COLLINS SOFTBACK ENGLISH DICTIONARY

General Consultant

J M Sinclair
Professor, Department of English Language and Literature
University of Birmingham

Special Consultants

AUSTRALIAN ENGLISH

G A Wilkes
Challis Professor of English Literature
University of Sydney

W A Krebs
Associate Professor in Literature and Communication
Bond University, Queensland

BRITISH REGIONAL ENGLISH, URBAN DIALECTS

Harold Orton
Professor Emeritus, Department of English
University of Leeds

CANADIAN ENGLISH

R J Gregg
Formerly Professor, Department of Linguistics
University of British Columbia

Patrick Drysdale
Editor, *A Dictionary of Canadianisms on Historical Principles*

CARIBBEAN ENGLISH

S R R Allsopp
Coordinator, Caribbean Lexicography Project
University of the West Indies, Barbados

EAST AFRICAN ENGLISH

J Kalema
Department of Linguistic Science
University of Reading

INDIAN ENGLISH

R K Bansal
Professor, Department of Phonetics and Spoken English
Central Institute of English and Foreign Languages
Hyderabad

IRISH ENGLISH

R J Gregg
Formerly Professor, Department of Linguistics
University of British Columbia

T de Bhaldraithe
Professor, Department of Irish Dialectology
University College, Dublin

NEW ZEALAND ENGLISH

Ian A Gordon
Professor Emeritus
University of Wellington

SCOTTISH ENGLISH

A J Aitken
Department of English Language
University of Edinburgh
Formerly Editor, *Dictionary of the Older Scottish Tongue*

SOUTH AFRICAN ENGLISH

L W Lanham
Professor, Department of Phonetics and General Linguistics
University of the Witwatersrand

M V Aldridge
Professor, Department of Phonetics and General Linguistics
University of the Witwatersrand

WEST AFRICAN ENGLISH

J Spencer
Director, Institute of Modern English Language Studies
University of Leeds

PRONUNCIATION

A C Gimson
Formerly Professor, Department of Phonetics and Linguistics
University College
University of London

COLLINS
SOFTBACK ENGLISH DICTIONARY

This edition published exclusively for
The Softback Preview
by HarperCollins Publishers
PO Box, Glasgow G4 0NB
1992

First Edition 1979
Second Edition 1986
Third Edition 1991

ISBN 0 00 470144-5

Prepared in conjunction with Market House Books Ltd., Aylesbury, England
Computer typeset by Barbers Ltd., Wrotham, England
Printed in Great Britain by HarperCollins Manufacturing

Contents

Editorial Staff

For the Third Edition

MANAGING EDITOR
Marian Makins

EDITORIAL CONSULTANT
Alan Isaacs

SENIOR EDITOR
Diana Adams

EDITORS
Alice Grandison Danielle McGinley Tom Shearer Lorna Knight Elspeth Summers Catherine Lyons Catherine Forde

COMPUTER STAFF
Colette Clenaghan Raymond Carrick

COLLINS COBUILD
Tim Lane

MARKET HOUSE EDITORS
John Daintith Elizabeth Martin Jonathan Law David Pickering Hazel Egerton Anne Stibbs

COMPUTERS
Edmund Wright

KEYBOARDERS
Jessica Scholes Elizabeth Bonham Sandra McQueen Linda Wells Gwynneth Shaw Brenda Tomkins

For Previous Editions

Patrick Hanks
EDITOR

Laurence Urdang
EDITORIAL DIRECTOR

Thomas Hill Long
MANAGING EDITOR

William T McLeod
MANAGING EDITOR

GENERAL CONTRIBUTORS

Paul Procter
CHIEF DEFINING EDITOR
Della Summers
DEPUTY DEFINING EDITOR
Alan Dingle
William Gould
Christopher Hotten
John Huggins
Bernard James
Catherine Limm
Lucy Liddell
Edwin Riddell
Michael Scherk
Clare Vickers
Eileen Williams
John D Wright

CONTENT EDITORS

Barbara Barrett
Jonathan Hunt
Catherine Hutton
Martin Manser
Judith Ravenscroft
Mary Shields
Maurice Waite
Judith Wardman
Rosalind Williams

SCIENCE CONTRIBUTORS

Alan Isaacs
CHIEF SCIENCE EDITOR
Elizabeth Martin
DEPUTY SCIENCE EDITOR
Edward R Brace
John Daintith
Martin Elliott
Anthony Lee
Stephanie Pain
Valerie H Pitt
Stella E Stiegeler

PRONUNCIATION CONTRIBUTORS

Carolyn Herzog
CHIEF PRONUNCIATION EDITOR
Judith Scott
William Gould
Jill Douglas Graham
Hope Liebersohn
Vera Steiner

ETYMOLOGY CONTRIBUTORS

Thomas Hill Long
CHIEF ETYMOLOGIST
Yvonne Shorthouse
Eva Wagner

COMPUTER SYSTEMS AND OPERATIONS

Barry Evans
DATA PROCESSING MANAGER
Allistair Bywater
Jeremy Knight

Foreword

The **Collins Softback English Dictionary** presents a fresh, revised, and augmented description of contemporary English, in which the work of specialist contributors and editorial staff combines with the latest computational techniques to provide a truly comprehensive survey of language today. In so doing it both continues and improves on the new standards set in the first edition of the *Collins English Dictionary* for its range of coverage, its description of contemporary English as it is actually used, and the clarity with which information is presented.

In deciding what to include in the dictionary, the criterion for the editors has always been: is the general reader likely to come across this word and want to look it up? Given the sophistication of the "general reader" today, and the constant proliferation of new information, and hence new terminology, in so many walks of life, this is not as simplistic as it may at first appear. It has led us to review, and in many cases expand, the areas of specialist coverage that form such an important element of the dictionary, and to add new vocabulary from subject fields, such as education, that have changed or developed rapidly in very recent years; sport, where increasing television coverage has brought to wider audiences the terminology of, for instance, snooker and American football; the environment where public interest in green issues is reflected in an increasing number of ecology-oriented words and concepts; business, where the different areas of the financial world — banking, insurance, investment, marketing — all contribute their specialist jargon to the general language; and many others.

The various subject fields which we refer to collectively as "science and technology" have been a main element in the dictionary since its first publication, and one to which special attention has been paid in this edition. Specialist contributors have provided updated material and new vocabulary, and areas of rapid development have been reassessed. Life science and medicine have been revised in line with the latest research, as have physics and chemistry and modern nomenclature and terminology is scrupulously followed.

To ensure that the dictionary contains a balanced and comprehensive coverage of new words that have entered the language in recent years, we have developed an editorial programme of language monitoring, which has become an important part of the work of our in-house editorial team. Many thousands of citations are studied and discussed in order to arrive at the new words, new meanings of existing words, new concepts, new usages, that are recorded in the dictionary. Increasingly, the human work of reading, listening, and researching to monitor language change is now augmented by the evidence of vast resources of computerized data, enabling the lexicographer to record with greater accuracy than ever before the living language of today.

Altogether, over six thousand new words and meanings have been added, and many thousands of existing entries revised. But, in preparing the third edition, we have taken care to keep all the features which proved so successful in the earlier editions: clarity of typeface, modern page layout, definitions worded in straightforward English, avoidance of puzzling symbols or abbreviations. The characteristic Collins Dictionaries style ensures that this edition is as user-friendly and practical in everyday use as its predecessors. The result is a book which, we are confident, will serve its user well and faithfully, containing as it does a fully revised and modernized text in a tried-and-tested dictionary style.

The creation of a dictionary is a long and complex task, and the editors would like to thank all those who, over the years, have contributed to it. The names of our specialist consultants and contributors are listed on pages ii, viii, and ix. We are grateful for the work of the specialist computing staff at Collins Cobuild, University of Birmingham, who provided corpus data; and for the extensive work on technical terminology of the Market House Books editorial team. But we would also like to record our gratitude to the hundreds of users of the Dictionary who have taken the trouble to write to us with suggestions for improvements or additions. Their letters, often with citations, are always of interest and have yielded much valuable material. They are too numerous to list, but we would especially thank some who have contributed regularly over the years: E M Bettenson, Stephen Corrin, Bernard Kramrisch, Don McLeod, Donald Miller, Vincent Petti, P Pledger, Sanzo Tsuboi, Naotoshi Yamagishi.

And, finally, we must record our thanks to the various organizations and individuals who have helped us with information on a variety of queries.

Specialist Contributors

AERONAUTICS

T C Wooldridge
Angus Boyd
Senior Lecturer in Aerodynamics, The College of Aeronautics, Cranfield

ARCHITECTURE; CIVIL ENGINEERING

Bruce Martin

AUSTRALIAN ENGLISH

Steve Higgs
Melbourne Grammar School

BROADCASTING, FILM, ETC.

Patrick Leggatt
Chief Engineer, External Relations, British Broadcasting Corporation

BUSINESS

Alan Isaacs

CHEMISTRY

John Daintith

COMPUTERS

Richard Fryer
Department of Computer Science, University of Strathclyde

CONSTRUCTION

M J Walker
Construction Industry Research and Information Association

EARTH SCIENCES

Peter J Smith
Reader in Earth Sciences, The Open University

ECONOMICS

P Donaldson
Ruskin College, Oxford

EDUCATION

Catherine Hodgetts
Teacher

ENGINEERING

J P Quayle
Editor, *Kempe's Engineering Year-Book*

INDUSTRIAL RELATIONS

Professor Angela M Bowey
Strathclyde Business School, University of Strathclyde
Alexander Purdie
Scottish College of Textiles, Galashiels

INFORMATION TECHNOLOGY

Professor Thomas Carbery
Andrew Doswell
Catherine M Young
Department of Information Science, University of Strathclyde

JUDAISM

Ephraim Borowski
Department of Philosophy, University of Glasgow

LANGUAGES & PEOPLES

David Kilby
Formerly, Department of Language and Linguistics, University of Essex

LAW

Richard Latham
Barrister-at-Law
Brian Russell Davis
Barrister-at-Law
Sandra Clarke

LIFE SCIENCES

Miranda Robertson
Life Sciences Editor, *Nature*
Dr W Gratzer
MRC Cell Biophysics Unit

LINGUISTICS

Professor Yorick Wilks
New Mexico State University

LINGUISTICS AND GRAMMAR

Lloyd Humberstone

LOGIC

Ephraim Borowski
Department of Philosophy, University of Glasgow

MALAYSIAN ENGLISH

U Yong-ee

MARKETING

Professor M Christopher
Department of Marketing and Logistics Systems, Cranfield School of Management

METALLURGY

Stanley White

MILITARY

Major S R Elliot
Colonel Andrew Duncan
The International Institute for Strategic Studies

Specialist Contributors

MILITARY AND NAUTICAL TERMS
Cmdr I Johnston RN

PHILOSOPHY
Christopher Sion
Ephraim Borowski
Department of Philosophy,
University of Glasgow

PHYSICAL SCIENCES
R Cutler

PHYSICS
J W Warren
Department of Physics,
Brunel University

PIDGINS AND CREOLES
Loreto Todd
The School of English,
University of Leeds

PLANTS
Sandra Holmes

POP MUSIC
Ingrid von Essen

PRINTING
C H Parsons
Laurence Chizlett

PSYCHOLOGY
Dr Eric Taylor
Professor Stuart Sutherland
Director, Centre for Research
on Perception and Cognition,
University of Sussex

RAILWAYS
James Barnes

RELIGION
The Rev D Lancashire
University of Essex

RELIGIOUS TERMS
David Bourke
Rev Canon D W Gundry
Chancellor of Leicester Cathedral

SOCIAL WELFARE
Bob Marsden
Harrow Social Services Department

SPORT
Stuart Bathgate
Freelance Journalist

STATISTICS
Ephraim Borowski
Department of Philosophy,
University of Glasgow

TOOLS
N J Smail
Associate of the Institute of
Marine Engineers

Other Contributors

Jane Bartholomew ANIMALS
Jenny Baster COOKERY; CLOTHING AND FASHION; TEXTILES
Denise Bown PLACE NAMES
Ron Brown JAZZ
Daphne Butler CHEMISTRY
Christopher L Clarke HOROLOGY
Brian Dalgleish METALLURGY
Carolyn Eardley ANTIQUES; FURNITURE; TEXTILES
R J Edwards PSYCHOLOGY
Dennis Exton FILMS, TV, AND RADIO
Ian Fuller PSYCHOLOGY
C Gallon PLANTS
Cherry McDonald-Taylor EDUCATION; LIBRARY SCIENCE
Mary Marshall CARDS; DANCING AND BALLET
David Martin PSYCHOLOGY
Peter Miller SPORTS
Stewart Murray METALLURGY
Serena Penman ART
H G Procter PSYCHOLOGY
David H Shaw ENGINEERING
Brian Street ANTHROPOLOGY
Andrew Treacher PSYCHOLOGY
Ralph Tyler FILMS, TV, AND RADIO; LITERATURE; MYTHOLOGY; THEATRE
Jennifer Wearden ARCHAEOLOGY
Irene Wise BIOCHEMISTRY

Guide to the Use of the Dictionary

Collins Softback English Dictionary is designed to be easy to use so that you can go straight to the word you want. The Guide that follows sets out the main principles on which the Dictionary is arranged and enables you to make full use of the Dictionary by showing the range of information that it contains.

1 HEADWORD

All main entries, including abbreviations, prefixes, and suffixes, are printed in large boldface type and are listed in strict alphabetical order. This applies even if the headword consists of more than one word.

1.1 Order of entries

Words that have the same spelling but are derived from different sources (homographs) are entered separately with superscript numbers after the headwords.

saw[1] (sɔː) *n.* **1.** any of various hand tools ...
saw[2] (sɔː) *vb.* the past tense of **see**[1].
saw[3] (sɔː) *n.* a wise saying, maxim, or proverb. ...

A word with a capital initial letter, if entered separately, follows the lower-case form. For example, **Catholic** follows **catholic**.

1.2 Abbreviations, acronyms, and symbols

Abbreviations, acronyms, and symbols are entered as headwords in the main alphabetical list. In line with modern practice, full stops are generally not used with symbols (**Ga**), nor for most abbreviations that are either strings of initials (**MA, mph**) or contractions (**St, Mr**). However, stops are used for an abbreviation of a word that is not a contraction (**Brig.**) and for strings of lower-case initials that could form a word (**c.o.d.**). Alternative forms with stops are only shown for certain standard abbreviations (**e.g.** *or* **eg**) but it can be assumed that nearly all abbreviations are equally acceptable with or without stops.

1.3 Prefixes, suffixes, and combining forms

Prefixes (e.g. **in-**, **pre-**, **sub-**), suffixes (e.g. **-able**, **-ation**, **-ity**), and combining forms (e.g. **psycho-**, **-iatry**) have been entered as headwords if they are still used freely to produce new words in English.

1.4 Plural headwords

Words that have a standard use or uses in the plural may be entered as separate headwords at both singular and plural forms, with a cross-reference to the plural form at the singular entry if other headwords intervene.

affair (ə'fɛə). *n.* **1.** a thing to be done or attended to ... ~ See also **affairs.**
affairs (ə'fɛəz). *pl. n.* **1.** personal or business interests ...

1.5 Variant spellings

Common acceptable variant spellings of English words are given as alternative forms of the headword.

capitalize *or* **capitalise** ('kæpɪtəˌlaɪz) *vb.* ...

2 PRONUNCIATION

Pronunciations of words in this Dictionary represent those that are common in educated speech. They are transcribed in the International Phonetic Alphabet (IPA). A *Key to the Pronunciation Symbols* is printed at the end of this Guide. See also the article on *The Pronunciation of British English* by Professor Gimson on p.xxii. The pronunciation is normally given in brackets immediately after the headword.

abase (ə'beɪs) *vb.* (*tr.*) **1.** to humble ...

The stress pattern is marked by the symbols ' for primary stress and ˌ for secondary stress. The stress mark precedes the syllable to which it applies.

2.1 Variant pronunciations

When a headword has an acceptable variant pronunciation or stress pattern, the variant is given by repeating only the syllable or syllables that change.

economic (ˌiːkə'nɒmɪk, ˌɛkə-) *adj.* **1.** of or relating to ...

Guide to the Use of the Dictionary

2.2 Pronunciations with different parts of speech

When two or more parts of speech of a word have different pronunciations, the pronunciations are shown in brackets before the relevant group of senses.

> **record** *n.* (ˈrɛkɔːd). **1.** an account in permanent form, ... ~ *vb.* (rɪkˈɔːd). (*mainly tr.*) **19.** to set down in some permanent form ...

2.3 Pronunciation of individual senses

If one sense of a headword has a different pronunciation from that of the rest, the pronunciation is given in brackets after the sense number.

> **conjure** (ˈkʌndʒə) *vb.* **1.** (*intr.*) to practise conjuring or to be a conjurer. **2.** (*intr.*) to call upon supposed supernatural forces by spells and incantations. **3.** (kənˈdʒʊə). (*tr.*) to appeal earnestly or strongly to: *I conjure you to help me ...*

2.4 Foreign words and phrases

Foreign words or phrases are printed in boldface italic type and are given foreign-language pronunciations only, unless they are regarded as having become accepted in English.

> ***haut monde*** *French* (o mɔ̃d) *n.* ...

3 INFLECTED FORMS

Inflected forms of nouns, verbs, and adjectives are shown immediately after the part-of-speech label if they are irregular or, in certain cases, if they are regular but might cause confusion.

3.1 Regular inflections

Where inflections are not shown, it may be assumed that they are formed as follows:

nouns. Regular plurals are formed by the addition of *-s* (e.g. *pencils, monkeys*)
or, in the case of nouns ending in *-s, -x, -z, -ch,* or *-sh,* by the addition of *-es* (e.g. *losses*).

verbs. In regularly inflected verbs:
the third person singular of the present tense is formed by the addition of *-s* to the infinitive (e.g. *plays*)
or, for verbs ending in *-s, -x, -z, -ch,* or *-sh,* by the addition of *-es* (e.g. *passes, reaches*)
the past tense and past participle are formed by the addition of *-ed* to the infinitive (e.g. *played*)
the present participle is formed by the addition of *-ing* to the infinitive (e.g. *playing*).
Verbs that end in a consonant plus *-e* (e.g. *locate, snare*) regularly lose the final *-e* before the addition of *-ed* and *-ing.*

adjectives. The regular comparatives and superlatives of adjectives are formed by adding *-er* and *-est* to the base (e.g. *short, shorter, shortest*).
Adjectives that end in a consonant plus *-e* regularly lose the *-e* before *-er* and *-est* (e.g. *fine, finer, finest*).

3.2 Irregular and unfamiliar inflections

Inflected forms are shown for the following:

Nouns and verbs whose inflections involve a change in internal spelling.

> **goose**[1] (guːs) *n., pl.* **geese** ...
>
> **drive** (draɪv) *vb.* **drives, driving, drove** (drəʊv), **driven.** ...

Nouns, verbs, and adjectives that end in a consonant plus *-y*, where *y* is changed to *i* before inflectional endings.

> **augury** (ˈɔːgjʊrɪ) *n., pl.* **-ries** ...

Nouns having identical singular and plural forms.

sheep (ʃi:p) *n., pl.* **sheep** ...

Nouns that closely resemble others but form their plurals differently.

mongoose ('mɒŋˌgu:s) *n., pl.* **-gooses** ...

Nouns that end in *-ful*, *-o*, and *-us*

handful ('hændfʊl) *n., pl.* **-fuls** ...
tomato (tə'mɑ:təʊ) *n., pl.* **-toes** ...
prospectus (prə'spɛktəs) *n., pl.* **-tuses** ...

Nouns whose plurals are not regular English inflections.

basis ('beɪsɪs) *n., pl.* **-ses** (-si:z) ...

Plural nouns whose singulars are not regular English forms.

bacteria (bæk'tɪərɪə) *pl. n., sing.* **-rium** (-rɪəm) ...

Nouns whose plurals have regular spellings but involve a change in pronunciation.

house (haʊs) *n., pl.* **houses** ('haʊzɪz) ...

Multiword nouns when it is not obvious which word takes a plural inflection.

attorney-at-law *n., pl.* **attorneys-at-law** ...

Adjectives that change their roots to form comparatives and superlatives.

good (gʊd) *adj.* **better, best** ...

Adjectives and verbs that double their final consonant before adding endings.

fat (fæt) ... ~*adj.* **fatter, fattest** ...
control (kən'trəʊl) *vb.* **-trols, -trolling, -trolled** ...

Verbs that are regular and do not (as might be expected) double their final consonant before adding endings.

focus ('fəʊkəs) ... ~*vb.* **-cuses, -cusing, -cused** ...

Verbs and adjectives that end in a vowel plus *-e*.

canoe (kə'nu:) ... ~*vb.* **-noes, -noeing, -noed** ...
free (fri:) *adj.* **freer, freest** ... ~*vb.* **frees, freeing, freed** ...

4 PARTS OF SPEECH

A part-of-speech label in italics precedes the sense or senses relating to that part of speech.

4.1 Standard parts of speech

The standard parts of speech, with the abbreviations used, are as follows:

adjective (*adj.*), adverb (*adv.*), conjunction (*conj.*), interjection (*interj.*), noun (*n.*), preposition (*prep.*), pronoun (*pron.*), verb (*vb.*).

4.2 Less traditional parts of speech

Certain other less traditional parts of speech have been used in this Dictionary. They are as follows:

determiners. Such words as *that, this, my, his*, etc.,which used to be classed as demonstrative and possessive adjectives and/or pronouns, have been classified in this Dictionary as determiners.
The label *determiner* also replaces the traditional classification for words like *the, a, some, any*, as well as the numerals, and possessives such as *my* and *your*. Many determiners can have a pronoun function without change of meaning, and this is indicated as in the following example:

some (sʌm; *unstressed* səm) *determiner.* ... **2. a.** an unknown or unspecified quantity or amount of: *there's some rice on the table; he owns some horses.* **b.** (*as pron.*; *functioning as sing. or pl.*): *we'll buy some* ...

sentence connectors. This description replaces the traditional classification of certain words, such as *therefore* and *however*, as adverbs or conjunctions. These words link sentences together rather in the manner of conjunctions; however, they are not confined to the first position in a clause as conjunctions are.

sentence substitutes. Sentence substitutes are words such as *yes, no, perhaps, definitely*, and *maybe*. They can stand as meaningful utterances by themselves. They are distinguished in this Dictionary from interjections such as *ouch, ah, damn*, etc., which are expressions of emotional reaction rather than meaningful utterances.

4.3 Words used as more than one part of speech

If a word can be used as more than one part of speech, the senses of one part of speech are separated from the others by a swung dash.

> **lure** (lʊə) *vb.* (*tr.*) ... **2.** *Falconry.* to entice (a hawk or falcon) from the air to the falconer by a lure. ~*n.* **3.** a person or thing that lures ...

5 GRAMMATICAL INFORMATION

Grammatical information is provided in brackets and typically in italics to distinguish it from other types of information.

5.1 Adjectives and determiners

Some adjectives and determiners are restricted by usage to a particular position relative to the nouns they qualify. This is indicated by the following labels:

postpositive (used predicatively or after the noun, but not before the noun):

> **ablaze** (əˈbleɪz) *adj.* (*postpositive*), *adv.* **1.** on fire; burning ...

immediately postpositive (always used immediately following the noun qualified and never used predicatively):

> **galore** (gəˈlɔː) *determiner.* (*immediately postpositive*) in great numbers or quantity: *there were daffodils galore in the park* ...

prenominal (used before the noun, and never used predicatively):

> **chief** (tʃiːf) ... ~*adj.* **5.** (*prenominal*) **a.** most important; principal. **b.** highest in rank or authority ...

5.2 Intensifiers

Adjectives and adverbs that perform an exclusively intensifying function, with no addition of meaning, are described as (intensifier) without further explanation.

> **blooming** (ˈbluːmɪŋ) *adv., adj. Brit. informal.* (intensifier): *a blooming genius; blooming painful.*

5.3 Conjunctions

Conjunctions are divided into two classes, marked by the following labels placed in brackets:

coordinating. Coordinating conjunctions connect words, phrases, or clauses that perform an identical function and are not dependent on each other. They include *and, but*, and *or*.

subordinating. Subordinating conjunctions introduce clauses that are dependent on a main clause in a complex sentence. They include *where, until*, and *or*.

Some conjunctions, such as *while* and *whereas*, can function as either coordinating or subordinating conjunctions.

5.4 Singular and plural labelling of nouns

Headwords and senses that are apparently plural in form but that take a singular verb, etc., are marked '*functioning as sing.*'

> **physics** ('fɪzɪks) *n. (functioning as sing.)* **1.** the branch of science ...

Headwords and senses that appear to be singular, such as collective nouns, but that take a plural verb, etc., are marked '*functioning as pl.*'

> **cattle** ('kætᵊl) *n. (functioning as pl.)* **1.** bovid mammals of the tribe *Bovini* ...

Headwords and senses that may take either a singular or a plural verb, etc., are marked '*functioning as sing. or pl.*'

> **bellows** ('bɛləʊz) *n. (functioning as sing. or pl.)* **1.** Also: **pair of bellows.** an instrument consisting of an air chamber ...

5.5 Modifiers

A noun that is commonly used as if it were an adjective is labelled *modifier*. If the sense of the modifier can be understood from the sense of the noun, the modifier is shown without further explanation, with an example to illustrate its use.

> **denim** ('dɛnɪm) *n.Textiles.* **1. a.** a hard-wearing twill-weave cotton fabric used for trousers, work clothes, etc. **b.** (*as modifier*); *a denim jacket* ...

If the sense of the modifier cannot be understood from the sense of the noun, or if it is related to more than one of the noun senses, its meaning and/or usage is explained separately.

> **key**[1] (kiː) *n.* ... **8.** (*modifier*) of great importance: *a key issue* ...

5.6 Verbs

The principal parts given are: 3rd person singular of the present tense; present participle; past tense; past participle if different from the past tense.

5.7 Intransitive and transitive verbs

When a sense of a verb (*vb.*) is restricted to transitive use, it is labelled (*tr.*); if it is intransitive only, it is labelled (*intr.*). If all the senses of a verb are transitive or all are intransitive, the appropriate label appears before the first numbered sense and is not repeated.

Absence of a label is significant: it indicates that the sense may be used both transitively and intransitively.

If nearly all the senses of a verb are transitive, the label (*mainly tr.*) appears immediately before the first numbered sense. An individual sense may then be labelled (*also intr.*) to show that it is both transitive and intransitive, or it may be labelled (*intr.*) to show that it is intransitive only.

> **carry** ('kærɪ) *vb.* (*mainly tr.*) **1.** (*also intr.*) to take or bear (something) from one place to another: *to carry a baby in one's arms.* **2.** to transfer for consideration; take: *he carried his complaints to her superior* ... **27.** (*intr.*) (of a ball, projectile, etc.) to travel through the air or reach a specified point: *his first drive carried to the green.*

Similarly, all the senses of a verb may be labelled (*mainly intr.*) and the labels (*also tr.*) and (*tr.*) introduced before individual senses as required.

When a sense of a verb may be transitive or intransitive, a direct object that would typically follow its transitive use is sometimes shown in brackets. The brackets should be ignored in order to obtain the intransitive use.

> **act** (ækt) ... ~*vb.* ... **11.** to perform (a part or role) in a play ...

When the object of the transitive use of a verb constitutes the subject of the intransitive use, this is shown as follows:

> **fire** (faɪə) ... ~*vb.* ... **25.** to discharge (a firearm or projectile) or (of a firearm, etc.) to be discharged ...

When the intransitive verb functions with a preposition but the transitive use does not, an equivalent preposition is given in brackets.

> **differentiate** (ˌdɪfəˈrɛnʃɪˌeɪt) *vb.* ... **2.** (when *intr.*, often foll. by *between*) to perceive, show, or make a difference (in or between); discriminate.

5.8 **Copulas**

A verb that takes a complement is labelled *copula*.

> **seem** (siːm) *vb.* (may take an infinitive) **1.** *(copula)* to appear to the mind or eye; look: *this seems nice; the car seems to be running well.*

5.9 **Phrasal verbs**

Verbal constructions consisting of a verb and a prepositional or an adverbial particle are given headword status if the meaning of the phrasal verb cannot be deduced from the separate meanings of the verb and the particle.

Phrasal verbs are labelled to show four possible distinctions:
a transitive verb with an adverbial particle (*tr.*, *adv.*); a transitive verb with a prepositional particle (*tr.*, *prep.*); an intransitive verb with an adverbial particle (*intr.*, *adv.*); an intransitive verb with a prepositional particle (*intr.*, *prep.*):

> **turn on** ... **4.** (*tr.*, *adv.*) *Informal* to produce (charm, tears, etc.) suddenly or automatically.
>
> **take for** *vb.* (*tr.*, *prep.*) *Informal* to consider or suppose to be, esp. mistakenly: *the fake coins were taken for genuine; who do you take me for?*
>
> **break off** ... **3.** (*intr.*, *adv.*) to stop abruptly: *he broke off in the middle of his speech.*
>
> **turn on** ... **2.** (*intr.*, *prep.*) to depend or hinge on: *the success of the party turns on you.*

As with the labelling of other verbs, the absence of a label is significant. If there is no label (*tr.*) or (*intr.*), the verb may be used either transitively or intransitively. If there is no label (*adv.*) or (*prep.*), the particle may be either adverbial or prepositional.

Any noun, adjective, or modifier formed from a phrasal verb is entered under the phrasal-verb headword. In some cases, where the noun or adjective is more common than the verb, the phrasal verb is entered after the noun or adjective form:

> **breakaway** (ˈbreɪkəˌweɪ) *n.* **1. a.** loss or withdrawal of a group of members from an association, club, etc. **b.** *(as modifier)*: *a breakaway faction.* ... ~*vb.* **break away.** (*intr.*, *adv.*) ... **4.** to withdraw or secede.

A cross-reference is given at the main verb when related phrasal verbs are entered as headwords but are separated from it by more than five intervening entries.

> **fit**[1] (fɪt) *vb.* See also **fit in, fit out, fit up.** [C14: probably from Middle Dutch *vitten*] ...

6 **RESTRICTIVE LABELS**

If a particular sense is restricted as to appropriateness, connotation, subject field, etc., an italic label is placed immediately before the relevant definition.

> **hang on** *vb.* (*intr.*) ... **5.** (*adv.*) *Informal.* to wait or remain: *hang on for a few minutes.*

If a label applies to all senses of one part of speech, it is placed immediately after the part-of-speech label.

> **assured** (əˈʃʊəd) *adj.* ... ~*n.* **4.** *Chiefly Brit.* **a.** the beneficiary under a life assurance policy. **b.** the person whose life is insured. ...

If a label applies to all senses of a headword, it is placed immediately after the pronunciation (or inflections).

> **con**[1] (kɒn) *Inf.* ~*n.* **1. a.** short for **confidence trick. b.** (*as modifier*): *con man.* ~*vb.* **cons, conning, conned. 2.** (*tr.*) to swindle or defraud ...

6.1 Usage labels

Slang. This refers to words or senses that are racy or extremely informal. The appropriate contexts in which slang is used are restricted, for example, to members of a particular social group or those engaged in a particular activity. Slang words are inappropriate in formal speech or writing.

Informal. This label applies to words or senses that may be widely used, especially in conversation, letter-writing, etc., but that are not common in formal writing. Such words are subject to fewer contextual restrictions than slang words.

Taboo. This label applies to words that are not acceptable in polite use. The reader is advised to avoid the use of such words if he or she wishes to be sure of avoiding social disapproval.

Offensive. This label indicates that a word might be regarded as offensive by the person described or referred to, even if the speaker uses the word without any malicious intention.

Derogatory. This implies that the connotations of a word are unpleasant with intent on the part of the speaker or writer.

Not standard. This label is given to words or senses that are frequently encountered but widely regarded as incorrect and therefore avoided by careful speakers and writers.

Archaic. This label denotes a word or sense that is no longer in common use but that may be found in literary works or used to impart a historical colour to contemporary writing.

Obsolete. This label denotes a word or sense that is no longer in use. In specialist or technical fields the label often implies that the term has been superseded.

The word 'formerly' is placed in brackets before a sense or set of senses when the practice, concept, etc., being described, rather than the word itself, is obsolete or out-of-date.

A number of other usage labels, such as *Ironic, Facetious,* and *Euphemistic,* are used where appropriate.

More extended help on usage is provided in usage notes after certain entries. See section 14 of the *Guide to the Use of the Dictionary.*

6.2 Subject-field labels

A number of italic labels are used to indicate that a word or sense is used in a particular specialist or technical field. Subject-field labels are given either in full (e.g. *Astronomy, Philosophy*) or only slightly abbreviated, so that the full label may be easily understood.

6.3 National and regional labels

Words or senses restricted to or associated with a particular country or region are labelled accordingly. The following labels are the ones most frequently used: *Austral.* (Australian), *Brit.* (British), *Canadian, Caribbean, Irish, N.Z.* (New Zealand), *S. African, Scot.* (Scottish), *U.S.* (United States).

The label *Brit.* is used mainly to distinguish a particular word or sense from its North American equivalent or to identify a term or concept that does not exist in North American English. The North American equivalent may be given in boldface type after the appropriate numbered sense.

Regional dialects (*Scot. and northern English dialect, Midland dialect,* etc.) have been specified as precisely as possible, even at the risk of overrestriction, in order to give the reader an indication of the appropriate regional flavour.

7 MEANING

The meaning of each headword in this Dictionary is explained in one or more definitions, together with information about context, typical use, and other relevant facts.

Where a headword has more than one sense, each sense is given separately and numbered in order to avoid confusion.

Example sentences and phrases illustrating the use of a sense are given at the end of many definitions.

7.1 Order of senses

As a general rule, where a headword has more than one sense, the first sense given is the one most common in current usage.

> **complexion** (kəmˈplɛkʃən) *n.* **1.** the colour and general appearance of a person's skin, esp. of the face. **2.** aspect, character or nature: *the general complexion of a nation's finances.* **3.** *Obsolete.* **a.** the temperament of a person ...

Where the editors consider that a current sense is the 'core meaning' in that it illuminates the meaning of other senses, the core meaning may be placed first.

> **competition** (ˌkɒmˈpɪtɪʃən) *n.* **1.** the act of competing; rivalry. **2.** a contest in which a winner is selected from among two or more entrants. **3.** a series of games, sports events, etc. **4.** the opposition offered by competitors ...

Subsequent senses are arranged so as to give a coherent account of the meaning of a headword. If a word is used as more than one part of speech, all the senses of each part of speech are grouped together in a single block. Within a part-of-speech block, closely related senses are grouped together; technical senses generally follow general senses; archaic and obsolete senses follow technical senses; idioms and fixed phrases are generally placed last.

7.2 Scientific and technical definitions

Units, physical quantities, formulas, etc. In accordance with the recommendations of the International Standards Organization, all scientific measurements are expressed in SI units (*Système International d'Unités*). Measurements and quantities in more traditional units are often given as well as SI units. The entries for chemical compounds give the systematic names as well as the more familiar popular names.

Plants and animals. When the scientific (Latin) name of phyla, divisions, classes, orders, families, genera, and species are used in definitions, they are printed in italic type and all except the specific name have an initial capital letter. Taxonomic information is always given.

> **moss** (mɒs) *n.* **1.** any bryophyte of the class *Musci*, typically growing in dense mats on trees ...
>
> **capybara** (ˌkæpɪˈbɒːrə) *n.* the largest rodent: a pig-sized amphibious hystricomorph, *Hydrochoerus hydrochaeris* ...

8 CROSS-REFERENCES

The main entry is always given at the most common spelling or form of the word. Cross-reference entries refer to this main entry. Thus the entry for **deoxyribonucleic acid** cross-refers to **DNA,** where the full explanation is given.

8.1 **Comparisons**

Cross-references introduced by the words 'See also' or 'Compare' refer the reader to additional information elsewhere in the Dictionary. If the cross-reference is preceded by a swung dash (~), it applies to all senses of the headword that have gone before it, unless otherwise stated. If there is no swung dash, the cross-reference applies only to the sense immediately preceding it.

8.2 **Variant spellings**

Variant spellings (e.g. **foetus** ... a variant spelling of **fetus**) are generally entered as cross-references if their place in the alphabetical list is more than ten entries distant from the main entry.

8.3 **Alternative names**

Alternative names or terms are printed in boldface type and introduced by the words 'Also' or 'Also called'. If the alternative name or term is preceded by a swung dash, it applies to the entire entry.

9 **RELATED ADJECTIVES**

Certain nouns, especially of Germanic origin, have related adjectives that are derived from Latin or French. For example, *mural* (from Latin) is an adjective related in meaning to *wall*. Such adjectives are shown in a number of cases after the sense (or part-of-speech block) to which they are related.

> **wall** (wɔːl) *n.* **1. a.** a vertical construction made of stone, brick, wood, etc. ... Related adj.: **mural** ...

10 **IDIOMS**

Fixed noun phrases, such as **dark horse,** and certain other idioms are given full headword status. Other idioms are placed under the key word of the idiom, as a separate sense, generally at the end of the appropriate part-of-speech block.

> **ground**[1] (graʊnd) *n.* ... **21. break new ground.** to do something that has not been done before ...

11 **ETYMOLOGIES**

Etymologies are placed in square brackets after the definition. They are given for all headwords except those that are derivative forms (consisting of a base word and a suffix or prefix), compound words, inflected forms, and proper names. Thus, the headword **manage** has been given an etymology but the related headwords **manageable** (equivalent to *manage* plus the suffix *-able*), **management** (*manage* plus *-ment*), **manager** (*manage* plus *-er*), **manageress** (*manager* plus *-ess*), etc., do not have etymologies.

Inflected forms such as **saw** (the past tense of *see*) and obvious compounds such as **mothball** are not given an etymology. Many headwords, such as **enlighten** and **preposses,** consist of a prefix and a base word and are not accompanied by etymologies since the essential etymological information is shown for the component parts, all of which are entered in the Dictionary as headwords in their own right (in this instance, **en-, light, -en** and **pre-, possess**).

The purpose of the etymologies is to trace briefly the history of the word back from the present day, through its first recorded appearance in English, to its origin, often in some source language other than English. The etymologies show the history of the word both in English (wherever there has been significant change in form or sense) and in its pre-English source languages. Since records of both Latin and Ancient Greek exist, it is usually possible to show the actual Latin or Greek form of the source of an English word. In the case of English words of Germanic origin, cognate forms in one or more Germanic languages are shown. These cognate forms are words from the same (lost) Germanic originals, and the chief cognate languages cited are Old Norse, Swedish, Danish, German, Dutch and Old Saxon.

All the languages and linguistic terminology used in the etymologies are entries in their own right in the Dictionary. Words printed in SMALL CAPITALS refer the reader to other headwords where relevant or additional information, either in the definition or in the etymology, may be found.

11.1 Dating

The etymology records the first known occurrence (a written citation) of a word in English. Words first appearing in the language during the Middle English period or later are dated by century, abbreviated C.

> **mantis** ... [C17: New Latin, from Greek: prophet, alluding to its praying posture]

This indicates that there is a written citation for **mantis** in the seventeenth century. The absence of a New Latin or Greek form in the etymology means that the form of the word was the same in those languages as in English.

11.2 Old English

Native words from Old English are not dated, written records of Old English being comparatively scarce, but are simply identified as being of Old English origin.

> **mar** (mɒː) *vb.* **mars, marring, marred.** ... [Old English *merran*; compare Old Saxon *merrian* to hinder, Old Norse *merja* to bruise]

12 DERIVED WORDS

Words derived from a base word by the addition of suffixes such as *-ly*, *-ness*, etc., are entered in boldface type immediately after the etymology or after the last definition if there is no etymology. The meanings of such words may be deduced from the meanings of the suffix and the headword.

13 LISTED ENTRIES

In English many words are formed by adding productive prefixes such as *non-*, *over-*, *un-*, etc., to existing words. In most cases, the meanings of these words are obvious. Such words are included, without definition, at the foot of the appropriate page in the alphabetical sequence.

14 USAGE NOTES

A brief note introduced by the symbol ▷ and the label **Usage** has been added at the end of a number of entries in order to comment on matters of usage. These comments are based on the observed practice or preference of the majority of educated speakers and writers.

> **ain't** (eɪnt) *Not standard. contraction of* am not, is not, are not, have not *or* has not: *I ain't seen it.*
>
> ▷ **Usage** Although the interrogative form *ain't I?* would be a natural contraction of *am not I?*, it is generally avoided in spoken English and never used in formal English.

Pronunciation Key

The symbols used in the pronunciation transcriptions are those of the International Phonetic Alphabet. The following consonant symbols have their usual English values: *b, d, f, h, k, l, m, n, p, r, s, t, v, w, z*. The remaining symbols and their interpretations are listed in the tables below.

English Sounds

ɑː as in *father* (ˈfɑːðə), *alms* (ɑːmz), *clerk* (klɑːk), *heart* (hɑːt), *sergeant* (ˈsɑːdʒənt)

æ as in *act* (ækt), *Caedmon* (ˈkædmən), *plait* (plæt)

aɪ as in *dive* (daɪv), *aisle* (aɪl), *guy* (gaɪ), *might* (maɪt), *rye* (raɪ)

aɪə as in *fire* (ˈfaɪə), *buyer* (ˈbaɪə), *liar* (ˈlaɪə), *tyre* (ˈtaɪə)

aʊ as in *out* (aʊt), *bough* (baʊ), *crowd* (kraʊd), *slouch* (slaʊtʃ)

aʊə as in *flour* (ˈflaʊə), *cower* (ˈkaʊə), *flower* (ˈflaʊə), *sour* (ˈsaʊə)

ɛ as in *bet* (bɛt), *ate* (ɛt), *bury* (ˈbɛrɪ), *heifer* (ˈhɛfə), *said* (sɛd), *says* (sɛz)

eɪ as in *paid* (peɪd), *day* (deɪ), *deign* (deɪn), *gauge* (geɪdʒ), *grey* (greɪ), *neigh* (neɪ)

ɛə as in *bear* (bɛə), *dare* (dɛə), *prayer* (prɛə), *stairs* (stɛəz), *where* (wɛə)

g as in *get* (gɛt), *give* (gɪv), *ghoul* (guːl), *guard* (gɑːd), *examine* (ɪgˈzæmɪn)

ɪ as in *pretty* (ˈprɪtɪ), *build* (bɪld), *busy* (ˈbɪzɪ), *nymph* (nɪmf), *pocket* (ˈpɒkɪt), *sieve* (sɪv), *women* (ˈwɪmɪn)

iː as in *see* (siː), *aesthete* (ˈiːsθiːt), *evil* (ˈiːvᵊl), *magazine* (ˌmægəˈziːn), *receive* (rɪˈsiːv), *siege* (siːdʒ)

ɪə as in *fear* (fɪə), *beer* (bɪə), *mere* (mɪə), *tier* (tɪə)

j as in *yes* (jɛs), *onion* (ˈʌnjən), *vignette* (vɪˈnjɛt)

ɒ as in *pot* (pɒt), *botch* (bɒtʃ), *sorry* (ˈsɒrɪ)

əʊ as in *note* (nəʊt), *beau* (bəʊ), *dough* (dəʊ), *hoe* (həʊ), *slow* (sləʊ), *yeoman* (ˈjəʊmən)

ɔː as in *thaw* (θɔː), *broad* (brɔːd), *drawer* (ˈdrɔːə), *fault* (fɔːlt), *halt* (hɔːlt), *organ* (ˈɔːgən)

ɔɪ as in *void* (vɔɪd), *boy* (bɔɪ), *destroy* (dɪˈstrɔɪ)

ʊ as in *pull* (pʊl), *good* (gʊd), *should* (ʃʊd), *woman* (ˈwʊmən)

uː as in *zoo* (zuː), *do* (duː), *queue* (kjuː), *shoe* (ʃuː), *spew* (spjuː), *true* (truː), *you* (juː)

ʊə as in *poor* (pʊə), *skewer* (ˈskjʊə), *sure* (ʃʊə)

ə as in *potter* (ˈpɒtə), *alone* (əˈləʊn), *furious* (ˈfjʊərɪəs), *nation* (ˈneɪʃən), *the* (ðə)

ɜː as in *fern* (fɜːn), *burn* (bɜːn), *fir* (fɜː), *learn* (lɜːn), *term* (tɜːm), *worm* (wɜːm)

ʌ as in *cut* (kʌt), *flood* (flʌd), *rough* (rʌf), *son* (sʌn)

ʃ as in *ship* (ʃɪp), *election* (ɪˈlɛkʃən), *machine* (məˈʃiːn), *mission* (ˈmɪʃən), *pressure* (ˈprɛʃə), *schedule* (ˈʃɛdjuːl), *sugar* (ˈʃʊgə)

ʒ as in *treasure* (ˈtrɛʒə), *azure* (ˈæʒə), *closure* (ˈkləʊʒə), *evasion* (ɪˈveɪʒən)

tʃ as in *chew* (tʃuː), *nature* (ˈneɪtʃə)

dʒ as in *jaw* (dʒɔː), *adjective* (ˈædʒɪktɪv), *lodge* (lɒdʒ), *soldier* (ˈsəʊldʒə), *usage* (ˈjuːsɪdʒ)

θ as in *thin* (θɪn), *strength* (strɛŋθ), *three* (θriː)

ð as in *these* (ðiːz), *bathe* (beɪð), *lather* (ˈlɑːðə)

ŋ as in *sing* (sɪŋ), *finger* (ˈfɪŋgə), *sling* (slɪŋ)

ᵊ indicates that the following consonant (*l* or *n*) is syllabic, as in *bundle* (ˈbʌndᵊl) and *button* (ˈbʌtᵊn)

x as in Scottish *loch* (lɒx). See also below

əɪ as in Scottish *aye* (əɪ), *bile* (bəɪl), *byke* (bəɪk).

Foreign Sounds

The symbols above are also used to represent foreign sounds where these are similar to English sounds. However, certain common foreign sounds require symbols with markedly different values, as follows:

a *a* in French *ami*, German *Mann*, Italian *pasta*: a sound between English (æ) and (ɑː), similar to the vowel in Northern English *cat* or London *cut*.

ɑ *a* as in French *bas*: a sound made with a tongue position similar to that of English (ɑː), but shorter.

e *é* in French *été*, *eh* in German *sehr*, *e* in Italian *che*: a sound similar to the first part of the English diphthong (eɪ) in *day* or to the Scottish vowel in *day*.

i *i* in French *il*, German *Idee*, Spanish *filo*, Italian *signor*: a sound made with a tongue position similar to that of English (iː), but shorter.

ɔ *o* in Italian *no*, French *bonne*, German *Sonne*: a vowel resembling English (ɒ), but with a higher tongue position and more rounding of the lips.

o *o* in French *rose*, German *so*, Italian *voce*: a sound between English (ɔː) and (uː) with closely rounded lips, similar to the Scottish vowel in *so*.

u *ou* in French *genou*, *u* in German *kulant*, Spanish *puna*: a sound made with a tongue position similar to that of English (uː), but shorter.

y *u* in French *tu*, *ü* in German *über* or *fünf*: a sound made with a tongue position similar to that of English (iː), but with closely rounded lips.

ø *eu* in French *deux*, *ö* in German *schön*: a sound made with the tongue position of (e), but with closely rounded lips.

œ *œu* in French *œuf*, *ö* in German *zwölf*: a sound made with a tongue position similar to that of English (ɛ), but with open rounded lips.

~ above a vowel indicates nasalization, as in French *un* (œ̃), *bon* (bɔ̃), *vin* (vɛ̃), *blanc* (blɑ̃).

x *ch* in German *Buch*, *j* in Spanish *Juan*.

ç *ch* in German *ich:* a (j) sound as in *yes*, said without voice; similar to the first sound in *huge*.

β *b* in Spanish *Habana:* a voiced fricative sound similar to (v), but made by the two lips.

ʎ *ll* in Spanish *llamar*, *gl* in Italian *consiglio:* similar to the (lj) sequence in *million*, but with the tongue tip lowered and the sounds said simultaneously.

ɥ *u* in French *lui:* a short (y).

ɲ *gn* in French *vigne*, Italian *gnocchi*, *ñ* in Spanish *España:* similar to the (nj) sequence in *onion*, but with the tongue tip lowered and the two sounds said simultaneously.

ɣ *g* in Spanish *luego:* a weak (g) made with voiced friction.

Length

The symbol ː denotes length and is shown together with certain vowel symbols when the vowels are typically long.

Stress

Three grades of stress are shown in the transcriptions by the presence or absence of marks placed immediately *before* the affected syllable. Primary or strong stress is shown by ˈ, while secondary or weak stress is shown by ˌ. Unstressed syllables are not marked. In *photographic* (ˌfəʊtəˈɡræfɪk), for example, the first syllable carries secondary stress and the third primary stress, while the second and fourth are unstressed.

List of Abbreviations

abbrev.	abbreviation	**N**	north(ern)
adj.	adjective	**n.**	noun
adv.	adverb(ial)	**NE**	northeast(ern)
approx.	approximate(ly)	**no.**	number
Austral.	Australian	**NW**	northwest(ern)
Brit.	British	**N.Z.**	New Zealand
C	century (e.g. C14 = 14th century)	**p.**	page
°C	degrees Celsius	**pl.**	plural
cap(s).	capital initial(s)	**Pop.**	population
cf.	compare	**pp.**	pages
conj.	conjunction	**prep.**	preposition(al)
E	east(ern)	**pron.**	pronoun
e.g.	for example	**pt.**	point
esp.	especially	**RP**	Received Pronunciation
est.	estimate	**S**	south(ern)
etc.	et cetera	**S. African**	South African
fem.	feminine	**Scot.**	Scottish, Scots
foll.	followed	**SE**	southeast(ern)
ft.	foot *or* feet	**sing.**	singular
i.e.	that is	**sq.**	square
in.	inch(es)	**SW**	southwest(ern)
interj.	interjection	**tr.**	transitive
intr.	intransitive	**U.S.**	United States
IPA	International Phonetic Alphabet	**vb.**	verb
km	kilometres	**vol.**	volume
m	metre(s)	**W**	west(ern)
masc.	masculine	**wt.**	weight

The Pronunciation of British English

by A C Gimson

The Origins

English has been spoken in Britain for some fourteen centuries. During this time, it has undergone such fundamental changes (affecting grammar, vocabulary, and pronunciation) that the speech of an inhabitant of the London region of the 7th century would be totally unintelligible to the modern Londoner. The earliest form of English, brought by Germanic invaders from the 5th century onwards, is known as *Old English* and extends up to about the 11th century. This general term itself embraces a number of separate dialects deriving from the different geographical origins of the invaders. It was the West Saxon form of the South and the Southwest of the country that ultimately became regarded as a standard language, and it is in this form that most of the extant texts are written. From about the 7th century, Old English began to be written with the Latin alphabet, probably introduced into England by Irish missionaries. The Latin alphabet was, however, inadequate to express the more complex phonological system of the dialects of Old English. New letters, such as 'æ,' were added to indicate a value between that of Italian *e* and *a*; digraphs, such as 'th,' had to be used for consonant sounds that were unknown in Italian. Although there was a good deal of agreement about the orthography to be applied to the Old English sound system, there are in the texts of the period considerable variations in spelling forms as between one dialect and another and also between scribes. In fact, English has had a standardized form of spelling for not much more than two hundred years, the present apparent inconsistencies in our orthography reflecting the historical development of the language.

It can be said that the next major influence on our language — that of the French dominance from the 11th century onwards — affected spelling more than pronunciation (although it added enormously to our stock of words). During this period of *Middle English* (roughly 1100–1450), English remained the language of the people, but French was used by the aristocracy as well as in administrative and legal proceedings. It was not until the end of this era that English became re-established as the language used by all sections of society. By then, various French spelling forms had been taken over, e.g. *u* was replaced by *ou* in a word like *house* because of the different value attributed to *u* in French borrowings; and the *ch* sound of a word like *chin* (originally spelt with *c*) took on the French spelling of words such as *chamber*. By the time of Chaucer, the language began to look more like Modern English and would be to a large extent intelligible to the modern ear.

In the following period, *Early Modern English* (1450–1600), the pronunciation of the language became increasingly similar to that of today. A modern Londoner would have little difficulty in understanding the speech used in the plays performed at Shakespeare's *Globe*, although it would make a somewhat rustic impression on his ear. Nevertheless, he would notice that there was still considerable variation in the spelling forms used, to some extent in printed works (where the styles depended upon the conventions adopted by individual printers) but more particularly in the handwritten letters of individuals (who continued to spell largely according to their own phonetic principles and thus provided us with a good deal of information about contemporary pronunciation). It is not until the end of the 18th century that English began to sound more completely like the language we speak today. What is more, with the appearance of the great dictionaries of that century, the orthography was standardized into a form almost identical with our present one. However, even in the last two centuries, there have been notable pronunciation changes, which demonstrate that the sound system of the language is constantly undergoing evolution. The ambiguities of spelling that reflect fourteen centuries of linguistic history remain to puzzle the native user and to frustrate the foreign learner.

The Present Situation

With so many influences at work on the language for so long, it is hardly surprising that the pronunciation of English in Britain today presents an extremely complex picture. It is possible to discern three main causes for variation, relating to the speaker's regional origin, his place in society, and his generation.

Elements of regional differences of pronunciation are evident today, to such an extent that a cockney and a Glaswegian may still have serious difficulties of communication in speech. Englishmen are still readily able to identify the part of the country from which a person comes simply by listening to his speech, despite the fears of those who predict that dialect forms will soon disappear completely. Indeed, these regional forms of speech are often related to gross statements of regional prejudice— the Southerner who regards the speech of the Northerner as overblunt, and the Northerner who characterizes the speaker with a Southern accent as affected. Dialect differences of pronunciation are therefore still important both for reasons of intelligibility and also in social terms. It is worth remarking too that, of all the various accents of British English, that of the London region has developed most rapidly, the speech of the other regions remaining closer to the historical origins of the language.

But the pronunciation of English in Britain has also a more purely social significance. As has been stated, at one time the upper classes would speak French whereas the rest of the people spoke English. In more recent centuries, when English was in universal use, there emerged different types of pronunciation in any region relating to the speaker's position in society, e.g. the popular speech forms of the working man, full of the historical characteristics of the region, as opposed to the pronunciation used by the professional and upper classes, which was modified towards a general standard. It can be said that the notion of a socially prestigious standard of pronunciation arose explicitly in the 16th century, when grammarians began to recommend that the only acceptable form of pronunciation was that used in London and at the Court, i.e. the speech of educated people in the Southeast of England. Such a notion of standard pronunciation, based on social criteria, became increasingly accepted during the next three centuries, so that in the middle of the 19th century the philologist Alexander J Ellis was able to characterize it as 'received pronunciation' — a term which is used to this day (often in an abbreviated form as RP). A century ago, people of the ruling classes would pronounce English in the same way wherever they lived in Britain. This form of pronunciation had the advantage, therefore, of being widely intelligible. Moreover, it was important for the ambitious, who might wish to move upwards in society, to change their pronunciation. This was the sociolinguistic climate in which Bernard Shaw wrote his *Pygmalion*, a play which had a greater social significance at the time of its first production than it can possibly have now. In the first half of this century, this standard was adopted as a model by more and more of the population, despite vigorous opposition from a number of interests, notably the Poet Laureate, Robert Bridges, and his Society for Pure English, who advocated a standard based on a more Northern type. It was on the grounds of wide intelligibility that, in the 1930s, the BBC decided to adopt 'received pronunciation' as the form to be used by announcers. Indeed, the British public became so accustomed to this style of speech that they were suspicious of any attempt by the BBC to introduce news readers with a regional pronunciation. Moreover, the broadcasting media exposed more and more of the population to the Southern-based standard, with the result that a greater number of people began to use it, at least in a modified form.

Within the last twenty-five years, however, a considerable change of attitude seems to have taken place. The social divisions in the country have become noticeably less rigid, and the movement between classes has become easier. In particular, the young tend to reject the former 'received' pronunciation as the voice of outmoded authority, preferring new speech styles related to their own culture, such as the popular speech of London and Liverpool, as well as non-British accents such as those of America and Australia. It is too early to say whether this reaction by the young will have lasting consequences for the line of development of the traditional standard. But it is already clear that it is no longer possible to define the standard form as simply the variety of speech used by a particular section of society, since in a diluted form its use is more widespread than was the case even fifty years ago. It is no longer thought of as the 'best' pronunciation, but as one which has advantages on account of its wide intelligibility; it is for this reason that it remains the form taught to foreign learners, although it is not the simplest system for them to acquire. It continues to have as its basis the speech of the London region, but, being no longer socially determined, must rely for definition on phonetic and phonological criteria. In the remarks on the sound system given below, 20 vowels and 24 consonants are listed. In addition, certain characteristics of usage identify the accent, e.g. different vowels are used in *cat* and *calm*; the vowels of *cot* and *caught* are distinguished; the vowel of *book* is the same as that in *good* rather than that in *food*; an *r* is not pronounced in words like *farm*, despite the spelling, nor is the final *g* sounded in *sing*, etc. Other characteristics are of a more phonetic kind, i.e. are concerned with the quality of the sounds, e.g. the vowels of *day* and *go* are clearly diphthongal, though the more open onset typical of cockney is excluded; the two *l* sounds of *little* have different qualities, the first being 'clear' and the second 'dark,' thus excluding some Scottish accents where both are 'dark' and some Irish accents where both tend to be 'clear,' etc.

Nevertheless, even when a theoretical basis for the standard has been decided upon, account has to be taken of changes in pronunciation, especially in respect of vowels, reflected in the speech of different generations. Thus, older speakers (and those with conservative attitudes to life) use the vowel of *saw* in words like *off, clock*, and *cross*, rather than that of *hot*, which is of almost universal currency amongst the younger generation. Consonantal change is typified by the treatment of words beginning with *wh-*, such as *where, which* as opposed to *wear, witch.*

The distinction between such pairs began to be lost, on a large scale, in the London region as early as the 18th century. Today, it may be regarded as an optional extra to the system (often advocated by elocutionists) but almost totally abandoned by the young. The pronunciation shown in this dictionary represents the form used by the middle generations, avoiding the archaisms of the old and the possibly ephemeral eccentricities of the young.

It will be clear from what has been said that there remains a great diversity in the pronunciation of English in Britain, reflecting differences of region, social class, and generation. It is possible that modern facility of communication, in all its senses, is levelling out some of the extreme forms of pronunciation which even a century ago led to lack of intelligibility. But complete standardization is unlikely to be achieved. However far we proceed along the road to a standard pronunciation, there will always remain slight differences as between one individual and another, and between the various speech styles which an individual will use in different situations.

The Sound System

The infinite number of sounds produced in speaking a language can be reduced for linguistic purposes to a finite set of distinctive terms known as *phonemes.* Thus, the meaningful oppositions illustrated by the English series *seat, sit, set, sat*, etc., demonstrate the operation of vowel phonemes; similarly, *pin, tin, kin, bin, fin*, etc., exemplify the distinctive use of consonant phonemes. The realization of a phoneme may differ considerably according to its situation, e.g. the /p/ of *pin* is different from the /p/ of *nip*, the sound of /l/ in *leaf* differs from that in *feel.* But these differences of phonetic quality, of which the speaker is usually unaware, do not distinguish meaning. A phoneme may therefore be regarded as the smallest linguistic unit that can bring about a change of meaning. It should be noted, however, that English tolerates a certain degree of variability in the incidence of phonemes in particular words, even within the standard pronunciation, e.g. the short or long vowel in *room.* This dictionary recommends the form that has the most extensive current usage and is most widely understood. It is not a form which is intrinsically 'better' than any other nor can it be thought of as synonymous with 'educated': many highly educated people speak in a way that is easily identifiable as regional, e.g. with a type of Scottish, Northern, Southwestern, or even cockney English.

(a) Vowels

The standard Southern English form of pronunciation operates with 20 basic vowel phonemes:
5 long vowels: /iː/ *feed*, /uː/ *food*, /ɑː/ *calm*, /ɔː/ *saw*, /ɜː/ *bird* (where ː indicates length)
7 short vowels: /ɪ/ *bit*, /ɛ/ *bet*, /æ/ *bat*, /ʌ/ bud, /ɒ/ *hot*, /ʊ/ *foot*; and the unstressed vowel /ə/ as in the first syllable of *above*
8 diphthongs: /eɪ/ *late*, /aɪ/ *five*, /ɔɪ/ *boy*, /əʊ/ *home*, /aʊ/ *house*, /ɪə/ *dear*, /ɛə/ *fair*, /ʊə/ *poor*

Notes:

(i) The length of so-called long vowels and diphthongs varies considerably. Thus, the /iː/ sound of *seat* is very much shorter than those in *seed* and *sea*; the diphthong in *plate* is shorter than those in *played* or *play.* In such cases the duration of the vowel is a prime cue in distinguishing between a pair like *seat* and *seed* — more important than the final consonants. The actual length of long vowels and diphthongs is conditioned by the type of syllable closure involved: when a 'voiceless' consonant (e.g. /s/ or /t/) closes the syllable, the long vowel or diphthong is much shorter than when it is followed by a 'voiced' consonant (e.g. /z/ or /d/) or when it is an open syllable (e.g. in *see*). The result is that, in fact, the shortened 'long'

/iː/ of *seat* may be no longer than the short /ɪ/ of *sit*.
(ii) The vowels /iː, ɪ, uː, ʊ/ are traditionally paired as long and short. However, the difference of quality between /iː/ and /ɪ/ and between /uː/ and /ʊ/ is more important than that of length. In an opposition such as *bead — bid*, both length and quality operate as distinctive features; but, as was noted above, *seat* and *sit* exhibit an opposition which relies entirely upon a quality difference. In this dictionary, the notations /iː/ - /ɪ/ and /uː/ - /ʊ/ indicate the quality distinction by means of different symbols.
(iii) /ɪ/ frequently occurs in unstressed syllables, e.g. in *pocket, waited, savage*, etc. However, there is a tendency for the traditional /ɪ/ to be replaced by /ə/ in many cases, e.g. in words like *hopeless, goodness, secret*, etc. This use of /ə/, characteristic of regional forms of English, is extended by some even to cases like *boxers* v. *boxes*, where a meaningful opposition is lost. In this dictionary, the use of /ɪ/ in such cases, typical of the middle generations of English speakers, is retained.
(iv) Considerable variation between the use of /juː/ and /uː/ is found in words like *lurid, revolution, suit*, and the prefix *super-*. The /j/-less form, which is increasingly common in such cases, is the first form given in this dictionary.
(v) Similarly, it is possible to use /æ/ or /ɑː/ in the prefix *trans-* (e.g. *translation*) or the suffix *-graph* (e.g. *autograph*). The most common forms, shown in the dictionary, are /æ/ for the prefix and /ɑː/ for the suffix.
(vi) The old-fashioned /ɔː/ in words like *off, clock, cross*, is abandoned in favour of /ɒ/.
(vii) Since the distinction between *pour* and *paw* is now rarely made, /ɔː/ is shown in both.
(viii) The sequences /aɪə, aʊə/ as in *tyre, tower* have, for at least a century, been reduced to /aə/ or /ɑː/, so that for many speakers the opposition is lost. Since this merger is by no means completely established in the language, the full forms /aɪə, aʊə/ are retained.
(ix) Certain monosyllables, having a grammatical function, e.g. *and, was, for*, have different pronunciations according to whether or not they carry stress, e.g. stressed /ænd, wɒz, fɔː/, unstressed /ən(d), wəz, fə/. The citation (stressed) form is given first in the dictionary, although in normal discourse the weaker form has a much higher frequency of occurrence.

(b) Consonants

There are 24 consonant phonemes:
/p/ *pin*, /t/ *tin*, /k/ *kin*
/b/ *bay*, /d/ *day*, /g/ *gay*
/tʃ/ *choke*, /dʒ/ *joke*
/m/ *some*, /n/ *sun*, /ŋ/ *sung*
/r/ *red*, /l/ *led*
/f/ *fine*, /v/ *vine*, /θ/ *thing*, /ð/ *this*
/s/ *seal*, /z/ *zeal*, /ʃ/ *shoe*, /ʒ/ *measure*, /h/ *hat*
/w/ *wet*, /j/ *yet*

Note:

(i) Some consonant phonemes have a restricted distribution, e.g. /ŋ/ occurs only in syllable-final positions; /ʒ/ occurs typically only in medial positions. In the case of words borrowed comparatively recently from French, such as *prestige, beige, camouflage*, both /ʒ/ and /dʒ/ are possible, the more common form being given in the dictionary.
(ii) Words ending in *r*, e.g. *father, far*, have no /r/ in the pronunciation when a consonant or a pause follows. However, it is normal for a 'linking' /r/ to be pronounced when a vowel follows, e.g. in *father and mother, far off*. (This usage is extended by many speakers to cases where no *r* exists in the spelling, e.g. *the idea* /r/ *of it*.)
(iii) Variant pronunciations occur in words like *issue* (/sj/ or /ʃ/), *actual* (/tj/ or /tʃ/). The commonest form is given.
(iv) /l/ and /n/, in particular, are frequently sounded as syllabic, without an accompanying vowel. Such cases are shown with raised ᵊ, e.g. *mutton* /ˈmʌtᵊn/.

(c) Stress

What is here referred to as 'stress,' for the sake of brevity, is in English a complex of several factors, including stress (i.e. intensity for the speaker and loudness for the listener), pitch, quality (some sounds being more prominent to the listener than others), and length. The effect of this combination of factors is to render a syllable more or less prominent amongst its neighbours. The situation of the stressed syllable has always been an important feature of English pronunciation both in the word and in connected speech. Indeed, there are some pairs of words that are distinguished entirely or mainly by the placing of the stress-accent, e.g. *insult* (*vb.*) v. *insult* (*n.*), *object* (*vb.*) v. *object* (*n.*). In short words, there is usually only one stress-accent, e.g. *over* and *above*. This is shown by placing before the stressed syllable, e.g. /ˈəʊvə/ and /əˈbʌv/. However, in addition to this type of primary (tonic) stress, there may occur secondary stresses, e.g. *consideration*, where the secondary stress on *-sid-* is shown by ˌ before the syllable e.g. /kənˌsɪdəˈreɪʃən/.

The stress patterns given in the dictionary will always be those of the isolate, predicative forms, although in the case of double-stressed words and compounds there may be a shift of primary and secondary stressing when the word or compound is used attributively, e.g. *afternoon* (predicative) /ˌ--ˈ-/; but attributive in *afternoon tea* /ˌ--ˈ-/.

Finally, as was the case with vowels and, to a lesser extent with consonants, word stress patterns are liable to change in time; e.g. *character* was once stressed on the second syllable, whereas now the first syllable carries the stress-accent. Today, some instability of stressing may be observed in certain words, e.g. *controversy* (ˈkɒntrəˌvɜːsɪ, kənˈtrɒvəsɪ). There are also stressing variants that are characteristic of regional forms of English, e.g. Scottish English *realize* with /-ˈ-/ rather than the Southern /ˈ--/. As with the sounds, the most common Southern form is given.

Selected Bibliography

D C Brazil, *The Communicative Value of Intonation* (Birmingham University, ELR), 1985.
A Campbell, *Old English Grammar* (Oxford University Press), 1959.
E J Dobson, *English Pronunciation 1500–1700* (Oxford University Press), 1957.
A C Gimson, *An Introduction to the Pronunciation of English* (Edward Arnold), 3rd edition 1980.
D Jones, *The Pronunciation of English* (Cambridge University Press), 4th edition 1956.
D Jones, *An English Pronouncing Dictionary*, ed. A C Gimson (Dent), 14th edition 1977.
R Kingdon, *Groundwork of English Stress* (Longman), 1958.
J S Wells, *Longman Pronunciation Dictionary* (Longman), 1990.
H C Wyld, *A History of Modern Colloquial English* (Blackwell), 3rd edition 1936.

The Development of English as a World Language

The Making of English

by David Brazil

English Around the World

by A J Aitken, S R R Allsopp, R K Bansal, D Brazil, R J Gregg, L W Lanham, T H Long, Harold Orton, J M Sinclair, John Spencer, Loreto Todd, and G A Wilkes

Over the last five hundred years, the English language, formerly the language of a mere five or six million people living within the confines of the British Isles, has expanded to become the everyday speech of over three hundred million. Among the results of this expansion is the present status of English as the mother tongue of most of the inhabitants of the vast ethnically diverse society of the United States of America and as the most important second language of some fifty millions in Southern Asia and a number of the new nations of Africa. The expansion has, however, for practical purposes been a feature of the most recent of the three major phases of development into which linguistic scholarship customarily divides the recorded history of the language. Although our principal concern here is with that geographical extension that has led to the label 'English' being applied to many simultaneously existing varieties round the world, we can achieve a proper perspective only if we consider briefly the historical dimension of its variation.

'New English' or 'Modern English', which has been so pre-eminently an article for export, is distinguished from the earlier variety, 'Middle English', and the latter from the still earlier variety 'Old English'. The three periods are separated by two watersheds, one associated with the Norman Conquest, and the other with those complex developments to which historians apply the terms Renaissance and Reformation. At each of these times there occurred marked accelerations in the process of continuous change that all living language is subject to. The response of the language to historical pressures resulted on each occasion in the emergence of a form significantly different from that which preceded it, so that Old English must now be learned by the native speaker of English almost as a foreign language, and Middle English, the language of Chaucer and Langland, is today fully intelligible only to the specialist scholar.

Old English was the language of the heathen invaders who began to appear along the Eastern coast of Britain in the third century A.D., and who, after the withdrawal of the Roman legions, settled all but the North and West, where a Celtic language continued to be used. They were by no means homogeneous culturally, speaking different dialects of a common Germanic tongue, and the geographical disposition which tradition assigns to them, the Jutes in the Southeast, the Saxons in Wessex, and the two major divisions of the Angles in the Midlands and the North, set up at the outset many of the regional differences that still persist in the popular speech of the British Isles.

The earliest written records date from after the Christian conversion of the English instigated by Pope Gregory in or around 597. The West Saxon dialect, which is most often used in the texts that survive, acquired a special status as a literary medium. By this time, the warlike habits of the English had, for the most part, given way to agricultural pursuits, and one can create a pleasant, if somewhat romanticized, picture of their agrarian life from a stock of words that have often been spoken of approvingly as 'short', 'simple', and 'Anglo-Saxon' — eg *man* and *child*; *eat*, *drink*, and *sleep*; *love* and *hate*; *land*, *harvest*, and *crops*.

Old English had a facility, comparable with that of modern German, for meeting the need for new vocabulary by compounding or redefining existing words: *daisy* is picturesquely derived from 'day's eye' and *nostril* from 'nose hole'. When the conversion to Christianity created new needs, many of these were supplied from indigenous resources. Thus *Easter* was adopted from the pagan vocabulary and applied to the new Christian festival while the compound *godspell* (good news) was preferred to the Latin *evangelium*. Native material did not supply all the needs, however, and it was the Latin of the new clerics that provided the first large-scale input of foreign loans we know of. Apart from words of obvious ecclesiastical significance, like *priest*, *monk*, *hymn*, and *altar*, others like *master* and *grammar*, *plaster* and *fever*, reflect the Church's commitment to learning and medical care.

The arrival of the Vikings, who, until King Alfred's victory in 878, threatened to subjugate the newly Christianized English, resulted in further augmentation of the vocabulary. But the language they spoke, which had a strong influence upon English speech, particularly in the Danelaw, the area lying to the northeast of a line drawn from Chester to London, was closely related to it. The results of its admixture were more subtle and elusive. Pairs of words, differentiated by a single sound, like *skirt* and *shirt*, *whole* and *hale*, have survived. Instead of a quasi-technical vocabulary associated with a new field of interest or endeavour, we have Old Norse borrowings that are every bit as commonplace as native Old English words: *husband*, *ugly*, *call*, *want*, and, most surprisingly, the pronouns *they*, *them*, and *their* to go alongside Old English *he*, *him*, and *her*.

The effects of this kind of merging are not evident until we come to examine texts of the early Middle English period, and its thoroughness is such that we cannot always be sure to which of the two Germanic languages a particular word should be traced.

When William, Duke of Normandy, defeated the English king at Hastings in 1066, he inaugurated a period of rule by French-speaking kings and of pervasive domination by a nobility and clergy whose interests were predominantly in things French. Until King John lost the last of the continental possessions in 1205, Norman French was the language of the Court, of business, and of lay culture, while Latin remained the ecclesiastical language. English seems virtually to have been reduced to the role of a patois. Further contact with France, through royal marriages and through participation in the wider European cultural scene, of which French was the unchallenged medium, ensured that that language retained its privileged position in the upper reaches of society right up to Chaucer's time, but alongside this the thirteenth century saw a gradual reinstatement of English.

By this time, the language had undergone radical changes, some of which can be directly related to the long break in the literary tradition. The elaborate inflection system that had been so conspicuous a feature of Old English, manifested, for instance, in the six different forms of the noun *stan* (stone), may well have been undergoing simplification in the spoken language before the Norman Conquest. Absence of the conservative influence of the written form would undoubtedly accelerate the process: although some vestiges of inflectional endings survive until after Chaucer's time, Middle English is essentially without this refinement. Instead, the relations between content words are specified by a freer use of prepositions. Another change was largely due to the fact that the French-trained scribes, who now replaced those trained in the Old English tradition, introduced new orthographic conventions and in so doing were responsible for much of the inconsistency for which modern English spelling is notorious. (Cf. Professor Gimson's comments, *The Pronunciation of British English*, p. xxii.) New characters — k, g, q, v, w, z — were brought into use. As a consequence, the two pronunciations of Old English 'c' could now be differentiated, as in the modern spelling of *king* (from *cyning*) and *choose* (from *ceosan*). But the retention of 'c' in words like *cat* and its use to represent /s/ in *nice* have left the confusing results: *king, can, cent.* The characteristic Old English letters þ and ð were gradually replaced by *th*, and the loss of ʒ resulted in the sound it represented (a sound which was itself subsequently lost) being spelt as *gh* in words like *night, daughter*, and *laugh*. Finally, because of the similarity of a number of characters such as *u, v, n, m*, and *w* in the Carolingian script used by the scribes, *u* was replaced by *o* in many words like *come, son*, and *wonder*.

But by far the most noticeable feature of English, as it re-emerges after the period of the supremacy of French, was the very large number of French words that had been absorbed into the common stock. Many of these can be sorted into sets that correspond with activities in which the indigenous English speakers are thought to have played only minor parts. For instance, they include much of the modern vocabulary of government and law, of ecclesiastical and military matters, of art, learning, and medicine. Other words reflect an upper-class preoccupation with fashion, polite social life, and refined feeding habits. A measure of the degree of assimilation of the new French words is the speed of their occurrence in derivatives, often taking English endings as in *gently* and *gentleness*, and forming hybrid compounds like *gentleman*. The early borrowings were naturally from Norman French, but later the source was predominantly the culturally more prestigious dialect of Central France. The borrowing, at different times, of related words from both dialects provided such differentiated forms as *cattle* and *chattel, warden* and *guard*. Generally, the massive accession of loan words seems to have inhibited the language's facility for creating new, self-explanatory compounds, a practice that was not revived extensively until the nineteenth century, when scientific and technological advances generated new needs.

A characteristic of Middle English was its very considerable regional variation. Contemporary writers testify that the speech of one area was frequently unintelligible to inhabitants of another. Amid the confusion, it is possible to distinguish five major areas: the North, extending as far as the Humber; the East and West Midlands, together extending from the Humber to the Thames; the South; and Kent. Each of these is represented in some part of the literary output that has survived, a situation that contrasts with the near monopoly of West Saxon as a literary dialect in the earlier, Old English, period. The end of the fourteenth century, however, saw the rise of Standard English, a result largely of the commercial supremacy of the East Midlands. In particular the growing importance of London as a political, judicial, social, and intellectual centre led to the elevation of one particular variety of the East Midland dialect, namely London English, to a position of prestige that it has enjoyed ever since. It was this dialect that was to be used overwhelmingly when the invention of printing opened up unprecedented opportunities for disseminating the written word.

The printing press was one of the factors that, around 1500, resulted in the second great change in English. The need and the possibility of what we can properly think of as mass circulation placed a high premium on the use of the vernacular. As in other parts of Europe, the latter made incursions into territories in which Latin had formerly held sway: law, medicine, and religion in particular. And one aspect of the revival of interest in classical antiquity was the very considerable translating activity that gave Shakespeare, for instance, with his 'little Latin and less Greek', access to much of the classical heritage. Engagement with Latin and Greek had effects upon English — upon both vocabulary and grammar. The effects on vocabulary were more immediately noticeable and led to a further accession of new words, often those of a learned and polysyllabic kind, which, when carried to excess, earned contemporary castigation as 'inkhorn' terms. In this way, the classical experience may be said to have been a potent instrument of change. Its effect upon grammar, though less immediate, was, by contrast, conservative.

The increasing use of English in more scholarly contexts after 1500 resulted in misgivings about its ability to survive. Compared with the fixity and predictability of Ciceronian Latin — by now a well and truly 'dead' language — it seemed all too subject to change. The desire to 'fix' English, so that matter expressed in it would have the same chances of survival as that expressed in the ancient languages, led to attempts by grammarians to legislate for the user; the basis of their legislation was, understandably, the well-known syntax of Latin. A similar concern for durability and respectability underlay the new preoccupation with orthography. Early spelling reformers, especially printers, sought to replace the largely idiosyncratic practices that had sufficed in the preprinting era with a common system that seemed to them to be related to the sound system in a more consistent way. They were not helped in this enterprise—an enterprise that, incidentally, has continued to exercise the minds of language teachers ever since—by the fact that some of the sounds were themselves currently undergoing major changes. A complex process that led to an altered distribution of all the long vowels of English, known to philologists as the Great Vowel Shift, began in the latter part of the Middle English period but was not completed until after Shakespeare's time. For his audiences *Rome* rhymed with *room*, and *raisin* with *reason*.

In bringing this sketch of the development of English up to the beginning of the Modern English period, we have already reached the stage where its internal history and its external history react upon each other. The astonishing — and as some thought — excessive openness of English to new vocabulary resulted in the adoption of words not only from every major European language, but also from the exotic languages of remoter lands to which it was now being carried. In the following paragraphs we note something of the effects of local languages and local conditions upon the speech of English-speaking settlers across the world; they were felt not only in vocabulary, but in grammar and pronunciation also. An important aspect of the more recent development of British English has been its absorption of features from the new regional varieties to which geographical dispersion gave rise. Since no account of language development, however brief, can legitimately omit reference to attitudes, we must recognize that this last tendency has by no means always been welcomed by purists. And if a desire to protect the home-grown product from the effects of outside interference is questionable, the wish to prescribe standards for the much greater number of people who speak English outside the British Isles is even more so.

In the various forms that Standard English now takes,

there are, in fact, only very slight differences in grammar, and the variations in pronunciation—the numerous local accents—represent no insuperable barrier to intelligibility, however forcibly they may impress themselves upon the listener. As for vocabulary, there is a central core of ordinary, most frequently used words that all geographically distinguished varieties of the standard language share. There is also a shared and continually growing lexicon of highly specialized and technical terms. Between these two lies a considerable body of moderately common words and idioms, and it is here that the major national and local distinctions are to be found: Americanisms, Australianisms, Scotticisms, and so on, all having their own peculiarities of usage.

The differences and distinctions we find in the use of English round the world seem hardly likely to wither away. Present conditions seem rather to indicate a gradual increase. Common sense seems to suggest willing acceptance of them as natural and interesting aspects of the language and of the individualities of the people who use it.

The Regional Dialects of England

The question of the existence of a standard pronunciation of English has been the occasion for controversy nowhere more than in the context of discussions of the local and social varieties of the language that coexist within England. Before World War II many believed that a standard form did exist but that it was a class dialect rather than a regional one, flourishing in the public schools, the older universities, the law courts, the higher ranks of the armed forces and the civil service, the BBC, and of course the Royal Court. Having a well-recognized sound system, it was also characterized by the use of a pleasing voice quality, a rhythmical unhurried speech tempo, and a good articulation that was not staccato or too precise and lacked a glottal stop or any trace of regional intonation. This they called 'Received Pronunciation' or RP.

Between the World Wars, linguistic historians recognized the existence of modified forms of RP. Having penetrated into the provinces, the socially prestigious speech of London and the Home Counties was modified by local speech habits, which differed from county to county and even from town to town. These modified varieties have since achieved much greater prominence and standing partly through changed attitudes to English used in broadcasts and partly through the emergence of an influential group from the provincial grammar schools and universities, who have been inclined to resent the stigmatization of their own regional accents. A widely held belief that any pronunciation is good provided it is intelligible and appropriate to its geographical context has also perhaps helped, though a reaction, in the form of a returning preference for RP, is now discernible.

The sounds of RP vary in their realizations within acceptable limits. They also undergo changes. Recently these changes have been less extensive and have been rather obscured by phonological features of educated London English. Nevertheless, the traditional long /ɔː/ before /s/, /f/, and /θ/, as in *cross, off,* and *cloth,* has now given way to the more open vowel /ɒ/; the long /ɑː/ that developed before the same sounds, as in *pass, path,* and *chaff,* has been extended by some speakers to other words such as *plastic, mass,* and *raffia*; the *-ing* of present participles and verbal nouns (*hunting, shooting*) has recovered its /ŋ/; and initial *wh-*, as in *white,* often persists as /hw/.

Among modern trends that seem definitely attributable to the influence of London English is the treatment of the vowels /ɛ/ and /æ/, which, in words like *set* and *sat,* may sound very similar. Many young people in the public eye tend in their speech to retract /æ/ to a type of /a/ similar to a sound long assumed to characterize Northern and Midland English. In so doing they reduce the distinction from the /ʌ/ of hut, a sound very similar in quality to /a/. Other London traits involve the pronunciation of /əʊ/ in *boat* rather like /u/, the diphthongization of /iː/ and /uː/, as in *feet* and *boot,* and the representation of /aʊ/ in *mouse* and /aɪ/ in *mice* with an advanced and a retracted first element respectively.

Some of the sounds that serve to differentiate the regional dialects of England can be traced back to Old English. Initial *wh-* is still a vigorous /hw/ in Northumbrian speech; in South Lancashire and the West Midlands a characteristic /g/ ends words like *ring* and *long*; in Northumberland /l/ is clear (like the first *l* in *little*) in all positions, while further south it becomes darker (like the second *l* in *little*) until it almost becomes /u/ in the Home Counties. In the eastern part of the country /r/ before a consonant disappears or is faintly articulated (farm, fort), in the south and west it is pronounced with the tongue turned back or reverted, and in Northumbria it is characteristically 'throaty' (the Northumberland burr). The pronunciation of the *u* of *cup* and *bun* as /u/, as in Standard English *pull,* is a trait commonly found in dialects of much of the north of England (except for the extreme northeast). The absence of initial /h/ is frequently assumed to characterize regional dialects generally; it is, however, still preserved in the extreme north, in East Anglia and Essex, and in Somerset and Wiltshire.

Historical factors have conditioned the lexicon and grammar of the modified forms of Standard English as well as their sounds. Many educated northerners do not hesitate to use local vernacular items like *beck, burn,* and *gill* (streams). *Bonny* and *canny* (agreeable) are frequently encountered, as are *body* (a person), *lad, lass, pikelet* (a crumpet), and *scallion* (a spring onion). The word stock of large parts of Northern England, the East Midlands, and East Anglia was greatly enriched as a result of the Viking invasions. Local words like *band* (string), *lop* (flea), *nay, sile, stoop* (a post) and *teem* (pour) come from this source. The ubiquity of *bairn* is due to its double descent from both the Old English and the Old Norse word for *child.* The extent of the choice that may be provided by dialectal variants can be illustrated by the variety of the terms *drawing room, front room, lounge, parlour,* and *sitting room*; and tea may be *made, brewed, mashed, scalded,* or *steeped.*

Dialect usages characteristic of the regions also seem sometimes to spread into varieties of the language that are nearer to high prestige forms. Educated Northerners may use expressions like *I'll be away then*; *I want this letter posting*; *The dog wants out*; and *The boy got wrong off* (was punished by) *his father.*

Local historical dialects in England are disappearing faster than ever before, regional peculiarities of pronunciation being supplanted by the sounds of RP or of one of its locally modified varieties. Provincial vocabulary seems, however, more likely to survive, except for the names of things that have themselves become obsolete, such as terms relating to equipment used for thatching harvesting, or blacksmithing.

The English of Scotland

Until the seventeenth century the national literary and spoken language of Scotland was the Northern English dialect known as Older Scots, the ancestor of the modern dialects of the Lowlands, but with the accession of the Stuarts to the English throne in 1603 this began to give way to Standard English as the language of writing. The use of something approximating to educated Standard English as the spoken language of polite society began a little later. But this new Scottish English was shaped and modified by the native Scots that the gentry and intelligentsia had previously spoken. The distinctiveness of the Scots variety of present-day Standard English is attributable to this underlying native tradition.

Its peculiarities include the free use of a very considerable body of Scots vocabulary. Many words associated with special cultural features of Scottish society, like *laird, kirk, ceilidh,* and *Hogmanay,* are as likely to be used by anyone who writes or talks of Scotland as they are by a Scotsman and are hardly to be considered peculiarities of Scottish usage. Neither are the many Scotticisms that have passed into general English usage, largely through the influence of Burns, Scott, and Carlyle, such as *cuddle, eerie, gloaming,* and *greed* (all from Old English) and *clan, pet, slogan,* and *whisky* (from Gaelic). More peculiarly Scottish are those native locutions with which speakers are apt to pepper their English, especially when adopting an informal or explicitly Scottish role: *He's a right old sweetiewife*; *It's back to auld claes* (old clothes) *and parritch* (porridge) *tomorrow; like a hen on a het* (hot) *girdle*; or similarly used 'couthy' words like *dreich, peely-wally,* and *scunner.* But in addition to such obvious and deliberate Scotticisms, most Scottish speakers of English also employ usages the Scottishness of which they may be scarcely aware of: *Is that you away then*? (Are you about to leave?); *I put her gas at a peep* (I deflated her); *to come up one's back* (occur to one), and, of course, the ubiquitous preposition *outwith.*

The grammar of spoken Scottish English has one or two minor rules of its own, such as the avoidance of *isn't* and *won't,* for which *'s not* and *'ll not* are regularly substituted, and the use of the form *mines* in *that's mines.*

The variety is most Scottish, however, in its pronunciation. Characteristic forms are /lənθ/ and /strɛnθ/ (for *length* and *strength*), and /lʌdʒ/ and /ˈlʌdʒər/ (for *lodge* and *lodger*); the 'full' pronunciation of items like *raspberry, Wednesday,* and *tortoise*; and disyllabic versions of words like *elm, burn,* and *whirl.* Many sounds, particularly the vowels and *wh-, r,* and *l* have special Scottish pronunciations, and there is an extra consonant, /x/, heard in words like *loch, Buchan,* and *Brechin.* Whereas *aunt* and *ant* are usually pronounced alike, *oar, or,* and *awe,* which are indistinguishable in the speech of London and certain other kinds of English, are quite distinct in Scots.

Scottish English is exceptional among other kinds of English in having no true long vowels: the vowel in *seed* and *seat* is short. On the other hand, there is marked lengthening of certain vowels in particular positions: the verb *close* ending with /z/ has a much longer vowel than the adjective *close* which ends in /s/. Related to this is the long diphthong in words like *five* and *rise,* which can be compared with the short diphthong in *fife* and *rice.* This last phenomenon, which is observable also in Ulster Scots (Scotch-Irish standard speech), can be shown to result from sound changes occurring around the year 1600.

Apart from the educated Scottish English to which the foregoing notes apply, many other types exist, particularly among rural speakers, who have additional dialect features in their pronunciations. Working-class people in Glasgow and Edinburgh also have features that are widely regarded, by speakers who do not have them, as debased or slovenly. They include pronunciation habits like the tendency to replace noninitial /p/, /k/, or /t/ by the glottal stop, and special usages of vocabulary and grammar: *You'll be away to the bingo, eh, no*?; *She's awfie tattie-peelin* (stuck-up); *I shouldnae never went.* At the other extreme are the varieties of Scottish speech that have been strongly influenced by the RP of the Scottish gentry and by broadcasting, of which the 'Morningside' and 'Kelvinside' types are regarded by many Scots as comical. Yet another set of distinguishing features separates the 'Highland English' and 'Island English' from all these dialects, which share a typically Lowland provenance. The most important of such features are those that derive from speech habits originally native to Scottish Gaelic and from the fact that English was for so long a 'schoolbook' language in the Highlands and Islands.

The influence of the earlier Celtic tongue is by and large less noticeable in the English used in Wales. However, its effect on Irish English merits greater attention.

Irish English

All the varieties of English currently heard in Ireland have their origins in the Elizabethan period. The English that developed in the Pale around Dublin at that time is frequently called Anglo-Irish. It was based mainly on the northwest Midland dialects of England. This was the type of English that, encroaching everywhere on the native Gaelic, spread south and west and as far north as the Ulster border. The survival of Gaelic dialects there stopped its advance and separated it from a northern version of Anglo-Irish, which had similarly originated in the English Midlands but entered Ireland by way of Belfast and the Lagan valley. The differences that are nowadays observable between the northern and southern dialects arise for the most part from differences in the substratum of Gaelic speech.

Similarities include many characteristically Irish vocabulary items that are widely distributed throughout the whole island: *blarney, galore, slug* (swig, drink), *smithereens,* and *twig* (to understand, find out) are all of Gaelic origin. Some of the special vocabulary — *banshee* and *keen* (lament for the dead), for instance — is naturally related to Irish folk culture and has thus attained wider currency. Syntactic peculiarities shared by North and South are exemplified in: *He is just after finishing his work*; *She has a desperate cold on her*; *I have a terrible drooth* (drought) *on me* (I am very thirsty); *I wonder will she go.* All these arise from a literal translation of the Gaelic. Among the distinctive phonological features is the universal retention of final and preconsonantal /r/, which has a semivocalic articulation that seems to have arisen in Elizabethan times. Irish English further agrees in giving the lateral /l/ a 'bright' or 'clear' resonance as in French. 'Pure' long vowels generally occur where many other varieties of English have diphthongs: thus /deː/ is preferred to /deɪ/ as a pronunciation of *day,* and /goː/ to /gəʊ/ for *go.* The vowel in words like *pat* and *mat* is pronounced with the tongue lower in the mouth than in most other regional types. The slight lip-rounding observable everywhere in the Irish English vowel in words like *putt* is paralleled in some Northern English dialects.

Northern Anglo-Irish was considerably influenced by its contacts with Lowland Scottish dialects that were introduced into Ulster during the Jacobean period. The influence has been sufficiently strong to give rise to the expression *Scotch Irish,* used originally in North America to distinguish all types of Ulster accents from the so-called southern Irish brogue. Much of the distinctive vocabulary of the North is of Scottish origin. It includes *byre* (cow house), *corn* (oats), *dander* or *danner* (stroll), *lift* (steal), and *mind* (remember). Ulster speakers resemble some Scots also in pronouncing words like *too* or *prove* with a very advanced central vowel somewhat like that in the French word *tu*.

The southern variety is often distinguished from that of the north by the use of a different dialectal form, or set of forms, for a particular notion. Thus the concept 'left-handed' — including all the social and superstitious implications proper to the Irish environment — is expressed by *clootie*, *flyuggy*, etc., in the north, but by *kittagh*, *kittogue*, etc., in the south. The most conspicuous pronunciation trait of the south is the treatment of the fricatives /θ/ and /ð/, a dental variety of /t/ or /d/ being used at the beginning of words like *thin* and *then*. These sounds are, however, quite distinct from the alveolar /t/ and /d/ that are regularly used in *tin* and *den*. Ulster speakers normally have the usual English fricatives.

An interesting feature of the English of most parts of Ireland is the survival of pronunciations characteristic of earlier stages in the development of the language in England. We can instance /teː/ (*tea*), /ˈdeːsənt/ (*decent*), /kürs/ (*course*), /ˈlɑːndrɪ/ (*laundry*), and /ˈsoːdʒər/ (*soldier*).

American English

The development of English in the United States may be traced in three historical stages. The first of these, the colonial period, dates from the settlement of Jamestown in 1607 (followed shortly, in 1620, by the arrival of the Puritans in New England) to about 1790, the date of the ratification of the Constitution of an independent United States. The settlers in Virginia and New England spoke a seventeenth-century English that was predominantly that of the southern counties of England. Although regional dialects never developed the distinctive characteristics they have in England, some of the local variation that does exist can be traced to this time. Subsequent settlement of the Middle Atlantic States was influenced by the ideals of William Penn, and the population of these areas, in particular colonial Pennsylvania, was less uniformly Anglo-Saxon in origin. The presence there of a large number of immigrants from Ulster and, after an agreement made with Penn in 1683, of Palatinate Germans, has been a factor of continuing linguistic significance.

The second stage of development runs from 1790 to about the time of the Civil War (1860). This period saw two important developments. There was an expansion southwards and westwards from the thirteen original Atlantic colonies, across the Appalachian Mountains that had temporarily confined them, and on to the Pacific. In addition, new waves of immigrants arrived, this time from Ireland, after the famine of 1845, and from Germany after 1848. At the end of this period, the population was still predominantly British by origin, as it had been at the beginning, but it now included a higher proportion of other northern European immigrants.

The most recent phase, from about 1860 to the present, witnessed massive immigration from southern Europe and from the Slavonic countries. This last development seems to have had little effect on American English with the exception of New York and its environs, where certain influences on speech and vocabulary are discernible.

The first of these three periods is responsible for certain archaisms that survive in American English. Forms like *gotten* (the past participle of *get*), *sick*, with its general instead of its restrictive sense, and *I guess* meaning *I suppose*, exemplify this linguistic conservatism, the latter having been standard in England as early as the fourteenth century. Such evidences of conservatism are, however, far less representative than developments that show the facility of the language for innovation. Contemporary American speech differs as much from the language of the colonists as modern British English differs from the seventeenth- and eighteenth-century speech of England.

The vocabulary of American English began to change at first contact with the new environment. Words were borrowed from Indians and from other Europeans, and native English words were adapted to new meanings. From the Indian languages came a number of words for flora and fauna and other terms relating to Indian life: *canoe, caucus, hickory, hominy, moccasin, opossum, pecan, raccoon, skunk, squash* (a vegetable marrow), *tapioca*, and *toboggan*. From Dutch settlers the colonists borrowed *boss, cookie*, and *coleslaw*, and from the French *chowder* and *bureau*. Perhaps the most famous example of an existing English word being borrowed for a new use is *corn*, a development that occurred when the adjective was dropped from the colonists' original phrase, *Indian corn*. The term *maize* entered British English as a Spanish loan word at the same time as the specialized use of *corn* was becoming established in America.

The pattern of settlement in the seventeenth and eighteenth centuries has left its mark on the dialects of present-day America. Three large speech areas are conventionally distinguished: Northern (New England and New York State), Midland (Pennsylvania and New Jersey and along the Blue Ridge Mountains south to Georgia), and Southern (southern Delaware and Virginia along the Atlantic coast and west to the foothills in the Carolinas and Georgia). Within these large areas, eighteen dialects have been identified. Discussion of the sound patterns of American English involves reference not only to the way they differ from British English but also consideration of how the dialects — at least the three major ones — differ from each other.

The retention of final and preconsonantal /r/, which tends to be dropped in England, for instance, is characteristic of Midland American but is not a feature of Eastern New England or of all Southern dialects. Another feature of American speech, sometimes wrongly assumed to characterize all dialects, is the vowel /æ/ in such words as *fast, laugh, grass*, etc. In Eastern New England and Virginia, a so-called broad *a* /ɑ/ is often used, the quality of which more closely resembles that of the comparable vowel in southern British English. A distinction that does hold between British English and most American English is in the treatment of *o*, which American English tends to make unrounded as /ɑ/ in such words as *rob, stop*, and *hop*. This, like the use of /iː/ in *either* and *neither*, is a survival of the pronunciation that was current in Britain at the time of colonization. Finally, we may note the tendency, which has increased in America in recent years, to pronounce words like *duke, new*, and *Tuesday* with /uː/ instead of /juː/, in sharp contrast with British usage.

Two further characteristics that differentiate much American speech from British may be noted. One is that the Northern American dialects have less variety in pitch-pattern. The second is the preservation of the secondary accent in polysyllabic words, especially those ending in *-ory, -ary*, or *-ery*. The contrast with British pronunciation in *ordinary, dictionary, secretary, temporary*, etc., is noticeable in all American speech.

Many specific differences between American and British English were listed by H L Mencken in *The American Language* (first edition 1919). Since the publication of that book, various influences have operated to reduce these differences, among them films, radio, television, and the growth since the 1950s and 1960s of an international youth culture grounded in a common popular music (rock). Most often, resulting changes have been in favour of terminology originating in America. Nevertheless, much of the diversity represented by Mencken's list still exists:

US	UK
apartment	flat
baby carriage	pram
broiled (meat)	grilled
candy	sweets
cookie	biscuit
cotton (absorbent)	cotton wool
daylight-saving time	summer time
druggist	chemist
elevator	lift
installment plan	hire-purchase
oatmeal (boiled)	porridge
second floor	first floor
sidewalk	pavement
spigot (or faucet)	tap
suspenders (men's)	braces
undershirt	vest or singlet
water heater	geyser
checkers (game)	draughts
deck (cards)	pack
gasoline, gas	petrol
hood (car)	bonnet
intermission (theatre)	interval
legal holiday	bank holiday

Finally, there are minor differences between preferred spellings. Among them are the American preference for *-er* in *center, fiber,* and *theater*; *-or* in *honor, color, humor*; *-se* instead of *-ce* in *defense* and *offense*; and undoubled intervocalic consonants in certain words such as *jeweler, marvelous,* and *traveling.* The majority of these differences are traceable to the lexicographer Noah Webster's interest in spelling reform. Although his earlier writings on the subject argued for radical changes based on phonetic spelling, he gradually modified his view. The system used in his American Dictionary (1828) was adopted in America and accounts for most of the distinguishing features of modern American orthography.

Canadian English

The early history of Canadian English resembles that of American English. In the early days of settlement the language used was that of contemporary Britain. Features have persisted from this time, supplying a conservative element in present-day speech. Innovations, subsequently made in response to the new environment, led to differentiation that eventually produced a distinctive brand of English that is said to sound like American to Britons and like British to Americans. After the War of American Independence a political boundary separating Canada from the United States encouraged linguistic differentiation. Since then, the continuous contacts to the south on the one hand and the uninterrupted flow of immigrants to Canada from Britain on the other have maintained cultural and linguistic links with both countries.

Many additions to the lexicon resulted from the contacts the Canadians made with the various indigenous Indian and Eskimo peoples, as well as the languages of other groups of settlers from many parts of the Old World. In pioneer days they borrowed many words from Canadian French: *bateau* (flat-bottomed riverboat), *brulé* (area of forest destroyed by fire), *coureur de bois, habitant* (a French Canadian, esp. a farmer), *mush* (a command to sled dogs, from French *marché!*), *charivari* or *shivaree,* and *snye* (side channel of a river, from Canadian French *chenail*). More recent borrowings from Canadian French include *anglophone* and *francophone* (referring respectively to English and French speakers) and *tuque* (a long knitted woollen cap, as worn by skiers).

From the native Indian languages came many terms, including the following ultimately from Algonquian sources in Eastern and Central Canada: *babiche* (thongs of rawhide), *bogan,* otherwise *pokelogan* or *logan* (a sluggish sidestream), *carcajou, caribou, kinnikinnick, muskeg, pemmican,* and *totem.* The contributions of the languages of British Columbia frequently came in through the Chinook Jargon, an Indian-based trade or contact language current in pioneer days west of the Rockies and as far north as the Yukon. Among them were: *chuck* (a body of water), *klahanie* (the great outdoors), *mowitch* (deer), and *tillicum* (friend). The Tlingit language has contributed *hooch,* shortened from *hootchinoo,* which has now passed into general English. From Eskimo Canadian English acquired *anorak, Inuit* (Eskimo), *komatik, malamute, mukluk, Nanook, parka, igloo,* and *kayak.*

Educated Canadian English probably still reflects the spoken norms of the eighteenth century to a large extent. It shares with Midland American the conservative habit of articulating final and preconsonantal /r/. Another early feature is the voicing of medial /t/ in words like *better, patio,* and *little* ('bɛdər/, /'pædiou/, /'lɪdᵊl/); and yet another is the loss of /t/ following /n/, as in *winter* /'wɪnər/ and *Toronto* /'trɑnou/.

The Canadian vocalic system is on the whole very similar to that of General American, but has normally only ten vowels, as illustrated in the following series of words: *beet, bit, bait, bet, bat, bought, butt, boat, boot.* The tenth vowel, that of *pull,* is in contrast with that in *pool* (which is the same as that in *boot*). The words *cot* and *caught* usually rhyme in Canada.

Most characteristic, however, is the Canadian treatment of diphthongs. Speakers in England and the U.S. have generally only one type of diphthong in words like *rye, ride,* and *right,* namely /aɪ/. Canadians agree for the first two items, but have a different diphthong, [əi], for the third, which occurs in all such cases where the following consonant is voiceless, for instance *ripe, hike, life,* and *ice.* Similarly, in words like *now, loud,* and *lout,* Canadian English resembles other types in having /aʊ/ for the first two, but differs in having [ʌu] for the last.

Americans will also notice that the choice of vowel is different in *docile,* /'dousəil/ not /'dɒsᵊl/, and in *lever,* /'liːvər/ not /'lɛ̄vər/. Britons, on the other hand, will notice the use of /'mɪsᵊl/ instead of /'mɪsaɪl/ for *missile.*

English of the Caribbean

The history of the English language in the Caribbean dates from the settlement of St Christopher (St Kitts) in 1624 and Barbados in 1627. The core of Caribbean English is British English. Modified by the African background of many of its speakers since that first settlement, it has also been subjected to the linguistic influences of French, Spanish, Dutch, and Asian Indian. Portuguese and Chinese have also left their marks. In more recent times, the nearness of the United States, its economic prestige, its cinema and broadcasting, and its Black ethnic and cultural sympathies have produced further considerable effects.

All these ingredients mix to produce local varieties at the social bottom of a continuum, the top end of which is the national form of the standard language we may call *Caribbean English*, the variety aspired to by educated speakers. Vocabulary items show the effect of these many influences well. They include survivals from British dialects such as *fig* (a segment of an orange), *gie* (give), and *kerfuffle*; older English words (*glebe land, proven*); and everyday expressions whose use may be related to the influence of the Anglican Church (*beforetime, bounden duty, whosoever*). From African sources have come such items as *ackee, bakra, kokobeh*, and *Quashi*, and many calques (literal translations) based on African substructures, such as *cut one's eye on, dayclean*, and *forceripe*. Many plant and animal names are of Amerindian origin (*cassava, manatee*, etc.). European elements other than those of British English include, from French, *crapaud* and *dasheen* (from *chou de Chine*), while *pannier* replaces *basket* in many areas. From Dutch come *mawger* and *paal*, and from Spanish *mamaguy* and *mustee* (from *mestizo*). The postslavery immigrations of workers have introduced many Hindu, Muslim, and Chinese terms to do with food, clothing, etc. (*dhoti, chow mein*). Other recent acquisitions have come from informal American English.

The Caribbean life style and culture have produced lexical and idiomatic forms of their own: *Berbice chair, jump-up* (a celebration or dance), *good hair*, etc. Some are now international: *calypso, reggae, steel band, obeah, Rastafarian*. Moreover, in the Caribbean some Standard English words take on different meanings. *Breakfast*, among older people, means the midday meal; *bath* and *bathe* refer chiefly to showering; *galvanise* is used as a noun meaning corrugated iron sheeting; and *wares* regularly means crockery.

The pronunciation of Caribbean English is remarkable for its characteristically wide-ranging intonation patterns, probably the result of early phonological influences from African languages. A peculiarity of the distribution of stress in relation to pitch treatment is illustrated in the pronunciation of a word like *biscuit*, which often is pronounced with the main stress on the first syllable (as in Standard English) but with a higher pitch level in the second. A few of the many distinguishing segmental features may be singled out. There are fewer vowels and diphthongs than in Standard English. The vowel in *fat* is /a/, intermediate between the RP pronunciation of ɑ in *fat* and *father*. The RP diphthongs in *bare, beer*, and *bait* are replaced by the same pure vowel /eː/. The vowels in *hot* and *fall* are more open than their RP counterparts. The ending *-ing* is pronounced /ɪn/, and forms of /t/ and /d/ replace the fricatives /θ/ and /ð/.

Nonstandard Caribbean English is a form of creole, noticed in more detail at the end of this article. In it, inflections and tense distinctions may be abandoned, and this, combined with functional shifts in syntax, results in sentences like: *de two son tek de fader car go Georgetown las' night* (the two sons took their father's car and went to Georgetown last night); *dey unfairin you* (they're cheating you). Echoic interjections abound, and language at all levels is enlivened by gestures.

The English of Australia and New Zealand

The types of English spoken in Australia and New Zealand have much in common, chiefly because of links in the histories of the two countries, their geographical propinquity, and the continual close contact that has existed between them. Yet the two varieties are distinct from each other in certain details of pronunciation and vocabulary.

The settlement established in New South Wales in 1788 inherited the language of England, Scotland, Ireland, and Wales, including its dialect forms, but Australian English soon began to take a different direction. This was partly because of the new vocabulary supplied by the environment, partly because existing words acquired new senses and applications, and partly because some words, especially those from dialect, survived in Australia after they fell into disuse in Britain. The first source of the new vocabulary was the aboriginal languages, which were responsible for the names of various animals (*kangaroo, dingo, wallaby, wombat*, and the mythical *bunyip*), of birds (*brolga, corella*), of fish (*barramundi, morwong*), of trees (*kurrajong, belah*), of natural features (*billabong, bombora*), and of some artefacts (*waddy, dilly bag, gunyah*). Some of these terms, like *boomerang*, have become part of international English.

Another source of Australian vocabulary was the convict system itself, which gave new meaning to words like *assignment* and *special*. The argot of the convicts introduced such words as *shake* in the sense of 'steal' and *scale* in the sense of 'defraud.' Various English dialects were the sources for terms regarded as Australian in origin, such as *dinkum* in the sense of 'authentic' or 'genuine,' *cobber, larrikin, bowyangs, wowser, barrack, bodger, barney, dunny, skerrick*, and *sollicker*.

With the extension of settlement, new terms naturally arose to describe new conditions, and the occupations of rural Australia had a marked effect on vocabulary. *Spinney, coppice*, and *dell* were replaced by more appropriate terms such as *outback, backblocks*, and *back country*, with *stockman, boundary rider*, and *squatter* for those who inhabited such regions. The sheep or cattle *station, pastoral* management, *rouseabout, wood-and-water joey, sundowner* or *remittance man, swagman*, and *bushranger* also originated in rural or bush life.

The gold discoveries of the mid-nineteenth century brought an influx of immigrants and the terminology of another industry, producing terms like *mullock, fossick, nuggety*, and *duffer*. The immigrants from North America brought some terms that became established as Australianisms — by adoption, not origin — especially *digger* (for any miner) and the expressions *up a gumtree* and *stir the possum*. The influx of Chinese gave currency to the derogatory term *chow*.

A distinctive language of city life was slower to emerge. What passed as 'Sydney' and 'Australian' slang in the 1890s was still predominantly English. An exception might be found in a handful of terms with criminal associations, like *bludger, drum* (for brothel), *keep nit*, and later *stand over*, but even these are in the nature of extensions of existing words. Most of the 'rhyming slang' heard in Australia even now is English rather than Australian. Instances of Australian inventions in this field are rare: *on one's pat* for 'alone' (Pat Malone), *babbler* for 'cook' (babbling brook), *oscar* for 'cash' (Oscar Asche, the actor), and more recently *septic* for 'Yank' (septic tank).

Of the words with social or nationalistic overtones, the most interesting is *pommy*. Although its origin is uncertain immigrants from England in the early nineteenth century were already being called *jimmygrants*, or *jimmies* for short. Before the First World War *jimmygrant* had become associated with *pomegranate*, and Xavier Herbert in his autobiography *Disturbing Element* recalls in his childhood jeering at newly arrived migrants in heavy British clothing: '*Jimmygrants, Pommygranates, Pommies!*' It has never been a favourable term.

World War II was responsible for more additions to Australian English. Some of them, like *choco* (for 'chocolate soldier') or *munga* (for 'food') were revivals from the past, but experience in new theatres of war gave rise to *troppo* (nervously affected by conditions in the tropics) and *jungle juice* (improvised alcoholic drink). To *come the raw prawn* in the sense of seeking an advantage, trying to impose on someone, dates from the war years, as do *ear-basher* and *spine-basher,* with *jack up* for a collective refusal of orders and *pull your head* in for 'come off it.'

The formation of words by abbreviation, often to produce a diminutive ending in *-ie* or *-o,* is a common feature of Australian English. The *bottle-o* and the *milko* go back to the turn of the century, as does the *rabbito.* The *schoolie,* the *postie,* and the *trammie* were established by the 1920s, though the habit of taking a *sickie* has grown since, and the *hostie* had to wait the development of commercial aviation. In Australia the abbreviation *super* can refer to the superintendent on a station, to superphosphate, or to superannuation benefits, and a *semi* can be a semidetached house, a semitrailer, or a semifinal in a sporting competition.

Some misunderstandings can arise from the way in which Australian English has drawn away from British English, when words held in common have come to denote different things. The *never-never* in Australia refers to regions remote from settlement, not to hire-purchase. A *spell* is an interval of rest, not another turn of work. A *scallop* in Australia is not only a shellfish and a dressmaking term, but also a flat slice of potato cooked in batter. *Maggoty* means angry or irritated; *snags* are sausages. A *theatre* is commonly a 'picture theatre,' or what is elsewhere a *cinema.* A *radiator* may be a portable electric fire, not a fixed heating system. To be *crook* is to be ill, not dishonest. *Hooray* has the meaning of 'goodbye.'

In New Zealand — in which, incidentally, a Scottish linguistic element survives in the predominantly Scottish settlement of Otago — borrowings from the languages of the indigenous populations have been even more numerous than those adopted in Australia. This is a consequence of the Maori's readier adaptation to European social institutions. New Zealand's pattern of settlement by separate groupings of free settlers has resulted in a degree of regional conservation, which contrasts with the dialectal homogeneity of Australia, the result of the mobility of the work force during the gold rush and subsequent seasonal employment.

Differences in the vocabularies reflect the differences in the two countries: *bush* has a different significance in the two countries because of dissimilarities in flora and terrain; *farm,* respectable enough in New Zealand, implies *smallholding* in Australia. *Football* in New Zealand usually implies rugby, while in Australia it means rugby league or soccer or, especially in Victoria and South Australia, *Australian Rules.*

A pronunciation feature that distinguishes both Australian and New Zealand English from British varieties is the treatment of /ɑː/ in words like *part,* the tongue being brought further forward than for the corresponding RP vowel. In New Zealand only, a point of divergence is found in the pronunciation of /ɪ/ in pit, for which the tongue is more retracted and slightly lower in the mouth than it is in Australia. What is popularly known as 'the Australian accent' (designated Broad Australian by phoneticians) is most readily identified by six sounds:

/eɪ/ as in *praise.* In Broad Australian this tends towards /ʌɪ/, so that praise may be heard (though not by another speaker of Broad Australian) as *prize.*

/əʊ/ as in *dough.* This tends towards /ʌʊ/ in Broad Australian.

/iː/ as in *me.* This tends towards the diphthong /əɪ/.

/uː/ as in *boot.* This tends towards the diphthong /əʊ/.

/aɪ/ as in *buy.* This tends towards /ɑɪ/, so that *buy* may be heard as *boy.*

/aʊ/ as in *house.* This tends towards /æʊ/, sometimes with nasalization.

English in Africa

English as a mother tongue was not fully and firmly established on the African continent until the 19th century. Notably instrumental in this process were the 1820 settlers, a group of some four thousand British colonists who took up residence along the eastern borders of the Cape Colony. They were a heterogeneous group representing several social and regional British dialects, but within two generations a distinctive South African English had emerged, in which the original speech variations had coalesced into a more or less uniform dialect characterized particularly by speech habits derived from those of the working and lower middle classes of Southeast England, especially London. For example, the tongue positions for the vowels /æ/ and /ɛ/, being higher and more advanced than they are for RP, reflect even in present-day South African English a feature of later 18th-century London pronunciation that is also evident in the semiliterate phonetic spellings of early colonists: *yis* for *yes, kittle* for *kettle, eksel* for *axle.*

These early colonists adapted themselves to their new environment by borrowing from the already implanted Dutch (later Afrikaans) language and to a lesser extent from the indigenous Bantu languages and Khoisan (Hottentot, etc.).

The early efforts of educators were vigorously in the direction of inculcating the grammar and usage prescribed by the middle-class doctrine of correctness that prevailed in late eighteenth- and nineteenth-century Britain. The grammar of South African English differs little, therefore, from the standard southern British form of the language. In vocabulary and usage the more picturesque colloquialisms and slang words disappeared early on, as did those socially stigmatized features of pronunciation that were probably present in the speech of the settlers.

The industrial changes consequent upon the discovery of gold and diamonds significantly changed linguistic attitudes during the late nineteenth and early twentieth centuries. In the new mining and industrial cities, a high social value was placed upon the RP of the British middle classes, to the detriment of both South African English and other British dialects. This attitude, characteristic of urban rather than rural society, continued to prevail among the most influential groups until World War II. Since then, South African English, which had been preserved in the rural areas of its origin, has once again been heard in all sections of society.

Generally, however, rural society was and has remained predominantly Afrikaner. Since the 1920s, the contact between speakers of English and speakers of Afrikaans has resulted in further vocabulary acquisitions, like *platteland* and *verkrampte;* and pronunciation changes such as the rendering of *sin* and *did* with a vowel like the second one of *enter* are probably due to the same cause. The influence of Afrikaans grammar is evident in locutions like *Will you come with?* and *I will throw you with a stone* (I will hit you with a stone). The influence of Bantu and other indigenous African languages has continued to be comparatively weak.

In addition to the one and three-quarter million Whites and some half-million Indians who use English as a mother tongue in South Africa, several million Africans and Afrikaans-speaking Whites employ it competently as a second language. The Indian population share with the latter groups a distinctive dialect and accent, which makes its own contribution to the richness and vitality of South African English.

West Africa is the first of the regions considered so far in which the chief importance of English is associated with its status as a second language. It has this status for many speakers in The Gambia, Liberia, Sierra Leone, Ghana, Nigeria, and Cameroon. (These states are themselves interspersed between other West African countries that were formerly French colonies and in which French is a lingua franca.) In the first five of these states English is the sole medium of education beyond the first few years of primary school, the main administrative and legislative language, the medium for journalism and broadcasting, and the vehicle for science, technology, large-scale business, and international communication. In the western sector of the Republic of Cameroon it fulfils a similar range of functions, sharing them with French elsewhere in that country. The whole of West Africa is extremely fragmented linguistically, several hundred indigenous languages being in use in the area. In consequence, English serves as a lingua franca for mobile educated West Africans both within and between these states. It is, therefore, de facto, if not always de jure, a national language for each of them and for their combined population of nearly 100 million.

Historically, English was first used along the West African coast as a contact language between English traders and the Africans with whom they had dealings. The first recorded instance of West Africans being taught English was in 1554, when an English merchant from Bristol took back five inhabitants of the Guinea coast to learn the language, later returning with them to act as interpreters. As the slave trade increased in the seventeenth and eighteenth centuries, a pidginized variety of English developed along the coast, used not only between European and African but also among the Africans themselves. Freed slaves were settled in Freetown (Sierra Leone) from the end of the eighteenth century, and in Liberia they brought with them a creolized English developed in the slave plantations of the New World. Pidginized and creolized forms continue to be used today alongside Standard English. The spread of the western type of education through missionary effort and colonial rule from the nineteenth century onwards gradually extended literacy in English, encouraged the use of the standard form, and gave it high prestige.

Some of the terms peculiar to West African English have resulted from calques or loan translations, especially those for institutions or objects of a traditional kind, as for instance *outdooring*, the traditional ceremony of naming a baby on its first appearance out of doors, practised particularly in Ghana. Others are compounds such as *palm wine*, the drink produced by tapping the palm tree, or *headtie*, a cloth tied in traditional fashion on the heads of women. Some common English words have special collocations and senses: *on seat* means available for consultation, and is normally used of officials; *beento*, used either as a noun or attributively, signifies someone who has studied in Britain. Words borrowed from local languages include *kente*, a handwoven cloth from Ghana. Many words in colloquial use have come from pidginized English: *chop* (food or to eat), *pass* (to serve drinks or food), *pickin* (small child—from Portuguese), etc.

The pronunciation of English in West Africa is variable, depending on the degree to which the phonetic imprint of the first language has been eradicated. There is thus as yet no stable, homogeneous pronunciation. Such general phonetic characteristics as have begun to emerge are mainly distinctive prosodic features relating to syllabification and rhythm.

English is so extensively used in West Africa that slang and colloquial idioms are constantly created and local languages drawn upon for special use. In its written form, however, the language tends to conform to the norms of Standard English. Only in Liberia, which has a long history of contact with the United States, is the American variety preferred to the British.

As an expanding second language, the future development of West African English and the processes whereby it accommodates itself to local needs seem unlikely to follow precisely the pattern of change and adaptation observed among native English-speaking communities. While colloquial English is likely to be marked in varying degrees by the continuing contact with African languages and pidginized English, formal and written usage may be expected to conform to internationally accepted norms, except where creative demands or special semantic needs force the language to extend its resources in particular situations.

The present status of English elsewhere on the African continent can usually be related to the availability or non-availability of an indigenous language enjoying sufficiently general currency to serve as a lingua franca. In Zambia, for instance, a survey conducted in 1970-71 by the local broadcasting service identified eleven different language groups; in this situation English serves as the language of education and public life in spite of objections by Zambian teachers, academics, and publicists. By contrast, the linguistically homogeneous state of Lesotho, though ranking English as a second official language, uses Sesotho for many official and semiofficial purposes, including its national newspapers. In Malawi, although Chichewa is used as a lingua franca by the majority of the population, English holds a prestigious position among an educated minority. The government of Tanzania has actively promoted the replacement of English by Swahili for all public matters since 1974. In neighbouring Kenya, the very firmly established role of English as a school subject and as a gateway to professional preferment will probably make a similar policy more difficult to implement.

The linguistic complexity that results from the needs — often conflicting ones — for effective communication and the satisfaction of national aspirations makes it difficult to identify particular varieties of English in these countries. It means also that any useful attempt to relate distinctive features, whether of lexis, grammar, or pronunciation, to historical development or the influence of local languages is far beyond the scope of such an introductory article as this.

English in Asia

The situation in Asia is no easier to describe in summary terms, although the use of English in Asia, as in Africa, is best established in those areas that were formerly part of the British Empire. In the nineteenth century English became the medium of higher education, the language of administration, and the lingua franca among the educated population of the whole of the Indo-Pakistan subcontinent. Since the end of British rule in 1947 it has been in competition, to differing degrees, with Hindi in India, with Urdu in Pakistan and, more recently, with Bengali in Bangladesh. In India it has retained the status of associate official language and is still widely used by educated people. In Pakistan it is the language in which the business of government, the higher courts of law, and higher academic studies are normally conducted. Since the political separation of Bangladesh from Pakistan, the teaching and use of English in the former has declined sharply, partly because it is no longer necessary as a link between the two areas of what was formerly a single Muslim state.

The English of India itself shares a number of features with the versions in use in the neighbouring states, all of which resulted ultimately from the influence of the British

Raj. Its special vocabulary includes on the one hand words from Indian languages commonly used in English-language books, journals, and newspapers published in India and on the other words that relate particularly to Indian contexts or that have acquired a special form of meaning in India. In the first category are words having mythological, philosophical, or religious reference: *Buddha, Ram, Siva, yoga,* etc. Others are concerned with political activity (*bandh, hartal, Naxalite, satyagraha*), sociology (*adivasi, Harijan, Sarvodaya, Swadeshi*), clothing (*dhoti, sari*), administration (*Panchayat, Pradesh, Zila*), titles (*mahatma, sahib, sardar*), food (*dal, puree, pan*), and music (*sarangi, tabla*). In the second category are, firstly, words like *Anglo-Indian, Aryan, betel, cardamom, caste, chariot, chilli,* and *turban,* and secondly words and phrases like *Akademi, basic education, Gandhi cap, Congress, gazetted officer, mass leave,* and *quarters.*

The pronunciation of English in India differs from other varieties very considerably. Here, only some of the more noticeable differences can be indicated. For example, vowel length is not maintained consistently. Words like *cot* and *caught* are pronounced alike; the vowels in the two syllables of a word like *butter* have a similar pronunciation; pairs like *shot/short, coat/court,* and *shut/shirt* are distinguished only by the presence of /r/ in the second.

There are also differences in the distribution of stress between Indian English and British varieties. This affects both the occurrence of stressed syllables within words and the way stress is related to word classes: grammatical words like articles, pronouns, auxiliary verbs, and prepositions are sometimes stressed while content words may lack stress. A feature related to this is the intonation pattern, which often imposes different groupings of sentence constituents from those that a speaker of British English would expect, and distributes the emphasis among words in a way that can sound confusing. Another related feature is the tendency for unstressed syllables to retain their 'full' value instead of being reduced to /ə/ or /ɪ/.

Indian speakers often use a weak /ʊ/ for both /v/ and /w/. /p/, /t/, and /k/ are always unaspirated. Dental forms of aspirated /t/ and unaspirated /d/ replace the fricatives /θ/ and /ð/ in words like *thin* and *then,* while the sounds /t/ and /d/ are sometimes retroflex.

Grammatical divergences can be illustrated by the following example from Indian English: *They want that the number should be fixed* (They want the number to be fixed). *Would* is often used where standard usage would have *will,* and there are characteristic differences in the use of the definite article.

Further east, English has an important role in Malaysia and Singapore. In the latter its increasing use in higher education is recognized in the emphasis on bilingualism in schools. In Malaysia its use is still widespread, in spite of its being officially superseded by Bahasa Malaysia as the language used in government offices and official correspondence. The popular tendency to lump together the English of Singapore with that of, for instance, Kuala Lumpur, is probably an oversimplification. Research yet to be undertaken is likely to reveal systematic differences due to the predominant Chinese and Malaysian influences respectively. Vocabulary differences reflect cultural differences — as for example the Chinese custom of giving red packets at the Chinese New Year. English is also important as a language of business and administration in Hong Kong, and as a second language in Japan and the Philippines. In the latter two countries the influence of American English may be detected, in contrast with the countries where English is a legacy of the British Empire.

Creoles and Pidgins

English is in fact now used as a lingua franca of business, science, and sport almost everywhere in the world, whether or not it is spoken as a native language. Its status as a world language has been developing for several centuries, and in the process many exotic varieties, widely different from the native tongue of London, have grown up in places where the influence of the source country has been slight. One such language is Neo-Melanesian, the official language of Papua New Guinea, which is in origin an English pidgin, although to the casual listener its English antecedents are no longer apparent.

A pidgin is a trade or vehicular language of limited vocabulary and structure. It arises to facilitate communication between people with no common language, drawing its vocabulary almost exclusively from a single language. There are two types of pidgin: the first is *restricted pidgin,* a minimal contact language like Korean 'Bamboo English' that dies out when contact ceases; the second, *developed pidgin* like Cameroon pidgin, remains in existence after the removal of the contact that initiated it and becomes a lingua franca between indigenous peoples with no mutually intelligible language. The latter type may eventually become the mother tongue of the community and so acquire the status *creole.*

The above process accounts for one of the ways in which a creole may arise. The other is when communities with mutually intelligible languages are kept apart, as was the case with African Negroes in the Americas, who were separated to prevent insurrection. In this situation the community resorts to a pidgin as the only viable lingua franca, and this then becomes a creole.

All the pidgins and creoles examined to date share certain characteristics. They are syntactically simpler than the languages upon which they are based: inflections are minimal, distinctions being made by varying word order; reduplication is common (Jamaica Creole *small-small,* Neo-Melanesian *talk-talk*), as is serial verb structure, giving sentences like this from Cameroon pidgin: *dat chief he woman go start begin teach he.*

Creoles and pidgins based on English exist in all six continents and can be divided into two main groups: *Atlantic* varieties, showing certain West African features, and *Pacific* varieties, related to the English used, especially in the late nineteenth and early twentieth centuries, on the China Coast. While most of the vocabulary comes from English, it also includes Portuguese words such as *savvy* and *piccaninny,* which have passed into Standard English.

Selected Bibliography

A C Baugh, *A History of the English Language* (Routledge), 3rd edition 1978.

G L Brook, *English Dialects* (André Deutsch), 1963.

W Nelson Francis, *The Structure of American English* (Oxford University Press), 1958.

Otto Jespersen, *Growth and Structure of the English Language* (Basil Blackwell), 9th edition 1956.

L W Lanham and K Prinsloo, *Language and Communication Studies in South Africa* (Oxford University Press), 1978.

Angus McIntosh, *Introduction to a Survey of Scottish Dialects* (Thomas Nelson), 1961.

A M Marckwardt, *American English* (Oxford University Press), 1958.

J Spencer (ed.), *The English Language in West Africa* (Longman), 1971.

Barbara M H Strang, *A History of English* (Methuen), 1970.

C W Turner, *The English Language in Australia and New Zealand* (Longman), revised edition l972.

DICTIONARY

a *or* **A** (eɪ) *n., pl.* **a's, A's,** *or* **As.** **1.** the first letter and first vowel of the modern English alphabet. **2.** any of several speech sounds represented by this letter, in English as in *take, bag, calm, shortage,* or *cobra.* **3.** Also called: **alpha.** the first in a series, esp. the highest grade or mark, as in an examination. **4. from A to Z.** from start to finish, thoroughly and in detail.

a[1] (ə; *emphatic* eɪ) *determiner.* (*indefinite article;* used before an initial consonant. Compare **an**[1]) **1.** used preceding a singular countable noun, if the noun is not previously specified or known: *a dog; a terrible disappointment.* **2.** used preceding a proper noun to indicate that a person or thing has some of the qualities of the one named: *a Romeo; a Shylock.* **3.** used preceding a noun or determiner of quantity: *a cupful; a dozen eggs; a great many; to read a lot.* **4.** used preceding a noun indicating a concrete or abstract thing capable of being divided: *half a loaf; a quarter of a minute.* **5.** (preceded by *once, twice, several times,* etc.) each or every; per: *once a day; fifty pence a pound.* **6.** a certain; one: *to change policy at a stroke; a Mr Jones called.* **7.** (preceded by *not*) any at all: *not a hope.* ~Compare **the**[1].

a[2] (ə) *vb.* an informal or dialect word for **have:** *they'd a said if they'd known.*

a[3] (ə) *prep.* (usually linked to the preceding noun) an informal form of **of:** *sorta sad; a kinda waste.*

a[4] *symbol for:* **1.** acceleration. **2.** are(s) (metric measure of land). **3.** atto-. **4.** *Chess.* See **algebraic notation.**

A *symbol for:* **1.** *Music.* **a.** a note having a frequency of 440 hertz (**A above middle C**) or this value multiplied or divided by any power of 2; the sixth note of the scale of C major. **b.** a key, string, or pipe producing this note. **c.** the major or minor key having this note as its tonic. **2.** a human blood type of the ABO group, containing the A antigen. **3.** (in Britain) a major arterial road: *the A3 runs from London to Portsmouth.* **4.** (in Britain, formerly) **a.** a film certified for viewing by anyone, but which contains material that some parents may not wish their children to see. **b.** (*as modifier*): *an A film.* **5.** mass number. **6.** the number 10 in hexadecimal notation. **7.** *Cards.* ace. **8.** argon (now superseded by **Ar**). **9.** ampere(s). **10.** Also: **at.** ampere-turn. **11.** absolute (temperature). **12.** (in circuit diagrams) ammeter. **13.** area. **14.** (*in combination*) atomic: *an A-bomb; an A-plant.* **15.** *Chem.* affinity. **16.** *Logic.* a universal affirmative categorical proposition, such as *all men are mortal:* often symbolized as **SaP.** Compare **E, I, O.** [from Latin *a(ffirmo)* I affirm] **17. a.** a person whose job is in top management, or who holds a senior administrative or professional position. **b.** (*as modifier*): *A worker.* ~See also **occupation groupings.** ~**18.** *international car registration for* Austria.

Å *symbol for* angstrom unit.

a. *abbrev. for:* **1.** acre(s) or acreage. **2.** alto. **3.** amateur. **4.** answer.

A. *abbrev. for:* **1.** acre(s) or acreage. **2.** America(n). **3.** answer.

a', aa, *or* **aw** (ɔː) *determiner. Scot.* variants of **all.**

a-[1] *or before a vowel* **an-** *prefix.* not; without; opposite to: *atonal; asocial.* [from Greek *a-, an-* not, without]

a-[2] *prefix.* **1.** on; in; towards: *afoot; abed; aground; aback.* **2.** *Literary or archaic.* (*used before a present participle*) in the act or process of: *come a-running; go a-hunting.* **3.** in the condition or state of: *afloat; alive; asleep.*

A1, A-1, *or* **A-one** (ˈeɪˈwʌn) *adj.* **1.** in good health; physically fit. **2.** *Informal.* first class; excellent. **3.** (of a vessel) with hull and equipment in first-class condition.

A4 *n.* **a.** a standard paper size, 210 × 297 mm. **b.** (*as adj.*): *an A4 book.* ~See also **A sizes.**

A5 *n.* **a.** a standard paper size (half A4), 148 × 210 mm. **b.** (*as adj.*): *A5 notepaper.* ~See also **A sizes.**

aa[1] (ˈɑːɑː) *n.* a volcanic rock consisting of angular blocks of lava with a very rough surface. [Hawaiian]

aa[2] *abbrev. for* **ana**[1].

AA *abbrev. for:* **1.** Alcoholics Anonymous. **2.** anti-aircraft. **3.** Architectural Association. **4.** (in Britain) Automobile Association. ~*symbol for:* **5.** (in Britain, formerly) a film that may not be shown publicly to a child under fourteen.

AAA *abbrev. for:* **1.** *Brit.* Amateur Athletic Association. **2.** Australian Association of Accountants. **3.** *U.S.* Automobile Association of America.

aalii (ɑːˈliːiː) *n.* a bushy sapindaceous shrub, *Dodonaea viscosa,* of Australia, Hawaii, Africa, and tropical America, having small greenish flowers and sticky foliage. [Hawaiian]

AAM *abbrev. for* air-to-air missile.

A & M *abbrev. for:* **1.** Agricultural and Mechanical. **2.** Ancient and Modern (hymn book).

A & P (in New Zealand) *abbrev. for* Agricultural and Pastoral (Association, Show, etc.).

A & R *abbrev. for* artists and repertoire.

AAP *abbrev. for* Australian Associated Press.

aardvark (ˈɑːdˌvɑːk) *n.* a nocturnal mammal, *Orycteropus afer,* the sole member of its family (*Orycteropodidae*) and order (*Tubulidentata*). It inhabits the grasslands of Africa, has long ears and snout, and feeds on termites. Also called: **ant bear.** [C19: from obsolete Afrikaans, from *aarde* earth + *varken* pig]

aardwolf (ˈɑːdˌwʊlf) *n., pl.* **-wolves.** a nocturnal mammal, *Proteles cristatus,* that inhabits the plains of southern Africa and feeds on termites and insect larvae: family *Hyaenidae* (hyenas), order *Carnivora* (carnivores). [C19: from Afrikaans, from *aarde* earth + *wolf* wolf]

Aaron's beard (ˈɛərənz) *n.* another name for **rose of Sharon** (sense 1).

Aaron's rod *n.* a widespread Eurasian scrophulariaceous plant, *Verbascum thapsus,* having woolly leaves and tall erect spikes of yellow flowers.

A'asia *abbrev. for* Australasia.

Ab (æb) *n.* a variant of **Av.**

AB *abbrev. for:* **1.** Also: **a.b.** able-bodied seaman. **2.** (in the U.S.) Bachelor of Arts. **3.** Alberta (Canada). ~**4.** *symbol for* a human blood type of the ABO group, containing both the A antigen and the B antigen.

ab-[1] *prefix.* away from; off; outside of; opposite to: *abnormal; abaxial; aboral.* [from Latin *ab* away from]

ab-[2] *prefix.* denoting a cgs unit of measurement in the electromagnetic system: *abvolt.* [abstracted from ABSOLUTE]

aba (ˈæbə) *n.* **1.** a type of cloth from Syria, made of goat hair or camel hair. **2.** a sleeveless outer garment of such cloth. [from Arabic]

ABA *abbrev. for:* **1.** (in Britain) Amateur Boxing Association. **2.** American Booksellers Association.

abac (ˈeɪbæk) *n.* another name for **nomogram.** [C20: from French, from Latin ABACUS]

abaca (ˈæbəkə) *n.* **1.** a Philippine plant, *Musa textilis,* related to the banana: family *Musaceae.* Its leafstalks are the source of Manila hemp. **2.** another name for **Manila hemp.** [via Spanish from Tagalog *abaká*]

aback (əˈbæk) *adv.* **1. taken aback. a.** startled or disconcerted. **b.** *Nautical.* (of a vessel or sail) having the wind against the forward side so as to prevent forward motion. **2.** *Rare.* towards the back; backwards. [Old English *on bæc* to the back]

abactinal (æbˈæktɪnᵊl) *adj. Zoology.* (of organisms showing radial symmetry) situated away from or opposite to the mouth; aboral. —**abˈactinally** *adv.*

abacus (ˈæbəkəs) *n., pl.* **-ci** (-ˌsaɪ) *or* **-cuses.** **1.** a counting device that consists of a frame holding rods on which a specific number of beads are free to move. Each rod designates a given denomination, such as units, tens, hundreds, etc., in the decimal system, and each bead represents a digit or a specific number of digits. **2.** *Architect.* the flat upper part of the capital of a column. [C16: from Latin, from Greek *abax* board covered with sand for tracing calculations, from Hebrew *ābhāq* dust]

abaft (əˈbɑːft) *Nautical.* ~*adv., adj.* (*postpositive*) **1.** closer to the stern than to another place on a vessel: *with the wind abaft.* ~*prep.* **2.** behind; aft of: *abaft the mast.* [C13: *on baft; baft* from Old English *beæftan,* from *be* by + *æftan* behind]

abalone (ˌæbəˈləʊnɪ) *n.* any of various edible marine gastropod molluscs of the genus *Haliotis,* having an ear-shaped shell that is perforated with a row of respiratory holes. The shells are used for ornament or decoration. Also called: **ear shell.** See also **ormer.** [C19: from American Spanish *abulón;* origin unknown]

abampere (æbˈæmpɛə) *n.* the cgs unit of current in the electromagnetic system; the constant current that, when flowing through two parallel straight infinitely long conductors 1 centimetre apart, will produce a force between them of 2 dynes per centimetre: equivalent to 10 amperes. Abbrev.: **abamp.**

abandon (əˈbændən) *vb.* (*tr.*) **1.** to forsake completely; desert; leave behind: *to abandon a baby; drivers had to abandon their cars.* **2. abandon ship.** the order given to the crew of a ship that is about to sink to take to the lifeboats. **3.** to give up completely: *to abandon a habit; to abandon hope.* **4.** to yield control of or concern in; relinquish: *to abandon office.* **5.** to give up (something begun) before completion: *to abandon a job; the game was abandoned.* **6.** to surrender (oneself) to emotion without restraint. **7.** to give (insured property that has suffered partial loss or damage) to the insurers in order that a claim for a total loss may be made. ~*n.* **8.** freedom from inhibitions, restraint, concern, or worry: *she danced with abandon.* [C14: *abandounen* (vb.), from Old French, from *a bandon* under one's control, in one's power, from *a* at, to + *bandon* control, power] —**aˈbandonment** *n.*

abandoned (ə'bændənd) *adj.* **1.** deserted: *an abandoned windmill.* **2.** forsaken: *an abandoned child.* **3.** unrestrained; uninhibited: *wild, abandoned dancing.* **4.** depraved; profligate.

abandonee (ə,bændə'niː) *n. Law.* a person to whom something is formally relinquished, esp. an insurer having the right to salvage a wreck.

abapical (æb'eɪpɪkᵊl) *adj. Biology.* away from or opposite the apex.

à bas *French.* (a bɑ) *interj.* down with!

abase (ə'beɪs) *vb. (tr.)* **1.** to humble or belittle (oneself, etc.). **2.** to lower or reduce, as in rank or estimation. [C15 *abessen,* from Old French *abaissier* to make low. See BASE[2]] —**a'basement** *n.*

abash (ə'bæʃ) *vb. (tr.; usually passive)* to cause to feel ill at ease, embarrassed, or confused; make ashamed. [C14: via Norman French from Old French *esbair* to be astonished, from *es-* out + *bair* to gape, yawn] —**abashedly** (ə'bæʃɪdlɪ) *adv.* —**a'bashment** *n.*

abate (ə'beɪt) *vb.* **1.** to make or become less in amount, intensity, degree, etc.: *the storm has abated.* **2.** *(tr.) Law.* **a.** to remove, suppress, or terminate (a nuisance). **b.** to suspend or extinguish (a claim or action). **c.** to annul (a writ). **3.** *(intr.) Law.* (of a writ, legal action, etc.) to become null and void. **4.** *(tr.)* to subtract or deduct, as part of a price. [C14: from Old French *abatre* to beat down, fell]

abatement (ə'beɪtmənt) *n.* **1.** diminution or alleviation; decrease. **2.** suppression or termination: *the abatement of a nuisance.* **3.** the amount by which something is reduced, such as the cost of an article. **4.** *Property law.* a decrease in the payment to creditors or legatees when the assets of the debtor or estate are insufficient to meet all payments in full. **5.** *Property law.* (formerly) a wrongful entry on land by a stranger who takes possession after the death of the owner and before the heir has entered into possession.

abatis *or* **abattis** ('æbətɪs, 'æbətiː) *n. Fortifications.* **1.** a rampart of felled trees bound together placed with their branches outwards. **2.** a barbed-wire entanglement before a position. [C18: from French, from *abattre* to fell]

abator (ə'beɪtə) *n. Law.* a person who effects an abatement.

abattoir ('æbə,twɑː) *n.* another name for **slaughterhouse.** [C19: French, from *abattre* to fell]

abaxial (æb'æksɪəl) *adj.* facing away from the axis, as the surface of a leaf. Compare **adaxial.**

Abba ('æbə) *n.* a title given to bishops and patriarchs in the Syrian, Coptic, and Ethiopian Churches. [from Aramaic]

abbacy ('æbəsɪ) *n., pl.* **-cies.** the office, term of office, or jurisdiction of an abbot or abbess. [C15: from Church Latin *abbātia,* from *abbāt-* ABBOT]

Abbasid ('æbə,sɪd, ə'bæsɪd) *n.* **a.** any caliph of the dynasty that ruled the Muslim empire from Baghdad (750–1258) and claimed descent from Abbas, uncle of Mohammed. **b.** *(as modifier): the Abbasid dynasty.*

abbatial (ə'beɪʃəl) *adj.* of or relating to an abbot, abbess, or abbey. [C17: from Church Latin *abbātiālis,* from *abbāt-* ABBOT; see -AL[1]]

abbé ('æbeɪ; *French* abe) *n.* **1.** a French abbot. **2.** a title used in addressing any other French cleric, such as a priest.

abbess ('æbɪs) *n.* the female superior of a convent. [C13: from Old French, from Church Latin *abbātissa*]

Abbevillian (æb'vɪlɪən, -jən) *Archaeol.* ~*n.* **1.** the period represented by Lower Palaeolithic European sites containing the earliest hand axes, dating from the Mindel glaciation. See also **Acheulian.** ~*adj.* **2.** of or relating to this period. [C20: after *Abbeville,* town in N France, where the stone tools were discovered]

abbey ('æbɪ) *n.* **1.** a building inhabited by a community of monks or nuns governed by an abbot or abbess. **2.** a church built in conjunction with such a building. **3.** such a community of monks or nuns. [C13: via Old French *abeie* from Church Latin *abbātia* ABBACY]

abbot ('æbət) *n.* the superior of an abbey of monks. [Old English *abbod,* from Church Latin *abbāt-* (stem of *abbas*), ultimately from Aramaic *abbā* ABBA] —**'abbot,ship** *or* **'abbotcy** *n.*

abbrev. *or* **abbr.** *abbrev. for* abbreviation.

abbreviate (ə'briːvɪ,eɪt) *vb. (tr.)* **1.** to shorten (a word or phrase) by contraction or omission of some letters or words. **2.** to shorten (a speech or piece of writing) by omitting sections, paraphrasing, etc. **3.** to cut short; curtail. [C15: from the past participle of Late Latin *abbreviāre,* from Latin *brevis* brief] —**ab'brevi,ator** *n.*

abbreviation (ə,briːvɪ'eɪʃən) *n.* **1.** a shortened or contracted form of a word or phrase used in place of the whole. **2.** the process or result of abbreviating.

ABC[1] *n.* **1.** *(pl. in U.S.)* the rudiments of a subject. **2.** an alphabetical guide to a subject. **3.** *(often pl. in U.S.)* the alphabet.

ABC[2] *abbrev. for:* **1.** (formerly, of weapons or warfare) atomic, biological, and chemical. **2.** Australian Broadcasting Corporation. **3.** American Broadcasting Company.

abcoulomb (æb'kuːlɒm) *n.* the cgs unit of electric charge in the electromagnetic system; the charge per second passing any cross section of a conductor through which a steady current of 1 abampere is flowing: equivalent to 10 coulombs.

abdicate ('æbdɪ,keɪt) *vb.* to renounce (a throne, power, responsibility, rights, etc.), esp. formally. [C16: from the past participle of Latin *abdicāre* to proclaim away, disclaim] —**abdicable** ('æbdɪkəbᵊl) *adj.* —**,abdi'cation** *n.* —**abdicative** (æb'dɪkətɪv) *adj.* —**'abdi,cator** *n.*

abdomen ('æbdəmən, æb'dəʊ-) *n.* **1.** the region of the body of a vertebrate that contains the viscera other than the heart and lungs. In mammals it is separated from the thorax by the diaphragm. **2.** the front or surface of this region; belly. **3.** (in arthropods) the posterior part of the body behind the thorax, consisting of up to ten similar segments. [C16: from Latin; origin obscure] —**abdominal** (æb'dɒmɪnᵊl) *adj.* —**ab'dominally** *adv.*

abdominal thrust *n.* another name for **Heimlich manoeuvre.**

abdominous (æb'dɒmɪnəs) *adj. Rare.* having a large belly.

abducens nerve (æb'djuːsənz) *n.* either of the sixth pair of cranial nerves, which supply the lateral rectus muscle of the eye. [see ABDUCENT]

abducent (æb'djuːsᵊnt) *adj.* (of a muscle) abducting. [C18: from Latin *abdūcent-, abdūcens* leading away, from *abdūcere,* from *ab-* away + *dūcere* to lead, carry]

abduct (æb'dʌkt) *vb. (tr.)* **1.** to remove (a person) by force or cunning; kidnap. **2.** (of certain muscles) to pull away (a leg, arm, etc.) from the median axis of the body. Compare **adduct.** [C19: from the past participle of Latin *abdūcere* to lead away] —**ab'duction** *n.* —**ab'ductor** *n.*

abeam (ə'biːm) *adv., adj. (postpositive)* at right angles to the length and directly opposite the centre of a vessel or aircraft. [C19: A-[2] + BEAM]

abecedarian (,eɪbiːsiː'dɛərɪən) *n.* **1.** a person who is learning the alphabet or the rudiments of a subject. ~*adj.* **2.** alphabetically arranged. [C17: from Late Latin *abecedarius,* from the letters *a, b, c, d*]

abed (ə'bɛd) *adv. Archaic.* in bed.

abele (ə'biːl, 'eɪbᵊl) *n.* another name for **white poplar.** [C16: from Dutch *abeel,* ultimately related to Latin *albus* white]

Abelian group (ə'biːlɪən) *n.* a group the defined binary operation of which is commutative: if *a* and *b* are members of an Abelian group then $ab = ba$. [C19: named after Niels Henrik *Abel* (1802–29), Norwegian mathematician]

abelmosk ('eɪbᵊl,mɒsk) *n.* a tropical bushy malvaceous plant, *Hibiscus abelmoschus,* cultivated for its yellow-and-crimson flowers and for its musk-scented seeds, which yield an oil used in perfumery. Also called: **musk mallow.** [New Latin, from Arabic *abu'l misk* father of musk]

Aberdeen Angus ('æbədiːn 'æŋgəs) *n.* a black hornless breed of beef cattle originating in Scotland.

Aberdeen terrier *n.* a former name for **Scottish terrier.**

aberdevine (,æbədɪ'viːn) *n.* a former name for the **siskin** (sense 1), esp. as a cagebird. [C18: of unknown origin]

Aberdonian (,æbə'dəʊnɪən) *n.* **1.** a native or inhabitant of Aberdeen, a city in NE Scotland. ~*adj.* **2.** of or relating to Aberdeen. [from Medieval Latin *Aberdonia* Aberdeen]

abernethy (,æbə'nɛθɪ) *n.* a crisp unleavened biscuit. [C19: perhaps named after Dr. John *Abernethy* (1764–1831), English surgeon interested in diet]

aberrant (æ'bɛrənt) *adj.* **1.** deviating from the normal or usual type, as certain animals from the group in which they are classified. **2.** behaving in an abnormal or untypical way. **3.** deviating from truth, morality, etc. [rare before C19: from the present participle of Latin *aberrāre* to wander away] —**ab'errance** *or* **ab'errancy** *n.*

aberration (,æbə'reɪʃən) *n.* **1.** deviation from what is normal, expected, or usual. **2.** departure from truth, morality, etc. **3.** a lapse in control of one's mental faculties. **4.** *Optics.* a defect in a lens or mirror that causes the formation of either a distorted image (see **spherical aberration**) or one with coloured fringes (see **chromatic aberration**). **5.** *Astronomy.* the apparent displacement of a celestial body due to the motion of the observer with the earth.

abet (ə'bɛt) *vb.* **abets, abetting, abetted.** *(tr.)* to assist or encourage, esp. in crime or wrongdoing. [C14: from Old French *abeter* to lure on, entice, from *beter* to bait] —**a'betment** *or* **a'bettal** *n.* —**a'better** *or (esp. Law)* **a'bettor** *n.*

abeyance (ə'beɪəns) *n.* **1.** (usually preceded by *in* or *into*) a state of being suspended or put aside temporarily. **2.** (usually preceded by *in*) *Law.* an indeterminate state of ownership, as when the person entitled to an estate has not been ascertained. [C16–17: from Anglo-French, from Old French *abeance* expectation, literally a gaping after, a reaching towards] —**a'beyant** *adj.*

abfarad (æb'færæd, -əd) *n.* the cgs unit of capacitance in the electromagnetic system; the capacitance of a capacitor having a charge of 1 abcoulomb and a potential difference of 1 abvolt between its conductors: equivalent to 10^9 farads.

abhenry (æb'hɛnrɪ) *n., pl.* **-ries.** the cgs unit of inductance in the electromagnetic system; the inductance that results when a rate of change of current of 1 abampere per second generates an induced emf of 1 abvolt: equivalent to 10^{-9} henry.

abhor (əb'hɔː) *vb.* **-hors, -horring, -horred.** *(tr.)* to detest vehemently; find repugnant; reject. [C15: from Latin *abhorrēre* to shudder at, shrink from, from *ab-* away from + *horrēre* to bristle, shudder] —**ab'horrer** *n.*

abhorrence (əb'hɒrəns) *n.* **1.** a feeling of extreme loathing or aversion. **2.** a person or thing that is loathsome.

abhorrent (əb'hɒrənt) *adj.* **1.** repugnant; loathsome. **2.** (when *postpositive,* foll. by *of*) feeling extreme aversion or loathing (for):

abhorrent of vulgarity. **3.** (usually *postpositive* and foll. by *to*) conflicting (with): *abhorrent to common sense.* —**ab'horrently** *adv.*

Abib (*Hebrew* ɑ'biːb) *n. Judaism.* an older name for the month of **Nisan** (Exodus 13:4). [Hebrew *ābhībh* ear of grain, hence the month when grain was fresh]

abide (ə'baɪd) *vb.* **abides, abiding, abode** *or* **abided. 1.** (*tr.*) to tolerate; put up with. **2.** (*tr.*) to accept or submit to; suffer: *to abide the court's decision.* **3.** (*intr.*; foll. by *by*) **a.** to comply (with): *to abide by the decision.* **b.** to remain faithful (to): *to abide by your promise.* **4.** (*intr.*) to remain or continue. **5.** (*intr.*) *Archaic.* to dwell. **6.** (*tr.*) *Archaic.* to await in expectation. **7.** (*tr.*) *Archaic.* to withstand or sustain; endure: *to abide the onslaught.* [Old English *ābīdan,* from *a-* (intensive) + *bīdan* to wait, bide] —**a'bidance** *n.* —**a'bider** *n.*

abiding (ə'baɪdɪŋ) *adj.* permanent; enduring: *an abiding belief.* —**a'bidingly** *adv.*

abietic acid (ˌæbɪ'ɛtɪk) *n.* a yellowish powder occurring naturally as a constituent of rosin and used in lacquers, varnishes, and soap. Formula: $C_{19}H_{29}COOH$; melting pt.: 173°C. [C19 *abietic,* from Latin *abiēt-,* from *abiēs* silver fir (the acid originally being extracted from the resin)]

abigail ('æbɪˌgeɪl) *n.* (*sometimes cap.*) *Archaic.* a lady's maid. [C17: after the name of a lady's maid in Beaumont and Fletcher's play, *The Scornful Lady* (1610)]

ability (ə'bɪlɪtɪ) *n., pl.* **-ties. 1.** possession of the qualities required to do something; necessary skill, competence, or power: *the ability to cope with a problem.* **2.** considerable proficiency; natural capability: *a man of ability.* **3.** (*pl.*) special talents. [C14: from Old French from Latin *habilitās* aptitude, handiness, from *habilis* ABLE]

ab initio *Latin.* (æb ɪ'nɪʃɪˌəʊ) from the start.

abiogenesis (ˌeɪbaɪəʊ'dʒɛnɪsɪs) *n.* the hypothetical process by which living organisms arise from inanimate matter: formerly thought to explain the origin of microorganisms. Also called: **spontaneous generation, autogenesis.** Compare **biogenesis.** [C19: New Latin, from A-[1] + BIO- + GENESIS] —ˌ**abioge'netic** *adj.* —**abiogenist** (ˌeɪbaɪ'ɒdʒɪnɪst) *n.*

abiosis (ˌeɪbaɪ'əʊsɪs) *n.* absence of life. [C20: from A-[1] + Greek *biōsis* a way of living] —**abiotic** (ˌeɪbaɪ'ɒtɪk) *adj.*

abirritant (æb'ɪrɪtənt) *adj.* **1.** relieving irritation. ~*n.* **2.** any drug or agent that relieves irritation.

abirritate (æb'ɪrɪˌteɪt) *vb.* (*tr.*) *Med.* to soothe or make less irritable.

abject ('æbdʒɛkt) *adj.* **1.** utterly wretched or hopeless. **2.** miserable; forlorn; dejected. **3.** indicating humiliation; submissive: *an abject apology.* **4.** contemptible; despicable; servile: *an abject liar.* [C14 (in the sense: rejected, cast out): from Latin *abjectus* thrown or cast away, from *abjicere,* from *ab-* away + *jacere* to throw] —**ab'jection** *n.* —**'abjectly** *adv.* —**'abjectness** *n.*

abjure (əb'dʒʊə) *vb.* (*tr.*) **1.** to renounce or retract, esp. formally, solemnly, or under oath. **2.** to abstain from or reject. [C15: from Old French *abjurer* or Latin *abjurāre* to deny on oath] —ˌ**abju'ration** *n.* —**ab'jurer** *n.*

Abkhaz (æb'kɑːz) *n.* **1.** (*pl.* **-khaz**) Also called: **Abkhazi, Abkhazian.** a member of a Georgian people living east of the Black Sea. **2.** the language of this people, belonging to the North-West Caucasian family.

abl. *abbrev. for* ablative.

ablactation (ˌæblæk'teɪʃən) *n.* **1.** the weaning of an infant. **2.** the cessation of milk secretion in the breasts.

ablate (æb'leɪt) *vb.* (*tr.*) to remove by ablation. [C20: back formation from ABLATION]

ablation (æb'leɪʃən) *n.* **1.** the surgical removal of an organ, structure, or part. **2.** the melting or wearing away of an expendable part, such as the heat shield of a space re-entry vehicle on passing through the earth's atmosphere. **3.** the wearing away of a rock or glacier. [C15: from Late Latin *ablatiōn-,* from Latin *auferre* to carry away, remove]

ablative ('æblətɪv) *Grammar.* ~*adj.* **1.** (in certain inflected languages such as Latin) denoting a case of nouns, pronouns, and adjectives indicating the agent in passive sentences or the instrument, manner, or place of the action described by the verb. ~*n.* **2. a.** the ablative case. **b.** a word or speech element in the ablative case.

ablative absolute *n.* an absolute construction in Latin grammar in which a governor noun and a modifier in the ablative case function as a sentence modifier; for example, *hostibus victis,* "the enemy having been beaten".

ablator (æb'leɪtə) *n.* the heat shield of a space vehicle, which melts or wears away during re-entry into the earth's atmosphere. [C20: from ABLATION]

ablaut ('æblaʊt; *German* 'aplaut) *n. Linguistics.* vowel gradation, esp. in Indo-European languages. See **gradation** (sense 5). [German, coined 1819 by Jakob Grimm from *ab* off + *Laut* sound]

ablaze (ə'bleɪz) *adj.* (*postpositive*), *adv.* **1.** on fire; burning. **2.** brightly illuminated. **3.** emotionally aroused.

able ('eɪbᵊl) *adj.* **1.** (*postpositive*) having the necessary power, resources, skill, time, opportunity, etc., to do something: *able to swim.* **2.** capable; competent; talented: *an able teacher.* **3.** *Law.* qualified, competent, or authorized to do some specific act. [C14: ultimately from Latin *habilis* easy to hold, manageable, apt, from *habēre* to have, hold + *-ilis* -ILE]

-able *suffix forming adjectives.* **1.** capable of, suitable for, or deserving of (being acted upon as indicated): *enjoyable; pitiable; readable; separable; washable.* **2.** inclined to; given to; able to; causing: *comfortable; reasonable; variable.* [via Old French from Latin *-ābilis, -ībilis,* forms of *-bilis,* adjectival suffix] —**-ably** *suffix forming adverbs.* —**-ability** *suffix forming nouns.*

able-bodied *adj.* physically strong and healthy; robust.

able-bodied seaman *n.* an ordinary seaman, esp. one in the merchant navy, who has been trained in certain skills. Also: **able seaman.** Abbrevs.: **AB, a.b.**

able rating *n.* (esp. in the Royal Navy) a rating who is qualified to perform certain duties of seamanship.

abloom (ə'bluːm) *adj.* (*postpositive*) in flower; blooming.

ablution (ə'bluːʃən) *n.* **1.** the ritual washing of a priest's hands or of sacred vessels. **2.** (*often pl.*) the act of washing (esp. in the phrase **perform one's ablutions**). **3.** (*pl.*) *Military informal.* a washing place. [C14: ultimately from Latin *ablūere* to wash away] —**ab'lutionary** *adj.*

ably ('eɪblɪ) *adv.* in a competent or skilful manner.

ABM *abbrev. for* antiballistic missile.

Abnaki (æb'nɑːkɪ) *n.* **1.** (*pl.* **-ki** *or* **-kis**) a member of a North American Indian people formerly living in Maine and Quebec. **2.** the language of this people, belonging to the Algonquian family.

abnegate ('æbnɪˌgeɪt) *vb.* (*tr.*) to deny to oneself; renounce (privileges, pleasure, etc.). [C17: from Latin *abnegāre* to deny] —ˌ**abne'gation** *n.* —**'abneˌgator** *n.*

Abney level ('æbnɪ) *n.* a surveying instrument consisting of a spirit level and a sighting tube, used to measure the angle of inclination of a line from the observer to another point. [C20: named after Sir William *Abney* (1843–1920), British chemist and physicist]

abnormal (æb'nɔːməl) *adj.* **1.** not normal; deviating from the usual or typical; extraordinary. **2.** *Informal.* odd in behaviour or appearance; strange. [C19: AB-[1] + NORMAL, replacing earlier *anormal* from Medieval Latin *anormalus,* a blend of Late Latin *anōmalus* ANOMALOUS + Latin *abnormis* departing from a rule] —**ab'normally** *adv.*

abnormality (ˌæbnɔː'mælɪtɪ) *n., pl.* **-ties. 1.** an abnormal feature, event, etc. **2.** a physical malformation; deformity. **3.** deviation from the typical or usual; irregularity.

abnormal psychology *n.* the study of behaviour patterns that diverge widely from generally accepted norms, esp. those of a pathological nature.

Abo ('æbəʊ) *n., pl.* **Abos.** (*sometimes not cap.*) *Austral. informal, often derogatory.* **a.** short for **Aborigine. b.** (*as modifier*): *an Abo reserve.*

aboard (ə'bɔːd) *adv., adj.* (*postpositive*), *prep.* **1.** on, in, onto, or into (a ship, train, aircraft, etc.). **2.** *Nautical.* alongside (a vessel). **3. all aboard!** a warning to passengers to board a vehicle, ship, etc.

abode[1] (ə'bəʊd) *n.* a place in which one lives; one's home. [C17: n. formed from ABIDE]

abode[2] (ə'bəʊd) *vb.* a past tense and past participle of **abide.**

abohm (æb'əʊm, 'æbˌəʊm) *n.* the cgs unit of resistance in the electromagnetic system: equivalent to 10^{-9} ohm.

aboideau ('æbəˌdəʊ) *or* **aboiteau** ('æbəˌtəʊ) *n., pl.* **-deaus, -deaux** (-ˌdəʊz) *or* **-teaus, -teaux** (-ˌtəʊz). (in the Canadian Maritimes) **1.** a dyke with a sluice gate that allows flood water to drain off while keeping the sea water out. **2.** a sluice gate in a dyke. [Canadian French]

abolish (ə'bɒlɪʃ) *vb.* (*tr.*) to do away with (laws, regulations, customs, etc.); put an end to. [C15: from Old French *aboliss-* (lengthened stem of *abolir*), ultimately from Latin *abolēre* to destroy] —**a'bolishable** *adj.* —**a'bolisher** *n.* —**a'bolishment** *n.*

abolition (ˌæbə'lɪʃən) *n.* **1.** the act of abolishing or the state of being abolished; annulment. **2.** (*often cap.*) (in British territories) the ending of the slave trade (1807) or the ending of slavery (1833): accomplished after a long campaign led by William Wilberforce. **3.** (*often cap.*) (in the U.S.) the emancipation of the slaves, accomplished by the Emancipation Proclamation issued in 1863 and ratified in 1865. [C16: from Latin *abolitio,* from *abolēre* to destroy] —ˌ**abo'litionary** *adj.* —ˌ**abo'litionism** *n.* —ˌ**abo'litionist** *n., adj.*

abomasum (ˌæbə'meɪsəm) *n.* the fourth and last compartment of the stomach of ruminants, which receives and digests food from the psalterium and passes it on to the small intestine. [C18: New Latin, from AB-[1] + *omāsum* bullock's tripe]

A-bomb *n.* short for **atom bomb.**

abominable (ə'bɒmɪnəbᵊl) *adj.* **1.** offensive; loathsome; detestable. **2.** *Informal.* very bad, unpleasant, or inferior: *abominable weather; abominable workmanship.* [C14: from Latin *abōminābilis,* from *abōminārī* to ABOMINATE] —**a'bominably** *adv.*

abominable snowman *n.* a large legendary manlike or apelike creature, alleged to inhabit the Himalayan Mountains. Also called: **yeti.** [a translation of Tibetan *metohkangmi,* from *metoh* foul + *kangmi* snowman]

abominate (ə'bɒmɪˌneɪt) *vb.* (*tr.*) to dislike intensely; loathe; detest. [C17: from the past participle of Latin *abōminārī* to regard as an ill omen, from *ab-* away from + *ōmin-,* from OMEN] —**a'bomiˌnator** *n.*

abomination (əˌbɒmɪˈneɪʃən) *n.* **1.** a person or thing that is disgusting or loathsome. **2.** an action that is vicious, vile, etc. **3.** intense loathing or disgust.

abondance (*French* abɔ̃dɑ̃s) *n. Cards.* a variant spelling of **abundance** (sense 6).

à bon marché *French.* (a bɔ̃ marʃe) *adv.* at a bargain price.

aboral (æbˈɔːrəl) *adj. Zoology.* away from or opposite the mouth.

aboriginal (ˌæbəˈrɪdʒɪnəl) *adj.* existing in a place from the earliest known period; indigenous; autochthonous. —**ˌaboˈriginally** *adv.*

Aboriginal (ˌæbəˈrɪdʒɪnəl) *adj.* **1.** of, relating to, or characteristic of the Aborigines of Australia. ~*n.* **2.** another word for an Australian **Aborigine.**

Aboriginality (ˌæbəˌrɪdʒɪˈnælɪtɪ) *n.* the state of being Aboriginal, esp. with regard to having a common Aboriginal culture.

aborigine (ˌæbəˈrɪdʒɪnɪ) *n.* an original inhabitant of a country or region who has been there from the earliest known times. [C16: back formation from *aborigines,* from Latin: inhabitants of Latium in pre-Roman times, probably representing some tribal name but associated in folk etymology with *ab origine* from the beginning]

Aborigine (ˌæbəˈrɪdʒɪnɪ) *n.* **1.** Also called: **native Australian, Aboriginal,** (Austral.) **native,** (Austral.) **Black.** a member of a dark-skinned hunting and gathering people who were living in Australia when European settlers arrived. Often shortened to **Abo. 2.** any of the languages of this people. See also **Australian** (sense 3).

aborning (əˈbɔːnɪŋ) *adv. U.S.* while being born, developed, or realized (esp. in the phrase **die aborning**). [C20: from A-[2] + *borning,* from BORN]

abort (əˈbɔːt) *vb.* **1.** to undergo or cause (a woman) to undergo the termination of pregnancy before the fetus is viable. **2.** (*tr.*) to cause (a fetus) to be expelled from the womb before it is viable. **3.** (*intr.*) to fail to come to completion; go wrong. **4.** (*tr.*) to stop the development of; cause to be abandoned. **5.** (*intr.*) to give birth to a dead or nonviable fetus. **6.** (of a space flight, military operation, etc.) to fail or terminate prematurely. **7.** (*intr.*) (of an organism or part of an organism) to fail to develop into the mature form. ~*n.* **8.** the premature termination or failure of (a space flight, military operation, etc.). [C16: from Latin *abortāre,* from the past participle of *aborīrī* to miscarry, from *ab-* wrongly, badly + *orīrī* to appear, arise, be born]

abortifacient (əˌbɔːtɪˈfeɪʃənt) *adj.* **1.** causing abortion. ~*n.* **2.** a drug or agent that causes abortion.

abortion (əˈbɔːʃən) *n.* **1.** an operation or other procedure to terminate pregnancy before the fetus is viable. **2.** the premature termination of pregnancy by spontaneous or induced expulsion of a nonviable fetus from the uterus. **3.** the products of abortion; an aborted fetus. **4.** the arrest of development of an organ. **5.** a failure to develop to completion or maturity: *the project proved an abortion.* **6.** a person or thing that is deformed. —**aˈbortional** *adj.*

abortionist (əˈbɔːʃənɪst) *n.* **1.** a person who performs abortions, esp. illegally. **2.** a person who is in favour of abortion on demand.

abortive (əˈbɔːtɪv) *adj.* **1.** failing to achieve a purpose; fruitless. **2.** (of organisms) imperfectly developed; rudimentary. **3.** causing abortion; abortifacient.

ABO system *n.* a system for classifying human blood on the basis of the presence or absence of two antigens in the red cells: there are four such blood types (A, B, AB, and O).

aboulia (əˈbuːlɪə, -ˈbjuː-) *n.* a variant spelling of **abulia.**

abound (əˈbaʊnd) *vb.* (*intr.*) **1.** to exist or occur in abundance; be plentiful: *a swamp in which snakes abound.* **2.** (foll. by *with* or *in*) to be plentifully supplied (with); teem (with): *the gardens abound with flowers; the fields abound in corn.* [C14: via Old French from Latin *abundāre* to overflow, from *undāre* to flow, from *unda* wave]

about (əˈbaʊt) *prep.* **1.** relating to; concerning; on the subject of. **2.** near or close to (in space or time). **3.** carried on: *I haven't any money about me.* **4.** on every side of; all the way around. **5.** active in or engaged in: *she is about her business.* **6. about to. a.** on the point of; intending to: *she was about to jump.* **b.** (*with a negative*) determined not to: *nobody is about to miss it.* ~*adv.* **7.** approximately; near in number, time, degree, etc.: *about 50 years old.* **8.** nearby. **9.** here and there; from place to place; in no particular direction: *walk about to keep warm.* **10.** all around; on every side. **11.** in or to the opposite direction: *he turned about and came back.* **12.** in rotation or revolution: *turn and turn about.* **13.** used in informal phrases to indicate understatement: *I've had just about enough of your insults; it's about time you stopped.* **14.** *Archaic.* in circumference; around. ~*adj.* **15.** (*predicative*) active; astir after sleep: *up and about.* **16.** (*predicative*) in existence, current, or in circulation: *there aren't many about nowadays.* [Old English *abūtan, onbūtan* on the outside of, around, from ON + *būtan* outside]

about-ship *vb.* **-ships, -shipping, -shipped.** (*intr.*) *Nautical.* to manoeuvre a vessel onto a new tack.

about turn *or U.S.* **about face** *interj.* **1.** a military command to a formation of men to reverse the direction in which they are facing. ~*n.* **about-turn** *or U.S.* **about-face. 2.** a complete change or reversal, as of opinion, attitude, direction, etc. ~*vb.* **about-turn** *or U.S.* **about-face. 3.** (*intr.*) to perform an about-turn.

above (əˈbʌv) *prep.* **1.** on top of or higher than; over: *the sky above the earth.* **2.** greater than in quantity or degree: *above average in weight.* **3.** superior to or prior to: *to place honour above wealth.* **4.** too honourable or high-minded for: *above petty gossiping.* **5.** too respected for; beyond: *above suspicion; above reproach.* **6.** too difficult to be understood by: *the talk was above me.* **7.** louder or higher than (other noise): *I heard her call above the radio.* **8.** in preference to: *I love you above all others.* **9.** north of: *which town lies just above London?* **10.** upstream from. **11. above all.** most of all; especially. **12. above and beyond.** in addition to. **13. above oneself.** presumptuous or conceited. ~*adv.* **14.** in or to a higher place: *the sky above.* **15. a.** in a previous place (in something written). **b.** (*in combination*): *the above-mentioned clause.* **16.** higher in rank or position. **17.** in or concerned with heaven: *seek the things that are above.* ~*n.* **18. the above.** something that is above or previously mentioned. ~*adj.* **19.** mentioned or appearing in a previous place (in something written). [Old English *abufan,* from *a-* on + *bufan* above]

above board *adj.* (**aboveboard** *when prenominal*), *adv.* in the open; without dishonesty, concealment, or fraud.

ab ovo *Latin.* (æb ˈəʊvəʊ) from the beginning. [literally: from the egg]

Abp *or* **abp** *abbrev. for* archbishop.

abr. *abbrev. for:* **1.** abridged. **2.** abridgment.

abracadabra (ˌæbrəkəˈdæbrə) *interj.* **1.** a spoken formula, used esp. by conjurors. ~*n.* **2.** a word used in incantations, etc., considered to possess magic powers. **3.** gibberish; nonsense. [C17: from Latin: magical word used in certain Gnostic writings, perhaps related to Greek *Abraxas;* see ABRAXAS]

abrade (əˈbreɪd) *vb.* (*tr.*) to scrape away or wear down by friction; erode. [C17: from Latin *abrādere* to scrape away, from AB-[1] + *rādere* to scrape] —**aˈbradant** *n.* —**aˈbrader** *n.*

abranchiate (əˈbræŋkɪɪt, -ˌeɪt) *or* **abranchial** *adj. Zoology.* having no gills. [C19: A-[1] + BRANCHIATE]

abrasion (əˈbreɪʒən) *n.* **1.** the process of scraping or wearing down by friction. **2.** a scraped area or spot; graze. **3.** *Geography.* the effect of mechanical erosion of rock, esp. a river bed, by rock fragments scratching and scraping it; wearing down. Compare **attrition** (sense 4), **corrasion.** [C17: from Medieval Latin *abrāsiōn-,* from the past participle of Latin *abrādere* to ABRADE]

abrasive (əˈbreɪsɪv) *n.* **1.** a substance or material such as sandpaper, pumice, or emery, used for cleaning, grinding, smoothing, or polishing. ~*adj.* **2.** causing abrasion; grating; rough. **3.** irritating in manner or personality; causing tension or annoyance.

abraxas (əˈbræksəs) *or* **abrasax** (əˈbræsəks) *n.* an ancient charm composed of Greek letters: originally believed to have magical powers and inscribed on amulets, etc., but from the second century A.D. personified by Gnostics as a deity, the source of divine emanations. [from Greek: invented word]

abreact (ˌæbrɪˈækt) *vb.* (*tr.*) *Psychoanal.* to alleviate (emotional tension) through abreaction.

abreaction (ˌæbrɪˈækʃən) *n. Psychoanal.* the release and expression of emotional tension associated with repressed ideas by bringing those ideas into consciousness.

abreast (əˈbrɛst) *adj.* (*postpositive*) **1.** alongside each other and facing in the same direction. **2.** (foll. by *of* or *with*) up to date (with); fully conversant (with).

abri (æˈbriː) *n.* a shelter or place of refuge, esp. in wartime. [French, from Latin *apricum* an open place]

abridge (əˈbrɪdʒ) *vb.* (*tr.*) **1.** to reduce the length of (a written work) by condensing or rewriting. **2.** to curtail; diminish. **3.** *Archaic.* to deprive of (privileges, rights, etc.). [C14: via Old French *abregier* from Late Latin *abbreviāre* to shorten] —**aˈbridgable** *or* **aˈbridgeable** *adj.* —**aˈbridger** *n.*

abridgment *or* **abridgement** (əˈbrɪdʒmənt) *n.* **1.** a shortened version of a written work. **2.** the act of abridging or state of being abridged.

abroach (əˈbrəʊtʃ) *adj.* (*postpositive*) (of a cask, barrel, etc.) tapped; broached. [C14: from Old French *abrochier* from *a-* to + *brochier* to BROACH]

abroad (əˈbrɔːd) *adv.* **1.** to or in a foreign country or countries. ~*adj.* (*postpositive*) **2.** (of news, rumours, etc.) in general circulation; current. **3.** out in the open. **4.** over a wide area. **5.** *Archaic.* in error. [C13: from A-[2] + BROAD]

abrogate (ˈæbrəʊˌgeɪt) *vb.* (*tr.*) to cancel or revoke formally or officially; repeal; annul. [C16: from Latin *abrogātus* repealed, from AB-[1] + *rogāre* to propose (a law)] —ˌ**abroˈgation** *n.* —ˈ**abroˌgator** *n.*

abrupt (əˈbrʌpt) *adj.* **1.** sudden; unexpected. **2.** brusque or brief in speech, manner, etc.; curt. **3.** (of a style of writing or speaking) making sharp transitions from one subject to another; disconnected. **4.** precipitous; steep. **5.** *Botany.* shaped as though a part has been cut off; truncate. **6.** *Geology.* (of strata) cropping out suddenly. [C16: from Latin *abruptus* broken off, from AB-[1] + *rumpere* to break] —**abˈruptly** *adv.* —**abˈruptness** *n.*

abruption (əˈbrʌpʃən) *n.* a breaking off of a part or parts from a mass. [C17: from Latin *abruptio;* see ABRUPT]

ABS *abbrev. for* acrylonitrile–butadiene–styrene: any of a range of tough copolymers used esp. for making moulded articles.

ABS brake *n.* another name for **antilock brake.** [from German *antiblockier System*]
abscess (ˈæbsɛs, -sɪs) *n.* **1.** a localized collection of pus formed as the product of inflammation and often caused by bacteria. ~*vb.* **2.** (*intr.*) to form such a collection of pus. [C16: from Latin *abscessus* a going away, a throwing off of bad humours, hence an abscess, from *abscēdere* to go away] —ˈ**abscessed** *adj.*
abscise (æbˈsaɪz) *vb.* to separate or be separated by abscission. [C17: from Latin *abscīsus*, from *abscīdere* to cut off]
abscissa (æbˈsɪsə) *n., pl.* **-scissas** *or* **-scissae** (-ˈsɪsiː). the horizontal or *x*-coordinate of a point in a two-dimensional system of Cartesian coordinates. It is the distance from the *y*-axis measured parallel to the *x*-axis. Compare **ordinate** (sense 1). [C17: New Latin, originally *linea abscissa* a cut-off line]
abscission (æbˈsɪʒən, -ˈsɪʃ-) *n.* **1.** the separation of leaves, branches, flowers, and bark from plants by the formation of an abscission layer. **2.** the act of cutting off. [C17: from Latin *abscissiōn-*, from AB-[1] + *scissiō* a cleaving]
abscission layer *n.* a layer of parenchyma cells, bounded on both sides by cork, that is formed at the base of fruit, flower, and leaf stems and under bark before abscission. As the parenchyma disintegrates the organ becomes separated from the plant.
abscond (əbˈskɒnd) *vb.* (*intr.*) to run away secretly, esp. from an open institution or to avoid prosecution or punishment. [C16: from Latin *abscondere* to hide, put away, from *abs-* AB-[1] + *condere* to stow] —**abˈsconder** *n.*
abseil (ˈæbsaɪl) *vb.* (*intr.*) **1.** *Mountaineering.* to descend a steep slope or vertical drop by a rope secured from above and coiled around one's body or through karabiners attached to one's body in order to control the speed of descent. **2.** to descend by rope from a helicopter. ~*n.* **3.** an instance or the technique of abseiling. ~Also called: **rappel.** [C20: from German *abseilen* to descend by a rope, from *ab-* down + *Seil* rope]
absence (ˈæbsəns) *n.* **1.** the state of being away. **2.** the time during which a person or thing is away. **3.** the fact of being without something; lack. [C14: via Old French from Latin *absentia*, from *absēns* a being away]
absent *adj.* (ˈæbsənt). **1.** away or not present. **2.** lacking; missing. **3.** inattentive; absent-minded. ~*vb.* (æbˈsent). **4.** (*tr.*) to remove (oneself) or keep away. [C14: from Latin *absent-*, stem of *absēns*, present participle of *abesse* to be away] —**abˈsenter** *n.*
absentee (ˌæbsənˈtiː) *n.* **a.** a person who is absent. **b.** (*as modifier*): *an absentee voter.*
absenteeism (ˌæbsənˈtiːɪzəm) *n.* persistent absence from work, school, etc.
absentee landlord *n.* a landlord who does not live in or near a property from which he draws an income.
absente reo (æbˈsɛntɪ ˈriːəʊ) *Law.* in the absence of the defendant. [Latin, literally: the defendant being absent]
absently (ˈæbsəntlɪ) *adv.* in an absent-minded or preoccupied manner; inattentively.
absent-minded *adj.* preoccupied; forgetful; inattentive. —ˌ**absent-ˈmindedly** *adv.* —ˌ**absent-ˈmindedness** *n.*
absent without leave *Military.* the full form of **AWOL.**
absinthe *or* **absinth** (ˈæbsɪnθ) *n.* **1.** a potent green alcoholic drink, technically a gin, originally having high wormwood content. **2.** another name for **wormwood** (the plant). [C15: via French and Latin from Greek *apsinthion* wormwood]
absinthism (ˈæbsɪnˌθɪzəm) *n. Pathol.* a diseased condition resulting from excessive drinking of absinthe.
absit omen *Latin.* (ˈæbsɪt ˈəʊmɛn) may the presentiment not become real or take place. [literally: may the (evil) omen be absent]
absolute (ˈæbsəˌluːt) *adj.* **1.** complete; perfect. **2.** free from limitations, restrictions, or exceptions; unqualified: *an absolute choice.* **3.** having unlimited authority; despotic: *an absolute ruler.* **4.** undoubted; certain: *the absolute truth.* **5.** not dependent on, conditioned by, or relative to anything else; independent: *an absolute term in logic; the absolute value of a quantity in physics.* **6.** pure; unmixed: *absolute alcohol.* **7.** (of a grammatical construction) syntactically independent of the main clause, as for example the construction *Joking apart* in the sentence *Joking apart, we'd better leave now.* **8.** *Grammar.* (of a transitive verb) used without a direct object, as the verb *intimidate* in the sentence *His intentions are good, but his rough manner tends to intimidate.* **9.** *Grammar.* (of an adjective) used as a noun, as for instance *young* and *aged* in the sentence *The young care little for the aged.* **10.** *Physics.* **a.** (*postpositive*) (of a pressure measurement) not relative to atmospheric pressure: *the pressure was 5 bar absolute.* Compare **gauge** (sense 18). **b.** denoting absolute or thermodynamic temperature. **11.** *Maths.* **a.** Also: **numerical.** (of a value) having a magnitude but no sign. **b.** (of a constant) never changing in value. **c.** (of an inequality) unconditional. **d.** (of a term) not containing a variable. **12.** *Law.* (of a court order or decree) coming into effect immediately and not liable to be modified; final. See **decree absolute.** **13.** *Law.* (of a title to property, etc.) not subject to any encumbrance or condition. ~*n.* **14.** something that is absolute. [C14: from Latin *absolūtus* unconditional, freed from, from *absolvere.* See ABSOLVE]
Absolute (ˈæbsəˌluːt) *n.* (*sometimes not cap.*) **1.** *Philosophy.* **a.** the ultimate basis of reality. **b.** that which is totally unconditioned, unrestricted, pure, perfect, or complete. **2.** (in Hegelian philosophy) that towards which all things evolve dialectically.
absolute alcohol *n.* a liquid containing at least 99 per cent of pure ethanol by weight.
absolute ceiling *n.* the maximum height above sea level, usually measured in feet or metres, at which an aircraft can maintain horizontal flight. Compare **service ceiling.**
absolute configuration *n. Chem.* the spatial arrangement of atoms or groups in a chemical compound about an asymmetric atom. See **chirality.**
absolute humidity *n.* the humidity of the atmosphere expressed as the number of grams of water contained in 1 cubic metre of air. Compare **relative humidity.**
absolute judgment *n. Psychol.* any judgment about a single stimulus, e.g. about the value of one of its properties or about whether it is present or absent. Compare **comparative judgment.**
absolutely (ˌæbsəˈluːtlɪ) *adv.* **1.** in an absolute manner, esp. completely or perfectly. ~*sentence substitute.* **2.** yes; certainly; unquestionably.
absolute magnitude *n.* the magnitude a given star would have if it were situated at a distance of 10 parsecs (32.6 light years) from the earth.
absolute majority *n.* a number of votes totalling over 50 per cent, such as the total number of votes or seats obtained by a party that beats the combined opposition. Compare **relative majority.**
absolute monarchy *n.* a monarchy without constitutional limits. Compare **constitutional monarchy.**
absolute music *n.* music that is not designed to depict or evoke any scene or event. Compare **programme music.**
absolute pitch *n.* **1.** Also called (not in technical usage): **perfect pitch.** the ability to identify exactly the pitch of a note without comparing it to another. **2.** the exact pitch of a note determined by vibration per second.
absolute temperature *n.* another name for **thermodynamic temperature.**
absolute threshold *n. Psychol.* the minimum intensity of a stimulus at which it can just be perceived. Compare **difference threshold.**
absolute unit *n.* **1.** a unit of measurement forming part of the electromagnetic cgs system, such as an abampere or abcoulomb. **2.** a unit of measurement forming part of a system of units that includes a unit of force defined so that it is independent of the acceleration of free fall.
absolute value *n. Maths.* **1.** the positive real number equal to a given real but disregarding its sign. Written $|x|$. Where r is positive, $|r| = r = |-r|$. **2.** Also called: **modulus.** a measure of the magnitude of a complex number, represented by the length of a vector in the Argand diagram: $|x + iy| = \sqrt{(x^2 + y^2)}$, so $|4 + 3i| = 5$.
absolute viscosity *n.* a full name for **viscosity,** used to distinguish it from kinematic viscosity and specific viscosity.
absolute zero *n.* the lowest temperature theoretically attainable, at which the particles constituting matter would be in the lowest energy states available; the zero of thermodynamic temperature; zero on the International Practical Scale of Temperature: equivalent to −273.15°C or −459.67°F.
absolution (ˌæbsəˈluːʃən) *n.* **1.** the act of absolving or the state of being absolved; release from guilt, obligation, or punishment. **2.** *Christianity.* **a.** a formal remission of sin pronounced by a priest in the sacrament of penance. **b.** the prescribed form of words granting such a remission. [C12: from Latin *absolūtiōn-* acquittal, forgiveness of sins, from *absolvere* to ABSOLVE] —**absolutory** (æbˈsɒljʊtərɪ, -trɪ) *adj.*
absolutism (ˈæbsəluːˌtɪzəm) *n.* **1.** the principle or practice of a political system in which unrestricted power is vested in a monarch, dictator, etc.; despotism. **2.** *Philosophy.* **a.** any theory which holds that truth or moral or aesthetic value is absolute and universal and not relative to individual or social differences. Compare **relativism.** **b.** the doctrine that reality is unitary and unchanging and that change and diversity are mere illusion. See also **monism** (sense 2). **3.** *Christianity.* an uncompromising form of the doctrine of predestination. —ˈ**absoˌlutist** *n., adj.*
absolve (əbˈzɒlv) *vb.* (*tr.*) **1.** (usually foll. by *from*) to release from blame, sin, punishment, obligation, or responsibility. **2.** to pronounce not guilty; acquit; pardon. [C15: from Latin *absolvere* to free from, from AB-[1] + *solvere* to make loose] —**abˈsolvable** *adj.* —**abˈsolver** *n.*
absonant (ˈæbsənənt) *adj. Archaic.* discordant or inharmonious. [C16: Medieval Latin, from Latin AB-[1] + *sonant-*, from *sonāns* sounding. Compare CONSONANT]
absorb (əbˈsɔːb, -ˈzɔːb) *vb.* (*tr.*) **1.** to soak or suck up (liquids). **2.** to engage or occupy (the interest, attention, or time) of (someone); engross. **3.** to receive or take in (the energy of an impact). **4.** *Physics.* to take in (all or part of incident radiated energy) and retain it without reflection or transmission. **5.** to take in or assimilate; incorporate. **6.** to accept and find a market for (goods, etc.). **7.** to pay for as part of a commercial transaction: *the distributor absorbed the cost of transport.* **8.** *Chem.* to cause to undergo a process in which one substance, usually a liquid or gas, permeates into or is dissolved by a liquid or solid: *porous solids absorb water; hydrochloric acid absorbs carbon dioxide.*

Compare **adsorb.** [C15: via Old French from Latin *absorbēre* to suck, swallow, from AB-[1] + *sorbēre* to suck] —**abˌsorbaˈbility** *n.* —**abˈsorbable** *adj.*

absorbance (əbˈsɔːbəns, -ˈzɔː-) *n. Physics.* **a.** the logarithm to base ten of internal transmittance. **b.** another term for **transmission density.**

absorbed (əbˈsɔːbd, -ˈzɔːbd) *adj.* engrossed; deeply interested. —**absorbedly** (əbˈsɔːbɪdlɪ, -ˈzɔː-) *adv.*

absorbed dose *n.* the amount of energy transferred by nuclear or ionizing radiation to a unit mass of absorbing material.

absorbefacient (əbˌsɔːbɪˈfeɪʃənt, -ˌzɔː-) *Med.* ~*n.* **1.** a medicine or other agent that promotes absorption. ~*adj.* **2.** causing or promoting absorption.

absorbent (əbˈsɔːbənt, -ˈzɔː-) *adj.* **1.** able to absorb. ~*n.* **2.** a substance that absorbs. —**abˈsorbency** *n.*

absorbent cotton *n.* the usual U.S. term for **cotton wool** (sense 1).

absorber (əbˈsɔːbə, -ˈzɔː-) *n.* **1.** a person or thing that absorbs. **2.** *Physics.* a material, esp. in a nuclear reactor, that absorbs radiation or causes it to lose energy.

absorbing (əbˈsɔːbɪŋ, -ˈzɔːb-) *adj.* occupying one's interest or attention; engrossing; gripping. —**abˈsorbingly** *adv.*

absorptance (əbˈsɔːptəns, -ˈzɔːp-) *or* **absorption factor** *n. Physics.* a measure of the ability of an object or surface to absorb radiation, equal to the ratio of the absorbed flux to the incident flux. For a plate of material the ratio of the flux absorbed between the entry and exit surfaces to the flux leaving the entry surface is the **internal absorptance.** Symbol: α Compare **reflectance, transmittance.** [C20: ABSORPTION + -ANCE]

absorption (əbˈsɔːpʃən, -ˈzɔːp-) *n.* **1.** the process of absorbing or the state of being absorbed. **2.** *Physiol.* **a.** normal assimilation by the tissues of the products of digestion. **b.** the process of taking up various gases, fluids, drugs, etc., through the mucous membranes or skin. **3.** *Physics.* a reduction of the intensity of any form of radiated energy as a result of energy conversion in a medium, such as the conversion of sound energy into heat. **4.** *Immunol.* the process of removing superfluous antibodies or antigens from a mixture using a reagent. [C16: from Latin *absorptiōn-*, from *absorbēre* to ABSORB] —**abˈsorptive** *adj.*

absorption spectrum *n.* the characteristic pattern of dark lines or bands that occurs when electromagnetic radiation is passed through an absorbing medium into a spectroscope. The same pattern occurs as coloured lines or bands in the emission spectrum of that medium.

absorptivity (ˌæbsɔːpˈtɪvɪtɪ, -zɔːp-) *n. Physics.* a measure of the ability of a material to absorb radiation, equal to the internal absorptance of a homogeneous plate of the material under conditions in which the path of the radiation has unit length and the boundaries of the plate have no influence.

absquatulate (æbˈskwɒtjʊˌleɪt) *vb.* (*intr.*) to leave; decamp. [C19: humorous formation as if from Latin]

abstain (əbˈsteɪn) *vb.* (*intr.*; usually foll. by *from*) **1.** to choose to refrain: *he abstained from alcohol.* **2.** to refrain from voting, esp. in a committee, legislature, etc. [C14: via Old French from Latin *abstinēre*, from *abs-* AB-[1] + *tenēre* to hold, keep] —**abˈstainer** *n.*

abstemious (əbˈstiːmɪəs) *adj.* moderate or sparing, esp. in the consumption of alcohol or food; temperate. [C17: from Latin *abstēmius*, from *abs-* AB-[1] + *tēm-*, from *tēmētum* intoxicating drink] —**abˈstemiously** *adv.* —**abˈstemiousness** *n.*

abstention (əbˈstɛnʃən) *n.* **1.** a voluntary decision not to act; the act of refraining or abstaining. **2.** the act of withholding one's vote. [C16: from Late Latin *abstentiōn-*, from Latin *abstinēre*. See ABSTAIN] —**abˈstentious** *adj.*

abstergent (əbˈstɜːdʒənt) *adj.* cleansing or scouring. [C17: from Latin *abstergent-*, *abstergens* wiping off, from *abs-* away, off + *tergēre* to wipe]

abstinence (ˈæbstɪnəns) *n.* **1.** the act or practice of refraining from some action or from the use of something, esp. alcohol. **2.** *Chiefly R.C. Church.* the practice of refraining from specific kinds of food or drink, esp. from meat, as an act of penance. [C13: via Old French from Latin *abstinentia*, from *abstinēre* to ABSTAIN] —ˈ**abstinent** *adj.*

abstract *adj.* (ˈæbstrækt). **1.** having no reference to material objects or specific examples; not concrete. **2.** not applied or practical; theoretical. **3.** hard to understand; recondite; abstruse. **4.** denoting art characterized by geometric, formalized, or otherwise nonrepresentational qualities. **5.** defined in terms of its formal properties: *an abstract machine.* **6.** *Philosophy* (of an idea) functioning for some empiricists as the meaning of a general term: *the word "man" does not name all men but the abstract idea of manhood.* ~*n.* (ˈæbstrækt) **7.** a condensed version of a piece of writing, speech, etc.; summary. **8.** an abstract term or idea. **9.** an abstract painting, sculpture, etc. **10. in the abstract.** without reference to specific circumstances or practical experience. ~*vb.* (æbˈstrækt). (*tr.*) **11.** to think of (a quality or concept) generally without reference to a specific example; regard theoretically. **12.** to form (a general idea) by abstraction. **13.** (ˈæbstrækt). (*also intr.*) to summarize or epitomize. **14.** to remove or extract. **15.** *Euphemistic.* to steal. [C14 (in the sense: extracted): from Latin *abstractus* drawn off, removed from (something specific), from *abs-* AB-[1] + *trahere* to draw]

abstracted (æbˈstræktɪd) *adj.* **1.** lost in thought; preoccupied. **2.** taken out or separated; extracted. —**abˈstractedly** *adv.* —**abˈstractedness** *n.*

abstract expressionism *n.* a school of painting in New York in the 1940s that combined the spontaneity of expressionism with abstract forms in unpremeditated, apparently random, compositions. See also **action painting, tachisme.**

abstraction (æbˈstrækʃən) *n.* **1.** absence of mind; preoccupation. **2.** the process of formulating generalized ideas or concepts by extracting common qualities from specific examples. **3.** an idea or concept formulated in this way: *good and evil are abstractions.* **4.** *Logic.* an operator that forms a class name or predicate from any given expression. See also **lambda-calculus. 5.** an abstract painting, sculpture, etc. **6.** the act of withdrawing or removing. —**abˈstractive** *adj.* —**abˈstractively** *adv.*

abstractionism (æbˈstrækʃəˌnɪzəm) *n.* the theory and practice of the abstract, esp. of abstract art. —**abˈstractionist** *n.*

abstract noun *n.* a noun that refers to an abstract concept. Compare **concrete noun.**

abstract of title *n. Property law.* a summary of the ownership of land, showing the original grant, conveyances, and any incumbrances.

abstriction (æbˈstrɪkʃən) *n.* the separation and release of a mature spore from a sporophore by the formation of a septum. This process occurs in some fungi. [C17: from Latin AB-[1] + *strictio* a binding, from *stringere* to bind]

abstruse (əbˈstruːs) *adj.* not easy to understand; recondite; esoteric. [C16: from Latin *abstrūsus* thrust away, concealed, from *abs-* AB-[1] + *trūdere* to thrust] —**abˈstrusely** *adv.* —**abˈstruseness** *n.*

absurd (əbˈsɜːd) *adj.* **1.** at variance with reason; manifestly false. **2.** ludicrous; ridiculous. ~*n.* **3.** *Philosophy.* (*sometimes cap.*; often preceded by *the*) the conception of the world, esp. in Existentialist thought, as neither designed nor predictable but irrational and meaningless. ~See also **theatre of the absurd.** [C16: via French from Latin *absurdus* dissonant, senseless, from AB-[1] (intensive) + *surdus* dull-sounding, indistinct] —**abˈsurdity** *or* **abˈsurdness** *n.* —**abˈsurdly** *adv.*

ABTA (ˈæbtə) *n. acronym for* Association of British Travel Agents.

abulia *or* **aboulia** (əˈbuːlɪə, -ˈbjuː-) *n. Psychiatry.* a pathological inability to take decisions. [C19: New Latin, from Greek *aboulia* lack of resolution, from A-[1] + *boulē* will] —**aˈbulic** *adj.*

abundance (əˈbʌndəns) *n.* **1.** a copious supply; great amount. **2.** fullness or benevolence: *from the abundance of my heart.* **3.** degree of plentifulness. **4.** *Chem.* the extent to which an element occurs in the earth's crust or some other specified environment: expressed in parts per million or as a percentage. **5.** *Physics.* the ratio of the number of atoms of a specific isotope in a mixture of isotopes of an element to the total number of atoms present: often expressed as a percentage: *the abundance of neon-22 in natural neon is 8.82 per cent.* **6.** Also called: **abondance.** a call in solo whist undertaking to make nine tricks. **7.** affluence. [C14: via Old French from Latin *abundantia*, from *abundāre* to ABOUND]

abundant (əˈbʌndənt) *adj.* **1.** existing in plentiful supply. **2.** (*postpositive*; foll. by *in*) having a plentiful supply (of). **3.** (of a chemical element or mineral) occurring to an extent specified in relation to other elements or minerals in the earth's crust or some other specified environment. **4.** (of an isotope) occurring to an extent specified in relation to other isotopes in a mixture of isotopes. [C14: from Latin *abundant-*, present participle of *abundāre* to ABOUND] —**aˈbundantly** *adv.*

ab urbe condita *Latin.* (æb ˈɜːbɪ ˈkɒndɪtə) the full form of **AUC** (sense 1). [literally: from the founding of the city]

A bursary *n. N.Z.* the higher of two bursaries available for students entering university, polytechnic, etc. Compare **B bursary.**

abuse *vb.* (əˈbjuːz). (*tr.*) **1.** to use incorrectly or improperly; misuse. **2.** to maltreat, esp. physically or sexually. **3.** to speak insultingly or cruelly to; revile. **4.** (*reflexive*) to masturbate. ~*n.* (əˈbjuːs). **5.** improper, incorrect, or excessive use; misuse. **6.** maltreatment of a person; injury. **7.** insulting, contemptuous, or coarse speech. **8.** an evil, unjust, or corrupt practice. **9.** See **child abuse. 10.** *Archaic.* a deception. [C14 (vb.): via Old French from Latin *abūsus*, past participle of *abūtī* to misuse, from AB-[1] + *ūtī* to USE] —**aˈbuser** *n.*

abusive (əˈbjuːsɪv) *adj.* **1.** characterized by insulting or coarse language. **2.** characterized by maltreatment. **3.** incorrectly used; corrupt. —**aˈbusively** *adv.* —**aˈbusiveness** *n.*

abut (əˈbʌt) *vb.* **abuts, abutting, abutted.** (usually foll. by *on*, *upon*, or *against*) to adjoin, touch, or border on (something) at one end. [C15: from Old French *abouter* to join at the ends, border on; influenced by *abuter* to touch at an end, buttress]

abutilon (əˈbjuːtɪlən) *n.* any shrub or herbaceous plant of the malvaceous genus *Abutilon*, such as the flowering maple, that have showy white, yellow, or red flowers. [C18: New Latin from Arabic]

abutment (əˈbʌtmənt) *or* **abuttal** *n.* **1.** the state or process of abutting. **2. a.** something that abuts. **b.** the thing on which something abuts. **c.** the point of junction between them. **3.** *Architect., civil engineering.* a construction that takes the thrust of an arch or vault or supports the end of a bridge.

abuttals (əˈbʌtəlz) *pl. n. Property law.* the boundaries of a plot of land where it abuts against other property.

abutter (əˈbʌtə) *n. Property law.* the owner of adjoining property.

abuzz (əˈbʌz) *adj.* (*postpositive*) humming, as with conversation, activity, etc.; buzzing.

abvolt (ˈæbˌvəʊlt) *n.* the cgs unit of potential difference in the electromagnetic system; the potential difference between two points when work of 1 erg must be done to transfer 1 abcoulomb of charge from one point to the other: equivalent to 10^{-8} volt.

abwatt (ˈæbˌwɒt) *n.* the cgs unit of power in the electromagnetic system, equal to the power dissipated when a current of 1 abampere flows across a potential difference of 1 abvolt: equivalent to 10^{-7} watt.

aby *or* **abye** (əˈbaɪ) *vb.* **abys** *or* **abyes, abying, abought.** (*tr.*) *Archaic.* to pay the penalty for; redeem. [Old English *ābycgan* to pay for, atone for, from *bycgan* to buy]

abysm (əˈbɪzəm) *n.* an archaic word for **abyss.** [C13: via Old French from Medieval Latin *abysmus* ABYSS]

abysmal (əˈbɪzməl) *adj.* **1.** immeasurable; very great: *abysmal stupidity.* **2.** *Informal.* extremely bad: *an abysmal film.* —**aˈbysmally** *adv.*

abyss (əˈbɪs) *n.* **1.** a very deep or unfathomable gorge or chasm. **2.** anything that appears to be endless or immeasurably deep, such as time, despair, or shame. **3.** hell or the infernal regions conceived of as a bottomless pit. [C16: via Late Latin from Greek *abussos* bottomless (as in the phrase *abussos limnē* bottomless lake), from A-[1] + *bussos* depth]

abyssal (əˈbɪsəl) *adj.* **1.** of or belonging to the ocean depths, esp. below 2000 metres (6500 feet): *abyssal zone.* **2.** *Geology.* another word for **plutonic.**

Abyssinian cat (ˌæbɪˈsɪnɪən) *n.* a variety of cat with a long body and a short brown coat with black or dark brown markings. [named after *Abyssinia,* former name for Ethiopia]

abyssopelagic (əˌbɪsəʊpɛˈlædʒɪk) *adj.* referring to or occurring in the region of deep water above the floor of the ocean.

Ac *the chemical symbol for* actinium.

AC *abbrev. for:* **1.** alternating current. Compare **DC. 2.** ante Christum. [Latin: before Christ] **3.** Air Corps. **4.** athletic club. **5.** Companion of the Order of Australia.

a.c. *abbrev. for* (in prescriptions) ante cibum. [Latin: before meals]

a/c *Book-keeping. abbrev. for:* **1.** account. **2.** account current.

ACA *abbrev. for* Associate of the Institute of Chartered Accountants.

acacia (əˈkeɪʃə) *n.* **1.** any shrub or tree of the tropical and subtropical mimosaceous genus *Acacia,* having compound or reduced leaves and small yellow or white flowers. See also **wattle** (sense 4). **2. false acacia.** another name for **locust** (senses 2, 3). **3. gum acacia.** another name for **gum arabic.** [C16: from Latin, from Greek *akakia,* perhaps related to *akē* point]

academe (ˈækəˌdiːm) *n. Literary.* **1.** any place of learning, such as a college or university. **2. the grove(s) of Academe.** the academic world. [C16: first used by Shakespeare in *Love's Labour's Lost* (1588); see ACADEMY]

academia (ˌækəˈdiːmɪə) *n.* the academic world.

academic (ˌækəˈdɛmɪk) *adj.* **1.** belonging or relating to a place of learning, esp. a college, university, or academy. **2.** of purely theoretical or speculative interest: *an academic argument.* **3.** excessively concerned with intellectual matters and lacking experience of practical affairs. **4.** (esp. of a schoolchild) having an aptitude for study. **5.** conforming to set rules and traditions; conventional: *an academic painter.* **6.** relating to studies such as languages, philosophy, and pure science, rather than applied, technical, or professional studies. ~*n.* **7.** a member of a college or university. —ˌ**acaˈdemically** *adv.*

academicals (ˌækəˈdɛmɪkəlz) *pl. n.* another term for **academic dress.**

academic dress *n.* formal dress, usually comprising cap, gown, and hood, worn by university staff and students.

academician (əˌkædəˈmɪʃən, ˌækədə-) *n.* a member of an academy (sense 1).

academicism (ˌækəˈdɛmɪˌsɪzəm) *or* **academism** (əˈkædəˌmɪzəm) *n.* adherence to rules and traditions in art, literature, etc.; conventionalism.

academy (əˈkædəmɪ) *n., pl.* **-mies. 1.** an institution or society for the advancement of literature, art, or science. **2.** a school for training in a particular skill or profession: *a military academy.* **3.** a secondary school: now used only as part of a name, and often denoting a private school. [C16: via Latin from Greek *akadēmeia* name of the grove where Plato taught, named after the legendary hero *Akadēmos*]

Academy Award *n.* the official name for an **Oscar.**

Acadian (əˈkeɪdɪən) *adj.* **1.** denoting or relating to Acadia, a region of E Canada, or its inhabitants. ~*n.* **2.** any of the early French settlers in Nova Scotia, many of whom were deported to Louisiana in the 18th century. See also **Cajun.**

acajou (ˈækəˌʒuː) *n.* **1.** a type of mahogany used by cabinet-makers in France. **2.** a less common name for **cashew.** [C18: via French from Portuguese *acajú,* from Tupi]

acalculia (ˌækælˈkjuːlɪə) *n. Psychol.* an inability to make simple mathematical calculations. [C20: from A-[1] + Latin *calculare* to calculate]

acaleph (ˈækəˌlɛf) *n. Obsolete.* any of the coelenterates of the former taxonomic group *Acalephae,* which included the jellyfishes. [C18: from New Latin, from Greek *akalēphē* a sting]

acanthaceous (ˌækənˈθeɪʃəs) *adj.* **1.** of or relating to the *Acanthaceae,* a mainly tropical and subtropical family of flowering plants that includes the acanthus. **2.** having spiny or prickly outgrowths.

acanthine (əˈkænθaɪn, -θiːn) *adj.* **1.** of or resembling an acanthus. **2.** decorated with acanthus leaves.

acantho- *or before a vowel* **acanth-** *combining form.* indicating a spine or thorn: *acanthocephalan.* [New Latin from Greek *akanthos* thorn plant, from *akantha* thorn]

acanthocephalan (əˌkænθəʊˈsɛfələn) *n.* **1.** any of the parasitic wormlike invertebrates of the phylum *Acanthocephala,* the adults of which have a spiny proboscis and live in the intestines of vertebrates. ~*adj.* **2.** of, relating to, or belonging to the *Acanthocephala.*

acanthoid (əˈkænθɔɪd) *adj.* resembling a spine; spiny.

acanthopterygian (ˌækənˌθɒptəˈrɪdʒɪən) *adj.* **1.** of, relating to, or belonging to the *Acanthopterygii,* a large group of teleost fishes having spiny fin rays. The group includes most saltwater bony fishes. ~*n.* **2.** any fish belonging to the *Acanthopterygii.* ~Compare **malacopterygian.** [C19: from New Latin *Acanthopterygii,* from ACANTHO- + Greek *pterúgion* fin]

acanthous (əˈkænθəs) *adj.* another term for **spinous.**

acanthus (əˈkænθəs) *n., pl.* **-thuses** *or* **-thi** (-θaɪ). **1.** any shrub or herbaceous plant of the genus *Acanthus,* native to the Mediterranean region but widely cultivated as ornamental plants, having large spiny leaves and spikes of white or purplish flowers: family *Acanthaceae.* See also **bear's-breech. 2.** a carved ornament based on the leaves of the acanthus plant, esp. as used on the capital of a Corinthian column. [C17: New Latin, from Greek *akanthos,* from *akantha* thorn, spine]

a cappella (ɑː kəˈpɛlə) *adj., adv. Music.* without instrumental accompaniment. [Italian: literally, according to (the style of the) chapel]

acariasis (ˌækəˈraɪəsɪs) *n.* infestation of the hair follicles and skin with acarids, esp. mites. [C19: New Latin. See ACARUS, -IASIS]

acaricide (əˈkærɪˌsaɪd) *n.* any preparation for killing acarids.

acarid (ˈækərɪd) *or* **acaridan** (əˈkærɪdən) *n.* **1.** any of the small arachnids of the order *Acarina* (or *Acari),* which includes the ticks and mites. ~*adj.* **2.** of or relating to the order *Acarina.* [C19: from ACARUS]

acaroid (ˈækəˌrɔɪd) *adj.* resembling a mite or tick. [C19: see ACARUS, -OID]

acaroid gum *or* **resin** *n.* a red alcohol-soluble resin that exudes from various species of grass tree, esp. *Xanthorrhoea hastilis,* and is used in varnishes, for coating paper, etc. Also called: **gum accroides.** [C19 *acaroid,* of uncertain origin (apparently not related to ACARUS)]

acarology (ˌækəˈrɒlədʒɪ) *n.* the study of mites and ticks.

acarpellous *or U.S.* **acarpelous** (eɪˈkɑːpələs) *adj.* (of flowers) having no carpels.

acarpous (eɪˈkɑːpəs) *adj.* (of plants) producing no fruit. [from Greek *akarpos,* from A-[1] + *karpos* fruit]

acarus (ˈækərəs) *n., pl.* **-ri** (-ˌraɪ). any of the free-living mites of the widely distributed genus *Acarus,* several of which, esp. *A. siro,* are serious pests of stored flour, grain, etc. [C17: New Latin, from Greek *akari* a small thing, a mite]

ACAS *or* **Acas** (ˈeɪkæs) *n.* (in Britain) *acronym for* Advisory Conciliation and Arbitration Service.

acatalectic (æˌkætəˈlɛktɪk) *Prosody.* ~*adj.* **1.** having the necessary number of feet or syllables, esp. having a complete final foot. ~*n.* **2.** a verse having the full number of syllables. [C16: via Late Latin from Greek *akatalēktikos.* See A-[1], CATALECTIC]

acaudal (eɪˈkɔːdəl) *or* **acaudate** *adj. Zoology.* having no tail.

acaulescent (ˌækɔːˈlɛsənt) *adj.* having no visible stem or a very short one.

acauline (ˈækɔːˌlaɪn) *or* **acaulose** *adj. Biology.* having no stem.

ACC (in New Zealand) *abbrev. for* Accident Compensation Corporation.

acc. *abbrev. for:* **1.** *Commerce.* acceptance. **2.** accompanied. **3.** according. **4.** *Book-keeping.* account. **5.** *Grammar.* accusative.

ACCA *abbrev. for* Associate of the Chartered Association of Certified Accountants.

accede (ækˈsiːd) *vb.* (*intr.;* usually foll. by *to*) **1.** to assent or give one's consent; agree. **2.** to enter upon or attain (to an office, right, etc.): *the prince acceded to the throne.* **3.** *International law.* to become a party (to an agreement between nations, etc.), as by signing a treaty. [C15: from Latin *accēdere* to approach, agree, from *ad-* to + *cēdere* to go, yield] —**acˈcedence** *n.* —**acˈceder** *n.*

accel. *abbrev. for* accelerando.

accelerando (ækˌsɛləˈrændəʊ) *Music.* ~*adj., adv.* **1.** (to be performed) with increasing speed. ~*n., pl.* **-dos. 2.** an increase in speed. [Italian]

accelerant (ækˈsɛlərənt) *n. Chem.* another name for **accelerator** (sense 3). [C20: from Latin from *accelerāns,* present participle of *accelerāre* to go faster]

accelerate (ækˈsɛləˌreɪt) *vb.* **1.** to go, occur, or cause to go or occur more quickly; speed up. **2.** (*tr.*) to cause to happen sooner than expected. **3.** (*tr.*) to increase the velocity of (a body, reaction, etc.); cause acceleration. [C16: from Latin *accelerātus*, from *accelerāre* to go faster, from *ad-* (intensive) + *celerāre* to hasten, from *celer* swift] —**ac'celerable** *adj.* —**ac'celerative** *or* **ac'celeratory** *adj.*

acceleration (æk,sɛlə'reɪʃən) *n.* **1.** the act of accelerating or the state of being accelerated. **2.** the rate of increase of speed or the rate of change of velocity. Symbol: *a*

acceleration of free fall *n.* the acceleration of a body falling freely in a vacuum in the earth's gravitational field: the standard value is 9.806 65 metres per second per second or 32.174 feet per second per second. Symbol: *g* Also called: **acceleration due to gravity, acceleration of gravity.**

accelerator (æk'sɛlə,reɪtə) *n.* **1.** a device for increasing speed, esp. a pedal for controlling the fuel intake in a motor vehicle; throttle. **2.** Also called (not in technical usage): **atom smasher.** *Physics.* a machine for increasing the kinetic energy of subatomic particles or atomic nuclei and focusing them on a target. **3.** *Chem.* a substance that increases the speed of a chemical reaction, esp. one that increases the rate of vulcanization of rubber, the rate of development in photography, the rate of setting of synthetic resins, or the rate of setting of concrete; catalyst. **4.** *Economics.* (in an economy) the relationship between the rate of change in output or sales and the consequent change in the level of investment. **5.** *Anatomy.* a muscle or nerve that increases the rate of a function.

accelerometer (æk,sɛlə'rɒmɪtə) *n.* an instrument for measuring acceleration, esp. of an aircraft or rocket.

accent *n.* ('æksənt). **1.** the characteristic mode of pronunciation of a person or group, esp. one that betrays social or geographical origin. **2.** the relative prominence of a spoken or sung syllable, esp. with regard to stress or pitch. Compare **pitch**[1] (sense 27), **stress** (sense 3). **3.** a mark (such as ', ,, ˊ or ˋ) used in writing to indicate the stress or prominence of a syllable. Such a mark may also be used to indicate that a written syllable is to be pronounced, esp. when such pronunciation is not usual, as in *turnèd*. **4.** any of various marks or symbols conventionally used in writing certain languages to indicate the quality of a vowel, or for some other purpose, such as differentiation of homographs. See **acute** (sense 9), **grave**[2] (sense 5), **circumflex.** **5.** (in some languages, such as Chinese) any of the tones that have phonemic value in distinguishing one word from another. Compare **tone** (sense 7). **6.** rhythmical stress in verse or prose. **7.** *Music.* **a.** stress placed on certain notes in a piece of music, indicated by a symbol printed over the note concerned. **b.** the rhythmical pulse of a piece or passage, usually represented as the stress on the first beat of each bar. See also **syncopation.** **8.** *Maths.* either of two superscript symbols indicating a specific unit, such as feet (′), inches (″), minutes of arc (′), or seconds of arc (″). **9.** a distinctive characteristic of anything, such as taste, pattern, style, etc. **10.** particular attention or emphasis: *an accent on learning.* **11.** a strongly contrasting detail: *a blue rug with red accents.* ~*vb.* (æk'sɛnt). (*tr.*) **12.** to mark with an accent in writing, speech, music, etc. **13.** to lay particular emphasis or stress on. [C14: via Old French from Latin *accentus*, from *ad-* to + *cantus* chant, song. The Latin is a rendering of Greek *prosōidia* a song sung to music, the tone of a syllable]

accentor (æk'sɛntə) *n.* any small sparrow-like songbirds of the genus *Prunella*, family *Prunellidae*, which inhabit mainly mountainous regions of Europe and Asia. See also **hedge sparrow.**

accentual (æk'sɛntʃʊəl) *adj.* **1.** of, relating to, or having accents; rhythmical. **2.** *Prosody.* of or relating to verse based on the number of stresses in a line rather than on the number of syllables. Compare **quantitative.** —**ac'centually** *adv.*

accentuate (æk'sɛntʃʊ,eɪt) *vb.* (*tr.*) to stress or emphasize. —**ac,centu'ation** *n.*

accept (ək'sɛpt) *vb.* (*mainly tr.*) **1.** to take or receive (something offered). **2.** to give an affirmative reply to: *to accept an invitation.* **3.** to take on the responsibilities, duties, etc., of: *he accepted office.* **4.** to tolerate or accommodate oneself to. **5.** to consider as true or believe in (a philosophy, theory, etc.): *I cannot accept your argument.* **6.** (*may take a clause as object*) to be willing to grant or believe: *you must accept that he lied.* **7.** to receive with approval or admit, as into a community, group, etc. **8.** *Commerce.* to agree to pay (a bill, draft, shipping document, etc.), esp. by signing. **9.** to receive as adequate, satisfactory, or valid. **10.** to receive, take, or hold (something applied, inserted, etc.). **11.** (*intr.*; sometimes foll. by *of*) *Archaic.* to take or receive an offer, invitation, etc. [C14: from Latin *acceptāre*, from *ad-* to + *capere* to take] —**ac'cepter** *n.*

acceptable (ək'sɛptəbᵊl) *adj.* **1.** satisfactory; adequate. **2.** pleasing; welcome. **3.** tolerable. —**ac,cepta'bility** *or* **ac'ceptableness** *n.* —**ac'ceptably** *adv.*

acceptance (ək'sɛptəns) *n.* **1.** the act of accepting or the state of being accepted or acceptable. **2.** favourable reception; approval. **3.** (often foll. by *of*) belief (in) or assent (to). **4.** *Commerce.* **a.** a formal agreement by a debtor to pay a draft, bill, etc. **b.** the document so accepted. Compare **bank acceptance.** **5.** (*pl.*) *Austral. and N.Z.* a list of horses accepted as starters in a race. **6.** *Contract law.* words or conduct by which a person signifies his assent to the terms and conditions of an offer or agreement.

acceptant (ək'sɛptənt) *adj.* receiving willingly; receptive.

acceptation (,æksɛp'teɪʃən) *n.* the accepted meaning, as of a word, phrase, etc.

accepted (ək'sɛptɪd) *adj.* commonly approved or recognized; customary; established. —**ac'ceptedly** *adv.*

accepting house *n.* a financial institution that guarantees a bill of exchange, as a result of which it can be discounted on more favourable terms.

acceptor (ək'sɛptə) *n.* **1.** *Commerce.* the person or organization on which a draft or bill of exchange is drawn after liability has been accepted, usually by signature. **2.** Also called: **acceptor impurity.** *Electronics.* an impurity, such as gallium, added to a semiconductor material to increase its p-type conductivity by increasing the number of holes in the semiconductor. Compare **donor** (sense 5). **3.** *Electronics.* a circuit tuned to accept a particular frequency. **4.** *Chem.* the atom or group that accepts electrons in a coordinate bond.

access ('æksɛs) *n.* **1.** the act of approaching or entering. **2.** the condition of allowing entry, esp. (of a building or room) allowing entry by wheelchairs, prams, etc. **3.** the right or privilege to approach, reach, enter, or make use of something. **4.** a way or means of approach or entry. **5.** (*modifier*) designating programmes made by the general public as distinguished from those made by professional broadcasters: *access television.* **6.** a sudden outburst or attack, as of rage or disease. ~*vb.* **7.** to gain access to; make accessible or available. **8.** (*tr.*) *Computer technol.* **a.** to obtain or retrieve (information) from a storage device. **b.** to place (information) in a storage device. See also **direct access, sequential access.** [C14: from Old French or from Latin *accessus* an approach, from *accēdere* to ACCEDE]

accessary (ək'sɛsərɪ) *n., pl.* **-ries,** *adj.* *Law.* a less common spelling of **accessory.** —**ac'cessarily** *adv.* —**ac'cessariness** *n.*

accessible (ək'sɛsəbᵊl) *adj.* **1.** easy to approach, enter, or use. **2. accessible to.** likely to be affected by; open to; susceptible to. **3.** obtainable; available. **4.** *Logic.* (of a possible world) surveyable from some other world so that the truth value of statements about it can be known. A statement *possibly p* is true in a world W if and only if *p* is true in some worlds accessible to W. —**ac,cessi'bility** *n.* —**ac'cessibly** *adv.*

accession (ək'sɛʃən) *n.* **1.** the act of entering upon or attaining to an office, right, condition, etc. **2.** an increase due to an addition. **3.** an addition, as to a collection. **4.** *Property law.* **a.** an addition to land or property by natural increase or improvement. **b.** the owner's right to the increased value of such land. **5.** *International law.* the formal acceptance of a convention or treaty. **6.** agreement; consent. **7.** a less common word for **access** (sense 1). ~*vb.* **8.** (*tr.*) to make a record of (additions to a collection). —**ac'cessional** *adj.*

accession number *n.* *Library science.* the number given to record a new addition to a collection.

accessorius (,æksɛs'ɔːrɪəs) *n.* *Anatomy.* a muscle or nerve that has an augmenting action.

accessorize *or* **accessorise** (ək'sɛsə,raɪz) *vb.* (*tr.*) to add accessories to: *accessorize a plain jacket with feminine jewellery.*

accessory (ək'sɛsərɪ) *n., pl.* **-ries.** **1.** a supplementary part or object, as of a car, appliance, etc. **2.** (*often pl.*) a small accompanying item of dress, esp. of women's dress. **3.** (formerly) a person involved in a crime although absent during its commission, either a person who incites or encourages or otherwise assists the planning of a crime (**accessory before the fact**) or a person who knowingly conceals, comforts, or assists after the commission of a crime (**accessory after the fact**). ~*adj.* **4.** supplementary; additional; subordinate. **5.** assisting in or having knowledge of an act, esp. a crime. [C17: from Late Latin *accessōrius*: see ACCESS] —**accessorial** (,æksɛ'sɔːrɪəl) *adj.* —**ac'cessorily** *adv.* —**ac'cessoriness** *n.*

accessory fruit *n.* another name for **pseudocarp.**

accessory nerve *n.* either one of the eleventh pair of cranial nerves, which supply the muscles of the head, shoulders, larynx, and pharynx and the viscera of the abdomen and thorax.

accessory shoe *n.* *Photog.* a bracket on top of a camera to which a flash unit or other accessory may be fitted.

access road *n.* a road providing a means of entry into a region or of approach to another road, esp. a motorway.

access time *n.* *Computer technol.* the time required to retrieve a piece of stored information.

acciaccatura (ɑː,tʃɑːkɑː'tʊərə) *n., pl.* **-ras** *or* **-re** (-reɪ, -riː). **1.** a small grace note melodically adjacent to a principal note and played simultaneously with or immediately before it. **2.** (in modern music) a very short appoggiatura. [C18: Italian: literally, a crushing sound]

accidence ('æksɪdəns) *n.* inflectional morphology; the part of grammar concerned with changes in the form of words by internal modification or by affixation, for the expression of tense, person, case, number, etc. [C15: from Latin *accidentia* accidental matters, hence inflections of words, from *accidere* to happen. See ACCIDENT]

accident ('æksɪdənt) *n.* **1.** an unforeseen event or one without an apparent cause. **2.** anything that occurs unintentionally or by chance; chance; fortune: *I met him by accident.* **3.** a misfortune or mishap, esp. one causing injury or death. **4.** Also called: **adjunct.** *Logic, philosophy.* a nonessential attribute or characteristic of something (as opposed to substance). **5.** *Metaphysics.* a property as contrasted with the substance in which it inheres. **6.** *Geology.* a surface irregularity in a natural formation, esp. in a rock formation or a river system [C14: via Old French from Latin *accident-* chance, happening, from the present participle of *accidere* to befall, happen, from *ad-* to + *cadere* to fall]

accidental (ˌæksɪˈdɛntᵊl) *adj.* **1.** occurring by chance, unexpectedly, or unintentionally. **2.** nonessential; incidental. **3.** *Music.* denoting sharps, flats, or naturals that are not in the key signature of a piece. **4.** *Logic.* (of a property) not essential; contingent. ~*n.* **5.** an incidental, nonessential, or supplementary circumstance, factor, or attribute. **6.** *Music.* a symbol denoting a sharp, flat, or natural that is not a part of the key signature. —ˌacciˈ**dentally** *adv.*

accident insurance *n.* insurance providing compensation for accidental injury or death.

accident proneness *n.* the unconscious tendency, thought to exist in some people, to involve themselves in a large number of accidents. —ˈ**accident-**ˌ**prone** *adj.*

accidie (ˈæksɪdɪ) *or* **acedia** *n.* spiritual sloth; apathy; indifference. [in use C13 to C16 and revived C19: via Late Latin from Greek *akēdia,* from A-[1] + *kēdos* care]

accipiter (ækˈsɪpɪtə) *n.* any hawk of the genus *Accipiter,* typically having short rounded wings and a long tail. [C19: New Latin, from Latin: hawk]

accipitrine (ækˈsɪpɪˌtraɪn, -trɪn) *adj.* **1.** Also: **accipitral** (ækˈsɪpɪtrəl). of, relating to, or resembling a hawk; rapacious. **2.** of, relating to, or belonging to the subfamily *Accipitrinae,* which includes the hawks.

acclaim (əˈkleɪm) *vb.* **1.** (*tr.*) to acknowledge publicly the excellence of (a person, act, etc.). **2.** to salute with cheering, clapping, etc.; applaud. **3.** (*tr.*) to acknowledge publicly that (a person) has (some position, quality, etc.): *they acclaimed him king.* ~*n.* **4.** an enthusiastic approval, expression of enthusiasm, etc. [C17: from Latin *acclāmāre* to shout at, shout applause, from *ad-* to + *clamāre* to shout] —**ac**ˈ**claimer** *n.*

acclamation (ˌækləˈmeɪʃən) *n.* **1.** an enthusiastic reception or exhibition of welcome, approval, etc. **2.** an expression of approval by a meeting or gathering through shouts or applause. **3.** *Canadian.* an instance of electing or being elected without opposition: *there were two acclamations in the 1985 election.* **4. by acclamation. a.** by an overwhelming majority without a ballot. **b.** *Canadian.* (of an election or electoral victory) without opposition: *he won by acclamation.* —**acclamatory** (əˈklæmətərɪ, -trɪ) *adj.*

acclimatize, acclimatise (əˈklaɪməˌtaɪz), *or* **acclimate** (əˈklaɪmeɪt, ˈæklɪˌmeɪt) *vb.* to adapt or become accustomed to a new climate or environment. —**ac**ˈ**clima**ˌ**tizable, ac**ˈ**clima**ˌ**tisable,** *or* **ac**ˈ**climatable** *adj.* —**ac**ˌ**climati**ˈ**zation, ac**ˌ**climati**ˈ**sation,** *or* ˌ**accli**ˈ**mation** *n.* —**ac**ˈ**clima**ˌ**tizer** *or* **ac**ˈ**clima**ˌ**tiser** *n.*

acclivity (əˈklɪvɪtɪ) *n., pl.* **-ties.** an upward slope, esp. of the ground. Compare **declivity.** [C17: from Latin *acclīvitās,* from *acclīvis* sloping up, steep] —**ac**ˈ**clivitous** *or* **acclivous** (əˈklaɪvəs) *adj.*

accolade (ˈækəˌleɪd, ˌækəˈleɪd) *n.* **1.** strong praise or approval; acclaim. **2.** an award or honour. **3.** the ceremonial gesture used to confer knighthood, originally an embrace, now a touch on the shoulder with a sword. **4.** a rare word for **brace** (sense 7). **5.** *Architect.* a curved ornamental moulding, esp. one having the shape of an ogee arch. [C17: via French and Italian from Vulgar Latin *accollāre* (unattested) to hug; related to Latin *collum* neck]

accommodate (əˈkɒməˌdeɪt) *vb.* **1.** (*tr.*) to supply or provide, esp. with lodging or board and lodging. **2.** (*tr.*) to oblige or do a favour for. **3.** to adjust or become adjusted; adapt. **4.** (*tr.*) to bring into harmony; reconcile. **5.** (*tr.*) to allow room for; contain. **6.** (*tr.*) to lend money to, esp. on a temporary basis until a formal loan has been arranged. [C16: from Latin *accommodāre* to make fit, from *ad-* to + *commodus* having the proper measure] —**ac**ˈ**commo**ˌ**dative** *adj.*

accommodating (əˈkɒməˌdeɪtɪŋ) *adj.* willing to help; kind; obliging. —**ac**ˈ**commo**ˌ**datingly** *adv.*

accommodation (əˌkɒməˈdeɪʃən) *n.* **1.** lodging or board and lodging. **2.** adjustment, as of differences or to new circumstances; adaptation, settlement, or reconciliation. **3.** something fulfilling a need, want, etc.; convenience or facility. **4.** *Physiol.* the automatic or voluntary adjustment of the thickness of the lens of the eye for far or near vision. **5.** willingness to help or oblige. **6.** *Commerce.* a loan, usually made as an act of favour by a bank before formal credit arrangements are agreed.

accommodation address *n.* an address on letters, etc., to a person or business that does not wish or is not able to receive post at a permanent or actual address.

accommodation bill *n. Commerce.* a bill of exchange cosigned by a guarantor: designed to strengthen the acceptor's credit.

accommodation ladder *n. Nautical.* a flight of stairs or a ladder for lowering over the side of a ship for access to and from a small boat, pier, etc.

accommodation platform *or* **rig** *n.* a platform or semisubmersible rig specially built or adapted to act as living accommodation for offshore personnel in the oil industry.

accompaniment (əˈkʌmpənɪmənt, əˈkʌmpnɪ-) *n.* **1.** something that accompanies or is served or used with something else. **2.** something inessential or subsidiary that is added, as for ornament or symmetry. **3.** *Music.* a subordinate part for an instrument, voices, or an orchestra.

accompanist (əˈkʌmpənɪst, əˈkʌmpnɪst) *or U.S.* (*sometimes*) **accompanyist** (əˈkʌmpəniːɪst) *n.* a person who plays a musical accompaniment for another performer, esp. a pianist accompanying a singer.

accompany (əˈkʌmpənɪ, əˈkʌmpnɪ) *vb.* **-nies, -nying, -nied. 1.** (*tr.*) to go along with, so as to be in company with or escort. **2.** (*tr.;* foll. by *with*) to supplement: *he accompanied his tirade with gestures.* **3.** (*tr.*) to occur, coexist, or be associated with. **4.** to provide a musical accompaniment for (a performer). [C15: from Old French *accompaignier,* from *compaing* COMPANION[1]] —**ac**ˈ**companier** *n.*

accomplice (əˈkɒmplɪs, əˈkʌm-) *n.* a person who helps another in committing a crime. [C15: from *a complice,* interpreted as one word. See COMPLICE]

accomplish (əˈkɒmplɪʃ, əˈkʌm-) *vb.* (*tr.*) **1.** to manage to do; achieve. **2.** to conclude successfully; complete. [C14: from Old French *acomplir* to complete, ultimately from Latin *complēre* to fill up. See COMPLETE] —**ac**ˈ**complishable** *adj.* —**ac**ˈ**complisher** *n.*

accomplished (əˈkɒmplɪʃt, əˈkʌm-) *adj.* **1.** successfully completed; achieved. **2.** expert; proficient.

accomplishment (əˈkɒmplɪʃmənt, əˈkʌm-) *n.* **1.** the act of carrying out or achieving. **2.** something achieved or successfully completed. **3.** (*often pl.*) skill or talent. **4.** (*often pl.*) social grace, style, and poise.

accord (əˈkɔːd) *n.* **1.** agreement; conformity; accordance (esp. in the phrase **in accord with**). **2.** consent or concurrence of opinion. **3. with one accord.** unanimously. **4.** pleasing relationship between sounds, colours, etc.; harmony. **5.** a settlement of differences, as between nations; compromise. **6. of one's own accord.** voluntarily. ~*vb.* **7.** to be or cause to be in harmony or agreement. **8.** (*tr.*) to grant; bestow. [C12: via Old French from Latin *ad-* to + *cord-,* stem of *cor* heart] —**ac**ˈ**cordable** *adj.* —**ac**ˈ**corder** *n.*

accordance (əˈkɔːdəns) *n.* **1.** conformity; agreement; accord (esp. in the phrase **in accordance with**). **2.** the act of granting; bestowal: *accordance of rights.*

accordant (əˈkɔːdᵊnt) *adj.* (*usually postpositive* and foll. by *with*) in conformity or harmony. —**ac**ˈ**cordantly** *adv.*

according (əˈkɔːdɪŋ) *adj.* **1.** (foll. by *to*) in proportion; in relation: *salary will be according to age and experience.* **2.** (foll. by *to*) on the report (of); as stated (by). **3.** (foll. by *to*) in conformity (with); in accordance (with): *everything went according to plan.* **4.** (foll. by *as*) depending (on whether). **5.** *Not standard.* dependent on: *it's all according where you want to go.*

accordingly (əˈkɔːdɪŋlɪ) *adv.* **1.** in an appropriate manner; suitably. ~*sentence connector.* **2.** consequently.

accordion (əˈkɔːdɪən) *n.* **1.** a portable box-shaped instrument of the reed organ family, consisting of metallic reeds that are made to vibrate by air from a set of bellows controlled by the player's hands. Notes are produced by means of studlike keys. **2.** short for **piano accordion.** [C19: from German *Akkordion,* from *Akkord* harmony, chord] —**ac**ˈ**cordionist** *n.*

accordion pleats *pl. n.* tiny knife pleats.

accost (əˈkɒst) *vb.* **1.** (*tr.*) to approach, stop, and speak to (a person), as to ask a question, confront with a crime, solicit sexually, etc. ~*n.* **2.** *Rare.* a greeting. [C16: from Late Latin *accostāre* to place side by side, from Latin *costa* side, rib] —**ac**ˈ**costable** *adj.*

accouchement *French.* (akuʃmɑ̃; *English* əˈkuːʃmənt) *n.* childbirth or the period of confinement. [C19: from *accoucher* to put to bed, to give birth. See COUCH]

accoucheur *French.* (akuʃœr) *or* (*fem.*) ***accoucheuse*** (akuʃøz) *n.* an obstetrician or midwife. [literally: one who is present at the bedside]

account (əˈkaʊnt) *n.* **1.** a verbal or written report, description, or narration of some occurrence, event, etc. **2.** an explanation of conduct, esp. one made to someone in authority. **3.** ground; basis; consideration (often in the phrases **on this (that, every, no,** etc.) **account, on account of**). **4.** importance, consequence, or value: *of little account.* **5.** assessment; judgment. **6.** profit or advantage: *to turn an idea to account.* **7.** part or behalf (only in the phrase **on one's** *or* **someone's account**). **8.** *Finance.* **a.** a business relationship between a bank, department store, stockbroker, etc., and a depositor, customer, or client permitting the latter certain banking or credit services. **b.** the sum of money deposited at a bank. **c.** the amount of credit available to the holder of an account. **d.** a record of these. **9.** a statement of monetary transactions with the resulting balance. **10.** (on the London Stock Exchange) the period, ordinarily of a fortnight's duration, in which transactions take place and at the end of which settlements are made. **11.** *Book-keeping.* a chronological list of debits and credits relating to a specified asset, liability, expense, or income of a business and forming part of the ledger. **12. a.** a regular client or customer, esp. a firm that purchases commodities on credit. **b.** an area of business assigned to another: *they transferred their publicity account to a new agent.* **13. call** (*or* **bring**) **to account. a.** to insist on explanation. **b.** to rebuke; reprimand. **c.** to hold responsible. **14. give a good (bad,** etc.) **account of oneself.** to perform well (badly, etc.): *he gave a poor account of himself in the examination.* **15. on account. a.** on credit. **b.** Also: **to account.** as partial payment. **16. on account of.** (*prep.*) because of; by reason of. **17. take**

account of *or* **take into account.** to take into consideration; allow for. **18. settle** *or* **square accounts with. a.** to pay or receive a balance due. **b.** to get revenge on (someone). **19.** See **bank account** or **credit account.** ~*vb.* **20.** (*tr.*) to consider or reckon: *he accounts himself poor.* [C13: from Old French *acont*, from *conter, compter* to COUNT[1]]

accountable (ə'kaʊntəbᵊl) *adj.* **1.** responsible to someone or for some action; answerable. **2.** able to be explained. —**ac,counta'bility** *n.* —**ac'countably** *adv.*

accountancy (ə'kaʊntənsɪ) *n.* the profession or business of an accountant.

accountant (ə'kaʊntənt) *n.* a person concerned with the maintenance and audit of business accounts and the preparation of consultant reports in tax and finance.

account day *n.* (on the London Stock Exchange) the day on which deliveries and payments relating to transactions made during the preceding account are made.

account for *vb.* (*intr., prep.*) **1.** to give reasons for (an event, act, etc.). **2.** to make or provide a reckoning of (expenditure, payments, etc.). **3.** to be responsible for destroying, killing, or putting (people, aircraft, etc.) out of action.

accounting (ə'kaʊntɪŋ) *n.* the skill or practice of maintaining and auditing accounts and preparing reports on the assets, liabilities, etc., of a business.

account payable *n. Accounting, U.S. and Canadian.* a current liability account showing amounts payable by a firm to suppliers for purchases of materials, stocks, or services on credit.

account receivable *n. Accounting, U.S. and Canadian.* a current asset account showing amounts payable to a firm by customers who have made purchases of goods and services on credit.

accouplement (ə'kʌpᵊlmənt) *n.* a timber joist or beam that serves as a tie or support. [C15: French, from *accoupler*, from Latin *copulāre* to COUPLE]

accoutre *or U.S.* **accouter** (ə'ku:tə) *vb.* (*tr.; usually passive*) to provide with equipment or dress, esp. military. [C16: from Old French *accoustrer* to equip with clothing, ultimately related to Latin *consuere* to sew together]

accoutrement (ə'ku:trəmənt, ə'ku:tə-) *or U.S.* **accouterment** (ə'ku:tərmənt) *n.* **1.** equipment worn by soldiers in addition to their clothing and weapons. **2.** (*usually pl.*) clothing, equipment, etc.; trappings: *the correct accoutrements for any form of sport.*

accredit (ə'krɛdɪt) *vb.* (*tr.*) **1.** to ascribe or attribute. **2.** to give official recognition to; sanction; authorize. **3.** to certify or guarantee as meeting required standards. **4.** (often foll. by *at* or *to*) **a.** to furnish or send (an envoy, etc.) with official credentials. **b.** to appoint (someone) as an envoy, etc. **5.** *N.Z.* to pass (a candidate) for university entrance on school recommendation without external examination: *there are six accrediting schools in the area.* [C17: from French *accréditer*, from the phrase *mettre à crédit* to put to CREDIT] —**ac,credi'tation** *n.*

accrescent (æ'krɛsᵊnt) *adj. Botany.* (of a calyx or other part) continuing to grow after flowering. [C18: from Latin *accrēscere* to continue to grow, from *crēscere* to grow]

accrete (ə'kri:t) *vb.* **1.** to grow or cause to grow together; be or become fused. **2.** to make or become bigger, as by addition. ~*adj.* **3.** (of plant organs) grown together. [C18: back formation from ACCRETION]

accretion (ə'kri:ʃən) *n.* **1.** any gradual increase in size, as through growth or external addition. **2.** something added, esp. extraneously, to cause growth or an increase in size. **3.** the growing together of normally separate plant or animal parts. **4.** *Pathol.* **a.** abnormal union or growing together of parts; adhesion. **b.** a mass of foreign matter collected in a cavity. **5.** *Law.* an increase in the share of a beneficiary in an estate, as when a co-beneficiary fails to take his share. **6.** *Astronomy.* the process in which matter under the influence of gravity is attracted to and increases the size of a celestial body. **7.** *Geology.* the process in which a continent is enlarged by the tectonic movement and deformation of the earth's crust. [C17: from Latin *accretiō* increase, from *accrēscere*. See ACCRUE] —**ac'cretive** *or* **ac'cretionary** *adj.*

accretionary wedge *or* **prism** *n. Geology* a body of deformed sediments, wedge-shaped in two dimensions or prism-shaped in three dimensions, that has been scraped off the surface of the oceanic lithosphere as it moves downward beneath a continent. The sediments are added to the continental edge.

accrual (ə'kru:əl) *n.* **1.** the act of accruing. **2.** something that has accrued. **3.** *Accounting* a charge incurred in one accounting period that has not been paid by the end of it.

accrue (ə'kru:) *vb.* **-crues, -cruing, -crued.** (*intr.*) **1.** to increase by growth or addition, esp. (of capital) to increase by periodic addition of interest. **2.** (often foll. by *to*) to fall naturally (to); come into the possession (of); result (for). **3.** *Law.* (of a right or demand) to become capable of being enforced. [C15: from Old French *accreue* growth, ultimately from Latin *accrēscere* to increase, from *ad-* to, in addition + *crēscere* to grow]

ACCT *abbrev. for* Association of Cinematograph, Television, and Allied Technicians.

acculturate (ə'kʌltʃə,reɪt) *vb.* (of a cultural or social group) to assimilate the cultural traits of another group. [C20: from AD- + CULTURE + -ATE[1]] —**ac,cultur'ation** *n.*

accumbent (ə'kʌmbənt) *adj.* **1.** *Botany.* (of plant parts and plants) lying against some other part or thing. **2.** a rare word for recumbent. [C18: from Latin *accumbere* to recline] —**ac'cumbency** *n.*

accumulate (ə'kju:mjʊ,leɪt) *vb.* to gather or become gathered together in an increasing quantity; amass; collect. [C16: from Latin *accumulātus*, past participle of *accumulāre* to heap up, from *cumulus* a heap] —**ac'cumulable** *adj.* —**ac'cumulative** *adj.* —**ac'cumulatively** *adv.* —**ac'cumulativeness** *n.*

accumulation (ə,kju:mjʊ'leɪʃən) *n.* **1.** the act or process of collecting together or becoming collected. **2.** something that has been collected, gathered, heaped, etc. **3.** *Finance.* **a.** the continuous growth of capital by retention of interest or earnings. **b.** (in computing the yield on a bond purchased at a discount) the amount that is added to each yield to bring the cost of the bond into equality with its par value over its life. Compare **amortization** (sense 2). **4.** the taking of a first and an advanced university degree simultaneously.

accumulation point *n. Maths.* another name for **limit point.**

accumulator (ə'kju:mjʊ,leɪtə) *n.* **1.** Also called: **battery, storage battery.** a rechargeable device for storing electrical energy in the form of chemical energy, consisting of one or more separate secondary cells. **2.** *Horse racing, Brit.* a collective bet, esp. on four or more races, in which the stake and winnings on each successive race are carried forward to become the stake on the next, so that both stakes and winnings accumulate progressively so long as the bet continues to be a winning one. **3. a.** a register in a computer or calculator used for holding the results of a computation or data transfer. **b.** a location in a computer store in which arithmetical results are produced.

accuracy ('ækjʊrəsɪ) *n., pl.* **-cies. 1.** faithful measurement or representation of the truth; correctness; precision. **2.** *Physics, chem.* the degree of agreement between a measured value and the standard or accepted value for that measurement.

accurate ('ækjərɪt) *adj.* **1.** faithfully representing or describing the truth. **2.** showing a negligible or permissible deviation from a standard: *an accurate ruler.* **3.** without error; precise; meticulous. **4.** *Maths.* **a.** (to *n* significant digits) correctly representing the first *n* digits of the given number following the first nonzero digit, but approximating to the nearest digit in the final position: *since* $\pi = 3.14159...$, *the approximation 3.1416 is accurate to 5 significant digits.* **b.** (to *n* decimal places) giving the first *n* digits after the decimal point without further approximation: $\pi = 3.1415$ *is in this sense accurate to 4 decimal places.* [C16: from Latin *accūrātus*, past participle of *accūrāre* to perform with care, from *cūra* care] —**'accurately** *adv.* —**'accurateness** *n.*

accursed (ə'kɜ:sɪd, ə'kɜ:st) *or* **accurst** (ə'kɜ:st) *adj.* **1.** under or subject to a curse; doomed. **2.** (*prenominal*) hateful; detestable; execrable. [Old English *ācursod*, past participle of *ācursian* to put under a CURSE] —**accursedly** (ə'kɜ:sɪdlɪ) *adv.* —**ac'cursedness** *n.*

accusal (ə'kju:zᵊl) *n.* another word for **accusation.**

accusation (,ækjʊ'zeɪʃən) *n.* **1.** an allegation that a person is guilty of some fault, offence, or crime; imputation. **2.** a formal charge brought against a person stating the crime that he is alleged to have committed.

accusative (ə'kju:zətɪv) *adj.* **1.** *Grammar.* denoting a case of nouns, pronouns, and adjectives in inflected languages that is used to identify the direct object of a finite verb, of certain prepositions, and for certain other purposes. See also **objective** (sense 5). **2.** another word for **accusatorial.** ~*n.* **3.** *Grammar.* **a.** the accusative case. **b.** a word or speech element in the accusative case. [C15: from Latin; in grammar, from the phrase *cāsus accūsātīvus* accusative case, a mistaken translation of Greek *ptōsis aitiatikē* the case indicating causation. See ACCUSE] —**accusatival** (ə,kju:zə'taɪvᵊl) *adj.* —**ac'cusatively** *adv.*

accusatorial (ə,kju:zə'tɔ:rɪəl) *or* **accusatory** (ə'kju:zətərɪ, -trɪ, ,ækjʊ'zeɪtərɪ) *adj.* **1.** containing or implying blame or strong criticism. **2.** *Law.* denoting criminal procedure in which the prosecutor is distinct from the judge and the trial is conducted in public. Compare **inquisitorial** (sense 3).

accuse (ə'kju:z) *vb.* to charge (a person or persons) with some fault, offence, crime, etc.; impute guilt or blame. [C13: via Old French from Latin *accūsare* to call to account, from *ad-* to + *causa* lawsuit] —**ac'cuser** *n.* —**ac'cusing** *adj.* —**ac'cusingly** *adv.*

accused (ə'kju:zd) *n.* (preceded by *the*) *Law.* the defendant or defendants appearing on a criminal charge.

accustom (ə'kʌstəm) *vb.* (*tr.;* usually foll. by *to*) to make (oneself) familiar (with) or used (to), as by practice, habit, or experience. [C15: from Old French *acostumer*, from *costume* CUSTOM]

accustomed (ə'kʌstəmd) *adj.* **1.** usual; customary. **2.** (*postpositive;* foll. by *to*) used or inured (to). **3.** (*postpositive;* foll. by *to*) in the habit (of): *accustomed to walking after meals.*

Accutron ('ækju:,trɒn) *n. Trademark.* a type of watch in which the balance wheel and hairspring are replaced by a tuning fork kept in vibration by a tiny internal battery.

AC/DC *adj. Informal.* (of a person) bisexual. [C20: humorous reference to electrical apparatus that is adaptable for ALTERNATING CURRENT and DIRECT CURRENT]

ace (eɪs) *n.* **1.** any die, domino, or any of four playing cards with one spot. **2.** a single spot or pip on a playing card, die, etc. **3.** *Tennis.* a winning serve that the opponent fails to reach. **4.** *Golf, chiefly U.S.* a hole in one. **5.** a fighter pilot accredited with destroying several enemy aircraft. **6.** *Informal.* an expert or highly skilled person: *an ace at driving.* **7. an ace up one's sleeve** *or* **an ace in the hole.** a hidden and powerful advantage. *~adj.* **8.** *Informal.* superb; excellent. *~vb.* **9.** (*tr.*) *Tennis.* to serve an ace against. **10.** *Golf.* to play (a hole) in one stroke. [C13: via Old French from Latin *as* a unit, perhaps from a Greek variant of *heis* one]

ACE (eɪs) *n. acronym for:* **1.** (in Britain) Advisory Centre for Education; a private organization offering advice on schools to parents. **2.** Allied Command Europe.

-acea *suffix forming plural proper nouns.* denoting animals belonging to a class or order: *Crustacea* (class); *Cetacea* (order). [New Latin, from Latin, neuter plural of *-āceus* -ACEOUS]

-aceae *suffix forming plural proper nouns.* denoting plants belonging to a family: *Liliaceae; Ranunculaceae.* [New Latin, from Latin, feminine plural of *-āceus* -ACEOUS]

acedia (əˈsiːdɪə) *n.* another word for **accidie.**

acellular (eɪˈsɛljʊlə) *adj. Biology.* not made up of or containing cells.

acentric (eɪˈsɛntrɪk) *adj.* **1.** without a centre. **2.** not on centre; eccentric. **3.** *Genetics.* (of a chromosome or chromosome fragment) lacking a centromere. *~n.* **4.** an acentric chromosome or fragment.

-aceous *suffix forming adjectives.* relating to, belonging to, having the nature of, or resembling: *herbaceous; larvaceous.* [New Latin, from Latin *-āceus* of a certain kind; related to *-āc, -āx,* adjectival suffix]

acephalous (əˈsɛfələs) *adj.* **1.** having no head or one that is reduced and indistinct, as certain insect larvae. **2.** having or recognizing no ruler or leader. [C18: via Medieval Latin from Greek *akephalos.* See A-[1], -CEPHALIC]

acer (ˈeɪsə) *n.* any tree or shrub of the genus *Acer,* often cultivated for their brightly coloured foliage. See also **maple.**

ACER *abbrev. for* Australian Council for Educational Research.

acerate (ˈæsəˌreɪt, -rɪt) *adj.* another word for **acerose.** [C19: from Latin *ācer* sharp + -ATE[1]]

acerbate (ˈæsəˌbeɪt) *vb.* (*tr.*) **1.** to embitter or exasperate. **2.** to make sour or bitter. [C18: from Latin *acerbātus,* past participle of *acerbāre* to make sour]

acerbic (əˈsɜːbɪk) *adj.* harsh, bitter, or astringent; sour. [C17: from Latin *acerbus* sour, bitter]

acerbity (əˈsɜːbɪtɪ) *n., pl.* **-ties. 1.** vitriolic or embittered speech, temper, etc. **2.** sourness or bitterness of taste.

acerose (ˈæsəˌrəʊs, -ˌrəʊz) *or* **acerous** *adj.* shaped like a needle, as pine leaves. [C18: from Latin *acerōsus* full of chaff (erroneously used by Linnaeus as if derived from *ācer* sharp)]

acervate (əˈsɜːvɪt, -ˌveɪt) *adj. Botany.* growing in heaps or clusters. [C19: from Latin *acervātus,* from *acervāre* to heap up, from *acervus* a heap] —**aˈcervately** *adv.*

acescent (əˈsɛsᵊnt) *adj.* slightly sour or turning sour. [C18: from Latin *acēscent-,* from *acēscere* to become sour, from *ācer* sharp] —**aˈcescence** *or* **aˈcescency** *n.*

acetabulum (ˌæsɪˈtæbjʊləm) *n., pl.* **-la** (-lə). **1.** the deep cuplike cavity on the side of the hipbone that receives the head of the thighbone. **2.** a round muscular sucker in flatworms, leeches, and cephalopod molluscs. **3.** the aperture in the thorax of an insect that holds the leg. [Latin: vinegar cup, hence a cuplike cavity, from *acētum* vinegar + *-abulum,* suffix denoting a container]

acetal (ˈæsɪˌtæl) *n.* **1.** a colourless volatile liquid used as a solvent and in perfumes. Formula: $CH_3CH(OC_2H_5)_2$. **2.** any organic compound containing the group $-CH(OR_1)OR_2$, where R_1 and R_2 are other organic groups. [C19: from German *Azetal,* from ACETO- + ALCOHOL]

acetaldehyde (ˌæsɪˈtældɪˌhaɪd) *n.* a colourless volatile pungent liquid, miscible with water, used in the manufacture of organic compounds and as a solvent and reducing agent. Formula: CH_3CHO. Systematic name: **ethanal.**

acetamide (ˌæsɪˈtæmaɪd, əˈsɛtɪˌmaɪd) *or* **acetamid** (ˌæsɪˈtæmɪd, əˈsɛtɪmɪd) *n.* a white or colourless soluble deliquescent crystalline compound, used in the manufacture of organic chemicals. Formula: CH_3CONH_2. [C19: from German *Azetamid,* from ACETO- + AMIDE]

acetanilide (ˌæsɪˈtænɪˌlaɪd) *or* **acetanilid** (ˌæsɪˈtænɪlɪd) *n.* a white crystalline powder used in the manufacture of dyes and rubber and as an analgesic in medicine. Formula: $C_6H_5NHCOCH_3$. [C19: from ACETO- + ANILINE + -IDE]

acetate (ˈæsɪˌteɪt) *n.* **1.** any salt or ester of acetic acid, containing the monovalent ion CH_3COO^- or the group CH_3COO-. Systematic name: **ethanoate. 2.** (*modifier*) consisting of, containing, or concerned with the group CH_3COO-: *acetate group or radical.* **3.** short for **acetate rayon** *or* **cellulose acetate. 4.** a sound recording disc composed of an acetate lacquer coating on an aluminium or plastic base: used for demonstration or other short-term purposes. [C19: from ACETIC + -ATE[1]] —**ˈaceˌtated** *adj.*

acetate rayon *n.* a synthetic textile fibre made from cellulose acetate. Also called: **acetate.**

acetic (əˈsiːtɪk, əˈsɛt-) *adj.* of, containing, producing, or derived from acetic acid or vinegar. [C19: from Latin *acētum* vinegar]

acetic acid *n.* a colourless pungent liquid, miscible with water, widely used in the manufacture of acetic anhydride, vinyl acetate, plastics, pharmaceuticals, dyes, etc. Formula: CH_3COOH. Systematic name: **ethanoic acid.** See also **glacial acetic acid, vinegar.**

acetic anhydride *n.* a colourless pungent liquid used in the manufacture of cellulose and vinyl acetates for synthetic fabrics. Formula: $(CH_3CO)_2O$.

acetify (əˈsɛtɪˌfaɪ) *vb.* **-fies, -fying, -fied.** to become or cause to become acetic acid or vinegar. —**aˌcetifiˈcation** *n.* —**aˈcetiˌfier** *n.*

aceto- *or before a vowel* **acet-** *combining form.* containing an acetyl group or derived from acetic acid: *acetone.* [from Latin *acētum* vinegar]

acetometer (ˌæsɪˈtɒmɪtə) *n.* a device for measuring the concentration of acetic acid in a solution, esp. in vinegar.

acetone (ˈæsɪˌtəʊn) *n.* a colourless volatile flammable pungent liquid, miscible with water, used in the manufacture of chemicals and as a solvent and thinner for paints, varnishes, and lacquers. Formula: CH_3COCH_3. Systematic name: **propanone.** [C19: from German *Azeton,* from ACETO- + -ONE] —**acetonic** (ˌæsɪˈtɒnɪk) *adj.*

acetone body *n.* another name for **ketone body.**

acetophenetidin (əˌsiːtəʊfəˈnɛtɪdɪn) *n.* another name for **phenacetin.**

acetous (ˈæsɪtəs, əˈsiː-) *or* **acetose** (ˈæsɪˌtəʊs, -ˌtəʊz) *adj.* **1.** containing, producing, or resembling acetic acid or vinegar. **2.** tasting like vinegar. [C18: from Late Latin *acētōsus* vinegary, from *acētum* vinegar]

acetum (əˈsiːtəm) *n.* **1.** another name for **vinegar. 2.** a solution that has dilute acetic acid as solvent. [Latin]

acetyl (ˈæsɪˌtaɪl, əˈsiːtaɪl) *n.* (*modifier*) of, consisting of, or containing the monovalent group CH_3CO-: *acetyl group or radical.* [C19: from ACET(IC) + -YL] —**acetylic** (ˌæsɪˈtɪlɪk) *adj.*

acetylate (əˈsɛtɪˌleɪt) *vb.* **1.** (*tr.*) to introduce an acetyl group into (a chemical compound). **2.** (*intr.*) (of a chemical compound) to gain or suffer substitution of an acetyl group. —**aˌcetyˈlation** *n.*

acetyl chloride *n.* a colourless pungent liquid used as an acetylating agent. Formula: CH_3COCl. Also called: **ethanoyl chloride.**

acetylcholine (ˌæsɪtaɪlˈkəʊliːn, -lɪn) *n.* a chemical substance secreted at the ends of many nerve fibres, esp. in the autonomic nervous system, and responsible for the transmission of nervous impulses. Formula: $C_7H_{17}NO_3$.

acetylcholinesterase (əˈsiːtaɪlˌkəʊliːnˈɛstərˌeɪz, ˈæsɪtaɪl-) *n.* an enzyme in nerve cells that is responsible for the destruction of acetylcholine and thus for switching off excitation of the nerve.

acetylene (əˈsɛtɪˌliːn) *n.* **1.** a colourless soluble flammable gas used in the manufacture of organic chemicals and in cutting and welding metals. Formula: C_2H_2. Systematic name: **ethyne. 2. a.** another name for **alkyne. b.** (*as modifier*): *acetylene series.* —**acetylenic** (əˌsɛtɪˈlɛnɪk) *adj.*

acetylide (əˈsɛtɪˌlaɪd) *n.* any of a class of carbides in which the carbon is present as a diatomic divalent ion (C_2^{2-}). They are formally derivatives of acetylene.

acetylsalicylic acid (ˌæsɪtaɪlˌsælɪˈsɪlɪk, əˈsiːtaɪl-) *n.* the chemical name for **aspirin.**

acey-deucy (ˈeɪsɪˈdjuːsɪ) *n.* a form of backgammon.

ACGI *abbrev. for* Associate of the City and Guilds Institute.

ach (ɑːx) *interj. Scot.* an expression of surprise, impatience, disgust, etc. Also: **och.**

Achaean (əˈkiːən) *or* **Achaian** (əˈkaɪən) *n.* **1.** a member of a principal Greek tribe in the Mycenaean era. **2.** a native or inhabitant of the later Greek province of Achaea. *~adj.* **3.** of or relating to Achaea or the Achaeans.

Achaemenid (əˈkiːmənɪd, əˈkɛm-) *n., pl.* **Achaemenids, Achaemenidae** (ˌækɪˈmɛnɪˌdiː), *or* **Achaemenides** (ˌækɪˈmɛnɪˌdiːz). any member of a Persian dynasty of kings, including Cyrus the Great, that ruled from about 550 to 331 B.C., when Darius III was overthrown by Alexander the Great. [from Greek, after *Akhaimenēs,* name of the founder]

achalasia (ˌækəˈleɪzɪə) *n. Pathol.* failure of the cardiac sphincter of the oesophagus to relax, resulting in difficulty in swallowing. [New Latin, from A-[1] + Greek *chalasis* relaxation]

Achates (əˈkeɪtiːz) *n.* a loyal friend [from Aeneas' faithful companion in Vergil's *Aeneid*]

ache (eɪk) *vb.* (*intr.*) **1.** to feel, suffer, or be the source of a continuous dull pain. **2.** to suffer mental anguish. *~n.* **3.** a continuous dull pain. [Old English *ācan* (vb.), *æce* (n.), Middle English *aken* (vb.), *ache* (n.). Compare BAKE, BATCH] —**ˈaching** *adj.* —**ˈachingly** *adv.*

achene *or* **akene** (əˈkiːn) *n.* a dry one-seeded indehiscent fruit with the seed distinct from the fruit wall. It may be smooth, as in the buttercup, or feathery, as in clematis. [C19: from New Latin *achaenium* that which does not yawn or open, from A-[1] + Greek *khainein* to yawn] —**aˈchenial** *or* **aˈkenial** *adj.*

Achernar (ˈeɪkəˌnɑː) *n.* the brightest star in the constellation Eridanus, visible only in the S hemisphere. Visual magnitude: 0.6; spectral type: B5; distance: 66 light years. [from Arabic *ākhīr al-nahr,* literally: end of the river, alluding to the star's location in the constellation]

Acheulian *or* **Acheulean** (əˈʃuːlɪən, -ʃən) *Archaeol.* *~n.* **1.** (in Europe) the period in the Lower Palaeolithic following the Abbevillian, represented by the use of soft hammerstones in hand axe production made of chipped stone, bone, antler, or wood. The Acheulian dates from the Riss glaciation. **2.** (in

Africa) the period represented by every stage of hand axe development. ~*adj.* 3. of or relating to this period. [C20: after *St. Acheul,* town in northern France]

à cheval *French.* (a ʃəval) *adv.* (of a bet, esp. in roulette) made on two adjacent numbers, cards, etc. [literally: on horseback]

achieve (əˈtʃiːv) *vb. (tr.)* **1.** to bring to a successful conclusion; accomplish; attain. **2.** to gain as by hard work or effort: *to achieve success.* [C14: from Old French *achever* to bring to an end, from the phrase *a chef* to a head, to a conclusion] —**aˈchievable** *adj.* —**aˈchiever** *n.*

achievement (əˈtʃiːvmənt) *n.* **1.** something that has been accomplished, esp. by hard work, ability, or heroism. **2.** successful completion; accomplishment. **3.** *Heraldry.* a less common word for **hatchment.**

achievement age *n. Psychol.* the age at which a child should be able to perform a standardized test successfully. Compare **mental age.**

achievement quotient *n. Psychol.* a measure of ability derived by dividing an individual's achievement age by his actual age. Abbrev.: **AQ.**

achievement test *n. Psychol.* a test designed to measure the effects that learning and teaching have on individuals.

achillea (ˌækɪˈliːə) *n.* any plant of the southern temperate genus *Achillea,* with white, yellow, or purple flowers, some species of which are widely grown as garden plants: family *Compositae.* See also **sneezewort, yarrow.** [from *Achilles,* who was credited with discovering medicinal properties in the plant]

Achilles heel (əˈkɪliːz) *n.* a small but fatal weakness. [named after *Achilles,* hero in Greek mythology, invulnerable except for his heel]

Achilles tendon *n.* the fibrous cord that connects the muscles of the calf to the heelbone.

achimenes (ˌækɪˈmiːniːz) *n.* any plant of the S American tuberous-rooted perennial genus *Achimenes,* with showy red, blue, or white tubular flowers, some of which are grown as greenhouse plants: family *Gesneriaceae.* [from Latin *achaemenis,* from Greek *achaimenis,* a species of euphorbia]

achlamydeous (ˌækləˈmɪdɪəs) *adj.* (of flowers such as the willow) having neither petals nor sepals. [C19: from Greek *a-* not, without + *chlamys* cloak]

ach-laut (ˈæklaʊt, ˈæx-) *n.* (*sometimes cap.*) *Phonetics.* the voiceless velar fricative sound that is written as *ch* in Scottish *loch* or in German *ach,* often allophonic with the ich-laut. See also **ich-laut.** [from German, from *ach* ah + *Laut* sound]

achlorhydria (ˌeɪklɔːˈhaɪdrɪə) *n.* a marked reduction or virtual absence of free hydrochloric acid from the gastric juice. [C20: New Latin; see A-[1], CHLORO-, HYDRO-]

achondrite (eɪˈkɒndraɪt) *n.* a rare stony meteorite that consists mainly of silicate minerals and has the texture of igneous rock but contains no chondrules. Compare **chondrite.** —**achondritic** (ˌeɪkɒnˈdrɪtɪk) *adj.*

achondroplasia (eɪˌkɒndrəʊˈpleɪzɪə) *n.* a skeletal disorder, characterized by failure of normal conversion of cartilage into bone, that begins during fetal life and results in dwarfism. [C20: New Latin; see A-[1], CHONDRO-, -PLASIA] —**achondroplastic** (eɪˌkɒndrəʊˈplæstɪk) *adj.*

achromat (ˈækrəˌmæt) *n.* **1.** Also called: **achromatic lens.** a lens designed to bring light of two chosen wavelengths to the same focal point, thus reducing chromatic aberration. Compare **apochromat.** **2.** a person who has no colour vision at all and can distinguish only black, white, and grey. The condition is very rare.

achromatic (ˌækrəˈmætɪk) *adj.* **1.** without colour. **2.** capable of reflecting or refracting light without chromatic aberration. **3.** *Cytology.* **a.** not staining with standard dyes. **b.** of or relating to achromatin. **4.** *Music.* **a.** involving no sharps or flats. **b.** another word for **diatonic.** **5.** denoting a person who is an achromat. —ˌ**achroˈmatically** *adv.* —**achromatism** (əˈkrəʊməˌtɪzəm) *or* **achromaticity** (əˌkrəʊməˈtɪsɪtɪ) *n.*

achromatic colour *n. Physics.* colour, such as white, black, and grey, that is devoid of hue. See **colour** (sense 2).

achromatin (əˈkrəʊmətɪn) *n.* the material of the nucleus of a cell that does not stain with basic dyes. Compare **chromatin.**

achromatize *or* **achromatise** (əˈkrəʊmətaɪz) *vb. (tr.)* to make achromatic; to remove colour from. —**aˌchromatiˈzation** *or* **aˌchromatiˈsation** *n.*

achromatous (əˈkrəʊmətəs) *adj.* having little or no colour or less than is normal.

achromic (əˈkrəʊmɪk) *or* **achromous** *adj.* colourless.

achy (ˈeɪkɪ) *adj.* **achier, achiest.** affected by a continuous dull pain; aching.

ach-y-fi (ˌaxəˈviː, ˌʌx-) *interj. Welsh dialect.* an expression of disgust or abhorrence. [Welsh, probably from *ach, achy* general exclamation of disgust + *fi* I, me]

acicula (əˈsɪkjʊlə) *n., pl.* **-lae** (-ˌliː). a needle-shaped part, such as a spine, prickle, or crystal. [C19: New Latin, diminutive of *acus* needle] —**aˈcicular** *adj.*

aciculate (əˈsɪkjʊlɪt, -ˌleɪt) *or* **aciculated** *adj.* **1.** having aciculae. **2.** marked with or as if with needle scratches.

aciculum (əˈsɪkjʊləm) *n., pl.* **-lums** *or* **-la** (-lə). a needle-like bristle that provides internal support for the appendages (chaetae) of some polychaete worms. [C19: New Latin; see ACICULA]

acid (ˈæsɪd) *n.* **1.** any substance that dissociates in water to yield a sour corrosive solution containing hydrogen ions, having a pH of less than 7, and turning litmus red. See also **Lewis acid.** **2.** a sour-tasting substance. **3.** a slang name for **LSD.** **4. put the acid on (someone).** *Austral. and N.Z. informal.* to apply pressure to (someone), usually when seeking a favour. ~*adj.* **5.** *Chem.* **a.** of, derived from, or containing acid: *an acid radical.* **b.** being or having the properties of an acid: *sodium bicarbonate is an acid salt.* **6.** sharp or sour in taste. **7.** cutting, sharp, or hurtful in speech, manner, etc.; vitriolic; caustic. **8.** (of rain, snow, etc.) containing pollutant acids in solution. **9.** (of igneous rocks) having a silica content of more than two thirds the total and containing at least one tenth quartz. **10.** *Metallurgy.* of or made by a process in which the furnace or converter is lined with an acid material: *acid steel.* [C17 (first used by Francis Bacon): from French *acide* or Latin *acidus,* from *acēre* to be sour or sharp] —ˈ**acidly** *adv.* —ˈ**acidness** *n.* —ˈ**acidy** *adj.*

acid anhydride *n.* another name for **anhydride** (sense 3).

acidanthera (ˌæsɪˈdænθərə) *n.* any plant of the African cormous genus *Acidanthera,* cultivated for its graceful tubular white and red or white and purple flowers, often scented: family *Iridaceae.* [from Greek *akis* point + New Latin *anthera* anther, from the shape of the anthers]

acid drop *n.* a boiled sweet with a sharp taste.

acid dye *n.* a dye in which the chromophore is part of a negative ion usually applied from an acidic solution.

acid-fast *adj.* (of bacteria and tissues) resistant to decolorization by mineral acids after staining.

acid-forming *adj.* **1.** (of an oxide or element) yielding an acid when dissolved in water or having an oxide that forms an acid in water; acidic. **2.** (of foods) producing an acid residue following digestion.

acid halide *n.* another name for **acyl halide.**

acidhead (ˈæsɪdˌhɛd) *n. Slang.* a person who uses LSD.

Acid House *or* **Acid** *n.* a type of funk-based electronically edited disco music of the late 1980s, which has hypnotic sound effects and is associated with hippie culture and the use of the drug ecstasy. [C20: perhaps from ACID (LSD) + HOUSE (MUSIC)]

Acid-House party *n.* a professionally organized large-scale party for young people, usually held in a field or a disused building, with Acid-House music. Compare **warehouse party.**

acidic (əˈsɪdɪk) *adj.* **1.** another word for **acid.** **2.** (of an oxide) yielding an acid in aqueous solution.

acidify (əˈsɪdɪˌfaɪ) *vb.* **-fies, -fying, -fied.** to convert into or become acid. —**aˈcidiˌfiable** *adj.* —**aˌcidifiˈcation** *n.* —**aˈcidiˌfier** *n.*

acidimeter (ˌæsɪˈdɪmɪtə) *n.* **1.** any instrument for determining the amount of acid in a solution. **2.** another name for **acidometer.**

acidimetry (ˌæsɪˈdɪmɪtrɪ) *n.* the determination of the amount of acid present in a solution, measured by an acidimeter or by volumetric analysis. —**acidimetric** (ˌæsɪdɪˈmɛtrɪk) *or* ˌ**acidiˈmetrical** *adj.* —ˌ**acidiˈmetrically** *adv.*

acidity (əˈsɪdɪtɪ) *n., pl.* **-ties.** **1.** the quality or state of being acid. **2.** the amount of acid present in a solution, often expressed in terms of pH. **3.** another name for **hyperacidity.**

acidometer (ˌæsɪˈdɒmɪtə) *n.* a type of hydrometer for measuring the relative density of an acid solution, esp. the acid in a battery. Also called: **acidimeter.**

acidophil (ˈæsɪdəʊˌfɪl, əˈsɪdə-) *or* **acidophile** (ˈæsɪdəʊˌfaɪl, əˈsɪdə-) *adj. also* **acidophilic** (ˌæsɪdəʊˈfɪlɪk, əˌsɪdə-) *or* **acidophilous** (ˌæsɪˈdɒfɪləs). **1.** (of cells or cell contents) easily stained by acid dyes. **2.** (of microorganisms) growing well in an acid environment. ~*n.* **3.** an acidophil organism. [C20: see ACID, -PHILE]

acidophilus milk (ˌæsɪˈdɒfɪləs) *n. Med.* milk fermented by bacteria of the species *Lactobacillus acidophilus,* used in treating disorders of the gastrointestinal tract.

acidosis (ˌæsɪˈdəʊsɪs) *n.* a condition characterized by an abnormal increase in the acidity of the blood and extracellular fluids. —**acidotic** (ˌæsɪˈdɒtɪk) *adj.*

acid rain *n.* rain that contains a high concentration of pollutants, chiefly sulphur dioxide and nitrogen oxide, released into the atmosphere by the burning of fossil fuels such as coal or oil.

acid rock *n.* a type of rock music characterized by electronically amplified bizarre instrumental effects. [C20: from ACID (sense 3), alluding to its supposed inspiration by drug-induced states of consciousness]

acid salt *n. Chem.* a salt formed by partial replacement of the acidic hydrogen atoms of the parent acid.

acid soil *n.* a soil that gives a pH reaction of below 7.2, found especially in cool moist areas where soluble bases are leached away.

acid test *n.* a rigorous and conclusive test to establish worth or value: *the play passed the critic's acid test.* [C19: from the testing of gold with nitric acid]

acidulate (əˈsɪdjʊˌleɪt) *vb.* *(tr.)* to make slightly acid or sour. [C18: ACIDULOUS + -ATE[1]] —**aˌciduˈlation** *n.*

acidulous (əˈsɪdjʊləs) *or* **acidulent** *adj.* **1.** rather sour. **2.** sharp or sour in speech, manner, etc.; acid. [C18: from Latin *acidulus* sourish, diminutive of *acidus* sour]

acid value *n.* the number of milligrams of potassium hydroxide required to neutralize the free fatty acid in one gram of a fat, oil, resin, etc.

acierate ('æsɪə,reɪt) *vb.* (*tr.*) to change (iron) into steel. [C19: from French *acier* steel, from Latin *aciēs* sharpness] —**,acier'ation** *n.*

ACII *abbrev. for* Associate of the Chartered Insurance Institute.

acinaciform (,æsɪ'næsɪ,fɔːm) *adj.* (of leaves) shaped like a scimitar; curved. [C19: via Latin *acīnacēs,* from Greek *akinakēs* short sword, ultimately from Iranian + -FORM]

aciniform (ə'sɪnɪ,fɔːm) *adj.* shaped like a bunch of grapes. [C19: from New Latin *aciniformis;* see ACINUS]

acinus ('æsɪnəs) *n., pl.* **-ni** (-,naɪ). **1.** *Anatomy.* any of the terminal saclike portions of a compound gland. **2.** *Botany.* any of the small drupes that make up the fruit of the blackberry, raspberry, etc. **3.** *Botany, obsolete.* a collection of berries, such as a bunch of grapes. [C18: New Latin, from Latin: grape, berry] —**acinic** (ə'sɪnɪk), **'acinous,** *or* **'acinose** *adj.*

ack-ack ('æk,æk) *n. Military.* **1. a.** anti-aircraft fire. **b.** (*as modifier*): *ack-ack guns.* **2.** anti-aircraft arms. [C20: British army World War I phonetic alphabet for AA, abbreviation of *anti-aircraft*]

ackee *or* **akee** ('ækiː) *n.* **1. a.** a sapindaceous tree, *Blighia sapida,* native to tropical Africa and cultivated in the West Indies for its fruit, edible when cooked. **b.** the red pear-shaped fruit of this tree. **2.** a sapindaceous tree, *Melicoccus bijugatus,* that grows on some Caribbean islands and is valued for its timber and edible fruit. **3.** the green tough-skinned berry of this tree. [C18: of African origin]

ack-emma ('æk'ɛmə) *adv. Old-fashioned.* in the morning; a.m. [World War I phonetic alphabet for A, M]

acknowledge (ək'nɒlɪdʒ) *vb.* (*tr.*) **1.** (*may take a clause as object*) to recognize or admit the existence, truth, or reality of. **2.** to indicate recognition or awareness of, as by a greeting, glance, etc. **3.** to express appreciation or thanks for: *to acknowledge a gift.* **4.** to make the receipt of known to the sender: *to acknowledge a letter.* **5.** to recognize, esp. in legal form, the authority, rights, or claims of. [C15: probably from earlier *knowledge,* on the model of Old English *oncnāwan,* Middle English *aknowen* to confess, recognize] —**ac'knowledgeable** *adj.* —**ac'knowledger** *n.*

acknowledgment *or* **acknowledgement** (ək'nɒlɪdʒmənt) *n.* **1.** the act of acknowledging or state of being acknowledged. **2.** something done or given as an expression of thanks, as a reply to a message, etc. **3.** (*pl.*) an author's statement acknowledging his use of the works of other authors, usually printed at the front of a book.

aclinic line (ə'klɪnɪk) *n.* another name for **magnetic equator.** [C19 *aclinic,* from Greek *aklinēs* not bending, from A-[1] + *klinein* to bend, lean]

ACM *abbrev. for* air chief marshal.

acme ('ækmɪ) *n.* the culminating point, as of achievement or excellence; summit; peak. [C16: from Greek *akmē*]

acme screw thread *n.* a type of screw thread having inclined flat flanks and a flat top and bottom: used in machine tools.

acne ('æknɪ) *n.* a chronic skin disease common in adolescence, involving inflammation of the sebaceous glands and characterized by pustules on the face, neck, and upper trunk. [C19: New Latin, from a misreading of Greek *akmē* eruption on the face. See ACME]

acnode ('æk,nəʊd) *n.* a point whose coordinates satisfy the equation of a curve although it does not lie on the curve; an isolated point. The origin is an acnode of the curve $y^2 + x^2 = x^3$. [C19: from Latin *acus* a needle + NODE] —**ac'nodal** *adj.*

Acol ('ækᵊl) *n. Bridge.* a popular British bidding system favouring light opening bids and a flexible approach. [C20: named after a club in *Acol* Road, London]

acolyte ('ækə,laɪt) *n.* **1.** a follower or attendant. **2.** *Christianity.* an officer who attends or assists a priest. [C16: via Old French and Medieval Latin from Greek *akolouthos* a follower]

aconite ('ækə,naɪt) *or* **aconitum** (,ækə'naɪtəm) *n.* **1.** any of various N temperate plants of the ranunculaceous genus *Aconitum,* such as monkshood and wolfsbane, many of which are poisonous. Compare **winter aconite. 2.** the dried poisonous root of many of these plants, sometimes used as a narcotic and analgesic. [C16: via Old French or Latin from Greek *akoniton* aconite, monkshood] —**aconitic** (,ækə'nɪtɪk) *adj.*

acorn ('eɪkɔːn) *n.* the fruit of the oak tree, consisting of a smooth thick-walled nut in a woody scaly cuplike base. [C16: a variant (through influence of *corn*) of Old English *æcern* the fruit of a tree, acorn; related to Gothic *akran* fruit, yield]

acorn barnacle *or* **shell** *n.* any of various barnacles, such as *Balanus balanoides,* that live attached to rocks and have a volcano-shaped shell from the top of which protrude feathery food-catching appendages (cirri).

acorn valve *or U.S.* **tube** *n.* a small electronic valve, approximately acorn-shaped with small closely-spaced electrodes, used in ultrahigh-frequency applications.

acorn worm *n.* any of various small burrowing marine animals of the genus *Balanoglossus* and related genera, having an elongated wormlike body with an acorn-shaped eversible proboscis at the head end: subphylum *Hemichordata* (hemichordates).

acotyledon (ə,kɒtɪ'liːdᵊn) *n.* any plant, such as a fern, moss, or fungus, that does not possess cotyledons. —**a,coty'ledonous** *adj.*

acouchi *or* **acouchy** (ə'kuːʃɪ) *n., pl.* **-chis** *or* **-chies.** any of several South American rodents of the genus *Myoprocta,* closely related to the agoutis but much smaller, with a white-tipped tail: family *Dasyproctidae.* [C19: via French from a native name in Guiana]

acoustic (ə'kuːstɪk) *or* **acoustical** *adj.* **1.** of or related to sound, the sense of hearing, or acoustics. **2.** designed to respond to, absorb, or control sound: *an acoustic tile.* **3.** (of a musical instrument or recording) without electronic amplification: *an acoustic bass; an acoustic guitar.* [C17: from Greek *akoustikos,* from *akouein* to hear] —**a'coustically** *adv.*

acoustic coupler *n. Computer technol.* a device converting computer-data signals into acoustic form for transmission down a telephone line, through the handset microphone. See also **modem.**

acoustic feature *n. Phonetics.* any of the acoustic components or elements present in a speech sound and capable of being experimentally observed, recorded, and reproduced.

acoustic guitar *n.* an ordinary guitar, which produces its normal sound through the sounding board and is not amplified in any way. Compare **electric guitar.**

acoustician (,ækʊ'stɪʃən) *n.* an expert in acoustics.

acoustic nerve *n.* either one of the eighth pair of cranial nerves, which supply the cochlea and semicircular canals of the internal ear and contribute to the sense of hearing.

acoustic phonetics *n.* (*functioning as sing.*) the branch of phonetics concerned with the acoustic properties of human speech. Compare **auditory phonetics, articulatory phonetics.**

acoustics (ə'kuːstɪks) *n.* **1.** (*functioning as sing.*) the scientific study of sound and sound waves. **2.** (*functioning as pl.*) the characteristics of a room, auditorium, etc., that determine the fidelity with which sound can be heard within it.

acoustoelectronic (ə,kuːstəʊ,ɪlɛk'trɒnɪk) *adj.* denoting a device in which electronic signals are converted into acoustic waves, esp. in delay lines, etc. Also: **electroacoustic.** —**a,cousto,elec'tronics** *n.*

acpt. *Commerce. abbrev. for* acceptance.

acquaint (ə'kweɪnt) *vb.* (*tr.*) **1.** (foll. by *with* or *of*) to make (a person) familiar or conversant (with); inform (of). **2.** (foll. by *with*) *Chiefly U.S.* to introduce (to); bring into contact (with). [C13: via Old French and Medieval Latin from Latin *accognitus,* from *accognōscere* to know perfectly, from *ad-* (intensive) + *cognōscere* to know]

acquaintance (ə'kweɪntəns) *n.* **1.** a person with whom one has been in contact but who is not a close friend. **2.** knowledge of a person or thing, esp. when slight. **3. make the acquaintance of.** to come into social contact with. **4.** those persons collectively whom one knows. **5.** *Philosophy.* the relation between a knower and the object of his knowledge, as contrasted with knowledge by description (esp. in the phrase **knowledge by acquaintance**). —**ac'quaintance,ship** *n.*

acquainted (ə'kweɪntɪd) *adj.* (*postpositive*) **1.** (sometimes foll. by *with*) on terms of familiarity but not intimacy. **2.** (foll. by *with*) having knowledge or experience (of); familiar (with).

acquiesce (,ækwɪ'ɛs) *vb.* (*intr.;* often foll. by *in* or *to*) to comply (with); assent (to) without protest. [C17: from Latin *acquiēscere* to remain at rest, agree without protest, from *ad-* at + *quiēscere* to rest, from *quiēs* QUIET] —**,acqui'escence** *n.* —**,acqui'escent** *adj.* —**,acqui'escently** *adv.*

acquire (ə'kwaɪə) *vb.* (*tr.*) to get or gain (something, such as an object, trait, or ability), esp. more or less permanently. [C15: via Old French from Latin *acquīrere,* from *ad-* in addition + *quaerere* to get, seek] —**ac'quirable** *adj.* —**ac'quirement** *n.* —**ac'quirer** *n.*

acquired behaviour *n. Psychol.* the behaviour of an organism resulting from the effects of the environment.

acquired characteristic *n.* a characteristic of an organism resulting from increased use or disuse of an organ or the effects of the environment. See also **Lamarckism.**

acquired drive *n. Psychol.* a drive, like the desire for money, that has not been inherited but is learned, presumably because it leads to the satisfaction of innate drives.

acquired immune deficiency syndrome *or* **acquired immunodeficiency syndrome** *n.* the full name for **AIDS.**

acquired immunity *n.* the immunity produced by exposure of an organism to antigens, which stimulates the production of antibodies.

acquired taste *n.* **1.** a liking for something that is at first considered unpleasant. **2.** the thing so liked.

acquisition (,ækwɪ'zɪʃən) *n.* **1.** the act of acquiring or gaining possession. **2.** something acquired. **3.** a person or thing of special merit added to a group. **4.** *Astronautics.* **a.** the re-establishment of communications between a spacecraft and a ground control station after a temporary blackout. **b.** the process of locating a spacecraft, satellite, etc., esp. by radar, in order to gather tracking and telemetric information. [C14: from Latin *acquīsītiōn-,* from *acquīrere* to ACQUIRE]

acquisition accounting *n.* an accounting procedure in which the assets of a company that has recently been taken over are changed from the book value to the fair market value.

acquisitive (əˈkwɪzɪtɪv) *adj.* inclined or eager to acquire things, esp. material possessions. —**acˈquisitively** *adv.* —**acˈquisitiveness** *n.*
acquit (əˈkwɪt) *vb.* **-quits, -quitting, -quitted.** (*tr.*) **1.** (foll. by *of*) **a.** to free or release (from a charge of crime). **b.** to pronounce not guilty. **2.** (foll. by *of*) to free or relieve (from an obligation, duty, responsibility, etc.). **3.** to repay or settle (something, such as a debt or obligation). **4.** to perform (one's part); conduct (oneself). [C13: from Old French *aquiter*, from *quiter* to release, free from, QUIT] —**acˈquitter** *n.*
acquittal (əˈkwɪtᵊl) *n.* **1.** *Criminal law.* the deliverance and release of a person appearing before a court on a charge of crime, as by a finding of not guilty. **2.** a discharge or release from an obligation, duty, debt, etc.
acquittance (əˈkwɪtəns) *n.* **1.** a release from or settlement of a debt, etc. **2.** a record of this, such as a receipt.
acre (ˈeɪkə) *n.* **1.** a unit of area used in certain English-speaking countries, equal to 4840 square yards or 4046.86 square metres. **2.** (*pl.*) **a.** land, esp. a large area. **b.** *Informal.* a large amount: *he has acres of space in his room.* **3. farm the long acre.** *N.Z.* to graze cows on the verge of a road. [Old English *æcer* field, acre; related to Old Norse *akr*, German *Acker*, Latin *ager* field, Sanskrit *ajra* field]
acreage (ˈeɪkərɪdʒ) *n.* land area in acres.
acred (ˈeɪkəd) *adj.* (*usually in combination*) having acres of land: *a many-acred farm; a well-acred nobleman.*
acre-foot *n., pl.* **-feet.** the volume of water that would cover an area of 1 acre to a depth of 1 foot: equivalent to 43 560 cubic feet or 1233.5 cubic metres.
acre-inch *n.* the volume of water that would cover an area of 1 acre to a depth of 1 inch; one twelfth of an acre-foot: equivalent to 3630 cubic feet or 102.8 cubic metres.
acrid (ˈækrɪd) *adj.* **1.** unpleasantly pungent or sharp to the smell or taste. **2.** sharp or caustic, esp. in speech or nature. [C18: from Latin *ācer* sharp, sour; probably formed on the model of ACID] —**acridity** (əˈkrɪdɪtɪ) *or* **ˈacridness** *n.* —**ˈacridly** *adv.*
acridine (ˈækrɪˌdiːn) *n.* a colourless crystalline solid used in the manufacture of dyes. Formula: $C_{13}H_9N$.
acriflavine (ˌækrɪˈfleɪvɪn, -viːn) *n.* a brownish or orange-red powder used in medicine as an antiseptic and bacteriostat. Formula: $C_{14}H_{14}N_3Cl$. [C20: from ACRIDINE + FLAVIN]
acriflavine hydrochloride *n.* a red crystalline water-soluble solid substance obtained from acriflavine and used as an antiseptic. Also called: **flavine.**
Acrilan (ˈækrɪˌlæn) *n. Trademark.* an acrylic fibre or fabric, characterized by strength, softness, and crease-resistance and used for clothing, upholstery, carpets, etc.
acrimony (ˈækrɪmənɪ) *n., pl.* **-nies.** bitterness or sharpness of manner, speech, temper, etc. [C16: from Latin *ācrimōnia*, from *ācer* sharp, sour] —**acrimonious** (ˌækrɪˈməʊnɪəs) *adj.* —ˌ**acriˈmoniously** *adv.* —ˌ**acriˈmoniousness** *n.*
acro- *combining form.* **1.** denoting something at a height, summit, top, tip, beginning, or end: *acropolis; acrogen.* **2.** denoting an extremity of the human body: *acromegaly.* [from Greek *akros* extreme, topmost]
acrobat (ˈækrəˌbæt) *n.* **1.** an entertainer who performs acts that require skill, agility, and coordination, such as tumbling, swinging from a trapeze, or walking a tightrope. **2.** a person noted for his frequent and rapid changes of position or allegiances: *a political acrobat.* [C19: via French from Greek *akrobatēs* acrobat, one who walks on tiptoe, from ACRO- + *bat-*, from *bainein* to walk] —ˌ**acroˈbatic** *adj.* —ˌ**acroˈbatically** *adv.*
acrobatics (ˌækrəˈbætɪks) *n.* **1.** (*functioning as pl.*) the skills or feats of an acrobat. **2.** (*functioning as sing.*) the art of an acrobat. **3.** (*functioning as pl.*) any activity requiring agility and skill: *mental acrobatics.*
acrocarpous (ˌækrəʊˈkɑːpəs) *adj.* (of ferns, mosses, etc.) having the reproductive parts at the tip of a stem. [C19: from New Latin, from Greek *akrokarpos*]
acrocentric (ˌækrəʊˈsɛntrɪk) *adj.* **1.** (of a chromosome) having the centromere at one end. ~*n.* **2.** an acrocentric chromosome.
acrocyanosis (ˌækrəʊˌsaɪəˈnəʊsɪs) *n.* persistent cyanosis of the hands and feet due to poor circulation of the blood.
acrodont (ˈækrəˌdɒnt) *adj.* **1.** (of the teeth of some reptiles) having no roots and being fused at the base to the margin of the jawbones. See also **pleurodont** (sense 1). **2.** having acrodont teeth. [C19: from ACRO- + -ODONT]
acrodrome (ˈækrəˌdrəʊm) *adj.* (of the veins of a leaf) running parallel to the edges of the leaf and fusing at the tip. Also: **acrodromous** (əˈkrɒdrəməs). [from ACRO- + -DROMOUS]
acrogen (ˈækrədʒən) *n.* any flowerless plant, such as a fern or moss, in which growth occurs from the tip of the main stem. [C19: from ACRO- + Greek *genēs* born; see -GEN] —**acrogenic** (ˌækrəˈdʒɛnɪk) *or* **acrogenous** (əˈkrɒdʒɪnəs) *adj.* —**aˈcrogenously** *adv.*
acrolein (əˈkrəʊlɪɪn) *n.* a colourless or yellowish flammable poisonous pungent liquid used in the manufacture of resins and pharmaceuticals. Formula: CH_2:CHCHO. [C19: from Latin *ācer* sharp + *olēre* to smell + -IN]
acrolith (ˈækrəlɪθ) *n.* (esp. in ancient Greek sculpture) a wooden, often draped figure with only the head, hands, and feet in stone. [C19: via Latin *acrolithus* from Greek *akrolithos* having stone extremities] —ˌ**acroˈlithic** *adj.*
acromegaly (ˌækrəʊˈmɛgəlɪ) *n.* a chronic disease characterized by enlargement of the bones of the head, hands, and feet. It is caused by excessive secretion of growth hormone by the pituitary gland. Compare **gigantism.** [C19: from French *acromégalie*, from ACRO- + Greek *megal-*, stem of *megas* big] —**acromegalic** (ˌækrəʊmɪˈgælɪk) *adj., n.*
acromion (əˈkrəʊmɪən) *n., pl.* **-mia** (-mɪə). the outermost edge of the spine of the shoulder blade. [C17: New Latin, from Greek *akrōmion* the point of the shoulder, from ACRO- + *ōmion*, diminutive of *ōmos* shoulder]
acronychal, acronycal, *or U.S.* **acronical** (əˈkrɒnɪkᵊl) *adj.* occurring at sunset: *the star has an acronychal rising.* [C16: from Greek *akronychos* at sunset, from ACRO- + *nykh-*, *nyx* night] —**aˈcronychally, aˈcronycally,** *or U.S.* **aˈcronically** *adv.*
acronym (ˈækrənɪm) *n.* a pronounceable name made up of a series of initial letters or parts of words; for example, *UNESCO* for the *United Nations Educational, Scientific, and Cultural Organization.* [C20: from ACRO- + -ONYM] —ˌ**acroˈnymic** *or* **acronymous** (əˈkrɒnɪməs) *adj.*
acroparaesthesia (ˌækrəʊˌpæresˈθiːzɪə) *or U.S.* **acroparesthesia** *n. Pathol.* a persistent sensation of numbness and tingling in the hands and feet.
acropetal (əˈkrɒpɪtᵊl) *adj.* (of leaves and flowers) produced in order from the base upwards so that the youngest are at the apex. Compare **basipetal.**
acrophobia (ˌækrəˈfəʊbɪə) *n.* abnormal fear or dread of being at a great height. [C19: from ACRO- + -PHOBIA] —ˌ**acroˈphobic** *adj.*
acropolis (əˈkrɒpəlɪs) *n.* the citadel of an ancient Greek city. [C17: from Greek, from ACRO- + *polis* city]
acrospire (ˈækrəˌspaɪə) *n.* the first shoot developing from the plumule of a germinating grain seed. [C17: from obsolete *akerspire*, from *aker* EAR² + *spire* sprout, SPIRE¹; the modern form is influenced by ACRO-]
across (əˈkrɒs) *prep.* **1.** from one side to the other side of. **2.** on or at the other side of. **3.** so as to transcend boundaries or barriers: *people united across borders by religion and history; the study of linguistics across cultures.* ~*adv.* **4.** from one side to the other. **5.** on or to the other side. [C13 *on croice, acros*, from Old French *a croix* crosswise]
across-the-board *adj.* **1.** (of salary increases, taxation cuts, etc.) affecting all levels or classes equally. **2.** *Horse racing.* the U.S. term for **each way.**
acrostic (əˈkrɒstɪk) *n.* **a.** a number of lines of writing, such as a poem, certain letters of which form a word, proverb, etc. A **single acrostic** is formed by the initial letters of the lines, a **double acrostic** by the initial and final letters, and a **triple acrostic** by the initial, middle, and final letters. **b.** the word, proverb, etc., so formed. **c.** (*as modifier*): *an acrostic sonnet.* [C16: via French from Greek *akrostikhis*, from ACRO- + *stikhos* line of verse, STICH] —**aˈcrostically** *adv.*
acroter (əˈkrəʊtə, ˈækrətə) *n. Architect.* a plinth bearing a statue, etc., at either end or at the apex of a pediment. [C18: from French, from Latin *acroterium*, from Greek *akrōtērion* summit, from *akros* extreme]
acrylic (əˈkrɪlɪk) *adj.* **1.** of, derived from, or concerned with acrylic acid. ~*n.* **2.** short for **acrylic fibre, acrylic resin. 3.** a paint or colour containing acrylic resin. [C20: from ACROLEIN + -YL + -IC]
acrylic acid *n.* a colourless corrosive pungent liquid, miscible with water, used in the manufacture of acrylic resins. Formula: CH_2:CHCOOH. Systematic name: **propenoic acid.**
acrylic fibre *n.* a textile fibre, such as Orlon or Acrilan, produced from acrylonitrile.
acrylic resin *n.* any of a group of polymers or copolymers of acrylic acid, its esters, or amides, used as synthetic rubbers, textiles, paints, adhesives, and as plastics such as Perspex.
acrylonitrile (ˌækrɪləʊˈnaɪtraɪl) *n.* a colourless liquid that is miscible with water and has toxic fumes: used in the manufacture of acrylic fibres and resins, rubber, and thermoplastics. Formula: CH_2:CHCN. [C20: from ACRYLIC + NITRILE]
acrylyl (ˈækrɪlɪl) *n.* (*modifier*) of, consisting of, or containing the monovalent group CH_2:CHCO-: *acrylyl group or radical.*
a/cs pay. *abbrev. for* accounts payable.
a/cs rec. *abbrev. for* accounts receivable.
act (ækt) *n.* **1.** something done or performed; a deed. **2.** the performance of some physical or mental process; action. **3.** (*cap. when part of a name*) the formally codified result of deliberation by a legislative body; a law, edict, decree, statute, etc. **4.** (*often pl.*) a formal written record of transactions, proceedings, etc., as of a society, committee, or legislative body. **5.** a major division of a dramatic work. **6. a.** a short performance of skill, a comic sketch, dance, etc., esp. one that is part of a programme of light entertainment. **b.** those giving such a performance. **7.** an assumed attitude or pose, esp. one intended to impress. **8.** *Philosophy.* an occurrence effected by the volition of a human agent, usually opposed at least as regards its explanation to one which is causally determined. Compare **event** (sense 4). ~*vb.* **9.** (*intr.*) to do something; carry out an action. **10.** (*intr.*) to function in a specified way; operate; react: *his mind acted quickly.* **11.** to perform (a part or role) in a play, etc. **12.** (*tr.*) to present (a play, etc.) on stage. **13.** (*intr.*; usually foll. by *for* or *as*) to be a substitute (for); function in place (of). **14.** (*intr.*; foll. by *as*) to

serve the function or purpose (of): *the glass acted as protection.* **15.** (*intr.*) to conduct oneself or behave (as if one were): *she usually acts like a lady.* **16.** (*intr.*) to behave in an unnatural or affected way. **17.** (*copula*) to pose as; play the part of: *to act the fool.* **18.** (*copula*) to behave in a manner appropriate to (esp. in the phrase **act one's age**). **19.** (*copula*) *Not standard.* to seem or pretend to be: *to act tired.* **20. get in on the act.** *Informal.* to become involved in a profitable undertaking or advantageous situation in order to share in the benefits. **21. get one's act together.** *Informal.* to become organized or prepared. ~See also **act on, act out, act up.** [C14: from Latin *actus* a doing, performance, and *actum* a thing done, from the past participle of *agere* to do] —**ˈactable** *adj.* —**ˌactaˈbility** *n.*

ACT *abbrev. for:* **1.** Australian Capital Territory. **2.** advance corporation tax.

actant (ˈæktənt) *n. Linguistics.* (in valency grammar) a noun phrase functioning as the agent of the main verb of a sentence.

actg *abbrev. for* acting.

ACTH *n.* adrenocorticotrophic hormone; a polypeptide hormone, secreted by the anterior lobe of the pituitary gland, that stimulates growth of the adrenal gland and the synthesis and secretion of corticosteroids. It is used in treating rheumatoid arthritis, allergic and skin diseases, and many other disorders. Also called: **corticotrophin.**

actin (ˈæktɪn) *n.* a protein that participates in many kinds of cell movement, including muscle contraction, during which it interacts with filaments of a second protein, myosin. [C20: from ACT + -IN]

actinal (ˈæktɪn^{ə}l, ækˈtaɪn^{ə}l) *adj.* **1.** of or denoting the oral part of a radiate animal, such as a jellyfish, sea anemone, or sponge, from which the rays, tentacles, or arms grow. **2.** possessing rays or tentacles, as a jellyfish. [C19: see ACTINO-, -AL[1]] —**ˈactinally** *adv.*

acting (ˈæktɪŋ) *adj.* (*prenominal*) **1.** taking on duties temporarily, esp. as a substitute for another: *the acting president.* **2.** operating or functioning: *an acting order.* **3.** intended for stage performance; provided with directions for actors: *an acting version of "Hedda Gabler".* ~*n.* **4.** the art or profession of an actor.

actinia (ækˈtɪnɪə) *n., pl.* **-tiniae** (-ˈtɪnɪˌiː) *or* **-tinias.** any sea anemone of the genus *Actinia,* which are common in rock pools. [C18: New Latin, literally: things having a radial structure. See ACTINO-, -IA]

actinic (ækˈtɪnɪk) *adj.* (of radiation) producing a photochemical effect. [C19: from ACTINO- + -IC] —**acˈtinically** *adv.* —**ˈactinˌism** *n.*

actinide (ˈæktɪˌnaɪd) *n.* a member of the actinide series. Also called: **actinon.** [C19: from ACTINO- + -IDE]

actinide series *n.* a series of 15 radioactive elements with increasing atomic numbers from actinium to lawrencium.

actiniform (ækˈtɪnɪˌfɔːm) *adj.* another word for **actinoid.** [C20: from ACTINO- + -FORM]

actinium (ækˈtɪnɪəm) *n.* a radioactive element of the actinide series, occurring as a decay product of uranium. It is used as an alpha-particle source and in neutron production. Symbol: Ac; atomic no.: 89; half-life of most stable isotope, ^{227}Ac: 22 years; relative density: 10.07; melting pt.: 1050°C; boiling pt.: 3200°C (est.). [C19: New Latin, from ACTINO- + -IUM]

actinium series *n.* a radioactive series that starts with uranium-235 and ends with lead-207.

actino- *or before a vowel* **actin-** *combining form.* **1.** indicating a radial structure: *actinomorphic.* **2.** indicating radioactivity or radiation: *actinometer.* [from Greek *aktino-,* from *aktis* beam, ray]

actinobiology (ˌæktɪnəʊbaɪˈɒlədʒɪ) *n.* the branch of biology concerned with the effects of radiation on living organisms.

actinochemistry (ækˌtɪnəʊˈkɛmɪstrɪ) *n.* another name for **photochemistry.**

actinodermatitis (ˌæktɪnəʊˌdɜːməˈtaɪtɪs) *n.* dermatitis from exposure to radiation, esp. ultraviolet light or x-rays.

actinoid (ˈæktɪˌnɔɪd) *adj.* having a radiate form, as a sea anemone or starfish.

actinolite (ækˈtɪnəˌlaɪt) *n.* a green mineral of the amphibole group consisting of calcium magnesium iron silicate. Formula: $Ca_2(Mg,Fe)_5Si_8O_{22}(OH)_2$. [C19: from ACTINO- (from the radiating crystals in some forms) + -LITE]

actinomere (ˈæktɪnəʊˌmɪə) *n.* another name for **antimere.**

actinometer (ˌæktɪˈnɒmɪtə) *n.* an instrument for measuring the intensity of radiation, esp. of the sun's rays. —**actinometric** (ˌæktɪnəʊˈmɛtrɪk) *or* **ˌactinoˈmetrical** *adj.* —**ˌactiˈnometry** *n.*

actinomorphic (ˌæktɪnəʊˈmɔːfɪk) *or* **actinomorphous** *adj. Botany.* (esp. of a flower) having radial symmetry, as buttercups; capable of being cut vertically through the axis in any of two or more planes so that the two cut halves are mirror images of each other. See also **zygomorphic.** —**ˈactinoˌmorphy** *n.*

actinomycete (ˌæktɪnəʊmaɪˈsiːt) *n.* any microorganism of the group *Actinomycetes,* usually regarded as filamentous bacteria. [C20: from ACTINO- + -MYCETE]

actinomycin (ˌæktɪnəʊˈmaɪsɪn) *n.* any of several toxic antibiotics obtained from bacteria of the genus *Streptomyces,* used in treating some cancers.

actinomycosis (ˌæktɪnəʊmaɪˈkəʊsɪs) *n.* a fungal disease of cattle, sometimes transmitted to man, characterized by a swelling of the affected part, most often the jaw. Nontechnical name: **lumpy jaw.** —**actinomycotic** (ˌæktɪnəʊmaɪˈkɒtɪk) *adj.*

actinon (ˈæktɪˌnɒn) *n.* **1.** a radioisotope of radon that is a decay product of radium. Symbol: An or ^{219}Rn; atomic no.: 86; half-life: 3.92s. **2.** another name for **actinide.** [C20: New Latin, from ACTINIUM + -ON]

actinopod (ækˈtɪnəˌpɒd) *n.* any protozoan of the subclass *Actinopoda,* such as a radiolarian or a heliozoan, having stiff radiating pseudopodia.

actinotherapy (ˌæktɪnəʊˈθɛrəpɪ) *n.* another name for **radiotherapy.**

actinouranium (ˌæktɪnəʊjʊˈreɪnɪəm) *n.* the isotope of uranium that has a mass number of 235.

actinozoan (ˌæktɪnəʊˈzəʊən) *n., adj.* another word for **anthozoan.**

action (ˈækʃən) *n.* **1.** the state or process of doing something or being active; operation. **2.** something done, such as an act or deed. **3.** movement or posture during some physical activity. **4.** activity, force, or energy: *a man of action.* **5.** (*usually pl.*) conduct or behaviour. **6.** *Law.* **a.** a legal proceeding brought by one party against another, seeking redress of a wrong or recovery of what is due; lawsuit. **b.** the right to bring such a proceeding. **7.** the operating mechanism, esp. in a piano, gun, watch, etc. **8.** (of a guitar) the distance between the strings and the fingerboard. **9.** (of keyboard instruments) the sensitivity of the keys to touch. **10.** the force applied to a body: *the reaction is equal and opposite to the action.* **11.** the way in which something operates or works. **12.** *Physics.* **a.** a property of a system expressed as twice the mean kinetic energy of the system over a given time interval multiplied by the time interval. **b.** the product of work or energy and time, usually expressed in joule seconds: *Planck's constant of action.* **13.** the events that form the plot of a story, film, play, or other composition. **14.** *Military.* **a.** a minor engagement. **b.** fighting at sea or on land: *he saw action in the war.* **15.** *Philosophy.* behaviour which is voluntary and explicable in terms of the agent's reasons, as contrasted with that which is coerced or determined causally. **16.** *Brit.* short for **industrial action.** **17.** *Informal.* the profits of an enterprise or transaction (esp. in the phrase **a piece of the action**). **18.** *Slang.* the main activity, esp. social activity. ~*vb.* (*tr.*) **19.** to put into effect; take action concerning: *matters decided at the meeting cannot be actioned until the following week.* ~*interj.* **20.** a command given by a film director to indicate that filming is to begin. See also **cue**[1] (senses 1, 8). [C14 *accioun,* ultimately from Latin *āctiōn-,* stem of *āctiō,* from *agere* to do, act]

actionable (ˈækʃənəb^{ə}l) *adj. Law.* affording grounds for legal action. —**ˈactionably** *adv.*

action at a distance *n. Physics.* the supposed interaction of two separated bodies without any intervening medium. In modern theories all interactions are assumed to require a field of force.

actioner (ˈækʃənə) *n. Informal.* a film with a fast-moving plot, usually containing scenes of violence.

action painting *n.* a development of abstract expressionism evolved in the 1940s, characterized by broad vigorous brush strokes and accidental effects of thrown, smeared, dripped, or spattered paint. Also called: **tachisme.** See also **abstract expressionism.**

action potential *n.* a localized change in electrical potential, from −70 mV to +30 mV, that occurs across a nerve fibre during transmission of a nerve impulse.

action replay *n.* the rerunning of a small section of a television film or tape of a match or other sporting contest, often in slow motion. U.S. and Canadian name: **instant replay.**

action stations *pl. n.* **1.** *Military.* the positions taken up by individuals in preparation for or during a battle. ~*interj.* **2.** *Military.* a command to take up such positions. **3.** *Informal.* a warning to get ready for something.

activate (ˈæktɪˌveɪt) *vb.* (*tr.*) **1.** to make active or capable of action. **2.** *Physics.* to make radioactive. **3.** *Chem.* **a.** to increase the rate of (a reaction). **b.** to treat (a substance, such as carbon or alumina) so as to increase powers of adsorption. **4.** *Physiol.* to prepare by arousal (the body or one of its organs (e.g. the brain)) for action. **5.** to purify (sewage) by aeration. **6.** *U.S. military.* to create, mobilize, or organize (a unit). —**ˌactiˈvation** *n.* —**ˈactiˌvator** *n.*

activated alumina *n.* a granular highly porous and adsorptive form of aluminium oxide, used for drying gases and as an oil-filtering material and catalyst.

activated carbon *n.* a porous highly adsorptive form of carbon used to remove colour or impurities from liquids and gases, in the separation and extraction of chemical compounds, and in the recovery of solvents. Also called: **activated charcoal, active carbon.**

activated sludge *n.* a mass of aerated precipitated sewage added to untreated sewage to bring about purification by hastening bacterial decomposition.

active (ˈæktɪv) *adj.* **1.** in a state of action; moving, working, or doing something. **2.** busy or involved: *an active life.* **3.** physically energetic. **4.** exerting influence; effective: *an active ingredient.* **5.** *Grammar.* **a.** denoting a voice of verbs used to indicate that the subject of a sentence is performing the action or causing the event or process described by the verb, as *kicked* in *The boy kicked the football.* Compare **passive** (sense 5). **b.** another word for **nonstative.** 6. being fully engaged in military service (esp. in the phrase **on active service**). 7. (of a volcano) erupting periodically; not extinct. Compare **dormant** (sense 3), **extinct** (sense 3). 8. *Astronomy.* (of the sun) exhibiting a large number of sunspots, solar flares, etc., and a marked variation in intensity and frequency of radio emission. Compare **quiet** (sense 8). 9. *Commerce.* producing or being used to produce profit, esp. in the form of interest: *active balances.* 10. *Electronics.* **a.** containing a source of power: *an active network.* **b.** capable of amplifying a signal or controlling some function: *an active component; an active communication satellite.* ~*n.* 11. *Grammar.* **a.** the active voice. **b.** an active verb. 12. *Chiefly U.S. and Canadian.* a member of an organization who participates in its activities. [C14: from Latin *āctīvus.* See ACT, -IVE] —**'actively** *adv.* —**'activeness** *n.*

active centre *n. Biochem.* the region in an enzyme molecule in which the reactive groups that participate in its action are juxtaposed.

active list *n. Military.* a list of officers available for full duty.

active service *or esp. U.S.* **active duty** *n.* military duty in an operational area.

active transport *n. Biochem., physiol.* a process by which molecules are enabled to pass across a membrane from a region where they are in a low concentration to one of high concentration; this requires the expenditure of energy in metabolism and is assisted by enzymes, commonly referred to as pumps.

active vocabulary *n.* the total number of words a person uses in his own speech and writing. Compare **passive vocabulary.**

activism ('æktɪˌvɪzəm) *n.* a policy of taking direct and often militant action to achieve an end, esp. a political or social one. —**'activist** *n.*

activity (æk'tɪvɪtɪ) *n., pl.* **-ties.** 1. the state or quality of being active. 2. lively action or movement. 3. any specific deed, action, pursuit, etc.: *recreational activities.* 4. the number of disintegrations of a radioactive substance in a given unit of time, usually expressed in curies or disintegrations per second. 5. **a.** the capacity of a substance to undergo chemical change. **b.** the effective concentration of a substance in a chemical system. The **absolute activity** of a substance B, λ_B, is defined as exp (μ_B/RT) where μ_B is the chemical potential.

act of contrition *n. Christianity.* a short prayer of penitence.

act of faith *n. Christianity.* an act that demonstrates or tests a person's religious beliefs.

act of God *n. Law.* a sudden and inevitable occurrence caused by natural forces and not by the agency of man, such as a flood, earthquake, or a similar catastrophe.

act of war *n.* an aggressive act, usually employing military force, which constitutes an immediate threat to peace.

actomyosin (ˌæktəʊ'maɪəsɪn) *n.* a complex protein in skeletal muscle that is formed by actin and myosin and which, when stimulated, shortens to cause muscle contraction.

acton ('æktən) *n.* (in medieval Europe) 1. a jacket or jerkin, originally of quilted cotton, worn under a coat of mail. 2. a leather jacket padded with mail. [C14: from Old French *auqueton,* probably ultimately from Arabic *alqutun* the cotton]

act on *or* **upon** *vb. (intr., prep.)* 1. to regulate one's behaviour in accordance with (advice, information, etc.). 2. to have an effect on (illness, a part of the body, etc.).

actor ('æktə) *or (fem.)* **actress** ('æktrɪs) *n.* 1. a person who acts in a play, film, broadcast, etc. 2. *Informal.* a person who puts on a false manner in order to deceive others (often in the phrase **bad actor**).

act out *vb. (adv.)* 1. *(tr.)* to reproduce (an idea, former event, etc.) in actions, often by mime. 2. *Psychiatry.* to express unconsciously (a repressed impulse or experience) in overt behaviour.

actressy ('æktrɪsɪ) *adj.* exaggerated and affected in manner; theatrical.

ACTT *abbrev. for* Association of Cinematograph and Television Technicians.

ACTU *abbrev. for* Australian Council of Trade Unions.

actual ('æktʃʊəl) *adj.* 1. existing in reality or as a matter of fact. 2. real or genuine. 3. existing at the present time; current. 4. (usually preceded by *your*) *Brit. informal, often facetious.* (intensifier): *that music's by your actual Mozart, isn't it?* ~See also **actuals.** [C14 *actuel* existing, from Late Latin *āctuālis* relating to acts, practical, from Latin *āctus* ACT]

▷**Usage.** The excessive use of *actual* and *actually* should be avoided. They are unnecessary in sentences such as *in actual fact, he is forty-two,* and *he did actually go to the play but did not enjoy it.*

actuality (ˌæktʃʊ'ælɪtɪ) *n., pl.* **-ties.** 1. true existence; reality. 2. *(sometimes pl.)* a fact or condition that is real.

actualize *or* **actualise** ('æktʃʊəˌlaɪz) *vb. (tr.)* 1. to make actual or real. 2. to represent realistically. —ˌ**actuali'zation** *or* ˌ**actuali'sation** *n.*

actually ('æktʃʊəlɪ) *adv.* 1. **a.** as an actual fact; really. **b.** *(as sentence modifier): actually, I haven't seen him.* 2. at present. 3. *Informal.* a parenthetic filler used to add slight emphasis: *I don't know, actually.*

actuals ('æktʃʊəlz) *n.* See **physicals.**

actual sin *n. Christianity.* any sin that a person commits of his own free will and for which he is personally responsible. Compare **original sin.**

actuary ('æktʃʊərɪ) *n., pl.* **-aries.** a statistician, esp. one employed by insurance companies to calculate risks, policy premiums and dividends, and annuity rates. [C16 (meaning: registrar): from Latin *āctuārius* one who keeps accounts, from *actum* public business, and *acta* documents, deeds. See ACT, -ARY] —**actuarial** (ˌæktʃʊ'ɛərɪəl) *adj.*

actuate ('æktʃʊˌeɪt) *vb. (tr.)* 1. to put into action or mechanical motion. 2. to motivate or incite into action: *actuated by unworthy desires.* [C16: from Medieval Latin *actuātus,* from *actuāre* to incite to action, from Latin *āctus* ACT] —ˌ**actu'ation** *n.* —**'actuˌator** *n.*

act up *vb. (intr., adv.) Informal.* to behave in a troublesome way: *the engine began to act up.*

acuity (ə'kjuːɪtɪ) *n.* 1. keenness or acuteness, esp. in vision or thought. 2. the capacity of the eye to see fine detail measured by determining the finest detail that can just be detected. [C15: from Old French, from Latin *acūtus* ACUTE]

aculeate (ə'kjuːlɪɪt, -ˌeɪt) *or* **aculeated** *adj.* 1. cutting; pointed. 2. having prickles or spines, as a rose. 3. having a sting, as bees, wasps, and ants. [C17: from Latin *acūleātus;* see ACULEUS]

aculeus (ə'kjuːlɪəs) *n.* 1. a prickle or spine, such as the thorn of a rose. 2. a sting or ovipositor. [C19: from Latin, diminutive of *acus* needle]

acumen ('ækjʊˌmɛn, ə'kjuːmən) *n.* the ability to judge well; keen discernment; insight. [C16: from Latin: sharpness, from *acuere* to sharpen, from *acus* needle] —**a'cuminous** *adj.*

acuminate *adj.* (ə'kjuːmɪnɪt, -ˌneɪt). 1. narrowing to a sharp point, as some types of leaf. ~*vb.* (ə'kjuːmɪˌneɪt). 2. *(tr.)* to make pointed or sharp. [C17: from Latin *acūmināre* to sharpen; see ACUMEN] —**aˌcumi'nation** *n.*

acupressure ('ækjʊˌprɛʃə) *n.* another name for **shiatsu.** [C19: from ACU(PUNCTURE) + PRESSURE]

acupuncture ('ækjʊˌpʌŋktʃə) *n.* the insertion of the tips of needles into the skin at specific points for the purpose of treating various disorders by stimulating nerve impulses. Originally Chinese, this method of treatment is practised in many parts of the world. Also called: **stylostixis.** [C17: from Latin *acus* needle + PUNCTURE] —**'acuˌpunctural** *adj.* —**'acuˌpuncturist** *n.*

acutance (ə'kjuːtᵊns) *n.* a physical rather than subjective measure of the sharpness of a photographic image.

acute (ə'kjuːt) *adj.* 1. penetrating in perception or insight. 2. sensitive to details; keen. 3. of extreme importance; crucial. 4. sharp or severe; intense: *acute pain; an acute drought.* 5. having a sharp end or point. 6. *Maths.* **a.** (of an angle) less than 90°. **b.** (of a triangle) having all its interior angles less than 90°. 7. (of a disease) **a.** arising suddenly and manifesting intense severity. **b.** of relatively short duration. Compare **chronic** (sense 2). 8. *Phonetics.* **a.** (of a vowel or syllable in some languages with a pitch accent, such as ancient Greek) spoken or sung on a higher musical pitch relative to neighbouring syllables or vowels. **b.** of or relating to an accent (é) placed over vowels, denoting that the vowel is pronounced with higher musical pitch (as in ancient Greek), with a certain special quality (as in French), etc. Compare (for a. and b.) **grave**[2] (sense 5), **circumflex.** ~*n.* 9. an acute accent. [C14: from Latin *acūtus,* past participle of *acuere* to sharpen, from *acus* needle] —**a'cutely** *adv.* —**a'cuteness** *n.*

acute accent *n.* the diacritical mark (é), used in the writing system of some languages to indicate that the vowel over which it is placed has a special quality (as in French *été*) or that it receives the strongest stress in the word (as in Spanish *hablé*).

acute arch *n.* another name for **lancet arch.**

acute dose *n.* a total dose of radiation received over such a short period that biological recovery is impossible.

ACW *abbrev. for* aircraftwoman.

acyclic (eɪ'saɪklɪk, eɪ'sɪklɪk) *adj.* 1. *Chem.* not cyclic; having an open chain structure. 2. *Botany.* having flower parts arranged in a spiral rather than a whorl.

acyl ('eɪsaɪl) *n.* 1. *(modifier)* of, denoting, or containing the monovalent group of atoms RCO-, where R is an aliphatic group: *acyl group or radical; acyl substitution.* 2. an organometallic compound in which a metal atom is directly bound to an acyl group. [C20: from ACID + -YL]

acyl anhydride *n.* another name for **anhydride** (sense 3).

acylation (ˌeɪsaɪ'leɪʃən) *n.* the introduction into a chemical compound of an acyl group.

acyl halide *n.* any derivative of carboxylic acid in which the hydroxyl group has been replaced by a halogen atom. Also called: **acid halide.**

ad[1] (æd) *n.* short for **advertisement.**

ad[2] (æd) *n. Tennis, U.S. and Canadian.* short for **advantage.** Brit. equivalent: **van.**

AD *abbrev. for:* 1. same as **A.D.** 2. *Military.* active duty. 3. *Military.* air defence.

A.D. *or* **AD** (indicating years numbered from the supposed year of the birth of Christ) *abbrev. for* anno Domini: *70 A.D.* Compare **B.C.** [Latin: in the year of the Lord]

▷**Usage.** In strict usage, A.D. is only employed with specific years: *he died in 1621 A.D.,* but *he died in the 17th century* (and not *the 17th century A.D.*). Formerly the practice was to write A.D. preceding the date (*A.D. 1621*), and it is also strictly correct to omit *in* when A.D. is used, since this is already contained in the meaning of the Latin *anno Domini* (in the year of Our Lord), but this is no longer general practice. B.C. is used with both specific dates and indications of the period: *Heraclitus was born about 540 B.C.; the battle took place in the 4th century B.C.*

ad- *prefix.* **1.** to; towards: *adsorb; adverb.* **2.** near; next to: *adrenal.* [from Latin: to, towards. As a prefix in words of Latin origin, *ad-* became *ac-, af-, ag-, al-, an-, acq-, ar-, as-*, and *at-* before *c, f, g, l, n, q, r, s*, and *t*, and became *a-* before *gn, sc, sp, st*]

-ad[1] *suffix forming nouns.* **1.** a group or unit (having so many parts or members): *triad.* **2.** an epic poem concerning (the subject indicated by the stem): *Dunciad.* [via Latin from Greek *-ad-* (plural *-ades*), originally forming adjectives; names of epic poems are all formed on the model of the *Iliad*]

-ad[2] *suffix forming adverbs.* denoting direction towards a specified part in anatomical descriptions: *cephalad.* [from Latin *ad* to, towards]

Ada ('eɪdə) *n.* a high-level computer programming language designed for dealing with real-time processing problems: used for military and other systems. [C20: named after *Ada* Lovelace (1815–52), who worked with Charles Babbage on the first computing machine]

adactylous (eɪ'dæktɪləs) *adj.* possessing no fingers or toes. [C19: from A-[1] + DACTYL + -OUS]

adage ('ædɪdʒ) *n.* a traditional saying that is accepted by many as true or partially true; proverb. [C16: via Old French from Latin *adagium;* related to *āio* I say]

adagio (ə'dɑːdʒɪˌəʊ; *Italian* a'dadʒo) *Music.* ~*adj., adv.* **1.** (to be performed) slowly. ~*n., pl.* **-gios. 2.** a movement or piece to be performed slowly. **3.** *Ballet.* a slow section of a pas de deux. [C18: Italian, from *ad* at + *agio* ease]

Adam[1] ('ædəm) *n.* **1.** *Old Testament.* the first man, created by God. **2. not know (someone) from Adam.** to have no knowledge of or acquaintance with (someone). **3. the old Adam.** the evil supposedly inherent in human nature. **4. Adam's ale** *or* **wine.** water.

Adam[2] *adj.* in the neoclassical style made popular by Robert Adam (1728–92), British architect and furniture designer.

Adam-and-Eve *n.* another name for **puttyroot.**

adamant ('ædəmənt) *adj.* **1.** unshakable in purpose, determination, or opinion; unyielding. **2.** a less common word for **adamantine** (sense 1). ~*n.* **3.** any extremely hard or apparently unbreakable substance. **4.** a legendary stone said to be impenetrable, often identified with the diamond or loadstone. [Old English: from Latin *adamant-*, stem of *adamas,* from Greek; literal meaning perhaps: unconquerable, from A-[1] + *daman* to tame, conquer] —'**adamantly** *adv.*

adamantine (ˌædə'mæntaɪn) *adj.* **1.** very hard; unbreakable or unyielding. **2.** having the lustre of a diamond.

Adamawa (ˌædə'mɑːwə) *n.* a small group of languages of W Africa, spoken chiefly in E Nigeria, N Cameroon, the Central African Republic, and N Zaïre, forming a branch of the Niger-Congo family.

Adamite ('ædəˌmaɪt) *n.* **1.** a human being. **2.** a nudist, esp. a member of an early Christian sect who sought to imitate Adam. —**Adamitic** (ˌædə'mɪtɪk) *adj.*

Adam's apple *n.* the visible projection of the thyroid cartilage of the larynx at the front of the neck.

adamsite ('ædəmˌzaɪt) *n.* a yellow poisonous crystalline solid that readily sublimes; diphenylaminechlorarsine. It is used in chemical warfare as a vomiting agent. Formula: $C_6H_4AsClNHC_6H_4$; relative density: 1.65; melting pt.: 195°C; boiling pt.: 410°C. [C20: named after Roger *Adams* (1899–1971), American chemist]

Adam's-needle *n.* a North American liliaceous plant, *Yucca filamentosa,* that has a tall woody stem, stiff pointed leaves, and large clusters of white flowers arranged in spikes. It is cultivated as an ornamental plant. See also **Spanish bayonet.**

Adams-Stokes syndrome *n.* another term for **heart block.** [C19: named after R. *Adams* (1791–1875) and W. *Stokes* (1804–78), Irish physicians]

adapt (ə'dæpt) *vb.* **1.** (often foll. by *to*) to adjust (someone or something, esp. oneself) to different conditions, a new environment, etc. **2.** (*tr.*) to fit, change, or modify to suit a new or different purpose: *to adapt a play for use in schools.* [C17: from Latin *adaptāre,* from *ad-* to + *aptāre* to fit, from *aptus* APT] —**a'daptable** *adj.* —**aˌdapta'bility** *or* **a'daptableness** *n.* —**a'daptive** *adj.*

adaptation (ˌædæp'teɪʃən, ˌædæp-) *n.* **1.** the act or process of adapting or the state of being adapted; adjustment. **2.** something that is produced or created by adapting something else. **3.** something that is changed or modified to suit new conditions or needs. **4.** *Biology.* an inherited or acquired modification in organisms that makes them better suited to survive and reproduce in a particular environment. **5.** *Physiol.* the decreased response of a sense organ to a repeated or sustained stimulus. **6.** *Psychol.* (in learning theory) the weakening of a response to a stimulus with repeated presentation of the stimulus without reinforcement; applied mainly to innate responses. **7.** *Social welfare.* alteration to a dwelling to make it more convenient for a disabled person, as by replacing steps with ramps.

adapter *or* **adaptor** (ə'dæptə) *n.* **1.** a person or thing that adapts. **2.** any device for connecting two parts, esp. ones that are of different sizes or have different mating fitments. **3. a.** a plug used to connect an electrical device to a mains supply when they have different types of terminals. **b.** a device used to connect several electrical appliances to a single mains socket.

adaption (æ'dæpʃən) *n.* another word for **adaptation.**

adaptive radiation *n.* the development of many different forms from an originally homogeneous group of animals as a result of the increase of the original stock and its spread and adaptation to different environments. This type of evolution occurred in the Tertiary mammals and the Mesozoic reptiles.

Adar (a'dar) *n.* (in the Jewish calendar) the twelfth month of the year according to biblical reckoning and the sixth month of the civil year, usually falling within February and March. In a leap year, an additional month **Adar Rishon** (first Adar) is intercalated between Shevat and Adar, and the latter is known as **Adar Sheni** (second Adar). [from Hebrew]

adaxial (æd'æksɪəl) *adj.* facing towards the axis, as the surface of a leaf that faces the stem. Compare **abaxial.**

ADC *abbrev. for:* **1.** aide-de-camp. **2.** analogue-digital converter.

add (æd) *vb.* **1.** to combine (two or more numbers or quantities) by addition. **2.** (*tr.;* foll. by *to*) to increase (a number or quantity) by another number or quantity using addition. **3.** (*tr.;* often foll. by *to*) to join (something) to something else in order to increase the size, quantity, effect, or scope; unite (with): *to add insult to injury.* **4.** (*intr.;* foll. by *to*) to have an extra and increased effect (on): *her illness added to his worries.* **5.** (*tr.*) to say or write further. **6.** (*tr.;* foll. by *in*) to include. ~See also **add up.** [C14: from Latin *addere,* literally: to put to, from *ad-* to + *-dere* to put]

add. *abbrev. for:* **1.** addendum. **2.** addition. **3.** additional. **4.** address.

addax ('ædæks) *n.* a large light-coloured antelope, *Addax nasomaculatus,* having ribbed loosely spiralled horns and inhabiting desert regions in N Africa: family *Bovidae,* order *Artiodactyla.* [C17: Latin, from an unidentified ancient N African language]

added sixth *n.* a chord much used esp. in jazz, consisting of a triad with an added sixth above the root. Also called: **added sixth chord.** Compare **sixth chord.**

addend ('ædɛnd, ə'dɛnd) *n.* any of a set of numbers that is to be added. Compare **sum** (sense 1). [C20: short for ADDENDUM]

addendum (ə'dɛndəm) *n., pl.* **-da** (-də). **1.** something added; an addition. **2.** a supplement or appendix to a book, magazine, etc. **3.** the radial distance between the inner and outer pitch circles of a screw thread. **4.** the radial distance between the pitch circle and tip of a gear tooth. [C18: from Latin, literally: a thing to be added, neuter gerundive of *addere* to ADD]

adder[1] ('ædə) *n.* **1.** Also called: **viper.** a common viper, *Vipera berus,* that is widely distributed in Europe, including Britain, and Asia and is typically dark greyish in colour with a black zigzag pattern along the back. **2.** any of various similar venomous or nonvenomous snakes. ~See also **death adder, puff adder.** [Old English *nǣdre* snake; in Middle English *a naddre* was mistaken for *an addre,* whence the modern form; related to Old Norse *nathr,* Gothic *nadrs*]

adder[2] ('ædə) *n.* a person or thing that adds, esp. a single element of an electronic computer, the function of which is to add a single digit of each of two inputs.

adder's-meat *n.* another name for the **greater stitchwort** (see **stitchwort).**

adder's-mouth *n.* any of various orchids of the genus *Malaxis* that occur in all parts of the world except Australia and New Zealand and have clusters of small usually greenish flowers. See also **bog orchid.**

adder's-tongue *n.* **1.** any of several terrestrial ferns of the genus *Ophioglossum,* esp. *O. vulgatum,* that grow in the N hemisphere and have a narrow spore-bearing body that sticks out like a spike from the leaf: family *Ophioglossaceae.* **2.** another name for **dogtooth violet.**

addict *vb.* (ə'dɪkt). **1.** (*tr.; usually passive;* often foll. by *to*) to cause (someone or oneself) to become dependent (on something, esp. a narcotic drug). ~*n.* ('ædɪkt). **2.** a person who is addicted, esp. to narcotic drugs. **3.** *Informal.* a person who is devoted to something: *a jazz addict.* [C16 (as adj. and as vb.; n. use C20): from Latin *addictus* given over, from *addīcere* to give one's assent to, from *ad-* to + *dīcere* to say]

addiction (ə'dɪkʃən) *n.* the condition of being abnormally dependent on some habit, esp. compulsive dependency on narcotic drugs.

addictive (ə'dɪktɪv) *adj.* of, relating to, or causing addiction.

adding ('ædɪŋ) *n.* **1.** an act or instance of addition. ~*adj.* **2.** of, for, or relating to addition. **3.** (in systemic grammar) denoting a bound clause that qualifies the meaning of an antecedent noun rather than of the sentence as a whole. Compare **contingency** (sense 4).

adding machine *n.* a mechanical device, operated manually or electrically, for adding and often subtracting, multiplying, and dividing.

Addison's disease *n.* a disease characterized by deep bronzing of the skin, anaemia, and extreme weakness, caused by underactivity of the adrenal glands. Also called: **adrenal insufficiency.** [C19: named after Thomas *Addison* (1793–1860), British physician who identified it]

addition (ə'dɪʃən) *n.* **1.** the act, process, or result of adding. **2.** a person or thing that is added or acquired. **3.** a mathematical operation in which the sum of two numbers or quantities is calculated. Usually indicated by the symbol + **4.** *Chiefly U.S. and Canadian.* a part added to a building or piece of land; annexe. **5.** *Obsolete.* a title following a person's name. **6. in addition.** (*adv.*) also; as well; besides. **7. in addition to.** (*prep.*) besides; as well as. [C15: from Latin *additiōn-*, from *addere* to ADD]

additional (əˈdɪʃənᵊl) *adj.* added or supplementary.

Additional Member System *n.* a system of voting in which people vote separately for the candidate and the party of their choice. Parties are allocated extra seats if the number of constituencies they win does not reflect their overall share of the vote. See also **proportional representation.**

additive (ˈædɪtɪv) *adj.* **1.** characterized or produced by addition; cumulative. ~*n.* **2.** any substance added to something to improve it, prevent deterioration, etc. **3.** short for **food additive.** [C17: from Late Latin *additīvus*, from *addere* to ADD]

additive process *n.* a photographic process in which the desired colours are produced by adding together appropriate proportions of three primary colours. Compare **subtractive process.**

addle[1] (ˈædᵊl) *vb.* **1.** to make or become confused or muddled. **2.** to make or become rotten. ~*adj.* **3.** (*in combination*) indicating a confused or muddled state: *addle-brained; addle-pated.* [C18 (vb.), back formation from *addled*, from C13 *addle* rotten, from Old English *adela* filth; related to dialect German *Addel* liquid manure]

addle[2] (ˈædᵊl) *vb. Northern English dialect.* to earn (money or one's living). [C13 *addlen*, from Old Norse *öthlask* to gain possession of property, from *ōthal* property]

add-on *n. Computer technol.* a circuit, hardware, etc., that can be added to a computer to increase its capacity or performance.

address (əˈdrɛs) *n.* **1.** the conventional form by which the location of a building is described. **2.** the written form of this, as on a letter or parcel, preceded by the name of the person or organization for whom it is intended. **3.** the place at which someone lives. **4.** a speech or written communication, esp. one of a formal nature. **5.** skilfulness or tact. **6.** *Archaic.* manner or style of speaking or conversation. **7.** *Computer technol.* a number giving the location of a piece of stored information. See also **direct access.** **8.** *Brit. government.* a statement of the opinions or wishes of either or both Houses of Parliament that is sent to the sovereign. **9.** the alignment or position of a part, component, etc., that permits correct assembly or fitting. **10.** *Rare.* the act of dispatching or directing a ship. **11.** (*usually pl.*) expressions of affection made by a man in courting a woman. ~*vb.* **-dresses, -dressing; -dressed** *or* (*obsolete or poetic*) **-drest.** (*tr.*) **12.** to mark (a letter, parcel, etc.) with an address. **13.** to speak to, refer to in speaking, or deliver a speech to. **14.** (used reflexively; foll. by *to*) **a.** to speak or write to: *he addressed himself to the chairman.* **b.** to apply oneself to: *he addressed himself to the task.* **15.** to direct (a message, warning, etc.) to the attention of. **16.** to consign or entrust (a ship or a ship's cargo) to a factor, merchant, etc. **17.** to adopt a position facing (the ball in golf, a partner in a dance, the target in archery, etc.). **18.** to treat of; deal with: *chapter 10 addresses the problem of transitivity.* **19.** an archaic word for **woo.** [C14 (in the sense: to make right, adorn) and C15 (in the modern sense: to direct words): via Old French from Vulgar Latin *addrictiāre* (unattested) to make straight, direct oneself towards, from Latin *ad-* to + *dīrectus* DIRECT] —**adˈdresser** *or* **adˈdressor** *n.*

addressable (əˈdrɛsəbᵊl) *adj. Computer technol.* possessing or capable of being reached by an address. —ˈ**ad,dressaˈbility** *n.*

addressee (ˌædrɛˈsiː) *n.* a person or organization to whom a letter, parcel, etc., is addressed.

Addressograph (əˈdrɛsəʊˌgrɑːf, -ˌgræf) *n. Trademark.* a machine for addressing envelopes, etc.

adduce (əˈdjuːs) *vb.* (*tr.*) to cite (reasons, examples, etc.) as evidence or proof. [C15: from Latin *addūcere* to lead or bring to] —**adˈducent** *adj.* —**adˈducible** *or* **adˈduceable** *adj.* —**adduction** (əˈdʌkʃən) *n.*

adduct (əˈdʌkt) *vb.* (*tr.*) **1.** (of a muscle) to draw or pull (a leg, arm, etc.) towards the median axis of the body. Compare **abduct** (sense 2). ~*n.* **2.** *Chem.* a compound formed by direct combination of two or more different compounds or elements. [C19: from Latin *addūcere*; see ADDUCE] —**adˈduction** *n.*

adductor (əˈdʌktə) *n.* a muscle that adducts.

add up *vb.* (*adv.*) **1.** to find the sum (of). **2.** (*intr.*) to result in a correct total. **3.** (*intr.*) *Informal.* to make sense. **4.** (*intr.*; foll. by *to*) to amount to.

-ade *suffix forming nouns.* a sweetened drink made of various fruits: *lemonade; limeade.* [from French, from Latin *-āta* made of, feminine past participle of verbs ending in *-āre*]

ademption (əˈdɛmpʃən) *n. Property law.* the failure of a specific legacy, as by a testator disposing of the subject matter in his lifetime. [C16: from Latin *ademptiōn-* a taking away, from *adimere* to take away, take to (oneself), from *ad-* to + *emere* to buy, take]

adenectomy (ˌædəˈnɛktəmɪ) *n., pl.* **-mies.** **1.** surgical removal of a gland. **2.** another name for **adenoidectomy.** [C19: from ADENO- + -ECTOMY]

adenine (ˈædənɪn, -ˌniːn, -ˌnaɪn) *n.* a purine base present in animal and plant tissues as a constituent of the nucleic acids DNA and RNA and of certain coenzymes; 6-aminopurine. Formula: $C_5H_5N_5$; melting pt.: 360–365°C.

adenitis (ˌædəˈnaɪtɪs) *n.* inflammation of a gland or lymph node. [C19: New Latin, from ADENO- + -ITIS]

adeno- *or before a vowel* **aden-** *combining form.* gland or glandular: *adenoid; adenology.* [New Latin, from Greek *adēn* gland]

adenocarcinoma (ˌædɪnəʊˌkɑːsɪˈnəʊmə) *n., pl.* **-mas** *or* **-mata** (-mətə). **1.** a malignant tumour originating in glandular tissue. **2.** a malignant tumour with a glandlike structure.

adenohypophysis (ˌædɪnəʊhaɪˈpɒfɪsɪs) *n.* the anterior lobe of the pituitary gland. Compare **neurohypophysis.**

adenoid (ˈædɪˌnɔɪd) *adj.* **1.** of or resembling a gland. **2.** of or relating to lymphoid tissue, as that found in the lymph nodes, spleen, tonsils, etc. **3.** of or relating to the adenoids. [C19: from Greek *adenoeidēs.* See ADENO-, -OID]

adenoidal (ˌædɪˈnɔɪdᵊl) *adj.* **1.** having the nasal tones or impaired breathing of one with enlarged adenoids. **2.** another word for **adenoid** (for all senses).

adenoidectomy (ˌædɪnɔɪˈdɛktəmɪ) *n., pl.* **-mies.** surgical removal of the adenoids.

adenoids (ˈædɪˌnɔɪdz) *pl. n.* a mass of lymphoid tissue at the back of the throat behind the uvula: when enlarged it often restricts nasal breathing, esp. in young children. Technical name: **pharyngeal tonsil.**

adenoma (ˌædɪˈnəʊmə) *n., pl.* **-mas** *or* **-mata** (-mətə). **1.** a tumour, usually benign, occurring in glandular tissue. **2.** a tumour having a glandlike structure.

adenopathy (ˌædɪˈnɒpəθɪ) *n. Pathol.* **1.** enlargement of the lymph nodes. **2.** enlargement of a gland.

adenosine (æˈdɛnəˌsiːn, ˌædɪˈnəʊsiːn) *n. Biochem.* a nucleoside formed by the condensation of adenine and ribose. It is present in all living cells in a combined form, as in ribonucleic acids. Formula: $C_{10}H_{13}N_5O_4$. [C20: a blend of ADENINE + RIBOSE]

adenosine monophosphate (ˌmɒnəʊˈfɒsfeɪt) *n.* another term for **adenylic acid.** Abbrev.: **AMP.**

adenosine triphosphate *n.* the full name of **ATP.**

adenovirus (ˌædɪnəʊˈvaɪrəs) *n.* any of a group of viruses that may cause upper respiratory diseases in man. Compare **enterovirus, myxovirus.**

adenylic acid (ˌædəˈnɪlɪk) *n.* a nucleotide consisting of adenine, ribose or deoxyribose, and a phosphate group. It is a constituent of DNA or RNA. Also called: **adenosine monophosphate.**

adept *adj.* (əˈdɛpt). **1.** very proficient in something requiring skill or manual dexterity. **2.** skilful; expert. ~*n.* (ˈædɛpt). **3.** a person who is skilled or proficient in something. [C17: from Medieval Latin *adeptus*, from Latin *adipiscī* to attain, from *ad-* to + *apiscī* to attain] —**aˈdeptly** *adv.* —**aˈdeptness** *n.*

adequate (ˈædɪkwɪt) *adj.* able to fulfil a need or requirement without being abundant, outstanding, etc. [C17: from Latin *adaequāre* to equalize, from *ad-* to + *aequus* EQUAL] —**adequacy** (ˈædɪkwəsɪ) *n.* —ˈ**adequately** *adv.*

à deux *French.* (a dø) *adj., adv.* of or for two persons.

ADH *abbrev. for* antidiuretic hormone. See **vasopressin.**

adhere (ədˈhɪə) *vb.* (*intr.*) **1.** (usually foll. by *to*) to stick or hold fast. **2.** (foll. by *to*) to be devoted (to a political party, cause, religion, etc.); be a follower (of). **3.** (foll. by *to*) to follow closely or exactly: *adhere to the rules.* [C16: via Medieval Latin *adhērēre* from Latin *adhaerēre* to stick to] —**adˈherence** *n.*

adherent (ədˈhɪərənt) *n.* **1.** (usually foll. by *of*) a supporter or follower. ~*adj.* **2.** sticking, holding fast, or attached.

adhesion (ədˈhiːʒən) *n.* **1.** the quality or condition of sticking together or holding fast. **2.** ability to make firm contact without skidding or slipping. **3.** attachment or fidelity, as to a political party, cause, etc. **4.** an attraction or repulsion between the molecules of unlike substances in contact: distinguished from *cohesion.* **5.** *Pathol.* abnormal union of structures or parts. **6.** *Rare.* concurrence; assent. [C17: from Latin *adhaesiōn-* a sticking. See ADHERE]

adhesive (ədˈhiːsɪv) *adj.* **1.** able or designed to adhere; sticky: *adhesive tape.* **2.** tenacious or clinging. ~*n.* **3.** a substance used for sticking objects together, such as glue, cement, or paste. —**adˈhesively** *adv.* —**adˈhesiveness** *n.*

adhibit (ədˈhɪbɪt) *vb.* (*tr.*) *Rare.* **1.** to administer or apply. **2.** to affix; attach. [C16: from Latin *adhibēre* to bring to, from *ad-* to + *habēre* to have, hold] —**adhibition** (ˌædhɪˈbɪʃən) *n.*

ad hoc (æd ˈhɒk) *adj., adv.* for a particular purpose only; lacking generality or justification: *an ad hoc decision; an ad hoc committee.* [Latin, literally: to this]

ad hominem *Latin.* (æd ˈhɒmɪˌnɛm) *adj., adv.* **1.** directed against a person rather than against his arguments. **2.** based on or appealing to emotion rather than reason. ~Compare **ad rem.** See also **argumentum ad hominem.** [literally: to the man]

adiabatic (ˌædɪəˈbætɪk, ˌeɪ-) *adj.* **1.** (of a thermodynamic process) taking place without loss or gain of heat. ~*n.* **2.** a curve on a graph representing the changes in two characteristics (such as pressure and volume) of a system undergoing an adiabatic process. [C19: from Greek *adiabatos* not to be crossed, impassable (to heat), from A-[1] + *diabatos* passable, from *dia-* across + *bainein* to go]

adiactinic (ˌædɪækˈtɪnɪk) *adj. Physics.* denoting a substance that does not transmit radiation affecting photochemically sensitive materials, such as a safelight in a photographic darkroom.

adiaphorism (ˌædɪˈæfəˌrɪzəm) *n.* a Christian Protestant theological theory that certain rites and actions are matters of indifference in religion since not forbidden by the Scriptures. [C19: see ADIAPHOROUS] —ˌadiˈaphorist *n.* —ˌadiˌaphoˈristic *adj.*

adiaphorous (ˌædɪˈæfərəs) *adj. Med.* having no effect for good or ill, as a drug or placebo. [C17: from Greek *adiaphoros* indifferent, from A-[1] + *diaphoros* different]

adiathermancy (ˌædɪəˈθɜːmənsɪ) *n.* another name for **athermancy.** —ˌ**adiaˈthermanous** *adj.*

adieu (əˈdjuː; *French* adjø) *sentence substitute, n., pl.* **adieus** *or* **adieux** (əˈdjuːz; *French* adjø). goodbye; farewell. [C14: from Old French, from *a* to + *dieu* God]

ad infinitum (æd ˌɪnfɪˈnaɪtəm) *adv.* without end; endlessly; to infinity. Abbrev.: **ad inf.** [Latin]

ad interim (æd ˈɪntərɪm) *adj., adv.* for the meantime; for the present: *ad interim measures.* Abbrev.: **ad int.** [Latin]

adios (ˌædɪˈɒs; *Spanish* aˈðjos) *sentence substitute.* goodbye; farewell. [literally: to God]

adipic acid (əˈdɪpɪk) *n.* a colourless crystalline solid used in the preparation of nylon. Formula: $HOOC(CH_2)_4COOH$. [C19: from New Latin *adiposus* fat + -IC]

adipocere (ˌædɪpəʊˈsɪə, ˈædɪpəʊˌsɪə) *n.* a waxlike fatty substance formed during the decomposition of corpses. Nontechnical name: **grave-wax.** [C19: via French from New Latin *adiposus* fat (see ADIPOSE) + French *cire* wax] —**adipocerous** (ˌædɪˈpɒsərəs) *adj.*

adipocyte (ˈædɪpəʊˌsaɪt) *n.* a fat cell that accumulates and stores fats.

adipose (ˈædɪˌpəʊs, -ˌpəʊz) *adj.* **1.** of, resembling, or containing fat; fatty. ~*n.* **2.** animal fat. [C18: from New Latin *adiposus,* from Latin *adeps* fat]

adipose fin *n.* a posterior dorsal fin occurring in the salmon and related fishes.

Adiprene (ˈædɪpriːn) *n. Trademark.* a polyurethane elastomer with exceptional abrasion resistance and strength.

adipsia (eɪˈdɪpsɪə) *n.* **1.** complete lack of thirst. **2.** abnormal abstinence from drinking. [C20: from A-[1] + Greek *dipsa* thirst]

adit (ˈædɪt) *n.* an almost horizontal shaft into a mine, for access or drainage. [C17: from Latin *aditus* an approach, from *adīre,* from *ad-* towards + *īre* to go]

Adivasi (ˈɑːdɪˌvɑːsɪ) *n.* a member of any of the aboriginal peoples of India. [Sanskrit, from *adi* beginning + *vasi* dweller]

adj. *abbrev. for:* **1.** adjective. **2.** *Maths.* adjoint. **3.** adjunct. **4.** adjourned. **5.** *Insurance, banking, etc.* adjustment. **6.** Also: **adjt.** adjutant.

adjacent (əˈdʒeɪsᵊnt) *adj.* **1.** being near or close, esp. having a common boundary; adjoining; contiguous. **2.** *Maths.* **a.** (of a pair of vertices in a graph) joined by a common edge. **b.** (of a pair of edges in a graph) meeting at a common vortex. ~*n.* **3.** *Geometry.* the side lying between a specified angle and a right angle in a right-angled triangle. [C15: from Latin *adjacēre* to lie next to, from *ad-* near + *jacēre* to lie] —**adˈjacency** *n.* —**adˈjacently** *adv.*

adjacent angles *pl. n.* two angles that have the same vertex and a side in common.

adjective (ˈædʒɪktɪv) *n.* **1. a.** a word imputing a characteristic to a noun or pronoun. **b.** (*as modifier*): *an adjective phrase.* Abbrev.: **adj.** ~*adj.* **2.** additional or dependent. **3.** (of law) relating to court practice and procedure, as opposed to the principles of law dealt with by the courts. Compare **substantive** (sense 7). [C14: from Late Latin *adjectīvus* attributive, from *adjicere* to throw to, add, from *ad-* to + *jacere* to throw; in grammatical sense, from the Latin phrase *nōmen adjectīvum* attributive noun] —**adjectival** (ˌædʒɪkˈtaɪvᵊl) *adj.*

adjoin (əˈdʒɔɪn) *vb.* **1.** to be next to (an area of land, etc.). **2.** (*tr.;* foll. by *to*) to join; affix or attach. [C14: via Old French from Latin *adjungere,* from *ad-* to + *jungere* to join]

adjoining (əˈdʒɔɪnɪŋ) *adj.* being in contact; connected or neighbouring.

adjoint (ˈædˌdʒɔɪnt) *n. Maths.* **a.** another name for **Hermitian conjugate. b.** a generalization in category theory of this notion.

adjourn (əˈdʒɜːn) *vb.* **1.** (*intr.*) (of a court, etc.) to close at the end of a session. **2.** to postpone or be postponed, esp. temporarily or to another place. **3.** (*tr.*) to put off (a problem, discussion, etc.) for later consideration; defer. **4.** (*intr.*) *Informal.* **a.** to move elsewhere: *let's adjourn to the kitchen.* **b.** to stop work. [C14: from Old French *ajourner* to defer to an arranged day, from *a-* to + *jour* day, from Late Latin *diurnum,* from Latin *diurnus* daily, from *diēs* day] —**adˈjournment** *n.*

adjt. *or* **adj.** *abbrev. for* adjutant.

adjudge (əˈdʒʌdʒ) *vb.* (*tr.; usually passive*) **1.** to pronounce formally; declare: *he was adjudged the winner.* **2. a.** to determine judicially; judge. **b.** to order or pronounce by law; decree: *he was adjudged bankrupt.* **c.** to award (costs, damages, etc.). **3.** *Archaic.* to sentence or condemn. [C14: via Old French from Latin *adjūdicāre.* See ADJUDICATE]

adjudicate (əˈdʒuːdɪˌkeɪt) *vb.* **1.** (when *intr.,* usually foll. by *upon*) to give a decision (on), esp. a formal or binding one. **2.** (*intr.*) to act as an adjudicator. **3.** (*tr.*) *Chess.* to determine the likely result of (a game) by counting relative value of pieces, positional strength, etc. **4.** (*intr.*) to serve as a judge or arbiter, as in a competition. [C18: from Latin *adjūdicāre* to award something to someone, from *ad-* to + *jūdicāre* to act as a judge, from *jūdex* judge] —**adˌjudiˈcation** *n.* —**adjudicative** (əˈdʒuːdɪkətɪv) *adj.*

adjudicator (əˈdʒuːdɪˌkeɪtə) *n.* **1.** a judge, esp. in a competition. **2.** an arbitrator, esp. in a dispute.

adjunct (ˈædʒʌŋkt) *n.* **1.** something incidental or not essential that is added to something else. **2.** a person who is subordinate to another. **3.** *Grammar.* **a.** part of a sentence other than the subject or the predicate. **b.** (in systemic grammar) part of a sentence other than the subject, predicator, object, or complement; usually a prepositional or adverbial group. **c.** part of a sentence that may be omitted without making the sentence ungrammatical; a modifier. **4.** *Logic.* another name for **accident** (sense 4). ~*adj.* **5.** added or connected in a secondary or subordinate position; auxiliary. [C16: from Latin *adjunctus,* past participle of *adjungere* to ADJOIN] —**adjunctive** (əˈdʒʌŋktɪv) *adj.* —ˈ**adjunctly** *adv.*

adjunction (əˈdʒʌŋkʃən) *n.* (in phrase-structure grammar) the relationship between a branch of a tree representing a sentence to other branches to its left or right that descend from the same node immediately above.

adjure (əˈdʒʊə) *vb.* (*tr.*) **1.** to command, often by exacting an oath; charge. **2.** to appeal earnestly to. [C14: from Latin *adjūrāre* to swear to, from *ad-* to + *jūrāre* to swear, from *jūs* oath] —**adjuration** (ˌædʒʊəˈreɪʃən) *n.* —**adˈjuratory** *adj.* —**adˈjurer** *or* **adˈjuror** *n.*

adjust (əˈdʒʌst) *vb.* **1.** (*tr.*) to alter slightly, esp. to achieve accuracy; regulate: *to adjust the television.* **2.** to adapt, as to a new environment, etc. **3.** (*tr.*) to put into order. **4.** (*tr.*) *Insurance.* to determine the amount payable in settlement of (a claim). [C17: from Old French *adjuster,* from *ad-* to + *juste* right, JUST] —**adˈjustable** *adj.* —**adˈjustably** *adv.* —**adˈjuster** *n.*

adjustment (əˈdʒʌstmənt) *n.* **1.** the act of adjusting or state of being adjusted. **2.** a control for regulating: *the adjustment for volume is beside the speaker.*

adjutant (ˈædʒətənt) *n.* **1.** an officer who acts as administrative assistant to a superior officer. Abbrevs.: **adjt., adj. 2.** short for **adjutant bird.** [C17: from Latin *adjūtāre* to AID] —ˈ**adjutancy** *n.*

adjutant bird *or* **stork** *n.* either of two large carrion-eating storks, *Leptoptilos dubius* or *L. javanicus,* which are closely related and similar to the marabou and occur in S and SE Asia. [so called for its supposedly military gait]

adjutant general *n., pl.* **adjutants general. 1.** *Brit. Army.* **a.** a member of the Army Board responsible for personnel and administrative functions. **b.** a general's executive officer. **2.** *U.S. Army.* the adjutant of a military unit with general staff.

adjuvant (ˈædʒəvənt) *adj.* **1.** aiding or assisting. ~*n.* **2.** something that aids or assists; auxiliary. **3.** *Med.* a drug or other substance that enhances the activity of another. **4.** *Immunol.* a substance that enhances the immune response stimulated by an antigen when injected with the antigen. [C17: from Latin *adjuvāns,* present participle of *adjuvāre,* from *juvāre* to help]

Adlerian (ædˈlɪərɪən) *adj.* of or relating to Alfred Adler (1870–1937), Austrian psychiatrist.

ad-lib (ædˈlɪb) *vb.* **-libs, -libbing, -libbed. 1.** to improvise and deliver without preparation (a speech, musical performance, etc.). ~*adj.* (**ad lib** when predicative) **2.** improvised; impromptu. ~*adv.* **ad lib. 3.** without restraint; freely. **4.** *Music.* short for **ad libitum.** ~*n.* **5.** an improvised performance, often humorous. [C18: short for Latin *ad libitum,* literally: according to pleasure] —**ad-ˈlibber** *n.*

ad libitum (ˈlɪbɪtum, -təm) *adj., adv. Music.* (to be performed) at the performer's discretion. Often shortened to **ad lib.** [See AD-LIB]

ad litem *Latin.* (æd ˈlaɪtɛm) *adj.* (esp. of a guardian) appointed for a lawsuit.

Adm. *abbrev. for:* **1.** Admiral. **2.** Admiralty.

adman (ˈædˌmæn, -mən) *n., pl.* **-men.** *Informal.* a person who works in advertising.

admass (ˈædmæs) *n.* **a.** the section of the public that is susceptible or responsive to advertising, publicity, etc. **b.** (*as modifier*): *the admass society.* [C20: from AD[1] + MASS]

admeasure (ædˈmɛʒə) *vb.* **1.** to measure out (land, etc.) as a share; apportion. **2.** (*tr.*) to determine the dimensions, capacity, weight, and other details of (a vessel), as for an official registration, documentation, or yacht handicap rating. [C14 *amesuren,* from Old French *amesurer,* from *mesurer* to MEASURE; the modern form derives from AD- + MEASURE] —**adˈmeasurement** *n.*

admin (ˈædmɪn) *n. Informal.* short for **administration.**

adminicle (ædˈmɪnɪkᵊl) *n. Law.* something contributing to prove a point without itself being complete proof. [C16: from Latin *adminiculum* support]

administer (ədˈmɪnɪstə) *vb.* (*mainly tr.*) **1.** (*also intr.*) to direct or control (the affairs of a business, government, etc.). **2.** to put into execution; dispense: *administer justice.* **3.** (when *intr.,* foll. by *to*) to give or apply (medicine, assistance, etc.) as a remedy or relief. **4.** to apply formally; perform: *to administer extreme unction.* **5.** to supervise or impose the taking of (an oath, etc.). **6.** to manage or distribute (an estate, property, etc.). [C14 *amynistre,* via Old French from Latin *administrare,* from *ad-* to + *ministrāre* to MINISTER]

administrate (ədˈmɪnɪˌstreɪt) *vb.* to manage or direct (the affairs of a business, institution, etc.).

administration (ədˌmɪnɪ'streɪʃən) *n.* **1.** management of the affairs of an organization, such as a business or institution. **2.** the duties of an administrator. **3.** the body of people who administer an organization. **4.** the conduct of the affairs of government. **5.** term of office: often used of presidents, governments, etc. **6.** the executive branch of government along with the public service; the government as a whole. **7.** (*often cap.*) *Chiefly U.S.* the political executive, esp. of the U.S.; the government. **8.** *Chiefly U.S.* a government board, agency, authority, etc. **9.** *Property law.* **a.** the conduct or disposal of the estate of a deceased person. **b.** the management by a trustee of an estate subject to a trust. **10. a.** the administering of something, such as a sacrament, oath, or medical treatment. **b.** the thing that is administered. —**ad'ministrative** *adj.* —**ad'ministratively** *adv.*

administration order *n. Law.* **1.** an order by a court appointing a person to manage a company that is in financial difficulty, in an attempt to ensure the survival of the company or achieve the best realization of its assets. **2.** an order by a court for the administration of the estate of a debtor who has been ordered by the court to pay money that he owes.

administrator (əd'mɪnɪˌstreɪtə) *n.* **1.** a person who administers the affairs of an organization, official body, etc. **2.** *Property law.* a person authorized to manage an estate, esp. when the owner has died intestate or without having appointed executors. —**adˌminis'tratrix** *fem. n.*

admirable ('ædmərəbəl) *adj.* deserving or inspiring admiration; excellent. —**'admirably** *adv.*

admiral ('ædmərəl) *n.* **1.** the supreme commander of a fleet or navy. **2.** Also called: **admiral of the fleet, fleet admiral.** a naval officer of the highest rank, equivalent to general of the army or field marshal. **3.** a senior naval officer entitled to fly his own flag. See also **rear admiral, vice admiral. 4.** *Chiefly Brit.* the master of a fishing fleet. **5.** any of various nymphalid butterflies, esp. the red admiral or white admiral. [C13 *amyral,* from Old French *amiral* emir, and from Medieval Latin *admīrālis* (the spelling with *d* probably influenced by *admīrābilis* admirable); both from Arabic *amīr* emir, commander, esp. in the phrase *amīr-al* commander of, as in *amīr-al-bahr* commander of the sea] —**'admiralˌship** *n.*

admiralty ('ædmərəltɪ) *n., pl.* **-ties. 1.** the office or jurisdiction of an admiral. **2. a.** jurisdiction over naval affairs. **b.** (*as modifier*): *admiralty law.*

Admiralty Board *n.* **the.** a department of the British Ministry of Defence, responsible for the administration and planning of the Royal Navy.

Admiralty mile *n.* another name for **nautical mile.**

admiration (ˌædmə'reɪʃən) *n.* **1.** pleasurable contemplation or surprise. **2.** a person or thing that is admired: *she was the admiration of the court.* **3.** *Archaic.* wonder.

admire (əd'maɪə) *vb.* (*tr.*) **1.** to regard with esteem, respect, approval, or pleased surprise. **2.** *Archaic.* to wonder at. [C16: from Latin *admīrārī* to wonder at, from *ad-* to, at + *mīrārī* to wonder, from *mīrus* wonderful] —**ad'mirer** *n.* —**ad'miring** *adj.* —**ad'miringly** *adv.*

admissible (əd'mɪsəbəl) *adj.* **1.** able or deserving to be considered or allowed. **2.** deserving to be admitted or allowed to enter. **3.** *Law.* (esp. of evidence) capable of being or bound to be admitted in a court of law. —**adˌmissi'bility** *or* **ad'missibleness** *n.*

admission (əd'mɪʃən) *n.* **1.** permission to enter or the right, authority, etc., to enter. **2.** the price charged for entrance. **3.** acceptance for a position, office, etc. **4.** a confession, as of a crime, mistake, etc. **5.** an acknowledgment of the truth or validity of something. [C15: from Latin *admissiōn-,* from *admittere* to ADMIT] —**ad'missive** *adj.*

admit (əd'mɪt) *vb.* **-mits, -mitting, -mitted.** (*mainly tr.*) **1.** (*may take a clause as object*) to confess or acknowledge (a crime, mistake, etc.). **2.** (*may take a clause as object*) to concede (the truth or validity of something). **3.** to allow to enter; let in. **4.** (foll. by *to*) to allow participation (in) or the right to be part (of): *to admit to the profession.* **5.** (when *intr.*, foll. by *of*) to allow (of); leave room (for). **6.** (*intr.*) to give access: *the door admits onto the lawn.* [C14: from Latin *admittere* to let come or go to, from *ad-* to + *mittere* to send]

admittance (əd'mɪtəns) *n.* **1.** the right or authority to enter. **2.** the act of giving entrance. **3.** *Electrical engineering.* the reciprocal of impedance, usually measured in siemens. It can be expressed as a complex quantity, the real part of which is the conductance and the imaginary part the susceptance. Symbol: *y*

admittedly (əd'mɪtɪdlɪ) *adv.* (*sentence modifier*) willingly conceded: *admittedly I am afraid.*

admix (əd'mɪks) *vb.* (*tr.*) *Rare.* to mix or blend. [C16: back formation from obsolete *admixt,* from Latin *admīscēre* to mix with]

admixture (əd'mɪkstʃə) *n.* **1.** a less common word for **mixture. 2.** anything added in mixing; ingredient.

admonish (əd'mɒnɪʃ) *vb.* (*tr.*) **1.** to reprove firmly but not harshly. **2.** to advise to do or against doing something; warn; caution. [C14: via Old French from Vulgar Latin *admonestāre* (unattested), from Latin *admonēre* to put one in mind of, from *monēre* to advise] —**ad'monisher** *or* **ad'monitor** *n.* —**admo'nition** (ˌædmə'nɪʃən) *n.* —**ad'monitory** *adj.*

adnate ('ædneɪt) *adj. Botany.* growing closely attached to an adjacent part or organ. [C17: from Latin *adnātus,* a variant form of *agnātus* AGNATE]

ad nauseam (æd 'nɔːzɪˌæm, -sɪ-) *adv.* to a disgusting extent. [Latin: to (the point of) nausea]

adnexa (æd'nɛksə) *pl. n. Anat.* adjoining organs, esp. of the uterus. [C19: New Latin: appendages] —**ad'nexal** *adj.*

adnominal (əd'nɒmɪnəl) *Grammar.* ~*n.* **1.** a word modifying a noun. ~*adj.* **2.** of or relating to an adnoun.

adnoun ('ædnaʊn) *n.* an adjective used as a noun; absolute adjective. [C18: from Latin *ad* to + NOUN, formed on the model of ADVERB]

ado (ə'duː) *n.* bustling activity; fuss; bother; delay (esp. in the phrases **without more ado, with much ado**). [C14: from the phrase *at do* a to-do, from Old Norse *at* to (marking the infinitive) + DO[1]]

adobe (ə'dəʊbɪ) *n.* **1. a.** a sun-dried brick used for building. **b.** (*as modifier*): *an adobe house.* **2.** a building constructed of such bricks. **3.** the clayey material from which such bricks are made. [C19: from Spanish]

adobe flat *n. Chiefly U.S.* a gently sloping clayey plain formed by a short-lived stream or flood water.

adolescence (ˌædə'lɛsəns) *n.* the period in human development that occurs between the beginning of puberty and adulthood. [C15: via Old French from Latin *adolēscentia,* from *adolēscere* to grow up, from *alēscere* to grow, from *alere* to feed, nourish]

adolescent (ˌædə'lɛsənt) *adj.* **1.** of or relating to adolescence. **2.** *Informal.* behaving in an immature way; puerile. ~*n.* **3.** an adolescent person.

Adonic (ə'dɒnɪk) *adj.* **1.** (in classical prosody) of or relating to a verse line consisting of a dactyl (-˘˘) followed by a spondee (--) or by a trochee (-˘), thought to have been first used in laments for Adonis, the handsome youth loved by Aphrodite in Greek mythology. **2.** of or relating to Adonis. ~*n.* **3.** an Adonic line or verse.

Adonis (ə'dəʊnɪs) *n.* a handsome young man. [C16: from Latin, via Greek *Adōnis* from Phoenician *adōni* my lord, a title of the god Tammuz]

adopt (ə'dɒpt) *vb.* (*tr.*) **1.** *Law.* to bring (a person) into a specific relationship, esp. to take (another's child) as one's own child. **2.** to choose and follow (a plan, technique, etc.). **3.** to take over (an idea, etc.) as if it were one's own. **4.** to take on; assume: *to adopt a title.* **5.** to accept (a report, etc.). [C16: from Latin *adoptāre* to choose for oneself, from *optāre* to choose] —**a'doption** *n.*

adopted (ə'dɒptɪd) *adj.* having been adopted: *an adopted child.* Compare **adoptive.**

adoption panel *n. Social welfare.* (in Britain) a committee appointed by an adoption agency, such as a local authority, to make recommendations concerning the suitability of prospective adoption cases.

adoptive (ə'dɒptɪv) *adj.* **1.** acquired or related by adoption: *an adoptive father.* **2.** of or relating to adoption. Compare **adopted.**

adorable (ə'dɔːrəbəl) *adj.* **1.** very attractive; charming; lovable. **2.** *Becoming rare.* deserving or eliciting adoration. —**a'dorably** *adv.*

adoration (ˌædə'reɪʃən) *n.* **1.** deep love or esteem. **2.** the act of worshipping.

adore (ə'dɔː) *vb.* **1.** (*tr.*) to love intensely or deeply. **2.** to worship (a god) with religious rites. **3.** (*tr.*) *Informal.* to like very much: *I adore chocolate.* [C15: via French from Latin *adōrāre,* from *ad-* to + *ōrāre* to pray] —**a'dorer** *n.* —**a'doring** *adj.* —**a'doringly** *adv.*

adorn (ə'dɔːn) *vb.* (*tr.*) **1.** to decorate: *she adorned her hair with flowers.* **2.** to increase the beauty, distinction, etc., of. [C14: via Old French from Latin *adōrnāre,* from *ōrnāre* to furnish, prepare] —**a'dornment** *n.*

ADP[1] *n. Biochem.* adenosine diphosphate; a nucleotide derived from ATP with the liberation of energy that is then used in the performance of muscular work.

ADP[2]**, A.D.P.,** *or* **a.d.p.** *abbrev. for* automatic data processing.

Adrastea (ə'dræstɪə) *n.* a small satellite of Jupiter, discovered in 1979.

ad rem *Latin.* (æd 'rɛm) *adj., adv.* to the point; without digression: *to reply ad rem; an ad rem discussion.* Compare **ad hominem.**

adrenal (ə'driːnəl) *adj.* **1.** on or near the kidneys. **2.** of or relating to the adrenal glands or their secretions. ~*n.* **3.** an adrenal gland. [C19: from AD- (near) + RENAL]

adrenal gland *n.* an endocrine gland at the anterior end of each kidney. Its medulla secretes adrenaline and noradrenaline and its cortex secretes several steroid hormones. Also called: **suprarenal gland.**

Adrenalin (ə'drɛnəlɪn) *n. Trademark.* a brand of **adrenaline.**

adrenaline (ə'drɛnəlɪn, -ˌliːn) *n.* a hormone that is secreted by the adrenal medulla in response to stress and increases heart rate, pulse rate, and blood pressure, and raises the blood levels of glucose and lipids. It is extracted from animals or synthesized for such medical uses as the treatment of asthma. Chemical name: aminohydroxyphenylpropionic acid; formula: $C_9H_{13}NO_3$. U.S. name: **epinephrine.**

adrenal insufficiency *n.* another name for **Addison's disease.**

adrenergic (ˌædrəˈnɜːdʒɪk) *adj.* releasing or activated by adrenaline or an adrenaline-like substance. [C20: ADRENALINE + Greek *ergon* work]
adrenocorticotrophic (əˌdriːnəʊˌkɔːtəkəʊˈtrɒfɪk) *or* **adrenocorticotropic** (əˌdriːnəʊˌkɔːtəkəʊˈtrɒpɪk) *adj.* stimulating the adrenal cortex.
adrenocorticotrophic hormone *n.* the full name of **ACTH.**
Adriatic (ˌeɪdrɪˈætɪk) *adj.* of or relating to the Adriatic Sea, or to the inhabitants of its coast or islands.
adrift (əˈdrɪft) *adj. (postpositive), adv.* **1.** floating without steering or mooring; drifting. **2.** without purpose; aimless. **3.** *Informal.* off course or amiss: *the project went adrift.*
adroit (əˈdrɔɪt) *adj.* **1.** skilful or dexterous. **2.** quick in thought or reaction. [C17: from French *à droit* according to right, rightly] —**aˈdroitly** *adv.* —**aˈdroitness** *n.*
adscititious (ˌædsɪˈtɪʃəs) *adj.* added or supplemental; additional. [C17: from Latin *adscītus* admitted (from outside), from *adscīscere* to admit, from *scīscere* to seek to know, from *scīre* to know] —ˌ**adsciˈtitiously** *adv.*
adscription (ədˈskrɪpʃən) *n.* a less common word for **ascription.**
adsorb (ədˈsɔːb, -ˈzɔːb) *vb.* to undergo or cause to undergo a process in which a substance, usually a gas, accumulates on the surface of a solid forming a thin film, often only one molecule thick: *to adsorb hydrogen on nickel; oxygen adsorbs on tungsten.* Compare **absorb** (sense 8). [C19: AD- + *-sorb* as in ABSORB] —**adˈsorbable** *adj.* —**adˌsorbaˈbility** *n.* —**adˈsorption** *n.*
adsorbate (ədˈsɔːbeɪt, -bɪt, -ˈzɔː-) *n.* a substance that has been or is to be adsorbed on a surface.
adsorbent (ədˈsɔːbənt, -ˈzɔː-) *adj.* **1.** capable of adsorption. ~*n.* **2.** a material, such as activated charcoal, on which adsorption can occur.
adsuki bean (ædˈzuːkɪ) *n.* a variant spelling of **adzuki bean.**
adsum (ˈædˌsʊm) *sentence substitute.* I am present. [Latin]
adularescent (əˌdjʊləˈrɛsənt) *adj.* (of minerals, such as moonstone) having or emitting a milky or bluish iridescence. [C19: from ADULAR(IA) + -ESCENT] —**aˌdulaˈrescence** *n.*
adularia (ˌædjʊˈlɛərɪə) *n.* a white or colourless glassy variety of orthoclase in the form of prismatic crystals. It occurs in metamorphic rocks and is a minor gemstone. Formula: $KAlSi_3O_8$. [C18: via Italian from French *adulaire,* after *Adula,* a group of mountains in Switzerland]
adulate (ˈædjʊˌleɪt) *vb. (tr.)* to flatter or praise obsequiously. [C17: back formation from C15 *adulation,* from Latin *adūlāri* to flatter] —ˌ**aduˈlation** *n.* —ˈ**aduˌlator** *n.* —**adulatory** (ˌædjʊˈleɪtərɪ, ˈædjʊˌleɪtərɪ) *adj.*
Adullamite (əˈdʌləˌmaɪt) *n.* a person who has withdrawn from a political group and joined with a few others to form a dissident group. [C19: originally applied to members of the British House of Commons who withdrew from the Liberal party (1866); alluding to the cave of *Adullam* in the Bible, to which David and others fled (1 Samuel 22: 1–2)]
adult (ˈædʌlt, əˈdʌlt) *adj.* **1.** having reached maturity; fully developed. **2.** of or intended for mature people: *adult education.* **3.** regarded as suitable only for adults, because of being pornographic: *adult films.* ~*n.* **4.** a person who has attained maturity; a grownup. **5.** a mature fully grown animal or plant. **6.** *Law.* a person who has attained the age of legal majority (18 years for most purposes). Compare **infant.** [C16: from Latin *adultus,* from *adolēscere* to grow up, from *alēscere* to grow, from *alēre* to feed, nourish] —**aˈdulthood** *n.*
adulterant (əˈdʌltərənt) *n.* **1.** a substance or ingredient that adulterates. ~*adj.* **2.** adulterating.
adulterate *vb.* (əˈdʌltəˌreɪt). **1.** *(tr.)* to debase by adding inferior material: *to adulterate milk with water.* ~*adj.* (əˈdʌltərɪt, -ˌreɪt). **2.** adulterated; debased or impure. **3.** a less common word for **adulterous.** [C16: from Latin *adulterāre* to corrupt, commit adultery, probably from *alter* another, hence to approach another, commit adultery] —**aˌdulterˈation** *n.* —**aˈdulterˌator** *n.*
adulterer (əˈdʌltərə) *or (fem.)* **adulteress** *n.* a person who has committed adultery. [C16: originally also *adulter,* from Latin *adulter,* back formation from *adulterāre* to ADULTERATE]
adulterine (əˈdʌltərɪn, -ˌriːn, -ˌraɪn) *adj.* **1.** of or made by adulteration; fake. **2.** conceived in adultery: *an adulterine child.*
adulterous (əˈdʌltərəs) *adj.* **1.** of, characterized by, or inclined to adultery. **2.** an obsolete word for **adulterate** (sense 2). —**aˈdulterously** *adv.*
adultery (əˈdʌltərɪ) *n., pl.* **-teries.** voluntary sexual intercourse between a married man or woman and partner other than the legal spouse. [C15 *adulterie,* altered (as if directly from Latin *adulterium*) from C14 *avoutrie,* via Old French from Latin *adulterium,* from *adulter,* back formation from *adulterāre.* See ADULTERATE]
Adult Training Centre *n. Social welfare.* a day centre, run by a local authority, for mentally handicapped people to gain work experience.
adumbral (ædˈʌmbrəl) *adj. Usually poetic.* shadowy. [C19: from AD- (in the sense: in) + Latin *umbra* shadow]
adumbrate (ˈædʌmˌbreɪt) *vb. (tr.)* **1.** to outline; give a faint indication of. **2.** to foreshadow. **3.** to overshadow; obscure. [C16: from Latin *adumbrātus* represented only in outline, from *adumbrāre* to cast a shadow on, from *umbra* shadow] —ˌ**adumˈbration** *n.* —**adumbrative** (ædˈʌmbrətɪv) *adj.* —**adˈumbratively** *adv.*
adust (əˈdʌst) *adj. Archaic.* **1.** dried up or darkened by heat; burnt or scorched. **2.** gloomy or melancholy. [C14 (in the sense: gloomy): from Latin *adūstus,* from *adūrere* to set fire to, from *ūrere* to burn]
adv. *abbrev. for:* **1.** adverb. **2.** adverbial. **3.** adversus. [Latin: against] **4.** advertisement. **5.** advocate.
ad val. *abbrev. for* ad valorem.
ad valorem (æd vəˈlɔːrəm) *adj., adv.* (of taxes) in proportion to the estimated value of the goods taxed. Abbrevs.: **ad val., a.v., A/V.** [from Latin]
advance (ədˈvɑːns) *vb.* **1.** to go or bring forward in position. **2.** (foll. by *on*) to move (towards) in a threatening manner. **3.** *(tr.)* to present for consideration; suggest. **4.** to bring or be brought to a further stage of development; improve; further. **5.** *(tr.)* to cause (an event) to occur earlier. **6.** *(tr.)* to supply (money, goods, etc.) beforehand, either for a loan or as an initial payment. **7.** to increase (a price, value, rate of occurrence, etc.) or (of a price, etc.) to be increased. **8.** *(intr.)* to improve one's position; be promoted: *he advanced rapidly in his job.* **9.** *(tr.) Archaic.* to promote in rank, status, or position. ~*n.* **10.** forward movement; progress in time or space. **11.** improvement; progress in development. **12.** *Commerce.* **a.** the supplying of commodities or funds before receipt of an agreed consideration. **b.** the commodities or funds supplied in this manner. **c.** *(as modifier): an advance supply.* **13.** Also called: **advance payment.** a money payment made before it is legally due. **14.** a loan of money. **15.** an increase in price, value, rate of occurrence, etc. **16.** a less common word for **advancement** (sense 1). **17. in advance. a.** beforehand: *payment in advance.* **b.** (foll. by *of*) ahead in time or development: *ideas in advance of the time.* **18.** *(modifier)* forward in position or time: *advance booking; an advance warning.* ~See also **advances.** [C15 *advauncen,* altered (on the model of words beginning with Latin *ad-*) from C13 *avauncen,* via Old French from Latin *abante* from before, from *ab-* away from + *ante* before] —**adˈvancer** *n.* —**adˈvancingly** *adv.*
advance corporation tax *n.* a UK tax in which a company paying a dividend must deduct the basic rate of income tax from the grossed-up value of the dividend and pay it to the Inland Revenue. Abbrev.: **ACT.**
advanced (ədˈvɑːnst) *adj.* **1.** being ahead in development, knowledge, progress, etc.: *advanced studies.* **2.** having reached a comparatively late stage: *a man of advanced age.* **3.** ahead of the times: *advanced views on religion.*
advanced gas-cooled reactor *n.* a nuclear reactor using carbon dioxide as the coolant, graphite as the moderator, and ceramic uranium dioxide cased in stainless steel as the fuel. Abbrev.: **AGR.**
Advanced level *n.* (in Britain) the formal name for **A level.**
advance guard *n.* **1.** a military unit sent ahead of a main body to find gaps in enemy defences, clear away minor opposition, and prevent unexpected contact. **2.** a temporary military detachment sent ahead of a force to prepare for a landing or other operation, esp. by making reconnaissance.
advance man *n. U.S.* an agent of a political candidate or other public figure who travels in advance of the candidate to organize publicity, arrange meetings, and make security checks.
advancement (ədˈvɑːnsmənt) *n.* **1.** promotion in rank, status, etc.; preferment. **2.** a less common word for **advance** (senses 10, 11). **3.** *Property law.* the use during a testator's lifetime of money or property for the benefit of a child or other person who is a prospective beneficiary in the testator's will.
advance notice *n.* See **notice** (sense 6).
advance poll *n. Canadian.* (in an election) a poll held prior to election day to permit voters who expect to be absent then to cast their ballots.
advance ratio *n. Aeronautics.* **1.** the ratio of wind speed along the axis of a rotor or propeller to the speed of the blade tip. **2.** the ratio of forward flight speed to the speed of the rotor tip of a helicopter.
advances (ədˈvɑːnsɪz) *pl. n. (sometimes sing.;* often foll. by *to* or *towards)* personal overtures made in an attempt to become friendly, gain a favour, etc.
advantage (ədˈvɑːntɪdʒ) *n.* **1.** (often foll. by *over* or *of*) superior or more favourable position or power: *he had an advantage over me because of his experience.* **2.** benefit or profit (esp. in the phrase **to one's advantage**). **3.** *Tennis.* **a.** the point scored after deuce. **b.** the resulting state of the score. **4. take advantage of. a.** to make good use of. **b.** to impose upon the weakness, good nature, etc., of; abuse. **c.** to seduce. **5. to advantage.** to good effect: *he used his height to advantage at the game.* **6. you have the advantage of me.** you know me but I do not know you. ~*vb.* **7.** *(tr.)* to put in a better position; favour. [C14 *avantage* (later altered to *advantage* on the model of words beginning with Latin *ad-*), from Old French *avant* before, from Latin *abante* from before, away. See ADVANCE]
advantageous (ˌædvənˈteɪdʒəs) *adj.* producing advantage. —ˌ**advanˈtageously** *adv.* —ˌ**advanˈtageousness** *n.*
advection (ədˈvɛkʃən) *n.* the transference of heat energy in a horizontal stream of gas, esp. of air. [C20: from Latin *advectiō* conveyance, from *advehere,* from *ad-* to + *vehere* to carry]

advent ('ædvɛnt, -vənt) *n.* an arrival or coming, esp. one which is awaited. [C12: from Latin *adventus*, from *advenīre*, from *ad-* to + *venīre* to come]

Advent ('ædvɛnt, -vənt) *n. Christianity.* the season including the four Sundays preceding Christmas.

Advent calendar *n. Brit.* a large card with a brightly coloured sometimes tinselled design on it that contains small numbered doors for children to open on each of the days of Advent, revealing pictures beneath them.

Adventist ('ædvɛntɪst, 'ædvən-) *n.* a member of any of the Christian groups, such as the **Seventh-Day Adventists,** that hold that the Second Coming of Christ is imminent.

adventitia (ˌædvɛn'tɪʃɪə, -'tɪʃə) *n.* the outermost covering of an organ or part, esp. the outer coat of a blood vessel. [C19: New Latin, from the neuter plural of Latin *adventīcius*; see ADVENTITIOUS]

adventitious (ˌædvɛn'tɪʃəs) *adj.* **1.** added or appearing accidentally or unexpectedly. **2.** (of a plant or animal part) developing in an abnormal position, as a root that grows from a stem. [C17: from Latin *adventīcius* coming from outside, from *adventus* a coming] —ˌ**adven'titiously** *adv.*

adventive (əd'vɛntɪv) *Biology.* ~*adj.* **1.** introduced to an area by chance and not yet established there; exotic. ~*n.* **2.** such a plant or animal. ~Also called: **casual.**

Advent Sunday *n.* the first of the four Sundays of Advent, and the one that falls nearest to November 30.

adventure (əd'vɛntʃə) *n.* **1.** a risky undertaking of unknown outcome. **2.** an exciting or unexpected event or course of events. **3.** a hazardous financial operation; commercial speculation. **4.** *Obsolete.* **a.** danger or misadventure. **b.** chance. ~*vb.* **5.** to take a risk or put at risk. **6.** (*intr.*; foll. by *into, on, upon*) to dare to go or enter (into a place, dangerous activity, etc.). **7.** to dare to say (something): *he adventured his opinion.* [C13 *aventure* (later altered to *adventure* after the Latin spelling), via Old French ultimately from Latin *advenīre* to happen to (someone), arrive] —**ad'ventureful** *adj.*

adventure playground *n. Brit.* a playground for children that contains building materials, discarded industrial parts, etc., used by the children to build with, hide in, climb on, etc.

adventurer (əd'vɛntʃərə) *or* (*fem.*) **adventuress** *n.* **1.** a person who seeks adventure, esp. one who seeks success or money through daring exploits. **2.** a person who seeks money or power by unscrupulous means. **3.** a speculator.

adventurism (əd'vɛntʃəˌrɪzəm) *n.* recklessness, esp. in politics and finance. —**ad'venturist** *n.*

adventurous (əd'vɛntʃərəs) *adj.* **1.** Also: **adventuresome.** daring or enterprising. **2.** dangerous; involving risk. —**ad'venturously** *adv.*

adverb ('ædˌvɜːb) *n.* **a.** a word or group of words that serves to modify a whole sentence, a verb, another adverb, or an adjective; for example, *probably, easily, very,* and *happily* respectively in the sentence *They could probably easily envy the very happily married couple.* **b.** (*as modifier*): *an adverb marker.* Abbrev.: **adv.** [C15–C16: from Latin *adverbium* adverb, literally: added word, a translation of Greek *epirrhēma* a word spoken afterwards]

adverbial (æd'vɜːbɪəl) *n.* **1.** a word or group of words playing the grammatical role of an adverb, such as *in the rain* in the sentence *I'm singing in the rain.* ~*adj.* **2.** of or relating to an adverb or adverbial. —**ad'verbially** *adv.*

adversarial (ˌædvɜː'sɛərɪəl) *adj.* **1.** pertaining to or characterized by antagonism and conflict. **2.** *Brit.* having or involving opposing parties or interests in a legal contest. U.S. term: **adversary.**

adversary ('ædvəsərɪ) *n., pl.* **-saries.** **1.** a person or group that is hostile to someone; enemy. **2.** an opposing contestant in a game or sport. ~*adj.* **3.** the U.S. term for **adversarial** (sense 2). [C14: from Latin *adversārius*, from *adversus* against. See ADVERSE]

adversative (əd'vɜːsətɪv) *Grammar.* ~*adj.* **1.** (of a word, phrase, or clause) implying opposition or contrast. *But* and *although* are adversative conjunctions introducing adversative clauses. ~*n.* **2.** an adversative word or speech element.

adverse ('ædvɜːs, æd'vɜːs) *adj.* **1.** antagonistic or inimical; hostile: *adverse criticism.* **2.** unfavourable to one's interests: *adverse circumstances.* **3.** contrary or opposite in direction or position: *adverse winds.* **4.** (of leaves, flowers, etc.) facing the main stem. Compare **averse** (sense 2). [C14: from Latin *adversus* opposed to, hostile, from *advertere* to turn towards, from *ad-* to, towards + *vertere* to turn] —**ad'versely** *adv.* —**ad'verseness** *n.*

adverse possession *n. Property law.* the occupation or possession of land by a person not legally entitled to it. If continued unopposed for a period specifed by law, such occupation extinguishes the title of the rightful owner.

adverse pressure gradient *n. Aerodynamics.* an increase of pressure in the direction of flow.

adversity (əd'vɜːsɪtɪ) *n., pl.* **-ties.** **1.** distress; affliction; hardship. **2.** an unfortunate event or incident.

advert[1] (əd'vɜːt) *vb.* (*intr.*; foll. by *to*) to draw attention (to); refer (to). [C15: from Latin *advertere* to turn one's attention to. See ADVERSE]

advert[2] ('ædvɜːt) *n. Brit. informal.* short for **advertisement.**

advertence (əd'vɜːtəns) *or* **advertency** *n.* heedfulness or attentiveness. —**ad'vertent** *adj.* —**ad'vertently** *adv.*

advertise *or U.S.* (*sometimes*) **advertize** ('ædvəˌtaɪz) *vb.* **1.** to present or praise (goods, a service, etc.) to the public, esp. in order to encourage sales. **2.** to make (something, such as a vacancy, article for sale, etc.) publicly known, as to possible applicants, buyers, etc.: *to advertise a job.* **3.** (*intr.*; foll. by *for*) to make a public request (for), esp. in a newspaper, etc.: *she advertised for a cook.* **4.** *Obsolete.* to warn; caution. [C15: from a lengthened stem of Old French *avertir*, ultimately from Latin *advertere* to turn one's attention to. See ADVERSE] —'**adverˌtiser** *or U.S.* (*sometimes*) '**adverˌtizer** *n.*

advertisement *or U.S.* (*sometimes*) **advertizement** (əd'vɜːtɪsmənt, -tɪz-) *n.* any public notice, as a printed display in a newspaper, short film on television, announcement on radio, etc., designed to sell goods, publicize an event, etc. Shortened forms: **ad, advert.**

advertising *or U.S.* (*sometimes*) **advertizing** ('ædvəˌtaɪzɪŋ) *n.* **1.** the promotion of goods or services for sale through impersonal media, such as radio or television. **2.** the business that specializes in creating such publicity. **3.** advertisements collectively; publicity.

advertising agency *n.* an organization that creates advertising material, contracts for publication space, and undertakes market research on behalf of its clients.

Advertising Standards Authority *n.* an independent UK body set up by the advertising industry to ensure that all advertisements comply with the British Code of Advertising Practice. Abbrev.: **ASA.**

advice (əd'vaɪs) *n.* **1.** recommendation as to appropriate choice of action; counsel. **2.** (*sometimes pl.*) formal notification of facts, esp. when communicated from a distance. [C13 *avis* (later *advise*), via Old French from a Vulgar Latin phrase based on Latin *ad* to, according to + *vīsum* view (hence: according to one's view, opinion)]

advice note *n.* a document sent by a supplier to a customer to inform him that goods he ordered have been dispatched. It usually gives details such as the quantity of goods and how they have been sent.

advisable (əd'vaɪzəbᵊl) *adj.* worthy of recommendation; prudent; sensible. —**ad'visably** *adv.* —**adˌvisa'bility** *or* **ad'visableness** *n.*

advise (əd'vaɪz) *vb.* (*when tr., may take a clause as object or an infinitive*) **1.** to offer advice (to a person or persons); counsel: *he advised the king; to advise caution; he advised her to leave.* **2.** (*tr.*; sometimes foll. by *of*) to inform or notify. **3.** (*intr.*; foll. by *with*) *Chiefly U.S., obsolete in Brit.* to consult or discuss. [C14: via Old French from Vulgar Latin *advīsāre* (unattested) to consider, from Latin *ad-* to + *visāre* (unattested), from *vīsere* to view, from *vidēre* to see]

▷**Usage.** *Advise* is often used in the same sense as *inform*: *as we advised you in our last communication, the order is being dealt with.* This use is accepted and common in business correspondence. Careful users of English prefer *inform, notify,* or *tell* in general English: *when he returned home, the police informed him* (not *advised him*) *that his car had been stolen.*

advised (əd'vaɪzd) *adj.* resulting from deliberation. See also **ill-advised, well-advised.** —**advisedly** (əd'vaɪzɪdlɪ) *adv.*

advisement (əd'vaɪzmənt) *n. Chiefly U.S., archaic in Britain.* consultation; deliberation.

adviser *or* **advisor** (əd'vaɪzə) *n.* **1.** a person who advises. **2.** *Education.* a person responsible for advising students on academic matters, career guidance, etc. **3.** *Brit. education.* a subject specialist who advises heads of schools on current teaching methods and facilities.

advisory (əd'vaɪzərɪ) *adj.* giving advice; empowered to make recommendations: *an advisory body.*

advisory teacher *n. Brit.* a teacher who visits schools to advise teachers on curriculum developments within a particular subject area.

advocaat ('ædvəʊˌkɑː, -ˌkɑːt, 'ædvə-) *n.* a liqueur having a raw egg base. [C20: Dutch, from *advocatenborrel*, from *advocaat* ADVOCATE (n.) + *borrel* drink]

advocacy ('ædvəkəsɪ) *n., pl.* **-cies.** active support, esp. of a cause.

advocate *vb.* ('ædvəˌkeɪt). **1.** (*tr.*; *may take a clause as object*) to support or recommend publicly; plead for or speak in favour of. ~*n.* ('ædvəkɪt, -ˌkeɪt). **2.** a person who upholds or defends a cause; supporter. **3.** a person who intercedes on behalf of another. **4.** a person who pleads his client's cause in a court of law. See also **barrister, solicitor, counsellor.** **5.** *Scots Law.* the usual word for **barrister.** [C14: via Old French from Latin *advocātus* legal witness, advocate, from *advocāre* to call as witness, from *vocāre* to call] —ˌ**advo'catory** *adj.*

Advocate Depute *n.* a Scottish law officer with the functions of public prosecutor.

advocation (ˌædvə'keɪʃən) *n. Scots Law, papal law.* the transfer to itself by a superior court of an action pending in a lower court.

advocatus diaboli *Latin.* (ˌædvə'kɑːtəs daɪ'æbəˌlaɪ) *n.* another name for the **devil's advocate.**

advowson (əd'vaʊzᵊn) *n. English ecclesiastical law.* the right of presentation to a vacant benefice. [C13: via Anglo-French and

Old French from Latin *advocātiōn-* the act of summoning, from *advocāre* to summon]

advt *abbrev. for* advertisement.

Adygei *or* **Adyghe** ('ɑːdɪˌgeɪ, ˌɑːdɪ'geɪ, ˌɑːdɪ'gɛ) *n.* **1.** (*pl.* **-gei, -geis** *or* **-ghe, -ghes**) a member of a Circassian people of the Northwest Caucasus. **2.** the Circassian language, esp. its Western dialect. Compare **Kabardian.**

adynamia (ˌædɪ'neɪmɪə) *n.* loss of vital power or strength, esp. as the result of illness; weakness or debility. [C19: New Latin, from A-[1] + *-dynamia,* from Greek *dunamis* strength, force] —**adynamic** (ˌædɪ'næmɪk) *adj.*

adytum ('ædɪtəm) *n., pl.* **-ta** (-tə). the most sacred place of worship in an ancient temple from which the laity was prohibited. [C17: Latin, from Greek *aduton* a place not to be entered, from A-[1] + *duein* to enter]

adze *or U.S.* **adz** (ædz) *n.* a heavy hand tool with a steel cutting blade attached at right angles to a wooden handle, used for dressing timber. [Old English *adesa*]

adzuki bean *or* **adsuki bean** (æd'zuːkɪ) *n.* **1.** a papilionaceous plant, *Phaseolus angularis,* that has yellow flowers and pods containing edible brown seeds and is widely cultivated as a food crop in China and Japan. **2.** the seed of this plant. [*adzuki,* from Japanese: red bean]

æ *or* **Æ** **1.** a digraph in Latin representing either a native diphthong, as in *æquus,* or a Greek αι (*ai*) in Latinized spellings, as in *Æschylus*: now usually written *ae,* or *e* in some words, such as *demon.* **2.** a ligature used in Old and early Middle English to represent the vowel sound of *a* in *cat.* **3.** a ligature used in modern phonetic transcription also representing the vowel sound *a* in *cat.*

ae (e) *or* **yae** *determiner. Scot.* one; a single. [from Old English *ān*]

ae. *abbrev. for* aetatis. [Latin: at the age of; aged]

AEA (in Britain) *abbrev. for* Atomic Energy Authority.

AE & P *abbrev. for* Ambassador Extraordinary and Plenipotentiary.

AEC (in the U.S.) *abbrev. for* Atomic Energy Commission.

aeciospore ('iːsɪəˌspɔː) *n.* any of the spores produced in an aecium of the rust fungi, which spread to and infect the primary host. Also called: **aecidospore.** [C20: from AECIUM + SPORE]

aecium ('iːsɪəm) *or* **aecidium** (iː'sɪdɪəm) *n., pl.* **-cia** (-sɪə) *or* **-cidia** (-'sɪdɪə). a globular or cup-shaped structure in some rust fungi in which aeciospores are produced. [C19: New Latin, from Greek *aikia* injury (so called because of the damage the fungi cause)]

aedes (eɪ'iːdiːz) *n.* any mosquito of the genus *Aedes* (formerly *Stegomyia*) of tropical and subtropical regions, esp. *A. aegypti,* which transmits yellow fever and dengue. [C20: New Latin, from Greek *aēdēs* unpleasant, from A-[1] + *ēdos* pleasant]

aedile *or U.S.* (*sometimes*) **edile** ('iːdaɪl) *n.* a magistrate of ancient Rome in charge of public works, games, buildings, and roads. [C16: from Latin *aedīlis* concerned with buildings, from *aedēs* a building]

Aegean (iː'dʒiːən) *adj.* **1.** of or relating to the Aegean Sea or Islands. **2.** of or relating to the Bronze Age civilization of Greece, Asia Minor, and the Aegean Islands.

aegis *or U.S.* (*sometimes*) **egis** ('iːdʒɪs) *n.* **1.** sponsorship or protection; auspices (esp. in the phrase **under the aegis of**). **2.** *Greek myth.* the shield of Zeus, often represented in art as a goatskin. [C18: from Latin, from Greek *aigis* shield of Zeus, perhaps related to *aig-,* stem of *aix* goat]

aegrotat ('aɪgrəʊˌtæt, 'iː-; iː'grəʊtæt) *n.* **1.** (in British and certain other universities, and, sometimes, schools) a certificate allowing a candidate to pass an examination although he has missed all or part of it through illness. **2.** a degree or other qualification obtained in such circumstances. [C19: Latin, literally: he is ill]

-aemia, -haemia, *or U.S.* **-emia, -hemia** *n. combining form.* denoting blood, esp. a specified condition of the blood in names of diseases: *leukaemia.* [New Latin, from Greek *-aimia,* from *haima* blood]

Aeneid (ɪ'niːɪd) *n.* an epic poem in Latin by Virgil relating the experiences of Aeneas after the fall of Troy, written chiefly to provide an illustrious historical background for Rome.

aeneous (eɪ'iːnɪəs) *adj. Rare.* of a lustrous bronze colour. [C19: from Latin *aēneus* of bronze, from *aes* bronze]

aeolian (iː'əʊlɪən) *adj.* **1.** of or relating to the wind; produced or carried by the wind. **2.** (*often cap.*) denoting or relating to an authentic mode represented by the ascending natural diatonic scale from A to A: the basis of the modern minor key. See also **Hypo-. [C18: from** *Aeolus,* Greek god of the winds]

aeolian deposits *pl. n. Geology.* sediments, such as loess, made up of windblown grains of sand or dust.

aeolian harp *n.* a stringed instrument that produces a musical sound when a current of air or wind passes over the strings. Also called: **wind harp.**

aeolian tone *n.* the musical tone produced by the passage of a current of air over a stretched string, etc., as in an aeolian harp.

Aeolic *or* **Eolic** (iː'ɒlɪk, iː'əʊlɪk) *adj.* **1.** of or relating to the Aeolians, a Hellenic people, or their dialect. ~*n.* **2.** one of four chief dialects of Ancient Greek, spoken chiefly in Thessaly, Boeotia, and Aeolis. ~Compare **Arcadic, Doric, Ionic.** See also **Attic** (sense 3).

aeolipile (iː'ɒlɪˌpaɪl) *n.* a device illustrating the reactive forces of a gas jet: usually a spherical vessel mounted so as to rotate and equipped with angled exit pipes from which steam within it escapes. [C17: from Latin *aeolīpilae* balls of *Aeolus,* Greek god of the winds, or *aeolīpylae* gates of *Aeolius*]

aeolotropic (ˌiːələʊ'trɒpɪk) *adj.* a less common word for **anisotropic.** [C19: from Greek *aiolos* fickle + -TROPIC]

aeon *or esp. U.S.* **eon** ('iːən, 'iːɒn) *n.* **1.** an immeasurably long period of time; age. **2.** *Astron.* a period of one thousand million years. **3.** (*often cap.*) *Gnosticism.* one of the powers emanating from the supreme being and culminating in the demiurge. [C17: from Greek *aiōn* an infinitely long time]

aeonian *or* **eonian** (iː'əʊnɪən) *adj. Literary.* everlasting.

aepyornis (ˌiːpɪ'ɔːnɪs) *n.* any of the large extinct flightless birds of the genus *Aepyornis,* remains of which have been found in Madagascar. [C19: New Latin, from Greek *aipus* high + *ornis* bird]

aer- *combining form.* a variant of **aero-** before a vowel.

aerate ('ɛəreɪt) *vb.* (*tr.*) **1.** to charge (a liquid) with a gas, esp. carbon dioxide, as in the manufacture of effervescent drink. **2.** to expose to the action or circulation of the air, so as to purify. —**aer'ation** *n.* —**'aerator** *n.*

aeri- *combining form.* a variant of **aero-.**

aerial ('ɛərɪəl) *adj.* **1.** of, relating to, or resembling air. **2.** existing, occurring, moving, or operating in the air: *aerial cable car; aerial roots of a plant.* **3.** ethereal; light and delicate. **4.** imaginary; visionary. **5.** extending high into the air; lofty. **6.** of or relating to aircraft: *aerial combat.* ~*n.* **7.** Also called: **antenna.** the part of a radio or television system having any of various shapes, such as a dipole, Yagi, long-wire, or vertical aerial, by means of which radio waves are transmitted or received. [C17: via Latin from Greek *aērios,* from *aēr* air]

aerialist ('ɛərɪəlɪst) *n. Chiefly U.S.* a trapeze artist or tightrope walker.

aerial ladder *n.* the U.S. and Canadian term for **turntable ladder.**

aerial perspective *n.* a means of indicating relative distance in terms of a gradation of clarity, tone, and colour, esp. blue. Also called: **atmospheric perspective.**

aerial pingpong *n. Austral., facetious.* Australian Rules football.

aerial top dressing *n.* the process of spreading lime, fertilizer, etc. over farmland from an aeroplane.

aerie ('ɛərɪ, 'ɪərɪ) *n.* a variant spelling (esp. U.S.) of **eyrie.**

aeriform ('ɛərɪˌfɔːm) *adj.* **1.** having the form of air; gaseous. **2.** unsubstantial.

aerify ('ɛərɪˌfaɪ) *vb.* **-fies, -fying, -fied. 1.** to change or cause to change into a gas. **2.** to mix or combine with air. —ˌ**aerifi'cation** *n.*

aero ('ɛərəʊ) *n.* (*modifier*) of or relating to aircraft or aeronautics: *an aero engine.*

aero-, aeri-, *or before a vowel* **aer-** *combining form.* **1.** denoting air, atmosphere, or gas: *aerodynamics.* **2.** denoting aircraft: *aeronautics.* [ultimately from Greek *aēr* air]

aeroacoustics (ˌɛərəʊə'kuːstɪks) *n.* (*functioning as sing.*) the study of the generation and transmittance of sound by fluid flow.

aeroballistics (ˌɛərəʊbə'lɪstɪks) *n.* (*functioning as sing.*) the ballistics of projectiles dropped, launched, or fired from aircraft.

aerobatics (ˌɛərəʊ'bætɪks) *n.* (*functioning as sing. or pl.*) spectacular or dangerous manoeuvres, such as loops or rolls, performed in an aircraft or glider; stunt flying. [C20: from AERO- + (ACRO)BATICS]

aerobe ('ɛərəʊb) *or* **aerobium** (ɛə'rəʊbɪəm) *n., pl.* **-obes** *or* **-obia** (-'əʊbɪə). an organism that requires free oxygen or air for respiration. Compare **anaerobe.** [C19: from AERO- + Greek *bios* life. Compare MICROBE]

aerobic (ɛə'rəʊbɪk) *adj.* **1.** (of an organism or process) depending on free oxygen or air. **2.** of or relating to aerobes. **3.** designed for or relating to aerobics: *aerobic shoes; aerobic dances.* ~Compare **anaerobic.**

aerobics (ɛə'rəʊbɪks) *n.* (*functioning as sing.*) any system of sustained exercises designed to increase the amount of oxygen in the blood and strengthen the heart and lungs. —**aer'obicist** *n.*

aerobiology (ˌɛərəʊbaɪ'ɒlədʒɪ) *n.* the study of airborne microorganisms, spores, etc., esp. those causing disease. —ˌ**aerobio'logical** *adj.* —ˌ**aerobio'logically** *adv.* —ˌ**aerobi'ologist** *n.*

aerobiosis (ˌɛərəʊbaɪ'əʊsɪs) *n.* life in the presence of free oxygen. —**aerobiotic** (ˌɛərəʊbaɪ'ɒtɪk) *adj.*

aerobraking ('ɛərəʊˌbreɪkɪŋ) *n.* the use of aerodynamic braking in extremely low-density atmospheres in space at hypersonic Mach numbers.

aerodonetics (ˌɛərəʊdə'nɛtɪks) *n.* (*functioning as sing.*) the study of soaring or gliding flight, esp. the study of gliders. [C20: from Greek *aerodonetos* tossed in the air, from AERO- + *donētos,* past participle of *donein* to toss]

aerodrome ('ɛərəˌdrəʊm) *or U.S.* **airdrome** ('ɛəˌdrəʊm) *n.* a landing area, esp. for private aircraft, that is usually smaller than an airport.

aerodynamic braking *n.* **1.** the use of aerodynamic drag to slow spacecraft re-entering the atmosphere. **2.** the use of airbrakes to retard flying vehicles or objects. **3.** the use of a parachute or reversed thrust to decelerate an aircraft before landing.

aerodynamics (ˌɛərəʊdaɪˈnæmɪks) *n.* (*functioning as sing.*) the study of the dynamics of gases, esp. of the forces acting on a body passing through air. Compare **aerostatics** (sense 1). —ˌ**aerodyˈnamic** *adj.* —ˌ**aerodyˈnamically** *adv.*

aerodyne (ˈɛərəʊˌdaɪn) *n.* any heavier-than-air machine, such as an aircraft, that derives the greater part of its lift from aerodynamic forces. [C20: back formation from AERODYNAMIC; see DYNE]

aeroembolism (ˌɛərəʊˈɛmbəˌlɪzəm) *n.* the presence in the tissues and blood of nitrogen bubbles, caused by an abrupt and substantial reduction in atmospheric pressure. See **decompression sickness.**

aero engine *n.* an engine for powering an aircraft.

aerofoil (ˈɛərəʊˌfɔɪl) *or U.S. and Canadian* **airfoil** (ˈɛəˌfɔɪl) *n.* a cross section of an aileron, wing, tailplane, or rotor blade.

aerogel (ˈɛərəˌdʒɛl) *n.* a colloid that has a continuous solid phase containing dispersed gas.

aerogram *or* **aerogramme** (ˈɛərəˌgræm) *n.* **1.** Also called: **air letter.** an air-mail letter written on a single sheet of lightweight paper that folds and is sealed to form an envelope. **2.** another name for **radiotelegram.**

aerography (ɛəˈrɒgrəfɪ) *n.* the description of the character of the atmosphere.

aerolite (ˈɛərəˌlaɪt) *n.* a stony meteorite consisting of silicate minerals. —**aerolitic** (ˌɛərəˈlɪtɪk) *adj.*

aerology (ɛəˈrɒlədʒɪ) *n.* the study of the atmosphere, including its upper layers. —**aerologic** (ˌɛərəˈlɒdʒɪk) *or* ˌ**aeroˈlogical** *adj.* —**aerˈologist** *n.*

aeromechanic (ˌɛərəʊmɪˈkænɪk) *n.* **1.** an aircraft mechanic. ~*adj.* **2.** of or relating to aeromechanics.

aeromechanics (ˌɛərəʊmɪˈkænɪks) *n.* (*functioning as sing.*) the mechanics of gases, esp. air. —ˌ**aeromeˈchanical** *adj.*

aerometeorograph (ˌɛərəʊˈmiːtɪərəˌgrɑːf, -ˌgræf) *n. Chiefly U.S.* an aircraft instrument that records temperature, humidity, and atmospheric pressure.

aerometer (ɛəˈrɒmɪtə) *n.* an instrument for determining the mass or density of a gas, esp. air. —**aerometric** (ˌɛərəˈmɛtrɪk) *adj.*

aerometry (ɛəˈrɒmɪtrɪ) *n.* another name for **pneumatics.**

aeron. *abbrev. for:* **1.** aeronautics. **2.** aeronautical.

aeronaut (ˈɛərəˌnɔːt) *n.* a person who flies in a lighter-than-air craft, esp. the pilot or navigator.

aeronautical (ˌɛərəˈnɔːtɪkəl) *adj.* of or relating to aeronauts or aeronautics. —ˌ**aeroˈnautically** *adv.*

aeronautical engineering *n.* the branch of engineering concerned with the design, production, and maintenance of aircraft. —**aeronautical engineer** *n.*

aeronautics (ˌɛərəˈnɔːtɪks) *n.* (*functioning as sing.*) the study or practice of all aspects of flight through the air.

aeroneurosis (ˌɛərəʊnjʊˈrəʊsɪs) *n.* a functional disorder of aeroplane pilots characterized by anxiety and various psychosomatic disturbances, caused by insufficient oxygen at high altitudes and the emotional tension of flying.

aero-optics (ˌɛərəʊˈɒptɪks) *n.* (*functioning as sing.*) the study of the effect of aircraft-induced and atmospheric disturbances on the efficiency of laser weapons.

aeropause (ˈɛərəˌpɔːz) *n.* the region of the upper atmosphere above which aircraft cannot fly.

aerophagia (ˌɛərəˈfeɪdʒɪə, -dʒə) *n.* spasmodic swallowing of air, a fairly common neurotic habit that may lead to belching and stomach pain.

aerophobia (ˌɛərəˈfəʊbɪə) *n.* a pathological fear of draughts of air. —ˌ**aeroˈphobic** *adj.*

aerophyte (ˈɛərəˌfaɪt) *n.* another name for **epiphyte.**

aeroplane (ˈɛərəˌpleɪn) *or U.S. and Canadian* **airplane** (ˈɛəˌpleɪn) *n.* a heavier-than-air powered flying vehicle with fixed wings. [C19: from French *aéroplane,* from AERO- + Greek *-planos* wandering, related to PLANET]

aeroplane cloth *or* **fabric** *n.* **1.** a strong fabric made from cotton, linen, and nylon yarns, used for some light aircraft fuselages and wings. **2.** a similar lightweight fabric used for clothing. ~Also called: **aircraft fabric.**

aeroplane spin *n.* a wrestling attack in which a wrestler lifts his opponent onto his shoulders and spins around, leaving the opponent dizzy.

aerosol (ˈɛərəˌsɒl) *n.* **1.** a colloidal dispersion of solid or liquid particles in a gas; smoke or fog. **2.** a substance, such as a paint, polish, or insecticide, dispensed from a small metal container by a propellant under pressure. **3.** Also called: **air spray.** such a substance together with its container. [C20: from AERO- + SOL(UTION)]

aerospace (ˈɛərəˌspeɪs) *n.* **1.** the atmosphere and space beyond. **2.** (*modifier*) of or relating to rockets, missiles, space vehicles, etc., that fly or operate in aerospace: *the aerospace industry.*

aerosphere (ˈɛərəˌsfɪə) *n.* the entire atmosphere surrounding the earth.

aerostat (ˈɛərəˌstæt) *n.* a lighter-than-air craft, such as a balloon. [C18: from French *aérostat,* from AERO- + Greek *-statos* standing] —ˌ**aeroˈstatic** *or* ˌ**aeroˈstatical** *adj.*

aerostatics (ˌɛərəˈstætɪks) *n.* (*functioning as sing.*) **1.** the study of gases in equilibrium and bodies held in equilibrium in gases. Compare **aerodynamics. 2.** the study of lighter-than-air craft, such as balloons.

aerostation (ˈɛərəˌsteɪʃən) *n.* the science of operating lighter-than-air craft.

aerostructure (ˈɛərəʊˌstrʌktʃə) *n.* any separately manufactured unit, component, or section of an aircraft or other vehicle capable of flight.

aerothermodynamics (ˌɛərəʊˌθɜːməʊdaɪˈnæmɪks) *n.* (*functioning as sing.*) the study of the exchange of heat between solids and gases, esp. of the heating effect on aircraft flying through the air at very high speeds. —ˌ**aeroˌthermodyˈnamic** *adj.*

aerugo (ɪˈruːgəʊ) *n.* (esp. of old bronze) another name for **verdigris.** [C18: from Latin, from *aes* copper, bronze] —**aeruginous** (ɪˈruːdʒɪnəs) *adj.*

aery[1] (ˈɛərɪ, ˈeɪərɪ) *adj. Poetic.* **1.** a variant spelling of **airy. 2.** lofty, insubstantial, or visionary. [C16: via Latin from Greek *aērios,* from *aēr* AIR]

aery[2] (ˈɛərɪ, ˈɪərɪ) *n., pl.* **aeries.** a variant spelling of **eyrie.**

Aeschylean (ˌiːskəˈliːən) *adj.* of or relating to the works of Aeschylus, 5th-century B.C. Greek dramatist.

Aesculapian (ˌiːskjʊˈleɪpɪən) *adj.* of or relating to Aesculapius, the Roman god of medicine, or to the art of medicine.

aesthesia *or U.S.* **esthesia** (iːsˈθiːzɪə) *n.* the normal ability to experience sensation, perception, or sensitivity. [C20: back formation from ANAESTHESIA]

aesthete *or U.S.* **esthete** (ˈiːsθiːt) *n.* a person who has or who affects a highly developed appreciation of beauty, esp. in poetry and the visual arts. [C19: back formation from AESTHETICS]

aesthetic (iːsˈθɛtɪk, ɪs-), **aesthetical** *or U.S.* (*sometimes*) **esthetic, esthetical** *adj.* **1.** connected with aesthetics or its principles. **2. a.** relating to pure beauty rather than to other considerations. **b.** artistic or relating to good taste: *an aesthetic consideration.* —**aesˈthetically** *or U.S.* (*sometimes*) **esˈthetically** *adv.*

aesthetician *or U.S.* (*sometimes*) **esthetician** (ˌiːsθɪˈtɪʃən, ˌɛs-) *n.* a student of aesthetics.

aestheticism *or U.S.* (*sometimes*) **estheticism** (iːsˈθɛtɪˌsɪzəm, ɪs-) *n.* **1.** the doctrine that aesthetic principles are of supreme importance and that works of art should be judged accordingly. **2.** sensitivity to beauty, esp. in art, music, literature, etc.

aesthetics *or U.S.* (*sometimes*) **esthetics** (iːsˈθɛtɪks, ɪs-) *n.* (*functioning as sing.*) **1.** the branch of philosophy concerned with the study of such concepts as beauty, taste, etc. **2.** the study of the rules and principles of art. [C18: from Greek *aisthētikos* perceptible by the senses, from *aisthesthai* to perceive]

aestival *or U.S.* **estival** (iːˈstaɪvəl, ˈɛstɪ-) *adj. Rare.* of or occurring in summer. [C14: from French, from Late Latin *aestīvālis,* from Latin *aestās* summer]

aestivate *or U.S.* **estivate** (ˈiːstɪˌveɪt, ˈɛs-) *vb.* (*intr.*) **1.** to pass the summer. **2.** (of animals such as the lungfish) to pass the summer or dry season in a dormant condition. Compare **hibernate.** [C17: from Latin *aestīvātus,* from *aestīvāre* to stay during the summer, from *aestās* summer] —ˈ**aestiˌvator** *or U.S.* ˈ**estiˌvator** *n.*

aestivation *or U.S.* **estivation** (ˌiːstɪˈveɪʃən, ˌɛs-) *n.* **1.** the act or condition of aestivating. **2.** the arrangement of the parts of a flower bud, esp. the sepals and petals.

aet. *or* **aetat.** *abbrev. for* aetatis. [Latin: at the age of]

aether (ˈiːθə) *n.* a variant spelling of **ether** (senses 3–5).

aethereal (ɪˈθɪərɪəl) *adj.* a variant spelling of **ethereal** (senses 1, 2, 3). —**aethereality** (ɪˌθɪərɪˈælɪtɪ) *n.* —**aeˈthereally** *adv.*

aetiological *or* **etiological** (ˌiːtɪˈɒlədʒɪkəl) *adj.* **1.** of or relating to aetiology. **2.** *Philosophy.* (of an explanation) in terms of causal precedents, as opposed, for instance, to the intentions of an agent. —ˌ**aetioˈlogically** *or* ˌ**etioˈlogically** *adv.*

aetiology *or* **etiology** (ˌiːtɪˈɒlədʒɪ) *n., pl.* **-gies. 1.** the philosophy or study of causation. **2.** the study of the causes of diseases. **3.** the cause of a disease. [C16: from Late Latin *aetologia,* from Greek *aitiologia,* from *aitia* cause] —ˌ**aetiˈologist** *or* ˌ**etiˈologist** *n.*

AEU (in Britain) *abbrev. for* Amalgamated Engineering Union.

AEW *abbrev. for* airborne early warning (aircraft).

AF *abbrev. for* Anglo-French.

Af. *abbrev. for* Africa(n).

a.f. *abbrev. for* audio frequency.

A/F (in auction catalogues, etc.) *abbrev. for* as found.

afar (əˈfɑː) *adv.* **1.** at, from, or to a great distance. ~*n.* **2.** a great distance (esp. in the phrase **from afar**). [C14 *a fer,* altered from earlier *on fer* and *of fer;* see A-[2], FAR]

AFB *abbrev. for* (U.S.) Air Force Base.

AFC *abbrev. for:* **1.** Air Force Cross. **2.** Association Football Club. **3.** automatic flight control. **4.** automatic frequency control.

afeard *or* **afeared** (əˈfɪəd) *adj.* (*postpositive*) an archaic or dialect word for **afraid.** [Old English *āfǣred,* from *afǣran* to frighten, from *fǣran* to FEAR]

afebrile (æˈfiːbraɪl, eɪ-) *adj.* without fever.

aff (æf) *Scot.* ~*adv.* **1.** off. ~*prep.* **2.** off. **3.** from; out of. [Old English *of;* Old Norse *af*]

affable (ˈæfəbəl) *adj.* **1.** showing warmth and friendliness; kindly; mild; benign. **2.** easy to converse with; approachable; amicable. [C16: from Latin *affābilis* easy to talk to, from *affārī* to talk to, from *ad-* to + *fārī* to speak; compare FABLE, FATE] —ˌ**affaˈbility** *n.* —ˈ**affably** *adv.*

affair (əˈfɛə) *n.* **1.** a thing to be done or attended to; matter; business: *this affair must be cleared up.* **2.** an event or happening: *a strange affair.* **3.** (*qualified by an adjective or descriptive phrase*) something previously specified, esp. a man-made object; thing: *our house is a tumbledown affair.* **4.** a sexual relationship between two people who are not married to each other. ~See also **affairs.** [C13: from Old French, from *à faire* to do]

affaire *French.* (afɛr) *n.* a love affair.

affaire d'amour *French.* (afɛr damur) *n., pl.* ***affaires d'amour*** (afɛr damur). a love affair.

affaire de coeur *French.* (afɛr də kœr) *n., pl.* ***affaires de coeur*** (afɛr də kœr). an affair of the heart; love affair.

affaire d'honneur *French.* (afɛr dɔnœr) *n., pl.* ***affaires d'honneur*** (afɛr dɔnœr). a duel.

affairs (əˈfɛəz) *pl. n.* **1.** personal or business interests: *his affairs were in disorder.* **2.** matters of public interest: *current affairs.*

affect[1] *vb.* (əˈfɛkt). (*tr.*) **1.** to act upon or influence, esp. in an adverse way: *damp affected the sparking plugs.* **2.** to move or disturb emotionally or mentally: *her death affected him greatly.* **3.** (of pain, disease, etc.) to attack. ~*n.* (ˈæfɛkt, əˈfɛkt). **4.** *Psychol.* the emotion associated with an idea or set of ideas. See also **affection.** [C17: from Latin *affectus,* past participle of *afficere* to act upon, from *ad-* to + *facere* to do]

affect[2] (əˈfɛkt) *vb.* (*mainly tr.*) **1.** to put on an appearance or show of; make a pretence of: *to affect ignorance.* **2.** to imitate or assume, esp. pretentiously: *to affect an accent.* **3.** to have or use by preference: *she always affects funereal clothing.* **4.** to adopt the character, manner, etc., of: *he was always affecting the politician.* **5.** (of plants or animals) to live or grow in: *penguins affect an arctic climate.* **6.** to incline naturally or habitually towards: *falling drops of liquid affect roundness.* [C15: from Latin *affectāre* to strive after, pretend to have; related to *afficere* to AFFECT[1]]

affectation (ˌæfɛkˈteɪʃən) *n.* **1.** an assumed manner of speech, dress, or behaviour, esp. one that is intended to impress others. **2.** (often foll. by *of*) deliberate pretence or false display: *affectation of nobility.* [C16: from Latin *affectātiōn-* an aiming at, striving after, from *affectāre;* see AFFECT[2]]

affected[1] (əˈfɛktɪd) *adj.* (*usually postpositive*) **1.** deeply moved, esp. by sorrow or grief: *he was greatly affected by her departure.* **2.** changed, esp. detrimentally. [C17: from AFFECT[1] + -ED[2]]

affected[2] (əˈfɛktɪd) *adj.* **1.** behaving, speaking, etc., in an artificial or assumed way, esp. in order to impress others. **2.** feigned: *affected indifference.* **3.** *Archaic.* inclined; disposed. [C16: from AFFECT[2] + -ED[2]] —**afˈfectedly** *adv.* —**afˈfectedness** *n.*

affecting (əˈfɛktɪŋ) *adj.* evoking feelings of pity, sympathy, or pathos; moving. —**afˈfectingly** *adv.*

affection (əˈfɛkʃən) *n.* **1.** a feeling of fondness or tenderness for a person or thing; attachment. **2.** (*often pl.*) emotion, feeling, or sentiment: *to play on a person's affections.* **3.** *Pathol.* any disease or pathological condition. **4.** *Psychol.* any form of mental functioning that involves emotion. See also **affect**[1]. **5.** the act of affecting or the state of being affected. **6.** *Archaic.* inclination or disposition. [C13: from Latin *affectiōn-* disposition, from *afficere* to AFFECT[1]] —**afˈfectional** *adj.*

affectionate (əˈfɛkʃənɪt) *adj.* having or displaying tender feelings, affection, or warmth: *an affectionate mother; an affectionate letter.* —**afˈfectionately** *adv.*

affective (əˈfɛktɪv) *adj.* **1.** *Psychol.* relating to affects. **2.** concerned with or arousing the emotions or affection. —**affectivity** (ˌæfɛkˈtɪvɪtɪ) *or* **afˈfectiveness** *n.*

affective psychosis *n.* a severe mental disorder characterized by extreme moods of either depression or mania.

affenpinscher (ˈæfənˌpɪnʃə) *n.* a small wire-haired breed of dog of European origin, having tufts of hair on the muzzle. [German, literally: monkey-terrier, so called because its face resembles a monkey's]

afferent (ˈæfərənt) *adj.* bringing or directing inwards to a part or an organ of the body, esp. towards the brain or spinal cord. Compare **efferent.** [C19: from Latin *afferre* to carry to, from *ad-* to + *ferre* to carry]

affettuoso (æˌfɛtʃuːˈəʊsəʊ) *adj., adv. Music.* with feeling. [C18: from Italian]

affiance (əˈfaɪəns) *vb.* **1.** (*tr.*) to bind (a person or oneself) in a promise of marriage; betroth. ~*n.* **2.** *Archaic.* a solemn pledge, esp. a marriage contract. [C14: via Old French from Medieval Latin *affīdāre* to trust (oneself) to, from *fīdāre* to trust, from *fīdus* faithful]

affiant (əˈfaɪənt) *n. U.S. law.* a person who makes an affidavit. [C19: Old French, from *affier* to trust to, from Medieval Latin *affīdāre;* see AFFIANCE]

affiche *French.* (afiʃ) *n.* a poster or advertisement, esp. one drawn by an artist, as for the opening of an exhibition. [C18: from *afficher* to post]

affidavit (ˌæfɪˈdeɪvɪt) *n. Law.* a declaration in writing made upon oath before a person authorized to administer oaths. [C17: from Medieval Latin, literally: he declares on oath, from *affīdare* to trust (oneself) to; see AFFIANCE]

affiliate *vb.* (əˈfɪlɪˌeɪt). **1.** (*tr.;* foll. by *to* or *with*) to receive into close connection or association (with a larger body, group, organization, etc.); adopt as a member, branch, etc. **2.** (foll. by *with*) to associate (oneself) or be associated, esp. as a subordinate or subsidiary; bring or come into close connection: *he affiliated himself with the Union.* ~*n.* (əˈfɪlɪɪt, -ˌeɪt). **3. a.** a person or organization that is affiliated with another. **b.** (*as modifier*): *an affiliate member.* [C18: from Medieval Latin *affīliātus* adopted as a son, from *affīliāre,* from Latin *filius* son] —**afˌfiliˈation** *n.*

affiliation order *n. Law.* an order made by a magistrates' court that a man adjudged to be the father of an illegitimate child shall contribute a specified periodic sum towards the child's maintenance.

affiliation proceedings *pl. n.* legal proceedings, usually initiated by an unwed mother, claiming legal recognition that a particular man is the father of her child, often associated with a claim for financial support.

affine (ˈæfaɪn) *adj. Maths.* of, characterizing, or involving transformations which preserve collinearity, esp. in classical geometry, those of translation, rotation and reflection in an axis. [C16: via French from Latin *affīnis* bordering on, related]

affined (əˈfaɪnd) *adj.* closely related; connected.

affinity (əˈfɪnɪtɪ) *n., pl.* **-ties. 1.** a natural liking, taste, or inclination for a person or thing. **2.** the person or thing so liked. **3.** a close similarity in appearance or quality; inherent likeness. **4.** relationship by marriage or by ties other than of blood, as by adoption. Compare **consanguinity. 5.** similarity in structure, form, etc., between different animals, plants, or languages. **6.** *Chem.* **a.** the force holding atoms together in a molecule; chemical attraction. **b.** a measure of the tendency of a chemical reaction to take place expressed in terms of the free energy change. Symbol: *A* **7.** *Immunol.* a measure of the degree of interaction between an antigen and an antibody. [C14: via Old French from Latin *affīnitāt-* connected by marriage, from *affīnis* bordering on, related] —**afˈfinitive** *adj.*

affirm (əˈfɜːm) *vb.* (*mainly tr.*) **1.** (*may take a clause as object*) to declare to be true; assert positively. **2.** to uphold, confirm, or ratify. **3.** (*intr.*) *Law.* to make an affirmation. [C14: via Old French from Latin *affirmāre* to present (something) as firm or fixed, assert, from *ad-* to + *firmāre* to make FIRM] —**afˈfirmer** *or* **afˈfirmant** *n.*

affirmation (ˌæfəˈmeɪʃən) *n.* **1.** the act of affirming or the state of being affirmed. **2.** a statement of the existence or truth of something; assertion. **3.** *Law.* a solemn declaration permitted on grounds of conscientious objection to taking an oath.

affirmative (əˈfɜːmətɪv) *adj.* **1.** confirming or asserting something as true or valid: *an affirmative statement.* **2.** indicating agreement or assent: *an affirmative answer.* **3.** *Logic.* **a.** (of a categorial proposition) affirming the satisfaction by the subject of the predicate, as in *all birds have feathers; some men are married.* **b.** not containing negation. Compare **negative** (sense 12). ~*n.* **4.** a positive assertion. **5.** a word or phrase stating agreement or assent, such as *yes* (esp. in the phrase **answer in the affirmative**). **6.** *Logic.* an affirmative proposition. **7. the affirmative.** *Chiefly U.S. and Canadian.* the side in a debate that supports the proposition. ~*sentence substitute.* **8.** *Military, etc.* a signal codeword used to express assent or confirmation. —**afˈfirmatively** *adv.*

affirmative action *n. U.S.* a policy or programme designed to counter discrimination against minority groups and women in areas such as employment and education. Brit. equivalent: **positive discrimination.**

affix *vb.* (əˈfɪks). (*tr.;* usually foll. by *to* or *on*) **1.** to attach, fasten, join, or stick: *to affix a poster to the wall.* **2.** to add or append: *to affix a signature to a document.* **3.** to attach or attribute (guilt, blame, etc.). ~*n.* (ˈæfɪks). **4.** a linguistic element added to a word or root to produce a derived or inflected form: *-ment* in *establishment* is a derivational affix; *-s* in *drowns* is an inflectional affix. See also **prefix, suffix, infix. 5.** something fastened or attached; appendage. [C15: from Medieval Latin *affixāre,* from *ad-* to + *fixāre* to FIX] —**affixation** (ˌæfɪkˈseɪʃən) *or* **affixture** (əˈfɪkstʃə) *n.*

afflatus (əˈfleɪtəs) *n.* an impulse of creative power or inspiration, esp. in poetry, considered to be of divine origin (esp. in the phrase **divine afflatus**). [C17: Latin, from *afflātus,* from *afflāre* to breathe or blow on, from *flāre* to blow]

afflict (əˈflɪkt) *vb.* (*tr.*) to cause suffering or unhappiness to; distress greatly. [C14: from Latin *afflictus,* past participle of *affligere* to knock against, from *fligere* to knock, to strike] —**afˈflictive** *adj.*

afflicting (əˈflɪktɪŋ) *adj.* deeply distressing; painful.

affliction (əˈflɪkʃən) *n.* **1.** a condition of great distress, pain, or suffering. **2.** something responsible for physical or mental suffering, such as a disease, grief, etc.

affluence (ˈæfluəns) *n.* **1.** an abundant supply of money, goods, or property; wealth. **2.** *Rare.* abundance or profusion.

affluent (ˈæfluənt) *adj.* **1.** rich; wealthy. **2.** abundant; copious. **3.** flowing freely. ~*n.* **4.** a tributary stream. [C15: from Latin *affluent-,* present participle of *affluere* to flow towards, from *fluere* to flow]

affluent society *n.* a society in which the material benefits of prosperity are widely available.

afflux (ˈæflʌks) *n.* a flowing towards a point: *an afflux of blood to the head.* [C17: from Latin *affluxus,* from *fluxus* FLUX]

afford (əˈfɔːd) *vb.* **1.** (preceded by *can, could,* etc.) to be able to do or spare something, esp. without incurring financial difficulties or without risk of undesirable consequences: *we can afford to buy a small house; I can afford to give you one of my chess sets; we can't afford to miss this play.* **2.** to give, yield, or supply: *the meeting afforded much useful information.* [Old English *geforthian* to further, promote, from *forth* FORTH; the Old English prefix *ge-* was later reduced to *a-*, and the modern spelling (C16) is influenced by words beginning *aff-*] —**af'fordable** *adj.* —**af,ford-a'bility** *n.*

afforest (ə'fɒrɪst) *vb.* (*tr.*) to plant trees on; convert into forested land. [C15: from Medieval Latin *afforestāre*, from *forestis* FOREST] —**af,forest'ation** *n.*

affranchise (ə'fræntʃaɪz) *vb.* (*tr.*) to release from servitude or an obligation. [C15: from Old French *afranchiss-*, a stem of *afranchir*, from *franchir* to free; see FRANK] —**af'franchisement** *n.*

affray (ə'freɪ) *n.* **1.** *Law.* a fight, noisy quarrel, or disturbance between two or more persons in a public place. ~*vb.* **2.** (*tr.*) *Archaic.* to frighten. [C14: via Old French from Vulgar Latin *exfridāre* (unattested) to break the peace; compare German *Friede* peace]

affreightment (ə'freɪtmənt) *n.* a contract hiring a ship to carry goods. [C19: from French *affréter* to charter a ship, from *fret* FREIGHT]

affricate ('æfrɪkɪt) *n.* a composite speech sound consisting of a stop and a fricative articulated at the same point, such as the sound written *ch*, as in *chair*. [C19: from Latin *affricāre* to rub against, from *fricāre* to rub; compare FRICTION]

affricative (ə'frɪkətɪv, 'æfrə,keɪ-) *n.* **1.** another word for **affricate.** ~*adj.* **2.** of, relating to, or denoting an affricate.

affright (ə'fraɪt) *Archaic or poetic.* ~*vb.* **1.** (*tr.*) to frighten. ~*n.* **2.** a sudden terror. [Old English *āfyrhtan*, from *a-*, a prefix indicating the beginning or end of an action + *fyrhtan* to FRIGHT]

affront (ə'frʌnt) *n.* **1.** a deliberate insult. ~*vb.* (*tr.*) **2.** to insult, esp. openly. **3.** to offend the pride or dignity of. **4.** *Obsolete.* to confront defiantly. [C14: from Old French *afronter* to strike in the face, from Vulgar Latin *affrontāre* (unattested), from the Latin phrase *ad frontem* to the face]

affusion (ə'fjuːʒən) *n.* the baptizing of a person by pouring water onto his head. Compare **aspersion** (sense 3), **immersion.** [C17: from Late Latin *affūsiōn-* a pouring upon, from *affundere*, from *fundere* to pour]

Afg. *or* **Afgh.** *abbrev. for* Afghanistan.

afghan ('æfgæn, -gən) *n.* **1.** a knitted or crocheted wool blanket or shawl, esp. one with a geometric pattern. **2.** a sheepskin coat, often embroidered and having long fur trimming around the edges.

Afghan ('æfgæn, -gən) *or* **Afghani** (æf'gænɪ, -'gɑː-) *n.* **1.** a native or inhabitant of Afghanistan, a republic in central Asia. **2.** another name for **Pashto** (the language). **3.** (formerly) an Indian camel driver employed in the outback of Australia. ~*adj.* **4.** denoting or relating to Afghanistan, its people, or their language.

Afghan hound *n.* a tall graceful breed of hound with a long silky coat.

afghani (æf'gɑːnɪ) *n.* the standard monetary unit of Afghanistan, divided into 100 puls.

aficionado (ə,fɪʃjə'nɑːdəʊ; *Spanish* afiθjo'naðo) *n., pl.* **-dos** (-dəʊz; *Spanish* -ðos). **1.** an ardent supporter or devotee: *a jazz aficionado.* **2.** a devotee of bullfighting. [Spanish, from *aficionar* to arouse affection, from *afición* AFFECTION]

afield (ə'fiːld) *adv., adj.* (*postpositive*) **1.** away from one's usual surroundings or home (esp. in the phrase **far afield**). **2.** off the subject; away from the point (esp. in the phrase **far afield**). **3.** in or to the field, esp. the battlefield.

afire (ə'faɪə) *adv., adj.* (*postpositive*) **1.** on fire; ablaze. **2.** intensely interested or passionate: *he was afire with enthusiasm for the new plan.*

aflame (ə'fleɪm) *adv., adj.* (*postpositive*) **1.** in flames; ablaze. **2.** deeply aroused, as with passion: *he was aflame with desire.* **3.** (of the face) red or inflamed.

aflatoxin (,æflə'tɒksɪn) *n.* a toxin produced by the fungus *Aspergillus flavus* growing on peanuts, maize, etc., causing liver disease (esp. cancer) in man. [C20: from *A(spergillus) fla(vus)* + TOXIN]

AFL-CIO *abbrev. for* American Federation of Labor and Congress of Industrial Organizations; a federation of independent American trade unions formed by the union of these two groups in 1955.

afloat (ə'fləʊt) *adj.* (*postpositive*), *adv.* **1.** floating. **2.** aboard ship; at sea. **3.** covered with water; flooded. **4.** aimlessly drifting: *afloat in a sea of indecision.* **5.** in circulation; afoot: *nasty rumours were afloat.* **6.** free of debt; solvent.

aflutter (ə'flʌtə) *adj.* (*postpositive*), *adv.* in or into a nervous or excited state.

AFM *abbrev. for* Air Force Medal.

AFNOR *abbrev. for* Association Française de Normalisation: the standards organization of France.

afoot (ə'fʊt) *adj.* (*postpositive*), *adv.* **1.** in circulation or operation; astir: *mischief was afoot.* **2.** on or by foot.

afore (ə'fɔː) *adv., prep., conj.* an archaic or dialect word for **before.**

aforementioned (ə'fɔː,mɛnʃənd) *adj.* (*usually prenominal*) (chiefly in legal documents) stated or mentioned before or already.

aforesaid (ə'fɔː,sɛd) *adj.* (*usually prenominal*) (chiefly in legal documents) spoken of or referred to previously.

aforethought (ə'fɔː,θɔːt) *adj.* (*immediately postpositive*) premeditated (esp. in the phrase **malice aforethought**).

aforetime (ə'fɔː,taɪm) *adv. Archaic.* formerly.

a fortiori (eɪ ,fɔːtɪ'ɔːraɪ, -rɪ; ɑː) *adv.* for similar but more convincing reasons: *if Britain cannot afford a space programme, then, a fortiori, neither can India.* [Latin]

afoul (ə'faʊl) *adv., adj.* (*postpositive*) **1.** (usually foll. by *of*) in or into a state of difficulty, confusion, or conflict (with). **2.** (often foll. by *of*) in or into an entanglement or collision (with) (often in the phrase **run afoul of**): *a yacht with its sails afoul; the boat ran afoul of a steamer.*

afp *abbrev. for* alpha-fetoprotein.

Afr. *abbrev. for* Africa(n).

AFRAeS (in Britain) *abbrev. for* Associate Fellow of the Royal Aeronautical Society.

afraid (ə'freɪd) *adj.* (*postpositive*) **1.** (often foll. by *of*) feeling fear or apprehension; frightened: *he was afraid of cats.* **2.** reluctant (to do something), as through fear or timidity: *he was afraid to let himself go.* **3.** (often foll. by *that*; used to lessen the effect of an unpleasant statement) regretful: *I'm afraid that I shall have to tell you to go.* [C14 *affraied*, past participle of AFFRAY (to frighten)]

A-frame *adj.* (of a house) constructed with an A-shaped elevation.

afreet *or* **afrit** ('æfriːt, ə'friːt) *n. Arabian myth.* a powerful evil demon or giant monster. [C19: from Arabic *'ifrīt*]

afresh (ə'frɛʃ) *adv.* once more; once again; anew.

African ('æfrɪkən) *adj.* **1.** denoting or relating to Africa or any of its peoples, languages, nations, etc. ~*n.* **2.** a native, inhabitant, or citizen of any of the countries of Africa. **3.** a member or descendant of any of the peoples of Africa, esp. a Negro.

African-American *n.* **1.** an American of African descent. ~*adj.* **2.** of or relating to Americans of African descent.

Africanism ('æfrɪkə,nɪzəm) *n.* something characteristic of Africa or Africans, esp. a characteristic feature of an African language when introduced into a non-African language.

Africanist ('æfrɪkənɪst) *n.* a person specializing in the study of African affairs or culture.

Africanize *or* **Africanise** ('æfrɪkə,naɪz) *vb.* (*tr.*) to make African, esp. to give control of (policy, government, etc.) to Africans. —**,Africani'zation** *or* **,Africani'sation** *n.*

African lily *n.* a liliaceous plant, *Agapanthus africanus*, of southern Africa, having rounded clusters of blue or white funnel-shaped flowers.

African mahogany *n.* **1.** any of several African trees of the meliaceous genus *Khaya*, esp. *K. ivorensis*, that have wood similar to that of true mahogany. **2.** the wood of any of these trees, used for furniture, etc. **3.** any of various other African woods that resemble true mahogany.

African time *n. S. African slang.* unpunctuality.

African violet *n.* any of several tropical African plants of the genus *Saintpaulia*, esp. *S. ionantha*, cultivated as house plants, with violet, white, or pink flowers and hairy leaves: family *Gesneriaceae*.

Afrikaans (,æfrɪ'kɑːns, -'kɑːnz) *n.* an official language of all the Republic of South Africa, closely related to Dutch and Flemish. Sometimes called: **South African Dutch, Taal.** [C20: from Dutch: African]

Afrikander *or* **Africander** (afri'kandə, ,æfrɪ'kændə) *n.* **1.** a breed of humpbacked beef cattle originally raised in southern Africa. **2.** a southern African breed of fat-tailed sheep. **3.** a former name for an **Afrikaner.** [C19: from South African Dutch, formed on the model of *Hollander*]

Afrikaner (afri'kaːnə, ,æfrɪ'kɑːnə) *n.* a White native of the Republic of South Africa whose mother tongue is Afrikaans. See also **Boer.**

Afrikanerdom (afri'kaːnədəm, ,æfrɪ'kɑːnədəm) *n.* (in South Africa) Afrikaner nationalism based on pride in the Afrikaans language and culture, conservative Calvinism, and a sense of heritage as pioneers.

Afrikanerize *or* **Afrikanerise** (afri'kaːnə,raɪz, ,æfrɪ'kɑːnə,raɪz) *vb.* (*tr.*) *Chiefly S. African.* to make (a person) Afrikaans in attitudes, language, etc. —**,Afrikaneri'zation** *or* **,Afrikaneri'sation** *n.*

afrit ('æfriːt, ə'friːt) *n.* a variant spelling of **afreet.**

Afro ('æfrəʊ) *n., pl.* **-ros.** a hairstyle in which the hair is shaped into a wide frizzy bush, popular esp. among Negroes. [C20: independent use of AFRO-]

Afro- *combining form.* indicating Africa or African: *Afro-Asiatic.*

Afro-American *n., adj.* another word for **African-American.**

Afro-Asian *adj.* of or relating to both Africa and Asia, esp. as part of the Third World.

Afro-Asiatic *n.* **1.** Also called: **Semito-Hamitic.** a family of languages of SW Asia and N Africa, consisting of the Semitic, ancient Egyptian, Berber, Cushitic, and Chadic subfamilies. ~*adj.* **2.** denoting, belonging to, or relating to this family of languages.

Afro-chain *n.* (in the Caribbean) a large chain necklace with a central pendant: usually worn with a dashiki by men.

Afro-comb *n.* a comb with a handle and long teeth used esp. on curly hair.

Afro-Cuban *adj.* of or relating to a type of jazz influenced by Cuban variants of African rhythms. Compare **Cu-bop.**

afrormosia (,æfrɔː'məʊzɪə) *n.* a hard teaklike wood obtained from tropical African trees of the leguminous genus *Pericopsis*. [C20: from AFRO- + *Ormosia* (genus name)]

AFSLAET *abbrev. for* Associate Fellow of the Society of Licensed Aircraft Engineers and Technologists.

aft (ɑːft) *adv., adj. Chiefly nautical.* towards or at the stern or rear: *the aft deck; aft of the engines.* [C17: perhaps a shortened form of earlier ABAFT]

after ('ɑːftə) *prep.* **1.** following in time; in succession to: *after dinner; time after time.* **2.** following; behind: *they entered one after another.* **3.** in pursuit or search of: *chasing after a thief; he's only after money.* **4.** concerning: *to inquire after his health.* **5.** considering: *after what you have done, you shouldn't complain.* **6.** next in excellence or importance to: *he ranked Jonson after Shakespeare.* **7.** in imitation of; in the manner of: *a statue after classical models.* **8.** in accordance with or in conformity to: *a man after her own heart.* **9.** with a name derived from: *Mary was named after her grandmother.* **10.** *U.S.* past (the hour of): *twenty after three.* **11. after all. a.** in spite of everything: *it's only a game, after all.* **b.** in spite of expectations, efforts, etc.: *he won the race after all!* **12. after you.** please go, enter, etc., before me. ~*adv.* **13.** at a later time; afterwards. **14.** coming afterwards; in pursuit. **15.** *Nautical.* further aft; sternwards. ~*conj.* **16.** (*subordinating*) at a time later than that at which: *he came after I had left.* ~*adj.* **17.** *Nautical.* further aft: *the after cabin.* [Old English *æfter;* related to Old Norse *aptr* back, *eptir* after, Old High German *aftar*]

afterbirth ('ɑːftəˌbɜːθ) *n.* the placenta and fetal membranes expelled from the uterus after the birth of offspring.

afterbody ('ɑːftəˌbɒdɪ) *n., pl.* **-bodies.** any discarded part that continues to trail a satellite, rocket, etc., in orbit.

afterbrain ('ɑːftəˌbreɪn) *n.* a nontechnical name for **myelencephalon.**

afterburner ('ɑːftəˌbɜːnə) *n.* **1.** a device in the exhaust system of an internal-combustion engine for removing or rendering harmless potentially dangerous components in the exhaust gases. **2.** a system of fuel injection and combustion located behind the turbine of an aircraft jet engine to produce additional thrust.

afterburning ('ɑːftəˌbɜːnɪŋ) *n.* **1.** Also called: **reheat.** a process in which additional fuel is ignited in the exhaust gases of a jet engine to produce additional thrust. **2.** irregular burning of fuel in a rocket motor after the main burning has ceased. **3.** persistence of combustion in an internal-combustion engine, either in an incorrect part of the cycle or after the ignition has been switched off.

aftercare ('ɑːftəˌkɛə) *n.* **1.** support services by a welfare agency for a person discharged from an institution, such as hospital, hostel, prison, or borstal. **2.** *Med.* the care before discharge from hospital of a patient recovering from an illness or operation. **3.** any system of maintenance or upkeep of an appliance or product: *contact lens aftercare.*

afterdamp ('ɑːftəˌdæmp) *n.* a poisonous gas, consisting mainly of carbon monoxide, formed after the explosion of firedamp in coal mines. See also **whitedamp.**

afterdeck ('ɑːftəˌdɛk) *n. Nautical.* the unprotected deck behind the bridge of a ship.

aftereffect ('ɑːftərɪˌfɛkt) *n.* **1.** any result occurring some time after its cause. **2.** *Med.* any delayed response to a stimulus or agent. Compare **side effect. 3.** *Psychol.* any illusory sensation caused by a stimulus that has ceased.

afterglow ('ɑːftəˌgləʊ) *n.* **1.** the glow left after a light has disappeared, such as that sometimes seen after sunset. **2.** the glow of an incandescent metal after the source of heat has been removed. **3.** *Physics.* luminescence persisting on the screen of a cathode-ray tube or in a gas-discharge tube after the power supply has been disconnected. **4.** a trace, impression, etc., of past emotion, brilliance, etc.

afterheat ('ɑːftəˌhiːt) *n.* the heat generated in a nuclear reactor after it has been shut down, produced by residual radioactivity in the fuel elements.

afterimage ('ɑːftərˌɪmɪdʒ) *n.* a sustained or renewed sensation, esp. visual, after the original stimulus has ceased. Also called: **aftersensation, photogene.**

afterlife ('ɑːftəˌlaɪf) *n.* life after death or at a later time in a person's lifetime.

aftermath ('ɑːftəˌmɑːθ, -ˌmæθ) *n.* **1.** signs or results of an event or occurrence considered collectively, esp. of a catastrophe or disaster: *the aftermath of war.* **2.** *Agriculture.* a second mowing or crop of grass from land that has already yielded one crop earlier in the same year. [C16: AFTER + *math* a mowing, from Old English *mæth*]

aftermost ('ɑːftəˌməʊst) *adj.* closer or closest to the rear or (in a vessel) the stern; last.

afternoon (ˌɑːftə'nuːn) *n.* **1. a.** the period of the day between noon and evening. **b.** (*as modifier*): *afternoon tea.* **2.** a middle or later part: *the afternoon of life.*

afternoons (ˌɑːftə'nuːnz) *adv. Informal.* during the afternoon, esp. regularly.

afterpains ('ɑːftəˌpeɪnz) *pl. n.* cramplike pains caused by contraction of the uterus after childbirth.

afterpeak ('ɑːftəˌpiːk) *n. Nautical.* the space behind the aftermost bulkhead, often used for storage.

afterpiece ('ɑːftəˌpiːs) *n.* a brief usually comic dramatic piece presented after a play.

after-ripening *n. Botany.* the period of internal change that is necessary in some apparently mature seeds before germination can occur.

afters ('ɑːftəz) *n.* (*functioning as sing. or pl.*) *Brit. informal.* dessert; sweet.

aftersensation ('ɑːftəsɛnˌseɪʃən) *n.* another word for **afterimage.**

aftershaft ('ɑːftəˌʃɑːft) *n. Ornithol.* a secondary feather arising near the base of a contour feather.

aftershave lotion ('ɑːftəˌʃeɪv) *n.* a lotion, usually styptic and perfumed, for application to the face after shaving. Often shortened to **aftershave.**

aftershock ('ɑːftəˌʃɒk) *n.* one of a series of minor tremors occurring after the main shock of an earthquake. Compare **foreshock.**

aftertaste ('ɑːftəˌteɪst) *n.* **1.** a taste that lingers on after eating or drinking. **2.** a lingering impression or sensation.

afterthought ('ɑːftəˌθɔːt) *n.* **1.** a comment, reply, etc., that occurs to one after the opportunity to deliver it has passed. **2.** an addition to something already completed.

afterwards ('ɑːftəwədz) *or* **afterward** *adv.* after an earlier event or time; subsequently. [Old English *æfterweard, æfteweard,* from AFT + WARD]

afterword ('ɑːftəˌwɜːd) *n.* an epilogue or postscript in a book, etc.

afterworld ('ɑːftəˌwɜːld) *n.* a world inhabited after death.

AFTN *abbrev. for* Aeronautical Fixed Telecommunications Network: a worldwide system of radio and cable links for transmitting and recording messages.

AFV *abbrev. for* armoured fighting vehicle.

Ag *the chemical symbol for* silver. [from Latin *argentum*]

AG *abbrev. for:* **1.** Adjutant General. **2.** Attorney General. **3.** Aktiengesellschaft. [German: joint-stock company]

aga *or* **agha** ('ɑːgə) *n.* (in the Ottoman Empire) **1.** a title of respect, often used with the title of a senior position. **2.** a military commander. [C17: Turkish, literally: lord]

again (ə'gɛn, ə'geɪn) *adv.* **1.** another or second time; once more; anew: *he had to start again.* **2.** once more in a previously experienced or encountered place, state, or condition: *he is ill again; he came back again.* **3.** in addition to the original amount, quantity, etc. (esp. in the phrases **as much again; half as much again**). **4.** (*sentence modifier*) on the other hand: *he might come and then again he might not.* **5.** besides; also: *she is beautiful and, again, intelligent.* **6.** *Archaic.* in reply; back: *he answered again to the questioning voice.* **7. again and again.** continuously; repeatedly. **8.** (*used with a negative*) *Caribbean.* any more; any longer: *I don't eat pumpkin again.* ~*sentence connector.* **9.** moreover; furthermore: *again, it could be said that he is not dead.* [Old English *ongegn* opposite to, from A-[2] + *gegn* straight]

against (ə'gɛnst, ə'geɪnst) *prep.* **1.** opposed to; in conflict or disagreement with: *they fought against the legislation.* **2.** standing or leaning beside or in front of: *a ladder against the wall.* **3.** coming in contact with: *the branches of a tree brushed against the bus.* **4.** in contrast to: *silhouettes are outlines against a light background.* **5.** having an adverse or unfavourable effect on: *the economic system works against small independent companies.* **6.** as a protection from or means of defence from the adverse effects of: *a safeguard against contaminated water.* **7.** in exchange for or in return for. **8.** *Now rare.* in preparation for: *he gave them warm clothing against their journey through the night.* **9. as against.** as opposed to or as compared with: *he had two shots at him this time as against only one last time.* [C12 *ageines,* from *again, ageyn,* etc., AGAIN + *-es* genitive ending; the spelling with *-t* (C16) was probably due to confusion with superlatives ending in *-st*]

Aga Khan ('ɑːgə 'kɑːn) *n.* the hereditary title of the head of the Ismaili sect of Muslims.

agalactia (ˌægə'læktɪə) *n. Pathol.* absence or failure of secretion of milk. [C19: New Latin, from A-[1] + Greek *galaktos* milk]

agalloch (ə'gæləək) *n.* another name for **eaglewood.** [C17: from Greek *agallokhon*]

agama ('ægəmə, ə'gæmə) *n.* **1.** any small terrestrial lizard of the genus *Agama,* which inhabit warm regions of the Old World: family *Agamidae.* **2.** Also called: **agamid** ('ægəmɪd, ə'gæmɪd). any other lizard of the family *Agamidae,* which occur in the Old World and Australia and show a wide range of habits and diversity of structure. [C19: Carib]

agamete (ə'gæmiːt) *n.* a reproductive cell, such as the merozoite of some protozoans, that develops into a new form without fertilization. [C19: from Greek *agametos* unmarried; see A-[1], GAMETE]

agamic (ə'gæmɪk) *adj.* asexual; occurring or reproducing without fertilization. [C19: from Greek *agamos* unmarried, from A-[1] + *gamos* marriage] —**a'gamically** *adv.*

agamogenesis (ˌægəməʊ'dʒɛnɪsɪs) *n.* asexual reproduction, such as fission or parthenogenesis. [C19: AGAMIC + GENESIS] —**agamogenetic** (ˌægəməʊdʒə'nɛtɪk) *adj.* —ˌ**agamoge'netically** *adv.*

agamogony (ˌægə'mɒgənɪ) *n.* another name for **schizogony.**

agamont ('ægəmɒnt) *n.* another name for **schizont.**

agamospermy ('ægəməʊˌspɜːmɪ) *n. Botany.* formation of seeds in the absence of fertilization; a form of apomixis. [C19: AGAMIC + Greek *sperma* seed]

agapanthus (ˌægə'pænθəs) *n.* a South African liliaceous plant with blue funnel-shaped flowers, widely cultivated for ornament. [C19: New Latin, from Greek *agapē* love + *anthos* flower]

agape (ə'geɪp) *adj.* (*postpositive*) **1.** (esp. of the mouth) wide open. **2.** very surprised, expectant, or eager, esp. as indicated by a wide open mouth. [C17: A-[2] + GAPE]

Agape (ˈæɡəpɪ) *n. Christianity.* **1.** Christian love, esp. as contrasted with erotic love; charity. **2.** a communal meal in the early Church taken in commemoration of the Last Supper; love feast. [C17: Greek *agapē* love]

agar (ˈeɪɡə) *n.* a complex gelatinous carbohydrate obtained from seaweeds, esp. those of the genus *Gelidium,* used as a culture medium for bacteria, a laxative, in food such as ice cream as a thickening agent (**E406**), etc. Also called: **agar-agar.** [C19: Malay]

agaric (ˈæɡərɪk, əˈɡærɪk) *n.* **1.** any saprophytic basidiomycetous fungus of the family *Agaricaceae,* having gills on the underside of the cap. The group includes both the edible mushrooms and poisonous forms, such as the fly agaric. **2.** the dried spore-producing bodies of certain fungi, esp. *Polyphorus officinalis* (or *Boletus laricis*), formerly used in medicine. [C16: via Latin *agaricum,* from Greek *agarikon,* perhaps named after *Agaria,* a town in Sarmatia] —**agaricaceous** (əˌɡærɪˈkeɪʃəs) *adj.*

agate (ˈæɡɪt) *n.* **1.** an impure microcrystalline form of quartz consisting of a variegated, usually banded chalcedony, used as a gemstone and in making pestles and mortars, burnishers, and polishers. Formula: SiO_2. **2.** a playing marble of this quartz or resembling it. **3.** *Printing.* the U.S. and Canadian name for **ruby** (sense 5). [C16: via French from Latin *achātēs,* from Greek *akhatēs*]

agate line *n. U.S. and Canadian.* a measure of advertising space, one column wide and one fourteenth of an inch deep. Sometimes shortened to **line.**

agateware (ˈæɡɪtˌwɛə) *n.* ceramic ware made to resemble agate or marble.

agave (əˈɡeɪvɪ, ˈæɡeɪv) *n.* any plant of the genus *Agave* native to tropical America with tall flower stalks rising from thick fleshy leaves: family *Agavaceae.* Some species are the source of fibres such as sisal or of alcoholic beverages such as pulque and tequila. See also **century plant.** [C18: New Latin, from Greek *agauē,* feminine of *agauos* illustrious, probably alluding to the height of the plant]

AGC *abbrev. for* automatic gain control.

agcy *abbrev. for* agency.

age (eɪdʒ) *n.* **1.** the period of time that a person, animal, or plant has lived or is expected to live: *the age of a tree; what age was he when he died? the age of a horse is up to thirty years.* **2.** the period of existence of an object, material, group, etc.: *the age of this table is 200 years.* **3. a.** a period or state of human life: *he should know better at his age; she had got beyond the giggly age.* **b.** (*as modifier*): *age group.* **4.** the latter part of life. **5. a.** a period of history marked by some feature or characteristic; era. **b.** (*cap. when part of a name*): *the Middle Ages; the Space Age.* **6.** generation: *the Edwardian age.* **7.** *Geology, palaeontol.* **a.** a period of the earth's history distinguished by special characteristics: *the age of reptiles.* **b.** the period during which a stage of rock strata is formed; a subdivision of an epoch. **8.** *Myth.* any of the successive periods in the legendary history of man, which were, according to Hesiod, the golden, silver, bronze, heroic, and iron ages. **9.** (*often pl.*) *Informal.* a relatively long time: *she was an age washing her hair; I've been waiting ages.* **10.** *Psychol.* the level in years that a person has reached in any area of development, such as mental or emotional, compared with the normal level for his chronological age. See also **achievement age, mental age. 11. age before beauty.** (often said humorously when yielding precedence) older people take precedence over younger people. **12. of age.** adult and legally responsible for one's actions (usually at 18 or, formerly, 21 years). ~*vb.* **ages, ageing** *or* **aging, aged. 13.** to grow or make old or apparently old; become or cause to become old or aged. **14.** to begin to seem older: *to have aged a lot in the past year.* **15.** *Brewing.* to mature or cause to mature. [C13: via Old French from Vulgar Latin *aetāticum* (unattested), from Latin *aetās,* ultimately from *aevum* lifetime; compare AEON]

-age *suffix forming nouns.* **1.** indicating a collection, set, or group: *acreage; baggage.* **2.** indicating a process or action or the result of an action: *haulage; passage; breakage.* **3.** indicating a state, condition, or relationship: *bondage; parentage.* **4.** indicating a house or place: *orphanage.* **5.** indicating a charge or fee: *postage.* **6.** indicating a rate: *dosage; mileage.* [from Old French, from Late Latin *-āticum,* noun suffix, neuter of *-āticus,* adjectival suffix, from *-ātus* -ATE^{1} + *-icus* -IC]

aged (ˈeɪdʒɪd) *adj.* **1. a.** advanced in years; old. **b.** (*as collective n.;* preceded by *the*): *the aged.* **2.** of, connected with, or characteristic of old age. **3.** (eɪdʒd). (*postpositive*) having the age of: *a woman aged twenty.* **4.** *Geography.* having reached an advanced stage of erosion.

agee *or* **ajee** (əˈdʒiː) *Scot. and English dialect.* ~*adj.* **1.** awry, crooked, or ajar. ~*adv.* **2.** awry; at an angle. [C19: A-^{2} + GEE^{1}]

age hardening *n.* the hardening of metals by spontaneous structural changes over a period of time. See also **precipitation hardening.**

ageing *or* **aging** (ˈeɪdʒɪŋ) *n.* **1.** the process of growing old or developing the appearance and characteristics of old age. **2.** the change of properties that occurs in some metals after heat treatment or cold working. ~*adj.* **3.** becoming or appearing older or elderly: *an ageing car.* **4.** giving or creating the appearance of age or elderliness: *that dress is really ageing on her.*

ageism *or* **agism** (ˈeɪdʒɪzəm) *n.* discrimination against people on the grounds of age; specifically, discrimination against the elderly. —ˈ**ageist** *or* ˈ**agist** *adj.*

ageless (ˈeɪdʒlɪs) *adj.* **1.** apparently never growing old. **2.** timeless; eternal: *an ageless quality.* —ˈ**agelessness** *n.*

agency (ˈeɪdʒənsɪ) *n., pl.* **-cies. 1.** a business or other organization providing a specific service: *an employment agency.* **2.** the place where an agent conducts business. **3.** the business, duties, or functions of an agent. **4.** action, power, or operation: *the agency of fate.* **5.** intercession or mediation. **6.** *Chiefly U.S.* one of the administrative organizations of a government. [C17: from Medieval Latin *agentia,* from Latin *agere* to do]

agenda (əˈdʒɛndə) *n.* **1.** (*functioning as sing.*) Also called: **agendum.** a schedule or list of items to be attended to. **2.** (*functioning as pl.*) Also called: **agendas, agendums.** matters to be attended to, as at a meeting of a committee. [C17: Latin, literally: things to be done, from *agere* to do]

agenesis (eɪˈdʒɛnɪsɪs) *n.* **1.** (of an animal or plant) imperfect development. **2.** impotence or sterility. —**agenetic** (ˌeɪdʒəˈnɛtɪk) *adj.*

agent (ˈeɪdʒənt) *n.* **1.** a person who acts on behalf of another person, group, business, government, etc.; representative. **2.** a person or thing that acts or has the power to act. **3.** a phenomenon, substance, or organism that exerts some force or effect: *a chemical agent.* **4.** the means by which something occurs or is achieved; instrument: *wind is an agent of plant pollination.* **5.** a person representing a business concern, esp. a travelling salesman. **6.** *Brit.* short for **estate agent. 7.** short for **secret agent.** [C15: from Latin *agent-,* noun use of the present participle of *agere* to do] —**agential** (eɪˈdʒɛnʃəl) *adj.*

agent-general *n., pl.* **agents-general.** a representative in London of a Canadian province or an Australian state.

agentive (ˈeɪdʒəntɪv) *or* **agential** (eɪˈdʒɛnʃəl) *Grammar.* ~*adj.* **1.** (in some inflected languages) denoting a case of nouns, etc., indicating the agent described by the verb. **2.** (of a speech element) indicating agency: *"-er" in "worker" is an agentive suffix.* ~*n.* **3. a.** the agentive case. **b.** a word or element in the agentive case.

agent of production *n.* another name for **factor of production.**

Agent Orange *n.* a highly poisonous herbicide used as a spray for defoliation and crop destruction, esp. by U.S. forces during the Vietnam War. [C20: named after the identifying colour stripe on its container]

agent provocateur *French.* (aʒɑ̃ prɔvɔkatœr) *n., pl.* ***agents provocateurs*** (aʒɑ̃ prɔvɔkatœr). a secret agent employed to provoke suspected persons to commit illegal acts and so be discredited or liable to punishment.

age of consent *n.* **1.** the age at which a person, esp. a female, is considered legally competent to consent to marriage or sexual intercourse. **2.** the age at which a person can enter into a legally binding contract.

Age of Reason *n.* (usually preceded by *the*) the 18th century in W Europe. See also **Enlightenment.**

age-old *or* **age-long** *adj.* very old or of long duration; ancient.

ageratum (ˌædʒəˈreɪtəm) *n.* any tropical American plant of the genus *Ageratum,* such as *A. houstonianum* and *A. conyzoides,* which have thick clusters of purplish-blue flowers. [C16: New Latin, via Latin from Greek *agēraton* that which does not age, from A-^{1} + *gērat-,* stem of *gēras* old age; the flowers of the plant remain vivid for a long time]

ageusia (eɪˈɡjuːsɪə) *n. Pathol.* lack or impairment of the sense of taste. [C20: from A-^{1} + Greek *geusis* taste]

Aggadah (əɡəˈda) *n., pl.* **Aggadoth** (-ˈdɔːt, -ˈdəʊt). *Judaism.* **1. a.** a homiletic passage of the Talmud. **b.** collectively, the homiletic part of traditional Jewish literature, as contrasted with Halacha, consisting of elaborations on the biblical narratives or tales from the lives of the ancient Rabbis. **2.** any traditional homiletic interpretation of scripture. ~Also called: **Aggadatah** (əˈɡadəta), **Haggadah.** [from Hebrew]

agger (ˈædʒə) *n.* an earthwork or mound forming a rampart, esp. in a Roman military camp. [C14: from Latin *agger* a heap, from *ad-* to + *gerere* to carry, bring]

aggiornamento *Italian.* (addʒornaˈmɛnto) *n., pl.* ***-ti*** (-ti). *R.C. Church.* the process of bringing up to date methods, ideas, etc.

agglomerate *vb.* (əˈɡlɒməˌreɪt). **1.** to form or be formed into a mass or cluster; collect. ~*n.* (əˈɡlɒmərɪt, -ˌreɪt). **2.** a confused mass. **3.** a volcanic rock consisting of angular fragments within a groundmass of lava. Compare **conglomerate** (sense 2). ~*adj.* (əˈɡlɒmərɪt, -ˌreɪt). **4.** formed into a mass. [C17: from Latin *agglomerāre,* from *glomerāre* to wind into a ball, from *glomus* ball, mass] —**agˌglomerˈation** *n.* —**agˈglomerative** *adj.*

agglutinate *vb.* (əˈɡluːtɪˌneɪt). **1.** to adhere or cause to adhere, as with glue. **2.** *Linguistics.* to combine or be combined by agglutination. **3.** (*tr.*) to cause (bacteria, red blood cells, etc.) to clump together. ~*adj.* (əˈɡluːtɪnɪt, -ˌneɪt). **4.** united or stuck, as by glue. [C16: from Latin *agglūtināre* to glue to, from *gluten* glue] —**agˌglutinaˈbility** *n.* —**agˈglutinable** *adj.* —**agˈglutinant** *adj.*

agglutination (əˌɡluːtɪˈneɪʃən) *n.* **1.** the act or process of agglutinating. **2.** the condition of being agglutinated; adhesion. **3.** a united mass or group of parts. **4.** *Chemistry.* the formation of clumps of particles in a suspension. **5.** *Immunol.* the formation of a mass of particles, such as erythrocytes, by the action of antibodies. **6.** *Linguistics.* the building up of words from component morphemes in such a way that these undergo little or no change of form or meaning in the process of combination.

agglutinative (əˈgluːtɪnətɪv) *adj.* **1.** tending to join or capable of joining. **2.** Also: **agglomerative.** *Linguistics.* denoting languages, such as Hungarian, whose morphology is characterized by agglutination. Compare **analytic** (sense 3), **synthetic** (sense 3), **polysynthetic.**

agglutinin (əˈgluːtɪnɪn) *n.* an antibody that causes agglutination. [C19: AGGLUTINATE + -IN]

agglutinogen (ˌæglʊˈtɪnədʒən) *n.* an antigen that reacts with or stimulates the formation of a specific agglutinin. [C20: from AGGLUTINATE + -GEN]

aggrade (əˈgreɪd) *vb.* (*tr.*) to build up the level of (any land surface) by the deposition of sediment. Compare **degrade** (sense 4). —**aggradation** (ˌægrəˈdeɪʃən) *n.*

aggrandize *or* **aggrandise** (ˈægrənˌdaɪz, əˈgrænˌdaɪz) *vb.* (*tr.*) **1.** to increase the power, wealth, prestige, scope, etc., of. **2.** to cause (something) to seem greater; magnify; exaggerate. [C17: from Old French *aggrandiss-*, long stem of *aggrandir* to make bigger, from Latin *grandis* GRAND; the ending *-ize* is due to the influence of verbs ending in *-ise, -ize*] —**aggrandizement** *or* **aggrandisement** (əˈgrændɪzmənt) *n.* —ˈ**aggranˌdizer** *or* ˈ**aggranˌdiser** *n.*

aggravate (ˈægrəˌveɪt) *vb.* (*tr.*) **1.** to make (a disease, situation, problem, etc.) worse or more severe. **2.** *Informal.* to annoy; exasperate, esp. by deliberate and persistent goading. [C16: from Latin *aggravāre* to make heavier, from *gravis* heavy] —ˈ**aggraˌvating** *adj.* —ˌ**aggraˈvation** *n.*

▷**Usage.** The use of *aggravate, aggravating,* and *aggravation* for *annoy, annoying,* and *annoyance* is usually avoided in formal English.

aggregate *adj.* (ˈægrɪgɪt, -ˌgeɪt). **1.** formed of separate units collected into a whole; collective; corporate. **2.** (of fruits and flowers) composed of a dense cluster of carpels or florets. ~*n.* (ˈægrɪgɪt, -ˌgeɪt). **3.** a sum or assemblage of many separate units; sum total. **4.** *Geology.* a rock, such as granite, consisting of a mixture of minerals. **5.** the sand and stone mixed with cement and water to make concrete. **6. in the aggregate.** taken as a whole. ~*vb.* (ˈægrɪˌgeɪt). **7.** to combine or be combined into a body, etc. **8.** (*tr.*) to amount to (a number). [C16: from Latin *aggregāre* to add to a flock or herd, attach (oneself) to, from *grex* flock] —ˈ**aggregately** *adv.* —**aggregative** (ˈægrɪˌgeɪtɪv) *adj.*

aggregation (ˌægrɪˈgeɪʃən) *n.* **1.** the act or process of aggregating. **2.** *Ecology.* dispersion in which the individuals of a species are closer together than if they were randomly dispersed.

aggress (əˈgrɛs) *vb.* (*intr.*) to attack first or begin a quarrel. [C16: from Medieval Latin *aggressāre* to attack, from Latin *aggredī* to attack, approach]

aggression (əˈgrɛʃən) *n.* **1.** an attack or harmful action, esp. an unprovoked attack by one country against another. **2.** any offensive activity, practice, etc.: *an aggression against personal liberty.* **3.** *Psychol.* a hostile or destructive mental attitude or behaviour. [C17: from Latin *aggression-*, from *aggrēdi* to attack] —**aggressor** (əˈgrɛsə) *n.*

aggressive (əˈgrɛsɪv) *adj.* **1.** quarrelsome or belligerent: *an aggressive remark.* **2.** assertive; vigorous: *an aggressive businessman.* —**agˈgressively** *adv.* —**agˈgressiveness** *n.*

aggrieve (əˈgriːv) *vb.* (*tr.*) **1.** (*often impersonal or passive*) to grieve; distress; afflict: *it aggrieved her much that she could not go.* **2.** to injure unjustly, esp. by infringing a person's legal rights. [C14 *agreven,* via Old French from Latin *aggravāre* to AGGRAVATE] —**agˈgrieved** *adj.* —**aggrievedly** (əˈgriːvɪdlɪ) *adv.*

aggro (ˈægrəʊ) *n.* *Brit. slang.* aggressive behaviour, esp. by youths in a gang. [C20: from AGGRAVATION]

agha (ˈɑːgə) *n.* a variant spelling of **aga.**

aghast (əˈgɑːst) *adj.* (*postpositive*) overcome with amazement or horror. [C13 *agast,* from Old English *gæstan* to frighten. The spelling with *gh* is on the model of GHASTLY]

agile (ˈædʒaɪl) *adj.* **1.** quick in movement; nimble. **2.** mentally quick or acute. [C15: from Latin *agilis,* from *agere* to do, act] —ˈ**agilely** *adv.* —**agility** (əˈdʒɪlɪtɪ) *n.*

agin (əˈgɪn) *prep.* an informal, facetious, or dialect word for **against.** [C19: from obsolete *again* AGAINST]

agio (ˈædʒɪəʊ) *n., pl.* **-ios. 1. a.** the difference between the nominal and actual values of a currency. **b.** the charge payable for conversion of the less valuable currency. **2.** a percentage payable for the exchange of one currency into another. **3.** an allowance granted to compensate for differences in currency values, as on foreign bills of exchange. **4.** an informal word for **agiotage.** [C17: from Italian, literally: ease]

agiotage (ˈædʒətɪdʒ) *n.* **1.** the business of exchanging currencies. **2.** speculative dealing in stock exchange securities or foreign exchange. [C19: French, from AGIO]

agist (əˈdʒɪst) *vb.* (*tr.*) *Law.* **1.** to care for and feed (cattle or horses) for payment. **2.** to assess and charge (land or its owner) with a public burden, such as a tax. [C14: from Old French *agister,* from *gister* to lodge, ultimately from Latin *jacēre* to lie down]

agitate (ˈædʒɪˌteɪt) *vb.* **1.** (*tr.*) to excite, disturb, or trouble (a person, the mind or feelings); worry. **2.** (*tr.*) to cause to move vigorously; shake, stir, or disturb. **3.** (*intr.;* often foll. by *for* or *against*) to attempt to stir up public opinion for or against something. **4.** (*tr.*) to discuss or debate in order to draw attention to or gain support for (a cause, etc.): *to agitate a political cause.* [C16: from Latin *agitātus,* from *agitāre* to move to and fro, set into motion, from *agere* to act, do] —ˈ**agiˌtated** *adj.* —ˈ**agiˌtatedly** *adv.* —ˌ**agiˈtation** *n.* —ˌ**agiˈtational** *adj.*

agitated depression *n.* severe depression accompanied by extreme anxiety and agitation. Also called: **agitated melancholia.**

agitato (ˌædʒɪˈtɑːtəʊ) *adj., adv.* *Music.* (to be performed) in an agitated manner.

agitator (ˈædʒɪˌteɪtə) *n.* **1.** a person who agitates for or against a cause, etc. **2.** a device, machine, or part used for mixing, shaking, or vibrating a material.

agitpop (ˈædʒɪtˌpɒp) *n.* the use of pop music to promote political propaganda.

agitprop (ˈædʒɪtˌprɒp) *n.* **1.** (*often cap.*) a bureau of the Central Committee of the Communist Party of the Soviet Union, in charge of agitation and propaganda on behalf of Communism. **2. a.** any promotion, as in the arts, of political propaganda, esp. of a Communist nature. **b.** (*as modifier*): *agitprop theatre.* [C20: short for Russian *Agitpropbyuro,* from *agit(atsiya)* agitation + *prop(aganda)* propaganda]

agleam (əˈgliːm) *adj.* (*postpositive*) glowing; gleaming.

aglet (ˈæglɪt) *or* **aiglet** *n.* **1.** a metal sheath or tag at the end of a shoelace, ribbon, etc. **2.** a variant spelling of **aiguillette. 3.** any ornamental pendant. [C15: from Old French *aiguillette* a small needle]

agley (əˈgleɪ, əˈglaɪ, əˈgliː) *or* **aglee** (əˈgliː) *adv., adj.* *Scot.* awry; askew. [from *gley* squint]

aglimmer (əˈglɪmə) *adj.* (*postpositive*) glimmering.

aglitter (əˈglɪtə) *adj.* (*postpositive*) sparkling; glittering.

aglossia (əˈglɒsɪə) *n.* *Pathol.* congenital absence of the tongue. [C19: from A-[1] + GLOSSA + -IA] —**aˈglossal** *adj.* —**aˈglossate** *adj.*

aglow (əˈgləʊ) *adj.* (*postpositive*) glowing.

aglu *or* **agloo** (ˈægluː) *n.* *Canadian.* a breathing hole made in ice by a seal. [C19: from Eskimo]

AGM *abbrev. for* annual general meeting.

agma (ˈægmə) *n.* *Phonetics.* the symbol (ŋ), used to represent a velar nasal consonant, as in *long* (lɒŋ) or *tank* (tæŋk).

agminate (ˈægmɪnɪt, -ˌneɪt) *adj.* gathered or clustered together. [C19: from Latin *agmen* a moving throng]

agnail (ˈægˌneɪl) *n.* another name for **hangnail.**

agnate (ˈægneɪt) *adj.* **1.** related by descent from a common male ancestor. **2.** related in any way; cognate. ~*n.* **3.** a male or female descendant by male links from a common male ancestor. [C16: from Latin *agnātus* born in addition, added by birth, from *agnāsci,* from *ad-* in addition + *gnāsci* to be born] —**agnatic** (ægˈnætɪk) *adj.* —**agˈnation** *n.*

agnathan (ægˈneɪθən) *n.* **1.** any jawless eel-like aquatic vertebrate of the superclass *Agnatha,* which includes the lampreys and hagfishes. ~*adj.* **2.** of, relating to, or belonging to the superclass *Agnatha.* See also **cyclostome.** [C19: from New Latin *agnatha,* from A-[1] + Greek *gnathos* jaw]

agnathous (ægˈneɪθəs) *adj.* *Zoology.* (esp. of lampreys and hagfishes) lacking jaws.

agnomen (ægˈnəʊmɛn) *n., pl.* **-nomina** (-ˈnɒmɪnə). **1.** the fourth name or second cognomen occasionally acquired by an ancient Roman. See also **cognomen, nomen, praenomen. 2.** another word for **nickname.** [C18: from Late Latin, from *ad-* in addition to + *nōmen* name] —**agnominal** (ægˈnɒmɪnᵊl) *adj.*

agnosia (ægˈnəʊzɪə) *n.* *Psychol.* loss or diminution of the power to recognize familiar objects or people, usually as a result of brain damage. [C20: New Latin, from Greek *agnōsia,* from *a-* without + *gnōsis* knowledge] —**agˈnosic** *adj.*

agnostic (ægˈnɒstɪk) *n.* **1.** a person who holds that knowledge of a Supreme Being, ultimate cause, etc., is impossible. Compare **atheist, theist. 2.** a person who claims, with respect to any particular question, that the answer cannot be known with certainty. ~*adj.* **3.** of or relating to agnostics. [C19: coined 1869 by T. H. Huxley (1825–95), British biologist, from A-[1] + GNOSTIC] —**agˈnosticism** *n.*

Agnus Dei (ˈægnʊs ˈdeɪɪ) *n.* *Christianity.* **1.** the figure of a lamb bearing a cross or banner, emblematic of Christ. **2.** a chant beginning with these words or a translation of them, forming part of the Roman Catholic Mass or sung as an anthem in the Anglican liturgy. **3.** a wax medallion stamped with a lamb as emblem of Christ and blessed by the pope. [Latin: Lamb of God]

ago (əˈgəʊ) *adv.* in the past: *five years ago; long ago.* [C14 *ago,* from Old English *āgān* to pass away]

▷**Usage.** The use of *ago* with *since* (*it's ten years ago since he wrote the novel*) is redundant and is therefore avoided in careful English. *Ago* should be followed by *that: it was ten years ago that he wrote the novel.*

agog (əˈgɒg) *adj.* (*postpositive*) highly impatient, eager, or curious. [C15: perhaps from Old French *en gogues* in merriments, origin unknown]

à gogo (ə ˈgəʊˌgəʊ) *adj., adv.* *Informal.* as much as one likes; galore: *champagne à gogo.* [C20: from French]

-agogue *or esp. U.S.* **-agog** *n. combining form.* **1.** indicating a person or thing that leads or incites to action: *pedagogue; demagogue.* **2.** denoting a substance that stimulates the secretion of something: *galactagogue.* [via Late Latin from Greek *agōgos* leading, from *agein* to lead] —**-agogic** *adj. combining form.* —**-agogy** *n. combining form.*

agon (ˈægəʊn, -gɒn) *n., pl.* **agones** (əˈgəʊniːz). (in ancient Greece) a festival at which competitors contended for prizes. Among the best known were the Olympic, Pythian, Nemean, and Isthmian Games. [C17: Greek: contest, from *agein* to lead]

agone (əˈgɒn) *adv.* an archaic word for **ago.**

agonic (əˈgɒnɪk, eɪˈgɒnɪk) *adj.* forming no angle. [C19: from Greek *agōnos,* from A-[1] + *gōnia* angle]

agonic line *n.* an imaginary line on the surface of the earth connecting points of zero magnetic declination.

agonist (ˈægənɪst) *n.* **1.** any muscle that is opposed in action by another muscle. Compare **antagonist** (sense 2). **2.** a competitor, as in an agon. [C17: from Greek *agōn* AGON]

agonistic (ˌægəˈnɪstɪk) *adj.* **1.** striving for effect; strained. **2.** eager to win in discussion or argument; competitive. [C17: via Late Latin from Greek *agōnistikos,* from *agōn* contest]

agonize *or* **agonise** (ˈægəˌnaɪz) *vb.* **1.** to suffer or cause to suffer agony. **2.** (*intr.*) to make a desperate effort; struggle; strive. [C16: via Medieval Latin from Greek *agōnizesthai* to contend for a prize, from *agōn* AGON] —ˈ**agoˌnizingly** *or* ˈ**agoˌnisingly** *adv.*

agony (ˈægənɪ) *n., pl.* **-nies. 1.** acute physical or mental pain; anguish. **2.** the suffering or struggle preceding death. **3. pile, put,** *or* **turn on the agony.** *Brit. informal.* to exaggerate one's distress for sympathy or greater effect. **4.** (*modifier*) relating to or advising on personal problems about which people have written to the media: *agony column; agony writer.* [C14: via Late Latin from Greek *agōnia* struggle, from *agōn* contest]

agony aunt *n.* (*sometimes cap.*) a person who writes the replies to readers' letters in an **agony column** (sense 1).

agony column *n.* **1.** a magazine or newspaper feature in which advice is offered to readers who have sent in letters about their personal problems. **2.** a part of a newspaper containing advertisements for lost relatives, personal messages, etc.

agora[1] (ˈægərə) *n., pl.* **-rae** (-riː, -raɪ) *or* **-ras.** (*often cap.*) **a.** the marketplace in Athens, used for popular meetings, or any similar place of assembly in ancient Greece. **b.** the meeting itself. [from Greek, from *agorein* to gather]

agora[2] (ˌægəˈrɑː) *n., pl.* **-rot** (-ˈrɒt). an Israeli monetary unit worth one hundredth of a shekel. [Hebrew, from *āgōr* to collect]

agoraphobia (ˌægərəˈfəʊbɪə) *n.* a pathological fear of open or public spaces that may result in the sufferer becoming housebound. —ˌ**agoraˈphobic** *adj., n.*

agouti (əˈguːtɪ) *n., pl.* **-tis** *or* **-ties. 1.** any hystricomorph rodent of the genus *Dasyprocta,* of Central and South America and the West Indies: family *Dasyproctidae.* Agoutis are agile and long-legged, with hooflike claws, and are valued for their meat. **2.** a pattern of fur in certain rodents, characterized by irregular stripes. [C18: via French and Spanish from Guarani]

AGR *abbrev. for* advanced gas-cooled reactor.

agr. *or* **agric.** *abbrev. for:* **1.** agricultural. **2.** agriculture. **3.** agricultur(al)ist.

agraffe *or U.S.* (*sometimes*) **agrafe** (əˈgræf) *n.* **1.** a fastening consisting of a loop and hook, formerly used in armour and clothing. **2.** a metal cramp used to connect stones. [C18: from French, from *grafe* a hook]

agranulocytosis (əˌgrænjʊləʊsaɪˈtəʊsɪs) *n.* a serious and sometimes fatal illness characterized by a marked reduction of leucocytes, usually caused by hypersensitivity to certain drugs. [C20: New Latin; see A-[1], GRANULE, -CYTE, -OSIS]

agrapha (ˈægrəfə) *pl. n. Christianity.* sayings of Jesus not recorded in the canonical Gospels. [Greek: things not written, from A-[1] + *graphein* to write]

agraphia (əˈgræfɪə) *n.* loss of the ability to write, resulting from a brain lesion. [C19: New Latin, from A-[1] + Greek *graphein* to write]

agrarian (əˈgrɛərɪən) *adj.* **1.** of or relating to land or its cultivation or to systems of dividing landed property. **2.** of or relating to rural or agricultural matters. **3.** (of plants) growing wild. ~*n.* **4.** a person who favours the redistribution of landed property. [C16: from Latin *agrārius,* from *ager* field, land] —**aˈgrarianism** *n.*

agree (əˈgriː) *vb.* **agrees, agreeing, agreed.** (*mainly intr.*) **1.** (often foll. by *with*) to be of the same opinion; concur. **2.** (*also tr.;* when *intr.,* often foll. by *to;* when *tr., takes a clause as object or an infinitive*) to give assent; consent: *she agreed to go home; I'll agree to that.* **3.** (*also tr.;* when *intr.,* foll. by *on* or *about;* when *tr., may take a clause as object*) to come to terms (about); arrive at a settlement (on): *they agreed a price; they agreed on the main points.* **4.** (foll. by *with*) to be similar or consistent; harmonize; correspond. **5.** (foll. by *with*) to be agreeable or suitable (to one's health, temperament, etc.). **6.** (*tr.; takes a clause as object*) to concede or grant; admit: *they agreed that the price they were asking was too high.* **7.** (*tr.*) to make consistent with: *to agree the balance sheet with the records by making adjustments, writing off, etc.* **8.** *Grammar.* to undergo agreement. [C14: from Old French *agreer,* from the phrase *a gre* at will or pleasure]

agreeable (əˈgrɪəbᵊl) *adj.* **1.** pleasing; pleasant. **2.** prepared to consent. **3.** (foll. by *to* or *with*) in keeping; consistent: *salaries agreeable with current trends.* **4.** (foll. by *to*) to one's liking: *the terms were not agreeable to him.* —**aˈgreeableness** *n.* —**aˈgreeably** *adv.*

agreed (əˈgriːd) *adj.* **1.** determined by common consent: *the agreed price.* ~*interj.* **2.** an expression of agreement or consent.

agreement (əˈgriːmənt) *n.* **1.** the act of agreeing. **2.** a settlement, esp. one that is legally enforceable; covenant; treaty. **3.** a contract or document containing such a settlement. **4.** the state of being of the same opinion; concord; harmony. **5.** the state of being similar or consistent; correspondence; conformity. **6.** *Grammar.* the determination of the inflectional form of one word by some grammatical feature, such as number or gender, of another word, esp. one in the same sentence. Also called: **concord. 7.** See **collective agreement, national agreement.** [C14: from Old French]

agrestal (əˈgrɛstəl) *adj.* (of uncultivated plants such as weeds) growing on cultivated land.

agrestic (əˈgrɛstɪk) *adj.* **1.** rural; rustic. **2.** unpolished; uncouth. [C17: from Latin *agrestis,* from *ager* field]

agribusiness (ˈægrɪˌbɪznɪs) *n.* the various businesses collectively that process, distribute, and support farm products. [C20: from AGRI(CULTURE) + BUSINESS]

agric. *or* **agr.** *abbrev. for:* **1.** agricultural. **2.** agriculture. **3.** agricultur(al)ist.

agriculture (ˈægrɪˌkʌltʃə) *n.* the science or occupation of cultivating land and rearing crops and livestock; farming; husbandry. [C17: from Latin *agricultūra,* from *ager* field, land + *cultūra* CULTURE] —ˌ**agriˈcultural** *adj.* —ˌ**agriˈculturally** *adv.* —ˌ**agriˈculturist** *or* ˌ**agriˈculturalist** *n.*

agrimony (ˈægrɪmənɪ) *n.* **1.** any of various temperate rosaceous plants of the genus *Agrimonia,* which have compound leaves, long spikes of small yellow flowers, and bristly burlike fruits. **2.** any of several other plants, such as hemp agrimony. [C15: altered from *egrimonie* (C14), via Old French from Latin *agrimōnia,* variant of *argemōnia* from Greek *argemōnē* poppy]

agro- *combining form.* denoting fields, soil, or agriculture: *agronomy.* [from Greek *agros* field]

agrobiology (ˌægrəʊbaɪˈɒlədʒɪ) *n.* the science of plant growth and nutrition in relation to agriculture. —**agrobiological** (ˌægrəʊˌbaɪəˈlɒdʒɪkᵊl) *adj.* —ˌ**agrobiˈologist** *n.*

agrochemical (ˌægrəʊˈkɛmɪkᵊl) *n.* a chemical, such as a pesticide, used for agricultural purposes.

agroforestry (ˌægrəʊˈfɒrɪstrɪ) *n.* a method of farming integrating herbaceous and tree crops.

agrology (əˈgrɒlədʒɪ) *n.* the scientific study of soils and their potential productivity. —**agrological** (ˌægrəˈlɒdʒɪkᵊl) *adj.*

agron. *abbrev. for* agronomy.

agronomics (ˌægrəˈnɒmɪks) *n.* (*functioning as sing.*) the branch of economics dealing with the distribution, management, and productivity of land. —ˌ**agroˈnomic** *or* ˌ**agroˈnomical** *adj.*

agronomy (əˈgrɒnəmɪ) *n.* the science of cultivation of land, soil management, and crop production. —**aˈgronomist** *n.*

agrostemma (ˌægrəʊˈstɛmə) *n.* **1.** See **corncockle. 2.** See **silene.** [New Latin, from Greek *agros* a field + *stemma* a garland]

agrostology (ˌægrəˈstɒlədʒɪ) *n.* the branch of botany concerned with the study of grasses. [C19: from Greek *agrōstis* a type of grass + -LOGY]

aground (əˈgraʊnd) *adv., adj.* (*postpositive*) on or onto the ground or bottom, as in shallow water.

agrypnotic (ˌægrɪpˈnɒtɪk) *adj.* **1.** inducing, relating to, or characterized by insomnia. ~*n.* **2.** a drug or agent that induces insomnia. [C20: from Greek *agrupnos* wakeful, from *agrein* to pursue + *hupnos* sleep]

agt *abbrev. for:* **1.** agent. **2.** agreement.

aguardiente *Spanish.* (aɣwarˈðjente) *n.* any inferior brandy or similar spirit, esp. from Spain, Portugal, or South America. [C19: Spanish: burning water]

ague (ˈeɪgjuː) *n.* **1.** malarial fever with successive stages of fever and chills. **2.** a fit of shivering. [C14: from Old French (*fievre*) *ague* acute fever; see ACUTE] —ˈ**aguish** *adj.*

agueweed (ˈeɪgjuːˌwiːd) *n.* **1.** a North American gentianaceous plant, *Gentiana quinquefolia,* that has clusters of pale blue-violet or white flowers. **2.** another name for **boneset.**

ah (ɑː) *interj.* an exclamation expressing pleasure, pain, sympathy, etc., according to the intonation of the speaker.

AH (indicating years in the Muslim system of dating, numbered from the Hegira (622 A.D.)) *abbrev. for* anno Hegirae. [Latin]

a.h. *abbrev. for* ampere-hour.

aha (ɑːˈhɑː) *interj.* an exclamation expressing triumph, surprise, etc., according to the intonation of the speaker.

AHA *abbrev. for* Australian Hotels Association.

ahead (əˈhɛd) *adj.* **1.** (*postpositive*) in front; in advance. ~*adv.* **2.** at or in the front; in advance; before. **3.** onwards; forwards: *go straight ahead.* **4. ahead of. a.** in front of; at a further advanced position than. **b.** *Stock Exchange.* in anticipation of: *the share price rose ahead of the annual figures.* **5.** *Informal.* **be ahead.** to have an advantage; be winning: *to be ahead on points.* **6. get ahead.** to advance or attain success.

ahem (əˈhɛm) *interj.* a clearing of the throat, used to attract attention, express doubt, etc.

ahemeral (æˈhɛmərᵊl, eɪ-) *adj.* not constituting a full 24-hour day. [C20: from Greek *a-* not + *hēmera* a day]

ahimsa (ɑːˈhɪmsɑː) *n.* (in Hindu, Buddhist, and Jainist philosophy) the law of reverence for, and nonviolence to, every form of life. [Sanskrit, from A-[1] + *himsā* injury]

ahistorical (ˌeɪhɪsˈtɒrɪkəl) *or* **ahistoric** *adj.* not related to history; not historical.

A horizon *n.* the top layer of a soil profile, usually dark coloured and containing humus, from which the soluble salts have been leached. See **B horizon, C horizon.**
ahoy (əˈhɔɪ) *interj. Nautical.* a hail used to call a ship or to attract attention.
AHQ *abbrev. for* Army Headquarters.
Ahriman (ˈɑːrɪmən) *n. Zoroastrianism.* the supreme evil spirit and diabolical opponent of Ormazd.
Ahura Mazda (əˈhʊərə ˈmæzdə) *n. Zoroastrianism.* another name for **Ormazd.**
ai (ˈɑːɪ) *n., pl.* **ais.** another name for **three-toed sloth** (see **sloth** (sense 1)). [C17: from Portuguese, from Tupi]
AI *abbrev. for:* **1.** artificial insemination. **2.** artificial intelligence.
AIA *abbrev. for* Associate of the Institute of Actuaries.
AICC *abbrev. for* All India Congress Committee: the national assembly of the Indian National Congress.
aid (eɪd) *vb.* **1.** to give support to (someone to do something); help or assist. **2.** (*tr.*) to assist financially. ~*n.* **3.** assistance; help; support. **4.** a person, device, etc., that helps or assists: *a teaching aid.* **5.** Also: **artificial aid.** *Mountaineering.* any of various devices such as piton or nut when used as a direct help in the ascent. **6.** (in medieval Europe; in England after 1066) a feudal payment made to the king or any lord by his vassals, usually on certain occasions such as the marriage of a daughter or the knighting of an eldest son. **7. in aid of.** *Brit. informal.* in support of; for the purpose of. [C15: via Old French *aidier* from Latin *adjūtāre* to help, from *juvāre* to help] —ˈ**aider** *n.*
Aid *or* **-aid** *n. combining form.* denoting a charitable organization or function that raises money for a cause: *Band Aid*; *Ferryaid*.
AID *abbrev. for:* **1.** acute infectious disease. **2.** Agency for International Development. **3.** artificial insemination (by) donor: former name for Donor Insemination (DI).
aid climbing *n. Mountaineering.* climbing that employs mechanical devices (aids) to accomplish difficult manoeuvres (artificial moves). Also called: **peg climbing, pegging, artificial climbing.**
aide (eɪd) *n.* **1.** an assistant. **2.** *Social welfare.* an unqualified assistant to a professional welfare worker. **3.** short for **aide-de-camp.**
aide-de-camp *or* **aid-de-camp** (ˈeɪd də ˈkɒŋ) *n., pl.* **aides-de-camp** *or* **aids-de-camp.** a military officer serving as personal assistant to a senior. Abbrev.: **ADC.** [C17: from French: camp assistant]
aide-mémoire *French.* (ɛdmemwar; *English* ˈeɪd mɛmˈwɑː) *n., pl.* ***aides-mémoire*** (ɛdmemwar; *English* ˈeɪdz mɛmˈwɑː). a memorandum or summary of the items of an agreement, etc. [from *aider* to help + *mémoire* memory]
AIDS *or* **Aids** (eɪdz) *n. acronym for* acquired immune (or immuno-) deficiency syndrome: a condition, caused by a virus, in which certain white blood cells (lymphocytes) are destroyed, resulting in loss of the body's ability to protect itself against disease. AIDS is transmitted by sexual intercourse, through infected blood and blood products, and through the placenta.
AIDS-related complex *n.* See **ARC.**
AIF (formerly) *abbrev. for* Australian Imperial Force.
aiglet (ˈeɪglɪt) *n.* a variant of **aglet.**
aigrette *or* **aigret** (ˈeɪgrɛt, eɪˈgrɛt) *n.* **1.** a long plume worn on hats or as a headdress, esp. one of long egret feathers. **2.** an ornament or piece of jewellery in imitation of a plume of feathers. [C19: French]
aiguille (eɪˈgwiːl, ˈeɪgwiːl) *n.* **1.** a rock mass or mountain peak shaped like a needle. **2.** an instrument for boring holes in rocks or masonry. [C19: French, literally: needle]
aiguillette (ˌeɪgwɪˈlɛt) *n.* **1.** an ornamentation worn by certain military officers, consisting of cords with metal tips. **2.** a variant of **aglet.**
AIH *abbrev. for* artificial insemination (by) husband.
aikido (ˈaɪkɪdəʊ) *n.* a Japanese system of self-defence employing similar principles to judo, but including blows from the hands and feet. [from Japanese, from *ai* to join, receive + *ki* spirit, force + *do* way]
aikona (ˈaɪkɔːnə) *interj. S. African.* an informal word expressing strong negation. [from Nguni]
ail (eɪl) *vb.* **1.** (*tr.*) to trouble; afflict. **2.** (*intr.*) to feel unwell. [Old English *eglan* to trouble, from *egle* troublesome, painful, related to Gothic *agls* shameful]
ailanthus (eɪˈlænθəs) *n., pl.* **-thuses.** an E Asian simaroubaceous deciduous tree, *Ailanthus altissima,* planted in Europe and North America, having pinnate leaves, small greenish flowers, and winged fruits. Also called: **tree of heaven.** [C19: New Latin, from native name (in Amboina) *ai lanto* tree (of) the gods]
aileron (ˈeɪlərɒn) *n.* a flap hinged to the trailing edge of an aircraft wing to provide lateral control, as in a bank or roll. [C20: from French, diminutive of *aile* wing]
ailing (ˈeɪlɪŋ) *adj.* unwell, esp. over a long period.
ailment (ˈeɪlmənt) *n.* a slight but often persistent illness.
ailurophile (aɪˈlʊərəˌfaɪl) *n.* a person who likes cats. [C20: facetious coinage from Greek *ailuros* cat + -PHILE] —**ailurophilia** (aɪˌlʊərəˈfɪlɪə) *n.*
ailurophobe (aɪˈlʊərəˌfəʊb) *n.* a person who dislikes or is afraid of cats. [C20: from Greek *ailuros* cat + -PHOBE]
aim (eɪm) *vb.* **1.** to point (a weapon, missile, etc.) or direct (a blow) at a particular person or object; level. **2.** (*tr.*) to direct (satire, criticism, etc.) at a person, object, etc. **3.** (*intr.*; foll. by *at* or an infinitive) to propose or intend: *we aim to leave early.* **4.** (*intr.*; often foll. by *at* or *for*) to direct one's efforts or strive (towards): *to aim at better communications; to aim high.* ~*n.* **5.** the action of directing something at an object. **6.** the direction in which something is pointed; line of sighting (esp. in the phrase **to take aim**). **7.** the object at which something is aimed; target. **8.** intention; purpose. [C14: via Old French *aesmer* from Latin *aestimāre* to ESTIMATE]
aimless (ˈeɪmlɪs) *adj.* having no goal, purpose, or direction. —ˈ**aimlessly** *adv.* —ˈ**aimlessness** *n.*
ain[1] (eɪn) *determiner.* a Scot. word for **own.**
ain[2] (ˈɑːjɪn) *n.* a variant of **ayin.**
ain't (eɪnt) *Not standard. contraction of* am not, is not, are not, have not, *or* has not: *I ain't seen it.*
▷**Usage.** Although the interrogative form *ain't I?* would be a natural contraction of *am not I?,* it is generally avoided in spoken English and never used in formal English.
Ainu (ˈaɪnuː) *n.* **1.** (*pl.* **-nus** *or* **-nu**) a member of the aboriginal people of Japan, now mostly intermixed with Mongoloid immigrants whose skin colour is more yellowish. **2.** the language of this people, sometimes tentatively associated with Altaic, still spoken in parts of Hokkaido and elsewhere. [Ainu: man]
aïoli (aɪˈəʊlɪ, eɪ-) *n.* garlic mayonnaise. [from French *ail* garlic]
air (ɛə) *n.* **1.** the mixture of gases that forms the earth's atmosphere. At sea level dry air has a density of 1.226 kilograms per cubic metre and consists of 78.08 per cent nitrogen, 20.95 per cent oxygen, 0.93 per cent argon, 0.03 per cent carbon dioxide, with smaller quantities of ozone and inert gases; water vapour varies between 0 and 4 per cent and in industrial areas sulphur gases may be present as pollutants. **2.** the space above and around the earth; sky. Related adj.: **aerial. 3.** breeze; slight wind. **4.** public expression; utterance: *to give air to one's complaints.* **5.** a distinctive quality: *an air of mystery.* **6.** a person's distinctive appearance, manner, or bearing. **7.** *Music.* **a.** a simple tune for either vocal or instrumental performance. **b.** another word for **aria. 8.** transportation in aircraft (esp. in the phrase **by air). 9.** an archaic word for **breath** (senses 1–3). **10. clear the air.** to rid a situation of tension or discord by settling misunderstandings, etc. **11. give (someone) the air.** *Slang.* to reject or dismiss (someone). **12. in the air. a.** in circulation; current. **b.** in the process of being decided; unsettled. **13. into thin air.** leaving no trace behind. **14. on** (*or* **off) the air.** (not) in the act of broadcasting or (not) being broadcast on radio or television. **15. take the air.** to go out of doors, as for a short walk or ride. **16. up in the air. a.** uncertain. **b.** *Informal.* agitated or excited. **17. walk on air.** to feel elated or exhilarated. **18.** (*modifier*) *Astrology.* of or relating to a group of three signs of the zodiac, Gemini, Libra, and Aquarius. Compare **earth** (sense 10), **fire** (sense 24), **water** (sense 12). ~*vb.* **19.** to expose or be exposed to the air so as to cool or freshen; ventilate: *to air a room.* **20.** to expose or be exposed to warm or heated air so as to dry: *to air linen.* **21.** (*tr.*) to make known publicly; display; publicize: *to air one's opinions.* ~See also **airs.** [C13: via Old French and Latin from Greek *aēr* the lower atmosphere]
AIR *abbrev. for* All India Radio.
air alert *n. Military.* **1.** the condition in which combat aircraft are airborne and ready for an operation. **2.** a signal to prepare for this.
air bag *n.* a safety device in a car, consisting of a bag that inflates automatically in an accident and prevents the passengers from being thrown forwards.
air base *n.* a centre from which military aircraft operate. Also called: **air station.**
air bed *n.* an inflatable mattress.
air bladder *n.* **1.** *Ichthyol.* an air-filled sac, lying above the alimentary canal in bony fishes, that regulates buoyancy at different depths by a variation in the pressure of the air. Also called: **swim bladder. 2.** any air-filled sac, such as one of the bladders of seaweeds.
airboat (ˈɛəˌbəʊt) *n.* another name for **swamp boat.**
airborne (ˈɛəˌbɔːn) *adj.* **1.** conveyed by or through the air. **2.** (of aircraft) flying; in the air.
air brake *n.* **1.** a brake operated by compressed air, esp. in heavy vehicles and trains. **2.** Also called: **dive brake.** an articulated flap or small parachute for reducing the speed of an aircraft. **3.** a rotary fan or propeller connected to a shaft to reduce its speed.
airbrick (ˈɛəˌbrɪk) *n. Chiefly Brit.* a brick with holes in it, put into the wall of a building for ventilation.
air bridge *n. Brit.* a link by air transport between two places, esp. two places separated by a stretch of sea.
airbrush (ˈɛəˌbrʌʃ) *n.* **1.** an atomizer for spraying paint or varnish by means of compressed air. ~*vb.* (*tr.*) **2.** to paint or varnish (something) by using an airbrush.
airburst (ˈɛəˌbɜːst) *n.* the explosion of a bomb, shell, etc., in the air.
Airbus (ˈɛəˌbʌs) *n. Trademark.* a commercial aircraft manufactured and marketed by an international consortium of aerospace companies.

air chief marshal *n.* a senior officer of the Royal Air Force and certain other air forces, of equivalent rank to admiral in the Royal Navy. Abbrev.: **ACM.**
air cleaner *n.* a filter that prevents dust and other particles from entering the air-intake of an internal-combustion engine. Also called: **air filter.**
air commodore *n.* a senior officer of the Royal Air Force and certain other air forces, of equivalent rank to brigadier in the Army.
air-condition *vb.* (*tr.*) to apply air conditioning to.
air conditioning *n.* a system or process for controlling the temperature and sometimes the humidity and purity of the air in a house, etc. —**air conditioner** *n.*
air-cool *vb.* (*tr.*) to cool (an engine) by a flow of air. Compare **water-cool.**
air corridor *n.* an air route along which aircraft are allowed to fly.
air cover *n.* **a.** the use of aircraft to provide aerial protection for ground forces against enemy air attack. **b.** the aircraft used in this. ~Also called: **air support.**
aircraft ('ɛəˌkrɑːft) *n., pl.* **-craft.** any machine capable of flying by means of buoyancy or aerodynamic forces, such as a glider, helicopter, or aeroplane.
aircraft carrier *n.* a warship built with an extensive flat deck space for the launch and recovery of aircraft.
aircraft cloth *or* **fabric** *n.* variants of **aeroplane cloth.**
aircraftman ('ɛəˌkrɑːftmən) *n., pl.* **-men.** a serviceman of the most junior rank in the RAF. Also (not in official use): **aircraftsman.** —'**aircraftˌwoman** *or* (not in official use) '**aircraftsˌwoman** *fem. n.*
aircrew ('ɛəˌkruː) *n.* (*sometimes functioning as pl.*) the crew of an aircraft.
air curtain *n.* an air stream across a doorway to exclude draughts, etc.
air cushion *n.* **1.** an inflatable cushion, usually made of rubber or plastic. **2.** the pocket of air that supports a hovercraft. **3.** a form of pneumatic suspension consisting of an enclosed volume of air. See also **air spring.**
air cylinder *n.* a cylinder containing air, esp. one fitted with a piston and used for damping purposes.
air dam *n.* any device, such as a spoiler, that reduces air resistance and increases the stability of a car, aircraft, etc.
airdrome ('ɛəˌdrəʊm) *n.* the U.S. name for **aerodrome.**
airdrop ('ɛəˌdrɒp) *n.* **1.** a delivery of supplies, troops, etc., from an aircraft by parachute. ~*vb.* **-drops, -dropping, -dropped.** **2.** (*tr.*) to deliver (supplies, etc.) by an airdrop.
air-dry *vb.* **-dries, -drying, -dried.** (*tr.*) to dry by exposure to the air.
Airedale ('ɛəˌdeɪl) *n.* a large rough-haired tan-coloured breed of terrier characterized by a black saddle-shaped patch covering most of the back. Also called: **Airedale terrier.** [C19: name of a district in Yorkshire]
air embolism *n.* another name for **aeroembolism.**
air engine *n.* **1.** an engine that uses the expansion of heated air to drive a piston. **2.** a small engine that uses compressed air to drive a piston.
air-entrained concrete *n.* a type of concrete throughout which small air bubbles are dispersed in order to increase its frost resistance: used for making roads.
airfield ('ɛəˌfiːld) *n.* a landing and taking-off area for aircraft, usually with permanent buildings.
air filter *n.* another name for **air cleaner.**
airflow ('ɛəˌfləʊ) *n.* the flow of air in a wind tunnel or past a moving aircraft, car, train, etc.; airstream.
airfoil ('ɛəˌfɔɪl) *n.* the U.S. and Canadian name for **aerofoil.**
air force *n.* **1. a.** the branch of a nation's armed services primarily responsible for air warfare. **b.** (*as modifier*): *an air-force base.* **2.** a formation in the U.S. and certain other air forces larger than an air division but smaller than an air command.
airframe ('ɛəˌfreɪm) *n.* the body of an aircraft, excluding its engines.
air gas *n.* another name for **producer gas.**
airglow ('ɛəˌgləʊ) *n.* the faint light from the upper atmosphere in the night sky, esp. in low latitudes.
air guitar *n.* an imaginary guitar played while miming to rock music.
air gun *n.* a gun discharged by means of compressed air.
air hardening *n.* a process of hardening high-alloy steels by heating and cooling in a current of air. Compare **oil hardening.**
airhead[1] ('ɛəˌhɛd) *n. Military.* an area secured in hostile territory, used as a base for the supply and evacuation of troops and equipment by air. [C20: modelled on BEACHHEAD]
airhead[2] ('ɛəˌhɛd) *n. Slang.* a stupid or simple-minded person; idiot. [C20: from AIR + HEAD]
air hole *n.* **1.** a hole that allows the passage of air, esp. for ventilation. **2.** a section of open water in a frozen surface. **3.** a less common name for **air pocket** (sense 1).
air hostess *n.* a stewardess on an airliner.
airily ('ɛərɪlɪ) *adv.* **1.** in a jaunty or high-spirited manner. **2.** in a light or delicate manner.
airiness ('ɛərɪnɪs) *n.* **1.** the quality or condition of being fresh, light, or breezy. **2.** lightness of heart; gaiety.
airing ('ɛərɪŋ) *n.* **1. a.** exposure to air or warmth, as for drying or ventilation. **b.** (*as modifier*): *airing cupboard.* **2.** an excursion in the open air. **3.** exposure to public debate.
air-intake *n.* **1. a.** an opening in an aircraft through which air is drawn, esp. for the engines. **b.** the amount of air drawn in. **2.** the part of a carburettor or similar device through which air enters an internal-combustion engine. **3.** any opening, etc., through which air enters.
air jacket *n.* **1.** an air-filled envelope or compartment surrounding a machine or part to reduce the rate at which heat is transferred to or from it. Compare **water jacket.** **2.** a less common name for **life jacket.**
airless ('ɛəlɪs) *adj.* **1.** lacking fresh air; stuffy or sultry. **2.** devoid of air. —'**airlessness** *n.*
air letter *n.* another name for **aerogram** (sense 1).
airlift ('ɛəˌlɪft) *n.* **1.** the transportation by air of passengers, troops, cargo, etc., esp. when other routes are blocked. ~*vb.* **2.** (*tr.*) to transport by an airlift.
air-lift pump *n.* a pump that pumps liquid by injecting air into the lower end of an open pipe immersed in the liquid: often used in boreholes.
airline ('ɛəˌlaɪn) *n.* **1. a.** a system or organization that provides scheduled flights for passengers or cargo. **b.** (*as modifier*): *an airline pilot.* **2.** a hose or tube carrying air under pressure. **3.** *Chiefly U.S.* a beeline.
airliner ('ɛəˌlaɪnə) *n.* a large passenger aircraft.
airlock ('ɛəˌlɒk) *n.* **1.** a bubble in a pipe causing an obstruction or stoppage to the flow. **2.** an airtight chamber with regulated air pressure used to gain access to a space that has air under pressure.
air mail *n.* **1.** the system of conveying mail by aircraft. **2.** mail conveyed by aircraft. ~*adj.* **air-mail.** **3.** of, used for, or concerned with air mail. ~*vb.* **air-mail.** **4.** (*tr.*) to send by air mail.
airman ('ɛəmən) *n., pl.* **-men.** an aviator, esp. a man who serves in his country's air force. —'**airˌwoman** *fem. n.*
air marshal *n.* **1.** a senior Royal Air Force officer of equivalent rank to a vice admiral in the Royal Navy. **2.** a Royal Australian Air Force officer of the highest rank. **3.** a Royal New Zealand Air Force officer of the highest rank when chief of defence forces.
air mass *n.* a large body of air having characteristics of temperature, moisture, and pressure that are approximately uniform horizontally.
air mile *n.* another name for **nautical mile** (sense 1).
air-minded *adj.* interested in or promoting aviation or aircraft. —'**air-ˌmindedness** *n.*
air miss *n.* a situation in which two aircraft pass very close to one another in the air; near miss.
Air Officer *n.* a term used to denote the appointment of any officer in the Royal Air Force above the rank of Air Commodore to a position of command: *Air Officer commanding....*
airplane ('ɛəˌpleɪn) *n.* the U.S. and Canadian name for **aeroplane.**
air plant *n.* a name given to some epiphytes grown as greenhouse or house plants, esp. orchids of the large Old World tropical genus *Aerides,* grown for their white scented flowers spotted with red, purple, or rose.
airplay ('ɛəˌpleɪ) *n.* (of a gramophone record) radio exposure.
air pocket *n.* **1.** a localized region of low air density or a descending air current, causing an aircraft to suffer an abrupt decrease in height. **2.** any pocket of air that prevents the flow of a liquid or gas, as in a pipe.
airport ('ɛəˌpɔːt) *n.* a landing and taking-off area for civil aircraft, usually with surfaced runways and aircraft maintenance and passenger facilities.
air power *n.* the strength of a nation's air force.
air pump *n.* a device for pumping air in or out of something.
air raid *n.* **a.** an attack by hostile aircraft. **b.** (*as modifier*): *an air-raid shelter.*
air-raid warden *n.* a member of a civil defence organization responsible for enforcing regulations, etc., during an air attack.
air rifle *n.* a rifle discharged by compressed air.
airs (ɛəz) *pl. n.* affected manners intended to impress others (esp. in the phrases **give oneself airs, put on airs**).
air sac *n.* **1.** any of the membranous air-filled extensions of the lungs of birds, which increase the efficiency of gaseous exchange in the lungs. **2.** any of the thin-walled extensions of the tracheae of insects having a similar function.
air scoop *n.* a device fitted to the surface of an aircraft to provide air pressure or ventilation from the airflow.
Air Scout *n.* a scout belonging to a scout troop that specializes in flying, gliding, etc. See **Scout.**
airscrew ('ɛəˌskruː) *n. Brit.* an aircraft propeller.
air-sea rescue *n.* an air rescue at sea.
air shaft *n.* a shaft for ventilation, esp. in a mine or tunnel.
airship ('ɛəˌʃɪp) *n.* a lighter-than-air self-propelled craft. Also called: **dirigible.**
air shot *n. Golf.* a shot that misses the ball completely but counts as a stroke.
airshow ('ɛəˌʃəʊ) *n.* an occasion when an air base is open to the public and a flying display and, usually, static exhibitions are held.
airsick ('ɛəˌsɪk) *adj.* sick or nauseated from travelling in an aircraft. —'**airˌsickness** *n.*

airside (ˈɛəˌsaɪd) *n.* the part of an airport nearest the aircraft, the boundary of which is the security check, customs, passport control, etc. Compare **landside** (sense 1).
air sock *n.* another name for **windsock.**
airspace (ˈɛəˌspeɪs) *n.* the atmosphere above the earth or part of the earth, esp. the atmosphere above a country deemed to be under its jurisdiction.
airspeed (ˈɛəˌspiːd) *n.* the speed of an aircraft relative to the air in which it moves. Compare **groundspeed.**
air spray *n.* another name for **aerosol** (sense 3).
air spring *n. Mechanical engineering.* an enclosed pocket of air used to absorb shock or sudden fluctuations of load.
air station *n.* an airfield, usually smaller than an airport but having facilities for the maintenance of aircraft.
airstream (ˈɛəˌstriːm) *n.* **1.** a wind, esp. at a high altitude. **2.** a current of moving air.
airstrip (ˈɛəˌstrɪp) *n.* a cleared area for the landing and taking off of aircraft; runway. Also called: **landing strip.**
airt (ɛət; *Scot.* ert) *or* **airth** (ɛəθ; *Scot.* erθ) *n. Scot.* a direction or point of the compass, esp. the direction of the wind; quarter; region. [C14: from Scots Gaelic *aird* point of the compass, height]
air terminal *n. Brit.* a building in a city from which air passengers are taken by road or rail to an airport.
airtight (ˈɛəˌtaɪt) *adj.* **1.** not permitting the passage of air either in or out. **2.** having no weak points; rigid or unassailable: *this categorization is hardly airtight.*
airtime (ˈɛəˌtaɪm) *n.* **1.** the time allocated to a particular programme, item, topic, or type of material on radio or television. **2.** the time of the start of a radio or television broadcast.
air-to-air *adj.* operating between aircraft in flight.
air traffic *n.* **1.** the organized movement of aircraft within a given space. **2.** the passengers, cargo, or mail carried by aircraft.
air-traffic control *n.* an organization that determines the altitude, speed, and direction at which planes fly in a given area, giving instructions to pilots by radio. —**air-traffic controller** *n.*
air turbine *n.* a small turbine driven by compressed air, esp. one used as a starter for engines.
air valve *n.* **1.** a device for controlling the flow of air in a pipe. **2.** a valve for exhausting air from a fluid system, esp. from a central-heating installation. See also **bleed valve.**
air vesicle *or* **cavity** *n.* **1.** a large air-filled intercellular space in some aquatic plants. **2.** a large intercellular space in a leaf into which a stoma opens.
air vice-marshal *n.* **1.** a senior Royal Air Force officer of equivalent rank to a rear admiral in the Royal Navy. **2.** a Royal Australian Air Force officer of the second highest rank. **3.** a Royal New Zealand Air Force officer of the highest rank. Abbrev.: **AVM.**
airwaves (ˈɛəˌweɪvz) *pl. n. Informal.* radio waves used in radio and television broadcasting.
airway (ˈɛəˌweɪ) *n.* **1.** an air route, esp. one that is fully equipped with emergency landing fields, navigational aids, etc. **2.** a passage for ventilation, esp. in a mine. **3.** the passage of air from the nose or mouth to the lungs. **4.** *Med.* a tubelike device inserted via the throat to keep open the airway of an unconscious patient.
airworthy (ˈɛəˌwɜːðɪ) *adj.* (of an aircraft) safe to fly.
airy (ˈɛərɪ) *adj.* **airier, airiest. 1.** abounding in fresh air. **2.** spacious or uncluttered. **3.** nonchalant; superficial. **4.** visionary; fanciful: *airy promises; airy plans.* **5.** of or relating to air. **6.** weightless and insubstantial: *an airy gossamer.* **7.** light and graceful in movement. **8.** buoyant and gay; lively. **9.** having no material substance: *airy spirits.* **10.** high up in the air; lofty. **11.** performed in the air; aerial.
airy-fairy (ˈɛərɪˈfɛərɪ) *adj.* **1.** *Informal.* fanciful and unrealistic: *an airy-fairy scheme.* **2.** delicate to the point of being insubstantial; light. [C19: from a poem *Lillian* (1830) by the British poet Alfred, Lord Tennyson (1809–92), in which the central figure is described as "Airy, fairy Lillian"]
aisle (aɪl) *n.* **1.** a passageway separating seating areas in a theatre, church, etc.; gangway. **2.** a lateral division in a church flanking the nave or chancel. **3. (rolling) in the aisles.** *Informal.* (of an audience) overcome with laughter. [C14 *ele* (later *aile, aisle,* through confusion with *isle* (island)), via Old French from Latin *āla* wing] —**aisled** *adj.* —ˈ**aisleless** *adj.*
ait (eɪt) *or* **eyot** *n. Dialect.* an islet, esp. in a river. [Old English *ȳgett* small island, from *ieg* ISLAND]
aitch (eɪtʃ) *n.* the letter *h* or the sound represented by it: *he drops his aitches.* [C16: a phonetic spelling]
aitchbone (ˈeɪtʃˌbəʊn) *n.* **1.** the rump bone or floor of the pelvis in cattle. **2.** a cut of beef from or including the rump bone. [C15 hach-boon, altered from earlier *nache-bone, nage-bone* (*a nache* mistaken for *an ache, an aitch;* compare ADDER[1]); *nache* buttock, via Old French from Late Latin *natica,* from Latin *natis* buttock]
AJA *abbrev. for* Australian Journalists' Association.
ajar[1] (əˈdʒɑː) *adj.* (*postpositive*), *adv.* (esp. of a door or window) slightly open. [C18: altered form of obsolete *on char,* literally: on the turn; *char,* from Old English *cierran* to turn]
ajar[2] (əˈdʒɑː) *adj.* (*postpositive*) not in harmony. [C19: altered form of *at jar* at discord. See JAR[2]]
AJC *abbrev. for* Australian Jockey Club.
AK *abbrev. for* Alaska.
a.k.a. *or* **AKA** *abbrev. for* also known as.
Akademi (əˈkɑːdəmɪ) *n.* (in India) a learned society.
Akan (ˈɑːkɑːn) *n.* **1.** (*pl.* **-kan** *or* **-kans**) a member of a people of Ghana and the E Ivory Coast. **2.** the language of this people, having two chief dialects, Fanti and Twi, and belonging to the Kwa branch of the Niger-Congo family.
akaryote (eɪˈkærɪəʊt) *n. Biology.* a cell without a nucleus. [from A-[1] + KARYO- + *-ote* as in *zygote*] —**aˌkaryˈotic** *adj.*
Akela (ɑːˈkeɪlə) *n. Brit.* the adult leader of a pack of Cub Scouts. U.S. equivalent: **Den Mother.** [C20: after the leader of a wolfpack in *The Jungle Book* (1894–95), by the British poet and writer Rudyard Kipling (1865–1936)]
akene (əˈkiːn) *n.* a variant spelling of **achene.**
akhara (əˈkɑːrɑː) *n.* (in India) a gymnasium.
akimbo (əˈkɪmbəʊ) *adj., adv.* **(with) arms akimbo.** with hands on hips and elbows projecting outwards. [C15 *in kenebowe,* literally: in keen bow, that is, in a sharp curve]
akin (əˈkɪn) *adj.* (*postpositive*) **1.** related by blood; of the same kin. **2.** (often foll. by *to*) having similar characteristics, properties, etc.
Akkadian *or* **Accadian** (əˈkædɪən, əˈkeɪ-) *n.* **1.** a member of an ancient Semitic people who lived in central Mesopotamia in the third millennium B.C. **2.** the extinct language of this people, belonging to the E Semitic subfamily of the Afro-Asiatic family. ~*adj.* **3.** of or relating to this people or their language.
akrasia (əˈkreɪzɪə) *n. Philosophy.* weakness of will; acting in a way contrary to one's sincerely held moral values. [C20: from A-[2] + Greek *kratos* power] —**aˈkratic** *adj.*
Akubra (əˈkuːbrə) *n. Trademark.* a brand of Australian hat.
akvavit (ˈɑːkvɑːˌviːt) *n.* a variant spelling of **aquavit.**
Al *the chemical symbol for* aluminium.
AL *abbrev. for:* **1.** Alabama. **2.** Anglo-Latin. ~**3.** *international car registration for* Albania.
al. *abbrev. for:* **1.** alcohol. **2.** alcoholic.
-al[1] *suffix forming adjectives.* of; related to; connected with: *functional; sectional; tonal.* [from Latin *-ālis*]
-al[2] *suffix forming nouns.* the act or process of doing what is indicated by the verb stem: *rebuttal; recital; renewal.* [via Old French *-aille, -ail,* from Latin *-ālia,* neuter plural used as substantive, from *-ālis* -AL[1]]
-al[3] *suffix forming nouns.* **1.** indicating an aldehyde: *ethanal.* **2.** indicating a pharmaceutical product: *phenobarbital.* [shortened from ALDEHYDE]
ala (ˈeɪlə) *n., pl.* **alae** (ˈeɪliː). **1.** *Zoology.* a wing or flat winglike process or structure, such as a part of some bones and cartilages. **2.** *Botany.* a winglike part, such as one of the wings of a sycamore seed or one of the flat petals of a sweet pea flower. [C18: from Latin *āla* a wing]
à la (ɑː lɑː, æ lə; *French* a la) *prep.* **1.** in the manner or style of. **2.** as prepared in (a particular place) or by or for (a particular person). [C17: from French, short for *à la mode de* in the style of]
Ala. *abbrev. for* Alabama.
alabaster (ˈæləˌbɑːstə, -ˌbæstə) *n.* **1.** a fine-grained usually white, opaque, or translucent variety of gypsum used for statues, vases, etc. **2.** a variety of hard semitranslucent calcite, often banded like marble. ~*adj.* **3.** of or resembling alabaster. [C14: from Old French *alabastre,* from Latin *alabaster,* from Greek *alabastros*] —ˌ**alaˈbastrine** *adj.*
à la carte (ɑː lɑː ˈkɑːt, æ lə; *French* a la kart) *adj., adv.* **1.** (of a menu or a section of a menu) having dishes listed separately and individually priced. Compare **table d'hôte. 2.** (of a dish) offered on such a menu. [C19: from French, literally: according to the card]
alack (əˈlæk) *or* **alackaday** (əˈlækəˌdeɪ) *interj.* an archaic or poetic word for **alas.** [C15: from *a* ah! + *lack* loss, LACK]
alacrity (əˈlækrɪtɪ) *n.* liveliness or briskness. [C15: from Latin *alacritās,* from *alacer* lively] —**aˈlacritous** *adj.*
Aladdin's cave (əˈlædɪnz) *n.* a place containing fabulous riches. [named after *Aladdin,* mythical oriental youth]
à la king (ɑː lɑː ˈkɪŋ, æ lə) *adj.* (*usually postpositive*) cooked in a cream sauce with mushrooms and green peppers.
alalia (æˈleɪlɪə) *n.* a complete inability to speak; mutism. [A-[1] + -LALIA]
alameda (ˌæləˈmeɪdə) *n. Chiefly southwestern U.S.* a public walk or promenade lined with trees, often poplars.
à la mode (ɑː lɑː ˈməʊd, æ lə; *French* a la mɔd) *adj.* **1.** fashionable in style, design, etc. **2.** (of meats) braised with vegetables in wine. **3.** *Chiefly U.S. and Canadian.* (of desserts) served with ice cream. [C17: from French: according to the fashion]
alamode (ˈæləˌməʊd) *n.* a soft light silk used for shawls and dresses, esp. in the 19th century. See also **surah.** [C17: from À LA MODE]
alanine (ˈæləˌniːn, -ˌnaɪn) *n.* a nonessential aliphatic amino acid that occurs in many proteins. [C19: from German *Alanin,* from AL(DEHYDE) + *-an-* (euphonic infix) + *-in* -INE[2]]
alannah (əˈlænə) *interj. Irish.* my child: used as a term of address or endearment. [from Irish Gaelic *a leanbh*]
Alaouite *or* **Alawite** (ˈæləˌwiːt) *n.* **1.** a member of a Shiite sect of Syrian Muslims. ~*adj.* **2.** of or relating to this sect. [via French from Arabic, from *'alaoui* upper, celestial, from *'ala* (vb.) to excel, surpass]

alap (ə'lɑːp) *n.* Indian vocal music without words.

alar ('eɪlə) *adj.* relating to, resembling, or having wings or alae. [C19: from Latin *āla* a wing]

Alar ('eɪlɑː) *n.* a chemical sprayed on cultivated apple trees in certain countries, to increase fruit set. Also called: **daminozide.**

alarm (ə'lɑːm) *vb.* (*tr.*) **1.** to fill with apprehension, anxiety, or fear. **2.** to warn about danger; alert. **3.** to fit or activate a burglar alarm on a house, car, etc. ~*n.* **4.** fear or terror aroused by awareness of danger; fright. **5.** apprehension or uneasiness: *the idea of failing filled him with alarm.* **6.** a noise, signal, etc., warning of danger. **7.** any device that transmits such a warning: *a burglar alarm.* **8. a.** the device in an alarm clock that triggers off the bell or buzzer. **b.** short for **alarm clock. 9.** *Archaic.* a call to arms. **10.** *Fencing.* a warning or challenge made by stamping the front foot. [C14: from Old French *alarme,* from Old Italian *all'arme* to arms; see ARM[2]] —**a'larming** *adj.* —**a'larmingly** *adv.*

alarm clock *n.* a clock with a mechanism that sounds at a set time: used esp. for waking a person up.

alarmist (ə'lɑːmɪst) *n.* **1.** a person who alarms or attempts to alarm others needlessly or without due grounds. **2.** a person who is easily alarmed. ~*adj.* **3.** characteristic of an alarmist. —**a'larmism** *n.*

alarum (ə'lærəm, -'lɑːr-, -'lɛər-) *n.* **1.** *Archaic.* an alarm, esp. a call to arms. **2.** (used as a stage direction, esp. in Elizabethan drama) a loud disturbance or conflict (esp. in the phrase **alarums and excursions**). [C15: variant of ALARM]

alary ('eɪlərɪ, 'æ-) *adj.* of, relating to, or shaped like wings. [C17: from Latin *ālārius,* from *āla* wing]

alas (ə'læs) *interj.* an exclamation of grief, compassion, or alarm. [C13: from Old French *ha las!* oh wretched!; *las* from Latin *lassus* weary]

Alas. *abbrev. for* Alaska.

alate ('eɪleɪt) *adj.* having wings or winglike extensions. [C17: from Latin *ālātus,* from *āla* wing]

alb (ælb) *n. Christianity.* a long white linen vestment with sleeves worn by priests and others. [Old English *albe,* from Medieval Latin *alba* (*vestis*) white (clothing)]

Alb. *abbrev. for* Albania(n).

albacore ('ælbəˌkɔː) *n.* a tunny, *Thunnus alalunga,* occurring mainly in warm regions of the Atlantic and Pacific. It has very long pectoral fins and is a valued food fish. Also called: **long-fin tunny.** [C16: from Portuguese *albacor,* from Arabic *al-bakrah,* from *al* the + *bakr* young camel]

Albanian (æl'beɪnɪən) *n.* **1.** the official language of Albania: of uncertain relationship within the Indo-European family, but thought to be related to ancient Illyrian. **2. a.** a native, citizen, or inhabitant of Albania. **b.** a native speaker of Albanian. ~*adj.* **3.** of or relating to Albania, its people, or their language.

albata (æl'beɪtə) *n.* a variety of German silver consisting of nickel, copper, and zinc. [C19: from Latin, literally: clothed in white, from *albus* white]

albatross ('ælbəˌtrɒs) *n.* **1.** any large oceanic bird of the genera *Diomedea* and *Phoebetria,* family *Diomedeidae,* of cool southern oceans: order *Procellariiformes* (petrels). They have long narrow wings and are noted for a powerful gliding flight. See also **wandering albatross. 2.** a constant and inescapable burden or handicap: *an albatross of debt.* **3.** *Golf.* a score of three strokes under par for a hole. [C17: from Portuguese *alcatraz* pelican, from Arabic *al-ghattās,* from *al* the + *ghattās* white-tailed sea eagle; influenced by Latin *albus* white: C20 in sense 2, from *The Rime of the Ancient Mariner* by the British poet S. T. Coleridge (1772–1834)]

albedo (æl'biːdəʊ) *n.* **1.** the ratio of the intensity of light reflected from an object, such as a planet, to that of the light it receives from the sun. **2.** *Physics.* the probability that a neutron passing through a surface will return through that surface. [C19: from Church Latin: whiteness, from Latin *albus* white]

albeit (ɔːl'biːɪt) *conj.* even though. [C14 *al be it,* that is, although it be (that)]

albert ('ælbət) *n.* **1.** a kind of watch chain usually attached to a waistcoat. **2.** *Brit.* a standard size of notepaper, 6 × 3⅞ inches. [C19: named after Prince *Albert* (1819–61), Consort of Queen Victoria]

Albertan (æl'bɜːtən) *adj.* **1.** of or denoting Alberta, a province of W Canada. ~*n.* **2.** a native or inhabitant of Alberta.

albertite ('ælbəˌtaɪt) *n.* a black solid variety of bitumen that has a conchoidal fracture and occurs in veins in oil-bearing strata. [C19: named after *Albert* county, New Brunswick, Canada, where it is mined]

albescent (æl'bɛsᵊnt) *adj.* shading into, growing, or becoming white. [C19: from Latin *albēscere* to grow white, from *albus* white] —**al'bescence** *n.*

Albigenses (ˌælbɪ'dʒɛnsiːz) *pl. n.* members of a Manichean sect that flourished in S France from the 11th to the 13th century. [from Medieval Latin: inhabitants of *Albi,* S France] —**ˌAlbi'gensian** *adj.* —**ˌAlbi'gensianism** *n.*

albino (æl'biːnəʊ) *n., pl.* **-nos. 1.** a person with congenital absence of pigmentation in the skin, eyes, and hair. **2.** any animal or plant that is deficient in pigment. [C18: via Portuguese from Spanish, from *albo* white, from Latin *albus*] —**albinic** (æl'bɪnɪk) *or* **ˌalbin'istic** *adj.* —**albinism** ('ælbɪˌnɪzəm) *n.* —**albinotic** (ˌælbɪ'nɒtɪk) *adj.*

Albion ('ælbɪən) *n. Archaic or poetic.* Britain or England. [C13: from Latin, of Celtic origin]

albite ('ælbaɪt) *n.* a colourless, milky-white, yellow, pink, green, or black mineral of the feldspar group and plagioclase series, found in igneous sedimentary and metamorphic rocks. It is used in the manufacture of glass and ceramics. Composition: sodium aluminium silicate. Formula: $NaALSi_3O_8$. Crystal structure: triclinic. [C19: from Latin *albus* white] —**albitic** (æl'bɪtɪk) *adj.*

album ('ælbəm) *n.* **1.** a book or binder consisting of blank pages, pockets, or envelopes for keeping photographs, stamps, autographs, drawings, poems, etc. **2.** one or more long-playing records released as a single item. **3.** a booklike holder containing sleeves for gramophone records. **4.** *Chiefly Brit.* an anthology, usually large and illustrated. [C17: from Latin: blank tablet, from *albus* white]

albumblatt ('ælbəmˌblæt) *n. Music.* a short occasional instrumental composition, usually light in character. [C19: German: album-leaf]

albumen ('ælbjʊmɪn, -mɛn) *n.* **1.** the white of an egg; the nutritive and protective gelatinous substance, mostly an albumin, that surrounds the yolk. **2.** a rare name for **endosperm. 3.** a variant spelling of **albumin.** [C16: from Latin: white of an egg, from *albus* white]

albumenize *or* **albumenise** (æl'bjuːmɪˌnaɪz) *vb.* (*tr.*) to coat with a solution containing albumen or albumin.

albumin *or* **albumen** ('ælbjʊmɪn) *n.* any of a group of simple water-soluble proteins that are coagulated by heat and are found in blood plasma, egg white, etc. [C19: from ALBUMEN + -IN]

albuminate (æl'bjuːmɪˌneɪt) *n. Now rare.* any of several substances formed from albumin by the action of acid or alkali.

albuminoid (æl'bjuːmɪˌnɔɪd) *adj.* **1.** resembling albumin. ~*n.* **2.** another name for **scleroprotein.**

albuminous (æl'bjuːmɪnəs) *adj.* of or containing albumin.

albuminuria (ælˌbjuːmɪ'njʊərɪə) *n. Pathol.* the presence of albumin in the urine. Also called: **proteinuria.**

albumose ('ælbjʊˌməʊs, -ˌməʊz) *n.* the U.S. name for **proteose.** [C19: from ALBUMIN + -OSE[2]]

alburnum (æl'bɜːnəm) *n.* a former name for **sapwood.** [C17: from Latin: sapwood, from *albus* white]

alcahest ('ælkəˌhɛst) *n.* a variant spelling of **alkahest.**

Alcaic (æl'keɪɪk) *adj.* **1.** of or relating to a metre used by the poet Alcaeus, consisting of a strophe of four lines each with four feet. ~*n.* **2.** (*usually pl.*) verse written in the Alcaic form. [C17: from Late Latin *Alcaicus* of *Alcaeus,* 7th-century B.C. Greek poet]

alcaide (æl'keɪd; *Spanish* al'kaɪðe) *n.* (in Spain and Spanish America) **1.** the commander of a fortress or castle. **2.** the governor of a prison. [C16: from Spanish, from Arabic *al-qā'id* the captain, commander, from *qād* to give orders]

alcalde (æl'kældɪ; *Spanish* al'kalde) *or* **alcade** (æl'keɪd) *n.* (in Spain and Spanish America) the mayor or chief magistrate in a town. [C17: from Spanish, from Arabic *al-qādī* the judge, from *qadā* to judge]

alcazar (ˌælkə'zɑː; *Spanish* al'kaθar) *n.* any of various palaces or fortresses built in Spain by the Moors. [C17: from Spanish, from Arabic *al-qasr* the castle]

alchemist ('ælkəmɪst) *n.* a person who practises alchemy.

alchemize *or* **alchemise** ('ælkəˌmaɪz) *vb.* (*tr.*) to alter (an element, metal, etc.) by alchemy; transmute.

alchemy ('ælkəmɪ) *n., pl.* **-mies. 1.** the pseudoscientific predecessor of chemistry that sought a method of transmuting base metals into gold, an elixir to prolong life indefinitely, a panacea or universal remedy, and an alkahest or universal solvent. **2.** a power like that of alchemy: *her beauty had a potent alchemy.* [C14 *alkamye,* via Old French from Medieval Latin *alchimia,* from Arabic *al-kīmiyā',* from *al* the + *kīmiyā'* transmutation, from Late Greek *khēmeia* the art of transmutation] —**alchemic** (æl'kɛmɪk), **al'chemical,** *or* **ˌalchem'istic** *adj.*

alcheringa (ˌæltʃə'rɪŋgə) *n.* (in the mythology of Australian Aboriginal peoples) a mythical Golden Age of the past. Also called: **alchera** ('æltʃərə), **dream time.** [from a native Australian language, literally: dream time]

alcidine ('ælsɪˌdaɪn) *adj.* of, relating to, or belonging to the *Alcidae,* a family of sea birds including the auks, guillemots, puffins, and related forms. [C20: from New Latin *Alcidae,* from *Alca* type genus]

ALCM *abbrev. for* air-launched cruise missile: a type of cruise missile that can be launched from an aircraft.

alcohol ('ælkəˌhɒl) *n.* **1.** a colourless flammable liquid, the active principle of intoxicating drinks, produced by the fermentation of sugars, esp. glucose, and used as a solvent and in the manufacture of organic chemicals. Formula: C_2H_5OH. Also called: **ethanol, ethyl alcohol. 2.** a drink or drinks containing this substance. **3.** *Chem.* any one of a class of organic compounds that contain one or more hydroxyl groups bound to carbon atoms that are not part of an aromatic ring. The simplest alcohols have the formula ROH, where R is an alkyl group. Compare **phenol** (sense 2). See also **diol, triol.** [C16: via New Latin from Medieval Latin, from Arabic *al-kuhl* powdered antimony; see KOHL]

alcoholic (ˌælkə'hɒlɪk) *n.* **1.** a person affected by alcoholism. ~*adj.* **2.** of, relating to, containing, or resulting from alcohol.

alcoholicity (ˌælkəhɒ'lɪsɪtɪ) *n.* the strength of an alcoholic liquor.

Alcoholics Anonymous *n.* an association of alcoholics who try, esp. by mutual assistance, to overcome alcoholism.

alcoholism ('ælkəhɒˌlɪzəm) *n.* a condition in which dependence on alcohol harms a person's health, social functioning, or family life.

alcoholize *or* **alcoholise** ('ælkəhɒˌlaɪz) *vb.* (*tr.*) to turn into alcoholic drink, as by fermenting or mixing with alcohol. —ˌ**alcoˌholiˈzation** *or* ˌ**alcoˌholiˈsation** *n.*

alcoholometer (ˌælkəhɒˈlɒmɪtə) *n.* an instrument, such as a specially calibrated hydrometer, for determining the percentage of alcohol in a liquid.

Alcoran *or* **Alkoran** (ˌælkɒˈrɑːn) *n.* another name for the **Koran.** —ˌ**Alcoˈranic** *or* ˌ**Alkoˈranic** *adj.*

alcove ('ælkəʊv) *n.* **1.** a recess or niche in the wall of a room, as for a bed, books, etc. **2.** any recessed usually vaulted area, as in a garden wall. **3.** any covered or secluded spot, such as a summerhouse. [C17: from French *alcôve,* from Spanish *alcoba,* from Arabic *al-qubbah* the vault, arch]

Alcyone (ælˈsaɪənɪ) *n.* the brightest star in the Pleiades, located in the constellation Taurus.

Ald. *or* **Aldm.** *abbrev. for* Alderman.

Aldebaran (ælˈdɛbərən) *n.* a binary star, one component of which is a red giant, the brightest star in the constellation Taurus. It is situated close to the star cluster Hyades. Visual magnitude: 1.06; spectral type: K5; distance: 55 light years. [C14: via Medieval Latin from Arabic *al-dabarān* the follower (of the Pleiades)]

aldehyde ('ældɪˌhaɪd) *n.* **1.** any organic compound containing the group -CHO. Aldehydes are oxidized to carboxylic acids and take part in many addition reactions. **2.** (*modifier*) consisting of, containing, or concerned with the group -CHO: *aldehyde group or radical.* [C19: from New Latin *al(cohol) dehyd(rogenātum)* dehydrogenated alcohol] —**aldehydic** (ˌældəˈhɪdɪk) *adj.*

al dente *Italian.* (al ˈdɛnte) *adj.* (of a pasta dish) cooked so as to be firm when eaten. [literally: to the tooth]

alder ('ɔːldə) *n.* **1.** any N temperate betulaceous shrub or tree of the genus *Alnus,* having toothed leaves and conelike fruits. The bark is used in dyeing and tanning and the wood for bridges, etc. because it resists underwater rot. **2.** any of several similar trees or shrubs. [Old English *alor;* related to Old High German *elira,* Latin *alnus*]

alder buckthorn *n.* a Eurasian rhamnaceous shrub, *Frangula alnus,* with small greenish flowers and black berry-like fruits.

alder fly *n.* any of various neuropterous insects of the widely distributed group *Sialoidea,* such as *Sialis lutaria,* that have large broad-based hind wings, produce aquatic larvae, and occur near water.

alderman ('ɔːldəmən) *n., pl.* **-men. 1.** (in England and Wales until 1974) one of the senior members of a local council, elected by other councillors. **2.** (in the U.S., Canada, Australia, etc.) a member of the governing body of a municipality. **3.** *History.* a variant spelling of **ealdorman.** ~Abbrevs. (for senses 1, 2): **Ald., Aldm.** [Old English *aldormann,* from *ealdor* chief (comparative of *eald* OLD) + *mann* MAN] —**aldermanic** (ˌɔːldəˈmænɪk) *adj.* —ˈ**aldermanry** *n.* —ˈ**aldermanˌship** *n.*

Alderney ('ɔːldənɪ) *n.* any of a breed of dairy cattle. [named after *Alderney,* an island in the English Channel, where it originated]

Aldine ('ɔːldaɪn, -diːn) *adj.* **1.** relating to the Italian printer Aldus Manutius (1450–1515) or to his editions of the classics. ~*n.* **2.** a book printed by the Aldine press. **3.** any of the several typefaces designed by Aldus Manutius.

Aldis lamp ('ɔːldɪs) *n.* a portable lamp used to transmit Morse code. [C20: originally a trademark, after A. C. W. *Aldis,* its inventor]

aldohexose (ˌældəʊˈhɛksəʊs, -əʊz) *n.* any aldose containing six carbon atoms, such as glucose or mannose.

aldol ('ældɒl) *n.* **1.** a colourless or yellowish oily liquid, miscible with water, used in the manufacture of rubber accelerators, as an organic solvent, in perfume, and as a hypnotic and sedative. Formula: $CH_3CHOHCH_2CHO$. **2.** any organic compound containing the group $-CHOHCH_2CHO$. **3.** (*modifier*) consisting of, containing, or concerned with the group $-CHOHCH_2CHO$: *aldol group or radical; aldol reaction.* [C19: from ALD(EHYDE) + -OL[1]]

aldose ('ældəʊs, -dəʊz) *n.* a sugar that contains the aldehyde group or is a hemiacetal. [C20: from ALD(EHYDE) + -OSE[2]]

aldosterone (ælˈdɒstəˌrəʊn) *n.* the principal mineralocorticoid secreted by the adrenal cortex. A synthesized form is used in the treatment of Addison's disease. [C20: from ALD(EHYDE) + -O- + STER(OL) + -ONE]

aldoxime (ælˈdɒksiːm) *n.* an oxime formed by reaction between hydroxylamine and an aldehyde.

aldrin ('ɔːldrɪn) *n.* a brown to white poisonous crystalline solid, more than 95 per cent of which consists of the compound $C_{12}H_8Cl_6$, which is used as an insecticide. Melting pt.: 105°C. [C20: named after K. *Alder* (1902–58), German chemist]

ale (eɪl) *n.* **1.** an alcoholic drink made by fermenting a cereal, esp. barley, originally differing from beer by being unflavoured by hops. Compare **beer. 2.** *U.S. and Canadian.* a drink made from hops fermented rapidly at a high temperature. **3.** *Chiefly Brit.* another word for **beer.** [Old English *alu, ealu;* related to Old Norse *öl,* Old Saxon *alofat*]

aleatory ('eɪlɪətərɪ, -trɪ) *or* **aleatoric** (ˌeɪlɪəˈtɒrɪk) *adj.* **1.** dependent on chance. **2.** (esp. of a musical composition) involving elements chosen at random by the performer. [C17: from Latin *āleātōrius,* from *āleātor* gambler, from *ālea* game of chance, dice, of uncertain origin]

alec *or* **aleck** ('ælɪk) *n. Austral. slang.* a stupid person; silly fool.

alecithal (eɪˈlɛsɪθəl) *n. Zoology.* (of an ovum) having little or no yolk. [from A-[1] + Greek *lekithos* egg yolk]

ale conner *n. English history.* a local official appointed to examine the measure and quality of ale, beer, and bread. [C14: from ALE + *conner,* from Old English *cunnere* one who tests]

alecost ('eɪlˌkɒst) *n.* another name for **costmary.**

alee (əˈliː) *adv., adj.* (*postpositive*) *Nautical.* on or towards the lee: *with the helm alee.* Compare **aweather.**

alegar ('eɪlɪgə, 'æ-) *n.* malt vinegar. [C14: from ALE + VINEGAR]

alehouse ('eɪlˌhaʊs) *n.* **1.** *Archaic.* a place where ale was sold; tavern. **2.** *Informal.* another name for **pub.**

Alemanni (ˌæləˈmɑːnɪ) *n.* a West Germanic people who settled in the 4th century A.D. between the Rhine, the Main, and the Danube. [C18: from Latin, of Germanic origin; related to Gothic *alamans* a totality of people]

Alemannic (ˌæləˈmænɪk) *n.* **1. a.** the group of High German dialects spoken in Alsace, Switzerland, and SW Germany. **b.** the language of the ancient Alemanni, from which these modern dialects have developed. See also **Old High German.** ~*adj.* **2.** of or relating to the Alemanni, their speech, or the High German dialects descended from it. [C18: from Late Latin *Alamannicus,* of Germanic origin]

alembic (əˈlɛmbɪk) *n.* **1.** an obsolete type of retort used for distillation. **2.** anything that distils or purifies. [C14: from Medieval Latin *alembicum,* from Arabic *al-anbīq* the still, from Greek *ambix* cup]

alembicated (əˈlɛmbɪˌkeɪtɪd) *adj.* (of a literary style) excessively refined; precious. —**aˌlembiˈcation** *n.*

Alençon lace (*French* alɑ̃sɔ̃) *n.* an elaborate lace worked on a hexagonal mesh and used as a border, or a machine-made copy of this. [named after *Alençon,* NW France]

aleph ('ɑːlɪf; *Hebrew* ˈaːlɛf) *n.* the first letter in the Hebrew alphabet (א) articulated as a glottal stop and transliterated with a superior comma (ʼ). [Hebrew: ox]

aleph-bet ('ɑlefˈbet) *or* **aleph-beis** ('ɑlefˈbeis) *n.* the Hebrew alphabet. [from the first two letters]

aleph-null *or* **aleph-zero** *n.* the smallest infinite cardinal number; the cardinal number of the set of positive integers. Symbol: $\aleph_0$.

Aleppo gall *n.* a type of nutgall occurring in oaks in W Asia and E Europe.

alerce (əˈlɜːs, æˈlɜːsɪ) *n.* **1.** the wood of the sandarac tree. **2.** a cupressus-like Chilean pine, *Fitzroya cupressoides,* cut for timber. [Spanish: larch, from Latin *larix,* influenced by Arabic *al-arz*]

alert (əˈlɜːt) *adj.* (*usually postpositive*) **1.** vigilantly attentive: *alert to the problems.* **2.** brisk, nimble, or lively. ~*n.* **3.** an alarm or warning, esp. a siren warning of an air raid. **4.** the period during which such a warning remains in effect. **5. on the alert. a.** on guard against danger, attack, etc. **b.** watchful; ready: *on the alert for any errors.* ~*vb.* (*tr.*) **6.** to warn or signal (troops, police, etc.) to prepare for action. **7.** to warn of danger, an attack, etc. [C17: from Italian *all'erta* on the watch, from *erta* lookout post, from *ergere* to build up, from Latin *ērigere;* see ERECT] —**aˈlertly** *adv.* —**aˈlertness** *n.*

-ales *suffix forming plural proper nouns.* denoting plants belonging to an order: *Rosales; Filicales.* [New Latin, from Latin, plural of *-ālis* -AL[1]]

alethic (əˈliːθɪk) *adj. Logic.* **a.** of or relating to such philosophical concepts as truth, necessity, possibility, contingency, etc. **b.** designating the branch of modal logic that deals with the formalization of these concepts. [C20: from Greek *alētheia* truth]

aleurone (əˈlʊərən, -ˌrəʊn) *or* **aleuron** (əˈlʊərɒn, -rən) *n.* an albuminoid protein that occurs in the form of storage granules in plant cells, esp. in seeds such as maize. [C19: from Greek *aleuron* flour]

Aleut (æˈluːt, ˈæliːˌʊt) *n.* **1.** a member of a people inhabiting the Aleutian Islands and SW Alaska, related to the Eskimos. **2.** the language of this people, related to Eskimo. [from Russian *aleút,* probably of Chukchi origin]

Aleutian (əˈluːʃən) *adj.* **1.** of, denoting, or relating to the Aleutian Islands, the Aleuts, or their language. ~*n.* **2.** another word for **Aleut.**

A level *n.* (in Britain) **1. a.** the advanced level of a subject taken for General Certificate of Education (**GCE**). **b.** (*as modifier*): *A level maths.* **2.** a pass in a particular subject at A level: *she has three A levels.*

alevin ('ælɪvɪn) *n.* a young fish, esp. a young salmon or trout. [C19: from French, from Old French *alever* to rear (young), from Latin *levāre* to raise]

alewife ('eɪlˌwaɪf) *n., pl.* **-wives.** a North American fish, *Pomolobus pseudoharengus,* similar to the herring *Clupea harengus:* family *Clupeidae* (herrings). [C19: perhaps an alteration (through influence of *alewife,* that is, a large rotund woman, alluding to the fish's shape) of French *alose* shad]

alexanders (ˌælɪgˈzɑːndəz) *n.* **1.** a biennial umbelliferous plant, *Smyrnium olusatrum,* native to S Europe, with dense umbels of yellow-green flowers and black fruits. **2. golden alexanders.** an umbelliferous plant, *Zizia aurea,* of North America, having yellow flowers in compound umbels. [Old English, from Medieval Latin *alexandrum,* probably (through association in folk etymology with *Alexander* the Great) changed from Latin *holus atrum* black vegetable]

Alexander technique *n.* a technique for developing awareness of one's posture and movement in order to improve it. [C20: named after Frederick Matthias *Alexander* (died 1955), Australian actor who originated it]

Alexandrian (ˌælɪɡˈzændrɪən, -ˈzɑːn-) *adj.* **1.** of or relating to Alexandria in Egypt. **2.** relating to the Hellenistic philosophical, literary, and scientific ideas that flourished in Alexandria in the last three centuries B.C. **3.** (of writers, literary works, etc.) erudite and imitative rather than original or creative. ~*n.* **4.** a native or inhabitant of Alexandria.

Alexandrine (ˌælɪɡˈzændraɪn, -drɪn, -ˈzɑːn-) *Prosody.* ~*n.* **1.** a line of verse having six iambic feet, usually with a caesura after the third foot. ~*adj.* **2.** of, characterized by, or written in Alexandrines. [C16: from French *alexandrin,* from *Alexandre,* title of 15th-century poem written in this metre]

alexandrite (ˌælɪɡˈzændraɪt) *n.* a green variety of chrysoberyl used as a gemstone. [C19: named after *Alexander* I of Russia (1777–1825); see -ITE[1]]

alexia (əˈlɛksɪə) *n.* a disorder of the central nervous system characterized by impaired ability to read. Nontechnical name: **word blindness.** Compare **aphasia.** [C19: from New Latin, from A-[1] + Greek *lexis* speech; influenced in meaning by Latin *legere* to read]

alexin (əˈlɛksɪn) *n. Immunol.* a former word for **complement** (sense 9). [C19: from German, from Greek *alexein* to ward off] —**alexinic** (ˌælɪkˈsɪnɪk) *adj.*

alexipharmic (əˌlɛksɪˈfɑːmɪk) *Med.* ~*adj.* **1.** acting as an antidote. ~*n.* **2.** an antidote. [C17: from Greek *alexipharmakon* antidote, from *alexein* to avert + *pharmakon* drug]

alf (ælf) *n. Austral. slang.* an uncultivated Australian. [from shortening of the name *Alfred*]

ALF (in Britain) *abbrev. for* Animal Liberation Front.

Alfa (ˈælfə) *n.* a variant spelling of **Alpha** (sense 2).

alfalfa (ælˈfælfə) *n.* a papilionaceous plant, *Medicago sativa,* of Europe and Asia, having compound leaves with three leaflets and clusters of small purplish flowers. It is widely cultivated for forage and used as a commercial source of chlorophyll. Also called: **lucerne.** [C19: from Spanish, from Arabic *al-fasfasah,* from *al* the + *fasfasah* the best sort of fodder]

alfilaria *or* **alfileria** (ˌælfɪˈlɛərɪə) *n.* a geraniaceous plant, *Erodium cicutarium,* native to Europe, with finely divided leaves and small pink or purplish flowers. It is widely naturalized in North America and is used as fodder. Also called: **pin clover.** [via American Spanish from Spanish *alfilerillo,* from *alfiler* pin, from Arabic *al-khilāl* the thorn]

alforja (ælˈfɔːdʒə) *n. Southwestern U.S.* a saddlebag made of leather or canvas. [C17: from Spanish, from Arabic *al-khurj* the saddlebag]

alfresco (ælˈfrɛskəʊ) *adj., adv.* in the open air. [C18: from Italian: in the cool]

Alfvén wave *n.* a magnetohydrodynamic wave that is propagated in a plasma. [C20: named after Hannes *Alfvén* (born 1908), Swedish physicist]

alg. *abbrev. for* algebra *or* algebraic.

Alg. *abbrev. for* Algeria(n).

algae (ˈældʒiː) *pl. n., sing.* **alga** (ˈælɡə). unicellular or multicellular plants, occurring in fresh or salt water or moist ground, that have chlorophyll and other pigments but lack true stems, roots, and leaves. The group includes the seaweeds, diatoms, and spirogyra. See also **thallophyte.** [C16: from Latin, plural of *alga* seaweed, of uncertain origin] —**algal** (ˈælɡəl) *adj.*

algarroba *or* **algaroba** (ˌælɡəˈrəʊbə) *n.* **1.** another name for **mesquite** or **carob. 2.** the edible pod of these trees. [C19: from Spanish, from Arabic *al* the + *kharrūbah* CAROB]

algebra (ˈældʒɪbrə) *n.* **1.** a branch of mathematics in which arithmetical operations and relationships are generalized by using alphabetic symbols to represent unknown numbers or members of specified sets of numbers. **2.** any abstract calculus, a formal language in which functions and operations can be defined and their properties studied. Thus the **algebra of clauses** is another name for **set theory,** and the **algebra of logic** for **formal logic.** [C14: from Medieval Latin, from Arabic *al-jabr* the bone-setting, reunification, mathematical reduction] —**algebraist** (ˌældʒɪˈbreɪɪst) *n.*

algebraic (ˌældʒɪˈbreɪɪk) *or* **algebraical** *adj.* **1.** of or relating to algebra: *an algebraic expression.* **2.** using or relating to finite numbers, operations, or relationships. —ˌ**algeˈbraically** *adv.*

algebraic function *n. Maths.* any function which can be constructed in a finite number of steps from the elementary operations and the inverses of any function already constructed. Compare **transcendental function.**

algebraic notation *n. Chess.* the standard method of denoting the squares on the chessboard, by allotting a letter, a, b, c, up to h, to each of the files running up the board from White's side, starting from the left, and a number to each of the ranks across the board, starting with White's first rank.

algebraic number *n.* any number that is a root of a polynominal equation having rational coefficients such as $\sqrt{2}$ but not π. Compare **transcendental number.**

algerine (ˌældʒəˈriːn) *n.* a soft striped woollen cloth. [C19: from French, from *algérien* Algerian: because the cloth was originally made in Algeria]

algesia (ælˈdʒiːzɪə, -sɪə) *n. Physiol.* the capacity to feel pain. [New Latin from Greek *algēsis* sense of pain] —**alˈgesic** *or* **alˈgetic** *adj.*

-algia *n. combining form.* denoting pain or a painful condition of the part specified: *neuralgia; odontalgia.* [from Greek *algos* pain] —**-algic** *adj. combining form.*

algicide (ˈældʒɪˌsaɪd) *n.* any substance that kills algae.

algid (ˈældʒɪd) *adj. Med.* chilly or cold. [C17: from Latin *algidus,* from *algēre* to be cold] —**alˈgidity** *n.*

algin (ˈældʒɪn) *n.* alginic acid or one of its esters or salts, esp. the gelatinous solution obtained as a by-product in the extraction of iodine from seaweed, used in mucilages and for thickening jellies.

alginate (ˈældʒɪˌneɪt) *n.* a salt or ester of alginic acid.

alginic acid (ælˈdʒɪnɪk) *n.* a white or yellowish powdery polysaccharide having marked hydrophilic properties. Extracted from kelp, it is used mainly in the food and textile industries and in cosmetics and pharmaceuticals. Formula: $(C_6H_8O_6)_n$; molecular wt.: 32 000–250 000.

algo- *combining form.* denoting pain: *algometer; algophobia.* [from Greek *algos* pain]

algoid (ˈælɡɔɪd) *adj.* resembling or relating to algae.

Algol[1] (ˈælɡɒl) *n.* the second brightest star in Perseus, the first known eclipsing binary. Visual magnitude: 2.2–3.5; period: 68.8 hours; spectral type (brighter component): B8. [C14: from Arabic *al ghūl* the GHOUL]

Algol[2] (ˈælɡɒl) *n.* a computer programming language designed for mathematical and scientific purposes; a high-level language. [C20 *alg(orithmic) o(riented) l(anguage)*]

algolagnia (ˌælɡəˈlæɡnɪə) *n.* a perversion in which sexual pleasure is gained from the experience or infliction of pain. See also **sadism, masochism.** —ˌ**algoˈlagnic** *adj.* —ˌ**algoˈlagnist** *n.*

algology (ælˈɡɒlədʒɪ) *n.* the branch of botany concerned with the study of algae. —**algological** (ˌælɡəˈlɒdʒɪkəl) *adj.* —ˌ**algoˈlogically** *adv.* —**alˈgologist** *n.*

algometer (ælˈɡɒmɪtə) *n.* an instrument for measuring sensitivity to pressure (**pressure algometer**) or to pain. —**alˈgometry** *n.*

Algonkian (ælˈɡɒŋkɪən) *n., adj.* **1.** an obsolete term for **Proterozoic. 2.** a variant of **Algonquian.**

Algonquian (ælˈɡɒŋkɪən, -kwɪ-) *or* **Algonkian** *n.* **1.** a family of North American Indian languages whose speakers ranged over an area stretching from the Atlantic between Newfoundland and Delaware to the Rocky Mountains, including Micmac, Mahican, Ojibwa, Fox, Blackfoot, Cheyenne, and Shawnee. Some linguists relate it to Muskogean in a Macro-Algonquian phylum. **2.** (*pl.* **-ans** *or* **-an**) a member of any of the North American Indian peoples that speak one of these languages. ~*adj.* **3.** denoting, belonging to, or relating to this linguistic family or its speakers.

Algonquin (ælˈɡɒŋkɪn, -kwɪn) *or* **Algonkin** (ælˈɡɒŋkɪn) *n.* **1.** (*pl.* **-quins, -quin** *or* **-kins, -kin**) a member of a North American Indian people formerly living along the St Lawrence and Ottawa Rivers in Canada. **2.** the language of this people, a dialect of Ojibwa. ~*n., adj.* **3.** a variant of **Algonquian.** [C17: from Canadian French, earlier written as *Algoumequin;* perhaps related to Micmac *algoomaking* at the fish-spearing place]

algophobia (ˌælɡəˈfəʊbɪə) *n. Psychiatry.* an acute fear of experiencing or witnessing bodily pain.

algor (ˈælɡɔː) *n. Med.* chill. [C15: from Latin]

algorism (ˈælɡəˌrɪzəm) *n.* **1.** the Arabic or decimal system of counting. **2.** the skill of computation using any system of numerals. **3.** another name for **algorithm.** [C13: from Old French *algorisme,* from Medieval Latin *algorismus,* from Arabic *al-khuwārizmi,* from the name of abu-Ja'far Mohammed ibn-Mūsa *al-Khuwārizmi,* ninth-century Persian mathematician] —ˌ**alˈgoˈrismic** *adj.*

algorithm (ˈælɡəˌrɪðəm) *n.* **1.** a logical arithmetical or computational procedure that if correctly applied ensures the solution of a problem. Compare **heuristic. 2.** *Logic, maths.* a recursive procedure whereby an infinite sequence of terms can be generated. ~Also called: **algorism.** [C17: changed from ALGORISM, through influence of Greek *arithmos* number] —ˌ**algoˈrithmic** *adj.* —ˌ**algoˈrithmically** *adv.*

Al Hijrah *or* **Al Hijra** (æl ˈhɪdʒrə) *n.* an annual Muslim festival marking the beginning of the Muslim year. It commemorates Mohammed's move from Mecca to Medina and involves the exchange of gifts and the telling of stories about Mohammed. See also **Hegira.** [from Arabic, *hijrah* emigration or flight]

alias (ˈeɪlɪəs) *adv.* **1.** at another time or place known as or named: *Dylan, alias Zimmerman.* ~*n., pl.* **-ases. 2.** an assumed name. [C16: from Latin *aliās* (adv.) otherwise, at another time, from *alius* other]

aliasing (ˈeɪlɪəsɪŋ) *n. Radio, television.* the error in a vision or sound signal arising from limitations in the system that generates or processes the signal.

alibi (ˈælɪˌbaɪ) *n., pl.* **-bis. 1.** *Law.* **a.** a defence by an accused person that he was elsewhere at the time the crime in question was committed. **b.** the evidence given to prove this. **2.** *Informal.* an excuse. ~*vb.* **3.** (*tr.*) to provide with an alibi. [C18: from Latin *alibī* elsewhere, from *alius* other + *-bī* as in *ubī* where]

alible ('æləbᵊl) *adj. Archaic.* nourishing; nutritive. [C17: from Latin *alibilis* nutritious, from *alere* to nourish]

Alice band ('ælɪs) *n.* an ornamental band worn across the front of the hair to hold it back from the face.

Alice-in-Wonderland *adj.* fantastic; irrational. [C20: alluding to the absurdities of Wonderland in the book by Lewis Carroll (1832–98)]

alicyclic (ˌælɪ'saɪklɪk, -'sɪk-) *adj.* (of an organic compound) having essentially aliphatic properties, in spite of the presence of a ring of carbon atoms. [C19: from German *alicyclisch,* from ALI(PHATIC) + CYCLIC]

alidade ('ælɪˌdeɪd) *or* **alidad** ('ælɪˌdæd) *n.* **1.** a surveying instrument used in plane-tabling for drawing lines of sight on a distant object and taking angular measurements. **2.** the upper rotatable part of a theodolite, including the telescope and its attachments. [C15: from French, from Medieval Latin *allidada,* from Arabic *al-'idāda* the revolving radius of a circle]

alien ('eɪljən, 'eɪlɪən) *n.* **1.** a person owing allegiance to a country other than that in which he lives; foreigner. **2.** any being or thing foreign to the environment in which it now exists. **3.** (in science fiction) a being from another world, sometimes specifically an extraterrestrial. ~*adj.* **4.** unnaturalized; foreign. **5.** having foreign allegiance: *alien territory.* **6.** unfamiliar; strange: *an alien quality in a work of art.* **7.** (*postpositive* and foll. by *to*) repugnant or opposed (to): *war is alien to his philosophy.* **8.** (in science fiction) of or from another world. ~*vb.* **9.** (*tr.*) *Rare.* to transfer (property, etc.) to another. [C14: from Latin *aliēnus* foreign, from *alius* other] —**alienage** ('eɪljənɪdʒ, 'eɪlɪə-) *n.*

alienable ('eɪljənəbᵊl, 'eɪlɪə-) *adj. Law.* (of property) transferable to another owner. —ˌ**aliena'bility** *n.*

alienate ('eɪljəˌneɪt, 'eɪlɪə-) *vb.* (*tr.*) **1.** to cause (a friend, sympathizer, etc.) to become indifferent, unfriendly, or hostile; estrange. **2.** to turn away; divert: *to alienate the affections of a person.* **3.** *Law.* to transfer the ownership of (property, title, etc.) to another person. —'**alienˌator** *n.*

alienation (ˌeɪljə'neɪʃən, ˌeɪlɪə-) *n.* **1.** a turning away; estrangement. **2.** the state of being an outsider or the feeling of being isolated, as from society. **3.** *Psychiatry.* a state in which a person's feelings are inhibited so that eventually both the self and the external world seem unreal. **4.** *Law.* **a.** the transfer of property, as by conveyance or will, into the ownership of another. **b.** the right of an owner to dispose of his property.

alienee (ˌeɪljə'niː, ˌeɪlɪə-) *n. Law.* a person to whom a transfer of property is made.

alienism ('eɪljəˌnɪzəm, 'eɪlɪə-) *n. Obsolete.* the study and treatment of mental illness.

alienist ('eɪljənɪst, 'eɪlɪə-) *n.* **1.** *U.S.* a psychiatrist who specializes in the legal aspects of mental illness. **2.** *Obsolete.* a person who practises alienism.

alienor ('eɪljənə, 'eɪlɪə-) *n. Law.* a person who transfers property to another.

aliform ('ælɪˌfɔːm, 'eɪlɪ-) *adj.* wing-shaped; alar. [C19: from New Latin *āliformis,* from Latin *āla* a wing]

alight[1] (ə'laɪt) *vb.* **alights, alighting, alighted** *or* **alit.** (*intr.*) **1.** (usually foll. by *from*) to step out (of) or get down (from): *to alight from a taxi.* **2.** to come to rest; settle; land: *a thrush alighted on the wall.* [Old English *ālīhtan,* from A-[2] + *līhtan* to make less heavy, from *līht* LIGHT[2]]

alight[2] (ə'laɪt) *adj.* (*postpositive*), *adv.* **1.** burning; on fire. **2.** illuminated; lit up. [Old English *ālīht* lit up, from *ālīhtan* to light up; see LIGHT[1]]

alighting gear *n.* another name for **undercarriage** (sense 1).

align (ə'laɪn) *vb.* **1.** to place or become placed in a line. **2.** to bring (components or parts, such as the wheels of a car) into proper or desirable coordination or relation. **3.** (*tr.;* usually foll. by *with*) to bring (a person, country, etc.) into agreement or cooperation with the policy, etc. of another person or group. [C17: from Old French *aligner,* from *à ligne* into line]

alignment (ə'laɪnmənt) *n.* **1.** arrangement in a straight line. **2.** the line or lines formed in this manner. **3.** alliance or union with a party, cause, etc. **4.** proper or desirable coordination or relation of components. **5.** a ground plan of a railway, motor road, etc. **6.** *Archaeol.* an arrangement of one or more ancient rows of standing stones, of uncertain significance.

alike (ə'laɪk) *adj.* (*postpositive*) **1.** possessing the same or similar characteristics: *they all look alike to me.* ~*adv.* **2.** in the same or a similar manner, way, or degree: *they walk alike.* [Old English *gelīc;* see LIKE[1]]

aliment *n.* ('ælɪmənt). **1.** something that nourishes, supports, or sustains the body or mind. **2.** *Scots. Law.* another term for **alimony.** ~*vb.* ('ælɪˌmɛnt). **3.** (*tr.*) *Obsolete.* to support or sustain. [C15: from Latin *alimentum* food, from *alere* to nourish] —ˌ**ali'mental** *adj.*

alimentary (ˌælɪ'mɛntərɪ, -trɪ) *adj.* **1.** of or relating to nutrition. **2.** providing sustenance or nourishment. **3.** *Scots. Law.* free from the claims of creditors: *an alimentary trust.*

alimentary canal *n.* the tubular passage extending from the mouth to the anus, through which food is passed and digested.

alimentation (ˌælɪmɛn'teɪʃən) *n.* **1.** nourishment. **2.** sustenance; support. —ˌ**ali'mentative** *adj.*

alimony ('ælɪmənɪ) *n. Law.* (formerly) an allowance paid under a court order by one spouse to another when they are separated but not divorced. See also **maintenance.** [C17: from Latin *alimōnia* sustenance, from *alere* to nourish]

aline (ə'laɪn) *vb.* a rare spelling of **align.** —**a'linement** *n.* —**a'liner** *n.*

A-line *adj.* (of a garment, esp. a skirt or dress) flaring slightly from the waist or shoulders.

aliped ('ælɪˌpɛd) *adj.* **1.** (of bats and similar animals) having the digits connected by a winglike membrane. ~*n.* **2.** an aliped animal. [C19: from Latin *ālipēs* having winged feet, from *āla* wing + -PED]

aliphatic (ˌælɪ'fætɪk) *adj.* (of an organic compound) not aromatic, esp. having an open chain structure, such as alkanes, alkenes, and alkynes. [C19: from Greek *aleiphat-, aleiphar* oil]

aliquant ('ælɪkwənt) *adj. Maths.* of, signifying, or relating to a quantity or number that is not an exact divisor of a given quantity or number: *5 is an aliquant part of 12.* Compare **aliquot** (sense 1). [C17: from New Latin, from Latin *aliquantus* somewhat, a certain quantity of]

aliquot ('ælɪˌkwɒt) *adj.* **1.** *Maths.* of, signifying, or relating to an exact divisor of a quantity or number: *3 is an aliquot part of 12.* Compare **aliquant.** **2.** consisting of equal quantities: *the sample was divided into five aliquot parts.* ~*n.* **3.** an aliquot part. [C16: from Latin: several, a few]

alison ('ælɪsᵊn) *n.* **1. sweet alison.** another name for **sweet alyssum.** **2. small alison.** a rare compact cruciferous annual, *Alyssum alyssoides,* having small yellow flowers. [altered from ALYSSUM]

alit (ə'lɪt) *vb.* a rare past tense and past participle of **alight**[1].

aliterate (eɪ'lɪtərɪt) *n.* **1.** a person who is able to read but disinclined to do so. ~*adj.* **2.** of or relating to aliterates.

aliunde (ˌeɪlɪ'ʌndɪ) *adv., adj.* from a source extrinsic to the matter, document, or instrument under consideration: *evidence aliunde.* [Latin: from elsewhere]

alive (ə'laɪv) *adj.* (*postpositive*) **1.** (of people, animals, plants, etc.) living; having life. **2.** in existence; active: *they kept hope alive; the tradition was still alive.* **3.** (*immediately postpositive and usually used with a superlative*) of those living; now living: *the happiest woman alive.* **4.** full of life; lively: *she was wonderfully alive for her age.* **5.** (usually foll. by *with*) animated: *a face alive with emotion.* **6.** (foll. by *to*) aware (of); sensitive (to). **7.** (foll. by *with*) teeming (with): *the mattress was alive with fleas.* **8.** *Electronics.* another word for **live**[2] (sense 11). **9. alive and kicking.** (of a person) active and in good health. **10. look alive!** hurry up! get busy! [Old English *on līfe* in LIFE] —**a'liveness** *n.*

aliyah *n. Judaism.* **1.** (ali'ja). (*pl.* **-yoth** (-'jɒt)) immigration to the Holy Land. **2.** (ə'liːə). the honour of being called to read from the Torah. [from Hebrew, literally: act of going up, ascent]

alizarin (ə'lɪzərɪn) *n.* a brownish-yellow powder or orange-red crystalline solid used as a dye and in the manufacture of other dyes. Formula: $C_6H_4(CO)_2C_6H_2(OH)_2$. [C19: probably from French *alizarine,* probably from Arabic *al-'asārah* the juice, from *'asara* to squeeze]

alk. *abbrev. for* alkali.

alkahest *or* **alcahest** ('ælkəˌhɛst) *n.* the hypothetical universal solvent sought by alchemists. [C17: apparently coined by the alchemist Paracelsus on the model of Arabic words]

alkali ('ælkəˌlaɪ) *n., pl.* **-lis** *or* **-lies.** **1.** *Chemistry.* a soluble base or a solution of a base. **2.** a soluble mineral salt that occurs in arid soils and some natural waters. [C14: from Medieval Latin, from Arabic *al-qili* the ashes (of the plant saltwort)]

alkalic (æl'kælɪk) *adj.* **1.** (of igneous rocks) containing large amounts of alkalis, esp. caustic soda and caustic potash. **2.** another word for **alkaline.**

alkali flat *n.* an arid plain encrusted with alkaline salts derived from the streams draining into it.

alkalify ('ælkəlɪˌfaɪ, æl'kæl-) *vb.* **-fies, -fying, -fied.** to make or become alkaline.

alkali metal *n.* any of the monovalent metals lithium, sodium, potassium, rubidium, caesium, and francium, belonging to group 1A of the periodic table. They are all very reactive and electropositive.

alkalimeter (ˌælkə'lɪmɪtə) *n.* **1.** an apparatus for determining the concentration of alkalis in solution. **2.** an apparatus for determining the quantity of carbon dioxide in carbonates. —**alkalimetric** (ˌælkəlɪ'mɛtrɪk) *adj.*

alkalimetry (ˌælkə'lɪmɪtrɪ) *n.* determination of the amount of alkali or base in a solution, measured by an alkalimeter or by volumetric analysis.

alkaline ('ælkəˌlaɪn) *adj.* having the properties of or containing an alkali.

alkaline earth *n.* **1.** Also called: **alkaline earth metal** *or* **alkaline earth element.** any of the divalent electropositive metals beryllium, magnesium, calcium, strontium, barium, and radium, belonging to group 2A of the periodic table. **2.** an oxide of one of the alkaline earth metals.

alkalinity (ˌælkə'lɪnɪtɪ) *n.* **1.** the quality or state of being alkaline. **2.** the amount of alkali or base in a solution, often expressed in terms of pH.

alkali soil *n.* a soil that gives a pH reaction of 8.5 or above, found esp. in dry areas where the soluble salts, esp. of sodium, have not been leached away but have accumulated in the B horizon of the soil profile.

alkalize *or* **alkalise** ('ælkəˌlaɪz) *vb.* (*tr.*) to make alkaline. —'**alkaˌlizable** *or* '**alkaˌlisable** *adj.*

alkaloid ('ælkəˌlɔɪd) *n.* any of a group of nitrogenous basic compounds found in plants, typically insoluble in water and physiologically active. Common examples are morphine, strychnine, and quinine.

alkalosis (ˌælkə'ləʊsɪs) *n.* an abnormal increase in alkalinity of the blood and extracellular fluids.

alkane ('ælkeɪn) *n.* **a.** any saturated aliphatic hydrocarbon with the general formula C_nH_{2n+2}. **b.** (*as modifier*): *alkane series.* ~Also called: **paraffin.**

alkanet ('ælkəˌnɛt) *n.* **1.** a European boraginaceous plant, *Alkanna tinctoria,* the roots of which yield a red dye. **2.** Also called: **anchusin, alkannin.** the dye obtained from this plant. **3.** any of certain hairy blue-flowered Old World plants of the boraginaceous genus *Anchusa* (or *Pentaglottis*), such as *A. sempervirens* of Europe. See also **bugloss. 4.** another name for **puccoon** (sense 1). [C14: from Spanish *alcaneta,* diminutive of *alcana* henna, from Medieval Latin *alchanna,* from Arabic *al* the + *hinnā'* henna]

alkene ('ælkiːn) *n.* **a.** any unsaturated aliphatic hydrocarbon with the general formula C_nH_{2n}. **b.** (*as modifier*): *alkene series.* ~Also called: **olefine.**

Alkoran *or* **Alcoran** (ˌælkɒ'rɑːn) *n.* a less common name for the **Koran.**

alky *or* **alkie** ('ælkɪ) *n., pl.* **-kies.** *Slang.* a heavy drinker or alcoholic.

alkyd resin ('ælkɪd) *n.* any synthetic resin made from a dicarboxylic acid, such as phthalic acid, and diols or triols: used in paints and adhesives.

alkyl ('ælkɪl) *n.* **1.** (*modifier*) of, consisting of, or containing the monovalent group C_nH_{2n+1}: *alkyl group or radical.* **2.** an organometallic compound, such as tetraethyl lead, containing an alkyl group bound to a metal atom. [C19: from German, from *Alk(ohol)* ALCOHOL + -YL]

alkylating agent ('ælkɪˌleɪtɪŋ) *n.* any cytotoxic drug containing alkyl groups that acts by damaging DNA; widely used in chemotherapy.

alkylation (ˌælkɪ'leɪʃən) *n.* **1.** the replacement of a hydrogen atom in an organic compound by an alkyl group. **2.** the addition of an alkane hydrocarbon to an alkene in producing high-octane fuels.

alkyne ('ælkaɪn) *n.* **a.** any unsaturated aliphatic hydrocarbon that has a formula of the type C_nH_{2n-2}. **b.** (*as modifier*): *alkyne series.* ~Also called: **acetylene.**

all (ɔːl) *determiner.* **1. a.** the whole quantity or amount of; totality of; every one of a class: *all the rice; all men are mortal.* **b.** (*as pronoun; functioning as sing. or pl.*): *is that all there are? all of it is nice; all are welcome.* **c.** (*in combination with a noun used as a modifier*): *an all-ticket match; an all-amateur tournament; an all-night sitting.* **2.** the greatest possible: *in all earnestness.* **3.** any whatever: *to lose all hope of recovery; beyond all doubt.* **4. above all.** most of all; especially. **5. after all.** see **after** (sense 11). **6. all along.** all the time. **7. all but.** almost; nearly: *all but dead.* **8. all of.** no less or smaller than: *she's all of thirteen years.* **9. all over. a.** finished; at an end: *the affair is all over between us.* **b.** over the whole area (of something); everywhere (in, on, etc.): *all over England.* **c.** Also (Irish): **all out.** typically; representatively (in the phrase **that's me (you, him, us, them,** *etc.*) **all over**). **d.** unduly effusive towards. **e.** *Sports.* in a dominant position over. **10.** See **all in. 11. all in all. a.** everything considered: *all in all, it was a great success.* **b.** the object of one's attention or interest: *you are my all in all.* **12. all that.** Also: **that.** (*usually used with a negative*) *Informal.* (intensifier): *she's not all that intelligent.* **13. all the.** (foll. by a comparative adjective or adverb) so much (more or less) than otherwise: *we must work all the faster now.* **14. all too.** definitely but regrettably: *it's all too true.* **15. and all.** *Brit. informal.* as well; too: *and you can take that smile off your face and all.* **16. and all that.** *Informal.* **a.** and similar or associated things; et cetera: *coffee, tea, and all that will be served in the garden.* **b.** used as a filler or to make what precedes more vague: in this sense, it often occurs with concessive force: *she was sweet and pretty and all that, but I still didn't like her.* **c.** See **that** (sense 4). **17. as all that.** as one might expect or hope: *she's not as pretty as all that, but she has personality.* **18. at all. a.** (*used with a negative or in a question*) in any way whatsoever or to any extent or degree: *I didn't know that at all.* **b.** even so; anyway: *I'm surprised you came at all.* **19. be all for.** *Informal.* to be strongly in favour of. **20. for all. a.** in so far as; to the extent that: *for all anyone knows, he was a baron.* **b.** notwithstanding: *for all my pushing, I still couldn't move it.* **21. for all that.** in spite of that: *he was a nice man for all that.* **22. in all.** altogether: *there were five of them in all.* ~*adv.* **23.** (in scores of games) apiece; each: *the score at half time was three all.* ~*n.* **24.** (preceded by *my, your, his,* etc.) (one's) complete effort or interest: *to give your all; you are my all.* **25.** totality or whole. [Old English *eall;* related to Old High German *al,* Old Norse *allr,* Gothic *alls* all]

all- *combining form.* a variant of **allo-** before a vowel.

alla breve ('ælə 'breɪvɪ; *Italian* 'alla 'brɛːve) *n.* **1.** a musical time signature indicating two or four minims to a bar. ~*adj., adv.* **2.** twice as fast as normal. Musical symbol: ¢ [C19: Italian, literally: (according) to the breve]

Allah ('ælə) *n. Islam.* the principal Muslim name for God; the one Supreme Being. [C16: from Arabic, from *al* the + *Ilāh* god; compare Hebrew *elōah*]

allanite ('æləˌnaɪt) *n.* a rare black or brown mineral consisting of the hydrated silicate of calcium, aluminium, iron, cerium, lanthanum, and other rare earth minerals. It occurs in granites and other igneous rocks. Formula: $(Ca,Ce,La,Na)_2(Al,Fe,Be,Mn,Mg)_3(SiO_4)_3(OH)$. [C19: named after T. *Allan* (1777–1833), British mineralogist]

allantoid (ə'læntɔɪd) *adj.* **1.** relating to or resembling the allantois. **2.** *Botany.* shaped like a sausage. ~*n.* **3.** another name for **allantois.** [C17: from Greek *allantoeidēs* sausage-shaped, from *allas* sausage + -OID] —**allantoidal** (ˌælən'tɔɪdᵊl) *adj.*

allantois (ˌælən'təʊɪs, ə'læntɔɪs) *n.* a membranous sac growing out of the ventral surface of the hind gut of embryonic reptiles, birds, and mammals. It combines with the chorion to form the mammalian placenta. [C17: New Latin, irregularly from Greek *allantoeidēs* sausage-shaped, ALLANTOID] —**allantoic** (ˌælən'təʊɪk) *adj.*

alla prima ('ɑːlɑː 'priːmə) *adj.* (of a painting) painted with a single layer of paint, in contrast to paintings built up layer by layer. [C19: from Italian: at once]

allargando (ˌɑːlɑː'gændəʊ). *adj., adv. Music.* (to be performed) with increasing slowness. [Italian, from *allargare* to make slow or broad]

all-around *adj.* (*prenominal*) the U.S. equivalent of **all-round.**

allay (ə'leɪ) *vb.* **1.** to relieve (pain, grief, etc.) or be relieved. **2.** (*tr.*) to reduce (fear, anger, etc.). [Old English *ālecgan* to put down, from *lecgan* to LAY[1]]

All Blacks *pl. n.* **the.** the international Rugby Union football team of New Zealand. [so named because of the players' black playing strip]

all clear *n.* **1.** a signal, usually a siren, indicating that some danger, such as an air raid, is over. **2.** an indication that obstacles are no longer present; permission to proceed: *he received the all clear on the plan.*

allegation (ˌælɪ'geɪʃən) *n.* **1.** the act of alleging. **2.** an unproved statement or assertion, esp. one in an accusation.

allege (ə'lɛdʒ) *vb.* (*tr.; may take a clause as object*) **1.** to declare in or as if in a court of law; state without or before proof: *he alleged malpractice.* **2.** to put forward (an argument or plea) for or against an accusation, claim, etc. **3.** *Archaic.* to cite or quote, as to confirm. [C14 *aleggen,* ultimately from Latin *allēgāre* to dispatch on a mission, from *lēx* law]

alleged (ə'lɛdʒd) *adj.* (*prenominal*) **1.** stated or described to be such; presumed: *the alleged murderer.* **2.** dubious: *an alleged miracle.* —**allegedly** (ə'lɛdʒɪdlɪ) *adv.*

allegiance (ə'liːdʒəns) *n.* **1.** loyalty, as of a subject to his sovereign or of a citizen to his country. **2.** (in feudal society) the obligations of a vassal to his liege lord. See also **fealty, homage** (sense 2). [C14: from Old French *ligeance,* from *lige* LIEGE]

allegorical (ˌælɪ'gɒrɪkᵊl) *or* **allegoric** *adj.* used in, containing, or characteristic of allegory. —ˌ**alle'gorically** *adv.*

allegorize *or* **allegorise** ('ælɪgəˌraɪz) *vb.* **1.** to transform (a story, narrative, fable, etc.) into or compose in the form of allegory. **2.** (*tr.*) to interpret allegorically. —ˌ**allegori'zation** *or* ˌ**allegori'sation** *n.*

allegory ('ælɪgərɪ) *n., pl.* **-ries. 1.** a poem, play, picture, etc., in which the apparent meaning of the characters and events is used to symbolize a deeper moral or spiritual meaning. **2.** the technique or genre that this represents. **3.** use of such symbolism to illustrate truth or a moral. **4.** anything used as a symbol or emblem. [C14: from Old French *allegorie,* from Latin *allēgoria,* from Greek, from *allēgorein* to speak figuratively, from *allos* other + *agoreuein* to make a speech in public, from *agora* a public gathering] —'**allegorist** *n.*

allegretto (ˌælɪ'grɛtəʊ) *Music.* ~*adj., adv.* **1.** (to be performed) fairly quickly or briskly. ~*n., pl.* **-tos. 2.** a piece or passage to be performed in this manner. [C19: diminutive of ALLEGRO]

allegro (ə'leɪgrəʊ, -'lɛg-) *Music.* ~*adj., adv.* **1.** (to be performed) quickly, in a brisk lively manner. ~*n., pl.* **-gros. 2.** a piece or passage to be performed in this manner. [C17: from Italian: cheerful, from Latin *alacer* brisk, lively]

allele (ə'liːl) *n.* any of two or more genes that have the same relative position on homologous chromosomes and are responsible for alternative characteristics, such as smooth or wrinkled seeds in peas. Also called: **allelomorph** (ə'liːləˌmɔːf). See also **multiple alleles.** [C20: from German *Allel,* shortened from *allelomorph,* from Greek *allēl-* one another + *morphē* form] —**al'lelic** *adj.* —**al'lelism** *n.*

allelopathy (ˌælɪ'lɒpəθɪ) *n.* the effect of one living plant upon another, either harmful, as by exuding toxic substances, or beneficial, as by assisting the intake of nutrients. [from French *allélopathie,* from Greek *allēl-* one another + *pathos* suffering]

alleluia (ˌælɪ'luːjə) *interj.* **1.** praise the Lord! Used more commonly in liturgical contexts in place of *hallelujah.* ~*n.* **2.** a song of praise to God. [C14: via Medieval Latin from Hebrew *hallelūyāh*]

allemande ('ælɪmænd; *French* almɑ̃d) *n.* **1.** the first movement of the classical suite, composed in a moderate tempo in a time signature of four-four. **2.** any of several German dances. **3.** a figure in country dancing or square dancing by means of which couples change position in the set. [C17: from French *danse allemande* German dance]

Allen key *n.* an L-shaped tool consisting of a rod having a hexagonal cross section, used to turn a screw (**Allen screw**) with a hexagonal recess in the head. A different size of key is required for each size of screw.

allergen ('ælə,dʒɛn) *n.* any substance, usually a protein, capable of inducing an allergy. —,**aller'genic** *adj.*

allergic (ə'lɜːdʒɪk) *adj.* **1.** of, relating to, having, or caused by an allergy. **2.** (*postpositive;* foll. by *to*) *Informal.* having an aversion (to): *he's allergic to work.*

allergist ('ælədʒɪst) *n.* a physician skilled in the diagnosis and treatment of diseases or conditions caused by allergy.

allergy ('ælədʒɪ) *n., pl.* **-gies. 1.** a hypersensitivity to a substance that causes the body to react to any contact with that substance. Hay fever is an allergic reaction to pollen. **2.** *Informal.* aversion: *he has an allergy to studying.* [C20: from German *Allergie* (indicating a changed reaction), from Greek *allos* other + *ergon* activity]

allethrin (æ'lɛθrɪn) *n.* a clear viscous amber-coloured liquid used as an insecticide and synergist. Formula: $C_{19}H_{26}O_3$; relative density: 1.005. [C20: from ALL(YL) + (PYR)ETHRIN]

alleviate (ə'liːvɪ,eɪt) *vb.* (*tr.*) to make (pain, sorrow, etc.) easier to bear; lessen; relieve. [C15: from Late Latin *alleviāre* to mitigate, from Latin *levis* light] —**al,levi'ation** *n.* —**al'leviative** *adj.* —**al'levi,ator** *n.*

alley[1] ('ælɪ) *n.* **1.** a narrow lane or passage, esp. one between or behind buildings. **2.** See **bowling alley. 3.** *Tennis, chiefly U.S.* the space between the singles and doubles sidelines. **4.** a walk in a park or garden, esp. one lined with trees or bushes. **5. up** (*or* **down**) **one's alley.** a variant of **up one's street** (see **street** (sense 8)). [C14: from Old French *alee,* from *aler* to go, ultimately from Latin *ambulāre* to walk]

alley[2] ('ælɪ) *n.* a large playing marble. [C18: shortened and changed from ALABASTER]

alley cat *n. U.S. and Canadian.* a homeless cat that roams in back streets.

alleyway ('ælɪ,weɪ) *n.* a narrow passage; alley.

all-fired *Slang, chiefly U.S.* ~*adj.* **1.** (*prenominal*) excessive; extreme. ~*adv.* **2.** (intensifier): *don't be so all-fired sure of yourself!* [altered from *hell-fired*]

all-flying tail *n.* a type of aircraft tailplane in which the whole of the tailplane is moved for control purposes.

All Fools' Day *n.* another name for **April Fools' Day** (see **April fool**).

all fours *n.* **1.** both the arms and legs of a person or all the legs of a quadruped (esp. in the phrase **on all fours**). **2.** another name for **seven-up.**

all hail *interj.* an archaic greeting or salutation. [C14, literally: all health (to someone)]

Allhallows (,ɔːl'hæləʊz) *n.* **1.** a less common term for **All Saints' Day. 2. Allhallows Eve.** a less common name for **Hallowe'en.**

Allhallowtide (,ɔːl'hæləʊ,taɪd) *n.* the season of All Saints' Day (Allhallows).

allheal ('ɔːl,hiːl) *n.* any of several plants reputed to have healing powers, such as selfheal and valerian.

alliaceous (,ælɪ'eɪʃəs) *adj.* **1.** of or relating to *Allium,* a genus of liliaceous plants that have a strong onion or garlic smell and often have bulbs. The genus occurs in the N hemisphere and includes onion, garlic, leek, chive, and shallot. **2.** tasting or smelling like garlic or onions. [C18: from Latin *allium* garlic; see -ACEOUS]

alliance (ə'laɪəns) *n.* **1.** the act of allying or state of being allied; union; confederation. **2.** a formal agreement or pact, esp. a military one, between two or more countries to achieve a particular aim. **3.** the countries involved in such an agreement. **4.** a union between families through marriage. **5.** affinity or correspondence in qualities or characteristics. **6.** *Botany.* a taxonomic category consisting of a group of related families; subclass. [C13: from Old French *aliance,* from *alier* to ALLY]

allied (ə'laɪd, 'ælaɪd) *adj.* **1.** joined, as by treaty, agreement, or marriage; united. **2.** of the same type or class; related.

Allied ('ælaɪd) *adj.* of or relating to the Allies.

allies ('ælaɪz) *n.* the plural of **ally.**

Allies ('ælaɪz) *pl. n.* **1.** (in World War I) the powers of the Triple Entente (France, Russia, and Britain) together with the nations allied with them. **2.** (in World War II) the countries that fought against the Axis and Japan. The main Allied powers were Britain and the Commonwealth countries, the U.S., the Soviet Union, France, China, and Poland. See also **Axis.**

alligator ('ælɪ,geɪtə) *n.* **1.** a large crocodilian, *Alligator mississipiensis,* of the southern U.S., having powerful jaws and sharp teeth and differing from the crocodiles in having a shorter and broader snout: family *Alligatoridae* (alligators and caymans). **2.** a similar but smaller species, *A. sinensis,* occurring in China near the Yangtse River. **3.** any crocodilian belonging to the family *Alligatoridae.* **4.** any of various tools or machines having adjustable toothed jaws, used for gripping, crushing, or compacting. [C17: from Spanish *el lagarto* the lizard, from Latin *lacerta*]

alligator pear *n.* another name for **avocado.**

alligator pepper *n. Chiefly W African.* **1.** a tropical African zingiberaceous plant, *Amomum melegueta,* having red or orange spicy seed capsules. **2.** the capsules or seeds of this plant, used as a spice.

all-important *adj.* crucial; vital.

all in *adj.* **1.** (*postpositive*) *Informal.* completely exhausted; tired out. ~*adv., adj.* (**all-in** *when prenominal*). **2. a.** with all expenses or costs included in the price: *the flat is twenty pounds a week all in.* **b.** (*prenominal*): *the all-in price is thirty pounds.*

all-inclusive *adj.* including everything; comprehensive.

all-in wrestling *n.* another name for **freestyle** (sense 2b).

alliterate (ə'lɪtə,reɪt) *vb.* **1.** to contain or cause to contain alliteration. **2.** (*intr.*) to speak or write using alliteration.

alliteration (ə,lɪtə'reɪʃən) *n.* the use of the same consonant (**consonantal alliteration**) or of a vowel, not necessarily the same vowel (**vocalic alliteration**), at the beginning of each word or each stressed syllable in a line of verse, as in *around the rock the ragged rascal ran.* [C17: from Medieval Latin *alliterātiō* (from Latin *al-* (see AD-) + *litera* letter), on the model of *obliterātiō* OBLITERATION] —**al'literative** *adj.*

allium ('ælɪəm) *n.* any liliaceous plant of the genus *Allium,* such as the onion, garlic, shallot, leek, and chive. [C19: from Latin: garlic]

all-nighter (,ɔːl'naɪtə) *n.* an entertainment, such as a pop concert or film screening, that lasts all night.

allo- *or before a vowel* **all-** *combining form.* indicating difference, variation, or opposition: *allopathy; allomorph; allophone; allonym.* [from Greek *allos* other, different]

allocate ('ælə,keɪt) *vb.* (*tr.*) **1.** to assign or allot for a particular purpose. **2.** a less common word for **locate** (sense 2). [C17: from Medieval Latin *allocāre,* from Latin *locāre* to place, from *locus* a place] —'**allo,catable** *adj.*

allocation (,ælə'keɪʃən) *n.* **1.** the act of allocating or the state of being allocated. **2.** a part that is allocated; share. **3.** *Accounting, Brit.* a system of dividing overhead expenses between the various departments of a business. **4.** *Social welfare.* (in a Social Services Department) the process of assigning **referrals** to individual workers, thus changing their status to **cases.**

allochthonous (ə'lɒkθənəs) *adj.* (of rocks, deposits, etc.) found in a place other than where they or their constituents were formed. Compare **autochthonous** (sense 1). [C20: from Greek *allokhthon,* from ALLO- + *khthōn* (genitive *khthonos*) earth]

allocution (,ælə'kjuːʃən) *n. Rhetoric.* a formal or authoritative speech or address, esp. one that advises, informs, or exhorts. [C17: from Late Latin *allocūtiō,* from Latin *alloquī* to address, from *loquī* to speak]

allodial (ə'ləʊdɪəl) *adj.* **1.** (of land) held as an allodium. **2.** (of tenure) characterized by or relating to the system of holding land in absolute ownership: *the allodial system.* **3.** (of people) holding an allodium.

allodium (ə'ləʊdɪəm) *or* **allod** ('ælɒd) *n., pl.* **-lodia** (-'ləʊdɪə) *or* **-lods.** *History.* lands held in absolute ownership, free from such obligations as rent or services due to an overlord. Also: **alodium.** [C17: from Medieval Latin, from Old German *allōd* (unattested) entire property, from *al-* ALL + *-ōd* property; compare Old High German *ōt,* Old English *ēad* property]

allogamy (ə'lɒgəmɪ) *n.* cross-fertilization in flowering plants. —**al'logamous** *adj.*

allograft ('æləʊ,grɑːft) *n.* a tissue graft from a donor genetically unrelated to the recipient.

allograph ('ælə,grɑːf) *n.* **1.** a document written by a person who is not a party to it. **2.** a signature made by one person on behalf of another. Compare **autograph. 3.** *Linguistics.* any of the written symbols that constitute a single grapheme: m *and* M *are allographs in the Roman alphabet.* —**allographic** (,ælə'græfɪk) *adj.*

allomerism (ə'lɒmə,rɪzəm) *n.* similarity of crystalline structure in substances of different chemical composition. —**allomeric** (,ælə'mɛrɪk) *or* **al'lomerous** *adj.*

allometry (ə'lɒmɪtrɪ) *n.* **1.** the study of the growth of part of an organism in relation to the growth of the entire organism. **2.** a change in proportion of any of the parts of an organism that occurs during growth. —**allometric** (,ælə'mɛtrɪk) *adj.*

allomone ('ælə,məʊn) *n.* a chemical substance secreted externally by certain animals, such as insects, affecting the behaviour or physiology of another species. Compare **pheromone.**

allomorph ('ælə,mɔːf) *n.* **1.** *Linguistics.* any of the phonological representations of a single morpheme. For example, the final (s) and (z) sounds of *bets* and *beds* are allomorphs of the English noun-plural morpheme. **2.** any of two or more different crystalline forms of a chemical compound, such as a mineral. —,**allo'morphic** *adj.*

allomorphism (,ælə'mɔːfɪzəm) *n.* variation in the crystalline form of a chemical compound.

allonym ('ælənɪm) *n.* a name, often one of historical significance or that of another person, assumed by a person, esp. an author.

allopath ('ælə,pæθ) *or* **allopathist** (ə'lɒpəθɪst) *n.* a person who practises or is skilled in allopathy.

allopathy (ə'lɒpəθɪ) *n.* the usual method of treating disease, by inducing a condition different from the cause of the disease. Compare **homeopathy.** —**allopathic** (,ælə'pæθɪk) *adj.* —,**allo'pathically** *adv.*

allopatric (,ælə'pætrɪk) *adj.* (of biological speciation or species) taking place or existing in areas that are geographically isolated from one another. Compare **sympatric.** [C20: from ALLO- + *-patric*, from Greek *patris* native land] —ˌ**allo'patrically** *adv.*

allophane ('ælәˌfeɪn) *n.* a variously coloured amorphous mineral consisting of hydrated aluminium silicate and occurring in cracks in some sedimentary rocks. [C19: from Greek *allophanēs* appearing differently, from ALLO- + *phainesthai* to appear]

allophone ('ælәˌfәʊn) *n.* any of several speech sounds that are regarded as contextual or environmental variants of the same phoneme. In English the aspirated initial (p) in *pot* and the unaspirated (p) in *spot* are allophones of the phoneme /p/. —**allophonic** (ˌælә'fɒnɪk) *adj.*

alloplasm ('ælәˌplæzәm) *n. Biology.* part of the cytoplasm that is specialized to form cilia, flagella, and similar structures. —ˌ**allo'plasmic** *adj.*

allopolyploid (ˌælә'pɒlɪˌplɔɪd) *adj.* **1.** (of cells, organisms, etc.) having more than two sets of haploid chromosomes inherited from different species. ~*n.* **2.** an interspecific hybrid of this type that is therefore fertile. ~See also **autopolyploid, polyploid.** —ˌ**allo'polyˌploidy** *n.*

allopurinol (ˌælәʊ'pjʊәrәˌnɒl) *n.* a synthetic drug that reduces blood levels of uric acid and is administered orally in the treatment of gout. Formula: $C_5H_4N_4O$. [C20: from ALLO- + PURINE + -OL[1]]

allosteric (ˌælәʊ'stɪәrɪk) *adj. Biochem.* of, relating to, or designating a function of an enzyme in which the structure and activity of the enzyme are modified by the binding of a metabolic molecule.

allot (ә'lɒt) *vb.* **-lots, -lotting, -lotted.** (*tr.*) **1.** to assign or distribute (shares, etc.). **2.** to designate for a particular purpose: *money was allotted to cover expenses.* **3.** (foll. by *to*) apportion: *we allotted two hours to the case.* [C16: from Old French *aloter*, from *lot* portion, LOT]

allotment (ә'lɒtmәnt) *n.* **1.** the act of allotting; apportionment. **2.** a portion or amount allotted. **3.** *Brit.* a small piece of usually public land rented by an individual for cultivation.

allotrope ('ælәˌtrәʊp) *n.* any of two or more physical forms in which an element can exist: *diamond and graphite are allotropes of carbon.*

allotropous (ә'lɒtrәpәs) *adj.* (of flowers) having the nectar accessible to any species of insect.

allotropy (ә'lɒtrәpɪ) *or* **allotropism** *n.* the existence of an element in two or more physical forms. The most common elements having this property are phosphorus, carbon, and sulphur. —**allotropic** (ˌælә'trɒpɪk) *adj.* —ˌ**allo'tropically** *adv.*

all'ottava (ælә'tɑːvә) *adj., adv. Music.* to be played an octave higher or lower than written. Symbol: 8va [Italian: at the octave]

allottee (әlɒt'iː) *n.* a person to whom something is allotted.

allotype ('ælәˌtaɪp) *n. Biology.* an additional type specimen selected because of differences from the original type specimen, such as opposite sex or morphological details.

all-out *Informal.* ~*adj.* **1.** using one's maximum powers: *an all-out effort.* ~*adv.* **all out. 2.** to one's maximum effort or capacity: *he went all out on the home stretch.*

all-over *adj.* covering the entire surface.

allow (ә'laʊ) *vb.* **1.** (*tr.*) to permit (to do something); let. **2.** (*tr.*) to set aside: *five hours were allowed to do the job.* **3.** (*tr.*) to let enter or stay: *they don't allow dogs.* **4.** (*tr.*) to acknowledge or concede (a point, claim, etc.). **5.** (*tr.*) to let have; grant: *he was allowed few visitors.* **6.** (*intr.*; foll. by *for*) to take into account: *allow for delays.* **7.** (*intr.*; often foll. by *of*) to permit; admit: *a question that allows of only one reply.* **8.** (*tr.*; *may take a clause as object*) *U.S. dialect.* to assert; maintain. **9.** (*tr.*) *Archaic.* to approve; accept. [C14: from Old French *alouer*, from Late Latin *allaudāre* to extol, influenced by Medieval Latin *allocāre* to assign, ALLOCATE]

allowable (ә'laʊәbᵊl) *adj.* permissible; admissible. —**al'lowably** *adv.*

allowance (ә'laʊәns) *n.* **1.** an amount of something, esp. money or food, given or allotted usually at regular intervals. **2.** a discount, as in consideration for something given in part exchange or to increase business; rebate. **3.** (in Britain) an amount of a person's income that is not subject to income tax and is therefore deducted before his liability to taxation is assessed. **4.** a portion set aside to compensate for something or to cover special expenses. **5.** *Brit. Education.* a salary supplement given to a teacher who is appointed to undertake extra duties and responsibilities. **6.** admission; concession. **7.** the act of allowing; sanction; toleration. **8.** something allowed. **9. make allowances** (*or* **allowance**). (usually foll. by *for*) **a.** to take mitigating circumstances into account in consideration (of). **b.** to allow (for). ~*vb.* (*tr.*) **10.** to supply (something) in limited amounts.

allowedly (ә'laʊɪdlɪ) *adv.* (*sentence modifier*) by general admission or agreement; admittedly.

alloy *n.* ('ælɔɪ, ә'lɔɪ). **1.** a metallic material, such as steel, brass, or bronze, consisting of a mixture of two or more metals or of metallic elements with nonmetallic elements. Alloys often have physical properties markedly different from those of the pure metals. **2.** something that impairs the quality or reduces the value of the thing to which it is added. ~*vb.* (ә'lɔɪ). (*tr.*) **3.** to add (one metal or element to another metal or element) to obtain a substance with a desired property. **4.** to debase (a pure substance) by mixing with an inferior element. **5.** to diminish or impair. [C16: from Old French *aloi* a mixture, from *aloier* to combine, from Latin *alligāre*, from *ligāre* to bind]

alloyed junction *n.* a semiconductor junction used in some junction transistors and formed by alloying metal contacts, functioning as emitter and collector regions, to a wafer of semiconductor that acts as the base region. Compare **diffused junction.**

all-powerful *adj.* possessing supreme power; omnipotent.

all right *adj.* (*postpositive except in slang use*), *adv.* **1.** adequate; satisfactory. **2.** unharmed; safe. **3. all-right.** *U.S. slang.* **a.** acceptable: *an all-right book.* **b.** reliable: *an all-right guy.* ~*sentence substitute.* **4.** very well: used to express assent. ~*adv.* **5.** satisfactorily; adequately: *the car goes all right.* **6.** without doubt: *he's a bad one, all right.* ~Also: **alright.**

▷**Usage.** See at **alright.**

all-round *adj.* **1.** efficient in all respects, esp. in sport; versatile: *an all-round player.* **2.** comprehensive; many-sided; not narrow: *an all-round education.*

all-rounder *n.* a versatile person, esp. in a sport.

All Saints' Day *n.* a Christian festival celebrated on Nov. 1 to honour all the saints.

allseed ('ɔːlˌsiːd) *n.* any of several plants that produce many seeds, such as knotgrass.

all-sorts *pl. n.* a mixture, esp. a mixture of liquorice sweets.

All Souls' Day *n. R.C. Church.* a day of prayer (Nov. 2) for the dead in purgatory.

allspice ('ɔːlˌspaɪs) *n.* **1.** a tropical American myrtaceous tree, *Pimenta officinalis*, having small white flowers and aromatic berries. **2.** the whole or powdered seeds of this berry used as a spice, having a flavour said to resemble a mixture of cinnamon, cloves, and nutmeg. ~Also called: **pimento, Jamaica pepper.**

all square *adj.* (*postpositive*) **1.** mutually clear of all debts or obligations. **2.** (of contestants or teams in sports) having equal scores.

all-star *adj.* (*prenominal*) consisting of star performers.

all-time *adj.* (*prenominal*) *Informal.* unsurpassed in some respect at a particular time: *an all-time record.*

▷**Usage.** *All-time* is an imprecise superlative and is avoided by careful writers as being superfluous: *his high jump was a record* (not *an all-time record*).

all told *adv.* (*sentence modifier*) taking every one into account; in all: *we were seven all told.*

allude (ә'luːd) *vb.* (*intr.*; foll. by *to*) **1.** to refer indirectly, briefly, or implicitly. **2.** (loosely) to mention. [C16: from Latin *allūdere*, from *lūdere* to sport, from *lūdus* a game]

allure (ә'ljʊә, ә'lʊә) *vb.* **1.** (*tr.*) to entice or tempt (someone) to a person or place or to a course of action; attract. ~*n.* **2.** attractiveness; appeal: *the cottage's allure was its isolation.* [C15: from Old French *alurer*, from *lure* bait, LURE] —**al'lurement** *n.* —**al'lurer** *n.*

alluring (ә'ljʊәrɪŋ, ә'lʊә-) *adj.* enticing; fascinating; attractive. —**al'luringly** *adv.*

allusion (ә'luːʒәn) *n.* **1.** the act of alluding. **2.** a passing reference; oblique or obscure mention. [C16: from Late Latin *allūsiō*, from Latin *allūdere* to sport with, ALLUDE]

allusive (ә'luːsɪv) *adj.* containing or full of allusions. —**al'lusively** *adv.* —**al'lusiveness** *n.*

alluvial (ә'luːvɪәl) *adj.* **1.** of or relating to alluvium. ~*n.* **2.** another name for **alluvium. 3.** *Austral. and N.Z.* alluvium containing any heavy mineral, esp. gold.

alluvial fan *or* **cone** *n.* a fan-shaped accumulation of silt, sand, gravel, and boulders deposited by fast-flowing mountain rivers when they reach flatter land.

alluvial mining *n.* a method of extracting minerals by dredging alluvial deposits.

alluvion (ә'luːvɪәn) *n.* **1. a.** the wash of the sea or of a river. **b.** an overflow or flood. **c.** matter deposited as sediment; alluvium. **2.** *Law.* the gradual formation of new land, as by the recession of the sea or deposit of sediment on a riverbed. [C16: from Latin *alluviō* an overflowing, from *luere* to wash]

alluvium (ә'luːvɪәm) *n., pl.* **-viums** *or* **-via** (-vɪә). a fine-grained fertile soil consisting of mud, silt, and sand deposited by flowing water on flood plains, in river beds, and in estuaries. [C17: from Latin; see ALLUVION]

ally *vb.* (ә'laɪ), **-lies, -lying, -lied.** (usually foll. by *to* or *with*) **1.** to unite or be united, esp. formally, as by treaty, confederation, or marriage. **2.** (*tr.*; *usually passive*) to connect or be related, as through being similar or compatible. ~*n.* ('ælaɪ, ә'laɪ), *pl.* **-lies. 3.** a country, person, or group allied with another. **4.** a plant, animal, substance, etc., closely related to another in characteristics or form. [C14: from Old French *alier* to join, from Latin *alligāre* to bind to, from *ligāre* to bind]

allyl ('ælaɪl, 'ælɪl) *n.* (*modifier*) of, consisting of, or containing the monovalent group $CH_2{:}CHCH_2^-$: *allyl group or radical; allyl resin.* [C19: from Latin *allium* garlic + -YL; first distinguished in a compound isolated from garlic]

allyl alcohol *n.* a colourless pungent poisonous liquid used in the manufacture of resins, plasticizers, and other organic chemicals. Formula: $CH_2{:}CHCH_2OH$; relative density: 0.85; melting pt.: –129°C; boiling pt.: 96.9°C.

allyl resin *n.* any of several thermosetting synthetic resins made by polymerizing esters of allyl alcohol with a dibasic acid. They are used as adhesives.

allyl sulphide *n.* a colourless liquid that smells like garlic and is used as a flavouring. Formula: $(CH_2{:}CHCH_2)_2S$; relative density: 0.888; boiling pt.: 139°C.

allyou ('ɔːlˌjuː, 'ɔːˌjʊ) *pron.* (*used in addressing more than one person*) *Caribbean informal.* all of you.

Almagest ('ælməˌdʒɛst) *n.* **1.** a work on astronomy compiled by Ptolemy in the 2nd century A.D. containing a description of the geocentric system of the universe and a star catalogue. **2.** (*sometimes not cap.*) any of various similar medieval treatises on astrology, astronomy, or alchemy. [C14: from Old French, from Arabic *al-majisti,* from *al* the + *majisti,* from Greek *megistē* greatest (treatise)]

alma mater ('ælmə 'mɑːtə, 'meɪtə) *n.* (*often caps.*) one's school, college, or university. [C17: from Latin: bountiful mother]

almanac ('ɔːlməˌnæk) *n.* a yearly calendar giving statistical information on events and phenomena, such as the phases of the moon, times of sunrise and sunset, tides, anniversaries, etc. Also (archaic): **almanack.** [C14: from Medieval Latin *almanachus,* perhaps from Late Greek *almenikhiaka*]

almandine ('ælməndɪn, -ˌdaɪn) *n.* a deep violet-red garnet that consists of iron aluminium silicate and is used as a gemstone. Formula: $Fe_3Al_2(SiO_4)_3$. [C17: from French, from Medieval Latin *alabandīna,* from *Alabanda,* ancient city of Asia Minor where these stones were cut]

almemar (æl'miːmɑː) *n. Judaism.* (in Ashkenazic usage) the raised platform in a synagogue on which the reading desk stands. Also called: **bema, bimah, bima.** [from Hebrew, from Arabic *al-minbar* the pulpit, platform]

almighty (ɔːl'maɪtɪ) *adj.* **1.** all-powerful; omnipotent. **2.** *Informal.* (intensifier): *an almighty row.* ~*adv.* **3.** *Informal.* (intensifier): *an almighty loud bang.* —**al'mightily** *adv.* —**al'mightiness** *n.*

Almighty (ɔːl'maɪtɪ) *n.* **the.** another name for **God.**

Almohade ('ælməˌheɪd, -ˌheɪdiː) *or* **Almohad** ('ælməˌhæd) *n., pl.* **-hades** *or* **-hads.** a member of a group of puritanical Muslims, originally Berbers, who arose in S Morocco in the 12th century as a reaction against the corrupt Almoravides and who ruled Spain and all Maghrib from about 1147 to after 1213. [from Arabic *al-muwahhid*]

almond ('ɑːmənd) *n.* **1.** a small widely cultivated rosaceous tree, *Prunus amygdalus,* that is native to W Asia and has pink flowers and a green fruit containing an edible nutlike seed. **2.** the oval-shaped nutlike edible seed of this plant, which has a yellowish-brown shell. **3.** (*modifier*) made of or containing almonds: *almond cake.* **4. a.** a pale yellowish-brown colour. **b.** (*as adj.*): *almond wallpaper.* **5.** Also called: **almond green. a.** a yellowish-green colour. **b.** (*as adj.*): *an almond skirt.* **6.** anything shaped like an almond nut. [C13: from Old French *almande,* from Medieval Latin *amandula,* from Latin *amygdala,* from Greek *amugdalē*]

almond-eyed *adj.* having narrow oval eyes.

almoner ('ɑːmənə) *n.* **1.** *Brit., obsolete.* a trained hospital social worker responsible for the welfare of patients. **2.** (formerly) a person who distributes alms or charity on behalf of a household or institution. [C13: from Old French *almosnier,* from *almosne* alms, from Vulgar Latin *alemosina* (unattested), from Late Latin *eleēmosyna;* see ALMS]

almonry ('ɑːmənrɪ) *n., pl.* **-ries.** *History.* the house of an almoner, usually the place where alms were given. [C15: from Old French *almosnerie;* see ALMONER, ALMS]

Almoravide (æl'mɔːrəˌvaɪd) *or* **Almoravid** (æl'mɔːrəvɪd) *n.* a member of a fanatical people of Berber origin and Islamic faith, who founded an empire in N Africa that spread over much of Spain in the 11th century A.D. [from Arabic *al-murābitūn* the holy ones]

almost ('ɔːlməʊst) *adv.* little short of being; very nearly.

alms (ɑːmz) *pl. n.* charitable donations of money or goods to the poor or needy. [Old English *ælmysse,* from Late Latin *eleēmosyna,* from Greek *eleēmosunē* pity; see ELEEMOSYNARY]

almshouse ('ɑːmzˌhaʊs) *n.* **1.** *Brit.* a privately supported house offering accommodation to the aged or needy. **2.** *Chiefly Brit.* another name for **poorhouse.**

almsman ('ɑːmzmən) *or* (*fem.*) **almswoman** *n., pl.* **-men** *or* **-women.** *Archaic.* a person who gives or receives alms.

almucantar *or* **almacantar** (ˌælmə'kæntə) *n.* **1.** a circle on the celestial sphere parallel to the horizontal plane. **2.** an instrument for measuring altitudes. [C14: from French, from Arabic *almukantarāt* sundial]

almuce ('ælmjuːs) *n.* a fur-lined hood or cape formerly worn by members of certain religious orders, more recently by canons of France. [C15: from Old French *aumusse,* from Medieval Latin *almucia,* of unknown origin]

Alnico ('ælnɪˌkəʊ) *n. Trademark.* an alloy of aluminium, nickel, cobalt, iron, and copper, used to make permanent magnets.

alodium (ə'ləʊdɪəm) *n., pl.* **-dia** (-dɪə). a variant spelling of **allodium.** —**a'lodial** *adj.*

aloe ('æləʊ) *n., pl.* **-oes. 1.** any plant of the liliaceous genus *Aloe,* chiefly native to southern Africa, with fleshy spiny-toothed leaves and red or yellow flowers. **2. American aloe.** another name for **century plant.** [C14: from Latin *aloē,* from Greek] —**aloetic** (ˌæləʊ'ɛtɪk) *adj.*

aloes ('æləʊz) *n.* (*functioning as sing.*) **1.** Also called: **aloes wood.** another name for **eaglewood. 2. bitter aloes.** a bitter purgative drug made from the leaves of several species of aloe.

aloft (ə'lɒft) *adv., adj.* (*postpositive*) **1.** in or into a high or higher place; up above. **2.** *Nautical.* in or into the rigging of a vessel. [C12: from Old Norse *ā lopt* in the air; see LIFT[1], LOFT]

aloha (ə'ləʊə, ɑː'ləʊhɑː) *n., sentence substitute.* a Hawaiian word for **hello** or **goodbye.**

aloin ('æləʊɪn) *n.* a bitter crystalline compound derived from various species of aloe and used medicinally as a laxative. [C19: from ALOE + -IN]

alone (ə'ləʊn) *adj.* (*postpositive*), *adv.* **1.** apart from another or others; solitary. **2.** without anyone or anything else: *one man alone could lift it.* **3.** without equal; unique: *he stands alone in the field of microbiology.* **4.** to the exclusion of others; only: *she alone believed him.* **5. leave** *or* **let alone** *or* **be.** to refrain from annoying or interfering with. **6. leave** *or* **let well (enough) alone.** to refrain from interfering with something that is satisfactory. **7. let alone.** much less; not to mention: *he can't afford beer, let alone whisky.* [Old English *al one,* literally: all (entirely) one]

along (ə'lɒŋ) *prep.* **1.** over or for the length of, esp. in a more or less horizontal plane: *along the road.* ~*adv.* **2.** continuing over the length of some specified thing. **3.** in accompaniment; together with some specified person or people: *he says he'd like to come along.* **4.** forward: *the horse trotted along at a steady pace.* **5.** to a more advanced state: *he got the work moving along.* **6. along with.** accompanying; together with: *consider the advantages along with the disadvantages.* [Old English *andlang,* from *and-* against + *lang* LONG[1]; compare Old Frisian *andlinga,* Old Saxon *antlang*]

▷**Usage.** See at **plus.**

alongshore (əˌlɒŋ'ʃɔː) *adv., adj.* (*postpositive*) close to, by, or along a shore.

alongside (ə'lɒŋˌsaɪd) *prep.* **1.** (often foll. by *of*) along the side of; along beside: *alongside the quay.* ~*adv.* **2.** along the side of some specified thing: *come alongside.*

aloof (ə'luːf) *adj.* distant, unsympathetic, or supercilious in manner, attitude, or feeling. [C16: from A-[1] + *loof,* a variant of LUFF] —**a'loofly** *adv.* —**a'loofness** *n.*

alopecia (ˌælə'piːʃɪə) *n.* loss of hair, esp. on the head; baldness. [C14: from Latin, from Greek *alōpekia,* originally: mange in foxes, from *alōpēx* fox]

aloud (ə'laʊd) *adv., adj.* (*postpositive*) **1.** in a normal voice; not in a whisper. **2.** in a spoken voice; not silently. **3.** *Archaic.* in a loud voice.

alow (ə'ləʊ) *adv., adj.* (*postpositive*) *Nautical.* in or into the lower rigging of a vessel, near the deck.

alp (ælp) *n.* **1.** (in Switzerland) a pasture on a mountain side. **2.** a high mountain. [C14: back formation from *Alps,* from French *Alpes* (pl.), from Latin *Alpēs,* from Greek *Alpeis*]

ALP *abbrev. for* Australian Labor Party.

alpaca[1] (æl'pækə) *n.* **1.** a domesticated cud-chewing artiodactyl mammal, *Lama pacos,* closely related to the llama and native to South America: family *Camelidae.* Its dark shaggy hair is a source of wool and cloth. **2.** the wool or cloth obtained from this animal. **3.** a glossy fabric simulating this, used for linings, etc. [C18: via Spanish from Aymara *allpaca*]

alpaca[2] *or* (*sometimes*) **alpacca** (æl'pækə) *n.* a type of nickel silver used in jewellery. [of uncertain origin]

alpenglow ('ælpənˌgləʊ) *n.* a reddish light on the summits of snow-covered mountain peaks at sunset or sunrise. [partial translation of German *Alpenglühen,* from *Alpen* Alps + *glühen* to GLOW]

alpenhorn ('ælpənˌhɔːn) *n.* another name for **alphorn.**

alpenstock ('ælpənˌstɒk) *n.* an early form of ice axe, consisting of a stout stick with an iron tip and sometimes having a pick and adze at the head, formerly used by mountain climbers. [C19: from German, from *Alpen* Alps + *Stock* STICK[1]]

alpestrine (æl'pɛstrɪn) *adj.* (of plants) growing at high altitudes; subalpine. [C19: from Medieval Latin *alpestris,* from Latin *Alpēs* the Alps]

alpha ('ælfə) *n.* **1.** the first letter in the Greek alphabet (Α, α), a vowel transliterated as *a.* **2.** *Brit.* the highest grade or mark, as in an examination. **3.** (*modifier*) **a.** involving or relating to helium nuclei: *an alpha particle.* **b.** relating to one of two or more allotropes or crystal structures of a solid: *alpha iron.* **c.** relating to one of two or more isomeric forms of a chemical compound, esp. one in which a group is attached to the carbon atom to which the principal group is attached. [via Latin from Greek, of Phoenician origin; related to Hebrew *āleph,* literally: ox]

Alpha ('ælfə) *n.* **1.** (*foll. by the genitive case of a specified constellation*) usually the brightest star in a constellation: *Alpha Centauri.* **2.** *Communications.* a code word for the letter *a.*

alpha and omega *n.* **1.** the first and last, a phrase used in Revelation 1:8 to signify God's eternity. **2.** the basic reason or meaning; most important part.

alphabet ('ælfəˌbɛt) *n.* **1.** a set of letters or other signs used in a writing system, usually arranged in a fixed order, each letter or sign being used to represent one or sometimes more than one phoneme in the language being transcribed. **2.** any set of symbols or characters, esp. one representing sounds of speech. **3.** basic principles or rudiments, as of a subject. [C15: from Late Latin *alphabētum*, from Greek *alphabētos*, from the first two letters of the Greek alphabet; see ALPHA, BETA]

alphabetical (ˌælfəˈbɛtɪkᵊl) *or* **alphabetic** *adj.* **1.** in the conventional order of the letters or symbols of an alphabet. **2.** of, characterized by, or expressed by an alphabet. —ˌ**alphaˈbetically** *adv.*

alphabetize *or* **alphabetise** (ˈælfəbəˌtaɪz) *vb.* (*tr.*) **1.** to arrange in conventional alphabetical order. **2.** to express by an alphabet. —ˌ**alphabetiˈzation** *or* ˌ**alphabetiˈsation** *n.* —ˈ**alphabetˌizer** *or* ˈ**alphabetˌiser** *n.*

Alpha Centauri (sɛnˈtɔːrɪ) *n.* a binary star that is the brightest in the constellation Centaurus and is the second nearest star to the sun. Visual magnitude: 0.0 (A), 1.4 (B); spectral type: G4 (A), K1 (B); distance from earth: 4.3 light years. Also called: **Rigil Kent.** See also **Proxima.**

alpha decay *n.* the radioactive decay process resulting in emission of alpha particles.

alpha emitter *n.* a radioactive isotope that emits alpha particles.

alpha-fetoprotein (ˌælfəˌfiːtəʊˈprəʊtiːn) *n.* a protein that forms in the liver of the human fetus. Excessive quantities in the amniotic fluid and maternal blood may indicate spina bifida in the fetus; low levels may point to Down's syndrome. Abbrev.: **afp.**

alpha helix *n. Biochem.* a helical conformation of a polypeptide chain, found abundantly in the structure of proteins.

alpha iron *n.* a magnetic allotrope of iron that is stable below 910°C; ferrite.

alphanumeric (ˌælfənjuːˈmɛrɪk) *or* **alphameric** (ˌælfəˈmɛrɪk) *adj.* (of a character set, code, or file of data) consisting of alphabetical and numerical symbols. —ˌ**alphanuˈmerically** *or* ˌ**alphaˈmerically** *adv.*

alpha particle *n.* a helium nucleus, containing two neutrons and two protons, emitted during some radioactive transformations.

alpha privative *n.* (in Greek grammar) the letter alpha (or *an-* before vowels) used as a negative or privative prefix. It appears in English words derived from Greek, as in *atheist, anaesthetic.*

alpha radiation *n.* alpha particles emitted from a radioactive isotope.

alpha ray *n.* ionizing radiation consisting of a stream of alpha particles.

alpha rhythm *or* **wave** *n. Physiol.* the normal bursts of electrical activity from the cerebral cortex of a drowsy or inactive person, occurring at a frequency of 8 to 12 hertz and detectable with an electroencephalograph. See also **brain wave.**

alpha stock *n.* any of the most active securities on the Stock Exchange of which there are between 100 and 200; at least ten market makers must continuously display the prices of an alpha stock and all transactions in them must be published immediately.

alpha-test *n.* **1.** an in-house test of a new or modified piece of computer software. ~*vb.* (*tr.*) **2.** to test (software) in this way. Compare **beta-test.**

alphorn (ˈælpˌhɔːn) *or* **alpenhorn** *n. Music.* a wind instrument used in the Swiss Alps, consisting of a very long tube of wood or bark with a cornet-like mouthpiece. [C19: from German *Alpenhorn* Alps horn]

alphosis (ælˈfəʊsɪs) *n. Pathol.* absence of skin pigmentation, as in albinism. [C19: from New Latin, from Greek *alphos* leprosy]

alpine (ˈælpaɪn) *adj.* **1.** of or relating to high mountains. **2.** (of plants) growing on mountains above the limit for tree growth. **3.** connected with or used in mountaineering in medium-sized glaciated mountain areas such as the Alps. **4.** *Skiing.* of or relating to racing events on steep prepared slopes, such as the slalom and downhill. Compare **nordic.** ~*n.* **5.** a plant that is native or suited to alpine conditions.

Alpine (ˈælpaɪn) *adj.* **1.** of or relating to the Alps or their inhabitants. **2.** *Geology.* of or relating to an episode of mountain building in the Tertiary period during which the European Alps were formed.

alpine-style *adj., adv. Mountaineering.* of or in an ascent (esp. in high mountains like the Himalayas) in which the climbers carry all their equipment with them in a single ascent from base to summit.

alpinist (ˈælpɪnɪst) *n.* a mountaineer who climbs in medium-sized glaciated mountain areas such as the Alps. —ˈ**alpinism** *n.*

already (ɔːlˈrɛdɪ) *adv.* **1.** by or before a stated or implied time: *he is already here.* **2.** at a time earlier than expected: *is it ten o'clock already?*

alright (ɔːlˈraɪt) *adv., sentence substitute, adj.* a variant spelling of **all right.**

▷**Usage.** The form *alright,* though very commonly encountered, is still considered by many careful users of English to be wrong or less acceptable than *all right.*

ALS *abbrev. for* autograph letter signed.

Alsatian (ælˈseɪʃən) *n.* **1.** a large wolflike breed of dog often used as a guard or guide dog and by the police. Also called: **German shepherd, German shepherd dog.** **2.** a native or inhabitant of Alsace, a region of NE France. **3.** (in the 17th century) a criminal or debtor who took refuge in the Whitefriars area of London, known as Alsatia. ~*adj.* **4.** of or relating to Alsace or its inhabitants.

alsike (ˈælsaɪk, -sɪk, ˈɔːl-) *n.* a clover, *Trifolium hybridum,* native to Europe and Asia but widely cultivated as a forage crop. It has trifoliate leaves and pink or whitish flowers. Also called: **alsike clover.** [C19: named after *Alsike,* Sweden]

Al Sirat (ˌæl sɪˈræt) *n. Islam.* **1.** the correct path of religion. **2.** the razor-edged bridge by which all who enter paradise must pass. [from Arabic: the road, from Latin *via strāta* paved way]

also (ˈɔːlsəʊ) *adv.* **1.** (*sentence modifier*) in addition; as well; too. ~*sentence connector.* **2.** besides; moreover. [Old English *alswā;* related to Old High German *alsō,* Old Frisian *alsa;* see ALL, SO[1]]

also-ran *n.* **1.** a contestant, horse, etc., failing to finish among the first three in a race. **2.** an unsuccessful person; loser or nonentity.

alstroemeria (ˌælstrəˈmiːrɪə) *n.* any plant of the tuberous perennial genus *Alstroemeria,* originally S American, grown for their brightly coloured orchid-like flowers: family *Amaryllidaceae.* Also called: **Peruvian lily.** [named by Linnaeus for his friend Baron Klas von *Alstroemer*]

alt[1] (ælt) *Music.* ~*adj.* **1.** (esp. of vocal music) high in pitch. **2.** of or relating to the octave commencing with the G above the top line of the treble staff. ~*n.* **3. in alt.** in the octave directly above the treble staff. [C16: from Provençal, from Latin *altus* high, deep]

alt[2] (ɔːlt) *n. Austral. slang.* a follower of an alternative lifestyle.

alt. *abbrev. for:* **1.** alternate. **2.** altitude. **3.** alto.

Alta. *abbrev. for* Alberta.

Altaic (ælˈteɪɪk) *n.* **1.** a postulated family of languages of Asia and SE Europe, consisting of the Turkic, Mongolic, and Tungusic branches, and perhaps also Japanese, Korean, and Ainu. See also **Ural-Altaic.** ~*adj.* **2.** denoting, belonging to, or relating to this linguistic family or its speakers.

Altair (ˈæltɛə) *n.* the brightest star in the constellation Aquila. Visual magnitude: 0.9; spectral type: A5; distance: 15.7 light years. [Arabic, from *al* the + *tā'ir* bird]

altar (ˈɔːltə) *n.* **1.** a raised place or structure where sacrifices are offered and religious rites performed. **2.** (in Christian churches) the communion table. **3.** a step in the wall of a dry dock upon which structures supporting a vessel can stand. **4. lead to the altar.** *Informal.* to marry. [Old English, from Latin *altāria* (plural) altar, from *altus* high]

altar boy *n. R.C. Church, Church of England.* a boy serving as an acolyte.

altar cloth *n. Christianity.* the cloth used for covering an altar: often applied also to the frontal.

altarpiece (ˈɔːltəˌpiːs) *n.* a work of art set above and behind an altar; a reredos.

altazimuth (ælˈtæzɪməθ) *n.* **1.** an instrument for measuring the altitude and azimuth of a celestial body by the horizontal and vertical rotation of a telescope. **2.** a surveying instrument for measuring horizontal and vertical angles that is similar to but more accurate than a theodolite. [C19: from ALT(ITUDE) + AZIMUTH]

alter (ˈɔːltə) *vb.* **1.** to make or become different in some respect; change. **2.** (*tr.*) *Informal, chiefly U.S.* a euphemistic word for **castrate** or **spay.** [C14: from Old French *alterer,* from Medieval Latin *alterāre* to change, from Latin *alter* other] —ˈ**alterable** *adj.* —ˈ**alterably** *adv.* —ˌ**alteraˈbility** *n.*

alteration (ˌɔːltəˈreɪʃən) *n.* **1.** an adjustment, change, or modification. **2.** the act of altering or state of being altered.

alterative (ˈɔːltərətɪv) *adj.* **1.** likely or able to produce alteration. **2.** (of a drug) able to restore normal health. ~*n.* **3.** a drug that restores normal health.

altercate (ˈɔːltəˌkeɪt) *vb.* (*intr.*) to argue, esp. heatedly; dispute. [C16: from Latin *altercārī* to quarrel with another, from *alter* other]

altercation (ˌɔːltəˈkeɪʃən) *n.* an angry or heated discussion or quarrel; argument.

altered chord *n. Music.* a chord in which one or more notes are chromatically changed by the introduction of accidentals.

alter ego (ˈæltər ˈiːgəʊ, ˈɛgəʊ) *n.* **1.** a second self. **2.** a very close and intimate friend. [Latin: other self]

alternant (ɔːlˈtɜːnənt) *adj.* alternating. [C17: from French, from Latin *alternāre* to ALTERNATE]

alternate *vb.* (ˈɔːltəˌneɪt). **1.** (often foll. by *with*) to occur or cause to occur successively or by turns: *day and night alternate.* **2.** (*intr.;* often foll. by *between*) to swing repeatedly from one condition, action, etc., to another: *he alternates between success and failure.* **3.** (*tr.*) to interchange regularly or in succession. **4.** (*intr.*) (of an electric current, voltage, etc.) to reverse direction or sign at regular intervals, usually sinusoidally, the instantaneous value varying continuously. **5.** (*intr.;* often foll. by *for*) *Theatre.* to understudy another actor or actress. ~*adj.* (ɔːlˈtɜːnɪt). **6.** occurring by turns: *alternate feelings of love and hate.* **7.** every other or second one of a series: *he came to work on alternate days.* **8.** being a second or further choice; alternative. **9.** *Botany.* **a.** (of leaves, flowers, etc.) arranged singly at different heights on either side of the stem. **b.** (of parts of a flower) arranged opposite the spaces between other parts. Compare **opposite** (sense 4). ~*n.* (ˈɔːltənɪt, ɔːlˈtɜːnɪt). **10.** *U.S. and Canadian.* a person who substitutes for another in his absence; stand-in. [C16: from Latin *alternāre* to do one thing and then another, from *alternus* one after the other, from *alter* other]

alternate angles *pl. n.* two angles at opposite ends and on opposite sides of a transversal cutting two lines.

alternately (ɔːlˈtɜːnɪtlɪ) *adv.* in an alternating sequence or position.

alternating current *n.* a continuous electric current that periodically reverses direction, usually sinusoidally. Abbrev.: **AC.** Compare **direct current.**

alternating-gradient focusing *n. Physics.* a method of focusing beams of charged particles in high-energy accelerators, in which a series of magnetic or electrostatic lenses alternately converge and diverge the beam, producing a net focusing effect and thus preventing the beam from spreading.

alternation (ˌɔːltəˈneɪʃən) *n.* **1.** successive change from one condition or action to another and back again repeatedly. **2.** *Logic.* another name for **disjunction** (sense 3).

alternation of generations *n.* the production within the life cycle of an organism of alternating asexual and sexual reproductive forms. It occurs in many plants and lower animals. Also called: **metagenesis, heterogenesis, digenesis, xenogenesis.**

alternative (ɔːlˈtɜːnətɪv) *n.* **1.** a possibility of choice, esp. between two things, courses of action, etc. **2.** either of such choices: *we took the alternative of walking.* ~*adj.* **3.** presenting a choice, esp. between two possibilities only. **4.** (of two things) mutually exclusive. **5.** denoting a lifestyle, culture, art form, etc., regarded by its adherents as preferable to that of contemporary society because it is less conventional, materialistic, or institutionalized, and, often, more in harmony with nature. **6.** *Logic.* another word for **disjunctive** (sense 3). —**alˈternatively** *adv.* —**alˈternativeness** *n.*

alternative curriculum *n. Brit. Education.* any course of study offered as an alternative to the National Curriculum.

alternative energy *n.* a form of energy derived from a natural source, such as the sun, wind, tides, or waves. Also called: **renewable energy.**

alternative hypothesis *n. Statistics.* the hypothesis that given data do not conform with a given null hypothesis: accepted only if its probability exceeds a predetermined significance level. See **hypothesis testing.** Compare **null hypothesis.**

alternative medicine *n.* the treatment, alleviation, or prevention of disease by techniques such as osteopathy and acupuncture, allied with attention to factors such as diet and emotional stability, which affect a person's general wellbeing. Also called: **complementary medicine.** See also **holism** (sense 2).

Alternative Vote *n. (modifier)* of or relating to a system of voting in which voters list the candidates in order of preference. If no candidate obtains more than 50% of first-preference votes, the votes for the bottom candidate are redistributed according to the voters' next preference. See **proportional representation.**

alternator (ˈɔːltəˌneɪtə) *n.* an electrical machine that generates an alternating current.

althaea *or U.S.* **althea** (ælˈθiːə) *n.* **1.** any Eurasian plant of the malvaceous genus *Althaea,* such as the hollyhock, having tall spikes of showy white, yellow, or red flowers. **2.** another name for **rose of Sharon** (sense 2). [C17: from Latin *althaea,* from Greek *althaia* marsh mallow (literally: healing plant), from Greek *althein* to heal]

Althing (ˈælθɪŋ) *n.* the bicameral parliament of Iceland.

althorn (ˈæltˌhɔːn) *n.* a valved brass musical instrument belonging to the saxhorn or flügelhorn families.

although (ɔːlˈðəʊ) *conj. (subordinating)* despite the fact that; even though: *although she was ill, she worked hard.*

alti- *combining form.* indicating height or altitude: *altimeter.* [from Latin *altus* high]

altimeter (ælˈtɪmɪtə, ˈæltɪˌmiːtə) *n.* an instrument that indicates height above sea level, esp. one based on an aneroid barometer and fitted to an aircraft.

altimetry (ælˈtɪmɪtrɪ) *n.* the science of measuring altitudes, as with an altimeter. —**altimetrical** (ˌæltɪˈmɛtrɪkᵊl) *adj.* —ˌ**altiˈmetrically** *adv.*

altissimo (ælˈtɪsɪˌməʊ) *adj.* **1.** (of music) very high in pitch. **2.** of or relating to the octave commencing on the G lying an octave above the treble clef. ~*n.* **3. in altissimo.** in the octave commencing an octave above the treble clef. [Italian, literally: highest]

altitude (ˈæltɪˌtjuːd) *n.* **1.** the vertical height of an object above some chosen level, esp. above sea level; elevation. **2.** *Geometry.* the perpendicular distance from the vertex to the base of a geometrical figure or solid. **3.** Also called: **elevation.** *Astronomy, navigation.* the angular distance of a celestial body from the horizon measured along the vertical circle passing through the body. Compare **azimuth** (sense 1). **4.** *Surveying.* the angle of elevation of a point above the horizontal plane of the observer. **5.** (*often pl.*) a high place or region. [C14: from Latin *altitūdō,* from *altus* high, deep] —ˌ**altiˈtudinal** *adj.*

altitude sickness *n.* another name for **mountain sickness.**

alto (ˈæltəʊ) *n., pl.* **-tos. 1.** the highest adult male voice; countertenor. **2.** (in choral singing) a shortened form of **contralto. 3.** a singer with such a voice. **4.** another name for **viola**[1] (sense 1). **5.** a flute, saxophone, etc., that is the third or fourth highest instrument in its group. ~*adj.* **6.** denoting a flute, saxophone, etc., that is the third or fourth highest instrument in its group. [C18: from Italian: high, from Latin *altus*]

alto- *combining form.* high: *altocumulus; altostratus.* [from Latin *altus* high]

alto clef *n.* the clef that establishes middle C as being on the third line of the staff. Also called: **viola clef.** See also **C clef.**

altocumulus (ˌæltəʊˈkjuːmjʊləs) *n., pl.* **-li** (-laɪ). a globular cloud at an intermediate height of about 2400 to 6000 metres (8000 to 20 000 feet).

altogether (ˌɔːltəˈgɛðə, ˈɔːltəˌgɛðə) *adv.* **1.** with everything included: *altogether he owed me sixty pounds.* **2.** completely; utterly; totally: *he was altogether mad.* **3.** on the whole: *altogether it was a very good party.* ~*n.* **4. in the altogether.** *Informal.* naked.

alto horn *n.* another term for **althorn.**

altoist (ˈæltəʊɪst) *n.* a person who plays the alto saxophone.

alto-relievo *or* **alto-rilievo** (ˌæltəʊrɪˈliːvəʊ) *n., pl.* **-vos.** another name for **high relief.** [C18: from Italian]

altostratus (ˌæltəʊˈstreɪtəs, -ˈstrɑː-) *n., pl.* **-ti** (-taɪ). a layer cloud at an intermediate height of about 2400 to 6000 metres (8000 to 20 000 feet).

altrices (ˈæltrɪsiːz) *pl. n.* altricial birds.

altricial (ælˈtrɪʃəl) *adj.* **1.** (of the young of some species of birds after hatching) naked, blind, and dependent on the parents for food. ~*n.* **2.** an altricial bird, such as a pigeon. ~Compare **precocial.** [C19: from New Latin *altriciālis,* from Latin *altrix* a nurse, from *alere* to nourish]

altruism (ˈæltruːˌɪzəm) *n.* **1.** the principle or practice of unselfish concern for the welfare of others. **2.** the philosophical doctrine that right action is that which produces the greatest benefit to others. ~Compare **egoism.** See also **utilitarianism.** [C19: from French *altruisme,* from Italian *altrui* others, from Latin *alterī,* plural of *alter* other] —ˈ**altruist** *n.* —ˌ**altruˈistic** *adj.* —ˌ**altruˈistically** *adv.*

ALU *Computer technol. abbrev. for* arithmetic and logic unit.

aludel (ˈæljuˌdɛl) *n. Chem.* a pear-shaped vessel, open at both ends, formerly used with similar vessels for collecting condensates, esp. of subliming mercury. [C16: via Old French from Spanish, from Arabic *al-uthāl* the vessel]

alula (ˈæljʊlə) *n., pl.* **-lae** (-liː). another name for **bastard wing.** [C18: New Latin: a little wing, from Latin *āla* a wing] —ˈ**alular** *adj.*

alum (ˈæləm) *n.* **1.** Also called: **potash alum.** a colourless soluble hydrated double sulphate of aluminium and potassium used in the manufacture of mordants and pigments, in dressing leather and sizing paper, and in medicine as a styptic and astringent. Formula: $K_2SO_4.Al_2(SO_4)_3.24H_2O$. **2.** any of a group of isomorphic double sulphates of a monovalent metal or group and a trivalent metal. Formula: $X_2SO_4.Y_2(SO_4)_3.24H_2O$, where X is monovalent and Y is trivalent. [C14: from Old French, from Latin *alūmen*]

alum. *abbrev. for* aluminium.

alumina (əˈluːmɪnə) *n.* another name for **aluminium oxide.** [C18: from New Latin, plural of Latin *alūmen* ALUM]

aluminate (əˈluːmɪneɪt) *n.* a salt of the ortho or meta acid forms of aluminium hydroxide containing the ions AlO_2^- or AlO_3^{3-}.

aluminiferous (əˌluːmɪˈnɪfərəs) *adj.* containing or yielding aluminium or alumina.

aluminium (ˌæljʊˈmɪnɪəm) *or U.S. and Canadian* **aluminum** (əˈluːmɪnəm) *n.* a light malleable ductile silvery-white metallic element that resists corrosion; the third most abundant element in the earth's crust (8.1 per cent), occurring only as a compound, principally in bauxite. It is used, esp. in the form of its alloys, in aircraft parts, kitchen utensils, etc. Symbol: Al; atomic no.: 13; atomic wt.: 26.981; valency: 3; relative density: 2.699; melting pt.: 660.2°C; boiling pt.: 2467°C.

aluminium bronze *n.* any of a range of copper alloys that contain between 5 and 10 per cent aluminium.

aluminium hydroxide *n.* a white crystalline powder derived from bauxite and used in the manufacture of glass and ceramics, aluminium and its salts, and in dyeing. Formula: $Al(OH)_3$ or $Al_2O_3.3H_2O$.

aluminium oxide *n.* a white or colourless insoluble powder occurring naturally as corundum and used in the production of aluminium and its compounds, abrasives, glass, and ceramics. Formula: Al_2O_3. Also called: **alumina.** See also **activated alumina.**

aluminium sulphate *n.* a white crystalline salt used in the paper, textile, and dyeing industries and in the purification of water. Formula: $Al_2(SO_4)_3$.

aluminize *or* **aluminise** (əˈluːmɪˌnaɪz) *vb. (tr.)* to cover with aluminium or aluminium paint.

aluminosilicate (əˌluːmɪnəʊˈsɪlɪkɪt) *n.* a silicate in which some of the silicon in the tetrahedral unit SiO_4 has been replaced by aluminium.

aluminothermy (əˌluːmɪnəʊˈθɜːmɪ) *n.* a process for reducing metallic oxides using finely divided aluminium powder. The mixture of aluminium and oxide is ignited, causing the aluminium to be oxidized and the metal oxide to be reduced to the metal. Also called: **thermite process.**

aluminous (əˈluːmɪnəs) *adj.* **1.** resembling aluminium. **2.** another word for **aluminiferous.** —**aluminosity** (əˌluːmɪˈnɒsɪtɪ) *n.*

aluminous cement *n.* another term for **Ciment Fondu.**

alumnus (ə'lʌmnəs) *or* (*fem.*) **alumna** (ə'lʌmnə) *n., pl.* **-ni** (-naɪ) *or* **-nae** (-niː). *Chiefly U.S. and Canadian.* a graduate of a school, college, etc. [C17: from Latin: nursling, pupil, foster son, from *alere* to nourish]
alumroot ('æləmˌruːt) *n.* **1.** any of several North American plants of the saxifragaceous genus *Heuchera,* having small white, reddish, or green bell-shaped flowers and astringent roots. **2.** the root of such a plant.
Alundum (ə'lʌndəm) *n. Trademark.* a hard material composed of fused alumina, used as an abrasive and a refractory.
alunite ('æljuˌnaɪt) *n.* a white, grey, or reddish mineral consisting of hydrated aluminium sulphate. It occurs in volcanic igneous rocks and is a source of potassium and aluminium compounds. Formula: $KAl_3(SO_4)_2(OH)_6$. [C19: from French *alun* alum (from Latin *alūmen*) + -ITE[1]]
alveolar (æl'vɪələ, ˌælvɪ'əʊlə) *adj.* **1.** *Anatomy.* of, relating to, or resembling an alveolus. **2.** denoting the part of the jawbone containing the roots of the teeth. **3.** (of a consonant) articulated with the tongue in contact with the projecting part of the jawbone immediately behind the upper teeth. ~*n.* **4.** an alveolar consonant, such as the speech sounds written *t, d,* and *s* in English.
alveolate (æl'vɪəlɪt, -ˌleɪt) *adj.* **1.** having many alveoli. **2.** resembling the deep pits of a honeycomb. [C19: from Late Latin *alveolātus* forming a channel, hollowed, from Latin: ALVEOLUS] —**ˌalveo'lation** *n.*
alveolus (æl'vɪələs) *n., pl.* **-li** (-ˌlaɪ). **1.** any small pit, cavity, or saclike dilation, such as a honeycomb cell. **2.** any of the sockets in which the roots of the teeth are embedded. **3.** any of the tiny air sacs in the lungs at the end of the bronchioles, through which oxygen is taken into the blood. [C18: from Latin: a little hollow, diminutive of *alveus*]
alvine ('ælvɪn, -vaɪn) *adj. Obsolete.* of or relating to the intestines or belly. [C18: from Latin *alvus* belly]
always ('ɔːlweɪz, -wɪz) *adv.* **1.** without exception; on every occasion; every time: *he always arrives on time.* **2.** continually; repeatedly. **3.** in any case: *you could always take a day off work.* **4. for always.** *Informal.* for ever; without end: *our marriage is for always.* ~Also (archaic): **alway.** [C13 *alles weiss,* from Old English *ealne weg,* literally: all the way; see ALL, WAY]
alyssum ('ælɪsəm) *n.* any widely cultivated herbaceous garden plant of the genus *Alyssum,* having clusters of small yellow or white flowers: family *Cruciferae* (crucifers). See also **sweet alyssum, alison.** [C16: from New Latin, from Greek *alusson,* from *alussos* (adj.) curing rabies, referring to the ancient belief in the plant's healing properties]
Alzheimer's disease ('æltsˌhaɪməz) *n.* a disorder of the brain resulting in a progressive decline in intellectual and physical abilities and eventual senility. Often shortened to **Alzheimer's.** [C20: named after A. *Alzheimer* (1864–1915), German physician who first identified it]
am[1] (æm; *unstressed* əm) *vb.* (used with *I*) a form of the present tense (indicative mood) of **be.** [Old English *eam;* related to Old Norse *em,* Gothic *im,* Old High German *bim,* Latin *sum,* Greek *eimi,* Sanskrit *asmi*]
am[2] See **1. AM** (sense 4). **2. a.m.**
Am *the chemical symbol for* americium.
AM *abbrev. for:* **1.** associate member. **2.** Albert Medal. **3.** *U.S.* Master of Arts. **4.** Also: **am.** amplitude modulation. **5.** See **a.m. 6.** Member of the Order of Australia.
Am. *abbrev. for* America(n).
a.m., A.M., am, *or* **AM** (indicating the time period from midnight to midday) *abbrev. for* ante meridiem. Compare **p.m.** [Latin: before noon]
AMA *abbrev. for:* **1.** American Medical Association. **2.** Australian Medical Association.
amadavat (ˌæmədə'væt) *n.* another name for **avadavat.**
amadou ('æməˌduː) *n.* a spongy substance made from certain fungi, such as *Polyporus* (or *Fomes*) *fomentarius* and related species, used as tinder to light fires, in medicine to stop bleeding, and, esp. formerly, by anglers to dry off dry flies between casts. [C18: from French, from Provençal: lover, from Latin *amātor,* from *amāre* to love; so called because it readily ignites]
amah ('ɑːmə, 'æmə) *n.* (in the East, esp. formerly) a nurse or maidservant, esp. one of Chinese origin. Compare **ayah.** [C19: from Portuguese *ama* nurse, wet nurse]
amain (ə'meɪn) *adv. Archaic or poetic.* with great strength, speed, or haste. [C16: from A-[2] + MAIN[1]]
Amalekite (ə'mæləˌkaɪt) *n. Old Testament.* a member of a nomadic tribe descended from Esau (Genesis 36:12), dwelling in the desert between Sinai and Canaan and hostile to the Israelites: they were defeated by Saul and destroyed by David (I Samuel 15–30).
amalgam (ə'mælgəm) *n.* **1.** an alloy of mercury with another metal, esp. with silver: *dental amalgam.* **2.** a rare white metallic mineral that consists of silver and mercury and occurs in deposits of silver and cinnabar. **3.** a blend or combination. [C15: from Medieval Latin *amalgama,* of obscure origin]
amalgamate (ə'mælgəˌmeɪt) *vb.* **1.** to combine or cause to combine; unite. **2.** to alloy (a metal) with mercury.
amalgamation (əˌmælgə'meɪʃən) *n.* **1.** the action or process of amalgamating. **2.** the state of being amalgamated. **3.** a method of extracting precious metals from their ores by treatment with mercury to form an amalgam. **4.** *Commerce.* another word for **merger** (sense 1).
amanita (ˌæmə'naɪtə) *n.* any of various saprophytic agaricaceous fungi constituting the genus *Amanita,* having white gills and a broken membranous ring (volva) around the stalk. The genus includes several highly poisonous species, such as death cap, destroying angel, and fly agaric. [C19: from Greek *amanitai* (plural) a variety of fungus]
amanuensis (əˌmænju'ɛnsɪs) *n., pl.* **-ses** (-siːz). a person employed to take dictation or to copy manuscripts. [C17: from Latin *āmanuensis,* from the phrase *servus ā manū* slave at hand (that is, handwriting)]
amaranth ('æməˌrænθ) *n.* **1.** *Poetic.* an imaginary flower that never fades. **2.** any of numerous tropical and temperate plants of the genus *Amaranthus,* having tassel-like heads of small green, red, or purple flowers: family *Amaranthaceae.* See also **love-lies-bleeding, tumbleweed, pigweed** (sense 1). **3.** a synthetic red food colouring **(E123),** used in packet soups, cake mixes, etc. [C17: from Latin *amarantus,* from Greek *amarantos* unfading, from A-[1] + *marainein* to fade]
amaranthaceous (ˌæməræn'θeɪʃəs) *adj.* of, relating to, or belonging to the *Amaranthaceae* (or *Amarantaceae*), a family of tropical and temperate herbaceous or shrubby flowering plants that includes the amaranths and cockscomb.
amaranthine (ˌæmə'rænθaɪn) *adj.* **1.** of a dark reddish-purple colour. **2.** of or resembling the amaranth.
amarelle ('æməˌrɛl) *n.* a variety of sour cherry that has pale red fruit and colourless juice. Compare **morello.** [C20: from German, from Medieval Latin *amārellum,* from Latin *amārus* bitter; compare MORELLO]
amaretto (æmə'rɛtəʊ) *n.* an Italian liqueur with a flavour of almonds. [C20: from Italian *amaro* bitter]
amaryllidaceous (ˌæməˌrɪlɪ'deɪʃəs) *adj.* of, relating to, or belonging to the *Amaryllidaceae,* a family of widely cultivated flowering plants having bulbs and including the amaryllis, snowdrop, narcissus, and daffodil.
amaryllis (ˌæmə'rɪlɪs) *n.* **1.** Also called: **belladonna lily.** an amaryllidaceous plant, *Amaryllis belladonna,* native to southern Africa and having large lily-like reddish or white flowers. **2.** any of several related plants. [C18: from New Latin, from Latin: named after AMARYLLIS]
Amaryllis (ˌæmə'rɪlɪs) *n.* (in pastoral poetry) a name for a shepherdess or country girl.
amass (ə'mæs) *vb.* **1.** (*tr.*) to accumulate or collect (esp. riches, etc.). **2.** to gather in a heap; bring together. [C15: from Old French *amasser,* from *masse* MASS] —**a'masser** *n.*
amateur ('æmətə, -tʃə, -ˌtjʊə; ˌæmə'tɜː) *n.* **1.** a person who engages in an activity, esp. a sport, as a pastime rather than professionally or for gain. **2.** an athlete or sportsman. **3.** a person unskilled in or having only a superficial knowledge of a subject or activity. **4.** a person who is fond of or admires something. **5.** (*modifier*) consisting of or for amateurs: *an amateur event.* ~*adj.* **6.** amateurish; not professional or expert: *an amateur approach.* [C18: from French, from Latin *amātor* lover, from *amāre* to love] —**'amateurism** *n.*
amateurish ('æmətərɪʃ, -tʃər-, -ˌtʃʊər-; ˌæmə'tɜːrɪʃ) *adj.* lacking professional skill or expertise. —**'amateurishly** *adv.* —**'amateurishness** *n.*
Amati (ə'mɑːtɪ) *n.* (*pl.* **Amatis**) a violin or other stringed instrument made by any member of the Amati family of Cremona, N Italy, in the 16th and 17th centuries.
amative ('æmətɪv) *adj.* a rare word for **amorous.** [C17: from Medieval Latin *amātīvus,* from Latin *amāre* to love] —**'amatively** *adv.* —**'amativeness** *n.*
amatol ('æməˌtɒl) *n.* an explosive mixture of ammonium nitrate and TNT, used in shells and bombs. [C20: from AM(MONIUM) + (TRINITRO) TOL(UENE)]
amatory ('æmətərɪ) *or* **amatorial** (ˌæmə'tɔːrɪəl) *adj.* of, relating to, or inciting sexual love or desire. [C16: from Latin *amātōrius,* from *amāre* to love]
amaurosis (ˌæmɔː'rəʊsɪs) *n. Pathol.* blindness, esp. when occurring without observable damage to the eye. [C17: via New Latin from Greek: darkening, from *amauroun* to dim, darken] —**amaurotic** (ˌæmɔː'rɒtɪk) *adj.*
amaut *or* **amowt** (ə'maʊt) *n. Canadian.* a hood on an Eskimo woman's parka for carrying a child. [from Eskimo]
amaze (ə'meɪz) *vb.* (*tr.*) **1.** to fill with incredulity or surprise; astonish. **2.** an obsolete word for **bewilder.** ~*n.* **3.** an archaic word for **amazement.** [Old English *āmasian*]
amazement (ə'meɪzmənt) *n.* **1.** incredulity or great astonishment; complete wonder or surprise. **2.** *Obsolete.* bewilderment or consternation.
amazing (ə'meɪzɪŋ) *adj.* causing wonder or astonishment: *amazing feats.* —**a'mazingly** *adv.*
amazon ('æməzᵊn) *n.* any of various tropical American parrots of the genus *Amazona,* such as *A. farinosa* (green amazon), having a short tail and mainly green plumage.
Amazon ('æməzᵊn) *n.* **1.** *Greek myth.* one of a race of women warriors of Scythia near the Black Sea. **2.** one of a legendary tribe of female warriors of South America. **3.** (*often not cap.*) any tall, strong, or aggressive woman. [C14: via Latin from Greek *Amazōn,* of uncertain origin]

Amazonian (ˌæməˈzəʊnɪən) *adj.* 1. of or relating to the river Amazon: *Amazonian rainforest.* 2. of, denoting, or characteristic of an Amazon warrior.

amazon ant *n.* any of several small reddish ants of the genus *Polyergus,* esp. *P. rufescens,* that enslave the young of other ant species.

amazonite (ˈæməzəˌnaɪt) *n.* a green variety of microcline used as a gemstone. Formula: $KAlSi_3O_8$. Also called: **Amazon stone.**

ambage (ˈæmbɪdʒ) *n., pl.* **ambages** (ˈæmbɪdʒɪz, æmˈbeɪdʒiːz). *Archaic.* (*often pl.*) circuitous, secret, or tortuous paths, ways, thoughts, etc. [C14: via Old French from Latin *ambāges* a going around, from *ambi-* around + *agere* to lead] —**ambagious** (æmˈbeɪdʒəs) *adj.*

ambary *or* **ambari** (æmˈbɑːrɪ) *n., pl.* **-ries** *or* **-ris.** 1. a tropical Asian malvaceous plant, *Hibiscus cannabinus,* that yields a fibre similar to jute. 2. the fibre derived from this plant. ~Also called: **kenaf.** [C20: from Hindi *ambārī*]

ambassador (æmˈbæsədə) *n.* 1. short for **ambassador extraordinary and plenipotentiary;** a diplomatic minister of the highest rank, accredited as permanent representative to another country or sovereign. 2. **ambassador extraordinary.** a diplomatic minister of the highest rank sent on a special mission. 3. **ambassador plenipotentiary.** a diplomatic minister of the first rank with treaty-signing powers. 4. **ambassador-at-large.** *U.S.* an ambassador with special duties who may be sent to more than one government. 5. an authorized representative or messenger. [C14: from Old French *ambassadeur,* from Italian *ambasciator,* from Old Provençal *ambaisador,* from *ambaisa* (unattested) mission, errand; see EMBASSY] —**amˈbassadress** *fem. n.* —**ambassadorial** (æmˌbæsəˈdɔːrɪəl) *adj.* —**amˈbassadorˌship** *n.*

ambatch *or* **ambach** (ˈæmˌbætʃ) *n.* a tree or shrub of the Nile Valley, *Aeschynomene elaphroxylon,* valued for its light-coloured pithlike wood. [C19: probably from the Ethiopian name]

amber (ˈæmbə) *n.* 1. **a.** a yellow or yellowish-brown hard translucent fossil resin derived from extinct coniferous trees that occurs in Tertiary deposits and often contains trapped insects. It is used for jewellery, ornaments, etc. **b.** (*as modifier*): *an amber necklace.* 2. **fly in amber.** a strange relic or reminder of the past. 3. **a.** a medium to dark brownish-yellow colour, often somewhat orange, similar to that of the resin. **b.** (*as adj.*): *an amber dress.* 4. an amber traffic light used as a warning between red and green. [C14: from Medieval Latin *ambar,* from Arabic *ʽanbar* ambergris]

amber fluid *n. Austral. slang.* beer.

amber gambler *n. Brit. informal.* a driver who races through traffic lights when they are at amber.

ambergris (ˈæmbəˌgriːs, -grɪs) *n.* a waxy substance consisting mainly of cholesterol secreted by the intestinal tract of the sperm whale and often found floating in the sea: used in the manufacture of perfumes. [C15: from Old French *ambre gris* grey amber]

amberjack (ˈæmbəˌdʒæk) *n.* any of several large carangid fishes of the genus *Seriola,* esp. *S. dumerili,* with golden markings when young, occurring in tropical and subtropical Atlantic waters. [C19: from AMBER + JACK[1]]

amberoid (ˈæmbəˌrɔɪd) *or* **ambroid** *n.* a synthetic amber made by compressing pieces of amber and other resins together at a high temperature.

ambi- *combining form.* indicating both: *ambidextrous; ambivalence; ambiversion.* [from Latin: round, on both sides, both, from *ambo* both; compare AMPHI-]

ambidentate (ˌæmbɪˈdenteɪt) *adj. Chem.* another word for **amphidentate.**

ambidextrous (ˌæmbɪˈdɛkstrəs) *adj.* 1. equally expert with each hand. 2. *Informal.* highly skilled or adept. 3. underhanded; deceitful. —**ambidexterity** (ˌæmbɪdɛkˈstɛrɪtɪ) *or* ˌ**ambiˈdextrousness** *n.* —ˌ**ambiˈdextrously** *adv.*

ambience *or* **ambiance** (ˈæmbɪəns; *French* ɑ̃bjɑ̃s) *n.* the atmosphere of a place. [C19: from French *ambiance,* from *ambiant* surrounding; see AMBIENT]

ambient (ˈæmbɪənt) *adj.* of or relating to the immediate surroundings: *the ambient temperature was 15°C.* [C16: from Latin *ambiēns* going round, from *ambīre,* from AMBI- + *īre* to go]

ambient noise *n.* the level of the total noise in an area.

ambiguity (ˌæmbɪˈgjuːɪtɪ) *n., pl.* **-ties.** 1. the possibility of interpreting an expression in two or more distinct ways. 2. an instance of this, as in the sentence *they are cooking apples.* 3. vagueness or uncertainty of meaning: *there are several ambiguities in the situation.*

ambiguous (æmˈbɪgjʊəs) *adj.* 1. having more than one possible interpretation or meaning. 2. difficult to understand or classify; obscure. [C16: from Latin *ambiguus* going here and there, uncertain, from *ambigere* to go around, from AMBI- + *agere* to lead, act] —**amˈbiguously** *adv.* —**amˈbiguousness** *n.*

ambiophony (ˌæmbɪˈɒfənɪ) *n.* the reproduction of sound to create an illusion to a listener of being in a spacious room, such as a concert hall.

ambipolar (ˌæmbɪˈpəʊlə) *adj. Electronics.* (of plasmas and semiconductors) involving both positive and negative charge carriers.

ambisexual (ˌæmbɪˈsɛksjʊəl) *or* **ambosexual** *adj. Biology.* relating to or affecting both the male and female sexes.

ambisonics (ˌæmbɪˈsɒnɪks) *n.* (*functioning as sing.*) the technique of reproducing and transmitting surround sound. See **surround sound.**

ambit (ˈæmbɪt) *n.* 1. scope or extent. 2. limits, boundary, or circumference. [C16: from Latin *ambitus* a going round, from *ambīre* to go round, from AMBI- + *īre* to go]

ambition (æmˈbɪʃən) *n.* 1. strong desire for success, achievement, or distinction. 2. something so desired; goal; aim. [C14: from Old French, from Latin *ambitiō* a going round (of candidates), a striving to please, from *ambīre* to go round; see AMBIT]

ambitious (æmˈbɪʃəs) *adj.* 1. having a strong desire for success or achievement; wanting power, money, etc. 2. necessitating extraordinary effort or ability: *an ambitious project.* 3. (often foll. by *of*) having a great desire (for something or to do something). —**amˈbitiously** *adv.* —**amˈbitiousness** *n.*

ambivalence (æmˈbɪvələns) *or* **ambivalency** *n.* the simultaneous existence of two opposed and conflicting attitudes, emotions, etc. —**amˈbivalent** *adj.*

ambivert (ˈæmbɪˌvɜːt) *n. Psychol.* a person who is intermediate between an extrovert and an introvert. —**ambiversion** (ˌæmbɪˈvɜːʃən) *n.*

amble (ˈæmbᵊl) *vb.* (*intr.*) 1. to walk at a leisurely relaxed pace. 2. (of a horse) to move slowly, lifting both legs on one side together. 3. to ride a horse at an amble or leisurely pace. ~*n.* 4. a leisurely motion in walking. 5. a leisurely walk. 6. the ambling gait of a horse. [C14: from Old French *ambler,* from Latin *ambulāre* to walk] —ˈ**ambler** *n.*

amblygonite (æmˈblɪgəˌnaɪt) *n.* a white or greyish mineral consisting of lithium aluminium fluophosphate in triclinic crystalline form. It is a source of lithium. Formula: $LiAl(PO_4)(F,OH)$. [C16: from Greek *amblugōnios,* from *amblus* blunt + *gōnia* angle; referring to the obtuse angles in its crystals]

amblyopia (ˌæmblɪˈəʊpɪə) *n.* impaired vision with no discernible damage to the eye or optic nerve. [C18: New Latin, from Greek *ambluōpia,* from *amblus* dull, dim + *ōps* eye] —**amblyopic** (ˌæmblɪˈɒpɪk) *adj.*

ambo (ˈæmbəʊ) *n., pl.* **ambos** *or* **ambones** (æmˈbəʊniːz). either of two raised pulpits from which the gospels and epistles were read in early Christian churches. [C17: from Medieval Latin, from Greek *ambōn* raised rim, pulpit]

amboceptor (ˈæmbəʊˌsɛptə) *n.* an immune body formed in the blood during infection or immunization that serves to link the complement to the antigen. [C20: from Latin *ambō* both (see AMBI-) + (RE)CEPTOR]

amboyna *or* **amboina** (æmˈbɔɪnə) *n.* the mottled curly-grained wood of an Indonesian papilionaceous tree, *Pterocarpus indicus,* used in making furniture. [C19: from the island of *Amboina* in Indonesia]

ambroid (ˈæmbrɔɪd) *n.* a variant of **amberoid.**

ambrosia (æmˈbrəʊzɪə) *n.* 1. *Classical myth.* the food of the gods, said to bestow immortality. Compare **nectar** (sense 2). 2. anything particularly delightful to taste or smell. 3. another name for **beebread.** 4. any of various herbaceous plants constituting the genus *Ambrosia,* mostly native to America but widely naturalized: family *Compositae* (composites). The genus includes the ragweeds. [C16: via Latin from Greek: immortality, from *ambrotos,* from A-[1] + *brotos* mortal] —**amˈbrosial** *or* **amˈbrosian** *adj.* —**amˈbrosially** *adv.*

ambrosia beetle *n.* any of various small beetles of the genera *Anisandrus, Xyleborus,* etc., that bore tunnels into solid wood, feeding on fungi growing in the tunnels: family *Scolytidae* (bark beetles).

ambrotype (ˈæmbrəʊˌtaɪp) *n. Photog.* an early type of glass negative that could be made to appear as a positive by backing it with black varnish or paper. [C19: from Greek *ambrotos* immortal + -TYPE; see AMBROSIA]

ambry (ˈæmbrɪ) *or* **aumbry** (ˈɔːmbrɪ) *n., pl.* **-bries.** 1. a recessed cupboard in the wall of a church near the altar, used to store sacred vessels, etc. 2. *Obsolete.* a small cupboard or other storage space. [C14: from Old French *almarie,* from Medieval Latin *almārium,* from Latin *armārium* chest for storage, from *arma* arms]

ambsace *or* **amesace** (ˈeɪmzˌeɪs, ˈæmz-) *n.* 1. double ace, the lowest throw at dice. 2. bad luck. [C13: from Old French *ambes as,* both aces; *as* from Latin: unit]

ambulacrum (ˌæmbjʊˈleɪkrəm) *n., pl.* **-ra** (-rə). any of five radial bands on the ventral surface of echinoderms, such as the starfish and sea urchin, on which the tube feet are situated. [C19: from Latin: avenue, from *ambulāre* to walk] —ˌ**ambuˈlacral** *adj.*

ambulance (ˈæmbjʊləns) *n.* a motor vehicle designed to carry sick or injured people. [C19: from French, based on (*hôpital*) *ambulant* mobile or field (hospital), from Latin *ambulāre* to walk]

ambulance chaser *n. U.S. slang.* a lawyer who seeks to encourage and profit from the lawsuits of accident victims. —**ambulance chasing** *n.*

ambulance stocks *pl. n.* high performance stocks and shares recommended by a broker to a dissatisfied client to improve their relationship.

ambulant (ˈæmbjʊlənt) *adj.* 1. moving about from place to place. 2. *Med.* another word for **ambulatory** (sense 3).

ambulate (ˈæmbjʊˌleɪt) *vb.* (*intr.*) to wander about or move from one place to another. [C17: from Latin *ambulāre* to walk, AMBLE] —ˌ**ambuˈlation** *n.*

ambulatory ('æmbjulətərɪ) *adj.* **1.** of, relating to, or designed for walking. **2.** changing position; not fixed. **3.** Also: **ambulant.** able to walk. **4.** *Law.* (esp. of a will) capable of being altered or revoked. ~*n., pl.* **-ries. 5.** *Architect.* **a.** an aisle running around the east end of a church, esp. one that passes behind the sanctuary. **b.** a place for walking, such as an aisle or a cloister.

ambuscade (ˌæmbə'skeɪd) *n.* **1.** an ambush. ~*vb.* **2.** to ambush or lie in ambush. [C16: from French *embuscade,* from Old Italian *imboscata,* probably of Germanic origin; compare AMBUSH]

ambush ('æmbuʃ) *n.* **1.** the act of waiting in a concealed position in order to launch a surprise attack. **2.** a surprise attack from such a position. **3.** the concealed position from which such an attack is launched. **4.** the person or persons waiting to launch such an attack. ~*vb.* **5.** to lie in wait (for). **6.** (*tr.*) to attack suddenly from a concealed position. [C14: from Old French *embuschier* to position in ambush, from *em-* IM- + *-buschier,* from *busche* piece of firewood, probably of Germanic origin; see BUSH[1]]

AMDG *abbrev. for* ad majorem Dei gloriam (the Jesuit motto). [Latin: to the greater glory of God]

ameba (ə'miːbə) *n., pl.* **-bae** (-biː) *or* **-bas.** the usual U.S. spelling of **amoeba.** —**a'mebic** *adj.*

ameer (ə'mɪə) *n.* **1.** a variant spelling of **emir. 2.** (formerly) the ruler of Afghanistan; amir.

ameiosis (ˌeɪmaɪ'əusɪs) *n.* *Biology.* the nonpairing of chromosomes during meiosis.

amelia (ə'miːlɪə) *n.* *Pathol.* the congenital absence of arms or legs. [from A-[1] + Greek *melos* limb + -IA]

ameliorate (ə'miːljəˌreɪt) *vb.* to make or become better; improve. [C18: from MELIORATE, influenced by French *améliorer* to improve, from Old French *ameillorer* to make better, from *meillor* better, from Latin *melior*] —**ameliorable** (ə'miːljərəbᵊl) *adj.* —**a'meliorant** *n.* —**a'meliorative** *adj.* —**a'melioˌrator** *n.*

amelioration (əˌmiːljə'reɪʃən) *n.* **1.** the act or an instance of ameliorating or the state of being ameliorated. **2.** something that ameliorates; an improvement. **3.** Also called: **elevation.** *Linguistics.* (of the meaning of a word) a change from pejorative to neutral or positively pleasant. The word *nice* has achieved its modern meaning by amelioration from the earlier sense *foolish, silly.*

ameloblast (ə'miːləublæst, -blɑːst) *n.* a type of cell involved in forming dental enamel. [C19: from (EN)AMEL + -O- + -BLAST]

amelogenesis (əˌmiːləu'dʒɛnɪsɪs) *n.* the production of enamel by ameloblasts.

amen (ˌeɪ'mɛn, ˌɑː'mɛn) *interj.* **1.** so be it!: a term used at the end of a prayer or religious statement. ~*n.* **2.** the use of the word *amen,* as at the end of a prayer. **3. say amen to.** to express strong approval of or support for (an assertion, hope, etc.). [C13: via Late Latin via Greek from Hebrew *āmēn* certainly]

amenable (ə'miːnəbᵊl) *adj.* **1.** open or susceptible to suggestion; likely to listen, cooperate, etc. **2.** accountable for behaviour to some authority; answerable. **3.** capable of being or liable to be tested, judged, etc. [C16: from Anglo-French, from Old French *amener* to lead up, from Latin *mināre* to drive (cattle), from *minārī* to threaten] —**aˌmena'bility** *or* **a'menableness** *n.* —**a'menably** *adv.*

amen corner *n.* **the.** *U.S.* the part of a church, usually to one side of the pulpit, occupied by people who lead the responsive amens during the service.

amend (ə'mɛnd) *vb.* (*tr.*) **1.** to improve; change for the better. **2.** to remove faults from; correct. **3.** to alter or revise (legislation, a constitution, etc.) by formal procedure. [C13: from Old French *amender,* from Latin *ēmendāre* to EMEND] —**a'mendable** *adj.* —**a'mender** *n.*

amendatory (ə'mɛndətərɪ, -trɪ) *adj.* *U.S.* serving to amend; corrective.

amende honorable *French.* (amɑ̃d ɔnɔrablə) *n., pl.* ***amendes honorables*** (amɑ̃d ɔnɔrablə). a public apology and reparation made to satisfy the honour of the person wronged. Sometimes shortened to ***amende.*** [C18: literally: honourable compensation]

amendment (ə'mɛndmənt) *n.* **1.** the act of amending; correction. **2.** an addition, alteration, or improvement to a motion, document, etc.

amends (ə'mɛndz) *n.* (*functioning as sing.*) recompense or compensation given or gained for some injury, insult, etc.: *to make amends.* [C13: from Old French *amendes* fines, from *amende* compensation, from *amender* to EMEND]

amenity (ə'miːnɪtɪ) *n., pl.* **-ties. 1.** (*often pl.*) a useful or pleasant facility or service: *a swimming pool was just one of the amenities.* **2.** the fact or condition of being pleasant or agreeable. **3.** (*usually pl.*) a social courtesy or pleasantry. [C14: from Latin *amoenitās* pleasantness, from *amoenus* agreeable]

amenity bed *n.* (in Britain) a hospital bed whose occupant receives free treatment but pays for nonmedical advantages, such as privacy. Also called (informal): **pay bed.**

amenorrhoea *or esp. U.S.* **amenorrhea** (æˌmɛnə'rɪə, eɪ-) *n.* abnormal absence of menstruation. [C19: from A-[1] + MENO- + -RRHOEA]

a mensa et thoro (eɪ 'mɛnsə ɛt 'θɔːrəu) *adj.* *Law.* denoting or relating to a form of divorce in which the parties remain married but do not cohabit: abolished in England in 1857. [Latin: from table and bed]

ament[1] ('æmənt, 'eɪmənt) *n.* another name for **catkin.** Also called: **amentum** (ə'mɛntəm). [C18: from Latin *āmentum* strap, thong] —ˌ**amen'taceous** *adj.* —ˌ**amen'tiferous** *adj.*

ament[2] (æ'mɛnt, 'eɪmənt) *n.* *Psychiatry.* a mentally deficient person. [C19: from Latin *āment-, āmens* without mind; see AMENTIA]

amentia (ə'mɛnʃə) *n.* severe mental deficiency, usually congenital. Compare **dementia.** [C14: from Latin: insanity, from *āmēns* mad, from *mēns* mind]

Amer. *abbrev. for* America(n).

amerce (ə'mɜːs) *vb.* (*tr.*) *Obsolete.* **1.** *Law.* to punish by a fine. **2.** to punish with any arbitrary penalty. [C14: from Anglo-French *amercier,* from Old French *à merci* at the mercy (because the fine was arbitrarily fixed); see MERCY] —**a'merceable** *adj.* —**a'mercement** *n.* —**a'mercer** *n.*

American (ə'mɛrɪkən) *adj.* **1.** of or relating to the United States of America, its inhabitants, or their form of English. **2.** of or relating to the American continent. **3.** *Rare.* of or relating to the American Indians. ~*n.* **4.** a native or citizen of the U.S. **5.** a native or inhabitant of any country of North, Central, or South America. **6.** the English language as spoken or written in the United States. [C16: from *America,* from *Americus* Vespucius, Latin form of *Amerigo* Vespucci (?1454–1512), Florentine navigator after whom the continent was named]

Americana (əˌmɛrɪ'kɑːnə) *n.* objects, such as books, documents, relics, etc., relating to America, esp. in the form of a collection.

American aloe *n.* another name for **century plant.**

American chameleon *n.* another name for **anole.**

American cheese *n.* a type of smooth hard white or yellow cheese similar to a mild Cheddar.

American cloth *n.* a glazed or waterproofed cotton cloth.

American Dream *n.* **the.** the notion that the American social, economic, and political system makes success possible for every individual.

American eagle *n.* another name for **bald eagle,** esp. when depicted as the national emblem of the U.S.

American Expeditionary Forces *pl. n.* the troops sent to Europe by the U.S. during World War I.

American Federation of Labor *n.* the first permanent national labour movement in America, founded in 1886. It amalgamated with the Congress of Industrial Organizations in 1955. See also **AFL-CIO.**

American football *n.* **1.** a team game similar to rugby, with 11 players on each side. Forward passing is allowed and planned strategies and formations for play are decided during the course of the game. **2.** the oval-shaped inflated ball used in this game.

American Indian *n.* **1.** Also called: **Indian, Red Indian, Amerindian.** a member of any of the indigenous peoples of North, Central, or South America, having Mongoloid affinities, notably straight black hair and a yellow to brown skin. ~*adj.* **2.** Also: **Amerindian.** of or relating to any of these peoples, their languages, or their cultures.

American Indian Movement *n.* a militant movement or grouping of American Indians, organized in 1968 to combat discrimination, injustice, etc.

Americanism (ə'mɛrɪkəˌnɪzəm) *n.* **1.** a custom, linguistic usage, or other feature peculiar to or characteristic of the United States, its people, or their culture. **2.** loyalty to the United States, its people, customs, etc.

Americanist (ə'mɛrɪkənɪst) *n.* a person who studies some aspect of America, such as its history or languages.

Americanize *or* **Americanise** (ə'mɛrɪkəˌnaɪz) *vb.* to make or become American in outlook, attitudes, etc. —**Aˌmericani'zation** *or* **Aˌmericani'sation** *n.* —**A'mericanˌizer** *or* **A'mericanˌiser** *n.*

American pit bull terrier *n.* another name for **pit bull terrier.**

American plan *n.* *U.S.* a hotel rate in which the charge includes meals. Compare **European plan.**

American Revolution *n.* the usual U.S. term for **War of American Independence.**

American sign language *n.* See **Ameslan.**

American Standard Version *n.* a revised version of the Authorized (King James) Version of the Bible, published by a committee of American scholars in 1901.

American trypanosomiasis *n.* *Pathol.* another name for **Chagas' disease.**

American Wake *n.* *Irish.* an all-night farewell party for a person about to emigrate to America.

America's Cup *n.* an international yachting trophy, first won by the schooner *America* in 1851 and held as a challenge trophy by the New York Yacht Club until 1983.

americium (ˌæmə'rɪsɪəm) *n.* a white metallic transuranic element artificially produced from plutonium. It is used as an alpha-particle source. Symbol: Am; atomic no.: 95; half-life of most stable isotope, ^{243}Am: 7.4×10^3 years; valency: 3,4,5, or 6; relative density: 13.67; melting pt.: 995°C; boiling pt.: 2607°C (est.). [C20: from *America* (because it was discovered at Berkeley, California) + -IUM]

Amerindian (ˌæmə'rɪndɪən) *n. also* **Amerind** ('æmərɪnd), *adj.* another word for **American Indian.** —ˌ**Amer'indic** *adj.*

amesace ('eɪmzˌeɪs, 'æmz-) *n.* a variant spelling of **ambsace.**

Ameslan ('æməs,læn) *n.* American sign language: a communications system in which meaning is conveyed by hand gestures and their position in relation to the upper part of the body. Abbrev.: **ASL.** [C20: from *Ame(rican) s(ign) lan(guage)*]
Ames test (eɪmz) *n.* a method of preliminary screening for carcinogens, based on their ability to cause mutations in bacteria. [named after Bruce *Ames* (born 1928), U.S. biochemist who invented the test]
ametabolic (ə,mɛtə'bɒlɪk) *adj.* (of certain insects) having no obvious metamorphosis.
amethyst ('æmɪθɪst) *n.* **1.** a purple or violet transparent variety of quartz used as a gemstone. Formula: SiO_2. **2.** a purple variety of sapphire; oriental amethyst. **3.** the purple colour of amethyst. [C13: from Old French *amatiste,* from Latin *amethystus,* from Greek *amethustos,* literally: not drunken, from A-[1] + *methuein* to make drunk; referring to the belief that the stone could prevent intoxication] —**amethystine** (,æmɪ'θɪstaɪn) *adj.*
ametropia (,æmɪ'trəʊpɪə) *n.* loss of ability to focus images on the retina, caused by an imperfection in the refractive function of the eye. [C19: New Latin, from Greek *ametros* unmeasured (from A-[1] + *metron* measure) + *ōps* eye]
AMF *abbrev. for* Australian Military Forces.
Amharic (æm'hærɪk) *n.* **1.** the official language of Ethiopia, belonging to the SE Semitic subfamily of the Afro-Asiatic family. ~*adj.* **2.** denoting or relating to this language.
ami French. (ami) *n.* a male friend.
amiable ('eɪmɪəbᵊl) *adj.* having or displaying a pleasant or agreeable nature; friendly. [C14: from Old French, from Late Latin *amīcābilis* AMICABLE] —,**amia'bility** *or* '**amiableness** *n.* —'**amiably** *adv.*
amianthus (,æmɪ'ænθəs) *n.* any of the fine silky varieties of asbestos. [C17: from Latin *amiantus,* from Greek *amiantos* unsullied, from A-[1] + *miainein* to pollute] —,**ami'anthine,** ,**ami'anthoid,** *or* ,**amian'thoidal** *adj.*
amicable ('æmɪkəbᵊl) *adj.* characterized by friendliness: *an amicable agreement.* [C15: from Late Latin *amīcābilis,* from Latin *amīcus* friend; related to *amāre* to love] —,**amica'bility** *or* '**amicableness** *n.* —'**amicably** *adv.*
amice[1] ('æmɪs) *n. Christianity.* a rectangular piece of white linen worn by priests around the neck and shoulders under the alb or, formerly, on the head. [C15: from Old French *amis,* plural of *amit,* or from Medieval Latin *amicia,* both from Latin *amictus* cloak, from *amicīre* to clothe, from *am-* AMBI- + *iacere* to throw]
amice[2] ('æmɪs) *n.* another word for **almuce.**
AMICE *abbrev. for* Associate Member of the Institution of Civil Engineers.
AMIChemE *abbrev. for* Associate Member of the Institution of Chemical Engineers.
amicus curiae (æ'miːkʊs 'kjʊərɪ,iː) *n., pl.* **amici curiae** (æ'miːkaɪ) *Law.* a person not directly engaged in a case who advises the court. [Latin, literally: friend of the court]
amid (ə'mɪd) *or* **amidst** *prep.* in the middle of; among. [Old English *on middan* in the middle; see MID[1]]
Amidah (ami'daː, a'midə) *n. Judaism.* the central prayer in each of the daily services, recited silently and standing. Also called: **Shemona Esrei.**
amide ('æmaɪd) *n.* **1.** any organic compound containing the group -$CONH_2$. **2.** (*modifier*) consisting of, containing, or concerned with the group -$CONH_2$: *amide group or radical.* **3.** an inorganic compound having the general formula $M(NH_2)_x$, where M is a metal atom. [C19: from AM(MONIA) + -IDE] —**amidic** (ə'mɪdɪk) *adj.*
amido- *combining form.* (in chemistry) indicating the presence of an amide group. [from AMIDE]
Amidol ('æmɪdɒl) *n. Trademark.* a grey to colourless soluble crystalline solid that is used as a photographic developer; 2,4-diaminophenol dihydrochloride. Formula: $C_6H_3(NH_2)_2(OH).2HCl$.
amidships (ə'mɪdʃɪps) *adv., adj.* (*postpositive*) *Nautical.* at, near, or towards the centre of a vessel.
amie French. (ami) *n.* a female friend.
AMIEE (in Britain) *abbrev. for* Associate Member of the Institution of Electrical Engineers.
amigo (æ'miːgəʊ, ə-) *n., pl.* **-gos.** a friend; comrade. [Spanish, from Latin *amicus*]
AMIMechE (in Britain) *abbrev. for* Associate Member of the Institution of Mechanical Engineers.
amine (ə'miːn, 'æmɪn) *n.* an organic base formed by replacing one or more of the hydrogen atoms of ammonia by organic groups. [C19: from AM(MONIUM) + -INE[2]]
-amine *n. combining form.* indicating an amine: *histamine; methylamine.*
amino (ə'maɪnəʊ, -'miː-) *n.* (*modifier*) of, consisting of, or containing the group of atoms -NH_2: *amino group or radical; amino acid.*
amino- *combining form.* indicating the presence of an amino group: *aminobenzoic acid.* [from AMINE]
amino acid *n.* any of a group of organic compounds containing one or more amino groups, -NH_2, and one or more carboxyl groups, -COOH. The alpha-amino acids $RCH(NH_2)COOH$ (where R is either hydrogen or an organic group) are the component molecules of proteins; some can be synthesized in the body (**nonessential amino acids**) and others cannot and are thus essential components of the diet (**essential amino acids**).
amino acid sequence *n.* the unique sequence of amino acids that characterizes a given protein.
aminobenzoic acid (ə,maɪnəʊbɛn'zəʊɪk, -,miː-) *n.* a derivative of benzoic acid existing in three isomeric forms, the *para-* form being used in the manufacture of dyes and sunburn preventatives. Formula: $NH_2C_6H_4COOH$.
aminophenol (ə,maɪnəʊ'fiːnɒl, -,miː-) *n. Chem.* any of three isomeric forms that are white soluble crystalline solids, used as a dye intermediate (meta- and ortho-), in dyeing hair, fur, and textiles (ortho- and para-), and as a photographic developer (para-). Formula: $C_6H_4NH_2OH$.
aminopyrine (ə,maɪnəʊ'paɪriːn, -,miː-) *n.* a crystalline compound used to reduce pain and fever. Formula: $C_{13}H_{17}N_3O$.
amino resin *n.* any thermosetting synthetic resin formed by copolymerization of amines with aldehydes. Amino resins are used as adhesives and as coatings for paper and textiles. See also **urea-formaldehyde resin, melamine.**
amir (ə'mɪə) *n.* **1.** a variant spelling of **emir. 2.** (formerly) the ruler of Afghanistan; ameer. [C19: from Arabic, variant of EMIR] —**a'mirate** *n.*
Amish ('ɑːmɪʃ, 'æ-) *adj.* **1.** of or relating to a U.S. and Canadian Mennonite sect that traces its origin to Jakob Amman. ~*n.* **2.** **the.** the Amish people. [C19: from German *Amisch,* after Jakob *Amman,* 17th-century Swiss Mennonite bishop]
amiss (ə'mɪs) *adv.* **1.** in an incorrect, inappropriate, or defective manner. **2. take (something) amiss.** to be annoyed or offended by (something). ~*adj.* **3.** (*postpositive*) wrong, incorrect, or faulty. [C13 *a mis,* from *mis* wrong; see MISS[1]]
amitosis (,æmɪ'təʊsɪs) *n.* an unusual form of cell division in which the nucleus and cytoplasm divide by constriction without the formation of chromosomes; direct cell division. [C19: A[1] + MITOSIS] —**amitotic** (,æmɪ'tɒtɪk) *adj.* —,**ami'totically** *adv.*
amitriptyline (,æmɪ'trɪptɪ,liːn, -lɪn) *n.* a tricyclic antidepressant drug: a mild tranquillizer. Formula: $C_{20}H_{23}N$. [C20: from AMINO + TRYPTAMINE + METHYL + -INE[2]]
amity ('æmɪtɪ) *n., pl.* **-ties.** friendship; cordiality. [C15: from Old French *amité,* from Medieval Latin *amīcitās* friendship, from Latin *amīcus* friend]
AMMA (in Britain) *abbrev. for* Assistant Masters' and Mistresses' Association.
ammeter ('æm,miːtə) *n.* an instrument for measuring an electric current in amperes. [C19: AM(PERE) + -METER]
ammine ('æmiːn, ə'miːn) *n.* a compound that has molecules containing one or more ammonia molecules bound to another molecule, group, or atom by coordinate bonds. Also called: **ammoniate, ammonate.** [C19: from AMM(ONIA) + -INE[2]]
ammo ('æməʊ) *n. Informal.* short for **ammunition.**
ammocoete ('æmə,siːt) *n.* the larva of primitive jawless vertebrates, such as the lamprey, that lives buried in mud and feeds on microorganisms. [C19: from New Latin *ammocoetēs,* literally: that lie in sand, from Greek *ammos* sand + *koitē* bed, from *keisthai* to lie]
ammonal ('æmənᵊl) *n.* an explosive made by mixing TNT, ammonium nitrate, and aluminium powder. [C20: from AMMON(IUM) + AL(UMINIUM)]
ammonate ('æmə,neɪt) *n.* another name for **ammine.**
ammonia (ə'məʊnɪə, -njə) *n.* **1.** a colourless pungent highly soluble gas mainly used in the manufacture of fertilizers, nitric acid, and other nitrogenous compounds, and as a refrigerant and solvent. Formula: NH_3. **2.** a solution of ammonia in water, containing the compound ammonium hydroxide. [C18: from New Latin, from Latin *(sal) ammōniacus* (sal) AMMONIAC]
ammoniac[1] (ə'məʊnɪ,æk) *adj.* a variant of **ammoniacal.**
ammoniac[2] (ə'məʊnɪ,æk) *n.* a strong-smelling gum resin obtained from the stems of the N Asian umbelliferous plant *Dorema ammoniacum* and formerly used as an expectorant, stimulant, perfume, and in porcelain cement. Also called: **gum ammoniac.** [C14: from Latin *ammōniacum,* from Greek *ammōniakos* belonging to Ammon (apparently the gum resin was extracted from plants found in Libya near the temple of Ammon)]
ammoniacal (,æmə'naɪəkᵊl) *adj.* of, containing, using, or resembling ammonia. Also: **ammoniac.**
ammonia clock *n.* an atomic clock based on the frequency of inversion of the ammonia molecule.
ammoniate (ə'məʊnɪ,eɪt) *vb.* **1.** to unite or treat with ammonia. ~*n.* **2.** another name for **ammine.** —**am,moni'ation** *n.*
ammonic (ə'mɒnɪk, ə'məʊnɪk) *adj.* of or concerned with ammonia or ammonium compounds. —**am'monical** *adj.*
ammonify (ə'mɒnɪ,faɪ, ə'məʊnɪ-) *vb.* **-fies, -fying, -fied.** to treat or impregnate with ammonia or a compound of ammonia. —**am,monifi'cation** *n.*
ammonite[1] ('æmə,naɪt) *n.* **1.** any extinct marine cephalopod mollusc of the order *Ammonoidea,* which were common in Mesozoic times and had a coiled partitioned shell. Their closest modern relative is the pearly nautilus. **2.** the shell of any of these animals, commonly occurring as a fossil. [C18: from New Latin *Ammōnītēs,* from Medieval Latin *cornū Ammōnis,* literally: horn of Ammon (Jupiter)] —**ammonitic** (,æmə'nɪtɪk) *adj.*
ammonite[2] ('æmə,naɪt) *n.* **1.** an explosive consisting mainly of ammonium nitrate with smaller amounts of other substances,

such as TNT. **2.** a nitrogenous fertilizer made from animal wastes. [C20: from AMMO(NIUM) + NI(TRA)TE]

Ammonites ('æməˌnaɪts) *pl. n. Old Testament.* a nomadic tribe living east of the Jordan: a persistent enemy of the Israelites.

ammonium (ə'məʊnɪəm, -njəm) *n.* (*modifier*) of, consisting of, or containing the monovalent group NH_4^- or the ion NH_4^+: *ammonium compounds.*

ammonium carbamate *n.* a white soluble crystalline compound produced by reaction between dry ammonia and carbon dioxide and used as a nitrogen fertilizer. Formula: $(NH_4)CO_2NH_2$.

ammonium carbonate *n.* **1.** an unstable pungent soluble white powder that is a double salt of ammonium bicarbonate and ammonium carbamate: used in the manufacture of baking powder, smelling salts, and ammonium compounds. Formula: $(NH_4)HCO_3.(NH_4)CO_2NH_2$. **2.** an unstable substance that is produced by treating this compound with ammonia. Formula: $(NH_4)_2CO_3$.

ammonium chloride *n.* a white soluble crystalline solid used chiefly as an electrolyte in dry batteries and as a mordant and soldering flux. Formula: NH_4Cl. Also called: **sal ammoniac.**

ammonium hydroxide *n.* a compound existing only in aqueous solution, formed when ammonia dissolves in water to form ammonium ions and hydroxide ions. Formula: NH_4OH.

ammonium ion *n.* the ion NH_4^+, formed from ammonia and present in aqueous solutions of ammonia and in many salts.

ammonium nitrate *n.* a colourless highly soluble crystalline solid used mainly as a fertilizer and in explosives and pyrotechnics. Formula: NH_4NO_3.

ammonium sulphate *n.* a white soluble crystalline solid used mainly as a fertilizer and in water purification. Formula: $(NH_4)_2SO_4$.

ammonolysis (ˌæmə'nɒlɪsɪs) *n. Chem.* solvolysis in liquid ammonia.

ammunition (ˌæmjʊ'nɪʃən) *n.* **1.** any projectiles, such as bullets, rockets, etc., that can be discharged from a weapon. **2.** bombs, missiles, chemicals, biological agents, nuclear materials, etc., capable of use as weapons. **3.** any means of defence or attack, as in an argument. [C17: from obsolete French *amunition*, by mistaken division from earlier *la munition;* see MUNITION]

amnesia (æm'niːzjə, -ʒjə, -zɪə) *n.* a defect in memory, esp. one resulting from pathological cause, such as brain damage or hysteria. [C19: via New Latin from Greek: forgetfulness, probably from *amnēstia* oblivion; see AMNESTY] **—amnesiac** (æm'niːzɪˌæk) *or* **amnesic** (æm'niːsɪk, -zɪk) *adj., n.*

amnesty ('æmnɪstɪ) *n., pl.* **-ties.** **1.** a general pardon, esp. for offences against a government. **2.** a period during which a law is suspended to allow offenders to admit their crime without fear of prosecution. **3.** *Law.* a pardon granted by the Crown and effected by statute, effective for a limited period of time. *~vb.* **-ties, -tying, -tied. 4.** (*tr.*) to overlook or forget (an offence). [C16: from Latin *amnēstia*, from Greek: oblivion, from *amnēstos* forgetting, from A-[1] + *-mnēstos*, from *mnasthai* to remember]

Amnesty International *n.* an international organization founded in Britain in 1961 that works to secure the release of people imprisoned for their beliefs, to ban the use of torture, and to abolish the death penalty. Abbrev.: **AI.**

amniocentesis (ˌæmnɪəʊsɛn'tiːsɪs) *n., pl.* **-ses** (-siːz). removal of some amniotic fluid by the insertion into the womb of a hollow needle, for therapeutic or diagnostic purposes. [C20: from AMNION + *centesis*, from Greek *kentēsis* a puncture, from *kentein* to prick]

amnion ('æmnɪən) *n., pl.* **-nions** *or* **-nia** (-nɪə). the innermost of two membranes (see also **chorion**) enclosing an embryonic reptile, bird, or mammal. [C17: via New Latin from Greek: a little lamb, from *amnos* a lamb] **—amniotic** (ˌæmnɪ'ɒtɪk) *adj.*

amniote ('æmnɪəʊt) *n.* any vertebrate animal, such as a reptile, bird, or mammal, that possesses an amnion, chorion, and allantois during embryonic development. Compare **anamniote.**

amniotic fluid *n.* the fluid surrounding the fetus in the womb.

amoeba *or U.S.* **ameba** (ə'miːbə) *n., pl.* **-bae** (-biː) *or* **-bas.** any protozoan of the order *Amoebida*, esp. any of the genus *Amoeba*, able to change shape because of the movements of cell processes (pseudopodia): class *Sarcodina*. They live in fresh water or soil or as parasites in man and animals. [C19: from New Latin, from Greek *amoibē* change, from *ameibein* to change, exchange] **—a'moebic** *or U.S.* **a'mebic** *adj.*

amoebaean *or* **amoebean** (ˌæmɪ'biːən) *adj. Prosody.* of or relating to lines of verse dialogue that answer each other alternately.

amoebiasis (ˌæmɪ'baɪəsɪs) *n., pl.* **-ses** (-ˌsiːz). infection, esp. of the intestines, caused by the parasitic amoeba *Endamoeba histolytica.*

amoebic dysentery *n.* inflammation of the intestines caused by the parasitic amoeba *Endamoeba histolytica.*

amoebocyte *or U.S.* **amebocyte** (ə'miːbəˌsaɪt) *n.* any amoeboid cell found in the blood and body fluids. Some kinds, such as the phagocytic white blood cell, can engulf foreign particles.

amoeboid *or U.S.* **ameboid** (ə'miːbɔɪd) *adj.* of, related to, or resembling amoebae.

amok (ə'mʌk, ə'mɒk) *or* **amuck** (ə'mʌk) *n.* **1.** a state of murderous frenzy, originally observed among Malays. *~adv.* **2. run amok.** to run about with or as if with a frenzied desire to kill. [C17: from Malay *amoq* furious assault]

among (ə'mʌŋ) *or* **amongst** *prep.* **1.** in the midst of: *he lived among the Indians.* **2.** to each of: *divide the reward among yourselves.* **3.** in the group, class, or number of: *ranked among the greatest writers.* **4.** taken out of (a group): *he is only one among many.* **5.** with one another within a group; by the joint action of: *a lot of gossip among the women employees; decide it among yourselves.* [Old English *amang*, contracted from *on gemang* in the group of, from ON + *gemang* crowd; see MINGLE, MONGREL]

▷**Usage.** See at **between.**

amontillado (əˌmɒntɪ'lɑːdəʊ) *n.* a medium dry Spanish sherry, not as pale in colour as a fino. [C19: from Spanish *vino amontillado* wine of *Montilla*, town in Spain]

amoral (eɪ'mɒrəl) *adj.* **1.** having no moral quality; nonmoral. **2.** without moral standards or principles. **—amorality** (ˌeɪmɒ'rælɪtɪ) *n.* **—a'morally** *adv.*

▷**Usage.** *Amoral* is frequently and incorrectly used where *immoral* is meant. In careful usage, however, *immoral* is applied to that which infringes moral rules and *amoral* is only used of that to which considerations of morality are irrelevant or of persons who lack any moral code.

amoretto (ˌæmə'rɛtəʊ) *or* **amorino** (ˌæmɔː'riːnəʊ) *n., pl.* **-retti** (-'rɛtɪ) *or* **-rini** (-'riːnɪ). (esp. in painting) a small chubby naked boy representing a cupid. Also called: **putto.** [C16: from Italian, diminutive of *Amore* Cupid, from Latin *Amor* Love]

amorist ('æmərɪst) *n.* a lover or a writer about love.

amoroso (ˌæmə'rəʊsəʊ) *adj., adv.* **1.** *Music.* (to be played) lovingly. *~n.* **2.** a rich sweetened sherry of a dark colour. [from Italian and Spanish: AMOROUS]

amorous ('æmərəs) *adj.* **1.** inclined towards or displaying love or desire. **2.** in love. **3.** of or relating to love. [C14: from Old French, from Medieval Latin *amōrōsus*, from Latin *amor* love] **—'amorously** *adv.* **—'amorousness** *n.*

amor patriae *Latin.* ('æmɔː 'pætrɪˌiː) *n.* love of one's country; patriotism.

amorphous (ə'mɔːfəs) *adj.* **1.** lacking a definite shape; formless. **2.** of no recognizable character or type. **3.** (of chemicals, rocks, etc.) not having a crystalline structure. [C18: from New Latin, from Greek *amorphos* shapeless, from A-[1] + *morphē* shape] **—a'morphism** *n.* **—a'morphously** *adv.* **—a'morphousness** *n.*

amortization *or* **amortisation** (əˌmɔːtaɪ'zeɪʃən) *n.* **1. a.** the process of amortizing a debt. **b.** the money devoted to amortizing a debt. **2.** (in computing the redemption yield on a bond purchased at a premium) the amount that is subtracted from the annual yield. Compare **accumulation** (sense 3b). **—amortizement** *or* **amortisement** (ə'mɔːtɪzmənt) *n.*

amortize *or* **amortise** (ə'mɔːtaɪz) *vb.* (*tr.*) **1.** *Finance.* to liquidate (a debt, mortgage, etc.) by instalment payments or by periodic transfers to a sinking fund. **2.** to write off (a wasting asset) by annual transfers to a sinking fund. **3.** *Property law.* (formerly) to transfer (lands, etc.) in mortmain. [C14: from Medieval Latin *admortizāre*, from Old French *amortir* to reduce to the point of death, ultimately from Latin *ad* to + *mors* death] **—a'mortizable** *or* **a'mortisable** *adj.*

amount (ə'maʊnt) *n.* **1.** extent; quantity; supply. **2.** the total of two or more quantities; sum. **3.** the full value, effect, or significance of something. **4.** a principal sum plus the interest on it, as in a loan. *~vb.* **5.** (*intr.;* usually foll. by *to*) to be equal or add up in effect, meaning, or quantity. [C13: from Old French *amonter* to go up, from *amont* upwards, from *a* to + *mont* mountain (from Latin *mōns*)]

amount of substance *n.* a measure of the number of entities (atoms, molecules, ions, electrons, etc.) present in a substance, expressed in moles.

amour (ə'mʊə) *n.* a love affair, esp. a secret or illicit one. [C13: from Old French, from Latin *amor* love]

amour-propre *French.* (amurprɔprə) *n.* self-respect.

amowt (ə'maʊt) *n.* a variant spelling of **amaut.**

amp (æmp) *n.* **1.** an ampere. **2.** *Informal.* an amplifier.

AMP *abbrev. for* **1.** adenosine monophosphate. **2.** Australian Mutual Provident Society.

amp. *abbrev. for:* **1.** amperage. **2.** ampere.

ampelopsis (ˌæmpɪ'lɒpsɪs) *n.* any woody vine of the vitaceous genus *Ampelopsis*, of tropical and subtropical Asia and America. [C19: from New Latin, from Greek *ampelos* grapevine]

amperage ('æmpərɪdʒ) *n.* the strength of an electric current measured in amperes, esp. the rated current of an electrical component or device.

ampere ('æmpɛə) *n.* **1.** the basic SI unit of electric current; the constant current that, when maintained in two parallel conductors of infinite length and negligible cross section placed 1 metre apart in free space, produces a force of 2×10^{-7} newton per metre between them. 1 ampere is equivalent to 1 coulomb per second. **2.** a former unit of electric current (**international ampere**); the current that, when passed through a solution of silver nitrate, deposits silver at the rate of 0.001118 gram per second. 1 international ampere equals 0.999835 ampere. ~Abbrev.: **amp.** Symbol: A [C19: named after A. M. *Ampère* (1775–1836), French physicist and mathematician]

ampere-hour *n.* a practical unit of quantity of electricity; the quantity that flows in one hour through a conductor carrying a current of 1 ampere. 1 ampere-hour is equivalent to 3600 coulombs. Abbrev.: **a.h.**

ampere-turn *n.* a unit of magnetomotive force; the magnetomotive force produced by a current of 1 ampere passing through one complete turn of a coil. 1 ampere-turn is equivalent to 4π/10 or 1.257 gilberts. Abbrevs.: **At, A.**

ampersand ('æmpəˌsænd) *n.* the character (&), meaning *and: John Brown & Co.* [C19: shortened from *and per se and,* that is, the symbol & by itself (represents) *and*]

amphetamine (æm'fɛtəˌmiːn, -mɪn) *n.* a synthetic colourless volatile liquid used medicinally as the white crystalline sulphate, mainly for its stimulant action on the central nervous system, although it also stimulates the sympathetic nervous system. It can have unpleasant or dangerous side effects and drug dependence can occur; 1-phenyl-2-aminopropane. Formula: $C_6H_5CH_2CH(NH_2)CH_3$. [C20: from A(LPHA) + M(ETHYL) + PH(ENYL) + ET(HYL) + -AMINE]

amphi- *prefix of nouns and adjectives.* **1.** on both sides; at both ends; of both kinds: *amphipod; amphitrichous; amphibious.* **2.** around: *amphibole.* [from Greek]

amphiarthrosis (ˌæmfɪɑː'θrəʊsɪs) *n., pl.* **-ses** (-siːz). *Anatomy.* a type of articulation permitting only slight movement, as between the vertebrae of the backbone. [C19: from AMPHI- + Greek *arthrōsis* articulation, from *arthron* a joint]

amphiaster ('æmfɪˌæstə) *n. Cytology.* the structure that occurs in a cell undergoing mitosis, consisting of a spindle with an aster at each end. [C19: from AMPHI- + New Latin *aster;* see ASTER]

amphibian (æm'fɪbɪən) *n.* **1.** any cold-blooded vertebrate of the class *Amphibia,* typically living on land but breeding in water. Their aquatic larvae (tadpoles) undergo metamorphosis into the adult form. The class includes the newts and salamanders, frogs and toads, and caecilians. **2.** a type of aircraft able to land and take off from both water and land. **3.** any vehicle able to travel on both water and land. ~*adj.* **4.** another word for **amphibious. 5.** of, relating to, or belonging to the class *Amphibia.*

amphibiotic (ˌæmfɪbaɪ'ɒtɪk) *adj.* having an aquatic larval form and a terrestrial adult form, as amphibians.

amphibious (æm'fɪbɪəs) *adj.* **1.** able to live both on land and in the water, as frogs, toads, etc. **2.** designed for operation on or from both water and land. **3.** relating to military forces and equipment organized for operations launched from the sea against an enemy shore. **4.** having a dual or mixed nature. [C17: from Greek *amphibios,* literally: having a double life, from AMPHI- + *bios* life] —**am'phibiously** *adv.* —**am'phibiousness** *n.*

amphiblastic (ˌæmfɪ'blæstɪk) *adj.* (of animal ova) showing complete but unequal cleavage after fertilization.

amphiblastula (ˌæmfɪ'blæstjʊlə) *n.* the free-swimming larva of certain sponges, which consists of a hollow spherical mass of cells some of which have flagella.

amphibole ('æmfɪˌbəʊl) *n.* any of a large group of minerals consisting of the silicates of calcium, iron, magnesium, sodium, and aluminium, usually in the form of long slender dark-coloured crystals. Members of the group, including hornblende, actinolite, and tremolite, are common constituents of igneous rocks. [C17: from French, from Greek *amphibolos* uncertain; so called from the large number of varieties in the group]

amphibolite (æm'fɪbəˌlaɪt) *n.* a metamorphic rock consisting mainly of amphibole and plagioclase.

amphibology (ˌæmfɪ'bɒlədʒɪ) *or* **amphiboly** (æm'fɪbəlɪ) *n., pl.* **-gies** *or* **-lies.** ambiguity of expression, esp. when due to a grammatical construction, as in *save rags and waste paper.* [C14: from Late Latin *amphibologia,* ultimately from Greek *amphibolos* ambiguous; see AMPHIBOLE, -LOGY] —ˌ**amphi'bolic** *or* **amphibolous** (æm'fɪbələs) *adj.* —**amphibological** (æmˌfɪbə'lɒdʒɪkᵊl) *adj.* —**amˌphibo'logically** *adv.*

amphibrach ('æmfɪˌbræk) *n. Prosody.* a metrical foot consisting of a long syllable between two short syllables (⏑–⏑). Compare **cretic.** [C16: from Latin, from Greek *amphibrakhus,* literally: both ends being short, from AMPHI- + *brakhus* short] —ˌ**amphi'brachic** *adj.*

amphichroic (ˌæmfɪ'krəʊɪk) *or* **amphichromatic** (ˌæmfɪkrəʊ'mætɪk) *adj.* producing two colours, one on reacting with an acid, the other on reacting with a base.

amphicoelous (ˌæmfɪ'siːləs) *adj.* (of the vertebrae of most fishes and some amphibians) concave at the anterior and posterior ends. [C19: from AMPHI- + Greek *koilos* hollow]

amphictyon (æm'fɪktɪən) *n.* a delegate to an amphictyonic council. [C16: back formation from *amphictyons,* from Greek *amphiktiones* neighbours, from AMPHI- + *ktizein* to found]

amphictyony (æm'fɪktɪənɪ) *n., pl.* **-nies.** (in ancient Greece) a religious association of states for the maintenance of temples and the cults connected with them. —**amphictyonic** (æmˌfɪktɪ'ɒnɪk) *adj.*

amphidentate (ˌæmfɪ'dɛnteɪt) *adj.* (of a ligand) able to coordinate through either of two different atoms, as in CN^-. Also: **ambidentate.**

amphidiploid (ˌæmfɪ'dɪplɔɪd) *n.* a hybrid plant in which the chromosome number is the sum of the chromosome numbers of both parental species.

amphigory ('æmfɪgərɪ) *or* **amphigouri** ('æmfɪˌgʊərɪ) *n., pl.* **-ries** *or* **-ris.** a piece of nonsensical writing in verse or, less commonly, prose. [C19: from French *amphigouri,* of unknown origin] —**amphigoric** (ˌæmfɪ'gɒrɪk) *adj.*

amphimacer (æm'fɪməsə) *n. Prosody.* another word for **cretic.** [C16: from Latin *amphimacrus,* from Greek *amphimakros* both ends being long, from AMPHI- + *makros* long]

amphimixis (ˌæmfɪ'mɪksɪs) *n., pl.* **-mixes** (-'mɪksiːz). true sexual reproduction, esp. the fusion of gametes from two organisms. Compare **apomixis.** [C19: from AMPHI- + Greek *mixis* a blending, from *mignunai* to mingle] —**amphimictic** (ˌæmfɪ'mɪktɪk) *adj.*

amphioxus (ˌæmfɪ'ɒksəs) *n., pl.* **-oxi** (-'ɒksaɪ) *or* **-oxuses.** another name for the **lancelet.** [C19: from New Latin: both ends being sharp, from AMPHI- + Greek *oxus* sharp]

amphipathic (ˌæmfɪ'pæθɪk) *or* **amphipath** ('æmfɪˌpæθ) *adj. Chem., biochem.* of or relating to a molecule that possesses both hydrophobic and hydrophilic elements, such as are found in detergents, or phospholipids of biological membranes.

amphipod ('æmfɪˌpɒd) *n.* **1.** any marine or freshwater crustacean of the order *Amphipoda,* such as the sand hoppers, in which the body is laterally compressed: subclass *Malacostraca.* ~*adj.* **2.** of, relating to, or belonging to the *Amphipoda.*

amphipodous (æm'fɪpədəs) *adj.* (of certain invertebrates, such as sand hoppers) having both swimming and jumping appendages.

amphiprostyle (æm'fɪprəˌstaɪl, ˌæmfɪ'prəʊstaɪl) *adj.* **1.** (esp. of a classical temple) having a set of columns at both ends but not at the sides. ~*n.* **2.** a temple of this kind. —**amˌphipro'stylar** *adj.*

amphiprotic (ˌæmfɪ'prəʊtɪk) *adj.* another word for **amphoteric.**

amphisbaena (ˌæmfɪs'biːnə) *n., pl.* **-nae** (-niː) *or* **-nas. 1.** any worm lizard of the genus *Amphisbaena.* **2.** *Classical myth.* a poisonous serpent having a head at each end and able to move forwards or backwards. [C16: via Latin from Greek *amphisbaina,* from *amphis* both ways + *bainein* to go] —ˌ**amphis'baenic** *adj.*

amphistomatal (ˌæmfɪ'stəʊmətᵊl) *or* **amphistomatic** (ˌæmfɪstə'mætɪk) *adj.* (of a leaf) having stomata on both surfaces.

amphistomous (ˌæmfɪ'stəʊməs) *adj.* (of certain animals, such as leeches) having a sucker at either end of the body.

amphistylar (ˌæmfɪ'staɪlə) *adj.* **1.** (esp. of a classical temple) having a set of columns at both ends or at both sides. ~*n.* **2.** a temple of this kind.

amphitheatre *or U.S.* **amphitheater** ('æmfɪˌθɪətə) *n.* **1.** a building, usually circular or oval, in which tiers of seats rise from a central open arena, as in those of ancient Rome. **2.** a place where contests are held; arena. **3.** any level circular area of ground surrounded by higher ground. **4. a.** the first tier of seats in the gallery of a theatre. **b.** any similarly designated seating area in a theatre. **5.** a lecture room in which seats are tiered away from a central area. —**amphitheatric** (ˌæmfɪθɪ'ætrɪk) *or* ˌ**amphithe'atrical** *adj.* —ˌ**amphithe'atrically** *adv.*

amphithecium (ˌæmfɪ'θiːsɪəm) *n., pl.* **-cia** (-sɪə). the outer layer of cells of the embryo of mosses and liverworts that develops into the outer parts of the spore-bearing capsule. [C19: from New Latin, from AMPHI- + Greek *thēkion* a little case, from *thēkē* case]

amphitricha (æm'fɪtrɪkə) *pl. n.* bacteria that have flagella at both ends. [C20: from AMPHI- + *-tricha,* from Greek *thrix* hair] —**am'phitrichous** *adj.*

amphitropous (æm'fɪtrəpəs) *adj.* (of a plant ovule) partially inverted so that the base and the micropyle at the apex are the same distance from the funicle.

amphora ('æmfərə) *n., pl.* **-phorae** (-fəˌriː) *or* **-phoras.** an ancient Greek or Roman two-handled narrow-necked jar for oil, wine, etc. [C17: from Latin, from Greek *amphoreus,* from AMPHI- + *phoreus* bearer, from *pherein* to bear]

amphoric (æm'fɒrɪk) *adj.* resembling the sound produced by blowing into a bottle. Amphoric breath sounds are heard through a stethoscope placed over a cavity in the lung.

amphoteric (ˌæmfə'tɛrɪk) *adj. Chem.* able to function as either a base or an acid. Also: **amphiprotic.** [C19: from Greek *amphoteros* each of two (from *amphō* both) + -IC]

ampicillin (ˌæmpɪ'sɪlɪn) *n.* a semisynthetic penicillin used to treat various infections.

ample ('æmpᵊl) *adj.* **1.** more than sufficient; abundant: *an ample helping.* **2.** large in size, extent, or amount: *of ample proportions.* [C15: from Old French, from Latin *amplus* spacious] —'**ampleness** *n.*

amplexicaul (æm'plɛksɪˌkɔːl) *adj.* (of some sessile leaves, stipules, etc.) having an enlarged base that encircles the stem. [C18: from New Latin *amplexicaulis,* from Latin *amplectī* to embrace + *caulis* stalk]

amplification (ˌæmplɪfɪ'keɪʃən) *n.* **1.** the act or result of amplifying. **2.** material added to a statement, story, etc., in order to expand or clarify it. **3.** a statement, story, etc., with such additional material. **4.** *Electronics.* **a.** the increase in strength of an electrical signal by means of an amplifier. **b.** another word for **gain**[1] (sense 13). **5.** *Genetics.* Also called: **gene amplification.** the production of multiple copies of a particular gene or DNA sequence. It can occur naturally or artificially, by genetic engineering techniques.

amplifier ('æmplɪˌfaɪə) *n.* **1.** an electronic device used to increase the strength of the current or voltage signal fed into it. **2.** such a device used for the amplification of sound signals in a radio, record player, etc. 3. *Photog.* an additional lens for altering the focal length of a camera lens. 4. a person or thing that amplifies.

amplify ('æmplɪˌfaɪ) *vb.* **-fies, -fying, -fied.** 1. (*tr.*) to increase in size, extent, effect, etc., as by the addition of extra material; augment; enlarge; expand. 2. *Electronics.* to produce amplification of (electrical signals); increase the amplitude of (signals). 3. (*tr.*) *U.S.* to exaggerate. 4. (*intr.*) to expand or enlarge a speech, narrative, etc. [C15: from Old French *amplifier,* ultimately from Latin *amplificāre* to enlarge, from *amplus* spacious + *facere* to make] —'**ampliˌfiable** *adj.*

amplitude ('æmplɪˌtjuːd) *n.* 1. greatness of extent; magnitude. 2. abundance or copiousness. 3. breadth or scope, as of the mind. 4. *Astronomy.* the angular distance along the horizon measured from true east or west to the point of intersection of the vertical circle passing through a celestial body. 5. Also called: **argument.** *Maths.* (of a complex number) the angle that the vector representing the complex number makes with the positive real axis. If the point (x, y) has polar coordinates (r, θ), the amplitude of $x + iy$ is θ, that is, $\arctan Y/x$. Compare **modulus** (sense 2). See also **Argand diagram.** 6. *Physics.* the maximum displacement from the zero or mean position of a periodic motion or curve. [C16: from Latin *amplitūdō* breadth, from *amplus* spacious]

amplitude modulation *n.* 1. one of the principal methods of transmitting audio, visual, or other types of information using radio waves, the relevant signal being superimposed onto a radio-frequency carrier wave. The frequency of the carrier wave remains unchanged but its amplitude is varied in accordance with the amplitude of the input signal. Abbrevs.: **AM, am.** Compare **frequency modulation.** 2. a wave that has undergone this process.

amply ('æmplɪ) *adv.* more than sufficiently; fully; generously: *he was amply rewarded.*

ampoule ('æmpuːl, -pjuːl) *or esp. U.S.* **ampule** *n. Med.* a small glass vessel in which liquids for injection are hermetically sealed.

ampulla (æm'pʊlə) *n., pl.* **-pullae** (-'pʊliː). 1. *Anatomy.* the dilated end part of certain ducts or canals, such as the end of a uterine tube. 2. *Christianity.* **a.** a vessel for containing the wine and water used at the Eucharist. **b.** a small flask for containing consecrated oil. 3. a Roman two-handled bottle for oil, wine, or perfume. [C16: from Latin, diminutive of AMPHORA] —**ampullaceous** (ˌæmpʊ'leɪʃəs) *or* ˌ**ampul'laceal** *adj.* —**ampullar** (æm'pʊlə) *or* **ampullary** (æm'pʊlərɪ) *adj.*

amputate ('æmpjʊˌteɪt) *vb. Surgery.* to remove (all or part of a limb, esp. an arm or leg). [C17: from Latin *amputāre,* from *am-* around + *putāre* to trim, prune] —ˌ**ampu'tation** *n.* —'**ampuˌtator** *n.*

amputee (ˌæmpjʊ'tiː) *n.* a person who has had a limb amputated.

amrita *or* **amreeta** (æm'riːtə) *n. Hindu myth.* 1. the ambrosia of the gods that bestows immortality. 2. the immortality it confers. [from Sanskrit *amrta* immortal, from *a-* without + *mrta* death]

amt *abbrev. for* amount.

amu *abbrev. for* atomic mass unit.

amuck (ə'mʌk) *n., adv.* a variant of **amok.**

amulet ('æmjʊlɪt) *n.* a trinket or piece of jewellery worn as a protection against evil; charm. [C17: from Latin *amulētum,* of unknown origin]

amuse (ə'mjuːz) *vb.* (*tr.*) 1. to keep pleasantly occupied; entertain; divert. 2. to cause to laugh or smile. [C15: from Old French *amuser* to cause to be idle, from *muser* to MUSE]

amusement (ə'mjuːzmənt) *n.* 1. something that amuses, such as a game or other pastime. 2. a mechanical device used for entertainment, as at a fair. 3. the act of amusing or the state or quality of being amused.

amusement arcade *n. Brit.* a covered area having coin-operated game machines.

amusement park *n.* an open-air entertainment area consisting of stalls, side shows, etc.

amusing (ə'mjuːzɪŋ) *adj.* mildly entertaining; pleasantly diverting; causing a smile or laugh. —**a'musingly** *adv.*

amygdala (ə'mɪgdələ) *n., pl.* **-lae** (-ˌliː). *Anatomy.* an almond-shaped part, such as a tonsil or a lobe of the cerebellum. [C16: from Medieval Latin: ALMOND]

amygdalate (ə'mɪgdəlɪt, -ˌleɪt) *adj.* relating to, having, or bearing almonds.

amygdale (ə'mɪgdeɪl) *n.* an oval vesicle in a volcanic rock, formed from a bubble of escaping gas, that has become filled with a light-coloured mineral, such as quartz. Also called: **amygdule** (ə'mɪgdjuːl). [C19: from Greek: ALMOND]

amygdalin (ə'mɪgdəlɪn) *n.* a white soluble bitter-tasting crystalline glycoside extracted from bitter almonds and used as an expectorant. Formula: $C_6H_5CHCNOC_{12}H_{21}O_{10}$.

amygdaline (ə'mɪgdəlɪn, -ˌlaɪn) *adj.* 1. *Anatomy.* of or relating to a tonsil. 2. of or resembling almonds.

amygdaloid (ə'mɪgdəˌlɔɪd) *n.* 1. a volcanic igneous rock containing amygdales. ~*adj.* 2. having the shape of an almond. 3. a less common form of **amygdaloidal** (sense 1).

amygdaloidal (əˌmɪgdə'lɔɪdᵊl) *adj.* 1. (of a volcanic rock) containing amygdales. 2. a less common form of **amygdaloid** (sense 2).

amyl ('æmɪl) *n.* (*modifier*) (*no longer in technical usage*) of, consisting of, or containing any of eight isomeric forms of the monovalent group C_5H_{11}-: *amyl group or radical.* See also **pentyl.** [C19: from Latin: AMYLUM]

amylaceous (ˌæmɪ'leɪʃəs) *adj.* of or resembling starch.

amyl acetate *n.* another name (no longer in technical usage) for **pentyl acetate.**

amyl alcohol *n.* a colourless flammable liquid existing in eight isomeric forms that is used as a solvent and in the manufacture of organic compounds and pharmaceuticals. Formula: $C_5H_{11}OH$.

amylase ('æmɪˌleɪz) *n.* any of several enzymes that hydrolyse starch and glycogen to simple sugars, such as glucose. They are present in saliva.

amylene ('æmɪˌliːn) *n.* another name (no longer in technical usage) for **pentene.**

amyl nitrite *n.* a yellowish unstable volatile fragrant liquid used in medicine as a vasodilator and in perfumes. Formula: $(CH_3)_2CHCH_2CH_2NO_2$.

amylo- *or before a vowel* **amyl-** *combining form.* indicating starch: *amylolysis; amylase.* [from Latin: AMYLUM]

amyloid ('æmɪˌlɔɪd) *n.* 1. *Pathol.* a complex protein resembling starch, deposited in tissues in some degenerative diseases. 2. any substance resembling starch. ~*adj.* 3. starchlike.

amyloidosis (ˌæmɪlɔɪ'dəʊsɪs) *n. Pathol.* the deposition of amyloid in various tissues of the body, as occurs in certain chronic infections.

amylolysis (ˌæmɪ'lɒlɪsɪs) *n.* the conversion of starch into sugar. —**amylolytic** (əˌmaɪləʊ'lɪtɪk) *adj.*

amylopectin (ˌæmɪləʊ'pɛktɪn) *n.* the major component of starch (about 80 per cent), consisting of branched chains of glucose units. It is insoluble and gives a red-brown colour with iodine. Compare **amylose.**

amylopsin (ˌæmɪ'lɒpsɪn) *n.* an enzyme of the pancreatic juice that converts starch into sugar; pancreatic amylase. [C19: from AMYLO(LYSIS) + (PE)PSIN]

amylose ('æmɪˌləʊz, -ləʊs) *n.* the minor component (about 20 per cent) of starch, consisting of long unbranched chains of glucose units. It is soluble in water and gives an intense blue colour with iodine. Compare **amylopectin.**

amylum ('æmɪləm) *n.* another name for **starch** (sense 2). [Latin, from Greek *amulon* fine meal, starch, from *amulos* not ground at the mill, from A-[1] + *mulē* mill]

amyotonia (ˌeɪmaɪə'təʊnɪə) *n.* another name for **myotonia.**

amyotrophy (ˌæmɪ'ɒtrəfɪ) *n. Pathol.* wasting of muscles, caused by disease of the nerves supplying them.

Amytal ('æmɪˌtæl) *n. Trademark.* a crystalline compound used as a sedative and hypnotic; sodium amytal.

an[1] (æn; *unstressed* ən) *determiner.* (*indefinite article*) a form of **a**[1], used before an initial vowel sound: *an old car; an elf; an honour.* [Old English *ān* ONE]

▷ **Usage.** *An* was formerly often used before words that begin with *h* and are unstressed on the first syllable: *an hotel; an historic meeting:* sometimes the initial *h* was not pronounced. In British English this usage is now obsolescent.

an[2] *or* **an'** (æn; *unstressed* ən) *conj.* (*subordinating*) an obsolete or dialect word for **if.** See **and** (sense 9).

An *the chemical symbol for* actinon.

AN *abbrev. for* Anglo-Norman.

an. *abbrev. for* anno. [Latin: in the year]

an- *or before a consonant* **a-** *prefix.* not; without: *anaphrodisiac.* [from Greek]

-an, -ean, *or* **-ian** *suffix.* 1. (*forming adjectives and nouns*) belonging to or relating to; a person belonging to or coming from: *European.* 2. (*forming adjectives and nouns*) typical of or resembling; a person typical of: *Elizabethan.* 3. (*forming adjectives and nouns*) adhering to or following; an adherent of: *Christian.* 4. (*forming nouns*) a person who specializes or is expert in: *dietitian; phonetician.* [from Latin *-ānus,* suffix of adjectives]

ana[1] ('ɑːnə, 'ɑːnə) *adv. Pharmacol.* (of ingredients in a prescription) in equal quantities. Abbrev.: **aa.** [C16: via Medieval Latin from Greek: of every one similarly]

ana[2] ('ɑːnə) *n.* 1. a collection of reminiscences, sketches, etc., of or about a person or place. 2. an item of or for such a collection. [C18: independent use of -ANA]

ANA *Commerce. abbrev. for* Article Number Association: (in Britain) an organization of manufacturers, retailers, and wholesalers that provides a system (**article numbering**) by which a product is identified by a unique machine-readable number (see **bar code**) compatible with article-numbering systems used in other countries.

ana- *or before a vowel* **an-** *prefix.* 1. up; upwards: *anadromous.* 2. again: *anagram.* 3. back; backwards: *anatropous.* [from Greek *ana*]

-ana *or* **-iana** *suffix forming nouns.* denoting a collection of objects or information relating to a particular individual, subject, or place: *Shakespeareana; Victoriana; Americana.* [New Latin, from Latin *-āna,* literally: matters relating to, neuter plural of *-ānus;* see -AN]

anabaena (ˌænə'biːnə) *n., pl.* **-nas.** any freshwater alga of the genus *Anabaena,* sometimes occurring in drinking water, giving it a fishy taste and smell. [New Latin, from Greek *anabainein* to shoot up, go up, from ANA- + *bainein* to go; so called because they rise to the surface at intervals]

anabantid (ˌænəˈbæntɪd) *n.* **1.** any of various spiny-finned fishes constituting the family *Anabantidae* and including the fighting fish, climbing perch, and gourami. See also **labyrinth fish.** ~*adj.* **2.** of, relating to, or belonging to the family Anabantidae.

Anabaptist (ˌænəˈbæptɪst) *n.* **1.** a member of any of various 16th-century Protestant movements that rejected infant baptism, insisted that adults be rebaptized, and sought to establish Christian communism. **2.** a member of a later Protestant sect holding the same doctrines, esp. with regard to baptism. ~*adj.* **3.** of or relating to these movements or sects or their doctrines. [C16: from Ecclesiastical Latin *anabaptista*, from *anabaptīzāre* to baptize again, from Late Greek *anabaptizein;* see ANA-, BAPTIZE] —ˌ**Anaˈbaptism** *n.*

anabas (ˈænəˌbæs) *n.* any of several labyrinth fishes of the genus *Anabas*, esp. the **climbing fish.** [C19: from New Latin, from Greek *anabainein* to go up; see ANABAENA]

anabasis (əˈnæbəsɪs) *n., pl.* **-ses** (-ˌsiːz). **1.** the march of Cyrus the Younger and his Greek mercenaries from Sardis to Cunaxa in Babylonia in 401 B.C., described by Xenophon in his *Anabasis.* Compare **katabasis. 2.** any military expedition, esp. one from the coast to the interior. [C18: from Greek: a going up, ascent, from *anabainein* to go up; see ANABAENA]

anabatic (ˌænəˈbætɪk) *adj. Meteorol.* (of air currents) rising upwards, esp. up slopes. Compare **katabatic.** [C19: from Greek *anabatikos* relating to ascents, from *anabainein* to go up; see ANABASIS]

anabiosis (ˌænəbaɪˈəʊsɪs) *n.* the ability to return to life after apparent death; suspended animation. [C19: via New Latin from Greek, from *anabioein* to come back to life, from ANA- + *bios* life] —**anabiotic** (ˌænəbaɪˈɒtɪk) *adj.*

anableps (ˈænəˌblɛps) *n., pl.* **-bleps.** any of various cyprinodont fishes constituting the genus *Anableps*, which includes the four-eyed fishes. [New Latin, literally: one who looks up, from Greek, from *anablepein* to look up]

anabolic steroid (ˌænəˈbɒlɪk) *n.* any of a group of synthetic steroid hormones (androgens) used to stimulate muscle and bone growth for athletic or therapeutic purposes.

anabolism (əˈnæbəˌlɪzəm) *n.* a metabolic process in which complex molecules are synthesized from simpler ones with the storage of energy; constructive metabolism. Compare **catabolism.** [C19: from ANA- + (META)BOLISM] —**anabolic** (ˌænəˈbɒlɪk) *adj.*

anabolite (əˈnæbəˌlaɪt) *n.* a product of anabolism. —**anabolitic** (əˌnæbəˈlɪtɪk) *adj.*

anabranch (ˈɑːnəˌbrɑːntʃ) *n.* a stream that leaves a river and enters it again further downstream. [C19: from *ana(stomosing) branch*]

anacardiaceous (ˌænəˌkɑːdɪˈeɪʃəs) *adj.* of, relating to, or belonging to the *Anacardiaceae*, a chiefly tropical family of trees and shrubs many of which have edible drupes. The family includes the cashew, mango, pistachio, and sumach. [C19: from New Latin *Anacardiăceae*, from ANA- + Greek *kardia* heart; so called from the shape of the top of the fruit stem]

anachorism (əˈnækəˌrɪzəm) *n.* a geographical misplacement; something located in an incongruous position. Compare **anachronism.** [C19: from ANA- + *khōros* place]

anachronic (ˌænəˈkrɒnɪk) *or* **anachronical** *adj.* out of chronological order or out of date. [C19: see ANACHRONISM] —ˌ**anaˈchronically** *adv.*

anachronism (əˈnækrəˌnɪzəm) *n.* **1.** the representation of an event, person, or thing in a historical context in which it could not have occurred or existed. **2.** a person or thing that belongs or seems to belong to another time. [C17: from Latin *anachronismus*, from Greek *anakhronismos* a mistake in chronology, from *anakhronizein* to err in a time reference, from ANA- + *khronos* time] —**aˌnachroˈnistic** *adj.* —**aˌnachroˈnistically** *adv.*

anaclinal (ˌænəˈklaɪnᵊl) *adj.* (of valleys and similar formations) progressing in a direction opposite to the dip of the surrounding rock strata. [C19: see ANA-, -CLINE]

anaclitic (ˌænəˈklɪtɪk) *adj. Psychoanal.* of or relating to relationships that are characterized by the strong dependence of one person on others or another. [C20: from Greek *anaklitos* for leaning upon; see ANA-, -CLINE] —**anaclisis** (ˌænəˈklaɪsɪs) *n.*

anacoluthia (ˌænəkəˈluːθɪə) *n. Rhetoric.* lack of grammatical sequence, esp. within a single sentence. —ˌ**anacoˈluthic** *adj.*

anacoluthon (ˌænəkəˈluːθɒn) *n., pl.* **-tha** (-θə). *Rhetoric.* a construction that involves the change from one grammatical sequence to another within a single sentence; an example of anacoluthia. [C18: from Late Latin, from Greek *anakolouthon*, from *anakolouthos* not consistent, from AN- + *akolouthos* following]

anaconda (ˌænəˈkɒndə) *n.* a very large nonvenomous arboreal and semiaquatic snake, *Eunectes murinus*, of tropical South America, which kills its prey by constriction: family *Boidae* (boas). [C18: probably changed from Sinhalese *henakandayā* whip snake, from *hena* lightning + *kanda* stem; originally referring to a snake of Sri Lanka]

anacoustic (ˌænəˈkuːstɪk) *adj.* unable to support the propagation of sound; soundless.

Anacreontic (əˌnækrɪˈɒntɪk) (*sometimes not cap.*) ~*adj.* **1.** (of verse) in praise of love or wine; amatory or convivial. ~*n.* **2.** an Anacreontic poem. [after *Anacreon* (?572–?488 B.C.), Greek lyric poet] —**Aˌnacreˈontically** *adv.*

anacrusis (ˌænəˈkruːsɪs) *n., pl.* **-ses** (-siːz). **1.** *Prosody.* one or more unstressed syllables at the beginning of a line of verse. **2.** *Music.* **a.** an unstressed note or group of notes immediately preceding the strong first beat of the first bar. **b.** another word for **upbeat.** [C19: from Greek *anakrousis* prelude, from *anakrouein* to strike up, from ANA- + *krouein* to strike] —**anacrustic** (ˌænəˈkrʌstɪk) *adj.*

anadem (ˈænəˌdɛm) *n. Poetic.* a garland for the head. [C17: from Latin *anadēma* wreath, from Greek *anadēma*, from *anadein* to wreathe, from ANA- + *dein* to bind]

anadiplosis (ˌænədɪˈpləʊsɪs) *n. Rhetoric.* repetition of the words or phrase at the end of one sentence, line, or clause at the beginning of the next. [C16: via Latin from Greek: repetition, from *anadiploun* to double back, from ANA- + *diploun* to double]

anadromous (əˈnædrəməs) *adj.* (of fishes such as the salmon) migrating up rivers from the sea in order to breed. Compare **catadromous.** [C18: from Greek *anadromos* running upwards, from ANA- + *dromos* a running]

anaemia *or U.S.* **anemia** (əˈniːmɪə) *n.* **1.** a deficiency in the number of red blood cells or in their haemoglobin content, resulting in pallor, shortness of breath, and lack of energy. **2.** lack of vitality or vigour. **3.** pallid complexion. [C19: from New Latin, from Greek *anaimia* lack of blood, from AN- + *haima* blood]

anaemic *or U.S.* **anemic** (əˈniːmɪk) *adj.* **1.** relating to or suffering from anaemia. **2.** pale and sickly looking; lacking vitality.

anaerobe (æˈnɛərəʊb, ˈænərəʊb) *or* **anaerobium** (ˌænɛəˈrəʊbɪəm) *n., pl.* **-obes** *or* **-obia** (-ˈəʊbɪə). an organism that does not require free oxygen or air for respiration. Compare **aerobe.**

anaerobic (ˌænɛəˈrəʊbɪk) *adj.* **1.** (of an organism or process) requiring the absence of or not dependent on the presence of free oxygen or air. **2.** of or relating to anaerobes. ~Compare **aerobic.** —ˌ**anaerˈobically** *adv.*

anaerobiosis (ˌænɛərəʊbaɪˈəʊsɪs) *n.* life in the absence of free oxygen.

anaesthesia *or U.S.* **anesthesia** (ˌænɪsˈθiːzɪə) *n.* **1.** local or general loss of bodily sensation, esp. of touch, as the result of nerve damage or other abnormality. **2.** loss of sensation, esp. of pain, induced by drugs: called **general anaesthesia** when consciousness is lost and **local anaesthesia** when only a specific area of the body is involved. **3.** a general dullness or lack of feeling. [C19: from New Latin, from Greek *anaisthēsia* absence of sensation, from AN- + *aisthēsis* feeling]

anaesthesiology *or U.S.* **anesthesiology** (ˌænɪsˌθiːzɪˈɒlədʒɪ) *n.* the U.S. name for **anaesthetics.**

anaesthetic *or U.S.* **anesthetic** (ˌænɪsˈθɛtɪk) *n.* **1.** a substance that causes anaesthesia. ~*adj.* **2.** causing or characterized by anaesthesia.

anaesthetics (ˌænɪsˈθɛtɪks) *n.* (*functioning as sing.*) the science, study, and practice of anaesthesia and its application. U.S. name: **anesthesiology.**

anaesthetist (əˈniːsθətɪst) *n.* **1.** *Brit.* a qualified doctor specializing in the administration of anaesthetics. U.S. name: **anesthesiologist. 2.** *U.S.* a person qualified to administer anaesthesia, often a nurse or someone other than a physician. Compare **anesthesiologist.**

anaesthetize, anaesthetise, *or U.S.* **anesthetize** (əˈniːsθəˌtaɪz) *vb.* (*tr.*) to render insensible to pain by administering an anaesthetic. —**aˌnaesthetiˈzation, aˌnaesthetiˈsation,** *or U.S.* **aˌnesthetiˈzation** *n.*

anaglyph (ˈænəˌglɪf) *n.* **1.** *Photog.* a stereoscopic picture consisting of two images of the same object, taken from slightly different angles, in two complementary colours, usually red and cyan (green-blue). When viewed through spectacles having one red and one cyan lens, the images merge to produce a stereoscopic sensation. **2.** anything cut to stand in low relief, such as a cameo. [C17: from Greek *anagluphē* carved in low relief, from ANA- + *gluphē* carving, from *gluphein* to carve] —ˌ**anaˈglyphic,** ˌ**anaˈglyphical** *or* **anaglyptic** (ˌænəˈglɪptɪk), ˌ**anaˈglyptical** *adj.* —**anaglyphy** (əˈnægləfɪ, ˈænəˌglɪfɪ) *n.*

Anaglypta (ˌænəˈglɪptə) *n. Trademark.* a type of thick embossed wallpaper. [C19: from Greek *anagluptos;* see ANAGLYPH]

anagnorisis (ˌænəgˈnɒrɪsɪs) *n., pl.* **-ses** (-ˌsiːz). (in Greek tragedy) the recognition or discovery by the protagonist of the identity of some character or the nature of his own predicament, which leads to the resolution of the plot; denouement. [from Greek: recognition]

anagoge *or* **anagogy** (ˈænəˌgɒdʒɪ) *n.* **1.** allegorical or spiritual interpretation, esp. of sacred works such as the Bible. **2.** *Christianity.* allegorical interpretation of the Old Testament as typifying or foreshadowing subjects in the New Testament. [C18: via Late Latin from Greek *anagōgē* a lifting up, from *anagein*, from ANA- + *agein* to lead] —**anagogic** (ˌænəˈgɒdʒɪk) *or* ˌ**anaˈgogical** *adj.* —ˌ**anaˈgogically** *adv.*

anagram (ˈænəˌgræm) *n.* a word or phrase the letters of which can be rearranged into another word or phrase. [C16: from New Latin *anagramma*, shortened from Greek *anagrammatismos*, from *anagrammatizein* to transpose letters, from ANA- + *gramma* a letter] —**anagrammatic** (ˌænəgrəˈmætɪk) *or* ˌ**anagramˈmatical** *adj.* —ˌ**anagramˈmatically** *adv.*

anagrammatize *or* **anagrammatise** (ˌænəˈɡræməˌtaɪz) *vb.* to arrange into an anagram. —ˌ**anaˈgrammaˌtism** *n.* —ˌ**anaˈgrammatist** *n.*

anal (ˈeɪnəl) *adj.* **1.** of, relating to, or near the anus. **2.** *Psychoanal.* **a.** relating to a stage of psychosexual development during which the child's interest is concentrated on the anal region and excremental functions. **b.** designating personality traits in the adult, such as orderliness, meanness, stubbornness, etc., due to fixation at the anal stage of development. Compare **oral** (sense 7). [C18: from New Latin *ānālis*; see ANUS] —ˈ**anally** *adv.*

anal. *abbrev. for:* **1.** analogous. **2.** analogy. **3.** analysis. **4.** analytic.

anal canal *n.* the terminal part of the rectum forming the passage to the anus.

analcite (æˈnælsaɪt; ˈænəlˌsaɪt, -sɪt) *or* **analcime** (æˈnælsɪm, -saɪm, -siːm) *n.* a white, grey, or colourless zeolite mineral consisting of hydrated sodium aluminium silicate in cubic crystalline form. Formula: $NaAlSi_2O_6.H_2O$. [C19: from Greek *analkimos* weak (from AN- + *alkimos* strong, from *alkē* strength) + -ITE[1]]

analects (ˈænəˌlɛkts) *or* **analecta** (ˌænəˈlɛktə) *pl. n.* selected literary passages from one or more works. [C17: via Latin from Greek *analekta*, from *analegein* to collect up, from *legein* to gather] —ˌ**anaˈlectic** *adj.*

analemma (ˌænəˈlɛmə) *n., pl.* **-mas** *or* **-mata** (-mətə). a graduated scale shaped like a figure eight that indicates the daily declination of the sun. [C17: from Latin: sundial, pedestal of sundial, from Greek *analēmma* pedestal, from *analambanein* to support] —**analemmatic** (ˌænəlɛˈmætɪk) *adj.*

analeptic (ˌænəˈlɛptɪk) *adj.* **1.** (of a drug, etc.) restorative or invigorating. ~*n.* **2.** a restorative remedy or drug. [C17: from New Latin *analēpticus*, from Greek *analēptikos* stimulating, from *analambanein* to take up; see ANALEMMA]

anal erotic *n.* a person with anal personality traits.

anal fin *n.* a median ventral unpaired fin, situated between the anus and the tail fin in fishes, that helps to maintain stable equilibrium.

analgesia (ˌænəlˈdʒiːzɪə, -sɪə) *or* **analgia** (ænˈældʒɪə) *n.* inability to feel pain. [C18: via New Latin from Greek: insensibility, from AN- + *algēsis* sense of pain]

analgesic (ˌænəlˈdʒiːzɪk, -sɪk) *adj.* **1.** of or causing analgesia. ~*n.* **2.** a substance that produces analgesia.

anal intercourse *n.* a form of sexual intercourse in which the penis is inserted into the anus.

analog (ˈænəˌlɒɡ) *n.* a variant spelling of **analogue.**

▷**Usage.** The spelling *analog* is a U.S. variant of *analogue* in all its senses, and is also the generally preferred spelling in the computer industry.

analog computer *n.* a mechanical, electrical, or electronic computer that performs arithmetical operations by using some variable physical quantity, such as mechanical movement or voltage, to represent numbers.

analogize *or* **analogise** (əˈnæləˌdʒaɪz) *vb.* **1.** (*intr.*) to make use of analogy, as in argument; draw comparisons. **2.** (*tr.*) to make analogous or reveal analogy in.

analogous (əˈnæləɡəs) *adj.* **1.** similar or corresponding in some respect. **2.** *Biology.* (of organs and parts) having the same function but different evolutionary origin: *the paddle of a whale and the fin of a fish are analogous.* Compare **homologous** (sense 4). **3.** *Linguistics.* formed by analogy: *an analogous plural.* [C17: from Latin *analogus*, from Greek *analogos* proportionate, from ANA- + *logos* speech, ratio] —**aˈnalogously** *adv.* —**aˈnalogousness** *n.*

analogue *or U.S.* (*sometimes*) **analog** (ˈænəˌlɒɡ) *n.* **1. a.** a physical object or quantity, such as a pointer on a dial or a voltage, used to measure or represent another quantity. **b.** (*as modifier*): *analogue watch; analogue recording.* **2.** something analogous to something else. **3.** *Biology.* an analogous part or organ. **4.** *Chem.* an organic chemical compound related to another by substitution of hydrogen atoms with alkyl groups: *toluene is an analogue of benzene.*

▷**Usage.** See at **analog.**

analogue clock *or* **watch** *n.* a clock or watch in which the hours, minutes, and sometimes seconds are indicated by hands on a dial. Compare **digital clock.**

analogue-digital converter *n.* a device converting an analogue electrical signal into its digital representation so that it can be processed by a digital system. Abbrev.: **ADC.**

analogy (əˈnælədʒɪ) *n., pl.* **-gies.** **1.** agreement or similarity, esp. in a certain limited number of features or details. **2.** a comparison made to show such a similarity: *to draw an analogy between an atom and the solar system.* **3.** *Biology.* the relationship between analogous organs or parts. **4.** *Logic, maths.* a form of reasoning in which a similarity between two or more things is inferred from a known similarity between them in other respects. **5.** *Linguistics.* imitation of existing models or regular patterns in the formation of words, inflections, etc.: *a child may use "sheeps" as the plural of "sheep" by analogy with "dog," "dogs," "cat," "cats," etc.* [C16: from Greek *analogia* ratio, correspondence, from *analogos* ANALOGOUS] —**analogical** (ˌænəˈlɒdʒɪkəl) *or* ˌ**anaˈlogic** *adj.* —ˌ**anaˈlogically** *adv.* —**aˈnalogist** *n.*

analphabetic (ˌænælfəˈbɛtɪk, ænˌæl-) *adj.* **1.** not in alphabetical order. ~*n., adj.* **2.** a less common word for **illiterate.** [C20: from Greek *analphabētos*; see AN-, ALPHABET] —ˌ**analphaˈbetically** *adv.*

analysand (əˈnælɪˌsænd) *n.* any person who is undergoing psychoanalysis. [C20: from ANALYSE + *-and*, on the model of *multiplicand*]

analyse *or U.S.* **analyze** (ˈænəˌlaɪz) *vb.* **1.** (*tr.*) to examine in detail in order to discover meaning, essential features, etc. **2.** (*tr.*) to break down into components or essential features: *to analyse a financial structure.* **3.** (*tr.*) to make a mathematical, chemical, grammatical, etc., analysis of. **4.** another word for **psychoanalyse.** [C17: back formation from ANALYSIS] —ˌ**anaˈlysable** *or U.S.* ˌ**anaˈlyzable** *adj.* —ˌ**analyˈsation** *or U.S.* ˌ**analyˈzation** *n.* —ˈ**anaˌlyser** *or U.S.* ˈ**anaˌlyzer** *n.*

analysis (əˈnælɪsɪs) *n., pl.* **-ses** (-ˌsiːz). **1.** the division of a physical or abstract whole into its constituent parts to examine or determine their relationship or value. Compare **synthesis** (sense 1). **2.** a statement of the results of this. **3.** short for **psychoanalysis.** **4.** *Chem.* **a.** the decomposition of a substance into its elements, radicals, or other constituents in order to determine the kinds of constituents present (**qualitative analysis**) or the amount of each constituent (**quantitative analysis**). **b.** the result obtained by such a determination. **5.** *Linguistics.* the use of word order together with word function to express syntactic relations in a language, as opposed to the use of inflections. Compare **synthesis** (sense 4). **6.** *Maths.* the branch of mathematics principally concerned with the properties of functions, largely arising out of calculus. **7.** *Philosophy.* (in the writings of Kant) the separation of a concept from another that contains it. Compare **synthesis** (sense 6). **8. in the last, final,** *or* **ultimate analysis.** after everything has been given due consideration. [C16: from New Latin, from Greek *analusis*, literally: a dissolving, from *analuein*, from ANA- + *luein* to loosen]

analysis of variance *n. Statistics.* any of a number of techniques for resolving the observed variance between sets of data into components, esp. to determine whether the difference between two samples is explicable as random sampling variation with the same underlying population.

analysis situs *n.* a former name for **topology** (sense 2).

analyst (ˈænəlɪst) *n.* **1.** a person who analyses or is skilled in analysis. **2.** short for **psychoanalyst.**

analytic (ˌænəˈlɪtɪk) *or* **analytical** (ˌænəˈlɪtɪkəl) *adj.* **1.** relating to analysis. **2.** capable of or given to analysing: *an analytic mind.* **3.** Also: **isolating.** *Linguistics.* denoting languages, such as Chinese, whose morphology is characterized by analysis. Compare **synthetic** (sense 3), **agglutinative** (sense 2), **polysynthetic.** **4.** *Logic.* (of a proposition) **a.** true by virtue of the meanings of the words alone without reference to the facts, as *all spinsters are unmarried.* **b.** true or false by virtue of meaning alone; so *all spinsters are married* is analytically false. ~Compare **synthetic** (sense 4), **a priori.** **5.** Also: **regular, holomorphic.** *Maths.* (of a function of a complex variable) having a derivative at each point of its domain. [C16: via Late Latin from Greek *analutikos* from *analuein* to dissolve, break down; see ANALYSIS] —ˌ**anaˈlytically** *adv.*

analytical geometry *n.* the branch of geometry that uses algebraic notation and analysis to locate a geometric point in terms of a coordinate system; coordinate geometry.

analytical philosophy *n.* a school of philosophy which flourished in the first half of the 20th century and which sought to resolve philosophical problems by analysing the language in which they are expressed, esp. in terms of formal logic as in Russell's theory of descriptions. Compare **linguistic philosophy.**

analytical reagent *n.* a chemical compound of a known high standard of purity.

analytic psychology *n.* a school of psychoanalysis founded by Jung as a result of disagreements with Freud. See also **archetype, collective unconscious.**

anamnesis (ˌænæmˈniːsɪs) *n., pl.* **-ses** (-siːz). **1.** the ability to recall past events; recollection. **2.** the case history of a patient. [C17: via New Latin from Greek, from *anamimnēskein* to recall, from *mimnēskein* to call to mind]

anamnestic (ˌænæmˈnɛstɪk) *adj.* **1.** of or relating to anamnesis. **2.** *Immunol.* denoting a response to antigenic stimulation characterized by the production of large amounts of antibody specific to a different antigen from that which elicited the response. —ˌ**anamˈnestically** *adv.*

anamniote (ænˈæmnɪəʊt) *n.* any vertebrate animal, such as a fish or amphibian, that lacks an amnion, chorion, and allantois during embryonic development. Compare **amniote.** —**anamniotic** (ænˌæmnɪˈɒtɪk) *adj.*

anamorphic (ˌænəˈmɔːfɪk) *adj.* of, relating to, or caused by anamorphosis or anamorphism.

anamorphic lens *n.* a component in the optical system of a film projector for converting standard 35mm film images into wide-screen format.

anamorphism (ˌænəˈmɔːˌfɪzəm) *n.* metamorphism of a rock in which complex minerals are formed from simpler ones.

anamorphoscope (ˌænəˈmɔːfəˌskəʊp) *n.* an optical device, such as a cylindrical lens, for correcting an image that has been distorted by anamorphosis.

anamorphosis (ˌænəˈmɔːfəsɪs, -mɔːˈfəʊsɪs) *n., pl.* **-ses** (-ˌsiːz). **1.** *Optics.* **a.** an image or drawing distorted in such a way that it becomes recognizable only when viewed in a specified manner or through a special device. **b.** the process by which such images or drawings are produced. **2.** the evolution of one type of organism from another by a series of gradual changes. [C18: from Greek, from *anamorphoun* to transform, from *morphē* form, shape]

ananas (əˈnænəs) *n.* another name for the **pineapple,** or for a related tropical American bromeliaceous plant, the pinguin, that has an edible plum-shaped fruit. [C17: from the native name in Peru]

anandrous (ænˈændrəs) *adj.* (of flowers) having no stamens. [C19: from Greek *anandros* lacking males, from AN- + *anēr* man]

Ananias (ˌænəˈnaɪəs) *n.* a liar. [after *Ananias,* a New Testament character who was struck dead for lying]

ananthous (ænˈænθəs) *adj.* (of higher plants) having no flowers. [C19: from Greek *ananthēs,* from AN- + *anthos* flower]

anapaest *or* **anapest** (ˈænəpɛst, -piːst) *n. Prosody.* a metrical foot of three syllables, the first two short, the last long (⏑⏑–). [C17: via Latin from Greek *anapaistos* reversed (that is, a dactyl reversed), from *anapaiein,* from *ana-* back + *paiein* to strike] —ˌ**anaˈpaestic** *or* ˌ**anaˈpestic** *adj.*

anaphase (ˈænəˌfeɪz) *n.* **1.** the third stage of mitosis, during which the chromatids separate and migrate towards opposite ends of the spindle. See also **prophase, metaphase, telophase.** **2.** the corresponding stage of the first division of meiosis. [C19: from ANA- + PHASE]

anaphora (əˈnæfərə) *n.* **1.** *Grammar.* the use of a word such as a pronoun that has the same reference as a word previously used in the same discourse. In the sentence *John wrote the essay in the library but Peter did it at home,* both *did* and *it* are examples of anaphora. Compare **cataphora, exophoric.** **2.** *Rhetoric.* the repetition of a word or phrase at the beginning of successive clauses. [C16: via Latin from Greek: repetition, from *anapherein,* from ANA- + *pherein* to bear] —**anaphoric** (ˌænəˈfɒrɪk) *adj.* —ˌ**anaˈphorically** *adv.*

anaphoresis (ˌænəfəˈriːsɪs) *n. Chem.* the movement of suspended particles towards the anode in an electric field.

anaphrodisiac (ˌænæfrəˈdɪzɪˌæk) *adj.* **1.** tending to lessen sexual desire. ~*n.* **2.** an anaphrodisiac drug. —ˌ**anaphroˈdisia** *n.*

anaphylaxis (ˌænəfɪˈlæksɪs) *n.* extreme sensitivity to an injected antigen, esp. a protein, following a previous injection. [C20: from ANA- + (PRO)PHYLAXIS] —ˌ**anaphyˈlactic** *or* ˌ**anaphyˈlactoid** *adj.* —ˌ**anaphyˈlactically** *adv.*

anaplasia (ˌænəˈpleɪsɪə) *n.* reversion of plant or animal cells to a simpler less differentiated form.

anaplasmosis (ˌænəplæzˈməʊsɪs) *n.* another name for **gallsickness.**

anaplastic (ˌænəˈplæstɪk) *adj.* **1.** of or relating to anaplasia. **2.** relating to plastic surgery.

anaplasty (ˈænəˌplæstɪ) *n. Surgery.* another name for **plastic surgery.**

anaptyxis (ˌænæpˈtɪksɪs) *n., pl.* **-tyxes** (-ˈtɪksiːz). the insertion of a short vowel between consonants in order to make a word more easily pronounceable. [C19: via New Latin from Greek *anaptuxis,* from *anaptussein* to unfold, from ANA- + *ptussein* to fold] —**anaptyctic** (ˌænæpˈtɪktɪk) *or* ˌ**anapˈtyctical** *adj.*

anarch (ˈænɑːk) *n. Archaic.* an instigator or personification of anarchy.

anarchism (ˈænəˌkɪzəm) *n.* **1.** *Political theory.* a doctrine advocating the abolition of government. **2.** the principles or practice of anarchists.

anarchist (ˈænəkɪst) *n.* **1.** a person who advocates the abolition of government and a social system based on voluntary cooperation. **2.** a person who causes disorder or upheaval. —ˌ**anarˈchistic** *adj.*

anarchy (ˈænəkɪ) *n.* **1.** general lawlessness and disorder, esp. when thought to result from an absence or failure of government. **2.** the absence or lack of government. **3.** the absence of any guiding or uniting principle; disorder; chaos. **4.** the theory or practice of political anarchism. [C16: from Medieval Latin *anarchia,* from Greek *anarkhia,* from *anarkhos* without a ruler, from AN- + *arkh-* leader, from *arkhein* to rule] —**anarchic** (ænˈɑːkɪk) *or* **anˈarchical** *adj.* —**anˈarchically** *adv.*

anarthria (ænˈɑːθrɪə) *n. Pathol.* loss of the ability to speak coherently. [C19: New Latin, from Greek *anarthros* lacking vigour, from AN- + *arthros* joint]

anarthrous (ænˈɑːθrəs) *adj.* **1.** (of a noun) used without an article. **2.** having no joints or articulated limbs. [C19: from Greek *anarthros,* from AN- + *arthros* joint, definite article] —**anˈarthrously** *adv.* —**anˈarthrousness** *n.*

anasarca (ˌænəˈsɑːkə) *n. Pathol.* a generalized accumulation of serous fluid within the subcutaneous connective tissue, resulting in oedema. [C14: from New Latin, from ANA- (puffed up) + Greek *sarx* flesh] —ˌ**anaˈsarcous** *adj.*

anastigmat (æˈnæstɪgˌmæt, ˌænəˈstɪgmæt) *n.* a lens or system of lenses designed to be free of astigmatism.

anastigmatic (ˌænəstɪgˈmætɪk) *adj.* (of a lens or optical device) not astigmatic. Also: **stigmatic.**

anastomose (əˈnæstəˌməʊz) *vb.* to join (two parts of a blood vessel, etc.) by anastomosis.

anastomosis (əˌnæstəˈməʊsɪs) *n., pl.* **-ses** (-siːz). **1.** a natural connection between two tubular structures, such as blood vessels. **2.** the surgical union of two hollow organs or parts that are normally separate. **3.** a reticulate pattern, as in the veins of a leaf. [C16: via New Latin from Greek: opening, from *anastomoun* to equip with a mouth, from *stoma* mouth] —**anastomotic** (əˌnæstəˈmɒtɪk) *adj.*

anastrophe (əˈnæstrəfɪ) *n. Rhetoric.* another term for **inversion** (sense 3). [C16: from Greek, from *anastrephein* to invert]

anat. *abbrev. for:* **1.** anatomical. **2.** anatomy.

anatase (ˈænəˌteɪz) *n.* a rare blue or black mineral that consists of titanium oxide in tetragonal crystalline form and occurs in veins in igneous rocks. Formula: TiO_2. Also called: **octahedrite.** [C19: from French, from Greek *anatasis* an extending (referring to the length of the crystals), from *anateinein* to stretch out]

anathema (əˈnæθəmə) *n., pl.* **-mas.** **1.** a detested person or thing: *he is anathema to me.* **2.** a formal ecclesiastical curse of excommunication or a formal denunciation of a doctrine. **3.** the person or thing so cursed. **4.** a strong curse; imprecation. [C16: via Church Latin from Greek: something accursed, dedicated (to evil), from *anatithenai* to dedicate, from ANA- + *tithenai* to set]

anathematize *or* **anathematise** (əˈnæθɪməˌtaɪz) *vb.* to pronounce an anathema (upon a person, etc.); curse. —**aˌnathematiˈzation** *or* **aˌnathematiˈsation** *n.*

Anatolian (ˌænəˈtəʊlɪən) *adj.* **1.** of or relating to Anatolia, the Asian part of Turkey, or its inhabitants. **2.** denoting, belonging to, or relating to an ancient family of languages related to the Indo-European family and including Hittite. ~*n.* **3.** this family of languages, sometimes regarded as a branch of Indo-European. **4.** a native or inhabitant of Anatolia.

anatomical (ˌænəˈtɒmɪkᵊl) *adj.* of or relating to anatomy. —ˌ**anatomically** *adv.*

anatomical snuffbox *n.* the triangular depression on the back of the hand between the thumb and the index finger.

anatomist (əˈnætəmɪst) *n.* an expert in anatomy.

anatomize *or* **anatomise** (əˈnætəˌmaɪz) *vb.* (*tr.*) **1.** to dissect (an animal or plant). **2.** to examine in minute detail. —**aˌnatomiˈzation** *or* **aˌnatomiˈsation** *n.* —**aˈnatoˌmizer** *or* **aˈnatoˌmiser** *n.*

anatomy (əˈnætəmɪ) *n., pl.* **-mies.** **1.** the science concerned with the physical structure of animals and plants. **2.** the physical structure of an animal or plant or any of its parts. **3.** a book or treatise on this subject. **4.** dissection of an animal or plant. **5.** any detailed analysis: *the anatomy of a crime.* **6.** *Informal.* the human body. [C14: from Latin *anatomia,* from Greek *anatomē,* from *anatemnein* to cut up, from ANA- + *temnein* to cut]

anatropous (əˈnætrəpəs) *adj.* (of a plant ovule) inverted during development by a bending of the stalk (funicle) attaching it to the carpel wall. Compare **orthotropous.** [C19: from ANA- (inverted) + -TROPOUS]

anatto (əˈnætəʊ) *n., pl.* **-tos.** a variant spelling of **annatto.**

anaxial (ænˈæksɪəl) *adj. Biology.* asymmetrical.

anbury (ˈænbərɪ) *n., pl.* **-buries.** **1.** a soft spongy tumour in horses and oxen. **2.** a disease of cruciferous plants, esp. root crops, in which the roots are clubbed. [C16: of uncertain origin]

ANC *abbrev. for* African National Congress.

-ance *or* **-ancy** *suffix forming nouns.* indicating an action, state or condition, or quality: *hindrance; tenancy; resemblance.* Compare **-ence.** [via Old French from Latin *-antia;* see -ANCY]

ancestor (ˈænsɛstə) *n.* **1.** (*often pl.*) a person from whom another is directly descended, esp. someone more distant than a grandparent; forefather. **2.** an early type of animal or plant from which a later, usually dissimilar, type has evolved. **3.** a person or thing regarded as a forerunner of a later person or thing: *the ancestor of the modern camera.* [C13: from Old French *ancestre,* from Late Latin *antecēssor* one who goes before, from Latin *antecēdere;* see ANTECEDE] —ˈ**ancestress** *fem. n.*

ancestral (ænˈsɛstrəl) *adj.* **1.** of, inherited from, or derived from ancestors. ~*n.* **2.** *Logic.* a relation that holds between x and y if there is a chain of instances of a given relation leading from x to y. Thus the ancestral of *parent of* is *ancestor of,* since x is the ancestor of y if and only if x is a parent of ... a parent of ... a parent of y. —**anˈcestrally** *adv.*

ancestry (ˈænsɛstrɪ) *n., pl.* **-tries.** **1.** lineage or descent, esp. when ancient, noble, or distinguished. **2.** ancestors collectively.

anchor (ˈæŋkə) *n.* **1.** any of several devices, usually of steel, attached to a vessel by a cable and dropped overboard so as to grip the bottom and restrict the vessel's movement. **2.** an object used to hold something else firmly in place: *the rock provided an anchor for the rope.* **3.** a source of stability or security: *religion was his anchor.* **4. a.** a metal cramp, bolt, or similar fitting, esp. one used to make a connection to masonry. **b.** (*as modifier*): *anchor bolt; anchor plate.* **5. a.** the rear person in a tug-of-war team. **b.** short for **anchorman** or **anchorwoman.** **6. at anchor.** (of a vessel) anchored. **7. cast, come to,** *or* **drop anchor.** to anchor a vessel. **8. drag anchor.** See **drag** (sense 12). **9. ride at anchor.** to be anchored. **10. weigh anchor.** to raise a vessel's anchor or (of a vessel) to have its anchor raised in preparation for departure. ~*vb.* **11.** to use an anchor to hold (a vessel) in one place. **12.** to fasten or be fastened securely; fix or become fixed firmly. **13.** (*tr.*) *Radio, television.* to act as an anchorman on. [Old English *ancor,* from Latin *ancora,* from

Greek *ankura;* related to Greek *ankos* bend; compare Latin *uncus* bent, hooked]

anchorage[1] ('æŋkərɪdʒ) *n.* **1.** the act of anchoring. **2.** any place where a vessel is anchored. **3.** a place designated for vessels to anchor. **4.** a fee imposed for anchoring. **5.** anything used as an anchor. **6.** a source of security or strength. **7.** something that supplies a secure hold for something else.

anchorage[2] ('æŋkərɪdʒ) *n.* the cell or retreat of an anchorite.

anchorite ('æŋkəˌraɪt) *n.* a person who lives in seclusion, esp. a religious recluse; hermit. [C15: from Medieval Latin *anchorīta,* from Late Latin *anachōrēta,* from Greek *anakhōrētēs,* from *anakhōrein* to retire, withdraw, from *khōra* a space] —'**anchoress** *fem. n.*

anchorman ('æŋkəmæn) *n., pl.* **-men. 1.** *Sport.* the last person in a team to compete, esp. in a relay race. **2.** (in broadcasting) a person in a central studio who links up and maintains contact with various outside camera units, reporters, etc. —'**anchorˌwoman** *fem. n.*

anchor ring *n.* a ring made from an iron bar of circular cross-section.

anchoveta (ˌæntʃə'vɛtə) *n.* a small anchovy, *Cetengraulis mysticetus,* of the American Pacific, used as bait by tuna fishermen. [C20: Spanish, diminutive of *anchova* ANCHOVY]

anchovy ('æntʃəvɪ) *n., pl.* **-vies** *or* **-vy.** any of various small marine food fishes of the genus *Engraulis* and related genera, esp. *E. encrasicolus* of S Europe: family *Clupeidae* (herrings). They have a salty taste and are often tinned or made into a paste or essence. [C16: from Spanish *anchova,* perhaps ultimately from Greek *aphuē* small fish]

anchovy pear *n.* a West Indian tree, *Grias cauliflora,* bearing edible fruit that taste like the mango: family *Lecythidaceae.* [C18: so called from the use of the fruit as an hors d'oeuvre]

anchusa (æŋ'kjuːsə) *n.* any Eurasian plant of the boraginaceous genus *Anchusa,* having rough hairy stems and leaves and blue flowers. See also **alkanet** (sense 3), **bugloss.** [C18: from Latin]

anchusin (æŋ'kjuːsɪn) *n.* another name for **alkanet** (sense 2).

anchylose ('æŋkɪˌləʊz) *vb.* a variant spelling of **ankylose.** —ˌ**anchy'losis** *n.* —**anchylotic** (ˌæŋkɪ'lɒtɪk) *adj.*

anchylostomiasis (ˌæŋkɪˌlɒstə'maɪəsɪs) *n.* a variant of **ancylostomiasis.**

ancien régime *French.* (ɑ̃sjɛ̃ reʒim) *n., pl.* ***anciens régimes*** (ɑ̃sjɛ̃ reʒim). **1.** the political and social system of France before the Revolution of 1789. **2.** a former or outdated regime. [literally: old regime]

ancient[1] ('eɪnʃənt) *adj.* **1.** dating from very long ago: *ancient ruins.* **2.** very old; aged. **3.** of the far past, esp. before the collapse of the Western Roman Empire (476 A.D.). Compare **medieval, modern. 4.** *Law.* having existed since before the time of legal memory. ~*n.* **5.** (*often pl.*) a member of a civilized nation in the ancient world, esp. a Greek, Roman, or Hebrew. **6.** (*often pl.*) one of the classical authors of Greek or Roman antiquity. **7.** *Archaic.* an old man. [C14: from Old French *ancien,* from Vulgar Latin *anteanus* (unattested), from Latin *ante* before] —'**ancientness** *n.*

ancient[2] ('eɪnʃənt) *n. Archaic.* **1.** a flag or other banner; standard. **2.** a standard-bearer; ensign. [C16: changed from ENSIGN through the influence of ANCIENT[1]]

Ancient Greek *n.* the Greek language from the earliest records to about 300 B.C., the chief dialect areas of which were Aeolic, Arcadic, Doric, and Ionic (including Attic). Compare **Koine, Late Greek, Medieval Greek.**

ancient history *n.* **1.** the history of the **ancient world,** from the earliest known civilizations to the collapse of the Western Roman Empire in 476 A.D.. **2.** *Informal.* a recent event or fact sufficiently familiar to have lost its pertinence.

ancient lights *n.* (*usually functioning as sing.*) the legal right to receive, by a particular window or windows, adequate and unobstructed daylight.

anciently ('eɪnʃəntlɪ) *adv.* in ancient times.

ancient monument *n. Brit.* a historical building or the remains of one, usually dating from no later than the medieval period, that has been designated as worthy of preservation and is often in the care of a government department.

ancillary (æn'sɪlərɪ) *adj.* **1.** subsidiary. **2.** auxiliary; supplementary: *ancillary services.* ~*n., pl.* **-laries. 3.** a subsidiary or auxiliary thing or person: *the company has an ancillary abroad.* [C17: from Latin *ancillāris* concerning maidservants, from *ancilla,* diminutive of *ancūla* female servant]

ancipital (æn'sɪpɪtᵊl) *or* **ancipitous** (æn'sɪpɪtəs) *adj. Biology.* flattened and having two edges: *ancipital stems.* [C18: from Latin *anceps* two-headed]

ancon ('æŋkɒn) *or* **ancone** ('æŋkəʊn) *n., pl.* **ancones** (æŋ'kəʊniːz). **1.** *Architect.* a projecting bracket or console supporting a cornice. **2.** a former technical name for **elbow.** [C18: from Greek *ankōn* a bend] —**anconal** (æŋ'kəʊnᵊl) *or* **anconeal** (æŋ'kəʊnɪəl) *adj.*

-ancy *suffix forming nouns.* a variant of **-ance,** indicating condition or quality: *expectancy; poignancy.*

ancylostomiasis (ˌænsɪˌlɒstə'maɪəsɪs), **ankylostomiasis,** *or* **anchylostomiasis** *n.* infestation of the human intestine with blood-sucking hookworms, causing progressive anaemia. Also called: **hookworm disease.** [from New Latin, from *Ancylostoma* genus of hookworms, from Greek *ankulos* hooked, crooked + *stoma* mouth]

and (ænd; *unstressed* ənd, ən) *conj.* (*coordinating*) **1.** along with; in addition to: *boys and girls.* **2.** as a consequence: *he fell down and cut his knee.* **3.** afterwards: *we pay the man and go through that door.* **4.** (preceded by *good* or *nice*) (intensifier): *the sauce is good and thick.* **5.** plus: *two and two equals four.* **6.** used to join identical words or phrases to give emphasis or indicate repetition or continuity: *better and better; we ran and ran; it rained and rained.* **7.** used to join two identical words or phrases to express a contrast between instances of what is named: *there are jobs and jobs.* **8.** *Informal.* used in place of *to* in infinitives after verbs such as *try, go,* and *come: try and see it my way.* **9.** an obsolete word for **if:** *and it please you.* Informal spellings: **an, an', 'n.** ~*n.* **10.** (*usually pl.*) an additional matter or problem: *ifs, ands, or buts.* [Old English *and;* related to Old Frisian *anda,* Old Saxon *ande,* Old High German *anti,* Sanskrit *atha*]

▷**Usage.** See at **to.**

AND *international car registration for* Andorra.

-and *or* **-end** *suffix forming nouns.* indicating a person or thing that is to be dealt with in a specified way: *analysand; dividend; multiplicand.* [from Latin gerundives ending in *-andus, -endus*]

andalusite (ˌændə'luːsaɪt) *n.* a grey, pink, or brown hard mineral consisting of aluminium silicate in orthorhombic crystalline form. It occurs in metamorphic rocks and is used as a refractory and as a gemstone. Formula: Al_2SiO_5.

andante (æn'dæntɪ) *Music.* ~*adj., adv.* **1.** (to be performed) at a moderately slow tempo. ~*n.* **2.** a passage or piece to be performed in this manner. [C18: Italian: going, from *andare* to go, from Latin *ambulāre* to walk]

andantino (ˌændæn'tiːnəʊ) *Music.* ~*adj., adv.* **1.** (to be performed) slightly faster, or slightly more slowly, than andante. ~*n., pl.* **-nos. 2.** a passage or piece to be performed in this manner. [C19: diminutive of ANDANTE]

AND circuit *or* **gate** (ænd) *n. Computer technol.* a logic circuit having two or more input wires and one output wire that has a high-voltage output signal if and only if all input signals are at a high voltage simultaneously: used extensively as a basic circuit in computers. Compare **NAND circuit, NOR circuit, OR circuit.** [C20: so named because the action performed on electrical signals is similar to the operation of the conjunction *and* in logical constructions]

Andean (æn'diːən, 'ændɪən) *adj.* of, relating to, or resembling the Andes.

Anderson shelter ('ændəsᵊn) *n. Brit.* a small prefabricated air-raid shelter of World War II consisting of an arch of corrugated metal and designed to be partly buried in people's gardens and covered with earth for protection. [C20: so named because its use was adopted while Sir John *Anderson* was Home Secretary (1939–40)]

andesine ('ændɪˌziːn, -zɪn) *n.* a rare feldspar mineral of the plagioclase series consisting of an aluminium silicate of sodium and calcium. Formula: $NaAlSi_3O_8.CaAl_2Si_2O_8$. [C19: from the *Andes* (where it is found) + -INE[1]]

andesite ('ændɪˌzaɪt) *n.* a fine-grained grey volcanic rock consisting of plagioclase feldspar, esp. andesine, amphibole, and pyroxene. [C19: from *Andes* + -ITE[1]]

andiron ('ændˌaɪən) *n.* either of a pair of decorative metal stands in a hearth for supporting logs. [C14: from Old French *andier,* of unknown origin; influenced by IRON]

and/or *conj.* (*coordinating*) used to join terms when either one or the other or both is indicated: *passports and/or other means of identification.*

▷**Usage.** *And/or* is not universally accepted as being appropriate in good usage outside legal and commercial contexts. It is never used by careful writers and speakers where *or* is meant: *he must bring his car or his bicycle* (not *his car and/or his bicycle*).

andradite ('ændrəˌdaɪt) *n.* a yellow, green, or brownish-black garnet that consists of calcium iron silicate and is used as a gemstone. Formula: $Ca_3Fe_2(SiO_4)_3$. [C19: named after J. B. d'*Andrada* e Silva (1763–1838), Brazilian mineralogist; see -ITE[1]]

andro- *or before a vowel* **andr-** *combining form.* **1.** male; masculine: *androsterone.* **2.** (in botany) stamen or anther: *androecium.* [from Greek *anēr* (genitive *andros*) man]

androcentric (ˌændrəʊ'sɛntrɪk) *adj.* having or regarding man or the male sex as central or primary. —ˌ**andro'centrism** *n.*

androclinium (ˌændrə'klɪnɪəm) *n., pl.* **-clinia** (-'klɪnɪə). another name for **clinandrium.** [C19: New Latin, from ANDRO- + *-clinium,* from Greek *klinē* slope; see CLINO-]

androdioecious (ˌændrəʊdaɪ'iːʃəs) *adj.* (of a plant species) having hermaphrodite and male flowers on separate plants.

androecium (æn'driːsɪəm) *n., pl.* **-cia** (-sɪə). the stamens of a flowering plant collectively. [C19: from New Latin, from ANDRO- + Greek *oikion* a little house] —**an'droecial** *adj.*

androgen ('ændrədʒən) *n.* any of several steroids, produced as hormones by the testes or made synthetically, that promote development of male sexual organs and male secondary sexual characteristics. —**androgenic** (ˌændrə'dʒɛnɪk) *adj.*

androgenous (æn'drɒdʒɪnəs) *adj. Biology.* producing only male offspring.

androgyne ('ændrəˌdʒaɪn) *n.* another word for **hermaphrodite.** [C17: from Old French, via Latin from Greek *androgunos,* from *anēr* man + *gunē* woman]

androgynophore (ˌændrəʊˈgaɪnəʊfɔː) *n.* another name for **androphore.**

androgynous (ænˈdrɒdʒɪnəs) *adj.* **1.** *Botany.* having male and female flowers in the same inflorescence, as plantain. **2.** having male and female characteristics; hermaphrodite. —**anˈdrogyny** *n.*

android (ˈændrɔɪd) *n.* **1.** (in science fiction) a robot resembling a human being. ~*adj.* **2.** resembling a human being. [C18: from Late Greek *androeidēs* manlike; see ANDRO-, -OID]

Andromeda (ænˈdrɒmɪdə) *n., Latin genitive* **Andromedae** (ænˈdrɒmɪˌdiː). a constellation in the N hemisphere lying between Cassiopeia and Pegasus, the three brightest stars being of the second magnitude. It contains the **Andromeda Galaxy,** a spiral galaxy 2.2 million light years away. [C18: from *Andromeda* in Greek mythology, who was the daughter of Cassiopeia]

andromonoecious (ˌændrəʊmɒˈniːʃəs) *adj.* (of a plant species) having hermaphrodite and male flowers on the same plant.

androphore (ˈændrəʊfɔː) *n. Botany.* an extension of the receptacle carrying the stamens. Also called: **androgynophore.**

androsphinx (ˈændrəˌsfɪŋks) *n., pl.* **-sphinxes** *or* **-sphinges** (-ˌsfɪndʒiːz). a sphinx having the head of a man.

androsterone (ænˈdrɒstəˌrəʊn) *n.* an androgenic steroid hormone produced in the testes. Formula: $C_{19}H_{30}O_2$.

-androus *adj. combining form.* (in botany) indicating number or type of stamens: *diandrous.* [from New Latin *-andrus,* from Greek *-andros,* from *anēr* man]

-andry *n. combining form.* indicating number of husbands: *polyandry.* [from Greek *-andria,* from *anēr* man]

ane (eɪn) *determiner, pron., n.* a Scot. word for **one.**

-ane *suffix forming nouns.* indicating an alkane hydrocarbon: *hexane.* [coined to replace *-ene, -ine,* and *-one*]

anear (əˈnɪə) *Archaic.* ~*prep.* **1.** near. ~*adv.* **2.** nearly.

anecdotage (ˈænɪkˌdəʊtɪdʒ) *n.* **1.** anecdotes collectively. **2.** *Humorous.* talkative or garrulous old age.

anecdotal (ˌænɛkˈdəʊtᵊl) *adj.* containing or consisting exclusively of anecdotes rather than connected discourse or research conducted under controlled conditions.

anecdote (ˈænɪkˌdəʊt) *n.* a short usually amusing account of an incident, esp. a personal or biographical one. [C17: from Medieval Latin *anecdota* unpublished items, from Greek *anekdotos* unpublished, from AN- + *ekdotos* published, from *ekdidonai,* from *ek-* out + *didonai* to give] —ˌ**anecˈdotic** *adj.* —ˌ**anecˈdotalist** *or* ˈ**anecˌdotist** *n.*

anecdysis (ˌænɛkˈdaɪsɪs) *n.* the period between moults in arthropods.

anechoic (ˌænɪˈkəʊɪk) *adj.* having a low degree of reverberation of sound: *an anechoic recording studio.*

anelace (ˈænəˌleɪs) *n.* a variant spelling of **anlace.**

anele (əˈniːl) *vb. (tr.) Archaic.* to anoint, esp. to give extreme unction to. [C14 *anelen,* from *an-* (from Old English *an-* ON) + *elen* to anoint (from *ele* oil, from Latin *oleum*)]

anemia (əˈniːmɪə) *n.* the usual U.S. spelling of **anaemia.** [C19: from New Latin, from Greek *anaimia* lack of blood]

anemic (əˈniːmɪk) *adj.* the usual U.S. spelling of **anaemic.**

anemo- *combining form.* indicating wind: *anemometer; anemophilous.* [from Greek *anemos* wind]

anemochore (əˈniːməʊˌkɔː) *n.* a plant in which the fruits or seeds are dispersed by wind. —**aˌnemoˈchorous** *adj.*

anemograph (əˈnɛməʊˌgrɑːf) *n.* a self-recording anemometer. —**anemographic** (əˌnɛməʊˈgræfɪk) *adj.* —**aˌnemoˈgraphically** *adv.*

anemography (ˌænɪˈmɒgrəfɪ) *n. Meteorol.* the technique of recording wind measurements.

anemology (ˌænɪˈmɒlədʒɪ) *n.* the study of winds.

anemometer (ˌænɪˈmɒmɪtə) *n.* **1.** Also called: **wind gauge.** an instrument for recording the speed and often the direction of winds. **2.** any instrument that measures the rate of movement of a fluid. —**anemometric** (ˌænɪməʊˈmɛtrɪk) *or* ˌ**anemoˈmetrical** *adj.*

anemometry (ˌænɪˈmɒmɪtrɪ) *n. Meteorol.* the technique of measuring wind speed and direction.

anemone (əˈnɛmənɪ) *n.* any ranunculaceous woodland plant of the genus *Anemone* of N temperate regions, such as the white-flowered *A. nemorosa* (**wood anemone** or **windflower**). Some cultivated anemones have lilac, pale blue, pink, purple, or red flowers. See also **pasqueflower.** Compare **sea anemone** (an animal). [C16: via Latin from Greek: windflower, from *anemos* wind]

anemone fish *n.* any of various damselfishes of the genus *Amphiprion,* such as *A. percula* (clown anemone fish), that usually live closely associated with sea anemones.

anemophilous (ˌænɪˈmɒfɪləs) *adj.* (of flowering plants such as grasses) pollinated by the wind. Compare **entomophilous.** —ˌ**aneˈmophily** *n.*

anemoscope (əˈnɛməˌskəʊp) *n. Meteorol.* any device that shows the presence and direction of a wind.

anencephalic (ˌænɛnsəˈfælɪk) *adj.* born with no or only a partial brain. [AN- + ENCEPHALIC] —**anencephaly** (ˌænɛnˈsɛfəlɪ) *n.*

anent (əˈnɛnt) *prep. Archaic or Scot.* **1.** lying against; alongside. **2.** concerning; about. [Old English *on efen,* literally: on even (ground)]

anergy (ˈænədʒɪ) *n.* **1.** lack of energy. **2.** *Immunol.* diminution or lack of immunity to an antigen. [from New Latin *anergia,* from AN- + Greek *ergon* work] —**anergic** (æˈnɜːdʒɪk) *adj.*

aneroid (ˈænəˌrɔɪd) *adj.* not containing a liquid. [C19: from French, from AN- + Greek *nēros* wet + -OID]

aneroid barometer *n.* a device for measuring atmospheric pressure without the use of fluids. It consists of a partially evacuated metal chamber, the thin corrugated lid of which is displaced by variations in the external air pressure. This displacement is magnified by levers and made to operate a pointer.

anesthesia (ˌænɪsˈθiːzɪə) *n.* the usual U.S. spelling of **anaesthesia.**

anesthesiologist *or* **anaesthesiologist** (ˌænɪsˌθiːzɪˈɒlədʒɪst) *n.* the U.S. name for an **anaesthetist;** in the U.S., a qualified doctor specializing in the administration of anaesthesia. Compare **anesthetist.**

anesthetic (ˌænɪsˈθɛtɪk) *n., adj.* the usual U.S. spelling of **anaesthetic.**

anesthetist (əˈnɛsθətɪst) *n.* (in the U.S.) a person qualified to administer anaesthesia, often a nurse or someone other than a physician. Compare **anesthesiologist.**

anestrus (ænˈiːstrəs) *n.* a variant spelling (esp. U.S.) of **anoestrus.** —**anˈestrous** *adj.*

anethole (ˈænɪˌθəʊl) *n.* a white water-soluble crystalline substance with a liquorice-like odour, used as a flavouring and a sensitizer in the processing of colour photographs. Formula: $CH_3CH{:}CHC_6H_4OCH_3$. [C19: from Latin *anēthum* dill, anise, from Greek *anēthon*]

aneuploid (ˈænjʊˌplɔɪd) *adj.* **1.** (of polyploid cells or organisms) having a chromosome number that is not an exact multiple of the haploid number, caused by one chromosome set being incomplete. ~*n.* **2.** a cell or individual of this type. ~Compare **euploid.**

aneurin (əˈnjʊərɪn) *n.* a less common name for **thiamine.** [C20: from A(NTI-) + (POLY)NEUR(ITIS) + (VITAM)IN]

aneurysm *or* **aneurism** (ˈænjəˌrɪzəm) *n.* a sac formed by abnormal dilation of the weakened wall of a blood vessel. [C15: from Greek *aneurusma,* from *aneurunein* to dilate, from *eurunein* to widen] —ˌ**aneuˈrysmal,** ˌ**aneuˈrismal,** ˌ**aneurysˈmatic,** *or* ˌ**aneurisˈmatic** *adj.* —ˌ**aneuˈrysmally,** ˌ**aneuˈrismally,** ˌ**aneurysˈmatically,** *or* ˌ**aneurisˈmatically** *adv.*

anew (əˈnjuː) *adv.* **1.** over again; once more. **2.** in a different way; afresh. [Old English *of nīwe;* see OF, NEW]

anfractuosity (ˌænfræktʃʊˈɒsɪtɪ) *n.* **1.** the condition or quality of being anfractuous. **2.** a winding, circuitous, or intricate passage, surface, process, etc.

anfractuous (ænˈfræktʃʊəs) *adj.* characterized by twists and turns; convoluted. [C17: from Late Latin *anfractuōsus,* from Latin *anfractus* a digression, literally: a bending]

angary (ˈæŋgərɪ) *n. International law.* the right of a belligerent state to use the property of a neutral state or to destroy it if necessary, subject to payment of full compensation to the owners. [C19: from French *angarie,* from Late Latin *angaria* enforced service, from Greek *angareia* office of a courier, from *angaros* courier, of Persian origin]

angashore (ˈæŋɪʃoːr) *n. Irish.* a miserable person given to complaining. [from Irish Gaelic *ainniseoir*]

angel (ˈeɪndʒəl) *n.* **1.** *Theol.* one of a class of spiritual beings attendant upon God. In medieval angelology they are divided by rank into nine orders: seraphim, cherubim, thrones, dominations (or dominions), virtues, powers, principalities (or princedoms), archangels, and angels. **2.** a divine messenger from God. **3.** a guardian spirit. **4.** a conventional representation of any of these beings, depicted in human form with wings. **5.** *Informal.* a person, esp. a woman, who is kind, pure, or beautiful. **6.** *Informal.* an investor in a venture, esp. a backer of a theatrical production. **7.** Also called: **angel-noble.** a former English gold coin with a representation of the archangel Michael on it, first minted in Edward IV's reign. **8.** *Informal.* an unexplained signal on a radar screen. [Old English, from Late Latin *angelus,* from Greek *angelos* messenger]

angel cake *or esp. U.S.* **angel food cake** *n.* a very light sponge cake made without egg yolks.

angel dust *n.* a slang name for **PCP.**

Angeleno (ˌændʒəˈliːnəʊ) *n., pl.* **-nos.** a native or inhabitant of Los Angeles.

angelfish (ˈeɪndʒəlˌfɪʃ) *n., pl.* **-fish** *or* **-fishes. 1.** any of various small tropical marine percoid fishes of the genus *Pomacanthus* and related genera, which have a deep flattened brightly coloured body and brushlike teeth: family *Chaetodontidae.* See also **butterfly fish. 2.** Also called: **scalare.** a South American cichlid, *Pterophyllum scalare,* of the Amazon region, having a compressed body and large dorsal and anal fins: a popular aquarium fish. **3.** another name for **angel shark.**

angelic (ænˈdʒɛlɪk) *adj.* **1.** of or relating to angels. **2.** Also: **anˈgelical.** resembling an angel in beauty, purity, power, etc. —**anˈgelically** *adv.*

angelica (ænˈdʒɛlɪkə) *n.* **1.** Also called: **archangel.** any tall umbelliferous plant of the genus *Angelica,* having compound leaves and clusters of small white or greenish flowers, esp. *A. archangelica,* the aromatic seeds, leaves, and stems of which are used in medicine and cookery. **2.** the candied stems of this plant, used for decorating and flavouring sweet dishes. [C16: from Medieval Latin (*herba*) *angelica* angelic herb]

angelology (ˌeɪndʒəˈlɒlədʒɪ) *n.* a doctrine or theory treating of angels.

angel shark *or* **angelfish** *n.* any of several sharks constituting the family *Squatinidae,* such as *Squatina squatina,* that have very large flattened pectoral fins and occur in the Atlantic and Pacific Oceans. Also called: **monkfish.**

angels-on-horseback *n. Brit.* a savoury of oysters wrapped in bacon slices and served on toast.

angel's tears *n.* (*functioning as sing.*) another name for **moonflower** (sense 2).

Angelus (ˈændʒɪləs) *n. R.C. Church.* **1.** a series of prayers recited in the morning, at midday, and in the evening, commemorating the Annunciation and Incarnation. **2.** the bell (**Angelus bell**) signalling the times of these prayers. [C17: Latin, from the phrase *Angelus domini nuntiavit Mariae* the angel of the Lord brought tidings to Mary]

anger (ˈæŋgə) *n.* **1.** a feeling of great annoyance or antagonism as the result of some real or supposed grievance; rage; wrath. ~*vb.* (*tr.*) **2.** to make angry; enrage. [C12: from Old Norse *angr* grief; related to Old English *enge,* Old High German *engi* narrow, Latin *angere* to strangle]

Angevin (ˈændʒɪvɪn) *n.* **1.** a native or inhabitant of Anjou in France. **2.** *History.* a member of the Plantagenet royal line descended from Geoffrey, Count of Anjou, esp. one of the kings of England from Henry II to John (1154–1216). ~*adj.* **3.** of or relating to Anjou or its inhabitants. **4.** of or relating to the Plantagenet kings of England between 1154 and 1216.

angina (ænˈdʒaɪnə) *n.* **1.** any disease marked by painful attacks of spasmodic choking, such as Vincent's angina and quinsy. **2.** short for **angina pectoris.** [C16: from Latin: quinsy, from Greek *ankhonē* a strangling] —**anˈginal** *adj.* —**anginose** (ænˈdʒaɪnəʊs, -nəʊz) *or* **anˈginous** *adj.*

angina pectoris (ˈpɛktərɪs) *n.* a sudden intense pain in the chest, often accompanied by feelings of suffocation, caused by momentary lack of adequate blood supply to the heart muscle. Sometimes shortened to **angina.** [C18: New Latin: angina of the chest]

angio- *or before a vowel* **angi-** *combining form.* indicating a blood or lymph vessel; seed vessel: *angiology; angiosperm; angioma.* [from Greek *angeion* vessel]

angiogenesis (ˌændʒɪəˈgɛnɪsɪs) *n.* the induction of blood-vessel growth, often in association with a particular organ or tissue, or with a tumour.

angiogram (ˈændʒɪəʊˌgræm) *n.* an x-ray picture obtained by angiography.

angiography (ˌændʒɪˈɒgrəfɪ) *n.* a method of obtaining an x-ray of blood vessels by injecting into them a substance, such as iodine, that shows up as opaque on an x-ray picture.

angiology (ˌændʒɪˈɒlədʒɪ) *n.* the branch of medical science concerned with the blood vessels and the lymphatic system.

angioma (ˌændʒɪˈəʊmə) *n., pl.* **-mas** *or* **-mata** (-mətə). a tumour consisting of a mass of blood vessels (**haemangioma**) or a mass of lymphatic vessels (**lymphangioma**). —ˌ**angiˈomatous** *adj.*

angioplasty (ˈændʒɪəˌplæstɪ) *n.* a surgical technique for restoring normal blood flow through an artery narrowed or blocked by atherosclerosis, either by inserting a balloon into the narrowed section and inflating it or by using a laser beam.

angiosperm (ˈændʒɪəˌspɜːm) *n.* any seed-bearing plant of the division *Angiospermae,* in which the ovules are enclosed in an ovary, which develops into the fruit after fertilization; any flowering plant. Compare **gymnosperm.** —ˌ**angioˈspermous** *adj.*

angiotensin (ˌændʒɪəˈtɛnsɪn) *n.* a peptide of physiological importance that is capable of causing constriction of blood vessels, which raises blood pressure. [from ANGIO- + TENSE + -IN]

Angl. *abbrev. for* Anglican.

angle[1] (ˈæŋgᵊl) *n.* **1.** the space between two straight lines that diverge from a common point or between two planes that extend from a common line. **2.** the shape formed by two such lines or planes. **3.** the extent to which one such line or plane diverges from another, measured in degrees or radians. **4.** an angular projection or recess; corner. **5.** standpoint; point of view: *look at the question from another angle; the angle of a newspaper article.* **6.** *Informal.* a selfish or devious motive or purpose. **7.** See **angle iron.** ~*vb.* **8.** to move in or bend into angles or an angle. **9.** (*tr.*) to produce (an article, statement, etc.) with a particular point of view. **10.** (*tr.*) to present, direct, or place at an angle. **11.** (*intr.*) to turn or bend in a different direction: *the path angled sharply to the left.* [C14: from French, from Old Latin *angulus* corner]

angle[2] (ˈæŋgᵊl) *vb.* (*intr.*) **1.** to fish with a hook and line. **2.** (often foll. by *for*) to attempt to get: *he angled for a compliment.* ~*n.* **3.** *Obsolete.* any piece of fishing tackle, esp. a hook. [Old English *angul* fish-hook; related to Old High German *ango,* Latin *uncus,* Greek *onkos*]

Angle (ˈæŋgᵊl) *n.* a member of a West Germanic people from N Germany who invaded and settled large parts of E and N England in the 5th and 6th centuries A.D. [from Latin *Anglus,* from Germanic (compare ENGLISH), an inhabitant of *Angul,* a district in Schleswig (now *Angeln*), a name identical with Old English *angul* hook, ANGLE[2], referring to its shape]

angle bracket *n.* either of a pair of brackets having the shapes < and >.

angle iron *n.* **1.** Also called: **angle, angle bar.** an iron or a steel structural bar that has an L-shaped cross section. **2.** any piece of iron or steel forming an angle, esp. a right angle.

angle of advance *n. Engineering.* **1.** the angle in excess of 90° that a steam-engine valve gear is in advance of the crank. **2.** the angle between the point of ignition and bottom dead-centre in a spark-ignition engine.

angle of attack *n.* the acute angle between the chord line of an aerofoil and the undisturbed relative airflow. Also called: **angle of incidence.**

angle of bank *n.* the angle between the lateral axis of an aircraft in flight and the horizontal.

angle of deviation *n.* the angle between the direction of the refracted ray and the direction of the incident ray when a ray of light passes from one medium to another.

angle of dip *n.* the full name for **dip** (sense 27).

angle of friction *n. Physics.* the angle of a plane to the horizontal when a body placed on the plane will just start to slide. The tangent of the angle of friction is the **coefficient of friction.**

angle of incidence *n.* **1.** the angle that a line or beam of radiation makes with a line perpendicular to the surface at the point of incidence. **2.** another name for **angle of attack. 3.** Also called: **rigging angle of incidence.** the angle between the chord line of an aircraft wing or tailplane and the aircraft's longitudinal axis.

angle of reflection *n.* the angle that a beam of reflected radiation makes with the normal to a surface at the point of reflection.

angle of refraction *n.* the angle that a refracted beam of radiation makes with the normal to the surface between two media at the point of refraction.

angle of repose *n.* the maximum angle to the horizontal at which rocks, soil, etc., will remain without sliding.

angle plate *n.* a steel structural plate, esp. one in the shape of a right-angled triangle, used to connect structural members and stiffen frameworks.

angler (ˈæŋglə) *n.* **1.** a person who fishes with a rod and line. **2.** *Informal.* a person who schemes or uses devious methods to secure an advantage. **3.** Also called: **angler fish.** any spiny-finned fish of the order *Pediculati* (or *Lophiiformes*). They live at the bottom of the sea and typically have a long spiny movable dorsal fin with which they lure their prey.

anglesite (ˈæŋgᵊlˌsaɪt) *n.* a white or grey secondary mineral consisting of lead sulphate in orthorhombic crystalline form. It occurs in lead-ore deposits and is a source of lead. Formula: $PbSO_4$. [C19: from the island of *Anglesey,* N Wales, where it was first found]

angleworm (ˈæŋgᵊlˌwɜːm) *n.* an earthworm used as bait by anglers.

Anglian (ˈæŋglɪən) *adj.* **1.** of or relating to the Angles or to the Anglian dialects of Old English. ~*n.* **2.** the group of Old and Middle English dialects spoken in the Midlands and the north of England, divided into Mercian and Northumbrian. See also **Kentish, West Saxon.**

Anglican (ˈæŋglɪkən) *adj.* **1.** denoting or relating to the Anglican communion. ~*n.* **2.** a member of the Church of England or one of the Churches in full communion with it. [C17: from Medieval Latin *Anglicānus,* from *Anglicus* English, from Latin *Anglī* the Angles]

Anglican Church *n.* any Church of the Anglican Communion or the Anglican Communion itself.

Anglican Communion *n.* a group of Christian Churches including the Church of England, the Church of Ireland, the Episcopal Church in Scotland, the Church in Wales, the Episcopal Church in the U.S., and certain other Churches, all of which are in full communion with each other.

Anglicanism (ˈæŋglɪkəˌnɪzəm) *n.* the doctrine and practice of the Church of England and other Anglican Churches.

Anglice (ˈæŋglɪsɪ) *adv.* in English: *Roma, Anglice Rome.* [from Medieval Latin]

Anglicism (ˈæŋglɪˌsɪzəm) *n.* **1.** a word, phrase, or idiom peculiar to the English language, esp. as spoken in England. **2.** an English attitude, mannerism, custom, etc. **3.** the fact or quality of being English.

Anglicist (ˈæŋglɪsɪst) *or* **Anglist** *n. Rare.* an expert in or student of English literature or language.

anglicize, anglicise (ˈæŋglɪˌsaɪz), *or* **anglify** (ˈæŋglɪˌfaɪ) *vb.* **-cizes, -cizing, -cized, -cises, -cising, -cised** *or* **-fies, -fying, -fied.** (*sometimes cap.*) to make or become English in outlook, attitude, form, etc. —ˌ**angliciˈzation** *or* ˌ**angliciˈsation** *n.*

angling (ˈæŋglɪŋ) *n.* **a.** the art or sport of catching fish with a rod and line and a baited hook or other lure, such as a fly; fishing. **b.** (*as modifier*): *an angling contest.*

Anglo (ˈæŋgləʊ) *n., pl.* **-glos. 1.** *U.S.* a White inhabitant of the United States who is not of Latin extraction. **2.** *Austral., often derogatory.* an Australian of Anglo-Celtic descent.

Anglo- (ˈæŋgləʊ-) *combining form.* denoting English or England: *Anglo-Saxon.* [from Medieval Latin *Anglī*]

Anglo-American *adj.* **1.** of or relating to relations between England and the United States or their peoples. ~*n.* **2.** *Chiefly U.S.* an inhabitant or citizen of the United States who was or whose ancestors were born in England.

Anglo-Catholic *adj.* **1.** of or relating to a group within the Church of England or the Anglican Communion that emphasizes the Catholic elements in its teaching and practice. *~n.* **2.** a member of this group. —ˌ**Anglo-Ca'tholiˌcism** *n.*
Anglo-French *adj.* **1.** of or relating to England and France. **2.** of or relating to Anglo-French. *~n.* **3.** the Norman-French language of medieval England.
Anglo-Indian *adj.* **1.** of or relating to England and India. **2.** denoting or relating to Anglo-Indians. **3.** (of a word) introduced into English from an Indian language. *~n.* **4.** a person of mixed English and Indian descent. **5.** an Englishman who lives or has lived for a long time in India.
Anglo-Irish *n.* **1.** (preceded by *the; functioning as pl.*) the inhabitants of Ireland of English birth or descent. **2.** the English language as spoken in Ireland. *~adj.* **3.** of or relating to the Anglo-Irish. **4.** of or relating to English and Irish. **5.** of or relating to the English language as spoken in Ireland.
Anglomania (ˌæŋgləʊ'meɪnɪə) *n.* excessive respect for English customs, etc. —ˌ**Anglo'maniˌac** *n.*
Anglo-Norman *adj.* **1.** *History.* relating to the Norman conquerors of England, their society, or their language. *~n.* **2.** *History.* a Norman inhabitant of England after 1066. **3.** the Anglo-French language.
Anglophile ('æŋgləʊfɪl, -ˌfaɪl) *or* **Anglophil** *n.* **1.** a person having admiration for England or the English. *~adj.* **2.** marked by or possessing such admiration. —**Anglophilia** (ˌæŋgləʊ'fɪlɪə) *n.* —**Anglophiliac** (ˌæŋgləʊ'fɪlɪˌæk) *or* **Anglophilic** (ˌæŋgləʊ'fɪlɪk) *adj.*
Anglophobe ('æŋgləʊˌfəʊb) *n.* a person who hates or fears England or its people. —ˌ**Anglo'phobia** *n.*
Anglophone ('æŋgləˌfəʊn) (*often not cap.*) *n.* **1.** a person who speaks English, esp. a native speaker. *~adj.* **2.** speaking English.
Anglo-Saxon *n.* **1.** a member of any of the West Germanic tribes (Angles, Saxons, and Jutes) that settled in Britain from the 5th century A.D. and were dominant until the Norman conquest. **2.** the language of these tribes. See **Old English. 3.** any White person whose native language is English and whose cultural affiliations are those common to Britain and the U.S. **4.** *Informal.* plain blunt English, esp. English containing taboo words. *~adj.* **5.** forming part of the Germanic element in Modern English: *"forget" is an Anglo-Saxon word.* **6.** of or relating to the Anglo-Saxons or the Old English language. **7.** of or relating to the White Protestant culture of Britain, Australia, and the U.S. **8.** *Informal.* (of English speech or writing) plain and blunt.
Angolan ('æŋˌgəʊlən) *adj.* of or relating to Angola, a republic in SW Africa.
angora (æŋ'gɔːrə) *n.* (*sometimes cap.*) **1. a.** the long soft hair of the outer coat of the Angora goat or the fur of the Angora rabbit. **b.** yarn, cloth, or clothing made from this hair. **c.** a material made to resemble this yarn or cloth. **d.** (*as modifier*): *an angora sweater.* See also **mohair. 2.** *Austral. slang.* an idiot; fool. [from *Angora*, former name of Ankara in Turkey]
Angora (æŋ'gɔːrə) *n.* short for **Angora cat, Angora goat,** or **Angora rabbit.**
Angora cat *n.* a former long-haired variety of cat, similar to the Persian.
Angora goat *n.* a breed of domestic goat with long soft hair.
Angora rabbit *n.* a breed of rabbit with long usually white silky hair.
angostura bark (ˌæŋgə'stjʊərə) *n.* the bitter aromatic bark of certain South American rutaceous trees of the genus *Cusparia* or *Galipea,* formerly used medicinally to reduce fever. [from *Angostura*, former name for Ciudad Bolívar, town in Venezuela]
angostura bitters *pl. n.* (*often cap.*) *Trademark.* a bitter aromatic tonic made from gentian and various spices and vegetable colourings, used as a flavouring in alcoholic drinks.
angry ('æŋgrɪ) *adj.* **-grier, -griest. 1.** feeling or expressing annoyance, animosity, or resentment; enraged. **2.** suggestive of anger: *angry clouds.* **3.** severely inflamed: *an angry sore.* —'**angrily** *adv.*
angry young man *n.* **1.** (*often caps.*) one of several British novelists and playwrights of the 1950s who shared a hostility towards the established traditions and ruling elements of their country. **2.** any similarly rebellious person.
angst (æŋst; *German* aŋst) *n.* **1.** an acute but nonspecific sense of anxiety or remorse. **2.** (in Existentialist philosophy) the dread caused by man's awareness that his future is not determined but must be freely chosen. [German]
angstrom ('æŋstrʌm, -strəm) *n.* a unit of length equal to 10^{-10} metre, used principally to express the wavelengths of electromagnetic radiations. It is equivalent to 0.1 nanometre. Symbol: Å or A Also called: **angstrom unit.** [C20: named after Anders J. *Ångström* (1814–74), Swedish physicist]
anguilliform (æŋ'gwɪlɪˌfɔːm) *adj.* having the shape or form of an eel. [C17: from Latin *anguilla* eel, diminutive of *anguis* snake]
anguine ('æŋgwɪn) *adj.* of, relating to, or similar to a snake. [C17: from Latin *anguīnus,* from *anguis* snake]
anguish ('æŋgwɪʃ) *n.* **1.** extreme pain or misery; mental or physical torture; agony. *~vb.* **2.** to afflict or be afflicted with anguish. [C13: from Old French *angoisse* a strangling, from Latin *angustia* narrowness, from *angustus* narrow]
anguished ('æŋgwɪʃt) *adj.* feeling or expressing anguish.
angular ('æŋgjʊlə) *adj.* **1.** lean or bony. **2.** awkward or stiff in manner or movement. **3.** having an angle or angles. **4.** placed at an angle. **5.** measured by an angle or by the rate at which an angle changes. [C15: from Latin *angulāris,* from *angulus* ANGLE[1]] —'**angularly** *adv.* —'**angularness** *n.*
angular acceleration **1.** *n.* the rate of change of angular velocity. **2.** *Astronautics.* the acceleration of a space vehicle around an axis.
angular displacement *n. Physics.* the angle through which a point, line, or body is rotated about a specific axis in a given direction.
angular frequency *n. Physics.* the frequency of a periodic process, wave system, etc., expressed in radians per second.
angularity (ˌæŋgjʊ'lærɪtɪ) *n., pl.* **-ties. 1.** the condition of being angular. **2.** an angular form or shape.
angular magnification *n. Physics.* the ratio of the angle subtended at the eye by an image formed by an optical instrument to the angle subtended at the unaided eye by the object.
angular momentum *n.* a measure of the momentum of a body caused by its circular motion around an axis of rotation, equal to the product of its mass and its angular velocity.
angular velocity *n.* the velocity of a body rotating about a fixed point measured as the rate of change of the angle subtended at that fixed point by the path of the body. Symbol: ω
angulate *adj.* ('æŋgjʊlɪt, -ˌleɪt). **1.** having angles or an angular shape. *~vb.* ('æŋgjʊˌleɪt). **2.** to make or become angular. [C18: from Late Latin *angulāre* to make angled, from Latin *angulus* ANGLE[1]] —'**anguˌlated** *adj.*
angulation (ˌæŋgjʊ'leɪʃən) *n.* **1.** an angular formation. **2.** the precise measurement of angles.
angwantibo (æŋ'gwæntɪˌbəʊ) *n., pl.* **-bos.** a rare gold-coloured prosimian primate of tropical Africa, *Arctocebus calabarensis,* having digits that are specialized as a pair of pincers for climbing: family *Lorisidae* (lorises). Also called: **golden potto.** [C19: from Efik]
anharmonic (ˌænhɑː'mɒnɪk) *adj. Physics.* of or concerned with an oscillation whose frequency is not an integral factor or multiple of the base frequency.
anhedral (æn'hiːdrəl) *n.* the downward inclination of an aircraft wing in relation to the lateral axis. Compare **dihedral** (sense 4).
anhidrosis (ˌænhɪ'drəʊsɪs) *or* **anidrosis** *n. Pathol.* the absence of sweating. [from AN- + Greek *hidrōs* sweat + -OSIS]
anhidrotic (ˌænhɪ'drɒtɪk) *Med. ~adj.* **1.** curbing the secretion of sweat. *~n.* **2.** a substance that suppresses sweating.
anhinga (æn'hɪŋgə) *n.* another name for **darter** (the bird). [C18: via Portuguese from Tupi]
anhydride (æn'haɪdraɪd, -drɪd) *n.* **1.** a compound that has been formed from another compound by dehydration. **2.** a compound that forms an acid or base when added to water. **3.** Also called: **acid anhydride** or **acyl anhydride.** any organic compound containing the group -CO.O.CO- formed by removal of one water molecule from two carboxyl groups. [C19: from ANHYDR(OUS) + -IDE]
anhydrite (æn'haɪdraɪt) *n.* a colourless or greyish-white mineral, found in sedimentary rocks. It is used in the manufacture of cement, fertilizers, and chemicals. Composition: anhydrous calcium sulphate. Formula: $CaSO_4$. Crystal structure: orthorhombic. [C19: from ANHYDR(OUS) + -ITE[1]]
anhydrous (æn'haɪdrəs) *adj.* containing no water, esp. no water of crystallization. [C19: from Greek *anudros;* see AN-, HYDRO-]
ani ('ɑːnɪ) *n., pl.* **anis.** any of several gregarious tropical American birds of the genus *Crotophaga:* family *Cuculidae* (cuckoos). They have a black plumage, long square-tipped tail, and heavily hooked bill. [Spanish *ani,* from Tupi]
aniconic (ˌænaɪ'kɒnɪk) *adj.* (of images of deities, symbols, etc.) not portrayed in a human or animal form. [C19: from AN- + ICONIC]
anil ('ænɪl) *n.* a leguminous West Indian shrub, *Indigofera suffruticosa:* a source of indigo. Also called: **indigo.** [C16: from Portuguese, from Arabic *an-nīl,* the indigo, from Sanskrit *nīla* dark blue]
anile ('ænaɪl, 'eɪnaɪl) *adj.* of or like a feeble old woman. [C17: from Latin *anīlis,* from *anus* old woman] —**anility** (ə'nɪlɪtɪ) *n.*
aniline ('ænɪlɪn, -ˌliːn) *n.* a colourless oily pungent poisonous liquid used in the manufacture of dyes, plastics, pharmaceuticals, and explosives. Formula: $C_6H_5NH_2$. Also called: **phenylamine.**
aniline dye *n.* any synthetic dye originally made from raw materials, such as aniline, obtained from coal tar.
anilingus (ˌeɪnɪ'lɪŋgəs) *n.* sexual stimulation involving oral contact with the anus. [C20: from *ani-* ANUS + *-lingus,* as in CUNNILINGUS]
anim. *abbrev. for* animato.
anima ('ænɪmə) *n.* (in Jungian psychology) **a.** the feminine principle as present in the male unconscious. **b.** the inner personality, which is in communication with the unconscious. See also **animus.** [Latin: air, breath, spirit, feminine of ANIMUS]
animadversion (ˌænɪmæd'vɜːʃən) *n.* **1.** criticism or censure. **2.** a carefully considered observation.
animadvert (ˌænɪmæd'vɜːt) *vb.* (*intr.*) **1.** (usually foll. by *on* or *upon*) to comment with strong criticism (upon); make censorious remarks (about). **2.** to make an observation or comment. [C16:

from Latin *animadvertere* to notice, pay attention, from *animus* mind + *advertere* to turn to, from *vertere* to turn]

animal ('ænɪməl) *n.* **1.** *Zoology.* any living organism characterized by voluntary movement, the possession of cells with noncellulose cell walls and specialized sense organs enabling rapid response to stimuli, and the ingestion of complex organic substances such as plants and other animals. **2.** any mammal, esp. any mammal except man. **3.** a brutish person. **4.** *Facetious.* a person or thing (esp. in the phrase **no such animal**). *~adj.* **5.** of, relating to, or derived from animals: *animal products; an animal characteristic.* **6.** of or relating to the physical needs or desires; carnal; sensual. [C14: from Latin *animal* (n.), from *animālis* (adj.) living, breathing; see ANIMA]

animalcule (ˌænɪ'mælkjuːl) *or* **animalculum** (ˌænɪ'mælkjʊləm) *n., pl.* **-cules** *or* **-cula** (-kjʊlə). a microscopic animal such as an amoeba or rotifer. [C16: from New Latin *animalculum* a small ANIMAL] —ˌ**ani'malcular** *adj.*

animal husbandry *n.* the science of breeding, rearing, and caring for farm animals.

animalier ('ænɪməˌlɪə, ˌænɪ'mælɪeɪ) *n.* **a.** a painter or sculptor of animal subjects, esp. a member of a group of early 19th-century French sculptors who specialized in realistic figures of animals, usually in bronze. **b.** (*as modifier*): *an animalier bronze.* [from French]

animalism ('ænɪməˌlɪzəm) *n.* **1.** satisfaction of or preoccupation with physical matters; sensuality. **2.** the doctrine or belief that man lacks a spiritual nature. **3.** a trait or mode of behaviour typical of animals. —'**animalist** *n.*

animality (ˌænɪ'mælɪtɪ) *n.* **1.** the animal side of man, as opposed to the intellectual or spiritual. **2.** the fact of being or having the characteristics of an animal.

animalize *or* **animalise** ('ænɪməˌlaɪz) *vb.* (*tr.*) to rouse to brutality or sensuality or make brutal or sensual. —ˌ**animali'zation** *or* ˌ**animali'sation** *n.*

animal kingdom *n.* a category of living organisms comprising all animals. Compare **plant kingdom, mineral kingdom.**

Animal Liberation Front *n.* (in Britain) an animal-rights movement often using direct action. Abbrev.: **ALF.**

animal magnetism *n.* **1.** *Sometimes facetious.* the quality of being attractive, esp. to members of the opposite sex. **2.** *Obsolete.* hypnotism.

animal rights *pl. n.* **a.** the rights of animals to be protected from exploitation and abuse by humans. **b.** (*as modifier*): *the animal-rights lobby.*

animal spirits *pl. n.* cheerful and exuberant boisterousness. [originally, referring to a vital force believed to be dispatched throughout the body by the brain]

animal starch *n.* a less common name for **glycogen.**

animate *vb.* ('ænɪˌmeɪt). (*tr.*) **1.** to give life to or cause to come alive. **2.** to make gay or lively; enliven. **3.** to encourage or inspire. **4.** to impart motion to; move to action or work. **5.** to record on film or video tape so as to give movement to: *an animated cartoon.* *~adj.* ('ænɪmɪt). **6.** being alive or having life. **7.** gay, spirited, or lively. [C16: from Latin *animāre* to fill with breath, make alive, from *anima* breath, spirit]

animated ('ænɪˌmeɪtɪd) *adj.* **1.** full of vivacity and spirit; lively. **2.** characterized by movement and activity: *an animated scene met her eye.* **3.** possessing life; animate. **4.** moving or appearing to move as if alive: *an animated display.* **5.** pertaining to cinematographic animation. —'**aniˌmatedly** *adv.*

animated cartoon *n.* a film produced by photographing a series of gradually changing drawings, etc., which give the illusion of movement when the series is projected rapidly.

animation (ˌænɪ'meɪʃən) *n.* **1.** liveliness; vivacity. **2.** the condition of being alive. **3. a.** the techniques used in the production of animated cartoons. **b.** a variant of **animated cartoon.**

animatism ('ænɪməˌtɪzəm) *n.* the belief that inanimate objects have consciousness.

animato (ˌænɪ'mɑːtəʊ) *adj., adv. Music.* (to be performed) in a lively manner. [Italian]

animator *or* **animater** ('ænɪˌmeɪtə) *n.* an artist who produces animated cartoons.

animé[1] ('ænɪˌmeɪ, -mɪ) *n.* any of various resins, esp. that obtained from the tropical American leguminous tree *Hymenaea courbaril.* [French: of uncertain origin]

animé[2] ('ænɪˌmeɪ) *adj., adv. Music.* the French word for **animato.**

animism ('ænɪˌmɪzəm) *n.* **1.** the belief that natural objects, phenomena, and the universe itself have desires and intentions. **2.** (in the philosophies of Plato and Pythagoras) the hypothesis that there is an immaterial force that animates the universe. [C19: from Latin *anima* vital breath, spirit] —'**animist** *n.* —**animistic** (ˌænɪ'mɪstɪk) *adj.*

animosity (ˌænɪ'mɒsɪtɪ) *n., pl.* **-ties.** a powerful and active dislike or hostility; enmity. [C15: from Late Latin *animōsitās,* from Latin *animōsus* spirited, from ANIMUS]

animus ('ænɪməs) *n.* **1.** intense dislike; hatred; animosity. **2.** motive, intention, or purpose. **3.** (in Jungian psychology) the masculine principle present in the female unconscious. See also **anima.** [C19: from Latin: mind, spirit]

anion ('ænˌaɪən) *n.* a negatively charged ion; an ion that is attracted to the anode during electrolysis. Compare **cation.** [C19: from ANA- + ION] —**anionic** (ˌænaɪ'ɒnɪk) *adj.*

anise ('ænɪs) *n.* a Mediterranean umbelliferous plant, *Pimpinella anisum,* having clusters of small yellowish-white flowers and liquorice-flavoured seeds (see **aniseed).** [C13: from Old French *anis,* via Latin from Greek *anison*]

aniseed ('ænɪˌsiːd) *n.* the liquorice-flavoured aromatic seeds of the anise plant, used medicinally for expelling intestinal gas and in cookery as a flavouring, esp. in cakes. Also called: **anise.**

aniseikonia (ˌænaɪsaɪ'kəʊnɪə) *n.* a condition caused by a defect in the lens of the eye in which the images produced in the two eyes differ in size or shape. [C20: New Latin, from ANISO- + Greek *eikon* image] —ˌ**anisei'konic** *adj.*

anisette (ˌænɪ'zɛt, -'sɛt) *n.* a liquorice-flavoured liqueur made from aniseed. [C19: from French; see ANISE, -ETTE]

aniso- *or before a vowel* **anis-** *combining form.* not equal: *anisogamy.* [New Latin, from Greek *anisos;* see AN-, ISO-]

anisocercal (ænˌaɪsəʊ'sɜːkᵊl) *adj.* (of fish) having unequal tail-fin lobes. [C19: from ANISO- + Greek *kerkos* tail]

anisodactyl (ænˌaɪsəʊ'dæktɪl, ˌænaɪ-) *adj. also* **anisodactylous.** **1.** (of the feet of passerine birds) having the first toe directed backwards and the other three toes directed forwards. *~n.* **2.** a bird having this type of feet.

anisogamy (ˌænaɪ'sɒgəmɪ) *n.* a type of sexual reproduction in which the gametes are dissimilar, either in size alone or in size and form. —ˌ**ani'sogamous** *adj.*

anisole ('ænɪˌsəʊl) *n.* a colourless pleasant-smelling liquid used as a solvent and vermicide and in perfume and flavouring. Formula: $C_6H_5OCH_3$; relative density: 0.996; melting pt.: –37.5°C; boiling pt.: 155°C. [C19: from ANISE + -OLE[1]]

anisomeric (ænˌaɪsəʊ'mɛrɪk) *adj.* (of a chemical compound) lacking isomers.

anisomerous (ˌænɪ'sɒmərəs) *adj.* (of flowers) having floral whorls that differ in the number of their parts. Compare **isomerous** (sense 2).

anisometric (ænˌaɪsəʊ'mɛtrɪk) *adj.* **1.** not isometric; having unsymmetrical parts or unequal measurements. **2.** (of a crystal) having unequal axes.

anisometropia (ænˌaɪsəʊmə'trəʊpɪə, ˌænaɪ-) *n.* an imbalance in the power of the two eyes to refract light.

anisomorphic (ænˌaɪsəʊ'mɔːfɪk) *adj. Linguistics.* differing in the semantic scope of terms referring to the real world: for instance, English and Russian are anisomorphic with regard to colour terms, English treating light blue and navy blue as shades of one colour but Russian treating these two shades as unrelated.

anisophyllous (æˌnaɪsəʊ'fɪləs) *adj.* another word for **heterophyllous.** —**an'isoˌphylly** *n.*

anisotropic (ænˌaɪsəʊ'trɒpɪk, ˌænaɪ-) *adj.* **1.** not isotropic; having different physical properties in different directions: *anisotropic crystals.* **2.** (of a plant) responding unequally to an external stimulus in different parts of the plant. —**anˌiso'tropically** *adv.* —**anisotropy** (ˌænaɪ'sɒtrəpɪ) *n.*

ankerite ('æŋkəˌraɪt) *n.* a greyish to brown mineral that resembles dolomite and consists of a carbonate of calcium, magnesium, and iron. Formula: $(Ca,Mg,Fe)CO_3$. [C19: named after M. J. *Anker* (died 1843), Austrian mineralogist]

ankh (æŋk) *n.* a tau cross with a loop on the top, symbolizing eternal life: often appearing in Egyptian personal names, such as Tutankhamen. Also called: **ansate cross, crux ansata.** [from Egyptian *'nh* life, soul]

ankle ('æŋkᵊl) *n.* **1.** the joint connecting the leg and the foot. See **talus**[1]. **2.** the part of the leg just above the foot. [C14: from Old Norse; related to German, Dutch *enkel,* Latin *angulus* ANGLE[1]]

ankle biter *n. Austral slang.* a child.

anklebone ('æŋkᵊlˌbəʊn) *n.* the nontechnical name for **talus**[1].

ankle sock *n.* (*often pl.*) *Brit.* a short sock coming up to the ankle. U.S. term: **anklet.**

anklet ('æŋklɪt) *n.* **1.** an ornamental chain worn around the ankle. **2.** the U.S. word for **ankle sock.**

ankus ('æŋkəs) *n., pl.* **-kus** *or* **-kuses.** a stick used, esp. in India, for goading elephants. [from Hindi]

ankylosaur ('æŋkɪləʊˌsɔː) *n.* any of various quadrupedal herbivorous ornithischian dinosaurs constituting the suborder *Ankylosauria,* which were most abundant in upper Cretaceous times and had a very heavily armoured tanklike body. [C20: from New Latin, from Greek *ankulos* crooked + -SAUR]

ankylose *or* **anchylose** ('æŋkɪˌləʊs, -ˌləʊz) *vb.* (of bones in a joint, etc.) to fuse or stiffen by ankylosis.

ankylosis *or* **anchylosis** (ˌæŋkɪ'ləʊsɪs) *n.* abnormal adhesion or immobility of the bones in a joint, as by a direct joining of the bones, a fibrous growth of tissues within the joint, or surgery. [C18: from New Latin, from Greek *ankuloun* to crook] —**ankylotic** *or* **anchylotic** (ˌæŋkɪ'lɒtɪk) *adj.*

ankylostomiasis (ˌæŋkɪˌlɒstə'maɪəsɪs) *n.* a variant of **ancylostomiasis.**

anlace ('ænlɪs) *or* **anelace** *n.* a medieval short dagger with a broad tapering blade. [C13: of unknown origin]

anlage ('ænˌlɑːgə) *n., pl.* **-gen** (-gən) *or* **-ges.** another word for **primordium.** [German: predisposition, layout]

ann. *abbrev. for:* **1.** annals (periodical publications). **2.** annual. **3.** annuity.

anna ('ænə) *n.* a former Indian copper coin, worth one sixteenth of a rupee. [C18: from Hindi *ānā*]

annabergite ('ænəˌbɜːgaɪt) *n.* a rare green secondary mineral consisting of hydrated nickel arsenate in monoclinic crystalline form. Formula: $Ni_3(AsO_4)_2.8H_2O$. Also called: **nickel bloom.** [C19: named after *Annaberg* in Saxony, where it was discovered; see -ITE[1]]

annal ('ænᵊl) *n.* the recorded events of one year. See also **annals.**

annals ('ænᵊlz) *pl. n.* **1.** yearly records of events, generally in chronological order. **2.** history or records of history in general. **3.** regular reports of the work of a society, learned body, etc. [C16: from Latin (*librī*) *annālēs* yearly (books), from *annus* year] —'**annalist** *n.* —ˌ**annal'istic** *adj.*

Annamese (ˌænə'mi:z) *adj.* **1.** of or relating to Annam, now part of Vietnam. ~*adj., n.* **2.** a former word for **Vietnamese.**

annates ('æneɪts, -əts) *pl. n. R.C. Church.* the first year's revenue of a see, an abbacy, or a minor benefice, paid to the pope. [C16: plural of French *annate,* from Medieval Latin *annāta,* from Latin *annus* year]

annatto *or* **anatto** (ə'nætəʊ) *n., pl.* **-tos. 1.** a small tropical American tree, *Bixa orellana,* having red or pinkish flowers and pulpy seeds that yield a dye: family *Bixaceae.* **2.** the yellowish-red dye obtained from the pulpy outer layer of the coat of the seeds of this tree, used for colouring fabrics, butter, varnish, etc. [from Carib]

anneal (ə'ni:l) *vb.* **1.** to temper or toughen (something) by heat treatment. **2.** to subject to or undergo some physical treatment, esp. heating, that removes internal stress, crystal defects, and dislocations. **3.** (*tr.*) to toughen or strengthen (the will, determination, etc.). **4.** (often foll. by *out*) *Physics.* to disappear or cause to disappear by a rearrangement of atoms: *defects anneal out at different temperatures.* ~*n.* **5.** an act of annealing. [Old English *onǣlan,* from ON + *ǣlan* to burn, from *āl* fire] —**an'nealer** *n.*

annelid ('ænəlɪd) *n.* **1.** any worms of the phylum *Annelida,* in which the body is divided into segments both externally and internally. The group includes the earthworms, lugworm, ragworm, and leeches. ~*adj.* **2.** of, relating to, or belonging to the *Annelida.* [C19: from New Latin *Annelida,* from French *annelés,* literally: the ringed ones, from Old French *annel* ring, from Latin *ānellus,* from *ānulus* ring] —**annelidan** (ə'nɛlɪdən) *n., adj.*

annex *vb.* (æ'nɛks). (*tr.*) **1.** to join or add, esp. to something larger; attach. **2.** to add (territory) by conquest or occupation. **3.** to add or append as a condition, warranty, etc. **4.** to appropriate without permission. ~*n.* ('ænɛks). **5.** a variant spelling (esp. U.S.) of **annexe.** [C14: from Medieval Latin *annexāre,* from Latin *annectere* to attach to, from *nectere* to join] —**an'nexable** *adj.*

annexation (ˌænɪk'seɪʃən, -ɛk-) *n.* **1.** the act of annexing, esp. territory, or the condition of being annexed. **2.** something annexed. —ˌ**annex'ational** *adj.* —ˌ**annex'ationism** *n.* —ˌ**annex'ationist** *n.*

annexe *or esp. U.S.* **annex** ('ænɛks) *n.* **1. a.** an extension to a main building. **b.** a building used as an addition to a main building nearby. **2.** something added or annexed, esp. a supplement to a document.

annihilate (ə'naɪəˌleɪt) *vb.* **1.** (*tr.*) to destroy completely; extinguish. **2.** (*tr.*) *Informal.* to defeat totally, as in debate or argument. **3.** (*intr.*) *Physics.* to undergo annihilation. [C16: from Late Latin *annihilāre* to bring to nothing, from Latin *nihil* nothing] —**annihilable** (ə'naɪələbᵊl) *adj.* —**an'nihilative** *adj.* —**an'nihiˌlator** *n.*

annihilation (əˌnaɪə'leɪʃən) *n.* **1.** total destruction. **2.** the act of annihilating. **3.** *Physics.* the destruction of a particle and its antiparticle when they collide. The annihilation of an electron with a positron generates two or, very rarely, three photons of **annihilation radiation.** The annihilation of a nucleon with its antiparticle generates several pions.

anniversary (ˌænɪ'vɜ:sərɪ) *n., pl.* **-ries. 1.** the date on which an event occurred in some previous year: *a wedding anniversary.* **2.** the celebration of this. ~*adj.* **3.** of or relating to an anniversary. **4.** recurring every year, esp. on the same date. [C13: from Latin *anniversārius* returning every year, from *annus* year + *vertere* to turn]

Anniversary Day *n.* **1.** another name for **Australia Day. 2.** (*not caps.*) *N.Z.* a day for celebrating the foundation date of one of the former Provinces.

anno Domini ('ænəʊ 'dɒmɪˌnaɪ, -ˌni:) *adv.* **1.** the full form of **A.D.** or **AD.** ~*n.* **2.** *Informal.* advancing old age. [Latin: in the year of our Lord]

anno regni *Latin.* ('ænəʊ 'rɛgnaɪ) in the year of the reign.

annotate ('ænəʊˌteɪt, 'ænə-) *vb.* to supply (a written work, such as an ancient text) with critical or explanatory notes. [C18: from Latin *annotāre,* from *nota* mark] —'**annoˌtatable** *adj.* —'**annoˌtative** *adj.* —'**annoˌtator** *n.*

annotation (ˌænəʊ'teɪʃən, ˌænə-) *n.* **1.** the act of annotating. **2.** a note added in explanation, etc., esp. of some literary work.

announce (ə'naʊns) *vb.* **1.** (*tr.; may take a clause as object*) to make known publicly; proclaim. **2.** (*tr.*) to declare the arrival of: *to announce a guest.* **3.** (*tr.; may take a clause as object*) to reveal to the mind or senses; presage: *the dark clouds announced rain.* **4.** (*intr.*) to work as an announcer, as on radio or television. **5.** *U.S.* to make known (one's intention to run as a candidate): *to announce for the presidency.* [C15: from Old French *anoncer,* from Latin *annuntiāre,* from *nuntius* messenger]

announcement (ə'naʊnsmənt) *n.* **1.** a public statement. **2.** a brief item or advertisement, as in a newspaper. **3.** a formal printed or written invitation. **4.** the act of announcing.

announcer (ə'naʊnsə) *n.* a person who announces, esp. one who reads the news, introduces programmes, etc., on radio or television.

anno urbis conditae *Latin.* ('ænəʊ 'ɜ:bɪs 'kɒndɪˌti:) the full form of **AUC** (sense 1). [literally: in the year of the founding of the city]

annoy (ə'nɔɪ) *vb.* **1.** to irritate or displease. **2.** to harass with repeated attacks. [C13: from Old French *anoier,* from Late Latin *inodiāre* to make hateful, from Latin *in odiō (esse)* (to be) hated, from *odium* hatred] —**an'noyer** *n.* —**an'noying** *adj.* —**an'noyingly** *adv.*

annoyance (ə'nɔɪəns) *n.* **1.** the feeling of being annoyed. **2.** the act of annoying. **3.** a person or thing that annoys.

annual ('ænjʊəl) *adj.* **1.** occurring, done, etc., once a year or every year; yearly: *an annual income.* **2.** lasting for a year: *an annual subscription.* ~*n.* **3.** a plant that completes its life cycle in one year. Compare **perennial** (sense 3), **biennial** (sense 3). **4.** a book, magazine, etc., published once every year. [C14: from Late Latin *annuālis,* from Latin *annuus* yearly, from *annus* year] —'**annually** *adv.*

annual general meeting *n. Brit.* the statutory meeting of the directors and shareholders of a company or of the members of a society, held once every financial year, at which the annual report is presented. Abbrev.: **AGM.**

annualize *or* **annualise** ('ænjʊəˌlaɪz) *vb.* (*tr.*) to convert (a rate of interest) to an annual rate when it is quoted for a period of less than a year: *credit card companies are obliged to quote an annualized percentage rate to borrowers.*

annual parallax *n.* See under **parallax** (sense 2).

annual report *n.* a report presented by the directors of a company to its shareholders each year, containing the profit-and-loss account, the balance sheet, and details of the past year's activity.

annual ring *n.* a ring of wood indicating one year's growth, seen in the transverse section of stems and roots of woody plants growing in temperate climates. Also called: **tree ring.**

annuitant (ə'nju:ɪtənt) *n.* a person in receipt of or entitled to an annuity.

annuity (ə'nju:ɪtɪ) *n., pl.* **-ties. 1.** a fixed sum payable at specified intervals, esp. annually, over a period, such as the recipient's life, or in perpetuity, in return for a premium paid either in instalments or in a single payment. **2.** the right to receive or the duty to pay such a sum. [C15: from French *annuité,* from Medieval Latin *annuitās,* from Latin *annuus* ANNUAL]

annul (ə'nʌl) *vb.* **-nuls, -nulling, -nulled.** (*tr.*) to make (something, esp. a law or marriage) void; cancel the validity of; abolish. [C14: from Old French *annuller,* from Late Latin *annullāre* to bring to nothing, from Latin *nullus* not any; see NULL] —**an'nullable** *adj.*

annular ('ænjʊlə) *adj.* ring-shaped; of or forming a ring. [C16: from Latin *annulāris,* from *annulus, ānulus* ring] —**annularity** (ˌænjʊ'lærɪtɪ) *n.* —'**annularly** *adv.*

annular eclipse *n.* an eclipse of the sun in which the moon does not cover the entire disc of the sun, so that a ring of sunlight surrounds the shadow of the moon. Compare **total eclipse, partial eclipse.**

annular ligament *n. Anatomy.* any of various ligaments that encircle a part, such as the wrist, ankle, or trachea.

annulate ('ænjʊlɪt, -ˌleɪt) *adj.* having, composed of, or marked with rings. [C19: from Latin *ānulātus,* from *ānulus* a ring] —'**annuˌlated** *adj.*

annulation (ˌænjʊ'leɪʃən) *n.* **1.** the formation of rings. **2.** a ringlike formation or part.

annulet ('ænjʊlɪt) *n.* **1.** *Architect.* a moulding in the form of a ring, as at the top of a column adjoining the capital. **2.** *Heraldry.* a ring-shaped device on a shield; hollow roundel. **3.** a little ring. [C16: from Latin *ānulus* ring + -ET]

annulment (ə'nʌlmənt) *n.* **1.** a formal invalidation, as of a marriage, judicial proceeding, etc. **2.** the act of annulling.

annulose ('ænjʊˌləʊs, -ˌləʊz) *adj.* (of earthworms, crustaceans, and similar animals) having a body formed of a series of rings; segmented. [C19: from New Latin *annulōsus;* see ANNULUS]

annulus ('ænjʊləs) *n., pl.* **-li** (-ˌlaɪ) *or* **-luses. 1.** the area between two concentric circles. **2.** a ring-shaped part, figure, or space. [C16: from Latin, variant of *ānulus* ring]

annunciate (ə'nʌnsɪˌeɪt, -ʃɪ-) *vb.* (*tr.*) a less common word for **announce.** [C16: from *annunciātus,* Medieval Latin misspelling of *annuntiātus,* past participle of Latin *annuntiāre;* see ANNOUNCE] —**anˌnunci'ation** *n.* —**annunciative** (ə'nʌnsɪətɪv, -ʃətɪv) *or* **annunciatory** (ə'nʌnsɪətərɪ, -ʃə-) *adj.*

Annunciation (əˌnʌnsɪ'eɪʃən) *n.* **1. the.** *New Testament.* the announcement of the Incarnation by the angel Gabriel to the Virgin Mary (Luke 1:26–38). **2.** Also called: **Annunciation Day.** the festival commemorating this, held on March 25 (Lady Day).

annunciator (ə'nʌnsɪˌeɪtə) *n.* **1.** a device that gives a visual indication as to which of a number of electric circuits has operated, such as an indicator in a hotel showing in which room a bell has been rung. **2.** a device giving an audible signal indicating the position of a train. **3.** a less common word for **announcer.**

annus mirabilis *Latin.* ('ænʊs mɪ'ræbɪlɪs) *n., pl.* ***anni mirabiles*** ('ænaɪ mɪ'ræbɪliːz). a year of wonders, catastrophes, or other notable events.

anoa (ə'nəʊə) *n.* the smallest of the cattle tribe *Anoa depressicornis,* having small straight horns and inhabiting the island of Celebes in Indonesia. Compare **tamarau.** [from a native name in Celebes]

anobiid (ə'nəʊbɪɪd) *n.* any coleopterous beetle of the family *Anobiidae,* in which the pronotum characteristically forms a hood that more or less covers the head. The family includes such notorious pests as the **furniture beetle** (*Anobium punctatum*) and the **deathwatch beetle,** the larvae of which attack furniture and beams. See also **deathwatch.**

anode ('ænəʊd) *n.* **1.** the positive electrode in an electrolytic cell. **2.** Also called (esp. U.S.): **plate.** the positively charged electrode in an electronic valve or tube. **3.** the negative terminal of a primary cell. Compare **cathode.** [C19: from Greek *anodos* a way up, from *hodos* a way; alluding to the movement of the current to or from the positive pole] —**anodal** (eɪ'nəʊdᵊl) *or* **anodic** (ə'nɒdɪk) *adj.*

anodize *or* **anodise** ('ænəˌdaɪz) *vb.* to coat (a metal, such as aluminium or magnesium) with a protective oxide film by electrolysis.

anodontia (ˌænəʊ'dɒnʃɪə) *n.* the congenital absence of teeth. [from AN- + Greek *odōn* tooth + -IA]

anodyne ('ænəˌdaɪn) *n.* **1.** a drug that relieves pain; analgesic. **2.** anything that alleviates mental distress. ~*adj.* **3.** capable of relieving pain or distress. [C16: from Latin *anōdynus,* from Greek *anōdunos* painless, from AN- + *odunē* pain]

anoestrus *or U.S.* **anestrus** (æn'iːstrəs) *n.* a period of sexual inactivity between two periods of oestrus in many mammals. [C20: New Latin; see AN-, OESTRUS] —**an'oestrous** *or U.S.* **an'estrous** *adj.*

anoint (ə'nɔɪnt) *vb. (tr.)* **1.** to smear or rub over with oil or an oily liquid. **2.** to apply oil to as a sign of consecration or sanctification in a sacred rite. [C14: from Old French *enoint,* from *enoindre,* from Latin *inunguere,* from IN-[2] + *unguere* to smear with oil] —**a'nointer** *n.* —**a'nointment** *n.*

anointing of the sick *n. R.C. Church.* a sacrament in which a person who is seriously ill or dying is anointed by a priest with consecrated oil. Former name: **extreme unction.**

anole (ə'nəʊlɪ) *n.* any small arboreal tropical American insectivorous lizards of the genus *Anolis,* such as *A. carolinensis* (**green anole**): family *Iguanidae* (iguanas). They are able to change the colour of their skin. Also called: **American chameleon.** [C18 *annolis,* from French *anolis,* from Carib *anoli*]

anomalistic month *n.* the interval between two successive passages of the moon through perigee; 27.55455 days.

anomalistic year *n.* the interval between two successive passages of the earth through perihelion; 365.25964 mean solar days.

anomalous (ə'nɒmələs) *adj.* deviating from the normal or usual order, type, etc.; irregular, abnormal, or incongruous. [C17: from Late Latin *anōmalus,* from Greek *anōmalos* uneven, inconsistent, from AN- + *homalos* even, from *homos* one and the same] —**a'nomalously** *adv.* —**a'nomalousness** *n.*

anomalous monism *n.* the philosophical doctrine that although all mental states consist merely in states of the brain, there exist no regular correspondences between classes of mental and physical states, and so no psychophysical laws. See also **identity theory.**

anomaly (ə'nɒməlɪ) *n., pl.* **-lies. 1.** something anomalous. **2.** deviation from the normal or usual order, type, etc.; irregularity. **3.** *Astronomy.* the angle between a planet, the sun, and the previous perihelion of the planet. **4.** *Geology.* **a.** Also called: **gravity anomaly.** a deviation from the normal value of gravity at the earth's surface, caused by density differences at depth, for example those caused by a buried mineral body. **b.** Also called: **magnetic anomaly.** a magnetic field, for example one produced by a buried mineral body, that deviates from an expected or standard value, usually that of the earth's magnetic field. —**aˌnoma'listic** *adj.* —**aˌnoma'listically** *adv.*

anomie *or* **anomy** ('ænəʊmɪ) *n. Sociol.* lack of social or moral standards in an individual or society. [from Greek *anomia* lawlessness, from A-[1] + *nomos* law] —**anomic** (ə'nɒmɪk) *adj.*

anon (ə'nɒn) *adv. Archaic or literary.* **1.** in a short time; soon. **2. ever and anon.** now and then. [Old English *on āne,* literally: in one, that is, immediately]

anon. *abbrev. for* anonymous.

anonym ('ænənɪm) *n.* **1.** a less common word for **pseudonym. 2.** an anonymous person or publication.

anonymous (ə'nɒnɪməs) *adj.* **1.** from or by a person, author, etc., whose name is unknown or withheld: *an anonymous letter.* **2.** having no known name. **3.** lacking individual characteristics; unexceptional. [C17: via Late Latin from Greek *anōnumos,* from AN- + *onoma* name] —**anonymity** (ˌænə'nɪmɪtɪ) *n.* —**a'nonymously** *adv.* —**a'nonymousness** *n.*

anopheles (ə'nɒfɪˌliːz) *n., pl.* **-les.** any of various mosquitoes constituting the genus *Anopheles,* some species of which transmit the malaria parasite to man. [C19: via New Latin from Greek *anōphelēs* useless, from AN- + *ōphelein* to help, from *ophelos* help]

anorak ('ænəˌræk) *n.* a warm waterproof hip-length jacket usually with a hood, originally worn in polar regions, but now worn for any outdoor activity. [from Eskimo *ánorâq*]

anorexia (ˌænɒ'rɛksɪə) *n.* **1.** loss of appetite. **2.** Also called: **anorexia nervosa** (nɜː'vəʊsə). a disorder characterized by fear of becoming fat and refusal of food, leading to debility and even death. [C17: via New Latin from Greek, from AN- + *orexis* appetite] —ˌ**ano'rectic** *or* ˌ**ano'rexic** *adj., n.*

anorthic (æn'ɔːθɪk) *adj.* another word for **triclinic.** [C19: from AN- + ORTHO- + -IC]

anorthite (æn'ɔːθaɪt) *n.* a white to greyish-white or reddish-white mineral of the feldspar group and plagioclase series, found chiefly in igneous rocks and more rarely in metamorphic rocks. It is used in the manufacture of glass and ceramics. Composition: calcium aluminium silicate. Formula: $CaAl_2Si_2O_8$. Crystal structure: triclinic. [C19: from AN- + ORTHO- + -ITE[1]] —**anorthitic** (ˌænɔː'θɪtɪk) *adj.*

anorthosite (æn'ɔːθəˌsaɪt) *n.* a coarse-grained plutonic igneous rock consisting almost entirely of plagioclase feldspar. [C19: from French *anorthose* (see AN-, ORTHO-) + -ITE[1]]

anosmia (æn'ɒzmɪə, -'ɒs-) *n. Pathol.* loss of the sense of smell, usually as the result of a lesion of the olfactory nerve, disease in another organ or part, or obstruction of the nasal passages. [C19: from New Latin, from AN- + Greek *osmē* smell, from *ozein* to smell] —**anosmatic** (ˌænɒz'mætɪk) *or* **an'osmic** *adj.*

another (ə'nʌðə) *determiner.* **1. a.** one more; an added: *another chance.* **b.** (*as pronoun*): *help yourself to another.* **2. a.** a different; alternative: *another era from ours.* **b.** (*as pronoun*): *to try one path, then another.* **3. a.** a different example of the same sort: *another Beethoven.* **b.** (*as pronoun*): *we got rid of one loafer, but I think this new man's another.* **4. another place.** the other House of Parliament (used in the House of Commons to refer to the House of Lords and vice versa). [C14: originally *an other*]

A.N. Other *n. Brit.* an unnamed person: used in team lists, etc., to indicate a place that remains to be filled.

anoxaemia *or U.S.* **anoxemia** (ˌænɒk'siːmɪə) *n.* a deficiency in the amount of oxygen in the arterial blood. [C19: from New Latin, from AN- + OX(YGEN) + -AEMIA] —ˌ**anox'aemic** *or U.S.* ˌ**anox'emic** *adj.*

anoxia (æn'ɒksɪə) *n.* **1.** lack or absence of oxygen. **2.** a deficiency of oxygen in tissues and organs. Compare **hypoxia.** [C20: from AN- + OX(YGEN) + -IA] —**an'oxic** *adj.*

ansate ('ænseɪt) *adj.* having a handle or handle-like part. [C19: from Latin *ansātus,* from *ansa* handle]

Anschluss ('ænʃlʊs) *n.* a political or economic union, esp. the annexation of Austria by Nazi Germany (1938). [German: from *anschliessen* to join]

anserine ('ænsəˌraɪn, -rɪn) *or* **anserous** ('ænsərəs) *adj.* **1.** of or resembling a goose. **2.** of, relating to, or belonging to the subfamily *Anserinae,* which includes geese, swans, and certain ducks: family *Anatidae,* order *Anseriformes.* **3.** silly; foolish. [C19: from Latin *anserīnus,* from *anser* goose]

ANSI *abbrev. for* American National Standards Institution.

answer ('ɑːnsə) *n.* **1.** a reply, either spoken or written, as to a question, request, letter, or article. **2.** a reaction or response in the form of an action: *drunkenness was his answer to disappointment.* **3.** a solution, esp. of a mathematical problem. **4.** *Law.* **a.** a party's written reply to his opponent's interrogatories. **b.** (in divorce law) the respondent's written reply to the petition. **5.** a musical phrase that follows the subject of a fugue, reproducing it a fifth higher or a fourth lower. ~*vb.* **6.** (when *tr., may take a clause as object*) to reply or respond (to) by word or act: *to answer a question; he answered; to answer the door; he answered that he would come.* **7.** (*tr.*) to reply correctly to; solve or attempt to solve: *I could answer only three questions.* **8.** (*intr.;* usually foll. by *to*) to respond or react (to a stimulus, command, etc.): *the steering answers to the slightest touch.* **9.** (*tr.*) to pay off (a debt, obligation, etc.); discharge. **10.** (when *intr.,* often foll. by *for*) to meet the requirements (of); be satisfactory (for); serve the purpose (of): *this will answer his needs; this will answer for a chisel.* **11.** (when *intr.,* foll. by *to*) to match or correspond (esp. in the phrase **answer** (or **answer to**) **the description**). **12.** (*tr.*) to give a defence or refutation of (a charge) or in (an argument). [Old English *andswaru* an answer; related to Old Frisian *ondser,* Old Norse *andsvar;* see SWEAR]

answerable ('ɑːnsərəbᵊl) *adj.* **1.** (*postpositive;* foll. by *for* or *to*) responsible or accountable: *answerable for someone's safety; answerable to one's boss.* **2.** able to be answered. —ˌ**answera'bility** *or* '**answerableness** *n.* —'**answerably** *adv.*

answer back *vb.* (*adv.*) to reply rudely to (a person, esp. someone in authority) when one is expected to remain silent.

answer for *vb.* (*intr., prep.*) **1.** to be liable or responsible for (a person's actions, behaviour, etc.). **2.** to vouch for or speak on behalf of (a person). **3.** to suffer or atone for (one's wrongdoing).

answering machine *n.* a device by means of which a telephone call is answered automatically and the caller enabled to leave a recorded message. In full: **telephone answering machine.**

ant (ænt) *n.* **1.** any small social insect of the widely distributed hymenopterous family *Formicidae,* typically living in highly organized colonies of winged males, wingless sterile females (workers), and fertile females (queens), which are winged until after mating. See also **army ant, fire ant, slave ant, wood ant.** Related adj.: **formic. 2. white ant.** another name for a **termite. 3. have ants in one's pants.** *Slang.* to be restless or impatient. [Old English *ǣmette;* related to Old High German *āmeiza,* Old Norse *meita;* see EMMET]

ant. *abbrev. for* antonym.

an't *Chiefly Brit.* **1.** (ɑːnt). a rare variant spelling of **aren't. 2.** (eɪnt). *Dialect.* a variant spelling of **ain't.**

ant- *prefix.* a variant of **anti-**: *antacid.*

-ant *suffix forming adjectives and nouns.* causing or performing an action or existing in a certain condition; the agent that performs an action: *pleasant; claimant; deodorant; protestant; servant.* [from Latin *-ant,* ending of present participles of the first conjugation]

anta ('æntə) *n., pl.* **antae** ('æntiː). *Architect.* a pilaster attached to the end of a side wall or sometimes to the side of a doorway.

Antabuse ('æntəˌbjuːs) *n. Trademark.* a drug used in the treatment of alcoholism that acts by inducing nausea following ingestion of alcohol; tetraethylthiuram disulphide.

antacid (ænt'æsɪd) *n.* **1.** a substance used to treat acidity, esp. in the stomach. ~*adj.* **2.** having the properties of this substance.

antagonism (æn'tægəˌnɪzəm) *n.* **1.** openly expressed and usually mutual opposition. **2.** the inhibiting or nullifying action of one substance or organism on another. **3.** *Physiol.* the normal opposition between certain muscles. **4.** *Biology.* the inhibition or interference of growth of one kind of organism by another.

antagonist (æn'tægənɪst) *n.* **1.** an opponent or adversary, as in a contest, drama, sporting event, etc. **2.** any muscle that opposes the action of another. Compare **agonist** (sense 1). **3.** a drug that neutralizes or counteracts the effects of another drug. Compare **synergist** (sense 1).

antagonistic (ænˌtægə'nɪstɪk) *adj.* **1.** in active opposition. **2.** mutually opposed. —**anˌtago'nistically** *adv.*

antagonize *or* **antagonise** (æn'tægəˌnaɪz) *vb. (tr.)* **1.** to make hostile; annoy or irritate. **2.** to act in opposition to or counteract. [C17: from Greek *antagōnizesthai,* from ANTI- + *agōnizesthai* to strive, from *agōn* contest] —**an'tagoˌnizable** *or* **an'tagoˌnisable** *adj.* —**anˌtagoni'zation** *or* **anˌtagoni'sation** *n.*

antalkali (ænt'ælkəˌlaɪ) *n., pl.* **-lis** *or* **-lies.** a substance that neutralizes alkalis, esp. one used to treat alkalosis. —**antalkaline** (ænt'ælkəˌlaɪn, -lɪn) *adj., n.*

Antarctic (ænt'ɑːktɪk) *adj.* of or relating to the south polar regions. [C14: via Latin from Greek *antarktikos;* see ANTI-, ARCTIC]

Antarctic Circle *n.* the imaginary circle around the earth, parallel to the equator, at latitude 66° 32′ S.

Antarctic prion *n.* another name for **dove prion.**

Antares (æn'tɛəriːz) *n.* the brightest star in the constellation Scorpius. It is a variable binary star whose main component, a red supergiant, is associated with a fainter green component. Visual magnitude: 1.2 (red), 6.8 (green); spectral type: MO (red); distance: 250 light years. [from Greek *Antarēs,* literally: simulating Mars (in colour), from ANTI- + *Arēs* Mars]

ant bear *n.* another name for **aardvark.**

ant bird *n.* any of various dull-coloured South American passerine birds of the family *Formicariidae,* such as *Hylophylax naevioides* (spotted ant bird), that typically feed on ants. Also called: **bush shrike, ant thrush.**

ant cow *n.* an insect, esp. an aphid, that excretes a sweet honeylike substance that is collected and eaten by ants.

ante ('æntɪ) *n.* **1.** the gaming stake put up before the deal in poker by the players. **2.** *Informal.* a sum of money representing a person's share, as in a syndicate. ~*vb.* **-tes, -teing; -ted** *or* **-teed. 3.** to place (one's stake) in poker. **4.** (usually foll. by *up*) *Informal, chiefly U.S.* to pay.

ante- *prefix.* before in time or position; previous to; in front of: *antedate; antechamber.* [from Latin]

anteater ('æntˌiːtə) *n.* **1.** any toothless edentate mammal of the family *Myrmecophagidae* of Central and South America, esp. *Myrmecophaga tridactyla* (or *jubata*) **(giant anteater),** having a long tubular snout used for eating termites. See also **tamandua. 2. scaly anteater.** another name for **pangolin. 3. spiny anteater.** another name for **echidna. 4. banded anteater.** another name for **numbat.**

antebellum (ˌæntɪ'bɛləm) *adj.* of or during the period before a war, esp. the American Civil War: *the antebellum South.* [Latin *ante bellum,* literally: before the war]

antecede (ˌæntɪ'siːd) *vb. (tr.)* to go before, as in time, order, etc.; precede. [C17: from Latin *antecēdere,* from *cēdere* to go]

antecedence (ˌæntɪ'siːdᵊns) *n.* **1.** precedence; priority. **2.** *Astronomy.* retrograde motion.

antecedent (ˌæntɪ'siːdᵊnt) *n.* **1.** an event, circumstance, etc., that happens before another. **2.** *Grammar.* a word or phrase to which a pronoun refers. In the sentence "People who live in glass houses shouldn't throw stones," *people* is the antecedent of *who.* **3.** *Logic.* the hypothetical clause, usually introduced by "if", in a conditional statement: that which implies the other. **4.** *Maths.* an obsolescent name for **numerator** (sense 1). **5. denying the antecedent.** *Logic.* the fallacy of inferring the falsehood of the consequent of a conditional statement, given the truth of the conditional and the falsehood of its antecedent, as *if there are five of them, there are more than four: there are not five, so there are not more than four.* ~*adj.* **6.** preceding in time or order; prior. ~See also **antecedents.**

antecedents (ˌæntɪ'siːdᵊnts) *pl. n.* **1.** ancestry. **2.** a person's past history.

antechamber ('æntɪˌtʃeɪmbə) *n.* another name for **anteroom.** [C17: from Old French, from Italian *anticamera;* see ANTE-, CHAMBER]

antechoir ('æntɪˌkwaɪə) *n.* the part of a church in front of the choir, usually enclosed by screens, tombs, etc.

antedate *vb.* ('æntɪˌdeɪt, ˌæntɪ'deɪt). *(tr.)* **1.** to be or occur at an earlier date than. **2.** to affix a date to (a document, etc.) that is earlier than the actual date. **3.** to assign a date to (an event, etc.) that is earlier than its previously assigned date. **4.** to cause to occur sooner. ~*n.* ('æntɪˌdeɪt). **5.** an earlier date.

antediluvian (ˌæntɪdɪ'luːvɪən, -daɪ-) *adj.* **1.** belonging to the ages before the biblical Flood (Genesis 7, 8). **2.** old-fashioned or antiquated. ~*n.* **3.** an antediluvian person or thing. [C17: from ANTE- + Latin *dīluvium* flood]

antefix ('æntɪˌfɪks) *n., pl.* **-fixes** *or* **-fixa** (-ˌfɪksə). a carved ornament at the eaves of a roof to hide the joint between the tiles. [C19: from Latin *antefixa* (things) fastened in front, from *fīgere* to FIX] —**antefixal** (ˌæntɪ'fɪksəl) *adj.*

antelope ('æntɪˌləʊp) *n., pl.* **-lopes** *or* **-lope. 1.** any bovid mammal of the subfamily *Antilopinae,* of Africa and Asia. They are typically graceful, having long legs and horns, and include the gazelles, springbok, impala, gerenuk, blackbuck, and dik-diks. **2.** any of various similar bovids of Africa and Asia. **3. American antelope.** another name for **pronghorn.** [C15: from Old French *antelop,* from Medieval Latin *antalopus,* from Late Greek *antholops* a legendary beast]

antemeridian (ˌæntɪmə'rɪdɪən) *adj.* before noon; in the morning. [C17: from Latin *antemerīdiānus;* see ANTE-, MERIDIAN]

ante meridiem ('æntɪ mə'rɪdɪəm) the full form of **a.m.** [Latin, from ANTE- + *merīdiēs* midday]

ante-mortem *adj., adv.* (esp. in legal or medical contexts) before death. [Latin]

antenatal (ˌæntɪ'neɪtᵊl) *adj.* **1.** occurring or present before birth; during pregnancy. ~*n.* **2.** Also called: **prenatal.** *Informal.* an examination during pregnancy. —ˌ**ante'natally** *adv.*

antenna (æn'tɛnə) *n.* **1.** (*pl.* **-nae** (-niː)) one of a pair of mobile appendages on the heads of insects, crustaceans, etc., that are often whiplike and respond to touch and taste but may be specialized for swimming or attachment. **2.** (*pl.* **-nas**) another name for **aerial** (sense 7). [C17: from Latin: sail yard, of obscure origin] —**an'tennal** *or* **an'tennary** *adj.*

antennule (æn'tɛnjuːl) *n.* one of a pair of small mobile appendages on the heads of crustaceans in front of the antennae, usually having a sensory function. [C19: from French, diminutive of ANTENNA]

antependium (ˌæntɪ'pɛndɪəm) *n., pl.* **-dia** (-dɪə). a covering hung over the front of an altar. [C17: from Medieval Latin, from Latin ANTE- + *pendēre* to hang]

antepenult (ˌæntɪpɪ'nʌlt) *n.* the third last syllable in a word. [C16: shortened from Latin *(syllaba) antepaenultima;* see ANTE-, PENULT]

antepenultimate (ˌæntɪpɪ'nʌltɪmɪt) *adj.* **1.** third from last. ~*n.* **2.** anything that is third from last.

anteposition ('æntɪpəˌzɪʃən) *n. Botany.* the position opposite a given part of a plant.

anterior (æn'tɪərɪə) *adj.* **1.** situated at or towards the front. **2.** earlier in time. **3.** *Zoology.* of or near the head end. **4.** *Botany.* (of part of a flower or leaf) situated farthest away from the main stem. ~Compare **posterior.** [C17: from Latin, comparative of *ante* before] —**anteriority** (ænˌtɪərɪ'ɒrɪtɪ) *n.*

anterograde amnesia ('æntərəʊˌgreɪd) *n.* amnesia caused by brain damage in which the memory loss relates to events occurring after the damage. Compare **retrograde amnesia.** [from Latin *anterior* previous + -GRADE]

anteroom ('æntɪˌruːm, -ˌrʊm) *n.* a room giving entrance to a larger room, often used as a waiting room.

antetype ('æntɪˌtaɪp) *n.* an earlier form; prototype.

anteversion (ˌæntɪ'vɜːʃən) *n.* abnormal forward tilting of a bodily organ, esp. the uterus.

antevert (ˌæntɪ'vɜːt) *vb. (tr.)* to displace (an organ or part) by tilting forward. [C17: from Latin *antevertere* to go in front, from *vertere* to turn]

anthelion (ænt'hiːlɪən, æn'θiː-) *n., pl.* **-lia** (-lɪə). **1.** a faint halo sometimes seen in polar or high altitude regions around the shadow of an object cast onto a thick cloud bank or fog. **2.** a white spot occasionally appearing on the parhelic circle at the same height as and opposite to the sun. [C17: from Late Greek, from *anthēlios* opposite the sun, from ANTE- + *hēlios* sun]

anthelix (ænt'hiːlɪks, æn'θiː-) *or* **antihelix** *n., pl.* **-helices** (-'hiːlɪsiːz) *or* **-helixes.** *Anatomy.* a prominent curved fold of cartilage just inside the outer rim of the external ear.

anthelmintic (ˌænθɛl'mɪntɪk) *or* **anthelminthic** (ˌænθɛl'mɪnθɪk) *n. Med.* another name for **vermifuge.**

anthem ('ænθəm) *n.* **1.** a song of loyalty or devotion, as to a nation or college: *a national anthem.* **2.** a musical composition for a choir, usually set to words from the Bible, sung as part of a church service. **3.** a religious chant sung antiphonally. [Old English *antemne,* from Late Latin *antiphōna* ANTIPHON]

anthemion (æn'θiːmɪən) *n., pl.* **-mia** (-mɪə). a floral design, used esp. in ancient Greek and Roman architecture and decoration, usually consisting of honeysuckle, lotus, or palmette leaf motifs. [from Greek: a little flower, from *anthos* flower]

anther ('ænθə) *n.* the terminal part of a stamen consisting of two lobes each containing two sacs in which the pollen matures. [C18: from New Latin *anthēra,* from Latin: a remedy prepared from flowers, from Greek, from *anthēros* flowery, from *anthos* flower] —'**antheral** *adj.*

antheridium (ˌænθəˈrɪdɪəm) *n., pl.* **-ia** (-ɪə). the male sex organ of algae, fungi, mosses, and ferns, which produces antherozoids. [C19: from New Latin, diminutive of *anthēra* ANTHER] —ˌ**antherˈidial** *adj.*

antherozoid (ˌænθərəˈzəʊɪd, -ˈzɔɪd) *n.* one of many small male gametes produced in an antheridium. [C19: see ANTHER, ZO(O)ID]

anthesis (ænˈθiːsɪs) *n.* the process of flowering in plants. [C19: via New Latin from Greek: full bloom, from *anthein* to bloom, from *anthos* flower]

ant hill *n.* a mound of soil, leaves, etc., near the entrance of an ants' nest, carried and deposited there by the ants while constructing the nest.

antho- *combining form.* denoting a flower: *anthophore; anthotaxy; anthozoan.* [from Greek *anthos*]

anthocyanin (ˌænθəʊˈsaɪənɪn) *or* **anthocyan** (ˌænθəʊˈsaɪən) *n.* any of a class of water-soluble glycosidic pigments, esp. those responsible for the red and blue colours in flowers. They are closely related to vitamins E and P. [C19: from ANTHO- + *-cyanin,* from Greek *kuanos* dark blue]

anthodium (ænˈθəʊdɪəm) *n., pl.* **-dia** (-dɪə). *Botany.* another name for **capitulum** (sense 1). [C19: from New Latin, from Greek *anthōdēs* flower-like, from *anthos* flower + *-ōdēs* -OID]

anthologize *or* **anthologise** (ænˈθɒləˌdʒaɪz) *vb.* to compile or put into an anthology.

anthology (ænˈθɒlədʒɪ) *n., pl.* **-gies.** **1.** a collection of literary passages or works, esp. poems, by various authors. **2.** any printed collection of literary pieces, songs, works of art, etc. [C17: from Medieval Latin *anthologia,* from Greek, literally: a flower gathering, from *anthos* flower + *legein* to collect] —**anthological** (ˌænθəˈlɒdʒɪkᵊl) *adj.* —**anˈthologist** *n.*

anthophilous (ænˈθɒfɪləs) *adj.* **1.** (esp. of insects) frequenting flowers. **2.** feeding on flowers.

anthophore (ˈænθəʊˌfɔː, -θə-) *n.* an elongation of the receptacle of a flower between the calyx and corolla.

anthotaxy (ˈænθəˌtæksɪ) *n.* the arrangement of flowers on a stem or parts on a flower.

anthozoan (ˌænθəˈzəʊən) *n.* **1.** any of the solitary or colonial sessile marine coelenterates of the class *Anthozoa,* including the corals, sea anemones, and sea pens, in which the body is in the form of a polyp. ~*adj.* **2.** Also: **actinozoan.** of or relating to the class *Anthozoa.*

anthracene (ˈænθrəˌsiːn) *n.* a colourless tricyclic crystalline solid having a slight blue fluorescence, used in the manufacture of chemicals, esp. diphenylamine and alizarin, and as crystals in scintillation counters. Formula: $C_6H_4(CH)_2C_6H_4$. [C19: from ANTHRAX + -ENE]

anthracite (ˈænθrəˌsaɪt) *n.* a hard jet-black coal that burns slowly with a nonluminous flame giving out intense heat. Fixed carbon content: 86–98 per cent; calorific value: 3.14×10^7–3.63×10^7 J/kg. Also called: **hard coal.** [C19: from Latin *anthracītes* type of bloodstone, from Greek *anthrakitēs* coal-like, from *anthrax* coal, ANTHRAX] —**anthracitic** (ˌænθrəˈsɪtɪk) *adj.*

anthracnose (ænˈθræknəʊs) *n.* any of several fungus diseases of plants, such as vines and beans, characterized by oval dark depressed spots on the fruit and elsewhere. [C19: from French, from Greek *anthrax* coal, carbuncle + *nosos* disease]

anthracoid (ˈænθrəˌkɔɪd) *adj.* **1.** resembling anthrax. **2.** resembling carbon, coal, or charcoal.

anthracosis (ˌænθrəˈkəʊsɪs) *n.* a lung disease due to inhalation of coal dust. Informal name: **coal miner's lung.**

anthraquinone (ˌænθrəkwɪˈnəʊn, -ˈkwɪnəʊn) *n.* a yellow crystalline solid used in the manufacture of dyes, esp. **anthraquinone dyes,** which have excellent colour properties. Formula: $C_6H_4(CO)_2C_6H_4$. [C19: ANTHRA(CENE) + QUINONE]

anthrax (ˈænθræks) *n., pl.* **-thraces** (-θrəˌsiːz). **1.** a highly infectious disease of animals, esp. cattle and sheep, characterized by fever, enlarged spleen and swelling of the throat. It is caused by the bacterium *Bacillus anthracis* and can be transmitted to man. **2.** a pustule or other lesion caused by this disease. [C19: from Late Latin, from Greek: carbuncle]

anthrop. *abbrev. for:* **1.** anthropological. **2.** anthropology.

anthropic (ænˈθrɒpɪk) *adj.* of or relating to human beings.

anthropo- *combining form.* indicating man or human: *anthropology; anthropomorphism.* [from Greek *anthrōpos*]

anthropocentric (ˌænθrəpəʊˈsɛntrɪk) *adj.* regarding man as the most important and central factor in the universe. —ˌ**anthropoˈcentrism** *n.*

anthropogenesis (ˌænθrəpəʊˈdʒɛnɪsɪs) *or* **anthropogeny** (ˌænθrəˈpɒdʒɪnɪ) *n.* the study of the origins of man. —ˌ**anthropogeˈnetic** *or* ˌ**anthropoˈgenic** *adj.*

anthropoid (ˈænθrəˌpɔɪd) *adj.* **1.** resembling man. **2.** resembling an ape; apelike. **3.** of or relating to the suborder *Anthropoidea.* ~*n.* **4.** any primate of the suborder *Anthropoidea,* including monkeys, apes, and man. Compare **prosimian.** —ˌ**anthroˈpoidal** *adj.*

anthropoid ape *n.* any primate of the family *Pongidae,* having no tail, elongated arms, and a highly developed brain. The group includes gibbons, orang-utans, chimpanzees, and gorillas.

anthropol. *abbrev. for* anthropology.

anthropology (ˌænθrəˈpɒlədʒɪ) *n.* the study of man, his origins, physical characteristics, institutions, religious beliefs, social relationships, etc. See also **cultural anthropology, ethnology, physical anthropology, social anthropology.** —**anthropological** (ˌænθrəpəˈlɒdʒɪkᵊl) *adj.* —ˌ**anthropoˈlogically** *adv.* —ˌ**anthroˈpologist** *n.*

anthropometry (ˌænθrəˈpɒmɪtrɪ) *n.* the comparative study of sizes and proportions of the human body. —**anthropometric** (ˌænθrəpəˈmɛtrɪk) *or* ˌ**anthropoˈmetrical** *adj.* —ˌ**anthropoˈmetrically** *adv.* —ˌ**anthroˈpometrist** *n.*

anthropomorphic (ˌænθrəpəˈmɔːfɪk) *adj.* **1.** of or relating to anthropomorphism. **2.** resembling the human form. —ˈ**anthropoˌmorph** *n.* —ˌ**anthropoˈmorphically** *adv.*

anthropomorphism (ˌænθrəpəˈmɔːfɪzəm) *n.* the attribution of human form or behaviour to a deity, animal, etc. —ˌ**anthropoˈmorphist** *n.*

anthropomorphize *or* **anthropomorphise** (ˌænθrəpəˈmɔːfaɪz) *vb.* to attribute or ascribe human form or behaviour to (a god, animal, object, etc.).

anthropomorphosis (ˌænθrəpəˈmɔːfəsɪs) *n.* transformation into human form.

anthropomorphous (ˌænθrəpəˈmɔːfəs) *adj.* **1.** shaped like a human being. **2.** another word for **anthropomorphic.** —ˌ**anthropoˈmorphously** *adv.*

anthropopathy (ˌænθrəˈpɒpəθɪ) *or* **anthropopathism** *n.* the attribution of human passions, etc., to a deity, object, etc. —**anthropopathic** (ˌænθrəpəˈpæθɪk) *adj.*

anthropophagi (ˌænθrəˈpɒfəˌgaɪ) *pl. n., sing.* **-gus** (-gəs). cannibals. [C16: from Latin, from Greek *anthrōpophagos;* see ANTHROPO-, -PHAGY]

anthropophagite (ˌænθrəˈpɒfəˌgaɪt) *n.* a rare word for **cannibal.** —**anthropophagy** (ˌænθrəˈpɒfədʒɪ) *n.* —**anthropophagic** (ˌænθrəpəˈfædʒɪk) *adj.* —ˌ**anthroˈpophagous** *adj.*

anthropophyte (ænˈθrɒpəˌfaɪt) *n.* a plant species accidentally introduced during the cultivation of another.

anthroposophy (ˌænθrəˈpɒsəfɪ) *n.* the spiritual and mystical teachings of the philosopher Rudolph Steiner (1861–1925), based on the belief that creative activities such as myth making, which formed a part of life in earlier times, are psychologically valuable, esp. for educational and therapeutic purposes. —**anthroposophic** (ˌænθrəpəʊˈsɒfɪk) *adj.* —ˌ**anthroˈposophist** *n.*

anthurium (ænˈθjʊərɪəm) *n.* any of various tropical American aroid plants constituting the genus *Anthurium,* many of which are cultivated as house plants for their showy foliage and their flowers, which have a long-stalked spike surrounded by a flaring heart-shaped white or red bract. [C19: New Latin, from ANTHO- + Greek *oura* a tail]

anti (ˈæntɪ) *Informal.* ~*adj.* **1.** opposed to a party, policy, attitude, etc.: *he won't join because he is rather anti.* ~*n.* **2.** an opponent of a party, policy, etc.

anti- *prefix.* **1.** against; opposing: *anticlerical; antisocial.* **2.** opposite to: *anticlimax; antimere.* **3.** rival; false: *antipope.* **4.** counteracting, inhibiting, or neutralizing: *antifreeze; antihistamine.* [from Greek *anti*]

anti-aircraft (ˌæntɪˈɛəkrɑːft) *n.* (*modifier*) of or relating to defence against aircraft attack: *anti-aircraft batteries.*

antiar (ˈæntɪˌɑː) *n.* another name for **upas** (senses 1, 2). [from Javanese]

antibaryon (ˌæntɪˈbærɪɒn) *n. Physics.* the antiparticle of any of the baryons.

antibiosis (ˌæntɪbaɪˈəʊsɪs) *n.* an association between two organisms, esp. microorganisms, that is harmful to one of them.

antibiotic (ˌæntɪbaɪˈɒtɪk) *n.* **1.** any of various chemical substances, such as penicillin, streptomycin, neomycin, and tetracycline, produced by various microorganisms, esp. fungi, or made synthetically and capable of destroying or inhibiting the growth of microorganisms, esp. bacteria. ~*adj.* **2.** of or relating to antibiotics.

antibody (ˈæntɪˌbɒdɪ) *n., pl.* **-bodies.** any of various proteins produced in the blood in response to the presence of an antigen. By becoming attached to antigens on infectious organisms antibodies can render them harmless or cause them to be destroyed. See also **immunoglobulin.**

antic (ˈæntɪk) *n.* **1.** *Archaic.* an actor in a ludicrous or grotesque part; clown; buffoon. ~*adj.* **2.** *Archaic.* fantastic; grotesque. ~See also **antics.** [C16: from Italian *antico* something ancient, or grotesque (from its application to fantastic carvings found in ruins of ancient Rome); see ANTIQUE]

ˌ**anti-aˈbortion** *adj.*
ˌ**anti-aˈbrasion** *adj.*
ˌ**anti-ˈageing** *adj.*
ˌ**anti-ˈalien** *adj.*
ˌ**anti-Aˈmerican** *adj.*
ˌ**anti-aˈpartheid** *adj.*
ˌ**anti-ˌaristoˈcratic** *adj.*
ˌ**antibacˈterial** *adj.*
ˌ**antibalˈlistic** *adj.*
ˌ**antiˈbiblical** *adj.*
ˌ**anti-ˈBolshevik** *n., adj.*
ˌ**anti-ˈBolshevism** *n.*
ˌ**anti-ˈBolshevist** *n., adj.*
ˌ**anti-ˈBritish** *adj.*
ˌ**antiˈcapitalist** *n., adj.*
ˌ**antiˌcapitalˈistic** *adj.*
ˌ**anti-ˈCatholic** *adj., n.*
ˌ**anti-Caˈtholiˌcism** *n.*
ˌ**antiˈcensorˌship** *adj., n.*
ˌ**antiˈchurch** *adj.*

anticatalyst (ˌæntɪˈkætəlɪst) *n.* **1.** a substance that destroys or diminishes the activity of a catalyst. **2.** another name for **inhibitor** (sense 2).
anticathode (ˌæntɪˈkæθəʊd) *n.* the target electrode for the stream of electrons in a vacuum tube, esp. an x-ray tube.
antichlor (ˈæntɪˌklɔː) *n.* a substance used to remove chlorine from a material after bleaching. [C19: from ANTI- + CHLOR(INE)] —ˌ**antichloˈristic** *adj.*
anticholinergic (ˌæntɪˌkɒlɪˈnɜːdʒɪk) *adj.* **1.** *Physiol.* blocking nerve impulses through the parasympathetic nerves. ~*n.* **2.** *Med.* a drug or agent that blocks these nerve impulses, used esp. to control intestinal spasm.
anticholinesterase (ˌæntɪˌkɒləˈnɛstəˌreɪz) *n.* any of a group of substances that inhibit the action of cholinesterase.
Antichrist (ˈæntɪˌkraɪst) *n.* (*sometimes not cap.*) an enemy of Christ or Christianity. —ˌ**Antiˈchristian** *adj.*
anticipant (ænˈtɪsɪpənt) *adj.* **1.** operating in advance; expectant. ~*n.* **2.** a person who anticipates.
anticipate (ænˈtɪsɪˌpeɪt) *vb.* (*mainly tr.*) **1.** (*may take a clause as object*) to foresee and act in advance of: *he anticipated the fall in value by selling early.* **2.** to thwart by acting in advance of; forestall: *I anticipated his punch by moving out of reach.* **3.** (*also intr.*) to mention (something) before its proper time: *don't anticipate the climax of the story.* **4.** (*may take a clause as object*) to regard as likely; expect; foresee: *he anticipated that it would happen.* **5.** to make use of in advance of possession: *he anticipated his salary in buying a house.* **6.** to pay (a bill, etc.) before it falls due. **7.** to cause to happen sooner: *the spread of nationalism anticipated the decline of the Empire.* [C16: from Latin *anticipāre* to take before, realize beforehand, from *anti-* ANTE- + *capere* to take] —**anˈticiˌpator** *n.* —**anˈticipatory** *or* **anˈticipative** *adj.* —**anˈticipatorily** *or* **anˈticipatively** *adv.*
▷**Usage.** The use of *anticipate* to mean *expect,* while very common, is avoided by careful writers and speakers of English.
anticipation (ænˌtɪsɪˈpeɪʃən) *n.* **1.** the act of anticipating; expectation, premonition, or foresight. **2.** the act of taking or dealing with funds before they are legally available or due. **3.** *Music.* an unstressed, usually short note introduced before a downbeat and harmonically related to the chord immediately following it. Compare **suspension** (sense 11).
anticlastic (ˌæntɪˈklæstɪk) *adj.* *Maths.* (of a surface) having a curvature, at a given point and in a particular direction, that is of the opposite sign to the curvature at that point in a perpendicular direction. Compare **synclastic.**
anticlerical (ˌæntɪˈklɛrɪkᵊl) *adj.* **1.** opposed to the power and influence of the clergy, esp. in politics. ~*n.* **2.** a supporter of an anticlerical party. —ˌ**antiˈclericalism** *n.*
anticlimax (ˌæntɪˈklaɪmæks) *n.* **1.** a disappointing or ineffective conclusion to a series of events, etc. **2.** a sudden change from a serious subject to one that is disappointing or ludicrous. **3.** *Rhetoric.* a descent in discourse from the significant or important to the trivial, inconsequential, etc. —**anticlimactic** (ˌæntɪklaɪˈmæktɪk) *adj.* —ˌ**anticliˈmactically** *adv.*
anticlinal (ˌæntɪˈklaɪnᵊl) *adj.* **1.** of, relating to, or resembling an anticline. **2.** *Botany.* of or relating to the plane at right angles to the surface of an organ.
anticline (ˈæntɪˌklaɪn) *n.* a formation of stratified rock raised up, by folding, into a broad arch so that the strata slope down on both sides from a common crest. Compare **syncline.**
anticlinorium (ˌæntɪklaɪˈnɔːrɪəm) *n., pl.* **-noria** (-ˈnɔːrɪə). a vast elongated anticline with its strata further folded into anticlines and synclines.
anticlockwise (ˌæntɪˈklɒkˌwaɪz) *adv., adj.* in the opposite direction to the rotation of the hands of a clock. U.S. equivalent: **counterclockwise.**
anticoagulant (ˌæntɪkəʊˈægjʊlənt) *adj.* **1.** acting to prevent or retard coagulation, esp. of blood. ~*n.* **2.** an agent that prevents or retards coagulation.
anticoincidence (ˌæntɪkəʊˈɪnsɪdəns) *n.* (*modifier*) of or relating to an electronic circuit that produces an output pulse if one but not both of its input terminals receives a pulse within a specified interval of time. Compare **coincidence** (sense 3).
anticonvulsant (ˌæntɪkənˈvʌlsənt) *n.* **1.** any of a class of drugs used to relieve convulsions. ~*adj.* **2.** of or relating to this class of drugs.
antics (ˈæntɪks) *pl. n.* absurd or grotesque acts or postures.
anticyclone (ˌæntɪˈsaɪkləʊn) *n.* *Meteorol.* a body of moving air of higher pressure than the surrounding air, in which the pressure decreases away from the centre. Winds circulate around the centre in a clockwise direction in the N hemisphere and anticlockwise in the S hemisphere. Also called: **high.** —**anticyclonic** (ˌæntɪsaɪˈklɒnɪk) *adj.*
antidazzle mirror (ˈæntɪˌdæzᵊl) *n.* a rear-view mirror for road vehicles that only partially reflects headlights behind.
antidepressant (ˌæntɪdɪˈprɛsᵊnt) *n.* **1.** any of a class of drugs used to alleviate depression. ~*adj.* **2.** of or relating to this class of drugs.
antidiuretic hormone (ˌæntɪˌdaɪjʊˈrɛtɪk) *n.* another name for **vasopressin.** Abbrev.: **ADH.**
antidote (ˈæntɪˌdəʊt) *n.* **1.** *Med.* a drug or agent that counteracts or neutralizes the effects of a poison. **2.** anything that counteracts or relieves a harmful or unwanted condition; remedy. [C15: from Latin *antidotum,* from Greek *antidoton* something given as a countermeasure, from ANTI- + *didonai* to give] —ˌ**antiˈdotal** *adj.*
antidromic (ˌæntɪˈdrɒmɪk) *adj.* **1.** (of nerve fibres) conducting nerve impulses in a direction opposite to normal. **2.** (of plants) showing twining to the left and right in members of the same species. [from ANTI- + Greek *dromos* course]
antidune (ˈæntɪˌdjuːn) *n.* a sand hill or inclined bedding plane that forms a steep slope against the direction of a fast-flowing current.
antiemetic (ˌæntɪɪˈmɛtɪk) *adj.* **1.** preventing vomiting. ~*n.* **2.** any antiemetic drug, such as promethazine.
antifebrile (ˌæntɪˈfiːbraɪl) *adj.* **1.** reducing fever; antipyretic. ~*n.* **2.** an antifebrile agent or drug.
Antifederalist (ˌæntɪˈfɛdərəlɪst, -ˈfɛdrə-) *n.* **1.** *U.S. history.* a person who opposed the ratification of the Constitution in 1789 and thereafter allied with Thomas Jefferson's Antifederal Party, which opposed extension of the powers of the federal Government. **2.** (*often not cap.*) any person who opposes federalism.
antiferromagnetism (ˌæntɪˌfɛrəʊˈmægnɪˌtɪzəm) *n.* *Physics.* the phenomenon exhibited by substances that resemble paramagnetic substances in the value of their relative permeability but that behave like ferromagnetic substances when their temperature is varied. See also **ferrimagnetism.**
antifouling (ˌæntɪˈfaʊlɪŋ) *adj.* **1.** (of a paint or other coating) inhibiting the growth of barnacles and other marine organisms on a ship's bottom. ~*n.* **2.** an antifouling paint or other coating.
antifreeze (ˈæntɪˌfriːz) *n.* a liquid, usually ethylene glycol (ethanediol), added to cooling water to lower its freezing point, esp. for use in an internal-combustion engine.
antifriction metal (ˌæntɪˈfrɪkʃən) *n.* another name for **white metal.**
antigen (ˈæntɪdʒən, -ˌdʒɛn) *n.* a substance that stimulates the production of antibodies. [C20: from ANTI(BODY) + -GEN] —ˌ**antiˈgenic** *adj.* —ˌ**antiˈgenically** *adv.*
antigenic determinant *n.* the specific part of an antigen molecule to which an antibody becomes attached.
antiglobulin (ˌæntɪˈglɒbjʊlɪn) *n.* a serum containing antibody specific to an immunoglobulin.
anti-G suit *n.* another name for **G-suit.**
antihalation (ˌæntɪhəˈleɪʃən) *n.* *Photog.* **a.** a process by which light, passing through the emulsion on a film or plate, is not reflected back into it but is absorbed by a layer of dye or pigment, usually on the back of the film, thus preventing halation. **b.** (*as modifier*): *antihalation backing.*
antihelix (ˌæntɪˈhiːlɪks) *n., pl.* **-helices** (-ˈhiːlɪsiːz) *or* **-helixes.** a variant spelling of **anthelix.**
antihero (ˈæntɪˌhɪərəʊ) *n., pl.* **-roes.** a central character in a novel, play, etc., who lacks the traditional heroic virtues.
antihistamine (ˌæntɪˈhɪstəˌmiːn, -mɪn) *n.* any drug that neutralizes the effects of histamine, used esp. in the treatment of allergies.
anti-icer *n.* a device fitted to an aircraft to prevent the formation of ice. Compare **de-icer.**
anti-inflammatory *adj.* **1.** reducing inflammation. ~*n.* **2.** any anti-inflammatory drug, such as cortisone, aspirin, or ibuprofen.
antiknock (ˌæntɪˈnɒk) *n.* a compound, such as lead tetraethyl, added to petrol to reduce knocking in the engine.
antilepton (ˌæntɪˈlɛptən) *n.* *Physics.* the antiparticle of any of the leptons.
antilock brake (ˈæntɪˌlɒk) *n.* a brake fitted to some road vehicles that prevents skidding and improves control by sensing and compensating for overbraking. Also called: **ABS brake.**
antilog (ˈæntɪˌlɒg) *n.* short for **antilogarithm.**
antilogarithm (ˌæntɪˈlɒgəˌrɪðəm) *n.* a number whose logarithm to a given base is a given number: *100 is the antilogarithm of 2 to base 10.* Often shortened to **antilog.** —ˌ**antiˌlogaˈrithmic** *adj.*
antilogy (ænˈtɪlədʒɪ) *n., pl.* **-gies.** a contradiction in terms. [C17: from Greek *antilogia*]
antimacassar (ˌæntɪməˈkæsə) *n.* a cloth covering the back and arms of chairs, etc., to prevent soiling or as decoration. [C19: from ANTI- + MACASSAR (OIL)]

ˌ**antiˈclassical** *adj.*
ˌ**anticoˈaguˌlating** *adj.*
ˌ**anti-ˈCommunist** *n., adj.*
ˌ**anticonˈscription** *adj.*
ˌ**antiˌconstiˈtutional** *adj.*
ˌ**anticorˈrosive** *adj.*
ˌ**anti-Darˈwinian** *adj., n.*
ˌ**antiˌdemoˈcratic** *adj.*
ˌ**antiˌdiuˈretic** *adj., n.*
ˌ**anti-ecˌclesiˈastical** *adj.*
ˌ**anti-ecˌclesiˈastically** *adv.*
ˌ**anti-eˈpiscopal** *adj., n.*
ˌ**anti-eˈrosion** *adj.*
ˌ**anti-Esˈtablishment** *adj.*
ˌ**anti-ˌevoˈlution** *adj.*
ˌ**anti-ˌevoˈlutionist** *n., adj.*
ˌ**antiˈfaction** *adj.*
ˌ**antiˈfascist** *n., adj.*
ˌ**anti-ˈFreudian** *adj., n.*
ˌ**antiˌfundaˈmentalist** *n., adj.*
ˌ**antiˈhumanism** *n.*
ˌ**antiˈhumanist** *adj., n.*
ˌ**anti-imˈperialˌism** *n.*
ˌ**anti-imˈperialist** *adj., n.*
ˌ**anti-inˈflationary** *adj.*
ˌ**antiˈlabour** *adj.*
ˌ**antiliˈturgical** *adj.*

antimagnetic (ˌæntɪmæɡˈnɛtɪk) *adj.* of or constructed of a material that does not acquire permanent magnetism when exposed to a magnetic field: *an antimagnetic watch.*
antimalarial (ˌæntɪməˈlɛərɪəl) *adj.* **1.** effective in the treatment of malaria. ~*n.* **2.** an antimalarial drug or agent.
antimasque (ˈæntɪˌmɑːsk) *n.* a comic or grotesque dance, presented between the acts of a masque.
antimatter (ˈæntɪˌmætə) *n.* a hypothetical form of matter composed of antiparticles.
antimere (ˈæntɪˌmɪə) *n.* a part or organ of a bilaterally or radially symmetrical organism that corresponds to a similar structure on the other side of the axis, such as the right or left limb of a four-legged animal. Also called: **actinomere.** —**antimeric** (ˌæntɪˈmɛrɪk) *adj.* —**antimerism** (ænˈtɪməˌrɪzəm) *n.*
antimetabolite (ˌæntɪmɪˈtæbəˌlaɪt) *n.* any drug that acts by disrupting the normal growth of a cell. Antimetabolites are used in cancer treatment.
antimissile (ˌæntɪˈmɪsaɪl) *adj.* **1.** relating to defensive measures against missile attack: *an antimissile system.* ~*n.* **2.** Also called: **antimissile missile.** a defensive missile used to intercept and destroy attacking missiles.
antimonial (ˌæntɪˈməʊnɪəl) *adj.* **1.** of or containing antimony. ~*n.* **2.** a drug or agent containing antimony.
antimonic (ˌæntɪˈmɒnɪk) *adj.* of or containing antimony in the pentavalent state.
antimonous (ˈæntɪmənəs) *adj.* of or containing antimony in the trivalent state.
antimony (ˈæntɪmənɪ) *n.* a toxic metallic element that exists in two allotropic forms and occurs principally in stibnite. The stable form is a brittle silvery-white crystalline metal that is added to alloys to increase their strength and hardness and is used in semiconductors. Symbol: Sb; atomic no.: 51; atomic wt.: 121.75; valency: 3 or 5; relative density: 6.684; melting pt.: 630.5°C; boiling pt.: 1640°C. [C15: from Medieval Latin *antimōnium,* of uncertain origin]
antimonyl (ˈæntɪmənɪl, ænˈtɪm-) *n.* (*modifier*) of, consisting of, or containing the monovalent group SbO-: *an antimonyl group or radical.*
antimony potassium tartrate *n.* a colourless odourless poisonous crystalline salt used as a mordant for textiles and leather, as an insecticide, and as an anthelmintic. Formula: $K(SbO)C_4H_4O_6$. Also called: **tartar emetic.**
antimuon (ˌæntɪˈmjuːɒn) *n.* the antiparticle of a muon.
antimutagen (ˌæntɪˈmjuːtədʒən) *n.* any substance that acts against a mutagen.
antimycotic (ˌæntɪmaɪˈkɒtɪk) *adj.* **1.** inhibiting the growth of fungi. ~*n.* **2.** any antimycotic drug, used to treat fungal infections.
antineutrino (ˌæntɪnjuːˈtriːnəʊ) *n., pl.* **-nos.** the antiparticle of a neutrino; a particle having the opposite spin to a neutrino.
antineutron (ˌæntɪˈnjuːtrɒn) *n.* the antiparticle of a neutron; a particle having the same mass as the neutron but a magnetic moment of opposite sign.
anting (ˈæntɪŋ) *n.* the placing or rubbing of ants by birds on their feathers. The body fluids of the ants are thought to repel parasites.
antinode (ˈæntɪˌnəʊd) *n. Physics.* a point at which the amplitude of one of the two kinds of displacement in a standing wave has maximum value. Generally the other kind of displacement has its minimum value at this point. See also **standing wave.** Compare **node.** —ˌ**antiˈnodal** *adj.*
antinoise (ˈæntɪˌnɔɪz) *n.* sound generated so that it is out of phase with a noise, such as that made by an engine, in order to reduce the noise level by interference.
antinomian (ˌæntɪˈnəʊmɪən) *adj.* **1.** relating to the doctrine that by faith and the dispensation of grace a Christian is released from the obligation of adhering to any moral law. ~*n.* **2.** a member of a Christian sect holding such a doctrine. —ˌ**antiˈnomianism** *n.*
antinomy (ænˈtɪnəmɪ) *n., pl.* **-mies. 1.** opposition of one law, principle, or rule to another; contradiction within a law. **2.** *Philosophy.* contradiction existing between two apparently indubitable propositions; paradox. [C16: from Latin *antinomia,* from Greek: conflict between laws, from ANTI- + *nomos* law] —**antinomic** (ˌæntɪˈnɒmɪk) *adj.* —ˌ**antiˈnomically** *adv.*
antinovel (ˈæntɪˌnɒvᵊl) *n.* a type of prose fiction in which conventional or traditional novelistic elements are rejected. Also called: **anti-roman, nouveau roman.**
antinuclear (ˌæntɪˈnjuːklɪə) *adj.* opposed to nuclear weapons. —ˌ**antiˈnuclearist** *n.*
antinucleon (ˌæntɪˈnjuːklɪˌɒn) *n.* an antiproton or an antineutron.
antioxidant (ˌæntɪˈɒksɪdənt) *n.* any substance that retards deterioration by oxidation, esp. of fats, oils, foods, petroleum products, or rubber.
antiparallel (ˌæntɪˈpærəˌlɛl) *adj.* **1.** *Physics.* parallel but pointing or rotating in opposite directions. **2.** *Maths.* (of two lines) cutting two given lines so that in the quadrilateral formed the interior opposite angles are supplementary. **3.** *Maths.* (of vectors) parallel but having opposite directions.
antiparticle (ˈæntɪˌpɑːtɪkᵊl) *n.* any of a group of elementary particles that have the same mass as their corresponding particle but have a charge, baryon number, strangeness, and isospin quantum number, I_3, of equal magnitude but opposite sign. When a particle collides with its antiparticle mutual annihilation occurs.
antipasto (ˌæntɪˈpɑːstəʊ, -ˈpæs-) *n., pl.* **-tos.** a course of hors d'oeuvres in an Italian meal. [Italian: before food]
antipathetic (ænˌtɪpəˈθɛtɪk, ˌæntɪpə-) *or* **antipathetical** *adj.* (often foll. by *to*) having or arousing a strong aversion. —ˌ**antipaˈthetically** *adv.*
antipathy (ænˈtɪpəθɪ) *n., pl.* **-thies. 1.** a feeling of intense aversion, dislike, or hostility. **2.** the object of such a feeling. [C17: from Latin *antipathia,* from Greek *antipatheia,* from ANTI- + *patheia* feeling]
antiperiodic (ˌæntɪˌpɪərɪˈɒdɪk) *Med.* ~*adj.* **1.** efficacious against recurring attacks of a disease. ~*n.* **2.** an antiperiodic drug or agent.
antiperistalsis (ˌæntɪˌpɛrɪˈstælsɪs) *n. Physiol.* contractions of the intestine that force the contents in the opposite direction to the normal. —ˌ**antiˌperiˈstaltic** *adj.*
antipersonnel (ˌæntɪˌpɜːsəˈnɛl) *adj.* (of weapons, etc.) designed to cause casualties to personnel rather than to destroy equipment or defences.
antiperspirant (ˌæntɪˈpɜːspərənt) *n.* **1.** an astringent substance applied to the skin to reduce or prevent perspiration. ~*adj.* **2.** reducing or preventing perspiration.
antiphlogistic (ˌæntɪfləˈdʒɪstɪk) *adj.* **1.** of or relating to the prevention or alleviation of inflammation. ~*n.* **2.** an antiphlogistic agent or drug.
antiphon (ˈæntɪfən) *n.* **1.** a short passage, usually from the Bible, recited or sung as a response after certain parts of a liturgical service. **2.** a psalm, hymn, etc., chanted or sung in alternate parts. **3.** any response or answer. [C15: from Late Latin *antiphōna* sung responses, from Late Greek, plural of *antiphōnon* (something) responsive, from *antiphōnos,* from ANTI- + *phōnē* sound]
antiphonal (ænˈtɪfənəl) *adj.* **1.** sung or recited in alternation. ~*n.* **2.** another word for **antiphonary.** —**anˈtiphonally** *adv.*
antiphonary (ænˈtɪfənərɪ) *n., pl.* **-naries. 1.** a bound collection of antiphons, esp. for use in the divine office. ~*adj.* **2.** of or relating to such a book.
antiphony (ænˈtɪfənɪ) *n., pl.* **-nies. 1.** the antiphonal singing of a musical composition by two choirs. **2.** any musical or other sound effect that answers or echoes another.
antiphrasis (ænˈtɪfrəsɪs) *n. Rhetoric.* the use of a word in a sense opposite to its normal one, esp. for ironic effect. [C16: via Late Latin from Greek, from ANTI- + *phrasis,* from *phrazein* to speak]
antipodal (ænˈtɪpədᵊl) *adj.* **1.** of or relating to diametrically opposite points on the earth's surface. **2.** exactly or diametrically opposite.
antipode (ˈæntɪpəʊd) *n.* the exact or direct opposite.
antipodes (ænˈtɪpəˌdiːz) *pl. n.* **1.** either or both of two points, places, or regions that are situated diametrically opposite to one another on the earth's surface, esp. the country or region opposite one's own. **2.** the people who live there. **3.** (*often cap.*) **the.** Australia and New Zealand. **4.** (*sometimes functioning as sing.*) the exact or direct opposite. [C16: via Late Latin from Greek, plural of *antipous* having the feet opposite, from ANTI- + *pous* foot] —**antipodean** (ænˌtɪpəˈdiːən) *adj.*
antipope (ˈæntɪˌpəʊp) *n.* a rival pope elected in opposition to one who has been canonically chosen.
antiproton (ˈæntɪˌprəʊtɒn) *n.* the antiparticle of the proton; a particle having the same mass as the proton but an equal and opposite charge.
antipsychiatry (ˌæntɪsaɪˈkaɪətrɪ) *n.* an approach to mental disorders that makes use of concepts derived from existentialism, psychoanalysis, and sociological theory.
antipyretic (ˌæntɪpaɪˈrɛtɪk) *adj.* **1.** preventing or alleviating fever. ~*n.* **2.** an antipyretic remedy or drug. —**antipyresis** (ˌæntɪpaɪˈriːsɪs) *n.*
antipyrine (ˌæntɪˈpaɪrɪn, -riːn) *n.* a white powder formerly used medicinally to reduce pain and fever. Formula: $C_{11}H_{12}N_2O$.
antiq. *abbrev. for:* **1.** antiquarian. **2.** antiquity.
antiquarian (ˌæntɪˈkwɛərɪən) *adj.* **1.** concerned with the study of antiquities or antiques. ~*n.* **2.** the largest size of handmade drawing paper, 53 × 31 inches. **3.** a less common name for **antiquary.** —ˌ**antiˈquarianism** *n.*
antiquark (ˈæntɪkwɑːk) *n.* the antiparticle of a quark.

ˌ**antimaˌterialˈistic** *adj.*
ˌ**antimiˈcrobial** *adj.*
ˌ**antiˈmilitarˌism** *n.*
ˌ**antiˈmilitarist** *n., adj.*
ˌ**antiˌmilitaˈristic** *adj.*
ˌ**antiˈmodernist** *n., adj.*
ˌ**antimoˈnarchical** *adj.*
ˌ**antiˈmonarchist** *adj., n.*
ˌ**antinarˈcotic** *adj., n.*
ˌ**antiˈnationalist** *n., adj.*
ˌ**antiˌnationalˈistic** *adj.*
ˌ**anti-ˈNazi** *adj., n.*
ˌ**antiˈnoise** *adj.*
ˌ**antiˈpacifist** *n., adj.*
ˌ**antiˈpathogen** *n.*
ˌ**antiˌpathoˈgenic** *adj.*
ˌ**antipoˈlitical** *adj.*
ˌ**antipolˈlution** *adj., n.*
ˌ**antiˌprohiˈbition** *n., adj.*
ˌ**antiˌprohiˈbitionist** *n., adj.*
ˌ**anti-ˈProtestant** *adj., n.*
ˌ**antiˈpuritan** *n., adj.*

antiquary ('æntɪkwərɪ) *n., pl.* **-quaries.** a person who collects, deals in, or studies antiques, ancient works of art, or ancient times. Also called: **antiquarian.**

antiquate ('æntɪˌkweɪt) *vb.* (*tr.*) **1.** to make obsolete or old-fashioned. **2.** to give an old or antique appearance to. [C15: from Latin *antīquāre* to make old, from *antīquus* ancient]

antiquated ('æntɪˌkweɪtɪd) *adj.* **1.** outmoded; obsolete. **2.** aged; ancient. —**'antiˌquatedness** *n.*

antique (æn'tiːk) *n.* **1. a.** a decorative object, piece of furniture, or other work of art created in an earlier period, that is collected and valued for its beauty, workmanship, and age. **b.** (*as modifier*): *an antique shop.* **2.** any object made in an earlier period. **3. the.** the style of ancient art, esp. Greek or Roman art, or an example of it. **4.** *Printing.* a family of typefaces having all lines of nearly equal thickness. ~*adj.* **5.** made in or in the style of an earlier period. **6.** of or belonging to the distant past, esp. of or in the style of ancient Greece or Rome. **7.** *Informal.* old-fashioned; out-of-date. **8.** *Archaic.* aged or venerable. **9.** (of paper) not calendered or coated; having a rough surface. ~*vb.* **10.** (*tr.*) to give an antique appearance to. [C16: from Latin *antīquus* ancient, from *ante* before]

antiquities (æn'tɪkwɪtɪz) *pl. n.* remains or relics, such as statues, buildings, or coins, that date from ancient times.

antiquity (æn'tɪkwɪtɪ) *n., pl.* **-ties.** **1.** the quality of being ancient or very old: *a vase of great antiquity.* **2.** the far distant past, esp. the time preceding the Middle Ages in Europe. **3.** the people of ancient times collectively; the ancients.

antirachitic (ˌæntɪrə'kɪtɪk) *adj.* **1.** preventing or curing rickets. ~*n.* **2.** an antirachitic remedy or agent.

antiracism (ˌæntɪ'reɪsɪzəm) *n.* the policy of challenging racism and promoting racial tolerance. —**ˌanti'racist** *n., adj.*

anti-roll bar *n.* a crosswise rubber-mounted bar in the suspension of a motor vehicle, which counteracts the movement downward on one side when cornering.

anti-roman *French.* (ɑ̃tirɔmɑ̃) *n., pl.* ***anti-romans*** (ɑ̃tirɔmɑ̃) another term for **antinovel.** [literally: anti-novel]

antirrhinum (ˌæntɪ'raɪnəm) *n.* any scrophulariaceous plant of the genus *Antirrhinum,* esp. the snapdragon, which have two-lipped flowers of various colours. [C16: via Latin from Greek *antirrhinon,* from ANTI- (imitating) + *rhis* nose; so called from a fancied likeness to an animal's snout]

antiscorbutic (ˌæntɪskɔː'bjuːtɪk) *adj.* **1.** preventing or curing scurvy. ~*n.* **2.** an antiscorbutic remedy or agent.

anti-Semite *n.* a person who persecutes or discriminates against Jews. —**ˌanti-Se'mitic** *adj.* —**ˌanti-Se'mitically** *adv.* —**ˌanti-'Semitism** *n.*

antisepsis (ˌæntɪ'sɛpsɪs) *n.* **1.** destruction of undesirable microorganisms, such as those that cause disease or putrefaction. Compare **asepsis.** **2.** the state or condition of being free from such microorganisms.

antiseptic (ˌæntɪ'sɛptɪk) *adj.* **1.** of, relating to, or effecting antisepsis. **2.** entirely free from contamination. **3.** *Informal.* lacking spirit or excitement; clinical. ~*n.* **4.** an antiseptic agent or substance. —**ˌanti'septically** *adv.*

antiserum (ˌæntɪ'sɪərəm) *n., pl.* **-rums** *or* **-ra** (-rə). blood serum containing antibodies against a specific antigen, used to treat or provide immunity to a disease.

antislavery (ˌæntɪ'sleɪvərɪ) *adj.* opposed to slavery, esp. Negro slavery.

antisocial (ˌæntɪ'səʊʃəl) *adj.* **1.** avoiding the company of other people; unsociable. **2.** contrary or injurious to the interests of society in general. —**ˌanti'socially** *adv.*

antispasmodic (ˌæntɪspæz'mɒdɪk) *adj.* **1.** preventing or arresting spasms. ~*n.* **2.** an antispasmodic drug.

antistatic (ˌæntɪ'stætɪk) *adj.* (of a substance, textile, etc.) retaining sufficient moisture to provide a conducting path, thus avoiding the effects of static electricity.

antistrophe (æn'tɪstrəfɪ) *n.* **1.** (in ancient Greek drama) **a.** the second of two movements made by a chorus during the performance of a choral ode. **b.** the second part of a choral ode sung during this movement. **2.** (in classical prosody) the second of two metrical systems used alternately within a poem. ~See **strophe.** [C17: via Late Latin from Greek *antistrophē* an answering turn, from ANTI- + *strophē* a turning] —**antistrophic** (ˌæntɪ'strɒfɪk) *adj.* —**ˌanti'strophically** *adv.*

antisymmetric (ˌæntɪsɪ'mɛtrɪk) *adj. Logic.* (of a relation) never holding between a pair of arguments x and y when it holds between y and x except when $x = y$, as "*... is no younger than ....*" Compare **asymmetric, symmetric** (sense 1), **nonsymmetric.**

antitank (ˌæntɪ'tæŋk) *adj.* designed to immobilize or destroy armoured vehicles: *antitank weapons.*

antithesis (æn'tɪθɪsɪs) *n., pl.* **-ses** (-ˌsiːz). **1.** the exact opposite. **2.** contrast or opposition. **3.** *Rhetoric.* the juxtaposition of contrasting ideas, phrases, or words so as to produce an effect of balance, such as *my words fly up, my thoughts remain below.* **4.** *Philosophy.* the second stage in the **Hegelian dialectic,** contradicting the **thesis** before resolution by the **synthesis.** [C15: via Latin from Greek: a setting against, from ANTI- + *tithenai* to place]

antithetical (ˌæntɪ'θɛtɪkəl) *or* **antithetic** *adj.* **1.** of the nature of antithesis. **2.** directly contrasted.

antitoxin (ˌæntɪ'tɒksɪn) *n.* **1.** an antibody that neutralizes a toxin. **2.** blood serum that contains a specific antibody. —**ˌanti'toxic** *adj.*

antitrades ('æntɪˌtreɪdz) *pl. n.* winds in the upper atmosphere blowing in the opposite direction from and above the trade winds.

antitragus (æn'tɪtrəgəs) *n., pl.* **-gi** (-ˌdʒaɪ). a cartilaginous projection of the external ear opposite the tragus. [C19: from New Latin, from Greek *antitragos;* see ANTI-, TRAGUS]

antitranspirant (ˌæntɪ'trænspɪrənt) *n.* any substance that decreases transpiration and, usually, photosynthesis.

antitrust (ˌæntɪ'trʌst) *n.* (*modifier*) *Chiefly U.S.* regulating or opposing trusts, monopolies, cartels, or similar organizations, esp. in order to prevent unfair competition.

antitussive (ˌæntɪ'tʌsɪv) *adj.* **1.** alleviating or suppressing coughing. ~*n.* **2.** an antitussive drug. [from ANTI- + Latin *tussis* a cough]

antitype ('æntɪˌtaɪp) *n.* **1.** a person or thing that is foreshadowed or represented by a type or symbol, esp. a character or event in the New Testament prefigured in the Old Testament. **2.** an opposite type. —**antitypic** (ˌæntɪ'tɪpɪk) *or* **ˌanti'typical** *adj.* —**ˌanti'typically** *adv.*

antivenin (ˌæntɪ'vɛnɪn) *or* **antivenene** (ˌæntɪvɪ'niːn) *n.* an antitoxin that counteracts a specific venom, esp. snake venom. [C19: from ANTI- + VEN(OM) + -IN]

antiworld ('æntɪˌwɜːld) *n.* a hypothetical or supposed world or universe composed of antimatter.

antler ('æntlə) *n.* one of a pair of bony outgrowths on the heads of male deer and some related species of either sex. The antlers are shed each year and grow more branches as the animal ages. [C14: from Old French *antoillier,* from Vulgar Latin *anteoculare* (unattested) (something) in front of the eye]

antler moth *n.* a European noctuid moth, *Cerapteryx* (or *Charaeas*) *graminis,* that has white antler-like markings on the forewings and produces larvae that periodically cause great damage to pastures and grasslands.

Antlia ('æntlɪə) *n., Latin genitive* **Antliae** ('æntlɪˌiː). a faint constellation in the S hemisphere close to Hydra and Vela. [C19: from Latin, from Greek: bucket]

antlike ('æntˌlaɪk) *adj.* **1.** of or like an ant or ants. **2.** characterized by scurrying activity or teeming restlessness.

antlion ('æntˌlaɪən) *n.* **1.** Also called: **antlion fly.** any of various neuropterous insects of the family *Myrmeleontidae,* which typically resemble dragonflies and are most common in tropical regions. **2.** Also called (U.S.): **doodlebug.** the larva of this insect, which has very large jaws and buries itself in the sand to await its prey.

antonomasia (ˌæntənə'meɪzɪə) *n. Rhetoric.* **1.** the substitution of a title or epithet for a proper name, such as *his highness.* **2.** the use of a proper name for an idea: *he is a Daniel come to judgment.* [C16: via Latin from Greek, from *antonomazein* to name differently, from *onoma* name] —**antonomastic** (ˌæntənə'mæstɪk) *adj.* —**ˌantono'mastically** *adv.*

Anton Piller order ('æntɒn 'pɪlə) *n. Law.* an injunction allowing a person to enter the premises of another to search for and take copies of evidence required for a court case, used esp. in cases of infringement of copyright. [C20: named after the plaintiff in a case (1976) in which such an order was made]

antonym ('æntənɪm) *n.* a word that means the opposite of another word: *"empty" is an antonym of "full".* [C19: from Greek *antōnumia,* from ANTI- + *onoma* name] —**antonymous** (æn'tɒnɪməs) *adj.*

antre ('æntə) *n. Rare.* a cavern or cave. [C17: from French, from Latin *antrum,* from Greek *antron*]

antrorse (æn'trɔːs) *adj. Biology.* directed or pointing upwards or forwards. [C19: from New Latin *antrorsus,* from *antero-* front + *-orsus,* as in Latin *introrsus;* see INTRORSE] —**an'trorsely** *adv.*

antrum ('æntrəm) *n., pl.* **-tra** (-trə). *Anatomy.* a natural cavity, hollow, or sinus, esp. in a bone. [C14: from Latin: cave, from Greek *antron*] —**'antral** *adj.*

ANU *abbrev. for* Australian National University.

anuran (ə'njʊərən) *n.* **1.** any of the vertebrates of the order *Anura* (or *Salientia*), characterized by absence of a tail and very long hind legs specialized for hopping: class *Amphibia* (amphibians). The group includes the frogs and toads. ~*adj.* **2.** of, relating to, or belonging to the order *Anura.* ~Also: **salientian.** [C20: from New Latin *Anura,* from AN- + Greek *oura* tail]

ˌanti'rational *adj.*
ˌanti'rationalism *n.*
ˌantire'ligious *adj.*
ˌantire'publican *adj., n.*
ˌantiˌrevo'lutionary *adj., n., pl.* **-aries.**
ˌanti'riot *adj.*
ˌanti'rust *adj.*
ˌantiˌscien'tific *adj.*
ˌanti'shock *adj.*
ˌanti'skid *adj.*
ˌanti-'Soviet *adj., n.*
ˌanti'spiritual *adj.*
ˌantiˌsubma'rine *adj.*
ˌanti'tarnishing *adj.*
ˌanti'terrorist *adj.*
ˌanti'theft *adj.*
ˌanti'theism *n.*
ˌanti'theist *n.*
ˌantiˌtrini'tarian *n.*
ˌanti'virus *adj.*
ˌantiˌvivi'section *adj.*
ˌantiˌvivi'sectionist *n., adj.*
ˌanti'war *adj.*
ˌanti-'Zionism *n.*
ˌanti-'Zionist *n., adj.*

anuresis (ˌænjʊˈriːsɪs) *n. Pathol.* inability to urinate even though urine is formed by the kidneys and retained in the urinary bladder. Compare **anuria.** [C20: New Latin, from AN- + Greek *ouresis* urination, from *ouron* urine]

anuria (əˈnjʊərɪə) *n. Pathol.* complete suppression of urine formation, often as the result of a kidney disorder. Compare **anuresis, oliguria.** [C19: from New Latin, from AN- + Greek *ouron* urine]

anurous (æˈnjʊərəs) *adj. Zoology.* lacking a tail; tailless; acaudate. [C19: from AN- + Greek *oura* tail]

anus (ˈeɪnəs) *n.* the excretory opening at the end of the alimentary canal. [C16: from Latin]

anvil (ˈænvɪl) *n.* **1.** a heavy iron or steel block on which metals are hammered during forging. **2.** any part having a similar shape or function, such as the lower part of a telegraph key. **3.** the fixed jaw of a measurement device against which the piece to be measured is held. **4.** *Anatomy.* the nontechnical name for **incus.** [Old English *anfealt;* related to Old High German *anafalz,* Middle Dutch *anvilte;* see ON, FELT[2]]

anxiety (æŋˈzaɪɪtɪ) *n., pl.* **-ties. 1.** a state of uneasiness or tension caused by apprehension of possible future misfortune, danger, etc.; worry. **2.** intense desire; eagerness. **3.** *Psychol.* a state of intense apprehension or worry often accompanied by physical symptoms such as shaking, intense feelings in the gut, etc., common in mental illness or after a very distressing experience. See also **angst.** [C16: from Latin *anxietas;* see ANXIOUS]

anxiety neurosis *n.* a relatively mild form of mental illness characterized by extreme distress and agitation, often occurring without any obvious cause.

anxiolytic (ˌæŋksɪəʊˈlɪtɪk) *n.* **1.** any of a class of drugs that reduce anxiety. *~adj.* **2.** of or relating to this class of drugs.

anxious (ˈæŋkʃəs, ˈæŋʃəs) *adj.* **1.** worried and tense because of possible misfortune, danger, etc.; uneasy. **2.** fraught with or causing anxiety; worrying; distressing: *an anxious time.* **3.** intensely desirous; eager: *anxious for promotion.* [C17: from Latin *anxius;* related to Latin *angere* to torment; see ANGER, ANGUISH] —ˈ**anxiously** *adv.* —ˈ**anxiousness** *n.*

any (ˈɛnɪ) *determiner.* **1. a.** one, some, or several, as specified, no matter how much or many, what kind or quality, etc.: *any cheese in the cupboard is yours; you may take any clothes you like.* **b.** (*as pronoun; functioning as sing. or pl.*): *take any you like.* **2.** (*usually used with a negative*) **a.** even the smallest amount or even one: *I can't stand any noise.* **b.** (*as pronoun; functioning as sing. or pl.*): *don't give her any.* **3.** whatever or whichever; no matter what or which: *any dictionary will do; any time of day.* **4.** an indefinite or unlimited amount or number (esp. in the phrases **any amount** or **number**): *any number of friends.* *~adv.* **5.** (*usually used with a negative*) **a.** (foll. by a comparative adj.) to even the smallest extent: *it isn't any worse now.* **b.** *Not standard.* at all: *he doesn't care any.* [Old English *ǣnig;* related to Old Frisian *ēnig,* Old High German *einag,* Old Norse *einigr* anyone, Latin *ūnicus* unique; see AN[1], ONE]

anybody (ˈɛnɪˌbɒdɪ, -bədɪ) *pron.* **1.** any person; anyone. **2.** (*usually used with a negative or a question*) a person of any importance: *he isn't anybody in this town.* *~n., pl.* **-bodies. 3.** (often preceded by *just*) any person at random; no matter who.

anyhow (ˈɛnɪˌhaʊ) *adv.* **1.** in any case; at any rate. **2.** in any manner or by any means whatever. **3.** in a haphazard manner; carelessly.

any more *or esp. U.S.* **anymore** (ˌɛnɪˈmɔː) *adv.* any longer; still; now or from now on; nowadays: *he does not work here any more.*

anyone (ˈɛnɪˌwʌn, -wən) *pron.* **1.** any person; anybody. **2.** (*used with a negative or a question*) a person of any importance: *is he anyone in this town?* **3.** (often preceded by *just*) any person at random; no matter who.

anyplace (ˈɛnɪˌpleɪs) *adv. U.S. and Canadian informal.* in, at, or to any unspecified place.

anyroad (ˈɛnɪˌrəʊd) *adv.* a northern English dialect word for **anyway.**

anything (ˈɛnɪˌθɪŋ) *pron.* **1.** any object, event, action, etc., whatever: *anything might happen.* *~n.* **2.** a thing of any kind: *have you anything to declare?* *~adv.* **3.** in any way: *he wasn't anything like his father.* **4. anything but.** by no means; not in the least: *she was anything but happy.* **5. like anything.** (intensifier; usually euphemistic): *he ran like anything.*

anyway (ˈɛnɪˌweɪ) *adv.* **1.** in any case; at any rate; nevertheless; anyhow. **2.** in a careless or haphazard manner. **3.** Usually **any way.** in any manner; by any means.

anyways (ˈɛnɪˌweɪz) *adv. U.S.* a nonstandard word for **anyway.**

anywhere (ˈɛnɪˌwɛə) *adv.* **1.** in, at, or to any place. **2. get anywhere.** to be successful: *it took three years before he got anywhere.* **3. anywhere from.** any quantity, time, degree, etc., above a specified limit: *he could be anywhere from 40 to 50 years old.*

anywheres (ˈɛnɪˌwɛəz) *adv. U.S.* a nonstandard word for **anywhere.**

anywise (ˈɛnɪˌwaɪz) *adv. Chiefly U.S.* in any way or manner; at all.

ANZAAS (ˈænzəs, -zæs) *n. acronym for* Australian and New Zealand Association for the Advancement of Science.

Anzac (ˈænzæk) *n.* **1.** (in World War I) a soldier serving with the Australian and New Zealand Army Corps. **2.** (now) any Australian or New Zealand soldier. **3.** the Anzac landing at Gallipoli in 1915. **4.** *Austral. informal.* a typical Australian.

Anzac Day *n.* 25 April, a public holiday in Australia and New Zealand commemorating the Anzac landing at Gallipoli in 1915.

ANZUS (ˈænzəs) *n. acronym for* Australia, New Zealand, and the United States, with reference to the security alliance between them.

AO *abbrev. for:* **1.** Officer of the Order of Australia. **2.** Australian Opera.

A/O *or* **a/o** *Account., etc. abbrev. for* account of.

AOB *or* **a.o.b.** *abbrev. for* any other business.

AOC *abbrev. for* appellation d'origine contrôlée: the highest French wine classification; indicates that the wine meets strict requirements concerning area of production, strength, etc. Compare **VDQS, vin de pays.**

AOCB *abbrev. for* any other competent business.

AOH *abbrev. for* Ancient Order of Hibernians: an Irish Catholic nationalist association founded in the 19th century; an important political force up to the founding of the Irish Free State (1922).

A-OK *or* **A-okay** *adj. Informal, chiefly U.S.* in perfect working order; excellent. [C20: from *a(ll systems) OK*]

AOR *Music. abbrev. for:* **1.** album-oriented rock. **2.** adult-oriented rock. **3.** *U.S.* album-oriented radio.

aorist (ˈeɪərɪst, ˈɛərɪst) *n. Grammar.* a tense of the verb in classical Greek and in certain other inflected languages, indicating past action without reference to whether the action involved was momentary or continuous. Compare **perfect** (sense 8), **imperfect** (sense 4). [C16: from Greek *aoristos* not limited, from A-[1] + *horistos* restricted, from *horizein* to define] —ˌ**aoˈristic** *adj.* —ˌ**aoˈristically** *adv.*

aorta (eɪˈɔːtə) *n., pl.* **-tas** *or* **-tae** (-tiː). the main vessel in the arterial network, which conveys oxygen-rich blood from the heart to all parts of the body except the lungs. [C16: from New Latin, from Greek *aortē,* literally: something lifted, from *aeirein* to raise] —**aˈortic** *or* **aˈortal** *adj.*

aortitis (ˌeɪɔːˈtaɪtɪs) *n.* inflammation of the aorta.

aoudad (ˈɑːʊˌdæd) *n.* a wild mountain sheep, *Ammotragus lervia,* of N Africa, having horns curved in a semicircle and long hair covering the neck and forelegs. Also called: **Barbary sheep.** [from French, from Berber *audad*]

AP *abbrev. for:* **1.** Air Police. **2.** Associated Press.

a.p. *abbrev. for:* **1.** additional premium. **2.** (in prescriptions, etc.) ante prandium. [Latin: before a meal]

ap- *prefix.* a variant of **apo-:** *aphelion.*

apace (əˈpeɪs) *adv.* quickly; rapidly. [C14: probably from Old French *à pas,* at a (good) pace]

apache (əˈpɑːʃ, -ˈpæʃ; *French* apaʃ) *n.* a Parisian gangster or ruffian. [from French: APACHE]

Apache (əˈpætʃɪ) *n.* **1.** (*pl.* **Apaches** *or* **Apache**) a member of a North American Indian people, formerly nomadic and warlike, inhabiting the southwestern U.S. and N Mexico. **2.** the language of this people, belonging to the Athapascan group of the Na-Dene phylum. [from Mexican Spanish, probably from Zuñi *Apachu,* literally: enemy]

apache dance *n.* a fast violent dance in French vaudeville, supposedly between a Parisian gangster and his girl.

apanage (ˈæpənɪdʒ) *n.* a variant spelling of **appanage.**

aparejo *Spanish.* (apaˈrexo) *n., pl.* **-jos** (-xos). *Southwestern U.S.* a kind of packsaddle made of stuffed leather cushions. [American Spanish: equipment, from *aparejar* to make ready; see APPAREL]

apart (əˈpɑːt) *adj.* (*postpositive*), *adv.* **1.** to pieces or in pieces: *he had the television apart on the floor.* **2.** placed or kept separately or to one side for a particular purpose, reason, etc.; aside (esp. in the phrases **set** or **put apart**). **3.** separate in time, place, or position; at a distance: *he stood apart from the group; two points three feet apart.* **4.** not being taken into account; aside: *these difficulties apart, the project ran smoothly.* **5.** individual; distinct; separate: *a race apart.* **6.** separately or independently in use, thought, or function: *considered apart, his reasoning was faulty.* **7. apart from.** (*prep.*) besides; other than. *~*See also **take apart, tell apart.** [C14: from Old French *a part* at (the) side]

apartheid (əˈpɑːthaɪt, -heɪt) *n.* (in South Africa) the former official government policy of racial segregation. [C20: Afrikaans, from *apart* APART + *-heid* -HOOD]

apartment (əˈpɑːtmənt) *n.* **1.** (*often pl.*) any room in a building, usually one of several forming a suite, esp. one that is spacious and well furnished and used as living accommodation, offices, etc. **2. a.** another name (esp. U.S. and Canadian) for **flat**[2] (sense 1). **b.** (*as modifier*): *apartment building; apartment house.* [C17: from French *appartement,* from Italian *appartamento,* from *appartare* to set on one side, separate]

apatetic (ˌæpəˈtɛtɪk) *adj.* of or relating to coloration that disguises and protects an animal. [C19: from Greek *apatētikos* deceitful, from *apateuein* to deceive]

apathetic (ˌæpəˈθɛtɪk) *adj.* having or showing little or no emotion; indifferent. [C18: from APATHY + PATHETIC] —ˌ**apaˈthetically** *adv.*

apathy (ˈæpəθɪ) *n.* **1.** absence of interest in or enthusiasm for things generally considered interesting or moving. **2.** absence of emotion. [C17: from Latin, from Greek *apatheia,* from *apathēs* without feeling, from A-[1] + *pathos* feeling]

apatite (ˈæpəˌtaɪt) *n.* a pale green to purple mineral, found in igneous rocks and metamorphosed limestones. It is used in the manufacture of phosphorus, phosphates, and fertilizers. Composition: calcium fluorophosphate or calcium chlorophosphate. General formula: $Ca_5(PO_4,CO_3)_3(F,OH,Cl)$. Crystal structure: hexagonal. [C19: from German *Apatit,* from Greek *apatē* deceit; from its misleading similarity to other minerals]

APC *n.* acetylsalicylic acid, phenacetin, and caffeine; the mixture formerly used in headache and cold tablets.

ape (eɪp) *n.* **1.** any of various primates, esp. those of the family *Pongidae* (see **anthropoid ape**), in which the tail is very short or absent. **2.** (*not in technical use*) any monkey. **3.** an imitator; mimic. **4.** *U.S. informal.* a coarse, clumsy, or rude person. ~*vb.* **5.** (*tr.*) to imitate. [Old English *apa;* related to Old Saxon *ape,* Old Norse *api,* Old High German *affo*] —**'ape,like** *adj.*

apeak (ə'piːk) *adv., adj.* *Nautical.* in a vertical or almost vertical position: *with the oars apeak.*

apeman ('eɪp,mæn) *n., pl.* **-men.** any of various extinct apelike primates thought to have been the forerunners, or closely related to the forerunners, of modern man.

aperçu *French.* (apɛrsy) *n.* **1.** an outline; summary. **2.** an insight. [from *apercevoir* to PERCEIVE]

aperient (ə'pɪərɪənt) *Med.* ~*adj.* **1.** laxative. ~*n.* **2.** a mild laxative. [C17: from Latin *aperīre* to open]

aperiodic (,eɪpɪərɪ'ɒdɪk) *adj.* **1.** not periodic; not occurring at regular intervals. **2.** *Physics.* **a.** (of a system or instrument) being damped sufficiently to reach equilibrium without oscillation. **b.** (of an oscillation or vibration) not having a regular period. **c.** (of an electrical circuit) not having a measurable resonant frequency. —**,aperi'odically** *adv.* —**aperiodicity** (,eɪpɪərɪə'dɪsɪtɪ) *n.*

apéritif (ɑː,pɛrɪ'tiːf, ə,pɛr-) *n.* an alcoholic drink, esp. a wine, drunk before a meal to whet the appetite. [C19: from French, from Medieval Latin *aperitīvus,* from Latin *aperīre* to open]

aperture ('æpətʃə) *n.* **1.** a hole, gap, crack, slit, or other opening. **2.** *Physics.* **a.** a usually circular and often variable opening in an optical instrument or device that controls the quantity of radiation entering or leaving it. **b.** the diameter of such an opening. See also **relative aperture.** [C15: from Late Latin *apertūra* opening, from Latin *aperīre* to open]

aperture priority *n.* *Photog.* an automatic exposure system in which the photographer selects the aperture and the camera then automatically sets the correct shutter speed. Compare **shutter priority.**

apery ('eɪpərɪ) *n., pl.* **-eries.** imitative behaviour; mimicry.

apetalous (eɪ'pɛtələs) *adj.* (of flowering plants such as the wood anemone) having no petals. [C18: from New Latin *apetalus,* see A-[1], PETAL] —**a'petaly** *n.*

apex ('eɪpɛks) *n., pl.* **apexes** *or* **apices** ('æpɪ,siːz, 'eɪ-). **1.** the highest point; vertex. **2.** the pointed end or tip of something. **3.** a pinnacle or high point, as of a career, etc. **4.** Also called: **solar apex.** *Astronomy.* the point on the celestial sphere, lying in the constellation Hercules, towards which the sun appears to move at a velocity of 7.5 kilometres per second relative to the nearest stars. [C17: from Latin: point]

APEX ('eɪpɛks) *n. acronym for:* **1.** Advance Purchase Excursion: a reduced airline or long-distance rail fare that must be paid a specified number of days in advance. **2.** (in Britain) Association of Professional, Executive, Clerical, and Computer Staff.

Apex Club *n.* (in Australia) an association of business and professional men founded to promote community welfare. —**Apexian** (eɪ'pɛksɪən) *adj., n.*

apgar score *or* **rating** ('æpgɑː) *n.* a system for determining the condition of an infant at birth by allotting a maximum of 2 points to each of the following: heart rate, breathing effort, muscle tone, response to stimulation, and colour. [C20: named after V. *Apgar* (born 1909), U.S. anaesthetist]

aphaeresis *or* **apheresis** (ə'fɪərɪsɪs) *n.* the omission of a letter or syllable at the beginning of a word. [C17: via Late Latin from Greek, from *aphairein* to remove] —**aphaeretic** *or* **apheretic** (,æfə'rɛtɪk) *adj.*

aphagia (ə'feɪdʒɪə) *n.* *Pathol.* refusal or inability to swallow. [C20: from A-[1] + Greek *aphagein* to consume]

aphakia (ə'feɪkɪə) *n.* absence of the lens of an eye, congenital or otherwise. [from A-[1] + Greek *phakos* lentil + -IA]

aphanite ('æfə,naɪt) *n.* any fine-grained rock, such as a basalt, containing minerals that cannot be distinguished with the naked eye. [C19: from Greek *aphanēs* invisible]

aphasia (ə'feɪzɪə) *n.* a disorder of the central nervous system characterized by partial or total loss of the ability to communicate, esp. in speech or writing. Compare **alexia.** [C19: via New Latin from Greek, from A-[1] + *-phasia,* from *phanai* to speak] —**a'phasi,ac** *or* **a'phasic** *adj., n.*

aphelandra (,æfə'lændrə) *n.* any shrub of the evergreen genus *Aphelandra,* originally from tropical America, widely grown as a house plant for its variegated shiny leaves and brightly coloured flowers: family *Acanthaceae.* [from Greek *aphelēs* simple + *andros,* genitive of *anēr* man, male, because the anthers are single celled]

aphelion (æp'hiːlɪən, ə'fiː-) *n., pl.* **-lia** (-lɪə). the point in its orbit when a planet or comet is at its greatest distance from the sun. Compare **perihelion.** [C17: from New Latin *aphēlium* (with pseudo-Greek ending *-ion*) from AP- + Greek *hēlios* sun] —**ap'helian** *adj.*

apheliotropic (æp,hiːlɪə'trɒpɪk, ə,fiː-) *adj.* *Biology.* growing in a direction away from the sunlight, as the roots of plants. [C19: see APO-, HELIOTROPIC] —**apheliotropism** (æp,hiːlɪ'ɒtrə,pɪzəm) *n.*

aphesis ('æfɪsɪs) *n.* the gradual disappearance of an unstressed vowel at the beginning of a word, as in *squire* from *esquire.* [C19: from Greek, from *aphienai* to set free, send away] —**aphetic** (ə'fɛtɪk) *adj.* —**a'phetically** *adv.*

aphid ('eɪfɪd) *n.* any of the small homopterous insects of the family *Aphididae,* which feed by sucking the juices from plants. Also called: **plant louse.** See also **greenfly, blackfly.** [C19: back formation from *aphides,* plural of APHIS] —**aphidian** (ə'fɪdɪən) *adj., n.* —**a'phidious** *adj.*

aphis ('eɪfɪs) *n., pl.* **aphides** ('eɪfɪ,diːz). **1.** any of various aphids constituting the genus *Aphis,* such as the blackfly. **2.** any other aphid. [C18: from New Latin (coined by Linnaeus for obscure reasons)]

aphonia (ə'fəʊnɪə) *or* **aphony** ('æfənɪ) *n.* loss of the voice caused by damage to the vocal tract. [C18: via New Latin from Greek, from A-[1] + *phōnē* sound, voice]

aphonic (ə'fɒnɪk) *adj.* **1.** affected with aphonia. **2.** *Phonetics.* **a.** not representing a spoken sound, as *k* in *know.* **b.** voiceless or devoiced.

aphorism ('æfə,rɪzəm) *n.* a short pithy saying expressing a general truth; maxim. [C16: from Late Latin *aphorismus,* from Greek *aphorismos* definition, from *aphorizein* to define, set limits to, from *horos* boundary] —**'aphorist** *n.*

aphoristic (,æfə'rɪstɪk) *adj.* **1.** of, relating to, or resembling an aphorism. **2.** tending to write or speak in aphorisms.

aphorize *or* **aphorise** ('æfə,raɪz) *vb.* (*intr.*) to write or speak in aphorisms.

aphotic (ə'fɒtɪk) *adj.* **1.** characterized by or growing in the absence of light: *an aphotic plant.* **2.** of or relating to the zone of an ocean below about 90m (300 ft.), the lowest level at which photosynthesis can take place. [C20: from A-[1] + *-photic,* from Greek *phōs* light]

aphrodisiac (,æfrə'dɪzɪæk) *n.* **1.** a drug, food, etc., that excites sexual desire. ~*adj.* **2.** exciting or heightening sexual desire. [C18: from Greek *aphrodisiakos,* from *aphrodisios* belonging to *Aphrodite* goddess of love]

aphtha ('æfθə) *n., pl.* **-thae** (-θiː). a small ulceration on a mucous membrane, as in thrush, caused by a fungal infection. [C17: via Latin from Greek: mouth-sore, thrush] —**'aphthous** *adj.*

aphyllous (ə'fɪləs) *adj.* (of plants) having no leaves. [C19: from New Latin *aphyllus,* from Greek *aphullos,* from A-[1] + *phullon* leaf] —**a'phylly** *n.*

apian ('eɪpɪən) *adj.* of, relating to, or resembling bees. [C19: from Latin *apiānus,* from *apis* bee]

apiarian (,eɪpɪ'ɛərɪən) *adj.* of or relating to the breeding and care of bees.

apiarist ('eɪpɪərɪst) *n.* a person who studies or keeps bees.

apiary ('eɪpɪərɪ) *n., pl.* **-aries.** a place where bees are kept, usually in beehives. [C17: from Latin *apiārium* from *apis* bee]

apical ('æpɪkəl, 'eɪ-) *adj.* **1.** of, at, or being the apex. **2.** of or denoting a consonant articulated with the tip of the tongue, such as (t) or (d). [C19: from New Latin *apicālis,* from Latin: APEX] —**'apically** *adv.*

apices ('æpɪ,siːz, 'eɪ-) *n.* a plural of **apex.**

apiculate (ə'pɪkjʊlɪt, -,leɪt) *adj.* (of leaves) ending in a short sharp point. [C19: from New Latin *apiculātus,* from *apiculus* a short point, from APEX]

apiculture ('eɪpɪ,kʌltʃə) *n.* the breeding and care of bees. [C19: from Latin *apis* bee + CULTURE] —**,api'cultural** *adj.* —**,api'culturist** *n.*

apiece (ə'piːs) *adv.* for, to, or from each one: *they were given two apples apiece.*

à pied *French.* (a pje) *adv., adj.* (*postpositive*) on foot.

Apiezon (,æpɪ'eɪzɒn) *adj.* *Trademark.* designating any of a number of hydrocarbon oils, greases, or waxes, characterized by a low vapour pressure and used in vacuum equipment.

API gravity scale *n.* the American Petroleum Institute gravity scale: a universally accepted scale of the relative density of fluids that is used in fuel technology and is measured in degrees API. One degree API is equal to $(141.5/d)$–13.5, where d = relative density at 288.7K. See also **Baumé scale.**

apish ('eɪpɪʃ) *adj.* **1.** stupid; foolish. **2.** resembling an ape. **3.** slavishly imitative. —**'apishly** *adv.* —**'apishness** *n.*

apivorous (eɪ'pɪvərəs) *adj.* eating bees: *apivorous birds.* [C19: from Latin *apis* bee + -VOROUS]

aplacental (,eɪplə'sɛntəl, ,æplə-) *adj.* (of monotremes and marsupials) having no placenta.

aplanatic (,æplə'nætɪk) *adj.* (of a lens or mirror) free from spherical aberration. [C18: from Greek *aplanētos* prevented from wandering, from A-[1] + *planētos,* from *planaein* to wander] —**,apla'natically** *adv.*

aplanetic (,æplə'nɛtɪk) *adj.* (esp. of some algal and fungal spores) nonmotile or lacking a motile stage. [variant of APLANATIC]

aplanospore (ə'pleɪnəʊ,spɔː) *n.* a nonmotile asexual spore produced by certain algae and fungi. [C20: from A-[1] + Greek *planos* wandering + SPORE]

aplasia (ə'pleɪzɪə) *n.* *Pathol.* congenital absence or abnormal development of an organ or part. [C19: New Latin, from A-[1] + *-plasia,* from Greek *plassein* to form]

aplastic (eɪ'plæstɪk) *adj.* **1.** relating to or characterized by aplasia. **2.** failing to develop into new tissue; defective in the regeneration of tissue, as of blood cells: *aplastic anaemia.*

aplenty (ə'plentɪ) *adj. (postpositive), adv.* in plenty.

aplite ('æplaɪt) *or* **haplite** *n.* a light-coloured fine-grained acid igneous rock with a sugary texture, consisting of quartz and feldspars. [C19: from German *Aplit,* from Greek *haploos* simple + -ITE[1]] —**aplitic** (æp'lɪtɪk) *or* **hap'litic** *adj.*

aplomb (ə'plɒm) *n.* equanimity, self-confidence, or self-possession. [C18: from French: rectitude, uprightness, from *à plomb* according to the plumb line, vertically]

apneusis (æp'nu:sɪs) *n. Pathol.* protracted gasping inhalation followed by short inefficient exhalation, which can cause asphyxia. [from A-[1] + Greek *pnein* to breathe]

apneustic (æp'nu:stɪk) *adj.* **1.** of or relating to apneusis. **2.** (of certain animals) having no specialized organs for respiration.

apnoea *or U.S.* **apnea** (æp'nɪə) *n.* a temporary inability to breathe. [C18: from New Latin, from Greek *apnoia,* from A-[1] + *pnein* to breathe]

apo- *or* **ap-** *prefix.* **1.** away from; off: *apogee.* **2.** indicating separation of: *apocarpous.* **3.** indicating a lack or absence of: *apogamy.* **4.** indicating derivation from or relationship to: *apomorphine.* [from Greek *apo* away, off]

Apoc. *abbrev. for:* **1.** Apocalypse. **2.** Apocrypha or Apocryphal.

apocalypse (ə'pɒkəlɪps) *n.* **1.** a prophetic disclosure or revelation. **2.** an event of great importance, violence, etc., such as the events described in the biblical Apocalypse. [C13: from Late Latin *apocalypsis,* from Greek *apokalupsis,* from *apokaluptein* to disclose, from APO- + *kaluptein* to hide]

apocalyptic (əˌpɒkə'lɪptɪk) *adj.* **1.** outstanding in revelation, prophecy, or significance. **2.** of or like an apocalypse. —**aˌpoca'lyptically** *adv.*

apocarp ('æpəˌkɑ:p) *n.* an apocarpous gynoecium or fruit.

apocarpous (ˌæpə'kɑ:pəs) *adj.* (of the ovaries of flowering plants such as the buttercup) consisting of separate carpels. Compare **syncarpous.**

apochromat (ˌæpə'krəʊmæt) *or* **apochromatic lens** *n.* a lens, consisting of three or more elements of different types of glass, that is designed to bring light of three colours to the same focal point, thus reducing its chromatic aberration. Compare **achromat.**

apochromatic (ˌæpəkrə'mætɪk) *adj.* (of a lens) almost free from spherical and chromatic aberration. —**apochromatism** (ˌæpə'krəʊməˌtɪzəm) *n.*

apocopate (ə'pɒkəˌpeɪt) *vb. (tr.)* to omit the final sound or sounds of (a word). —**aˌpoco'pation** *n.*

apocope (ə'pɒkəpɪ) *n.* omission of the final sound or sounds of a word. [C16: via Late Latin from Greek *apokopē,* from *apokoptein* to cut off]

Apocr. *abbrev. for* Apocrypha.

apocrine ('æpəkraɪn, -krɪn) *adj.* denoting a type of glandular secretion in which part of the secreting cell is lost with the secretion, as in mammary glands. Compare **merocrine, holocrine.** [C20: from APO- + *-crine,* from Greek *krinein* to separate]

Apocrypha (ə'pɒkrɪfə) *n.* **the.** *(functioning as sing. or pl.)* **1.** the 14 books included as an appendix to the Old Testament in the Septuagint and the Vulgate but not included in the Hebrew canon. They are not printed in Protestant versions of the Bible. **2.** *R.C. Church.* another name for the **Pseudepigrapha.** [C14: via Late Latin *apocrypha (scripta)* hidden (writings), from Greek, from *apokruptein* to hide away]

apocryphal (ə'pɒkrɪfəl) *adj.* **1.** of questionable authenticity. **2.** *(sometimes cap.)* of or like the Apocrypha. **3.** untrue; counterfeit. —**a'pocryphally** *adv.*

apocynaceous (əˌpɒsɪ'neɪʃəs) *adj.* of, relating to, or belonging to the *Apocynaceae,* a family of mostly tropical flowering plants with latex in their stems, including the dogbane, periwinkle, oleander, and some lianas. [C19: from New Latin *Apocynum* type genus, from Latin: dogbane, from Greek *apokunon,* from *kuōn* dog]

apocynthion (ˌæpə'sɪnθɪən) *n.* the point at which a spacecraft in lunar orbit is farthest from the moon. Compare **apolune, pericynthion.** [C20: from APO- (away) + *cynthion,* from Latin *Cynthia* goddess of the moon]

apodal ('æpəd[ə]l) *or* **apodous** *adj.* (of snakes, eels, etc.) without feet; having no obvious hind limbs or pelvic fins. [C18: from Greek *apous* from A-[1] + *pous* foot]

apodeictic (ˌæpə'daɪktɪk) *or* **apodictic** (ˌæpə'dɪktɪk) *adj.* **1.** unquestionably true by virtue of demonstration. **2.** *Logic, archaic.* **a.** necessarily true. **b.** asserting that a property holds necessarily. ~Compare **problematic** (sense 2), **assertoric.** [C17: from Latin *apodīcticus,* from Greek *apodeiktikos* clearly demonstrating, from *apodeiknunai* to demonstrate] —ˌ**apo'deictically** *or* ˌ**apo'dictically** *adv.*

apodosis (ə'pɒdəsɪs) *n., pl.* **-ses** (-ˌsi:z). *Logic, grammar.* the consequent of a conditional statement, as *the game will be cancelled* in *if it rains the game will be cancelled.* Compare **protasis.** [C17: via Late Latin from Greek: a returning or answering (clause), from *apodidonai* to give back]

apoenzyme (ˌæpəʊ'ɛnzaɪm) *n.* a protein component that together with a coenzyme forms an enzyme.

apogamy (ə'pɒgəmɪ) *n.* a type of reproduction, occurring in some ferns, in which the sporophyte develops from the gametophyte without fusion of gametes. —**apogamic** (ˌæpə'gæmɪk) *adj.* —**a'pogamous** *adj.*

apogee ('æpəˌdʒi:) *n.* **1.** the point in its orbit around the earth when the moon or an artificial satellite is at its greatest distance from the earth. Compare **perigee. 2.** the highest point. [C17: from New Latin *apogaeum* (influenced by French *apogée*), from Greek *apogaion,* from *apogaios* away from the earth, from APO- + *gaia* earth] —ˌ**apo'gean** *adj.*

apogeotropism (ˌæpədʒɪ'ɒtrəˌpɪzəm) *n.* negative geotropism, as shown by plant stems. [C19: from Greek *apogaios* away from the earth + *tropos* a turn] —**apogeotropic** (ˌæpəˌdʒɪə'trɒpɪk) *adj.*

apolitical (ˌeɪpə'lɪtɪk[ə]l) *adj.* politically neutral; without political attitudes, content, or bias.

Apollinaris (əˌpɒlɪ'nɛərɪs) *n.* an effervescent mineral water. [C19: named after *Apollinarisburg,* near Bonn, Germany]

apollo (ə'pɒləʊ) *n., pl.* **-los. 1.** a strikingly handsome youth. **2.** a handsome Eurasian mountain butterfly, *Parnassius apollo,* with palish wings and prominent red ocelli. [after *Apollo,* Greek god of light]

Apollo (ə'pɒləʊ) *n.* any of a series of manned U.S. spacecraft designed to explore the moon and surrounding space. **Apollo 11** made the first moon landing in July 1969.

Apollonian (ˌæpə'ləʊnɪən) *adj.* **1.** of or relating to Apollo, Greek god of light, poetry, music, healing, and prophecy, or the cult of Apollo. **2.** *(sometimes not cap.)* (in the philosophy of Nietzsche) denoting or relating to the set of static qualities that encompass form, reason, harmony, sobriety, etc. **3.** *(often not cap.)* harmonious; serene; ordered. ~Compare **Dionysian.**

apologetic (əˌpɒlə'dʒɛtɪk) *adj.* **1.** expressing or anxious to make apology; contrite. **2.** protecting or defending in speech or writing. —**aˌpolo'getically** *adv.*

apologetics (əˌpɒlə'dʒɛtɪks) *n. (functioning as sing.)* **1.** the branch of theology concerned with the defence and rational justification of Christianity. **2.** a defensive method of argument.

apologia (ˌæpə'ləʊdʒɪə) *n.* a formal written defence of a cause or one's beliefs or conduct.

apologist (ə'pɒlədʒɪst) *n.* a person who offers a defence by argument.

apologize *or* **apologise** (ə'pɒləˌdʒaɪz) *vb. (intr.)* **1.** to express or make an apology; acknowledge failings or faults. **2.** to make a formal defence in speech or writing. —**a'poloˌgizer** *or* **a'poloˌgiser** *n.*

apologue ('æpəˌlɒg) *n.* an allegory or moral fable. [C17: from Latin, from Greek *apologos*]

apology (ə'pɒlədʒɪ) *n., pl.* **-gies. 1.** a verbal or written expression of regret or contrition for a fault or failing. **2.** a poor substitute or offering. **3.** another word for **apologia.** [C16: from Old French *apologie,* from Late Latin *apologia,* from Greek: a verbal defence, from APO- + *logos* speech]

apolune ('æpəˌlu:n) *n.* the point in a lunar orbit when a spacecraft is at its greatest distance from the moon. Compare **apocynthion, perilune.** [C20: from APO- + *-lune,* from Latin *lūna* moon]

apomict ('æpəˌmɪkt) *n.* an organism, esp. a plant, produced by apomixis.

apomixis (ˌæpə'mɪksɪs) *n., pl.* **-mixes** (-'mɪksi:z). any of several types of asexual reproduction, such as parthenogenesis and apogamy, in which fertilization does not take place. Compare **amphimixis.** [C20: New Latin, from Greek APO- + *mixis* a mixing] —ˌ**apo'mictic** *adj.*

apomorphine (ˌæpə'mɔ:fi:n, -fɪn) *n.* a white crystalline alkaloid, derived from morphine but less strong in action, that is used medicinally as an emetic, expectorant, and hypnotic. Formula: $C_{17}H_{17}NO_2$.

aponeurosis (ˌæpənjʊə'rəʊsɪs) *n., pl.* **-ses** (-si:z). *Anatomy.* a white fibrous sheet of tissue by which certain muscles are attached to bones. [C17: via New Latin from Greek, from *aponeurousthai* to change into a tendon, from *neuron* tendon] —**aponeurotic** (ˌæpənjʊə'rɒtɪk) *adj.*

apopemptic (ˌæpə'pɛmptɪk) *Archaic.* ~*adj.* **1.** relating to leave-taking or farewell; valedictory. ~*n.* **2.** a speech or poem made on departure. [C18: from Greek *apopemptikos* concerning dismissal, from *apopempein* to dismiss, from *pempein* to send]

apophasis (ə'pɒfəsɪs) *n. Rhetoric.* the device of mentioning a subject by stating that it will not be mentioned: *I shall not discuss his cowardice or his treachery.* [C17: via Latin from Greek: denial, from APO- + *phanai* to say]

apophthegm *or* **apothegm** ('æpəˌθɛm) *n.* a short cryptic remark containing some general or generally accepted truth; maxim. [C16: from Greek *apophthegma,* from *apophthengesthai* to speak one's opinion frankly, from *phthengesthai* to speak] —**apophthegmatic** *or* **apothegmatic** (ˌæpəθɛg'mætɪk) *adj.*

apophyge (ə'pɒfɪdʒɪ) *n. Architect.* the outward curve at each end of the shaft of a column, adjoining the base or capital. Also called: **hypophyge.** [C16: from Greek *apophugē,* literally: escape, from *apopheugein* to escape from]

apophyllite (ə'pɒfɪˌlaɪt, ˌæpə'fɪlaɪt) *n.* a white, colourless, pink, or green mineral consisting of a hydrated silicate of calcium, potassium, and fluorine in tetragonal crystalline form. It occurs in cracks in volcanic rocks. Formula: $KCa_4FSi_4O_{10}.8H_2O$. [C19:

from French, from APO- + Greek *phullon* leaf + -ITE[1]; referring to its tendency to exfoliate]

apophysis (ə'pɒfɪsɪs) *n., pl.* **-ses** (-ˌsiːz). **1.** a process, outgrowth, or swelling from part of an animal or plant. **2.** *Geology.* a tapering offshoot from a larger igneous intrusive mass. [C17: via New Latin from Greek *apophusis* a sideshoot, from APO- + *phusis* growth] —**apophysate** (ə'pɒfɪsɪt, -seɪt) *adj.* —**apophysial** (ˌæpə'fɪzɪəl) *adj.*

apoplast ('æpəˌplæst) *n. Botany.* the nonprotoplasmic component of a plant, including the cell walls and intercellular material.

apoplectic (ˌæpə'plɛktɪk) *adj.* **1.** of or relating to apoplexy. **2.** *Informal.* furious. ~*n.* **3.** a person having apoplexy. —ˌ**apo'plectically** *adv.*

apoplexy ('æpəˌplɛksɪ) *n.* sudden loss of consciousness, often followed by paralysis, caused by rupture or occlusion of a blood vessel in the brain. [C14: from Old French *apoplexie,* from Late Latin *apoplēxia,* from Greek: from *apoplēssein* to cripple by a stroke, from *plēssein* to strike]

apoprotein ('æpəˌprəʊtiːn) *n. Biochem.* any conjugated protein from which the prosthetic group has been removed, such as apohaemoglobin (the protein of haemoglobin without its haem group).

aporia (ə'pɔːrɪə) *n.* **1.** *Rhetoric.* a doubt, real or professed, about what to do or say. **2.** *Philosophy.* puzzlement occasioned by the raising of philosophical objections without any proffered solutions, esp. in the works of Socrates. [C16: from Greek, literally: a state of being at a loss] —**aporetic** (ˌæpə'rɛtɪk) *adj.*

aport (ə'pɔːt) *adv., adj.* (*postpositive*) *Nautical.* on or towards the port side: *with the helm aport.*

aposematic (ˌæpəsɪ'mætɪk) *adj.* (of the coloration of certain distasteful or poisonous animals) characterized by bright conspicuous markings, which predators recognize and learn to avoid; warning. [C19: from APO- + Greek *sēma* sign]

aposiopesis (ˌæpəʊˌsaɪə'piːsɪs) *n., pl.* **-ses** (-siːz). *Rhetoric.* the device of suddenly breaking off in the middle of a sentence as if unwilling to continue. [C16: via Late Latin from Greek, from *aposiōpaein* to be totally silent, from *siōpaein* to be silent] —**aposiopetic** (ˌæpəʊˌsaɪə'pɛtɪk) *adj.*

apospory ('æpəˌspɔːrɪ) *n. Botany.* development of the gametophyte from the sporophyte without the formation of spores. [C19: from APO- + SPORE + -Y[1]]

apostasy (ə'pɒstəsɪ) *n., pl.* **-sies.** abandonment of one's religious faith, party, a cause, etc. [C14: from Church Latin *apostasia,* from Greek *apostasis* desertion, from *apostanai* to stand apart from, desert]

apostate (ə'pɒsteɪt, -tɪt) *n.* **1.** a person who abandons his religion, party, cause, etc. ~*adj.* **2.** guilty of apostasy. —**apostatical** (ˌæpə'stætɪk°l) *adj.*

apostatize *or* **apostatise** (ə'pɒstəˌtaɪz) *vb.* (*intr.*) to forsake or abandon one's belief, faith, or allegiance.

a posteriori (eɪ pɒsˌtɛrɪ'ɔːraɪ, -rɪ; ɑː) *adj. Logic.* **1.** relating to or involving inductive reasoning from particular facts or effects to a general principle. **2.** derived from or requiring evidence for its validation or support; empirical; open to revision. **3.** *Statistics.* See **posterior probability.** ~Compare **a priori, synthetic** (sense 4). [C18: from Latin, literally: from the latter (that is, from effect to cause)]

apostil (ə'pɒstɪl) *n.* a marginal note. [C16: from French *apostille,* from Old French *apostiller* to make marginal notes, from Medieval Latin *postilla,* probably from Latin *post illa* (*verba*) after those (words)]

apostle (ə'pɒs°l) *n.* **1.** (*often cap.*) one of the 12 disciples chosen by Christ to preach his gospel. **2.** any prominent Christian missionary, esp. one who first converts a nation or people. **3.** an ardent early supporter of a cause, reform movement, etc. **4.** *Mormon Church.* a member of a council of twelve officials appointed to administer and preside over the Church. [Old English *apostol,* from Church Latin *apostolus,* from Greek *apostolos* a messenger, from *apostellein* to send forth]

Apostles' Creed *n.* a concise statement of Christian beliefs dating from about 500 A.D., traditionally ascribed to the Apostles.

apostle spoon *n.* a silver spoon with a figure of one of the Apostles on the handle.

apostolate (ə'pɒstəlɪt, -ˌleɪt) *n.* the office, authority, or mission of an apostle.

apostolic (ˌæpə'stɒlɪk) *adj.* **1.** of, relating to, deriving from, or contemporary with the Apostles. **2.** of or relating to the teachings or practice of the Apostles. **3.** of or relating to the pope regarded as chief successor of the Apostles. —ˌ**apos'tolical** *adj.* —ˌ**apos'tolically** *adv.*

apostolic delegate *n. R.C. Church.* a representative of the pope sent to countries that do not have full or regular diplomatic relations with the Holy See.

Apostolic Fathers *pl. n.* the Fathers of the early Church who immediately followed the Apostles.

Apostolic See *n.* **1.** *R.C. Church.* the see of the pope regarded as the successor to Saint Peter. **2.** (*often not caps.*) a see established by one of the Apostles.

Apostolic succession *n.* the doctrine that the authority of Christian bishops derives from the Apostles through an unbroken line of consecration.

apostrophe[1] (ə'pɒstrəfɪ) *n.* the punctuation mark ' used to indicate the omission of a letter or number, such as *he's* for *he has* or *he is,* also used in English to form the possessive, as in *John's father* and *twenty pounds' worth.* [C17: from Late Latin, from Greek *apostrophos* mark of elision, from *apostrephein* to turn away]

apostrophe[2] (ə'pɒstrəfɪ) *n. Rhetoric.* a digression from a discourse, esp. an address to an imaginary or absent person or a personification. [C16: from Latin *apostrophē,* from Greek: a turning away, digression] —**apostrophic** (ˌæpə'strɒfɪk) *adj.*

apostrophize *or* **apostrophise** (ə'pɒstrəˌfaɪz) *vb.* (*tr.*) *Rhetoric.* to address an apostrophe to.

apothecaries' measure *n.* a system of liquid volume measure used in pharmacy in which 60 minims equal 1 fluid drachm, 8 fluid drachms equal 1 fluid ounce, and 20 fluid ounces equal 1 pint.

apothecaries' weight *n.* a system of weights formerly used in pharmacy based on the Troy ounce, which contains 480 grains. 1 grain is equal to 0.065 gram.

apothecary (ə'pɒθɪkərɪ) *n., pl.* **-caries. 1.** an archaic word for **chemist. 2.** *Law.* a chemist licensed by the Society of Apothecaries of London to prescribe, prepare, and sell drugs. [C14: from Old French *apotecaire,* from Late Latin *apothēcārius* warehouseman, from *apothēca,* from Greek *apothēkē* storehouse]

apothecium (ˌæpə'θiːsɪəm) *n., pl.* **-cia** (-sɪə). *Botany.* a cup-shaped structure that contains the asci; a type of ascocarp. [C19: from New Latin, from APO- + Greek *thēkion* a little case] —**apothecial** (ˌæpə'θiːsɪəl) *adj.*

apothegm ('æpəˌθɛm) *n.* a variant spelling of **apophthegm.**

apothem ('æpəˌθɛm) *n.* the perpendicular line or distance from the centre of a regular polygon to any of its sides. [C20: from APO- + Greek *thema,* from *tithenai* to place]

apotheosis (əˌpɒθɪ'əʊsɪs) *n., pl.* **-ses** (-siːz). **1.** the elevation of a person to the rank of a god; deification. **2.** glorification of a person or thing. **3.** a glorified ideal. [C17: via Late Latin from Greek: deification, from *theos* god]

apotheosize *or* **apotheosise** (ə'pɒθɪəˌsaɪz) *vb.* (*tr.*) **1.** to deify. **2.** to glorify or idealize.

apotropaic (ˌæpəʊtrə'peɪɪk) *adj.* preventing or intended to prevent evil. [C19: from Greek *apotropaios* turning away (evil), from *apotrepein;* see APO-, TROPE]

app. *abbrev. for:* **1.** apparatus. **2.** appendix (of a book). **3.** applied. **4.** appointed. **5.** apprentice. **6.** approved. **7.** approximate.

appal *or U.S.* **appall** (ə'pɔːl) *vb.* **-pals, -palling, -palled** *or U.S.* **-palls, -palling, -palled.** (*tr.*) to fill with horror; shock or dismay. [C14: from Old French *appalir* to turn pale]

Appalachian (ˌæpə'leɪtʃɪən) *adj.* **1.** of, from, or relating to the Appalachian Mountains, E North America. **2.** *Geology.* of or relating to an episode of mountain building in the late Palaeozoic era during which the Appalachian Mountains were formed.

appalling (ə'pɔːlɪŋ) *adj.* causing extreme dismay, horror, or revulsion. —**ap'pallingly** *adv.*

Appaloosa (ˌæpə'luːsə) *n.* a breed of horse, originally from America, typically having a spotted rump. [C19: perhaps from *Palouse,* river in Idaho]

appanage *or* **apanage** ('æpənɪdʒ) *n.* **1.** land or other provision granted by a king for the support of a member of the royal family, esp. a younger son. **2.** a natural or customary accompaniment or perquisite, as to a job or position. [C17: from Old French, from Medieval Latin *appanāgium,* from *appanāre* to provide for, from Latin *pānis* bread]

apparat (ˌæpə'rɑːt) *n.* (formerly) the Communist Party organization in the Soviet Union and other states. [Russian, literally: APPARATUS]

apparatchik (ˌæpə'rɑːtʃɪk) *n.* **1.** a member of a Communist apparat. **2.** an official or bureaucrat in any organization.

apparatus (ˌæpə'reɪtəs, -'rɑːtəs, 'æpəˌreɪtəs) *n., pl.* **-ratus** *or* **-ratuses. 1.** a collection of instruments, machines, tools, parts, or other equipment used for a particular purpose. **2.** a machine having a specific function: *breathing apparatus.* **3.** the means by which something operates; organization: *the apparatus of government.* **4.** *Anatomy.* any group of organs having a specific function. [C17: from Latin, from *apparāre* to make ready]

apparatus criticus ('krɪtɪkəs) *n.* textual notes, list of variant readings, etc., relating to a document, esp. in a scholarly edition of a text. [Latin: critical apparatus]

apparel (ə'pærəl) *n.* **1.** something that covers or adorns, esp. outer garments or clothing. **2.** *Nautical.* a vessel's gear and equipment. ~*vb.* **-els, -elling, -elled** *or U.S.* **-els, -eling, -eled. 3.** *Archaic.* (*tr.*) to clothe, adorn, etc. [C13: from Old French *apareillier* to make ready, from Vulgar Latin *appariculāre* (unattested), from Latin *apparāre,* from *parāre* to prepare]

apparent (ə'pærənt, ə'pɛər-) *adj.* **1.** readily seen or understood; evident; obvious. **2.** (*usually prenominal*) seeming, as opposed to real: *his apparent innocence belied his complicity in the crime.* **3.** *Physics.* as observed but ignoring such factors as the motion of the observer, changes in the environment, etc. Compare **true** (sense 9). [C14: from Latin *apparēns,* from *apparēre* to APPEAR] —**ap'parently** *adv.* —**ap'parentness** *n.*

apparent magnitude *n.* another name for **magnitude** (sense 4).

apparent movement *n. Psychol.* the sensation of seeing movement when nothing actually moves in the environment, as when two neighbouring lights are switched on and off in rapid succession.

apparition (ˌæpəˈrɪʃən) *n.* **1.** an appearance, esp. of a ghost or ghostlike figure. **2.** the figure so appearing; phantom; spectre. **3.** the act of appearing or being visible. [C15: from Late Latin *appāritiō*, from Latin: attendance, from *appārēre* to APPEAR]

apparitor (əˈpærɪtə) *n.* an officer who summons witnesses and executes the orders of an ecclesiastical and (formerly) a civil court. [C15: from Latin: public servant, from *appārēre* to APPEAR]

appassionato (əˌpæsjəˈnɑːtəʊ) *adj., adv. Music.* (to be performed) in an impassioned manner.

appeal (əˈpiːl) *n.* **1.** a request for relief, aid, etc. **2.** the power to attract, please, stimulate, or interest: *a dress with appeal.* **3.** an application or resort to another person or authority, esp. a higher one, as for a decision or confirmation of a decision. **4.** *Law.* **a.** the judicial review by a superior court of the decision of a lower tribunal. **b.** a request for such review. **c.** the right to such review. **5.** *Cricket.* a verbal request to the umpire from one or more members of the fielding side to declare a batsman out. **6.** *English law.* (formerly) a formal charge or accusation: *appeal of felony.* ~*vb.* **7.** (*intr.*) to make an earnest request for relief, support, etc. **8.** (*intr.*) to attract, please, stimulate, or interest. **9.** *Law.* to apply to a superior court to review (a case or particular issue decided by a lower tribunal). **10.** (*intr.*) to resort to (to), as for a decision or confirmation of a decision. **11.** (*intr.*) *Cricket.* to ask the umpire to declare a batsman out. **12.** (*intr.*) to challenge the umpire's or referee's decision. [C14: from Old French *appeler*, from Latin *appellāre* to entreat (literally: to approach), from *pellere* to push, drive] —**apˈpealable** *adj.* —**apˈpealer** *n.* —**apˈpealing** *adj.* —**apˈpealingly** *adv.*

appear (əˈpɪə) *vb.* (*intr.*) **1.** to come into sight or view. **2.** (*copula; may take an infinitive*) to seem or look: *the evidence appears to support you.* **3.** to be plain or clear, as after further evidence, etc.: *it appears you were correct after all.* **4.** to develop or come into being; occur: *faults appeared during testing.* **5.** to become publicly available; be published: *his biography appeared last month.* **6.** to perform or act: *he has appeared in many London productions.* **7.** to be present in court before a magistrate or judge: *he appeared on two charges of theft.* [C13: from Old French *aparoir*, from Latin *appārēre* to become visible, attend upon, from *pārēre* to appear]

appearance (əˈpɪərəns) *n.* **1.** the act or an instance of appearing, as to the eye, before the public, etc. **2.** the outward or visible aspect of a person or thing: *her appearance was stunning; it has the appearance of powdered graphite.* **3.** an outward show; pretence: *he gave an appearance of working hard.* **4.** (*often pl.*) one of the outward signs or indications by which a person or thing is assessed: *first appearances are deceptive.* **5.** *Law.* **a.** the formal attendance in court of a party in an action. **b.** formal notice that a party or his legal representative intends to maintain or contest the issue: *to enter an appearance.* **6.** *Philosophy.* **a.** the outward or phenomenal manifestation of things. **b.** the world as revealed by the senses, as opposed to its real nature. Compare **reality** (sense 4). **7. keep up appearances.** to maintain the public impression of wellbeing or normality. **8. put in** *or* **make an appearance.** to come or attend briefly, as out of politeness. **9. to all appearances.** to the extent that can easily be judged; apparently.

appearance money *n.* money paid by a promoter of an event to a particular celebrity in order to ensure that the celebrity takes part in the event.

appease (əˈpiːz) *vb.* (*tr.*) **1.** to calm, pacify, or soothe, esp. by acceding to the demands of. **2.** to satisfy or quell (an appetite or thirst, etc.). [C16: from Old French *apaisier*, from *pais* peace, from Latin *pax*] —**apˈpeasable** *adj.* —**apˈpeaser** *n.*

appeasement (əˈpiːzmənt) *n.* **1.** the policy of acceding to the demands of a potentially hostile nation in the hope of maintaining peace. **2.** the act of appeasing.

appel (əˈpɛl; *French* apɛl) *n. Fencing.* **1.** a stamp of the foot, used to warn of one's intent to attack. **2.** a sharp blow with the blade made to procure an opening. [from French: challenge]

appellant (əˈpɛlənt) *n.* **1.** a person who appeals. **2.** *Law.* the party who appeals to a higher court from the decision of a lower tribunal. ~*adj.* **3.** *Law.* another word for **appellate.** [C14: from Old French; see APPEAL]

appellate (əˈpɛlɪt) *adj. Law.* **1.** of or relating to appeals. **2.** (of a tribunal) having jurisdiction to review cases on appeal and to reverse decisions of inferior courts. [C18: from Latin *appellātus* summoned, from *appellāre* to APPEAL]

appellation (ˌæpɪˈleɪʃən) *n.* **1.** an identifying name or title. **2.** the act of naming or giving a title to.

appellative (əˈpɛlətɪv) *n.* **1.** an identifying name or title; appellation. **2.** *Grammar.* another word for **common noun.** ~*adj.* **3.** of or relating to a name or title. **4.** (of a proper noun) used as a common noun. —**apˈpellatively** *adv.*

appellee (ˌæpɛˈliː) *n. Law.* a person who is accused or appealed against. [C16: from Old French *apele* summoned; see APPEAL]

append (əˈpɛnd) *vb.* (*tr.*) **1.** to add as a supplement: *to append a footnote.* **2.** to attach; hang on. [C15: from Late Latin *appendere* to hang (something) from, from Latin *pendere* to hang]

appendage (əˈpɛndɪdʒ) *n.* **1.** an ancillary or secondary part attached to a main part; adjunct. **2.** *Zoology.* any organ that projects from the trunk of animals such as arthropods. **3.** *Botany.* any subsidiary part of a plant, such as a branch or leaf.

appendant (əˈpɛndənt) *adj.* **1.** attached, affixed, or added. **2.** attendant or associated as an accompaniment or result. **3.** a less common word for **pendent.** **4.** *Law.* relating to another right. ~*n.* **5.** a person or thing attached or added. **6.** *Property law.* a subordinate right or interest, esp. in or over land, attached to a greater interest and automatically passing with the sale of the latter.

appendicectomy (əˌpɛndɪˈsɛktəmɪ) *or esp. U.S. and Canadian* **appendectomy** (ˌæpənˈdɛktəmɪ) *n., pl.* **-mies.** surgical removal of any appendage, esp. the vermiform appendix.

appendicitis (əˌpɛndɪˈsaɪtɪs) *n.* inflammation of the vermiform appendix.

appendicle (əˈpɛndɪkᵊl) *n.* a small appendage. [C17: from Latin *appendicula;* see APPENDIX]

appendicular (ˌæpənˈdɪkjʊlə) *adj.* **1.** relating to an appendage or appendicle. **2.** *Anatomy.* of or relating to the vermiform appendix.

appendix (əˈpɛndɪks) *n., pl.* **-dixes** *or* **-dices** (-dɪˌsiːz). **1.** a body of separate additional material at the end of a book, magazine, etc., esp. one that is documentary or explanatory. **2.** any part that is dependent or supplementary in nature or function; appendage. **3.** *Anatomy.* See **vermiform appendix.** [C16: from Latin: an appendage, from *appendere* to APPEND]

apperceive (ˌæpəˈsiːv) *vb.* (*tr.*) **1.** to be aware of perceiving. **2.** *Psychol.* to comprehend by assimilating (a perception) to ideas already in the mind. [C19: from Old French *aperceveir*, from Latin *percipere* to PERCEIVE]

apperception (ˌæpəˈsɛpʃən) *n. Psychol.* **1.** the attainment of full awareness of a sensation or idea. **2.** the act or process of apperceiving. —ˌ**apperˈceptive** *adj.*

appertain (ˌæpəˈteɪn) *vb.* (*intr.;* usually foll. by *to*) to belong (to) as a part, function, right, etc.; relate (to) or be connected (with). [C14: from Old French *apertenir* to belong, from Late Latin *appertinēre*, from Latin AD- + *pertinēre* to PERTAIN]

appestat (ˈæpɪstæt) *n.* a neural control centre within the hypothalamus of the brain that regulates the sense of hunger and satiety. [C20: from APPE(TITE) + -STAT]

appetence (ˈæpɪtəns) *or* **appetency** *n., pl.* **-tences** *or* **-tencies.** **1.** a natural craving or desire. **2.** a natural or instinctive inclination. **3.** an attraction or affinity. [C17: from Latin *appetentia*, from *appetere* to crave]

appetite (ˈæpɪˌtaɪt) *n.* **1.** a desire for food or drink. **2.** a desire to satisfy a bodily craving, as for sexual pleasure. **3.** (usually foll. by *for*) a desire, liking, or willingness: *a great appetite for work.* [C14: from Old French *apetit*, from Latin *appetītus* a craving, from *appetere* to desire ardently] —**appetitive** (əˈpɛtɪtɪv, ˈæpɪˌtaɪtɪv) *adj.*

appetizer *or* **appetiser** (ˈæpɪˌtaɪzə) *n.* **1.** a small amount of food or drink taken to stimulate the appetite. **2.** any stimulating foretaste.

appetizing *or* **appetising** (ˈæpɪˌtaɪzɪŋ) *adj.* pleasing or stimulating to the appetite; delicious; tasty.

applaud (əˈplɔːd) *vb.* **1.** to indicate approval of (a person, performance, etc.) by clapping the hands. **2.** (*usually tr.*) to offer or express approval or praise of (an action, person, or thing): *I applaud your decision.* [C15: from Latin *applaudere* to clap, from *plaudere* to beat, applaud] —**apˈplauder** *n.* —**apˈplauding** *adj.* —**apˈplaudingly** *adv.*

applause (əˈplɔːz) *n.* appreciation or praise, esp. as shown by clapping the hands.

apple (ˈæpᵊl) *n.* **1.** a rosaceous tree, *Malus pumila* (or *Pyrus malus*), widely cultivated in temperate regions in many varieties, having pink or white fragrant flowers and firm rounded edible fruits. **2.** the fruit of this tree, having red, yellow, or green skin and crisp whitish flesh. **3.** the wood of this tree. **4.** any of several unrelated trees that have fruit similar to the apple, such as the custard apple, sugar apple, and May apple. See also **love apple, oak apple, thorn apple.** **5. apple of one's eye.** a person or thing that is very precious or much loved. ~See also **apples.** [Old English *æppel;* related to Old Saxon *appel*, Old Norse *apall*, Old High German *apful*]

apple blight *n.* an aphid, *Eriosoma lanigera*, that is covered with a powdery waxy secretion and infests apple trees. Also called: **American blight.**

apple box *n.* an ornamental Australian tree, *Eucalyptus bridgesiana*, having heart-shaped juvenile leaves, large lanceolate adult leaves, and conical fruits. Also called: **apple gum.**

apple butter *n.* a jam made from stewed spiced apples.

applecart (ˈæpᵊlˌkɑːt) *n.* **1.** a cart or barrow from which apples and other fruit are sold in the street. **2. upset the** *or* **one's applecart.** to spoil plans or arrangements.

apple green *n.* **a.** a bright light green or moderate yellowish-green. **b.** (*as adj.*): *an apple-green carpet.*

applejack (ˈæpᵊlˌdʒæk) *n.* a brandy made from apples; distilled cider. Also called: **applejack brandy, apple brandy.**

apple maggot *n.* a fruit fly, *Rhagoletis pomonella*, the larvae of which bore into and feed on the fruit of apple trees: family *Trypetidae.*

apple-pie bed *n. Brit.* a way of making a bed so as to prevent the person from entering it.

apple-pie order *n. Informal.* perfect order or condition.

apple polisher *n. U.S. and Canadian informal.* a sycophant; toady.

apples ('æpᵊlz) *pl. n.* **1.** See **apples and pears. 2. she's apples.** *Austral. and N.Z. informal.* all is going well.
apples and pears *pl. n. Cockney rhyming slang.* stairs. Often shortened to **apples.**
apple sauce *n.* **1.** a purée of stewed apples often served with pork. **2.** *U.S. and Canadian slang.* nonsense; rubbish.
applesnits ('æpᵊl,snɪts) *n. Canadian W coast.* a dish consisting of apple slices. [from German *Apfelschnitzel*]
Appleton layer *n.* another name for **F region** (of the ionosphere). [C20: named after Sir Edward *Appleton* (1892–1965), British physicist]
appliance (ə'plaɪəns) *n.* **1.** a machine or device, esp. an electrical one used domestically. **2.** any piece of equipment having a specific function. **3.** a device fitted to a machine or tool to adapt it for a specific purpose. **4.** another name for a **fire engine.**
applicable ('æplɪkəbᵊl, ə'plɪkə-) *adj.* being appropriate or relevant; able to be applied; fitting. —ˌ**applica'bility** *or* '**applicableness** *n.* —'**applicably** *adv.*
applicant ('æplɪkənt) *n.* a person who applies, as for a job, grant, support, etc.; candidate. [C15: from Latin *applicāns,* from *applicāre* to APPLY]
application (ˌæplɪ'keɪʃən) *n.* **1.** the act of applying to a particular purpose or use. **2.** relevance or value: *the practical applications of space technology.* **3.** the act of asking for something: *an application for leave.* **4.** a verbal or written request, as for a job, etc.: *he filed his application.* **5.** diligent effort or concentration: *a job requiring application.* **6.** something, such as a healing agent or lotion, that is applied, esp. to the skin. **7.** *Logic, maths.* the process of determining the value of a function for a given argument.
application program *n.* a computer program that is written and designed for a specific need or purpose.
applications package *n. Computer technol.* a specialized program or set of specialized programs and associated documentation designed to carry out a particular task.
applicative (ə'plɪkətɪv) *adj.* relevant or applicable. —**ap'plicatively** *adv.*
applicator ('æplɪˌkeɪtə) *n.* a device, such as a spatula or rod, for applying a medicine, glue, etc.
applicatory ('æplɪkətərɪ) *adj.* suitable for application.
applied (ə'plaɪd) *adj.* related to or put to practical use: *applied mathematics.* Compare **pure** (sense 5).
appliqué (æ'pliːkeɪ) *n.* **1.** a decoration or trimming of one material sewn or otherwise fixed onto another. **2.** the practice of decorating in this way. ~*vb.* **-qués, -quéing, -quéd. 3.** (*tr.*) to sew or fix (a decoration) on as an appliqué. [C18: from French, literally: applied]
apply (ə'plaɪ) *vb.* **-plies, -plying, -plied. 1.** (*tr.*) to put to practical use; utilize; employ. **2.** (*intr.*) to be relevant, useful, or appropriate. **3.** (*tr.*) to cause to come into contact with; put onto. **4.** (*intr.;* often foll. by *for*) to put in an application or request. **5.** (*tr.;* often foll. by *to*) to devote (oneself, one's efforts) with diligence. **6.** (*tr.*) to bring into operation or use: *the police only applied the law to aliens.* **7.** (*tr.*) to refer (a word, epithet, etc.) to a person or thing. [C14: from Old French *aplier,* from Latin *applicāre* to attach to] —**ap'plier** *n.*
appoggiatura (əˌpɒdʒə'tʊərə) *n., pl.* **-ras** *or* **-re** (-rɛ). *Music.* an ornament consisting of a nonharmonic note (short or long) preceding a harmonic one either before or on the stress. See also **acciaccatura** (sense 2). [C18: from Italian, literally: a propping, from *appoggiare* to prop, support]
appoint (ə'pɔɪnt) *vb.* (*mainly tr.*) **1.** (*also intr.*) to assign officially, as for a position, responsibility, etc.: *he was appointed manager.* **2.** to establish by agreement or decree; fix: *a time was appointed for the duel.* **3.** to prescribe or ordain: *laws appointed by tribunal.* **4.** *Property law.* to nominate (a person), under a power granted in a deed or will, to take an interest in property. **5.** to equip with necessary or usual features; furnish: *a well-appointed hotel.* [C14: from Old French *apointer* to put into a good state, from *a point* in good condition, literally: to a POINT] —**ap'pointer** *n.*
appointee (əpɔɪn'tiː, ˌæp-) *n.* **1.** a person who is appointed. **2.** *Property law.* a person to whom property is granted under a power of appointment.
appointive (ə'pɔɪntɪv) *adj. Chiefly U.S.* relating to or filled by appointment: *an appointive position.*
appointment (ə'pɔɪntmənt) *n.* **1.** an arrangement to meet a person or be at a place at a certain time. **2.** the act of placing in a job or position. **3.** the person who receives such a job or position. **4.** the job or position to which such a person is appointed. **5.** (*usually pl.*) a fixture or fitting. **6.** *Property law.* nomination to an interest in property under a deed or will.
appointor (ə'pɔɪntə, əpɔɪn'tɔː) *n. Property law.* a person to whom a power to nominate persons to take property is given by deed or will. See also **power of appointment.**
apport (ə'pɔːt) *n.* **1. a.** the production of objects by apparently supernatural means at a spiritualists' seance. **b.** the objects produced. **2.** *Obsolete.* bearing; demeanour. **3.** (*pl.*) *Obsolete.* things brought as offerings; revenues. [C15: from Old French *aport,* from *aporter* (vb.), from Latin AD- + *portāre* to carry]
apportion (ə'pɔːʃən) *vb.* (*tr.*) to divide, distribute, or assign appropriate shares of; allot proportionally: *to apportion the blame.* —**ap'portionable** *adj.* —**ap'portioner** *n.*
apportionment (ə'pɔːʃənmənt) *n.* **1.** the act of apportioning. **2.** *U.S. government.* the proportional distribution of the seats in a legislative body, esp. the House of Representatives, on the basis of population.
apposable (ə'pəʊzəbᵊl) *adj.* **1.** capable of being apposed or brought into apposition. **2.** *Anatomy.* another word for **opposable** (sense 2).
appose (ə'pəʊz) *vb.* (*tr.*) **1.** to place side by side or near to each other. **2.** (usually foll. by *to*) to place (something) near or against another thing. [C16: from Old French *apposer,* from *poser* to put, from Latin *pōnere*]
apposite ('æpəzɪt) *adj.* well suited for the purpose; appropriate; apt. [C17: from Latin *appositus* placed near, from *appōnere,* from *pōnere* to put, place] —'**appositely** *adv.* —'**appositeness** *n.*
apposition (ˌæpə'zɪʃən) *n.* **1.** a putting into juxtaposition. **2.** a grammatical construction in which a word, esp. a noun phrase, is placed after another to modify its meaning. **3.** *Biology.* growth in the thickness of a cell wall by the deposition of successive layers of material. Compare **intussusception** (sense 2). —ˌ**ap-po'sitional** *adj.*
appositive (ə'pɒzɪtɪv) *adj.* **1.** *Grammar.* **a.** standing in apposition. **b.** another word for **nonrestrictive. 2.** of or relating to apposition. ~*n.* **3.** an appositive word or phrase. —**ap'positively** *adv.*
appraisal (ə'preɪzᵊl) *or* **appraisement** *n.* **1.** an assessment or estimation of the worth, value, or quality of a person or thing. See also **performance appraisal. 2.** a valuation of property or goods.
appraisal drilling *n.* (in the oil industry) drilling carried out once oil or gas has been discovered in order to assess the extent of the field, the reserves, the possible rate of production, and the properties of the oil or gas.
appraise (ə'preɪz) *vb.* (*tr.*) **1.** to assess the worth, value, or quality of. **2.** to make a valuation of, as for taxation purposes. [C15: from Old French *aprisier,* from *prisier* to PRIZE[2]] —**ap'praisable** *adj.* —**ap'praiser** *n.* —**ap'praisingly** *adv.* —**ap'praisive** *adj.* —**ap'praisively** *adv.*
appreciable (ə'priːʃɪəbᵊl, -ʃəbᵊl) *adj.* sufficient to be easily seen, measured, or noticed. —**ap'preciably** *adv.*
appreciate (ə'priːʃɪˌeɪt, -sɪ-) *vb.* (*mainly tr.*) **1.** to feel thankful or grateful for: *to appreciate a favour.* **2.** (*may take a clause as object*) to take full or sufficient account of: *to appreciate a problem.* **3.** to value highly: *to appreciate Shakespeare.* **4.** (*usually intr.*) to raise or increase in value. [C17: from Medieval Latin *appretiāre* to value, prize, from Latin *pretium* PRICE] —**ap'preciˌator** *n.*
appreciation (əˌpriːʃɪ'eɪʃən, -sɪ-) *n.* **1.** thanks or gratitude. **2.** assessment of the true worth or value of persons or things. **3.** perceptive recognition of qualities, as in art. **4.** an increase in value, as of goods or property. **5.** a written review of a book, etc., esp. when favourable.
appreciative (ə'priːʃɪətɪv, -ʃə-) *or* **appreciatory** *adj.* feeling, expressing, or capable of appreciation. —**ap'preciatively** *or* **ap'preciatorily** *adv.* —**ap'preciativeness** *n.*
apprehend (ˌæprɪ'hɛnd) *vb.* **1.** (*tr.*) to arrest and escort into custody; seize. **2.** to perceive or grasp mentally; understand. **3.** (*tr.*) to await with fear or anxiety; dread. [C14: from Latin *apprehendere* to lay hold of]
apprehensible (ˌæprɪ'hɛnsɪbᵊl) *adj.* capable of being comprehended or grasped mentally. —ˌ**appreˌhensi'bility** *n.* —ˌ**appre'hensibly** *adv.*
apprehension (ˌæprɪ'hɛnʃən) *n.* **1.** fear or anxiety over what may happen. **2.** the act of capturing or arresting. **3.** the faculty of comprehending; understanding. **4.** a notion or conception.
apprehensive (ˌæprɪ'hɛnsɪv) *adj.* **1.** fearful or anxious. **2.** (*usually postpositive* and foll. by *of*) *Archaic.* intelligent, perceptive, or appreciative. —ˌ**appre'hensively** *adv.* —ˌ**appre'hensiveness** *n.*
apprentice (ə'prɛntɪs) *n.* **1.** someone who works for a skilled or qualified person in order to learn a trade or profession, esp. for a recognized period. **2.** any beginner or novice. ~*vb.* **3.** (*tr.*) to take, place, or bind as an apprentice. [C14: from Old French *aprentis,* from Old French *aprendre* to learn, from Latin *apprehendere* to APPREHEND] —**ap'prenticeˌship** *n.*
appressed (ə'prɛst) *adj.* pressed closely against, but not joined to, a surface: *leaves appressed to a stem.* [C18: from Latin *appressus,* from *apprimere,* from *premere* to press]
appressorium (ˌæprɛ'sɔːrɪəm) *n., pl.* **-ria** (-rɪə). *Botany.* a flattened hypha of a parasitic fungus that penetrates the host tissues. [from New Latin, from Latin *appressus*; see APPRESSED]
apprise *or* **apprize** (ə'praɪz) *vb.* (*tr.;* often foll. by *of*) to make aware; inform. [C17: from French *appris,* from *apprendre* to teach; learn; see APPREHEND]
appro ('æprəʊ) *n.* an informal shortening of **approval:** *on appro.*
approach (ə'prəʊtʃ) *vb.* **1.** to come nearer in position, time, quality, character, etc., to (someone or something). **2.** (*tr.*) to make advances to, as with a proposal, suggestion, etc. **3.** (*tr.*) to begin to deal with: *to approach a problem.* **4.** (*tr.*) *Rare.* to cause to come near. ~*n.* **5.** the act of coming towards or drawing close or closer. **6.** a close approximation. **7.** the way or means of entering or leaving; access. **8.** (*often pl.*) an advance or overture to a person. **9.** a means adopted in tackling a problem, job of work, etc. **10.** Also called: **approach path.** the course fol-

lowed by an aircraft preparing for landing. [C14: from Old French *aprochier*, from Late Latin *appropiāre* to draw near, from Latin *prope* near]

approachable (əˈprəʊtʃəbᵊl) *adj.* **1.** capable of being approached; accessible. **2.** (of a person) friendly. —**apˌproachaˈbility** *or* **apˈproachableness** *n.*

approach shot *n.* **1.** *Golf.* Also called: **approach.** a shot made to or towards the green after a tee shot. **2.** *Tennis.* a deep drive, usually hit with underspin to keep the ball low, designed to enable the player to make an approach to the net.

approbate (ˈæprəˌbeɪt) *vb.* (*tr.*) **1.** *Scots Law.* to accept as valid. **2. approbate and reprobate.** *Scots Law.* to accept part of a document and reject those parts unfavourable to one's interests. **3.** *Chiefly U.S.* to sanction officially. [C15: from Latin *approbāre* to approve, from *probāre* to test]

approbation (ˌæprəˈbeɪʃən) *n.* **1.** commendation; praise. **2.** official recognition or approval. **3.** an obsolete word for **proof.** —ˈ**approˌbative** *or* ˈ**approˌbatory** *adj.*

appropriacy (əˈprəʊprɪəsɪ) *n.* the condition of delicate and precise fittingness of a word or expression to its context, even when it is chosen from a number of close synonyms.

appropriate *adj.* (əˈprəʊprɪɪt). **1.** right or suitable; fitting. **2.** *Rare.* particular; own: *they had their appropriate methods.* ~*vb.* (əˈprəʊprɪˌeɪt). (*tr.*) **3.** to take for one's own use, esp. illegally or without permission. **4.** to put aside (funds, etc.) for a particular purpose or person. [C15: from Late Latin *appropriāre* to make one's own, from Latin *proprius* one's own; see PROPER] —**apˈpropriable** *adj.* —**apˈpropriately** *adv.* —**apˈpropriateness** *n.* —**apˈpropriative** *adj.* —**apˈpropriˌator** *n.*

appropriation (əˌprəʊprɪˈeɪʃən) *n.* **1.** the act of setting apart or taking for one's own use. **2.** a sum of money set apart for a specific purpose, esp. by a legislature.

approval (əˈpruːvᵊl) *n.* **1.** the act of approving. **2.** formal agreement; sanction. **3.** a favourable opinion; commendation. **4. on approval.** (of articles for sale) for examination with an option to buy or return.

approve[1] (əˈpruːv) *vb.* **1.** (when *intr.*, often foll. by *of*) to consider fair, good, or right; commend (a person or thing). **2.** (*tr.*) to authorize or sanction. **3.** (*tr.*) *Obsolete.* to demonstrate or prove by trial. [C14: from Old French *aprover*, from Latin *approbāre* to approve, from *probāre* to test, PROVE]

approve[2] (əˈpruːv) *vb.* (*tr.*) *Law.* to improve or increase the value of (waste or common land), as by enclosure. [C15: from Old French *approuer* to turn to advantage, from *prou* advantage]

approved school *n.* (in Britain) a former name for **community home.**

approved social worker *n.* *Social welfare.* (in England) a qualified social worker specially trained in mental-health work, who is approved by his employing local authority to apply for a mentally disordered person to be admitted to hospital and detained there, or to apply for the person to be received into the guardianship of the local authority.

approx. *abbrev. for* approximate(ly).

approximal (əˈprɒksɪməl) *adj.* *Anatomy.* situated side by side; close together: *approximal teeth or fillings.*

approximate *adj.* (əˈprɒksɪmɪt). **1.** almost accurate or exact. **2.** inexact; rough; loose: *only an approximate fit.* **3.** much alike; almost the same. **4.** near; close together. ~*vb.* (əˈprɒksɪˌmeɪt). **5.** (usually foll. by *to*) to come or bring near or close; be almost the same (as). **6.** *Maths.* to find an expression for (some quantity) accurate to a specified degree. See **accurate** (sense 4). [C15: from Late Latin *approximāre*, from Latin *proximus* nearest, from *prope* near] —**apˈproximately** *adv.* —**apˈproximative** *adj.*

approximation (əˌprɒksɪˈmeɪʃən) *n.* **1.** the process or result of making a rough calculation, estimate, or guess: *he based his conclusion on his own approximation of the fuel consumption.* **2.** an imprecise or unreliable record or version: *an approximation of what really happened.* **3.** *Maths.* an inexact number, relationship, or theory that is sufficiently accurate for a specific purpose. **4.** *Maths.* **a.** an estimate of the value of some quantity to a desired degree of accuracy. **b.** an expression in simpler terms than a given expression which approximates to it.

APPU *abbrev. for* Australian Primary Producers' Union.

appulse (əˈpʌls) *n.* a very close approach of two celestial bodies so that they are in conjunction but no eclipse or occultation occurs. [C17: from Latin *appulsus* brought near, from *appellere* to drive towards, from *pellere* to drive] —**apˈpulsive** *adj.* —**apˈpulsively** *adv.*

appurtenance (əˈpɜːtɪnəns) *n.* **1.** a secondary or less significant thing or part. **2.** (*pl.*) accessories or equipment. **3.** *Property law.* a minor right, interest, or privilege which passes when the title to the principal property is transferred. [C14: from Anglo-French *apurtenance*, from Old French *apartenance*, from *apartenir* to APPERTAIN]

appurtenant (əˈpɜːtɪnənt) *adj.* **1.** relating, belonging, or accessory. ~*n.* **2.** another word for **appurtenance.**

APR *abbrev. for:* **1.** annualized (or annual) percentage rate. See **annualize.** **2.** Annual Purchase Rate (in connection with hire-purchase schemes).

Apr. *abbrev. for* April.

apraxia (əˈpræksɪə) *n.* a disorder of the central nervous system caused by brain damage and characterized by impaired ability to carry out purposeful muscular movements. [C19: via New Latin from Greek: inactivity, from A-[1] + *praxis* action] —**aˈpraxic** *or* **aˈpractic** *adj.*

après-ski (ˌæpreɪˈskiː) *n.* **a.** social activity following a day's skiing. **b.** (*as modifier*): *an après-ski outfit.* [French, literally: after ski]

apricot (ˈeɪprɪˌkɒt) *n.* **1.** a rosaceous tree, *Prunus armeniaca*, native to Africa and W Asia, but widely cultivated for its edible fruit. **2.** the downy yellow juicy edible fruit of this tree, which resembles a small peach. [C16: earlier *apricock*, from Portuguese (*albricoque*) or Spanish, from Arabic *al-birqūq* the apricot, from Late Greek *praikokion*, from Latin *praecox* early-ripening; see PRECOCIOUS]

April (ˈeɪprəl) *n.* the fourth month of the year, consisting of 30 days. [C14: from Latin *Aprīlis*, probably of Etruscan origin]

April fool *n.* an unsuspecting victim of a practical joke or trick traditionally performed on the first of April (**April Fools' Day** *or* **All Fools' Day**).

a priori (eɪ praɪˈɔːraɪ, ɑː prɪˈɔːrɪ) *adj.* **1.** *Logic.* relating to or involving deductive reasoning from a general principle to the expected facts or effects. **2.** *Logic.* known to be true independently of or in advance of experience of the subject matter; requiring no evidence for its validation or support. **3.** *Statistics.* See **prior probability, mathematical probability.** ~Compare **a posteriori, analytic** (sense 4). [C18: from Latin, literally: from the previous (that is, from cause to effect)] —**apriority** (ˌeɪpraɪˈɒrɪtɪ) *n.*

apriorism (eɪˈpraɪəˌrɪzəm) *n.* the philosophical doctrine that there may be genuine knowledge independent of experience. Compare **rationalism** (sense 2), **sensationalism** (sense 3).

apron (ˈeɪprən) *n.* **1.** a protective or sometimes decorative or ceremonial garment worn over the front of the body and tied around the waist. **2.** the part of a stage extending in front of the curtain line; forestage. **3.** a hard-surfaced area in front of or around an aircraft hangar, terminal building, etc., upon which aircraft can stand. **4.** a continuous conveyor belt composed of metal slats linked together. **5.** a protective plate screening the operator of a machine, artillery piece, etc. **6.** a ground covering of concrete or other material used to protect the underlying earth from water erosion. **7.** a panel or board between a window and a skirting in a room. **8.** *Geology.* a sheet of sand, gravel, etc., deposited at the front of a moraine. **9.** *Golf.* the part of the fairway leading onto the green. **10.** *Machinery.* the housing for the lead screw gears of a lathe. **11.** another name for **skirt** (sense 3). **12. tied to someone's apron strings.** dependent on or dominated by someone, esp. a mother or wife. ~*vb.* **13.** (*tr.*) to protect or provide with an apron. [C16: mistaken division (as if *an apron*) of earlier *a napron*, from Old French *naperon* a little cloth, from *nape* cloth, from Latin *mappa* napkin]

apron stage *n.* a stage that projects into the auditorium so that the audience sit on three sides of it.

apropos (ˌæprəˈpəʊ) *adj.* **1.** appropriate; pertinent. ~*adv.* **2.** appropriately or pertinently. **3.** by the way; incidentally. **4. apropos of.** (*prep.*) with regard to; in respect of. [C17: from French *à propos* to the purpose]

aprotic (eɪˈprəʊtɪk) *adj.* *Chem.* (of solvents) neither accepting nor donating hydrogen ions.

apse (æps) *n.* **1.** Also called: **apsis.** a domed or vaulted semicircular or polygonal recess, esp. at the east end of a church. **2.** *Astronomy.* another name for **apsis** (sense 1). [C19: from Latin *apsis*, from Greek: a fitting together, arch, from *haptein* to fasten] —**apsidal** (æpˈsaɪdᵊl, ˈæpsɪdᵊl) *adj.*

apsis (ˈæpsɪs) *n., pl.* **apsides** (æpˈsaɪdiːz, ˈæpsɪˌdiːz). **1.** Also called: **apse.** either of two points lying at the extremities of an eccentric orbit of a planet, satellite, etc., such as the aphelion and perihelion of a planet or the apogee and perigee of the moon. The **line of apsides** connects two such points and is the principal axis of the orbit. **2.** another name for **apse** (sense 1). [C17: via Latin from Greek; see APSE] —**apsidal** (æpˈsaɪdᵊl, ˈæpsɪdᵊl) *adj.*

apt (æpt) *adj.* **1.** suitable for the circumstance or purpose; appropriate. **2.** (*postpositive*; foll. by an infinitive) having a tendency (to behave as specified). **3.** having the ability to learn and understand easily; clever (esp. in the phrase **an apt pupil**). [C14: from Latin *aptus* fitting, suitable, from *apere* to fasten] —ˈ**aptly** *adv.* —ˈ**aptness** *n.*

APT *abbrev. for* Advanced Passenger Train.

apt. *pl.* **apts.** *abbrev. for* apartment.

apteral (ˈæptərəl) *adj.* **1.** (esp. of a classical temple) not having columns at the sides. **2.** (of a church) having no aisles. [C19: from Greek *apteros* wingless; see APTEROUS]

apterous (ˈæptərəs) *adj.* **1.** (of insects) without wings, as silverfish and springtails. **2.** without winglike expansions, as some plant stems, seeds, and fruits. [C18: from Greek *apteros* wingless, from A-[1] + *pteron* wing] —ˈ**apterˌism** *n.*

apterygial (ˌæptəˈrɪdʒɪəl) *adj.* (of eels, certain insects, etc.) lacking such paired limbs as wings or fins. [C20: from New Latin *apteryx* wingless creature; see APTEROUS]

apteryx (ˈæptərɪks) *n.* another name for **kiwi** (the bird). [C19: from New Latin: wingless creature; see APTEROUS]

aptitude (ˈæptɪˌtjuːd) *n.* **1.** inherent or acquired ability. **2.** ease in learning or understanding; intelligence. **3.** the condition or quality of being apt. [C15: via Old French from Late Latin *aptitūdō*, from Latin *aptus* APT]

aptitude test *n.* a test designed to assess a person's ability to do a particular type of work.

APU (in Britain) *abbrev. for* Assessment of Performance Unit: a research unit founded by the Department of Education and Science in 1975 to monitor pupil performance and report upon findings in subject areas such as mathematics, English Language, and modern languages.

Apus ('eɪpəs) *n., Latin genitive* **Apodis** ('æpədɪs). a constellation in the S hemisphere situated near Musca and Octans. [New Latin, from Greek *apous,* literally: footless, from A-[1] + *pous* foot]

apyrexia (ˌæpaɪ'rɛksɪə) *n.* absence of fever. [C19: from A-[1] + Greek *puretos* fever] —ˌ**apy'retic** *adj.*

AQ *abbrev. for* achievement quotient.

aq. *or* **Aq.** *abbrev. for:* **1.** aqua. [Latin: water] **2.** aqueous.

aqua ('ækwə) *n., pl.* **aquae** ('ækwiː) *or* **aquas. 1.** water: used in compound names of certain liquid substances (as in **aqua regia**) or solutions of substances in water (as in **aqua ammoniae),** esp. in the names of pharmacological solutions. ~*adj.* **2.** short for **aquamarine** (sense 2). [Latin: water]

aquaculture ('ækwəˌkʌltʃə) *or* **aquiculture** *n.* the cultivation of freshwater and marine resources, both plant and animal, for human consumption or use.

aquaerobics (ˌækwə'rəʊbɪks) *n. (functioning as sing.)* the practice of exercising to music in a swimming pool. [C20: from Latin *aqua* water + AEROBICS]

aqua fortis ('fɔːtɪs) *n.* an obsolete name for **nitric acid.** [C17: from Latin, literally: strong water]

aqualung ('ækwəˌlʌŋ) *n.* breathing apparatus used by divers, etc., consisting of a mouthpiece attached to air cylinders strapped to the back.

aquamarine (ˌækwəmə'riːn) *n.* **1.** a pale greenish-blue transparent variety of beryl used as a gemstone. **2. a.** a pale blue to greenish-blue colour. **b.** *(as adj.): an aquamarine dress.* [C19: from New Latin *aqua marīna,* from Latin: sea water (referring to the gem's colour)]

aquanaut ('ækwənɔːt) *n.* **1.** a person who lives and works underwater. **2.** a person who swims or dives underwater. [C20: from AQUA + *-naut,* as in ASTRONAUT]

aquaphobia (ˌækwə'fəʊbɪə) *n.* an abnormal fear of water, esp. because of the possibility of drowning. Compare **hydrophobia** (sense 2).

aquaplane ('ækwəˌpleɪn) *n.* **1.** a single board on which a person stands and is towed by a motorboat at high speed, as in water skiing. ~*vb. (intr.)* **2.** to ride on an aquaplane. **3.** (of a motor vehicle travelling at high speeds in wet road conditions) to rise up onto a thin film of water between the tyres and road surface so that actual contact with the road is lost.

aqua regia ('riːdʒɪə) *n.* a yellow fuming corrosive mixture of one part nitric acid and three to four parts hydrochloric acid, used in metallurgy for dissolving metals, including gold. Also called: **nitrohydrochloric acid.** [C17: from New Latin: royal water; referring to its use in dissolving gold, the royal metal]

aquarelle (ˌækwə'rɛl) *n.* **1.** a method of watercolour painting in transparent washes. **2.** a painting done in this way. [C19: from French] —ˌ**aqua'rellist** *n.*

aquarist ('ækwərɪst) *n.* **1.** the curator of an aquarium. **2.** a person who studies aquatic life.

aquarium (ə'kwɛərɪəm) *n., pl.* **-riums** *or* **-ria** (-rɪə). **1.** a tank, bowl, or pool in which aquatic animals and plants are kept for pleasure, study, or exhibition. **2.** a building housing a collection of aquatic life, as for exhibition. [C19: from Latin *aquārius* relating to water, on the model of VIVARIUM]

Aquarius (ə'kwɛərɪəs) *n., Latin genitive* **Aquarii** (ə'kwɛərɪˌaɪ). **1.** *Astronomy.* a zodiacal constellation in the S hemisphere lying between Pisces and Capricorn on the ecliptic. **2.** *Astrology.* **a.** Also called: the **Water Carrier.** the eleventh sign of the zodiac, symbol ♒, having a fixed air classification and ruled by the planets Saturn and Uranus. The sun is in this sign between about Jan. 20 and Feb. 18. **b.** a person born during a period when the sun is in this sign. ~*adj.* **3.** *Astrology.* born under or characteristic of Aquarius. ~Also (for senses 2b, 3): **Aquarian** (ə'kwɛərɪən). [Latin]

aquashow ('ækwəˌʃəʊ) *or U.S.* **aquacade** ('ækwəˌkeɪd) *n.* an exhibition of swimming and diving, often accompanied by music.

aquatic (ə'kwætɪk, ə'kwɒt-) *adj.* **1.** growing, living, or found in water. **2.** *Sport.* performed in or on water. ~*n.* **3.** a marine animal or plant. [C15: from Latin *aquāticus,* from *aqua* water]

aquatics (ə'kwætɪks, ə'kwɒt-) *pl. n.* sports or pastimes performed in or on the water.

aquatint ('ækwəˌtɪnt) *n.* **1.** a technique of etching copper with acid to produce an effect resembling the flat tones of wash or watercolour. The tone or tint is obtained by acid (aqua) biting through the pores of a ground that only partially protects the copper. **2.** an etching made in this way. ~*vb.* **3.** *(tr.)* to etch (a block, etc.) in aquatint. [C18: from Italian *acqua tinta:* dyed water]

aquavit ('ækwəˌvɪt) *n.* a grain- or potato-based spirit from the Scandinavian countries, flavoured with aromatic seeds and spices, esp. caraway. Also called: **akvavit.** [from Scandinavian; see AQUA VITAE]

aqua vitae ('viːtaɪ, 'vaɪtiː) *n.* an archaic name for **brandy.** [Medieval Latin: water of life]

aqueduct ('ækwɪˌdʌkt) *n.* **1.** a conduit used to convey water over a long distance. **2.** a structure, often a bridge, that carries such a conduit or a canal across a valley or river. **3.** a channel in an organ or part of the body, esp. one that conveys a natural body fluid. [C16: from Latin *aquaeductus,* from *aqua* water + *dūcere* to convey]

aqueous ('eɪkwɪəs, 'ækwɪ-) *adj.* **1.** of, like, or containing water. **2.** dissolved in water: *aqueous ammonia.* **3.** (of rocks, deposits, etc.) formed from material laid down in water. [C17: from Medieval Latin *aqueus,* from Latin *aqua* water]

aqueous humour *n. Physiol.* the watery fluid within the eyeball between the cornea and the lens.

aquiculture ('eɪkwɪˌkʌltʃə, 'ækwɪ-) *n.* **1.** another name for **hydroponics. 2.** a variant of **aquaculture.** —'**aquiˌcultural** *adj.* —'**aquiˌculturist** *n.*

aquifer ('ækwɪfə) *n.* a deposit of rock, such as a sandstone, containing water that can be used to supply wells.

Aquila ('ækwɪlə, ə'kwɪlə) *n., Latin genitive* **Aquilae** ('ækwɪˌliː). a constellation lying in the Milky Way close to Cygnus and situated on the celestial equator. The brightest star is Altair. [from Latin: eagle]

aquilegia (ˌækwɪ'liːdʒɪə) *n.* another name for **columbine**[1]. [C19: from Medieval Latin, of uncertain origin]

aquiline ('ækwɪˌlaɪn) *adj.* **1.** (of a nose) having the curved or hooked shape of an eagle's beak. **2.** of or resembling an eagle. [C17: from Latin *aquilīnus,* from *aquila* eagle]

Ar *the chemical symbol for* argon.

AR *abbrev. for:* **1.** Arkansas. **2.** Autonomous Region.

ar. *abbrev. for:* **1.** arrival. **2.** arrive(s).

Ar. *abbrev. for:* **1.** Arabia(n). **2.** Also: **Ar** Arabic. **3.** Aramaic.

a.r. *abbrev. for* anno regni. [Latin: in the year of the reign]

-ar *suffix forming adjectives.* of; belonging to; like: *linear; polar; minuscular.* [via Old French *-er* from Latin *-āris,* replacing *-ālis* (-AL[1]) after stems ending in *l*]

Ara ('ɑːrə) *n., Latin genitive* **Arae** ('ɑːriː). a constellation in the S hemisphere near Scorpius. [from Latin: altar]

ARA *abbrev. for:* **1.** (in Britain) Associate of the Royal Academy. **2.** (in Britain) Aircraft Research Association. **3.** (in New Zealand) Auckland Regional Authority.

Arab ('ærəb) *n.* **1.** a member of a Semitic people originally inhabiting Arabia, who spread throughout the Middle East, N Africa, and Spain during the seventh and eighth centuries A.D. **2.** a small lively intelligent breed of horse, mainly used for riding. **3.** *(modifier)* of or relating to the Arabs: *the Arab nations.* [C14: from Latin *Arabs,* from Greek *Araps,* from Arabic *'Arab*]

Arab. *abbrev. for:* **1.** Arabia(n). **2.** Arabic.

arabesque (ˌærə'bɛsk) *n.* **1.** *Ballet.* a classical position in which the dancer has one leg raised behind and both arms stretched out in one of several conventional poses. **2.** *Music.* a piece or movement with a highly ornamented or decorated melody. **3.** *Arts.* **a.** a type of curvilinear decoration in painting, metalwork, etc., with intricate intertwining leaf, flower, animal, or geometrical designs. **b.** a design of flowing lines. ~*adj.* **4.** designating, of, or decorated in this style. [C18: from French, from Italian *arabesco* in the Arabic style]

Arabian (ə'reɪbɪən) *adj.* **1.** of or relating to Arabia or the Arabs. ~*n.* **2.** another word for **Arab.**

Arabian camel *n.* a domesticated camel, *Camelus dromedarius,* having one hump on its back and used as a beast of burden in the hot deserts of N Africa and SW Asia. See also **dromedary.** Compare **Bactrian camel.**

Arabic ('ærəbɪk) *n.* **1.** the language of the Arabs, spoken in a variety of dialects; the official language of Algeria, Egypt, Iraq, Jordan, the Lebanon, Libya, Morocco, Saudi Arabia, the Sudan, Syria, Tunisia, and Yemen. It is estimated to be the native language of some 75 million people throughout the world. It belongs to the Semitic subfamily of the Afro-Asiatic family of languages and has its own alphabet, which has been borrowed by certain other languages such as Urdu. ~*adj.* **2.** denoting or relating to this language, any of the peoples that speak it, or the countries in which it is spoken.

arabica bean (ə'ræbɪkə) *n.* a type of coffee bean obtained from the tree *Coffea arabica.*

Arabic numeral *n.* one of the numbers 0,1,2,3,4,5,6,7,8,9 (opposed to *Roman numerals*).

arabinose (ə'ræbɪˌnəʊz, -ˌnəʊs) *n.* a pentose sugar in plant gums, esp. of cedars and pines. It is used as a culture medium in bacteriology. Formula: $C_5H_{10}O_5$. [C19: from *arabin* (from (GUM) ARAB(IC) + -IN) + -OSE[2]]

arabis ('ærəbɪs) *n.* any plant of the annual or perennial genus *Arabis* that forms low-growing mats with downy grey foliage and white flowers: family *Cruciferae.* Also called: **rock cress.** [New Latin, from Greek *arabis* (fem.) of Arabia]

Arabist ('ærəbɪst) *n.* a student or expert in Arabic culture, language, history, etc.

arable ('ærəb[ə]l) *adj.* **1.** (of land) being or capable of being tilled for the production of crops. **2.** of, relating to, or using such land: *arable farming.* ~*n.* **3.** arable land or farming. [C15: from Latin *arābilis* that can be ploughed, from *arāre* to plough]

araceous (ə'reɪʃəs) *adj.* another word for **aroid** (sense 1). [C19: from New Latin *Arāceae;* see ARUM]

arachidonic acid (ˌærəkəˈdɒnɪk) *n.* a fatty acid occurring in animal cells: the metabolic precursor of several groups of biologically active substances, including prostaglandins.

arachnid (əˈræknɪd) *n.* any terrestrial chelicerate arthropod of the class *Arachnida,* characterized by simple eyes and four pairs of legs. The group includes the spiders, scorpions, ticks, mites, and harvestmen. [C19: from New Latin *Arachnida,* from Greek *arakhnē* spider] —**aˈrachnidan** *adj., n.*

arachnoid (əˈræknɔɪd) *n.* **1.** the middle of the three membranes (see **meninges**) that cover the brain and spinal cord. **2.** another name for **arachnid.** ~*adj.* **3.** of or relating to the middle of the three meninges. **4.** *Botany.* consisting of or covered with soft fine hairs or fibres. **5.** of or relating to the arachnids.

arachnology (ˌærækˈnɒlədʒɪ) *n.* the study of arachnids. —ˌ**arachˈnologist** *n.*

aragonite (əˈrægəˌnaɪt) *n.* a generally white or grey mineral, found in sedimentary rocks and as deposits from hot springs. Composition: calcium carbonate. Formula: $CaCO_3$. Crystal structure: orthorhombic. [C19: from *Aragon,* region of NE Spain, + -ITE[1]]

arak (ˈærək) *n.* a variant spelling of **arrack.**

Araldite (ˈærəlˌdaɪt) *n. Trademark.* a strong epoxy resin best known as a glue or adhesive.

aralia (əˈreɪlɪə) *n.* any plant of the genus *Aralia* of trees, shrubs, and herbaceous plants. The greenhouse and house plant generally known as aralia is *Dizygotheca elegantissima* of a related genus, grown for its decorative evergreen crinkled foliage: family *Araliaceae.* [New Latin, of uncertain origin]

araliaceous (əˌreɪlɪˈeɪʃəs) *adj.* of, relating to, or belonging to the *Araliaceae,* a chiefly tropical family of trees, shrubs, or woody climbers having small clusters of whitish or greenish flowers. The family includes the ivy and ginseng.

Aram. *abbrev. for* Aramaic.

Aramaic (ˌærəˈmeɪɪk) *n.* **1.** an ancient language of the Middle East, still spoken in parts of Syria and the Lebanon, belonging to the NW Semitic subfamily of the Afro-Asiatic family. Originally the speech of Aram (ancient Syria), in the 5th century B.C. it spread to become the lingua franca of the Persian empire. See also **Biblical Aramaic.** ~*adj.* **2.** of, relating to, or using this language.

Aran (ˈærən) *adj.* **1.** of or relating to the Aran Islands, off the W coast of Ireland. **2.** made of thick undyed wool with its natural oils retained: *an Aran sweater.*

Aranda (ˈærəndə) *n.* **1.** an Aboriginal people of S central Australia. **2.** the language of this people.

araneid (əˈreɪnɪɪd) *n.* any of numerous arachnids constituting the order *Araneae* (or *Araneida),* which comprises the spiders. [C19: from New Latin *Araneida,* from Latin *arānea* spider]

Arapaho (əˈræpəˌhəʊ) *n.* **1.** (*pl.* **-hos** *or* **-ho**) a member of a North American Indian people of the Plains, now living chiefly in Oklahoma and Wyoming. **2.** the language of this people, belonging to the Algonquian family.

arapaima (ˌærəˈpaɪmə) *n.* a very large primitive freshwater teleost fish, *Arapaima gigas,* that occurs in tropical South America and can attain a length of 4.5 m (15 ft.) and a weight of 200 kg (440 lbs): family *Osteoglossidae.* [via Portuguese from Tupi]

araroba (ˌærəˈrəʊbə) *n.* **1.** a Brazilian leguminous tree, *Andira araroba.* **2.** Also called: **Goa powder.** a bitter yellow powder obtained from cavities in the wood of this tree, used in medicine to treat skin ailments. See also **chrysarobin.** [from Portuguese, probably from Tupi, from *arara* parrot + *yba* tree]

Araucanian (ˌærɔːˈkeɪnɪən) *n.* **1.** a South American Indian language; thought to be an isolated branch of the Penutian phylum, spoken in Chile and W Argentina. **2.** a member of the people who speak this language. ~*adj.* **3.** of or relating to this people or their language.

araucaria (ˌærɔːˈkeərɪə) *n.* any tree of the coniferous genus *Araucaria* of South America, Australia, and Polynesia, such as the monkey puzzle and bunya-bunya. [C19: from New Latin (*arbor*) *Araucaria* (tree) from *Arauco,* a province in Chile]

Arawakan (ˌærəˈwækən) *n.* **1.** a family of American Indian languages found throughout NE South America. ~*adj.* **2.** of or relating to the peoples speaking these languages.

arbalest *or* **arbalist** (ˈɑːbəlɪst) *n.* a large medieval crossbow, usually cocked by mechanical means. [C11: from Old French *arbaleste,* from Late Latin *arcuballista,* from Latin *arcus* bow + BALLISTA]

arbiter (ˈɑːbɪtə) *n.* **1.** a person empowered to judge in a dispute; referee; arbitrator. **2.** a person having complete control of something. [C15: from Latin, of obscure origin] —ˈ**arbitress** *fem. n.*

arbitrage (ˈɑːbɪˌtrɑːʒ, ˈɑːbɪtrɪdʒ) *n. Finance.* **a.** the purchase of currencies, securities, or commodities in one market for immediate resale in others in order to profit from unequal prices. **b.** (*as modifier*): *arbitrage operations.* [C15: from French, from *arbitrer* to ARBITRATE] —**arbitrageur** (ˌɑːbɪtræˈʒɜː) *n.*

arbitral (ˈɑːbɪtrəl) *adj.* of or relating to arbitration.

arbitrament (ɑːˈbɪtrəmənt) *n.* **1.** the decision or award made by an arbitrator upon a disputed matter. **2.** the power or authority to pronounce such a decision. **3.** another word for **arbitration.**

arbitrary (ˈɑːbɪtrərɪ) *adj.* **1.** founded on or subject to personal whims, prejudices, etc.; capricious. **2.** having only relative application or relevance; not absolute. **3.** (of a government, ruler, etc.) despotic or dictatorial. **4.** *Maths.* not representing any specific value: *an arbitrary constant.* **5.** *Law.* (esp. of a penalty or punishment) not laid down by statute; within the court's discretion. ~*n., pl.* **-traries.** **6.** *Printing.* a less common name for **peculiar** (sense 4). [C15: from Latin *arbitrārius* arranged through arbitration, uncertain] —ˈ**arbitrarily** *adv.* —ˈ**arbitrariness** *n.*

arbitrate (ˈɑːbɪˌtreɪt) *vb.* **1.** to settle or decide (a dispute); achieve a settlement between parties. **2.** to submit to or settle by arbitration. [C16: from Latin *arbitrārī* to give judgment; see ARBITER] —ˈ**arbitrable** *adj.* —ˈ**arbiˌtrator** *n.*

arbitration (ˌɑːbɪˈtreɪʃən) *n.* **1.** *Law.* the hearing and determination of a dispute, esp. an industrial dispute, by an impartial referee selected or agreed upon by the parties concerned. **2.** *International law.* the procedure laid down for the settlement of international disputes.

arbitress (ˈɑːbɪtrɪs) *n.* a female arbitrator.

arbor[1] (ˈɑːbə) *n.* the U.S. spelling of **arbour.**

arbor[2] (ˈɑːbə) *n.* **1.** a rotating shaft in a machine or power tool on which a milling cutter or grinding wheel is fitted. **2.** a rotating shaft or mandrel on which a workpiece is fitted for machining. **3.** *Foundry.* a part, piece, or structure used to reinforce the core of a mould. [C17: from Latin: tree, mast]

arboraceous (ˌɑːbəˈreɪʃəs) *adj. Literary.* **1.** resembling a tree. **2.** wooded.

arboreal (ɑːˈbɔːrɪəl) *adj.* **1.** of, relating to, or resembling a tree. **2.** living in or among trees: *arboreal monkeys.*

arboreous (ɑːˈbɔːrɪəs) *adj.* **1.** thickly wooded; having many trees. **2.** another word for **arborescent.**

arborescent (ˌɑːbəˈresᵊnt) *adj.* having the shape or characteristics of a tree. —ˌ**arboˈrescence** *n.*

arboretum (ˌɑːbəˈriːtəm) *n., pl.* **-ta** (-tə) *or* **-tums.** a place where trees or shrubs are cultivated for their scientific or educational interest. [C19: from Latin, from *arbor* tree]

arboriculture (ˈɑːbərɪˌkʌltʃə) *n.* the cultivation of trees or shrubs, esp. for the production of timber. —ˌ**arboriˈcultural** *adj.* —ˌ**arboriˈculturist** *n.*

arborist (ˈɑːbərɪst) *n.* a specialist in the cultivation of trees.

arborization *or* **arborisation** (ˌɑːbəraɪˈzeɪʃən) *n.* a branching treelike appearance in certain fossils and minerals.

arbor vitae (ˈɑːbɔː ˈviːtaɪ, ˈvaɪtiː) *n.* any of several Asian and North American evergreen coniferous trees of the genera *Thuja* and *Thujopsis,* esp. *Thuja occidentalis,* having tiny scalelike leaves and egglike cones. See also **red cedar.** [C17: from New Latin, literally: tree of life]

arbour (ˈɑːbə) *n.* **1.** a leafy glade or bower shaded by trees, vines, shrubs, etc., esp. when trained about a trellis. **2.** *Obsolete.* an orchard, garden, or lawn. [C14 *erber,* from Old French *herbier,* from Latin *herba* grass]

arbutus (ɑːˈbjuːtəs) *n., pl.* **-tuses.** **1.** any of several temperate ericaceous shrubs of the genus *Arbutus,* esp. the strawberry tree of S Europe. They have clusters of white or pinkish flowers, broad evergreen leaves, and strawberry-like berries. **2.** See **trailing arbutus.** [C16: from Latin; related to *arbor* tree]

arc (ɑːk) *n.* **1.** something curved in shape. **2.** part of an unbroken curved line. **3.** a luminous discharge that occurs when an electric current flows between two electrodes or any other two surfaces separated by a small gap and a high potential difference. **4.** *Astronomy.* a circular section of the apparent path of a celestial body. **5.** *Maths.* a section of a curve, graph, or geometric figure. ~*vb.* **arcs, arcing, arced** *or* **arcs, arcking, arcked.** **6.** (*intr.*) to form an arc. ~*prefix.* **7.** *Maths.* specifying an inverse trigonometric function: usually written **arcsin, arctanh, arcsec,** etc., or sometimes $\sin^{-1}$, $\tanh^{-1}$, $\sec^{-1}$, etc. [C14: from Old French, from Latin *arcus* bow, arch]

ARC *abbrev. for* AIDS-related complex: an early condition in which a person infected with the AIDS virus may suffer from such mild symptoms as loss of weight, fever, etc.

arcade (ɑːˈkeɪd) *n.* **1.** a set of arches and their supporting columns. **2.** a covered and sometimes arched passageway, usually with shops on one or both sides. **3.** a building, or part of a building, with an arched roof. [C18: from French, from Italian *arcata,* from *arco,* from Latin *arcus* bow, arch]

Arcadia (ɑːˈkeɪdɪə) *or* **Arcady** (ˈɑːkədɪ) *n.* the traditional idealized rural setting of Greek and Roman bucolic poetry and later in the literature of the Renaissance. [C16: from *Arcadia,* rural district of Ancient Greece]

Arcadian (ɑːˈkeɪdɪən) *adj.* **1.** of or relating to the idealized Arcadia of pastoral poetry. **2.** rustic or bucolic: *a life of Arcadian simplicity.* ~*n.* **3.** an inhabitant of Arcadia. **4.** a person who leads or prefers a quiet simple rural life. —**Arˈcadianism** *n.*

Arcadic (ɑːˈkeɪdɪk) *adj.* **1.** of or relating to the Arcadians or to their dialect of Ancient Greek. ~*n.* **2.** one of four chief dialects of Ancient Greek; the dialect spoken by the Arcadians. See also **Attic** (sense 3). ~Compare **Aeolic, Doric, Ionic.**

arcana (ɑːˈkeɪnə, -ˈkɑː-) *n.* either of the two divisions (the **minor arcana** and the **major arcana**) of a pack of tarot cards.

arcane (ɑːˈkeɪn) *adj.* requiring secret knowledge to be understood; mysterious; esoteric. [C16: from Latin *arcānus* secret, hidden, from *arcēre* to shut up, keep safe] —**arˈcanely** *adv.* —**arˈcaneness** *n.*

arcanum (ɑːˈkeɪnəm) *n., pl.* **-na** (-nə). **1.** (*sometimes pl.*) a profound secret or mystery known only to initiates. **2.** a secret of nature sought by alchemists. [C16: from Latin; see ARCANE]
arcature (ˈɑːkətʃə) *n.* **1.** a small-scale arcade. **2.** a set of blind arches attached to the wall of a building as decoration.
arc-boutant *French.* (arkbutɑ̃) *n., pl.* ***arcs-boutants*** (arkbutɑ̃). another name for **flying buttress.**
arc furnace *n.* a furnace in which the charge is heated by an electric arc.
arch[1] (ɑːtʃ) *n.* **1.** a curved structure, normally in the vertical plane, that spans an opening. **2.** Also called: **archway.** a structure in the form of an arch that serves as a gateway. **3.** something curved like an arch. **4. a.** any of various parts or structures of the body having a curved or archlike outline, such as the transverse portion of the aorta (**arch of the aorta**) or the raised bony vault formed by the tarsal and metatarsal bones (**arch of the foot**). **b.** one of the basic patterns of the human fingerprint, formed by several curved ridges one above the other. Compare **loop**[1] (sense 10), **whorl** (sense 3). *~vb.* **5.** (*tr.*) to span (an opening) with an arch. **6.** to form or cause to form an arch or a curve resembling that of an arch: *the cat arched its back.* **7.** (*tr.*) to span or extend over: *the bridge arched the flooded stream.* [C14: from Old French *arche,* from Vulgar Latin *arca* (unattested), from Latin *arcus* bow, ARC]
arch[2] (ɑːtʃ) *adj.* **1.** (*prenominal*) chief; principal; leading: *his arch rival.* **2.** (*prenominal*) very experienced; expert: *an arch criminal.* **3.** knowing or superior. **4.** playfully or affectedly roguish or mischievous. [C16: independent use of ARCH-] —ˈ**archly** *adv.* —ˈ**archness** *n.*
arch. *abbrev. for:* **1.** archaic. **2.** archaism. **3.** archery. **4.** archipelago. **5.** architect. **6.** architectural. **7.** architecture.
Arch. *abbrev. for* Archbishop.
arch- *or* **archi-** *combining form.* **1.** chief; principal; of highest rank: *archangel; archbishop; archduke.* **2.** eminent above all others of the same kind; extreme: *archenemy; archfiend; archfool.* [ultimately from Greek *arkhi-,* from *arkhein* to rule]
-arch *n. combining form.* leader; ruler; chief: *patriarch; monarch; heresiarch.* [from Greek *-arkhēs,* from *arkhein* to rule; compare ARCH-]
Archaean *or esp. U.S.* **Archean** (ɑːˈkiːən) *adj.* of or relating to the highly metamorphosed rocks formed in the early Precambrian era.
archaeo- *or* **archeo-** *combining form.* **1.** indicating ancient or primitive time or condition: *archaeology; archaeopteryx.* **2.** of, involving, or denoting the study of remains from archaeological sites: *archaeozoology.* [from Greek *arkhaio-,* from *arkhaios,* from *arkhein* to begin]
archaeoastronomy *or* **archeoastronomy** (ˌɑːkɪəʊəˈstrɒnəmɪ) *n.* the scientific study of the beliefs and practices concerning astronomy that existed in ancient and prehistoric civilizations. —ˌ**archaeoasˈtronomer** *or* ˌ**archeoasˈtronomer** *n.*
archaeobotany *or* **archeobotany** (ˌɑːkɪəʊˈbɒtənɪ) *n.* the analysis and interpretation of plant remains found at archaeological sites. —ˌ**archaeoˈbotanist** *or* ˌ**archeoˈbotanist** *n.*
archaeol. *abbrev. for* archaeology.
archaeology *or* **archeology** (ˌɑːkɪˈɒlədʒɪ) *n.* the study of man's past by scientific analysis of the material remains of his cultures. See also **prehistory, protohistory.** [C17: from Late Latin *archaeologia,* from Greek *arkhaiologia* study of what is ancient, from *arkhaios* ancient (from *arkhē* beginning)] —ˌ**archaeological** *or* **archeological** (ˌɑːkɪəˈlɒdʒɪkᵊl) *adj.* —ˌ**archaeoˈlogically** *or* ˌ**archeoˈlogically** *adv.* —ˌ**archaeˈologist** *or* ˌ**archeˈologist** *n.*
archaeomagnetism *or* **archeomagnetism** (ˌɑːkɪəʊˈmægnɪˌtɪzəm) *n.* an archaeological technique for dating certain clay objects by measuring the extent to which they have been magnetized by the earth's magnetic field.
archaeopteryx (ˌɑːkɪˈɒptərɪks) *n.* any of several extinct primitive birds constituting the genus *Archaeopteryx,* esp. *A. lithographica,* which occurred in Jurassic times and had teeth, a long tail, well-developed wings, and a body covering of feathers. [C19: from ARCHAEO- + Greek *pterux* winged creature]
archaeornis (ˌɑːkɪˈɔːnɪs) *n.* an extinct primitive Jurassic bird, formerly placed in the genus *Archaeornis* but now thought to be a species of archaeopteryx. [C19: New Latin, from ARCHAEO- + Greek *ornis* bird]
Archaeozoic *or esp. U.S.* **Archeozoic** (ˌɑːkɪəˈzəʊɪk) *adj.* **1.** of or formed in the early Precambrian era. *~n.* **2.** the earlier of two divisions of the Precambrian era, during which the earliest forms of life are assumed to have appeared. Compare **Proterozoic.**
archaeozoology *or* **archeozoology** (ˌɑːkɪəʊzəʊˈɒlədʒɪ, -zuː-) *n.* the analysis and interpretation of animal remains found at archaeological sites. —ˌ**archaeozoˈologist** *or* ˌ**archeozoˈologist** *n.*
archaic (ɑːˈkeɪɪk) *adj.* **1.** belonging to or characteristic of a much earlier period; ancient. **2.** out of date; antiquated: *an archaic prison system.* **3.** (of idiom, vocabulary, etc.) characteristic of an earlier period of a language and not in ordinary use. [C19: from French *archaïque,* from Greek *arkhaïkos,* from *arkhaios* ancient, from *arkhē* beginning, from *arkhein* to begin] —**arˈchaically** *adv.*
archaism (ˈɑːkɪˌɪzəm, -keɪ-) *n.* **1.** the adoption or imitation of something archaic, such as a word or an artistic or literary style. **2.** an archaic word, expression, style, etc. [C17: from New Latin *archaismus,* from Greek *arkhaïsmos,* from *arkhaizein* to model one's style upon that of ancient writers; see ARCHAIC] —ˈ**archaist** *n.* —ˌ**archaˈistic** *adj.*
archaize *or* **archaise** (ˈɑːkɪˌaɪz, -keɪ-) *vb.* (*tr.*) to give an archaic appearance or character to, as by the use of archaisms. —ˈ**archaˌizer** *or* ˈ**archaˌiser** *n.*
archangel (ˈɑːkˌeɪndʒəl) *n.* **1.** a principal angel, a member of the order ranking immediately above the angels in medieval angelology. **2.** another name for **angelica** (sense 1). **3. yellow archangel.** a Eurasian herbaceous plant, *Galeobdolon luteum* (or *Lamium galeobdolon*), that occurs in woodlands and has yellow helmet-shaped flowers: family *Labiatae* (labiates). **4.** a bronze-coloured breed of domestic pigeon with black markings. —**archangelic** (ˌɑːkænˈdʒɛlɪk) *adj.*
archbishop (ˈɑːtʃˈbɪʃəp) *n.* a bishop of the highest rank. Abbrevs.: **abp, Abp, Arch., Archbp.**
archbishopric (ˈɑːtʃˈbɪʃəprɪk) *n.* **1.** the rank, office, or jurisdiction of an archbishop. **2.** the area governed by an archbishop.
Archbp *abbrev. for* archbishop.
Archd. *abbrev. for:* **1.** archdeacon. **2.** archduke.
archdeacon (ˈɑːtʃˈdiːkən) *n.* **1.** an Anglican clergyman ranking just below a bishop and having supervisory duties under the bishop. **2.** a clergyman of similar rank in other Churches.
archdeaconry (ˈɑːtʃˈdiːkənrɪ) *n., pl.* **-ries.** **1.** the office, rank, or duties of an archdeacon. **2.** the residence of an archdeacon.
archdiocese (ˌɑːtʃˈdaɪəˌsiːs, -sɪs) *n.* the diocese of an archbishop. —**archdiocesan** (ˌɑːtʃdaɪˈɒsɪsᵊn) *adj.*
archducal (ˈɑːtʃˈdjuːkᵊl) *adj.* of or relating to an archduke, archduchess, or archduchy.
archduchess (ˈɑːtʃˈdʌtʃɪs) *n.* **1.** the wife or widow of an archduke. **2.** (since 1453) a princess of the Austrian imperial family, esp. a daughter of the Austrian emperor.
archduchy (ˈɑːtʃˈdʌtʃɪ) *n., pl.* **-duchies.** the territory ruled by an archduke or archduchess.
archduke (ˈɑːtʃˈdjuːk) *n.* a chief duke, esp. (since 1453) a prince of the Austrian imperial dynasty.
Archean (ɑːˈkiːən) *adj.* a variant spelling (esp. U.S.) of **Archaean.**
arched (ɑːtʃt) *adj.* **1.** provided with or spanned by an arch or arches. **2.** shaped like an arch; curved.
archegonium (ˌɑːkɪˈgəʊnɪəm) *n., pl.* **-nia** (-nɪə). a female sex organ, occurring in mosses, ferns, and evergreen trees, that produces a single egg cell in its swollen base. [C19: from New Latin, from Greek *arkhegonos* original parent, from *arkhe-* chief, first + *gonos* seed, race] —ˌ**archeˈgoniate** *adj.*
archenemy (ˈɑːtʃˈɛnɪmɪ) *n., pl.* **-mies.** **1.** a chief enemy. **2.** (*often cap.; preceded by the*) the devil.
archenteron (ɑːˈkɛntəˌrɒn) *n.* the cavity within an embryo at the gastrula stage of development that eventually becomes the digestive cavity. [C19: from Greek *arkhē* beginning + *enteron* intestine] —**archenteric** (ˌɑːkənˈtɛrɪk) *adj.*
archeology (ˌɑːkɪˈɒlədʒɪ) *n.* a variant spelling of **archaeology.**
Archeozoic (ˌɑːkɪəˈzəʊɪk) *adj.* a variant spelling (esp. U.S.) of **Archaeozoic.**
archer (ˈɑːtʃə) *n.* a person skilled in the use of a bow and arrow. [C13: from Old French *archier,* from Late Latin *arcārius,* from Latin *arcus* bow]
Archer (ˈɑːtʃə) *n.* **the.** the constellation Sagittarius, the ninth sign of the zodiac.
archerfish (ˈɑːtʃəˌfɪʃ) *n., pl.* **-fish** *or* **-fishes.** any freshwater percoid fish of the family *Toxotidae* of S and SE Asia and Australia, esp. *Toxotes jaculatrix,* that catch insects by spitting water at them.
archery (ˈɑːtʃərɪ) *n.* **1.** the art or sport of shooting with bows and arrows. **2.** archers or their weapons collectively.
Arches (ˈɑːtʃɪz) *pl. n.* **Court of.** *Church of England.* the court of appeal of the Province of Canterbury, formerly held under the arches of Bow Church.
archespore (ˈɑːkɪˌspɔː) *or* **archesporium** (ˌɑːkɪˈspɔːrɪəm) *n., pl.* **-spores** *or* **-sporia** (-ˈspɔːrɪə). *Botany.* the cell or group of cells in a sporangium that gives rise to spores. —ˌ**archeˈsporial** *adj.*
archetype (ˈɑːkɪˌtaɪp) *n.* **1.** a perfect or typical specimen. **2.** an original model or pattern; prototype. **3.** *Psychoanal.* one of the inherited mental images postulated by Jung as the content of the collective unconscious. **4.** a constantly recurring symbol or motif in literature, painting, etc. [C17: from Latin *archetypum* an original, from Greek *arkhetupon,* from *arkhetupos* first-moulded; see ARCH-, TYPE] —ˌ**archeˈtypal** *or* **archetypical** (ˌɑːkɪˈtɪpɪkᵊl) *adj.* —ˌ**archeˈtypally** *or* ˌ**archeˈtypically** *adv.*
archfiend (ˌɑːtʃˈfiːnd) *n.* (*often cap.*) **the.** the chief of fiends or devils; Satan.
archi- *combining form.* a variant of **arch-.**
Archibald prize (ˈɑːtʃɪbɔːld) *n. Austral.* an annual prize awarded by the Trustees of the Art Gallery of New South Wales since 1921, for outstanding contributions to art, letters, science, and politics. [named after Jules François *Archibald* (1856–1919), Australian journalist]
archicarp (ˈɑːkɪˌkɑːp) *n.* a female reproductive structure in ascomycetous fungi that consists of a cell or hypha and develops into the ascogonium.

archidiaconal (ˌɑːkɪdaɪˈækənᵊl) *adj.* of or relating to an archdeacon or his office.
archidiaconate (ˌɑːkɪdaɪˈækənɪt) *n.* the office, term of office, or area of jurisdiction of an archdeacon.
archiepiscopal (ˌɑːkɪɪˈpɪskəpᵊl) *adj.* of or associated with an archbishop.
archiepiscopate (ˌɑːkɪɪˈpɪskəpɪt, -ˌpeɪt) *or* **archiepiscopacy** (ˌɑːkɪɪˈpɪskəpəsɪ) *n.* the rank, office, or term of office of an archbishop.
archil (ˈɑːtʃɪl) *n.* a variant spelling of **orchil.**
Archilochian (ˌɑːkɪˈləʊkɪən) *adj.* denoting or relating to Archilochus, 7th century B.C. Greek poet, or his verse, esp. the iambic trimeters or trochaic tetrameters used by him.
archimage (ˈɑːkɪˌmeɪdʒ) *n.* a great magician or wizard. [C16: from ARCHI- + *mage,* from Latin *magus* magician]
archimandrite (ˌɑːkɪˈmændraɪt) *n. Greek Orthodox Church.* the head of a monastery or a group of monasteries. [C16: from Late Latin *archimandrīta,* from Late Greek *arkhimandritēs,* from ARCHI- + *mandra* monastery]
Archimedes' principle (ˌɑːkɪmˈiːdiːz) *n.* a law of physics stating that the apparent loss in weight of a body immersed in a fluid is equal to the weight of the displaced fluid. [named after *Archimedes* (?287–212 B.C.), Greek mathematician and physicist]
Archimedes' screw *or* **Archimedean screw** (ˌɑːkɪˈmiːdɪən, -mɪˈdiːən) *n.* an ancient type of water-lifting device making use of a spiral passage in an inclined cylinder. The water is raised when the spiral is rotated.
archine (ɑːˈʃiːn) *n.* a Russian unit of length equal to about 71 cm. [from Russian *arshin,* of Turkic origin]
archipelago (ˌɑːkɪˈpɛlɪˌgəʊ) *n., pl.* **-gos** *or* **-goes. 1.** a group of islands. **2.** a sea studded with islands. [C16 (meaning: the Aegean Sea): from Italian *arcipelago,* literally: the chief sea (perhaps originally a mistranslation of Greek *Aigaion pelagos* the Aegean Sea), from ARCHI- + *pelago* sea, from Latin *pelagus,* from Greek *pelagos*] —**archipelagic** (ˌɑːkɪpəˈlædʒɪk) *or* **archipelagian** (ˌɑːkɪpəˈleɪdʒɪən) *adj.*
archiphoneme (ˈɑːkɪˌfəʊniːm, ˌɑːkɪˈfəʊniːm) *n. Phonetics* an abstract linguistic unit representing two or more phonemes when the distinction between these has been neutralized: conventionally shown by a capital letter within slashes, as /T/ for /t/ and /d/ in German *Rat* and *Rad.*
archiplasm (ˈɑːkɪˌplæzəm) *n.* a variant spelling of **archoplasm.** —ˌ**archiˈplasmic** *adj.*
archit. *abbrev. for* architecture.
architect (ˈɑːkɪˌtɛkt) *n.* **1.** a person qualified to design buildings and to superintend their erection. **2.** a person similarly qualified in another form of construction: *a naval architect.* **3.** any planner or creator: *the architect of the expedition.* [C16: from French *architecte,* from Latin *architectus,* from Greek *arkhitektōn* director of works, from ARCHI- + *tektōn* workman; related to *tekhnē* art, skill]
architectonic (ˌɑːkɪtɛkˈtɒnɪk) *adj.* **1.** denoting, relating to, or having architectural qualities. **2.** *Metaphysics.* of or relating to the systematic classification of knowledge. [C16: from Late Latin *architectonicus* concerning architecture; see ARCHITECT] —ˌ**architecˈtonically** *adv.*
architectonics (ˌɑːkɪtɛkˈtɒnɪks) *n. (functioning as sing.)* **1.** the science of architecture. **2.** *Metaphysics.* the scientific classification of knowledge.
architecture (ˈɑːkɪˌtɛktʃə) *n.* **1.** the art and science of designing and superintending the erection of buildings and similar structures. **2.** a style of building or structure: *Gothic architecture.* **3.** buildings or structures collectively. **4.** the structure or design of anything: *the architecture of the universe.* **5.** the internal organization of a computer's components with particular reference to the way in which data is transmitted. **6.** the arrangement of the various devices in a complete computer system or network. —ˌ**archiˈtectural** *adj.* —ˌ**archiˈtecturally** *adv.*
architrave (ˈɑːkɪˌtreɪv) *n. Architect.* **1.** the lowest part of an entablature that bears on the columns. **2.** a moulding around a doorway, window opening, etc. [C16: via French from Italian, from ARCHI- + *trave* beam, from Latin *trabs*]
archival storage *n.* a method of retaining information outside of the internal memory of a computer.
archive (ˈɑːkaɪv) *n. (often pl.)* **1.** a collection of records of or about an institution, family, etc. **2.** a place where such records are kept. ~*vb. (tr.)* **3.** to store (documents, data, etc.) in an archive or other repository. [C17: from Late Latin *archīvum,* from Greek *arkheion* repository of official records, from *arkhē* government] —**arˈchival** *adj.*
archivist (ˈɑːkɪvɪst) *n.* a person in charge of archives, their collection, and cataloguing.
archivolt (ˈɑːkɪˌvəʊlt) *n. Architect.* **1.** a moulding around an arch, sometimes decorated. **2.** the under surface of an arch. [C18: from Italian *archivolto;* see ARC, VAULT[1]]
archon (ˈɑːkɒn, -kən) *n.* (in ancient Athens) one of the nine chief magistrates. [C17: from Greek *arkhōn* ruler, from *arkhein* to rule] —ˈ**archonˌship** *n.*
archoplasm (ˈɑːkəˌplæzəm) *or* **archiplasm** *n.* the protoplasmic material surrounding the centrosome, formerly thought to be involved in the formation of the asters and spindle during mitosis. —ˌ**archoˈplasmic** *adj.*
archpriest (ˈɑːtʃˈpriːst) *n. Christianity.* **1.** (formerly) a chief assistant to a bishop, performing many of his sacerdotal functions during his absence. **2.** a senior priest. —ˈ**archˈpriestˌhood** *or* ˈ**archˈpriestˌship** *n.*
archt *abbrev. for* architect.
archway (ˈɑːtʃˌweɪ) *n.* a passageway or entrance under an arch or arches.
-archy *n. combining form.* government; rule: *anarchy; monarchy.* [from Greek *-arkhia;* see -ARCH] —**-archic** *adj. combining form.* —**-archist** *n. combining form.*
arc light *n.* a light source in which an arc between two electrodes, usually carbon, produces intense white illumination. Also called: **arc lamp.**
ARCM *abbrev. for* Associate of the Royal College of Music.
arcograph (ˈɑːkəˌgrɑːf, -ˌgræf) *n. Geometry.* an instrument used for drawing arcs without using a central point. Also called: **cyclograph.**
arcos (ˈɑːˌkɒs) *Maths. abbrev. for* arc-cosine: the function the value of which for a given argument between −1 and 1 is the angle in radians (between 0 and π), the cosine of which is that argument: the inverse of the cosine function.
ARCS *abbrev. for* Associate of the Royal College of Science.
arcsin (ˈɑːkˌsaɪn) *Maths. abbrev. for* arcsine: the function the value of which for a given argument between −1 and 1 is the angle in radians (between −π/2 and π/2), the sine of which is that argument: the inverse of the sine function.
arctan (ˈɑːkˌtæn) *Maths. abbrev. for* arctangent: the function the value of which for a given argument is the angle in radians (between −π and π) the tangent of which is that argument: the inverse of the tangent function.
arctic (ˈɑːktɪk) *adj.* **1.** *(often cap.)* of or relating to the regions north of the Arctic Circle: *Arctic Ocean, arctic temperatures.* **2.** *Informal.* cold; freezing: *the weather at Christmas was arctic.* ~*n.* **3.** *U.S.* a high waterproof overshoe with buckles. **4.** *(modifier)* designed or suitable for conditions of extreme cold: *arctic clothing.* [C14: from Latin *arcticus,* from Greek *arktikos* northern, literally: pertaining to (the constellation of) the Bear, from *arktos* bear]
arctic char *n.* a char, *Salvelinus alpinus,* that occurs in northern and arctic seas.
Arctic Circle *n.* the imaginary circle round the earth, parallel to the equator, at latitude 66° 32′ N.
arctic fox *n.* a fox, *Alopex lagopus,* of arctic regions, whose fur is dark grey in the summer and white in the winter. See also **blue fox.**
arctic hare *n.* a large hare, *Lepus arcticus,* of the Canadian Arctic whose fur is white in winter.
arctic tern *n.* a black-capped tern, *Sterna paradisea,* that breeds in the Arctic and then migrates as far south as the Antarctic.
arctic willow *n.* a low-growing shrub, *Salix arctica,* of the Canadian tundra.
arctiid (ˈɑːktɪɪd) *n.* any moth of the family *Arctiidae,* which includes the footman, ermine, and tiger moths.
arctophile (ˈɑːktəʊˌfaɪl) *n.* a person who collects teddy bears or is fond of them. [C20: from Greek *arktos* bear + -PHILE]
Arcturus (ɑːkˈtjʊərəs) *n.* the brightest star in the constellation Boötes: a red giant. Visual magnitude: 0.24; spectral type: KO; distance: 36 light years. [C14: from Latin, from Greek *Arktouros,* from *arktos* bear + *ouros* guard, keeper] —**Arcˈturian** *adj.*
arcuate (ˈɑːkjuːɪt, -ˌeɪt) *adj.* shaped or bent like an arc or bow: *arcuate leaves; arcuate fibres of the cerebrum.* Also: **arcuated.** [C17: from Latin *arcuāre,* from *arcus* ARC] —ˈ**arcuately** *adv.*
arcuation (ˌɑːkjʊˈeɪʃən) *n.* **1.** the use of arches or vaults in buildings. **2.** an arrangement of arches. [C17: from Late Latin *arcuātiō* arch, from Latin *arcuāre* to curve]
arcus senilis (ˈɑːkəs sɪˈnaɪlɪs) *n.* an opaque circle around the cornea of the eye, often seen in elderly people. [Latin: senile bow]
arc welding *n.* a technique in which metal is welded by heat generated by an electric arc struck between two electrodes or between one electrode and the metal workpiece. —**arc welder** *n.*
-ard *or* **-art** *suffix forming nouns.* indicating a person who does something, esp. to excess, or is characterized by a certain quality: *braggart; drunkard; dullard.* [via Old French from Germanic *-hard* (literally: hardy, bold), the final element in many Germanic masculine names, such as *Bernhard* Bernard, *Gerhart* Gerard, etc.]
ardeb (ˈɑːdɛb) *n.* a unit of dry measure used in Egypt and other Middle Eastern countries. In Egypt it is approximately equal to 0.195 cubic metres. [C19: from Arabic *ardabb,* from Greek *artabē* a Persian measure]
ardent (ˈɑːdᵊnt) *adj.* **1.** expressive of or characterized by intense desire or emotion; passionate: *ardent love.* **2.** intensely enthusiastic; eager: *an ardent longing.* **3.** glowing, flashing, or shining: *ardent eyes.* **4.** *Rare.* burning: *an ardent fever.* [C14: from Latin *ārdēre* to burn] —ˈ**ardency** *n.* —ˈ**ardently** *adv.*
ardent spirits *pl. n.* spirits, such as rum, whisky, etc.
ardour *or U.S.* **ardor** (ˈɑːdə) *n.* **1.** feelings of great intensity and warmth; fervour. **2.** eagerness; zeal. **3.** *Rare.* burning heat. [C14: from Old French *ardour,* from Latin *ārdor,* from *ārdēre* to burn]

arduous (ˈɑːdjʊəs) *adj.* **1.** requiring great physical or mental effort; difficult to accomplish; strenuous. **2.** hard to endure; harsh: *arduous conditions.* **3.** hard to overcome or surmount; steep or difficult: *an arduous track.* [C16: from Latin *arduus* steep, difficult] —ˈ**arduously** *adv.* —ˈ**arduousness** *n.*

are[1] (ɑː; *unstressed* ə) *vb.* the plural form of the present tense (indicative mood) of **be** and the singular form used with *you.* [Old English *aron,* second person plural of *bēon* to BE]

are[2] (ɑː) *n.* a unit of area equal to 100 sq. metres or 119.599 sq. yards; one hundredth of a hectare. Symbol: a. [C19: from French, from Latin *ārea* piece of ground; see AREA]

area (ˈɛərɪə) *n.* **1.** any flat, curved, or irregular expanse of a surface. **2. a.** the extent of a two-dimensional surface enclosed within a specified boundary or geometric figure: *the area of Ireland; the area of a triangle.* **b.** the two-dimensional extent of the surface of a solid, or of some part thereof, esp. one bounded by a closed curve: *the area of a sphere.* **3.** a section, portion, or part: *an area of the body; an area of the sky.* **4.** region; district; locality: *a mountainous area.* **5. a.** a geographical division of administrative responsibility. **b.** (*as modifier*): *area manager.* **6.** a part or section, as of a building, town, etc., having some specified function or characteristic: *reception area; commercial area; slum area.* **7.** Also called: **areaway.** a sunken area, usually enclosed, giving light, air, and sometimes access to a cellar or basement. **8.** the range, extent, or scope of anything. **9.** a subject field or field of study. **10.** any unoccupied or unused flat open piece of ground. **11.** the ground on which a building stands, or the ground surrounding a building. **12.** *Anatomy.* any of the various regions of the cerebral cortex. **13.** *Computer technol.* any part of a computer memory assigned to store data of a specified type. [C16: from Latin: level ground, open space for play, threshing-floor; related to *ārēre* to be dry] —ˈ**areal** *adj.*

area code *n. U.S. and Canadian.* a three-digit number prefixed to an individual telephone number: used in making long-distance calls.

areaway (ˈɛərɪəˌweɪ) *n.* **1.** a passageway between parts of a building or between different buildings. **2.** See **area** (sense 7).

areca (ˈærɪkə, əˈriːkə) *n.* any of various tall palms of the genus *Areca,* which are native to SE Asia and have white flowers and orange or red egg-shaped nuts. [C16: from Portuguese, from Malayalam *adekka*]

areg (əˈrɛg) *n.* a plural of **erg**[2].

arena (əˈriːnə) *n.* **1. a.** an enclosure or platform, usually surrounded by seats on all sides, in which sports events, contests, entertainments, etc., take place: *a boxing arena.* **b.** (*as modifier*): *arena stage.* **2.** the central area of an ancient Roman amphitheatre, in which gladiatorial contests and other spectacles were held. **3.** a sphere or scene of conflict or intense activity: *the political arena.* [C17: from Latin *harēna* sand, place where sand was strewn for the combats]

arenaceous (ˌærɪˈneɪʃəs) *adj.* **1.** (of sedimentary rocks and deposits) composed of sand or sandstone. Compare **argillaceous** and **rudaceous. 2.** (of plants) growing best in a sandy soil. [C17: from Latin *harēnāceus* sandy, from *harēna* sand]

arena theatre *n.* another term for **theatre-in-the-round.**

arene (ˈæriːn) *n.* an aromatic hydrocarbon. [C20: from AR(OMATIC) + -ENE]

arenicolous (ˌærɪˈnɪkələs) *adj.* growing or living in sand or sandy places: *arenicolous plants.* [C19: from Latin *harēna* sand + *colere* to inhabit]

arenite (ˈærəˌnaɪt, əˈriː-) *n.* any arenaceous rock; a sandstone. [C20: from Latin *harēna* sand + -ITE[1]] —**arenitic** (ˌærəˈnɪtɪk) *adj.*

aren't (ɑːnt) **1.** *contraction of* are not. **2.** *Informal, chiefly Brit.* (used in interrogative sentences) *contraction of* am not.

areography (ˌɛərɪˈɒgrəfɪ) *n.* the description of the physical features, such as the surface, atmosphere, etc., of the planet Mars. [C19: from Greek *Areos* Mars + -GRAPHY]

areola (əˈrɪələ) *n., pl.* **-lae** (-ˌliː) *or* **-las.** *Anatomy.* any small circular area, such as the pigmented ring around the human nipple or the inflamed area surrounding a pimple. [C17: from Latin: diminutive of AREA] —**aˈreolar** *or* **areolate** (əˈrɪəlɪt, -ˌleɪt) *adj.* —**areolation** (əˌrɪəˈleɪʃən) *n.*

areole (ˈærɪəʊl) *n.* **1.** *Biology.* a space outlined on a surface, such as an area between veins on a leaf or on an insect's wing. **2.** a sunken area on a cactus from which spines, hairs, etc., arise. —ˈ**areoˌlate** *adj.*

Areopagus (ˌærɪˈɒpəgəs) *n.* **1.** (in ancient Athens) the judicial council whose members (Areopagites) met on Areopagus, a hill in Athens. **2.** *Literary.* any high court. [via Latin from Greek *Areiopagus,* contracted from *Areios pagos,* hill of Ares] —**Areopagite** (ˌærɪˈɒpədʒaɪt) *n.*

arête (əˈreɪt, əˈrɛt) *n.* a sharp ridge separating two cirques or glacial valleys in mountainous regions. [C19: from French: fishbone, backbone (of a fish), ridge, sharp edge, from Latin *arista* ear of corn, fishbone]

arethusa (ˌærɪˈθjuːzə) *n.* a North American orchid, *Arethusa bulbosa,* having one long narrow leaf and one rose-purple flower fringed with yellow.

Arg. *abbrev. for* Argentina.

argal (ˈɑːgəl) *n.* another name for **argol.**

argali (ˈɑːgəlɪ) *or* **argal** *n., pl.* **-gali** *or* **-gals.** a wild sheep, *Ovis ammon,* inhabiting semidesert regions in central Asia: family *Bovidae,* order *Artiodactyla.* It is the largest of the sheep, having massive horns in the male, which may almost form a circle. [C18: from Mongolian]

Argand diagram (ˈɑːgænd) *n. Maths.* a diagram in which complex numbers are represented by the points in the plane the coordinates of which are respectively the real and imaginary parts of the number, so that the number $x + iy$ is represented by the point (x, y), or by the corresponding vector $\langle x, y\rangle$. If the polar coordinates of (x, y) are (r, θ), r is the modulus and θ the amplitude of $x + iy$. [C19: named after Jean-Robert *Argand* (1768–1822), French mathematician]

argent (ˈɑːdʒənt) *n.* **a.** an archaic or poetic word for **silver. b.** (*as adj.; often postpositive, esp. in heraldry*): *a bend argent.* [C15: from Old French, from Latin]

argentic (ɑːˈdʒɛntɪk) *adj. Chem.* of or containing silver in the divalent or trivalent state.

argentiferous (ˌɑːdʒənˈtɪfərəs) *adj.* containing or bearing silver.

argentine (ˈɑːdʒənˌtaɪn) *adj.* **1.** of, relating to, or resembling silver. ~*n.* **2.** any of various small marine salmonoid fishes, such as *Argentina sphyraena,* that constitute the family *Argentinidae* and are characterized by a long silvery body.

Argentine (ˈɑːdʒənˌtiːn, -ˌtaɪn) *or* **Argentinian** (ˌɑːdʒənˈtɪnɪən) *n.* **1.** a native or inhabitant of Argentina. ~*adj.* **2.** of or relating to Argentina.

argentite (ˈɑːdʒənˌtaɪt) *n.* a dark grey mineral that consists of silver sulphide, usually in cubic crystalline forms, and occurs in veins, often with native silver. It is found esp. in Mexico, Nevada, and Saxony and is an important source of silver. Formula: Ag_2S.

argentous (ɑːˈdʒɛntəs) *adj. Chem.* of or containing silver in the monovalent state.

argentum (ɑːˈdʒɛntəm) *n.* an obsolete name for **silver.** [Latin]

argie-bargie (ˈɑːdʒɪˈbɑːdʒɪ) *n.* a variant spelling of **argy-bargy.**

argil (ˈɑːdʒɪl) *n.* clay, esp. potters' clay. [C16: from Latin *argilla* white clay, from Greek *argillos*]

argillaceous (ˌɑːdʒɪˈleɪʃəs) *adj.* (of sedimentary rocks and deposits) composed of very fine-grained material, such as clay, shale, etc. Compare **arenaceous** (sense 1) and **rudaceous.**

argilliferous (ˌɑːdʒɪˈlɪfərəs) *adj.* containing or yielding clay: *argilliferous rocks.*

argillite (ˈɑːdʒɪˌlaɪt) *n.* any argillaceous rock, esp. a hardened mudstone. [C18: from Latin *argilla* clay (from Greek *argillos*) + -ITE[1]] —**argillitic** (ˌɑːdʒɪˈlɪtɪk) *adj.*

arginine (ˈɑːdʒɪˌnaɪn) *n.* an essential amino acid of plant and animal proteins, necessary for nutrition and for the production of excretory urea. [C19: from German *Arginin,* of uncertain origin]

Argive (ˈɑːdʒaɪv, -gaɪv) *adj.* **1.** (in Homer, Virgil, etc.) of or relating to the Greeks besieging Troy, esp. those from the ancient Greek city of Argos. **2.** of or relating to Argos or the Peloponnese region of Argolis. **3.** a literary word for **Greek.** ~*n.* **4.** an ancient Greek, esp. one from Argos or Argolis.

argle-bargle (ˌɑːgᵊlˈbɑːgᵊl) *n.* another word for **argy-bargy.**

Argo (ˈɑːgəʊ) *n., Latin genitive* **Argus** (ˈɑːgəs). an extensive constellation in the S hemisphere now subdivided into the smaller constellations of **Puppis, Vela, Carina,** and **Pyxis.** Also called: **Argo Navis** (ˈneɪvɪs).

argol (ˈɑːgɒl) *or* **argal** *n.* crude potassium hydrogentartrate, deposited as a crust on the sides of wine vats. [C14: from Anglo-French *argoil,* of unknown origin]

argon (ˈɑːgɒn) *n.* an extremely unreactive colourless odourless element of the rare gas series that forms almost 1 per cent (by volume) of the atmosphere. It is used in electric lights. Symbol: Ar; atomic no.: 18; atomic wt.: 39.95; density: 1.78 kg/m^3; freezing pt.: –189.2°C; boiling pt.: –185.7°C. [C19: from Greek, from *argos* idle, inactive, from A-[1] + *ergon* work]

Argonaut (ˈɑːgəˌnɔːt) *n.* **1.** a person who took part in the Californian gold rush of 1849. **2.** another name for the **paper nautilus.** [C16: from Greek *Argonautēs,* from *Argō* the name of Jason's ship + *nautēs* sailor] —ˌ**Argoˈnautic** *adj.*

argonon (ˈɑːgəˌnɒn) *n.* another name for **inert gas** (sense 1). [C20: from ARGON + -ON (indicating an inert gas)]

argosy (ˈɑːgəsɪ) *n., pl.* **-sies.** *Archaic or poetic.* a large abundantly laden merchant ship, or a fleet of such ships. [C16: from Italian *Ragusea (nave)* (ship) of Ragusa]

argot (ˈɑːgəʊ) *n.* slang or jargon peculiar to a particular group, esp. (formerly) a group of thieves. [C19: from French, of unknown origin] —**argotic** (ɑːˈgɒtɪk) *adj.*

arguable (ˈɑːgjʊəbᵊl) *adj.* **1.** capable of being disputed; doubtful. **2.** capable of being supported by argument; plausible. —ˈ**arguably** *adv.*

argue (ˈɑːgjuː) *vb.* **-gues, -guing, -gued. 1.** (*intr.*) to quarrel; wrangle: *they were always arguing until I arrived.* **2.** (*intr.; often foll. by for or against*) to present supporting or opposing reasons or cases in a dispute; reason. **3.** (*tr.; may take a clause as object*) to try to prove by presenting reasons; maintain. **4.** (*tr.; often passive*) to debate or discuss: *the case was fully argued before agreement was reached.* **5.** (*tr.*) to persuade: *he argued me into going.* **6.** (*tr.*) to give evidence of; suggest: *her looks argue despair.* [C14: from Old French *arguer* to assert, charge with, from Latin *arguere* to make clear, accuse; related to Latin *argūtus* clear, *argentum* silver] —ˈ**arguer** *n.*

argufy ('ɑːgjʊˌfaɪ) *vb.* **-fies, -fying, -fied.** *Facetious or dialect.* to argue or quarrel, esp. over something trivial.
argument ('ɑːgjʊmənt) *n.* **1.** a quarrel; altercation. **2.** a discussion in which reasons are put forward in support of and against a proposition, proposal, or case; debate: *the argument on birth control will never be concluded.* **3.** (*sometimes pl.*) a point or series of reasons presented to support or oppose a proposition. **4.** a summary of the plot or subject of a book, etc. **5.** *Logic.* **a.** a process of deductive or inductive reasoning that purports to show its conclusion to be true. **b.** formally a sequence of statements one of which is the conclusion and the remainder the premises. **6.** *Logic.* an obsolete name for the middle term of a syllogism. **7.** *Maths.* **a.** an element to which an operation, function, predicate, etc., applies, esp. the independent variable of a function. **b.** another name for **amplitude** (sense 5) of a complex number.
argumentation (ˌɑːgjʊmɛn'teɪʃən) *n.* **1.** the process of reasoning methodically. **2.** a less common word for **argument** (senses 2, 3).
argumentative (ˌɑːgjʊ'mɛntətɪv) *adj.* **1.** given to arguing; contentious. **2.** characterized by argument; controversial. —ˌ**argu'mentatively** *adv.* —ˌ**argu'mentativeness** *n.*
argument from design *n.* another name for **teleological argument.**
argumentum ad hominem *Latin.* (ˌɑːgjʊ'mɛntʊm æd 'hɒmɪˌnɛm) *n. Logic.* **1.** fallacious argument that attacks not an opponent's beliefs but his motives or character. **2.** argument that shows an opponent's statement to be inconsistent with his other beliefs. **3.** an instance of either of these. [literally: argument to the person]
argus ('ɑːgəs) *n.* any of various brown butterflies, esp. the **Scotch argus** (*Erebia aethiops*) found on moorland and in forests up to a height of 2000 m.
Argus ('ɑːgəs) *n.* a vigilant person; guardian. [after *Argus*, a giant with a hundred eyes who was made guardian of the heifer Io]
Argus-eyed *adj.* keen-sighted; observant; vigilant.
argus pheasant *n.* either of two pheasants, *Argusianus argus* (great argus) or *Rheinardia ocellata* (crested argus), occurring in SE Asia and Indonesia. The males have very long tails marked with eyelike spots.
argy-bargy *or* **argie-bargie** ('ɑːdʒɪ'bɑːdʒɪ) *n., pl.* **-bargies.** *Brit. informal.* a wrangling argument or verbal dispute. Also called: **argle-bargle.** [C19: from Scottish, compound based on dialect *argle*, probably from ARGUE]
argyle (ɑː'gaɪl) *adj.* **1.** made of knitted or woven material with a diamond-shaped pattern of two or more colours. ~*n.* **2.** (*often pl.*) a sock made of this. [C20: after Campbell of *Argyle* (Argyll), the pattern being an adaptation of the tartan of this clan]
Argyrol ('ɑːdʒɪˌrɒl, ɑː'dʒɪərɒl) *n. Trademark.* a dark brown compound of silver and a protein, used medicinally as a local antiseptic.
Arhat ('ɑːhət) *n.* a Buddhist, esp. a monk who at death passes to nirvana. Compare **Bodhisattva.** [from Sanskrit: worthy of respect, from *arhati* he deserves]
aria ('ɑːrɪə) *n.* an elaborate accompanied song for solo voice from a cantata, opera, or oratorio. See also **da capo.** [C18: from Italian: tune, AIR]
Arian ('ɛərɪən) *adj.* **1.** of, relating to, or characterizing Arianism or Arius. ~*n.* **2.** an adherent of Arianism. ~*adj., n.* **3.** a variant spelling of **Aryan.**
-arian *suffix forming nouns.* indicating a person or thing that advocates, believes, or is associated with something: *vegetarian; millenarian; librarian.* [from Latin *-ārius* -ARY + -AN]
Arianism ('ɛərɪəˌnɪzəm) *n.* the doctrine of Arius (?250–336 A.D.), Greek Christian theologian. It was pronounced heretical at the Council of Nicaea, which asserted that Christ was not of one substance with the Father, but a creature raised by the Father to the dignity of Son of God.
arid ('ærɪd) *adj.* **1.** having little or no rain; dry; parched with heat. **2.** devoid of interest. [C17: from Latin *āridus*, from *ārēre* to be dry] —**aridity** (ə'rɪdɪtɪ) *or* '**aridness** *n.* —'**aridly** *adv.*
arid zone *n.* either of the zones of latitude 15–30° N and S characterized by very low rainfall and desert or semidesert terrain.
ariel ('ɛərɪəl) *n.* an Arabian gazelle, *Gazella arabica* (or *dama*). [C19: from Arabic *aryal*]
Aries ('ɛəriːz) *n., Latin genitive* **Arietis** (ə'raɪɪtɪs). **1.** *Astronomy.* a small zodiacal constellation in the N hemisphere lying between Taurus and Pisces on the ecliptic and having a second-magnitude star. **2.** *Astrology.* **a.** Also called: the **Ram.** the first sign of the zodiac, symbol ♈, having a cardinal fire classification, ruled by the planet Mars. The sun is in this sign between about March 21 and April 19. **b.** a person born during the period when the sun is in this sign. ~*adj.* **3.** *Astrology.* born under or characteristic of Aries. ~Also (for senses 2b, 3): **Arien** ('ɛərɪən). [C14: from Latin: ram]
arietta (ˌærɪ'ɛtə; *Italian* ari'etta) *or* **ariette** (ˌærɪ'ɛt) *n., pl.* **-ettas, -ette** (-'ette), *or* **-ettes.** a short relatively uncomplicated aria. [C18: from Italian, diminutive of ARIA]
aright (ə'raɪt) *adv.* correctly; rightly; properly.
ariki ('ɑːrɪkɪ) *n., pl.* **ariki.** *N.Z.* the first-born male or female in a notable family; chief. [Maori]
aril ('ærɪl) *n.* an appendage on certain seeds, such as those of the yew and nutmeg, developed from or near the funicle of the ovule and often brightly coloured and fleshy. [C18: from New Latin *arillus*, from Medieval Latin *arilli* raisins, pips of grapes] —'**arilˌlate** *adj.*
arillode ('ærɪˌləʊd) *n.* a structure in certain seeds, such as the nutmeg, that resembles an aril but is developed from the micropyle of the ovule. [C19: from ARIL + -ODE[1]]
ariose ('ɑːrɪˌəʊs, 'æ-; ˌɑːrɪ'əʊs, ˌæ-) *adj. Rare.* melodic or songlike. [C18: from Italian ARIOSO]
arioso (ˌɑːrɪ'əʊzəʊ, ˌæ-) *n., pl.* **-sos** *or* **-si** (-siː). *Music.* a recitative with the lyrical quality of an aria. [C18: from Italian, from ARIA]
arise (ə'raɪz) *vb.* **arises, arising, arose, arisen.** (*intr.*) **1.** to come into being; originate. **2.** (foll. by *from*) to spring or proceed as a consequence; result. **3.** to get or stand up, as from a sitting, kneeling, or lying position. **4.** to come into notice. **5.** to move upwards; ascend. [Old English *ārīsan*; related to Old Saxon *arīsan*, Old High German *irrīsan*; see RISE]
arista (ə'rɪstə) *n., pl.* **-tae** (-tiː). **1.** a stiff bristle such as the awn of some grasses and cereals. **2.** a bristle-like appendage on the antennae of some insects. [C17: from Latin: ear of corn, fishbone] —**a'ristate** *adj.*
aristocracy (ˌærɪ'stɒkrəsɪ) *n., pl.* **-cies.** **1.** a privileged class of people usually of high birth; the nobility. **2.** such a class as the ruling body of a state. **3.** government by such a class. **4.** a state governed by such a class. **5.** a class of people considered to be outstanding in a sphere of activity. [C16: from Late Latin *aristocratia*, from Greek *aristokratia* rule by the best-born, from *aristos* best; see -CRACY]
aristocrat ('ærɪstəˌkræt) *n.* **1.** a member of the aristocracy; a noble. **2.** a person who has the manners or qualities of a member of a privileged or superior class. **3.** a person who advocates aristocracy as a form of government.
aristocratic (ˌærɪstə'krætɪk) *adj.* **1.** relating to or characteristic of aristocracy or an aristocrat. **2.** elegant or stylish in appearance and behaviour. —ˌ**aristo'cratically** *adv.*
Aristotelian (ˌærɪstə'tiːlɪən) *adj.* **1.** of or relating to Aristotle (?448–?380 B.C.), Greek philosopher, or his philosophy. **2.** (of a philosophical position) derived from that of Aristotle, or incorporating such of his major doctrines as the distinctions between matter and form, and substance and accident, or the primacy of individuals over universals. ~*n.* **3.** a follower of Aristotle.
Aristotelian logic *n.* the logical theories of Aristotle as developed in the Middle Ages, concerned mainly with syllogistic reasoning: traditional as opposed to modern or symbolic logic.
arithmetic (ə'rɪθmətɪk) *n.* **1.** the branch of mathematics concerned with numerical calculations, such as addition, subtraction, multiplication, and division. **2.** one or more calculations involving numerical operations. **3.** knowledge of or skill in using arithmetic: *his arithmetic is good.* ~*adj.* (ˌærɪθ'mɛtɪk), *also* ˌ**arith'metical.** **4.** of, relating to, or using arithmetic. [C13: from Latin *arithmētica*, from Greek *arithmētikē*, from *arithmein* to count, from *arithmos* number] —ˌ**arith'metically** *adv.* —**aˌrithme'tician** *n.*
arithmetic mean *n.* the average value of a set of integers, terms, or quantities, expressed as their sum divided by their number: *the arithmetic mean of 3, 4, and 8 is 5.* Often shortened to **mean.** Also called: **average.** Compare **geometric mean.**
arithmetic progression *n.* a sequence of numbers or quantities, each term of which differs from the succeeding term by a constant amount, such as 3,6,9,12. Compare **geometric progression.**
-arium *suffix forming nouns.* indicating a place for or associated with something: *aquarium; planetarium; solarium.* [from Latin *-ārium*, neuter of *-ārius* -ARY]
Ariz. *abbrev. for* Arizona.
ark (ɑːk) *n.* **1.** the vessel that Noah built and in which he saved himself, his family, and a number of animals and birds during the Flood (Genesis 6–9). **2. out of the ark.** *Informal.* very old; out of date. **3.** a place or thing offering shelter or protection. **4.** *Dialect.* a chest, box, or coffer. [Old English *arc*, from Latin *arca* box, chest]
Ark (ɑːk) *n. Judaism.* **1.** Also called: **Holy Ark.** the cupboard at the front of a synagogue, usually in the eastern wall, in which the Torah scrolls are kept. **2.** Also called: **Ark of the Covenant.** the most sacred symbol of God's presence among the Hebrew people, carried in their journey from Sinai to the Promised Land (Canaan) and eventually enshrined in the holy of holies of the Temple in Jerusalem.
Ark. *abbrev. for* Arkansas.
arkose ('ɑːkəʊs) *n.* a sandstone consisting of grains of feldspar and quartz cemented by a mixture of quartz and clay minerals. [C19: from French]
arm[1] (ɑːm) *n.* **1.** (in man) either of the upper limbs from the shoulder to the wrist. Related adj.: **brachial.** **2.** the part of either of the upper limbs from the elbow to the wrist; forearm. **3. a.** the corresponding limb of any other vertebrate. **b.** an armlike appendage of some invertebrates. **4.** an object that covers or supports the human arm, esp. the sleeve of a garment or the side of a chair, sofa, etc. **5.** anything considered to resemble an arm in appearance, position, or function, esp. something that branches out from a central support or larger mass: *an*

arm of the sea; the arm of a record player. **6.** an administrative subdivision of an organization: *an arm of the government.* **7.** power; authority: *the arm of the law.* **8.** any of the specialist combatant sections of a military force, such as cavalry, infantry, etc. **9.** *Nautical.* See **yardarm.** **10.** *Sport, esp. ball games.* ability to throw or pitch: *he has a good arm.* **11. arm in arm.** with arms linked. **12. at arm's length.** at a distance; away from familiarity with or subjection to another. **13. in the arms of Morpheus.** sleeping. **14. with open arms.** with great warmth and hospitality: *to welcome someone with open arms.* ~*vb.* **15.** (*tr.*) *Archaic.* to walk arm in arm with. [Old English; related to German *Arm,* Old Norse *armr* arm, Latin *armus* shoulder, Greek *harmos* joint] —'**armless** *adj.* —'**arm,like** *adj.*

arm[2] (ɑːm) *vb.* (*tr.*) **1.** to equip with weapons as a preparation for war. **2.** to provide (a person or thing) with something that strengthens, protects, or increases efficiency: *he armed himself against the cold.* **3. a.** to activate (a fuse) so that it will explode at the required time. **b.** to prepare (an explosive device) for use by introducing a fuse or detonator. **4.** *Nautical.* to pack arming into (a sounding lead). ~*n.* **5.** (*usually pl.*) a weapon, esp. a firearm. ~See also **arms.** [C14: (n.) back formation from *arms,* from Old French *armes,* from Latin *arma;* (vb.) from Old French *armer* to equip with arms, from Latin *armāre,* from *arma* arms, equipment]

Arm. *abbrev. for* Armenia(n).

armada (ɑːˈmɑːdə) *n.* a large number of ships or aircraft. [C16: from Spanish, from Medieval Latin *armāta* fleet, armed forces, from Latin *armāre* to provide with arms]

armadillo (ˌɑːməˈdɪləʊ) *n., pl.* **-los.** **1.** any edentate mammal of the family *Dasypodidae* of Central and South America and S North America, such as *Priodontes giganteus* (**giant armadillo**). They are burrowing animals, with peglike rootless teeth and a covering of strong horny plates over most of the body. **2. fairy armadillo.** another name for **pichiciego.** [C16: from Spanish, diminutive of *armado* armed (man), from Latin *armātus* armed; compare ARMADA]

Armageddon (ˌɑːməˈgɛdᵊn) *n.* a catastrophic and extremely destructive conflict, esp. World War I viewed as this. [C19: from Late Latin *Armagedōn,* from Greek, from Hebrew *har megiddōn,* mountain district of *Megiddo,* in N Palestine, site of various battles in the Old Testament]

Armagnac (ˈɑːmənˌjæk) *n.* a dry brown brandy distilled in the French district of Gers. [from *Armagnac,* the former name of this region]

Armalite (ˈɑːməlaɪt) *n. Trademark.* a lightweight high-velocity automatic rifle of various calibres. [C20: from *Armalite* Division, Fairchild Engine and Airplane Company, manufacturers]

armament (ˈɑːməmənt) *n.* **1.** the weapon equipment of a military vehicle, ship, or aircraft. **2.** a military force raised and armed ready for war. **3.** preparation for war involving the production of equipment and arms. [C17: from Latin *armāmenta* utensils, from *armāre* to equip]

armamentarium (ˌɑːməmɛnˈtɛərɪəm) *n., pl.* **-iums** *or* **-ia** (-ɪə). the items that comprise the material and equipment used by a physician in his professional practice.

armature (ˈɑːmətjʊə) *n.* **1.** a revolving structure in an electric motor or generator, wound with the coils that carry the current. **2.** any part of an electric machine or device that moves under the influence of a magnetic field or within which an electromotive force is induced. **3.** Also called: **keeper.** a soft iron or steel bar placed across the poles of a permanent magnet to close the magnetic circuit. **4.** such a bar placed across the poles of an electromagnet to transmit mechanical force. **5.** *Sculpture.* a framework to support the clay or other material used in modelling. **6.** the protective outer covering of an animal or plant. **7.** *Archaic.* armour. [C15: from Latin *armātūra* armour, equipment, from *armāre* to furnish with equipment; see ARM[2]]

armband (ˈɑːmˌbænd) *n.* a band of material worn round the arm, such as one bearing an identifying mark, etc., or a black one indicating mourning.

armchair (ˈɑːmˌtʃɛə) *n.* **1.** a chair, esp. an upholstered one, that has side supports for the arms or elbows. **2.** (*modifier*) taking no active part; lacking practical experience; theoretical: *an armchair strategist.* **3.** (*modifier*) participated in away from the place of action or in the home: *armchair theatre.*

Armco (ˈɑːmkəʊ) *n. Trademark.* a metal safety barrier erected at the side of motor-racing circuits, esp. on corners.

armed[1] (ɑːmd) *adj.* **1.** equipped with or supported by arms, armour, etc. **2.** prepared for conflict or any difficulty. **3.** (of an explosive device) prepared for use; having a fuse or detonator installed. **4.** (of plants) having the protection of thorns, spines, etc.

armed[2] (ɑːmd) *adj.* **a.** having an arm or arms. **b.** (*in combination*): *long-armed; one-armed.*

armed forces *pl. n.* the military forces of a nation or nations, including the army, navy, air force, marines, etc.

Armenian (ɑːˈmiːnɪən) *n.* **1.** a native or inhabitant of Armenia, a republic in SE Europe, or an Armenian-speaking person elsewhere. **2.** the language of the Armenians: an Indo-European language probably belonging to the Thraco-Phrygian branch, but containing many non-Indo-European elements. **3.** an adherent of the Armenian Church or its doctrines. ~*adj.* **4.** of or relating to Armenia, its inhabitants, their language, or the Armenian Church.

Armenian Church *n.* the national Church of Armenia, founded in the early fourth century A.D., the dogmas and liturgy of which are similar to those of the Orthodox Church.

armeria (ɑːˈmɪːrɪə) *n.* the generic name for **thrift** (sense 2). [New Latin, from *flos armeriae,* a species of dianthus]

armes parlantes (*French* arm parlɑ̃t) *pl. n. Heraldry.* arms using devices to illustrate the name of the bearers, such as a rose and a wall to illustrate the name *Rosewall.* [literally: speaking arms]

armet (ˈɑːmɛt) *n.* a close-fitting medieval visored helmet with a neck guard. [C16: from Old French, from Old Spanish *almete,* from Old French HELMET]

armful (ˈɑːmfʊl) *n., pl.* **-fuls.** the amount that can be held by one or both arms.

armhole (ˈɑːmˌhəʊl) *n.* the opening in an article of clothing through which the arm passes and to which a sleeve is often fitted.

armiger (ˈɑːmɪdʒə) *n.* **1.** a person entitled to bear heraldic arms, such as a sovereign or nobleman. **2.** a squire carrying the armour of a medieval knight. [C16: from Medieval Latin: squire, from Latin: armour-bearer, from *arma* arms + *gerere* to carry, bear] —**armigerous** (ɑːˈmɪdʒərəs) *adj.*

armillary (ˈɑːmɪlərɪ, ɑːˈmɪlərɪ) *adj.* of or relating to bracelets. [C17: from New Latin *armillaris,* from Latin *armilla* bracelet]

armillary sphere *n.* a model of the celestial sphere consisting of rings representing the relative positions of the celestial equator, ecliptic, etc., used by early astronomers for determining the positions of stars.

arming (ˈɑːmɪŋ) *n.* **1.** the act of taking arms or providing with arms. **2.** *Nautical.* a greasy substance, such as tallow, packed into the recess at the bottom of a sounding lead to pick up samples of sand, gravel, etc., from the bottom.

Arminian (ɑːˈmɪnɪən) *adj.* **1.** denoting, relating to, or believing in the Christian Protestant doctrines of Dutch theologian Jacobus Arminius (1560–1609), which rejected absolute predestination and insisted that the sovereignty of God is compatible with free will in man. These doctrines deeply influenced Wesleyan and Methodist theology. ~*n.* **2.** a follower of such doctrines. —**Ar'minian,ism** *n.*

armipotent (ɑːˈmɪpətənt) *adj. Literary.* strong in arms or war. [C14: from Latin *armipotēns,* from *arma* arms + *potēns* powerful, from *posse* to be able] —**ar'mipotence** *n.*

armistice (ˈɑːmɪstɪs) *n.* an agreement between opposing armies to suspend hostilities in order to discuss peace terms; truce. [C18: from New Latin *armistitium,* from Latin *arma* arms + *sistere* to stop, stand still]

Armistice Day *n.* the anniversary of the signing of the armistice that ended World War I, on Nov. 11, 1918, now kept on Remembrance Sunday. See also **Remembrance Sunday.** U.S. name: **Veterans Day.**

armlet (ˈɑːmlɪt) *n.* **1.** a small arm, as of a lake, the sea, etc. **2.** a band or bracelet worn round the arm for ornament, identification, etc. **3.** a very short sleeve on a garment.

armoire (ɑːmˈwɑː) *n.* a large cabinet, originally used for storing weapons. [C16: from French, from Old French *armaire,* from Latin *armārium* chest, closet; see AMBRY]

armor (ˈɑːmə) *n.* the U.S. spelling of **armour.**

armorial (ɑːˈmɔːrɪəl) *adj.* **1.** of or relating to heraldry or heraldic arms. ~*n.* **2.** a book of coats of arms.

armory (ˈɑːmərɪ) *n., pl.* **-mories.** **1.** *Rare.* another name for **heraldry.** **2.** the usual U.S. spelling of **armoury.** —'**armorist** *n.*

armour *or U.S.* **armor** (ˈɑːmə) *n.* **1.** any defensive covering, esp. that of metal, chain mail, etc., worn by medieval warriors to prevent injury to the body in battle. **2.** the protective metal plates on a tank, warship, etc. **3.** *Military.* armoured fighting vehicles in general; military units equipped with these. **4.** any protective covering, such as the shell of certain animals. **5.** *Nautical.* the watertight suit of a diver. **6.** *Engineering.* permanent protection for an underwater structure. **7.** heraldic insignia; arms. ~*vb.* **8.** (*tr.*) to equip or cover with armour. [C13: from Old French *armure,* from Latin *armātūrā* armour, equipment]

armour-bearer *n. History.* a retainer who carried the arms or armour of a warrior.

armoured *or U.S.* **armored** (ˈɑːməd) *adj.* **1.** having a protective covering, such as armour or bone. **2.** comprising units making use of armoured vehicles: *an armoured brigade.* **3.** (of glass) toughened.

armoured car *n.* **1.** *Military.* a fast lightly armed and armoured vehicle, mainly used for reconnaissance. **2.** any vehicle strengthened by armoured plate, esp. a security van for transporting cash and valuables.

armourer *or U.S.* **armorer** (ˈɑːmərə) *n.* **1.** a person who makes or mends arms and armour. **2.** a person employed in the maintenance of small arms and weapons in a military unit.

armour plate *n.* a tough heavy steel, usually containing chromium, nickel, and molybdenum and often hardened on the surface, used for protecting warships, tanks, etc.

armoury *or U.S.* **armory** (ˈɑːmərɪ) *n., pl.* **-mouries** *or* **-mories.** **1.** a secure place for the storage of weapons. **2.** armour generally. **3. a.** *U.S.* a building in which training in the use of arms and drill takes place; drill hall. **b.** (*pl.*) *Canadian.* such a building used for training and as headquarters by a reserve unit of the armed forces. **4.** resources, as of arguments or objections, on which to draw: *they thought they had proved him wrong, but he still had a few weapons in his armoury.* **5.** *U.S.* a place where arms are made.

armpit ('ɑːmˌpɪt) *n.* the small depression beneath the arm where it joins the shoulder. Technical name: **axilla.**

armrest ('ɑːmˌrɛst) *n.* the part of a chair, sofa, etc., that supports the arm. Sometimes shortened to **arm.**

arms (ɑːmz) *pl. n.* **1.** weapons collectively. See also **small arms.** **2.** military exploits: *prowess in arms.* **3.** the official heraldic symbols of a family, state, etc., including a shield with distinctive devices, and often supports, a crest, or other insignia. **4. bear arms. a.** to carry weapons. **b.** to serve in the armed forces. **c.** to have a coat of arms. **5. in** *or* **under arms.** armed and prepared for war. **6. lay down one's arms.** to stop fighting; surrender. **7. present arms.** *Military.* **a.** a position of salute in which the rifle is brought up to a position vertically in line with the body, muzzle uppermost and trigger guard to the fore. **b.** the command for this drill. **8. take (up) arms.** to prepare to fight. **9. to arms!** arm yourselves! **10. up in arms.** indignant; prepared to protest strongly. [C13: from Old French *armes,* from Latin *arma;* see ARM[2]]

arm's-length *adj.* **1.** lacking intimacy or friendliness, esp. when possessing some special connection, such as previous closeness: *we now have an arm's-length relationship.* **2.** (of commercial transactions) in accordance with market values, disregarding any connection such as common ownership of the companies involved.

arms race *n.* the continuing competitive attempt by two or more nations each to have available to it more and more powerful weapons than the other(s).

armure ('ɑːmjʊə) *n.* a silk or wool fabric with a small cobbled pattern. [C19: from French: ARMOUR]

arm wrestling *n.* a contest in which two people sit facing each other each with one elbow resting on a table, clasp hands, and each tries to force the other's arm flat onto the table while keeping his own elbow touching the table.

army ('ɑːmɪ) *n., pl.* **-mies. 1.** the military land forces of a nation. **2.** a military unit usually consisting of two or more corps with supporting arms and services. **3.** (*modifier*) of, relating to, or characteristic of an army: *army rations.* **4.** any large body of people united for some specific purpose. **5.** a large number of people, animals, etc.; multitude. [C14: from Old French *armee,* from Medieval Latin *armāta* armed forces; see ARMADA]

army ant *n.* any of various mainly tropical American predatory ants of the subfamily *Dorylinae,* which live in temporary nests and travel in vast hordes preying on other animals. Also called: **legionary ant.** See also **driver ant.**

Army List *n. Brit.* an official list of all serving commissioned officers of the army and reserve officers liable for recall.

army worm *n.* **1.** the caterpillar of a widely distributed noctuid moth, *Leucania unipuncta,* which travels in vast hordes and is a serious pest of cereal crops in North America. **2.** any of various similar caterpillars.

arnica ('ɑːnɪkə) *n.* **1.** any N temperate or arctic plant of the genus *Arnica,* typically having yellow flowers: family *Compositae* (composites). **2.** the tincture of the dried flower heads of any of these plants, esp. *A. montana,* used in treating bruises. [C18: from New Latin, of unknown origin]

aroha ('ɑːrɒhə) *n. N.Z.* love, compassion, or affectionate regard. [Maori]

aroid ('ærɔɪd, 'ɛər-) *adj.* **1.** Also: **araceous.** of, relating to, or belonging to the *Araceae,* a family of plants having small flowers massed on a spadix surrounded by a large petaloid spathe. The family includes arum, calla, and anthurium. ~*n.* **2.** any plant of the *Araceae.* [C19: from New Latin *Arum* type genus + -OID; see ARUM]

aroint thee *or* **ye** (ə'rɔɪnt) *sentence substitute. Archaic.* away! begone! [C17: of unknown origin]

aroma (ə'rəʊmə) *n.* **1.** a distinctive usually pleasant smell, esp. of spices, wines, and plants. **2.** a subtle pervasive quality or atmosphere. [C18: via Latin from Greek: spice]

aromatherapy (əˌrəʊmə'θɛrəpɪ) *n.* the massaging of the skin with oils or creams containing fragrant plant extracts: a treatment in alternative medicine designed to relieve tension and cure certain skin disorders. —**aˌroma'therapist** *n.*

aromatic (ˌærə'mætɪk) *adj.* **1.** having a distinctive, usually fragrant smell. **2.** (of an organic compound) having an unsaturated ring containing alternating double and single bonds, esp. containing a benzene ring; exhibiting aromaticity. Compare **aliphatic.** ~*n.* **3.** something, such as a plant or drug, giving off a fragrant smell. —**ˌaro'matically** *adv.*

aromaticity (əˌrəʊmə'tɪsɪtɪ) *n.* **1.** the property of certain planar cyclic conjugated molecules, esp. benzene, of behaving like unsaturated molecules and undergoing substitution reactions rather than addition. **2.** the quality or state of having an aroma.

aromatize *or* **aromatise** (ə'rəʊməˌtaɪz) *vb.* **1.** (*tr.*) to make aromatic. **2.** to convert (an aliphatic compound) to an aromatic compound. —**aˌromati'zation** *or* **aˌromati'sation** *n.*

arose (ə'rəʊz) *vb.* the past tense of **arise.**

around (ə'raʊnd) *prep.* **1.** situated at various points in: *a lot of shelves around the house.* **2.** from place to place in: *driving around Ireland.* **3.** somewhere in or near: *to stay around the house.* **4.** *Chiefly U.S.* approximately in: *it happened around 1957, I think.* ~*adv.* **5.** in all directions from a point of reference: *he owns the land for ten miles around.* **6.** in the vicinity, esp. restlessly but idly: *to wait around; stand around.* **7.** here and there; in no particular place or direction: *dotted around.* **8.** *Informal.* (of people) active and prominent in a particular area or profession: *some pop stars are around for only a few years.* **9.** *Informal.* present in some place (the exact location being inexact): *he's around here somewhere.* **10.** *Informal.* in circulation; available: *that type of phone has been around for some years now.* **11.** *Informal.* to many places, so as to have gained considerable experience, often of a worldly or social nature: *he gets around; I've been around.* [C17 (rare earlier): from A-[2] + ROUND]

▷**Usage.** In American English, *around* is usually used instead of *round* in adverbial and prepositional senses, except in a few fixed phrases such as *all year round.* Such uses of *around* are less common in British English.

arouse (ə'raʊz) *vb.* **1.** (*tr.*) to evoke or elicit (a reaction, emotion, or response); stimulate. **2.** to awaken from sleep. —**a'rousal** *n.* —**a'rouser** *n.*

arpeggio (ɑː'pɛdʒɪəʊ) *n., pl.* **-gios. 1.** a chord whose notes are played in rapid succession rather than simultaneously. **2.** an ascending and descending figuration used in practising the piano, voice, etc. [C18: from Italian, from *arpeggiare* to perform on the harp, from *arpa* HARP]

arpent ('ɑːpənt; *French* arpɑ̃) *n.* **1.** a former French unit of length equal to 190 feet (approximately 58 metres). **2.** an old French unit of land area equal to about one acre: still used in Quebec and Louisiana. [C16: from Old French, probably from Late Latin *arepennis* half an acre, of Gaulish origin; related to Middle Irish *airchenn* unit of land measure]

arquebus ('ɑːkwɪbəs) *or* **harquebus** *n.* a portable long-barrelled gun dating from the 15th century: fired by a wheel-lock or matchlock. Also called: **hackbut, hagbut.** [C16: via Old French *harquebuse* from Middle Dutch *hakebusse,* literally: hook gun, from the shape of the butt, from *hake* hook + *busse* box, gun, from Late Latin *busis* box]

arr. *abbrev. for:* **1.** arranged (by). **2.** arrival. **3.** arrive(d).

arrack *or* **arak** ('ærək) *n.* a coarse spirit distilled in various Eastern countries from grain, rice, sugar cane, etc. [C17: from Arabic *'araq* sweat, sweet juice, liquor]

arraign (ə'reɪn) *vb.* **1.** (*tr.*) to bring (a prisoner) before a court to answer an indictment. **2.** (*tr.*) to call to account; complain about; accuse. [C14: from Old French *araisnier* to speak, accuse, from A-[2] + *raisnier,* from Vulgar Latin *ratiōnāre* (unattested) to talk, argue, from Latin *ratiō* a reasoning] —**ar'raigner** *n.* —**ar'raignment** *n.*

arrange (ə'reɪndʒ) *vb.* **1.** (*tr.*) to put into a proper, systematic, or decorative order. **2.** (*tr.; may take a clause as object or an infinitive*) to arrive at an agreement or understanding about; settle. **3.** (when *intr.,* often foll. by *for;* when *tr., may take a clause as object or an infinitive*) to make plans or preparations in advance (for something): *we arranged for her to be met.* **4.** (*tr.*) to adapt (a musical composition) for performance in a different way, esp. on different instruments. **5.** (*tr.*) to adapt (a play, etc.) for broadcasting. **6.** (*intr.;* often foll. by *with*) to come to an agreement. [C14: from Old French *arangier,* from A-[2] + *rangier* to put in a row, RANGE] —**ar'rangeable** *adj.* —**ar'ranger** *n.*

arrangement (ə'reɪndʒmənt) *n.* **1.** the act of arranging or being arranged. **2.** the form in which things are arranged: *he altered the arrangement of furniture in the room.* **3.** a thing composed of various ordered parts; the result of arranging: *a flower arrangement.* **4.** (*often pl.*) a preparatory measure taken or plan made; preparation. **5.** an agreement or settlement; understanding. **6.** an adaptation of a piece of music for performance in a different way, esp. on different instruments from those for which it was originally composed. **7.** an adaptation (of a play, etc.) for broadcasting.

arrant ('ærənt) *adj.* utter; out-and-out: *an arrant fool.* [C14: a variant of ERRANT (wandering, vagabond); sense developed from its frequent use in phrases like *arrant thief* (hence: notorious)] —**'arrantly** *adv.*

arras ('ærəs) *n.* a wall hanging, esp. of tapestry. [from *Arras,* a town in N France formerly famous for tapestry]

array (ə'reɪ) *n.* **1.** an impressive display or collection. **2.** an orderly or regular arrangement, esp. of troops in battle order. **3.** *Poetic.* rich clothing; apparel. **4.** *Maths.* a sequence of numbers or symbols in a specified order. **5.** *Maths.* a set of numbers or symbols arranged in rows and columns, as in a determinant or matrix. **6.** *Electronics.* an arrangement of aerials spaced to give desired directional characteristics, used esp. in radar. **7.** *Law.* a panel of jurors. **8.** the arming of military forces. **9.** *Computer technol.* a regular data structure in which individual elements may be located by reference to one or more integer index variables, the number of such indices being the number of dimensions in the array. ~*vb.* (*tr.*) **10.** to dress in rich attire; adorn. **11.** to arrange in order (esp. troops for battle); marshal. **12.** *Law.* to draw up (a panel of jurors). [C13: from Old French *aroi* arrangement, from *arayer* to arrange, of Germanic origin; compare Old English *arǣdan* to make ready] —**ar'rayal** *n.*

arrears (ə'rɪəz) *n.* **1.** (*sometimes sing.*) Also called: **arrearage** (ə'rɪərɪdʒ). something outstanding or owed. **2. in arrears** *or* **arrear.** late in paying a debt or meeting an obligation. [C18: from obsolete *arrear* (adv.) behindhand, from Old French *arere,* from Medieval Latin *adretrō,* from Latin *ad* to + *retrō* backwards]

arrest (ə'rɛst) *vb.* (*tr.*) **1.** to deprive (a person) of liberty by taking him into custody, esp. under lawful authority. **2.** to seize (a ship) under lawful authority. **3.** to slow or stop the development or progress of (a disease, growth, etc.). **4.** to catch and hold (one's attention, sight, etc.). **5. arrest judgment.** *Law.* to stay proceedings after a verdict, on the grounds of error or possible error. ~*n.* **6.** the act of taking a person into custody, esp. under lawful authority. **7.** the act of seizing and holding a ship under lawful authority. **8.** the state of being held, esp. under lawful authority: *under arrest.* **9.** Also called: **arrestation** (ˌærɛs'teɪʃən). the slowing or stopping of the development or progress of something. **10.** the stopping or sudden cessation of motion of something: *a cardiac arrest.* [C14: from Old French *arester,* from Vulgar Latin *arrestāre* (unattested), from Latin *ad* at, to + *restāre* to stand firm, stop]

arrestable (ə'rɛstəbᵊl) *adj.* **1.** liable to be arrested. **2.** (of an offence) such that an offender may be arrested without a warrant.

arrester (ə'rɛstə) *n.* **1.** a person who arrests. **2.** a thing that stops or checks motion, esp. a mechanism of wires for slowing aeroplanes as they land on an aircraft carrier.

arresting (ə'rɛstɪŋ) *adj.* attracting attention; striking. —**ar'restingly** *adv.*

arrestment (ə'rɛstmənt) *n. Scots Law.* the seizure of money or property to prevent a debtor paying one creditor in advance of another.

arrest of judgment *n. Law.* a stay of proceedings after a verdict, on the grounds of error or possible error.

Arretine ware ('ærɪˌtaɪn) *n.* another term for **Samian ware** (sense 2). [from *Arretium,* ancient Latin name of *Arezzo,* city in central Italy]

arrhythmia (ə'rɪðmɪə) *n.* any variation from the normal rhythm in the heartbeat. [C19: New Latin, from Greek *arrhuthmia,* from A-[1] + *rhuthmos* RHYTHM]

arrière-ban *French.* (arjɛrbɑ̃) *n.* **1.** (in medieval France) a summons to the king's vassals to do military service. **2.** the vassals so assembled for military service. [C16: changed from Old French *herban* call to arms, of Germanic origin; compare Old High German *heriban,* from *heri* army + *ban* summons, BAN[2]]

arrière-pensée *French.* (arjɛrpɑ̃se) *n.* an unrevealed thought or intention. [C19: literally: behind thought]

arris ('ærɪs) *n., pl.* **-ris** *or* **-rises.** a sharp edge at the meeting of two surfaces at an angle with one another, as at two adjacent sides of a stone block. [C17: apparently from Old French *areste* beard of grain, sharp ridge; see ARÊTE]

arrival (ə'raɪvᵊl) *n.* **1.** the act or time of arriving. **2.** a person or thing that arrives or has arrived. **3.** the reaching of a condition or objective.

arrive (ə'raɪv) *vb.* (*intr.*) **1.** to come to a certain place during or after a journey; reach a destination. **2.** (foll. by *at*) to agree upon; reach: *to arrive at a decision.* **3.** to occur eventually: *the moment arrived when pretence was useless.* **4.** *Informal.* (of a baby) to be born. **5.** *Informal.* to attain success or gain recognition. [C13: from Old French *ariver,* from Vulgar Latin *arrīpāre* (unattested) to land, reach the bank, from Latin *ad* to + *rīpa* river bank] —**ar'river** *n.*

arrivederci *Italian.* (arrive'dertʃi) *sentence substitute.* goodbye.

arrivisme (ˌæriː'viːzmə; *French* arivism) *n.* unscrupulous ambition.

arriviste (ˌæriː'viːst; *French* arivist) *n.* a person who is unscrupulously ambitious. [French: see ARRIVE, -IST]

arroba (ə'rəʊbə) *n., pl.* **-bas.** **1.** a unit of weight, approximately equal to 11 kilograms, used in some Spanish-speaking countries. **2.** a unit of weight, approximately equal to 15 kilograms, used in some Portuguese-speaking countries. **3.** a liquid measure used in some Spanish-speaking countries with different values, but in Spain used as a wine-measure, approximately equal to 16 litres. [C16: from Spanish, from Arabic *ar-rub'* the quarter (of a quintal)]

arrogant ('ærəgənt) *adj.* having or showing an exaggerated opinion of one's own importance, merit, ability, etc.; conceited; overbearingly proud: *an arrogant teacher; an arrogant assumption.* [C14: from Latin *arrogāre* to claim as one's own; see ARROGATE] —'**arrogance** *n.* —'**arrogantly** *adv.*

arrogate ('ærəˌgeɪt) *vb.* **1.** (*tr.*) to claim or appropriate for oneself presumptuously or without justification. **2.** (*tr.*) to attribute or assign to another without justification. [C16: from Latin *arrogāre,* from *rogāre* to ask] —ˌ**arro'gation** *n.* —**arrogative** (ə'rɒgətɪv) *adj.* —'**arroˌgator** *n.*

arrondissement (*French* arɔ̃dismɑ̃) *n.* (in France) **1.** the largest administrative subdivision of a department. **2.** a municipal district of certain large cities, esp. Paris. [C19: from *arrondir* to make round, from AB-[1] + *-rondir* from *rond* ROUND]

arrow ('ærəʊ) *n.* **1.** a long slender pointed weapon, usually having feathers fastened at the end as a balance, that is shot from a bow. **2.** any of various things that resemble an arrow in shape, function, or speed, such as a sign or symbol indicating direction or position. ~See also **arrows.** [Old English *arwe;* related to Old Norse *ör,* Gothic *arhvazna,* Latin *arcus* bow, ARCH[1]]

arrowgrass ('ærəʊˌgrɑːs) *n.* either of two species, **sea arrowgrass** (*Triglochin maritima*) or **marsh arrowgrass** (*T. palustris*), of monocotyledonous perennials having long thin fleshy leaves and spikes of inconspicuous flowers. [C18: named from the shape of the fruits when open]

arrowhead ('ærəʊˌhɛd) *n.* **1.** the pointed tip of an arrow, often removable from the shaft. **2.** something that resembles the head of an arrow in shape, such as a triangular decoration on garments used to reinforce joins. **3.** any aquatic herbaceous plant of the genus *Sagittaria,* esp. *S. sagittifolia,* having arrow-shaped aerial leaves and linear submerged leaves: family *Alismataceae.*

arrowroot ('ærəʊˌruːt) *n.* **1.** a white-flowered West Indian plant, *Maranta arundinacea,* whose rhizomes yield an easily digestible starch: family *Marantaceae.* **2.** the starch obtained from this plant. **3.** any of several other plants whose rhizomes or roots yield starch.

arrows ('ærəʊz) *n.* (*functioning as sing.*) *Brit.* an informal name for **darts.**

arrowwood ('ærəʊˌwʊd) *n.* any of various trees or shrubs, esp. certain viburnums, having long straight tough stems formerly used by North American Indians to make arrows.

arrowworm ('ærəʊˌwɜːm) *n.* any small marine invertebrate of the genus *Sagitta,* having an elongated transparent body with fins and prehensile oral bristles: phylum *Chaetognatha* (chaetognaths).

arroyo (ə'rɔɪəʊ) *n., pl.* **-os.** *Chiefly southwestern U.S.* a steep-sided stream bed that is usually dry except after heavy rain. [C19: from Spanish]

arse (ɑːs) *or U.S. and Canadian* **ass** *n. Taboo.* **1.** the buttocks. **2.** the anus. **3.** a stupid person; fool. **4.** *Slang.* sexual intercourse. **5.** *Austral. slang.* effrontery; cheek. ~Also called (for senses 2, 3): **arsehole** ('ɑːsˌhəʊl), (U.S., Canadian) **asshole.**

arse *or U.S. and Canadian* **ass about** *or* **around** *vb.* (*intr., adv.*) *Taboo slang.* to play the fool; act stupidly, esp. in an irritating manner.

arse *or U.S. and Canadian* **ass licker** *n. Taboo slang.* a person who curries favour. —'**arse-ˌlicking** *or U.S. and Canadian* '**ass-ˌlicking** *adj., n.*

arsenal ('ɑːsənᵊl) *n.* **1.** a store for arms, ammunition, and other military items. **2.** a workshop or factory that produces munitions. **3.** a store of anything regarded as weapons: *an arsenal of destructive arguments.* [C16: from Italian *arsenale* dockyard, from the original Venetian *arsenal* dockyard and naval store, from Arabic *dār sinā'ah,* from *dār* house + *sinā'ah* manufacture]

arsenate ('ɑːsəˌneɪt, -nɪt) *n.* a salt or ester of arsenic acid.

arsenic *n.* ('ɑːsnɪk). **1.** a toxic metalloid element, existing in several allotropic forms, that occurs principally in realgar and orpiment and as the free element. It is used in transistors, lead-based alloys, and high-temperature brasses. Symbol: As; atomic no.: 33; atomic wt.: 74.92; valency: 3 or 5; relative density: 5.73 grey; melting pt.: 817°C at a pressure of $3MN/m^2$ (grey); sublimes at 613°C (grey). **2.** a nontechnical name for **arsenic trioxide.** ~*adj.* (ɑː'sɛnɪk). **3.** of or containing arsenic, esp. in the pentavalent state. [C14: from Latin *arsenicum,* from Greek *arsenikon* yellow orpiment, from Syriac *zarnīg* (influenced in form by Greek *arsenikos* virile)]

arsenic acid *n.* a white poisonous soluble crystalline solid used in the manufacture of arsenates and insecticides. Formula: H_3AsO_4.

arsenical (ɑː'sɛnɪkᵊl) *adj.* **1.** of or containing arsenic. ~*n.* **2.** a drug or insecticide containing arsenic.

arsenic trioxide *n.* a white poisonous powder used in the manufacture of glass and as an insecticide, rat poison, and weedkiller. Also called: **arsenic.** Formula: As_2O_3.

arsenide ('ɑːsəˌnaɪd) *n.* a compound in which arsenic is the most electronegative element.

arsenious (ɑː'siːnɪəs) *or* **arsenous** ('ɑːsɪnəs) *adj.* of or containing arsenic in the trivalent state.

arsenite ('ɑːsɪˌnaɪt) *n.* a salt or ester of arsenous acid.

arsenopyrite (ˌɑːsɪnəʊ'paɪraɪt, ɑːˌsɛnə-) *n.* a white or grey metallic mineral consisting of a sulphide of iron and arsenic in monoclinic crystalline form: an ore of arsenic. Formula: FeAsS. Also called: **mispickel.**

arsine ('ɑːsiːn) *n.* a colourless poisonous gas used in the manufacture of organic compounds, to dope transistors, and as a military poisonous gas. Formula: AsH_3.

arsis ('ɑːsɪs) *n., pl.* **-ses** (-siːz). (in classical prosody) the long syllable or part on which the ictus falls in a metrical foot. Compare **thesis** (sense 6). [C18: via Late Latin from Greek, from *airein* to raise]

ARSM (in Britain) *abbrev. for* Associate of the Royal School of Mines.

ars nova ('ɑːz 'nəʊvə) *n.* a style of music of the 14th century, characterized by great freedom and variety of rhythm and melody contrasted with the strictness of the music of the 13th century. [Latin, literally: new art]

arson ('ɑːsᵊn) *n. Criminal law.* the act of intentionally or recklessly setting fire to another's property or to one's own property for some improper reason. [C17: from Old French, from Medieval Latin *ārsiō,* from Latin *ārdēre* to burn; see ARDENT] —'**arsonist** *n.*

arsphenamine (ɑːs'fɛnəmɪn, -ˌmiːn) *n.* a drug containing arsenic, formerly used in the treatment of syphilis and related infections.

ars poetica ('ɑːz pəʊ'ɛtɪkə) *n.* the art of poetry.

arsy-versy ('ɑːsɪ'vɜːsɪ) *adv. Slang.* **1.** backwards or upside down. **2.** in reverse. [C16: from ARSE + Latin *versus* turned, modelled on compounds like *hurly-burly*]

art[1] (ɑːt) *n.* **1. a.** the creation of works of beauty or other special significance. **b.** (*as modifier*): *an art movement.* **2.** the exercise of human skill (as distinguished from *nature*). **3.** imaginative skill as applied to representations of the natural world or figments of the imagination. **4. a.** the products of man's creative activities; works of art collectively, esp. of the visual arts, sometimes also music, drama, dance, and literature. **b.** (*as modifier*): *an art gallery.* See also **arts, fine art. 5.** excellence or aesthetic merit of conception or execution as exemplified by such works. **6.** any branch of the visual arts, esp. painting. **7.** (*modifier*) intended to be artistic or decorative: *art needlework.* **8. a.** any field using the techniques of art to display artistic qualities: *advertising art.* **b.** (*as modifier*): *an art film.* **9.** *Journalism.* photographs or other illustrations in a newspaper, etc. **10.** method, facility, or knack: *the art of threading a needle; the art of writing letters.* **11.** the system of rules or principles governing a particular human activity: *the art of government.* **12.** artfulness; cunning. **13. get something down to a fine art.** to become highly proficient at something through practice. ~See also **arts.** [C13: from Old French, from Latin *ars* craftsmanship]

art[2] (ɑːt) *vb. Archaic.* (used with the pronoun *thou*) a singular form of the present tense (indicative mood) of **be.** [Old English *eart*, part of *bēon* to BE]

art. *abbrev. for:* **1.** article. **2.** artificial. **3.** Also: **arty.** artillery.

-art *suffix forming nouns.* a variant of **-ard.**

artal ('ɑːtɑːl) *n.* a plural of **rotl.**

Art Deco ('dɛkəʊ) *n.* **a.** a style of interior decoration, jewellery, architecture, etc., at its height in the 1930s and characterized by geometrical shapes, stylized natural forms, and symmetrical utilitarian designs adapted to mass production. **b.** (*as modifier*): *an Art-Deco carpet.* [C20: shortened from *art décoratif*, after the *Exposition des arts décoratifs* held in Paris in 1925]

art director *n.* a person responsible for the sets and costumes in a film.

artefact *or* **artifact** ('ɑːtɪˌfækt) *n.* **1.** something made or given shape by man, such as a tool or a work of art, esp. an object of archaeological interest. **2.** anything man-made, such as a spurious experimental result. **3.** *Cytology.* a structure seen in tissue after death, fixation, staining, etc., that is not normally present in the living tissue. [C19: from Latin phrase *arte factum*, from *ars* skill + *facere* to make]

artel (ɑː'tɛl) *n.* **1.** (in the Soviet Union) a cooperative union or organization, esp. of producers, such as peasants. **2.** (in prerevolutionary Russia) a quasi-cooperative association of people engaged in the same activity. [from Russian *artel'*, from Italian *artieri* art sans, from *arte* work, from Latin *ars* ART[1]]

artemisia (ˌɑːtɪ'miːzɪə) *n.* any herbaceous perennial plant of the genus *Artemisia*, of the N hemisphere, such as mugwort, sagebrush, and wormwood: family *Compositae* (composites). [C14: via Latin from Greek, probably from *Artemis*, goddess of the hunt and the moon]

Arte Povera (*Italian* ˌarte po'vera) *n.* a style of minimal art originating in Italy in the late 1960s, making use of cheap and commonly available materials such as stones, newspapers etc. [C20: Italian, literally: poor art]

arterial (ɑː'tɪərɪəl) *adj.* **1.** of, relating to, or affecting an artery or arteries: *arterial disease.* **2.** denoting or relating to the usually bright red reoxygenated blood returning from the lungs or gills that circulates in the arteries. **3.** being a major route, esp. one with many minor branches: *an arterial road.* —**ar'terially** *adv.*

arterialize *or* **arterialise** (ɑː'tɪərɪəˌlaɪz) *vb.* (*tr.*) **1.** to change (venous blood) into arterial blood by replenishing the depleted oxygen. **2.** to vascularize (tissues). **3.** to provide with arteries. —**arˌteriali'zation** *or* **arˌteriali'sation** *n.*

arterio- *combining form.* artery or arteries: *arteriosclerosis.* [from Greek; see ARTERY]

arteriography (ɑːˌtɪərɪ'ɒgrəfɪ) *n.* the x-ray examination of an artery or arterial system after injection of a contrast medium into the bloodstream.

arteriole (ɑː'tɪərɪˌəʊl) *n. Anat.* any of the small subdivisions of an artery that form thin-walled vessels ending in capillaries. [C19: from New Latin *arteriola*, from Latin *artēria* ARTERY]

arteriosclerosis (ɑːˌtɪərɪəʊsklɪə'rəʊsɪs) *n., pl.* **-ses** (-siːz). a pathological condition of the circulatory system characterized by thickening and loss of elasticity of the arterial walls. Nontechnical name: **hardening of the arteries.** —**arteriosclerotic** (ɑːˌtɪərɪəʊsklɪə'rɒtɪk) *adj.*

arteriovenous (ɑːˌtɪərɪəʊ'viːnəs) *adj.* of, relating to, or affecting an artery and a vein.

arteritis (ˌɑːtə'raɪtɪs) *n. Pathol.* inflammation of an artery.

artery ('ɑːtərɪ) *n., pl.* **-teries. 1.** any of the tubular thick-walled muscular vessels that convey oxygenated blood from the heart to various parts of the body. Compare **pulmonary artery, vein. 2.** a major road or means of communication in any complex system. [C14: from Latin *artēria*, related to Greek *aortē* the great artery, AORTA]

artesian well (ɑː'tiːzɪən, -ʒən) *n.* a well sunk through impermeable strata into strata receiving water from an area at a higher altitude than that of the well, so that there is sufficient pressure to force water to flow upwards. [C19: from French *artésien*, from Old French *Arteis* Artois, old province, where such wells were common]

Artex ('ɑːtɛks) *n. Trademark.* a brand of coating for walls and ceilings that gives a textured finish.

art form *n.* **1.** a conventionally established form of artistic composition, such as the symphony or the sonnet. **2.** a genre or activity viewed or treated as an art form.

artful ('ɑːtfʊl) *adj.* **1.** cunning or tricky. **2.** skilful in achieving a desired end. **3.** *Archaic.* characterized by skill or art. **4.** *Archaic.* artificial. —'**artfully** *adv.* —'**artfulness** *n.*

arthralgia (ɑː'θrældʒə) *n. Pathol.* pain in a joint. —**ar'thralgic** *adj.*

arthrectomy (ɑː'θrɛktəmɪ) *n., pl.* **-mies.** surgical excision of a joint.

arthritis (ɑː'θraɪtɪs) *n.* inflammation of a joint or joints characterized by pain and stiffness of the affected parts, caused by gout, rheumatic fever, etc. See also **rheumatoid arthritis.** [C16: via Latin from Greek: see ARTHRO-, -ITIS] —**arthritic** (ɑː'θrɪtɪk) *adj., n.*

arthro- *or before a vowel* **arthr-** *combining form.* indicating a joint: *arthritis; arthropod.* [from Greek *arthron*]

arthrodia (ɑː'θrəʊdɪə) *n. Anatomy, zoology.* a joint. —**ar'throdial** *adj.*

arthrography (ɑː'θrɒgrəfɪ) *n.* the x-ray examination of a joint after injection of a contrast medium into the joint space.

arthromere ('ɑːθrəˌmɪə) *n.* any of the segments of the body of an arthropod. —**arthromeric** (ˌɑːθrə'mɛrɪk) *adj.*

arthroplasty ('ɑːθrəˌplæstɪ) *n.* surgical repair of a diseased joint.

arthropod ('ɑːθrəˌpɒd) *n.* any invertebrate of the phylum *Arthropoda*, having jointed limbs, a segmented body, and an exoskeleton made of chitin. The group includes the crustaceans, insects, arachnids, and centipedes. —**arthropodous** (ɑː'θrɒpədəs) *or* **ar'thropodal** *adj.*

arthroscope ('ɑːθrəˌskəʊp) *n.* a tubular instrument that is inserted into the capsule of a joint to examine the joint, extract tissue, etc. —ˌ**arthro'scopic** *adj.* —**arthroscopy** (ɑː'θrɒskəpɪ) *n.*

arthrospore ('ɑːθrəˌspɔː) *n.* **1.** a sporelike cell of ascomycetous fungi and some algae produced by a breaking of the hyphae. **2.** a resting sporelike cell produced by some bacteria. —ˌ**arthro'sporic** *or* ˌ**arthro'sporous** *adj.*

Arthurian (ɑː'θjʊərɪən) *adj.* of or relating to the legendary King Arthur and his Knights of the Round Table.

artic (ɑː'tɪk) *n. Informal.* short for **articulated lorry.**

artichoke ('ɑːtɪˌtʃəʊk) *n.* **1.** Also called: **globe artichoke.** a thistle-like Eurasian plant, *Cynara scolymus*, cultivated for its large edible flower head containing many fleshy scalelike bracts: family *Compositae* (composites). **2.** the unopened flower head of this plant, which can be cooked and eaten. **3.** See **Jerusalem artichoke.** [C16: from Italian *articiocco*, from Old Spanish *alcarchofa*, from Arabic *al-kharshūf*]

article ('ɑːtɪkᵊl) *n.* **1.** one of a class of objects; item: *an article of clothing.* **2.** an unspecified or previously named thing, esp. a small object: *he put the article on the table.* **3.** a distinct part of a subject or action. **4.** a written composition on a subject, often being one of several found in a magazine, newspaper, etc. **5.** *Grammar.* a kind of determiner, occurring in many languages including English, that lacks independent meaning but may serve to indicate the specificity of reference of the noun phrase with which it occurs. See also **definite article, indefinite article. 6.** a clause or section in a written document such as a treaty, contract, statute, etc. **7. in articles.** undergoing training, according to the terms of a written contract, in the legal profession. **8.** (*often cap.*) *Christianity.* See **article of faith, Thirty-nine Articles. 9.** *Archaic.* a topic or subject. ~*vb.* (*tr.*) **10.** to bind by a written contract, esp. one that governs a period of training: *an articled clerk in a solicitor's office.* **11.** *Archaic.* to accuse. [C13: from Old French, from Latin *articulus* small joint, from *artus* joint]

articled clerk *n.* a person who is being trained as a solicitor while working in a solicitor's office.

article numbering *n. Commerce.* See **ANA.**

article of faith *n.* **1.** *Christianity.* any of the clauses or propositions into which a creed or other statement of doctrine is divided. **2.** a deeply held belief.

articles of association *pl. n.* **1.** the constitution and regulations of a registered company as required by the British Companies Acts. **2.** the document containing these.

articular (ɑː'tɪkjʊlə) *adj.* of or relating to joints or to the structural components in a joint. [C15: from Latin *articulāris* concerning the joints, from *articulus* small joint; see ARTICLE]

articulate *adj.* (ɑː'tɪkjʊlɪt). **1.** able to express oneself fluently and coherently: *an articulate lecturer.* **2.** having the power of speech. **3.** distinct, clear, or definite; well-constructed: *an articulate voice; an articulate document.* **4.** *Zoology.* (of arthropods and higher vertebrates) possessing joints or jointed segments. ~*vb.* (ɑː'tɪkjʊˌleɪt). **5.** to speak or enunciate (words, syllables, etc.) clearly and distinctly. **6.** (*tr.*) to express coherently in words. **7.** (*intr.*) *Zoology.* to be jointed or form a joint. **8.** (*tr.*) to separate into jointed segments. [C16: from Latin *articulāre* to divide into joints; see ARTICLE] —**ar'ticulately** *adv.* —**ar'ticulateness** *or* **ar'ticulacy** *n.*

articulated lorry *n.* a large lorry made in two separate sections, a tractor and a trailer, connected by a pivoted bar.

articulation (ɑːˌtɪkjʊ'leɪʃən) *n.* **1.** the act or process of speaking or expressing in words. **2. a.** the process of articulating a speech sound. **b.** the sound so produced, esp. a consonant. **3.** the act or the state of being jointed together. **4.** the form or manner in which something is jointed. **5.** *Zoology.* **a.** a joint such as that between bones or arthropod segments. **b.** the way in which jointed parts are connected. **6.** *Botany.* the part of a plant at which natural separation occurs, such as the joint between leaf and stem. **7.** a joint or jointing. —**ar'ticulatory** *adj.*

articulator (ɑː'tɪkjʊˌleɪtə) *n.* **1.** a person or thing that articulates. **2.** *Phonetics.* any vocal organ that takes part in the production of a speech sound. Such organs are of two types: those that can move, such as the tongue, lips, etc. (**active articulators**), and those that remain fixed, such as the teeth, the hard palate, etc. (**passive articulators**).

articulatory loop *n. Psychol.* a short-term memory system that enables a person to remember short strings of words by rehearsing them repeatedly in his head.

articulatory phonetics *n.* (*functioning as sing.*) the branch of phonetics concerned with the production of speech sounds. Compare **acoustic phonetics, auditory phonetics.**

artifact ('ɑːtɪˌfækt) *n.* a variant spelling of **artefact.**

artifice ('ɑːtɪfɪs) *n.* **1.** a clever expedient; ingenious stratagem. **2.** crafty or subtle deception. **3.** skill; cleverness. **4.** a skilfully contrived device. **5.** *Obsolete.* craftsmanship. [C16: from Old French, from Latin *artificium* skill, from *artifex* one possessed of a specific skill, from *ars* skill + *-fex,* from *facere* to make]

artificer (ɑː'tɪfɪsə) *n.* **1.** a skilled craftsman. **2.** a clever or inventive designer. **3.** a serviceman trained in mechanics.

artificial (ˌɑːtɪ'fɪʃəl) *adj.* **1.** produced by man; not occurring naturally: *artificial materials of great strength.* **2.** made in imitation of a natural product, esp. as a substitute; not genuine: *artificial cream.* **3.** pretended; assumed; insincere: *an artificial manner.* **4.** lacking in spontaneity; affected: *an artificial laugh.* **5.** *Biology.* relating to superficial characteristics not based on the interrelationships of organisms: *an artificial classification.* [C14: from Latin *artificiālis* belonging to art, from *artificium* skill, ARTIFICE] —**artificiality** (ˌɑːtɪˌfɪʃɪ'ælɪtɪ) *n.* —ˌ**arti'ficially** *adv.*

artificial aid *n. Mountaineering.* another name for **aid** (sense 5).

artificial climbing *n.* another name for **aid climbing.**

artificial daylight *n. Physics.* artificial light having approximately the same spectral characteristics as natural daylight.

artificial disintegration *n. Physics.* radioactive transformation of a substance by bombardment with high-energy particles, such as alpha particles or neutrons.

artificial feel *n.* a system, used in aircraft that have fully powered control surfaces, providing the pilot with simulated aerodynamic forces on the controls.

artificial horizon *n.* **1.** Also called: **gyro horizon.** an aircraft instrument, using a gyroscope, that indicates the aircraft's attitude in relation to the horizontal. **2.** *Astronomy.* a level reflecting surface, such as one of mercury, that measures the altitude of a celestial body as half the angle between the body and its reflection.

artificial insemination *n.* introduction of spermatozoa into the vagina or uterus by means other than sexual union. See **AI, AIH, DI.**

artificial intelligence *n.* the study of the modelling of human mental functions by computer programs. Abbrev.: **AI.**

artificialize *or* **artificialise** (ˌɑːtɪ'fɪʃəˌlaɪz) *vb.* (*tr.*) to render artificial.

artificial kidney *n. Med.* a mechanical apparatus for performing haemodialysis.

artificial language *n.* an invented language, esp. one intended as an international medium of communication or for use with computers. Compare **natural language.**

artificial respiration *n.* **1.** any of various methods of restarting breathing after it has stopped, by manual rhythmic pressure on the chest, mouth-to-mouth breathing, etc. **2.** any method of maintaining respiration artificially, as by use of an iron lung.

artillery (ɑː'tɪlərɪ) *n.* **1.** guns, cannon, howitzers, mortars, etc., of calibre greater than 20 mm. **2.** troops or military units specializing in using such guns. **3.** the science dealing with the use of guns. **4.** devices for discharging heavy missiles, such as catapults or slings. [C14: from Old French *artillerie,* from *artillier* to equip with weapons, of uncertain origin]

artilleryman (ɑː'tɪlərɪmən) *n., pl.* **-men.** a serviceman who serves in an artillery unit.

artillery plant *n.* any of various tropical urticaceous plants of the genus *Pilea,* such as *P. microphylla,* all having stamens that discharge their pollen explosively.

artiodactyl (ˌɑːtɪəʊ'dæktɪl) *n.* **1.** any placental mammal of the order *Artiodactyla,* having hooves with an even number of toes; an even-toed ungulate. The order includes pigs, hippopotamuses, camels, deer, cattle, and antelopes. ~*adj.* **2.** of, relating to, or belonging to the order *Artiodactyla.* [C19: from New Latin *artiodactylus,* from Greek *ártios* even + *daktulos* digit] —ˌ**artio'dactylous** *adj.*

artisan ('ɑːtɪˌzæn, ˌɑːtɪ'zæn) *n.* **1.** a skilled workman; craftsman. **2.** *Obsolete.* an artist. [C16: from French, from Old Italian *artigiano,* from *arte* ART[1]] —**artisanal** (ɑː'tɪzənᵊl, 'ɑːtɪzənᵊl) *adj.*

artist ('ɑːtɪst) *n.* **1.** a person who practises or is skilled in an art, esp. painting, drawing, or sculpture. **2.** a person who displays in his work qualities required in art, such as sensibility and imagination. **3.** a person whose profession requires artistic expertise, esp. a designer: *a commercial artist.* **4.** a person skilled in some task or occupation: *an artist at bricklaying.* **5.** *Obsolete.* an artisan. **6.** *Slang.* a person devoted to or proficient in something: *a booze artist; a con artist.*

artiste (ɑː'tiːst; *French* artist) *n.* **1.** an entertainer, such as a singer or dancer. **2.** a person who is highly skilled in some occupation: *a hair artiste.*

artistic (ɑː'tɪstɪk) *adj.* **1.** of or characteristic of art or artists. **2.** performed, made, or arranged decoratively and tastefully; aesthetically pleasing. **3.** appreciative of and sensitive to beauty in art. **4.** naturally gifted with creative skill. —**ar'tistically** *adv.*

artistry ('ɑːtɪstrɪ) *n.* **1.** artistic workmanship, ability, or quality. **2.** artistic pursuits. **3.** great skill.

artless ('ɑːtlɪs) *adj.* **1.** free from deceit, guile, or artfulness; ingenuous: *an artless remark.* **2.** natural, without artifice; unpretentious: *artless elegance.* **3.** without art or skill. —**'artlessly** *adv.* —**'artlessness** *n.*

art music *n.* music written by a composer rather than passed on by oral tradition. Compare **folk music.**

Art Nouveau (ɑː nuː'vəʊ; *French* ar nuvo) *n.* **a.** a style of art and architecture of the 1890s, characterized by swelling sinuous outlines and stylized natural forms, such as flowers and leaves. **b.** (*as modifier*): *an Art-Nouveau mirror.* [French, literally: new art]

art paper *n.* a high-quality type of paper having a smooth coating of china clay or similar substance on it.

arts (ɑːts) *pl. n.* **1. a. the.** imaginative, creative, and nonscientific branches of knowledge considered collectively, esp. as studied academically. **b.** (*as modifier*): *an arts degree.* **2.** See **fine art.** **3.** cunning or crafty actions or plots; schemes.

art union *n. Austral. and N.Z.* a lottery, usually with prizes other than cash.

artwork ('ɑːtˌwɜːk) *n.* all the original nontextual matter in a publication, esp. the illustrations.

arty ('ɑːtɪ) *adj.* **artier, artiest.** *Informal.* having an ostentatious or affected interest in or desire to imitate artists or artistic standards. —**'artiness** *n.*

arty-crafty *adj. Informal.* affectedly artistic, esp. in a homespun or rural style.

arum ('ɛərəm) *n.* **1.** any plant of the aroid genus *Arum,* of Europe and the Mediterranean region, having arrow-shaped leaves and a typically white spathe. See also **cuckoopint.** **2.** **arum lily.** another name for **calla** (sense 1). [C16: from Latin, a variant of *aros* wake-robin, from Greek *aron*]

arundinaceous (əˌrʌndɪ'neɪʃəs) *adj. Botany.* resembling a reed. [C17: from Latin *harundināceus,* from *harundō* a reed]

aruspex (ə'rʌspɛks) *n., pl.* **-pices** (-pɪˌsiːz). a variant spelling of **haruspex.**

arvo ('ɑːvəʊ) *n. Austral. informal.* afternoon.

-ary *suffix.* **1.** (*forming adjectives*) of; related to; belonging to: *cautionary; rudimentary.* **2.** (*forming nouns*) **a.** a person connected with or engaged in: *missionary.* **b.** a thing relating to; a place for: *commentary; aviary.* [from Latin *-ārius, -āria, -ārium*]

Aryan *or* **Arian** ('ɛərɪən) *n.* **1.** (in Nazi ideology) a Caucasian of non-Jewish descent, esp. of the Nordic type. **2.** a member of any of the peoples supposedly descended from the Indo-Europeans, esp. a speaker of an Iranian or Indic language in ancient times. ~*adj.* **3.** of, relating to, or characteristic of an Aryan or Aryans. ~*adj., n.* **4.** *Archaic.* Indo-European. [C19: from Sanskrit *ārya* of noble birth]

Aryanize *or* **Aryanise** ('ɛərɪəˌnaɪz) *vb.* (*tr.*) (in Nazi ideology) to purge (politics and society) of all non-Aryan elements or people; make characteristically Aryan.

aryl ('ærɪl) *n.* **1.** (*modifier*) *Chem.* of, consisting of, or containing an aromatic group: *aryl group or radical.* **2.** an organometallic compound in which a metal atom is bound to an aryl or molecule. [C20: from AR(OMATIC) + -YL]

arytenoid *or* **arytaenoid** (ˌærɪ'tiːnɔɪd) *adj. also* **arytenoidal.** **1.** denoting either of two small cartilages of the larynx that are attached to the vocal cords. **2.** denoting any of three small muscles of the larynx that narrow the space between the vocal cords. ~*n.* **3.** an arytenoid cartilage or muscle. [C18: from New Latin *arytaenoīdes,* from Greek *arutainoeidēs* shaped like a ladle, from *arutaina* ladle]

as[1] (æz; *unstressed* əz) *conj.* (*subordinating*) **1.** (often preceded by *just*) while; when; at the time that: *he caught me as I was leaving.* **2.** in the way that: *dancing as only she can.* **3.** that which; what: *I did as I was told.* **4.** (of) which fact, event, etc. (referring to the previous statement): *to become wise, as we all know, is not easy.* **5. as it were.** in a way; so to speak; as if it were really so. **6. as you were. a.** a military command to return to the previous position. **b.** a statement to withdraw something just said. **7.**

since; seeing that: *as you're in charge here, you'd better tell me where to wait.* **8.** in the same way that: *he died of cancer, as his father had done.* **9.** in spite of the extent to which: *intelligent as you are, I suspect you will fail.* **10.** for instance: *capital cities, as London.* ~*adv., conj.* **11. a.** used correlatively before an adjective or adverb and before a noun phrase or a clause to indicate identity of extent, amount, etc.: *she is as heavy as her sister; she is as heavy now as she used to be.* **b.** used with this sense after a noun phrase introduced by *the same: the same height as her sister.* ~*prep.* **12.** in the role of; being: *as his friend, I am probably biased.* **13. as for** *or* **to.** with reference to: *as for my past, I'm not telling you anything.* **14. as from** *or U.S. and Canadian* **of.** *Formal.* (in expressions of time) from: *fares will rise as from January 11.* **15. as if** *or* **though.** as it would be if: *he talked as if he knew all about it.* **16. as (it) is.** in the existing state of affairs: *as it is, I shall have difficulty finishing all this work, without any more.* **17. as per.** See **per** (sense 3). **18. as regards.** See **regard** (sense 6). **19. as such.** See **such** (sense 3). **20. such as.** See **such** (sense 5). **21. as was.** in a previous state. **22. as well.** See **well**[1] (sense 13). **23. as yet.** up to now; so far. [Old English *alswā* likewise; see ALSO]

as[2] (æs) *n.* **1.** an ancient Roman unit of weight approximately equal to 1 pound troy (373 grams). **2.** the standard monetary unit and copper coin of ancient Rome. [C17: from Latin *ās* unity, probably of Etruscan origin]

As *symbol for:* **1.** *Chemistry.* arsenic. **2.** altostratus.

AS *abbrev. for:* **1.** Also: **A.S.** Anglo-Saxon. **2.** antisubmarine.

As. *abbrev. for:* **1.** Asia(n). **2.** Asiatic.

ASA *abbrev. for:* **1.** (in Britain) Amateur Swimming Association. **2.** (in Britain) Advertising Standards Authority. **3.** (in the U.S.) American Standards Association.

ASA/BS *abbrev.* an expression of the speed of a photographic film, given as 0.8/*E*, where *E* is the exposure of a point 0.1 density units above the fog level on the characteristic curve of a particular sensitized material. Compare **DIN** (sense 1), **ISO rating.** [C20: from *American Standards Association/British Standard*]

asafoetida *or* **asafetida** (ˌæsəˈfɛtɪdə) *n.* a bitter resin with an unpleasant onion-like smell, obtained from the roots of some umbelliferous plants of the genus *Ferula:* formerly used to treat flatulence, etc. [C14: from Medieval Latin, from *asa* gum (compare Persian *azā* mastic) + Latin *foetidus* evil-smelling, FETID]

asana (ˈɑːsənə) *n.* any of various postures in yoga. See also **hatha yoga.** [Sanskrit]

Asantehene (æˈʃæntɪˌhɛnɪ) *n.* the ruler of the Ashanti people of Ghana.

a.s.a.p. *abbrev. for* as soon as possible.

asarabacca (ˌæsərəˈbækə) *n.* a perennial evergreen Eurasian plant, *Asarum europaeum,* having kidney-shaped leaves and a single brownish flower: family *Aristolochiaceae.*

asarum (ˈæsərəm) *n.* the dried strong-scented root of the wild ginger plant: a flavouring agent and source of an aromatic oil used in perfumery, formerly used in medicine. [C19: via New Latin from Latin: hazelwort, from Greek *asaron*]

asbestos (æsˈbɛstɒs, -təs) *n.* **a.** any of the fibrous amphibole and serpentine minerals, esp. chrysotile and tremolite, that are incombustible and resistant to chemicals. It was formerly widely used in the form of fabric or board as a heat-resistant structural material. **b.** (*as modifier*): *asbestos matting.* [C14 (originally applied to a mythical stone the heat of which could not be extinguished): via Latin from Greek: from *asbestos* inextinguishable, from A-[1] + *sbennunai* to extinguish] —**asˈbestine** *adj.*

asbestosis (ˌæsbɛsˈtəʊsɪs) *n.* inflammation of the lungs resulting from chronic inhalation of asbestos particles.

ASBSBSW (in Britain) *abbrev. for* Amalgamated Society of Boilermakers, Shipwrights, Blacksmiths, and Structural Workers.

Asc. *Astrology. abbrev. for* Ascendant.

ASCAP (ˈæskæp) *n. acronym for* American Society of Composers, Authors, and Publishers.

ascariasis (ˌæskəˈraɪəsɪs) *n.* infestation of the intestines with the roundworm *Ascaris lumbricoides,* causing abdominal pain, nausea and vomiting, weight loss, etc.

ascarid (ˈæskərɪd) *n.* any parasitic nematode worm of the family *Ascaridae,* such as the common roundworm of man and pigs. [C14: from New Latin *ascaridae,* from Greek *askarides,* plural of *askaris*]

ascend (əˈsɛnd) *vb.* **1.** to go or move up (a ladder, hill, slope, etc.); mount; climb. **2.** (*intr.*) to slope or incline upwards. **3.** (*intr.*) to rise to a higher point, level, degree, etc. **4.** to follow (a river) upstream towards its source. **5.** to trace (a genealogy, etc.) back in time. **6.** to sing or play (a scale, arpeggio, etc.) from the lower to higher notes. **7. ascend the throne.** to become king or queen. [C14: from Latin *ascendere,* from *scandere*]

ascendancy, ascendency (əˈsɛndənsɪ) *or* **ascendance, ascendence** *n.* the condition of being dominant, esp. through superior economic or political power.

ascendant *or* **ascendent** (əˈsɛndənt) *adj.* **1.** proceeding upwards; rising. **2.** dominant, superior, or influential. **3.** *Botany.* another term for **ascending.** ~*n.* **4.** *Rare.* an ancestor. **5.** a position or condition of dominance, superiority or control. **6.** *Astrology.* (*sometimes cap.*) **a.** a point on the ecliptic that rises on the eastern horizon at a particular moment and changes as the earth rotates on its axis. **b.** the sign of the zodiac containing this point. **7. in the ascendant.** increasing in influence, prosperity, etc.

ascender (əˈsɛndə) *n.* **1.** *Printing.* **a.** the part of certain lowercase letters, such as *b* or *h,* that extends above the body of the letter. **b.** any letter having such a part. **2.** a person or thing that ascends. **3.** another word for **ascendeur.**

ascendeur (*French* asɑ̃dœr) *n. Mountaineering.* a metal grip that is threaded on a rope and can be alternately tightened and slackened as an aid to climbing the rope: used attached to slings for the feet and waist. Also called: **ascender.** [C20]

ascending (əˈsɛndɪŋ) *adj.* **1.** moving upwards; rising. **2.** *Botany.* sloping or curving upwards: *the ascending stem of a vine.*

ascension (əˈsɛnʃən) *n.* **1.** the act of ascending. **2.** *Astronomy.* the rising of a star above the horizon. —**asˈcensional** *adj.*

Ascension (əˈsɛnʃən) *n. New Testament.* the passing of Jesus Christ from earth into heaven (Acts 1:9); celebrated on **Ascension Day,** the 40th day after Easter.

Ascension Day *n. Christianity.* the 40th day after Easter, when the Ascension of Christ into heaven is celebrated.

ascensionist (əˈsɛnʃənɪst) *n. Mountaineering.* a person who has completed a mountain ascent, esp. a notable one.

Ascensiontide (əˈsɛnʃənˌtaɪd) *n.* the ten days from Ascension Day to the day before Whit Sunday.

ascent (əˈsɛnt) *n.* **1.** the act of ascending; climb or upward movement: *the ascent of hot gases.* **2.** an upward slope; incline or gradient. **3.** movement back through time, as in tracing of earlier generations (esp. in the phrase **line of ascent**).

ascertain (ˌæsəˈteɪn) *vb.* (*tr.*) **1.** to determine or discover definitely. **2.** *Archaic.* to make certain. [C15: from Old French *acertener* to make certain] —ˌ**ascerˈtainable** *adj.* —ˌ**ascerˈtainably** *adv.* —ˌ**ascerˈtainment** *n.*

ascesis (əˈsiːsɪs) *n., pl.* **-ses** (-siːz). the exercise of self-discipline. [C19: from Greek, from *askein* to exercise]

ascetic (əˈsɛtɪk) *n.* **1.** a person who practises great self-denial and austerities and abstains from worldly comforts and pleasures, esp. for religious reasons. **2.** (in the early Christian Church) a monk. ~*adj. also* **asˈcetical.** **3.** rigidly abstinent or abstemious; austere. **4.** of or relating to ascetics or asceticism. **5.** intensely rigorous in religious austerities. [C17: from Greek *askētikos,* from *askētēs,* from *askein* to exercise] —**asˈcetically** *adv.*

asceticism (əˈsɛtɪˌsɪzəm) *n.* **1.** the behaviour, discipline, or outlook of an ascetic, esp. of a religious ascetic. **2.** the principles of ascetic practices, esp. in the early Christian Church. **3.** the theory and system of ascetic practices.

asci (ˈæsaɪ, ˈæskaɪ) *n.* the plural of **ascus.**

ascidian (əˈsɪdɪən) *n.* **1.** any minute marine invertebrate animal of the class *Ascidiacea,* such as the sea squirt, the adults of which are degenerate and sedentary: subphylum *Tunicata* (tunicates). **2. ascidian tadpole.** the free-swimming larva of an ascidian, having a tadpole-like tail containing the notochord and nerve cord. ~*adj.* **3.** of, relating to, or belonging to the *Ascidiacea.*

ascidium (əˈsɪdɪəm) *n., pl.* **-cidia** (-ˈsɪdɪə). part of a plant that is shaped like a pitcher, such as the modified leaf of the pitcher plant. [C18: from New Latin, from Greek *askidion* a little bag, from *askos* bag]

ASCII (ˈæskiː) *n. acronym for* American standard code for information interchange: a computer code for representing alphanumeric characters.

ascites (əˈsaɪtiːz) *n., pl.* **ascites.** *Pathol.* accumulation of serous fluid in the peritoneal cavity. [C14: from Latin: a kind of dropsy, from Greek *askitēs,* from *askos* wineskin] —**ascitic** (əˈsɪtɪk) *adj.*

asclepiadaceous (æˌskliːpɪəˈdeɪʃəs) *adj.* of, relating to, or belonging to the *Asclepiadaceae,* a family of mostly tropical and subtropical flowering plants, including the milkweed and swallowwort, having pollen in the form of a waxy mass (pollinium). [C19: from New Latin *Asclēpias* genus name, from Latin, from Greek *asklēpias,* named after *Asclepius,* god of healing]

Asclepiadean (æˌskliːpɪəˈdiːən) *Prosody.* ~*adj.* **1.** of or relating to a type of classical verse line consisting of a spondee, two or three choriambs, and an iamb. ~*n.* **2.** Also called: **Asclepiad.** an Asclepiadean verse. [C17: via Latin from Greek *Asklēpiadēs* (about 270 B.C.), who invented the verse form]

asclepias (əˈskliːpɪəs) *n.* any plant of the perennial mostly tuberous genus *Asclepias;* some are grown as garden or greenhouse plants for their showy orange-scarlet or purple flowers: family *Asclepiadaceae.* Sometimes called also: **milkweed.** [Greek *asklēpias* swallowwort]

asco- *combining form.* indicating a bladder or ascus: *ascomycete.* [from Greek *askos* bladder]

ascocarp (ˈæskəˌkɑːp) *n.* (in some ascomycetous fungi) a globular structure containing the asci. See **apothecium, perithecium.**

ascogonium (ˌæskəˈgəʊnɪəm) *n., pl.* **-nia** (-nɪə). a female reproductive body in some ascomycetous fungi in which, after fertilization, the asci develop.

ascomycete (ˌæskəmaɪˈsiːt) *n.* any fungus of the class *Ascomycetes,* in which the spores (ascospores) are formed inside a club-shaped cell (ascus). The group includes yeast, penicillium, aspergillus, truffles, and certain mildews. —ˌ**ascomyˈcetous** *adj.*

ascorbic acid (əˈskɔːbɪk) *n.* a white crystalline vitamin present in plants, esp. citrus fruits, tomatoes, and green vegetables. A deficiency in the diet of man leads to scurvy. Formula: $C_6H_8O_6$. Also called: **vitamin C.** [C20: *ascorbic* from A-[1] + SCORB(UT)IC]

ascospore ('æskəˌspɔː) *n.* one of the spores (usually eight in number) that are produced in an ascus.

ascot ('æskət) *n.* a cravat with wide square ends, usually secured with an ornamental stud. [C20: named after *Ascot*, a town in S England, where it was probably first worn at horse race meetings]

ascribe (əˈskraɪb) *vb.* (*tr.*) **1.** to credit or assign, as to a particular origin or period: *to ascribe parts of a play to Shakespeare.* **2.** to attribute as a quality; consider as belonging to: *to ascribe beauty to youth.* [C15: from Latin *ascrībere* to enrol, from *ad* in addition + *scrībere* to write] —**asˈcribable** *adj.*

ascription (əˈskrɪpʃən) *or* **adscription** (ədˈskrɪpʃən) *n.* **1.** the act of ascribing. **2.** a statement ascribing something to someone, esp. praise to God. [C16: from Latin *ascrīptiō*, from *ascrībere* to ASCRIBE]

ascus ('æskəs) *n., pl.* **asci** ('æsaɪ, 'æskaɪ). a saclike structure that produces (usually) eight ascospores during sexual reproduction in ascomycetous fungi such as yeasts and mildews. [C19: from New Latin, from Greek *askos* bag]

ASDE *abbrev. for* Airport Surface Detection Equipment: a radar system that is used by aircraft controllers to assist in the safe manoeuvring of aircraft on the ground.

asdic ('æzdɪk) *n.* an early form of **sonar.** [C20: from *A(nti-)S(ubmarine) D(etection) I(nvestigation) C(ommittee)*]

-ase *suffix forming nouns.* indicating an enzyme: *oxidase.* [abstracted from DIASTASE]

ASEAN ('æsɪˌæn) *n. acronym for* Association of Southeast Asian Nations.

aseismic (eɪˈsaɪzmɪk) *adj.* **1.** denoting a region free of earthquakes. **2.** (*not in technical use*) denoting a region free of all but a few small earthquakes. **3.** (of buildings, etc.) designed to withstand earthquakes.

aseity (eɪˈsiːɪtɪ) *n. Philosophy.* existence derived from itself, having no other source. [C17: from Medieval Latin *aseitas*, from Latin *ā* from + *sē* oneself]

asepalous (æˈsɛpələs) *adj.* (of a plant or flower) having no sepals.

asepsis (əˈsɛpsɪs, eɪ-) *n.* **1.** the state of being free from living pathogenic organisms. **2.** the methods of achieving a germ-free condition. —**aˈseptic** *adj.*

aseptate (eɪˈsɛpteɪt) *adj. Biology.* not divided into cells or sections by septa.

asexual (eɪˈsɛksjʊəl, æ-) *adj.* **1.** having no apparent sex or sex organs. **2.** (of reproduction) not involving the fusion of male and female gametes, as in vegetative reproduction, fission, and budding. —**ˌasexuˈality** *n.* —**aˈsexually** *adv.*

ash[1] (æʃ) *n.* **1.** the nonvolatile products and residue formed when matter is burnt. **2.** any of certain compounds formed by burning. See **soda ash. 3.** fine particles of lava thrown out by an erupting volcano. **4.** a light silvery grey colour, often with a brownish tinge. ~See also **ashes.** [Old English *æsce;* related to Old Norse, Old High German *aska*, Gothic *azgō*, Latin *aridus* dry]

ash[2] (æʃ) *n.* **1.** any oleaceous tree of the genus *Fraxinus*, esp. *F. excelsior* of Europe and Asia, having compound leaves, clusters of small greenish flowers, and winged seeds. **2.** the close-grained durable wood of any of these trees, used for tool handles, etc. **3.** any of several trees resembling the ash, such as the mountain ash. [Old English *æsc;* related to Old Norse *askr*, Old Saxon, Old High German *ask*, Lithuanian *uosis*]

ash[3] (æʃ) *n.* the digraph *æ*, as in Old English, representing a front vowel approximately like that of the *a* in Modern English *hat.* The character is also used to represent this sound in the International Phonetic Alphabet.

ASH (æʃ) *n.* (in Britain) *acronym for* Action on Smoking and Health.

ashamed (əˈʃeɪmd) *adj.* (*usually postpositive*) **1.** overcome with shame, guilt, or remorse. **2.** (foll. by *of*) suffering from feelings of inferiority or shame in relation to (a person, thing, or deed). **3.** (foll. by *to*) unwilling through fear of humiliation, shame, etc. [Old English *āscamod*, past participle of *āscamian* to shame, from *scamu* SHAME] —**ashamedly** (əˈʃeɪmɪdlɪ) *adv.*

Ashanti (əˈʃæntɪ) *n., pl.* **-ti** *or* **-tis.** a native or inhabitant of Ashanti, a region of central Ghana.

A shares *pl. n. Brit.* those ordinary shares in a company which carry restricted voting rights or other restrictions.

ash blond *n.* **1. a.** a very light blond colour. **b.** (*as adj.*): *ash-blond hair.* **2.** a person whose hair is this colour. ~Also: **ash blonde** *fem.*

ash can *n.* a U.S. word for **dustbin.** Also called: **garbage can, ash bin, trash can.**

Ash Can School *n.* a group of U.S. painters including Robert Henri and later George Bellows, founded in 1907, noted for their depiction of the sordid aspects of city life.

ashen[1] ('æʃən) *adj.* **1.** drained of colour; pallid. **2.** consisting of or resembling ashes. **3.** of a pale greyish colour.

ashen[2] ('æʃən) *adj.* of, relating to, or made from the ash tree or its timber.

ashes ('æʃɪz) *pl. n.* **1.** ruins or remains, as after destruction or burning: *the city was left in ashes.* **2.** the remains of a human body after cremation.

Ashes ('æʃɪz) *pl. n.* **the.** a cremated cricket bail in a pottery urn now preserved at Lord's. Victory or defeat in test matches between England and Australia is referred to as winning, losing, or retaining the Ashes. [from the mock obituary of English cricket in *The Times* in 1882 after a great Australian victory at the Oval, in which it was said that the body would be cremated and the ashes taken to Australia]

ashet ('æʃɪt) *n. Scot. and northern English dialect.* a shallow oval dish or large plate. [C16: from French *assiette*]

Ashkenazi (ˌæʃkəˈnɑːzɪ) *n., pl.* **-zim** (-zɪm). **1.** (*modifier*) of or relating to the Jews of Germany and E Europe. **2.** a Jew of German or E European descent. **3.** the pronunciation of Hebrew used by these Jews. ~ Compare **Sephardi.** [C19: Late Hebrew, from Hebrew *Ashkenaz*, the son of Gomer (Genesis 10:3; I Chronicles 1:6), a descendant of Noah through Japheth, and hence taken to be identified with the ancient Ascanians of Phrygia and, in the medieval period, the Germans]

ashkey ('æʃkiː) *n.* the winged fruit of the ash.

ashlar *or* **ashler** ('æʃlə) *n.* **1.** a block of hewn stone with straight edges for use in building. **2.** Also called: **ashlar veneer.** a thin dressed stone with straight edges, used to face a wall. **3.** masonry made of ashlar. [C14: from Old French *aisselier* crossbeam, from *ais* board, from Latin *axis* axletree; see AXIS[1]]

ashlaring ('æʃlərɪŋ) *n.* **1.** ashlars collectively. **2.** a number of short upright boards forming the wall of a garret, cutting off the acute angle between the rafters and the floor.

ashore (əˈʃɔː) *adv.* **1.** towards or onto land from the water: *we swam ashore.* ~*adj.* (*postpositive*), *adv.* **2.** on land, having come from the water: *a day ashore before sailing.*

ashplant ('æʃˌplɑːnt) *n.* a walking stick made from an ash sapling.

ashram ('æʃrəm, 'ɑːʃ-) *n.* **1.** a religious retreat or community where a Hindu holy man lives. **2.** a house that provides accommodation for destitute people. [from Sanskrit *āśrama*, from *ā-* near + *śrama* religious exertion]

ashtray ('æʃˌtreɪ) *n.* a receptacle for tobacco ash, cigarette butts, etc.

Ash Wednesday *n.* the first day of Lent, named from the practice of Christians of placing ashes on their heads as a sign of penitence.

ashy ('æʃɪ) *adj.* **ashier, ashiest. 1.** of a pale greyish colour; ashen. **2.** consisting of, covered with, or resembling ash.

Asian ('eɪʃən, 'eɪʒən) *adj.* **1.** of or relating to Asia, the largest of the continents, or to any of its peoples or languages. ~*n.* **2.** a native or inhabitant of Asia or a descendant of one.

▷**Usage.** *Asian* is used in formal writing as a noun indicating a person from Asia. The use of the word *Asiatic* in this sense is regarded by some people as offensive.

Asian flu *n.* a type of influenza recurring in worldwide epidemics, caused by a virus (A2 strain or subsequent antigenic variants), which apparently originated in China in 1957.

Asian pear *n.* **1.** a tropical pear tree, esp. any of several varieties of Japanese pear *Pyrus serotina.* **2.** Also called: **nashi.** the fruit of the Japanese pear, which resembles a large yellow apple, has crisp juicy flesh, and is cultivated in Japan, Korea, the U.S., and New Zealand.

Asiatic (ˌeɪʃɪˈætɪk, -zɪ-) *n., adj.* another word for **Asian.**

▷**Usage.** See at **Asian.**

Asiatic beetle *n.* a Japanese scarabaeid beetle, *Anomala orientalis*, introduced into Hawaii and the northeastern U.S.: a serious pest of sugar cane and cereal crops because it destroys the roots.

Asiatic cholera *n.* another name for **cholera.**

aside (əˈsaɪd) *adv.* **1.** on or to one side: *they stood aside to let him pass.* **2.** out of hearing; in or into seclusion: *he took her aside to tell her of his plan.* **3.** away from oneself: *he threw the book aside.* **4.** out of mind or consideration: *he put aside all fears.* **5.** in or into reserve: *to put aside money for old age.* **6. aside from.** (*prep.*) *Chiefly U.S. and Canadian.* **a.** besides: *he has money aside from his possessions.* **b.** except for: *he has nothing aside from the clothes he stands in.* Compare **apart** (sense 7). ~*n.* **7.** something spoken by an actor, intended to be heard by the audience, but not by the others on stage. **8.** any confidential statement spoken in undertones. **9.** a digression.

A-side *n.* the side of a gramophone record regarded as the more important one.

asinine ('æsɪˌnaɪn) *adj.* **1.** obstinate or stupid. **2.** resembling an ass. [C16: from Latin *asinīnus*, from *asinus* ASS[1]] —**ˈasiˌninely** *adv.* —**asininity** (ˌæsɪˈnɪnɪtɪ) *n.*

ASIO *abbrev. for* Australian Security Intelligence Organization.

-asis *suffix forming nouns.* a variant of **-iasis.**

A sizes *or* **A series** *n.* a series of paper sizes approved by the International Standards Organization, running from 2AO to A7, each size (defined in mm) being half as large as the one preceding it, as follows: **2AO,** 1189 × 1682; **AO,** 841 × 1189; **A1,** 594 × 841; **A2,** 420 × 594; **A3,** 297 × 420; **A4,** 210 × 297; **A5,** 148 × 210; **A6,** 105 × 148; **A7,** 74 × 105.

ask (ɑːsk) *vb.* **1.** (often foll. by *about*) to put a question (to); request an answer (from): *she asked (him) about God.* **2.** (*tr.*) to inquire about: *she asked him the time of the train; she asked the way.* **3.** (*tr.*) to direct or put (a question). **4.** (*may take a clause as object or an infinitive;* often foll. by *for*) to make a request or demand: *she asked (him) for information; they asked for a deposit.* **5.** (*tr.*) to demand or expect (esp. in the phrases **ask a lot of, ask too much of**). **6.** (*tr.*) Also: **ask out, ask over.** to request (a person) politely to come or go to a place; invite: *he asked her to the* *party.* 7. (*tr.*) to need; require: *the job asks both time and patience.* 8. (*tr.*) *Archaic.* to proclaim (marriage banns). ~See also **ask after, ask for.** [Old English *āscian;* related to Old Frisian *āskia,* Old Saxon *ēscon,* Old High German *eiscōn*] —'**asker** *n.*

ask after *or* (*Scot.*) **ask for** *vb.* (*prep.*) to make inquiries about the health of (someone): *he asked after her mother.*

askance (ə'skæns) *or* **askant** (ə'skænt) *adv.* 1. with an oblique glance. 2. with doubt or mistrust. [C16: of unknown origin]

askari (as'kaːri) *n.* (in East Africa) a soldier or policeman. [C19: from Arabic: soldier]

askew (ə'skjuː) *adv., adj.* at an oblique angle; towards one side; awry.

ask for *vb.* (*prep.*) 1. to try to obtain by requesting: *he asked for help.* 2. (*intr.*) *Informal.* to behave in a provocative manner that is regarded as inviting (trouble): *she's asking for trouble; you're asking for it.* 3. *Scot.* to ask after.

asking price *n.* the price suggested by a seller but usually considered to be subject to bargaining.

ASL *abbrev. for* American Sign Language. See **Ameslan.**

aslant (ə'slɑːnt) *adv.* 1. at a slant. ~*prep.* 2. at a slant across or athwart.

asleep (ə'sliːp) *adj.* (*postpositive*) 1. in or into a state of sleep. 2. in or into a dormant or inactive state. 3. (of limbs, esp. when the blood supply to them has been restricted) numb; lacking sensation. 4. *Euphemistic.* dead.

ASLEF ('æzlɛf) *n.* (in Britain) *acronym for* Associated Society of Locomotive Engineers and Firemen.

A/S level *n. Brit.* 1. **a.** an advanced level of a subject taken for the General Certificate of Education, with a smaller course content than an A level. **b.** (*as modifier*): *A/S-level English.* 2. a pass in a subject at A/S level: *I've got three A/S levels.*

ASLIB ('æzlɪb) *n. acronym for* Association of Special Libraries and Information Bureaux.

aslope (ə'sləʊp) *adv., adj.* (*postpositive*) sloping.

ASM *abbrev. for* air-to-surface missile.

asocial (eɪ'səʊʃəl) *adj.* 1. avoiding contact; not gregarious. 2. unconcerned about the welfare of others. 3. hostile to society or social practices.

asp[1] (æsp) *n.* 1. the venomous snake, probably *Naja haje* (Egyptian cobra), that caused the death of Cleopatra and was formerly used by the Pharaohs as a symbol of their power over life and death. See also **uraeus.** 2. Also called: **asp viper.** a viper, *Vipera aspis,* that occurs in S Europe and is very similar to but smaller than the adder. 3. **horned asp.** another name for **horned viper.** [C15: from Latin *aspis,* from Greek]

asp[2] (æsp) *n.* an archaic name for the **aspen.** [Old English *æspe;* related to Old Norse *ösp,* Old High German *aspa*]

asparagine (ə'spærəˌdʒiːn, -dʒɪn) *n.* a nonessential amino acid, a component of proteins. [C19: from French, from Latin *asparagus* ASPARAGUS + -INE[2]]

asparagus (ə'spærəgəs) *n.* 1. any Eurasian liliaceous plant of the genus *Asparagus,* esp. the widely cultivated *A. officinalis,* having small scaly or needle-like leaves. 2. the succulent young shoots of *A. officinalis,* which may be cooked and eaten. 3. **asparagus fern.** a fernlike species of asparagus, *A. plumosus,* native to southern Africa. [C15: from Latin, from Greek *asparagos,* of obscure origin]

aspartame (ə'spɑːˌteɪm) *n.* an artificial sweetener produced from aspartic acid. Formula: $C_{14}H_{18}N_2O_5$. [C20: from ASPART(IC ACID) + (*phenyl*)*a*(*lanine*) *m*(*ethyl*) *e*(*ster*)]

aspartic acid (ə'spɑːtɪk) *n.* a nonessential amino acid that is a component of proteins and acts as a neurotransmitter. [C19: from ASPAR(AGUS) + -IC]

aspect ('æspɛkt) *n.* 1. appearance to the eye; visual effect: *the physical aspect of the landscape.* 2. a distinct feature or element in a problem, situation, etc.; facet: *to consider every aspect of a problem.* 3. the way in which a problem, idea, etc., may be considered: *to consider a problem from every aspect.* 4. a facial expression; manner of appearing: *a severe aspect.* 5. a position facing a particular direction; outlook: *the southern aspect of a house.* 6. a view in a certain direction: *a good aspect of the village from the tower.* 7. a surface that faces in a given direction: *the ventral aspect of a fish.* 8. *Astrology.* any of several specific angular distances between two planets or a planet and the Ascendant or Midheaven measured, from the earth, in degrees along the ecliptic. 9. *Grammar.* a category of verbs or verbal inflections that expresses such features as the continuity, repetition, or completedness of the action described. Compare **perfective** (sense 2), **progressive** (senses 8, 10). 10. *Botany.* **a.** the extent to which a plant habitat is exposed to the sun, wind, etc. **b.** the effect of the seasons on the appearance of plants. 11. *Archaic.* glance or gaze. [C14: from Latin *aspectus* a sight, from *aspicere,* from *ad-* to, at + *specere* to look]

aspect ratio *n.* 1. the ratio of width to height of a picture on a television or cinema screen. 2. *Aeronautics.* the ratio of the span of a wing to its mean chord.

aspectual (æ'spɛktjʊəl) *adj.* of or relating to grammatical aspect.

aspen ('æspən) *n.* 1. any of several trees of the salicaceous genus *Populus,* such as *P. tremula* of Europe, in which the leaves are attached to the stem by long flattened stalks so that they quiver in the wind. Archaic name: **asp.** ~*adj.* 2. *Archaic, chiefly literary.* trembling. [Old English *æspe;* see ASP[2]]

asper ('æspə) *n.* a Turkish monetary unit, formerly a silver coin, worth 1/20 of a piastre. [from Turkish, ultimately from Latin: rough, harsh]

asperate ('æspəˌreɪt) *or* **asperous** ('æspərəs) *adj.* (of plant parts) having a rough surface due to a covering of short stiff hairs.

Asperges (æ'spɜːdʒiːz) *n. R.C. Church.* 1. a short rite preceding Mass, in which the celebrant sprinkles those present with holy water to the accompaniment of the chant *Asperges me, Domine.* 2. the chant opening with these words. [C16: from Latin *Asperges* (*me hyssopo*) Thou shalt purge (me with hyssop)]

aspergillosis (æˌspɜːdʒɪ'ləʊsɪs) *n., pl.* **-ses** (-siːz). a rare fungal infection, esp. of the mucous membranes or lungs, caused by various species of *Aspergillus.* [C19: from New Latin, from ASPERGILLUS]

aspergillum (ˌæspə'dʒɪləm) *or* **aspergill** ('æspədʒɪl) *n., pl.* **-gilla** (-'dʒɪlə), **-gillums,** *or* **-gills.** another term for **aspersorium** (sense 2). [C17: from New Latin *aspergillum,* from Latin *aspergere,* from *spargere* to sprinkle]

aspergillus (ˌæspə'dʒɪləs) *n., pl.* **-gilli** (-'dʒɪlaɪ). any ascomycetous fungus of the genus *Aspergillus,* having chains of spores attached like bristles to a club-shaped stalk: family *Aspergillaceae.* [C19: from New Latin: *aspergillum* (from its similar appearance)]

asperity (æ'spɛrɪtɪ) *n., pl.* **-ties.** 1. roughness or sharpness of temper. 2. roughness or harshness of a surface, sound, taste, etc. 3. a condition hard to endure; affliction. 4. *Physics.* the elastically compressed region of contact between two surfaces caused by the normal force. [C16: from Latin *asperitās,* from *asper* rough]

aspermia (ə'spɜːmɪə) *n. Pathol.* the failure to form or emit semen.

asperse (ə'spɜːs) *vb.* (*tr.*) 1. to spread false rumours about; defame. 2. *Rare.* to sprinkle, as with water in baptism. [C15: from Latin *aspersus,* from *aspergere* to sprinkle] —**as'perser** *n.* —**as'persive** *adj.* —**as'persively** *adv.*

aspersion (ə'spɜːʃən) *n.* 1. a disparaging or malicious remark; slanderous accusation (esp. in the phrase **cast aspersions (on)**). 2. the act of defaming. 3. *Rare.* the act of sprinkling, esp. of water in baptism.

aspersorium (ˌæspə'sɔːrɪəm) *n., pl.* **-ria** (-rɪə) *or* **-riums.** *R.C. Church.* 1. a basin containing holy water with which worshippers sprinkle themselves. 2. Also called: **aspergillum.** a perforated instrument used to sprinkle holy water.

asphalt ('æsfælt, 'æʃ-, -fɔːlt) *n.* 1. any of several black semisolid substances composed of bitumen and inert mineral matter. They occur naturally in parts of America and as a residue from petroleum distillation: used as a waterproofing material and in paints, dielectrics, and fungicides. 2. a mixture of this substance with gravel, used in road-surfacing and roofing materials. 3. (*modifier*) containing or surfaced with asphalt. ~*vb.* 4. (*tr.*) to cover with asphalt. [C14: from Late Latin *aspaltus,* from Greek *asphaltos,* probably from A-[1] + *sphallein* to cause to fall; referring to its use as a binding agent] —**as'phaltic** *adj.*

asphaltite (æs'fæltaɪt) *n.* any of various naturally occurring hydrocarbons that resemble asphalt but have a higher melting point.

asphodel ('æsfəˌdɛl) *n.* 1. any of various S European liliaceous plants of the genera *Asphodelus* and *Asphodeline,* having clusters of white or yellow flowers. Compare **bog asphodel.** 2. any of various other plants, such as the daffodil. 3. an unidentified flower of Greek legend, probably a narcissus, said to cover the Elysian fields. [C16: from Latin *asphodelus,* from Greek *asphodelos,* of obscure origin]

asphyxia (æs'fɪksɪə) *n.* lack of oxygen in the blood due to restricted respiration; suffocation. If severe enough and prolonged, it causes death. [C18: from New Latin, from Greek *asphuxia* a stopping of the pulse, from A-[1] + *sphuxis* pulse, from *sphuzein* to throb] —**as'phyxial** *adj.*

asphyxiant (æs'fɪksɪənt) *adj.* 1. causing asphyxia. ~*n.* 2. anything that causes asphyxia: *carbon monoxide is an asphyxiant.*

asphyxiate (æs'fɪksɪˌeɪt) *vb.* to cause asphyxia in or undergo asphyxia; smother; suffocate. —**asˌphyxi'ation** *n.* —**as'phyxiˌator** *n.*

aspic[1] ('æspɪk) *n.* a savoury jelly based on meat or fish stock, used as a relish or as a mould for meat, vegetables, etc. [C18: from French: aspic (jelly), ASP[1]; variously explained as referring to its colour or coldness as compared to that of the snake]

aspic[2] ('æspɪk) *n.* an archaic word for **asp**[1]. [C17: from French, from Old Provençal *espic* spike, from Latin *spīca,* head (of flower); compare SPIKENARD]

aspic[3] ('æspɪk) *n.* either of two species of lavender, *Lavandula spica* or *L. latifolia,* that yield an oil used in perfumery: family *Labiatae* (labiates). [C16: from Old French, a variant of *aspe* ASP[2]]

aspidistra (ˌæspɪ'dɪstrə) *n.* any Asian plant of the liliaceous genus *Aspidistra,* esp. *A. lurida,* a popular house plant with long tough evergreen leaves and small brownish flowers. [C19: from New Latin, from Greek *aspis* shield, on the model of *Tupistra* genus of liliaceous plants]

aspirant ('æspɪrənt, ə'spaɪərənt) *n.* 1. a person who aspires, as to a high position. ~*adj.* 2. aspiring or striving.

aspirate *vb.* ('æspɪˌreɪt). (*tr.*) 1. *Phonetics.* **a.** to articulate (a stop) with some force, so that breath escapes with audible friction as the stop is released. **b.** to pronounce (a word or syllable) with an initial *h*. **2.** to draw in or remove by inhalation or suction, esp. to suck (air or fluid) from a body cavity or to inhale (fluid) into the lungs after vomiting. **3.** to supply air to (an internal-combustion engine). ~*n*. ('æspɪrɪt). **4.** *Phonetics.* **a.** a stop pronounced with an audible release of breath. **b.** the glottal fricative represented in English and several other languages as *h*. ~*adj*. ('æspɪrɪt). **5.** *Phonetics.* (of a stop) pronounced with a forceful and audible expulsion of breath.

aspiration (ˌæspɪ'reɪʃən) *n*. **1.** strong desire to achieve something, such as success. **2.** the aim of such desire. **3. a.** the act of breathing. **b.** a breath. **4.** *Phonetics.* **a.** the pronunciation of a stop with an audible and forceful release of breath. **b.** the friction of the released breath. **c.** an aspirated consonant. **5.** removal of air or fluid from a body cavity by suction. **6.** *Med.* **a.** the sucking of fluid or foreign matter into the air passages of the body. **b.** the removal of air or fluid from the body by suction. —**aspiratory** (ə'spaɪrətərɪ, -trɪ; 'æspɪrətərɪ, -trɪ) *adj*.

aspirator ('æspɪˌreɪtə) *n*. a device employing suction, such as a jet pump or one for removing fluids from a body cavity.

aspire (ə'spaɪə) *vb*. (*intr*.) **1.** (usually foll. by *to* or *after*) to yearn (for) or have a powerful or ambitious plan, desire, or hope (to do or be something): *to aspire to be a great leader.* **2.** to rise to a great height. [C15: from Latin *aspīrāre* to breathe upon, from *spīrāre* to breathe] —**as'pirer** *n*. —**as'piring** *adj*.

aspirin ('æsprɪn) *n*., *pl*. **-rin** *or* **-rins. 1.** a white crystalline compound widely used in the form of tablets to relieve pain, fever, and colds and to reduce inflammation. Formula: $CH_3COOC_6H_4COOH$. Chemical name: **acetylsalicylic acid. 2.** a tablet of aspirin. [C19: from German, from *A(cetyl)* + *Spir(säure)* spiraeic acid (modern salicylic acid) + -IN; see also SPIRAEA]

asplanchnic (eɪ'splæŋknɪk) *adj*. *Zoology.* having no gut.

asplenium (æ'spliːnɪəm) *n*. any fern of the very large genus *Asplenium*, of worldwide distribution. Some, esp. the bird's nest fern (*A. nidus*), are grown as greenhouse or house plants for their decorative deeply-cut evergreen fronds: family *Polypodiaceae*. See also **spleenwort.** [New Latin, from Latin *asplēnum*, from Greek *asplēnon* spleenwort, from *a-* not + *splēn* spleen (from its reputed medicinal properties)]

asquint (ə'skwɪnt) *adv*., *adj*. (*postpositive*) with a glance from the corner of the eye, esp. a furtive one. [C13: perhaps from Dutch *schuinte* slant, of obscure origin]

ass[1] (æs) *n*. **1.** either of two perissodactyl mammals of the horse family (*Equidae*), *Equus asinus* (**African wild ass**) or *E. hemionus* (**Asiatic wild ass**). They are hardy and sure-footed, having longer ears than the horse. **2.** (*not in technical use*) the domesticated variety of the African wild ass; donkey. **3.** a foolish or ridiculously pompous person. **4. not within an ass's roar of.** *Irish informal.* not close to obtaining, winning, etc.: *she wasn't within an ass's roar of it.* [Old English *assa*, probably from Old Irish *asan*, from Latin *asinus*; related to Greek *onos* ass]

ass[2] (æs) *n*. **1.** the usual U.S. and Canadian word for **arse. 2.** *U.S. and Canadian slang, offensive, taboo.* sexual intercourse or a woman considered sexually (esp. in the phrase **piece of ass**). [Old English *ærs*; see ARSE]

assagai ('æsəˌgaɪ) *n*., *pl*. **-gais.** a variant spelling of **assegai.**

assai[1] (æ'saɪ) *adv*. *Music.* (usually preceded by a musical direction) very: *allegro assai.* [Italian: enough]

assai[2] (æ'saɪ) *n*. **1.** any of several Brazilian palm trees of the genus *Euterpe*, esp. *E. edulis*, that have small dark purple fleshy edible fruit. **2.** a beverage made from the fruit of this tree. [via Brazilian Portuguese from Tupi]

assail (ə'seɪl) *vb*. (*tr*.) **1.** to attack violently; assault. **2.** to criticize or ridicule vehemently, as in argument. **3.** to beset or disturb: *his mind was assailed by doubts.* **4.** to encounter with the intention of mastering: *to assail a problem; to assail a difficult mountain ridge.* [C13: from Old French *asalir*, from Vulgar Latin *assalīre* (unattested) to leap upon, from Latin *assilīre*, from *salīre* to leap] —**as'sailable** *adj*. —**as'sailer** *n*. —**as'sailment** *n*.

assailant (ə'seɪlənt) *n*. a person who attacks another, either physically or verbally.

assam ('æsæm; *Malay* 'asam) *n*. (in Malaysia) tamarind as used in cooking. **Assam ikan** is a dish of fish cooked with tamarind. [from Malay *asam* sour]

Assamese (ˌæsə'miːz) *n*. **1.** the state language of Assam, NE India, belonging to the Indic branch of the Indo-European family and closely related to Bengali. **2.** (*pl*. **-mese**) a native or inhabitant of Assam. ~*adj*. **3.** of or relating to Assam, its people, or their language.

assassin (ə'sæsɪn) *n*. a murderer, esp. one who kills a prominent political figure. [C16: from Medieval Latin *assassīnus*, from Arabic *hashshāshīn*, plural of *hashshāsh* one who eats HASHISH]

assassinate (ə'sæsɪˌneɪt) *vb*. (*tr*.) **1.** to murder (a person, esp. a public or political figure), usually by a surprise attack. **2.** to ruin or harm (a person's reputation, etc.) by slander. —**asˌsassi'nation** *n*.

assassin bug *n*. any long-legged predatory, often blood-sucking, insect of the heteropterous family *Reduviidae*.

assassin fly *n*. another name for **robber fly.**

assault (ə'sɔːlt) *n*. **1.** a violent attack, either physical or verbal. **2.** *Law.* an intentional or reckless act that causes another person to expect to be subjected to immediate and unlawful violence. Compare **battery** (sense 4), **assault and battery. 3. a.** the culmination of a military attack, in which fighting takes place at close quarters. **b.** (*as modifier*): *assault troops.* **4.** rape or attempted rape. ~*vb*. (*tr*.) **5.** to make an assault upon. **6.** to rape or attempt to rape. [C13: from Old French *asaut*, from Vulgar Latin *assaltus* (unattested), from *assalīre* (unattested) to leap upon; see ASSAIL] —**as'saulter** *n*. —**as'saultive** *adj*.

assault and battery *n*. *Criminal law.* a threat of attack to another person followed by actual attack, which need amount only to touching with hostile intent.

assault course *n*. an obstacle course designed to give soldiers practice in negotiating hazards in making an assault.

assay *vb*. (ə'seɪ). **1.** to subject (a substance, such as silver or gold) to chemical analysis, as in the determination of the amount of impurity. **2.** (*tr*.) to attempt (something or to do something). **3.** (*tr*.; *may take a clause as object*) to test, analyse, or evaluate: *to assay the significance of early childhood experience.* ~*n*. (ə'seɪ, 'æseɪ). **4. a.** an analysis, esp. a determination of the amount of metal in an ore or the amounts of impurities in a precious metal. **b.** (*as modifier*): *an assay office.* **5.** a substance undergoing an analysis. **6.** a written report on the results of an analysis. **7.** a test. **8.** *Archaic.* an attempt. [C14: from Old Northern French *assai*; see ESSAY] —**as'sayable** *adj*. —**as'sayer** *n*.

assegai *or* **assagai** ('æsəˌgaɪ) *n*., *pl*. **-gais. 1.** a southern African cornaceous tree, *Curtisia faginea*, the wood of which is used for making spears. **2.** a sharp light spear, esp. one made of this wood. [C17: from Portuguese *azagaia*, from Arabic *az zaghāyah*, from *al* the + *zaghāyah* assegai, from Berber]

assemblage (ə'sɛmblɪdʒ) *n*. **1.** a number of things or persons assembled together; collection; assembly. **2.** a list of dishes served at a meal or the dishes themselves. **3.** the act or process of assembling or the state of being assembled. **4.** (ˌæsəm'blɑːʒ). a three-dimensional work of art that combines various objects into an integrated whole.

assemble (ə'sɛmbᵊl) *vb*. **1.** to come or bring together; collect or congregate. **2.** to fit or join together (the parts of something, such as a machine): *to assemble the parts of a kit.* **3.** to run (a computer program) that converts a set of symbolic data, usually in the form of specific single-step instructions, into machine language. [C13: from Old French *assembler*, from Vulgar Latin *assimulāre* (unattested) to bring together, from Latin *simul* together]

assemblé *French.* (asɑ̃ble) *n*. *Ballet.* a sideways leap in which the feet come together in the air in preparation for landing. [literally: brought together]

assembler (ə'sɛmblə) *n*. **1.** a type of computer program that converts a program written in assembly language into machine code. Compare **compiler** (sense 2). **2.** another name for **assembly language.**

assembly (ə'sɛmblɪ) *n*., *pl*. **-blies. 1.** a number of people gathered together, esp. for a formal meeting held at regular intervals. **2.** the act of assembling or the state of being assembled. **3.** the process of putting together a number of parts to make a machine or other product. **4.** *Machinery.* a group of mating components before or after fitting together. **5.** *Military.* **a.** a signal for personnel to assemble, as by drum, bugle, etc. **b.** (*as modifier*): *an assembly area.*

Assembly (ə'sɛmblɪ) *n*., *pl*. **-blies. 1.** the lower chamber in various American state legislatures. See also **House of Assembly, legislative assembly. 2.** *N.Z.* short for **General Assembly.**

assembly language *n*. *Computer technol.* a low-level programming language that allows a programmer complete control of the machine code to be generated.

assembly line *n*. a sequence of machines, tools, operations, workers, etc., in a factory, arranged so that at each stage a further process is carried out.

assemblyman (ə'sɛmblɪmən) *n*., *pl*. **-men.** (*sometimes cap*.) a member of an assembly, esp. a legislature.

assent (ə'sɛnt) *n*. **1.** agreement, as to a statement, proposal, etc.; acceptance. **2.** hesitant agreement; compliance. **3.** sanction. ~*vb*. (*intr*.; usually foll. by *to*) **4.** to agree or express agreement. **5.** *Archaic.* to concede. [C13: from Old French *assenter*, from Latin *assentīrī*, from *sentīre* to think]

assentation (ˌæsɛn'teɪʃən) *n*. servile or hypocritical agreement.

assentient (ə'sɛnʃɪənt) *adj*. **1.** approving or agreeing. ~*n*. **2.** a person who assents.

assentor (ə'sɛntə) *n*. *Brit. government.* any of the eight voters legally required to endorse the nomination of a candidate in a parliamentary or local election in addition to the nominator and seconder.

assert (ə'sɜːt) *vb*. (*tr*.) **1.** to insist upon (rights, claims, etc.). **2.** (*may take a clause as object*) to state to be true; declare categorically. **3.** to put (oneself) forward in an insistent manner. [C17: from Latin *asserere* to join to oneself, from *serere* to join] —**as'serter** *or* **as'sertor** *n*. —**as'sertible** *adj*.

assertion (ə'sɜːʃən) *n*. **1.** a positive statement, usually made without an attempt at furnishing evidence. **2.** the act of asserting.

assertive (ə'sɜːtɪv) *adj*. given to making assertions or bold demands; dogmatic or aggressive. —**as'sertively** *adv*. —**as'sertiveness** *n*.

assertoric (ˌæsɜːˈtɒrɪk) *adj. Logic.* **1.** (of a statement) stating a fact, as opposed to expressing an evaluative judgment. **2.** *Obsolete.* judging what is rather than what may or must be. ~Compare **apodeictic** (sense 2), **problematic** (sense 2).

assess (əˈsɛs) *vb.* (*tr.*) **1.** to judge the worth, importance, etc., of; evaluate. **2.** (foll. by *at*) to estimate the value of (income, property, etc.) for taxation purposes: *the estate was assessed at three thousand pounds.* **3.** to determine the amount of (a fine, tax, damages, etc.). **4.** to impose a tax, fine, etc., on (a person or property). [C15: from Old French *assesser*, from Latin *assidēre* to sit beside, from *sedēre* to sit] —**asˈsessable** *adj.*

assessment (əˈsɛsmənt) *n.* **1.** the act of assessing, esp. (in Britain) the evaluation of a student's achievement on a course. **2.** an amount determined as payable. **3.** a valuation set on taxable property, income, etc. **4.** evaluation; estimation.

assessment arrangements *pl. n. Brit. Education.* nationally standardized plans for pupil assessment in different subjects based on attainment targets at the end of each key stage in the National Curriculum.

assessor (əˈsɛsə) *n.* **1.** a person who evaluates the merits, importance, etc., of something, esp. (in Britain) work prepared as part of a course of study. **2.** a person who values property for taxation. **3.** a person who estimates the value of damage to property for insurance purposes. **4.** a person with technical expertise called in to advise a court on specialist matters. **5.** a person who shares another's position or rank, esp. in an advisory capacity. —**assessorial** (ˌæsɛˈsɔːrɪəl) *adj.*

asset (ˈæsɛt) *n.* anything valuable or useful: *experience is their main asset.* See also **assets.** [C19: back formation from ASSETS]

assets (ˈæsɛts) *pl. n.* **1.** *Accounting.* the property and claims against debtors that a business enterprise may apply to discharge its liabilities. Assets may be fixed, current, liquid, or intangible and are shown balanced against liabilities. Compare **liabilities.** **2.** *Law.* the property available to an executor or administrator for settlement of the debts and payment of legacies of a deceased person's estate. **3.** any property owned by a person or firm. [C16 (in the sense: enough to discharge one's liabilities): via Anglo-French from Old French *asez* enough, from Vulgar Latin *ad satis* (unattested), from Latin *ad* up to + *satis* enough]

asset-stripping *n. Commerce.* the practice of taking over a failing company at a low price and then selling the assets piecemeal. —ˈ**asset-ˌstripper** *n.*

asseverate (əˈsɛvəˌreɪt) *vb.* (*tr.*) to assert or declare emphatically or solemnly. [C18: from Latin *assevērāre* to do (something) earnestly, from *sevērus* SEVERE] —**asˌseverˈation** *n.*

assez (ˈæseɪ) *adv. Music.* (as part of a musical direction) fairly; rather. [C19: French: enough]

asshole (ˈæsˌhəul) *n. Slang, derogatory.* the usual U.S. and Canadian word for **arsehole** (see **arse**).

assibilate (əˈsɪbɪˌleɪt) *vb. Phonetics.* **1.** (*intr.*) (of a speech sound) to be changed into a sibilant. **2.** (*tr.*) to pronounce (a speech sound) with or as a sibilant. [C19: from Late Latin *assībilāre* to hiss at, from *sībilāre* to hiss; see SIBILANT] —**asˌsibiˈlation** *n.*

assiduity (ˌæsɪˈdjuːɪtɪ) *n., pl.* **-ties. 1.** constant and close application. **2.** (*often pl.*) devoted attention.

assiduous (əˈsɪdjuəs) *adj.* **1.** hard-working; persevering: *an assiduous researcher.* **2.** undertaken with perseverance and care: *assiduous editing.* [C16: from Latin *assiduus* sitting down to (something), from *assidēre* to sit beside, from *sedēre* to sit] —**asˈsiduously** *adv.* —**asˈsiduousness** *n.*

assign (əˈsaɪn) *vb.* (*mainly tr.*) **1.** to select for and appoint to a post, etc.: *to assign an expert to the job.* **2.** to give out or allot (a task, problem, etc.): *to assign advertising to an expert.* **3.** to set apart (a place, person, time, etc.) for a particular function or event: *to assign a day for the meeting.* **4.** to attribute to a specified cause, origin, or source; ascribe: *to assign a stone cross to the Vikings.* **5.** to transfer (one's right, interest, or title to property) to someone else. **6.** (*also intr.*) *Law.* (formerly) to transfer (property) to trustees so that it may be used for the benefit of creditors. **7.** *Military.* to allocate (men or materials) on a permanent basis. Compare **attach** (sense 6). **8.** *Computer technol.* to place (a value corresponding to a variable) in a memory location. ~*n.* **9.** *Law.* a person to whom property is assigned; assignee. [C14: from Old French *assigner*, from Latin *assignāre*, from *signāre* to mark out] —**asˈsignable** *adj.* —**asˌsignaˈbility** *n.* —**asˈsignably** *adv.* —**asˈsigner** *n.*

assignat (ˈæsɪgˌnæt, ˌæsɪˈnjɑː; *French* asinja) *n. French history.* the paper money issued by the Constituent Assembly in 1789, backed by the confiscated land of the Church and the émigrés. [C18: from French, from Latin *assignātum* something appointed; see ASSIGN]

assignation (ˌæsɪgˈneɪʃən) *n.* **1.** a secret or forbidden arrangement to meet, esp. one between lovers. **2.** the act of assigning; assignment. **3.** *Law, chiefly Scot.* another word for **assignment.** [C14: from Old French, from Latin *assignātiō* a marking out; see ASSIGN]

assignee (ˌæsaɪˈniː) *n.* **1.** *Law.* a person to whom some right, interest, or property is transferred. **2.** *Austral. history.* a convict who had undergone assignment.

assignment (əˈsaɪnmənt) *n.* **1.** something that has been assigned, such as a mission or task. **2.** a position or post to which a person is assigned. **3.** the act of assigning or state of being assigned. **4.** *Law.* **a.** the transfer to another of a right, interest, or title to property, esp. personal property: *assignment of a lease.* **b.** the document effecting such a transfer. **c.** the right, interest, or property transferred. **5.** *Law.* (formerly) the transfer, esp. by an insolvent debtor, of property in trust for the benefit of his creditors. **6.** *Logic.* a function that associates specific values with each variable in a formal expression. **7.** *Austral. history.* a system (1789–1841) whereby a convict could become the unpaid servant of a freeman.

assignor (ˌæsɪˈnɔː) *n. Law.* a person who transfers or assigns property.

assimilate (əˈsɪmɪˌleɪt) *vb.* **1.** (*tr.*) to learn (information, a procedure, etc.) and understand it thoroughly. **2.** (*tr.*) to absorb (food) and incorporate it into the body tissues. **3.** (*intr.*) to become absorbed, incorporated, or learned and understood. **4.** (usually foll. by *into* or *with*) to bring or come into harmony; adjust or become adjusted: *the new immigrants assimilated easily.* **5.** (usually foll. by *to* or *with*) to become or cause to become similar. **6.** (usually foll. by *to*) *Phonetics.* to change (a consonant) or (of a consonant) to be changed into another under the influence of one adjacent to it: (*n*) often assimilates to (ŋ) before (k), as in "include". [C15: from Latin *assimilāre* to make one thing like another, from *similis* like, SIMILAR] —**asˈsimilable** *adj.* —**asˌsimilably** *adv.* —**asˌsimiˈlation** *n.* —**asˈsimilative** *or* **asˈsimilatory** *adj.* —**asˈsimiˌlator** *n.* —**asˈsimilatively** *adv.*

Assiniboine (əˈsɪnəˌbɔɪn) *n.* **1.** (*pl.* **-boine** *or* **-boines**) a member of a North American Indian people living in Alberta, Saskatchewan, and Montana; one of the Sioux peoples. **2.** the language of this people, belonging to the Siouan family.

assist (əˈsɪst) *vb.* **1.** to give help or support to (a person, cause, etc.); aid. **2.** to work or act as an assistant or subordinate to (another). **3.** *Ice hockey.* to help (a team-mate) to score, as by passing the puck. **4.** (*intr.*; foll. by *at*) *Archaic.* to be present; attend. ~*n.* **5.** *U.S. and Canadian.* the act of helping; aid; assistance. **6.** *Baseball.* the act of a player who throws or deflects a batted ball in such a way that a team is enabled to put out an opponent. **7.** *Ice hockey.* **a.** an action, such as a breakaway or a pass of the puck, that enables a team-mate to score. **b.** a credit given for such an action. [C15: from French *assister* to be present, from Latin *assistere* to stand by, from *sistere* to cause to stand, from *stāre* to stand] —**asˈsister** *n.*

assistance (əˈsɪstəns) *n.* **1.** help; support. **2.** the act of assisting. **3.** *Brit. informal.* See **national assistance.**

assistant (əˈsɪstənt) *n.* **1. a.** a person who assists, esp. in a subordinate position. **b.** (*as modifier*): *assistant manager.* **2.** See **shop assistant.** ~*adj.* **3.** *Archaic.* helpful or useful as an aid.

assistant professor *n. U.S. and Canadian.* a university teacher lower in rank than an associate professor.

assize (əˈsaɪz) *n.* **1.** (in the U.S.) **a.** a sitting of a legislative assembly or administrative body. **b.** an enactment or order of such an assembly. **2.** *English history.* a trial or judicial inquest, the writ instituting such inquest, or the verdict. **3.** *Scots Law.* **a.** trial by jury. **b.** another name for **jury.** [C13: from Old French *assise* session, from *asseoir* to seat, from Latin *assidēre* to sit beside; see ASSESS]

assizes (əˈsaɪzɪz) *pl. n.* (formerly in England and Wales) the sessions, usually held four times a year, of the principal court in each county, exercising civil and criminal jurisdiction, attended by itinerant judges: replaced in 1971 by crown courts.

assn *abbrev. for* association.

assoc. *abbrev. for:* **1.** associate(d). **2.** association.

associate *vb.* (əˈsəuʃɪˌeɪt, -sɪ-). (usually foll. by *with*) **1.** (*tr.*) to link or connect in the mind or imagination: *to associate Christmas with fun.* **2.** (*intr.*) to keep company; mix socially: *to associate with writers.* **3.** (*intr.*) to form or join an association, group, etc. **4.** (*tr.; usually passive*) to consider in conjunction; connect: *rainfall is associated with humidity.* **5.** (*tr.*) to bring (a person, esp. oneself) into friendship, partnership, etc. **6.** (*tr.; often passive*) to express agreement or allow oneself to be connected (with): *Bertrand Russell was associated with the peace movement.* ~*n.* (əˈsəuʃɪɪt, -ˌeɪt, -sɪ-). **7.** a person joined with another or others in an enterprise, business, etc.; partner; colleague. **8.** a companion or friend. **9.** something that usually accompanies another thing; concomitant: *hope is an associate to happiness.* **10.** a person having a subordinate position in or admitted to only partial membership of an institution, association, etc. ~*adj.* (əˈsəuʃɪɪt, -ˌeɪt, -sɪ-). (*prenominal*) **11.** joined with another or others in an enterprise, business, etc.; having equal or nearly equal status: *an associate director.* **12.** having partial rights and privileges or subordinate status: *an associate member.* **13.** accompanying; concomitant. [C14: from Latin *associāre* to ally with, from *sociāre* to join, from *socius* an ally] —**asˈsociable** *adj.* —**asˈsociˌator** *n.* —**asˈsociatory** *adj.* —**asˈsociateˌship** *n.*

associate professor *n.* **1.** (in the U.S. and Canada) a university teacher lower in rank than a full professor but higher than an assistant professor. **2.** (in New Zealand) a senior lecturer holding the rank below professor.

association (əˌsəusɪˈeɪʃən, -ʃɪ-) *n.* **1.** a group of people having a common purpose or interest; a society or club. **2.** the act of associating or the state of being associated. **3.** friendship or companionship: *their association will not last.* **4.** a mental connection of ideas, feelings, or sensations: *association of revolution with bloodshed.* **5.** *Psychol.* the mental process of linking ideas so that the recurrence of one idea automatically recalls the other. See also **free association.** **6.** *Chem.* the formation of groups of molecules and ions, esp. in liquids, held together by weak chemical bonds. **7.** *Ecology.* a group of similar plants that grow in a uniform environment and contain one or more dominant species.

association football *n.* **1.** a more formal name for **soccer.** **2.** *Austral.* an Australian Rules competition conducted within a football association rather than a league. Compare **league football** (sense 2).

associationism (əˌsəʊsɪ'eɪʃəˌnɪzəm) *n. Psychol.* a theory that all mental activity is based on connections between basic mental events, such as sensations and feelings.

association law *n. Psychol.* any law governing the association of ideas.

associative (ə'səʊʃɪətɪv) *adj.* **1.** of, relating to, or causing association or union. **2.** *Maths, logic.* **a.** being independent of the grouping of numbers, symbols, or terms within a given set, as in conjunction or in an expression such as (2 × 3) × 4 = 2 × (3 × 4). **b.** referring to this property: *the associative laws of arithmetic.*

associative cortex *n. Anatomy.* the part of the cortex that does not have direct connections to the senses or motor system and is thought to be involved in higher mental processes.

associative storage *n. Computer technol.* a storage device in which the information is identified by content rather than by an address. Also called: **content-addressable storage.**

assoil (ə'sɔɪl) *vb.* (*tr.*) *Archaic.* **1.** to absolve; set free. **2.** to atone for. [C13: from Old French *assoldre,* from Latin *absolvere* to ABSOLVE]

assonance ('æsənəns) *n.* **1.** the use of the same vowel sound with different consonants or the same consonant with different vowels in successive words or stressed syllables, as in a line of verse. Examples are *time* and *light* or *mystery* and *mastery.* **2.** partial correspondence; rough similarity. [C18: from French, from Latin *assonāre* to sound, from *sonāre* to sound] —**'assonant** *adj., n.* —**assonantal** (ˌæsə'næntəl) *adj.*

assort (ə'sɔːt) *vb.* **1.** (*tr.*) to arrange or distribute into groups of the same type; classify. **2.** (*intr.;* usually foll. by *with*) to fit or fall into a class or group; match. **3.** (*tr.*) to supply with an assortment of merchandise. **4.** (*tr.*) to put in the same category as others; group. **5.** (*intr.;* usually foll. by *with*) *Rare.* to keep company; consort. [C15: from Old French *assorter,* from *sorte* SORT] —**as'sortative** *or* **as'sortive** *adj.* —**as'sortatively** *adv.* —**as'sorter** *n.*

assorted (ə'sɔːtɪd) *adj.* **1.** consisting of various kinds mixed together; miscellaneous: *assorted sweets.* **2.** arranged in sorts; classified: *assorted categories.* **3.** matched; suited (esp. in the combinations **well-assorted, ill-assorted**).

assortment (ə'sɔːtmənt) *n.* **1.** a collection or group of various things or sorts. **2.** the act of assorting.

asst *abbrev. for* assistant.

assuage (ə'sweɪdʒ) *vb.* (*tr.*) **1.** to soothe, moderate, or relieve (grief, pain, etc.). **2.** to give relief to (thirst, appetite, etc.); satisfy. **3.** to pacify; calm. [C14: from Old French *assouagier,* from Vulgar Latin *assuāviāre* (unattested) to sweeten, from Latin *suāvis* pleasant; see SUAVE] —**as'suagement** *n.* —**as'suager** *n.* —**assuasive** (ə'sweɪsɪv) *adj.*

assume (ə'sjuːm) *vb.* (*tr.*) **1.** (*may take a clause as object*) to take for granted; accept without proof; suppose: *to assume that someone is sane.* **2.** to take upon oneself; undertake or take on or over (a position, responsibility, etc.): *to assume office.* **3.** to pretend to; feign: *he assumed indifference, although the news affected him deeply.* **4.** to take or put on; adopt: *the problem assumed gigantic proportions.* **5.** to appropriate or usurp (power, control, etc.); arrogate: *the revolutionaries assumed control of the city.* **6.** *Christianity.* (of God) to take up (the soul of a believer) into heaven. [C15: from Latin *assūmere* to take up, from *sūmere* to take up, from SUB- + *emere* to take] —**as'sumable** *adj.* —**as'sumer** *n.*

assumed (ə'sjuːmd) *adj.* **1.** false; fictitious: *an assumed name.* **2.** taken for granted: *an assumed result.* **3.** usurped; arrogated: *an assumed authority.*

assuming (ə'sjuːmɪŋ) *adj.* **1.** expecting too much; presumptuous; arrogant. *~conj.* **2.** (often foll. by *that*) if it is assumed or taken for granted (that): *even assuming he understands the problem, he will never take any action.*

assumpsit (ə'sʌmpsɪt) *n. Law.* (before 1875) an action to recover damages for breach of an express or implied contract or agreement that was not under seal. [C17: from Latin, literally: he has undertaken, from *assūmere* to ASSUME]

assumption (ə'sʌmpʃən) *n.* **1.** the act of taking something for granted or something that is taken for granted. **2.** an assuming of power or possession of something. **3.** arrogance; presumption. **4.** *Logic.* a statement that is used as the premise of a particular argument but may not be otherwise accepted. Compare **axiom** (sense 4). [C13: from Latin *assūmptiō* a taking up, from *assūmere* to ASSUME] —**as'sumptive** *adj.* —**as'sumptively** *adv.*

Assumption (ə'sʌmpʃən) *n. Christianity.* **1.** the taking up of the Virgin Mary (body and soul) into heaven when her earthly life was ended. **2.** the feast commemorating this, celebrated by Roman Catholics on Aug. 15.

assurance (ə'ʃʊərəns) *n.* **1.** a statement, assertion, etc., intended to inspire confidence or give encouragement: *she was helped by his assurance that she would cope.* **2.** a promise or pledge of support: *he gave an assurance of help when needed.* **3.** freedom from doubt; certainty: *his assurance about his own superiority infuriated her.* **4.** forwardness; impudence. **5.** *Chiefly Brit.* insurance providing for certainties such as death as contrasted with fire or theft.

assure (ə'ʃʊə) *vb.* (*tr.; may take a clause as object*) **1.** to cause to feel sure or certain; convince: *to assure a person of one's love.* **2.** to promise; guarantee: *he assured us that he would come.* **3.** to state positively or with assurance. **4.** to make (an event) certain; ensure. **5.** *Chiefly Brit.* to insure against loss, esp. of life. **6.** *Property law.* another word for **convey.** [C14: from Old French *aseürer* to assure, from Medieval Latin *assēcūrāre* to secure or make sure, from *sēcūrus* SECURE] —**as'surable** *adj.* —**as'surer** *n.*

assured (ə'ʃʊəd) *adj.* **1.** made certain; sure; guaranteed. **2.** self-assured. **3.** *Chiefly Brit.* insured, esp. by a life assurance policy. *~n.* **4.** *Chiefly Brit.* **a.** the beneficiary under a life assurance policy. **b.** the person whose life is insured. —**assuredly** (ə'ʃʊərɪdlɪ) *adv.* —**as'suredness** *n.*

assured tenancy *n. Brit.* an agreement between a government-approved body such as a housing association and a tenant for occupation of a newly-built house or flat at an agreed market rent, under which the tenant has security of tenure. Compare **regulated tenancy.**

assurgent (ə'sɜːdʒənt) *adj.* (of leaves, stems, etc.) curving or growing upwards; rising. [C16: from Latin *assurgere* to rise up, from *surgere* to rise] —**as'surgency** *n.*

Assyr. *abbrev. for* Assyrian.

Assyrian (ə'sɪrɪən) *n.* **1.** an inhabitant of ancient Assyria, a kingdom of Mesopotamia in SW Asia. **2.** the extinct language of the Assyrians, belonging to the E Semitic subfamily of the Afro-Asiatic family and regarded as a dialect of Akkadian. *~adj.* **3.** of, relating to, or characteristic of the ancient Assyrians, their language, or culture.

Assyriology (əˌsɪrɪ'ɒlədʒɪ) *n.* the study of the culture, history, and archaeological remains of ancient Assyria. —**Asˌsyri'ologist** *n.*

AST *abbrev. for* Atlantic Standard Time.

astable (eɪ'steɪbəl) *adj.* **1.** not stable. **2.** *Electronics.* capable of oscillating between two states.

astatic (æ'stætɪk, eɪ-) *adj.* **1.** not static; unstable. **2.** *Physics.* **a.** having no tendency to assume any particular position or orientation. **b.** (of a galvanometer) having two mutually compensating magnets arranged so that the instrument is independent of the earth's magnetic field. [C19: from Greek *astatos* unsteady; see A-[1], STATIC] —**a'statically** *adv.* —**a'statiˌcism** *n.*

astatide ('æstəˌtaɪd) *n. Chem.* a binary compound of astatine with a more electropositive element.

astatine ('æstəˌtiːn, -tɪn) *n.* a radioactive element of the halogen series: a decay product of uranium and thorium that occurs naturally in minute amounts and is artificially produced by bombarding bismuth with alpha particles. Symbol: At; atomic no.: 85; half-life of most stable isotope, ^{210}At: 8.3 hours; valency: 1,3,5, or 7. [C20: from Greek *astatos* unstable (see ASTATIC) + -INE[2]]

aster ('æstə) *n.* **1.** any plant of the genus *Aster,* having white, blue, purple, or pink daisy-like flowers: family *Compositae* (composites). Compare **golden aster.** **2. China aster.** a related Chinese plant, *Callistephus chinensis,* widely cultivated for its showy brightly coloured flowers. **3.** *Cytology.* a group of radiating cytoplasmic threads that surrounds the centrosome before and during mitosis. [C18: from New Latin, from Latin *aster* star, from Greek]

-aster *suffix forming nouns.* a person or thing that is inferior or bears only a poor resemblance to what is specified: *poetaster.* [from Latin: suffix indicating imperfect resemblance]

astereognosis (əˌsterɪəʊ'gnəʊsɪs) *n.* inability to recognize objects by touch. [A-[1] + STEREO- + -GNOSIS]

asteriated (æ'stɪərɪˌeɪtɪd) *adj.* (of a crystal, esp. a gemstone) exhibiting a star-shaped figure in transmitted or reflected light.

asterisk ('æstərɪsk) *n.* **1.** a star-shaped character (*) used in printing or writing to indicate a cross-reference to a footnote, an omission, etc. **2. a.** (in historical linguistics) this sign used to indicate an unattested reconstructed form. **b.** (in descriptive linguistics) this sign used to indicate that an expression is ungrammatical or in some other way unacceptable. *~vb.* **3.** (*tr.*) to mark with an asterisk. [C17: from Late Latin *asteriscus* a small star, from Greek *asteriskos,* from *astēr* star]

asterism ('æstəˌrɪzəm) *n.* **1.** three asterisks arranged in a triangle (⁂ or ⁂), to draw attention to the text that follows. **2.** a starlike effect seen in some minerals and gemstones when viewed by reflected or transmitted light. **3.** a cluster of stars or a constellation. [C16: from Greek *asterismos* arrangement of constellations, from *astēr* star]

astern (ə'stɜːn) *adv., adj.* (*postpositive*) *Nautical.* **1.** at or towards the stern. **2.** with the stern first: *full speed astern!* **3.** aft of the stern of a vessel.

asternal (æ'stɜːnəl, eɪ-) *adj. Anatomy.* **1.** not connected or joined to the sternum. **2.** lacking a sternum.

asteroid (ˈæstəˌrɔɪd) *n.* **1.** Also called: **minor planet, planetoid.** any of numerous small celestial bodies that move around the sun mainly between the orbits of Mars and Jupiter. Their diameters range from 670 kilometres (Ceres) to less than one kilometre. **2.** Also called: **asteroidean** (ˌæstəˈrɔɪdɪən). any echinoderm of the class *Asteroidea;* a starfish. *~adj. also* **asteroidal** (ˌæstəˈrɔɪdᵊl). **3.** of, relating to, or belonging to the class *Asteroidea.* **4.** shaped like a star. [C19: from Greek *asteroeidēs* starlike, from *astēr* a star]
asthenia (æsˈθiːnɪə) *or* **astheny** (ˈæsθənɪ) *n. Pathol.* an abnormal loss of strength; debility. [C19: via New Latin from Greek *astheneia* weakness, from A-[1] + *sthenos* strength]
asthenic (æsˈθɛnɪk) *adj.* **1.** of, relating to, or having asthenia; weak. **2.** (in constitutional psychology) referring to a physique characterized by long limbs and a small trunk: claimed to be associated with a schizoid personality. See also **somatotype.** *~n.* **3.** a person having long limbs and a small trunk.
asthenopia (ˌæsθɪˈnəʊpɪə) *n.* a technical name for **eyestrain.** [C19: from New Latin, from Greek *asthenēs* weak (from A-[1] + *sthenos* strength) + *ōps* eye] —**asthenopic** (ˌæsθɪˈnɒpɪk) *adj.*
asthenosphere (əsˈθiːnəˌsfɪə, -ˈθɛn-) *n.* a thin semifluid layer of the earth (100–200 km thick), below the outer rigid lithosphere, forming part of the mantle and thought to be able to flow vertically and horizontally, enabling sections of lithosphere to subside, rise, and undergo lateral movement. See also **isostasy.** [C20: from *astheno-,* from Greek *asthenēs* weak + SPHERE]
asthma (ˈæsmə) *n.* a respiratory disorder, often of allergic origin, characterized by difficulty in breathing, wheezing, and a sense of constriction in the chest. [C14: from Greek: laborious breathing, from *azein* to breathe hard]
asthmatic (æsˈmætɪk) *adj.* **1.** of, relating to, or having asthma. *~n.* **2.** a person who has asthma. —**asthˈmatically** *adv.*
astigmatic (ˌæstɪgˈmætɪk) *adj.* **1.** of, relating to, having, correcting, or corrected for astigmatism. *~n.* **2.** a person who has astigmatism. [C19: from A-[1] + Greek *stigmat-, stigma* spot, focus; see STIGMA] —ˌ**astigˈmatically** *adv.*
astigmatism (əˈstɪgməˌtɪzəm) *or* **astigmia** (əˈstɪgmɪə) *n.* **1.** a defect of a lens resulting in the formation of distorted images; caused by the curvature of the lens being different in different planes. **2.** faulty vision resulting from astigmatism of the lens of the eye.
astilbe (əˈstɪlbɪ) *n.* any perennial saxifragaceous plant of the genus *Astilbe* of E Asia and North America: cultivated for their ornamental spikes or panicles of pink or white flowers. [C19: New Latin, from Greek: not glittering, from A-[1] + *stilbē,* from *stilbein* to glitter; referring to its inconspicuous individual flowers]
astir (əˈstɜː) *adj.* (*postpositive*) **1.** awake and out of bed. **2.** in motion; on the move.
ASTM *abbrev. for* American Society for Testing Materials.
astomatous (æˈstɒmətəs, -ˈstəʊ-) *adj.* **1.** (of animals) having no mouth. **2.** (of plants) having no stomata.
astonied (əˈstɒnɪd) *adj. Archaic.* stunned; dazed. [C14: from *astonyen* to ASTONISH]
astonish (əˈstɒnɪʃ) *vb.* (*tr.*) to fill with amazement; surprise greatly. [C15: from earlier *astonyen* (see ASTONIED), from Old French *estoner,* from Vulgar Latin *extonāre* (unattested) to strike with thunder, from Latin *tonāre* to thunder] —**aˈstonishing** *adj.* —**aˈstonishingly** *adv.*
astonishment (əˈstɒnɪʃmənt) *n.* **1.** extreme surprise; amazement. **2.** a cause of amazement.
astound (əˈstaʊnd) *vb.* (*tr.*) to overwhelm with amazement and wonder; bewilder. [C17: from *astoned* amazed, from Old French *estoné,* from *estoner* to ASTONISH] —**aˈstounding** *adj.* —**aˈstoundingly** *adv.*
astr. *or* **astron.** *abbrev. for:* **1.** astronomer. **2.** astronomical. **3.** astronomy.
astraddle (əˈstrædᵊl) *adj.* **1.** (*postpositive*) with a leg on either side of something. *~prep.* **2.** astride.
astragal (ˈæstrəgᵊl) *n.* **1.** *Architect.* **a.** Also called: **bead.** a small convex moulding, usually with a semicircular cross section. **b.** a moulding having the form of a string of beads. **2.** *Furniture.* a glazing bar, esp. in a bookcase. **3.** *Anatomy.* the ankle or anklebone. [C17: from Latin *astragalus,* from Greek *astragalos* anklebone, hence, small round moulding]
astragalus (æˈstrægələs) *n., pl.* **-li** (-ˌlaɪ). *Anatomy.* another name for **talus.** [C16: via New Latin from Latin: ASTRAGAL]
astrakhan (ˌæstrəˈkæn, -ˈkɑːn) *n.* **1.** a fur, usually black or grey, made of the closely curled wool of lambs from Astrakhan in Russia. **2.** a cloth with curled pile resembling this. **3.** (*modifier*) made of such fur or cloth: *an astrakhan collar.*
astral (ˈæstrəl) *adj.* **1.** relating to, proceeding from, consisting of, or resembling the stars: *an astral body.* **2.** *Biology.* of or relating to the aster occurring in dividing cells. **3.** *Theosophy.* denoting or relating to a supposed supersensible substance believed to form the material of a second body for each person, taking the form of an aura discernible to certain gifted individuals. [C17: from Late Latin *astrālis,* from Latin *astrum* star, from Greek *astron*] —**ˈastrally** *adv.*
astraphobia *or* **astrophobia** (ˌæstrəˈfəʊbɪə) *n.* an exaggerated fear of thunder and lightning. [C20: see ASTRO-, -PHOBIA] —ˌ**astraˈphobic** *or* ˌ**astroˈphobic** *adj.*
astray (əˈstreɪ) *adj.* (*postpositive*), *adv.* **1.** out of the correct path or direction. **2.** out of the right, good, or expected way; into error. [C13: from Old French *estraie* roaming, from *estraier* to STRAY]
astrict (əˈstrɪkt) *vb.* (*tr.*) *Archaic.* to bind, confine, or constrict. [C16: from Latin *astrictus* drawn closely together, from *astringere* to tighten, from *stringere* to bind] —**asˈtriction** *n.* —**asˈtrictive** *adj.* —**asˈtrictively** *adv.*
astride (əˈstraɪd) *adj.* (*postpositive*) **1.** with a leg on either side. **2.** with the legs far apart. *~prep.* **3.** with a leg on either side of. **4.** with a part on both sides of; spanning.
astringent (əˈstrɪndʒənt) *adj.* **1.** severe; harsh. **2.** sharp or invigorating. **3.** causing contraction of body tissues, checking blood flow, or restricting secretions of fluids; styptic. *~n.* **4.** an astringent drug or lotion. [C16: from Latin *astringēns* drawing together; see ASTRICT] —**asˈtringency** *or* **asˈtringence** *n.* —**asˈtringently** *adv.*
astro- *combining form.* **1.** indicating a heavenly body, star, or star-shaped structure: *astrology; astrocyte.* **2.** indicating outer space: *astronautics.* [from Greek, from *astron* star]
astrobiology (ˌæstrəʊbaɪˈɒlədʒɪ) *n.* the branch of biology that investigates the possibility of life on other planets.
astrobleme (ˈæstrəˌbliːm) *n.* a mark on the earth's surface, usually circular, formed by a large ancient meteorite impact. [C20: from ASTRO- + Greek *blēma* shot, wound]
astrobotany (ˌæstrəʊˈbɒtənɪ) *n.* the branch of botany that investigates the possibility that plants grow on other planets.
astrochemistry (ˌæstrəʊˈkɛmɪstrɪ) *n.* the study of the chemistry of celestial bodies and space, esp. by means of spectroscopy.
astrocompass (ˌæstrəʊˈkʌmpəs) *n.* a navigational instrument for giving directional bearings from the centre of the earth to a particular star. It is carried in long-range aircraft, ships, spacecraft, etc.
astrocyte (ˈæstrəʊˌsaɪt) *n.* any of the star-shaped cells in the tissue supporting the brain and spinal cord (neuroglia).
astrodome (ˈæstrəˌdəʊm) *n.* a transparent dome on the top of an aircraft, through which observations can be made, esp. of the stars. Also called: **astrohatch.**
astrodynamics (ˌæstrəʊdaɪˈnæmɪks) *n.* (*functioning as sing.*) the study of the motion of natural and artificial bodies in space.
astrogeology (ˌæstrəʊdʒɪˈɒlədʒɪ) *n.* the study of the structure, composition, and history of other planets and other bodies in the solar system.
astroid (ˈæstrɔɪd) *n. Maths.* a hypocycloid having four cusps. [C19: from ASTRO- + -OID]
astrol. *abbrev. for:* **1.** astrologer. **2.** astrological. **3.** astrology.
astrolabe (ˈæstrəˌleɪb) *n.* an instrument used by early astronomers to measure the altitude of stars and planets and also as a navigational aid. It consists of a graduated circular disc with a movable sighting device. Compare **sextant.** [C13: via Old French and Medieval Latin from Greek, from *astrolabos* (adj.), literally: star-taking, from *astron* star + *lambanein* to take]
astrology (əˈstrɒlədʒɪ) *n.* **1.** the study of the motions and relative positions of the planets, sun, and moon, interpreted in terms of human characteristics and activities. **2.** the primitive study of celestial bodies, which formed the basis of astronomy. [C14: from Old French *astrologie,* from Latin *astrologia,* from Greek, from *astrologos* (originally: astronomer); see ASTRO-, -LOGY] —**asˈtrologer** *or* **asˈtrologist** *n.* —**astrological** (ˌæstrəˈlɒdʒɪkᵊl) *adj.* —ˌ**astroˈlogically** *adv.*
astrometry (əˈstrɒmɪtrɪ) *n.* the branch of astronomy concerned with the measurement of the position and motion of celestial bodies. —**astrometric** (ˌæstrəˈmɛtrɪk) *or* ˌ**astroˈmetrical** *adj.*
astronaut (ˈæstrəˌnɔːt) *n.* a person trained for travelling in space. See also **cosmonaut.** [C20: from ASTRO- + *-naut* from Greek *nautēs* sailor, on the model of *aeronaut*]
astronautics (ˌæstrəˈnɔːtɪks) *n.* (*functioning as sing.*) the science and technology of space flight. —ˌ**astroˈnautic** *or* ˌ**astroˈnautical** *adj.* —ˌ**astroˈnautically** *adv.*
astronavigation (ˌæstrəʊˌnævɪˈgeɪʃən) *n.* another term for **celestial navigation.** —ˌ**astroˈnaviˌgator** *n.*
astronomer (əˈstrɒnəmə) *n.* a scientist who studies astronomy.
astronomical (ˌæstrəˈnɒmɪkᵊl) *or* **astronomic** *adj.* **1.** enormously large; immense. **2.** of or relating to astronomy. —ˌ**astroˈnomically** *adv.*
astronomical clock *n.* **1.** a complex clock showing astronomical phenomena, such as the phases of the moon. **2.** any clock showing sidereal time used in observatories.
astronomical telescope *n.* any telescope designed and mounted for use in astronomy. Such telescopes usually form inverted images. See **Cassegrainian telescope, Newtonian telescope, equatorial telescope.**
astronomical unit *n.* a unit of distance used in astronomy equal to the mean distance between the earth and the sun. 1 astronomical unit is equivalent to 1.495×10^{11} metres or about 9.3×10^{7} miles.
astronomical year *n.* another name for **solar year.** See **year** (sense 4).
astronomy (əˈstrɒnəmɪ) *n.* the scientific study of the individual celestial bodies (excluding the earth) and of the universe as a whole. Its various branches include astrometry, astrodynamics, cosmology, and astrophysics. [C13: from Old French *astronomie,* from Latin *astronomia,* from Greek; see ASTRO-, -NOMY]

astrophotography (ˌæstrəʊfəˈtɒɡrəfɪ) *n.* the photography of celestial bodies used in astronomy. **—astrophotographic** (ˌæstrəʊˌfəʊtəˈɡræfɪk) *adj.*

astrophysics (ˌæstrəʊˈfɪzɪks) *n.* (*functioning as sing.*) the branch of physics concerned with the physical and chemical properties, origin, and evolution of the celestial bodies. **—ˌastroˈphysical** *adj.* **—ˌastroˈphysicist** *n.*

astrosphere (ˈæstrəˌsfɪə) *n. Cytology.* **1.** another name for **centrosome. 2.** Also called: **attraction sphere.** the part of the aster excluding the centrosome.

astute (əˈstjuːt) *adj.* having insight or acumen; perceptive; shrewd. [C17: from Latin *astūtus* cunning, from *astus* (n.) cleverness] **—asˈtutely** *adv.* **—asˈtuteness** *n.*

astylar (æˈstaɪlə, eɪ-) *adj. Architect.* without columns or pilasters. [C19: from A-^{1} + Greek *stulos* pillar]

asunder (əˈsʌndə) *adv., adj.* (*postpositive*) **1.** in or into parts or pieces; apart: *to tear asunder.* **2.** *Archaic.* in or into a position apart or separate. [Old English *on sundran* apart; see SUNDER]

ASW *abbrev. for* antisubmarine warfare.

aswarm (əˈswɔːm) *adj.* (*postpositive*) filled, esp. with moving things; swarming: *flower beds aswarm with bees.*

asyllabic (ˌæsɪˈlæbɪk, ˌeɪ-) *adj.* not functioning in the manner of a syllable.

asylum (əˈsaɪləm) *n.* **1.** a safe or inviolable place of refuge, esp. as formerly offered by the Christian Church to criminals, outlaws, etc.; sanctuary (often in the phrase **give asylum to**). **2.** shelter; refuge. **3.** *International law.* refuge afforded to a person whose extradition is sought by a foreign government: *political asylum.* **4.** *Obsolescent.* an institution for the shelter, treatment, or confinement of individuals, esp. a mental hospital (formerly termed **lunatic asylum**). [C15: via Latin from Greek *asulon* refuge, from *asulos* that may not be seized, from A-^{1} + *sulon* right of seizure]

asymmetric (ˌæsɪˈmɛtrɪk, ˌeɪ-) *or* **asymmetrical** *adj.* **1.** not symmetrical; lacking symmetry; misproportioned. **2.** *Chem.* **a.** (of a molecule) having its atoms and radicals arranged unsymmetrically. **b.** (of a carbon atom) attached to four different atoms or radicals so that stereoisomerism results. **c.** involving the isolation of an optically active compound from a racemic mixture: *asymmetric synthesis.* **3.** *Electrical engineering.* (of conductors) having different conductivities depending on the direction of current flow, as of diodes. **4.** *Aeronautics.* having unequal thrust, as caused by an inoperative engine in a twin-engined aircraft. **5.** *Logic, maths.* (of a relation) never holding between a pair of values *x* and *y* when it holds between *y* and *x*, as "*... is the father of ...*". Compare **symmetric** (sense 1), **antisymmetric, nonsymmetric. —ˌasymˈmetrically** *adv.*

asymmetric time *n.* musical time consisting of an odd number of beats in each bar divided into uneven combinations, such as 3 + 2, 4 + 3, 2 + 3 + 2, etc.

asymmetry (æˈsɪmɪtrɪ, eɪ-) *n.* lack or absence of symmetry in spatial arrangements or in mathematical or logical relations.

asymptomatic (æˌsɪmptəˈmætɪk, eɪ-) *adj.* (of a disease or suspected disease) without symptoms; providing no subjective evidence of existence. **—aˌsymptoˈmatically** *adv.*

asymptote (ˈæsɪmˌtəʊt) *n.* a straight line that is closely approached by a plane curve so that the perpendicular distance between them decreases to zero as the distance from the origin increases to infinity. [C17: from Greek *asumptōtos* not falling together, from A-^{1} + SYN- + *ptōtos* inclined to fall, from *piptein* to fall]

asymptotic (ˌæsɪmˈtɒtɪk) *or* **asymptotical** *adj.* **1.** of or referring to an asymptote. **2.** (of a function, series, formula, etc.) approaching a given value or condition, as a variable or an expression containing a variable approaches a limit, usually infinity. **—ˌasympˈtotically** *adv.*

asynapsis (ˌeɪsɪnˈæpsɪs) *n. Biology.* failure of pairing of chromosomes at meiosis.

asynchronism (æˈsɪŋkrəˌnɪzəm, eɪ-) *n.* a lack of synchronism; occurrence at different times. **—aˈsynchronous** *adj.* **—aˈsynchronously** *adv.*

asyndetic (ˌæsɪnˈdɛtɪk) *adj.* **1.** (of a catalogue or index) without cross references. **2.** (of a linguistic construction) having no conjunction, as in *I came, I saw, I conquered.* **—ˌasynˈdetically** *adv.*

asyndeton (æˈsɪndɪtən) *n., pl.* **-deta** (-dɪtə). **1.** the omission of a conjunction between the parts of a sentence. **2.** an asyndetic construction. Compare **syndeton.** [C16: from New Latin, from Greek *asundeton,* from *asundetos* unconnected, from A-^{1} + *sundein* to bind together]

asynergia (ˌæsɪˈnɜːdʒɪə) *or* **asynergy** (əˌsɪnədʒɪ) *n. Pathol.* lack of coordination between muscles or parts, as occurs in cerebellar disease.

asystole (əˈsɪstəlɪ) *n. Pathol.* the absence of heartbeat; cardiac arrest. **—asystolic** (ˌæsɪsˈtɒlɪk) *adj.*

at^{1} (æt) *prep.* **1.** used to indicate location or position: *are they at the table?; staying at a small hotel.* **2.** towards; in the direction of: *looking at television; throwing stones at windows.* **3.** used to indicate position in time: *come at three o'clock.* **4.** engaged in; in a state of (being): *children at play; stand at ease; he is at his most charming today.* **5.** (in expressions concerned with habitual activity) during the passing of (esp. in the phrase **at night**): *he used to work at night.* **6.** for; in exchange for: *it's selling at four pounds.* **7.** used to indicate the object of an emotion: *angry at the driver; shocked at his behaviour.* **8. where it's at.** *Slang.* the real place of action. [Old English *æt;* related to Old Norse *at* to, Latin *ad* to]

at^{2} (ɑːt, æt) *n., pl.* **at.** a Laotian monetary unit worth one hundredth of a kip. [from Thai]

At **1.** *the chemical symbol for* astatine. **2.** Also: **A** *symbol for* ampere-turn.

AT *abbrev. for* attainment target.

at. *abbrev. for:* **1.** Also: **atm.** atmosphere (unit of pressure). **2.** atomic.

Atabrine (ˈætəˌbriːn, -brɪn) *n.* See **Atebrin.**

atactic (eɪˈtæktɪk) *adj.* **1.** *Chem.* (of a polymer) having random sequence of the stereochemical arrangement of groups on carbon atoms in the chain; not stereospecific. **2.** *Pathol.* relating to or displaying ataxia.

ataghan (ˈætəˌɡæn) *n.* a variant of **yataghan.**

ataman (ˈætəmən) *n., pl.* **-mans.** an elected leader of the Cossacks; hetman. [from Russian, from Polish *hetman,* from German *Hauptmann* (literally: head man)]

ataractic (ˌætəˈræktɪk) *or* **ataraxic** (ˌætəˈræksɪk) *adj.* **1.** able to calm or tranquillize. *~n.* **2.** an ataractic drug.

ataraxia (ˌætəˈræksɪə) *or* **ataraxy** (ˈætəˌræksɪ) *n.* calmness or peace of mind; emotional tranquillity. [C17: from Greek: serenity, from *ataraktos* undisturbed, from A-^{1} + *tarassein* to trouble]

atavism (ˈætəˌvɪzəm) *n.* **1.** the recurrence in a plant or animal of certain primitive characteristics that were present in an ancestor but have not occurred in intermediate generations. **2.** reversion to a former or more primitive type. [C19: from French *atavisme,* from Latin *atavus* strictly: great-grandfather's grandfather, probably from *atta* daddy + *avus* grandfather] **—ˈatavist** *n.* **—ˌataˈvistic** *or* **atavic** (əˈtævɪk) *adj.* **—ˌataˈvistically** *adv.*

ataxia (əˈtæksɪə) *or* **ataxy** (əˈtæksɪ) *n. Pathol.* lack of muscular coordination. [C17: via New Latin from Greek: lack of coordination, from A-^{1} + *-taxia,* from *tassein* to put in order] **—aˈtaxic** *or* **aˈtactic** *adj.*

ATC *abbrev. for:* **1.** air-traffic control. **2.** (in Britain) Air Training Corps.

ate (ɛt, eɪt) *vb.* the past tense of **eat.**

-ate^{1} *suffix.* **1.** (*forming adjectives*) possessing; having the appearance or characteristics of: *fortunate; palmate; Latinate.* **2.** (*forming nouns*) a chemical compound, esp. a salt or ester of an acid: *carbonate; stearate.* **3.** (*forming nouns*) the product of a process: *condensate.* **4.** forming verbs from nouns and adjectives: *hyphenate; rusticate.* [from Latin *-ātus,* past participial ending of verbs ending in *-āre*]

-ate^{2} *suffix forming nouns.* denoting office, rank, or a group having a certain function: *episcopate; electorate.* [from Latin *-ātus,* suffix (fourth declension) of collective nouns]

Atebrin (ˈætəbrɪn) *or U.S.* **Atabrine** (ˈætəˌbriːn, -brɪn) *n. Trademark.* proprietary names for **mepacrine.**

atelectasis (ˌætəˈlɛktəsɪs) *n.* **1.** failure of the lungs to expand fully at birth. **2.** collapse of the lung or a part of the lung, usually caused by bronchial obstruction. [C19: New Latin, from Greek *atelēs* imperfect + *ektasis* extension]

atelier (ˈætəlˌjeɪ; *French* atəlje) *n.* an artist's studio or workshop. [C17: from Old French *astelier* workshop, from *astele* chip of wood, from Latin *astula* splinter, from *assis* board]

a tempo (ɑː ˈtɛmpəʊ) *Music.* *~adj., adv.* **1.** to the original tempo. *~n.* **2.** a passage thus marked. *~*Also: **tempo primo.** [Italian: in (the original) time]

Athanasian Creed (ˌæθəˈneɪʃən) *n. Christianity.* a profession of faith widely used in the Western Church which, though formerly attributed to Saint Athanasius (?296–373 A.D.), probably originated in Gaul between 381 and 428 A.D.

Athapascan, Athapaskan (ˌæθəˈpæskən) *or* **Athabascan, Athabaskan** (ˌæθəˈbæskən) *n.* **1.** a group of North American Indian languages belonging to the Na-Dene phylum, including Apache and Navaho. **2.** a speaker of one of these languages. [from Cree *athapaskaaw* scattered grass or reeds]

Atharva-Veda (əˈtɑːvəˈveɪdə) *n. Hinduism.* the fourth and latest Veda, largely consisting of priestly spells and incantations.

atheism (ˈeɪθɪˌɪzəm) *n.* **1.** rejection of belief in God or gods. **2.** *Archaic.* behaviour or attitudes regarded as evil or sinful; godlessness. [C16: from French *athéisme,* from Greek *atheos* godless, from A-^{1} + *theos* god] **—ˈatheist** *n., adj.* **—ˌatheˈistic** *or* **ˌatheˈistical** *adj.* **—ˌatheˈistically** *adv.*

atheling (ˈæθəlɪŋ) *n.* (in Anglo-Saxon England) a prince of any of the royal dynasties. [Old English *ætheling,* from *æthelu* noble family + -ING^{3}; related to Old High German *adaling,* Old Norse *öthlingr*]

athematic (ˌæθɪˈmætɪk) *adj.* **1.** *Music.* not based on themes. **2.** *Linguistics.* (of verbs) having a suffix attached immediately to the stem, without an intervening vowel.

athenaeum *or U.S.* **atheneum** (ˌæθɪˈniːəm) *n.* **1.** an institution for the promotion of learning. **2.** a building containing a reading room or library, esp. one used by such an institution. [C18: from Late Latin, from Greek *Athēnaion* temple of Athena (goddess of wisdom), frequented by poets and teachers]

Athenian (əˈθiːnɪən) *n.* **1.** a native or inhabitant of Athens, capital of Greece. *~adj.* **2.** of or relating to Athens.

athermancy (æˈθɜːmənsɪ) *n.* an inability to transmit radiant heat or infrared radiation. Also called: **adiathermancy.** [C19: from

Greek *athermantos* not heated, from A-[1] + *thermainein* to heat, from *thermē* heat; compare DIATHERMANCY]

athermanous (æ'θɜːmənəs) *adj.* capable of stopping radiant heat or infrared radiation.

atherogenic (ˌæθərəʊ'dʒɛnɪk) *adj.* causing atheroma. —ˌ**athero'genesis** *n.*

atheroma (ˌæθə'rəʊmə) *n., pl.* **-mas** *or* **-mata** (-mətə). *Pathol.* a fatty deposit on or within the inner lining of an artery, often causing an obstruction to the blood flow. [C18: via Latin from Greek *athērōma* tumour full of matter resembling gruel, from *athēra* gruel] —**atheromatous** (ˌæθə'rɒmətəs, -'rəʊ-) *adj.*

atherosclerosis (ˌæθərəʊsklɪə'rəʊsɪs) *n., pl.* **-ses** (-siːz). a degenerative disease of the arteries characterized by patchy thickening of the inner lining of the arterial walls, caused by deposits of fatty material; a form of arteriosclerosis. See **atheroma.** [C20: from New Latin, from Greek *athēra* gruel (see ATHEROMA) + SCLEROSIS] —**atherosclerotic** (ˌæθərəʊsklɪə'rɒtɪk) *adj.*

athetosis (ˌæθə'təʊsɪs) *n. Pathol.* a condition characterized by uncontrolled rhythmical writhing movement, esp. of fingers, hands, head, and tongue, caused by cerebral lesion. [C19: from Greek *athetos* not in place, from A-[1] + *tithenai* to place] —'**atheˌtoid** *adj.*

athirst (ə'θɜːst) *adj.* (*postpositive*) **1.** (often foll. by *for*) having an eager desire; longing. **2.** *Archaic.* thirsty.

athlete ('æθliːt) *n.* **1.** a person trained to compete in sports or exercises involving physical strength, speed, or endurance. **2.** a person who has a natural aptitude for physical activities. **3.** *Chiefly Brit.* a competitor in track and field events. [C18: from Latin via Greek *athlētēs*, from *athlein* to compete for a prize, from *athlos* a contest]

athlete's foot *n.* a fungal infection of the skin of the foot, esp. between the toes and on the soles. Technical name: **tinea pedis.**

athletic (æθ'lɛtɪk) *adj.* **1.** physically fit or strong; muscular or active. **2.** of, relating to, or suitable for an athlete or for athletics. **3.** of or relating to a person with a muscular and well-proportioned body. See also **somatotype.** —**ath'letically** *adv.* —**ath'leticism** *n.*

athletics (æθ'lɛtɪks) *n.* (*functioning as pl. or sing.*) **1. a.** track and field events. **b.** (*as modifier*): *an athletics meeting.* **2.** sports or exercises engaged in by athletes. **3.** the theory or practice of athletic activities and training.

athletic support *n.* a more formal term for **jockstrap.**

athodyd ('æθəʊˌdaɪd) *n.* another name for **ramjet.** [C20: from *a(ero)-th(erm)ody(namic) d(uct)*]

Atholl brose ('æθəl) *n. Scot.* a mixture of whisky and honey left to ferment before consumption. [C19: after *Atholl*, a district of central Scotland]

at-home *n.* **1.** another name for **open day. 2.** a social gathering in a person's home.

athwart (ə'θwɔːt) *adv.* **1.** transversely; from one side to another. *~prep.* **2.** across the path or line of (esp. a ship). **3.** in opposition to; against. [C15: from A-[2] + THWART]

athwartships (ə'θwɔːtˌʃɪps) *adv. Nautical.* from one side to the other of a vessel at right angles to the keel.

-atic *suffix forming adjectives.* of the nature of the thing specified: *problematic.* [from French *-atique*, from Greek *-atikos*]

atilt (ə'tɪlt) *adv., adj.* (*postpositive*) **1.** in a tilted or inclined position. **2.** *Archaic.* in or as if in a joust.

-ation *suffix forming nouns.* indicating an action, process, state, condition, or result: *arbitration; cogitation; hibernation; moderation.* Compare **-ion, -tion.** [from Latin *-ātiōn-*, suffix of abstract nouns, from *-ātus* -ATE[1] + *-iōn* -ION]

-ative *suffix forming adjectives.* of, relating to, or tending to: *authoritative; decorative; informative.* [from Latin *-ātīvus*, from *ātus* -ATE[1] + *īvus* -IVE]

Atlantean (ˌætlæn'tiːən, æt'læntɪən) *adj. Literary.* of, relating to, or like Atlas, a Titan in Greek mythology; extremely strong.

atlantes (ət'læntiːz) *n.* the plural of **atlas** (sense 4).

Atlantic (ət'læntɪk) *adj.* of or relating to or bordering the Atlantic Ocean. [C15: from Latin *Atlanticus*, from Greek (*pelagos*) *Atlantikos* (the sea) of Atlas (so called because it lay beyond the Atlas Mountains of N Africa)]

Atlanticism (ət'læntɪˌsɪzəm) *n.* advocacy of close cooperation in military, political, and economic matters between Western Europe, esp. the UK, and the U.S. —**At'lanticist** *n.*

Atlantic Standard Time *n.* the local time used in eastern Canada, four hours behind Greenwich Mean Time. Abbrev.: **AST.**

atlas ('ætləs) *n.* **1.** a collection of maps, usually in book form. **2.** a book of charts, graphs, etc., illustrating aspects of a subject: *an anatomical atlas.* **3.** *Anatomy.* the first cervical vertebra, attached to and supporting the skull in man. Compare **axis**[1] (sense 3). **4.** (*pl.* **atlantes**) *Architect.* another name for **telamon. 5.** a standard size of drawing paper, 26 × 17 inches. [C16: via Latin from Greek; first applied to maps, from depictions of Atlas supporting the heavens in 16th-century collections of maps]

Atlas ('ætləs) *n.* a U.S. intercontinental ballistic missile, also used in launching spacecraft. [C20: after *Atlas*, a Titan in Greek mythology]

ATM *abbrev. for* automated telling machine.

atm. *abbrev. for:* **1.** Also: **at.** atmosphere (unit of pressure). **2.** atmospheric.

atman ('ɑːtmən) *n. Hinduism.* **1.** the personal soul or self; the thinking principle as manifested in consciousness. **2.** Brahman considered as the Universal Soul, the great Self or Person that dwells in the entire created order. [from Sanskrit *ātman* breath; compare Old High German *ātum* breath]

atmo- *combining form.* air or vapour: *atmometer; atmosphere.* [via New Latin from Greek *atmos* vapour]

atmolysis (æt'mɒlɪsɪs) *n., pl.* **-ses** (-ˌsiːz). a method of separating gases that depends on their differential rates of diffusion through a porous substance.

atmometer (æt'mɒmɪtə) *n.* an instrument for measuring the rate of evaporation of water into the atmosphere. Also called: **evaporimeter, evaporometer.** —**at'mometry** *n.*

atmosphere ('ætməsˌfɪə) *n.* **1.** the gaseous envelope surrounding the earth or any other celestial body. See also **troposphere, stratosphere, mesosphere,** and **ionosphere. 2.** the air or climate in a particular place: *the atmosphere was thick with smoke.* **3.** a general pervasive feeling or mood: *an atmosphere of elation.* **4.** the prevailing tone or mood of a novel, symphony, painting, or other work of art. **5.** a special mood or character associated with a place. **6.** any local gaseous environment or medium: *an inert atmosphere.* **7.** Abbrevs.: **at., atm.** a unit of pressure; the pressure that will support a column of mercury 760 mm high at 0°C at sea level. 1 atmosphere is equivalent to 101 325 newtons per square metre or 14.72 pounds per square inch. —ˌ**atmos'pheric** *or* ˌ**atmos'pherical** *adj.* —ˌ**atmos'pherically** *adv.*

atmospheric perspective *n.* another term for **aerial perspective.**

atmospheric pressure *n.* the pressure exerted by the atmosphere at the earth's surface. It has an average value of 1 atmosphere.

atmospherics (ˌætməs'fɛrɪks) *pl. n.* **1.** electrical disturbances produced in the atmosphere by natural causes such as lightning. **2.** radio interference, heard as crackling or hissing in receivers, caused by electrical disturbance.

ATN *abbrev. for:* **1.** arc tangent. **2.** augmented transition network.

at. no. *abbrev. for* atomic number.

atoll ('ætɒl, ə'tɒl) *n.* a circular coral reef or string of coral islands surrounding a lagoon. [C17: from *atollon*, native name in the Maldive Islands]

atom ('ætəm) *n.* **1. a.** the smallest quantity of an element that can take part in a chemical reaction. **b.** this entity as a source of nuclear energy: *the power of the atom.* See also **atomic structure. 2.** any entity regarded as the indivisible building block of a theory. **3.** the hypothetical indivisible particle of matter postulated by certain ancient philosophers as the fundamental constituent of matter. See also **atomism. 4.** a very small amount or quantity; minute fragment: *to smash something to atoms; there is not an atom of truth in his allegations.* [C16: via Old French and Latin, from Greek *atomos* (n.), from *atomos* (adj.) that cannot be divided, from A-[1] + *temnein* to cut]

atom bomb *or* **atomic bomb** *n.* a type of bomb in which the energy is provided by nuclear fission. Uranium-235 and plutonium-239 are the isotopes most commonly used in atom bombs. Also called: **A-bomb, fission bomb.** Compare **fusion bomb.**

atomic (ə'tɒmɪk) *adj.* **1.** of, using, or characterized by atom bombs or atomic energy: *atomic warfare.* **2.** of, related to, or comprising atoms: *atomic hydrogen.* **3.** extremely small; minute. **4.** *Logic.* (of a sentence, formula, etc.) having no internal structure at the appropriate level of analysis. In predicate calculus, *Fa* is an **atomic sentence** and *Fx* an **atomic predicate.** —**a'tomically** *adv.*

atomic age *n.* **the.** the current historical period, initiated by the development of the first atomic bomb towards the end of World War II and now marked by a balance of power between nations possessing the hydrogen bomb and the use of nuclear power as a source of energy.

atomic clock *n.* an extremely accurate clock in which an electrical oscillator is controlled by the natural vibrations of an atomic or molecular system such as caesium or ammonia.

atomic cocktail *n.* an aqueous solution of radioactive substance, such as sodium iodide, administered orally as part of the treatment for cancer.

atomic energy *n.* another name for **nuclear energy.**

Atomic Energy Authority *n.* (in Britain) a government body established in 1954 to control research and development in atomic energy. Abbrev.: **AEA.**

Atomic Energy Commission *n.* (in the U.S.) a federal board established in 1946 to administer and develop domestic atomic energy programmes. Abbrev.: **AEC.**

atomic heat *n.* the product of an element's atomic weight and its specific heat (capacity).

atomicity (ˌætə'mɪsɪtɪ) *n.* **1.** the state of being made up of atoms. **2.** the number of atoms in the molecules of an element. **3.** a less common name for **valency.**

atomic mass *n. Chem.* **1.** the mass of an isotope of an element in atomic mass units. **2.** short for **relative atomic mass;** see **atomic weight.**

atomic mass unit *n.* a unit of mass used to express atomic and molecular weights that is equal to one twelfth of the mass of an atom of carbon-12. It is equivalent to 1.66×10^{-27} kg. Abbrev.: **amu.** Also called: **unified atomic mass unit, dalton.**

atomic number *n.* the number of protons in the nucleus of an atom of an element. Abbrev.: **at. no.** Symbol: *Z* Also called: **proton number.**

atomic pile *n.* the original name for a **nuclear reactor.**

atomic power *n.* another name for **nuclear power.**

atomic structure *n.* the concept of an atom as a central positively charged nucleus consisting of protons and neutrons surrounded by a number of electrons. The number of electrons is equal to the number of protons: the whole entity is thus electrically neutral.

atomic theory *n.* **1.** any theory in which matter is regarded as consisting of atoms, esp. that proposed by John Dalton (1766–1844), British chemist, postulating that elements are composed of atoms that can combine in definite proportions to form compounds. **2.** the current concept of the atom as an entity with a definite structure. See **atomic structure.**

atomic volume *n.* the atomic weight (relative atomic mass) of an element divided by its density.

atomic weight *n.* the former name for **relative atomic mass.** Abbrev.: **at. wt.**

atomism ('ætəˌmɪzəm) *n.* **1.** an ancient philosophical theory that the ultimate constituents of the universe are atoms: see **atom** (sense 3). **2. a.** any of a number of theories that hold that some objects or phenomena can be explained as constructed out of a small number of distinct types of simple indivisible entities. **b.** any theory that holds that an understanding of the parts is logically prior to an understanding of the whole. Compare **holism** (sense 1). **3.** *Psychol.* the theory that experiences and mental states are composed of elementary units. —**'atomist** *n., adj.* —**ˌatom'istic** *or* **ˌatom'istical** *adj.* —**ˌatom'istically** *adv.*

atomize *or* **atomise** ('ætəˌmaɪz) *vb.* **1.** to separate or be separated into free atoms. **2.** to reduce (a liquid or solid) to fine particles or spray or (of a liquid or solid) to be reduced in this way. **3.** (*tr.*) to destroy by weapons, esp. nuclear weapons. —**ˌatomi'zation** *or* **ˌatomi'sation** *n.*

atomizer *or* **atomiser** ('ætəˌmaɪzə) *n.* a device for reducing a liquid to a fine spray, such as the nozzle used to feed oil into a furnace or an enclosed bottle with a fine outlet used to spray perfumes or medicines.

atom smasher *n. Physics.* the nontechnical name for **accelerator** (sense 2).

atomy[1] ('ætəmɪ) *n., pl.* **-mies.** *Archaic.* **1.** an atom or minute particle. **2.** a minute creature. [C16: from Latin *atomī* atoms, but used as if singular; see ATOM]

atomy[2] ('ætəmɪ) *n., pl.* **-mies.** an obsolete word for **skeleton.** [C16: from mistaken division of ANATOMY (as if *an atomy*)]

atonal (eɪ'təʊnᵊl, æ-) *adj. Music.* having no established key. Compare **tonal** (sense 2). —**a'tonalism** *n.* —**a'tonally** *adv.*

atonality (ˌeɪtəʊ'nælɪtɪ, ˌæ-) *n.* **1.** absence of or disregard for an established musical key in a composition. **2.** the principles of composition embodying this and providing a radical alternative to the diatonic system. ~Compare **tonality.**

atone (ə'təʊn) *vb.* **1.** (*intr.*; foll. by *for*) to make amends or reparation (for a crime, sin, etc.). **2.** (*tr.*) to expiate: *to atone a guilt with repentance.* **3.** *Obsolete.* to be in or bring into agreement. [C16: back formation from ATONEMENT] —**a'tonable** *or* **a'toneable** *adj.* —**a'toner** *n.*

atonement (ə'təʊnmənt) *n.* **1.** satisfaction, reparation, or expiation given for an injury or wrong. **2.** (*often cap.*) *Christian theology.* **a.** the reconciliation of man with God through the life, sufferings, and sacrificial death of Christ. **b.** the sufferings and death of Christ. **3.** *Christian Science.* the state in which the attributes of God are exemplified in man. **4.** *Obsolete.* reconciliation or agreement. [C16: from Middle English phrase *at onement* in harmony]

atonic (eɪ'tɒnɪk, æ-) *adj.* **1.** (of a syllable, word, etc.) carrying no stress; unaccented. **2.** *Pathol.* relating to or characterized by atony. ~*n.* **3.** an unaccented or unstressed syllable, word, etc., such as *for* in *food for thought.* [C18: from Latin *atonicus,* from Greek *atonos* lacking tone; see ATONY] —**atonicity** (ˌætə'nɪsɪtɪ, ˌeɪtəʊ-) *n.*

atony ('ætənɪ) *n.* **1.** *Pathol.* lack of normal tone or tension, as in muscles; abnormal relaxation of a muscle. **2.** *Phonetics.* lack of stress or accent on a syllable or word. [C17: from Latin *atonia,* from Greek: tonelessness, from *atonos* slack, from A-[1] + *tonos* TONE]

atop (ə'tɒp) *adv.* **1.** on top; at the top. ~*prep.* **2.** on top of; at the top of.

atopy ('ætəʊpɪ) *n. Immunol.* a hereditary tendency to be hypersensitive to certain allergens. —**atopic** (ə'tɒpɪk) *adj.*

-ator *suffix forming nouns.* a person or thing that performs a certain action: *agitator; escalator; radiator.* [from Latin *-ātor;* see -ATE[1], -OR[1]]

-atory *suffix forming adjectives.* of, relating to, characterized by, or serving to: *circulatory; exploratory; migratory; explanatory.* [from Latin *-ātōrius;* see -ATE[1], -ORY[2]]

ATP *n.* adenosine triphosphate; a nucleotide found in the mitochondria of all plant and animal cells. It is the major source of energy for cellular reactions, this energy being released during its conversion to ADP. Formula: $C_{10}H_{16}N_5O_{13}P_3$.

ATPase (ˌeɪtiː'piːˌeɪz) *n.* adenosine triphosphatase; an enzyme that converts ATP to ADP.

atrabilious (ˌætrə'bɪljəs) *or* **atrabiliar** *adj. Rare.* irritable. [C17: from Latin *ātra bīlis* black bile, from *āter* black + *bīlis* BILE] —**ˌatra'biliousness** *n.*

atrazine ('ætrəziːn) *n.* a white crystalline compound widely used as a weedkiller. Formula: $C_8H_{14}N_5Cl$. [C20: from A(MINO) TR(I)AZINE]

atresia (ə'triːʒɪə, -ʒə) *n.* absence of or unnatural narrowing of a body channel. [C19: New Latin, from Greek *atrētos* not perforated]

atrioventricular (ˌeɪtrɪəʊvɛn'trɪkjʊlə) *adj. Anatomy.* of, relating to, or affecting both the atria and the ventricles of the heart: *atrioventricular disease.* [C19: from *atrio-*, from New Latin *atrium* heart chamber (see ATRIUM) + VENTRICULAR]

atrip (ə'trɪp) *adj.* (*postpositive*) *Nautical.* (of an anchor) no longer caught on the bottom; tripped; aweigh.

atrium ('eɪtrɪəm, 'ɑː-) *n., pl.* **atria** ('eɪtrɪə, 'ɑː-). **1.** the open main court of a Roman house. **2.** a central often glass-roofed hall that extends through several storeys in a building, such as a shopping centre or hotel. **3.** a court in front of an early Christian or medieval church, esp. one flanked by colonnades. **4.** *Anatomy.* a cavity or chamber in the body, esp. the upper chamber of each half of the heart. [C17: from Latin; related to *āter* black, perhaps originally referring to the part of the house that was blackened by smoke from the hearth] —**'atrial** *adj.*

atrocious (ə'trəʊʃəs) *adj.* **1.** extremely cruel or wicked; ruthless: *atrocious deeds.* **2.** horrifying or shocking: *an atrocious road accident.* **3.** *Informal.* very bad; detestable: *atrocious writing.* [C17: from Latin *ātrōx* dreadful, from *āter* black] —**a'trociously** *adv.* —**a'trociousness** *n.*

atrocity (ə'trɒsɪtɪ) *n., pl.* **-ties. 1.** behaviour or an action that is wicked or ruthless. **2.** the fact or quality of being atrocious. **3.** (*usually pl.*) acts of extreme cruelty, esp. against prisoners or civilians in wartime.

atrophy ('ætrəfɪ) *n., pl.* **-phies. 1.** a wasting away of an organ or part, or a failure to grow to normal size as the result of disease, faulty nutrition, etc. **2.** any degeneration or diminution, esp. through lack of use. ~*vb.* **-phies, -phying, -phied. 3.** to waste away or cause to waste away. [C17: from Late Latin *atrophia,* from Greek, from *atrophos* ill-fed, from A-[1] + *-trophos* from *trephein* to feed] —**atrophic** (ə'trɒfɪk) *adj.*

atropine ('ætrəˌpiːn, -pɪn) *or* **atropin** ('ætrəpɪn) *n.* a poisonous alkaloid obtained from deadly nightshade, having an inhibitory action on the autonomic nervous system. It is used medicinally in preanaesthetic medication, to treat peptic ulcers, biliary and renal colic, etc., and as an emergency first-aid counter to exposure to chemical warfare nerve agents. Formula: $C_{17}H_{23}NO_3$. [C19: from New Latin *atropa* deadly nightshade, from Greek *atropos* unchangeable, inflexible]

att. *abbrev. for:* **1.** attached. **2.** attorney.

attaboy ('ætəˌbɔɪ) *sentence substitute. Slang, chiefly U.S.* an expression of approval or exhortation.

attach (ə'tætʃ) *vb.* (*mainly tr.*) **1.** to join, fasten, or connect. **2.** (*reflexive or passive*) to become associated with or join, as in a business or other venture: *he attached himself to the expedition.* **3.** (*intr.*; foll. by *to*) to be inherent (in) or connected (with): *responsibility attaches to the job.* **4.** to attribute or ascribe: *to attach importance to an event.* **5.** to include or append, esp. as a condition: *a proviso is attached to the contract.* **6.** (*usually passive*) *Military.* to place on temporary duty with another unit. **7.** (*usually passive*) to put (a member of an organization) to work in a different unit or agency, either with an expectation of reverting to, or while retaining some part of, the original working arrangement. **8.** to appoint officially. **9.** *Law.* to arrest or take (a person, property, etc.) with lawful authority. **10.** *Obsolete.* to seize. [C14: from Old French *atachier* to fasten, changed from *estachier* to fasten with a stake, from *estache* STAKE[1]] —**at'tachable** *adj.* —**at'tacher** *n.*

attaché (ə'tæʃeɪ; *French* ataʃe) *n.* **1.** a specialist attached to a diplomatic mission: *military attaché.* **2.** *Brit.* a junior member of the staff of an embassy or legation. [C19: from French: someone attached (to a mission), from *attacher* to ATTACH]

attaché case *n.* a small flat rectangular briefcase used for carrying documents, papers, etc.

attached (ə'tætʃt) *adj.* **1.** (foll. by *to*) fond (of); full of regard (for): *he was very attached to the old lady.* **2.** married, engaged, or associated in an exclusive sexual relationship: *it's no good dancing with her, she's already attached.*

attachment (ə'tætʃmənt) *n.* **1.** a means of securing; a fastening. **2.** (often foll. by *to*) affection or regard (for); devotion (to): *attachment to a person or to a cause.* **3.** an object to be attached, esp. a supplementary part: *an attachment for an electric drill.* **4.** the act of attaching or the state of being attached. **5. a.** the arrest of a person for disobedience to a court order. **b.** the lawful seizure of property and placing of it under control of a court. **c.** a writ authorizing such arrest or seizure. **6.** *Law.* the binding of a debt in the hands of a garnishee until its disposition has been decided by the court.

attachment of earnings *n.* (in Britain) a court order requiring an employer to deduct amounts from an employee's wages to pay debts or honour financial obligations.

attack (ə'tæk) *vb.* **1.** to launch a physical assault (against) with or without weapons; begin hostilities (with). **2.** (*intr.*) to take the initiative in a game, sport, etc.: *after a few minutes, the team* *began to attack.* **3.** (*tr.*) to direct hostile words or writings at; criticize or abuse vehemently. **4.** (*tr.*) to turn one's mind or energies vigorously to (a job, problem, etc.). **5.** (*tr.*) to begin to injure or affect adversely; corrode, corrupt, or infect: *rust attacked the metal.* **6.** (*tr.*) to attempt to rape. ~*n.* **7.** the act or an instance of attacking. **8.** strong criticism or abuse: *an unjustified attack on someone's reputation.* **9.** an offensive move in a game, sport, etc. **10.** commencement of a task, etc. **11.** any sudden and usually severe manifestation of a disease or disorder: *a heart attack; an attack of indigestion.* **12. the attack.** *Ball games.* the players in a team whose main role is to attack the opponents' goal or territory. **13.** *Music.* decisiveness in beginning a passage, movement, or piece. **14.** *Music.* the speed with which a note reaches its maximum volume. **15.** an attempted rape. [C16: from French *attaquer,* from Old Italian *attaccare* to attack, attach, from *estaccare* to attach, from *stacca* STAKE[1]; compare ATTACH] —**at'tackable** *adj.* —**at'tacker** *n.*

attain (ə'teɪn) *vb.* **1.** (*tr.*) to achieve or accomplish (a task, goal, aim, etc.). **2.** (*tr.*) to reach or arrive at in space or time: *to attain old age.* **3.** (*intr.;* often foll. by *to*) to arrive (at) with effort or exertion: *to attain to glory.* [C14: from Old French *ateindre,* from Latin *attingere* to reach, from *tangere* to touch] —**at'tainable** *adj.* —**at,taina'bility** *or* **at'tainableness** *n.*

attainder (ə'teɪndə) *n.* **1.** (formerly) the extinction of a person's civil rights resulting from a sentence of death or outlawry on conviction for treason or felony. See also **bill of attainder.** **2.** *Obsolete.* dishonour. ~Archaic equivalent: **attainture** (ə'teɪntʃə). [C15: from Anglo-French *attaindre* to convict, from Old French *ateindre* to ATTAIN]

attainment (ə'teɪnmənt) *n.* an achievement or the act of achieving; accomplishment.

attainment target *n. Brit. Education.* a general defined level of ability that a pupil is expected to achieve in every subject at each key stage in the National Curriculum. Abbrev.: **AT.**

attaint (ə'teɪnt) *vb.* (*tr.*) *Archaic.* **1.** to pass judgment of death or outlawry upon (a person); condemn by bill of attainder. **2.** to dishonour or disgrace. **3.** to accuse or prove to be guilty. **4.** (of sickness) to affect or strike (somebody). ~*n.* **5.** a less common word for **attainder. 6.** a dishonour; taint. [C14: from Old French *ateint* convicted, from *ateindre* to ATTAIN]

attar ('ætə), **otto** ('ɒtəʊ), *or* **ottar** ('ɒtə) *n.* an essential oil from flowers, esp. the damask rose, used pure or as a base for perfume: *attar of roses.* [C18: from Persian *'atir* perfumed, from *'itr* perfume, from Arabic]

attemper (ə'tɛmpə) *vb.* (*tr.*) *Archaic.* **1.** to modify by blending; temper. **2.** to moderate or soothe. **3.** to accommodate or bring into harmony. —**at'temperment** *n.*

attempt (ə'tɛmpt) *vb.* (*tr.*) **1.** to make an effort (to do something) or to achieve (something); try. **2.** to try to surmount (an obstacle). **3.** to try to climb: *they will attempt the north wall of the Eiger.* **4.** *Archaic.* to attack. **5.** *Archaic.* to tempt. ~*n.* **6.** an endeavour to achieve something; effort. **7.** a result of an attempt or endeavour. **8.** an attack, esp. with the intention to kill: *an attempt on his life.* [C14: from Old French *attempter,* from Latin *attemptāre* to strive after, from *tentāre* to try] —**at'temptable** *adj.* —**at'tempter** *n.*

attend (ə'tɛnd) *vb.* **1.** to be present at (an event, meeting, etc.). **2.** (when *intr.,* foll. by *to*) to give care; minister. **3.** (when *intr.,* foll. by *to*) to pay attention; listen. **4.** (*tr.; often passive*) to accompany or follow: *a high temperature attended by a severe cough.* **5.** (*intr.;* foll. by *on* or *upon*) to follow as a consequence (of). **6.** (*intr.;* foll. by *to*) to devote one's time; apply oneself: *to attend to the garden.* **7.** (*tr.*) to escort or accompany. **8.** (*intr.;* foll. by *on* or *upon*) to wait (on); serve; provide for the needs (of): *to attend on a guest.* **9.** (*tr.*) *Archaic.* to wait for; expect. **10.** (*intr.*) *Obsolete.* to delay. [C13: from Old French *atendre,* from Latin *attendere* to stretch towards, from *tendere* to extend] —**at'tender** *n.*

attendance (ə'tɛndəns) *n.* **1.** the act or state of attending. **2.** the number of persons present: *an attendance of 5000 at the festival.* **3.** *Obsolete.* attendants collectively; retinue.

attendance allowance *n.* (in Britain) a tax-free noncontributory welfare benefit for children over two years old and adults who are so severely disabled that they need frequent attention or continual supervision.

attendance centre *n.* (in Britain) a place at which young offenders are required to attend regularly instead of going to prison.

attendant (ə'tɛndənt) *n.* **1.** a person who accompanies or waits upon another. **2.** a person employed to assist, guide, or provide a service for others, esp. for the general public: *a lavatory attendant.* **3.** a person who is present. **4.** a logical consequence or natural accompaniment: *hatred is often an attendant of jealousy.* ~*adj.* **5.** being in attendance. **6.** associated; accompanying; related: *attendant problems.*

attention (ə'tɛnʃən) *n.* **1.** concentrated direction of the mind, esp. to a problem or task. **2.** consideration, notice, or observation: *a new matter has come to our attention.* **3.** detailed care or special treatment: *to pay attention to one's appearance.* **4.** (*usually pl.*) an act of consideration, courtesy, or gallantry indicating affection or love: *attentions given to a lover.* **5.** the motionless position of formal military alertness, esp. in drill when an upright position is assumed with legs and heels together, arms to the sides, head and eyes facing to the front. **6.** *Psychol.* the act of concentrating on any one of a set of objects or thoughts. See also **selective attention.** ~*sentence substitute.* **7.** the order to be alert or to adopt a position of formal military alertness. [C14: from Latin *attentiō,* from *attendere* to apply the mind to; see ATTEND]

attentive (ə'tɛntɪv) *adj.* **1.** paying attention; listening carefully; observant. **2.** (*postpositive;* often foll. by *to*) careful to fulfil the needs or wants (of); considerate (about): *she was always attentive to his needs.* —**at'tentively** *adv.* —**at'tentiveness** *n.*

attenuant (ə'tɛnjʊənt) *adj.* **1.** causing dilution or thinness, esp. of the blood. ~*n.* **2.** an attenuant drug or agent.

attenuate *vb.* (ə'tɛnjʊ,eɪt). **1.** to weaken or become weak; reduce in size, strength, density, or value. **2.** to make or become thin or fine; extend. **3.** (*tr.*) to make (a pathogenic bacterium, virus, etc.) less virulent, as by culture in special media or exposure to heat. ~*adj.* (ə'tɛnjʊɪt, -,eɪt). **4.** diluted, weakened, slender, or reduced. **5.** *Botany.* tapering gradually to a point. [C16: from Latin *attenuāre* to weaken, from *tenuis* thin]

attenuation (ə,tɛnjʊ'eɪʃən) *n.* **1.** the act of attenuating or the state of being attenuated. **2.** the loss of energy suffered by radiation as it passes through matter, esp. as a result of absorption or scattering.

attenuator (ə'tɛnjʊ,eɪtə) *n.* **1.** *Physics.* any device designed to reduce the power of a wave or electrical signal without distorting it. **2.** a person or thing that attenuates.

attest (ə'tɛst) *vb.* **1.** (*tr.*) to affirm the correctness or truth of. **2.** (when *intr.,* usually foll. by *to*) to witness (an act, event, etc.) or bear witness to (an act, event, etc.) as by signature or oath. **3.** (*tr.*) to make evident; demonstrate: *his life of luxury attests his wealth.* **4.** (*tr.*) to provide evidence for: *the marks in the ground attested the presence of a fossil.* [C16: from Latin *attestārī* to prove, from *testārī* to bear witness, from *testis* a witness] —**at'testable** *adj.* —**at'testant, at'tester** *or esp. in legal usage* **at'testor, at'testator** *n.* —**attestation** (,ætɛ'steɪʃən) *n.*

attested (ə'tɛstɪd) *adj. Brit.* (of cattle, etc.) certified to be free from a disease, esp. from tuberculosis.

Att. Gen. *or* **Atty. Gen.** *abbrev. for* Attorney General.

attic ('ætɪk) *n.* **1.** a space or room within the roof of a house. **2.** *Architect.* a storey or low wall above the cornice of a classical façade. [C18: special use of ATTIC, from the use of Attic-style pilasters to adorn the façade of the top storey]

Attic ('ætɪk) *adj.* **1.** of or relating to Attica, the area around Athens, its inhabitants, or the dialect of Greek spoken there, esp. in classical times. **2.** (*often not cap.*) classically elegant, simple, or pure: *an Attic style.* ~*n.* **3.** the dialect of Ancient Greek spoken and written in Athens: the chief literary dialect of classical Greek. See also **Aeolic, Arcadic, Doric, Ionic.**

Atticism ('ætɪ,sɪzəm) *n.* **1.** the idiom or character of the Attic dialect of Ancient Greek, esp. in the Hellenistic period. **2.** an elegant, simple, and clear expression. —**'Atticist** *n.*

Attic order *n.* a low pilaster of any order set into the cornice of a building.

Attic salt *or* **wit** *n.* refined incisive wit.

attire (ə'taɪə) *vb.* **1.** (*tr.*) to dress, esp. in fine elegant clothes; array. ~*n.* **2.** clothes or garments, esp. if fine or decorative. **3.** the antlers of a mature male deer. [C13: from Old French *atirier* to put in order, from *tire* row; see TIER[1]]

attitude ('ætɪ,tjuːd) *n.* **1.** the way a person views something or tends to behave towards it, often in an evaluative way. **2.** a theatrical pose created for effect (esp. in the phrase **strike an attitude**). **3.** a position of the body indicating mood or emotion. **4.** *Informal.* a hostile manner: *don't give me attitude, my girl.* **5.** the orientation of an aircraft's axes in relation to some plane, esp. the horizontal. See also **axis**[1] (sense 1). **6.** the orientation of a spacecraft in relation to its direction of motion. **7.** *Ballet.* a classical position in which the body is upright and one leg raised and bent behind. [C17: from French, from Italian *attitudine* disposition, from Late Latin *aptitūdō* fitness, from Latin *aptus* APT] —**,atti'tudinal** *adj.*

attitudinize *or* **attitudinise** (,ætɪ'tjuːdɪ,naɪz) *vb.* (*intr.*) to adopt a pose or opinion for effect; strike an attitude. —**,atti'tudi,nizer** *or* **,atti'tudi,niser** *n.*

attn *abbrev. for* attention.

atto- *prefix.* denoting 10^{-18}: *attotesla.* Symbol: a [from Norwegian, Danish *atten* eighteen]

attorn (ə'tɜːn) *vb.* **1.** (*intr.*) *Law.* to acknowledge a new owner of land as one's landlord. **2.** (*intr.*) *Feudal history.* to transfer allegiance or do homage to a new lord. **3.** (*tr.*) *Rare.* to transfer. [C15: from Old French *atourner* to direct to, from *tourner* to TURN] —**at'tornment** *n.*

attorney (ə'tɜːnɪ) *n.* **1.** a person legally appointed or empowered to act for another. **2.** *U.S.* a lawyer qualified to represent clients in legal proceedings. [C14: from Old French *atourné,* from *atourner* to direct to; see ATTORN] —**at'torney,ship** *n.*

attorney-at-law *n., pl.* **attorneys-at-law.** *Law.* **1.** *Now chiefly U.S.* a lawyer qualified to represent in court a party to a legal action. **2.** *Brit. obsolete.* a solicitor.

attorney general *n., pl.* **attorneys general** *or* **attorney generals. 1.** a country's chief law officer and senior legal adviser to its government. **2.** (in the U.S.) the chief law officer and legal adviser of a state government. **3.** (in some states of the U.S.) a public prosecutor.

Attorney General *n.* **1.** (in the United Kingdom except Scotland) the senior law officer and chief legal counsel of the Crown: a member of the government and of the House of Commons. **2.** (in the U.S.) the chief law officer and legal adviser to the Administration: head of the Department of Justice and member of the cabinet. **3.** (in Australia and New Zealand) the chief government law officer: a member of Parliament and usually a cabinet minister.

attract (əˈtrækt) *vb.* (*mainly tr.*) **1.** to draw (notice, a crowd of observers, etc.) to oneself by conspicuous behaviour or appearance (esp. in the phrase **attract attention**). **2.** (*also intr.*) to exert a force on (a body) that tends to cause an approach or oppose a separation: *the gravitational pull of the earth attracts objects to it.* **3.** to possess some property that pulls or draws (something) towards itself: *jam attracts wasps.* **4.** (*also intr.*) to exert a pleasing, alluring, or fascinating influence (upon); be attractive (to). [C15: from Latin *attrahere* to draw towards, from *trahere* to pull] —**atˈtractable** *adj.* —**atˈtractor** *or* **atˈtracter** *n.*

attractant (əˈtræktənt) *n.* a substance that attracts, esp. a chemical (**sex attractant**) produced by an insect and attracting insects of the same species. See also **pheromone.**

attraction (əˈtrækʃən) *n.* **1.** the act, power, or quality of attracting. **2.** a person or thing that attracts or is intended to attract. **3.** a force by which one object attracts another, such as the gravitational or magnetic force. **4.** a change in the form of one linguistic element caused by the proximity of another element.

attraction sphere *n.* another name for **astrosphere** (sense 2).

attractive (əˈtræktɪv) *adj.* **1.** appealing to the senses or mind through beauty, form, character, etc. **2.** arousing interest: *an attractive opportunity.* **3.** possessing the ability to draw or pull: *an attractive force.* —**atˈtractively** *adv.* —**atˈtractiveness** *n.*

attrib. *abbrev. for:* **1.** attribute. **2.** attributive.

attribute *vb.* (əˈtrɪbjuːt). **1.** (*tr.;* usually foll. by *to*) to regard as belonging (to), produced (by), or resulting (from); ascribe (to): *to attribute a painting to Picasso.* ~*n.* (ˈætrɪˌbjuːt). **2.** a property, quality, or feature belonging to or representative of a person or thing. **3.** an object accepted as belonging to a particular office or position. **4.** *Grammar.* **a.** an adjective or adjectival phrase. **b.** an attributive adjective. **5.** *Logic.* the property, quality, or feature that is affirmed or denied concerning the subject of a proposition. [C15: from Latin *attribuere* to associate with, from *tribuere* to give] —**atˈtributable** *adj.* —**atˈtributer** *or* **atˈtributor** *n.* —**attribution** (ˌætrɪˈbjuːʃən) *n.*

attribution theory *n.* *Psychol.* the theory that tries to explain how people link actions and emotions to particular causes, both internal and external.

attributive (əˈtrɪbjʊtɪv) *adj.* **1.** relating to an attribute. **2.** *Grammar.* (of an adjective or adjectival phrase) modifying a noun and constituting part of the same noun phrase, in English normally preceding the noun, as *black* in *Fido is a black dog* (as opposed to *Fido is black*). Compare **predicative. 3.** *Philosophy.* relative to an understood domain, as *small* in *that elephant is small.* ~*n.* **4.** an attributive adjective. —**atˈtributively** *adv.* —**atˈtributiveness** *n.*

attrit (əˈtrɪt) *vb.* (*tr.*) **-trits, -tritting, -tritted.** *U.S. slang.* **1.** to wear down or dispose of gradually. **2. to kill. [C18: back formation from** ATTRITION]

attrition (əˈtrɪʃən) *n.* **1.** the act of wearing away or the state of being worn away, as by friction. **2.** constant wearing down to weaken or destroy (often in the phrase **war of attrition**). **3.** Also called: **natural wastage.** a decrease in the size of the workforce of an organization achieved by not replacing employees who retire or resign. **4.** *Geography.* the grinding down of rock particles by friction during transportation by water, wind, or ice. Compare **abrasion** (sense 3), **corrasion. 5.** *Theol.* sorrow for sin arising from fear of damnation, esp. as contrasted with contrition, which arises purely from love of God. [C14: from Late Latin *attrītiō* a rubbing against something, from Latin *atterere* to weaken, from *terere* to rub] —**atˈtritional** *adj.* —**attritive** (əˈtraɪtɪv) *adj.*

attune (əˈtjuːn) *vb.* (*tr.*) **1.** to adjust or accustom (a person or thing); acclimatize. **2.** to tune (a musical instrument).

atty *abbrev. for* attorney.

atua (ˈɑːtuːə) *n. N.Z.* a spirit or demon. [Maori]

atween (əˈtwiːn) *prep.* an archaic or Scot. word for **between.**

at. wt. *abbrev. for* atomic weight.

atypical (eɪˈtɪpɪkᵊl) *adj.* not typical; deviating from or not conforming to type. —**aˈtypically** *adv.*

Au *the chemical symbol for* gold. [from New Latin *aurum*]

AU *or* **a.u.** *abbrev. for:* **1.** angstrom unit. **2.** astronomical unit.

aubade (*French* obad) *n.* **1.** a song or poem appropriate to or greeting the dawn. **2.** a romantic or idyllic prelude or overture. ~Compare **serenade.** [C19: from French, from Old Provençal *aubada* (unattested), from *auba* dawn, ultimately from Latin *albus* white]

auberge (*French* obɛrʒ) *n.* an inn or tavern. [C17: from French, from Old Provençal *alberga,* of Germanic origin; compare Old Saxon *heriberga* army shelter]

aubergine (ˈəʊbəˌʒiːn) *n.* **1.** a tropical Old World solanaceous plant, *Solanum melongena,* widely cultivated for its egg-shaped typically dark purple fruit. U.S., Canadian, and Australian name: **eggplant. 2.** the fruit of this plant, which is cooked and eaten as a vegetable. **3. a.** a dark purple colour. **b.** (*as adj.*): *an aubergine dress.* [C18: from French, from Catalan *alberginia,* from Arabic *al-bādindjān,* ultimately from Sanskrit *vatinganah,* of obscure origin]

aubrietia, aubrieta, *or* **aubretia** (ɔːˈbriːʃə) *n.* any trailing purple-flowered plant of the genus *Aubrietia,* native to European mountains but widely planted in rock gardens: family *Cruciferae* (crucifers). [C19: from New Latin, named after Claude *Aubriet,* 18th-century French painter of flowers and animals]

auburn (ˈɔːbᵊn) *n.* **a.** a moderate reddish-brown colour. **b.** (*as adj.*): *auburn hair.* [C15 (originally meaning: blond): from Old French *alborne* blond, from Medieval Latin *alburnus* whitish, from Latin *albus* white]

Aubusson (*French* obysɔ̃) *adj.* denoting or relating to a type of flat woven carpet or tapestry. [C16: from *Aubusson,* a town in central France]

AUC *abbrev. for:* **1.** (indicating years numbered from the founding of Rome, taken as 753 B.C.) **a.** ab urbe condita. **b.** anno urbis conditae. **2.** Australian Universities Commission.

au contraire *French.* (o kɔ̃trɛr) *adv.* on the contrary.

au courant *French.* (o kurɑ̃) *adj.* up-to-date, esp. in knowledge of current affairs. [literally: in the current]

auction (ˈɔːkʃən) *n.* **1.** a public sale of goods or property, esp. one in which prospective purchasers bid against each other until the highest price is reached. Compare **Dutch auction. 2.** the competitive calls made in bridge and other games before play begins, undertaking to win a given number of tricks if a certain suit is trumps. **3.** See **auction bridge.** ~*vb.* **4.** (*tr.;* often foll. by *off*) to sell by auction. [C16: from Latin *auctiō* an increasing, from *augēre* to increase]

auction bridge *n.* a variety of bridge, now generally superseded by contract bridge, in which all the tricks made score towards game.

auctioneer (ˌɔːkʃəˈnɪə) *n.* **1.** a person who conducts an auction by announcing the lots and controlling the bidding. ~*vb.* **2.** (*tr.*) to sell by auction.

auctorial (ɔːkˈtɔːrɪəl) *adj.* of or relating to an author. [C19: from Latin *auctor* AUTHOR]

aud. *abbrev. for:* **1.** audit. **2.** auditor.

audacious (ɔːˈdeɪʃəs) *adj.* **1.** recklessly bold or daring; fearless. **2.** impudent or presumptuous. [C16: from Latin *audāx* bold, from *audēre* to dare] —**auˈdaciously** *adv.* —**auˈdaciousness** *or* **audacity** (ɔːˈdæsɪtɪ) *n.*

audible (ˈɔːdɪbᵊl) *adj.* **1.** perceptible to the hearing; loud enough to be heard. ~*n.* **2.** *American football.* a change of playing tactics called by the quarterback when the offense is lined up at the line of scrimmage. [C16: from Late Latin *audibilis,* from Latin *audīre* to hear] —ˌ**audiˈbility** *or* ˈ**audibleness** *n.* —ˈ**audibly** *adv.*

audience (ˈɔːdɪəns) *n.* **1.** a group of spectators or listeners, esp. at a public event such as a concert or play. **2.** the people reached by a book, film, or radio or television programme. **3.** the devotees or followers of a public entertainer, lecturer, etc.; regular public. **4.** an opportunity to put one's point of view, such as a formal interview with a monarch or head of state. [C14: from Old French, from Latin *audientia* a hearing, from *audīre* to hear]

audile (ˈɔːdɪl, ˈɔːdaɪl) *Psychol.* ~*n.* **1.** a person who possesses a faculty for auditory imagery that is more distinct than his visual or other imagery. ~*adj.* **2.** of or relating to such a person. [C19: from AUD(ITORY) + -ILE]

audio (ˈɔːdɪˌəʊ) *n.* (*modifier*) **1.** of or relating to sound or hearing: *audio frequency.* **2.** relating to or employed in the transmission, reception, or reproduction of sound. **3.** of, concerned with, or operating at audio frequencies. ~Compare **video.** [C20: independent use of AUDIO-]

audio- *combining form.* indicating hearing or sound: *audiometer; audiovisual.* [from Latin *audīre* to hear]

audio conference *n.* a meeting that is conducted by the use of audio telecommunications.

audio frequency *n.* a frequency in the range 20 hertz to 20 000 hertz. A sound wave of this frequency would be audible to the human ear.

audiogenic (ˌɔːdɪəʊˈdʒɛnɪk) *adj.* caused or produced by sound or an audio frequency: *an audiogenic epileptic fit.*

audiogram (ˈɔːdɪəʊˌɡræm) *n.* a graphic record of the acuity of hearing of a person obtained by means of an audiometer.

audiology (ˌɔːdɪˈɒlədʒɪ) *n.* the scientific study of hearing, often including the treatment of persons with hearing defects. —**audiological** (ˌɔːdɪəˈlɒdʒɪkᵊl) *adj.* —ˌ**audioˈlogically** *adv.* —ˌ**audiˈologist** *n.*

audiometer (ˌɔːdɪˈɒmɪtə) *n.* an instrument for testing the intensity and frequency range of sound that is capable of detection by the human ear. —**audiometric** (ˌɔːdɪəʊˈmɛtrɪk) *adj.* —ˌ**audioˈmetrically** *adv.* —ˌ**audiˈometrist** *n.* —ˌ**audiˈometry** *n.*

audiophile (ˈɔːdɪəʊˌfaɪl) *n.* a person who has a great interest in high-fidelity sound reproduction.

audio response *n.* a computer response that is audible rather than textual or graphical.

audiotypist (ˈɔːdɪəʊˌtaɪpɪst) *n.* a typist trained to type from a dictating machine. —ˈ**audioˌtyping** *n.*

audiovisual (ˌɔːdɪəʊˈvɪzjʊəl, -ʒʊəl) *adj.* (esp. of teaching aids) involving or directed at both hearing and sight: *the language class had new audiovisual equipment.* —ˌ**audioˈvisually** *adv.*

audiphone ('ɔːdɪˌfəʊn) *n.* a type of hearing aid consisting of a diaphragm that, when placed against the upper teeth, conveys sound vibrations to the inner ear.

audit ('ɔːdɪt) *n.* **1. a.** an inspection, correction, and verification of business accounts by a qualified accountant. **b.** (*as modifier*): *audit report.* **2.** *U.S.* an audited account. **3.** any thoroughgoing check or examination. **4.** *Archaic.* a hearing. ~*vb.* **5.** to inspect, correct, and certify (accounts, etc.). **6.** *U.S. and Canadian.* to attend (classes, etc.) as an auditor. [C15: from Latin *audītus* a hearing, from *audīre* to hear]

audition (ɔːˈdɪʃən) *n.* **1.** a test at which a performer or musician is asked to demonstrate his ability for a particular role, etc. **2.** the act, sense, or power of hearing. ~*vb.* **3.** to judge by means of or be tested in an audition. [C16: from Latin *audītiō* a hearing, from *audīre* to hear]

auditor ('ɔːdɪtə) *n.* **1.** a person qualified to audit accounts. **2.** a person who hears or listens. **3.** *U.S. and Canadian.* a registered student who attends a class that is not an official part of his course of study. [C14: from Old French *auditeur,* from Latin *audītor* a hearer] —ˌ**audi'torial** *adj.*

auditorium (ˌɔːdɪˈtɔːrɪəm) *n., pl.* **-toriums** *or* **-toria** (-ˈtɔːrɪə). **1.** the area of a concert hall, theatre, etc., in which the audience sits. **2.** *U.S. and Canadian.* a building for public gatherings or meetings. [C17: from Latin: a judicial examination, from *audītōrius* concerning a hearing; see AUDITORY]

auditory ('ɔːdɪtərɪ, -trɪ) *adj. also* **auditive** ('ɔːdɪtɪv). **1.** of or relating to hearing, the sense of hearing, or the organs of hearing. ~*n.* **2.** an archaic word for **audience** or **auditorium.** [C14: from Latin *audītōrius* relating to hearing, from *audīre* to hear]

auditory phonetics *n.* (*functioning as sing.*) the branch of phonetics concerned with the perception of speech sounds by humans. Compare **acoustic phonetics, articulatory phonetics.**

AUEW (in Britain) *abbrev. for* Amalgamated Union of Engineering Workers.

au fait *French.* (o fɛ; *English* əʊ 'feɪ) *adj.* fully informed; in touch or expert. [C18: literally: to the point]

Aufklärung *German.* ('aufklɛːrʊŋ) *n.* the Enlightenment, esp. in Germany.

au fond *French.* (o fɔ̃) *adv.* fundamentally; essentially. [literally: at the bottom]

auf Wiedersehen *German.* (auf 'viːdərzeːən) *sentence substitute.* goodbye, until we see each other again.

aug. *abbrev. for* augmentative.

Aug. *abbrev. for* August.

Augean (ɔːˈdʒiːən) *adj.* extremely dirty or corrupt. [C16: after *Augeas* in Greek mythology, whose stables remained uncleaned for 30 years]

augend ('ɔːdʒɛnd, ɔːˈdʒɛnd) *n.* a number to which another number, the addend, is added. [from Latin *augendum* that is to be increased, from *augēre* to increase]

auger ('ɔːgə) *n.* **1.** a hand tool with a bit shaped like a corkscrew, for boring holes in wood. **2.** a larger tool of the same kind for boring holes in the ground. [C15 *an augur,* resulting from mistaken division of earlier *a nauger,* from Old English *nafugār* nave (of a wheel) spear (that is, tool for boring hubs of wheels), from *nafu* NAVE[2] + *gār* spear; see GORE[2]]

Auger effect ('augə) *n.* the emission of an electron instead of a photon by an excited ion as a result of a vacancy being filled in an inner electron shell. [C20: named after Pierre *Auger* (born 1899), French physicist]

aught[1] *or* **ought** (ɔːt) (*used with a negative or in conditional or interrogative sentences or clauses*) *Archaic or literary.* ~*pron.* **1.** anything at all; anything whatever (esp. in the phrase **for aught I know**). ~*adv.* **2.** *Dialect.* in any least part; to any degree. [Old English *āwiht,* from *ā* ever, AY[1] + *wiht* thing; see WIGHT[1]]

aught[2] *or* **ought** (ɔːt) *n.* a less common word for **nought** (zero).

augite ('ɔːgaɪt) *n.* a black or greenish-black mineral of the pyroxene group, found in igneous rocks. Composition: calcium magnesium iron aluminium silicate. General formula: $(Ca,Mg,Fe,Al)(Si,Al)_2O_6$. Crystal structure: monoclinic. [C19: from Latin *augītēs,* from Greek, from *augē* brightness] —**augitic** (ɔːˈgɪtɪk) *adj.*

augment *vb.* (ɔːgˈmɛnt). **1.** to make or become greater in number, amount, strength, etc.; increase. **2.** (*tr.*) *Music.* to increase (a major or perfect interval) by a semitone. Compare **diminish** (sense 3). **3.** (*tr.*) (in Greek and Sanskrit grammar) to prefix a vowel or diphthong to (a verb) to form a past tense. ~*n.* ('ɔːgmɛnt). **4.** (in Greek and Sanskrit grammar) a vowel or diphthong prefixed to a verb to form a past tense. [C15: from Late Latin *augmentāre* to increase, from *augmentum* growth, from Latin *augēre* to increase] —**aug'mentable** *adj.* —**aug'mentor** *or* **aug'menter** *n.*

augmentation (ˌɔːgmɛnˈteɪʃən) *n.* **1.** the act of augmenting or the state of being augmented. **2.** the amount by which something is increased. **3.** *Music.* the presentation of a subject of a fugue, in which the note values are uniformly increased. Compare **diminution** (sense 2).

augmentative (ɔːgˈmɛntətɪv) *adj.* **1.** tending or able to augment. **2.** *Grammar.* **a.** denoting an affix that may be added to a word to convey the meaning *large* or *great;* for example, the suffix *-ote* in Spanish, where *hombre* means man and *hombrote* big man. **b.** denoting a word formed by the addition of an augmentative affix. ~*n.* **3.** *Grammar.* an augmentative word or affix. ~Compare (for senses 2, 3) **diminutive.** —**aug'mentatively** *adv.*

augmented (ɔːgˈmɛntɪd) *adj.* **1.** *Music.* (of an interval) increased or expanded from the state of being perfect or major by the raising of the higher note or the dropping of the lower note by one semitone: *C to G is a perfect fifth, but C to G sharp is an augmented fifth.* Compare **diminished** (sense 2). **2.** *Music.* **a.** denoting a chord based upon an augmented triad: *an augmented seventh chord.* **b.** denoting a triad consisting of the root plus a major third and an augmented fifth. **c.** (*postpositive*) (esp. in jazz) denoting a chord having as its root the note specified: *D augmented.* **3.** having been increased, esp. in number: *an augmented orchestra.*

augmented transition network *n.* (in certain schools of linguistics) a formalism, usually expressed as a diagram, having the power of a Turing machine, used as the basis of processes transforming sentences into their syntactic representations. Abbrev.: **ATN.**

au gratin (*French* o gratɛ̃) *adj.* covered and cooked with browned breadcrumbs and sometimes cheese. [French, literally: with the grating]

augur ('ɔːgə) *n.* **1.** Also called: **auspex.** (in ancient Rome) a religious official who observed and interpreted omens and signs to help guide the making of public decisions. **2.** any prophet or soothsayer. ~*vb.* **3.** to predict (some future event), as from signs or omens. **4.** (*tr.; may take a clause as object*) to be an omen (of); presage. **5.** (*intr.*) to foreshadow future events to be as specified; bode: *this augurs well for us.* [C14: from Latin: a diviner, perhaps from *augēre* to increase] —**augural** ('ɔːgjurəl) *adj.* —'**augurship** *n.*

augury ('ɔːgjʊrɪ) *n., pl.* **-ries.** **1.** the art of or a rite conducted by an augur. **2.** a sign or portent; omen.

august (ɔːˈgʌst) *adj.* **1.** dignified or imposing: *an august presence.* **2.** of noble birth or high rank: *an august lineage.* [C17: from Latin *augustus;* related to *augēre* to increase] —**au'gustly** *adv.* —**au'gustness** *n.*

August ('ɔːgəst) *n.* the eighth month of the year, consisting of 31 days. [Old English, from Latin, named after the Roman emperor *Augustus* (63 B.C.–14 A.D.)]

Augustan (ɔːˈgʌstən) *adj.* **1.** characteristic of, denoting, or relating to the Roman emperor Augustus Caesar, his period, or the poets writing during his reign. **2.** of, relating to, or characteristic of any literary period noted for refinement and classicism, esp. the late 17th century in France or the 18th century in England. ~*n.* **3.** an author in an Augustan Age. **4.** a student of or specialist in Augustan literature.

auguste *or* **august** (aʊˈguːst, 'aʊˌgʊst) *n.* (*often cap.*) a type of circus clown who usually wears battered ordinary clothes and is habitually maladroit or unlucky. [C20: French, from German]

Augustinian (ˌɔːgəˈstɪnɪən) *adj.* **1.** of or relating to Saint Augustine of Hippo (354–430 A.D.), his doctrines, or any of the Christian religious orders founded on his doctrines. ~*n.* **2.** a member of any of several religious orders, such as the **Augustinian Canons, Augustinian Hermits,** and **Austin Friars,** which are governed by the rule of Saint Augustine. **3.** a person who follows the doctrines of Saint Augustine.

au jus (*French* o ʒy) *adj.* (of meat) served in its own gravy. [literally: with the juice]

auk (ɔːk) *n.* **1.** any of various diving birds of the family *Alcidae* of northern oceans having a heavy body, short tail, narrow wings, and a black-and-white plumage: order *Charadriiformes.* See also **great auk, razorbill.** **2. little auk.** Also called: **dovekie.** a small short-billed auk, *Plautus alle,* abundant in Arctic regions. [C17: from Old Norse *ālka;* related to Swedish *alka,* Danish *alke*]

auklet ('ɔːklɪt) *n.* any of various small auks of the genera *Aethia* and *Ptychoramphus.*

au lait (əʊ 'leɪ; *French* o lɛ) *adj.* prepared or served with milk. [French, literally: with milk]

auld (ɔːld) *adj.* a Scot. word for **old.** [Old English *āld*]

auld lang syne ('ɔːld læŋ 'səɪn, 'saɪn, 'zaɪn) *n.* old times; times past, esp. those remembered with affection or nostalgia. [Scottish, literally: old long since]

aulic ('ɔːlɪk) *adj. Rare.* relating to a royal court. [C18: from Latin *aulicus,* from Greek *aulikos* belonging to a prince's court, from *aulē* court]

AULLA ('aulə) *n. acronym for* Australasian Universities Language and Literature Association.

au naturel *French.* (o natyrɛl) *adj., adv.* **1.** naked; nude. **2.** uncooked or plainly cooked. [literally: in (a) natural (condition)]

aunt (ɑːnt) *n.* (*often cap., esp. as a term of address*) **1.** a sister of one's father or mother. **2.** the wife of one's uncle. **3.** a term of address used by children for any woman, esp. for a friend of the parents. **4. my (sainted) aunt!** an exclamation of surprise or amazement. [C13: from Old French *ante,* from Latin *amita* a father's sister]

auntie *or* **aunty** ('ɑːntɪ) *n., pl.* **-ies.** a familiar or diminutive word for **aunt.**

Auntie ('ɑːntɪ) *n. Brit.* an informal name for the **BBC.**

auntie man *n. Caribbean informal.* an effeminate or homosexual male.

Aunt Sally ('sælɪ) *n., pl.* **-lies.** *Brit.* **1.** a figure of an old woman's head, typically with a clay pipe, used in fairgrounds and fêtes as a target for balls or other objects. **2.** any person who is a target for insults or criticism. **3.** something set up as a target for disagreement or attack.

au pair (əʊ 'pɛə; *French* o pɛr) *n.* **1. a.** a young foreigner, usually a girl, who undertakes housework in exchange for board and lodging, esp. in order to learn the language. **b.** *(as modifier): an au pair girl.* **2.** a young person who lives temporarily with a family abroad in exchange for a reciprocal arrangement with his or her own family. *~vb.* **3.** *(intr.)* to work as an au pair. *~adv.* **4.** as an au pair: *she worked au pair in Greece.* [C20: from French: on an equal footing]

aura ('ɔːrə) *n., pl.* **auras** *or* **aurae** ('ɔːriː). **1.** a distinctive air or quality considered to be characteristic of a person or thing. **2.** any invisible emanation, such as a scent or odour. **3.** *Pathol.* strange sensations, such as noises in the ears or flashes of light, that immediately precede an attack, esp. of epilepsy. **4.** (in parapsychology) an invisible emanation produced by and surrounding a person or object: alleged to be discernible by individuals of supernormal sensibility. [C18: via Latin from Greek: breeze]

aural[1] ('ɔːrəl) *adj.* of or relating to the sense or organs of hearing; auricular. [C19: from Latin *auris* ear] —**'aurally** *adv.*

aural[2] ('ɔːrəl) *adj.* of or relating to an aura.

aurar ('ɔːrɑː) *n.* the plural of **eyrir.**

aureate ('ɔːrɪɪt, -ˌeɪt) *adj.* **1.** covered with gold; gilded. **2.** of a golden colour. **3.** (of a style of writing or speaking) excessively elaborate or ornate; florid. [C15: from Late Latin *aureātus* gilded, from Latin *aureus* golden, from *aurum* gold] —**'aureately** *adv.* —**'aureateness** *n.*

aureole ('ɔːrɪˌəʊl) *or* **aureola** (ɔː'riːələ) *n.* **1.** (esp. in paintings of Christian saints and the deity) a border of light or radiance enveloping the head or sometimes the whole of a figure represented as holy. **2.** a less common word for **halo. 3.** another name for **corona** (sense 2). [C13: from Old French *auréole,* from Medieval Latin *(corōna) aureola* golden (crown), from Latin *aureolus* golden, from *aurum* gold]

Aureomycin (ˌɔːrɪəʊ'maɪsɪn) *n. Trademark.* a brand of **chlortetracycline.**

aureus ('ɔːrɪəs) *n., pl.* **aurei** ('ɔːrɪˌaɪ). a gold coin of the Roman Empire. [Latin: golden; see AUREATE]

au revoir *French.* (o rəvwar) *sentence substitute.* goodbye. [literally: to the seeing again]

auric ('ɔːrɪk) *adj.* of or containing gold in the trivalent state. [C19: from Latin *aurum* gold]

auricle ('ɔːrɪkᵊl) *n.* **1. a.** the upper chamber of the heart; atrium. **b.** a small sac in the atrium of the heart. **2.** Also called: **pinna.** *Anat.* the external part of the ear. **3.** Also called: **auricula.** *Biology.* an ear-shaped part or appendage, such as that occurring at the base of some leaves. [C17: from Latin *auricula* the external ear, from *auris* ear] —**'auricled** *adj.*

auricula (ɔː'rɪkjʊlə) *n., pl.* **-lae** (-ˌliː) *or* **-las. 1.** Also called: **bear's-ear.** a widely cultivated alpine primrose, *Primula auricula,* with leaves shaped like a bear's ear. **2.** another word for **auricle** (sense 3). [C17: from New Latin, from Latin: external ear; see AURICLE]

auricular (ɔː'rɪkjʊlə) *adj.* **1.** of, relating to, or received by the sense or organs of hearing; aural. **2.** shaped like an ear. **3.** of or relating to an auricle of the heart. **4.** (of feathers) occurring in tufts surrounding the ears of owls and similar birds. *~n.* **5.** *(usually pl.)* an auricular feather. —**au'ricularly** *adv.*

auriculate (ɔː'rɪkjʊlɪt, -ˌleɪt) *or* **auriculated** *adj.* **1.** having ears. **2.** *Botany.* having ear-shaped parts or appendages. **3.** Also: **auriform** ('ɔːrɪˌfɔːm). shaped like an ear; auricular. —**au'riculately** *adv.*

auriferous (ɔː'rɪfərəs) *adj.* (of rock) containing gold; gold-bearing. [C18: from Latin *aurifer* gold-bearing, from *aurum* gold + *ferre* to bear]

Auriga (ɔː'raɪgə) *n., Latin genitive* **Aurigae** (ɔː'raɪdʒiː). a conspicuous constellation in the N hemisphere between the Great Bear and Orion, at the edge of the Milky Way. It contains the first magnitude star Capella and the binary star **Epsilon Aurigae,** which is the largest known star. [Latin: charioteer]

Aurignacian (ˌɔːrɪg'neɪʃən) *adj.* of, relating to, or produced during a flint culture of the Upper Palaeolithic type characterized by the use of bone and antler tools, pins, awls, etc., and also by cave art and evidence of the beginnings of religion. [C20: from French *Aurignacien,* after *Aurignac,* France, in the Pyrenees, near which is the cave where remains were discovered]

aurist ('ɔːrɪst) *n.* an ear specialist.

aurochs ('ɔːrɒks) *n., pl.* **-rochs.** a recently extinct member of the cattle tribe, *Bos primigenius,* that inhabited forests in N Africa, Europe, and SW Asia. It had long horns and is thought to be one of the ancestors of modern cattle. Also called: **urus.** [C18: from German, from Old High German *ūrohso,* from *ūro* bison + *ohso* OX]

aurora (ɔː'rɔːrə) *n., pl.* **-ras** *or* **-rae** (-riː). **1.** an atmospheric phenomenon consisting of bands, curtains, or streamers of light, usually green, red, or yellow, that move across the sky in polar regions. It is caused by collisions between air molecules and charged particles from the sun that are trapped in the earth's magnetic field. **2.** *Poetic.* the dawn. [C14: from Latin: dawn; see EAST] —**au'roral** *adj.* —**au'rorally** *adv.*

aurora australis (ɒ'streɪlɪs) *n.* *(sometimes cap.)* the aurora seen around the South Pole. Also called: **southern lights.** [New Latin: southern aurora]

aurora borealis (ˌbɔːrɪ'eɪlɪs) *n.* *(sometimes cap.)* the aurora seen around the North Pole. Also called: **northern lights.** [C17: New Latin: northern aurora]

aurous ('ɔːrəs) *adj.* of or containing gold, esp. in the monovalent state. [C19: apparently from French *aureux,* from Late Latin *aurōsus* gold-coloured, from Latin *aurum* gold]

aurum ('ɔːrəm) *n. Obsolete.* gold. [C16: Latin]

AUS *international car registration for* Australia.

Aus. *abbrev. for:* **1.** Australia(n). **2.** Austria(n).

auscultate ('ɔːskəlˌteɪt) *vb.* to examine (a patient) by means of auscultation. —**'auscultator** *n.*

auscultation (ˌɔːskəl'teɪʃən) *n.* **1.** the diagnostic technique in medicine of listening to the various internal sounds made by the body, usually with the aid of a stethoscope. **2.** the act of listening. [C19: from Latin *auscultātiō* a listening, from *auscultāre* to listen attentively; related to Latin *auris* ear] —**auscultatory** (ɔː'skʌltətərɪ) *or* **auscultative** (ɔː'skʌltətɪv, 'ɔːskəlˌteɪtɪv) *adj.*

ausforming ('aʊsˌfɔːmɪŋ) *n.* a treatment to strengthen hard steels, prior to quenching, in which the specimen is plastically deformed while it is in the austenite temperature range. [C20: from AUS(TENITIC) + (DE)FORM]

auspex ('ɔːspɛks) *n., pl.* **auspices** ('ɔːspɪˌsiːz). *Roman history.* another word for **augur** (sense 1). [C16: from Latin: observer of birds, from *avis* bird + *specere* to look]

auspicate ('ɔːspɪˌkeɪt) *vb. (tr.) Archaic.* to begin.

auspice ('ɔːspɪs) *n., pl.* **-pices** (-pɪsɪz). **1.** *(usually pl.)* patronage or guidance (esp. in the phrase **under the auspices of**). **2.** *(often pl.)* a sign or omen, esp. one that is favourable. [C16: from Latin *auspicium* augury from birds; see AUSPEX]

auspicious (ɔː'spɪʃəs) *adj.* **1.** favourable or propitious. **2.** *Archaic.* prosperous or fortunate. —**aus'piciously** *adv.* —**aus'piciousness** *n.*

Aussat ('ɒsæt, 'ɒzæt) *n.* the Australian-owned communications satellite launched in 1985.

Aussie ('ɒzɪ) *adj., n.* an informal word for **Australian.**

Aust. *abbrev. for:* **1.** Australia(n). **2.** Austria(n).

austenite ('ɔːstəˌnaɪt) *n.* **1.** a solid solution of carbon in face-centred-cubic gamma iron, usually existing above 723°C. **2.** the gamma phase of iron, stabilized at low temperatures by the addition of such elements as nickel. [C20: named after Sir William C. Roberts-*Austen* (1843–1902), British metallurgist] —**austenitic** (ˌɔːstə'nɪtɪk) *adj.*

austenitic stainless steel *n.* an alloy of iron, usually containing at least 8 per cent of nickel and 18 per cent of chromium, used where corrosion resistance, heat resistance, creep resistance, or nonmagnetic properties are required.

Auster ('ɔːstə) *n. Poetic.* the south wind. [C14: Latin]

austere (ɒ'stɪə) *adj.* **1.** stern or severe in attitude or manner: *an austere schoolmaster.* **2.** grave, sober, or serious: *an austere expression.* **3.** self-disciplined, abstemious, or ascetic: *an austere life.* **4.** severely simple or plain: *an austere design.* [C14: from Old French *austère,* from Latin *austērus* sour, from Greek *austēros* astringent; related to Greek *hauein* to dry] —**aus'terely** *adv.* —**aus'tereness** *n.*

austerity (ɒ'stɛrɪtɪ) *n., pl.* **-ties. 1.** the state or quality of being austere. **2.** *(often pl.)* an austere habit, practice, or act. **3. a.** reduced availability of luxuries and consumer goods, esp. when brought about by government policy. **b.** *(as modifier): an austerity budget.*

Austin ('ɒstɪn) *adj., n.* another word for **Augustinian.** [C14: shortened form of *Augustine*]

austral[1] ('ɔːstrəl) *adj.* of or coming from the south: *austral winds.* [C14: from Latin *austrālis,* from *auster* the south wind]

austral[2] (aʊ'strɑːl) *n., pl.* **-trales.** the standard monetary unit of Argentina equal to 100 centavos. [from Spanish; see AUSTRAL[1]]

Austral. *abbrev. for:* **1.** Australasia. **2.** Australia(n).

Australasian (ˌɒstrə'leɪzɪən) *n.* **1.** a native or inhabitant of Australasia, comprising Australia, New Zealand, and the neighbouring islands. *~adj.* **2.** of or relating to Australasia. **3.** (of organizations) having members in Australasia.

Australia Day *n.* a public holiday in Australia, commemorating the landing of the British in 1788: observed on the first Monday after January 26.

Australian (ɒ'streɪlɪən) *n.* **1.** a native or inhabitant of Australia, the smallest continent. **2.** the form of English spoken in Australia. **3.** a linguistic phylum consisting of the languages spoken by the Aborigines of Australia. *~adj.* **4.** of, relating to, or characteristic of Australia, the Australians, or their form of English. **5.** of, relating to, or belonging to the phylum of languages spoken by the Australian Aborigines. **6.** of or denoting a zoogeographical region consisting of Australia, New Zealand, Polynesia, New Guinea, and the Moluccas.

Australiana (ɒˌstreɪlɪ'ɑːnə) *n.* objects or documents relating to Australia and its history or culture esp. in the form of a collection.

Australianism (ɒ'streɪlɪəˌnɪzəm) *n.* **1.** the Australian national character or spirit. **2.** loyalty to Australia, its political independence, culture, etc. **3.** a linguistic usage, custom, or other feature peculiar to or characteristic of Australia, its people, or their culture.

Australianize *or* **Australianise** (ɒ'streɪlɪəˌnaɪz) *vb.* (esp. of a new immigrant) to adopt or cause to adopt Australian habits and attitudes; integrate into Australian society.

Australian Rules *n.* (*functioning as sing.*) a game resembling rugby football, played in Australia between teams of 18 men each on an oval pitch, with a ball resembling a large rugby ball. Players attempt to kick the ball between posts (without cross-bars) at either end of the pitch, scoring six points for a goal (between the two main posts) and one point for a behind (between either of two outer posts and the main posts). They may punch or kick the ball and run with it provided that they bounce it every ten yards. Also called: **national code.**

Australian salmon *n.* another name for **kahawai.**

Australian terrier *n.* a small wire-haired breed of terrier similar to the cairn.

Australoid ('ɒstrəˌlɔɪd) *adj.* **1.** denoting, relating to, or belonging to a racial group that includes the Australian Aborigines and certain other peoples of southern Asia and the Pacific islands, characterized by dark skin, flat retreating forehead, and medium stature. ~*n.* **2.** any member of this racial group.

australopithecine (ˌɒstrələʊ'pɪθɪˌsiːn) *n.* **1.** any of various extinct apelike primates of the genus *Australopithecus* and related genera, remains of which have been discovered in southern and E Africa. Some species are estimated to be over 4.5 million years old. See also **zinjanthropus.** ~*adj.* **2.** of or relating to any of these primates. [C20: from New Latin *Australopithecus,* from Latin *austrālis* southern, AUSTRAL + Greek *pithēkos* ape]

Australorp ('ɒstrəˌlɔːp) *n.* a heavy black breed of domestic fowl laying brown eggs. [shortened from *Austral(ian Black) Orp(ington)*]

Austro-Hungarian *adj.* of or relating to the Dual Monarchy of Austria-Hungary (1867–1918).

Austrian ('ɒstrɪən) *adj.* **1.** of or relating to Austria, a republic in central Europe. ~*n.* **2.** a native or inhabitant of Austria.

Austrian blind *n.* a window blind consisting of rows of vertically gathered fabric that may be drawn up to form a series of ruches.

Austro-[1] ('ɒstrəʊ-) *combining form.* southern: *Austro-Asiatic.* [from Latin *auster* the south wind]

Austro-[2] ('ɒstrəʊ-) *combining form.* Austrian: *Austro-Hungarian.*

Austro-Asiatic *n.* a hypothetical phylum or superfamily of languages consisting of Mon-Khmer and certain other languages of India and South-East Asia. Links with Malayo-Polynesian have also been suggested.

Austronesian (ˌɒstrəʊ'niːʒən, -ʃən) *adj.* **1.** of or relating to Austronesia (S Pacific islands including Indonesia, Melanesia, Micronesia, and Polynesia), its peoples, or their languages. ~*n.* **2.** another name for **Malayo-Polynesian.**

AUT *abbrev. for* Association of University Teachers.

aut- *combining form.* a variant of **auto-** before a vowel.

autacoid ('ɔːtəˌkɔɪd) *n. Physiol.* any natural internal secretion, esp. one that exerts an effect similar to a drug. [C20: from AUTO- + Greek *akos* cure + -OID]

autarchy[1] ('ɔːtɑːkɪ) *n., pl.* **-chies. 1.** unlimited rule; autocracy. **2.** self-government; self-rule. [C17: from Greek *autarkhia,* from *autarkhos* autocratic; see AUTO-, -ARCHY] —**au'tarchic** *or* **au'tarchical** *adj.*

autarchy[2] ('ɔːtɑːkɪ) *n., pl.* **-chies.** a variant spelling (now rare) of **autarky.**

autarky ('ɔːtɑːkɪ) *n., pl.* **-kies. 1.** (esp. of a political unit) a system or policy of economic self-sufficiency aimed at removing the need for imports. **2.** an economically self-sufficient country. [C17: from Greek *autarkeia,* from *autarkēs* self-sufficient, from AUTO- + *arkein* to suffice] —**au'tarkic** *adj.* —**'autarkist** *n.*

autecious (ɔː'tiːʃəs) *adj.* a variant spelling of **autoecious.**

autecology (ˌɔːtɪ'kɒlədʒɪ) *n.* the ecological study of an individual organism or species. Compare **synecology.** —ˌ**auteco'logical** *adj.*

auteur (ɔː'tɜː) *n.* a film director, esp. one considered as having a dominant creative role. [French: author]

auth. *abbrev. for:* **1.** author. **2.** authority. **3.** authorized.

authentic (ɔː'θɛntɪk) *adj.* **1.** of undisputed origin or authorship; genuine: *an authentic signature.* **2.** accurate in representation of the facts; trustworthy; reliable: *an authentic account.* **3.** (of a deed or other document) duly executed, any necessary legal formalities having been complied with. **4.** *Music.* **a.** using period instruments and historically researched scores and playing techniques in an attempt to perform a piece as it would have been played at the time it was written. **b.** (*in combination*): *an authentic-instrument performance.* **5.** *Music.* **a.** (of a mode as used in Gregorian chant) commencing on the final and ending an octave higher. **b.** (of a cadence) progressing from a dominant to a tonic chord. Compare **plagal.** [C14: from Late Latin *authenticus* coming from the author, from Greek *authentikos,* from *authentēs* one who acts independently, from AUTO- + *hentēs* a doer] —**au'thentically** *adv.* —**authenticity** (ˌɔːθɛn'tɪsɪtɪ) *n.*

authenticate (ɔː'θɛntɪˌkeɪt) *vb.* (*tr.*) **1.** to establish as genuine or valid. **2.** to give authority or legal validity to. —**auˌthenti'cation** *n.* —**au'thentiˌcator** *n.*

authigenic (ˌɔːθɪ'dʒɛnɪk) *adj.* (of minerals) having crystallized in a sediment during or after deposition. [C19: from German *authigene* from Greek *authigenēs* native + -IC]

author ('ɔːθə) *n.* **1.** a person who composes a book, article, or other written work. Related adj.: **auctorial. 2.** a person who writes books as a profession; writer. **3.** the writings of such a person: *reviewing a postwar author.* **4.** an originator or creator: *the author of this plan.* ~*vb.* (*tr.*) **5.** to write or originate. [C14: from Old French *autor,* from Latin *auctor* author, from *augēre* to increase] —**authorial** (ɔː'θɔːrɪəl) *adj.*

authoress ('ɔːθəˌrɛs) *n. Now usually disparaging.* a female author.

authoritarian (ɔːˌθɒrɪ'tɛərɪən) *adj.* **1.** favouring, denoting, or characterized by strict obedience to authority. **2.** favouring, denoting, or relating to government by a small elite with wide powers. **3.** despotic; dictatorial; domineering. ~*n.* **4.** a person who favours or practises authoritarian policies. —**auˌthori'tarianism** *n.*

authoritative (ɔː'θɒrɪtətɪv) *adj.* **1.** recognized or accepted as being true or reliable: *an authoritative article on drugs.* **2.** exercising or asserting authority; commanding: *an authoritative manner.* **3.** possessing or supported by authority; official: *an athoritative communiqué.* —**au'thoritatively** *adv.* —**au'thoritativeness** *n.*

authority (ɔː'θɒrɪtɪ) *n., pl.* **-ties. 1.** the power or right to control, judge, or prohibit the actions of others. **2.** (*often pl.*) a person or group of people having this power, such as a government, police force, etc. **3.** a position that commands such a power or right (often in the phrase **in authority**). **4.** such a power or right delegated, esp. from one person to another; authorization: *she has his authority.* **5.** the ability to influence or control others: *a man of authority.* **6.** an expert or an authoritative written work in a particular field: *he is an authority on Ming china.* **7.** evidence or testimony: *we have it on his authority that she is dead.* **8.** confidence resulting from great expertise: *the violinist lacked authority in his cadenza.* **9.** (*cap. when part of a name*) a public board or corporation exercising governmental authority in administering some enterprise: *Independent Broadcasting Authority.* **10.** *Law.* **a.** a judicial decision, statute, or rule of law that establishes a principle; precedent. **b.** legal permission granted to a person to perform a specified act. [C14: from French *autorité,* from Latin *auctōritas,* from *auctor* AUTHOR]

authorize *or* **authorise** ('ɔːθəˌraɪz) *vb.* (*tr.*) **1.** to confer authority upon (someone to do something); empower. **2.** to permit (someone to do or be something) with official sanction: *a dealer authorized by a manufacturer to retail his products.* —ˌ**authori'zation** *or* ˌ**authori'sation** *n.* —**'authorˌizer** *or* **'authorˌiser** *n.*

Authorized Version *n.* **the.** an English translation of the Bible published in 1611 under James I. Also called: **King James Version, King James Bible.**

authorship ('ɔːθəˌʃɪp) *n.* **1.** the origin or originator of a written work, plan, etc.: *a book of unknown authorship.* **2.** the profession of writing books.

Auth. Ver. *abbrev. for* Authorized Version (of the Bible).

autism ('ɔːtɪzəm) *n. Psychiatry.* abnormal self-absorption, usually affecting children, characterized by lack of response to people and actions and limited ability to communicate: children suffering from autism often do not learn to speak. [C20: from Greek *autos* self + -ISM] —**au'tistic** *adj., n.*

auto ('ɔːtəʊ) *n., pl.* **-tos.** *U.S. and Canadian informal.* **a.** short for **automobile. b.** (*as modifier*): *auto parts.*

auto. *abbrev. for:* **1.** automatic. **2.** automobile. **3.** automotive.

auto- *or sometimes before a vowel* **aut-** *combining form.* **1.** self; same; of or by the same one: *autobiography.* **2.** acting from or occurring within; self-caused: *autohypnosis.* **3.** self-propelling; automatic: *automobile.* [from Greek *autos* self]

autoallogamy (ˌɔːtəʊə'lɒgəmɪ) *n.* the ability of some plants of a species to cross-pollinate and others to self-pollinate.

autoantibody (ˌɔːtəʊ'æntɪˌbɒdɪ) *n., pl.* **-bodies.** an antibody reacting with an antigen that is a part of the organism in which the antibody is formed.

autobahn ('ɔːtəˌbɑːn) *n.* a motorway in German-speaking countries. [from German, from *Auto* car + *Bahn* road]

autobiographical (ˌɔːtəˌbaɪə'græfɪkᵊl) *adj.* **1.** of or concerned with one's own life. **2.** of or relating to an autobiography. —ˌ**autoˌbio'graphically** *adv.*

autobiography (ˌɔːtəʊbaɪ'ɒgrəfɪ, ˌɔːtəbaɪ-) *n., pl.* **-phies.** an account of a person's life written or otherwise recorded by that person. —ˌ**autobi'ographer** *n.*

autocade ('ɔːtəʊˌkeɪd) *n. U.S.* another name for **motorcade.**

autocatalysis (ˌɔːtəʊkə'tælɪsɪs) *n., pl.* **-ses** (-ˌsiːz). the catalysis of a reaction in which the catalyst is one of the products of the reaction.

autocephalous (ˌɔːtəʊ'sɛfələs) *adj.* **1.** (of an Eastern Christian Church) governed by its own national synods and appointing its own patriarchs or prelates. **2.** (of a bishop) independent of any higher governing body. —**autocephalic** (ˌɔːtəʊsɪ'fælɪk) *adj.* —ˌ**auto'cephaly** *n.*

autochanger ('ɔːtəʊˌtʃeɪndʒə) *n.* **1.** a device in a record player that enables a small stack of records to be dropped automatically onto the turntable one at a time and played separately. **2.** a record player with such a device.

autochthon (ɔːˈtɒkθən, -θɒn) *n., pl.* **-thons** *or* **-thones** (-θəˌniːz). **1.** (*often pl.*) one of the earliest known inhabitants of any country; aboriginal. **2.** an animal or plant that is native to a particular region. [C17: from Greek *autokhthōn* from the earth itself, from AUTO- + *khthōn* the earth]

autochthonous (ɔːˈtɒkθənəs), **autochthonic** (ˌɔːtɒkˈθɒnɪk), *or* **autochthonal** *adj.* **1.** (of rocks, deposits, etc.) found where they and their constituents were formed. Compare **allochthonous.** **2.** inhabiting a place or region from earliest known times; aboriginal. **3.** *Physiol.* (of some functions, such as heartbeat) originating within an organ rather than from external stimulation. —**auˈtochthonism** *or* **auˈtochthony** *n.* —**auˈtochthonously** *adv.*

autocidal (ˌɔːtəʊˈsaɪdᵊl) *adj.* (of insect pest control) effected by the introduction of sterile or genetically altered individuals into the wild population.

autoclave (ˈɔːtəˌkleɪv) *n.* **1.** a strong sealed vessel used for chemical reactions at high pressure. **2.** an apparatus for sterilizing objects (esp. surgical instruments) or for cooking by means of steam under pressure. **3.** *Civil engineering.* a vessel in which freshly cast concrete or sand-lime bricks are cured very rapidly in high-pressure steam. *~vb.* **4.** (*tr.*) to put in or subject to the action of an autoclave. [C19: from French AUTO- + *-clave,* from Latin *clāvis* key]

autocorrelation (ˌɔːtəʊˌkɒrɪˈleɪʃən) *n. Statistics.* the condition occurring when successive items in a series are correlated so that their covariance is not zero and they are not independent. Also called: **serial correlation.**

autocracy (ɔːˈtɒkrəsɪ) *n., pl.* **-cies.** **1.** government by an individual with unrestricted authority. **2.** the unrestricted authority of such an individual. **3.** a country, society, etc., ruled by an autocrat.

autocrat (ˈɔːtəˌkræt) *n.* **1.** a ruler who possesses absolute and unrestricted authority. **2.** a domineering or dictatorial person. —ˌ**autoˈcratic** *adj.* —ˌ**autoˈcratically** *adv.*

autocross (ˈɔːtəʊˌkrɒs) *n.* a form of motor sport in which cars race over a half-mile circuit of rough grass. See also **motocross, rallycross.**

Autocue (ˈɔːtəʊˌkjuː) *n. Trademark.* an electronic television prompting device whereby a prepared script, unseen by the audience, is enlarged line by line for the speaker. U.S. and Canadian name (trademark): **Teleprompter.**

autocycle (ˈɔːtəʊˌsaɪkᵊl) *n. Obsolete.* a bicycle powered or assisted by a small engine.

auto-da-fé (ˌɔːtəʊdəˈfeɪ) *n., pl.* **autos-da-fé.** **1.** *History.* a ceremony of the Spanish Inquisition including the pronouncement and execution of sentences passed on sinners or heretics. **2.** the burning to death of people condemned as heretics by the Inquisition. [C18: from Portuguese, literally: act of the faith]

autodestruct (ˌɔːtəʊdɪˈstrʌkt) *adj. also* **autodestructive.** **1.** likely to or possessing the power to destroy or obliterate itself or its possessor: *autodestruct mechanism.* *~vb.* (*intr.*) **2.** (of a missile, machine, etc.) to destroy itself.

autodidact (ˈɔːtəʊˌdaɪdækt) *n.* a person who is self-taught. [C16: from Greek *autodidaktos* self-taught, from *autos* self + *didaskein* to teach] —ˌ**autodiˈdactic** *adj.*

autodyne (ˈɔːtəʊˌdaɪn) *adj. Electronics.* denoting or relating to an electrical circuit in which the same elements and valves are used as oscillator and detector.

autoecious *or U.S.* (*sometimes*) **autecious** (ɔːˈtiːʃəs) *adj.* (of parasites, esp. the rust fungi) completing the entire life cycle on a single species of host. Compare **heteroecious.** [C19: from AUTO- + *-oecious,* from Greek *oikia* house] —**auˈtoecism** *or U.S.* (*sometimes*) **auˈtecism** *n.*

autoeroticism (ˌɔːtəʊɪˈrɒtɪˌsɪzəm) *or* **autoerotism** (ˌɔːtəʊˈɛrəˌtɪzəm) *n. Psychol.* the arousal and use of one's own body as a sexual object, as through masturbation. —ˌ**autoeˈrotic** *adj.*

autogamy (ɔːˈtɒgəmɪ) *n.* **1.** self-fertilization in flowering plants. **2.** a type of sexual reproduction, occurring in some protozoans, in which the uniting gametes are derived from the same cell. —**auˈtogamous** *or* **autogamic** (ˌɔːtəˈgæmɪk) *adj.*

autogenesis (ˌɔːtəʊˈdʒɛnɪsɪs) *or* **autogeny** (ɔːˈtɒdʒɪnɪ) *n.* another word for **abiogenesis.** —**autogenetic** (ˌɔːtəʊdʒɪˈnɛtɪk) *adj.*

autogenic training (ˌɔːtəʊˈdʒɛnɪk) *n.* a technique for reducing stress through mental exercises to produce physical relaxation. Also called: **autogenics.**

autogenous (ɔːˈtɒdʒɪnəs) *adj.* **1. a.** originating within the body. Compare **heterogenous.** **b.** denoting a vaccine made from bacteria obtained from the patient's own body. **2.** self-generated; self-produced. **3.** denoting a weld in which the filler metal and the parent metal are of similar composition. —**auˈtogenously** *adv.*

autogiro *or* **autogyro** (ˌɔːtəʊˈdʒaɪrəʊ) *n., pl.* **-ros.** a self-propelled aircraft supported in flight mainly by unpowered rotating horizontal blades. Also called: **gyroplane.** Compare **helicopter.** [C20: originally a trademark]

autograft (ˈɔːtəˌgrɑːft) *n. Surgery.* a tissue graft obtained from one part of a patient's body for use on another part.

autograph (ˈɔːtəˌgrɑːf, -ˌgræf) *n.* **1. a.** a handwritten signature, esp. that of a famous person. **b.** (*as modifier*): *an autograph album.* **2.** a person's handwriting. **3. a.** a book, document, etc., handwritten by its author; original manuscript; holograph. **b.** (*as modifier*): *an autograph letter.* *~vb.* (*tr.*) **4.** to write one's signature on or in; sign. **5.** to write with one's own hand. [C17: from Late Latin, from Greek *autographos,* from *autos* self + *graphein* to write] —**autographic** (ˌɔːtəˈgræfɪk) *or* ˌ**autoˈgraphical** *adj.* —ˌ**autoˈgraphically** *adv.*

autography (ɔːˈtɒgrəfɪ) *n.* **1.** the writing of something in one's own handwriting; something handwritten. **2.** the precise reproduction of an illustration or of writing.

Autoharp (ˈɔːtəʊˌhɑːp) *n. Trademark.* a zither-like musical instrument used in country-and-western music, equipped with button-controlled dampers that can prevent selected strings from sounding, thus allowing chords to be played. It is plucked with the fingers or a plectrum.

autohypnosis (ˌɔːtəʊhɪpˈnəʊsɪs) *n. Psychol.* the process or result of self-induced hypnosis. —**autohypnotic** (ˌɔːtəʊhɪpˈnɒtɪk) *adj.* —ˌ**autohypˈnotically** *adv.*

autoicous (ɔːˈtɔɪkəs) *adj.* (of plants, esp. mosses) having male and female reproductive organs on the same plant. [C19: from AUTO- + Greek *oikos* dwelling]

autoimmune (ˌɔːtəʊɪˈmjuːn) *adj.* (of a disease) caused by the action of antibodies produced against substances normally present in the body. —ˌ**autoimˈmunity** *n.*

autoinfection (ˌɔːtəʊɪnˈfɛkʃən) *n.* infection by a pathogenic agent already within the body or infection transferred from one part of the body to another.

autoinoculation (ˌɔːtəʊɪˌnɒkjʊˈleɪʃən) *n.* the inoculation of micro-organisms (esp. viruses) from one part of the body into another, usually in the form of a vaccine.

autointoxication (ˌɔːtəʊɪnˌtɒksɪˈkeɪʃən) *n.* self-poisoning caused by absorption of toxic products originating within the body. Also called: **autotoxaemia.**

autoionization *or* **autoionisation** (ˌɔːtəʊˌaɪənaɪˈzeɪʃən) *n. Physics.* the process in which the decay of excited atoms or molecules results in emission of electrons, rather than photons.

autokinetic (ˌɔːtəʊkɪˈnɛtɪk, -kaɪ-) *adj.* automatically self-moving.

autokinetic phenomenon *n. Psychol.* the apparent movement of a fixed point of light when observed in a darkened room. The effect is produced by small eye movements for which the brain is unable to compensate, having no other reference points.

autoloading (ˈɔːtəʊˌləʊdɪŋ) *adj.* self-loading.

autologous (ɔːˈtɒləgəs) *adj.* (of a tissue graft, blood transfusion, etc.) originating from the recipient rather than from a donor.

autolyse *or U.S.* **autolyze** (ˈɔːtəˌlaɪz) *vb. Biochem.* to undergo or cause to undergo autolysis.

autolysin (ˌɔːtəˈlaɪsɪn, ɔːˈtɒlɪ-) *n.* any agent that produces autolysis.

autolysis (ɔːˈtɒlɪsɪs) *n.* the destruction of cells and tissues of an organism by enzymes produced by the cells themselves. [C20: via German from Greek *autos* self + *lusis* loosening, release] —**autolytic** (ˌɔːtəˈlɪtɪk) *adj.*

automat (ˈɔːtəˌmæt) *n.* **1.** Also called: **vending machine.** a machine that automatically dispenses goods, such as cigarettes, when money is inserted. **2.** *Chiefly U.S.* an area or room, sometimes having restaurant facilities, where food and other goods are supplied from vending machines.

automata (ɔːˈtɒmətə) *n.* a plural of **automaton.**

automata theory *n.* the formal study of the power of computation of abstract machines.

automate (ˈɔːtəˌmeɪt) *vb.* to make (a manufacturing process, factory, etc.) automatic, or (of a manufacturing process, etc.) to be made automatic.

automated telling machine *n.* a computerized cash dispenser.

automatic (ˌɔːtəˈmætɪk) *adj.* **1.** performed from force of habit or without conscious thought; lacking spontaneity; mechanical: *an automatic smile.* **2. a.** (of a device, mechanism, etc.) able to activate, move, or regulate itself. **b.** (of an act or process) performed by such automatic equipment. **3.** (of the action of a muscle, gland, etc.) involuntary or reflex. **4.** occurring as a necessary consequence: *promotion is automatic after a year.* **5.** (of a firearm) **a.** utilizing some of the force of each explosion to eject the empty shell, replace it with a new one, and fire continuously until release of the trigger. Compare **semiautomatic** (sense 2). **b.** short for **semiautomatic** (sense 2). *~*See also **machine** (sense 5). *~n.* **6.** an automatic firearm. **7.** a motor vehicle having automatic transmission. **8.** a machine that operates automatically. [C18: from Greek *automatos* acting independently] —ˌ**autoˈmatically** *adv.* —**automaticity** (ˌɔːtəʊməˈtɪsɪtɪ) *n.*

automatic camera *n.* a camera in which the lens aperture or the shutter speed or both are automatically adjusted to the prevailing conditions.

automatic data processing *n.* data processing performed by automatic electromechanical devices. Abbrevs.: **ADP, A.D.P., a.d.p.** Compare **electronic data processing.**

automatic door *n.* a self-opening door.

automatic exposure *n.* the automatic adjustment of the lens aperture and shutter speed of a camera by a control mechanism.

automatic frequency control *n.* a system in a radio or television receiver by which the tuning of an incoming signal is accurately maintained. Abbrev.: **AFC.**

automatic gain control *n.* control of a radio receiver in which the gain varies inversely with the magnitude of the input, thus maintaining the output at an approximately constant level. Abbrev.: **AGC.**

automatic pilot *n.* a device that automatically maintains an aircraft on a preset course. Also called: **autopilot.**
automatic repeat *n.* a key on the keyboard of a typewriter, computer, etc., which, when depressed continuously, produces the character repeatedly until the key is released.
automatic transmission *n.* a transmission system in a motor vehicle, usually incorporating a fluid clutch, in which the gears change automatically.
automatic typesetting *n.* another name for **computer typesetting.**
automation (ˌɔːtəˈmeɪʃən) *n.* **1.** the use of methods for controlling industrial processes automatically, esp. by electronically controlled systems, often reducing manpower. **2.** the extent to which a process is so controlled.
automatism (ɔːˈtɒməˌtɪzəm) *n.* **1.** the state or quality of being automatic; mechanical or involuntary action. **2.** *Law, philosophy* the explanation of an action, or of action in general, as determined by the physiological states of the individual, admissible in law as a defence. **3.** *Psychol.* the performance of actions, such as sleepwalking, without conscious knowledge or control. **4.** the suspension of consciousness sought or achieved by certain artists and writers to allow free flow of uncensored thoughts. —**auˈtomatist** *n.*
automatize *or* **automatise** (ɔːˈtɒməˌtaɪz) *vb.* to make (a process, etc.) automatic or (of a process, etc.) to be made automatic. —**auˌtomatiˈzation** *or* **auˌtomatiˈsation** *n.*
automaton (ɔːˈtɒməˌtɒn, -tᵊn) *n., pl.* **-tons** *or* **-ta** (-tə). **1.** a mechanical device operating under its own hidden power; robot. **2.** a person who acts mechanically or leads a routine monotonous life. [C17: from Latin, from Greek, from *automatos* spontaneous, self-moving] —**auˈtomatous** *adj.*
autometer (ˈɔːtəʊˌmiːtə) *n.* a small device inserted in a photocopier to enable the process of copying to begin and to record the number of copies made.
automobile (ˈɔːtəməˌbiːl) *n.* another word (esp. U.S.) for **car** (sense 1). —**automobilist** (ˌɔːtəməˈbiːlɪst, -ˈməʊbɪlɪst) *n.*
automobilia (ˌɔːtəməˈbiːlɪə) *pl. n.* items connected with cars and motoring of interest to the collector.
automotive (ˌɔːtəˈməʊtɪv) *adj.* **1.** relating to motor vehicles. **2.** self-propelling.
autonomic (ˌɔːtəˈnɒmɪk) *adj.* **1.** occurring involuntarily or spontaneously. **2.** of or relating to the autonomic nervous system. **3.** Also: **autonomous.** (of plant movements) occurring as a result of internal stimuli. —ˌ**autoˈnomically** *adv.*
autonomic nervous system *n.* the section of the nervous system of vertebrates that controls the involuntary actions of the smooth muscles, heart, and glands. Compare **somatic nervous system.**
autonomics (ˌɔːtəˈnɒmɪks) *n. (functioning as sing.) Electronics.* the study of self-regulating systems for process control.
autonomous (ɔːˈtɒnəməs) *adj.* **1.** (of a community, country, etc.) possessing a large degree of self-government. **2.** of or relating to an autonomous community. **3.** independent of others. **4.** *Philosophy.* **a.** acting or able to act in accordance with rules and principles of one's own choosing. **b.** (in the moral philosophy of Kant, of an individual's will) directed to duty rather than to some other end. Compare **heteronomous** (sense 3). See also **categorical imperative.** **5.** *Biol.* existing as an organism independent of other organisms or parts. **6.** a variant spelling of **autonomic** (sense 3). [C19: from Greek *autonomos* living under one's own laws, from AUTO- + *nomos* law] —**auˈtonomously** *adv.*
autonomy (ɔːˈtɒnəmɪ) *n., pl.* **-mies.** **1.** the right or state of self-government, esp. when limited. **2.** a state, community, or individual possessing autonomy. **3.** freedom to determine one's own actions, behaviour, etc. **4.** *Philosophy.* **a.** the doctrine that the individual human will is or ought to be governed only by its own principles and laws. See also **categorical imperative.** **b.** the state in which one's actions are autonomous. [C17: from Greek *autonomia* freedom to live by one's own laws; see AUTONOMOUS] —**auˈtonomist** *n.*
autophyte (ˈɔːtəˌfaɪt) *n.* an autotrophic plant, such as any green plant. —**autophytic** (ˌɔːtəˈfɪtɪk) *adj.* —ˌ**autoˈphytically** *adv.*
autopilot (ˌɔːtəˈpaɪlət, -təʊ-) *n.* short for **automatic pilot.**
autopista (ˌɔːtəˈpiːstə) *n.* a Spanish motorway. [from Spanish: auto(mobile) track]
autoplasty (ˈɔːtəˌplæstɪ) *n.* surgical repair of defects by grafting or transplanting tissue from the patient's own body. —ˌ**autoˈplastic** *adj.*
autopolyploid (ˌɔːtəʊˈpɒlɪˌplɔɪd) *adj.* **1.** (of cells, organisms, etc.) having more than two sets of haploid chromosomes inherited from a single species. ~*n.* **2.** an organism or cell of this type. ~See also **allopolyploid, polyploid.** —ˌ**autoˈpolyˌploidy** *n.*
autopsy (ˈɔːtəpsɪ, ɔːˈtɒp-) *n., pl.* **-sies.** **1.** Also called: **necropsy, postmortem examination.** dissection and examination of a dead body to determine the cause of death. **2.** an eyewitness observation. **3.** any critical analysis. [C17: from New Latin *autopsia,* from Greek: seeing with one's own eyes, from AUTO- + *opsis* sight]
autoput (ˈɔːtəʊˌpʊt) *n.* a Yugoslavian motorway. [from Serbo-Croat: auto(mobile) road]
autoradiograph (ˌɔːtəʊˈreɪdɪəˌgrɑːf, -ˌgræf) *n.* a photograph showing the distribution of a radioactive substance in a specimen. The photographic plate is exposed by radiation from the specimen. Also called: **radioautograph.** —**autoradiographic** (ˌɔːtəʊˌreɪdɪəˈgræfɪk) *adj.* —**autoradiography** (ˌɔːtəʊˌreɪdɪˈɒgrəfɪ) *n.*
autorickshaw (ˈɔːtəʊˈrɪkʃɔː) *n.* (in India) a light three-wheeled vehicle driven by a motorcycle engine.
autorotation (ˌɔːtəʊrəʊˈteɪʃən) *n.* the continuous rotation of a body in an airflow, such as that of the rotor blades of a helicopter in an unpowered descent.
autoroute (ˈɔːtəʊˌruːt) *n.* a French motorway. [from French, from *auto* car + *route* road]
autosome (ˈɔːtəˌsəʊm) *n.* any chromosome that is not a sex chromosome. —ˌ**autoˈsomal** *adj.*
autospore (ˈɔːtəʊˌspɔː) *n.* a nonmotile algal spore that develops adult characteristics before being released.
autostability (ˌɔːtəʊstəˈbɪlɪtɪ) *n.* the property of being stable either as a result of inherent characteristics or of built-in devices.
autostrada (ˈɔːtəʊˌstrɑːdə) *n.* an Italian motorway. [from Italian, from *auto* car + *strada* road]
autosuggestion (ˌɔːtəʊsəˈdʒɛstʃən) *n.* a process of suggestion in which the person unconsciously supplies or consciously attempts to supply the means of influencing his own behaviour or beliefs. —ˌ**autosugˈgestive** *adj.*
autotimer (ˈɔːtəʊˌtaɪmə) *n.* a device for turning an electric cooker on and off automatically at times predetermined by advance setting.
autotomize *or* **autotomise** (ɔːˈtɒtəˌmaɪz) *vb.* to cause (a part of the body) to undergo autotomy.
autotomy (ɔːˈtɒtəmɪ) *n., pl.* **-mies.** the casting off by an animal of a part of its body, to facilitate escape when attacked. —**autotomic** (ˌɔːtəˈtɒmɪk) *adj.*
autotoxaemia *or U.S.* **autotoxemia** (ˌɔːtəʊtɒkˈsiːmɪə) *n.* another name for **autointoxication.**
autotoxin (ˌɔːtəˈtɒksɪn) *n.* any poison or toxin formed in the organism upon which it acts. See **autointoxication.** —ˌ**autoˈtoxic** *adj.*
autotransformer (ˌɔːtəʊtrænsˈfɔːmə) *n.* a transformer in which part of the winding is common to both primary and secondary circuits.
autotrophic (ˌɔːtəˈtrɒfɪk) *adj.* (of organisms such as green plants) capable of manufacturing complex organic nutritive compounds from simple inorganic sources such as carbon dioxide, water, and nitrates. Compare **heterotrophic.** —**autotroph** (ˈɔːtəˌtrəʊf) *n.*
autotype (ˈɔːtəˌtaɪp) *n.* **1.** a photographic process for producing prints in black and white, using a carbon pigment. **2.** an exact copy of a manuscript, etc.; facsimile. —**autotypic** (ˌɔːtəˈtɪpɪk) *adj.* —ˈ**autoˌtypy** *n.*
autowinder (ˈɔːtəʊˌwaɪndə) *n. Photog.* a battery-operated device for advancing the film in a camera automatically after each exposure. Compare **motor drive.**
autoxidation (ɔːˌtɒksɪˈdeɪʃən) *n. Chem.* **a.** oxidation by exposure to atmospheric oxygen. **b.** oxidation that will only occur when another oxidation reaction is taking place in the same system.
autumn (ˈɔːtəm) *n.* **1.** (*sometimes cap.*) **a.** Also called (esp. U.S. and Canadian): **fall.** the season of the year between summer and winter, astronomically from the September equinox to the December solstice in the N hemisphere and from the March equinox to the June solstice in the S hemisphere. **b.** (*as modifier*): *autumn leaves.* **2.** a period of late maturity, esp. one followed by a decline. [C14: from Latin *autumnus,* perhaps of Etruscan origin]
autumnal (ɔːˈtʌmnᵊl) *adj.* of, occurring in, or characteristic of autumn. —**auˈtumnally** *adv.*
autumnal equinox *n.* **1.** the time at which the sun crosses the plane of the equator away from the relevant hemisphere, making day and night of equal length. It occurs about Sept. 23 in the N hemisphere (March 21 in the S hemisphere). **2.** *Astronomy.* the point on the celestial sphere, lying in the constellation of Virgo, at which the ecliptic intersects the celestial equator.
autumn crocus *n.* a liliaceous plant, *Colchicum autumnale,* of Europe and N Africa having pink or purplish autumn flowers. Also called: **meadow saffron.** Compare **saffron.**
autunite (ˈɔːtəˌnaɪt) *n.* a yellowish fluorescent radioactive mineral consisting of a hydrated calcium uranium phosphate in tetragonal crystalline form. It is found in uranium ores. Formula: $Ca(UO_2)_2(PO_4)_2.10–12H_2O$. [C19: named after *Autun* in France, one of the places where it was found, + -ITE[1]]
aux. *abbrev. for* auxiliary.
auxanometer (ˌɔːksəˈnɒmɪtə) *n.* an instrument that measures the linear growth of plant shoots. [C19: from Greek *auxanein* to increase + -METER]
auxesis (ɔːgˈziːsɪs, ɔːkˈsiː-) *n.* growth in animal or plant tissues resulting from an increase in cell size without cell division. [C16: via Latin from Greek: increase, from *auxein* to increase, grow]
auxiliaries (ɔːgˈzɪljərɪz, -ˈzɪlə-) *pl. n.* foreign or allied troops serving another nation; mercenaries.
auxiliary (ɔːgˈzɪljərɪ, -ˈzɪlə-) *adj.* **1.** secondary or supplementary. **2.** supporting. **3.** *Nautical.* (of a sailing vessel) having an engine: *an auxiliary sloop.* ~*n., pl.* **-ries.** **4.** a person or thing that supports or supplements; subordinate or assistant. **5.** *Nautical.*

a. a sailing vessel with an engine. b. the engine of such a vessel. 6. *Navy.* a vessel such as a tug, hospital ship, etc., not used for combat. [C17: from Latin *auxiliārius* bringing aid, from *auxilium* help, from *augēre* to increase, enlarge, strengthen]

auxiliary note *n. Music.* a nonharmonic note occurring between two harmonic notes.

auxiliary power unit *n.* an additional engine fitted to an aircraft to operate when the main engines are not in use.

auxiliary rotor *n.* the tail rotor of a helicopter, used for directional and rotary control.

auxiliary verb *n.* a verb used to indicate the tense, voice, mood, etc., of another verb where this is not indicated by inflection, such as English *will* in *he will go, was* in *he was eating* and *he was eaten, do* in *I do like you,* etc.

auxin ('ɔːksɪn) *n.* any of various plant hormones, such as indoleacetic acid, that promote growth and control fruit and flower development. Synthetic auxins are widely used in agriculture and horticulture. [C20: from Greek *auxein* to grow]

auxochrome ('ɔːksəˌkrəʊm) *n.* a group of atoms that can be attached to a chromogen to convert it into a dye.

auxocyte ('ɔːksəˌsaɪt) *n.* any cell undergoing meiosis, esp. an oocyte or spermatocyte.

auxospore ('ɔːksəˌspɔː) *n.* the protoplasm of a diatom before its cell wall is formed.

auxotonic (ˌɔːksə'tɒnɪk) *adj.* (of muscle contraction) occurring against increasing force.

auxotroph ('ɔːksətrəʊf) *n.* a mutant strain of microorganism requiring growth factors not needed by the normal organism. —ˌ**auxo'trophic** *adj.*

Av (æv) *or* **Ab** *n.* (in the Jewish calendar) the fifth month of the year according to biblical reckoning and the eleventh month in the civil year, usually falling within July and August. [from Hebrew]

AV *abbrev. for* Authorized Version (of the Bible).

av. *abbrev. for:* 1. average. 2. avoirdupois.

Av. *or* **av.** *abbrev. for* avenue.

a.v. *or* **A/V** *abbrev. for* ad valorem.

a-v, A-V, *or* **AV** *abbrev. for* audiovisual.

ava (ə'vɔː) *adv. Scot.* at all. [Scot. form of *of all*]

avadavat (ˌævədə'væt) *or* **amadavat** (ˌæmədə'væt) *n.* either of two Asian weaverbirds of the genus *Estrilda,* esp. *E. amandava,* having a red plumage: often kept as cagebirds. [C18: from *Ahmadabad,* Indian city from which these birds were brought to Europe]

avail (ə'veɪl) *vb.* 1. to be of use, advantage, profit, or assistance (to). 2. **avail oneself of.** to make use of to one's advantage. ~*n.* 3. use or advantage (esp. in the phrases **of no avail, to little avail**). [C13 *availen,* from *vailen,* from Old French *valoir,* from Latin *valēre* to be strong, prevail] —**a'vailingly** *adv.*

available (ə'veɪləbᵊl) *adj.* 1. obtainable or accessible; capable of being made use of; at hand. 2. *U.S. politics, derogatory.* suitable for public office, usually as a result of having an inoffensive character: *Smith was a particularly available candidate.* 3. *Archaic.* advantageous. —**aˌvaila'bility** *or* **a'vailableness** *n.* —**a'vailably** *adv.*

avalanche ('ævəˌlɑːntʃ) *n.* 1. a. a fall of large masses of snow and ice down a mountain. b. a fall of rocks, sand, etc. 2. a sudden or overwhelming appearance of a large quantity of things: *an avalanche of letters.* 3. *Physics.* a group of ions produced by a single ion as a result of a collision with some other form of matter. ~*vb.* 4. to come down overwhelmingly (upon). [C18: from French, by mistaken division from *la valanche,* from *valanche,* from (northwestern Alps) dialect *lavantse;* related to Old Provençal *lavanca,* of obscure origin]

avant- *prefix.* of or belonging to the avant-garde of a specified field.

avant-garde (ˌævɒŋ'gɑːd; *French* avɑ̃gard) *n.* 1. those artists, writers, musicians, etc., whose techniques and ideas are markedly experimental or in advance of those generally accepted. ~*adj.* 2. of such artists, etc., their ideas, or techniques. 3. radical; daring. [from French: VANGUARD] —ˌ**avant-'gardism** *n.* —ˌ**avant-'gardist** *n.*

avantist (æ'vɒntɪst) *n.* short for **avant-gardist.**

Avar ('eɪvɑː, 'ævɑː) *n.* 1. a member of a people of unknown origin in E Europe from the 6th to the early 9th century A.D.: crushed by Charlemagne around 800. 2. a member of a people of the Caucasas. 3. the language of this people, belonging to the North-East Caucasian family.

avarice ('ævərɪs) *n.* extreme greed for riches; cupidity. [C13: from Old French, from Latin *avaritia,* from *avārus* covetous, from *avēre* to crave] —ˌ**ava'ricious** *adj.* —ˌ**ava'riciously** *adv.* —ˌ**ava'riciousness** *n.*

avascular (ə'væskjʊlə) *adj.* (of certain tissues, such as cartilage) lacking blood vessels.

avast (ə'vɑːst) *sentence substitute. Nautical.* stop! cease! [C17: perhaps from Dutch *hou'vast* hold fast]

avatar ('ævəˌtɑː) *n.* 1. *Hinduism.* the manifestation of a deity, notably Vishnu, in human, superhuman, or animal form. 2. a visible manifestation or embodiment of an abstract concept; archetype. [C18: from Sanskrit *avatāra* a going down, from *avatarati* he descends, from *ava* down + *tarati* he passes over]

avaunt (ə'vɔːnt) *sentence substitute. Archaic.* go away! depart! [C15: from Old French *avant!* forward!, from Late Latin *ab ante* forward, from Latin *ab* from + *ante* before]

avdp. *abbrev. for* avoirdupois.

ave ('ɑːvɪ, 'ɑːveɪ) *sentence substitute.* welcome or farewell. [Latin]

Ave[1] ('ɑːvɪ) *n. R.C. Church.* 1. short for **Ave Maria:** see **Hail Mary.** 2. the time for the Angelus to be recited, so called because of the threefold repetition of the Ave Maria in this devotion. 3. the beads of the rosary used to count the number of Ave Marias said. [C13: from Latin: hail!]

Ave[2] *or* **ave** *abbrev. for* avenue.

avel ('avɛl) *n. Judaism.* a variant of **ovel.**

Ave Maria (mə'riːə) *n.* another name for **Hail Mary.** [C14: from Medieval Latin: hail, Mary!]

avenge (ə'vɛndʒ) *vb.* (*usually tr.*) to inflict a punishment in retaliation for (harm, injury, etc.) done to (a person or persons); take revenge for or on behalf of: *to avenge a crime; to avenge a murdered friend.* [C14: from Old French *avengier,* from *vengier,* from Latin *vindicāre;* see VENGEANCE, VINDICATE] —**a'venger** *n.*

avens ('ævɪnz) *n., pl.* **-ens.** (*functioning as sing.*) 1. any of several temperate or arctic rosaceous plants of the genus *Geum,* such as *G. rivale* (**water avens**), which has a purple calyx and orange-pink flowers. See also **herb bennet.** 2. **mountain avens.** a trailing evergreen white-flowered rosaceous shrub, *Dryas octopetala,* that grows on mountains in N temperate regions. [C15: from Old French *avence,* from Medieval Latin *avencia* variety of clover]

aventurine, aventurin (ə'vɛntjʊrɪn), *or* **avanturine** (ə'væntjʊrɪn) *n.* 1. a dark-coloured glass, usually green or brown, spangled with fine particles of gold, copper, or some other metal. 2. Also called: **sunstone.** a light-coloured translucent variety of orthoclase feldspar containing reddish-gold particles of iron compounds. 3. a variety of quartz containing red or greenish particles of iron oxide or mica: a gemstone. [C19: from French, from Italian *avventurina,* from *avventura* chance; so named because usually found by accident; see ADVENTURE]

avenue ('ævɪˌnjuː) *n.* 1. a. a broad street, often lined with trees. b. (*cap. as part of a street name*) a road, esp. in a built-up area: *Shaftesbury Avenue.* 2. a main approach road, as to a country house. 3. a way bordered by two rows of trees: *an avenue of oaks.* 4. a line of approach: *explore every avenue.* [C17: from French, from *avenir* to come to, from Latin *advenīre,* from *venīre* to come]

aver (ə'vɜː) *vb.* **avers, averring, averred.** (*tr.*) 1. to state positively; assert. 2. *Law.* to allege as a fact or prove to be true. [C14: from Old French *averer,* from Medieval Latin *advērāre,* from Latin *vērus* true] —**a'verment** *n.*

average ('ævərɪdʒ, 'ævrɪdʒ) *n.* 1. the typical or normal amount, quality, degree, etc.: *above average in intelligence.* 2. Also called: **arithmetic mean.** the result obtained by adding the numbers or quantities in a set and dividing the total by the number of members in the set: *the average of 3, 4, and 8 is 5.* 3. (of a continuously variable ratio, such as speed) the quotient of the differences between the initial and final values of the two quantities that make up the ratio: *his average over the journey was 30 miles per hour.* 4. *Maritime law.* a. a loss incurred or damage suffered by a ship or its cargo at sea. b. the equitable apportionment of such loss among the interested parties. 5. (*often pl.*) *Stock exchange.* a simple or weighted average of the prices of a selected group of securities computed in order to facilitate market comparisons. 6. **on (the** *or* **an) average.** usually; typically: *on average, he goes twice a week.* ~*adj.* 7. usual or typical. 8. mediocre or inferior: *his performance was only average.* 9. constituting a numerical average: *the average age; an average speed.* 10. approximately typical of a range of values: *the average contents of a matchbox.* ~*vb.* 11. (*tr.*) to obtain or estimate a numerical average of. 12. (*tr.*) to assess the general quality of. 13. (*tr.*) to perform or receive a typical number of: *to average eight hours' work a day.* 14. (*tr.*) to divide up proportionately: *they averaged the profits among the staff.* 15. (*tr.*) to amount to or be on average: *the children averaged 15 years of age.* 16. (*intr.*) *Stock Exchange.* to purchase additional securities in a holding whose price has fallen (**average down**) or risen (**average up**) in anticipation of a speculative profit after further increases in price. [C15 *averay* loss arising from damage to ships or cargoes (shared equitably among all concerned, hence the modern sense), from Old Italian *avaria,* ultimately from Arabic *awār* damage, blemish] —'**averagely** *adv.*

average adjuster *n.* a person who calculates average claims, esp. for marine insurance. See **average** (sense 4).

average deviation *n. Statistics.* another name for **mean deviation.**

Averroism (ˌævə'rəʊɪzəm, ə'vɛrəʊ-) *n.* the teachings of Averroës (1126–88), Arab philosopher and physician), esp. his attempts to reconcile Aristotelian philosophy with Islamic religion. —ˌ**Aver'roist** *n.* —ˌ**Averro'istic** *adj.*

averse (ə'vɜːs) *adj.* 1. (*postpositive;* usually foll. by *to*) opposed, disinclined, or loath. 2. (of leaves, flowers, etc.) turned away from the main stem. Compare **adverse** (sense 4). [C16: from Latin *āversus,* from *āvertere* to turn from, from *vertere* to turn] —**a'versely** *adv.* —**a'verseness** *n.*

▷**Usage.** *To* is the preposition now normally used with *averse* (*he was averse to giving any assistance*), although *from* is often used with *averse* and *aversion* and was at one time considered to be grammatically correct.

aversion (ə'vɜːʃən) *n.* **1.** (usually foll. by *to* or *for*) extreme dislike or disinclination; repugnance. **2.** a person or thing that arouses this: *he is my pet aversion.*

aversion therapy *n. Psychiatry.* a method of suppressing an undesirable habit, such as excessive smoking, by causing the subject to associate an unpleasant effect, such as an electric shock or nausea, with the habit.

aversive (ə'vɜːsɪv) *adj.* tending to dissuade or repel. —**a'versively** *adv.*

avert (ə'vɜːt) *vb. (tr.)* **1.** to turn away or aside: *to avert one's gaze.* **2.** to ward off; prevent from occurring: *to avert danger.* [C15: from Old French *avertir,* from Latin *āvertere;* see AVERSE] —**a'vertible** *or* **a'vertable** *adj.*

Aves ('eɪviːz) *pl. n.* the class of vertebrates comprising the birds. See **bird** (sense 1). [pl. of Latin *avis* bird]

Avesta (ə'vɛstə) *n.* a collection of sacred writings of Zoroastrianism, including the Songs of Zoroaster.

Avestan (ə'vɛstən) *or* **Avestic** (ə'vɛstɪk) *n.* **1.** the oldest recorded language of the Iranian branch of the Indo-European family; the language of the Avesta. Formerly called: **Zend.** ~*adj.* **2.** of or relating to the Avesta or its language.

avg. *abbrev. for* average.

avgolemono (ˌævgə'lɛmənəʊ) *n.* a Greek soup made with eggs, lemon juice, and rice. [C20: from Modern Greek]

avian ('eɪvɪən) *adj.* of, relating to, or resembling a bird. [C19: from Latin *avis* bird]

aviarist ('eɪvjərɪst) *n.* a person who keeps an aviary.

aviary ('eɪvjərɪ) *n., pl.* **aviaries.** a large enclosure in which birds are kept. [C16: from Latin *aviārium,* from *aviārius* concerning birds, from *avis* bird]

aviate ('eɪvɪˌeɪt) *vb.* to pilot or fly in an aircraft.

aviation (ˌeɪvɪ'eɪʃən) *n.* **1. a.** the art or science of flying aircraft. **b.** the design, production, and maintenance of aircraft. **2.** *U.S.* military aircraft collectively. [C19: from French, from Latin *avis* bird]

aviation medicine *n.* the branch of medicine concerned with the effects on man of flight in the earth's atmosphere. Compare **space medicine.**

aviator ('eɪvɪˌeɪtə) *n. Old-fashioned.* the pilot of an aeroplane or airship; flier. —'**aviˌatrix** *or* '**aviˌatress** *fem. n.*

aviculture ('eɪvɪˌkʌltʃə) *n.* the keeping and rearing of birds. —ˌ**avi'culturist** *n.*

avid ('ævɪd) *adj.* **1.** very keen; enthusiastic: *an avid reader.* **2.** (*postpositive;* often foll. by *for* or *of*) eager (for); desirous (of); greedy (for): *avid for revenge.* [C18: from Latin *avidus,* from *avēre* to long for] —'**avidly** *adv.*

avidin ('ævɪdɪn, ə'vɪdɪn) *n.* a protein, found in egg-white, that combines with biotin to form a stable compound that cannot be absorbed, leading to a biotin deficiency in the consumer. [C20: from AVID + (BIOT)IN; from its characteristic avidity for biotin]

avidity (ə'vɪdɪtɪ) *n.* **1.** the quality or state of being avid. **2. a.** eagerness. **b.** greed; avarice. **3.** *Chem.* **a.** the strength of an acid or base in proportion to its degree of dissociation. **b.** another term for **affinity** (sense 6b). **4.** *Immunol.* a measure of antigen-to-antibody binding, based on the rate of formation of the complex.

avifauna (ˌeɪvɪ'fɔːnə) *n.* all the birds in a particular region. —ˌ**avi'faunal** *adj.*

avionics (ˌeɪvɪ'ɒnɪks) *n.* **1.** (*functioning as sing.*) the science and technology of electronics applied to aeronautics and astronautics. **2.** (*functioning as pl.*) the electronic circuits and devices of an aerospace vehicle. [C20: from *avi(ation electr)onics*] —ˌ**avi'onic** *adj.*

avirulent (æ'vɪrʊlənt) *adj.* (esp. of bacteria) not virulent.

avitaminosis (æˌvɪtəmɪn'əʊsɪs, ˌævɪˌtæmɪ'nəʊsɪs) *n., pl.* **-ses** (-siːz). any disease caused by a vitamin deficiency in the diet.

avizandum (ˌævɪ'zændəm) *n. Scots Law.* **a.** a judge's or court's decision to consider a case privately before giving judgment. **b.** a judge's or court's private consideration of a case before giving judgment. **c.** the period during which judgment is delayed in these circumstances. A judge or court makes avizandum when time is needed to consider arguments or submissions made. ~Compare **CAV.** [from Medieval Latin, from *avizare* to consider; see ADVISE]

AVM (in Britain) *abbrev. for* Air Vice-Marshal.

avn *abbrev. for* aviation.

avocado (ˌævə'kɑːdəʊ) *n., pl.* **-dos.** **1.** a pear-shaped fruit having a leathery green or blackish skin, a large stony seed, and a greenish-yellow edible pulp. **2.** the tropical American lauraceous tree, *Persea americana,* that bears this fruit. **3.** a dull greenish colour resembling that of the fruit. ~Also called (for senses 1 & 2): **avocado pear, alligator pear.** [C17: from Spanish *aguacate,* from Nahuatl *ahuacatl* testicle, alluding to the shape of the fruit]

avocation (ˌævə'keɪʃən) *n. Archaic.* **1.** a minor occupation undertaken as a diversion. **2.** a person's regular job or vocation. [C17: from Latin *āvocātiō* a calling away, diversion from, from *āvocāre* to distract, from *vocāre* to call]

avocet ('ævəˌsɛt) *n.* any of several long-legged shore birds of the genus *Recurvirostra,* such as the European *R. avosetta,* having black-and-white plumage and a long slender upward-curving bill: family *Recurvirostridae,* order *Charadriiformes.* [C18: from French *avocette,* from Italian *avocetta,* of uncertain origin]

Avogadro constant *or* **number** (ˌævə'gɑːdrəʊ) *n.* the number of atoms or molecules in a mole of a substance, equal to 6.022 52 × 10^{23} per mole. Symbol: L or N_A [named after Amedeo *Avogadro* (1776–1856), Italian physicist]

Avogadro's law *or* **hypothesis** *n.* the principle that equal volumes of all gases contain the same number of molecules at the same temperature and pressure.

avoid (ə'vɔɪd) *vb. (tr.)* **1.** to keep out of the way of. **2.** to refrain from doing. **3.** to prevent from happening: *to avoid damage to machinery.* **4.** *Law.* to make (a plea, contract, etc.) void; invalidate; quash. **5.** *Obsolete.* to expel. **6.** *Obsolete.* to depart from. [C14: from Anglo-French *avoider,* from Old French *esvuidier,* from *vuidier* to empty, VOID] —**a'voidable** *adj.* —**a'voidably** *adv.* —**a'voider** *n.*

avoidance (ə'vɔɪdəns) *n.* **1.** the act of keeping away from or preventing from happening. **2.** *Law.* **a.** the act of annulling or making void. **b.** the countering of an opponent's plea with fresh evidence. **3.** *Ecclesiastical law.* the state of a benefice having no incumbent.

avoir. *abbrev. for* avoirdupois.

avoirdupois *or* **avoirdupois weight** (ˌævədə'pɔɪz, ˌævwɑːdjuː'pwɑː) *n.* a system of weights used in many English-speaking countries. It is based on the pound, which contains 16 ounces or 7000 grains. 100 pounds (U.S.) or 112 pounds (Brit.) is equal to 1 hundredweight and 20 hundredweights equals 1 ton. Abbrevs.: **avdp., avoir.** [C14: from Old French *aver de peis* goods of weight]

avouch (ə'vaʊtʃ) *vb. (tr.) Archaic.* **1.** to vouch for; guarantee. **2.** to acknowledge. **3.** to assert. [C16: from Old French *avochier* to summon, call on, from Latin *advocāre;* see ADVOCATE] —**a'vouchment** *n.*

avow (ə'vaʊ) *vb. (tr.)* **1.** to state or affirm. **2.** to admit openly. **3.** *Law, rare.* to justify or maintain (some action taken). [C13: from Old French *avouer* to confess, from Latin *advocāre* to appeal to, call upon; see AVOUCH, ADVOCATE] —**a'vowable** *adj.* —**a'vowal** *n.* —**avowed** (ə'vaʊd) *adj.* —**avowedly** (ə'vaʊɪdlɪ) *adv.* —**a'vower** *n.*

avulsion (ə'vʌlʃən) *n.* **1.** a forcible tearing away or separation of a bodily structure or part, either as the result of injury or as an intentional surgical procedure. **2.** *Law.* the sudden removal of soil from one person's land to that of another, as by flooding. [C17: from Latin *āvulsiō,* from *āvellere* to pluck away, from *vellere* to pull, pluck]

avuncular (ə'vʌŋkjʊlə) *adj.* **1.** of or concerned with an uncle. **2.** resembling an uncle; friendly; helpful. [C19: from Latin *avunculus* (maternal) uncle, diminutive of *avus* grandfather]

avunculate (ə'vʌŋkjʊlɪt) *n.* **1.** the custom in some societies of assigning rights and duties to a maternal uncle concerning his sister's son. ~*adj.* **2.** of, relating to, or governed by this custom.

aw[1] (ɔː) *determiner. Scot.* a variant spelling of **a'** (all).

aw[2] (ɔː) *interj. Informal, chiefly U.S.* an expression of disapproval, commiseration, or appeal.

a.w. *abbrev. for* all water (shipping).

AWA *abbrev. for* Amalgamated Wireless (Australasia) Ltd.

awa' (ə'wɔː) *adv. Scot.* away; departed; onward.

AWACS *or* **Awacs** ('eɪwæks) *n. acronym for* airborne warning and control system.

await (ə'weɪt) *vb.* **1.** (*tr.*) to wait for; expect. **2.** (*tr.*) to be in store for. **3.** (*intr.*) to wait, esp. with expectation. **4.** (*tr.*) *Obsolete.* to wait for in order to ambush.

awake (ə'weɪk) *vb.* **awakes, awaking; awoke** *or* **awaked; awoken** *or* **awaked.** **1.** to emerge or rouse from sleep; wake. **2.** to become or cause to become alert. **3.** (usually foll. by *to*) to become or make aware (of): *to awake to reality.* **4.** Also: **awaken.** (*tr.*) to arouse (feelings, etc.) or cause to remember (memories, etc.). ~*adj.* (*postpositive*) **5.** not sleeping. **6.** (sometimes foll. by *to*) lively or alert. [Old English *awacian, awacan;* see WAKE[1]]

▷**Usage.** See at **wake**[1].

award (ə'wɔːd) *vb. (tr.)* **1.** to give (something due), esp. as a reward for merit: *to award prizes.* **2.** *Law.* to declare to be entitled, as by decision of a court of law or an arbitrator. ~*n.* **3.** something awarded, such as a prize or medal: *an award for bravery.* **4.** (in Australia and New Zealand) the amount of an award wage (esp. in the phrase **above award**). **5.** *Law.* **a.** the decision of an arbitrator. **b.** a grant made by a court of law, esp. of damages in a civil action. [C14: from Anglo-Norman *awarder,* from Old Northern French *eswarder* to decide after investigation, from *es-* EX-[1] + *warder* to observe; see WARD] —**a'wardable** *adj.* —**aˌward'ee** *n.* —**a'warder** *n.*

award wage *n.* (in Australia and New Zealand) statutory minimum pay for a particular group of workers. Sometimes shortened to **award.**

aware (ə'wɛə) *adj.* **1.** (*postpositive;* foll. by *of*) having knowledge; cognizant: *aware of his error.* **2.** informed of current developments: *politically aware.* [Old English *gewær;* related to Old Saxon, Old High German *giwar* Latin *verērī* to be fearful; see BEWARE, WARY] —**a'wareness** *n.*

awash (ə'wɒʃ) *adv., adj.* (*postpositive*) *Nautical.* **1.** at a level even with the surface of the sea. **2.** washed over by the waves.

away (ə'weɪ) *adv.* **1.** from a particular place; off: *to swim away.* **2.** in or to another, usual, or proper place: *to put toys away.* **3.**

apart; at a distance: *to keep away from strangers.* **4.** out of existence: *the music faded away.* **5.** indicating motion, displacement, transfer, etc., from a normal or proper place, from a person's own possession, etc.: *to turn one's head away; to give away money.* **6.** indicating activity that is wasteful or designed to get rid of something: *to sleep away the hours.* **7.** continuously: *laughing away; fire away.* **8. away with.** a command for a person to go or be removed: *away with you; away with him to prison!* **9. far and away.** by a very great margin: *far and away the biggest meal he'd ever eaten.* ~*adj.* (*usually postpositive*) **10.** not present: *away from school.* **11.** distant: *he is a good way away.* **12.** having started; released: *he was away before sunrise; bombs away!* **13.** (*also prenominal*) *Sport.* played on an opponent's ground: *an away game.* **14.** *Golf.* (of a ball or player) farthest from the hole. **15.** *Baseball.* (of a player) having been put out. **16.** *Horse racing.* relating to the outward portion or first half of a race. ~*n.* **17.** *Sport.* a game played or won at an opponent's ground. ~*interj.* **18.** an expression of dismissal. [Old English *on weg* on way]

awe (ɔː) *n.* **1.** overwhelming wonder, admiration, respect, or dread. **2.** *Archaic.* power to inspire fear or reverence. ~*vb.* **3.** (*tr.*) to inspire with reverence or dread. [C13: from Old Norse *agi;* related to Gothic *agis* fear, Greek *akhesthai* to be grieved] —**'aweless** *or U.S.* **'awless** *adj.*

aweather (ə'wɛðə) *adv., adj.* (*postpositive*) *Nautical.* towards the weather: *with the helm aweather.* Compare **alee.**

aweigh (ə'weɪ) *adj.* (*postpositive*) *Nautical.* (of an anchor) no longer hooked into the bottom; hanging by its rode.

awe-inspiring *adj.* causing or worthy of admiration or respect; amazing or magnificent.

awesome ('ɔːsəm) *adj.* inspiring or displaying awe. —**'awesomely** *adv.* —**'awesomeness** *n.*

awe-stricken *or* **awe-struck** *adj.* overcome or filled with awe.

awful ('ɔːfʊl) *adj.* **1.** nasty or ugly. **2.** *Archaic.* inspiring reverence or dread. **3.** *Archaic.* overcome with awe; reverential. ~*adv.* **4.** *Not standard.* (intensifier): *an awful cold day.* [C13: see AWE, -FUL] —**'awfulness** *n.*

awfully ('ɔːfəlɪ, 'ɔːflɪ) *adv.* **1.** in an unpleasant, bad, or reprehensible manner. **2.** *Informal.* (intensifier): *I'm awfully keen to come.* **3.** *Archaic.* so as to express or inspire awe.

awheel (ə'wiːl) *adv.* on wheels.

awhile (ə'waɪl) *adv.* for a brief period.

awkward ('ɔːkwəd) *adj.* **1.** lacking dexterity, proficiency, or skill; clumsy; inept: *the new recruits were awkward in their exercises.* **2.** ungainly or inelegant in movements or posture. **3.** unwieldy; difficult to use: *an awkward implement.* **4.** embarrassing: *an awkward moment.* **5.** embarrassed: *he felt awkward about leaving.* **6.** difficult to deal with; requiring tact: *an awkward situation; an awkward customer.* **7.** deliberately uncooperative or unhelpful. **8.** dangerous or difficult: *an awkward ascent of the ridge.* **9.** *Obsolete.* perverse. [C14 *awk,* from Old Norse *öfugr* turned the wrong way round + -WARD] —**'awkwardly** *adv.* —**'awkwardness** *n.*

awl (ɔːl) *n.* a pointed hand tool with a fluted blade used for piercing wood, leather, etc. See also **bradawl.** [Old English *ǣl;* related to Old Norse *alr,* Old High German *āla,* Dutch *aal,* Sanskrit *ārā*]

awlwort ('ɔːlˌwɜːt) *n.* a small stemless aquatic plant, *Subularia aquatica,* of the N hemisphere, having slender sharp-pointed leaves and minute submerged white flowers: family *Cruciferae* (crucifers).

awn (ɔːn) *n.* any of the bristles growing from the flowering parts of certain grasses and cereals. [Old English *agen* ear of grain; related to Old Norse *ögn* chaff, Gothic *ahana,* Old High German *agana,* Greek *akōn* javelin] —**awned** *adj.* —**'awnless** *adj.*

awning ('ɔːnɪŋ) *n.* a roof of canvas or other material supported by a frame to provide protection from the weather, esp. one placed over a doorway or part of a deck of a ship. [C17: of uncertain origin]

awoke (ə'wəʊk) *vb.* a past tense or (now rare or dialectal) past participle of **awake.**

AWOL ('eɪwɒl) *or* **A.W.O.L.** *adj. Military.* absent without leave; absent from one's post or duty without official permission but without intending to desert.

AWRE *abbrev. for* Atomic Weapons Research Establishment.

awry (ə'raɪ) *adv., adj.* (*postpositive*) **1.** with a slant or twist to one side; askew. **2.** away from the appropriate or right course; amiss. [C14 *on wry;* see A-[2], WRY]

AWU *abbrev. for* Australian Workers' Union.

ax. *abbrev. for* axiom.

axe *or U.S.* **ax** (æks) *n., pl.* **axes.** **1.** a hand tool with one side of its head forged and sharpened to a cutting edge, used for felling trees, splitting timber, etc. See also **hatchet.** **2. an axe to grind. a.** an ulterior motive. **b.** a grievance. **c.** a pet subject. **3. the axe.** *Informal.* **a.** dismissal, esp. from employment; the sack (esp. in the phrase **get the axe**). **b.** *Brit.* severe cutting down of expenditure, esp. the removal of unprofitable sections of a public service. **4.** *U.S. slang.* any musical instrument, esp. a guitar or horn. ~*vb.* (*tr.*) **5.** to chop or trim with an axe. **6.** *Informal.* to dismiss (employees), restrict (expenditure or services), or terminate (a project). [Old English *æx;* related to Old Frisian *axa,* Old High German *acchus,* Old Norse *öx,* Latin *ascia,* Greek *axinē*]

axe-breaker *n. Austral.* an Australian oleaceous tree, *Notelaea longifolia,* yielding very hard timber.

axel ('æksəl) *n. Skating.* a jump in which the skater takes off from the forward outside edge of one skate, makes one and a half, two and a half, or three and a half turns in the air, and lands on the backward outside edge of the other skate. [C20: named after *Axel* Paulsen (died 1938), Norwegian skater]

axeman *or U.S.* **axman** ('æksmən) *n., pl.* **-men.** **1.** a man who wields an axe, esp. to cut down trees. **2.** a person who makes cuts in expenditure or services, esp. on behalf of another: *the chancellor's axeman.* **3.** *U.S. slang.* a man who plays a musical instrument, esp. a guitar.

axenic (eɪ'ziːnɪk) *adj.* (of a biological culture or culture medium) free from undesirable microorganisms; uncontaminated. [C20: see A-[1], XENO-, -IC]

axes[1] ('æksiːz) *n.* the plural of **axis**[1].

axes[2] ('æksɪz) *n.* the plural of **axe.**

axial ('æksɪəl) *adj.* **1.** relating to, forming, or characteristic of an axis. **2.** situated in, on, or along an axis. —ˌ**axi'ality** *n.* —**'axially** *adv.*

axial-flow compressor *n.* a device for compressing a gas by accelerating it tangentially by means of bladed rotors, to increase its kinetic energy, and then diffusing it through static vanes (stators), to increase its pressure.

axial skeleton *n.* the bones that together comprise the skull and the vertebral column.

axial vector *n.* another name for **pseudovector.**

axil ('æksɪl) *n.* the angle between the upper surface of a branch or leafstalk and the stem from which it grows. [C18: from Latin *axilla* armpit]

axile ('æksɪl, -saɪl) *adj. Botany.* of, relating to, or attached to the axis: *axile placentation.*

axilemma (ˌæksɪ'lɛmə) *n.* a variant spelling of **axolemma.**

axilla (æk'sɪlə) *n., pl.* **-lae** (-liː). **1.** the technical name for the **armpit.** **2.** the area on the undersurface of a bird's wing corresponding to the armpit. [C17: from Latin: armpit]

axillary (æk'sɪlərɪ) *adj.* **1.** of, relating to, or near the armpit. **2.** *Botany.* growing in or related to the axil: *an axillary bud.* ~*n., pl.* **-laries.** **3.** (*usually pl.*) Also called: **axillar** (æk'sɪlə, 'æksɪlə). one of the feathers growing from the axilla of a bird's wing.

axinite ('æksɪˌnaɪt) *n.* a brilliant brown mineral with wedge-shaped triclinic crystals, a complex borosilicate of calcium and aluminium containing some iron and manganese. Formula: $H(Ca,Fe,Mn)_3Al_2B(SiO_4)_3$.

axiology (ˌæksɪ'ɒlədʒɪ) *n. Philosophy.* the theory of values, moral or aesthetic. [C20: from Greek *axios* worthy] —**axiological** (ˌæksɪə'lɒdʒɪkəl) *adj.* —ˌ**axio'logically** *adv.* —ˌ**axi'ologist** *n.*

axiom ('æksɪəm) *n.* **1.** a generally accepted proposition or principle, sanctioned by experience; maxim. **2.** a universally established principle or law that is not a necessary truth: *the axioms of politics.* **3.** a self-evident statement. **4.** *Logic, maths.* a statement or formula that is stipulated to be true for the purpose of a chain of reasoning: the foundation of a formal deductive system. Compare **assumption** (sense 4). [C15: from Latin *axiōma* a principle, from Greek, from *axioun* to consider worthy, from *axios* worthy]

axiomatic (ˌæksɪə'mætɪk) *or* **axiomatical** *adj.* **1.** relating to or resembling an axiom; self-evident. **2.** containing maxims; aphoristic. **3.** (of a logical system) consisting of a set of axioms from which theorems are derived by **transformation rules.** Compare **natural deduction.** —ˌ**axio'matically** *adv.*

axion ('æksɪˌɒn) *n. Physics.* a hypothetical neutral elementary particle postulated to account for certain conservation laws in the strong interaction. [C20: from AXI(OM) + -ON]

axis[1] ('æksɪs) *n., pl.* **axes** ('æksiːz). **1.** a real or imaginary line about which a body, such as an aircraft, can rotate or about which an object, form, composition, or geometrical construction is symmetrical. **2.** one of two or three reference lines used in coordinate geometry to locate a point in a plane or in space. **3.** *Anatomy.* the second cervical vertebra. Compare **atlas** (sense 3). **4.** *Botany.* the main central part of a plant, typically consisting of the stem and root, from which secondary branches and other parts develop. **5.** an alliance between a number of states to coordinate their foreign policy. **6.** Also called: **principal axis.** *Optics.* the line of symmetry of an optical system, such as the line passing through the centre of a lens. **7.** *Geology.* an imaginary line along the crest of an anticline or the trough of a syncline. **8.** *Crystallog.* one of three lines passing through the centre of a crystal and used to characterize its symmetry. [C14: from Latin: axletree, earth's axis; related to Greek *axōn* axis]

axis[2] ('æksɪs) *n., pl.* **axises.** any of several S Asian deer of the genus *Axis,* esp. *A. axis.* They typically have a reddish-brown white-spotted coat and slender antlers. [C18: from Latin: Indian wild animal, of uncertain identity]

Axis ('æksɪs) *n.* **a. the.** the alliance of Nazi Germany, Fascist Italy, and Japan, established in 1936 and lasting until their defeat in World War II. **b.** (*as modifier*): *the Axis powers.*

axle ('æksəl) *n.* a bar or shaft on which a wheel, pair of wheels, or other rotating member revolves. [C17: from Old Norse *öxull;* related to German *Achse;* see AXIS[1]]

axletree ('æksəlˌtriː) *n.* a bar fixed across the underpart of a wagon or carriage that has rounded ends on which the wheels revolve.

Axminster carpet (ˈæksˌmɪnstə) *n.* a type of patterned carpet with a cut pile. Often shortened to **Axminster.** [after *Axminster,* in Devon, where such carpets are made]

axolemma (ˌæksəˈlɛmə) *or* **axilemma** *n.* the membrane that encloses the axon of a nerve cell.

axolotl (ˈæksəˌlɒtᵊl) *n.* **1.** any of several aquatic salamanders of the North American genus *Ambystoma,* esp. *A. mexicanum* (**Mexican axolotl**), in which the larval form (including external gills) is retained throughout life under natural conditions (see **neoteny**): family *Ambystomidae.* **2.** any of various other North American salamanders in which neoteny occurs or is induced. [C18: from Nahuatl, from *atl* water + *xolotl* servant, doll]

axon (ˈæksɒn) *or* **axone** (ˈæksəʊn) *n.* the long threadlike extension of a nerve cell that conducts nerve impulses from the cell body. Compare **dendrite.** [C19: via New Latin from Greek: axis, axle, vertebra] —ˈ**axonal** *adj.*

axonometric projection (ˌæksənəˈmɛtrɪk) *n.* a geometric drawing of an object, such as a building, in three dimensions showing the verticals and horizontals projected to scale but with diagonals and curves distorted, so that the whole appears inclined.

axonometry (ˌæksəˈnɒmɪtrɪ) *n.* the branch of crystallography concerned with measurement of the axes of crystals.

axseed (ˈæksˌsiːd) *n.* another name for **crown vetch.**

ay[1] (eɪ) *adv. Archaic, poetic.* ever; always. [C12 *ai,* from Old Norse *ei;* related to Old English *ā* always, Latin *aevum* an age, Greek *aiōn*]

ay[2] *or* **aye** (eɪ) *interj. Archaic, poetic.* an expression of misery or surprise. [C14 *ey:* from an involuntary cry of surprise]

ayah (ˈaɪə) *n.* (in the East, Africa, and other parts of the former British Empire) a maidservant, nursemaid, or governess, esp. one of Indian or Malay origin. Compare **amah.** [C18: from Hindi *āyā,* from Portuguese *aia,* from Latin *avia* grandmother]

ayahuasca (ˌaɪəˈwɑːskə) *n.* a Brazilian plant, *Banisteriopsis caapi,* that has winged fruits and yields a powerful hallucinogenic alkaloid sometimes used to treat certain disorders of the central nervous system: family *Malpighiaceae.* [C20: from Quechua]

ayatollah (ˌaɪəˈtɒlə) *n.* one of a class of Iranian Shiite religious leaders. [via Persian from Arabic, from *aya* sign + *Allah* god]

aye[1] *or* **ay** (aɪ) *sentence substitute.* **1.** yes: archaic or dialectal except in voting by voice. **2. aye aye. a.** an expression of compliance, esp. used by seamen. **b.** *Brit.* an expression of amused surprise, esp. at encountering something that confirms one's suspicions, expectations, etc. ~*n.* **3. a.** a person who votes in the affirmative. **b.** an affirmative vote. ~Compare **nay.** [C16: probably from pronoun *I,* expressing assent]

aye[2] (əɪ) *adv. Scot.* always; still. [Old Norse *ei* ever; Old English *ā;* compare Latin *aevum* an age, Greek *aion* aeon, *aiei* ever, always]

aye-aye (ˈaɪˌaɪ) *n.* a rare nocturnal arboreal prosimian primate of Madagascar, *Daubentonia madagascariensis,* related to the lemurs: family *Daubentoniidae.* It has long bony fingers and rodent-like incisor teeth adapted for feeding on insect larvae and bamboo pith. [C18: from French, from Malagasy *aiay,* probably of imitative origin]

ayin (ˈɑːjɪn; *Hebrew* ˈajiːn) *n.* the 16th letter in the Hebrew alphabet (ע), originally a pharyngeal fricative, that is now silent and transliterated by a raised inverted comma (ʻ). [Hebrew]

Aymara (ˌaɪməˈrɑː) *n.* **1.** (*pl.* **-ras** *or* **-ra**) a member of a South American Indian people of Bolivia and Peru. **2.** the language of this people, probably related to Quechua. [from Spanish *aimará,* of American Indian origin] —ˌ**Aymaˈran** *adj.*

ayont (əˈjɒnt) *adv., prep. Scot.* beyond. [*a,* from Old English *an* on + *yont* YOND]

Ayurveda (ˈɑːjʊˌveɪdə, -ˌviːdə) *n. Hinduism.* an ancient medical treatise on the art of healing and prolonging life, sometimes regarded as a fifth Veda. [from Sanskrit, from *āyur* life + *veda* knowledge] —ˌ**Ayurˈvedic** *adj.*

az. *abbrev. for* azimuth.

aza- *or before a vowel* **az-** *combining form.* denoting the presence of nitrogen, esp. a nitrogen atom in place of a $-CH$ group or an $-NH$ group in place of a $-CH_2$ group: *azathioprine.* [C20: from AZ(O)- + *-a-*]

azalea (əˈzeɪljə) *n.* any ericaceous plant of the group *Azalea,* formerly a separate genus but now included in the genus *Rhododendron:* cultivated for their showy pink or purple flowers. [C18: via New Latin from Greek, from *azaleos* dry; from its supposed preference for a dry situation]

azan (ɑːˈzɑːn) *n. Islam.* the call to prayer five times a day, usually by a muezzin from a minaret. [from Arabic *adhān,* from *adhina* to proclaim, invite; see MUEZZIN]

azathioprine (ˌæzəˈθaɪəˌpriːn) *n.* a synthetic drug that suppresses the normal immune responses of the body and is administered orally during and after organ transplantation and also in certain types of anaemia and rheumatoid arthritis. Formula: $C_9H_7N_7O_2S$. [C20: from AZA- + THIO- + P(U)RINE]

azedarach (əˈzɛdəˌræk) *n.* **1.** the astringent bark of the chinaberry tree, formerly used as an emetic and cathartic. **2.** another name for **chinaberry** (sense 1). [C18: from French *azédarac,* from Persian *āzād dirakht,* from *āzād* free, noble + *dirakht* tree]

azeotrope (əˈziːəˌtrəʊp) *n.* a mixture of liquids that boils at a constant temperature, at a given pressure, without change of composition. [C20: from A-[1] + *zeo-,* from Greek *zein* to boil + -TROPE] —**azeotropic** (ˌeɪzɪəˈtrɒpɪk) *adj.*

Azerbaijani (ˌæzəbaɪˈdʒɑːnɪ) *n.* **1.** (*pl.* **-ni** *or* **-nis**) a native or inhabitant of the former Soviet Socialist Republic of Azerbaijan or of the region of Azerbaijan in NW Iran. Sometimes shortened to **Azeri. 2.** the language of this people, belonging to the Turkic branch of the Altaic family.

Azeri (əˈzɛərɪ) *n.* short for **Azerbaijani** (sense 1).

azerty *or* **AZERTY keyboard** (əˈzɜːtɪ) *n.* a common European version of typewriter keyboard layout with the characters a, z, e, r, t, and y positioned on the top row of alphabetic characters at the left side of the keyboard.

azide (ˈeɪzaɪd) *n.* **1.** any compound containing the monovalent group $-N_3$ or the monovalent ion N_3^-. **2.** (*modifier*) consisting of, containing, or concerned with the group $-N_3$ or the ion N_3^-: *azide group or radical.*

Azilian (əˈzɪlɪən) *n.* **1.** a Palaeolithic culture of Spain and SW France that can be dated to the 10th millennium B.C., characterized by flat bone harpoons and schematically painted pebbles. ~*adj.* **2.** of or relating to this culture. [C19: named after Mas d'*Azil,* France, where artefacts were found]

azimuth (ˈæzɪməθ) *n.* **1.** *Astronomy, navigation.* the angular distance usually measured clockwise from the south point of the horizon in astronomy or from the north point in navigation to the intersection with the horizon of the vertical circle passing through a celestial body. Compare **altitude** (sense 3). **2.** *Surveying.* the horizontal angle of a bearing clockwise from a standard direction, such as north. [C14: from Old French *azimut,* from Arabic *as-sumūt,* plural of *as-samt* the path, from Latin *semita* path] —**azimuthal** (ˌæzɪˈmʌθəl) *adj.* —ˌ**aziˈmuthally** *adv.*

azimuthal projection *n.* another term for **zenithal projection.**

azine (ˈeɪziːn, -zɪn) *n.* any organic compound having a six-membered ring containing at least one nitrogen atom. See also **diazine, triazine.**

azo (ˈeɪzəʊ, ˈæ-) *adj.* of, consisting of, or containing the divalent group $-N{:}N-$: *an azo group or radical.* See also **diazo.** [independent use of AZO-]

azo- *or before a vowel* **az-** *combining form.* indicating the presence of an azo group: *azobenzene.* [from French *azote* nitrogen, from Greek *azōos* lifeless, from A-[1] + *zōē* life]

azobenzene (ˌeɪzəʊˈbɛnziːn, -bɛnˈziːn) *n.* **1.** a yellow or orange crystalline solid used mainly in the manufacture of dyes. Formula: $C_6H_5N{:}NC_6H_5$. **2.** any organic compound that is a substituted derivative of azobenzene.

azo dye *n.* any of a class of artificial dyes that contain the azo group. They are usually red, brown, or yellow and are obtained from aromatic amines.

azoic (əˈzəʊɪk, eɪ-) *adj.* without life; characteristic of the ages that have left no evidence of life in the form of organic remains. [C19: from Greek *azōos* lifeless; see AZO-]

azole (ˈeɪzəʊl, əˈzəʊl) *n.* **1.** an organic five-membered ring compound containing one or more atoms in the ring, the number usually being specified by a prefix: *diazole; triazole.* **2.** a less common name for **pyrrole.** [from AZO- + -OLE[1], on the model of *diazole*]

azonal soil (eɪˈzəʊnᵊl) *n.* soil that has a profile determined predominantly by factors other than local climate and vegetation. Azonal soils include some mountain, alluvial, marine, glacial, windblown, and volcanic soils. Compare **intrazonal soil, zonal soil.**

azoospermia (eɪˌzəʊəˈspɜːmɪə) *n. Pathol.* absence of spermatozoa in the semen.

azotaemia *or esp. U.S.* **azotemia** (ˌæzəˈtiːmɪə) *n. Pathol.* a less common name for **uraemia.** [C20: see AZOTE, -AEMIA] —**azotaemic** *or esp. U.S.* **azotemic** (ˌæzəˈtiːmɪk) *adj.*

azote (ˈeɪzəʊt, əˈzəʊt) *n.* an obsolete name for **nitrogen.** [C18: from French, from Greek *azōtos* ungirded, intended for Greek *azōos* lifeless]

azoth (ˈæzɒθ) *n.* **1.** the alchemical name for **mercury,** regarded as the first principle of all metals. **2.** the panacea postulated by Paracelsus. [from Arabic *az-zā'ūq* the mercury]

azotic (eɪˈzɒtɪk) *adj.* of, containing, or concerned with nitrogen.

azotize *or* **azotise** (ˈeɪzəˌtaɪz) *vb.* a less common word for **nitrogenize.**

azotobacter (əˈzəʊtəʊˌbæktə) *n.* any bacterium of the family *Azotobacteriaceae,* important in nitrogen fixation in the soil. [New Latin; see AZOTE, BACTERIA]

AZT *abbrev. for* azidothymidine: also called **zidovudine.**

Aztec (ˈæztɛk) *n.* **1.** a member of a Mexican Indian people who established a great empire, centred on the valley of Mexico, that was overthrown by Cortés and his followers in the early 16th century. **2.** the language of the Aztecs. See also **Nahuatl.** ~*adj. also* **Aztecan. 3.** of, relating to, or characteristic of the Aztecs, their civilization, or their language. [C18: from Spanish *Azteca,* from Nahuatl *Aztecatl,* from *Aztlan,* their traditional place of origin, literally: near the cranes, from *azta* cranes + *tlan* near]

azure (ˈæʒə, -ʒʊə, ˈeɪ-) *n.* **1.** a deep blue, occasionally somewhat purple, similar to the colour of a clear blue sky. **2.** *Poetic.* a clear blue sky. ~*adj.* **3.** of the colour azure; serene. **4.** (*usually postpositive*) *Heraldry.* of the colour blue. [C14: from Old French

azur, from Old Spanish, from Arabic *lāzaward* lapis lazuli, from Persian *lāzhuward*]
azurite ('æʒʊˌraɪt) *n.* an azure-blue mineral associated with copper deposits. It is a source of copper. Composition: copper carbonate. Formula: $Cu_3(CO_3)_2(OH)_2$. Crystal structure: monoclinic.
azygospore (ə'zaɪgəʊˌspɔː) *n.* a thick-walled spore produced by parthenogenesis in certain algae and fungi. Also called: **parthenospore.**
azygous ('æzɪgəs) *adj. Biology.* developing or occurring singly. [C17: via New Latin from Greek *azugos*, from A-[1] + *zugon* YOKE]

b *or* **B** (biː) *n., pl.* **b's, B's,** *or* **Bs. 1.** the second letter and first consonant of the modern English alphabet. **2.** a speech sound represented by this letter, usually a voiced bilabial stop, as in *bell.* **3.** Also: **beta.** the second in a series, esp. the second highest grade in an examination.

b *Chess.* See **algebraic notation.**

B *symbol for:* **1.** *Music.* **a.** a note having a frequency of 493.88 hertz (**B above middle C**) or this value multiplied or divided by any power of 2; the seventh note of the scale of C major. **b.** a key, string, or pipe producing this note. **c.** the major or minor key having this note as its tonic. **2.** the supporting or less important of two things: *the B side of a record.* **3.** a human blood type of the ABO group, containing the B antigen. **4.** (in Britain) a secondary road. **5.** the number 11 in hexadecimal notation. **6.** *Chem.* boron. **7.** magnetic flux density. **8.** *Chess.* bishop. **9.** (on Brit. pencils, signifying degree of softness of lead) black: *B; 2B; 3B.* Compare **H** (sense 5). **10.** Also: **b** *Physics.* bel. **11.** *Physics.* baryon number. **12.** balboa. **13.** belga. **14.** bolivar. **15.** *Photog.* B-setting. **16. a.** a person whose job is in middle management, or who holds an intermediate administrative or professional position. **b.** (*as modifier*): *B worker.* ~See also **occupation groupings.** ~**17.** *international car registration for* Belgium.

b. *abbrev. for:* **1.** born. **2.** *Cricket.* bowled. **3.** *Cricket.* bye.

b. *or* **B.** *abbrev. for:* **1.** *Music.* bass *or* basso. **2.** billion. **3.** book. **4.** breadth.

B. *abbrev. for:* **1.** (on maps, etc.) bay. **2.** Bible. **3.** British.

B- (of U.S. military aircraft) *abbrev. for* bomber: *B-52.*

Ba *the chemical symbol for* barium.

BA *abbrev. for:* **1.** Bachelor of Arts. **2.** British Academy. **3.** British Airways. **4.** British Association (for the Advancement of Science). **5.** British Association screw thread.

baa (bɑː) *vb.* **baas, baaing, baaed. 1.** (*intr.*) to make the cry of a sheep; bleat. ~*n.* **2.** the cry made by sheep.

BAA *abbrev. for* British Airports Authority.

BAAB *abbrev. for* British Amateur Athletic Board.

Baal (bɑːl) *n.* (*sometimes not cap.*) any false god or idol. [from Hebrew *bá'al* lord, master]

baalebos ('baləbɔs) *n. Yiddish.* **1.** the master of the house. **2.** the proprietor of a business, etc. **3.** *Slang.* an officious person. [from Hebrew *ba'al La-bayis* master of the house]

baas (bɑːs) *n.* a South African word for **boss:** used by Africans and Coloureds in addressing European managers or overseers. [C17: from Afrikaans, from Middle Dutch *baes* master; see BOSS[1]]

baaskap *or* **baasskap** ('bɑːsˌkap) *n.* (*sometimes cap.*) (in South Africa) control by Whites of non-Whites. [from Afrikaans, from BAAS + *-skap* -SHIP]

Ba'athist (bɑː'ɑːθɪst) *n.* a variant of **Ba'thist.**

Bab (bɑːb) *n.* **the.** title of Mirza Ali Mohammed (1819–50), Persian religious leader who founded Babism. [from Persian *bāb* gate, from Arabic]

baba ('bɑːbɑː; *French* baba) *n.* a small cake of leavened dough, sometimes mixed with currants and usually soaked in rum (**rum baba**). [C19: from French, from Polish, literally: old woman]

babaco ('bæbəˌkəʊ, bə'bɑːkəʊ) *n., pl.* **-cos. 1.** a subtropical parthenocarpic tree, *Carica pentagona,* originating in South America and cultivated for its fruit: family *Caricaceae.* **2.** the greenish-yellow egg-shaped fruit of this tree, having a delicate fragrance and no pips.

babassu (ˌbɑːbə'suː) *n.* a Brazilian palm tree, *Orbignya martiana* (or *O. speciosa*), having hard edible nuts that yield an oil used in making soap, margarine, etc. [from Portuguese *babaçú,* from a native Amerindian word]

babbitt ('bæbɪt) *vb.* (*tr.*) to line (a bearing) or face (a surface) with Babbitt metal or a similar soft alloy.

Babbitt ('bæbɪt) *n. U.S. derogatory.* a narrow-minded and complacent member of the middle class. [C20: after George *Babbitt,* central character in the novel *Babbitt* (1922) by Sinclair Lewis] —'**Babbittry** *n.*

Babbitt metal *n.* any of a number of alloys originally based on tin, antimony, and copper but now often including lead: used esp. in bearings. Sometimes shortened to **Babbitt.** [C19: named after Isaac *Babbitt* (1799–1862), American inventor]

babble ('bæbəl) *vb.* **1.** to utter (words, sounds, etc.) in an incoherent or indistinct jumble. **2.** (*intr.*) to talk foolishly, incessantly, or irrelevantly. **3.** (*tr.*) to disclose (secrets, confidences, etc.) carelessly or impulsively. **4.** (*intr.*) (of streams, birds, etc.) to make a low murmuring or bubbling sound. ~*n.* **5.** incoherent or foolish speech; chatter. **6.** a murmuring or bubbling sound. [C13: compare Dutch *babbelen,* Swedish *babbla,* French *babiller* to prattle, Latin *babulus* fool; probably all of imitative origin] —'**babblement** *n.* —'**babbling** *n., adj.*

babbler[1] ('bæblə) *n.* **1.** a person who babbles. **2.** any of various insect-eating birds of the Old World tropics and subtropics that have a loud incessant song: family *Muscicapidae* (warblers, thrushes, etc.).

babbler[2] ('bæblə) *n. Austral. slang.* a cook or chef. [C20: from *babbling brook,* rhyming slang for *cook*]

babe (beɪb) *n.* **1.** a baby. **2.** *Informal.* a naive, gullible, or unsuspecting person (often in the phrase **a babe in arms**). **3.** *Slang, chiefly U.S.* a girl or young woman.

Babel ('beɪbəl) *n.* (*often not cap.*) **1.** a confusion of noises or voices. **2.** a scene of noise and confusion. [from the Tower of *Babel* (Genesis 11:1–10), from Hebrew *Bābhél,* from Akkadian *Bāb-ilu,* literally: gate of God]

Babi ('bɑːbɪ) *n.* **1.** a disciple of the Bab. **2.** another word for **Babism.**

babiche (bɑː'biːʃ) *n. Canadian.* thongs or lacings of rawhide. [C19: from Canadian French, of Algonquian origin]

babies'-breath *n.* a variant of **baby's-breath.**

Babinski effect (bə'bɪnskɪ) *n. Physiol.* the reflex curling upwards of the toes (instead of inwards) when the sole of the foot is stroked, normal in infants below the age of two but a pathological condition in adults. [after Joseph *Babinski* (1857–1932), French neuropathologist]

babirusa (ˌbɑːbɪ'ruːsə) *n.* a wild pig, *Babyrousa babyrussa,* inhabiting marshy forests in Indonesia. It has an almost hairless wrinkled skin and enormous curved canine teeth. [C17: from Malay, from *bābī* hog + *rūsa* deer]

Babism ('bɑːbɪzəm) *n.* a pantheistic Persian religious sect, founded in 1844 by the Bab, forbidding polygamy, concubinage, begging, trading in slaves, and indulgence in alcohol and drugs. Compare **Baha'ism.**

baboon (bə'buːn) *n.* any of several medium-sized omnivorous Old World monkeys of the genus *Papio* (or *Chaeropithecus*) and related genera, inhabiting open rocky ground or wooded regions of Africa. They have an elongated muzzle, large teeth, and a fairly long tail. See also **hamadryas, gelada.** [C14 *babewyn* gargoyle, later, baboon, from Old French *babouin,* from *baboue* grimace; related to Old French *babine* a thick lip]

Babo's law ('bæbəʊz) *n. Chem.* the law stating that the vapour pressure of a solution is reduced in proportion to the amount of solute added. [C19: named after Lambert von *Babo* (1818–99), German chemist who formulated it]

babu ('bɑːbuː) *n.* (in India) a title or form of address more or less equivalent to *Mr,* placed before a person's full name or after his first name. [Hindi, literally: father]

babul (bɑː'buːl, 'bɑːbuːl) *n.* any of several mimosaceous trees of the genus *Acacia,* esp. *A. arabica* of N Africa and India, which bear small yellow flowers and are a source of gum arabic, tannin, and hardwood. [from Persian *babūl;* related to Sanskrit *babbūla*]

babushka (bə'buːʃkə) *n.* **1.** a headscarf tied under the chin, worn by Russian peasant women. **2.** (in Russia) an old woman. [Russian: grandmother, from *baba* old woman]

baby ('beɪbɪ) *n., pl.* **-bies. 1. a.** a newborn or recently born child; infant. **b.** (*as modifier*): *baby food.* **2.** the youngest or smallest of a family or group. **3. a.** a newborn or recently born animal. **b.** (*as modifier*): *baby rabbits.* **4.** *Usually derogatory.* an immature person. **5.** *Slang.* a young woman or sweetheart: often used as a term of address expressing affection. **6.** a project of personal concern. **7. be left holding the baby.** to be left with the responsibility. **8. throw the baby out with the bath water.** to lose the essential element by indiscriminate rejection. ~*adj.* **9.** (*prenominal*) comparatively small of its type: *a baby car.* ~*vb.* **-bies, -bying, -bied.** (*tr.*) **10.** to treat with love and attention. **11.** to treat (someone) like a baby; pamper or overprotect. [C14: probably childish reduplication; compare MAMA, PAPA] —'**babyhood** *n.* —'**babyish** *adj.*

baby bonus *n. Canadian informal.* family allowance.

baby boom *n.* a sharp increase in the birth rate of a population, esp. the one that occurred after World War II. Also called (esp. Brit.): **the bulge.**

baby-boomer *n.* a person born during a baby boom, esp. (in Britain and the U.S.) one born during the years 1945–55.

Baby-bouncer *n. Trademark.* a seat on springs suspended from a door frame, etc., in which a baby may be placed for exercise.

baby break *n.* a break in a woman's career during which she has children.

baby buggy *n.* **1.** *Brit. Trademark.* a kind of child's light pushchair. **2.** *U.S. and Canadian informal.* a small pram.

baby carriage *n.* Also: **baby buggy.** the U.S. and Canadian name for **pram**[1].

baby-face *n.* **1.** a smooth round face like a baby's. **2.** a person with such a face.

baby grand *n.* a small grand piano, approximately 5 feet long. Compare **boudoir grand, concert grand.**

Babylon ('bæbɪlən) *n. Derogatory.* **1.** (in Protestant polemic) the Roman Catholic Church, regarded as the seat of luxury and corruption. **2.** any society or group in a society considered as corrupt or as a place of exile by another society or group, esp. White Britain as viewed by some West Indians. [from the city of *Babylon* in ancient Mesopotamia, via Latin and Greek from Hebrew *Bābhel;* see BABEL]

Babylonian (ˌbæbɪ'ləʊnɪən) *n.* **1.** an inhabitant of the ancient city of Babylon or the ancient Mesopotamian kingdom of Babylonia. **2.** the extinct language of Babylonia, belonging to the E Semitic subfamily of the Afro-Asiatic family: a dialect of Akkadian. ~*adj.* **3.** of, relating to, or characteristic of ancient Babylon or Babylonia, its people, or their language. **4.** decadent or depraved.

Babylonian captivity *n.* **1.** the exile of the Jews in Babylonia from 597 to about 538 B.C. **2.** the exile of the seven popes in Avignon (1309–77).

baby-minder *n.* a person who is paid to look after other people's babies or very young children. —**'baby-ˌminding** *n.*

baby's-breath *or* **babies'-breath** *n.* **1.** a tall Eurasian caryophyllaceous plant, *Gypsophila paniculata,* bearing small white or pink fragrant flowers. **2.** any of several other plants, such as the grape hyacinth and certain bedstraws, that have small scented flowers.

baby-sit *vb.* **-sits, -sitting, -sat.** (*intr.*) to act or work as a baby-sitter. —**'baby-ˌsitting** *n., adj.*

baby-sitter *n.* a person who takes care of a child or children while the parents are out.

baby snatcher *n. Informal.* **1.** a person who steals a baby from its pram. **2.** someone who marries or has an affair with a much younger person.

baby talk *n.* **1.** the speech of very young children learning to talk. **2.** an adult's imitation of this.

baby tooth *n.* another term for **milk tooth.**

baby-walker *n.* a light frame on casters or wheels to help a baby learn to walk. U.S. equivalent: **go-cart.**

baby wipe *n.* a disposable moistened medicated paper towel supplied in a plastic drum and used for cleaning babies.

baccalaureate (ˌbækə'lɔːrɪɪt) *n.* **1.** the university degree of Bachelor or Arts, Bachelor of Science, etc. **2.** an internationally recognized programme of study, comprising different subjects, offered as an alternative to a course of A levels in Britain. **3.** *U.S.* a farewell sermon delivered at the commencement ceremonies in many colleges and universities. [C17: from Medieval Latin *baccalaureātus,* from *baccalaureus* advanced student, alteration of *baccalārius* BACHELOR; influenced in folk etymology by Latin *bāca* berry + *laureus* laurel]

baccarat ('bækəˌrɑː, ˌbækə'rɑː; *French* bakara) *n.* a card game in which two or more punters gamble against the banker. [C19: from French *baccara,* of unknown origin]

baccate ('bækeɪt) *adj. Botany.* **1.** like a berry in form, texture, etc. **2.** bearing berries. [C19: from Latin *bāca* berry]

bacchanal ('bækənᵊl) *n.* **1.** a follower of Bacchus, the Greek god of wine. **2.** a drunken and riotous celebration. **3.** a participant in such a celebration; reveller. ~*adj.* **4.** of or relating to Bacchus. [C16: from Latin *Bacchānālis,* from Greek *Bakkhos;* related to Latin *bāca* small round fruit, berry]

bacchanalia (ˌbækə'neɪlɪə) *pl. n.* **1.** (*often cap.*) orgiastic rites associated with Bacchus. **2.** any drunken revelry. —**ˌbaccha'nalian** *adj., n.*

bacchant ('bækənt) *or* (*fem.*) **bacchante** (bə'kæntɪ) *n., pl.* **bacchants, bacchantes** (bə'kæntɪz) *or* (*fem.*) **bacchantes.** **1.** a priest, priestess, or votary of Bacchus. **2.** a drunken reveller. [C17: from Latin *bacchāns,* from *bacchārī* to celebrate the BACCHANALIA]

Bacchic ('bækɪk) *adj.* **1.** of or relating to Bacchus. **2.** (*often not cap.*) riotously drunk.

bacchius (bæ'kaɪəs) *n., pl.* **-chii** (-'kaɪaɪ). *Prosody.* a metrical foot of one short syllable followed by two long ones (⏑––). Compare **dactyl.** [C16: from Latin, from Greek *Bakkheios* (*pous*) a Bacchic (foot)]

bacciferous (bæk'sɪfərəs) *adj.* bearing berries. [C17: from Latin *bācifer,* from *bāca* berry + *ferre* to bear]

bacciform ('bæksɪˌfɔːm) *adj. Botany.* shaped like a berry.

baccivorous (bæk'sɪvərəs) *adj.* feeding on berries.

baccy ('bækɪ) *n. Brit.* an informal name for **tobacco.**

bach[1] (bax, bɑːk) *n. Welsh.* a term of friendly address: used esp. after a person's name. [Welsh, literally: little one]

bach[2] (bætʃ) *vb.* a variant spelling of **batch**[2].

bachelor ('bætʃələ, 'bætʃlə) *n.* **1. a.** an unmarried man. **b.** (*as modifier*): *a bachelor flat.* **2. a.** a person who holds the degree of Bachelor of Arts, Bachelor of Education, Bachelor of Science, etc. **b.** the degree itself. **3.** Also called: **bachelor-at-arms.** (in the Middle Ages) a young knight serving a great noble. **4. bachelor seal.** a young male seal, esp. a fur seal, that has not yet mated. [C13: from Old French *bacheler* youth, squire, from Vulgar Latin *baccalāris* (unattested) farm worker, of Celtic origin; compare Irish Gaelic *bachlach* peasant] —**'bachelorhood** *n.*

bachelor girl *n.* a young unmarried woman, esp. one who is self-supporting.

Bachelor of Arts *n.* **1.** a degree conferred on a person who has successfully completed his undergraduate studies, usually in a branch of the liberal arts or humanities. **2.** a person who holds this degree.

Bachelor of Science *n.* **1.** a degree conferred on a person who has successfully completed his undergraduate studies in a branch of the sciences. **2.** a person who holds this degree.

bachelor's-buttons *n.* (*functioning as sing. or pl.*) any of various plants of the daisy family with button-like flower heads, esp. a double-flowered buttercup.

Bach trumpet (bɑːx) *n.* a modern small three-valved trumpet for playing clarino passages in the music of Johann Sebastian Bach (1685–1750).

bacillaemia *or U.S.* **bacillemia** (ˌbæsɪ'liːmɪə) *n. Pathol.* the presence of bacilli in the blood.

bacillary (bə'sɪlərɪ) *or* **bacillar** (bə'sɪlə) *adj.* **1.** of, relating to, or caused by bacilli. **2.** Also: **bacilliform** (bə'sɪlɪˌfɔːm). shaped like a short rod.

bacilluria (ˌbæsɪ'ljʊərɪə) *n. Pathol.* the presence of bacilli in the urine.

bacillus (bə'sɪləs) *n., pl.* **-cilli** (-'sɪlaɪ). **1.** any rod-shaped bacterium, such as a clostridium bacterium. Compare **coccus** (sense 1), **spirillum** (sense 1). **2.** any of various rodlike spore-producing bacteria constituting the family *Bacillaceae,* esp. of the genus *Bacillus.* [C19: from Latin: a small staff, from *baculum* walking stick]

bacitracin (ˌbæsɪ'treɪsɪn) *n.* an antibiotic used mainly in treating bacterial skin infections: obtained from the bacterium *Bacillus subtilis.* [C20: BACI(LLUS) + *-trac-* from Margaret *Tracy* (born 1936), American girl in whose blood *Bacillus subtilis* was found; see -IN]

back[1] (bæk) *n.* **1.** the posterior part of the human body, extending from the neck to the pelvis. **2.** the corresponding or upper part of an animal. **3.** the spinal column. **4.** the part or side of an object opposite the front. **5.** the part or side of anything less often seen or used: *the back of a carpet; the back of a knife.* **6.** the part or side of anything that is furthest from the front or from a spectator: *the back of the stage.* **7.** the convex part of something: *the back of a hill; the back of a ship.* **8.** something that supports, covers, or strengthens the rear of an object. **9.** *Ball games.* **a.** a mainly defensive player behind a forward. **b.** the position of such a player. **10.** the part of a book to which the pages are glued or that joins the covers. **11.** *Mining.* **a.** the side of a passage or layer nearest the surface. **b.** the earth between that level and the next. **12.** the upper surface of a joist, rafter, slate, tile, etc., when in position. Compare **bed** (sense 13). **13. at one's back.** behind, esp. in support or pursuit. **14. at the back of one's mind.** not in one's conscious thoughts. **15. behind one's back.** without one's knowledge; secretly or deceitfully. **16. break one's back.** to overwork or work very hard. **17. break the back of.** to complete the greatest or hardest part of (a task). **18. (flat) on one's back.** incapacitated, esp. through illness. **19. get off someone's back.** *Informal.* to stop criticizing or pestering someone. **20. have on one's back.** to be burdened with. **21. put one's back into.** to devote all one's strength to (a task). **22. put** (*or* **get**) **someone's back up.** to annoy someone. **23. see the back of.** to be rid of. **24. back of beyond. a. the.** a very remote place. **b.** *Austral.* in such a place (esp. in the phrase **out back of beyond**). **25. turn one's back on. a.** to turn away from in anger or contempt. **b.** to refuse to help; abandon. **26. with one's back to the wall.** in a difficult or desperate situation. ~*vb.* (*mainly tr.*) **27.** (*also intr.*) to move or cause to move backwards. **28.** to provide support, money, or encouragement for (a person, enterprise, etc.). **29.** to bet on the success of: *to back a horse.* **30.** to provide with a back, backing, or lining. **31.** to provide with a music accompaniment: *a soloist backed by an orchestra.* **32.** to provide a background for; be at the back of: *mountains back the town.* **33.** to countersign or endorse. **34.** *Archaic.* to mount the back of. **35.** (*intr.;* foll. by *on* or *onto*) to have the back facing (towards): *the house backs onto a river.* **36.** (*intr.*) (of the wind) to change direction in an anticlockwise direction. Compare **veer**[1] (sense 3a.). **37.** *Nautical.* to position (a sail) so that the wind presses on its opposite side. **38. back and fill. a.** *Nautical.* to manoeuvre the sails by alternately filling and emptying them of wind to navigate in a narrow place. **b.** to vacillate in one's opinion. ~*adj.* (*prenominal*) **39.** situated behind: *a back lane.* **40.** of the past: *back issues of a magazine.* **41.** owing from an earlier date: *back rent.* **42.** *Chiefly U.S., Austral., and N.Z.* remote: *back country.* **43.** (of a road) not direct. **44.** moving in a backward direction: *back current.* **45.** *Phonetics.* of, relating to, or denoting a vowel articulated with the tongue retracted towards the soft palate, as for the vowels in English *hard, fall, hot, full, fool.* ~*adv.* **46.** at, to, or towards the rear; away from something considered to be the front; backwards; behind. **47.** in, to, or towards the original starting point, place, or condition: *to go back home; put the book back; my headache has come back.* **48.** in or into the past: *to look back on one's childhood.* **49.** in reply, repayment, or retaliation: *to hit someone back; pay back a debt; to answer back.* **50.** in check: *the dam holds back the water.* **51.** in concealment; in reserve: *to keep something back; to hold back information.* **52. back and forth.** to and fro. **53. back to front. a.** in reverse. **b.** in disorder. ~See also **back down,**

back out, back up. [Old English *bæc;* related to Old Norse *bak,* Old Frisian *bek,* Old High German *bah*]

back[2] (bæk) *n.* a large tub or vat, esp. one used by brewers. [C17: from Dutch *bak* tub, cistern, from Old French *bac,* from Vulgar Latin *bacca* (unattested) vessel for liquids]

backache (ˈbækˌeɪk) *n.* an ache or pain in one's back.

backbeat (ˈbækˌbiːt) *n.* the second and fourth beats in music written in even time or, in more complex time signatures, the last beat of the bar. Compare **downbeat** (sense 1).

backbencher (ˈbækˈbɛntʃə) *n. Brit., Austral., and N.Z., etc.* a Member of Parliament who does not hold office in the government or opposition.

backbend (ˈbækˌbɛnd) *n.* a gymnastic exercise in which the trunk is bent backwards until the hands touch the floor.

backbite (ˈbækˌbaɪt) *vb.* **-bites, -biting, -bit; -bitten** *or* **-bit.** to talk spitefully about (an absent person). —ˈ**backˌbiter** *n.*

backblocks (ˈbækˌblɒks) *pl. n. Austral. and N.Z.* bush or remote farming area far distant from city amenities. —ˈ**backˌblock** *adj.* —ˈ**backˌblocker** *n.*

backboard (ˈbækˌbɔːd) *n.* **1.** a board that is placed behind something to form or support its back. **2.** a board worn to straighten or support the back, as after surgery. **3.** (in basketball) a flat upright surface supported on a high frame, under which the basket is attached.

back boiler *n.* a tank or series of pipes at the back of a fireplace for heating water. U.S. name: **water back.**

backbone (ˈbækˌbəʊn) *n.* **1.** a nontechnical name for **spinal column.** **2.** something that resembles the spinal column in function, position, or appearance. **3.** strength of character; courage. **4.** the main or central mountain range of a country or region. **5.** *Printing.* a less common name for **spine** (sense 4). **6.** *Nautical.* the main longitudinal members of a vessel, giving structural strength.

backbreaker (ˈbækˌbreɪkə) *n.* **1.** a wrestling hold in which a wrestler uses his knee or shoulder as a fulcrum to bend his opponent's body backwards. **2.** *Informal.* an extremely arduous task.

backbreaking (ˈbækˌbreɪkɪŋ) *adj.* demanding great effort; exhausting.

backburn (ˈbækˌbɜːn) *Austral. and N.Z.* ~*vb.* (*tr.*) **1.** to clear (an area of scrub, bush, etc.) by creating a new fire that burns in the opposite direction to the line of advancing fire. ~*n.* **2.** the act or result of backburning.

back burner *n.* **on the back burner.** put aside for the time being, as a subject that is not of immediate concern but that may be activated later; postponed.

backchat (ˈbækˌtʃæt) *n. Informal.* the act of answering back, esp. impudently.

backcloth (ˈbækˌklɒθ) *n.* a large painted curtain hanging at the back of a stage set. Also called: **backdrop.**

backcomb (ˈbækˌkəʊm) *vb.* to comb the under layers of (the hair) towards the roots to give more bulk to a hairstyle. Also: **tease.**

back country *n. Austral. and N.Z.* land remote from a town or settled area.

backcourt (ˈbækˌkɔːt) *n.* **1.** *Tennis, chiefly U.S.* the part of the court between the service line and the baseline. **2.** (in various court games) the area nearest the back boundary line.

backcross (ˈbækˌkrɒs) *vb.* **1.** to mate (a hybrid of the first generation) with one of its parents. ~*n.* **2.** the offspring so produced. **3.** the act or process of backcrossing.

backdate (ˌbækˈdeɪt) *vb.* (*tr.*) to make effective from an earlier date: *the pay rise was backdated to August.*

back door *n.* **1.** a door at the rear or side of a building. **2.** a means of entry to a job, position, etc., that is secret, underhand, or obtained through influence.

back down *vb.* **1.** (*intr., adv.*) to withdraw an earlier claim. **2.** (*tr.*) *Rowing.* to cause (a boat) to move backwards by pushing rather than pulling on the oars. ~*n.* **backdown.** **3.** abandonment of an earlier claim.

backdrop (ˈbækˌdrɒp) *n.* **1.** another name for **backcloth.** **2.** the background to any scene or situation.

backed (bækt) *adj.* **a.** having a back or backing. **b.** (*in combination*): *high-backed; black-backed.*

back emf *n. Electrical engineering.* an electromagnetic force appearing in an inductive circuit in such a direction as to oppose any change of current in the circuit.

back emission *n. Electronics.* the secondary emission of electrons from an anode.

back end *n. Northern English dialect.* autumn. [from the phrase *the back end of the year*]

backer (ˈbækə) *n.* **1.** a person who gives financial or other support. **2.** a person who bets on a competitor or contestant.

backfield (ˈbækˌfiːld) *n. American football.* **1.** (usually preceded by *the*) the quarterback and running backs in a team. **2.** the area behind the line of scrimmage from which the backfield begin each play.

backfile (ˈbækˌfaɪl) *n.* the archives of a newspaper or magazine.

backfill (ˈbækˌfɪl) *vb.* **1.** (*tr.*) to refill an excavated trench, esp. (in archaeology) at the end of an investigation. ~*n.* **2.** the soil used to do this.

backfire (ˌbækˈfaɪə) *vb.* (*intr.*) **1.** (of an internal-combustion engine) to emit a loud noise as a result of an explosion in the inlet manifold or exhaust system. **2.** to fail to have the desired or expected effect: *his plans backfired on him.* **3.** to start a controlled fire in order to halt an advancing forest or prairie fire by creating a barren area. ~*n.* **4.** (in an internal-combustion engine) **a.** an explosion of unburnt gases in the exhaust system. **b.** a premature explosion in a cylinder or inlet manifold. **5.** a controlled fire started to create a barren area that will halt an advancing forest or prairie fire.

back formation *n.* **1.** the unwitting invention of a new word on the assumption that a familiar word is derived from it. The verbs *edit* and *burgle* in English were so created from *editor* and *burglar.* **2.** a word formed by this process.

back four *n. Soccer.* the defensive players in many modern team formations: usually two fullbacks and two centre backs.

backgammon (ˈbækˌgæmən, bækˈgæmən) *n.* **1.** a game for two people played on a board with pieces moved according to throws of the dice. **2.** the most complete form of win in this game. [C17: BACK[1] + *gammon,* variant of GAME]

back green *n. Central Scot. urban dialect.* grass or a garden at the back of a house, esp. a tenement.

background (ˈbækˌgraʊnd) *n.* **1.** the part of a scene or view furthest from the viewer. **2. a.** an inconspicuous or unobtrusive position (esp. in the phrase **in the background**). **b.** (*as modifier*): *a background influence.* **3.** *Art.* **a.** the plane or ground in a picture upon which all other planes or forms appear superimposed. **b.** the parts of a picture that appear most distant. Compare **foreground, middle-distance.** **4.** a person's social class, education, training, or experience. **5. a.** the social, historical, or technical circumstances that lead up to or help to explain something: *the background to the French Revolution.* **b.** (*as modifier*): *background information.* **6. a.** a low level of sound, lighting, etc., whose purpose is to be an unobtrusive or appropriate accompaniment to something else, such as a social activity, conversation, or the action of a film. **b.** (*as modifier*): *background music.* **7.** Also called: **background radiation.** *Physics.* low-intensity radiation from small amounts of radioisotopes in soil, air, building materials, etc. **8.** *Electronics.* **a.** unwanted effects, such as noise, occurring in a measuring instrument, electronic device, etc. **b.** (*as modifier*): *background interference.*

background processing *n. Computer technol.* the ability of a system to handle two or more processes virtually simultaneously so that it appears to be printing one document while editing another document.

backhand (ˈbækˌhænd) *n.* **1.** *Tennis, squash, etc.* **a.** a stroke made across the body with the back of the hand facing the direction of the stroke. **b.** (*as modifier*): *a backhand return.* **2.** the side on which backhand strokes are made. **3.** handwriting slanting to the left. ~*adv.* **4.** with a backhand stroke. ~*vb.* (*tr.*) **5.** *Sport.* to play (a shot) backhand.

backhanded (ˌbækˈhændɪd) *adj.* **1.** (of a blow, shot, stroke, etc.) performed with the arm moving across the body. **2.** double-edged; equivocal: *a backhanded compliment.* **3.** (of handwriting) slanting to the left. **4.** (of a rope) twisted in the opposite way from the normal right-handed direction. ~*adv.* **5.** in a backhanded manner. —ˌ**backˈhandedly** *adv.* —ˌ**backˈhandedness** *n.*

backhander (ˈbækˌhændə) *n.* **1.** a backhanded stroke or blow. **2.** *Informal.* an indirect attack. **3.** *Slang.* a bribe.

backing (ˈbækɪŋ) *n.* **1.** support given to a person, cause, or enterprise. **2.** a body of supporters. **3.** something that forms, protects, supports, or strengthens the back of something. **4.** *Theatre.* a scenic cloth or flat placed behind a window, door, etc., in a set to mask the offstage space. **5.** musical accompaniment, esp. for a pop singer. **6.** the support in gold or precious metals for a country's issue of money in notes. **7.** *Meteorol.* an anticlockwise change in wind direction.

backing dog *n. N.Z.* a dog that moves a flock of sheep by jumping on their backs.

backing store *n.* a computer storage device, such as a disk, drum, or magnetic tape, that has a larger capacity but longer access time than a computer memory.

backlash (ˈbækˌlæʃ) *n.* **1.** a reaction or recoil between interacting worn or badly fitting parts in a mechanism. **2.** the excessive play between such parts. **3.** a sudden and adverse reaction, esp. to a political or social development: *the White backlash to the Black Power movement.*

backless (ˈbæklɪs) *adj.* (of a dress) low-cut at the back.

back light *n.* light falling on a photographic or television subject from the rear.

back list *n.* a publisher's previously published books that are still available.

backlog (ˈbækˌlɒg) *n.* **1.** an accumulation of uncompleted work, unsold stock, etc., to be dealt with. **2.** *Chiefly U.S. and Canadian.* a large log at the back of a fireplace.

back marker *n.* a competitor who is at the back of a field in a race.

back matter *n.* the parts of a book, such as the index and appendixes, that follow the main text. Also called: **end matter.**

backmost (ˈbækˌməʊst) *adj.* furthest back.

back mutation *n. Genetics.* the reversion of a mutant to the original phenotype.

back number *n.* **1.** an issue of a newspaper, magazine, etc., that appeared on a previous date. **2.** *Informal.* a person or thing considered to be old-fashioned.

back o' Bourke (bɜːk) *adv. Austral.* in a remote or backward place. [from *Bourke,* a town in New South Wales]

back out *vb.* (*intr., adv.;* often foll. by *of*) to withdraw (from an agreement, etc.).

backpack ('bæk,pæk) *n.* **1.** a rucksack or knapsack. **2.** a pack carried on the back of an astronaut, containing oxygen cylinders, essential supplies, etc. ~*vb.* **3.** (*intr.*) to travel about or go hiking with a backpack. **4.** (*tr.*) to transport (food or equipment) by backpack. —'**back,packer** *n.* —'**back,packing** *n.*

back passage *n.* **1.** the rectum. **2.** an interior passageway towards the back of a building.

back pay *n.* pay received by an employee from an increase awarded retrospectively.

back-pedal *vb.* **-pedals, -pedalling, -pedalled** *or U.S.* **-pedals, -pedaling, -pedaled.** (*intr.*) **1.** to turn the pedals of a bicycle backwards. **2.** to retract or modify a previous opinion, principle, etc. **3.** *Boxing.* to take backward steps.

back pressure *n.* **1.** *Engineering.* the pressure that opposes the motion of a piston on its exhaust stroke in an internal-combustion engine. **2.** *Med.* the local pressure that builds up when fluid flow is obstructed in the cardiovascular or urinary systems.

back projection *n.* a method of projecting pictures onto a translucent screen so that they are viewed from the opposite side, used esp. in films to create the illusion that the actors in the foreground are moving. Also called: **background projection.**

back rest *n.* a support for the back of something.

back room *n.* **a.** a place where research or planning is done, esp. secret research in wartime. **b.** (*as modifier*): *back-room boys.*

back saw *n.* a small handsaw stiffened along its upper edge by a metal section.

back scatter *n. Physics.* **1.** the scattering of radiation, such as x-rays or alpha-particles, by the atoms of the medium through which it passes, a proportion of this radiation emerging from the surface through which it entered. **2.** the radiation so scattered. **3.** a technique whereby very long-range radars locate targets hidden by the curvature of the earth. Radar beams are reflected off the underside of the troposphere onto the target and the return beams, similarly reflected, are measured.

backscratcher ('bæk,skrætʃə) *n.* **1.** an implement with a long handle, used for scratching one's own back. **2.** *Informal.* a person who provides a service, corporate or public money etc., for another, in order to receive a similar service or reward in return. —'**back,scratching** *n.*

back seat *n.* **1.** a seat at the back, esp. of a vehicle. **2.** *Informal.* a subordinate or inconspicuous position (esp. in the phrase **take a back seat**).

back-seat driver *n. Informal.* **1.** a passenger in a car who offers unwanted advice to the driver. **2.** a person who offers advice on or tries to direct matters that are not his concern.

backsheesh ('bækʃiːʃ) *n.* a variant spelling of **baksheesh.**

back shift *n. Brit.* the second shift of the working day.

backside (,bæk'saɪd) *n.* **1.** the back of something. **2.** ('bæk,saɪd) *Informal.* the buttocks.

backsight ('bæk,saɪt) *n.* **1.** the sight of a rifle nearer the stock. **2.** *Surveying.* a reading taken looking backwards to a previously occupied station. Compare **foresight** (sense 4).

back slang *n.* a type of slang in which words are spelled and, as far as possible, pronounced backwards.

back-slapping *adj.* energetically jovial; hearty.

backslide ('bæk,slaɪd) *vb.* **-slides, -sliding, -slid; -slid** *or* **-slidden.** (*intr.*) to lapse into bad habits or vices from a state of virtue, religious faith, etc. —'**back,slider** *n.*

backspace ('bæk,speɪs) *vb.* **1.** to move a (typewriter carriage) backwards. ~*n.* **2.** a typewriter key that can effect such a movement.

backspin ('bæk,spɪn) *n. Sport.* a backward spinning motion imparted to a ball to reduce its speed at impact. Compare **topspin.**

backstage (,bæk'steɪdʒ) *adv.* **1.** behind the part of the theatre in view of the audience; in the dressing rooms, wings, etc. **2.** towards the rear of the stage. ~*adj.* **3.** situated backstage. **4.** *Informal.* away from public view.

backstairs ('bæk'stɛəz) *pl. n.* **1.** a secondary staircase in a house, esp. one originally for the use of servants. ~*adj. also* **backstair.** **2.** underhand: *backstairs gossip.*

backstay ('bæk,steɪ) *n.* **1.** *Nautical.* a stay leading aft from the upper part of a mast to the deck or stern. **2.** *Machinery.* a supporting piece or arresting part. **3.** anything that supports or strengthens the back of something, such as leather covering the back seam of a shoe.

backstitch ('bæk,stɪtʃ) *n.* **1.** a strong sewing stitch made by starting the next stitch at the middle or beginning of the preceding one. ~*vb.* **2.** to sew using this stitch.

backstop ('bæk,stɒp) *n.* **1.** *Sport.* a screen or fence to prevent balls leaving the playing area. **2.** a block or catch to prevent excessive backward movement, such as one on the sliding seat of a rowing boat. ~*vb.* **-stops, -stopping, -stopped.** (*tr.*) **3.** *U.S.* to provide with backing or support.

back straight *n.* a straight part of a circuit, esp. of an athletics track, furthest from the finishing point.

backstreet ('bæk,striːt) *n.* **1.** a street in a town remote from the main roads. **2.** (*modifier*) denoting illicit activities regarded as likely to take place in such a street: *a backstreet abortion.*

back stretch *n.* a horse-racing term for **back straight.**

backstroke ('bæk,strəʊk) *n.* **1.** Also called: **back crawl.** *Swimming.* **a.** a stroke performed on the back, using backward circular strokes of each arm and flipper movements of the feet. **b.** (*as modifier*): *the backstroke champion.* **2.** a return stroke or blow. **3.** *Chiefly U.S.* a backhanded stroke. **4.** *Bell-ringing.* the upward movement of the bell rope as the bell swings back and forth. Compare **handstroke.** ~*vb.* **5.** (*intr.*) to swim the backstroke.

backswept ('bæk,swɛpt) *adj.* **1.** slanting backwards. **2.** another word for **sweptback.**

backsword ('bæk,sɔːd) *n.* **1.** another name for **broadsword.** **2.** Also called: '**back,swordsman.** a person who uses the backsword. **3.** a fencing stick with a basket-like protective hilt.

back-to-back *adj.* (*usually postpositive*) **1.** facing in opposite directions, often with the backs touching. **2.** *Chiefly Brit.* (of urban houses) built so that their backs are joined or separated only by a narrow alley. **3.** *Informal.* consecutive. ~*n.* **4.** a house or terrace built in back-to-back style.

backtrack ('bæk,træk) *vb.* (*intr.*) **1.** to return by the same route by which one has come. **2.** to retract or reverse one's opinion, action, policy, etc. —'**back,tracking** *n.*

back up *vb.* (*adv.*) **1.** (*tr.*) to support or assist. **2.** (*intr.*) *Cricket.* (of a nonstriking batsman) to move down the wicket in readiness for a run as a ball is bowled. **3.** (of water) to accumulate. **4.** *Printing.* to print the second side of (a sheet). **5.** *Computer technol.* to make a copy of (a data file), esp. for storage in another place as a security copy. **6.** (*intr.*, usually foll. by *on*) *Austral.* to repeat an action immediately. ~*n.* **backup.** **7.** a support or reinforcement. **8. a.** a reserve or substitute. **b.** (*as modifier*): *backup troops.* **9.** the overflow from a blocked drain or pipe.

back-up light *n.* a U.S. and Canadian name for **reversing light.**

backveld ('bækfɛlt, -vɛlt) *n. S. African informal.* a remote sparsely populated rural area. [Afrikaans, from *back* BACK[1] + *velt* field] —'**backvelder** *n.*

backward ('bækwəd) *adj.* **1.** (*usually prenominal*) directed towards the rear: *a backward glance.* **2.** retarded in physical, material, or intellectual development: *backward countries; a backward child.* **3. a.** of or relating to the past; conservative or reactionary. **b.** (*in combination*): *backward-looking.* **4.** reluctant or bashful: *a backward lover.* **5.** *Chess.* (of a pawn) behind neighbouring pawns and unable to be supported by them. ~*adv.* **6.** a variant of **backwards.** —'**backwardly** *adv.* —'**backwardness** *n.*

backwardation (,bækwə'deɪʃən) *n. Commerce.* **1.** the difference between the spot price for a commodity, including rent and interest, and the forward price. **2.** (formerly, on the Stock Exchange) postponement of delivery by a seller of securities until the next settlement period.

backwards ('bækwədz) *or* **backward** *adv.* **1.** towards the rear. **2.** with the back foremost. **3.** in the reverse of usual order or direction. **4.** to or towards the past. **5.** into a worse state: *the patient was slipping backwards.* **6.** towards the point of origin. **7. bend, lean,** *or* **fall over backwards.** *Informal.* to make a special effort, esp. in order to please. **8. know backwards.** *Informal.* to understand completely.

backwash ('bæk,wɒʃ) *n.* **1.** a dashing movement of water, such as that of retreating waves. Compare **swash.** **2.** water washed backwards by the motion of oars or other propelling devices. **3.** the backward flow of air set up by an aircraft's engines. **4.** a condition resulting from a previous event; repercussion. ~*vb.* **5.** (*tr.*) to remove oil from (combed wool).

backwater ('bæk,wɔːtə) *n.* **1.** a body of stagnant water connected to a river. **2.** water held or driven back, as by a dam, flood, or tide. **3.** an isolated, backward, or intellectually stagnant place or condition. ~*vb.* **back water.** **4.** (*intr.*) to reverse the direction of a boat, esp. to push the oars of a rowing boat.

backwoods ('bækwʊdz) *pl. n.* **1.** *Chiefly U.S. and Canadian.* partially cleared, sparsely populated forests. **2.** any remote sparsely populated place. **3.** (*modifier*) of, from, or like the backwoods. **4.** (*modifier*) uncouth; rustic.

backwoodsman ('bæk,wʊdzmən) *n., pl.* **-men.** **1.** a person from the backwoods. **2.** *U.S. informal.* an uncouth or rustic person. **3.** *Brit. informal.* a peer who rarely attends the House of Lords.

backword ('bæk,wɜːd) *n. Brit. dialect.* the act or an instance of failing to keep a promise or commitment (esp. in the phrase **give (someone) backword**).

back yard *n.* **1.** a yard at the back of a house, etc. **2. in one's own back yard. a.** close at hand. **b.** involving or implicating one.

baclava ('bɑːklə,vɑː) *n.* a variant spelling of **baklava.**

bacon ('beɪkən) *n.* **1.** meat from the back and sides of a pig, dried, salted, and usually smoked. **2. bring home the bacon.** *Informal.* **a.** to achieve success. **b.** to provide material support. **3. save one's bacon.** *Brit. informal.* to escape from a dangerous or difficult situation. [C12: from Old French *bacon,* from Old High German *bahho;* related to Old Saxon *baco;* see BACK[1]]

bacon-and-eggs *n.* another name for **bird's-foot trefoil.**

bacon beetle *n.* See **dermestid.**

baconer ('beɪkənə) *n.* a pig that weighs between 83 and 101 kg, from which bacon is cut.

Baconian (beɪ'kəʊnɪən) *adj.* **1.** of or relating to Francis Bacon (1561–1626), English philosopher, or his inductive method of reasoning. ~*n.* **2.** a follower of Bacon's philosophy. **3.** one who believes that plays attributed to Shakespeare were written by Bacon.

bact. *abbrev. for* bacteria(l).

bacteraemia *or U.S.* **bacteremia** (ˌbæktə'riːmɪə) *n. Pathol.* the presence of bacteria in the blood.

bacteria (bæk'tɪərɪə) *pl. n., sing.* **-rium** (-rɪəm). a large group of typically unicellular microorganisms, usually classified as plants. Most bacteria are parasites (many of which cause disease) or saprophytes and reproduce by fission. [C19: plural of New Latin *bacterium,* from Greek *baktērion,* literally: a little stick, from *baktron* rod, staff] —**bac'terial** *adj.* —**bac'terially** *adv.*

bacteria bed *n.* a layer of sand or gravel used to expose sewage effluent, in its final stages, to air and the action of microorganisms. Compare **filter bed** (sense 1).

bacterial plaque *n.* another term for **dental plaque.**

bactericide (bæk'tɪərɪˌsaɪd) *n.* a substance able to destroy bacteria. —**bacˌteri'cidal** *adj.*

bacterin ('bæktərɪn) *n.* a vaccine prepared from bacteria.

bacterio-, bacteri-, *or sometimes before a vowel* **bacter-** *combining form.* indicating bacteria or an action or condition relating to bacteria: *bacteriology; bactericide; bacteroid.* [New Latin, from BACTERIA]

bacteriol. *abbrev. for:* **1.** bacteriological. **2.** bacteriology.

bacteriological warfare *n.* another term for **germ warfare.**

bacteriology (bækˌtɪərɪ'ɒlədʒɪ) *n.* the branch of science that is concerned with the study of bacteria. —**bacteriological** (bækˌtɪərɪə'lɒdʒɪk^{ə}l) *adj.* —**bacˌterio'logically** *adv.* —**bacˌteri'ologist** *n.*

bacteriolysis (bækˌtɪərɪ'ɒlɪsɪs) *n.* the destruction of bacteria, esp. by antibodies. —**bacteriolytic** (bækˌtɪərɪə'lɪtɪk) *adj.*

bacteriophage (bæk'tɪərɪəˌfeɪdʒ) *n.* a virus that is parasitic in a bacterium and multiplies within its host, which is destroyed when the new viruses are released. Often shortened to **phage.** —**bacteriophagic** (bækˌtɪərɪə'fædʒɪk) *adj.* —**bacteriophagous** (bækˌtɪərɪ'ɒfəgəs) *adj.*

bacteriostasis (bækˌtɪərɪəʊ'steɪsɪs, -'stæsɪs) *n., pl.* **-stases** (-'steɪsiːz, -'stæsiːz). inhibition of the growth and reproduction of bacteria, esp. by the action of a chemical agent. —**bacteriostatic** (bækˌtɪərɪəʊ'stætɪk) *adj.* —**bacˌterio'statically** *adv.*

bacteriostat (bæk'tɪərɪəʊˌstæt) *n.* any substance that arrests the growth or reproduction of bacteria but does not kill them.

bacteriotoxin (bækˌtɪərɪəʊ'tɒksɪn) *n.* **1.** any toxin that kills bacteria. **2.** a toxin produced by a bacterium.

bacterium (bæk'tɪərɪəm) *n.* the singular of **bacteria.**

bacteriuria (bækˌtɪərɪ'jʊərɪə) *or* **bacteruria** (ˌbæktə'rjʊərɪə) *n.* the presence of bacteria in the urine.

bacteroid ('bæktəˌrɔɪd) *adj.* **1.** resembling a bacterium. ~*n.* **2.** any rodlike bacterium of the genus *Bacteroides,* occurring in the gut of man and animals.

Bactrian camel ('bæktrɪən) *n.* a two-humped camel, *Camelus bactrianus,* used as a beast of burden in the cold deserts of central Asia. Compare **Arabian camel.** [from *Bactria,* ancient country of SW Asia]

baculiform (bə'kjuːlɪˌfɔːm, 'bækjuː-) *adj. Biology.* shaped like a rod: *baculiform fungal spores.* [C19: from *baculi-,* from Latin *baculum* walking stick + -FORM]

baculum ('bækjʊləm) *n., pl.* **-la** (-lə) *or* **-lums.** a bony support in the penis of certain mammals, esp. the carnivores. [C20: New Latin, from Latin: stick, staff]

bad[1] (bæd) *adj.* **worse, worst. 1.** not good; of poor quality; inadequate; inferior: *bad workmanship; bad soil; bad light for reading.* **2.** (often foll. by *at*) lacking skill or talent; incompetent: *a bad painter; bad at sports.* **3.** (often foll. by *for*) harmful: *bad air; smoking is bad for you.* **4.** immoral; evil: *a bad life.* **5.** naughty; mischievous; disobedient: *a bad child.* **6.** rotten; decayed; spoiled: *a bad egg.* **7.** severe; intense: *a bad headache.* **8.** incorrect; wrong; faulty: *bad pronunciation.* **9.** ill or in pain (esp. in the phrase **feel bad**). **10.** regretful, sorry, or upset (esp. in the phrase **feel bad about**). **11.** unfavourable; distressing: *bad news; a bad business.* **12.** offensive; unpleasant; disagreeable: *bad language; bad temper.* **13.** not valid or sound; void: *a bad cheque.* **14.** not recoverable: *a bad debt.* **15. (badder, baddest)** *Slang.* good; excellent. **16. go from bad to worse.** to deteriorate even more. **17. go bad.** to putrefy; spoil. **18. in a bad way.** *Informal.* **a.** seriously ill, through sickness or injury. **b.** in trouble of any kind. **19. in someone's bad books.** See **book** (sense 20). **20. make the best of a bad job.** to manage as well as possible in unfavourable circumstances. **21. not bad** *or* **not so bad.** *Informal.* passable; fair; fairly good. **22. not half bad.** *Informal.* very good. **23. too bad.** *Informal.* (often used dismissively) regrettable. ~*n.* **24.** unfortunate or unpleasant events collectively (often in the phrase **take the bad with the good**). **25.** an immoral or degenerate state (often in the phrase **go to the bad**). **26.** the debit side of an account: *£200 to the bad.* **27. in bad with.** *Informal.* out of favour with. ~*adv.* **28.** *Not standard.* badly: *to want something bad.* [C13: probably from *bæd-,* as the first element of Old English *bǣddel* hermaphrodite, *bǣdling* sodomite] —**'baddish** *adj.* —**'badness** *n.*

▷**Usage.** See at **good.**

bad[2] (bæd) *vb.* a variant of **bade.**

bad blood *n.* a feeling of intense hatred or hostility; enmity.

baddeleyite ('bædlɪˌaɪt) *n.* a mineral consisting largely of zirconium dioxide: a source of zirconium. Formula: ZrO_2. [C19: named after J. *Baddeley,* British geologist]

badderlocks ('bædəˌlɒks) *n.* a seaweed, *Alaria esculenta,* that has long brownish-green fronds and is eaten in parts of N Europe. [C18: of unknown origin]

baddie *or* **baddy** ('bædɪ) *n., pl.* **-dies.** *Informal.* a bad character in a story, film, etc., esp. an opponent of the hero.

bade (bæd, beɪd) *or* **bad** *vb.* past tense of **bid.**

bad faith *n.* **1.** intention to deceive; treachery or dishonesty (esp. in the phrase **in bad faith**). **2.** Also called: **mauvaise foi.** (in the philosophy of Sartre) self-deception, as when an agent regards his actions as conditioned by circumstances or conventions in order to evade his own responsibility for choosing them freely.

badge (bædʒ) *n.* **1.** a distinguishing emblem or mark worn to signify membership, employment, achievement, etc. **2.** any revealing feature or mark. [C14: from Norman French *bage;* related to Anglo-Latin *bagia*]

badger ('bædʒə) *n.* **1.** any of various stocky omnivorous musteline mammals of the subfamily *Melinae,* such as *Meles meles* **(Eurasian badger)**, occurring in Europe, Asia, and North America: order *Carnivora* (carnivores). They are typically large burrowing animals, with strong claws and a thick coat striped black and white on the head. Compare **ferret badger, hog badger. 2. honey badger.** another name for **ratel.** ~*vb.* **3.** (*tr.*) to pester or harass. [C16: variant of *badgeard,* probably from BADGE (from the white mark on its forehead) + -ARD]

badinage ('bædɪˌnɑːʒ) *n.* playful or frivolous repartee or banter. [C17: from French, from *badiner* to jest, banter, from Old Provençal *badar* to gape]

badinerie (bəˌdɪnə'riː) *n. Music.* a name given in the 18th century to a type of quick, light movement in a suite. [French: a pleasantry]

badlands ('bædˌlændz) *pl. n.* any deeply eroded barren area.

badly ('bædlɪ) *adv.* **worse, worst. 1.** poorly; defectively; inadequately: *the chair is badly made.* **2.** unfavourably; unsuccessfully; unfortunately: *our scheme worked out badly.* **3.** severely; gravely: *he was badly hurt.* **4.** incorrectly or inaccurately: *to speak German badly.* **5.** improperly; naughtily; wickedly: *to behave badly.* **6.** without humanity; cruelly: *to treat badly.* **7.** very much (esp. in the phrases **need badly, badly in need of, want badly**). **8.** regretfully: *he felt badly about it.* **9. badly off.** poor; impoverished. ~*adj.* **10.** (*postpositive*) *Northern English dialect.* ill; poorly.

badman ('bædˌmæn) *n., pl.* **-men.** *Chiefly U.S.* a hired gunman, outlaw, or criminal.

badminton ('bædmɪntən) *n.* **1.** a game played with rackets and a shuttlecock, which is hit back and forth across a high net. **2.** Also called: **badminton cup.** a long refreshing drink of claret with soda water and sugar. [C19: named after *Badminton* House in SW England, where the game was first played]

bad-mouth *vb.* (*tr.*) *Slang, chiefly U.S. and Canadian.* to speak unfavourably about.

bad news *n. Slang.* someone or something regarded as undesirable: *he's bad news around here.*

bad-tempered *adj.* angry, irritable, or ungracious.

BAe *abbrev. for* British Aerospace.

Baedeker ('beɪdɪkə) *n.* **1.** any of a series of travel guidebooks issued by the German publisher Karl Baedeker (1801–59) or his firm. **2.** any guidebook.

Baedeker raid *n. Informal.* one of the German air raids in 1942 on places of cultural and historical importance in England.

bael ('beɪəl) *n.* **1.** a spiny Indian rutaceous tree, *Aegle marmelos.* **2.** the edible thick-shelled fruit of this tree. [C17: from Hindi *bel*]

baffle ('bæf^{ə}l) *vb.* (*tr.*) **1.** to perplex; bewilder; puzzle. **2.** to frustrate (plans, efforts, etc.). **3.** to check, restrain, or regulate (the flow of a fluid or the emission of sound or light). **4.** to provide with a baffle. **5.** *Obsolete.* to cheat or trick. ~*n.* **6.** Also called: **baffle board, baffle plate.** a plate or mechanical device designed to restrain or regulate the flow of a fluid, the emission of light or sound, or the distribution of sound, esp. in a loudspeaker or microphone. [C16: perhaps from Scottish dialect *bachlen* to condemn publicly; perhaps related to French *bafouer* to disgrace] —**'bafflement** *n.* —**'baffler** *n.* —**'baffling** *adj.* —**'bafflingly** *adv.*

BAFTA ('bæftə) *n. acronym for* British Academy of Film and Television Arts.

bag (bæg) *n.* **1.** a flexible container with an opening at one end. **2.** Also called: **bagful.** the contents of or amount contained in such a container. **3.** any of various measures of quantity, such as a bag containing 1 hundredweight of coal. **4.** a piece of portable luggage. **5.** short for **handbag. 6.** anything that hangs loosely, sags, or is shaped like a bag, such as a loose fold of skin under the eyes or the bulging part of a sail. **7.** any pouch or sac forming part of the body of an animal, esp. the udder of a cow. **8.** *Hunting.* the quantity of quarry taken in a single hunting trip or by a single hunter. **9.** *Derogatory slang.* an ugly or bad-tempered woman or girl (often in the phrase **old bag**). **10.** *Slang.* a measure of marijuana, heroin, etc., in folded paper. **11.** *Slang.* a person's particular taste, field of skill, interest, activity, etc.: *blues is his bag.* **12. bag and baggage.** *Informal.* **a.** with all one's belongings. **b.** entirely. **13. a bag of bones.** a lean creature. **14. in the bag.** *Slang.* almost assured of succeeding or being obtained. **15. the (whole) bag of tricks.** *Informal.* every device; everything. ~*vb.* **bags, bagging, bagged. 16.** (*tr.*) to put into a bag. **17.** to bulge or cause to bulge; swell. **18.** (*tr.*) to capture or kill, as in hunting. **19.** (*tr.*) to catch, seize, or steal. **20.** (*intr.*) to hang loosely; sag. **21.** (*tr.*) *Brit. informal.* to reserve or secure the right to do or to have something: *he bagged the best chair.* **22.** (*tr.*) *Austral. slang.* to criticize; disparage. ~See also **bags.** [C13: probably from Old Norse *baggi;* related to Old French *bague* bundle, pack, Medieval Latin *baga* chest, sack, Flemish *bagge*]

Baganda (bəˈgændə, -ˈgɑːn-) *n.* (*functioning as pl.*) a Negroid people of E Africa living chiefly in Uganda. See also **Ganda, Luganda.**

bagasse (bəˈgæs) *n.* **1.** the dry pulp remaining after the extraction of juice from sugar cane or other similar plants: used as fuel, for making fibreboard, paper, etc. **2.** Also called: **megass, megasse.** a type of paper made from bagasse fibres. [C19: from French, from Spanish *bagazo* dregs, refuse, from *baga* husk, from Latin *bāca* berry]

bagassosis (ˌbægəˈsəʊsɪs) *n.* an allergic response to the dust of bagasse, causing breathlessness and fever.

bagatelle (ˌbægəˈtɛl) *n.* **1.** something of little value or significance; trifle. **2.** a board game in which balls are struck into holes, with pins as obstacles; pinball. **3.** another name for **bar billiards. 4.** a short light piece of music, esp. for piano. [C17: from French, from Italian *bagattella,* from (dialect) *bagatta* a little possession, from *baga* a possession, probably from Latin *bāca* berry]

bagel *or* **beigel** (ˈbeɪgᵊl) *n.* a hard ring-shaped bread roll, characteristic of Jewish baking. [C20: from Yiddish *beygel,* ultimately from Old High German *boug* ring]

baggage (ˈbægɪdʒ) *n.* **1. a.** suitcases, bags, etc., packed for a journey; luggage. **b.** *Chiefly U.S. and Canadian.* (*as modifier*): *baggage car.* **2.** an army's portable equipment. **3.** *Informal, old-fashioned.* **a.** a pert young woman. **b.** an immoral woman or prostitute. **4.** *Irish informal.* a cantankerous old woman. [C15: from Old French *bagage,* from *bague* a bundle, perhaps of Scandinavian origin; compare Old Norse *baggi* BAG]

bagging (ˈbægɪŋ) *n.* coarse woven cloth; sacking.

baggy[1] (ˈbægɪ) *adj.* **-gier, -giest.** (of clothes) hanging loosely; puffed out. —ˈ**baggily** *adv.* —ˈ**bagginess** *n.*

baggy[2] (ˈbægɪ) *n., pl.* **-gies.** a variant spelling of **bagie.**

bagh (bɑːg) *n.* (in India and Pakistan) a garden. [Urdu]

bagie (ˈbeɪgɪ) *or* **baggy** *n., pl.* **-gies.** *Northumbrian dialect.* a turnip. [perhaps from RUTABAGA]

bag lady *n. Chiefly U.S.* a woman who is homeless and wanders city streets with all her possessions in shopping bags. Also called (in full): **shopping bag lady.**

bagman (ˈbægmən) *n., pl.* **-men. 1.** *Brit. informal.* a travelling salesman. **2.** *Slang, chiefly U.S.* a person who collects or distributes money for racketeers. **3.** *Informal, chiefly Canadian.* a person who solicits money or subscriptions for a political party. **4.** *Austral.* a tramp or swagman, esp. one on horseback.

bag moth *n. N.Z.* a moth, the larvae of which develop in bags or cases.

bagnette (ˈbægnɛt) *n.* a variant of **baguette** (sense 3).

bagnio (ˈbɑːnjəʊ) *n., pl.* **-ios. 1.** a brothel. **2.** *Obsolete.* an oriental prison for slaves. **3.** *Obsolete.* an Italian or Turkish bathhouse. [C16: from Italian *bagno,* from Latin *balneum* bath, from Greek *balaneion*]

bagpipe (ˈbægˌpaɪp) *n.* (*modifier*) of or relating to the bagpipes: *a bagpipe maker.*

bagpipes (ˈbægˌpaɪps) *pl. n.* any of a family of musical wind instruments in which sounds are produced in reed pipes supplied with air from a bag inflated either by the player's mouth, as in the **Irish bagpipes** or **Highland bagpipes** of Scotland, or by arm-operated bellows, as in the **Northumbrian bagpipes.**

bags (bægz) *pl. n.* **1.** *Informal.* a lot; a great deal. **2.** short for **Oxford bags. 3.** *Brit. informal.* any pair of trousers. ~*interj.* **4.** Also: **bags I.** *Children's slang, Brit.* an indication of the desire to do, be, or have something. **5. rough as bags** *or* **sacks.** *Austral. and N.Z.* uncouth.

baguette *or* **baguet** (bæˈgɛt) *n.* **1.** a small gem cut as a long rectangle. **2.** the shape of such a gem. **3.** *Architect.* a small moulding having a semicircular cross section. **4.** a narrow French stick loaf. [C18: from French, from Italian *bacchetta* a little stick, from *bacchio* rod, from Latin *baculum* walking stick]

bagwash (ˈbægˌwɒʃ) *n. Old-fashioned.* **1.** a laundry that washes clothes without drying or pressing them. **2.** the clothes so washed.

bagwig (ˈbægˌwɪg) *n.* an 18th-century wig with hair pushed back into a bag.

bagworm (ˈbægˌwɜːm) *n.* **1.** the larva of moths of the family *Psychidae,* which typically constructs and inhabits a protective case of silk covered with grass, leaves, etc. **2. bagworm moth.** any moth of the family *Psychidae.*

bah (bɑː, bæ) *interj.* an expression of contempt or disgust.

bahadur (bəˈhɑːdə) *n.* (*often in combination*) a title formerly conferred by the British on distinguished Indians. [C18: from Hindi *bahādur* hero, from Persian: valiant]

Baha'i (bəˈhɑːɪ) *n.* **1.** an adherent of Baha'ism. ~*adj.* **2.** of or relating to Baha'ism. [from Persian *bahā'ī,* literally: of glory, from *bahā' u'llāh* glory of God, from Arabic]

Baha'ism (bəˈhɑːˌɪzəm) *n.* a religious system founded in 1863 by Baha'ullah, based on Babism and emphasizing the value of all religions and the spiritual unity of all mankind. —**Baˈha'ist** *or* **Baˈha'ite** *adj., n.*

Bahamian (bəˈheɪmɪən, -ˈhɑː-) *adj.* **1.** of or relating to the Bahamas, a country in the West Indies. ~*n.* **2.** a native or inhabitant of the Bahamas.

Bahasa Indonesia (bɑːˈhɑːsə) *n.* the official language of Indonesia: developed from the form of Malay formerly widely used as a trade language in SE Asia.

Baha'ullah (ˌbɑːhɑːˈʊlə) *n.* title of Mirza Hosein Ali (1817–92), Persian religious leader who founded Baha'ism.

baht (bɑːt) *n., pl.* **bahts** *or* **baht.** the standard monetary unit of Thailand, divided into 100 satangs. [from Thai *bāt*]

bahuvrihi (ˌbɑːhuːˈvriːhiː) *n. Linguistics.* **1.** a class of compound words consisting of two elements the first of which is a specific feature of the second. **2.** a compound word of this type, such as *hunchback, bluebell, highbrow.* [C19: from Sanskrit *bahuvrīhi,* itself this type of compound, from *bahu* much + *vrīh* rice]

bail[1] (beɪl) *Law.* ~*n.* **1.** a sum of money by which a person is bound to take responsibility for the appearance in court of another person or himself, forfeited if the person fails to appear. **2.** the person or persons so binding themselves; surety. **3.** the system permitting release of a person from custody where such security has been taken: *he was released on bail.* **4. jump bail** *or* (*formal*) **forfeit bail.** to fail to appear in court to answer to a charge. **5. stand** *or* **go bail.** to act as surety (for someone). ~*vb.* (*tr.*) **6.** (often foll. by *out*) to release or obtain the release of (a person) from custody, security having been made. ~See also **bale out.** [C14: from Old French: custody, from *baillier* to hand over, from Latin *bāiulāre* to carry burdens, from *bāiulus* carrier, of obscure origin]

bail[2] *or* **bale** (beɪl) *vb.* (often foll. by *out*) to remove (water) from (a boat). [C13: from Old French *baille* bucket, from Latin *bāiulus* carrier] —ˈ**bailer** *or* ˈ**baler** *n.*

bail[3] (beɪl) *n.* **1.** *Cricket.* either of two small wooden bars placed across the tops of the stumps to form the wicket. **2.** *Agriculture.* **a.** a partition between stalls in a stable or barn, for horses. **b.** a portable dairy house built on wheels or skids. **3.** *Austral. and N.Z.* a framework in a cowshed used to secure the head of a cow during milking. ~*vb.* **4.** See **bail up.** [C18: from Old French *baile* stake, fortification, probably from Latin *baculum* stick]

bail[4] *or* **bale** (beɪl) *n.* **1.** the semicircular handle of a kettle, bucket, etc. **2.** a semicircular support for a canopy. **3.** a movable bar on a typewriter that holds the paper against the platen. [C15: probably of Scandinavian origin; compare Old Norse *beygja* to bend]

bailable (ˈbeɪləbᵊl) *adj. Law.* **1.** eligible for release on bail. **2.** admitting of bail: *a bailable offence.*

bail bond *n.* a document in which a prisoner and one or more sureties guarantee that the prisoner will attend the court hearing of the charges against him if he is released on bail.

bailee (beɪˈliː) *n. Contract law.* a person to whom goods are entrusted under a contract of bailment.

bailey (ˈbeɪlɪ) *n.* the outermost wall or court of a castle. [C13: from Old French *baille* enclosed court, from *bailler* to enclose; see BAIL[3]]

Bailey bridge (ˈbeɪlɪ) *n.* a temporary bridge made of prefabricated steel parts that can be rapidly assembled. [C20: named after Sir Donald Coleman *Bailey* (1901–85), its British designer]

bailie (ˈbeɪlɪ) *n.* **1.** (in Scotland) a municipal magistrate. **2.** an obsolete or dialect spelling of **bailiff.** [C13: from Old French *bailli,* from earlier *baillif* BAILIFF]

bailiff (ˈbeɪlɪf) *n.* **1.** *Brit.* the agent or steward of a landlord or landowner. **2.** a sheriff's officer who serves writs and summonses, makes arrests, and ensures that the sentences of the court are carried out. **3.** *Chiefly Brit.* (formerly) a high official having judicial powers. **4.** *Chiefly U.S.* an official having custody of prisoners appearing in court. [C13: from Old French *baillif,* from *bail* custody; see BAIL[1]]

bailiwick (ˈbeɪlɪwɪk) *n.* **1.** *Law.* the area over which a bailiff has jurisdiction. **2.** a person's special field of interest, authority, or skill. [C15: from BAILIE + WICK[2]]

bailment (ˈbeɪlmənt) *n.* **1.** *Contract law.* a contractual delivery of goods in trust to a person for a specific purpose. **2.** *Criminal law.* the act of granting bail.

bailor (ˈbeɪlə, beɪˈlɔː) *n. Contract law.* a person who delivers goods to another under a contract of bailment.

bailsman (ˈbeɪlzmən) *n., pl.* **-men.** *Rare.* a person who stands bail for another; surety.

bail up *vb.* (*adv.*) **1.** *Austral and N.Z.* to confine (a cow) or (of a cow) to be confined by the head in a bail. See **bail**[3]. **2.** (*tr.*) *Austral.* (of a bushranger) to tie up or hold under guard in order to rob. **3.** (*intr.*) *Austral.* to submit to robbery without offering resistance. **4.** (*tr.*) *Austral. informal.* to accost or detain, esp. in conversation; buttonhole.

Baily's beads (ˈbeɪlɪz) *pl. n.* the brilliant points of sunlight that appear briefly around the moon, just before and after a total eclipse. [C19: named after Francis *Baily* (died 1844), British astronomer who described them]

báinín *or* **bawneen** (ˈbɑːniːn) *n. Irish.* **1.** a collarless revers-less unlined man's jacket made of white close-woven wool. **2.** the material for such a jacket. **3. báinín skirt.** a skirt made of this material. **4. báinín wool.** white woollen thread. [C20: from Irish Gaelic *báinín,* diminutive of *bán* white]

bainite (ˈbeɪnaɪt) *n.* a mixture of iron and iron carbide found in incompletely hardened steels, produced when austenite is transformed at temperatures between the pearlite and martensite ranges. [C20: named after Edgar C. *Bain* (1891–1971), American physicist; see -ITE[1]]

bain-marie *French.* (bɛ̃mari) *n., pl.* ***bains-marie*** (bɛ̃mari). a vessel for holding hot water, in which sauces and other dishes are gently cooked or kept warm. [C19: from French, from Medieval Latin *balneum Mariae,* literally: bath of Mary, inaccurate translation of Medieval Greek *kaminos Marios,* literally: furnace of *Miriam,* alleged author of a treatise on alchemy]

Bairam (baɪˈræm, ˈbaɪræm) *n.* either of two Muslim festivals, one (**Lesser Bairam**) falling at the end of Ramadan, the other (**Greater Bairam**) 70 days later at the end of the Islamic year. [from Turkish *bayrām*]

bairn (bɛən; *Scot.* bern) *n. Scot. and northern English.* a child. [Old English *bearn;* related to *bearm* lap, Old Norse, Old High German *barn* child]

Baisakhi (baɪˈsækiː) *n.* an annual Sikh festival commemorating the founding (1699) of the Order of the Khalsa by Gobind Singh. [from Sanskrit, *Baisakh* (month of the year)]

bait[1] (beɪt) *n.* **1.** something edible, such as soft bread paste, worms, pieces of meat, etc., fixed to a hook or in a trap to attract fish or animals. **2.** an enticement; temptation. **3.** a variant spelling of **bate**[4]. **4.** *Northern English dialect.* food, esp. a packed lunch. **5.** *Archaic.* a short stop for refreshment during a journey. ~*vb.* **6.** (*tr.*) to put a piece of food on or in (a hook or trap). **7.** (*tr.*) to persecute or tease. **8.** (*tr.*) to entice; tempt. **9.** (*tr.*) to set dogs upon (a bear, etc.). **10.** (*tr.*) *Archaic.* to feed (a horse), esp. during a break in a journey. **11.** (*intr.*) *Archaic.* to stop for rest and refreshment during a journey. [C13: from Old Norse *beita* to hunt, persecute; related to Old English *bǣtan* to restrain, hunt, Old High German *beizen*]

bait[2] (beɪt) *vb.* a variant spelling of **bate**[2].

baize (beɪz) *n.* **1.** a woollen fabric resembling felt, usually green, used mainly for the tops of billiard tables. ~*vb.* **2.** (*tr.*) to line or cover with such fabric. [C16: from Old French *baies,* plural of *baie* baize, from *bai* reddish brown, BAY[5], perhaps the original colour of the fabric]

Bajan (ˈbeɪdʒən) *Caribbean informal.* ~*n.* **1.** a native of Barbados. ~*adj.* **2.** of or relating to Barbados or its inhabitants. [C20: variant of *Badian,* a shortened form of BARBADIAN]

bake (beɪk) *vb.* **1.** (*tr.*) to cook by dry heat in or as if in an oven. **2.** (*intr.*) to cook bread, pastry, etc., in an oven. **3.** to make or become hardened by heat. **4.** (*intr.*) *Informal.* to be extremely hot, as in the heat of the sun. ~*n.* **5.** *U.S.* a party at which the main dish is baked. **6.** a batch of things baked at one time. **7.** *Scot.* a kind of biscuit. **8.** *Caribbean.* a small flat fried cake. [Old English *bacan;* related to Old Norse *baka,* Old High German *bahhan* to bake, Greek *phōgein* to parch, roast]

bakeapple (ˈbeɪkˌæpᵊl) *n. Canadian.* the fruit of the cloudberry.

baked Alaska *n.* a dessert consisting of cake and ice cream covered with meringue and cooked very quickly in a hot oven.

baked beans *pl. n.* haricot beans, baked and tinned in tomato sauce.

bakehouse (ˈbeɪkˌhaʊs) *n.* another word for **bakery.**

Bakelite (ˈbeɪkəˌlaɪt) *n. Trademark.* any one of a class of thermosetting resins used as electric insulators and for making plastic ware, telephone receivers, etc. [C20: named after L. H. *Baekeland* (1863–1944), Belgian-born U.S. inventor; see -ITE[1]]

baker (ˈbeɪkə) *n.* **1.** a person whose business or employment is to make or sell bread, cakes, etc. **2.** a portable oven. **3. on the baker's list.** *Irish informal.* in good health.

baker's dozen *n.* thirteen. [C16: from the bakers' former practice of giving thirteen rolls where twelve were requested, to protect themselves against accusations of giving light weight]

bakery (ˈbeɪkərɪ) *n., pl.* **-eries.** **1.** Also called: **bakehouse.** a room or building equipped for baking. **2.** a shop in which bread, cakes, etc., are sold.

Bakewell tart (ˈbeɪkwɛl) *n. Brit.* an open tart having a pastry base and a layer of jam and filled with almond-flavoured sponge cake. [C19: named after *Bakewell,* Derbyshire]

baking (ˈbeɪkɪŋ) *n.* **1. a.** the process of cooking bread, cakes, etc. **b.** (*as modifier*): *a baking dish.* **2.** the bread, cakes, etc., cooked at one time. ~*adj.* **3.** (esp. of weather) very hot and dry.

baking powder *n.* any of various powdered mixtures that contain sodium bicarbonate, starch (usually flour), and one or more slightly acidic compounds, such as cream of tartar: used in baking as a substitute for yeast.

baklava *or* **baclava** (ˈbɑːkləˌvɑː) *n.* a rich cake of Middle Eastern origin consisting of thin layers of pastry filled with nuts and honey. [from Turkish]

bakra (ˈbækrə) *Caribbean.* ~*n., pl.* **-ra** *or* **-ras.** **1.** a White person, esp. one from Britain. ~*adj.* **2.** (of people) White, esp. British. [of African origin]

baksheesh *or* **backsheesh** (ˈbækʃiːʃ) (in some Eastern countries, esp. formerly) ~*n.* **1.** money given as a tip, a present, or alms. ~*vb.* **2.** to give such money to (a person). [C17: from Persian *bakhshīsh,* from *bakhshīdan* to give; related to Sanskrit *bhaksati* he enjoys]

BAL *abbrev. for* British anti-lewisite. See **dimercaprol.**

bal. *Book-keeping. abbrev. for* balance.

Balaclava helmet (ˌbæləˈklɑːvə) *n.* a close-fitting woollen hood that covers the ears and neck, as originally worn by soldiers in the Crimean War. [C19: named after *Balaklava,* a port in Ukraine, scene of a battle (1854) during the Crimean War]

balalaika (ˌbæləˈlaɪkə) *n.* a plucked musical instrument, usually having a triangular body and three strings: used chiefly for Russian folk music. [C18: from Russian]

balance (ˈbæləns) *n.* **1.** a weighing device, generally consisting of a horizontal beam pivoted at its centre, from the ends of which two pans are suspended. The substance to be weighed is placed in one pan and known weights are placed in the other until the beam returns to the horizontal. See also **microbalance.** **2.** an imagined device for events, actions, motives, etc., in relation to each other (esp. in the phrases **weigh in the balance, hang in the balance**). **3.** a state of equilibrium. **4.** something that brings about such a state. **5.** equilibrium of the body; steadiness: *to lose one's balance.* **6.** emotional stability; calmness of mind. **7.** harmony in the parts of a whole: *balance in an artistic composition.* **8.** the act of weighing factors, quantities, etc., against each other. **9.** the power to influence or control: *he held the balance of power.* **10.** something that remains or is left: *let me have the balance of what you owe me.* **11.** *Accounting.* **a.** equality of debit and credit totals in an account. **b.** a difference between such totals. **12.** *Chem.* the state of a chemical equation in which the number, kind, electrical charges, etc., of the atoms on opposite sides are equal. **13.** a balancing movement. **14.** short for **spring balance.** **15. in the balance.** in an uncertain or undecided condition. **16. on balance.** after weighing up all the factors. **17. strike a balance.** to make a compromise. ~*vb.* **18.** (*tr.*) to weigh in or as if in a balance. **19.** (*intr.*) to be or come into equilibrium. **20.** (*tr.*) to bring into or hold in equilibrium. **21.** (*tr.*) to assess or compare the relative weight, importance, etc., of. **22.** (*tr.*) to act so as to equalize; be equal to. **23.** (*tr.*) to compose or arrange so as to create a state of harmony. **24.** (*tr.*) to bring (a chemical or mathematical equation) into balance. **25.** (*tr.*) *Accounting.* **a.** to compute the credit and debit totals of (an account) in order to determine the difference. **b.** to equalize the credit and debit totals of (an account) by making certain entries. **c.** to settle or adjust (an account) by paying any money due. **26.** (*intr.*) (of a business account, balance sheet, etc.) to have the debit and credit totals equal. **27.** to match or counter (one's dancing partner or his or her steps) by moving towards and away from him or her. [C13: from Old French, from Vulgar Latin *bilancia* (unattested), from Late Latin *bilanx* having two scalepans, from BI-[1] + *lanx* scale] —ˈ**balanceable** *adj.*

Balance (ˈbæləns) *n.* **the.** the constellation Libra, the seventh sign of the zodiac.

balance bridge *n.* another name for **bascule bridge** (see **bascule** (sense 1)).

balanced (ˈbælənst) *adj.* **1.** having weight equally distributed. **2.** (of a person) mentally and emotionally stable. **3.** (of a discussion, programme, etc.) presenting opposing points of view fairly and without bias. **4.** (of a diet) consisting of all essential nutrients in suitable form and amounts to maintain health. **5.** (of a budget) having expenditure no greater than income. **6.** *Electronics.* (of signals or circuitry) symmetrically disposed about earth or other reference potential. **7.** (of a chemical equation) having the correct relative number of moles of reactants and products.

balance of nature *n.* the stable state in which natural communities of animals and plants exist, maintained by adaptation, competition, and other interactions between members of the community and their nonliving environment.

balance of payments *n.* the difference over a given time between total payments to foreign nations, arising from imports of goods and services and transfers abroad of capital, interest, grants, etc., and total receipts from foreign nations, arising from exports of goods and services and transfers from abroad of capital, interest, grants, etc.

balance of power *n.* **1.** the distribution of power among countries so that no one nation can seriously threaten the fundamental interests of another. **2.** any similar distribution of power or influence.

balance of trade *n.* the difference in value between total exports and total imports of goods. Also called: **visible balance.** Compare **invisible balance.**

balance pipe *n. Engineering.* a pipe between two points used to equalize pressure.

balancer (ˈbælənsə) *n.* **1.** a person or thing that balances. **2.** *Entomol.* another name for **haltere.**

balance sheet *n.* a statement that shows the financial position of a business enterprise at a specified date by listing the asset balances and the claims on such assets.

balance weight *n. Engineering.* a weight used in machines to counterbalance a part, as of a crankshaft. Also called: **bob-weight.**

balance wheel *n.* a wheel oscillating against the hairspring of a timepiece, thereby regulating its beat.

balanitis (ˌbæləˈnaɪtɪs) *n. Med.* inflammation of the glans penis, usually due to infection. [from New Latin *balanus,* from Greek *balanos* acorn + -ITIS]
balas (ˈbæləs, ˈbeɪ-) *n.* a red variety of spinel, used as a gemstone. Also called: **balas ruby.** [C15: from Old French *balais,* from Arabic *bālakhsh,* from *Badhakhshān,* region in Afghanistan where the gem is found]
balata (ˈbælətə) *n.* **1.** a tropical American sapotaceous tree, *Manilkara bidentata,* yielding a latex-like sap. **2.** a rubber-like gum obtained from this sap: used as a substitute for gutta-percha. [from American Spanish, of Carib origin]
balboa (bælˈbəʊə) *n.* the standard currency unit of Panama, divided into 100 centesimos. [named after Vasco Núñez de *Balboa* (?1475–1519), Spanish explorer]
balbriggan (bælˈbrɪgən) *n.* **1.** a knitted unbleached cotton fabric. **2.** (*often pl.*) underwear made of this. [C19: from *Balbriggan,* Ireland, where it was originally made]
balcony (ˈbælkənɪ) *n., pl.* **-nies. 1.** a platform projecting from the wall of a building with a balustrade or railing along its outer edge, often with access from a door or window. **2.** a gallery in a theatre or auditorium, above the dress circle. **3.** *U.S. and Canadian.* any circle or gallery in a theatre or auditorium including the dress circle. [C17: from Italian *balcone,* probably from Old High German *balko* beam; see BALK] —ˈ**balconied** *adj.*
bald (bɔːld) *adj.* **1.** having no hair or fur, esp. (of a man) having no hair on all or most of the scalp. **2.** lacking natural growth or covering. **3.** plain or blunt: *a bald statement.* **4.** bare or simple; unadorned. **5.** Also: **baldfaced.** (of certain birds and other animals) having white markings on the head and face. **6.** (of a tyre) having a worn tread. [C14 *ballede* (literally: having a white spot); related to Danish *bældet,* Greek *phalaros* having a white spot] —ˈ**baldish** *adj.* —ˈ**baldly** *adv.* —ˈ**baldness** *n.*
baldachin, baldaquin (ˈbɔːldəkɪn), *or* **baldachino** (ˌbɔːldəˈkiːnəʊ) *n.* **1.** a richly ornamented silk and gold brocade. **2.** a canopy of fabric or stone over an altar, shrine, or throne in a Christian church or carried in Christian religious processions over an object of veneration. [Old English *baldekin,* from Italian *baldacchino,* literally: stuff from Baghdad, from *Baldacco* Baghdad, noted for its brocades]
bald cypress *n.* another name for **swamp cypress.**
bald eagle *n.* a large eagle, *Haliaeetus leucocephalus,* of North America, having a white head and tail, a yellow bill, and dark wings and body. It is the U.S. national bird (see also **American eagle**).
balderdash (ˈbɔːldəˌdæʃ) *n.* stupid or illogical talk; senseless rubbish. [C16: of unknown origin]
baldhead (ˈbɔːldˌhɛd) *n.* a person with a bald head.
baldheaded (ˌbɔːldˈhɛdɪd) *adj.* **1.** having a bald head. **2. go baldheaded.** (usually foll. by *into, for,* or *at*) *Informal.* to act impetuously without regard to the consequences.
balding (ˈbɔːldɪŋ) *adj.* somewhat bald or becoming bald.
baldmoney (ˈbɔːldˌmʌnɪ) *n.* another name for **spignel.**
baldpate (ˈbɔːldˌpeɪt) *n.* **1.** a person with a bald head. **2.** another name for the **American wigeon** (see **wigeon** (sense 2)).
baldric (ˈbɔːldrɪk) *n.* a wide silk sash or leather belt worn over the right shoulder to the left hip for carrying a sword, etc. [C13: from Old French *baudrei,* of Frankish origin]
bale[1] (beɪl) *n.* **1.** a large bundle, esp. of a raw or partially processed material, bound by ropes, wires, etc., for storage or transportation: *bale of hay.* **2.** a large package or carton of goods. **3.** *U.S.* 500 pounds of cotton. **4.** a group of turtles. **5.** *Austral. and N.Z.* See **wool bale.** ~*vb.* **6.** to make (hay, etc.) into a bale or bales. **7.** to put (goods) into packages or cartons. **8.** *Austral. and N.Z.* to pack and compress (wool) into wool bales. ~See also **bale out.** [C14: probably from Old French *bale,* from Old High German *balla* BALL[1]]
bale[2] (beɪl) *n. Archaic.* **1.** evil; injury. **2.** woe; suffering; pain. [Old English *bealu;* related to Old Norse *böl* evil, Gothic *balwa,* Old High German *balo*]
bale[3] (beɪl) *vb.* a variant spelling of **bail**[2].
bale[4] (beɪl) *n.* a variant spelling of **bail**[4].
baleen (bəˈliːn) *n.* whalebone. [C14: from Latin *bālaena* whale; related to Greek *phalaina* whale]
baleen whale *n.* another name for **whalebone whale.**
balefire (ˈbeɪlˌfaɪə) *n. Archaic.* **1.** a bonfire. **2.** a beacon fire. **3.** a funeral pyre. [C14 *bale,* from Old English *bǣl* pyre; related to Old Norse *bāl* flame, pyre, Sanskrit *bhāla* brightness]
baleful (ˈbeɪlfʊl) *adj.* **1.** harmful, menacing, or vindictive. **2.** *Archaic.* dejected. —ˈ**balefully** *adv.* —ˈ**balefulness** *n.*
bale out *or* **bail out** *vb.* (*adv.*) **1.** (*intr.*) to make an emergency parachute jump from an aircraft. **2.** (*tr.*) *Informal.* to help (a person, organization, etc.) out of a predicament: *the government baled the company out.* **3.** (*intr.*) *Informal.* to escape from a predicament.
baler (ˈbeɪlə) *n.* an agricultural machine for making bales of hay, etc. Also called: **baling machine.**
balibuntal (ˌbælɪˈbʌntᵊl) *n.* **1.** closely woven fine straw, used for making hats in the Philippines. **2.** a hat of this straw. [C20: changed from *Baliuag buntal,* from *Baliuag* in the Philippines, where such hats were made]
Balinese (ˌbɑːlɪˈniːz) *adj.* **1.** of or relating to the Indonesian island of Bali, its people, or their language. ~*n.* **2.** (*pl.* **-nese**) a native or inhabitant of Bali. **3.** the language of the people of Bali, belonging to the Malayo-Polynesian family.
balk *or* **baulk** (bɔːk, bɔːlk) *vb.* **1.** (*intr.;* usually foll. by *at*) to stop short, esp. suddenly or unexpectedly; jib: *the horse balked at the jump.* **2.** (*intr.;* foll. by *at*) to turn away abruptly; recoil: *he balked at the idea of murder.* **3.** (*tr.*) to thwart, check, disappoint, or foil: *he was balked in his plans.* **4.** (*tr.*) to avoid deliberately: *he balked the question.* **5.** (*tr.*) to miss unintentionally. ~*n.* **6.** a roughly squared heavy timber beam. **7.** a timber tie beam of a roof. **8.** an unploughed ridge to prevent soil erosion or mark a division on common land. **9.** an obstacle; hindrance; disappointment. **10.** *Baseball.* an illegal motion by a pitcher towards the plate or towards the base when there are runners on base, esp. without delivering the ball. ~See also **baulk.** [Old English *balca;* related to Old Norse *bálkr* partition, Old High German *balco* beam] —ˈ**balker** *or* ˈ**baulker** *n.*
Balkan (ˈbɔːlkən) *adj.* of, denoting, or relating to a large peninsula in SE Europe between the Adriatic and Aegean Seas, or to its inhabitants, countries, etc.
Balkanize *or* **Balkanise** (ˈbɔːlkəˌnaɪz) *vb.* (*tr.*) to divide (a territory) into small warring states. —ˌ**Balkaniˈzation** *or* ˌ**Balkaniˈsation** *n.*
balky *or* **baulky** (ˈbɔːkɪ, ˈbɔːlkɪ) *adj.* **balkier, balkiest** *or* **baulkier, baulkiest.** inclined to stop abruptly and unexpectedly: *a balky horse.* —ˈ**balkily** *or* ˈ**baulkily** *adv.* —ˈ**balkiness** *or* ˈ**baulkiness** *n.*
ball[1] (bɔːl) *n.* **1.** a spherical or nearly spherical body or mass: *a ball of wool.* **2.** a round or roundish body, either solid or hollow, of a size and composition suitable for any of various games, such as football, golf, billiards, etc. **3.** a ball propelled in a particular way in a sport: *a high ball.* **4.** any of various rudimentary games with a ball: *to play ball.* **5.** *Cricket.* a single delivery of the ball by the bowler to the batsman. **6.** *Baseball.* a single delivery of the ball by a pitcher outside certain limits and not swung at by the batter. **7. a.** a solid nonexplosive projectile for a firearm. Compare **shell** (sense 6). **b.** such projectiles collectively. **8.** any more or less rounded part or protuberance: *the ball of the foot.* **9.** *Taboo slang.* a testicle. See **balls. 10.** *Vet. science.* another word for **bolus. 11.** *Horticulture.* the hard mass of roots and earth removed with the rest of the plant during transplanting. **12. ball of muscle.** *Austral.* a very strong, fit, or forceful person. **13. have the ball at one's feet.** to have the chance of doing something. **14. keep the ball rolling.** to maintain the progress of a project, plan, etc. **15. on the ball.** *Informal.* alert; informed. **16. play ball.** *Informal.* to cooperate. **17. start** *or* **set the ball rolling.** to open or initiate (an action, discussion, movement, etc.). **18. the ball is in your court.** you are obliged to make the next move. ~*vb.* **19.** (*tr.*) to make, form, wind, etc., into a ball or balls: *to ball wool.* **20.** (*intr.*) to gather into a ball or balls. [C13: from Old Norse *böllr;* related to Old High German *balla,* Italian *palla,* French *balle*]
ball[2] (bɔːl) *n.* **1.** a social function for dancing, esp. one that is lavish or formal. **2.** *Informal.* a very enjoyable time (esp. in the phrase **have a ball**). ~*vb.* **3.** *Taboo slang, chiefly U.S.* to copulate (with). [C17: from French *bal* (n.), from Old French *baller* (vb.), from Late Latin *ballāre* to dance, from Greek *ballizein*]
ballad (ˈbæləd) *n.* **1.** a narrative song with a recurrent refrain. **2.** a narrative poem in short stanzas of popular origin, originally sung to a repeated tune. **3.** a slow sentimental song, esp. a pop song. [C15: from Old French *balade,* from Old Provençal *balada* song accompanying a dance, from *balar* to dance, from Late Latin *ballāre;* see BALL[2]]
ballade (bæˈlɑːd; *French* balad) *n.* **1.** *Prosody.* a verse form consisting of three stanzas and an envoy, all ending with the same line. The first three stanzas commonly have eight or ten lines each and the same rhyme scheme. **2.** *Music.* an instrumental composition, esp. for piano, based on or intended to evoke a narrative.
balladeer (ˌbæləˈdɪə) *n.* a singer of ballads.
ballad metre *n.* the metre of a ballad stanza.
balladmonger (ˈbælədˌmʌŋgə) *n.* **1.** (formerly) a seller of ballads, esp. on broadsheets. **2.** *Derogatory.* a writer of mediocre poetry.
ballad opera *n.* an opera consisting of popular tunes to which appropriate words have been set, interspersed with spoken dialogue.
balladry (ˈbælədrɪ) *n.* **1.** ballad poetry or songs. **2.** the art of writing, composing, or performing ballads.
ballad stanza *n.* a four-line stanza, often used in ballads, in which the second and fourth lines rhyme and have three stresses each and the first and third lines are unrhymed and have four stresses each.
ball and chain *n.* **1.** (formerly) a heavy iron ball attached to a chain and fastened to a prisoner. **2.** a heavy restraint. **3.** *Slang.* one's wife.
ball-and-socket joint *n.* **1.** a coupling between two rods, tubes, etc., that consists of a spherical part fitting into a spherical socket, allowing free movement and rotation. **2.** Also called: **multiaxial joint.** *Anatomy.* a bony joint, such as the hip joint, in which a rounded head fits into a rounded cavity, allowing a wide range of movement.
ballast (ˈbæləst) *n.* **1.** any dense heavy material, such as lead or iron pigs, used to stabilize a vessel, esp. one that is not carrying

cargo. **2.** crushed rock, broken stone, etc., used for the foundation of a road or railway track. **3.** coarse aggregate of sandy gravel, used in making concrete. **4.** anything that provides stability or weight. **5.** *Electronics.* a device for maintaining the current in a circuit. ~*vb.* (*tr.*) **6.** to give stability or weight to. [C16: probably from Low German; related to Old Danish, Old Swedish *barlast,* literally: bare load (without commercial value), from *bar* bare, mere + *last* load, burden]

ball bearing *n.* **1.** a bearing consisting of a number of hard steel balls rolling between a metal sleeve fitted over the rotating shaft and an outer sleeve held in the bearing housing, so reducing friction between moving parts. **2.** a metal ball, esp. one used in such a bearing.

ball boy *n.* (esp. in tennis) a person who retrieves balls that go out of play.

ballbreaker ('bɔːlˌbreɪkə) *n. Slang.* a woman whose character and behaviour may be regarded as threatening a man's sense of power. [C20: from BALL[1] (in the sense: testicle) + BREAKER[1]]

ball cock *n.* a device for regulating the flow of a liquid into a tank, cistern, etc., consisting of a floating ball mounted at one end of an arm and a valve on the other end that opens and closes as the ball falls and rises.

ballerina (ˌbæləˈriːnə) *n.* **1.** a female ballet dancer. **2.** *U.S.* the principal female dancer of a ballet company. [C18: from Italian, feminine of *ballerino* dancing master, from *ballare* to dance, from Late Latin *ballāre;* see BALL[2]]

ballet ('bæleɪ, bæ'leɪ) *n.* **1. a.** a classical style of expressive dancing based on precise conventional steps with gestures and movements of grace and fluidity. **b.** (*as modifier*): *ballet dancer.* **2.** a theatrical representation of a story or theme performed to music by ballet dancers. **3.** a troupe of ballet dancers. **4.** a piece of music written for a ballet. [C17: from French, from Italian *balletto,* literally: a little dance, from *ballare* to dance; see BALL[2]] —**balletic** (bæ'lɛtɪk) *adj.*

balletomania (ˌbælɪtəʊ'meɪnɪə) *n.* passionate enthusiasm for ballet. [C20: from BALLET + -O- + -MANIA] —**balletomane** ('bælɪtəʊˌmeɪn) *n.*

ballflower ('bɔːlˌflaʊə) *n. Architect.* a carved ornament in the form of a ball enclosed by the three petals of a circular flower.

ball game *n.* **1.** any game played with a ball. **2.** *U.S. and Canadian.* a game of baseball. **3.** *Informal.* a situation; state of affairs (esp. in the phrase **a whole new ball game**).

ballista (bə'lɪstə) *n., pl.* **-tae** (-tiː). **1.** an ancient catapult for hurling stones, etc. **2.** an ancient form of large crossbow used to propel a spear. [C16: from Latin, ultimately from Greek *ballein* to throw]

ballistic (bə'lɪstɪk) *adj.* **1.** of or relating to ballistics. **2.** denoting or relating to the flight of projectiles after power has been cut off, moving under their own momentum and the force of gravity. **3.** (of a measurement or measuring instrument) depending on a brief impulse or current that causes a movement related to the quantity to be measured: *a ballistic pendulum.* —**bal'listically** *adv.*

ballistic galvanometer *n. Physics.* a type of galvanometer for measuring surges of current. After deflection the instrument returns slowly to its original reading.

ballistic missile *n.* a missile that has no wings or fins and that follows a ballistic trajectory when its propulsive power is discontinued.

ballistics (bə'lɪstɪks) *n.* (*functioning as sing.*) the study of the flight dynamics of projectiles, either through the interaction of the forces of propulsion, the aerodynamics of the projectile, atmospheric resistance, and gravity (**exterior ballistics**), or through these forces along with the means of propulsion, and the design of the propelling weapon and projectile (**interior ballistics**).

ballistospore (bə'lɪstəˌspɔː) *n. Botany.* a spore, esp. a fungal spore, that is forcefully ejected from its source.

ball lightning *n. Meteorol.* a slow-moving luminous ball occasionally seen during electrical storms.

ball mill *n. Engineering.* a horizontal cylinder or cone in which a substance, such as a mineral, is ground by rotation with steel or ceramic balls.

ballocks ('bɒləks, 'bæl-) *pl. n., interj., vb.* a variant spelling of **bollocks.**

ball of fire *n. Informal.* a very lively person.

ballon d'essai (bæ'lõ dɛ'seɪ) *n., pl.* **ballons d'essai** (bæ'lõ dɛ'seɪ). a project or policy put forward experimentally to gauge reactions to it. Compare **trial balloon.** [C19: from French, literally: trial balloon]

ballonet (ˌbælə'nɛt) *n.* an air or gas compartment in a balloon or nonrigid airship, used to control buoyancy and shape. [C20: from French *ballonnet* a little BALLOON]

balloon (bə'luːn) *n.* **1.** an inflatable rubber bag of various sizes, shapes, and colours: usually used as a plaything or party decoration. **2.** a large impermeable bag inflated with a lighter-than-air gas, designed to rise and float in the atmosphere. It may have a basket or gondola for carrying passengers, etc. See also **barrage balloon, hot-air balloon. 3.** a circular or elliptical figure containing the words or thoughts of a character in a cartoon. **4.** *Brit.* **a.** a kick or stroke that propels a ball high into the air. **b.** (*as modifier*): *a balloon shot.* **5.** *Chem.* a round-bottomed flask. **6.** a large rounded brandy glass. **7.** *Commerce.* **a.** a large sum paid as an irregular instalment of a loan repayment. **b.** (*as modifier*): *a balloon loan.* **8.** *Surgery.* **a.** an inflatable plastic tube used for dilating obstructed blood vessels or parts of the alimentary canal. **b.** (*as modifier*): *balloon angioplasty.* **9. when the balloon goes up.** *Informal.* when the action starts. ~*vb.* **10.** (*intr.*) to go up or fly in a balloon. **11.** to inflate or be inflated; distend; swell: *the wind ballooned the sails.* **12.** (*tr.*) *Brit.* to propel (a ball) high into the air. [C16 (in the sense: ball, ball game): from Italian dialect *ballone,* from *balla,* of Germanic origin; compare Old High German *balla* BALL[1]] —**bal'looning** *n.* —**bal'loonist** *n.* —**bal'loon-ˌlike** *adj.*

balloon loan *n.* a loan in respect of which interest and capital are paid off in instalments at regular intervals.

balloon sail *n. Nautical.* a large light bellying sail used in light winds. Compare **spinnaker.**

balloon sleeve *n.* a sleeve fitting tightly from wrist to elbow and becoming fully rounded from elbow to shoulder.

balloon tyre *n.* a pneumatic tyre containing air at a relatively low pressure and having a wide tread.

balloon vine *n.* a tropical tendril-climbing sapindaceous plant, *Cardiospermum halicacabum,* cultivated for its ornamental balloon-like seed capsules.

ballot ('bælət) *n.* **1.** the democratic practice of selecting a representative, a course of action, or deciding some other choice by submitting the options to a vote of all qualified persons. **2.** an instance of voting, usually in secret using ballot papers or a voting machine. **3.** the paper on which a vote is recorded. **4.** a list of candidates standing for office. **5.** the number of votes cast in an election. **6.** a random selection of successful applicants for something in which the demand exceeds the supply, esp. for shares in an oversubscribed new issue. **7.** *N.Z.* the allocation by ballot of farming land among eligible candidates, such as ex-servicemen. **8.** *N.Z.* a low-interest housing loan allocated by building societies by drawing lots among its eligible members. **9.** *Archaic.* a drawing of lots. ~*vb.* **-lots, -loting, -loted. 10.** to vote or elicit a vote from: *we balloted the members on this issue.* **11.** (*tr.;* usually foll. by *for*) to select (officials, etc.) by lot or ballot or to select (successful applicants) at random. **12.** (*tr.;* often foll. by *for*) to vote or decide (on an issue, etc.). [C16: from Italian *ballotta,* literally: a little ball, from *balla* BALL[1]]

ballot box *n.* a box into which ballot papers are dropped after voting.

ballotini (ˌbælə'tiːnɪ) *pl. n.* small glass beads used in reflective paints. [C20: from Italian *ballottini,* small balls]

ballot paper *n.* a paper used for voting in a ballot, esp. (in a parliamentary or local government election) one having the names of the candidates printed on it.

ballottement (bə'lɒtmənt) *n. Med.* a technique of feeling for a movable object in the body, esp. confirmation of pregnancy by feeling the rebound of the fetus following a quick digital tap on the wall of the uterus. [C19: from French, literally: a tossing, shaking, from *ballotter* to toss, from *ballotte* a little ball, from Italian *ballotta;* see BALLOT]

ballpark ('bɔːlˌpɑːk) *n.* **1.** *U.S. and Canadian.* a stadium used for baseball games. **2.** *Informal.* **a.** approximate range: *in the right ballpark.* **b.** (*as modifier*): *a ballpark figure.* **3.** *Informal.* a situation; state of affairs: *its a whole new ballpark for him.*

ball-peen hammer *n.* a hammer that has one end of its head shaped in a hemisphere for beating metal, etc.

ballplayer ('bɔːlˌpleɪə) *n.* **1.** a player, esp. in soccer, with outstanding ability to control the ball. **2.** *U.S. and Canadian.* a baseball player, esp. a professional.

ballpoint, ballpoint pen ('bɔːlˌpɔɪnt), *or* **ball pen** *n.* a pen having a small ball bearing as a writing point. Also called (Brit.): **Biro.**

ball race *n. Engineering.* **1.** a ball bearing. **2.** one of the metal rings having a circular track within which the balls of the bearing roll.

ballroom ('bɔːlˌruːm, -ˌrʊm) *n.* a large hall for dancing.

ballroom dancing *n.* social dancing, popular since the beginning of the 20th century, to dances in conventional rhythms (**ballroom dances**) such as the foxtrot and the quickstep.

balls (bɔːlz) *Slang.* ~*pl. n.* **1.** *Taboo.* the testicles. **2. by the balls.** *Taboo.* so as to be rendered powerless. **3.** *Taboo.* nonsense; rubbish. **4.** *Taboo.* courage; forcefulness. ~*interj.* **5.** *Taboo.* an exclamation of strong disagreement, contempt, annoyance, etc.

balls-up *or U.S.* **ballup** ('bɔːlʌp) *Taboo slang.* ~*n.* **1.** something botched or muddled. ~*vb.* **balls up** *or U.S.* **ball up. 2.** (*tr., adv.*) to muddle or botch.

ball tearer *n. Austral. slang.* something exceptional in its class, for good or bad qualities.

ball valve *n.* a one-way valve consisting of a metal ball fitting into a concave seat over an opening.

bally ('bælɪ) *adj., adv.* (intensifier) *Brit. slang.* a euphemistic word for **bloody** (sense 6).

ballyhoo (ˌbælɪ'huː) *n. Informal.* **1.** a noisy, confused, or nonsensical situation or uproar. **2.** sensational or blatant advertising or publicity. ~*vb.* **-hoos, -hooing, -hooed. 3.** (*tr.*) *Chiefly U.S.* to advertise or publicize by sensational or blatant methods. [C19: of uncertain origin]

ballyrag ('bælɪˌræg) *vb.* **-rags, -ragging, -ragged.** a variant of **bullyrag.**

balm (bɑːm) *n.* **1.** any of various oily aromatic resinous substances obtained from certain tropical trees and used for healing and soothing. See also **balsam** (sense 1). **2.** any plant yielding such a substance, esp. the balm of Gilead. **3.** something comforting or soothing: *soft music is a balm.* **4.** any aromatic or oily substance used for healing or soothing. **5.** Also called: **lemon balm.** an aromatic Eurasian herbaceous plant, *Melissa officinalis,* having clusters of small fragrant white two-lipped flowers: family *Labiatae* (labiates). **6.** a pleasant odour. [C13: from Old French *basme,* from Latin *balsamum* BALSAM] —ˈ**balmˌlike** *adj.*

balmacaan (ˌbælməˈkɑːn) *n.* a man's knee-length loose flaring overcoat with raglan sleeves. [C19: after *Balmacaan,* near Inverness, Scotland]

balm of Gilead (ˈgɪlɪæd) *n.* **1.** any of several trees of the burseraceous genus *Commiphora,* esp. *C. opobalsamum* of Africa and W Asia, that yield a fragrant oily resin (see **balm** (sense 1)). Compare **myrrh** (sense 1). **2.** the resin exuded by these trees. **3.** a North American hybrid female poplar tree, *Populus gileadensis* (or *P. candicans*), with broad heart-shaped leaves. **4.** a fragrant resin obtained from the balsam fir. See also **Canada balsam.** [from *Gilead,* historic region E of the River Jordan]

Balmoral (bælˈmɒrəl) *n.* (*sometimes not cap.*) **1.** a laced walking shoe. **2.** a 19th-century woollen petticoat, worn showing below the skirt. **3.** Also called: **bluebonnet.** a Scottish brimless hat traditionally of dark blue wool with a cockade and plume on one side. [C19: named after *Balmoral* Castle in NE Scotland]

balmy (ˈbɑːmɪ) *adj.* **balmier, balmiest. 1.** (of weather) mild and pleasant. **2.** having the qualities of balm; fragrant or soothing. **3.** a variant spelling of **barmy.** —ˈ**balmily** *adv.* —ˈ**balminess** *n.*

balneal (ˈbælnɪəl) *or* **balneary** (ˈbælnɪərɪ) *adj. Rare.* of or relating to baths or bathing. [C17: from Latin *balneum* bath, from Greek *balaneion*]

balneology (ˌbælnɪˈɒlədʒɪ) *n.* the branch of medical science concerned with the therapeutic value of baths, esp. those taken with natural mineral waters. [C19: from Latin *balneum* bath] —**balneological** (ˌbælnɪəˈlɒdʒɪkᵊl) *adj.* —ˌ**balneˈologist** *n.*

balneotherapy (ˌbælnɪəˈθɛrəpɪ) *n.* the treatment of disease by bathing, esp. to improve limb mobility in arthritic and neuromuscular disorders.

baloney *or* **boloney** (bəˈləʊnɪ) *n.* **1.** *Informal.* foolish talk; nonsense. **2.** *Chiefly U.S.* another name for **bologna sausage.** [C20: changed from *Bologna* (sausage)]

BALPA (ˈbælpə) *n. acronym for* British Airline Pilots' Association.

balsa (ˈbɔːlsə) *n.* **1.** a bombacaceous tree, *Ochroma lagopus,* of tropical America. **2.** Also called: **balsawood.** the very light wood of this tree, used for making rafts, etc. **3.** a light raft. [C18: from Spanish: raft]

balsam (ˈbɔːlsəm) *n.* **1.** any of various fragrant oleoresins, such as balm or tolu, obtained from any of several trees and shrubs and used as a base for medicines and perfumes. **2.** any of various similar substances used as medicinal or ceremonial ointments. **3.** any of certain aromatic resinous turpentines. See also **Canada balsam. 4.** any plant yielding balsam. **5.** Also called: **busy Lizzie.** any of several balsaminaceous plants of the genus *Impatiens,* esp. *I. balsamina,* cultivated for its brightly coloured flowers. **6.** anything healing or soothing. [C15: from Latin *balsamum,* from Greek *balsamon,* from Hebrew *bāśām* spice] —**balsamic** (bɔːlˈsæmɪk) *adj.* —ˈ**balsamy** *adj.*

balsam apple *n.* an ornamental cucurbitaceous vine, *Momordica balsamina,* of the Old World tropics, with yellow flowers and orange egg-shaped fruits.

balsam fir *n.* a fir tree, *Abies balsamea,* of NE North America, that yields Canada balsam. Also called: **balsam, Canada balsam.** See also **balm of Gilead.**

balsamiferous (ˌbɔːlsəˈmɪfərəs) *adj.* yielding or producing balsam.

balsaminaceous (ˌbɔːlsəmɪˈneɪʃəs) *adj.* of, relating to, or belonging to the *Balsaminaceae,* a family of flowering plants, including balsam and touch-me-not, that have irregular flowers and explosive capsules.

balsam of Peru (pəˈruː) *n.* an aromatic balsam that is obtained from the tropical South American leguminous tree *Myroxylon pereirae* and is similar to balsam of Tolu. Also called: **Peru balsam.**

balsam of Tolu *n.* the full name of **tolu.**

balsam poplar *n.* a poplar tree, *Populus balsamifera,* of NE North America, having resinous buds and broad heart-shaped leaves. See also **tacamahac.**

balsam spruce *n.* either of two North American coniferous trees of the genus *Picea, P. pungens* (the blue spruce) or *P. engelmanni.*

Balt (bɔːlt) *n.* **1.** a member of any of the Baltic-speaking peoples of the Baltic States. **2.** *Austral. slang, derogatory.* an immigrant to Australia from the Baltic countries.

Balt. *abbrev. for* Baltic.

Balthazar (ˈbælθəˌzɑː, bælˈθæzə) *n.* a wine bottle holding the equivalent of sixteen normal bottles (approximately 12 litres). [C20: named after *Balthazar* (Belshazzar) from his drinking wine at a great feast (Daniel 5:1)]

Baltic (ˈbɔːltɪk) *adj.* **1.** denoting or relating to the Baltic Sea in N Europe or the Baltic States bordering on it. **2.** of, denoting, or characteristic of Baltic as a group of languages. ~*n.* **3.** a branch of the Indo-European family of languages consisting of Lithuanian, Latvian, and Old Prussian. **4.** Also called: **Baltic Exchange.** a commodity and freight-chartering market in the City of London.

Baltimore oriole (ˈbɔːltɪˌmɔː) *n.* a North American oriole, *Icterus galbula,* the male of which has orange and black plumage. [named after *Baltimore,* port in Maryland]

Balto-Slavonic *or* **Balto-Slavic** *n.* a hypothetical subfamily of Indo-European languages consisting of Baltic and Slavonic. It is now generally believed that similarities between them result from geographical proximity rather than any special relationship.

Baluchi (bəˈluːtʃɪ) *or* **Balochi** (bəˈləʊtʃɪ) *n.* **1.** (*pl.* **-chis** *or* **-chi**) a member of a Muslim people living chiefly in coastal Pakistan and Iran. **2.** the language of this people, belonging to the West Iranian branch of the Indo-European family. ~*adj.* **3.** of or relating to Baluchistan, a region of SW Asia, SW Pakistan, and SE Iran, or to its inhabitants or their language.

balun (ˈbælən) *n. Electronics.* a device for coupling two electrical circuit elements, such as an aerial and its feeder cable, where one is balanced and the other is unbalanced. [C20: shortened from *bal*(*ance to*) *un*(*balance transformer*)]

baluster (ˈbæləstə) *n.* **1.** any of a set of posts supporting a rail or coping. ~*adj.* **2.** (of a shape) swelling at the base and rising in a concave curve to a narrow stem or neck: *a baluster stem on a goblet.* [C17: from French *balustre,* from Italian *balaustro* pillar resembling a pomegranate flower, ultimately from Greek *balaustion*]

balustrade (ˈbæləˌstreɪd) *n.* an ornamental rail or coping with its supporting set of balusters. [C17: from French, from *balustre* BALUSTER]

Bambara (bɑːmˈbɑːrə) *n.* **1.** (*pl.* **-ra** *or* **-ras**) a member of a Negroid people of W Africa living chiefly in Mali and by the headwaters of the River Niger in Guinea. **2.** the language of this people, belonging to the Mande branch of the Niger-Congo family.

bambino (bæmˈbiːnəʊ) *n., pl.* **-nos** *or* **-ni** (-niː). **1.** *Informal.* a young child, esp. an Italian one. **2.** a representation of the infant Jesus. [C18: from Italian]

bamboo (bæmˈbuː) *n.* **1.** any tall treelike tropical or semitropical fast-growing grass of the genus *Bambusa,* having hollow woody-walled stems with ringed joints and edible young shoots (**bamboo shoots**). **2.** the stem of any of these plants, used for building, poles, and furniture. **3.** any of various bamboo-like grasses of the genera *Arundinaria, Phyllostachys,* or *Dendrocalamus.* **4.** (*modifier*) made of bamboo: *a bamboo pipe; a bamboo fence.* [C16: probably from Malay *bambu*]

bamboo curtain *n.* (esp. in the 1950s and 1960s) the political and military barrier to communications around the People's Republic of China.

bamboozle (bæmˈbuːzᵊl) *vb.* (*tr.*) *Informal.* **1.** to cheat; mislead. **2.** to confuse. [C18: of unknown origin] —**bamˈboozler** *n.* —**bamˈboozlement** *n.*

ban[1] (bæn) *vb.* **bans, banning, banned. 1.** (*tr.*) to prohibit, esp. officially, from action, display, entrance, sale, etc.; forbid: *to ban a book; to ban smoking.* **2.** (*tr.*) (in South Africa) to place (a person suspected of illegal political activity) under a government order restricting his movement and his contact with other people. **3.** *Archaic.* to curse. ~*n.* **4.** an official prohibition or interdiction. **5.** *Law.* an official proclamation or public notice, esp. of prohibition. **6.** a public proclamation or edict, esp. of outlawry. **7.** *Archaic.* public censure or condemnation. **8.** *Archaic.* a curse; imprecation. [Old English *bannan* to proclaim; compare Old Norse *banna* to forbid, Old High German *bannan* to command]

ban[2] (bæn) *n.* (in feudal England) the summoning of vassals to perform their military obligations. [C13: from Old French *ban,* of Germanic origin; related to Old High German *ban* command, Old Norse *bann* BAN[1]]

ban[3] (bæn) *n., pl.* **bani** (ˈbɑːnɪ). a Romanian monetary unit worth one hundredth of a leu. [from Romanian, from Serbo-Croatian *bān* lord]

banak (ˈbænək) *n.* **1.** a tree of the genus *Virola,* of Central America: family *Myristicaceae.* **2.** the timber of this tree, used esp. in Honduras for turning and general construction. [C20: Honduran name]

banal (bəˈnɑːl) *adj.* lacking force or originality; trite; commonplace. [C18: from Old French: relating to compulsory feudal service, hence common to all, commonplace, from *ban* BAN[2]] —**banality** (bəˈnælɪtɪ) *n.* —**baˈnally** *adv.*

banana (bəˈnɑːnə) *n.* **1.** any of several tropical and subtropical herbaceous treelike plants of the musaceous genus *Musa,* esp. *M. sapientum,* a widely cultivated species propagated from suckers and having hanging clusters of edible fruit. **2.** the crescent-shaped fruit of any of these plants. ~Compare **plantain**[2]. [C16: from Spanish or Portuguese, of African origin]

banana belt *n. Canadian informal.* a region with a warm climate, esp. one in Canada.

Banana bender *n. Austral. informal, offensive.* a native or inhabitant of Queensland. Also called: **Bananalander** (bəˈnɑːnəˌlændə).

banana oil *n.* **1.** a solution of cellulose nitrate in pentyl acetate or a similar solvent, which has a banana-like smell. **2.** a nontechnical name for **pentyl acetate.**

banana plug *n. Electrical engineering.* a small single-conductor electrical plug having a curved metal spring along its shank used to hold it in its socket.

banana republic *n. Informal and derogatory.* a small country, esp. in Central America, that is politically unstable and has an economy dominated by foreign interest, usually dependent on one export, such as bananas.

bananas (bəˈnɑːnəz) *adj. Slang.* crazy.

banana skin *n.* **1.** the soft outer covering of a banana. **2.** *Informal.* something unforeseen that causes an obvious and embarrassing mistake. [sense 2 from the common slapstick joke of a person slipping after treading on a banana skin]

banana split *n.* a dish of ice cream and banana cut in half lengthwise, usually topped with syrup, nuts, whipped cream, etc.

banausic (bəˈnɔːsɪk) *adj.* merely mechanical; materialistic; utilitarian. [C19: from Greek *banausikos* for mechanics, from *baunos* forge]

Banbury cake (ˈbænbərɪ) *n. Brit.* a cake consisting of a pastry base filled with currants, raisins, candied peel, and sugar, with a criss-cross pattern on the top. [named after *Banbury*, a town in central England]

banc (bæŋk) *n.* **in banc.** *Law.* sitting as a full court. [C18: from Anglo-French: bench]

banco (ˈbæŋkəʊ) *interj.* a call in gambling games such as chemin de fer and baccarat by a player or bystander who wishes to bet against the entire bank. [C18: from French from Italian: bank]

band[1] (bænd) *n.* **1.** a company of people having a common purpose; group: *a band of outlaws.* **2.** a group of musicians playing either brass and percussion instruments only (**brass band**) or brass, woodwind, and percussion instruments (**concert band** or **military band**). **3.** a group of musicians who play popular music, jazz, etc., often for dancing. **4.** a group of instrumentalists generally; orchestra. **5.** *Canadian.* a formally recognized group of Indians on a reservation. **6.** *Anthropol.* a division of a tribe; a family group or camp group. **7.** *U.S. and Canadian.* a flock or herd. *~vb.* **8.** (usually foll. by *together*) to unite; assemble. [C15: from French *bande,* probably from Old Provençal *banda,* of Germanic origin; compare Gothic *bandwa* sign, BANNER]

band[2] (bænd) *n.* **1.** a thin flat strip of some material, used esp. to encircle objects and hold them together: *a rubber band.* **2. a.** a strip of fabric or other material used as an ornament, distinguishing mark, or to reinforce clothing. **b.** (*in combination*): *waistband; hairband; hatband.* **3.** a stripe of contrasting colour or texture. See also **chromosome band.** **4.** a driving belt in machinery. **5.** a range of values that are close or related in number, degree, or quality. **6. a.** *Physics.* a range of frequencies or wavelengths between two limits. **b.** *Radio.* such a range allocated to a particular broadcasting station or service. **7.** short for **energy band.** **8.** *Computer technol.* one or more tracks on a magnetic disk or drum. **9.** *Anatomy.* any structure resembling a ribbon or cord that connects, encircles, or binds different parts. **10.** the cords to which the folded sheets of a book are sewn. **11.** a thin layer or seam of ore. **12.** *Architect.* a strip of flat panelling, such as a fascia or plinth, usually attached to a wall. **13.** a large white collar, sometimes edged with lace, worn in the 17th century. **14.** either of a pair of hanging extensions of the collar, forming part of academic, legal, or (formerly) clerical dress. **15.** (of a gramophone record) another word for **track** (sense 11). **16.** a ring for the finger (esp. in phrases such as **wedding band, band of gold,** etc.). *~vb.* (*tr.*) **17.** to fasten or mark with a band. **18.** *U.S. and Canadian.* to ring (birds). See **ring**[1] (sense 22). [C15: from Old French *bende,* of Germanic origin; compare Old High German *binda* fillet; see BAND[3]]

band[3] (bænd) *n.* an archaic word for **bond** (senses 1, 3, 4). [C13: from Old Norse *band;* related to Old High German *bant* fetter; see BEND[1], BOND]

bandage (ˈbændɪdʒ) *n.* **1.** a piece of material used to dress a wound, bind a broken limb, etc. **2.** a strip of any soft material used for binding, etc. *~vb.* **3.** to cover or bind with a bandage. [C16: from French, from *bande* strip, BAND[2]]

bandanna *or* **bandana** (bænˈdænə) *n.* a large silk or cotton handkerchief or neckerchief. [C18: from Hindi *bāndhnū* tie-dyeing, from *bāndhnā* to tie, from Sanskrit *bandhnāti* he ties]

b. and b. *or* **B & B** *abbrev. for* bed and breakfast.

bandbox (ˈbændˌbɒks) *n.* a lightweight usually cylindrical box used for holding small articles, esp. hats.

bandeau (ˈbændəʊ) *n., pl.* **-deaux** (-dəʊz). a narrow band of ribbon, velvet, etc., worn round the head. [C18: from French, from Old French *bandel* a little BAND[2]]

banderilla (ˌbændəˈriːə, -ˈriːljə) *n. Bullfighting.* a decorated barbed dart, thrust into the bull's neck or shoulder. [Spanish, literally: a little banner, from *bandera* BANNER]

banderillero (ˌbændəriːˈɛərəʊ, -riːˈljɛərəʊ) *n., pl.* **-ros.** a bullfighter's assistant who sticks banderillas into the bull.

banderole, banderol (ˈbændəˌrəʊl), *or* **bannerol** *n.* **1.** a long narrow flag, usually with forked ends, esp. one attached to the masthead of a ship; pennant. **2.** a square flag draped over a tomb or carried at a funeral. **3.** a ribbon-like scroll or sculptured band bearing an inscription, found esp. in Renaissance architecture. **4.** a streamer on a knight's lance. [C16: from Old French, from Italian *banderuola,* literally: a little banner, from *bandiera* BANNER]

band-gala (ˈbʌndgəlɑː) *adj.* (in India) (of a coat) closed at the neck. [from Hindi]

bandh *or* **bundh** (bʌnd) *n.* (in India) a general strike. [Hindi, literally: a tying up]

bandicoot (ˈbændɪˌkuːt) *n.* **1.** any agile terrestrial marsupial of the family *Peramelidae* of Australia and New Guinea. They have a long pointed muzzle and a long tail and feed mainly on small invertebrates. **2. bandicoot rat.** Also called: **mole rat.** any of three burrowing rats of the genera *Bandicota* and *Nesokia,* of S and SE Asia: family *Muridae. ~vb.* **3.** *Austral.* to dig up (potatoes), leaving the plant intact above the ground. [C18: from Telugu *pandikokku,* from *pandi* pig + *kokku* bandicoot]

banding (ˈbændɪŋ) *n. Brit.* the practice of grouping schoolchildren according to ability to ensure a balanced intake at different levels of ability to secondary school.

bandit (ˈbændɪt) *n., pl.* **-dits** *or* **-ditti** (-ˈdɪtɪ). a robber, esp. a member of an armed gang; brigand. [C16: from Italian *bandito,* literally: banished man, from *bandire* to proscribe, from *bando* edict, BAN[1]] —ˈ**banditry** *n.*

bandmaster (ˈbændˌmɑːstə) *n.* the conductor of a band.

bandobust *or* **bundobust** (ˈbʌndəʊbəst) *n.* (in India and Pakistan) arrangements. [Hindi *band-o-bast* tying and binding, from Persian]

Band of Hope *n.* a society promoting lifelong abstention from alcohol among young people: founded in Britain in 1847.

bandoleer *or* **bandolier** (ˌbændəˈlɪə) *n.* a soldier's broad shoulder belt having small pockets or loops for cartridges. [C16: from Old French *bandouliere,* from Old Spanish *bandolera, bandolero* guerrilla, from Catalan *bandoler,* from *bandol* band, from Spanish *bando;* see BAND[1]]

bandoline (ˈbændəˌliːn) *n.* a glutinous hair dressing, used (esp. formerly) to keep the hair in place. [C19: *bando-,* from French BANDEAU + *-line,* from Latin *linere* to smear]

bandore (bænˈdɔː, ˈbændɔː) *n.* a 16th-century plucked musical instrument resembling a lute but larger and fitted with seven pairs of metal strings. Also called: **pandore, pandora.** [C16: from Spanish *bandurria,* from Late Latin *pandūra* three-stringed instrument, from Greek *pandoura*]

band-pass filter *n.* **1.** *Electronics.* a filter that transmits only those currents having a frequency lying within specified limits. Compare **high-pass filter, low-pass filter.** **2.** an optical device, consisting of absorbing filters, for transmitting electromagnetic waves of predetermined wavelengths.

band saw *n.* a power-operated saw consisting of an endless toothed metal band running over and driven by two wheels.

bandsman (ˈbændzmən) *n., pl.* **-men.** a player in a musical band, esp. a brass or military band.

band spectrum *n.* a spectrum consisting of a number of bands of closely spaced lines that are associated with emission or absorption of radiation by molecules.

bandspreading (ˈbændˌsprɛdɪŋ) *n.* an additional tuning control in some radio receivers whereby a selected narrow band of frequencies can be spread over a wider frequency band, in order to give finer control of tuning.

bandstand (ˈbændˌstænd) *n.* a platform for a band, usually out of doors and roofed.

band theory *n. Physics.* a theory of the electrical properties of metals, semiconductors, and insulators based on energy bands.

bandwagon (ˈbændˌwægən) *n.* **1.** *U.S.* a wagon, usually high and brightly coloured, for carrying the band in a parade. **2. climb, jump,** *or* **get on the bandwagon.** to join or give support to a party or movement that seems to be assured of success.

bandwidth (ˈbændˌwɪdθ) *n.* **1.** the range of frequencies within a given waveband used for a particular radio transmission. **2.** the range of frequencies over which a receiver or amplifier should not differ appreciably from its maximum value. **3.** the range of frequencies used in a specific telecommunications signal.

bandy (ˈbændɪ) *adj.* **-dier, -diest.** **1.** Also: **bandy-legged.** having legs curved outwards at the knees. **2.** (of legs) curved outwards at the knees. **3. knock (someone) bandy.** *Austral. informal.* to amaze or astound. *~vb.* **-dies, -dying, -died.** (*tr.*) **4.** to exchange (words) in a heated or hostile manner. **5.** to give and receive (blows). **6.** (often foll. by *about*) to circulate (a name, rumour, etc.). **7.** to throw or strike to and fro; toss about. *~n., pl.* **-dies.** **8.** an early form of hockey, often played on ice. **9.** a stick, curved at one end, used in the game of bandy. **10.** an old form of tennis. [C16: probably from Old French *bander* to hit the ball back and forth at tennis]

bandy-bandy (ˈbændɪˈbændɪ) *n., pl.* **-bandies.** a small Australian elapid snake, *Vermicella annulata,* ringed with black and yellow.

bandy legs *pl. n.* another term for **bow legs.**

bane[1] (beɪn) *n.* **1.** a person or thing that causes misery or distress (esp. in the phrase **bane of one's life**). **2.** something that causes death or destruction. **3. a.** a fatal poison. **b.** (*in combination*): *ratsbane.* **4.** *Archaic.* ruin or distress. [Old English *bana;* related to Old Norse *bani* death, Old High German *bano* destruction, death]

bane[2] (ben, beɪn) *n.* a Scot. word for **bone.**

baneberry ('beɪnbərɪ) *n., pl.* **-ries.** **1.** Also called: **herb Christopher** (Brit.), **cohosh** (U.S.). any ranunculaceous plant of the genus *Actaea*, esp. *A. spicata*, which has small white flowers and red or white poisonous berries. **2.** a berry of any of these plants.

baneful ('beɪnfʊl) *adj. Archaic.* destructive, poisonous, or fatal. —'**banefully** *adv.* —'**banefulness** *n.*

bang[1] (bæŋ) *n.* **1.** a short loud explosive noise, as of the bursting of a balloon or the report of a gun. **2.** a hard blow or knock, esp. a noisy one; thump: *he gave the ball a bang.* **3.** *Informal.* a startling or sudden effect: *he realized with a bang that he was late.* **4.** *U.S. and Canadian slang.* thrill; excitement. **5.** *Slang.* an injection of heroin or other narcotic. **6.** *Taboo slang.* an act of sexual intercourse. **7.** **with a bang.** successfully: *the party went with a bang.* ~*vb.* **8.** to hit or knock, esp. with a loud noise; bump: *to bang one's head.* **9.** to move noisily or clumsily: *to bang about the house.* **10.** to close (a door, window, etc.) or (of a door, etc.) be closed noisily; slam. **11.** (*tr.*) to cause to move by hitting vigorously: *he banged the ball over the fence.* **12.** to make or cause to make a loud noise, as of an explosion. **13.** (*tr.*) *Brit.* **a.** to cause (stock prices) to fall by rapid selling. **b.** to sell rapidly in (a stock market), thus causing prices to fall. **14.** *Taboo slang.* to have sexual intercourse with. **15.** (*intr.*) *Slang.* to inject heroin, etc. **16.** **bang one's head against a brick wall.** to try to achieve something impossible. ~*adv.* **17.** with a sudden impact or effect: *bang went his hopes of winning; the car drove bang into a lamp-post.* **18.** precisely: *bang in the middle of the road.* **19.** **bang to rights.** *Slang.* caught red-handed. **20.** **go bang.** to burst, shut, etc., with a loud noise. ~See also **bang up.** [C16: from Old Norse *bang, banga* hammer; related to Low German *bangen* to beat; all of imitative origin]

bang[2] (bæŋ) *n.* **1.** a fringe or section of hair cut straight across the forehead. ~*vb.* (*tr.*) **2.** to cut (the hair) in such a style. **3.** to dock (the tail of a horse, etc.). [C19: probably short for *bangtail* short tail]

bang[3] (bæŋ) *n.* a variant spelling of **bhang.**

bangalore torpedo (ˌbæŋgə'lɔː) *n.* an explosive device in a long metal tube, used to blow gaps in barbed-wire barriers. [C20: named after *Bangalore in S India,* where it was used]

banger ('bæŋə) *n. Brit.* **1.** *Slang.* a sausage. **2.** *Informal* **a.** an old decrepit car. **b.** (*as modifier*): *banger racing.* **3.** a type of firework that explodes loudly.

Bangla ('bæŋlə) *n.* another name for **Bengali** (sense 2).

Bangladeshi (ˌbæŋglə'dɛʃɪ) *adj.* **1.** of or relating to Bangladesh, a republic in S Asia. ~*n.* **2.** a native or inhabitant of Bangladesh.

bangle ('bæŋgᵊl) *n.* **1.** a bracelet, usually without a clasp, often worn high up round the arm or sometimes round the ankle. **2.** a disc or charm hanging from a bracelet, necklace, etc. [C19: from Hindi *bangrī*]

bang on *adj., adv. Brit. informal.* **1.** with absolute accuracy. **2.** excellent or excellently. ~Also (U.S.): **bang up.**

bangtail ('bæŋˌteɪl) *n.* **1.** a horse's tail cut straight across but not through the bone. **2.** a horse with a tail cut in this way. [C19: from *bangtail* short tail]

bangtail muster *n. Austral.* a roundup of cattle to be counted, each one having the hairs on its tail docked as it is counted.

bang up *vb.* (*tr., adv.*) *Prison slang.* to lock up (a prisoner) in his cell, esp. for the night.

bani ('bɑːnɪ) *n.* the plural of **ban**[3].

banian ('bænjən) *n.* a variant spelling of **banyan.**

banish ('bænɪʃ) *vb.* (*tr.*) **1.** to expel from a place, esp. by an official decree as a punishment. **2.** to drive away: *to banish gloom.* [C14: from Old French *banir,* of Germanic origin; compare Old High German *ban* BAN[2]] —'**banishment** *n.*

banisters *or* **bannisters** ('bænɪstəz) *pl. n.* the railing and supporting balusters on a staircase; balustrade. [C17: altered from BALUSTER]

banjo ('bændʒəʊ) *n., pl.* **-jos** *or* **-joes.** **1.** a stringed musical instrument with a long neck (usually fretted) and a circular drumlike body overlaid with parchment, plucked with the fingers or a plectrum. **2.** *Slang.* any banjo-shaped object, esp. a frying pan. **3.** *Austral. and N.Z. slang.* a long-handled shovel with a wide blade. **4.** (*modifier*) banjo-shaped: *a banjo clock.* [C18: variant (U.S. Southern pronunciation) of BANDORE] —'**banjoist** *n.*

bank[1] (bæŋk) *n.* **1.** an institution offering certain financial services, such as the safekeeping of money, conversion of domestic into and from foreign currencies, lending of money at interest, and acceptance of bills of exchange. **2.** the building used by such an institution. **3.** a small container used at home for keeping money. **4.** the funds held by a gaming house or a banker or dealer in some gambling games. **5.** (in various games) **a.** the stock, as of money, pieces, tokens, etc., on which players may draw. **b.** the player holding this stock. **6.** any supply, store, or reserve, for future use: *a data bank; a blood bank.* ~*vb.* **7.** (*tr.*) to deposit (cash, cheques, etc.) in a bank. **8.** (*intr.*) to transact business with a bank. **9.** (*intr.*) to engage in the business of banking. **10.** (*intr.*) to hold the bank in some gambling games. ~See also **bank on.** [C15: probably from Italian *banca* bench, moneychanger's table, of Germanic origin; compare Old High German *banc* BENCH]

bank[2] (bæŋk) *n.* **1.** a long raised mass, esp. of earth; mound; ridge. **2.** a slope, as of a hill. **3.** the sloping side of any hollow in the ground, esp. when bordering a river: *the left bank of a river is on a spectator's left looking downstream.* **4.** **a.** an elevated section, rising to near the surface, of the bed of a sea, lake, or river. **b.** (*in combination*): *sandbank; mudbank.* **5.** **a.** the area around the mouth of the shaft of a mine. **b.** the face of a body of ore. **6.** the lateral inclination of an aircraft about its longitudinal axis during a turn. **7.** Also called: **banking, camber, cant, superelevation.** a bend on a road or on a railway, athletics, cycling, or other track having the outside built higher than the inside in order to reduce the effects of centrifugal force on vehicles, runners, etc., rounding it at speed. **8.** the cushion of a billiard table. ~*vb.* **9.** (when *tr.*, often foll. by *up*) to form into a bank or mound. **10.** (*tr.*) to border or enclose (a road, etc.) with a bank. **11.** (*tr.;* sometimes foll. by *up*) to cover (a fire) with ashes, fresh fuel, etc., so that it will burn slowly. **12.** to cause (an aircraft) to tip laterally about its longitudinal axis or (of an aircraft) to tip in this way, esp. while turning. **13.** to travel round a bank, esp. at high speed. **14.** (*tr.*) *Billiards.* to drive (a ball) into the cushion. [C12: of Scandinavian origin; compare Old Icelandic *bakki* hill, Old Danish *banke,* Swedish *backe*]

bank[3] (bæŋk) *n.* **1.** an arrangement of objects, esp. similar objects, in a row or in tiers: *a bank of dials.* **2.** **a.** a tier of oars in a galley. **b.** a bench for the rowers in a galley. **3.** *Printing.* lines of type under a headline. **4.** *Telephony.* (in automatic switching) an assembly of fixed electrical contacts forming a rigid unit in a selector or similar device. ~*vb.* **5.** (*tr.*) to arrange in a bank. [C17: from Old French *banc* bench, of Germanic origin; see BANK[1]]

bankable ('bæŋkəbᵊl) *adj.* **1.** appropriate for receipt by a bank. **2.** dependable or reliable: *a bankable promise.* **3.** *U.S.* (esp. of a star) likely to ensure the financial success of a film.

bank acceptance *n.* a bill of exchange or draft drawn on and endorsed by a bank. Also called: **banker's acceptance.**

bank account *n.* **1.** an account created by the deposit of money at a bank by a customer. **2.** the amount of money credited to a depositor at a bank.

bank annuities *pl. n.* another term for **consols.**

bank bill *n.* **1.** Also called: **bank draft.** a bill of exchange drawn by one bank on another. **2.** Also called: **banker's bill.** *U.S.* a banknote.

bankbook ('bæŋkˌbʊk) *n.* a book held by depositors at certain banks, in which the bank enters a record of deposits, withdrawals, and earned interest. Also called: **passbook.**

bank clerk *n. Brit.* an employee of a bank.

bank discount *n.* interest on a loan deducted from the principal amount when the loan is made and based on the loan's face value.

banker[1] ('bæŋkə) *n.* **1.** a person who owns or is an executive in a bank. **2.** an official or player in charge of the bank in any of various games, esp. gambling games. **3.** a result that has been forecast identically in a series of entries on a football pool coupon.

banker[2] ('bæŋkə) *n.* **1.** a fishing vessel of Newfoundland. **2.** a fisherman in such a vessel. **3.** *Austral. and N.Z. informal.* a stream almost overflowing its banks (esp. in the phrase **run a banker**). **4.** Also called: **bank engine.** *Brit.* a locomotive that is used to help a heavy train up a steep gradient.

banker[3] ('bæŋkə) *n.* **1.** a craftsman's workbench. **2.** a timber board used as a base for mixing building materials.

banker's order *n.* another name for **standing order** (sense 1).

banket ('bæŋkɪt) *n.* a gold-bearing conglomerate found in South Africa. [C19: from Dutch: a kind of almond hardbake, alluding to its appearance]

Bank Giro *n.* a British giro system operated by clearing banks to enable customers to pay sums of money to others by credit transfer.

bank holiday *n.* (in Britain) any of several weekdays on which banks are closed by law and which are observed as national holidays.

banking[1] ('bæŋkɪŋ) *n.* the business engaged in by a bank.

banking[2] ('bæŋkɪŋ) *n.* **1.** an embankment of a river. **2.** another word for **bank**[2] (sense 7). **3.** fishing on a sea bank, esp. off the coast of Newfoundland. **4.** the manoeuvre causing an aircraft to bank.

bank manager *n.* a person who directs the business of a local branch of a bank.

banknote ('bæŋkˌnəʊt) *n.* a promissory note issued by a central bank, serving as money.

Bank of England *n.* the central bank of the United Kingdom, which acts as banker to the government and the commercial banks. It is responsible for managing the government's debt and implementing its policy on interest rates and other monetary matters: established in 1694, nationalized in 1946.

bank on *vb.* (*intr., prep.*) to expect or rely with confidence on: *you can bank on him always arriving on time.*

bankroll ('bæŋkˌrəʊl) *U.S. and Canadian.* ~*n.* **1.** a roll of currency notes. **2.** the financial resources of a person, organization, etc. ~*vb.* **3.** (*tr.*) *Slang.* to provide the capital for; finance.

bankrupt ('bæŋkrʌpt, -rəpt) *n.* **1.** a person adjudged insolvent by a court, his property being transferred to a trustee and administered for the benefit of his creditors. **2.** any person unable to discharge all his debts. **3.** a person whose resources in a certain field are exhausted or nonexistent: *a spiritual bankrupt.* ~*adj.* **4.** adjudged insolvent. **5.** financially ruined. **6.** depleted in resources or having completely failed: *spiritually bankrupt.* **7.** (foll. by *of*) *Brit.* lacking: *bankrupt of intelligence.* ~*vb.* **8.** (*tr.*) to make bankrupt. [C16: from Old French *banqueroute,* from Old Italian *bancarotta,* from *banca* BANK[1] + *rotta* broken, from Latin *ruptus,* from *rumpere* to break]

bankruptcy ('bæŋkrʌptsɪ, -rəptsɪ) *n., pl.* **-cies.** the state, condition, or quality of being or becoming bankrupt.

banksia ('bæŋksɪə) *n.* any shrub or tree of the Australian genus *Banksia,* having long leathery evergreen leaves and dense cylindrical heads of flowers that are often yellowish: family *Proteaceae.* See also **honeysuckle** (sense 3). [C19: New Latin, named after Sir Joseph *Banks* (1743–1820), British botanist]

banksman ('bæŋksmən) *n.* a crane driver's helper, who signals instructions to the driver for the movement of the crane and its jib.

bank statement *n.* a statement of transactions in a bank account, esp. one of a series sent at regular intervals to the depositor.

banlieue *French.* (bɑ̃ljø) *n.* a suburb of a city.

banner ('bænə) *n.* **1.** a long strip of flexible material displaying a slogan, advertisement, etc., esp. one suspended between two points. **2.** a placard or sign carried in a procession or demonstration. **3.** something that represents a belief or principle: *a commitment to nationalization is the banner of British socialism.* **4.** the flag of a nation, army, etc., used as a standard or ensign. **5.** (formerly) the standard of an emperor, knight, etc. **6.** Also called: **banner headline.** a large headline in a newspaper, etc., extending across the page, esp. the front page. **7.** a square flag, often charged with the arms of its bearer. ~*adj.* **8.** *U.S.* outstandingly successful: *a banner year for orders.* [C13: from Old French *baniere,* of Germanic origin; compare Gothic *bandwa* sign; influenced by Medieval Latin *bannum* BAN[1], *bannīre* to BANISH] —'**bannered** *adj.*

banneret ('bænərɪt, -ə,rɛt) *n.* (in the Middle Ages) **1.** Also called: **knight banneret.** a knight who was entitled to command other knights and men-at-arms under his own banner. **2.** a title of knighthood conferred by the king for valour on the battlefield. [C14: from Old French *banerete* a small BANNER]

bannerette *or* **banneret** (,bænə'rɛt) *n.* a small banner. [C13: from Old French *baneret,* from *banere* BANNER]

bannerol ('bænə,rəʊl) *n.* a variant of **banderole.**

bannisters ('bænɪstəz) *pl. n.* a variant spelling of **banisters.**

bannock ('bænək) *n.* a round flat unsweetened cake originating in Scotland, made from oatmeal or barley and baked on a griddle. [Old English *bannuc;* of Celtic origin; compare Gaelic *bannach,* Cornish *banna* a drop, bit; perhaps related to Latin *pānicium,* from *pānis* bread]

banns *or* **bans** (bænz) *pl. n.* **1.** the public declaration of an intended marriage, usually formally announced on three successive Sundays in the parish churches of both the betrothed. **2.** **forbid the banns.** to raise an objection to a marriage announced in this way. [C14: plural of *bann* proclamation; see BAN[1]]

banquet ('bæŋkwɪt) *n.* **1.** a lavish and sumptuous meal; feast. **2.** a ceremonial meal for many people, often followed by speeches. ~*vb.* **-quets, -queting, -queted.** **3.** (*intr.*) to hold or take part in a banquet. **4.** (*tr.*) to entertain or honour (a person) with a banquet. [C15: from Old French, from Italian *banchetto,* from *banco* a table, of Germanic origin; see BANK[1]] —'**banqueter** *n.*

banquette (bæŋ'kɛt) *n.* **1.** (formerly) a raised part behind a parapet. **2.** a footbridge. **3.** *Chiefly U.S. and Canadian.* an upholstered bench. [C17: from French, from Provençal *banqueta,* literally: a little bench, from *banc* bench; see BANK[3]]

bans (bænz) *pl. n.* a variant spelling of **banns.**

bansela (ban'sɛlə) *n.* a variant of **bonsela.**

banshee ('bænʃiː, bæn'ʃiː) *n.* (in Irish folklore) a female spirit whose wailing warns of impending death. [C18: from Irish Gaelic *bean sidhe,* literally: woman of the fairy mound]

bant (bænt) *n. Lancashire dialect.* string. [probably a dialect pronunciation of BAND[2]]

bantam ('bæntəm) *n.* **1.** any of various very small breeds of domestic fowl. **2.** a small but aggressive person. **3.** *Boxing.* short for **bantamweight.** [C18: after *Bantam,* village in Java, said to be the original home of this fowl]

bantamweight ('bæntəm,weɪt) *n.* **1. a.** a professional boxer weighing 112–118 pounds (51–53.5 kg). **b.** an amateur boxer weighing 51–54 kg (112–119 pounds). **c.** (*as modifier*): *the bantamweight champion.* **2.** a wrestler in a similar weight category (usually 115–126 pounds (52–57 kg)).

banter ('bæntə) *vb.* **1.** to speak to or tease lightly or jokingly. ~*n.* **2.** light, teasing, or joking language or repartee. [C17: of unknown origin] —'**banterer** *n.*

banting ('bæntɪŋ) *n. Obsolete.* slimming by avoiding eating sugar, starch, and fat. [C19: named after William *Banting* (1797–1878), London undertaker who popularized this diet]

bantling ('bæntlɪŋ) *n. Archaic, disparaging.* a young child; brat. [C16: perhaps from German *Bänkling* illegitimate child, from *Bank* bench + -LING[1]]

Bantoid ('bɑːntɔɪd, 'bæn-) *adj.* denoting or relating to languages, esp. in Cameroon and Nigeria, that possess certain Bantu characteristics. See also **Semi-Bantu.**

Bantu ('bɑːntʊ, 'bæntuː, bæn'tuː) *n.* **1.** a group of languages of Africa, including most of the principal languages spoken from the equator to the Cape of Good Hope, but excluding the Khoisan family: now generally regarded as part of the Benue-Congo branch of the Niger-Congo family. **2.** (*pl.* **-tu** *or* **-tus**) a member of any of the indigenous Negroid peoples who inhabit southern, eastern, and central Africa and speak any of these languages. ~*adj.* **3.** denoting, relating to, or belonging to this group of peoples or to any of their languages. [C19: from Bantu *Ba-ntu* people]

Bantu beer *n. S. African.* a malted drink made from partly fermented and germinated millet.

Bantustan ('bɑːntʊ,stɑːn, ,bæntʊ'stɑːn) *n.* (in South Africa) an area reserved for occupation by a Black African people, with limited self-government. Official name: **homeland.**

banyan *or* **banian** ('bænjən) *n.* **1.** a moraceous tree, *Ficus benghalensis,* of tropical India and the East Indies, having aerial roots that grow down into the soil forming additional trunks. **2.** a member of the Hindu merchant caste of N and W India. **3.** a loose-fitting shirt, jacket, or robe, worn originally in India. [C16: from Hindi *baniyā,* from Sanskrit *vānija* merchant]

banzai ('bɑːnzaɪ, bɑːn'zaɪ) *interj.* a patriotic cheer, battle cry, or salutation. [Japanese: literally, (may you live for) ten thousand years]

banzai attack *n.* a mass attack of troops, without concern for casualties, as practised by the Japanese in World War II.

baobab ('beɪəʊ,bæb) *n.* a bombacaceous tree, *Adansonia digitata,* native to Africa and northern Australia that has a very thick trunk, large white flowers, and a gourdlike fruit with an edible pulp called monkey bread. Also called: **bottle tree, monkey bread tree.** [C17: probably from a native African word]

BAOR *abbrev. for* British Army of the Rhine.

bap (bæp) *n. Brit.* a large soft bread roll. [C16: of unknown origin]

bapt. *abbrev. for:* **1.** baptism. **2.** baptized.

Bapt. *abbrev. for* Baptist.

baptism ('bæp,tɪzəm) *n.* **1.** a Christian religious rite consisting of immersion in or sprinkling with water as a sign that the subject is cleansed from sin and constituted as a member of the Church. **2.** the act of baptizing or of undergoing baptism. **3.** any similar experience of initiation, regeneration, or dedication. —**bap'tismal** *adj.* —**bap'tismally** *adv.*

baptism of fire *n.* **1.** a soldier's first experience of battle. **2.** any initiating ordeal or experience. **3.** *Christianity.* the penetration of the Holy Ghost into the human spirit to purify, consecrate, and strengthen it, as was believed to have occurred initially at Pentecost.

Baptist ('bæptɪst) *n.* **1.** a member of any of various Christian sects that affirm the necessity of baptism (usually of adults and by immersion) following a personal profession of the Christian faith. ~*adj.* **2.** denoting, relating to, or characteristic of any Christian sect that affirms the necessity of baptism following a personal profession of the Christian faith.

baptistry *or* **baptistery** ('bæptɪstrɪ) *n., pl.* **-ries** *or* **-eries.** **1.** a part of a Christian church in which baptisms are carried out. **2.** a tank in a Baptist church in which baptisms are carried out.

baptize *or* **baptise** (bæp'taɪz) *vb.* **1.** *Christianity.* to immerse (a person) in water or sprinkle water on (a person) as part of the rite of baptism. **2.** (*tr.*) to give a name to; christen. **3.** (*tr.*) to cleanse; purify. [C13: from Late Latin *baptīzāre,* from Greek *baptizein,* from *baptein* to bathe, dip]

bar[1] (bɑː) *n.* **1.** a rigid usually straight length of metal, wood, etc., that is longer than it is wide or thick, used esp. as a barrier or as a structural or mechanical part: *a bar of a gate.* **2.** a solid usually rectangular block of any material: *a bar of soap.* **3.** anything that obstructs or prevents. **4. a.** an offshore ridge of sand, mud, or shingle lying near the shore and parallel to it, across the mouth of a river, bay, or harbour, or linking an island to the mainland. **b.** *U.S. and Canadian.* an alluvial deposit in a stream, river, or lake. **5.** a counter or room where alcoholic drinks are served. **6.** a counter, room, or establishment where a particular range of goods, food, services, etc., are sold: *a coffee bar; a heel bar.* **7.** a narrow band or stripe, as of colour or light. **8.** a heating element in an electric fire. **9.** (in England) the area in a court of law separating the part reserved for the bench and Queen's Counsel from the area occupied by junior barristers, solicitors, and the general public. See also **Bar.** **10.** the place in a court of law where the accused stands during his trial: *the prisoner at the bar.* **11.** a particular court of law. **12.** *Brit.* (in the House of Lords and House of Commons) the boundary where nonmembers wishing to address either House appear and where persons are arraigned. **13.** a plea showing that a plaintiff has no cause of action, as when the case has already been adjudicated upon or the time allowed for bringing the action has passed. **14.** anything referred to as an authority or tribunal: *the bar of decency.* **15.** Also called: **measure.** *Music.* **a.** a group of beats that is repeated with a consistent rhythm throughout a piece or passage of music. The number of beats in the bar is indicated by the time signature. **b.** another word for **bar line.** **16. a.** *Brit.* insignia added to a decoration indicating a second award. **b.** *U.S.* a strip of metal worn with uniform, esp. to signify rank or as an award for service. **17.** a variant spelling of **barre.** **18.** *Football, etc.* See **crossbar.** **19.** *Gymnastics.* See **horizontal**

bar. **20. a.** part of the metal mouthpiece of a horse's bridle. **b.** the space between the horse's teeth in which such a part fits. **21.** either of two horny extensions that project forwards and inwards from the rear of the outer layer of a horse's hoof. **22.** See **crowbar** and **glazing-bar.** **23.** *Lacemaking, needlework.* another name for **bride**[2]. **24.** *Heraldry.* an ordinary consisting of a horizontal line across a shield, typically narrower than a fesse, and usually appearing in twos or threes. **25. behind bars.** in prison. **26. won't** (*or* **wouldn't) have a bar of.** *Austral. and N.Z. informal.* cannot tolerate; dislike. ~*vb.* **bars, barring, barred.** (*tr.*) **27.** to fasten or secure with a bar: *to bar the door.* **28.** to shut in or out with or as if with barriers: *to bar the entrances.* **29.** to obstruct; hinder: *the fallen tree barred the road.* **30.** (usually foll. by *from*) to prohibit; forbid: *to bar a couple from meeting.* **31.** (usually foll. by *from*) to keep out; exclude: *to bar a person from membership.* **32.** to mark with a bar or bars. **33.** *Law.* to prevent or halt (an action) by showing that the plaintiff has no cause. **34.** to mark off (music) into bars with bar lines. ~*prep.* **35.** except for: *the best recital bar last night's.* **36. bar none.** without exception. [C12: from Old French *barre,* from Vulgar Latin *barra* (unattested) bar, rod, of unknown origin]

bar[2] (bɑː) *n.* a cgs unit of pressure equal to 10^6 dynes per square centimetre. 1 bar is equivalent to 10^5 newtons per square metre. [C20: from Greek *baros* weight]

bar[3] (bɑː) *Southwest English dialect.* ~*n.* **1.** immunity from being caught or otherwise penalized in a game. ~*interj.* **2.** a cry for such immunity. [variant of BARLEY[2]]

Bar (bɑː) *n.* **the. 1.** (in England and elsewhere) barristers collectively. **2.** *U.S.* the legal profession collectively. **3. be called to** *or* **go to the Bar.** *Brit.* to become a barrister. **4. be called within the Bar.** *Brit.* to be appointed as a Queen's Counsel.

BAR *abbrev. for* Browning Automatic Rifle.

bar. *abbrev. for:* **1.** barometer. **2.** barometric. **3.** barrel (container or unit of measure). **4.** barrister.

Bar- (bar, bɑː) *prefix.* (before Jewish patronymic names) son of: *Bar-Kochba.*

baraesthesia *or U.S.* **baresthesia** (ˌbærɪsˈθiːzɪə) *n.* *Physiol.* the ability to sense pressure. [C20: from Greek *baros* weight + AESTHESIA]

barathea (ˌbærəˈθɪə) *n.* a fabric made of silk and wool or cotton and rayon, used esp. for coats. [C19: of unknown origin]

baraza (baˈraza) *n. E African.* **1.** a place where public meetings are held. **2.** a palaver or meeting. [C19: from Swahili]

barb[1] (bɑːb) *n.* **1.** a subsidiary point facing in the opposite direction to the main point of a fish-hook, harpoon, arrow, etc., intended to make extraction difficult. **2.** any of various pointed parts, as on barbed wire. **3.** a cutting remark; gibe. **4.** any of the numerous hairlike filaments that form the vane of a feather. **5.** a beardlike growth in certain animals. **6.** a hooked hair or projection on certain fruits. **7.** any small cyprinid fish of the genus *Barbus* (or *Puntius*) and related genera, such as *B. conchonius* (**rosy barb**). **8.** (*usually pl.*) any of the small fleshy protuberances beneath the tongue in horses and cattle. **9.** a white linen cloth forming part of a headdress extending from the chin to the upper chest, originally worn by women in the Middle Ages, now worn by nuns of some orders. **10.** *Obsolete.* a beard. ~*vb.* **11.** (*tr.*) to provide with a barb or barbs. [C14: from Old French *barbe* beard, point, from Latin *barba* beard] —**barbed** *adj.*

barb[2] (bɑːb) *n.* a breed of horse of North African origin, similar to the Arab but less spirited. [C17: from French *barbe,* from Italian *barbero* a Barbary (horse)]

barb[3] (bɑːb) *n. Austral.* a black kelpie (see **kelpie**[1]). [C19: named after one that was named *Barb* after a winning racehorse]

BARB (bɑːb) *n.* (in Britain) *acronym for* Broadcasters' Audience Research Board.

Barbadian (bɑːˈbeɪdɪən) *n.* **1.** a native or inhabitant of Barbados, an island in the West Indies. ~*adj.* **2.** of Barbados, its people, culture, etc.

Barbados earth (bɑːˈbeɪdəʊs, -dəʊz, -dɒs) *n.* a diatomaceous marl found in Barbados.

barbarian (bɑːˈbɛərɪən) *n.* **1.** a member of a primitive or uncivilized people. **2.** a coarse, insensitive, or uncultured person. **3.** a vicious person. ~*adj.* **4.** of an uncivilized culture. **5.** insensitive, uncultured, or brutal. [C16: see BARBAROUS] —**barˈbarianism** *n.*

barbaric (bɑːˈbærɪk) *adj.* **1.** of or characteristic of barbarians. **2.** primitive or unsophisticated; unrestrained. **3.** brutal. [C15: from Latin *barbaricus* foreign, outlandish; see BARBAROUS] —**barˈbarically** *adv.*

barbarism (ˈbɑːbəˌrɪzəm) *n.* **1.** a brutal, coarse, or ignorant act. **2.** the condition of being backward, coarse, or ignorant. **3.** a substandard or erroneously constructed or derived word or expression; solecism. **4.** any act or object that offends against accepted taste. [C16: from Latin *barbarismus* error of speech, from Greek *barbarismos,* from *barbaros* BARBAROUS]

barbarity (bɑːˈbærɪtɪ) *n., pl.* **-ties. 1.** the state or condition of being barbaric or barbarous. **2.** a brutal or vicious act. **3.** a crude or unsophisticated quality, style, expression, etc.

barbarize *or* **barbarise** (ˈbɑːbəˌraɪz) *vb.* **1.** to make or become barbarous. **2.** to use barbarisms in (language). —ˌ**barbariˈzation** *or* ˌ**barbariˈsation** *n.*

barbarous (ˈbɑːbərəs) *adj.* **1.** uncivilized; primitive. **2.** brutal or cruel. **3.** lacking refinement. [C15: via Latin from Greek *barbaros* barbarian, non-Greek, in origin imitative of incomprehensible speech; compare Sanskrit *barbara* stammering, non-Aryan] —ˈ**barbarously** *adv.* —ˈ**barbarousness** *n.*

Barbary ape (ˈbɑːbərɪ) *n.* a tailless macaque, *Macaca sylvana,* that inhabits rocky cliffs and forests in the Barbary region of N Africa and Gibraltar: family *Cercopithecidae,* order *Primates.*

barbastelle (ˌbɑːbəˈstɛl) *n.* an insectivorous forest bat, *Barbastella barbastellus,* widely distributed across Eurasia, having a wrinkled face and prominent ears: roosts in trees or caves. [French: from Italian *barbastello,* from Latin *vespertilio* bat; see PIPISTRELLE]

barbate (ˈbɑːbeɪt) *adj. Chiefly biology.* having tufts of long hairs; bearded. [C19: from Latin *barba* a beard]

barbecue (ˈbɑːbɪˌkjuː) *n.* **1.** a meal cooked out of doors over an open fire. **2.** an outdoor party or picnic at which barbecued food is served. **3.** a grill or fireplace used in barbecuing. **4.** the food so cooked. ~*vb.* **-cues, -cuing, -cued.** (*tr.*) **5.** to cook (meat, fish, etc.) on a grill, usually over charcoal and often with a highly seasoned sauce. **6.** to cook (meat, fish, etc.) in a highly seasoned sauce. [C17: from American Spanish *barbacoa,* probably from Taino: frame made of sticks]

barbed wire *n.* strong wire with sharply pointed barbs at close intervals. Also called (U.S.): **barbwire.**

barbed-wire grass *n. Austral.* an aromatic grass, *Cymbopogon refractus,* with groups of seed heads resembling barbed wire.

barbel (ˈbɑːbᵊl) *n.* **1.** any of several slender tactile spines or bristles that hang from the jaws of certain fishes, such as the catfish and carp. **2.** any of several European cyprinid fishes of the genus *Barbus,* esp. *B. barbus,* that resemble the carp but have a longer body and pointed snout. [C14: from Old French, from Latin *barbus,* from *barba* beard]

barbell (ˈbɑːˌbɛl) *n.* a metal rod to which heavy discs are attached at each end for weightlifting exercises.

barbellate (ˈbɑːbɪˌleɪt; bɑːˈbɛlɪt, -eɪt) *adj.* **1.** (of plants or plant organs) covered with barbs, hooks, or bristles. **2.** (of animals) possessing bristles or barbels. [C19: from New Latin *barbellātus,* from *barbella* short stiff hair, from Latin *barbula* a little beard, from *barba* beard]

barber (ˈbɑːbə) *n.* **1.** a person whose business is cutting men's hair and shaving or trimming beards. ~*vb.* (*tr.*) **2.** to cut the hair of. **3.** to shave or trim the beard of. [C13: from Old French *barbeor,* from *barbe* beard, from Latin *barba*]

barberry (ˈbɑːbərɪ) *n., pl.* **-ries. 1.** any spiny Asian berberidaceous shrub of the genus *Berberis,* esp. *B. vulgaris,* having clusters of yellow flowers and orange or red berries: widely cultivated as hedge plants. **2.** the fruit of any of these plants. [C15: from Old French *berberis,* from Arabic *barbāris*]

barbershop (ˈbɑːbəˌʃɒp) *n.* **1.** *Now chiefly U.S.* the premises of a barber. **2.** (*modifier*) denoting or characterized by a type of close four-part harmony for male voices, popular in romantic and sentimental songs of the 1920s and 1930s: *a barbershop quartet.*

barber's itch *or* **rash** *n.* any of various fungal infections of the bearded portion of the neck and face. Technical name: **tinea barbae.**

barber's pole *n.* a sign outside a barber's shop consisting of a pole painted with red and white spiral stripes.

barbet (ˈbɑːbɪt) *n.* any small tropical brightly coloured bird of the family *Capitonidae,* having short weak wings and a sharp stout bill with tuftlike feathers at its base: order *Piciformes* (woodpeckers, etc.). [C18: from French, ultimately from Latin *barbātus* bearded, BARBATE]

barbette (bɑːˈbɛt) *n.* **1.** (formerly) an earthen platform inside a parapet, from which heavy guns could fire over the top. **2.** an armoured cylinder below a turret on a warship that protects the revolving structure and foundation of the turret. [C18: from French, diminutive of *barbe* a nun's BARB[1], from a fancied similarity between the earthwork around a cannon and this part of a nun's habit]

barbican (ˈbɑːbɪkən) *n.* **1.** a walled outwork or tower to protect a gate or drawbridge of a fortification. **2.** a watchtower projecting from a fortification. [C13: from Old French *barbacane,* from Medieval Latin *barbacana,* of unknown origin]

barbicel (ˈbɑːbɪˌsɛl) *n. Ornithol.* any of the minute hooks on the barbules of feathers that interlock with those of adjacent barbules. [C19: from New Latin *barbicella,* literally: a small beard, from Latin *barba* beard]

barbie (ˈbɑːbɪ) *n. Austral. slang.* short for **barbecue.**

bar billiards *n.* (*functioning as sing.*) *Brit.* a table game in pubs, etc., in which short cues are used to pocket balls into holes scoring various points and guarded by wooden pegs that incur penalties if they are knocked over.

barbitone (ˈbɑːbɪˌtəʊn) *or U.S.* **barbital** (ˈbɑːbɪˌtæl) *n.* a long-acting barbiturate used medicinally, usually in the form of the sodium salt, as a sedative or hypnotic. [C20: from BARBIT(URIC ACID) + -ONE]

barbiturate (bɑːˈbɪtjʊrɪt, -ˌreɪt) *n.* a derivative of barbituric acid, such as barbitone or phenobarbitone, used in medicine as a sedative or hypnotic.

barbituric acid (ˌbɑːbɪˈtjʊərɪk) *n.* a white crystalline solid used in the preparation of barbiturate drugs. Formula: $C_4H_4N_2O_3$. Also called: **malonylurea.** [C19: partial translation of German

Barbitursäure, perhaps from the name *Barbara* + URIC + *Säure* acid]

barbule ('bɑːbjuːl) *n.* **1.** a very small barb. **2.** *Ornithol.* any of the minute hairs that project from a barb and in some feathers interlock by hooks and grooves, forming a flat vane. [C19: from Latin *barbula* a little beard, from *barba* beard]

barcarole *or* **barcarolle** ('bɑːkəˌrəʊl, -ˌrɒl; ˌbɑːkə'rəʊl) *n.* **1.** a Venetian boat song in a time of six or twelve quaver beats to the bar. **2.** an instrumental composition resembling this. [C18: from French, from Italian *barcarola,* from *barcaruolo* boatman, from *barca* boat; see BARQUE]

BArch *abbrev. for* Bachelor of Architecture.

barchan, barkhan, barchane, *or* **barkan** (bɑː'kɑːn) *n.* a crescent-shaped shifting sand dune, convex on the windward side and steeper and concave on the leeward.

bar chart *n.* another name for **bar graph.**

bar code *n. Commerce.* a machine-readable arrangement of numbers and parallel lines of different widths printed on a package, which can be electronically scanned at a checkout to register the price of the goods and to activate computer stock-checking and reordering.

Barcoo salute (bɑː'kuː) *n. Austral. informal.* a movement of the hand to brush flies away from the face. [from *Barcoo* River, E central Australia]

bard[1] (bɑːd) *n.* **1. a.** (formerly) one of an ancient Celtic order of poets who recited verses about the exploits, often legendary, of their tribes. **b.** (in modern times) a poet who wins a verse competition at a Welsh eisteddfod. **2.** *Archaic or literary.* any poet, esp. one who writes lyric or heroic verse or is of national importance. [C14: from Scottish Gaelic; related to Welsh *bardd*] —'**bardic** *adj.*

bard[2] *or* **barde** (bɑːd) *n.* **1.** a piece of larding bacon or pork fat placed on game or lean meat during roasting to prevent drying out. **2.** an ornamental caparison for a horse. ~*vb.* (*tr.*) **3.** to place a bard on. [C15: from Old French *barde,* from Old Italian *barda,* from Arabic *barda'ah* packsaddle]

bar diagram *n.* another name for **bar graph.**

bardie ('bɑːdiː) *n.* **1.** an edible white wood-boring grub of Australia. **2. starve the bardies!** *Austral.* an exclamation of surprise or protest. [from a native Australian language]

bardolatry (bɑː'dɒlətrɪ) *n. Facetious.* idolatry or excessive admiration of William Shakespeare (1564–1616). [from *the Bard,* an epithet of Shakespeare]

bare[1] (bɛə) *adj.* **1.** unclothed; exposed: used esp. of a part of the body. **2.** without the natural, conventional, or usual covering or clothing: *a bare tree.* **3.** lacking appropriate furnishings, etc.: *a bare room.* **4.** unembellished; simple: *the bare facts.* **5.** (*prenominal*) just sufficient; mere: *he earned the bare minimum.* **6. with one's bare hands.** without a weapon or tool. ~*vb.* **7.** (*tr.*) to make bare; uncover; reveal. [Old English *bær;* compare Old Norse *berr,* Old High German *bar* naked, Old Slavonic *bosŭ* barefoot] —'**bareness** *n.*

bare[2] (bɛə) *vb. Archaic.* a past tense of **bear**[1].

bareback ('bɛəˌbæk) *or* **barebacked** *adj., adv.* (of horse-riding) without a saddle.

barefaced ('bɛəˌfeɪst) *adj.* **1.** unconcealed or shameless: *a barefaced lie.* **2.** with the face uncovered or shaven. —**barefacedly** ('bɛəˌfeɪsɪdlɪ) *adv.* —'**bareˌfacedness** *n.*

barefoot ('bɛəˌfʊt) *or* **barefooted** *adj., adv.* with the feet uncovered.

barefoot doctor *n.* (esp. in China) a worker trained as a medical auxiliary in a rural area who dispenses medicine, gives first aid, assists at childbirth, etc. [C20: translation of Chinese *chijiao yisheng,* officially translated as primary health worker]

barège *French.* (barɛʒ) *n.* **1.** a light silky gauze fabric made of wool. ~*adj.* **2.** made of such a fabric. [C19: named after *Barèges,* France, where it was originally made]

barehanded (ˌbɛə'hændɪd) *adv., adj.* **1.** without weapons, tools, etc. **2.** with hands uncovered.

bareheaded (ˌbɛə'hɛdɪd) *adj., adv.* with head uncovered.

barely ('bɛəlɪ) *adv.* **1.** only just; scarcely: *barely enough for their needs.* **2.** *Informal.* not quite; nearly: *barely old enough.* **3.** scantily; poorly: *barely furnished.* **4.** *Archaic.* openly.

▷**Usage.** See at **hardly.**

baresark ('bɛəˌsɑːk) *n.* **1.** another word for **berserk** (sense 2). ~*adv.* **2.** *Archaic.* without armour. [C19: literally: bare shirt]

bar fly *n. Informal, chiefly U.S. and Canadian.* a person who frequents bars.

bargain ('bɑːgɪn) *n.* **1.** an agreement or contract establishing what each party will give, receive, or perform in a transaction between them. **2.** something acquired or received in such an agreement. **3. a.** something bought or offered at a low price: *a bargain at an auction.* **b.** (*as modifier*): *a bargain price.* **4. into** *or* (*U.S.*) **in the bargain.** in excess of what has been stipulated; besides. **5. make** *or* **strike a bargain.** to agree on terms. ~*vb.* **6.** (*intr.*) to negotiate the terms of an agreement, transaction, etc. **7.** (*tr.*) to exchange, as in a bargain. **8.** to arrive at (an agreement or settlement). [C14: from Old French *bargaigne,* from *bargaignier* to trade, of Germanic origin; compare Medieval Latin *barcāniāre* to trade, Old English *borgian* to borrow] —'**bargainer** *n.* —'**bargaining** *n., adj.*

bargain away *vb.* (*tr., adv.*) to lose or renounce (freedom, rights, etc.) in return for something valueless or of little value.

bargain basement *n.* part of a shop where goods are sold at reduced prices.

bargain for *vb.* (*intr., prep.*) to expect; anticipate (a style of behaviour, change in fortune, etc.): *he got more than he bargained for.*

bargaining agent *n.* an organization, usually a trade union, that acts or bargains on behalf of a group of employees in collective bargaining.

bargaining level *n.* the level within an organizational hierarchy, such as company level, national level, etc., at which collective bargaining takes place.

bargaining scope *n.* the range of topics within the scope of a particular set of negotiations leading to a collective agreement.

bargaining unit *n.* a specific group of employees who are covered by the same collective agreement or set of agreements and represented by the same bargaining agent or agents.

bargain on *vb.* (*intr., prep.*) to rely or depend on (something): *he bargained on her support.*

barge (bɑːdʒ) *n.* **1.** a vessel, usually flat-bottomed and with or without its own power, used for transporting freight, esp. on canals. **2.** a vessel, often decorated, used in pageants, for state occasions, etc. **3.** *Navy.* a boat allocated to a flag officer, used esp. for ceremonial occasions and often carried on board his flagship. **4.** *Informal and derogatory.* any vessel, esp. an old or clumsy one. ~*vb.* **5.** (*intr.;* foll. by *into*) *Informal.* to bump (into). **6.** *Informal.* to push (someone or one's way) violently. **7.** (*intr.;* foll. by *into* or *in*) *Informal.* to interrupt rudely or clumsily: *to barge into a conversation.* **8.** *Sailing.* to bear down on (another boat or boats) at the start of a race. **9.** (*tr.*) to transport by barge. **10.** (*intr.*) *Informal.* to move slowly or clumsily. [C13: from Old French, from Medieval Latin *barga,* probably from Late Latin *barca* a small boat; see BARQUE]

bargeboard ('bɑːdʒˌbɔːd) *n.* a board, often decorated with carved ornaments, placed along the gable end of a roof. Also called: **vergeboard.**

barge couple *n.* either of a pair of outside rafters along the gable end of a roof.

barge course *n.* **1.** the overhang of the gable end of a roof. **2.** a course of bricks laid on edge to form the coping of a wall.

bargee (bɑː'dʒiː) *or U.S. and Canadian.* **bargeman** ('bɑːdʒmən) *n., pl.* **bargees** *or* **bargemen.** a person employed on or in charge of a barge.

bargepole ('bɑːdʒˌpəʊl) *n.* **1.** a long pole used to propel a barge. **2. not touch with a bargepole.** *Informal.* to refuse to have anything to do with.

bar girl *n. Chiefly U.S.* an attractive girl employed by the management of a bar to befriend male customers and encourage them to buy drinks.

bar graph *n.* a graph consisting of vertical or horizontal bars whose lengths are proportional to amounts or quantities. Also called: **bar chart, bar diagram.**

baric[1] ('bɛərɪk, 'bærɪk) *adj.* of or containing barium.

baric[2] ('bærɪk) *adj.* of or concerned with weight, esp. that of the atmosphere as indicated by barometric pressure.

barilla (bə'rɪlə) *n.* **1.** an impure mixture of sodium carbonate and sodium sulphate obtained from the ashes of certain plants, such as the saltworts. **2.** either of two chenopodiaceous plants, *Salsola kali* (or *soda*) or *Halogeton soda,* formerly burned to obtain a form of sodium carbonate. See also **saltwort.** [C17: from Spanish *barrilla,* literally: a little bar, from *barra* BAR[1]]

barit. *abbrev. for* baritone.

barite ('bɛəraɪt) *n.* the usual U.S. and Canadian name for **barytes.** [C18: from BAR(IUM) + -ITE[1]]

baritone ('bærɪˌtəʊn) *n.* **1.** the second lowest adult male voice, having a range approximately from G an eleventh below middle C to F a fourth above it. **2.** a singer with such a voice. **3.** the second lowest instrument in the families of the saxophone, horn, oboe, etc. ~*adj.* **4.** relating to or denoting a baritone: *a baritone part.* **5.** denoting the second lowest instrument in a family: *the baritone horn.* [C17: from Italian *baritono* a deep voice, from Greek *barutonos* deep-sounding, from *barus* heavy, low + *tonos* TONE]

barium ('bɛərɪəm) *n.* a soft silvery-white metallic element of the alkaline earth group. It is used in bearing alloys and compounds are used as pigments. Symbol: Ba; atomic no.: 56; atomic wt.: 137.34; valency: 2; relative density: 3.5; melting pt.: 725°C; boiling pt.: 1140°C. [C19: from BAR(YTA) + -IUM]

barium enema *n.* an injection into the rectum of a preparation of barium sulphate, which is opaque to x-rays, before x-raying the lower alimentary canal.

barium hydroxide *n.* a white poisonous crystalline solid, used in the manufacture of organic compounds and in the preparation of beet sugar. Formula: $Ba(OH)_2$. Also called: **baryta.**

barium meal *n.* a preparation of barium sulphate, which is opaque to x-rays, swallowed by a patient before x-ray examination of the upper part of his alimentary canal.

barium oxide *n.* a white or yellowish-white poisonous heavy powder used esp. as a dehydrating agent. Formula: BaO. Also called: **baryta.**

barium sulphate *n.* a white insoluble fine heavy powder, used as a pigment, as a filler for paper, rubber, etc., and in barium meals. Formula: $BaSO_4$. Also called: **blanc fixe.**

barium titanate *n.* a crystalline ceramic used in capacitors and piezoelectric devices. Formula: $BaTiO_3$.

bark[1] (bɑːk) *n.* **1.** the loud abrupt usually harsh or gruff cry of a dog or any of certain other animals. **2.** a similar sound, such as one made by a person, gun, etc. **3. his bark is worse than his bite.** he is bad-tempered but harmless. ~*vb.* **4.** (*intr.*) (of a dog or any of certain other animals) to make its typical loud abrupt cry. **5.** (*intr.*) (of a person, gun, etc.) to make a similar loud harsh sound. **6.** to say or shout in a brusque, peremptory, or angry tone: *he barked an order.* **7.** *U.S. informal.* to advertise (a show, merchandise, etc.) by loudly addressing passers-by. **8. bark up the wrong tree.** *Informal.* to misdirect one's attention, efforts, etc.; be mistaken. [Old English *beorcan;* related to Lithuanian *burgėti* to quarrel, growl]

bark[2] (bɑːk) *n.* **1.** a protective layer of dead corky cells on the outside of the stems of woody plants. **2.** any of several varieties of this substance that can be used in tanning, dyeing, or in medicine. **3.** an informal name for **cinchona.** ~*vb.* (*tr.*) **4.** to scrape or rub off skin, as in an injury. **5.** to remove the bark or a circle of bark from (a tree or log). **6.** to cover or enclose with bark. **7.** to tan (leather), principally by the tannins in barks. [C13: from Old Norse *börkr;* related to Swedish, Danish *bark,* German *Borke;* compare Old Norse *björkr* BIRCH]

bark[3] (bɑːk) *n.* a variant spelling (esp. U.S.) of **barque.**

bark beetle *n.* any small beetle of the family *Scolytidae,* which bore tunnels in the bark and wood of trees, causing great damage. They are closely related to the weevils.

bark cloth *n.* a papery fabric made from the fibrous inner bark of various trees, esp. of the moraceous genus *Ficus* and the leguminous genus *Brachystegia.*

barkeeper (ˈbɑːˌkiːpə) *n.* another name (esp. U.S.) for **barman.**

barkentine *or* **barkantine** (ˈbɑːkənˌtiːn) *n.* the usual U.S. and Canadian spellings of **barquentine.**

barker[1] (ˈbɑːkə) *n.* **1.** an animal or person that barks. **2.** a person who stands at a show, fair booth, etc., and loudly addresses passers-by to attract customers.

barker[2] (ˈbɑːkə) *n.* a person or machine that removes bark from trees or logs or prepares it for tanning.

barkhan *or* **barkan** (bɑːˈkɑːn) *n.* variant spellings of **barchan.**

barking (ˈbɑːkɪŋ) *Slang.* ~*adj.* **1.** mad; crazy. ~*adv.* **2.** (intensifier): *barking mad.*

barking deer *n.* another name for **muntjac.**

barley[1] (ˈbɑːlɪ) *n.* **1.** any of various erect annual temperate grasses of the genus *Hordeum,* esp. *H. vulgare,* that have short leaves and dense bristly flower spikes and are widely cultivated for grain and forage. **2.** the grain of any of these grasses, used in making beer and whisky and for soups, puddings, etc. See also **pearl barley.** [Old English *bærlīc* (adj.); related to *bere* barley, Old Norse *barr* barley, Gothic *barizeins* of barley, Latin *farīna* flour]

barley[2] (ˈbɑːlɪ) *sentence substitute. Dialect.* a cry for truce or respite from the rules of a game. [C18: probably changed from PARLEY]

barleycorn (ˈbɑːlɪˌkɔːn) *n.* **1.** a grain of barley, or barley itself. **2.** an obsolete unit of length equal to one third of an inch.

barley sugar *n.* a brittle clear amber-coloured sweet made by boiling sugar, originally with a barley extract.

barley water *n.* a drink made from an infusion of barley, usually flavoured with lemon or orange.

barley wine *n. Brit.* an exceptionally strong beer.

bar line *or* **bar** *n. Music.* the vertical line marking the boundary between one bar and the next.

barm (bɑːm) *n.* **1.** the yeasty froth on fermenting malt liquors. **2.** an archaic or dialect word for **yeast.** [Old English *beorma;* related to *beran* to BEAR, Old Norse *barmr* barm, Gothic *barms,* Old High German *barm;* see FERMENT]

barmaid (ˈbɑːˌmeɪd) *n.* a woman who serves in a pub.

barman (ˈbɑːmən) *n., pl.* **-men.** a man who serves in a pub.

barm cake *n. Lancashire dialect.* a round flat soft bread roll.

Barmecide (ˈbɑːmɪˌsaɪd) *or* **Barmecidal** *adj.* lavish or plentiful in imagination only; illusory; sham: *a Barmecide feast.* [C18: from the name of a prince in *The Arabian Nights* who served empty plates to beggars, alleging that they held sumptuous food]

Bar Mitzvah (bɑː ˈmɪtsvə) (*sometimes not caps.*) *Judaism.* ~*adj.* **1.** (of a Jewish boy) having assumed full religious obligations, being at least thirteen years of age. ~*n.* **2.** the occasion, ceremony, or celebration of that event. **3.** the boy himself on that day. [Hebrew: son of the law]

barmy (ˈbɑːmɪ) *adj.* **-mier, -miest.** *Slang.* insane. Also: **balmy.** [C16: originally, full of BARM, hence frothing, excited, flighty, etc.]

barn[1] (bɑːn) *n.* **1.** a large farm outbuilding, used chiefly for storing hay, grain, etc., but also for housing livestock. **2.** *U.S. and Canadian.* a large shed for sheltering railroad cars, trucks, etc. **3.** any large building, esp. an unattractive one. [Old English *beren,* from *bere* barley + *ærn* room; see BARLEY[1]]

barn[2] (bɑːn) *n.* a unit of nuclear cross section equal to 10^{-28} square metre. Symbol: b [C20: from BARN[1]; so called because of the relatively large cross section]

barnacle (ˈbɑːnəkᵊl) *n.* **1.** any of various marine crustaceans of the subclass *Cirripedia* that, as adults, live attached to rocks, ship bottoms, etc. They have feathery food-catching cirri protruding from a hard shell. See **acorn barnacle, goose barnacle. 2.** a person or thing that is difficult to get rid of. [C16: related to Late Latin *bernicla,* of obscure origin] —ˈ**barnacled** *adj.*

barnacle goose *n.* **1.** a N European goose, *Branta leucopsis,* that has a black-and-white head and body and grey wings. **2.** a former name for **brent goose.** [C13 *bernekke,* related to Late Latin *bernaca,* from the belief that the goose developed from a shellfish; ultimate origin obscure]

Barnard's star (ˈbɑːnɑːdz) *n.* a red dwarf star in the constellation Ophiuchus having the largest proper motion known. [C20: named after E. E. *Barnard* (1857–1923), U.S. astronomer]

barn-brack (ˈbɑːnˌbræk) *n. Irish.* a loaf of bread with currants in it. [from Irish Gaelic *bairín breac* speckled loaf]

barn dance *n.* **1.** *Brit.* a progressive round country dance. **2.** *U.S. and Canadian.* a party with hoedown music and square-dancing. **3.** a party featuring country dancing. **4.** a disco or party held in a barn.

barn door *n.* **1.** the door of a barn. **2.** *Informal.* a target so large that it cannot be missed. **3.** *Photog., television, etc.* an adjustable flap over the front of a studio or theatre lamp.

barney (ˈbɑːnɪ) *Informal.* ~*n.* **1.** a noisy argument. ~*vb.* (*intr.*) **2.** *Chiefly Austral. and N.Z.* to argue or quarrel. [C19: of unknown origin]

barn owl *n.* any owl of the genus *Tyto,* esp. *T. alba,* having a pale brown and white plumage, long slender legs, and a heart-shaped face: family *Tytonidae.*

barnstorm (ˈbɑːnˌstɔːm) *vb.* (*intr.*) **1.** to tour rural districts putting on shows, esp. theatrical, athletic, or acrobatic shows. **2.** *Chiefly U.S. and Canadian.* to tour rural districts making speeches in a political campaign. [C19: from BARN[1] + STORM (*vb.*); from the performances often being in barns] —ˈ**barnˌstormer** *n.* —ˈ**barnˌstorming** *n., adj.*

barn swallow *n.* the U.S. and Canadian name for the common swallow, *Hirundo rustica.* See **swallow**[2].

barnyard (ˈbɑːnˌjɑːd) *n.* **1.** a yard adjoining a barn, in which farm animals are kept. **2.** (*modifier*) belonging to or characteristic of a barnyard. **3.** (*modifier*) crude or earthy: *barnyard humour.*

baro- *combining form.* indicating weight or pressure: *barometer.* [from Greek *baros* weight; related to Latin *gravis* heavy]

barognosis (ˌbærɒgˈnəʊsɪs) *n. Physiol.* the ability to judge weight. [C20: from Greek *baros* weight + *gnosis* knowledge]

barogram (ˈbærəˌgræm) *n. Meteorol.* the record of atmospheric pressure traced by a barograph or similar instrument.

barograph (ˈbærəˌgrɑːf, -ˌgræf) *n. Meteorol.* a self-recording aneroid barometer. —**barographic** (ˌbærəˈgræfɪk) *adj.*

barometer (bəˈrɒmɪtə) *n.* **1.** an instrument for measuring atmospheric pressure, usually to determine altitude or weather changes. **2.** anything that shows change or impending change: *the barometer of social change.* —**barometric** (ˌbærəˈmɛtrɪk) *or* ˌ**baroˈmetrical** *adj.* —ˌ**baroˈmetrically** *adv.* —**baˈrometry** *n.*

barometric pressure *n.* atmospheric pressure as indicated by a barometer.

baron (ˈbærən) *n.* **1.** a member of a specific rank of nobility, esp. the lowest rank in the British Isles. **2.** (in Europe from the Middle Ages) originally any tenant-in-chief of a king or other overlord, who held land from his superior by honourable service; a land-holding nobleman. **3.** a powerful businessman or financier: *a press baron.* **4.** *English law.* (formerly) the title held by judges of the Court of Exchequer. **5.** short for **baron of beef.** [C12: from Old French, of Germanic origin; compare Old High German *baro* freeman, Old Norse *berjask* to fight]

baronage (ˈbærənɪdʒ) *n.* **1.** barons collectively. **2.** the rank or dignity of a baron.

baroness (ˈbærənɪs) *n.* **1.** the wife or widow of a baron. **2.** a woman holding the rank of baron in her own right.

baronet (ˈbærənɪt, -ˌnɛt) *n.* (in Britain) a commoner who holds the lowest hereditary title of honour, ranking below a baron. Abbrevs.: **Bart.** or **Bt.** [C15: order instituted 1611, from BARON + -ET]

baronetage (ˈbærənɪtɪdʒ) *n.* **1.** the order of baronets; baronets collectively. **2.** the rank of a baronet; baronetcy.

baronetcy (ˈbærənɪtsɪ, -ˌnɛt-) *n., pl.* **-cies.** the rank, position, or patent of a baronet.

barong (bæˈrɒŋ) *n.* a broad-bladed cleaver-like knife used in the Philippines. [from Moro; see PARANG]

baronial (bəˈrəʊnɪəl) *adj.* of, relating to, or befitting a baron or barons.

baron of beef *n.* a cut of beef consisting of a double sirloin joined at the backbone.

barony (ˈbærənɪ) *n., pl.* **-nies. 1. a.** the domain of a baron. **b.** (in Ireland) a division of a county. **c.** (in Scotland) a large estate or manor. **2.** the rank or dignity of a baron. **3.** a sphere of influence dominated by an industrial magnate or other powerful individual.

barophilic (ˌbærəˈfɪlɪk) *adj.* (of bacteria) able to tolerate or growing best in conditions of high atmospheric pressure. —**barophile** (ˈbærəˌfaɪl) *n.*

barophoresis (ˌbærəfəˈriːsɪs) *n. Chem.* the diffusion of suspended particles at a rate dependent on external forces.

baroque (bəˈrɒk, bəˈrəʊk) *n.* (*often cap.*) **1.** a style of architecture and decorative art that flourished throughout Europe from the late 16th to the early 18th century, characterized by extensive ornamentation. **2.** a 17th-century style of music characterized by extensive use of the thorough bass and of ornamentation. **3.** any ornate or heavily ornamented style. *~adj.* **4.** denoting, being in, or relating to the baroque. **5.** (of pearls) irregularly shaped. [C18: from French, from Portuguese *barroco* a rough or imperfectly shaped pearl]

baroreceptor (ˈbærəʊrɪˌseptə) *or* **baroceptor** *n.* a collection of sensory nerve endings, principally in the carotid sinuses and the aortic arch, that monitor blood pressure changes in the body.

baroscope (ˈbærəˌskəʊp) *n.* any instrument for measuring atmospheric pressure, esp. a manometer with one side open to the atmosphere. —**baroscopic** (ˌbærəˈskɒpɪk) *adj.*

barostat (ˈbærəʊˌstæt) *n.* a device for maintaining constant pressure, such as one used in an aircraft cabin.

Barotse (bəˈrɒtsɪ) *n.* **1.** (*pl.* **-se** *or* **-ses**) a member of a Negroid people of central Africa living chiefly in SW Zambia. **2.** the language spoken by this people; Lozi.

barouche (bəˈruːʃ) *n.* a four-wheeled horse-drawn carriage, popular in the 19th century, having a retractable hood over the rear half, seats inside for two couples facing each other, and a driver's seat outside at the front. [C19: from German (dialect) *Barutsche,* from Italian *baroccio,* from Vulgar Latin *birotium* (unattested) vehicle with two wheels, from Late Latin *birotus* two-wheeled, from BI-[1] + *rota* wheel]

barperson (ˈbɑːˌpɜːsᵊn) *n., pl.* **-persons.** a person who serves in a pub: used esp. in advertisements.

barque *or esp. U.S.* **bark** (bɑːk) *n.* **1.** a sailing ship of three or more masts having the foremasts rigged square and the aftermast rigged fore-and-aft. **2.** *Poetic.* any boat, esp. a small sailing vessel. [C15: from Old French, from Old Provençal *barca,* from Late Latin, of unknown origin]

barquentine *or* **barquantine** (ˈbɑːkənˌtiːn) *n.* a sailing ship of three or more masts rigged square on the foremast and fore-and-aft on the others. Usual U.S. and Canadian spelling: **barkentine.** [C17: from BARQUE + (BRIG)ANTINE]

barrack[1] (ˈbærək) *vb.* to house (people, esp. soldiers) in barracks.

barrack[2] (ˈbærək) *vb. Brit., Austral., and N.Z. informal.* **1.** to criticize loudly or shout against (a player, team, speaker, etc.); jeer. **2.** (*intr.*; foll. by *for*) to shout support (for). [C19: from northern Irish: to boast] —ˈ**barracker** *n.* —ˈ**barracking** *n., adj.*

barrack-room lawyer *n.* a person who freely offers opinions, esp. in legal matters, that he is unqualified to give.

barracks (ˈbærəks) *pl. n.* (*sometimes sing.; when pl., sometimes functions as sing.*) **1.** a building or group of buildings used to accommodate military personnel. **2.** any large building used for housing people, esp. temporarily. **3.** a large and bleak building. [C17: from French *baraque,* from Old Catalan *barraca* hut, of uncertain origin]

barracoon (ˌbærəˈkuːn) *n.* (formerly) a temporary place of confinement for slaves or convicts, esp. those awaiting transportation. [C19: from Spanish *barracón,* from *barraca* hut, from Catalan]

barracouta (ˌbærəˈkuːtə) *n.* a large predatory Pacific fish, *Thyrsites atun,* with a protruding lower jaw and strong teeth: family *Gempylidae.* [C17: variant of BARRACUDA]

barracuda (ˌbærəˈkjuːdə) *n., pl.* **-da** *or* **-das.** any predatory marine teleost fish of the mostly tropical family *Sphyraenidae,* esp. *Sphyraena barracuda.* They have an elongated body, strong teeth, and a protruding lower jaw. [C17: from American Spanish, of unknown origin]

barrage (ˈbærɑːʒ) *n.* **1.** *Military.* the firing of artillery to saturate an area, either to protect against an attack or to support an advance. **2.** an overwhelming and continuous delivery of something, as words, questions, or punches. **3.** a construction across a watercourse, esp. one to increase the depth of water to assist navigation or irrigation. **4.** *Fencing.* a heat or series of bouts in a competition. *~vb.* **5.** (*tr.*) to attack or confront with a barrage: *the speaker was barraged with abuse.* [C19: from French, from *barrer* to obstruct; see BAR[1]]

barrage balloon *n.* one of a number of tethered balloons with cables or net suspended from them, used to deter low-flying air attack.

barramunda (ˌbærəˈmʌndə) *n., pl.* **-das** *or* **-da.** the edible Australian lungfish, *Neoceratodus forsteri,* having paddle-like fins and a long body covered with large scales. [from a native Australian language]

barramundi (ˌbærəˈmʌndɪ) *n., pl.* **-dis, -dies,** *or* **-di.** any of several edible Australian fishes, esp. the percoid species *Lates calcarifer* (family Centropomidae) of NE coastal waters or the freshwater species *Scleropages leichardti* (family Osteoglossidae) of Queensland.

barranca (bəˈræŋkə) *or* **barranco** (bəˈræŋkəʊ) *n., pl.* **-cas** *or* **-cos.** *Southwestern U.S.* a ravine or precipice. [C19: from Spanish, of uncertain origin]

barrator (ˈbærətə) *n.* a person guilty of barratry. [C14: from Old French *barateor,* from *barater* to BARTER]

barratry *or* **barretry** (ˈbærətrɪ) *n.* **1.** *Criminal law.* (formerly) the vexatious stirring up of quarrels or bringing of lawsuits. **2.** *Maritime law.* a fraudulent practice committed by the master or crew of a ship to the prejudice of the owner or charterer. **3.** *Scots Law.* the crime committed by a judge in accepting a bribe. **4.** the purchase or sale of public or Church offices. [C15: from Old French *baraterie* deception, from *barater* to BARTER] —ˈ**barratrous** *or* ˈ**barretrous** *adj.* —ˈ**barratrously** *or* ˈ**barretrously** *adv.*

barre *French.* (bar) *n.* a rail at hip height used for ballet practice. [literally: bar]

barré (ˈbæreɪ) *n.* **1.** the act of laying the index finger over some or all of the strings of a guitar, lute, or similar instrument, so that the pitch of each stopped string is simultaneously raised. Compare **capo**[1]. **2.** the playing of chords in this manner. *~vb.* **3.** to execute (chords) in this manner. *~adv.* **4.** by using the barré. [C19: from French, from *barrer* BAR[1]]

barrel (ˈbærəl) *n.* **1.** a cylindrical container usually bulging outwards in the middle and held together by metal hoops; cask. **2.** Also called: **barrelful.** the amount that a barrel can hold. **3.** a unit of capacity used in brewing, equal to 36 Imperial gallons. **4.** a unit of capacity used in the oil and other industries, normally equal to 42 U.S. gallons or 35 Imperial gallons. **5.** a thing or part shaped like a barrel, esp. a tubular part of a machine. **6.** the tube through which the projectile of a firearm is discharged. **7.** *Horology.* the cylindrical drum in a watch or clock that is rotated by the mainspring. **8.** the trunk of a four-legged animal: *the barrel of a horse.* **9.** the quill of a feather. **10.** *Informal.* a large measure; a great deal (esp. in the phrases **barrel of fun, barrel of laughs**). **11. over a barrel.** *Informal.* powerless. **12. scrape the barrel.** *Informal.* to be forced to use one's last and weakest resource. *~vb.* **-rels, -relling, -relled** *or U.S.* **-rels, -reling, -reled. 13.** (*tr.*) to put into a barrel or barrels. **14.** (*intr.*; usually foll. by *along*) *Informal, chiefly U.S. and Canadian.* to travel or move very fast. [C14: from Old French *baril,* perhaps from *barre* BAR[1]]

barrel-chested *adj.* having a large rounded chest.

barrelhouse (ˈbærəlˌhaʊs) *n.* **1.** *U.S.* a cheap and disreputable drinking establishment. **2. a.** a vigorous and unpolished style of jazz for piano, originating in the barrelhouses of New Orleans. **b.** (*as modifier*): *barrelhouse blues.*

barrel organ *n.* **1.** an instrument consisting of a cylinder turned by a handle and having pins on it that interrupt the air flow to certain pipes, thereby playing any of a number of tunes. See also **hurdy-gurdy. 2.** a similar instrument in which the projections on a rotating barrel pluck a set of strings.

barrel roll *n.* **1.** a flight manoeuvre in which an aircraft rolls about its longitudinal axis while following a spiral course in line with the direction of flight. *~vb.* **barrel-roll. 2.** (*intr.*) (of an aircraft) to perform a barrel roll.

barrel vault *n. Architect.* a vault in the form of a half cylinder. Also called: **wagon vault, tunnel vault.**

barren (ˈbærən) *adj.* **1.** incapable of producing offspring, seed, or fruit; sterile: *a barren tree.* **2.** unable to support the growth of crops, etc.; unproductive; bare: *barren land.* **3.** lacking in stimulation or ideas; dull: *a rather barren play.* **4.** not producing worthwhile results; unprofitable: *a barren period in a writer's life.* **5.** (foll. by *of*) totally lacking (in); devoid (of): *his speech was barren of wit.* **6.** (of rock strata) having no fossils. [C13: from Old French *brahain,* of uncertain origin] —ˈ**barrenly** *adv.* —ˈ**barrenness** *n.*

barrens (ˈbærənz) *pl. n.* (*sometimes sing.*) (in North America) a stretch of usually level land that is sparsely vegetated or barren.

barrenwort (ˈbærənˌwɜːt) *n.* a herbaceous European berberidaceous plant, *Epimedium alpinum,* having red-and-yellow star-shaped flowers.

barret (ˈbærɪt) *n.* a small flat cap resembling a biretta. [C19: from French *barrette,* from Italian *berretta* BIRETTA; compare BERET]

barrette (bəˈrɛt) *n.* a clasp or pin for holding women's hair in place. [C20: from French: a little bar, from *barre* BAR[1]]

barricade (ˌbærɪˈkeɪd, ˈbærɪˌkeɪd) *n.* **1.** a barrier for defence, esp. one erected hastily, as during street fighting. *~vb.* (*tr.*) **2.** to erect a barricade across (an entrance, passageway, etc.) or at points of access to (a room, district of a town, etc.): *they barricaded the door.* **3.** (*usually passive*) to obstruct; block: *his mind was barricaded against new ideas.* [C17: from Old French, from *barriquer* to barricade, from *barrique* a barrel, from Spanish *barrica,* from *barril* BARREL] —ˈ**barriˌcader** *n.*

barrier (ˈbærɪə) *n.* **1.** anything serving to obstruct passage or to maintain separation, such as a fence or gate. **2.** anything that prevents or obstructs passage, access, or progress: *a barrier of distrust.* **3.** anything that separates or hinders union: *a language barrier.* **4. a.** an exposed offshore sand bar separated from the shore by a lagoon. **b.** (*as modifier*): *a barrier beach.* **5.** (*sometimes cap.*) that part of the Antarctic icecap extending over the sea. [C14: from Old French *barriere,* from *barre* BAR[1]]

barrier cream *n.* a cream used to protect the skin, esp. the hands, from dirt and from the action of oils or solvents.

barrier-nurse *vb.* (*tr.*) to tend (infectious patients) in isolation, to prevent the spread of infection. —**barrier nursing** *n.*

barrier of ideas *n. Philosophy.* the representations of objects which certain accounts of perception interpose between the objects themselves and our awareness of them, so that, as critics argue, we can never know whether there is in reality anything which resembles our perceptions. See **representationalism** (sense 1).

barrier reef *n.* a long narrow coral reef near and lying parallel to the shore, separated from it by deep water.

barring (ˈbɑːrɪŋ) *prep.* unless (something) occurs; except for: *barring rain, the match will be held tomorrow.*

barrio ('bærɪəʊ; *Spanish* 'barrjo) *n., pl.* **-rios.** **1.** a Spanish-speaking quarter in a town or city, esp. in the U.S. **2.** a Spanish-speaking community. [from Spanish, from Arabic *barrī* of open country, from *barr* open country]

barrister ('bærɪstə) *n.* **1.** Also called: **barrister-at-law.** (in England) a lawyer who has been called to the bar and is qualified to plead in the higher courts. Compare **solicitor.** See also **advocate, counsel.** **2.** (in Canada) a lawyer who pleads in court. **3.** *U.S.* a less common word for **lawyer.** [C16: from BAR[1]]

barroom ('bɑːˌruːm, -ˌrʊm) *n. U.S.* a room or building where alcoholic drinks are served over a counter.

barrow[1] ('bærəʊ) *n.* **1.** See **wheelbarrow, handbarrow.** **2.** Also called: **barrowful.** the amount contained in or on a barrow. **3.** *Chiefly Brit.* a handcart, typically having two wheels and a canvas roof, used esp. by street vendors. **4.** *Northern English dialect.* concern or business (esp. in the phrases **that's not my barrow, that's just my barrow**). **5. into one's barrow.** *Irish and Scot. dialect.* suited to one's interests or desires. [Old English *bearwe;* related to Old Norse *barar* BIER, Old High German *bāra*]

barrow[2] ('bærəʊ) *n.* a heap of earth placed over one or more prehistoric tombs, often surrounded by ditches. **Long barrows** are elongated Neolithic mounds usually covering stone burial chambers; **round barrows** are Bronze Age, covering burials or cremations. [Old English *beorg;* related to Old Norse *bjarg,* Gothic *bairgahei* hill, Old High German *berg* mountain]

barrow[3] ('bærəʊ) *n.* a castrated pig. [Old English *bearg;* related to Old Norse *börgr,* Old High German *barug*]

barrow boy *n. Brit.* a man who sells his wares from a barrow; street vendor.

Barsac ('bɑːsæk; *French* barsak) *n.* a sweet French white wine produced around the town of Barsac in the Gironde.

bar sinister *n.* **1.** (not in heraldic usage) another name for **bend sinister.** **2.** the condition, implication, or stigma of being of illegitimate birth.

Bart. *abbrev. for* Baronet.

bartender ('bɑːˌtɛndə) *n.* another name (esp. U.S. and Canadian) for **barman.**

barter ('bɑːtə) *vb.* **1.** to trade (goods, services, etc.) in exchange for other goods, services, etc., rather than for money: *the refugees bartered for food.* **2.** (*intr.*) to haggle over the terms of such an exchange; bargain. ~*n.* **3.** trade by the exchange of goods. [C15: from Old French *barater* to cheat; perhaps related to Greek *prattein* to do] —**'barterer** *n.*

Barthian ('bɑːtɪən, -θɪən) *adj.* **1.** of or relating to the Swiss theologian Karl Barth (1886–1968) or his ideas. ~*n.* **2.** a person who supports or believes in the ideas of Karl Barth.

Bartholin's glands ('bɑːθəlɪnz) *pl. n. Anatomy.* two small reddish-yellow glands, one on each side of the vaginal orifice, that secrete a mucous lubricating substance during sexual stimulation in females. Compare **Cowper's glands.** [named by Caspar *Bartholin* (1655–1738), Danish anatomist, in honour of his father, Thomas]

bartizan ('bɑːtɪzən, ˌbɑːtɪ'zæn) *n.* a small turret projecting from a wall, parapet, or tower. [C19: variant of *bertisene,* erroneously for *bretising,* from *bretasce* parapet; see BRATTICE] —**bartizaned** ('bɑːtɪzənd, ˌbɑːtɪ'zænd) *adj.*

Bartlett *or* **Bartlett pear** ('bɑːtlɪt) *n.* another name for **Williams pear:** used esp. in the U.S. and generally of tinned pears. [named after Enoch *Bartlett* (1779–1860), of Dorchester, Mass., who marketed it in the U.S.]

barton ('bɑːt[ə]n) *n. Archaic.* a farmyard. [Old English *beretūn,* from *bere* barley + *tūn* stockade; see TOWN]

bartsia ('bɑːtsɪə) *n.* any of several species of semiparasitic scrophulariaceous perennials, including **red bartsia** (*Odontites verna*), a pink-flowered weed of cornfields. [C18: New Latin, named after Johann *Bartsch* (died 1738), German botanist]

barycentre ('bærɪˌsɛntə) *n.* a centre of mass, esp. of the earth-moon system. [C20: from Greek *barus* heavy + CENTRE] —ˌ**bary'centric** *adj.*

barye ('bærɪ) *n.* a unit of pressure in the cgs system equal to one dyne per square centimetre. 1 barye is equivalent to 1 microbar. [C19: from French, from Greek *barus* heavy]

baryon ('bærɪˌɒn) *n.* any of a class of elementary particles that have a mass greater than or equal to that of the proton, participate in strong interactions, and have a spin of ½. Baryons are either nucleons or hyperons. The **baryon number** is the number of baryons in a system minus the number of antibaryons. [C20: *bary-,* from Greek *barus* heavy + -ON] —ˌ**bary'onic** *adj.*

barysphere ('bærɪˌsfɪə) *n.* the central portion of the earth, thought to consist chiefly of iron and nickel. [C20: from Greek *barus* heavy + SPHERE]

baryta (bə'raɪtə) *n.* another name for **barium oxide** or **barium hydroxide.** [C19: New Latin, from Greek *barutēs* weight, from *barus* heavy] —**barytic** (bə'rɪtɪk) *adj.*

barytes (bə'raɪtiːz) *n.* a colourless or white mineral consisting of barium sulphate in rhombic crystalline form, occurring in sedimentary rocks and with sulphide ores: a source of barium. Formula: $BaSO_4$. Also called: **barite** (esp. U.S. and Canadian), **heavy spar.** [C18: from Greek *barus* heavy + *-itēs* -ITE[1]]

baryton ('bærɪˌtəʊn) *n.* a bass viol with sympathetic strings as well as its six main strings. [C18: from French: BARITONE]

barytone[1] ('bærɪˌtəʊn) *n.* a less common spelling of **baritone.**

barytone[2] ('bærɪˌtəʊn) (in ancient Greek) ~*adj.* **1.** having the last syllable unaccented. ~*n.* **2.** a word in which the last syllable is unaccented. ~Compare **oxytone.** [C19: from Greek *barutonos* heavy-sounding, from *barus* heavy + *tonos* TONE]

basal ('beɪs[ə]l) *adj.* **1.** at, of, or constituting a base. **2.** of or constituting a foundation or basis; fundamental; essential. —**'basally** *adv.*

basal anaesthesia *n.* preliminary and incomplete anaesthesia induced to prepare a surgical patient for total anaesthesia with another agent.

basal ganglia *pl. n.* the thalamus together with other closely related masses of grey matter, situated near the base of the brain.

basal metabolic rate *n.* the rate at which heat is produced by the body at rest, 12 to 14 hours after eating, measured in kilocalories per square metre of body surface per hour. Abbrev.: **BMR.**

basal metabolism *n.* the amount of energy required by an individual in the resting state, for such functions as breathing and circulation of the blood. See **basal metabolic rate.**

basalt ('bæsɔːlt) *n.* **1.** a fine-grained dark basic igneous rock consisting of plagioclase feldspar, a pyroxene, and olivine: the most common volcanic rock and usually extrusive. See **flood basalt.** **2.** a form of black unglazed pottery resembling basalt. [C18: from Late Latin *basaltēs,* variant of *basanītēs,* from Greek *basanitēs* touchstone, from *basanos,* of Egyptian origin] —**ba'saltic** *adj.*

basaltware ('bæsɔːltˌwɛə, 'beɪsɔːlt-) *n.* hard fine-grained black stoneware, made in Europe, esp. in England, in the late 18th century.

basanite ('bæsəˌnaɪt) *n.* a black basaltic rock containing plagioclase, augite, olivine, and nepheline, leucite, or analcite, formerly used as a touchstone.

bas bleu *French.* (bɑ blø) *n., pl.* ***bas bleus*** (bɑ blø). a bluestocking; intellectual woman. [C18: from French translation of English BLUESTOCKING]

bascinet (ˌbæsɪ'nɛt, 'bæsɪˌnɛt) *n. Armour.* a variant spelling of **basinet.**

bascule ('bæskjuːl) *n.* **1.** Also called: **balance bridge, counterpoise bridge.** a bridge with a movable section hinged about a horizontal axis and counterbalanced by a weight. Compare **drawbridge.** **2.** a movable roadway forming part of such a bridge: *Tower Bridge has two bascules.* [C17: from French: see-saw, from *bas* low + *cul* rump; see BASE[2], CULET]

base[1] (beɪs) *n.* **1.** the bottom or supporting part of anything. **2.** the fundamental or underlying principle or part, as of an idea, system, or organization; basis. **3. a.** a centre of operations, organization, or supply: *the climbers made a base at 8000 feet.* **b.** (*as modifier*): *base camp.* **4.** a centre from which military activities are coordinated. **5.** anything from which a process, as of measurement, action, or thought, is or may be begun; starting point: *the new discovery became the base for further research.* **6.** the main ingredient of a mixture: *to use rice as a base in cookery.* **7.** a chemical compound that combines with an acid to form a salt and water. A solution of a base in water turns litmus paper blue, produces hydroxyl ions, and has a pH greater than 7. Bases are metal oxides or hydroxides or amines. See also **Lewis base.** **8.** a medium such as oil or water in which the pigment is dispersed in paints, inks, etc.; vehicle. **9.** the inorganic material on which the dye is absorbed in lake pigments; carrier. **10.** *Biology.* **a.** the part of an organ nearest to its point of attachment. **b.** the point of attachment of an organ or part. **11.** the bottommost layer or part of anything. **12.** *Architect.* **a.** the lowest division of a building or structure. **b.** the lower part of a column or pier. **13.** another word for **baseline** (sense 2). **14.** the lower side or face of a geometric construction. **15.** *Maths.* **a.** the number of distinct single-digit numbers in a counting system, and so the number represented as *10* in a place-value system: *the binary system has two digits, 0 and 1, and 10 to base two represents 2.* See **place-value.** **b.** (of a logarithm or exponential) the number whose powers are expressed: *since* $1000 = 10^3$, the logarithm of 1000 to base 10 is 3. **c.** (of a mathematical structure) a substructure from which the given system can be generated. **d.** the initial instance from which a generalization is proven by mathematical induction. **16.** *Logic, maths.* Also called: **base clause.** the initial element of a recursive definition, that defines the first element of the infinite sequence generated thereby. **17.** *Linguistics.* **a.** a root or stem. **b.** See **base component.** **18.** *Electronics.* the region in a transistor between the emitter and collector. **19.** *Photog.* the glass, paper, or cellulose-ester film that supports the sensitized emulsion with which it is coated. **20.** *Heraldry.* the lower part of the shield. **21.** *Jewellery.* the quality factor used in pricing natural pearls. **22.** a starting or finishing point in any of various games. **23.** *Baseball.* any of the four corners of the diamond, which runners have to reach in order to score. **24. get to first base.** *U.S. and Canadian informal.* to accomplish the first stage in a project or a series of objectives. **25. off base.** *U.S. and Canadian informal.* wrong or badly mistaken. ~*vb.* **26.** (*tr.;* foll. by *on* or *upon*) to use as a basis (for); found (on): *your criticisms are based on ignorance.* **27.** (often foll. by *at* or *in*) to station, post, or place (a person or oneself). [C14: from Old French, from Latin *basis* pedestal; see BASIS]

base[2] (beɪs) *adj.* **1.** devoid of honour or morality; ignoble; contemptible. **2.** of inferior quality or value. **3.** debased; alloyed; counterfeit: *base currency.* **4.** *English history.* **a.** (of land tenure) held by villein or other ignoble service. **b.** holding land by villein or other ignoble service. **5.** *Archaic.* born of humble parents; plebeian. **6.** *Archaic.* illegitimate. ~*adj., n.* **7.** *Music.* an obsolete spelling of **bass**[1]. [C14: from Old French *bas,* from Late Latin *bassus* of low height, perhaps from Greek *bassōn* deeper] —'**basely** *adv.* —'**baseness** *n.*
baseball ('beɪsˌbɔːl) *n.* **1.** a team game with nine players on each side, played on a field with four bases connected to form a diamond. The object is to score runs by batting the ball and running round the bases. **2.** the hard rawhide-covered ball used in this game.
baseball cap *n.* a close-fitting thin cap with a deep peak.
baseband ('beɪsˌbænd) *n.* a transmission technique using a narrow range of frequencies that allows only one message to be telecommunicated at a time. See also **broadband.**
baseboard ('beɪsˌbɔːd) *n.* **1.** a board functioning as the base of anything. **2.** the usual U.S. and Canadian word for **skirting board.**
baseborn ('beɪsˌbɔːn) *adj. Archaic.* **1.** born of humble parents. **2.** illegitimate. **3.** mean; contemptible.
baseburner ('beɪsˌbɜːnə) *n. U.S.* a stove into which coal is automatically fed from a hopper above the fire chamber.
base component *n.* the system of rules in a transformational grammar that specify the deep structure of the language.
base hospital *n. Austral.* a hospital serving a large rural area.
baseless ('beɪslɪs) *adj.* not based on fact; unfounded: *a baseless supposition.* —'**baselessly** *adv.* —'**baselessness** *n.*
base level *n.* the lowest level to which a land surface can be eroded by streams, which is, ultimately, sea level.
baseline ('beɪsˌlaɪn) *n.* **1.** *Surveying.* a measured line through a survey area from which triangulations are made. **2.** an imaginary line, standard of value, etc., by which things are measured or compared. **3.** a line at each end of a tennis court that marks the limit of play.
base load *n.* the more or less constant part of the total load on an electrical power-supply system. Compare **peak load.**
baseman ('beɪsmən) *n., pl.* **-men.** *Baseball.* a fielder positioned near a base.
basement ('beɪsmənt) *n.* **1. a.** a partly or wholly underground storey of a building, esp. the one immediately below the main floor. Compare **cellar. b.** (*as modifier*): *a basement flat.* **2.** the foundation or substructure of a wall or building. **3.** *Geology.* a part of the earth's crust formed of hard igneous or metamorphic rock that lies beneath the cover of soft sedimentary rock, sediment, and soil.
base metal *n.* any of certain common metals such as copper, lead, zinc, and tin, as distinct from the precious metals, gold, silver, and platinum.
basenji (bəˈsɛndʒɪ) *n.* a small smooth-haired breed of dog of African origin having a tightly curled tail and an inability to bark. [C20: from a Bantu language]
base pairing *n. Biochem.* the hydrogen bonding that occurs between complementary nitrogenous bases in the two polynucleotide chains of a DNA molecule.
base period *n. Statistics.* a neutral period used as a standard for comparison in constructing an index to express a variable factor: 100 is usually taken as the index number for the variable in the base period.
base rate *n.* **1.** *Brit.* the rate of interest used by individual commercial banks as a basis for their lending rates. **2.** *Brit. informal.* the rate at which the Bank of England lends to the discount houses, which effectively controls the interest rates charged throughout the banking system. **3.** *Statistics.* the average number of times an event occurs divided by the average number of times on which it might occur.
base rate fallacy *n. Statistics.* the tendency, when making judgments of the probability with which an event will occur, to ignore the base rate and to concentrate on other information.
bases[1] ('beɪsiːz) *n.* the plural of **basis.**
bases[2] ('beɪsɪz) *n.* the plural of **base**[1].
base station *n.* a fixed transmitter that forms part of an otherwise mobile radio network.
base unit *n. Physics.* any of the fundamental units in a system of measurement. The base SI units are the metre, kilogram, second, ampere, kelvin, candela, and mole.
bash (bæʃ) *Informal.* ~*vb.* **1.** (*tr.*) to strike violently or crushingly. **2.** (*tr.;* often foll. by *in, down,* etc.) to smash, break, etc., with a crashing blow: *to bash a door down.* **3.** (*intr.;* foll. by *into*) to crash (into); collide (with): *to bash into a lamppost.* **4.** to dent or be dented: *this tin is bashed; this cover won't bash easily.* ~*n.* **5.** a heavy blow, as from a fist. **6.** a dent; indentation. **7.** a party. **8. have a bash.** *Informal.* to make an attempt. ~See also **bash up.** [C17: of uncertain origin]
bashaw (bəˈʃɔː) *n.* **1.** a rare spelling of **pasha. 2.** an important or pompous person. [C16: from Turkish *başa,* from *bas* head, chief]
bashful ('bæʃfʊl) *adj.* **1.** disposed to attempt to avoid notice through shyness or modesty; diffident; timid. **2.** indicating or characterized by shyness or modesty. [C16: from *bash,* short for ABASH + -FUL] —'**bashfully** *adv.* —'**bashfulness** *n.*
bashibazouk (ˌbæʃɪbəˈzuːk) *n.* (in the 19th century) one of a group of irregular Turkish soldiers notorious for their brutality. [C19: from Turkish *başibozuk* irregular soldier, from *bas* head + *bozuk* corrupt]
-bashing *n. and adj. combining form. Informal or slang.* **a.** indicating a malicious attack on members of a group: *queer-bashing; union-bashing.* **b.** indicating any of various other activities: *Bible-bashing; spud-bashing; square-bashing.* —**-basher** *n. combining form.*
Bashkir (bæʃˈkɪə) *n.* **1.** (*pl.* **-kir** *or* **-kirs**) a member of a Mongoloid people of E central Russia, living chiefly in the former Bashkir ASSR. **2.** the language of this people, belonging to the Turkic branch of the Altaic family.
bash up *vb.* (*tr., adv.*) *Brit. slang.* to thrash; beat violently.
basic ('beɪsɪk) *adj.* **1.** of, relating to, or forming a base or basis; fundamental; underlying. **2.** elementary or simple: *a few basic facts.* **3.** excluding additions or extras: *basic pay.* **4.** *Chem.* **a.** of, denoting, or containing a base; alkaline. **b.** (of a salt) containing hydroxyl or oxide groups not all of which have been replaced by an acid radical: *basic lead carbonate,* $2PbCO_3.Pb(OH)_2$. **5.** *Metallurgy.* of, concerned with, or made by a process in which the furnace or converter is made of a basic material, such as magnesium oxide. **6.** (of such igneous rocks as basalt) containing between 52 and 45 per cent silica. **7.** *Military.* primary or initial: *basic training.* ~*n.* **8.** (*usually pl.*) a fundamental principle, fact, etc. —'**basically** *adv.*
BASIC *or* **Basic** ('beɪsɪk) *n.* a computer programming language that uses common English terms. [C20: acronym of *b(eginner's) a(ll-purpose) s(ymbolic) i(nstruction) c(ode)*]
Basic Curriculum *n. Brit. Education.* the National Curriculum plus religious education.
basic education *n.* (in India) education in which all teaching is correlated with the learning of a craft.
basic English *n.* a simplified form of English, proposed by C. K. Ogden and I. A. Richards, containing a vocabulary of approximately 850 of the commonest English words, intended as an international language.
basic industry *n.* an industry which is highly important in a nation's economy.
basicity (beɪˈsɪsɪtɪ) *n. Chem.* **a.** the state of being a base. **b.** the extent to which a substance is basic.
basicranial (ˌbæsɪˈkreɪnɪᵊl) *adj. Anatomy.* of or relating to the base of the skull.
basic rate *n.* the standard or lowest level on a scale of money payable, esp. in taxation.
basic slag *n.* a furnace slag produced in steel-making, containing large amounts of calcium phosphate: used as a fertilizer.
basidiocarp (bæˈsɪdɪəʊˌkɑːp) *n.* the fruiting body of basidiomycetous fungi; the mushroom of agarics.
basidiomycete (bæˌsɪdɪəʊmaɪˈsiːt) *n.* any fungus of the class *Basidiomycetes,* in which the spores are produced in basidia. The group includes puffballs, smuts, and rusts. [C19: from BASIDI(UM) + -MYCETE] —**baˌsidiomyˈcetous** *adj.*
basidiospore (bæˈsɪdɪəʊˌspɔː) *n.* one of the spores, usually four in number, produced in a basidium. —**baˌsidioˈsporous** *adj.*
basidium (bæˈsɪdɪəm) *n., pl.* **-ia** (-ɪə). the structure, produced by basidiomycetous fungi after sexual reproduction, in which spores are formed at the tips of projecting slender stalks. [C19: from New Latin, from Greek *basidion;* see BASIS, -IUM] —**baˈsidial** *adj.*
basifixed ('beɪsɪˌfɪxt) *adj. Botany.* (of an anther) attached to the filament by its base.
basifugal (beɪˈsɪfjʊgᵊl) *adj. Botany.* a less common word for **acropetal.**
basify ('beɪsɪˌfaɪ) *vb.* **-fies, -fying, -fied.** (*tr.*) to make basic.
basil ('bæzᵊl) *n.* **1.** Also called: **sweet basil.** a Eurasian plant, *Ocimum basilicum,* having spikes of small white flowers and aromatic leaves used as herbs for seasoning: family *Labiatae* (labiates). **2.** Also called: **wild basil.** a European plant, *Satureja vulgaris* (or *Clinopodium vulgare*), with dense clusters of small pink or whitish flowers: family *Labiatae.* **3. basil-thyme.** a European plant, *Acinos arvensis,* having clusters of small violet-and-white flowers: family *Labiatae.* [C15: from Old French *basile,* from Late Latin *basilicum,* from Greek *basilikon,* from *basilikos* royal, from *basileus* king]
basilar ('bæsɪlə) *adj. Chiefly anatomy.* of or situated at a base: *basilar artery* (at the base of the skull). Also: **basilary** ('bæsɪlərɪ, -sɪlrɪ). [C16: from New Latin *basilaris,* from Latin *basis* BASE[1]; compare Medieval Latin *bassile* pelvis]
Basilian (bəˈzɪlɪən) *n.* a monk of the Eastern Christian order of St. Basil, founded in Cappadocia in the 4th century A.D.
basilica (bəˈzɪlɪkə) *n.* **1.** a Roman building, used for public administration, having a large rectangular central nave with an aisle on each side and an apse at the end. **2.** a rectangular early Christian or medieval church, usually having a nave with clerestories, two or four aisles, one or more vaulted apses, and a timber roof. **3.** a Roman Catholic church having special ceremonial rights. [C16: from Latin, from Greek *basilikē* hall, from *basilikē oikia* the king's house, from *basileus* king; see BASIL] —**baˈsilican** *or* **baˈsilic** *adj.*
basilic vein (bəˈzɪlɪk) *n.* a large vein situated on the inner side of the arm. [C18: from Latin *basilicus* kingly; see BASIL]

basilisk ('bæzɪˌlɪsk) *n.* **1.** (in classical legend) a serpent that could kill by its breath or glance. **2.** any small arboreal semiaquatic lizard of the genus *Basiliscus* of tropical America: family *Iguanidae* (iguanas). The males have an inflatable head crest, used in display. **3.** a 16th-century medium cannon, usually which is made of brass. [C14: from Latin *basiliscus,* from Greek *basiliskos* royal child, from *basileus* king]

basin ('beɪsᵊn) *n.* **1.** a round container open and wide at the top with sides sloping inwards towards the bottom or base, esp. one in which liquids are mixed or stored. **2.** Also called: **basinful.** the amount a basin will hold. **3.** a washbasin or sink. **4.** any partially enclosed or sheltered area where vessels may be moored or docked. **5.** the catchment area of a particular river and its tributaries or of a lake or sea. **6.** a depression in the earth's surface. **7.** *Geology.* a part of the earth's surface consisting of rock strata that slope down to a common centre. [C13: from Old French *bacin,* from Late Latin *bacchīnon,* from Vulgar Latin *bacca* (unattested) container for water; related to Latin *bāca* berry]

basinet *or* **bascinet** ('bæsɪnɪt, -ˌnɛt) *n.* a close-fitting medieval helmet of light steel usually with a visor. [C14: from Old French *bacinet,* a little basin, from *bacin* BASIN]

basion ('beɪsɪən) *n. Anatomy.* the midpoint on the forward border of the foramen magnum. [C19: from New Latin, from Latin *basis* BASE[1]]

basipetal (beɪ'sɪpɪtᵊl) *adj.* (of leaves and flowers) produced in order from the apex downwards so that the youngest are at the base. Compare **acropetal.**

basis ('beɪsɪs) *n., pl.* **-ses** (-siːz). **1.** something that underlies, supports, or is essential to something else, esp. an abstract idea. **2.** a principle on which something depends or from which something has issued. **3.** *Maths.* (of a Euclidean space) a maximal set of mutually perpendicular vectors, in terms of which all the elements of the space are uniquely expressible, and the number of which is the dimension of the space: *the vectors* **x, y** *and* **z** *form a basis of the 3-dimensional space all members of which can be written as a***x** + *b***y** + *c***z**. [C14: via Latin from Greek: step, from *bainein* to step, go]

bask (bɑːsk) *vb.* (*intr.;* usually foll. by *in*) **1.** to lie in or be exposed to pleasant warmth, esp. that of the sun. **2.** to flourish or feel secure under some benevolent influence or favourable condition. [C14: from Old Norse *bathask* to BATHE]

Baskerville ('bæskəˌvɪl) *n.* a style of type. [C18: named after John *Baskerville* (1706–75), English printer]

basket ('bɑːskɪt) *n.* **1.** a container made of interwoven strips of pliable materials, such as cane, straw, thin wood, or plastic, and often carried by means of a handle or handles. **2.** Also called: **basketful.** the amount a basket will hold. **3.** something resembling such a container in appearance or function, such as the structure suspended from a balloon. **4.** *Basketball.* **a.** an open horizontal metal hoop fixed to the backboard, through which a player must throw the ball to score points. **b.** a point or points scored in this way. **5.** a group or collection of similar of related things: *a basket of currencies.* **6.** *Informal.* a euphemism for **bastard** (senses 2, 3). [C13: probably from Old Northern French *baskot* (unattested), from Latin *bascauda* basketwork holder, of Celtic origin]

basketball ('bɑːskɪtˌbɔːl) *n.* **1.** a game played by two opposing teams of five men (or six women) each, usually on an indoor court. Points are scored by throwing the ball through an elevated horizontal metal hoop. **2.** the inflated ball used in this game.

basket case *n. Slang, chiefly U.S. and Canadian.* **1.** a person who has had both arms and both legs amputated. **2.** someone who is completely incapacitated. **3.** a person who is suffering from extreme nervous strain; nervous wreck.

basket chair *n.* a chair made of wickerwork; a wicker chair.

basket clause *n.* an all-inclusive or comprehensive clause in a contract.

basket hilt *n.* a hilt fitted to a broadsword, with a generally padded basket-shaped guard to protect the hand. —'**basketˌhilted** *adj.*

Basket Maker *n.* a member of an early American Indian people of the southwestern U.S., preceding the Pueblo people, known for skill in basket-making.

basketry ('bɑːskɪtrɪ) *n.* **1.** the art or practice of making baskets. **2.** baskets collectively.

basket-star *n.* any of several echinoderms of the genus *Gorgonocephalus,* in which long slender arms radiate from a central disc: order *Ophiuroidea* (brittle-stars).

basket weave *n.* a weave of two or more yarns together, resembling that of a basket, esp. in wool or linen fabric.

basketwork ('bɑːskɪtˌwɜːk) *n.* another word for **wickerwork.**

basking shark *n.* a very large plankton-eating shark, *Cetorhinus maximus,* often floating at the sea surface: family *Cetorhinidae.* Also called: **sailfish.**

basmati rice (bəz'mætɪ) *n.* a variety of long-grain rice with slender aromatic grains, used for savoury dishes. [from Hindi, literally: aromatic]

Bas Mitzvah (bɑːs 'mɪtsvə) *n.* (*sometimes not caps.*) a variant of **Bat Mitzvah.**

basophil ('beɪsəfɪl) *or* **basophile** *adj. also* **basophilic** (ˌbeɪsə'fɪlɪk). **1.** (of cells or cell contents) easily stained by basic dyes. ~*n.* **2.** a basophil cell, esp. a leucocyte. [C19: from Greek; see BASE[1] + -PHILE]

basophilia (ˌbeɪsə'fɪlɪə) *n.* **1.** an abnormal increase of basophil leucocytes in the blood. **2.** the affinity of a microscope specimen for basic dyes.

Basotho (bə'suːtuː, -'səʊtəʊ) *n., pl.* **-tho** *or* **-thos.** a member of the subgroup of the Sotho people who chiefly inhabit Lesotho. Former name: **Basuto.**

basque (bæsk, bɑːsk) *n.* **1.** a short extension below the waist to the bodice of a woman's jacket, etc. **2.** a tight-fitting bodice for women. [C19: perhaps from BASQUE]

Basque (bæsk, bɑːsk) *n.* **1.** a member of a people of unknown origin living around the W Pyrenees in France and Spain. **2.** the language of this people, of no known relationship with any other language. ~*adj.* **3.** relating to, denoting, or characteristic of this people or their language. [C19: from French, from Latin *Vascō* a Basque]

bas-relief (ˌbɑːrɪ'liːf, ˌbæs-; 'bɑːrɪˌliːf, 'bæs-) *n.* sculpture in low relief, in which the forms project slightly from the background but no part is completely detached from it. Also called (Italian): **basso rilievo.** [C17: from French, from Italian *basso rilievo* low relief; see BASE[2], RELIEF]

bass[1] (beɪs) *n.* **1.** the lowest adult male voice usually having a range from E a 13th below middle C to D a tone above it. **2.** a singer with such a voice. **3. the bass.** the lowest part in a piece of harmony. See also **thorough bass.** **4.** *Informal.* short for **bass guitar, double bass.** **5. a.** the low-frequency component of an electrical audio signal, esp. in a record player or tape recorder. **b.** the knob controlling this on such an instrument. ~*adj.* **6.** relating to or denoting the bass: *bass pitch; the bass part.* **7.** denoting the lowest and largest instrument in a family: *a bass clarinet.* [C15 *bas* BASE[1]; modern spelling influenced by BASSO]

bass[2] (bæs) *n.* **1.** any of various sea perches, esp. *Morone labrax,* a popular game fish with one large spiny dorsal fin separate from a second smaller one. See also **sea bass, stone bass.** **2.** another name for the **European perch** (see **perch**[2] (sense 1)). **3.** any of various predatory North American freshwater percoid fishes, such as *Micropterus salmoides* (**largemouth bass**): family *Centrarchidae* (sunfishes, etc.). See also **black bass, rock bass.** [C15: changed from BASE[2], influenced by Italian *basso* low]

bass[3] (bæs) *n.* **1.** another name for **bast.** **2.** short for **basswood.** **3.** Also called: **fish bass.** a bast fibre bag for holding an angler's catch. [C17: changed from BAST]

bass clef (beɪs) *n.* the clef that establishes F a fifth below middle C on the fourth line of the staff. Symbol: 𝄢 Also called: **F clef.**

bass drum (beɪs) *n.* a large shallow drum of low and indefinite pitch. Also called: **gran cassa.**

basset[1] ('bæsɪt) *n.* a long low smooth-haired breed of hound with short strong legs and long ears. Also called: **basset hound.** [C17: from French, from *basset* short, from *bas* low; see BASE[2]]

basset[2] ('bæsɪt) *vb.* **-sets, -seting, -seted,** *n.* a less common word for **outcrop.** [C17: perhaps from French: low stool, see BASSET[1]]

basset horn *n.* an obsolete woodwind instrument of the clarinet family. [C19: probably from German *Bassetthorn,* from Italian *bassetto,* diminutive of BASSO + HORN]

bass guitar (beɪs) *n.* a guitar that has the same pitch and tuning as a double bass, usually electrically amplified.

bassinet (ˌbæsɪ'nɛt) *n.* a wickerwork or wooden cradle or pram, usually hooded. [C19: from French: little basin, from *bassin* BASIN; associated in folk etymology with French *barcelonnette* a little cradle, from *berceau* cradle]

bassist ('beɪsɪst) *n.* a player of a double bass, esp. in a jazz band.

basso ('bæsəʊ) *n., pl.* **-sos** *or* **-si** (-sɪ). (esp. in operatic or solo singing) a singer with a bass voice. [C19: from Italian, from Late Latin *bassus* low; see BASE[2]]

basso continuo *n.* another term for **thorough bass.** Often shortened to **continuo.** [Italian, literally: continuous bass]

bassoon (bə'suːn) *n.* **1.** a woodwind instrument, the tenor of the oboe family. Range: about three and a half octaves upwards from the B flat below the bass staff. **2.** an orchestral musician who plays the bassoon. [C18: from French *basson,* from Italian *bassone,* from *basso* deep; see BASE[2]] —**bas'soonist** *n.*

basso profundo (prəʊ'fʌndəʊ; *Italian* pro'fundo) *n., pl.* **-dos.** (esp. in operatic solo singing) a singer with a very deep bass voice. [Italian, literally: deep bass]

basso rilievo (*Italian* 'basso ri'ljevo) *n., pl.* **-vos.** Italian name for **bas-relief.**

bass response (beɪs) *n.* the response of an audio reproduction system or component to low frequencies.

bass viol (beɪs) *n.* **1.** another name for **viola da gamba.** **2.** *U.S.* a less common name for **double bass** (sense 1).

basswood ('bæsˌwʊd) *n.* **1.** any of several North American linden trees, esp. *Tilia americana.* Sometimes shortened to **bass.** **2.** the soft light-coloured wood of any of these trees, used for furniture. [C19: from BASS[3]; see BAST]

bast (bæst) *n.* **1.** *Botany.* another name for **phloem.** **2.** fibrous material obtained from the phloem of jute, hemp, flax, lime, etc., used for making rope, matting, etc. ~Also called: **bass.** [Old English *bæst;* related to Old Norse, Middle High German *bast*]

bastard ('bɑːstəd, 'bæs-) *n.* **1.** a person born of unmarried parents; an illegitimate baby, child, or adult. **2.** *Informal, offensive.* an obnoxious or despicable person. **3.** *Informal, often humorous or affectionate.* a person, esp. a man: *lucky bastard.* **4.** *Informal.*

something extremely difficult or unpleasant: *that job is a real bastard.* **5.** something irregular, abnormal, or inferior. **6.** a hybrid, esp. an accidental or inferior one. ~*adj.* (*prenominal*) **7.** illegitimate by birth. **8.** irregular, abnormal, or inferior in shape, size, or appearance. **9.** resembling a specified thing, but not actually being such: *a bastard cedar.* **10.** counterfeit; spurious. [C13: from Old French *bastart,* perhaps from *bast* in the phrase *fils de bast* son of the packsaddle (that is, of an unlawful and not the marriage bed), from Medieval Latin *bastum* packsaddle, of uncertain origin] —'**bastardly** *adj.*

bastard cut *adj. Mechanical engineering.* (of a file) having medium teeth; intermediate between a coarse cut and a fine cut.

bastardization *or* **bastardisation** (ˌbɑːstədaɪˈzeɪʃən, ˌbæs-) *n.* **1.** the act of bastardizing. **2.** *Austral.* **a.** an initiation ceremony in a school or military unit, esp. one involving brutality. **b.** brutality or bullying.

bastardize *or* **bastardise** (ˈbɑːstəˌdaɪz, ˈbæs-) *vb.* (*tr.*) **1.** to debase; corrupt. **2.** to declare illegitimate.

bastard measles *n. Pathol.* an informal name for **rubella.**

bastardry (ˈbɑːstədrɪ, ˈbæs-) *n. Chiefly Austral.* malicious or cruel behaviour.

bastard title *n.* another name for **half-title** (of a book).

bastard wing *n.* a tuft of feathers attached to the first digit of a bird, distinct from the wing feathers attached to the other digits and the ulna. Also called: **alula.**

bastardy (ˈbɑːstədɪ, ˈbæs-) *n.* the condition of being a bastard; illegitimacy.

baste[1] (beɪst) *vb.* (*tr.*) to sew with loose temporary stitches. [C14: from Old French *bastir* to build, of Germanic origin; compare Old High German *besten* to sew with BAST]

baste[2] (beɪst) *vb.* to moisten (meat) during cooking with hot fat and the juices produced. [C15: of uncertain origin]

baste[3] (beɪst) *vb.* (*tr.*) to beat thoroughly; thrash. [C16: probably from Old Norse *beysta*]

basti, bustee, *or* **busti** (ˈbʌstɪ) *n.* (in India) a slum inhabited by poor people. [Urdu: settlement]

Bastille Day (bæˈstiːl; *French* bastij) *n.* (in France) an annual holiday on July 14, commemorating the fall of the Bastille prison in 1789, at the beginning of the French Revolution.

bastinado (ˌbæstɪˈneɪdəʊ) *n., pl.* **-does. 1.** punishment or torture in which the soles of the feet are beaten with a stick. **2.** a blow or beating with a stick. **3.** a stick; cudgel. ~*vb.* **-does, -doing, -doed.** (*tr.*) **4.** to beat (a person) on the soles of the feet. [C16: from Spanish *bastonada,* from *baston* stick, from Late Latin *bastum;* see BATON]

basting (ˈbeɪstɪŋ) *n.* **1.** loose temporary stitches; tacking. **2.** sewing with such stitches.

bastion (ˈbæstɪən) *n.* **1.** a projecting work in a fortification designed to permit fire to the flanks along the face of the wall. **2.** any fortified place. **3.** a thing or person regarded as upholding or defending an attitude, principle, etc.: *the last bastion of opposition.* [C16: from French, from earlier *bastillon* bastion, from *bastile* fortress, from Old Provençal *bastir* to build]

bastnaesite *or* **bastnasite** (ˈbæstnəˌsaɪt) *n.* a rare yellow to reddish-brown mineral consisting of a carbonate of fluorine and several lanthanide metals. It occurs in association with zinc and is a source of the lanthanides. Formula: $LaFCO_3$. [C19: from Swedish *bastnäsit,* after *Bastnäs,* Sweden, where it was found]

Basuto (bəˈsuːtəʊ) *n., pl.* **-tos** *or* **-to.** a former name for **Sotho** (senses 3, 4).

BASW (ˈbæzwə) *n.* (in Britain) *acronym for* British Association of Social Workers.

bat[1] (bæt) *n.* **1.** any of various types of club with a handle, used to hit the ball in certain sports, such as cricket, baseball, or table tennis. **2.** a flat round club with a short handle, resembling a table-tennis bat, used by a man on the ground to guide the pilot of an aircraft when taxiing. **3.** *Cricket.* short for **batsman. 4.** any stout stick, esp. a wooden one. **5.** *Informal.* a blow from such a stick. **6.** *Austral.* a small board used for tossing the coins in the game of two-up. **7.** *U.S. and Canadian slang.* a drinking spree; binge. **8.** *Slang.* speed; rate; pace: *they went at a fair bat.* **9.** another word for **batting** (sense 1). **10. carry one's bat.** *Cricket.* (of a batsman) to reach the end of an innings without being dismissed. **11. off one's own bat. a.** of one's own accord; without being prompted by someone else. **b.** by one's own unaided efforts. **12. (right) off the bat.** *U.S. and Canadian informal.* immediately; without hesitation. ~*vb.* **bats, batting, batted. 13.** (*tr.*) to strike with or as if with a bat. **14.** (*intr.*) *Cricket, etc.* (of a player or a team) to take a turn at batting. ~See also **bat around.** [Old English *batt* club, probably of Celtic origin; compare Gaelic *bat,* Russian *bat*]

bat[2] (bæt) *n.* **1.** any placental mammal of the order *Chiroptera,* being a nocturnal mouselike animal flying with a pair of membranous wings (patagia). The group is divided into the *Megachiroptera* (**fruit bats**) and *Microchiroptera* (**insectivorous bats**). **2. blind as a bat.** having extremely poor eyesight. **3. have bats in the** (*or* **one's**) **belfry.** *Informal.* to be mad or eccentric; have strange ideas. **4. like a bat out of hell.** *Slang.* very quickly. [C14 *bakke,* probably of Scandinavian origin; compare Old Norse *ledhrblaka* leather-flapper, Swedish dialect *natt-batta* night bat] —ˈ**batlike** *adj.*

bat[3] (bæt) *vb.* **bats, batting, batted.** (*tr.*) **1.** to wink or flutter (one's eyelids). **2. not bat an eye** (*or* **eyelid**). *Informal.* to show no surprise or concern. [C17: probably a variant of BATE[2]]

bat around *vb.* **1.** (*tr., adv.*) *U.S. and Canadian slang.* to discuss (an idea, proposition, etc.) informally. **2.** (*intr.*) Also: **bat along.** *Dialect, U.S. and Canadian slang.* to wander or move about.

batata (bəˈtɑːtə) *n.* another name for **sweet potato.** [C16: from Spanish, from Taino]

batch[1] (bætʃ) *n.* **1.** a group or set of usually similar objects or people, esp. if sent off, handled, or arriving at the same time. **2.** the bread, cakes, etc., produced at one baking. **3.** the amount of a material needed for an operation. **4.** Also called: **batch loaf.** a tall loaf having a close texture and a thick crust on the top and bottom, baked as part of a batch: the sides of each loaf are greased so that they will pull apart after baking to have pale crumby sides; made esp. in Scotland and Ireland. Compare **pan loaf.** ~*vb.* (*tr.*) **5.** to group (items) for efficient processing. **6.** to handle by batch processing. [C15 *bache;* related to Old English *bacan* to BAKE; compare Old English *gebæc* batch, German *Gebäck*]

batch[2] *or* **bach** (bætʃ) *vb.* (*intr.*) *Austral. and N.Z. informal.* (of a man) to do his own cooking and housekeeping.

Bat Chayil (bɑːt ˈxajil) *n.* (*sometimes not caps.*) *Judaism.* **1.** (in some congregations) a ceremony of confirmation for a girl of at least Bat Mitzvah age. **2.** the girl herself. ~Also: **Bat Hayil.** [from Hebrew, literally: daughter of valour]

batch processing *n.* a system by which the computer programs of a number of individual users are submitted to the computer as a single batch. Compare **time sharing** (sense 2).

bate[1] (beɪt) *vb.* **1.** another word for **abate. 2. with bated breath.** holding one's breath in suspense or fear.

bate[2] (beɪt) *vb.* (*intr.*) (of hawks) to jump violently from a perch or the falconer's fist, often hanging from the leash while struggling to escape. [C13: from Old French *batre* to beat, from Latin *battuere;* related to BAT[1]]

bate[3] (beɪt) *vb.* (*tr.*) **1.** to soak (skin or hides) in a special solution to soften them and remove chemicals used in previous treatments. ~*n.* **2.** the solution used. [Old English *bǣtan* to BAIT[1]]

bate[4] (beɪt) *n. Brit. slang.* a bad temper or rage. [C19: from BAIT[1], alluding to the mood of a person who is being baited]

bateau (bæˈtəʊ; *French* bato) *n., pl.* **-teaux** (-təʊz; *French* -to). a light flat-bottomed boat used on rivers in Canada and the northern U.S. [C18: from French: boat, from Old French *batel,* from Old English *bāt;* see BOAT]

bateleur eagle (ˈbætələː) *n.* an African crested bird of prey, *Terathopius ecaudatus,* with a short tail and long wings: subfamily *Circaetinae,* family *Accipitridae* (hawks, etc.). [C19: from French *bateleur* juggler]

Batesian mimicry (ˈbeɪtsɪən) *n. Zoology.* mimicry in which a harmless species is protected from predators by means of its resemblance to a harmful or inedible species. [C19: named after H. W. *Bates* (1825–92), British naturalist and explorer]

batfish (ˈbætˌfɪʃ) *n., pl.* **-fish** *or* **-fishes.** any angler of the family *Ogcocephalidae,* having a flattened scaleless body and moving on the sea floor by means of fleshy pectoral and pelvic fins.

batfowl (ˈbætˌfaʊl) *vb.* (*intr.*) to catch birds by temporarily blinding them with light. —ˈ**batˌfowler** *n.*

bath[1] (bɑːθ) *n., pl.* **baths** (bɑːðz). **1.** a large container, esp. one made of enamelled iron or plastic, used for washing or medically treating the body. Related adj.: **balneal. 2.** the act or an instance of washing in such a container. **3.** the amount of liquid contained in a bath. **4. run a bath.** to turn on the taps to fill a bath with water for bathing oneself. **5.** (*usually pl.*) a place having baths or a swimming pool for public use. **6. a.** a vessel in which something is immersed to maintain it at a constant temperature, to process it photographically, electrolytically, etc., or to lubricate it. **b.** the liquid used in such a vessel. ~*vb.* **7.** *Brit.* to wash in a bath. [Old English *bæth;* compare Old High German *bad,* Old Norse *bath;* related to Swedish *basa* to clean with warm water, Old High German *bāen* to warm]

bath[2] (bæθ) *n.* an ancient Hebrew unit of liquid measure equal to about 8.3 Imperial gallons or 10 U.S. gallons. [Hebrew]

Ba'thist (ˈbɑːθɪst) *or* **Ba'athist** *n.* a member of an Arab Socialist party, esp. in Iraq and Syria, that attempts to combine Marxism with pan-Islamic nationalism. [C20: from Arabic *Ba'th* resurgence] —ˈ**Ba'thism** *n.*

Bat Hayil (bɑːt ˈxajil) *n.* a variant spelling of **Bat Chayil.**

bath bun *n. Brit.* a sweet bun containing spices and dried fruit. [C19: from *Bath,* the city in SW England where it was originally made]

Bath chair *n.* a wheelchair for invalids, often with a hood.

Bath chap *n.* the lower part of the cheek of a pig, cooked and eaten, usually cold.

bath cube *n.* a cube of soluble scented material for use in a bath.

bathe (beɪð) *vb.* **1.** (*intr.*) to swim or paddle in a body of open water or a river, esp. for pleasure. **2.** (*tr.*) to apply liquid to (skin, a wound, etc.) in order to cleanse or soothe. **3.** to immerse or be immersed in a liquid: *to bathe machine parts in oil.* **4.** *Chiefly U.S. and Canadian.* to wash in a bath. **5.** (*tr.; often passive*) to suffuse: *her face was bathed with radiance.* **6.** (*tr.*) (of water, the sea, etc.) to lap; wash: *waves bathed the shore.* ~*n.* **7.** *Brit.* a swim or paddle in a body of open water or a river. [Old English

bathian; related to Old Norse *batha,* Old High German *badōn*] —'**bather** *n.*
bathers ('beɪðəz) *pl. n. Austral.* a swimming costume.
bathetic (bə'θɛtɪk) *adj.* containing or displaying bathos.
bathhouse ('bɑːθˌhaʊs) *n.* a building containing baths, esp. for public use.
bathing beauty ('beɪðɪŋ) *n.* an attractive girl in a swimming costume. Also called (old-fashioned): **bathing belle.**
bathing cap ('beɪðɪŋ) *n.* a tight rubber cap worn by a swimmer to keep the hair dry.
bathing costume ('beɪðɪŋ) *n.* another name for **swimming costume.**
bathing machine ('beɪðɪŋ) *n.* a small hut, on wheels so that it could be pulled to the sea, used in the 18th and 19th centuries for bathers to change their clothes.
bathing suit ('beɪðɪŋ) *n.* **1.** a garment worn for bathing, esp. an old-fashioned one that covers much of the body. **2.** another name for **swimming costume.**
batho- *combining form.* a variant of **bathy-.**
bathochromic (ˌbæθə'krəʊmɪk) *adj. Chem.* denoting or relating to a shift to a longer wavelength in the absorption spectrum of a compound. —'**bathoˌchrome** *n.*
batholith ('bæθəlɪθ) *or* **batholite** ('bæθəˌlaɪt) *n.* a very large irregular-shaped mass of igneous rock, esp. granite, formed from an intrusion of magma at great depth, esp. one exposed after erosion of less resistant overlying rocks. —ˌ**batho'lithic** *or* ˌ**batho'litic** *adj.*
Bath Oliver *n. Brit.* a kind of unsweetened biscuit. [C19: named after William *Oliver* (1695–1764), a physician at Bath]
bathometer (bə'θɒmɪtə) *n.* an instrument for measuring the depth of water. —**bathometric** (ˌbæθə'mɛtrɪk) *adj.* —ˌ**batho'metrically** *adv.* —**bathometry** (bə'θɒmɪtrɪ) *n.*
Bathonian (bə'θəʊnɪən) *adj.* **1.** of or relating to Bath. **2.** *Geology.* of or denoting a stage of the Jurassic system in NW Europe. ~*n.* **3.** a native or resident of Bath. **4.** the Bathonian period or rock system.
bathophilous (bæ'θɒfɪləs) *adj.* (of an organism) living in very deep water.
bathos ('beɪθɒs) *n.* **1.** a sudden ludicrous descent from exalted to ordinary matters or style in speech or writing. **2.** insincere or excessive pathos. **3.** triteness; flatness. **4.** the lowest point; nadir. [C18: from Greek: depth, from *bathus* deep]
bathrobe ('bɑːθˌrəʊb) *n.* **1.** a loose-fitting garment of towelling, for wear before or after a bath or swimming. **2.** *U.S. and Canadian.* a dressing gown.
bathroom ('bɑːθˌruːm, -ˌrʊm) *n.* **1.** a room containing a bath or shower and usually a washbasin and lavatory. **2.** *U.S. and Canadian.* another name for **lavatory.**
bath salts *pl. n.* soluble scented salts for use in a bath.
Bath stone *n. Brit.* a kind of limestone used as a building material, esp. at Bath in England.
bathtub ('bɑːθˌtʌb) *n.* a bath, esp. one not permanently fixed.
Bathurst burr ('bæθəst) *n.* an Australian plant, *Xanthium spinosum,* having numerous hooked burrs that became entangled in sheep's wool. [C19: from the *Bathurst* region of New South Wales]
bathy- *or* **batho-** *combining form.* indicating depth: *bathysphere; bathometer.* [from Greek *bathus* deep]
bathyal ('bæθɪəl) *adj.* denoting or relating to an ocean depth of between 200 and 2000 metres (about 100 and 1000 fathoms), corresponding to the continental slope.
bathylimnetic (ˌbæθɪlɪm'nɛtɪk) *adj.* (of an organism) living in the depths of lakes and marshes.
bathymetry (bə'θɪmɪtrɪ) *n.* measurement of the depth of an ocean or other large body of water. —**bathymetric** (ˌbæθɪ'mɛtrɪk) *adj.* —ˌ**bathy'metrically** *adv.*
bathypelagic (ˌbæθɪpə'lædʒɪk) *adj.* of, relating to, or inhabiting the lower depths of the ocean between approximately 1000 and 4000 metres.
bathyscaph ('bæθɪˌskæf), **bathyscaphe** ('bæθɪˌskeɪf, -ˌskæf), *or* **bathyscape** *n.* a submersible vessel having a flotation compartment with an observation capsule underneath, capable of reaching ocean depths of over 10 000 metres (about 5000 fathoms). [C20: from BATHY- + *-scaph,* from Greek *skaphē* light boat]
bathysphere ('bæθɪˌsfɪə) *n.* a strong steel deep-sea diving sphere, lowered by cable.
batik *or* **battik** ('bætɪk) *n.* **a.** a process of printing fabric in which parts not to be dyed are covered by wax. **b.** fabric printed in this way. **c.** (*as modifier*): *a batik shirt.* [C19: via Malay from Javanese: painted]
batiste (bæ'tiːst) *n.* a fine plain-weave cotton fabric: used esp. for shirts and dresses. [C17: from French, from Old French *toile de baptiste,* probably after *Baptiste* of Cambrai, 13th-century French weaver, its reputed inventor]
batman ('bætmən) *n., pl.* **-men.** an officer's personal servant in any of the armed forces. [C18: from Old French *bat, bast,* from Medieval Latin *bastum* packsaddle]
Bat Mitzvah (bɑːt 'mɪtsvə) (*sometimes not caps.*) ~*adj.* **1.** (of a Jewish girl) having attained religious majority at the age of twelve. ~*n.* **2.** the date of, or, in some congregations, a ceremony marking, this event. **3.** the girl herself on that day. ~Also called: **Bas Mitzvah.** [from Hebrew, literally: daughter of the commandment]
baton ('bætən, -tɒn) *n.* **1.** a thin stick used by the conductor of an orchestra, choir, etc., to indicate rhythm or expression. **2. a.** a short stick carried for use as a weapon, as by a policeman; truncheon. **b.** (*as modifier*): *a baton charge.* **3.** *Athletics.* a short bar carried by a competitor in a relay race and transferred to the next runner at the end of each stage. **4.** a long stick with a knob on one end, carried, twirled, and thrown up and down by a drum major or drum majorette, esp. at the head of a parade. **5.** a staff or club carried by an official as a symbol of authority. **6.** *Heraldry.* a single narrow diagonal line superimposed on all other charges, esp. one curtailed at each end, signifying a bastard line. [C16: from French *bâton,* from Late Latin *bastum* rod, probably ultimately from Greek *bastazein* to lift up, carry]
bâton de commandement *French.* (bɑtɔ̃ də kɔmɑ̃dmɑ̃) *n.* an antler object found in Upper Palaeolithic sites from the Aurignacian period onwards, consisting of a rod, often ornately decorated, with a hole through the thicker end. [literally: baton of command, although the object was probably actually used in making shafts for arrows and spears]
baton round *n.* the official name for **plastic bullet.**
batrachian (bə'treɪkɪən) *n.* **1.** any amphibian, esp. a frog or toad. ~*adj.* **2.** of or relating to the frogs and toads. [C19: from New Latin *Batrachia,* from Greek *batrakhos* frog]
bats (bæts) *adj. Informal.* crazy; very eccentric. [from BATS-IN-THE-BELFRY (sense 2)]
bats-in-the-belfry *n.* (*functioning as sing.*) **1.** a hairy Eurasian campanulaceous plant, *Campanula trachelium,* with bell-shaped blue-purple flowers. ~*adj.* **2.** *Slang.* mad; demented.
batsman ('bætsmən) *n., pl.* **-men.** **1.** *Cricket, etc.* **a.** a person who bats or whose turn it is to bat. **b.** a player who specializes in batting. **2.** a person on the ground who uses bats to guide the pilot of an aircraft when taxiing. —'**batsmanˌship** *n.*
batt (bæt) *n.* **1.** *Textiles.* another word for **batting** (sense 1). **2.** *Austral. and N.Z.* a slab-shaped piece of insulating material used in building houses.
battalion (bə'tæljən) *n.* **1.** a military unit comprised of three or more companies or formations of similar size. **2.** (*usually pl.*) any large array. [C16: from French *bataillon,* from Old Italian *battaglione,* from *battaglia* company of soldiers, BATTLE]
battels ('bætᵊlz) *pl. n.* (at Oxford University) the account of a member of a college for board, provisions, and other college expenses. [C16: perhaps from obsolete *battle* to feed, fatten, of uncertain origin]
battement (*French* batmɑ̃) *n. Ballet.* extension of one leg forwards, sideways, or backwards, either once or repeatedly. [C19: French, literally: beating]
batten[1] ('bætᵊn) *n.* **1.** a sawn strip of wood used in building to cover joints, provide a fixing for tiles or slates, support lathing, etc. **2.** a long narrow board used for flooring. **3.** a narrow flat length of wood or plastic inserted in pockets of a sail to give it proper shape. **4.** a lath used for holding a tarpaulin along the side of a raised hatch on a ship. **5.** *Theatre.* **a.** a row of lights. **b.** the strip or bar supporting them. **6.** Also called: **dropper.** *N.Z.* an upright part of a fence made of wood or other material, designed to keep wires at equal distances apart. ~*vb.* **7.** (*tr.*) to furnish or strengthen with battens. **8. batten down the hatches. a.** to use battens in nailing a tarpaulin over a hatch on a ship to make it secure. **b.** to prepare for action, a crisis, etc. [C15: from French *bâton* stick; see BATON] —'**battening** *n.*
batten[2] ('bætᵊn) *vb.* (*intr.*) (usually foll. by *on*) to thrive, esp. at the expense of someone else: *to batten on the needy.* [C16: probably from Old Norse *batna* to improve; related to Old Norse *betr* BETTER, Old High German *bazzen* to get better]
Battenburg ('bætᵊnˌbɜːg) *n.* an oblong sponge cake divided longitudinally into four square sections, two coloured pink and two yellow, with an outer coating of marzipan. [perhaps named after *Battenberg,* a village in Prussia]
batten plate *n.* (in structural design) a horizontal rectangular plate that is used to connect pairs of steel sections by being riveted or welded across them to form a composite section.
batter[1] ('bætə) *vb.* **1.** to hit (someone or something) repeatedly using heavy blows, as with a club or other heavy instrument; beat heavily. **2.** (*tr.; often passive*) to damage or injure, as by blows, heavy wear, etc. **3.** (*tr.*) *Social welfare.* to subject (a person, esp. a close relative living in the same house) to oppressive physical violence, esp. persistently and intermittently. **4.** (*tr.*) to subject (a person, opinion, or theory) to harsh criticism; attack. ~*n.* **5.** printing type or a printing plate that is damaged or worn. **6.** the defective impression produced by such type or such a plate. [C14 *bateren,* probably from *batten* to BAT[1]]
batter[2] ('bætə) *n.* a mixture of flour, eggs, and milk, used to make cakes, pancakes, etc., and to coat certain foods before frying. [C15 *bater,* probably from *bateren* to BATTER[1]]
batter[3] ('bætə) *n. Baseball, etc.* a player who bats.
batter[4] ('bætə) *n.* **1.** the slope of the face of a wall that recedes gradually backwards and upwards. ~*vb.* **2.** (*intr.*) to have such a slope. [C16 (vb.: to incline): of uncertain origin]
batter[5] ('bætə) *n.* a spree or debauch. [C19: of unknown origin]
batterer ('bætərə) *n.* **a.** a person who batters someone. **b.** (*in combination*): *baby-batterer; wife-batterer.*
batterie de cuisine *French.* (batri də kɥizin) *n.* cooking utensils collectively; pots and pans, etc. [C18: literally: battery of kitchen]

battering ('bætərɪŋ) *n.* **a.** the act or practice of battering someone. **b.** *(in combination): baby-battering; granny-battering.*

battering ram *n.* (esp. formerly) a large beam used to break down the walls or doors of fortifications.

battery ('bætərɪ) *n., pl.* **-teries. 1. a.** two or more primary cells connected together, usually in series, to provide a source of electric current. **b.** short for **dry battery. 2.** another name for **accumulator** (sense 1). **3.** a number of similar things occurring together: *a battery of questions.* **4.** *Criminal law.* unlawful beating or wounding of a person or mere touching in a hostile or offensive manner. See also **assault and battery. 5.** a fortified structure on which artillery is mounted. **6.** a group of guns, missile launchers, searchlights, or torpedo tubes of similar type or size operated as a single entity. **7.** a small tactical unit of artillery usually consisting of two or more troops, each of two, three or four guns. **8.** *Chiefly Brit.* **a.** a large group of cages for intensive rearing of poultry. **b.** *(as modifier): battery hens.* **9.** *Psychol.* a series of tests. **10.** *Chess.* two men of the same colour placed so that one can unmask an attack by the other by moving. **11.** the percussion section in an orchestra. **12.** *Baseball.* the pitcher and the catcher considered together. [C16: from Old French *batterie* beating, from *battre* to beat, from Latin *battuere*]

battik ('bætɪk) *n.* a variant spelling of **batik.**

batting ('bætɪŋ) *n.* **1.** Also called: **batt.** cotton or woollen wadding used in quilts, mattresses, etc. **2.** the action of a person or team that hits with a bat, esp. in cricket or baseball.

battle ('bætᵊl) *n.* **1.** a fight between large armed forces; military or naval engagement; combat. **2.** conflict; contention; struggle: *his battle for recognition.* **3. do, give,** *or* **join battle.** to start fighting. *~vb.* **4.** *(intr.;* often foll. by *against, for,* or *with)* to fight in or as if in military combat; contend. **5.** to struggle in order to achieve something or arrive somewhere: *he battled through the crowd.* **6.** *(intr.) Austral.* to scrape a living, esp. by doing odd jobs. [C13: from Old French *bataile,* from Late Latin *battālia* exercises performed by soldiers, from *battuere* to beat] —'**battler** *n.*

battle-axe *n.* **1.** (formerly) a large broad-headed axe. **2.** *Informal.* an argumentative domineering woman.

battle-axe block *n. Austral.* a block of land behind another, with access from the street through a narrow drive.

battle cruiser *n.* a warship of battleship size but with lighter armour and fewer guns and capable of high speed.

battle cry *n.* **1.** a shout uttered by soldiers going into battle. **2.** a slogan used to rally the supporters of a campaign, movement, etc.

battledore ('bætᵊlˌdɔː) *n.* **1.** Also called: **battledore and shuttlecock.** an ancient racket game. **2.** a light racket, smaller than a tennis racket, used for striking the shuttlecock in this game. **3.** (formerly) a wooden utensil used for beating clothes, in baking, etc. *~vb.* **4.** *Rare.* to hurl or volley (something) back and forth. [C15 *batyldoure,* perhaps from Old Provençal *batedor* a beater, from Old French *battre* to beat, BATTER[1]]

battledress ('bætᵊlˌdrɛs) *n.* the ordinary uniform of a soldier, consisting of tunic and trousers.

battle fatigue *n. Psychol.* a type of mental disorder, characterized by anxiety, depression, and loss of motivation, caused by the stress of active warfare. Also called: **combat fatigue.** See also **shell shock.**

battlefield ('bætᵊlˌfiːld) *or* **battleground** ('bætᵊlˌgraʊnd) *n.* the place where a battle is fought; an area of conflict.

battlement ('bætᵊlmənt) *n.* a parapet or wall with indentations or embrasures, originally for shooting through. [C14: from Old French *batailles,* plural of *bataille* BATTLE] —'**battlemented** *adj.*

battlepiece ('bætᵊlˌpiːs) *n.* a painting, relief, mosaic, etc., depicting a battle, usually commemorating an actual event.

battle royal *n.* **1.** a fight, esp. with fists or cudgels, involving more than two combatants; melee. **2.** a long violent argument.

battleship ('bætᵊlˌʃɪp) *n.* **1.** a heavily armoured warship of the largest type having many large-calibre guns. **2.** (formerly) a warship of sufficient size and armament to take her place in the line of battle; ship of the line.

battue (bæ'tuː, -'tjuː; *French* baty) *n.* **1.** the beating of woodland or cover to force game to flee in the direction of hunters. **2. a.** an organized shooting party using this method. **b.** the game disturbed or shot by this method. **3.** indiscriminate slaughter, as of a defenceless crowd. [C19: from French, feminine of *battu* beaten, from *battre* to beat, from Latin *battuere*]

batty ('bætɪ) *adj.* **-tier, -tiest.** *Slang.* **1.** insane; crazy. **2.** odd; eccentric. [C20: from BAT[2]; compare the phrase *have bats in the belfry*]

batwing ('bætˌwɪŋ) *adj.* shaped like the wings of a bat, as a black tie, collar, etc.

batwing sleeve *n.* a sleeve of a garment with a deep armhole and a tight wrist.

batwoman ('bætwʊmən) *n., pl.* **-women.** a female servant in any of the armed forces.

bauble ('bɔːbᵊl) *n.* **1.** a showy toy or trinket of little value; trifle. **2.** (formerly) a mock staff of office carried by a court jester. [C14: from Old French *baubel* plaything, of obscure origin]

bauchle ('bɒxᵊl) *n. Scot.* **1.** an old worn shoe. **2.** a worthless or clumsy person. **3.** a useless object. **4.** a trout-fisher's term for a **perch**[2]. [C18: of unknown origin]

baud (bɔːd) *n.* a unit used to measure the speed of electronic code transmissions, equal to one unit interval per second. [C20: named after J. M. E. *Baudot* (1845–1903), French inventor]

baudekin *or* **baudikin** ('bɔːdɪkɪn) *n. Archaic.* other words for **baldachin** (sense 1).

Bauhaus ('baʊˌhaʊs) *n.* **a.** a German school of architecture and applied arts (1919–33) founded on experimental principles of functionalism and truth to materials. **b.** *(as modifier): Bauhaus wallpaper.* [C20: German, literally: building house]

bauhinia (bɔː'hɪnɪə, bəʊ-) *n.* any climbing leguminous plant of the genus *Bauhinia,* of tropical and warm regions, widely cultivated for ornament. [C18: New Latin, named after Jean and Gaspard *Bauhin,* 16th-century French herbalists]

baulk (bɔːk; *usually for sense 1* bɔːlk) *n.* **1.** Also (U.S.): **balk.** *Billiards.* **a.** (in billiards) the space, usually 29 inches deep, between the baulk line and the bottom cushion. **b.** (in baulk-line games) one of the spaces between the cushions and the baulk lines. **c. in baulk.** inside one of these spaces. **2.** *Archaeol.* a strip of earth left between excavation trenches for the study of the complete stratigraphy of a site. **3.** *Croquet.* either of two lines (**A baulk** and **B baulk**) at diagonally opposite ends of the court, from which the ball is struck into play. *~vb., n.* **4.** a variant spelling of **balk.**

baulk line *or U.S.* **balk line** *n. Billiards.* **1.** Also called: **string line.** a straight line across a billiard table behind which the cue balls are placed at the start of a game. **2. a.** one of four lines parallel to the cushions dividing the table into a central panel and eight smaller ones (the baulks). **b.** a type of game using these lines as restrictions.

Baumé scale (bəʊ'meɪ, 'bəʊmeɪ) *n.* a scale for calibrating hydrometers used for measuring the specific gravity of liquids. 1 degree Baumé is equal to $144.3((s-1)/s)$, where s is specific gravity. [C19: named after Antoine *Baumé* (1728–1804), French chemist]

bauxite ('bɔːksaɪt) *n.* a white, red, yellow, or brown amorphous claylike substance comprising aluminium oxides and hydroxides, often with such impurities as iron oxides. It is the chief ore of aluminium. General formula: $Al_2O_3.nH_2O$. [C19: from French, from *(Les) Baux* in southern France, where it was originally found]

Bav. *abbrev. for* Bavaria(n).

Bavarian (bə'veərɪən) *n.* **1.** a native or inhabitant of Bavaria, a state in S Germany. *~adj.* **2.** of Bavaria, its people, culture, etc.

Bavarian cream *n.* a cold dessert consisting of a rich custard set with gelatine and flavoured in various ways. Also called: **bavarois** (*French* bavarwa).

bawbee (bɔː'biː) *n.* **1.** a former Scottish silver coin. **2.** *Scot.* an informal word for **halfpenny** (sense 2). [C16: named after Alexander Orok of *Sillebawby,* master of the mint from 1538]

bawcock ('bɔːˌkɒk) *n. Archaic.* a fine fellow. [C16: from French *beau coq,* from *beau* handsome + *coq* COCK[1]]

bawd (bɔːd) *n. Archaic.* **1.** a person who runs a brothel, esp. a woman. **2.** a prostitute. [C14: from Old French *baude,* feminine of *baud* merry, of Germanic origin; compare Old High German *bald* BOLD]

bawdry ('bɔːdrɪ) *n. Archaic.* obscene talk or language.

bawdy ('bɔːdɪ) *adj.* **bawdier, bawdiest. 1.** (of language, plays, etc.) containing references to sex, esp. to be humorous. *~n.* **2.** obscenity or eroticism, esp. in writing or drama. —'**bawdily** *adv.* —'**bawdiness** *n.*

bawdyhouse ('bɔːdɪˌhaʊs) *n.* an archaic word for **brothel.**

bawl (bɔːl) *vb.* **1.** *(intr.)* to utter long loud cries, as from pain or frustration; wail. **2.** to shout loudly, as in anger. *~n.* **3.** a loud shout or cry. [C15: probably from Icelandic *baula* to low; related to Medieval Latin *baulāre* to bark, Swedish *böla* to low; all of imitative origin] —'**bawler** *n.* —'**bawling** *n.*

bawl out *vb. (tr., adv.) Informal.* to scold loudly.

bawneen ('bɑniːn) *n. Irish.* a variant spelling of **báinín.**

bay[1] (beɪ) *n.* **1.** a wide semicircular indentation of a shoreline, esp. between two headlands or peninsulas. **2.** an extension of lowland into hills that partly surround it. **3.** *U.S.* an extension of prairie into woodland. [C14: from Old French *baie,* perhaps from Old French *baer* to gape, from Medieval Latin *batāre* to yawn]

bay[2] (beɪ) *n.* **1.** an alcove or recess in a wall. **2.** any partly enclosed compartment, as one in which hay is stored in a barn. **3.** See **bay window. 4.** an area off a road in which vehicles may park or unload, esp. one adjacent to a shop, factory, etc. **5.** a compartment in an aircraft, esp. one used for a specified purpose: *the bomb bay.* **6.** *Nautical.* a compartment in the forward part of a ship between decks, often used as the ship's hospital. **7.** *Brit.* a tracked recess in the platform of a railway station, esp. one forming the terminus of a branch line. [C14: from Old French *baee* gap or recess in a wall, from *baer* to gape; see BAY[1]]

bay[3] (beɪ) *n.* **1.** a deep howl or growl, esp. of a hound on the scent. **2. at bay. a.** (of a person or animal) forced to turn and face attackers: *the dogs held the deer at bay.* **b.** at a distance: *to keep a disease at bay.* **3. bring to bay.** to force into a position from which retreat is impossible. *~vb.* **4.** *(intr.)* to howl (at) in deep prolonged tones. **5.** *(tr.)* to utter in a loud prolonged tone. **6.** *(tr.)* to drive to or hold at bay. [C13: from Old French *abaiier* to bark, of imitative origin]

bay[4] (beɪ) *n.* **1.** a Mediterranean laurel, *Laurus nobilis.* See **laurel** (sense 1). **2.** any of several magnolias. See **sweet bay** (sense 1). **3.** any of certain other trees or shrubs, esp. bayberry. **4.** (*pl.*) a wreath of bay leaves. See **laurel** (sense 6). [C14: from Old French *baie* laurel berry, from Latin *bāca* berry]

bay[5] (beɪ) *n.* **1. a.** a moderate reddish-brown colour. **b.** (*as adj.*): *a bay horse.* **2.** an animal of this colour, esp. a horse. [C14: from Old French *bai,* from Latin *badius*]

bayadere (ˌbaɪəˈdɪə, -ˈdɛə) *n.* **1.** a dancing girl, esp. one serving in a Hindu temple. **2.** a fabric or design with horizontal stripes, esp. of a bright colour. *~adj.* **3.** (of fabric, etc.) having horizontal stripes. [C18: via French from Portuguese *bailadeira* dancing girl, from *bailar* to dance, from Latin *ballāre;* see BALL[2]]

bayard (ˈbeɪəd) *Archaic.* *~n.* **1.** a bay horse. *~adj.* **2.** bay-coloured. [C14: from Old French, from BAY[5] + -ARD]

bayberry (ˈbeɪbərɪ) *or* **bay** *n., pl.* **-ries. 1.** any of several North American aromatic shrubs or small trees of the genus *Myrica,* that bear grey waxy berries: family *Myricaceae.* See also **wax myrtle. 2.** Also called: **bay rum tree.** a tropical American myrtaceous tree, *Pimenta acris,* that yields an oil used in making bay rum. **3.** the fruit of any of these plants.

Bayesian (ˈbeɪzɪən) *adj.* (of a theory) presupposing known a priori probabilities which may be subjectively assessed and which can be revised in the light of experience in accordance with Bayes' theorem. A hypothesis is thus confirmed by an experimental observation which is likely given the hypothesis and unlikely without it. Compare **maximum likelihood.**

Bayes' theorem (beɪz) *n. Statistics.* the fundamental result which expresses the conditional probability $P(E/A)$ of an event E given an event A as $P(A/E).P(E)/P(A)$; more generally, where E_n is one of a set of E_i which partition the sample space, $P(E_n/A) = P(A/E_n)P(E_n)/\Sigma_i P(A/E_i)P(E_i)$. This enables prior estimates of probability to be continually revised in the light of observations. [C20: named after Thomas *Bayes* (1702–61), English mathematician and Presbyterian minister]

bay leaf *n.* a leaf, usually dried, of the Mediterranean laurel, *Laurus nobilis,* used in cooking to flavour soups and stews.

bay lynx *n.* another name for **bobcat.**

bayonet (ˈbeɪənɪt) *n.* **1.** a blade for stabbing that can be attached to the muzzle of a firearm. **2.** a type of fastening in which a cylindrical member is inserted into a socket against spring pressure and turned so that pins on its side engage in slots in the socket. *~vb.* **-nets, -neting, -neted,** *or* **-nets, -netting, -netted. 3.** (*tr.*) to stab or kill with a bayonet. [C17: from French *baïonnette,* from *Bayonne,* SW France, where it originated]

bayou (ˈbaɪuː) *n.* (in the southern U.S.) a sluggish marshy tributary of a lake or river. [C18: from Louisiana French, from Choctaw *bayuk*]

bay rum *n.* **1.** an aromatic liquid, used in medicines and cosmetics, originally obtained by distilling the leaves of the bayberry tree (*Pimenta acris*) with rum: now also synthesized from alcohol, water, and various oils. **2. bay rum tree.** another name for **bayberry** (sense 2).

Bay Street *n.* (in Canada) **1.** the financial centre of Toronto, in which Canada's largest stock exchange is situated. **2.** the financial interests and powers of Toronto.

bay tree *n.* another name for **bay**[4] (sense 1).

bay window *n.* a window projecting from the wall of a building and forming an alcove of a room. Sometimes shortened to **bay.** See also **bow window, oriel.**

baywood (ˈbeɪˌwʊd) *n.* the light soft wood of a tropical American mahogany tree, *Swietenia macrophylla,* of the bay region of SE Mexico.

bazaar *or* **bazar** (bəˈzɑː) *n.* **1.** (esp. in the Orient) a market area, esp. a street of small stalls. **2.** a sale in aid of charity, esp. of miscellaneous secondhand or handmade articles. **3.** a shop where a large variety of goods is sold. [C16: from Persian *bāzār,* from Old Persian *abēcharish*]

bazoo (bəˈzuː) *n.* a U.S. slang word for **mouth.** [C19: of unknown origin]

bazooka (bəˈzuːkə) *n.* a portable tubular rocket-launcher that fires a projectile capable of piercing armour: used by infantrymen as a short-range antitank weapon. [C20: named after a pipe instrument invented by Bob Burns (1896–1956), American comedian]

BB 1. *abbrev. for* Boys' Brigade. **2.** (on Brit. pencils) *symbol for* double black: denoting a very soft lead.

BBBC *abbrev. for* British Boxing Board of Control.

BBC *abbrev. for* British Broadcasting Corporation.

BBFC *abbrev. for* British Board of Film Censors.

bbl. *abbrev. for* barrel (container or unit of measure).

B-boy (ˈbiːˌbɔɪ) *n.* a male rap-music fan, who typically can be identified by his casual style of dress. [C20: from *Bronx boy*]

B bursary *n. N.Z.* the lower of two bursaries available for students entering university, polytechnic, etc. Compare **A bursary.**

BC *abbrev. for* British Columbia.

B.C. *or* **BC** *abbrev. for* (indicating years numbered back from the supposed year of the birth of Christ) before Christ: *in 54* B.C. *Caesar came.* Compare **A.D.**

▷**Usage.** See at **A.D.**

BCA (in New Zealand) *abbrev. for* Bachelor of Commerce and Administration.

BCAR *abbrev. for* British Civil Airworthiness Requirements.

BCC *abbrev. for* British Coal Corporation (formerly the National Coal Board).

BCD *abbrev. for* binary-coded decimal.

BCE *abbrev. for* Before Common Era (used, esp. by non-Christians, in numbering years B.C.).

B-cell *n.* another name for **B-lymphocyte.**

BCF *abbrev. for:* **1.** British Chess Federation. **2.** British Cycling Federation.

BCG *abbrev. for* bacille Calmette-Guérin (antituberculosis vaccine).

BCh *abbrev. for* Bachelor of Surgery. [from Latin *Baccalaureus Chirurgiae*]

BCL *abbrev. for* Bachelor of Civil Law.

BCNZ *abbrev. for* Broadcasting Corporation of New Zealand.

BCom *abbrev. for* Bachelor of Commerce.

B complex *n.* short for **vitamin B complex.**

bd *abbrev. for:* **1.** board. **2.** *Insurance, finance, etc.* bond. **3.** *Bookbinding.* bound. **4.** bundle.

BD *abbrev. for:* **1.** Bachelor of Divinity. **2.** *Commerce.* bills discounted.

B/D *abbrev. for:* **1.** bank draft. **2.** *Commerce.* bills discounted. **3.** Also: **b/d** *Book-keeping.* brought down.

BDA *abbrev. for* British Dental Association.

Bde *or* **bde** *abbrev. for* brigade.

bdellium (ˈdɛlɪəm) *n.* **1.** any of several African or W Asian trees of the burseraceous genus *Commiphora* that yield a gum resin. **2.** the aromatic gum resin, similar to myrrh, produced by any of these trees. [C16: from Latin, from Greek *bdellion,* perhaps from Hebrew *bĕdhōlah*]

bd.ft. *abbrev. for* board foot.

bdl *abbrev. for* bundle.

bds *abbrev. for:* **1.** *Bookbinding.* (bound in) boards. **2.** bundles.

BDS 1. *abbrev. for* Bachelor of Dental Surgery. **2.** *international car registration for* Barbados.

be (biː; *unstressed* bɪ) *vb. pres. sing. 1st pers.* **am;** *2nd pers.* **are;** *3rd pers.* **is.** *pres. pl.* **are.** *past sing. 1st pers.* **was;** *2nd pers.* **were;** *3rd pers.* **was.** *past pl.* **were.** *pres. part.* **being.** *past part.* **been.** (*intr.*) **1.** to have presence in the realm of perceived reality; exist; live: *I think, therefore I am; not all that is can be understood.* **2.** (*used in the perfect or past perfect tenses only*) to pay a visit; go: *have you been to Spain?* **3.** to take place; occur: *my birthday was last Thursday.* **4.** (*copula*) used as a linking verb between the subject of a sentence and its noun or adjective complement or complementing phrase. *Be* has no intrinsic meaning of its own but rather expresses the relationship of either essential or incidental equivalence or identity (*John is a man; John is a musician*) or specifies an essential or incidental attribute (*honey is sweet; Susan is angry*). It is also used with an adverbial complement to indicate a relationship of location in space or time (*Bill is at the office; the dance is on Saturday*). **5.** (*takes a present participle*) forms the progressive present tense: *the man is running.* **6.** (*takes a past participle*) forms the passive voice of all transitive verbs and (archaically) certain intransitive ones: *a good film is being shown on television tonight; I am done.* **7.** (*takes an infinitive*) expresses intention, expectation, supposition, or obligation: *the president is to arrive at 9.30; you are not to leave before I say so.* **8.** (*takes a past participle*) forms the perfect or past perfect tense of certain intransitive verbs of motion, such as **go** or **come:** *the last train is gone.* **9. be that as it may.** the facts concerning (something) are of no importance. [Old English *bēon;* related to Old High German *bim* am, Latin *fui* I have been, Greek *phuein* to bring forth, Sanskrit *bhavati* he is]

Be *chemical symbol for* beryllium.

Bé *abbrev. for* Baumé.

BE *abbrev. for:* **1.** bill of exchange. **2.** (in the U.S.) Board of Education. **3.** Bachelor of Education. **4.** Bachelor of Engineering.

be- *prefix forming transitive verbs.* **1.** (*from nouns*) to surround completely; cover on all sides: *befog.* **2.** (*from nouns*) to affect completely or excessively: *bedazzle.* **3.** (*from nouns*) to consider as or cause to be: *befool; befriend.* **4.** (*from nouns*) to provide or cover with: *bejewel.* **5.** (*from verbs*) at, for, against, on, or over: *bewail; berate.* [Old English *be-, bi-,* unstressed variant of *bī* BY]

B/E, BE, *or* **b.e.** *abbrev. for* bill of exchange.

BEA (formerly) *abbrev. for* British European Airways.

BEAB *abbrev. for* British Electrical Approvals Board.

beach (biːtʃ) *n.* **1.** an extensive area of sand or shingle sloping down to a sea or lake, esp. the area between the high- and low-water marks on a seacoast. Related adj.: **littoral.** *~vb.* **2.** to run or haul (a boat) onto a beach. [C16: perhaps related to Old English *bæce* river, BECK[2]]

beach ball *n.* a large light brightly coloured ball for playing with on a beach.

beach buggy *n.* a low car, often open and with balloon tyres, for driving on sand. Also called: **dune buggy.**

beachcomber (ˈbiːtʃˌkəʊmə) *n.* **1.** a person who searches shore debris for anything of worth, esp. a vagrant living on a beach. **2.** a long high wave rolling onto a beach. —ˈ**beachˌcombing** *n.*

beach flea *n.* another name for the **sand hopper.**

beachhead (ˈbiːtʃˌhɛd) *n. Military.* **1.** an area on a beach that has been captured from the enemy and on which troops and equipment are landed. **2.** the object of an amphibious operation. [C20: modelled on BRIDGEHEAD]

beachie ('biːtʃɪ) *n. Austral. informal.* **1.** a beach fisherman. **2.** a young unemployed vagrant who frequents beaches.

Beach-la-Mar (ˌbiːtʃlə'mɑː) *n.* an English-based creole language spoken in Vanuatu and Fiji, and formerly much more widespread. Also called: **Biche-la-mar.** [C19: quasi-French, from BÊCHE-DE-MER (trepang, this being a major trading commodity in the SW Pacific; hence the name was applied to the trading language)]

beach plum *n.* **1.** a rosaceous shrub, *Prunus maritima,* of coastal regions of E North America. **2.** its edible plumlike fruit.

beacon ('biːkən) *n.* **1.** a signal fire or light on a hill, tower, etc., esp. one used formerly as a warning of invasion. **2.** a hill on which such fires were lit. **3.** a lighthouse, signalling buoy, etc., used to warn or guide ships in dangerous waters. **4.** short for **radio beacon. 5.** a radio or other signal marking a flight course in air navigation. **6.** short for **Belisha beacon. 7.** a person or thing that serves as a guide, inspiration, or warning. *~vb.* **8.** to guide or warn. **9.** (*intr.*) to shine. [Old English *beacen* sign; related to Old Frisian *bāken,* Old Saxon *bōcan,* Old High German *bouhhan*]

bead (biːd) *n.* **1.** a small usually spherical piece of glass, wood, plastic, etc., with a hole through it by means of which it may be strung with others to form a necklace, etc. **2.** a small drop of moisture: *a bead of sweat.* **3.** a small bubble in or on a liquid. **4.** a small metallic knob acting as the sight of a firearm. **5. draw a bead on.** to aim a rifle or pistol at. **6.** Also called: **astragal.** *Architect., furniture.* a small convex moulding having a semicircular cross section. **7.** *Chem.* a small solid globule made by fusing a powdered sample with borax or a similar flux on a platinum wire. The colour of the globule serves as a test for the presence of certain metals (**bead test**). **8.** *Metallurgy.* a deposit of welding metal on the surface of a metal workpiece, often used to examine the structure of the weld zone. **9.** *R.C. Church.* one of the beads of a rosary. **10. count, say,** *or* **tell one's beads.** to pray with a rosary. *~vb.* **11.** (*tr.*) to decorate with beads. **12.** to form into beads or drops. [Old English *bed* prayer; related to Old High German *gibet* prayer] —'**beaded** *adj.*

beadblast ('biːdˌblɑːst) *n.* **1.** a jet of small glass beads blown from a nozzle under air or steam pressure. *~vb.* (*tr.*) to clean or treat (a surface) with a beadblast. —'**bead,blaster** *n.*

beading ('biːdɪŋ) *n.* **1.** another name for **bead** (sense 6). **2.** Also called: **beadwork** ('biːdˌwɜːk). a narrow strip of some material used for edging or ornamentation.

beadle ('biːdᵊl) *n.* **1.** (formerly, in the Church of England) a minor parish official who acted as an usher and kept order. **2.** (in Scotland) a church official attending on the minister. **3.** *Judaism.* **a.** a synagogue attendant. See also **shammes. 4.** an official in certain British universities and other institutions. [Old English *bydel;* related to Old High German *butil* bailiff] —'**beadleship** *n.*

beadledom ('biːdᵊldəm) *n.* petty officialdom.

beadroll ('biːdˌrəʊl) *n. Archaic.* a list of persons for whom prayers are to be offered.

bead-ruby *n., pl.* **-bies.** a N temperate liliaceous plant, *Maianthemum canadense,* with small white bell-shaped flowers and small red berries.

beadsman *or* **bedesman** ('biːdzmən) *n., pl.* **-men.** *Archaic.* **1.** a person who prays for another's soul, esp. one paid or fed for doing so. **2.** a person kept in an almshouse.

beady ('biːdɪ) *adj.* **beadier, beadiest. 1.** small, round, and glittering: used esp. of eyes. **2.** resembling or covered with beads. —'**beadily** *adv.* —'**beadiness** *n.*

beady eye *n. Informal.* keen watchfulness that may be somewhat hostile: *he's got his beady eye on you.* —ˌ**beady-'eyed** *adj.*

beagle ('biːgᵊl) *n.* **1.** a small sturdy breed of hound, having a smooth dense coat usually of white, tan, and black; often used (esp. formerly) for hunting hares. **2.** *Archaic.* a person who spies on others. *~vb.* **3.** (*intr.*) to hunt with beagles, normally on foot. [C15: of uncertain origin]

beak[1] (biːk) *n.* **1.** the projecting jaws of a bird, covered with a horny sheath; bill. **2.** any beaklike mouthpart in other animals, such as turtles. **3.** *Slang.* a person's nose, esp. one that is large, pointed, or hooked. **4.** any projecting part, such as the pouring lip of a bucket. **5.** *Architect.* the upper surface of a cornice, which slopes out to throw off water. **6.** *Chem.* the part of a still or retort through which vapour passes to the condenser. **7.** *Nautical.* another word for **ram** (sense 5). [C13: from Old French *bec,* from Latin *beccus,* of Gaulish origin] —**beaked** (biːkt) *adj.* —'**beakless** *adj.* —'**beak,like** *adj.* —'**beaky** *adj.*

beak[2] (biːk) *n.* a Brit. slang word for **judge, magistrate, headmaster,** or **schoolmaster.** [C19: originally thieves' jargon]

beaker ('biːkə) *n.* **1.** a cup usually having a wide mouth: *a plastic beaker.* **2.** a cylindrical flat-bottomed container used in laboratories, usually made of glass and having a pouring lip. **3.** the amount a beaker holds. [C14: from Old Norse *bikarr;* related to Old High German *behhāri,* Middle Dutch *bēker* beaker, Greek *bikos* earthenware jug]

Beaker folk *n.* a prehistoric people thought to have originated in the Iberian peninsula and spread to central Europe and Britain during the second millennium B.C. [C20: named after the beakers found among their remains]

be-all and end-all *n. Informal.* **1.** the ultimate aim or justification: *to provide help for others is the be-all and end-all of this group.* **2.** *Often humorous.* a person or thing considered to be beyond improvement.

beam (biːm) *n.* **1.** a long thick straight-sided piece of wood, metal, concrete, etc., esp. one used as a horizontal structural member. **2.** any rigid member or structure that is loaded transversely. **3.** the breadth of a ship or boat taken at its widest part, usually amidships. **4.** a ray or column of light, as from a beacon. **5.** a broad smile. **6.** one of the two cylindrical rollers on a loom, one of which holds the warp threads before weaving, the other the finished work. **7.** the main stem of a deer's antler from which the smaller branches grow. **8.** the central shaft of a plough to which all the main parts are attached. **9.** a narrow unidirectional flow of electromagnetic radiation or particles: *a beam of light; an electron beam.* **10.** the horizontal centrally pivoted bar in a balance. **11.** *Informal.* the width of the hips (esp. in the phrase **broad in the beam). 12. a beam in one's eye.** a fault or grave error greater in oneself than in another person. **13. off (the) beam. a.** not following a radio beam to maintain a course. **b.** *Informal.* wrong, mistaken, or irrelevant. **14. on the beam. a.** following a radio beam to maintain a course. **b.** *Nautical.* opposite the beam of a vessel; abeam. **c.** *Informal.* correct, relevant, or appropriate. *~vb.* **15.** to send out or radiate (rays of light). **16.** (*tr.*) to divert or aim (a radio signal or broadcast, light, etc.) in a certain direction: *to beam a programme to Tokyo.* **17.** (*intr.*) to smile broadly with pleasure or satisfaction. [Old English *beam;* related to Gothic *bagms* tree, Old High German *boum* tree] —**beamed** *adj.* —'**beaming** *adj., n.* —'**beamless** *adj.* —'**beam,like** *adj.* —'**beamy** *adj.*

beam aerial *n.* an aerial system, such as a Yagi aerial, having directional properties. Also called (esp. U.S.): **beam antenna.**

beam compass *n.* an instrument for drawing large circles or arcs, consisting of a horizontal beam along which two vertical legs slide. Also called: **trammel.**

beam-ends *pl. n.* **1.** the ends of a vessel's beams. **2. on her beam-ends.** (of a vessel) heeled over through an angle of 90°. **3. on one's beam-ends. a.** out of resources; destitute. **b.** desperate.

beam engine *n.* an early type of steam engine, in which a pivoted beam is vibrated by a vertical steam cylinder at one end, so that it transmits motion to the workload, such as a pump, at the other end.

beam hole *n.* a hole in the shield of a nuclear reactor through which a beam of radiation, esp. of neutrons, is allowed to escape for experimental purposes.

beam riding *n.* a method of missile guidance in which the missile steers itself along the axis of a conically scanned microwave beam. —**beam rider** *n.*

beam splitter *n.* a system that divides a beam of light, electrons, etc., into two or more paths.

bean (biːn) *n.* **1.** any of various papilionaceous plants of the widely cultivated genus *Phaseolus* producing edible seeds in pods. See **French bean, lima bean, scarlet runner, string bean. 2.** any of several other papilionaceous plants that bear edible pods or seeds, such as the broad bean and soya bean. **3.** any of various other plants whose seeds are produced in pods or podlike fruits. **4.** the seed or pod of any of these plants. **5.** any of various beanlike seeds, such as coffee. **6.** *U.S. and Canadian slang* another word for **head. 7. not have a bean.** *Slang.* to be without money: *I haven't got a bean.* **8. full of beans.** *Informal.* **a.** full of energy and vitality. **b.** *U.S.* mistaken; erroneous. **9. spill the beans.** *Informal.* to disclose something confidential. *~vb.* **10.** *Chiefly U.S. and Canadian slang.* (*tr.*) to hit (a person) on the head. [Old English *bēan;* related to Old Norse *baun,* Old Frisian *bāne,* Old High German *bōna* bean]

beanbag ('biːnˌbæg) *n.* **1.** a small cloth bag filled with dried beans and thrown in games. **2.** a very large cushion loosely filled with foam rubber or polystyrene granules so that it moulds into a comfortable shape: used as an informal low seat.

bean caper *n.* a shrub, *Zygophyllum fabago,* of E Mediterranean regions, whose flower buds are eaten as a substitute for capers: family *Zygophyllaceae.*

beanery ('biːnərɪ) *n., pl.* **-eries.** *U.S. informal.* a cheap restaurant.

beanfeast ('biːnˌfiːst) *n. Brit. informal.* **1.** an annual dinner given by employers to employees. **2.** any festive or merry occasion.

beanie *or* **beany** ('biːnɪ) *n., pl.* **beanies.** *Chiefly U.S.* a round close-fitting hat resembling a skullcap.

beano ('biːnəʊ) *n., pl.* **beanos.** *Brit. slang.* a celebration, party, or other enjoyable time.

beanpole ('biːnˌpəʊl) *n.* **1.** a tall stick or pole used to support bean plants. **2.** *Slang.* a tall thin person.

bean sprout *n.* the sprout of a newly germinated mung bean, eaten as a vegetable, esp. in Chinese dishes.

beanstalk ('biːnˌstɔːk) *n.* the stem of a bean plant.

bean tree *n.* any of various trees having beanlike pods, such as the catalpa and carob.

bear[1] (bɛə) *vb.* **bears, bearing, bore, borne.** (*mainly tr.*) **1.** to support or hold up; sustain. **2.** to bring or convey: *to bear gifts.* **3.** to take, accept, or assume the responsibility of: *to bear an expense.* **4.** (*past participle* **born** in passive use except when foll. by *by*) to give birth to: *to bear children.* **5.** (*also intr.*) to produce by or as if by natural growth: *to bear fruit.* **6.** to tolerate or endure: *she couldn't bear him.* **7.** to admit of; sustain: *his story does not bear scrutiny.* **8.** to hold in the conscious mind or in one's feelings: *to bear a grudge; I'll bear that idea in mind.* **9.** to show or be marked with: *he still bears the scars.* **10.** to transmit or spread: *to bear gossip.* **11.** to render or supply (esp. in the phrase **bear witness**). **12.** to conduct or manage (oneself, the body, etc.): *she bore her head high.* **13.** to have, be, or stand in (relation or comparison): *his account bears no relation to the facts.* **14.** (*intr.*) to move, be located, or lie in a specified direction: *the way bears east.* **15.** to have by right; be entitled to (esp. in the phrase **bear title**). **16. bear a hand.** to give assistance. **17. bring to bear.** to bring into operation or effect: *he brought his knowledge to bear on the situation.* ~See also **bear down, bear off, bear on, bear out, bear up, bear with, born.** [Old English *beran;* related to Old Norse *bera,* Old High German *beran* to carry, Latin *ferre,* Greek *pherein* to bear, Sanskrit *bharati* he carries]

bear[2] (bɛə) *n., pl.* **bears** *or* **bear. 1.** any plantigrade mammal of the family *Ursidae:* order *Carnivora* (carnivores). Bears are typically massive omnivorous animals with a large head, a long shaggy coat, and strong claws. See also **black bear, brown bear, polar bear. 2.** any of various bearlike animals, such as the koala and the ant bear. **3.** a clumsy, churlish, or ill-mannered person. **4.** a teddy bear. **5.** *Stock Exchange.* **a.** a speculator who sells in anticipation of falling prices to make a profit on repurchase. **b.** (*as modifier*): *a bear market.* Compare **bull**[1] (sense 5). ~*vb.* **bears, bearing, beared. 6.** (*tr.*) to lower or attempt to lower the price or prices of (a stock market or a security) by speculative selling. [Old English *bera;* related to Old Norse *bjorn,* Old High German *bero*]

Bear (bɛə) *n.* **the.** the English name for either **Ursa Major (Great Bear)** or **Ursa Minor (Little Bear).**

bearable ('bɛərəbəl) *adj.* endurable; tolerable. —'**bearably** *adv.*

bear-baiting *n.* (formerly) an entertainment in which dogs attacked and enraged a chained bear.

bearberry ('bɛəbərɪ) *n., pl.* **-ries. 1.** a trailing evergreen ericaceous shrub, *Arctostaphylos uva-ursi,* with small pinkish-white flowers, red berries, and astringent leaves. **2. alpine** or **black bearberry.** a related species, *A. alpina* of European mountains, having black berries.

bearcat ('bɛəˌkæt) *n.* another name for **lesser panda** (see **panda** (sense 2)).

beard (bɪəd) *n.* **1.** the hair growing on the lower parts of a man's face. **2.** any similar growth in animals. **3.** a tuft of long hairs in plants such as barley and wheat; awn. **4.** the gills of an oyster. **5.** a barb, as on an arrow or fish-hook. **6.** *Printing.* the part of a piece of type that connects the face with the shoulder. ~*vb.* (*tr.*) **7.** to oppose boldly or impertinently. **8.** to pull or grasp the beard of. [Old English *beard;* related to Old Norse *barth,* Old High German *bart,* Latin *barba*] —'**bearded** *adj.*

bearded collie *n.* a medium-sized breed of dog having a profuse long straight coat, usually grey or fawn and often with white on the head, legs, and chest, a long tail, and a distinctive beard.

bearded lizard *or* **dragon** *n.* another name for **jew lizard.**

bearded tit *n.* another name for **reedling.**

bearded vulture *n.* another name for **lammergeier.**

beardless ('bɪədlɪs) *adj.* **1.** without a beard. **2.** too young to grow a beard; immature. —'**beardlessness** *n.*

bear down *vb.* (*intr., adv.;* often foll. by *on* or *upon*) **1.** to press or weigh down. **2.** to approach in a determined or threatening manner. **3.** (of a vessel) to make an approach (to another vessel, obstacle, etc.) from windward. **4.** (of a woman during childbirth) to exert a voluntary muscular pressure to assist delivery.

bearer ('bɛərə) *n.* **1.** a person or thing that bears, presents, or upholds. **2.** a person who presents a note or bill for payment. **3.** (in Africa, India, etc., formerly) **a.** a native carrier, esp. on an expedition. **b.** a native servant. **4.** See **pallbearer. 5.** the holder of a rank, position, office, etc. **6.** (*modifier*) *Finance.* payable to the person in possession: *bearer bonds.*

bear garden *n.* **1.** (formerly) a place where bears were exhibited and where bear-baiting took place. **2.** a place or scene of tumult and disorder.

bear hug *n.* **1.** a wrestling hold in which the arms are locked tightly round an opponent's chest and arms. **2.** any similar tight embrace. **3.** *Commerce.* an approach to the board of one company by another to indicate that an offer is to be made for their shares.

bearing ('bɛərɪŋ) *n.* **1.** a support, guide, or locating piece for a rotating or reciprocating mechanical part. **2.** (foll. by *on* or *upon*) relevance (to): *it has no bearing on this problem.* **3.** a person's general social conduct, esp. in manners, dress, and behaviour. **4. a.** the act, period, or capability of producing fruit or young. **b.** an amount produced; yield. **5.** the part of a beam or lintel that rests on a support. **6.** anything that carries weight or acts as a support. **7.** the angular direction of a line, point, or course measured from true north or south **(true bearing),** magnetic north or south **(magnetic bearing),** or one's own position. **8.** (*usually pl.*) the position or direction, as of a ship, fixed with reference to two or more known points. **9.** (*usually pl.*) a sense of one's relative position or situation; orientation (esp. in the phrases **lose, get,** *or* **take one's bearings**). **10.** *Heraldry.* **a.** a device or emblem on a heraldic shield; charge. **b.** another name for **coat of arms.**

bearing pedestal *n.* an independent support for a bearing, usually incorporating a bearing housing.

bearing pile *n.* a foundation pile that supports weight vertically. Compare **sheet pile.**

bearing rein *n. Chiefly Brit.* a rein from the bit to the saddle, designed to keep the horse's head in the desired position. Usual U.S. word: **checkrein.**

bearish ('bɛərɪʃ) *adj.* **1.** like a bear; rough; clumsy; churlish. **2.** *Stock Exchange.* causing, expecting, or characterized by a fall in prices: *a bearish market.* —'**bearishly** *adv.* —'**bearishness** *n.*

Béarnaise (ˌbeɪəˈneɪz) *n.* a rich sauce made from egg yolks, lemon juice or wine vinegar, butter, shallots, herbs, and seasoning. [C19: French, from *Béarn* in SW France]

bear off *vb.* (*adv.*) *Nautical.* (of a vessel) to avoid hitting an obstacle, another vessel, etc., by swerving onto a different course.

bear on *vb.* (*intr., prep.*) **1.** to be relevant to; relate to. **2.** to be burdensome to or afflict: *his misdeeds bore heavily on his conscience.*

bear out *vb.* (*tr., adv.*) to show to be true or truthful; confirm: *the witness will bear me out.*

bear raid *n.* an attempt to force down the price of a security or commodity by sustained selling.

bear's-breech *or* **bear's-breeches** *n.* a widely cultivated S European acanthus plant, *Acanthus mollis,* having whitish purple-veined flowers.

bear's-ear *n.* another name for **auricula** (sense 1).

bear's-foot *n.* either of two Eurasian hellebore plants, *Helleborus foetidus* or *H. viridis,* having leaves shaped like the foot and claws of a bear.

bearskin ('bɛəˌskɪn) *n.* **1.** the pelt of a bear, esp. when used as a rug. **2.** a tall helmet of black fur worn by certain regiments in the British Army. **3.** a rough shaggy woollen cloth, used for overcoats.

bear up *vb.* (*intr., adv.*) to endure cheerfully.

bear with *vb.* (*intr., prep.*) to be patient with: *bear with me while I tell you my story.*

bearwood ('bɛəˌwʊd) *n.* another name for **cascara** (sense 2).

beast (biːst) *n.* **1.** any animal other than man, esp. a large wild quadruped. **2.** savage nature or characteristics: *the beast in man.* **3.** a brutal, uncivilized, or filthy person. [C13: from Old French *beste,* from Latin *bestia,* of obscure origin]

beastie ('biːstɪ) *n.* **1.** *Scot.* a small animal. **2.** *Informal.* an insect.

beastings ('biːstɪŋz) *n.* a U.S. spelling of **beestings.**

beastly ('biːstlɪ) *adj.* **-lier, -liest. 1.** *Informal.* unpleasant; disagreeable; nasty: *beastly weather.* **2.** *Obsolete.* of or like a beast; bestial. ~*adv.* **3.** *Informal.* (intensifier): *the weather is so beastly hot.* —'**beastliness** *n.*

beast of burden *n.* an animal, such as a donkey or ox, used for carrying loads.

beast of prey *n.* any animal that hunts other animals for food.

beat (biːt) *vb.* **beats, beating, beat; beaten** *or* **beat. 1.** (when *intr.,* often foll. by *against, on,* etc.) to strike with or as if with a series of violent blows; dash or pound repeatedly (against). **2.** (*tr.*) to punish by striking; flog. **3.** to move or cause to move up and down; flap: *the bird beat its wings heavily.* **4.** (*intr.*) to throb rhythmically; pulsate: *her heart beat fast.* **5.** (*tr.*) to make (one's way) by or as if by blows: *she beat her way out of the crowd.* **6.** (*tr.;* sometimes foll. by *up*) *Cookery.* to stir or whisk (an ingredient or mixture) vigorously. **7.** (*tr.;* sometimes foll. by *out*) to shape, make thin, or flatten (a piece of metal) by repeated blows. **8.** (*tr.*) *Music.* to indicate (time) by the motion of one's hand, baton, etc., or by the action of a metronome. **9.** (when *tr.,* sometimes foll. by *out*) to produce (a sound or signal) by or as if by striking a drum. **10.** to sound or cause to sound, by or as if by beating: *beat the drums!* **11.** to overcome (an opponent) in a contest, battle, etc. **12.** (*tr.;* often foll. by *back, down, off,* etc.) to drive, push, or thrust. **13.** (*tr.*) to arrive or finish before (someone or something); anticipate or forestall: *they set off early to beat the rush hour.* **14.** (*tr.*) to form (a path or track) by repeatedly walking or riding over it. **15.** to scour (woodlands, coverts, or undergrowth) so as to rouse game for shooting. **16.** (*tr.*) *Slang.* to puzzle or baffle: *it beats me how he can do that.* **17.** (*intr.*) *Physics.* (of sounds or electrical signals) to combine and produce a pulsating sound or signal. **18.** (*intr.*) *Nautical.* to steer a sailing vessel as close as possible to the direction from which the wind is blowing. **19.** (*tr.*) *Slang, chiefly U.S.* to cheat or defraud: *he beat his brother out of the inheritance.* **20. beat about the bush.** to avoid the point at issue; prevaricate. **21. beat a retreat.** to withdraw or depart in haste. **22. beat it.** *Slang.* (*often imperative*) to go away. **23. beat one's brains (out).** to try to find ideas, a solution, etc. **24. beat one's breast.** See **breast** (sense 10). **25. beat someone's brains out.** *Slang.* to kill by knocking severely about the head. **26. beat someone to it.** *Informal.* to reach a place or achieve an objective before someone else. **27. beat the bounds. a.** *Brit.* (formerly) to define the boundaries of a parish by making a procession around them and hitting the ground with rods. **b.** to define the scope or limit, as of a topic or discussion. **28. can you beat it** *or* **that?** *Slang.* an expression of utter amazement or surprise. ~*n.* **29.** a stroke or blow. **30.** the sound made by a stroke or blow. **31.** a regular sound or stroke; throb. **32. a.** an assigned or habitual round or route, as of a policeman or sentry. **b.** (*as modifier*): *beat police officers.* **33.** the basic rhythmic unit in a piece of music, usually grouped in twos, threes, or fours. **34. a.** pop or rock music characterized by a heavy rhythmic beat. **b.** (*as modifier*): *a beat group.* **35.** *Physics.* one of the regular pulses produced by combining two sounds or electrical signals that have similar frequencies. **36.** *Horology.* the impulse given to the balance wheel by the action of the escapement. **37.** *Prosody.* the accent, stress, or ictus in a metrical foot. **38.** *Nautical.* a course that steers a sailing vessel as close as possible to the direction from which the wind is blowing. **39. a.** the act of scouring for game by beating. **b.** the organized scouring of a particular woodland so as to rouse the game in it. **c.** the woodland where game is so roused. **40.** short for **beatnik. 41.** *Fencing.* a sharp tap with one's blade on an opponent's blade to deflect it. **42.** (*modifier*) (*often cap.*) of, characterized by, or relating to the Beat Generation: *a beat poet; beat philosophy.* ~*adj.* **43.** (*postpositive*) *Slang.* totally exhausted. ~See also **beat down, beat up.** [Old English *bēatan;* related to Old Norse *bauta,* Old High German *bōzan*] —'**beatable** *adj.*

beatbox ('biːtˌbɒks) *n. Informal.* a drum machine.

beat down *vb.* (*adv.*) **1.** (*tr.*) *Informal.* to force or persuade (a seller) to accept a lower price: *I beat him down three pounds.* **2.** (*intr.*) (of the sun) to shine intensely; be very hot.

beaten ('biːtᵊn) *adj.* **1.** defeated or baffled. **2.** shaped or made thin by hammering: *a bowl of beaten gold.* **3.** much travelled; well trodden (esp. in the phrase **the beaten track**). **4. off the beaten track. a.** in or into unfamiliar territory. **b.** out of the ordinary; unusual. **5.** (of food) mixed by beating; whipped. **6.** tired out; exhausted. **7.** *Hunting.* (of woods, undergrowth, etc.) scoured so as to rouse game.

beater ('biːtə) *n.* **1.** a person who beats or hammers: *a panel beater.* **2.** an instrument or device used for beating: *a carpet beater.* **3.** a person who rouses wild game from woodland, undergrowth, etc.

Beat Generation *n.* (*functioning as sing. or pl.*) members of the generation that came to maturity in the 1950s, whose rejection of the social and political systems of the West was expressed through contempt for regular work, possessions, traditional dress, etc., and espousal of anarchism, communal living, drugs, etc.

beatific (ˌbiːə'tɪfɪk) *adj.* **1.** displaying great happiness, calmness, etc.: *a beatific smile.* **2.** of, conferring, or relating to a state of celestial happiness. [C17: from Late Latin *beātificus,* from Latin *beātus,* from *beāre* to bless + *facere* to make] —ˌ**bea'tifically** *adv.*

beatify (bɪ'ætɪˌfaɪ) *vb.* **-fies, -fying, -fied. 1.** (*tr.*) *R.C. Church.* (of the pope) to declare formally that (a deceased person) showed a heroic degree of holiness in his or her life and therefore is worthy of public veneration: the first step towards canonization. **2.** (*tr.*) to make extremely happy. [C16: from Old French *beatifier,* from Late Latin *beātificāre* to make blessed; see BEATIFIC] —**beatification** (bɪˌætɪfɪ'keɪʃən) *n.*

beating ('biːtɪŋ) *n.* **1.** a whipping or thrashing, as in punishment. **2.** a defeat or setback. **3. take some** *or* **a lot of beating.** to be difficult to improve upon.

beatitude (bɪ'ætɪˌtjuːd) *n.* **1.** supreme blessedness or happiness. **2.** an honorific title of the Eastern Christian Church, applied to those of patriarchal rank. [C15: from Latin *beātitūdō,* from *beātus* blessed; see BEATIFIC]

beatnik ('biːtnɪk) *n.* **1.** a member of the Beat Generation. **2.** *Informal.* any person with long hair and shabby clothes. [C20: from BEAT (n.) + -NIK, by analogy with SPUTNIK]

beat up *Informal.* ~*vb.* **1.** (*tr., adv.*) to strike or kick (a person), usually repeatedly, so as to inflict severe physical damage. ~*adj.* **beat-up. 2.** worn-out; dilapidated.

beau (bəʊ) *n., pl.* **beaus** (bəʊz) *or* **beaux** (bəʊ, bəʊz). **1.** a lover, sweetheart, or escort of a girl or woman. **2.** a man who is greatly concerned with his clothes and appearance; dandy. [C17: from French, from Old French *biau,* from Latin *bellus* handsome, charming]

Beaufort scale ('bəʊfət) *n. Meteorol.* an international scale of wind velocities ranging for practical purposes from 0 (calm) to 12 (hurricane force). In the U.S. an extension of the scale, from 13 to 17 for winds over 64 knots, is used. [C19: after Sir Francis *Beaufort* (1774–1857), British admiral and hydrographer who devised it]

beau geste *French.* (bo ʒɛst) *n., pl.* ***beaux gestes*** (bo ʒɛst). a noble or gracious gesture or act, esp. one that is meaningless. [literally: beautiful gesture]

beau idéal *French.* (bo ideal) *n., pl.* ***beaux idéals*** (boz ideal). perfect beauty or excellence. [literally: ideal beauty]

beaujolais ('bəʊʒəˌleɪ) *n.* (*sometimes cap.*) a popular fresh-tasting red or white wine from southern Burgundy in France.

beau monde ('bəʊ 'mɒnd; *French* bo mɔ̃d) *n.* the world of fashion and society. [C18: French, literally: fine world]

Beaune (bəʊn) *n.* a wine from the district around Beaune in E France.

beaut (bjuːt) *Slang, chiefly Austral. and N.Z.* ~*n.* **1.** a person or thing that is outstanding or distinctive. ~*adj., interj.* **2.** good or excellent: an expression of approval.

beauteous ('bjuːtɪəs) *adj.* a poetic word for **beautiful.** —'**beauteously** *adv.* —'**beauteousness** *n.*

beautician (bjuː'tɪʃən) *n.* a person who works in or manages a beauty salon.

beautiful ('bjuːtɪfʊl) *adj.* **1.** possessing beauty; aesthetically pleasing. **2.** highly enjoyable; very pleasant: *the party was beautiful.* —'**beautifulness** *n.*

beautifully ('bjuːtɪflɪ) *adv.* **1.** in a beautiful manner. **2.** *Informal.* (intensifier): *you did beautifully well in the race.*

beautiful people *pl. n.* (*sometimes caps.;* preceded by *the*) rich, fashionable people in international high society.

beautify ('bjuːtɪˌfaɪ) *vb.* **-fies, -fying, -fied.** to make or become beautiful. —**beautification** (ˌbjuːtɪfɪ'keɪʃən) *n.* —'**beautiˌfier** *n.*

beauty ('bjuːtɪ) *n., pl.* **-ties. 1.** the combination of all the qualities of a person or thing that delight the senses and please the mind. **2.** a very attractive and well-formed girl or woman. **3.** *Informal.* an outstanding example of its kind: *the horse is a beauty.* **4.** *Informal.* an advantageous feature: *one beauty of the job is the short hours.* **5.** *Informal, old-fashioned.* a light-hearted and affectionate term of address: *hello, my old beauty!* ~*interj.* **6.** (*N.Z.* 'bjuːdɪ) *Austral. and N.Z. slang.* an expression of approval or agreement. Also (Scot., Austral., and N.Z.): **you beauty.** [C13: from Old French *biauté,* from *biau* beautiful; see BEAU]

beauty queen *n.* an attractive young woman, esp. one who has won a beauty contest.

beauty salon *or* **parlour** *n.* an establishment providing women with services to improve their beauty, such as hairdressing, manicuring, facial treatment, and massage.

beauty sleep *n. Informal.* sleep, esp. sleep before midnight.

beauty spot *n.* **1.** a place of outstanding beauty. **2.** a small dark-coloured patch or spot worn on a lady's face as an adornment or as a foil to her complexion. **3.** a mole or other similar natural mark on the skin.

beaux (bəʊ, bəʊz) *n.* a plural of **beau.**

beaux-arts (bəʊ'zɑː) *pl. n.* **1.** another word for **fine art. 2.** (*modifier*) relating to the classical decorative style, esp. that of the École des Beaux-Arts in Paris: *beaux-arts influences.* [C19: French, literally: fine arts]

beaver[1] ('biːvə) *n.* **1.** a large amphibious rodent, *Castor fiber,* of Europe, Asia, and North America: family *Castoridae.* It has soft brown fur, a broad flat hairless tail, and webbed hind feet, and constructs complex dams and houses (lodges) in rivers. **2.** the fur of this animal. **3. mountain beaver.** a burrowing rodent, *Aplodontia rufa,* of W North America: family *Aplodontidae.* **4.** a tall hat of beaver fur or a fabric resembling it, worn, esp. by men, during the 19th century. **5.** a woollen napped cloth resembling beaver fur, formerly much used for overcoats, etc. **6.** a greyish- or yellowish-brown. **7.** *Obsolete.* a full beard. **8.** a bearded man. **9.** (*modifier*) having the colour of beaver or made of beaver fur or some similar material: *a beaver lamb coat; a beaver stole.* ~*vb.* **10.** (*intr.;* usually foll. by *away*) to work industriously or steadily. [Old English *beofor;* compare Old Norse *biōrr,* Old High German *bibar,* Latin *fiber,* Sanskrit *babhrú* red-brown]

beaver[2] ('biːvə) *n.* a movable piece on a medieval helmet used to protect the lower part of the face. [C15: from Old French *baviere,* from *baver* to dribble]

Beaver ('biːvə) *n.* a member of a **Beaver Colony,** the youngest group of boys (aged 6–8 years) in the Scout Association.

Beaverboard ('biːvəˌbɔːd) *n. Trademark.* a stiff light board of compressed wood fibre, used esp. to surface partitions.

bebeerine (bə'bɪəriːn, -rɪn) *n.* an alkaloid, resembling quinine, obtained from the bark of the greenheart and other plants. [C19: from German *Bebeerin;* see BEBEERU, -INE[2]]

bebeeru (bə'bɪəruː) *n.* another name for **greenheart** (sense 1). [C19: from Spanish *bibirú,* of Carib origin]

bebop ('biːbɒp) *n.* the full name for **bop**[1] (sense 1). [C20: imitative of the rhythm of the music] —'**bebopper** *n.*

becalmed (bɪ'kɑːmd) *adj.* (of a sailing boat or ship) motionless through lack of wind.

became (bɪ'keɪm) *vb.* the past tense of **become.**

because (bɪ'kɒz, -'kəz) *conj.* **1.** (*subordinating*) on account of the fact that; on account of being; since: *because it's so cold we'll go home.* **2. because of.** (*prep.*) on account of: *I lost my job because of her.* [C14 *bi cause,* from *bi* BY + CAUSE]

▷**Usage.** See at **reason.**

beccafico (ˌbɛkə'fiːkəʊ) *n., pl.* **-cos.** any of various European songbirds, esp. warblers of the genus *Sylvia,* eaten as a delicacy in Italy and other countries. [C17: from Italian, from *beccare* to peck + *fico* fig, from Latin *ficus*]

béchamel sauce (ˌbeɪʃə'mɛl) *n.* a thick white sauce flavoured with onion and seasonings. [C18: named after the Marquis of *Béchamel,* steward of Louis XIV of France and its inventor]

bechance (bɪ'tʃɑːns) *vb.* (*intr.*) *Archaic.* to happen (to).

bêche-de-mer (ˌbɛʃdə'mɛə) *n., pl.* **bêches-de-mer** (ˌbɛʃdə'mɛə) *or* **bêche-de-mer. 1.** another name for **trepang. 2.** See **Beach-la-Mar.** [C19: quasi-French, from earlier English *biche de mer,* from Portuguese *bicho do mar* worm of the sea]

Bechuana (bɛ'tʃwɑːnə; ˌbɛtʃʊ'ɑːnə, ˌbɛkjʊ-) *n., pl.* **-na** *or* **-nas. 1.** a former name for **Tswana. 2.** a former name for a member of the Bantu people of Botswana.

beck[1] (bɛk) *n.* **1.** a nod, wave, or other gesture or signal. **2. at (someone's) beck and call.** ready to obey (someone's) orders instantly; subject to (someone's) slightest whim. [C14: short for *becnen* to BECKON]

beck[2] (bɛk) *n.* (in N England) a stream, esp. a swiftly flowing one. [Old English *becc,* from Old Norse *bekkr;* related to Old English *bece,* Old Saxon *beki,* Old High German *bah* brook, Sanskrit *bhanga* wave]

becket ('bɛkɪt) *n. Nautical.* **1.** a clevis forming part of one end of a sheave, used for securing standing lines by means of a thimble. **2.** a short line with a grommet or eye at one end and a knot at the other, used for securing spars or other gear in place. [C18: of unknown origin]

becket bend *n.* another name for **sheet bend.**

beckon ('bɛkən) *vb.* **1.** to summon with a gesture of the hand or head. **2.** to entice or lure. ~*n.* **3.** a summoning gesture. [Old English *bīecnan,* from *bēacen* sign; related to Old Saxon *bōknian;* see BEACON] —'**beckoner** *n.* —'**beckoning** *adj., n.*

becloud (bɪ'klaʊd) *vb. (tr.)* **1.** to cover or obscure with a cloud. **2.** to confuse or muddle: *to becloud the issues.*

become (bɪ'kʌm) *vb.* **-comes, -coming, -came, -come.** (*mainly intr.*) **1.** (*copula*) to come to be; develop or grow into: *he became a monster.* **2.** (foll. by *of; usually used in a question*) to fall to or be the lot (of); happen (to): *what became of him?* **3.** (*tr.*) (of clothes, etc.) to enhance the appearance of (someone); suit: *that dress becomes you.* **4.** (*tr.*) to be appropriate; befit: *it ill becomes you to complain.* [Old English *becuman* to happen; related to Old High German *biqueman* to come to, Gothic *biquiman* to appear suddenly]

becoming (bɪ'kʌmɪŋ) *adj.* **1.** suitable; appropriate. ~*n.* **2.** any process of change. **3.** (in the philosophy of Aristotle) any change from the lower level of potentiality to the higher level of actuality. —**be'comingly** *adv.* —**be'comingness** *n.*

becquerel (ˌbɛkə'rɛl) *n.* the derived SI unit of radioactivity equal to one disintegration per second. Symbol: **Bq** [C20: named after A. H. *Becquerel* (1852–1908), French physicist]

bed (bɛd) *n.* **1.** a piece of furniture on which to sleep. **2.** the mattress and bedclothes on such a piece of furniture: *an unmade bed.* **3.** sleep or rest: *time for bed.* **4.** any place in which a person or animal sleeps or rests. **5.** *Med.* a unit of potential occupancy in a hospital or residential institution. **6.** *Informal.* a place for sexual intercourse. **7.** *Informal.* sexual intercourse. **8.** a plot of ground in which plants are grown, esp. when considered together with the plants in it: *a flower bed.* **9.** the bottom of a river, lake, or sea. **10.** a part of this used for cultivation of a plant or animal: *oyster beds.* **11.** a layer of crushed rock, gravel, etc., used as a foundation for a road, railway, etc. **12.** a layer of mortar in a masonry wall. **13.** the underside of a brick, tile, slate, etc., when in position. Compare **back**[1] (sense 12). **14.** any underlying structure or part. **15.** a layer of rock, esp. sedimentary rock. **16.** the flat part of a letterpress printing press onto or against which the type forme is placed. **17.** a layer of solid particles of an absorbent, catalyst, or reagent through which a fluid is passed during the course of a chemical reaction or other process. **18.** a machine base on which a moving part carrying a tool or workpiece slides: *lathe bed.* **19. a bed of roses.** a situation of comfort or ease. **20. be brought to bed (of).** *Archaic.* to give birth (to). **21. bed of nails. a.** a situation or position of extreme difficulty. **b.** a bed studded with nails on which a fakir lies. **22. get out of bed on the wrong side.** *Informal.* to be ill-tempered from the start of the day. **23. go to bed. a.** (often foll. by *with*) to have sexual intercourse (with). **b.** *Journalism, printing.* (of a newspaper, magazine, etc.) to go to press; start printing. **24. put to bed. a.** *Journalism.* to finalize work on (a newspaper, magazine, etc.) so that it is ready to go to press. **b.** *Letterpress printing.* to lock up the type forme of (a publication) in the press before printing. **25. take to one's bed.** to remain in bed, esp. because of illness. ~*vb.* **beds, bedding, bedded. 26.** (usually foll. by *down*) to go to or put into a place to sleep or rest. **27.** (*tr.*) to have sexual intercourse with. **28.** (*tr.*) to place, fix, or sink firmly into position; embed. **29.** *Geology.* to form or be arranged in a distinct layer; stratify. **30.** (*tr.*; often foll. by *out*) to plant in a bed of soil. ~ See also **bed in.** [Old English *bedd;* related to Old Norse *bethr,* Old High German *betti,* Gothic *badi*]

BEd *abbrev. for* Bachelor of Education.

bed and board *n.* **1.** sleeping accommodation and meals. **2. divorce from bed and board.** *U.S. law.* a form of divorce whereby the parties are prohibited from living together but the marriage is not dissolved.

bed and breakfast *Chiefly Brit.* ~*n.* **1.** (in a hotel, boarding house, etc.) overnight accommodation and breakfast. ~*adj.* **2.** (of a stock-exchange transaction) establishing a loss for tax purposes, shares being sold after hours one evening and bought back the next morning when the market opens.

bedaub (bɪ'dɔːb) *vb. (tr.)* **1.** to smear all over with something thick, sticky, or dirty. **2.** to ornament in a gaudy or vulgar fashion.

bedazzle (bɪ'dæzᵊl) *vb. (tr.)* to dazzle or confuse, as with brilliance. —**be'dazzlement** *n.*

bed bath *n.* another name for **blanket bath.**

bedbug ('bɛdˌbʌg) *n.* any of several bloodsucking insects of the heteropterous genus *Cimex,* esp. *C. lectularius* of temperate regions, having an oval flattened wingless body and infesting dirty houses: family *Cimicidae.*

bedchamber ('bɛdˌtʃeɪmbə) *n.* an archaic word for **bedroom.**

bedclothes ('bɛdˌkləʊðz) *pl. n.* sheets, blankets, and other coverings of a bed.

beddable ('bɛdəbᵊl) *adj.* sexually attractive.

bedder ('bɛdə) *n.* **1.** *Brit.* (at Cambridge University) a college servant employed to keep students' rooms in order. **2.** a plant that may be grown in a garden bed.

bedding ('bɛdɪŋ) *n.* **1.** bedclothes, sometimes considered together with a mattress. **2.** litter, such as straw, for animals. **3.** something acting as a foundation, such as mortar under a brick. **4.** the arrangement of a mass of rocks into distinct layers; stratification.

bedding plant *n.* a plant that may be grown in a garden bed.

bedeck (bɪ'dɛk) *vb. (tr.)* to cover with decorations; adorn.

bedel *or* **bedell** ('biːdᵊl) *n.* archaic spellings of **beadle** (sense 4).

bedesman ('biːdzmən) *n., pl.* **-men.** a variant spelling of **beadsman.**

bedevil (bɪ'dɛvᵊl) *vb.* **-ils, -illing, -illed** *or U.S.* **-ils, -iling, -iled.** (*tr.*) **1.** to harass or torment. **2.** to throw into confusion. **3.** to possess, as with a devil. —**be'devilment** *n.*

bedew (bɪ'djuː) *vb. (tr.)* to wet or cover with or as if with drops of dew.

bedfast ('bɛdˌfɑːst) *adj.* an archaic word for **bedridden.**

bedfellow ('bɛdˌfɛləʊ) *n.* **1.** a person with whom one shares a bed. **2.** a temporary ally or associate.

Bedford cord ('bɛdfəd) *n.* a heavy corded cloth, similar to corduroy. [C19: named after *Bedford,* a town in SE central England]

bedight (bɪ'daɪt) *Archaic.* ~*vb.* **-dights, -dighting, -dight** *or* **-dighted. 1.** (*tr.*) to array or adorn. ~*adj.* **2.** (*past participle of the verb*) adorned or bedecked. [C14: from DIGHT]

bedim (bɪ'dɪm) *vb.* **-dims, -dimming, -dimmed.** (*tr.*) to make dim or obscure.

bed in *vb. (prep.) Engineering.* to fit (parts) together accurately or (of parts) to be fitted together, either through machining or use, as in fitting a bearing to its shaft.

bedizen (bɪ'daɪzᵊn, -'dɪzᵊn) *vb. (tr.) Archaic.* to dress or decorate gaudily or tastelessly. [C17: from BE- + obsolete *dizen* to dress up, of uncertain origin] —**be'dizenment** *n.*

bed jacket *n.* a woman's short upper garment worn over a nightgown when sitting up in bed.

bedlam ('bɛdləm) *n.* **1.** a noisy confused place or situation; state of uproar: *his speech caused bedlam.* **2.** *Archaic.* a lunatic asylum; madhouse. [C13 *bedlem, bethlem,* after the Hospital of St Mary of *Bethlehem* in London]

bedlamite ('bɛdləˌmaɪt) *n. Archaic.* a lunatic; insane person.

bed linen *n.* sheets and pillowcases for a bed.

Bedlington terrier ('bɛdlɪŋtən) *n.* a lithe, graceful breed of terrier having a long tapering head with no stop and a thick fleecy coat. Often shortened to **Bedlington.** [C19: named after the town *Bedlington* in Northumberland, where they were first bred]

bed moulding *n. Architect.* **1.** a moulding in an entablature between the corona and the frieze. **2.** any moulding below a projection.

Bedouin *or* **Beduin** ('bɛdʊɪn) *n.* **1.** (*pl.* **-ins** *or* **-in**) a member of any of the nomadic tribes of Arabs inhabiting the deserts of Arabia, Jordan, and Syria, as well as parts of the Sahara. **2.** a wanderer or rover. ~*adj.* **3.** of or relating to the Bedouins. **4.** wandering or roving. [C14: from Old French *beduin,* from Arabic *badāwi,* plural of *badwi,* from *badw* desert]

bedpan ('bɛdˌpæn) *n.* **1.** a shallow vessel placed under a bedridden patient to collect his faeces and urine. **2.** another name for **warming pan.**

bedplate ('bɛdˌpleɪt) *n.* a heavy metal platform or frame to which an engine or machine is attached.

bedpost ('bɛdˌpəʊst) *n.* **1.** any of the four vertical supports at the corners of a bedstead. **2. between you and me and the bedpost.** *Informal.* confidentially; in secret.

bedraggle (bɪ'drægᵊl) *vb. (tr.)* to make (hair, clothing, etc.) limp, untidy, or dirty, as with rain or mud. —**be'draggled** *adj.*

bedrail ('bɛdˌreɪl) *n.* a rail or board along the side of a bed that connects the headboard with the footboard.

bedridden ('bɛdˌrɪdᵊn) *adj.* confined to bed because of illness, esp. for a long or indefinite period. [Old English *bedreda,* from *bedd* BED + *-rida* rider, from *rīdan* to RIDE]

bedrock ('bɛdˌrɒk) *n.* **1.** the solid unweathered rock that lies beneath the loose surface deposits of soil, alluvium, etc. **2.** basic principles or facts (esp. in the phrase **get down to bedrock). 3.** the lowest point, level, or layer.

bedroll ('bɛdˌrəʊl) *n.* a portable roll of bedding, such as a sleeping bag, used esp. for sleeping in the open.

bedroom ('bɛdˌruːm, -ˌrʊm) *n.* **1.** a room furnished with beds or used for sleeping. **2.** (*modifier*) containing references to sex: *a bedroom comedy.*

Beds *abbrev. for* Bedfordshire.

bedside ('bɛdˌsaɪd) *n.* **a.** the space by the side of a bed, esp. of a sick person. **b.** (*as modifier*): *a bedside lamp; a doctor's bedside manner.*

bedsitter (ˌbɛd'sɪtə, 'bɛdˌsɪtə) *n.* a furnished sitting room containing sleeping accommodation and sometimes cooking and washing facilities. Also called: ˌ**bed'sitting room,** '**bedˌsit.**

bedsore ('bɛdˌsɔː) *n.* the nontechnical name for **decubitus ulcer.**

bedspread ('bɛdˌsprɛd) *n.* a top cover on a bed over other bedclothes.

bedstead (ˈbɛd,stɛd) *n.* the framework of a bed, usually including a headboard and springs but excluding the mattress and other coverings.

bedstraw (ˈbɛd,strɔː) *n.* any of numerous rubiaceous plants of the genus *Galium*, which have small white or yellow flowers and prickly or hairy fruits: formerly used as *Galium*, which have small white or yellow flowers and prickly or hairy fruits: formerly used as straw for beds. See also **lady's bedstraw.**

bed tea *n.* (in Pakistan) tea served to a guest in bed in the morning.

bedtime (ˈbɛd,taɪm) *n.* **a.** the time when one usually goes to bed. **b.** (*as modifier*): *a bedtime story*.

bedwarmer (ˈbɛd,wɔːmə) *n.* a metal pan containing hot coals, formerly used to warm a bed.

bed-wetting *n.* the act or habit of involuntarily urinating in bed. Technical term: **enuresis.** —ˈ**bed-,wetter** *n.*

bee[1] (biː) *n.* **1.** any hymenopterous insect of the superfamily *Apoidea*, which includes social forms such as the honeybee and solitary forms such as the carpenter bee. See also **bumblebee, mason bee. 2. busy bee.** a person who is industrious or has many things to do. **3. have a bee in one's bonnet.** to be preoccupied or obsessed with an idea. [Old English *bīo*; related to Old Norse *bȳ*, Old High German *bīa*, Dutch *bij*, Swedish *bi*]

bee[2] (biː) *n.* **1.** a social gathering for a specific purpose, as to carry out a communal task or hold competitions: *quilting bee.* **2.** See **spelling bee.** [C18: perhaps from dialect *bean* neighbourly help, from Old English *bēn* boon]

bee[3] (biː) *n. Nautical.* a small sheave with one cheek removed and the pulley and other cheek fastened flat to a boom or another spar, used for reeving outhauls or stays. [Old English *bēag* related to Old High German *boug* ring, Old Norse *bogi* a bow]

Beeb (biːb) *n.* **the.** an informal name for the **BBC.**

bee beetle *n.* a European beetle, *Trichodes apiarius*, that is often parasitic in beehives: family *Cleridae*.

beebread (ˈbiː,brɛd) *n.* a mixture of pollen and nectar prepared by worker bees and fed to the larvae. Also called: **ambrosia.**

beech (biːtʃ) *n.* **1.** any N temperate tree of the genus *Fagus*, esp. *F. sylvatica* of Europe, having smooth greyish bark: family *Fagaceae*. **2.** any tree of the related genus *Nothofagus*, of temperate Australasia and South America. **3.** the hard wood of any of these trees, used in making furniture, etc. **4.** See **copper beech.** [Old English *bēce*; related to Old Norse *bók*, Old High German *buohha*, Middle Dutch *boeke*, Latin *fāgus* beech, Greek *phēgos* edible oak] —ˈ**beechen** *or* ˈ**beechy** *adj.*

beech fern *n.* a fern, *Thelypteris phegopteris*, that grows in damp N temperate woods: family *Polypodiaceae*.

beech marten *n.* another name for **stone marten.**

beechnut (ˈbiːtʃ,nʌt) *n.* the small brown triangular edible nut of the beech tree. Collectively, the nuts are often termed **beech mast,** esp. when lying on the ground.

bee-eater *n.* any insectivorous bird of the family *Meropidae* of tropical and subtropical regions of the Old World, having a long downward-curving bill and long pointed wings and tail: order *Coraciiformes* (kingfishers, etc.).

beef (biːf) *n.* **1.** the flesh of various bovine animals, esp. the cow, when killed for eating. **2.** (*pl.* **beeves** (biːvz)) an adult ox, bull, cow, etc., reared for its meat. **3.** *Informal.* human flesh, esp. when muscular. **4.** (*pl.* **beefs**) *Slang.* a complaint. ~*vb.* **5.** (*intr.*) *Slang.* to complain, esp. repeatedly: *he was beefing about his tax.* **6.** (*tr.*; often foll. by *up*) *Informal.* to strengthen; reinforce. [C13: from Old French *boef*, from Latin *bōs* ox; see COW[1]]

beefburger (ˈbiːf,bɜːgə) *n.* a flat fried cake of minced beef; hamburger.

beefcake (ˈbiːf,keɪk) *n. Slang.* men displayed for their muscular bodies, esp. in photographs. Compare **cheesecake** (sense 2).

beefeater (ˈbiːf,iːtə) *n.* a yeoman warder of the Tower of London.

bee fly *n.* any hairy beelike nectar-eating dipterous fly of the family *Bombyliidae*, whose larvae are parasitic on those of bees and related insects.

beef road *n. Austral.* a road used for transporting cattle.

beefsteak (ˈbiːf,steɪk) *n.* a piece of beef that can be grilled, fried, etc., cut from any lean part of the animal.

beefsteak fungus *n.* an edible reddish bracket fungus, *Fistulina hepatica*, that grows esp. on oak trees and oozes a bloodlike juice.

beefsteak tomato *n.* a very large fleshy variety of tomato. Also called: **beef tomato.**

beef stroganoff *n.* a dish of thin strips of beef cooked with onions, mushrooms, and seasonings, served in a sour-cream sauce. [C19: named after Count Paul *Stroganoff*, 19th-century Russian diplomat]

beef tea *n.* a drink made by boiling pieces of lean beef: often given to invalids to stimulate the appetite.

beefwood (ˈbiːf,wʊd) *n.* **1.** any of various trees that produce very hard wood, esp. the Australian tree *Casuarina equisetifolia* (see **casuarina**), widely planted in warm regions. **2.** the wood of any of these trees. [from the red colour and grain]

beefy (ˈbiːfɪ) *adj.* **beefier, beefiest. 1.** like beef. **2.** *Informal.* muscular; brawny. **3.** *Informal.* fleshy; obese. —ˈ**beefily** *adv.* —ˈ**beefiness** *n.*

bee glue *n.* another name for **propolis.**

beehive (ˈbiː,haɪv) *n.* **1.** a man-made receptacle used to house a swarm of bees. **2.** a dome-shaped hair style in which the hair is piled high on the head. **3.** a place where busy people are assembled.

beehive house *n.* a prehistoric circular building found in various parts of Europe, usually of stone and having a dome-shaped roof.

beekeeper (ˈbiː,kiːpə) *n.* a person who keeps bees for their honey; apiarist. —ˈ**bee,keeping** *n.*

bee killer *n.* another name for **robber fly.**

beeline (ˈbiː,laɪn) *n.* the most direct route between two places (esp. in the phrase **make a beeline for**).

Beelzebub (bɪˈɛlzɪ,bʌb) *n.* Satan or any devil or demon. [Old English *Belzebub*, ultimately from Hebrew *báʻal zebūb*, literally: lord of flies]

bee moth *n.* any of various pyralid moths, such as the wax moth, whose larvae live in the nests of bees or wasps, feeding on nest materials and host larvae.

been (biːn, bɪn) *vb.* the past participle of **be.**

beento (ˈbiːntuː, ˈbɪntʊ) *W African informal.* ~*n., pl.* **-tos. 1.** a person who has resided in Britain, esp. during part of his education. ~*adj.* **2.** of, relating to, or characteristic of such a person. [C20: from BEEN + TO]

bee orchid *n.* a European orchid, *Ophrys apifera*, whose flower resembles a bumble bee in shape and colour.

beep (biːp) *n.* **1.** a short high-pitched sound, esp. one made by the horn of a car, bicycle, etc., or by electronic apparatus. ~*vb.* **2.** to make or cause to make such a noise. [C20: of imitative origin] —ˈ**beeper** *n.*

bee plant *n.* any of various plants much visited by bees for nectar and pollen.

beer (bɪə) *n.* **1.** an alcoholic drink brewed from malt, sugar, hops, and water and fermented with yeast. Compare **ale. 2.** a slightly fermented drink made from the roots or leaves of certain plants: *ginger beer; nettle beer.* **3.** (*modifier*) relating to or used in the drinking of beer: *beer glass; beer mat.* **4.** (*modifier*) in which beer is drunk, esp. (of licensed premises) having a licence to sell beer but not spirits: *beer house; beer cellar; beer garden.* [Old English *beor*; related to Old Norse *björr*, Old Frisian *biār*, Old High German *bior*]

beer and skittles *n.* (*functioning as sing.*) *Informal.* enjoyment or pleasure.

beer-up *n. Austral. slang.* a drinking bout.

beery (ˈbɪərɪ) *adj.* **beerier, beeriest. 1.** smelling or tasting of beer. **2.** given to drinking beer. —ˈ**beerily** *adv.* —ˈ**beeriness** *n.*

bee's knees *n.* **the** (*functioning as sing.*) *Informal.* an excellent or ideally suitable person or thing.

beestings, biestings *or U.S.* **beastings** (ˈbiːstɪŋz) *n.* (*functioning as sing.*) the first milk secreted by the mammary glands of a cow or similar animal immediately after giving birth; colostrum. [Old English *bȳsting*, from *bēost* beestings; related to Middle Dutch *biest*]

beeswax (ˈbiːz,wæks) *n.* **1. a.** a yellowish or dark brown wax secreted by honeybees for constructing honeycombs. **b.** this wax after refining, purifying, etc., used in polishes, ointments, and for modelling. ~*vb.* **2.** (*tr.*) to polish with such wax.

beeswing (ˈbiːz,wɪŋ) *n.* **1.** a light filmy crust of tartar that forms in port and some other wines after long keeping in the bottle. **2.** a port or other wine containing beeswing.

beet (biːt) *n.* **1.** any chenopodiaceous plant of the genus *Beta*, esp. the Eurasian species *B. vulgaris*, widely cultivated in such varieties as the sugar beet, mangelwurzel, beetroot, and spinach beet. See also **chard. 2.** the leaves of any of several varieties of this plant, which are cooked and eaten as a vegetable. **3. red beet.** the U.S. name for **beetroot.** [Old English *bēte*, from Latin *bēta*]

beetfly (ˈbiːt,flaɪ) *n., pl.* **-flies.** a muscid fly, *Pegomyia hyoscyami*: a common pest of beets and mangel-wurzels. Also called: **mangold fly.**

beetle[1] (ˈbiːtᵊl) *n.* **1.** any insect of the order *Coleoptera*, having biting mouthparts and forewings modified to form shell-like protective elytra. **2.** a game played with dice in which the players draw or assemble a beetle-shaped form. ~*vb.* (*intr.*; foll. by *along, off*, etc.) **3.** *Informal.* to scuttle or scurry; hurry. [Old English *bitela*; related to *bitol* teeth, BIT, *bītan* to BITE]

beetle[2] (ˈbiːtᵊl) *n.* **1.** a heavy hand tool, usually made of wood, used for ramming, pounding, or beating. **2.** a machine used to finish cloth by stamping it with wooden hammers. ~*vb.* (*tr.*) **3.** to beat or pound with a beetle. **4.** to finish (cloth) by means of a beetle. [Old English *bīetel*, from *bēatan* to BEAT; related to Middle Low German *bētel* chisel, Old Norse *beytill* penis]

beetle[3] (ˈbiːtᵊl) *vb.* **1.** (*intr.*) to overhang; jut. ~*adj.* **2.** overhanging; prominent. [C14: perhaps related to BEETLE[1]] —ˈ**beetling** *adj.*

beetle-browed *adj.* **1.** having bushy or overhanging eyebrows. **2.** sullen in appearance; scowling.

beetle drive *n.* a social occasion at which a progressive series of games of beetle is played. See **beetle**[1] (sense 2).

beetroot (ˈbiːt,ruːt) *n.* **1.** a variety of the beet plant, *Beta vulgaris*, that has a bulbous dark red root that may be eaten as a vegetable, in salads, or pickled. **2.** the root of this plant. ~U.S. name: **red beet.**

beet sugar *n.* the sucrose obtained from sugar beet, identical in composition to cane sugar.

beeves (biːvz) *n.* the plural of **beef** (sense 2).

beezer (ˈbiːzə) *Slang.* ~*n.* **1.** *Brit., old fashioned.* a person or chap. **2.** *Brit., old fashioned.* the nose. **3.** *Scot.* an extreme example of its kind. ~*adj.* **4.** *Brit., old fashioned.* excellent; most attractive. [C20: of uncertain origin]
BEF *abbrev. for* British Expeditionary Force, the British army that served in France 1939–40.
befall (bɪˈfɔːl) *vb.* **-falls, -falling, -fell, -fallen.** *Archaic or literary.* **1.** (*intr.*) to take place; come to pass. **2.** (*tr.*) to happen to. **3.** (*intr.*; usually foll. by *to*) to be due, as by right. [Old English *befeallan;* related to Old High German *bifallan,* Dutch *bevallen;* see BE-, FALL]
befit (bɪˈfɪt) *vb.* **-fits, -fitting, -fitted.** (*tr.*) to be appropriate to or suitable for. [C15: from BE- + FIT[1]] —**beˈfitting** *adj.* —**beˈfittingly** *adv.*
befog (bɪˈfɒg) *vb.* **-fogs, -fogging, -fogged.** (*tr.*) **1.** to surround with fog. **2.** to make confused, vague, or less clear.
befool (bɪˈfuːl) *vb.* (*tr.*) **1.** to make a fool of. **2.** *Archaic.* to treat or regard as a fool.
before (bɪˈfɔː) *conj.* (*subordinating*) **1.** earlier than the time when. **2.** rather than: *he'll resign before he agrees to it.* ~*prep.* **3.** preceding in space or time; in front of; ahead of: *standing before the altar.* **4.** when confronted by: *to withdraw before one's enemies.* **5.** in the presence of: *to be brought before a judge.* **6.** in preference to: *to put friendship before money.* ~*adv.* **7.** at an earlier time; previously; beforehand; in front. [Old English *beforan;* related to Old Frisian *befara,* Old High German *bifora*]
beforehand (bɪˈfɔːˌhænd) *adj.* (*postpositive*), *adv.* early; in advance; in anticipation: *she came an hour beforehand.*
beforetime (bɪˈfɔːˌtaɪm) *adv. Archaic.* formerly.
befoul (bɪˈfaʊl) *vb.* (*tr.*) to make dirty or foul; soil; defile. —**beˈfouler** *n.* —**beˈfoulment** *n.*
befriend (bɪˈfrɛnd) *vb.* (*tr.*) to be a friend to; assist; favour.
befuddle (bɪˈfʌdᵊl) *vb.* (*tr.*) **1.** to confuse, muddle, or perplex. **2.** to make stupid with drink. —**beˈfuddlement** *n.*
beg[1] (bɛg) *vb.* **begs, begging, begged.** **1.** (when *intr.*, often foll. by *for*) to solicit (for money, food, etc.), esp. in the street. **2.** to ask (someone) for (something or leave to do something) formally, humbly, or earnestly: *I beg forgiveness; I beg to differ.* **3.** (*intr.*) (of a dog) to sit up with forepaws raised expectantly. **4.** to leave unanswered or unresolved: *to beg a point.* **5. beg the question.** **a.** to evade the issue. **b.** to assume the thing under examination as proved. **6. go (a-)begging.** to be unwanted or unused. ~See also **beg off.** [C13: probably from Old English *bedecian;* related to Gothic *bidagwa* BEGGAR]
beg[2] (bɛg) *n.* a variant of **bey.**
begad (bɪˈgæd) *interj. Archaic slang.* an emphatic exclamation. [C18: euphemistic alteration of *by God!*]
began (bɪˈgæn) *vb.* the past tense of **begin.**
begat (bɪˈgæt) *vb. Archaic.* a past tense of **beget.**
beget (bɪˈgɛt) *vb.* **-gets, -getting, -got** *or* **-gat; -gotten** *or* **-got.** (*tr.*) **1.** to father. **2.** to cause or create. [Old English *begietan;* related to Old Saxon *bigetan,* Old High German *pigezzan,* Gothic *bigitan* to find; see BE-, GET] —**beˈgetter** *n.*
beggar (ˈbɛgə) *n.* **1.** a person who begs, esp. one who lives by begging. **2.** a person who has no money or resources; pauper. **3.** *Ironic or jocular, chiefly Brit.* fellow: *lucky beggar!* ~*vb.* (*tr.*) **4.** to be beyond the resources of (esp. in the phrase **to beggar description**). **5.** to impoverish; reduce to begging. —**ˈbeggarˌhood** *or* **ˈbeggardom** *n.*
beggarly (ˈbɛgəlɪ) *adj.* meanly inadequate; very poor: *beggarly living conditions.* —**ˈbeggarliness** *n.*
beggar-my-neighbour *n.* **1.** a card game in which one player tries to win all the cards of the other player. **2.** (*modifier*) relating to or denoting an advantage gained by one side at the expense of the other: *beggar-my-neighbour policies.*
beggar's-lice *n.* (*functioning as sing.*) **1.** any of several plants, esp. the stickseed, having small prickly fruits that adhere to clothing, fur, etc. **2.** the seed or fruit of any of these plants.
beggar-ticks *or* **beggar's-ticks** *n.* (*functioning as sing.*) **1.** any of various plants, such as the bur marigold and tick trefoil, having fruits or seeds that cling to clothing, fur, etc. **2.** the seed or fruit of any of these plants.
beggarweed (ˈbɛgəˌwiːd) *n.* any of various leguminous plants of the genus *Desmodium,* esp. *D. purpureum* of the West Indies, grown in the southern U.S. as forage plants and to improve the soil. See also **tick trefoil.**
beggary (ˈbɛgərɪ) *n.* **1.** extreme poverty or need. **2.** the condition of being a beggar.
begging bowl *n.* a bowl carried by a beggar, esp. a Franciscan or other friar or a Buddhist monk, to receive food or alms.
begging letter *n.* a letter asking for money sent esp. by a stranger to someone known to be rich.
Beghard (ˈbɛgəd, bɪˈgɑːd) *n.* a member of a Christian brotherhood that was founded in Flanders in the 13th century and followed a life based on that of the Beguines. Also called: **Beguin.** [C17: from Medieval Latin *beghardus,* from BEG(UINE) + -ARD; compare Old French *bégard,* Middle Dutch *beggaert,* Middle High German *beghart*]
begin (bɪˈgɪn) *vb.* **-gins, -ginning, -gan, -gun.** **1.** to start or cause to start (something or to do something). **2.** to bring or come into being for the first time; arise or originate. **3.** to start to say or speak. **4.** (*used with a negative*) to have the least capacity (to do something): *he couldn't begin to compete with her.* **5. to begin with.** in the first place. [Old English *beginnan;* related to Old High German *biginnan,* Gothic *duginnan*]
beginner (bɪˈgɪnə) *n.* a person who has just started to do or learn something; novice.
beginning (bɪˈgɪnɪŋ) *n.* **1.** a start; commencement. **2.** (*often pl.*) a first or early part or stage. **3.** the place where or time when something starts. **4.** an origin; source.
begird (bɪˈgɜːd) *vb.* **-girds, -girding, -girt** *or* **-girded.** (*tr.*) *Poetic.* **1.** to surround; gird around. **2.** to bind. [Old English *begierdan;* see BE-, GIRD[1]]
beg off *vb.* (*intr., adv.*) to ask to be released from an engagement, obligation, etc.
begone (bɪˈgɒn) *sentence substitute* go away! [C14: from BE (imperative) + GONE]
begonia (bɪˈgəʊnjə) *n.* any plant of the genus *Begonia,* of warm and tropical regions, widely cultivated for their ornamental leaves and waxy flowers: family *Begoniaceae.* [C18: New Latin, named after Michel *Bégon* (1638–1710), French patron of science]
begorra (bɪˈgɒrə) *interj.* an emphatic exclamation, regarded as a characteristic utterance of Irishmen. [C19: euphemistic alteration of *by God!*]
begot (bɪˈgɒt) *vb.* a past tense and past participle of **beget.**
begotten (bɪˈgɒtᵊn) *vb.* a past participle of **beget.**
begrime (bɪˈgraɪm) *vb.* (*tr.*) to make dirty; soil.
begrudge (bɪˈgrʌdʒ) *vb.* (*tr.*) **1.** to give, admit, or allow unwillingly or with a bad grace. **2.** to envy (someone) the possession of (something). —**beˈgrudgingly** *adv.*
beguile (bɪˈgaɪl) *vb.* **-guiles, -guiling, -guiled.** (*tr.*) **1.** to charm; fascinate. **2.** to delude; influence by slyness. **3.** (often foll. by *of* or *out of*) to deprive (someone) of something by trickery; cheat (someone) of. **4.** to pass pleasantly; while away. —**beˈguilement** *n.* —**beˈguiler** *n.* —**beˈguiling** *adj.* —**beˈguilingly** *adv.*
Beguin (ˈbɛgɪn; *French* begɛ̃) *n.* another word for **Beghard.**
beguine (bɪˈgiːn) *n.* **1.** a dance of South American origin in bolero rhythm. **2.** a piece of music in the rhythm of this dance. **3.** a variant of **biggin**[1]. [C20: from Louisiana French, from French *béguin* flirtation]
Beguine (ˈbɛgiːn) *n.* a member of a Christian sisterhood that was founded in Liège in the 12th century, and, though not taking religious vows, followed an austere life. [C15: from Old French, perhaps after *Lambert le Bègue* (the Stammerer), 12th-century priest of Liège, who founded the sisterhood]
begum (ˈbeɪgəm) *n.* (in Pakistan and certain other Muslim countries) a woman of high rank, esp. the widow of a prince. [C18: from Urdu *begam,* from Turkish *begim;* see BEY]
begun (bɪˈgʌn) *vb.* the past participle of **begin.**
behalf (bɪˈhɑːf) *n.* interest, part, benefit, or respect (only in the phrases **on (someone's) behalf, on** *or U.S. and Canadian* **in behalf of, in this** (*or* **that**) **behalf**). [Old English *be halfe* from *be* by + *halfe* side; compare Old Norse *af halfu*]
behave (bɪˈheɪv) *vb.* **1.** (*intr.*) to act or function in a specified or usual way. **2.** to conduct (oneself) in a specified way: *he behaved badly towards her.* **3.** to conduct (oneself) properly or as desired: *the child behaved himself all day.* [C15: see BE-, HAVE]
behaviour *or U.S.* **behavior** (bɪˈheɪvjə) *n.* **1.** manner of behaving or conducting oneself. **2. on one's best behaviour.** behaving with careful good manners. **3.** *Psychol.* **a.** the aggregate of all the responses made by an organism in any situation. **b.** a specific response of a certain organism to a specific stimulus or group of stimuli. **4.** the action, reaction, or functioning of a machine, chemical substance, etc., under normal or specified circumstances. [C15: from BEHAVE; influenced in form by Middle English *havior,* from Old French *havoir,* from Latin *habēre* to have] —**beˈhavioural** *or U.S.* **beˈhavioral** *adj.*
behavioural contagion *n.* the spread of a particular type of behaviour, such as crying, through a crowd or group of people.
behavioural science *n.* the application of scientific methods to the study of the behaviour of organisms.
behavioural sink *n. Psychol.* a small area in which people or animals live in overcrowded conditions.
behaviourism *or U.S.* **behaviorism** (bɪˈheɪvjəˌrɪzəm) *n.* **1.** a school of psychology that regards the objective observation of the behaviour of organisms (usually by means of automatic recording devices) as the only proper subject for study, and the only item to be referred to in a theory, and that often refuses to postulate any intervening mechanisms between the stimulus and the response. **2.** the doctrine that the mind has no separate existence but that statements about the mind and mental states can be analysed into statements about actual and potential behaviour. Compare **materialism** (sense 2). See also **mind-body problem.** —**beˈhaviourist** *or U.S.* **beˈhaviorist** *adj., n.* —**beˌhaviourˈistic** *or U.S.* **beˌhaviorˈistic** *adj.*
behaviour therapy *n.* any of various means of treating psychological disorders, such as desensitization, aversion therapy, and instrumental conditioning, that depend on the patient systematically learning new modes of behaviour.
behead (bɪˈhɛd) *vb.* (*tr.*) to remove the head from; decapitate. [Old English *behēafdian,* from BE- + *heafod* HEAD; related to Middle High German *behoubeten*]
beheld (bɪˈhɛld) *vb.* the past tense and past participle of **behold.**
behemoth (bɪˈhiːmɒθ) *n.* **1.** *Old Testament.* a gigantic beast, probably a hippopotamus, described in Job 40:15. **2.** a huge or

monstrous person or thing. [C14: from Hebrew *bĕhēmōth*, plural of *bĕhēmāh* beast]

behest (bɪˈhɛst) *n.* an authoritative order or earnest request. [Old English *behǣs*, from *behātan;* see BE-, HEST]

behind (bɪˈhaɪnd) *prep.* **1.** in or to a position further back than; at the rear of; at the back of. **2.** in the past in relation to: *I've got the exams behind me now.* **3.** late according to; not keeping up with: *running behind schedule.* **4.** concerning the circumstances surrounding: *the reasons behind his departure.* **5.** backing or supporting: *I'm right behind you in your application.* ~*adv.* **6.** in or to a position further back; following. **7.** remaining after someone's departure: *he left his books behind.* **8.** in debt; in arrears: *to fall behind with payments.* ~*adj.* **9.** (*postpositive*) in a position further back; retarded: *the man behind asked me to give you this.* ~*n.* **10.** *Informal.* the buttocks. **11.** *Australian Rules football.* a score of one point made by kicking the ball over the **behind line** between a goalpost and one of the smaller outer posts (**behind posts**). [Old English *behindan*]

behindhand (bɪˈhaɪnd,hænd) *adj.* (*postpositive*), *adv.* **1.** remiss in fulfilling an obligation. **2.** in debt; in arrears. **3.** delayed in development; backward. **4.** late; behind time.

behold (bɪˈhəʊld) *vb.* **-holds, -holding, -held.** (often used in the imperative to draw attention to something) *Archaic or literary.* to look (at); observe. [Old English *bihealdan;* related to Old High German *bihaltan*, Dutch *behouden;* see BE-, HOLD] —**beˈholder** *n.*

beholden (bɪˈhəʊldᵊn) *adj.* indebted; obliged; under a moral obligation. [Old English *behealden*, past participle of *behealdan* to BEHOLD]

behoof (bɪˈhuːf) *n., pl.* **-hooves.** *Rare.* advantage or profit. [Old English *behōf;* related to Middle High German *behuof* something useful; see BEHOVE]

behove (bɪˈhəʊv) *or U.S.* **behoove** (bɪˈhuːv) *vb.* (*tr.; impersonal*) *Archaic.* to be necessary or fitting for: *it behoves me to arrest you.* [Old English *behōfian;* related to Middle Low German *behōven*]

beige (beɪʒ) *n.* **1. a.** a very light brown, sometimes with a yellowish tinge, similar to the colour of undyed wool. **b.** (*as adj.*): *beige gloves.* **2.** a fabric made of undyed or unbleached wool. [C19: from Old French, of obscure origin]

beigel (ˈbeɪgᵊl) *n.* a variant spelling of **bagel.**

being (ˈbiːɪŋ) *n.* **1.** the state or fact of existing; existence. **2.** essential nature; self: *she put her whole being into the part.* **3.** something that exists or is thought to exist, esp. something that cannot be assigned to any category: *a being from outer space.* **4.** a person; human being. **5.** (in the philosophy of Aristotle) actuality. Compare **becoming** (sense 3).

Beit Knesset *or* **Beth Knesseth** (bɛt ˈknɛsɛt) *n.* a synagogue: often used in the names of congregations. [from Hebrew, literally: house of assembly]

bejabers (bɪˈdʒeɪbəz) *or* **bejabbers** (bɪˈdʒæbəz) *interj.* an exclamation of surprise, emphasis, etc., regarded as a characteristic utterance of Irishmen. [C19: alteration of *by Jesus!*]

bejewel (bɪˈdʒuːəl) *vb.* **-els, -elling, -elled** *or U.S.* **-els, -eling, -eled.** (*tr.*) to decorate with or as if with jewels. —**beˈjewelled** *or U.S.* **beˈjeweled** *adj.*

bel (bɛl) *n.* a unit for comparing two power levels, equal to the logarithm to the base ten of the ratio of the two powers. Symbols: **B, b** See also **decibel.** [C20: named after A. G. *Bell* (1847–1922), U.S. scientist and inventor of the telephone]

belabour *or U.S.* **belabor** (bɪˈleɪbə) *vb.* (*tr.*) **1.** to beat severely; thrash. **2.** to attack verbally; criticize harshly. **3.** an obsolete word for **labour.**

belah *or* **belar** (ˈbiːlɑː) *n.* an Australian casuarina tree, *Casuarina glauca*, yielding a useful timber.

belated (bɪˈleɪtɪd) *adj.* late or too late: *belated greetings.* —**beˈlatedly** *adv.* —**beˈlatedness** *n.*

belay (bɪˈleɪ) *vb.* **-lays, -laying, -layed.** **1.** *Nautical.* to make fast (a line) by securing to a pin, cleat, or bitt. **2.** (*usually imperative*) *Nautical.* to stop; cease. **3.** (ˈbiː,leɪ). *Mountaineering.* to secure (a climber) to a mountain by tying the rope off round a rock spike, piton, nut, etc. ~*n.* **4.** (ˈbiː,leɪ). *Mountaineering.* the attachment (of a climber) to a mountain by tying the rope off round a rock spike, piton, nut, etc., to safeguard the party in the event of a fall. See also **running belay.** [Old English *belecgan;* related to Old High German *bileggen*, Dutch *beleggen*]

belaying pin *n. Nautical.* a cylindrical, sometimes tapered pin, usually of metal or wood, that fits into a hole in a pin or fife rail: used for belaying.

bel canto (ˈbɛl ˈkæntəʊ) *n. Music.* **a.** a style of singing characterized by beauty of tone rather than dramatic power. **b.** (*as modifier*): *a bel canto aria.* [C19: Italian, literally: beautiful singing]

belch (bɛltʃ) *vb.* **1.** (*usually intr.*) to expel wind from the stomach noisily through the mouth; eructate. **2.** to expel or be expelled forcefully from inside: *smoke belching from factory chimneys.* **3.** to say (curses, insults, etc.) violently or bitterly. ~*n.* **4.** an act of belching; eructation. [Old English *bialcan;* related to Middle Low German *belken* to shout, Dutch *balken* to bray]

beldam *or* **beldame** (ˈbɛldəm) *n.* **1.** *Archaic.* an old woman, esp. an ugly or malicious one; hag. **2.** an obsolete word for **grandmother.** [C15: from *bel-* grand (as in *grandmother*), from Old French *bel* beautiful, from Latin *bellus* + *dam* mother, variant of DAME]

beleaguer (bɪˈliːgə) *vb.* (*tr.*) **1.** to trouble persistently; harass. **2.** to lay siege to. [C16: from BE- + LEAGUER[1]]

belemnite (ˈbɛləm,naɪt) *n.* **1.** any extinct marine cephalopod mollusc of the order *Belemnoidea*, related to the cuttlefish. **2.** the long pointed conical internal shell of any of these animals: a common Mesozoic fossil. [C17: from Greek *belemnon* dart]

belemnoid (ˈbɛləm,nɔɪd) *adj. Anatomy, zoology.* shaped like a dart.

bel esprit *French.* (bɛl ɛspri) *n., pl.* ***beaux esprits*** (boz ɛspri). a witty or clever person. [literally: fine wit]

belfry (ˈbɛlfrɪ) *n., pl.* **-fries.** **1.** the part of a tower or steeple in which bells are hung. **2.** a tower or steeple. Compare **campanile.** **3.** the timber framework inside a tower or steeple on which bells are hung. **4.** (formerly) a movable tower for attacking fortifications. [C13: from Old French *berfrei*, of Germanic origin; compare Middle High German *bercfrit* fortified tower, Medieval Latin *berfredus* tower]

Belg. *or* **Bel.** *abbrev. for:* **1.** Belgian. **2.** Belgium.

belga (ˈbɛlgə) *n.* a former Belgian monetary unit worth five francs.

Belgae (ˈbɛldʒiː, ˈbɛlgaɪ) *n.* an ancient Celtic people who in Roman times inhabited present-day Belgium and N France. —**ˈBelgic** *adj.*

Belgian (ˈbɛldʒən) *n.* **1.** a native, citizen, or inhabitant of Belgium, a kingdom in NW Europe. See also **Fleming, Walloon.** ~*adj.* **2.** of, relating to, or characteristic of Belgium or the Belgians. **3.** of or relating to the Walloon French or the Flemish languages.

Belgian hare *n.* a large red breed of domestic rabbit.

belie (bɪˈlaɪ) *vb.* **-lies, -lying, -lied.** (*tr.*) **1.** to show to be untrue; contradict. **2.** to misrepresent; disguise the nature of: *the report belied the real extent of the damage.* **3.** to fail to justify; disappoint. [Old English *belēogan;* related to Old Frisian *biliuga*, Old High German *biliugan;* see BE-, LIE[1]] —**beˈlier** *n.*

belief (bɪˈliːf) *n.* **1.** a principle, proposition, idea, etc., accepted as true. **2.** opinion; conviction. **3.** religious faith. **4.** trust or confidence, as in a person or a person's abilities, probity, etc.

believe (bɪˈliːv) *vb.* **1.** (*tr.; may take a clause as object*) to accept (a statement, supposition, or opinion) as true: *I believe God exists.* **2.** (*tr.*) to accept the statement or opinion of (a person) as true. **3.** (*intr.;* foll. by *in*) to be convinced of the truth or existence (of): *to believe in fairies.* **4.** (*intr.*) to have religious faith. **5.** (*when tr., takes a clause as object*) to think, assume, or suppose: *I believe that he has left already.* **6.** (*tr.;* foll. by *of; used with can, could, would, etc.*) to think that someone is able to do (a particular action): *I wouldn't have believed it of him.* [Old English *beliefan*] —**be,lievaˈbility** *n.* —**beˈlievable** *adj.* —**beˈlievably** *adv.* —**beˈliever** *n.* —**beˈlieving** *n., adj.*

belike (bɪˈlaɪk) *adv. Archaic or dialect.* perhaps; maybe.

Belisha beacon (bəˈliːʃə) *n.* a flashing light in an orange globe mounted on a post, indicating a pedestrian crossing on a road. [C20: named after Leslie Hore-*Belisha* (1893–1957), British politician]

belittle (bɪˈlɪtᵊl) *vb.* (*tr.*) **1.** to consider or speak of (something) as less valuable or important than it really is; disparage. **2.** to cause to make small; dwarf. —**beˈlittlement** *n.* —**beˈlittler** *n.* —**beˈlittlingly** *adv.*

bell[1] (bɛl) *n.* **1.** a hollow, usually metal, cup-shaped instrument that emits a musical ringing sound when struck, often by a clapper hanging inside it. **2.** the sound made by such an instrument or device, as for showing the hours or marking the beginning or end of a period of time. **3.** an electrical device that rings or buzzes as a signal. **4.** the bowl-shaped termination of the tube of certain musical wind instruments, such as the trumpet or oboe. **5.** any musical percussion instrument emitting a ringing tone, such as a glockenspiel, one of a set of hand bells, etc. Compare **chime**[1] (sense 3). **6.** *Nautical.* a signal rung on a ship's bell to count the number of half-hour intervals during each of six four-hour watches reckoned from midnight. Thus, one bell may signify 12.30, 4.30, or 8.30 a.m. or p.m. **7.** See **diving bell.** **8.** *Biology.* a structure resembling a bell in shape, such as the corolla of certain flowers or the body of a jellyfish. **9.** *Brit. slang.* a telephone call (esp. in the phrase **give someone a bell**). **10. bell, book, and candle. a.** instruments used formerly in excommunications and other ecclesiastical acts. **b.** *Informal.* the solemn ritual ratification of such acts. **11. ring a bell.** to sound familiar; recall to the mind something previously experienced, esp. indistinctly. **12. sound as a bell.** in perfect condition. **13. the bells.** the ringing of bells, in a church or other public building, at midnight on December 31st, symbolizing the beginning of a new year. ~*vb.* **14.** to be or cause to be shaped like a bell. **15.** (*tr.*) to attach a bell or bells to. **16. bell the cat.** to undertake a dangerous mission. [Old English *belle;* related to Old Norse *bjalla*, Middle Low German *bell;* see BELL[2]]

bell[2] (bɛl) *n.* **1.** a bellowing or baying cry, esp. that of a hound or a male deer in rut. ~*vb.* **2.** to utter (such a cry). [Old English *bellan;* related to Old Norse *belja* to bellow, Old High German *bellan* to roar, Sanskrit *bhāsate* he talks; see BELLOW]

belladonna (,bɛləˈdɒnə) *n.* **1.** either of two alkaloid drugs, atropine or hyoscyamine, obtained from the leaves and roots of the deadly nightshade. **2.** another name for **deadly nightshade.** [C16: from Italian, literally: beautiful lady; supposed to refer to its use by women as a cosmetic]

belladonna lily *n.* another name for **amaryllis.**
bellarmine ('bɛlɑːˌmiːn) *n.* a large stoneware or earthenware jug for ale or spirits, bearing a bearded mask. [C18: named after Robert *Belarmine* (1542–1621), Italian Jesuit cardinal, whom these jugs were intended to caricature]
Bellatrix ('bɛlətrɪks) *n.* the third brightest star in the constellation Orion.
bellbird ('bɛlˌbɜːd) *n.* **1.** any of several tropical American passerine birds of the genus *Procnias* having a bell-like call: family *Cotingidae* (cotingas). **2.** either of two other birds with a bell-like call: an Australian flycatcher, *Oreoica gutturalis* **(crested bellbird)**, or a New Zealand honeyeater, *Anthornis melanura.*
bell-bottoms *pl. n.* trousers that flare from the knee and have wide bottoms. —**'bell-ˌbottomed** *adj.*
bellboy ('bɛlˌbɔɪ) *n. Chiefly U.S. and Canadian* a man or boy employed in a hotel, club, etc., to carry luggage and answer calls for service; page; porter. Also called (U.S. and Canadian): **bellhop.**
bell bronze *n.* an alloy of copper and tin that contains a high proportion (at least 20 per cent) of tin: used for bell founding.
bell buoy *n.* a navigational buoy fitted with a bell, the clapper of which strikes when the waves move the buoy.
bell crank *n. Engineering.* a lever with two arms having a common fulcrum at their junction.
belle (bɛl) *n.* **1.** a beautiful girl or woman. **2.** the most attractive or admired girl or woman at a place, function, etc. (esp. in the phrase **the belle of the ball**). [C17: from French, feminine of BEAU]
Belleek (bə'liːk) *n.* **a.** a kind of thin fragile porcelain with a lustrous glaze. **b.** (*as modifier*): *a Belleek vase.* [named after *Belleek,* a town in Northern Ireland where such porcelain is made]
belle époque *French.* (bɛl epɔk) *n.* the period of comfortable well-established life before World War I. [literally: fine period]
belles-lettres (*French* bɛllɛtrə) *n.* (*functioning as sing.*) literary works, esp. essays and poetry, valued for their aesthetic rather than their informative or moral content. [C17: from French: fine letters]
belletrist (bɛl'lɛtrɪst) *n.* a writer of belles-lettres. —**bel'letrism** *n.* —**belletristic** (ˌbɛlɪ'trɪstɪk) *adj.*
bellflower ('bɛlˌflaʊə) *n.* another name for **campanula.**
bellfounder ('bɛlˌfaʊndə) *n.* a foundry worker who casts bells. —**'bellˌfoundry** *n.*
bell glass *n.* another name for **bell jar.**
bell heather *n.* an ericaceous shrub, *Erica cinerea.* See **heath** (sense 2).
bellhop ('bɛlˌhɒp) *n. U.S. and Canadian.* another name for **bellboy.**
bellicose ('bɛlɪˌkəʊs, -ˌkəʊz) *adj.* warlike; aggressive; ready to fight. [C15: from Latin *bellicōsus,* from *bellum* war] —**'belliˌcosely** *adv.* —**bellicosity** (ˌbɛlɪ'kɒsɪtɪ) *n.*
belligerence (bɪ'lɪdʒərəns) *n.* the act or quality of being belligerent or warlike; aggressiveness.
belligerency (bɪ'lɪdʒərənsɪ) *n.* the state of being at war.
belligerent (bɪ'lɪdʒərənt) *adj.* **1.** marked by readiness to fight or argue; aggressive: *a belligerent tone.* **2.** relating to or engaged in a legally recognized war or warfare. ~*n.* **3.** a person or country engaged in fighting or war. [C16: from Latin *belliger,* from *bellum* war + *gerere* to wage]
bell jar *n.* a bell-shaped glass cover used to protect flower arrangements or fragile ornaments or to cover apparatus in experiments, esp. to prevent gases escaping.
bell magpie *n.* another name for **currawong.**
bellman ('bɛlmən) *n., pl.* **-men.** a man who rings a bell, esp. (formerly) a town crier.
bell metal *n.* an alloy of copper and tin, with some zinc and lead, used in casting bells.
bell moth *n.* any moth of the family *Tortricidae,* which when at rest resemble the shape of a bell.
bellow ('bɛləʊ) *vb.* **1.** (*intr.*) to make a loud deep raucous cry like that of a bull; roar. **2.** to shout (something) unrestrainedly, as in anger or pain; bawl. ~*n.* **3.** the characteristic noise of a bull. **4.** a loud deep sound, as of pain or anger. [C14: probably from Old English *bylgan;* related to *bellan* to BELL[2]] —**'bellower** *n.*
bellows ('bɛləʊz) *n.* (*functioning as sing. or pl.*) **1.** Also called: **pair of bellows.** an instrument consisting of an air chamber with flexible sides, a means of compressing it, an inlet valve, and a constricted outlet that is used to create a stream of air, as for producing a draught for a fire or for sounding organ pipes. **2.** *Photog.* a telescopic light-tight sleeve, connecting the lens system of some cameras to the body of the instrument. **3.** a flexible corrugated element used as an expansion joint, pump, or means of transmitting axial motion. [C16: from plural of Old English *belig* BELLY]
bellows fish *n.* another name for **snipefish.**
bell pull *n.* a handle, rope, or cord pulled to operate a doorbell or servant's bell.
bell punch *n.* a machine that issues or stamps a ticket, etc., ringing a bell as it does so.
bell push *n.* a button pressed to operate an electric bell.
bell-ringer *n.* **1.** a person who rings church bells. **2.** a person who plays musical handbells. —**'bell-ˌringing** *n.*
bell sheep *n. Austral.* a sheep that a shearer is just starting to shear (and which he is allowed to finish) as the bell rings for the end of a work period. Also called: **catch.**
bells of Ireland *n.* (*functioning as sing.*) an annual garden plant, *Moluccella laevis,* whose flowers have a green cup-shaped calyx: family *Labiatae* (labiates).
Bell's palsy *n.* a usually temporary paralysis of the muscles of the face, normally on one side. [C19: named after Sir Charles *Bell* (1774–1842), British anatomist]
bell tent *n.* a cone-shaped tent having a single central supporting pole.
bell-topper *n. N.Z. obsolete, informal.* a tall silk hat.
bellwether ('bɛlˌwɛðə) *n.* **1.** a sheep that leads the herd, often bearing a bell. **2.** a leader, esp. one followed blindly.
bellwort ('bɛlˌwɜːt) *n. U.S.* **1.** any plant of the North American liliaceous genus *Uvularia,* having slender bell-shaped yellow flowers. **2.** another name for **campanula.**
belly ('bɛlɪ) *n., pl.* **-lies. 1.** the lower or front part of the body of a vertebrate, containing the intestines and other abdominal organs; abdomen. **2.** the stomach, esp. when regarded as the seat of gluttony. **3.** a part, line, or structure that bulges deeply: *the belly of a sail.* **4.** the inside or interior cavity of something: *the belly of a ship.* **5.** the front or inner part or underside of something. **6.** the surface of a stringed musical instrument over which the strings are stretched. **7.** the thick central part of certain muscles. **8.** *Austral. and N.Z.* **a.** the wool from a sheep's belly. **b.** (*as modifier*): *belly wool.* **9.** *Tanning.* the portion of a hide or skin on the underpart of an animal. **10.** *Archery.* the surface of the bow next to the bowstring. **11.** *Archaic.* the womb. ~*vb.* **-lies, -lying, -lied. 12.** to swell out or cause to swell out; bulge. [Old English *belig;* related to Old High German *balg,* Old Irish *bolg* sack, Sanskrit *barhi* chaff]
bellyache ('bɛlɪˌeɪk) *n.* **1.** an informal term for **stomachache.** ~*vb.* **2.** (*intr.*) *Slang.* to complain repeatedly. —**'bellyˌacher** *n.*
bellyband ('bɛlɪˌbænd) *n.* a strap around the belly of a draught animal, holding the shafts of a vehicle.
bellybutton ('bɛlɪˌbʌtᵊn) *n.* an informal name for the **navel.**
belly dance *n.* **1.** a sensuous and provocative dance of Middle Eastern origin, performed by women, with undulating movements of the hips and abdomen. ~*vb.* **belly-dance. 2.** (*intr.*) to perform such a dance. —**belly dancer** *n.*
belly flop *n.* **1.** a dive into water in which the body lands horizontally. **2.** another name for **belly landing.** ~*vb.* **belly-flop, -flops, -flopping, -flopped. 3.** (*intr.*) to perform a belly flop.
bellyful ('bɛlɪˌfʊl) *n.* **1.** as much as one wants or can eat. **2.** *Slang.* more than one can tolerate.
belly landing *n.* the landing of an aircraft on its fuselage without use of its landing gear.
belly laugh *n.* a loud deep hearty laugh.
belong (bɪ'lɒŋ) *vb.* (*intr.*) **1.** (foll. by *to*) to be the property or possession (of). **2.** (foll. by *to*) to be bound to (a person, place, or club) by ties of affection, dependence, allegiance, or membership. **3.** (foll. by *to, under, with,* etc.) to be classified (with): *this plant belongs to the daisy family.* **4.** (foll. by *to*) to be a part or adjunct (of): *this top belongs to the smaller box.* **5.** to have a proper or usual place: *that plate belongs in the cupboard.* **6.** *Informal.* to be suitable or acceptable, esp. socially: *although they were rich, they just didn't belong.* [C14 *belongen,* from BE- (intensive) + *longen;* related to Old High German *bilangēn* to reach; see LONG[3]]
belonging (bɪ'lɒŋɪŋ) *n.* secure relationship; affinity (esp. in the phrase **a sense of belonging**).
belongings (bɪ'lɒŋɪŋz) *pl. n.* (*sometimes sing.*) the things that a person owns or has with him; possessions; effects.
Belorussian (ˌbjɛləʊ'rʌʃən, ˌbɛl-) *n., adj.* a variant spelling of **Byelorussian.**
beloved (bɪ'lʌvɪd, -'lʌvd) *adj.* **1.** dearly loved. ~*n.* **2.** a person who is dearly loved, such as a wife or husband.
below (bɪ'ləʊ) *prep.* **1.** at or to a position lower than; under. **2.** less than in quantity or degree. **3.** south of. **4.** downstream of. **5.** unworthy of; beneath. ~*adv.* **6.** at or to a lower position or place. **7.** at a later place (in something written): *see below.* **8.** *Archaic.* beneath heaven; on earth or in hell. [C14: *bilooghe,* from *bi* BY + *looghe* LOW[1]]
below stairs *adv.* (formerly) at or in the basement of a large house, considered as the place where the servants live and work.
Bel Paese ('bɛl pɑː'eɪzɪ) *n.* a mild creamy Italian cheese. [C20: from Italian, literally: beautiful country]
belt (bɛlt) *n.* **1.** a band of cloth, leather, etc., worn, usually around the waist, to support clothing, carry tools, weapons, or ammunition, or as decoration. **2.** a narrow band, circle, or stripe, as of colour. **3.** an area, esp. an elongated one, where a specific thing or specific conditions are found; zone: *the town belt; a belt of high pressure.* **4.** a belt worn as a symbol of rank (as by a knight or an earl), or awarded as a prize (as in boxing or wrestling), or to mark particular expertise (as in judo or karate). **5.** See **seat belt. 6.** a band of flexible material between rotating shafts or pulleys to transfer motion or transmit goods: *a fan belt; a conveyer belt.* **7.** short for **beltcourse** (see **cordon** (sense 4)). **8.** *Informal.* a sharp blow, as with a bat or the fist. **9. below the belt. a.** *Boxing.* below the waist, esp. in the groin. **b.** *Informal.*

in an unscrupulous or cowardly way. **10. tighten one's belt.** to take measures to reduce expenditure. **11. under one's belt. a.** (of food or drink) in one's stomach. **b.** in one's possession. **c.** as part of one's experience: *he had a linguistics degree under his belt.* ~*vb.* **12.** (*tr.*) to fasten or attach with or as if with a belt. **13.** (*tr.*) to hit with a belt. **14.** (*tr.*) *Slang.* to give a sharp blow; punch. **15.** (*intr.*; often foll. by *along*) *Slang.* to move very fast, esp. in a car: *belting down the motorway.* **16.** (*tr.*) *Rare.* to mark with belts, as of colour. **17.** (*tr.*) *Rare.* to encircle; surround. ~See also **belt out, belt up.** [Old English, from Latin *balteus*]

Beltane ('bɛlteɪn, -tən) *n.* an ancient Celtic festival with a sacrificial bonfire on May Day. [C15: from Scottish Gaelic *bealltainn*]

beltcourse ('bɛltˌkɔːs) *n.* another name for **cordon** (sense 4).

belt drive *n. Engineering.* a transmission system using a flexible belt to transfer power.

belter ('bɛltə) *n. Slang.* a rousing or spirited popular song that is sung loudly and enthusiastically.

belting ('bɛltɪŋ) *n.* **1.** the material used to make a belt or belts. **2.** belts collectively. **3.** *Informal.* a beating.

belt man *n. Austral. and N.Z.* the member of a beach life-saving team who swims out with a line attached to his belt.

belt out *vb.* (*tr., adv.*) *Informal.* to sing loudly or emit (sound, esp. pop music) loudly: *a jukebox belting out the latest hits.*

belt up *vb.* (*adv.*) **1.** *Slang.* to become or cause to become silent; stop talking: often used in the imperative. **2.** to fasten with or by a belt, esp. a seat belt.

beltway ('bɛltˌweɪ) *n.* the usual U.S. name for a **ring road.**

beluga (bɪ'luːgə) *n.* **1.** a large white sturgeon, *Acipenser* (or *Huso*) *huso,* of the Black and Caspian Seas: a source of caviar and isinglass. **2.** another name for **white whale.** [C18: from Russian *byeluga,* from *byely* white]

belvedere ('bɛlvɪˌdɪə, ˌbɛlvɪ'dɪə) *n.* a building, such as a summerhouse or roofed gallery, sited to command a fine view. See also **gazebo.** [C16: from Italian: beautiful sight]

BEM *abbrev. for* British Empire Medal.

bema, bimah, *or* **bima** ('biːmə) *n.* **1.** the speaker's platform in the assembly in ancient Athens. **2.** *Christian Orthodox Church.* a raised area surrounding the altar in a church; the sanctuary. **3.** *Judaism.* another word for **almemar.** [C17: via Late Latin, from Greek *bēma,* from *bainein* to go]

Bemba ('bɛmbə) *n.* **1.** (*pl.* **-ba** *or* **-bas**) a member of a Negroid people of Africa, living chiefly in Zambia on a high infertile plateau. **2.** the language of this people, belonging to the Bantu group of the Niger-Congo family.

Bembo ('bɛmbəʊ) *n.* a style of type. [C20: named after the Italian scholar Pietro *Bembo* (1470–1547) because the design of the typeface was based on one used for an edition of his tract *De Ætna* by the printer Aldus Manutius]

bemean (bɪ'miːn) *vb.* a less common word for **demean**[1].

bemire (bɪ'maɪə) *vb.* (*tr.*) **1.** to soil with or as if with mire. **2.** (*usually passive*) to stick fast in mud or mire.

bemoan (bɪ'məʊn) *vb.* to grieve over (a loss, etc.); mourn; lament (esp. in the phrase **bemoan one's fate**). [Old English *bemǣnan;* see BE-, MOAN]

bemuse (bɪ'mjuːz) *vb.* (*tr.*) to confuse; bewilder. —**be'musement** *n.* —**be'musing** *adj.*

bemused (bɪ'mjuːzd) *adj.* preoccupied; lost in thought. —**bemusedly** (bɪ'mjuːzɪdlɪ) *adv.*

ben[1] (bɛn) *Scot.* ~*n.* **1.** an inner room in a house or cottage. ~*prep., adv.* **2.** in; within; inside; into the inner part (of a house). ~*adj.* **3.** inner. Compare **but**[2]. [Old English *binnan,* from BE- + *innan* inside]

ben[2] (bɛn) *n.* **1.** any of several Asiatic trees of the genus *Moringa,* esp. *M. oleifera* of Arabia and India, whose seeds yield **oil of ben,** used in manufacturing perfumes and cosmetics, lubricating delicate machinery, etc.: family *Moringaceae.* **2.** the seed of such a tree. [C15: from Arabic *bān*]

ben[3] (bɛn) *n. Scot., Irish.* a mountain peak (esp. in place names): *Ben Lomond.* [C18: from Gaelic *beinn,* from *beann*]

Benadryl ('bɛnədrɪl) *n. Trademark.* an antihistamine drug used in sleeping pills; diphenhydramine. Formula: $C_{17}H_{21}NO$.

bename (bɪ'neɪm) *vb.* **-names, -naming, -named; -named** *or* **-nempt.** an archaic word for **name** (sense 11). [Old English *benemnan;* see BE-, NAME]

bench (bɛntʃ) *n.* **1.** a long seat for more than one person, usually lacking a back or arms. **2.** a plain stout worktable. **3. the bench.** (*sometimes cap.*) **a.** a judge or magistrate sitting in court in a judicial capacity. **b.** judges or magistrates collectively. **4.** *Sport.* the seat on which reserve players and officials sit during a game. **5.** *Geology.* a flat narrow platform of land, esp. one marking a former shoreline. **6.** a ledge in a mine or quarry from which work is carried out. **7.** a platform on which dogs or other domestic animals are exhibited at shows. **8.** *N.Z.* a flattened-out ledge on a hillside. **9.** *N.Z.* a hollow on a hillside formed by sheep. ~*vb.* (*tr.*) **10.** to provide with benches. **11.** to exhibit (a dog, etc.) at a show. **12.** *N.Z.* to form (a track) up a hill by excavating a flattened area. [Old English *benc;* related to Old Norse *bekkr,* Old High German *bank,* Danish, Swedish *bänk;* see BANK[3]]

bencher ('bɛntʃə) *n.* (*often pl.*) *Brit.* **1.** a member of the governing body of one of the Inns of Court, usually a judge or a Queen's Counsel. **2.** See **backbencher.**

bench mark *n.* **1.** a mark on a stone post or other permanent feature, at a point whose exact elevation and position is known: used as a reference point in surveying. Abbrev.: **BM. 2.** Also: **'benchˌmark. a.** a criterion by which to measure something; standard; reference point. **b.** (*as modifier*): *a benchmark test.*

bench mark position *n. N.Z.* a public service job used for comparison with a similar position, such as a position in commerce, for wage settlements.

bench test *n.* the critical evaluation of a new or repaired component, device, apparatus, etc., prior to installation to ensure that it is in perfect condition.

bench warrant *n.* a warrant issued by a judge or court directing that an offender be apprehended.

benchy ('bɛntʃɪ) *adj. N.Z.* (of a hillside) hollowed out in benches.

bend[1] (bɛnd) *vb.* **bends, bending, bent. 1.** to form or cause to form a curve, as by pushing or pulling. **2.** to turn or cause to turn from a particular direction: *the road bends left past the church.* **3.** (*intr.*; often foll. by *down,* etc.) to incline the body; stoop; bow. **4.** to submit or cause to submit: *to bend before superior force.* **5.** (*tr.*) to turn or direct (one's eyes, steps, attention, etc.). **6.** (*tr.*) to concentrate (the mind); apply oneself closely. **7.** (*tr.*) *Nautical.* to attach or fasten, as a sail to a boom or a line to a cleat. **8. bend over backwards.** *Informal.* to make a special effort, esp. in order to please: *he bends over backwards to accommodate his customers.* **9. bend (someone's) ear.** *Informal.* to speak at length to an unwilling listener, esp. to voice one's troubles. **10. bend the rules.** *Informal.* to ignore rules or change them to suit one's own convenience. ~*n.* **11.** a curved part, as in a road or river. **12.** *Nautical.* a knot or eye in a line for joining it to another or to an object. **13.** the act or state of bending. **14. round the bend.** *Brit. slang.* mad; crazy; eccentric. ~See also **bends.** [Old English *bendan;* related to Old Norse *benda,* Middle High German *benden;* see BIND, BAND[3]]

bend[2] (bɛnd) *n. Heraldry.* an ordinary consisting of a diagonal line traversing a shield. [Old English *bend* BAND[2]; see BEND[1]]

Ben Day process *n. Printing.* a method of adding texture, shading, or detail to line drawings by overlaying a transparent sheet of dots or any other pattern during platemaking. [C20: named after *Benjamin Day* (1838–1916), American printer]

bender ('bɛndə) *n. Informal.* a drinking bout.

bends (bɛndz) *pl. n.* **the.** (*functioning as sing. or pl.*) a nontechnical name for **decompression sickness.**

bend sinister *n. Heraldry.* a diagonal line bisecting a shield from the top right to the bottom left, typically indicating a bastard line.

bendy[1] ('bɛndɪ) *adj.* **bendier, bendiest. 1.** flexible or pliable. **2.** having many bends: *a bendy road.*

bendy[2] *or* **bendee** ('bɛndɪ) *adj.* (*usually postpositive*) *Heraldry.* striped diagonally.

beneath (bɪ'niːθ) *prep.* **1.** below, esp. if covered, protected, or obscured by. **2.** not as great or good as would be demanded by: *beneath his dignity.* ~*adv.* **3.** below; underneath. [Old English *beneothan,* from BE- + *neothan* low; see NETHER]

benedicite (ˌbɛnɪ'daɪsɪtɪ) *n.* **1.** (esp. in Christian religious orders) a blessing or grace. ~*interj.* **2.** *Obsolete.* an expression of surprise. [C13: from Latin, from *benedīcere,* from *bene* well + *dīcere* to speak]

Benedicite (ˌbɛnɪ'daɪsɪtɪ) *n. Christianity.* a canticle that originated as part of the *Song of the Three Holy Children* in the secondary addition to the Book of Daniel, beginning *Benedicite omnia opera Domini Domino* in Latin, and *O all ye Works of the Lord* in English.

Benedictine *n.* **1.** (ˌbɛnɪ'dɪktɪn, -taɪn). a monk or nun who is a member of a Christian religious community founded by or following the rule of Saint Benedict (?480–?547 A.D.). **2.** (ˌbɛnɪ'dɪktiːn). a greenish-yellow liqueur made from a secret formula developed at the Benedictine monastery at Fécamp in France in about 1510. ~*adj.* **3.** (ˌbɛnɪ'dɪktɪn, -taɪn). of or relating to Saint Benedict, his order, or his rule.

benediction (ˌbɛnɪ'dɪkʃən) *n.* **1.** an invocation of divine blessing, esp. at the end of a Christian religious ceremony. **2.** a Roman Catholic service in which the congregation is blessed with the sacrament. **3.** the state of being blessed. [C15: from Latin *benedictio,* from *benedīcere* to bless; see BENEDICITE] —ˌ**bene'dictory** *adj.*

Benedict's solution *or* **reagent** ('bɛnɪˌdɪkts) *n.* a chemical solution used to detect the presence of glucose and other reducing sugars. Medically, it is used to test the urine of diabetics. [named after S. R. *Benedict* (1884–1936), U.S. chemist]

Benedictus (ˌbɛnɪ'dɪktəs) *n.* (*sometimes not cap.*) *Christianity.* **1.** a short canticle beginning *Benedictus qui venit in nomine Domini* in Latin and *Blessed is he that cometh in the name of the Lord* in English. **2.** a canticle beginning *Benedictus Dominus Deus Israel* in Latin and *Blessed be the Lord God of Israel* in English.

benefaction (ˌbɛnɪ'fækʃən) *n.* **1.** the act of doing good, esp. by giving a donation to charity. **2.** the donation or help given. [C17: from Late Latin *benefactiō,* from Latin *bene* well + *facere* to do]

benefactor ('bɛnɪˌfæktə, ˌbɛnɪ'fæk-) *n.* a person who supports or helps a person, institution, etc., esp. by giving money; patron. —'**beneˌfactress** *fem. n.*

benefic (bɪ'nɛfɪk) *adj.* a rare word for **beneficent.**

benefice ('bɛnɪfɪs) *n.* **1.** *Christianity.* an endowed Church office yielding an income to its holder; a Church living. **2.** the property or revenue attached to such an office. **3.** (in feudal society) a tenement (piece of land) held by a vassal from a landowner on easy terms or free, esp. in return for military support. See also **vassalage.** ~*vb.* **4.** (*tr.*) to provide with a benefice. [C14: from Old French, from Latin *beneficium* benefit, from *beneficus,* from *bene* well + *facere* to do]

beneficence (bɪ'nɛfɪsəns) *n.* **1.** the act of doing good; kindness. **2.** a charitable act or gift.

beneficent (bɪ'nɛfɪsᵊnt) *adj.* charitable; generous. [C17: from Latin *beneficent-,* from *beneficus;* see BENEFICE] —**be'neficently** *adv.*

beneficial (ˌbɛnɪ'fɪʃəl) *adj.* **1.** (sometimes foll. by *to*) causing a good result; advantageous. **2.** *Law.* entitling a person to receive the profits or proceeds of property: *a beneficial interest in land.* [C15: from Late Latin *beneficiālis,* from Latin *beneficium* kindness] —ˌ**bene'ficially** *adv.*

beneficiary (ˌbɛnɪ'fɪʃərɪ) *n., pl.* **-ciaries.** **1.** a person who gains or benefits in some way from something. **2.** *Law.* a person entitled to receive funds or other property under a trust, will, or insurance policy. **3.** the holder of an ecclesiastical or other benefice. **4.** *N.Z.* a person who receives government assistance: *social security beneficiary.* ~*adj.* **5.** of or relating to a benefice or the holder of a benefice.

benefit ('bɛnɪfɪt) *n.* **1.** something that improves or promotes. **2.** advantage or sake: *this is for your benefit.* **3. a.** *Brit.* an allowance paid by the government as for sickness, unemployment, etc., to which a person is entitled under social security or the national insurance scheme. **b.** any similar allowance in various other countries. **4.** (*sometimes pl.*) a payment or series of payments made by an institution, such as an insurance company or trade union, to a person who is ill, unemployed, etc. **5.** a theatrical performance, sports event, etc., to raise money for a charity. ~*vb.* **-fits, -fiting, -fited** *or esp. U.S.* **-fits, -fitting, -fitted.** **6.** to do or receive good; profit. [C14: from Anglo-French *benfet,* from Latin *benefactum,* from *bene facere* to do well]

benefit of clergy *n. Christianity.* **1.** sanction by the church: *marriage without benefit of clergy.* **2.** (in the Middle Ages) a privilege that placed the clergy outside the jurisdiction of secular courts and entitled them to trial in ecclesiastical courts.

benefit society *n.* a U.S. term for **friendly society.**

benempt (bɪ'nɛmpt) *vb. Archaic.* a past participle of **bename.**

benevolence (bɪ'nɛvələns) *n.* **1.** inclination or tendency to help or do good to others; charity. **2.** an act of kindness. **3.** (in the Middle Ages) a forced loan or contribution exacted by English kings from their nobility and subjects.

benevolent (bɪ'nɛvələnt) *adj.* **1.** intending or showing goodwill; kindly; friendly: *a benevolent smile; a benevolent old man.* **2.** doing good or giving aid to others, rather than making profit; charitable: *a benevolent organization.* [C15: from Latin *benevolēns,* from *bene* well + *velle* to wish] —**be'nevolently** *adv.*

BEng *abbrev. for* Bachelor of Engineering.

Beng. *abbrev. for* Bengal(i).

Bengali (bɛn'gɔːlɪ, bɛŋ-) *n.* **1.** a member of a people living chiefly in Bangladesh and in Indian West Bengal. The West Bengalis are mainly Hindus; the East Bengalis of Bangladesh are mainly Muslims. **2.** the language of this people: the official language of Bangladesh and the chief language of West Bengal; it belongs to the Indic branch of the Indo-European family. Also called: **Bangla.** ~*adj.* **3.** of or relating to Bengal, the Bengalis, or their language.

bengaline ('bɛŋgəˌliːn, ˌbɛŋgə'liːn) *n.* a heavy corded fabric, esp. silk with woollen or cotton cord. [C19: from French; first produced in *Bengal;* see -INE[1]]

Bengal light (bɛn'gɔːl) *n.* a firework or flare that burns with a steady bright blue light, formerly used as a signal.

benighted (bɪ'naɪtɪd) *adj.* **1.** lacking cultural, moral, or intellectual enlightenment; ignorant. **2.** *Archaic.* overtaken by night. —**be'nightedly** *adv.* —**be'nightedness** *n.*

benign (bɪ'naɪn) *adj.* **1.** showing kindliness; genial. **2.** (of soil, climate, etc.) mild; gentle. **3.** favourable; propitious. **4.** *Pathol.* (of a tumour, etc.) not threatening to life or health; not malignant. [C14: from Old French *benigne,* from Latin *benignus,* from *bene* well + *gignere* to produce] —**be'nignly** *adv.*

benignant (bɪ'nɪgnənt) *adj.* **1.** kind; gracious, as a king to his subjects. **2.** a less common word for **benign** (senses 3, 4). —**be'nignancy** *n.* —**be'nignantly** *adv.*

benignity (bɪ'nɪgnɪtɪ) *n., pl.* **-ties.** **1.** the quality of being benign; favourable attitude. **2.** a kind or gracious act.

Benioff zone ('bɛnɪəf) *n.* a long narrow region, usually adjacent to a continent, along which earthquake foci lie on a plane which dips downwards at about 45° and along which the oceanic lithosphere is thought to be descending into the earth's interior. Also called: **subduction zone.** [C20: named after Hugo *Benioff* (1899–1968), American seismologist, who first discovered the phenomenon]

benison ('bɛnɪzᵊn, -sᵊn) *n. Archaic.* a blessing, esp. a spoken one. [C13: from Old French *beneison,* from Latin *benedictiō* BENEDICTION]

benjamin ('bɛndʒəmɪn) *n.* **1.** another name for **benzoin** (sense 1). **2. benjamin bush.** another name for **spicebush.** [C16: variant of *benzoin;* influenced in form by the name *Benjamin*]

benne ('bɛnɪ) *n.* **1.** another name for **sesame.** **2. benne oil.** the edible oil obtained from sesame seeds. [C18: from Malay *bene;* compare Bambara *bene*]

bennet ('bɛnɪt) *n.* short for **herb bennet.**

benny[1] ('bɛnɪ) *n., pl.* **-nies.** *Dated slang.* an amphetamine tablet, esp. benzedrine: a stimulant. [C20: shortened from BENZEDRINE]

benny[2] ('bɛnɪ) *n., pl* **-nies.** *U.S. slang.* a man's overcoat. [C19: from *Benjamin,* perhaps from a tailor's name]

bent[1] (bɛnt) *adj.* **1.** not straight; curved. **2.** (foll. by *on*) fixed (on a course of action); resolved (to); determined (to). **3.** *Slang.* **a.** dishonest; corrupt. **b.** (of goods) stolen. **c.** crazy; mad. **d.** sexually deviant, esp. homosexual. ~*n.* **4.** personal inclination, propensity, or aptitude. **5.** capacity of endurance (esp. in the phrase **to the top of one's bent**). **6.** *Civil engineering.* a framework placed across a structure to stiffen it.

bent[2] (bɛnt) *n.* **1.** short for **bent grass.** **2.** a stalk of bent grass. **3.** *Archaic.* any stiff grass or sedge. **4.** *Archaic or Scot. and northern English dialect.* heath or moorland. [Old English *bionot;* related to Old Saxon *binet,* Old High German *binuz* rush]

bent grass *n.* any perennial grass of the genus *Agrostis,* esp. *A. tenuis,* which has a spreading panicle of tiny flowers. Some species are planted for hay or in lawns. Sometimes shortened to **bent.**

Benthamism ('bɛnθəˌmɪzəm) *n.* the philosophy of utilitarianism as first expounded by the British philosopher Jeremy Bentham (1748–1832) in terms of an action being good that has a greater tendency to augment the happiness of the community than to diminish it. —'**Benthaˌmite** *n., adj.*

benthos ('bɛnθɒs) *or* **benthon** *n.* **1.** the animals and plants living at the bottom of a sea or lake. **2.** the bottom of a sea or lake. [C19: from Greek: depth; related to *bathus* deep] —'**benthic,** '**benthal,** *or* **ben'thonic** *adj.*

bentonite ('bɛntəˌnaɪt) *n.* a valuable clay, formed by the decomposition of volcanic ash, that swells as it absorbs water: used as a filler in the building, paper, and pharmaceutical industries. [C19: from Fort *Benton,* Montana, U.S.A., where found, + -ITE[1]]

bentwood ('bɛntˌwʊd) *n.* **a.** wood bent in moulds after being heated by steaming, used mainly for furniture. **b.** (*as modifier*): *a bentwood chair.*

Benue-Congo ('bɛnuˌeɪ'kɒŋgəʊ) *n.* **1.** a branch of the Niger-Congo family of African languages, consisting of the Bantu languages together with certain other languages of W Africa. ~*adj.* **2.** relating or belonging to this group of languages.

benumb (bɪ'nʌm) *vb.* (*tr.*) **1.** to make numb or powerless; deaden physical feeling in, as by cold. **2.** (*usually passive*) to make inactive; stupefy (the mind, senses, will, etc.). —**be'numbingly** *adv.*

benzaldehyde (bɛn'zældɪˌhaɪd) *n.* a yellowish fragrant volatile oil occurring in almond kernels and used in the manufacture of dyes, perfumes, and flavourings and as a solvent for oils and resins. Formula: C_6H_5CHO. Systematic name: **benzenecarbaldehyde.**

Benzedrine ('bɛnzɪˌdriːn, -drɪn) *n.* a trademark for **amphetamine.**

benzene ('bɛnziːn, bɛn'ziːn) *n.* a colourless flammable poisonous aromatic liquid used in the manufacture of styrene, phenol, etc., as a solvent for fats, resins, etc., and as an insecticide. Formula: C_6H_6. See also **benzene ring.**

benzenecarbaldehyde (ˌbɛnziːnkɑː'bældɪˌhaɪd) *n.* the systematic name for **benzaldehyde.**

benzenecarbonyl (ˌbɛnziːn'kɑːbɒnaɪl) *n.* (*modifier*) the systematic name for **benzoyl.**

benzenecarboxylate (ˌbɛnziːnkɑː'bɒksɪˌleɪt) *n.* the systematic name for **benzoate.**

benzenecarboxylic acid (ˌbɛnziːnˌkɑːbɒk'sɪlɪk) *n.* the systematic name for **benzoic acid.**

benzene hexachloride *n.* another name for **hexachlorocyclohexane.**

benzene ring *n.* the hexagonal ring of bonded carbon atoms in the benzene molecule or its derivatives. Also called: **benzene nucleus.** See also **Kekulé formula.**

benzidine ('bɛnzɪˌdiːn, -dɪn) *n.* a grey or reddish poisonous crystalline powder used mainly in the manufacture of dyes, esp. Congo red. Formula: $NH_2(C_6H_4)_2NH_2$.

benzine ('bɛnziːn, bɛn'ziːn) *or* **benzin** ('bɛnzɪn) *n.* **1.** a volatile mixture of the lighter aliphatic hydrocarbon constituents of petroleum. See **ligroin, petroleum ether.** **2.** *Austral. and N.Z.* a rare name for **petrol.**

benzo- *or sometimes before a vowel* **benz-** *combining form.* **1.** indicating a benzene ring fused to another ring in a polycyclic compound: *benzofuran.* **2.** indicating derivation from benzene or benzoic acid or the presence of phenyl groups: *benzophenone.* [from BENZOIN]

benzoate ('bɛnzəʊˌeɪt, -ɪt) *n.* any salt or ester of benzoic acid, containing the group C_6H_5COO- or the ion $C_6H_5COO^-$. Systematic name: **benzenecarboxylate.**

benzoate of soda *n.* another name for **sodium benzoate.**

benzocaine ('bɛnzəʊˌkeɪn) *n.* a white crystalline ester used as a local anaesthetic; ethyl *para*-aminobenzoate. Formula: $C_9H_{11}NO_2$.

benzodiazepine (ˌbɛnzəʊdaɪ'eɪzəˌpiːn) *n.* any of a group of chemical compounds that are used as minor tranquillizers, such as diazepam (Valium) and chlordiazepoxide (Librium). [C20: from BENZO- + DI-[1] + AZ- + EP- + -INE[2]]

benzofuran (ˌbɛnzəʊˈfjʊəræn) *n.* a colourless insoluble aromatic liquid obtained from coal tar and used in the manufacture of synthetic resins. Formula: C_8H_6O. Also called: **coumarone, cumarone.**

benzoic (bɛnˈzəʊɪk) *adj.* of, containing, or derived from benzoic acid or benzoin.

benzoic acid *n.* a white crystalline solid occurring in many natural resins, used in the manufacture of benzoates, plasticizers, and dyes and as a food preservative (**E210**). Formula: C_6H_5COOH. Systematic name: **benzenecarboxylic acid.**

benzoin (ˈbɛnzɔɪn, -zəʊɪn; bɛnˈzəʊɪn) *n.* **1.** Also called: **benjamin.** a gum resin containing benzoic acid, obtained from various trees of the genus *Styrax,* esp. *S. benzoin* of Java and Sumatra, and used in ointments, perfume, etc. **2.** a white or yellowish crystalline compound with a camphor-like odour used as an antiseptic and flavouring; 2-hydroxy-2-phenylacetophenone. Formula: $C_6H_5CHO{+}HCOC_6H_5$. **3.** any lauraceous aromatic shrub or tree of the genus *Lindera,* esp. *L. benzoin* (spicebush). [C16: from French *benjoin,* from Old Catalan *benjui,* from Arabic *lubān jāwī,* literally: frankincense of Java]

benzol *or* **benzole** (ˈbɛnzɒl) *n.* **1.** a crude form of benzene, containing toluene, xylene, and other hydrocarbons, obtained from coal tar or coal gas and used as a fuel. **2.** an obsolete name for **benzene.**

benzophenone (ˌbɛnzəʊfɪˈnəʊn) *n.* a white sweet-smelling crystalline solid used mainly in the manufacture of organic compounds and in perfume. Formula: $C_6H_5COC_6H_5$.

benzoquinone (ˌbɛnzəʊkwɪˈnəʊn, -ˈkwɪnəʊn) *n.* a yellow crystalline water-soluble unsaturated ketone manufactured from aniline and used in the production of dyestuffs. Formula: $C_6H_4O_2$. Also called: **quinone.** Systematic name: **cyclohexadiene-1,4-quinone.**

benzoyl (ˈbɛnzəʊɪl) *n.* (*modifier*) of, consisting of, or containing the monovalent group C_6H_5CO-: *benzoyl group or radical.* Systematic name: **benzenecarbonyl.**

benzyl (ˈbɛnzaɪl) *n.* (*modifier*) of, consisting of, or containing the monovalent group $C_6H_5CH_2$-: *benzyl alcohol.* Systematic name: **phenylmethyl.**

bequeath (bɪˈkwiːð, -ˈkwiːθ) *vb.* (*tr.*) **1.** *Law.* to dispose of (property, esp. personal property) by will. Compare **devise** (sense 2). **2.** to hand down; pass on, as to following generations. [Old English *becwethan;* related to Old Norse *kvetha* to speak, Gothic *qithan,* Old High German *quethan*] —**beˈqueather** *n.*

bequest (bɪˈkwɛst) *n.* **1. a.** the act of bequeathing. **b.** something that is bequeathed. **2.** *Law.* a gift of property by will, esp. personal property. Compare **devise** (senses 4, 5). [C14: BE- + Old English *-cwiss* degree; see BEQUEATH]

berate (bɪˈreɪt) *vb.* (*tr.*) to scold harshly.

Berber (ˈbɜːbə) *n.* **1.** a member of a Caucasoid Muslim people of N Africa. **2.** the language of this people, forming a subfamily of the Afro-Asiatic family of languages. There are extensive differences between dialects. ~*adj.* **3.** of or relating to this people or their language.

berberidaceous (ˌbɜːbərɪˈdeɪʃəs) *adj.* of, relating to, or belonging to the *Berberidaceae,* a mainly N temperate family of flowering plants (mostly shrubs), including barberry and barrenwort. [C19: from Medieval Latin *berberis,* from Arabic *barbārīs* BARBERRY]

berberine (ˈbɜːbəˌriːn) *n.* a yellow bitter-tasting alkaloid obtained from barberry and other plants and used medicinally, esp. in tonics. Formula: $C_{20}H_{19}NO_5$. [C19: from German *Berberin,* from New Latin *berberis* BARBERRY]

berberis (ˈbɜːbərɪs) *n.* any shrub of the berberidaceous genus *Berberis.* See **barberry.** [C19: from Medieval Latin, of unknown origin]

berbice chair (ˈbɜːbiːs) *n.* a large armchair with long arms that can be folded inwards to act as leg rests. [C20: named after *Berbice,* a river and county in Guyana]

berceuse (*French* bɛrsøz) *n.* **1.** a cradlesong or lullaby. **2.** an instrumental piece suggestive of this, in six-eight time. [C19: from French: lullaby, from *bercer* to rock]

bereave (bɪˈriːv) *vb.* (*tr.*) **1.** (usually foll. by *of*) to deprive (of) something or someone valued, esp. through death. **2.** *Obsolete.* to remove by force. ~See also **bereft.** [Old English *bereafian;* see REAVE[1]] —**beˈreavement** *n.*

bereft (bɪˈrɛft) *adj.* (usually foll. by *of*) deprived; parted (from): *bereft of hope.*

beret (ˈbɛreɪ) *n.* a round close-fitting brimless cap of soft wool material or felt. [C19: from French *béret,* from Old Provençal *berret,* from Medieval Latin *birrettum* cap; see BIRETTA]

berg[1] (bɜːg) *n.* short for **iceberg.**

berg[2] (bɜːg) *n.* a South African word for **mountain.**

bergamot (ˈbɜːgəˌmɒt) *n.* **1.** Also called: **bergamot orange.** a small Asian spiny rutaceous tree, *Citrus bergamia,* having sour pear-shaped fruit. **2. essence of bergamot.** a fragrant essential oil from the fruit rind of this plant, used in perfumery. **3.** a Mediterranean mint, *Mentha citrata,* that yields an oil similar to essence of bergamot. **4. a. wild bergamot.** a North American plant, *Monarda fistulosa,* with clusters of purple flowers: family *Labiatae* (labiates). **b.** a garden plant of the same genus, usually *M. didyma* (bee balm), grown for its scarlet or pink flowers. **5.** a variety of pear. [C17: from French *bergamote,* from Italian *bergamotta,* of Turkic origin; related to Turkish *bey-armudu* prince's pear; see BEY]

Bergdama (ˌbɜːgˈdɑːmə) *n.* another name for a **Damara.**

bergère (bɜːˈʒɛə) *n.* **1.** a type of French armchair made from about 1725 having a wide deep seat and upholstered sides and back. In later examples, woven cane is often used instead of upholstery. **2.** a sofa of a similar design. [French, literally: shepherdess]

Bergie (ˈbɜːgɪ) *n. S. African informal.* a vagabond, esp. one living on the slopes of Table Mountain in the Western Cape of South Africa. [from Afrikaans *berg* mountain]

bergschrund (ˈbɛrkʃrʊnt, ˈbɜːgʃruːnd) *n.* a crevasse at the head of a glacier. Also called: **rimaye.** [C19: German: mountain crack]

Bergsonism (ˈbɜːgsəˌnɪzəm) *n.* the philosophy of the French philosopher Henri Bergson (1859–1941), which emphasizes duration as the basic element of experience and asserts the existence of a life-giving force that permeates the entire natural order. Compare **élan vital.**

berg wind *n.* a hot dry wind in South Africa blowing from the plateau down to the coast.

beriberi (ˌbɛrɪˈbɛrɪ) *n.* a disease, endemic in E and S Asia, caused by dietary deficiency of thiamine (vitamin B_1). It affects the nerves to the limbs, producing pain, paralysis, and swelling. [C19: from Sinhalese, by reduplication from *beri* weakness]

berk (bɜːk) *n. Brit. slang.* a variant spelling of **burk.**

Berkeleian (bɑːˈkliːən) *adj.* **1.** denoting or relating to the philosophy of George Berkeley. See **Berkelianism.** ~*n.* **2.** a follower of his teachings.

Berkeleianism (bɑːˈkliːəˌnɪzəm) *n.* the philosophical system of the Irish philosopher and Anglican bishop, George Berkeley (1685–1753). This holds that objects exist only when perceived, that God's perception sustains the universe, and that there is no independent substratum or substance in which these perceptions inhere.

berkelium (bɜːˈkiːlɪəm, ˈbɜːklɪəm) *n.* a metallic transuranic element produced by bombardment of americium. Symbol: Bk; atomic no.: 97; half-life of most stable isotope, ^{247}Bk: 1400 years. [C20: named after *Berkeley,* California, where it was discovered]

Berks (bɑːks) *abbrev. for* Berkshire.

berley *or* **burley** (ˈbɜːlɪ) *Austral.* ~*n.* **1.** groundbait. **2.** *Slang.* rubbish; nonsense. ~*vb.* (*tr.*) **3.** to scatter groundbait over. **4.** to hurry (someone); urge on. [origin unknown]

berlin (bəˈlɪn, ˈbɜːlɪn) *n.* **1.** (*sometimes cap.*) Also called: **berlin wool.** a fine wool yarn used for tapestry work, etc. **2.** a four-wheeled two-seated covered carriage, popular in the 18th century. **3.** a limousine with a glass partition between the front and rear seats. ~Also called (for senses 2, 3): **berline** (bəˈliːn, ˈbɜːliːn). [C18: named after *Berlin*]

Berliner (bɜːˈlɪnə) *n.* a native or inhabitant of Berlin, the capital of Germany.

berm *or* **berme** (bɜːm) *n.* **1.** a narrow path or ledge at the edge of a slope, road, or canal. **2.** *N.Z.* the grass verge of a suburban street, usually kept mown. **3.** *Fortifications.* a narrow path or ledge between a moat and a rampart. **4.** *Military.* a man-made ridge of sand, designed as an obstacle to tanks, which, in crossing it, have to expose their vulnerable underparts. [C18: from French *berme,* from Dutch *berm,* probably from Old Norse *barmr* BRIM]

Bermuda grass (bəˈmjuːdə) *n.* a widely distributed grass, *Cynodon dactylon,* with wiry creeping rootstocks and several purplish spikes of flowers arising from a single point: used for lawns, pasturage, binding sand dunes, etc. Also called: **scutch grass, wire grass.**

Bermudan *or* **Bermudian** (bəˈmjuːdæn, -dɪən) *n.* **1.** a native or inhabitant of Bermuda, a British colony of islands in the NW Atlantic. ~*adj.* **2.** of Bermuda, its people, culture, etc.

Bermuda rig *n.* a fore-and-aft sailing boat rig characterized by a tall mainsail (**Bermudian mainsail**) that tapers to a point. —**Berˈmuda-ˈrigged** *adj.*

Bermuda shorts *pl. n.* close-fitting shorts that come down to the knees. Also called: **Berˈmudas.**

Bernardine (ˈbɜːnədɪn, -ˌdiːn) *n.* **1.** a monk of one of the reformed and stricter branches of the Cistercian order. ~*adj.* **2. a** of or relating to this branch of the Cistercians. **b.** of or relating to Saint Bernard of Clairvaux (?1090–1153), founder of the branch.

bernicle goose (ˈbɜːnɪkᵊl) *n.* a former name for the **brent goose** or **barnacle goose.**

Bernoulli's principle *or* **law** (bɜːˈnuːliːz) *n. Physics.* the principle that in a liquid flowing through a pipe the pressure difference that accelerates the flow when the bore changes is equal to the product of half the density times the change of the square of the speed, provided friction is negligible. [C19: named after Daniel *Bernoulli* (1700–82), Swiss mathematician and physicist]

Bernoulli trial *n. Statistics.* one of a sequence of independent experiments each of which has the same probability of success, such as successive throws of a die, the outcome of which is described by a binomial distribution. See also **binomial experiment.** [named after Jacques *Bernoulli* (1654–1705), Swiss mathematician]

berretta (bɪˈrɛtə) *n.* a variant spelling of **biretta.**

berry (ˈbɛrɪ) *n., pl.* **-ries.** **1.** any of various small edible fruits such as the blackberry and strawberry. **2.** *Botany.* an indehiscent fruit with two or more seeds and a fleshy pericarp, such as the grape or gooseberry. **3.** any of various seeds or dried kernels, such as a coffee bean. **4.** the egg of a lobster, crayfish, or similar animal. ~*vb.* **-ries, -rying, -ried.** (*intr.*) **5.** to bear or produce berries. **6.** to gather or look for berries. [Old English *berie;* related to Old High German *beri,* Dutch *bezie*] —'**berried** *adj.*

bersagliere (ˌbɛəsɑːˈljɛərɪ) *n., pl.* **-ri** (-riː). a member of a rifle regiment in the Italian Army. [C19: from Italian, from *bersaglio* target, from Old French *bersail,* from *berser* to fire at]

berseem (bɜːˈsiːm) *n.* a Mediterranean clover, *Trifolium alexandrinum,* grown as a forage crop and to improve the soil in the southwestern U.S. and the Nile valley. Also called: **Egyptian clover.** [C20: from Arabic *barsīm,* from Coptic *bersīm*]

berserk (bəˈzɜːk, -ˈsɜːk) *adj.* **1.** frenziedly violent or destructive (esp. in the phrase **go berserk**). ~*n.* **2.** Also called: **berserker.** a member of a class of ancient Norse warriors who worked themselves into a frenzy before battle and fought with insane fury and courage. [C19: Icelandic *berserkr,* from *björn* bear + *serkr* shirt]

berth (bɜːθ) *n.* **1.** a bed or bunk in a vessel or train, usually narrow and fixed to a wall. **2.** *Nautical.* a place assigned to a ship at a mooring. **3.** *Nautical.* sufficient distance from the shore or from other ships or objects for a ship to manoeuvre. **4. give a wide berth to.** to keep clear of; avoid. **5.** *Nautical.* accommodation on a ship. **6.** *Informal.* a job, esp. as a member of a ship's crew. ~*vb.* **7.** (*tr.*) *Nautical.* to assign a berth to (a vessel). **8.** *Nautical.* to dock (a vessel). **9.** (*tr.*) to provide with a sleeping place, as on a vessel or train. **10.** (*intr.*) *Nautical.* to pick up a mooring in an anchorage. [C17: probably from BEAR[1] + -TH[1]]

bertha (ˈbɜːθə) *n.* a wide deep capelike collar, often of lace, usually to cover up a low neckline. [C19: from French *berthe,* from *Berthe,* 8th-century Frankish queen, mother of Charlemagne]

Bertillon system (ˈbɜːtɪˌlɒn; *French* bɛrtijɔ̃) *n.* a system formerly in use for identifying persons, esp. criminals, by means of a detailed record of physical characteristics. [C19: named after Alphonse *Bertillon* (1853–1914), French criminal investigator]

beryl (ˈbɛrɪl) *n.* a white, blue, yellow, green, or pink mineral, found in coarse granites and igneous rocks. It is a source of beryllium and used as a gemstone; the green variety is emerald, the blue is aquamarine. Composition: beryllium aluminium silicate. Formula: $Be_3Al_2Si_6O_{18}$. Crystal structure: hexagonal. [C13: from Old French, from Latin *bēryllus,* from Greek *bērullos,* of Indic origin] —'**beryline** *adj.*

beryllium (bɛˈrɪlɪəm) *n.* a corrosion-resistant toxic silvery-white metallic element that occurs chiefly in beryl and is used mainly in x-ray windows and in the manufacture of alloys. Symbol: Be; atomic no.: 4; atomic wt.: 9.012; valency: 2; relative density: 1.85; melting pt.: 1278°C; boiling pt.: 2970°C. Former names: **glucinum, glucinium.** [C19: from Latin *bēryllus,* from Greek *bērullos*]

beseech (bɪˈsiːtʃ) *vb.* **-seeches, -seeching, -sought** *or* **-seeched.** (*tr.*) to ask (someone) earnestly (to do something *or* for something); beg. [C12: see BE-, SEEK; related to Old Frisian *besēka*] —**be'seecher** *n.* —**be'seeching** *adj.* —**be'seechingly** *adv.*

beseem (bɪˈsiːm) *vb. Archaic.* to be suitable for; befit.

beset (bɪˈsɛt) *vb.* **-sets, -setting, -set.** (*tr.*) **1.** (esp. of dangers, temptations, or difficulties) to trouble or harass constantly. **2.** to surround or attack from all sides. **3.** *Archaic.* to cover with, esp. with jewels. —**be'setter** *n.*

besetting (bɪˈsɛtɪŋ) *adj.* tempting, harassing, or assailing (esp. in the phrase **besetting sin**).

beshrew (bɪˈʃruː) *vb.* (*tr.*) *Archaic.* to wish evil on; curse (used in mild oaths such as **beshrew me**). [C14: see BE-, SHREW]

beside (bɪˈsaɪd) *prep.* **1.** next to; at, by, or to the side of. **2.** as compared with. **3.** away from; wide of: *beside the point.* **4.** *Archaic.* besides. **5. beside oneself.** (*postpositive;* often foll. by *with*) overwhelmed; overwrought: *beside oneself with grief.* ~*adv.* **6.** at, by, to, or along the side of something or someone. [Old English *be sīdan;* see BY, SIDE]

besides (bɪˈsaɪdz) *prep.* **1.** apart from; even considering: *besides costing too much, the scheme is impractical.* ~*sentence connector.* **2.** anyway; moreover. ~*adv.* **3.** as well.

besiege (bɪˈsiːdʒ) *vb.* (*tr.*) **1.** to surround (a fortified area, esp. a city) with military forces to bring about its surrender. **2.** to crowd round; hem in. **3.** to overwhelm, as with requests or queries. —**be'sieger** *n.*

besmear (bɪˈsmɪə) *vb.* (*tr.*) **1.** to smear over; daub. **2.** to sully; defile (often in the phrase **besmear (a person's) reputation).**

besmirch (bɪˈsmɜːtʃ) *vb.* (*tr.*) **1.** to make dirty; soil. **2.** to reduce the brightness or lustre of. **3.** to sully (often in the phrase **besmirch (a person's) name).**

besom[1] (ˈbiːzəm) *n.* **1.** a broom, esp. one made of a bundle of twigs tied to a handle. **2.** *Curling.* a broom or brush used to sweep the ice in front of the stone to make it slide farther. ~*vb.* (*tr.*) **3.** to sweep with a besom. [Old English *besma;* related to Old High German *besmo* broom]

besom[2] (ˈbɪzəm, ˈbizəm) *n. Scot. and northern English dialect.* a derogatory term for a **woman.** [perhaps from Old English *bysen* example; related to Old Norse *bysn* wonder]

besotted (bɪˈsɒtɪd) *adj.* **1.** stupefied with drink; intoxicated. **2.** infatuated; doting. **3.** foolish; muddled.

besought (bɪˈsɔːt) *vb.* the past tense and past participle of **beseech.**

bespangle (bɪˈspæŋgəl) *vb.* (*tr.*) to cover or adorn with or as if with spangles.

bespatter (bɪˈspætə) *vb.* (*tr.*) **1.** to splash all over, as with dirty water. **2.** to defile; slander; besmirch.

bespeak (bɪˈspiːk) *vb.* **-speaks, -speaking, -spoke; -spoken** *or* **-spoke.** (*tr.*) **1.** to engage, request, or ask for in advance. **2.** to indicate or suggest: *this act bespeaks kindness.* **3.** *Poetic.* to speak to; address. **4.** *Archaic.* to foretell.

bespectacled (bɪˈspɛktəkəld) *adj.* wearing spectacles.

bespoke (bɪˈspəʊk) *adj. Chiefly Brit.* **1.** (esp. of a suit, jacket, etc.) made to the customer's specifications. **2.** making or selling such suits, jackets, etc.: *a bespoke tailor.*

bespread (bɪˈsprɛd) *vb.* **-spreads, -spreading, -spread.** (*tr.*) to cover (a surface) with something.

besprent (bɪˈsprɛnt) *adj. Poetic.* sprinkled over. [C14: past participle of Old English *besprengan* to BESPRINKLE]

besprinkle (bɪˈsprɪŋkəl) *vb.* (*tr.*) to sprinkle all over with liquid, powder, etc.

Bessemer converter (ˈbɛsɪmə) *n.* a refractory-lined furnace used to convert pig iron into steel by the Bessemer process.

Bessemer process *n.* **1.** (formerly) a process for producing steel by blowing air through molten pig iron at about 1250°C in a Bessemer converter: silicon, manganese, and phosphorus impurities are removed and the carbon content is controlled. **2.** a similar process for removing sulphur and iron from copper matte. [C19: named after Sir Henry *Bessemer* (1813–98), British engineer]

best (bɛst) *adj.* **1.** the superlative of **good. 2.** most excellent of a particular group, category, etc. **3.** most suitable, advantageous, desirable, attractive, etc. **4. the best part of.** most of: *the best part of an hour.* **5. put one's best foot forward. a.** to do one's utmost to make progress. **b.** to hurry. ~*adv.* **6.** the superlative of **well. 7.** in a manner surpassing all others; most excellently, advantageously, attractively, etc. **8.** (*in combination*) in or to the greatest degree or extent; most: *the best-loved hero.* **9. as best one can** *or* **may.** as effectively as possible within one's limitations. **10. had best.** would be wise, sensible, etc., to: *you had best go now.* ~*n.* **11. the best.** the most outstanding or excellent person, thing, or group in a category. **12.** (often preceded by *at*) the most excellent, pleasing, or skilled quality or condition: *journalism at its best.* **13.** the most effective effort of which a person or group is capable: *even their best was inadequate.* **14.** a winning majority: *the best of three games.* **15.** Also: **all the best.** best wishes: *she sent him her best.* **16.** a person's smartest outfit of clothing. **17. at best. a.** in the most favourable interpretation. **b.** under the most favourable conditions. **18. for the best. a.** for an ultimately good outcome. **b.** with good intentions: *he meant it for the best.* **19. get** *or* **have the best of.** to surpass, defeat, or outwit; better. **20. give (someone) the best.** to concede (someone's) superiority. **21. make the best of.** to cope as well as possible in the unfavourable circumstances of (often in the phrases **make the best of a bad job, make the best of it**). **22. six of the best.** *Informal.* six strokes with a cane on the buttocks or hand. ~*vb.* **23.** (*tr.*) to gain the advantage over or defeat. [Old English *betst;* related to Gothic *batista,* Old High German *bezzist*]

best-ball *adj. Golf.* of, relating to, or denoting a match in which one player competes against the best individual totals of two or more other players at each hole.

best boy *n. Chiefly U.S.* the assistant to the senior electrician or to the key grip in a film crew.

bestead (bɪˈstɛd) *Archaic.* ~*vb.* **-steads, -steading, -steaded; -steaded** *or* **-stead. 1.** (*tr.*) to help; avail. ~*adj. also* **bested. 2.** placed; situated. [C13: see BE-, STEAD]

best end *n.* the end of the neck of lamb, pork, etc., nearest to the ribs.

best girl *n. Archaic.* one's sweetheart.

bestial (ˈbɛstɪəl) *adj.* **1.** brutal or savage. **2.** sexually depraved; carnal. **3.** lacking in refinement; brutish. **4.** of or relating to a beast. [C14: from Late Latin *bestiālis,* from Latin *bestia* BEAST] —'**bestially** *adv.*

bestiality (ˌbɛstɪˈælɪtɪ) *n., pl.* **-ties. 1.** bestial behaviour, character, or action. **2.** sexual activity between a person and an animal.

bestialize *or* **bestialise** (ˈbɛstɪəˌlaɪz) *vb.* (*tr.*) to make bestial or brutal.

bestiary (ˈbɛstɪərɪ) *n., pl.* **-aries.** a moralizing medieval collection of descriptions of real and/or mythical animals.

bestir (bɪˈstɜː) *vb.* **-stirs, -stirring, -stirred.** (*tr.*) to cause (oneself, or, rarely, another person) to become active; rouse.

best man *n.* the (male) attendant of the bridegroom at a wedding.

bestow (bɪˈstəʊ) *vb.* (*tr.*) **1.** to present (a gift) or confer (an award or honour). **2.** *Archaic.* to apply (energy, resources, etc.). **3.** *Archaic.* to house (a person) or store (goods). —**be'stowal** *or* **be'stowment** *n.* —**be'stower** *n.*

bestrew (bɪˈstruː) *vb.* **-strews, -strewing, -strewed; -strewn** *or* **-strewed.** (*tr.*) to scatter or lie scattered over (a surface).

bestride (bɪˈstraɪd) *vb.* **-strides, -striding, -strode** *or* (*Archaic*) **-strid; -stridden** *or* (*Archaic*) **-strid.** (*tr.*) **1.** to have or put a leg on either side of. **2.** to extend across; span. **3.** to stride over or across.

best seller *n.* **1.** a book, gramophone record, or other product that has sold in great numbers, esp. over a short period. **2.** the author of one or more such books, etc. —ˌ**best-'selling** *adj.*

bet (bɛt) *n.* **1.** an agreement between two parties that a sum of money or other stake will be paid by the loser to the party who correctly predicts the outcome of an event. **2.** the money or stake risked. **3.** the predicted result in such an agreement: *his bet was that the horse would win.* **4.** a person, event, etc., considered as likely to succeed or occur: *it's a good bet that they will succeed.* **5.** a course of action (esp. in the phrase **one's best bet**). **6.** *Informal.* an opinion; view: *my bet is that you've been up to no good.* ~*vb.* **bets, betting, bet** *or* **betted. 7.** (when *intr.* foll. by *on* or *against*) to make or place a bet with (a person or persons). **8.** (*tr.*) to stake (money, etc.) in a bet. **9.** (*tr.; may take a clause as object*) *Informal.* to predict (a certain outcome): *I bet she fails.* **10. you bet.** *Informal.* of course; naturally. [C16: probably short for ABET]

bet. *abbrev. for* between.

beta ('bi:tə) *n.* **1.** the second letter in the Greek alphabet (Β or β), a consonant, transliterated as *b.* **2.** the second highest grade or mark, as in an examination. **3.** (*modifier*) **a.** involving or relating to electrons: *beta emitter.* **b.** relating to one of two or more allotropes or crystal structures of a solid: *beta iron.* **c.** relating to one of two or more isomeric forms of a chemical compound. [from Greek *bēta*, from Hebrew; see BETH]

Beta ('bi:tə) *n.* (*foll. by the genitive case of a specified constellation*) the second brightest star in a constellation: *Beta Persei.*

beta-blocker *n.* any of a class of drugs, such as propranolol, that inhibit the activity of the nerves that stimulate secretions of adrenaline and that therefore decrease the activity of the heart: used in the treatment of high blood pressure and angina pectoris.

betacarotene (ˌbi:tə'kærəˌti:n) *n.* the most important form of the plant pigment carotene, which occurs in milk, vegetables, and other foods and, when eaten by man and animals, is converted in the body to vitamin A.

betacyanin (ˌbi:tə'saɪənɪn) *n.* any one of a group of red nitrogenous pigments found in certain plants, such as beetroot.

beta decay *n.* the radioactive transformation of an atomic nucleus accompanying the emission of an electron. It involves unit change of atomic number but none in mass number. Also called: **beta transformation** *or* **process.**

beta globulin *n.* another name for **transferrin.**

betaine ('bi:təˌi:n, -ɪn, bɪ'teɪi:n, -ɪn) *n.* **1.** a sweet-tasting alkaloid that occurs in the sugar beet and other plants and in animals. Formula: $C_5H_{11}NO_2$. **2.** (*pl.*) a group of chemical compounds that resemble betaine and are slightly basic zwitterions. [C19: from New Latin *Bēta* beet + -INE[2]]

beta iron *n.* a nonmagnetic allotrope of pure iron stable between 770°C and 910°C.

betake (bɪ'teɪk) *vb.* **-takes, -taking, -took, -taken.** (*tr.*) **1. betake oneself.** to go; move. **2.** *Archaic.* to apply (oneself) to.

beta particle *n.* a high-speed electron or positron emitted by a nucleus during radioactive decay or nuclear fission.

beta ray *n.* a stream of beta particles.

beta rhythm *or* **wave** *n.* *Physiol.* the normal electrical activity of the cerebral cortex, occurring at a frequency of 13 to 30 hertz and detectable with an electroencephalograph. See also **brain wave.**

beta stock *n.* any of the second rank of active securities on the Stock Exchange, of which there are about 500. Continuous display of prices by market makers is required but not immediate publication of transactions.

beta-test *n.* **1.** a test of a new or modified piece of computer software by customers who volunteer to do so. ~*vb.* (*tr.*) **2.** to test (software) in this way. Compare **alpha-test.**

betatopic (ˌbi:tə'tɒpɪk) *adj.* (of atoms) differing in proton number by one, theoretically as a result of emission of a beta particle.

betatron ('bi:təˌtrɒn) *n.* a type of particle accelerator for producing high-energy beams of electrons, having an alternating magnetic field to keep the electrons in a circular orbit of fixed radius and accelerate them by magnetic induction. It produces energies of up to about 300 MeV.

betel ('bi:tᵊl) *n.* an Asian piperaceous climbing plant, *Piper betle,* the leaves of which are chewed, with the betel nut, by the peoples of SE Asia. [C16: from Portuguese, from Malayalam *vettila*]

Betelgeuse *or* **Betelgeux** (ˌbi:tᵊl'dʒɜ:z, 'bi:tᵊlˌdʒɜ:z) *n.* a variable red supergiant, Alpha Orionis: the second brightest star in the constellation Orion. Distance: 260 light years; diameter: 330–460 times solar diameter. [C18: from French, from Arabic *bīt al-jauzā'*, literally: shoulder of the giant, that is, of Orion]

betel nut *n.* the seed of the betel palm, chewed with betel leaves and lime by people in S and SE Asia as a digestive stimulant and narcotic.

betel palm *n.* a tropical Asian feather palm, *Areca catechu,* with scarlet or orange fruits. See **betel nut.**

bête noire *French.* (bɛt nwar) *n., pl.* ***bêtes noires*** (bɛt nwar) a person or thing that one particularly dislikes or dreads. [literally: black beast]

beth (bɛt) *n.* the second letter of the Hebrew alphabet (ב) transliterated as *b.* [from Hebrew *bēth-, bayith* house]

Beth Din *or* **Bet Din** (bɛθ dɪn; *Hebrew* bet din) *n.* *Judaism.* a rabbinical court, consisting of at least three dayanim, and having authority over such matters as divorce and conversion and other communal ecclesiastical matters such as Kashruth. It may also try civil disputes with the consent of both parties. [from Hebrew, literally: house of judgment]

Bethel ('bɛθəl) *n.* **1.** a chapel of any of certain Nonconformist Christian sects. **2.** a seamen's chapel. [C17: from Hebrew *bēth 'Ēl* house of God]

Bethesda (bə'θɛzdə) *n.* a chapel of any of certain Nonconformist Christian sects. [from *Bethesda,* pool in Jerusalem reputed to have healing powers]

bethink (bɪ'θɪŋk) *vb.* **-thinks, -thinking, -thought.** *Archaic or dialect.* **1.** to cause (oneself) to consider or meditate. **2.** (*tr.; often foll. by of*) to remind (oneself).

bethought (bɪ'θɔ:t) *vb.* the past tense and past participle of **bethink.**

betide (bɪ'taɪd) *vb.* to happen or happen to; befall (often in the phrase **woe betide (someone)**). [C13: see BE-, TIDE[2]]

betimes (bɪ'taɪmz) *adv.* *Archaic.* **1.** in good time; early. **2.** in a short time; soon. [C14 *bitimes;* see BY, TIME]

bêtise (bɛ'ti:z) *n.* *Rare.* folly or lack of perception. [French, from *bête* foolish, from *bête* (n.) stupid person, BEAST]

betoken (bɪ'təʊkən) *vb.* (*tr.*) **1.** to indicate; signify: *black clothes betoken mourning.* **2.** to portend; augur.

betony ('bɛtənɪ) *n., pl.* **-nies. 1.** a Eurasian plant, *Betonica* (or *Stachys*) *officinalis,* with a spike of reddish-purple flowers, formerly used in medicine and dyeing: family *Labiatae* (labiates). **2.** any of several related plants of the genus *Stachys.* **3. wood betony.** a North American scrophulariaceous plant, *Pedicularis canadensis.* See also **lousewort.** [C14: from Old French *betoine,* from Latin *betonica,* variant of *vettonica,* probably named after the *Vettones,* an ancient Iberian tribe]

betook (bɪ'tʊk) *vb.* the past tense of **betake.**

betray (bɪ'treɪ) *vb.* (*tr.*) **1.** to aid an enemy of (one's nation, friend, etc.); be a traitor to: *to betray one's country.* **2.** to hand over or expose (one's nation, friend, etc.) treacherously to an enemy. **3.** to disclose (a secret, confidence, etc.) treacherously. **4.** to break (a promise) or be disloyal to (a person's trust). **5.** to disappoint the expectations of; fail: *his tired legs betrayed him.* **6.** to show signs of; indicate: *if one taps china, the sound betrays any faults.* **7.** to reveal unintentionally: *his grin betrayed his satisfaction.* **8. betray oneself.** to reveal one's true character, intentions, etc. **9.** to lead astray; deceive. **10.** *Euphemistic.* to seduce and then forsake (a woman). [C13: from BE- + *trayen,* from Old French *trair,* from Latin *trādere*] —**be'trayal** *n.* —**be'trayer** *n.*

betroth (bɪ'trəʊð) *vb.* (*tr.*) *Archaic.* to promise to marry or to give in marriage. [C14 *betreuthen,* from BE- + *treuthe* TROTH, TRUTH]

betrothal (bɪ'trəʊðəl) *n.* **1.** engagement to be married. **2.** a mutual promise to marry.

betrothed (bɪ'trəʊðd) *adj.* **1.** engaged to be married: *he was betrothed to her.* ~*n.* **2.** the person to whom one is engaged; fiancé or fiancée.

betta ('bɛtə) *n.* another name for **fighting fish.** [C19: from New Latin, of unknown origin]

better[1] ('bɛtə) *adj.* **1.** the comparative of **good. 2.** more excellent than other members of a particular group, category, etc. **3.** more suitable, advantageous, attractive, etc. **4.** improved in health. **5.** fully recovered in health. **6. better off.** in more favourable circumstances, esp. financially. **7. the better part of.** a large part of: *the better part of a day.* ~*adv.* **8.** the comparative of **well. 9.** in a more excellent manner; more advantageously, attractively, etc. **10.** in or to a greater degree or extent; more: *she is better loved than her sister.* **11. go one better.** (*Brit. intr.; U.S. tr.*) to outdo (a person) or improve upon (someone else's effort). **12. had better.** would be wise, sensible, etc. to: *I had better be off.* **13. know better than to.** not to be so stupid as to. **14. think better of. a.** to change one's course of action after reconsideration. **b.** to rate (a person) more highly. ~*n.* **15. the better.** something that is the more excellent, useful, etc., of two such things. **16.** (*usually pl.*) a person who is superior, esp. in social standing or ability. **17. all the better for.** improved as a result of. **18. all the better to.** more suitable to. **19. for better for worse.** whatever the subsequent events or changes may be. **20. for the better.** by way of improvement: *a change for the better.* **21. get the better of.** to defeat, outwit, or surpass. **22. the better of.** *Irish.* having recovered from: *I'm not the better of it yet.* ~*vb.* **23.** to make or become better. **24.** (*tr.*) to improve upon; surpass. [Old English *betera;* related to Old Norse *betri,* Gothic *batiza,* Old High German *beziro*]

better[2] *or esp. U.S.* **bettor** ('bɛtə) *n.* a person who bets.

better half *n.* *Humorous.* one's spouse.

betterment ('bɛtəmənt) *n.* **1.** a change for the better; improvement. **2.** *Property law.* an improvement effected on real property that enhances the value of the property.

betting shop *n.* (in Britain) a licensed bookmaker's premises not on a racecourse.

bettong (bɛ'tɒŋ) *n.* a species of rat kangaroo of Australia having a short nose. [C19: from a native Australian language]

betulaceous (ˌbɛtjʊ'leɪʃəs) *adj.* of, relating to, or belonging to the *Betulaceae,* a family of mostly N temperate catkin-bearing trees and shrubs such as birch and alder, some species of which reach the northern limits of tree growth. [C19: from Latin *betula* birch]

between (bɪˈtwiːn) *prep.* **1.** at a point or in a region intermediate to two other points in space, times, degrees, etc. **2.** in combination; together: *between them, they saved enough money to buy a car.* **3.** confined or restricted to: *between you and me.* **4.** indicating a reciprocal relation or comparison: *an argument between a man and his wife.* **5.** indicating two or more alternatives: *a choice between going now and staying all night.* ~*adv.* also **in between. 6.** between one specified thing and another: *two houses with a garage between.* [Old English *betwēonum;* related to Gothic *tweihnai* two together; see TWO, TWAIN]

▷**Usage.** In careful usage, *between* is restricted to cases where only two objects, possibilities, etc., are concerned. Where three or more are involved, *among* is used. An exception to this rule is made in cases when not more than two of the things covered by *between* need be involved at any one time: *treaties were drawn up between the nations.* Grammatically, *between* is a preposition and for this reason, *between you and I* is incorrect, although the mistake is usually the result of an attempt to be correct. The proper construction is *between you and me. And,* not *or,* is the connector that should be used after *between: she had to choose between staying and* (not *or*) *leaving immediately.*

between-subjects design *n.* (*modifier*) *Statistics.* (of an experiment) concerned with measuring the value of the dependent variable for distinct and unrelated groups subjected to each of the experimental conditions. Compare **within-subjects design, matched-pairs design.**

betweentimes (bɪˈtwiːnˌtaɪmz) *or* **betweenwhiles** (bɪˈtwiːnˌwaɪlz) *adv.* between other activities; during intervals.

betwixt (bɪˈtwɪkst) *prep., adv.* **1.** *Archaic.* another word for **between. 2. betwixt and between.** in an intermediate, indecisive, or middle position. [Old English *betwix;* related to Old High German *zwiski* two each]

BeV (in the U.S.) *abbrev. for* gigaelectronvolts (GeV). [C20: from *b(illion) e(lectron) v(olts)*]

Bevanite (ˈbɛvəˌnaɪt) *adj.* **1.** of or relating to the policies or ideals of the British Labour statesman Aneurin Bevan (1897–1960). ~*n.* **2.** a supporter of such policies or ideals.

bevatron (ˈbɛvəˌtrɒn) *n.* a proton synchrotron at the University of California. [C20: from BEV + -TRON]

bevel (ˈbɛvᵊl) *n.* **1. a.** Also called: **cant.** a surface that meets another at an angle other than a right angle. Compare **chamfer** (sense 1). **b.** (*as modifier*): *a bevel edge; bevel square.* ~*vb.* **-els, -elling, -elled** *or U.S.* **-els, -eling, -eled. 2.** (*intr.*) to be inclined; slope. **3.** (*tr.*) to cut a bevel on (a piece of timber, etc.). [C16: from Old French *bevel* (unattested), from *baïf,* from *baer* to gape; see BAY[1]] —**ˈbevelled** *or U.S.* **ˈbeveled** *adj.* —**ˈbeveller** *or U.S.* **ˈbeveler** *n.*

bevel gear *n.* a gear having teeth cut into a conical surface known as the pitch zone. Two such gears mesh together to transmit power between two shafts at an angle to each other.

bevel square *n.* a woodworker's square with an adjustable arm that can be set to mark out an angle or to check the slope of a surface.

beverage (ˈbɛvərɪdʒ, ˈbɛvrɪdʒ) *n.* any drink, usually other than water. [C13: from Old French *bevrage,* from *beivre* to drink, from Latin *bibere*]

Bevin boy (ˈbɛvɪn) *n.* (in Britain during World War II) a young man selected by ballot to work in a coal mine instead of doing conventional military service. [C20: named after Ernest *Bevin* (1881–1951), British Labour statesman who originated the scheme]

bevvy (ˈbɛvɪ) *Dialect.* ~*n., pl.* **-vies. 1.** a drink, esp. an alcoholic one: *we had a few bevvies last night.* **2.** a night of drinking. ~*vb.* **-vies, -vying, -vied.** (*intr.*) **3.** to drink alcohol. [probably from Old French *bevee, buvee* drinking] —**ˈbevvied** *adj.*

bevy (ˈbɛvɪ) *n., pl.* **bevies. 1.** a flock of quails. **2.** a group, esp. of girls. **3.** a group of roedeer. [C15: of uncertain origin]

bewail (bɪˈweɪl) *vb.* to express great sorrow over (a person or thing); lament. —**beˈwailed** *adj.* —**beˈwailer** *n.* —**beˈwailing** *n., adj.* —**beˈwailingly** *adv.*

beware (bɪˈwɛə) *vb.* (*usually used in the imperative or infinitive,* often foll. by *of*) to be cautious or wary (of); be on one's guard (against). [C13 *be war,* from BE (imperative) + *war* WARY]

bewhiskered (bɪˈwɪskəd) *adj.* having whiskers on the cheeks.

Bewick's swan (ˈbjuːɪks) *n.* a white Old World swan, *Cygnus bewickii,* having a black bill with a small yellow base. [named after Thomas *Bewick* (1753–1828), British wood engraver]

bewilder (bɪˈwɪldə) *vb.* (*tr.*) **1.** to confuse utterly; puzzle. **2.** *Archaic.* to cause to become lost. [C17: see BE-, WILDER] —**beˈwildering** *adj.* —**beˈwilderingly** *adv.* —**beˈwilderment** *n.*

bewitch (bɪˈwɪtʃ) *vb.* (*tr.*) **1.** to attract and fascinate; enchant. **2.** to cast a spell over. [C13 *bewicchen;* see BE-, WITCH] —**beˈwitching** *adj.* —**beˈwitchingly** *adv.*

bewray (bɪˈreɪ) *vb.* (*tr.*) an obsolete word for **betray.** [C13: from BE- + Old English *wrēgan* to accuse; related to Gothic *wrōhjan*] —**beˈwrayer** *n.*

bey (beɪ) *n.* **1.** (in the Ottoman Empire) a title given to senior officers, provincial governors, certain other officials or nobles, and (sometimes) Europeans. **2.** (in modern Turkey) a title of address, corresponding to *Mr.* ~Also called: **beg.** [C16: Turkish: lord]

beyond (bɪˈjɒnd) *prep.* **1.** at or to a point on the other side of; at or to the further side of: *beyond those hills there is a river.* **2.** outside the limits or scope of: *beyond this country's jurisdiction.* ~*adv.* **3.** at or to the other or far side of something. **4.** outside the limits of something. ~*n.* **5. the beyond.** the unknown; the world outside the range of man's perception, esp. life after death in certain religious beliefs. [Old English *begeondan;* see BY, YONDER]

bezant, bezzant (ˈbɛzᵊnt, bɪˈzænt), *or* **byzant** *n.* **1.** a medieval Byzantine gold coin. **2.** *Architect.* an ornament in the form of a flat disc. **3.** *Heraldry.* a small gold circle. [C13: from Old French *besant,* from Medieval Latin *Bȳzantius* Byzantine (coin)]

bezazz *or* **bezzazz** (bɪˈzæz) *n. Informal.* variants of **pizzazz.**

bezel (ˈbɛzᵊl) *n.* **1.** the sloping face adjacent to the working edge of a cutting tool. **2.** the upper oblique faces of a cut gem. **3.** a grooved ring or part holding a gem, watch crystal, etc. **4.** a retaining outer rim used in vehicle instruments, e.g. in tachometers and speedometers. **5.** a small indicator light used in vehicle instrument panels. [C17: probably from French *biseau,* perhaps from Latin *bis* twice]

bezique (bɪˈziːk) *n.* **1.** a card game for two or more players with tricks similar to whist but with additional points scored for honours and sequences: played with two packs with nothing below a seven. **2.** (in this game) the queen of spades and jack of diamonds declared together. [C19: from French *bésigue,* of unknown origin]

bezoar (ˈbiːzɔː) *n.* a hard mass, such as a stone or hairball, in the stomach and intestines of animals, esp. ruminants, and man: formerly thought to be an antidote to poisons. [C15: from Old French *bézoard,* from Arabic *bāzahr,* from Persian *bādzahr,* from *bād* against + *zahr* poison]

bezonian (bɪˈzəʊnɪən) *n. Archaic.* a knave or rascal. [C16: from Italian *bisogno* ill-equipped raw recruit; literally, need]

bf *abbrev. for:* **1.** *Brit. informal.* bloody fool. **2.** *Printing.* bold face.

B/F *or* **b/f** *Book-keeping. abbrev. for* brought forward.

BFI *abbrev. for* British Film Institute.

BFPO *abbrev. for* British Forces Post Office.

BG *international car registration for* Bulgaria.

BH *international car registration for* British Honduras.

Bhagavad-Gita (ˈbʌgəvədˈgiːtə) *n.* a sacred Hindu text composed about 200 B.C. and incorporated into the *Mahabharata,* a Sanskrit epic. [from Sanskrit: song of the Blessed One, from *bhaga* blessing + *gītā* a song]

Bhai (baɪ) *n.* a title or form of address prefixed to the names of distinguished Sikhs. [from Hindi *bhāī,* from Sanskrit *bhrātr* BROTHER]

bhaji (ˈbɑːdʒɪ) *n.* an Indian savoury made of chopped vegetables mixed in a spiced batter and deep-fried.

bhakti (ˈbʌktɪ) *n. Hinduism.* loving devotion to God leading to nirvana. [from Sanskrit: portion, from *bhajati* he allocates]

bhang *or* **bang** (bæŋ) *n.* a preparation of the leaves and flower tops of Indian hemp, which has psychoactive properties: much used in India. See also **cannabis.** [C16: from Hindi *bhāng*]

bhangra (ˈbæŋgrə) *n.* a type of Asian pop music that combines elements of traditional Punjabi music with Western pop. [C20: from Hindi]

bharal *or* **burhel** (ˈbʌrəl) *n.* a wild Himalayan sheep, *Pseudois nayaur,* with a bluish-grey coat and round backward-curving horns. [Hindi]

Bharatiya (ˈbɑːrəˌtiːjə) *adj.* of or relating to India; Indian.

Bharat Natyam (ˈbʌrət ˈnɑːtjəm) *n.* a form of Indian classical ballet. [from Sanskrit *bharatanātya* Bharata's dancing, from *Bharata* the sage supposed to have written of dramatic art and dancing + *nātya* dancing]

bhavan (ˈbʌvən) *or* **bhawan** *n.* (in India) a large house or building.

bhindi (ˈbɪndɪ) *n.* the okra as used in Indian cooking: its green pods are eaten as vegetables. Also called: **lady's finger.** [Hindi]

bhishti *or* **bheesty** (ˈbiːstɪ) *n., pl.* **-ties.** (formerly in India) a water-carrier. [C18: from Hindi *bhīstī,* from Persian *bihishtī* heavenly one, from *bihisht* paradise]

B horizon *n.* the layer of a soil profile immediately below the A horizon, containing deposits of leached material.

bhp *abbrev. for* brake horsepower.

BHP (in Australia) *abbrev. for* Broken Hill Proprietary.

bi (baɪ) *adj., n. Slang.* short for **bisexual** (senses 1, 6).

Bi *the chemical symbol for* bismuth.

bi-[1] *or sometimes before a vowel* **bin-** *combining form.* **1.** two; having two: *bifocal.* **2.** occurring every two; lasting for two: *biennial.* **3.** on both sides, surfaces, directions, etc.: *bilateral.* **4.** occurring twice during: *biweekly.* **5. a.** denoting an organic compound containing two identical cyclic hydrocarbon systems: *biphenyl.* **b.** (rare in technical usage) indicating an acid salt of a dibasic acid: *sodium bicarbonate.* **c.** (not in technical usage) equivalent of **di-[1]** (sense 2). [from Latin, from *bis* TWICE]

bi-[2] *combining form.* a variant of **bio-.**

biannual (baɪˈænjʊəl) *adj.* occurring twice a year. Compare **biennial.** —**biˈannually** *adv.*

biannulate (baɪˈænjʊlɪt, -ˌleɪt) *adj. Zoology.* having two bands, esp. of colour.

bias (ˈbaɪəs) *n.* 1. mental tendency or inclination, esp. an irrational preference or prejudice. 2. a diagonal line or cut across the weave of a fabric. 3. *Electronics.* the voltage applied to an electrode of a transistor or valve to establish suitable working conditions. 4. *Bowls.* a. a bulge or weight inside one side of a bowl. b. the curved course of such a bowl on the green. 5. *Statistics.* a. an extraneous latent influence on, unrecognized conflated variable in, or selectivity in a sample which influences its distribution and so renders it unable to reflect the desired population parameters. b. if *T* is an estimator of the parameter θ, the estimated value of (*T*-θ). 6. an inaudible high-frequency signal used to improve the quality of a tape recording. ~*adj.* 7. slanting obliquely; diagonal: *a bias fold.* ~*adv.* 8. obliquely; diagonally. ~*vb.* **-ases, -asing, -ased** *or* **-asses, -assing, -assed.** (*tr.*) 9. (*usually passive*) to cause to have a bias; prejudice; influence. [C16: from Old French *biais,* from Old Provençal, perhaps ultimately from Greek *epikarsios* oblique] —**ˈbiased** *or* **ˈbiassed** *adj.*

bias binding *n.* a strip of material cut on the bias for extra stretch and often doubled, used for binding hems, interfacings, etc., or for decoration.

biathlon (baɪˈæθlən, -lɒn) *n. Sport.* a contest in which skiers with rifles shoot at four targets along a 20-kilometre (12.5-mile) cross-country course.

biauriculate (ˌbaɪɔːˈrɪkjʊlɪt, -ˌleɪt) *or* **biauricular** *adj.* having two auricles or earlike parts.

biaxial (baɪˈæksɪəl) *adj.* (esp. of a crystal) having two axes.

bib (bɪb) *n.* 1. a piece of cloth or plastic worn, esp. by babies, to protect their clothes while eating. 2. the upper part of some aprons, dungarees, etc., that covers the upper front part of the body. 3. Also called: **pout, whiting pout.** a light-brown European marine gadoid food fish, *Gadus* (or *Trisopterus*) *luscus,* with a barbel on its lower jaw. 4. short for **bibcock.** 5. **stick one's bib in.** *Austral. informal.* to interfere. ~*vb.* **bibs, bibbing, bibbed.** 6. *Archaic.* to drink (something); tipple. [C14 *bibben* to drink, probably from Latin *bibere*]

Bib. *abbrev. for:* 1. Bible. 2. Biblical.

bib and brace *n.* a work garment consisting of trousers and an upper front part supported by straps over the shoulders.

bib and tucker *n. Informal.* an outfit of clothes (esp. in the phrase **best bib and tucker**).

bibb (bɪb) *n. Nautical.* a wooden support on a mast for the trestletrees. [C18: variant of BIB]

bibber (ˈbɪbə) *n.* a drinker; tippler (esp. in the expression **winebibber**).

bibcock (ˈbɪbˌkɒk) *or* **bib** *n.* a tap having a nozzle bent downwards and supplied from a horizontal pipe.

bibelot (ˈbɪbləʊ; *French* biblo) *n.* 1. an attractive or curious trinket. 2. a miniature book. [C19: from French, from Old French *beubelet,* perhaps from a reduplication of *bel* beautiful]

bibl. *abbrev. for:* 1. bibliographical. 2. bibliography.

Bibl. *abbrev. for* Biblical.

Bible (ˈbaɪbᵊl) *n.* 1. a. **the.** the sacred writings of the Christian religion, comprising the Old and New Testaments and, in the Roman Catholic Church, the Apocrypha. b. (*as modifier*): *a Bible reading.* 2. (*often not cap.*) any book containing the sacred writings of a religion. 3. (*usually not cap.*) a book regarded as authoritative: *the angler's bible.* [C13: from Old French, from Medieval Latin *biblia* books, from Greek, plural of *biblion* book, diminutive of *biblos* papyrus, from *Bublos* Phoenician port from which Greece obtained Egyptian papyrus]

Bible Belt *n.* **the.** certain regions of the U.S., esp. in the South or in western Canada, where Protestant fundamentalism is dominant.

Bible paper *n.* 1. a thin tough opaque paper used for Bibles, prayer books, and reference books. 2. (not in technical usage) another name for **India paper.**

Bible-thumper *n. Slang.* an enthusiastic or aggressive exponent of the Bible. Also called: **Bible-basher, Bible-pounder, Bible-puncher.** —**ˈBible-ˌthumping** *n., adj.*

biblical (ˈbɪblɪkᵊl) *adj.* 1. of, occurring in, or referring to the Bible. 2. resembling the Bible in written style. —**ˈbiblically** *adv.*

Biblical Aramaic *n.* the form of Aramaic that was the common language of Palestine in New Testament times. It was widespread throughout the Persian Empire from the 5th century and is found in the later books of the Old Testament (esp. Daniel 2:4–7:28).

Biblical Latin *n.* the form of Latin used in versions of the Bible, esp. the form used in the Vulgate. See also **Late Latin.**

Biblicist (ˈbɪblɪsɪst) *or* **Biblist** *n.* 1. a biblical scholar. 2. a person who takes the Bible literally.

biblio- *combining form.* indicating book or books: *bibliography; bibliomania.* [from Greek *biblion* book]

bibliog. *abbrev. for:* 1. bibliographer. 2. bibliography.

bibliography (ˌbɪblɪˈɒgrəfɪ) *n., pl.* **-phies.** 1. a list of books or other material on a subject. 2. a list of sources used in the preparation of a book, thesis, etc. 3. a list of the works of a particular author or publisher. 4. a. the study of the history, classification, etc., of literary material. b. a work on this subject. —**ˌbibliˈographer** *n.* —**bibliographic** (ˌbɪblɪəʊˈgræfɪk) *or* **ˌbiblioˈgraphical** *adj.* —**ˌbiblioˈgraphically** *adv.*

bibliolatry (ˌbɪblɪˈɒlətrɪ) *n.* 1. excessive devotion to or reliance on the Bible. 2. extreme fondness for books.

bibliomancy (ˈbɪblɪəʊˌmænsɪ) *n.* prediction of the future by interpreting a passage chosen at random from a book, esp. the Bible.

bibliomania (ˌbɪblɪəʊˈmeɪnɪə) *n.* extreme fondness for books. —**ˌbiblioˈmaniˌac** *n., adj.*

bibliophile (ˈbɪblɪəˌfaɪl) *or* **bibliophil** (ˈbɪblɪəfɪl) *n.* a person who collects or is fond of books. —**bibliophilism** (ˌbɪblɪˈɒfəˌlɪzəm) *n.* —**ˌbibliˌophiˈlistic** *adj.*

bibliopole (ˈbɪblɪəʊˌpəʊl) *or* **bibliopolist** (ˌbɪblɪˈɒpəlɪst) *n.* a dealer in books, esp. rare or decorative ones. [C18: from Latin *bibliopōla,* from Greek *bibliopōlēs* bookseller, from BIBLIO- + *pōlein* to sell] —**ˌbibliˈopoly** *n.*

bibliotheca (ˌbɪblɪəʊˈθiːkə) *n., pl.* **-cas** *or* **-cae** (-kiː). 1. a library or collection of books. 2. a printed catalogue compiled by a bibliographer. [Latin: library, from Greek *bibliothēkē,* from BIBLIO- + *thēkē* receptacle]

bibulous (ˈbɪbjʊləs) *adj.* addicted to alcohol. [C17: from Latin *bibulus,* from *bibere* to drink] —**ˈbibulously** *adv.* —**ˈbibulousness** *n.*

bicameral (baɪˈkæmərəl) *adj.* (of a legislature) consisting of two chambers [C19: from BI-[1] + Latin *camera* CHAMBER] —**biˈcameralˌism** *n.* —**biˈcameralist** *n.*

bicapsular (baɪˈkæpsjʊlə) *adj.* (of plants) having two capsules or one capsule with two chambers.

bicarb (ˈbaɪkɑːb) *n.* short for **bicarbonate of soda.** See **sodium bicarbonate.**

bicarbonate (baɪˈkɑːbənɪt, -ˌneɪt) *n.* 1. a salt of carbonic acid containing the ion HCO_3^-; an acid carbonate. 2. (*modifier*) consisting of, containing, or concerned with the ion HCO_3^-: *a bicarbonate compound.* Systematic name: **hydrogen carbonate.** 3. short for **bicarbonate of soda.**

bicarbonate of soda *n.* sodium bicarbonate, esp. when used as a medicine or as a raising agent in baking.

bicarpellary (ˌbaɪkɑːˈpɛlərɪ) *adj. Botany.* (of an ovary) having two carpels.

bice (baɪs) *n.* 1. Also called: **bice blue.** a medium blue colour; azurite. 2. Also called: **bice green.** a yellowish-green colour; malachite. [C14: from Old French *bis* dark grey, of uncertain origin]

bicentenary (ˌbaɪsɛnˈtiːnərɪ) *or U.S.* **bicentennial** (ˌbaɪsɛnˈtɛnɪəl) *adj.* 1. marking a 200th anniversary. 2. occurring every 200 years. 3. lasting 200 years. ~*n., pl.* **-naries.** 4. a 200th anniversary.

bicephalous (baɪˈsɛfələs) *adj.* 1. *Biology.* having two heads. 2. crescent-shaped.

biceps (ˈbaɪsɛps) *n., pl.* **-ceps.** *Anatomy.* any muscle having two heads or origins, esp. the muscle that flexes the forearm. [C17: from Latin: having two heads, from BI-[1] + *caput* head]

Biche-la-mar (ˌbiːtʃləˈmɑː) *n.* another name for **Beach-la-Mar.**

bichloride (baɪˈklɔːraɪd) *n.* another name for **dichloride.**

bichloride of mercury *n.* another name for **mercuric chloride.**

bichromate (baɪˈkrəʊˌmeɪt, -mɪt) *n.* another name for **dichromate.**

bicipital (baɪˈsɪpɪtᵊl) *adj.* 1. having two heads. 2. of or relating to a biceps muscle. [C17: see BICEPS, -AL[1]]

bicker (ˈbɪkə) *vb.* (*intr.*) 1. to argue over petty matters; squabble. 2. *Poetic.* a. (esp. of a stream) to run quickly. b. to flicker; glitter. ~*n.* 3. a petty squabble. [C13: of unknown origin] —**ˈbickerer** *n.* —**ˈbickering** *n., adj.*

bickie (ˈbɪkɪ) *n. Informal.* 1. short for **biscuit** (sense 1). 2. **big bickies.** *Austral. slang.* a large sum of money.

bicollateral (ˌbaɪkɒˈlætərəl) *adj. Botany.* (of a vascular bundle) having two phloem groups to the inside and outside, respectively, of the xylem.

bicolour (ˈbaɪˌkʌlə), **bicoloured** *or U.S.* **bicolor, bicolored** *adj.* two-coloured.

biconcave (baɪˈkɒnkeɪv, ˌbaɪkɒnˈkeɪv) *adj.* (of a lens) having concave faces on both sides; concavo-concave. —**biconcavity** (ˌbaɪkɒnˈkævɪtɪ) *n.*

biconditional (ˌbaɪkənˈdɪʃənᵊl) *n.* another name for **equivalence** (sense 2).

biconvex (baɪˈkɒnvɛks, ˌbaɪkɒnˈvɛks) *adj.* (of a lens) having convex faces on both sides; convexo-convex.

bicorn (ˈbaɪkɔːn), **bicornate** (baɪˈkɔːnɪt, -ˌneɪt), *or* **bicornuate** (baɪˈkɔːnjʊɪt, -ˌeɪt) *adj.* having two horns or hornlike parts. [C19: from Latin *bicornis,* from BI-[1] + *cornu* horn]

bicuspid (baɪˈkʌspɪd) *or* **bicuspidate** (baɪˈkʌspɪˌdeɪt) *adj.* 1. having or terminating in two cusps or points. ~*n.* 2. a bicuspid tooth; premolar.

bicuspid valve *n.* another name for **mitral valve.**

bicycle (ˈbaɪsɪkᵊl) *n.* 1. a vehicle with a tubular metal frame mounted on two spoked wheels, one behind the other. The rider sits on a saddle, propels the vehicle by means of pedals that drive the rear wheel through a chain, and steers with handlebars on the front wheel. Often shortened to **bike** (informal), **cycle.** ~*vb.* 2. (*intr.*) to ride a bicycle; cycle. [C19: from BI-[1] + Late Latin *cyclus,* from Greek *kuklos* wheel] —**ˈbicyclist** *or* **ˈbicycler** *n.*

bicycle chain *n.* a chain that transmits power from the pedals to the rear wheel of a bicycle.

bicycle clip *n.* one of a pair of clips worn around the ankles by cyclists to keep the trousers tight and out of the chain.

bicycle pump *n.* a hand pump for pumping air into the tyres of a bicycle.

bicyclic (baɪˈsaɪklɪk, -ˈsɪklɪk) *or* **bicyclical** *adj.* **1.** of, forming, or formed by two circles, cycles, etc. **2.** (of stamens, petals, etc.) arranged in two whorls. **3.** (of a chemical compound) having atoms arranged in two rings fused together with at least two atoms common to each ring: *naphthalene is bicyclic.*

bid (bɪd) *vb.* **bids; bidding; bad, bade,** *or* (esp. for senses 1, 2, 5, 7) **bid; bidden** *or* (esp. for senses 1, 2, 5, 7) **bid. 1.** (often foll. by *for* or *against*) to offer (an amount) in attempting to buy something, esp. in competition with others as at an auction. **2.** *Commerce.* to respond to an offer by a seller by stating (the more favourable terms) on which one is willing to make a purchase. **3.** (*tr.*) to say (a greeting, blessing, etc.): *to bid farewell.* **4.** to order; command: *do as you are bid!* **5.** (*intr.;* usually foll. by *for*) to attempt to attain power, etc. **6.** (*tr.*) to invite; ask kindly: *she bade him sit down.* **7.** *Bridge, etc.* to declare in the auction before play how many tricks one expects to make. **8. bid defiance.** to resist boldly. **9. bid fair.** to seem probable. ~*n.* **10. a.** an offer of a specified amount, as at an auction. **b.** the price offered. **11.** *Commerce.* **a.** a statement by a buyer, in response to an offer by a seller, of the more favourable terms that would be acceptable. **b.** the price or other terms so stated. **12.** an attempt, esp. an attempt to attain power. **13.** *Bridge, etc.* **a.** the number of tricks a player undertakes to make. **b.** a player's turn to make a bid. **14.** short for **bid price.** ~See also **bid in, bid up.** [Old English *biddan;* related to German *bitten*] —ˈ**bidder** *n.*

b.i.d. (in prescriptions) *abbrev. for* bis in die. [Latin: twice a day]

bidarka (baɪˈdɑːkə) *or* **bidarkee** (baɪˈdɑːkiː) *n.* a canoe covered in animal skins, esp. sealskin, used by the Eskimos of Alaska. [C19: from Russian *baidarka* diminutive of *baidara* umiak]

biddable (ˈbɪdəbᵊl) *adj.* **1.** having sufficient value to be bid on, as a hand or suit at bridge. **2.** docile; obedient. —ˈ**biddableness** *n.* —ˈ**biddably** *adv.*

bidden (ˈbɪdᵊn) *vb.* a past participle of **bid.**

bidding (ˈbɪdɪŋ) *n.* **1.** an order; command (often in the phrases **do** *or* **follow the bidding of, at someone's bidding**). **2.** an invitation; summons. **3.** the act of making bids, as at an auction or in bridge. **4.** *Bridge, etc.* a group of bids considered collectively, esp. those made on a particular deal.

biddy[1] (ˈbɪdɪ) *n., pl.* **-dies.** a dialect word for **chicken** or **hen.** [C17: perhaps imitative of calling chickens]

biddy[2] (ˈbɪdɪ) *n., pl.* **-dies.** *Informal.* a woman, esp. an old gossipy or interfering one. [C18: from pet form of *Bridget*]

biddy-biddy *or* **biddi-biddi** (ˈbɪdɪˌbɪdɪ) *n., pl.* **-biddies. 1.** a low-growing rosaceous plant, *Acaena viridior,* of New Zealand, having pricky burs. **2.** the burs of this plant. ~Also: (N.Z.) **biddy-bid,** (Austral.) **bidgee-widgee** (ˈbɪdʒɪˌwɪdʒɪ). [from Maori *piri piri*]

bide (baɪd) *vb.* **bides, biding, bided** *or* **bode, bided. 1.** (*intr.*) *Archaic or dialect.* to continue in a certain place or state; stay. **2.** (*intr.*) *Archaic or dialect.* to live; dwell. **3.** (*tr.*) *Archaic or dialect.* to tolerate; endure. **4. bide a wee.** *Scot.* to stay a little. **5. bide by.** *Scot.* to abide by. **6. bide one's time.** to wait patiently for an opportunity. ~Also (Scot.) **byde.** [Old English *bīdan;* related to Old Norse *bītha* to wait, Gothic *beidan,* Old High German *bītan*]

bidentate (baɪˈdɛnˌteɪt) *adj.* **1.** having two teeth or toothlike parts or processes. **2.** *Chem.* (of a ligand) having two atoms from which electrons can be donated to the central coordinated atom.

bidet (ˈbiːdeɪ) *n.* a small low basin for washing the genitals and anal area. [C17: from French: small horse, probably from Old French *bider* to trot]

bid in *vb.* (*adv.*) (in an auction) to outbid all previous offers for (one's own property) to retain ownership or increase the final selling price.

bidirectional (ˌbaɪdɪˈrɛkʃənᵊl) *adj. Computer technol.* (of a printhead) capable of printing from left to right and from right to left.

bid price *n. Stock Exchange.* the price at which a stockjobber is prepared to purchase a specific security. Compare **offer price.**

bid up *vb.* (*adv.*) to increase the market price of (a commodity) by making artificial bids.

Biedermeier (ˈbiːdəˌmaɪə) *adj.* **1.** of or relating to a decorative and furnishing style in mid-19th-century Germany, characterized by solidity and conventionality. **2.** boringly conventional in outlook; bourgeois. [C19: after Gottlieb *Biedermeier,* a fictitious character portrayed as a conventional unimaginative bourgeois and the author of poems actually written by several satirical poets]

bield (biːld) *Scot. and northern English dialect.* ~*n.* **1.** a shelter; house. ~*vb.* **2.** to shelter or take shelter. [Old English *bieldo, byldo* boldness (hence: refuge); related to Gothic *balthei,* Old English *beald* BOLD]

biennial (baɪˈɛnɪəl) *adj.* **1.** occurring every two years. **2.** lasting two years. Compare **biannual.** ~*n.* **3.** a plant, such as the carrot, that completes its life cycle in two years, developing vegetative storage parts during the first year. Compare **annual** (sense 3), **perennial** (sense 3). **4.** an event that takes place every two years. —**biˈennially** *adv.*

bien-pensant (bjɛ̃pɑ̃sɑ̃) *adj.* **1.** right-thinking; orthodox. ~*n.* ***bien pensant,*** *pl.* ***bien pensants*** (bjɛ̃pɑ̃sɑ̃). **2.** a right-thinking person. [French: well-thinking]

bier (bɪə) *n.* a platform or stand on which a corpse or a coffin containing a corpse rests before burial. [Old English *bǣr;* related to *beran* to BEAR[1], Old High German *bāra* bier, Sanskrit *bhārá* a burden]

bierkeller (ˈbɪəˌkɛlə) *n. Brit.* a public house decorated in German style, selling German beers. [C20: German, literally: beer cellar]

biestings (ˈbiːstɪŋz) *n.* a variant spelling of **beestings.**

bifacial (baɪˈfeɪʃəl) *adj.* **1.** having two faces or surfaces. **2.** *Botany.* (of leaves, etc.) having upper and lower surfaces differing from each other. **3.** *Archaeol.* (of flints) flaked by percussion from two sides along the chopping edge.

bifarious (baɪˈfɛərɪəs) *adj. Botany.* having parts arranged in two rows on either side of a central axis. [C17: from Latin *bifārius* double] —**biˈfariously** *adv.*

biff (bɪf) *Slang.* ~*n.* **1.** a blow with the fist. **2.** *Irish school slang.* a blow to the palm of the hand with a strap or cane as a punishment. ~*vb.* **3.** (*tr.*) to give (someone) such a blow. [C20: probably of imitative origin]

biffin (ˈbɪfɪn) *n. Brit.* a variety of red cooking apple. [C18: from *beefin* ox for slaughter, from BEEF; referring to the apple's colour]

bifid (ˈbaɪfɪd) *adj.* divided into two lobes by a median cleft: *bifid leaves.* [C17: from Latin *bifidus* from BI-[1] + *-fidus,* from *findere* to split] —**biˈfidity** *n.* —ˈ**bifidly** *adv.*

bifilar (baɪˈfaɪlə) *adj.* **1.** having two parallel threads, as in the suspension of certain measuring instruments. **2.** of or relating to a resistor in which the wire is wound in a loop around a coil, the two leads being parallel, to reduce the inductance. —**biˈfilarly** *adv.*

biflagellate (baɪˈflædʒɪˌleɪt, -lɪt) *adj. Biology.* having two flagella: *biflagellate protozoans.*

bifocal (baɪˈfəʊkᵊl) *adj.* **1.** *Optics.* having two different focuses. **2.** relating to a compound lens permitting near and distant vision.

bifocals (baɪˈfəʊkᵊlz) *pl. n.* a pair of spectacles with bifocal lenses.

bifoliate (baɪˈfəʊlɪˌeɪt, -ɪt) *adj.* having two leaves or leaflets.

bifoliolate (baɪˈfəʊlɪəʊˌleɪt, -lɪt) *adj.* (of compound leaves) consisting of two leaflets.

biforate (ˈbaɪfəˌreɪt) *adj. Biology.* having two openings, pores, or perforations. [C19: from New Latin *biforātus,* from BI-[1] + *forāre* to pierce]

biform (ˈbaɪˌfɔːm) *or* **biformed** *adj.* having or combining the characteristics of two forms, as a centaur.

bifurcate *vb.* (ˈbaɪfəˌkeɪt). **1.** to fork or divide into two parts or branches. ~*adj.* (ˈbaɪfəˌkeɪt, -kɪt). **2.** forked or divided into two sections or branches. [C17: from Medieval Latin *bifurcātus,* from Latin *bifurcus* from BI-[1] + *furca* fork] —ˌ**bifurˈcation** *n.*

big[1] (bɪg) *adj.* **bigger, biggest. 1.** of great or considerable size, height, weight, number, power, or capacity. **2.** having great significance; important: *a big decision.* **3.** important through having power, influence, wealth, authority, etc.: *the big four banks.* **4.** (intensifier usually qualifying something undesirable): *a big dope.* **5.** *Informal.* considerable in extent or intensity (esp. in the phrase **in a big way**). **6. a.** elder: *my big brother.* **b.** grown-up: *when you're big, you can stay up later.* **7. a.** generous; magnanimous: *that's very big of you.* **b.** (in combination): *big-hearted.* **8.** (often foll. by *with*) brimming; full: *my heart is big with sadness.* **9.** extravagant; boastful: *he's full of big talk.* **10. too big for one's boots** *or* **breeches.** conceited; unduly self-confident. **11.** in an advanced stage of pregnancy (esp. in the phrase **big with child**). **12. big on.** *Informal, chiefly U.S.* enthusiastic about: *that company is big on research.* ~*adv. Informal.* **13.** boastfully; pretentiously (esp. in the phrase **talk big**). **14.** in an exceptional way; well: *his talk went over big with the audience.* **15.** on a grand scale (esp. in the phrase **think big**). [C13: perhaps of Scandinavian origin; compare Norwegian dialect *bugge* big man] —ˈ**biggish** *adj.* —ˈ**bigness** *n.*

big[2] (bɪg) *vb.* **bigs, bigging, bigged** *or* **bug** (bʌg). *Scot.* **1.** to build. **2.** to excavate (earth) into a pile. [from Old Norse *byggja;* related to Old English *būian* to inhabit]

bigamy (ˈbɪgəmɪ) *n., pl.* **-mies.** the crime of marrying a person while one is still legally married to someone else. [C13: via French from Medieval Latin *bigamus;* see BI-[1], -GAMY] —ˈ**bigamist** *n.* —ˈ**bigamous** *adj.* —ˈ**bigamously** *adv.*

bigarreau (ˈbɪgəˌrəʊ, ˌbɪgəˈrəʊ) *n.* any of several heart-shaped varieties of sweet cherry that have firm flesh. [C17: from French, from *bigarré* mottled]

big band *n.* a large jazz or dance band, popular esp. in the 1930s to the 1950s.

big bang *n.* **1.** any sudden forceful beginning or radical change. **2.** (*modifier*) of or relating to the big-bang theory. **3.** (*sometimes caps.*) the major modernization that took place on the London Stock Exchange on Oct. 27 1986, after which the distinction between jobbers and brokers was abolished and operations became fully computerized.

big-bang theory *n.* a cosmological theory postulating that approximately 10 000 million years ago all the matter of the universe, packed into a small superdense mass, was hurled in all directions by a cataclysmic explosion. As the fragments slowed down, the galaxies and stars evolved but the universe is still expanding. Compare **steady-state theory.**

Big Bertha *n.* any of three large German guns of World War I used to bombard Paris. [C20: approximate translation of German *dicke Bertha:* fat Bertha; named after *Bertha* Krupp, at whose works in Essen a very effective 42 cm mortar was made]

Big Board *n. U.S. informal.* **1.** the quotation board in the New York Stock Exchange. **2.** the New York Stock Exchange.

Big Brother *n.* a person, organization, etc., that exercises total dictatorial control. [C20: after a character in George Orwell's novel *1984* (1949)]

big bucks *pl. n. Informal, chiefly U.S.* **1.** large quantities of money. **2.** the power and influence of people or organizations that control large quantities of money.

big bud *n.* a serious disease of plants, esp. of blackcurrants, in which the buds swell up as a result of attack by the gall mite *Cecidophyopsis ribis.*

big business *n.* large commercial organizations collectively, esp. when considered as exploitative or socially harmful.

big cheese *n. Slang, old-fashioned.* an important person.

big Chief *or* **big Daddy** *n. Informal.* other terms for **big White Chief.**

big deal *interj. Slang.* an exclamation of scorn, derision, etc., used esp. to belittle a claim or offer.

big dipper *n.* (in amusement parks) a narrow railway with open carriages that run swiftly over a route of sharp curves and steep inclines. Also called: **roller coaster.**

Big Dipper *n.* the U.S. and Canadian name for the **Plough** (constellation).

big end *n. Brit.* **1.** Also called (in vertical engines): **bottom end.** the larger end of a connecting rod in an internal-combustion engine. Compare **little end. 2.** the bearing surface between the larger end of a connecting rod and the crankpin of the crankshaft.

bigener ('baɪdʒɪnə) *n. Biology.* a hybrid between individuals of different genera. [C20: back formation from *bigeneric;* see BI-[1], GENUS]

bigeneric (ˌbaɪdʒəˈnɛrɪk) *adj.* (of a hybrid plant) derived from parents of two different genera.

bigeye ('bɪgˌaɪ) *n., pl.* **-eye** *or* **-eyes.** any tropical or subtropical red marine percoid fish of the family *Priacanthidae,* having very large eyes and rough scales.

big game *n.* **1.** large animals that are hunted or fished for sport. **2.** *Informal.* the objective of an important or dangerous undertaking.

biggin[1] *or* **biggon** ('bɪgɪn) *n.* a plain close-fitting cap, often tying under the chin, worn in the Middle Ages and by children in the 17th century. [C16: from French *béguin;* see BEGUINE]

biggin[2] ('bɪgən) *n. Scot.* a construction, esp. a house or cottage. [see BIG[2]]

big gun *n. Informal.* an important or influential person.

bighead ('bɪgˌhɛd) *n.* **1.** *Informal.* a conceited person. **2.** *U.S. and Canadian informal.* conceit; egotism. **3.** *Vet. science.* **a.** an abnormal bulging or increase in the size of an animal's skull, as from osteomalacia. **b.** any of various diseases of sheep characterized by swelling of the head, esp. any caused by infection with *Clostridium* bacteria. —ˌ**big'headed** *adj.* —ˌ**big'headedly** *adv.* —ˌ**big'headedness** *n.*

big-hearted *adj.* warmly generous. —ˌ**big-'heartedness** *n.*

bighorn ('bɪgˌhɔːn) *n., pl.* **-horns** *or* **-horn.** a large wild sheep, *Ovis canadensis,* inhabiting mountainous regions in North America and NE Asia: family *Bovidae,* order *Artiodactyla.* The male has massive curved horns, and the species is well adapted for climbing and leaping.

bight (baɪt) *n.* **1.** a wide indentation of a shoreline, or the body of water bounded by such a curve. **2.** the slack middle part of an extended rope. **3.** a curve or loop in a rope. *~vb.* **4.** (*tr.*) to fasten or bind with a bight. [Old English *byht;* see BOW[2]]

big money *n.* large sums of money: *there's big money in professional golf.*

bigmouth ('bɪgˌmaʊθ) *n. Slang.* a noisy, indiscreet, or boastful person. —'**big-ˌmouthed** *adj.*

big noise *n. Informal.* an important person.

bignonia (bɪg'nəʊnɪə) *n.* any tropical American bignoniaceous climbing shrub of the genus *Bignonia* (or *Doxantha*), cultivated for their trumpet-shaped yellow or reddish flowers. See also **cross vine.** [C19: from New Latin, named after the Abbé Jean-Paul *Bignon* (1662–1743)]

bignoniaceous (bɪgˌnəʊnɪ'eɪʃəs) *adj.* of, relating to, or belonging to the *Bignoniaceae,* a chiefly tropical family of trees, shrubs, and lianas, including jacaranda, bignonia, and catalpa.

big-note *vb. Austral. informal.* to boast about (oneself).

bigot ('bɪgət) *n.* a person who is intolerant of any ideas other than his own, esp. on religion, politics, or race. [C16: from Old French: name applied contemptuously to the Normans by the French, of obscure origin] —'**bigoted** *adj.*

bigotry ('bɪgətrɪ) *n., pl.* **-ries.** the attitudes, behaviour, or way of thinking of a bigot; prejudice; intolerance.

big science *n.* scientific research that requires a large investment of capital.

big screen *n.* an informal name for the **cinema.**

big shot *n. Informal.* an important or influential person.

Big Smoke *n.* **the.** *Informal.* a large city, esp. London.

big stick *n. Informal.* force or the threat of using force.

big time *n. Informal.* **a. the.** the highest or most profitable level of an occupation or profession, esp. the entertainment business. **b.** (*as modifier*): *a big-time comedian.* —'**big-'timer** *n.*

big top *n. Informal.* **1.** the main tent of a circus. **2.** the circus itself.

big tree *n.* a giant Californian coniferous tree, *Sequoiadendron giganteum,* with a wide tapering trunk and thick spongy bark: family *Taxodiaceae.* It often reaches a height of 90 metres. Also called: **giant sequoia.** See also **sequoia.**

biguanide (baɪ'gwɑːnaɪd) *n.* any of a class of compounds some of which are used in the treatment of certain forms of diabetes. See also **phenformin.** [C19: from BI-[1] + GUANIDINE + -IDE]

big wheel *n.* **1.** another name for a **Ferris wheel. 2.** *Informal.* an important person.

big White Chief *n. Informal.* an important person, boss, or leader. Also called: **big Chief, big Daddy.**

bigwig ('bɪgˌwɪg) *n. Informal.* an important person.

Bihari (bɪ'hɑːrɪ) *n.* **1.** (*pl.* **Bihari** *or* **Biharis**) a member of an Indian people living chiefly in the NE Indian state of Bihar but also in Bangladesh and Pakistan. **2.** the language of this people, comprising a number of highly differentiated dialects, belonging to the Indic branch of the Indo-European family. *~adj.* **3.** of or relating to this people, their language, or Bihar.

bijection (baɪ'dʒɛkʃən) *n.* a mathematical function or mapping that is both an injection and a surjection and therefore has an inverse.

bijective (baɪ'dʒɛktɪv) *adj. Maths.* (of a function, relation, etc.) associating two sets in such a way that every member of each set is uniquely paired with a member of the other: *the mapping from the set of married men to the set of married women is bijective in a monogamous society.* Compare **injective, surjective.**

bijou ('biːʒuː) *n., pl.* **-joux** (-ʒuːz). **1.** something small and delicately worked, such as a trinket. **2.** (*modifier*) *Often ironic.* small but elegant and tasteful: *a bijou residence.* [C19: from French, from Breton *bizou* finger ring, from *biz* finger; compare Welsh *bys* finger, Cornish *bis*]

bijouterie (biː'ʒuːtərɪ) *n.* **1.** jewellery esteemed for the delicacy of the work rather than the value of the materials. **2.** a collection of such jewellery.

bijugate ('baɪdʒʊˌgeɪt, baɪ'dʒuːgeɪt) *or* **bijugous** *adj.* (of compound leaves) having two pairs of leaflets.

bike[1] (baɪk) *n., vb.* **1.** *Informal.* short for **bicycle** or **motorcycle. 2. on your bike.** *Brit. slang.* away you go. **3. get off one's bike.** *Austral. and N.Z. slang.* to lose one's self-control. *~n.* **4.** *Slang.* a promiscuous woman: *the town bike.*

bike[2] *or* **byke** (bəɪk, baɪk) *Scot.* *~n.* **1.** a wasps' or bees' nest. *~vb.* (*intr.*) **2.** to swarm. [C14: of uncertain origin]

biker ('baɪkə) *n. Informal.* a member of a motorcycle gang.

bikie ('baɪkɪ) *n. Austral. and N.Z. slang.* a member of a motorcycle gang.

bikini (bɪ'kiːnɪ) *n., pl.* **-nis.** a woman's very brief two-piece swimming costume. [C20: after *Bikini* atoll, a U.S. atomic test site in the N Pacific; from a comparison between the devastating effect of the atom bomb and the effect caused by women wearing bikinis]

bilabial (baɪ'leɪbɪəl) *adj.* **1.** of, relating to, or denoting a speech sound articulated using both lips: *(p) is a bilabial stop, (w) a bilabial semivowel.* *~n.* **2.** a bilabial speech sound.

bilabiate (baɪ'leɪbɪˌeɪt, -ɪt) *adj. Botany.* divided into two lips: *the snapdragon has a bilabiate corolla.*

bilander ('bɪləndə) *n.* a small two-masted cargo ship. [C17: from Dutch, literally: by-lander, because used on canals]

bilateral (baɪ'lætərəl) *adj.* **1.** having or involving two sides. **2.** affecting or undertaken by two parties; mutual: *a bilateral treaty.* **3.** denoting or relating to bilateral symmetry. **4.** having identical sides or parts on each side of an axis; symmetrical. **5.** *Sociol.* relating to descent through both maternal and paternal lineage. Compare **unilateral** (sense 5). **6.** *Brit.* relating to an education that combines academic and technical courses. —**bi'laterally** *adv.*

bilateral symmetry *n.* the property of an organism or part of an organism such that, if cut in only one plane, the two cut halves are mirror images of each other. See also **radial symmetry.**

bilateral trade *n.* a system of trading between two countries in which each country attempts to balance its trade with that of the other.

bilberry ('bɪlbərɪ) *n., pl.* **-ries. 1.** any of several ericaceous shrubs of the genus *Vaccinium,* such as the whortleberry, having edible blue or blackish berries. See also **blueberry. 2. a.** the fruit of any of these plants. **b.** (*as modifier*): *bilberry pie.* [C16: probably of Scandinavian origin; compare Danish *böllebær,* from *bölle* bilberry + *bær* BERRY]

bilbo ('bɪlbəʊ) *n., pl.* **-bos** *or* **-boes.** (formerly) a sword with a marked temper and elasticity. [C16: from *Bilboa,* variant (in English) of *Bilbao,* Spain, noted for its blades]

bilboes ('bɪlbəʊz) *pl. n.* a long iron bar with two sliding shackles, formerly used to confine the ankles of a prisoner. [C16: perhaps changed from *Bilbao,* Spain]

bilby ('bɪlbɪ) *n., pl.* **-bies.** a burrowing marsupial of the genus *Macrotis* of Australia having long pointed ears and grey fur. Also called: **rabbit bandicoot, dalgyte.**

Bildungsroman *German.* ('bɪldʊŋsroma:n) *n.* a novel concerned with a person's formative years and development. [literally: education novel]

bile[1] (baɪl) *n.* **1.** a bitter greenish to golden brown alkaline fluid secreted by the liver and stored in the gall bladder. It is discharged during digestion into the duodenum, where it aids the emulsification and absorption of fats. **2.** irritability or peevishness. **3.** *Archaic.* either of two bodily humours, one of which (**black bile**) was thought to cause melancholy and the other (**yellow bile**) anger. [C17: from French, from Latin *bīlis,* probably of Celtic origin; compare Welsh *bustl* bile]

bile[2] (bəɪl) *n.* a Scot. word for **boil**[1].

bilection (baɪ'lɛkʃən) *n.* another word for **bolection.**

bilestone ('baɪlˌstəʊn) *n.* another name for **gallstone.**

bilge (bɪldʒ) *n.* **1.** *Nautical.* the parts of a vessel's hull where the vertical sides curve inwards to form the bottom. **2.** (*often pl.*) the parts of a vessel between the lowermost floorboards and the bottom. **3.** Also called: **bilge water.** the dirty water that collects in a vessel's bilge. **4.** *Informal.* silly rubbish; nonsense. **5.** the widest part of the belly of a barrel or cask. ~*vb.* **6.** (*intr.*) *Nautical.* (of a vessel) to take in water at the bilge. **7.** (*tr.*) *Nautical.* to damage (a vessel) in the bilge, causing it to leak. [C16: probably a variant of BULGE] —'**bilgy** *adj.*

bilge keel *n.* one of two keel-like projections along the bilges of some vessels to improve sideways stability.

bilharzia (bɪl'hɑ:tsɪə) *n.* **1.** another name for a **schistosome. 2.** another name for **schistosomiasis.** [C19: New Latin, named after Theodor *Bilharz* (1825–62), German parasitologist who discovered schistosomes]

bilharziasis (ˌbɪlhɑ:'tsaɪəsɪs) *or* **bilharziosis** (bɪlˌhɑ:tsɪ'əʊsɪs) *n.* another name for **schistosomiasis.**

biliary ('bɪlɪərɪ) *adj.* of or relating to bile, to the ducts that convey bile, or to the gall bladder.

bilinear (baɪ'lɪnɪə) *adj.* **1.** of or referring to two lines. **2.** of or relating to a function of two variables that is linear in each independently, as f(x, y) = xy.

bilingual (baɪ'lɪŋgwəl) *adj.* **1.** able to speak two languages, esp. with fluency. **2.** written or expressed in two languages. ~*n.* **3.** a bilingual person. —**bi'lingualˌism** *n.* —**bi'lingually** *adv.*

bilious ('bɪlɪəs) *adj.* **1.** of or relating to bile. **2.** affected with or denoting any disorder related to excess secretion of bile. **3.** *Informal.* (esp. of colours) extremely distasteful; nauseating: *a bilious green.* **4.** *Informal.* bad-tempered; irritable. [C16: from Latin *bīliōsus* full of BILE] —'**biliousness** *n.*

bilirubin (ˌbɪlɪ'ru:bɪn, ˌbaɪ-) *n.* an orange-yellow pigment in the bile formed as a breakdown product of haemoglobin. Excess amounts in the blood produce the yellow appearance associated with jaundice. Formula: $C_{32}H_{36}O_6N_4$. [C19: from BILE + Latin *ruber* red + -IN]

biliverdin (ˌbɪlɪ'vɜ:dɪn) *n.* a dark green pigment in the bile formed by the oxidation of bilirubin. Formula: $C_{33}H_{34}O_6N_4$. [C19: coined in Swedish, from Latin *bīlis* bile + Old French *verd* green + -IN]

bilk (bɪlk) *vb.* (*tr.*) **1.** to balk; thwart. **2.** (often foll. by *of*) to cheat or deceive, esp. to avoid making payment to. **3.** to escape from; elude. **4.** *Cribbage.* to play a card that hinders (one's opponent) from scoring in his crib. ~*n.* **5.** a swindle or cheat. **6.** a person who swindles or cheats. [C17: perhaps variant of BALK] —'**bilker** *n.*

bill[1] (bɪl) *n.* **1.** money owed for goods or services supplied: *an electricity bill.* **2.** a written or printed account or statement of money owed. **3.** *Chiefly Brit.* such an account for food and drink in a restaurant, hotel, etc. Usual U.S. and Canadian word: **check. 4.** any printed or written list of items, events, etc., such as a theatre programme: *who's on the bill tonight?* **5. fill the bill.** *Informal.* to serve or perform adequately. **6.** a statute in draft, before it becomes law. **7.** a printed notice or advertisement; poster. **8.** *U.S. and Canadian.* a piece of paper money; note. **9.** an obsolete name for **promissory note. 10.** *Law.* See **bill of indictment. 11.** See **bill of exchange. 12.** See **bill of fare. 13.** *Archaic.* any document. ~*vb.* (*tr.*) **14.** to send or present an account for payment to (a person). **15.** to enter (items, goods, etc.) on an account or statement. **16.** to advertise by posters. **17.** to schedule as a future programme: *the play is billed for next week.* [C14: from Anglo-Latin *billa,* alteration of Late Latin *bulla* document, BULL[3]]

bill[2] (bɪl) *n.* **1.** the mouthpart of a bird, consisting of projecting jaws covered with a horny sheath; beak. It varies in shape and size according to the type of food eaten and may also be used as a weapon. **2.** any beaklike mouthpart in other animals. **3.** a narrow promontory: *Portland Bill.* **4.** *Nautical.* the pointed tip of the fluke of an anchor. ~*vb.* (*intr.*) (esp. in the phrase **bill and coo**). **5.** (of birds, esp. doves) to touch bills together. **6.** (of lovers) to kiss and whisper amorously. [Old English *bile;* related to *bill* BILL[3]]

bill[3] (bɪl) *n.* **1.** a pike or halberd with a narrow hooked blade. **2.** short for **billhook.** [Old English *bill* sword, related to Old Norse *bīldr* instrument used in blood-letting, Old High German *bil* pickaxe]

bill[4] (bɪl) *n. Ornithol.* another word for **boom**[1] (sense 4). [C18: from dialect *beel* BELL[2] (vb.)]

billabong ('bɪləˌbɒŋ) *n. Austral.* **1.** a backwater channel that forms a lagoon or pool. **2.** a branch of a river running to a dead end. [C19: from a native Australian language, from *billa* river + *bong* dead]

billboard[1] ('bɪlˌbɔ:d) *n. Chiefly U.S. and Canadian.* another name for **hoarding.** [C19: from BILL[1] + BOARD]

billboard[2] ('bɪlˌbɔ:d) *n.* a fitting at the bow of a vessel for securing an anchor. [C19: from BILL[2] + BOARD]

bill broker *n.* a person whose business is the purchase and sale of bills of exchange.

billet[1] ('bɪlɪt) *n.* **1.** accommodation, esp. for a soldier, in civilian lodgings. **2.** the official requisition for such lodgings. **3.** a space or berth allocated, esp. for slinging a hammock, in a ship. **4.** *Informal.* a job. **5.** *Archaic.* a brief letter or document. ~*vb.* **-lets, -leting, -leted. 6.** (*tr.*) to assign a lodging to (a soldier). **7.** (*tr.*) *Informal.* to assign to a post or job. **8.** to lodge or be lodged. [C15: from Old French *billette,* from *bulle* a document; see BULL[3]] —ˌ**billet'ee** *n.* —'**billeter** *n.*

billet[2] ('bɪlɪt) *n.* **1.** a chunk of wood, esp. for fuel. **2.** *Metallurgy.* **a.** a metal bar of square or circular cross section. **b.** an ingot cast into the shape of a prism. **3.** *Architect.* a carved ornament in a moulding, with short cylinders or blocks evenly spaced. [C15: from Old French *billette* a little log, from *bille* log, probably of Celtic origin]

billet-doux (ˌbɪlɪ'du:; *French* bijɛdu) *n., pl.* **billets-doux** (ˌbɪlɪ'du:z; *French* bijɛdu). *Old-fashioned or jocular.* a love letter. [C17: from French, literally: a sweet letter, from *billet* (see BILLET[1]) + *doux* sweet, from Latin *dulcis*]

billfish ('bɪlˌfɪʃ) *n., pl.* **-fish** *or* **-fishes.** *U.S.* any of various fishes having elongated jaws, esp. any fish of the family *Istiophoridae,* such as the spearfish and marlin.

billfold ('bɪlˌfəʊld) *n.* a U.S. and Canadian word for **wallet.**

billhook ('bɪlˌhʊk) *n.* a cutting tool with a wooden handle and a curved blade terminating in a hook at its tip, used for pruning, chopping, etc. Also called: **bill.**

billiard ('bɪljəd) *n.* (*modifier*) of or relating to billiards: *a billiard table; a billiard cue; a billiard ball.*

billiards ('bɪljədz) *n.* (*functioning as sing.*) **1.** any of various games in which long cues are used to drive balls now made of composition or plastic. It is played on a rectangular table covered with a smooth tight-fitting cloth and having raised cushioned edges. **2.** a version of this, played on a rectangular table having six pockets let into the corners and the two longer sides. Points are scored by striking one of three balls with the cue to contact the other two or one of the two. Compare **pool**[2] (sense 5), **snooker.** [C16: from Old French *billard* curved stick, from Old French *bille* log; see BILLET[2]]

billing ('bɪlɪŋ) *n.* **1.** *Theatre.* the relative importance of a performer or act as reflected in the prominence given in programmes, advertisements, etc. **2.** *Chiefly U.S. and Canadian.* public notice or advertising (esp. in the phrase **advance billing).**

billingsgate ('bɪlɪŋzˌgeɪt) *n.* obscene or abusive language. [C17: after *Billingsgate* fish market, London, which was notorious for such language]

Billings method ('bɪlɪŋz) *n.* a natural method of birth control that involves examining the colour and viscosity of the cervical mucus to discover when ovulation is occurring. Also called: **ovulation method, mucus method.** [C20: devised by Drs John and Evelyn *Billings* in the 1960s]

billion ('bɪljən) *n., pl.* **-lions** *or* **-lion. 1.** one thousand million: written as 1 000 000 000 or 10^9. **2.** (formerly, in Britain) one million million: written as 1 000 000 000 000 or 10^{12}. **3.** (*often pl.*) any exceptionally large number. ~*determiner.* **4.** (preceded by *a* or a cardinal number) **a.** amounting to a billion: *it seems like a billion years ago.* **b.** (*as pronoun*): *we have a billion here.* [C17: from French, from BI-[1] + *-llion* as in *million*] —'**billionth** *adj., n.*

billionaire (ˌbɪljə'nɛə) *n.* a person whose assets are worth over a billion of the monetary units of his country.

bill of adventure *n.* a certificate made out by a merchant to show that goods handled by him and his agents are the property of another party at whose risk the dealing is done.

bill of attainder *n.* (formerly) a legislative act finding a person guilty without trial of treason or felony and declaring him attainted. See also **attainder** (sense 1).

bill of exchange *n.* (now chiefly in foreign transactions) a document, usually negotiable, containing an instruction to a third party to pay a stated sum of money at a designated future date or on demand.

bill of fare *n.* another name for **menu.**

bill of health *n.* **1.** a certificate, issued by a port officer, that attests to the health of a ship's company. **2. clean bill of health.** *Informal.* **a.** a good report of one's physical condition. **b.** a favourable account of a person's or a company's financial position.

bill of indictment *n. Criminal Law.* a formal document accusing a person or persons of crime, formerly presented to a grand jury for certification as a true bill but now signed by a court official.

bill of lading *n.* (in foreign trade) a document containing full particulars of goods shipped or for shipment. Usual U.S. and Canadian name: **waybill.**

Bill of Rights *n.* **1.** an English statute of 1689 guaranteeing the rights and liberty of the individual subject. **2.** the first ten amendments to the U.S. Constitution, added in 1791, which guarantee the liberty of the individual. **3.** (in Canada) a statement of basic human rights and freedoms enacted by Parliament in 1960. **4.** (*usually not caps.*) any charter or summary of basic human rights.

bill of sale *n. Law.* a deed transferring personal property, either outright or as security for a loan or debt.

billon ('bɪlən) *n.* **1.** an alloy consisting of gold or silver and a base metal, usually copper, used esp. for coinage. **2.** any coin made of such an alloy. [C18: from Old French: ingot, from *bille* log; see BILLET[2]]

billow ('bɪləʊ) *n.* **1.** a large sea wave. **2.** a swelling or surging mass, as of smoke or sound. **3.** (*pl.*) *Poetic.* the sea itself. ~*vb.* **4.** to rise up, swell out, or cause to rise up or swell out. [C16: from Old Norse *bylgja*; related to Swedish *bölja*, Danish *bölg*, Middle High German *bulge*; see BELLOW, BELLY] —'**billowing** *adj., n.*

billowy ('bɪləʊɪ) *adj.* full of or forming billows: *a billowy sea.* —'**billowiness** *n.*

billposter ('bɪlˌpəʊstə) *or* **billsticker** *n.* a person who is employed to stick advertising posters to walls, fences, etc. —'**bill,posting** *or* '**bill,sticking** *n.*

billy[1] ('bɪlɪ) *n., pl.* **-lies.** *U.S. and Canadian.* a wooden club esp. a policeman's truncheon. [C19: special use of the name *Billy*, pet form of *William*]

billy[2] ('bɪlɪ) *or* **billycan** ('bɪlɪˌkæn) *n., pl.* **-lies** *or* **-lycans. 1.** a metal can or pot for boiling water, etc., over a campfire. **2.** *Austral. and N.Z.* (*as modifier*): *billy-tea.* **3. boil the billy.** *Austral. and N.Z. informal.* to make tea. [C19: from Scot. *billypot* cooking vessel]

billy-bread *n. N.Z.* bread baked in a billy over a camp fire.

billycock ('bɪlɪkɒk) *n. Rare, chiefly Brit.* any of several round-crowned brimmed hats of felt, such as the bowler. [C19: named after *William Coke*, Englishman for whom it was first made]

billy goat *n.* a male goat. Compare **nanny goat.**

billyo *or* **billyoh** ('bɪlɪˌəʊ) *n.* **like billyo.** *Informal.* (intensifier): *snowing like billyo.* [C19: of unknown origin]

bilobate (baɪ'ləʊˌbeɪt) *or* **bilobed** ('baɪˌləʊbd) *adj.* divided into or having two lobes: *a bilobate leaf.*

bilocular (baɪ'lɒkjʊlə) *or* **biloculate** *adj. Biology.* divided into two chambers or cavities: *some flowering plants have bilocular ovaries.*

biltong ('bɪlˌtɒŋ) *n. S. African.* strips of meat dried and cured in the sun. [C19: Afrikaans, from Dutch *bil* buttock + *tong* TONGUE]

Bim (bɪm) *n. Informal.* a native or inhabitant of Barbados. [C19: of unknown origin]

BIM *abbrev. for* British Institute of Management.

bimah *or* **bima** ('biːmə) *n.* variant spellings of **bema.**

bimanous ('bɪmənəs, baɪ'meɪ-) *adj.* (of man and the higher primates) having two hands distinct in form and function from the feet. [C19: from New Latin *bimana* two handed, from BI-[1] + Latin *manus* hand]

bimanual (baɪ'mænjʊəl) *adj.* using or requiring both hands. —**bi'manually** *adv.*

bimbo ('bɪmbəʊ) *n., pl.* **-bos** *or* **-boes.** *Slang, usually derogatory.* **1.** an attractive but empty-headed young woman. **2.** a fellow; person esp. a foolish one. [C20: from Italian: little child, perhaps via Polari]

bimestrial (baɪ'mɛstrɪəl) *adj.* **1.** lasting for two months. **2.** a less common word for **bimonthly** (sense 1). [C19: from Latin *bimēstris*, from BI-[1] + *mēnsis* month] —**bi'mestrially** *adv.*

bimetallic (ˌbaɪmɪ'tælɪk) *adj.* **1.** consisting of two metals. **2.** of, relating to, or based on bimetallism.

bimetallic strip *n.* a strip consisting of two metals of different coefficients of expansion welded together so that it buckles on heating: used in thermostats, etc.

bimetallism (baɪ'mɛtəˌlɪzəm) *n.* **1.** the use of two metals, esp. gold and silver, in fixed relative values as the standard of value and currency. **2.** the economic policies or doctrine supporting a bimetallic standard. —**bi'metallist** *n.*

bimillenary (ˌbaɪmɪ'liːnərɪ, baɪ'mɪlɪnərɪ) *adj.* **1.** marking a two-thousandth anniversary. ~*n. pl.,* **-naries. 2.** a two-thousandth anniversary.

bimodal distribution (baɪ'məʊdᵊl) *n. Statistics.* a frequency distribution with two modes.

bimolecular (ˌbaɪmə'lɛkjʊlə) *adj.* (of a chemical complex, collision, etc.) having or involving two molecules.

bimonthly (baɪ'mʌnθlɪ) *adj., adv.* **1.** every two months. **2.** (often avoided because of confusion with sense 1) twice a month; semimonthly. See **bi-**[1]. ~*n., pl.* **-lies. 3.** a periodical published every two months.

bimorph ('baɪmɔːf) *or* **bimorph cell** *n. Electronics.* an assembly of two piezoelectric crystals cemented together so that an applied voltage causes one to expand and the other to contract, converting electrical signals into mechanical energy. Conversely, bending can generate a voltage: used in loudspeakers, gramophone pick-ups, etc.

bin (bɪn) *n.* **1.** a large container or enclosed space for storing something in bulk, such as coal, grain, or wool. **2.** Also called: **bread bin.** a small container for bread. **3.** Also called: **dustbin, rubbish bin.** a container for litter, rubbish, etc. **4.** *Brit.* **a.** a storage place for bottled wine. **b.** one particular bottling of wine. ~*vb.* **bins, binning, binned. 5.** (*tr.*) to store in a bin. **6.** (*tr.*) to put in a wastepaper bin. [Old English *binne* basket, probably of Celtic origin; related to *bindan* to BIND]

bin- *prefix.* a variant, esp. before a vowel, of **bi-**[1]: *binocular.*

binal ('baɪnᵊl) *adj.* twofold; double. [C17: from New Latin *bīnālis*; see BIN-]

binary ('baɪnərɪ) *adj.* **1.** composed of, relating to, or involving two; dual. **2.** *Maths, computer technol.* of, relating to, or expressed in binary notation or binary code. **3.** (of a compound or molecule) containing atoms of two different elements. **4.** *Metallurgy.* (of an alloy) consisting of two components or phases. **5.** (of an educational system) consisting of two parallel forms of education such as the grammar school and the secondary modern in Britain. **6.** *Maths, logic.* (of a relation, expression, or operation) applying to two elements of its domain; having two argument places; dyadic. ~*n., pl.* **-ries. 7.** something composed of two parts or things. **8.** *Astronomy.* See **binary star. 9.** short for **binary weapon.** [C16: from Late Latin *bīnārius*; see BIN-]

binary code *n. Computer technol.* the representation of each one of a set of numbers, letters, etc., as a unique sequence of bits, as in ASCII.

binary-coded decimal *n.* a number in binary code written in groups of four bits, each group representing one digit of the corresponding decimal number. Abbrev.: **BCD.**

binary digit *n.* either of the two digits 0 or 1, used in binary notation. See also: **bit**[4].

binary fission *n.* asexual reproduction in unicellular organisms by division into two similar daughter cells.

binary form *n. Music.* a structure consisting of two sections, each being played twice.

binary notation *or* **system** *n.* a number system having a base of two, numbers being expressed by sequences of the digits 0 and 1: used in computing, as 0 and 1 can be represented electrically as *off* and *on.*

binary number *n.* a number expressed in binary notation, as $1101.101 = 1 \times 2^3 + 1 \times 2^2 + 0 \times 2^1 + 1 \times 2^0 + 1 \times 2^{-1} + 0 \times 2^{-2} + 1 \times 2^{-3} = 13\frac{5}{8}$.

binary star *n.* a double star system containing two associated stars revolving around a common centre of gravity in different orbits. A **visual binary** can be seen through a telescope. A **spectroscopic binary** can only be observed by the spectroscopic Doppler shift as each star moves towards or away from the earth. Sometimes shortened to **binary.** See also **optical double star, eclipsing binary.**

binary weapon *n.* a chemical weapon consisting of a projectile containing two substances separately that mix to produce a lethal agent when the projectile is fired.

binate ('baɪˌneɪt) *adj. Botany.* occurring in two parts or in pairs: *binate leaves.* [C19: from New Latin *bīnātus*, probably from Latin *combīnātus* united] —'**bi,nately** *adv.*

binaural (baɪ'nɔːrəl, bɪn-) *adj.* **1.** relating to, having, or hearing with both ears. **2.** employing two separate channels for recording or transmitting sound; so creating an impression of depth: *a binaural recording.* —**bin'aurally** *adv.*

bind (baɪnd) *vb.* **binds, binding, bound. 1.** to make or become fast or secure with or as if with a tie or band. **2.** (*tr.*; often foll. by *up*) to encircle or enclose with a band: *to bind the hair.* **3.** (*tr.*) to place (someone) under obligation; oblige. **4.** (*tr.*) to impose legal obligations or duties upon (a person or party to an agreement). **5.** (*tr.*) to make (a bargain, agreement, etc.) irrevocable; seal. **6.** (*tr.*) to restrain or confine with or as if with ties, as of responsibility or loyalty. **7.** (*tr.*) to place under certain constraints; govern. **8.** (*tr.*; often foll. by *up*) to bandage or swathe: *to bind a wound.* **9.** to cohere or stick or cause to cohere or stick: *egg binds fat and flour.* **10.** to make or become compact, stiff, or hard: *frost binds the earth.* **11. a.** (*tr.*) to enclose and fasten (the pages of a book) between covers. **b.** (*intr.*) (of a book) to undergo this process. **12.** (*tr.*) to provide (a garment, hem, etc.) with a border or edging, as for decoration or to prevent fraying. **13.** (*tr.*; sometimes foll. by *out* or *over*) to employ as an apprentice; indenture. **14.** (*intr.*) *Slang.* to complain. **15.** (*tr.*) *Logic.* to bring (a variable) into the scope of an appropriate quantifier. See also **bound**[1] (sense 10). ~*n.* **16.** something that binds. **17.** the act of binding or state of being bound. **18.** *Informal.* a difficult or annoying situation. **19.** another word for **bine. 20.** *Music.* another word for **tie** (sense 17). **21.** *Mining.* clay between layers of coal. **22.** *Fencing.* a pushing movement with the blade made to force one's opponent's sword from one line into another. **23.** *Chess.* a position in which one player's pawns have a hold on the centre that makes it difficult for the opponent to advance there. ~See also **bind over.** [Old English *bindan*; related to Old Norse *binda*, Old High German *bintan*, Latin *offendix* BAND[2], Sanskrit *badhnāti* he binds]

binder ('baɪndə) *n.* **1.** a firm cover or folder with rings or clasps for holding loose sheets of paper together. **2.** a material used to bind separate particles together, give an appropriate consistency, or facilitate adhesion to a surface. **3.** a person who binds books; bookbinder. **4.** something used to fasten or tie, such as rope or twine. **5.** *N.Z. informal.* a square meal. **6.** Also called: **reaper binder.** *Obsolete.* a machine for cutting grain and binding it into bundles or sheaves. Compare **combine harvester. 7.** an informal agreement giving insurance coverage pending formal issue of a policy. **8.** a tie, beam, or girder, used to support floor joists. **9.** a stone for binding masonry; bondstone. **10.** the nonvolatile component of the organic media in which pigments are dispersed in paint. **11.** (in systemic grammar) a word that introduces a bound clause; a subordinating conjunction or a relative pronoun. Compare **linker** (sense 2).

bindery (ˈbaɪndərɪ) *n., pl.* **-eries.** a place in which books are bound.

bindi-eye (ˈbɪndɪˌaɪ) *n. Austral.* **1.** any of various small weedy Australian herbaceous plants of the genus *Calotis,* with burlike fruits: family *Compositae* (composites). **2.** any bur or prickle. [C20: perhaps from a native Australian language]

binding (ˈbaɪndɪŋ) *n.* **1.** anything that binds or fastens. **2.** the covering within which the pages of a book are bound. **3.** the material or tape used for binding hems, etc. *~adj.* **4.** imposing an obligation or duty: *a binding promise.* **5.** causing hindrance; restrictive.

binding energy *n. Physics.* **1.** the energy that must be supplied to a stable nucleus before it can undergo fission. It is equal to the mass defect. **2.** the energy required to remove a particle from a system, esp. an electron from an atom.

bind over *vb.* (*tr., adv.*) to place (a person) under a legal obligation, such as one to keep the peace.

bindweed (ˈbaɪndˌwiːd) *n.* **1.** any convolvulaceous plant of the genera *Convolvulus* and *Calystegia* that twines around a support. See also **convolvulus. 2.** any of various other trailing or twining plants, such as black bindweed.

bine (baɪn) *n.* **1.** the climbing or twining stem of any of various plants, such as the woodbine or bindweed. **2.** any plant with such a stem. [C19: variant of BIND]

Binet-Simon scale (ˈbiːneɪˈsaɪmən) *n. Psychol.* a test comprising questions and tasks, used to determine the mental age of subjects, usually children. Also called: **Binet scale** *or* **test.** See also **Stanford-Binet test.** [C20: named after Alfred *Binet* (1857–1911) + Théodore *Simon* (1873–1961), French psychologists]

bing (bɪŋ) *n. Dialect.* a heap or pile, esp. of spoil from a mine. [C16: from Old Norse *bingr* heap]

binge (bɪndʒ) *n. Informal.* **1.** a bout of excessive eating or drinking. **2.** excessive indulgence in anything: *a shopping binge. ~vb.* **binges, bingeing** *or* **binging, binged.** (*intr.*) **3.** to indulge in a binge (esp. of eating or drinking). [C19: probably Lincolnshire dialect *binge* to soak]

bingey *or* **bingy** (ˈbɪndʒɪ) *n., pl.* **bingeys** *or* **bingies.** *Austral. informal.* the stomach; belly. [C19: from a native Australian language]

binghi (ˈbɪŋgaɪ) *n. Austral. slang, often derogatory.* an Aborigine. [C19: from a native Australian language, literally: brother]

bingle (ˈbɪŋgᵊl) *n. Austral. informal.* a minor crash or upset, as in a car or on a surfboard. [C20: of uncertain origin]

bingo (ˈbɪŋgəʊ) *n., pl.* **-gos. 1.** a gambling game, usually played with several people, in which numbers selected at random are called out and the players cover the numbers on their individual cards. The first to cover a given arrangement of numbers is the winner. Compare **lotto.** *~sentence substitute.* **2.** a cry by the winner of a game of bingo. **3.** an expression of surprise at a sudden occurrence or the successful completion of something: *and bingo! the lights went out.* [C19: perhaps from *bing,* imitative of a bell ringing to mark the win]

Bini *or* **Beni** (bəˈniː) *n., pl.* **-ni** *or* **-nis.** other names for **Edo.**

binman (ˈbɪnˌmæn, ˈbɪnmən) *n., pl.* **-men.** another name for **dustman.**

binnacle (ˈbɪnəkᵊl) *n.* a housing for a ship's compass. [C17: changed from C15 *bitakle,* from Portuguese *bitácula,* from Late Latin *habitāculum* dwelling-place, from Latin *habitāre* to inhabit; spelling influenced by BIN]

binocular (bɪˈnɒkjʊlə, baɪ-) *adj.* involving, relating to, seeing with or intended for both eyes: *binocular vision.* [C18: from BI-[1] + Latin *oculus* eye]

binocular disparity *n. Physiol.* the small differences in the positions of the parts of the images falling on each eye as a result of each eye viewing the scene from a slightly different position; these differences make stereoscopic vision possible.

binocular rivalry *n. Psychol.* the inability to see simultaneously different images presented one to each eye; usually in some areas of the eye the image presented to the left eye is seen, in others that presented to the right eye. Also called: **retinal rivalry.**

binoculars (bɪˈnɒkjʊləz, baɪ-) *pl. n.* an optical instrument for use with both eyes, consisting of two small telescopes joined together. Also called: **field glasses.**

binomial (baɪˈnəʊmɪəl) *n.* **1.** a mathematical expression consisting of two terms, such as $3x + 2y$. **2.** a two-part taxonomic name for an animal or plant. See **binomial nomenclature.** *~adj.* **3.** referring to two names or terms. [C16: from Medieval Latin *binōmius* from BI-[1] + Latin *nōmen* NAME] **—biˈnomially** *adv.*

binomial coefficient *n. Maths.* any of the numerical factors which multiply the successive terms in a binomial expansion; any term of the form $n!/(n-k)!k!$: written $\binom{n}{k}$, ${}^nC_k$, or $C^n{}_k$. See also **combination** (sense 6).

binomial distribution *n.* a statistical distribution giving the probability of obtaining a specified number of successes in a specified number of independent trials of an experiment with a constant probability of success in each. Symbol: $Bi\ (n, p)$, where n is the number of trials and p the probability of success in each.

binomial experiment *n. Statistics.* an experiment consisting of a fixed number of independent trials each with two possible outcomes, success and failure, and the same probability of success. The probability of a given number of successes is described by a binominal distribution. See also **Bernoulli trial.**

binomial *or* **binominal nomenclature** *n.* a system for naming plants and animals by means of two Latin names: the first indicating the genus and the second the species to which the organism belongs, as in *Panthera leo* (the lion).

binomial theorem *n.* a mathematical theorem that gives the expansion of any binomial raised to a positive integral power, *n.* It contains $n + 1$ terms: $(x + a)^n = x^n + nx^{n-1}a + [n(n-1)/2]x^{n-2}a^2 + \ldots + \binom{n}{k}x^{n-k}a^k + \ldots + a^n$, where $\binom{n}{k} = n!/(n-k)!k!$, the number of combinations of k items selected from n.

binominal (baɪˈnɒmɪnᵊl) *Biology. ~adj.* **1.** of or denoting the binomial nomenclature. *~n.* **2.** a two-part taxonomic name; binomial.

binovular (bɪˈnɒvjʊlə) *adj. Physiol.* relating to or derived from two different ova: *binovular fertilization; binovular twins.*

bint (bɪnt) *n. Slang.* a derogatory term for **girl** or **woman.** [C19: from Arabic, literally: daughter]

binturong (ˈbɪntjʊˌrɒŋ, bɪnˈtjʊərɒŋ) *n.* an arboreal SE Asian viverrine mammal, *Arctictis binturong,* closely related to the palm civets but larger and having long shaggy black hair. [from Malay]

binucleate (baɪˈnjuːklɪˌeɪt, -ɪt) *adj. Biology.* having two nuclei: *a binucleate cell.* Also: **biˈnuclear, biˈnucleˌated.**

bio (ˈbaɪəʊ) *n., pl.* **bios.** *Informal.* short for **biography.**

bio- *or before a vowel* **bi-** *combining form.* **1.** indicating or involving life or living organisms: *biogenesis; biolysis.* **2.** indicating a human life or career: *biography; biopic.* [from Greek *bios* life]

bioaeration (ˌbaɪəʊɛəˈreɪʃən) *n.* the oxidative treatment of raw sewage by aeration.

bioaeronautics (ˌbaɪəʊˌɛərəˈnɔːtɪks) *n.* (*functioning as sing.*) the use of aircraft in the discovery, development, and protection of natural and biological resources.

bioassay *n.* (ˌbaɪəʊəˈseɪ, -ˈæseɪ). **1.** a method of determining the concentration, activity, or effect of a drug, hormone, or vitamin by testing its effect on a living organism and comparing this with the activity of an agreed standard. *~vb.* (ˌbaɪəʊəˈseɪ). **2.** (*tr.*) to subject to a bioassay.

bioastronautics (ˌbaɪəʊˌæstrəˈnɔːtɪks) *n.* (*functioning as sing.*) the study of the effects of space flight on living organisms. See **space medicine.**

bioavailability (ˌbaɪəʊəˌveɪləˈbɪlɪtɪ) *n.* the extent to which a drug or other substance is taken up by a specific tissue or organ after administration. **—ˌbioaˈvailable** *adj.*

biocatalyst (ˌbaɪəʊˈkætəlɪst) *n.* a chemical, esp. an enzyme, that initiates or modifies the rate of a biochemical reaction. **—biocatalytic** (ˌbaɪəʊˌkætəˈlɪtɪk) *adj.*

biocellate (baɪˈɒsɪˌleɪt, ˌbaɪəʊˈsɛlɪt) *adj.* (of animals and plants) marked with two eyelike spots or ocelli. [C19: from BI-[1] + *ocellate,* from Latin *ocellus,* diminutive of *oculus* eye]

biochemical oxygen demand *n.* a measure of the organic pollution of water: the amount of oxygen, in mg per litre of water, absorbed by a sample kept at 20°C for five days. Abbrev.: **BOD.**

biochemistry (ˌbaɪəʊˈkɛmɪstrɪ) *n.* the study of the chemical compounds, reactions, etc., that occur in living organisms. **—biochemical** (ˌbaɪəʊˈkɛmɪkᵊl) *adj.* **—ˌbioˈchemically** *adv.* **—ˌbioˈchemist** *n.*

biocide (ˈbaɪəˌsaɪd) *n.* a chemical, such as a pesticide, capable of killing living organisms. **—ˌbioˈcidal** *adj.*

bioclastic (ˌbaɪəʊˈklæstɪk) *adj.* (of deposits, esp. limestones) derived from shell fragments or similar organic remains.

bioclimatology (ˌbaɪəʊˌklaɪməˈtɒlədʒɪ) *n.* the study of the effects of climatic conditions on living organisms. **—ˌbioˌclimaˈtologist** *n.*

biocoenology *or* **biocenology** (ˌbaɪəʊsɪˈnɒlədʒɪ) *n.* the branch of ecology concerned with the relationships and interactions between the members of a natural community. [C20: from BIO- + *ceno-,* from Greek *koinos* common + -LOGY]

biocoenosis *or* **biocenosis** (ˌbaɪəʊsɪˈnəʊsɪs) *n.* a diverse community inhabiting a single biotope. **—ˌbiocoeˈnotic** *or* **ˌbioceˈnotic** *adj.*

bioconversion (ˌbaɪəʊkənˈvɜːʃən) *n.* the use of biological processes or materials to change organic substances into a new form, such as the conversion of waste into methane by fermentation.

biocycle (ˈbaɪəʊˌsaɪkᵊl) *n. Ecology.* any of the major regions of the biosphere, such as the land or sea, which are capable of supporting life.

biodegradable (ˌbaɪəʊdɪˈgreɪdəbᵊl) *adj.* (of sewage constituents, packaging material, etc.) capable of being decomposed by bacteria or other biological means. **—biodegradation** (ˌbaɪəʊˌdɛgrəˈdeɪʃən) *n.* **—biodegradability** (ˌbaɪəʊˌdɛgreɪdɪˈbɪlɪtɪ) *n.*

biodiversity (ˌbaɪəʊdaɪˈvɜːsɪtɪ) *n.* the existence of a wide variety of plant and animal species in their natural environments, which is the aim of conservationists concerned about the indiscriminate destruction of rain forests and other habitats.

biodot (ˈbaɪəʊˌdɒt) *n.* a temperature-sensitive device stuck to the skin in order to monitor stress levels.

biodynamics (ˌbaɪəʊdaɪˈnæmɪks, -dɪ-) *n.* (*functioning as sing.*) the branch of biology that deals with the energy production and activities of organisms. **—ˌbiodyˈnamic** *or* **ˌbiodyˈnamical** *adj.*

bioecology (ˌbaɪəʊɪˈkɒlədʒɪ) *n.* another word for **ecology** (sense 1). —**bioecological** (ˌbaɪəʊˌiːkəˈlɒdʒɪkəl) *adj.* —ˌ**bioˌecoˈlogically** *adv.* —ˌ**bioeˈcologist** *n.*

bioelectricity (ˌbaɪəʊˌɪlɛkˈtrɪsɪtɪ) *n.* electricity generated by a living organism. —ˌ**bioeˈlectric** *adj.*

bioenergetics (ˌbaɪəʊˌɛnəˈdʒɛtɪks) *n.* (*functioning as sing.*) the study of energy relationships in living organisms. —ˌ**bioˌenerˈgetic** *adj.*

bioengineering (ˌbaɪəʊˌɛndʒɪˈnɪərɪŋ) *n.* **1.** the design and manufacture of aids, such as artificial limbs, to rectify defective body functions. **2.** the design, manufacture, and maintenance of engineering equipment used in biosynthetic processes, such as fermentation. —ˌ**bioˌengiˈneer** *n.*

bioethics (ˌbaɪəʊˈɛθɪks) *n.* (*functioning as sing.*) the study of ethical problems arising from biological research and its applications in such fields as organ transplantation, genetic engineering, or artificial insemination. —ˌ**bioˈethical** *adj.*

biofeedback (ˌbaɪəʊˈfiːdˌbæk) *n. Physiol., psychol.* a technique for teaching the control of autonomic functions, such as the rate of heartbeat or breathing, by recording the activity and presenting it (usually visually) so that the person can know the state of the autonomic function he is learning to control.

bioflavonoid (ˌbaɪəʊˈfleɪvəˌnɔɪd) *n.* another name for **vitamin P.**

biog. *abbrev. for:* **1.** biographical. **2.** biography.

biogas (ˈbaɪəʊˌgæs) *n.* a gas that is produced by the action of bacteria on organic waste matter: used as a fuel.

biogen (ˈbaɪədʒən) *n.* a hypothetical protein assumed to be the basis of the formation and functioning of body cells and tissues.

biogenesis (ˌbaɪəʊˈdʒɛnɪsɪs) *n.* the principle that a living organism must originate from a parent organism similar to itself. Compare **abiogenesis.** —ˌ**biogeˈnetic**, ˌ**biogeˈnetical**, *or* **biogenous** (baɪˈɒdʒənəs) *adj.* —ˌ**biogeˈnetically** *adv.*

biogeography (ˌbaɪəʊdʒɪˈɒgrəfɪ) *n.* the branch of biology concerned with the geographical distribution of plants and animals. —**biogeographical** (ˌbaɪəʊˌdʒɪəˈgræfɪkəl) *adj.* —ˌ**bioˌgeoˈgraphically** *adv.*

biography (baɪˈɒgrəfɪ) *n., pl.* **-phies. 1.** an account of a person's life by another. **2.** such accounts collectively. —**biˈographer** *n.* —**biographical** (ˌbaɪəˈgræfɪkəl) *or* (*archaic*) ˌ**bioˈgraphic** *adj.* —ˌ**bioˈgraphically** *adv.*

biohazard (ˌbaɪəʊˈhæzəd) *n.* the risk of contracting a disease or contaminating the environment in the course of biological research. —ˌ**bioˈhazardous** *adj.*

bioherm (ˈbaɪəʊˌhɜːm) *n.* a mass of organic material, esp. a coral reef, surrounded by rocks of different origin. [C20: from BIO- + Greek *herma* submerged rock]

biol. *abbrev. for:* **1.** biological. **2.** biology.

biological (ˌbaɪəˈlɒdʒɪkəl) *or* (*archaic*) **biologic** *adj.* **1.** of or relating to biology. ~*n.* **2.** (of a detergent) containing enzymes said to be capable of removing stains of organic origin from items to be washed. **3.** (*usually pl.*) a drug, such as a vaccine, that is derived from a living organism. —ˌ**bioˈlogically** *adv.*

biological clock *n.* **1.** an inherent periodicity in the physiological processes of living organisms that is not dependent on the periodicity of external factors. **2.** the hypothetical mechanism responsible for this periodicity. ~See also **circadian.**

biological control *n.* the control of destructive organisms by nonchemical means, such as introducing a natural predator of the pest.

biological shield *n.* a protective shield impervious to radiation, esp. the thick concrete wall surrounding the core of a nuclear reactor.

biological warfare *n.* the use of living organisms or their toxic products to induce death or incapacity in humans and animals and damage to plant crops, etc. Abbrev.: **BW.**

biology (baɪˈɒlədʒɪ) *n.* **1.** the study of living organisms, including their structure, functioning, evolution, distribution, and interrelationships. **2.** the structure, functioning, etc., of a particular organism or group of organisms. **3.** the animal and plant life of a particular region. —**biˈologist** *n.*

bioluminescence (ˌbaɪəʊˌluːmɪˈnɛsəns) *n.* the production of light by living organisms as a result of the oxidation of a light-producing substance (luciferin) by the enzyme luciferase: occurs in many marine organisms, such insects as the glow-worm and firefly, etc. —ˌ**bioˌlumiˈnescent** *adj.*

biolysis (baɪˈɒlɪsɪs) *n.* **1.** the death and dissolution of a living organism. **2.** the disintegration of organic matter by the action of bacteria etc. —**biolytic** (ˌbaɪəˈlɪtɪk) *adj.*

biomass (ˈbaɪəʊˌmæs) *n.* **1.** the total number of living organisms in a given area, expressed in terms of living or dry weight per unit area. **2.** vegetable matter used as a source of energy.

biomathematics (ˌbaɪəʊˌmæθəˈmætɪks, -ˌmæθˈmæt-) *n.* (*functioning as sing.*) the study of the application of mathematics to biology.

biome (ˈbaɪˌəʊm) *n.* a major ecological community, extending over a large area and usually characterized by a dominant vegetation. See **formation** (sense 6). [C20: from BIO- + -OME]

biomedicine (ˌbaɪəʊˈmɛdɪsɪn, -ˈmɛdsɪn) *n.* **1.** the medical study of the effects of unusual environmental stress on human beings, esp. in connection with space travel. **2.** the study of herbal remedies. —ˌ**bioˈmedical** *adj.*

biometeorology (ˌbaɪəʊˌmiːtɪəˈrɒlədʒɪ) *n.* the study of the effect of weather conditions on living organisms.

biometry (baɪˈɒmɪtrɪ) *or* **biometrics** (ˌbaɪəˈmɛtrɪks) *n.* (*functioning as sing.*) **1.** the study of biological data by means of statistical analysis. **2.** the statistical calculation of the probable duration of human life. —**biometric** (ˌbaɪəˈmɛtrɪk) *adj.* —ˌ**bioˈmetrically** *adv.*

bionic (baɪˈɒnɪk) *adj.* **1.** of or relating to bionics. **2.** (in science fiction) having certain physiological functions augmented or replaced by electronic equipment: *the bionic man.*

bionics (baɪˈɒnɪks) *n.* (*functioning as sing.*) **1.** the study of certain biological functions, esp. those relating to the brain, that are applicable to the development of electronic equipment, such as computer hardware, designed to operate in a similar manner. **2.** the technique of replacing a limb or body part by an artificial limb or part that is electronically or mechanically powered. [C20: from BIO- + (ELECTR)ONICS]

bionomics (ˌbaɪəˈnɒmɪks) *n.* (*functioning as sing.*) a less common name for **ecology** (senses 1, 2). [C19: from BIO- + *nomics* on pattern of ECONOMICS] —ˌ**bioˈnomic** *adj.* —ˌ**bioˈnomically** *adv.* —**bionomist** (baɪˈɒnəmɪst) *n.*

biophysics (ˌbaɪəʊˈfɪzɪks) *n.* (*functioning as sing.*) the physics of biological processes and the application of methods used in physics to biology. —ˌ**bioˈphysical** *adj.* —ˌ**bioˈphysically** *adv.* —**biophysicist** (ˌbaɪəʊˈfɪzɪsɪst) *n.*

biopic (ˈbaɪəʊˌpɪk) *n. Informal.* a film based on the life of a famous person, esp. one giving a popular treatment. [C20: from *bio(graphical)* + *pic(ture)*]

bioplasm (ˈbaɪəʊˌplæzəm) *n.* living matter; protoplasm. —ˌ**bioˈplasmic** *adj.*

biopoiesis (ˌbaɪəʊpɔɪˈiːsɪs) *n.* the synthesis of living matter from nonliving matter, esp. considered as an evolutionary process.

biopsy (ˈbaɪɒpsɪ) *n., pl.* **-sies.** examination, esp. under a microscope, of tissue from a living body to determine the cause or extent of a disease. [C20: from BIO- + Greek *opsis* sight] —**bioptic** (baɪˈɒptɪk) *adj.*

biorhythm (ˈbaɪəʊˌrɪðəm) *n.* a cyclically recurring pattern of physiological states in an organism or organ, such as alpha rhythm or circadian rhythm; believed by some to affect physical and mental states and behaviour. —ˌ**bioˈrhythmic** *adj.* —ˌ**bioˈrhythmically** *adv.*

biorhythmics (ˌbaɪəʊˈrɪðmɪks) *n.* (*functioning as sing.*) the study of biorhythms.

bioscience (ˈbaɪəʊˌsaɪəns) *n.* the science of biology. —ˌ**bioscienˈtific** *adj.* —ˌ**bioˈscientist** *n.*

bioscope (ˈbaɪəˌskəʊp) *n.* **1.** a kind of early film projector. **2.** a South African word for **cinema.**

bioscopy (baɪˈɒskəpɪ) *n., pl.* **-pies.** examination of a body to determine whether it is alive.

-biosis *n. combining form.* indicating a specified mode of life: *symbiosis.* [New Latin, from Greek *biōsis;* see BIO-, -OSIS] —**-biotic** *adj. combining form.*

biosphere (ˈbaɪəˌsfɪə) *n.* the part of the earth's surface and atmosphere inhabited by living things.

biostatics (ˌbaɪəʊˈstætɪks) *n.* (*functioning as sing.*) the branch of biology that deals with the structure of organisms in relation to their function. —ˌ**bioˈstatic** *adj.* —ˌ**bioˈstatically** *adv.*

biostrome (ˈbaɪəˌstrəʊm) *n.* a thin rocky layer consisting of a deposit of organic material, such as fossils. [C20: from BIO- + Greek *strōma* covering]

biosynthesis (ˌbaɪəʊˈsɪnθɪsɪs) *n.* the formation of complex compounds from simple substances by living organisms. —**biosynthetic** (ˌbaɪəʊsɪnˈθɛtɪk) *adj.* —ˌ**biosynˈthetically** *adv.*

biosystematics (ˌbaɪəʊˌsɪstɪˈmætɪks) *n.* (*functioning as sing.*) the study of the variation and evolution of a population of organisms in relation to their taxonomic classification.

biota (baɪˈəʊtə) *n.* the plant and animal life of a particular region or period. [C20: from New Latin, from Greek *biotē* way of life, from *bios* life]

biotechnology (ˌbaɪəʊtɛkˈnɒlədʒɪ) *n.* **1.** (in industry) the technique of using microorganisms, such as bacteria, to perform chemical processing, such as waste recycling, or to produce other materials, such as beer and wine, cheese, antibiotics, and (using genetic engineering) hormones, vaccines, etc. **2.** another name for **ergonomics.** —**biotechnological** (ˌbaɪəʊˌtɛknəˈlɒdʒɪkəl) *adj.* —ˌ**bioˌtechnoˈlogically** *adv.* —ˌ**biotechˈnologist** *n.*

biotelemetry (ˌbaɪəʊtɪˈlɛmɪtrɪ) *n.* the monitoring of biological functions in humans or animals by means of a miniature transmitter that sends data to a distant point to be read by electronic instruments. —**biotelemetric** (ˌbaɪəʊtɛlɪˈmɛtrɪk) *adj.*

biotic (baɪˈɒtɪk) *adj.* **1.** of or relating to living organisms. **2.** (of a factor in an ecosystem) produced by the action of living organisms. Compare **edaphic.** [C17: from Greek *biotikos,* from *bios* life]

biotin (ˈbaɪətɪn) *n.* a vitamin of the B complex, abundant in egg yolk and liver, deficiency of which causes dermatitis and loss of hair. Formula: $C_{10}H_{16}N_2O_3S$. See also **avidin.** [C20: *biot-* from Greek *biotē* life, way of life + -IN]

biotite (ˈbaɪəˌtaɪt) *n.* a black or dark green mineral of the mica group, found in igneous and metamorphic rocks. Composition: hydrous magnesium iron potassium aluminium silicate. General formula: $K(Mg,Fe)_3(Al,Fe)Si_3O_{10}(OH)_2$. Crystal structure: monoclinic. —**biotitic** (ˌbaɪəˈtɪtɪk) *adj.*

biotope ('baɪəˌtəʊp) *n. Ecology.* a small area, such as the bark of a tree, that supports its own distinctive community. [C20: from BIO- + Greek *topos* place]
biotroph ('baɪəʊˌtrəʊf) *n.* a parasitic plant, esp. a fungus.
biotype ('baɪəˌtaɪp) *n.* a group of plants or animals within a species that resemble, but differ physiologically from, other members of the species. —**biotypic** (ˌbaɪə'tɪpɪk) *adj.*
biparietal (ˌbaɪpə'raɪɪtᵊl) *adj. Anatomy.* relating to or connected to both parietal bones.
biparous ('bɪpərəs) *adj.* **1.** *Zoology.* producing offspring in pairs. **2.** *Botany.* (esp. of an inflorescence) producing two branches from one stem.
bipartisan (ˌbaɪpɑːtɪ'zæn, baɪ'pɑːtɪˌzæn) *adj.* consisting of or supported by two political parties. —ˌ**biparti'sanship** *n.*
bipartite (baɪ'pɑːtaɪt) *adj.* **1.** consisting of or having two parts. **2.** affecting or made by two parties; bilateral: *a bipartite agreement.* **3.** *Botany.* (esp. of some leaves) divided into two parts almost to the base. —**bi'partitely** *adv.* —**bipartition** (ˌbaɪpɑː'tɪʃən) *n.*
biped ('baɪpɛd) *n.* **1.** any animal with two feet. ~*adj. also* **bipedal** (baɪ'piːdᵊl, -'pɛdᵊl). **2.** having two feet.
bipetalous (baɪ'pɛtələs) *adj.* having two petals.
biphasic (baɪ'feɪzɪk) *adj.* **1.** having two phases. **2.** See **two-phase.**
biphenyl (baɪ'fenᵊl, -'fiː-) *n.* **1.** a white or colourless crystalline solid used as a heat-transfer agent, as a fungicide, as an antifungal food preservative (**E230**) on the skins of citrus fruit, and in the manufacture of dyes, etc. Formula: $C_6H_5C_6H_5$. **2.** any substituted derivative of biphenyl. ~Also called: **diphenyl.**
bipinnate (baɪ'pɪnˌeɪt) *adj.* (of compound leaves) having both the leaflets and the stems bearing them arranged pinnately. —**bi'pinˌnately** *adv.*
biplane ('baɪˌpleɪn) *n.* an early type of aeroplane having two sets of wings, one above the other. Compare **monoplane.**
bipod ('baɪpɒd) *n.* a two-legged support or stand.
bipolar (baɪ'pəʊlə) *adj.* **1.** having two poles: *a bipolar dynamo; a bipolar neuron.* **2.** relating to or found at the North and South Poles. **3.** having or characterized by two opposed opinions, natures, etc. **4.** (of a transistor) utilizing both majority and minority charge carriers.
bipolar manic-depressive disorder *or* **bipolar syndrome** *n.* See **manic-depressive.**
biprism ('baɪˌprɪzəm) *n.* a prism having a highly obtuse angle to facilitate beam splitting.
bipropellant (ˌbaɪprə'pɛlənt) *n.* a rocket propellant consisting of two substances, usually a fuel and an oxidizer. Also called: **dipropellant.** Compare **monopropellant.**
bipyramid (ˌbaɪ'pɪrəmɪd) *n.* a geometrical form consisting of two pyramids with a common polygonal base.
biquadrate (baɪ'kwɒdreɪt, -rɪt) *n. Maths.* the fourth power.
biquadratic (ˌbaɪkwɒ'drætɪk) *Maths.* ~*adj. also* **quartic. 1.** of or relating to the fourth power. ~*n.* **2.** a biquadratic equation, such as $x^4 + x + 6 = 0$.
biquarterly (baɪ'kwɔːtəlɪ) *adj.* occurring twice every three months.
biracial (baɪ'reɪʃəl) *adj.* for, representing, or including members of two races, esp. White and Black. —**bi'racialism** *n.* —**bi'racially** *adv.*
biradial (baɪ'reɪdɪəl) *adj.* showing both bilateral and radial symmetry, as certain sea anemones.
biramous ('bɪrəməs) *adj.* divided into two parts, as the appendages of crustaceans.
birch (bɜːtʃ) *n.* **1.** any betulaceous tree or shrub of the genus *Betula,* having thin peeling bark. See also **silver birch. 2.** the hard close-grained wood of any of these trees. **3. the birch.** a bundle of birch twigs or a birch rod used, esp. formerly, for flogging offenders. ~*adj.* **4.** of, relating to, or belonging to the birch. **5.** consisting or made of birch. ~*vb.* **6.** (*tr.*) to flog with a birch. [Old English *bierce;* related to Old High German *birihha,* Sanskrit *bhūrja*] —'**birchen** *adj.*
Bircher ('bɜːtʃə), **Birchist,** *or* **Birchite** *n.* a member or supporter of the John Birch Society. —'**Birchˌism** *n.*
bird (bɜːd) *n.* **1.** any warm-blooded egg-laying vertebrate of the class *Aves,* characterized by a body covering of feathers and forelimbs modified as wings. Birds vary in size between the ostrich and the humming bird. Related adj.: **avian. 2.** *Informal.* a person (usually preceded by a qualifying adjective, as in the phrases **rare bird, odd bird, clever bird**). **3.** *Slang, chiefly Brit.* a girl or young woman, esp. one's girlfriend. **4.** *Slang.* prison or a term in prison (esp. in the phrase **do bird;** shortened from *birdlime,* rhyming slang for *time*). **5. a bird in the hand.** something definite or certain. **6. the bird has flown.** *Informal.* the person in question has fled or escaped. **7. birds of a feather.** people with the same characteristics, ideas, interests, etc. **8. get the bird.** *Informal.* **a.** to be fired or dismissed. **b.** (esp. of a public performer) to be hissed at, booed, or derided. **9. give (someone) the bird.** *Informal.* to tell (someone) rudely to depart; scoff at; hiss. **10. kill two birds with one stone.** to accomplish two things with one action. **11. like a bird.** without resistance or difficulty. **12. a little bird.** a (supposedly) unknown informant: *a little bird told me it was your birthday.* **13. (strictly) for the birds.** *Informal.* deserving of disdain or contempt; not important. [Old English *bridd,* of unknown origin] —'**birdlike** *adj.*
birdbath ('bɜːdˌbɑːθ) *n.* a small basin or trough for birds to bathe in, usually in a garden.
bird-brained *adj. Informal.* silly; stupid.
birdcage ('bɜːdˌkeɪdʒ) *n.* **1.** a wire or wicker cage in which captive birds are kept. **2.** any object of a similar shape, construction, or purpose. **3.** *Austral. and N.Z.* an area on a racecourse where horses parade before a race. **4.** *Austral. and N.Z. informal.* a second-hand car dealer's yard.
bird call *n.* **1.** the characteristic call or song of a bird. **2.** an imitation of this. **3.** an instrument imitating the call of a bird, used esp. by hunters or bird-catchers.
bird cherry *n.* a small Eurasian rosaceous tree, *Prunus padus,* with clusters of white flowers and small black fruits. See also **cherry** (sense 1).
bird dog *U.S. and Canadian.* ~*n.* **1.** *Hunting.* a dog used or trained to retrieve game birds after they are shot. ~*vb.* **bird-dog, -dogs, -dogging, -dogged. 2.** *Informal.* to control closely with unceasing vigilance.
birder ('bɜːdə) *n.* an informal name for a **bird-watcher.**
birdhouse ('bɜːdˌhaʊs) *n. U.S.* **1.** a small shelter or box for birds to nest in. **2.** an enclosure or large cage for captive birds; aviary.
birdie ('bɜːdɪ) *n.* **1.** *Golf.* a score of one stroke under par for a hole. **2.** *Informal.* a bird, esp. a small bird. ~*vb.* **3.** *(tr.) Golf.* to play (a hole) in one stroke under par.
birdlime ('bɜːdˌlaɪm) *n.* **1.** a sticky substance, prepared from holly, mistletoe, or other plants, smeared on twigs to catch small birds. ~*vb.* **2.** (*tr.*) to smear (twigs) with birdlime to catch (small birds).
birdman ('bɜːdˌmæn, -mən) *n., pl.* **-men. 1.** a man concerned with birds, such as a fowler or ornithologist. **2.** a man who attempts to fly using his own muscle power. **3.** an obsolete informal name for **airman.**
bird-nesting *or* **birds'-nesting** *n.* searching for birds' nests as a hobby, often to steal the eggs.
bird of paradise *n.* **1.** any songbird of the family *Paradisaeidae* of New Guinea and neighbouring regions, the males of which have brilliantly coloured ornate plumage. **2. bird-of-paradise flower.** any of various musaceous plants of the genus *Strelitzia,* esp. *S. reginae,* that are native to tropical southern Africa and South America *Strelitzia,* esp. *S. reginae,* that are native to tropical southern Africa and South America and have purple bracts and large orange or yellow flowers resembling birds' heads.
bird of passage *n.* **1.** a bird that migrates seasonally. **2.** a transient person or one who roams about.
bird of peace *n.* a figurative name for **dove**[1] (sense 1).
bird of prey *n.* a bird, such as a hawk, eagle, or owl, that hunts and kills other animals, esp. vertebrates, for food. It has strong talons and a sharp hooked bill.
bird pepper *n.* **1.** a tropical solanaceous plant, *Capsicum frutescens,* thought to be the ancestor of the sweet pepper and many hot peppers. **2.** the narrow podlike hot-tasting fruit of this plant.
birdseed ('bɜːdˌsiːd) *n.* a mixture of various kinds of seeds for feeding cagebirds. Also called: **canary seed.**
bird's-eye *adj.* **1. a.** seen or photographed from high above. **b.** summarizing the main points of a topic; summary (esp. in the phrase **bird's-eye view**). **2.** having markings resembling birds' eyes. ~*n.* **3. bird's-eye primrose.** a Eurasian primrose, *Primula farinosa,* having clusters of purplish flowers with yellow centres. **4. bird's-eye speedwell.** the usual U.S. name for **germander speedwell. 5.** any of several other plants having flowers of two contrasting colours. **6.** a pattern in linen and cotton fabrics, made up of small diamond shapes with a dot in the centre of each. **7.** a linen or cotton fabric with such a pattern.
bird's-foot *or* **bird-foot** *n., pl.* **-foots. 1.** a European papilionaceous plant, *Ornithopus perpusillus,* with red-veined white flowers and curved pods resembling a bird's claws. **2.** any of various other plants whose flowers, leaves, or pods resemble a bird's foot or claw.
bird's-foot trefoil *n.* a creeping papilionaceous Eurasian plant, *Lotus corniculatus,* with red-tipped yellow flowers and seed pods resembling the claws of a bird. Also called: **bacon-and-eggs.**
birdshot ('bɜːdˌʃɒt) *n.* small pellets designed for shooting birds.
bird's-nest *vb.* (*intr.*) to search for the nests of birds in order to collect the eggs.
bird's-nest fungus *n.* any fungus of the family *Nidulariaceae,* having a nestlike spore-producing body containing egglike spore-filled structures.
bird's-nest orchid *n.* a brown parasitic Eurasian orchid, *Neottia nidus-avis,* whose thick fleshy roots resemble a bird's nest and contain a fungus on which the orchid feeds.
bird's-nest soup *n.* a rich spicy Chinese soup made from the outer part of the nests of SE Asian swifts of the genus *Collocalia.*
birdsong ('bɜːdˌsɒŋ) *n.* the musical call of a bird or birds.
bird spider *n.* any large hairy predatory bird-eating spider of the family *Aviculariidae,* of tropical America.
bird strike *n.* a collision of an aircraft with a bird.
bird table *n.* a table or platform in the open on which food for birds may be placed.

bird-watcher *n.* a person who studies wild birds in their natural surroundings. —'**bird-,watching** *n.*
birefringence (,baɪrɪ'frɪndʒəns) *n.* another name for **double refraction.** —,**bire'fringent** *adj.*
bireme ('baɪriːm) *n.* an ancient galley having two banks of oars. [C17: from Latin *birēmus,* from BI-[1] + *-rēmus* oar]
biretta *or* **berretta** (bɪ'rɛtə) *n. R.C. Church.* a stiff clerical cap having either three or four upright pieces projecting outwards from the centre to the edge: coloured black for priests, purple for bishops, red for cardinals, and white for certain members of religious orders. [C16: from Italian *berretta,* from Old Provençal *berret,* from Late Latin *birrus* hooded cape]
biriani (,bɪrɪ'ɑːnɪ) *n.* a variant spelling of **biryani.**
birk (bɪrk, bɜːk) *Chiefly Scot.* ~*n.* **1.** a birch tree. **2.** (*pl.*) a birch wood. ~*adj.* **3.** consisting or made of birch. [C14: from Old Norse; compare BIRCH]
birkie ('bɪrkɪ) *n. Scot.* **1.** a spirited or lively person. **2.** a foolish posturer. [C18: perhaps related to Old English *beorcan* to bark; compare Old Norse *berkia*]
birl[1] (bɜːl; *Scot.* bɪrl) *vb.* **1.** *Scot.* to spin; twirl. **2.** *U.S. and Canadian.* to cause (a floating log) to spin using the feet, esp. as a sport among lumberjacks. ~*n.* **3.** a variant spelling of **burl**[2]. [C18: probably imitative and influenced by WHIRL and HURL]
birl[2] (bɜːl; *Scot.* bɪrl) *vb. Archaic, Scot.* to ply (one's guests, etc.) with drink. [Old English *byrelian;* related to *byrele* cup-bearer]
Biro ('baɪrəʊ) *n., pl.* **-ros.** *Trademark, Brit.* a kind of ballpoint. [C20: named after Laszlo *Biró* (1900–85), Hungarian inventor]
birr[1] (bɜː) *Chiefly U.S. and Scot.* ~*vb.* **1.** to make or cause to make a whirring sound. ~*n.* **2.** a whirring sound. **3.** force, as of wind. **4.** vigour; energy. [Old English *byre* storm, related to Old Norse *byrr* favourable wind]
birr[2] (bɜː) *n.* the standard monetary unit of Ethiopia, divided into 100 cents. [C20: from Amharic]
birth (bɜːθ) *n.* **1.** the process of bearing young; parturition; childbirth. Related adj.: **natal. 2.** the act or fact of being born; nativity. **3.** the coming into existence of something; origin. **4.** ancestry; lineage: *of high birth.* **5.** noble ancestry: *a man of birth.* **6.** natural or inherited talent: *an artist by birth.* **7.** *Archaic.* the offspring or young born at a particular time or of a particular mother. **8. give birth (to). a.** to bear (offspring). **b.** to produce, originate, or create (an idea, plan, etc.). ~*vb.* (*tr.*) *Rare.* **9.** to bear or bring forth (a child). [C12: from Old Norse *byrth;* related to Gothic *gabaurths,* Old Swedish *byrdh,* Old High German *berd* child; see BEAR[1], BAIRN]
birth certificate *n.* an official form giving details of the time and place of a person's birth, and his or her name, sex, mother's name and (usually) father's name.
birth control *n.* limitation of child-bearing by means of contraception. See also **family planning.**
birthday ('bɜːθ,deɪ) *n.* **1. a.** an anniversary of the day of one's birth. **b.** (*as modifier*): *birthday present.* **2.** the day on which a person was born. **3.** any anniversary.
Birthday honours *pl. n.* (in Britain) honorary titles conferred on the official birthday of the sovereign.
birthday suit *n. Informal, humorous.* a state of total nakedness, as at birth.
birthing chair ('bɜːθɪŋ) *n.* a chair constructed to allow a woman in labour to give birth in a sitting position.
birthmark ('bɜːθ,mɑːk) *n.* a blemish or new growth on skin formed before birth, usually brown or dark red; naevus.
birthplace ('bɜːθ,pleɪs) *n.* the place where someone was born or where something originated.
birth rate *n.* the ratio of live births in a specified area, group, etc., to the population of that area, etc., usually expressed per 1000 population per year.
birthright ('bɜːθ,raɪt) *n.* **1.** privileges or possessions that a person has or is believed to be entitled to as soon as he is born. **2.** the privileges or possessions of a first-born son. **3.** inheritance; patrimony.
birthroot ('bɜːθ,ruːt) *n.* any of several North American plants of the genus *Trillium,* esp. *T. erectum,* whose tuber-like roots were formerly used by the American Indians as an aid in childbirth: family *Trilliaceae.*
birthstone ('bɜːθ,stəʊn) *n.* a precious or semiprecious stone associated with a month or sign of the zodiac and thought to bring luck if worn by a person born in that month or under that sign.
birthwort ('bɜːθ,wɜːt) *n.* any of several climbing plants of the genus *Aristolochia,* esp. *A. clematitis* of Europe, once believed to ease childbirth: family *Aristolochiaceae.*
biryani *or* **biriani** (,bɪrɪ'ɑːnɪ) *n.* any of a variety of Indian dishes made with rice, highly flavoured and coloured with saffron or turmeric, mixed with meat or fish. [from Urdu]
bis (bɪs) *adv.* **1.** twice; for a second time (used in musical scores to indicate a part to be repeated). ~*sentence substitute* **2.** encore! again! [C19: via Italian from Latin, from Old Latin *duis*]
BIS *abbrev. for* Bank for International Settlements: an institution, based in Basel, Switzerland, that accepts deposits, makes loans for national central banks, and assists in offsetting speculative movements of funds between the major currencies; set up in 1930.
Bisayan (bɪ'sɑːjən) *n.* a variant of **Visayan.**
biscuit ('bɪskɪt) *n.* **1.** *Brit.* a small flat dry sweet or plain cake of many varieties, baked from a dough. U.S. and Canadian word: **cookie. 2.** *U.S. and Canadian.* a kind of small roll similar to a muffin. **3. a.** a pale brown or yellowish-grey colour. **b.** (*as adj.*): *biscuit gloves.* **4.** Also called: **bisque.** earthenware or porcelain that has been fired but not glazed. **5. take the biscuit.** *Slang.* to be regarded (by the speaker) as the most surprising thing that could have occurred. [C14: from Old French, from (*pain*) *bescuit* twice-cooked (bread), from *bes* BIS + *cuire* to cook, from Latin *coquere*]
bise (biːz) *n.* a cold dry northerly wind in Switzerland and the neighbouring parts of France and Italy, usually in the spring. [C14: from Old French, of Germanic origin; compare Old Swedish *bīsa* whirlwind]
bisect (baɪ'sɛkt) *vb.* **1.** (*tr.*) *Maths.* to divide into two equal parts. **2.** to cut or split into two. [C17: BI-[1] + *-sect* from Latin *secāre* to cut] —**bisection** (baɪ'sɛkʃən) *n.*
bisector (baɪ'sɛktə) *n. Maths.* **1.** a straight line or plane that bisects an angle. **2.** a line or plane that bisects another line.
bisectrix (baɪ'sɛktrɪks) *n., pl.* **bisectrices** (baɪ'sɛktrɪ,siːz). **1.** another name for **bisector. 2.** the bisector of the angle between the optic axes of a crystal.
biseriate (,baɪ'sɪərɪɪt) *adj.* (of plant parts, such as petals) arranged in two whorls, cycles, rows, or series.
biserrate (baɪ'sɛreɪt, -ɪt) *adj.* **1.** *Botany.* (of leaf margins, etc.) having serrations that are themselves serrated. **2.** *Zoology.* serrated on both sides, as the antennae of some insects.
bisexual (baɪ'sɛksjʊəl) *adj.* **1.** sexually attracted by both men and women. **2.** showing characteristics of both sexes: *a bisexual personality.* **3.** (of some plants and animals) having both male and female reproductive organs. **4.** of or relating to both sexes. ~*n.* **5.** a bisexual organism; a hermaphrodite. **6.** a bisexual person. —**bisexuality** (baɪ,sɛksjʊ'ælɪtɪ) *or esp. U.S.* **bi'sexualism** *n.* —**bi'sexually** *adv.*
bish (bɪʃ) *n. Brit. slang.* a mistake. [C20: of unknown origin]
bishop ('bɪʃəp) *n.* **1.** (in the Roman Catholic, Anglican, and Greek Orthodox Churches) a clergyman having spiritual and administrative powers over a diocese or province of the Church. See also **suffragan.** Related adj.: **episcopal. 2.** (in some Protestant Churches) a spiritual overseer of a local church or a number of churches. **3.** a chesspiece, capable of moving diagonally over any number of unoccupied squares of the same colour. **4.** mulled wine, usually port, spiced with oranges, cloves, etc. [Old English *biscop,* from Late Latin *episcopus,* from Greek *episkopos,* from EPI- + *skopos* watcher]
bishopbird ('bɪʃəp,bɜːd) *n.* any African weaverbird of the genus *Euplectes* (or *Pyromelana*), the males of which have black plumage marked with red or yellow.
bishopric ('bɪʃəprɪk) *n.* the see, diocese, or office of a bishop.
bishop's-cap *n.* another name for **mitrewort.**
bishop sleeve *n.* a full sleeve gathered at the wrist.
bishop's mitre *n.* a European heteropterous bug, *Aelia acuminata,* whose larvae are a pest of cereal grasses: family *Pentatomidae.*
bishop's weed *n.* another name for **goutweed.**
bisk (bɪsk) *n.* a less common spelling of **bisque**[1].
Bismarck herring ('bɪzmɑːk) *n.* marinaded herring, served cold.
bismuth ('bɪzməθ) *n.* a brittle pinkish-white crystalline metallic element having low thermal and electrical conductivity, which expands on cooling. It is widely used in alloys, esp. low-melting alloys in fire safety devices; its compounds are used in medicines. Symbol: Bi; atomic no.: 83; atomic wt.: 208.98; valency: 3 or 5; relative density: 9.75; melting pt.: 271.3°C; boiling pt.: 1560°C. [C17: from New Latin *bisemūtum,* from German *Wismut,* of unknown origin] —**bismuthal** ('bɪzməθəl) *adj.*
bismuthic (bɪz'mjuːθɪk, -'mʌθɪk) *adj.* of or containing bismuth in the pentavalent state.
bismuthinite (bɪz'mʌθɪ,naɪt) *or* **bismuth glance** *n.* a grey mineral consisting of bismuth sulphide in orthorhombic crystalline form. It occurs in veins associated with tin, copper, silver, lead, etc., and is a source of bismuth. Formula: Bi_2S_3.
bismuthous ('bɪzməθəs) *adj.* of or containing bismuth in the trivalent state.
bison ('baɪsən) *n., pl.* **-son. 1.** Also called: **American bison, buffalo.** a member of the cattle tribe, *Bison bison,* formerly widely distributed over the prairies of W North America but now confined to reserves and parks, with a massive head, shaggy forequarters, and a humped back. **2.** Also called: **wisent, European bison.** a closely related and similar animal, *Bison bonasus,* formerly widespread in Europe. [C14: from Latin *bisōn,* of Germanic origin; related to Old English *wesand,* Old Norse *vīsundr*]
bisque[1] (bɪsk) *n.* a thick rich soup made from shellfish. [C17: from French]
bisque[2] (bɪsk) *n.* **1. a.** a pink to yellowish tan colour. **b.** (*as adj.*): *a bisque tablecloth.* **2.** *Ceramics.* another name for **biscuit** (sense 4). [C20: shortened from BISCUIT]
bisque[3] (bɪsk) *n. Tennis, golf, croquet.* an extra point, stroke, or turn allowed to an inferior player, usually taken when desired. [C17: from French, of obscure origin]
bissextile (bɪ'sɛkstaɪl) *adj.* **1.** (of a month or year) containing the extra day of a leap year. ~*n.* **2.** a rare name for **leap year.** [C16: from Late Latin *bissextilis annus* leap year, from Latin *bissextus,* from BI-[1] + *sextus* sixth; referring to February 24, the 6th day before the Calends of March]

bist (bɪst) *vb. Southwest English dialect.* a form of the second person singular of **be.**

bistable (baɪˈsteɪbᵊl) *adj.* 1. having two stable states: *bistable circuit.* ~*n.* 2. *Computer technology.* another name for **flip-flop** (sense 2).

Bisto (ˈbɪstəʊ) *n. Trademark.* a preparation for thickening, flavouring, and browning gravy.

bistort (ˈbɪstɔːt) *n.* 1. Also called: **snakeroot, snakeweed, Easter-ledges.** a Eurasian polygonaceous plant, *Polygonum bistorta,* having leaf stipules fused to form a tube around the stem and a spike of small pink flowers. 2. Also called: **snakeroot.** a related plant, *Polygonum bistortoides,* of W North America, with oval clusters of pink or white flowers. 3. any of several other plants of the genus *Polygonum.* [C16: from French *bistorte,* from Latin *bis* twice + *tortus* from *torquēre* to twist]

bistoury (ˈbɪstərɪ) *n., pl.* **-ries.** a long surgical knife with a narrow blade. [C15: from Old French *bistorie* dagger, of unknown origin]

bistre *or U.S.* **bister** (ˈbɪstə) *n.* 1. a transparent water-soluble brownish-yellow pigment made by boiling the soot of wood, used for pen and wash drawings. 2. a. a yellowish-brown to dark brown colour. b. (*as adj.*): *bistre paint.* [C18: from French, of unknown origin]

bistro (ˈbiːstrəʊ) *n., pl.* **-tros.** a small restaurant. [French: of obscure origin; perhaps from Russian *bistro* fast]

bisulcate (baɪˈsʌlˌkeɪt) *adj.* 1. marked by two grooves. 2. *Zoology.* a. cleft or cloven, as a hoof. b. having cloven hoofs.

bisulphate (baɪˈsʌlˌfeɪt) *n.* 1. a salt or ester of sulphuric acid containing the monovalent group $-HSO_4$ or the ion HSO_4^-. 2. (*modifier*) consisting of, containing, or concerned with the group $-HSO_4$ or the ion HSO_4^-: *bisulphate ion.* ~Systematic name: **hydrogen sulphate.**

bisulphide (baɪˈsʌlfaɪd) *n.* another name for **disulphide.**

bisulphite (baɪˈsʌlfaɪt) *n.* 1. a salt or ester of sulphurous acid containing the monovalent group $-HSO_3$ or the ion HSO_3^-. 2. (*modifier*) consisting of or containing the group $-HSO_3$ or the ion HSO_3^-: *bisulphite ion.* ~Systematic name: **hydrogen sulphite.**

bisymmetric (ˌbaɪsɪˈmɛtrɪk) *or* **bisymmetrical** *adj.* 1. *Botany.* showing symmetry in two planes at right angles to each other. 2. (of plants and animals) showing bilateral symmetry. —ˌ**bisymˈmetrically** *adv.* —**bisymmetry** (baɪˈsɪmɪtrɪ) *n.*

bit[1] (bɪt) *n.* 1. a small piece, portion, or quantity. 2. a short time or distance. 3. *U.S. and Canadian informal.* the value of an eighth of a dollar: spoken of only in units of two: *two bits.* 4. any small coin. 5. short for **bit part.** 6. *Informal.* way of behaving, esp. one intended to create a particular impression: *she's doing the prima donna bit.* 7. **a bit.** rather; somewhat: *a bit dreary.* 8. **a bit of. a.** rather: *a bit of a dope.* b. a considerable amount: *that must take quite a bit of courage.* 9. **a bit of all right, bit of crumpet, bit of skirt, bit of stuff,** *or* **bit of tail.** *Brit. slang.* a sexually attractive woman. 10. **bit by bit.** gradually. 11. **bit on the side.** *Informal.* an extramarital affair. 12. **do one's bit.** to make one's expected contribution. 13. **every bit.** (foll. by *as*) to the same degree: *she was every bit as clever as her brother.* 14. **not a bit (of it).** not in the slightest; not at all. 15. **to bits.** completely apart: *to fall to bits.* [Old English *bite* action of biting; see BITE]

bit[2] (bɪt) *n.* 1. a metal mouthpiece, for controlling a horse on a bridle. 2. anything that restrains or curbs. 3. **take** *or* **have the bit in** *or* **between one's teeth. a.** to undertake a task with determination. b. to rebel against control. 4. a cutting or drilling tool, part, or head in a brace, drill, etc. 5. the blade of a plane. 6. the part of a pair of pincers designed to grasp an object. 7. the copper end of a soldering iron. 8. the part of a key that engages the levers of a lock. ~*vb.* **bits, bitting, bitted.** (*tr.*) 9. to put a bit in the mouth of (a horse). 10. to restrain; curb. [Old English *bita;* related to Old English *bītan* to BITE]

bit[3] (bɪt) *vb.* the past tense and (archaic) past participle of **bite.**

bit[4] (bɪt) *n. Maths., computer technology.* 1. a single digit of binary notation, represented either by 0 or by 1. 2. the smallest unit of information, indicating the presence or absence of a single feature. 3. a unit of capacity of a computer, consisting of an element of its physical structure capable of being in either of two states, such as a switch with *on* and *off* positions, or a microscopic magnet capable of alignment in two directions. [C20: from abbreviation of BINARY DIGIT]

bitartrate (baɪˈtɑːˌtreɪt) *n.* (not in technical usage) a salt or ester of tartaric acid containing the monovalent group $-HC_4H_4O_6$ or the ion $HC_4H_4O_6^-$. Also called: **hydrogen tartrate.**

bitch (bɪtʃ) *n.* 1. a female dog or other female canine animal, such as a wolf. 2. *Slang, derogatory.* a malicious, spiteful, or coarse woman. 3. *Informal.* a complaint. 4. *Informal.* a difficult situation or problem. ~*vb. Informal.* 5. (*intr.*) to complain; grumble. 6. to behave (towards) in a spiteful or malicious manner. 7. (*tr.,* often foll. by *up*) to botch; bungle. [Old English *bicce*]

bitchy (ˈbɪtʃɪ) *adj.* **bitchier, bitchiest.** *Informal.* characteristic of or behaving like a bitch; malicious; snide. —ˈ**bitchily** *adv.* —ˈ**bitchiness** *n.*

bite (baɪt) *vb.* **bites, biting, bit, bitten.** 1. to grip, cut off, or tear with or as if with the teeth or jaws. 2. (of animals, insects, etc.) to injure by puncturing or tearing (the skin or flesh) with the teeth, fangs, etc., esp. as a natural characteristic. 3. (*tr.*) to cut or penetrate, as with a knife. 4. (of corrosive material such as acid) to eat away or into. 5. to smart or cause to smart; sting: *mustard bites the tongue.* 6. (*intr.*) *Angling.* (of a fish) to take or attempt to take the bait or lure. 7. to take firm hold of or act effectively upon. 8. to grip or hold (a workpiece) with a tool or chuck. 9. (of a screw, thread, etc.) to cut into or grip (an object, material, etc.). 10. (*tr.*) *Informal.* to annoy or worry: *what's biting her?* 11. (*often passive*) *Slang.* to cheat. 12. (*tr.;* often foll. by *for*) *Austral. and N.Z. slang.* to ask (for); scrounge from. 13. **bite off more than one can chew.** *Informal.* to attempt a task beyond one's capability. 14. **bite on the bullet.** to face up to (pain, trouble, etc.) with fortitude; be stoical. 15. **bite someone's head off.** to respond harshly and rudely (to). 16. **bite the dust. a.** to fall down dead. b. to be defeated: *another good idea bites the dust.* 17. **bite the hand that feeds one.** to repay kindness with injury or ingratitude. 18. **once bitten, twice shy.** after an unpleasant experience one is cautious in similar situations. 19. **put the bite on (someone).** *Austral. slang.* to ask (someone) for money. ~*n.* 20. the act of biting. 21. a thing or amount bitten off. 22. a wound, bruise, or sting inflicted by biting. 23. *Angling.* an attempt by a fish to take the bait or lure. 24. *Informal.* an incisive or penetrating effect or quality: *that's a question with a bite.* 25. a light meal; snack. 26. a cutting, stinging, or smarting sensation. 27. the depth of cut of a machine tool. 28. the grip or hold applied by a tool or chuck to a workpiece. 29. *Dentistry.* the angle or manner of contact between the upper and lower teeth when the mouth is closed naturally. 30. the surface of a file or rasp with cutting teeth. 31. the corrosive action of acid, as on a metal etching plate. [Old English *bītan;* related to Latin *findere* to split, Sanskrit *bhedati* he splits] —ˈ**biter** *n.*

bite back *vb.* (*tr., adv.*) to restrain (a hurtful, embarrassing, or indiscreet remark); avoid saying.

biting (ˈbaɪtɪŋ) *adj.* 1. piercing; keen: *a biting wind.* 2. sarcastic; incisive: *a biting comment.* —ˈ**bitingly** *adv.*

biting *or* **bird louse** *n.* See **louse** (sense 2).

biting midge *n.* any small fragile dipterous fly of the family *Ceratopogonidae,* most of which suck the blood of mammals, birds, or other insects.

bit part *n.* a very small acting role with few lines to speak.

bit rate *n. Computer technol.* the rate of flow of binary digits in a digital data-processing system.

bitser (ˈbɪtsə) *n. Austral. informal.* a mongrel dog. [C20: from *bits o'* bits of, as in *his dog is bits o' this and bits o' that*]

bit slice *adj. Computer technol.* (of central processing units) able to be built up in sections to form complete central processing units with various word lengths.

bitstock (ˈbɪtˌstɒk) *n.* the handle or stock of a tool into which a drilling bit is fixed.

bitt (bɪt) *Nautical.* ~*n.* 1. one of a pair of strong posts on the deck of a ship for securing mooring and other lines. 2. another word for **bollard** (sense 1). ~*vb.* 3. (*tr.*) to secure (a line) by means of a bitt. [C14: probably of Scandinavian origin; compare Old Norse *biti* cross beam, Middle High German *bizze* wooden peg]

bitten (ˈbɪtᵊn) *vb.* the past participle of **bite.**

bitter (ˈbɪtə) *adj.* 1. having or denoting an unpalatable harsh taste, as the peel of an orange or coffee dregs. Compare **sour** (sense 1). 2. showing or caused by strong unrelenting hostility or resentment: *he was still bitter about the divorce.* 3. difficult or unpleasant to accept or admit: *a bitter blow.* 4. cutting; sarcastic: *bitter words.* 5. bitingly cold: *a bitter night.* ~*adv.* 6. very; extremely (esp. in the phrase **bitter cold**). ~*n.* 7. a thing that is bitter. 8. *Brit.* draught beer with a high hop content, with a slightly bitter taste. ~*vb.* 9. to make or become bitter. ~See also **bitters.** [Old English *biter;* related to *bītan* to BITE] —ˈ**bitterly** *adv.* —ˈ**bitterness** *n.*

bitter apple *n.* another name for **colocynth.**

bittercress (ˈbɪtəˌkrɛs) *n.* one of several perennial or annual cruciferous plants of the genus *Cardamine,* that are related to lady's-smock, including **hairy bittercress** (*C. hirsuta*), a common weed resembling shepherd's purse, with which it is often confused.

bitter end *n.* 1. *Nautical.* the end of a line, chain, or cable, esp. the end secured in the chain locker of a vessel. 2. **to the bitter end. a.** until the finish of a task, job, etc., however unpleasant or difficult. b. until final defeat or death. [C19: in both senses perhaps from BITT]

bitterling (ˈbɪtəlɪŋ) *n.* a small brightly coloured European freshwater cyprinid fish, *Rhodeus sericeus:* a popular aquarium fish. [C19: from German; see BITTER + -LING[1]]

bittern[1] (ˈbɪtən) *n.* any wading bird of the genera *Ixobrychus* and *Botaurus,* related and similar to the herons but with shorter legs and neck, a stouter body, and a booming call: family *Ardeidae,* order *Ciconiiformes.* [C14: from Old French *butor,* perhaps from Latin *būtiō* bittern + *taurus* bull; referring to its cry]

bittern[2] (ˈbɪtən) *n.* the bitter liquid remaining after common salt has been crystallized out of sea water: a source of magnesium, bromine, and iodine compounds. [C17: variant of *bittering;* see BITTER]

bitternut (ˈbɪtəˌnʌt) *n.* 1. an E North American hickory tree, *Carya cordiformis,* with thin-shelled nuts and bitter kernels. 2. the nut of this plant.

bitter orange *n.* another name for **Seville orange.**

bitter principle *n.* any of various bitter-tasting substances, such as aloin, usually extracted from plants.
bitters ('bɪtəz) *pl. n.* **1.** bitter-tasting spirits of varying alcoholic content flavoured with plant extracts. **2.** a similar liquid containing a bitter-tasting substance, used as a tonic to stimulate the appetite or improve digestion.
bittersweet ('bɪtəˌswiːt) *n.* **1.** any of several North American woody climbing plants of the genus *Celastrus*, esp. *C. scandens*, having orange capsules that open to expose scarlet-coated seeds: family *Celastraceae*. **2.** another name for **woody nightshade.** ~*adj.* **3.** tasting of or being a mixture of bitterness and sweetness. **4.** pleasant but tinged with sadness.
bitterweed ('bɪtəˌwiːd) *n.* any of various plants that contain a bitter-tasting substance.
bitterwood ('bɪtəˌwʊd) *n.* any of several simaroubaceous trees of the genus *Picrasma* of S and SE Asia and the West Indies, whose bitter bark and wood are used in medicine *Picrasma* of S and SE Asia and the West Indies, whose bitter bark and wood are used in medicine as a substitute for quassia.
bitty ('bɪtɪ) *adj.* **-tier, -tiest.** **1.** lacking unity; disjointed. **2.** containing bits, sediment, etc. —'**bittiness** *n.*
bitumen ('bɪtjʊmɪn) *n.* **1.** any of various viscous or solid impure mixtures of hydrocarbons that occur naturally in asphalt, tar, mineral waxes, etc.: used as a road surfacing and roofing material. **2.** the constituents of coal that can be extracted by an organic solvent. **3. the bitumen. a.** *Austral. and N.Z. informal.* any road with a bitumen surface. **b.** (*cap.*) *Austral.* the road in the Northern Territory between Darwin and Alice Springs. **4.** a transparent brown pigment or glaze made from asphalt. [C15: from Latin *bitūmen*, perhaps of Celtic origin] —**bituminous** (bɪ'tjuːmɪnəs) *adj.*
bituminize *or* **bituminise** (bɪ'tjuːmɪˌnaɪz) *vb.* (*tr.*) to treat with or convert into bitumen. —**biˌtumini'zation** *or* **biˌtumini'sation** *n.*
bituminous coal *n.* a soft black coal, rich in volatile hydrocarbons, that burns with a smoky yellow flame. Fixed carbon content: 46–86 per cent; calorific value: $1.93 \times 10^7 - 3.63 \times 10^7$ J/kg. Also called: **soft coal.**
bivalence *n. Logic, philosophy.* the semantic principle that there are exactly two truth values, so that every meaningful statement is either true of false. Compare **many-valued logic.**
bivalent (baɪ'veɪlənt, 'bɪvə-) *adj.* **1.** *Chem.* another word for **divalent. 2.** (of homologous chromosomes) associated together in pairs. ~*n.* **3.** a structure formed during meiosis consisting of two homologous chromosomes associated together. —**bi'valency** *n.*
bivalve ('baɪˌvælv) *n.* **1.** Also called: **lamellibranch, pelecypod.** any marine or freshwater mollusc of the class *Bivalvia* (or *Lamellibranchia, Pelecypoda*), having a laterally compressed body, a shell consisting of two hinged valves, and gills for respiration. The group includes clams, cockles, oysters, and mussels. ~*adj.* **2.** Also: **lamellibranch, pelecypod.** of, relating to, or belonging to the *Bivalvia*. **3.** Also: **bivalvate** (baɪ'vælveɪt). *Biology.* having or consisting of two valves or similar parts: *a bivalve seed capsule.* —**bi'valvular** *adj.*
bivariate (baɪ'vɛərɪɪt) *adj. Statistics.* (of a distribution) involving two random variables, not necessarily independent of one another.
bivouac ('bɪvʊˌæk, 'bɪvwæk) *n.* **1.** a temporary encampment with few facilities, as used by soldiers, mountaineers, etc. ~*vb.* **-acs, -acking, -acked. 2.** (*intr.*) to make such an encampment. [C18: from French *bivuac*, probably from Swiss German *Beiwacht*, literally: BY + WATCH]
bivvy ('bɪvɪ) *n., pl.* **-vies.** *Slang.* a small tent or shelter. [C20: shortened from BIVOUAC]
biweekly (baɪ'wiːklɪ) *adj., adv.* **1.** every two weeks. **2.** (often avoided because of confusion with sense 1) twice a week; semiweekly. See **bi-**[1]. ~*n., pl.* **-lies. 3.** a periodical published every two weeks.
biyearly (baɪ'jɪəlɪ) *adj., adv.* **1.** every two years; biennial or biennially. **2.** (often avoided because of confusion with sense 1) twice a year; biannual or biannually. See **bi-**[1].
biz (bɪz) *n. Informal.* short for **business.**
bizarre (bɪ'zɑː) *adj.* odd or unusual, esp. in an interesting or amusing way. [C17: from French: from Italian *bizzarro* capricious, of uncertain origin] —**bi'zarrely** *adv.* —**bi'zarreness** *n.*
bizarrerie (bɪ'zɑːrərɪ) *n.* **1.** the quality of being bizarre. **2.** a bizarre act.
bk *abbrev. for:* **1.** bank. **2.** book.
Bk *the chemical symbol for* berkelium.
bkcy *abbrev. for* bankruptcy.
bkg *abbrev. for* banking.
bkpt *abbrev. for* bankrupt.
bks *abbrev. for:* **1.** barracks. **2.** books.
bl *abbrev. for* barrel.
BL *abbrev. for:* **1.** Bachelor of Law. **2.** Bachelor of Letters. **3.** Barrister-at-Law. **4.** British Leyland. **5.** British Library.
bl. *abbrev. for:* **1.** bale. **2.** black. **3.** blue.
B/L, b/l, *or* **b.l.** *pl.* **Bs/L, bs/l,** *or* **bs.l.** *abbrev. for* bill of lading.
blab (blæb) *vb.* **blabs, blabbing, blabbed. 1.** to divulge (secrets) indiscreetly. **2.** (*intr.*) to chatter thoughtlessly; prattle. ~*n.* **3.** a less common word for **blabber** (senses 1, 2). [C14: of Germanic origin; compare Old High German *blabbizōn*, Icelandic *blabbra*] —'**blabbing** *n., adj.*
blabber ('blæbə) *n.* **1.** a person who blabs. **2.** idle chatter. ~*vb.* **3.** (*intr.*) to talk without thinking; chatter. [C15 *blabberen*, probably of imitative origin]
blabbermouth ('blæbəˌmaʊθ) *n. Informal.* a person who talks too much or indiscreetly.
black (blæk) *adj.* **1.** of the colour of jet or carbon black, having no hue due to the absorption of all or nearly all incident light. Compare **white** (sense 1). **2.** without light; completely dark. **3.** without hope or alleviation; gloomy: *the future looked black.* **4.** very dirty or soiled: *black factory chimneys.* **5.** angry or resentful: *she gave him black looks.* **6.** (of a play or other work) dealing with the unpleasant realities of life, esp. in a pessimistic or macabre manner: *black comedy.* **7.** (of coffee or tea) without milk or cream. **8.** causing, resulting from, or showing great misfortune: *black areas of unemployment.* **9. a.** wicked or harmful: *a black lie.* **b.** (*in combination*): *black-hearted.* **10.** causing or deserving dishonour or censure: *a black crime.* **11.** (of the face) purple, as from suffocation. **12.** *Brit.* (of goods, jobs, works, etc.) being subject to boycott by trade unionists, esp. in support of industrial action elsewhere. ~*n.* **13.** a black colour. **14.** a dye or pigment of or producing this colour. **15.** black clothing, worn esp. as a sign of mourning. **16.** *Chess, draughts.* **a.** a black or dark-coloured piece or square. **b.** (*usually cap.*) the player playing with such pieces. **17.** complete darkness: *the black of the night.* **18.** a black ball in snooker, etc. **19.** (in roulette and other gambling games) one of two colours on which players may place even bets, the other being red. **20. in the black.** in credit or without debt. **21.** *Archery.* a black ring on a target, between the outer and the blue, scoring three points. ~*vb.* **22.** another word for **blacken. 23.** (*tr.*) to polish (shoes, etc.) with blacking. **24.** (*tr.*) to bruise so as to make black: *he blacked her eye.* **25.** (*tr.*) *Brit., Austral., and N.Z.* (of trade unionists) to organize a boycott of (specified goods, jobs, work, etc.), esp. in support of industrial action elsewhere. ~See also **blackout.** [Old English *blæc*; related to Old Saxon *blak* ink, Old High German *blakra* to blink] —'**blackish** *adj.* —'**blackishly** *adv.* —'**blackly** *adv.* —'**blackness** *n.*
Black (blæk) *n.* **1.** a member of a dark-skinned race, esp. a Negro or an Australian Aborigine. ~*adj.* **2.** of or relating to a Black or Blacks: *a Black ghetto.*
blackamoor ('blækəˌmʊə, -ˌmɔː) *n. Archaic.* a Negro or other person with dark skin. [C16: see BLACK, MOOR]
black-and-blue *adj.* **1.** (of the skin) discoloured, as from a bruise. **2.** feeling pain or soreness, as from a beating.
black and tan *n.* a mixture of stout or porter and ale.
Black and Tans *pl. n.* **the.** a specially recruited armed auxiliary police force sent to Ireland in 1921 by the British Government to combat Sinn Féin. [name suggested by the colour of their uniforms and the *Black and Tans* hunt in Munster]
black-and-tan terrier *n.* a less common name for **Manchester terrier.**
black-and-white *n.* **1. a.** a photograph, picture, sketch, etc., in black, white, and shades of grey rather than in colour. **b.** (*as modifier*): *black-and-white film.* **2.** the neutral tones of black, white, and intermediate shades of grey. Compare **colour** (sense 2). **3. in black and white. a.** in print or writing. **b.** in extremes: *he always saw things in black and white.*
black art *n.* **the.** another name for **black magic.**
black-backed gull *n.* either of two common black-and-white European coastal gulls, *Larus fuscus* (**lesser black-backed gull**) and *L. marinus* (**great black-backed gull**).
blackball ('blækˌbɔːl) *n.* **1.** a negative vote or veto. **2.** a black wooden ball used to indicate disapproval or to veto in a vote. ~*vb.* (*tr.*) **3.** to vote against in a ballot. **4.** to exclude (someone) from a group, profession, etc.; ostracize. [C18: see sense 2]
black bass (bæs) *n.* any of several predatory North American percoid freshwater game fishes of the genus *Micropterus:* family *Centrarchidae* (sunfishes, etc.).
black bean *n.* an Australian leguminous tree, *Castanospermum australe*, having thin smooth bark and yellow or reddish flowers: used in furniture manufacture. Also called: **Moreton Bay chestnut.**
black bear *n.* **1. American black bear.** a bear, *Euarctos* (or *Ursus*) *americanus*, inhabiting forests of North America. It is smaller and less ferocious than the brown bear. **2. Asiatic black bear.** a bear, *Selenarctos thibetanus*, of central and E Asia, whose coat is black with a pale V-shaped mark on the chest.
black beetle *n.* another name for the **oriental cockroach** (see **cockroach**).
black belt *n. Judo, karate.* **1.** a black belt worn by an instructor or expert competitor in the dan grades, usually from first to fifth dan. **2.** a person entitled to wear this.
blackberry ('blækbərɪ) *n., pl.* **-ries. 1.** Also called: **bramble.** any of several woody plants of the rosaceous genus *Rubus*, esp. *R. fruticosus*, that have thorny stems and black or purple glossy edible berry-like fruits (drupelets). **2. a.** the fruit of any of these plants. **b.** (*as modifier*): *blackberry jam.* **3. blackberry lily.** an ornamental Chinese iridaceous plant, *Belamcanda chinensis*, that has red-spotted orange flowers and clusters of black seeds that resemble blackberries. ~*vb.* **-ries, -rying, -ried. 4.** (*intr.*) to gather blackberries.

black bile *n. Archaic.* one of the four bodily humours; melancholy. See **humour** (sense 8).
black bindweed *n.* a twining polygonaceous European plant, *Polygonum convolvulus,* with heart-shaped leaves and triangular black seed pods.
blackbird ('blækˌbɜːd) *n.* **1.** a common European thrush, *Turdus merula,* in which the male has a black plumage and yellow bill and the female is brown. **2.** any of various American orioles having a dark plumage, esp. any of the genus *Agelaius.* **3.** (formerly) a person, esp. a South Sea Islander, who was kidnapped and sold as a slave, esp. in Australia. ~*vb.* **4.** (*tr.*) (formerly) to kidnap and sell into slavery.
blackboard ('blækˌbɔːd) *n.* a hard or rigid surface made of a smooth usually dark substance, used for writing or drawing on with chalk, esp. in teaching.
black body *n. Physics.* a hypothetical body that would be capable of absorbing all the electromagnetic radiation falling on it. Also called: **full radiator.**
black book *n.* **1.** a book containing the names of people to be punished, blacklisted, etc. **2. in someone's black books.** *Informal.* out of favour with someone.
black bottom *n.* a dance of the late 1920s that originated in America, involving a sinuous rotation of the hips.
black box *n.* **1.** a self-contained unit in an electronic or computer system whose circuitry need not be known to understand its function. **2.** an informal name for **flight recorder.**
blackboy ('blækˌbɔɪ) *n.* another name for **grass tree** (sense 1).
black bread *n.* a kind of very dark coarse rye bread.
black bryony *n.* a climbing herbaceous Eurasian plant, *Tamus communis,* having small greenish flowers and poisonous red berries: family *Dioscoreaceae.*
blackbuck ('blækˌbʌk) *n.* an Indian antelope, *Antilope cervicapra,* the male of which has spiral horns, a dark back, and a white belly.
black bun *n. Scot.* a very rich dark fruitcake, usually in a pastry case. Also called **currant bun.**
blackbutt ('blækˌbʌt) *n.* any of various Australian eucalyptus trees having rough fibrous bark and hard wood used as timber.
blackcap ('blækˌkæp) *n.* **1.** a brownish-grey Old World warbler, *Sylvia atricapilla,* the male of which has a black crown. **2.** any of various similar birds, such as the black-capped chickadee (*Parus atricapillus*). **3.** *U.S.* a popular name for **raspberry** (sense 3). **4.** *Brit.* (formerly) the cap worn by a judge when passing a death sentence.
black-coated *adj. Brit.* (esp. formerly) (of a worker) clerical or professional, as distinguished from commercial or industrial.
blackcock ('blækˌkɒk) *n.* the male of the black grouse. Also called: **heath cock.** Compare **greyhen.**
blackcurrant (ˌblæk'kʌrənt) *n.* **1.** a N temperate shrub, *Ribes nigrum,* having red or white flowers and small edible black berries: family *Grossulariaceae.* **2. a.** the fruit of this shrub. **b.** (*as modifier*): *blackcurrant jelly.*
blackdamp ('blækˌdæmp) *n.* air that is low in oxygen content and high in carbon dioxide as a result of an explosion in a mine. Also called: **chokedamp.**
Black Death *n.* **the.** a form of bubonic plague pandemic in Europe and Asia during the 14th century, when it killed over 50 million people. See **bubonic plague.**
black diamond *n.* **1.** another name for **carbonado**[2]. **2.** (*usually pl.*) a figurative expression for **coal.**
black disc *n.* a conventional black vinyl gramophone record as opposed to a compact disc.
black earth *n.* another name for **chernozem.**
black economy *n.* that portion of the income of a nation that remains illegally undeclared either as a result of payment in kind or as a means of tax avoidance.
blacken ('blækən) *vb.* **1.** to make or become black or dirty. **2.** (*tr.*) to defame; slander (esp. in the phrase **blacken someone's name**).
black eye *n.* bruising round the eye.
black-eyed pea *n.* another name for **cowpea** (sense 2).
black-eyed Susan *n.* **1.** any of several North American plants of the genus *Rudbeckia,* esp. *R. hirta,* having flower heads of orange-yellow rays and brown-black centres: family *Compositae* (composites). **2.** a tropical African climbing plant, *Thunbergia alata,* having yellow flowers with purple centres, grown as a greenhouse annual.
blackface ('blækˌfeɪs) *n.* **1. a.** a performer made up to imitate a Negro. **b.** the make-up used by such a performer, usually consisting of burnt cork. **2.** a breed of sheep having a dark face. **3.** *Printing.* a less common name for **Gothic** (sense 10).
blackfish ('blækˌfɪʃ) *n., pl.* **-fish** *or* **-fishes. 1.** a minnow-like Alaskan freshwater fish, *Dallia pectoralis,* related to the pikes and thought to be able to survive prolonged freezing. **2.** a female salmon that has recently spawned. Compare **redfish** (sense 1). **3.** any of various other dark fishes, esp. a common edible Australian estuary fish. **4.** another name for **pilot whale.**
black flag *n.* another name for the **Jolly Roger.**
blackfly ('blækˌflaɪ) *n., pl.* **-flies.** a black aphid, *Aphis fabae,* that infests beans, sugar beet, and other plants. Also called: **bean aphid.**
black fly *n.* any small blackish stout-bodied dipterous fly of the family *Simuliidae,* which suck the blood of man, mammals, and birds. See also **buffalo gnat.**
Blackfoot ('blækˌfʊt) *n.* **1.** (*pl.* **-feet** *or* **-foot**) a member of a warlike group of North American Indian peoples formerly living in the northwestern Plains. **2.** any of the languages of these peoples, belonging to the Algonquian family. [C19: translation of Blackfoot *Siksika*]
Black Friar *n.* a Dominican friar.
black frost *n.* a frost without snow or rime that is severe enough to blacken vegetation.
black game *n.* another name for **black grouse** (sense 1).
black grouse *n.* **1.** Also called: **black game.** a large N European grouse, *Lyrurus tetrix,* the male of which has a bluish-black plumage and lyre-shaped tail. **2.** a related and similar species, *Lyrurus mlokosiewiczi,* of W Asia.
blackguard ('blægɑːd, -gəd) *n.* **1. a.** an unprincipled contemptible person; scoundrel. **b.** (*as modifier*): *blackguard language.* ~*vb.* **2.** (*tr.*) to ridicule or denounce with abusive language. **3.** (*intr.*) to behave like a blackguard. [C16: originally a collective noun referring to the lowest menials in court, camp followers, vagabonds; see BLACK, GUARD] —'**blackguardism** *n.* —'**blackguardly** *adj.*
black guillemot *n.* a common guillemot, *Cepphus grylle:* its summer plumage is black with white wing patches and its winter plumage white with greyish wings.
blackhead ('blækˌhɛd) *n.* **1.** a black-tipped plug of fatty matter clogging a pore of the skin, esp. the duct of a sebaceous gland. Technical name: **comedo. 2.** an infectious and often fatal disease of turkeys and some other fowl caused by parasitic protozoa. Technical name: **infectious enterohepatitis. 3.** any of various birds, esp. gulls or ducks, with black plumage on the head.
blackheart ('blækˌhɑːt) *n.* **1.** an abnormal darkening of the woody stems of some plants, thought to be caused by extreme cold. **2.** any of various diseases of plants, such as the potato, in which the central tissues are blackened. **3.** a variety of cherry that has large sweet fruit with purplish flesh and an almost black skin.
black heat *n.* heat emitted by an electric element made from low-resistance thick wire that does not glow red.
black hole *n.* **1.** *Astronomy.* a hypothetical region of space resulting from the gravitational collapse of a star following the exhaustion of its nuclear fuel. The gravitational field around the region would be so high that neither matter nor radiation could escape from it. **2.** any place regarded as resembling a black hole in that items or information entering it cannot be retrieved.
Black Hole of Calcutta *n.* **1.** a small dungeon in which in 1756 the Nawab of Bengal reputedly confined 146 English prisoners, of whom only 23 survived. **2.** *Informal, chiefly Brit.* any uncomfortable or overcrowded place.
black horehound *n.* a hairy unpleasant-smelling chiefly Mediterranean plant, *Ballota nigra,* having clusters of purple flowers: family *Labiatae* (labiates).
black ice *n.* a thin transparent layer of new ice on a road or similar surface.
blacking ('blækɪŋ) *n.* any preparation, esp. one containing lampblack, for giving a black finish to shoes, metals, etc.
blackjack[1] ('blækˌdʒæk) *Chiefly U.S. and Canadian.* ~*n.* **1.** a truncheon of leather-covered lead with a flexible shaft. ~*vb.* **2.** (*tr.*) to hit with or as if with a blackjack. **3.** (*tr.*) to compel (a person) by threats. [C19: from BLACK + JACK[1] (implement)]
blackjack[2] ('blækˌdʒæk) *n. Cards.* **1.** pontoon or any of various similar card games. **2.** the ace of spades. [C20: from BLACK + JACK[1] (the knave)]
blackjack[3] ('blækˌdʒæk) *n.* a dark iron-rich variety of the mineral sphalerite. [C18: from BLACK + JACK[1] (originally a miner's name for this useless ore)]
blackjack[4] ('blækˌdʒæk) *n.* a small oak tree, *Quercus marilandica,* of the southeastern U.S., with blackish bark and fan-shaped leaves. Also called: **blackjack oak.** [C19: from BLACK + JACK[1] (from the proper name, popularly used in many plant names)]
blackjack[5] ('blækˌdʒæk) *n.* a tarred leather tankard or jug. [C16: from BLACK + JACK[3]]
black japan *n.* a black bituminous varnish.
black knight *n. Commerce.* a person or firm that makes an unwelcome takeover bid for a company. Compare **grey knight, white knight.**
black knot *n.* a fungal disease of plums and cherries caused by *Dibotryon morbosum,* characterized by rough black knotlike swellings on the twigs and branches.
black lead (lɛd) *n.* another name for **graphite.**
blackleg ('blækˌlɛg) *n.* **1.** Also called: **scab.** *Brit.* **a.** a person who acts against the interests of a trade union, as by continuing to work during a strike or taking over a striker's job. **b.** (*as modifier*): *blackleg labour.* **2.** an acute infectious disease of cattle, sheep, and pigs, characterized by gas-filled swellings, esp. on the legs, caused by *Clostridium* bacteria. **3.** *Plant pathol.* **a.** a fungal disease of cabbages and related plants caused by *Phoma lingam,* characterized by blackening and decay of the lower stems. **b.** a similar disease of potatoes, caused by bacteria. **4.** a person who cheats in gambling, esp. at cards or in racing. ~*vb.*

-legs, -legging, -legged. **5.** *Brit.* to act against the interests of a trade union, esp. by refusing to join a strike.

black letter *n. Printing.* another name for **Gothic** (sense 10).

black light *n.* the invisible electromagnetic radiation in the ultraviolet and infrared regions of the spectrum.

blacklist ('blæk,lɪst) *n.* **1.** a list of persons or organizations under suspicion, or considered untrustworthy, disloyal, etc., esp. one compiled by a government or an organization. *~vb.* **2.** (*tr.*) to put on a blacklist. —'**black,listing** *n.*

black lung *n.* another name for **pneumoconiosis.**

black magic *n.* magic used for evil purposes by invoking the power of the devil.

blackmail ('blæk,meɪl) *n.* **1.** the act of attempting to obtain money by intimidation, as by threats to disclose discreditable information. **2.** the exertion of pressure or threats, esp. unfairly, in an attempt to influence someone's actions. *~vb.* (*tr.*) **3.** to exact or attempt to exact (money or anything of value) from (a person) by threats or intimidation; extort. **4.** to attempt to influence the actions of (a person), esp. by unfair pressure or threats. [C16: see BLACK, MAIL[3]] —'**blackmailer** *n.*

Black Maria (mə'raɪə) *n.* a police van for transporting prisoners.

black mark *n.* an indication of disapproval, failure, etc.

black market *n.* **1. a.** any system in which goods or currencies are sold and bought illegally, esp. in violation of controls or rationing. **b.** (*as modifier*): *black market lamb.* **2.** the place where such a system operates. *~vb.* **black-market.** **3.** to sell (goods) on the black market. —**black marketeer** *n.*

black mass *n.* (*sometimes caps.*) a blasphemous travesty of the Christian Mass, performed by practitioners of black magic.

black measles *pl. n.* (*often functioning as sing.*) a severe form of measles characterized by dark eruptions caused by bleeding under the skin.

black medick *n.* a small European papilionaceous plant, *Medicago lupulina,* with trifoliate leaves, small yellow flowers, and black pods. Also called: **nonesuch.**

black money *n.* **1.** that part of a nation's income that relates to its black economy. **2.** any money that a person or organization acquires illegally, as by a means that involves tax evasion. **3.** *U.S.* money to fund a government project that is concealed in the cost of some other project.

Black Monk *n.* a Benedictine monk.

black mould *n.* another name for **bread mould.**

Black Muslim *n.* (esp. in the U.S.) a member of a political and religious movement of Black people who adopt the religious practices of Islam and seek to establish a new Black nation. Official name: **Nation of Islam.**

black mustard *n.* a Eurasian cruciferous plant, *Brassica* (or *Sinapsis*) *nigra,* with clusters of yellow flowers and pungent seeds from which the condiment mustard is made.

black nightshade *n.* a poisonous solanaceous plant, *Solanum nigrum,* a common weed in cultivated land, having small white flowers with backward-curved petals and black berry-like fruits.

black opal *n.* any opal of a dark coloration, not necessarily black.

blackout ('blækaʊt) *n.* **1.** the extinguishing or hiding of all artificial light, esp. in a city visible to an enemy attack from the air. **2.** a momentary loss of consciousness, vision, or memory. **3.** a temporary electrical power failure or cut. **4.** *Electronics.* a temporary loss of sensitivity in a valve following a short strong pulse. **5.** a temporary loss of radio communications between a spacecraft and earth, esp. on re-entry into the earth's atmosphere. **6.** the suspension of radio or television broadcasting, as by a strike or for political reasons. *~vb.* **black out.** (*adv.*) **7.** (*tr.*) to obliterate or extinguish (lights). **8.** (*tr.*) to create a blackout in (a city etc.). **9.** (*intr.*) to lose vision, consciousness, or memory temporarily. **10.** (*tr., adv.*) to stop (news, a television programme) from being released or broadcast.

Black Panther *n.* (in the U.S.) a member of a militant Black political party founded in 1965 to end the political dominance of Whites.

black pepper *n.* a pungent condiment made by grinding the dried unripe berries, together with their black husks, of the pepper plant *Piper nigrum.*

black pine *n.* See **matai.**

blackpoll ('blæk,pəʊl) *n.* a North American warbler, *Dendroica striata,* the male of which has a black-and-white head.

black powder *n.* another name for **gunpowder.**

Black Power *n.* a social, economic, and political movement of Black people, esp. in the U.S. and Australia, to obtain equality with Whites.

black pudding *n.* a kind of black sausage made from minced pork fat, pig's blood, and other ingredients. Also called: **blood pudding.** Usual U.S. and Canadian name: **blood sausage.**

black rat *n.* a common rat, *Rattus rattus:* a household pest that has spread from its native Asia to all countries.

Black Rod *n.* **1.** (in Britain) an officer of the House of Lords and of the Order of the Garter, whose main duty is summoning the Commons at the opening and proroguing of Parliament. **2.** a similar officer in any of certain other legislatures.

black rot *n.* any of various plant diseases of fruits and vegetables, producing blackening, rotting, and shrivelling and caused by bacteria (including *Xanthomonas campestris*) and fungi (such as *Physalospora malorum*).

black rust *n.* a stage in any of several diseases of cereals and grasses caused by rust fungi in which black masses of spores appear on the stems or leaves.

black section *n.* (in Britain) an unofficial group within the Labour Party in any constituency that represents the interests of local Black people.

black sheep *n.* a person who is regarded as a disgrace or failure by his family or peer group.

Blackshirt ('blæk,ʃɜːt) *n.* (in Europe) a member of a fascist organization, esp. a member of the Italian Fascist party before and during World War II.

blacksmith ('blæk,smɪθ) *n.* an artisan who works iron with a furnace, anvil, hammer, etc. [C14: see BLACK, SMITH]

blacksnake ('blæk,sneɪk) *n.* **1.** any of several Old World black venomous elapid snakes, esp. *Pseudechis porphyriacus* (**Australian blacksnake**). **2.** any of various dark nonvenomous snakes, such as *Coluber constrictor* (black racer). **3.** *U.S. and Canadian.* a long heavy pliant whip of braided leather or rawhide.

black spot *n.* **1.** a place on a road where accidents frequently occur. **2.** any dangerous or difficult place. **3.** a disease of roses, *Diplocarpon rosae,* that causes circular black blotches on the leaves.

black spruce *n.* a coniferous tree, *Picea mariana,* of the northern regions of North America, growing mostly in cold bogs and having dark green needles. Also called: **spruce pine.**

blackstrap molasses ('blæk,stræp) *pl. n.* (*functioning as sing.*) the molasses remaining after the maximum quantity of sugar has been extracted from the raw material.

black stump *n.* **1. the.** *Austral.* an imaginary marker of the extent of civilization (esp. in the phrase **beyond the black stump**). **2.** *N.Z.* a long way off.

black swan *n.* a large Australian swan, *Cygnus atratus,* that has a black plumage and red bill.

blacktail ('blæk,teɪl) *n.* a variety of mule deer having a black tail.

blackthorn ('blæk,θɔːn) *n.* **1.** Also called: **sloe.** a thorny Eurasian rosaceous shrub, *Prunus spinosa,* with black twigs, white flowers, and small sour plumlike fruits. **2.** a walking stick made from its wood.

black tie *n.* **1.** a black bow tie worn with a dinner jacket. **2.** (*modifier*) denoting an occasion when a dinner jacket should be worn. ~Compare **white tie.**

blacktop ('blæk,tɒp) *n. Chiefly U.S. and Canadian.* **1.** a bituminous mixture used for paving. **2.** a road paved with this mixture.

black tracker *n. Austral.* an Aboriginal tracker working for the police.

black treacle *n. Brit.* another term for **treacle** (sense 1).

black velvet *n.* **1.** a mixture of stout and champagne in equal proportions. **2.** *Austral. slang.* Aboriginal women as sexual partners.

black vomit *n.* **1.** vomit containing blood, often a manifestation of disease, such as yellow fever. **2.** *Informal.* yellow fever.

Blackwall hitch ('blæk,wɔːl) *n.* a knot for hooking tackle to the end of a rope, holding fast when pulled but otherwise loose. [C19: named after *Blackwall,* former docks in London]

black walnut *n.* **1.** a North American walnut tree, *Juglans nigra,* with hard dark wood and edible oily nuts. **2.** the valuable wood of this tree, used for cabinet work. **3.** the nut of this tree. ~Compare **butternut** (senses 1–4).

blackwater fever ('blæk,wɔːtə) *n.* a rare and serious complication of chronic malaria caused by *Plasmodium falciparum,* characterized by massive destruction of red blood cells, producing dark red or blackish urine.

black whale *n.* another name for **pilot whale.**

black widow *n.* an American spider, *Latrodectus mactans,* the female of which is black with red markings, highly venomous, and commonly eats its mate.

blackwood ('blæk,wʊd) *n.* a tall Australian acacia tree, *A. melanoxylon,* having small clusters of flowers and curved pods and yielding highly valued black timber. Also called: **Sally Wattle.**

Blackwood ('blæk,wʊd) *n. Bridge.* a conventional bidding sequence of four and five no-trumps, which are requests to the partner to show aces and kings respectively. [C20: named after Easeley F. *Blackwood,* its American inventor]

bladder ('blædə) *n.* **1.** *Anatomy.* a distensible membranous sac, usually containing liquid or gas, esp. the urinary bladder. Related adj.: **vesical.** **2.** an inflatable part of something. **3.** a blister, cyst, vesicle, etc., usually filled with fluid. **4.** a hollow vesicular or saclike part or organ in certain plants, such as the bladderwrack. [Old English *blǣdre*] —'**bladdery** *adj.*

bladder campion *n.* a European caryophyllaceous plant, *Silene vulgaris,* having white flowers with an inflated calyx.

bladder fern *n.* a small fern, *Cystoperis fragilis,* with graceful lanceolate leaves, typically growing on limestone rocks and walls. [C19: named from the bladder-shaped indusium]

bladder ketmia ('kɛtmɪə) *n.* another name for **flower-of-an-hour.**

bladdernose ('blædə,nəʊz) *n.* another name for **hooded seal.**

bladdernut ('blædə,nʌt) *n.* **1.** any temperate shrub or small tree of the genus *Staphylea,* esp. *S. pinnata* of S Europe, that has bladder-like seed pods: family *Staphyleaceae.* **2.** the pod of any such tree.

bladder senna *n.* a Eurasian papilionaceous plant, *Colutea arborescens,* with yellow and red flowers and membranous inflated pods.

bladder worm *n.* an encysted saclike larva of the tapeworm. The main types are cysticercus, hydatid and coenurus.

bladderwort ('blædəˌwɜːt) *n.* any aquatic plant of the genus *Utricularia,* some of whose leaves are modified as small bladders to trap minute aquatic animals: family *Lentibulariaceae.*

bladderwrack ('blædəˌræk) *n.* any of several seaweeds of the genera *Fucus* and *Ascophyllum,* esp. *F. vesiculosus,* that grow in the intertidal regions of rocky shores and have branched brown fronds with air bladders.

blade (bleɪd) *n.* **1.** the part of a sharp weapon, tool, etc., that forms the cutting edge. **2.** (*pl.*) *Austral. and N.Z.* hand shears used for shearing sheep. **3.** the thin flattish part of various tools, implements, etc., as of a propeller, turbine, etc. **4.** the flattened expanded part of a leaf, sepal, or petal. **5.** the long narrow leaf of a grass or related plant. **6.** the striking surface of a bat, club, stick, or oar. **7.** the metal runner on an ice skate. **8.** *Archaeol.* a long thin flake of flint, possibly used as a tool. **9.** the upper part of the tongue lying directly behind the tip. **10.** *Archaic.* a dashing or swaggering young man. **11.** short for **shoulder blade. 12.** a poetic word for a **sword** or **swordsman.** [Old English *blæd;* related to Old Norse *blath* leaf, Old High German *blat,* Latin *folium* leaf] —'**bladed** *adj.*

blade grader *n.* another name for **grader** (sense 2).

blade-shearing *n. N.Z.* the shearing of sheep using hand shears. —'**blade-ˌshearer** *n.*

blade slap *n.* the regular noise beat generated by a helicopter rotor.

blae (ble, bleɪ) *adj. Scot.* bluish-grey; slate-coloured. [from Old Norse *blár*]

blaeberry ('bleɪbərɪ) *n., pl.* **-ries.** *Brit.* another name for **whortleberry** (senses 1, 2). [C15: from BLAE + BERRY]

blaes (blez, bleɪz) *n. Scot.* **a.** hardened clay or shale, esp. when crushed and used to form the top layer of a sports pitch: bluish-grey or reddish in colour. **b.** (*as modifier*): *a blaes pitch.* [C18: from BLAE]

blag (blæg) *Slang.* ~*n.* **1.** a robbery, esp. with violence. ~*vb.* **blags, blagging, blagged.** (*tr.*) **2.** to snatch (wages, someone's handbag, etc.); steal. **3.** to rob (esp. a bank or post office). [C19: of unknown origin] —'**blagger** *n.*

blague (blɑːg) *n.* pretentious but empty talk; nonsense. [C19: from French] —'**blaguer** *n.*

blah *or* **blah blah** (blɑː) *Slang.* ~*n.* **1.** worthless or silly talk; claptrap. ~*adj.* **2.** uninteresting; insipid. ~*vb.* **3.** (*intr.*) to talk nonsense or boringly.

blain (bleɪn) *n.* a blister, blotch, or sore on the skin. [Old English *blegen;* related to Middle Low German *bleine*]

blame (bleɪm) *n.* **1.** responsibility for something that is wrong or deserving censure; culpability. **2.** an expression of condemnation; reproof. **3. be to blame.** to be at fault or culpable. ~*vb.* (*tr.*) **4.** (usually foll. by *for*) to attribute responsibility to; accuse: *I blame him for the failure.* **5.** (usually foll. by *on*) to ascribe responsibility for (something) to: *I blame the failure on him.* **6.** to find fault with. [C12: from Old French *blasmer,* ultimately from Late Latin *blasphēmāre* to BLASPHEME] —'**blamable** *or* '**blameable** *adj.* —'**blamably** *or* '**blameably** *adv.*

blamed (bleɪmd) *adj., adv. Chiefly U.S.* a euphemistic word for **damned** (senses 2, 3).

blameful ('bleɪmfʊl) *adj.* deserving blame; guilty. —'**blamefully** *adv.* —'**blamefulness** *n.*

blameless ('bleɪmlɪs) *adj.* free from blame; innocent. —'**blamelessly** *adv.* —'**blamelessness** *n.*

blameworthy ('bleɪmˌwɜːðɪ) *adj.* deserving disapproval or censure. —'**blameˌworthiness** *n.*

blanc fixe *French.* (blɑ̃ fiks) *n.* another name for **barium sulphate.** [literally: fixed white]

blanch (blɑːntʃ) *vb.* (*mainly tr.*) **1.** (*also intr.*) to remove colour from, or (of colour) to be removed; whiten; fade: *the sun blanched the carpet; over the years the painting blanched.* **2.** (*usually intr.*) to become or cause to become pale, as with sickness or fear. **3.** to plunge tomatoes, nuts, etc., into boiling water to loosen the skin. **4.** to plunge (meat, green vegetables, etc.) in boiling water or bring to the boil in water in order to whiten, preserve the natural colour, or reduce or remove a bitter or salty taste. **5.** to cause (celery, chicory, etc.) to grow free of chlorophyll by the exclusion of sunlight. **6.** *Metallurgy.* to whiten (a metal), usually by treating it with an acid or by coating it with tin. **7.** (*tr.,* usually foll. by *over*) to attempt to conceal something. [C14: from Old French *blanchir* from *blanc* white; see BLANK]

blancmange (blə'mɒnʒ) *n.* a jelly-like dessert, stiffened usually with cornflour and set in a mould. [C14: from Old French *blanc manger,* literally: white food]

bland (blænd) *adj.* **1.** devoid of any distinctive or stimulating characteristics; uninteresting; dull: *bland food.* **2.** gentle and agreeable; suave. **3.** (of the weather) mild and soothing. **4.** unemotional or unmoved: *a bland account of atrocities.* [C15: from Latin *blandus* flattering] —'**blandly** *adv.* —'**blandness** *n.*

blandish ('blændɪʃ) *vb.* (*tr.*) to seek to persuade or influence by mild flattery; coax. [C14: from Old French *blandir* from Latin *blandīrī*]

blandishments ('blændɪʃmənts) *pl. n.* (*rarely sing.*) flattery intended to coax or cajole.

blank (blæŋk) *adj.* **1.** (of a writing surface) bearing no marks; not written on. **2.** (of a form, etc.) with spaces left for details to be filled in. **3.** without ornament or break; unrelieved: *a blank wall.* **4.** not filled in; empty; void: *a blank space.* **5.** exhibiting no interest or expression: *a blank look.* **6.** lacking understanding; confused: *he looked blank even after the explanations.* **7.** absolute; complete: *blank rejection.* **8.** devoid of ideas or inspiration: *his mind went blank in the exam.* **9.** unproductive; barren. ~*n.* **10.** an emptiness; void; blank space. **11.** an empty space for writing in, as on a printed form. **12.** a printed form containing such empty spaces. **13.** something characterized by incomprehension or mental confusion: *my mind went a complete blank.* **14.** a mark, often a dash, in place of a word, esp. a taboo word. **15.** short for **blank cartridge. 16.** a plate or plug used to seal an aperture. **17.** a piece of material prepared for stamping, punching, forging, or some other operation. **18.** *Archery.* the white spot in the centre of a target. **19. draw a blank. a.** to choose a lottery ticket that fails to win. **b.** to get no results from something. ~*vb.* (*tr.*) **20.** (usually foll. by *out*) to cross out, blot, or obscure. **21.** to forge, stamp, punch, or cut (a piece of material) in preparation for forging, die-stamping, or drawing operations. **22.** (often foll. by *off*) to seal (an aperture) with a plate or plug. **23.** *U.S. and Canadian.* to prevent (an opponent) from scoring in a game. [C15: from Old French *blanc* white, of Germanic origin; related to Old English *blanca* a white horse] —'**blankly** *adv.* —'**blankness** *n.*

blank cartridge *n.* a cartridge containing powder but no bullet: used in battle practice or as a signal.

blank cheque *n.* **1.** a cheque that has been signed but on which the amount payable has not been specified. **2.** complete freedom of action.

blank endorsement *n.* an endorsement on a bill of exchange, cheque, etc., naming no payee and thus making the endorsed sum payable to the bearer. Also called: **endorsement in blank.**

blanket ('blæŋkɪt) *n.* **1.** a large piece of thick cloth for use as a bed covering, animal covering, etc., enabling a person or animal to retain much of his natural body heat. **2.** a concealing cover or layer, as of smoke, leaves, or snow. **3.** a rubber or plastic sheet wrapped round a cylinder, used in offset printing to transfer the image from the plate, stone, or forme to the paper. **4.** *Physics.* a layer of a fertile radioactive substance placed round the core of a nuclear reactor as a reflector and often to breed new fissionable fuel. **5.** (*modifier*) applying to or covering a wide group or variety of people, conditions, situations, etc.: *blanket insurance against loss, injury, and theft.* **6. (born) on the wrong side of the blanket.** *Informal.* illegitimate. **7. on the blanket.** *Irish.* (of an imprisoned terrorist) wearing only a blanket instead of prison uniform, as a protest against not being recognized as a political prisoner. ~*vb.* (*tr.*) **8.** to cover with or as if with a blanket; overlie. **9.** to cover a very wide area, as in a publicity campaign; give blanket coverage. **10.** (usually foll. by *out*) to obscure or suppress: *the storm blanketed out the television picture.* **11.** *Nautical.* to prevent wind from reaching the sails of (another sailing vessel) by passing close to windward of it. [C13: from Old French *blancquete,* from *blanc;* see BLANK]

blanket bath *n.* an all-over wash given to a person confined to bed.

blanket bog *n.* a very acid peat bog, low in nutrients, extending widely over a flat terrain, found in cold wet climates.

blanket finish *n. Athletics, horse racing.* a finish so close that a blanket would cover all the contestants involved.

blanket stitch *n.* a strong reinforcing stitch for the edges of blankets and other thick material.

blankety ('blæŋkɪtɪ) *adj., adv.* a euphemism for any taboo word. [C20: from BLANK]

blank verse *n. Prosody.* unrhymed verse, esp. in iambic pentameters.

blanquette de veau (blæŋ'kɛt də 'vəʊ) *n.* a ragout or stew of veal in a white sauce. [French]

blare (blɛə) *vb.* **1.** to sound loudly and harshly. **2.** to proclaim loudly and sensationally. ~*n.* **3.** a loud and usually harsh or grating noise. [C14: from Middle Dutch *bleren;* of imitative origin]

blasé ('blɑːzeɪ) *adj.* **1.** indifferent to something because of familiarity or surfeit. **2.** lacking enthusiasm; bored. [C19: from French, past participle of *blaser* to cloy]

blaspheme (blæs'fiːm) *vb.* **1.** (*tr.*) to show contempt or disrespect for (God, a divine being, or sacred things), esp. in speech. **2.** (*intr.*) to utter profanities, curses, or impious expressions. [C14: from Late Latin *blasphēmāre,* from Greek *blasphēmein* from *blasphēmos* BLASPHEMOUS] —**blas'phemer** *n.*

blasphemous ('blæsfɪməs) *adj.* expressing or involving impiousness or gross irreverence towards God, a divine being, or something sacred. [C15: via Late Latin, from Greek *blasphēmos* evil-speaking, from *blapsis* evil + *phēmē* speech] —'**blasphemously** *adv.*

blasphemy ('blæsfɪmɪ) *n., pl.* **-mies. 1.** blasphemous behaviour or language. **2.** Also called: **blasphemous libel.** *Law.* the crime committed if a person insults, offends, or vilifies the deity, Christ, or the Christian religion.

blast (blɑːst) *n.* **1.** an explosion, as of dynamite. **2. a.** the rapid movement of air away from the centre of an explosion, combustion of rocket fuel, etc. **b.** a wave of overpressure caused by an explosion; shock wave. **3.** the charge of explosive used in a single explosion. **4.** a sudden strong gust of wind or air. **5.** a sudden loud sound, as of a trumpet. **6.** a violent verbal outburst, as of criticism. **7.** a forcible jet or stream of air, esp. one used to intensify the heating effect of a furnace, increase the draught in a steam engine, or break up coal at a coalface. **8.** any of several diseases of plants and animals, esp. one producing withering in plants. **9. (at) full blast.** at maximum speed, volume etc. ~*interj.* **10.** *Slang.* an exclamation of annoyance (esp. in phrases such as **blast it! blast him!**). ~*vb.* **11.** to destroy or blow up with explosives, shells, etc. **12.** to make or cause to make a loud harsh noise. **13.** (*tr.*) to remove, open, etc., by an explosion: *to blast a hole in a wall.* **14.** (*tr.*) to ruin; shatter: *the rain blasted our plans for a picnic.* **15.** to wither or cause to wither; blight or be blighted. **16.** to criticize severely. **17.** to shoot or shoot at: *he blasted the hat off her head; he blasted away at the trees.* ~See also **blastoff.** [Old English *blǣst,* related to Old Norse *blāstr*] —'**blaster** *n.*

-blast *n. combining form.* (in biology) indicating an embryonic cell or formative layer: *mesoblast.* [from Greek *blastos* bud]

blasted ('blɑːstɪd) *adj.* **1.** blighted or withered. ~*adj.* (*prenominal*), *adv.* **2.** *Slang.* (intensifier): *a blasted idiot.*

blastema (blæ'stiːmə) *n., pl.* **-mas** *or* **-mata** (-mətə). a mass of undifferentiated animal cells that will develop into an organ or tissue: present at the site of regeneration of a lost part. [C19: from New Latin, from Greek: offspring, from *blastos* bud] —**blastemic** (blæ'stiːmɪk, -'stɛm-) *adj.*

blast furnace *n.* a vertical cylindrical furnace for smelting iron, copper, lead, and tin ores. The ore, scrap, solid fuel, and slag-forming materials are fed through the top and a blast of preheated air is forced through the charge from the bottom. Metal and slag are run off from the base.

blast-furnace cement *n.* a type of cement made from a blend of ordinary Portland cement and crushed slag from a blast furnace. It has lower setting properties than ordinary Portland cement.

blasting ('blɑːstɪŋ) *n.* a distortion of sound caused by overloading certain components of a radio system.

blast injection *n.* the injection of liquid fuel directly into the cylinder of an internal-combustion engine using a blast of high-pressure air to atomize the spray of fuel. Compare **solid injection.**

blasto- *combining form.* (in biology) indicating an embryo or bud or the process of budding: *blastoderm.* [from Greek *blastos.* See -BLAST]

blastochyle ('blæstəʊˌkaɪl) *n. Embryol.* the fluid in a blastocoel.

blastocoel *or* **blastocoele** ('blæstəʊˌsiːl) *n. Embryol.* the cavity within a blastula. Also called: **segmentation cavity.**

blastocyst ('blæstəʊˌsɪst) *n. Embryol.* **1.** Also called: **blastosphere.** the blastula of mammals: a sphere of cells (trophoblast) enclosing an inner mass of cells and a fluid-filled cavity (blastocoel). **2.** another name for **germinal vesicle.**

blastoderm ('blæstəʊˌdɜːm) *n. Embryol.* **1.** a flat disc of cells formed after cleavage in a heavily yolked egg, such as a bird's egg. **2.** a layer of cells on the inside of the blastula surrounding the blastocoel. —ˌ**blasto'dermic** *adj.*

blastoff ('blɑːstˌɒf) *n.* **1.** the launching of a rocket under its own power. **2.** the time at which this occurs. ~*vb.* **blast off. 3.** (*adv.; when tr., usually passive*) (of a rocket, spacemen, etc.) to be launched.

blastogenesis (ˌblæstəʊ'dʒɛnɪsɪs) *n.* **1.** the theory that inherited characteristics are transmitted only by germ plasm. See also **pangenesis. 2.** asexual reproduction, esp. budding. —ˌ**blasto'genic** *or* ˌ**blastoge'netic** *adj.*

blastoma (ˌblæs'təʊmə) *n., pl.* **-mata** *or* **-mas.** *Pathol.* **a.** a tumour composed of embryonic tissue that has not yet developed a specialized function. **b.** (*in combination*): *neuroblastoma* [C20: New Latin, from BLASTO- + -OMA]

blastomere ('blæstəʊˌmɪə) *n. Embryol.* any of the cells formed by cleavage of a fertilized egg. —**blastomeric** (ˌblæstəʊ'mɛrɪk) *adj.*

blastopore ('blæstəʊˌpɔː) *n. Embryol.* the opening of the archenteron in the gastrula that develops into the anus of some animals. —ˌ**blasto'poric** *or* ˌ**blasto'poral** *adj.*

blastosphere ('blæstəʊˌsfɪə) *n.* **1.** another name for **blastula. 2.** another name for **blastocyst** (sense 1).

blastospore ('blæstəʊˌspɔː) *n. Botany.* a spore formed by budding, as in certain fungi.

blastula ('blæstjʊlə) *n., pl.* **-las** *or* **-lae** (-liː). an early form of an animal embryo that develops from a morula, consisting of a sphere of cells with a central cavity. Also called: **blastosphere.** [C19: New Latin; see BLASTO-] —'**blastular** *adj.*

blastulation (ˌblæstjʊ'leɪʃən) *n. Embryol.* the process of blastula formation.

blat (blæt) *vb.* **blats, blatting, blatted.** *U.S. and Canadian.* **1.** (*intr.*) to cry out or bleat like a sheep. **2.** (*tr.*) to utter indiscreetly in a loud voice. [C19: of imitative origin]

blatant ('bleɪtᵊnt) *adj.* **1.** glaringly conspicuous or obvious: *a blatant lie.* **2.** offensively noticeable: *blatant disregard for a person's feelings.* **3.** offensively noisy. **4.** *Archaic.* (of animals) bleating. [C16: coined by Edmund Spenser; probably influenced by Latin *blatīre* to babble; compare Middle Low German *pladderen*] —'**blatancy** *n.* —'**blatantly** *adv.*

blather ('blæðə) *vb., n.* a variant spelling (esp. U.S.) of **blether.** [C15: from Old Norse *blathra,* from *blathr* nonsense]

blatherskite ('blæðəˌskaɪt) *n.* **1.** a talkative silly person. **2.** foolish talk; nonsense. [C17: see BLATHER, SKATE[3]]

blaubok ('blaʊˌbɒk) *n., pl.* **-bok** *or* **-boks.** a large blue-haired antelope, *Hippotragus leucophaeus,* of southern Africa: extinct since 1800. Also called: **blue buck.** [C18: via Afrikaans from Dutch *blauwbok*]

blaze[1] (bleɪz) *n.* **1.** a strong fire or flame. **2.** a very bright light or glare. **3.** an outburst (of passion, acclaim, patriotism, etc.). **4.** brilliance; brightness. ~*vb.* (*intr.*) **5.** to burn fiercely. **6.** to shine brightly. **7.** (often foll. by *up*) to become stirred, as with anger or excitement. **8.** (usually foll. by *away*) to shoot continuously. ~See also **blazes.** [Old English *blæse*]

blaze[2] (bleɪz) *n.* **1.** a mark, usually indicating a path, made on a tree, esp. by chipping off the bark. **2.** a light-coloured marking on the face of a domestic animal, esp. a horse. ~*vb.* (*tr.*) **3.** to indicate or mark (a tree, path, etc.) with a blaze. **4. blaze a trail.** to explore new territories, areas of knowledge, etc., in such a way that others can follow. [C17: probably from Middle Low German *bles* white marking; compare BLEMISH]

blaze[3] (bleɪz) *vb.* (*tr;* often foll. by *abroad*) to make widely known; proclaim. [C14: from Middle Dutch *blāsen,* from Old High German *blāsan;* related to Old Norse *blāsa*]

blazer ('bleɪzə) *n.* a fairly lightweight jacket, often striped or in the colours of a sports club, school, etc.

blazes ('bleɪzɪz) *pl. n.* **1.** *Slang.* a euphemistic word for **hell** (esp. in the phrase **go to blazes**). **2.** *Informal.* (intensifier): *to run like blazes; what the blazes are you doing?*

blazing star *n. U.S.* **1.** a North American plant, *Chamaelirium luteum,* with a long spike of small white flowers: family *Compositae* (composites). **2.** any plant of the related North American genus *Liatris,* having clusters of small red or purple flowers.

blazon ('bleɪzᵊn) *vb.* (*tr.*) **1.** (often foll. by *abroad*) to proclaim loudly and publicly. **2.** *Heraldry.* to describe (heraldic arms) in proper terms. **3.** to draw and colour (heraldic arms) conventionally. ~*n.* **4.** *Heraldry.* a conventional description or depiction of heraldic arms. **5.** any description or recording, esp. of good qualities. [C13: from Old French *blason* coat of arms] —'**blazoner** *n.*

blazonry ('bleɪzənrɪ) *n., pl.* **-ries. 1.** the art or process of describing heraldic arms in proper form. **2.** heraldic arms collectively. **3.** colourful or ostentatious display.

bldg *abbrev. for* building.

bleach (bliːtʃ) *vb.* **1.** to make or become white or colourless, as by exposure to sunlight, by the action of chemical agents, etc. ~*n.* **2.** a bleaching agent. **3.** the degree of whiteness resulting from bleaching. **4.** the act of bleaching. [Old English *blǣcan;* related to Old Norse *bleikja,* Old High German *bleih* pale] —'**bleachable** *adj.* —'**bleacher** *n.*

bleachers ('bliːtʃəz) *pl. n.* **1.** (*sometimes sing.*) a tier of seats in a sports stadium, etc., that are unroofed and inexpensive. **2.** the people occupying such seats.

bleaching powder *n.* a white powder with the odour of chlorine, consisting of chlorinated calcium hydroxide with an approximate formula $CaCl(OCl).4H_2O$. It is used in solution as a bleaching agent and disinfectant. Also called: **chloride of lime, chlorinated lime.**

bleak[1] (bliːk) *adj.* **1.** exposed and barren; desolate. **2.** cold and raw. **3.** offering little hope or excitement; dismal: *a bleak future.* [Old English *blāc* bright, pale; related to Old Norse *bleikr* white, Old High German *bleih* pale] —'**bleakly** *adv.* —'**bleakness** *n.*

bleak[2] (bliːk) *n.* any slender silvery European cyprinid fish of the genus *Alburnus,* esp. *A. lucidus,* occurring in slow-flowing rivers. [C15: probably from Old Norse *bleikja* white colour; related to Old High German *bleiche* BLEACH]

blear (blɪə) *Archaic.* ~*vb.* **1.** (*tr.*) to make (eyes or sight) dim with or as if with tears; blur. ~*adj.* **2.** a less common word for **bleary.** [C13: *blere* to make dim; related to Middle High German *blerre* blurred vision]

bleary ('blɪərɪ) *adj.* **blearier, bleariest. 1.** (of eyes or vision) dimmed or blurred, as by tears or tiredness. **2.** indistinct or unclear. **3.** exhausted; tired. —'**blearily** *adv.* —'**bleariness** *n.*

bleary-eyed *or* **blear-eyed** *adj.* **1.** with eyes blurred, as with old age or after waking. **2.** physically or mentally unperceptive.

bleat (bliːt) *vb.* **1.** (*intr.*) (of a sheep, goat, or calf) to utter its characteristic plaintive cry. **2.** (*intr.*) to speak with any similar sound. **3.** to whine; whimper. ~*n.* **4.** the characteristic cry of sheep, goats, and young calves. **5.** any sound similar to this. **6.** a weak complaint or whine. [Old English *blǣtan;* related to Old High German *blāzen,* Dutch *blaten,* Latin *flēre* to weep; see BLARE] —'**bleater** *n.* —'**bleating** *n., adj.*

bleb (blɛb) *n.* **1.** a fluid-filled blister on the skin. **2.** a small air bubble. [C17: variant of BLOB] —'**blebby** *adj.*

bleed (bliːd) *vb.* **bleeds, bleeding, bled. 1.** (*intr.*) to lose or emit blood. **2.** (*tr.*) to remove or draw blood from (a person or animal). **3.** (*intr.*) to be injured or die, as for a cause or one's country. **4.** (of plants) to exude (sap or resin), esp. from a cut. **5.** (*tr.*) *Informal.* to obtain relatively large amounts of money, goods, etc., esp. by extortion. **6.** (*tr.*) to draw liquid or gas from (a container or enclosed system): *to bleed the hydraulic brakes.* **7.** (*intr.*) (of dye or paint) to run or become mixed, as when wet. **8.**

to print or be printed so that text, illustrations, etc., run off the trimmed page. **9.** (*tr.*) to trim (the edges of a printed sheet) so closely as to cut off some of the printed matter. **10.** (*intr.*) *Civil engineering, building trades.* (of a mixture) to exude (a liquid) during compaction, such as water from cement. **11. one's heart bleeds.** used to express sympathetic grief, but often used ironically. ~*n.* **12.** *Printing.* **a.** an illustration or sheet trimmed so that some matter is bled. **b.** (*as modifier*): *a bleed page.* **13.** *Printing.* the trimmings of a sheet that has been bled. [Old English *blēdan;* see BLOOD]

bleeder ('bliːdə) *n.* **1.** *Slang.* **a.** *Derogatory.* a despicable person: *a rotten bleeder.* **b.** any person; fellow: *where's the bleeder gone?* **2.** *Pathol.* a nontechnical name for a **haemophiliac.**

bleeder resistor *n.* a resistor connected across the output terminals of a power supply in order to improve voltage regulation and to discharge filter capacitors.

bleeder's disease *n.* a nontechnical name for **haemophilia.**

bleeding ('bliːdɪŋ) *adj., adv. Brit. slang.* (intensifier): *a bleeding fool; it's bleeding beautiful.*

bleeding heart *n.* **1.** any of several plants of the genus *Dicentra,* esp. the widely cultivated Japanese species *D. spectabilis,* which has finely divided leaves and heart-shaped nodding pink flowers: family *Fumariaceae.* **2.** *Informal.* **a.** a person who is excessively softhearted. **b.** (*as modifier*): *a bleeding-heart liberal.*

bleed valve *n.* a valve for running off a liquid from a tank, tube, etc., or for allowing accumulations of gas in a liquid to blow off. Also called: **bleed nipple.**

bleep (bliːp) *n.* **1.** a single short high-pitched signal made by an electronic apparatus; beep. **2.** Also called: '**bleeper.** a small portable radio receiver, worn esp. by doctors, that sounds a coded bleeping signal to call the wearer. ~*vb.* **3.** (*intr.*) to make such a noise. **4.** (*tr.*) to call (someone) by triggering the bleep he is wearing. [C20: of imitative origin]

blemish ('blɛmɪʃ) *n.* **1.** a defect; flaw; stain. ~*vb.* **2.** (*tr.*) to flaw the perfection of; spoil; tarnish. [C14: from Old French *blemir* to make pale, probably of Germanic origin.]

blench[1] (blɛntʃ) *vb.* (*intr.*) to shy away, as in fear; quail. [Old English *blencan* to deceive.]

blench[2] (blɛntʃ) *vb.* to make or become pale or white. [C19: variant of BLANCH]

blend (blɛnd) *vb.* **1.** to mix or mingle (components) together thoroughly. **2.** (*tr.*) to mix (different grades or varieties of tea, whisky, tobacco, etc.) to produce a particular flavour, consistency, etc. **3.** (*intr.*) to look good together; harmonize. **4.** (*intr.*) (esp. of colours) to shade imperceptibly into each other. ~*n.* **5.** a mixture or type produced by blending. **6.** the act of blending. **7.** Also called: **portmanteau word.** a word formed by joining together the beginning and the end of two other words: *"brunch" is a blend of "breakfast" and "lunch."* [Old English *blandan;* related to *blendan* to deceive, Old Norse *blanda,* Old High German *blantan*]

blende (blɛnd) *n.* **1.** another name for **sphalerite.** **2.** any of several sulphide ores, such as antimony sulphide. [C17: German *Blende,* from *blenden* to deceive, BLIND; so called because it is easily mistaken for galena]

blender ('blɛndə) *n.* **1.** a person or thing that blends. **2.** Also called: **liquidizer.** a kitchen appliance with blades used for puréeing vegetables, blending liquids, etc.

Blenheim ('blɛnɪm) *n.* **1.** a type of King Charles spaniel having red-and-white markings. **2.** Also called: **Blenheim orange. a.** a type of apple tree bearing gold-coloured apples. **b.** the fruit of this tree. [C19: named after *Blenheim* Palace, Oxfordshire]

blennioid ('blɛnɪˌɔɪd) *adj.* **1.** of, relating to, or belonging to the *Blennioidea,* a large suborder of small mainly marine spiny-finned fishes having an elongated body with reduced pelvic fins. The group includes the blennies, butterfish, and gunnel. ~*n.* **2.** any fish belonging to the *Blennioidea.*

blennorrhoea *or U.S.* **blennorrhea** (ˌblɛnəˈrɪə) *n. Pathol.* an excessive discharge of watery mucus, esp. from the urethra or the vagina.

blenny ('blɛnɪ) *n., pl.* **-nies.** **1.** any blennioid fish of the family *Blenniidae* of coastal waters, esp. of the genus *Blennius,* having a tapering scaleless body, a long dorsal fin, and long raylike pelvic fins. **2.** any of various related fishes. [C18: from Latin *blennius,* from Greek *blennos* slime; from the mucus that coats its body]

blent (blɛnt) *vb. Archaic or literary.* a past participle of **blend.**

blepharism ('blɛfərɪzəm) *n.* spasm of the eyelids, causing rapid involuntary blinking.

blepharitis (ˌblɛfəˈraɪtɪs) *n.* inflammation of the eyelids. [C19: from Greek *blephar(on)* eyelid + -ITIS] —**blepharitic** (ˌblɛfəˈrɪtɪk) *adj.*

blesbok *or* **blesbuck** ('blɛsˌbʌk) *n., pl.* **-boks, -bok** *or* **-bucks, -buck.** an antelope, *Damaliscus dorcas* (or *albifrons*), of southern Africa. The coat is a deep reddish-brown with a white blaze between the eyes; the horns are lyre-shaped. [C19: Afrikaans, from Dutch *bles* BLAZE[2] + *bok* goat, BUCK[1]]

bless (blɛs) *vb.* **blesses, blessing, blessed** *or* **blest.** (*tr.*) **1.** to consecrate or render holy, beneficial, or prosperous by means of a religious rite. **2.** to give honour or glory to (a person or thing) as divine or holy. **3.** to call upon God to protect; give a benediction to. **4.** to worship or adore (God); call or hold holy. **5.** (*often passive*) to grant happiness, health, or prosperity to: *they were blessed with perfect peace.* **6.** (*usually passive*) to endow with a talent, beauty, etc.: *she was blessed with an even temper.* **7.** *Rare.* to protect against evil or harm. **8. bless you!** (*interj.*) **a.** a traditional phrase said to a person who has just sneezed. **b.** an exclamation of well-wishing or surprise. **9. bless me!** *or* **(God) bless my soul!** (*interj.*) an exclamation of surprise. **10. not have a penny to bless oneself with.** to be desperately poor. [Old English *blǣdsian* to sprinkle with sacrificial blood; related to *blōd* BLOOD]

blessed ('blɛsɪd, blɛst) *adj.* **1.** made holy by religious ceremony; consecrated. **2.** worthy of deep reverence or respect. **3.** *R.C. Church.* (of a person) beatified by the pope. **4.** characterized by happiness or good fortune: *a blessed time.* **5.** bringing great happiness or good fortune. **6.** a euphemistic word for **damned,** used in mild oaths: *I'm blessed if I know.* ~*n.* **7. the blessed.** *Christianity.* the dead who are already enjoying heavenly bliss. —'**blessedly** *adv.* —'**blessedness** *n.*

Blessed Sacrament *n. Chiefly R.C. Church.* the consecrated elements of the Eucharist.

blessing ('blɛsɪŋ) *n.* **1.** the act of invoking divine protection or aid. **2.** the words or ceremony used for this. **3.** a short prayer of thanksgiving before or after a meal; grace. **4.** *Judaism.* Also called: **brachah, brocho. a.** a short prayer prescribed for a specific occasion and beginning "Blessed art thou, O Lord ...". **b.** a section of the liturgy including a similar formula. **5.** approval; good wishes: *her father gave his blessing to the marriage.* **6.** the bestowal of a divine gift or favour. **7.** a happy event or state of affairs: *a blessing in disguise.*

blest (blɛst) *vb.* a past tense and past participle of **bless.**

blet (blɛt) *n.* a state of softness or decay in certain fruits, such as the medlar, brought about by overripening. [C19: from French *blettir* to become overripe]

blether ('blɛðə) *or esp. U.S.* **blather** *Scot.* ~*vb.* **1.** (*intr.*) to speak foolishly. ~*n.* **2.** foolish talk; nonsense. **3.** a person who blethers. [C16: from Old Norse *blathra,* from *blathr* nonsense]

blew (bluː) *vb.* the past tense of **blow**[1].

blewits ('bluːɪts) *n.* (*functioning as sing.*) an edible saprophytic agaricaceous fungus, *Tricholoma saevum,* having a pale brown cap and bluish stalk. [C19: probably based on BLUE]

blight (blaɪt) *n.* **1.** any plant disease characterized by withering and shrivelling without rotting. **2.** any factor, such as bacterial attack or air pollution, that causes the symptoms of blight in plants. **3.** a person or thing that mars or prevents growth, improvement, or prosperity. **4.** an ugly urban district. **5.** the state or condition of being blighted or spoilt. ~*vb.* **6.** to cause or suffer a blight. **7.** (*tr.*) to frustrate or disappoint. **8.** (*tr.*) to spoil; destroy. [C17: perhaps related to Old English *blǣce* rash; compare BLEACH]

blighter ('blaɪtə) *n. Brit. informal.* **1.** a fellow: *where's the blighter gone?* **2.** a despicable or irritating person or thing.

blighty *or* **blighty bird** ('blaɪtɪ) *n. N.Z.* another name for **white-eye.**

Blighty ('blaɪtɪ) *n.* (*sometimes not cap.*) *Brit. slang.* (used esp. by troops serving abroad) **1.** England; home. **2.** (esp. in World War I) **a.** Also called: **a blighty one.** a slight wound that causes the recipient to be sent home to England. **b.** leave in England. [C20: from Hindi *bilāyatī* foreign land, England, from Arabic *wilāyat* country, from *waliya* he rules]

blimey ('blaɪmɪ) *interj. Brit. slang.* an exclamation of surprise or annoyance. [C19: short for *gorblimey* God blind me]

blimp[1] (blɪmp) *n.* **1.** a small nonrigid airship, esp. one used for observation or as a barrage balloon. **2.** *Films.* a soundproof cover fixed over a camera during shooting. [C20: probably from (*type*) *B-limp*]

blimp[2] (blɪmp) *n.* (*often cap.*) *Chiefly Brit.* a person, esp. a military officer, who is stupidly complacent and reactionary. Also called: **Colonel Blimp.** [C20: after a character created by David Low (1891–1963), British cartoonist]

blin (blɪn) *adj.* a Scot. word for **blind.**

blind (blaɪnd) *adj.* **1. a.** unable to see; sightless. **b.** (*as collective n.; preceded by the*): *the blind.* **2.** (usually foll. by *to*) unable or unwilling to understand or discern. **3.** not based on evidence or determined by reason: *blind hatred.* **4.** acting or performed without control or preparation. **5.** done without being able to see, relying on instruments for information. **6.** hidden from sight: *a blind corner; a blind stitch.* **7.** closed at one end: *a blind alley.* **8.** completely lacking awareness or consciousness: *a blind stupor.* **9.** *Informal.* very drunk. **10.** having no openings or outlets: *a blind wall.* **11.** without having been seen beforehand: *a blind purchase.* **12.** (of cultivated plants) having failed to produce flowers or fruits. **13.** (intensifier): *not a blind bit of notice.* **14. turn a blind eye (to).** to disregard deliberately or pretend not to notice (something, esp. an action of which one disapproves). ~*adv.* **15.** without being able to see ahead or using only instruments: *to drive blind; flying blind.* **16.** without adequate knowledge or information; carelessly: *to buy a house blind.* **17.** (intensifier) (in the phrase **blind drunk**). **18. bake blind.** to bake (the empty crust of a pie, pastry, etc.) by half filling with dried peas, crusts of bread, etc., to keep it in shape. ~*vb.* (*mainly tr.*) **19.** to deprive of sight permanently or temporarily. **20.** to deprive of good sense, reason, or judgment. **21.** to darken; conceal. **22.** (foll. by *with*) to overwhelm by showing detailed knowledge: *to blind somebody with science.* **23.** (*intr.*) *Brit. slang.* to drive very fast. **24.** (*intr.*) *Brit. slang.* to curse (esp. in the phrase **effing and blinding**). ~*n.* **25.** (*modifier*) for or intended to help the blind: *a blind school.* **26.** a shade for a window, usually on a roller. **27.** any obstruction or hindrance to sight, light, or air. **28.** a person, action, or thing that serves to deceive or conceal the truth. **29.** a person who acts on behalf of someone who does not wish his identity or actions to be known. **30.** *Brit. slang.* Also called: **blinder.** a drunken orgy; binge. **31.** *Poker.* a stake put up by a player before he examines his cards. **32.** *Hunting, chiefly U.S. and Canadian.* a screen of brush or undergrowth, in which hunters hide to shoot their quarry. Brit. name: **hide. 33.** *Military.* a round or demolition charge that fails to explode. [Old English *blind;* related to Old Norse *blindr,* Old High German *blint;* Lettish *blendu* to see dimly; see BLUNDER] —**'blindly** *adv.* —**'blindness** *n.*

blindage ('blaɪndɪdʒ) *n. Military.* (esp. formerly) a protective screen or structure, as over a trench.

blind alley *n.* **1.** an alley open at one end only; cul-de-sac. **2.** *Informal.* a situation in which no further progress can be made.

blind date *n. Informal.* **1.** a social meeting between a man and a woman who have not met before. **2.** either of the persons involved.

blinder ('blaɪndə) *n.* **1.** an outstanding performance in sport. **2.** *Brit. slang.* another name for **blind** (sense 30).

blinders ('blaɪndəz) *pl. n.* the usual U.S. and Canadian word for **blinkers.**

blindfish ('blaɪnd,fɪʃ) *n., pl.* **-fish** *or* **-fishes.** any of various small fishes, esp. the cavefish, that have rudimentary or functionless eyes and occur in subterranean streams.

blindfold ('blaɪnd,fəʊld) *vb.* (*tr.*) **1.** to prevent (a person or animal) from seeing by covering (the eyes). **2.** to prevent from perceiving or understanding. ~*n.* **3.** a piece of cloth, bandage, etc., used to cover the eyes. **4.** any interference to sight. ~*adj., adv.* **5.** having the eyes covered with a cloth or bandage. **6.** *Chess.* not seeing the board and pieces. **7.** rash; inconsiderate. [changed (C16) through association with FOLD[1] from Old English *blindfellian* to strike blind; see BLIND, FELL[2]]

Blind Freddie *n. Austral. informal.* an imaginary person representing the highest degree of incompetence (esp. in the phrase **Blind Freddie could see that!**).

blind gut *n. Informal.* another name for the **caecum.**

blinding ('blaɪndɪŋ) *n.* **1.** sand or grit spread over a road surface to fill up cracks. **2.** the process of laying blinding. **3.** Also called: **mattress.** a layer of concrete made with little cement spread over soft ground to seal it so that reinforcement can be laid on it. ~*adj.* **4.** making one blind or as if blind: *blinding snow.* **5.** most noticeable; brilliant or dazzling: *a blinding display of skill.* —**'blindingly** *adv.*

blind man's buff *n.* a game in which a blindfolded person tries to catch and identify the other players. [C16: *buff,* perhaps from Old French *buffe* a blow; see BUFFET[2]]

blind register *n.* (in the UK) a list of those who are blind and are therefore entitled to financial and other benefits.

blindsight ('blaɪnd,saɪt) *n.* the ability to respond to visual stimuli without having any conscious visual experience; it can occur after some forms of brain damage.

blind snake *n.* any burrowing snake of the family *Typhlopidae* and related families of warm and tropical regions, having very small or vestigial eyes.

blind spot *n.* **1.** a small oval-shaped area of the retina in which vision is not experienced. It marks the nonphotosensitive site of entrance into the eyeball of the optic nerve. See **optic disc. 2.** a place or area, as in an auditorium or part of a road, where vision is completely or partially obscured or hearing is difficult or impossible. **3.** a subject about which a person is ignorant or prejudiced, or an occupation in which he is inefficient. **4.** a location within the normal range of a radio transmitter with weak reception.

blind staggers *n.* (*functioning as sing.*) *Vet. science.* another name for **staggers.**

blind stamping *n. Bookbinding.* an impression on a book cover without using colour or gold leaf. Also called: **book tooling.**

blindstorey *or* **blindstory** ('blaɪnd,stɔːrɪ) *n., pl.* **-reys** *or* **-ries.** a storey without windows, such as a gallery in a Gothic church. Compare **clerestory.**

blindworm ('blaɪnd,wɜːm) *n.* another name for **slowworm.**

blini ('blɪnɪ) *or* **blinis** ('blɪnɪz) *pl. n.* Russian pancakes made of buckwheat flour and yeast. [C19: from Russian: plural of *blin,* from Old Russian *mlinŭ,* related to Russian *molot'* to grind]

blink (blɪŋk) *vb.* **1.** to close and immediately reopen (the eyes or an eye), usually involuntarily. **2.** (*intr.*) to look with the eyes partially closed, as in strong sunlight. **3.** to shine intermittently, as in signalling, or unsteadily. **4.** (*tr.;* foll. by *away, from,* etc.) to clear the eyes of (dust, tears, etc.). **5.** (when *tr.,* usually foll. by *at*) to be surprised or amazed: *he blinked at the splendour of the ceremony.* **6.** (when *intr.,* foll. by *at*) to pretend not to know or see (a fault, injustice, etc.). ~*n.* **7.** the act or an instance of blinking. **8.** a glance; glimpse. **9.** short for **iceblink** (sense 1). **10. on the blink.** *Slang.* not working properly. [C14: variant of BLENCH[1]; related to Middle Dutch *blinken* to glitter, Danish *blinke* to wink, Swedish *blinka*]

blinker ('blɪŋkə) *n.* **1.** a flashing light for sending messages, as a warning device, etc., such as a direction indicator on a road vehicle. **2.** (*often pl.*) a slang word for **eye.** ~*vb.* (*tr.*) **3.** to provide (a horse) with blinkers. **4.** to obscure with or as if with blinkers. —**'blinkered** *adj.*

blinkers ('blɪŋkəz) *pl. n.* **1.** (*sometimes sing.*) *Chiefly Brit.* leather sidepieces attached to a horse's bridle to prevent sideways vision. Usual U.S. and Canadian word: **blinders. 2.** a slang word for **goggle** (sense 4).

blinking ('blɪŋkɪŋ) *adj., adv. Informal.* (intensifier): *a blinking fool; a blinking good film.*

blinks (blɪŋks) *n.* (*functioning as sing.*) a small temperate portulacaceous plant, *Montia fontana* with small white flowers. [C19: from BLINK, because the flowers do not fully open and thus seem to blink at the light]

blintz *or* **blintze** (blɪnts) *n.* a thin pancake folded over a filling usually of apple, cream cheese, or meat. [C20: from Yiddish *blintse,* from Russian *blinyets* little pancakes; see BLINI]

blip (blɪp) *n.* **1.** a repetitive sound, such as that produced by an electronic device, by dripping water, etc. **2.** Also called: **pip.** the spot of light or a sharply peaked pulse on a radar screen indicating the position of an object. **3.** a temporary irregularity recorded in performance of something. ~*vb.* **blips, blipping, blipped. 4.** (*intr.*) to produce such a noise. [C20: of imitative origin]

bliss (blɪs) *n.* **1.** perfect happiness; serene joy. **2.** the ecstatic joy of heaven. [Old English *blīths;* related to *blīthe* BLITHE, Old Saxon *blīdsea* bliss] —**'blissless** *adj.*

blissful ('blɪsfʊl) *adj.* **1.** serenely joyful or glad. **2. blissful ignorance.** unawareness or inexperience of something unpleasant. —**'blissfully** *adv.* —**'blissfulness** *n.*

blister ('blɪstə) *n.* **1.** a small bubble-like elevation of the skin filled with serum, produced as a reaction to a burn, mechanical irritation, etc. **2.** a swelling containing air or liquid, as on a painted surface. **3.** a transparent dome or any bulge on the fuselage of an aircraft, such as one used for observation. **4.** *Slang.* an irritating person. **5. a.** *N.Z. slang.* a rebuke. **b.** *Austral. and N.Z. slang.* a summons to court. ~*vb.* **6.** to have or cause to have blisters. **7.** (*tr.*) to attack verbally with great scorn or sarcasm. [C13: from Old French *blestre,* probably from Middle Dutch *bluyster* blister; see BLAST] —**'blistered** *adj.* —**'blistery** *adj.*

blister beetle *n.* any beetle of the family *Meloidae,* many of which produce a secretion that blisters the skin. See also **Spanish fly.**

blister copper *n.* an impure form of copper having a blister-like surface due to the release of gas during cooling.

blistering ('blɪstərɪŋ, -trɪŋ) *adj.* **1.** (of weather) extremely hot. **2.** (of criticism) extremely harsh. —**'blisteringly** *adv.*

blister pack *n.* a type of packet in which small items are displayed and sold, consisting of a transparent dome of plastic or similar material mounted on a firm backing such as cardboard. Also called: **bubble pack.**

blister rust *n.* a disease of certain pines caused by rust fungi of the genus *Cronartium,* causing swellings on the bark from which orange masses of spores are released.

BLit *abbrev. for* Bachelor of Literature.

blithe (blaɪð) *adj.* **1.** very happy or cheerful; gay. **2.** heedless; casual and indifferent. [Old English *blīthe*] —**'blithely** *adv.* —**'blitheness** *n.*

blithering ('blɪðərɪŋ) *adj.* **1.** talking foolishly; jabbering. **2.** *Informal.* stupid; foolish: *you blithering idiot.* [C19: variant of BLATHER + -ING[2]]

blithesome ('blaɪðsəm) *adj. Literary.* cheery; merry. —**'blithesomely** *adv.* —**'blithesomeness** *n.*

BLitt *abbrev. for* Bachelor of Letters. [Latin *Baccalaureus Litterarum*]

blitz (blɪts) *n.* **1.** a violent and sustained attack, esp. with intensive aerial bombardment. **2.** any sudden intensive attack or concerted effort. **3.** *American football.* a defensive charge on the quarterback. ~*vb.* **4.** (*tr.*) to attack suddenly and intensively. [C20: shortened from German *Blitzkrieg* lightning war]

Blitz (blɪts) *n.* **the.** the systematic night-time bombing of the British in 1940–41 by the German Luftwaffe.

blitzkrieg ('blɪts,kriːg) *n.* a swift intensive military attack designed to defeat the opposition quickly. [C20: from German: lightning war]

blizzard ('blɪzəd) *n.* a strong bitterly cold wind accompanied by a widespread heavy snowfall. [C19: of uncertain origin]

blk *abbrev. for:* **1.** black. **2.** block. **3.** bulk.

BLL *abbrev. for* Bachelor of Laws.

bloat (bləʊt) *vb.* **1.** to swell or cause to swell, as with a liquid, air, or wind. **2.** to become or cause to be puffed up, as with conceit. **3.** (*tr.*) to cure (fish, esp. herring) by half-drying in smoke. ~*n.* **4.** *Vet. science.* an abnormal distention of the abdomen in cattle, sheep, etc., caused by accumulation of gas in the stomach. [C17: probably related to Old Norse *blautr* soaked, Old English *blāt* pale] —**'bloated** *adj.*

bloater ('bləʊtə) *n.* a herring, or sometimes a mackerel, that has been salted in brine, smoked, and cured.

blob (blɒb) *n.* **1.** a soft mass or drop, as of some viscous liquid. **2.** a spot, dab, or blotch of colour, ink, etc. **3.** an indistinct or shapeless form or object. **4.** *Cricket slang.* a score of nought; a duck. ~*vb.* **blobs, blobbing, blobbed.** 5. (*tr.*) to put blobs, as of ink or paint, on. [C15: perhaps of imitative origin; compare BUBBLE] —'**blobby** *adj.*

bloc (blɒk) *n.* a group of people or countries combined by a common interest or aim: *the Soviet bloc.* [C20: from French: BLOCK]

block (blɒk) *n.* **1.** a large solid piece of wood, stone, or other material with flat rectangular sides, as for use in building. **2.** any large solid piece of wood, stone, etc., usually having at least one face fairly flat. **3.** such a piece on which particular tasks may be done, as chopping, cutting, or beheading. **4.** Also called: **building block.** one of a set of wooden or plastic cubes as a child's toy. **5.** a form on which things are shaped or displayed: *a wig block.* **6.** *Slang.* a person's head (esp. in the phrase **knock someone's block off**). **7. do one's block.** *Austral. and N.Z. slang.* to become angry. **8.** a dull, unemotional, or hardhearted person. **9.** a large building of offices, flats, etc. **10. a.** a group of buildings in a city bounded by intersecting streets on each side. **b.** the area or distance between such intersecting streets. **11.** *Austral. and N.Z.* an area of land, usually extensive, taken up for farming, settlement, etc. **12.** *N.Z.* an area of bush reserved by licence for a trapper or hunter. **13.** *Austral. and N.Z.* a log, usually a willow, fastened to a timber base and used in a wood-chopping competition. **14. put (someone) on the block.** *N.Z. taboo slang.* to gang rape (someone). **15.** an area of land, esp. one to be divided for building or settling. **16.** See **cylinder block.** **17. a.** a piece of wood, metal, or other material having an engraved, cast, or carved design in relief, used either for printing or for stamping book covers, etc. **b.** *Brit.* a letterpress printing plate, esp. one mounted type-high on wood or metal. **18.** a casing housing one or more freely rotating pulleys. See also **block and tackle.** **19. on the block.** *Chiefly U.S. and Canadian.* up for auction. **20.** the act of obstructing or condition of being obstructed, as in sports. **21.** an obstruction or hindrance. **22.** *Pathol.* **a.** interference in the normal physiological functioning of an organ or part. **b.** See **heart block.** **c.** See **nerve block.** **23.** *Psychol.* a short interruption of perceptual or thought processes. **24.** obstruction of an opponent in a sport. **25. a.** a section or quantity, as of tickets or shares, handled or considered as a single unit. **b.** (*as modifier*): *a block booking; block voting.* **26. a.** a stretch of railway in which only one train may travel at a time. **b.** (*as modifier*): *a block signal.* **27.** an unseparated group of four or more postage stamps. Compare **strip**[2] (sense 3). **28.** a pad of paper. **29.** *Computer technol.* a group of words on magnetic tape treated as a unit of data. **30.** *Athletics.* short for **starting block.** **31.** *Cricket.* a mark made near the popping crease by a batsman to indicate his position in relation to the wicket. **32. a chip off the old block.** *Informal.* a person who resembles one of his or her parents in behaviour. ~*vb.* (*mainly tr.*) **33.** to shape or form (something) into a block. **34.** to fit with or mount on a block. **35.** to shape by use of a block: *to block a hat.* **36.** (often foll. by *up*) to obstruct (a passage, channel, etc.) or prevent or impede the motion or flow of (something or someone) by introducing an obstacle: *to block the traffic; to block up a pipe.* **37.** to impede, retard, or prevent (an action, procedure, etc.). **38.** to stamp (a title, design, etc.) on (a book cover, etc.) by means of a block (see sense 17a.), esp. using gold leaf or other foil. **39.** (esp. of a government or central bank) to limit the use or conversion of assets or currency. **40.** (*also intr.*) *Sports.* to obstruct or impede movement by (an opponent). **41.** (*intr.*) to suffer a psychological block. **42.** to interrupt a physiological function, as by use of an anaesthetic. **43.** (*also intr.*) *Cricket.* to play (a ball) defensively. ~See also **block in, block out.** [C14: from Old French *bloc,* from Dutch *blok;* related to Old High German *bloh*] —'**blocker** *n.*

blockade (blɒ'keɪd) *n.* **1.** *Military.* the interdiction of a nation's sea lines of communications, esp. of an individual port by the use of sea power. **2.** something that prevents access or progress. **3.** *Med.* the inhibition of the effect of a hormone or the action of a nerve by a drug. ~*vb.* (*tr.*) **4.** to impose a blockade on. **5.** to obstruct the way to. [C17: from BLOCK + *-ade,* as in AMBUSCADE] —**block'ader** *n.*

blockage ('blɒkɪdʒ) *n.* **1.** the act of blocking or state of being blocked. **2.** an object causing an obstruction.

block and tackle *n.* a hoisting device in which a rope or chain is passed around a pair of blocks containing one or more pulleys. The upper block is secured overhead and the lower block supports the load, the effort being applied to the free end of the rope or chain.

blockboard ('blɒk,bɔːd) *n.* a type of plywood in which soft wood strips are bonded together and sandwiched between two layers of veneer.

blockbuster ('blɒk,bʌstə) *n. Informal.* **1.** a large bomb used to demolish extensive areas or strengthened targets. **2.** a very forceful, successful person, thing, etc.

blockbusting ('blɒk,bʌstɪŋ) *n. U.S. informal.* the act or practice of inducing the sale of property cheaply by exploiting the owners' fears of lower prices if racial minorities live in the area.

block capital *n.* another term for **block letter** (sense 2).

block diagram *n.* **1.** a diagram showing the interconnections between the parts of an industrial process. **2.** a three-dimensional drawing representing a block of the earth's crust, showing geological structure. **3.** *Computer technol.* a diagram showing the interconnections between electronic components or parts of a program.

blocked (blɒkt) *adj. Slang.* functionally impeded by amphetamine.

blocked shoe *n.* a dancing shoe with a stiffened toe that enables a ballet dancer to dance on the tips of the toes.

block grant *n.* (in Britain) an annual grant made by the government to a local authority to help to pay for the public services it provides, such as health, education, and housing.

blockhead ('blɒk,hɛd) *n. Derogatory.* a stupid person. —'**block,headed** *adj.* —'**block,headedly** *adv.* —'**block,headedness** *n.*

blockhouse ('blɒk,haʊs) *n.* **1.** (formerly) a wooden fortification with ports or loopholes for defensive fire, observation, etc. **2.** a concrete structure strengthened to give protection against enemy fire, with apertures to allow defensive gunfire. **3.** a building constructed of logs or squared timber. **4.** a reinforced concrete building close to a rocket-launching site for protecting personnel and equipment during launching.

block in *vb.* (*tr., adv.*) to sketch in outline, with little detail.

blocking ('blɒkɪŋ) *n. Electronics.* the interruption of anode current in a valve because of the application of a high negative voltage to the grid.

blockish ('blɒkɪʃ) *adj.* lacking vivacity or imagination; stupid. —'**blockishly** *adv.* —'**blockishness** *n.*

block lava *n.* volcanic lava occurring as rough-surfaced jagged blocks.

block letter *n.* **1.** *Printing.* a less common name for **sans serif.** **2.** Also called: **block capital.** a plain capital letter.

block out *vb.* (*tr., adv.*) **1.** to plan or describe (something) in a general fashion. **2.** to prevent the entry or consideration of (something). **3.** *Photography, printing.* to mask part of (a negative), in order that light may not pass through it.

block plane *n.* a carpenter's small plane used to cut across the end grain of wood.

block printing *n.* printing from hand engraved or carved blocks of wood or linoleum.

block release *n. Brit.* the release of industrial trainees from work for study at a college for several weeks.

block sampling *n.* the selection of a corpus for statistical literary analysis by random selection of a starting point and consideration of the continuous passage following it. Compare **spread sampling.**

block tin *n.* pure tin, esp. when cast into ingots.

block vote *n. Brit.* (at a conference, esp. of trade unionists) the system whereby each delegate's vote has a value in proportion to the number of people he represents.

bloke (bləʊk) *n.* **1.** *Brit.* an informal word for **man.** **2. the Old Bloke.** *Austral. informal.* God. [C19: from Shelta]

blokeish *or* **blokish** ('bləʊkɪʃ) *adj. Informal, sometimes derogatory.* denoting or exhibiting the characteristics believed typical of an ordinary man. —'**blokeishness** *or* '**blokishness** *n.*

blonde *or* (*masc.*) **blond** (blɒnd) *adj.* **1.** (of hair) of a light colour; fair. **2.** (of a person, people or a race) having fair hair, a light complexion, and, typically, blue or grey eyes. **3.** (of soft furnishings, wood, etc.) light in colour. ~*n.* **4.** a person having light-coloured hair and skin. **5.** Also called: **blonde lace.** a French pillow lace, originally of unbleached cream-coloured Chinese silk, later of bleached or black-dyed silk. [C15: from Old French *blond* (fem. *blonde*), probably of Germanic origin; related to Late Latin *blundus* yellow, Italian *biondo,* Spanish *blondo*] —'**blondeness** *or* '**blondness** *n.*

blood (blʌd) *n.* **1.** a reddish fluid in vertebrates that is pumped by the heart through the arteries and veins, supplies tissues with nutrients, oxygen, etc., and removes waste products. It consists of a fluid (see **blood plasma**) containing cells (erythrocytes and leucocytes) and platelets. **2.** a similar fluid in such invertebrates as annelids and arthropods. **3.** bloodshed, esp. when resulting in murder. **4.** the guilt or responsibility for killing or injuring (esp. in the phrase **to have blood on one's hands** *or* **head**). **5.** life itself; lifeblood. **6.** relationship through being of the same family, race, or kind; kinship. **7. flesh and blood. a.** near kindred or kinship, esp. that between a parent and child. **b.** human nature (esp. in the phrase **it's more than flesh and blood can stand**). **8.** ethnic or national descent: *of Spanish blood.* **9. in one's blood.** as a natural or inherited characteristic or talent. **10. the blood.** royal or noble descent: *a prince of the blood.* **11.** temperament; disposition; temper. **12. a.** good or pure breeding; pedigree. **b.** (*as modifier*): *blood horses.* **13.** people viewed as members of a group, esp. as an invigorating force (in the phrases **new blood, young blood**). **14.** *Chiefly Brit., rare.* a dashing young man; dandy; rake. **15.** the sensual or carnal nature of man. **16.** *Obsolete.* one of the four bodily humours. See **humour** (sense 8). **17. bad blood.** hatred; ill feeling. **18. blood is thicker than water.** family duties and loyalty outweigh other ties. **19. have** *or* **get one's blood up.** to be or cause to be angry or inflamed. **20. in cold blood.** showing no passion; deliberately; ruthlessly. **21. make one's blood boil.** to cause to be angry or indignant. **22. make one's blood run cold.** to fill with horror. ~*vb.* (*tr.*) **23.** *Hunting.* to cause (young hounds) to taste the blood of a freshly killed quarry and so become keen to hunt. **24.** *Hunting.* to smear the cheeks or forehead of (a person) with the blood of the kill as an initiation in hunting. **25.** to initiate (a person) to war. [Old English *blōd;* related to Old Norse *blōth,* Old High German *bluot*]

blood-and-thunder *adj.* denoting or relating to a melodramatic adventure story.

blood bank *n.* a place where whole blood or blood plasma is stored until required in transfusion.

blood bath *n.* indiscriminate slaughter; a massacre.

blood brother *n.* **1.** a brother by birth. **2.** a man or boy who has sworn to treat another as his brother, often in a ceremony in which their blood is mingled.

blood cell *n.* any of the cells that circulate in the blood. See **erythrocyte, leucocyte.**

blood count *n.* determination of the number of red and white blood corpuscles in a specific sample of blood. See **haemocytometer.**

bloodcurdling ('blʌdˌkɜːdlɪŋ) *adj.* terrifying; horrifying. —'**bloodˌcurdlingly** *adv.*

blood donor *n.* a person who gives his blood to be used for transfusion.

blood doping *n.* the illegal practice of removing a quantity of blood from an athlete long before a race and reinjecting it shortly before a race, so boosting oxygenation of the blood.

blood-drop emlets ('ɛmlɪts) *n.* (*functioning as sing.*) a Chilean scrophulariaceous plant, *Mimulus luteus,* naturalized in central Europe, having red-spotted yellow flowers. See also **monkey flower, musk** (sense 3).

blooded ('blʌdɪd) *adj.* **1.** (of horses, cattle, etc.) of good breeding. **2.** (*in combination*) having blood or temperament as specified: *hot-blooded, cold-blooded, warm-blooded, red-blooded, blue-blooded.*

blood feud *n.* a feud in which the members of hostile families or clans murder each other.

bloodfin ('blʌdˌfɪn) *n.* a silvery red-finned South American freshwater fish, *Aphyocharax rubripinnis:* a popular aquarium fish: family *Characidae* (characins).

blood fluke *n.* any parasitic flatworm, such as a schistosome, that lives in the blood vessels of man and other vertebrates: class *Digenea.* See also **trematode.**

blood group *n.* any one of the various groups into which human blood is classified on the basis of its agglutinogens. Also called: **blood type.**

blood guilt *n.* guilt of murder or shedding blood. —'**blood-ˌguilty** *adj.* —'**blood-ˌguiltiness** *n.*

blood heat *n.* the normal temperature of the human body, 98.4°F or 37°C.

bloodhound ('blʌdˌhaʊnd) *n.* **1.** a large breed of hound having a smooth glossy coat of red, tan, or black and loose wrinkled skin on its head: formerly much used in tracking and police work. **2.** *Informal.* a detective.

bloodhouse ('blʌdˌhaʊs) *n. Austral. slang.* a public house with an unsavoury reputation.

bloodless ('blʌdlɪs) *adj.* **1.** without blood. **2.** conducted without violence (esp. in the phrase **bloodless revolution).** **3.** anaemic-looking; pale. **4.** lacking vitality; lifeless. **5.** lacking in emotion; cold; unfeeling. —'**bloodlessly** *adv.* —'**bloodlessness** *n.*

blood-letting ('blʌdˌlɛtɪŋ) *n.* **1.** the therapeutic removal of blood, as in relieving congestive heart failure. See also **phlebotomy.** **2.** bloodshed, esp. in a blood feud.

bloodline ('blʌdˌlaɪn) *n.* all the members of a family group over generations, esp. regarding characteristics common to that group; pedigree.

bloodmobile ('blʌdməˌbiːl) *n. U.S.* a motor vehicle equipped for collecting blood from donors.

blood money *n.* **1.** compensation paid to the relatives of a murdered person. **2.** money paid to a hired murderer. **3.** a reward for information about a criminal, esp. a murderer.

blood orange *n.* a variety of orange all or part of the pulp of which is dark red when ripe.

blood plasma *n.* **1.** the pale yellow fluid portion of the blood; blood from which blood cells and platelets have been removed. **2.** a sterilized preparation of this fluid that is used in transfusions.

blood poisoning *n.* a nontechnical term for **septicaemia.**

blood pressure *n.* the pressure exerted by the blood on the inner walls of the arteries, being relative to the elasticity and diameter of the vessels and the force of the heartbeat.

blood pudding *n.* another name for **black pudding.**

blood red *n.* **a.** a deep red colour. **b.** (*as adj.*): *blood-red roses.*

blood relation *or* **relative** *n.* a person related to another by birth, as distinct from one related by marriage.

bloodroot ('blʌdˌruːt) *n.* **1.** Also called: **red puccoon.** a North American papaveraceous plant, *Sanguinaria canadensis,* having a single whitish flower and a fleshy red root that yields a red dye. **2.** another name for **tormentil.**

blood sausage *n.* another term (esp. U.S. and Canadian) for **black pudding.**

blood serum *n.* blood plasma from which the clotting factors have been removed.

bloodshed ('blʌdˌʃɛd) *n.* slaughter; killing.

bloodshot ('blʌdˌʃɒt) *adj.* (of an eye) inflamed.

blood sport *n.* any sport involving the killing of an animal, esp. hunting.

bloodstain ('blʌdˌsteɪn) *n.* a dark discoloration caused by blood, esp. dried blood. —'**bloodˌstained** *adj.*

bloodstock ('blʌdˌstɒk) *n.* thoroughbred horses, esp. those bred for racing.

bloodstock industry *n.* the breeding and training of racehorses.

bloodstone ('blʌdˌstəʊn) *n.* a dark-green variety of chalcedony with red spots: used as a gemstone. Also called: **heliotrope.**

bloodstream ('blʌdˌstriːm) *n.* the flow of blood through the vessels of a living body.

blood substitute *n.* a mixture of plasma, albumin, and dextran used to replace lost blood to increase the blood volume.

bloodsucker ('blʌdˌsʌkə) *n.* **1.** an animal that sucks blood, esp. a leech or mosquito. **2.** a person or thing that preys upon another person, esp. by extorting money.

blood sugar *n. Med.* the glucose circulating in the blood: the normal fasting level is between 3.9 and 5.6 mmol/l.

blood test *n.* analysis of a blood sample to determine blood group, alcohol level, etc.

bloodthirsty ('blʌdˌθɜːstɪ) *adj.* **-thirstier, -thirstiest.** **1.** murderous; cruel. **2.** taking pleasure in bloodshed or violence. **3.** describing or depicting killing and violence; gruesome: *a bloodthirsty film.* —'**bloodˌthirstily** *adv.* —'**bloodˌthirstiness** *n.*

blood type *n.* another name for **blood group.**

blood vessel *n.* an artery, capillary, or vein.

blood volume *n. Med.* the total quantity of blood in the body.

bloodwood ('blʌdˌwʊd) *n.* any of several species of Australian eucalyptus that exude a red sap.

bloodworm ('blʌdˌwɜːm) *n.* **1.** the red wormlike aquatic larva of the midge, *Chironomus plumosus,* which lives at the bottom of stagnant pools and ditches. **2.** a freshwater oligochaete tubifex worm. **3.** any of several small reddish worms used as angling bait.

bloody ('blʌdɪ) *adj.* **bloodier, bloodiest.** **1.** covered or stained with blood. **2.** resembling or composed of blood. **3.** marked by much killing and bloodshed: *a bloody war.* **4.** cruel or murderous: *a bloody tyrant.* **5.** of a deep red colour; blood-red. ~*adv., adj.* **6.** *Slang, chiefly Brit.* (intensifier): *a bloody fool; bloody fine food.* ~*vb.* **bloodies, bloodying, bloodied.** **7.** (*tr.*) to stain with blood. —'**bloodily** *adv.* —'**bloodiness** *n.*

Bloody Mary *n.* a drink consisting of tomato juice and vodka.

bloody-minded *adj. Brit. informal.* deliberately obstructive and unhelpful.

bloody-nosed beetle *n.* a beetle, *Timarcha tenebricosa,* that exudes bright red blood when alarmed: family *Chrysomelidae.*

bloom[1] (bluːm) *n.* **1.** a blossom on a flowering plant; a flower. **2.** the state, time, or period when flowers open (esp. in the phrases **in bloom, in full bloom).** **3.** open flowers collectively: *a tree covered with bloom.* **4.** a healthy, vigorous, or flourishing condition; prime (esp. in the phrase **the bloom of youth).** **5.** youthful or healthy rosiness in the cheeks or face; glow. **6.** a fine whitish coating on the surface of fruits, leaves, etc., consisting of minute grains of a waxy substance. **7.** any coating similar in appearance, such as that on new coins. **8.** *Ecology.* a visible increase in the algal constituent of plankton, which may be seasonal or due to excessive organic pollution. **9.** Also called: **chill.** a dull area formed on the surface of gloss paint, lacquer, or varnish. ~*vb.* (*mainly intr.*) **10.** (of flowers) to open; come into flower. **11.** to bear flowers; blossom. **12.** to flourish or grow. **13.** to be in a healthy, glowing, or flourishing condition. **14.** (*tr.*) *Physics.* to coat (a lens) with a thin layer of a substance, often magnesium fluoride, to eliminate surface reflection. [C13: of Germanic origin; compare Old Norse *blōm* flower, Old High German *bluomo,* Middle Dutch *bloeme;* see BLOW[3]] —'**bloomy** *adj.*

bloom[2] (bluːm) *n.* **1.** a rectangular mass of metal obtained by rolling or forging a cast ingot. See also **billet**[2] (sense 2). ~*vb.* **2.** (*tr.*) to convert (an ingot) into a bloom by rolling or forging. [Old English *blōma* lump of metal]

bloomed (bluːmd) *adj. Photog., optics.* (of a lens) coated with a thin film of magnesium fluoride or some other substance to reduce the amount of light lost by reflection. Also: **coated.**

bloomer[1] ('bluːmə) *n.* a plant that flowers, esp. in a specified way: *a night bloomer.*

bloomer[2] ('bluːmə) *n. Brit. informal.* a stupid mistake; blunder. [C20: from BLOOMING]

bloomer[3] ('bluːmə) *n. Brit.* a medium-sized loaf, baked on the sole of the oven, glazed and notched on top. [C20: of uncertain origin]

bloomers ('bluːməz) *pl. n.* **1.** *Informal.* women's or girls' baggy knickers. **2.** (formerly) loose trousers gathered at the knee worn by women for cycling and athletics. **3.** *History.* Also called: **rational dress.** long loose trousers gathered at the ankle and worn under a shorter skirt. [from *bloomer,* a garment introduced in about 1850 and publicized by Mrs A. *Bloomer* (1818–94), U.S. social reformer]

bloomery ('bluːmərɪ) *n., pl.* **-eries.** a place in which malleable iron is produced directly from iron ore.

blooming ('bluːmɪŋ) *adv., adj. Brit. informal.* (intensifier): *a blooming genius; blooming painful.* [C19: euphemistic for BLOODY]

Bloomsbury ('bluːmzbərɪ, -brɪ) *~adj.* relating to or characteristic of the a group of writers, artists, and intellectuals living and working in and around Bloomsbury in London from about 1907 to 1930: *a Bloomsbury writer.*

blooper ('bluːpə) *n. Informal, chiefly U.S. and Canadian.* a blunder; bloomer; stupid mistake. [C20: from *bloop* (imitative of an embarrassing sound) + -ER[1]]

blossom ('blɒsəm) *n.* **1.** the flower or flowers of a plant, esp. conspicuous flowers producing edible fruit. **2.** the time or period of flowering (esp. in the phrases **in blossom, in full blossom**). *~vb. (intr.)* **3.** (of plants) to come into flower. **4.** to develop or come to a promising stage: *youth had blossomed into maturity.* [Old English *blōstm;* related to Middle Low German *blōsem,* Latin *flōs* flower] —'**blossoming** *n., adj.* —'**blossomless** *adj.* —'**blossomy** *adj.*

blot[1] (blɒt) *n.* **1.** a stain or spot of ink, paint, dirt, etc. **2.** something that spoils or detracts from the beauty or worth of something. **3.** a blemish or stain on one's character or reputation. *~vb.* **blots, blotting, blotted. 4.** (of ink, dye, etc.) to form spots or blobs on (a material) or (of a person) to cause such spots or blobs to form on (a material). **5. blot one's copybook.** *Informal.* to spoil one's reputation by making a mistake, offending against social customs, etc. **6.** *(intr.)* to stain or become stained or spotted. **7.** *(tr.)* to cause a blemish in or on; disgrace. **8.** to soak up (excess ink, etc.) by using blotting paper or some other absorbent material. **9.** (of blotting paper or some other absorbent material) to absorb (excess ink, etc.). **10.** *(tr.;* often foll. by *out)* **a.** to darken or hide completely; obscure; obliterate. **b.** to destroy; annihilate. [C14: probably of Germanic origin; compare Middle Dutch *bluyster* BLISTER]

blot[2] (blɒt) *n.* **1.** *Backgammon.* a man exposed by being placed alone on a point and therefore able to be taken by the other player. **2.** *Archaic.* a weak spot. [C16: perhaps from Middle Dutch *bloot* poor]

blot analysis *n. Biochem.* a technique for analysing biological molecules, such as proteins (**Western blot analysis**), DNA (**Southern blot analysis**), and RNA (**Northern blot analysis**), involving their separation by gel electrophoresis, transfer to a nitrocellulose sheet, and subsequent analysis by autoradiography. Also called: **blotting.**

blotch (blɒtʃ) *n.* **1.** an irregular spot or discoloration, esp. a dark and relatively large one such as an ink stain. *~vb.* **2.** to become or cause to become marked by such discoloration. **3.** *(intr.)* (of a pen or ink) to write or flow unevenly in blotches. [C17: probably from BOTCH, influenced by BLOT[1]] —'**blotchy** *adj.* —'**blotchily** *adv.* —'**blotchiness** *n.*

blotter ('blɒtə) *n.* **1.** something used to absorb excess ink or other liquid, esp. a sheet of blotting paper with a firm backing. **2.** *U.S.* a daily record of events, such as arrests, in a police station (esp. in the phrase **police blotter**).

blotting paper *n.* a soft absorbent unsized paper, used esp. for soaking up surplus ink.

blotto ('blɒtəʊ) *adj. Slang.* unconscious, esp. through drunkenness. [C20: from BLOT[1] (vb.); compare *blot out*]

blouse (blaʊz) *n.* **1.** a woman's shirtlike garment made of cotton, nylon, etc. **2.** a loose-fitting smocklike garment, often knee length and belted, worn esp. by E European peasants. **3.** a loose-fitting waist-length belted jacket worn by soldiers. *~vb.* **4.** to hang or make so as to hang in full loose folds. [C19: from French, of unknown origin]

blouson ('bluːzɒn) *n.* a short jacket or top having the shape of a blouse. [C20: French]

blow[1] (bləʊ) *vb.* **blows, blowing, blew, blown. 1.** (of a current of air, the wind, etc.) to be or cause to be in motion. **2.** *(intr.)* to move or be carried by or as if by wind or air: *a feather blew in through the window.* **3.** to expel (air, cigarette smoke, etc.) through the mouth or nose. **4.** to force or cause (air, dust, etc.) to move (into, in, over, etc.) by using an instrument or by expelling breath. **5.** *(intr.)* to breathe hard; pant. **6.** (sometimes foll. by *up)* to inflate with air or the breath. **7.** *(intr.)* (of wind, a storm, etc.) to make a roaring or whistling sound. **8.** to cause (a whistle, siren, etc.) to sound by forcing air into it, as a signal, or (of a whistle, etc.) to sound thus. **9.** *(tr.)* to force air from the lungs through (the nose) to clear out mucus or obstructing matter. **10.** (often foll. by *up, down, in,* etc.) to explode, break, or disintegrate completely: *the bridge blew down in the gale.* **11.** *Electronics.* to burn out (a fuse, valve, etc.) because of excessive current or (of a fuse, valve, etc.) to burn out. **12. blow a fuse.** *Slang, chiefly U.S.* to lose one's temper. **13.** *(intr.)* (of a whale) to spout water or air from the lungs. **14.** *(tr.)* to wind (a horse) by making it run excessively. **15.** to cause (a wind instrument) to sound by forcing one's breath into the mouthpiece, or (of such an instrument) to sound in this way. **16.** *(intr.) Jazz slang.* to play in a jam session. **17.** *(intr.)* (of flies) to lay eggs (in). **18.** to shape (glass, ornaments, etc.) by forcing air or gas through the material when molten. **19.** *(intr.) Chiefly Scot., Austral., and N.Z.* to boast or brag. **20.** *(tr.) Slang.* **a.** to spend (money) freely. **b.** *U.S.* to treat or entertain. **21.** *(tr.) Slang.* to use (an opportunity) ineffectively. **22.** *Slang.* to go suddenly away (from). **23.** *(tr.) Slang.* to expose or betray (a person or thing meant to be kept secret). **24.** *(tr.) U.S. slang.* to inhale (a drug). **25.** *(intr.) Slang.* to masturbate. **26.** (past participle: **blowed**). *Informal.* another word for **damn** (esp. in the phrases **I'll be blowed, blow it! blow me down!**). **27.** *Draughts.* another word for **huff** (sense 4). **28. blow hot and cold.** to vacillate. **29. blow a kiss** *or* **kisses.** to kiss one's hand, then blow across it as if to carry the kiss through the air to another person. **30. blow one's own trumpet.** to boast of one's own skills or good qualities. **31. blow someone's mind.** *Slang.* **a.** (of a drug, esp. LSD) to alter someone's mental state. **b.** to astound or surprise someone. **32. blow one's top** *or* (esp. U.S. and Canadian) **lid** *or* **stack.** *Informal.* to lose one's temper. *~n.* **33.** the act or an instance of blowing. **34.** the sound produced by blowing. **35.** a blast of air or wind. **36.** *Metallurgy.* **a.** a stage in the Bessemer process in which air is blasted upwards through molten pig iron. **b.** the quantity of metal treated in a Bessemer converter. **37.** *Mining.* **a.** a rush of air into a mine. **b.** the collapse of a mine roof. **38.** *Jazz slang.* a jam session. **39. a.** *Brit.* a slang name for **cannabis** (sense 2). **b.** *U.S.* a slang name for **cocaine.** ~See also **blow away, blow in, blow into, blow off, blow on, blow out, blow over, blow through, blow up.** [Old English *blāwan,* related to Old Norse *blǣr* gust of wind, Old High German *blāen,* Latin *flāre*]

blow[2] (bləʊ) *n.* **1.** a powerful or heavy stroke with the fist, a weapon, etc. **2. at one** *or* **a blow.** by or with only one action; all at one time. **3.** a sudden setback; unfortunate event: *to come as a blow.* **4. come to blows. a.** to fight. **b.** to result in a fight. **5.** an attacking action: *a blow for freedom.* **6.** *Austral. and N.Z.* a stroke of the shears in sheep-shearing. [C15: probably of Germanic origin; compare Old High German *bliuwan* to beat]

blow[3] (bləʊ) *vb.* **blows, blowing, blew, blown. 1.** *(intr.)* (of a plant or flower) to blossom or open out. **2.** *(tr.)* to produce (flowers). *~n.* **3.** a mass of blossoms. **4.** the state or period of blossoming (esp. in the phrase **in full blow**). [Old English *blōwan;* related to Old Frisian *blōia* to bloom, Old High German *bluoen,* Latin *flōs* flower; see BLOOM[1]]

blow away *vb. (tr., adv.) Slang, chiefly U.S.* **1.** to kill (someone) by shooting. **2.** to defeat decisively.

blowback ('bləʊˌbæk) *n.* **1.** the escape to the rear of gases formed during the firing of a weapon or in a boiler, internal-combustion engine, etc. **2.** the action of a light automatic weapon in which the expanding gases of the propellant force back the bolt, thus reloading the weapon.

blow-by-blow *adj. (prenominal)* explained in great detail: *a blow-by-blow account of the argument.*

blowdown ('bləʊˌdaʊn) *n.* an accident in a nuclear reactor in which a cooling pipe bursts causing the loss of essential coolant.

blow-dry *vb.* **-dries, -drying, -dried.** *(tr.)* **1.** to style (one's own or somebody else's hair) while drying it with a hand-held hair dryer. *~n.* **2.** this method of styling the hair.

blower ('bləʊə) *n.* **1.** a mechanical device, such as a fan, that blows. **2.** a low-pressure compressor, esp. in a furnace or internal-combustion engine. See also **supercharger. 3.** an informal name for **telephone. 4.** an informal name for **speaking tube. 5.** an informal name for a **whale. 6.** *Mining.* a discharge of firedamp from a crevice.

blowfish ('bləʊˌfɪʃ) *n., pl.* **-fish** *or* **-fishes.** a popular name for **puffer** (sense 2).

blowfly ('bləʊˌflaɪ) *n., pl.* **-flies.** any of various dipterous flies of the genus *Calliphora* and related genera that lay their eggs in rotting meat, dung, carrion, and open wounds: family *Calliphoridae.* Also called: **bluebottle.**

blowgun ('bləʊˌgʌn) *n.* the U.S. word for **blowpipe** (sense 1).

blowhard ('bləʊˌhɑːd) *Informal. ~n.* **1.** a boastful person. *~adj.* **2.** blustering or boastful.

blowhole ('bləʊˌhəʊl) *n.* **1.** the nostril, paired or single, of whales, situated far back on the skull. **2.** a hole in ice through which whales, seals, etc., breathe. **3. a.** a vent for air or gas, esp. to release fumes from a tunnel, passage, etc. **b.** *N.Z.* a hole emitting gas or steam in a volcanic region. **4.** a bubble-like defect in an ingot resulting from gas being trapped during solidification. **5.** *Geology.* a hole in a cliff top leading to a sea cave through which air is forced by the action of the sea.

blowie ('bləʊɪ) *n. Austral. informal.* a blowfly.

blow in *vb. (intr., adv.) Informal.* to arrive or enter suddenly.

blow-in *n. Austral. informal.* an unwelcome newcomer or stranger.

blow into *vb. (intr., prep.) Informal.* to arrive in or enter (a room, etc.) suddenly.

blow job *n. Taboo.* a slang term for **fellatio.**

blowlamp ('bləʊˌlæmp) *n.* a small burner that produces a very hot flame, used to remove old paint, melt soft metal, etc. U.S. and Canadian name: **blowtorch.**

blow moulding *n.* a process for moulding single-piece plastic objects in which a thermoplastic is extruded into a split mould and blown against its sides.

blown (bləʊn) *vb.* the past participle of **blow**[1] and **blow**[3].

blow off *vb. (adv.)* **1.** to permit (a gas under pressure, esp. steam) to be released. **2.** *(intr.) Brit. slang.* to emit wind noisily from the anus. **3. blow off steam.** See **let off** (sense 7). *~n.* **blow-off. 4.** a discharge of a surplus fluid, such as steam, under pressure. **5.** a device through which such a discharge is made.

blow on *vb. (intr., prep.)* to defame or discredit (a person).

blow out *vb. (adv.)* **1.** to extinguish (a flame, candle, etc.) or (of a flame, candle, etc.) to become extinguished. **2.** *(intr.)* (of a tyre) to puncture suddenly, esp. at high speed. **3.** *(intr.)* (of a fuse) to melt suddenly. **4.** *(tr.; often reflexive)* to diminish or use up the energy of: *the storm blew itself out.* **5.** (*intr.*) (of an oil or gas well) to lose oil or gas in an uncontrolled manner. **6.** (*tr.*) *Slang.* to cancel: *the band had to blow out the gig.* **7. blow one's brains out.** to kill oneself by shooting oneself in the head. ~*n.* **blow-out. 8.** the sudden melting of an electrical fuse. **9.** a sudden burst in a tyre. **10.** the uncontrolled escape of oil or gas from an oil or gas well. **11.** the failure of a jet engine, esp. when in flight. **12.** *Slang.* a large filling meal or lavish entertainment.

blow over *vb.* (*intr., adv.*) **1.** to cease or be finished: *the storm blew over.* **2.** to be forgotten: *the scandal will blow over.*

blowpipe ('bləʊˌpaɪp) *n.* **1.** a long tube from which pellets, poisoned darts, etc., are shot by blowing. U.S. word: **blowgun. 2.** Also called: **blow tube.** a tube for blowing air or oxygen into a flame to intensify its heat and direct it onto a small area. **3.** a long narrow iron pipe used to gather molten glass and blow it into shape.

blow through *vb.* (*intr., adv.*) *Austral. informal.* to leave; make off.

blowtorch ('bləʊˌtɔːtʃ) *n.* the U.S. and Canadian name for **blowlamp.**

blow up *vb.* (*adv.*) **1.** to explode or cause to explode. **2.** (*tr.*) to increase the importance of (something): *they blew the whole affair up.* **3.** (*intr.*) to come into consideration: *we lived well enough before this thing blew up.* **4.** (*intr.*) to come into existence with sudden force: *a storm had blown up.* **5.** *Informal.* to lose one's temper (with a person). **6.** (*tr.*) *Informal.* to reprimand (someone). **7.** (*tr.*) *Informal.* to enlarge the size or detail of (a photograph). ~*n.* **blow-up. 8.** an explosion. **9.** *Informal.* an enlarged photograph or part of a photograph. **10.** *Informal.* a fit of temper or argument. **11.** Also called: **blowing up.** *Informal.* a reprimand.

blowy ('bləʊɪ) *adj.* **blowier, blowiest.** another word for **windy** (sense 1).

blowzy *or* **blowsy** ('blaʊzɪ) *adj.* **blowzier, blowziest** *or* **blowsier, blowsiest. 1.** (esp. of a woman) untidy in appearance; slovenly or sluttish. **2.** (of a woman) ruddy in complexion; red-faced. [C18: from dialect *blowze* beggar girl, of unknown origin] —'**blowzily** *or* '**blowsily** *adv.* —'**blowziness** *or* '**blowsiness** *n.*

blub (blʌb) *vb.* **blubs, blubbing, blubbed.** *Brit.* a slang word for **blubber** (senses 1-3).

blubber ('blʌbə) *vb.* **1.** to sob without restraint. **2.** to utter while sobbing. **3.** (*tr.*) to make (the face) wet and swollen or disfigured by crying. ~*n.* **4.** a thick insulating layer of fatty tissue below the skin of aquatic mammals such as the whale: used by man as a source of oil. **5.** *Informal.* excessive and flabby body fat. **6.** the act or an instance of weeping without restraint. ~*adj.* **7.** (*often in combination*) swollen or fleshy: *blubber-faced; blubber-lips.* [C12: perhaps from Low German *blubbern* to BUBBLE, of imitative origin] —'**blubberer** *n.* —'**blubbery** *adj.*

blucher ('bluːkə, -tʃə) *n.* *Obsolete.* a high shoe with laces over the tongue. [C19: named after Gebhard von *Blücher* (1742–1819), Prussian field marshal]

bludge (blʌdʒ) *Austral. and N.Z. informal.* ~*vb.* **1.** (when *intr.*, often foll. by *on*) to scrounge from (someone). **2.** (*intr.*) to evade work. ~*n.* **3.** a very easy task; undemanding employment. [C19: back formation from slang *bludger* pimp, from BLUDGEON]

bludgeon ('blʌdʒən) *n.* **1.** a stout heavy club, typically thicker at one end. **2.** a person, line of argument, etc., that is effective but unsubtle. ~*vb.* (*tr.*) **3.** to hit or knock down with or as with a bludgeon. **4.** (often foll. by *into*) to force; bully; coerce: *they bludgeoned him into accepting the job.* [C18: of uncertain origin] —'**bludgeoner** *n.*

bludger ('blʌdʒə) *n.* *Austral. and N.Z. informal.* **1.** a person who scrounges. **2.** a person who avoids work. **3.** a person in authority regarded as ineffectual by those working under him.

blue (bluː) *n.* **1.** any of a group of colours, such as that of a clear unclouded sky, that have wavelengths in the range 490–445 nanometres. Blue is the complementary colour of yellow and with red and green forms a set of primary colours. **2.** a dye or pigment of any of these colours. **3.** blue cloth or clothing: *dressed in blue.* **4. a.** a sportsman who represents or has represented Oxford or Cambridge University and has the right to wear the university colour (dark blue for Oxford, light blue for Cambridge): *an Oxford blue.* **b.** the honour of so representing one's university. **5.** *Brit.* an informal name for **Tory. 6.** any of numerous small blue-winged butterflies of the genera *Lampides, Polyommatus,* etc.: family *Lycaenidae.* **7.** *Archaic.* short for **bluestocking. 8.** *Slang.* a policeman. **9.** *Archery.* a blue ring on a target, between the red and the black, scoring five points. **10.** a blue ball in snooker, etc. **11.** another name for **blueing. 12.** *Austral. and N.Z. slang.* an argument or fight: *he had a blue with a taxi driver.* **13.** Also: **bluey.** *Austral. and N.Z. informal.* a court summons, esp. for a traffic offence. **14.** *Austral. and N.Z. informal.* a mistake; error. **15. out of the blue.** apparently from nowhere; unexpectedly: *the opportunity came out of the blue.* **16. into the blue.** into the unknown or the far distance. ~*adj.* **bluer, bluest. 17.** of the colour blue. **18.** (of the flesh) having a purple tinge, as from cold or contusion. **19.** depressed, moody, or unhappy. **20.** dismal or depressing: *a blue day.* **21.** indecent, titillating, or pornographic: *blue films.* **22.** bluish in colour or having parts or marks that are bluish: *a blue fox; a blue whale.* **23.** *Rare.* aristocratic; noble; patrician: *a blue family.* See **blue blood.** ~*vb.* **blues, blueing** *or* **bluing, blued. 24.** to make, dye, or become blue. **25.** (*tr.*) to treat (laundry) with blueing. **26.** (*tr.*) *Slang.* to spend extravagantly or wastefully; squander. ~See also **blues.** [C13: from Old French *bleu,* of Germanic origin; compare Old Norse *blār,* Old High German *blāo,* Middle Dutch *blā;* related to Latin *flāvus* yellow] —'**bluely** *adv.* —'**blueness** *n.*

Blue (bluː) *n.* *Austral. informal.* a person with red hair.

blue baby *n.* a baby born with a bluish tinge to the skin because of lack of oxygen in the blood, esp. caused by a congenital defect of the heart.

blue bag *n.* (in Britain) **1.** a fabric bag for a barrister's robes. **2.** a small bag containing blueing for laundering.

bluebeard ('bluːˌbɪəd) *n.* a man who has had several wives. [named after a villain of European folklore who marries and murders several wives]

bluebeat ('bluːˌbiːt) *n.* a type of West Indian pop music of the 1960s; a precursor of reggae.

bluebell ('bluːˌbel) *n.* **1.** Also called: **wild** or **wood hyacinth.** a European liliaceous woodland plant, *Endymion* (or *Scilla*) *non-scriptus,* having a one-sided cluster of blue bell-shaped flowers. **2.** a Scot. name for **harebell. 3.** any of various other plants with blue bell-shaped flowers.

blueberry ('bluːbərɪ, -brɪ) *n., pl.* **-ries. 1.** Also called: **huckleberry.** any of several North American ericaceous shrubs of the genus *Vaccinium,* such as *V. pennsylvanicum,* that have blue-black edible berries with tiny seeds. See also **bilberry. 2. a.** the fruit of any of these plants. **b.** (*as modifier*): *blueberry pie.*

bluebill ('bluːˌbɪl) *n.* *U.S.* another name for **scaup.**

blue billy *n.* *N.Z.* an informal name for **dove prion.** [probably from the name *Billy*]

bluebird ('bluːˌbɜːd) *n.* **1.** any North American songbird of the genus *Sialia,* having a blue or partly blue plumage: subfamily *Turdinae* (thrushes). **2. fairy bluebird.** any songbird of the genus *Irena,* of S and SE Asia, having a blue-and-black plumage: family *Irenidae.* **3.** any of various other birds having a blue plumage.

blue blood *n.* royal or aristocratic descent. [C19: translation of Spanish *sangre azul*] —'**blue-'blooded** *adj.*

bluebonnet ('bluːˌbɒnɪt) *or* **bluecap** ('bluːˌkæp) *n.* other names for **Balmoral** (sense 3).

bluebook ('bluːˌbʊk) *n.* **1.** (in Britain) a government publication bound in a stiff blue paper cover: usually the report of a royal commission or a committee. **2.** *Informal, chiefly U.S.* a register of well-known people. **3.** (in Canada) an annual statement of government accounts.

bluebottle ('bluːˌbɒtᵊl) *n.* **1.** another name for the **blowfly. 2.** any of various blue-flowered plants, esp. the cornflower. **3.** *Brit.* an informal word for a **policeman. 4.** *Austral. and N.Z.* an informal name for **Portuguese man-of-war.**

blue buck *n.* another name for the **blaubok.**

blue cheese *n.* cheese containing a blue mould, esp. Stilton, Roquefort, or Danish blue. Also called (Austral., N.Z.): **blue vein.**

blue chip *n.* **1.** a gambling chip with the highest value. **2.** *Finance.* **a.** a stock considered reliable with respect to both dividend income and capital value. **3.** (*modifier*) denoting something considered to be a valuable asset.

blue cod *n.* a common marine spiny-finned food fish, *Parapercis colias,* of the sub-Antarctic waters of New Zealand, esp. at the Chatham Islands, which is greenish blue with brown marbling and inhabits rocky bottoms. Its smoked flesh is considered a delicacy. Also called: **rock cod, rawaru, pakirikiri, patutuki.**

blue-collar *adj.* of, relating to, or designating manual industrial workers: *a blue-collar union.* Compare **white-collar.**

blue devils *pl. n.* **1.** a fit of depression or melancholy. **2.** an attack of delirium tremens.

blue duck *n.* a mountain duck, *Hymenolaimus malacorhynchos,* of New Zealand having a mostly lead-blue plumage.

Blue Ensign *n.* an ensign having the Union Jack on a blue background at the upper corner of the vertical edge alongside the hoist: flown by Royal Navy auxiliary vessels, and, with some extra distinguishing mark or insignia, by certain yacht clubs. Compare **Red Ensign, White Ensign.**

blue-eyed boy *n.* *Informal, chiefly Brit.* the favourite or darling of a person or group. Usual U.S. equivalent: **fair-haired boy.**

blue-eyed grass *n.* any of various mainly North American iridaceous marsh plants of the genus *Sisyrinchium* that have grasslike leaves and small flat starlike blue flowers.

blue-eyed Mary *n.* a blue-flowered boraginaceous plant, *Omphalodes verna,* native to S Europe and cultivated in Britain.

blue-eyed soul *n.* *Informal.* soul music written and performed by White singers in a style derived from the blues.

bluefish ('bluːˌfɪʃ) *n., pl.* **-fish** *or* **-fishes. 1.** Also called: **snapper.** a bluish marine percoid food and game fish, *Pomatomus saltatrix,* related to the horse mackerel: family *Pomatomidae.* **2.** any of various other bluish fishes.

Blue Flag *n.* an award given to a seaside resort that meets EC standards of cleanliness of beaches and purity of water in bathing areas.

blue fox *n.* **1.** a variety of the arctic fox that has a pale grey winter coat and is bred for its fur. **2.** the fur of this animal.

blue funk *n.* *Slang.* a state of great terror or loss of nerve.

bluegill ('bluːˌgɪl) *n.* a common North American freshwater sunfish, *Lepomis macrochirus:* an important food and game fish.

blue goose *n.* a variety of the snow goose that has a bluish-grey body and white head and neck.
bluegrass ('bluːˌgrɑːs) *n.* **1.** any of several North American bluish-green grasses of the genus *Poa*, esp. *P. pratensis* (**Kentucky bluegrass**), grown for forage. **2.** a type of folk music originating in Kentucky, characterized by a simple harmonized accompaniment.
blue-green algae *pl. n.* microorganisms, formerly classified as algae but now regarded as bacteria, including nostoc, which contain a blue pigment in addition to chlorophyll.
blue ground *n. Mineralogy.* another name for **kimberlite.**
blue grouse *n.* a grouse, *Dendragapus obscurus,* of W North America, having a bluish-grey plumage with a black tail.
blue gum *n.* **1.** a tall fast-growing widely cultivated Australian myrtaceous tree, *Eucalyptus globulus,* having aromatic leaves containing a medicinal oil, bark that peels off in shreds, and hard timber. The juvenile leaves are bluish in colour. **2.** any of several other eucalyptus trees. ~See also **red gum** (sense 1).
blue heeler *n. Austral. and N.Z.* a cattle dog that controls cattle by biting their heels. Also called: **heeler.**
blueing *or* **bluing** ('bluːɪŋ) *n.* **1.** a blue material, such as indigo, used in laundering to counteract yellowing. **2.** the formation of a film of blue oxide on a steel surface.
bluejacket ('bluːˌdʒækɪt) *n.* a sailor in the Navy.
blue jay *n.* a common North American jay, *Cyanocitta cristata,* having bright blue plumage with greyish-white underparts.
blue john *n.* a blue or purple fibrous variety of fluorspar occurring only in Derbyshire: used for vases, etc.
blue laws *pl. n. U.S. history.* a number of repressive puritanical laws of the colonial period, forbidding any secular activity on Sundays.
blue lias *n.* a type of rock composed of alternating layers of bluish shale or clay and grey argillaceous limestone. See also **Lias.**
Blue Mantle *n.* one of the four pursuivants of the British College of Arms.
blue merle *n.* See **merle**[2].
blue moon *n.* **once in a blue moon.** *Informal.* very rarely; almost never.
blue mould *n.* **1.** Also called: **green mould.** any fungus of the genus *Penicillium* that forms a bluish mass on decaying food, leather, etc. **2.** any fungal disease of fruit trees characterized by necrosis and a bluish growth on the affected tissue: mostly caused by *Penicillium* species.
blue murder *n. Informal.* a great outcry, noise; horrible din (esp. in such phrases as **cry, howl, scream,** etc., **blue murder**).
bluenose ('bluːˌnəʊz) *n.* **1.** *U.S. slang.* a puritanical or prudish person. **2.** (*often cap.*) *Informal.* a native or inhabitant of Nova Scotia.
blue note *n. Jazz.* a flattened third or seventh, used frequently in the blues.
blue pencil *n.* **1.** deletion, alteration, or censorship of the contents of a book or other work. ~*vb.* **blue-pencil, -cils, -cilling, -cilled** *or U.S.* **-cils, -ciling, -ciled.** **2.** (*tr.*) to alter or delete parts of (a book, film, etc.), esp. to censor.
blue peter *n.* a signal flag of blue with a white square at the centre, displayed by a vessel about to leave port. [C19: from the name *Peter*]
blue pointer *n.* a large shark, *Isuropsis mako,* of Australian coastal waters, having a blue back and pointed snout.
blueprint ('bluːˌprɪnt) *n.* **1.** Also called: **cyanotype.** a photographic print of plans, technical drawings, etc., consisting of white lines on a blue background. **2.** an original plan or prototype that influences subsequent design or practice: *the Montessori method was the blueprint for education in the 1940s.* ~*vb.* **3.** (*tr.*) to make a blueprint of (a plan).
blue racer *n.* a long slender blackish-blue fast-moving colubrid snake, *Coluber constrictor flaviventris,* of the U.S.
blue riband *or* **ribband** *n.* **1.** (*sometimes caps.*) Also called (esp. U.S.) **blue ribbon.** the record for the fastest sea journey between two places, esp. (in the 1920s and 30s) for a passenger liner between New York and Southampton. **2. a.** the most distinguished achievement in any field. **b.** (*as modifier*): *the blue-riband event of the meeting.*
blue ribbon *n.* **1.** (in Britain) a badge of blue silk worn by members of the Order of the Garter. **2.** a badge awarded as the first prize in a competition. **3.** *U.S.* a badge worn by a member of a temperance society.
blue-ribbon jury *n.* a U.S. name for a **special jury.**
blue rinse *n.* **1.** a rinse for tinting grey hair a silvery-blue colour. ~*adj.* **blue-rinse.** **2.** denoting or typifying an elderly, well-groomed, socially active, and comparatively wealthy woman.
Blue Rod *n. Brit.* officer of the Order of St Michael and St George. Full title: **Gentleman Usher of the Blue Rod.**
blues (bluːz) *pl. n.* (*sometimes functioning as sing.*) **the.** **1.** a feeling of depression or deep unhappiness. **2.** a type of folk song originating among Black Americans at the beginning of the 20th century, usually employing a basic 12-bar chorus, the tonic, subdominant, and dominant chords, frequent minor intervals, and blue notes. —'**bluesy** *adj.*
Blues (bluːz) *pl. n.* **the.** *Brit.* the Royal Horse Guards.
blue schist *n.* a metamorphic rock formed under conditions of high pressure and relatively low temperature.
blue shift *n.* a shift in the spectral lines of a stellar spectrum towards the blue end of the visible region relative to the wavelengths of these lines in the terrestrial spectrum: thought to be a result of the **Doppler effect** caused by stars approaching the solar system. Compare **red shift.**
blue-sky *n.* (*modifier*) of or denoting theoretical research without regard to any future application of its result: *a blue-sky project.*
blue-sky law *n. U.S.* a state law regulating the trading of securities: intended to protect investors from fraud.
blue spruce *n.* a spruce tree, *Picea pungens glauca,* native to the Rocky Mountains of North America, having blue-green needle-like leaves. Also called: **balsam spruce.**
blue stain *n. Forestry.* a bluish discoloration of sapwood caused by growth of fungi.
bluestocking ('bluːˌstɒkɪŋ) *n. Usually disparaging.* a scholarly or intellectual woman. [from the blue worsted stockings worn by members of a C18 literary society]
bluestone ('bluːˌstəʊn) *n.* **1.** a blue-grey sandstone containing much clay, used for building and paving. **2.** the blue crystalline form of copper sulphate. **3.** a blue variety of basalt found in Australia and used as a building stone.
bluet ('bluːɪt) *n.* a North American rubiaceous plant, *Houstonia caerulea,* with small four-petalled blue flowers.
bluethroat ('bluːˌθrəʊt) *n.* a small brownish European songbird, *Cyanosylvia svecica,* related to the thrushes, the male of which has a blue throat: family *Muscicapidae.*
bluetit ('bluːˌtɪt) *n.* a common European tit, *Parus caeruleus,* having a blue crown, wings, and tail, yellow underparts, and a black and grey head.
bluetongue ('bluːˌtʌŋ) *n.* an Australian lizard, *Tiliqua scincoides,* having a cobalt-blue tongue.
blue vein *n. Austral. and N.Z.* another name for **blue cheese.**
blue vitriol *n.* the fully hydrated blue crystalline form of copper sulphate.
blueweed ('bluːˌwiːd) *n. U.S.* another name for **viper's bugloss.**
blue whale *n.* the largest mammal: a widely distributed bluish-grey whalebone whale, *Sibbaldus* (or *Balaenoptera*) *musculus,* closely related and similar to the rorquals: family *Balaenopteridae.* Also called: **sulphur-bottom.**
bluey ('bluːɪ) *n. Austral. informal.* **1.** a blanket. **2.** a swagman's bundle. **3. hump (one's) bluey.** to carry one's bundle; tramp. **4.** a variant of **blue** (sense 13). **5.** a cattle dog. [(for senses 1, 2, 5) C19: from BLUE (on account of their colour) + -Y[2]]
Bluey ('bluːɪ) *n.* a variant of **Blue.**
bluff[1] (blʌf) *vb.* **1.** to pretend to be confident about an uncertain issue or to have undisclosed resources, in order to influence or deter (someone). ~*n.* **2.** deliberate deception intended to create the impression of a stronger position or greater resources than one actually has. **3. call someone's bluff.** to challenge someone to give proof of his claims. [C19: originally U.S. poker-playing term, from Dutch *bluffen* to boast] —'**bluffer** *n.*
bluff[2] (blʌf) *n.* **1.** a steep promontory, bank, or cliff, esp. one formed by river erosion on the outside bend of a meander. **2.** *Canadian.* a clump of trees on the prairie; copse. ~*adj.* **3.** good-naturedly frank and hearty. **4.** (of a bank, cliff, etc.) presenting a steep broad face. [C17 (in the sense: nearly perpendicular): perhaps from Middle Dutch *blaf* broad] —'**bluffly** *adv.* —'**bluffness** *n.*
bluish *or* **blueish** ('bluːɪʃ) *adj.* somewhat blue. —'**bluishness** *or* '**blueishness** *n.*
blunder ('blʌndə) *n.* **1.** a stupid or clumsy mistake. **2.** a foolish tactless remark. ~*vb.* (*mainly intr.*) **3.** to make stupid or clumsy mistakes. **4.** to make foolish tactless remarks. **5.** (*often foll. by about, into,* etc.) to act clumsily; stumble: *he blundered into a situation he knew nothing about.* **6.** (*tr.*) to mismanage; botch. [C14: of Scandinavian origin; compare Old Norse *blunda* to close one's eyes, Norwegian dialect *blundra;* see BLIND] —'**blunderer** *n.* —'**blundering** *n., adj.* —'**blunderingly** *adv.*
blunderbuss ('blʌndəˌbʌs) *n.* **1.** an obsolete short musket with large bore and flared muzzle, used to scatter shot at short range. **2.** *Informal.* a clumsy unsubtle person. [C17: changed (through the influence of BLUNDER) from Dutch *donderbus;* from *donder* THUNDER + obsolete *bus* gun]
blunge (blʌndʒ) *vb.* (*tr.*) to mix (clay or a similar substance) with water in order to form a suspension for use in ceramics. [C19: probably from BLEND + PLUNGE]
blunger ('blʌndʒə) *n.* a large vat in which the contents, esp. clay and water, are mixed by rotating arms.
blunt (blʌnt) *adj.* **1.** (esp. of a knife or blade) lacking sharpness or keenness; dull. **2.** not having a sharp edge or point: *a blunt instrument.* **3.** (of people, manner of speaking, etc.) lacking refinement or subtlety; straightforward and uncomplicated. **4.** outspoken; direct and to the point: *a blunt Yorkshireman.* ~*vb.* (*tr.*) **5.** to make less sharp. **6.** to diminish the sensitivity or perception of; make dull. [C12: probably of Scandinavian origin; compare Old Norse *blundr* dozing, *blunda* to close one's eyes; see BLUNDER, BLIND] —'**bluntly** *adv.* —'**bluntness** *n.*
blur (blɜː) *vb.* **blurs, blurring, blurred.** **1.** to make or become vague or less distinct: *heat haze blurs the hills; education blurs class distinctions.* **2.** to smear or smudge. **3.** (*tr.*) to make (the judgment, memory, or perception) less clear; dim. ~*n.* **4.** some-

thing vague, hazy, or indistinct. **5.** a smear or smudge. [C16: perhaps variant of BLEAR] —**blurred** (blɜːd) *adj.* —**blurredly** (ˈblɜːrɪdlɪ, ˈblɜːd-) *adv.* —ˈ**blurredness** *n.* —ˈ**blurriness** *n.* —ˈ**blurry** *adj.*

blurb (blɜːb) *n.* a promotional description, as found on the jackets of books. [C20: coined by Gelett Burgess (1866–1951), U.S. humorist and illustrator]

blurt (blɜːt) *vb.* (*tr.*; often foll. by *out*) to utter suddenly and involuntarily. [C16: probably of imitative origin]

blush (blʌʃ) *vb.* **1.** (*intr.*) to become suddenly red in the face from embarrassment, shame, modesty, or guilt; redden. **2.** to make or become reddish or rosy. ~*n.* **3.** a sudden reddening of the face from embarrassment, shame, modesty, or guilt. **4.** a rosy glow: *the blush of a peach.* **5.** a reddish or pinkish tinge. **6.** a cloudy area on the surface of freshly applied gloss paint. **7. at first blush.** when first seen; as a first impression. [Old English *blȳscan;* related to *blȳsian* to burn, Middle Low German *blüsen* to light a fire] —ˈ**blushful** *adj.* —ˈ**blushing** *n., adj.* —ˈ**blushingly** *adv.*

blusher (ˈblʌʃə) *n.* a cosmetic applied to the face to give a rosy colour.

bluster (ˈblʌstə) *vb.* **1.** to speak or say loudly or boastfully. **2.** to act in a bullying way. **3.** (*tr.*, foll. by *into*) to force or attempt to force (a person) into doing something by behaving thus. **4.** (*intr.*) (of the wind) to be noisy or gusty. ~*n.* **5.** boisterous talk or action; swagger. **6.** empty threats or protests. **7.** a strong wind; gale. [C15: probably from Middle Low German *blüsteren* to storm, blow violently] —ˈ**blusterer** *n.* —ˈ**blustering** *n., adj.* —ˈ**blusteringly** *or* ˈ**blusterously** *adv.* —ˈ**blustery** *or* ˈ**blusterous** *adj.*

Blvd *abbrev. for* Boulevard.

B-lymphocyte *n.* a type of lymphocyte, originating in bone marrow, that produces antibodies. Also called: **B-cell.** See also **T-lymphocyte.**

bm *abbrev. for:* **1.** board measure. **2.** bowel movement.

BM *abbrev. for:* **1.** Bachelor of Medicine. **2.** *Surveying.* bench mark. **3.** British Museum.

BMA *abbrev. for* British Medical Association.

BMI *abbrev. for* Broadcast Music Incorporated.

BMJ *abbrev. for* British Medical Journal.

B-movie *n.* a film originally made (esp. in Hollywood in the 1940s and 50s) as a supporting film, now often considered as a genre in its own right.

BMR *abbrev. for* basal metabolic rate.

BMus *abbrev. for* Bachelor of Music.

BMX *abbrev. for:* **1.** bicycle motocross; stunt riding on rough ground or over an obstacle course on a bicycle. **2.** a bicycle designed for bicycle motocross.

bn *abbrev. for* billion.

Bn *abbrev. for:* **1.** Baron. **2.** Also: **bn** Battalion.

BNFL *abbrev. for* British Nuclear Fuels Limited.

bo *or* **boh** (bəʊ) *interj.* an exclamation uttered to startle or surprise someone, esp. a child in a game.

BO *abbrev. for:* **1.** *Informal.* body odour. **2.** box office.

b.o. *abbrev. for:* **1.** back order. **2.** branch office. **3.** broker's order. **4.** buyer's option.

B/O *abbrev. for:* **1.** *Book-keeping.* brought over. **2.** buyer's option.

boa (ˈbəʊə) *n.* **1.** any large nonvenomous snake of the family *Boidae,* most of which occur in Central and South America and the West Indies. They have vestigial hind limbs and kill their prey by constriction. **2.** a woman's long thin scarf, usually of feathers or fur. [C19: from New Latin, from Latin: a large Italian snake, water snake]

boab (ˈbəʊæb) *n. Austral.* short for **baobab.**

BOAC (formerly) *abbrev. for* British Overseas Airways Corporation.

boa constrictor *n.* a very large snake, *Constrictor constrictor,* of tropical America and the West Indies, that kills its prey by constriction: family *Boidae* (boas).

boak (bok, bəʊk) *vb., n.* a variant spelling of **boke.**

Boanerges (ˌbəʊəˈnɜːdʒiːz) *n.* a fiery preacher, esp. one with a powerful voice. [C17: from Hebrew *benē reghesh* sons of thunder]

boar (bɔː) *n.* **1.** an uncastrated male pig. **2.** See **wild boar.** [Old English *bār;* related to Old High German *bēr*]

board (bɔːd) *n.* **1.** a long wide flat relatively thin piece of sawn timber. **2. a.** a smaller flat piece of rigid material for a specific purpose: *ironing board.* **b.** (*in combination*): *breadboard; cheeseboard.* **3.** a person's food or meals, provided regularly for money or sometimes as payment for work done (esp. in the phrases **full board, board and lodging**). **4.** *Archaic.* a table, esp. one used for eating at, and esp. when laden with food. **5. a.** (*sometimes functioning as pl.*) a group of people who officially administer a company, trust, etc.: *a board of directors.* **b.** (*as modifier*): *a board meeting.* **6.** any other committee or council: *a board of interviewers.* **7. the boards.** (*pl.*) the acting profession; the stage. **8.** short for **blackboard, chessboard, notice board, printed circuit board** (see **printed circuit**), **springboard,** or **surfboard.** **9.** stiff cardboard or similar material covered with paper, cloth, etc., used for the outside covers of a book. **10.** a flat thin rectangular sheet of composite material, such as plasterboard or chipboard. **11.** *Chiefly U.S.* **a.** a list on which stock-exchange securities and their prices are posted. **b.** *Informal.* the stock exchange itself. **12.** *Nautical.* **a.** the side of a ship. **b.** the leg that a sailing vessel makes on a beat to windward. **13.** *Austral. and N.Z.* the part of the floor of a sheep-shearing shed, esp. a raised part, where the shearers work. **14.** *N.Z.* the killing floor of an abattoir or freezing works. **15. a.** any of various portable surfaces specially designed for indoor games such as chess, backgammon, etc. **b.** (*as modifier*): *board games.* **16. a.** a set of hands in duplicate bridge. **b.** a wooden or metal board containing four slots, or often nowadays, a plastic wallet, in which the four hands are placed so that the deal may be replayed with identical hands. **17.** the hull of a sailboard, usually made of plastic, to which the mast is jointed and on which a windsurfer stands. **18.** See **above board.** **19. go by the board.** to be in disuse, neglected, or lost: *in these days courtesy goes by the board.* **20. on board.** on or in a ship, boat, aeroplane, or other vehicle. **21. sweep the board. a.** (in gambling) to win all the cards or money. **b.** to win every event or prize in a contest. **22. take on board.** to accept (new ideas, situations, theories, etc.). ~*vb.* **23.** to go aboard (a vessel, train, aircraft, or other vehicle). **24.** *Nautical.* to come alongside (a vessel) before attacking or going aboard. **25.** to attack (a ship) by forcing one's way aboard. **26.** (*tr.*; often foll. by *up, in,* etc.) to cover or shut with boards. **27.** (*intr.*) to give or receive meals or meals and lodging in return for money or work. **28.** (sometimes foll. by *out*) to receive or arrange for (someone, esp. a child) to receive food and lodging away from home, usually in return for payment. [Old English *bord;* related to Old Norse *borth* ship's side, table, Old High German *bort* ship's side, Sanskrit *bardhaka* a cutting off] —ˈ**boardable** *adj.*

board-and-shingle *n. Caribbean.* a small peasant dwelling with wooden walls and a shingle roof.

board bridge *n.* another name for **duplicate bridge.**

boarder (ˈbɔːdə) *n.* **1.** *Brit.* a pupil who lives at school during term time. **2.** *U.S.* a child who lives away from its parents and is cared for by a person or organization receiving payment. **3.** another word for **lodger.** **4.** a person who boards a ship, esp. one who forces his way aboard in an attack: *stand by to repel boarders.*

board foot *n.* a unit of board measure: the cubic content of a piece of wood one foot square and one inch thick.

boarding (ˈbɔːdɪŋ) *n.* **1.** a structure of boards, such as a floor or fence. **2.** timber boards collectively. **3. a.** the act of embarking on an aircraft, train, ship, etc. **b.** (*as modifier*): *a boarding pass.* **4.** a process used in tanning to accentuate the natural grain of hides, in which the surface of a softened leather is lightly creased by folding grain to grain and the fold is worked to and fro across the leather.

boarding house *n.* **1.** a private house in which accommodation and meals are provided for paying guests. **2.** *Austral.* a house for boarders at a school. See also **house** (sense 10).

boarding out *n. Social welfare, Brit.* **a.** the local-authority practice of placing a client in a foster family or voluntary establishment and paying for it. **b.** (*as modifier*): *a boarding-out allowance.*

boarding school *n.* a school providing living accommodation for some or all of its pupils.

board measure *n.* a system of units for measuring wood based on the board foot. 1980 board feet equal one standard.

board of trade *n. U.S. and Canadian.* another name for a **chamber of commerce.**

Board of Trade *n.* (in the United Kingdom) a ministry within the Department of Trade: responsible for the supervision of commerce and the promotion of export trade.

Board of Trade Unit *n.* a unit of electrical energy equal to 1 kilowatt-hour. Abbrev.: **BTU.**

boardroom (ˈbɔːdˌruːm, -ˌrʊm) *n.* **a.** a room where the board of directors of a company meets. **b.** (*as modifier*): *a boardroom power struggle.*

board rule *n.* a measuring device for estimating the number of board feet in a quantity of wood.

boardsailing (ˈbɔːdˌseɪlɪŋ) *n.* another name for **windsurfing.** —ˈ**boardˌsailor** *n.*

board school *n. Brit.* (formerly) a school managed by a board elected by local ratepayers.

boardwalk (ˈbɔːdˌwɔːk) *n. U.S. and Canadian.* a promenade, esp. along a beach, usually made of planks.

boarfish (ˈbɔːˌfɪʃ) *n., pl.* **-fish** *or* **-fishes.** any of various spiny-finned marine teleost fishes of the genera *Capros, Antigonia,* etc., related to the dories, having a deep compressed body, a long snout, and large eyes.

boarish (ˈbɔːrɪʃ) *adj.* coarse, cruel, or sensual. —ˈ**boarishly** *adv.* —ˈ**boarishness** *n.*

boart (bɔːt) *n.* a variant spelling of **bort.**

boast[1] (bəʊst) *vb.* **1.** (*intr.*; sometimes foll. by *of* or *about*) to speak in exaggerated or excessively proud terms of one's possessions, skills, or superior qualities; brag. **2.** (*tr.*) to possess (something to be proud of): *the city boasts a fine cathedral.* ~*n.* **3.** a bragging statement. **4.** a possession, attribute, attainment, etc., that is or may be bragged about. [C13: of uncertain origin] —ˈ**boaster** *n.* —ˈ**boasting** *n., adj.* —ˈ**boastingly** *adv.*

boast[2] (bəʊst) *vb.* (*tr.*) to shape or dress (stone) roughly with a broad chisel. [C19: of unknown origin]

boast[3] (bəʊst) *Squash.* ~*n.* **1.** a stroke in which the ball is hit on to one of the side walls before hitting the front wall. ~*vb.* **2.** to hit (the ball) in this way or make such a stroke. [C19: perhaps from French *bosse* the place where the ball hits the wall] —'**boasted** *adj.*

boastful ('bəʊstfʊl) *adj.* tending to boast; characterized by boasting. —'**boastfully** *adv.* —'**boastfulness** *n.*

boat (bəʊt) *n.* **1.** a small vessel propelled by oars, paddle, sails, or motor for travelling, transporting goods, etc., esp. one that can be carried aboard a larger vessel. **2.** (not in technical use) another word for **ship. 3.** *Navy.* a submarine. **4.** a container for gravy, sauce, etc. **5.** a small boat-shaped container for incense, used in some Christian churches. **6. in the same boat.** sharing the same problems. **7. burn one's boats.** See **burn**[1] (sense 18). **8. miss the boat.** to lose an opportunity. **9. push the boat out.** *Brit. informal.* to celebrate, esp. lavishly and expensively. **10. rock the boat.** *Informal.* to cause a disturbance in the existing situation. ~*vb.* **11.** (*intr.*) to travel or go in a boat, esp. as a form of recreation. **12.** (*tr.*) to transport or carry in a boat. [Old English *bāt;* related to Old Norse *beit* boat]

boatbill ('bəʊtˌbɪl) *or* **boat-billed heron** *n.* a nocturnal tropical American wading bird, *Cochlearius cochlearius,* similar to the night herons but with a broad flattened bill: family *Ardeidae,* order *Ciconiiformes.*

boat deck *n.* the deck of a ship on which the lifeboats are kept.

boat drill *n.* practice in launching the lifeboats and taking off the passengers and crew of a ship.

boatel *or* **botel** (bəʊ'tɛl) *n.* **1.** a waterside hotel catering for boating people. **2.** a ship that functions as a hotel. [C20: from BOAT + (HOT)EL]

boater ('bəʊtə) *n.* a stiff straw hat with a straight brim and flat crown.

boathook ('bəʊtˌhʊk) *n.* a pole with a hook at one end, used aboard a vessel for fending off other vessels or obstacles or for catching a line or mooring buoy.

boathouse ('bəʊtˌhaʊs) *n.* a shelter by the edge of a river, lake, etc., for housing boats.

boatie ('bəʊtɪ) *n. Austral. and N.Z. informal.* a boating enthusiast.

boating ('bəʊtɪŋ) *n.* the practice of rowing, sailing, or cruising in boats as a form of recreation.

boatload ('bəʊtˌləʊd) *n.* the amount of cargo or number of people held by a boat or ship.

boatman ('bəʊtmən) *n., pl.* **-men. 1.** a man who works on, hires out, repairs, or operates a boat or boats. **2.** short for **water boatman.**

boat neck *n.* a high slitlike neckline of a garment that extends onto the shoulders. Also called: **bateau neckline.**

boat people *pl. n.* refugees, esp. from Vietnam in the late 1970s, who leave by boat hoping to be picked up by ships of another country.

boat race *n.* **the.** *Brit.* a rowing event held annually in the spring, in which an eight representing Oxford University rows against one representing Cambridge on the Thames between Putney and Mortlake.

boat sheep *n. Austral.* sheep for winter shipment to the Middle East for Ramadan.

boatswain, bo's'n, *or* **bosun** ('bəʊsᵊn) *n.* a petty officer on a merchant ship or a warrant officer on a warship who is responsible for the maintenance of the ship and its equipment. [Old English *bātswegen;* see BOAT, SWAIN]

boatswain's chair *n. Nautical.* a seat consisting of a short flat board slung from ropes, used to support a man working on the side of a vessel or in its rigging.

boat train *n.* a train scheduled to take passengers to or from a particular ship.

bob[1] (bɒb) *vb.* **bobs, bobbing, bobbed. 1.** to move or cause to move up and down repeatedly, as while floating in water. **2.** to move or cause to move with a short abrupt movement, as of the head. **3.** to make (a bow or curtsy): *the little girl bobbed before the visitor.* **4.** (*intr.;* usually foll. by *up*) to appear or emerge suddenly. **5.** (*intr.;* foll. by *under, below,* etc.) to disappear suddenly, as beneath a surface. **6.** (*intr.;* usually foll. by *for*) to attempt to get hold (of a floating or hanging object, esp. an apple) in the teeth as a game. ~*n.* **7.** a short abrupt movement, as of the head. **8.** a quick curtsy or bow. **9.** *Changeringing.* a particular set of changes. **10.** *Angling.* **a.** short for **bobfloat. b.** the topmost fly on a cast of three, often fished bobbing at the surface. **c.** this position on a wet-fly cast. [C14: of uncertain origin]

bob[2] (bɒb) *n.* **1.** a hairstyle for women and children in which the hair is cut short evenly all round the head. **2.** a dangling or hanging object, such as the weight on a pendulum or on a plumb line. **3.** a polishing disc on a rotating spindle. It is usually made of felt, leather, etc., impregnated with an abrasive material. **4.** short for **bob skate** or **bobsleigh. 5.** a runner or pair of runners on a bobsled. **6.** *Angling.* a small knot of worms, maggots, etc., used as bait. **7.** a very short line of verse at the end of a stanza or preceding a rhyming quatrain (the wheel) at the end of a stanza. **8.** a refrain or burden with such a short line or lines. **9.** a docked tail, esp. of a horse. **10.** *Brit. dialect.* a hanging cluster, as of flowers or ribbons. ~*vb.* **bobs, bobbing, bobbed. 11.** (*tr.*) to cut (the hair) in a bob. **12.** (*tr.*) to cut short (something, esp. the tail of an animal); dock or crop. **13.** (*intr.*) to ride on a bobsled. [C14 *bobbe* bunch of flowers, perhaps of Celtic origin]

bob[3] (bɒb) *vb.* **bobs, bobbing, bobbed. 1.** to tap or cause to tap or knock lightly (against). ~*n.* **2.** a light knock; tap. [C13 *bobben* to rap, beat; see BOP[2]]

bob[4] (bɒb) *n., pl.* **bob.** *Brit.* (formerly) an informal word for a **shilling.** [C19: of unknown origin]

Bob (bɒb) *n.* **Bob's your uncle.** *Slang.* everything is or will turn out all right. [C19: perhaps from pet form of *Robert*]

bobbejaan ('bɒbəˌjɑːn) *n. S. African* a baboon. [Afrikaans]

bobbejaan spanner *n. S. African.* a monkey wrench. [from Afrikaans BOBBEJAAN + SPANNER]

bobbery ('bɒbərɪ) *n., pl.* **-beries. 1.** Also called: **bobbery pack.** a mixed pack of hunting dogs, often not belonging to any of the hound breeds. **2.** *Informal.* a noisy commotion. ~*adj.* **3.** *Informal.* noisy or excitable. [C19: from Hindi *bāp re,* literally: oh father!]

bobbin ('bɒbɪn) *n.* **1.** a spool or reel on which thread or yarn is wound, being unwound as required; spool; reel. **2.** narrow braid or cord used as binding or for trimming. **3.** a device consisting of a short bar and a length of string, used to control a wooden door latch. **4. a.** a spool on which insulated wire is wound to form the coil of a small electromagnetic device, such as a bell or buzzer. **b.** the coil of such a spool. [C16: from Old French *bobine,* of unknown origin]

bobbinet (ˌbɒbɪ'nɛt) *n.* a netted fabric of hexagonal mesh, made on a lace machine. [C19: see BOBBIN, NET[1]]

bobbin lace *n.* lace made with bobbins rather than with needle and thread (needlepoint lace); pillow lace.

bobble ('bɒbᵊl) *n.* **1.** a short jerky motion, as of a cork floating on disturbed water; bobbing movement. **2.** a tufted ball, usually for ornament, as on a knitted hat. **3.** any small dangling ball or bundle. ~*vb.* **4.** *U.S. informal.* to handle (something) ineptly; muff; bungle: *he bobbled the ball and lost the game.* [C19: from BOB[1] (vb.)]

bobby ('bɒbɪ) *n., pl.* **-bies.** *Informal.* a British policeman. [C19: from *Bobby,* after Sir *Robert Peel* (1788–1850), who, as Home Secretary, set up the Metropolitan Police Force in 1828]

bobby calf *n.* an unweaned calf culled for slaughter.

bobby-dazzler *n. Dialect.* anything outstanding, striking, or showy, esp. an attractive girl. [C19: expanded form of *dazzler* something striking or attractive]

bobby pin *n. U.S., Canadian, Austral., and N.Z.* a metal hairpin bent in order to hold the hair in place. Brit. terms: **hairgrip, kirby grip.**

bobby socks *pl. n.* ankle-length socks worn by teenage girls, esp. in the U.S. in the 1940s.

bobbysoxer ('bɒbɪˌsɒksə) *n. Informal, chiefly U.S.* an adolescent girl wearing bobby socks, esp. in the 1940s.

bobcat ('bɒbˌkæt) *n.* a North American feline mammal, *Lynx rufus,* closely related to but smaller than the lynx, having reddish-brown fur with dark spots or stripes, tufted ears, and a short tail. Also called: **bay lynx.** [C19: from BOB[2] (referring to its short tail) + CAT]

bobfloat ('bɒbˌfləʊt) *n. Angling.* a small buoyant float, usually consisting of a quill stuck through a piece of cork.

boblet ('bɒblɪt) *n.* a two-man bobsleigh. [C20: from BOB[2] + -LET]

bobol ('bʌbɔːl) *E Caribbean.* ~*n.* **1.** a fraud carried out by one or more persons with access to public funds in collusion with someone in a position of authority. ~*vb.* **2.** (*intr.*) to commit a bobol. [C20: of uncertain origin]

bobolink ('bɒbəˌlɪŋk) *n.* an American songbird, *Dolichonyx oryzivorus,* the male of which has a white back and black underparts in the breeding season: family *Icteridae* (American orioles). Also called (U.S.): **reedbird, ricebird.** [C18: of imitative origin]

bobotie (bʊ'bʊtɪ) *n.* a South African dish consisting of curried mincemeat with a topping of beaten egg baked to a crust. [C19: from Afrikaans, probably from Malay]

bobowler ('bɒbˌaʊlə) *n. Midland English dialect.* a large moth. [of uncertain origin]

bob skate *n. Chiefly U.S. and Canadian.* an ice skate with two parallel blades. [C20: from *bob(sled)* + SKATE[1]]

bobsleigh ('bɒbˌsleɪ) *n.* **1.** a racing sledge for two or more people, with a steering mechanism enabling the driver to direct it down a steeply banked ice-covered run. **2.** (esp. formerly) **a.** a sleigh made of two short sledges joined one behind the other. **b.** one of these two short sledges. ~*vb.* **3.** (*intr.*) to ride on a bobsleigh. ~Also called (esp. U.S. and Canadian): **bobsled** ('bɒbˌslɛd). [C19: BOB[2] + SLEIGH]

bobstay ('bɒbˌsteɪ) *n.* a strong stay between a bowsprit and the stem of a vessel for holding down the bowsprit. [C18: perhaps from BOB[1] + STAY[3]]

bobsy-die ('bɒbzɪˌdaɪ) *n. N.Z. informal.* fuss; confusion; pandemonium (esp. in the phrases **kick up bobsy-die, play bobsy-die**). [from C19 *bob's a-dying*]

bobtail ('bɒbˌteɪl) *n.* **1.** a docked or diminutive tail. **2.** an animal with such a tail. ~*adj. also* **bobtailed. 3.** having the tail cut short. ~*vb.* (*tr.*) **4.** to dock the tail of. **5.** to cut short; curtail. [C16: from BOB[2] + TAIL[1]]

bobweight ('bɒbˌweɪt) *n.* another name for **balance weight.**

bobwhite ('bɒbˌwaɪt) *n.* a brown North American quail, *Colinus virginianus,* the male of which has white markings on the head: a popular game bird. [C19: of imitative origin]

bocage (bɒˈkɑːʒ) *n.* **1.** the wooded countryside characteristic of northern France, with small irregular-shaped fields and many hedges and copses. **2.** woodland scenery represented in ceramics. [C17: from French, from Old French *bosc;* see BOSCAGE]

boccie, bocci, bocce (ˈbɒtʃiː), *or* **boccia** (ˈbɒtʃə) *n.* an Italian version of bowls played on a lawn shorter and narrower than a bowling green. [from Italian *bocce* bowls, plural of *boccia* ball; see BOSS[2]]

Boche (bɒʃ) *n. Derogatory slang.* (esp. in World Wars I and II) **1.** a German, esp. a German soldier. **2. the.** (*usually functioning as pl.*) Germans collectively, esp. German soldiers regarded as the enemy. [C20: from French, probably shortened from *alboche* German, from *allemand* German + *caboche* pate]

bock (bok, bəʊk) *vb., n.* a variant spelling of **boke.**

bock beer *or* **bock** (bɒk) *n.* **1.** *U.S. and Canadian.* heavy dark strong beer. **2.** (in France) a light beer. [C19: from German *Bock bier,* literally: buck beer, name given through folk etymology to beer brewed in *Einbeck,* near Hanover]

bockedy (ˈbɒkədɪ) *adj. Irish.* (of a structure, piece of furniture, etc.) unsteady. [from Irish Gaelic *bacaideach* limping]

bod (bɒd) *n. Informal.* **1.** a fellow; chap: *he's a queer bod.* **2.** another word for **body** (sense 1). [C18: short for BODY]

BOD *abbrev. for* biochemical oxygen demand.

bode[1] (bəʊd) *vb.* **1.** to be an omen of (good or ill, esp. of ill); portend; presage. **2.** (*tr.*) *Archaic.* to predict; foretell. [Old English *bodian;* related to Old Norse *botha* to proclaim, Old Frisian *bodia* to invite] —ˈ**boding** *n., adj.* —ˈ**bodement** *n.*

bode[2] (bəʊd) *vb.* the past tense of **bide.**

bodega (bəʊˈdiːgə; *Spanish* boˈðeγa) *n.* a shop selling wine and sometimes groceries, esp. in a Spanish-speaking country. [C19: from Spanish, ultimately from Greek *apothēkē* storehouse, from *apotithenai* to store, put away]

Bode's law (bəʊdz) *n. Astronomy.* an empirical rule relating the distances of the planets from the sun, based on the numerical sequence 0, 3, 6, 12, 24, ... Adding 4 to each number and dividing by 10 gives the sequence 0.4, 0.7, 1, 1.6, 2.8, ..., which is a reasonable representation of distances in astronomical units for most planets if the minor planets are counted as a single entity at 2.8. [named after Johann Elert *Bode* (1747–1826), who in 1772 published the law, formulated by Johann Titius in 1766]

bodge (bɒdʒ) *vb. Informal.* to make a mess of; botch. [C16: changed from BOTCH]

bodger (ˈbɒdʒə) *adj. Austral. informal.* worthless or second-rate. [C20: from BODGE]

bodgie (ˈbɒdʒɪ) *n. Austral. and N.Z.* an unruly or uncouth young man, esp. in the 1950s; teddy boy. [C20: from BODGE]

Bodhisattva (ˌbəʊdɪˈsætvə, -wə, ˌbɒd-; ˌbəʊdiːˈsʌtvə) *n.* (in Mahayana Buddhism) a divine being worthy of nirvana who remains on the human plane to help men to salvation. Compare **Arhat.** [Sanskrit, literally: one whose essence is enlightenment, from *bodhi* enlightenment + *sattva* essence]

bodhrán (baʊˈrɑːn, ˈbɔːrɑːn) *n.* a shallow one-sided drum popular in Irish and Scottish folk music. [Irish Gaelic]

bodice (ˈbɒdɪs) *n.* **1.** the upper part of a woman's dress, from the shoulder to the waist. **2.** a tight-fitting corset worn laced over a blouse, as in certain European national costumes, or (formerly) as a woman's undergarment. [C16: originally Scottish *bodies,* plural of BODY]

bodice ripper *n. Informal.* a romantic novel, usually on a historical theme, that involves some sex and violence.

Bo Diddley beat (ˌbəʊ ˈdɪdlɪ ˈbiːt) *n.* a type of syncopated Black rhythm, frequently used in rock music. [C20: named after *Bo Diddley* (born 1929), U.S. rhythm-and-blues performer and songwriter]

-bodied *adj.* (*in combination*) having a body or bodies as specified: *able-bodied; long-bodied; many-bodied.*

bodiless (ˈbɒdɪlɪs) *adj.* having no body or substance; incorporeal or insubstantial.

bodily (ˈbɒdɪlɪ) *adj.* **1.** relating to or being a part of the human body. ~*adv.* **2.** by taking hold of the body: *he threw him bodily from the platform.* **3.** in person; in the flesh.

bodkin (ˈbɒdkɪn) *n.* **1.** a blunt large-eyed needle used esp. for drawing tape through openwork. **2.** *Archaic.* a dagger. **3.** *Printing.* a pointed steel tool used for extracting characters when correcting metal type. **4.** *Archaic.* a long ornamental hairpin. [C14: probably of Celtic origin; compare Gaelic *biodag* dagger]

Bodoni (bəˈdəʊnɪ) *n.* a style of type designed by the Italian printer Giambattista Bodoni (1740–1813).

body (ˈbɒdɪ) *n., pl.* **bodies. 1. a.** the entire physical structure of an animal or human being. Related adj.: **corporeal. b.** (*as modifier*): *body odour.* **2.** the flesh, as opposed to the spirit: *while we are still in the body.* **3.** the trunk or torso, not including the limbs, head, or tail. **4.** a dead human or animal; corpse. **5.** the largest or main part of anything: *the body of a vehicle; the body of a plant.* **6.** a separate or distinct mass of water or land. **7.** the main part; majority: *the body of public opinion was against the plan.* **8.** the central part of a written work or document: *the body of a thesis as opposed to the footnotes.* **9.** a number of individuals regarded as a single entity; group: *the student body; they marched in a body to London.* **10.** *Maths.* a three-dimensional region with an interior. **11.** *Physics.* an object or substance that has three dimensions, a mass, and is distinguishable from surrounding objects. **12.** the characteristic full quality of certain wines, determined by the density and the content of alcohol or tannin: *a Burgundy has a heavy body.* **13.** substance or firmness, esp. of cloth. **14.** the sound box of a guitar, violin, or similar stringed instrument. **15.** a woman's close-fitting one-piece garment for the torso. **16.** the part of a dress covering the body from the shoulders to the waist. **17.** another name for **shank** (sense 11). **18. a.** the pigment contained in or added to paint, dye, etc. **b.** the opacity of a paint in covering a surface. **c.** the apparent viscosity of a paint. **19.** (in watercolour painting) **a.** a white filler mixed with pigments to make them opaque. **b.** (*as modifier*): *body colour.* See also **gouache. 20.** *Printing.* the measurement from top to bottom of a piece of type, usually ascender to descender. **21.** an informal or dialect word for a **person. 22. keep body and soul together.** to manage to keep alive; survive. **23.** (*modifier*) of or relating to the main reading matter of a book as distinct from headings, illustrations, appendices, etc.: *the body text.* ~*vb.* **bodies, bodying, bodied.** (*tr.*) **24.** (usually foll. by *forth*) to give a body or shape to. [Old English *bodig;* related to Old Norse *buthkr* box, Old High German *botah* body]

body bag *n. Military.* a large heavy plastic bag used to contain and transport human remains, esp. those of battle casualties.

body blow *n.* **1.** *Boxing.* Also called: **body punch.** a blow to the body of an opponent. **2.** a severe disappointment or setback: *unavailability of funds was a body blow to the project.*

body building *n.* the practice of performing regular exercises designed to make the muscles of the body conspicuous.

body cavity *n.* the internal cavity of any multicellular animal that contains the digestive tract, heart, kidneys, etc. In vertebrates it develops from the coelom.

body-centred *adj.* (of a crystal) having a lattice point at the centre of each unit cell as well as at the corners. Compare **face-centred.**

bodycheck (ˈbɒdɪˌtʃɛk) *n.* **1.** *Ice hockey.* obstruction of another player. **2.** *Wrestling.* the act of blocking a charging opponent with the body. ~*vb.* **3.** (*tr.*) to deliver a bodycheck to (an opponent).

body corporate *n. Law.* a group of persons incorporated to carry out a specific enterprise. See **corporation** (sense 1).

bodyguard (ˈbɒdɪˌgɑːd) *n.* a man or group of men who escort and protect someone, esp. a political figure.

body image *n. Psychol.* an individual's concept of his own body.

body language *n.* the nonverbal imparting of information by means of conscious or subconscious bodily gestures, posture, etc.

body-line *adj. Cricket.* denoting or relating to fast bowling aimed at the batsman's body.

Body of Christ *n.* the Christian Church.

body politic *n.* **the.** the people of a nation or the nation itself considered as a political entity; the state.

body popping *n.* a dance of the 1980s, characterized by snakelike arm and head movements. —**body popper** *n.*

body shop *n.* a place where the bodywork of motor vehicles is built or repaired.

body snatcher *n.* (formerly) a person who robbed graves and sold the corpses for dissection. —**body snatching** *n.*

body stocking *n.* a one-piece undergarment for women, usually of nylon, covering the torso.

bodysuit (ˈbɒdɪˌsuːt, -ˌsjuːt) *n.* **1.** another name for **body** (sense 15). **2.** a one-piece undergarment for a baby.

body-surf *vb.* (*intr.*) to ride a wave by lying on it without a surfboard. —ˈ**body-ˌsurfer** *n.* —ˈ**body-ˌsurfing** *n.*

body swerve *n.* **1.** *Sport.* (esp. in football games) the act or an instance of swerving past an opponent. **2.** *Scot.* the act or an instance of avoiding (a situation considered unpleasant): *I think I'll give the meeting a body swerve.* ~*vb.* **body-swerve. 3.** *Sport.* (esp. in football games) to pass (an opponent) using a body swerve. **4.** *Scot.* to avoid (a situation or person considered unpleasant).

body warmer *n.* a sleeveless type of jerkin, usually quilted, worn as an outer garment for extra warmth.

bodywork (ˈbɒdɪˌwɜːk) *n.* the external shell of a motor vehicle.

Boehmite (ˈbɜːmaɪt) *n.* a grey, red, or brown mineral that consists of alumina in rhombic crystalline form and occurs in bauxite. Formula: AlO(OH). [C20: from German *Böhmit,* after J. *Böhm,* 20th-century German scientist]

Boer (bʊə, ˈbəʊə, bɔː) *n., adj.* **a.** a descendant of any of the Dutch or Huguenot colonists who settled in South Africa, mainly in Cape Colony, the Orange Free State, and the Transvaal. **b.** (*as modifier*): *a Boer farm.* [C19: from Dutch *Boer;* see BOOR]

boerbul (ˈbʊəˌbʊl) *n. S. African.* a crossbred mastiff used esp. as a watchdog. [from Afrikaans *boerboel* a breed of mastiff]

boeremusiek (ˈbʊərəˌmjuːzɪk) *n. S. African.* a special variety of light music associated with the culture of the Afrikaners. [Afrikaans]

boerewors (ˈbʊərəˌvɒs) *n. S. African.* a highly seasoned traditional sausage made from minced or pounded meat. [Afrikaans]

boer goat *n. S. African.* a hardy indigenous breed of goat. [from Afrikaans *boer* + GOAT]

boerperd (ˈbʊəˌpɛət) *n., pl.* **-perde** (-ˌpɛədə). *S. African.* a particularly rugged breed of horse, often palomino. [from Afrikaans *boer* + *perd* horse]

boeuf bourguignon (*French* bœf burgiɲɔ̃) *n.* a casserole of beef, vegetables, herbs, etc., cooked in red wine. Also called: **boeuf à la bourguignonne.** [French: Burgundy beef]

boffin ('bɒfɪn) *n. Brit. informal.* a scientist, esp. one carrying out military research. [C20: of uncertain origin]

boffo ('bɒfəʊ) *adj. Slang.* very good; highly successful. [C20: of uncertain origin]

Bofors gun ('bəʊfəz) *n.* an automatic single- or double-barrelled anti-aircraft gun with 40 millimetre bore. [C20: named after *Bofors,* Sweden, where it was first made]

bog (bɒg) *n.* **1.** wet spongy ground consisting of decomposing vegetation, which ultimately forms peat. **2.** an area of such ground. **3.** a place or thing that prevents or slows progress or improvement. **4.** a slang word for **lavatory** (sense 1). **5.** *Austral. slang.* the act or an instance of defecating. ~See also **bog down, bog in.** [C13: from Gaelic *bogach* swamp, from *bog* soft] —'**boggy** *adj.* —'**bogginess** *n.*

bogan[1] ('bəʊgən) *n. Canadian.* (esp. in the Maritime Provinces) a sluggish side stream. Also called: **logan, pokelogan.** [of Algonquian origin]

bogan[2] ('bəʊgən) *n. Austral. slang.* a stupid and feeble person. [origin unknown]

bog asphodel *n.* either of two liliaceous plants, *Narthecium ossifragum* of Europe or *N. americanum* of North America, that grow in boggy places and have small yellow flowers and grasslike leaves.

bogbean ('bɒg,biːn) *n.* another name for **buckbean.**

bog cotton *n.* another name for **cotton grass.**

bog deal *n.* pine wood found preserved in peat bogs.

bog down *vb.* **bogs, bogging, bogged.** (*adv.;* when *tr., often passive*) to impede or be impeded physically or mentally.

bogey[1] *or* **bogy** ('bəʊgɪ) *n.* **1.** an evil or mischievous spirit. **2.** something that worries or annoys. **3.** *Golf.* **a.** a standard score for a hole or course, regarded as one that a good player should make. **b.** *U.S.* a score of one stroke over par on a hole. Compare **par** (sense 5). **4.** *Slang.* a piece of dried mucus discharged from the nose. **5.** *Air Force slang.* an unidentified or hostile aircraft. **6.** *Slang.* a detective; policeman. [C19: probably related to BUG[2] and BOGLE; compare BUGABOO]

bogey[2] *or* **bogie** ('bəʊgɪ) *Austral.* ~*vb.* **1.** to bathe or swim. ~*n.* **2.** a bathe or swim. [C19: from a native Australian language]

bogey hole *n. Austral.* a natural pool used for swimming.

bogeyman ('bəʊgɪ,mæn) *n., pl.* **-men.** a person, real or imaginary, used as a threat, esp. to children.

boggart ('bɒgət) *n. Northern English dialect.* a ghost or poltergeist. [perhaps from *bog,* variant of BUG[2] + -ARD]

boggle ('bɒgᵊl) *vb.* (*intr.;* often foll. by *at*) **1.** to be surprised, confused, or alarmed (esp. in the phrase **the mind boggles**). **2.** to hesitate or be evasive when confronted with a problem. [C16: probably variant of BOGLE]

bogie[1] *or* **bogy** ('bəʊgɪ) *n.* **1.** an assembly of four or six wheels forming a pivoted support at either end of a railway coach. It provides flexibility on curves. **2.** *Chiefly Brit.* a small railway truck of short wheelbase, used for conveying coal, ores, etc. **3.** *Scot.* another word for **soapbox** (sense 3). [C19: of unknown origin]

bogie[2] ('bəʊgɪ) *n.* a variant spelling of **bogey**[2].

bog in *vb.* (*intr., adv.*) *Austral. and N.Z. informal.* **1.** to start energetically on a task. **2.** to start eating; tuck in. ~Also (prep.): **bog into.**

bogle ('bəʊgᵊl, 'bɒg-) *n.* **1.** a dialect or archaic word for **bogey**[1] (sense 1). **2.** *Scot.* a scarecrow. [C16: from Scottish *bogill,* perhaps from Gaelic; compare Welsh *bygel;* see BUG[2]]

bogman ('bɒg,mæn) *n., pl.* **-men.** *Archaeol.* the body of a person found preserved in a peat bog.

bog moss *n.* another name for **peat moss.**

bog myrtle *n.* another name for **sweet gale.**

bog oak *n.* oak or other wood found preserved in peat bogs; bogwood.

bogong ('bəʊ,gɒŋ) *or* **bugong** ('buː,gɒŋ) *n.* an edible dark-coloured Australian noctuid moth, *Agrotis infusa.*

bog orchid *n.* an orchid, *Hammarbya* (or *Malaxis*) *paludosa,* growing in sphagnum bogs in the N hemisphere. It has greenish-yellow flowers and its leaves bear a fringe of tiny bulbils.

bog rush *n.* a blackish tufted cyperaceous plant, *Schoenus nigricans,* growing on boggy ground.

bogtrotter ('bɒg,trɒtə) *n.* a derogatory term for an Irishman, esp. an Irish peasant.

bogus ('bəʊgəs) *adj.* spurious or counterfeit; not genuine: *a bogus note.* [C19: from *bogus* apparatus for making counterfeit money; perhaps related to BOGEY[1]] —'**bogusly** *adv.* —'**bogusness** *n.*

bogwood ('bɒg,wʊd) *n.* another name for **bog oak.**

bogy ('bəʊgɪ) *n., pl.* **-gies.** a variant spelling of **bogey**[1] or **bogie**[1].

boh (bəʊ) *interj.* a variant spelling of **bo.**

bohea (bəʊ'hiː) *n.* a black Chinese tea, once regarded as the choicest, but now as an inferior grade. [C18: from Chinese (Fukien dialect) *bu-i,* from Mandarin Chinese *Wu-i Shan* range of hills on which this tea was grown]

Bohemian (bəʊ'hiːmɪən) *n.* **1.** a native or inhabitant of Bohemia, esp. of the old kingdom of Bohemia; a Czech. **2.** (*often not cap.*) a person, esp. an artist or writer, who lives an unconventional life. **3.** the Czech language. ~*adj.* **4.** of, relating to, or characteristic of Bohemia, its people, or their language. **5.** unconventional in appearance, behaviour, etc.

Bohemian Brethren *pl. n.* a Protestant Christian sect formed in the 15th century from various Hussite groups, which rejected oaths and military service and advocated a pure and disciplined spiritual life. It was reorganized in 1722 as the Moravian Church. Also called: **Unitas Fratrem** ('juːnɪtæs 'frætrɛm).

Bohemianism (bəʊ'hiːmɪə,nɪzəm) *n.* (*sometimes not cap.*) unconventional behaviour or appearance, esp. of an artist.

Böhm flute (*German* bøːm) *n.* a type of flute in which the holes are covered with keys; the standard type of modern flute. [C19: named after Theobald *Böhm* (1793–1881), German flautist who invented it]

Bohr theory (bɔː; *Danish* boːr) *n.* a theory of atomic structure that explains the spectrum of hydrogen atoms. It assumes that the electron orbiting around the nucleus can exist only in certain energy states, a jump from one state to another being accompanied by the emission or absorption of a quantum of radiation. [C20: after Niels *Bohr* (1885–1962), Danish physicist]

bohunk ('bəʊ,hʌŋk) *n. U.S. and Canadian, derogatory slang.* a labourer from east or central Europe. [C20: blend of *Bo(hemian)* + *Hung(arian),* with alteration of *g* to *k*]

boil[1] (bɔɪl) *vb.* **1.** to change or cause to change from a liquid to a vapour so rapidly that bubbles of vapour are formed copiously in the liquid. Compare **evaporate. 2.** to reach or cause to reach boiling point. **3.** to cook or be cooked by the process of boiling. **4.** (*intr.*) to bubble and be agitated like something boiling; seethe: *the ocean was boiling.* **5.** (*intr.*) to be extremely angry or indignant (esp. in the phrase **make one's blood boil**): *she was boiling at his dishonesty.* **6.** (*intr.*) to contain a boiling liquid: *the pot is boiling.* ~*n.* **7.** the state or action of boiling (esp. in the phrases **on the boil, off the boil**). ~See also **boil away, boil down, boil off, boil over, boil up.** [C13: from Old French *boillir,* from Latin *bullīre* to bubble, from *bulla* a bubble] —'**boilable** *adj.*

boil[2] (bɔɪl) *n.* a red painful swelling with a hard pus-filled core caused by bacterial infection of the skin and subcutaneous tissues, esp. at a hair follicle. Technical name: **furuncle.** [Old English *bȳle;* related to Old Norse *beyla* swelling, Old High German *būlla* bladder, Gothic *ufbauljan* to inflate]

boil away *vb.* (*adv.*) to cause (liquid) to evaporate completely by boiling or (of liquid) to evaporate completely.

boil down *vb.* (*adv.*) **1.** to reduce or be reduced in quantity and usually altered in consistency by boiling: *to boil a liquid down to a thick glue.* **2. boil down to. a.** (*intr.*) to be the essential element in something. **b.** (*tr.*) to summarize; reduce to essentials.

boiled shirt *n. Informal.* a dress shirt with a stiff front.

boiled sweet *n. Brit.* a hard sticky sweet of boiled sugar with any of various flavourings.

boiler ('bɔɪlə) *n.* **1.** a closed vessel or arrangement of enclosed tubes in which water is heated to supply steam to drive an engine or turbine or provide heat. **2.** a domestic device burning solid fuel, gas, or oil, to provide hot water, esp. for central heating. **3.** a large tub for boiling laundry. **4.** a tough old chicken for cooking by boiling.

boilermaker ('bɔɪlə,meɪkə) *n.* **1.** a person who works with metal in heavy industry; plater or welder. **2.** *Brit. slang.* a beer drink consisting half of draught mild and half of bottled brown ale. **3.** *U.S. slang.* a drink of whisky followed by a beer chaser.

boilerplate ('bɔɪlə,pleɪt) *n.* **1.** a form of mild-steel plate used in the production of boiler shells. **2.** a copy made with the intention of making other copies from it. **3.** a set of instructions incorporated in several places in a computer program or a standard form of words used repeatedly in drafting contracts, guarantees, etc. **4.** a draft contract that can easily be modified to cover various types of transaction.

boiler suit *n. Brit.* a one-piece work garment consisting of overalls and a shirt top usually worn over ordinary clothes to protect them.

boiling ('bɔɪlɪŋ) *adj., adv.* **1.** very warm: *a boiling hot day.* ~*n.* **2. the whole boiling.** *Slang.* the whole lot.

boiling point *n.* **1.** the temperature at which a liquid boils at a given pressure, usually atmospheric pressure at sea level; the temperature at which the vapour pressure of a liquid equals the external pressure. **2.** *Informal.* the condition of being angered or highly excited.

boiling-water reactor *n.* a nuclear reactor using water as coolant and moderator, steam being produced in the reactor itself: enriched uranium oxide cased in zirconium is the fuel. Abbrev.: **BWR.**

boil off *vb.* to remove or be removed (from) by boiling: *to boil off impurities.*

boilover ('bɔɪl,əʊvə) *n. Austral.* a surprising result in a sporting event, esp. in a horse race.

boil over *vb.* (*adv.*) **1.** to overflow or cause to overflow while boiling. **2.** (*intr.*) to burst out in anger or excitement: *she boiled over at the mention of his name.*

boil up *vb.* (*intr., adv.*) *Austral. and N.Z.* to make tea.

bois-brûlé (,bwɑːbruː'leɪ) *n.* (*sometimes cap.*) *Canadian archaic.* a half-breed of Indian and White (usually French Canadian) ancestry; Métis. Also called: **Brule.** [French, literally: burnt wood]

boisterous ('bɔɪstərəs, -strəs) *adj.* **1.** noisy and lively; unrestrained or unruly. **2.** (of the wind, sea, etc.) turbulent or stormy. [C13 *boistuous,* of unknown origin] —'**boisterously** *adv.* —'**boisterousness** *n.*

boke, boak, *or* **bock** (bok, bəʊk) *Scot.* ~*vb.* **1.** to retch or vomit. ~*n.* **2.** a retch; vomiting fit. [Middle English *bolken;* related to BELCH, German *bölken* to roar]

bokmakierie (ˌbɒkməˈkɪərɪ) *n. S. African.* a large yellow shrike, *Telephorus zeylonus,* of southern Africa, known for its melodious song. [C19: from Afrikaans, imitative of its call]

Bokmål (*Norwegian* ˈbuːkmoːl) *n.* one of the two official forms of written Norwegian, closely related to Danish. Also called: **Dano-Norwegian.** Formerly called: **Riksmål.** Compare **Nynorsk.** [Norwegian, literally: book language]

Bol. *abbrev. for* Bolivia(n).

bola (ˈbəʊlə) *or* **bolas** (ˈbəʊləs) *n., pl.* **-las** *or* **-lases.** a missile used by gauchos and Indians of South America, consisting of two or more heavy balls on a cord. It is hurled at a running quarry, such as an ox or emu, so as to entangle its legs. [Spanish: ball, from Latin *bulla* knob]

bold (bəʊld) *adj.* **1.** courageous, confident, and fearless; ready to take risks. **2.** showing or requiring courage: *a bold plan.* **3.** immodest or impudent: *she gave him a bold look.* **4.** standing out distinctly; conspicuous: *a figure carved in bold relief.* **5.** very steep: *the bold face of the cliff.* **6.** imaginative in thought or expression: *the novel's bold plot.* **7.** *Printing.* set in bold face. ~*n.* **8.** *Printing.* short for **bold face.** [Old English *beald;* related to Old Norse *ballr* dangerous, terrible, *baldinn* defiant, Old High German *bald* bold] —ˈ**boldly** *adv.* —ˈ**boldness** *n.*

bold face *n.* **1.** *Printing.* a weight of type characterized by thick heavy lines, as the entry words in this dictionary. Compare **light face.** ~*adj.* **boldface. 2.** (of type) having this weight.

bole[1] (bəʊl) *n.* the trunk of a tree. [C14: from Old Norse *bolr;* related to Middle High German *bole* plank]

bole[2] (bəʊl) *or* **bolus** *n.* **1.** a reddish soft variety of clay used as a pigment. **2.** a moderate reddish-brown colour. [C13: from Late Latin *bōlus* lump, from Greek *bōlos*]

bolection (bəʊˈlɛkʃən) *n. Architect.* a stepped moulding covering and projecting beyond the joint between two members having surfaces at different levels. Also called: **bilection.** [C18: of unknown origin]

bolero (bəˈlɛərəʊ) *n., pl.* **-ros. 1.** a Spanish dance, often accompanied by the guitar and castanets, usually in triple time. **2.** a piece of music composed for or in the rhythm of this dance. **3.** (*also* ˈbɒlərəʊ) a kind of short jacket not reaching the waist, with or without sleeves and open at the front: worn by men in Spain and by women elsewhere. [C18: from Spanish; perhaps related to *bola* ball]

boletus (bəʊˈliːtəs) *n., pl.* **-tuses** *or* **-ti** (-ˌtaɪ). any saprophytic basidiomycetous fungus of the genus *Boletus,* having a brownish umbrella-shaped cap with spore-bearing tubes in the underside: family *Boletineae.* Many species are edible. [C17: from Latin: variety of mushroom, from Greek *bōlitēs;* perhaps related to Greek *bōlos* lump]

bolide (ˈbəʊlaɪd, -lɪd) *n.* a large exceptionally bright meteor that often explodes. Also called: **fireball.** [C19: from French, from *bolis* missile; see BALLISTA]

bolivar (ˈbɒlɪˌvɑː; *Spanish* boˈliβar) *n., pl.* **-vars** *or* **-vares** (-βares) the standard monetary unit of Venezuela, equal to 100 centimos. [named after Simon *Bolivar* (1783–1830), South American soldier and liberator]

Bolivian (bəˈlɪvɪən) *n.* **1.** a native or inhabitant of Bolivia, a country in central S America. ~*adj.* **2.** of Bolivia, its people, culture, etc.

boliviano (bəˌlɪvɪˈɑːnəʊ; *Spanish* boliˈvjano) *n., pl.* **-nos** (-nəʊz; *Spanish* -nos). (until 1963 and from 1987) the standard monetary unit, comprising 100 centavos, of Bolivia.

boll (bəʊl) *n.* the fruit of such plants as flax and cotton, consisting of a rounded capsule containing the seeds. [C13: from Dutch *bolle;* related to Old English *bolla* BOWL[1]]

bollard (ˈbɒlɑːd, ˈbɒləd) *n.* **1.** a strong wooden or metal post mounted on a wharf, quay, etc., used for securing mooring lines. **2.** *Brit.* a small post or marker placed on a kerb or traffic island to make it conspicuous to motorists. **3.** *Mountaineering.* an outcrop of rock or pillar of ice that may be used to belay a rope. [C14: perhaps from BOLE[1] + -ARD]

bollocking (ˈbɒləkɪŋ) *n. Slang.* a severe telling-off; dressing-down. [from *bollock* (vb.) in the sense "to reprimand"]

bollocks (ˈbɒləks), **ballocks,** *or U.S.* **bollix** (ˈbɒlɪks) *Taboo slang.* ~*pl. n.* **1.** another word for **testicles.** ~*interj.* **2.** an exclamation of annoyance, disbelief, etc. ~*vb.* (usually foll. by *up*) **3.** to muddle or botch. [Old English *beallucas,* diminutive (pl.) of *beallu* (unattested); see BALL[1]]

boll weevil *n.* a greyish weevil, *Anthonomus grandis,* of the southern U.S. and Mexico, whose larvae live in and destroy cotton bolls. See also **weevil** (sense 1).

bollworm (ˈbəʊlˌwɜːm) *n.* any of various moth caterpillars, such as *Pectinophora* (or *Platyedra*) *gossypiella* (**pink bollworm**), that feed on and destroy cotton bolls.

bolo (ˈbəʊləʊ) *n., pl.* **-los.** a large single-edged knife, originating in the Philippines. [Philippine Spanish, probably from a native word]

bologna sausage (bəˈləʊnjə) *n. Chiefly U.S. and Canadian.* a large smoked sausage made of seasoned mixed meats. Also called: **baloney, boloney,** (esp. Brit.) **polony.**

Bolognese (ˌbɒləˈniːz, -ˈneɪz) *adj.* **1.** of the city of Bologna, N Italy, or its inhabitants, customs, cuisine, etc.: *bolognese sauce.* ~*n.* **2.** (*pl.* **-gnese**) a native or inhabitant of Bologna.

bolometer (bəʊˈlɒmɪtə) *n.* a sensitive instrument for measuring radiant energy by the increase in the resistance of an electrical conductor. [C19: from *bol-,* from Greek *bolē* ray of light, stroke, from *ballein* to throw + -METER] —**bolometric** (ˌbəʊləˈmɛtrɪk) *adj.* —ˌ**boloˈmetrically** *adv.* —**boˈlometry** *n.*

boloney (bəˈləʊnɪ) *n.* **1.** a variant spelling of **baloney. 2.** *Chiefly U.S.* another name for **bologna sausage.**

Bolshevik (ˈbɒlʃɪvɪk) *n., pl.* **-viks** *or* **-viki** (-ˈviːkɪ). **1.** (formerly) a Russian Communist. Compare **Menshevik. 2.** any Communist. **3.** (*often not cap.*) *Informal and derogatory.* any political radical, esp. a revolutionary. [C20: from Russian *Bol'shevik* majority, from *bol'shoi* great; from the fact that this group formed a majority of the Russian Social Democratic Party in 1903] —ˈ**Bolsheˌvism** *n.* —ˈ**Bolshevist** *adj., n.* —ˌ**Bolsheˈvistic** *adj.*

bolshie *or* **bolshy** (ˈbɒlʃɪ) (*sometimes cap.*) *Brit. informal.* ~*adj.* **1.** difficult to manage; rebellious. **2.** politically radical or left-wing. ~*n., pl.* **-shies. 3.** *Derogatory.* any political radical. [C20: shortened from BOLSHEVIK]

bolson (bəʊlˈsəʊn) *n. Southwestern U.S.* a desert valley surrounded by mountains, with a shallow lake at the centre. [C19: from American Spanish *bolsón,* from Spanish *bolsa* purse, from Late Latin *bursa* bag; see PURSE]

bolster (ˈbəʊlstə) *vb.* (*tr.*). **1.** (often foll. by *up*) to support or reinforce; strengthen: *to bolster morale.* **2.** to prop up with a pillow or cushion. **3.** to add padding to: *to bolster a dress.* ~*n.* **4.** a long narrow pillow or cushion. **5.** any pad or padded support. **6.** *Architect.* a short horizontal length of timber fixed to the top of a post to increase the bearing area and reduce the span of the supported beam. **7.** a cold chisel having a broad blade splayed towards the cutting edge, used for cutting stone slabs, etc. [Old English *bolster;* related to Old Norse *bolstr,* Old High German *bolstar,* Dutch *bulster*] —ˈ**bolsterer** *n.* —ˈ**bolstering** *n., adj.*

bolt[1] (bəʊlt) *n.* **1.** a bar that can be slid into a socket to lock a door, gate, etc. **2.** a bar or rod that forms part of a locking mechanism and is moved by a key or a knob. **3.** a metal rod or pin that has a head at one end and a screw thread at the other to take a nut. **4.** a sliding bar in a breech-loading firearm that ejects the empty cartridge, replaces it with a new one, and closes the breech. **5.** a flash of lightning. **6.** a sudden start or movement, esp. in order to escape: *they made a bolt for the door.* **7.** *U.S.* a sudden desertion, esp. from a political party. **8.** a roll of something, such as cloth, wallpaper, etc. **9.** an arrow, esp. for a crossbow. **10.** *Printing.* a folded edge on a sheet of paper that is removed when cutting to size. **11.** *Mountaineering.* short for **expansion bolt. 12. a bolt from the blue.** a sudden, unexpected, and usually unwelcome event. **13. shoot one's bolt.** to exhaust one's efforts: *the runner had shot his bolt.* ~*vb.* **14.** (*tr.*) to secure or lock with or as with a bolt or bolts: *bolt your doors.* **15.** (*tr.*) to eat hurriedly: *don't bolt your food.* **16.** (*intr.;* usually foll. by *from* or *out*) to move or jump suddenly: *he bolted from the chair.* **17.** (*intr.*) (esp. of a horse) to start hurriedly and run away without warning. **18.** (*tr.*) to roll or make (cloth, wallpaper, etc.) into bolts. **19.** *U.S.* to desert (a political party, etc.). **20.** (*intr.*) (of cultivated plants) to produce flowers and seeds prematurely. **21.** (*tr.*) to cause (a wild animal) to leave its lair; start: *terriers were used for bolting rats.* ~*adv.* **22.** stiffly, firmly, or rigidly (archaic except in the phrase **bolt upright**). [Old English *bolt* arrow; related to Old High German *bolz* bolt for a crossbow]

bolt[2] *or* **boult** (bəʊlt) *vb.* (*tr.*) **1.** to pass (flour, a powder, etc.) through a sieve. **2.** to examine and separate. [C13: from Old French *bulter,* probably of Germanic origin; compare Old High German *būtil* bag] —ˈ**bolter** *or* ˈ**boulter** *n.*

bolter (ˈbəʊltə) *n. Austral. informal.* **1.** an outsider in a contest or race. **2.** *Archaic.* an escaped convict; bushranger.

bolt hole *n.* a place of escape from danger.

boltonia (bəʊlˈtəʊnɪə) *n.* any North American plant of the genus *Boltonia,* having daisy-like flowers with white, violet, or pinkish rays: family *Compositae* (composites). [C18: New Latin, named after James *Bolton,* C18 English botanist]

boltrope (ˈbəʊltˌrəʊp) *n. Nautical.* a rope sewn to the foot or luff of a sail to strengthen it. [C17: from BOLT[1] + ROPE]

Boltzmann constant (ˈbəʊltsmən) *n. Physics.* the ratio of the gas constant to the Avogadro constant, equal to 1.380 622 × 10^{-23} joule per kelvin. Symbol: *k* [C20: named after L. *Boltzmann* (1844–1906), Austrian physicist]

bolus (ˈbəʊləs) *n., pl.* **-luses. 1.** a small round soft mass, esp. of chewed food. **2.** a large pill or tablet used in veterinary and clinical medicine. **3.** another word for **bole**[2]. [C17: from New Latin, from Greek *bōlos* clod, lump]

boma (ˈboːma) *n.* (in central and E Africa) **1.** an enclosure, esp. a palisade or fence of thorn bush, set up to protect a camp, herd of animals, etc. **2. a.** a police post. **b.** a magistrate's office. [C19: from Swahili]

bomb (bɒm) *n.* **1. a.** a hollow projectile containing explosive, incendiary, or other destructive substance, esp. one carried by aircraft. **b.** (*as modifier*): *bomb disposal; a bomb bay.* **c.** (*in combination*): *a bombload; bombproof.* **2.** any container filled with explosive: *a car bomb; a letter bomb.* **3. the bomb.** a hydrogen or atom bomb considered as the ultimate destructive weapon. **4.** a round or pear-shaped mass of volcanic rock, solidified from molten lava that has been thrown into the air. **5.** *Med.* a container for radioactive material, applied therapeutically to any part of the body: *a cobalt bomb.* **6.** *Brit. slang.* a large sum of money (esp. in the phrase **make a bomb**). **7.** *U.S. and Canadian slang.* a disastrous failure: *the new play was a total bomb.* **8.** *Austral. and N.Z. slang.* an old or dilapidated motorcar. **9.** *American football.* a very long high pass. **10. like a bomb.** *Brit. and N.Z. informal.* with great speed or success; very well (esp. in the phrase **go like a bomb**). ~*vb.* **11.** to attack with or as if with a bomb or bombs; drop bombs (on). **12.** (*intr.*; often foll. by *off, along,* etc.) *Informal.* to move or drive very quickly. **13.** (*intr.*) *U.S. and Canadian slang.* to fail disastrously; be a flop: *the new play bombed.* ~See also **bomb out.** [C17: from French *bombe,* from Italian *bomba,* probably from Latin *bombus* a booming sound, from Greek *bombos,* of imitative origin; compare Old Norse *bumba* drum]

bombacaceous (ˌbɒmbəˈkeɪʃəs) *adj.* of, relating to, or belonging to the *Bombacaceae,* a family of tropical trees, including the kapok tree and baobab, that have very thick stems, often with water-storing tissue. [C19: from New Latin *Bombācāceae,* from Medieval Latin *bombāx* cotton, from Latin *bombyx* silkworm, silk, from Greek *bombux*]

bombard *vb.* (bɒmˈbɑːd). (*tr.*) **1.** to attack with concentrated artillery fire or bombs. **2.** to attack with vigour and persistence: *the boxer bombarded his opponent with blows to the body.* **3.** to attack verbally, esp. with questions: *the journalists bombarded her with questions.* **4.** *Physics.* to direct high-energy particles or photons against (atoms, nuclei, etc.), esp. to produce ions or nuclear transformations. ~*n.* (ˈbɒmbɑːd). **5.** an ancient type of cannon that threw stone balls. [C15: from Old French *bombarder* to pelt, from *bombarde* stone-throwing cannon, probably from Latin *bombus* booming sound; see BOMB] —**bomˈbardment** *n.*

bombardier[1] (ˌbɒmbəˈdɪə) *n.* **1.** the member of a bomber aircrew responsible for aiming and releasing the bombs. **2.** *Brit.* a noncommissioned rank below the rank of sergeant in the Royal Artillery. **3.** Also called: **bombardier beetle.** any of various small carabid beetles of the genus *Brachinus,* esp. *B. crepitans* of Europe, which defend themselves by ejecting a jet of volatile fluid. [C16: from Old French: one directing a bombard; see BOMBARD]

bombardier[2] (ˌbɒmbəˈdɪə) *n. Canadian.* a snow tractor, typically having caterpillar tracks at the rear and skis at the front. [C20: named after J. A. *Bombardier,* Canadian inventor and manufacturer]

bombardon (ˈbɒmbədən, bɒmˈbɑːdᵊn) *n.* **1.** a brass instrument of the tuba type, similar to a sousaphone. **2.** a 16-foot bass reed stop on an organ. [C19: from Italian *bombardone;* see BOMBARD]

bombast (ˈbɒmbæst) *n.* **1.** pompous and grandiloquent language. **2.** *Obsolete.* material used for padding. [C16: from Old French *bombace,* from Medieval Latin *bombāx* cotton; see BOMBACACEOUS] —**bomˈbastic** *adj.* —**bomˈbastically** *adv.*

Bombay duck (bɒmˈbeɪ) *n.* a teleost fish, *Harpodon nehereus,* that resembles and is related to the lizard fishes: family *Harpodontidae.* It is eaten dried with curry dishes as a savoury. Also called: **bummalo.** [C19: changed from *bombil* (see BUMMALO) through association with *Bombay,* India, from which it was exported]

bombazine *or* **bombasine** (ˌbɒmbəˈziːn, ˈbɒmbəˌziːn) *n.* a twilled fabric, esp. one with a silk warp and worsted weft, formerly worn dyed black for mourning. [C16: from Old French *bombasin,* from Latin *bombȳcinus* silken, from *bombyx* silkworm, silk; see BOMBACACEOUS]

bomb calorimeter *n. Chem.* a device for determining heats of combustion by igniting a sample in a high pressure of oxygen in a sealed vessel and measuring the resulting rise in temperature: used for measuring the calorific value of foods.

bombe (bɒmb) *n.* **1.** Also called: **bombe glacée.** a dessert of ice cream lined or filled with custard, cake crumbs, etc. **2.** a mould shaped like a bomb in which this dessert is made. [C19: from French, literally: BOMB; from its rounded shape]

bombé (bɒmˈbeɪ; *French* bɔ̃be) *adj.* (of furniture) having a projecting swollen shape. [French, literally: bomb-shaped, from *bombe* BOMB]

bombed (bɒmd) *adj. Slang.* under the influence of alcohol or drugs (esp. in the phrase **bombed out of one's mind** *or* **skull**).

bomber (ˈbɒmə) *n.* **1.** a military aircraft designed to carry out bombing missions. **2.** a person who plants bombs. **3.** *Navy slang.* a Polaris submarine.

bomber jacket *n.* a short jacket finishing at the waist with an elasticated band, usually having a zip front and cuffed sleeves.

bombinate (ˈbɒmbɪˌneɪt) *vb.* (*intr.*) *Literary.* to make a buzzing noise. Also (rare): **bombilate.** [C19: from Latin *bombināre,* variant of *bombilāre* to buzz] —ˌ**bombiˈnation** *n.*

bombing run *n.* an approach by a bomber to a target.

bombora (bɒmˈbɔːrə) *n. Austral.* **1.** a submerged reef. **2.** a turbulent area of sea over such a reef. [from a native Australian language]

bomb out *vb.* (*adv.; tr., usually passive*) to make homeless by bombing: *24 families in this street have been bombed out.*

bombshell (ˈbɒmˌʃɛl) *n.* **1.** (esp. formerly) a bomb or artillery shell. **2.** a shocking or unwelcome surprise: *the news of his death was a bombshell.* **3.** *Informal.* an attractive girl or woman (esp. in the phrase **blonde bombshell**).

bombsight (ˈbɒmˌsaɪt) *n.* a mechanical or electronic device in an aircraft for aiming bombs.

bomb site *n.* an area where the buildings have been destroyed by bombs.

bombycid (ˈbɒmbɪsɪd) *n.* **1.** any moth, including the silkworm moth, of the family *Bombycidae,* most of which occur in Africa and SE Asia. ~*adj.* **2.** of, relating to, or belonging to the *Bombycidae.* [C19: from Latin *bombyx* silkworm]

Bon (bɔːn) *n.* **1.** Also called: **Feast** (*or* **Festival**) **of Lanterns.** an annual festival celebrated by Japanese Buddhists. **2. a.** the pre-Buddhist priests of Tibet or one such priest. **b.** their religion. [from Japanese *bon* bowl, lantern]

bona fide *adj.* (ˈbəʊnə ˈfaɪdɪ). **1.** real or genuine: *a bona fide manuscript.* **2.** undertaken in good faith: *a bona fide agreement.* ~*n.* (ˈbɔːnə fɑɪd). **3.** *Irish informal.* a public house licensed to remain open after normal hours to serve bona fide travellers. [C16: from Latin]

bona fides (ˈbəʊnə ˈfaɪdiːz) *n. Law.* good faith; honest intention. [Latin]

bonanza (bəˈnænzə) *n.* **1.** a source, usually sudden and unexpected, of luck or wealth. **2.** *U.S. and Canadian.* a mine or vein rich in ore. [C19: from Spanish, literally: calm sea, hence, good luck, from Medieval Latin *bonacia,* from Latin *bonus* good + *malacia* dead calm, from Greek *malakia* softness]

Bonapartism (ˈbəʊnəpɑːˌtɪzəm) *n.* **1.** a political system resembling the rule of Napoleon I (1769–1821), Emperor of the French (1804–15): centralized government by a military dictator, who enjoys popular support given expression in plebiscites. **2.** (esp. in France) support for the government or dynasty of Napoleon Bonaparte. —ˈ**Bonaˌpartist** *n.*

bona vacantia (ˈbəʊnə vəˈkæntɪə) *pl. n. Law.* unclaimed goods.

bonbon (ˈbɒnbɒn) *n.* a sweet. [C19: from French, originally a children's word from *bon* good]

bonce (bɒns) *n. Brit. slang.* the head. [C19 (originally: a type of large playing marble): of unknown origin]

bond (bɒnd) *n.* **1.** something that binds, fastens, or holds together, such as a chain or rope. **2.** (*often pl.*) something that brings or holds people together; tie: *a bond of friendship.* **3.** (*pl.*) something that restrains or imprisons; captivity or imprisonment. **4.** something that governs behaviour; obligation; duty. **5.** a written or spoken agreement, esp. a promise: *marriage bond.* **6.** adhesive quality or strength. **7.** *Finance.* a certificate of debt issued in order to raise funds. It carries a fixed rate of interest and is repayable with or without security at a specified future date. **8.** *Law.* a written acknowledgment of an obligation to pay a sum or to perform a contract. **9.** *Insurance, U.S. and Canadian.* a policy guaranteeing payment of a stated sum to an employer in compensation for financial losses incurred through illegal or unauthorized acts of an employee. **10.** any of various arrangements of bricks or stones in a wall in which they overlap so as to provide strength. **11.** See **chemical bond.** **12.** See **bond paper.** **13. in bond.** *Commerce.* deposited in a bonded warehouse. ~*vb.* (*mainly tr.*) **14.** (*also intr.*) to hold or be held together, as by a rope or an adhesive; bind; connect. **15.** *Aeronautics.* to join (metallic parts of an aircraft) together such that they are electrically interconnected. **16.** to put or hold (goods) in bond. **17.** *Law.* to place under bond. **18.** *Finance.* to issue bonds on; mortgage. **19.** to arrange (bricks, etc.) in a bond. [C13: from Old Norse *band;* see BAND[2]]

bondage (ˈbɒndɪdʒ) *n.* **1.** slavery or serfdom; servitude. **2.** Also called: **villeinage.** (in medieval Europe) the condition and status of unfree peasants who provided labour and other services for their lord in return for holdings of land. **3.** a sexual practice in which one partner is physically bound.

bonded (ˈbɒndɪd) *adj.* **1.** *Finance.* consisting of, secured by, or operating under a bond or bonds. **2.** *Commerce.* deposited in a bonded warehouse; placed or stored in bond.

bonded warehouse *n.* a warehouse in which dutiable goods are deposited until duty is paid or the goods are cleared for export.

bondholder (ˈbɒndˌhəʊldə) *n.* an owner of one or more bonds issued by a company or other institution.

bonding (ˈbɒndɪŋ) *n.* the process by which individuals become emotionally attached to one another. See also **pair bond.**

bondmaid (ˈbɒndˌmeɪd) *n.* an unmarried female serf or slave.

bond paper *n.* a superior quality of strong white paper, used esp. for writing and typing.

bondservant (ˈbɒndˌsɜːvənt) *n.* a serf or slave.

bondsman (ˈbɒndzmən) *n., pl.* **-men.** **1.** *Law.* a person bound by bond to act as surety for another. **2.** another word for **bondservant.**

bondstone (ˈbɒndˌstəʊn) *n.* a long stone or brick laid in a wall as a header. Also called: ˈ**bonder.**

bond washing *n.* a series of illegal deals in bonds made with the intention of avoiding taxation.

bone (bəʊn) *n.* **1.** any of the various structures that make up the skeleton in most vertebrates. **2.** the porous rigid tissue of which these parts are made, consisting of a matrix of collagen and inorganic salts, esp. calcium phosphate, interspersed with canals and small holes. **3.** something consisting of bone or a bonelike substance. **4.** (*pl.*) the human skeleton or body: *they laid his bones to rest; come and rest your bones.* **5.** a thin strip of whalebone, light metal, plastic, etc., used to stiffen corsets and brassieres. **6.** (*pl.*) the essentials (esp. in the phrase **the bare bones**): *to explain the bones of a situation.* **7.** (*pl.*) dice. **8.** (*pl.*) an informal nickname for a **doctor.** **9. feel in one's bones.** to have an intuition of. **10. have a bone to pick.** to have grounds for a quarrel. **11. make no bones about. a.** to be direct and candid about. **b.** to have no scruples about. **12. near** *or* **close to the bone. a.** risqué or indecent: *his jokes are rather near the bone.* **b.** in poverty; destitute. **13. (never) make old bones.** (not) live to a ripe old age. **14. point the bone.** (often foll. by *at*) *Austral.* **a.** to wish bad luck (on). **b.** to threaten to bring about the downfall (of). ~*vb.* (*mainly tr.*) **15.** to remove the bones from (meat for cooking, etc.). **16.** to stiffen (a corset, etc.) by inserting bones. **17.** to fertilize with bone meal. **18.** *Brit.* a slang word for **steal.** ~See also **bone up.** [Old English *bān;* related to Old Norse *béin,* Old Frisian *bēn,* Old High German *bein*] —'**boneless** *adj.*

bone ash *n.* the residue obtained when bones are burned in air, consisting mainly of calcium phosphate. It is used as a fertilizer and in the manufacture of bone china.

bone bed *n. Geology.* a sediment containing large quantities of fossilized animal remains, such as bones, teeth, scales, etc.

boneblack ('bəʊnˌblæk) *n.* a black residue from the destructive distillation of bones, containing about 10 per cent carbon and 80 per cent calcium phosphate, used as a decolorizing agent and pigment.

bone china *n.* porcelain containing bone ash.

bone-dry *adj. Informal.* **a.** completely dry: *a bone-dry well.* **b.** (*postpositive*): *the well was bone dry.*

bonefish ('bəʊnˌfɪʃ) *n., pl.* **-fish** *or* **-fishes. 1.** a silvery marine clupeoid game fish, *Albula vulpes,* occurring in warm shallow waters: family *Albulidae.* **2.** a similar related fish, *Dixonina nemoptera,* of the Pacific Ocean.

bonehead ('bəʊnˌhɛd) *n. Slang.* a stupid or obstinate person. —ˌ**bone'headed** *adj.*

bone idle *adj.* very idle; extremely lazy.

bone marrow *n.* See **marrow**[1] (sense 1).

bone meal *n.* the product of dried and ground animal bones, used as a fertilizer or in stock feeds.

bone of contention *n.* the grounds or subject of a dispute.

bone oil *n.* a dark brown pungent oil, containing pyridine and hydrocarbons, obtained by the destructive distillation of bones.

boner ('bəʊnə) *n.* **1.** *Slang.* a blunder. **2.** *N.Z.* a low-grade slaughtered animal suitable for use in pies, sausages, etc.

boneset ('bəʊnˌsɛt) *n.* any of various North American plants of the genus *Eupatorium,* esp. *E. perfoliatum,* which has flat clusters of small white flowers: family *Compositae* (composites). Also called: **agueweed, feverwort, thoroughwort.**

bonesetter ('bəʊnˌsɛtə) *n.* a person who sets broken or dislocated bones, esp. one who has no formal medical qualifications.

boneshaker ('bəʊnˌʃeɪkə) *n.* **1.** an early type of bicycle having solid tyres and no springs. **2.** *Slang.* any decrepit or rickety vehicle.

bone turquoise *n.* fossilized bone or tooth stained blue with iron phosphate and used as a gemstone. Also called: **odontolite.**

bone up *vb.* (*adv.;* when *intr.,* usually foll. by *on*) *Informal.* to study intensively.

boneyard ('bəʊnˌjɑːd) *n.* an informal name for a **cemetery.**

bonfire ('bɒnˌfaɪə) *n.* a large outdoor fire. [C15: alteration (through influence of French *bon* good) of *bone-fire;* from the use of bones as fuel]

bong (bɒŋ) *n.* **1.** a deep reverberating sound, as of a large bell. ~*vb.* (*intr.*) **2.** to make a deep reverberating sound. [C20: of imitative origin]

bongo[1] ('bɒŋgəʊ) *n., pl.* **-go** *or* **-gos.** a rare spiral-horned antelope, *Boocercus* (or *Taurotragus*) *eurycerus,* inhabiting forests of central Africa. The coat is bright red-brown with narrow cream stripes. [of African origin]

bongo[2] ('bɒŋgəʊ) *n., pl.* **-gos** *or* **-goes.** a small bucket-shaped drum, usually one of a pair, played by beating with the fingers. [American Spanish, probably of imitative origin]

bonham ('bɒnəv) *n. Irish.* a piglet. [C19: from Irish Gaelic *banbh*]

bonhomie ('bɒnəmiː; *French* bɔnɔmi) *n.* exuberant friendliness. [C18: from French, from *bonhomme* good-humoured fellow, from *bon* good + *homme* man]

bonhomous ('bɒnəməs) *adj.* exhibiting bonhomie.

bonism ('bəʊˌnɪzəm) *n.* the doctrine that the world is good, although not the best of all possible worlds. [C19: from Latin *bonus* good + -ISM] —'**bonist** *n., adj.*

bonito (bə'niːtəʊ) *n., pl.* **-tos. 1.** any of various small tunny-like marine food fishes of the genus *Sarda,* of warm Atlantic and Pacific waters: family *Scombridae* (tunnies and mackerels). **2.** any of various similar or related fishes, such as *Katsuwonus pelamis* (**oceanic bonito**), the flesh of which is dried and flaked and used in Japanese cookery. [C16: from Spanish *bonito,* from Latin *bonus* good]

bonk (bɒŋk) *vb. Informal.* **1.** (*tr.*) to hit. **2.** to have sexual intercourse (with). [C20: probably of imitative origin] —'**bonking** *n.*

bonkers ('bɒŋkəz) *adj. Slang, chiefly Brit.* mad; crazy. [C20 (originally in the sense: slightly drunk, tipsy): of unknown origin]

bon mot (*French* bɔ̃ mo) *n., pl.* **bons mots** (bɔ̃ mo). a clever and fitting remark. [French, literally: good word]

bonne *French.* (bɔn) *n.* a housemaid or female servant. [C18: from feminine of *bon* good]

bonne bouche *French.* (bɔn buʃ) *n., pl.* ***bonnes bouches*** (bɔn buʃ). a tasty titbit or morsel. [literally: good mouth(ful)]

bonnet ('bɒnɪt) *n.* **1.** any of various hats worn, esp. formerly, by women and girls, usually framing the face and tied with ribbons under the chin. **2.** (in Scotland) Also called: **bunnet** ('bʌnɪt). **a.** a soft cloth cap. **b.** formerly, a flat brimless cap worn by men. **3.** the hinged metal part of a motor vehicle body that provides access to the engine, or to the luggage space in a rear-engined vehicle. **4.** a cowl on a chimney. **5.** *Nautical.* a piece of sail laced to the foot of a foresail to give it greater area in light winds. **6.** (in the U.S. and Canada) a headdress of feathers worn by some tribes of American Indians, esp. formerly as a sign of war. [C14: from Old French *bonet,* from Medieval Latin *abonnis,* of unknown origin]

bonnet monkey *n.* an Indian macaque, *Macaca radiata,* with a bonnet-like tuft of hair.

bonnet rouge *French.* (bɔnɛ ruʒ) *n.* **1.** a red cap worn by ardent supporters of the French Revolution. **2.** an extremist or revolutionary. [literally: red cap]

bonny ('bɒnɪ) *adj.* **-nier, -niest. 1.** *Scot. and northern English dialect.* beautiful or handsome: *a bonny lass.* **2.** merry or lively: *a bonny family.* **3.** good or fine: *a bonny house.* **4.** (esp. of babies) plump. **5.** *Scot. and northern English dialect.* considerable; to be reckoned with: *cost a bonny penny.* **6.** *Scot. and northern English dialect.* terrible: *a bonny mess.* ~*adv.* **7.** *Informal.* agreeably or well: *to speak bonny.* [C15: of uncertain origin; perhaps from Old French *bon* good, from Latin *bonus*] —'**bonnily** *adv.*

bonsai ('bɒnsaɪ) *n., pl.* **-sai. 1.** the art of growing dwarfed ornamental varieties of trees or shrubs in small shallow pots or trays by selective pruning, etc. **2.** a tree or shrub grown by this method. [C20: Japanese: plant grown in a pot, from *bon* basin, bowl + *sai* to plant]

bonsela (bɒn'sɛlə) *n. S. African.* a small gift to a Black African. Also called: **bansela, pasela** (pə'sɛlə). [from a Bantu language]

bonspiel ('bɒnˌspiːl, -spəl) *n.* a curling match. [C16: probably from Low German; compare Flemish *bonespel* children's game; see SPIEL]

bontebok ('bɒntɪˌbʌk) *n., pl.* **-boks** *or* **-bok.** an antelope, *Damaliscus pygargus* (or *dorcas*), of southern Africa, having a deep reddish-brown coat with a white blaze, tail, and rump patch. [C18: Afrikaans, from *bont* pied + *bok* BUCK[1]]

bon ton *French.* (bɔ̃ tɔ̃) *n. Literary.* **1.** sophisticated manners or breeding. **2.** fashionable society. [literally: good tone]

bonus ('bəʊnəs) *n.* **1.** something given, paid, or received above what is due or expected: *a Christmas bonus for all employees.* **2.** *Chiefly Brit.* an extra dividend allotted to shareholders out of profits. **3.** *Insurance, Brit.* a dividend, esp. a percentage of net profits, distributed to policyholders either annually or when the policy matures. **4.** *Brit.* a slang word for a **bribe.** [C18: from Latin *bonus* (adj.) good]

bonus issue *n. Brit.* an issue of shares made by a company without charge and distributed pro rata among existing shareholders. Also called: **scrip issue.**

bon vivant *French.* (bɔ̃ vivɑ̃) *n., pl.* ***bons vivants*** (bɔ̃ vivɑ̃). a person who enjoys luxuries, esp. good food and drink. Also called (but not in French): **bon viveur** (ˌbɒn viː'vɜː). [literally: good living (man)]

bon voyage (*French* bɔ̃ vwajaʒ) *sentence substitute.* a phrase used to wish a traveller a pleasant journey. [French, literally: good journey]

bonxie ('bɒŋksɪ) *n.* a name, originally Shetland, for the **great skua** (see **skua**). [C19: probably of Scandinavian origin: compare Norwegian *bunke* heap, something dumpy]

bony ('bəʊnɪ) *adj.* **bonier, boniest. 1.** resembling or consisting of bone or bones. **2.** having many bones. **3.** having prominent bones: *bony cheeks.* **4.** thin or emaciated: *a bony old woman.* **5.** (of fishes) having a skeleton of bone, rather than of cartilage. —'**boniness** *n.*

bonze (bɒnz) *n.* a Chinese or Japanese Buddhist priest or monk. [C16: from French, from Portuguese *bonzo,* from Japanese *bonsō,* from Chinese *fan sêng,* from *fan* Buddhist (from Sanskrit *brāhmanas* BRAHMAN) + *sêng* MONK]

bonzer ('bɒnzə) *adj. Austral. and N.Z. slang, archaic.* excellent; very good. [C20: of uncertain origin; perhaps from BONANZA]

boo (buː) *interj.* **1.** an exclamation uttered to startle or surprise someone, esp. a child. **2.** a shout uttered to express disgust, dissatisfaction, or contempt, esp. at a theatrical production, political meeting, etc. **3. would not say boo to a goose.** is extremely timid or diffident. ~*vb.* **boos, booing, booed. 4.** to shout "boo" at (someone or something), esp. as an expression of disgust, dissatisfaction, or disapproval: *to boo the actors.*

boob (buːb) *Slang.* ~*n.* **1.** an ignorant or foolish person; booby. **2.** *Brit.* an embarrassing mistake; blunder. **3.** a female breast. ~*vb.* **4.** (*intr.*) *Brit.* to make a blunder. [C20: back formation from BOOBY]

boobialla (ˌbuːbɪ'ælə) *n. Austral.* **1.** another name for **golden wattle** (sense 2). **2.** any of various trees or shrubs of the genus *Myoporum,* esp. *M. insulare.* [from a native Australian language]

boo-boo *n., pl.* **-boos.** *Informal.* an embarrassing mistake; blunder. [C20: perhaps from nursery talk; compare BOOHOO]
boobook ('buːbʊk) *n.* a small spotted brown Australian owl, *Ninox boobook.*
boob tube *n. Slang.* **1.** a close-fitting strapless top, worn by women. **2.** *Austral.* a strapless, boneless, shapeless brassiere made of a stretch fabric. **3.** *Chiefly U.S. and Canadian.* a television receiver.
booby ('buːbɪ) *n., pl.* **-bies.** **1.** an ignorant or foolish person. **2.** *Brit.* the losing player in a game. **3.** any of several tropical marine birds of the genus *Sula:* family *Sulidae,* order *Pelecaniformes* (pelicans, cormorants, etc.). They have a straight stout bill and the plumage is white with darker markings. Compare **gannet.** [C17: from Spanish *bobo,* from Latin *balbus* stammering]
booby hatch *n.* **1.** a hoodlike covering for a hatchway on a ship. **2.** *U.S. slang.* a mental hospital.
booby prize *n.* a mock prize given to the person having the lowest score or giving the worst performance in a competition.
booby trap *n.* **1.** a hidden explosive device primed in such a way as to be set off by an unsuspecting victim. **2.** a trap for an unsuspecting person, esp. one intended as a practical joke, such as an object balanced above a door to fall on the person who opens it. *~vb.* **booby-trap, -traps, -trapping, -trapped.** **3.** (*tr.*) to set a booby trap in or on (a building or object) or for (a person).
boodle ('buːdᵊl) *Slang.* *~n.* **1.** money or valuables, esp. when stolen, counterfeit, or used as a bribe. **2.** *Chiefly U.S.* another word for **caboodle.** *~vb.* **3.** to give or receive money or valuables corruptly or illegally. [C19: from Dutch *boedel* all one's possessions, from Old Frisian *bōdel* movable goods, inheritance; see CABOODLE]
boofhead ('bʊfhɛd) *n. Slang, chiefly Austral.* **1.** a stupid person. **2.** a person or animal with a large head.
boogie ('buːgɪ) *Slang.* *~vb.* **-gies, -gieing, -gied.** (*intr.*) **1.** to dance to pop music. **2.** to make love. *~n.* **3.** a session of dancing to pop music. [C20: originally American Negro slang, perhaps from Kongo *mbugi* devilishly good]
boogie-woogie ('bʊgɪ'wʊgɪ, 'buːgɪ'wuːgɪ) *n.* a style of piano jazz using a dotted bass pattern, usually with eight notes in a bar and the harmonies of the 12-bar blues.
boohai (buː'haɪ) *n.* **up the boohai.** *N.Z. informal.* thoroughly lost. [from the remote township of *puhoi*]
boohoo (ˌbuː'huː) *vb.* **-hoos, -hooing, -hooed.** **1.** to sob or pretend to sob noisily. *~n., pl.* **-hoos.** **2.** (*sometimes pl.*) distressed or pretended sobbing. [C20: nursery talk]
boo-hurrah theory *n. Philosophy.* an informal term for **emotivism.**
book (bʊk) *n.* **1.** a number of printed or written pages bound together along one edge and usually protected by thick paper or stiff pasteboard covers. See also **hardback, paperback.** **2. a.** a written work or composition, such as a novel, technical manual, or dictionary. **b.** (*as modifier*): *the book trade; book reviews.* **c.** (*in combination*): *bookseller; bookshop; bookshelf; bookrack.* **3.** a number of blank or ruled sheets of paper bound together, used to record lessons, keep accounts, etc. **4.** (*pl.*) a record of the transactions of a business or society. **5.** the script of a play or the libretto of an opera, musical, etc. **6.** a major division of a written composition, as of a long novel or of the Bible. **7.** a number of tickets, sheets, stamps, etc., fastened together along one edge. **8.** *Bookmaking.* a record of the bets made on a horse race or other event. **9.** (in card games) the number of tricks that must be taken by a side or player before any trick has a scoring value: *in bridge, six of the 13 tricks form the book.* **10.** strict or rigid regulations, rules, or standards (esp. in the phrases **according to the book, by the book**). **11.** a source of knowledge or authority: *the book of life.* **12.** a telephone directory (in the phrase **in the book**). **13. the book.** (*sometimes cap.*) the Bible. **14. an open book.** a person or subject that is thoroughly understood. **15. a closed book.** a person or subject that is unknown or beyond comprehension: *chemistry is a closed book to him.* **16. bring to book.** to reprimand or require (someone) to give an explanation of his conduct. **17. close the books.** *Book-keeping.* to balance accounts in order to prepare a statement or report. **18. cook the books.** *Informal.* to make fraudulent alterations to business or other accounts. **19. in my book.** according to my view of things. **20. in someone's good** (*or* **bad**) **books.** regarded by someone with favour (or disfavour). **21. keep the books.** to keep written records of the finances of a business or other enterprise. **22. on the books. a.** enrolled as a member. **b.** registered or recorded. **23. read (someone) like a book.** to understand (a person, his motives, character, etc.) thoroughly and clearly. **24. suit one's book.** to be pleasing or acceptable to one. **25. throw the book at. a.** to charge with every relevant offence. **b.** to inflict the most severe punishment on. *~vb.* **26.** to reserve (a place, passage, etc.) or engage the services of (a performer, driver, etc.) in advance: *to book a flight; to book a band.* **27.** (*tr.*) to take the name and address of (a person guilty of a minor offence) with a view to bringing a prosecution: *he was booked for ignoring a traffic signal.* **28.** (*tr.*) (of a football referee) to take the name of (a player) who grossly infringes the rules while playing, three such acts resulting in the player's dismissal from the field. **29.** (*tr.*) *Archaic.* to record in a book. ~See also **book in, book into, book out, book up.** [Old English *bōc;* related to Old Norse *bōk,* Old High German *buoh* book, Gothic *bōka* letter; see BEECH (the bark of which was used as a writing surface)]
bookbinder ('bʊkˌbaɪndə) *n.* a person whose business or craft is binding books. —**'bookˌbinding** *n.*
bookbindery ('bʊkˌbaɪndərɪ) *n., pl.* **-eries.** a place in which books are bound. Often shortened to **bindery.**
bookcase ('bʊkˌkeɪs) *n.* a piece of furniture containing shelves for books, often fitted with glass doors.
book club *n.* a club that sells books at low prices to members, usually by mail order, esp. on condition that they buy a minimum number.
booked up *adj.* unable to offer any appointments or accept any reservations, etc.; fully booked; full up.
book end *n.* one of a pair of usually ornamental supports for holding a row of books upright.
Booker Prize ('bʊkə) *n.* an annual prize for a work of British, Commonwealth, or Irish fiction of £15,000, awarded since 1969 by the Booker McConnell engineering company.
bookie ('bʊkɪ) *n. Informal.* short for **bookmaker.**
book in *vb.* (*adv.*) **1.** to reserve a room for (oneself or someone else) at a hotel. **2.** *Chiefly Brit.* to record something in a book or register, esp. one's arrival at a hotel.
booking ('bʊkɪŋ) *n.* **1.** *Chiefly Brit.* **a.** a reservation, as of a table or room in a hotel, seat in a theatre, or seat on a train, aircraft, etc. **b.** (*as modifier*): *the booking office at a railway station.* **2.** *Theatre.* an engagement for the services of an actor or acting company.
book into *vb.* (*prep.*) to reserve a room for (oneself or someone else) at (a hotel).
bookish ('bʊkɪʃ) *adj.* **1.** fond of reading; studious. **2.** consisting of or forming opinions or attitudes through reading rather than direct personal experience; academic: *a bookish view of life.* **3.** of or relating to books: *a bookish career in publishing.* —**'bookishly** *adv.* —**'bookishness** *n.*
book-keeping *n.* the skill or occupation of systematically recording business transactions. —**'book-ˌkeeper** *n.*
book-learning *n.* **1.** knowledge gained from books rather than from direct personal experience. **2.** formal education.
booklet ('bʊklɪt) *n.* a thin book, esp. one having paper covers; pamphlet.
booklouse ('bʊkˌlaʊs) *n., pl.* **-lice.** any small insect of the order *Psocoptera,* esp. *Trogium pulsatorium* (**common booklouse**), a wingless species that feeds on bookbinding paste, etc.
bookmaker ('bʊkˌmeɪkə) *n.* a person who as an occupation accepts bets, esp. on horseraces, and pays out to winning betters. —**'bookˌmaking** *n.*
bookmark ('bʊkˌmɑːk) *or* **bookmarker** *n.* a strip or band of some material, such as leather or ribbon, put between the pages of a book to mark a place.
bookmobile ('bʊkməˌbiːl) *n.* the U.S. and Canadian word for **mobile library.**
book of account *n.* another name for **journal** (sense 4a).
Book of Common Prayer *n.* the official book of church services of the Church of England, until 1980, when the Alternative Service Book was sanctioned.
book of hours *n.* (*often caps.*) a book used esp. in monasteries during the Middle Ages that contained the prayers and offices of the canonical hours.
Book of Mormon *n.* a sacred book of the Mormon Church, believed by Mormons to be a history of certain ancient peoples in America, written on golden tablets (now lost) and revealed by the prophet Mormon to Joseph Smith.
book of original entry *n.* another name for **journal** (sense 4a.).
book out *vb.* (*usually intr., adv.*) to leave or cause to leave a hotel.
bookplate ('bʊkˌpleɪt) *n.* a label bearing the owner's name and an individual design or coat of arms, pasted into a book.
book scorpion *n.* any of various small arachnids of the order *Pseudoscorpionida* (false scorpions), esp. *Chelifer cancroides,* which are sometimes found in old books, etc.
bookstall ('bʊkˌstɔːl) *n.* a stall or stand where periodicals, newspapers, or books are sold. U.S. word: **newsstand.**
booksy ('bʊksɪ) *adj.* inclined to be bookish or literary.
book token *n. Brit.* a gift token to be exchanged for books.
book up *vb.* (*adv.*) **1.** to make a reservation (for); book. **2.** See **booked up.**
book value *n.* **1.** the value of an asset of a business according to its books. **2. a.** the net capital value of an enterprise as shown by the excess of book assets over book liabilities. **b.** the value of a share computed by dividing the net capital value of an enterprise by its issued shares. Compare **par value, market value.**
bookworm ('bʊkˌwɜːm) *n.* **1.** any of various small insects that feed on the binding paste of books, esp. the book louse. **2.** a person excessively devoted to studying.
bool (bʊl) *Scot.* *~n.* **1.** a bowling bowl. **2.** a playing marble. **3.** (*pl.*) the game of bowls or marbles. *~vb.* (*intr.*) **4.** to play bowls. [Scot. variant of BOWL[2]]
Boolean algebra ('buːlɪən) *n.* a system of symbolic logic devised by the British mathematician George Boole (1815–64) to codify nonmathematical logical operations. It is used in computers.

boom[1] (bu:m) *vb.* **1.** to make a deep prolonged resonant sound, as of thunder or artillery fire. **2.** to prosper or cause to prosper vigorously and rapidly: *business boomed.* ~*n.* **3.** a deep prolonged resonant sound: *the boom of the sea.* **4.** the cry of certain animals, esp. the bittern. **5.** a period of high economic growth characterized by rising wages, profits, and prices, full employment, and high levels of investment, trade, and other economic activity. Compare **depression** (sense 5). [C15: perhaps from Dutch *bommen,* of imitative origin]

boom[2] (bu:m) *n.* **1.** *Nautical.* a spar to which a sail is fastened to control its position relative to the wind. **2.** a beam or spar pivoting at the foot of the mast of a derrick, controlling the distance from the mast at which a load is lifted or lowered. **3.** a pole, usually extensible, carrying an overhead microphone and projected over a film or television set. **4. a.** a barrier across a waterway, usually consisting of a chain of connected floating logs, to confine free-floating logs, protect a harbour from attack, etc. **b.** the area so barred off. [C16: from Dutch *boom* tree, BEAM]

boomer ('bu:mə) *n.* **1.** *Austral.* a large male kangaroo. **2.** *Austral. and N.Z. informal.* anything exceptionally large. [from English dialect]

boomerang ('bu:məˌræŋ) *n.* **1.** a curved flat wooden missile of Australian aborigines, which can be made to return to the thrower. **2.** an action or statement that recoils on its originator. ~*vb.* **3.** (*intr.*) to recoil or return unexpectedly, causing harm to its originator; backfire. [C19: from a native Australian language]

boomkin ('bu:mkɪn) *n. Nautical.* a short boom projecting from the deck of a ship, used to secure the main-brace blocks or to extend the lower edge of the foresail. [C17: from Dutch *boomken,* from *boom* tree; see BEAM, -KIN]

boomslang ('bu:mˌslæŋ) *n.* a large greenish venomous arboreal colubrid snake, *Dispholidus typus,* of southern Africa. [C18: from Afrikaans, from *boom* tree + *slang* snake]

boom town *n.* a town that is enjoying sudden prosperity or has grown rapidly.

boon[1] (bu:n) *n.* **1.** something extremely useful, helpful, or beneficial; a blessing or benefit: *the car was a boon to him.* **2.** *Archaic.* a favour; request: *he asked a boon of the king.* [C12: from Old Norse *bōn* request; related to Old English *bēn* prayer]

boon[2] (bu:n) *adj.* **1.** close, special, or intimate (in the phrase **boon companion**). **2.** *Archaic.* jolly or convivial. [C14: from Old French *bon,* from Latin *bonus* good]

boondocks ('bu:nˌdɒks) *pl. n.* **the.** *U.S. and Canadian slang.* **1.** wild, desolate, or uninhabitable country. **2.** a remote rural or provincial area. ~Sometimes shortened to **the Boonies.** [C20: from Tagalog *bundok* mountain]

boondoggle ('bu:nˌdɒgᵊl) *Informal, chiefly U.S. and Canadian.* ~*vb.* **1.** (*intr.*) to do futile and unnecessary work. ~*n.* **2.** a futile and unnecessary project or work. [C20: said to have been coined by R. H. Link, American scoutmaster] —**'boonˌdoggler** *n.*

boong (bu:ŋ) *n. Austral. offensive.* a Black person. [C20: perhaps of native Australian origin]

boongary ('bu:ŋgærɪ) *n.* a tree kangaroo, *Dendrolagus lumholtzi,* of northeastern Queensland. [from a native Australian language]

boor (bʊə) *n.* an ill-mannered, clumsy, or insensitive person. [Old English *gebūr;* related to Old High German *gibūr* farmer, dweller, Albanian *būr* man; see NEIGHBOUR] —**'boorish** *adj.* —**'boorishly** *adv.* —**'boorishness** *n.*

boost (bu:st) *n.* **1.** encouragement, improvement, or help: *a boost to morale.* **2.** an upward thrust or push: *he gave him a boost over the wall.* **3.** an increase or rise: *a boost in salary.* **4.** a publicity campaign; promotion. **5.** the amount by which the induction pressure of a supercharged internal-combustion engine exceeds that of the ambient pressure. ~*vb.* (*tr.*) **6.** to encourage, assist, or improve: *to boost morale.* **7.** to lift by giving a push from below or behind. **8.** to increase or raise: *to boost the voltage in an electrical circuit.* **9.** to cause to rise; increase: *to boost sales.* **10.** to advertise on a big scale. **11.** to increase the induction pressure of (an internal-combustion engine) above that of the ambient pressure; supercharge. [C19: of unknown origin]

booster ('bu:stə) *n.* **1.** a person or thing that supports, assists, or increases power or effectiveness. **2.** Also called: **launching vehicle.** the first stage of a multistage rocket. **3.** *Radio, television.* **a.** a radio-frequency amplifier connected between an aerial and a receiver to amplify weak incoming signals. **b.** a radio-frequency amplifier that amplifies incoming signals, retransmitting them at higher power. **4.** another name for **supercharger.** **5.** short for **booster shot.** **6.** *Slang, chiefly U.S.* a shoplifter.

booster shot *n.* a supplementary injection of a vaccine given to maintain the immunization provided by an earlier dose.

boot[1] (bu:t) *n.* **1.** a strong outer covering for the foot; shoe that extends above the ankle, often to the knee. See also **chukka boot, top boot, Wellington boot, surgical boot.** **2.** *Brit.* an enclosed compartment of a car for holding luggage, etc., usually at the rear. U.S. and Canadian name: **trunk.** **3.** a protective covering over a mechanical device, such as a rubber sheath protecting a coupling joining two shafts. **4.** *U.S. and Canadian.* a rubber patch used to repair a puncture in a tyre. **5.** an instrument of torture used to crush the foot and lower leg. **6.** a protective covering for the lower leg of a horse. **7.** a kick: *he gave the door a boot.* **8.** *Brit. slang.* an ugly person (esp. in the phrase **old boot**). **9.** *U.S. slang.* a navy or marine recruit, esp. one in training. **10.** *Computer technol.* short for **bootstrap** (sense 4a). **11. bet one's boots.** to be certain: *you can bet your boots he'll come.* **12.** See **boots and all.** **13. die with one's boots on. a.** to die while still active. **b.** to die in battle. **14. lick the boots of.** to be servile, obsequious, or flattering towards. **15. put the boot in.** *Slang.* **a.** to kick a person, esp. when he is already down. **b.** to harass someone or aggravate a problem. **c.** to finish off (something) with unnecessary brutality. **16. the boot.** *Slang.* dismissal from employment; the sack. **17. the boot is on the other foot** *or* **leg.** the situation is or has now reversed. **18. too big for one's boots.** self-important or conceited. ~*vb.* (*tr.*) **19.** (esp. in football) to kick. **20.** to equip with boots. **21.** *Informal.* **a.** (often foll. by *out*) to eject forcibly. **b.** to dismiss from employment. ~See also **boots.** [C14 *bote,* from Old French, of uncertain origin]

boot[2] (bu:t) *vb.* (*usually impersonal*) **1.** *Archaic.* to be of advantage or use to (a person): *what boots it to complain?* ~*n.* **2.** *Obsolete.* an advantage. **3.** *Dialect.* something given in addition, esp. to equalize an exchange: *a ten pound boot to settle the bargain.* **4. to boot.** as well; in addition: *it's cold and musty, and damp to boot.* [Old English *bōt* compensation; related to Old Norse *bōt* remedy, Gothic *bōta,* Old High German *buoza* improvement]

bootblack ('bu:tˌblæk) *n. Chiefly U.S.* another word for **shoeblack.**

boot camp *n. U.S. slang.* a basic training camp for new recruits to the U.S. Navy or Marine Corps.

booted ('bu:tɪd) *adj.* **1.** wearing boots. **2.** *Ornithol.* **a.** (of birds) having an undivided tarsus covered with a horny sheath. **b.** (of poultry) having a feathered tarsus.

bootee ('bu:ti:, bu:'ti:) *n.* **1.** a soft shoe for a baby, esp. a knitted one. **2.** a boot for women and children, esp. an ankle-length one.

Boötes (bəʊ'əʊti:z) *n., Latin genitive* **Boötis** (bəʊ'əʊtɪs). a constellation in the N hemisphere lying near Ursa Major and containing the first magnitude star Arcturus. [C17: via Latin from Greek: ploughman, from *boōtein* to plough, from *bous* ox]

booth (bu:ð, bu:θ) *n., pl.* **booths** (bu:ðz). **1.** a stall for the display or sale of goods, esp. a temporary one at a fair or market. **2.** a small enclosed or partially enclosed room or cubicle, such as one containing a telephone (**telephone booth**) or one in which a person casts his vote at an election (**polling booth**). **3.** two long high-backed benches with a long table between, used esp. in bars and inexpensive restaurants. **4.** (formerly) a temporary structure for shelter, dwelling, storage, etc. [C12: of Scandinavian origin; compare Old Norse *buth,* Swedish, Danish *bod* shop, stall; see BOWER[1]]

bootie ('bu:tɪ) *n. Brit. slang.* a Royal Marine. [C20: from *bootneck,* so called from the leather tab used to close their tunic collars]

bootjack ('bu:tˌdʒæk) *n.* a device that grips the heel of a boot to enable the foot to be withdrawn easily.

bootlace ('bu:tˌleɪs) *n.* a strong lace for fastening a boot.

bootlace fungus *n.* another name for **honey fungus.**

bootlace worm *n.* a nemertean worm, *Linens longissimus,* that inhabits shingly shores and attains lengths of over 6 m (20 ft.).

bootleg ('bu:tˌleg) *vb.* **-legs, -legging, -legged.** **1.** to make, carry, or sell (illicit goods, esp. alcohol). ~*n.* **2.** something made or sold illicitly, such as alcohol during Prohibition in the U.S. ~*adj.* **3.** produced, distributed, or sold illicitly: *bootleg whisky; a bootleg record.* [C17: see BOOT[1], LEG; from the practice of smugglers of carrying bottles of liquor concealed in their boots] —**'bootˌlegger** *n.*

bootless ('bu:tlɪs) *adj.* of little or no use; vain; fruitless: *a bootless search.* [Old English *bōtlēas,* from *bōt* compensation; Old Norse *bótalauss*] —**'bootlessly** *adv.*

bootlick ('bu:tˌlɪk) *vb. Informal.* to seek favour by servile or ingratiating behaviour towards (someone, esp. someone in authority); toady. —**'bootˌlicker** *n.*

bootloader ('bu:tˌləʊdə) *n. Computer technol.* short for **bootstrap loader:** see **bootstrap** (sense 4).

boots (bu:ts) *n., pl.* **boots.** *Brit.* (formerly) a shoeblack who cleans the guests' shoes in a hotel.

boot sale *n.* a sale of goods from car boots in a car park hired for the occasion. Also called **car-boot sale.**

boots and all *Austral. and N.Z.* ~*adv.* **1.** making every effort; with no holds barred. ~*adj.* (**boots-and-all** *when prenominal*) **2.** behaving or conducted in such a manner.

boots and saddles *n.* a bugle call formerly used in the U.S. Cavalry to summon soldiers to mount.

bootstrap ('bu:tˌstræp) *n.* **1.** a leather or fabric loop on the back or side of a boot for pulling it on. **2. by one's (own) bootstraps.** by one's own efforts; unaided. **3.** (*modifier*) self-acting or self-sufficient, as an electronic amplifier that uses its output voltage to bias its input or a self-consistent theory of nuclear interactions. **4. a.** a technique for loading the first few program instructions into a computer main store to enable the rest of the program to be introduced from an input device. **b.** (*as modifier*): *a bootstrap loader.* **5.** *Commerce.* an offer to purchase a controlling interest in a company, esp. with the intention of purchasing the remainder of the equity at a lower price.

boot tapping *n. Nautical.* the line separating the two main colours painted on a ship's hull.

boot tree *n.* **1.** a shoetree for a boot, often having supports to stretch the leg of the boot. **2.** a last for making boots.

booty ('bu:tɪ) *n., pl.* **-ties.** any valuable article or articles, esp. when obtained as plunder. [C15: from Old French *butin,* from Middle Low German *buite* exchange; related to Old Norse *býta* to exchange, *býti* barter]

boo-word ('bu:ˌwɜ:d) *n.* any word that seems to cause irrational fear: *"communism" became a boo-word in the McCarthy era.*

booze (bu:z) *Informal.* ~*n.* **1.** alcoholic drink. **2.** a drinking bout or party. ~*vb.* **3.** (*usually intr.*) to drink (alcohol), esp. in excess. [C13: from Middle Dutch *būsen*] —**boozed** *adj.* —'**boozing** *n.*

boozer ('bu:zə) *n. Informal.* **1.** a person who is fond of drinking. **2.** *Brit., Austral., and N.Z.* a bar or pub.

booze-up *n. Brit., Austral., and N.Z. slang.* a drinking spree.

boozy ('bu:zɪ) *adj.* **boozier, booziest.** *Informal.* inclined to or involving excessive drinking of alcohol; drunken: *a boozy lecturer; a boozy party.* —'**booziness** *n.*

bop[1] (bɒp) *n.* **1.** a form of jazz originating in the 1940s, characterized by rhythmic and harmonic complexity and instrumental virtuosity. Originally called: **bebop. 2.** *Informal.* a session of dancing to pop music. ~*vb.* **bops, bopping, bopped. 3.** (*intr.*) *Informal.* to dance to pop music, as at a disco. [C20: shortened from BEBOP] —'**bopper** *n.*

bop[2] (bɒp) *Informal.* ~*vb.* **bops, bopping, bopped. 1.** (*tr.*) to strike; hit. ~*n.* **2.** a blow. [C19: of imitative origin]

bo-peep (ˌbəʊ'pi:p) *n.* **1.** a game for very young children, in which one hides (esp. hiding one's face in one's hands) and reappears suddenly. **2.** *Austral. and N.Z. informal.* a look (esp. in the phrase **have a bo-peep**).

bor. *abbrev. for* borough.

bora[1] ('bɔ:rə) *n.* (*sometimes cap.*) a violent cold north wind blowing from the mountains to the E coast of the Adriatic, usually in winter. [C19: from Italian (Venetian dialect), from Latin *boreās* the north wind]

bora[2] ('bɔ:rə) *n.* an initiation ceremony of Australian Aborigines, introducing youths to manhood. [from a native Australian language]

boracic (bə'ræsɪk) *adj.* another word for **boric.**

boracite ('bɔ:rəˌsaɪt) *n.* a white mineral that forms salt deposits of magnesium borate and chloride in cubic crystalline form. Formula: $Mg_6Cl_2B_{14}O_{26}$.

borage ('bɒrɪdʒ, 'bʌrɪdʒ) *n.* **1.** a Mediterranean boraginaceous plant, *Borago officinalis,* with star-shaped blue flowers. The young leaves have a cucumber-like flavour and are sometimes used in salads or as seasoning. **2.** any of several related plants. [C13: from Old French *bourage,* perhaps from Arabic *abū 'āraq* literally: father of sweat, from its use as a diaphoretic]

boraginaceous (bəˌrædʒɪ'neɪʃəs) *adj.* of, relating to, or belonging to the *Boraginaceae,* a family of temperate and tropical typically hairy-leaved flowering plants that includes forget-me-not, lungwort, borage, comfrey, and heliotrope. [C19: from New Latin *Borāginācеae,* from *Borāgō* genus name; see BORAGE]

borak ('bɔ:rək) *or* **borax** ('bɔ:ræks) *n. Austral. and N.Z. slang.* **1.** rubbish; nonsense. **2. poke borak at (someone).** to jeer at (someone). [from a native Australian language]

borane ('bɔ:reɪn) *n.* any compound of boron and hydrogen, used in the synthesis of other boron compounds and as high-energy fuels. [C20: from BOR(ON) + -ANE]

borate *n.* ('bɔ:reɪt, -ɪt). **1.** a salt or ester of boric acid. Salts of boric acid consist of BO_3 and BO_4 units linked together. ~*vb.* ('bɔ:reɪt). **2.** (*tr.*) to treat with borax, boric acid, or borate.

borax ('bɔ:ræks) *n., pl.* **-raxes** *or* **-races** (-rəˌsi:z). **1.** Also called: **tincal.** a soluble readily fusible white mineral consisting of impure hydrated disodium tetraborate in monoclinic crystalline form, occurring in alkaline soils and salt deposits. Formula: $Na_2B_4O_7.10H_2O$. **2.** pure disodium tetraborate. [C14: from Old French *boras,* from Medieval Latin *borax,* from Arabic *būraq,* from Persian *būrah*]

borazon ('bɔ:rəˌzɒn, -zᵊn) *n.* an extremely hard form of boron nitride. [C20: from BOR(ON) + AZO- + -ON]

borborygmus (ˌbɔ:bə'rɪgməs) *n., pl.* **-mi** (-maɪ). rumbling of the stomach. [C18: from Greek] —ˌ**borbo'rygmal** *or* ˌ**borbo'rygmic** *adj.*

Bordeaux (bɔ:'dəʊ; *French* bɔrdo) *n.* any of several red, white, or rosé wines produced around Bordeaux, SW France.

Bordeaux mixture *n. Horticulture.* a fungicide consisting of a solution of equal quantities of copper sulphate and quicklime. [C19: loose translation of French *bouillie bordelaise,* from *bouillir* to boil + *bordelais* of Bordeaux]

Bordelaise (ˌbɔ:də'leɪz; *French* bɔrdəlɛz) *adj. Cookery.* denoting a brown sauce flavoured with red wine and sometimes mushrooms. [French: of Bordeaux]

bordello (bɔ:'dɛləʊ) *n., pl.* **-los.** a brothel. Also called (archaic): **bordel** ('bɔ:dᵊl). [C16: from Italian, from Old French *borde* hut, cabin]

border ('bɔ:də) *n.* **1.** a band or margin around or along the edge of something. **2.** the dividing line or frontier between political or geographic regions. **3. a.** a region straddling such a boundary. **b.** (*as modifier*): *border country.* **4. a.** a design or ornamental strip around the edge or rim of something, such as a printed page or dinner plate. **b.** (*as modifier*): *a border illustration.* **5.** a long narrow strip of ground planted with flowers, shrubs, trees, etc., that skirts a path or wall or surrounds a lawn or other area: *a herbaceous border.* ~*vb.* **6.** (*tr.*) to decorate or provide with a border. **7.** (when *intr.,* foll. by *on* or *upon*) **a.** to be adjacent (to); lie along the boundary (of): *his land borders on mine.* **b.** to be nearly the same (as); verge (on): *his stupidity borders on madness.* [C14: from Old French *bordure,* from *border* to border, from *bort* side of a ship, of Germanic origin; see BOARD]

Border collie ('bɔ:də) *n.* a medium-sized breed of collie with a silky usually black-and-white coat: used mainly as sheepdogs.

bordereau (ˌbɔ:də'rəʊ; *French* bɔrdəro) *n., pl.* **-reaux** (-'rəʊ, -'rəʊz; *French* -ro). a memorandum or invoice prepared for a company by an underwriter, containing a list of reinsured risks. [C20: from French]

borderer ('bɔ:dərə) *n.* a person who lives in a border area, esp. the border between England and Scotland.

borderland ('bɔ:dəˌlænd) *n.* **1.** land located on or near a frontier or boundary. **2.** an indeterminate region: *the borderland between intellect and intelligence.*

Border Leicester *n.* a breed of sheep originally developed in the border country between Scotland and England by crossing English Leicesters with Cheviots, characterized by high fertility: popular in Scotland for crossing purpose: also found in large numbers in Australia and New Zealand. It has a long white fleece with no wool on the head.

borderline ('bɔ:dəˌlaɪn) *n.* **1.** a border; dividing line; line of demarcation. **2.** an indeterminate position between two conditions or qualities: *the borderline between friendship and love.* ~*adj.* **3.** on the edge of one category and verging on another: *a borderline failure in the exam.*

border terrier *n.* a small rough-coated breed of terrier.

bordure ('bɔ:djʊə) *n. Heraldry.* the outer edge of a shield, esp. when decorated distinctively. [C15: from Old French; see BORDER]

bore[1] (bɔ:) *vb.* **1.** to produce (a hole) in (a material) by use of a drill, auger, or rotary cutting tool. **2.** to increase the diameter of (a hole), as by an internal turning operation on a lathe or similar machine. **3.** (*tr.*) to produce (a hole in the ground, tunnel, mine shaft, etc.) by digging, drilling, cutting, etc. **4.** (*intr.*) *Informal.* (of a horse or athlete in a race) to push other competitors, esp. in order to try to get them out of the way. ~*n.* **5.** a hole or tunnel in the ground, esp. one drilled in search of minerals, oil, etc. **6. a.** a circular hole in a material produced by drilling or turning. **b.** the diameter of such a hole. **7. a.** the hollow part of a tube or cylinder, esp. of a gun barrel. **b.** the diameter of such a hollow part; calibre. **8.** *Austral.* an artesian well. [Old English *borian;* related to Old Norse *bora,* Old High German *borōn* to bore, Latin *forāre* to pierce, Greek *pharos* ploughing, *pharunx* PHARYNX]

bore[2] (bɔ:) *vb.* **1.** (*tr.*) to tire or make weary by being dull, repetitious, or uninteresting. ~*n.* **2.** a dull, repetitious, or uninteresting person, activity, or state. [C18: of unknown origin] —**bored** *adj.*

bore[3] (bɔ:) *n.* a high steep-fronted wave moving up a narrow estuary, caused by the tide. [C17: from Old Norse *bāra* wave, billow]

bore[4] (bɔ:) *vb.* the past tense of **bear**[1].

boreal ('bɔ:rɪəl) *adj.* of or relating to the north or the north wind. [C15: from Latin *boreās* the north wind]

Boreal ('bɔ:rɪəl) *adj.* **1.** of or denoting the coniferous forests in the north of the N hemisphere. **2.** designating a climatic zone having snowy winters and short summers. **3.** designating a dry climatic period from about 7500 to 5500 B.C., characterized by cold winters, warm summers, and a flora dominated by pines and hazels.

borecole ('bɔ:kəʊl) *n.* another name for **kale.**

boredom ('bɔ:dəm) *n.* the state of being bored; tedium.

boree ('bɔ:ri:) *n. Austral.* another name for **myall.** [from a native Australian language]

boreen ('bɔ:ri:n) *n. Irish.* a country lane or narrow road. [C19: from Irish Gaelic *bóithrín,* diminutive of *bóthar* road]

borehole ('bɔ:ˌhəʊl) *n.* a hole driven into the ground to obtain geological information, release water, etc.

borer ('bɔ:rə) *n.* **1.** a machine or hand tool for boring holes. **2.** any of various insects, insect larvae, molluscs, or crustaceans that bore into rock or plant material, esp. wood. See also **woodborer, corn borer, marine borer, rock borer.**

borer bomb *n. N.Z.* a device that emits pesticide fumes.

boric ('bɔ:rɪk) *adj.* of or containing boron. Also: **boracic.**

boric acid *n.* **1.** Also called: **orthoboric acid.** Systematic name: **trioxoboric(III) acid.** a white soluble weakly acid crystalline solid used in the manufacture of heat-resistant glass and porcelain enamels, as a fireproofing material, and as a mild antiseptic. Formula: H_3BO_3. **2.** any other acid containing boron.

boride ('bɔ:raɪd) *n.* a compound in which boron is the most electronegative element. [C19: from BOR(ON) + -IDE]

boring[1] ('bɔ:rɪŋ) *n.* **1. a.** the act or process of making or enlarging a hole. **b.** the hole made in this way. **2.** (*often pl.*) a fragment, particle, chip, etc., produced during boring.

boring[2] ('bɔ:rɪŋ) *adj.* dull; repetitious; uninteresting. —'**boringly** *adv.*

boring mill *n. Engineering.* a large vertical lathe having a rotating table on which work is secured. Tools are held on a fixed post and the work is rotated around it. Also called (informal): **round-about.**

borlotti bean (bɔːˈlɒtɪ) *n.* a variety of kidney bean with a pinkish-brown speckled skin that turns brown when cooked: grown in southern Europe, East Africa, and Taiwan. [from Italian, plural of *borlotto* kidney bean]

born (bɔːn) *vb.* **1.** the past participle (in most passive uses) of **bear**[1] (sense 4). **2. was not born yesterday.** is not gullible or foolish. *~adj.* **3.** possessing or appearing to have possessed certain qualities from birth: *a born musician.* **4. a.** being at birth in a particular social status or other condition as specified: *ignobly born.* **b.** (*in combination*): *lowborn.* **5. in all one's born days.** *Informal.* so far in one's life.

born-again (ˈbɔːnəˌgen) *adj.* **1.** having experienced conversion, esp. to evangelical Christianity. **2.** showing the enthusiasm of one newly converted to any cause: *a born-again monetarist.*

borne (bɔːn) *vb.* **1.** the past participle of **bear**[1] (for all active uses of the verb; also for all passive uses except sense 4 unless foll. by *by*). **2. be borne in on** *or* **upon.** (of a fact) to be realized by (someone): *it was borne in on us how close we had been to disaster.*

Bornean (ˈbɔːnɪən) *n.* **1.** a native or inhabitant of Borneo, an island in the W Pacific. *~adj.* **2.** of Borneo, its people, culture, etc.

borneol (ˈbɔːnɪˌɒl) *n.* a white solid terpene alcohol extracted from the Malaysian tree *Dryobalanops aromatica,* used in perfume and in the manufacture of organic esters. Formula: $C_{10}H_{17}OH$. [C19: from *Borne(o)* + -OL[1]]

Bornholm disease (ˈbɔːnˌhɒlm) *n.* an epidemic virus infection characterized by pain round the base of the chest. [C20: named after *Bornholm,* an island in the Baltic Sea, where it was first described]

bornite (ˈbɔːnaɪt) *n.* a mineral consisting of a sulphide of copper and iron that tarnishes to purple or dark red. It occurs in copper deposits. Formula: Cu_5FeS_4. Also called: **peacock ore.** [C19: named after I. von *Born* (1742–91), Austrian mineralogist; see -ITE[1]]

boron (ˈbɔːrɒn) *n.* a very hard almost colourless crystalline metalloid element that in impure form exists as a brown amorphous powder. It occurs principally in borax and is used in hardening steel. The naturally occurring isotope **boron-10** is used in nuclear control rods and neutron detection instruments. Symbol: B; atomic no.: 5; atomic wt.: 10.81; valency: 3; relative density: 2.34 (crystalline), 2.37 (amorphous); melting pt.: 2300°C; boiling pt.: 2550°C. [C19: from BOR(AX) + (CARB)ON]

boron carbide *n.* a black extremely hard inert substance having a high capture cross section for thermal neutrons. It is used as an abrasive and refractory and in control rods in nuclear reactors. Formula: B_4C.

boronia (bəˈrəʊnɪə) *n.* any aromatic rutaceous shrub of the Australian genus *Boronia.*

boron nitride *n.* a white inert crystalline solid existing both in a graphite-like form and in an extremely hard diamond-like form (borazon). It is used as a refractory, high temperature lubricant and insulator, and heat shield. Formula BN.

borosilicate (ˌbɔːrəʊˈsɪlɪkɪt, -ˌkeɪt) *n.* a salt of boric and silicic acids.

borosilicate glass *n.* any of a range of heat- and chemical-resistant glasses, such as Pyrex, prepared by fusing together boron(III) oxide, silicon dioxide, and, usually, a metal oxide.

borough (ˈbʌrə) *n.* **1.** a town, esp. (in Britain) one that forms the constituency of an MP or that was originally incorporated by royal charter. See also **burgh.** **2.** any of the 32 constituent divisions that together with the City of London make up Greater London. **3.** any of the five constituent divisions of New York City. **4.** (in the U.S.) a self-governing incorporated municipality. **5.** (in medieval England) a fortified town or village or a fort. **6.** (in New Zealand) a small municipality with a governing body. [Old English *burg;* related to *beorgan* to shelter, Old Norse *borg* wall, Gothic *baurgs* city, Old High German *burg* fortified castle]

borough-English *n. English law.* (until 1925) a custom in certain English boroughs whereby the youngest son inherited land to the exclusion of his older brothers. Compare **primogeniture, gavelkind.** [C14: from Anglo-French *tenure en burgh Engloys* tenure in an English borough; so called because the custom was unknown in France]

borrow (ˈbɒrəʊ) *vb.* **1.** to obtain or receive (something, such as money) on loan for temporary use, intending to give it, or something equivalent or identical, back to the lender. **2.** to adopt (ideas, words, etc.) from another source; appropriate. **3.** *Not standard.* to lend. **4.** *Golf.* to putt the ball uphill of the direct path to the hole: *make sure you borrow enough.* **5.** (*intr.*) *Golf.* (of a ball) to deviate from a straight path because of the slope of the ground. *~n.* **6.** *Golf.* a deviation of a ball from a straight path because of the slope of the ground: *a left borrow.* **7.** material dug from a borrow pit to provide fill at another. **8. living on borrowed time. a.** living an unexpected extension of life. **b.** close to death. [Old English *borgian;* related to Old High German *borgēn* to take heed, give security] —ˈ**borrower** *n.*

▷**Usage.** See at **lend.**

borrowed time *n.* an unexpected extension of the time allowed one, esp. a prolongation of one's life during the course of a disease (esp. in the phrase **living on borrowed time**).

borrow pit *n. Civil engineering.* an excavation dug to provide fill to make up ground elsewhere.

borsch, borsh (bɔːʃ), **borscht** (bɔːʃt), *or* **borshch** (bɔːʃtʃ) *n.* a Russian and Polish soup based on beetroot. [C19: from Russian *borshch*]

borsic (ˈbɔːsɪk) *n. Aeronautics.* a strong light composite material of boron fibre and silicon carbide used in aviation.

borstal (ˈbɔːstəl) *n.* **1.** (formerly in Britain) an informal name for an establishment in which offenders aged 15 to 21 could be detained for corrective training. Since the Criminal Justice Act 1982, they have been replaced by **youth custody centres.** **2.** a similar establishment in Australia and New Zealand. [C20: named after *Borstal,* village in Kent where the first institution was founded]

bort, boart (bɔːt), *or* **bortz** (bɔːts) *n.* an inferior grade of diamond used for cutting and drilling or, in powdered form, as an industrial abrasive. [Old English *gebrot* fragment; related to Old Norse *brot* piece, Old High German *broz* bud] —ˈ**borty** *adj.*

borzoi (ˈbɔːzɔɪ) *n., pl.* **-zois.** a tall graceful fast-moving breed of dog with a long silky coat, originally used in Russia for hunting wolves. Also called: **Russian wolfhound.** [C19: from Russian *borzoi,* literally: swift; related to Old Slavonic *brŭzŭ* swift]

boscage *or* **boskage** (ˈbɒskɪdʒ) *n. Literary.* a mass of trees and shrubs; thicket. [C14: from Old French *bosc,* probably of Germanic origin; see BUSH[1], -AGE]

boschbok (ˈbɒʃˌbʌk) *n., pl.* **-boks** *or* **-bok.** *S. African.* another name for **bushbuck.** [Afrikaans]

Bosch process (bɒʃ) *n.* an industrial process for manufacturing hydrogen by the catalytic reduction of steam with carbon monoxide. [C20: named after Carl *Bosch* (1874–1940), German chemist]

boschvark (ˈbɒʃˌvɑːk) *n. S. African.* another name for **bushpig.** [Afrikaans]

Bose-Einstein statistics (ˈbəʊsˈaɪnstaɪn) *pl. n.* (*functioning as sing.*) *Physics.* the branch of quantum statistics applied to systems of particles that do not obey the exclusion principle. Compare **Fermi-Dirac statistics.** [named after Satyendra Nath *Bose* (1894–1974), Indian physicist, and Albert *Einstein* (1879–1955), U.S. physicist]

bosh[1] (bɒʃ) *n. Informal.* empty or meaningless talk or opinions; nonsense. [C19: from Turkish *boş* empty]

bosh[2] (bɒʃ) *n.* **1.** the lower tapering portion of a blast furnace, situated immediately above the air-inlet tuyères. **2.** the deposit of siliceous material that occurs on the surfaces of vessels in which copper is refined. **3.** a water tank for cooling glass-making tools, etc. **4.** *South Wales dialect.* a kitchen sink or wash basin. [C17: probably from German; compare *böschen* to slope, *Böschung* slope]

bosk (bɒsk) *n. Literary.* a small wood of bushes and small trees. [C13: variant of *busk* BUSH[1]]

bosket *or* **bosquet** (ˈbɒskɪt) *n.* a clump of small trees or bushes; thicket. [C18: from French *bosquet,* from Italian *boschetto,* from *bosco* wood, forest; see BUSH[1]]

Boskop (ˈbɒskɒp) *n.* **a.** a prehistoric race of the late Pleistocene period in sub-Saharan Africa. **b.** (*as modifier*): *Boskop man.* [C20: named after *Boskop,* in the Transvaal, where remains of this race were first discovered]

bosky (ˈbɒskɪ) *adj.* **boskier, boskiest.** *Literary.* containing or consisting of bushes or thickets: *a bosky wood.*

bo's'n (ˈbəʊsᵊn) *n. Nautical.* a variant spelling of **boatswain.**

Bosnian (ˈbɒznɪən) *adj.* **1.** of or relating to Bosnia, a former Yugoslav republic. *~n.* **2.** a native or inhabitant of Bosnia.

bosom (ˈbʊzəm) *n.* **1.** the chest or breast of a person, esp. the female breasts. **2.** the part of a woman's dress, coat, etc., that covers the chest. **3.** a protective centre or part: *the bosom of the family.* **4.** the breast considered as the seat of emotions. **5.** (*modifier*) very dear; intimate: *a bosom friend.* *~vb.* (*tr.*) **6.** to embrace. **7.** to conceal or carry in the bosom. [Old English *bōsm;* related to Old High German *buosam*]

bosomy (ˈbʊzəmɪ) *adj.* (of a woman) having large breasts.

boson (ˈbəʊzɒn) *n.* any of a group of elementary particles, such as a photon or pion, that has zero or integral spin and obeys the rules of Bose-Einstein statistics. Compare **fermion.** [C20: named after Satyendra Nath *Bose* (1894–1974), Indian physicist]

bosquet (ˈbɒskɪt) *n.* a variant spelling of **bosket.**

boss[1] (bɒs) *Informal.* *~n.* **1.** a person in charge of or employing others. **2.** *Chiefly U.S.* a professional politician who controls a party machine or political organization, often using devious or illegal methods. *~vb.* **3.** to employ, supervise, or be in charge of. **4.** (usually foll. by *around* or *about*) to be domineering or overbearing towards (others). *~adj.* **5.** *Slang.* excellent; fine: *a boss hand at carpentry; that's boss!* [C19: from Dutch *baas* master; probably related to Old High German *basa* aunt, Frisian *baes* master]

boss[2] (bɒs) *n.* **1.** a knob, stud, or other circular rounded protuberance, esp. an ornamental one on a vault, a ceiling, or a shield. **2.** *Biology.* any of various protuberances or swellings in plants and animals. **3. a.** an area of increased thickness, usually cylindrical, that strengthens or provides room for a locating device on a shaft, hub of a wheel, etc. **b.** a similar projection around a hole in a casting or fabricated component. **4.** a rounded mass of igneous rock, esp. the uppermost part of an underlying batholith. *~vb.* (*tr.*) **5.** to ornament with bosses;

emboss. [C13: from Old French *boce,* from Vulgar Latin *bottia* (unattested); related to Italian *bozza* metal knob, swelling]
boss[3] (bɒs) *or* **bossy** *n., pl.* **bosses** *or* **bossies.** *U.S.* a calf or cow. [C19: from dialect *buss* calf, perhaps ultimately from Latin *bōs* cow, ox]
BOSS (bɒs) *n. acronym for* Bureau of State Security; a branch of the South African security police.
bossa nova ('bɒsə 'nəʊvə) *n.* **1.** a dance similar to the samba, originating in Brazil. **2.** a piece of music composed for or in the rhythm of this dance. [C20: Portuguese, literally: new voice]
bossboy ('bɒs,bɔɪ) *n. S. African.* a Black African foreman of a gang of workers.
boss cocky *n. Austral. informal.* a boss or person in power, esp. an overbearing one.
bosset ('bɒsɪt) *n.* either of the rudimentary antlers found in young deer. [C19: from French *bossette* a small protuberance, from *bosse* BOSS[2]]
boss-eyed *adj. Informal.* having a squint. [C19: from *boss* to miss or bungle a shot at a target (dialect)]
bossing ('bɒsɪŋ) *n. Civil engineering.* the act of shaping malleable metal, such as lead cladding, with mallets to fit a surface.
bossism ('bɒs,ɪzəm) *n. U.S.* the domination or the system of domination of political organizations by bosses.
bossy[1] ('bɒsɪ) *adj.* **bossier, bossiest.** *Informal.* domineering, overbearing, or authoritarian. —'**bossily** *adv.* —'**bossiness** *n.*
bossy[2] ('bɒsɪ) *adj.* (of furniture) ornamented with bosses.
bosthoon ('bɒsdu:n) *n. Irish.* a boor. [C19: from Irish Gaelic *bastún,* from Old French *baston* penis]
boston ('bɒstən) *n.* **1.** a card game for four, played with two packs. **2.** *Chiefly U.S.* a slow gliding dance, a variation of the waltz.
Boston crab ('bɒstən) *n.* a wrestling hold in which a wrestler seizes both or one of his opponent's legs, turns him face downwards, and exerts pressure over his back.
Boston ivy *n.* the U.S. name for **Virginia creeper** (sense 2).
Boston terrier *or* **bull terrier** *n.* a short stocky smooth-haired breed of terrier with a short nose, originally developed by crossing the French and English bulldogs with the English bull terrier.
bosun ('bəʊsᵊn) *n. Nautical.* a variant spelling of **boatswain.**
Boswellian (bɒz'welɪən) *adj.* of or relating to the works of James Boswell (1740–95), Scottish author, lawyer, and biographer of Samuel Johnson.
bot[1] *or* **bott** (bɒt) *n.* **1.** the larva of a botfly, which typically develops inside the body of a horse, sheep, or man. **2.** any similar larva. ~See also **bots.** [C15: probably from Low German; related to Dutch *bot,* of obscure origin]
bot[2] (bɒt) *Austral. informal.* ~*vb.* **1.** to scrounge or borrow. **2.** (*intr.;* often foll. by *on*) to scrounge (from); impose (on). ~*n.* **3.** a scrounger. **4. on the bot (for).** wanting to scrounge: *he's on the bot for a cigarette.* [C20: perhaps from BOTFLY, alluding to the creature's bite; see BITE (sense 12)]
BOT *abbrev. for* Board of Trade.
bot. *abbrev. for:* **1.** botanical. **2.** botany. **3.** bottle.
botanical (bə'tænɪkᵊl) *or* **botanic** *adj.* **1.** of or relating to botany or plants. ~*n.* **2.** any drug or pesticide that is made from parts of a plant. [C17: from Medieval Latin *botanicus,* from Greek *botanikos* relating to plants, from *botanē* plant, pasture, from *boskein* to feed; perhaps related to Latin *bōs* ox, cow] —**bo'tanically** *adv.*
botanic garden *n.* a place in which plants are grown, studied, and exhibited.
botanize *or* **botanise** ('bɒtə,naɪz) *vb.* **1.** (*intr.*) to collect or study plants. **2.** (*tr.*) to explore and study the plants in (an area or region).
botany ('bɒtənɪ) *n., pl.* **-nies. 1.** the study of plants, including their classification, structure, physiology, ecology, and economic importance. **2.** the plant life of a particular region or time. **3.** the biological characteristics of a particular group of plants. [C17: from BOTANICAL; compare ASTRONOMY, ASTRONOMICAL] —'**botanist** *n.*
Botany wool *n.* a fine wool from the merino sheep. [C19: from *Botany* Bay, SE Australia, where the wool came from originally]
botargo (bə'tɑ:gəʊ) *n., pl.* **-gos** *or* **-goes.** a relish consisting of the roe of mullet or tunny, salted and pressed into rolls. [C15: from obsolete Italian, from Arabic *butarkhah*]
BOTB *abbrev. for* British Overseas Trade Board.
botch (bɒtʃ) *vb.* (*tr.;* often foll. by *up*) **1.** to spoil through clumsiness or ineptitude. **2.** to repair badly or clumsily. ~*n.* **3.** Also called: **botch-up.** a badly done piece of work or repair (esp. in the phrase **make a botch of (something)**). [C14: of unknown origin] —'**botcher** *n.*
botchy ('bɒtʃɪ) *adj.* **botchier, botchiest.** clumsily done or made. —'**botchily** *adv.* —'**botchiness** *n.*
botel (bəʊ'tel) *n.* a variant spelling of **boatel.**
botfly ('bɒt,flaɪ) *n., pl.* **-flies.** any of various stout-bodied hairy dipterous flies of the families *Oestridae* and *Gasterophilidae,* the larvae of which are parasites of man, sheep, and horses.
both (bəʊθ) *determiner.* **1. a.** the two; two considered together: *both dogs were dirty.* **b.** (*as pronoun*): *both are to blame.* ~*conj.* **2.** (*coordinating*) used preceding words, phrases, or clauses joined by *and,* used to emphasize that not just one, but also the other of the joined elements is included: *both Ellen and Keith enjoyed the play; both new and exciting.* [C12: from Old Norse *bāthir;* related to Old High German *bēde,* Latin *ambō,* Greek *amphō*]
bother ('bɒðə) *vb.* **1.** (*tr.*) to give annoyance, pain, or trouble to; irritate: *his bad leg is bothering him again.* **2.** (*tr.*) to trouble (a person) by repeatedly disturbing; pester: *stop bothering your father!* **3.** (*intr.*) to take the time or trouble; concern oneself: *don't bother to come with me.* **4.** (*tr.*) to make (a person) alarmed or confused: *the thought of her husband's return clearly bothered her.* ~*n.* **5.** a state of worry, trouble, or confusion. **6.** a person or thing that causes fuss, trouble, or annoyance. **7.** *Informal.* a disturbance or fight; trouble (esp. in the phrase **a spot of bother**). ~*interj.* **8.** *Chiefly Brit.* an exclamation of slight annoyance. [C18: perhaps from Irish Gaelic *bodhar* deaf, vexed; compare Irish Gaelic *buairim* I vex]
botheration (,bɒðə'reɪʃən) *n., interj. Informal.* another word for **bother** (senses 5, 8).
bothersome ('bɒðəsəm) *adj.* causing bother; troublesome.
both ways *adj., adv.* **1.** another term for **each way. 2. have it both ways.** (*usually with a negative*) to try to get the best of a situation, argument, etc., by chopping and changing between alternatives or opposites.
bothy ('bɒθɪ) *n., pl.* **bothies.** *Chiefly Scot.* **1.** a cottage or hut. **2.** (esp. in NE Scotland) a farmworker's summer quarters. **3.** a mountain shelter. [C18: perhaps related to BOOTH]
bothy ballad *n. Scot.* a folk song, esp. one from the farming community of NE Scotland.
bo tree (bəʊ) *n.* another name for the **peepul.** [C19: from Sinhalese, from Pali *bodhitaru* tree of wisdom, from Sanskrit *bodhi* wisdom, awakening; see BODHISATTVA]
botryoidal (,bɒtrɪ'ɔɪdᵊl) *or* **botryose** ('bɒtrɪ,əʊs, -,əʊz) *adj.* (of minerals, parts of plants, etc.) shaped like a bunch of grapes. [C18: from Greek *botruoeidēs,* from *botrus* cluster of grapes; see -OID]
bots (bɒts) *n.* (*functioning as sing.*) a digestive disease of horses and some other animals caused by the presence of botfly larvae in the stomach.
bott (bɒt) *n.* a variant spelling of **bot**[1].
botte *French.* (bɔt) *n. Fencing.* a thrust or hit.
bottine (bɒ'ti:n) *n.* a light boot for women or children; half-boot. [C19: from French: little boot, from *botte* boot]
bottle[1] ('bɒtᵊl) *n.* **1. a.** a vessel, often of glass and typically cylindrical with a narrow neck that can be closed with a cap or cork, for containing liquids. **b.** (*as modifier*): *a bottle rack.* **2.** Also called: **bottleful.** the amount such a vessel will hold. **3. a.** a container equipped with a teat that holds a baby's milk or other liquid; nursing bottle. **b.** the contents of such a container: *the baby drank his bottle.* **4.** short for **magnetic bottle. 5.** *Brit. slang.* nerve; courage (esp. in the phrase **lose one's bottle**). **6.** *Brit. slang.* money collected by street entertainers or buskers. **7. the bottle.** *Informal.* drinking of alcohol, esp. to excess. ~*vb.* (*tr.*) **8.** to put or place (wine, beer, jam, etc.) in a bottle or bottles. **9.** to store (gas) in a portable container under pressure. **10.** *Slang.* to injure by thrusting a broken bottle into (a person). **11.** *Brit. slang.* (of a busker) to collect money from the bystanders. ~See also **bottle out, bottle up.** [C14: from Old French *botaille,* from Medieval Latin *butticula,* literally: a little cask, from Late Latin *buttis* cask, BUTT[4]]
bottle[2] ('bɒtᵊl) *n. Dialect.* a bundle, esp. of hay. [C14: from Old French *botel,* from *botte* bundle, of Germanic origin]
bottle bank *n.* a large container into which the public may throw glass bottles for recycling.
bottlebrush ('bɒtᵊl,brʌʃ) *n.* **1.** Also called: **callistemon.** any of various Australian myrtaceous shrubs or trees of the genera *Callistemon* and *Melaleuca,* having dense spikes of large red flowers with protruding brushlike stamens. **2.** any of various similar trees or shrubs. **3.** a cylindrical brush on a thin shaft, used for cleaning bottles.
bottled *or* **bottle gas** *n.* butane or propane gas liquefied under pressure in portable containers and used in camping stoves, blowlamps, etc.
bottle-feed *vb.* **-feeds, -feeding, -fed.** to feed (a baby) with milk from a bottle instead of breast-feeding.
bottle glass *n.* glass used for making bottles, comprised of silicon dioxide, sodium oxide, calcium oxide, and aluminium oxide.
bottle gourd *n.* **1.** an Old World cucurbitaceous climbing plant, *Lagenaria siceraria,* having large hard-shelled gourds as fruits. **2.** the fruit of this plant. ~Also called: **calabash.**
bottle green *n., adj.* **a.** a dark green colour. **b.** (*as adj.*): *a bottle-green car.*
bottle-jack *n. N.Z.* a large jack used for heavy lifts.
bottleneck ('bɒtᵊl,nek) *n.* **1. a.** a narrow stretch of road or a junction at which traffic is or may be held up. **b.** the hold up. **2.** something that holds up progress, esp. of a manufacturing process. **3.** *Music.* **a.** the broken-off neck of a bottle placed over a finger and used to produce a buzzing effect in a style of guitar-playing originally part of the American blues tradition. **b.** the style of guitar playing using a bottleneck. ~*vb.* **4.** (*tr.*) *U.S.* to be or cause an obstruction in.
bottlenose dolphin ('bɒtᵊl,nəʊz) *n.* any dolphin of the genus *Tursiops,* esp. *T. truncatus,* some of which have been kept in captivity and trained to perform tricks.

bottle-o *or* **bottle-oh** *n. Austral. and N.Z. informal.* a dealer in empty bottles.

bottle out *vb. (intr., adv.) Brit. slang.* to lose one's nerve.

bottle party *n.* a party to which guests bring drink.

bottler ('bɒtᵊlə) *n. Austral. and N.Z. informal.* an excellent or outstanding person or thing.

bottle store *n. Austral. and N.Z.* a shop where alcohol is sold in unopened containers for consumption elsewhere. Also called (Austral.): **bottle shop.**

bottle tree *n.* any of several Australian sterculiaceous trees of the genus *Sterculia* (or *Brachychiton*) that have a bottle-shaped swollen trunk.

bottle up *vb. (tr., adv.)* **1.** to restrain (powerful emotion). **2.** to keep (an army or other force) contained or trapped: *the French fleet was bottled up in Le Havre.*

bottle-washer *n. Informal.* a menial or factotum.

bottom ('bɒtəm) *n.* **1.** the lowest, deepest, or farthest removed part of a thing: *the bottom of a hill.* **2.** the least important or successful position: *the bottom of a class.* **3.** the ground underneath a sea, lake, or river. **4. touch bottom.** to run aground. **5.** the inner depths of a person's true feelings (esp. in the phrase **from the bottom of one's heart**). **6.** the underneath part of a thing. **7.** *Nautical.* the parts of a vessel's hull that are under water. **8.** (in literary or commercial contexts) a boat or ship. **9.** *Billiards, etc.* a strike in the centre of the cue ball. **10.** a dry valley or hollow. **11.** the lowest level worked in a mine. **12.** (esp. of horses) staying power; stamina. **13.** importance, seriousness, or influence: *his views all have weight and bottom.* **14.** *Informal.* the buttocks. **15. at bottom.** in reality; basically or despite appearances to the contrary: *he's a kind man at bottom.* **16. be at the bottom of.** to be the ultimate cause of. **17. get to the bottom of.** to discover the real truth about. **18. knock the bottom out of. a.** to destroy or eliminate. **b.** to show to be of little or no value. ~*adj. (prenominal)* **19.** lowest or last: *the bottom price.* **20. bet** (*or* **put**) **one's bottom dollar on.** to be absolutely sure of (one's opinion, a person, project, etc.). **21.** of, relating to, or situated at the bottom or a bottom: *the bottom shelf.* **22.** fundamental; basic. ~*vb.* **23.** (*tr.*) to provide (a chair, etc.) with a bottom or seat. **24.** (*tr.*) to discover the full facts or truth of; fathom. **25.** (usually foll. by *on* or *upon*) to base or be founded (on an idea, etc.). **26.** (*intr.*) *Nautical.* to strike the ground beneath the water with a vessel's bottom. **27.** *Austral.* **a.** to mine (a hole, claim, etc.) deep enough to reach any gold there is. **b.** (*intr.;* foll. by *on*) to reach (gold, mud, etc.) on bottoming. **28.** *Electronics.* to saturate a transistor so that further increase of input produces no change in output. ~See also **bottom out.** [Old English *botm;* related to Old Norse *botn,* Old High German *bodam,* Latin *fundus,* Greek *puthmēn*]

bottom dead centre *n. Engineering.* the position of the crank of a reciprocating engine when the piston is at its nearest point to the crankshaft. Also called: **outer dead centre.**

bottom drawer *n. Brit.* a young woman's collection of clothes, linen, cutlery, etc., in anticipation of marriage. U.S., Canadian, and N.Z. equivalent: **hope chest.**

bottom end *n.* (in vertical engines) another name for **big end** (sense 1).

bottom house *n. Caribbean.* **1.** the open space beneath a house built upon high pillars. **2.** such a space partially enclosed and floored for use as servants' quarters.

bottoming ('bɒtəmɪŋ) *n.* the lowest level of foundation material for a road or other structure.

bottomless ('bɒtəmlɪs) *adj.* **1.** having no bottom. **2.** unlimited; inexhaustible. **3.** very deep.

bottom line *n.* **1.** the last line of a financial statement that shows the net profit or loss of a company or organization. **2.** the final outcome of a process, discussion, etc.

bottommost ('bɒtəmˌməʊst) *adj.* lowest or most fundamental.

bottom out *vb. (intr., adv.)* to reach the lowest point and level out: *the recession shows no sign of bottoming out.*

bottomry ('bɒtəmrɪ) *n., pl.* **-ries.** *Maritime law.* a contract whereby the owner of a ship borrows money to enable the vessel to complete the voyage and pledges the ship as security for the loan. [C16: from Dutch *bodemerij,* from *bodem* BOTTOM (hull of a ship) + *-erij* -RY]

bottomset bed ('bɒtəmˌsɛt) *n.* the fine sediment deposited at the front of a growing delta.

bottoms up *interj.* an informal drinking toast.

bottom-up processing *n.* a processing technique, either in the brain or in a computer, in which incoming information is analysed in successive steps and later-stage processing does not affect processing in earlier stages.

botulin ('bɒtjʊlɪn) *n.* a potent toxin produced by the bacterium *Clostridium botulinum* in imperfectly preserved food, etc., causing botulism. [C19: from BOTULINUS]

botulinus (ˌbɒtjʊ'laɪnəs) *n., pl.* **-nuses.** an anaerobic bacterium, *Clostridium botulinum,* whose toxins (botulins) cause botulism: family *Bacillaceae.* [C19: from New Latin, from Latin *botulus* sausage]

botulism ('bɒtjʊˌlɪzəm) *n.* severe poisoning from ingestion of botulin, which affects the central nervous system producing difficulty in swallowing, visual disturbances, and respiratory paralysis: often fatal. [C19: first formed as German *Botulismus* literally: sausage poisoning, from Latin *botulus* sausage]

boubou *or* **bubu** ('buːbuː) *n.* a long flowing garment worn by men and women in Mali, Nigeria, Senegal, and some other parts of Africa. [a native name in Mali]

bouchée (buː'ʃeɪ) *n.* a small pastry case filled with a savoury mixture, served hot with cocktails or as an hors d'oeuvre. [C19: from French: mouthful]

bouclé ('buːkleɪ) *n.* **1.** a curled or looped yarn or fabric giving a thick knobbly effect. ~*adj.* **2.** of or designating such a yarn or fabric: *a bouclé wool coat.* [C19: from French *bouclé* curly, from *boucle* a curl, BUCKLE]

bouclée ('buːkleɪ) *n.* a support for a cue in billiards formed by doubling the first finger so that its tip is aligned with the thumb at its second joint, to form a loop through which the cue may slide. [from French, literally: curled]

boudoir ('buːdwɑː, -dwɔː) *n.* a woman's bedroom or private sitting room. [C18: from French, literally: room for sulking in, from *bouder* to sulk]

boudoir grand *n.* a domestic grand piano between 5 and 6 feet in length. Compare **baby grand, concert grand.**

bouffant ('buːfɒŋ) *adj.* **1.** (of a hair style) having extra height and width through back-combing; puffed out. **2.** (of sleeves, skirts, etc.) puffed out. ~*n.* **3.** a bouffant hair style. [C20: from French, from *bouffer* to puff up]

bouffe (buːf) *n.* See **opéra bouffe.**

bougainvillea *or* **bougainvillaea** (ˌbuːgən'vɪlɪə) *n.* any tropical woody nyctaginaceous widely cultivated climbing plant of the genus *Bougainvillea,* having inconspicuous flowers surrounded by showy red or purple bracts. [C19: New Latin, named after L. A. de *Bougainville* (1729–1811), French navigator]

bough (baʊ) *n.* any of the main branches of a tree. [Old English *bōg* arm, twig; related to Old Norse *bōgr* shoulder, ship's bow, Old High German *buog* shoulder, Greek *pēkhus* forearm, Sanskrit *bāhu;* see BOW[3], ELBOW]

bought (bɔːt) *vb.* **1.** the past tense and past participle of **buy.** ~*adj.* **2.** purchased from a shop; not homemade.

boughten ('bɔːtᵊn) *adj.* a dialect word for **bought** (sense 2).

bougie ('buːʒiː, buː'ʒiː) *n. Med.* a long slender semiflexible cylindrical instrument for inserting into body passages such as the rectum or urethra to dilate structures, introduce medication, etc. [C18: from French, originally a wax candle from *Bougie* (Bujiya), Algeria]

bouillabaisse (ˌbuːjə'bɛs) *n.* a rich stew or soup of fish and vegetables flavoured with spices, esp. saffron. [C19: from French, from Provençal *bouiabaisso,* literally: boil down]

bouillon ('buːjɒn) *n.* a plain unclarified broth or stock. [C18: from French, from *bouillir* to BOIL[1]]

boulder ('bəʊldə) *n.* **1.** a smooth rounded mass of rock that has been shaped by erosion and transported by ice or water from its original position. **2.** *Geology.* a rock fragment with a diameter greater than 256 mm and thus bigger than a cobble. [C13: probably of Scandinavian origin; compare Swedish dialect *bullersten,* from Old Swedish *bulder* rumbling + *sten* STONE] —'**bouldery** *adj.*

boulder clay *n.* an unstratified glacial deposit consisting of fine clay, boulders, and pebbles. See also **till**[4].

bouldering ('bəʊldərɪŋ) *n.* rock climbing on large boulders or small outcrops either as practice or as a sport in its own right.

boule[1] ('buːliː) *n.* **1.** the parliament in modern Greece. **2.** the senate of an ancient Greek city-state. [C19: from Greek *boulē* senate]

boule[2] (buːl) *n.* a pear-shaped imitation ruby, sapphire, etc., made from synthetic corundum. [C19: from French: ball]

boules *French.* (bul) *pl. n. (functioning as sing.)* a game, popular in France, in which metal bowls are thrown to land as near as possible to a target ball. It is played on rough surfaces. [plural of *boule* BALL[1]; see BOWL[2]]

boulevard ('buːlvɑː, -vɑːd) *n.* **1. a.** a wide usually tree-lined road in a city, often used as a promenade. **b.** (*cap. as part of a street name*): *Sunset Boulevard.* **2.** *Chiefly Canadian.* **a.** a grass strip between the pavement and road. **b.** the centre strip of a road dividing traffic travelling in different directions. [C18: from French, from Middle Dutch *bolwerc* BULWARK; so called because originally often built on the ruins of an old rampart]

boulevardier (buːl'vɑːdɪˌeɪ) *n.* (originally in Paris) a fashionable man, esp. one who frequents public places.

boulle, boule, *or* **buhl** (buːl) *adj.* **1.** denoting or relating to a type of marquetry of patterned inlays of brass and tortoiseshell, occasionally with other metals such as pewter, much used on French furniture from the 17th century. ~*n.* **2.** Also called: '**boullework.** something ornamented with such marquetry. [C18: named after André Charles *Boulle* (1642–1732), French cabinet-maker]

boult (bəʊlt) *vb.* a variant spelling of **bolt**[2].

bounce (baʊns) *vb.* **1.** (*intr.*) (of an elastic object, such as a ball) to rebound from an impact. **2.** (*tr.*) to cause (such an object) to hit a solid surface and spring back. **3.** to rebound or cause to rebound repeatedly. **4.** to move or cause to move suddenly, excitedly, or violently; spring: *she bounced up from her chair.* **5.** *Slang.* (of a bank) to send (a cheque) back or (of a cheque) to be sent back unredeemed because of lack of funds in the drawer's account. **6.** (*tr.*) *Slang.* to force (a person) to leave (a place or job); throw out; eject. **7.** (*tr.*) *Brit.* to hustle (a person) into believing or doing something. ~*n.* **8.** the action of rebounding from an impact. **9.** a leap; jump; bound. **10.** the quality of being able to rebound; springiness. **11.** *Informal.* vitality; vigour; resilience. **12.** *Brit.* swagger or impudence. **13. the bounce.** *Australian Rules.* the start of play at the beginning of each quarter or after a goal. **14. get** *or* **give the bounce.** *U.S. informal.* to dismiss or be dismissed from a job. [C13: probably of imitative origin; compare Low German *bunsen* to beat, Dutch *bonken* to thump]

bounce back *vb.* (*intr., adv.*) to recover one's health, good spirits, confidence, etc., easily after a setback.

bouncer ('baʊnsə) *n.* **1.** *Slang.* a man employed at a club, pub, disco, etc., to throw out drunks or troublemakers and stop those considered undesirable from entering. **2.** *Slang.* a dishonoured cheque. **3.** *Cricket.* another word for **bumper**[1]. **4.** a person or thing that bounces.

bouncing ('baʊnsɪŋ) *adj.* (when *postpositive,* foll. by *with*) vigorous and robust (esp. in the phrase **a bouncing baby**).

bouncing Bet (bɛt) *n.* another name for **soapwort.**

bouncy ('baʊnsɪ) *adj.* **bouncier, bounciest. 1.** lively, exuberant, or self-confident. **2.** having the capability or quality of bouncing: *a bouncy ball.* **3.** responsive to bouncing; springy: *a bouncy bed.* —'**bouncily** *adv.* —'**bounciness** *n.*

bound[1] (baʊnd) *vb.* **1.** the past tense and past participle of **bind.** ~*adj.* **2.** in bonds or chains; tied with or as if with a rope: *a bound prisoner.* **3.** (*in combination*) restricted; confined: *housebound; fogbound.* **4.** (*postpositive,* foll. by an infinitive) destined; sure; certain: *it's bound to happen.* **5.** (*postpositive,* often foll. by *by*) compelled or obliged to act, behave, or think in a particular way, as by duty, circumstance, or convention. **6.** *Rare.* constipated. **7.** (of a book) secured within a cover or binding: *to deliver bound books.* See also **half-bound. 8.** (*postpositive,* foll. by *on*) *U.S.* resolved; determined: *bound on winning.* **9.** *Linguistics.* **a.** denoting a morpheme, such as the prefix *non-,* that occurs only as part of another word and not as a separate word in itself. Compare **free** (sense 21). **b.** (in systemic grammar) denoting a clause that has a nonfinite predicator or that is introduced by a binder, and that occurs only together with a freestanding clause. **10.** *Logic.* (of a variable) occurring within the scope of a quantifier that indicates the degree of generality of the open sentence in which the variable occurs: in $(x)\,(Fx \rightarrow bxy)$, x is bound and y is free. Compare **free** (sense 22). **11. bound up with.** closely or inextricably linked with: *his irritability is bound up with his work.* **12. I'll be bound.** I am sure (something) is true.

bound[2] (baʊnd) *vb.* **1.** to move forwards or make (one's way) by leaps or jumps. **2.** to bounce; spring away from an impact. ~*n.* **3.** a jump upwards or forwards. **4. by leaps and bounds.** with unexpectedly rapid progess: *her condition improved by leaps and bounds.* **5.** a sudden pronounced sense of excitement: *his heart gave a sudden bound when he saw her.* **6.** a bounce, as of a ball. [C16: from Old French *bond* a leap, from *bondir* to jump, resound, from Vulgar Latin *bombitīre* (unattested) to buzz, hum, from Latin *bombus* booming sound]

bound[3] (baʊnd) *vb.* **1.** (*tr.*) to place restrictions on; limit. **2.** (when *intr.,* foll. by *on*) to form a boundary of (an area of land or sea, political or administrative region, etc.). ~*n.* **3.** *Maths.* **a.** a number which is greater than all the members of a set of numbers (an **upper bound**), or less than all its members (a **lower bound**). See also **bounded** (sense 1). **b.** more generally, an element of an ordered set that has the same ordering relation to all the members of a given subset. **c.** whence, an estimate of the extent of some set. **4.** See **bounds.** [C13: from Old French *bonde,* from Medieval Latin *bodina,* of Gaulish origin]

bound[4] (baʊnd) *adj.* **a.** (*postpositive,* often foll. by *for*) going or intending to go towards; on the way to: *a ship bound for Jamaica; homeward bound.* **b.** (*in combination*): *northbound traffic.* [C13: from Old Norse *buinn,* past participle of *būa* to prepare]

boundary ('baʊndərɪ, -drɪ) *n., pl.* **-ries. 1.** something that indicates the farthest limit, as of an area; border. **2.** *Cricket.* **a.** the marked limit of the playing area. **b.** a stroke that hits the ball beyond this limit. **c.** the four runs scored with such a stroke, or the six runs if the ball crosses the boundary without touching the ground.

boundary layer *n.* the layer of fluid closest to the surface of a solid past which the fluid flows: it has a lower rate of flow than the bulk of the fluid because of its adhesion to the solid.

boundary rider *n. Austral.* an employee on a sheep or cattle station whose job is to maintain fences in good repair and to prevent stock from straying.

bounded ('baʊndɪd) *adj. Maths.* **1.** (of a set) having a bound, esp. where a measure is defined in terms of which all the elements of the set, or the differences between all pairs of members, are less than some value, or else all its members lie within some other well-defined set. **2.** (of an operator, function, etc.) having a bounded set of values.

bounden ('baʊndən) *adj.* morally obligatory (archaic except in the phrase **bounden duty**).

bounder ('baʊndə) *n.* **1.** *Old-fashioned Brit. slang.* a morally reprehensible person; cad. **2.** a person or animal that bounds.

boundless ('baʊndlɪs) *adj.* unlimited; vast: *boundless energy.* —'**boundlessly** *adv.* —'**boundlessness** *n.*

bounds (baʊndz) *pl. n.* **1.** (*sometimes sing.*) a limit; boundary (esp. in the phrase **know no bounds**). **2.** something that restrains or confines, esp. the standards of a society: *within the bounds of modesty.* **3. beat the bounds.** See **beat** (sense 27). ~See also **out of bounds.**

bounteous ('baʊntɪəs) *adj. Literary.* **1.** giving freely; generous: *the bounteous goodness of God.* **2.** plentiful; abundant. —'**bounteously** *adv.* —'**bounteousness** *n.*

bountiful ('baʊntɪfʊl) *adj.* **1.** plentiful; ample (esp. in the phrase **a bountiful supply**). **2.** giving freely; generous. —'**bountifully** *adv.* —'**bountifulness** *n.*

bounty ('baʊntɪ) *n., pl.* **-ties. 1.** generosity in giving to others; liberality. **2.** a generous gift; something freely provided. **3.** a payment made by a government, as, formerly, to a sailor on enlisting or to a soldier after a campaign. **4.** any reward or premium: *a bounty of 20p for every rat killed.* [C13 (in the sense: goodness): from Old French *bontet,* from Latin *bonitās* goodness, from *bonus* good]

bouquet *n.* **1.** (bəʊ'keɪ, buː-). a bunch of flowers, esp. a large carefully arranged one. **2.** (buː'keɪ). Also called: **nose.** the characteristic aroma or fragrance of a wine or liqueur. **3.** a compliment or expression of praise. [C18: from French: thicket, from Old French *bosc* forest, wood, probably of Germanic origin; see BUSH[1]]

bouquet garni ('buːkeɪ gɑː'niː) *n., pl.* **bouquets garnis** ('buːkeɪz gɑː'niː). a bunch of herbs tied together and used for flavouring soups, stews, etc. [C19: from French, literally: garnished bouquet]

bourbon ('bɜːbᵊn) *n.* a whiskey distilled, chiefly in the U.S., from maize, esp. one containing at least 51 per cent maize (the rest being malt and rye) and aged in charred white-oak barrels. [C19: named after *Bourbon* county, Kentucky, where it was first made]

Bourbon ('bʊəbᵊn; *French* burbɔ̃) *n.* **a.** a member of any of several European dynasties that ruled in France (1589–1793; 1815–48), Spain (1700–1808; 1813–1931), and Naples and Sicily (1734–1806; 1815–1860). **b.** (*as modifier*): *the Bourbon kings.*

Bourbon biscuit *n.* a rich chocolate-flavoured biscuit with a chocolate-cream filling.

Bourbonism ('bʊəbəˌnɪzəm) *n.* **1.** support for Bourbon rule. **2.** *U.S.* extreme political and social conservatism.

bourdon ('bʊədᵊn, 'bɔːdᵊn) *n.* **1.** a 16-foot organ stop of the stopped diapason type. **2.** the drone of a bagpipe. **3.** a drone or pedal point in the bass of a harmonized melody. [C14: from Old French: drone (of a musical instrument), of imitative origin]

Bourdon gauge *n.* a type of pressure gauge consisting of a flattened curved tube attached to a pointer that moves around a dial. As the pressure in the tube increases the tube tends to straighten and the pointer indicates the applied pressure. [C19: named after Eugène *Bourdon* (1808–84), French hydraulic engineer, who invented it]

bourg (bʊəg; *French* bur) *n.* a French market town, esp. one beside a castle. [C15: French, from Old French *borc,* from Late Latin *burgus* castle, of Germanic origin; see BOROUGH]

bourgeois[1] ('bʊəʒwɑː, bʊə'ʒwɑː) *Often disparaging.* ~*n., pl.* **-geois. 1.** a member of the middle class, esp. one regarded as being conservative and materialistic or (in Marxist thought) a capitalist exploiting the working class. **2.** a mediocre, unimaginative, or materialistic person. ~*adj.* **3.** characteristic of, relating to, or comprising the middle class. **4.** conservative or materialistic in outlook: *a bourgeois mentality.* **5.** (in Marxist thought) dominated by capitalists or capitalist interests. [C16: from Old French *borjois, burgeis* burgher, citizen, from *bourg* town; see BURGESS] —**bourgeoise** ('bʊəʒwɑːz, bʊə'ʒwɑːz) *fem. n.*

bourgeois[2] (bə'dʒɔɪs) *n.* (formerly) a size of printer's type approximately equal to 9 point. [C19: perhaps from its size, midway between long primer and brevier]

bourgeoisie (ˌbʊəʒwɑː'ziː) *n.* **the. 1.** the middle classes. **2.** (in Marxist thought) the ruling class of the two basic classes of capitalist society, consisting of capitalists, manufacturers, bankers, and other employers. The bourgeoisie owns the most important of the means of production, through which it exploits the working class.

bourgeon ('bɜːdʒən) *n., vb.* a variant spelling of **burgeon.**

bourn[1] *or* **bourne** (bɔːn) *n. Archaic.* **1.** a destination; goal. **2.** a boundary. [C16: from Old French *borne;* see BOUND[3]]

bourn[2] (bɔːn) *n. Chiefly southern Brit.* a stream, esp. an intermittent one in chalk areas. Compare **burn**[2]. [C16: from Old French *bodne* limit; see BOUND[3]]

bourrée ('bʊəreɪ) *n.* **1.** a traditional French dance in fast duple time, resembling a gavotte. **2.** a piece of music composed in the rhythm of this dance. [C18: from French *bourrée* a bundle of faggots (it was originally danced round a fire of faggots)]

Bourse (bʊəs) *n.* a stock exchange of continental Europe, esp. Paris. [C19: from French, literally: purse, from Medieval Latin *bursa,* ultimately from Greek: leather]

bouse *or* **bowse** (baʊz) *vb.* (*tr.*) *Nautical.* to raise or haul with a tackle. [C16: of unknown origin]

boustrophedon (ˌbuːstrə'fiːdᵊn, ˌbaʊ-) *adj.* having alternate lines written from right to left and from left to right. [C17: from Greek, literally: turning as in ploughing with oxen, from *bous* ox + *-strophēdon* from *strephein* to turn; see STROPHE]

bout (baʊt) *n.* **1. a.** a period of time spent doing something, such as drinking. **b.** a period of illness. **2.** a contest or fight, esp. a boxing or wrestling match. [C16: variant of obsolete *bought* turn; related to German *Bucht* BIGHT; see ABOUT]

boutade (buːˈtɑːd) *n.* an outburst; sally. [C17: from French, from *bouter* to thrust]

boutique (buːˈtiːk) *n.* **1.** a shop, esp. a small one selling fashionable clothes and other items. **2.** (*modifier*) of or denoting a small specialized producer or business: *a boutique operation*; *a boutique winery*. [C18: from French, probably from Old Provençal *botica*, ultimately from Greek *apothēkē* storehouse; see APOTHECARY]

boutonniere (ˌbuːtɒnɪˈɛə) *n.* another name for **buttonhole** (sense 2). [C19: from French: buttonhole, from *bouton* BUTTON]

bouvier (ˈbuːvɪeɪ) *n.* a large powerful dog of a Belgian breed, having a rough shaggy coat: used esp. for cattle herding and guarding. [C20: from French, literally: cowherd]

bouzouki (buːˈzuːkɪ) *n.* a Greek long-necked stringed musical instrument related to the mandolin. [C20: from Modern Greek *mpouzouki*, perhaps from Turkish *büjük* large]

bovid (ˈbəʊvɪd) *adj.* **1.** of, relating to, or belonging to the *Bovidae*, a family of ruminant artiodactyl hollow-horned mammals including sheep, goats, cattle, antelopes, and buffalo. ~*n.* **2.** any bovid animal. [C19: from New Latin *Bovidae*, from Latin *bōs* ox]

bovine (ˈbəʊvaɪn) *adj.* **1.** of, relating to, or belonging to the *Bovini* (cattle), a bovid tribe including domestic cattle. **2.** (of people) dull; sluggish; stolid. ~*n.* **3.** any animal belonging to the *Bovini*. [C19: from Late Latin *bovīnus* concerning oxen or cows, from Latin *bōs* ox, cow] —ˈ**bovinely** *adv.*

bovine somatotrophin *n.* the full name for **BST** (sense 1).

bovine spongiform encephalopathy *n.* the full name for **BSE.**

Bovril (ˈbɒvrɪl) *n. Trademark.* a concentrated beef extract, used for flavouring, as a stock, etc.

bovver (ˈbɒvə) *n. Brit. slang.* **a.** rowdiness, esp. caused by gangs of teenage youths. **b.** (*as modifier*): *a bovver boy.* [C20: slang pronunciation of BOTHER]

bovver boots *pl. n. Brit. slang.* heavy boots worn by some teenage youths in Britain, used in gang fights.

bow[1] (baʊ) *vb.* **1.** to lower (one's head) or bend (one's knee or body) as a sign of respect, greeting, assent, or shame. **2.** to bend or cause to bend; incline downwards. **3.** (*intr.*; usually foll. by *to* or *before*) to comply or accept: *bow to the inevitable.* **4.** (*tr.*; foll. by *in, out, to,* etc.) to usher (someone) into or out of a place with bows and deference: *the manager bowed us to our car.* **5.** (*tr.*; usually foll. by *down*) to bring (a person, nation, etc.) to a state of submission. **6. bow and scrape.** to behave in an excessively deferential or obsequious way. ~*n.* **7.** a lowering or inclination of the head or body as a mark of respect, greeting, or assent. **8. take a bow.** to acknowledge or receive applause or praise. ~See also **bow out.** [Old English *būgan*, related to Old Norse *bjūgr* bent, Old High German *biogan* to bend, Dutch *buigen*]

bow[2] (bəʊ) *n.* **1.** a weapon for shooting arrows, consisting of an arch of flexible wood, plastic, metal, etc. bent by a string (**bowstring**) fastened at each end. See also **crossbow. 2. a.** a long slightly curved stick across which are stretched strands of horsehair, used for playing the strings of a violin, cello, or related instrument. **b.** a stroke with such a stick. **3. a.** a decorative interlacing of ribbon or other fabrics, usually having two loops and two loose ends. **b.** the knot forming such an interlacing; bowknot. **4. a.** something that is curved, bent, or arched. **b.** (*in combination*): *rainbow; oxbow; saddlebow.* **5.** a person who uses a bow and arrow; archer. **6.** *U.S.* **a.** a frame of a pair of spectacles. **b.** a sidepiece of the frame of a pair of spectacles that curls round behind the ear. **7.** a metal ring forming the handle of a pair of scissors or of a large old-fashioned key. **8.** *Architect.* part of a building curved in the form of a bow. See also **bow window.** ~*vb.* **9.** to form or cause to form a curve or curves. **10.** to make strokes of a bow across (violin strings). [Old English *boga* arch, bow; related to Old Norse *bogi* a bow, Old High German *bogo*, Old Irish *bocc*, and BOW[1]]

bow[3] (baʊ) *n.* **1.** *Chiefly Nautical.* **a.** (*often pl.*) the forward end or part of a vessel. **b.** (*as modifier*): *the bow mooring line.* **2.** *Rowing.* short for **bowman**[2]. **3. on the port** (*or* **starboard**) **bow.** *Nautical.* within 45 degrees to the port (or starboard) of straight ahead. **4. a shot across someone's bows.** *Informal.* a warning. [C15: probably from Low German *boog*; related to Dutch *boeg*, Danish *bov* ship's bow, shoulder; see BOUGH]

bow collector (bəʊ) *n.* a sliding current collector, consisting of a bow-shaped strip mounted on a hinged framework, used on trains, etc., to collect current from an overhead-wire. Compare **skate**[1] (sense 4).

bow compass (bəʊ) *n. Geometry.* a compass in which the legs are joined by a flexible metal bow-shaped spring rather than a hinge, the angle being adjusted by a screw. Also called: **bow-spring compass.**

bowdlerize *or* **bowdlerise** (ˈbaʊdləˌraɪz) *vb.* (*tr.*) to remove passages or words regarded as indecent from (a play, novel, etc.); expurgate. [C19: after Thomas *Bowdler* (1754–1825), English editor who published an expurgated edition of Shakespeare] —ˌ**bowdleriˈzation** *or* ˌ**bowdleriˈsation** *n.* —ˈ**bowdlerˌizer** *or* ˈ**bowdlerˌiser** *n.* —ˈ**bowdlerism** *n.*

bowed (baʊd) *adj.* **1.** lowered; bent forward; curved: *bowed head; bowed back.* **2. bowed down.** (foll. by *by* or *with*) weighed down; troubled: *bowed down by grief.*

bowel (ˈbaʊəl) *n.* **1.** an intestine, esp. the large intestine in man. **2.** (*pl.*) innards; entrails. **3.** (*pl.*) the deep or innermost part (esp. in the phrase **the bowels of the earth**). **4.** (*pl.*) *Archaic.* the emotions, esp. of pity or sympathy. [C13: from Old French *bouel*, from Latin *botellus* a little sausage, from *botulus* sausage]

bowel movement *n.* **1.** the discharge of faeces; defecation. **2.** the waste matter discharged; faeces.

bower[1] (ˈbaʊə) *n.* **1.** a shady leafy shelter or recess, as in a wood or garden; arbour. **2.** *Literary.* a lady's bedroom or apartments, esp. in a medieval castle; boudoir. **3.** *Literary.* a country cottage, esp. one regarded as charming or picturesque. [Old English *būr* dwelling; related to Old Norse *būr* pantry, Old High German *būr* dwelling] —ˈ**bowery** *adj.*

bower[2] (ˈbaʊə) *n. Nautical.* a vessel's bow anchor. [C18: from BOW[3] + -ER[1]]

bower[3] (ˈbaʊə) *n.* a jack in euchre and similar card games. [C19: from German *Bauer* peasant, jack (in cards)]

bowerbird (ˈbaʊəˌbɜːd) *n.* **1.** any of various songbirds of the family *Ptilonorhynchidae*, of Australia and New Guinea. The males build bower-like display grounds in the breeding season to attract the females. **2.** *Informal, chiefly Austral.* a collector of unconsidered trifles.

bowfin (ˈbəʊˌfɪn) *n.* a primitive North American freshwater bony fish, *Amia calva*, with an elongated body and a very long dorsal fin: family *Amiidae*.

bowhead (ˈbəʊˌhɛd) *n.* a large-mouthed arctic whale, *Balaena mysticetus*, that has become rare through overfishing but is now a protected species.

bowie knife (ˈbəʊɪ) *n.* a stout hunting knife with a short hilt and a guard for the hand. [C19: named after Jim *Bowie* (1796–1836), U.S. frontiersman, who popularized it]

bowing (ˈbəʊɪŋ) *n.* the technique of using the bow in playing a violin, viola, cello, or related instrument.

bowknot (ˈbəʊˌnɒt) *n.* a decorative knot usually having two loops and two loose ends; bow.

bowl[1] (bəʊl) *n.* **1.** a round container open at the top, used for holding liquid, keeping fruit, serving food, etc. **2.** Also: **bowlful.** the amount a bowl will hold. **3.** the rounded or hollow part of an object, esp. of a spoon or tobacco pipe. **4.** any container shaped like a bowl, such as a sink or lavatory. **5.** *Chiefly U.S.* a bowl-shaped building or other structure, such as a football stadium or amphitheatre. **6.** a bowl-shaped depression of the land surface. See also **dust bowl. 7.** *Literary.* **a.** a drinking cup. **b.** intoxicating drink. [Old English *bolla*; related to Old Norse *bolli*, Old Saxon *bollo*]

bowl[2] (bəʊl) *n.* **1.** a wooden ball used in the game of bowls, having flattened sides, one side usually being flatter than the other in order to make it run on a curved course. **2.** a large heavy ball with holes for gripping with the fingers and thumb, used in tenpin bowling. ~*vb.* **3.** to roll smoothly or cause to roll smoothly, esp. by throwing underarm along the ground. **4.** (*intr.*; usually foll. by *along*) to move easily and rapidly, as in a car. **5.** *Cricket.* **a.** to send (a ball) down the pitch from one's hand towards the batsman, keeping the arm straight while doing so. **b.** Also: **bowl out.** to dismiss (a batsman) by delivering a ball that breaks his wicket. **6.** (*intr.*) to play bowls or tenpin bowling. **7.** (*tr.*) (in bowls) to score (a specified amount): *he bowled 120.* ~See also **bowl over, bowls.** [C15: from French *boule*, ultimately from Latin *bulla* bubble]

bow legs (bəʊ) *pl. n.* a condition in which the legs curve outwards like a bow between the ankle and the thigh. Also called: **bandy legs.** —**bow-legged** (bəʊˈlɛgɪd, bəʊˈlɛgd) *adj.*

bowler[1] (ˈbəʊlə) *n.* **1.** one who bowls in cricket. **2.** a player at the game of bowls.

bowler[2] (ˈbəʊlə) *n.* a stiff felt hat with a rounded crown and narrow curved brim. U.S. and Canadian name: **derby.** [C19: named after John *Bowler*, 19th-century London hatter]

bowler[3] (ˈbaʊlə) *n. Dublin dialect.* a dog. [perhaps from B(OW-WOW) + (H)OWLER]

bowline (ˈbəʊlɪn) *n. Nautical.* **1.** a line for controlling the weather leech of a square sail when a vessel is close-hauled. **2. on a bowline.** beating close to the wind. **3.** a knot used for securing a loop that will not slip at the end of a piece of rope. [C14: probably from Middle Low German *bōlīne*, equivalent to BOW[3] + LINE[1]]

bowling (ˈbəʊlɪŋ) *n.* **1.** any of various games in which a heavy ball is rolled down a special alley, usually made of wood, at a group of wooden pins, esp. the games of tenpin bowling (tenpins) and skittles (ninepins). **2.** the game of bowls. **3.** *Cricket.* the act of delivering the ball to the batsman. **4.** (*modifier*) of or relating to bowls or bowling: *a bowling team.*

bowling alley *n.* **1. a.** a long narrow wooden lane down which the ball is rolled in tenpin bowling. **b.** a similar lane or alley, usually with raised sides, for playing skittles (ninepins). **2.** a building having several lanes for tenpin bowling.

bowling crease *n. Cricket.* a line marked at the wicket, over which a bowler must not advance fully before delivering the ball.

bowling green *n.* an area of closely mown turf on which the game of bowls is played.

bowl over *vb.* (*tr., adv.*) **1.** *Informal.* to surprise (a person) greatly, esp. in a pleasant way; astound; amaze: *he was bowled over by our gift.* **2.** to knock (a person or thing) down; cause to fall over.

bowls (bəʊlz) *n.* (*functioning as sing.*) **1. a.** a game played on a bowling green in which a small bowl (the jack) is pitched from a mark and two opponents or opposing teams take turns to roll biased wooden bowls towards it, the object being to finish as near the jack as possible. **b.** (*as modifier*): *a bowls tournament.* **2.** skittles or tenpin bowling.

bowman[1] ('bəʊmən) *n., pl.* **-men.** *Archaic.* an archer.

bowman[2] ('baʊmən) *n., pl.* **-men.** *Nautical.* an oarsman at the bow of a boat. Also called: **bow oar.**

bow out (baʊ) *vb.* (*adv.; usually tr.;* often foll. by *of*) to retire or withdraw gracefully.

bowsaw ('bəʊˌsɔː) *n.* a saw with a thin blade in a bow-shaped frame, used for cutting curves.

bowse (baʊz) *vb.* a variant spelling of **bouse.**

bowser ('baʊzə) *n.* **1.** a tanker containing fuel for aircraft, military vehicles, etc. **2.** *Austral. and N.Z.* a petrol pump at a filling station. [originally a U.S. proprietary name, from S. F. *Bowser,* American inventor, who made the first one in 1885]

bowshot ('bəʊˌʃɒt) *n.* the distance an arrow travels from the bow.

bowsie ('baʊziː) *n. Irish.* a low-class mean or obstreperous person. [of unknown origin]

bowsprit ('bəʊsprɪt) *n. Nautical.* a spar projecting from the bow of a vessel, esp. a sailing vessel, used to carry the headstay as far forward as possible. [C13: from Middle Low German *bōchsprēt,* from *bōch* BOW[3] + *sprēt* pole]

Bow Street runner (bəʊ) *n.* (in Britain from 1749 to 1829) an officer at Bow Street magistrates' court, London, whose duty was to pursue and arrest criminals.

bowstring ('bəʊˌstrɪŋ) *n.* the string of an archer's bow, usually consisting of three strands of hemp.

bowstring hemp *n.* a hemplike fibre obtained from the sansevieria.

bow tie (bəʊ) *n.* a man's tie tied in a bow, now chiefly in plain black for formal evening wear.

bow weight (bəʊ) *n. Archery.* the poundage required to draw a bow to the full length of the arrow.

bow window (bəʊ) *n.* a bay window in the shape of a curve.

bow-wow ('baʊˌwaʊ, -'waʊ) *n.* **1.** a child's word for **dog.** **2.** an imitation of the bark of a dog. ~*vb.* **3.** (*intr.*) to bark or imitate a dog's bark.

bowyangs ('bəʊjæŋz) *pl. n. Austral. and N.Z.* a pair of strings or straps secured round each trouser leg below the knee, worn esp. by sheep-shearers and other labourers. [C19: from English dialect *bowy-yanks* leggings]

bowyer ('bəʊjə) *n.* a person who makes or sells archery bows.

box[1] (bɒks) *n.* **1.** a receptacle or container made of wood, cardboard, etc., usually rectangular and having a removable or hinged lid. **2.** Also called: **boxful.** the contents of such a receptacle or the amount it can contain: *he ate a whole box of chocolates.* **3.** any of various containers for a specific purpose: *a money box; letter box.* **4.** (*often in combination*) any of various small cubicles, kiosks, or shelters: *a telephone box or callbox; a sentry box; a signal box on a railway.* **5.** a separate compartment in a public place for a small group of people, as in a theatre or certain restaurants. **6.** an enclosure within a courtroom. See **jury box, witness box.** **7.** a compartment for a horse in a stable or a vehicle. See **loosebox, horsebox.** **8.** *Brit.* a small country house occupied by sportsmen when following a field sport, esp. shooting. **9. a.** a protective housing for machinery or mechanical parts. **b.** the contents of such a box. **c.** (*in combination*): *a gearbox.* **10.** a shaped device of light tough material worn by sportsmen to protect the genitals, esp. in cricket. **11.** a section of printed matter on a page, enclosed by lines, a border, or white space. **12.** a central agency to which mail is addressed and from which it is collected or redistributed: *a post-office box; to reply to a box number in a newspaper advertisement.* **13.** short for **penalty box.** **14.** *Baseball.* either of the designated areas for the batter or the pitcher. **15.** the raised seat on which the driver sits in a horse-drawn coach. **16.** *N.Z.* a wheeled container for transporting coal in a mine. **17.** *Austral. and N.Z.* an accidental mixing of herds or flocks. **18.** a hole cut into the base of a tree to collect the sap. **19.** short for **Christmas box.** **20.** a device for dividing water into two or more ditches in an irrigation system. **21.** an informal name for a **coffin.** **22.** *Austral. taboo slang.* the female genitals. **23. be a box of birds.** *N.Z.* to be very well indeed. **24. the box.** *Brit. informal.* television. **25. out of the box.** *Austral. informal.* outstanding or excellent: *a day out of the box.* ~*vb.* **26.** (*tr.*) to put into a box. **27.** (*tr.;* usually foll. by *in* or *up*) to prevent from moving freely; confine. **28.** (*tr.;* foll. by *in*) *Printing.* to enclose (text) within a ruled frame. **29.** (*tr.*) to make a cut in the base of (a tree) in order to collect the sap. **30.** (*tr.*) *Austral. and N.Z.* to mix (flocks or herds) accidentally. **31.** (*tr.;* sometimes foll. by *up*) *N.Z.* to confuse: *I am all boxed up.* **32.** *Nautical.* short for **boxhaul.** **33. box the compass.** *Nautical.* to name the compass points in order. **34. box the fox.** *Irish slang.* to rob an orchard. [Old English *box,* from Latin *buxus, from Greek puxos* BOX[3]] —'**box,like** *adj.*

box[2] (bɒks) *vb.* **1.** (*tr.*) to fight (an opponent) in a boxing match. **2.** (*intr.*) to engage in boxing. **3.** (*tr.*) to hit (a person) with the fist; punch or cuff. ~*n.* **4.** a punch with the fist, esp. on the ear. [C14: of uncertain origin; perhaps related to Dutch *boken* to shunt, push into position]

box[3] (bɒks) *n.* **1.** a dense slow-growing evergreen tree or shrub of the genus *Buxus,* esp. *B. sempervirens,* which has small shiny leaves and is used for hedges, borders, and garden mazes: family *Buxaceae.* **2.** the wood of this tree. See **boxwood** (sense 1). **3.** any of several trees the timber or foliage of which resembles this tree, esp. various species of *Eucalyptus* with rough bark. [Old English, from Latin *buxus*]

box beam *n.* another name for **box girder.**

boxberry ('bɒksbərɪ) *n., pl.* **-ries.** **1.** the fruit of the partridgeberry or wintergreen. **2.** another name for **partridgeberry** and **wintergreen** (sense 1).

boxboard ('bɒksˌbɔːd) *n.* a tough paperboard made from wood and wastepaper pulp: used for making boxes, etc.

box calf *n.* black calfskin leather, tanned with chromium salts, having a pattern of fine creases formed by boarding. [C20: named after Joseph *Box,* London shoemaker]

box camera *n.* a simple box-shaped camera having an elementary lens, shutter, and viewfinder.

box canyon *n. Western U.S.* a canyon with vertical or almost vertical walls.

boxcar ('bɒksˌkɑː) *n. U.S. and Canadian.* a closed railway van.

box chronometer *n. Nautical.* a ship's chronometer, supported on gimbals in a wooden box.

box coat *n.* **1.** a plain short coat that hangs loosely from the shoulders. **2.** a heavy overcoat, worn formerly by coachmen.

box elder *n.* a medium-sized fast-growing widely cultivated North American maple, *Acer negundo,* which has compound leaves with lobed leaflets. Also called: **ash-leaved maple.**

boxer ('bɒksə) *n.* **1.** a man who boxes, either professionally or as a hobby; pugilist. **2.** a medium-sized smooth-haired breed of dog with a short nose and a docked tail.

Boxer ('bɒksə) *n.* **a.** a member of a nationalistic Chinese secret society that led an unsuccessful rebellion in 1900 against foreign interests in China. **b.** (*as modifier*): *the Boxer Rebellion.* [C18: rough translation of Chinese *I Ho Ch'üan,* literally: virtuous harmonious fist, altered from *I Ho T'uan* virtuous harmonious society]

boxer shorts *pl. n.* men's underpants shaped like shorts but having a front opening. Also called: **boxers.**

boxfish ('bɒksˌfɪʃ) *n., pl.* **-fish** *or* **-fishes.** another name for **trunkfish.**

box girder *n.* **a.** a girder that is hollow and square or rectangular in shape. **b.** (*as modifier*): *a box-girder bridge.* ~Also called: **box beam.**

boxhaul ('bɒksˌhɔːl) *vb. Nautical.* to bring (a square-rigger) onto a new tack by backwinding the foresails and steering hard round.

boxing ('bɒksɪŋ) *n.* **a.** the act, art, or profession of fighting with the fists, esp. the modern sport practised under Queensberry rules. **b.** (*as modifier*): *a boxing enthusiast.*

Boxing Day *n. Brit.* the first weekday after Christmas, observed as a holiday. [C19: from the custom of giving Christmas boxes to tradesmen and staff on this day]

boxing glove *n.* one of a pair of thickly padded mittens worn for boxing.

box jellyfish *n.* any of various highly venomous jellyfishes of the order *Cubomedusae,* esp. *Chironex fleckeri,* of Australian tropical waters, having a cuboidal body with tentacles hanging from each of the lower corners. Also called (Austral.): **sea wasp.**

box junction *n.* (in Britain) a road junction having yellow cross-hatching painted on the road surface. Vehicles may only enter the hatched area when their exit is clear.

box kite *n.* a kite with a boxlike frame open at both ends.

box number *n.* **1.** the number of an individual pigeonhole at a newspaper to which replies to an advertisement may be addressed. **2.** the number of an individual pigeonhole at a post office from which mail may be collected.

box office *n.* **1.** an office at a theatre, cinema, etc., where tickets are sold. **2.** the receipts from a play, film, etc. **3. a.** the public appeal of an actor or production: *the musical was bad box office.* **b.** (*as modifier*): *a box-office success.*

box pleat *n.* a flat double pleat made by folding under the fabric on either side of it.

boxroom ('bɒksˌruːm, -ˌrʊm) *n.* a small room or large cupboard in which boxes, cases, etc., may be stored.

box seat *n.* **1.** a seat in a theatre box. **2. in the box seat.** *Austral. and N.Z.* in the best position.

box spanner *n.* a spanner consisting of a steel cylinder with a hexagonal end that fits over a nut: used esp. to turn nuts in positions that are recessed or difficult of access.

box spring *n.* a coiled spring contained in a boxlike frame, used as base for mattresses, chairs, etc.

boxthorn ('bɒksˌθɔːn) *n.* another name for **matrimony vine.**

boxwood ('bɒksˌwʊd) *n.* **1.** the hard close-grained yellow wood of the box tree, used to make tool handles, small turned or carved articles, etc. **2.** the box tree.

boxy ('bɒksɪ) *adj.* squarish or chunky in style or appearance: *a boxy square-cut jacket.*

boy (bɔɪ) *n.* **1.** a male child; lad; youth. **2.** a man regarded as immature or inexperienced: *he's just a boy when it comes to dealing with women.* **3.** See **old boy.** **4. the boys.** *Informal.* a group of men, esp. a group of friends. **5.** *Usually derogatory.* (esp. in former colonial territories) a Black or native male servant of any age. **6.** *Austral.* a jockey or apprentice. **7.** short for **boyfriend.** **8. boys will be boys.** youthful indiscretion or exuberance must be expected and tolerated. **9. jobs for the boys.** *Informal.* appointment of one's supporters to posts, without reference to their qualifications or ability. **10. the boy.**

Irish informal. the right tool for a particular task: *that's the boy to cut it.* ~*interj.* **11.** an exclamation of surprise, pleasure, contempt, etc. [C13 (in the sense: male servant; C14: young male): of uncertain origin; perhaps from Anglo-French *abuié* fettered (unattested), from Latin *boia* fetter]

boyar ('bəʊjɑː, 'bɔɪə) *n.* a member of an old order of Russian nobility, ranking immediately below the princes: abolished by Peter the Great. [C16: from Old Russian *boyarin,* from Old Slavic *boljarinŭ,* probably from Old Turkic *boila* a title]

boycott ('bɔɪkɒt) *vb.* **1.** (*tr.*) to refuse to have dealings with (a person, organization, etc.) or refuse to buy (a product) as a protest or means of coercion: *to boycott foreign produce.* ~*n.* **2.** an instance or the use of boycotting. [C19: after Captain C. C. *Boycott* (1832–97), Irish land agent for the Earl of Erne, County Mayo, Ireland, who was a victim of such practices for refusing to reduce rents]

boyfriend ('bɔɪˌfrɛnd) *n.* a male friend with whom a person is romantically or sexually involved; sweetheart or lover.

boyhood ('bɔɪhʊd) *n.* the state or time of being a boy: *his boyhood was happy.*

boyish ('bɔɪɪʃ) *adj.* of or like a boy in looks, behaviour, or character, esp. when regarded as attractive or endearing: *a boyish smile.* —**'boyishly** *adv.* —**'boyishness** *n.*

boyla ('bɔɪlə) *n. Austral.* an Aboriginal witch doctor. [from a native Australian language]

Boyle's law (bɔɪlz) *n.* the principle that the pressure of a gas varies inversely with its volume at constant temperature. [C18: named after Robert *Boyle* (1627–91), Irish scientist]

boy-meets-girl *adj.* conventionally or trivially romantic: *a boy-meets-girl story.*

boyo ('bɔɪəʊ) *n. Brit. informal.* a boy or young man: often used in direct address. [from Irish and Welsh]

Boys' Brigade *n.* (in Britain) an organization for boys, founded in 1883, with the aim of promoting discipline and self-respect.

boy scout *n.* See **Scout.**

boysenberry ('bɔɪzᵊnbərɪ) *n., pl.* **-ries.** **1.** a type of bramble: a hybrid of the loganberry and various blackberries and raspberries. **2.** the large red edible fruit of this plant. [C20: named after Rudolph *Boysen,* American botanist who developed it]

bozo ('bəʊzəʊ) *n., pl.* **-zos.** *U.S. slang.* a man, esp. a stupid one. [C20: of uncertain origin; perhaps based on BEAU]

bp *abbrev. for:* **1.** (of alcoholic density) below proof. **2.** boiling point. **3.** bishop. **4.** Also: **B/P.** bills payable.

BP *abbrev. for:* **1.** blood pressure. **2.** British Pharmacopoeia.

bp. *abbrev. for:* **1.** baptized. **2.** birthplace.

B/P *or* **bp** *abbrev. for* bills payable.

BPC *abbrev. for* British Pharmaceutical Codex.

BPharm *abbrev. for* Bachelor of Pharmacy.

BPhil *abbrev. for* Bachelor of Philosophy.

bpi *abbrev. for* bits per inch (used of a computer tape).

bps *Computer technol. abbrev. for* bits per second.

b.pt. *abbrev. for* boiling point.

Bq *symbol for* becquerel(s).

br *abbrev. for:* **1.** brother. **2.** Also: **B/R.** bills receivable.

Br **1.** *abbrev. for* (in a religious order) Brother. **2.** *the chemical symbol for* bromine.

BR **1.** *abbrev. for* British Rail (formerly British Railways). **2.** *international car registration for* Brazil.

br. *abbrev. for:* **1.** branch. **2.** bronze.

B/R *or* **br** *abbrev. for* bills receivable.

bra (brɑː) *n.* short for **brassiere.**

braai (braɪ) *S. African.* ~*vb.* **1.** to grill or roast (meat) over open coals. ~*n.* **2.** short for **braaivleis.** [Afrikaans]

braaivleis ('braɪˌfleɪs) *n. S. African.* a picnic at which meat is cooked over an open fire; a barbecue. [from Afrikaans *braai* roast + *vleis* meat]

braata ('brɑːtə) *or* **braatas** ('brɑːtəs) *n. Caribbean.* a small portion added to a purchase of food by a market vendor, to encourage the customer to return. Also called: **broughta, broughtas.** [perhaps from Spanish *barata* a bargain]

brabble ('bræbᵊl) *vb., n.* a rare word for **squabble.** [C16: from Middle Dutch *brabbelen* to jabber] —**'brabbler** *n.*

braccate ('brækeɪt) *adj.* (of birds) having feathered legs. [from Latin *braccātus,* from *brāccae* breeches + -ATE[1]]

brace (breɪs) *n.* **1.** in full: **hand brace.** a hand tool for drilling holes, with a socket to hold the drill at one end and a cranked handle by which the tool can be turned. See also **brace and bit.** **2.** something that steadies, binds, or holds up another thing. **3.** a structural member, such as a beam or prop, used to stiffen a framework. **4.** a sliding loop, usually of leather, attached to the cords of a drum: used to change its tension. **5.** a pair; two, esp. of game birds: *a brace of partridges.* **6.** either of a pair of characters, { }, used for connecting lines of printing or writing or as a third sign of aggregation in complex mathematical or logical expressions that already contain parentheses and square brackets. **7.** Also called: **accolade.** a line or bracket connecting two or more staves of music. **8.** (*often pl.*) an appliance of metal bands and wires that can be tightened to maintain steady pressure on the teeth for correcting uneven alignment. **9.** *Med.* any of various appliances for supporting the trunk or a limb. **10.** another word for **bracer**[2]. **11.** (in square-rigged sailing ships) a rope that controls the movement of a yard and thus the position of a sail. **12.** See **braces.** ~*vb.* (*mainly tr.*) **13.** to provide, strengthen, or fit with a brace. **14.** to steady or prepare (oneself or something) as before an impact. **15.** (*also intr.*) to stimulate; freshen; invigorate: *sea air is bracing.* **16.** to control the horizontal movement of (the yards of a square-rigged sailing ship). [C14: from Old French: the two arms, from Latin *bracchia* arms]

brace and bit *n.* a hand tool for boring holes, consisting of a cranked handle into which a drilling bit is inserted.

bracelet ('breɪslɪt) *n.* **1.** an ornamental chain worn around the arm or wrist. **2.** an expanding metal band for a wristwatch. [C15: from Old French, from *bracel,* literally: a little arm, from Latin *bracchium* arm; see BRACE]

bracelets ('breɪslɪts) *pl. n.* a slang name for **handcuffs.**

bracer[1] ('breɪsə) *n.* **1.** a person or thing that braces. **2.** *Informal.* a tonic, esp. an alcoholic drink taken as a tonic.

bracer[2] ('breɪsə) *n. Archery, fencing.* a leather guard worn to protect the arm. [C14: from Old French *braciere,* from *braz* arm, from Latin *bracchium* arm]

braces ('breɪsɪz) *pl. n. Brit.* a pair of straps worn over the shoulders by men for holding up the trousers. U.S. and Canadian word: **suspenders.**

brach (brætʃ) *or* **brachet** ('brætʃɪt) *n. Archaic.* a bitch hound. [C14: back formation from *brachez* hunting dogs, from Old French, plural of *brachet,* of Germanic origin; compare Old High German *braccho* hound]

brachah (bra'xa) *or* **brocho** *n. Judaism.* Hebrew terms usually translated as "blessing". See **blessing** (sense 4).

brachial ('breɪkɪəl, 'bræk-) *adj.* of or relating to the arm or to an armlike part or structure.

brachiate *adj.* ('breɪkɪɪt, -ˌeɪt, 'bræk-). **1.** *Botany.* having widely divergent paired branches. ~*vb.* ('breɪkɪˌeɪt, 'bræk-). **2.** (*intr.*) (of some arboreal apes and monkeys) to swing by the arms from one hold to the next. [C19: from Latin *bracchiātus* with armlike branches] —**ˌbrachi'ation** *n.*

brachio- *or before a vowel* **brachi-** *combining form.* indicating a brachium: *brachiopod.*

brachiocephalic (ˌbreɪkɪəʊsɪ'fælɪk) *adj.* of, relating to, or supplying the arm and head: *brachiocephalic artery.*

brachiopod ('breɪkɪəˌpɒd, 'bræk-) *n.* any marine invertebrate animal of the phylum *Brachiopoda,* having a ciliated feeding organ (lophophore) and a shell consisting of dorsal and ventral valves. Also called: **lamp shell.** See also **bryozoan.** [C19: from New Latin *Brachiopoda;* see BRACHIUM, -POD]

brachiosaurus (ˌbreɪkɪə'sɔːrəs, ˌbræk-) *n.* a dinosaur of the genus *Brachiosaurus,* up to 30 metres long: the largest land animal ever known. See also **sauropod.**

brachistochrone (brə'kɪstəˌkrəʊn) *n. Maths.* the curve between two points through which a body moves under the force of gravity in a shorter time than for any other curve; the path of quickest descent. [C18: from Greek *brakhistos,* superlative of *brakhus* short + *chronos* time]

brachium ('breɪkɪəm, 'bræk-) *n., pl.* **-chia** (-kɪə). **1.** *Anatomy.* the arm, esp. the upper part. **2.** a corresponding part, such as a wing, in an animal. **3.** *Biology.* a branching or armlike part. [C18: New Latin, from Latin *bracchium* arm, from Greek *brakhiōn*]

brachy- *combining form.* indicating something short: *brachycephalic.* [from Greek *brakhus* short]

brachycephalic (ˌbrækɪsɪ'fælɪk) *adj.* also **brachycephalous** (ˌbrækɪ'sɛfələs). **1.** having a head nearly as broad from side to side as from front to back, esp. one with a cephalic index over 80. ~*n.* **2.** an individual with such a head. ~Compare **dolichocephalic, mesocephalic.** —**ˌbrachy'cephaly** *or* **ˌbrachy'cephalism** *n.*

brachycerous (bræ'kɪsərəs) *adj.* (of insects) having short antennae.

brachydactylic (ˌbrækɪdæk'tɪlɪk) *or* **brachydactylous** (ˌbrækɪ'dæktɪləs) *adj.* having abnormally short fingers or toes. —**ˌbrachy'dactyly** *or* **ˌbrachy'dactylˌism** *n.*

brachylogy (bræ'kɪlədʒɪ) *n., pl.* **-gies.** **1.** a concise style in speech or writing. **2.** a colloquial shortened form of expression that is not the result of a regular grammatical process: *the omission of "good" in the expression "Afternoon" is a brachylogy.* —**bra'chylogous** *adj.*

brachyodont ('brækɪəˌdɒnt) *adj.* (of mammals, such as humans) having teeth with short crowns.

brachypterous (bræ'kɪptərəs) *adj.* having very short or incompletely developed wings: *brachypterous insects.* —**bra'chypterism** *n.*

brachyuran (ˌbrækɪ'jʊərən) *n.* **1.** any decapod crustacean of the group (formerly suborder) *Brachyura,* which includes the crabs. ~*adj.* **2.** of, relating to, or belonging to the *Brachyura.* [C19: from New Latin *Brachyura* (literally: short-tailed creatures), from BRACHY- + Greek *oura* tail]

bracing ('breɪsɪŋ) *adj.* **1.** refreshing; stimulating; invigorating: *the air here is bracing.* ~*n.* **2.** a system of braces used to strengthen or support: *the bracing supporting the building is perfectly adequate.* —**'bracingly** *adv.*

bracken ('brækən) *n.* **1.** Also called: **brake.** any of various large coarse ferns, esp. *Pteridium aquilinum,* having large fronds with spore cases along the undersides and extensive underground stems. **2.** a clump of any of these ferns. [C14: of Scandinavian origin; compare Swedish *bräken,* Danish *bregne*]

bracket ('brækɪt) *n.* **1.** an L-shaped or other support fixed to a wall to hold a shelf, etc. **2.** one or more wall shelves carried on brackets. **3.** *Architect.* a support projecting from the side of a wall or other structure. See also **corbel, ancon, console**[2]. **4.** Also called: **square bracket.** either of a pair of characters, [ ], used to enclose a section of writing or printing to separate it from the main text. **5.** a general name for **parenthesis, square bracket,** and **brace** (sense 6). **6.** a group or category falling within or between certain defined limits: *the lower income bracket.* **7.** the distance between two preliminary shots of artillery fire in range-finding. **8.** a skating figure consisting of two arcs meeting at a point, tracing the shape ⌣. *~vb.* (*tr.*) **-kets, -keting, -keted. 9.** to fix or support by means of a bracket or brackets. **10.** to put (written or printed matter) in brackets, esp. as being irrelevant, spurious, or bearing a separate relationship of some kind to the rest of the text. **11.** to couple or join (two lines of text, etc.) with a brace. **12.** (often foll. by *with*) to group or class together: *to bracket Marx with the philosophers.* **13.** to adjust (artillery fire) until the target is hit. [C16: from Old French *braguette* codpiece, diminutive of *bragues* breeches, from Old Provençal *braga,* from Latin *brāca* breeches]

bracket fungus *n.* any saprophytic or parasitic fungus of the basidiomycetous family *Polyporaceae,* growing as a shelflike mass (bracket) from tree trunks and producing spores in vertical tubes in the bracket.

bracketing ('brækɪtɪŋ) *n.* a set of brackets.

brackish ('brækɪʃ) *adj.* (of water) slightly briny or salty. [C16: from Middle Dutch *brac* salty; see -ISH] —'**brackishness** *n.*

bract (brækt) *n.* a specialized leaf with a single flower or inflorescence growing in its axil. [C18: from New Latin *bractea,* Latin: thin metal plate, gold leaf, variant of *brattea,* of obscure origin] —'**bracteal** *adj.* —'**bractless** *adj.*

bracteate ('bræktɪɪt, -ˌeɪt) *adj.* **1.** (of a plant) having bracts. *~n.* **2.** *Archaeol.* a fine decorated dish or plate of precious metal. [C19: from Latin *bracteātus* gold-plated; see BRACT]

bracteole ('bræktɪˌəʊl) *n.* a secondary or small bract. Also called: '**bractlet.** [C19: from New Latin *bracteola,* from *bractea* thin metal plate; see BRACT] —**bracteolate** ('bræktɪəlɪt, -ˌleɪt) *adj.*

brad (bræd) *n.* a small tapered nail having a small head that is either symmetrical or formed on one side only. [Old English *brord* point, prick; related to Old Norse *broddr* spike, sting, Old High German *brort* edge]

bradawl ('brædˌɔːl) *n.* an awl used to pierce wood, leather, or other materials for the insertion of brads, screws, etc.

Bradshaw ('brædˌʃɔː) *n.* a British railway timetable, published annually from 1839 to 1961. [C19: named after its original publisher, George *Bradshaw* (1801–53)]

brady- *combining form.* indicating slowness: *bradycardia.* [from Greek *bradus* slow]

bradycardia (ˌbrædɪ'kɑːdɪə) *n. Pathol.* an abnormally low rate of heartbeat. Compare **tachycardia.** —**bradycardiac** (ˌbrædɪ'kɑːdɪˌæk) *adj.*

bradykinesia (ˌbrædɪkɪ'niːzɪə) *n. Physiol.* abnormal slowness of physical movement, esp. as a symptom of Parkinson's disease. [C20: from BRADY- + Greek *kinēsis* motion]

bradykinin (ˌbrædɪ'kaɪnɪn, ˌbreɪdɪ-) *n.* a peptide in blood plasma that dilates blood vessels and causes contraction of smooth muscles. Formula: $C_{50}H_{73}N_{15}O_{11}$. [C20: from BRADY- + Greek *kin(ēsis)* motion + -IN]

brae (breɪ; *Scot.* bre) *n. Scot.* **1.** a hill or hillside; slope. **2.** (*pl.*) an upland area: *the Gleniffer braes.* [C14 *bra;* related to Old Norse *brā* eyelash, Old High German *brāwa* eyelid, eyebrow; compare BROW]

braeheid (bre'hiːd) *n. Scot.* the summit of a hill or slope.

brag (bræg) *vb.* **brags, bragging, bragged. 1.** to speak of (one's own achievements, possessions, etc.) arrogantly and boastfully. *~n.* **2.** boastful talk or behaviour, or an instance of this. **3.** something boasted of: *his brag was his new car.* **4.** a braggart; boaster. **5.** a card game: an old form of poker. [C13: of unknown origin] —'**bragger** *n.* —'**bragging** *n., adj.* —'**braggingly** *adv.*

braggadocio (ˌbrægə'dəʊtʃɪˌəʊ) *n., pl.* **-os. 1.** vain empty boasting. **2.** a person who boasts; braggart. [C16: from *Braggadocchio,* name of a boastful character in Spenser's *Faerie Queene*; probably from BRAGGART + Italian *-occhio* (augmentative suffix)]

braggart ('brægət) *n.* **1.** a person who boasts loudly or exaggeratedly; bragger. *~adj.* **2.** boastful. [C16: see BRAG]

Bragg's law (brægz) *n.* the principle that when a beam of x-rays of wavelength λ enters a crystal, the maximum intensity of the reflected ray occurs when $\sin \theta = n\lambda/2d$, where θ is the complement of the angle of incidence, *n* is a whole number, and *d* is the distance between layers of atoms. [C20: named after Sir William Henry *Bragg* (1862–1942) and his son, Sir William Lawrence *Bragg* (1890–1971), British physicists]

Brahma[1] ('brɑːmə) *n.* **1.** a Hindu god: in later Hindu tradition, the Creator who, with Vishnu, the Preserver, and Shiva, the Destroyer, constitutes the triad known as the Trimurti. **2.** another name for **Brahman** (sense 2). [from Sanskrit, from *brahman* praise]

Brahma[2] ('brɑːmə, 'breɪ-) *n.* a heavy breed of domestic fowl with profusely feathered legs and feet. [C19: shortened from *Brahmaputra* (river); from its having been imported originally from Lakhimpur, a town on the Brahmaputra]

Brahman ('brɑːmən) *n., pl.* **-mans. 1.** (*sometimes not cap.*) Also called (esp. formerly): **Brahmin.** a member of the highest or priestly caste in the Hindu caste system. **2.** *Hinduism.* the ultimate and impersonal divine reality of the universe, from which all being originates and to which it returns. **3.** another name for **Brahma**[1]. [C14: from Sanskrit *brāhmana,* from *brahman* prayer] —**Brahmanic** (brɑː'mænɪk) *or* **Brah'manical** *adj.*

Brahmana ('brɑːmənə) *n. Hinduism.* any of a number of sacred treatises added to each of the Vedas.

Brahmani ('brɑːmənɪ) *n., pl.* **-nis.** (*sometimes not cap.*) a woman of the Brahman caste.

Brahmanism ('brɑːməˌnɪzəm) *or* **Brahminism** *n.* (*sometimes not cap.*) **1.** the religious and social system of orthodox Hinduism, characterized by diversified pantheism, the caste system, and the sacrifices and family ceremonies of Hindu tradition. **2.** the form of Hinduism prescribed in the Vedas, Brahmanas, and Upanishads. —'**Brahmanist** *or* '**Brahminist** *n.*

Brahmin ('brɑːmɪn) *n., pl.* **-min** *or* **-mins. 1.** the older spelling of **Brahman** (a Hindu priest). **2.** (in the U.S.) a highly intelligent or socially exclusive person, esp. a member of one of the older New England families. **3.** an intellectual or social snob. —**Brah'minic** *or* **Brah'minical** *adj.*

Brahui (brɑː'huːɪ) *n.* **1.** a language spoken in Pakistan, forming an isolated branch of the Dravidian family. **2.** (*pl.* **-hui** *or* **-huis**) a member of the people that speaks this language.

braid[1] (breɪd) *vb.* (*tr.*) **1.** to interweave several strands of (hair, thread, etc.); plait. **2.** to make by such weaving: *to braid a rope.* **3.** to dress or bind (the hair) with a ribbon, etc. **4.** to decorate with an ornamental trim or border: *to braid a skirt.* *~n.* **5.** a length of hair, fabric, etc., that has been braided; plait. **6.** narrow ornamental tape of woven silk, wool, etc. [Old English *bregdan* to move suddenly, weave together; compare Old Norse *bregtha,* Old High German *brettan* to draw a sword] —'**braider** *n.*

braid[2] (bred, breɪd) *Scot.* *~adj.* **1.** broad. *~adv.* **2.** broadly; frankly. [Scot. variant of BROAD]

braided ('breɪdɪd) *adj.* (of a river or stream) flowing in several shallow interconnected channels separated by banks of deposited material.

braiding ('breɪdɪŋ) *n.* **1.** braids collectively. **2.** work done in braid. **3.** a piece of braid.

brail (breɪl) *Nautical.* *~n.* **1.** one of several lines fastened to the leech of a fore-and-aft sail to aid in furling it. *~vb.* **2.** (*tr.;* sometimes foll. by *up*) to furl (a fore-and-aft sail) using brails. [C15: from Old French *braiel,* from Medieval Latin *brācāle* belt for breeches, from Latin *brāca* breeches]

Braille (breɪl) *n.* **1.** a system of writing for the blind consisting of raised dots that can be interpreted by touch, each dot or group of dots representing a letter, numeral, or punctuation mark. **2.** any writing produced by this method. Compare **Moon.** *~vb.* **3.** (*tr.*) to print or write using this method. [C19: named after Louis *Braille* (1809–52), French inventor]

brain (breɪn) *n.* **1.** the soft convoluted mass of nervous tissue within the skull of vertebrates that is the controlling and coordinating centre of the nervous system and the seat of thought, memory, and emotion. It includes the cerebrum, brainstem, and cerebellum. Technical name: **encephalon.** Related adj.: **cerebral. 2.** the main neural bundle or ganglion of certain invertebrates. **3.** (*often pl.*) *Informal.* intellectual ability: *he's got brains.* **4.** *Informal.* shrewdness or cunning. **5.** *Informal.* an intellectual or intelligent person. **6.** (*usually pl.; functioning as sing.*) *Informal.* a person who plans and organizes an undertaking or is in overall control of an organization, etc. **7.** an electronic device, such as a computer, that performs apparently similar functions to the human brain. **8. on the brain.** constantly in mind: *I had that song on the brain.* **9. pick someone's brains.** to obtain information or ideas from someone. *~vb.* (*tr.*) **10.** to smash the skull of. **11.** *Slang.* to hit hard on the head. [Old English *brægen;* related to Old Frisian *brein,* Middle Low German *bregen,* Greek *brekhmos* forehead]

brainbox ('breɪnˌbɒks) *n. Slang.* **1.** the skull. **2.** a clever person.

brainchild ('breɪnˌtʃaɪld) *n., pl.* **-children.** *Informal.* an idea or plan produced by creative thought; invention.

brain coral *n.* a stony coral of the genus *Meandrina,* in which the polyps lie in troughlike thecae resembling the convoluted surface of a human brain.

braindead ('breɪnˌdɛd) *adj.* **1.** having suffered brain death. **2.** *Informal.* not using or showing intelligence; stupid.

brain death *n.* irreversible cessation of respiration due to irreparable brain damage, even though the heart may continue beating with the aid of a mechanical ventilator: widely considered as the criterion of death.

brain drain *n. Informal.* the emigration of scientists, technologists, academics, etc., for better pay, equipment, or conditions.

brain fever *n.* inflammation of the brain or its covering membranes.

brain-fever bird *n.* an Indian cuckoo, *Cuculus varius,* that utters a repetitive call.

brainless ('breɪnlɪs) *adj.* stupid or foolish. —'**brainlessly** *adv.* —'**brainlessness** *n.*

brainpan (ˈbreɪnˌpæn) *n. Informal.* the skull.

brainpower (ˈbreɪnˌpaʊə) *n.* intelligence; mental ability.

brainsick (ˈbreɪnˌsɪk) *adj.* relating to or caused by insanity; crazy; mad. —ˈ**brainˌsickly** *adv.* —ˈ**brainˌsickness** *n.*

brainstem (ˈbreɪnˌstɛm) *n.* the stalklike part of the brain consisting of the medulla oblongata, the midbrain, and the pons Varolii.

brainstorm (ˈbreɪnˌstɔːm) *n.* **1.** a severe outburst of excitement, often as the result of a transitory disturbance of cerebral activity. **2.** *Brit. informal.* a sudden mental aberration. **3.** *U.S. and Canadian informal.* another word for **brain wave** (sense 2).

brainstorming (ˈbreɪnˌstɔːmɪŋ) *n.* intensive discussion to solve problems or generate ideas.

brains trust *n.* **1.** a group of knowledgeable people who discuss topics in public or on radio or television. **2.** Also called: **brain trust.** *U.S.* a group of experts who advise the government.

brain-teaser *or* **brain-twister** *n. Informal.* a difficult problem.

brainwash (ˈbreɪnˌwɒʃ) *vb.* (*tr.*) to effect a radical change in the ideas and beliefs of (a person), esp. by methods based on isolation, sleeplessness, hunger, extreme discomfort, pain, and the alternation of kindness and cruelty. —ˈ**brainˌwasher** *n.* —ˈ**brainˌwashing** *n.*

brain wave *n.* **1.** any of the fluctuations of electrical potential in the brain as represented on an electroencephalogram. They vary in frequency from 1 to 30 hertz. See also **alpha rhythm, beta rhythm, delta rhythm. 2.** *Informal.* a sudden idea or inspiration.

brainy (ˈbreɪnɪ) *adj.* **brainier, brainiest.** *Informal.* clever; intelligent. —ˈ**brainily** *adv.* —ˈ**braininess** *n.*

braise (breɪz) *vb.* to cook (meat, vegetables, etc.) by lightly browning in fat and then cooking slowly in a closed pan with a small amount of liquid. [C18: from French *braiser,* from Old French *brese* live coals, probably of Germanic origin; compare Old English *brǣdan,* Old High German *brātan* to roast]

brake[1] (breɪk) *n.* **1. a.** (*often pl.*) a device for slowing or stopping a vehicle, wheel, shaft, etc., or for keeping it stationary, esp. by means of friction. See also **drum brake, disc brake, hydraulic brake, air brake, handbrake. b.** (*as modifier*): *the brake pedal.* **2.** a machine or tool for crushing or breaking flax or hemp to separate the fibres. **3.** Also called: **brake harrow.** a heavy harrow for breaking up clods. **4.** short for **brake van. 5.** short for **shooting brake. 6.** Also spelt: **break.** an open four-wheeled horse-drawn carriage. **7.** an obsolete word for the **rack** (an instrument of torture). ~*vb.* **8.** to slow down or cause to slow down, by or as if by using a brake. **9.** (*tr.*) to crush or break up using a brake. [C18: from Middle Dutch *braeke;* related to *breken* to BREAK] —ˈ**brakeless** *adj.*

brake[2] (breɪk) *n.* an area of dense undergrowth, shrubs, brushwood, etc.; thicket. [Old English *bracu;* related to Middle Low German *brake,* Old French *bracon* branch]

brake[3] (breɪk) *n.* another name for **bracken** (sense 1). See also **rock brake.**

brake[4] (breɪk) *vb. Archaic, chiefly biblical.* a past tense of **break.**

brake band *n.* a strip of fabric, leather, or metal tightened around a pulley or shaft to act as a brake.

brake drum *n.* the cast-iron drum attached to the hub of a wheel of a motor vehicle fitted with drum brakes. See also **brake shoe.**

brake-fade *n.* the decrease in efficiency of braking of a motor vehicle due to overheating of the brakes.

brake fluid *n.* an oily liquid used to transmit pressure in a hydraulic brake or clutch system.

brake horsepower *n.* the rate at which an engine does work, expressed in horsepower. It is measured by the resistance of an applied brake. Abbrev.: **bhp.**

brake light *n.* a red light attached to the rear of a motor vehicle that lights up when the brakes are applied, serving as a warning to following drivers. Also called: **stoplight.**

brake lining *n.* a curved thin strip of an asbestos composition riveted to a brake shoe to provide it with a renewable surface.

brakeman (ˈbreɪkmən) *n., pl.* **-men. 1.** *U.S. and Canadian.* a crew member of a goods or passenger train. His duties include controlling auxiliary braking power and inspecting the train. **2.** the man at the back of a two- or four-man bobsleigh, who operates the brake.

brake pad *n.* the flat metal casting, together with the bound friction material, in a disc brake.

brake parachute *n.* a parachute attached to the rear of a vehicle and opened to assist braking. Also called: **brake chute, parachute brake, parabrake.**

brake shoe *n.* **1.** the curved metal casting to which the brake lining is riveted in a drum brake. **2.** the curved metal casting together with the attached brake lining. Sometimes shortened (for both senses) to **shoe.**

brakesman (ˈbreɪksmən) *n., pl.* **-men.** a pithead winch operator.

brake van *n. Railways, Brit.* the coach or vehicle from which the guard applies the brakes; guard's van.

bramble (ˈbræmb^{ə}l) *n.* **1.** any of various prickly herbaceous plants or shrubs of the rosaceous genus *Rubus,* esp. the blackberry. See also **stone bramble. 2.** *Scot.* **a.** a blackberry. **b.** (*as modifier*): *bramble jelly.* **3.** any of several similar and related shrubs, such as the dog rose. ~*vb.* (*intr.*) **4.** to gather blackberries. [Old English *brǣmbel;* related to Old Saxon *brāmal,* Old High German *brāmo*] —ˈ**brambly** *adj.*

brambling (ˈbræmblɪŋ) *n.* a Eurasian finch, *Fringilla montifringilla,* with a speckled head and back and, in the male, a reddish brown breast and darker wings and tail.

Bramley (ˈbræmlɪ) *or* **Bramley's seedling** *n.* a variety of cooking apple having juicy firm flesh. [C19: named after Matthew *Bramley,* 19th-century British butcher, said to have first grown it]

bran (bræn) *n.* **1.** husks of cereal grain separated from the flour by sifting. **2.** food prepared from these husks. [C13: from Old French, probably of Gaulish origin]

branch (brɑːntʃ) *n.* **1.** a secondary woody stem arising from the trunk or bough of a tree or the main stem of a shrub. **2.** a subdivision of the stem or root of any other plant. **3.** an offshoot or secondary part: *a branch of a deer's antlers.* **4. a.** a subdivision or subsidiary section of something larger or more complex: *branches of learning; branch of the family.* **b.** (*as modifier*): *a branch office.* **5.** *U.S.* any small stream. **6.** *Maths.* a section of a curve separated from the rest of the curve by discontinuities or special points. **7.** Also called: **jump.** *Computer technol.* a departure from the normal sequence of programmed instructions into a separate program area. **8.** an alternative route in a radioactive decay series. ~*vb.* **9.** (*intr.*) (of a tree or other plant) to produce or possess branches. **10.** (*intr.;* usually foll. by *from*) (of stems, roots, etc.) to grow and diverge (from another part). **11.** to divide or be divided into subsidiaries or offshoots. **12.** (*intr.;* often foll. by *off*) to diverge from the main way, road, topic, etc. ~See also **branch out.** [C13: from Old French *branche,* from Late Latin *branca* paw, foot] —ˈ**branchless** *adj.* —ˈ**branchˌlike** *adj.* —ˈ**branchy** *adj.*

-branch *adj. and n. combining form.* (in zoology) indicating gills: *lamellibranch.* [from Latin: BRANCHIA]

branched chain *n. Chem.* an open chain of atoms with one or more side chains attached to it. Compare **straight chain.**

branchia (ˈbræŋkɪə) *n., pl.* **-chiae** (-kɪˌiː). a gill in aquatic animals. —ˈ**branchiˌate** *adj.*

branchial (ˈbræŋkɪəl) *adj.* **1.** of or relating to the gills of an aquatic animal, esp. a fish. **2.** of or relating to homologous structures in higher vertebrates: *branchial cyst.*

branching (ˈbrɑːntʃɪŋ) *n. Physics.* the occurrence of several decay processes (**branches**) in the disintegration of a particular nuclide. The **branching fraction** is the proportion of the disintegrating nuclei that follow a particular branch to the total number of disintegrating nuclides.

branch instruction *n. Computer technol.* a machine-language or assembly-language instruction that causes the computer to branch to another instruction.

branchiopod (ˈbræŋkɪəˌpɒd) *n.* any crustacean of the mainly freshwater subclass *Branchiopoda,* having flattened limblike appendages for swimming, feeding, and respiration. The group includes the water fleas.

branchiostegal (ˌbræŋkɪəˈstiːg^{ə}l) *adj. Zoology.* of or relating to the operculum covering the gill slits of fish: *branchiostegal membrane; branchiostegal rays.* [from BRANCHIA + Greek *stegos* roof]

branch line *n. Railways.* a secondary route to a place or places not served by a main line.

branch officer *n.* (in the British navy since 1949) any officer who holds warrant.

branch out *vb.* (*intr., adv.;* often foll. by *into*) to expand or extend one's interests: *our business has branched out into computers now.*

brand (brænd) *n.* **1.** a particular product or a characteristic that serves to identify a particular product. **2.** a trade name or trademark. **3.** a particular kind or variety: *he had his own brand of humour.* **4.** an identifying mark made, usually by burning, on the skin of animals or (formerly) slaves or criminals, esp. as a proof of ownership. **5.** an iron heated and used for branding animals, etc. **6.** a mark of disgrace or infamy; stigma: *he bore the brand of a coward.* **7.** a burning or burnt piece of wood, as in a fire. **8.** *Archaic or poetic.* **a.** a flaming torch. **b.** a sword. **9.** a fungal disease of garden plants characterized by brown spots on the leaves, caused by the rust fungus *Puccinia arenariae.* ~*vb.* (*tr.*) **10.** to label, burn, or mark with or as with a brand. **11.** to place indelibly in the memory: *the scene of slaughter was branded in their minds.* **12.** to denounce; stigmatize: *they branded him a traitor.* [Old English *brand-,* related to Old Norse *brandr,* Old High German *brant;* see BURN[1]] —ˈ**brander** *n.*

branded (ˈbrændɪd) *adj.* identifiable as being the product of a particular manufacturer or marketing company.

brand image *n.* the attributes of a brand as perceived by potential and actual customers.

brandish (ˈbrændɪʃ) *vb.* (*tr.*). **1.** to wave or flourish (a weapon) in a triumphant, threatening, or ostentatious way. ~*n.* **2.** a threatening or defiant flourish. [C14: from Old French *brandir,* from *brand* sword, of Germanic origin; compare Old High German *brant* weapon] —ˈ**brandisher** *n.*

brand leader *n. Marketing.* a product with the highest number of total sales within its category.

brandling (ˈbrændlɪŋ) *n.* a small red earthworm, *Eisenia foetida* (or *Helodrilus foetidus*), found in manure and used as bait by anglers. [C17: from BRAND + -LING[1]]

brand name *n.* another name for **brand** (sense 2).

brand-new *adj.* absolutely new. [C16: from BRAND (n.) + NEW, likened to newly forged iron]
brandy ('brændɪ) *n., pl.* **-dies.** **1.** an alcoholic drink consisting of spirit distilled from grape wine. **2.** a distillation of wines made from other fruits: *plum brandy.* [C17: from earlier *brandewine,* from Dutch *brandewijn,* burnt wine, from *bernen* to burn or distil + *wijn* WINE; compare German *Branntwein*]
brandy bottle *n.* another name for a **yellow water lily.**
brandy butter *n.* butter and sugar creamed together with brandy and served with Christmas pudding, etc.
brandy snap *n.* a crisp sweet biscuit, rolled into a cylinder after baking and often filled with whipped cream.
branks (bræŋks) *pl. n.* (formerly) an iron bridle used to restrain scolding women. [C16: of unknown origin]
branle ('bræn^əl) *n.* an old French country dance performed in a linked circle. [C17: from Old French *branler* to shake, variant of *brandir* to BRANDISH]
brant (brænt) *n., pl.* **brants** *or* **brant.** another name (esp. U.S. and Canadian) for **brent goose.**
bran tub *n.* (in Britain) a tub containing bran in which small wrapped gifts are hidden, used at parties, fairs, etc.
brash[1] (bræʃ) *adj.* **1.** tastelessly or offensively loud, showy, or bold. **2.** hasty; rash. **3.** impudent. [C19: perhaps influenced by RASH[1]] —'**brashly** *adv.* —'**brashness** *n.*
brash[2] (bræʃ) *n.* loose rubbish, such as broken rock, hedge clippings, etc.; debris. [C18: of unknown origin]
brash[3] (bræʃ) *n. Pathol.* another name for **heartburn.** [C16: perhaps of imitative origin]
brashy ('bræʃɪ) *adj.* **brashier, brashiest.** **1.** loosely fragmented; rubbishy. **2.** (of timber) brittle. —'**brashiness** *n.*
brasier ('breɪzɪə) *n.* a less common spelling of **brazier.**
brasil (brə'zɪl) *n.* a variant spelling of **brazil.**
brasilein (brə'zɪlɪɪn) *n.* a variant spelling of **brazilein.**
brasilin ('bræzɪlɪn) *n.* a variant spelling of **brazilin.**
brass (brɑːs) *n.* **1.** an alloy of copper and zinc containing more than 50 per cent of copper. **Alpha brass** (containing less than 35 per cent of zinc) is used for most engineering materials requiring forging, pressing, etc. **Alpha-beta brass** (35–45 per cent zinc) is used for hot working and extrusion. **Beta brass** (45–50 per cent zinc) is used for castings. Compare **bronze** (sense 1). **2.** an object, ornament, or utensil made of brass. **3. a.** the large family of wind instruments including the trumpet, trombone, French horn, etc., each consisting of a brass tube blown directly by means of a cup- or funnel-shaped mouthpiece. **b.** (*sometimes functioning as pl.*) instruments of this family forming a section in an orchestra. **c.** (*as modifier*): *a brass ensemble.* **4.** a renewable sleeve or bored semicylindrical shell made of brass or bronze, used as a liner for a bearing. **5.** (*functioning as pl.*) *Informal.* important or high-ranking officials, esp. military officers: *the top brass.* See also **brass hat.** **6.** *Northern English dialect.* money: *where there's muck, there's brass!* **7.** *Brit.* an engraved brass memorial tablet or plaque, set in the wall or floor of a church. **8.** *Informal.* bold self-confidence; cheek; nerve: *he had the brass to ask for more time.* **9.** *Slang.* a prostitute. **10.** (*modifier*) of, consisting of, or relating to brass or brass instruments: *a brass ornament; a brass band.* [Old English *bræs;* related to Old Frisian *bres* copper, Middle Low German *bras* metal]
brassard ('bræsɑːd) *or* **brassart** ('bræsət) *n.* **1.** an identifying armband or badge. **2.** a piece of armour for the upper arm. [C19: from French, from *bras* arm, from Latin BRACHIUM]
brass band *n.* See **band**[1] (sense 2).
brassbound ('brɑːsˌbaʊnd) *adj.* inflexibly entrenched: *brassbound traditions.*
brassed off *adj. Brit. slang.* fed up; disgruntled.
brasserie ('bræsərɪ) *n.* **1.** a bar in which drinks and often food are served. **2.** a small and usually cheap restaurant. [C19: from French, from *brasser* to stir, brew]
brass farthing *n. Brit. informal.* something of little or no value: *his opinion isn't worth a brass farthing.* [C18: probably coined when farthings were first minted in bronze rather than silver]
brass hat *n. Brit. informal.* a top-ranking official, esp. a military officer. [C20: from the gold leaf decoration on the peaks of caps worn by officers of high rank]
brassica ('bræsɪkə) *n.* any cruciferous plant of the genus *Brassica,* native to the Mediterranean region and grown widely as vegetables, such as cabbage, rape, swede, turnip, and mustard. [C19: from Latin: cabbage] —**brassicaceous** (ˌbræsɪ'keɪʃəs) *adj.*
brassie *or* **brassy** ('bræsɪ, 'brɑː-) *n., pl.* **brassies.** *Golf.* a former name for a club, a No. 2 wood, originally having a brass-plated sole and with a shallower face than a driver to give more loft.
brassiere ('bræsɪə, 'bræz-) *n.* a woman's undergarment for covering and supporting the breasts. Often shortened to **bra.** [C20: from C17 French: bodice, from Old French *braciere* a protector for the arm, from *braz* arm]
brass neck *n. Brit. informal.* effrontery; nerve.
brass rubbing *n.* **1.** the taking of an impression of an engraved brass tablet or plaque by placing a piece of paper over it and rubbing the paper with graphite, heelball, or chalk. **2.** an impression made in this way.
brass tacks *pl. n. Informal.* basic realities; hard facts (esp. in the phrase **get down to brass tacks**).
brassy ('brɑːsɪ) *adj.* **brassier, brassiest.** **1.** insolent; brazen. **2.** flashy; showy. **3.** (of sound) harsh, strident, or resembling the sound of a brass instrument. **4.** like brass, esp. in colour. **5.** decorated with or made of brass. —'**brassily** *adv.* —'**brassiness** *n.*
brat[1] (bræt) *n.* a child, esp. one who is dirty or unruly: used contemptuously or playfully. [C16: perhaps special use of earlier *brat* rag, from Old English *bratt* cloak, of Celtic origin; related to Old Irish *bratt* cloth, BRAT[2]]
brat[2] (bræt) *n. Northern English dialect.* an apron or overall. [from Old English *brat* cloak; related to Old Irish *bratt* cloth used to cover the body]
bratpack ('brætˌpæk) *n.* **1.** a group of precocious and successful young actors, writers, etc. **2.** a group of ill-mannered young people. —'**bratˌpacker** *n.*
brattice ('brætɪs) *n.* **1.** a partition of wood or treated cloth used to control ventilation in a mine. **2.** *Medieval fortifications.* a fixed wooden tower or parapet. ~*vb.* **3.** (*tr.*) *Mining.* to fit with a brattice. [C13: from Old French *bretesche* wooden tower, from Medieval Latin *breteschia,* probably from Latin *Britō* a Briton]
brattishing ('brætɪʃɪŋ) *n. Architect.* decorative work along the coping or on the cornice of a building. [C16: variant of *bratticing;* see BRATTICE]
bratwurst ('brɑːtˌwɜːst; *German* 'braːtvurst) *n.* a type of small pork sausage. [C20: German, from Old High German, from *brāto* meat + *wurst* sausage; related to Old Saxon *brādo* ham]
braunite ('braʊnaɪt) *n.* a brown or black mineral that consists of manganese oxide and silicate and is a source of manganese. Formula: Mn_7SiO_{12}. [C19: named after A. E. *Braun* (1809–56), German official in the treasury at Gotha]
bravado (brə'vɑːdəʊ) *n., pl.* **-does** *or* **-dos.** vaunted display of courage or self-confidence; swagger. [C16: from Spanish *bravada* (modern *bravata*), from Old Italian *bravare* to challenge, provoke, from *bravo* wild, BRAVE]
Bravais lattice ('brævəɪ, brə'veɪ) *n. Crystallog.* any of 14 possible space lattices found in crystals. [named after Auguste *Bravais,* 19th-century French physicist]
brave (breɪv) *adj.* **1. a.** having or displaying courage, resolution, or daring; not cowardly or timid. **b.** (*as collective n.* preceded by *the*): *the brave.* **2.** fine; splendid: *a brave sight; a brave attempt.* **3.** *Archaic.* excellent or admirable. ~*n.* **4.** a warrior of a North American Indian tribe. **5.** an obsolete word for **bully**[1]. ~*vb.* (*tr.*) **6.** to dare or defy: *to brave the odds.* **7.** to confront with resolution or courage: *to brave the storm.* **8.** *Obsolete.* to make splendid, esp. in dress. [C15: from French, from Italian *bravo* courageous, wild, perhaps ultimately from Latin *barbarus* BARBAROUS] —'**bravely** *adv.* —'**braveness** *n.* —'**bravery** *n.*
bravissimo (brɑː'vɪsɪˌməʊ) *interj.* very well done! excellent! [C18: from Italian, superlative of BRAVO]
bravo *interj.* **1.** (brɑː'vəʊ). well done! ~*n.* **2.** (brɑː'vəʊ), *pl.* **-vos.** a cry of "bravo." **3.** ('brɑːvəʊ), *pl.* **-voes** *or* **-vos.** a hired killer or assassin. [C18: from Italian: splendid!; see BRAVE]
Bravo ('brɑːvəʊ) *n. Communications.* a code word for the letter *b.*
bravura (brə'vjʊərə, -'vʊərə) *n.* **1.** a display of boldness or daring. **2.** *Music.* **a.** brilliance of execution. **b.** (*as modifier*): *a bravura passage.* [C18: from Italian: spirit, courage, from *bravare* to show off, see BRAVADO]
braw (brɔː, brɑː) *Chiefly Scot.* ~*adj.* **1.** fine or excellent, esp. in appearance or dress. ~*pl. n.* **2.** best clothes. [C16: Scottish variant of BRAVE] —'**brawly** *adv.*
brawl[1] (brɔːl) *n.* **1.** a loud disagreement or fight. **2.** *U.S. and Canadian slang.* an uproarious party. ~*vb.* (*intr.*) **3.** to quarrel or fight noisily; squabble. **4.** (esp. of water) to flow noisily. [C14: probably related to Dutch *brallen* to boast, behave aggressively] —'**brawler** *n.* —'**brawling** *n., adj.*
brawl[2] (brɔːl) *n.* a dance: the English version of the branle.
brawn (brɔːn) *n.* **1.** strong well-developed muscles. **2.** physical strength, esp. as opposed to intelligence. **3.** *Brit.* a seasoned jellied loaf made from the head and sometimes the feet of a pig or calf. [C14: from Old French *braon* slice of meat, of Germanic origin; compare Old High German *brāto,* Old English *brǣd* flesh]
brawny ('brɔːnɪ) *adj.* **brawnier, brawniest.** muscular and strong. —'**brawnily** *adv.* —'**brawniness** *n.*
braxy ('bræksɪ) *n.* an acute and usually fatal bacterial disease of sheep characterized by high fever, coma, and inflammation of the fourth stomach, caused by infection with *Clostridium septicum.* [C18: of unknown origin]
bray[1] (breɪ) *vb.* **1.** (*intr.*) (of a donkey) to utter its characteristic loud harsh sound; heehaw. **2.** (*intr.*) to make a similar sound, as in laughing: *he brayed at the joke.* **3.** (*tr.*) to utter with a loud harsh sound. ~*n.* **4.** the loud harsh sound uttered by a donkey. **5.** a similar loud cry or uproar: *a bray of protest.* [C13: from Old French *braire,* probably of Celtic origin] —'**brayer** *n.*
bray[2] (breɪ) *vb.* **1.** (*tr.*) to distribute (ink) over printing type or plates. **2.** (*tr.*) to pound into a powder, as in a mortar. **3.** *Northern English dialect.* to hit or beat (someone or something) hard; bang. [C14: from Old French *breier,* of Germanic origin; see BREAK] —'**brayer** *n.*
Braz. *abbrev. for* Brazil(ian).
braze[1] (breɪz) *vb.* (*tr.*) **1.** to decorate with or make of brass. **2.** to make like brass, as in hardness. [Old English *bræsen,* from *bræs* BRASS]

braze[2] (breɪz) *vb.* (*tr.*) to make a joint between (two metal surfaces) by fusing a layer of brass or high-melting solder between them. [C16: from Old French: to burn, of Germanic origin; see BRAISE] —'**brazer** *n.*

brazen ('breɪzᵊn) *adj.* **1.** shameless and bold. **2.** made of or resembling brass. **3.** having a ringing metallic sound like that of a brass trumpet. ~*vb.* (*tr.*) **4.** (usually foll. by *out* or *through*) to face and overcome boldly or shamelessly: *the witness brazened out the prosecutor's questions.* **5.** to make (oneself, etc.) bold or brash. [Old English *bræsen,* from *bræs* BRASS] —'**brazenly** *adv.* —'**brazenness** *n.*

brazen-faced *adj.* shameless or impudent.

brazier[1] *or* **brasier** ('breɪzɪə) *n.* a person engaged in brass-working or brass-founding. [C14: from Old English *bræsian* to work in brass + -ER[1]] —'**braziery** *n.*

brazier[2] *or* **brasier** ('breɪzɪə) *n.* a portable metal receptacle for burning charcoal or coal, used for cooking, heating, etc. [C17: from French *brasier,* from *braise* live coals; see BRAISE]

brazil *or* **brasil** (brə'zɪl) *n.* **1.** Also called: **brazil wood.** the red wood obtained from various caesalpiniaceous tropical trees of the genus *Caesalpinia,* such as *C. echinata* of America: used for cabinetwork. **2.** the red or purple dye extracted from any of these woods. See also **brazilin. 3.** short for **brazil nut.** [C14: from Old Spanish *brasil,* from *brasa* glowing coals, of Germanic origin; referring to the redness of the wood; see BRAISE]

brazilein *or* **brasilein** (brə'zɪlɪɪn) *n.* a red crystalline solid obtained by the oxidation of brazilin and used as a dye. Formula: $C_{16}H_{12}O_5$. [C19: from German *Brasilein,* from BRAZILIN]

Brazilian (brə'zɪlɪən) *adj.* **1.** of or relating to Brazil, a republic in South America, or to its people, culture, etc. ~*n.* **2.** a native or inhabitant of Brazil.

brazilin *or* **brasilin** ('bræzɪlɪn) *n.* a pale yellow soluble crystalline solid, turning red in alkaline solution, extracted from brazil wood and sappanwood and used in dyeing and as an indicator. Formula: $C_{16}H_{14}O_5$. [C19: from French *brésiline,* from *brésil* brazil wood]

brazil nut *n.* **1.** a tropical South American tree, *Bertholletia excelsa,* producing large globular capsules, each containing several closely packed triangular nuts: family *Lecythidaceae.* **2.** the nut of this tree, having an edible oily kernel and a woody shell. ~Often shortened to **brazil.**

BRCS *abbrev. for* British Red Cross Society.

BRE (in Britain) *abbrev. for* Building Research Establishment.

breach (briːtʃ) *n.* **1.** a crack, break, or rupture. **2.** a breaking, infringement, or violation of a promise, obligation, etc. **3.** any severance or separation: *there was a breach between the two factions of the party.* **4.** the act of a whale in breaking clear of the water. **5.** the breaking of sea waves on a shore or rock. **6.** an obsolete word for **wound**[1]. ~*vb.* **7.** (*tr.*) to break through or make an opening, hole, or incursion in. **8.** (*tr.*) to break a promise, law, etc. **9.** (*intr.*) (of a whale) to break clear of the water. [Old English *bræc;* influenced by Old French *brèche,* from Old High German *brecha,* from *brechan* to BREAK]

breach of promise *n. Law.* (formerly) failure to carry out one's promise to marry.

breach of the peace *n. Law.* an offence against public order causing an unnecessary disturbance of the peace.

breach of trust *n. Law.* a violation of duty by a trustee or any other person in a fiduciary position.

bread (brɛd) *n.* **1.** a food made from a dough of flour or meal mixed with water or milk, usually raised with yeast or baking powder and then baked. **2.** necessary food; nourishment: *give us our daily bread.* **3.** a slang word for **money. 4.** *Christianity.* a small loaf, piece of bread, or wafer of unleavened bread used in the Eucharist. **5. break bread.** See **break** (sense 46). **6. cast one's bread upon the waters.** to do good without expectation of advantage or return. **7. know which side one's bread is buttered.** to know what to do in order to keep one's advantages. **8. take the bread out of (someone's) mouth.** to deprive (someone) of a livelihood. ~*vb.* **9.** (*tr.*) to cover with breadcrumbs before cooking: *breaded veal.* [Old English *brēad;* related to Old Norse *braud,* Old Frisian *brād,* Old High German *brōt*]

bread and butter *Informal.* ~*n.* **1.** a means of support or subsistence; livelihood: *the inheritance was their bread and butter.* ~*modifier.* **2.** (**bread-and-butter**) **a.** providing a basic means of subsistence: *a bread-and-butter job.* **b.** solid, reliable, or practical: *a bread-and-butter player.* **c.** expressing gratitude, as for hospitality (esp. in the phrase **bread-and-butter letter**).

breadbasket ('brɛd,bɑːskɪt) *n.* **1.** a basket for carrying bread or rolls. **2.** a slang word for **stomach.**

breadboard ('brɛd,bɔːd) *n.* **1.** a wooden board on which dough is kneaded or bread is sliced. **2.** an experimental arrangement of electronic circuits giving access to components so that modifications can be carried out easily.

breadcrumb ('brɛd,krʌm) *n.* **1.** the soft inner part of bread. **2.** (*pl.*) bread crumbled into small fragments, as for use in cooking. ~*vb.* (*tr.*) **3.** to coat (food) with breadcrumbs: *egg and breadcrumb the escalopes.*

breadfruit ('brɛd,fruːt) *n., pl.* **-fruits** *or* **-fruit. 1.** a moraceous tree, *Artocarpus communis* (or *A. altilis*), of the Pacific Islands, having edible round, usually seedless, fruit. **2.** the fruit of this tree, which is eaten baked or roasted and has a texture like bread.

breadline ('brɛd,laɪn) *n.* **1.** a queue of people waiting for free food given out by a government agency or a charity organization. **2. on the breadline.** impoverished; living at subsistence level.

bread mould *or* **black mould** *n.* a black phycomycete fungus, *Rhizopus nigricans,* occurring on decaying bread and vegetable matter.

breadnut ('brɛd,nʌt) *n.* **1.** a moraceous tree, *Brosimum alicastrum,* of Central America and the West Indies. **2.** the nutlike fruit of this tree, ground to produce a substitute for wheat flour, esp. in the West Indies.

breadroot ('brɛd,ruːt) *n.* a papilionaceous plant, *Psoralea esculenta,* of central North America, having an edible starchy root. Also called: **prairie turnip.**

bread sauce *n.* a milk sauce thickened with breadcrumbs and served with roast poultry, esp. chicken.

breadth (brɛdθ, brɛtθ) *n.* **1.** the linear extent or measurement of something from side to side; width. **2.** a piece of fabric having a standard or definite width. **3.** distance, extent, size, or dimension. **4.** openness and lack of restriction, esp. of viewpoint or interest; liberality. [C16: from obsolete *brēde* (from Old English *brǣdu,* from *brād* BROAD) + -TH[1]; related to Gothic *braidei,* Old High German *breitī*]

breadthways ('brɛdθ,weɪz, 'brɛtθ-) *or esp. U.S.* **breadthwise** ('brɛdθ,waɪz, 'brɛtθ-) *adv.* from side to side.

breadwinner ('brɛd,wɪnə) *n.* a person supporting a family with his or her earnings. —'**bread,winning** *n., adj.*

break (breɪk) *vb.* **breaks, breaking, broke, broken. 1.** to separate or become separated into two or more pieces: *this cup is broken.* **2.** to damage or become damaged so as to be inoperative: *my radio is broken.* **3.** to crack or become cracked without separating. **4.** to burst or cut the surface of (skin, etc.). **5.** to discontinue or become discontinued: *they broke for lunch; to break a journey.* **6.** to disperse or become dispersed: *the clouds broke.* **7.** (*tr.*) to fail to observe (an agreement, promise, law, etc.): *to break one's word.* **8.** (foll. by *with*) to discontinue an association (with). **9.** to disclose or be disclosed: *he broke the news gently.* **10.** (*tr.*) to fracture (a bone) in (a limb, etc.). **11.** (*tr.*) to divide (something complete or perfect): *to break a set of books.* **12.** to bring or come to an end: *the summer weather broke at last.* **13.** (*tr.*) to bring to an end by or as if by force: *to break a strike.* **14.** (when *intr.,* often foll. by *out*) to escape (from): *he broke jail; he broke out of jail.* **15.** to weaken or overwhelm or be weakened or overwhelmed, as in spirit. **16.** (*tr.*) to cut through or penetrate: *a cry broke the silence.* **17.** (*tr.*) to improve on or surpass: *to break a record.* **18.** (*tr.;* often foll. by *in*) to accustom (a horse) to the bridle and saddle, to being ridden, etc. **19.** (*tr.;* often foll. by *of*) to cause (a person) to give up (a habit): *this cure will break you of smoking.* **20.** (*tr.*) to weaken the impact or force of: *this net will break his fall.* **21.** (*tr.*) to decipher: *to break a code.* **22.** (*tr.*) to lose the order of: *to break ranks.* **23.** (*tr.*) to reduce to poverty or the state of bankruptcy. **24.** (when *intr.,* foll. by *into*) to obtain, give, or receive smaller units in exchange for; change: *to break a pound note.* **25.** (*tr.*) *Chiefly military.* to demote to a lower rank. **26.** (*intr.;* often foll. by *from* or *out of*) to proceed suddenly. **27.** (*intr.*) to come into being: *light broke over the mountains.* **28.** (*intr.;* foll. by *into* or *out into*) to burst into song, laughter, etc. **29.** (*tr.*) to open with explosives: *to break a safe.* **30.** (*intr.*) (of waves) **a.** (often foll. by *against*) to strike violently. **b.** to collapse into foam or surf. **31.** (*intr.*) (esp. of fish) to appear above the surface of the water. **32.** (*intr.*). (of the amniotic fluid surrounding an unborn baby) to be released when the amniotic sac ruptures in the first stage of labour: *her waters have broken.* **33.** (*intr.*) *Informal, chiefly U.S.* to turn out in a specified manner: *things are breaking well.* **34.** (*intr.*) (of prices, esp. stock exchange quotations) to fall sharply. **35.** (*intr.*) to make a sudden effort, as in running, horse racing, etc. **36.** (*intr.*) *Cricket.* (of a ball) to change direction on bouncing. **37.** (*tr.*) *Cricket.* (of a player) to knock down at least one bail from (a wicket). **38.** (*intr.*) *Billiards, snooker.* to scatter the balls at the start of a game. **39.** (*intr.*) *Horse racing.* to commence running in a race: *they broke even.* **40.** (*intr.*) *Boxing, wrestling.* (of two fighters) to separate from a clinch. **41.** (*intr.*) *Music.* **a.** (of the male voice) to undergo a change in register, quality, and range at puberty. **b.** (of the voice or some instruments) to undergo a change in tone, quality, etc., when changing registers. **42.** (*intr.*) *Phonetics.* (of a vowel) to turn into a diphthong, esp. as a development in the language. **43.** (*tr.*) to open the breech of (certain firearms) by snapping the barrel away from the butt on its hinge. **44.** (*tr.*) to interrupt the flow of current in (an electrical circuit). Compare **make**[1] (sense 27). **45.** (*intr.*) *Informal, chiefly U.S.* to become successful; make a breakthrough. **46. break bread. a.** to eat a meal, esp. with others. **b.** *Christianity.* to administer or participate in Holy Communion. **47. break camp.** to pack up equipment and leave a camp. **48. break (new) ground.** to do something that has not been done before. **49. break one's back** *or* (*Taboo*) **balls.** to overwork or work very hard. **50. break the back of.** to complete the greatest or hardest part of (a task). **51. break the bank.** to ruin financially or deplete the resources of a bank (as in gambling). **52. break the ice. a.** to relieve shyness or reserve, esp. between strangers. **b.** to be the first of a group to do something. **53. break the mould.** to make a change that breaks an established habit, pattern, etc. **54. break service.** *Tennis.* to win a game in which an opponent is serving. **55.**

break wind. to emit wind from the anus. ~*n.* **56.** the act or result of breaking; fracture. **57.** a crack formed as the result of breaking. **58.** a brief respite: *a break from one's toil.* **59.** a sudden rush, esp. to escape: *to make a break for freedom.* **60.** a breach in a relationship: *she has made a break from her family.* **61.** any sudden interruption in a continuous action. **62.** *Brit.* a short period between classes at school. U.S. and Canadian equivalent: **recess. 63.** *Informal.* a fortunate opportunity, esp. to prove oneself. **64.** *Informal.* a piece of (good or bad) luck. **65.** (esp. in a stock exchange) a sudden and substantial decline in prices. **66.** *Prosody.* a pause in a line of verse; caesura. **67.** *Billiards, snooker.* **a.** a series of successful shots during one turn. **b.** the points scored in such a series. **68.** *Billiards, snooker.* **a.** the opening shot with the cue ball that scatters the placed balls. **b.** the right to take this first shot. **69.** Also called: **service break, break of serve.** *Tennis.* the act or instance of breaking an opponent's service. **70.** one of the intervals in a sporting contest. **71.** *Horse racing.* the start of a race: *an even break.* **72.** (in tenpin bowling) failure to knock down all the pins after the second attempt. **73. a.** *Jazz.* a short usually improvised solo passage. **b.** an instrumental passage in a pop song. **74.** a discontinuity in an electrical circuit. **75.** access to a radio channel by a citizen's band operator. **76.** a variant spelling of **brake**[1] (sense 6). ~*interj.* **77.** *Boxing, wrestling.* a command by a referee for two opponents to separate. ~See also **breakaway, break down, break even, break in, break into, break off, break out, break through, break up, break with.** [Old English *brecan;* related to Old Frisian *breka,* Gothic *brikan,* Old High German *brehhan,* Latin *frangere,* Sanskrit *bhráj* bursting forth]

breakable ('breɪkəbᵊl) *adj.* **1.** capable of being broken. ~*n.* **2.** (*usually pl.*) a fragile easily broken article.

breakage ('breɪkɪdʒ) *n.* **1.** the act or result of breaking. **2.** the quantity or amount broken: *the total breakage was enormous.* **3.** compensation or allowance for goods damaged while in use, transit, etc.

breakaway ('breɪkəˌweɪ) *n.* **1. a.** loss or withdrawal of a group of members from an association, club, etc. **b.** (*as modifier*): *a breakaway faction.* **2.** *Sport.* **a.** a sudden attack, esp. from a defensive position, in football, hockey, etc. **b.** an attempt to get away from the rest of the field in a race. ~*vb.* **break away.** (*intr., adv.*) **3.** (often foll. by *from*) to leave hastily or escape. **4.** to withdraw or secede. **5.** *Sport.* to make a breakaway. **6.** *Horse racing.* to start prematurely.

breakbone fever ('breɪkˌbəʊn) *n.* another name for **dengue.**

break dance *n.* **1.** an acrobatic dance style of the 1980s. ~*vb.* **break-dance.** (*intr.*) **2.** to perform a break dance. —**break dancer** *n.* —**break dancing** *n.*

break down *vb.* (*adv.*) **1.** (*intr.*) to cease to function; become ineffective: *communications had broken down.* **2.** to yield or cause to yield, esp. to strong emotion or tears: *she broke down in anguish.* **3.** (*tr.*) to crush or destroy. **4.** (*intr.*) to have a nervous breakdown. **5.** to analyse or be subjected to analysis. **6.** (*tr.*) *N.Z.* to saw (a large log) into planks. **7. break it down.** *Austral. and N.Z. informal.* **a.** stop it. **b.** don't expect me to believe that; come off it. ~*n.* **breakdown. 8.** an act or instance of breaking down; collapse. **9.** short for **nervous breakdown. 10.** an analysis or classification of something into its component parts: *he prepared a breakdown of the report.* **11.** the sudden electrical discharge through an insulator or between two electrodes in a vacuum or gas discharge tube. **12.** *Electrical engineering.* the sudden transition, dependent on the bias magnitude, from a high to a low dynamic resistance in a semiconductor device. **13.** a lively American country dance.

breakdown van *or* **truck** *n.* a motor vehicle equipped for towing away wrecked or disabled cars. U.S. and Canadian names: **wrecker, tow truck.**

breaker[1] ('breɪkə) *n.* **1.** a person or thing that breaks something, such as a person or firm that breaks up old cars, etc. **2.** a large wave with a white crest on the open sea or one that breaks into foam on the shore. **3.** *Electronics.* short for **circuit breaker. 4.** a machine or plant for crushing rocks or coal. **5.** Also called: **breaking plough.** a plough with a long shallow mouldboard for turning virgin land or sod land. **6.** *Textiles.* a machine for extracting fibre preparatory to carding. **7.** an operator on citizen's band radio.

breaker[2] ('breɪkə) *n.* a small water cask for use in a boat. [C19: anglicized variant of Spanish *barrica,* from French (Gascon dialect) *barrique*]

break even *vb.* **1.** (*intr., adv.*) to attain a level of activity, as in commerce, or a point of operation, as in gambling, at which there is neither profit nor loss. ~*n.* **breakeven. 2.** *Accounting.* **a.** the level of commercial activity at which the total cost and total revenue of a business enterprise are equal. **b.** (*as modifier*): *breakeven prices.*

breakeven chart ('breɪkˌiːvᵊn) *n. Accounting.* a graph measuring the value of an enterprise's revenue and costs against some index of its activity, such as percentage capacity. The intersection of the total revenue and total cost curves gives the breakeven point.

breakfast ('brɛkfəst) *n.* **1. a.** the first meal of the day. **b.** (*as modifier*): *breakfast cereal; a breakfast room.* **2.** the food at this meal. **3.** (in the West Indies) a midday meal. ~*vb.* **4.** to eat or supply with breakfast. [C15: from BREAK + FAST[2]] —**'breakfaster** *n.*

break feeding *n. N.Z.* the feeding of animals on paddocks where feeding space is controlled by the frequent movement of an electric fence.

breakfront ('breɪkˌfrʌnt) *adj.* (*prenominal*) (of a bookcase, bureau, etc.) having a slightly projecting central section.

break in *vb.* (*adv.*) **1.** (sometimes foll. by *on*) to interrupt. **2.** (*intr.*) to enter a house, etc., illegally, esp. by force. **3.** (*tr.*) to accustom (a person or animal) to normal duties or practice. **4.** (*tr.*) to use or wear (shoes, new equipment, etc.) until comfortable or running smoothly. **5.** (*tr.*) *Austral. and N.Z.* to bring (new land) under cultivation. ~*n.* **break-in. 6. a.** the illegal entering of a building, esp. by thieves. **b.** (*as modifier*): *the break-in plans.*

breaking ('breɪkɪŋ) *n. Linguistics.* (in Old English, Old Norse, etc.) the change of a vowel into a diphthong. [C19: translation of German *Brechung*]

breaking and entering *n.* (formerly) the gaining of unauthorized access to a building with intent to commit a crime or, having committed the crime, the breaking out of the building.

breaking point *n.* **1.** the point at which something or someone gives way under strain. **2.** the moment of crisis in a situation.

break into *vb.* (*intr., prep.*) **1.** to enter (a house, etc.) illegally, esp. by force. **2.** to change abruptly from a slower to a faster speed: *the horse broke into a gallop.* **3.** to consume (supplies held in reserve): *at the end of the exercise the soldiers had to break into their iron rations.*

breakneck ('breɪkˌnɛk) *adj.* (*prenominal*) (of speed, pace, etc.) excessive and dangerous.

break of day *n.* another term for **dawn** (sense 1).

break off *vb.* **1.** to sever or detach or be severed or detached: *it broke off in my hands; he broke a piece off the bar of chocolate.* **2.** (*adv.*) to end (a relationship, association, etc.) or (of a relationship, etc.) to be ended. **3.** (*intr., adv.*) to stop abruptly; halt: *he broke off in the middle of his speech.* ~*n.* **breakoff. 4.** the act or an instance of breaking off or stopping.

break out *vb.* (*intr., adv.*) **1.** to begin or arise suddenly: *panic broke out.* **2.** to make an escape, esp. from prison or confinement. **3.** (foll. by *in*) (of the skin) to erupt (in a rash, pimples, etc.). ~*n.* **break-out. 4.** an escape, esp. from prison or confinement.

breakpoint ('breɪkˌpɔɪnt) *n. Computer technol.* **a.** an instruction inserted by a debug program causing a return to the debug program. **b.** the point in a program at which such an instruction operates.

break through *vb.* **1.** (*intr.*) to penetrate. **2.** (*intr., adv.*) to achieve success, make a discovery, etc., esp. after lengthy efforts. ~*n.* **breakthrough. 3.** a significant development or discovery, esp. in science. **4.** the penetration of an enemy's defensive position or line in depth and strength.

break up *vb.* (*adv.*) **1.** to separate or cause to separate. **2.** to put an end to (a relationship) or (of a relationship) to come to an end. **3.** to dissolve or cause to dissolve; disrupt or be disrupted: *the meeting broke up at noon.* **4.** (*intr.*) *Brit.* (of a school) to close for the holidays. **5.** *Informal.* to lose or cause to lose control of the emotions: *the news of his death broke her up.* **6.** *Slang.* to be or cause to be overcome with laughter. ~*n.* **break-up. 7.** a separation or disintegration.

break-up value *n. Commerce.* **1.** the value of an organization assuming that it will not continue to trade. **2.** the value of a share in a company based only on the value of its assets.

breakwater ('breɪkˌwɔːtə) *n.* **1.** Also called: **mole.** a massive wall built out into the sea to protect a shore or harbour from the force of waves. **2.** another name for **groyne.**

break with *vb.* (*intr., prep.*) to end a relationship or association with (someone or an organization or social group).

bream[1] (briːm; *Austral.* brɪm) *or Austral.* **brim** (brɪm) *n., pl.* **bream** *or* **brim. 1.** any of several Eurasian freshwater cyprinid fishes of the genus *Abramis,* esp. *A. brama,* having a deep compressed body covered with silvery scales. **2. white** *or* **silver bream.** a similar cyprinid, *Blicca bjoerkna.* **3.** short for **sea bream.** [C14: from Old French *bresme,* of Germanic origin; compare Old High German *brahsema;* perhaps related to *brehan* to glitter]

bream[2] (briːm) *vb. Nautical.* (formerly) to clean debris from (the bottom of a vessel) by heating to soften the pitch. [C15: probably from Middle Dutch *bremme* broom; from using burning broom as a source of heat]

breast (brɛst) *n.* **1.** the front part of the body from the neck to the abdomen; chest. **2.** either of the two soft fleshy milk-secreting glands on the chest in sexually mature human females. **3.** a similar organ in certain other mammals. **4.** anything that resembles a breast in shape or position: *the breast of the hill.* **5.** a source of nourishment: *the city took the victims to its breast.* **6.** the source of human emotions. **7.** the part of a garment that covers the breast. **8.** a projection from the side of a wall, esp. that formed by a chimney. **9.** *Mining.* the face being worked at the end of a tunnel. **10. beat one's breast.** to display guilt and remorse publicly or ostentatiously. **11. make a clean breast of.** to make a confession of. ~*vb.* (*tr.*) **12.** to confront boldly; face: *breast the storm.* **13.** to oppose with the breast or meet at breast level: *breasting the waves.* **14.** to come alongside of: *breast the ship.* **15.** to reach the summit of: *breasting the mountain top.* [Old English *brēost;* related to Old Norse *brjōst,* Old

High German *brust,* Dutch *borst,* Swedish *bräss,* Old Irish *brū* belly, body]

breastbone ('brɛst,bəʊn) *n.* the nontechnical name for **sternum.**

breast-feed *vb.* **-feeds, -feeding, -fed.** to feed (a baby) with milk from the breast; suckle. —'**breast-,fed** *adj.* —'**breast-,feeding** *n.*

breastpin ('brɛst,pɪn) *n.* a brooch worn on the breast, esp. to close a garment.

breastplate ('brɛst,pleɪt) *n.* **1.** a piece of armour covering the chest. **2.** the strap of a harness covering a horse's breast. **3.** *Judaism.* an ornamental silver plate hung on the scrolls of the Torah. **4.** *Old Testament.* a square vestment ornamented with 12 precious stones, representing the 12 tribes of Israel, worn by the high priest when praying before the holy of holies. **5.** *Zoology.* a nontechnical name for **plastron.**

breaststroke ('brɛst,strəʊk) *n.* a swimming stroke in which the arms are extended in front of the head and swept back on either side while the legs are drawn up beneath the body and thrust back together.

breastwork ('brɛst,wɜːk) *n. Fortifications.* a temporary defensive work, usually breast-high. Also called: **parapet.**

breath (brɛθ) *n.* **1.** the intake and expulsion of air during respiration. **2.** the air inhaled or exhaled during respiration. **3.** a single respiration or inhalation of air, etc. **4.** the vapour, heat, or odour of exhaled air: *his breath on the window melted the frost.* **5.** a slight gust of air. **6.** a short pause or rest: *take a breath for five minutes.* **7.** a brief time: *it was done in a breath.* **8.** a suggestion or slight evidence; suspicion: *a breath of scandal.* **9.** a whisper or soft sound. **10.** life, energy, or vitality: *the breath of new industry.* **11.** *Phonetics.* the passage of air through the completely open glottis without vibration of the vocal cords, as in exhaling or pronouncing fricatives such as (f) or (h) or stops such as (p) or (k). Compare **voice** (sense 11). **12. catch one's breath.** to rest until breathing is normal, esp. after exertion. **13. in the same breath.** done or said at the same time. **14. out of breath.** gasping for air after exertion. **15. save one's breath.** to refrain from useless talk. **16. take one's breath away.** to overwhelm with surprise, etc. **17. under** *or* **below one's breath.** in a quiet voice or whisper. [Old English *brǣth;* related to *brǣdan* to burn, Old High German *brādam* heat, breath]

breathalyse *or U.S.* **breathalyze** ('brɛθə,laɪz) *vb.* (*tr.*) to apply a Breathalyzer test to (someone).

Breathalyzer *or* **Breathalyser** ('brɛθə,laɪzə) *n. Brit., trademark.* a device for estimating the amount of alcohol in the breath: used in testing people suspected of driving under the influence of alcohol. U.S. equivalent: **drunkometer.** [C20: BREATH + (AN)ALYSER]

breathe (briːð) *vb.* **1.** to take in oxygen from (the surrounding medium, esp. air) and give out carbon dioxide; respire. **2.** (*intr.*) to exist; be alive: *every animal that breathes on earth.* **3.** (*intr.*) to rest to regain breath, composure, etc.: *stop your questions, and give me a chance to breathe.* **4.** (*intr.*) (esp. of air) to blow lightly: *the wind breathed through the trees.* **5.** (*intr.*) *Machinery.* **a.** to take in air, esp. for combustion: *the engine breathes through this air filter.* **b.** to equalize the pressure within a container, chamber, etc., with atmospheric pressure: *the crankcase breathes through this duct.* **6.** (*tr.*) *Phonetics.* to articulate (a speech sound) without vibration of the vocal cords. Compare **voice** (sense 19). **7.** to exhale or emit: *the dragon breathed fire.* **8.** (*tr.*) to impart; instil: *to breathe confidence into the actors.* **9.** (*tr.*) to speak softly; whisper: *to breathe words of love.* **10.** (*tr.*) to permit to rest: *to breathe a horse.* **11. breathe again, freely,** *or* **easily.** to feel relief: *I could breathe again after passing the exam.* **12. breathe down (someone's) neck.** to stay close to (someone), esp. to oversee what they are doing. **13. breathe one's last.** to die or be finished or defeated. [C13: from BREATH]

breathed (brɛθt, briːðd) *adj. Phonetics.* relating to or denoting a speech sound for whose articulation the vocal cords are not made to vibrate. Compare **voiced.**

breather ('briːðə) *n.* **1.** *Informal.* a short pause for rest. **2.** a person who breathes in a specified way: *a deep breather.* **3.** a vent in a container to equalize internal and external pressure, such as the pipe in the crankcase of an internal-combustion engine. **4.** a small opening in a room, container, cover, etc., supplying air for ventilation.

breathing ('briːðɪŋ) *n.* **1.** the passage of air into and out of the lungs to supply the body with oxygen. **2.** a single breath: *a breathing between words.* **3.** an utterance: *a breathing of hate.* **4.** a soft movement, esp. of air. **5.** a rest or pause. **6.** *Phonetics.* **a.** expulsion of breath (**rough breathing**) or absence of such expulsion (**smooth breathing**) preceding the pronunciation of an initial vowel or rho in ancient Greek. **b.** either of two symbols indicating this.

breathing space *n.* **1.** enough area to permit freedom of movement: *the country gives us some breathing space.* **2.** a pause for rest, etc.: *a coffee break was their only breathing space.*

breathless ('brɛθlɪs) *adj.* **1.** out of breath; gasping, etc. **2.** holding one's breath or having it taken away by excitement, etc.: *a breathless confrontation.* **3.** (esp. of the atmosphere) motionless and stifling. **4.** *Rare.* lifeless; dead. —'**breathlessly** *adv.* —'**breathlessness** *n.*

breathtaking ('brɛθ,teɪkɪŋ) *adj.* causing awe or excitement: *a breathtaking view.* —'**breath,takingly** *adv.*

breath test *n. Brit.* a chemical test of a driver's breath to determine the amount of alcohol he has consumed.

breathy ('brɛθɪ) *adj.* **breathier, breathiest. 1.** (of the speaking voice) accompanied by an audible emission of breath. **2.** (of the singing voice) lacking resonance. —'**breathily** *adv.* —'**breathiness** *n.*

breccia ('brɛtʃɪə) *n.* a rock consisting of angular fragments embedded in a finer matrix, formed by erosion, volcanic activity, etc. [C18: from Italian, from Old High German *brecha* a fragment; see BREACH] —'**brecci,ated** *adj.*

Brechtian ('brɛxtɪən) *adj.* **1.** of or relating to the works of Bertolt Brecht (1898–1956), German dramatist and theatrical producer. ~*n.* **2.** a follower of Brecht, esp. his dramatic style.

bred (brɛd) *vb.* the past tense and past participle of **breed.**

brede (briːd) *n., vb.* an archaic spelling of **braid.**

bree[1] *or* **brie** (briː) *n. Scot.* broth, stock, or juice. [Old English *brīg,* variant of *brīw* pottage; related to Old High German *brīo* soup, Old English *brīwan* to cook, Middle Irish *brēo* flame]

bree[2] (briː) *n.* a Scottish word for **brunt.** [C19: perhaps from earlier *bree* brow]

breech *n.* (briːtʃ). **1.** the lower dorsal part of the human trunk; buttocks; rump. **2.** the lower part or bottom of something: *the breech of the bridge.* **3.** the lower portion of a pulley block, esp. the part to which the rope or chain is secured. **4.** the part of a firearm behind the barrel or bore. **5.** *Obstetrics.* short for **breech delivery.** ~*vb.* (briːtʃ, brɪtʃ). (*tr.*) **6.** to fit (a gun) with a breech. **7.** *Archaic.* to clothe in breeches or any other clothing. ~See also **breeches.** [Old English *brēc,* plural of *brōc* leg covering; related to Old Norse *brōk,* Old High German *bruoh*]

breechblock ('briːtʃ,blɒk) *n.* a metal block in breech-loading firearms that is withdrawn to insert the cartridge and replaced to close the breech before firing.

breechcloth ('briːtʃ,klɒθ) *or* **breechclout** ('briːtʃ,klaʊt) *n.* other names for **loincloth.**

breech delivery *n.* birth of a baby with the feet or buttocks appearing first.

breeches ('brɪtʃɪz, 'briː-) *pl. n.* **1.** trousers extending to the knee or just below, worn for riding, mountaineering, etc. **2.** *Informal or dialect.* any trousers. **3. too big for one's breeches.** conceited; unduly self-confident.

breeches buoy *n.* a ring-shaped life buoy with a support in the form of a pair of short breeches, in which a person is suspended for safe transfer from a ship.

breeching ('brɪtʃɪŋ, 'briː-) *n.* **1.** the strap of a harness that passes behind a horse's haunches. **2.** *Naval.* (formerly) the rope used to check the recoil run of a ship's guns or to secure them against rough weather. **3.** the parts comprising the breech of a gun.

breech-loader ('briːtʃ,ləʊdə) *n.* a firearm that is loaded at the breech. —'**breech-,loading** *adj.*

breed (briːd) *vb.* **breeds, breeding, bred. 1.** to bear (offspring). **2.** (*tr.*) to bring up; raise. **3.** to produce or cause to produce by mating; propagate. **4.** to produce and maintain new or improved strains of (domestic animals and plants). **5.** to produce or be produced; generate: *to breed trouble; violence breeds in densely populated areas.* ~*n.* **6.** a group of organisms within a species, esp. a group of domestic animals, originated and maintained by man and having a clearly defined set of characteristics. **7.** a lineage or race: *a breed of Europeans.* **8.** a kind, sort, or group: *a special breed of hatred.* [Old English *brēdan,* of Germanic origin; related to BROOD]

breeder ('briːdə) *n.* **1.** a person who breeds plants or animals. **2.** something that reproduces, esp. to excess: *rabbits are persistent breeders.* **3.** an animal kept for breeding purposes. **4.** a source or cause: *a breeder of discontent.* **5.** short for **breeder reactor.**

breeder reactor *n.* a type of nuclear reactor that produces more fissionable material than it consumes. Compare **converter reactor.** See also **fast-breeder reactor.**

breeding ('briːdɪŋ) *n.* **1.** the process of bearing offspring; reproduction. **2.** the process of producing plants or animals by hybridization, inbreeding, or other methods of reproduction. **3.** the result of good training, esp. the knowledge of correct social behaviour; refinement: *a man of breeding.* **4.** a person's line of descent: *his breeding was suspect.* **5.** *Physics.* a process occurring in a nuclear reactor as a result of which more fissionable material is produced than is used up.

breeks (briːks) *pl. n. Scot.* trousers. [Scot. variant of BREECHES]

breenge *or* **breinge** (briːndʒ) *Scot.* ~*vb.* (*intr.*) **1.** to lunge forward; move violently or dash. ~*n.* **2.** a violent movement. [of unknown origin]

breenger ('briːndʒə) *n. West central Scot. dialect.* an impetuous person. [from BREENGE]

breeze[1] (briːz) *n.* **1.** a gentle or light wind. **2.** *Meteorol.* a wind of force two to six inclusive on the Beaufort scale. **3.** *U.S. and Canadian informal.* an easy task or state of ease: *being happy here is a breeze.* **4.** *Informal, chiefly Brit.* a disturbance, esp. a lively quarrel. ~*vb.* (*intr.*) **5.** to move quickly or casually: *he breezed into the room.* **6.** (of wind) to blow: *the south wind breezed over the fields.* [C16: probably from Old Spanish *briza* northeast wind]

breeze[2] (briːz) *n.* an archaic or dialect name for the **gadfly.** [Old English *briosa,* of unknown origin]

breeze[3] (briːz) *n.* ashes of coal, coke, or charcoal used to make breeze blocks. [C18: from French *braise* live coals; see BRAISE]

breeze block *n.* a light building brick made from the ashes of coal, coke, etc., bonded together by cement and used esp. for walls that bear relatively small loads. Usual U.S. names: **cinder block, clinker block.**

breezeway ('bri:z,weɪ) *n.* a roofed passageway connecting two buildings, sometimes with the sides enclosed.

breezy ('bri:zɪ) *adj.* **breezier, breeziest.** **1.** fresh; windy: *a breezy afternoon.* **2.** casual or carefree; lively; light-hearted: *her breezy nature.* **3.** lacking substance; light: *a breezy conversation.* —'**breezily** *adv.* —'**breeziness** *n.*

bregma ('brɛgmə) *n., pl.* **-mata** (-mətə). the point on the top of the skull where the coronal and sagittal sutures meet: in infants this corresponds to the anterior fontanelle. [C16: New Latin from Greek: front part of the head]

brei (breɪ) *vb.* **breis, breiing, breid.** (*intr.*) *S. African informal.* to speak with a uvular *r*, esp. in Afrikaans. Also: **brey.** Compare **burr**[2]. [C20: from Afrikaans; compare BRAY[1]]

breid (bri:d) *n.* a Scot. word for **bread.**

breist *or* **breest** (bri:st) *n.* a Scot. word for **breast.**

brekky ('brɛkɪ) *n. Chiefly Austral.* a slang word for breakfast.

bremsstrahlung ('brɛmz,ʃtrɑ:ləŋ) *n.* the x-radiation produced when an electrically charged particle, such as an electron, is slowed down by the electric field of an atomic nucleus. [C20: German: braking radiation]

Bren gun (brɛn) *n.* an air-cooled gas-operated light machine gun taking .303 calibre ammunition: used by British and Commonwealth forces in World War II. [C20: after *Br(no)*, Czechoslovakia, where it was first made and *En(field)*, England, where manufacture was continued]

brent goose (brɛnt) *n.* a small goose, *Branta bernicla*, that has a dark grey plumage and short neck and occurs in most northern coastal regions. Also called: **brent,** (esp. U.S. and Canadian) **brant.** [C16: perhaps of Scandinavian origin; compare Old Norse *brandgās* sheldrake]

br'er (brɜ:, brɛə) *n. Southern U.S. Negro dialect.* brother: usually prefixed to a name: *Br'er Jones.*

brethren ('brɛðrɪn) *pl. n. Archaic except when referring to fellow members of a religion, sect, society, etc.* a plural of **brother.**

Breton ('brɛtᵊn; *French* brətɔ̃) *adj.* **1.** of or relating to Brittany, a region of NW France, or to its people, or their language. ~*n.* **2.** a native or inhabitant of Brittany, esp. one who speaks the Breton language. **3.** the indigenous language of Brittany, belonging to the Brythonic subgroup of the Celtic family of languages.

breunnerite ('brɔɪnə,raɪt) *n.* an iron-containing type of magnesite used in the manufacture of refractory bricks. [C19: named after Count *Breunner*, Austrian nobleman, + -ITE[1]]

breve (bri:v) *n.* **1.** an accent, ˘, placed over a vowel to indicate that it is of short duration or is pronounced in a specified way. **2.** *Music.* a note, now rarely used, equivalent in time value to two semibreves. **3.** *R.C. Church.* a less common word for **brief** (papal letter). [C13: from Medieval Latin *breve*, from Latin *brevis* short; see BRIEF]

brevet ('brɛvɪt) *n.* **1.** a document entitling a commissioned officer to hold temporarily a higher military rank without the appropriate pay and allowances. ~*vb.* **-vets, -vetting, -vetted** *or* **-vets, -veting, -veted.** **2.** (*tr.*) to promote by brevet. [C14: from Old French *brievet* a little letter, from *brief* letter; see BRIEF] —'**brevetcy** *n.*

breviary ('bri:vjərɪ) *n., pl.* **-ries.** **1.** *R.C. Church.* a book of psalms, hymns, prayers, etc., to be recited daily by clerics in major orders and certain members of religious orders as part of the divine office. **2.** a similar book in the Orthodox Church. [C16: from Latin *breviārium* an abridged version, from *breviāre* to shorten, from *brevis* short]

brevier (brə'vɪə) *n.* (formerly) a size of printer's type approximately equal to 8 point. [C16: probably from Dutch, literally: BREVIARY; so called because this type size was used for breviaries]

brevity ('brɛvɪtɪ) *n., pl.* **-ties.** **1.** conciseness of expression; lack of verbosity. **2.** a short duration; brief time. [C16: from Latin *brevitās* shortness, from *brevis* BRIEF]

brew (bru:) *vb.* **1.** to make (beer, ale, etc.) from malt and other ingredients by steeping, boiling, and fermentation. **2.** to prepare (a drink, such as tea) by boiling or infusing. **3.** (*tr.*) to devise or plan: *to brew a plot.* **4.** (*intr.*) to be in the process of being brewed: *the tea was brewing in the pot.* **5.** (*intr.*) to be impending or forming: *there's a storm brewing.* ~*n.* **6.** a beverage produced by brewing, esp. tea or beer: *a strong brew.* **7.** an instance or time of brewing: *last year's brew.* ~See also **brew up.** [Old English *brēowan* related to Old Norse *brugga*, Old Saxon *breuwan*, Old High German *briuwan*] —'**brewer** *n.*

brewage ('bru:ɪdʒ) *n.* **1.** a product of brewing; brew. **2.** the process of brewing.

brewer's yeast *n.* **1.** a yeast, *Saccharomyces cerevisiae*, used in brewing. See **yeast** (sense 2). **2.** yeast obtained as a by-product of brewing.

brewery ('brʊərɪ) *n., pl.* **-eries.** a place where beer, ale, etc., is brewed.

brewing ('bru:ɪŋ) *n.* a quantity of a beverage brewed at one time.

brewis ('bru:ɪs) *or* **brevis** ('brɛvɪs) *n. Dialect, chiefly northern English, Canadian, or U.S.* **1.** bread soaked in broth, gravy, etc. **2.** thickened broth. [C16: from Old French *broez*, from *broet*, diminutive of *breu* BROTH]

brew up *Brit. and N.Z. informal.* ~*vb.* (*intr., adv.*) **1.** to make tea, esp. out of doors or in informal circumstances. ~*n.* **brew-up.** **2.** a making of tea.

BRG *international car registration for* Guyana (formerly British Guiana).

briar[1] *or* **brier** ('braɪə) *n.* **1.** Also called: **tree heath.** an ericaceous shrub, *Erica arborea*, of S Europe, having a hard woody root (briarroot). **2.** a tobacco pipe made from the root of this plant. [C19: from French *bruyère* heath, from Late Latin *brūcus*, of Gaulish origin] —'**briary** *or* '**briery** *adj.*

briar[2] ('braɪə) *n.* a variant spelling of **brier**[1].

briard (bri:'ɑ:d, bri:'ɑ:) *n.* a medium-sized dog of an ancient French sheep-herding breed having a long rough coat of a single colour. [French, literally: of *Brie* (region in N France)]

briarroot *or* **brierroot** ('braɪə,ru:t) *n.* **1.** the hard woody root of the briar, used for making tobacco pipes. **2.** any of several other woods used to make tobacco pipes. ~Also called: '**briar,wood,** '**brier,wood.**

bribe (braɪb) *vb.* **1.** to promise, offer, or give something, usually money, to (a person) to procure services or gain influence, esp. illegally. ~*n.* **2.** a reward, such as money or favour, given or offered for this purpose. **3.** any persuasion or lure. **4.** a length of flawed or damaged cloth removed from the main piece. [C14: from Old French *briber* to beg, of obscure origin] —'**bribable** *or* '**bribeable** *adj.* —'**briber** *n.*

bribery ('braɪbərɪ) *n., pl.* **-eries.** the process of giving or taking bribes.

bric-a-brac ('brɪkə,bræk) *n.* miscellaneous small objects, esp. furniture and curios, kept because they are ornamental or rare. [C19: from French; phrase based on *bric* piece]

bricht (brɪxt) *adj.* a Scot. word for **bright.**

brick (brɪk) *n.* **1. a.** a rectangular block of clay mixed with sand and fired in a kiln or baked by the sun, used in building construction. **b.** (*as modifier*): *a brick house.* **2.** the material used to make such blocks. **3.** any rectangular block: *a brick of ice.* **4.** bricks collectively. **5.** *Informal.* a reliable, trustworthy, or helpful person. **6.** *Brit.* a child's building block. **7.** short for **brick red.** **8. drop a brick.** *Brit. informal.* to make a tactless or indiscreet remark. **9. like a ton of bricks.** *Informal.* (used esp. of the manner of punishing or reprimanding someone) with great force; severely: *when he spotted my mistake he came down on me like a ton of bricks.* ~*vb.* **10.** (*tr.*; usually foll. by *in, up,* or *over*) to construct, line, pave, fill, or wall up with bricks: *to brick up a window; brick over a patio.* [C15: from Old French *brique*, from Middle Dutch *bricke*; related to Middle Low German *brike*, Old English *brecan* to BREAK] —'**bricky** *adj.*

brickbat ('brɪk,bæt) *n.* **1.** a piece of brick or similar material, esp. one used as a weapon. **2.** blunt criticism: *the critic threw several brickbats at the singer.*

brickearth ('brɪk,ɜ:θ) *n.* a clayey alluvium suitable for the making of bricks: specifically, such a deposit in southern England, yielding a fertile soil.

brickie ('brɪkɪ) *n. Brit. informal.* a bricklayer.

bricklayer ('brɪk,leɪə) *n.* a person trained or skilled in laying bricks.

bricklaying ('brɪk,leɪɪŋ) *n.* the technique or practice of laying bricks.

brickle ('brɪkᵊl) *adj. Scot. and northern English dialect.* brittle; fragile; breakable. [Old English *brycel*; related to *brecan* to BREAK, Middle Low German *brökel* fragile] —'**brickleness** *n.*

brick red *n., adj.* **a.** a reddish-brown colour. **b.** (*as adj.*): *a brick-red carpet.*

brick veneer *n.* (in Australia) a timber-framed house with a brick exterior.

brickwork ('brɪk,wɜ:k) *n.* **1.** a structure, such as a wall, built of bricks. **2.** construction using bricks.

brickyard ('brɪk,jɑ:d) *n.* a place in which bricks are made, stored, or sold.

bricole (brɪ'kəʊl, 'brɪkᵊl) *n.* **1.** *Billiards.* a shot in which the cue ball touches a cushion after striking the object ball and before touching another ball. **2.** (in ancient and medieval times) a military catapult for throwing stones, etc. **3.** (esp. formerly) a harness worn by soldiers for dragging guns. **4.** an indirect or unexpected stroke or action. [C16: from Old French: catapult, from Medieval Latin *bricola*, of uncertain origin]

bridal ('braɪdᵊl) *adj.* **1.** of or relating to a bride or a wedding; nuptial. ~*n.* **2.** *Obsolete.* a wedding or wedding feast. [Old English *brȳdealu*, literally: "bride ale", that is, wedding feast]

bridal wreath *n.* any of several N temperate rosaceous shrubs of the genus *Spiraea*, esp. *S. prunifolia*, cultivated for their sprays of small white flowers.

bride[1] (braɪd) *n.* a woman who has just been or is about to be married. [Old English *brȳd*; related to Old Norse *brūthr*, Gothic *brūths* daughter-in-law, Old High German *brūt*]

bride[2] (braɪd) *n. Lacemaking, needlework.* a thread or loop that joins parts of a pattern. Also called: **bar.** [C19: from French, literally: BRIDLE, probably of Germanic origin]

bridegroom ('braɪd,gru:m, -,grʊm) *n.* a man who has just been or is about to be married. [C14: changed (through influence of GROOM) from Old English *brȳdguma*, from *brȳd* BRIDE[1] + *guma* man; related to Old Norse *brūthgumi,* Old High German *brūtigomo*]

bride price *or* **wealth** *n.* (in some societies) money, property, or services given by a bridegroom to the kinsmen of his bride in order to establish his rights over the woman.

bridesmaid ('braɪdzˌmeɪd) *n.* a girl or young unmarried woman who attends a bride at her wedding. Compare **matron of honour, maid of honour.**

bridewell ('braɪdˌwɛl, -wəl) *n.* a house of correction; jail, esp. for minor offences. [C16: after *Bridewell* (originally, *St Bride's Well*), a house of correction in London]

bridge[1] (brɪdʒ) *n.* **1.** a structure that spans and provides a passage over a road, railway, river, or some other obstacle. **2.** something that resembles this in shape or function: *his letters provided a bridge across the centuries.* **3. a.** the hard ridge at the upper part of the nose, formed by the underlying nasal bones. **b.** any anatomical ridge or connecting structure. Compare **pons. 4.** the part of a pair of glasses that rests on the nose. **5.** Also called: **bridgework.** a dental plate containing one or more artificial teeth that is secured to the surrounding natural teeth. **6.** a platform athwartships and above the rail, from which a ship is piloted and navigated. **7.** a piece of wood, usually fixed, supporting the strings of a violin, guitar, etc., and transmitting their vibrations to the sounding board. **8.** Also called: **bridge passage.** a passage in a musical, literary, or dramatic work linking two or more important sections. **9.** Also called: **bridge circuit.** *Electronics.* any of several networks, such as a Wheatstone bridge, consisting of two branches across which a measuring device is connected. The resistance, capacitance, etc., of one component can be determined from the known values of the others when the voltage in each branch is balanced. **10.** *Billiards, snooker.* **a.** a support for a cue made by placing the fingers on the table and raising the thumb. **b.** a cue rest with a notched end for shots beyond normal reach. **11.** *Theatre.* **a.** a platform of adjustable height above or beside the stage for the use of stagehands, light operators, etc. **b.** *Chiefly Brit.* a part of the stage floor that can be raised or lowered. **12.** a partition in a furnace or boiler to keep the fuel in place. **13. burn one's bridges.** See **burn**[1] (sense 18). **14. cross a bridge when (one) comes to it.** to deal with a problem only when it arises; not to anticipate difficulties. ~*vb.* (*tr.*) **15.** to build or provide a bridge over something; span: *to bridge a river.* **16.** to connect or reduce the distance between: *let us bridge our differences.* [Old English *brycg;* related to Old Norse *bryggja* gangway, Old Frisian *bregge,* Old High German *brucka,* Danish, Swedish *bro*] —'**bridgeable** *adj.* —'**bridgeless** *adj.*

bridge[2] (brɪdʒ) *n.* a card game for four players, based on whist, in which one hand (the dummy) is exposed and the trump suit decided by bidding between the players. See also **contract bridge, duplicate bridge, rubber bridge, auction bridge.** [C19: of uncertain origin, but compare Turkish *bir-üç* (unattested phrase) one-three (said perhaps to refer to the one exposed hand and the three players' hands]

bridgeboard ('brɪdʒˌbɔːd) *n.* a board on both sides of a staircase that is cut to support the treads and risers. Also called: **cut string.**

bridgehead ('brɪdʒˌhɛd) *n. Military.* **1.** an area of ground secured or to be taken on the enemy's side of an obstacle. **2.** a fortified or defensive position at the end of a bridge nearest to the enemy. **3.** an advantageous position gained for future expansion.

bridge passage *n.* See **bridge** (sense 8).

bridge rectifier *n. Electrical engineering.* a full-wave rectifier consisting of a bridge with a rectifier in each of the four arms.

bridge roll *n. Brit.* a soft bread roll in a long thin shape. [C20: from BRIDGE[2] or perhaps BRIDGE[1]]

bridgework ('brɪdʒˌwɜːk) *n.* **1. a.** a partial denture attached to the surrounding teeth. See **bridge**[1] (sense 5). **b.** the technique of making such appliances. **2.** the process or occupation of constructing bridges.

bridging ('brɪdʒɪŋ) *n.* **1.** one or more timber struts fixed between floor or roof joists to stiffen the construction and distribute the loads. **2.** *Mountaineering.* a technique for climbing a wide chimney by pressing left hand and foot against one side of it and right hand and foot against the other side.

bridging loan *n.* a loan made to cover the period between two transactions, such as the buying of another house before the sale of the first is completed.

bridie ('braɪdɪ; *Scot.* 'brəɪdɪ) *n. Scot.* a semicircular pie containing meat and onions. [of unknown origin]

bridle ('braɪdᵊl) *n.* **1.** a headgear for a horse, etc., consisting of a series of buckled straps and a metal mouthpiece (bit) by which the animal is controlled through the reins. **2.** something that curbs or restrains; check. **3.** a Y-shaped cable, rope, or chain, used for holding, towing, etc. **4.** *Machinery.* a device by which the motion of a component is limited, often in the form of a linkage or flange. ~*vb.* **5.** (*tr.*) to put a bridle on (a horse, mule, etc.). **6.** (*intr.*) (of a horse) to respond correctly to the pull of the reins. **7.** (*tr.*) to restrain; curb: *he bridled his rage.* **8.** (*intr.*; often foll. by *at*) to show anger, scorn, or indignation. [Old English *brigdels;* related to *bregdan* to BRAID, Old High German *brittil,* Middle Low German *breidel*] —'**bridler** *n.*

bridle path *n.* a path suitable for riding or leading horses. Also called (N.Z.): **bridle track.**

bridlewise ('braɪdᵊlˌwaɪz) *adj. U.S.* (of a horse) obedient to the pressure of the reins on the neck rather than to the bit.

bridoon (brɪ'duːn) *n.* a horse's bit: a small snaffle used in double bridles. [C18: from French *bridon,* from *bride* bridle; compare Middle English *bride*]

brie (briː) *n.* a variant spelling of **bree**[1].

Brie (briː) *n.* a soft creamy white cheese, similar to Camembert but milder, from the Brie area of N France.

brief (briːf) *adj.* **1.** short in duration: *a brief holiday.* **2.** short in length or extent; scanty: *a brief bikini.* **3.** abrupt in manner; brusque: *the professor was brief with me this morning.* **4.** terse or concise; containing few words: *he made a brief statement.* ~*n.* **5.** a condensed or short statement or written synopsis; abstract. **6.** *Law.* a document containing all the facts and points of law of a case by which a solicitor instructs a barrister to represent a client. **7.** *R.C. Church.* a letter issuing from the Roman court written in modern characters, as contrasted with a papal bull; papal brief. **8.** short for **briefing. 9.** a paper outlining the arguments and information on one side of a debate. **10.** *Brit. slang.* a lawyer, esp. a barrister. **11. hold a brief for.** to argue for; champion. **12. in brief.** in short; to sum up. ~*vb.* (*tr.*) **13.** to prepare or instruct by giving a summary of relevant facts. **14.** to make a summary or synopsis of. **15.** *English law.* **a.** to instruct (a barrister) by brief. **b.** to retain (a barrister) as counsel. ~See also **briefs.** [C14: from Old French *bref,* from Latin *brevis;* related to Greek *brakhus*] —'**briefly** *adv.* —'**briefness** *n.*

briefcase ('briːfˌkeɪs) *n.* a flat portable case, often of leather, for carrying papers, books, etc.

briefing ('briːfɪŋ) *n.* **1.** a meeting at which detailed information or instructions are given, as for military operations, etc. **2.** the facts presented during such a meeting.

briefless ('briːflɪs) *adj.* (said of a barrister) without clients.

briefs (briːfs) *pl. n.* men's underpants or women's pants without legs.

brier[1] *or* **briar** ('braɪə) *n.* any of various thorny shrubs or other plants, such as the sweetbrier and greenbrier. [Old English *brēr, brǣr,* of obscure origin] —'**briery** *or* '**briary** *adj.*

brier[2] ('braɪə) *n.* a variant spelling of **briar**[1].

brierroot ('braɪəˌruːt) *n.* a variant spelling of **briarroot.** Also called: '**brierˌwood.**

brig[1] (brɪg) *n.* **1.** *Nautical.* a two-masted square-rigger. **2.** *Chiefly U.S.* a prison, esp. in a navy ship. [C18: shortened from BRIGANTINE]

brig[2] (brɪg) *n.* a Scot. and northern English word for a **bridge**[1].

Brig. *abbrev. for* Brigadier.

brigade (brɪ'geɪd) *n.* **1.** a formation of fighting units, together with support arms and services, smaller than a division and usually commanded by a brigadier. **2.** a group of people organized for a certain task: *a rescue brigade.* ~*vb.* (*tr.*) **3.** to organize into a brigade. **4.** to put or group together. [C17: from Old French, from Old Italian, from *brigare* to fight, perhaps of Celtic origin; see BRIGAND]

brigadier (ˌbrɪgə'dɪə) *n.* **1.** an officer of the British Army or Royal Marines who holds a rank junior to a major general but senior to a colonel, usually commanding a brigade. **2.** an equivalent rank in other armed forces. **3.** *U.S. Army.* short for **brigadier general. 4.** *History.* a noncommissioned rank in the armies of Napoleon I. [C17: from French, from BRIGADE]

brigadier general *n., pl.* **brigadier generals. 1.** an officer of the U.S. Army, Air Force, or Marine Corps who holds a rank junior to a major general but senior to a colonel, usually commanding a brigade. **2.** the former name for a **brigadier** (sense 1).

brigalow ('brɪgələʊ) *n. Austral.* **a.** any of various acacia trees. **b.** (*as modifier*): *brigalow country.* [C19: from a native Australian language]

brigand ('brɪgənd) *n.* a bandit or plunderer, esp. a member of a gang operating in mountainous areas. [C14: from Old French, from Old Italian *brigante* fighter, from *brigare* to fight, from *briga* strife, of Celtic origin] —'**brigandage** *or* '**brigandry** *n.*

brigandine ('brɪgənˌdiːn, -ˌdaɪn) *n.* a coat of mail, invented in the Middle Ages to increase mobility, consisting of metal rings or sheets sewn on to cloth or leather. [C15: from Old French, from BRIGAND + -INE[1]]

brigantine ('brɪgənˌtiːn, -ˌtaɪn) *n.* a two-masted sailing ship, rigged square on the foremast and fore-and-aft with square topsails on the mainmast. [C16: from Old Italian *brigantino* pirate ship, from *brigante* BRIGAND]

Brig. Gen. *abbrev. for* brigadier general.

bright (braɪt) *adj.* **1.** emitting or reflecting much light; shining. **2.** (of colours) intense or vivid. **3.** full of promise: *a bright future.* **4.** full of animation; cheerful: *a bright face.* **5.** *Informal.* quick witted or clever: *a bright child.* **6.** magnificent; glorious: *a bright victory.* **7.** polished; glistening: *a bright finish.* **8.** (of the voice) distinct and clear. **9.** (of a liquid) translucent and clear: *a circle of bright water.* **10. bright and early.** very early in the morning. ~*n.* **11.** a thin flat paintbrush with a straight sharp edge used for highlighting in oil painting. **12.** *Poetic.* brightness or splendour: *the bright of his armour.* ~*adv.* **13.** brightly: *the fire was burning bright.* ~See also **brights.** [Old

English *beorht;* related to Old Norse *bjartr,* Gothic *bairhts* clear, Old High German *beraht,* Norwegian *bjerk,* Swedish *brokig* pied] —'**brightly** *adv.*

brighten ('braɪtᵊn) *vb.* **1.** to make or become bright or brighter. **2.** to make or become cheerful. —'**brightener** *n.*

brightening agent *n.* a compound applied to a textile to increase its brightness by the conversion of ultraviolet radiation to visible (blue) light, used in detergents.

bright-eyed *adj.* **1.** eager; fresh and enthusiastic. **2. bright-eyed and bushy-tailed.** *Informal.* keen, confident, and alert.

bright lights *pl. n.* **the.** places of entertainment in a city.

brightness ('braɪtnɪs) *n.* **1.** the condition of being bright. **2.** *Physics.* a former name for **luminosity** (sense 4). **3.** *Psychol.* the experienced intensity of light.

brights (braɪts) *pl. n. U.S.* the high beam of the headlights of a motor vehicle.

Bright's disease (braɪts) *n.* chronic inflammation of the kidneys; chronic nephritis. [C19: named after Richard *Bright* (1789–1858), British physician]

brightwork ('braɪtˌwɜːk) *n.* **1.** shiny metal trimmings or fittings on ships, cars, etc. **2.** varnished or plain woodwork on a vessel.

brill (brɪl) *n., pl.* **brill** *or* **brills.** a European food fish, *Scophthalmus rhombus,* a flatfish similar to the turbot but lacking tubercles on the body: family *Bothidae.* [C15: probably from Cornish *brȳthel* mackerel, from Old Cornish *brȳth* speckled; related to Welsh *brith* spotted]

brilliance ('brɪljəns) *or* **brilliancy** *n.* **1.** great brightness; radiance. **2.** excellence or distinction in physical or mental ability; exceptional talent. **3.** splendour; magnificence: *the brilliance of the royal court.* **4.** *Physics.* a former term for **luminance.**

brilliant ('brɪljənt) *adj.* **1.** shining with light; sparkling. **2.** (of a colour) having a high saturation and reflecting a considerable amount of light; vivid. **3.** outstanding; exceptional: *a brilliant success.* **4.** splendid; magnificent: *a brilliant show.* **5.** of outstanding intelligence or intellect: *a brilliant mind; a brilliant idea.* **6.** *Music.* **a.** (of the tone of an instrument) having a large proportion of high harmonics above the fundamental. **b.** Also: **brilliant** (*French* brijɑ̃), **brilliante** (*French* brijɑ̃t). with spirit; lively. ~*n.* **7.** Also called: **brilliant cut. a.** a popular circular cut for diamonds and other gemstones in the form of two many-faceted pyramids (the top one truncated) joined at their bases. **b.** a diamond of this cut. **8.** (formerly) a size of a printer's type approximately equal to 4 point. [C17: from French *brillant* shining, from *briller* to shine, from Italian *brillare,* from *brillo* BERYL] —'**brilliantly** *adv.*

brilliantine ('brɪljənˌtiːn) *n.* **1.** a perfumed oil used to make the hair smooth and shiny. **2.** *Chiefly U.S.* a glossy fabric made of mohair and cotton. [C19: from French, from *brillant* shining]

brim (brɪm) *n.* **1.** the upper rim of a vessel: *the brim of a cup.* **2.** a projecting rim or edge: *the brim of a hat.* **3.** the brink or edge of something. ~*vb.* **brims, brimming, brimmed. 4.** to fill or be full to the brim: *eyes brimming with tears.* [C13: from Middle High German *brem,* probably from Old Norse *barmr;* see BERM] —'**brimless** *adj.*

brimful *or* **brimfull** (ˌbrɪm'fʊl) *adj.* (*postpositive,* foll. by *of*) filled up to the brim (with).

brimmer ('brɪmə) *n.* a vessel, such as a glass or bowl, filled to the brim.

brimstone ('brɪmˌstəʊn) *n.* **1.** an obsolete name for **sulphur. 2.** a common yellow butterfly, *Gonepteryx rhamni,* of N temperate regions of the Old World: family *Pieridae.* **3.** *Archaic.* a scolding nagging woman; virago. [Old English *brynstān;* related to Old Norse *brennistein;* see BURN[1], STONE]

brindle ('brɪndᵊl) *n.* **1.** a brindled animal. **2.** a brindled colouring. [C17: back formation from BRINDLED]

brindled ('brɪndᵊld) *adj.* brown or grey streaked or patched with a darker colour: *a brindled dog.* [C17: changed from C15 *brended,* literally: branded, probably of Scandinavian origin; compare Old Norse *bröndottr;* see BRAND]

brine (braɪn) *n.* **1.** a strong solution of salt and water, used for salting and pickling meats, etc. **2.** the sea or its water. **3.** *Chem.* any solution of a salt in water: *a potassium chloride brine.* ~*vb.* **4.** (*tr.*) to soak in or treat with brine. [Old English *brīne;* related to Middle Dutch *brīne,* Old Slavonic *bridŭ* bitter, Sanskrit *bibhrāya* burnt] —'**brinish** *adj.*

brinelling ('brɪnəlɪŋ) *n.* a localized surface corrosion; a cause of damage to bearings.

Brinell number (brɪ'nel) *n.* a measure of the hardness of a material obtained by pressing a hard steel ball into its surface; it is expressed as the ratio of the load on the ball in kilograms to the area of the depression made by the ball in square millimetres. [C19: named after Johann A. *Brinell* (1849–1925), Swedish engineer]

bring (brɪŋ) *vb.* **brings, bringing, brought.** (*tr.*) **1.** to carry, convey, or take (something or someone) to a designated place or person: *bring that book to me; will you bring Jessica to Tom's party?* **2.** to cause to happen or occur to (oneself or another): *to bring disrespect on oneself.* **3.** to cause to happen as a consequence: *responsibility brings maturity.* **4.** to cause to come to mind: *it brought back memories.* **5.** to cause to be in a certain state, position, etc.: *the punch brought him to his knees.* **6.** to force, persuade, or make (oneself): *I couldn't bring myself to do it.* **7.** to sell for; fetch: *the painting brought 20 pounds.* **8.** *Law.* **a.** to institute (proceedings, charges, etc.). **b.** to put (evidence, etc.) before a tribunal. **9. bring forth.** to give birth to. **10. bring home to. a.** to convince of: *his account brought home to us the gravity of the situation.* **b.** to place the blame on. **11. bring to bear.** See **bear**[1] (sense 17). ~See also **bring about, bring down, bring forward, bring in, bring off, bring on, bring out, bring over, bring round, bring to, bring up.** [Old English *bringan;* related to Gothic *briggan,* Old High German *bringan*] —'**bringer** *n.*

bring about *vb.* (*tr., adv.*) **1.** to cause to happen: *to bring about a change in the law.* **2.** to turn (a ship) around.

bring-and-buy sale *n. Brit. and N.Z.* an informal sale, often conducted for charity, to which people bring items for sale and buy those that others have brought.

bring down *vb.* (*tr., adv.*) **1.** to cause to fall: *the fighter aircraft brought the enemy down; the ministers agreed to bring down the price of oil.* **2.** (*usually passive*) *Slang.* to cause to be elated and then suddenly depressed, as from using drugs.

bring forward *vb.* (*tr., adv.*) **1.** to present or introduce (a subject) for discussion. **2.** *Book-keeping.* to transfer (a figure representing the sum of the figures on a page or in a column) to the top of the next page or column.

bring in *vb.* (*tr., adv.*) **1.** to yield (income, profit, or cash): *his investments brought him in £100.* **2.** to produce or return (a verdict). **3.** to put forward or introduce (a legislative bill, etc.).

bringing-up *n.* another term for **upbringing.**

bring off *vb.* (*tr., adv.*) **1.** to succeed in achieving (something), esp. with difficulty or contrary to expectations: *he managed to bring off the deal.* **2.** *Taboo.* to cause to have an orgasm.

bring on *vb.* (*tr., adv.*) **1.** to induce or cause: *these pills will bring on labour.* **2.** *Taboo.* to cause sexual excitement in; stimulate.

bring out *vb.* (*tr., adv.*) **1.** to produce or publish or have published: *when are you bringing out a new dictionary?* **2.** to expose, reveal, or cause to be seen: *she brought out the best in me.* **3.** to encourage (a shy person) to be less reserved (often in the phrase **bring (someone) out of himself** *or* **herself**). **4.** *Brit.* (of a trade union, provocative action by management, misunderstanding, etc.) to cause (workers) to strike. **5.** (foll. by *in*) to cause (a person) to become covered (with spots, a rash, etc.). **6.** *Brit.* to introduce (a girl) formally into society as a debutante.

bring over *vb.* (*tr., adv.*) to cause (a person) to change allegiances.

bring round *or* **around** *vb.* (*tr., adv.*) **1.** to restore (a person) to consciousness, esp. after a faint. **2.** to convince (another person, usually an opponent) of an opinion or point of view.

bring to *vb.* (*tr.*) **1.** (*adv.*) to restore (a person) to consciousness. **2.** (*adv.*) to cause (a ship) to turn into the wind and reduce her headway. **3.** (*prep.*) to make (something) equal to (an amount of money): *that brings your bill to £17.*

bring up *vb.* (*tr., adv.*) **1.** to care for and train (a child); rear: *we had been brought up to go to church.* **2.** to raise (a subject) for discussion; mention. **3.** to vomit (food). **4.** (foll. by *against*) to cause (a person) to face or confront. **5.** (foll. by *to*) to cause (something) to be of a required standard.

brinjal ('brɪndʒəl) *n.* (in India and Africa) another name for the **aubergine.** [C17: from Portuguese *berinjela,* from Arabic; see AUBERGINE]

brink (brɪŋk) *n.* **1.** the edge, border, or verge of a steep place: *the brink of the precipice.* **2.** the highest point; top: *the sun fell below the brink of the hill.* **3.** the land at the edge of a body of water. **4.** the verge of an event or state: *the brink of disaster.* [C13: from Middle Dutch *brinc,* of Germanic origin; compare Old Norse *brekka* slope, Middle Low German *brink* edge of a field]

brinkmanship ('brɪŋkmənˌʃɪp) *n.* the art or practice of pressing a dangerous situation, esp. in international affairs, to the limit of safety and peace in order to win an advantage from a threatening or tenacious foe.

brinny ('brɪnɪ) *n. Austral. children's slang.* a stone, esp. when thrown.

briny ('braɪnɪ) *adj.* **brinier, briniest. 1.** of or resembling brine; salty. ~*n.* **2.** (preceded by *the*) an informal name for the **sea.** —'**brininess** *n.*

brio ('briːəʊ) *n.* liveliness or vigour; spirit. See also **con brio.** [C19: from Italian, of Celtic origin]

brioche ('briːəʊʃ, -ɒʃ; *French* briɔʃ) *n.* a soft roll or loaf made from a very light yeast dough, sometimes mixed with currants. [C19: from Norman dialect, from *brier* to knead, of Germanic origin; compare French *broyer* to pound, BREAK]

briolette (ˌbriːəʊ'lɛt) *n.* a pear-shaped gem cut with long triangular facets. [C19: from French, alteration of *brillolette,* from *brignolette* little dried plum, after *Brignoles,* France, where these plums are produced]

briony ('braɪənɪ) *n., pl.* **-nies.** a variant spelling of **bryony.**

briquette *or* **briquet** (brɪ'kɛt) *n.* **1.** a small brick made of compressed coal dust, sawdust, charcoal, etc., used for fuel. **2.** a small brick of any substance: *an ice-cream briquette.* ~*vb.* **3.** (*tr.*) to make into the form of a brick or bricks: *to briquette clay.* [C19: from French: a little brick, from *brique* BRICK]

bris (bris) *or* **brith** *n. Judaism.* ritual circumcision of male babies, usually at eight days old, regarded as the formal entry of the child to the Jewish community. [from Hebrew, literally: covenant]

brisance ('bri:zəns; *French* brizɑ̃s) *n.* the shattering effect or power of an explosion or explosive. [C20: from French, from *briser* to break, ultimately of Celtic origin; compare Old Irish *brissim* I break] —'**brisant** *adj.*
brise-soleil (ˌbri:zsəʊ'leɪ) *n.* a structure used in hot climates to protect a window from the sun, usually consisting of horizontal or vertical strips of wood, concrete, etc. [C20: French: break-sun, from *briser* to break + *soleil* sun]
brisk (brɪsk) *adj.* **1.** lively and quick; vigorous: *a brisk walk; trade was brisk.* **2.** invigorating or sharp: *brisk weather.* ~*vb.* **3.** (often foll. by *up*) to enliven; make or become brisk. [C16: probably variant of BRUSQUE] —'**briskly** *adv.* —'**briskness** *n.*
brisken ('brɪskən) *vb.* to make or become more lively or brisk.
brisket ('brɪskɪt) *n.* **1.** the breast of a four-legged animal. **2.** the meat from this part, esp. of beef. [C14: probably of Scandinavian origin; related to Old Norse *brjōsk* gristle, Norwegian and Danish *brusk*]
brisling ('brɪslɪŋ) *n.* another name for a **sprat**, esp. a Norwegian sprat seasoned, smoked, and canned in oil. [C20: from Norwegian; related to obsolete Danish *bretling*, German *Breitling*]
bristle ('brɪsᵊl) *n.* **1.** any short stiff hair of an animal or plant, such as any of the hairs on a pig's back. **2.** something resembling these hairs: *toothbrush bristle.* ~*vb.* **3.** (when *intr.*, often foll. by *up*) to stand up or cause to stand up like bristles: *the angry cat's fur bristled.* **4.** (*intr.*; sometimes foll. by *up*) to show anger, indignation, etc.: *she bristled at the suggestion.* **5.** (*intr.*) to be thickly covered or set: *the target bristled with arrows.* **6.** (*intr.*) to be in a state of agitation or movement: *the office was bristling with activity.* **7.** (*tr.*) to provide with a bristle or bristles. [C13 *bristil, brustel*, from earlier *brust*, from Old English *byrst*; related to Old Norse *burst*, Old High German *borst*] —'**bristly** *adj.*
bristlecone pine ('brɪsᵊlˌkəʊn) *n.* a coniferous tree, *Pinus aristata*, of the western U.S., bearing cones with bristle-like prickles: the longest-lived known tree, useful in radiocarbon dating.
bristle-grass *n.* any of various grasses of the genus *Setaria*, such as *S. viridis*, having a bristly inflorescence.
bristletail ('brɪsᵊlˌteɪl) *n.* any primitive wingless insect of the orders *Thysanura* and *Diplura*, such as the silverfish and firebrat, having a flattened body and long tail appendages.
bristle worm *n.* a popular name for a **polychaete.**
Bristol board ('brɪstᵊl) *n.* a heavy smooth cardboard of fine quality, used for printing and drawing.
Bristol fashion *adv., adj.* (*postpositive*) **1.** *Nautical.* clean and neat, with newly painted and scrubbed surfaces, brass polished, etc. **2. shipshape and Bristol fashion.** in good order; efficiently arranged.
bristols ('brɪstᵊlz) *pl. n. Brit. slang.* a woman's breasts. [C20: short for *Bristol Cities*, rhyming slang for *titties*]
brit (brɪt) *n.* (*functioning as sing. or pl.*) **1.** the young of a herring, sprat, or similar fish. **2.** minute marine crustaceans, esp. copepods, forming food for many fishes and whales. [C17: perhaps from Cornish *brȳthel* mackerel; see BRILL]
Brit (brɪt) *n. Informal.* a British person.
Brit. *abbrev. for:* **1.** Britain. **2.** British.
Britannia (brɪ'tænɪə) *n.* **1.** a female warrior carrying a trident and wearing a helmet, personifying Great Britain or the British Empire. **2.** short for **Britannia coin.**
Britannia coin *n.* any of four British gold coins introduced in 1987 for investment purposes; their denominations are £100, £50, £25, and £10.
Britannia metal *n.* an alloy of low melting point consisting of tin with 5–10 per cent antimony, 1–3 per cent copper, and sometimes small quantities of zinc, lead, or bismuth: used for decorative purposes and for bearings.
Britannic (brɪ'tænɪk) *adj.* of Britain; British (esp. in the phrases **His** *or* **Her Britannic Majesty**).
britches ('brɪtʃɪz) *pl. n.* a variant spelling of **breeches.**
brith (brit) *n.* a variant of **bris.**
Briticism ('brɪtɪˌsɪzəm) *n.* a custom, linguistic usage, or other feature peculiar to Britain or its people.
British ('brɪtɪʃ) *adj.* **1.** relating to, denoting, or characteristic of Britain or any of the natives, citizens, or inhabitants of the United Kingdom. **2.** relating to or denoting the English language as spoken and written in Britain, esp. the S dialect generally regarded as standard. See also **Southern British English, Received Pronunciation. 3.** relating to or denoting the ancient Britons. ~*n.* **4. the British.** (*functioning as pl.*) the natives or inhabitants of Britain. **5.** the extinct Celtic language of the ancient Britons. See also **Brythonic.** —'**Britishness** *n.*
British Association screw thread *n. Engineering.* a system of screw sizes designated from 0 to 25. Now superseded by standard metric sizes. Abbrev.: **BA.**
British Civil Airworthiness Requirements *pl. n.* (in Britain) documents specifying aerodynamic, engineering design, construction, and performance requirements, which must be met before an aircraft is given permission to fly.
Britisher ('brɪtɪʃə) *n.* (not used by the British) **1.** a native or inhabitant of Great Britain. **2.** any British subject.
Britishism ('brɪtɪˌʃɪzəm) *n.* a variant of **Briticism.**
British Israelite *n.* a member of a religious movement claiming that the British people are descended from the lost tribes of Israel.
British Legion *n. Brit.* an organization founded in 1921 to provide services and assistance for former members of the armed forces.
British Standard brass thread *n. Engineering.* a Whitworth screw thread having 26 threads per inch, used for thin-walled tubing and designated by the diameter of the tubing. Abbrev.: **BSB.**
British Standard fine thread *n. Engineering.* a screw thread having a Whitworth profile but a finer pitch for a given diameter. Abbrev.: **BSF.**
British Standard pipe thread *n. Engineering.* a screw thread of Whitworth profile used for piping and designated by the bore of the pipe. Abbrev.: **BSP.**
British Standards Institution *n.* an association, founded in London in 1901, that establishes and maintains standards for units of measurements, clothes sizes, technical terminology, etc., as used in Britain. Abbrev.: **BSI.** Compare **National Bureau of Standards, International Standards Organization.**
British Standard Time *n.* the standard time used in Britain all the year round from 1968 to 1971, set one hour ahead of Greenwich Mean Time and equalling Central European Time.
British Standard Whitworth thread *n.* See **Whitworth screw thread.** Abbrev.: **BSW.**
British Summer Time *n.* time set one hour ahead of Greenwich Mean Time: used in Britain from the end of March to the end of October, providing an extra hour of daylight in the evening. Abbrev.: **BST.** Compare **daylight-saving time.**
British thermal unit *n.* a unit of heat in the fps system equal to the quantity of heat required to raise the temperature of 1 pound of water by 1°F. 1 British thermal unit is equivalent to 1055.06 joules or 251.997 calories. Abbrevs.: **btu, BThU.**
British warm *n.* an army officer's short thick overcoat.
Briton ('brɪtᵊn) *n.* **1.** a native or inhabitant of Britain. **2.** a citizen of the United Kingdom. **3.** *History.* any of the early Celtic inhabitants of S Britain who were largely dispossessed by the Anglo-Saxon invaders after the 5th century A.D. [C13: from Old French *Breton*, from Latin *Britto*, of Celtic origin]
brittle ('brɪtᵊl) *adj.* **1.** easily cracked, snapped, or broken; fragile. **2.** curt or irritable: *a brittle reply.* **3.** hard or sharp in quality. ~*n.* **4.** a crunchy sweet made with treacle and nuts: *peanut brittle.* [C14: from Old English *brytel* (unattested); related to *brytsen* fragment, *brēotan* to break] —'**brittlely** *or* '**brittly** *adv.*
brittleness ('brɪtᵊlnɪs) *n.* **1.** the quality of being brittle. **2.** *Metallurgy.* the tendency of a metal to break without being significantly distorted or exposed to a high level of stress. Compare **toughness** (sense 2), **softness** (sense 2).
brittle-star *n.* any echinoderm of the class *Ophiuroidea*, occurring on the sea bottom and having five long slender arms radiating from a small central disc. See also **basket-star.**
Brittonic (brɪ'tɒnɪk) *n., adj.* another word for **Brythonic.**
britzka *or* **britska** ('brɪtskə) *n.* a long horse-drawn carriage with a folding top over the rear seat and a rear-facing front seat. [C19: from German, variant of *Britschka*, from Polish *bryczka* a little cart, from *bryka* cart]
Brix scale (brɪks) *n.* a scale for calibrating hydrometers used for measuring the concentration and density of sugar solutions at a given temperature. [C19: named after A. F. W. *Brix*, 19th-century German inventor]
BRN *international car registration for* Bahrain.
bro. (brəʊ) *abbrev. for* brother.
broach[1] (brəʊtʃ) *vb.* **1.** (*tr.*) to initiate (a topic) for discussion: *to broach a dangerous subject.* **2.** (*tr.*) to tap or pierce (a container) to draw off (a liquid): *to broach a cask; to broach wine.* **3.** (*tr.*) to open in order to begin to use: *to broach a shipment.* **4.** (*intr.*) to break the surface of the water: *the trout broached after being hooked.* **5.** (*tr.*) *Machinery.* to enlarge and finish (a hole) by reaming. ~*n.* **6.** a long tapered toothed cutting tool for enlarging holes. **7.** a spit for roasting meat, etc. **8.** a roof covering the corner triangle on the top of a square tower having an octagonal spire. **9.** a pin, forming part of some types of lock, that registers in the hollow bore of a key. **10.** a tool used for tapping casks. **11.** a less common spelling of **brooch.** [C14: from Old French *broche*, from Vulgar Latin *brocca* (unattested), from Latin *brochus* projecting] —'**broacher** *n.*
broach[2] (brəʊtʃ) *vb. Nautical.* (usually foll. by *to*) to cause (a sailing vessel) to swerve sharply and dangerously or (of a sailing vessel) to swerve sharply and dangerously in a following sea, so as to be broadside to the waves. [C18: perhaps from BROACH[1] in obsolete sense of turn on a spit]
broad (brɔ:d) *adj.* **1.** having relatively great breadth or width. **2.** of vast extent; spacious: *a broad plain.* **3.** (*postpositive*) from one side to the other: *four miles broad.* **4.** of great scope or potential: *that invention had broad applications.* **5.** not detailed; general: *broad plans.* **6.** clear and open; full (esp. in the phrase **broad daylight**). **7.** obvious or plain: *broad hints.* **8.** liberal; tolerant: *a broad political stance.* **9.** widely spread; extensive: *broad support.* **10.** outspoken or bold: *a broad manner.* **11.** vulgar; coarse; indecent: *a broad joke.* **12.** unrestrained; free: *broad laughter.* **13.** (of a dialect or pronunciation) consisting of a large number of speech sounds characteristic of a particular geographical area: *a broad Yorkshire accent.* **14.** *Finance.* denoting an assessment of liquidity as including notes and coin in circulation with the public, banks' till money and balances, most

private-sector bank deposits, and sterling bank-deposit certificates: *broad money.* Compare **narrow** (sense 7). **15.** *Phonetics.* **a.** of or relating to a type of pronunciation transcription in which symbols correspond approximately to phonemes without taking account of allophonic variations. **b. broad a.** the long vowel in English words such as *father, half,* as represented in the received pronunciation of Southern British English. **16. as broad as it is long.** amounting to the same thing; without advantage either way. ~*n.* **17.** the broad part of something. **18.** *Slang, chiefly U.S. and Canadian.* **a.** a girl or woman. **b.** a prostitute. **19.** *Brit. dialect.* a river spreading over a lowland. **20.** *East Anglia dialect.* a shallow lake. **21.** a wood-turning tool used for shaping the insides and bottoms of cylinders. ~*adv.* **22.** widely or fully: *broad awake.* [Old English *brād;* related to Old Norse *breithr,* Old Frisian *brēd,* Old High German *breit,* Gothic *braiths*] —ˈ**broadly** *adv.* —ˈ**broadness** *n.*

B-road *n.* (in Britain) a secondary road.

broad arrow *n.* **1.** a mark shaped like a broad arrowhead designating British government property and formerly used on prison clothing. **2.** an arrow with a broad head.

broadband (ˈbrɔːdˌbænd) *n.* a transmission technique using a wide range of frequencies that enables messages to be telecommunicated simultaneously. See also **baseband.**

broad bean *n.* **1.** an erect annual Eurasian bean plant, *Vicia faba,* cultivated for its large edible flattened seeds, used as a vegetable. **2.** the seed of this plant. ~Also called: **horse bean.**

broadbill (ˈbrɔːdˌbɪl) *n.* **1.** any passerine bird of the family *Eurylaimidae,* of tropical Africa and Asia, having bright plumage and a short wide bill. **2.** *U.S.* any of various wide-billed birds, such as the scaup and shoveler. **3.** *U.S.* another name for **swordfish.**

broadbrim (ˈbrɔːdˌbrɪm) *n.* a broad-brimmed hat, esp. one worn by the Quakers in the 17th century.

broadbrush (ˈbrɔːdˌbrʌʃ) *adj.* lacking full detail or information; incomplete or rough: *anything other than a broadbrush strategy for the industry will be overloaded with detail.*

broadcast (ˈbrɔːdˌkɑːst) *vb.* **-casts, -casting, -cast** *or* **-casted. 1.** to transmit (announcements or programmes) on radio or television. **2.** (*intr.*) to take part in a radio or television programme. **3.** (*tr.*) to make widely known throughout an area: *to broadcast news.* **4.** (*tr.*) to scatter (seed, etc.) over an area, esp. by hand. ~*n.* **5. a.** a transmission or programme on radio or television. **b.** (*as modifier*): *a broadcast signal.* **6. a.** the act of scattering seeds. **b.** (*as modifier*): *the broadcast method of sowing.* ~*adj.* **7.** dispersed over a wide area: *broadcast seeds.* ~*adv.* **8.** far and wide: *seeds to be sown broadcast.* —ˈ**broadˌcaster** *n.* —ˈ**broadˌcasting** *n.*

Broad Church *n.* **1.** a party within the Church of England which favours a broad and liberal interpretation of Anglican formularies and rubrics and objects to positive definition in theology. Compare **High Church, Low Church.** ~*adj.* **Broad-Church. 2.** of or relating to this party.

broadcloth (ˈbrɔːdˌklɒθ) *n.* **1.** fabric woven on a wide loom. **2.** a closely woven fabric of wool, worsted, cotton, or rayon with lustrous finish, used for clothing.

broaden (ˈbrɔːdᵊn) *vb.* to make or become broad or broader; widen.

broad gauge *n.* **1.** a railway track with a greater distance between the lines than the standard gauge of 56½ inches (about 1.44 metres) used now by most mainline railway systems. ~*adj.* **broad-gauge. 2.** of, relating to, or denoting a railway having this track.

broad jump *n.* the usual U.S. and Canadian term for **long jump.**

broadleaf (ˈbrɔːdˌliːf) *n., pl.* **-leaves.** any tobacco plant having broad leaves, used esp. in making cigars.

broad-leaved *adj.* denoting trees other than conifers; having broad rather than needleshaped leaves.

broadloom (ˈbrɔːdˌluːm) *n.* (*modifier*) of or designating carpets or carpeting woven on a wide loom to obviate the need for seams.

broad-minded *adj.* **1.** tolerant of opposing viewpoints; not prejudiced; liberal. **2.** not easily shocked by permissive sexual habits, pornography, etc. —ˌ**broad-ˈmindedly** *adv.* —ˌ**broad-ˈmindedness** *n.*

broad seal *n.* the official seal of a nation and its government.

broadsheet (ˈbrɔːdˌʃiːt) *n.* **1.** a newspaper having a large format, approximately 15 by 24 inches (38 by 61 centimetres). Compare **tabloid. 2.** another word for **broadside** (sense 4).

broadside (ˈbrɔːdˌsaɪd) *n.* **1.** *Nautical.* the entire side of a vessel, from stem to stern and from waterline to rail. **2.** *Naval.* **a.** all the armament fired from one side of a warship. **b.** the simultaneous discharge of such armament. **3.** a strong or abusive verbal or written attack. **4.** Also called: **broadside ballad.** a ballad or popular song printed on one side of a sheet of paper and sold by hawkers, esp. in 16th-century England. **5.** any standard size of paper before cutting or folding: *demy broadside.* **6.** another name for **broadsheet** (sense 1). **7.** a large flat surface: *the broadside of the barn.* ~*adv.* **8.** with a broader side facing an object; sideways: *the train hit the lorry broadside.*

broad-spectrum *n.* (*modifier*) effective against a wide variety of diseases or microorganisms: *a broad-spectrum antibiotic.*

broadsword (ˈbrɔːdˌsɔːd) *n.* a broad-bladed sword used for cutting rather than stabbing. Also called: **backsword.**

broadtail (ˈbrɔːdˌteɪl) *n.* **1.** the highly valued black wavy fur obtained from the skins of newly born karakul lambs; caracul. **2.** another name for **karakul.**

Broadway (ˈbrɔːdˌweɪ) *adj.* of or relating to or suitable for the commercial theatre, esp. on Broadway, the thoroughfare in New York City famous for its theatres.

Brobdingnagian (ˌbrɒbdɪŋˈnægɪən) *adj.* gigantic; huge; immense. [C18: from *Brobdingnag,* an imaginary country of giants in Swift's *Gulliver's Travels* (1726)]

brocade (brəʊˈkeɪd) *n.* **1. a.** a rich fabric woven with a raised design, often using gold or silver threads. **b.** (*as modifier*): *brocade curtains.* ~*vb.* **2.** (*tr.*) to weave with such a design. [C17: from Spanish *brocado,* from Italian *broccato* embossed fabric, from *brocco* spike, from Latin *brochus* projecting; see BROACH]

Broca's area *or* **centre** (ˈbrɒkəz) *n.* the region of the cerebral cortex of the brain concerned with speech; the speech centre. [C19: named after Paul *Broca* (1824–80), French surgeon]

brocatelle *or U.S.* **brocatel** (ˌbrɒkəˈtɛl) *n.* **1.** a heavy brocade with the design in deep relief, used chiefly in upholstery. **2.** a type of variegated marble from France and Italy. [C17: from French, from Italian *broccatello,* diminutive of *broccato* BROCADE]

broccoli (ˈbrɒkəlɪ) *n.* **1.** a cultivated variety of cabbage, *Brassica oleracea italica,* having branched greenish flower heads. **2.** the flower head of this plant, eaten as a vegetable before the buds have opened. **3.** a variety of this plant that does not form a head, whose stalks are eaten as a vegetable. [C17: from Italian, plural of *broccolo* a little sprout, from *brocco* sprout, spike; see BROCADE]

broch (brɒk, brɒx) *n.* (in Scotland) a circular dry-stone tower large enough to serve as a fortified home; they date from the Iron Age and are found esp. in the north and the islands. [C17: from Old Norse *borg;* related to Old English *burh* settlement, burgh]

broché (brəʊˈʃeɪ; *French* brɔʃe) *adj.* woven with a raised design, as brocade. [C19: from French *brocher* to brocade, stitch; see BROACH]

brochette (brɒˈʃɛt; *French* brɔʃɛt) *n.* a skewer or small spit, used for holding pieces of meat, etc., while roasting or grilling. [C19: from Old French *brochete* small pointed tool; see BROACH]

brocho (ˈbrɒxɔ) *n.* a variant of **brachah.**

brochure (ˈbrəʊʃjʊə, -ʃə) *n.* a pamphlet or booklet, esp. one containing summarized or introductory information or advertising. [C18: from French, from *brocher* to stitch (a book)]

brock (brɒk) *n.* a Brit. name for **badger** (sense 1): used esp. as a form of address in stories, etc. [Old English *broc,* of Celtic origin; compare Welsh *broch*]

Brocken Bow *or* **Brocken Spectre** (*German* ˈbrɔkən) *n.* an atmospheric phenomenon in which an observer, when the sun is low, may see his enlarged shadow against the clouds, often surrounded by coloured lights. [named after the *Brocken* mountain in central Germany]

brocket (ˈbrɒkɪt) *n.* any small deer of the genus *Mazama,* of tropical America, having small unbranched antlers. [C15: from Anglo-French *broquet,* from *broque* horn, from Vulgar Latin *brocca* (unattested); see BROACH]

broddle (ˈbrɒdᵊl) *vb.* (*tr.*) *Yorkshire dialect.* to poke or pierce (something). [perhaps from BRADAWL]

broderie anglaise (ˌbrəʊdəriː ɑːŋˈglɛz) *n.* open embroidery on white cotton, fine linen, etc. [C19: French: English embroidery]

brog (brɒg, brɔːg, brog) *n. Scot.* a bradawl. [C19: of uncertain origin]

brogan (ˈbrəʊgən) *n.* a heavy laced usually ankle-high work boot. [C19: from Gaelic *brōgan* a little shoe, from *brōg* shoe; see BROGUE[2]]

brogue[1] (brəʊg) *n.* a broad gentle-sounding dialectal accent, esp. that used by the Irish in speaking English. [C18: probably from BROGUE[2], alluding to the footwear of the peasantry]

brogue[2] (brəʊg) *n.* **1.** a sturdy walking shoe, often with ornamental perforations. **2.** an untanned shoe worn formerly in Ireland and Scotland. [C16: from Irish Gaelic *bróg* boot, shoe, probably from Old Norse *brōk* leg covering]

broider (ˈbrɔɪdə) *vb.* (*tr.*) an archaic word for **embroider.** [C15: from Old French *brosder,* of Germanic origin; see EMBROIDER]

broil[1] (brɔɪl) *vb.* **1.** the usual U.S. and Canadian word for **grill**[1] (sense 1). **2.** to become or cause to become extremely hot. **3.** (*intr.*) to be furious. ~*n.* **4.** the process of broiling. **5.** something broiled. [C14: from Old French *bruillir* to burn, of uncertain origin]

broil[2] (brɔɪl) *Archaic.* ~*n.* **1.** a loud quarrel or disturbance; brawl. ~*vb.* **2.** (*intr.*) to brawl; quarrel. [C16: from Old French *brouiller* to mix, from *breu* broth; see BREWIS, BROSE]

broiler (ˈbrɔɪlə) *n.* **1.** a young tender chicken suitable for roasting. **2.** *Chiefly U.S.* a pan, grate, etc. for broiling food. **3.** a very hot day.

broiler house *n.* a building in which broiler chickens are reared in confined conditions.

broke (brəʊk) *vb.* **1.** the past tense of **break.** ~*adj.* **2.** *Informal.* having no money; bankrupt. **3. go for broke.** *Slang.* to risk everything in a gambling or other venture.

broken (ˈbrəʊkən) *vb.* **1.** the past participle of **break.** ~*adj.* **2.** fractured, smashed, or splintered: *a broken vase.* **3.** imperfect or incomplete; fragmentary: *a broken set of books.* **4.** interrupted;

disturbed; disconnected: *broken sleep.* **5.** intermittent or discontinuous: *broken sunshine.* **6.** varying in direction or intensity, as of pitch: *a broken note; a broken run.* **7.** not functioning: *a broken radio.* **8.** spoilt or ruined by divorce (esp. in the phrases **broken home, broken marriage**). **9.** (of a trust, promise, contract, etc.) violated; infringed. **10.** overcome with grief or disappointment: *a broken heart.* **11.** (of the speech of a foreigner) imperfect in grammar, vocabulary, and pronunciation: *broken English.* **12.** Also: **broken-in.** made tame or disciplined by training: *a broken horse; a broken recruit.* **13.** exhausted or weakened as through ill-health or misfortune. **14.** confused or disorganized: *broken ranks of soldiers.* **15.** breached or opened: *broken defensive lines.* **16.** irregular or rough; uneven: *broken ground.* **17.** bankrupt or out of money: *a broken industry.* **18.** (of colour) having a multicoloured decorative effect, as by stippling paint onto a surface. —**'brokenly** *adv.*

broken chord *n. Music.* a chord played as an arpeggio.

broken consort *n.* See **consort** (sense 4).

broken-down *adj.* **1.** worn out, as by age or long use; dilapidated: *a broken-down fence.* **2.** not in working order: *a broken-down tractor.* **3.** physically or mentally ill.

brokenhearted (ˌbrəʊkən'hɑːtɪd) *adj.* overwhelmed by grief or disappointment. —ˌ**broken'heartedly** *adv.* —ˌ**broken'heartedness** *n.*

broken wind (wɪnd) *n. Vet. science.* another name for **heaves** (sense 1).

broker ('brəʊkə) *n.* **1.** an agent who, acting on behalf of a principal, buys or sells goods, securities, etc., in return for a commission: *insurance broker.* **2.** short for **stockbroker.** **3.** a dealer in second-hand goods. ~*vb.* **4.** to act as a broker (in). [C14: from Anglo-French *brocour* broacher (of casks, hence, one who sells, agent), from Old Northern French *broquier* to tap a cask, from *broque* tap of a cask; see BROACH]

brokerage ('brəʊkərɪdʒ) *n.* **1.** commission charged by a broker to his principals. **2.** a broker's business or office.

broking ('brəʊkɪŋ) *adj.* **1.** acting as a broker. ~*n.* **2.** the business of a broker. [C16: from obsolete verb *broke;* see BROKER]

brolga ('brɒlgə) *n.* a large grey Australian crane, *Grus rubicunda,* having a red-and-green head and a trumpeting call. Also called: **Australian crane, native companion.** [C19: from a native Australian language]

brolly ('brɒlɪ) *n., pl.* **-lies.** an informal Brit. name for **umbrella** (sense 1).

bromal ('brəʊməl) *n.* a yellowish oily synthetic liquid used medicinally as a sedative and hypnotic; tribromoacetaldehyde. Formula: Br_3CCHO. [C19: from BROM(INE) + AL(COHOL)]

bromate ('brəʊmeɪt) *n.* **1.** any salt or ester of bromic acid, containing the monovalent group $-BrO_3$ or ion BrO_3^-. ~*vb.* **2.** another word for **brominate.** [C19: probably from German *Bromat;* see BROMO-, -ATE[1]]

brome grass *or* **brome** (brəʊm) *n.* any of various grasses of the genus *Bromus,* having small flower spikes in loose drooping clusters. Some species are used for hay. [C18: via Latin from Greek *bromos* oats, of obscure origin]

bromeliad (brəʊ'miːlɪˌæd) *n.* any plant of the tropical American family *Bromeliaceae,* typically epiphytes with a rosette of fleshy leaves. The family includes the pineapple and Spanish moss. [C19: from New Latin *Bromelia* type genus, after Olaf *Bromelius* (1639–1705), Swedish botanist] —**broˌmeli'aceous** *adj.*

bromeosin (brəʊ'miːəsɪn) *n. Chem.* another name for **eosin.** [C20: from BROMO- + EOSIN]

bromic ('brəʊmɪk) *adj.* of or containing bromine in the trivalent or pentavalent state.

bromic acid *n.* a colourless unstable water-soluble liquid used as an oxidizing agent in the manufacture of dyes and pharmaceuticals. Formula: $HBrO_3$.

bromide ('brəʊmaɪd) *n.* **1.** any salt of hydrobromic acid, containing the monovalent ion Br^- (**bromide ion**). **2.** any compound containing a bromine atom, such as methyl bromide. **3.** a dose of sodium or potassium bromide given as a sedative. **4.** **a.** a trite saying; platitude. **b.** a dull or boring person. [C19, C20 (cliché): from BROM(INE) + -IDE]

bromide paper *n.* a type of photographic paper coated with an emulsion of silver bromide usually containing a small quantity of silver iodide.

bromidic (brəʊ'mɪdɪk) *adj.* ordinary; dull.

brominate ('brəʊmɪˌneɪt) *vb.* to treat or react with bromine. Also: **bromate.** —ˌ**bromin'ation** *n.*

bromine ('brəʊmiːn, -mɪn) *n.* a pungent dark red volatile liquid element of the halogen series that occurs in brine and is used in the production of chemicals, esp. ethylene dibromide. Symbol: Br; atomic no.: 35; atomic wt.: 79.91; valency: 1, 3, 5, or 7; relative density 3.12; density (gas): 7.59 kg/m^3; melting pt.: −7.2°C; boiling pt.: 58.78°C. [C19: from French *brome* bromine, from Greek *brōmos* bad smell + -INE[2], of uncertain origin]

bromism ('brəʊˌmɪzəm) *or U.S.* **brominism** *n.* poisoning caused by the excessive intake of bromine or compounds containing bromine.

bromo- *or before a vowel* **brom-** *combining form.* indicating the presence of bromine: *bromoform.*

bromoform ('brəʊməˌfɔːm) *n.* a heavy colourless liquid substance with a sweetish taste and an odour resembling that of chloroform. Systematic name: **tribromomethane.** Formula: $CHBr_3$.

bronchi ('brɒŋkaɪ) *n.* the plural of **bronchus.**

bronchia ('brɒŋkɪə) *pl. n.* another name for **bronchial tubes.** [C17: from Late Latin, from Greek *bronkhia,* plural of *bronkhion,* diminutive of *bronkhus* windpipe, throat]

bronchial ('brɒŋkɪəl) *adj.* of or relating to the bronchi or the bronchial tubes. —**'bronchially** *adv.*

bronchial tubes *pl. n.* the bronchi or their smaller divisions.

bronchiectasis (ˌbrɒŋkɪ'ɛktəsɪs) *n.* chronic dilation of the bronchi or bronchial tubes, which often become infected. [C19: from BRONCHO- + Greek *ektasis* a stretching]

bronchiole ('brɒŋkɪˌəʊl) *n.* any of the smallest bronchial tubes, usually ending in alveoli. [C19: from New Latin *bronchiolum,* diminutive of Late Latin *bronchium,* singular of BRONCHIA] —**bronchiolar** (ˌbrɒŋkɪ'əʊlə) *adj.*

bronchitis (brɒŋ'kaɪtɪs) *n.* inflammation of the bronchial tubes, characterized by coughing, difficulty in breathing, etc., caused by infection or irritation of the respiratory tract. —**bronchitic** (brɒŋ'kɪtɪk) *adj., n.*

broncho- *or before a vowel* **bronch-** *combining form.* indicating or relating to the bronchi: *bronchitis.* [from Greek: BRONCHUS]

bronchodilator ('brɒŋkəʊdaɪˌleɪtə) *n.* any drug or other agent that causes dilation of the bronchial tubes by relaxing bronchial muscle: used, esp. in the form of aerosol sprays, for the relief of asthma and chronic bronchitis.

bronchography (brɒŋ'kɒgrəfɪ) *n.* radiography of the bronchial tubes after the introduction of a radiopaque medium into the bronchi.

bronchopneumonia (ˌbrɒŋkəʊnjuː'məʊnɪə) *n.* inflammation of the lungs, originating in the bronchioles.

bronchoscope ('brɒŋkəˌskəʊp) *n.* an instrument for examining and providing access to the interior of the bronchial tubes. —**bronchoscopic** (ˌbrɒŋkə'skɒpɪk) *adj.* —**bronchoscopist** (brɒŋ'kɒskəpɪst) *n.* —**bron'choscopy** *n.*

bronchus ('brɒŋkəs) *n., pl.* **-chi** (-kaɪ). either of the two main branches of the trachea, which contain cartilage within their walls. [C18: from New Latin, from Greek *bronkhos* windpipe]

bronco *or* **broncho** ('brɒŋkəʊ) *n., pl.* **-cos** *or* **-chos.** (in the U.S. and Canada) a wild or partially tamed pony or mustang of the western plains. [C19: from Mexican Spanish, short for Spanish *potro bronco* unbroken colt, probably from Latin *broccus* projecting (as knots on wood), hence, rough, wild]

broncobuster ('brɒŋkəʊˌbʌstə) *n.* (in the western U.S. and Canada) a cowboy who breaks in broncos or wild horses.

brontosaurus (ˌbrɒntə'sɔːrəs) *or* **brontosaur** ('brɒntəˌsɔː) *n.* any very large herbivorous quadrupedal dinosaur of the genus *Apatosaurus,* common in North America during Jurassic times, having a long neck and long tail: suborder *Sauropoda* (sauropods). [C19: from New Latin, from Greek *brontē* thunder + *sauros* lizard]

Bronx cheer (brɒŋks) *n. Chiefly U.S.* a loud noise, imitating a fart, made with the lips and tongue and expressing derision or contempt; raspberry. [C20: named after the *Bronx,* a borough of New York City]

bronze (brɒnz) *n.* **1. a.** any hard water-resistant alloy consisting of copper and smaller proportions of tin and sometimes zinc and lead. **b.** any similar copper alloy containing other elements in place of tin, such as aluminium bronze, beryllium bronze, etc. See also **phosphor bronze, gunmetal.** Compare **brass** (sense 1). **2.** a yellowish-brown colour or pigment. **3.** a statue, medal, or other object made of bronze. **4.** short for **bronze medal.** ~*adj.* **5.** made of or resembling bronze. **6.** of a yellowish-brown colour: *a bronze skin.* ~*vb.* **7.** (esp. of the skin) to make or become brown; tan. **8.** (*tr.*) to give the appearance of bronze to. [C18: from French, from Italian *bronzo,* perhaps ultimately from Latin *Brundisium* Brindisi, famed for its bronze] —**'bronzy** *adj.*

Bronze Age *n. Archaeol.* **a.** a technological stage between the Stone and Iron Ages, beginning in the Middle East about 4500 B.C. and lasting in Britain from about 2000 to 500 B.C., during which weapons and tools were made of bronze and there was intensive trading. **b.** (*as modifier*): *a Bronze-Age tool.*

bronze medal *n.* a medal of bronze, awarded to a competitor who comes third in a contest or race. Compare **gold medal, silver medal.**

bronzing ('brɒnzɪŋ) *n. Building trades.* **1.** blue pigment producing a metallic lustre when ground into paint media at fairly high concentrations. **2.** the application of a mixture of powdered metal or pigments of a metallic lustre, and a binding medium, such as gold size, to a surface.

bronzite ('brɒnzaɪt) *n.* a type of orthopyroxene often having a metallic sheen.

brooch (brəʊtʃ) *n.* an ornament with a hinged pin and catch, worn fastened to clothing. [C13: from Old French *broche;* see BROACH]

brood (bruːd) *n.* **1.** a number of young animals, esp. birds, produced at one hatching. **2.** all the offspring in one family: often used jokingly or contemptuously. **3.** a group of a particular kind; breed. **4.** (*as modifier*) kept for breeding: *a brood mare.* ~*vb.* **5.** (of a bird) **a.** to sit on or hatch (eggs). **b.** (*tr.*) to cover (young birds) protectively with the wings. **6.** (when *intr.,* often foll. by *on, over,* or *upon*) to ponder morbidly or persistently. [Old English *brōd;* related to Middle High German *bruot,* Dutch *broed;* see BREED] —**'brooding** *n., adj.* —**'broodingly** *adv.*

brooder ('bru:də) *n.* **1.** an enclosure or other structure, usually heated, used for rearing young chickens or other fowl. **2.** a person or thing that broods.
brood pouch *n.* **1.** a pouch or cavity in certain animals, such as frogs and fishes, in which their eggs develop and hatch. **2.** another name for **marsupium.**
broody ('bru:dɪ) *adj.* **broodier, broodiest. 1.** moody; meditative; introspective. **2.** (of poultry) wishing to sit on or hatch eggs. **3.** *Informal.* (of a woman) wishing to have a baby of her own. —'**broodiness** *n.*
brook[1] (brʊk) *n.* a natural freshwater stream smaller than a river. [Old English *brōc;* related to Old High German *bruoh* swamp, Dutch *broek*]
brook[2] (brʊk) *vb.* (*tr.*) (*usually used with a negative*) to bear; tolerate. [Old English *brūcan;* related to Gothic *brūkjan* to use, Old High German *brūhhan,* Latin *fruī* to enjoy] —'**brookable** *adj.*
brookite ('brʊkaɪt) *n.* a reddish-brown to black mineral consisting of titanium oxide in orthorhombic crystalline form: occurs in silica veins. Formula: TiO_2. [C19: named after Henry J. *Brooke* (died 1857), English mineralogist]
brooklet ('brʊklɪt) *n.* a small brook.
brooklime ('brʊk,laɪm) *n.* either of two blue-flowered scrophulariaceous trailing plants, *Veronica americana* of North America or *V. beccabunga* of Europe and Asia, growing in moist places. See also **speedwell.** [C16: variant of C15 *brokelemk* speedwell, from BROOK[1] + *-lemk,* from Old English *hleomoce;* influenced by *lime*]
brook trout *n.* a North American freshwater trout, *Salvelinus fontinalis,* introduced in Europe and valued as a food and game fish. Also called: **speckled trout.**
brookweed ('brʊk,wi:d) *n.* either of two white-flowered primulaceous plants, *Samolus valerandi* of Europe or *S. floribundus* of North America, growing in moist places. Also called: **water pimpernel.** See also **pimpernel.**
broom (bru:m, brʊm) *n.* **1.** an implement for sweeping consisting of a long handle to which is attached either a brush of straw, bristles, or twigs, bound together, or a solid head into which are set tufts of bristles or fibres. **2.** any of various yellow-flowered Eurasian papilionaceous shrubs of the genera *Cytisus* and *Sarothamnus,* esp. *S. scoparius.* **3.** any of various similar Eurasian plants of the related genera *Genista* and *Spartium.* **4. new broom.** a newly appointed official, etc., eager to make changes. ~*vb.* **5.** (*tr.*) to sweep with a broom. [Old English *brōm;* related to Old High German *brāmo,* Middle Dutch *bremme*]
broomcorn ('bru:m,kɔ:n, 'brʊm-) *n.* a variety of sorghum, *Sorghum vulgare technicum,* the long stiff flower stalks of which have been used for making brooms.
broomie ('bru:mɪ) *n. Austral. and N.Z. informal.* a person who sweeps the board in a shearing shed. Also called: **sweepo.**
broomrape ('bru:m,reɪp, 'brʊm-) *n.* any orobanchaceous plant of the genus *Orobanche:* brownish small-flowered leafless parasites on the roots of other plants, esp. on broom. [C16: adaptation and partial translation of Medieval Latin *rāpum genistae* tuber (hence: root nodule) of Genista (a type of broom plant); compare PLANTAGENET]
broomstick ('bru:m,stɪk, 'brʊm-) *n.* the long handle of a broom.
bros. *or* **Bros.** *abbrev. for* brothers.
brose (brəʊz) *n. Scot.* oatmeal or pease porridge, sometimes with butter or fat added. See also **Atholl brose.** [C13 *broys,* from Old French *broez,* from *breu* broth, of Germanic origin]
broth (brɒθ) *n.* **1.** a soup made by boiling meat, fish, vegetables, etc., in water. **2.** another name for **stock** (sense 19). [Old English *broth;* related to Old Norse *broth,* Old High German *brod,* German *brodeln* to boil; see BREW]
brothel ('brɒθəl) *n.* **1.** a house or other place where men pay to have sexual intercourse with prostitutes. **2.** *Austral. informal.* any untidy or messy place. [C16: short for *brothel-house,* from C14 *brothel* useless person, from Old English *brēothan* to deteriorate; related to *briethel* worthless]
brother ('brʌðə) *n., pl.* **brothers** *or* (*Archaic except when referring to fellow members of a religion, sect, society, etc.*) **brethren. 1.** a male person having the same parents as another person. **2.** short for **half-brother** or **stepbrother. 3. a.** a male person belonging to the same group, profession, nationality, trade union, etc., as another or others; fellow member. **b.** (*as modifier*): *brother workers.* **4.** comrade; friend: used as a form of address. **5.** *Christianity.* **a.** a member of a male religious order who undertakes work for the order without actually being in holy orders. **b.** a lay member of a male religious order. ~Related adj.: **fraternal.** ~*interj.* **6.** *Slang.* an exclamation of amazement, disgust, surprise, disappointment, etc. [Old English *brōthor;* related to Old Norse *brōthir,* Old High German *bruoder,* Latin *frāter,* Greek *phratēr,* Sanskrit *bhrātar*]
brotherhood ('brʌðə,hʊd) *n.* **1.** the state of being related as a brother or brothers. **2.** an association or fellowship, such as a trade union. **3.** all persons engaged in a particular profession, trade, etc. **4.** the belief, feeling, or hope that all men should regard and treat one another as brothers.
brother-in-law *n., pl.* **brothers-in-law. 1.** the brother of one's wife or husband. **2.** the husband of one's sister.
Brother Jonathan *n. Archaic.* the government or people of the United States. [C19: perhaps originally applied to a New Englander (perhaps alluding to the many Old Testament names among New England settlers)]
brotherly ('brʌðəlɪ) *adj.* **1.** of, resembling, or suitable to a brother, esp. in showing loyalty and affection; fraternal. ~*adv.* **2.** in a brotherly way; fraternally. —'**brotherliness** *n.*
brougham ('bru:əm, bru:m) *n.* **1.** a four-wheeled horse-drawn closed carriage having a raised open driver's seat in front. **2.** *Obsolete.* a large car with an open compartment at the front for the driver. **3.** *Obsolete.* an early electric car. [C19: named after Henry Peter, Lord *Brougham* (1778–1868)]
brought (brɔ:t) *vb.* the past tense and past participle of **bring.**
broughta ('brɔ:tə) *or* **broughtas** ('brɔ:təs) *n.* variants of **braata.**
brouhaha ('bru:hɑ:hɑ:) *n.* a loud confused noise; commotion; uproar. [French, of imitative origin]
brow (braʊ) *n.* **1.** the part of the face from the eyes to the hairline; forehead. **2.** short for **eyebrow. 3.** the expression of the face; countenance: *a troubled brow.* **4.** the top of a mine shaft; pithead. **5.** the jutting top of a hill, etc. **6.** *Northern English dialect.* a steep slope on a road. [Old English *brū;* related to Old Norse *brūn* eyebrow, Lithuanian *bruvis,* Greek *ophrus,* Sanskrit *bhrūs*]
browband ('braʊ,bænd) *n.* the strap of a horse's bridle that goes across the forehead.
browbeat ('braʊ,bi:t) *vb.* **-beats, -beating, -beat, -beaten.** (*tr.*) to discourage or frighten with threats or a domineering manner; intimidate. —'**brow,beater** *n.*
-browed *adj.* (*in combination*) having a brow or brows as specified: *dark-browed.*
brown (braʊn) *n.* **1.** any of various colours, such as those of wood or earth, produced by low intensity light in the wavelength range 620–585 nanometres. **2.** a dye or pigment producing these colours. **3.** brown cloth or clothing: *dressed in brown.* **4.** any of numerous mostly reddish-brown butterflies of the genera *Maniola, Lasiommata,* etc., such as *M. jurtina* (**meadow brown**): family *Satyridae.* ~*adj.* **5.** of the colour brown. **6.** (of bread) made from a flour that has not been bleached or bolted, such as wheatmeal or wholemeal flour. **7.** deeply tanned or sunburnt. ~*vb.* **8.** to make (esp. food as a result of cooking) brown or (esp. of food) to become brown. [Old English *brūn;* related to Old Norse *brūnn,* Old High German *brūn,* Greek *phrunos* toad, Sanskrit *babhru* reddish-brown] —'**brownish** *or* '**browny** *adj.* —'**brownness** *n.*
brown algae *pl. n.* any algae of the family *Phaeophyceae,* such as the wracks and kelps, which contain a brown pigment in addition to chlorophyll.
brown bear *n.* a large ferocious brownish bear, *Ursus arctos,* inhabiting temperate forests of North America, Europe, and Asia. See also **grizzly bear, Kodiak bear.**
brown bomber *n. Austral. informal.* a parking policeman in New South Wales. [from former khaki-coloured uniform]
brown coal *n.* another name for **lignite.**
brown creeper *n.* a small bush bird, *Finschia novaeseelandiae,* of South Island, New Zealand. Also called: **bush canary.**
brown dwarf *n.* a type of celestial body midway in size between a large planet and a small star, thought to be one possible explanation of dark matter in the universe.
brown earth *n.* an intrazonal soil of temperate humid regions typically developed under deciduous forest into a dark rich layer (mull): characteristic of much of southern and central England.
browned-off *adj. Informal.* thoroughly discouraged or disheartened; fed up.
brown fat *n.* tissue composed of a type of fat cell that dissipates as heat most of the energy released when food is oxidized; brown adipose tissue. It is present in hibernating animals and human babies and is thought to be important in adult weight control.
brown goods *pl. n. Marketing.* consumer goods such as televisions, radios, or videos. Compare **white goods** (sense 2).
Brownian movement ('braʊnɪən) *n.* random movement of microscopic particles suspended in a fluid, caused by bombardment of the particles by molecules of the fluid. First observed in 1827, it provided strong evidence in support of the kinetic theory of molecules. [C19: named after Robert *Brown* (1773–1858), Scottish botanist]
brownie ('braʊnɪ) *n.* **1.** (in folklore) an elf said to do helpful work at night, esp. household chores. **2.** a small square nutty chocolate cake. **3.** *Austral.* a bread made with currants. [C16: diminutive of BROWN (that is, a small brown man)]
Brownie ('braʊnɪ) *n.* **1.** another name for **Brownie Guide. 2.** *Trademark.* (formerly) a popular make of simple box camera.
Brownie Guide *or* **Brownie** ('braʊnɪ) *n.* a member of the junior branch of the Guides.
Brownie Guider *n.* the adult leader of a pack of Brownie Guides. Former name: **Brown Owl.**
Brownie point *n.* a notional mark to one's credit earned for being seen to do the right thing. [C20: from the mistaken notion that Brownie Guides earn points for good deeds]
browning ('braʊnɪŋ) *n. Brit.* a substance used to darken soups, gravies, etc.
Browning ('braʊnɪŋ) *n.* **1.** Also called: **Browning automatic rifle.** a portable gas-operated air-cooled automatic rifle using .30 calibre ammunition and capable of firing between 200 and 350 rounds per minute. Abbrev.: **BAR. 2.** Also called: **Browning machine gun.** a water-cooled automatic machine gun using .30

or .50 calibre ammunition and capable of firing over 500 rounds per minute. [C20: named after John M. *Browning* (1855–1926), American designer of firearms]

Brownist ('braʊnɪst) *n.* a person who supported the principles of church government advocated by Robert Browne and adopted in modified form by the Independents or Congregationalists. [C16: named after Robert *Browne* (?1550–1633), English Puritan] —'**Brownism** *n.*

brown lung disease *n.* another name for **byssinosis.**

brown-nose ('braʊn,nəʊz) *Taboo slang.* ~*vb.* **1.** to be abjectly subservient (to); curry favour (with). ~*n.* **2.** an abjectly subservient person; sycophant. [C20: from the notion that a subservient person kisses the backside of the person with whom he is currying favour]

brownout ('braʊn,aʊt) *n. Chiefly U.S.* **1.** a dimming or reduction in the use of electric lights in a city, esp. to conserve electric power or as a defensive precaution in wartime. **2.** a temporary reduction in electrical power. Compare **blackout** (sense 3).

brown owl *n.* another name for **tawny owl.**

Brown Owl *n.* a name (no longer in official use) for **Brownie Guider.**

brown paper *n.* a coarse unbleached paper used for wrapping.

brown rat *n.* a common brownish rat, *Rattus norvegicus:* a serious pest in all parts of the world. Also called: **Norway rat.**

brown rice *n.* unpolished rice, in which the grains retain the outer yellowish-brown layer (bran).

brown rot *n.* **1.** a disease of apples, peaches, etc., caused by fungi of the genus *Sclerotinia* and characterized by yellowish-brown masses of spores on the plant surface. **2.** decay of timber caused by the action of fungi on the cellulose.

brown seaweed *n.* another term for **brown algae.**

Brown Shirt *n.* **1.** (in Nazi Germany) a storm trooper. **2.** a member of any fascist party or group.

brown snake *n. Austral.* any of various common venomous snakes of the genus *Pseudonaja.*

brown-state *adj.* (of linen and lace fabrics) undyed.

brownstone ('braʊn,stəʊn) *n. U.S.* **1.** a reddish-brown iron-rich sandstone used for building. **2.** a house built of or faced with this stone.

brown study *n.* a mood of deep absorption or thoughtfulness; reverie.

brown sugar *n.* sugar that is unrefined or only partially refined.

brown-tail moth *n.* a small brown-and-white European moth, *Euproctis phaeorrhoea,* naturalized in the eastern U.S. where it causes damage to shade trees: family *Lymantriidae* (or *Liparidae*). See also **tussock moth.**

brown trout *n.* a common brownish variety of the trout *Salmo trutta* that occurs in the rivers of N Europe and has been successfully introduced in North America. Compare **sea trout** (sense 1).

browse (braʊz) *vb.* **1.** to look through (a book, articles for sale in a shop, etc.) in a casual leisurely manner. **2.** (of deer, goats, etc.) to feed upon (vegetation) by continual nibbling. ~*n.* **3.** the act or an instance of browsing. **4.** the young twigs, shoots, leaves, etc., on which certain animals feed. [C15: from French *broust, brost* (modern French *brout*) bud, of Germanic origin; compare Old Saxon *brustian* to bud] —'**browser** *n.*

BRS *abbrev. for* British Road Services.

Bruce (bru:s) *n. Brit.* a jocular name for an Australian man.

brucellosis (,bru:sɪ'ləʊsɪs) *n.* an infectious disease of cattle, goats, and pigs, caused by bacteria of the genus *Brucella* and transmittable to man (e.g. by drinking contaminated milk): symptoms include fever, chills, and severe headache. Also called: **undulant fever.** [C20: from New Latin *Brucella,* named after Sir David *Bruce* (1855–1931), Australian bacteriologist and physician]

brucine ('bru:si:n, -sin) *n.* a bitter poisonous alkaloid resembling strychnine and obtained from the tree *Strychnos nuxvomica:* used mainly in the denaturation of alcohol. Formula: $C_{23}H_{26}N_2O_4$. [C19: named after James *Bruce* (1730–94), Scottish explorer of Africa]

bruin ('bru:ɪn) *n.* a name for a bear, used in children's tales, fables, etc. [C17: from Dutch *bruin* brown, the name of the bear in the epic *Reynard the Fox*]

bruise (bru:z) *vb.* (*mainly tr.*) **1.** (*also intr.*) to injure (tissues) without breaking the skin, usually with discoloration, or (of tissues) to be injured in this way. **2.** to offend or injure (someone's feelings) by an insult, unkindness, etc. **3.** to damage the surface of (something), as by a blow. **4.** to crush (food, etc.) by pounding or pressing. ~*n.* **5.** a bodily injury without a break in the skin, usually with discoloration; contusion. [Old English *brȳsan,* of Celtic origin; compare Irish *brūigim* I bruise] —'**bruising** *n., adj.*

bruiser ('bru:zə) *n.* a strong tough person, esp. a boxer or a bully.

bruit (bru:t) *vb.* **1.** (*tr.; often passive;* usually foll. by *about*) to report; rumour: *it was bruited about that the king was dead.* ~*n.* **2.** *Med.* an abnormal sound heard within the body during auscultation, esp. a heart murmur. **3.** *Archaic.* **a.** a rumour. **b.** a loud outcry; clamour. [C15: via French from Medieval Latin *brūgītus,* probably from Vulgar Latin *bragere* (unattested) to yell + Latin *rugīre* to roar]

Brule *or* **Brûlé** (bru:'leɪ) *n.* (*sometimes not cap.*) short for **bois-brûlé.**

Brumaire *French.* (brymɛr) *n.* the month of mist: the second month of the French revolutionary calendar, extending from Oct. 23 to Nov. 21. [C19: from *brume* mist, from Latin *brūma* winter; see BRUME]

brumal ('bru:məl) *adj.* of, characteristic of, or relating to winter; wintry.

brumby ('brʌmbɪ) *n., pl.* **-bies.** *Austral.* **1.** a wild horse, esp. one descended from runaway stock. **2.** a disorderly person. [C19: of unknown origin]

brume (bru:m) *n. Poetic.* heavy mist or fog. [C19: from French: mist, winter, from Latin *brūma,* contracted from *brevissima diēs* the shortest day] —'**brumous** *adj.*

Brummagem ('brʌmədʒəm) *n.* **1.** (*sometimes not cap.*) something that is cheap and flashy, esp. imitation jewellery. ~*adj.* **2.** (*sometimes not cap.*) cheap and gaudy; tawdry. [C17: from earlier *Bromecham,* local variant of *Birmingham,* a city in central England]

Brummie ('brʌmɪ) *n. Informal.* a native or inhabitant of Birmingham. [C20: from BRUMMAGEM]

brunch (brʌntʃ) *n.* a meal eaten late in the morning, combining breakfast with lunch. [C20: from BR(EAKFAST) + (L)UNCH]

brunette (bru:'nɛt) *n.* **1.** a girl or woman with dark brown hair. ~*adj. also* **brunet. 2.** dark brown: *brunette hair.* [C17: from French, feminine of *brunet* dark, brownish, from *brun* brown, of Germanic origin; see BROWN]

brunt (brʌnt) *n.* **1.** the main force or shock of a blow, attack, etc. (esp. in the phrase **bear the brunt of**). **2.** *Archaic.* a violent blow or attack. [C14: of unknown origin]

brush[1] (brʌʃ) *n.* **1.** a device made of bristles, hairs, wires, etc., set into a firm back or handle: used to apply paint, clean or polish surfaces, groom the hair, etc. **2.** the act or an instance of brushing. **3.** a light stroke made in passing; graze. **4.** a brief encounter or contact, esp. an unfriendly one; skirmish. **5.** the bushy tail of a fox, often kept as a trophy after a hunt, or of certain breeds of dog. **6.** an electric conductor, esp. one made of carbon, that conveys current between stationary and rotating parts of a generator, motor, etc. **7.** a dark brush-shaped region observed when a biaxial crystal is viewed through a microscope, caused by interference between beams of polarized light. **8.** *Austral. slang.* **a.** a woman. **b.** Also: **the brush.** women collectively. ~*vb.* **9.** (*tr.*) to clean, polish, scrub, paint, etc., with a brush. **10.** (*tr.*) to apply or remove with a brush or brushing movement: *brush the crumbs off the table.* **11.** (*tr.*) to touch lightly and briefly. **12.** (*intr.*) to move so as to graze or touch something lightly. ~See also **brush aside, brush off, brush up.** [C14: from Old French *broisse,* perhaps from *broce* BRUSH[2]] —'**brusher** *n.* —'**brush,like** *or* '**brushy** *adj.*

brush[2] (brʌʃ) *n.* **1.** a thick growth of shrubs and small trees; scrub. **2.** land covered with scrub. **3.** broken or cut branches or twigs; brushwood. **4.** wooded sparsely populated country; backwoods. [C16 (dense undergrowth), C14 (cuttings of trees): from Old French *broce,* from Vulgar Latin *bruscia* (unattested) brushwood] —'**brushy** *adj.*

brush aside *or* **away** *vb.* (*tr., adv.*) to dismiss without consideration; disregard.

brush border *n. Physiol.* a layer of tightly packed minute finger-like protuberances on cells that line absorptive surfaces, such as those of the intestine and kidney. See also: **microvillus.**

brush discharge *n.* a slightly luminous electrical discharge between points of high charge density when the charge density is insufficient to cause a spark or around sharp points on a highly charged conductor because of ionization of air molecules in their vicinity.

brushed (brʌʃt) *adj. Textiles.* treated with a brushing process to raise the nap and give a softer, warmer finish: *brushed nylon.*

brush fire *n.* **1.** a fire in bushes and scrub. **2.** a minor local war.

brushmark ('brʌʃ,mɑ:k) *n.* the indented lines sometimes left by the bristles of a brush on a painted surface.

brush off *Slang.* ~*vb.* (*tr., adv.*) **1.** to dismiss and ignore (a person), esp. curtly. ~*n.* **brushoff. 2.** an abrupt dismissal or rejection.

brush-tailed phalanger *n. Austral.* another name for **tuan**[2].

brush turkey *n.* any of several gallinaceous birds, esp. *Alectura lathami,* of New Guinea and Australia, having a black plumage: family *Megapodidae* (megapodes).

brush up *vb.* (*adv.*). **1.** (*tr.;* often foll. by *on*) to refresh one's knowledge, skill, or memory of (a subject). **2.** to make (a person or oneself) tidy, clean, or neat as after a journey. ~*n.* **brush-up. 3.** *Brit.* the act or an instance of tidying one's appearance (esp. in the phrase **wash and brush-up**).

brushwood ('brʌʃ,wʊd) *n.* **1.** cut or broken-off tree branches, twigs, etc. **2.** another word for **brush**[2] (sense 1).

brushwork ('brʌʃ,wɜ:k) *n.* **1.** a characteristic manner of applying paint with a brush: *that is not Rembrandt's brushwork.* **2.** work done with a brush.

brusque (bru:sk, brʊsk) *adj.* blunt or curt in manner or speech. [C17: from French, from Italian *brusco* sour, rough, from Medieval Latin *bruscus* butcher's broom] —'**brusquely** *adv.* —'**brusqueness** *or* (*less commonly*) **brusquerie** ('bru:skərɪ) *n.*

Brussels carpet ('brʌsᵊlz) *n.* a worsted carpet with a heavy pile formed by uncut loops of wool on a linen warp.

Brussels lace *n.* a fine lace with a raised or appliqué design.

Brussels sprout *n.* **1.** a variety of cabbage, *Brassica oleracea gemmifera,* having a stout stem studded with budlike heads of tightly folded leaves, resembling tiny cabbages. **2.** the head of this plant, eaten as a vegetable.

brut (bruːt; *French* bryt) *adj.* (of champagne) not sweet; dry. [C19: from French raw, rough, from Latin *brūtus* heavy; see BRUTE]

brutal ('bruːtᵊl) *adj.* **1.** cruel; vicious; savage. **2.** extremely honest or coarse in speech or manner. **3.** harsh; severe; extreme: *brutal cold.* —**bru'tality** *n.* —**'brutally** *adv.*

brutalism ('bruːtəˌlɪzəm) *n.* an austere style of architecture characterized by emphasis on such structural materials as undressed concrete and unconcealed service pipes. Also called: **new brutalism.** —**'brutalist** *n., adj.*

brutalize *or* **brutalise** ('bruːtəˌlaɪz) *vb.* **1.** to make or become brutal. **2.** *(tr.)* to treat brutally. —ˌ**brutali'zation** *or* ˌ**brutali'sation** *n.*

brute (bruːt) *n.* **1. a.** any animal except man; beast; lower animal. **b.** *(as modifier): brute nature.* **2.** a brutal person. ~*adj. (prenominal)* **3.** wholly instinctive or physical (esp. in the phrases **brute strength, brute force**). **4.** without reason or intelligence. **5.** coarse and grossly sensual. [C15: from Latin *brūtus* heavy, irrational; related to *gravis* heavy]

brutify ('bruːtɪˌfaɪ) *vb.* **-fies, -fying, -fied.** a less common word for **brutalize** (sense 1).

brutish ('bruːtɪʃ) *adj.* **1.** of, relating to, or resembling a brute or brutes; animal. **2.** coarse; cruel; stupid. —**'brutishly** *adv.* —**'brutishness** *n.*

bruxism ('brʌksɪzəm) *n.* the habit of grinding the teeth, esp. unconsciously. [irregularly formed from Greek *brykein* to gnash the teeth + -ISM]

bryology (braɪ'ɒlədʒɪ) *n.* the branch of botany concerned with the study of bryophytes. —**bryological** (ˌbraɪə'lɒdʒɪkᵊl) *adj.* —**bry'ologist** *n.*

bryony *or* **briony** ('braɪənɪ) *n., pl.* **-nies.** any of several herbaceous climbing plants of the cucurbitaceous genus *Bryonia,* of Europe and N Africa. See also **black bryony, white bryony.** [Old English *bryōnia,* from Latin, from Greek *bruōnia*]

bryophyte ('braɪəˌfaɪt) *n.* any plant of the division *Bryophyta,* having stems and leaves but lacking true vascular tissue and roots and reproducing by spores: includes the mosses and liverworts. [C19: New Latin, from Greek *bruon* moss + -PHYTE] —**bryophytic** (ˌbraɪə'fɪtɪk) *adj.*

bryozoan (ˌbraɪə'zəʊən) *n.* **1.** any aquatic invertebrate animal of the phylum *Bryozoa,* forming colonies of polyps each having a ciliated feeding organ (lophophore). Popular name: **sea mat.** ~*adj.* **2.** of, relating to, or belonging to the *Bryozoa.* ~Also: **polyzoan, ectoproct.** [C19: from Greek *bruon* moss + *zōion* animal]

Brython ('brɪθən) *n.* a Celt who speaks a Brythonic language. Compare **Goidel.** [C19: from Welsh; see BRITON]

Brythonic (brɪ'θɒnɪk) *n.* **1.** the S group of Celtic languages, consisting of Welsh, Cornish, and Breton. ~*adj.* **2.** of, relating to, or characteristic of this group of languages. ~Also called: **Brittonic.**

bs *abbrev. for:* **1.** balance sheet. **2.** bill of sale.

BS *abbrev. for:* **1.** Bachelor of Surgery. **2.** British Standard(s) (indicating the catalogue or publication number of the British Standards Institution). ~**3.** *international car registration for* Bahamas.

B/S *or* **b/s** *abbrev. for:* **1.** bags. **2.** bales. **3.** bill of sale.

BSB *abbrev. for:* **1.** British Sky Broadcasting (formerly for British Satellite Broadcasting). **2.** British Standard brass thread.

BSc *abbrev. for* Bachelor of Science.

BSC *abbrev. for:* **1.** British Steel Corporation. **2.** British Sugar Corporation. **3.** (in Britain) Broadcasting Standards Council.

BSE *abbrev. for* bovine spongiform encephalopathy: a fatal slow-developing virus disease of cattle, affecting the nervous system. Informal name: **mad cow disease.**

B-setting *n. Photog.* a shutter setting in which the shutter remains open until the shutter control is released.

BSF *abbrev. for* British Standard fine thread.

BSI *abbrev. for* British Standards Institution.

B-side *n.* the less important side of a gramophone record. Also called: **flip side.**

Bs/L *abbrev. for* bills of lading.

BSP *abbrev. for* British Standard pipe thread.

B Special *n.* a member of a part-time largely Protestant police force formerly functioning in Northern Ireland.

BSS *abbrev. for* British Standards Specification.

BSSc *or* **BSocSc** *abbrev. for* Bachelor of Social Science

BST *abbrev. for:* **1.** bovine somatotrophin: a growth hormone that can be used to increase milk production in dairy cattle. **2.** British Summer Time.

BSW *abbrev. for* British Standard Whitworth thread.

Bt *abbrev. for* Baronet.

BT *abbrev. for* British Telecom. [C20: shortened from TELECOMMUNICATIONS]

BTG *abbrev. for* British Technology Group.

btl. *abbrev. for* bottle.

btu *or* **BThU** *abbrev. for* British thermal unit. U.S. abbrev.: **BTU.**

BTU *abbrev. for* Board of Trade Unit.

bty *or* **btry.** *Military. abbrev. for* battery.

bu. *abbrev. for* bushel.

bub (bʌb) *n.* **1.** *U.S. informal.* fellow; youngster: used as a form of address. **2.** *Austral. and N.Z. slang.* **a.** a baby. **b. bubs grade.** the first grade of schooling; nursery school. [C20: perhaps from German *Bube* boy]

bubal ('bjuːbᵊl) *or* **bubalis** ('bjuːbəlɪs) *n.* any of various antelopes, esp. an extinct N African variety of hartebeest. [C15: from Latin *būbalus* African gazelle, from Greek *boubalos,* from Greek *bous* ox]

bubaline ('bjuːbəˌlaɪn, -lɪn) *adj.* **1.** (of antelopes) related to or resembling the bubal. **2.** resembling or relating to the buffalo. [C19: from New Latin, from Latin *būbalus;* see BUBAL]

bubble ('bʌbᵊl) *n.* **1.** a thin film of liquid forming a hollow globule around air or a gas: *a soap bubble.* **2.** a small globule of air or a gas in a liquid or a solid, as in carbonated drinks, glass, etc. **3.** the sound made by a bubbling liquid. **4.** something lacking substance, stability, or seriousness. **5.** an unreliable scheme or enterprise. **6.** a dome, esp. a transparent glass or plastic one. ~*vb.* **7.** to form or cause to form bubbles. **8.** *(intr.)* to move or flow with a gurgling sound. **9.** *(intr.; often foll. by over)* to overflow (with excitement, anger, etc.). **10.** *(intr.) Scot.* to snivel; blubber. [C14: probably of Scandinavian origin; compare Swedish *bubbla,* Danish *boble,* Dutch *bobbel,* all of imitative origin]

bubble and squeak *n.* (in Britain and Australia) a dish of leftover boiled cabbage, potatoes, and sometimes cooked meat fried together. [C18: so called from the sounds of this dish cooking]

bubble bath *n.* **1.** a powder, liquid, or crystals used to scent, soften, and foam in bath water. **2.** a bath to which such a substance has been added.

bubble car *n.* (in Britain, formerly) a small car, often having three wheels, with a transparent bubble-shaped top.

bubble chamber *n.* a device that enables the tracks of ionizing particles to be photographed as a row of bubbles in a superheated liquid. Immediately before the particles enter the chamber the pressure is reduced so that the ionized particles act as centres for small vapour bubbles.

bubble float *n. Angling.* a hollow spherical float that can be weighted with water to aid casting.

bubble gum *n.* **1.** a type of chewing gum that can be blown into large bubbles. **2.** *Slang.* **a.** crassly commercial pop music aimed at the very young. **b.** *(as modifier): a bubble-gum hit.*

bubble memory *n. Computer technol.* a method of storing high volumes of data by the use of minute pockets of magnetism (bubbles) in a semiconducting material: the bubbles may be caused to migrate past a read head or to a buffer area for storage.

bubble pack *n.* another term for **blister pack.**

bubble point *n. Chem.* the temperature at which bubbles just start to appear in a heated liquid mixture.

bubbler ('bʌblə) *n.* **1.** a drinking fountain in which the water is forced in a stream from a small vertical nozzle. **2.** *Chem.* any device for bubbling gas through a liquid.

bubbly ('bʌblɪ) *adj.* **-blier, -bliest.** **1.** full of or resembling bubbles. **2.** lively; animated; excited: *a bubbly personality.* ~*n.* **3.** an informal name for **champagne.**

bubo ('bjuːbəʊ) *n., pl.* **-boes.** *Pathol.* inflammation and swelling of a lymph node, often with the formation of pus, esp. in the region of the armpit or groin. [C14: from Medieval Latin *bubō* swelling, from Greek *boubōn* groin, glandular swelling] —**bubonic** (bjuː'bɒnɪk) *adj.*

bubonic plague *n.* an acute infectious febrile disease characterized by chills, prostration, delirium, and formation of buboes: caused by the bite of a rat flea infected with the bacterium *Pasteurella pestis.* See also **plague.**

bubonocele (bjuː'bɒnəˌsiːl) *n.* an incomplete hernia in the groin; partial inguinal hernia. [C17: from Greek *boubōn* groin + *kēlē* tumour]

bubu ('buːbuː) *n.* a variant spelling of **boubou.**

buccal ('bʌkᵊl) *adj.* **1.** of or relating to the cheek. **2.** of or relating to the mouth; oral: *buccal lesion.* [C19: from Latin *bucca* cheek]

buccaneer (ˌbʌkə'nɪə) *n.* **1.** a pirate, esp. one who preyed on the Spanish colonies and shipping in America and the Caribbean in the 17th and 18th centuries. ~*vb. (intr.)* **2.** to be or act like a buccaneer. [C17: from French *boucanier,* from *boucaner* to smoke meat, from Old French *boucan* frame for smoking meat, of Tupian origin; originally applied to French and English hunters of wild oxen in the West Indies]

buccinator ('bʌksɪˌneɪtə) *n.* a thin muscle that compresses the cheeks and holds them against the teeth during chewing, etc. [C17: from Latin, from *buccināre* to sound the trumpet, from *buccina* trumpet]

bucentaur (bjuː'sentɔː) *n.* the state barge of Venice from which the doge and other officials dropped a ring into the sea on Ascension Day to symbolize the ceremonial marriage of the state with the Adriatic. [C17: from Italian *bucentoro,* of uncertain origin]

Buchmanism ('bʊkməˌnɪzəm) *n.* another name for **Moral Re-armament.** [C20: named after Frank *Buchman* (1878–1961), U.S. evangelist who founded it] —**'Buchmanˌite** *n., adj.*

Buchner funnel ('bʌknə) *n.* a laboratory filter funnel used under reduced pressure. It consists of a shallow porcelain cylinder with a flat base perforated with small holes. [named after its inventor, E. *Buchner* (1860–1917), German chemist]

buchu ('buːkuː) *n.* any of several S. African rutaceous shrubs of the genus *Barosma,* esp. *B. betulina,* whose leaves are used as an antiseptic and diuretic. [C18: from a South African Bantu name]

buck[1] (bʌk) *n.* **1. a.** the male of various animals including the goat, hare, kangaroo, rabbit, and reindeer. **b.** (*as modifier*): *a buck antelope.* **2.** *S. African.* an antelope or deer of either sex. **3.** *U.S. slang, derogatory.* a young male Indian or Negro. **4.** *Archaic.* a robust spirited young man. **5.** *Archaic.* a dandy; fop. **6.** the act of bucking. ~*vb.* **7.** (*intr.*) (of a horse or other animal) to jump vertically, with legs stiff and back arched. **8.** (*tr.*) (of a horse, etc.) to throw (its rider) by bucking. **9.** (when *intr.,* often foll. by *against*) *Informal, chiefly U.S. and Canadian.* to resist or oppose obstinately: *to buck against change; to buck change.* **10.** (*tr.; usually passive*) *Informal.* to cheer or encourage: *I was very bucked at passing the exam.* **11.** *U.S. and Canadian informal.* (esp. of a car) to move forward jerkily; jolt. **12.** *U.S. and Canadian.* to charge against (something) with the head down; butt. ~See also **buck up.** [Old English *bucca* he-goat; related to Old Norse *bukkr,* Old High German *bock,* Old Irish *bocc*] —'**bucker** *n.*

buck[2] (bʌk) *n. U.S., Canadian, and Austral. slang.* **1.** a dollar. **2. a fast buck.** easily gained money. [C19: of obscure origin]

buck[3] (bʌk) *n.* **1.** *Gymnastics.* a type of vaulting horse. **2.** a U.S. and Canadian word for **sawhorse.** [C19: short for SAWBUCK]

buck[4] (bʌk) *n.* **1.** *Poker.* a marker in the jackpot to remind the winner of some obligation when his turn comes to deal. **2. pass the buck.** *Informal.* to shift blame or responsibility onto another. [C19: probably from *buckhorn knife,* placed before a player in poker to indicate that he was the next dealer]

buck and wing *n. U.S.* a boisterous tap dance, derived from Negro and Irish clog dances.

buckaroo ('bʌkəˌruː, ˌbʌkə'ruː) *n., pl.* **-roos.** *Southwestern U.S.* a cowboy. [C19: variant of Spanish *vaquero,* from *vaca* cow, from Latin *vacca*]

buckbean ('bʌkˌbiːn) *n.* a marsh plant, *Menyanthes trifoliata,* with white or pink flowers: family *Menyanthaceae.* Also called: **bogbean.**

buckboard ('bʌkˌbɔːd) *n. U.S. and Canadian.* an open four-wheeled horse-drawn carriage with the seat attached to a flexible board between the front and rear axles.

buckeen (bʌ'kiːn) *n.* (in Ireland) a poor young man who aspires to the habits and dress of the wealthy. [C18: from Irish Gaelic *boicín,* diminutive of *boc* an important person]

bucket ('bʌkɪt) *n.* **1.** an open-topped roughly cylindrical container; pail. **2.** Also called: '**bucketful.** the amount a bucket will hold. **3.** any of various bucket-like parts of a machine, such as the scoop on a mechanical shovel. **4.** a cupped blade or bucket-like compartment on the outer circumference of a water wheel, paddle wheel, etc. **5.** *Computer technol.* a unit of storage on a direct-access device from which data can be retrieved. **6.** *Chiefly U.S.* a turbine rotor blade. **7.** *Austral. and N.Z.* an ice cream container. **8. kick the bucket.** *Slang.* to die. ~*vb.* **-kets, -keting, -keted. 9.** (*tr.*) to carry in or put into a bucket. **10.** (*intr.;* (often foll. by *along*) *Chiefly Brit.* to travel or drive fast. **11.** (*tr.*) *Chiefly Brit.* to ride (a horse) hard without consideration. **12.** (*tr.*) *Austral. slang.* to criticize severely. [C13: from Anglo-French *buket,* from Old English *būc;* compare Old High German *būh* belly, German *Bauch* belly]

bucket about *vb.* (*intr.*) *Brit.* (esp. of a boat in a storm) to toss or shake violently.

bucket down *vb.* (*intr.*) (of rain) to fall very heavily.

bucket ladder *n.* **a.** a series of buckets that move in a continuous chain, used to dredge riverbeds, etc., or to excavate land. **b.** (*as modifier*): *a bucket-ladder dredger.*

bucket out *vb.* (*tr.*) to empty out with or as if with a bucket.

bucket seat *n.* a seat in a car, aircraft, etc., having curved sides that partially enclose and support the body.

bucket shop *n.* **1.** an unregistered firm of stockbrokers that engages in fraudulent speculation with the funds of its clients. **2.** *Chiefly Brit.* any small business that cannot be relied upon to fulfil its obligations, esp. a firm specializing in cheap airline tickets.

buckeye ('bʌkˌaɪ) *n.* any of several North American trees of the genus *Aesculus,* esp. *A. glabra* (Ohio buckeye), having erect clusters of white or red flowers and *Aesculus,* esp. *A. glabra* (Ohio buckeye), having erect clusters of white or red flowers and prickly fruits: family *Hippocastanaceae.* See also **horse chestnut.**

buck fever *n.* nervous excitement felt by inexperienced hunters at the approach of game.

buckhorn ('bʌkˌhɔːn) *n.* **1. a.** horn from a buck, used for knife handles, etc. **b.** (*as modifier*): *a buckhorn knife.* **2.** Also called: **buck's horn plantain.** a small Eurasian plant, *Plantago coronopus,* having narrow leaves resembling a buck's horn: family *Plantaginaceae.*

buckhound ('bʌkˌhaʊnd) *n.* a hound, smaller than a staghound, used for hunting the smaller breeds of deer, esp. fallow deer.

buckie ('bʌkɪ) *n. Scot.* **1.** a whelk or its shell. **2.** a lively or boisterous person, esp. a youngster. [related to Latin *buc(c)inum* whelk, from *buc(c)ina* trumpet, horn]

buckish ('bʌkɪʃ) *adj. Archaic.* foppish; being a dandy. —'**buckishly** *adv.* —'**buckishness** *n.*

buckjumper ('bʌkˌdʒʌmpə) *n. Austral.* an untamed horse.

buckjumping ('bʌkˌdʒʌmpɪŋ) *n. Austral.* a competitive event for buckjumpers in a rodeo.

buckle ('bʌkəl) *n.* **1.** a clasp for fastening together two loose ends, esp. of a belt or strap, usually consisting of a frame with an attached movable prong. **2.** an ornamental representation of a buckle, as on a shoe. **3.** a kink, bulge, or other distortion: *a buckle in a railway track.* ~*vb.* **4.** to fasten or be fastened with a buckle. **5.** to bend or cause to bend out of shape, esp. as a result of pressure or heat. [C14: from Old French *bocle,* from Latin *buccula* a little cheek, hence, cheek strap of a helmet, from *bucca* cheek]

buckle down *vb.* (*intr., adv.*) *Informal.* to apply oneself with determination: *to buckle down to a job.*

buckler ('bʌklə) *n.* **1.** a small round shield worn on the forearm or held by a short handle. **2.** a means of protection; defence. ~*vb.* **3.** (*tr.*) *Archaic.* to defend. [C13: from Old French *bocler,* from *bocle* shield boss; see BUCKLE, BOSS[2]]

buckler fern *n.* any of various ferns of the genus *Dryopteris,* such as *D. dilatata* (broad buckler fern): family *Polypodiaceae.*

Buckley's chance ('bʌklɪz) *n. Austral. and N.Z. slang.* no chance at all. Often shortened to **Buckley's.** [C19: of obscure origin]

buckling ('bʌklɪŋ) *n.* another name for a **bloater.** [C20: from German *Bückling*]

bucko ('bʌkəʊ) *n., pl.* **-oes.** *Irish.* a lively young fellow: often a term of address.

buckra ('bʌkrə) *n.* (used contemptuously by Negroes, esp. in the southeastern U.S.) a white man. [C18: probably from Efik *mbakara* master]

buck rabbit *or* **rarebit** *n. Brit.* Welsh rabbit with either an egg or a piece of toast on top.

buckram ('bʌkrəm) *n.* **1. a.** cotton or linen cloth stiffened with size, etc., used in lining or stiffening clothes, bookbinding, etc. **b.** (*as modifier*): *a buckram cover.* **2.** *Archaic.* stiffness of manner. ~*vb.* **-rams, -raming, -ramed. 3.** (*tr.*) to stiffen with buckram. [C14: from Old French *boquerant,* from Old Provençal *bocaran,* ultimately from *Bukhara,* a city in Uzbekistan, central Asia, once an important source of textiles]

Bucks (bʌks) *abbrev. for* Buckinghamshire.

bucksaw ('bʌkˌsɔː) *n.* a woodcutting saw having its blade set in a frame and tensioned by a turnbuckle across the back of the frame.

buck's fizz *n.* a cocktail made of champagne and orange juice.

buckshee (ˌbʌk'ʃiː) *adj. Brit. slang.* without charge; free. [C20: from BAKSHEESH]

buckshot ('bʌkˌʃɒt) *n.* lead shot of large size used in shotgun shells, esp. for hunting game. [C15 (original sense: the distance at which a buck can be shot)]

buckskin ('bʌkˌskɪn) *n.* **1.** the skin of a male deer. **2. a.** a strong greyish-yellow suede leather, originally made from deerskin but now usually made from sheepskin. **b.** (*as modifier*): *buckskin boots.* **3.** *U.S.* (*sometimes cap.*) a person wearing buckskin clothes, esp. an American soldier of the Civil War. **4.** a stiffly starched cotton cloth. **5.** a strong and heavy satin-woven woollen fabric. ~*adj.* **6.** greyish-yellow.

buckskins ('bʌkˌskɪnz) *pl. n.* (in the U.S. and Canada) breeches, shoes, or a suit of buckskin.

buck's party *or* **night** *n.* the Australian name for a **stag party.**

buckthorn ('bʌkˌθɔːn) *n.* any of several thorny small-flowered shrubs of the genus *Rhamnus,* esp. the Eurasian species *R. cathartica,* whose berries were formerly used as a purgative: family *Rhamnaceae.* See also **sea buckthorn.** [C16: from BUCK[1] (from the spiny branches, imagined as resembling antlers) + THORN]

bucktooth ('bʌkˌtuːθ) *n., pl.* **-teeth.** *Derogatory.* a projecting upper front tooth. [C18: from BUCK[1] (deer) + TOOTH]

buck up *vb.* (*adv.*) *Informal.* **1.** to make or cause to make haste. **2.** to make or become more cheerful, confident, etc.

buckwheat ('bʌkˌwiːt) *n.* **1.** any of several polygonaceous plants of the genus *Fagopyrum,* esp. *F. esculentum,* which has fragrant white flowers and is cultivated, esp. in the U.S., for its seeds. **2.** the edible seeds of this plant, ground into flour or used as animal fodder. **3.** the flour obtained from these seeds. [C16: from Middle Dutch *boecweite,* from *boeke* BEECH + *weite* WHEAT, from the resemblance of their seeds to beechnuts]

bucolic (bjuː'kɒlɪk) *adj. also* **bucolical. 1.** of or characteristic of the countryside or country life; rustic. **2.** of or relating to shepherds; pastoral. ~*n.* **3.** (*sometimes pl.*) a pastoral poem, often in the form of a dialogue. **4.** a rustic; farmer or shepherd. [C16: from Latin *būcolicus,* from Greek *boukolikos,* from *boukolos* cowherd, from *bous* ox] —**bu'colically** *adv.*

bud[1] (bʌd) *n.* **1.** a swelling on a plant stem consisting of overlapping immature leaves or petals. **2. a.** a partially opened flower. **b.** (*in combination*): *rosebud.* **3.** any small budlike outgrowth: *taste buds.* **4.** something small or immature. **5.** an asexually produced outgrowth in simple organisms such as yeasts and the hydra that develops into a new individual. **6. in bud.** at the stage of producing buds. **7. nip in the bud.** to put an end to (an idea, movement, etc.) in its initial stages. ~*vb.* **buds, budding, budded. 8.** (*intr.*) (of plants and some animals) to produce buds. **9.** (*intr.*) to begin to develop or grow. **10.** (*tr.*) *Horticulture.* to graft (a bud) from one plant onto another, usually by insertion under the bark. [C14 *budde*, of Germanic origin; compare Icelandic *budda* purse, Dutch *buidel*]

bud[2] (bʌd) *n. Informal, chiefly U.S.* short for **buddy**: used as a term of address.

buddha ('bʊdə) *n.* **1.** *Buddhism.* (*often cap.*) a person who has achieved a state of perfect enlightenment. **2.** an image or picture of the Buddha. [C17: from Sanskrit: awakened, from *bōdhati* he awakes]

Buddha ('bʊdə) *n.* **the.** a title applied to Gautama Siddhartha (?563–483 B.C.), a nobleman and religious teacher of N India: the founder of Buddhism.

Buddhism ('bʊdɪzəm) *n.* a religious teaching propagated by the Buddha and his followers, which declares that by destroying greed, hatred, and delusion, which are the causes of all suffering, man can attain perfect enlightenment. See **nirvana.** —'**Buddhist** *n., adj.*

budding ('bʌdɪŋ) *adj.* at an early stage of development but showing promise or potential: *a budding genius.*

buddle ('bʌdᵊl) *n.* **1.** a sloping trough in which ore is washed. ~*vb.* **2.** (*tr.*) to wash (ore) in a buddle. [C16: of unknown origin]

buddleia ('bʌdlɪə) *n.* any ornamental shrub of the genus *Buddleia*, esp. *B. davidii*, which has long spikes of mauve flowers and is frequently visited by butterflies: family *Buddleiaceae.* Also called: **butterfly bush.** [C19: named after A. *Buddle* (died 1715), British botanist]

buddy ('bʌdɪ) *n., pl.* **-dies. 1.** *Chiefly U.S. and Canadian.* an informal word for **friend.** Also called (as a term of address): **bud. 2.** a volunteer who visits and gives help and support to a person suffering from AIDS. ~*vb.* **-dying, -died. 3.** (*intr.*) to act as a buddy to a person suffering from AIDS. [C19: probably a baby-talk variant (U.S.) of BROTHER]

buddy movie *or* **film** *n.* a genre of film dealing with the relationship and adventures of two friends.

budge[1] (bʌdʒ) *vb.* (*usually used with a negative*) **1.** to move, however slightly: *the car won't budge.* **2.** to change or cause to change opinions, etc. [C16: from Old French *bouger*, from Vulgar Latin *bullicāre* (unattested) to bubble, from Latin *bullīre* to boil, from *bulla* bubble]

budge[2] (bʌdʒ) *n.* a lambskin dressed for the fur to be worn on the outer side. [C14: from Anglo-French *bogee*, of obscure origin]

budgerigar ('bʌdʒərɪˌgɑː) *n.* a small green Australian parrot, *Melopsittacus undulatus:* a popular cagebird that is bred in many different coloured varieties. Often shortened (informal) to **budgie.** [C19: from a native Australian language]

budget ('bʌdʒɪt) *n.* **1.** an itemized summary of expected income and expenditure of a country, company, etc., over a specified period, usually a financial year. **2.** an estimate of income and a plan for domestic expenditure of an individual or a family, often over a short period, such as a month or a week. **3.** a restriction on expenditure (esp. in the phrase **on a budget**). **4.** (*modifier*) economical; inexpensive: *budget meals for a family.* **5.** the total amount of money allocated for a specific purpose during a specified period. **6.** *Archaic.* a stock, quantity, or supply. ~*vb.* **-gets, -geting, -geted. 7.** (*tr.*) to enter or provide for in a budget. **8.** to plan the expenditure of (money, time, etc.). **9.** (*intr.*) to make a budget. [C15 (meaning: leather pouch, wallet): from Old French *bougette*, diminutive of *bouge*, from Latin *bulga*, of Gaulish origin; compare Old English *bælg* bag] —'**budgetary** *adj.*

Budget ('bʌdʒɪt) *n.* **the.** an estimate of British government expenditures and revenues and the financial plans for the ensuing fiscal year presented annually to the House of Commons by the Chancellor of the Exchequer.

budget account *n.* **1.** an account with a department store, etc., enabling a customer to make monthly payments to cover his past and future purchases. **2.** a bank account for paying household bills, being credited with regular or equal monthly payments from the customer's current account.

budgetary control *n.* a system of managing a business by making forecasts of the different activities and applying a financial value to each forecast. Actual performance is subsequently compared with the estimates.

budget for *vb.* (*tr., prep.*) to allocate, save, or set aside money for (a particular purpose, period, etc.): *we need to budget for a fuel increase this winter.*

budgie ('bʌdʒɪ) *n. Informal.* short for **budgerigar.**

bud scale *n.* one of the hard protective sometimes hairy or resinous specialized leaves surrounding the buds of certain plants, such as the rhododendron.

bud sport *n. Horticulture.* a shoot, inflorescence, etc., that differs from another such structure on a plant and is caused by a mutation; the differences can be retained by vegetative propagation.

BUF *abbrev. for* British Union of Fascists.

buff[1] (bʌf) *n.* **1. a.** a soft thick flexible undyed leather made chiefly from the skins of buffalo, oxen, and elk. **b.** (*as modifier*): *a buff coat.* **2. a.** a dull yellow or yellowish-brown colour. **b.** (*as adj.*): *buff paint.* **3.** Also called: **buffer. a.** a cloth or pad of material used for polishing an object. **b.** a flexible disc or wheel impregnated with a fine abrasive for polishing metals, etc., with a power tool. **4.** *Informal.* one's bare skin (esp. in the phrase **in the buff**). ~*vb.* **5.** to clean or polish (a metal, floor, shoes, etc.) with a buff. **6.** to remove the grain surface of (a leather). [C16: from Old French *buffle*, from Old Italian *bufalo*, from Late Latin *būfalus* BUFFALO]

buff[2] (bʌf) *vb.* **1.** (*tr.*) to deaden the force of. ~*n.* **2.** *Archaic.* a blow or buffet (now only in the phrase **blind man's buff**). [C15: back formation from BUFFET[2]]

buff[3] (bʌf) *n. Informal.* an expert on or devotee of a given subject: *a cheese buff.* [C20: originally U.S.: an enthusiastic fire watcher, from the buff-coloured uniforms worn by volunteer firemen in New York City]

buffalo ('bʌfəˌləʊ) *n., pl.* **-loes** *or* **-lo. 1.** Also called: **Cape buffalo.** a member of the cattle tribe, *Syncerus caffer*, mostly found in game reserves in southern and eastern Africa and having upward-curving horns. **2.** short for **water buffalo. 3.** a U.S. and Canadian name for **bison** (sense 1). ~*vb.* (*tr.*) *U.S. and Canadian informal.* **4.** (*often passive*) to confuse. **5.** to intimidate or overawe. [C16: from Italian *bufalo*, from Late Latin *būfalus*, alteration of Latin *būbalus;* see BUBAL]

buffalo fish *n.* any of several freshwater North American humpbacked cyprinoid fishes of the genus *Ictiobus:* family *Catostomidae* (suckers).

buffalo gnat *n.* any of various small North American blood-sucking dipterous insects of the genus *Simulium* and related genera: family *Simuliidae.* Also called: **black fly.**

buffalo grass *n.* **1.** a short grass, *Buchloë dactyloides*, growing on the dry plains of the central U.S. **2.** *Austral.* a grass, *Stenotaphrum americanum*, introduced from North America.

buffer[1] ('bʌfə) *n.* **1.** one of a pair of spring-loaded steel pads attached at both ends of railway vehicles and at the end of a railway track to reduce shock due to contact. **2.** a person or thing that lessens shock or protects from damaging impact, circumstances, etc. **3.** *Chem.* **a.** an ionic compound, usually a salt of a weak acid or base, added to a solution to resist changes in its acidity or alkalinity and thus stabilize its pH. **b.** Also called: **buffer solution.** a solution containing such a compound. **4.** *Computer technol.* a memory device for temporarily storing data. **5.** *Electronics.* an isolating circuit used to minimize the reaction between a driving and a driven circuit. **6.** short for **buffer state.** ~*vb.* (*tr.*) **7.** to insulate against or protect from shock; cushion. **8.** *Chem.* to add a buffer to (a solution). [C19: from BUFF[2]]

buffer[2] ('bʌfə) *n.* **1.** any device used to shine, polish, etc.; buff. **2.** a person who uses such a device.

buffer[3] ('bʌfə) *n. Brit. informal.* a stupid or bumbling man (esp. in the phrase **old buffer**). [C18: perhaps from Middle English *buffer* stammerer]

buffer state *n.* a small and usually neutral state between two rival powers.

buffer stock *n. Commerce.* a stock of a commodity built up by a government or trade organization with the object of using it to stabilize prices.

buffet[1] *n.* **1.** ('bʊfeɪ). a counter where light refreshments are served. **2.** ('bʊfeɪ). **a.** a meal at which guests help themselves from a number of dishes and often eat standing up. **b.** (*as modifier*): *a buffet lunch.* **3.** ('bʌfɪt, 'bʊfeɪ). a piece of furniture used from medieval times to the 18th century for displaying plate, etc. and typically comprising one or more cupboards and some open shelves. **4.** ('bʌfɪ). *Scot. and northern English dialect.* a kind of low stool, pouffe, or hassock. [C18: from French, of unknown origin]

buffet[2] ('bʌfɪt) *vb.* **-fets, -feting, -feted. 1.** (*tr.*) to knock against or about; batter: *the wind buffeted the boat.* **2.** (*tr.*) to hit, esp. with the fist; cuff. **3.** to force (one's way), as through a crowd. **4.** (*intr.*) to struggle; battle. ~*n.* **5.** a blow, esp. with a fist or hand. **6.** aerodynamic excitation of an aircraft structure by separated flows. [C13: from Old French *buffeter*, from *buffet* a light blow, from *buffe*, of imitative origin] —'**buffeter** *n.*

buffet car ('bʊfeɪ) *n. Brit.* a railway coach where light refreshments are served.

buffeting ('bʌfɪtɪŋ) *n.* response of an aircraft structure to buffet, esp. an irregular oscillation of the tail.

buffing wheel *n.* a wheel covered with a soft material, such as lamb's wool or leather, used for shining and polishing. Also called: **buff wheel.**

bufflehead ('bʌfᵊlˌhɛd) *n.* a small North American diving duck, *Bucephala* (or *Glaucionetta*) *albeola:* the male has black-and-white plumage and a fluffy head. Also called: **butterball.** [C17 *buffle* from obsolete *buffle* wild ox (see BUFF[1]), referring to the duck's head]

buffo ('bʊfəʊ; *Italian* 'buffo) *n., pl.* **-fi** (-fɪ) *or* **-fos. 1.** (in Italian opera of the 18th century) a comic part, esp. one for a bass. **2.** Also called: **buffo bass, basso buffo** (*Italian* 'basso 'buffo). a bass singer who performs such a part. [C18: from Italian (adj.): comic, from *buffo* (n.) BUFFOON]

buffoon (bə'fuːn) *n.* **1.** a person who amuses others by ridiculous or odd behaviour, jokes, etc. **2.** a foolish person. [C16: from French *bouffon*, from Italian *buffone*, from Medieval Latin *būfō*, from Latin: toad] —**buf'foonery** *n.*

buff-tip moth *n.* a large European moth, *Phalera bucephala*, having violet-brown buff-tipped forewings held at rest around the body so that it resembles a snapped-off twig.

bug[1] (bʌg) *n.* **1.** any insect of the order *Hemiptera*, esp. any of the suborder *Heteroptera*, having piercing and sucking mouthparts specialized as a beak (rostrum). See also **assassin bug, bedbug, chinch bug. 2.** *Chiefly U.S. and Canadian.* any insect, such as the June bug or the Croton bug. 3. *Informal.* **a.** a microorganism, esp. a bacterium, that produces disease. **b.** a disease, esp. a stomach infection, caused by a microorganism. 4. *Informal.* an obsessive idea, hobby, etc.; craze. 5. *Informal.* a person having such a craze; enthusiast. 6. (*often pl.*) *Informal.* an error or fault, as in a machine or system, esp. in a computer or computer program. 7. *Informal.* a concealed microphone used for recording conversations, as in spying. 8. *U.S.* (in poker) a joker used as an ace or wild card to complete a straight or flush. ~*vb.* **bugs, bugging, bugged.** *Informal.* 9. (*tr.*) to irritate; bother. 10. (*tr.*) to conceal a microphone in (a room, etc.). 11. (*intr.*) *U.S.* (of eyes) to protrude. ~See also **bug out.** [C16: of uncertain origin; perhaps related to Old English *budda* beetle]

bug[2] (bʌg) *n. Obsolete.* an evil spirit or spectre; hobgoblin. [C14 *bugge,* perhaps from Middle Welsh *bwg* ghost. See also BUGBEAR, BUGABOO]

bug[3] (bʌg) *vb.* a past tense and past participle of **big**[2].

bugaboo (ˈbʌgəˌbuː) *n., pl.* **-boos.** an imaginary source of fear; bugbear; bogey. [C18: probably of Celtic origin; compare Cornish *buccaboo* the devil]

bugbane (ˈbʌgˌbeɪn) *n.* any of several ranunculaceous plants of the genus *Cimicifuga,* esp. *C. foetida* of Europe, whose flowers are reputed to repel insects.

bugbear (ˈbʌgˌbɛə) *n.* 1. a thing that causes obsessive fear or anxiety. 2. (in English folklore) a goblin said to eat naughty children and thought to be in the form of a bear. [C16: from BUG[2] + BEAR[2]; compare BUGABOO]

bugger (ˈbʌgə) *n.* 1. a person who practises buggery. 2. *Taboo slang.* a person or thing considered to be contemptible, unpleasant, or difficult. 3. *Slang.* a humorous or affectionate term for a man or child: *a silly old bugger; a friendly little bugger.* 4. **bugger all.** *Slang.* nothing. ~*vb.* 5. to practise buggery (with). 6. (*tr.*) *Slang, chiefly Brit.* to ruin, complicate, or frustrate. 7. *Slang.* to tire; weary: *he was absolutely buggered.* ~*interj.* 8. *Taboo slang.* an exclamation of annoyance or disappointment. [C16: from Old French *bougre,* from Medieval Latin *Bulgarus* Bulgarian; from the condemnation of the Eastern Orthodox Bulgarians as heretics]

bugger about *or* **around** *vb.* (*adv.*) *Brit. slang.* 1. (*intr.*) to fool about and waste time. 2. (*tr.*) to create difficulties or complications for (a person).

bugger off *vb.* (*intr., adv.*) *Brit. taboo slang.* to go away; depart.

buggery (ˈbʌgərɪ) *n.* anal intercourse between a man and another man, a woman, or an animal. Compare **sodomy.**

buggy[1] (ˈbʌgɪ) *n., pl.* **-gies.** 1. a light horse-drawn carriage having either four wheels (esp. in the U.S. and Canada) or two wheels (esp. in Britain and India). 2. short for **beach buggy.** 3. short for **baby buggy.** 4. a small motorized vehicle designed for a particular purpose: *golf buggy, moon buggy.* [C18: of unknown origin]

buggy[2] (ˈbʌgɪ) *adj.* **-gier, -giest.** 1. infested with bugs. 2. *U.S. slang.* insane. —ˈ**bugginess** *n.*

bughouse (ˈbʌgˌhaʊs) *Offensive slang, chiefly U.S.* ~*n.* 1. a mental hospital or asylum. ~*adj.* 2. insane; crazy. [C20: from BUG[1] + (MAD)HOUSE]

bugle[1] (ˈbjuːgᵊl) *n.* 1. *Music.* a brass instrument similar to the cornet but usually without valves: used for military fanfares, signal calls, etc. ~*vb.* 2. (*intr.*) to play or sound (on) a bugle. [C14: short for *bugle horn* ox horn (musical instrument), from Old French *bugle,* from Latin *būculus* young bullock, from *bōs* ox] —ˈ**bugler** *n.*

bugle[2] (ˈbjuːgᵊl) *n.* any of several Eurasian plants of the genus *Ajuga,* esp. *A. reptans,* having small blue or white flowers: family *Labiatae* (labiates). Also called: **bugleweed.** See also **ground pine.** [C13: from Late Latin *bugula,* of uncertain origin]

bugle[3] (ˈbjuːgᵊl) *n.* a tubular glass or plastic bead sewn onto clothes for decoration. [C16: of unknown origin]

bugleweed (ˈbjuːgᵊlˌwiːd) *n.* 1. Also called: **water horehound.** *U.S.* any aromatic plant of the genus *Lycopus,* having small whitish or pale blue flowers: family *Labiatae* (labiates). See also **gipsywort.** 2. another name for **bugle**[2].

bugloss (ˈbjuːglɒs) *n.* any of various hairy Eurasian boraginaceous plants of the genera *Anchusa, Lycopsis,* and *Echium,* esp. *L. arvensis,* having clusters of blue flowers. See also **viper's bugloss.** [C15: from Latin *būglōssa,* from Greek *bouglōssos* ox-tongued, from *bōs* ox + *glōssa* tongue]

bugong (ˈbuːgɒŋ) *n.* another name for **bogong.**

bug out *vb.* (*intr., adv.*) *Slang, chiefly U.S.* to depart hurriedly; run away; retreat.

buhl (buːl) *adj., n.* the usual U.S. spelling of **boulle.**

buhrstone, burstone, *or* **burrstone** (ˈbɜːˌstəʊn) *n.* 1. a hard tough rock containing silica, fossils, and cavities, formerly used as a grindstone. 2. a grindstone or millstone made of this rock. [C18 *burr,* perhaps identical to BURR[1] (alluding to roughness)]

buibui (ˈbuɪˈbuɪ) *n.* a piece of black cloth worn as a shawl by Muslim women, esp. on the E African coast. [from Swahili]

build (bɪld) *vb.* **builds, building, built.** 1. to make, construct, or form by joining parts or materials: *to build a house.* 2. (*intr.*) to be a builder by profession. 3. (*tr.*) to order the building of: *the government builds most of our hospitals.* 4. (foll. by *on* or *upon*) to base; found: *his theory was not built on facts.* 5. (*tr.*) to establish and develop: *it took ten years to build a business.* 6. (*tr.*) to make in a particular way or for a particular purpose: *the car was not built for speed.* 7. (*intr.;* often foll. by *up*) to increase in intensity: *the wind was building.* 8. *Card games.* **a.** to add cards to each other to form (a sequence or set). **b.** (*intr.*) to add to the layout of cards on the table from one's hand. ~*n.* 9. physical form, figure, or proportions: *a man with an athletic build.* ~See also **build in, build into, build up.** [Old English *byldan;* related to *bylda* farmer, *bold* building, Old Norse *bōl* farm, dwelling; see BOWER[1]]

builder (ˈbɪldə) *n.* 1. a person who builds, esp. one who contracts for and supervises the construction or repair of buildings. 2. a substance added to a soap or detergent as a filler or abrasive.

build in *vb.* (*tr., adv.*) to incorporate or construct as an integral part: *to build in safety features.*

building (ˈbɪldɪŋ) *n.* 1. something built with a roof and walls, such as a house or factory. 2. the act, business, occupation, or art of building houses, boats, etc.

building and loan association *n.* a U.S. name for **building society.**

building block *n.* 1. a block of stone or other material, larger than a brick, used in building. 2. a component that fits with others to form a whole: *standardized software building blocks.* 3. another name for **block** (sense 4) (the child's toy).

building line *n.* the boundary line along a street beyond which buildings must not project.

building paper *n.* any of various types of heavy-duty paper that usually consist of bitumen reinforced with fibre sandwiched between two sheets of kraft paper: used in damp-proofing or as insulation between the soil and a road surface.

building society *n.* a cooperative organization that accepts deposits of money from savers and uses them to make loans, secured by mortgages, to house buyers. Since 1986 they have been empowered to offer banking services.

build into *vb.* (*tr., prep.*) to make (something) a definite part of (a contract, agreement, etc.).

build up *vb.* (*adv.*) 1. (*tr.*) to construct gradually, systematically, and in stages. 2. to increase, accumulate, or strengthen, esp. by degrees: *the murmur built up to a roar.* 3. (*intr.*) to prepare for or gradually approach a climax. 4. (*tr.*) to improve the health or physique of (a person). 5. (*tr., usually passive*) to cover (an area) with buildings. 6. (*tr.*) to cause (a person, enterprise, etc.) to become better known; publicize: *they built several actresses up into stars.* ~*n.* **build-up.** 7. progressive increase in number, size, etc.: *the build-up of industry.* 8. a gradual approach to a climax or critical point. 9. extravagant publicity or praise, esp. in the form of a campaign. 10. *Military.* the process of attaining the required strength of forces and equipment, esp. prior to an operation.

built (bɪlt) *vb.* the past tense and past participle of **build.**

built cane *n. Angling.* another name for **split cane.**

built-in *adj.* 1. made or incorporated as an integral part: *a built-in cupboard; a built-in escape clause.* 2. essential; inherent. ~*n.* 3. *Austral.* a built-in cupboard or wardrobe.

built-in obsolescence *n.* See **planned obsolescence.**

built-up *adj.* 1. having many buildings (esp. in the phrase **built-up area**). 2. increased by the addition of parts: *built-up heels.*

Bukhara rug *or* **Bokhara rug** (bʊˈxɑːrə) *n.* a kind of rug, typically having a black-and-white geometrical pattern on a reddish ground. [named after *Bukhara* (or *Bokhara*), a former kingdom of central Asia]

Bul (buːl) *n.* the eighth month of the Old Hebrew calendar, corresponding to Heshvan of the Babylonian or post-exilic Jewish calendar: a period from mid-October to mid-November. [from Hebrew *būl,* of Canaanite origin]

bul. *abbrev. for* bulletin.

bulb (bʌlb) *n.* 1. a rounded organ of vegetative reproduction in plants such as the tulip and onion: a flattened stem bearing a central shoot surrounded by fleshy nutritive inner leaves and thin brown outer leaves. Compare **corm.** 2. a plant, such as a hyacinth or daffodil, that grows from a bulb. 3. See **light bulb.** 4. a rounded part of an instrument such as a syringe or thermometer. 5. *Anatomy.* a rounded expansion of a cylindrical organ or part, such as the medulla oblongata. 6. Also called: **bulbous bow.** a bulbous protuberance at the forefoot of a ship to reduce turbulence. [C16: from Latin *bulbus,* from Greek *bolbos* onion]

bulbar (ˈbʌlbə) *adj. Chiefly anatomy.* of or relating to a bulb, esp. the medulla oblongata.

bulb fly *n.* a hoverfly the larvae of which live in bulbs and can become serious pests, esp. the yellow and black **narcissus bulb fly** (*Meridon equestris*).

bulbiferous (bʌlˈbɪfərəs) *adj.* (of plants) producing bulbs.

bulbil (ˈbʌlbɪl) *or* **bulbel** (ˈbʌlbᵊl) *n.* 1. a small bulblike organ of vegetative reproduction growing in leaf axils or on flower stalks of plants such as the onion and tiger lily. 2. any small bulb of a plant. 3. any small bulblike structure in an animal. [C19: from New Latin *bulbillus,* from Latin *bulbus* BULB]

bulb mite *n.* a widespread mite, *Rhizaglophus eclinops,* that tunnels in the bulbs of lilies and other plants.

bulbous (ˈbʌlbəs) *adj.* 1. shaped like a bulb; swollen; bulging. 2. growing from or bearing bulbs. —ˈ**bulbously** *adv.*

bulbul (ˈbʊlbʊl) *n.* 1. any songbird of the family *Pycnonotidae* of tropical Africa and Asia, having brown plumage and, in many species, a distinct crest. 2. a songbird, taken to be the nightingale, often mentioned in Persian poetry. [C18: via Persian from Arabic]

Bulg. *abbrev. for* Bulgaria(n).

Bulgar ('bʌlgɑː, 'bʊl-) *n.* **1.** a member of a group of non-Indo-European peoples that settled in SE Europe in the late 7th century A.D. and adopted the language and culture of their Slavonic subjects. **2.** a rare name for a **Bulgarian.**

Bulgarian (bʌl'gɛərɪən, bʊl-) *adj.* **1.** of, relating to, or characteristic of Bulgaria, a republic in SE Europe, its people, or their language. ~*n.* **2.** the official language of Bulgaria, belonging to the S Slavonic branch of the Indo-European family. **3.** a native, inhabitant, or citizen of Bulgaria.

bulge (bʌldʒ) *n.* **1.** a swelling or an outward curve. **2.** a sudden increase in number or volume, esp. of population. **3. the bulge.** *Brit.* another name for **baby boom. 4.** *Brit.* the projecting part of an army's front line; salient. ~*vb.* **5.** to swell outwards. [C13: from Old French *bouge,* from Latin *bulga* bag, probably of Gaulish origin] —**'bulging** *adj.* —**'bulgingly** *adv.* —**'bulgy** *adj.* —**'bulginess** *n.*

bulgur ('bʌlgə) *n.* a kind of dried cracked wheat. [C20: from Turkish, from Arabic *burghul,* from Persian]

bulimia (bjuː'lɪmɪə) *n.* **1.** pathologically insatiable hunger, esp. when caused by a brain lesion. **2.** Also called: **bulimia nervosa.** a disorder characterized by compulsive overeating followed by vomiting: sometimes associated with anxiety about gaining weight. [C17: from New Latin, from Greek *boulimia,* from *bous* ox + *limos* hunger] —**bu'limic** *n., adj.*

bulk (bʌlk) *n.* **1.** volume, size, or magnitude, esp. when great. **2.** the main part: *the bulk of the work is repetitious.* **3.** a large body, esp. of a person: *he eased his bulk out of the chair.* **4.** unpackaged cargo or goods. **5.** a ship's cargo or hold. **6.** *Printing.* **a.** the thickness of a number of sheets of paper or cardboard. **b.** the thickness of a book excluding its covers. **7. in bulk. a.** in large quantities. **b.** (of a cargo, etc.) unpackaged. ~*vb.* **8.** to cohere or cause to cohere in a mass. **9.** to place, hold, or transport (several cargoes of goods) in bulk. **10. bulk large.** to be or seem important or prominent: *the problem bulked large in his mind.* [C15: from Old Norse *bulki* cargo]

bulk buying *n.* **1.** the purchase at one time, and often at a reduced price, of a large quantity of a particular commodity. **2.** the purchase of the whole or greater part of the output of a commodity of a country or state by a single buyer, usually another country or state; state trading.

bulk carrier *n.* a ship that carries unpackaged cargo, usually consisting of a single dry commodity, such as coal or grain. Also called: **'bulker.**

bulkhead ('bʌlk,hɛd) *n.* **1.** any upright wall-like partition in a ship, aircraft, vehicle, etc. **2.** a wall or partition built to hold back earth, fire, water, etc. [C15: probably from *bulk* projecting framework, from Old Norse *bálkr* partition + HEAD]

bulking ('bʌlkɪŋ) *n.* the expansion of excavated material to a volume greater than that of the excavation from which it came.

bulk modulus *n.* a coefficient of elasticity of a substance equal to minus the ratio of the applied stress (p) to the resulting fractional change in volume (dV/V) in a specified reference state (dV/V is the **bulk strain**). Symbol: K

bulk up *vb.* (*adv.*) to increase or cause to increase in size or importance.

bulky ('bʌlkɪ) *adj.* **bulkier, bulkiest.** very large and massive, esp. so as to be unwieldy. —**'bulkily** *adv.* —**'bulkiness** *n.*

bull[1] (bʊl) *n.* **1.** any male bovine animal, esp. one that is sexually mature. Related adj.: **taurine. 2.** the uncastrated adult male of any breed of domestic cattle. **3.** the male of various other animals including the elephant and whale. **4.** a very large, strong, or aggressive person. **5.** *Stock Exchange.* **a.** a speculator who buys in anticipation of rising prices in order to make a profit on resale. **b.** (*as modifier*): *a bull market.* Compare **bear**[2] (sense 5). **6.** *Chiefly Brit.* short for **bull's-eye** (senses 1, 2). **7.** *Slang.* short for **bullshit. 8.** short for **bulldog, bull terrier. 9. a bull in a china shop.** a clumsy person. **10. shoot the bull.** *U.S. and Canadian slang.* **a.** to pass time talking lightly. **b.** to boast or exaggerate. **11. take the bull by the horns.** to face and tackle a difficulty without shirking. ~*adj.* **12.** male; masculine: *a bull elephant.* **13.** large; strong. ~*vb.* **14.** (*tr.*) to raise or attempt to raise the price or prices of (a stock market or a security) by speculative buying. **15.** (*intr.*) (of a cow) to be on heat. **16.** (*intr.*) *U.S. slang.* to talk lightly or foolishly. [Old English *bula,* from Old Norse *boli;* related to Middle Low German *bulle,* Middle Dutch *bolle*]

bull[2] (bʊl) *n.* a ludicrously self-contradictory or inconsistent statement. Also called: **Irish bull.** [C17: of uncertain origin]

bull[3] (bʊl) *n.* a formal document issued by the pope, written in antiquated characters and often sealed with a leaden bulla. [C13: from Medieval Latin *bulla* seal attached to a bull, from Latin: round object]

Bull (bʊl) *n.* **the.** the constellation Taurus, the second sign of the zodiac.

bull. *abbrev. for* bulletin.

bulla ('bʊlə, 'bʌlə) *n., pl.* **-lae** (-liː). **1.** a leaden seal affixed to a papal bull, having a representation of Saints Peter and Paul on one side and the name of the reigning pope on the other. **2.** an ancient Roman rounded metal or leather box containing an amulet, worn around the neck. **3.** *Pathol.* another word for **blister** (sense 1). **4.** *Anatomy.* a rounded bony projection. [C19: from Latin: round object, bubble]

bullace ('bʊlɪs) *n.* a small Eurasian rosaceous tree, *Prunus domestica insititia* (or *P. insititia*), of which the damson is the cultivated form. See also **plum**[1] (sense 1). [C14: from Old French *beloce,* from Medieval Latin *bolluca,* perhaps of Gaulish origin]

Bullamakanka (,buːləmə'kæŋkə) *n. Austral.* an imaginary very remote and backward place.

bullate ('bʌleɪt, -ɪt, 'bʊl-) *adj. Botany, anatomy, etc.* puckered or blistered in appearance: *the bullate leaves of the primrose.* [C19: from Medieval Latin *bullātus* inflated, from Latin *bulla* bubble]

bullbat ('bʊl,bæt) *n.* another name for **nighthawk** (sense 1).

bulldog ('bʊl,dɒg) *n.* **1.** a sturdy thickset breed of dog with an undershot jaw, broad head, and a muscular body. **2.** (at Oxford University) an official who accompanies the proctors on ceremonial occasions. **3.** *Commerce.* a fixed-interest bond issued in Britain by a foreign borrower.

bulldog ant *n.* any large Australian ant of the genus *Myrmecia,* having a powerful stinging bite: subfamily *Ponerinae.* Sometimes shortened to **bull ant.**

bulldog clip *n.* a clip for holding papers together, consisting of two T-shaped metal clamps held in place by a cylindrical spring.

bulldoze ('bʊl,dəʊz) *vb.* (*tr.*) **1.** to move, demolish, flatten, etc., with a bulldozer. **2.** *Informal.* to force; push: *he bulldozed his way through the crowd.* **3.** *Informal.* to intimidate or coerce. [C19: probably from BULL[1] + DOSE]

bulldozer ('bʊl,dəʊzə) *n.* **1.** a powerful tractor fitted with caterpillar tracks and a blade at the front, used for moving earth, rocks, etc. **2.** *Informal.* a person who bulldozes.

bull dust *n. Austral.* **1.** fine dust. **2.** *Slang.* nonsense.

bullet ('bʊlɪt) *n.* **1. a.** a small metallic missile enclosed in a cartridge, used as the projectile of a gun, rifle, etc. **b.** the entire cartridge. **2.** something resembling a bullet, esp. in shape or effect. **3.** *Stock Exchange.* a fixed interest security with a single maturity date. **4.** *Commerce.* a security that offers a fixed interest and matures on a fixed date. **5.** *Commerce.* **a.** the final repayment of a loan that repays the whole of the sum borrowed, as interim payments have been for interest only. **b.** (*as modifier*): *a bullet loan.* **6.** *Brit. slang.* dismissal, sometimes without notice (esp. in the phrases **get** *or* **give the bullet**). **7. bite (on) the bullet.** See **bite** (sense 14). [C16: from French *boulette,* diminutive of *boule* ball; see BOWL[2]] —**'bullet-,like** *adj.*

bulletin ('bʊlɪtɪn) *n.* **1.** an official statement on a matter of public interest, such as the illness of a public figure. **2.** a broadcast summary of the news. **3.** a periodical publication of an association, etc. ~*vb.* **4.** (*tr.*) to make known by bulletin. [C17: from French, from Italian *bullettino,* from *bulletta,* diminutive of *bulla* papal edict, BULL[3]]

bulletin board *n.* the U.S. and Canadian name for **notice board.**

bullet loan *n.* a loan that is repaid with interest in a single payment at the end of a fixed term.

bulletproof ('bʊlɪt,pruːf) *adj.* **1.** not penetrable by bullets: *bulletproof glass.* ~*vb.* **2.** (*tr.*) to make bulletproof.

bulletwood ('bʊlɪt,wʊd) *n.* the wood of a tropical American sapotaceous tree, *Manilkara bidentata,* widely used for construction due to its durability and toughness.

bullfight ('bʊl,faɪt) *n.* a traditional Spanish, Portuguese, and Latin American spectacle in which a matador, assisted by banderilleros and mounted picadors, baits and usually kills a bull in an arena. —**'bull,fighter** *n.* —**'bull,fighting** *n.*

bullfinch[1] ('bʊl,fɪntʃ) *n.* **1.** a common European finch, *Pyrrhula pyrrhula:* the male has a bright red throat and breast, black crown, wings, and tail, and a grey-and-white back. **2.** any of various similar finches. [C14: see BULL[1], FINCH; probably so called from its stocky shape and thick neck]

bullfinch[2] ('bʊl,fɪntʃ) *n. Brit.* a high thick hedge too difficult for a horse and rider to jump. [C19: perhaps changed from the phrase *bull fence*]

bullfrog ('bʊl,frɒg) *n.* any of various large frogs, such as *Rana catesbeiana* (**American bullfrog**), having a loud deep croak.

bullhead ('bʊl,hɛd) *n.* **1.** any of various small northern mainly marine scorpaenoid fishes of the family *Cottidae* that have a large head covered with bony plates. **2.** any freshwater North American catfish of the genus *Ameiurus* (or *Ictalurus*), having a large head bearing several long barbels. **3.** a scorpion fish, *Scorpaena guttata,* of North American Pacific coastal waters. **4.** *Informal.* a stupidly stubborn or unintelligent person.

bull-headed *adj.* blindly obstinate; stubborn, headstrong, or stupid. —,**bull-'headedly** *adv.* —,**bull-'headedness** *n.*

bullhead rail *n. Railways.* a rail having a cross section with a bulbous top and bottom, the top being larger. Now largely superseded by **flat-bottomed rail.**

bullhorn ('bʊl,hɔːn) *n.* the U.S. and Canadian name for **loudhailer.**

bullion ('bʊljən) *n.* **1.** gold or silver in mass. **2.** gold or silver in the form of bars and ingots, suitable for further processing. **3.** Also called: **bullion fringe.** a thick gold or silver wire or fringed cord used as a trimming, as on military uniforms. [C14 (in the sense: melted gold or silver): from Anglo-French: mint, probably from Old French *bouillir* to boil, from Latin *bullīre*]

bullish ('bʊlɪʃ) *adj.* **1.** like a bull. **2.** *Stock Exchange.* causing, expecting, or characterized by a rise in prices: *a bullish market.*

3. *Informal.* cheerful and optimistic: *the prime minister was in a bullish mood.* —'**bullishness** *n.*

bull kelp *n.* any of various large brown seaweeds of Pacific and Antarctic waters.

bull mastiff *n.* a large powerful breed of dog with a short usually fawn or brindle coat, developed by crossing the bulldog with the mastiff.

bull-necked *adj.* having a short thick neck.

bull nose *n.* **1.** a disease of pigs caused by infection with the bacterium *Actinomyces necrophorus,* characterized by swelling of the snout. **2.** a rounded edge of a brick, step, etc. **3.** a rounded exterior angle, as where two walls meet.

bull-nosed *adj.* having a rounded end.

bullock ('bʊlək) *n.* **1.** a gelded bull; steer. **2.** *Archaic.* a bull calf. ~*vb.* **3.** (*intr.*) *Austral. and N.Z. informal.* to work hard and long. [Old English *bulluc;* see BULL[1], -OCK]

bullock's heart *n.* another name for **custard apple** (senses 1, 2).

bullocky ('bʊləkɪ) *n., pl.* **-ockies.** *Austral. and N.Z. informal.* the driver of a team of bullocks.

bullpen ('bʊlˌpɛn) *n.* **1.** *U.S. informal.* a large cell where prisoners are confined together temporarily. **2.** *Baseball.* a part of a baseball field where relief pitchers warm up.

bullring ('bʊlˌrɪŋ) *n.* an arena for bullfighting.

bullroarer ('bʊlˌrɔːrə) *n.* a wooden slat attached to a thong that makes a roaring sound when the thong is whirled: used esp. by Australian aborigines in religious rites.

bull session *n. Informal, chiefly U.S. and Canadian.* an informal discussion, often among men. [C20: from BULL[2]]

bull's-eye *n.* **1.** the small central disc of a target, usually the highest valued area. **2.** a shot hitting this. **3.** *Informal.* something that exactly achieves its aim. **4.** a small circular or oval window or opening. **5.** a thick disc of glass set into a ship's deck, etc., to admit light. **6.** the glass boss at the centre of a sheet of blown glass. **7. a.** a small thick plano-convex lens used as a condenser. **b.** a lamp or lantern containing such a lens. **8.** a peppermint-flavoured, usually striped, boiled sweet. **9.** *Nautical.* a circular or oval wooden block with a groove around it for the strop of a shroud and a hole at its centre for a line. Compare **deadeye. 10.** *Meteorol.* the eye or centre of a cyclone.

bullshit ('bʊlʃɪt) *Taboo slang.* ~*n.* **1.** exaggerated or foolish talk; nonsense. **2.** (in the British Army) exaggerated zeal, esp. for ceremonial drill, cleaning, polishing, etc. Usually shortened to **bull.** ~*vb.* **-shits, -shitting, -shitted. 3.** (*intr.*) to talk in an exaggerated or foolish manner. —'**bullshitter** *n.*

bull snake *n.* any burrowing North American nonvenomous colubrid snake of the genus *Pituophis,* typically having yellow and brown markings. Also called: **gopher snake.**

bull's wool *n. Austral. and N.Z. informal.* nonsense.

bull terrier *n.* a breed of terrier having a muscular body and thick neck, with a short smooth often white coat: developed by crossing the bulldog with various terriers. See also **pit bull terrier, Staffordshire bull terrier.**

bull tongue *n. Chiefly U.S.* **1.** a heavy plough used in growing cotton, having an almost vertical mouldboard. **2.** a plough or cultivator with a single shovel.

bull trout *n.* any large trout, esp. the salmon trout.

bullwhip ('bʊlˌwɪp) *n.* **1.** a long tapering heavy whip, esp. one of plaited rawhide. ~*vb.* **-whips, -whipping, -whipped. 2.** (*tr.*) to whip with a bullwhip.

bully[1] ('bʊlɪ) *n., pl.* **-lies. 1.** a person who hurts, persecutes, or intimidates weaker people. **2.** *Archaic.* a hired ruffian. **3.** *Obsolete.* a procurer; pimp. **4.** *Obsolete.* a fine fellow or friend. **5.** *Obsolete.* a sweetheart; darling. ~*vb.* **-lies, -lying, -lied. 6.** (when *tr.,* often foll. by *into*) to hurt, intimidate, or persecute (a weaker or smaller person), esp. to make him do something. ~*adj.* **7.** dashing; jolly: *my bully boy.* **8.** *Informal.* very good; fine. ~*interj.* **9.** Also: **bully for you, him,** etc. *Informal.* well done! bravo! [C16 (in the sense: sweetheart, hence fine fellow, hence swaggering coward): probably from Middle Dutch *boele* lover, from Middle High German *buole,* perhaps childish variant of *bruoder* BROTHER]

bully[2] ('bʊlɪ) *n.* any of various small freshwater fishes of the genera *Gobiomorphus* and *Philynodon* of New Zealand. Also called (N.Z.): **pakoko, titarakura, toitoi.** [C20: short for COCKABULLY]

bully beef *n.* tinned corned beef. Often shortened to **bully.** [C19 *bully,* anglicized version of French *bouilli,* from *boeuf bouilli* boiled beef]

bullyboy ('bʊlɪˌbɔɪ) *n.* **a.** a ruffian or tough, esp. a hired one. **b.** (*as modifier*): *bullyboy tactics.*

bully-off *Hockey.* ~*n.* **1.** the method by which a game is started. Two opposing players stand with the ball between them and alternately strike their sticks together and against the ground three times before trying to hit the ball. ~*vb.* **bully off. 2.** (*intr., adv.*) to start play with a bully-off. ~Often shortened to **bully.** Compare **face-off.** [C19: perhaps from *bully* scrum in Eton football; of unknown origin]

bullyrag ('bʊlɪˌræg) *vb.* **-rags, -ragging, -ragged.** (*tr.*) to bully, esp. by means of cruel practical jokes. Also: **ballyrag.** [C18: of unknown origin]

bulnbuln ('bʊln'bʊln) *n. Austral.* another name for **lyrebird.** [C19: from a native Australian language]

bulrush ('bʊlˌrʌʃ) *n.* **1.** a grasslike cyperaceous marsh plant, *Scirpus lacustris,* used for making mats, chair seats, etc. **2.** a popular name for **reed mace** (sense 1): the name derived from Alma-Tadema's painting of the finding of the infant Moses in the "bulrushes"—actually reed mace. **3.** a biblical word for **papyrus** (the plant). [C15 *bulrish, bul-* perhaps from BULL[1] + *rish* RUSH[2], referring to the largeness of the plant]

bulwark ('bʊlwək) *n.* **1.** a wall or similar structure used as a fortification; rampart. **2.** a person or thing acting as a defence against injury, annoyance, etc. **3.** (*often pl.*) *Nautical.* a solid vertical fencelike structure along the outward sides of a deck. **4.** a breakwater or mole. ~*vb.* **5.** (*tr.*) to defend or fortify with or as if with a bulwark. [C15: via Dutch from Middle High German *bolwerk,* from *bol* plank, BOLE[1] + *werk* WORK]

bum[1] (bʌm) *n. Brit. slang.* the buttocks or anus. [C14: of uncertain origin]

bum[2] (bʌm) *Informal.* ~*n.* **1.** a disreputable loafer or idler. **2.** a tramp; hobo. **3.** an irresponsible, unpleasant, or mean person. **4.** a person who spends a great deal of time on a specified sport: *baseball bum.* **5. on the bum. a.** living as a loafer or vagrant. **b.** out of repair; broken. ~*vb.* **bums, bumming, bummed. 6.** (*tr.*) to get by begging; cadge: *to bum a lift.* **7.** (*intr.;* often foll. by *around*) to live by begging or as a vagrant or loafer. **8.** (*intr.;* usually foll. by *around*) to spend time to no good purpose; loaf; idle. ~*adj.* **9.** (*prenominal*) of poor quality; useless. [C19: probably shortened from earlier *bummer* a loafer, probably from German *bummeln* to loaf]

bumbailiff (ˌbʌm'beɪlɪf) *n. Brit. derogatory.* (formerly) an officer employed to collect debts and arrest debtors for nonpayment. [C17: from BUM[1] + bailiff, so called because he follows hard behind debtors]

bumble[1] ('bʌmbəl) *vb.* **1.** to speak or do in a clumsy, muddled, or inefficient way: *he bumbled his way through his speech.* **2.** (*intr.*) to proceed unsteadily; stumble. ~*n.* **3.** a blunder or botch. [C16: perhaps a blend of BUNGLE + STUMBLE] —'**bumbler** *n.* —'**bumbling** *n., adj.*

bumble[2] ('bʌmbəl) *vb.* (*intr.*) to make a humming sound. [C14 *bomblen* to buzz, boom, of imitative origin]

bumblebee ('bʌmbəlˌbiː) *or* **humblebee** *n.* any large hairy social bee of the genus *Bombus* and related genera, of temperate regions: family *Apidae.* [C16: from BUMBLE[2] + BEE[1]]

bumbledom ('bʌmbəldəm) *n.* self-importance in a minor office. [C19: after *Bumble,* name of the beadle in Dickens' *Oliver Twist* (1837–38)]

bumble-puppy *n.* **1.** a game in which a ball, attached by string to a post, is hit so that the string winds round the post. **2.** (*modifier*) (of whist or bridge) played unskilfully.

bumboat ('bʌmˌbəʊt) *n.* any small boat used for ferrying supplies or goods for sale to a ship at anchor or at a mooring. [C17 (in the sense: scavenger's boat): *bum,* from Dutch *boomschip* canoe (from *bom* tree) + BOAT]

bumf (bʌmf) *n.* a variant spelling of **bumph.**

bumfreezer ('bʌmˌfriːzə) *n.* **1.** a slang name for an **Eton jacket. 2.** *Slang.* any of various similar styles of short jacket worn by men.

bumkin ('bʌmkɪn) *n.* a variant spelling of **boomkin.**

bummalo ('bʌməˌləʊ) *n., pl.* **-lo.** another name for **Bombay duck.** [C17: from Marathi *bombīla*]

bummaree (ˌbʌmə'riː) *n. Brit.* (formerly) **1.** a dealer at Billingsgate fish market. **2.** a porter at Smithfield meat market. [C18: of unknown origin]

bummer ('bʌmə) *n. Slang.* **1.** *Chiefly U.S.* a vagrant or idler. **2.** person or thing considered inferior. **3.** an adverse reaction to a drug, characterized by panic or fear.

bump (bʌmp) *vb.* **1.** (when *intr.,* usually foll. by *against* or *into*) to knock or strike with a jolt. **2.** (*intr.;* often foll. by *along*) to travel or proceed in jerks and jolts. **3.** (*tr.*) to hurt by knocking: *he bumped his head on the ceiling.* **4.** (*tr.*) to knock out of place; dislodge: *the crash bumped him from his chair.* **5.** (*tr.*) *Brit.* to throw (a child) into the air, one other child holding each limb, and let him down again to touch the ground. **6.** (in rowing races, esp. at Oxford and Cambridge) to catch up with and touch (another boat that started a fixed distance ahead). **7.** *Cricket.* to bowl (a ball) so that it bounces high on pitching or (of a ball) to bounce high when bowled. **8.** (*intr.*) *Chiefly U.S. and Canadian.* to dance erotically by thrusting the pelvis forward (esp. in the phrase **bump and grind**). **9.** (*tr.*) *Poker.* to raise (someone). **10.** (*tr.*) *Informal.* to exclude a ticket-holding passenger from a flight as a result of overbooking. ~*n.* **11.** an impact; knock; jolt; collision. **12.** a dull thud or other noise from an impact or collision. **13.** the shock of a blow or collision. **14.** a lump on the body caused by a blow. **15.** a protuberance, as on a road surface. **16.** any of the natural protuberances of the human skull, said by phrenologists to indicate underlying faculties and character. **17.** a rising current of air that gives an aircraft a severe upward jolt. **18.** (*pl.*) the act of bumping a child. See sense 5. **19.** *Rowing.* the act of bumping. See **bumping race. 20. bump ball.** *Cricket.* a ball that bounces into the air after being hit directly into the ground by the batsman. ~See also **bump into, bump off, bump up.** [C16: probably of imitative origin]

bumper[1] ('bʌmpə) *n.* **1.** a horizontal metal bar attached to the front or rear end of a car, lorry, etc., to protect against damage from impact. **2.** a person or machine that bumps. **3.** *Cricket.* a ball bowled so that it bounces high on pitching; bouncer.

bumper[2] (ˈbʌmpə) *n.* **1.** a glass, tankard, etc., filled to the brim, esp. as a toast. **2.** an unusually large or fine example of something. ~*adj.* **3.** unusually large, fine, or abundant: *a bumper crop.* ~*vb.* **4.** (*tr.*) to toast with a bumper. **5.** (*tr.*) to fill to the brim. **6.** (*intr.*) to drink bumpers. [C17 (in the sense: a brimming glass): probably from *bump* (obsolete vb.) to bulge; see BUMP]

bumper[3] (ˈbʌmpə) *n. Austral. informal.* a cigarette end. [C19: perhaps from a blend of BUTT[1] and STUMP]

bumper car *n.* a low-powered electrically propelled vehicle driven and bumped against similar cars in a special rink at a funfair. Also called: **Dodgem.**

bumph *or* **bumf** (bʌmf) *n. Brit.* **1.** *Informal, derogatory.* official documents, forms, etc. **2.** *Slang.* toilet paper. [C19: short for earlier *bumfodder;* see BUM[1]]

bumping race *n.* (esp. at Oxford and Cambridge) a race in which rowing eights start an equal distance one behind the other and each tries to bump the boat in front.

bump into *vb.* (*intr., prep.*) *Informal.* to meet by chance; encounter unexpectedly.

bumpkin[1] (ˈbʌmpkɪn) *n.* an awkward simple rustic person (esp. in the phrase **country bumpkin**). [C16 (perhaps originally applied to Dutchmen): perhaps from Dutch *boomken* small tree, or from Middle Dutch *boomekijn* small barrel, alluding to a short or squat person]

bumpkin[2] (ˈbʌmpkɪn) *or* **bumkin** *n.* variant spellings of **boomkin.**

bump off *vb.* (*tr., adv.*) *Slang.* to murder; kill.

bump start *Brit.* ~*n.* **1.** a method of starting a motor vehicle by engaging a low gear with the clutch depressed and pushing it or allowing it to run down a hill until sufficient momentum has been acquired to turn the engine by releasing the clutch. ~*vb.* **bump-start. 2.** (*tr.*) to start (a motor vehicle) using this method.

bumptious (ˈbʌmpʃəs) *adj.* offensively self-assertive or conceited. [C19: perhaps a blend of BUMP + FRACTIOUS] —**ˈbumptiously** *adv.* —**ˈbumptiousness** *n.*

bump up *vb.* (*tr., adv.*) *Informal.* to raise or increase: *prices are being bumped up daily.*

bumpy (ˈbʌmpɪ) *adj.* **bumpier, bumpiest. 1.** having an uneven surface: *a bumpy road.* **2.** full of jolts; rough: *a bumpy flight.* —**ˈbumpily** *adv.* —**ˈbumpiness** *n.*

bum rap *n. U.S. slang.* **1.** a trumped-up or false charge. **2.** an unjust punishment.

bum's rush *n. Slang.* **1.** forcible ejection, as from a gathering. **2.** rapid dismissal, as of an idea.

bum steer *n. Slang, chiefly U.S.* false or misleading information or advice.

bumsucking (ˈbʌmˌsʌkɪŋ) *n. Brit. taboo slang.* obsequious behaviour; toadying. —**ˈbumˌsucker** *n.*

bun (bʌn) *n.* **1.** a small roll, similar to bread but usually containing sweetening, currants, spices, etc. **2.** any of various types of small round sweet cakes. **3.** a hairstyle in which long hair is gathered into a bun shape at the back of the head. [C14: of unknown origin]

Buna (ˈbuːnə, ˈbjuː-) *n. Trademark.* a synthetic rubber formed by polymerizing butadiene or by copolymerizing it with such compounds as acrylonitride or styrene.

bunch (bʌntʃ) *n.* **1.** a number of things growing, fastened, or grouped together: a *bunch of grapes; a bunch of keys.* **2.** a collection; group: *a bunch of queries.* **3.** *Informal.* a group or company: *a bunch of boys.* **4.** *Archaic.* a protuberance. ~*vb.* **5.** (sometimes foll. by *up*) to group or be grouped into a bunch. ~See also **bunches.** [C14: of obscure origin]

bunches (ˈbʌntʃɪz) *pl. n. Brit.* a hairstyle in which hair is tied into two sections on either side of the head at the back.

bunchy (ˈbʌntʃɪ) *adj.* **bunchier, bunchiest. 1.** composed of or resembling bunches. **2.** bulging. —**ˈbunchiness** *n.*

bunco *or* **bunko** (ˈbʌŋkəʊ) *U.S. informal.* ~*n., pl.* **-cos** *or* **-kos. 1.** a swindle, esp. one by confidence tricksters. ~*vb.* **-cos, -coing, -coed** *or* **-kos, -koing, -koed. 2.** (*tr.*) to swindle; cheat. [C19: perhaps from Spanish *banca* bank (in gambling), from Italian *banca* BANK[1]]

buncombe (ˈbʌŋkəm) *n.* a variant spelling (esp. U.S.) of **bunkum.**

bund (bʌnd) *n.* (in India and the Far East) **1.** an embankment; dyke. **2.** an embanked road or quay. [C19: from Hindi *band,* from Persian; related to Sanskrit *bandha* BAND[1]]

Bund (bʊnd; *German* bʊnt) *n., pl.* **Bunds** *or* **Bünde** (*German* ˈbyndə). (*sometimes not cap.*) a federation or league. [C19: German; related to BAND[2], BIND]

Bundesrat (ˈbʊndəsˌrɑːt) *n.* **1.** (in Germany and formerly in West Germany) the council of state ministers with certain legislative and administrative powers, representing the state governments at federal level. **2.** (in Austria) an assembly with some legislative power that represents state interests at the federal level. **3.** (in Switzerland) the executive council of the confederation. **4.** (in the German empire from 1871–1918) the council representing the governments of the constituent states, with administrative, judicial, and legislative powers. [C19: German, from *Bund* federation + *Rat* council]

Bundestag (ˈbʊndəsˌtɑːg) *n.* (in Germany and formerly in West Germany) the legislative assembly, which is elected by universal adult suffrage and elects the federal chancellor. [C19: German, from *Bund* federation + *-tag,* from *tagen* to meet]

bundh (bʌnd) *n.* a variant spelling of **bandh.**

bundle (ˈbʌndᵊl) *n.* **1.** a number of things or a quantity of material gathered or loosely bound together: *a bundle of sticks.* Related adj.: **fascicular. 2.** something wrapped or tied for carrying; package. **3.** *Slang.* a large sum of money. **4. go a bundle on.** *Slang.* to be extremely fond of. **5.** *Biology.* a collection of strands of specialized tissue such as nerve fibres. **6.** *Botany.* short for **vascular bundle. 7.** *Textiles.* a measure of yarn or cloth; 60 000 yards of linen yarn; 5 or 10 pounds of cotton hanks. **8. drop one's bundle.** *Austral. and N.Z. slang.* to panic or give up hope. ~*vb.* **9.** (*tr.;* often foll. by *up*) to make into a bundle. **10.** (foll. by *out, off, into,* etc.) to go or cause to go, esp. roughly or unceremoniously: *we bundled him out of the house.* **11.** (*tr.;* usually foll. by *into*) to push or throw, esp. quickly and untidily: *to bundle shirts into a drawer.* **12.** (*tr.*) to sell (computer hardware and software) as one indivisible package. **13.** (*tr.*) to give away (a relatively cheap product) when selling an expensive one to attract business: *several free cassettes are often bundled with music centres.* **14.** (*intr.*) to sleep or lie in one's clothes on the same bed as one's betrothed: formerly a custom in New England, Wales, and elsewhere. [C14: probably from Middle Dutch *bundel;* related to Old English *bindele* bandage; see BIND, BOND] —**ˈbundler** *n.*

bundle up *vb.* (*adv.*) **1.** to dress (somebody) warmly and snugly. **2.** (*tr.*) to make (something) into a bundle or bundles, esp. by tying.

bundobust (ˈbʌndəbʌst) *n.* a variant spelling of **bandobust.**

bundu (ˈbʊndʊ) *n. S. African and Zimbabwean slang.* **a.** a largely uninhabited wild region far from towns. **b.** (*as modifier*): *a bundu hat.* [C20: from a Bantu language]

bundwall (ˈbʌndˌwɔːl) *n.* a concrete or earth wall surrounding a storage tank containing crude oil or its refined product, designed to hold the contents of the tank in the event of a rupture or leak. [C20: from BUND + WALL]

bundy (ˈbʌndɪ) *n., pl.* **-dies.** *Austral.* **1.** a time clock. ~*vb.* (*intr.*) **2.** (foll. by *on* or *off*) to arrive or depart from work, esp. when it involves registering the time of arrival or departure on a card. [from a trademark]

bun fight *n. Brit. slang.* **1.** a tea party. **2.** *Ironic.* an official function.

bung[1] (bʌŋ) *n.* **1.** a stopper, esp. of cork or rubber, for a cask, piece of laboratory glassware, etc. **2.** short for **bunghole.** ~*vb.* (*tr.*) **3.** (often foll. by *up*) to close or seal with or as with a bung: *the car's exhaust was bunged up with mud.* **4.** *Brit. slang.* to throw; sling. [C15: from Middle Dutch *bonghe,* from Late Latin *puncta* PUNCTURE]

bung[2] (bʌŋ) *Brit. slang.* ~*n.* **1.** a gratuity; tip. **2.** a bribe. ~*vb.* **3.** (*tr.*) to give (someone) a tip or bribe. [C16 (originally in the sense: a purse): perhaps from Old English *pung,* changed through the influence of BUNG[1]]

bung[3] (bʌŋ) *adj. Austral. and N.Z. slang.* **1.** dead. **2.** destroyed. **3.** useless. **4. go bung. a.** to fail or collapse. **b.** to die. [C19: from a native Australian language]

bungalow (ˈbʌŋgəˌləʊ) *n.* **1.** a one-storey house, sometimes with an attic. **2.** (in India) a one-storey house, usually surrounded by a veranda. [C17: from Hindi *banglā* (house) of the Bengal type]

bunger (ˈbʌŋə) *n. Austral. slang.* a firework.

bunghole (ˈbʌŋˌhəʊl) *n.* a hole in a cask, barrel, etc., through which liquid can be poured or drained.

bungle (ˈbʌŋgᵊl) *vb.* **1.** (*tr.*) to spoil (an operation) through clumsiness, incompetence, etc.; botch. ~*n.* **2.** a clumsy or unsuccessful performance or piece of work; mistake; botch. [C16: perhaps of Scandinavian origin; compare dialect Swedish *bangla* to work without results] —**ˈbungler** *n.* —**ˈbungling** *adj., n.*

bunion (ˈbʌnjən) *n.* swelling of the first joint of the big toe, which is displaced to one side. An inflamed bursa forms over the joint. [C18: perhaps from obsolete *bunny* a swelling, of uncertain origin]

bunk[1] (bʌŋk) *n.* **1.** a narrow shelflike bed fixed along a wall. **2.** short for **bunk bed. 3.** *Informal.* any place where one sleeps. ~*vb.* **4.** (*intr.;* often foll. by *down*) to prepare to sleep: *he bunked down on the floor.* **5.** (*intr.*) to occupy a bunk or bed. **6.** (*tr.*) to provide with a bunk or bed. [C19: probably short for BUNKER]

bunk[2] (bʌŋk) *n. Informal.* short for **bunkum** (sense 1).

bunk[3] (bʌŋk) *Brit. slang.* ~*n.* **1.** a hurried departure, usually under suspicious circumstances (esp. in the phrase **do a bunk**). ~*vb.* **2.** (*intr.*) to run away; scram. [C19: perhaps from BUNK[1] (in the sense: to occupy a bunk, hence a hurried departure, as on a ship)]

bunk bed *n.* one of a pair of beds constructed one above the other to save space.

bunker (ˈbʌŋkə) *n.* **1.** a large storage container or tank, as for coal. **2.** Also called (esp. U.S. and Canadian): **sand trap.** an obstacle on a golf course, usually a sand-filled hollow bordered by a ridge. **3.** an underground shelter, often of reinforced concrete and with a bank and embrasures for guns above ground. ~*vb.* **4.** (*tr.*) *Golf.* **a.** to drive (the ball) into a bunker. **b.** (*passive*) to have one's ball trapped in a bunker. **5.** (*tr.*) *Nautical.* **a.** to fuel (a ship). **b.** to transfer (cargo) from a ship to a storehouse. [C16 (in the sense: chest, box): from Scottish *bonkar,* of unknown origin]

bunkhouse (ˈbʌŋkˌhaʊs) *n.* (in the U.S. and Canada) a building containing the sleeping quarters of workers on a ranch.

bunko (ˈbʌŋkəʊ) *n., pl.* **-kos,** *vb.* **-kos, -koing, -koed.** a variant spelling of **bunco.**

bunkum *or* **buncombe** (ˈbʌŋkəm) *n.* **1.** empty talk; nonsense. **2.** *Chiefly U.S.* empty or insincere speechmaking by a politician to please voters or gain publicity. [C19: after *Buncombe,* a county in North Carolina, alluded to in an inane speech by its Congressional representative Felix Walker (about 1820)]

bunny (ˈbʌnɪ) *n., pl.* **-nies. 1.** Also called: **bunny rabbit.** a child's word for **rabbit** (sense 1). **2.** Also called: **bunny girl.** a night-club hostess whose costume includes rabbit-like tail and ears. **3.** *Austral. slang.* a mug; dupe. [C17: from Scottish Gaelic *bun* scut of a rabbit]

bunny hug *n.* **1.** a ballroom dance with syncopated rhythm, popular in America in the early 20th century. **2.** a piece of music in the rhythm of this dance.

bunodont (ˈbjuːnəˌdɒnt) *adj.* (of the teeth of certain mammals) having cusps that are separate and rounded. [from Greek *bounos* hill + -ODONT]

bunraku (bʊnˈrɑːkuː) *n.* a Japanese form of puppet theatre in which the puppets are usually about four feet high, with moving features as well as limbs and each puppet is manipulated by up to three puppeteers who remain onstage. [C20: Japanese]

Bunsen burner (ˈbʌnsᵊn) *n.* a gas burner, widely used in scientific laboratories, consisting of a metal tube with an adjustable air valve at the base. [C19: named after R. W. *Bunsen* (1811–99), German chemist]

bunt[1] (bʌnt) *vb.* **1.** (of an animal) to butt (something) with the head or horns. **2.** to cause (an aircraft) to fly in part of an inverted loop or (of an aircraft) to fly in such a loop. **3.** *U.S. and Canadian.* (in baseball) to hit (a pitched ball) very gently. ~*n.* **4.** the act or an instance of bunting. [C19: perhaps nasalized variant of BUTT[3]]

bunt[2] (bʌnt) *n. Nautical.* the baggy centre of a fishing net or other piece of fabric, such as a square sail. [C16: perhaps from Middle Low German *bunt* BUNDLE]

bunt[3] (bʌnt) *n.* a disease of cereal plants caused by smut fungi (genus *Tilletia*). [C17: of unknown origin]

buntal (ˈbʌntᵊl) *n.* straw obtained from leaves of the talipot palm. [C20: from Tagalog]

bunting[1] (ˈbʌntɪŋ) *n.* **1.** a coarse, loosely woven cotton fabric used for flags, etc. **2.** decorative flags, pennants, and streamers. **3.** flags collectively, esp. those of a boat. [C18: of unknown origin]

bunting[2] (ˈbʌntɪŋ) *n.* any of numerous seed-eating songbirds of the families *Fringillidae* (finches, etc.) or *Emberizidae,* esp. those of the genera *Emberiza* of the Old World and *Passerina* of North America. They all have short stout bills. [C13: of unknown origin]

buntline (ˈbʌntlɪn, -ˌlaɪn) *n. Nautical.* one of several lines fastened to the foot of a square sail for hauling it up to the yard when furling. [C17: from BUNT[2] + LINE[1]]

bunya (ˈbʌnjə) *n.* a tall dome-shaped Australian coniferous tree, *Araucaria bidwillii,* having edible cones (**bunya nuts**) and thickish flattened needles. Also called: **bunya-bunya.** [C19: from a native Australian language]

bunyip (ˈbʌnjɪp) *n. Austral.* a legendary monster said to inhabit swamps and lagoons of the Australian interior. [C19: from a native Australian language]

buoy (bɔɪ; *U.S.* ˈbuːɪ) *n.* **1.** a distinctively shaped and coloured float, anchored to the bottom, for designating moorings, navigable channels, or obstructions in a body of water. See also **life buoy.** ~*vb.* **2.** (*tr.;* usually foll. by *up*) to prevent from sinking: *the life belt buoyed him up.* **3.** (*tr.;* usually foll. by *up*) to raise the spirits of; hearten. **4.** (*tr.*) *Nautical.* to mark (a channel or obstruction) with a buoy or buoys. **5.** (*intr.*) to rise to the surface; float. [C13: probably of Germanic origin; compare Middle Dutch *boeie, boeye;* see BEACON]

buoyage (ˈbɔɪɪdʒ) *n.* **1.** a system of buoys. **2.** the buoys used in such a system. **3.** the providing of buoys.

buoyancy (ˈbɔɪənsɪ) *n.* **1.** the ability to float in a liquid or to rise in liquid, air, or other gas. **2.** the tendency of a fluid to exert a lifting effect on a body that is wholly or partly submerged in it. **3.** the ability to recover quickly after setbacks; resilience. **4.** cheerfulness.

buoyancy bags *pl. n.* another term for **flotation bags.**

buoyant (ˈbɔɪənt) *adj.* **1.** able to float in or rise to the surface of a liquid. **2.** (of a liquid or gas) able to keep a body afloat or cause it to rise. **3.** cheerful or resilient. [C16: probably from Spanish *boyante,* from *boyar* to float, from *boya* buoy, ultimately of Germanic origin]

bupivacaine (bjuːˈpɪvəkeɪn) *n.* a local anaesthetic of long duration, used for nerve blocks.

buprestid (bjuːˈprɛstɪd) *n.* **1.** any beetle of the mainly tropical family *Buprestidae,* the adults of which are brilliantly coloured and the larvae of which bore into and cause damage to trees, roots, etc. ~*adj.* **2.** of, relating to, or belonging to the family *Buprestidae.* [C19: from Latin *buprestis* poisonous beetle, causing the cattle who eat it to swell up, from Greek, from *bous* ox + *prēthein* to swell up]

bur (bɜː) *n.* **1.** a seed vessel or flower head, as of burdock, having hooks or prickles. **2.** any plant that produces burs. **3.** a person or thing that clings like a bur. **4.** a small surgical or dental drill. **5.** a variant spelling of **burr**[3], **burr**[4]. ~*vb.* **burs, burring, burred. 6.** (*tr.*) to remove burs from. ~Also (for senses 1–4, 6): **burr.** [C14: probably of Scandinavian origin; compare Danish *burre* bur, Swedish *kardborre* burdock]

BUR *international car registration for* Burma.

Bur. *abbrev. for* Burma.

buran (buːˈrɑːn) *or* **bura** (buːˈrɑː) *n.* (in central Asia) **1.** a blizzard, with the wind blowing from the north and reaching gale force. **2.** a summer wind from the north, causing dust storms. [C19: from Russian, of Turkic origin; related to Kazan Tatar *buran*]

Burberry (ˈbɜːbərɪ) *n., pl.* **-ries.** *Trademark.* a light good-quality raincoat, esp. of gabardine.

burble (ˈbɜːbᵊl) *vb.* **1.** to make or utter with a bubbling sound; gurgle. **2.** (*intr.;* often foll. by *away* or *on*) to talk quickly and excitedly. **3.** (*intr.*) (of the airflow around a body) to become turbulent. ~*n.* **4.** a bubbling or gurgling sound. **5.** a flow of excited speech. **6.** turbulence in the airflow around a body. [C14: probably of imitative origin; compare Spanish *borbollar* to bubble, gush, Italian *borbugliare*] —ˈ**burbler** *n.*

burbot (ˈbɜːbət) *n., pl.* **-bots** *or* **-bot.** a freshwater gadoid food fish, *Lota lota,* that has barbels around its mouth and occurs in Europe, Asia, and North America. [C14: from Old French *bourbotte,* from *bourbeter* to wallow in mud, from *bourbe* mud, probably of Celtic origin]

burden[1] (ˈbɜːdᵊn) *n.* **1.** something that is carried; load. **2.** something that is exacting, oppressive, or difficult to bear: *the burden of responsibility.* Related adj.: **onerous. 3.** *Nautical.* **a.** the cargo capacity of a ship. **b.** the weight of a ship's cargo. ~*vb.* (*tr.*) **4.** (sometimes foll. by *up*) to put or impose a burden on; load. **5.** to weigh down; oppress: *the old woman was burdened with cares.* [Old English *byrthen;* related to *beran* to BEAR[1], Old Frisian *berthene* burden, Old High German *burdin*]

burden[2] (ˈbɜːdᵊn) *n.* **1.** a line of words recurring at the end of each verse of a ballad or similar song; chorus or refrain. **2.** the principal or recurrent theme of a speech, book, etc. **3.** another word for **bourdon.** [C16: from Old French *bourdon* bass horn, droning sound, of imitative origin]

burden of proof *n. Law.* the obligation, in criminal cases resting initially on the prosecution, to provide evidence that will convince the court or jury of the truth of one's contention.

burdensome (ˈbɜːdᵊnsəm) *adj.* hard to bear; onerous.

burdock (ˈbɜːˌdɒk) *n.* a coarse weedy Eurasian plant of the genus *Arctium,* having large heart-shaped leaves, tiny purple flowers surrounded by hooked bristles, and burlike fruits: family *Compositae* (composites). [C16: from BUR + DOCK[4]]

bureau (ˈbjʊərəʊ) *n., pl.* **-reaus** *or* **-reaux** (-rəʊz). **1.** *Chiefly Brit.* a writing desk with pigeonholes, drawers, etc., against which the writing surface can be closed when not in use. **2.** *U.S.* a chest of drawers. **3.** an office or agency, esp. one providing services for the public. **4. a.** a government department. **b.** a branch of a government department. [C17: from French: desk, office, originally: type of cloth used for covering desks and tables, from Old French *burel,* from Late Latin *burra* shaggy cloth]

bureaucracy (bjʊəˈrɒkrəsɪ) *n., pl.* **-cies. 1.** a system of administration based upon organization into bureaus, division of labour, a hierarchy of authority, etc.: designed to dispose of a large body of work in a routine manner. **2.** government by such a system. **3.** government or other officials collectively. **4.** any administration in which action is impeded by unnecessary official procedures and red tape.

bureaucrat (ˈbjʊərəˌkræt) *n.* **1.** an official in a bureaucracy. **2.** an official who adheres to bureaucracy, esp. rigidly. —ˌ**bureauˈcratic** *adj.* —ˌ**bureauˈcratically** *adv.* —**bureaucratism** (bjʊəˈrɒkrəˌtɪzəm) *n.*

bureaucratize *or* **bureaucratise** (bjʊəˈrɒkrəˌtaɪz) *vb.* (*tr.*) to administer by or transform into a bureaucracy. —**buˌreaucratiˈzation** *or* **buˌreaucratiˈsation** *n.*

burette *or U.S.* **buret** (bjʊˈrɛt) *n.* a graduated glass tube with a stopcock on one end for dispensing and transferring known volumes of fluids, esp. liquids. [C15: from French: cruet, oil can, from Old French *buire* ewer, of Germanic origin; compare Old English *būc* pitcher, belly]

burg (bɜːg) *n.* **1.** *History.* a fortified town. **2.** *U.S. informal.* a town or city. [C18 (in the sense: fortress): from Old High German *burg* fortified town; see BOROUGH]

burgage (ˈbɜːgɪdʒ) *n. History.* **1.** (in England) tenure of land or tenement in a town or city, which originally involved a fixed money rent. **2.** (in Scotland) the tenure of land direct from the crown in Scottish royal burghs in return for watching and warding. [C14: from Medieval Latin *burgāgium,* from *burgus,* from Old English *burg;* see BOROUGH]

burgee (ˈbɜːdʒiː) *n. Nautical.* a triangular or swallow-tailed flag flown from the mast of a merchant ship for identification and from the mast of a yacht to indicate its owner's membership of a particular yacht club. [C18: perhaps from French (Jersey dialect) *bourgeais* shipowner, from Old French *borgeis;* see BOURGEOIS[1], BURGESS]

burgeon *or* **bourgeon** (ˈbɜːdʒən) *vb.* **1.** (often foll. by *forth* or *out*) (of a plant) to sprout (buds). **2.** (*intr.;* often foll. by *forth* or *out*) to develop or grow rapidly; flourish. ~*n.* **3.** a bud of a plant.

[C13: from Old French *burjon,* perhaps ultimately from Late Latin *burra* shaggy cloth; from the downiness of certain buds]

burger ('bɜːgə) *n. Informal.* **a.** short for **hamburger.** **b.** (*in combination*): *a cheeseburger.*

burgess ('bɜːdʒɪs) *n.* **1.** (in England) **a.** a citizen or freeman of a borough. **b.** any inhabitant of a borough. **2.** *English history.* a Member of Parliament from a borough, corporate town, or university. **3.** a member of the colonial assembly of Maryland or Virginia. [C13: from Old French *burgeis,* from *borc* town, from Late Latin *burgus,* of Germanic origin; see BOROUGH]

burgh ('bʌrə) *n.* **1.** (in Scotland) a town, esp. one incorporated by charter, that enjoyed a degree of self-government until the local-government reorganization of 1975. **2.** an archaic form of **borough** (sense 1). [C14: Scottish form of BOROUGH] —**burghal** ('bɜːgᵊl) *adj.*

burgher ('bɜːgə) *n.* **1.** a member of the trading or mercantile class of a medieval city. **2.** a respectable citizen; bourgeois. **3.** *Archaic.* a citizen or inhabitant of a corporate town, esp. on the Continent. **4.** *S. African history.* **a.** a citizen of the Cape Colony or of one of the Transvaal and Free State republics. **b.** (*as modifier*): *burgher troops.* [C16: from German *Bürger,* or Dutch *burger* freeman of a BOROUGH]

burglar ('bɜːglə) *n.* a person who commits burglary; housebreaker. [C15: from Anglo-French *burgler,* from Medieval Latin *burglātor,* probably from *burgāre* to thieve, from Latin *burgus* castle, fortress, of Germanic origin]

burglarize *or* **burglarise** ('bɜːgləˌraɪz) *vb.* (*tr.*) *U.S. and Canadian.* to break into (a place) and steal from (someone); burgle.

burglary ('bɜːglərɪ) *n., pl.* **-ries.** *English criminal law.* the crime of either entering a building as a trespasser with the intention of committing theft, rape, grievous bodily harm, or damage, or, having entered as a trespasser, of committing one or more of these offences. —**burglarious** (bɜː'glɛərɪəs) *adj.*

burgle ('bɜːgᵊl) *vb.* to commit burglary upon (a house, etc.).

burgomaster ('bɜːgəˌmɑːstə) *n.* **1.** the chief magistrate of a town in Austria, Belgium, Germany, or the Netherlands; mayor. **2.** a popular name for the **glaucous gull.** [C16: partial translation of Dutch *burgemeester;* see BOROUGH, MASTER]

burgonet ('bɜːgəˌnɛt) *n.* a light 16th-century helmet, usually made of steel, with hinged cheekpieces. [C16: from French *bourguignotte,* from *bourguignot* of Burgundy, from *Bourgogne* Burgundy]

burgoo ('bɜːguː, bɜː'guː) *n., pl.* **-goos.** **1.** *Nautical slang.* porridge. **2.** *Southern U.S.* **a.** a thick highly seasoned soup or stew of meat and vegetables. **b.** a picnic or gathering at which such soup is served. [C18: perhaps from Arabic *burghul* crushed grain]

burgrave ('bɜːgreɪv) *n.* **1.** the military governor of a German town or castle, esp. in the 12th and 13th centuries. **2.** a nobleman ruling a German town or castle by hereditary right. [C16: from German *Burggraf,* from Old High German *burg* BOROUGH + *grāve* count]

Burgundy ('bɜːgəndɪ) *n., pl.* **-dies.** **1.** any red or white wine produced in the region of Burgundy, around Dijon, E France. **2.** any heavy red table wine. **3.** (*often not cap.*) a blackish-purple to purplish-red colour. —**Burgundian** (bɜː'gʌndɪən) *adj.*

burhel ('bʌrəl) *n.* a variant spelling of **bharal.**

burial ('bɛrɪəl) *n.* the act of burying, esp. the interment of a dead body. [Old English *byrgels* burial place, tomb; see BURY, -AL[2]]

burial ground *n.* a graveyard or cemetery.

Buridan's ass ('bjʊərɪdənz) *n. Philosophy.* an example intended to show the deficiency of reason. An ass standing equidistant from two identical heaps of oats starves to death because reason provides no grounds for choosing to eat one rather than the other. [named after Jean *Buridan,* 14th-century French philosopher, to whom it was incorrectly attributed]

burier ('bɛrɪə) *n.* a person or thing that buries.

burin ('bjʊərɪn) *n.* **1.** a chisel of tempered steel with a sharp lozenge-shaped point, used for engraving furrows in metal, wood, or marble. **2.** an engraver's individual style. **3.** *Archaeol.* a prehistoric flint tool with a very small transverse edge. [C17: from French, perhaps from Italian *burino,* of Germanic origin: compare Old High German *boro* auger; see BORE[1]]

burk *or* **berk** (bɜːk) *n. Brit. slang.* a stupid person; fool. [C20: shortened from *Berkeley* or *Berkshire Hunt,* rhyming slang for *cunt*]

burka ('bɜːkə) *n.* a long enveloping garment worn by Muslim women in public. [C19: from Arabic]

burke (bɜːk) *vb.* (*tr.*) **1.** to murder in such a way as to leave no marks on the body, usually by suffocation. **2.** to get rid of, silence, or suppress. [C19: named after William BURKE, executed in Edinburgh for a murder of this type]

Burkitt lymphoma ('bɜːkɪt) *or* **Burkitt's lymphoma** ('bɜːkɪts) *n.* a rare type of tumour of the white blood cells, occurring mainly in Africa and associated with infection by Epstein-Barr virus. [named after Dennis *Burkitt* (born 1911), British surgeon who first described the tumour]

burl[1] (bɜːl) *n.* **1.** a small knot or lump in wool. **2.** a roundish warty outgrowth from the trunk, roots, or branches of certain trees. ~*vb.* **3.** (*tr.*) to remove the burls from (cloth). [C15: from Old French *burle* tuft of wool, probably ultimately from Late Latin *burra* shaggy cloth] —'**burler** *n.*

burl[2] *or* **birl** (bɜːl) *n. Informal.* **1.** *Scot., Austral., and N.Z.* an attempt; try (esp. in the phrase **give it a burl**). **2.** *Austral. and N.Z.* a ride in a car. [C20: perhaps from BIRL[1] in the Scot. sense: a twist or turn]

burlap ('bɜːlæp) *n.* a coarse fabric woven from jute, hemp, or the like. [C17: from *borel* coarse cloth, from Old French *burel* (see BUREAU) + LAP[1]]

burlesque (bɜː'lɛsk) *n.* **1.** an artistic work, esp. literary or dramatic, satirizing a subject by caricaturing it. **2.** a ludicrous imitation or caricature. **3.** a play of the 17th–19th centuries that parodied some contemporary dramatic fashion or event. **4.** Also: **burlesk.** *U.S. and Canadian theatre.* a bawdy comedy show of the late 19th and early 20th centuries: the striptease eventually became one of its chief elements. Slang name: **burleycue.** ~*adj.* **5.** of, relating to, or characteristic of a burlesque. ~*vb.* **-lesques, -lesquing, -lesqued.** **6.** to represent or imitate (a person or thing) in a ludicrous way; caricature. [C17: from French, from Italian *burlesco,* from *burla* a jest, piece of nonsense] —**bur'lesquer** *n.*

burley[1] ('bɜːlɪ) *n., vb.* a variant spelling of **berley.**

burley[2] ('bɜːlɪ) *n.* a light thin-leaved tobacco, grown esp. in Kentucky. [C19: probably from the name *Burley*]

burly ('bɜːlɪ) *adj.,* **-lier, -liest.** large and thick of build; sturdy; stout. [C13: of Germanic origin; compare Old High German *burlīh* lofty] —'**burliness** *n.*

bur marigold *n.* any plant of the genus *Bidens* that has yellow flowers and pointed fruits that cling to fur and clothing: family *Compositae* (composites). Also called: **beggar-ticks, sticktight.**

Burmese (bɜː'miːz) *adj. also* **Burman.** **1.** of, relating to, or characteristic of Burma (now Myanmar), a republic in SE Asia, its people, or their language. ~*n., pl.* **-mese.** **2.** a native or inhabitant of Burma. **3.** the official language of Burma, belonging to the Sino-Tibetan family.

Burmese cat *n.* a breed of cat similar in shape to the Siamese but typically having a dark brown or blue-grey coat.

burn[1] (bɜːn) *vb.* **burns, burning, burnt** *or* **burned.** **1.** to undergo or cause to undergo combustion. **2.** to destroy or be destroyed by fire. **3.** (*tr.*) to damage, injure, or mark by heat: *he burnt his hand; she was burnt by the sun.* **4.** to die or put to death by fire: *to burn at the stake.* **5.** (*intr.*) to be or feel hot: *my forehead burns.* **6.** to smart or cause to smart: *brandy burns one's throat.* **7.** (*intr.*) to feel strong emotion, esp. anger or passion. **8.** (*tr.*) to use for the purposes of light, heat, or power: *to burn coal.* **9.** (*tr.*) to form by or as if by fire: *to burn a hole.* **10.** to char or become charred: *the potatoes are burning in the saucepan.* **11.** (*tr.*) to brand or cauterize. **12.** (*tr.*) to cut (metal) with an oxygen-rich flame. **13.** to produce by or subject to heat as part of a process: *to burn charcoal.* **14.** *Card games, chiefly Brit.* to discard or exchange (one or more useless cards). **15.** (*tr.; usually passive*) *Informal.* to cheat, esp. financially. **16.** *Slang, chiefly U.S.* to electrocute or be electrocuted. **17.** (*tr.*) *Austral. slang.* to drive fast (esp. in the phrase **go for a burn**). **18. burn one's boats** *or* **bridges.** to commit oneself to a particular course of action with no possibility of turning back. **19. burn the candle at both ends.** See **candle** (sense 3). **20. burn one's fingers.** to suffer from having meddled or been rash. ~*n.* **21.** an injury caused by exposure to heat, electrical, chemical, or radioactive agents. Burns are classified according to the depth of tissue affected: **first-degree burn:** skin surface painful and red; **second-degree burn:** blisters appear on the skin; **third-degree burn:** destruction of both epidermis and dermis. **22.** a mark, e.g. on wood, caused by burning. **23.** a controlled use of rocket propellant, esp. for a course correction. **24.** a hot painful sensation in a muscle, experienced during vigorous exercise: *go for the burn!* **25.** *Austral. and N.Z.* a controlled fire to clear an area of scrub. **26.** *Slang.* tobacco or a cigarette. ~See also **burn in, burn off, burn out.** [Old English *beornan* (intr.), *bærnan* (tr.); related to Old Norse *brenna* (tr. or intr.), Gothic *brinnan* (intr.), Latin *fervēre* to boil, seethe]

burn[2] (bɜːn; *Scot.* bʌrn) *n. Scot.* a small stream; brook. [Old English *burna;* related to Old Norse *brunnr* spring, Old High German *brunno,* Lithuanian *briáutis* to burst forth]

burned (bɜːnd) *adj. Slang.* **1.** having been cheated in a sale of drugs. **2.** *Rare.* **a.** revealed as a drug-peddler by a police informer. **b.** revealed to drug-users as a police informer.

burner ('bɜːnə) *n.* **1.** the part of a stove, lamp, etc., that produces flame or heat. **2.** an apparatus for burning something, as fuel or refuse: *an oil burner.*

burnet ('bɜːnɪt) *n.* **1.** a plant of the rosaceous genus *Sanguisorba* (or *Poterium*), such as *S. minor* (or *P. sanguisorba*) (**salad burnet**), which has purple-tinged green flowers and leaves that are sometimes used for salads. **2. burnet rose.** Also called: **Scotch rose.** a very prickly Eurasian rose, *Rosa pimpinellifolia,* with white flowers and purplish-black fruits. **3. burnet saxifrage.** a Eurasian umbelliferous plant of the genus *Pimpinella,* having umbrella-like clusters of white or pink flowers. **4.** a moth of the genus *Zygaena,* having red-spotted dark green wings and antennae with enlarged tips: family *Zygaenidae.* [C14: from Old French *burnete,* variant of *brunete* dark brown (see BRUNETTE); so called from the colour of the flowers of some of the plants]

Burnham scale ('bɜːnəm) *n.* the salary scale for teachers in English state schools, which is revised periodically. [C20: named after Lord *Burnham* (1862–1933), chairman of the committee that originally set it up]

burn in *vb.* (*tr., adv.*) to darken (areas on a photographic print) by exposing them to light while masking other regions.

burning (ˈbɜːnɪŋ) *adj.* **1.** intense; passionate. **2.** urgent; crucial: *a burning problem.* ~*n.* **3.** a form of heat treatment used to harden and finish ceramic materials or to prepare certain ores for further treatment by calcination. **4.** overheating of an alloy during heat treatment in which local fusion or excessive oxide formation and penetration occur, weakening the alloy. **5.** the heat treatment of particular kinds of gemstones to change their colour. —ˈ**burningly** *adv.*

burning bush *n.* **1.** any of several shrubs or trees, esp. the wahoo, that have bright red fruits or seeds. **2.** another name for **gas plant.** **3.** any of several plants, esp. kochia, with a bright red autumn foliage.

burning glass *n.* a convex lens for concentrating the sun's rays into a small area to produce heat or fire.

burnish (ˈbɜːnɪʃ) *vb.* **1.** to make or become shiny or smooth by friction; polish. ~*n.* **2.** a shiny finish; lustre. [C14 *burnischen,* from Old French *brunir* to make brown, from *brun* BROWN] —ˈ**burnishable** *adj.* —ˈ**burnisher** *n.*

burn off *vb.* (*tr., adv.*) **1.** to clear (land) of vegetation by burning. **2.** to get rid of (unwanted gas at an oil well, etc.) by burning. ~*n.* **burn-off.** **3.** an act or the process of burning off.

burnous, burnouse, *or U.S.* **burnoose** (bɜːˈnuːs, -ˈnuːz) *n.* a long circular cloak with a hood attached, worn esp. by Arabs. [C17: via French *burnous* from Arabic *burnus,* from Greek *birros* cloak] —**burˈnoused** *or U.S.* **burˈnoosed** *adj.*

burn out *vb.* (*adv.*) **1.** to become or cause to become worn out or inoperative as a result of heat or friction: *the clutch burnt out.* **2.** (*intr.*) (of a rocket, jet engine, etc.) to cease functioning as a result of exhaustion of the fuel supply. **3.** (*tr.; usually passive*) to destroy by fire. **4.** to become or cause to become exhausted through overwork or dissipation. ~*n.* **burnout.** **5.** the failure of a mechanical device from excessive heating. **6.** a total loss of energy and interest and an inability to function effectively, experienced as a result of excessive demands upon one's resources or chronic overwork.

burnsides (ˈbɜːnˌsaɪdz) *pl. n. U.S.* thick side whiskers worn with a moustache and clean-shaven chin. [C19: named after General A. E. *Burnside* (1824–81), Union general in the U.S. Civil War]

burnt (bɜːnt) *vb.* **1.** a past tense and past participle of **burn**[1]. ~*adj.* **2.** affected by or as if by burning; charred. **3.** (of various pigments, such as ochre and orange) calcined, with a resultant darkening of colour.

burnt almond *n.* a sweet consisting of an almond enclosed in burnt sugar.

burnt offering *n.* a sacrificial offering burnt, usually on an altar, to honour, propitiate, or supplicate a deity.

burnt shale *n.* carbonaceous shale formed by destructive distillation of oil shale or by spontaneous combustion of shale after it has been some years in a tip: sometimes used in road making.

burnt sienna *n.* **1.** a reddish-brown dye or pigment obtained by roasting raw sienna in a furnace. **2.** a dark reddish-orange to reddish-brown colour.

burnt-tip orchid *n.* a small orchid, *Orchis ustulata,* resembling the lady orchid, having dark reddish-brown hoods that give a burnt look to the tip of the flower spike.

burnt umber *n.* **1.** a brown pigment obtained by heating umber. **2.** a dark brown colour.

burn-up *n. Slang.* a period of fast driving.

bur oak *n.* an E North American oak, *Quercus macrocarpa,* having fringed acorn cups and durable timber.

buroo (bəˈruː, bruː) *n., pl.* **-roos.** *Scot. and Irish dialect.* **1.** the government office from which unemployment benefit is distributed. **2.** the unemployment benefit itself (esp. in the phrase **on the buroo**). [C20: from BUREAU]

burp (bɜːp) *n.* **1.** *Informal.* a belch. ~*vb.* **2.** (*intr.*) *Informal.* to belch. **3.** (*tr.*) to cause (a baby) to burp to relieve flatulence after feeding. [C20: of imitative origin]

burp gun *n. U.S. slang.* an automatic pistol or submachine gun.

burr[1] (bɜː) *n.* **1.** a small power-driven hand-operated rotary file, esp. for removing burrs or for machining recesses. **2.** a rough edge left on a workpiece after cutting, drilling, etc. **3.** a rough or irregular protuberance, such as a burl on a tree. **4.** *Brit.* **a.** a burl on the trunk or root of a tree, sliced across for use as decorative veneer. **b.** (*as modifier*): *burr walnut.* ~*n., vb.* **5.** a variant spelling of **bur.** ~*vb.* (*tr.*) **6.** to form a rough edge on (a workpiece). **7.** to remove burrs from (a workpiece); deburr. [C14: variant of BUR]

burr[2] (bɜː) *n.* **1.** *Phonetics.* an articulation of (r) characteristic of certain English dialects, esp. the uvular fricative trill of Northumberland or the retroflex *r* of the West of England. **2.** a whirring sound. ~*vb.* **3.** to pronounce (words) with a burr. **4.** to make a whirring sound. [C18: either special use of BUR (in the sense: rough sound) or of imitative origin]

burr[3] *or* **bur** (bɜː) *n.* **1.** a washer fitting around the end of a rivet. **2.** a blank punched out of sheet metal. [C16 (in the sense: broad ring on a spear): variant of *burrow* (in obsolete sense: BOROUGH)]

burr[4], **buhr,** *or* **bur** (bɜː) *n.* **1.** short for **buhrstone.** **2.** a mass of hard siliceous rock surrounded by softer rock. [C18: probably from BUR, from its qualities of roughness]

burramys (ˈbʌrəmɪs) *n.* the very rare mountain pigmy possum, *Burramys parvus,* of Australia. It is about the size of a rat and restricted in habitat to very high altitudes, mainly Mt Hotham, Victoria. Until 1966 it was known only as a fossil.

burrawang (ˈbʌrəwæŋ) *n.* any of several Australian cycads of the genus *Macrozamia,* having an edible nut. [C19: from Mount *Budawang,* New South Wales]

bur reed *n.* a marsh plant of the genus *Sparganium,* having narrow leaves, round clusters of small green flowers, and round prickly fruit: family *Sparganiaceae.*

burrito (bəˈriːtəʊ) *n., pl.* **-tos.** *Mexican cookery.* a tortilla folded over a filling of minced beef, chicken, cheese, or beans. [C20: from Mexican Spanish, from Spanish: literally, a young donkey]

burro (ˈbʊrəʊ) *n., pl.* **-ros.** a donkey, esp. one used as a pack animal. [C19: Spanish, from Portuguese, from *burrico* donkey, ultimately from Latin *burrīcus* small horse]

burrow (ˈbʌrəʊ) *n.* **1.** a hole or tunnel dug in the ground by a rabbit, fox, or other small animal, for habitation or shelter. **2.** a small snug place affording shelter or retreat. ~*vb.* **3.** to dig (a burrow) in, through, or under (ground). **4.** (*intr.;* often foll. by *through*) to move through by or as by digging: *to burrow through the forest.* **5.** (*intr.*) to hide or live in a burrow. **6.** (*intr.*) to delve deeply: *he burrowed into his pockets.* **7.** to hide (oneself). [C13: probably a variant of BOROUGH] —ˈ**burrower** *n.*

burrstone (ˈbɜːˌstəʊn) *n.* a variant spelling of **buhrstone.**

burry (ˈbɜːrɪ) *adj.* **-rier, -riest.** **1.** full of or covered in burs. **2.** resembling burs; prickly.

bursa (ˈbɜːsə) *n., pl.* **-sae** (-siː) *or* **-sas.** **1.** a small fluid-filled sac that reduces friction between movable parts of the body, esp. at joints. **2.** *Zoology.* any saclike cavity or structure. [C19: from Medieval Latin: bag, pouch, from Greek: skin, hide; see PURSE] —ˈ**bursal** *adj.*

bursar (ˈbɜːsə) *n.* **1.** an official in charge of the financial management of a school, college, or university. **2.** *Chiefly Scot. and N.Z.* a student holding a bursary. [C13: from Medieval Latin *bursārius* keeper of the purse, from *bursa* purse]

bursarial (bɜːˈsɛərɪəl) *adj.* of, relating to, or paid by a bursar or bursary.

bursary (ˈbɜːsərɪ) *n., pl.* **-ries.** **1.** Also called: ˈ**bursarˌship.** a scholarship or grant awarded esp. in Scottish and New Zealand schools, universities etc. **2.** *Brit.* **a.** the treasury of a college, etc. **b.** the bursar's room in a college.

Burschenschaft *German.* (ˈburʃənʃaft) *n.* a students' fraternity, originally one concerned with Christian ideals, patriotism, etc. [literally: youth association]

burse (bɜːs) *n.* **1.** *Chiefly R.C. Church.* a flat case used at Mass as a container for the corporal. **2.** *Scot.* **a.** a fund providing allowances for students. **b.** the allowance provided. [C19: from Medieval Latin *bursa* purse]

burseraceous (ˌbɜːsəˈreɪʃəs) *adj.* of, relating to, or belonging to the *Burseraceae,* a tropical family of trees and shrubs having compound leaves and resin or balsam in their stems. The family includes bdellium and some balsams. [C19: from New Latin *Bursera* type genus, named after J. *Burser* (1593–1649), German botanist]

bursicon (ˈbɜːsɪkɒn) *n.* a hormone, produced by the insect brain, that regulates processes associated with ecdysis, such as darkening of the cuticle.

bursiform (ˈbɜːsɪˌfɔːm) *adj.* shaped like a pouch or sac. [C19: from Latin *bursa* bag + -FORM]

bursitis (bɜːˈsaɪtɪs) *n.* inflammation of a bursa, esp. one in the shoulder joint.

burst (bɜːst) *vb.* **bursts, bursting, burst.** **1.** to break or cause to break open or apart suddenly and noisily, esp. from internal pressure; explode. **2.** (*intr.*) to come, go, etc., suddenly and forcibly: *he burst into the room.* **3.** (*intr.*) to be full to the point of breaking open. **4.** (*intr.*) to give vent (to) suddenly or loudly: *to burst into song.* **5.** to cause or suffer the rupture of: *to burst a blood vessel.* ~*n.* **6.** a sudden breaking open or apart; explosion. **7.** a break; breach; rupture. **8.** a sudden display or increase of effort or action; spurt: *a burst of speed.* **9.** a sudden and violent emission, occurrence, or outbreak: *a burst of heavy rain; a burst of applause.* **10.** a volley of fire from a weapon or weapons. ~*adj.* **11.** broken apart; ruptured: *a burst pipe.* [Old English *berstan;* related to Old Norse *bresta,* Old Frisian *bersta,* Old High German *brestan;* compare BREAK] —ˈ**burster** *n.*

burstone (ˈbɜːˌstəʊn) *n.* a variant spelling of **buhrstone.**

burthen (ˈbɜːðən) *n., vb.* an archaic word for **burden**[1]. —ˈ**burthensome** *adj.*

burton (ˈbɜːtᵊn) *n.* **1.** *Nautical.* a kind of light hoisting tackle. **2.** **go for a burton.** *Brit. slang.* **a.** to be broken, useless, or lost. **b.** to die. [C15: of uncertain origin]

burweed (ˈbɜːˌwiːd) *n.* any of various plants that bear burs, such as the burdock.

bury (ˈbɛrɪ) *vb.* **buries, burying, buried.** (*tr.*) **1.** to place (a corpse) in a grave, usually with funeral rites; inter. **2.** to place in the earth and cover with soil. **3.** to lose through death. **4.** to cover from sight; hide. **5.** to embed; sink: *to bury a nail in plaster.* **6.** to occupy (oneself) with deep concentration; engross: *to be buried in a book.* **7.** to dismiss from the mind; abandon: *to bury old hatreds.* **8.** **bury the hatchet.** to cease hostilities and become reconciled. **9.** **bury one's head in the sand.** to refuse to face a problem. [Old English *byrgan* to bury, hide; related to Old Norse *bjarga* to save, preserve, Old English *beorgan* to defend]

Buryat *or* **Buriat** (bʊəˈjɑːt, bʊərɪˈɑːt) *n.* **1.** a member of a Mongoloid people living chiefly in SE central Russia, in the former Buryat ASSR. **2.** the language of this people, belonging to the Mongolic branch of the Altaic family.

burying beetle *n.* a beetle of the genus *Necrophorous,* which buries the dead bodies of small animals by excavating beneath them, using the corpses as food for themselves and their larvae: family *Silphidae.* Also called: **sexton.**

bus (bʌs) *n., pl.* **buses** *or* **busses. 1.** a large motor vehicle designed to carry passengers between stopping places along a regular route. More formal name: **omnibus.** Sometimes called: **motorbus. 2.** short for **trolleybus. 3.** (*modifier*) of or relating to a bus or buses: *a bus driver; a bus station.* **4.** *Informal.* a car or aircraft, esp. one that is old and shaky. **5.** *Electronics, computer technol.* short for **busbar. 6.** the part of a MIRV missile payload containing the re-entry vehicles and guidance and thrust devices. **7.** *Astronautics.* a platform in a space vehicle used for various experiments and processes. **8. miss the bus.** to miss an opportunity; be too late. ~*vb.* **buses, busing, bused** *or* **busses, bussing, bussed. 9.** to travel or transport by bus. **10.** *Chiefly U.S. and Canadian.* to transport (children) by bus from one area to a school in another in order to create racially integrated classes. [C19: short for OMNIBUS]

bus. *abbrev. for* business.

busbar (ˈbʌzˌbɑː) *n.* **1.** an electrical conductor, maintained at a specific voltage and capable of carrying a high current, usually used to make a common connection between several circuits in a system. **2.** a group of such electrical conductors maintained at a low voltage, used for carrying data in binary form between the various parts of a computer or its peripherals. ~Sometimes shortened to **bus.**

bus boy *n. U.S. and Canadian.* a waiter's assistant.

busby (ˈbʌzbɪ) *n., pl.* **-bies. 1.** a tall fur helmet with a bag hanging from the top to the right side, worn by certain soldiers, usually hussars, as in the British Army. **2.** (not in official usage) another name for **bearskin** (the hat). [C18 (in the sense: large bushy wig): perhaps from a proper name]

busera (bʊˈserə) *n.* **1.** an alcoholic drink of Uganda made from millet: sometimes mixed with honey. **2.** a porridge made out of millet. [from Rukiga, a language of SW Uganda]

bush[1] (bʊʃ) *n.* **1.** a dense woody plant, smaller than a tree, with many branches arising from the lower part of the stem; shrub. **2.** a dense cluster of such shrubs; thicket. **3.** something resembling a bush, esp. in density: *a bush of hair.* **4. a.** (often preceded by *the*) an uncultivated or sparsely settled area, esp. in Africa, Australia, New Zealand, or Canada: usually covered with trees or shrubs, varying from open shrubby country to dense rainforest. **b.** (*as modifier*): *bush flies.* **5.** *Canadian.* an area of land on a farm on which timber is grown and cut. Also called: **bush lot, woodlot. 6.** a forested area; woodland. **7.** (often preceded by *the*) *Informal.* the countryside, as opposed to the city: *out in the bush.* **8.** a fox's tail; brush. **9.** *Obsolete.* **a.** a bunch of ivy hung as a vintner's sign in front of a tavern. **b.** any tavern sign. **10. beat about the bush.** to avoid the point at issue; prevaricate. ~*adj.* **11.** *West African informal.* ignorant or stupid, esp. as considered typical of unwesternized rustic life. **12. go bush.** *Informal, Austral. and N.Z.* **a.** to abandon city amenities and live rough. **b.** to run wild. ~*vb.* **13.** (*intr.*) to grow thick and bushy. **14.** (*tr.*) to cover, decorate, support, etc., with bushes. [C13: of Germanic origin; compare Old Norse *buski,* Old High German *busc,* Middle Dutch *bosch;* related to Old French *bosc* wood, Italian *bosco*]

bush[2] (bʊʃ) *n.* **1.** Also called (esp. U.S. and Canadian): **bushing.** a thin metal sleeve or tubular lining serving as a bearing or guide. ~*vb.* **2.** to fit a bush to (a casing, bearing, etc.). [C15: from Middle Dutch *busse* box, bush; related to German *Büchse* tin, Swedish *hjulbössa* wheel-box, Late Latin *buxis* BOX[1]]

bushbaby (ˈbʊʃˌbeɪbɪ) *n., pl.* **-babies.** any agile nocturnal arboreal prosimian primate of the genera *Galago* and *Euoticus,* occurring in Africa south of the Sahara: family *Lorisidae* (lorises). They have large eyes and ears and a long tail. Also called: **galago.**

bush ballad *n.* an old Australian bush poem in a ballad metre dealing with aspects of life and characters in the bush.

bushbashing (ˈbʊʃˌbæʃɪŋ) *n. Austral. and N.Z. slang.* the process of forcing a path through the bush.

bushbuck (ˈbʊʃˌbʌk) *or* **boschbok** *n., pl.* **-bucks, -buck** *or* **-boks, -bok.** a small nocturnal spiral-horned antelope, *Tragelaphus scriptus,* of the bush and tropical forest of Africa. Its coat is reddish-brown with a few white markings.

bush canary *n. N.Z.* another name for **brown creeper.**

bush carpenter *n. Austral. and N.Z.* a rough-and-ready unskilled workman.

bushcraft (ˈbʊʃˌkrɑːft) *n. Austral. and N.Z.* ability and experience in matters concerned with living in the bush.

bushed (bʊʃt) *adj. Informal.* **1.** (*postpositive*) extremely tired; exhausted. **2.** *Canadian.* mentally disturbed from living in isolation, esp. in the north. **3.** *Austral. and N.Z.* lost or bewildered, as in the bush.

bushel[1] (ˈbʊʃəl) *n.* **1.** a Brit. unit of dry or liquid measure equal to 8 Imperial gallons. 1 Imperial bushel is equivalent to 0.036 37 cubic metres. **2.** a U.S. unit of dry measure equal to 64 U.S. pints. 1 U.S. bushel is equivalent to 0.035 24 cubic metres. **3.** a container with a capacity equal to either of these quantities. **4.** *U.S. informal.* a large amount; great deal. **5. hide one's light under a bushel.** to conceal one's abilities or good qualities. [C14: from Old French *boissel,* from *boisse* one sixth of a bushel, of Gaulish origin]

bushel[2] (ˈbʊʃəl) *vb.* **-els, -elling, -elled** *or* **-els, -eling, -eled.** (*tr.*) *U.S.* to alter or mend (a garment). [C19: probably from German *bosseln* to do inferior work, patch, from Middle High German *bōzeln* to beat, from Old High German *bōzan*] —ˈ**busheller,** ˈ**busheler,** *or* ˈ**bushelman** *n.*

bushfire (ˈbʊʃˌfaɪə) *n.* an uncontrolled fire in the bush; a scrub or forest fire.

bushfly (ˈbʊʃˌflaɪ) *n., pl.* **-flies.** any of various small black dipterous flies of Australia, esp. *Musca vetustissima,* that breed in faeces and dung: family *Calliphoridae.*

bush grass *n.* a coarse reedlike grass, *Calamagrostis epigejos,* 1–1½ metres (3–4½ ft.) high that grows on damp clay soils.

bushhammer (ˈbʊʃˌhæmə) *n.* a hammer with small pyramids projecting from its working face, used for dressing stone. [C19: from German *Bosshammer,* from *bossen* to beat + HAMMER]

bush house *n. Chiefly Austral.* a shed or hut in the bush or a garden.

Bushido (ˌbuːʃɪˈdəʊ) *n.* (*sometimes not cap.*) the feudal code of the Japanese samurai, stressing self-discipline, courage and loyalty. [C19: from Japanese *bushi* warrior (from Chinese *wushih*) + *dō* way (from Chinese *tao*)]

bushie (ˈbʊʃɪ) *n.* a variant spelling of **bushy**[2].

bushing (ˈbʊʃɪŋ) *n.* **1.** another word for **bush**[2] (sense 1). **2.** an adapter having ends of unequal diameters, often with internal screw threads, used to connect pipes of different sizes. **3.** a layer of electrical insulation enabling a live conductor to pass through an earthed wall, etc.

bush jacket *or* **shirt** *n.* a casual jacket or shirt having four patch pockets and a belt.

bush lawyer *n. Austral. and N.Z.* **1.** any of several prickly trailing plants of the genus *Rubus cissoides.* **2.** *Informal.* a person who gives opinions but is not qualified to do so.

bush-line *n. N.Z.* the contour at which the growth of the bush ceases.

bush lot *n. Canadian.* another name for **bush**[1] (sense 5).

bushman (ˈbʊʃmən) *n., pl.* **-men.** *Austral. and N.Z.* a person who lives or travels in the bush, esp. one versed in bush lore.

Bushman (ˈbʊʃmən) *n., pl.* **-man** *or* **-men. 1.** a member of a hunting and gathering people of southern Africa, esp. the Kalahari region, typically having leathery yellowish skin, short stature, and prominent buttocks. **2.** any language of this people, belonging to the Khoisan family. [C18: from Afrikaans *boschjesman*]

bushman's singlet *n. N.Z.* a sleeveless heavy black woollen singlet, used as working clothing by timber fellers.

bushmaster (ˈbʊʃˌmɑːstə) *n.* a large greyish-brown highly venomous snake, *Lachesis muta,* inhabiting wooded regions of tropical America: family *Crotalidae* (pit vipers).

bush oyster *n. Austral., euphemistic.* a bull's testicle when cooked and eaten.

bushpig (ˈbʊʃˌpɪg) *n.* a wild pig, *Potamochoerus porcus,* inhabiting forests in tropical Africa and Madagascar. It is brown or black, with pale markings on the face. Also called: **boschvark.**

bushranger (ˈbʊʃˌreɪndʒə) *n.* **1.** *Austral.* an escaped convict or robber living in the bush. **2.** *U.S.* a person who lives away from civilization; backwoodsman.

bush shrike *n.* **1.** any shrike of the African subfamily *Malaconotinae,* such as *Chlorophoneus nigrifrons* (**black-fronted bush shrike**). **2.** another name for **ant bird.**

bush sickness *n. N.Z.* an animal disease caused by mineral deficiency in old bush country. —ˈ**bush-**ˌ**sick** *adj.*

bush tea *n.* **1.** a leguminous shrub of the genus *Cyclopia,* of southern Africa. **2.** a beverage prepared from the dried leaves of any of these plants.

bush telegraph *n.* **1.** a means of communication between primitive peoples over large areas, as by drum beats. **2.** a means of spreading rumour, gossip, etc.

bushtit (ˈbʊʃˌtɪt) *n.* any small grey active North American songbird of the genus *Psaltriparus,* such as *P. minimus* (**common bushtit**): family *Paridae* (titmice).

bush tram *n. N.Z.* a railway line in the bush to facilitate the entry of workers and the removal of timber.

bushwalking (ˈbʊʃˌwɔːkɪŋ) *n. Austral.* an expedition on foot in the bush.

bushwhack (ˈbʊʃˌwæk) *vb.* **1.** (*tr.*) *U.S. and Canadian.* to ambush. **2.** (*intr.*) *U.S. and Canadian.* to cut or beat one's way through thick woods. **3.** (*intr.*) *U.S., Canadian, and Austral.* to range or move around in woods or the bush. **4.** (*intr.*) *U.S. and Canadian.* to fight as a guerrilla in wild or uncivilized regions. **5.** (*intr.*) *N.Z.* to work in the bush, esp. at timber felling.

bushwhacker (ˈbʊʃˌwækə) *n.* **1.** *U.S., Canadian, and Austral.* a person who travels around or lives in thinly populated woodlands. **2.** *Austral. slang.* an unsophisticated person; boor. **3.** a Confederate guerrilla during the American Civil War. **4.** *U.S.* any guerrilla. **5.** *N.Z.* a person who works in the bush, esp. at timber felling.

bush wren *n.* a wren, *Xenicus longipes,* occurring in New Zealand: family *Xenicidae.* See also **rifleman** (sense 2).

bushy[1] ('bʊʃɪ) *adj.* **bushier, bushiest.** **1.** covered or overgrown with bushes. **2.** thick and shaggy: *bushy eyebrows.* —'**bushily** *adv.* —'**bushiness** *n.*
bushy[2] *or* **bushie** ('bʊʃɪ) *n., pl.* **bushies.** *Austral. informal.* **1.** a person who lives in the bush. **2.** an unsophisticated uncouth person.
busily ('bɪzɪlɪ) *adv.* in a busy manner; industriously.
business ('bɪznɪs) *n.* **1.** a trade or profession. **2.** an industrial, commercial, or professional operation; purchase and sale of goods and services: *the tailoring business.* **3.** a commercial or industrial establishment, such as a firm or factory. **4.** commercial activity; dealings (esp. in the phrase **do business**). **5.** volume or quantity of commercial activity: *business is poor today.* **6.** commercial policy or procedure: *overcharging is bad business.* **7.** proper or rightful concern or responsibility (often in the phrase **mind one's own business**). **8.** a special task; assignment. **9.** a matter or matters to be attended to: *the business of the meeting.* **10.** an affair; matter: *a queer business; I'm tired of the whole business.* **11.** serious work or activity: *get down to business.* **12.** a complicated affair; rigmarole. **13.** *Informal.* a vaguely defined collection or area: *jets, fast cars, and all that business.* **14.** Also called: **stage business.** *Theatre.* an incidental action, such as lighting a pipe, performed by an actor for dramatic effect. **15.** **like nobody's business.** *Informal.* extremely well or fast. **16.** **mean business.** to be in earnest. **17.** a euphemistic word for **defecation** (esp. in the phrase **do one's business**). **18.** a slang word for **prostitution.** [Old English *bisignis* solicitude, attentiveness, from *bisig* BUSY + *-nis* -NESS]
business college *n.* a college providing courses in secretarial studies, business management, accounting, commerce, etc.
business cycle *n.* another name (esp. U.S. and Canadian) for **trade cycle.**
business end *n. Informal.* the part of a tool or weapon that does the work, as contrasted with the handle.
businesslike ('bɪznɪs,laɪk) *adj.* **1.** efficient and methodical. **2.** earnest or severe.
businessman ('bɪznɪs,mæn, -mən) *or* (*fem.*) **businesswoman** *n., pl.* **-men** *or* **-women.** a person engaged in commercial or industrial business, esp. as an owner or executive.
business park *n.* an area specially designated and landscaped to accommodate business offices, warehouses, light industry, etc.
business plan *n.* a detailed plan setting out the objectives of a business, the strategy and tactics planned to achieve them, and the expected profits, usually over a period of three to ten years.
busk[1] (bʌsk) *n.* **1.** a strip of whalebone, wood, steel, etc., inserted into the front of a corset to stiffen it. **2.** *Archaic or dialect.* the corset itself. [C16: from Old French *busc,* probably from Old Italian *busco* splinter, stick, of Germanic origin]
busk[2] (bʌsk) *vb.* (*intr.*) *Brit.* to make money by singing, dancing, acting, etc., in public places, as in front of theatre queues. [C20: of unknown origin] —'**busker** *n.* —'**busking** *n.*
busk[3] (bʌsk) *vb.* (*tr.*) *Scot. and archaic.* **1.** to make ready; prepare. **2.** to dress or adorn. [C14: from Old Norse *būask,* from *būa* to make ready, dwell; see BOWER[1]]
buskin ('bʌskɪn) *n.* **1.** (formerly) a sandal-like covering for the foot and leg, reaching the calf and usually laced. **2.** Also called: **cothurnus.** a thick-soled laced half boot resembling this, worn esp. by actors of ancient Greece. **3.** (usually preceded by *the*) *Chiefly literary.* tragic drama. [C16: perhaps from Spanish *borzeguí;* related to Old French *bouzequin,* Italian *borzacchino,* of obscure origin]
bus lane *n.* one track of a road marked for use by buses only.
busman's holiday ('bʌsmənz) *n. Informal.* a holiday spent doing the same sort of thing as one does at work. [C20: alluding to a bus driver having a driving holiday]
buss (bʌs) *n., vb.* an archaic or dialect word for **kiss.** [C16: probably of imitative origin; compare French *baiser,* German dialect *Bussi* little kiss]
bus shelter *n.* a covered structure at a bus stop providing protection against the weather for people waiting for a bus.
bus stop *n.* a place on a bus route, usually marked by a sign, at which buses stop for passengers to alight and board.
bust[1] (bʌst) *n.* **1.** the chest of a human being, esp. a woman's bosom. **2.** a sculpture of the head, shoulders, and upper chest of a person. [C17: from French *buste,* from Italian *busto* a sculpture, of unknown origin]
bust[2] (bʌst) *Informal.* ~*vb.* **busts, busting, busted** *or* **bust. 1.** to burst or break. **2.** to make or become bankrupt. **3.** (*tr.*) (of the police) to raid, search, or arrest: *the girl was busted for drugs.* **4.** (*tr.*) *U.S. and Canadian.* to demote, esp. in military rank. **5.** (*tr.*) *U.S. and Canadian.* to break or tame (a horse, etc.). **6.** (*tr.*) *Chiefly U.S.* to punch; hit. ~*n.* **7.** a raid, search, or arrest by the police. **8.** *Chiefly U.S.* a punch; hit. **9.** *U.S. and Canadian.* a failure, esp. a financial one; bankruptcy. **10.** a drunken party. ~*adj.* **11.** broken. **12.** bankrupt. **13.** **go bust.** to become bankrupt. [C19: from a dialect pronunciation of BURST]
bustard ('bʌstəd) *n.* any terrestrial bird of the family *Otididae,* inhabiting open regions of the Old World: order *Gruiformes* (cranes, rails, etc.). They have long strong legs, a heavy body, a long neck, and speckled plumage. [C15: from Old French *bistarde,* influenced by Old French *oustarde,* both from Latin *avis tarda* slow bird]
bustee *or* **busti** ('bʌstiː) *n.* variant spellings of **basti.**
buster ('bʌstə) *n. Slang.* **1.** (in combination) a person or thing destroying something as specified: *dambuster.* **2.** *U.S. and Canadian.* a term of address for a boy or man. **3.** *U.S. and Canadian.* a person who breaks horses. **4.** *Chiefly U.S. and Canadian.* a spree, esp. a drinking bout. **5.** *Austral.* short for **southerly buster.**
bustier ('buːstɪeɪ) *n.* a type of close-fitting usually strapless top worn by women.
bustle[1] ('bʌsᵊl) *vb.* **1.** (when *intr.,* often foll. by *about*) to hurry or cause to hurry with a great show of energy or activity. ~*n.* **2.** energetic and noisy activity. [C16: probably from obsolete *buskle* to make energetic preparation, from dialect *busk,* from Old Norse *būask* to prepare] —'**bustler** *n.* —'**bustling** *adj.*
bustle[2] ('bʌsᵊl) *n.* a cushion or a metal or whalebone framework worn by women in the late 19th century at the back below the waist in order to expand the skirt. [C18: of unknown origin]
bust-up *Informal.* ~*n.* **1.** a quarrel, esp. a serious one ending a friendship, etc. **2.** *Brit.* a disturbance or brawl. ~*vb.* **bust up** (*adv.*). **3.** (*intr.*) to quarrel and part. **4.** (*tr.*) to disrupt (a meeting), esp. violently.
busty ('bʌstɪ) *adj.* **bustier, bustiest.** (of a woman) having a prominent bust.
busuuti (buː'suːtɪ) *n.* a long garment with short sleeves and a square neckline, worn by Ugandan women, esp. in S Uganda. [C20: from Luganda]
busy ('bɪzɪ) *adj.* **busier, busiest. 1.** actively or fully engaged; occupied. **2.** crowded with or characterized by activity: *a busy day.* **3.** *Chiefly U.S. and Canadian.* (of a room, telephone line, etc.) in use; engaged. **4.** overcrowded with detail: *a busy painting.* **5.** meddlesome; inquisitive; prying. ~*vb.* **busies, busying, busied. 6.** (*tr.*) to make or keep (someone, esp. oneself) busy; occupy. [Old English *bisig;* related to Middle Dutch *besich,* perhaps to Latin *festīnāre* to hurry] —'**busyness** *n.*
busybody ('bɪzɪ,bɒdɪ) *n., pl.* **-bodies.** a meddlesome, prying, or officious person. —'**busy,bodying** *n.*
busy Lizzie ('lɪzɪ) *n.* a balsaminaceous plant, *Impatiens balsamina,* that has pink, red, or white flowers and is often grown as a pot plant.
busy signal *n.* U.S. and Canadian equivalent of **engaged tone.**
but[1] (bʌt; *unstressed* bət) *conj.* (*coordinating*) **1.** contrary to expectation: *he cut his knee but didn't cry.* **2.** in contrast; on the contrary: *I like opera but my husband doesn't.* **3.** (*usually used after a negative*) other than: *we can't do anything but wait.* **4.** only: *I can but try.* ~*conj.* (*subordinating*). **5.** (*usually used after a negative*) without it happening or being the case that: *we never go out but it rains.* **6.** (foll. by *that*) except that: *nothing is impossible but that we live forever.* **7.** *Archaic.* if not; unless. ~*sentence connector.* **8.** *Informal.* used to introduce an exclamation: *my, but you're nice.* ~*prep.* **9.** except; save: *they saved all but one of the pigs.* **10.** **but for.** were it not for: *but for you, we couldn't have managed.* ~*adv.* **11.** just; merely: *he was but a child.* **12.** *Dialect and Austral.* though; however: *it's a rainy day; warm, but.* **13.** **all but.** almost; practically: *he was all but dead when we found him.* ~*n.* **14.** an objection (esp. in the phrase **ifs and buts**). [Old English *būtan* without, outside, except, from *be* BY + *ūtan* OUT; related to Old Saxon *biūtan,* Old High German *biūzan*]
but[2] (bʌt) *Scot.* ~*n.* **1.** the outer room of a two-roomed cottage: usually the kitchen. ~*prep., adv.* **2.** in or into the outer part (of a house). Compare **ben**[1]. [C18: from *but* (adv.) outside, hence, outer room; see BUT[1]]
butadiene (,bjuːtə'daɪiːn) *n.* a colourless easily liquefiable flammable gas that polymerizes readily and is used mainly in the manufacture of synthetic rubbers. Formula: $CH_2{:}CHCH{:}CH_2$. Systematic name: **buta-1,3-diene.** [C20: from BUTA(NE) + DI-[1] + -ENE]
but and ben *n. Scot.* a two-roomed cottage consisting of an outer room or kitchen (**but**) and an inner room (**ben**).
butane ('bjuːteɪn, bjuː'teɪn) *n.* a colourless flammable gaseous alkane that exists in two isomeric forms, both of which occur in natural gas. The stable isomer, *n*-butane, is used mainly in the manufacture of rubber and fuels (such as Calor Gas). Formula: C_4H_{10}. [C19: from BUT(YL) + -ANE]
butanol ('bjuːtə,nɒl) *n.* a colourless substance existing in four isomeric forms. The three liquid isomers are used as solvents for resins, lacquers, etc., and in the manufacture of organic compounds. Formula: C_4H_9OH. Also called: **butyl alcohol.** [C19: from BUTAN(E) + -OL[1]]
butanone ('bjuːtə,nəʊn) *n.* a colourless soluble flammable liquid used mainly as a solvent for resins, as a paint remover, and in lacquers, cements, and adhesives. Formula: $CH_3COC_2H_5$. Also called: **methyl ethyl ketone.** [C20: from BUTAN(E) + -ONE]
butat (bʊ'tʊt) *n.* a Gambian monetary unit worth one hundredth of a dalasi.
butch (bʊtʃ) *Slang.* ~*adj.* **1.** (of a woman or man) markedly or aggressively masculine. ~*n.* **2.** a lesbian who is noticeably masculine. **3.** a strong rugged man. [C18: back formation from BUTCHER]
butcher ('bʊtʃə) *n.* **1.** a retailer of meat. **2.** a person who slaughters or dresses meat for market. **3.** an indiscriminate or brutal murderer. **4.** a person who destroys, ruins, or bungles something. ~*vb.* (*tr.*) **5.** to slaughter or dress (animals) for meat. **6.** to kill indiscriminately or brutally. **7.** to make a mess

of; botch; ruin. [C13: from Old French *bouchier,* from *bouc* he-goat, probably of Celtic origin; see BUCK[1]; compare Welsh *bwch* he-goat]

butcherbird ('bʊtʃəˌbɜːd) *n.* **1.** a shrike, esp. one of the genus *Lanius.* **2.** any of several Australian magpies of the genus *Cracticus* that impale their prey on thorns.

butcher's ('bʊtʃəz) *or* **butcher's hook** *n. Brit. slang.* a look. [C19: rhyming slang]

butcher's-broom *n.* a liliaceous evergreen shrub, *Ruscus aculeatus,* that has stiff prickle-tipped flattened green stems, which resemble and function as true leaves. The plant was formerly used for making brooms.

butchery ('bʊtʃərɪ) *n., pl.* **-eries. 1.** the business or work of a butcher. **2.** wanton and indiscriminate slaughter; carnage. **3.** a less common word for **slaughterhouse.**

butene ('bjuːtiːn) *n.* a pungent colourless gas existing in four isomeric forms, all of which are used in the manufacture of organic compounds. Formula: C_4H_8. Also called: **butylene.** [C20: from BUT(YL) + -ENE]

butenedioic acid (ˌbjuːtiːndaɪ'əʊɪk) *n.* either of two geometrical isomers with the formula HOOCCH:CHCOOH. See **fumaric acid, maleic acid.**

butler ('bʌtlə) *n.* the male servant of a household in charge of the wines, table, etc.: usually the head servant. [C13: from Old French *bouteillier,* from *bouteille* BOTTLE]

butlery ('bʌtlərɪ) *n., pl.* **-leries. 1.** a butler's room. **2.** another name for **buttery**[2] (sense 1).

butt[1] (bʌt) *n.* **1.** the thicker or blunt end of something, such as the end of the stock of a rifle. **2.** the unused end of something, esp. of a cigarette; stub. **3.** *Tanning.* the portion of a hide covering the lower backside of the animal. **4.** *U.S. and Canadian informal.* the buttocks. **5.** *U.S.* a slang word for **cigarette. 6.** *Building.* short for **butt joint** or **butt hinge.** [C15 (in the sense: thick end of something, buttock): related to Old English *buttuc* end, ridge, Middle Dutch *bot* stumpy]

butt[2] (bʌt) *n.* **1.** a person or thing that is the target of ridicule, wit, etc. **2.** *Shooting, archery.* **a.** a mound of earth behind the target on a target range that stops bullets or wide shots. **b.** the target itself. **c.** (*pl.*) the target range. **3.** a low barrier, usually of sods or peat, behind which sportsmen shoot game birds, esp. grouse. **4.** *Archaic.* goal; aim. ~*vb.* **5.** (usually foll. by *on* or *against*) to lie or be placed end on to; abut: *to butt a beam against a wall.* [C14 (in the sense: mark for archery practice): from Old French *but;* related to French *butte* knoll, target]

butt[3] (bʌt) *vb.* **1.** to strike or push (something) with the head or horns. **2.** (*intr.*) to project; jut. **3.** (*intr.;* foll. by *in* or *into*) to intrude, esp. into a conversation; interfere; meddle. ~*n.* **4.** a blow with the head or horns. [C12: from Old French *boter,* of Germanic origin; compare Middle Dutch *botten* to strike; see BEAT, BUTTON] —'**butter** *n.*

butt[4] (bʌt) *n.* **1.** a large cask, esp. one with a capacity of two hogsheads, for storing wine or beer. **2.** a U.S. unit of liquid measure equal to 126 U.S. gallons. [C14: from Old French *botte,* from Old Provençal *bota,* from Late Latin *buttis* cask, perhaps from Greek *butinē* chamber pot]

butte (bjuːt) *n. Western U.S. and Canadian.* an isolated steep-sided flat-topped hill. [C19: from French, from Old French *bute* mound behind a target, from *but* target; see BUTT[2]]

butter ('bʌtə) *n.* **1. a.** an edible fatty whitish-yellow solid made from cream by churning, for cooking and table use. **b.** (*as modifier*): *butter icing.* Related adj.: **butyraceous. 2.** any substance with a butter-like consistency, such as peanut butter or vegetable butter. **3. look as if butter wouldn't melt in one's mouth.** to look innocent, although probably not so. ~*vb.* (*tr.*) **4.** to put butter on or in. **5.** to flatter. ~See also **butter up.** [Old English *butere,* from Latin *būtyrum,* from Greek *bouturon,* from *bous* cow + *turos* cheese]

butter-and-eggs *n.* (*functioning as sing.*) any of various plants, such as toadflax, the flowers of which are of two shades of yellow.

butterball ('bʌtəˌbɔːl) *n. U.S.* **1.** another name for **bufflehead. 2.** *Informal.* a chubby or fat person.

butter bean *n.* a variety of lima bean that has large pale flat edible seeds and is grown in the southern U.S.

butterbur ('bʌtəˌbɜː) *n.* a plant of the Eurasian genus *Petasites* with fragrant whitish or purple flowers, woolly stems, and leaves formerly used to wrap butter: family *Compositae* (composites).

buttercup ('bʌtəˌkʌp) *n.* any of various yellow-flowered ranunculaceous plants of the genus *Ranunculus,* such as *R. acris* (meadow buttercup), which is native to Europe but common throughout North America. See also **crowfoot, goldilocks** (sense 2), **spearwort, lesser celandine.**

butterfat ('bʌtəˌfæt) *n.* the fatty substance of milk from which butter is made, consisting of a mixture of glycerides, mainly butyrin, olein, and palmitin.

butterfat cheque *n.* **the.** *N.Z.* the total annual cash return for operations on a dairy farm.

butterfingers ('bʌtəˌfɪŋgəz) *n.* (*functioning as sing.*) *Informal.* a person who drops things inadvertently or fails to catch things. —'**butterˌfingered** *adj.*

butterfish ('bʌtəˌfɪʃ) *n., pl.* **-fish** *or* **-fishes. 1.** an eel-like blennioid food fish, *Pholis gunnellus,* occurring in North Atlantic coastal regions: family *Pholidae* (gunnels). It has a slippery scaleless golden brown skin with a row of black spots along the base of the long dorsal fin. **2.** Also called: **greenbone,** (Maori) **koaea,** (Maori) **marari.** an edible reef fish, *Coridodax pullus,* of esp. S New Zealand. It has a slippery purplish-grey to olive-green skin and is often found browsing on kelp.

butterflies ('bʌtəˌflaɪz) *pl. n. Informal.* tremors in the stomach region due to nervousness.

butterfly ('bʌtəˌflaɪ) *n., pl.* **-flies. 1.** any diurnal insect of the order *Lepidoptera* that has a slender body with clubbed antennae and typically rests with the wings (which are often brightly coloured) closed over the back. Compare **moth. 2.** a person who never settles with one group, interest, or occupation for long. **3.** a swimming stroke in which the arms are plunged forward together in large circular movements. **4.** *Commerce.* the simultaneous purchase and sale of traded call options, at different exercise prices or with different expiry dates, on a stock exchange or commodity market. [Old English *buttorflēoge;* the name perhaps is based on a belief that butterflies stole milk and butter]

butterfly bush *n.* another name for **buddleia.**

butterfly collar *n.* the Irish name for **wing collar.**

butterfly diagram *n. Astronomy.* a graphical butterfly-shaped representation of the sunspot density in the 11-year sunspot cycle.

butterfly effect *n.* the idea, used in chaos theory, that a very small difference in the initial state of a physical system can make a significant difference to the state at some later time. [C20: from the theory that a butterfly flapping its wings in one part of the world might ultimately cause a hurricane in another part of the world]

butterfly fish *n.* any small tropical marine percoid fish of the genera *Chaetodon, Chelmon,* etc., that has a deep flattened brightly coloured body and brushlike teeth: family *Chaetodontidae.* See also **angelfish** (sense 1).

butterfly nut *n.* another name for **wing nut.**

butterfly valve *n.* **1.** a disc that acts as a valve by turning about a diameter, esp. one used as the throttle valve in a carburettor. **2.** a non-return valve consisting of two semicircular plates hinged about a common central spindle.

butterfly weed *n.* a North American asclepiadaceous plant, *Asclepias tuberosa* (or *A. decumbens*), having flat-topped clusters of bright orange flowers. Also called: **orange milkweed, pleurisy root.**

butterine ('bʌtəˌriːn, -rɪn) *n.* an artificial butter made partly from milk.

buttermilk ('bʌtəˌmɪlk) *n.* the sourish liquid remaining after the butter has been separated from milk, often used for making scones and soda bread.

butter muslin *n.* a fine loosely woven cotton material originally used for wrapping butter.

butternut ('bʌtəˌnʌt) *n.* **1.** a walnut tree, *Juglans cinerea* of E North America. Compare **black walnut. 2.** the oily edible egg-shaped nut of this tree. **3.** the hard brownish-grey wood of this tree. **4.** the bark of this tree or an extract from it, formerly used as a laxative. **5.** a brownish colour or dye. **6.** *N.Z.* short for **butternut pumpkin.** ~Also called (for senses 1–4): **white walnut.**

butternut pumpkin *n. Austral.* a variety of pumpkin, eaten as vegetable. Also called (N.Z.): **butternut.**

butterscotch ('bʌtəˌskɒtʃ) *n.* **1.** a kind of hard brittle toffee made with butter, brown sugar, etc. **2. a.** a flavouring made from these ingredients. **b.** (*as modifier*): *butterscotch icing.* [C19: perhaps first made in Scotland]

butter up *vb.* (*tr., adv.*) to flatter.

butterwort ('bʌtəˌwɜːt) *n.* a plant of the genus *Pinguicula,* esp. *P. vulgaris,* that grows in wet places and has violet-blue spurred flowers and fleshy greasy glandular leaves on which insects are trapped and digested: family *Lentibulariaceae.*

buttery[1] ('bʌtərɪ) *adj.* **1.** containing, like, or coated with butter. **2.** *Informal.* grossly or insincerely flattering; obsequious. —'**butteriness** *n.*

buttery[2] ('bʌtərɪ) *n., pl.* **-teries. 1.** a room for storing foods or wines. **2.** *Brit.* (in some universities) a room in which food is supplied or sold to students. [C14: from Anglo-French *boterie,* from Anglo-Latin *buteria,* probably from *butta* cask, BUTT[4]]

butt hinge *n.* a hinge made of two matching leaves, one recessed into a door and the other into the jamb so that they are in contact when the door is shut. Sometimes shortened to **butt.**

butt joint *n.* a joint between two plates, planks, bars, sections, etc., when the components are butted together and do not overlap or interlock. The joint may be strapped with jointing plates laid across it or welded (**butt weld**). Sometimes shortened to **butt.**

buttock ('bʌtək) *n.* **1.** either of the two large fleshy masses of thick muscular tissue that form the human rump. See also **gluteus.** Related adj.: **gluteal. 2.** the analogous part in some mammals. [C13: perhaps from Old English *buttuc* round slope, diminutive of *butt* (unattested) strip of land; see BUTT[1], -OCK]

button ('bʌtᵊn) *n.* **1.** a disc or knob of plastic, wood, etc., attached to a garment, etc., usually for fastening two surfaces together by passing it through a buttonhole or loop. **2.** a small round object, such as any of various sweets, decorations, or badges. **3.** a small disc that completes an electric circuit when pushed, as one that operates a doorbell or machine. **4.** *Biology.* any rounded knoblike part or organ, such as an unripe mushroom. **5.** *Fencing.* the protective knob fixed to the point of a foil. **6.** a small amount of metal, usually lead, with which gold or silver is fused, thus concentrating it during assaying. **7.** the piece of a weld that pulls out during the destructive testing of spot welds. **8.** *Rowing.* a projection around the loom of an oar that prevents it slipping through the rowlock. **9.** *Brit.* an object of no value (esp. in the phrase **not worth a button**). **10.** *Slang.* intellect; mental capacity (in such phrases as **a button short, to have all one's buttons,** etc.). **11. on the button.** *Informal.* exactly; precisely. ~*vb.* **12.** to fasten with a button or buttons. **13.** (*tr.*) to provide with buttons. **14.** (*tr.*) *Fencing.* to hit (an opponent) with the button of one's foil. **15. button (up) one's lip** *or* **mouth.** *Slang.* to stop talking: often imperative. ~See also **buttons, button up.** [C14: from Old French *boton,* from *boter* to thrust, butt, of Germanic origin; see BUTT[3]] —'**buttoner** *n.* —'**buttonless** *adj.* —'**buttony** *adj.*

buttonball ('bʌtᵊn,bɔːl) *n. U.S. and Canadian.* a North American plane tree, *Platanus occidentalis.* See **plane tree.**

button day *n. Austral.* the usual name for **flag day.**

buttonhole ('bʌtᵊn,həul) *n.* **1.** a slit in a garment, etc., through which a button is passed to fasten two surfaces together. **2.** a flower or small bunch of flowers worn pinned to the lapel or in the buttonhole, esp. at weddings, formal dances, etc. U.S. name: **boutonniere.** ~*vb.* (*tr.*) **3.** to detain (a person) in conversation. **4.** to make buttonholes in. **5.** to sew with buttonhole stitch.

buttonhole stitch *n.* a reinforcing looped stitch for the edge of material, such as around a buttonhole.

buttonhook ('bʌtᵊn,hʊk) *n.* a thin tapering hooked instrument formerly used for pulling buttons through the buttonholes of gloves, shoes, etc.

buttonmould ('bʌtᵊn,məuld) *n.* the small core of plastic, wood, or metal that is the base for buttons covered with fabric, leather, etc.

button quail *n.* any small quail-like terrestrial bird of the genus *Turnix,* such as *T. sylvatica* (striped button quail), occurring in tropical and subtropical regions of the Old World: family *Turnicidae,* order *Gruiformes* (cranes, rails, etc.). Also called: **hemipode.**

buttons ('bʌtᵊnz) *n.* (*functioning as sing.*) *Brit. informal.* a page boy.

button-through *adj.* (of a dress or skirt) fastened with buttons from top to hem.

button tow *n.* a kind of ski lift for one person consisting of a pole that has a circular plate at the bottom and is attached to a moving cable. The person places the pole between his legs so that the plate takes his weight.

button up *vb.* (*tr., adv.*) **1.** to fasten (a garment) with a button or buttons. **2.** *Informal.* to conclude (business) satisfactorily. **3. buttoned up.** *Slang.* taciturn; silent and somewhat tense.

buttonwood ('bʌtᵊn,wʊd) *or* **button tree** *n.* **1.** Also called: **buttonball.** a North American plane tree, *Platanus occidentalis.* See **plane tree.** **2.** a small West Indian tree, *Conocarpus erectus,* with button-like fruits and heavy hard compact wood: family *Combretaceae.*

butt plate *n.* a plate made usually of metal and attached to the butt end of a gunstock.

buttress ('bʌtrɪs) *n.* **1.** Also called: **pier.** a construction, usually of brick or stone, built to support a wall. See also **flying buttress.** **2.** any support or prop. **3.** something shaped like a buttress, such as a projection from a mountainside. **4.** either of the two pointed rear parts of a horse's hoof. ~*vb.* (*tr.*) **5.** to support (a wall) with a buttress. **6.** to support or sustain. [C13: from Old French *bouterez,* short for *ars bouterez* thrusting arch, from *bouter* to thrust, BUTT[3]]

buttress root *n.* a root that supports the trunk of a tree, usually growing from the stem, as in the mangrove.

buttress thread *n.* a screw thread having one flank that is vertical while the other is inclined, and a flat top and bottom: used in machine tools and designed to withstand heavy thrust in one direction.

butt shaft *n.* a blunt-headed unbarbed arrow.

butt weld *n.* See **butt joint.**

butty[1] ('bʌtɪ) *n., pl.* **-ties.** *Chiefly northern English dialect.* a sandwich: *a jam butty.* [C19: from *buttered* (*bread*)]

butty[2] ('bʌtɪ) *n., pl.* **-ties.** *English dialect.* (esp. in mining parlance) a friend or workmate. [C19: perhaps from obsolete *booty* sharing, from BOOT[2], later applied to a middleman in a mine]

butyl ('bjuː,taɪl, -tɪl) *n.* (*modifier*) of, consisting of, or containing any of four isomeric forms of the group C_4H_9-: *butyl rubber.* [C19: from BUT(YRIC ACID) + -YL]

butyl acetate *n.* a colourless liquid with a fruity odour, existing in four isomeric forms. Three of the isomers are important solvents for cellulose lacquers. Formula: $CH_3COOC_4H_9$.

butyl alcohol *n.* another name for **butanol.**

butylene ('bjuːtɪ,liːn) *n.* another name for **butene.**

butyl rubber *n.* a copolymer of isobutene and isoprene, used in tyres and as a waterproofing material.

butyraceous (,bjuːtɪ'reɪʃəs) *adj.* of, containing, or resembling butter. [C17 *butyr-,* from Latin *būtyrum* BUTTER + -ACEOUS]

butyraldehyde (,bjuːtɪ'rældɪ,haɪd) *n.* a colourless flammable pungent liquid used in the manufacture of resins. Formula: $CH_3(CH_2)_2CHO$. [C20: from BUTYR(IC ACID) + ALDEHYDE]

butyrate ('bjuːtɪ,reɪt) *n.* any salt or ester of butyric acid, containing the monovalent group C_3H_7COO- or ion $C_3H_7COO^-$.

butyric acid (bjuː'tɪrɪk) *n.* a carboxylic acid existing in two isomeric forms, one of which produces the smell in rancid butter. Its esters are used in flavouring. Formula: $CH_3(CH_2)_2COOH$. [C19 *butyric,* from Latin *būtyrum* BUTTER]

butyrin ('bjuːtɪrɪn) *n.* a colourless liquid ester or oil found in butter. It is formed from butyric acid and glycerin. [C20: from BUTYR(IC + GLYCER)IN]

buxom ('bʌksəm) *adj.* **1.** (esp. of a woman) healthily plump, attractive, and vigorous. **2.** (of a woman) full-bosomed. [C12: *buhsum* compliant, pliant, from Old English *būgan* to bend, BOW[1]; related to Middle Dutch *būchsam* pliant, German *biegsam*] —'**buxomly** *adv.* —'**buxomness** *n.*

buy (baɪ) *vb.* **buys, buying, bought.** (*mainly tr.*) **1.** to acquire by paying or promising to pay a sum of money or the equivalent; purchase. **2.** to be capable of purchasing: *money can't buy love.* **3.** to acquire by any exchange or sacrifice: *to buy time by equivocation.* **4.** (*intr.*) to act as a buyer. **5.** to bribe or corrupt; hire by or as by bribery. **6.** *Slang.* to accept as true, practical, etc. **7.** (*intr.;* foll. by *into*) to purchase shares of (a company): *we bought into General Motors.* **8.** (*tr.*) *Theol.* (esp. of Christ) to ransom or redeem (a Christian or the soul of a Christian). **9. have bought it.** *Slang.* to be killed. ~*n.* **10.** a purchase (often in the phrases **good** or **bad buy**). ~See also **buy in, buy into, buy off, buy out, buy up.** [Old English *bycgan;* related to Old Norse *byggja* to let out, lend, Gothic *bugjan* to buy]

buy-back ('baɪ,bæk) *n. Commerce.* the repurchase by a company of some or all of its shares from an investor, who acquired them by putting venture capital into the company when it was formed.

buyer ('baɪə) *n.* **1.** a person who buys; purchaser; customer. **2.** a person employed to buy merchandise, materials, etc., as for a shop or factory.

buyers' market *n.* a market in which supply exceeds demand and buyers can influence prices.

buy in *vb.* (*adv.*) **1.** (*tr.*) to buy back for the owner (an item in an auction) at or below the reserve price. **2.** (*intr.*) to purchase shares in a company. **3.** (*intr.*) to buy goods or securities on the open market against a defaulting seller, charging this seller with any market differences. **4.** (*tr.*) Also: **buy into.** *U.S. informal.* to pay money to secure a position or place for (someone, esp. oneself) in some organization, esp. a business or club. **5.** to purchase (goods, etc.) in large quantities: *to buy in for the winter.* ~*n.* **buy-in. 6.** the purchase of a company by a manager or group who does not work for that company.

buy into *vb.* (*intr., prep.*) *Austral. and N.Z.* to get involved in (an argument, fight, etc.).

buy off *vb.* (*tr., adv.*) to pay (a person or group) to drop a charge, end opposition, relinquish a claim, etc.

buy out *vb.* (*tr., adv.*) **1.** to purchase the ownership, controlling interest, shares, etc., of (a company, etc.). **2.** to gain the release of (a person) from the armed forces by payment of money. **3.** to pay (a person) once and for all to give up (property, interest, etc.). ~*n.* **buyout. 4.** the purchase of a company, esp. by its former management or staff. See also **leveraged buyout, management buyout.**

Buys Ballot's Law (baɪs bə'lɒts, bɔɪs) *n.* a law stating that if an observer stands with his back to the wind in the N hemisphere, atmospheric pressure is lower on his left, and vice versa in the S hemisphere. [named after C. H. D. *Buys Ballot* (1817–90), Dutch meteorologist]

buy up *vb.* (*tr., adv.*) **1.** to purchase all, or all that is available, of (something). **2.** *Commerce.* to purchase a controlling interest in (a company, etc.), as by the acquisition of shares.

buzz (bʌz) *n.* **1.** a rapidly vibrating humming sound, as that of a prolonged *z* or of a bee in flight. **2.** a low sound, as of many voices in conversation. **3.** a rumour; report; gossip. **4.** *Informal.* a telephone call: *I'll give you a buzz.* **5.** *Slang.* **a.** a pleasant sensation, as from a drug such as cannabis. **b.** a sense of excitement; kick. ~*vb.* **6.** (*intr.*) to make a vibrating sound like that of a prolonged *z.* **7.** (*intr.*) to talk or gossip with an air of excitement or urgency: *the town buzzed with the news.* **8.** (*tr.*) to utter or spread (a rumour). **9.** (*intr.;* often foll. by *about*) to move around quickly and busily; bustle. **10.** (*tr.*) to signal or summon with a buzzer. **11.** (*tr.*) *Informal.* to call by telephone. **12.** (*tr.*) *Informal.* **a.** to fly an aircraft very low over (an object): *to buzz a ship.* **b.** to fly an aircraft very close to or across the path of (another aircraft), esp. to warn or intimidate. **13.** (*tr.*) (esp. of insects) to make a buzzing sound with (wings, etc.). [C16: of imitative origin] —'**buzzing** *n., adj.*

buzzard ('bʌzəd) *n.* **1.** any diurnal bird of prey of the genus *Buteo,* typically having broad wings and tail and a soaring flight: family *Accipitridae* (hawks, etc.). See **honey buzzard.** Compare **turkey buzzard.** **2.** a mean or cantankerous person. [C13: from Old French *buisard,* variant of *buison* buzzard, from Latin *būteō* hawk, falcon]

buzz bomb *n.* another name for the **V-1.**

buzzer ('bʌzə) *n.* **1.** a person or thing that buzzes. **2.** a device that produces a buzzing sound, esp. one similar to an electric bell without a hammer or gong. **3.** *N.Z.* a wood planing machine.

buzz off *vb.* (*intr., adv.; often imperative*) *Informal, chiefly Brit.* to go away; leave; depart.

buzz saw *n. U.S. and Canadian.* a power-operated circular saw.

buzz word *n. Informal.* a word, often originating in a particular jargon, that becomes a vogue word in the community as a whole or among a particular group.
BV *abbrev. for:* **1.** Beata Virgo. [Latin: Blessed Virgin] **2.** bene vale. [Latin: farewell]
BVM *abbrev. for* Beata Virgo Maria. [Latin: Blessed Virgin Mary]
BW *abbrev. for* biological warfare.
B/W *Photog. abbrev. for* black and white.
bwana ('bwɑːnə) *n.* (in E Africa) a master, often used as a respectful form of address corresponding to *sir.* [Swahili, from Arabic *abūna* our father]
BWG *abbrev. for* Birmingham Wire Gauge: a notation for the diameters of metal rods, ranging from 0 (0.340 inch) to 36 (0.004 inch).
BWR *abbrev. for* boiling-water reactor.
BWV (*preceding a number*) *Music. abbrev. for* Bach Werke-Verzeichnis: indicating the serial number in the catalogue of the works of J. S. Bach made by Wolfgang Schmieder (born 1901), published in 1950.
bx *abbrev. for* box.
by (baɪ) *prep.* **1.** used to indicate the agent after a passive verb: *seeds eaten by the birds.* **2.** used to indicate the person responsible for a creative work: *this song is by Schubert.* **3.** via; through: *enter by the back door.* **4.** foll. by a gerund to indicate a means used: *he frightened her by hiding behind the door.* **5.** beside; next to; near: *a tree by the house.* **6.** passing the position of; past: *he drove by the old cottage.* **7.** not later than; before: *return the books by Tuesday.* **8.** used to indicate extent, after a comparative: *it is hotter by five degrees than it was yesterday.* **9.** (esp. in oaths) invoking the name of: *I swear by all the gods.* **10.** multiplied by: *four by three equals twelve.* **11.** (*in habitual sentences*) during the passing of (esp. in the phrases **by day, by night**). **12.** placed between measurements of the various dimensions of something: *a plank fourteen inches by seven.* ~*adv.* **13.** near: *the house is close by.* **14.** away; aside: *he put some money by each week for savings.* **15.** passing a point near something; past: *he drove by.* **16.** *Scot.* past; over and done with: *that's a' by now.* **17.** *Scot.* aside; behind one: *you must put that by you.* ~*n., pl.* **byes. 18.** a variant spelling of **bye.** [Old English *bī*; related to Gothic *bi*, Old High German *bī*, Sanskrit *abhi* to, towards]
by- *or* **bye-** *prefix.* **1.** near: *bystander.* **2.** secondary or incidental: *by-effect; by-election; by-path; by-product.* [from BY]
by and by *adv.* **1.** presently or eventually. ~*n.* **by-and-by. 2.** *U.S. and Canadian.* a future time or occasion.
by and large *adv.* in general; on the whole. [C17: originally nautical (meaning: to the wind and off it)]
by-bidder *n.* a bidder at an auction who bids up the price of an item for the benefit of a seller.
by-blow *n.* **1.** a passing or incidental blow. **2.** an archaic word for a **bastard.**
byde (bəɪd) *vb. Scot.* a variant spelling of **bide.**
bye (baɪ) *n.* **1.** *Sport.* the situation in which a player or team in an eliminatory contest wins a preliminary round by virtue of having no opponent. **2.** *Golf.* one or more holes of a stipulated course that are left unplayed after the match has been decided. **3.** *Cricket.* a run scored off a ball not struck by the batsman: allotted to the team as an extra and not to the individual batsman. See also **leg bye. 4.** something incidental or secondary. **5. by the bye.** incidentally; by the way: used as a sentence connector. [C16: a variant of BY]
bye-bye *sentence substitute. Brit informal.* goodbye.
bye-byes *n.* (*functioning as sing.*) an informal word for **sleep,** used esp. in addressing children (as in the phrase **go to bye-byes**).
by-election *or* **bye-election** *n.* **1.** (in Great Britain and other countries of the Commonwealth) an election held during the life of a parliament to fill a vacant seat in the lower chamber. **2.** (in the U.S.) a special election to fill a vacant elective position with an unexpired term.
Byelorussian *or* **Belorussian** (ˌbjɛləʊ'rʌʃən, ˌbɛl-) *adj.* **1.** of, relating to, or characteristic of the former Soviet republic of Byelorussia, its people, or their language. ~*n.* **2.** the official language of Byelorussia: an East Slavonic language closely related to Russian. **3.** a native or inhabitant of Byelorussia. ~Also called: **White Russian.**
by-form *n.* a subsidiary or variant form.
bygone ('baɪˌgɒn) *adj.* **1.** (*usually prenominal*) past; former. ~*n.* **2.** (*often pl.*) a past occurrence. **3.** (*often pl.*) an artefact, implement, etc., of former domestic or industrial use, now often collected for interest. **4. let bygones be bygones.** to agree to forget past quarrels.
byke (bəɪk, baɪk) *n. Scot.* a variant spelling of **bike**[2].
bylane ('baɪˌleɪn) *n.* a side lane or alley off a road.
bylaw *or* **bye-law** ('baɪˌlɔː) *n.* **1.** a rule made by a local authority for the regulation of its affairs or management of the area it governs. **2.** a regulation of a company, society, etc. **3.** a subsidiary law. [C13: probably of Scandinavian origin; compare Old Norse *býr* dwelling, town; see BOWER[1], LAW[1]]
by-line *n.* **1.** *Journalism.* a line under the title of a newspaper or magazine article giving the author's name. **2.** *Soccer.* another word for **touchline.**
BYO *n. Austral. and N.Z.* an unlicensed restaurant at which diners may drink their own wine, etc. [C20: from the phrase *bring your own*]
BYOB *abbrev. for:* **1.** bring your own beer. **2.** bring your own booze. **3.** bring your own bottle.
bypass ('baɪˌpɑːs) *n.* **1.** a main road built to avoid a city or other congested area. **2.** a means of redirecting the flow of a substance around an appliance through which it would otherwise pass. **3.** *Surgery.* **a.** the redirection of blood flow, either to avoid a diseased blood vessel or in order to perform heart surgery. See **coronary bypass. b.** (*as modifier*): *bypass surgery.* **4.** *Electronics.* **a.** an electrical circuit, esp. one containing a capacitor, connected in parallel around one or more components, providing an alternative path for certain frequencies. **b.** (*as modifier*): *a bypass capacitor.* ~*vb.* **-passes, -passing, -passed** *or* **-past.** (*tr.*) **5.** to go around or avoid (a city, obstruction, problem, etc.). **6.** to cause (traffic, fluid, etc.) to go through a bypass. **7.** to proceed without reference to (regulations, a superior, etc.); get round; avoid.
bypass engine *n.* a gas turbine in which a part of the compressor delivery bypasses the combustion zone, flowing directly into or around the main exhaust gas flow to provide additional thrust. Compare **turbofan.**
bypass ratio *n. Aeronautics.* the ratio of the amount of air that bypasses the combustion chambers of an aircraft gas turbine to that passing through them.
bypath ('baɪˌpɑːθ) *n.* a little-used path or track, esp. in the country.
by-play *n.* secondary action or talking carried on apart while the main action proceeds, esp. in a play.
by-product *n.* **1.** a secondary or incidental product of a manufacturing process. **2.** a side effect.
byre (baɪə) *n. Brit.* a shelter for cows. [Old English *býre*; related to *būr* hut, cottage; see BOWER[1]]
byrnie ('bɜːnɪ) *n.* an archaic word for **coat of mail.** [Old English *byrne*; related to Old Norse *brynja*, Gothic *brunjō*, Old High German *brunnia* coat of mail, Old Irish *bruinne* breast]
byroad ('baɪˌrəʊd) *n.* a secondary or side road.
Byronic (baɪ'rɒnɪk) *adj.* of, relating to, or characteristic of George Gordon, Lord Byron (1788–1824), British Romantic poet, or his style. —**By'ronically** *adv.* —**'Byronˌism** *n.*
byssinosis (ˌbɪsɪ'nəʊsɪs) *n.* a lung disease caused by prolonged inhalation of fibre dust in textile factories. [C19: from New Latin, from Greek *bussinos* of linen (see BYSSUS) + -OSIS]
byssus ('bɪsəs) *n., pl.* **byssuses** *or* **byssi** ('bɪsaɪ). a mass of strong threads secreted by a sea mussel or similar mollusc that attaches the animal to a hard fixed surface. [C17: from Latin, from Greek *bussos* linen, flax, ultimately of Egyptian origin]
bystander ('baɪˌstændə) *n.* a person present but not involved; onlooker; spectator.
bystander effect *n.* the phenomenon that when many people observe a crime or someone in trouble, each of them is less likely to intervene than when only one person is present.
bystreet ('baɪˌstriːt) *n.* an obscure or secondary street.
byte (baɪt) *n. Computer technol.* **1.** a group of bits, usually six or eight, processed as a single unit of data. **2.** the storage space in a memory or other storage device that is allocated to such a group of bits. **3.** a subdivision of a word. [C20: probably a blend of BIT[4] + BITE]
byway ('baɪˌweɪ) *n.* **1.** a secondary or side road, esp. in the country. **2.** an area, field of study, etc., that is very obscure or of secondary importance.
byword ('baɪˌwɜːd) *n.* **1.** a person, place, or thing regarded as a perfect or proverbial example of something: *their name is a byword for good service.* **2.** an object of scorn or derision. **3.** a common saying; proverb. [Old English *bīwyrde*; see BY, WORD; compare Old High German *pīwurti*, from Latin *prōverbium* proverb]
by-your-leave *n.* a request for permission (esp. in the phrase **without so much as a by-your-leave**).
Byz. *abbrev. for* Byzantine.
Byzantine (bɪ'zænˌtaɪn, -ˌtiːn, baɪ-; 'bɪzənˌtiːn, -ˌtaɪn) *adj.* **1.** of or relating to Byzantium, an ancient Greek city on the Bosphorus. **2.** of or relating to the Byzantine Empire, the continuation of the Roman Empire in the East. **3.** of, relating to, or characterizing the Orthodox Church or its rites and liturgy. **4.** of or relating to the highly coloured stylized form of religious art developed in the Byzantine Empire. **5.** of or relating to the style of architecture developed in the Byzantine Empire, characterized by massive domes with square bases, rounded arches, spires and minarets, and the extensive use of mosaics. **6.** denoting the Medieval Greek spoken in the Byzantine Empire. **7.** (of attitudes, etc.) inflexible or complicated. ~*n.* **8.** an inhabitant of Byzantium. —**Byzantinism** (bɪ'zæntaɪˌnɪzəm, -tiː-, baɪ-; 'bɪzəntiːˌnɪzəm, -taɪ-) *n.*
Byzantine Church *n.* another name for the **Orthodox Church.**
Bz *or* **bz.** *abbrev. for* benzene.

c *or* **C** (siː) *n., pl.* **c's, C's,** *or* **Cs.** **1.** the third letter and second consonant of the modern English alphabet. **2.** a speech sound represented by this letter, in English usually either a voiceless alveolar fricative, as in *cigar,* or a voiceless velar stop, as in *case.* **3.** the third in a series, esp. the third highest grade in an examination. **4. a.** something shaped like a C. **b.** *(in combination): a C-spring.*

c *symbol for:* **1.** centi-. **2.** cubic. **3.** cycle. **4.** *Maths.* constant. **5.** specific heat capacity. **6.** the speed of light and other types of electromagnetic radiation in a free space. **7.** *Chess.* See **algebraic notation.**

C *symbol for:* **1.** *Music.* **a.** a note having a frequency of 261.63 hertz (**middle C**) or this value multiplied or divided by any power of 2; the first degree of a major scale containing no sharps or flats (**C major**). **b.** a key, string, or pipe producing this note. **c.** the major or minor key having this note as its tonic. **d.** a time signature denoting four crotchet beats to the bar. See also **alla breve** (sense 2), **common time. 2.** *Chem.* carbon. **3.** capacitance. **4.** heat capacity. **5.** cold (water). **6.** *Physics.* compliance. **7.** Celsius. **8.** centigrade. **9.** century: *C20.* **10.** coulomb. ~**11.** *the Roman numeral for* 100. See **Roman numerals.** ~**12.** *international car registration for* Cuba. ~*n.* **13.** a computer programming language combining the advantages of a high-level language with the ability to address the computer at a level comparable with that of an assembly language.

c. *abbrev. for:* **1.** carat. **2.** carbon (paper). **3.** *Cricket.* caught. **4.** cent(s). **5.** century or centuries. **6.** *(pl.* **cc.**) chapter. **7.** (used esp. preceding a date) circa: *c. 1800.* [Latin: about] **8.** colt. **9.** contralto. **10.** copyright.

C. *abbrev. for:* **1.** (on maps as part of name) Cape. **2.** Catholic. **3.** Celtic. **4.** Conservative. **5.** Corps.

c/- *Austral.* (in addresses) *abbrev. for* care of.

C- (of U.S. military aircraft) *abbrev. for* cargo transport: *C-5.*

© *symbol for* copyright.

C1 ('siː'wʌn) *n.* **a.** a person whose job is supervisory or clerical, or who works in junior management. **b.** *(as adj.): C1 worker.* ~See also **occupation groupings.**

C2 ('siː'tuː) *n.* **a.** a skilled manual worker, or a manual worker with responsibility for other people. **b.** *(as adj.): C2 worker.* ~See also **occupation groupings.**

C3 *or* **C-3** ('siː'θriː) *adj.* **1.** in poor health or having a poor physique. **2.** *Informal.* inferior; worthless. Compare **A1.**

Ca *the chemical symbol for* calcium.

CA *abbrev. for:* **1.** California. **2.** Central America. **3.** chartered accountant. **4.** chief accountant. **5.** consular agent. **6.** (in Britain) Consumers' Association.

ca. *abbrev. for* circa. [Latin: about]

C/A *abbrev. for:* **1.** capital account. **2.** credit account. **3.** current account.

caa[1] *or* **ca'**[1] (kɔː) *vb., n.* a Scot. word for **call.**

caa[2] *or* **ca'**[2] (kɔː) *vb. Scot.* **1.** to drive or propel. **2.** to knock. **3. caa** *or* **ca' canny.** to proceed cautiously; go slow. **4. caa** *or* **ca' the feet frae.** to send (a person) sprawling. [see CAA[1]]

CAA (in Britain) *abbrev. for* Civil Aviation Authority.

cab[1] (kæb) *n.* **1. a.** a taxi. **b.** *(as modifier): a cab rank.* **2.** the enclosed compartment of a lorry, locomotive, crane, etc., from which it is driven or operated. **3.** (formerly) a light horse-drawn vehicle used for public hire. **4. first cab off the rank.** *Austral. informal.* the first person, etc., to do or take advantage of something. [C19: shortened from CABRIOLET]

cab[2] *or* **kab** (kæb) *n.* an ancient Hebrew measure equal to about 2.3 litres (4 pints). [C16: from Hebrew *qabh* container, something hollowed out]

CAB *abbrev. for:* **1.** (in Britain) Citizens' Advice Bureau. **2.** (in the U.S.) Civil Aeronautics Board.

cabal (kə'bæl) *n.* **1.** a small group of intriguers, esp. one formed for political purposes. **2.** a secret plot, esp. a political one; conspiracy; intrigue. **3.** a secret or exclusive set of people; clique. ~*vb.* **-bals, -balling, -balled.** *(intr.)* **4.** to form a cabal; conspire; plot. [C17: from French *cabale,* from Medieval Latin *cabala;* see CABBALA]

Cabal (kə'bæl) *n.* **the.** *English history.* a group of ministers of Charles II that governed from 1667–73: consisting of Clifford, Ashley, Buckingham, Arlington, and Lauderdale. [see CABBALA; by a coincidence, the initials of Charles II's ministers can be arranged to form this word]

cabala (kə'bɑːlə) *n.* a variant spelling of **cabbala.** —**cabalism** ('kæbəˌlɪzəm) *n.* —'**cabalist** *n.* —ˌ**caba'listic** *adj.*

caballero (ˌkæbə'ljɛərəʊ; *Spanish* kaβa'ʎero) *n., pl.* **-ros** (-rəʊz; *Spanish* -ros). **1.** a Spanish gentleman. **2.** a southwestern U.S. word for **horseman.** [C19: from Spanish: gentleman, horseman, from Late Latin *caballārius* rider, groom, from *caballus* horse; compare CAVALIER]

cabana (kə'bɑːnə) *n. Chiefly U.S.* a tent used as a dressing room by the sea. [from Spanish *cabaña:* CABIN]

cabaret ('kæbəˌreɪ) *n.* **1.** a floor show of dancing, singing, or other light entertainment at a nightclub or restaurant. **2.** *Chiefly U.S.* a nightclub or restaurant providing such entertainment. [C17: from Norman French: tavern, probably from Late Latin *camera* an arched roof, CHAMBER]

cabbage[1] ('kæbɪdʒ) *n.* **1.** Also called: **cole.** any of various cultivated varieties of the cruciferous plant *Brassica oleracea capitata,* typically having a short thick stalk and a large head of green or reddish edible leaves. See also **brassica, savoy.** Compare **skunk cabbage, Chinese cabbage. 2. wild cabbage.** a Mediterranean cruciferous plant, *Brassica oleracea,* with broad leaves and a long spike of yellow flowers: the plant from which the cabbages, cauliflower, broccoli, and Brussels sprout have been bred. **3. a.** the head of a cabbage. **b.** the edible leaf bud of the cabbage palm. **4.** *Informal.* a dull or unimaginative person. **5.** *Informal.* a person who has no mental faculties and is dependent on others for his subsistence. [C14: from Norman French *caboche* head; perhaps related to Old French *boce* hump, bump, Latin *caput* head]

cabbage[2] ('kæbɪdʒ) *Brit. slang.* ~*n.* **1.** snippets of cloth appropriated by a tailor from a customer's material. ~*vb.* **2.** to steal; pilfer. [C17: of uncertain origin; perhaps related to Old French *cabas* theft]

cabbage bug *n.* another name for the **harlequin bug.**

cabbage lettuce *n.* any of several varieties of lettuce that have roundish flattened heads resembling cabbages.

cabbage moth *n.* a common brownish noctuid moth, *Mamestra brassicae,* the larva of which is destructive of cabbages and other plants.

cabbage palm *or* **tree** *n.* **1.** a West Indian palm, *Roystonea* (or *Oreodoxa*) *oleracea,* whose leaf buds are eaten like cabbage. **2.** a similar Brazilian palm, *Euterpe oleracea.* **3.** an Australian palm tree, *Livistona australis.*

cabbage palmetto *n.* a tropical American fan palm, *Sabal palmetto,* with edible leaf buds and leaves used in thatching.

cabbage root fly *n.* a dipterous fly, *Erioischia brassicae,* whose larvae feed on the roots and stems of cabbages and other brassicas: family *Muscidae* (houseflies, etc.).

cabbage rose *n.* a rose, *Rosa centifolia,* with a round compact full-petalled head.

cabbagetown ('kæbɪdʒˌtaʊn) *n. Canadian.* a city slum. [C20: from *Cabbagetown,* a depressed area of Toronto, where the Anglo-Saxon population was thought to exist on cabbage]

cabbage tree *n.* a tree, *Cordyline australis,* of New Zealand having a tall branchless trunk and a palmlike top. Also called: **ti.**

cabbage white *n.* any large white butterfly of the genus *Pieris,* esp. the Eurasian species *P. brassicae,* the larvae of which feed on the leaves of cabbages and related vegetables: family *Pieridae.*

cabbageworm ('kæbɪdʒˌwɜːm) *n. U.S.* any caterpillar that feeds on cabbages, esp. that of the cabbage white.

cabbala, cabala, kabbala, *or* **kabala** (kə'bɑːlə) *n.* **1.** an ancient Jewish mystical tradition based on an esoteric interpretation of the Old Testament. **2.** any secret or occult doctrine or science. [C16: from Medieval Latin, from Hebrew *qabbālāh* tradition, what is received, from *qābal* to receive] —**cabbalism, cabalism, kabbalism,** *or* **kabalism** ('kæbəˌlɪzəm) *n.* —'**cabbalist,** '**cabalist,** '**kabbalist,** *or* '**kabalist** *n.* —ˌ**cabba'listic,** ˌ**caba'listic,** ˌ**kabba'listic,** *or* ˌ**kaba'listic** *adj.*

cabby *or* **cabbie** ('kæbɪ) *n., pl.* **-bies.** *Informal.* a cab driver.

caber ('keɪbə; *Scot.* 'kebər) *n. Scot.* a heavy section of trimmed tree trunk thrown in competition at Highland games (**tossing the caber**). [C16: from Gaelic *cabar* pole]

Cabernet Sauvignon ('kæbəneɪ 'səʊvɪnjɒn; *French* kabɛrnɛ soviɲɔ̃) *n. (sometimes not caps.)* **1.** a black grape grown in the Bordeaux area of France, Australia, California, Bulgaria, and elsewhere, used for making wine. **2.** any of various red wines made from this grape. [French]

cabezon ('kæbɪzɒn) *or* **cabezone** ('kæbɪˌzəʊn) *n.* a large food fish, *Scorpaenichthys marmoratus,* of North American Pacific coastal waters, having greenish flesh: family *Cottidae* (bullheads and sea scorpions). [Spanish, from *cabeza* head, ultimately from Latin *caput*]

cabin ('kæbɪn) *n.* **1.** a small simple dwelling; hut. **2.** a simple house providing accommodation for travellers or holiday-makers at a motel or holiday camp. **3.** a room used as an office or living quarters in a ship. **4.** a covered compartment used for shelter or living quarters in a small boat. **5.** (in a warship) the compartment or room reserved for the commanding officer. **6.** *Brit.* another name for **signal box. 7. a.** the enclosed part of a light aircraft in which the pilot and passengers sit. **b.** the part of an airliner in which the passengers are carried. **c.** the section of an aircraft used for cargo. ~*vb.* **8.** to confine in a small space. [C14: from Old French *cabane,* from Old Provençal *cabana,* from Late Latin *capanna* hut]

cabin boy *n.* a boy who waits on the officers and passengers of a ship.

cabin class *n.* a class of accommodation on a passenger ship between first class and tourist class.

cabin cruiser *n.* a power boat fitted with a cabin and comforts for pleasure cruising or racing.

cabinet ('kæbɪnɪt) *n.* **1. a.** a piece of furniture containing shelves, cupboards, or drawers for storage or display. **b.** (*as modifier*): *cabinet teak.* **2.** the outer case of a television, radio, etc. **3. a.** (*often cap.*) the executive and policy-making body of a country, consisting of all government ministers or just the senior ministers. **b.** (*sometimes cap.*) an advisory council to a president, sovereign, governor, etc. **c.** (*as modifier*): *a cabinet reshuffle; a cabinet minister.* **4. a.** a standard size of paper, 6 × 4 inches (15 × 10 cm) or 6½ × 4¼ inches (16.5 × 10.5 cm), for mounted photographs. **b.** (*as modifier*): *a cabinet photograph.* **5.** *Printing.* an enclosed rack for holding cases of type, etc. **6.** *Archaic.* a private room. **7.** (*modifier*) suitable in size, value, decoration, etc., for a display cabinet: *a cabinet edition of Shakespeare.* **8.** (*modifier*) (of a drawing or projection of a three-dimensional object) constructed with true horizontal and vertical representation of scale but with oblique distances reduced to about half scale to avoid the appearance of distortion. **9.** (*modifier*) (of a wine) specially selected and usually rare. [C16: from Old French, diminutive of *cabine,* of uncertain origin]

cabinet beetle *n.* See **dermestid.**

cabinet-maker *n.* a craftsman specializing in the making of fine furniture. —'**cabinet-ˌmaking** *n.*

cabinet pudding *n.* a steamed suet pudding enriched with dried fruit.

cabinetwork ('kæbɪnɪtˌwɜːk) *n.* **1.** the making of furniture, esp. of fine quality. **2.** an article made by a cabinet-maker.

cabin fever *n. Canadian.* acute depression resulting from being isolated or sharing cramped quarters in the wilderness, esp. during the long northern winter.

cable ('keɪbᵊl) *n.* **1.** a strong thick rope, usually of twisted hemp or steel wire. **2.** *Nautical.* an anchor chain or rope. **3.** Also called: **cable length, cable's length.** a unit of length in nautical use that has various values. It is most commonly taken as 120 fathoms (720 feet) in the U.S. and one tenth of a nautical mile (608 feet) in Britain. It is also sometimes taken as 100 fathoms (600 feet). **4.** a wire or bundle of wires that conducts electricity: *a submarine cable.* See also **coaxial cable. 5.** Also called: **overseas** *or* **international telegram, cablegram.** a telegram sent abroad by submarine cable, radio, communications satellite, or by telephone line. **6.** See **cable stitch.** ~*vb.* **7.** to send (a message) to (someone) by cable. **8.** (*tr.*) to fasten or provide with a cable or cables. **9.** (*tr.*) to supply (a place) with or link (a place) to cable television. [C13: from Old Norman French, from Late Latin *capulum* halter]

cable car *n.* **1.** a cabin suspended from and moved by an overhead cable in a mountain area. **2.** a cableway. **3.** a passenger car on a cable railway.

cablegram ('keɪbᵊlˌgræm) *n.* a more formal name for **cable** (sense 5).

cable-laid *adj.* (of a rope) made of three plain-laid ropes twisted together in a left-handed direction.

cable railway *n.* a railway on which individual cars are drawn along by a strong cable or metal chain operated by a stationary motor.

cable release *n.* a short length of flexible cable, used to operate the shutter of a camera without shaking it.

cable-stayed bridge *n.* a type of suspension bridge in which the supporting cables are connected directly to the bridge deck without the use of suspenders.

cable stitch *n.* **a.** a pattern or series of knitting stitches producing a design like a twisted rope. **b.** (*as modifier*): *a cable-stitch sweater.* Sometimes shortened to **cable.**

cablet ('keɪblɪt) *n.* a small cable, esp. a cable-laid rope that has a circumference of less than 25 centimetres (ten inches).

cable television *n.* a television service in which programmes are distributed to subscribers' televisions by cable rather than by broadcast transmission.

cableway ('keɪbᵊlˌweɪ) *n.* a system for moving people or bulk materials in which suspended cars, buckets, etc., run on cables that extend between terminal towers.

cabman ('kæbmən) *n., pl.* **-men.** the driver of a cab.

cabob (kə'bɒb) *n.* a variant of **kebab.**

cabochon ('kæbəˌʃɒn; *French* kabɔʃɔ̃) *n.* a smooth domed gem, polished but unfaceted. [C16: from Old French, from Old Norman French *caboche* head; see CABBAGE[1]]

caboodle (kə'buːdᵊl) *n. Informal.* a lot, bunch, or group (esp. in the phrases **the whole caboodle, the whole kit and caboodle**). [C19: probably contraction of KIT and BOODLE]

caboose (kə'buːs) *n.* **1.** *U.S. informal.* short for **calaboose. 2.** *Railways. U.S. and Canadian.* a guard's van, esp. one with sleeping and eating facilities for the train crew. **3.** *Nautical.* **a.** a deckhouse for a galley aboard ship or formerly in Canada, on a lumber raft. **b.** *Chiefly Brit.* the galley itself. **4.** *Canadian.* **a.** a mobile bunkhouse used by lumbermen, etc. **b.** an insulated cabin on runners, equipped with a stove. [C18: from Dutch *cabūse,* of unknown origin]

cabotage ('kæbəˌtɑːʒ) *n.* **1.** *Nautical.* coastal navigation or shipping, esp. within the borders of one country. **2.** reservation to a country's carriers of its internal traffic, esp. air traffic. [C19: from French, from *caboter* to sail near the coast, apparently from Spanish *cabo* CAPE[2]]

cabretta (kə'brɛtə) *n. Chiefly U.S.* a soft leather obtained from the skins of certain South American or African sheep. [from Spanish *cabra* she-goat]

cabrilla (kə'brɪlə) *n.* any of various serranid food fishes, esp. *Epinephelus analogus,* occurring in warm seas around Florida and the West Indies. [Spanish, literally: little goat]

cabriole ('kæbrɪˌəʊl) *n.* **1.** Also called: **cabriole leg.** a type of furniture leg, popular in the first half of the 18th century, in which an upper convex curve descends tapering to a concave curve. **2.** *Ballet.* a leap in the air with one leg outstretched and the other beating against it. [C18: from French, from *cabrioler* to caper; from its being based on the leg of a capering animal; see CABRIOLET]

cabriolet (ˌkæbrɪəʊ'leɪ) *n.* **1.** a small two-wheeled horse-drawn carriage with two seats and a folding hood. **2.** a former name for a **drophead coupé.** [C18: from French, literally: a little skip, from *cabriole,* from Latin *capreolus* wild goat, from *caper* goat; referring to the lightness of movement]

ca'canny (ˌkɔː'kænɪ) *n. Scot.* **1.** moderation or wariness. **2. a.** a policy of restricting the output of work; a go-slow. **b.** (*as modifier*): *a ca'canny policy.* See also **caa**[2]. [C19: literally, *call canny* to drive gently]

cacao (kə'kɑːəʊ, -'keɪəʊ) *n.* **1.** a small tropical American evergreen tree, *Theobroma cacao,* having yellowish flowers and reddish-brown seed pods from which cocoa and chocolate are prepared: family *Sterculiaceae.* **2. cacao bean.** another name for **cocoa bean. 3. cacao butter.** another name for **cocoa butter.** [C16: from Spanish, from Nahuatl *cacauatl* cacao beans]

cacciatore (ˌkɑːtʃə'tɔːrɪ, ˌkætʃ-) *or* **cacciatora** *adj.* (*immediately postpositive*) prepared with tomatoes, mushrooms, herbs, and other seasonings. [Italian, literally: hunter]

cachalot ('kæʃəˌlɒt) *n.* another name for **sperm whale.** [C18: from French, from Portuguese, *cachalote,* of unknown origin]

cache (kæʃ) *n.* **1.** a hidden store of provisions, weapons, treasure, etc. **2.** the place where such a store is hidden. ~*vb.* **3.** (*tr.*) to store in a cache. [C19: from French, from *cacher* to hide]

cachepot ('kæʃˌpɒt, ˌkæʃ'pəʊ) *n.* an ornamental container for a flowerpot. [French: pot-hider]

cachet ('kæʃeɪ) *n.* **1.** an official seal on a document, letter, etc. **2.** a distinguishing mark; stamp. **3.** prestige; distinction. **4.** *Philately.* **a.** a mark stamped by hand on mail for commemorative purposes. **b.** a small mark made by dealers and experts on the back of postage stamps. Compare **overprint** (sense 3), **surcharge** (sense 5). **5.** a hollow wafer, formerly used for enclosing an unpleasant-tasting medicine. [C17: from Old French, from *cacher* to hide]

cachexia (kə'kɛksɪə) *or* **cachexy** *n.* a generally weakened condition of body or mind resulting from any debilitating chronic disease. [C16: from Late Latin from Greek *kakhexia,* from *kakos* bad + *hexis* condition, habit] —**cachectic** (kə'kɛktɪk) *adj.*

cachinnate ('kækɪˌneɪt) *vb.* (*intr.*) to laugh loudly. [C19: from Latin *cacchināre,* probably of imitative origin] —ˌ**cachin'natory** *adj.*

cachinnation (ˌkækɪ'neɪʃən) *n.* **1.** raucous or convulsive laughter. **2.** *Psychiatry.* inappropriate laughter, sometimes found in schizophrenia.

cachou ('kæʃuː, kæ'ʃuː) *n.* **1.** a lozenge eaten to sweeten the breath. **2.** another name for **catechu.** [C18: via French from Portuguese, from Malay *kāchu*]

cachucha (kə'tʃuːtʃə) *n.* **1.** a graceful Spanish solo dance in triple time. **2.** music composed for this dance. [C19: from Spanish]

cacique (kə'siːk) *or* **cazique** (kə'ziːk) *n.* **1.** an American Indian chief in a Spanish-speaking region. **2.** (esp. in Spanish America) a local political boss. **3.** any of various tropical American songbirds of the genus *Cacicus* and related genera: family *Icteridae* (American orioles). [C16: from Spanish, of Arawak origin; compare Taino *cacique* chief]

caciquism (kə'siːkˌɪzəm) *n.* (esp. in Spanish America) government by local political bosses.

cack-handed (ˌkæk'hændɪd) *adj. Informal.* **1.** left-handed. **2.** clumsy. [from dialect *cack* excrement, from the fact that clumsy people usually make a mess; via Middle Low German or Middle Dutch from Latin *cacāre* to defecate]

cackle ('kækᵊl) *vb.* **1.** (*intr.*) (esp. of a hen that has just laid an egg) to squawk with shrill broken notes. **2.** (*intr.*) to laugh or chatter raucously and noisily. **3.** (*tr.*) to utter in a cackling manner. ~*n.* **4.** the noise or act of cackling. **5.** noisy chatter. **6. cut the cackle.** *Informal.* to stop chattering or giggling; be quiet. [C13: probably from Middle Low German *kākelen,* of imitative origin] —'**cackler** *n.*

caco- *combining form.* bad, unpleasant, or incorrect: *cacophony.* [from Greek *kakos* bad]

cacodemon *or* **cacodaemon** (ˌkækə'diːmən) *n.* an evil spirit or devil. [C16: from Greek *kakodaimōn* evil genius]

cacodyl ('kækədaɪl) *n.* an oily poisonous liquid with a strong garlic smell; tetramethyldiarsine. [C19: from Greek *kakōdēs* evil-smelling (from *kakos* CACO- + *ozein* to smell) + -YL] —**cacodylic** (ˌkækəˈdɪlɪk) *adj.*

cacoepy (kəˈkəʊɪpɪ) *n.* bad or mistaken pronunciation. [C19: from Greek *kakoepeia*] —**cacoepistic** (kəˌkəʊɪˈpɪstɪk) *adj.*

cacoethes (ˌkækəʊˈiːθiːz) *n.* an uncontrollable urge or desire, esp. for something harmful; mania: *a cacoethes for smoking.* [C16: from Latin *cacoēthes* malignant disease, from Greek *kakoēthēs* of an evil disposition, from *kakos* CACO- + *ēthos* character] —**cacoethic** (ˌkækəʊˈɛθɪk) *adj.*

cacogenics (ˌkækəʊˈdʒɛnɪks) *n.* another name for **dysgenics.** [C20: from CACO- + EUGENICS] —ˌ**cacoˈgenic** *adj.*

cacography (kæˈkɒgrəfɪ) *n.* **1.** bad handwriting. Compare **calligraphy. 2.** incorrect spelling. Compare **orthography.** —**caˈcographer** *n.* —**cacographic** (ˌkækəˈgræfɪk) *or* ˌ**cacoˈgraphical** *adj.*

cacology (kəˈkɒlədʒɪ) *n.* a bad choice of words; faulty speech. [C17 (in the sense: ill report): from Greek *kakologia*]

cacomistle (ˈkækəˌmɪsᵊl) *or* **cacomixle** (ˈkækəˌmɪksᵊl) *n.* **1.** a catlike omnivorous mammal, *Bassariscus astutus,* of S North America, related to but smaller than the raccoons: family *Procyonidae,* order *Carnivora* (carnivores). It has yellowish-grey fur and a long bushy tail banded in black and white. **2.** a related smaller animal, *Jentinkia* (or *Bassariscus*) *sumichrasti,* of Central America. [C19: from Mexican Spanish, from Nahuatl *tlacomiztli,* from *tlaco* half + *miztli* cougar]

cacophonous (kəˈkɒfənəs) *or* **cacophonic** (ˌkækəˈfɒnɪk) *adj.* jarring in sound; discordant; harsh. —**caˈcophonously** *or* ˌ**cacoˈphonically** *adv.*

cacophony (kəˈkɒfənɪ) *n., pl.* **-nies. 1.** harsh discordant sound; dissonance. **2.** the use of unharmonious or dissonant speech sounds in language. Compare **euphony.**

cactus (ˈkæktəs) *n., pl.* **-tuses** *or* **-ti** (-taɪ). **1.** any spiny succulent plant of the family *Cactaceae* of the arid regions of America. Cactuses have swollen tough stems, leaves reduced to spines or scales, and large brightly coloured flowers. **2. cactus dahlia.** a double-flowered variety of dahlia. [C17: from Latin: prickly plant, from Greek *kaktos* cardoon] —**cactaceous** (kækˈteɪʃəs) *adj.*

cacuminal (kæˈkjuːmɪnᵊl) *Phonetics.* ~*adj.* **1.** Also called: **cerebral.** relating to or denoting a consonant articulated with the tip of the tongue turned back towards the hard palate. ~*n.* **2.** a consonant articulated in this manner. [C19: from Latin *cacūmen* point, top]

cad (kæd) *n. Brit. informal; old-fashioned.* a man who does not behave in a gentlemanly manner towards others. [C18: shortened from CADDIE] —ˈ**caddish** *adj.*

CAD *acronym for* computer-aided design.

cadaster *or* **cadastre** (kəˈdæstə) *n.* an official register showing details of ownership, boundaries, and value of real property in a district, made for taxation purposes. [C19: from French, from Provençal *cadastro,* from Italian *catastro,* from Late Greek *katastikhon* register, from *kata stikhon* line by line, from *kata* (see CATA-) + *stikhos* line, STICH] —**caˈdastral** *adj.*

cadaver (kəˈdeɪvə, -ˈdɑːv-) *n. Med.* a corpse. [C16: from Latin, from *cadere* to fall] —**caˈdaveric** *adj.*

cadaverine (kəˈdævəˌriːn) *n.* a toxic diamine with an unpleasant smell, produced by protein hydrolysis during putrefaction of animal tissue. Formula: $NH_2(CH_2)_5NH_2$.

cadaverous (kəˈdævərəs) *adj.* **1.** of or like a corpse, esp. in being deathly pale; ghastly. **2.** thin and haggard; gaunt. —**caˈdaverously** *adv.* —**caˈdaverousness** *n.*

CADCAM (ˈkædˌkæm) *n. acronym for* computer-aided design and manufacture.

caddie *or* **caddy** (ˈkædɪ) *n., pl.* **-dies. 1.** *Golf.* an attendant who carries clubs, etc., for a player. ~*vb.* **-dies, -dying, -died. 2.** (*intr.*) to act as a caddie. [C17 (originally: a gentleman learning the military profession by serving in the army without a commission, hence C18 (Scottish): a person looking for employment, an errand-boy): from French CADET]

caddie car *or* **caddie cart** *n. Golf.* a small light two-wheeled trolley for carrying clubs.

caddis *or* **caddice** (ˈkædɪs) *n.* a type of coarse woollen yarn, braid, or fabric.

caddis fly *n.* any small mothlike insect of the order *Trichoptera,* having two pairs of hairy wings and aquatic larvae (caddis worms). [C17: of unknown origin]

caddis worm *or* **caddis** *n.* the aquatic larva of a caddis fly, which constructs a protective case around itself made of silk, sand, stones, etc. Also called: **caseworm, strawworm.**

Caddoan (ˈkædəʊən) *n.* a family of North American Indian languages, including Pawnee, formerly spoken in a wide area of the Midwest, and probably distantly related to Siouan.

caddy[1] (ˈkædɪ) *n., pl.* **-dies.** *Chiefly Brit.* a small container, esp. for tea. [C18: from Malay *kati;* see CATTY[2]]

caddy[2] (ˈkædɪ) *n., pl.* **-dies,** *vb.* **-dies, -dying, -died.** a variant spelling of **caddie.**

cade[1] (keɪd) *n.* a juniper tree, *Juniperus oxycedrus* of the Mediterranean region, the wood of which yields an oily brown liquid (**oil of cade**) used to treat skin ailments. [C16: via Old French from Old Provençal, from Medieval Latin *catanus*]

cade[2] (keɪd) *adj.* (of a young animal) left by its mother and reared by humans, usually as a pet. [C15: of unknown origin]

-cade *n. combining form.* indicating a procession of a specified kind: *motorcade.* [abstracted from CAVALCADE]

cadelle (kəˈdɛl) *n.* a widely distributed beetle, *Tenebroides mauritanicus,* that feeds on flour, grain, and other stored foods: family *Trogositidae.* [French, from Provençal *cadello,* from Latin *catellus* a little dog]

cadence (ˈkeɪdᵊns) *or* **cadency** *n., pl.* **-dences** *or* **-dencies. 1.** the beat or measure of something rhythmic. **2.** a fall in the pitch of the voice, as at the end of a sentence. **3.** modulation of the voice; intonation. **4.** a rhythm or rhythmical construction in verse or prose; measure. **5.** the close of a musical phrase or section. [C14: from Old French, from Old Italian *cadenza,* literally: a falling, from Latin *cadere* to fall]

cadency (ˈkeɪdᵊnsɪ) *n., pl.* **-cies. 1.** *Heraldry.* the line of descent from a younger member of a family. **2.** another word for **cadence.**

cadent (ˈkeɪdᵊnt) *adj.* **1.** having cadence; rhythmic. **2.** *Archaic.* falling; descending. [C16: from Latin *cadēns* falling, from *cadere* to fall]

cadenza (kəˈdɛnzə) *n.* a virtuoso solo passage occurring near the end of a piece of music, formerly improvised by the soloist but now usually specially composed. [C19: from Italian; see CADENCE]

cadet (kəˈdɛt) *n.* **1.** a young person undergoing preliminary training, usually before full entry to the uniformed services, police, etc., esp. for officer status. **2.** a school pupil receiving elementary military training in a school corps. **3.** (in England and in France before 1789) a gentleman, usually a younger son, who entered the army to prepare for a commission. **4.** a younger son or brother. **5. cadet branch.** the family or family branch of a younger son. **6.** (in New Zealand) a person learning sheep farming on a sheep station. [C17: from French, from dialect (Gascon) *capdet* captain, ultimately from Latin *caput* head] —**caˈdetship** *n.*

cadge (kædʒ) *vb.* **1.** to get (food, money, etc.) by sponging or begging. ~*n.* **2.** *Brit.* a person who cadges. **3. on the cadge.** *Brit. informal.* engaged in cadging. [C17: of unknown origin]

cadger *n.* **1.** (ˈkædʒə). *Brit.* a person who cadges. **2.** (ˈkædʒər). *Scot.* a pedlar or carrier.

cadi *or* **kadi** (ˈkɑːdɪ, ˈkeɪdɪ) *n., pl.* **-dis.** a judge in a Muslim community. [C16: from Arabic *qāḍī* judge]

Cadmean victory (ˈkædmɪən) *n.* another name for **Pyrrhic victory.** [after *Cadmus,* in Greek mythology, who sowed dragon's teeth from which sprang soldiers who began to kill each other]

cadmium (ˈkædmɪəm) *n.* a malleable ductile toxic bluish-white metallic element that occurs in association with zinc ores. It is used in electroplating, alloys, and as a neutron absorber in the control of nuclear fission. Symbol: Cd; atomic no.: 48; atomic wt.: 112.4; valency: 2; relative density: 8.65; melting pt.: 320.9°C; boiling pt.: 765°C. [C19: from New Latin, from Latin *cadmīa* zinc ore, CALAMINE, referring to the fact that both calamine and cadmium are found in the ore]

cadmium cell *n.* **1.** a photocell with a cadmium electrode that is especially sensitive to ultraviolet radiation. **2.** a former name for **Weston standard cell.**

cadmium sulphide *n.* an orange or yellow insoluble solid used as a pigment in paints, etc. (**cadmium yellow**). Formula: CdS.

cadre (ˈkɑːdə) *n.* **1.** the nucleus of trained professional servicemen forming the basis for the training of new units or other military expansion. **2.** a basic unit or structure, esp. of personnel; nucleus; core. **3.** a member of a cadre. [C19: from French, from Italian *quadro,* from Latin *quadrum* square]

caduceus (kəˈdjuːsɪəs) *n., pl.* **-cei** (-sɪˌaɪ). **1.** *Classical myth.* a staff entwined with two serpents and bearing a pair of wings at the top, carried by Hermes (Mercury) as messenger of the gods. **2.** an insignia resembling this staff used as an emblem of the medical profession. Compare **staff of Aesculapius.** [C16: from Latin, from Doric Greek *karukeion,* from *karux* herald]

caducibranchiate (kəˌdjuːsɪˈbræŋkɪˌeɪt) *adj.* (of many amphibians, such as frogs) having gills during one stage of the life cycle only. [from Latin *cadūcus* CADUCOUS + BRANCHIA]

caducity (kəˈdjuːsɪtɪ) *n.* **1.** perishableness. **2.** senility. [C18: from French, from Latin *cadūcus* CADUCOUS]

caducous (kəˈdjuːkəs) *adj. Biology.* (of parts of a plant or animal) shed during the life of the organism. [C17: from Latin *cadūcus* falling, from *cadere* to fall]

CAE *abbrev. for:* **1.** computer-aided engineering. **2.** *Austral.* College of Advanced Education.

caecilian (siːˈsɪlɪən) *n.* any tropical limbless cylindrical amphibian of the order *Apoda* (or *Gymnophiona*), resembling earthworms and inhabiting moist soil. [C19: from Latin *caecilia* a kind of lizard, from *caecus* blind]

caecum *or U.S.* **cecum** (ˈsiːkəm) *n., pl.* **-ca** (-kə). *Anatomy.* any structure or part that ends in a blind sac or pouch, esp. the pouch that marks the beginning of the large intestine. [C18: short for Latin *intestinum caecum* blind intestine, translation of Greek *tuphlon enteron*] —ˈ**caecal** *or U.S.* ˈ**cecal** *adj.*

Caelum (ˈsiːləm) *n., Latin genitive* **Caeli** (ˈsiːlaɪ). a small faint constellation in the S hemisphere close to Eridanus. [Latin: the sky, heaven]

caenogenesis (ˌsiːnəʊˈdʒɛnɪsɪs), **cainogenesis, kainogenesis** *or U.S.* **cenogenesis, kenogenesis** *n.* the development of structures and organs in an embryo or larva that are adaptations to its way of life and are not retained in the adult form. Compare **recapitulation** (sense 2). —**caenogenetic** (ˌsiːnəʊdʒəˈnɛtɪk), ˌ**cainogeˈnetic**, ˌ**kainogeˈnetic** *or U.S.* ˌ**cenogeˈnetic**, ˌ**kenogeˈnetic** *adj.* —ˌ**caenogeˈnetically**, ˌ**cainogeˈnetically**, ˌ**kainogeˈnetically** *or U.S.* ˌ**cenogeˈnetically**, ˌ**kenogeˈnetically** *adv.*

Caenozoic (ˌsiːnəˈzəʊɪk) *adj.* a variant spelling of **Cenozoic.**

caeoma (siːˈəʊmə) *n.* an aecium in some rust fungi that has no surrounding membrane. [New Latin, from Greek *kaiein* to burn; referring to its glowing colour]

Caerphilly (kɛəˈfɪlɪ) *n.* a creamy white mild-flavoured cheese, originally made in Caerphilly in SE Wales.

caesalpiniaceous (ˌsɛzælˌpɪnɪˈeɪʃəs) *adj.* of, relating to, or belonging to the *Caesalpiniaceae,* a mainly tropical family of leguminous plants that have irregular flowers: includes carob, senna, brazil, cassia, and poinciana. [from New Latin *Caesalpinia* type genus, named after Andrea *Cesalpino* (1519–1603), Italian botanist]

Caesar (ˈsiːzə) *n.* **1.** a Roman emperor. **2.** (*sometimes not cap.*) any emperor, autocrat, dictator, or other powerful ruler. **3.** a title of the Roman emperors from Augustus to Hadrian (27 B.C. to 138 A.D.). **4.** (in the Roman Empire) **a.** a title borne by the imperial heir from the reign of Hadrian. **b.** the heir, deputy, and subordinate ruler to either of the two emperors under Diocletian's system of government. [after Gaius Julius *Caesar* (100–44 B.C.), Roman general and statesman]

Caesarean, Caesarian, *or U.S.* **Cesarean, Cesarian** (sɪˈzɛərɪən) *adj.* **1.** of or relating to any of the Caesars, esp. Julius Caesar. ~*n.* **2.** (*sometimes not cap.*) *Surgery.* **a.** short for **Caesarean section. b.** (*as modifier*): *Caesarean birth; Caesarean operation.*

Caesarean section *n.* surgical incision through the abdominal and uterine walls in order to deliver a baby. [C17: from the belief that Julius Caesar was so delivered, the name allegedly being derived from *caesus,* past participle of *caedere* to cut]

Caesarism (ˈsiːzəˌrɪzəm) *n.* an autocratic system of government. See also **Bonapartism.** —ˈ**Caesarist** *n.* —ˌ**Caesarˈistic** *adj.*

caesious *or U.S.* **cesious** (ˈsiːzɪəs) *adj. Botany.* having a waxy bluish-grey coating. [C19: from Latin *caesius* bluish grey]

caesium *or U.S.* **cesium** (ˈsiːzɪəm) *n.* a ductile silvery-white element of the alkali metal group that is the most electropositive metal. It occurs in pollucite and lepidolite and is used in photocells. The radioisotope **caesium-137,** with a half-life of 30.2 years, is used in radiotherapy. Symbol: Cs; atomic no.: 55; atomic wt.: 132.905; valency: 1; relative density: 1.87; melting pt.: 28.5°C; boiling pt.: 690°C.

caesium clock *n.* a type of atomic clock that uses the frequency of radiation absorbed in changing the spin of electrons in caesium atoms. See also **second**[2].

caespitose *or U.S.* **cespitose** (ˈsɛspɪˌtəʊs) *adj. Botany.* growing in dense tufts. [C19: from New Latin *caespitōsus,* from *caespitem* turf] —ˈ**caespiˌtosely** *or U.S.* ˈ**cespiˌtosely** *adv.*

caesura (sɪˈzjʊərə) *n., pl.* **-ras** *or* **-rae** (-riː). **1.** (in modern prosody) a pause, esp. for sense, usually near the middle of a verse line. Usual symbol: ‖ **2.** (in classical prosody) a break between words within a metrical foot, usually in the third or fourth foot of the line. [C16: from Latin, literally: a cutting, from *caedere* to cut] —**caeˈsural** *adj.*

CAF *abbrev. for* cost and freight.

cafard (*French* kafar) *n.* a feeling of severe depression. [C20: from French, literally: cockroach, hypocrite]

café (ˈkæfeɪ, ˈkæfɪ) *n.* a small or inexpensive restaurant or coffee bar, serving light meals and refreshments. [C19: from French: COFFEE]

café au lait *French.* (kafe o lɛ) *n.* **1.** coffee with milk. **2.** a light brown colour.

café noir *French.* (kafe nwar) *n.* black coffee.

cafeteria (ˌkæfɪˈtɪərɪə) *n.* a self-service restaurant. [C20: from American Spanish: coffee shop]

cafetiere (ˌkæfəˈtjɛə, ˌkæfəˈtɪə) *n.* a kind of coffeepot in which boiling water is poured onto ground coffee and a plunger fitted with a metal filter is pressed down, forcing the grounds to the bottom. [C20: from French *cafetière* coffeepot]

caff (kæf) *n.* a slang word for **café.**

caffeine *or* **caffein** (ˈkæfiːn, ˈkæfɪˌiːn) *n.* a white crystalline bitter alkaloid responsible for the stimulant action of tea, coffee, and cocoa: a constituent of many tonics and analgesics. Formula: $C_8H_{10}N_4O_2$. See also **xanthine** (sense 2). [C19: from German *Kaffein,* from *Kaffee* COFFEE]

caftan (ˈkæfˌtæn, -ˌtɑːn) *n.* a variant spelling of **kaftan.**

cag (kæg) *n. Mountaineering.* short for **cagoule.**

cage (keɪdʒ) *n.* **1. a.** an enclosure, usually made with bars or wire, for keeping birds, monkeys, mice, etc. **b.** (*as modifier*): *cagebird.* **2.** a thing or place that confines or imprisons. **3.** something resembling a cage in function or structure: *the rib cage.* **4.** the enclosed platform of a lift, esp. as used in a mine. **5.** *Engineering.* a skeleton ring device that ensures that the correct amount of space is maintained between the individual rollers or balls in a rolling bearing. **6.** *Informal.* the basket used in basketball. **7.** *Informal.* the goal in ice hockey. **8.** *U.S.* a steel framework on which guns are supported. ~*vb.* **9.** (*tr.*) to confine in or as in a cage. [C13: from Old French, from Latin *cavea* enclosure, from *cavus* hollow]

cageling (ˈkeɪdʒlɪŋ) *n.* a bird kept in a cage.

cagey *or* **cagy** (ˈkeɪdʒɪ) *adj.* **-ier, -iest.** *Informal.* not open or frank; cautious; wary. [C20: of unknown origin] —ˈ**cagily** *adv.* —ˈ**caginess** *n.*

cag-handed (ˌkægˈhændɪd) *adj. Dialect.* a variant of **cack-handed.**

cagmag (ˈkægˌmæg) *Midland English dialect.* ~*adj.* **1.** done shoddily; left incomplete. ~*vb.* **-mags, -magging, -magged.** (*intr.*) **2.** to chat idly; gossip. [C18: of uncertain origin]

cagoule (kəˈguːl) *n.* a lightweight usually knee-length type of anorak. Also spelt: **kaˈgoul, kaˈgoule.** Sometimes shortened to **cag.** [C20: from French]

cahier *French.* (kaje) *n.* **1.** a notebook. **2.** a written or printed report, esp. of the proceedings of a meeting.

cahoots (kəˈhuːts) *pl. n.* (*sometimes sing.*) *Informal.* **1.** *U.S.* partnership; league (esp. in the phrases **go in cahoots with, go cahoot**). **2. in cahoots.** in collusion. [C19: of uncertain origin]

CAI *abbrev. for* computer-aided instruction.

cailleach (ˈkæljəx) *n. Scot.* an old woman. [Gaelic]

caiman (ˈkeɪmən) *n., pl.* **-mans.** a variant spelling of **cayman.**

cain *or* **kain** (keɪn) *n. History.* (in Scotland and Ireland) payment in kind, usually farm produce paid as rent. [C12: from Scottish Gaelic *cāin* rent, perhaps ultimately from Late Latin *canōn* tribute (see CANON); compare Middle Irish *cāin* law]

cainogenesis (ˌkaɪnəʊˈdʒɛnɪsɪs) *n.* a variant spelling of **caenogenesis.** —**cainogenetic** (ˌkaɪnəʊdʒəˈnɛtɪk) *adj.* —ˌ**cainogeˈnetically** *adv.*

Cainozoic (ˌkaɪnəʊˈzəʊɪk, ˌkeɪ-) *adj.* a variant of **Cenozoic.**

caïque (kaɪˈiːk) *n.* **1.** a long narrow light rowing skiff used on the Bosporus. **2.** a sailing vessel of the E Mediterranean with a sprit mainsail, square topsail, and two or more jibs or other sails. [C17: from French, from Italian *caicco,* from Turkish *kayik*]

caird (kɛəd; *Scot.* kerd) *n. Scot. obsolete.* a travelling tinker; vagrant. [C17: from Scottish Gaelic; related to Welsh *cerdd* craft]

cairn (kɛən) *n.* **1.** a mound of stones erected as a memorial or marker. **2.** Also called: **cairn terrier.** a small rough-haired breed of terrier originally from Scotland. [C15: from Gaelic *carn*]

cairngorm (ˈkɛənˌgɔːm, ˌkernˈgɒrm) *n.* a smoky yellow, grey, or brown variety of quartz, used as a gemstone. Also called: **smoky quartz.** [C18: from *Cairn Gorm* (literally: blue cairn), mountain in Scotland where it is found]

caisson (kəˈsuːn, ˈkeɪsᵊn) *n.* **1.** a watertight chamber open at the bottom and containing air under pressure, used to carry out construction work under water. **2.** a watertight float filled with air, used to raise sunken ships. See also **camel** (sense 2). **3.** a watertight structure placed across the entrance of a basin, dry dock, etc., to exclude water from it. **4. a.** a box containing explosives formerly used as a mine. **b.** an ammunition chest. **c.** a two-wheeled vehicle containing an ammunition chest. **5.** another name for **coffer** (sense 3). [C18: from French, assimilated to *caisse* CASE[2]]

caisson disease *n.* another name for **decompression sickness.**

caitiff (ˈkeɪtɪf) *Archaic or poetic.* ~*n.* **1.** a cowardly or base person. ~*adj.* **2.** cowardly; base. [C13: from Old French *caitif* prisoner, from Latin *captīvus* CAPTIVE]

cajeput (ˈkædʒəˌpʊt) *n.* a variant spelling of **cajuput.**

cajole (kəˈdʒəʊl) *vb.* to persuade (someone) by flattery or pleasing talk to do what one wants; wheedle; coax. [C17: from French *cajoler* to coax, of uncertain origin] —**caˈjolement** *n.* —**caˈjoler** *n.* —**caˈjolery** *n.* —**caˈjolingly** *adv.*

Cajun (ˈkeɪdʒən) *n.* **1.** a native of Louisiana descended from 18th-century Acadian immigrants. **2.** the dialect of French spoken by such people. **3.** the music of this ethnic group, combining blues and European folk music. ~*adj.* **4.** denoting or relating to such people, their language, or their music. [C19: alteration of ACADIAN; compare *Injun* for *Indian*]

cajuput *or* **cajeput** (ˈkædʒəˌpʊt) *n.* **1.** a small myrtaceous tree or shrub, *Melaleuca leucadendron,* native to the East Indies and Australia, with whitish flowers and leaves. **2.** a green aromatic oil derived from this tree, used to treat skin diseases. **3.** a lauraceous tree, *Umbellularia californica,* whose aromatic leaves are used in medicine. [C18: from Malay *kayu puteh,* from *kayu* wood + *puteh* white]

cake (keɪk) *n.* **1.** a baked food, usually in loaf or layer form, typically made from a mixture of flour, sugar, and eggs. **2.** a flat thin mass of bread, esp. unleavened bread. **3.** a shaped mass of dough or other food of similar consistency: *a fish cake.* **4.** a mass, slab, or crust of a solidified or compressed substance, as of soap or ice. **5. have one's cake and eat it.** to enjoy both of two desirable but incompatible alternatives. **6. go** *or* **sell like hot cakes.** *Informal.* to be sold very quickly or in large quantities. **7. piece of cake.** *Informal.* something that is easily achieved or obtained. **8. take the cake.** *Informal.* to surpass all others, esp. in stupidity, folly, etc. **9.** *Informal.* the whole or total of something that is to be shared or divided: *the miners are demanding a larger slice of the cake; that is a fair method of sharing the cake.* ~*vb.* **10.** (*tr.*) to cover with a hard layer; encrust: *the hull was caked with salt.* **11.** to form or be formed into a hardened mass. [C13: from Old Norse *kaka;* related to Danish *kage,* German *Kuchen*] —ˈ**cakey** *or* ˈ**caky** *adj.*

cakewalk (ˈkeɪkˌwɔːk) *n.* **1.** a dance based on a march with intricate steps, originally performed by American Negroes with the prize of a cake for the best performers. **2.** a piece of music composed for this dance. **3.** *Informal.* an easily accomplished task. ~*vb.* **4.** (*intr.*) to perform the cakewalk. —ˈ**cakeˌwalker** *n.*

CAL *abbrev. for* computer-aided (or -assisted) learning.

cal. *abbrev. for:* **1.** calibre. **2.** calorie (small).

Cal. *abbrev. for:* **1.** Calorie (large). **2.** California.

Calabar bean (ˌkæləˈbɑː, ˈkæləˌbɑː) *n.* the dark brown very poisonous seed of a leguminous woody climbing plant, *Physostigma venenosum* of tropical Africa, used as a source of the drug physostigmine. [named after *Calabar*, port in SE Nigeria]

calabash (ˈkæləˌbæʃ) *n.* **1.** Also called: **calabash tree.** a tropical American evergreen tree, *Crescentia cujete,* that produces large round gourds: family *Bignoniaceae.* **2.** another name for the **bottle gourd. 3.** the gourd of either of these plants. **4.** the dried hollow shell of a gourd used as the bowl of a tobacco pipe, a bottle, rattle, etc. **5. calabash nutmeg.** a tropical African shrub, *Monodora myristica,* whose oily aromatic seeds can be used as nutmegs: family *Annonaceae.* [C17: from obsolete French *calabasse,* from Spanish *calabaza,* perhaps from Arabic *qar'ah yābisah* dry gourd, from *qar'ah* gourd + *yābisah* dry]

calaboose (ˈkæləˌbuːs) *n. U.S. informal.* a prison; jail. [C18: from Creole French, from Spanish *calabozo* dungeon, of unknown origin]

calabrese (ˌkæləˈbreɪzɪ) *n.* a variety of green sprouting broccoli. [C20: from Italian: Calabrian (of *Calabria,* a region of SW Italy)]

caladium (kəˈleɪdɪəm) *n.* any of various tropical plants of the aroid genus *Caladium,* which are widely cultivated as potted plants for their colourful variegated foliage. [C19: from New Latin, from Malay *kĕladi* araceous plant]

calalu *or* **calaloo** (ˈkæləluː) *n. Caribbean.* the edible leaves of various plants, used as greens or in making thick soups. [probably of African origin]

calamanco (ˌkæləˈmæŋkəʊ) *n.* a glossy woollen fabric woven with a checked design that shows on one side only. [C16: of unknown origin]

calamander (ˈkæləˌmændə) *n.* the hard black-and-brown striped wood of several trees of the genus *Diospyros,* esp. *D. quaesita* of India and Sri Lanka, used in making furniture: family *Ebenaceae.* See also **ebony** (sense 2). [C19: metathetic variant of *coromandel* in *Coromandel* Coast in SE India]

calamine (ˈkæləˌmaɪn) *n.* **1.** a pink powder consisting of zinc oxide and ferric oxide, (iron(III) oxide), used medicinally in the form of soothing lotions or ointments. **2.** *U.S.* another name for **smithsonite.** [C17: from Old French, from Medieval Latin *calamīna,* from Latin *cadmīa;* see CADMIUM]

calamint (ˈkæləmɪnt) *n.* any aromatic Eurasian plant of the genus *Satureja* (or *Calamintha*), having clusters of purple or pink flowers: family *Labiatae* (labiates). [C14: from Old French *calament* (but influenced by English MINT[1]), from Medieval Latin *calamentum,* from Greek *kalaminthē*]

calamite (ˈkæləˌmaɪt) *n.* any extinct treelike pteridophyte plant of the genus *Calamites,* of Carboniferous times, related to the horsetails. [C19: from New Latin *Calamītes* type genus, from Greek *kalamitēs* reedlike, from *kalamos* reed]

calamitous (kəˈlæmɪtəs) *adj.* causing, involving, or resulting in a calamity; disastrous. —**caˈlamitously** *adv.* —**caˈlamitousness** *n.*

calamity (kəˈlæmɪtɪ) *n., pl.* **-ties. 1.** a disaster or misfortune, esp. one causing extreme havoc, distress, or misery. **2.** a state or feeling of deep distress or misery. [C15: from French *calamité,* from Latin *calamitās;* related to Latin *incolumis* uninjured]

calamondin (ˈkæləˌmʌndɪn) *or* **calamondin orange** *n.* **1.** a small citrus tree, *Citrus mitis,* of the Philippines. **2.** the acid-tasting fruit of this tree, resembling a small orange. [from Tagalog *kalamunding*]

calamus (ˈkæləməs) *n., pl.* **-mi** (-ˌmaɪ). **1.** any tropical Asian palm of the genus *Calamus,* some species of which are a source of rattan and canes. **2.** another name for **sweet flag. 3.** the aromatic root of the sweet flag. **4.** *Ornithol.* the basal hollow shaft of a feather; quill. [C14: from Latin, from Greek *kalamos* reed, cane, stem]

calando (kəˈlændəʊ) *adj., adv. Music.* (to be performed) with gradually decreasing tone and speed. [Italian: dropping, from *calare* to lower, to drop]

calandria (kəˈlændrɪə) *n.* a cylindrical vessel through which vertical tubes pass, esp. one forming part of an evaporator, heat exchanger, or nuclear reactor. [C20: arbitrarily named, from Spanish, literally: lark]

calash (kəˈlæʃ) *or* **calèche** *n.* **1.** a horse-drawn carriage with low wheels and a folding top. **2.** the folding top of such a carriage. **3.** a woman's folding hooped hood worn in the 18th century. [C17: from French *calèche,* from German *Kalesche,* from Czech *kolesa* wheels]

calathea (ˌkæləˈθɪə) *n.* any plant of the S. American perennial genus *Calathea,* many species of which are grown as greenhouse or house plants for their decorative variegated leaves, esp. the zebra plant (*C. zebrina*), the leaves of which are purplish below and dark green with lighter stripes above: family *Marantaceae.* [New Latin, from Greek *kalathos* a basket]

calathus (ˈkæləθəs) *n., pl.* **-thi** (-ˌθaɪ). a vase-shaped basket represented in ancient Greek art, used as a symbol of fruitfulness. [C18: from Latin, from Greek *kalathos*]

calaverite (kəˈlævəˌraɪt) *n.* a metallic pale yellow mineral consisting of a telluride of gold in the form of elongated striated crystals. It is a source of gold in Australia and North America. Formula: $AuTe_2$. [C19: named after *Calaveras,* county in California where it was discovered]

calc- *combining form.* a variant of **calci-** before a vowel.

calcaneus (kælˈkeɪnɪəs) *or* **calcaneum** *n., pl.* **-nei** (-nɪaɪ). **1.** the largest tarsal bone, forming the heel in man. Nontechnical name: **heel bone. 2.** the corresponding bone in other vertebrates. [C19: from Late Latin: heel, from Latin *calx* heel] —**calˈcaneal** *or* **calˈcanean** *adj.*

calcar (ˈkælˌkɑː) *n., pl.* **calcaria** (kælˈkɛərɪə). a spur or spurlike process, as on the leg of a bird or the corolla of a flower. [C19: from Latin, from *calx* heel]

calcareous (kælˈkɛərɪəs) *adj.* of, containing, or resembling calcium carbonate; chalky. [C17: from Latin *calcārius,* from *calx* lime]

calcariferous (ˌkælkəˈrɪfərəs) *adj. Biology.* having a spur or spurs.

calceiform (ˈkælsɪɪˌfɔːm, kælˈsiː-) *or* **calceolate** (ˈkælsɪəˌleɪt) *adj. Botany.* shaped like a shoe or slipper. [C19: from Latin *calceus* shoe]

calceolaria (ˌkælsɪəˈlɛərɪə) *n.* any tropical American scrophulariaceous plant of the genus *Calceolaria:* cultivated for its speckled slipper-shaped flowers. Also called: **slipperwort.** [C18: from Latin *calceolus* small shoe, from *calceus*]

calces (ˈkælsiːz) *n.* a plural of **calx.**

calci- *or before a vowel* **calc-** *combining form.* indicating lime or calcium: *calcify.* [from Latin *calx, calc-* limestone]

calcic (ˈkælsɪk) *adj.* of, containing, or concerned with lime or calcium. [C19: from Latin *calx* lime]

calcicole (ˈkælsɪˌkəʊl) *n.* any plant that thrives in lime-rich soils. [C20: from CALCI- + -*cole,* from Latin *colere* to dwell] —**calcicolous** (kælˈsɪkələs) *adj.*

calciferol (kælˈsɪfərɒl) *n.* a fat-soluble steroid, found esp. in fish-liver oils, produced by the action of ultraviolet radiation on ergosterol. It increases the absorption of calcium from the intestine and is used in the treatment of rickets. Formula: $C_{28}H_{43}OH$. Also called: **vitamin D_2.** [C20: from CALCIF(EROUS + ERGOST)EROL]

calciferous (kælˈsɪfərəs) *adj.* forming or producing salts of calcium, esp. calcium carbonate.

calcific (kælˈsɪfɪk) *adj.* forming or causing to form lime or chalk.

calcification (ˌkælsɪfɪˈkeɪʃən) *n.* **1.** the process of calcifying or becoming calcified. **2.** *Pathol.* a tissue hardened by deposition of lime salts. **3.** any calcified object or formation.

calcifuge (ˈkælsɪˌfjuːdʒ) *n.* any plant that thrives in acid soils. —**calcifugal** (ˌkælsɪˈfjuːgᵊl) *adj.* —**calcifugous** (kælˈsɪfjəgəs) *adj.*

calcify (ˈkælsɪˌfaɪ) *vb.* **-fies, -fying, -fied. 1.** to convert or be converted into lime. **2.** to harden or become hardened by impregnation with calcium salts.

calcimine (ˈkælsɪˌmaɪn, -mɪn) *or* **kalsomine** *n.* **1.** a white or pale tinted wash for walls. ~*vb.* **2.** (*tr.*) to cover with calcimine. [C19: changed from *Kalsomine,* a trademark]

calcine (ˈkælsaɪn, -sɪn) *vb.* **1.** (*tr.*) to heat (a substance) so that it is oxidized, reduced, or loses water. **2.** (*intr.*) to oxidize as a result of heating. [C14: from Medieval Latin *calcināre* to heat, from Latin *calx* lime] —**calcination** (ˌkælsɪˈneɪʃən) *n.*

calcinosis (ˌkælsɪˈnəʊsɪs) *n.* the abnormal deposition of calcium salts in the tissues of the body.

calcite (ˈkælsaɪt) *n.* a colourless or white mineral (occasionally tinged with impurities), found in sedimentary and metamorphic rocks, in veins, in limestone, and in stalagmites and stalactites. It is used in the manufacture of cement, plaster, paint, glass, and fertilizer. Composition: calcium carbonate. Formula: $CaCO_3$. Crystal structure: hexagonal (rhombohedral). —**calcitic** (kælˈsɪtɪk) *adj.*

calcitonin (ˌkælsɪˈtəʊnɪn) *n.* a hormone secreted by the thyroid that inhibits the release of calcium from the skeleton and prevents a build-up of calcium in the blood. Also called: **thyrocalcitonin.** Compare **parathyroid hormone.** [C20: from CALCI- + TON(IC) + -IN]

calcium (ˈkælsɪəm) *n.* a malleable silvery-white metallic element of the alkaline earth group; the fifth most abundant element in the earth's crust (3.6 per cent), occurring esp. as forms of calcium carbonate. It is an essential constituent of bones and teeth and is used as a deoxidizer in steel. Symbol: Ca; atomic no.: 20; atomic wt.: 40.08; valency: 2; relative density: 1.55; melting pt.: 842–8° C; boiling pt.: 1487° C. [C19: from New Latin, from Latin *calx* lime]

calcium antagonist *or* **blocker** *n.* any drug that prevents the influx of calcium ions into cardiac and smooth muscle: used to treat high blood pressure and angina.

calcium carbide *n.* a grey salt of calcium used in the production of acetylene (by its reaction with water) and calcium cyanamide. Formula: CaC_2. Sometimes shortened to **carbide.**

calcium carbonate *n.* a white crystalline salt occurring in limestone, chalk, marble, calcite, coral, and pearl: used in the production of lime and cement. Formula: $CaCO_3$.

calcium chloride *n.* a white deliquescent salt occurring naturally in seawater and used in the de-icing of roads and as a drying agent. Formula: $CaCl_2$.
calcium cyanamide *n.* a white crystalline compound formed by heating calcium carbide with nitrogen. It is important in the fixation of nitrogen and can be hydrolysed to ammonia or used as a fertilizer. Formula: $CaCN_2$.
calcium hydroxide *n.* a white crystalline slightly soluble alkali with many uses, esp. in cement, water softening, and the neutralization of acid soils. Formula: $Ca(OH)_2$. Also called: **lime, slaked lime, hydrated lime, calcium hydrate, caustic lime, lime hydrate.**
calcium light *n.* another name for **limelight.**
calcium oxide *n.* a white crystalline base used in the production of calcium hydroxide and bleaching powder and in the manufacture of glass, paper, and steel. Formula: CaO. Also called: **lime, quicklime, calx, burnt lime, calcined lime, fluxing lime.**
calcium phosphate *n.* **1.** the insoluble nonacid calcium salt of orthophosphoric acid (phosphoric(V) acid): it occurs in bones and is the main constituent of bone ash. Formula: $Ca_3(PO_4)_2$. **2.** any calcium salt of a phosphoric acid. Calcium phosphates are found in many rocks and used esp. in fertilizers.
calcsinter ('kælk,sɪntə) *n.* another name for **travertine.** [C19: from German *Kalksinter,* from *Kalk* lime + *sinter* dross; see CHALK, SINTER]
calcspar ('kælk,spɑː) *n.* another name for **calcite.** [C19: partial translation of Swedish *kalkspat,* from *kalk* lime (ultimately from Latin *calx*) + *spat* SPAR[3]]
calc-tufa ('kælk,tuːfə) *or* **calc-tuff** ('kælk,tʌf) *n.* another name for **tufa.**
calculable ('kælkjʊləbᵊl) *adj.* **1.** that may be computed or estimated. **2.** predictable; dependable. —,**calcula'bility** *n.* —'**calculably** *adv.*
calculate ('kælkjʊ,leɪt) *vb.* **1.** to solve (one or more problems) by a mathematical procedure; compute. **2.** (*tr.; may take a clause as object*) to determine beforehand by judgment, reasoning, etc.; estimate. **3.** (*tr.; usually passive*) to design specifically; aim: *the car was calculated to appeal to women.* **4.** (*intr.*; foll. by *on* or *upon*) to depend; rely. **5.** (*tr.; may take a clause as object*) *U.S. dialect.* **a.** to suppose; think. **b.** to intend (to do something). [C16: from Late Latin *calculāre,* from *calculus* pebble used as a counter; see CALCULUS] —**calculative** ('kælkjʊlətɪv) *adj.*
calculated ('kælkjʊ,leɪtɪd) *adj.* (*usually prenominal*) **1.** undertaken after considering the likelihood of success or failure: *a calculated risk.* **2.** deliberately planned; premeditated: *a calculated insult.*
calculating ('kælkjʊ,leɪtɪŋ) *adj.* **1.** selfishly scheming. **2.** shrewd; cautious. —'**calcu,latingly** *adv.*
calculation (,kælkjʊ'leɪʃən) *n.* **1.** the act, process, or result of calculating. **2.** an estimation of probability; forecast. **3.** careful planning or forethought, esp. for selfish motives.
calculator ('kælkjʊ,leɪtə) *n.* **1.** a device for performing mathematical calculations, esp. an electronic device that can be held in the hand. **2.** a person or thing that calculates. **3.** a set of tables used as an aid to calculations.
calculous ('kælkjʊləs) *adj. Pathol.* of or suffering from a calculus.
calculus ('kælkjʊləs) *n., pl.* **-luses. 1.** a branch of mathematics, developed independently by Newton and Leibnitz. Both **differential calculus** and **integral calculus** are concerned with the effect on a function of an infinitesimal change in the independent variable as it tends to zero. **2.** any mathematical system of calculation involving the use of symbols. **3.** *Logic.* an uninterpreted formal system. Compare **formal language** (sense 2). **4.** *pl.* **-li** (-,laɪ). *Pathol.* a stonelike concretion of minerals and salts found in ducts or hollow organs of the body. [C17: from Latin: pebble, stone used in reckoning, from *calx* small stone, counter]
calculus of variations *n.* a branch of calculus concerned with maxima and minima of definite integrals.
caldarium (kæl'dɛərɪəm) *n., pl.* **-daria** (-'dɛərɪə). (in ancient Rome) a room for taking hot baths. [C18: from Latin, from *calidus* warm, from *calēre* to be warm]
caldera (kæl'dɛərə, 'kɔːldərə) *n.* a large basin-shaped crater at the top of a volcano, formed by the collapse or explosion of the cone but not by glacial erosion. See **cirque.** [C19: from Spanish *Caldera* (literally: CAULDRON), name of a crater in the Canary Islands]
caldron ('kɔːldrən) *n.* a variant spelling of **cauldron.**
calèche (*French* kalɛʃ) *n.* a variant of **calash.**
Caledonian (,kælɪ'dəʊnɪən) *adj.* **1.** of or relating to Scotland. **2.** of or denoting a period of mountain building in NW Europe in the Palaeozoic era. ~*n.* **3.** *Literary.* a native or inhabitant of Scotland. [from Latin *Caledonia* Scotland]
calefacient (,kælɪ'feɪʃənt) *adj.* **1.** causing warmth. ~*n.* **2.** *Med.* an agent that warms, such as a mustard plaster. [C17: from Latin *calefaciēns,* from *calefacere* to heat] —**calefaction** (,kælɪ'fækʃən) *n.*
calefactory (,kælɪ'fæktərɪ, -trɪ) *adj.* **1.** giving warmth. ~*n., pl.* **-ries. 2.** a heated sitting room in a monastery. [C16: from Latin *calefactōrius,* from *calefactus* made warm; see CALEFACIENT]
calendar ('kælɪndə) *n.* **1.** a system for determining the beginning, length, and order of years and their divisions. See also **Gregorian calendar, Jewish calendar, Julian calendar, Revolutionary calendar, Roman calendar. 2.** a table showing any such arrangement, esp. as applied to one or more successive years. **3.** a list, register, or schedule of social events, pending court cases, appointments, etc. ~*vb.* **4.** (*tr.*) to enter in a calendar; schedule; register. [C13: via Norman French from Medieval Latin *kalendārium* account book, from *Kalendae* the CALENDS, when interest on debts became due] —**calendrical** (kæ'lɛndrɪkᵊl) *or* **ca'lendric** *adj.*
calendar day *n.* See **day** (sense 1).
calendar month *n.* See **month** (sense 1).
calendar year *n.* See **year** (sense 1).
calender[1] ('kælɪndə) *n.* **1.** a machine in which paper or cloth is glazed or smoothed by passing between rollers. ~*vb.* **2.** (*tr.*) to subject (material) to such a process. [C17: from French *calandre,* of unknown origin]
calender[2] ('kælɪndə) *n.* a member of a mendicant order of dervishes in Turkey, Iran, and India. [from Persian *kalandar*]
calends *or* **kalends** ('kælɪndz) *pl. n.* the first day of each month in the ancient Roman calendar. [C14: from Latin *kalendae;* related to Latin *calāre* to proclaim]
calendula (kæ'lɛndjʊlə) *n.* **1.** any Eurasian plant of the genus *Calendula,* esp. the pot marigold, having orange-and-yellow rayed flowers: family *Compositae* (composites). **2.** the dried flowers of the pot marigold, formerly used medicinally and for seasoning. [C19: from Medieval Latin, from Latin *kalendae* CALENDS; perhaps from its supposed efficacy in curing menstrual disorders]
calenture ('kælən,tjʊə) *n.* a mild fever of tropical climates, similar in its symptoms to sunstroke. [C16: from Spanish *calentura* fever, ultimately from Latin *calēre* to be warm]
calf[1] (kɑːf) *n., pl.* **calves. 1.** the young of cattle, esp. domestic cattle. **2.** the young of certain other mammals, such as the buffalo, elephant, giraffe, and whale. **3.** a large piece of ice detached from an iceberg, etc. **4. kill the fatted calf.** to celebrate lavishly, esp. as a welcome. **5.** another name for **calfskin.** [Old English *cealf;* related to Old Norse *kālfr,* Gothic *kalbō,* Old High German *kalba*]
calf[2] (kɑːf) *n., pl.* **calves.** the thick fleshy part of the back of the leg between the ankle and the knee. [C14: from Old Norse *kalfi*]
calf love *n.* temporary infatuation or love of an adolescent for a member of the opposite sex. Also called: **puppy love.**
calf's-foot jelly *n.* a jelly made from the stock of boiled calves' feet and flavourings, formerly often served to invalids.
calfskin ('kɑːf,skɪn) *n.* **1.** the skin or hide of a calf. **2.** Also called: **calf. a.** fine leather made from this skin. **b.** (*as modifier*): *calfskin boots.*
Calgon ('kælgɒn) *n. Trademark.* a chemical compound, sodium hexametaphosphate, with water-softening properties, used in detergents.
Caliban ('kælɪ,bæn) *n.* a brutish or brutalized man. [C19: after a character in Shakespeare's *The Tempest* (1610)]
calibrate ('kælɪ,breɪt) *vb.* (*tr.*) **1.** to measure the calibre of (a gun, mortar, etc.). **2.** to mark (the scale of a measuring instrument) so that readings can be made in appropriate units. **3.** to determine the accuracy of (a measuring instrument, etc.). **4.** to determine or check the range and accuracy of (a piece of artillery). —,**cali'bration** *n.* —'**cali,brator** *or* '**cali,brater** *n.*
calibre *or U.S.* **caliber** ('kælɪbə) *n.* **1.** the diameter of a cylindrical body, esp. the internal diameter of a tube or the bore of a firearm. **2.** the diameter of a shell or bullet. **3.** ability; distinction: *a musician of high calibre.* **4.** personal character: *a man of high calibre.* [C16: from Old French, from Italian *calibro,* from Arabic *qālib* shoemaker's last, mould] —'**calibred** *or U.S.* '**calibered** *adj.*
calices ('kælɪ,siːz) *n.* the plural of **calix.**
caliche (kæ'liːtʃɪ) *n.* **1.** a bed of sand or clay in arid regions that contains Chile saltpetre, sodium chloride, and other soluble minerals. **2.** a surface layer of soil encrusted with calcium carbonate, occurring in arid regions. [C20: from American Spanish, from Latin *calx* lime]
calicle ('kælɪkᵊl) *n.* a variant spelling of **calycle.** —**calicular** (kə'lɪkjʊlə) *adj.*
calico ('kælɪ,kəʊ) *n., pl.* **-coes** *or* **-cos. 1.** a white or unbleached cotton fabric with no printed design. **2.** *Chiefly U.S.* a coarse printed cotton fabric. **3.** (*modifier*) made of calico. [C16: based on *Calicut,* town in India]
calico bush *n.* another name for **mountain laurel.**
calif ('keɪlɪf, 'kæl-) *n.* a variant spelling of **caliph.**
Calif. *abbrev. for* California.
califate ('keɪlɪ,feɪt, -fɪt, 'kæl-) *n.* a variant spelling of **caliphate.**
califont ('kæləfɒnt) *n. N.Z.* a gas water heater. [from a trade name]
Californian (,kælɪ'fɔːnɪən) *adj.* **1.** of, relating to, or characteristic of California, a state on the W coast of the U.S., or its inhabitants. ~*n.* **2.** an inhabitant or native of California.
California poppy (,kælɪ'fɔːnɪə) *n.* a papaveraceous plant, *Eschscholtzia californica,* of the Pacific coast of North America, having yellow or orange flowers and finely divided bluish-green leaves.

californium (ˌkælɪˈfɔːnɪəm) *n.* a metallic transuranic element artificially produced from curium. Symbol: Cf; atomic no.: 98; half-life of most stable isotope, ^{251}Cf: 800 years (approx.). [C20: New Latin; discovered at the University of *California*]

caliginous (kəˈlɪdʒɪnəs) *adj. Archaic.* dark; dim. [C16: from Latin *cālīginōsus,* from *cālīgō* darkness] —**caliginosity** (kəˌlɪdʒɪˈnɒsɪtɪ) *n.*

calipash *or* **callipash** (ˈkælɪˌpæʃ) *n.* the greenish glutinous edible part of the turtle found next to the upper shell, considered a delicacy. [C17: perhaps changed from Spanish *carapacho* CARAPACE]

calipee (ˈkælɪˌpiː) *n.* the yellow glutinous edible part of the turtle found next to the lower shell, considered a delicacy. [C17: perhaps a variant of CALIPASH]

caliper (ˈkælɪpə) *n.* the usual U.S. spelling of **calliper.**

caliph, calif, kalif, *or* **khalif** (ˈkeɪlɪf, ˈkæl-) *n. Islam.* the title of the successors of Mohammed as rulers of the Islamic world, later assumed by the Sultans of Turkey. [C14: from Old French, from Arabic *khalīfa* successor]

caliphate, califate, *or* **kalifate** (ˈkeɪlɪˌfeɪt, -fɪt, ˈkæl-) *n.* the office, jurisdiction, or reign of a caliph.

calisaya (ˌkælɪˈseɪə) *n.* the bark of any of several tropical trees of the rubiaceous genus *Cinchona,* esp. *C. calisaya,* from which quinine is extracted. Also called: **calisaya bark, yellowbark, cinchona.** [C19: from Spanish, from the name of a Bolivian Indian who taught the uses of quinine to the Spanish]

calisthenics (ˌkælɪsˈθenɪks) *n.* a variant spelling (esp. U.S.) of **callisthenics.** —ˌ**calisˈthenic** *adj.*

calix (ˈkeɪlɪks, ˈkæ-) *n., pl.* **calices** (ˈkælɪˌsiːz). a cup; chalice. [C18: from Latin: CHALICE]

calk[1] (kɔːk) *vb.* a variant spelling of **caulk.**

calk[2] (kɔːk) *or* **calkin** (ˈkɔːkɪn, ˈkæl-) *n.* **1.** a metal projection on a horse's shoe to prevent slipping. **2.** *Chiefly U.S. and Canadian.* a set of spikes or a spiked plate attached to the sole of a boot, esp. by loggers, to prevent slipping. ~*vb.* (*tr.*) **3.** to provide with calks. **4.** to wound with a calk. [C17: from Latin *calx* heel]

calk[3] (kɔːk) *vb.* (*tr.*) to transfer (a design) by tracing it with a blunt point from one sheet backed with loosely fixed colouring matter onto another placed underneath. [C17: from French *calquer* to trace; see CALQUE]

call (kɔːl) *vb.* **1.** (often foll. by *out*) to speak or utter (words, sounds, etc.) loudly so as to attract attention: *he called out her name.* **2.** (*tr.*) to ask or order to come: *to call a policeman.* **3.** (*intr.*; sometimes foll. by *on*) to make a visit (to): *she called on him.* **4.** (often foll. by *up*) to telephone (a person): *he called back at nine.* **5.** (*tr.*) to summon to a specific office, profession, etc.: *he was called to the ministry.* **6.** (of animals or birds) to utter (a characteristic sound or cry). **7.** (*tr.*) to summon (a bird or animal) by imitating its cry. **8.** (*tr.*) to name or style: *they called the dog Rover.* **9.** (*tr.*) to designate: *they called him a coward.* **10.** (*tr.*) *Brit. dialect.* to speak ill of or scold. **11.** (*tr.*) to regard in a specific way: *I call it a foolish waste of time.* **12.** (*tr.*) to attract (attention). **13.** (*tr.*) to read (a list, register, etc.) aloud to check for omissions or absentees. **14.** (when *tr.*, usually foll. by *for*) to give an order (for): *to call a strike.* **15.** (*intr.*) to try to predict the result of tossing a coin. **16.** (*tr.*) to awaken: *I was called early this morning.* **17.** (*tr.*) to cause to assemble: *to call a meeting.* **18.** (*tr.*) *Sport.* (of an umpire, referee, etc.) to pass judgment upon (a shot, player, etc.) with a call. **19.** (*tr.*) *Austral. and N.Z.* to broadcast a commentary on (a horse race or other sporting event). **20.** (*tr.*) to demand repayment of (a loan, redeemable bond, security, etc.). **21.** (*tr.*; often foll. by *up*) *Company accounting.* to demand payment of (a portion of a share issue not yet paid by subscribers). **22.** (*tr.*) *Brit.* to award (a student at an Inn of Court) the degree of barrister (esp. in the phrase **call to the bar**). **23.** (*tr.*) *Computer technol.* to transfer control to (a named subprogram). **24.** (*tr.*) *Poker.* to demand that (a player) expose his hand, after equalling his bet. **25.** (*intr.*) *Bridge.* to make a bid. **26.** (in square-dancing) to call out (instructions) to the dancers. **27.** *Billiards.* to ask (a player) to say what kind of shot he will play or (of a player) to name his shot. **28.** (*intr.*; foll. by *for*) **a.** to require: *this problem calls for study.* **b.** to come or go (for) in order to fetch: *I will call for my book later.* **29.** (*intr.*; foll. by *on* or *upon*) to make an appeal or request (to): *they called upon him to reply.* **30. call into being.** to create. **31. call into play.** to begin to operate. **32. call in** *or* **into question.** See **question** (sense 12). **33. call it a day.** to stop work or other activity. **34. call to mind.** to remember or cause to be remembered. ~*n.* **35.** a cry or shout. **36.** the characteristic cry of a bird or animal. **37.** a device, such as a whistle, intended to imitate the cry of a bird or animal. **38.** a summons or invitation. **39.** a summons or signal sounded on a horn, bugle, etc. **40.** *Hunting.* any of several notes or patterns of notes, blown on a hunting horn as a signal **41.** *Hunting.* **a.** an imitation of the characteristic cry of a wild animal or bird to lure it to the hunter. **b.** an instrument for producing such an imitation. **42.** a short visit: *the doctor made six calls this morning.* **43.** an inner urge to some task or profession; vocation. **44.** allure or fascination, esp. of a place: *the call of the forest.* **45.** *Brit.* the summons to the bar of a student member of an Inn of Court. **46.** need, demand, or occasion: *there is no call to shout; we don't get much call for stockings these days.* **47.** demand or claim (esp. in the phrase **the call of duty**). **48.** *Theatre.* a notice to actors informing them of times of rehearsals. **49.** (in square dancing) an instruction to execute new figures. **50.** a conversation or a request for a connection by telephone. **51.** *Commerce.* **a.** a demand for repayment of a loan. **b.** (*as modifier*): *call money.* **52.** *Finance.* **a.** a demand for redeemable bonds or shares to be presented for repayment. **b.** a demand for an instalment payment on the issue price of bonds or shares. **53.** *Billiards.* a demand to an opponent to say what kind of shot he will play. **54.** *Poker.* a demand for a hand or hands to be exposed. **55.** *Bridge.* a bid, or a player's turn to bid. **56.** *Sport.* a decision of an umpire or referee regarding a shot, pitch, etc. **57.** *Austral.* a broadcast commentary on a horse race or other sporting event. **58.** Also called: **call option.** *Stock Exchange.* an option to buy a stated amount of securities at a specified price during a specified period. Compare **put** (sense 20). **59.** See **roll call. 60. call for margin.** *Stock Exchange.* a demand made by a stockbroker for partial payment of a client's debt due to decreasing value of the collateral. **61. call of nature.** See **nature** (sense 15). **62. on call. a.** (of a loan, etc.) repayable on demand. **b.** (of a doctor, etc.) available when summoned; on duty. **63. within call.** within range; accessible. ~See also **call down, call forth, call in, call off, call out, call up.** [Old English *ceallian;* related to Old Norse *kalla,* Old High German *kallōn,* Old Slavonic *glasŭ* voice]

calla (ˈkælə) *n.* **1.** Also called: **calla lily, arum lily.** any southern African plant of the aroid genus *Zantedeschia,* esp. *Z. aethiopica,* which has a white funnel-shaped spathe enclosing a yellow spadix. **2.** an aroid plant, *Calla palustris,* that grows in wet places and has a white spathe enclosing a greenish spadix, and red berries. [C19: from New Latin, probably from Greek *kalleia* wattles on a cock, probably from *kallos* beauty]

callable (ˈkɔːləbᵊl) *adj.* **1.** (of a security) subject to redemption before maturity. **2.** (of money loaned) repayable on demand.

callais (kəˈleɪɪs) *n.* a green stone found as beads and ornaments in the late Neolithic and early Bronze Age of W Europe. [C19: from Greek *kallais*]

call alarm *n.* **a.** an electronic device that sends an alarm signal, usually to a distant monitoring centre, when activated by a person in distress, often a handicapped or frail old person living alone. **b.** (*as modifier*): *a call-alarm system.*

Callanetics (ˌkæləˈnetɪks) *n.* (*functioning as sing.*) *Trademark.* a system of exercise involving frequent repetition of small muscular movements and squeezes, designed to improve muscle tone. [C20: named after *Callan* Pinckney (born 1939), its U.S. inventor]

callant (ˈkælənt) *or* **callan** (ˈkælən) *n. Scot.* a youth; lad. [C16: from Dutch or Flemish *kalant* customer, fellow]

call bird *n. Marketing.* a cheap article displayed in a shop to attract custom, in the hope of selling expensive items.

call box *n.* a soundproof enclosure for a public telephone. Also called: **telephone box, telephone kiosk.**

callboy (ˈkɔːlˌbɔɪ) *n.* a person who notifies actors when it is time to go on stage.

call down *vb.* (*tr., adv.*) to request or invoke: *to call down God's anger.*

caller[1] (ˈkɔːlə) *n.* a person or thing that calls, esp. a person who makes a brief visit.

caller[2] (ˈkælə; *Scot.* ˈkælər, ˈkɒlər) *adj. Scot.* **1.** (of food, esp. fish) fresh. **2.** cool: *a caller breeze.* [C14: perhaps a Scottish variant of *calver* to prepare fresh salmon or trout in a certain way; perhaps from Old English *calwer* curds, from a fancied resemblance with the flaked flesh of the fish]

call forth *vb.* (*tr., adv.*) to cause (something) to come into action or existence: *she called forth all her courage.*

call girl *n.* a prostitute with whom appointments are made by telephone.

calli- *combining form.* beautiful: *calligraphy.* [from Greek *kalli-,* from *kallos* beauty]

calligraphy (kəˈlɪɡrəfɪ) *n.* handwriting, esp. beautiful handwriting considered as an art. Also called: **chirography.** —**calˈligrapher** *or* **calˈligraphist** *n.* —**calligraphic** (ˌkælɪˈɡræfɪk) *adj.* —ˌ**calliˈgraphically** *adv.*

call in *vb.* (*adv.*) **1.** (*intr.*; often foll. by *on*) to pay a visit, esp. a brief or informal one: *call in if you are in the neighbourhood.* **2.** (*tr.*) to demand payment of: *to call in a loan.* **3.** (*tr.*) to take (something) out of circulation, because it is defective or no longer useful. **4.** (*tr.*) to summon to one's assistance: *they had to call in a specialist.*

calling (ˈkɔːlɪŋ) *n.* **1.** a strong inner urge to follow an occupation, etc.; vocation. **2.** an occupation, profession, or trade.

calling card *n.* the usual U.S. and Canadian term for **visiting card.**

calliope (kəˈlaɪəpɪ) *n. U.S. and Canadian.* a steam organ. [C19: after *Calliope,* the Muse of epic poetry (literally: beautiful-voiced)]

calliopsis (ˌkælɪˈɒpsɪs) *n.* another name for **coreopsis.**

callipash (ˈkælɪˌpæʃ) *n.* a variant spelling of **calipash.**

calliper *or U.S.* **caliper** (ˈkælɪpə) *n.* **1.** (*often pl.*) Also called: **calliper compasses.** an instrument for measuring internal or external dimensions, consisting of two steel legs hinged together. **2.** Also called: **calliper splint.** *Med.* a splint consisting of two metal rods with straps attached, for supporting or exerting tension on the leg. ~*vb.* **3.** (*tr.*) to measure the dimensions of (an object) with callipers. [C16: variant of CALIBRE]

calliper rule *n.* a measuring instrument having two parallel jaws, one fixed at right angles to the end of a calibrated scale and the other sliding along it.
callipygian (ˌkælɪˈpɪdʒɪən) *or* **callipygous** (ˌkælɪˈpaɪgəs) *adj.* having beautifully shaped buttocks. [C19: from Greek *kallipugos*, epithet of a statue of Aphrodite, from CALLI- + *pugē* buttocks]
callistemon (kəˈlɪstəmən) *n.* another name for **bottlebrush** (sense 1).
callisthenics *or* **calisthenics** (ˌkælɪsˈθɛnɪks) *n.* **1.** (*functioning as pl.*) light exercises designed to promote general fitness, develop muscle tone, etc. **2.** (*functioning as sing.*) the practice of callisthenic exercises. [C19: from CALLI- + Greek *sthenos* strength] —ˌ**callisˈthenic** *or* ˌ**calisˈthenic** *adj.*
call letters *pl. n.* the call sign of an American or Canadian radio station, esp. that of a commercial broadcasting station.
call loan *n.* a loan that is repayable on demand. Also called: **demand loan.** Compare **time loan.**
call money *n.* money loaned by banks and recallable on demand.
call number *n.* the number given to a book in a library, indicating its shelf location. Also called: **call mark.**
call off *vb.* (*tr., adv.*) **1.** to cancel or abandon: *the game was called off because of rain.* **2.** to order (an animal or person) to desist or summon away: *the man called off his dog.* **3.** to stop (something) or give the order to stop.
callop (ˈkæləp) *n.* an edible freshwater fish, *Plectroplites ambiguus*, of Australia, often golden or pale yellow in colour. [from a native Australian language]
callose (ˈkæləʊz) *n.* a carbohydrate, a polymer of glucose, found in plants, esp. in the sieve tubes.
callosity (kəˈlɒsɪtɪ) *n., pl.* **-ties. 1.** hardheartedness. **2.** another name for **callus** (sense 1).
callous (ˈkæləs) *adj.* **1.** unfeeling; insensitive. **2.** (of skin) hardened and thickened. ~*vb.* **3.** *Pathol.* to make or become callous. [C16: from Latin *callōsus*; see CALLUS] —ˈ**callously** *adv.* —ˈ**callousness** *n.*
call out *vb.* (*adv.*) **1.** to utter aloud, esp. loudly. **2.** (*tr.*) to summon. **3.** (*tr.*) to order (workers) to strike. **4.** (*tr.*) to summon (an employee) to work at a time outside his normal working hours, usually in an emergency.
callow (ˈkæləʊ) *adj.* **1.** lacking experience of life; immature. **2.** *Rare.* (of a young bird) unfledged and usually lacking feathers. [Old English *calu*; related to Old High German *kalo*, Old Slavonic *golú* bare, naked, Lithuanian *galva* head, Latin *calvus* bald] —ˈ**callowness** *n.*
call rate *n.* the interest rate on a call loan.
call sign *n.* a group of letters and numbers identifying a radio transmitting station, esp. an amateur radio station. Compare **call letters.**
call slip *n.* a form for requesting a library book by title and call number. Also called: **call card, requisition form.**
call up *vb.* (*adv.*) **1.** to summon to report for active military service, as in time of war. **2.** (*tr.*) to recall (something); evoke: *his words called up old memories.* **3.** (*tr.*) to bring or summon (people, etc.) into action: *to call up reinforcements.* ~*n.* **call-up. 4. a.** a general order to report for military service. **b.** the number of men so summoned.
callus (ˈkæləs) *n., pl.* **-luses. 1.** Also called: **callosity.** an area of skin that is hard or thick, esp. on the palm of the hand or sole of the foot, as from continual friction or pressure. **2.** an area of bony tissue formed during the healing of a fractured bone. **3.** *Botany.* **a.** a mass of hard protective tissue produced in woody plants at the site of an injury. **b.** an accumulation of callose in the sieve tubes. ~*vb.* **4.** to produce or cause to produce a callus. [C16: from Latin, variant of *callum* hardened skin]
calm (kɑːm) *adj.* **1.** almost without motion; still: *a calm sea.* **2.** *Meteorol.* of force 0 on the Beaufort scale; without wind. **3.** not disturbed, agitated, or excited; under control: *he stayed calm throughout the confusion.* **4.** tranquil; serene: *a calm voice.* ~*n.* **5.** an absence of disturbance or rough motion; stillness. **6.** absence of wind. **7.** tranquillity. ~*vb.* **8.** (often foll. by *down*) to make or become calm. [C14: from Old French *calme*, from Old Italian *calma*, from Late Latin *cauma* heat, hence a rest during the heat of the day, from Greek *kauma* heat, from *kaiein* to burn] —ˈ**calmly** *adv.* —ˈ**calmness** *n.*
calmative (ˈkælmətɪv, ˈkɑːmə-) *adj.* **1.** (of a remedy or agent) sedative. ~*n.* **2.** a sedative remedy or drug.
calmodulin (kælˈmɒdjʊlɪn) *n. Biochem.* a protein found in most living cells; it regulates many enzymic processes that are dependent on calcium. [from CAL(CIUM) + MODUL(ATE) + -IN]
calomel (ˈkæləˌmɛl, -məl) *n.* a colourless tasteless powder consisting chiefly of mercurous chloride, used medicinally, esp. as a cathartic. Formula: Hg_2Cl_2. [C17: perhaps from New Latin *calomelas* (unattested), literally: beautiful black (perhaps so named because it was originally sublimed from a black mixture of mercury and mercuric chloride), from Greek *kalos* beautiful + *melas* black]
calorescence (ˌkæləˈrɛsəns) *n. Physics.* the absorption of radiation by a body, subsequently re-emitted at a higher frequency (lower wavelength). —ˌ**caloˈrescent** *adj.*
Calor Gas (ˈkælə) *n. Trademark.* butane gas liquefied under pressure in portable containers for domestic use.
caloric (kəˈlɒrɪk, ˈkælərɪk) *adj.* **1.** of or concerned with heat or calories. ~*n.* **2.** *Obsolete.* a hypothetical elastic fluid formerly postulated as the embodiment of heat. —**caloricity** (ˌkæləˈrɪsɪtɪ) *n.*
calorie *or* **calory** (ˈkælərɪ) *n., pl.* **-ries.** a unit of heat, equal to 4.1868 joules (**International Table calorie**): formerly defined as the quantity of heat required to raise the temperature of 1 gram of water by 1°C under standard conditions. It has now largely been replaced by the joule for scientific purposes. Abbrev.: **cal.** Also called: **gram calorie, small calorie.** Compare **Calorie.** [C19: from French, from Latin *calor* heat]
Calorie (ˈkælərɪ) *n.* **1.** Also called: **kilogram calorie, kilocalorie, large calorie.** a unit of heat, equal to one thousand calories, often used to express the heat output of an organism or the energy value of food. Abbrev.: **Cal. 2.** the amount of a specific food capable of producing one thousand calories of energy.
calorific (ˌkæləˈrɪfɪk) *adj.* of, concerning, or generating heat. —ˌ**caloˈrifically** *adv.*
calorific value *n.* the quantity of heat produced by the complete combustion of a given mass of a fuel, usually expressed in joules per kilogram.
calorimeter (ˌkæləˈrɪmɪtə) *n.* an apparatus for measuring amounts of heat, esp. to find specific heat capacities, calorific values, etc. —**calorimetric** (ˌkælərɪˈmɛtrɪk) *or* ˌ**caloriˈmetrical** *adj.* —ˌ**caloriˈmetrically** *adv.* —ˌ**caloˈrimetry** *n.*
calorize (ˈkæləˌraɪz) *vb.* (*tr.*) to coat (a ferrous metal) by spraying with aluminium powder and then heating.
calotte (kəˈlɒt) *n.* **1.** a skullcap worn by Roman Catholic clergy. **2.** *Architect.* a concavity in the form of a niche or cup, serving to reduce the apparent height of an alcove or chapel. [C17: from French, from Provençal *calota*, perhaps from Greek *kaluptra* hood]
calotype (ˈkæləʊˌtaɪp) *n.* **1.** an early photographic process invented by W. H. Fox Talbot, in which the image was produced on paper treated with silver iodide and developed by sodium thiosulphite. **2.** a photograph made by this process. [C19: from Greek *kalos* beautiful + -TYPE]
caloyer (ˈkælɔɪə) *n.* a monk of the Greek Orthodox Church, esp. of the Basilian Order. [C17: from French, from Medieval Greek *kalogēros* venerable, from Greek *kalos* beautiful + *gēras* old age]
calpac, calpack, *or* **kalpak** (ˈkælpæk) *n.* a large black brimless hat made of sheepskin or felt, worn by men in parts of the Near East. [C16: from Turkish *kalpāk*]
calque (kælk) *n.* **1.** another word for **loan translation.** ~*vb.* **calques, calquing, calqued. 2.** (*tr.*) another word for **calk**[3]. [C20: from French: a tracing, from *calquer*, from Latin *calcāre* to tread]
caltrop, caltrap (ˈkæltrəp), *or* **calthrop** (ˈkælθrəp) *n.* **1.** any tropical or subtropical plant of the zygophyllaceous genera *Tribulus* and *Kallstroemia* that have spiny burs or bracts. **2. water caltrop.** another name for **water chestnut** (sense 1). **3.** another name for the **star thistle. 4.** *Military.* a four-spiked iron ball or four joined spikes laid upon the ground as a device to lame cavalry horses, puncture tyres, etc. [Old English *calcatrippe* (the plant), from Medieval Latin *calcatrippa*, probably from Latin *calx* heel + *trippa* TRAP[1]]
calumet (ˈkæljʊˌmɛt) *n.* a less common name for **peace pipe.** [C18: from Canadian French, from French (Normandy dialect): straw, from Late Latin *calamellus* a little reed, from Latin: CALAMUS]
calumniate (kəˈlʌmnɪˌeɪt) *vb.* (*tr.*) to slander. —**caˈlumniable** *adj.* —**caˌlumniˈation** *n.* —**caˈlumniˌator** *n.*
calumnious (kəˈlʌmnɪəs) *or* **calumniatory** (kəˈlʌmnɪətərɪ, -trɪ) *adj.* **1.** of or using calumny. **2.** (of a person) given to calumny.
calumny (ˈkæləmnɪ) *n., pl.* **-nies. 1.** the malicious utterance of false charges or misrepresentation; slander; defamation. **2.** such a false charge or misrepresentation. [C15: from Latin *calumnia* deception, slander]
calutron (ˈkæljʊˌtrɒn) *n.* a large mass spectrometer used for the separation of isotopes. [C20: from Cal(ifornia) U(niversity) + -TRON]
Calvados (ˈkælvəˌdɒs) *n.* an apple brandy distilled from cider in the Calvados region of Normandy, France.
calvaria (kælˈvɛərɪə) *n.* the top part of the skull of vertebrates. Nontechnical name: **skullcap.** [C14: from Late Latin: (human) skull, from Latin *calvus* bald]
calvary (ˈkælvərɪ) *n., pl.* **-ries. 1.** (*often cap.*) a representation of Christ's crucifixion, usually sculptured and in the open air. **2.** any experience involving great suffering. [from *Calvary*, the place where Jesus was crucified, from Late Latin *Calvāria*, translation of Greek *kranion* skull, translation of Aramaic *gulgulta* Golgotha]
Calvary cross *n.* a Latin cross with a representation of three steps beneath it.
calve (kɑːv) *vb.* **1.** to give birth to (a calf). **2.** (of a glacier or iceberg) to release (masses of ice) in breaking up.
calves (kɑːvz) *n.* the plural of **calf**[1] and **calf**[2].
Calvin cycle (ˈkælvɪn) *n. Botany.* a series of reactions, occurring during photosynthesis, in which glucose is synthesized from carbon dioxide. [C20: named after Melvin *Calvin* (born 1911), U.S. chemist, who elucidated it]
Calvinism (ˈkælvɪˌnɪzəm) *n.* the theological system of John Calvin (1509–64) and his followers, characterized by emphasis on the

doctrines of predestination, the irresistibility of grace, and justification by faith. —**'Calvinist** *n., adj.* —**ˌCalvin'istic** *or* **ˌCalvin'istical** *adj.*

calvities (kæl'vɪʃɪˌiːz) *n.* baldness. [C17: from Late Latin, from Latin *calvus* bald]

calx (kælks) *n., pl.* **calxes** *or* **calces** ('kælsiːz). **1.** the powdery metallic oxide formed when an ore or mineral is roasted. **2.** another name for **calcium oxide. 3.** *Anatomy.* the heel. [C15: from Latin: lime, from Greek *khalix* pebble]

calyces ('kælɪˌsiːz, 'keɪlɪ-) *n.* a plural of **calyx.**

calycine ('kælɪˌsaɪn) *or* **calycinal** (kə'lɪsɪnəl) *adj.* relating to, belonging to, or resembling a calyx.

calycle, calicle ('kælɪkəl) *or* **calyculus** (kə'lɪkjʊləs) *n.* **1.** *Zoology.* a cup-shaped structure, as in the coral skeleton. **2.** *Botany.* another name for **epicalyx.** [C18: from Latin, diminutive of CALYX] —**calycular** (kə'lɪkjʊlə) *adj.*

calypso[1] (kə'lɪpsəʊ) *n., pl.* **-sos. 1.** a popular type of satirical, usually topical, West Indian ballad, esp. from Trinidad, usually extemporized to a percussive syncopated accompaniment. **2.** a dance done to the rhythm of this song. [C20: probably from *Calypso,* a sea nymph in Greek mythology]

calypso[2] (kə'lɪpsəʊ) *n., pl.* **-sos.** a rare N temperate orchid, *Calypso* (or *Cytherea*) *bulbosa,* whose flower is pink or white with purple and yellow markings. [C19: named after *Calypso*]

calyptra (kə'lɪptrə) *n. Botany.* **1.** a membranous hood covering the spore-bearing capsule of mosses and liverworts. **2.** any hoodlike structure, such as a root cap. [C18: from New Latin, from Greek *kaluptra* hood, from *kaluptein* to cover] —**calyptrate** (kə'lɪpˌtreɪt) *adj.*

calyptrogen (kə'lɪptrədʒən) *n.* a layer of rapidly dividing cells at the tip of a plant root, from which the root cap is formed. It occurs in grasses and many other plants. [C19: from CALYPTRA + -GEN]

calyx ('keɪlɪks, 'kælɪks) *n., pl.* **calyxes** *or* **calyces** ('kælɪˌsiːz, 'keɪlɪ-). **1.** the sepals of a flower collectively, forming the outer floral envelope that protects the developing flower bud. Compare **corolla. 2.** any cup-shaped cavity or structure, esp. any of the divisions of the human kidney (**renal calyx**) that form the renal pelvis. [C17: from Latin, from Greek *kalux* shell, from *kaluptein* to cover, hide] —**calycate** ('kælɪˌkeɪt) *adj.*

calzone (kæl'tsəʊnɪ) *n.* a dish of Italian origin consisting of pizza dough folded over a filling of cheese and tomatoes, herbs, ham, etc. [C20: Italian, literally: trouser leg, from *calzoni* trousers]

cam (kæm) *n.* a rotating cylinder with an irregular profile, attached to a revolving shaft to give a reciprocating motion to a part in contact with it. [C18: from Dutch *kam* comb]

CAM *abbrev. for:* **1.** computer-aided manufacture. **2.** *Botany.* **a.** crassulacean acid metabolism: a form of photosynthesis, first described in crassulaceous plants, in which carbon dioxide is taken up only at night. **b.** (*as modifier*): *a CAM plant.*

camail ('kæmeɪl) *n. Armour.* a neck and shoulders covering of mail worn with and laced to the basinet.

camaraderie (ˌkæmə'rɑːdərɪ) *n.* a spirit of familiarity and trust existing between friends. [C19: from French, from COMRADE]

camarilla (ˌkæmə'rɪlə; *Spanish* kama'riʎa) *n.* a group of confidential advisers, esp. formerly, to the Spanish kings; cabal. [C19: from Spanish: literally: a little room]

camass *or* **camas** ('kæmæs) *n.* **1.** Also called: **quamash.** any of several North American plants of the liliaceous genus *Camassia,* esp. *C. quamash,* which has a cluster of blue or white flowers and a sweet edible bulb. **2. death camass.** any liliaceous plant of the genus *Zygadenus* (or *Zigadenus*), of the western U.S., that is poisonous to livestock, esp. sheep. [C19: from Chinook Jargon *kamass,* from Nootka *chamas* sweet]

Camb. *abbrev. for* Cambridge.

camber ('kæmbə) *n.* **1.** a slight upward curve to the centre of the surface of a road, ship's deck, etc. **2.** another name for **bank**[2] (sense 7). **3.** an outward inclination of the front wheels of a road vehicle so that they are slightly closer together at the bottom than at the top. **4.** Also called: **hog.** a small arching curve of a beam or girder provided to lessen deflection and improve appearance. **5.** aerofoil curvature expressed by the ratio of the maximum height of the aerofoil mean line to its chord. ~*vb.* **6.** to form or be formed with a surface that curves upwards to its centre. [C17: from Old French (northern dialect) *cambre* curved, from Latin *camurus;* related to *camera* CHAMBER]

Camberwell beauty ('kæmbəˌwɛl, -wəl) *n.* a nymphalid butterfly, *Nymphalis antiopa,* of temperate regions, having dark purple wings with cream-yellow borders. U.S. name: **mourning cloak.** [C19: named after *Camberwell,* a district of S London]

cambist ('kæmbɪst) *n. Finance.* **1.** a dealer or expert in foreign exchange. **2.** a manual of currency exchange rates and similar equivalents of weights and measures. [C19: from French *cambiste,* from Italian *cambista,* from *cambio* (money) exchange] —**'cambistry** *n.*

cambium ('kæmbɪəm) *n., pl.* **-biums** *or* **-bia** (-bɪə). *Botany.* a meristem that increases the girth of stems and roots by producing additional xylem and phloem. See also **cork cambium.** [C17: from Medieval Latin: exchange, from Late Latin *cambiāre* to exchange, barter] —**'cambial** *adj.*

Cambodian (kæm'bəʊdɪən) *adj.* **1.** of or relating to Cambodia, a country in SE Asia, or its people. ~*n.* **2.** a native or inhabitant of Cambodia.

cambogia (kæm'bəʊdʒɪə) *n.* another name for **gamboge** (senses 1, 2).

camboose (kæm'buːs) *n.* (formerly in Canada) **1.** a cabin built as living quarters for a gang of lumbermen. **2.** an open fireplace in such a cabin. [C19: from Canadian French, from French *cambuse* hut, store, from Dutch *kambuis*]

cambrel ('kæmbrəl) *n.* a variant of **gambrel.**

Cambrian ('kæmbrɪən) *adj.* **1.** of, denoting, or formed in the first 100 million years of the Palaeozoic era, during which marine invertebrates, esp. trilobites, flourished. **2.** of or relating to Wales. ~*n.* **3. the.** the Cambrian period or rock system. **4.** a Welshman. [from Medieval Latin *Cambria* Wales]

cambric ('keɪmbrɪk) *n.* a fine white linen or cotton fabric. [C16: from Flemish *Kamerijk* Cambrai a town in NE France where it was originally made]

Cambridge blue ('keɪmbrɪdʒ) *n.* **1. a.** a lightish blue colour. **b.** (*as adj.*): *a Cambridge-blue scarf.* **2.** a person who has been awarded a blue from Cambridge University.

camcorder ('kæmˌkɔːdə) *n.* a video camera and recorder combined in a portable unit.

came[1] (keɪm) *vb.* the past tense of **come.**

came[2] (keɪm) *n.* a grooved strip of lead used to join pieces of glass in a stained-glass window or a leaded light. [C17: of unknown origin]

camel ('kæməl) *n.* **1.** either of two cud-chewing artiodactyl mammals of the genus *Camelus* (see **Arabian camel, Bactrian camel**): family *Camelidae.* They are adapted for surviving long periods without food or water in desert regions, esp. by using humps on the back for storing fat. **2.** a float attached to a vessel to increase its buoyancy. See also **caisson** (sense 2). **3.** a raft or float used as a fender between a vessel and a wharf. **4. a.** a fawn colour. **b.** (*as adj.*): *a camel dress.* [Old English, from Latin *camēlus,* from Greek *kamēlos,* of Semitic origin; related to Arabic *jamal*]

cameleer (ˌkæmɪ'lɪə) *n.* a camel-driver.

camel hair *or* **camel's hair** *n.* **1.** the hair of the camel or dromedary, used in clothing, rugs, etc. **2. a.** soft cloth made of or containing this hair or a substitute, usually tan in colour. **b.** (*as modifier*): *a camelhair coat.* **3. a.** the hair of the squirrel's tail, used for paintbrushes. **b.** (*as modifier*): *a camelhair brush.*

camellia (kə'miːlɪə) *n.* any ornamental shrub of the Asian genus *Camellia,* esp. *C. japonica,* having glossy evergreen leaves and showy roselike flowers, usually white, pink or red in colour: family *Theaceae.* Also called: **japonica.** [C18: New Latin, named after Georg Josef *Kamel* (1661–1706), Moravian Jesuit missionary, who introduced it to Europe]

camelopard ('kæmɪləˌpɑːd, kə'mɛl-) *n.* an obsolete word for **giraffe.** [C14: from Medieval Latin *camēlopardus,* from Greek *kamēlopardalis,* from *kamēlos* CAMEL + *pardalis* LEOPARD, because the giraffe was thought to have a head like a camel's and spots like a leopard's]

Camelopardus (kəˌmɛlə'pɑːdəs) *or* **Camelopardalis** (kəˌmɛlə'pɑːdəlɪs) *n., Latin genitive* **Camelopardi** (kəˌmɛlə'pɑːdaɪ) or **Camelopardalis** (kəˌmɛlə'pɑːdəlɪs). a faint extensive constellation in the N hemisphere close to Ursa Major and Cassiopeia.

camel's hair *n.* See **camel hair.**

Camembert ('kæməmˌbɛə; *French* kamɑ̃bɛr) *n.* a rich soft creamy cheese. [French, from *Camembert,* a village in Normandy where it originated]

cameo ('kæmɪˌəʊ) *n., pl.* **cameos. 1. a.** a medallion, as on a brooch or ring, with a profile head carved in relief. **b.** (*as modifier*): *a cameo necklace.* **2.** an engraving upon a gem or other stone of at least two differently coloured layers, such as sardonyx, so carved that the background is of a different colour from the raised design. **3.** a stone with such an engraving. **4. a.** a single and often brief dramatic scene played by a well-known actor or actress in a film or television play. **b.** (*as modifier*): *a cameo performance.* **5. a.** a short literary work or dramatic sketch. **b.** (*as modifier*): *a cameo sketch.* [C15: from Italian *cammeo,* of uncertain origin]

cameo ware *n.* jasper ware with applied decoration of classical motifs, resembling a cameo.

camera ('kæmərə, 'kæmrə) *n.* **1.** an optical device consisting of a lens system set in a light-proof construction inside which a light-sensitive film or plate can be positioned. See also **cine camera. 2.** *Television.* the equipment used to convert the optical image of a scene being televised into the corresponding electrical signals. **3.** See **camera obscura. 4.** *pl.* **-erae** (-əˌriː). a judge's private room. **5. in camera. a.** *Law.* relating to a hearing from which members of the public are excluded. **b.** in private. **6. off camera.** not within an area being filmed. **7. on camera.** (esp. of an actor) being filmed. [C18: from Latin: vault, from Greek *kamara*]

cameral ('kæmərəl) *adj.* of or relating to a judicial or legislative chamber. [C18: from Medieval Latin *camerālis;* see CAMERA]

camera lucida ('luːsɪdə) *n.* an instrument attached to a microscope, etc. to enable an observer to view simultaneously the image and a drawing surface to facilitate the sketching of the image. [New Latin: light chamber]

cameraman ('kæmərəˌmæn, 'kæmrə-) *n., pl.* **-men.** a person who operates a film or television camera.

camera obscura (ɒb'skjʊərə) *n.* a darkened chamber or small building in which images of outside objects are projected onto a flat surface by a convex lens in an aperture. Sometimes shortened to **camera.** [New Latin: dark chamber]

camera-ready copy *n. Printing.* type matter ready to be photographed for plate-making without further alteration. Also called (U.S. and Canadian): **mechanical.**

camera-shy *adj.* having an aversion to being photographed or filmed.

caméra stylo (*French* kamera stilo) *n. Films.* the use of the camera as a means of personal expression, especially as practised by some directors of the New Wave. [French, literally: camera stylograph]

camera tube *n.* the part of a television camera that converts an optical image into electrical signals of video frequency. See also **image orthicon, vidicon, Plumbicon, iconoscope.**

camerlengo (ˌkæməˈlɛŋgəʊ) *or* **camerlingo** (ˌkæməˈlɪŋgəʊ) *n., pl.* **-gos.** *R.C. Church.* a cardinal who acts as the pope's financial secretary and the papal treasurer. [C17: from Italian *camerlingo,* of Germanic origin; compare CHAMBERLAIN]

cam follower *n. Engineering.* the slider or roller in contact with the cam that transmits the movement dictated by the cam profile.

camiknickers (ˈkæmɪˌnɪkəz) *pl. n.* women's knickers attached to a camisole top. Often shortened to **ˈcamiˌknicks.**

camion (ˈkæmɪən; *French* kamjɔ̃) *n.* a lorry, or, esp. formerly, a large dray. [C19: from French, of obscure origin]

camisado (ˌkæmɪˈsɑːdəʊ) *or* **camisade** (ˌkæmɪˈseɪd) *n., pl.* **-sados** *or* **-sades.** (formerly) an attack made under cover of darkness. [C16: from obsolete Spanish *camisada,* literally: an attack in one's shirt (worn over the armour as identification), from *camisa* shirt]

camise (kəˈmiːz) *n.* a loose light shirt, smock, or tunic originally worn in the Middle Ages. [C19: from Arabic *qamīs,* from Late Latin *camīsia*]

camisole (ˈkæmɪˌsəʊl) *n.* **1.** a woman's underbodice with shoulder straps, originally designed as a cover for a corset. **2.** a woman's dressing jacket or short negligée. **3.** (*modifier*) resembling a camisole (the underbodice), as in fitting snugly around the bust and having a straight neckline: *a camisole slip; a camisole top.* [C19: from French, from Provençal *camisola,* from *camisa* shirt, from Late Latin *camīsia*]

camlet (ˈkæmlɪt) *n.* **1.** a tough waterproof cloth. **2.** a garment or garments made from such cloth. **3.** a soft woollen fabric used in medieval Asia. [C14: from Old French *camelot,* perhaps from Arabic *hamlat* plush fabric]

camogie (kaˈmoːgiː) *n. Irish.* a form of hurling played by women. [from Irish Gaelic *camógaíocht,* from *camóg* crooked stick]

camomile *or* **chamomile** (ˈkæməˌmaɪl) *n.* **1.** any aromatic plant of the Eurasian genus *Anthemis,* esp. *A. nobilis,* whose finely dissected leaves and daisy-like flowers are used medicinally: family *Compositae* (composites). **2.** any plant of the related genus *Matricaria,* esp. *M. chamomilla* (**German** or **wild camomile**). **3. camomile tea.** a medicinal beverage made from the fragrant leaves and flowers of any of these plants. [C14: from Old French *camomille,* from Medieval Latin *chamomilla,* from Greek *khamaimēlon,* literally, earth-apple (referring to the apple-like scent of the flowers)]

camoodi (kæˈmuːdɪ) *n.* a Caribbean name for **anaconda.** [C19: from an American Indian language of Guyana]

Camorra (kəˈmɒrə) *n.* **1.** a secret society organized in about 1820 in Naples, which thrives on blackmail and extortion. **2.** any similar clandestine group. [C19: from Italian, probably from Spanish: quarrel]

camouflage (ˈkæməˌflɑːʒ) *n.* **1.** the exploitation of natural surroundings or artificial aids to conceal or disguise the presence of military units, equipment, etc. **2.** (*modifier*) (of fabric or clothing) having a design of irregular dull brown and green patches, as used in military camouflage. **3.** the means by which animals escape the notice of predators, usually because of a resemblance to their surroundings: includes cryptic and apatetic coloration. **4.** a device or expedient designed to conceal or deceive. *~vb.* **5.** (*tr.*) to conceal by camouflage. [C20: from French, from *camoufler,* from Italian *camuffare* to disguise, deceive, of uncertain origin]

camp[1] (kæmp) *n.* **1.** a place where tents, cabins, or other temporary structures are erected for the use of military troops, for training soldiers, etc. **2.** the military life. **3.** tents, cabins, etc., used as temporary lodgings by a group of travellers, holidaymakers, Scouts, Gypsies, etc. **4.** the group of people living in such lodgings. **5.** *S. African.* a field or paddock fenced off as pasture. **6.** a group supporting a given doctrine or theory: *the socialist camp.* **7.** (*modifier*) suitable for use in temporary quarters, on holiday, etc., esp. by being portable and easy to set up: *a camp bed; a camp chair.* *~vb.* **8.** (*intr.;* often foll. by *down*) to establish or set up a camp. **9.** (*intr.;* often foll. by *out*) to live temporarily in or as if in a tent. **10.** (*tr.*) to put in a camp. [C16: from Old French, ultimately from Latin *campus* field] —**ˈcamping** *n.*

camp[2] (kæmp) *Informal.* *~adj.* **1.** effeminate; affected in mannerisms, dress, etc. **2.** homosexual. **3.** consciously artificial, exaggerated, vulgar, or mannered; self-parodying, esp. when in dubious taste. *~vb.* **4.** (*tr.*) to perform or invest with a camp quality. **5. camp it up. a.** to seek to focus attention on oneself by making an ostentatious display, overacting, etc. **b.** to flaunt one's homosexuality. *~n.* **6.** a camp quality, style, etc. [C20: of uncertain origin] —**ˈcampy** *adj.*

campagna (kæmˈpɑːnjə) *n.* another word for **champaign** (sense 1).

campaign (kæmˈpeɪn) *n.* **1.** a series of coordinated activities, such as public speaking and demonstrating, designed to achieve a social, political, or commercial goal: *a presidential campaign; an advertising campaign.* **2.** *Military.* a number of complementary operations aimed at achieving a single objective, usually constrained by time or geographic area. *~vb.* **3.** (*intr.;* often foll. by *for*) to conduct, serve in, or go on a campaign. [C17: from French *campagne* open country, from Italian *campagna,* from Late Latin *campānia,* from Latin *campus* field] —**camˈpaigner** *n.*

campanile (ˌkæmpəˈniːlɪ) *n.* (esp. in Italy) a bell tower, not usually attached to another building. Compare **belfry.** [C17: from Italian, from *campana* bell]

campanology (ˌkæmpəˈnɒlədʒɪ) *n.* the art or skill of ringing bells musically. [C19: from New Latin *campānologia,* from Late Latin *campāna* bell] —**campanological** (ˌkæmpənəˈlɒdʒɪkəl) *adj.* —**ˌcampaˈnologist** *or* **ˌcampaˈnologer** *n.*

campanula (kæmˈpænjʊlə) *n.* any N temperate plant of the campanulaceous genus *Campanula,* typically having blue or white bell-shaped flowers. Also called: **bellflower.** See also **Canterbury bell, harebell.** [C17: from New Latin: a little bell, from Late Latin *campāna* bell; see CAMPANILE]

campanulaceous (kəmˌpænjʊˈleɪʃəs) *adj.* of, relating to, or belonging to the *Campanulaceae,* a family of temperate and subtropical plants, including the campanulas, having bell-shaped nodding flowers.

campanulate (kæmˈpænjʊlɪt, -ˌleɪt) *adj.* (esp. of flower corollas) shaped like a bell. [C17: from New Latin *campanulātus;* see CAMPANULA]

Campbell-Stokes recorder (ˌkæmbəlˈstəʊks) *n.* an instrument for recording hours of sunshine per day, consisting of a solid glass sphere that focuses rays of sunlight onto a light-sensitive card on which a line is traced.

camp-drafting *n. Austral.* a competitive test, esp. at an agricultural show, of horsemen's skill in drafting cattle.

camper (ˈkæmpə) *n.* **1.** a person who lives or temporarily stays in a tent, cabin, etc. **2.** *U.S. and Canadian.* a vehicle equipped for camping out.

camper van *n. N.Z.* a motor caravan.

campestral (kæmˈpɛstrəl) *adj.* of or relating to open fields or country. [C18: from Latin *campester,* from *campus* field]

campfire (ˈkæmpˌfaɪə) *n.* an outdoor fire in a camp, esp. one used for cooking or as a focal point for community events.

camp follower *n.* **1.** any civilian, esp. a prostitute, who unofficially provides services to military personnel. **2.** a nonmember who is sympathetic to a particular group, theory, etc.

camphene (ˈkæmfiːn) *n.* a colourless crystalline insoluble optically active terpene derived from pinene and present in many essential oils. Formula: $C_{10}H_{16}$. [C19: from CAMPH(OR) + -ENE]

camphire (ˈkæmfaɪə) *n.* an archaic name for **henna** (senses 1, 2).

camphor (ˈkæmfə) *n.* a whitish crystalline aromatic terpene ketone obtained from the wood of the camphor tree or made from pinene: used in the manufacture of celluloid and in medicine as a liniment and treatment for colds. Formula: $C_{10}H_{16}O$. [C15: from Old French *camphre,* from Medieval Latin *camphora,* from Arabic *kāfūr,* from Malay *kāpūr* chalk; related to Khmer *kāpōr* camphor] —**camphoric** (kæmˈfɒrɪk) *adj.*

camphorate (ˈkæmfəˌreɪt) *vb.* (*tr.*) to apply, treat with, or impregnate with camphor.

camphorated oil *n.* a liniment consisting of camphor and peanut oil, used as a counterirritant.

camphor ball *n.* another name for **mothball** (sense 1).

camphor ice *n.* an ointment consisting of camphor, white wax, spermaceti, and castor oil, used to treat skin ailments, esp. chapped skin.

camphor tree *n.* **1.** a lauraceous evergreen E Asian tree, *Cinnamomum camphora,* whose aromatic wood yields camphor. **2.** any similar tree, such as the dipterocarpaceous tree *Dryobalanops aromatica* of Borneo.

campimetry (kæmˈpɪmɪtrɪ) *n.* a technique for assessing the central part of the visual field. [C20: from New Latin, from Latin *campus* field + *-metry;* see -METER]

camping ground *n.* another word for **camp site.**

campion (ˈkæmpɪən) *n.* any of various caryophyllaceous plants of the genera *Silene* and *Lychnis,* having red, pink, or white flowers. See also **bladder campion.** [C16: probably from *campion,* obsolete variant of CHAMPION, perhaps so called because originally applied to *Lychnis coronaria,* the leaves of which were used to crown athletic champions]

CAM plant (kæm) *n.* any plant that undergoes a form of photosynthesis known as crassulacean acid metabolism, in which carbon dioxide is taken up only at night. [*C(rassulacean) A(cid) M(etabolism) plant*]

camp meeting *n. Chiefly U.S.* a religious meeting held in a large tent or outdoors, often lasting several days.

campo (ˈkæmpəʊ) *n., pl.* **-pos.** (*often pl.*) level or undulating savanna country, esp. in the uplands of Brazil. [American Spanish, from Latin *campus*]

camporee (ˌkæmpəˈriː) *n.* a local meeting or assembly of Scouts. [C20: from CAMP[1] + (JAMB)OREE]
camp oven *n. Austral. and N.Z.* a metal pot or box with a heavy lid, used for baking over an open fire.
camp pie *n. Austral.* tinned meat.
camp site *n.* an area on which holiday-makers may pitch a tent, etc. Also called: **camping site.**
campus (ˈkæmpəs) *n., pl.* **-puses.** **1.** the grounds and buildings of a university. **2.** *Chiefly U.S.* the outside area of a college, university, etc. [C18: from Latin: field]
campus university *n. Brit.* a university in which the buildings, often including shops and cafés, are all on one site. Compare **redbrick.**
campylobacter (ˌkæmpɪləʊˈbæktə) *n.* a rod-shaped bacterium that causes infections in cattle and man. Unpasteurized milk infected with campylobacter is a common cause of gastroenteritis. [from Greek *kampulos* bent + BACTER(IUM)]
CAMRA (ˈkæmrə) *n. acronym for* Campaign for Real Ale.
camshaft (ˈkæmˌʃɑːft) *n.* a shaft having one or more cams attached to it, esp. one used to operate the valves of an internal-combustion engine.
camwood (ˈkæmˌwʊd) *n.* **1.** a W African leguminous tree, *Baphia nitida,* whose hard wood was formerly used in making a red dye. **2.** the wood of this tree. [C20: perhaps from Temne]
can[1] (kæn; *unstressed* kən) *vb. past* **could.** (takes an infinitive without *to* or an implied infinitive) used as an auxiliary: **1.** to indicate ability, skill, or fitness to perform a task: *I can run a mile in under four minutes.* **2.** to indicate permission or the right to something: *can I have a drink?* **3.** to indicate knowledge of how to do something: *he can speak three languages fluently.* **4.** to indicate the possibility, opportunity, or likelihood: *my trainer says I can win the race if I really work hard.* [Old English *cunnan;* related to Old Norse *kunna,* Old High German *kunnan,* Latin *cognōscere* to know, Sanskrit *jānāti* he knows; see KEN, UNCOUTH]
▷ **Usage.** See at **may.**
can[2] (kæn) *n.* **1.** a container, esp. for liquids, usually of thin sheet metal: *a petrol can; milk can.* **2.** another name (esp. U.S.) for **tin** (metal container). **3.** Also called: **ˈcanful.** the contents of a can or the amount a can will hold. **4.** a slang word for **prison. 5.** *U.S. and Canadian.* a slang word for **toilet** or **buttocks. 6.** *U.S. Navy.* a slang word for **destroyer. 7.** *Naval slang.* a depth charge. **8.** a shallow cylindrical metal container of varying size used for storing and handling film. **9. can of worms.** *Informal.* a complicated problem. **10. in the can. a.** (of a film, piece of music, etc.) having been recorded, processed, edited, etc. **b.** *Informal.* arranged or agreed: *the contract is almost in the can.* **11. carry the can.** See **carry** (sense 37). *~vb.* **cans, canning, canned. 12.** to put (food, etc.) into a can or cans; preserve in a can. **13.** *(tr.) U.S. slang.* to dismiss from a job. **14.** *(tr.) U.S. informal.* to stop (doing something annoying or making an annoying noise) (esp. in the phrase **can it!**). [Old English *canne;* related to Old Norse, Old High German *kanna,* Irish *gann,* Swedish *kana* sled]
can. *abbrev. for:* **1.** *Music.* canon. **2.** canto.
Can. *abbrev. for:* **1.** Canada. **2.** Canadian.
Canaanite (ˈkeɪnəˌnaɪt) *n.* **1.** a member of an ancient Semitic people who occupied the land of Canaan, between the River Jordan and the Mediterranean, before the Israelite conquest. **2.** the extinct language of this people, belonging to the Canaanitic branch of the Semitic subfamily of the Afro-Asiatic family.
Canaanitic (ˌkeɪnəˈnɪtɪk) *n.* **1.** a group of ancient languages belonging to the Semitic subfamily of the Afro-Asiatic family and including Canaanite, Phoenician, Ugaritic, and Hebrew. *~adj.* **2.** denoting, relating to, or belonging to this group of languages.
Canad. *abbrev. for* Canadian.
Canada balsam (ˈkænədə) *n.* **1.** a yellow transparent resin obtained from the balsam fir. Because its refractive index is similar to that of glass, it is used as an adhesive in optical devices and as a mounting medium for microscope specimens. **2.** another name for **balsam fir.**
Canada Day *n.* (in Canada) July 1, the anniversary of the day in 1867 when Canada became the first British colony to receive dominion status: a bank holiday. Former name: **Dominion Day.**
Canada goose *n.* a large common greyish-brown North American goose, *Branta canadensis,* with a black neck and head and a white throat patch.
Canada lily *n.* a lily, *Lilium canadense,* of NE North America, with small orange funnel-shaped nodding flowers. Also called: **meadow lily.**
Canada thistle *n.* the U.S. and Canadian name for **creeping thistle.**
Canadian (kəˈneɪdɪən) *adj.* **1.** of or relating to Canada or its people. *~n.* **2.** a native, citizen, or inhabitant of Canada.
Canadian football *n.* a game resembling American football, played on a grass pitch between two teams of 12 players.
Canadian French *n.* **1.** the French language as spoken in Canada, esp. in Quebec. *~adj.* **2.** denoting this language or a French-speaking Canadian.
Canadianism (kəˈneɪdɪəˌnɪzəm) *n.* **1.** the Canadian national character or spirit. **2.** loyalty to Canada, its political independence, culture, etc. **3.** a linguistic usage, custom, or other feature peculiar to or characteristic of Canada, its people, or their culture.
Canadian pondweed *n.* a North American aquatic plant, *Elodea* (or *Anacharis*) *canadensis,* naturalized in Europe, having crowded dark green leaves: family *Hydrocharitaceae.* It is used in aquariums.
canaigre (kəˈnaɪgə) *n.* a dock, *Rumex hymenosepalus,* of the southern U.S., the root of which yields a substance used in tanning. [C19: from Mexican Spanish]
canaille French. (kanɑj) *n.* the masses; mob; rabble. [C17: from French, from Italian *canaglia* pack of dogs]
canakin (ˈkænɪkɪn) *n.* a variant spelling of **cannikin.**
canal (kəˈnæl) *n.* **1.** an artificial waterway constructed for navigation, irrigation, water power, etc. **2.** any of various tubular passages or ducts: *the alimentary canal.* **3.** any of various elongated intercellular spaces in plants. **4.** *Astronomy.* any of the indistinct surface features of Mars originally thought to be a network of channels but not seen on close-range photographs. They are caused by an optical illusion in which faint geological features appear to have a geometric structure. *~vb.* **-nals, -nalling, -nalled** *or U.S.* **-nals, -naling, -naled.** *(tr.)* **5.** to dig a canal through. **6.** to provide with a canal or canals. [C15 (in the sense: pipe, tube): from Latin *canālis* channel, water pipe, from *canna* reed, CANE[1]]
canal boat *n.* a long narrow boat used on canals, esp. for carrying freight.
canaliculus (ˌkænəˈlɪkjʊləs) *n., pl.* **-li** (-ˌlaɪ). a small channel, furrow, or groove, as in some bones and parts of plants. [C16: from Latin: a little channel, from *canālis* CANAL] —ˌ**canaˈlicular, canaliculate** (ˌkænəˈlɪkjʊlɪt, -ˌleɪt), *or* ˌ**canaˈlicuˌlated** *adj.*
canalize *or* **canalise** (ˈkænəˌlaɪz) *vb. (tr.)* **1.** to provide with or convert into a canal or canals. **2.** to give a particular direction to or provide an outlet for; channel. —ˌ**canaliˈzation** *or* ˌ**canaliˈsation** *n.*
canal ray *n. Physics.* a stream of positive ions produced in a discharge tube by allowing them to pass through holes in the cathode.
canapé (ˈkænəpɪ, -ˌpeɪ; *French* kanape) *n.* **1.** a small piece of bread, toast, etc., spread with a savoury topping. **2.** (in French cabinetwork) a sofa. [C19: from French: sofa]
canard (kæˈnɑːd; *French* kanar) *n.* **1.** a false report; rumour or hoax. **2.** an aircraft in which the tailplane is mounted in front of the wing. [C19: from French: a duck, hoax, from Old French *caner* to quack, of imitative origin]
Canarese (ˌkænəˈriːz) *n., pl.* **-rese,** *adj.* a variant spelling of **Kanarese.**
canary (kəˈnɛərɪ) *n., pl.* **-naries. 1.** a small finch, *Serinus canaria,* of the Canary Islands and Azores: a popular cagebird noted for its singing. Wild canaries are streaked yellow and brown, but most domestic breeds are pure yellow. **2.** See **canary yellow. 3.** *Austral.* (formerly) a convict. **4.** *Archaic.* a sweet wine from the Canary Islands similar to Madeira. [C16: from Old Spanish *canario* of or from the *Canary* Islands, off the NW coast of Africa]
canary creeper *n.* a climbing plant, *Tropaeolum peregrinum,* similar to the nasturtium but with smaller yellow flowers and lobed leaves.
canary grass *n.* **1.** any of various grasses of the genus *Phalaris,* esp. *P. canariensis,* that is native to Europe and N Africa and has straw-coloured seeds used as birdseed. **2. reed canary grass.** a related plant, *Phalaris arundinacea,* used as fodder throughout the N hemisphere.
canary seed *n.* another name for **birdseed.**
canary yellow *n.* **a.** a moderate yellow colour, sometimes with a greenish tinge. **b.** *(as adj.): a canary-yellow car.* Sometimes shortened to **canary.**
canasta (kəˈnæstə) *n.* **1.** a card game for two to six players who seek to amass points by declaring sets of cards. **2.** Also called: **meld.** a declared set in this game, containing seven or more like cards, worth 500 points if the canasta is pure or 300 if wild (containing up to three jokers). [C20: from Spanish: basket (because two packs, or a basketful, of cards are required), variant of *canastro,* from Latin *canistrum;* see CANISTER]
canaster (ˈkænəstə) *n.* coarsely broken dried tobacco leaves. [C19: (meaning: rush basket in which tobacco was packed): from Spanish *canastro;* see CANISTER]
can buoy *n.* a buoy with a flat-topped cylindrical shape above water. Compare **nun buoy.**
canc. *abbrev. for:* **1.** cancelled. **2.** cancellation.
cancan (ˈkænˌkæn) *n.* a high-kicking dance performed by a female chorus, originating in the music halls of 19th-century Paris. [C19: from French, of uncertain origin]
cancel (ˈkænsᵊl) *vb.* **-cels, -celling, -celled** *or U.S.* **-cels, -celing, -celed.** *(mainly tr.)* **1.** to order (something already arranged, such as a meeting or event) to be postponed indefinitely; call off. **2.** to revoke or annul: *the order for the new television set was cancelled.* **3.** to delete (writing, numbers, etc.); cross out: *he cancelled his name and substituted hers.* **4.** to mark (a cheque, postage stamp, ticket, etc.) with an official stamp or by a perforation to prevent further use. **5.** *(also intr.; usually foll. by out)* to counterbalance; make up for (a deficiency, etc.): *his generosity cancelled out his past unkindness.* **6. a.** to close (an account) by discharging any outstanding debts. **b.** (sometimes foll. by *out*)

Accounting. to eliminate (a debit or credit) by making an offsetting entry on the opposite side of the account. **7.** *Maths.* **a.** to eliminate (numbers, quantities, or terms) as common factors from both the numerator and denominator of a fraction or as equal terms from opposite sides of an equation. **b.** (*intr.*) to be able to be eliminated in this way. ~*n.* **8.** a new leaf or section of a book replacing a defective one, one containing errors, or one that has been omitted. **9.** a less common word for **cancellation. 10.** *Music.* a U.S. word for **natural** (sense 19a). [C14: from Old French *canceller,* from Medieval Latin *cancellāre,* from Late Latin: to strike out, make like a lattice, from Latin *cancellī* lattice, grating] —'**canceller** *or U.S.* '**canceler** *n.*

cancellate ('kænsɪˌleɪt), **cancellous** ('kænsɪləs), *or* **cancellated** *adj.* **1.** *Anatomy.* having a spongy or porous internal structure: *cancellate bones.* **2.** *Botany.* forming a network; reticulate: *a cancellate venation.* [C17: from Latin *cancellāre* to make like a lattice; see CANCEL]

cancellation (ˌkænsɪ'leɪʃən) *n.* **1.** the fact or an instance of cancelling. **2.** something that has been cancelled, such as a theatre ticket, esp. when it is available for another person to take: *we have a cancellation in the stalls.* **3.** the marks or perforation made by cancelling.

cancer ('kænsə) *n.* **1.** any type of malignant growth or tumour, caused by abnormal and uncontrolled cell division: it may spread through the lymphatic system or blood stream to other parts of the body. **2.** the condition resulting from this. **3.** an evil influence that spreads dangerously. [C14: from Latin: crab, a creeping tumour; related to Greek *karkinos* crab, Sanskrit *karkata*] —'**cancerous** *adj.* —'**cancerously** *adv.*

Cancer ('kænsə) *n., Latin genitive* **Cancri** ('kæŋkriː). **1.** *Astronomy.* a small faint zodiacal constellation in the N hemisphere, lying between Leo and Gemini on the ecliptic and containing the star cluster Praesepe. **2.** *Astrology.* **a.** Also called: the **Crab.** the fourth sign of the zodiac, symbol ♋, having a cardinal water classification and ruled by the moon. The sun is in this sign between about June 21 and July 22. **b.** a person born during a period when the sun is in this sign. **3. tropic of Cancer.** See **tropic** (sense 1). ~*adj.* **4.** *Astrology.* born under or characteristic of Cancer. ~Also (for senses 2b, 4): **Cancerian** (kæn'sɪərɪən).

cancerophobia (ˌkænsərəʊ'fəʊbɪə) *n.* a morbid dread of being afflicted by cancer.

cancer stick *n.* a slang name for **cigarette.**

cancrizans ('kænkrɪˌzæns, 'kæŋ-) *adj.* See **crab canon.** [Medieval Latin: moving backwards, from *cancrizāre* to move crabwise]

cancroid ('kæŋkrɔɪd) *adj.* **1.** resembling a cancerous growth. **2.** resembling a crab. ~*n.* **3.** a skin cancer, esp. one of only moderate malignancy.

c & b *Cricket. abbrev. for* caught and bowled (by).

candela (kæn'diːlə, -'deɪlə) *n.* the basic SI unit of luminous intensity; the luminous intensity in a given direction of a source that emits monochromatic radiation of frequency 540 × 10^{12} hertz and that has a radiant intensity in that direction of (1/683) watt per steradian. Symbol: cd Also called: **candle, standard candle.** [C20: from Latin: CANDLE]

candelabrum (ˌkændɪ'lɑːbrəm) *or* **candelabra** *n., pl.* **-bra** (-brə), **-brums,** *or* **-bras.** a large branched candleholder or holder for overhead lights. [C19: from Latin, from *candēla* CANDLE]

candent ('kændənt) *adj.* an archaic word for **incandescent.** [C16: from Latin *candēre* to shine]

candescent (kæn'dɛsᵊnt) *adj. Rare.* glowing or starting to glow with heat. [C19: from Latin *candescere,* from *candēre* to be white, shine] —**can'descence** *n.* —**can'descently** *adv.*

c & f *abbrev. for* cost and freight.

C & G *abbrev. for* City and Guilds.

candid ('kændɪd) *adj.* **1.** frank and outspoken: *he was candid about his dislike of our friends.* **2.** without partiality; unbiased. **3.** unposed or informal: *a candid photograph.* **4.** *Obsolete.* **a.** white. **b.** clear or pure. [C17: from Latin *candidus* white, from *candēre* to be white] —'**candidly** *adv.* —'**candidness** *n.*

candida ('kændɪdə) *n.* any yeastlike parasitic fungus of the genus *Candida,* esp. *C. albicans,* which causes thrush (**candidiasis**). [New Latin, feminine of *candidus* white]

candidate ('kændɪˌdeɪt, -dɪt) *n.* **1.** a person seeking or nominated for election to a position of authority or honour or selection for a job, promotion, etc. **2.** a person taking an examination or test. **3.** a person or thing regarded as suitable or likely for a particular fate or position: *this wine is a candidate for his cellar.* [C17: from Latin *candidātus* clothed in white (because the candidate wore a white toga), from *candidus* white] —**candidacy** ('kændɪdəsɪ) *or* **candidature** ('kændɪdətʃə) *n.*

candid camera *n.* **a.** a small camera that may be used to take informal photographs of people, usually without their knowledge. **b.** (*as modifier*): *a candid-camera photograph.*

candied ('kændɪd) *adj.* **1.** impregnated or encrusted with or as if with sugar or syrup: *candied peel.* **2.** (of sugar, honey, etc.) crystallized.

Candiot ('kændɪˌɒt) *or* **Candiote** ('kændɪˌəʊt) *adj.* **1.** of or relating to Crete; Cretan. ~*n.* **2.** a native or inhabitant of Crete; a Cretan. [from Italian *Candia* (Crete)]

candle ('kændᵊl) *n.* **1.** a cylindrical piece of wax, tallow, or other fatty substance surrounding a wick, which is burned to produce light. **2.** *Physics.* **a.** see **international candle. b.** another name for **candela. 3. burn the candle at both ends.** to exhaust oneself, esp. by being up late and getting up early to work. **4. not hold a candle to.** *Informal.* to be inferior or contemptible in comparison with: *your dog doesn't hold a candle to mine.* **5. not worth the candle.** *Informal.* not worth the price or trouble entailed (esp. in the phrase **the game's not worth the candle**). ~*vb.* **6.** (*tr.*) to examine (eggs) for freshness or the likelihood of being hatched by viewing them against a bright light. [Old English *candel,* from Latin *candēla,* from *candēre* to be white, glitter] —'**candler** *n.*

candleberry ('kændᵊlbərɪ) *n., pl.* **-ries.** another name for **wax myrtle.**

candlefish ('kændᵊlˌfɪʃ) *n., pl.* **-fish** *or* **-fishes.** a salmonoid food fish, *Thaleichthys pacificus,* that occurs in the N Pacific and has oily flesh. Also called: **eulachon.**

candlelight ('kændᵊlˌlaɪt) *n.* **1. a.** the light from a candle or candles: *they ate by candlelight.* **b.** (*as modifier*): *a candlelight dinner.* **2.** dusk; evening.

Candlemas ('kændᵊlməs) *n. Christianity.* Feb. 2, the Feast of the Purification of the Virgin Mary and the presentation of Christ in the Temple: the day on which the church candles are blessed. In Scotland it is one of the four quarter days.

candlenut ('kændᵊlˌnʌt) *n.* **1.** a euphorbiaceous tree, *Aleurites mollucana,* of tropical Asia and Polynesia. **2.** the nut of this tree, which yields an oil used in paints and varnishes. In their native regions the nuts are strung together and burned as candles.

candlepin ('kændᵊlˌpɪn) *n.* a bowling pin, as used in skittles, tenpin bowling, candlepins, etc.

candlepins ('kændᵊlˌpɪnz) *n.* (*functioning as sing.*) a type of bowling game, employing a smaller ball than tenpins, in which three balls are allowed to a frame and fallen pins are not removed from the alley.

candlepower ('kændᵊlˌpaʊə) *n.* the luminous intensity of a source of light in a given direction: now expressed in candelas but formerly in terms of the international candle.

candlestick ('kændᵊlˌstɪk) *or* **candleholder** ('kændᵊlˌhəʊldə) *n.* a holder, usually ornamental, with a spike or socket for a candle.

candle-tree *n.* another name for **wax myrtle.**

candlewick ('kændᵊlˌwɪk) *n.* **1.** unbleached cotton or muslin into which loops of yarn are hooked and then cut to give a tufted pattern. It is used for bedspreads, dressing gowns, etc. **2.** the wick of a candle. **3.** (*modifier*) being or made of candlewick fabric.

candlewood ('kændᵊlˌwʊd) *n.* **1.** the resinous wood of any of several trees, used for torches and candle substitutes. **2.** any tree or shrub, such as ocotillo, that produces this wood.

C & M *abbrev. for* care and maintenance.

candour *or U.S.* **candor** ('kændə) *n.* **1.** the quality of being open and honest; frankness. **2.** fairness; impartiality. **3.** *Obsolete.* purity or brightness. [C17: from Latin *candor,* from *candēre* to be white, shine]

C &W *abbrev. for* country and western.

candy ('kændɪ) *n., pl.* **-dies. 1.** *Chiefly U.S. and Canadian.* confectionery in general; sweets, chocolate, etc. ~*vb.* **-dies, -dying, -died. 2.** to cause (sugar, etc.) to become crystalline, esp. by boiling or (of sugar) to become crystalline through boiling. **3.** to preserve (fruit peel, ginger, etc.) by boiling in sugar. **4.** to cover with any crystalline substance, such as ice or sugar. [C18: from Old French *sucre candi* candied sugar, from Arabic *qandi* candied, from *qand* cane sugar, of Dravidian origin]

candyfloss ('kændɪˌflɒs) *n. Brit.* a very light fluffy confection made from coloured spun sugar, usually held on a stick. U.S. and Canadian name: **cotton candy.** Austral. name: **fairyfloss.**

candy store *n.* a U.S. and Canadian term for **sweet shop.**

candy-striped *adj.* (esp. of clothing fabric) having narrow coloured stripes on a white background. —**candy stripe** *n.*

candytuft ('kændɪˌtʌft) *n.* either of two species of *Iberis* grown as annual garden plants for their umbels ("tufts") of white, red, or purplish flowers. See **iberis.** [C17: from *Candy,* obsolete variant of *Candia* (Crete) + TUFT]

cane[1] (keɪn) *n.* **1. a.** the long jointed pithy or hollow flexible stem of the bamboo, rattan, or any similar plant. **b.** any plant having such a stem. **2. a.** strips of such stems, woven or interlaced to make wickerwork, the seats and backs of chairs, etc. **b.** (*as modifier*): *a cane chair.* **3.** the woody stem of a reed, young grapevine, blackberry, raspberry, or loganberry. **4.** any of several grasses with long stiff stems, esp. *Arundinaria gigantea* of the southeastern U.S. **5.** a flexible rod with which to administer a beating as a punishment, as to schoolboys. **6.** a slender rod, usually wooden and often ornamental, used for support when walking; walking stick. **7.** see **sugar cane. 8.** a slender rod or cylinder, as of glass. ~*vb.* (*tr.*) **9.** to whip or beat with or as if with a cane. **10.** to make or repair with cane. **11.** *Informal.* to defeat: *we got well caned in the match.* [C14: from Old French, from Latin *canna,* from Greek *kanna,* of Semitic origin; related to Arabic *qanāh* reed] —'**caner** *n.*

cane[2] (keɪn) *n. Dialect.* a female weasel. [C18: of unknown origin]

canebrake ('keɪnˌbreɪk) *n. U.S.* a thicket of canes.

cane grass *n. Austral.* any of several tall perennial hard-stemmed grasses, esp. *Eragrostis australasica,* of inland swamps.
canella (kəˈnɛlə) *n.* the fragrant cinnamon-like inner bark of a West Indian tree, *Canella winterana* (family *Canellaceae*) used as a spice and in medicine. [C17: from Medieval Latin: cinnamon, from Latin *canna* cane, reed]
cane piece *n.* (in the Caribbean) a field of sugar cane, esp. a peasant's isolated field.
cane rat *n.* **1.** Also called (in W Africa): **cutting grass.** a tropical African cavy-like hystricomorph rodent, *Thryonomys swinderianus,* that lives in swampy regions: family *Thryonomyidae.* **2.** a similar but smaller species, *T. gregorianus.*
canescent (kəˈnɛsənt) *adj.* **1.** *Biology.* white or greyish due to the presence of numerous short white hairs. **2.** becoming hoary, white, or greyish. [C19: from Latin *cānescere* to grow white, become hoary, from *cānēre* to be white] —**caˈnescence** *n.*
cane sugar *n.* **1.** the sucrose obtained from sugar cane, which is identical to that obtained from sugar beet. See also **beet sugar.** **2.** another name for **sucrose.**
Canes Venatici (ˈkɑːniːz vɪˈnætɪˌsaɪ) *n., Latin genitive* **Canum Venaticorum** (ˈkɑːnəm vɪˌnætɪˈkɔːrəm). a small faint constellation in the N hemisphere near Ursa Major that contains the globular cluster M3 and the spiral galaxy M51. [Latin: hunting dogs]
canfield (ˈkænˌfiːld) *n. Cards.* a gambling game adapted from a type of patience. [C20: named after R. A. *Canfield* (1855–1914), U.S. gambler]
cangue *or* **cang** (kæŋ) *n.* (formerly in China) a large wooden collar worn by petty criminals as a punishment. [C18: from French, from Portuguese *canga* yoke]
Canicula (kəˈnɪkjʊlə) *n.* another name for **Sirius.** [Latin, literally: little dog, from *canis* dog]
canicular (kəˈnɪkjʊlə) *adj.* of or relating to the star Sirius or its rising.
canikin (ˈkænɪkɪn) *n.* a variant spelling of **cannikin.**
canine (ˈkeɪnaɪn, ˈkæn-) *adj.* **1.** of or resembling a dog; doglike. **2.** of, relating to, or belonging to the *Canidae,* a family of mammals, including dogs, jackals, wolves, and foxes, typically having a bushy tail, erect ears, and a long muzzle: order *Carnivora* (carnivores). **3.** of or relating to any of the four teeth, two in each jaw, situated between the incisors and the premolars. ~ν. αλσο **canid** (ˈkænɪd). **4.** any animal of the family *Canidae.* **5.** a canine tooth. [C17: from Latin *canīnus,* from *canis* dog]
canine distemper *n.* See **distemper**[1].
caning (ˈkeɪnɪŋ) *n.* **1.** a beating with a cane as a punishment. **2.** *Informal.* a severe defeat.
Canis Major (ˈkeɪnɪs) *n., Latin genitive* **Canis Majoris** (məˈdʒɔːrɪs). a constellation in the S hemisphere close to Orion, containing Sirius, the brightest star in the sky. Also called: the **Great Dog.** [Latin: the greater dog]
Canis Minor *n., Latin genitive* **Canis Minoris** (maɪˈnɔːrɪs). a small constellation in the N hemisphere close to Orion, containing the first magnitude star Procyon. Also called: the **Little Dog.** [Latin: the lesser dog]
canister (ˈkænɪstə) *n.* **1.** a container, usually made of metal, in which dry food, such as tea or coffee, is stored. **2.** (formerly) **a.** a type of shrapnel shell for firing from a cannon. **b.** Also called: **canister shot, case shot.** the shot or shrapnel packed inside this. [C17: from Latin *canistrum* basket woven from reeds, from Greek *kanastron,* from *kanna* reed, CANE[1]]
canker (ˈkæŋkə) *n.* **1.** an ulceration, esp. of the lips or lining of the oral cavity. **2.** *Vet. science.* **a.** a disease of horses in which the horn of the hoofs becomes soft and spongy. **b.** an ulcerative disease of the lining of the external ear, esp. in dogs and cats. **c.** ulceration or abscess of the mouth, eyelids, ears, or cloaca of birds. **3.** an open wound in the stem of a tree or shrub, caused by injury or parasites. **4.** something evil that spreads and corrupts. ~*vb.* **5.** to infect or become infected with or as if with canker. [Old English *cancer,* from Latin *cancer* crab, cancerous sore]
cankerous (ˈkæŋkərəs) *adj.* **1.** having cankers. **2.** infectious; corrupting.
cankerworm (ˈkæŋkəˌwɜːm) *n.* the larva of either of two geometrid moths, *Paleacrita vernata* or *Alsophila pometaria,* which feed on and destroy fruit and shade trees in North America.
canna (ˈkænə) *n.* any of various tropical plants constituting the genus *Canna,* having broad leaves and red or yellow showy flowers for which they are cultivated: family *Cannaceae.* [C17: from New Latin CANE[1]]
cannabin (ˈkænəbɪn) *n.* a greenish-black poisonous resin obtained from the hemp plant and thought to be the active narcotic principle. Also called: **cannabis resin.**
cannabis (ˈkænəbɪs) *n.* **1.** another name for **hemp** (the plant), esp. Indian hemp (*Cannabis indica*). **2.** the drug obtained from the dried leaves and flowers of the hemp plant, which is smoked or chewed for its psychoactive properties. It produces euphoria and relaxation; repeated use may lead to psychological dependence. See also **cannabin, hashish, marijuana, bhang.** [C18: from Latin, from Greek *kannabis;* see HEMP] —**ˈcannabic** *adj.*
canned (kænd) *adj.* **1.** preserved and stored in airtight cans or tins: *canned meat.* **2.** *Informal.* prepared or recorded in advance; artificial; not spontaneous: *canned music.* **3.** a slang word for **drunk** (sense 1).
cannel coal *or* **cannel** (ˈkænəl) *n.* a dull coal having a high volatile content and burning with a smoky luminous flame. [C16: from northern English dialect *cannel* candle: so called from its bright flame]
cannelloni *or* **canneloni** (ˌkænɪˈləʊnɪ) *pl. n.* tubular pieces of pasta filled with meat or cheese. [Italian, plural of *cannellone,* from *cannello* stalk, from *canna* CANE[1]]
cannelure (ˈkænəˌlʊə) *n.* a groove or fluting, esp. one around the cylindrical part of a bullet. [C18: from French, ultimately from Latin *canālis* CANAL]
canner (ˈkænə) *n.* a person or organization whose job is to can foods.
cannery (ˈkænərɪ) *n., pl.* **-neries.** a place where foods are canned.
cannibal (ˈkænɪbəl) *n.* **1. a.** a person who eats the flesh of other human beings. **b.** (*as modifier*): *cannibal tribes.* **2.** an animal that feeds on the flesh of others of its kind. [C16: from Spanish *Canibales,* name used by Columbus (1451–1506) to designate the Caribs of Cuba and Haiti, from Arawak *caniba,* variant of CARIB]
cannibalism (ˈkænɪbəˌlɪzəm) *n.* **1.** the act of eating human flesh or the flesh of one's own kind. **2.** savage and inhuman cruelty. —**ˌcannibalˈistic** *adj.* —**ˌcannibalˈistically** *adv.*
cannibalize *or* **cannibalise** (ˈkænɪbəˌlaɪz) *vb.* (*tr.*) to use (serviceable parts from one machine or vehicle) to repair another, esp. as an alternative to using new parts. —**ˌcannibaliˈzation** *or* **ˌcannibaliˈsation** *n.*
cannikin, canakin, *or* **canikin** (ˈkænɪkɪn) *n.* a small can, esp. one used as a drinking vessel. [C16: from Middle Dutch *kanneken;* see CAN[2], -KIN]
canning (ˈkænɪŋ) *n.* the process or business of sealing food in cans or tins to preserve it.
cannon (ˈkænən) *n., pl.* **-nons** *or* **-non.** **1.** an automatic aircraft gun of large calibre. **2.** *History.* a heavy artillery piece consisting of a metal tube mounted on a carriage. **3.** a heavy tube or drum, esp. one that can rotate freely on the shaft by which it is supported. **4.** the metal loop at the top of a bell, from which it is suspended. **5.** See **cannon bone.** **6.** *Billiards.* **a.** a shot in which the cue ball is caused to contact one object ball after another. **b.** the points scored by this. Usual U.S. and Canadian word: **carom.** **7.** a rebound or bouncing back, as of a ball off a wall. **8.** either of the two parts of a vambrace. ~*vb.* **9.** (*intr.;* often foll. by *into*) to collide (with). **10.** short for **cannonade.** **11.** (*intr.*) *Billiards.* to make a cannon. [C16: from Old French *canon,* from Italian *cannone* cannon, large tube, from *canna* tube, CANE[1]]
cannonade (ˌkænəˈneɪd) *n.* **1.** an intense and continuous artillery bombardment. ~*vb.* **2.** to attack (a target) with cannon.
cannonball (ˈkænənˌbɔːl) *n.* **1.** a projectile fired from a cannon: usually a solid round metal shot. **2.** *Tennis.* **a.** a very fast low serve. **b.** (*as modifier*): *a cannonball serve.* **3.** a jump into water by a person who has his arms tucked into the body to form a ball. ~*vb.* (*intr.*) **4.** (often foll. by *along,* etc.) to rush along, like a cannonball. **5.** to execute a cannonball jump. ~*adj.* **6.** very fast or powerful.
cannon bone *n.* a bone in the legs of horses and other hoofed animals consisting of greatly elongated fused metatarsals or metacarpals.
cannoneer (ˌkænəˈnɪə) *n.* (formerly) a soldier who served and fired a cannon; artilleryman.
cannon fodder *n.* men regarded as expendable because they are part of a huge army.
cannonry (ˈkænənrɪ) *n., pl.* **-ries.** *Rare.* **1.** a volley of artillery fire. **2.** artillery in general.
cannot (ˈkænɒt, kæˈnɒt) *vb.* an auxiliary verb expressing incapacity, inability, withholding permission, etc.; can not.
cannula *or* **canula** (ˈkænjʊlə) *n., pl.* **-las** *or* **-lae** (-ˌliː). *Surgery.* a narrow tube for insertion into a bodily cavity, as for draining off fluid, introducing medication, etc. [C17: from Latin: a small reed, from *canna* a reed]
cannulate *or* **canulate** *vb.* (ˈkænjʊˌleɪt). **1.** to insert a cannula into. ~*adj.* (ˈkænjʊˌleɪt, -ˌlɪt), *also* **cannular** *or* **canular.** **2.** shaped like a cannula. —**ˌcannuˈlation** *or* **ˌcanuˈlation** *n.*
canny (ˈkænɪ) *adj.* **-nier, -niest.** **1.** shrewd, esp. in business; astute or wary; knowing. **2.** *Scot. and northeast English dialect.* good or nice: used as a general term of approval. **3.** *Scot.* lucky or fortunate. ~*adv.* **4.** *Scot. and northeast English dialect.* quite; rather: *a canny long while.* [C16: from CAN[1] (in the sense: to know how) + -Y[1]] —**ˈcannily** *adv.* —**ˈcanniness** *n.*
canoe (kəˈnuː) *n.* **1.** a light narrow open boat, propelled by one or more paddles. **2. in the same canoe.** *N.Z.* of the same tribe. ~*vb.* **-noes, -noeing, -noed.** **3.** to go in a canoe or transport by canoe. [C16: from Spanish *canoa,* of Carib origin] —**caˈnoeist** *n.*
canoewood (kəˈnuːˌwʊd) *n.* another name for the **tulip tree.**
canon[1] (ˈkænən) *n.* **1.** *Christianity.* a Church decree enacted to regulate morals or religious practices. **2.** (*often pl.*) a general rule or standard, as of judgment, morals, etc. **3.** (*often pl.*) a principle or accepted criterion applied in a branch of learning or art. **4.** *R.C. Church.* the complete list of the canonized saints. **5.** *R.C. Church.* the prayer in the Mass in which the Host is consecrated. **6.** a list of writings, esp. sacred writings, officially recognized as genuine. **7.** a piece of music in which an extended

melody in one part is imitated successively in one or more other parts. See also **round** (sense 31), **catch** (sense 33). **8.** a list of the works of an author that are accepted as authentic. **9.** (formerly) a size of printer's type equal to 48 point. [Old English, from Latin, from Greek *kanōn* rule, rod for measuring, standard; related to *kanna* reed, CANE[1]]

canon[2] ('kænən) *n.* **1.** one of several priests on the permanent staff of a cathedral, who are responsible for organizing services, maintaining the fabric, etc. **2.** *R.C. Church.* Also called: **canon regular.** a member of either of two religious orders, the Augustinian or Premonstratensian Canons, living communally as monks but performing clerical duties. [C13: from Anglo-French *canunie*, from Late Latin *canonicus* one living under a rule, from CANON[1]]

cañon ('kænjən) *n.* a variant spelling of **canyon.**

canoness ('kænənɪs) *n. R.C. Church.* a woman belonging to any one of several religious orders and living under a rule but not under a vow.

canonical (kə'nɒnɪk[ə]l) *or* **canonic** *adj.* **1.** belonging to or included in a canon of sacred or other officially recognized writings. **2.** belonging to or in conformity with canon law. **3.** according to recognized law; accepted. **4.** *Music.* in the form of a canon. **5.** of or relating to a cathedral chapter. **6.** of or relating to a canon (clergyman). —**ca'nonically** *adv.*

canonical hour *n.* **1.** *R.C. Church.* **a.** one of the seven prayer times appointed for each day by canon law. **b.** the services prescribed for these times, namely matins, prime, terce, sext, nones, vespers, and compline. **2.** *Church of England.* any time between 8:00 a.m. and 6:00 p.m. at which marriages may lawfully be celebrated.

canonicals (kə'nɒnɪk[ə]lz) *pl. n.* the vestments worn by clergy when officiating.

canonicate (kə'nɒnɪˌkeɪt, -kɪt) *n.* the office or rank of a canon; canonry.

canonicity (ˌkænə'nɪsɪtɪ) *n.* the fact or quality of being canonical.

canonist ('kænənɪst) *n.* a specialist in canon law.

canonize *or* **canonise** ('kænəˌnaɪz) *vb.* (*tr.*) **1.** *R.C. Church.* to declare (a person) to be a saint and thus admit to the canon of saints. **2.** to regard as holy or as a saint. **3.** to sanction by canon law; pronounce valid. —ˌ**canoni'zation** *or* ˌ**canoni'sation** *n.*

canon law *n.* the law governing the affairs of a Christian Church, esp. the law created or recognized by papal authority in the Roman Catholic Church.

canonry ('kænənrɪ) *n., pl.* **-ries.** **1.** the office, benefice, or status of a canon. **2.** canons collectively. [C15: from CANON[2] + -RY]

canoodle (kə'nuːd[ə]l) *vb.* (*intr.*; often foll. by *with*) *Slang.* to kiss and cuddle; pet; fondle. [C19: of unknown origin] —**ca'noodler** *n.*

can-opener *n.* another name for **tin-opener.**

Canopic jar, urn, *or* **vase** (kə'nəʊpɪk) *n.* (in ancient Egypt) one of four containers with tops in the form of animal heads of the gods, for holding the entrails of a mummy. [from *Canopus*, a port in ancient Egypt]

Canopus (kə'nəʊpəs) *n.* the brightest star in the constellation Carina and the second brightest star in the sky. Visual magnitude: -0.7; spectral type: F0; distance: 110 light years.

canopy ('kænəpɪ) *n., pl.* **-pies.** **1.** an ornamental awning above a throne or bed or held over a person of importance on ceremonial occasions. **2.** a rooflike covering over an altar, niche, etc. **3.** a roofed structure serving as a sheltered passageway or area. **4.** a large or wide covering, esp. one high above: *the sky was a grey canopy.* **5.** the nylon or silk hemisphere that forms the supporting surface of a parachute. **6.** the transparent cover of an aircraft cockpit. **7.** the highest level of branches and foliage in a forest, formed by the crowns of the trees. ~*vb.* **-pies, -pying, -pied.** **8.** (*tr.*) to cover with or as if with a canopy. [C14: from Medieval Latin *canōpeum* mosquito net, from Latin *cōnōpeum* gauze net, from Greek *kōnōpeion* bed with protective net, from *kōnōps* mosquito]

canorous (kə'nɔːrəs) *adj. Rare.* tuneful; melodious. [C17: from Latin *canōrus*, from *canere* to sing] —**ca'norously** *adv.* —**ca'norousness** *n.*

cans (kænz) *pl. n.* an informal name for **headphones.**

canst (kænst) *vb. Archaic.* the form of **can**[1] used with the pronoun *thou* or its relative form.

cant[1] (kænt) *n.* **1.** insincere talk, esp. concerning religion or morals; pious platitudes. **2.** stock phrases that have become meaningless through repetition. **3.** specialized vocabulary of a particular group, such as thieves, journalists, or lawyers; jargon. **4.** singsong whining speech, as used by beggars. ~*vb.* **5.** (*intr.*) to speak in or use cant. [C16: probably via Norman French *canter* to sing, from Latin *cantāre*; used disparagingly, from the 12th century, of chanting in religious services] —**'canter** *n.* —**'cantingly** *adv.*

cant[2] (kænt) *n.* **1.** inclination from a vertical or horizontal plane; slope; slant. **2.** a sudden movement that tilts or turns something. **3.** the angle or tilt thus caused. **4.** a corner or outer angle, esp. of a building. **5.** an oblique or slanting surface, edge, or line. ~*vb.* (*tr.*) **6.** to tip, tilt, or overturn, esp. with a sudden jerk. **7.** to set in an oblique position. **8.** another word for **bevel** (sense 1). ~*adj.* **9.** oblique; slanting. **10.** having flat surfaces and without curves. [C14 (in the sense: edge, corner): perhaps from Latin *canthus* iron hoop round a wheel, of obscure origin] —**'cantic** *adj.*

cant[3] (kɑːnt) *adj. Scot. and northern English dialect.* lusty; merry; hearty. [C14: related to Low German *kant* bold, merry]

Cant. *abbrev. for:* **1.** Canterbury. **2.** *Bible.* Canticles.

can't (kɑːnt) *vb. contraction of* cannot.

Cantab. (kæn'tæb) *abbrev. for* Cantabrigiensis. [Latin: of Cambridge]

cantabile (kæn'tɑːbɪlɪ) *Music.* ~*adj., adv.* **1.** (to be performed) in a singing style, i.e. flowingly and melodiously. ~*n.* **2.** a piece or passage performed in this way. [Italian, from Late Latin *cantābilis*, from Latin *cantāre* to sing]

Cantabrigian (ˌkæntə'brɪdʒɪən) *adj.* **1.** of, relating to, or characteristic of Cambridge or Cambridge University, or of Cambridge, Massachusetts, or Harvard University. ~*n.* **2.** a member or graduate of Cambridge University or Harvard University. **3.** an inhabitant or native of Cambridge. [C17: from Medieval Latin *Cantabrigia*]

Cantal (*French* kɑ̃tal) *n.* a hard strong cheese made in the region of Cantal in the Auvergne, central France.

cantala (kæn'tɑːlə) *n.* **1.** a tropical American plant, *Agave cantala*, similar to the century plant: family *Agavaceae* (agaves). **2.** the coarse tough fibre of this plant, used in making twine. [of unknown origin]

cantaloupe *or* **cantaloup** ('kæntəˌluːp) *n.* **1.** a cultivated variety of muskmelon, *Cucumis melo cantalupensis*, with ribbed warty rind and orange flesh. **2.** any of several other muskmelons. [C18: from French, from *Cantaluppi*, former papal villa near Rome, where it was first cultivated in Europe]

cantankerous (kæn'tæŋkərəs) *adj.* quarrelsome; irascible. [C18: perhaps from C14 (obsolete) *conteckour* a contentious person, from *conteck* strife, from Anglo-French *contek*, of obscure origin] —**can'tankerously** *adv.* —**can'tankerousness** *n.*

cantata (kæn'tɑːtə) *n.* a musical setting of a text, esp. a religious text, consisting of arias, duets, and choruses interspersed with recitatives. [C18: from Italian, from *cantare* to sing, from Latin]

cantatrice (*French* kɑ̃tatris) *n.* a female singer, esp. a professional soloist.

canteen (kæn'tiːn) *n.* **1.** a restaurant attached to a factory, school, etc., providing meals for large numbers of people. **2.** **a.** a small shop that provides a limited range of items, such as toilet requisites, to a military unit. **b.** a recreation centre for military personnel. **3.** a soldier's eating and drinking utensils. **4.** a temporary or mobile stand at which food is provided. **5.** **a.** a box in which a set of cutlery is laid out. **b.** the cutlery itself. **6.** a flask or canister for carrying water or other liquids, as used by soldiers or travellers. [C18: from French *cantine*, from Italian *cantina* wine cellar, from *canto* corner, from Latin *canthus* iron hoop encircling chariot wheel; see CANT[2]]

canter ('kæntə) *n.* **1.** an easy three-beat gait of horses, etc., between a trot and a gallop in speed. **2.** **at a canter.** easily; without effort: *he won at a canter.* ~*vb.* **3.** to move or cause to move at a canter. [C18: short for *Canterbury trot*, the supposed pace at which pilgrims rode to Canterbury]

canterbury ('kæntəbərɪ, -brɪ) *n. Antiques.* **1.** a late 18th-century low wooden stand with partitions for holding cutlery and plates: often mounted on casters. **2.** a similar 19th-century stand used for holding sheet music, music books, or magazines.

Canterbury bell ('kæntəbərɪ, -brɪ) *n.* a campanulaceous biennial European plant, *Campanula medium*, widely cultivated for its blue, violet, or white flowers.

Canterbury lamb *n.* New Zealand lamb exported chilled or frozen to the United Kingdom.

cantharid ('kænθərɪd) *n.* any beetle of the family *Cantharidae*, having a soft elongated body; though found frequenting flowers, they are carnivorous.

cantharides (kæn'θærɪˌdiːz) *pl. n., sing.* **cantharis** ('kænθərɪs). a diuretic and urogenital stimulant or irritant prepared from the dried bodies of Spanish fly (family *Meloidae*, not *Cantharidae*), once thought to be an aphrodisiac. Also called: **Spanish fly.** [C15: from Latin, plural of *cantharis*, from Greek *kantharis* Spanish fly]

cant hook *or* **dog** *n. Forestry.* a wooden pole with an adjustable hook at one end, used for handling logs.

canthus ('kænθəs) *n., pl.* **-thi** (-ˌθaɪ). the inner or outer corner or angle of the eye, formed by the natural junction of the eyelids. [C17: from New Latin, from Latin: iron tyre] —**'canthal** *adj.*

canticle ('kæntɪk[ə]l) *n.* **1.** a nonmetrical hymn, derived from the Bible and used in the liturgy of certain Christian churches. **2.** a song, poem, or hymn, esp. one that is religious in character. [C13: from Latin *canticulum*, diminutive of *canticus* a song, from *canere* to sing]

cantilena (ˌkæntɪ'leɪnə) *n.* a smooth flowing style in the writing of vocal music. [C18: Italian, from Latin *cantilēna* a song]

cantilever ('kæntɪˌliːvə) *n.* **1.** **a.** a beam, girder, or structural framework that is fixed at one end only. **b.** (*as modifier*): *a cantilever wing.* **2.** a wing or tailplane of an aircraft that has no external bracing or support. **3.** a part of a beam or a structure projecting outwards beyond its support. ~*vb.* **4.** (*tr.*) to construct (a building member, beam, etc.) so that it is fixed at one end only. **5.** (*intr.*) to project like a cantilever. [C17: perhaps from CANT[2] + LEVER]

cantilever bridge *n.* a bridge having spans that are constructed as cantilevers and often a suspended span or spans, each end of which rests on one end of a cantilever span.

cantillate ('kæntɪˌleɪt) *vb.* **1.** to chant (passages of the Hebrew Scriptures) according to the traditional Jewish melody. **2.** to intone or chant. [C19: from Late Latin *cantillāre* to sing softly, from Latin *cantāre* to sing]

cantillation (ˌkæntɪ'leɪʃən) *n.* **1.** the traditional notation representing the various traditional Jewish melodies to which scriptural passages are chanted. **2.** chanting or intonation.

cantina (kæn'tiːnə) *n.* a bar or wine shop, esp. in a Spanish-speaking country. [from Spanish]

canting arms *pl. n. Heraldry.* a coat of arms making visual reference to the surname of its owner.

cantle ('kæntᵊl) *n.* **1.** the back part of a saddle that slopes upwards. **2.** a slice; a broken-off piece. [C14: from Old Northern French *cantel,* from *cant* corner; see CANT²]

canto ('kæntəʊ) *n., pl.* **-tos. 1.** *Music.* **a.** *Archaic.* a melody or song. **b.** another word for **cantus** (sense 2). **2.** a main division of a long poem. [C16: from Italian: song, from Latin *cantus,* from *canere* to sing]

canto fermo ('kæntəʊ 'fɜːməʊ) *or* **cantus firmus** ('kæntəs 'fɜːməs) *n.* **1.** a melody that is the basis to which other parts are added in polyphonic music. **2.** the traditional plainchant as prescribed by use and regulation in the Christian Church. [Italian, from Medieval Latin, literally: fixed song]

canton *n.* ('kæntɒn, kæn'tɒn). **1.** any of the 23 political divisions of Switzerland. **2.** a subdivision of a French arrondissement. **3.** ('kæntən). *Heraldry.* a small square or oblong charge on a shield, usually in the top left corner. *~vb.* **4.** (kæn'tɒn). (*tr.*) to divide into cantons. **5.** (kən'tuːn). (esp. formerly) to allocate accommodation to (military personnel). [C16: from Old French: corner, division, from Italian *cantone,* from *canto* corner, from Latin *canthus* iron rim; see CANT²] —'**cantonal** *adj.*

Canton crepe ('kæntɒn, -tən) *n.* a fine crinkled silk or rayon crepe fabric, slightly heavier than crepe de Chine. [C19: named after *Canton,* a port in SE China, where it was originally made]

Cantonese (ˌkæntə'niːz) *n.* **1.** the Chinese language spoken in Canton, Kwangtung and Kwangsi provinces, Hong Kong, and elsewhere outside China. **2.** (*pl.* **-ese**) a native or inhabitant of Canton or Kwangtung province. *~adj.* **3.** of or relating to Canton, Kwangtung province, or the Chinese language spoken there.

Canton flannel ('kæntɒn, -tən) *n.* another name for **cotton flannel.**

cantonment (kən'tuːnmənt) *n. Military.* (esp. formerly) **1.** a large training camp. **2.** living accommodation, esp. the winter quarters of a campaigning army. **3.** *History.* a permanent military camp in British India.

cantor ('kæntɔː) *n.* **1.** *Judaism.* Also called: **chazan.** a man employed to lead synagogue services, esp. to traditional modes and melodies. **2.** *Christianity.* the leader of the singing in a church choir. [C16: from Latin: singer, from *canere* to sing]

cantorial (kæn'tɔːrɪəl) *adj.* **1.** of or relating to a precentor. **2.** (of part of a choir) on the same side of a cathedral, etc., as the precentor; on the N side of the choir. Compare **decanal.**

cantoris (kæn'tɔːrɪs) *adj.* (in antiphonal music) to be sung by the cantorial side of a choir. Compare **decani.** [Latin: genitive of *cantor* precentor]

Cantor's paradox ('kæntɔːz) *n. Logic.* the paradox derived from the supposition of an all-inclusive universal set, since every set has more subsets than members while every subset of such a universal set would be a member of it. [named after Georg *Cantor* (1845–1918), German mathematician, born in Russia]

cantrip ('kæntrɪp) *Scot.* *~n.* **1.** a magic spell. **2.** (*often pl.*) a mischievous trick. *~adj.* **3.** (of an effect) produced by black magic. [C18: Scottish, of unknown origin]

Cantuar. ('kæntjʊˌɑː) *abbrev. for* Cantuariensis. [Latin: (Archbishop) of Canterbury]

cantus ('kæntəs) *n., pl.* **-tus. 1.** a medieval form of church singing; chant. **2.** Also called: **canto.** the highest part in a piece of choral music. **3.** (in 15th- or 16th-century music) a piece of choral music, usually secular, in polyphonic style. [Latin: song, from *canere* to sing]

canty ('kæntɪ, 'kɑːn-) *adj.* **cantier, cantiest.** *Scot. and northern English dialect.* lively; brisk; in good spirits. [C18: see CANT³] —'**cantily** *adv.* —'**cantiness** *n.*

Canuck (kə'nʌk) *n. U.S. and Canadian informal.* **a.** a Canadian. **b.** (formerly) a French Canadian. [C19: of uncertain origin]

canula ('kænjʊlə) *n., pl.* **-las** *or* **-lae** (-ˌliː). *Surgery.* a variant spelling of **cannula.**

canvas ('kænvəs) *n.* **1. a.** a heavy durable cloth made of cotton, hemp, or jute, used for sails, tents, etc. **b.** (*as modifier*): *a canvas bag.* **2. a.** a piece of canvas or a similar material on which a painting is done, usually in oils. **b.** a painting on this material, esp. in oils. **3.** a tent or tents collectively. **4.** *Nautical.* any cloth of which sails are made. **5.** *Nautical.* the sails of a vessel collectively. **6.** any coarse loosely woven cloth on which embroidery, tapestry, etc., is done. **7.** (preceded by *the*) the floor of a boxing or wrestling ring. **8.** *Rowing.* the tapering covered part at either end of a racing boat, sometimes referred to as a unit of length: *to win by a canvas.* **9. under canvas. a.** in tents. **b.** *Nautical.* with sails unfurled. [C14: from Norman French *canevas,* ultimately from Latin *cannabis* hemp]

canvasback ('kænvəsˌbæk) *n., pl.* **-backs** *or* **-back.** a North American diving duck, *Aythyra valisineria,* the male of which has a white body and reddish-brown head.

canvass ('kænvəs) *vb.* **1.** to solicit votes, orders, advertising, etc., from. **2.** to determine the feelings and opinions of (voters before an election, etc.), esp. by conducting a survey. **3.** to investigate (something) thoroughly, esp. by discussion or debate. **4.** *Chiefly U.S.* to inspect (votes) officially to determine their validity. *~n.* **5.** a solicitation of opinions, votes, sales orders, etc. **6.** close inspection; scrutiny. [C16: probably from obsolete sense of CANVAS (to toss someone in a canvas sheet, hence, to harass, criticize); the development of current senses is unexplained] —'**canvasser** *n.*

canyon *or* **cañon** ('kænjən) *n.* a gorge or ravine, esp. in North America, usually formed by the down-cutting of a river in a dry area where there is insufficient rainfall to erode the sides of the valley. [C19: from Spanish *cañon,* from *caña* tube, from Latin *canna* cane]

canzona (kæn'zəʊnə) *n.* a type of 16th- or 17th-century contrapuntal music, usually for keyboard, lute, or instrumental ensemble. [C19: from Italian, from Latin *cantiō* song, from *canere* to sing]

canzone (kæn'zəʊnɪ) *n., pl.* **-ni** (-nɪ). **1.** a Provençal or Italian lyric, often in praise of love or beauty. **2. a.** a song, usually of a lyrical nature. **b.** (in 16th-century choral music) a polyphonic song from which the madrigal developed. [C16: from Italian: song, from Latin *cantiō,* from *canere* to sing]

canzonetta (ˌkænzə'nɛtə) *or* **canzonet** (ˌkænzə'nɛt) *n.* a short cheerful or lively song, typically of the 16th to 18th centuries. [C16: Italian *canzonetta,* diminutive of CANZONE]

caoutchouc ('kaʊtʃuːk, -tʃʊk; kaʊ'tʃuːk, -'tʃʊk) *n.* another name for **rubber**¹ (sense 1). [C18: from French, from obsolete Spanish *cauchuc,* from Quechua]

cap (kæp) *n.* **1.** a covering for the head, esp. a small close-fitting one made of cloth or knitted. **2.** such a covering serving to identify the wearer's rank, occupation, etc.: *a nurse's cap.* **3.** something that protects or covers, esp. a small lid or cover: *lens cap.* **4.** an uppermost surface or part: *the cap of a wave.* **5. a.** See **percussion cap. b.** a small amount of explosive enclosed in paper and used in a toy gun. **6.** *Sport, chiefly Brit.* **a.** an emblematic hat or beret given to someone chosen for a representative team: *he has won three England caps.* **b.** a player chosen for such a team. **7.** the upper part of a pedestal in a classical order. **8.** the roof of a windmill, sometimes in the form of a dome. **9.** *Botany.* the pileus of a mushroom or toadstool. **10.** *Hunting.* **a.** money contributed to the funds of a hunt by a follower who is neither a subscriber nor a farmer, in return for a day's hunting. **b.** a collection taken at a meet of hounds, esp. for a charity. **11.** *Anatomy.* **a.** the natural enamel covering a tooth. **b.** an artificial protective covering for a tooth. **12.** See **Dutch cap** (sense 2). **13.** a mortarboard when worn with a gown at an academic ceremony (esp. in the phrase **cap and gown**). **14.** *Meteorol.* **a.** the cloud covering the peak of a mountain. **b.** the transient top of detached clouds above an increasing cumulus. **15. set one's cap for** *or* **at.** (of a woman) to be determined to win as a husband or lover. **16. cap in hand.** humbly, as when asking a favour. *~vb.* **caps, capping, capped.** (*tr.*) **17.** to cover, as with a cap: *snow capped the mountain tops.* **18.** *Informal.* to outdo; excel: *your story caps them all; to cap an anecdote.* **19. cap it all.** to provide the finishing touch: *we had sun, surf, cheap wine, and to cap it all a free car.* **20.** *Sport, Brit.* to select (a player) for a representative team: *he was capped 30 times by Scotland.* **21.** to seal off (an oil or gas well). **22.** to impose an upper limit on the level of increase of (a tax, such as the community charge): *charge-capping.* **23.** *Hunting.* to ask (hunt followers) for a cap. **24.** *Chiefly Scot. and N.Z.* to award a degree to. [Old English *cæppe,* from Late Latin *cappa* hood, perhaps from Latin *caput* head] —'**capper** *n.*

CAP *abbrev. for* Common Agricultural Policy: (in the EC) the system for supporting farm incomes by maintaining agricultural prices at agreed levels.

cap. *abbrev. for:* **1.** capacity. **2.** capital. **3.** capitalize. **4.** capital letter. **5.** caput. [Latin: chapter]

capability (ˌkeɪpə'bɪlɪtɪ) *n., pl.* **-ties. 1.** the quality of being capable; ability. **2.** the quality of being susceptible to the use or treatment indicated: *the capability of a metal to be fused.* **3.** (*usually pl.*) a characteristic that may be developed; potential aptitude.

capable ('keɪpəbᵊl) *adj.* **1.** having ability, esp. in many different fields; competent. **2.** (*postpositive;* foll. by *of*) able or having the skill (to do something): *she is capable of hard work.* **3.** (*postpositive;* foll. by *of*) having the temperament or inclination (to do something): *he seemed capable of murder.* [C16: from French, from Late Latin *capābilis* able to take in, from Latin *capere* to take] —'**capableness** *n.* —'**capably** *adv.*

capacious (kə'peɪʃəs) *adj.* capable of holding much; roomy; spacious. [C17: from Latin *capāx,* from Latin *capere* to take] —**ca'paciously** *adv.* —**ca'paciousness** *n.*

capacitance (kə'pæsɪtəns) *n.* **1.** the property of a system that enables it to store electric charge. **2.** a measure of this, equal to the charge that must be added to such a system to raise its electrical potential by one unit. Symbol: *C* Former name:

capacity. [C20: from CAPACIT(Y) + -ANCE] —**ca'pacitive** *adj.* —**ca'pacitively** *adv.*

capacitate (kə'pæsɪˌteɪt) *vb. (tr.)* **1.** to make legally competent. **2.** *Rare.* to make capable. —**caˌpaci'tation** *n.*

capacitor (kə'pæsɪtə) *n.* a device for accumulating electric charge, usually consisting of two conducting surfaces separated by a dielectric. Former name: **condenser.**

capacity (kə'pæsɪtɪ) *n., pl.* **-ties. 1.** the ability or power to contain, absorb, or hold. **2.** the amount that can be contained; volume: *a capacity of six gallons.* **3. a.** the maximum amount something can contain or absorb (esp. in the phrase **filled to capacity**). **b.** (*as modifier*): *a capacity crowd.* **4.** the ability to understand or learn; aptitude; capability: *he has a great capacity for Greek.* **5.** the ability to do or produce (often in the phrase **at capacity**): *the factory's output was not at capacity.* **6.** a specified position or function: *he was employed in the capacity of manager.* **7.** a measure of the electrical output of a piece of apparatus such as a motor, generator, or accumulator. **8.** *Electronics.* a former name for **capacitance. 9.** *Computer technol.* **a.** the number of words or characters that can be stored in a particular storage device. **b.** the range of numbers that can be processed in a register. **10.** legal competence: *the capacity to make a will.* [C15: from Old French *capacite,* from Latin *capācitās,* from *capāx* spacious, from *capere* to take]

cap and bells *n.* the traditional garb of a court jester, including a cap with bells attached to it.

cap-a-pie (ˌkæpə'piː) *adv.* (dressed, armed, etc.) from head to foot. [C16: from Old French]

caparison (kə'pærɪsᵊn) *n.* **1.** a decorated covering for a horse or other animal, esp. (formerly) for a warhorse. **2.** rich or elaborate clothing and ornaments. *~vb.* **3.** (*tr.*) to put a caparison on. [C16: via obsolete French from Old Spanish *caparazón* saddlecloth, probably from *capa* CAPE[1]]

cape[1] (keɪp) *n.* **1.** a sleeveless garment like a cloak but usually shorter. **2.** a strip of material attached to a coat or other garment so as to fall freely, usually from the shoulders. [C16: from French, from Provençal *capa,* from Late Latin *cappa;* see CAP]

cape[2] (keɪp) *n.* a headland or promontory. [C14: from Old French *cap,* from Old Provençal, from Latin *caput* head]

Cape (keɪp) *n.* (*modifier*) of, relating to, or denoting the SW region of the Cape Province of South Africa or the Cape of Good Hope in SW South Africa.

Cape buffalo *n.* another name for **buffalo** (sense 1).

Cape cart *n. S. African.* a two-wheeled horse-drawn vehicle sometimes with a canvas hood.

Cape Cod *or* **Cape Cod cottage** (kɒd) *n.* a one-storey cottage of timber construction with a simple gable roof and a large central chimney: originated on Cape Cod, SE Massachusetts, in the 18th century.

Cape Coloured *n.* (in South Africa) another name for a **Coloured** (sense 2).

Cape doctor *n. S. African informal.* a strong fresh SE wind blowing in the vicinity of Cape Town, esp. in the summer.

Cape Dutch *n.* **1.** an obsolete name for **Afrikaans. 2.** (in South Africa) a distinctive style of furniture or architecture.

cape gooseberry *n.* another name for **strawberry tomato.**

Cape jasmine *n.* a widely cultivated gardenia shrub, *Gardenia jasminoides.* See **gardenia.**

capelin ('kæpəlɪn) *or* **caplin** *n.* a small marine food fish, *Mallotus villosus,* occurring in northern and Arctic seas: family *Osmeridae* (smelts). [C17: from French *capelan,* from Old Provençal, literally: CHAPLAIN]

Capella (kə'pɛlə) *n.* the brightest star in the constellation Auriga; it is a yellow giant and a spectroscopic binary. Visual magnitude: 0.1; spectral type: G8; distance: 46 light years. [C17: New Latin, from Latin, diminutive of *capra* she-goat, from *caper* goat]

capellmeister *or* **kapellmeister** (kæ'pɛlˌmaɪstə) *n.* a person in charge of an orchestra, esp. in an 18th-century princely household. See also **maestro di cappella.** [from German, from *Kapelle* chapel + *Meister* MASTER]

Cape pigeon *n.* a species of seagoing petrel, *Daption capensis,* with characteristic white wing patches: a common winter visitor off the coasts of southern Africa: family *Diomedeidae.* Also called: **pintado petrel.**

Cape primrose *n.* See **streptocarpus.**

caper[1] ('keɪpə) *n.* **1.** a playful skip or leap. **2.** a high-spirited escapade. **3. cut a caper** *or* **capers. a.** to skip or jump playfully. **b.** to act or behave playfully; frolic. **4.** *U.S. and Canadian slang.* a crime, esp. an organized robbery. *~vb.* **5.** (*intr.*) to leap or dance about in a light-hearted manner. [C16: probably from CAPRIOLE] —'**caperer** *n.* —'**caperingly** *adv.*

caper[2] ('keɪpə) *n.* **1.** a spiny trailing Mediterranean capparidaceous shrub, *Capparis spinosa,* with edible flower buds. **2.** any of various similar plants or their edible parts. See also **bean caper, capers.** [C15: from earlier *capers, capres* (assumed to be plural), from Latin *capparis,* from Greek *kapparis*]

capercaillie (ˌkæpə'keɪljɪ) *or* **capercailzie** (ˌkæpə'keɪljɪ, -'keɪlzɪ) *n.* a large European woodland grouse, *Tetrao urogallus,* having a black plumage and fan-shaped tail in the male. [C16: from Scottish Gaelic *capull coille* horse of the woods]

capers ('keɪpəz) *pl. n.* the flower buds of the caper plant, which are pickled and used as a condiment.

capeskin ('keɪpˌskɪn) *n.* **1.** a soft leather obtained from the skins of a type of lamb or sheep having hairlike wool. *~adj.* **2.** made of this leather. [C19: named after the *Cape of Good Hope*]

Cape sparrow *n.* a sparrow, *Passer melanurus,* very common in southern Africa: family *Ploceidae.* Also called (esp. S. African): **mossie.**

Capetian (kə'piːʃən) *n.* **1.** a member of the dynasty founded by Hugh Capet (?938–996 A.D.), which ruled France from 987–1328 A.D. *~adj.* **2.** of or relating to the Capetian kings or their rule.

capias ('keɪpɪˌæs, 'kæp-) *n. Law.* a writ directing a sheriff or other officer to arrest a named person. [C15: from Latin, literally: you must take, from *capere*]

capillaceous (ˌkæpɪ'leɪʃəs) *adj.* **1.** having numerous filaments resembling hairs or threads. **2.** resembling a hair; capillary. [C18: from Latin *capillāceus* hairy, from *capillus* hair]

capillarity (ˌkæpɪ'lærɪtɪ) *n.* a phenomenon caused by surface tension and resulting in the distortion, elevation, or depression of the surface of a liquid in contact with a solid. Also called: **capillary action.**

capillary (kə'pɪlərɪ) *adj.* **1.** resembling a hair; slender. **2.** (of tubes) having a fine bore. **3.** *Anatomy.* of or relating to any of the delicate thin-walled blood vessels that form an interconnecting network between the arterioles and the venules. **4.** *Physics.* of or relating to capillarity. *~n., pl.* **-laries. 5.** *Anatomy.* any of the capillary blood vessels. **6.** a fine hole or narrow passage in any substance. [C17: from Latin *capillāris,* from *capillus* hair]

capillary tube *n.* a glass tube with a fine bore and thick walls, used in thermometers, etc.

capita ('kæpɪtə) *n.* **1.** See **per capita. 2.** *Anatomy.* the plural of **caput.**

capital[1] ('kæpɪtᵊl) *n.* **1. a.** the seat of government of a country or other political unit. **b.** (*as modifier*): *a capital city.* **2.** material wealth owned by an individual or business enterprise. **3.** wealth available for or capable of use in the production of further wealth, as by industrial investment. **4. make capital (out) of.** to get advantage from. **5.** (*sometimes cap.*) the capitalist class or their interests: *capital versus labour.* **6.** *Accounting.* **a.** the ownership interests of a business as represented by the excess of assets over liabilities. **b.** the nominal value of the authorized or issued shares. **c.** (*as modifier*): *capital issues.* **7.** any assets or resources, esp. when used to gain profit or advantage. **8. a.** a capital letter. Abbrev.: **cap** *or* **cap. b.** (*as modifier*): *capital B.* **9. with a capital A, B,** etc. (used to give emphasis to a statement): *he is mean with a capital M.* *~adj.* **10.** (*prenominal*) *Law.* involving or punishable by death: *a capital offence.* **11.** very serious; fatal: *a capital error.* **12.** primary, chief, or principal: *our capital concern is that everyone be fed.* **13.** of, relating to, or designating the large modern majuscule letter used chiefly as the initial letter in personal names and place names and other uniquely specificatory nouns, and often for abbreviations and acronyms. Compare **small** (sense 9). See also **upper case. 14.** *Chiefly Brit.* excellent; first-rate: *a capital idea.* [C13: from Latin *capitālis* (adj.) concerning the head, chief, from *caput* head; compare Medieval Latin *capitāle* (n.) wealth, from *capitālis* (adj.)]

capital[2] ('kæpɪtᵊl) *n.* the upper part of a column or pier that supports the entablature. Also called: **chapiter, cap.** [C14: from Old French *capitel,* from Late Latin *capitellum,* diminutive of *caput* head]

capital account *n.* **1.** *Economics.* that part of a balance of payments composed of movements of capital and international loans and grants. Compare **current account** (sense 2). **2.** *Accounting.* a financial statement showing the net value of a company at a specified date. It is defined as total assets minus total liabilities and represents ownership interests. **3.** *U.S.* an account of fixed assets.

capital allowance *n.* the allowing of a certain amount of money spent by a company on fixed assets to be taken off the profits of the company before tax is imposed.

capital assets *pl. n.* another name for **fixed assets.**

capital expenditure *n.* expenditure on acquisitions of or improvements to fixed assets.

capital gain *n.* the amount by which the selling price of a financial asset exceeds its cost.

capital gains tax *n.* a tax on the profit made from the sale of an asset. Abbrev.: **CGT.**

capital goods *pl. n. Economics.* goods that are themselves utilized in the production of other goods rather than being sold to consumers. Also called: **producer goods.** Compare **consumer goods.**

capitalism ('kæpɪtəˌlɪzəm) *n.* an economic system based on the private ownership of the means of production, distribution, and exchange, characterized by the freedom of capitalists to operate or manage their property for profit in competitive conditions. Also called: **free enterprise, private enterprise.** Compare **socialism** (sense 1).

capitalist ('kæpɪtəlɪst) *n.* **1.** a person who owns capital, esp. capital invested in a business. **2.** *Politics.* a supporter of capitalism. **3.** *Informal, usually derogatory.* a rich person. *~adj.* **4.** of or relating to capital, capitalists, or capitalism. —ˌ**capital'istic** *adj.*

capitalization *or* **capitalisation** (ˌkæpɪtəlaɪ'zeɪʃən) *n.* **1. a.** the act of capitalizing. **b.** the sum so derived. **2.** *Accounting.* the par value of the total share capital issued by a company, includ-

ing the loan capital and sometimes reserves. **3.** the act of estimating the present value of future payments, earnings, etc. **4.** the act of writing or printing in capital letters.
capitalization issue *n.* another name for **rights issue.**
capitalize *or* **capitalise** ('kæpɪtəˌlaɪz) *vb.* (*mainly tr.*) **1.** (*intr.;* foll. by *on*) to take advantage (of); profit (by). **2.** to write or print (text) in capital letters or with the first letter of (a word or words) in capital letters. **3.** to convert (debt or retained earnings) into capital stock. **4.** to authorize (a business enterprise) to issue a specified amount of capital stock. **5.** to provide with capital. **6.** *Accounting.* to treat (expenditures) as assets. **7. a.** to estimate the present value of (a periodical income). **b.** to compute the present value of (a business) from actual or potential earnings.
capital levy *n.* a tax on capital or property as contrasted with a tax on income.
capitally ('kæpɪtəlɪ) *adv. Chiefly Brit.* in an excellent manner; admirably.
capital market *n.* the financial institutions collectively that deal with medium-term and long-term capital and loans. Compare **money market.**
capital punishment *n.* the punishment of death for a crime; death penalty.
capital ship *n.* one of the largest and most heavily armed ships in a naval fleet.
capital stock *n.* **1.** the par value of the total share capital that a company is authorized to issue. **2.** the total physical capital existing in an economy at any moment of time.
capital surplus *n.* another name (esp. U.S.) for **share premium.**
capital transfer tax *n.* (in Britain) a tax payable from 1974 to 1986 at progressive rates on the cumulative total of gifts of money or property made during the donor's lifetime or after his death. It was replaced by inheritance tax.
capitate ('kæpɪˌteɪt) *adj.* **1.** *Botany.* shaped like a head, as certain flowers or inflorescences. **2.** *Zoology.* having an enlarged head-like end: *a capitate bone.* [C17: from Latin *capitātus* having a (large) head, from *caput* head]
capitation (ˌkæpɪ'teɪʃən) *n.* **1.** a tax levied on the basis of a fixed amount per head. **2. capitation grant.** a grant of money given to every person who qualifies under certain conditions. **3.** the process of assessing or numbering by counting heads. [C17: from Late Latin *capitātiō,* from Latin *caput* head] —**'capitative** *adj.*
capitellum (ˌkæpɪ'tɛləm) *n., pl.* **-la** (-lə). Anatomy. an enlarged knoblike structure at the end of a bone that forms an articulation with another bone; capitulum. [C19: from Latin, diminutive of CAPITULUM]
capitular (kə'pɪtjʊlə) *adj.* **1.** of or associated with a cathedral chapter. **2.** of or relating to a capitulum. [C17: from Medieval Latin *capitulāris,* from *capitulum* CHAPTER] —**ca'pitularly** *adv.*
capitulary (kə'pɪtjʊlərɪ) *n., pl.* **-laries.** any of the collections of ordinances promulgated by the Frankish kings (8th–10th centuries A.D.). [C17: from Medieval Latin *capitulāris;* see CAPITULAR]
capitulate (kə'pɪtjʊˌleɪt) *vb.* (*intr.*) to surrender, esp. under agreed conditions. [C16 (meaning: to arrange under heads, draw up in order; hence, to make terms of surrender): from Medieval Latin *capitulare* to draw up under heads, from *capitulum* CHAPTER] —**ca'pituˌlator** *n.*
capitulation (kəˌpɪtjʊ'leɪʃən) *n.* **1.** the act of capitulating. **2.** a document containing terms of surrender. **3.** a statement summarizing the main divisions of a subject. —**ca'pitulatory** *adj.*
capitulum (kə'pɪtjʊləm) *n., pl.* **-la** (-lə). **1.** a racemose inflorescence in the form of a disc of sessile flowers, the youngest at the centre. It occurs in the daisy and related plants. **2.** *Anatomy, zoology.* a headlike part, esp. the enlarged knoblike terminal part of a long bone, antenna, etc. [C18: from Latin, literally: a little head, from *caput* head]
capiz ('kæpɪz) *n.* the bivalve shell of a mollusc (*Placuna placenta*) found esp. in the Philippines and having a smooth translucent shiny interior: used in jewellery, ornaments, lampshades, etc. Also called: **jingle shell, window shell.** [from the native name in the Philippines]
caplin ('kæplɪn) *n.* a variant of **capelin.**
capo[1] ('keɪpəʊ, 'kæpəʊ) *n., pl.* **-pos.** a device fitted across all the strings of a guitar, lute, etc., so as to raise the pitch of each string simultaneously. Compare **barré.** Also called: **capo tasto** ('kæpəʊ 'tæstəʊ). [from Italian *capo tasto* head stop]
capo[2] ('kæpəʊ; *Italian* 'kapo) *n., pl.* **-pos.** the presumed title of a leader in the Mafia. [Italian: head]
cap of maintenance *n.* a ceremonial cap or hat worn or carried as a symbol of office, rank, etc.
capon ('keɪpən) *n.* a castrated cock fowl fattened for eating. [Old English *capun,* from Latin *cāpō* capon; related to Greek *koptein* to cut off]
caponize *or* **caponise** ('keɪpəˌnaɪz) *vb.* (*tr.*) to make (a cock) into a capon.
caporal (ˌkæpə'rɑːl) *n.* a strong coarse dark tobacco. [C19: from French *tabac du caporal* corporal's tobacco, denoting its superiority to *tabac du soldat* soldier's tobacco]
capot (kə'pɒt) *n. Piquet.* the winning of all the tricks by one player. [C17: from French]
capote (kə'pəʊt; *French* kapɔt) *n.* a long cloak or soldier's coat, usually with a hood. [C19: from French: cloak, from *cape;* see CAPE[1]]
capparidaceous (ˌkæpərɪ'deɪʃəs) *adj.* of, relating to, or belonging to the *Capparidaceae,* a family of plants, mostly shrubs including the caper, of warm and tropical regions. [C19: from New Latin *Capparidaceae,* from Latin *capparis* caper]
cappie ('kæpɪ) *n. Central Scot. dialect.* an ice-cream cone. [C19: diminutive of C18 *cap* wooden drinking vessel, from Old English *copp* or Old Norse *koppr*]
cappuccino (ˌkæpʊ'tʃiːnəʊ) *n., pl.* **-nos.** coffee with steamed milk, sometimes served with whipped cream or sprinkled with powdered chocolate. [Italian: CAPUCHIN]
capreolate ('kæprɪəˌleɪt, kə'priː-) *adj. Biology.* possessing or resembling tendrils. [C18: from Latin *capreolus* tendril]
capric acid ('kæprɪk) *n.* another name for **decanoic acid.** [C19: from Latin *caper* goat, so named from its smell]
capriccio (kə'prɪtʃɪˌəʊ) *or* **caprice** *n., pl.* **-priccios, -pricci** (-'priːtʃɪ), *or* **-prices.** *Music.* a lively piece composed freely and without adhering to the rules for any specific musical form. [C17: from Italian: CAPRICE]
capriccioso (kəˌprɪtʃɪ'əʊzəʊ) *adv. Music.* to be played in a free and lively style. [Italian: from *capriccio* CAPRICE]
caprice (kə'priːs) *n.* **1.** a sudden or unpredictable change of attitude, behaviour, etc.; whim. **2.** a tendency to such changes. **3.** another word for **capriccio.** [C17: from French, from Italian *capriccio* a shiver, caprice, from *capo* head + *riccio* hedgehog, suggesting a convulsive shudder in which the hair stood on end like a hedgehog's spines; meaning also influenced by Italian *capra* goat, by folk etymology]
capricious (kə'prɪʃəs) *adj.* characterized by or liable to sudden unpredictable changes in attitude or behaviour; impulsive; fickle. —**ca'priciously** *adv.* —**ca'priciousness** *n.*
Capricorn ('kæprɪˌkɔːn) *n.* **1.** *Astrology.* **a.** Also called: the **Goat, Capricornus.** the tenth sign of the zodiac, symbol ♑, having a cardinal earth classification and ruled by the planet Saturn. The sun is in this sign between about Dec. 22 and Jan. 19. **b.** a person born during the period when the sun is in this sign. **2.** *Astronomy.* another name for **Capricornus. 3. tropic of Capricorn.** See **tropic** (sense 1). *~adj.* **4.** *Astrology.* born under or characteristic of Capricorn. ~Also (for senses 1b., 4): **Capricornean** (ˌkæprɪ'kɔːnɪən). [C14: from Latin *Capricornus* (translating Greek *aigokerōs* goat-horned), from *caper* goat + *cornū* horn]
Capricornus (ˌkæprɪ'kɔːnəs) *n., Latin genitive* **-ni** (-naɪ). a faint zodiacal constellation in the S hemisphere, lying between Sagittarius and Aquarius.
caprification (ˌkæprɪfɪ'keɪʃən) *n.* a method of pollinating the edible fig by hanging branches of caprifig flowers in edible fig trees. Parasitic wasps in the caprifig flowers transfer pollen to the edible fig flowers. [C17: from Latin *caprificātiō,* from *caprificāre* to pollinate figs by this method, from *caprificus* CAPRIFIG]
caprifig ('kæprɪˌfɪg) *n.* a wild variety of fig, *Ficus carica sylvestris,* of S Europe and SW Asia, used in the caprification of the edible fig. [C15: from Latin *caprificus* literally: goat fig, from *caper* goat + *ficus* FIG[1]]
caprifoliaceous (ˌkæprɪˌfəʊlɪ'eɪʃəs) *adj.* of, relating to, or belonging to the *Caprifoliaceae,* a family of N temperate shrubs or small trees including honeysuckle, elder, and guelder-rose. [C19: from New Latin *caprifoliāceae,* from *caprifolium* type genus, from Medieval Latin: honeysuckle, from Latin *caper* goat + *folium* leaf]
caprine ('kæpraɪn) *adj.* of or resembling a goat. [C17: from Latin *caprīnus,* from *caper* goat]
capriole ('kæprɪˌəʊl) *n.* **1.** *Dressage.* a high upward but not forward leap made by a horse with all four feet off the ground. **2.** *Dancing.* a leap from bent knees. *~vb.* **3.** (*intr.*) to perform a capriole. [C16: from French, from Old Italian *capriola,* from *capriolo* roebuck, from Latin *capreolus, caper* goat]
Capri pants *or* **Capris** (kə'priː) *pl. n.* women's tight-fitting trousers. [named after *Capri,* an island off W Italy]
cap rock *n.* **1.** a layer of rock that overlies a salt dome and consists of limestone, gypsum, etc. **2.** a layer of relatively impervious rock overlying an oil- or gas-bearing rock.
caproic acid (kə'prəʊɪk) *n.* another name for **hexanoic acid.** [C19: *caproic,* from Latin *caper* goat, alluding to its smell]
caprolactam (ˌkæprəʊ'læktæm) *n.* a white crystalline cyclic imine used in the manufacture of nylon. Formula: $C_5H_{10}NHCO$. [C20: from CAPRO(IC) + LACTAM]
caps. *abbrev. for:* **1.** capital letters. **2.** capsule.
capsaicin (kæp'seɪɪsɪn) *n.* a colourless crystalline bitter alkaloid found in capsicums and used as a flavouring in vinegar and pickles. Formula: $C_{18}H_{27}O_3N$. [C19 *capsicine,* from CAPSICUM + -INE[2]; modern form refashioned from Latin *capsa* box, case + -IN]
cap screw *n.* a screwed bolt with a cylindrical head having a hexagonal recess. The bolt is turned using a wrench of hexagonal cross section.
Capsian ('kæpsɪən) *n.* **1.** a late Palaeolithic culture, dating from about 12 000 B.C., found mainly around the salt lakes of Tunisia. The culture is characterized by the presence of microliths, backed blades, and engraved limestone slabs. *~adj.* **2.** of or relating to this culture. [C20: from French *capsien,* from *Capsa,* Latinized form of *Gafsa,* Tunisia]

capsicum ('kæpsɪkəm) *n.* 1. any tropical American plant of the solanaceous genus *Capsicum,* such as *C. frutescens,* having mild or pungent seeds enclosed in a pod-shaped or bell-shaped fruit. 2. the fruit of any of these plants, used as a vegetable or ground to produce a condiment. ~See also **pepper** (sense 4). [C18: from New Latin, from Latin *capsa* box, CASE[2]]

capsid[1] ('kæpsɪd) *n.* any heteropterous bug of the family *Miridae* (formerly *Capsidae*), most of which feed on plant tissues, causing damage to crops. [C19: from New Latin *Capsus* (genus)]

capsid[2] ('kæpsɪd) *n.* the outer protein coat of a mature virus. [C20: from French *capside,* from Latin *capsa* box]

capsize (kæp'saɪz) *vb.* to overturn accidentally; upset. [C18: of uncertain origin] —**cap'sizal** *n.*

capsomere ('kæpsə,mɪə) *n.* any of the protein units that together form the capsid of a virus.

capstan ('kæpstən) *n.* 1. a machine with a drum that rotates round a vertical spindle and is turned by a motor or lever, used for hauling in heavy ropes, etc. 2. any similar device, such as the rotating shaft in a tape recorder that pulls the tape past the head. [C14: from Old Provençal *cabestan,* from Latin *capistrum* a halter, from *capere* to seize]

capstan bar *n.* a lever, often wooden, for turning a capstan.

capstan lathe *n.* a lathe for repetitive work, having a rotatable turret resembling a capstan to hold tools for successive operations. Also called: **turret lathe.**

capstone ('kæp,stəʊn) *or* **copestone** ('kəʊp,stəʊn) *n.* 1. one of a set of slabs on the top of a wall, building, etc. 2. *Mountaineering.* a chockstone occurring at the top of a gully or chimney. 3. a crowning achievement; peak.

capsulate ('kæpsjʊ,leɪt, -lɪt) *or* **capsulated** *adj.* within or formed into a capsule. —**,capsu'lation** *n.*

capsule ('kæpsjuːl) *n.* 1. a soluble case of gelatin enclosing a dose of medicine. 2. a thin metal cap, seal, or cover, such as the foil covering the cork of a wine bottle. 3. *Botany.* **a.** a dry fruit that liberates its seeds by splitting, as in the violet, or through pores, as in the poppy. **b.** the spore-producing organ of mosses and liverworts. 4. *Bacteriol.* a gelatinous layer of polysaccharide or protein surrounding the cell wall of some bacteria: thought to be responsible for the virulence in pathogens. 5. *Anatomy.* **a.** a cartilaginous, fibrous, or membranous envelope surrounding any of certain organs or parts. **b.** a broad band of white fibres (**internal capsule**) near the thalamus in each cerebral hemisphere. 6. See **space capsule.** 7. an aeroplane cockpit that can be ejected in a flight emergency, complete with crew, instruments, etc. 8. (*modifier*) in a highly concise form: *a capsule summary.* 9. (*modifier*) (in the fashion industry) consisting of a few important representative items: *a capsule collection.* [C17: from French, from Latin *capsula,* diminutive of *capsa* box]

capsulize *or* **capsulise** ('kæpsjʊ,laɪz) *vb.* (*tr.*) 1. to state (information) in a highly condensed form. 2. to enclose in a capsule.

Capt. *abbrev. for* Captain.

captain ('kæptɪn) *n.* 1. the person in charge of and responsible for a vessel. 2. an officer of the navy who holds a rank junior to a rear admiral but senior to a commander. 3. an officer of the army, certain air forces, and the marine corps who holds a rank junior to a major but senior to a lieutenant. 4. the officer in command of a civil aircraft, usually the senior pilot. 5. the leader of a team in games. 6. a person in command over a group, organization, etc.; leader: *a captain of industry.* 7. *U.S.* a policeman in charge of a precinct. 8. *U.S. and Canadian.* a head waiter. 9. *U.S. and Canadian.* a supervisor of bellboys in a hotel. ~*vb.* 10. (*tr.*) to be captain of. [C14: from Old French *capitaine,* from Late Latin *capitāneus* chief, from Latin *caput* head] —'**captaincy** *or* '**captain,ship** *n.*

Captain Cooker ('kʊkə) *n. N.Z.* a wild pig. [from Captain James *Cook* (1728–79), British navigator, who first released pigs in the New Zealand bush]

captain's biscuit *n.* a type of hard fancy biscuit.

caption ('kæpʃən) *n.* 1. a title, brief explanation, or comment accompanying an illustration; legend. 2. a heading, title, or headline of a chapter, article, etc. 3. graphic material, usually containing lettering, used in television presentation. 4. another name for **subtitle** (sense 2). 5. the formal heading of a legal document stating when, where, and on what authority it was taken or made. ~*vb.* 6. to provide with a caption or captions. [C14 (meaning: seizure, an arrest; later, heading of a legal document): from Latin *captiō* a seizing, from *capere* to take]

captious ('kæpʃəs) *adj.* apt to make trivial criticisms; fault-finding; carping. [C14 (meaning: catching in error): from Latin *captiōsus,* from *captiō* a seizing; see CAPTION] —'**captiously** *adv.* —'**captiousness** *n.*

captivate ('kæptɪ,veɪt) *vb.* (*tr.*) 1. to hold the attention of by fascinating; enchant. 2. an obsolete word for **capture.** [C16: from Late Latin *captivāre,* from *captīvus* CAPTIVE] —'**capti,vatingly** *adv.* —**,capti'vation** *n.* —'**capti,vator** *n.*

captive ('kæptɪv) *n.* 1. a person or animal that is confined or restrained, esp. a prisoner of war. 2. a person whose behaviour is dominated by some emotion: *a captive of love.* ~*adj.* 3. held as prisoner. 4. held under restriction or control; confined: *captive water held behind a dam.* 5. captivated; enraptured. 6. unable by circumstances to avoid speeches, advertisements, etc. (esp. in the phrase **captive audience**). [C14: from Latin *captīvus,* from *capere* to take]

captive market *n.* a group of consumers who are obliged through lack of choice to buy a particular product, thus giving the supplier a monopoly.

captivity (kæp'tɪvɪtɪ) *n., pl.* **-ties.** 1. the condition of being captive; imprisonment. 2. the period of imprisonment.

captor ('kæptə) *n.* a person or animal that holds another captive. [C17: from Latin, from *capere* to take]

capture ('kæptʃə) *vb.* (*tr.*) 1. to take prisoner or gain control over: *to capture an enemy; to capture a town.* 2. (in a game or contest) to win control or possession of: *to capture a pawn in chess.* 3. to succeed in representing or describing (something elusive): *the artist captured her likeness.* 4. *Physics.* (of an atom, molecule, ion, or nucleus) to acquire (an additional particle). 5. to insert or transfer (data) into a computer. ~*n.* 6. the act of taking by force; seizure. 7. the person or thing captured; booty. 8. *Physics.* a process by which an atom, molecule, ion, or nucleus acquires an additional particle. 9. Also called: **piracy.** *Geography.* the process by which the headwaters of one river are diverted into another through erosion caused by the second river's tributaries. 10. the act or process of inserting or transferring data into a computer. [C16: from Latin *captūra* a catching, that which is caught, from *capere* to take] —'**capturer** *n.*

capuche *or* **capouch** (kə'puːʃ) *n.* a large hood or cowl, esp. that worn by Capuchin friars. [C17: from French, from Italian *cappuccio* hood, from Late Latin *cappa* cloak]

capuchin ('kæpjʊtʃɪn, -ʃɪn) *n.* 1. any agile intelligent New World monkey of the genus *Cebus,* inhabiting forests in South America, typically having a cowl of thick hair on the top of the head. 2. a woman's hooded cloak. 3. (*sometimes cap.*) a rare variety of domestic fancy pigeon. [C16: from French, from Italian *cappuccino,* from *cappuccio* hood; see CAPUCHE]

Capuchin ('kæpjʊtʃɪn, 'kæpjʊʃɪn) *n.* **a.** a friar belonging to a strict and autonomous branch of the Franciscan order founded in 1525. **b.** (*as modifier*): *a Capuchin friar.* [C16: from French; see CAPUCHE]

caput ('keɪpət, 'kæp-) *n., pl.* **capita** ('kæpɪtə). 1. *Anatomy.* a technical name for the **head.** 2. the main or most prominent part of an organ or structure. [C18: from Latin]

capybara (,kæpɪ'bɑːrə) *n.* the largest rodent: a pig-sized amphibious hystricomorph, *Hydrochoerus hydrochaeris,* resembling a guinea pig and inhabiting river banks in Central and South America: family *Hydrochoeridae.* [C18: from Portuguese *capibara,* from Tupi]

car (kɑː) *n.* 1. **a.** Also called: **motorcar, automobile.** a self-propelled road vehicle designed to carry passengers, esp. one with four wheels that is powered by an internal-combustion engine. **b.** (*as modifier*): *car coat.* 2. a conveyance for passengers, freight, etc., such as a cable car or the carrier of an airship or balloon. 3. *Brit.* a railway vehicle for passengers only, such as a sleeping car or buffet car. 4. *Chiefly U.S. and Canadian.* a railway carriage or van. 5. *Chiefly U.S.* the enclosed platform of a lift. 6. a poetic word for **chariot.** [C14: from Anglo-French *carre,* ultimately related to Latin *carra, carrum* two-wheeled wagon, probably of Celtic origin; compare Old Irish *carr*]

CAR *abbrev. for* compound annual return.

carabao (,kærə'beɪəʊ) *n., pl.* **-os.** another name for **water buffalo.** [from Visayan *karabáw;* compare Malay *karbaw*]

carabid ('kærəbɪd) *n.* 1. any typically dark-coloured beetle of the family *Carabidae,* including the bombardier and other ground beetles. ~*adj.* 2. of, relating to, or belonging to the *Carabidae.* [C19: from New Latin, from Latin *cārabus* a kind of crab (name applied to these beetles)]

carabin ('kærəbɪn) *or* **carabine** ('kærə,baɪn) *n.* variants of **carbine** (sense 2).

carabineer *or* **carabinier** (,kærəbɪ'nɪə) *n.* variants of **carbineer.**

carabiner (,kærə'biːnə) *n.* a variant spelling of **karabiner.**

carabiniere *Italian.* (karabi'njɛːre) *n., pl.* **-ri** (-ri). an Italian national policeman.

caracal ('kærə,kæl) *n.* 1. Also called: **desert lynx.** a lynxlike feline mammal, *Lynx caracal,* inhabiting deserts of N Africa and S Asia, having long legs, a smooth coat of reddish fur, and black-tufted ears. 2. the fur of this animal. [C18: from French, from Turkish *kara kūlāk,* literally: black ear]

caracara (,kɑːrə'kɑːrə) *n.* any of various large carrion-eating diurnal birds of prey of the genera *Caracara, Polyborus,* etc., of S North, Central, and South America, having long legs and naked faces: family *Falconidae* (falcons). [C19: from Spanish or Portuguese, from Tupi; of imitative origin]

caracole ('kærə,kəʊl) *or* **caracol** ('kærə,kɒl) *n.* 1. *Dressage.* a half turn to the right or left. 2. a spiral staircase. ~*vb.* (*intr.*) 3. *Dressage.* to execute a half turn to the right or left. [C17: from French, from Spanish *caracol* snail, spiral staircase, turn]

caracul ('kærə,kʌl) *n.* 1. Also called: **Persian lamb.** the black loosely curled fur obtained from the skins of newly born lambs of the karakul sheep. 2. a variant spelling of **karakul.**

carafe (kə'ræf, -'rɑːf) *n.* **a.** an open-topped glass container for serving water or wine at table. **b.** (*as modifier*): *a carafe wine.* [C18: from French, from Italian *caraffa,* from Spanish *garrafa,* from Arabic *gharrāfah* vessel]

carageen ('kærə,giːn) *n.* a variant spelling of **carrageen.**

carambola (,kærəm'bəʊlə) *n.* 1. a tree, *Averrhoa carambola,* probably native to Brazil but cultivated in the tropics, esp. SE Asia, for its edible fruit. 2. Also called: **star fruit.** the smooth-skinned yellow fruit of this tree, which is star-shaped on cross section. [Spanish, from Portuguese]

caramel ('kærəməl, -ˌmɛl) *n.* **1.** burnt sugar, used for colouring and flavouring food. **2.** a chewy sweet made from sugar, butter, milk, etc. ~See also **crème caramel.** [C18: from French, from Spanish *caramelo,* of uncertain origin]

caramelize *or* **caramelise** ('kærəməˌlaɪz) *vb.* to convert or be converted into caramel.

carangid (kə'rændʒɪd, -'ræŋgɪd) *or* **carangoid** (kə'ræŋgɔɪd) *n.* **1.** any marine percoid fish of the family *Carangidae,* having a compressed body and deeply forked tail. The group includes the jacks, horse mackerel, pompano, and pilot fish. ~*adj.* **2.** of, relating to, or belonging to the *Carangidae.* [C19: from New Latin *Carangidae,* from *Caranx* type genus, from French *carangue* shad, from Spanish *caranga,* of obscure origin]

carapace ('kærəˌpeɪs) *n.* the thick hard shield, made of chitin or bone, that covers part of the body of crabs, lobsters, tortoises, etc. [C19: from French, from Spanish *carapacho,* of unknown origin]

carat ('kærət) *n.* **1.** a measure of the weight of precious stones, esp. diamonds. It was formerly defined as 3.17 grains, but the international carat is now standardized as 0.20 grams. **2.** Usual U.S. spelling: **karat.** a measure of the proportion of gold in an alloy, expressed as the number of parts of gold in 24 parts of the alloy. [C16: from Old French, from Medieval Latin *carratus,* from Arabic *qīrāt* weight of four grains, carat, from Greek *keration* a little horn, from *keras* horn]

caravan ('kærəˌvæn) *n.* **1. a.** a large enclosed vehicle capable of being pulled by a car or lorry and equipped to be lived in. U.S. and Canadian name: **trailer. b.** (*as modifier*): *a caravan site.* **2.** (esp. in some parts of Asia and Africa) a company of traders or other travellers journeying together, often with a train of camels, through the desert. **3.** a group of wagons, pack mules, camels, etc., esp. travelling in single file. **4.** a large covered vehicle, esp. a gaily coloured one used by Gypsies, circuses, etc. ~*vb.* **-vans, -vanning, -vanned. 5.** (*intr.*) *Brit.* to travel or have a holiday in a caravan. [C16: from Italian *caravana,* from Persian *kārwān*]

caravanserai (ˌkærə'vænsəˌraɪ, -ˌreɪ) *or* **caravansary** (ˌkærə'vænsərɪ) *n., pl.* **-rais** *or* **-ries.** (in some Eastern countries, esp. formerly) a large inn enclosing a courtyard, providing accommodation for caravans. [C16: from Persian *kārwānsarāī* caravan inn]

caravel ('kærəˌvɛl) *or* **carvel** *n.* a two- or three-masted sailing ship, esp. one with a broad beam, high poop deck, and lateen rig that was used by the Spanish and Portuguese in the 15th and 16th centuries. [C16: from Portuguese *caravela,* diminutive of *caravo* ship, ultimately from Greek *karabos* crab, horned beetle]

caraway ('kærəˌweɪ) *n.* **1.** an umbelliferous Eurasian plant, *Carum carvi,* having finely divided leaves and clusters of small whitish flowers. **2. caraway seed.** the pungent aromatic one-seeded fruit of this plant, used in cooking and in medicine. [C14: probably from Medieval Latin *carvi,* from Arabic *karawyā,* from Greek *karon*]

carbamate ('kɑːbəˌmeɪt) *n.* a salt or ester of carbamic acid. The salts contain the monovalent ion NH_2COO^-, and the esters contain the group NH_2COO–.

carbamazepine (ˌkɑːbə'mæzəˌpiːn) *n.* an anticonvulsant drug used in the management of epilepsy.

carbamic acid (kɑː'bæmɪk) *n.* a hypothetical compound known only in the form of carbamate salts and esters. Formula: NH_2COOH.

carbamide ('kɑːbəˌmaɪd) *n.* another name for **urea.**

carbamidine (kɑː'bæmɪˌdaɪn) *n.* another name for **guanidine.**

carbanion (kɑː'bænaɪən) *n. Chem.* a negatively charged organic ion, such as H_3C^-, derived from a free radical by addition of one electron. Compare **carbonium ion.**

carbaryl ('kɑːbərɪl) *n.* an organic compound of the carbamate group: used as an insecticide, esp. to treat head lice.

carbazole ('kɑːbəˌzəʊl) *n.* a colourless insoluble solid obtained from coal tar and used in the production of some dyes. Formula: $C_{12}H_9N$. Also called: **diphenylenimine** (daɪˌfiːnaɪ'lɛnɪmiːn).

carbene ('kɑːbiːn) *n. Chem.* a neutral divalent free radical, such as methylene: CH_2.

carbide ('kɑːbaɪd) *n.* **1.** a binary compound of carbon with a metal. See also **acetylide. 2.** See **calcium carbide.**

carbimazole (kɑː'bɪməˌzəʊl) *n.* a drug that inhibits the synthesis of the hormone thyroxine, used in the management of hyperthyroidism.

carbine ('kɑːbaɪn) *n.* **1.** a light automatic or semiautomatic rifle of limited range. **2.** Also called: **carabin, carabine.** a light short-barrelled shoulder rifle formerly used by cavalry. [C17: from French *carabine,* from Old French *carabin* carabineer, perhaps variant of *escarrabin* one who prepares corpses for burial, from *scarabée,* from Latin *scarabaeus* SCARAB]

carbineer (ˌkɑːbɪ'nɪə), **carabineer,** *or* **carabinier** (ˌkærəbɪ'nɪə) *n.* (formerly) a soldier equipped with a carbine.

carbo- *or before a vowel* **carb-** *combining form.* carbon: *carbohydrate; carbonate.*

carbocyclic (ˌkɑːbəʊ'saɪklɪk) *adj.* (of a chemical compound) containing a closed ring of carbon atoms.

carbohydrate (ˌkɑːbəʊ'haɪdreɪt) *n.* any of a large group of organic compounds, including sugars, such as sucrose, and polysaccharides, such as cellulose, glycogen, and starch, that contain carbon, hydrogen, and oxygen, with the general formula $C_m(H_2O)_n$: an important source of food and energy for animals.

carbolated ('kɑːbəˌleɪtɪd) *adj.* containing carbolic acid.

carbolic acid (kɑː'bɒlɪk) *n.* another name for **phenol,** esp. when it is used as an antiseptic or disinfectant. [C19: *carbolic,* from CARBO- + -OL[1] + -IC]

carbolize *or* **carbolise** ('kɑːbəˌlaɪz) *vb.* (*tr.*) another word for **phenolate.**

carbon ('kɑːbᵊn) *n.* **1. a.** a nonmetallic element existing in the three allotropic forms: amorphous carbon, graphite, and diamond: occurring in carbon dioxide, coal, oil, and all organic compounds. The isotope **carbon-12** has been adopted as the standard for atomic wt.; **carbon-14,** a radioisotope with a half-life of 5700 years, is used in radiocarbon dating and as a tracer. Symbol: C; atomic no.: 6; atomic wt.: 12.011 15; valency: 2, 3, or 4; relative density: 1.8–2.1 (amorphous), 1.9–2.3 (graphite), 3.1–3.5 (diamond); sublimes above 3500°C; boiling pt.: 4827°C. **b.** (*as modifier*): *a carbon compound.* **2.** short for **carbon paper** or **carbon copy. 3.** a carbon electrode used in a carbon-arc light or in carbon-arc welding. **4.** a rod or plate, made of carbon, used in some types of battery. [C18: from French *carbone,* from Latin *carbō* charcoal, dead or glowing coal] —'**carbonous** *adj.*

carbonaceous (ˌkɑːbə'neɪʃəs) *adj.* of, resembling, or containing carbon.

carbonade (ˌkɑːbə'neɪd, -'nɑːd) *n.* a stew of beef and onions cooked in beer. [C20: from French]

carbonado[1] (ˌkɑːbə'neɪdəʊ, -'nɑːdəʊ) *n., pl.* **-does** *or* **-dos. 1.** a piece of meat, fish, etc., scored and grilled. ~*vb.* **-dos, -doing, -doed.** (*tr.*) **2.** to score and grill (meat, fish, etc.). **3.** *Archaic.* to hack or slash. [C16: from Spanish *carbonada,* from *carbón* charcoal; see CARBON]

carbonado[2] (ˌkɑːbə'neɪdəʊ, -'nɑːdəʊ) *n., pl.* **-dos** *or* **-does.** an inferior dark massive variety of diamond used in industry for polishing and drilling. Also called: **black diamond.** [Portuguese, literally: carbonated]

carbon arc *n.* **1. a.** an electric arc produced between two carbon electrodes, formerly used as a light source. **b.** (*as modifier*): *carbon-arc light.* **2. a.** an electric arc produced between a carbon electrode and material to be welded. **b.** (*as modifier*): *carbon-arc welding.*

carbonate *n.* ('kɑːbəˌneɪt, -nɪt). **1.** a salt or ester of carbonic acid. Carbonate salts contain the divalent ion CO_3^{2-}. ~*vb.* ('kɑːbəˌneɪt). **2.** to form or turn into a carbonate. **3.** (*tr.*) to treat with carbon dioxide or carbonic acid, as in the manufacture of soft drinks. [C18: from French, from *carbone* CARBON]

carbonation (ˌkɑːbə'neɪʃən) *n.* **1.** absorption of or reaction with carbon dioxide. **2.** another word for **carbonization.**

carbon bisulphide *n.* (not in technical usage) another name for **carbon disulphide.**

carbon black *n.* a black finely divided form of amorphous carbon produced by incomplete combustion of natural gas or petroleum: used to reinforce rubber and in the manufacture of pigments and ink.

carbon brush *n.* a small block of carbon used to convey current between the stationary and moving parts of an electric generator, motor, etc.

carbon copy *n.* **1.** a duplicate copy of writing, typewriting, or drawing obtained by using carbon paper. Often shortened to **carbon. 2.** *Informal.* a person or thing that is identical or very similar to another.

carbon cycle *n.* **1.** the circulation of carbon between living organisms and their surroundings. Carbon dioxide from the atmosphere is synthesized by plants into plant tissue, which is ingested and metabolized by animals and reduced to carbon dioxide again during respiration and decay. **2.** four thermonuclear reactions believed to be the source of energy in many stars. Carbon nuclei function as catalysts in the fusion of protons to form helium nuclei.

carbon dating *n.* short for **radiocarbon dating.**

carbon dioxide *n.* a colourless odourless incombustible gas present in the atmosphere and formed during respiration, the decomposition and combustion of organic compounds, and in the reaction of acids with carbonates: used in carbonated drinks, fire extinguishers, and as dry ice for refrigeration. Formula: CO_2. Also called: **carbonic-acid gas.**

carbon dioxide snow *n.* solid carbon dioxide, used as a refrigerant.

carbon disulphide *n.* a colourless slightly soluble volatile flammable poisonous liquid commonly having a disagreeable odour due to the presence of impurities: used as an organic solvent and in the manufacture of rayon and carbon tetrachloride. Formula: CS_2. Also called (not in technical usage): **carbon bisulphide.**

carbonette (ˌkɑːbə'nɛt) *n. N.Z.* a ball of compressed coal dust used as fuel.

carbon fibre *n.* a black silky thread of pure carbon made by heating and stretching textile fibres and used because of its lightness and strength at high temperatures for reinforcing resins, ceramics, and metals, esp. in turbine blades and for fishing rods.

carbon fixation *n.* the process by which plants assimilate carbon from carbon dioxide in the atmosphere to form metabolically active compounds.

carbon-14 dating *n.* another name for **radiocarbon dating.**
carbonic (kɑːˈbɒnɪk) *adj.* (of a compound) containing carbon, esp. tetravalent carbon.
carbonic acid *n.* a weak acid formed when carbon dioxide combines with water: obtained only in aqueous solutions, never in the pure state. Formula: H_2CO_3.
carbonic-acid gas *n.* another name for **carbon dioxide.**
carbonic anhydrase *n.* an enzyme in blood cells that catalyses the decomposition of carbonic acid into carbon dioxide and water, facilitating the transport of carbon dioxide from the tissues to the lungs.
carboniferous (ˌkɑːbəˈnɪfərəs) *adj.* yielding coal or carbon.
Carboniferous (ˌkɑːbəˈnɪfərəs) *adj.* **1.** of, denoting, or formed in the fifth period of the Palaeozoic era, between the Devonian and Permian periods, lasting for 80 million years during which coal measures were formed. ~*n.* **2. the.** the Carboniferous period or rock system.
carbonium ion (kɑːˈbəʊnɪəm) *n. Chem.* a positively charged organic ion, such as H_3C^+, derived from a free radical by removal of one electron. Compare **carbanion.**
carbonize *or* **carbonise** (ˈkɑːbəˌnaɪz) *vb.* **1.** to turn or be turned into carbon as a result of heating, fossilization, chemical treatment, etc. **2.** (*tr.*) to enrich or coat (a substance) with carbon. **3.** (*intr.*) to react or unite with carbon. ~Also (for senses 2, 3): **carburize.** —ˌ**carboniˈzation** *or* ˌ**carboniˈsation** *n.* —ˈ**carbonˌizer** *or* ˈ**carbonˌiser** *n.*
carbon microphone *n.* a microphone in which a diaphragm, vibrated by sound waves, applies a varying pressure to a container packed with carbon granules, altering the resistance of the carbon. A current flowing through the carbon is thus modulated at the frequency of the sound waves.
carbon monoxide *n.* a colourless odourless poisonous flammable gas formed when carbon compounds burn in insufficient air and produced by the action of steam on hot carbon: used as a reducing agent in metallurgy and as a fuel. Formula: CO.
carbon paper *n.* **1.** a thin sheet of paper coated on one side with a dark waxy pigment, often containing carbon, that is transferred by the pressure of writing or of typewriter keys onto the copying surface below. Often shortened to **carbon. 2.** another name for **carbon tissue.**
carbon process *or* **printing** *n.* a photographic process for producing positive prints by exposing sensitized carbon tissue to light passing through a negative. Washing removes the unexposed gelatin leaving the pigmented image in the exposed insoluble gelatin.
carbon steel *n.* steel whose characteristics are determined by the amount of carbon it contains.
carbon tetrachloride *n.* a colourless volatile nonflammable sparingly soluble liquid made from chlorine and carbon disulphide; tetrachloromethane. It is used as a solvent, cleaning fluid, and insecticide. Formula: CCl_4.
carbon tissue *n.* a sheet of paper coated with pigmented gelatin, used in the carbon process. Also called: **carbon paper.**
carbon value *n. Chem.* an empirical measurement of the tendency of a lubricant to form carbon when in use.
carbonyl (ˈkɑːbəˌnaɪl, -nɪl) *n. Chem.* **1.** (*modifier*) of, consisting of, or containing the divalent group =CO: *a carbonyl group or radical.* **2.** any one of a class of inorganic complexes in which carbonyl groups are bound directly to metal atoms. —**carbonylic** (ˌkɑːbəˈnɪlɪk) *adj.*
carbonyl chloride *n.* (not in technical usage) another name for **phosgene.**
car-boot sale *n.* another name for **boot sale.**
Carborundum (ˌkɑːbəˈrʌndəm) *n. Trademark.* **a.** any of various abrasive materials, esp. one consisting of silicon carbide. **b.** (*as modifier*): *a Carborundum wheel.*
carboxyhaemoglobin *or U.S.* **carboxyhemoglobin** (kɑːˌbɒksɪˌhiːməʊˈgləʊbɪn, -ˌhɛm-) *n.* haemoglobin coordinated with carbon monoxide, formed as a result of carbon monoxide poisoning. As carbon monoxide is bound in preference to oxygen, tissues are deprived of oxygen.
carboxylase (kɑːˈbɒksɪˌleɪz) *n.* any enzyme that catalyses the release of carbon dioxide from certain acids.
carboxylate (kɑːˈbɒksɪˌleɪt) *n.* any salt or ester of a carboxylic acid having a formula of the type $M(RCOO)_x$, where M is a metal and R an organic group, or R_1COOR_2, where R_1 and R_2 are organic groups.
carboxyl group *or* **radical** (kɑːˈbɒksaɪl, -sɪl) *n.* the monovalent group -COOH, consisting of a carbonyl group bound to a hydroxyl group: the functional group in organic acids. [C19 *carboxyl,* from CARBO- + OXY-[2] + -YL]
carboxylic acid (ˌkɑːbɒkˈsɪlɪk) *n.* any of a class of organic acids containing the carboxyl group. See also **fatty acid.**
carboy (ˈkɑːˌbɔɪ) *n.* a large glass or plastic bottle, usually protected by a basket or box, used for containing corrosive liquids such as acids. [C18: from Persian *qarāba*]
carbuncle (ˈkɑːˌbʌŋkᵊl) *n.* **1.** an extensive skin eruption, similar to but larger than a boil, with several openings: caused by staphylococcal infection. **2.** a rounded gemstone, esp. a garnet cut without facets. **3.** a dark reddish-greyish-brown colour. [C13: from Latin *carbunculus* diminutive of *carbō* coal] —ˈ**carˌbuncled** *adj.* —**carbuncular** (kɑːˈbʌŋkjʊlə) *adj.*
carburation (ˌkɑːbjʊˈreɪʃən) *n.* the process of mixing a hydrocarbon fuel with a correct amount of air to make an explosive mixture for an internal-combustion engine.
carburet (ˈkɑːbjʊˌrɛt, ˌkɑːbjʊˈrɛt, -bə-) *vb.* **-rets, -retting, -retted** *or U.S.* **-rets, -reting, -reted.** (*tr.*) to combine or mix (a gas) with carbon or carbon compounds. [C18: from CARB(ON) + -URET]
carburettor, carburetter (ˌkɑːbjʊˈrɛtə, ˈkɑːbjʊˌrɛtə, -bə-) *or U.S.* **carburetor** (ˈkɑːbjʊˌreɪtə, -bə-) *n.* a device used in petrol engines for atomizing the petrol, controlling its mixture with air, and regulating the intake of the air-petrol mixture into the engine. Compare **fuel injection.**
carburize *or* **carburise** (ˈkɑːbjʊˌraɪz, -bə-) *vb.* **1.** another word for **carbonize** (senses 2, 3). **2.** (*tr.*) to increase the carbon content of (the surface of a low-carbon steel) so that the surface can be hardened by heat treatment. —ˌ**carburiˈzation** *or* ˌ**carburiˈsation** *n.*
carby (ˈkɑːbɪ) *n., pl.* **-bies.** *Austral. informal.* short for **carburettor.**
carbylamine (ˌkɑːbɪləˈmiːn, -ˈæmɪn) *n.* another name for **isocyanide.**
carcajou (ˈkɑːkəˌdʒuː, -ˌʒuː) *n.* a North American name for **wolverine.** [C18: from Canadian French, from Algonquian *karkajou*]
carcanet (ˈkɑːkəˌnɛt, -nɪt) *n. Archaic.* a jewelled collar or necklace. [C16: from French *carcan,* of Germanic origin; compare Old Norse *kverkband* chin strap]
carcass *or* **carcase** (ˈkɑːkəs) *n.* **1.** the dead body of an animal, esp. one that has been slaughtered for food, with the head, limbs, and entrails removed. **2.** *Informal, usually facetious or derogatory.* a person's body. **3.** the skeleton or framework of a structure: *the carcass of an old tyre.* **4.** the remains of anything when its life or vitality is gone; shell. [C14: from Old French *carcasse,* of obscure origin]
carcass trade *n. Brit. slang.* the practice of reconstructing dilapidated pieces of old furniture with new veneer to pass them off as antiques.
carcinogen (kɑːˈsɪnədʒən, ˈkɑːsɪnəˌdʒɛn) *n. Pathol.* any substance that produces cancer. [C20: from Greek *karkinos* CANCER + -GEN] —ˌ**carcinoˈgenic** *adj.* —ˌ**carcinogenˈicity** *n.*
carcinogenesis (ˌkɑːsɪnəʊˈdʒɛnɪsɪs) *n. Pathol.* the development of cancerous cells from normal ones.
carcinoma (ˌkɑːsɪˈnəʊmə) *n., pl.* **-mas** *or* **-mata** (-mətə). *Pathol.* **1.** any malignant tumour derived from epithelial tissue. **2.** another name for **cancer** (sense 1). [C18: from Latin, from Greek *karkinōma,* from *karkinos* CANCER] —ˌ**carciˈnomaˌtoid** *or* ˌ**carciˈnomatous** *adj.*
carcinomatosis (ˌkɑːsɪˌnəʊməˈtəʊsɪs) *n. Pathol.* a condition characterized by widespread dissemination of carcinomas or by a carcinoma that affects a large area. Also called: **carcinosis** (ˌkɑːsɪˈnəʊsɪs).
card[1] (kɑːd) *n.* **1.** a piece of stiff paper or thin cardboard, usually rectangular, with varied uses, as for filing information in an index, bearing a written notice for display, entering scores in a game, etc. **2.** such a card used for identification, reference, proof of membership, etc.: *library card; identity card; visiting card.* **3.** such a card used for sending greetings, messages, or invitations, often bearing an illustration, printed greetings, etc.: *Christmas card; birthday card.* **4.** one of a set of small pieces of cardboard, variously marked with significant figures, symbols, etc., used for playing games or for fortune-telling. **5. a.** short for **playing card. b.** (*as modifier*): *a card game.* **c.** (*in combination*): *cardsharp.* **6.** *Informal.* a witty, entertaining, or eccentric person. **7.** short for **cheque card** or **credit card. 8.** See **compass card. 9.** Also called: **race card.** *Horse racing.* a daily programme of all the races at a meeting, listing the runners, riders, weights to be carried, distances to be run, and conditions of each race. **10.** a thing or action used in order to gain an advantage, esp. one that is concealed and kept in reserve until needed (esp. in the phrase **a card up one's sleeve**). **11.** *Computer technol.* See **punched card. 12.** short for **printed circuit card.** See **printed circuit.** ~See also **cards.** [C15: from Old French *carte,* from Latin *charta* leaf of papyrus, from Greek *khartēs,* probably of Egyptian origin]
card[2] (kɑːd) *vb.* **1.** (*tr.*) to comb out and clean fibres of wool or cotton before spinning. ~*n.* **2.** (formerly) a machine or comblike tool for carding fabrics or for raising the nap on cloth. [C15: from Old French *carde* card, teasel, from Latin *carduus* thistle] —ˈ**carding** *n.* —ˈ**carder** *n.*
Card. *abbrev. for* Cardinal.
cardamom, cardamum (ˈkɑːdəməm), *or* **cardamon** *n.* **1.** a tropical Asian zingiberaceous plant, *Elettaria cardamomum,* that has large hairy leaves. **2.** the seeds of this plant, used esp. as a spice or condiment. **3.** a related East Indian plant, *Amomum cardamomum,* whose seeds are used as a substitute for cardamom seeds. [C15: from Latin *cardamōmum,* from Greek *kardamōmon,* from *kardamon* cress + *amōmon* an Indian spice]
cardan joint (ˈkɑːdæn) *n. Engineering.* a type of universal joint in a shaft that enables it to rotate when out of alignment. [C20: named after Geronimo *Cardan* (1501–76), Italian mathematician]
cardboard (ˈkɑːdˌbɔːd) *n.* **1. a.** a thin stiff board made from paper pulp and used esp. for making cartons. **b.** (*as modifier*): *cardboard boxes.* ~*adj.* **2.** (*prenominal*) without substance: *a cardboard smile; a cardboard general.*

cardboard city *n. Informal.* an area of a city in which homeless people sleep rough, often in cardboard boxes.
card-carrying *adj.* being an official member of a specified organization: *a card-carrying union member; a card-carrying Communist.*
card catalogue *n.* a catalogue of books, papers, etc., filed on cards.
card file *n.* another term for **card index.**
cardiac (ˈkɑːdɪˌæk) *adj.* **1.** of or relating to the heart. **2.** of or relating to the portion of the stomach connected to the oesophagus. ~*n.* **3.** a person with a heart disorder. **4.** a drug that stimulates the heart muscle. [C17: from Latin *cardiacus,* from Greek, from *kardia* heart]
cardialgia (ˌkɑːdɪˈældʒɪə, -dʒə) *n.* **1.** pain in or near the heart. **2.** a technical name for **heartburn.** —ˌ**cardiˈalgic** *adj.*
cardie *or* **cardy** (ˈkɑːdɪ) *n. Informal.* short for **cardigan.**
cardigan (ˈkɑːdɪgən) *n.* a knitted jacket or sweater with buttons up the front. [C19: named after the 7th Earl of *Cardigan* (1797–1868), British cavalry officer]
Cardigan (ˈkɑːdɪgən) *n.* the larger variety of corgi, having a long tail. [named after *Cardigan* (Cardiganshire, former Welsh county)]
cardinal (ˈkɑːdɪnᵊl) *n.* **1.** *R.C. Church.* any of the members of the Sacred College, ranking next after the pope, who elect the pope and act as his chief counsellors. **2.** Also called: **cardinal red.** a deep vivid red colour. **3.** See **cardinal number. 4.** Also called: **cardinal grosbeak,** (U.S.) **redbird.** a crested North American bunting, *Richmondena* (or *Pyrrhuloxia*) *cardinalis,* the male of which has a bright red plumage and the female a brown one. **5.** a fritillary butterfly, *Pandoriana pandora,* found in meadows of southern Europe. **6.** a woman's hooded shoulder cape worn in the 17th and 18th centuries. ~*adj.* **7.** (*usually prenominal*) fundamentally important; principal. **8.** of a deep vivid red colour. **9.** *Astrology.* of or relating to the signs Aries, Cancer, Libra, and Capricorn. Compare **mutable** (sense 2), **fixed** (sense 10). [C13: from Latin *cardinālis,* literally: relating to a hinge, hence, that on which something depends, principal, from *cardō* hinge] —ˈ**cardinally** *adv.*
cardinalate (ˈkɑːdɪnᵊˌleɪt) *or* **cardinalship** *n.* **1.** the rank, office, or term of office of a cardinal. **2.** the cardinals collectively.
cardinal beetle *n.* any of various large N temperate beetles of the family *Pyrochroidae,* such as *Pyrochroa serraticornis,* typically scarlet or partly scarlet in colour.
cardinal flower *n.* a campanulaceous plant, *Lobelia cardinalis* of E North America, that has brilliant scarlet, pink, or white flowers.
cardinality (ˌkɑːdɪˈnælɪtɪ) *n.* **1.** *Maths.* the property of possessing a cardinal number. **2.** *Maths, logic.* (of a class) the cardinal number associated with the given class. Two classes have the same cardinality if they can be put in one-to-one correspondence.
cardinal number *or* **numeral** *n.* **1.** a number denoting quantity but not order in a group. Sometimes shortened to **cardinal. 2.** *Maths, logic.* **a.** a measure of the size of a set that does not take account of the order of its members. Compare **natural number. b.** a particular number having this function. ~Compare **ordinal number.**
cardinal points *pl. n.* the four main points of the compass: north, south, east, and west.
cardinal spider *n.* a large house spider, *Tegenaria parietina.*
cardinal virtues *pl. n.* the most important moral qualities, traditionally justice, prudence, temperance, and fortitude.
cardinal vowels *pl. n.* a set of theoretical vowel sounds, based on the shape of the mouth needed to articulate them, that can be used to classify the vowel sounds of any speaker in any language.
card index *or* **file** *n.* **1.** an index in which each item is separately listed on systematically arranged cards. ~*vb.* **card-index.** (*tr.*) **2.** to make such an index of (a book).
carding (ˈkɑːdɪŋ) *n.* the process of preparing the fibres of cotton, wool, etc., for spinning.
cardio- *or before a vowel* **cardi-** *combining form.* heart: *cardiogram.* [from Greek *kardia* heart]
cardiocentesis (ˌkɑːdɪəʊsɛnˈtiːsɪs) *n. Med.* surgical puncture of the heart.
cardiogram (ˈkɑːdɪəʊˌgræm) *n.* short for **electrocardiogram.**
cardiograph (ˈkɑːdɪəʊˌgrɑːf, -ˌgræf) *n.* **1.** an instrument used for recording the mechanical force and form of heart movements. **2.** short for **electrocardiograph.** —**cardiographer** (ˌkɑːdɪˈɒgrəfə) *n.* —**cardiographic** (ˌkɑːdɪəʊˈgræfɪk) *or* ˌ**cardioˈgraphical** *adj.* —ˌ**cardioˈgraphically** *adv.* —ˌ**cardiˈography** *n.*
cardioid (ˈkɑːdɪˌɔɪd) *n.* a heart-shaped curve generated by a fixed point on a circle as it rolls around another fixed circle of equal radius, *a.* Equation: $r = a(1 - \cos\phi)$, where r is the radius vector and ϕ is the polar angle.
cardiology (ˌkɑːdɪˈɒlədʒɪ) *n.* the branch of medical science concerned with the heart and its diseases. —**cardiological** (ˌkɑːdɪəˈlɒdʒɪkᵊl) *adj.* —ˌ**cardiˈologist** *n.*
cardiomegaly (ˌkɑːdɪəʊˈmɛgəlɪ) *n. Pathol.* another name for **megalocardia.**
cardiomyopathy (ˌkɑːdɪəʊmaɪˈɒpəθɪ) *n. Pathol.* a disease of the heart muscle usually caused by a biochemical defect or a toxin such as alcohol.
cardioplegia (ˌkɑːdɪəʊˈpliːdʒɪə) *n. Med.* deliberate arrest of the action of the heart, as by hypothermia or the injection of chemicals, to enable complex heart surgery to be carried out.
cardiopulmonary (ˌkɑːdɪəʊˈpʌlmənərɪ, -mənrɪ, -ˈpʊl-) *adj.* of, relating to, or affecting the heart and lungs.
cardiopulmonary resuscitation *n.* an emergency measure to revive a patient whose heart has stopped beating, in which compressions applied with the hands to the patient's chest are alternated with mouth-to-mouth respiration. Abbrev.: **CPR.**
cardiovascular (ˌkɑːdɪəʊˈvæskjʊlə) *adj.* of or relating to the heart and the blood vessels.
carditis (kɑːˈdaɪtɪs) *n.* inflammation of the heart.
cardoon (kɑːˈduːn) *n.* a thistle-like S European plant, *Cynara cardunculus,* closely related to the artichoke, with spiny leaves, purple flowers, and a leafstalk that may be blanched and eaten: family *Compositae* (composites). [C17: from French *cardon,* ultimately from Latin *carduus* thistle, artichoke]
card punch *n.* **1.** a device, controlled by a computer, for transferring information from the central processing unit onto punched cards. Compare **card reader. 2.** another name for **key punch.**
card reader *n.* a device for reading information on a punched card and transferring it to a computer or storage device. Compare **card punch.**
cards (kɑːdz) *n.* **1.** (*usually functioning as sing.*) **a.** any game or games played with cards, esp. playing cards. **b.** the playing of such a game. **2.** an employee's national insurance and other documents held by the employer. **3. ask for** *or* **get one's cards.** to ask or be told to terminate one's employment. **4. on the cards.** possible or likely. U.S. equivalent: **in the cards. 5. play one's cards.** to carry out one's plans; take action (esp. in the phrase **play one's cards right**). **6. put** *or* **lay one's cards on the table.** Also: **show one's cards.** to declare one's intentions, resources, etc.
cardsharp (ˈkɑːdˌʃɑːp) *or* **cardsharper** *n.* a professional card player who cheats. —ˈ**cardˌsharping** *n.*
carduaceous (ˌkɑːdjʊˈeɪʃəs) *adj.* of, relating to, or belonging to the *Carduaceae,* a subfamily of composite plants that includes the thistle. [C19: from New Latin *Carduācеae,* from *Carduus* type genus, from Latin: thistle]
card vote *n. Brit.* a vote by delegates, esp. at a trade-union conference, in which each delegate's vote counts as a vote by all his constituents.
cardy (ˈkɑːdɪ) *n., pl.* **-dies.** *Informal.* a variant spelling of **cardie.**
care (kɛə) *vb.* **1.** (when *tr., may take a clause as object*) to be troubled or concerned; be affected emotionally: *he is dying, and she doesn't care.* **2.** (*intr.;* foll. by *for* or *about*) to have regard, affection, or consideration (for): *he cares more for his hobby than his job.* **3.** (*intr.;* foll. by *for*) to have a desire or taste (for): *would you care for some tea?* **4.** (*intr.;* foll. by *for*) to provide physical needs, help, or comfort (for): *the nurse cared for her patients.* **5.** (*tr.*) to agree or like (to do something): *would you care to sit down, please?* **6. for all I care** *or* **I couldn't care less.** I am completely indifferent. ~*n.* **7.** careful or serious attention: *under her care the plant flourished; he does his work with care.* **8.** protective or supervisory control: *in the care of a doctor.* **9.** (*often pl.*) trouble; anxiety; worry. **10.** an object of or cause for concern: *the baby's illness was her only care.* **11.** caution: *handle with care.* **12. care of.** at the address of: written on envelopes. Usual abbrev.: **c/o. 13. in** (*or* **into**) **care.** *Social welfare.* made the legal responsibility of a local authority by order of a court. [Old English *cearu* (n.), *cearian* (vb.), of Germanic origin; compare Old High German *chara* lament, Latin *garrīre* to gossip]
CARE (kɛə) *n. acronym for* communicated authenticity, regard, empathy: the three qualities believed to be essential in the therapist practising client-centred therapy.
care and maintenance *n. Commerce.* the state of a building, ship, machinery, etc., that is not in current use although it is kept in good condition to enable it to be quickly brought into service if there is demand for it. Abbrev.: **C & M.**
care attendant *n. Social welfare.* (in Britain) a person who is paid to look after one or more severely handicapped people by visiting them frequently and staying when needed, but who does not live in.
careen (kəˈriːn) *vb.* **1.** to sway or cause to sway dangerously over to one side. **2.** (*tr.*) *Nautical.* to cause (a vessel) to keel over to one side, esp. in order to clean or repair its bottom. **3.** (*intr.*) *Nautical.* (of a vessel) to keel over to one side. [C17: from French *carène* keel, from Italian *carena,* from Latin *carīna* keel] —**caˈreenage** *n.* —**caˈreener** *n.*
career (kəˈrɪə) *n.* **1.** a path or progress through life or history. **2.** a profession or occupation chosen as one's life's work. **3.** (*modifier*) having or following a career as specified: *a career diplomat.* **4.** a course or path, esp. a swift or headlong one. ~*vb.* **5.** (*intr.*) to move swiftly along; rush in an uncontrolled way. [C16: from French *carrière,* from Late Latin *carrāria* carriage road, from Latin *carrus* two-wheeled wagon, CAR]
career girl *or* **woman** *n.* a girl or woman, often unmarried, who follows a career or profession.
careerist (kəˈrɪərɪst) *n.* a person who values success in his career above all else and seeks to advance it by any possible means. —**caˈreerism** *n.*

careers master *or (fem.)* **careers mistress** *n.* a teacher who gives advice and information about careers to his pupils.

Careers Officer *n.* a person trained in giving vocational advice, esp. to school leavers.

carefree ('kɛəˌfriː) *adj.* without worry or responsibility. —'**care**ˌ**freeness** *n.*

careful ('kɛəfʊl) *adj.* **1.** cautious in attitude or action; prudent; wary. **2.** painstaking in one's work; exact and thorough: *he wrote very careful script.* **3.** (*usually postpositive;* foll. by *of, in,* or *about*) solicitous; protective: *careful of one's reputation.* **4.** *Archaic.* full of care; anxious. **5.** *Brit.* mean or miserly. —'**carefully** *adv.* —'**carefulness** *n.*

careless ('kɛəlɪs) *adj.* **1.** done with or acting with insufficient attention; negligent. **2.** (often foll. by *in, of,* or *about*) unconcerned in attitude or action; heedless; indifferent (to): *she's very careless about her clothes.* **3.** (*usually prenominal*) carefree. **4.** (*usually prenominal*) unstudied; artless: *an impression of careless elegance.* —'**carelessly** *adv.* —'**carelessness** *n.*

carer ('kɛərə) *n. Social welfare.* a person who has accepted responsibility for looking after a vulnerable neighbour or relative. See also **caretaker** (sense 3).

caress (kə'rɛs) *n.* **1.** a gentle touch or embrace, esp. one given to show affection. ~*vb.* **2.** (*tr.*) to touch or stroke gently with affection or as with affection: *the wind caressed her face.* [C17: from French *caresse,* from Italian *carezza,* from Latin *cārus* dear] —**ca'resser** *n.* —**ca'ressingly** *adv.*

caret ('kærɪt) *n.* a symbol (‸) used to indicate the place in written or printed matter at which something is to be inserted. [C17: from Latin, literally: there is missing, from *carēre* to lack]

caretaker ('kɛəˌteɪkə) *n.* **1.** a person who is in charge of a place or thing, esp. in the owner's absence: *the caretaker of a school.* **2.** (*modifier*) holding office temporarily; interim: *a caretaker government.* **3.** *Social welfare.* a person who takes care of a vulnerable person, often a close relative. See also **carer.** —'**care**ˌ**taking** *n.*

careworn ('kɛəˌwɔːn) *adj.* showing signs of care, stress, worry, etc.: *a careworn face.*

Carey Street ('kɛərɪ) *n.* the state of bankruptcy. [named after the street in which the London bankruptcy court was situated]

carfare ('kɑːˌfɛə) *n. U.S. and Canadian.* the fare that a passenger is charged for a ride on a bus, etc.

carfax ('kɑːfæks) *n.* a place where principal roads or streets intersect, esp. a place in a town where four roads meet. [C14: from Anglo-French *carfuks,* from Old French *carrefures,* from Latin *quadrifurcus* four-forked]

carfuffle (kə'fʌfᵊl) *n. Informal, chiefly Brit.* a variant spelling of **kerfuffle.** [C20: of unknown origin]

cargo ('kɑːgəʊ) *n., pl.* **-goes** *or esp. U.S.* **-gos. 1. a.** goods carried by a ship, aircraft, or other vehicle; freight. **b.** (*as modifier*): *a cargo vessel.* **2.** any load: *the train pulled in with its cargo of new arrivals.* [C17: from Spanish: from *cargar* to load, from Late Latin *carricāre* to load a vehicle, from *carrus* CAR]

cargo cult *n.* a religious movement of the SW Pacific, characterized by expectation of the return of spirits in ships or aircraft carrying goods that will provide for the needs of the followers.

carhop ('kɑːˌhɒp) *n. U.S. and Canadian informal.* a waiter or waitress at a drive-in restaurant.

Carib ('kærɪb) *n.* **1.** (*pl.* **-ibs** *or* **-ib**) a member of a group of American Indian peoples of NE South America and the Lesser Antilles, a group of islands in the West Indies. **2.** the family of languages spoken by these peoples. [C16: from Spanish *Caribe,* from Arawak] —'**Cariban** *adj.*

Caribbean (ˌkærɪ'biːən; *U.S.* kə'rɪbɪən) *adj.* **1.** of or relating to the Caribbean Sea and its islands, lying off Central America and N South America. **2.** of or relating to the Carib or any of their languages. ~*n.* **3.** a member of any of the peoples inhabiting the islands of the Caribbean Sea, such as a West Indian or a Carib.

Caribbee bark ('kærɪˌbiː) *n.* the bark of any of various tropical American and West Indian rubiaceous trees of the genus *Exostema,* used as a substitute for cinchona bark.

caribou ('kærɪˌbuː) *n., pl.* **-bous** *or* **-bou.** a large deer, *Rangifer tarandus,* of Arctic regions of North America, having large branched antlers in the male and female: also occurs in Europe and Asia, where it is called a reindeer. Also called (Canadian): **tuktu.** [C18: from Canadian French, of Algonquian origin; compare Micmac *khalibu* literally: scratcher]

Caribou Eskimo *n.* a member of any of the Inuit peoples who inhabit the Barren Lands of N Canada.

caricature ('kærɪkəˌtjʊə) *n.* **1.** a pictorial, written, or acted representation of a person, which exaggerates his characteristic traits for comic effect. **2.** a ludicrously inadequate or inaccurate imitation: *he is a caricature of a statesman.* ~*vb.* **3.** (*tr.*) to represent in caricature or produce a caricature of. [C18: from Italian *caricatura* a distortion, exaggeration, from *caricare* to load, exaggerate; see CARGO] —'**carica**ˌ**tural** *adj.* —'**carica**ˌ**turist** *n.*

CARICOM ('kærɪˌkɒm) *n. acronym for* Caribbean Community and Common Market.

caries ('kɛəriːz) *n., pl.* **-ies.** progressive decay of a bone or a tooth. [C17: from Latin: decay; related to Greek *kēr* death]

CARIFTA (kæ'rɪftə) *n. acronym for* Caribbean Free Trade Area.

carillon (kə'rɪljən) *n. Music.* **1.** a set of bells usually hung in a tower and played either from a set of keys and pedals or mechanically. **2.** a tune played on such bells. **3.** a mixture stop on an organ giving the effect of a bell. **4.** a form of celesta or keyboard glockenspiel. ~*vb.* **-lons, -lonning, -lonned. 5.** (*intr.*) to play a carillon. [C18: from French: set of bells, from Old French *quarregnon,* ultimately from Latin *quattuor* four]

carillonneur (kəˌrɪljə'nɜː) *n.* a person who plays a carillon.

carina (kə'riːnə, -'raɪ-) *n., pl.* **-nae** (-niː) *or* **-nas.** a keel-like part or ridge, as in the breastbone of birds or the fused lower petals of a leguminous flower. [C18: from Latin: keel]

Carina (kə'riːnə, -'raɪ-) *n., Latin genitive* **Carinae** (kə'riːniː, -'raɪ-). a large conspicuous constellation in the S hemisphere close to the Southern Cross that contains Canopus, the second brightest star in the sky. It was originally considered part of the more extensive constellation of Argo.

carinate ('kærɪˌneɪt) *or* **carinated** *adj. Biology.* having a keel or ridge; shaped like a keel. [C17: from Latin *carīnāre* to furnish with a keel or shell, from *carīna* keel]

caring ('kɛərɪŋ) *adj.* **1.** feeling or showing care and compassion: *a caring attitude.* **2.** of or relating to professional social or medical care: *nursing is a caring job.* ~*n.* **3.** the practice or profession of providing social or medical care.

carioca (ˌkærɪ'əʊkə) *n.* **1.** a Brazilian dance similar to the samba. **2.** a piece of music composed for this dance. [C19: from Brazilian Portuguese]

Cariocan (ˌkærɪ'əʊkən) *or* **Carioca** *n.* a native of Rio de Janeiro, Brazil.

cariogenic (ˌkɛərɪəʊ'dʒɛnɪk) *adj.* (of a substance) producing caries, esp. in the teeth.

cariole *or* **carriole** ('kærɪˌəʊl) *n.* **1.** a small open two-wheeled horse-drawn vehicle. **2.** a covered cart. [C19: from French *carriole,* ultimately from Latin *carrus;* see CAR]

carious ('kɛərɪəs) *or* **cariose** ('kɛərɪˌəʊz) *adj.* (of teeth or bone) affected with caries; decayed. —**cariosity** (ˌkærɪ'ɒsɪtɪ, ˌkɛərɪ-) *or* '**cariousness** *n.*

cark[1] (kɑːk) *n., vb.* an archaic word for **worry** (senses 1, 2, 11, 13). [C13 *carken* to burden, from Old Northern French *carquier,* from Late Latin *carricāre* to load]

cark[2] (kɑːk) *vb.* (*intr.*) *Austral. slang.* to break down; die. [perhaps from the cry of the crow, as a carrion feeding bird]

carl *or* **carle** (kɑːl) *n. Archaic or Scot.* another word for **churl.** [Old English, from Old Norse *karl*]

carlin ('kɑːlɪn) *n.* another name for **pug**[1]. [C18: named after a French actor who played Harlequin, because of the resemblance of the dog's face to the black mask of the Harlequin]

carline[1] ('kɑːlɪn) *n.* a Eurasian thistle-like plant, *Carlina vulgaris,* having spiny leaves and flower heads surrounded by raylike whitish bracts: family *Compositae* (composites). Also called: **carline thistle.** [C16: from French, probably from Latin *cardō* thistle]

carline[2] *or* **carlin** ('kɑːlɪn) *n.* **1.** *Chiefly Scot.* an old woman, hag, or witch. **2.** a variant of **carling.** [C14: from Old Norse *kerling* old woman, diminutive of *karl* man, CHURL]

carling ('kɑːlɪŋ) *or* **carline** *n.* a fore-and-aft beam in a vessel, used for supporting the deck, esp. around a hatchway or other opening. [C14: from Old Norse *kerling* old woman, CARLINE[2]]

Carlist ('kɑːlɪst) *n.* **1.** (in Spain) a supporter of Don Carlos (1788–1855), pretender to the Spanish throne, or his descendants as the rightful kings of Spain. **2.** (in France) a supporter of Charles X (1757–1836), exiled king, or his descendants. —'**Carlism** *n.*

Carlovingian (ˌkɑːləʊ'vɪndʒɪən) *adj., n. History.* a variant of **Carolingian.**

carmagnole (ˌkɑːmən'jəʊl; *French* karmaɲɔl) *n.* **1.** a dance and song popular during the French Revolution. **2.** the costume worn by many French Revolutionaries, consisting of a short jacket with wide lapels, black trousers, a red liberty cap, and a tricoloured sash. [C18: from French, probably named after *Carmagnola,* Italy, taken by French Revolutionaries in 1792]

carman ('kɑːmən) *n., pl.* **-men. 1.** a man who drives a car or cart; carter. **2.** a man whose business is the transport of goods; haulier. **3.** *U.S. and Canadian.* a tram driver.

Carmelite ('kɑːməˌlaɪt) *n. R.C. Church.* **1.** a member of an order of mendicant friars founded about 1154; a White Friar. **2.** a member of a corresponding order of nuns founded in 1452, noted for its austere rule. **3.** (*modifier*) of or relating to the Carmelite friars or nuns. [C14: from French; named after Mount *Carmel* in NW Israel, where the order was founded]

carminative ('kɑːmɪnətɪv) *adj.* **1.** able to relieve flatulence. ~*n.* **2.** a carminative drug. [C15: from French *carminatif,* from Latin *carmināre* to card wool, remove impurities, from *cārere* to card]

carmine ('kɑːmaɪn) *n.* **1. a.** a vivid red colour, sometimes with a purplish tinge. **b.** (*as adj.*): *carmine paint.* **2.** a pigment of this colour obtained from cochineal. [C18: from Medieval Latin *carmīnus,* from Arabic *qirmiz* KERMES]

carnage ('kɑːnɪdʒ) *n.* extensive slaughter, esp. of human beings in battle. [C16: from French, from Italian *carnaggio,* from Medieval Latin *carnāticum,* from Latin *carō* flesh]

carnal ('kɑːnᵊl) *adj.* relating to the appetites and passions of the body; sensual; fleshly. [C15: from Late Latin: relating to flesh, from Latin *carō* flesh] —'**carnalist** *n.* —**car'nality** *n.* —'**carnally** *adv.*

carnal knowledge *n. Chiefly law.* **1.** sexual intercourse. **2. have carnal knowledge of.** to have sexual intercourse with.

carnallite ('kɑːnəˌlaɪt) *n.* a white or sometimes coloured mineral consisting of a hydrated chloride of potassium and magnesium in rhombic crystalline form: a source of potassium and also used as a fertilizer. Formula: $KCl.MgCl_2.6H_2O$. [C19: named after Rudolf von *Carnall* (1804–74), German mining engineer; see -ITE[1]]

carnassial (kɑːˈnæsɪəl) *adj.* **1.** *Zoology.* of, relating to, or designating the last upper premolar and first lower molar teeth of carnivores, which have sharp edges for tearing flesh. ~*n.* **2.** a carnassial tooth. [C19: from French *carnassier* meat-eating, from Provençal, from *carnasso* abundance of meat, from *carn* meat, flesh, from Latin *carō*]

carnation (kɑːˈneɪʃən) *n.* **1.** Also called: **clove pink.** a Eurasian caryophyllaceous plant, *Dianthus caryophyllus,* cultivated in many varieties for its white, pink, or red flowers, which have a fragrant scent of cloves. **2.** the flower of this plant. **3. a.** a pink or reddish-pink colour. **b.** (*as adj.*): *a carnation dress.* **4.** (*often pl.*) a flesh tint in painting. [C16: from French: flesh colour, from Late Latin *carnātiō* fleshiness, from Latin *carō* flesh]

carnauba (kɑːˈnaʊbə) *n.* **1.** Also called: **wax palm.** a Brazilian fan palm, *Copernicia cerifera.* **2.** Also called: **carnauba wax.** the wax obtained from the young leaves of this tree, used esp. as a polish. [from Brazilian Portuguese, probably of Tupi origin]

carnelian (kɑːˈniːljən) *n.* a red or reddish-yellow translucent variety of chalcedony, used as a gemstone. [C17: variant of *cornelian,* from Old French *corneline,* of uncertain origin; *car-* spelling influenced by Latin *carneus* flesh-coloured]

carnet (ˈkɑːneɪ) *n.* **1. a.** a customs licence authorizing the temporary importation of a motor vehicle. **b.** an official document permitting motorists to cross certain frontiers. **2.** a book of tickets, travel coupons, etc. [French: notebook, from Old French *quernet,* ultimately from Latin *quaternī* four at a time; see QUIRE[1]]

carnify (ˈkɑːnɪˌfaɪ) *vb.* **-fies, -fying, -fied.** (*intr.*) *Pathol.* (esp. of lung tissue, as the result of pneumonia) to be altered so as to resemble skeletal muscle. [C17: from Latin *carō* flesh + *facere* to make] —**carnification** (ˌkɑːnɪfɪˈkeɪʃən) *n.*

carnival (ˈkɑːnɪvᵊl) *n.* **1. a.** a festive occasion or period marked by merrymaking, processions, etc.: esp. in some Roman Catholic countries, the period just before Lent. **b.** (*as modifier*): *a carnival atmosphere.* **2.** a travelling fair having sideshows, merry-go-rounds, etc. **3.** a show or display arranged as an amusement. **4.** *Austral.* a sports meeting. [C16: from Italian *carnevale,* from Old Italian *carnelevare* a removing of meat (referring to the Lenten fast)]

carnivore (ˈkɑːnɪˌvɔː) *n.* **1.** any placental mammal of the order *Carnivora,* typically having large pointed canine teeth and sharp molars and premolars, specialized for eating flesh. The order includes cats, dogs, bears, raccoons, hyenas, civets, and weasels. **2.** any other animal or any plant that feeds on animals. [C19: probably back formation from CARNIVOROUS]

carnivorous (kɑːˈnɪvərəs) *adj.* **1.** (esp. of animals) feeding on flesh. **2.** (of plants such as the pitcher plant and sundew) able to trap and digest insects and other small animals. **3.** of or relating to the *Carnivora.* [C17: from Latin *carnivorus,* from *carō* flesh + *vorāre* to consume] —**carˈnivorously** *adv.* —**carˈnivorousness** *n.*

Carnot cycle (ˈkɑːnəʊ) *n.* an idealized reversible heat-engine cycle giving maximum efficiency and consisting of an isothermal expansion, an adiabatic expansion, an isothermal compression, and an adiabatic compression back to the initial state. [C19: named after Sadi *Carnot* (1796–1832), French physicist]

carnotite (ˈkɑːnəˌtaɪt) *n.* a radioactive yellow mineral consisting of hydrated uranium potassium vanadate: occurs in sedimentary rocks and is a source of uranium, radium, and vanadium. Formula: $K_2(UO_2)_2(V_2O_4)_2.3H_2O$. [C20: named after A. *Carnot* (died 1920), French inspector general of mines]

Carnot principle *n.* the principle that the efficiency of a reversible heat engine depends on the maximum and minimum temperatures of the working fluid during the operating cycle and not on the properties of the fluid.

carny[1] *or* **carney** (ˈkɑːnɪ) *vb.* **-nies, -nying, -nied** *or* **-neys, -neying, -neyed.** *Brit. informal.* to coax or cajole or act in a wheedling manner. [C19: of unknown origin]

carny[2], **carney,** *or* **carnie** (ˈkɑːnɪ) *n., pl.* **-nies.** *U.S. and Canadian slang.* **1.** short for **carnival. 2.** a person who works in a carnival.

carob (ˈkærəb) *n.* **1.** Also called: **algarroba.** an evergreen caesalpiniaceous Mediterranean tree, *Ceratonia siliqua,* with compound leaves and edible pods. **2.** Also called: **algarroba, Saint John's bread.** the long blackish sugary pod of this tree, used for animal fodder and sometimes for human food. [C16: from Old French *carobe,* from Medieval Latin *carrūbium,* from Arabic *al kharrūbah*]

caroche (kəˈrɒʃ) *n.* a stately ceremonial carriage used in the 16th and 17th centuries. [C16: from French, ultimately from Latin *carrus* CAR]

carol (ˈkærəl) *n.* **1.** a joyful hymn or religious song, esp. one (a **Christmas carol**) celebrating the birth of Christ. **2.** *Archaic.* an old English circular dance. ~*vb.* **-ols, -olling, -olled** *or U.S.* **-ols, -oling, -oled. 3.** (*intr.*) to sing carols at Christmas. **4.** to sing (something) in a joyful manner. [C13: from Old French, of uncertain origin] —ˈ**caroler** *or* ˈ**caroller** *n.* —ˈ**caroling** *or* ˈ**carolling** *n.*

Caroline (ˈkærəˌlaɪn) *or* **Carolean** (ˌkærəˈliːən) *adj.* **1.** Also called: **Carolinian.** characteristic of or relating to Charles I (1600–49) or Charles II (1630–85), kings of England, Scotland, and Ireland, the society over which they ruled, or their government. **2.** of or relating to any other king called Charles.

Carolingian (ˌkærəˈlɪndʒɪən) *adj.* **1.** of or relating to the Frankish dynasty founded by Pepin the Short (died 768 A.D.), son of Charles Martel (?688–741 A.D.), which ruled in France from 751–987 A.D. and in Germany until 911 A.D. ~*n.* **2.** a member of the dynasty of the Carolingian Franks. ~Also: **Carlovingian, Carolinian.**

Carolinian[1] (ˌkærəˈlɪnɪən) *adj., n.* a variant of **Caroline** or **Carolingian.**

Carolinian[2] (ˌkærəˈlɪnɪən) *adj.* **1.** of or relating to North or South Carolina, U.S. states. ~*n.* **2.** a native or inhabitant of North or South Carolina.

carolus (ˈkærələs) *n., pl.* **-luses** *or* **-li** (-ˌlaɪ). any of several coins struck in the reign of a king called Charles, esp. an English gold coin from the reign of Charles I (1625–49).

carom (ˈkærəm) *n. Billiards.* another word (esp. U.S. and Canadian) for **cannon** (sense 6). [C18: from earlier *carambole* (taken as *carom ball*), from Spanish *carambola* a sour greenish fruit, from Portuguese, from Marathi *karambal*]

Caro's acid (ˈkærəʊz, ˈkɑː-) *n.* another name for **peroxysulphuric acid.** [C19: named after Heinrich *Caro* (died 1910), German chemist]

carotene (ˈkærəˌtiːn) *or* **carotin** (ˈkærətɪn) *n.* any of four orange-red isomers of an unsaturated hydrocarbon present in many plants (β-carotene is the orange pigment of carrots) and converted to vitamin A in the liver. Formula: $C_{40}H_{56}$. [C19: *carotin,* from Latin *carōta* CARROT; see -ENE]

carotenoid *or* **carotinoid** (kəˈrɒtɪˌnɔɪd) *n.* **1.** any of a group of red or yellow pigments, including carotenes, found in plants and certain animal tissues. ~*adj.* **2.** of or resembling carotene or a carotenoid.

carotid (kəˈrɒtɪd) *n.* **1.** either one of the two principal arteries that supply blood to the head and neck. ~*adj.* **2.** of or relating to either of these arteries. [C17: from French, from Greek *karōtides,* from *karoun* to stupefy; so named by Galen (?130–?200 A.D.), Greek physician, because pressure on them produced unconsciousness] —**caˈrotidal** *adj.*

carousal (kəˈraʊzᵊl) *n.* a merry drinking party.

carouse (kəˈraʊz) *vb.* **1.** (*intr.*) to have a merry drinking spree; drink freely. ~*n.* **2.** another word for **carousal.** [C16: via French *carrousser* from German (*trinken*) *gar aus* (to drink) right out] —**caˈrouser** *n.*

carousel (ˌkærəˈsɛl, -ˈzɛl) *n.* **1.** a circular magazine in which slides for a projector are held: it moves round as each slide is shown. **2.** a rotating conveyor belt for luggage, as at an airport. **3.** the usual U.S. and Canadian name for **merry-go-round. 4.** *History.* a tournament in which horsemen took part in races and various manoeuvres in formation. [C17: from French *carrousel,* from Italian *carosello,* of uncertain origin]

carp[1] (kɑːp) *n., pl.* **carp** *or* **carps. 1.** a freshwater teleost food fish, *Cyprinus carpio,* having a body covered with cycloid scales, a naked head, one long dorsal fin, and two barbels on each side of the mouth: family *Cyprinidae.* **2.** any other fish of the family *Cyprinidae;* a cyprinid. [C14: from Old French *carpe,* of Germanic origin; compare Old High German *karpfo,* Old Norse *karfi*]

carp[2] (kɑːp) *vb.* (*intr.;* often foll. by *at*) to complain or find fault; nag pettily. [C13: from Old Norse *karpa* to boast; related to Latin *carpere* to pluck] —ˈ**carper** *n.*

-carp *n. combining form.* (in botany) fruit or a reproductive structure that develops into a particular part of the fruit: *epicarp.* [from New Latin *-carpium,* from Greek *-karpion,* from *karpos* fruit]

carpal (ˈkɑːpᵊl) *n.* **a.** any bone of the wrist. **b.** (*as modifier*): *carpal bones.* ~Also: **carpale** (kɑːˈpeɪlɪ). [C18: from New Latin *carpālis,* from Greek *karpos* wrist]

car park *n.* an area or building reserved for parking cars. Usual U.S. and Canadian term: **parking lot.**

carpe diem *Latin.* (ˈkɑːpɪ ˈdiːɛm) *sentence substitute.* enjoy the pleasures of the moment, without concern for the future. [literally: seize the day!]

carpel (ˈkɑːpᵊl) *n.* the female reproductive organ of flowering plants, consisting of an ovary, style, and stigma. The carpels are separate or fused to form a single pistil. [C19: from New Latin *carpellum,* from Greek *karpos* fruit] —ˈ**carpellary** *adj.* —**carpellate** (ˈkɑːpɪˌleɪt) *adj.*

carpenter (ˈkɑːpɪntə) *n.* **1.** a person skilled in woodwork, esp. in buildings, ships, etc. ~*vb.* **2.** (*intr.*) to do the work of a carpenter. **3.** (*tr.*) to make or fit together by or as if by carpentry. [C14: from Anglo-French, from Latin *carpentārius* wagon-maker, from *carpentum* wagon; of Celtic origin]

carpenter bee *n.* any large solitary bee of the genus *Xylocopa* and related genera that lays its eggs in tunnels bored into wood or in plant stems: family *Apidae.*

carpenter moth *n.* any of various large moths of the family *Cossidae,* the larvae of which bore beneath and cause damage to tree bark.

carpentry (ˈkɑːpɪntrɪ) *n.* **1.** the art or technique of working wood. **2.** the work produced by a carpenter; woodwork.

carpet (ˈkɑːpɪt) *n.* **1. a.** a heavy fabric for covering floors. **b.** (*as modifier*): *a carpet sale.* **2.** a covering like a carpet: *a carpet of leaves.* **3. on the carpet.** *Informal.* **a.** before authority to be reproved for misconduct or error. **b.** under consideration. ~*vb.* (*tr.*) **-pets, -peting, -peted. 4.** to cover with or as if with a carpet. **5.** *Informal.* to reprimand. [C14: from Old French *carpite,* from Old Italian *carpita,* from Late Latin *carpeta,* literally: (wool) that has been carded, from Latin *carpere* to pluck, card]

carpetbag (ˈkɑːpɪtˌbæg) *n.* a travelling bag originally made of carpeting.

carpetbagger (ˈkɑːpɪtˌbægə) *n.* **1.** a politician who seeks public office in a locality where he has no real connections. **2.** *U.S.* a Northern White who went to the South after the Civil War to profit from Reconstruction.

carpet beetle *or U.S.* **carpet bug** *n.* any of various beetles of the genus *Anthrenus,* the larvae of which feed on carpets, furnishing fabrics, etc.: family *Dermestidae.*

carpet bombing *n.* systematic intensive bombing of an area.

carpeting (ˈkɑːpɪtɪŋ) *n.* carpet material or carpets in general.

carpet knight *n. Disparaging.* a soldier who spends his life away from battle; idler.

carpet moth *n.* any of several geometrid moths with black- (or brown-)and-white mottled wings. [C19: so named from the patterns on their wings]

carpet plot *n. Maths.* the graphed values of a function of more than one variable, read from an ordinate at points located by the intersection of curves of constant values of each of the variables. [C20: from the shape of the graph, thought to resemble a flying carpet]

carpet shark *n.* any of various sharks of the family *Orectolobidae,* having two dorsal fins and a patterned back, typically marked with white and brown.

carpet slipper *n.* one of a pair of slippers, originally one made with woollen uppers resembling carpeting.

carpet snake *or* **python** *n.* a large nonvenomous Australian snake, *Morelia variegata,* having a carpetlike pattern on its back.

carpet-sweeper *n.* a household device with a revolving brush for sweeping carpets.

carpet tiles *pl. n.* small pieces of carpeting laid as tiles to cover a floor.

car phone *n.* a telephone that operates by cellular radio for use in a car.

carpi (ˈkɑːpaɪ) *n.* the plural of **carpus.**

-carpic *adj. combining form.* a variant of **-carpous.**

carping (ˈkɑːpɪŋ) *adj.* tending to make petty complaints; fault-finding. —ˈ**carpingly** *adv.*

carpo-[1] *combining form.* (in botany) indicating fruit or a reproductive structure that develops into part of the fruit: *carpophore; carpogonium.* [from Greek *karpos* fruit]

carpo-[2] *combining form.* carpus or carpal bones: *carpometacarpus.*

carpogonium (ˌkɑːpəˈgəʊnɪəm) *n., pl.* **-nia** (-nɪə). the female sex organ of red algae, consisting of a swollen base containing the ovum and a long neck down which the male gametes pass. —ˌ**carpoˈgonial** *adj.*

carpology (kɑːˈpɒlədʒɪ) *n.* the branch of botany concerned with the study of fruits and seeds. —**carpological** (ˌkɑːpəˈlɒdʒɪk^{ə}l) *adj.* —**carˈpologist** *n.*

carpometacarpus (ˌkɑːpəʊˌmɛtəˈkɑːpəs) *n.* a bone in the wing of a bird that consists of the metacarpal bones and some of the carpal bones fused together.

carpophagous (kɑːˈpɒfəgəs) *adj. Zoology.* feeding on fruit: *carpophagous bats.*

carpophore (ˈkɑːpəˌfɔː) *n.* **1.** an elongated part of the receptacle in flowers such as the geranium that bears the carpels and stamens. **2.** a spore-bearing structure in some of the higher fungi.

carport (ˈkɑːˌpɔːt) *n.* a shelter for a car usually consisting of a roof built out from the side of a building and supported by posts.

carpospore (ˈkɑːpəʊˌspɔː) *n.* a sexual spore produced by red algae after fertilization of the carpogonium.

-carpous *or* **-carpic** *adj. combining form.* (in botany) indicating a certain kind or number of fruit: *apocarpous.* [from New Latin *-carpus,* from Greek *karpos* fruit]

carpus (ˈkɑːpəs) *n., pl.* **-pi** (-paɪ). **1.** the technical name for **wrist. 2.** the eight small bones of the human wrist that form the joint between the arm and the hand. **3.** the corresponding joint in other tetrapod vertebrates. [C17: New Latin, from Greek *karpos*]

carr (kɑː) *n. Brit.* an area of bog or fen in which scrub, esp. willow, has become established. [C15: from Old Norse]

carrack (ˈkærək) *n.* a galleon sailed in the Mediterranean as a merchantman in the 15th and 16th centuries. [C14: from Old French *caraque,* from Old Spanish *carraca,* from Arabic *qarāqīr* merchant ships]

carrageen, carragheen, *or* **carageen** (ˈkærəˌgiːn) *n.* **1.** an edible red seaweed, *Chondrus crispus,* of rocky shores of North America and N Europe, used to make a beverage, medicine, and jelly, and as an emulsifying and gelling agent **(E407)** in various processed desserts and drinks. **2.** any product of this seaweed. ~Also called: **Irish moss.** [C19: from *Carragheen,* near Waterford, Ireland, where it is very plentiful]

carrefour (ˈkærəˌfɔː) *n.* **1.** a rare word for **crossroads. 2.** a public square, esp. one at the intersection of several roads. [C15: from Old French *quarrefour,* ultimately from Latin *quadrifurcus* having four forks]

carrel *or* **carrell** (ˈkærəl) *n.* a small individual study room or private desk, often in a library, where a student or researcher can work undisturbed. [C16: a variant of CAROL]

carriage (ˈkærɪdʒ) *n.* **1.** *Brit.* a railway coach for passengers. **2.** the manner in which a person holds and moves his head and body; bearing. **3.** a four-wheeled horse-drawn vehicle for persons. **4.** the moving part of a machine that bears another part: *a typewriter carriage; a lathe carriage.* **5.** (ˈkærɪdʒ, ˈkærɪɪdʒ). **a.** the act of conveying; carrying. **b.** the charge made for conveying (esp. in the phrases **carriage forward,** when the charge is to be paid by the receiver, and **carriage paid**). [C14: from Old Northern French *cariage,* from *carier* to CARRY]

carriage bolt *n. Chiefly U.S. and Canadian.* another name for **coach bolt.**

carriage clock *n.* a portable clock, usually in a rectangular case with a handle on the top, of a type originally used by travellers.

carriage dog *n.* a former name for **Dalmatian.**

carriage line *n.* another term for **coach line.**

carriage trade *n.* trade from the wealthy part of society.

carriageway (ˈkærɪdʒˌweɪ) *n. Brit.* the part of a road along which traffic passes in a single line moving in one direction only: *a dual carriageway.*

carrick bend (ˈkærɪk) *n.* a knot used for joining two ropes or cables together. [C19: perhaps variant of CARRACK]

carrick bitt *n. Nautical.* either of a pair of strong posts used for supporting a windlass.

carrier (ˈkærɪə) *n.* **1.** a person, thing, or organization employed to carry goods, passengers, etc. **2.** a mechanism by which something is carried or moved, such as a device for transmitting rotation from the faceplate of a lathe to the workpiece. **3.** *Pathol.* another name for **vector** (sense 2). **4.** *Pathol.* a person or animal that, without having any symptoms of a disease, is capable of transmitting it to others. **5.** Also called: **charge carrier.** *Physics.* an electron or hole that carries the charge in a conductor or semiconductor. **6.** short for **carrier wave. 7.** *Chem.* **a.** the inert solid on which a dyestuff is adsorbed in forming a lake. **b.** a substance, such as kieselguhr or asbestos, used to support a catalyst. **c.** an inactive substance containing a radioisotope used in radioactive tracing. **d.** an inert gas used to transport the sample through a gas-chromatography column. **e.** a catalyst that effects the transfer of an atom or group from one molecule to another. **8.** See **aircraft carrier. 9.** a breed of domestic fancy pigeon having a large walnut-shaped wattle over the beak; a distinct variety of pigeon from the homing or carrier pigeon. See also **carrier pigeon. 10.** a U.S. name for **roof rack.**

carrier bag *n. Brit.* a large paper or plastic bag for carrying shopping

carrier pigeon *n.* any homing pigeon, esp. one used for carrying messages.

carrier wave *n. Radio.* a wave of fixed amplitude and frequency that is modulated in amplitude, frequency, or phase in order to carry a signal in radio transmission, etc. See **amplitude modulation, frequency modulation.**

carriole (ˈkærɪˌəʊl) *n.* a variant spelling of **cariole.**

carrion (ˈkærɪən) *n.* **1.** dead and rotting flesh. **2.** (*modifier*) eating carrion: *carrion beetles.* **3.** something rotten or repulsive. [C13: from Anglo-French *caroine,* ultimately from Latin *carō* flesh]

carrion beetle *n.* any beetle of the family *Silphidae* that track carrion by a keen sense of smell: best known are the **burying** or **sexton beetles.**

carrion crow *n.* a common predatory and scavenging European crow, *Corvus corone,* similar to the rook but having a pure black bill. See also **hooded crow.**

carrion flower *n.* **1.** a liliaceous climbing plant, *Smilax herbacea* of E North America, whose small green flowers smell like decaying flesh. **2.** any of several other plants, esp. any of the genus *Stapelia,* whose flowers have an unpleasant odour.

carronade (ˌkærəˈneɪd) *n.* an obsolete naval gun of short barrel and large bore. [C18: named after *Carron,* Scotland, where it was first cast; see -ADE]

carron oil (ˈkærən) *n.* an ointment of limewater and linseed oil, formerly used to treat burns. [C19: named after *Carron,* Scotland, where it was used among the ironworkers]

carrot (ˈkærət) *n.* **1.** an umbelliferous plant, *Daucus carota sativa,* with finely divided leaves and flat clusters of small white flowers. See also **wild carrot. 2.** the long tapering orange root of this plant, eaten as a vegetable. **3. a.** something offered as a lure or incentive. **b. carrot and stick.** reward and punishment as methods of persuasion. [C16: from Old French *carotte,* from Late Latin *carōta,* from Greek *karōton;* perhaps related to Greek *karē* head]

carrot fly *n.* a dipterous insect, *Psila rosae,* that is a serious pest of carrots. The larvae tunnel into the root to feed.

carroty (ˈkærətɪ) *adj.* **1.** of a reddish or yellowish-orange colour. **2.** having red hair.

carrousel (ˌkærəˈsɛl, -ˈzɛl) *n.* a variant spelling of **carousel.**

carry (ˈkærɪ) *vb.* **-ries, -rying, -ried.** (*mainly tr.*) **1.** (*also intr.*) to take or bear (something) from one place to another: *to carry a baby in one's arms.* **2.** to transfer for consideration; take: *he* *carried his complaints to her superior.* **3.** to have on one's person: *he always carries a watch.* **4.** (*also intr.*) to be transmitted or serve as a medium for transmitting: *sound carries best over water.* **5.** to contain or be capable of containing: *the jug carries water.* **6.** to bear or be able to bear the weight, pressure, or responsibility of: *her efforts carry the whole production.* **7.** to have as an attribute or result: *this crime carries a heavy penalty.* **8.** to bring or communicate: *to carry news.* **9.** (*also intr.*) to be pregnant with (young): *she is carrying her third child.* **10.** to bear (the head, body, etc.) in a specified manner: *she carried her head high.* **11.** to conduct or bear (oneself) in a specified manner: *she carried herself well in a difficult situation.* **12.** to continue or extend: *the war was carried into enemy territory.* **13.** to cause to move or go: *desire for riches carried him to the city.* **14.** to influence, esp. by emotional appeal: *his words carried the crowd.* **15.** to secure the passage of (a bill, motion, etc.). **16.** to win (an election). **17.** to obtain victory for (a candidate or measure) in an election. **18.** *Chiefly U.S.* to win a plurality or majority of votes in (a district, legislative body, etc.): *the candidate carried 40 states.* **19.** to capture: *our troops carried the town.* **20.** (of communications media) to include as the content: *this newspaper carries no book reviews.* **21.** Also (esp. U.S.): **carry over.** *Book-keeping.* to transfer (an item) to another account, esp. to transfer to the following year's account instead of writing off against profit and loss: *to carry a loss.* **22.** *Maths.* to transfer (a number) from one column of figures to the next, as from units to tens in multiplication and addition. **23.** (of a shop, trader, etc.) to keep in stock: *to carry confectionery.* **24.** to support (a musical part or melody) against the other parts. **25.** to sustain (livestock): *this land will carry twelve ewes to the acre.* **26.** to maintain (livestock) in good health but without increasing their weight or obtaining any products from them. **27.** (*intr.*) (of a ball, projectile, etc.) to travel through the air or reach a specified point: *his first drive carried to the green.* **28.** *Sport, esp. golf.* (of a ball) to travel beyond: *the drive carried the trees.* **29.** (*intr.*) (of a gun) to have a range as specified: *this rifle carries for 1200 yards.* **30.** to retain contact with and pursue (a line of scent). **31.** (*intr.*) (of ground) to be in such a condition that scent lies well upon it. **32.** *Ice hockey.* to dribble. **33.** *Informal.* to imbibe (alcoholic drink) without showing ill effects. **34.** (*intr.*) *Slang.* to have drugs on one's person. **35. carry all before (one).** to win unanimous support or approval for (oneself). **36. carry a tune.** to be able to sing in tune. **37. carry the can (for).** *Informal.* to take the responsibility for some misdemeanour, etc. (on behalf of). **38. carry the day.** to win a contest or competition; succeed. ~*n., pl.* **-ries. 39.** the act of carrying. **40.** *U.S. and Canadian.* a portion of land over which a boat must be portaged. **41.** the range of a firearm or its projectile. **42.** the distance travelled by a ball, etc., esp. (in golf) the distance from where the ball is struck to where it first touches the ground. [C14 *carien,* from Old Northern French *carier* to move by vehicle, from *car,* from Latin *carrum* transport wagon; see CAR]

carryall[1] ('kærɪˌɔːl) *n.* a light four-wheeled horse-drawn carriage usually designed to carry four passengers.

carryall[2] ('kærɪˌɔːl) *n.* the usual U.S. and Canadian name for a **holdall.**

carry away *vb.* (*tr., adv.*) **1.** to remove forcefully. **2.** (usually passive) to cause (a person) to lose self-control. **3.** (usually passive) to delight or enrapture: *he was carried away by the music.*

carry back *Tax accounting.* ~*vb.* **1.** (*tr., adv.*) to apply (a legally permitted credit, esp. an operating loss) to the taxable income of previous years in order to ease the overall tax burden. ~*n.* **carry-back. 2.** an amount carried back.

carrycot ('kærɪˌkɒt) *n.* a light cot with handles, similar to but smaller than the body of a pram and often attachable to an unsprung wheeled frame.

carry forward *vb.* (*tr., adv.*) **1.** *Book-keeping.* to transfer (a balance) to the next page, column, etc. **2.** *Tax accounting.* to apply (a legally permitted credit, esp. an operating loss) to the taxable income of following years to ease the overall tax burden. ~Also: **carry over.** ~*n.* **carry-forward. 3.** Also called: **carry-over.** *Tax accounting.* an amount carried forward.

carrying capacity *n. Ecology.* the maximum number of individuals that an area of land can support, usually determined by their food requirements.

carrying charge *n.* the opportunity cost of unproductive assets, such as goods stored in a warehouse.

carrying-on *n., pl.* **carryings-on.** *Informal.* **1.** unconventional or questionable behaviour. **2.** excited or flirtatious behaviour, esp. when regarded as foolish.

carrying place *n. Canadian.* another name for **portage.**

carry off *vb.* (*tr., adv.*) **1.** to remove forcefully. **2.** to win: *he carried off all the prizes.* **3.** to manage or handle (a situation) successfully: *he carried off the introductions well.* **4.** to cause to die: *he was carried off by pneumonia.*

carry on *vb.* (*adv.*) **1.** (*intr.*) to continue or persevere: *we must carry on in spite of our difficulties.* **2.** (*tr.*) to manage or conduct: *to carry on a business.* **3.** (*intr.;* often foll. by *with*) *Informal.* to have an affair. **4.** (*intr.*) *Informal.* to cause a fuss or commotion. ~*n.* **carry-on. 5.** *Informal, chiefly Brit.* a fuss or commotion.

carry out *vb.* (*tr., adv.*) **1.** to perform or cause to be implemented: *I wish he could afford to carry out his plan.* **2.** to bring to completion; accomplish. ~*n.* **carry-out.** *Chiefly Scot.* **3.** alcohol bought at a pub or off-licence for consumption elsewhere. **4. a.** hot cooked food bought at a shop or restaurant for consumption elseshere. **b.** a shop or restaurant that sells such food: *we'll get something from the Chinese carry-out.* **c.** (*as modifier*): *a carry-out shop.*

carry over *vb.* (*tr., adv.*) **1.** to postpone or defer. **2.** *Book-keeping, tax accounting.* another term for **carry forward. 3.** (on the London Stock Exchange) to postpone (payment or settlement) until the next account day. ~*n.* **carry-over. 4.** something left over for future use, esp. goods to be sold. **5.** *Book-keeping.* a sum or balance carried forward. **6.** another name for **contango. 7.** *Tax accounting.* another name for **carry-forward.**

carry through *vb.* (*tr., adv.*) **1.** to bring to completion. **2.** to enable to endure (hardship, trouble, etc.); support.

carse (kɑːs; *Scot.* kærs) *n. Scot.* a riverside area of flat fertile alluvium. [C14: of uncertain origin; perhaps from a plural form of CARR]

carsick ('kɑːˌsɪk) *adj.* nauseated from riding in a car or other vehicle. —'**carˌsickness** *n.*

cart[1] (kɑːt) *n.* **1.** a heavy open vehicle, usually having two wheels and drawn by horses, used in farming and to transport goods. **2.** a light open horse-drawn vehicle having two wheels and springs, for business or pleasure. **3.** any small vehicle drawn or pushed by hand, such as a trolley. **4. in the cart. a.** in an unpleasant or awkward situation. **b.** in the lurch. **5. put the cart before the horse.** to reverse the usual or natural order of things. ~*vb.* **6.** (*usually tr.*) to use or draw a cart to convey (goods, etc.): *to cart groceries.* **7.** (*tr.*) to carry with effort; haul: *to cart wood home.* [C13: from Old Norse *kartr;* related to Old English *cræt* carriage, Old French *carete;* see CAR] —'**cartable** *adj.* —'**carter** *n.*

cart[2] (kɑːt) *n. Radio, television.* short for **cartridge** (sense 4).

cartage ('kɑːtɪdʒ) *n.* the process or cost of carting.

carte (kɑːt) *n.* a variant spelling of **quarte** (in fencing).

carte blanche ('kɑːt 'blɑːntʃ; *French* kart blɑ̃ʃ) *n., pl.* **cartes blanches** ('kɑːts 'blɑːntʃ; *French* kart blɑ̃ʃ). **1.** complete discretion or authority: *the government gave their negotiator carte blanche.* **2.** *Cards.* a piquet hand containing no court cards: scoring ten points. [C18: from French: blank paper]

carte du jour ('kɑːt də 'ʒʊə, duː; *French* kart dy ʒur) *n., pl.* **cartes du jour** ('kɑːts də 'ʒʊə, duː; *French* kart dy ʒur). a menu listing dishes available on a particular day. [French, literally: card of the day]

cartel (kɑː'tɛl) *n.* **1.** Also called: **trust.** a collusive international association of independent enterprises formed to monopolize production and distribution of a product or service, control prices, etc. **2.** *Politics.* an alliance of parties or interests to further common aims. [C20: from German *Kartell,* from French, from Italian *cartello* a written challenge, public notice, diminutive of *carta* CARD[1]]

cartelize *or* **cartelise** ('kɑːtəlaɪz) *vb.* to form or be formed into a cartel. —ˌ**carteli'zation** *or* ˌ**carteli'sation** *n.*

Cartesian (kɑː'tiːzɪən, -ʒjən) *adj.* **1.** of or relating to the works of René Descartes (1596–1650), French mathematician and philosopher. **2.** of, relating to, or used in Descartes' mathematical system: *Cartesian coordinates.* **3.** of, relating to, or derived from Descartes' philosophy, esp. his contentions that personal identity consists in the continued existence of a unique mind and that the mind and body are connected causally. See also **dualism** (sense 2). ~*n.* **4.** a follower of the teachings and methods of Descartes. —**Car'tesianˌism** *n.*

Cartesian coordinates *pl. n.* a system of representing points in space in terms of their distance from a given origin measured along a set of mutually perpendicular axes. Written (x,y,z) with reference to three axes.

Cartesian product *n. Maths, logic.* the set of all ordered pairs of members of two given sets. The product $A \times B$ is the set of all pairs $\langle a, b \rangle$ where a is a member of A and b is a member of B. Also called: **cross product.**

cartful ('kɑːtˌfʊl) *n.* the amount a cart can hold.

Carthaginian (ˌkɑːθə'dʒɪnɪən) *adj.* of or relating to Carthage, an ancient city state on the N African coast. ~*n. adj.* an inhabitant of Carthage.

carthorse ('kɑːtˌhɔːs) *n.* a large heavily built horse kept for pulling carts or carriages.

Carthusian (kɑː'θjuːzɪən) *n. R.C. Church.* **a.** a member of an austere monastic order founded by Saint Bruno in 1084 near Grenoble, France. **b.** (*as modifier*): *a Carthusian monastery.* [C14: from Medieval Latin *Carthusianus,* from Latin *Carthusia* Chartreuse, near Grenoble]

cartilage ('kɑːtɪlɪdʒ, 'kɑːtlɪdʒ) *n.* a tough elastic tissue composing most of the embryonic skeleton of vertebrates. In the adults of higher vertebrates it is mostly converted into bone, remaining only on the articulating ends of bones, in the thorax, trachea, nose, and ears. Nontechnical name: **gristle.** [C16: from Latin *cartilāgō*] —**cartilaginous** (ˌkɑːtɪ'lædʒɪnəs) *adj.*

cartilage bone *n.* any bone that develops within cartilage rather than in a fibrous tissue membrane. Compare **membrane bone.**

cartilaginous fish *n.* any fish of the class *Chondrichthyes,* including the sharks, skates, and rays, having a skeleton composed entirely of cartilage.

cartload (ˈkɑːtˌləʊd) *n.* **1.** the amount a cart can hold. **2.** a quantity of rubble, ballast, etc., of between one quarter and one half of a cubic yard.

cart off, away, *or* **out** *vb. (tr., adv.) Informal.* to carry or remove brusquely or by force.

cartogram (ˈkɑːtəˌgræm) *n.* a map showing statistical information in diagrammatic form. [C20: from French *cartogramme,* from *carte* map, CHART; see -GRAM]

cartography *or* **chartography** (kɑːˈtɒgrəfɪ) *n.* the art, technique, or practice of compiling or drawing maps or charts. [C19: from French *cartographie,* from *carte* map, CHART] —**carˈtographer** *or* **charˈtographer** *n.* —**cartographic** (ˌkɑːtəˈgræfɪk), ˌ**cartoˈgraphical** *or* ˌ**chartoˈgraphic,** ˌ**chartoˈgraphical** *adj.* —ˌ**cartoˈgraphically** *or* ˌ**chartoˈgraphically** *adv.*

cartomancy (ˈkɑːtəˌmænsɪ) *n.* the telling of fortunes with playing cards. [C19: from French *carte* card + -MANCY]

carton (ˈkɑːtən) *n.* **1.** a cardboard box for containing goods. **2.** a container of waxed paper or plastic in which liquids, such as milk, are sold. **3.** *Shooting.* **a.** a white disc at the centre of a target. **b.** a shot that hits this disc. ~*vb. (tr.)* **4.** to enclose (goods) in a carton. [C19: from French, from Italian *cartone* pasteboard, from *carta* CARD[1]]

cartoon (kɑːˈtuːn) *n.* **1.** a humorous or satirical drawing, esp. one in a newspaper or magazine, concerning a topical event. **2.** a sequence of drawings in a newspaper, magazine, etc., relating a comic or adventurous situation. Also called: **comic strip. 3.** See **animated cartoon. 4.** a full-size preparatory sketch for a fresco, tapestry, mosaic, etc., from which the final work is traced or copied. [C17: from Italian *cartone* pasteboard, sketch on stiff paper; see CARTON] —**carˈtoonist** *n.*

cartophily (kɑːˈtɒfɪlɪ) *n.* the hobby of collecting cigarette cards. [C20: from French *carte* card + -O- + *-phily* from Greek *philos* loving] —**carˈtophilist** *n.*

cartouche *or* **cartouch** (kɑːˈtuːʃ) *n.* **1.** a carved or cast ornamental tablet or panel in the form of a scroll, sometimes having an inscription. **2.** an oblong figure enclosing characters expressing royal or divine names in Egyptian hieroglyphics. **3.** the paper case holding combustible materials in certain fireworks. **4.** *Now rare.* a cartridge or a box for cartridges. [C17: from French: scroll, cartridge, from Italian *cartoccio,* from *carta* paper; see CARD[1]]

cartridge (ˈkɑːtrɪdʒ) *n.* **1.** a cylindrical, usually metal casing containing an explosive charge and often a bullet, for a rifle or other small arms. **2.** a case for an explosive, such as a blasting charge. **3.** an electromechanical transducer in the pick-up of a record player, usually either containing a piezoelectric crystal (**crystal cartridge**) or an electromagnet (**magnetic cartridge**). **4.** a container for magnetic tape that is inserted into a tape deck. It is about four times the size of a cassette. **5.** Also called: **cassette, magazine.** *Photog.* a light-tight film container that enables a camera to be loaded and unloaded in normal light. **6.** *Computer technol.* a removable unit in a computer, such as an integrated circuit, containing software. [C16: from earlier *cartage,* variant of CARTOUCHE (cartridge)]

cartridge belt *n.* a belt with pockets for cartridge clips or loops for cartridges.

cartridge clip *n.* a metallic container holding cartridges for an automatic firearm.

cartridge paper *n.* **1.** an uncoated type of drawing or printing paper, usually made from bleached sulphate wood pulp with an addition of esparto grass. **2.** a heavy paper used in making cartridges or as drawing or printing paper.

cartridge pen *n.* a pen having a removable ink reservoir that is replaced when empty.

cart track *n.* a rough track or road in a rural area. Also called: **cart road.**

cartulary (ˈkɑːtjʊlərɪ) *or* **chartulary** (ˈtʃɑːtjʊlərɪ) *n., pl.* **-laries.** *Law.* **a.** a collection of charters or records, esp. relating to the title to an estate or monastery. **b.** any place where records are kept. [C16: from Medieval Latin *cartulārium,* from Latin *chartula* a little paper, from *charta* paper; see CARD[1]]

cartwheel (ˈkɑːtˌwiːl) *n.* **1.** the wheel of a cart, usually having wooden spokes and metal tyres. **2.** an acrobatic movement in which the body makes a sideways revolution supported on the hands with arms and legs outstretched. **3.** *U.S. slang.* a large coin, esp. the silver dollar.

cartwheel flower *n.* another name for **giant hogweed.**

cartwright (ˈkɑːtˌraɪt) *n.* a person who makes carts.

caruncle (ˈkærəŋkəl, kəˈrʌŋ-) *n.* **1.** a fleshy outgrowth on the heads of certain birds, such as a cock's comb. **2.** an outgrowth near the hilum on the seeds of some plants. **3.** any small fleshy mass in or on the body, either natural or abnormal. [C17: from obsolete French *caruncule,* from Latin *caruncula* a small piece of flesh, from *carō* flesh] —**caruncular** (kəˈrʌŋkjʊlə) *or* **caˈrunculous** *adj.* —**caruncuIate** (kəˈrʌŋkjʊlɪt, -ˌleɪt) *or* **caˈruncuˌlated** *adj.*

carve (kɑːv) *vb.* **1.** *(tr.)* to cut or chip in order to form something: *to carve wood.* **2.** to decorate or form (something) by cutting or chipping: *to carve statues.* **3.** to slice (meat) into pieces: *to carve a turkey.* [Old English *ceorfan;* related to Old Frisian *kerva,* Middle High German *kerben* to notch]

carvel (ˈkɑːvəl) *n.* another word for **caravel.**

carvel-built *adj.* (of a vessel) having a hull with planks made flush at the seams. Compare **clinker-built.**

carven (ˈkɑːvən) *vb.* an archaic or literary past participle of **carve.**

carve out *vb. (tr., adv.)* to make or create (a career): *he carved out his own future.*

carver (ˈkɑːvə) *n.* **1.** a carving knife. **2.** *(pl.)* a large matched knife and fork for carving meat. **3.** *Brit.* a chair having arms that forms part of a set of dining chairs.

carvery (ˈkɑːvərɪ) *n., pl.* **-veries.** an eating establishment at which customers pay a set price and may then have unrestricted helpings of food from a variety of meats, salads, and other vegetables.

carve up *vb. (tr., adv.)* **1.** to cut (something) into pieces. **2.** to divide or dismember (a country, land, etc.). ~*n.* **carve-up. 3.** *Informal.* an act or instance of dishonestly prearranging the result of a competition. **4.** *Slang.* the distribution of something, as of booty.

carving (ˈkɑːvɪŋ) *n.* a figure or design produced by carving stone, wood, etc.

carving knife *n.* a long-bladed knife for carving cooked meat for serving.

caryatid (ˌkærɪˈætɪd) *n., pl.* **-ids** *or* **-ides** (-ɪˌdiːz). a column, used to support an entablature, in the form of a draped female figure. Compare **telamon.** [C16: from Latin *Caryātides,* from Greek *Karuatides* priestesses of the goddess Artemis at *Karuai* (Caryae), village in Laconia] —ˌ**caryˈatidal,** ˌ**caryˌatiˈdean,** ˌ**caryˈatic,** *or* **caryatidic** (ˌkærɪəˈtɪdɪk) *adj.*

caryo- *combining form.* a variant of **karyo-.**

caryophyllaceous (ˌkærɪəʊfɪˈleɪʃəs) *adj.* of, relating to, or belonging to the *Caryophyllaceae,* a family of flowering plants including the pink, carnation, sweet william, and chickweed. [C19: from New Latin *Caryophyllāceae,* from *Caryophyllus* former type genus, from Greek *karuophullon* clove tree, from *karuon* nut + *phullon* leaf]

caryopsis (ˌkærɪˈɒpsɪs) *n., pl.* **-ses** (-siːz) *or* **-sides** (-sɪˌdiːz). a dry seedlike fruit having the pericarp fused to the seed coat of the single seed: produced by the grasses. [C19: New Latin; see KARYO-, -OPSIS]

carzey *or* **carsey** (ˈkɑːzɪ) *n. Cockney slang.* a lavatory; toilet. [C19: from *casa, case* a brothel, from Italian *casa* a house]

casaba *or* **cassaba** (kəˈsɑːbə) *n.* a kind of winter muskmelon having a yellow rind and sweet juicy flesh. [from *Kassaba,* former name of Turgutlu, Turkey]

Casanova (ˌkæsəˈnəʊvə) *n. (sometimes not cap.)* a man noted for his amorous adventures; a rake. [after Giovanni *Casanova* (1725–98), Italian adventurer and womanizer]

casbah (ˈkæzbɑː) *n. (sometimes cap.)* a variant spelling of **kasbah.**

cascabel (ˈkæskəˌbɛl) *n.* **1.** a knoblike protrusion on the rear part of the breech of an obsolete muzzle-loading cannon. **2.** the rear part itself. [C17: from Spanish: small bell, rattle, of uncertain origin]

cascade (kæsˈkeɪd) *n.* **1.** a waterfall or series of waterfalls over rocks. **2.** something resembling this, such as folds of lace. **3. a.** a consecutive sequence of chemical or physical processes. **b.** *(as modifier): cascade liquefaction.* **4. a.** a series of stages in the processing chain of an electrical signal where each operates the next in turn. **b.** *(as modifier): a cascade amplifier.* **5.** the cumulative process responsible for the formation of an electrical discharge, cosmic-ray shower, or Geiger counter avalanche in a gas. ~*vb.* **6.** *(intr.)* to flow or fall in or like a cascade. [C17: from French, from Italian *cascata,* from *cascare* to fall, ultimately from Latin *cadere* to fall]

cascara (kæsˈkɑːrə) *n.* **1.** See **cascara sagrada. 2.** Also called: **cascara buckthorn, bearwood.** a shrub or small tree, *Rhamnus purshiana* of NW North America, whose bark is a source of cascara sagrada: family *Rhamnaceae.* [C19: from Spanish: bark, from *cascar* to break, from Vulgar Latin *quassicāre* (unattested) to shake violently, shatter, from Latin *quassāre* to dash to pieces]

cascara sagrada (səˈgrɑːdə) *n.* the dried bark of the cascara buckthorn, used as a laxative and stimulant. Often shortened to **cascara.** [Spanish, literally: sacred bark]

cascarilla (ˌkæskəˈrɪlə) *n.* **1.** a West Indian euphorbiaceous shrub, *Croton eluteria,* whose bitter aromatic bark is used as a tonic. **2.** the bark of this shrub. [C17: from Spanish, diminutive of *cáscara* bark; see CASCARA]

case[1] (keɪs) *n.* **1.** a single instance, occurrence, or example of something. **2.** an instance of disease, injury, hardship, etc. **3.** a question or matter for discussion: *the case before the committee.* **4.** a specific condition or state of affairs; situation. **5.** a set of arguments supporting a particular action, cause, etc. **6. a.** a person attended or served by a doctor, social worker, solicitor, etc.; patient or client. **b.** *(as modifier): a case study.* **7. a.** an action or suit at law or something that forms sufficient grounds for bringing an action: *he has a good case.* **b.** the evidence offered in court to support a claim. **8.** *Grammar.* **a.** a set of grammatical categories of nouns, pronouns, and adjectives, marked by inflection in some languages, indicating the relation of the noun, adjective, or pronoun to other words in the sentence. **b.** any one of these categories: *the nominative case.* **9.** *Informal.* a person in or regarded as being in a specified condition: *the accident victim was a hospital case; he's a mental case.* **10.** *Informal.* a person of a specified character (esp. in the phrase **a hard case**). **11.** *Informal.* an odd person; eccentric. **12.** *U.S.*

informal. love or infatuation. **13.** short for **case shot.** See **canister** (sense 2). **14. as the case may be.** according to the circumstances. **15. in any case.** (*adv.*) no matter what; anyhow: *we will go in any case.* **16. in case.** (*adv.*) **a.** in order to allow for eventualities. **b.** (*as conj.*) in order to allow for the possibility that: *take your coat in case it rains.* **c.** *U.S.* if. **17. in case of.** (*prep.*) in the event of. **18. in no case.** (*adv.*) under no circumstances: *in no case should you fight back.* [Old English *casus* (grammatical) case, associated also with Old French *cas* a happening; both from Latin *cāsus,* a befalling, occurrence, from *cadere* to fall]

case[2] (keɪs) *n.* **1. a.** a container, such as a box or chest. **b.** (*in combination*): *suitcase; briefcase.* **2.** an outer cover or sheath, esp. for a watch. **3.** a receptacle and its contents: *a case of ammunition.* **4.** a pair or brace, esp. of pistols. **5.** *Architect.* another word for **casing** (sense 3). **6.** a completed cover ready to be fastened to a book to form its binding. **7.** *Printing.* a tray divided into many compartments in which a compositor keeps individual metal types of a particular size and style. Cases were originally used in pairs, one (the **upper case**) for capitals, the other (the **lower case**) for small letters. **8.** *Metallurgy.* the surface of a piece of steel that has been case-hardened. ~*vb.* (*tr.*) **9.** to put into or cover with a case: *to case the machinery.* **10.** *Slang.* to inspect carefully (esp. a place to be robbed). [C13: from Old French *casse,* from Latin *capsa,* from *capere* to take, hold]

casease (ˈkeɪsɪˌeɪz) *n.* a proteolytic enzyme formed by certain bacteria that activates the solution of albumin and casein in milk and cheese. [C20: from CASE(IN) + -ASE]

caseate (ˈkeɪsɪˌeɪt) *vb.* (*intr.*) *Pathol.* to undergo caseation. [C19: from Latin *cāseus* CHEESE]

caseation (ˌkeɪsɪˈeɪʃən) *n.* **1.** the formation of cheese from casein during the coagulation of milk. **2.** *Pathol.* the degeneration of dead tissue into a soft cheeselike mass.

casebook (ˈkeɪsˌbʊk) *n.* a book in which records of legal or medical cases are kept.

casebound (ˈkeɪsˌbaʊnd) *adj.* another word for **hardback.**

casefy (ˈkeɪsɪˌfaɪ) *vb.* **-fies, -fying, -fied.** to make or become similar to cheese. [C20: from Latin *cāseus* CHEESE + -FY]

case grammar *n. Linguistics.* a system of grammatical description based on the functional relations that noun groups have to the main verb of a sentence. Compare **systemic grammar, transformational grammar.**

case-harden *vb.* (*tr.*) **1.** *Metallurgy.* to form a hard surface layer of high carbon content on (a steel component) by heating in a carburizing environment with subsequent quenching or heat treatment. **2.** to harden the spirit or disposition of; make callous: *experience had case-hardened the judge.*

case history *n.* a record of a person's background, medical history, etc., esp. one used for determining medical treatment.

casein (ˈkeɪsɪɪn, -siːn) *n.* a phosphoprotein, precipitated from milk by the action of rennin, forming the basis of cheese: used in the manufacture of plastics and adhesives. Also called (U.S.): **paracasein.** [C19: from Latin *cāseus* cheese + -IN]

caseinogen (ˌkeɪsɪˈɪnədʒən, keɪˈsiːnə-) *n.* the principal protein of milk, converted to casein by rennin. Sometimes called (U.S.) **casein.**

case knife *n.* another name for **sheath knife.**

case law *n.* law established by following judicial decisions given in earlier cases. Compare **statute law.** See also **precedent** (sense 1).

casemate (ˈkeɪsˌmeɪt) *n.* an armoured compartment in a ship or fortification in which guns are mounted. [C16: from French, from Italian *casamatta,* perhaps from Greek *khasmata* apertures, plural of *khasma* CHASM] —ˈ**caseˌmated** *adj.*

casement (ˈkeɪsmənt) *n.* **1.** a window frame that is hinged on one side. **2.** a window containing frames hinged at the side or at the top or bottom. **3.** a poetic word for **window.** [C15: probably from Old Northern French *encassement* frame, from *encasser* to frame, encase, from *casse* framework, crate, CASE[2]]

caseose (ˈkeɪsɪˌəʊz, -ˌəʊs) *n.* a peptide produced by the peptic digestion of casein. [C20: from Latin *cāseus* cheese + -OSE[2]]

caseous (ˈkeɪsɪəs) *adj.* of or like cheese. [C17: from Latin *cāseus* CHEESE]

casern *or* **caserne** (kəˈzɜːn) *n.* (formerly) a billet or accommodation for soldiers in a town. [C17: from French *caserne,* from Old Provençal *cazerna* group of four men, ultimately from Latin *quattuor* four]

case shot *n.* another name for **canister** (sense 2).

case stated *n. Law.* a statement of the facts of a case prepared by one court for the opinion or judgment of another court. Also called: **stated case.**

case study *n.* the act or an instance of analysing one or more particular cases or case histories with a view to making generalizations.

casework (ˈkeɪsˌwɜːk) *n.* social work based on close study of the personal histories and circumstances of individuals and families. —ˈ**caseˌworker** *n.*

caseworm (ˈkeɪsˌwɜːm) *n.* another name for a **caddis worm.**

cash[1] (kæʃ) *n.* **1.** banknotes and coins, esp. in hand or readily available; money or ready money. **2.** immediate payment, in full or part, for goods or services (esp. in the phrase **cash down**). **3.** (*modifier*) of, for, or paid by cash: *a cash transaction.* ~*vb.* **4.** (*tr.*) to obtain or pay ready money for: *to cash a cheque.* ~See also **cash in, cash up.** [C16: from Old Italian *cassa* money box, from Latin *capsa* CASE[2]] —ˈ**cashable** *adj.*

cash[2] (kæʃ) *n., pl.* **cash.** any of various Chinese, Indonesian, or Indian coins of low value. [C16: from Portuguese *caixa,* from Tamil *kāsu,* from Sanskrit *karsa* weight of gold or silver]

cash-and-carry *adj., adv.* **1.** sold or operated on a basis of cash payment for merchandise that is not delivered but removed by the purchaser. ~*n.* **2.** a wholesale store, esp. for groceries, that operates on this basis. **3.** an operation on a commodities futures market in which spot goods are purchased and sold at a profit on a futures contract.

cash-book *n. Book-keeping.* a journal in which all cash or cheque receipts and disbursements are recorded.

cash card *n.* an embossed plastic card bearing the name and account details of a bank or building-society customer, used with a personal identification number to obtain money from a cash dispenser. Also called: **cash-point card.**

cash cow *n.* a product, acquisition, etc., that produces a steady flow of cash, esp. one with a well-known brand name commanding a high market share.

cash crop *n.* a crop grown for sale rather than for subsistence.

cash desk *n.* a counter or till in a shop where purchases are paid for.

cash discount *n.* a discount granted to a purchaser who pays before a stipulated date.

cash dispenser *n.* a computerized device outside a bank that supplies cash or account information when the user inserts his cash card and keys in his identification number.

cashed up *adj. Austral. informal.* having plenty of money.

cashew (ˈkæʃuː, kæˈʃuː) *n.* **1.** a tropical American anacardiaceous evergreen tree, *Anacardium occidentale,* bearing kidney-shaped nuts that protrude from a fleshy receptacle. **2.** Also called: **cashew nut.** the edible nut of this tree. [C18: from Portuguese *cajú,* from Tupi *acajú*]

cash flow *n.* **1.** the movement of money into and out of a business. **2.** a prediction of such movement over a given period.

cashier[1] (kæˈʃɪə) *n.* **1.** a person responsible for receiving payments for goods, services, etc., as in a shop. **2.** Also called: **teller.** an employee of a bank responsible for receiving deposits, cashing cheques, and other financial transactions; bank clerk. **3.** any person responsible for handling cash or maintaining records of its receipt and disbursement. [C16: from Dutch *cassier* or French *caissier,* from *casse* money chest; see CASE[2]]

cashier[2] (kæˈʃɪə) *vb.* (*tr.*) **1.** to dismiss with dishonour, esp. from the armed forces. **2.** *Rare.* to put away or discard; reject. [C16: from Middle Dutch *kasseren,* from Old French *casser,* from Latin *quassāre* to QUASH]

cash in *vb.* (*adv.*) **1.** (*tr.*) to give (something) in exchange, esp. for money. **2.** (*intr.*; often foll. by *on*) *Informal.* **a.** to profit (from). **b.** to take advantage (of). **3.** (*intr.*) a slang expression for **die**[1].

cashless (ˈkæʃlɪs) *adj.* functioning, operated, or performed without using coins or banknotes for money transactions but instead using credit cards or electronic transfer of funds: *cashless shopping.*

cash limit *n.* (*often pl.*) a limit imposed as a method of curtailing overall expenditure without specifying the precise means of budgetary control.

cashmere *or* **kashmir** (ˈkæʃmɪə) *n.* **1.** a fine soft wool from goats of the Kashmir area of SW central Asia. **2. a.** cloth or knitted material made from this or similar wool. **b.** (*as modifier*): *a cashmere sweater.*

cash on delivery *n.* a service entailing cash payment to the carrier on delivery of merchandise.

cash point *n.* **1.** any retail outlet at which goods are bought for cash. **2.** a cash dispenser.

cash ratio *n.* the ratio of cash on hand to total deposits that by law or custom commercial banks must maintain.

cash register *n.* a till with a keyboard that operates a mechanism for displaying and adding the amounts of cash received in individual sales.

cash up *vb.* (*intr., adv.*) *Brit.* (of cashiers, shopkeepers, etc.) to add up the money taken, esp. at the end of a working day.

casimere (ˈkæsɪˌmɪə) *n.* a variant spelling of **cassimere.**

casing (ˈkeɪsɪŋ) *n.* **1.** a protective case or cover. **2.** material for a case or cover. **3.** Also called: **case.** a frame containing a door, window, or staircase. **4.** the intestines of cattle, pigs, etc., or a synthetic substitute, used as a container for sausage meat. **5.** the outer cover of a pneumatic tyre. **6.** a pipe or tube used to line a hole or shaft. **7.** the outer shell of a steam or gas turbine.

casino (kəˈsiːnəʊ) *n., pl.* **-nos.** **1.** a public building or room in which gaming takes place, esp. roulette and card games such as baccarat and chemin de fer. **2.** a variant spelling of **cassino.** [C18: from Italian, diminutive of *casa* house, from Latin]

cask (kɑːsk) *n.* **1.** a strong wooden barrel used mainly to hold alcoholic drink: *a wine cask.* **2.** any barrel. **3.** the quantity contained in a cask. **4.** *Engineering.* another name for **flask** (sense 6). [C15: from Spanish *casco* helmet, perhaps from *cascar* to break]

casket (ˈkɑːskɪt) *n.* **1.** a small box or chest for valuables, esp. jewels. **2.** *Chiefly U.S.* another name for **coffin** (sense 1). [C15: probably from Old French *cassette* little box; see CASE[2]]

Caslon (ˈkæzlən) *n.* a style of type designed by William Caslon, English type founder (1692–1766).

Casparian strip (kæˈspɛərɪən) *n. Botany.* a band of suberized material around the radial walls of endodermal cells: impervious to gases and liquids. [C20: named after Robert *Caspary,* 19th-century German botanist]

casque (kæsk) *n. Zoology.* a helmet or a helmet-like process or structure, as on the bill of most hornbills. [C17: from French, from Spanish *casco;* see CASK] —**casqued** *adj.*

cassaba (kəˈsɑːbə) *n.* a variant spelling of **casaba.**

Cassandra (kəˈsændrə) *n.* a person whose prophecies of doom are unheeded. [after *Cassandra,* prophetess in Greek mythology who was fated never to be believed]

cassareep (ˈkæsəˌriːp) *n.* the juice of the bitter cassava root, boiled down to a syrup and used as a flavouring, esp. in West Indian cookery. [C19: of Carib origin]

cassata (kəˈsɑːtə) *n.* an ice cream, originating in Italy, usually containing nuts and candied fruit. [from Italian]

cassation (kæˈseɪʃən) *n. Chiefly law.* (esp. in France) annulment, as of a judicial decision by a higher court. [C15: from Old French, from Medieval Latin *cassātiō,* from Late Latin *cassāre* to cancel, from Latin *quassāre* to QUASH]

cassava (kəˈsɑːvə) *n.* **1.** Also called: **manioc.** any tropical euphorbiaceous plant of the genus *Manihot,* esp. the widely cultivated American species *M. esculenta* (or *utilissima*) (**bitter cassava**) and *M. dulcis* (**sweet cassava**). **2.** a starch derived from the root of this plant: an important food in the tropics and a source of tapioca. [C16: from Spanish *cazabe* cassava bread, from Taino *caçábi*]

Cassegrainian telescope (ˌkæsɪˈgreɪnɪən) *n.* an astronomical reflecting telescope in which incident light is reflected from a large concave mirror onto a smaller convex mirror and then back through a hole in the concave mirror to form the image. [C19: named after N. *Cassegrain,* 17th-century French scientist who invented it]

casserole (ˈkæsəˌrəʊl) *n.* **1.** a covered dish of earthenware, glass, etc., in which food is cooked and served. **2.** any food cooked and served in such a dish: *chicken casserole.* ~*vb.* **3.** to cook or be cooked in a casserole. [C18: from French, from Old French *casse* ladle, pan for dripping, from Old Provençal *cassa,* from Late Latin *cattia* dipper, from Greek *kuathion,* diminutive of *kuathos* cup]

cassette (kæˈsɛt) *n.* **1. a.** a plastic container for magnetic tape, inserted into a tape deck to be played or used. **b.** (*as modifier*): *a cassette recorder.* **2.** *Photog.* another term for **cartridge** (sense 5). **3.** *Films.* a container for film used to facilitate the loading of a camera or projector, esp. when the film is used in the form of a loop. **4.** the injection of genes from one species into the fertilized egg of another species. [C18: from French: little box; see CASE[2]]

cassia (ˈkæsɪə) *n.* **1.** any plant of the mainly tropical caesalpiniaceous genus *Cassia,* esp. *C. fistula,* whose pods yield **cassia pulp,** a mild laxative. See also **senna. 2.** a lauraceous tree, *Cinnamomum cassia,* of tropical Asia. **3. cassia bark.** the cinnamon-like bark of this tree, used as a spice. [Old English, from Latin *casia,* from Greek *kasia,* of Semitic origin; related to Hebrew *qesī ʿāh* cassia]

cassimere *or* **casimere** (ˈkæsɪˌmɪə) *n.* a woollen suiting cloth of plain or twill weave. [C18: variant of *cashmere,* from *Kashmir*]

cassino *or* **casino** (kəˈsiːnəʊ) *n.* a card game for two to four players in which players pair cards from their hands with others exposed on the table.

Cassiopeia (ˌkæsɪəˈpiːə) *n., Latin genitive* **Cassiopeiae** (ˌkæsɪəˈpiːiː). a very conspicuous W-shaped constellation near the Pole Star. **Cassiopeia A** is a very strong radio and x-ray source, identified as faint nebulous filaments that are the remains of the supernova observed in 1572. [named after *Cassiopeia* in Greek mythology] —ˌ**Cassioˈpeian** *adj.*

cassis (kɑːˈsiːs) *n.* a blackcurrant cordial. [C19: from French]

cassiterite (kəˈsɪtəˌraɪt) *n.* a black or brown mineral, found in igneous rocks and hydrothermal veins. It is a source of tin. Composition: tin oxide. Formula: SnO_2. Crystal structure: tetragonal. Also called: **tinstone.** [C19: from Greek *kassiteros* tin]

cassock (ˈkæsək) *n. Christianity.* an ankle-length garment, usually black, worn by priests and choristers. [C16: from Old French *casaque,* from Italian *casacca* a long coat, of uncertain origin] —ˈ**cassocked** *adj.*

cassoulet (ˌkæsəˈleɪ) *n.* a stew originating from France, made from haricot beans and goose, duck, pork, etc. [French, related to *casse* saucepan, bowl]

cassowary (ˈkæsəˌwɛərɪ) *n., pl.* **-waries.** any large flightless bird of the genus *Casuarius,* inhabiting forests in NE Australia, New Guinea, and adjacent islands, having a horny head crest, black plumage, and brightly coloured neck and wattles: order *Casuariiformes* (see **ratite**). [C17: from Malay *kĕsuari*]

cast (kɑːst) *vb.* **casts, casting, cast.** (*mainly tr.*) **1.** to throw or expel with violence or force. **2.** to throw off or away: *she cast her clothes to the ground.* **3.** to reject or dismiss: *he cast the idea from his mind.* **4.** to shed or drop: *the snake cast its skin; the horse cast a shoe; the ship cast anchor.* **5. be cast.** *N.Z.* (of a sheep) to have fallen and been unable to rise. **6.** to cause to appear: *to cast a shadow.* **7.** to express (doubts, suspicions, etc.) or cause (them) to be felt. **8.** to direct (a glance, attention, etc.): *cast your eye over this.* **9.** to place, esp. in a violent manner: *he was cast into prison.* **10.** (*also intr.*) *Angling.* to throw (a line) into the water. **11.** to draw or choose (lots). **12.** to give or deposit (a vote). **13.** to select (actors) to play parts in (a play, film, etc.). **14. a.** to shape (molten metal, glass, etc.) by pouring or pressing it into a mould. **b.** to make (an object) by such a process. **15.** (*also intr.; often foll. by up*) to compute (figures or a total). **16.** to predict: *the old woman cast my fortune.* **17.** *Astrology.* to draw on (a horoscope) details concerning the positions of the planets in the signs of the zodiac at a particular time for interpretation in terms of human characteristics, behaviour, etc. **18.** to contrive (esp. in the phrase **cast a spell**). **19.** to formulate: *he cast his work in the form of a chart.* **20.** (*also intr.*) to twist or cause to twist. **21.** (*also intr.*) *Nautical.* to turn the head of (a sailing vessel) or (of a sailing vessel) to be turned away from the wind in getting under way. **22.** *Hunting.* to direct (a pack of hounds) over (ground) where their quarry may recently have passed. **23.** (*intr.*) (of birds of prey) to eject from the crop and bill a pellet consisting of the indigestible parts of birds or animals previously eaten. **24.** *Falconry.* to hold the body of a hawk between the hands so as to perform some operation upon it. **25.** *Printing.* to stereotype or electrotype. **26. cast** *or* **throw in one's lot with.** to share in the activities or fortunes of (someone else). ~*n.* **27.** the act of casting or throwing. **28. a.** Also called: **casting.** something that is shed, dropped, or egested, such as the coil of earth left by an earthworm. **b.** another name for **pellet** (sense 4). **29.** an object that is thrown. **30.** the distance an object is or may be thrown. **31. a.** a throw at dice. **b.** the resulting number shown. **32.** *Angling.* **a.** a trace with a fly or flies attached. **b.** the act or an instance of casting. **33.** the wide sweep made by a sheepdog to get behind a flock of sheep or by a hunting dog in search of a scent. **34. a.** the actors in a play collectively. **b.** (*as modifier*): *a cast list.* **35. a.** an object made of metal, glass, etc., that has been shaped in a molten state by being poured or pressed into a mould. **b.** the mould used to shape such an object. **36.** form or appearance. **37.** sort, kind, or style. **38.** a fixed twist or defect, esp. in the eye. **39.** a distortion of shape. **40.** *Surgery.* a rigid encircling casing, often made of plaster of Paris, for immobilizing broken bones while they heal. **41.** *Pathol.* a mass of fatty, waxy, cellular, or other material formed in a diseased body cavity, passage, etc. **42.** the act of casting a pack of hounds. **43.** *Falconry.* a pair of falcons working in combination to pursue the same quarry. **44.** *Archery.* the speed imparted to an arrow by a particular bow. **45.** a slight tinge or trace, as of colour. **46.** a computation or calculation. **47.** a forecast or conjecture. **48.** fortune or a stroke of fate. **49.** *Palaeontol.* a mineral representation of an organic object, esp. a lump of mineral that indicates the shape and internal structure of a shell. ~See also **cast about, castaway, cast back, cast down, cast-off, cast on, cast out, cast up.** [C13: from Old Norse *kasta*]

cast about *vb.* (*intr., adv.*) to make a mental or visual search: *to cast about for an idea for a book.*

castanets (ˌkæstəˈnɛts) *pl. n.* curved pieces of hollow wood, usually held between the fingers and thumb and made to click together: used esp. by Spanish dancers. [C17 *castanet,* from Spanish *castañeta,* diminutive of *castaña* CHESTNUT]

castaway (ˈkɑːstəˌweɪ) *n.* **1.** a person who has been shipwrecked. **2.** something thrown off or away; castoff. ~*adj.* (*prenominal*) **3.** shipwrecked or put adrift. **4.** thrown away or rejected. ~*vb.* **cast away. 5.** (*tr., adv.; often passive*) to cause (a ship, person, etc.) to be shipwrecked or abandoned.

cast back *vb.* (*adv.*) to turn (the mind) to the past.

cast down *vb.* (*tr., adv.*) to make (a person) discouraged or dejected.

caste (kɑːst) *n.* **1. a.** any of the four major hereditary classes, namely the **Brahman, Kshatriya, Vaisya,** and **Sudra,** into which Hindu society is divided. **b.** Also called: **caste system.** the system or basis of such classes. **c.** the social position or rank conferred by this system. **2.** any social class or system based on such distinctions as heredity, rank, wealth, profession, etc. **3.** the position conferred by such a system. **4. lose caste.** *Informal.* to lose one's social position. **5.** *Entomol.* any of various types of specialized individual, such as the worker, in social insects (hive bees, ants, etc.). [C16: from Portuguese *casta* race, breed, ancestry, from *casto* pure, chaste, from Latin *castus*]

castellan (ˈkæstɪlən) *n. Rare.* a keeper or governor of a castle. Also called: **chatelain.** [C14: from Latin *castellānus,* from *castellum* CASTLE]

castellany (ˈkæstɪˌleɪnɪ) *n., pl.* **-nies.** *Rare.* **1.** the office, rank, or jurisdiction of a castellan. **2.** land belonging to a castle.

castellated (ˈkæstɪˌleɪtɪd) *adj.* **1.** having turrets and battlements, like a castle. **2.** having indentations similar to battlements: *a castellated nut; a castellated filament.* [C17: from Medieval Latin *castellātus,* from *castellāre* to fortify as a CASTLE] —ˌ**castelˈlation** *n.*

caster (ˈkɑːstə) *n.* **1.** a person or thing that casts. **2.** Also: **castor.** a bottle with a perforated top for sprinkling sugar, etc., or a stand containing such bottles. **3.** Also: **castor.** a small wheel mounted on a swivel so that the wheel tends to turn into its plane of rotation.

caster action *n.* the tendency, caused by the design of the mounting, of a wheel to turn into its plane of rotation.

caster sugar (ˈkɑːstə) *n.* finely ground white sugar.

castigate (ˈkæstɪˌgeɪt) *vb.* (*tr.*) to rebuke or criticize in a severe manner; chastise. [C17: from Latin *castīgāre* to correct, punish, from *castum* pure + *agere* to compel (to be)] —ˌ**castiˈgation** *n.* —ˈ**castiˌgator** *n.* —ˌ**castiˈgatory** *adj.*

Castile soap (kæˈstiːl) *n.* a hard soap made from olive oil and sodium hydroxide.

Castilian (kæˈstɪljən) *n.* **1.** the Spanish dialect of Castile, the region comprising most of modern Spain; the standard form of European Spanish. **2.** a native or inhabitant of Castile. ~*adj.* **3.** denoting, relating to, or characteristic of Castile, its inhabitants, or the standard form of European Spanish.

casting (ˈkɑːstɪŋ) *n.* **1.** an object or figure that has been cast, esp. in metal from a mould. **2.** the process of transferring molten steel to a mould. **3.** the choosing of actors for a production. **4.** *Hunting.* the act of directing a pack of hounds over ground where their quarry may recently have passed so that they can quest for, discover, or recapture its scent. **5.** *Zoology.* another word for **cast** (sense 27) or **pellet** (sense 4).

casting couch *n. Informal.* a couch on which a casting director is said to seduce girls seeking a part in a film or play.

casting vote *n.* the deciding vote used by the presiding officer of an assembly when votes cast on both sides are equal in number.

cast iron *n.* **1.** iron containing so much carbon (1.7 to 4.5 per cent) that it cannot be wrought and must be cast into shape. ~*adj.* **cast-iron.** **2.** made of cast iron. **3.** rigid, strong, or unyielding: *a cast-iron decision.*

castle (ˈkɑːsᵊl) *n.* **1.** a fortified building or set of buildings, usually permanently garrisoned, as in medieval Europe. **2.** any fortified place or structure. **3.** a large magnificent house, esp. when the present or former home of a nobleman or prince. **4.** the citadel and strongest part of the fortifications of a medieval town. **5.** *Chess.* another name for **rook**[2]. ~*vb.* **6.** *Chess.* to move (the king) two squares laterally on the first rank and place the nearest rook on the square passed over by the king, either towards the king's side (**castling short**) or the queen's side (**castling long**). [C11: from Latin *castellum,* diminutive of *castrum* fort]

castled (ˈkɑːsᵊld) *adj.* **1.** like a castle in construction; castellated: *a castled mansion.* **2.** (of an area) having many castles.

castle in the air *or* **in Spain** *n.* a hope or desire unlikely to be realized; daydream.

castle nut *n.* a hexagonal nut with six slots in the head, two of which take a locking pin to hold it firmly in position.

cast-off *adj.* **1.** (*prenominal*) thrown away; abandoned: *cast-off shoes.* ~*n.* ˈ**castoff.** **2.** a person or thing that has been discarded or abandoned. **3.** *Printing.* an estimate of the amount of space that a piece of copy will occupy when printed in a particular size and style of type. ~*vb.* **cast off.** (*adv.*) **4.** to remove (mooring lines) that hold (a vessel) to a dock. **5.** to knot (a row of stitches, esp. the final row) in finishing off knitted or woven material. **6.** *Printing.* to estimate the amount of space that will be taken up by (a book, piece of copy, etc.) when it is printed in a particular size and style of type. **7.** (*intr.*) (in Scottish country dancing) to perform a progressive movement during which each partner of a couple dances separately behind one line of the set and then reunites with the other in their original position in the set or in a new position.

cast on *vb.* (*adv.*) to form (the first row of stitches) in knitting and weaving.

castor[1] (ˈkɑːstə) *n.* **1.** the brownish aromatic secretion of the anal glands of a beaver, used in perfumery and medicine. **2.** the fur of the beaver. **3.** a hat made of beaver or similar fur. **4.** a less common name for **beaver**[1] (sense 1). [C14: from Latin, from Greek *kastōr* beaver]

castor[2] (ˈkɑːstə) *n.* a variant spelling of **caster** (senses 2, 3).

castor[3] (ˈkɑːstə) *adj. Austral. slang.* good; fine.

Castor (ˈkɑːstə) *n.* the second brightest star, Alpha Geminorum, in the constellation Gemini: a multiple star consisting of six components lying close to the star Pollux. Distance: 46 light years. [named after *Castor* in classical mythology]

castor bean *n. U.S. and Canadian.* **1.** another name for **castor-oil plant.** **2.** the seed of this plant.

castor oil *n.* a colourless or yellow glutinous oil obtained from the seeds of the castor-oil plant and used as a fine lubricant and as a cathartic.

castor-oil plant *n.* a tall euphorbiaceous Indian plant, *Ricinus communis,* cultivated in tropical regions for ornament and for its poisonous seeds, from which castor oil is extracted. Also called (U.S. and Canadian): **castor bean.**

cast out *vb.* (*intr., adv.*) *Scot.* to quarrel; be no longer friends.

castrate (kæˈstreɪt) *vb.* (*tr.*) **1.** to remove the testicles of; emasculate; geld. **2.** to deprive of vigour, masculinity, etc. **3.** to remove the ovaries of; spay. **4.** to expurgate or censor (a book, play, etc.). [C17: from Latin *castrāre* to emasculate, geld] —**casˈtration** *n.* —**casˈtrator** *n.*

castration complex *n. Psychoanal.* an unconscious fear of having one's genitals removed, as a punishment for wishing to have sex with a parent.

castrato (kæˈstrɑːtəʊ) *n., pl.* **-ti** (-tɪ) *or* **-tos.** (in 17th- and 18th-century opera) a male singer whose testicles were removed before puberty, allowing the retention of a soprano or alto voice. [C18: from Italian, from Latin *castrātus* castrated]

cast steel *n.* steel containing varying amounts of carbon, manganese, phosphorus, silicon, and sulphur that is cast into shape rather than wrought.

cast stone *n. Building trades.* a building component, such as a block or lintel, made from cast concrete with a facing that resembles natural stone.

cast up *vb.* (*tr., adv.*) **1.** (of the sea) to cast ashore. **2.** to compute (figures or a total). **3.** to bring up as a reproach against a person.

casual (ˈkæʒjʊəl) *adj.* **1.** happening by accident or chance: *a casual meeting.* **2.** offhand; not premeditated: *a casual remark.* **3.** shallow or superficial: *a casual affair.* **4.** being or seeming unconcerned or apathetic: *he assumed a casual attitude.* **5.** (esp. of dress) for informal wear: *a casual coat.* **6.** occasional or irregular: *casual visits; a casual labourer.* **7.** *Biology.* another term for **adventive.** ~*n.* **8.** (*usually pl.*) an informal article of clothing or footwear. **9.** an occasional worker. **10.** *Biology.* another term for an **adventive.** **11.** (*usually pl.*) a young man dressed in expensive casual clothes who goes to football matches in order to start fights. [C14: from Late Latin *cāsuālis* happening by chance, from Latin *cāsus* event, from *cadere* to fall; see CASE[1]] —ˈ**casually** *adv.* —ˈ**casualness** *n.*

casualization *or* **casualisation** (ˌkæʒjʊəlaɪˈzeɪʃən) *n.* the altering of working practices so that regular workers are re-employed on a casual or short-term basis.

casualty (ˈkæʒjʊəltɪ) *n., pl.* **-ties.** **1.** a serviceman who is killed, wounded, captured, or missing as a result of enemy action. **2.** a person who is injured or killed in an accident. **3.** a hospital department where victims of accidents, violence, etc., are treated. **4.** anything that is lost, damaged, or destroyed as the result of an accident, etc.

casuarina (ˌkæsjʊəˈraɪnə) *n.* any tree of the genus *Casuarina,* of Australia and the East Indies, having jointed leafless branchlets: family *Casuarinaceae.* See also **beefwood, she-oak.** [C19: from New Latin, from Malay *kĕsuari* CASSOWARY, referring to the resemblance of the branches to the feathers of the cassowary]

casuist (ˈkæzjʊɪst) *n.* **1.** a person, esp. a theologian, who attempts to resolve moral dilemmas by the application of general rules and the careful distinction of special cases. **2.** a person who is oversubtle in his analysis of fine distinctions; sophist. [C17: from French *casuiste,* from Spanish *casuista,* from Latin *cāsus* CASE[1]] —ˌ**casuˈistic** *or* ˌ**casuˈistical** *adj.* —ˌ**casuˈistically** *adv.*

casuistry (ˈkæzjʊɪstrɪ) *n., pl.* **-ries.** **1.** *Philosophy.* the resolution of particular moral dilemmas, esp. those arising from conflicting general moral rules, by careful distinction of the cases to which these rules apply. **2.** reasoning that is specious, misleading, or oversubtle.

casus belli *Latin.* (ˈkɑːsʊs ˈbeliː) *n., pl.* ***casus belli*** (ˈkɑːsʊs ˈbeliː). **1.** an event or act used to justify a war. **2.** the immediate cause of a quarrel. [literally: occasion of war]

cat[1] (kæt) *n.* **1.** Also called: **domestic cat.** a small domesticated feline mammal, *Felis catus* (or *domesticus*), having thick soft fur and occurring in many breeds in which the colour of the fur varies greatly: kept as a pet or to catch rats and mice. **2.** Also called: **big cat.** any of the larger felines, such as a lion or tiger. **3.** any wild feline mammal of the genus *Felis,* such as the lynx or serval, resembling the domestic cat. **4.** *Informal.* a woman who gossips maliciously. **5.** *Slang.* a man; guy. **6.** *Nautical.* a heavy tackle for hoisting an anchor to the cathead. **7.** a short sharp-ended piece of wood used in the game of tipcat. **8.** short for **catboat.** **9.** *Informal.* short for **caterpillar** (the vehicle). **10.** short for **cat-o'-nine-tails.** **11. a bag of cats.** *Irish informal.* a bad-tempered person: *she's a real bag of cats this morning.* **12. fight like Kilkenny cats.** to fight until both parties are destroyed. **13. let the cat out of the bag.** to disclose a secret, often by mistake. **14. like a cat on a hot tin roof** *or* **on hot bricks.** in an uneasy or agitated state. **15. like cat and dog.** quarrelling savagely. **16. look like something the cat brought in.** to appear dishevelled or bedraggled. **17. not a cat in hell's chance.** no chance at all. **18. not have room to swing a cat.** to have very little space. **19. put, set,** etc., **the cat among the pigeons.** to introduce some violently disturbing new element. **20. play cat and mouse.** to play with a person or animal in a cruel or teasing way, esp. before a final act of cruelty or unkindness. **21. rain cats and dogs.** to rain very heavily. ~*vb.* **cats, catting, catted.** **22.** (*tr.*) to flog with a cat-o'-nine-tails. **23.** (*tr.*) *Nautical.* to hoist (an anchor) to the cathead. **24.** (*intr.*) a slang word for **vomit.** [Old English *catte,* from Latin *cattus;* related to Old Norse *köttr,* Old High German *kazza,* Old French *chat,* Russian *kot*] —ˈ**catˌlike** *adj.* —ˈ**cattish** *adj.*

cat[2] (kæt) *n. Informal.* short for **catamaran** (sense 1).

cat[3] (kæt) *n.* **1. a.** short for **catalytic converter. b.** (*as modifier*): *a cat car.* ~*adj.* **2.** short for **catalytic** *a cat cracker.*

CAT (in Britain) *abbrev. for:* **1.** College of Advanced Technology. **2.** computer-aided teaching. **3.** computer-assisted trading.

cat. *abbrev. for:* **1.** catalogue. **2.** catamaran. **3.** *Christianity.* catechism.

cata-, kata-, *before an aspirate* **cath-,** *or before a vowel* **cat-** *prefix.* **1.** down; downwards; lower in position: *catadromous; cataphyll.* **2.** indicating reversal, opposition, degeneration, etc.: *cataplasia; catatonia.* [from Greek *kata-,* from *kata.* In compound words borrowed from Greek, *kata-* means: down (*catabo-*

lism), away, off (*catalectic*), against (*category*), according to (*catholic*), and thoroughly (*catalogue*)]

catabasis (kəˈtæbəsɪs) *n., pl.* **-ses** (-ˌsiːz). **1.** a descent or downward movement. **2.** the decline of a disease. —**catabatic** (ˌkætəˈbætɪk) *adj.*

catabolism *or* **katabolism** (kəˈtæbəˌlɪzəm) *n.* a metabolic process in which complex molecules are broken down into simple ones with the release of energy; destructive metabolism. Compare **anabolism.** [C19 *katabolism,* from Greek *katabolē* a throwing down, from *kataballein,* from *kata-* down + *ballein* to throw] —**catabolic** *or* **katabolic** (ˌkætəˈbɒlɪk) *adj.* —ˌ**cataˈbolically** *or* ˌ**kataˈbolically** *adv.*

catabolite (kəˈtæbəˌlaɪt) *n.* a substance produced as a result of catabolism.

catacaustic (ˌkætəˈkɔːstɪk, -ˈkɒs-) *Physics.* ~*adj.* **1.** (of a caustic curve or surface) formed by reflected light rays. Compare **diacaustic.** ~*n.* **2.** a catacaustic curve or surface.

catachresis (ˌkætəˈkriːsɪs) *n.* the incorrect use of words, as *luxuriant* for *luxurious.* [C16: from Latin, from Greek *katakhrēsis* a misusing, from *katakhrēsthai,* from *khrēsthai* to use] —**catachrestic** (ˌkætəˈkrɛstɪk) *or* ˌ**cataˈchrestical** *adj.* —ˌ**cataˈchrestically** *adv.*

cataclasis (ˌkætəˈkleɪsɪs) *n., pl.* **-ses** (-siːz). *Geology.* the deformation of rocks by crushing and shearing. [C19: New Latin, from Greek, from CATA- + *klasis* a breaking] —**cataclastic** (ˌkætəˈklæstɪk) *adj.*

cataclinal (ˌkætəˈklaɪnᵊl) *adj.* (of streams, valleys, etc.) running in the direction of the dip of the surrounding rock strata.

cataclysm (ˈkætəˌklɪzəm) *n.* **1.** a violent upheaval, esp. of a political, military, or social nature. **2.** a disastrous flood; deluge. **3.** *Geology.* another name for **catastrophe** (sense 4). [C17: via French from Latin, from Greek *kataklusmos* deluge, from *katakluzein* to flood, from *kluzein* to wash] —ˌ**cataˈclysmic** *or* ˌ**cataˈclysmal** *adj.* —ˌ**cataˈclysmically** *adv.*

catacomb (ˈkætəˌkəʊm, -ˌkuːm) *n.* **1.** (*usually pl.*) an underground burial place, esp. the galleries at Rome, consisting of tunnels with vaults or niches leading off them for tombs. **2.** a series of underground tunnels or caves. [Old English *catacumbe,* from Late Latin *catacumbas* (singular), name of the cemetery under the Basilica of St Sebastian, near Rome; origin unknown]

catadromous (kəˈtædrəməs) *adj.* (of fishes such as the eel) migrating down rivers to the sea in order to breed. Compare **anadromous.** [C19: from Greek *katadromos,* from *kata-* down + *dromos,* from *dremein* to run]

catafalque (ˈkætəˌfælk) *n.* a temporary raised platform on which a body lies in state before or during a funeral. [C17: from French, from Italian *catafalco,* of uncertain origin; compare SCAFFOLD]

Catalan (ˈkætəˌlæn, -lən) *n.* **1.** a language of Catalonia in NE Spain, quite closely related to Spanish and Provençal, belonging to the Romance group of the Indo-European family. **2.** a native or inhabitant of Catalonia. ~*adj.* **3.** denoting, relating to, or characteristic of Catalonia, its inhabitants, or their language.

catalase (ˈkætəˌleɪs) *n.* an enzyme that catalyses the decomposition of hydrogen peroxide.

catalectic (ˌkætəˈlɛktɪk) *adj. Prosody.* (of a line of verse) having an incomplete final foot. [C16: via Late Latin from Greek *katalēktikos* incomplete, from *katalēgein,* from *kata-* off + *lēgein* to stop]

catalepsy (ˈkætəˌlɛpsɪ) *n.* a state of prolonged rigid posture, occurring for example in schizophrenia or in hypnotic trances. [C16: from Medieval Latin *catalēpsia,* variant of Late Latin *catalēpsis,* from Greek *katalēpsis,* literally: a seizing, from *katalambanein* to hold down, from *kata-* down + *lambanein* to grasp] —ˌ**cataˈleptic** *adj.*

catalo (ˈkætəˌləʊ) *n., pl.* **-loes** *or* **-los.** a variant spelling of **cattalo.**

catalogue *or U.S.* **catalog** (ˈkætəˌlɒg) *n.* **1.** a complete, usually alphabetical list of items, often with notes giving details. **2.** a book, usually illustrated, containing details of items for sale, esp. as used by mail-order companies. **3.** a list of all the books or resources of a library. **4.** *U.S. and Canadian.* a list of courses offered by a university, college, etc. **5.** *N.Z.* a list of wool lots prepared for auction. ~*vb.* **-logues, -loguing, -logued** *or U.S.* **-logs, -loging, -loged. 6.** to compile a catalogue of (a library). **7.** to add (books, items, etc.) to an existing catalogue. [C15: from Late Latin *catalogus,* from Greek *katalogos,* from *katalegein* to list, from *kata-* completely + *legein* to collect] —ˈ**cataˌloguer** *or* ˈ**cataˌloguist** *n.*

catalogue raisonné (*French* katalɔg rɛzɔne) *n.* a descriptive catalogue, esp. one covering works of art in an exhibition or collection.

catalpa (kəˈtælpə) *n.* any bignoniaceous tree of the genus *Catalpa* of North America and Asia, having large leaves, bell-shaped whitish flowers, and long slender pods. [C18: New Latin, from Carolina Creek *kutuhlpa,* literally: winged head, referring to the appearance of the flowers]

catalyse *or U.S.* **catalyze** (ˈkætəˌlaɪz) *vb.* (*tr.*) to influence (a chemical reaction) by catalysis. —ˈ**cataˌlyser** *or U.S.* ˈ**cataˌlyzer** *n.*

catalysis (kəˈtælɪsɪs) *n., pl.* **-ses** (-ˌsiːz). acceleration of a chemical reaction by the action of a catalyst. [C17: from New Latin, from Greek *katalusis,* from *kataluein* to dissolve] —**catalytic** (ˌkætəˈlɪtɪk) *adj.* —ˌ**cataˈlytically** *adv.*

catalyst (ˈkætəlɪst) *n.* **1.** a substance that increases the rate of a chemical reaction without itself suffering any permanent chemical change. Compare **inhibitor** (sense 2). **2.** a person or thing that causes a change.

catalytic converter *n.* a device using three-way catalysts to reduce the obnoxious and poisonous components of the products of combustion (mainly oxides of nitrogen, carbon monoxide, and unburnt hydrocarbons) from the exhausts of motor vehicles.

catalytic cracker *n.* a unit in an oil refinery in which mineral oils with high boiling points are converted to fuels with lower boiling points by a catalytic process. Often shortened to **cat cracker.**

catamaran (ˌkætəməˈræn) *n.* **1.** a sailing vessel with twin hulls held parallel by a rigid framework. **2.** a primitive raft made of logs lashed together. **3.** *Informal.* a quarrelsome woman. [C17: from Tamil *kattumaram* tied timber]

catamenia (ˌkætəˈmiːnɪə) *pl. n. Physiol.* another word for **menses.** [C18: from New Latin, from Greek *katamēnia* menses] —ˌ**cataˈmenial** *adj.*

catamite (ˈkætəˌmaɪt) *n.* a boy kept for homosexual purposes. [C16: from Latin *Catamītus,* variant of *Ganymēdēs* Ganymede, cupbearer of the gods]

catamount (ˈkætəˌmaʊnt) *or* **catamountain** *n.* any of various medium-sized felines, such as the puma or lynx. [C17: short for *cat of the mountain*]

catananche (ˌkætəˈnæŋkɪ) *n.* any of the hardy perennial genus *Catananche,* from S Europe; some, esp. *C. caerulea,* are grown for their blue-and-white flowers that can be dried as winter decoration: family *Compositae.* Also called **cupid's dart.** [from Greek *katanangkē* a spell (from their use in love potions)]

cataphora (kəˈtæfərə) *n. Grammar.* the use of a word such as a pronoun that has the same reference as a word used subsequently in the same discourse. Compare **anaphora.** [from CATA- + Greek *pherein* to bear] —**cataphoric** (ˌkætəˈfɒrɪk) *adj.*

cataphoresis (ˌkætəfəˈriːsɪs) *n.* another name for **electrophoresis.** —**cataphoretic** (ˌkætəfəˈrɛtɪk) *adj.* —ˌ**cataphoˈretically** *adv.*

cataphyll (ˈkætəˌfɪl) *n.* a simplified form of plant leaf, such as a scale leaf or cotyledon.

cataplasia (ˌkætəˈpleɪzɪə) *n.* the degeneration of cells and tissues to a less highly developed form. —**cataplastic** (ˌkætəˈplæstɪk) *adj.*

cataplasm (ˈkætəˌplæzəm) *n. Med.* another name for **poultice.** [C16: from Latin *cataplasma,* from Greek, from *kataplassein* to cover with a plaster, from *plassein* to shape]

cataplexy (ˈkætəˌplɛksɪ) *n.* **1.** sudden temporary paralysis, brought on by severe shock. **2.** a state of complete absence of movement assumed by animals while shamming death. [C19: from Greek *kataplēxis* amazement, from *kataplēssein* to strike down (with amazement), confound, from *kata-* down + *plēssein* to strike] —ˌ**cataˈplectic** *adj.*

catapult (ˈkætəˌpʌlt) *n.* **1.** a Y-shaped implement with a loop of elastic fastened to the ends of the two prongs, used mainly by children for shooting small stones, etc. U.S. and Canadian name: **slingshot. 2.** a heavy war engine used formerly for hurling stones, etc. **3.** a device installed in warships to launch aircraft. ~*vb.* **4.** (*tr.*) to shoot forth from or as if from a catapult. **5.** (foll. by *over, into,* etc.) to move precipitately: *she was catapulted to stardom overnight.* [C16: from Latin *catapulta,* from Greek *katapeltēs,* from *kata-* down + *pallein* to hurl]

cataract (ˈkætəˌrækt) *n.* **1.** a large waterfall or rapids. **2.** a deluge; downpour. **3.** *Pathol.* **a.** partial or total opacity of the crystalline lens of the eye. **b.** the opaque area. [C15: from Latin *catarracta,* from Greek *katarrhaktēs,* from *katarassein* to dash down, from *arassein* to strike]

catarrh (kəˈtɑː) *n.* inflammation of a mucous membrane with increased production of mucus, esp. affecting the nose and throat in the common cold. [C16: via French from Late Latin *catarrhus,* from Greek *katarrous,* from *katarrhein* to flow down, from *kata-* down + *rhein* to flow] —**caˈtarrhal** *or* **caˈtarrhous** *adj.*

catarrhine (ˈkætəˌraɪn) *adj.* **1.** (of apes and Old World monkeys) having the nostrils set close together and opening to the front of the face. **2.** Also: **leptorrhine.** (of humans) having a thin or narrow nose. ~*n.* **3.** an animal or person with this characteristic. ~Compare **platyrrhine.** [C19: from New Latin *Catarrhina* (for sense 1), all ultimately from Greek *katarrhin* having a hooked nose, from *kata-* down + *rhis* nose]

catastrophe (kəˈtæstrəfɪ) *n.* **1.** a sudden, extensive, or notable disaster or misfortune. **2.** the denouement of a play, esp. a classical tragedy. **3.** a final decisive event, usually causing a disastrous end. **4.** Also called: **cataclysm.** any sudden and violent change in the earth's surface caused by flooding, earthquake, or some other process. [C16: from Greek *katastrophē,* from *katastrephein* to overturn, from *strephein* to turn] —**catastrophic** (ˌkætəˈstrɒfɪk) *adj.* —ˌ**cataˈstrophically** *adv.*

catastrophe theory *n.* **a.** the mathematical theory that classifies surfaces according to their form. **b.** the popular application of this theory to the explanation of abruptly changing phenomena, as by the discontinuity of a line on the topmost fold of a folded surface.

catastrophism (kəˈtæstrəˌfɪzəm) *n.* **1.** an old doctrine, now discarded, that the earth was created and has subsequently been shaped by sudden divine acts which have no logical connection with each other rather than by gradual evolutionary processes. **2.** Also called: **neo-catastrophism.** a modern doctrine that the gradual evolutionary processes shaping the earth have been supplemented in the past by the effects of huge natural catastrophes. See **uniformitarianism.** Compare **gradualism** (sense 2). —**caˈtastrophist** *n.*

catatonia (ˌkætəˈtəʊnɪə) *n.* a state of muscular rigidity and stupor, sometimes found in schizophrenia. [C20: New Latin, from German *Katatonie,* from CATA- + *-tonia,* from Greek *tonos* tension] —**catatonic** (ˌkætəˈtɒnɪk) *adj., n.*

Catawba (kəˈtɔːbə) *n.* **1.** (*pl.* **-ba** *or* **-bas**) a member of a North American Indian people, formerly of South Carolina, now almost extinct. **2.** their language, belonging to the Siouan family. **3.** a cultivated variety of red North American grape, widely grown in the eastern U.S. **4.** the wine made from these grapes.

catbird (ˈkætˌbɜːd) *n.* **1.** any of several North American songbirds of the family *Mimidae* (mockingbirds), esp. *Dumetella carolinensis,* whose call resembles the mewing of a cat. **2.** any of several Australian bowerbirds of the genera *Ailuroedus* and *Scenopoeetes,* having a catlike call.

catboat (ˈkætˌbəʊt) *n.* a sailing vessel with a single mast, set well forward and often unstayed, and a large sail, usually rigged with a gaff. Shortened form: **cat.**

cat brier *n.* another name for **greenbrier.**

cat burglar *n.* a burglar who enters buildings by climbing through upper windows, skylights, etc.

catcall (ˈkætˌkɔːl) *n.* **1.** a shrill whistle or cry expressing disapproval, as at a public meeting, etc. ~*vb.* **2.** to utter such a call (at); deride with catcalls. —ˈ**catˌcaller** *n.*

catch (kætʃ) *vb.* **catches, catching, caught. 1.** (*tr.*) to take hold of so as to retain or restrain: *he caught the ball.* **2.** (*tr.*) to take, seize, or capture, esp. after pursuit. **3.** (*tr.*) to ensnare or deceive, as by trickery. **4.** (*tr.*) to surprise or detect in an act: *he caught the dog rifling the larder.* **5.** (*tr.*) to reach with a blow: *the stone caught him on the side of the head.* **6.** (*tr.*) to overtake or reach in time to board: *if we hurry we should catch the next bus.* **7.** (*tr.*) to see or hear; attend: *I didn't catch the Ibsen play.* **8.** (*tr.*) to be infected with: *to catch a cold.* **9.** to hook or entangle or become hooked or entangled: *her dress caught on a nail.* **10.** to fasten or be fastened with or as if with a latch or other device. **11.** (*tr.*) to attract or arrest: *she tried to catch his eye.* **12.** (*tr.*) to comprehend: *I didn't catch his meaning.* **13.** (*tr.*) to hear accurately: *I didn't catch what you said.* **14.** (*tr.*) to captivate or charm. **15.** (*tr.*) to perceive and reproduce accurately: *the painter managed to catch his model's beauty.* **16.** (*tr.*) to hold back or restrain: *he caught his breath in surprise.* **17.** (*intr.*) to become alight: *the fire won't catch.* **18.** (*tr.*) *Cricket.* to dismiss (a batsman) by intercepting and holding a ball struck by him before it touches the ground. **19.** (*intr.;* often foll. by *at*) **a.** to grasp or attempt to grasp. **b.** to take advantage (of), esp. eagerly: *he caught at the chance.* **20.** (*intr.; used passively*) *Informal.* to make pregnant. **21. catch it.** *Informal.* to be scolded or reprimanded. **22. catch oneself on.** *Slang.* to realize that one's actions are mistaken. ~*n.* **23.** the act of catching or grasping. **24.** a device that catches and fastens, such as a latch. **25.** anything that is caught, esp. something worth catching. **26.** the amount or number caught. **27.** *Informal.* a person regarded as an eligible matrimonial prospect. **28.** a check or break in the voice. **29.** a break in a mechanism. **30.** *Informal.* **a.** a concealed, unexpected, or unforeseen drawback or handicap. **b.** (*as modifier*): *a catch question.* **31.** a game in which a ball is thrown from one player to another. **32.** *Cricket.* the catching of a ball struck by a batsman before it touches the ground, resulting in him being out. **33.** *Music.* a type of round popular in the 17th, 18th, and 19th centuries, having a humorous text that is often indecent or bawdy and hard to articulate. See **round** (sense 31), **canon**[1] (sense 7). **34.** *Austral.* another name for **bell sheep. 35.** *Rare.* a fragment. ~See also **catch on, catch out, catch up.** [C13 *cacchen* to pursue, from Old Northern French *cachier,* from Latin *captāre* to snatch, from *capere* to seize] —ˈ**catchable** *adj.*

catch-all *n. Chiefly U.S. and Canadian.* **a.** something designed to cover a variety of situations or possibilities. **b.** (*as modifier*): *a catch-all clause.*

catch-as-catch-can *n.* **1.** a style of wrestling in which trips, holds below the waist, etc., are allowed. ~*adj., adv.* **2.** *Chiefly U.S. and Canadian.* using any method or opportunity that comes to hand.

catch basin *n.* the U.S. and Canadian name for **catch pit.**

catch crop *n.* a quick-growing crop planted between two regular crops grown in consecutive seasons, or between two rows of regular crops in the same season.

catcher (ˈkætʃə) *n.* **1.** a person or thing that catches, esp. in a game or sport. **2.** *Baseball.* a fielder who stands behind home plate and catches pitched balls not hit by the batter.

catchfly (ˈkætʃˌflaɪ) *n., pl.* **-flies.** any of several caryophyllaceous plants of the genus *Silene* that have sticky calyxes and stems on which insects are sometimes trapped.

catching (ˈkætʃɪŋ) *adj.* **1.** infectious. **2.** attractive; captivating.

catching pen *n. Austral. and N.Z.* a pen adjacent to a shearer's stand containing the sheep ready for shearing.

catchment (ˈkætʃmənt) *n.* **1.** the act of catching or collecting water. **2.** a structure in which water is collected. **3.** the water so collected. **4.** *Brit.* the intake of a school from one catchment area.

catchment area *n.* **1.** the area of land bounded by watersheds draining into a river, basin, or reservoir. Also called: **catchment basin, drainage area, drainage basin. 2.** the area from which people are allocated to a particular school, hospital, etc.

catch on *vb.* (*intr., adv.*) *Informal.* **1.** to become popular or fashionable. **2.** to grasp mentally; understand.

catch out *vb.* (*tr., adv.*) *Informal, chiefly Brit.* to trap (a person), esp. in an error or doing something reprehensible.

catchpenny (ˈkætʃˌpɛnɪ) *adj.* **1.** (*prenominal*) designed to have instant appeal, esp. in order to sell quickly and easily without regard for quality: *catchpenny ornaments.* ~*n., pl.* **-nies. 2.** an item or commodity that is cheap and showy.

catch phrase *n.* a well-known frequently used phrase, esp. one associated with a particular group, etc.

catch pit *n.* a pit in a drainage system in which matter is collected that might otherwise block a sewer. U.S. and Canadian name: **catch basin.**

catch points *pl. n.* railway points designed to derail a train running back in the wrong direction to prevent collision with a following train.

catchpole *or* **catchpoll** (ˈkætʃˌpəʊl) *n.* (in medieval England) a sheriff's officer who arrested debtors. [Old English *cæcepol,* from Medieval Latin *cacepollus* tax-gatherer, literally: chicken-chaser, from *cace-* CATCH + *pollus* (from Latin *pullus* chick)]

catch-22 *n.* **1.** a situation in which a person is frustrated by a paradoxical rule or set of circumstances that preclude any attempt to escape from them. **2.** a situation in which any move that a person can make will lead to trouble. [C20: from the title of a novel (1961) by the U.S. writer Joseph Heller (born 1923)]

catchup (ˈkætʃəp, ˈkɛtʃ-) *n.* a variant spelling (esp. U.S.) of **ketchup.**

catch up *vb.* (*adv.*) **1.** (*tr.*) to seize and take up (something) quickly. **2.** (when *intr.,* often foll. by *with*) to reach or pass (someone or something), after following: *he soon caught him up.* **3.** (*intr.;* usually foll. by *on* or *with*) to make up for lost ground or deal with a backlog (in some specified task or activity). **4.** (*tr.; often passive*) to absorb or involve: *she was caught up in her reading.* **5.** (*tr.*) to raise by or as if by fastening: *the hem of her dress was caught up with ribbons.*

catchwater drain (ˈkætʃˌwɔːtə) *n.* a channel cut along the edge of high ground to catch surface water from it and divert it away from low-lying ground.

catchweight (ˈkætʃˌweɪt) *adj. Wrestling.* of or relating to a contest in which normal weight categories have been waived by agreement.

catchword (ˈkætʃˌwɜːd) *n.* **1.** a word or phrase made temporarily popular, esp. by a political campaign; slogan. **2.** a word printed as a running head in a reference book. **3.** *Theatre.* an actor's cue to speak or enter. **4.** the first word of a printed or typewritten page repeated at the bottom of the page preceding.

catchy (ˈkætʃɪ) *adj.* **catchier, catchiest. 1.** (of a tune, etc.) pleasant and easily remembered or imitated. **2.** tricky or deceptive: *a catchy question.* **3.** irregular: *a catchy breeze.* —ˈ**catchiness** *n.*

cat cracker *n.* an informal name for **catalytic cracker.**

cat door *n.* a small door or flap in a larger door through which a cat can pass.

catechetical (ˌkætɪˈkɛtɪkᵊl) *or* **catechetic** *adj.* of or relating to teaching by question and answer. —ˌ**cateˈchetically** *adv.*

catechin (ˈkætəkɪn) *n.* a soluble yellow solid substance found in catechu and mahogany wood and used in tanning and dyeing. Formula: $C_{15}H_{14}O_6$. [C19: from CATECHU + -IN]

catechism (ˈkætɪˌkɪzəm) *n.* **1.** instruction by a series of questions and answers, esp. a book containing such instruction on the religious doctrine of a Christian Church. **2.** rigorous and persistent questioning, as in a test or interview. [C16: from Late Latin *catēchismus,* ultimately from Greek *katēkhizein* to CATECHIZE] —ˌ**cateˈchismal** *adj.*

catechize *or* **catechise** (ˈkætɪˌkaɪz) *vb.* (*tr.*) **1.** to teach or examine by means of questions and answers. **2.** to give oral instruction in Christianity, esp. by using a catechism. **3.** to put questions to (someone). [C15: from Late Latin *catēchizāre,* from Greek *katēkhizein,* from *katēkhein* to instruct orally, literally: to shout down, from *kata-* down + *ēkhein* to sound] —ˈ**catechist,** ˈ**cateˌchizer** *or* ˈ**cateˌchiser** *n.* —ˌ**cateˈchistic** *or* ˌ**cateˈchistical** *adj.* —ˌ**cateˈchistically** *adv.* —ˌ**catechiˈzation** *or* ˌ**catechiˈsation** *n.*

catechol (ˈkætɪˌtʃɒl, -ˌkɒl) *n.* a colourless crystalline phenol found in resins and lignins; 1,2-dihydroxybenzene. It is used as a photographic developer. Formula: $C_6H_4(OH)_2$. Also called: **pyrocatechol.** [C20: from CATECHU + -OL[1]]

catecholamine (ˌkætəˈkɒləˌmiːn) *n.* any of a group of hormones that are catechol derivatives, esp. adrenaline and noradrenaline. [C20: from CATECHU + -OL[1] + AMINE]

catechu (ˈkætɪˌtʃuː), **cachou,** *or* **cutch** *n.* a water-soluble astringent resinous substance obtained from any of certain tropical plants, esp. the leguminous tree *Acacia catechu* of S Asia, and used in medicine, tanning, and dyeing. See also **gambier.** [C17: probably from Malay *kachu,* of Dravidian origin]

catechumen (ˌkætɪˈkjuːmɛn) *n. Christianity.* a person, esp. in the early Church, undergoing instruction prior to baptism. [C15: via Old French, from Late Latin, from Greek *katēkhoumenos* one being instructed verbally, from *katēkhein;* see CATECHIZE] —ˌcateˈ**chumenal** *or* **catechumenical** (ˌkætəkjʊˈmɛnɪkᵊl) *adj.* —ˌcateˈ**chumenate** *n.* —ˌcateˈ**chumenism** *n.*

categorial (ˌkætɪˈgɔːrɪəl) *adj.* **1.** of or relating to a category. **2.** *Logic.* (of a statement) consisting of a subject, S, and a predicate, P, each of which denotes a class, and having one of the following forms: *all S are P* (universal affirmative); *some S are P* (particular affirmative); *some S are not P* (particular negative); *no S are P* (universal negative). See **syllogism.**

categorial grammar *n.* a theory that characterizes syntactic categories in terms of functions between classes of expressions. The basic classes are names (*N*) and sentences (*S*). Intransitive verbs are symbols for functions which take a name and yield a sentence (written: *S/N*), adverbs form compound verbs from verbs (for example, *run fast*) and so are *(S/N)/(S/N)*, etc.

categorical (ˌkætɪˈgɒrɪkᵊl) *or* **categoric** *adj.* **1.** unqualified; positive; unconditional: *a categorical statement.* **2.** relating to or included in a category. **3.** *Logic.* another word for **categorial.** —ˌcateˈ**gorically** *adv.* —ˌcateˈ**goricalness** *n.*

categorical imperative *n.* (in Kantian ethics) the unconditional moral principle that one's behaviour should accord with universalizable maxims which respect persons as ends in themselves; the obligation to do one's duty for its own sake and not in pursuit of further ends. Compare **hypothetical imperative.**

categorize *or* **categorise** (ˈkætɪgəˌraɪz) *vb.* (*tr.*) to place in a category; classify. —ˌ**categoriˈzation** *or* ˌ**categoriˈsation** *n.*

category (ˈkætɪgərɪ) *n., pl.* **-ries. 1.** a class or group of things, people, etc., possessing some quality or qualities in common; a division in a system of classification. **2.** *Metaphysics.* any one of the most basic classes into which objects and concepts can be analysed. **3. a.** (in Aristotelian philosophy) any one of ten most fundamental modes of being, such as quantity, quality, and substance. **b.** (in Kantian philosophy) one of twelve concepts required by human beings to interpret the empirical world. **c.** any set of objects, concepts, or expressions distinguished from others within some logical or linguistic theory by the intelligibility of a specific set of statements concerning them. See also **category mistake.** [C15: from Late Latin *catēgoria,* from Greek *katēgoria,* from *kategorein* to accuse, assert]

category mistake *n. Philosophy, logic.* a sentence that says of something in one category what can only intelligibly be said of something in another, as when speaking of the mind located in space.

catena (kəˈtiːnə) *n., pl.* **-nae** (-niː). a connected series, esp. of patristic comments on the Bible. [C17: from Latin: chain]

catenaccio (*Italian* kateˈnattʃo) *n. Football.* an extremely defensive style of play. [C20: from Latin *catena* chain]

catenane (ˈkætɪˌneɪn) *n.* a type of chemical compound in which the molecules have two or more rings that are interlocked like the links of a chain. [C20: from Latin *catena* chain + -ANE]

catenary (kəˈtiːnərɪ) *n., pl.* **-ries. 1.** the curve assumed by a heavy uniform flexible cord hanging freely from two points. When symmetrical about the *y*-axis and intersecting it at $y = a$, the equation is $y = a \cosh x/a$. **2.** the hanging cable between pylons along a railway track, from which the trolley wire is suspended. ~*adj. also* **catenarian** (ˌkætɪˈnɛərɪən). **3.** of, resembling, relating to, or constructed using a catenary or suspended chain. [C18: from Latin *catēnārius* relating to a chain]

catenate (ˈkætɪˌneɪt) *vb.* **1.** *Biology.* to arrange or be arranged in a series of chains or rings. ~*adj.* **2.** another word for **catenulate.** [C17: from Latin *catēnāre* to bind with chains] —ˌcateˈ**nation** *n.*

catenoid (ˈkætəˌnɔɪd) *n.* the geometrical surface generated by rotating a catenary about its axis.

catenulate (kəˈtɛnjʊˌleɪt, -lɪt) *adj.* (of certain spores) formed in a row or chain. [C19: from Latin *catēnula,* diminutive of *catēna* chain]

cater (ˈkeɪtə) *vb.* **1.** (*intr.;* foll. by *for* or *to*) to provide what is required or desired (for): *to cater for a need; cater to your tastes.* **2.** (when *intr.,* foll. by *for*) to provide food, services, etc. (for): *we cater for parties; to cater a banquet.* [C16: from earlier *catour* purchaser, variant of *acatour,* from Anglo-Norman *acater* to buy, ultimately related to Latin *acceptāre* to ACCEPT]

cateran (ˈkætərən) *n.* (formerly) a member of a band of brigands and marauders in the Scottish highlands. [C14: probably from Scottish Gaelic *ceathairneach* robber, plunderer]

cater-cornered (ˈkætəˌkɔːnəd) *adj., adv. U.S. and Canadian informal.* diagonally placed; diagonal. Also: **catty-cornered.** [C16 *cater,* from dialect *cater* (adv.) diagonally, from obsolete *cater* (n.) four-spot of dice, from Old French *quatre* four, from Latin *quattuor*]

cater-cousin (ˈkeɪtəˌkʌzᵊn) *n. Archaic.* a close friend. [C16: perhaps from obsolete *cater* caterer; for sense, compare FOSTER, as in *foster brother,* etc.]

caterer (ˈkeɪtərə) *n.* a person who caters, esp. one who as a profession provides food for large social events, etc.

catering (ˈkeɪtərɪŋ) *n.* **1.** the trade of a professional caterer. **2.** the food, etc., provided at a function by a caterer.

caterpillar (ˈkætəˌpɪlə) *n.* **1.** the wormlike larva of butterflies and moths, having numerous pairs of legs and powerful biting jaws. It may be brightly coloured, hairy, or spiny. **2.** *Trademark.* an endless track, driven by sprockets or wheels, used to propel a heavy vehicle and enable it to cross soft or uneven ground. **3.** *Trademark.* a vehicle, such as a tractor, tank, bulldozer, etc., driven by such tracks. [C15 *catyrpel,* probably from Old Northern French *catepelose,* literally: hairy cat]

caterpillar hunter *n.* any of various carabid beetles of the genus *Calosoma,* of Europe and North America, which prey on the larvae of moths and butterflies.

caterwaul (ˈkætəˌwɔːl) *vb.* (*intr.*) **1.** to make a yowling noise, as a cat on heat. ~*n.* **2.** a shriek or yell made by or sounding like a cat on heat. [C14: of imitative origin] —ˈ**caterˌwauler** *n.*

cates (keɪts) *pl. n.* (*sometimes sing.*) *Archaic.* choice dainty food; delicacies. [C15: variant of *acates* purchases, from Old Northern French *acater* to buy, from Vulgar Latin *accaptāre* (unattested); ultimately related to Latin *acceptāre* to ACCEPT]

catfall (ˈkætˌfɔːl) *n. Nautical.* the line used in a cat.

catfish (ˈkætˌfɪʃ) *n., pl.* **-fish** *or* **-fishes. 1.** any of numerous mainly freshwater teleost fishes having whisker-like barbels around the mouth, esp. the silurids of Europe and Asia and the horned pouts of North America. **2.** another name for **wolffish.**

catgut (ˈkætˌgʌt) *n.* a strong cord made from the dried intestines of sheep and other animals that is used for stringing certain musical instruments and sports rackets, and, when sterilized, as surgical ligatures. Often shortened to **gut.**

Cath. *abbrev. for:* **1.** Cathedral. **2.** Catholic.

cath- *prefix.* a variant of **cata-** before an aspirate: *cathode.*

Cathar (ˈkæθə) *or* **Catharist** (ˈkæθərɪst) *n., pl.* **-ars, -ari** (-ərɪ), *or* **-arists.** a member of a Christian sect in Provence in the 12th and 13th centuries who believed the material world was evil and only the spiritual was good. [from Medieval Latin *Cathari,* from Greek *katharoi* the pure] —ˈ**Catharˌism** *n.*

catharsis (kəˈθɑːsɪs) *n., pl.* **-ses. 1.** (in Aristotelian literary criticism) the purging or purification of the emotions through the evocation of pity and fear, as in tragedy. **2.** *Psychoanal.* the bringing of repressed ideas or experiences into consciousness, thus relieving tensions. See also **abreaction. 3.** purgation, esp. of the bowels. [C19: New Latin, from Greek *katharsis,* from *kathairein* to purge, purify]

cathartic (kəˈθɑːtɪk) *adj.* **1.** purgative. **2.** effecting catharsis. ~*n.* **3.** a purgative drug or agent. —**caˈthartically** *adv.*

cathead (ˈkætˌhɛd) *n.* a fitting at the bow of a vessel for securing the anchor when raised.

cathectic (kəˈθɛktɪk) *adj.* of or relating to cathexis.

cathedra (kəˈθiːdrə) *n.* **1.** a bishop's throne. **2.** the office or rank of a bishop. **3.** See **ex cathedra.** [from Latin: chair]

cathedral (kəˈθiːdrəl) *n.* **a.** the principal church of a diocese, containing the bishop's official throne. **b.** (*as modifier*): *a cathedral city; cathedral clergy.* [C13: from Late Latin (*ecclesia*) *cathedrālis* cathedral (church), from *cathedra* bishop's throne, from Greek *kathedra* seat]

cathepsin (kəˈθɛpsɪn) *n.* a proteolytic enzyme responsible for the autolysis of cells after death. [C20: from Greek *kathepsein* to boil down, soften]

Catherine wheel (ˈkæθrɪn) *n.* **1.** Also called: **pinwheel.** a type of firework consisting of a powder-filled spiral tube, mounted with a pin through its centre. When lit it rotates quickly, producing a display of sparks and coloured flame. **2.** a circular window having ribs radiating from the centre. [C16: named after St *Catherine* of Alexandria, who was tortured on a spiked wheel and beheaded (307 A.D.)]

catheter (ˈkæθɪtə) *n. Med.* a long slender flexible tube for inserting into a natural bodily cavity or passage for introducing or withdrawing fluid. [C17: from Late Latin, from Greek *kathetēr,* from *kathienai* to send down, insert]

catheterize *or* **catheterise** (ˈkæθɪtəˌraɪz) *vb.* (*tr.*) to insert a catheter into. —ˌ**catheteriˈzation** *or* ˌ**catheteriˈsation** *n.*

cathexis (kəˈθɛksɪs) *n., pl.* **-thexes** (-ˈθɛksiːz). *Psychoanal.* concentration of psychic energy on a single goal. [C20: from New Latin, from Greek *kathexis,* from *katekhein* to hold fast, intended to render German *Besetzung* a taking possession of]

cathiodermie (ˌkæθɪəʊˈdɜːmɪ) *n.* a cosmetic treatment in which an electric current is passed through a special gel applied to the face in order to cleanse and oxygenate the skin. [C20: from French: electrolysis of the skin]

cathode (ˈkæθəʊd) *n.* **1.** the negative electrode in an electrolytic cell; the electrode by which electrons enter a device from an external circuit. **2.** the negatively charged electron source in an electronic valve. **3.** the positive terminal of a primary cell. ~Compare **anode.** [C19: from Greek *kathodos* a descent, from *kata-* down + *hodos* way] —**cathodal** (kæˈθəʊdᵊl), **cathodic** (kæˈθɒdɪk, -ˈθəʊ-), *or* **caˈthodical** *adj.*

cathode rays *pl. n.* a stream of electrons emitted from the surface of a cathode in a vacuum tube.

cathode-ray tube *n.* a vacuum tube in which a beam of high-energy electrons is focused onto a fluorescent screen to give a visible spot of light. The device, with appropriate deflection equipment, is used in television receivers, visual display units, oscilloscopes, etc. Abbrev.: **CRT.**

cathodic protection *n. Metallurgy.* a technique for protecting metal structures, such as steel ships and pipelines, from electrolytic corrosion by making the structure the cathode in a cell, either by applying an electromotive force directly or by putting it into contact with a more electropositive metal. See also **sacrificial anode.**

cathodoluminescence (ˌkæθədəʊˌluːmɪˈnɛsəns) *n. Physics.* luminescence caused by irradiation with electrons (cathode rays).

cat hole *n.* one of a pair of holes in the after part of a ship through which hawsers are passed for steadying the ship or heaving astern.

catholic (ˈkæθəlɪk, ˈkæθlɪk) *adj.* **1.** universal; relating to all men; all-inclusive. **2.** comprehensive in interests, tastes, etc.; broad-minded; liberal. [C14: from Latin *catholicus,* from Greek *katholikos* universal, from *katholou* in general, from *kata-* according to + *holos* whole] —**catholically** *or* **catholicly** (kəˈθɒlɪklɪ) *adv.*

Catholic (ˈkæθəlɪk, ˈkæθlɪk) *adj. Christianity.* **1.** denoting or relating to the entire body of Christians, esp. to the Church before separation into the Greek or Eastern and Latin or Western Churches. **2.** denoting or relating to the Latin or Western Church after this separation. **3.** denoting or relating to the Roman Catholic Church. **4.** denoting or relating to any church, belief, etc., that claims continuity with or originates in the ancient undivided Church. *~n.* **5.** a member of any of the Churches regarded as Catholic, esp. the Roman Catholic Church.

Catholic Church *n.* **1.** short for **Roman Catholic Church. 2.** any of several Churches claiming to have maintained continuity with the ancient and undivided Church.

Catholicism (kəˈθɒlɪˌsɪzəm) *n.* **1.** short for **Roman Catholicism. 2.** the beliefs, practices, etc., of any Catholic Church.

catholicity (ˌkæθəˈlɪsɪtɪ) *n.* **1.** a wide range of interests, tastes, etc.; liberality. **2.** universality; comprehensiveness.

Catholicity (ˌkæθəˈlɪsɪtɪ) *n.* the beliefs, etc., of the Catholic Church.

catholicize *or* **catholicise** (kəˈθɒlɪˌsaɪz) *vb.* **1.** to make or become catholic. **2.** (*often cap.*) to convert to or become converted to Catholicism. —**caˌtholiciˈzation** *or* **caˌtholiciˈsation** *n.*

catholicon (kəˈθɒlɪkən) *n.* a remedy for all ills; panacea. [C15: from Medieval Latin; see CATHOLIC]

cathouse (ˈkætˌhaʊs) *n. U.S. and Canadian.* a slang word for **brothel.**

cation (ˈkætaɪən) *n.* a positively charged ion; an ion that is attracted to the cathode during electrolysis. Compare **anion.** [C19: from CATA- + ION] —**cationic** (ˌkætaɪˈɒnɪk) *adj.*

cationic detergent *n.* a type of detergent in which the active part of the molecule is a positive ion (cation). Cationic detergents are usually quaternary ammonium salts and often also have bactericidal properties.

catkin (ˈkætkɪn) *n.* an inflorescence consisting of a hanging spike of much reduced flowers of either sex: occurs in birch, hazel, etc. Also called: **ament.** [C16: from obsolete Dutch *katteken* kitten, identical in meaning with French *chaton,* German *Kätzchen*]

catling (ˈkætlɪŋ) *n.* **1.** a long double-edged surgical knife for amputations. **2.** *Rare.* catgut or a string made from it. **3.** an archaic word for **kitten.** [C17: from CAT + -LING[1]]

cat litter *n.* absorbent material, often in a granular form, that is used to line a receptacle in which a domestic cat can urinate and defecate indoors.

catmint (ˈkætˌmɪnt) *n.* a Eurasian plant, *Nepeta cataria,* having spikes of purple-spotted white flowers and scented leaves of which cats are fond: family *Labiatae* (labiates). Also called: **catnip.**

catnap (ˈkætˌnæp) *n.* **1.** a short sleep or doze. *~vb.* **-naps, -napping, -napped. 2.** (*intr.*) to sleep or doze for a short time or intermittently.

catnip (ˈkætˌnɪp) *n.* another name for **catmint.**

catolyte (ˈkætəʊˌlaɪt) *or* **catholyte** (ˈkæθəʊˌlaɪt) *n. Electronics.* the part of the electrolyte that surrounds the cathode in an electrolytic cell.

cat-o'-mountain *n.* another name for **catamount.**

cat-o'-nine-tails *n., pl.* **-tails.** a rope whip consisting of nine knotted thongs, used formerly to flog prisoners. Often shortened to **cat.**

catoptrics (kəˈtɒptrɪks) *n.* (*functioning as sing.*) the branch of optics concerned with reflection, esp. the formation of images by mirrors. [C18: from Greek *katoptrikos,* from *katoptron* mirror] —**caˈtoptric** *or* **caˈtoptrical** *adj.*

cat rig *n.* the rig of a catboat. —**ˈcatˌrigged** *adj.*

CATS (kæts) *acronym for* credit accumulation transfer scheme: a scheme enabling school-leavers and others to acquire transferable certificates for relevant work experience and study towards a recognized qualification.

CAT scanner (kæt) *n.* former name for **CT scanner.** [C20: *(C)omputerized (A)xial (T)omography*]

cat's cradle *n.* a game played by making intricate patterns with a loop of string between the fingers.

cat's-ear *n.* any of various European plants of the genus *Hypochoeris,* esp. *H. radicata,* having dandelion-like heads of yellow flowers: family *Compositae* (composites).

cat's-eye *n.* any of a group of gemstones, esp. a greenish-yellow variety of chrysoberyl, that reflect a streak of light when cut in a rounded unfaceted shape.

Catseye (ˈkætsˌaɪ) *n. Trademark, Brit.* a glass reflector set into a small fixture, placed at intervals along roads to indicate traffic lanes at night.

cat's-foot *n., pl.* **-feet.** a European plant, *Antennaria dioica,* with whitish woolly leaves and heads of typically white flowers: family *Compositae* (composites). Also called: **mountain everlasting.**

cat's-paw *n.* **1.** a person used by another as a tool; dupe. **2.** *Nautical.* a hitch in the form of two loops, or eyes, in the bight of a line, used for attaching it to a hook. **3.** a pattern of ripples on the surface of water caused by a light wind. [(sense 1) C18: so called from the tale of the monkey who used a cat's paw to draw chestnuts out of a fire]

cat's-tail *n.* **1.** another name for **reed mace** (sense 1). **2.** another name for **catkin.**

catsuit (ˈkætˌsuːt) *n.* a one-piece usually close-fitting trouser suit.

catsup (ˈkætsəp) *n.* a variant (esp. U.S.) of **ketchup.**

cat's whisker *n.* **1.** a pointed wire formerly used to make contact with the crystal in a crystal radio receiver. **2.** any wire used to make contact with a semiconductor.

cat's whiskers *or* **cat's pyjamas** *n.* **the.** *Slang.* a person or thing that is excellent or superior.

cattalo *or* **catalo** (ˈkætəˌləʊ) *n., pl.* **-loes** *or* **-los.** a hardy breed of cattle developed by crossing the American bison with domestic cattle. [C20: from CATT(LE + BUFF)ALO]

cattery (ˈkætərɪ) *n., pl.* **-teries.** a place where cats are bred or looked after.

cattle (ˈkætᵊl) *n.* (*functioning as pl.*) **1.** bovid mammals of the tribe *Bovini* (bovines), esp. those of the genus *Bos.* **2.** Also called: **domestic cattle.** any domesticated bovine mammals, esp. those of the species *Bos taurus* (domestic ox). [C13: from Old Northern French *catel,* Old French *chatel* CHATTEL]

cattle-cake *n.* concentrated food for cattle in the form of cakes.

cattle-grid *n.* a grid of metal bars covering a hollow or hole dug in a roadway, intended to prevent the passage of livestock while allowing vehicles, etc., to pass unhindered.

cattleman (ˈkætᵊlmən) *n., pl.* **-men. 1.** a person who breeds, rears, or tends cattle. **2.** *Chiefly U.S. and Canadian.* a person who owns or rears cattle on a large scale, usually for beef, esp. the owner of a cattle ranch.

cattle plague *n.* another name for **rinderpest.**

cattle-stop *n.* the N.Z. name for **cattle-grid.**

cattle truck *n.* a railway wagon designed for carrying livestock. U.S. and Canadian equivalent: **stock car.**

cattleya (ˈkætlɪə) *n.* any tropical American orchid of the genus *Cattleya,* cultivated for their purplish-pink or white showy flowers. [C19: New Latin, named after William *Cattley* (died 1832), English botanist]

cat-train *or* **cat-swing** *n. Canadian.* a train of sleds, cabooses, etc., pulled by a caterpillar tractor, used chiefly in the north during winter to transport freight.

catty[1] (ˈkætɪ) *or* **cattish** *adj.* **-tier, -tiest. 1.** *Informal.* spiteful: *a catty remark.* **2.** of or resembling a cat. —**ˈcattily** *or* **ˈcattishly** *adv.* —**ˈcattiness** *or* **ˈcattishness** *n.*

catty[2] *or* **cattie** (ˈkætɪ) *n., pl.* **-ties.** a unit of weight, used esp. in China, equal to about one and a half pounds or about 0.67 kilogram. [C16: from Malay *kati*]

catty-cornered *adj.* a variant of **cater-cornered.**

CATV *abbrev. for* community antenna television.

catwalk (ˈkætˌwɔːk) *n.* a narrow pathway over the stage of a theatre, along a bridge, etc.

catworm (ˈkætˌwɜːm) *n.* an active carnivorous polychaete worm, *Nephthys hombergi,* that is about 10cm (4in) long, having a pearly sheen to its body: often dug for bait. Also called: **white worm, white cat.**

Caucasian (kɔːˈkeɪzɪən, -ʒən) *or* **Caucasic** (kɔːˈkeɪzɪk) *adj.* **1.** another word for **Caucasoid. 2.** of or relating to the Caucasus Mountains or the region of Caucasia, between the Caspian Sea and the Black Sea in the former Soviet Union. *~n.* **3.** a member of the Caucasoid race; a white man. **4.** a native or inhabitant of Caucasia. **5.** any of three possibly related families of languages spoken in the Caucasus: **North-West Caucasian,** including Circassian and Abkhaz, **North-East Caucasian,** including Avar, and **South Caucasian,** including Georgian.

Caucasoid (ˈkɔːkəˌzɔɪd) *adj.* **1.** denoting, relating to, or belonging to the light-complexioned racial group of mankind, which includes the peoples indigenous to Europe, N Africa, SW Asia, and the Indian subcontinent and their descendants in other parts of the world. *~n.* **2.** a member of this racial group.

caucus (ˈkɔːkəs) *n., pl.* **-cuses. 1.** *Chiefly U.S. and Canadian.* **a.** a closed meeting of the members of one party in a legislative chamber, etc., to coordinate policy, choose candidates, etc. **b.** such a bloc of politicians: *the Democratic caucus in Congress.* **2.** *Chiefly U.S.* **a.** a group of leading politicians of one party. **b.** a meeting of such a group. **3.** *Chiefly U.S.* a local meeting of party members. **4.** *Brit.* a group or faction within a larger group, esp. a political party, who discuss tactics, choose candidates, etc. **5.** *Austral.* a meeting of the members of the Federal parliamentary Labor Party. **6.** *N.Z.* a formal meeting of all Members of Parliament belonging to one political party. *~vb.* **7.** (*intr.*) to hold a caucus. [C18: probably of Algonquian origin; related to *caucauasu* adviser]

cauda (ˈkɔːdə) *n.* **1.** *Zoology.* the area behind the anus of an animal; tail. **2.** *Anatomy.* **a.** any tail-like structure. **b.** the posterior part of an organ. [Latin: tail]

caudad (ˈkɔːdæd) *adv. Anatomy.* towards the tail or posterior part. Compare **cephalad.** [C19: from CAUDA + -AD]

caudal (ˈkɔːdᵊl) *adj.* **1.** *Anatomy.* of or towards the posterior part of the body. **2.** *Zoology.* relating to, resembling, or in the position of the tail. [C17: from New Latin *caudālis,* from CAUDA] —ˈ**caudally** *adv.*

caudal fin *n.* the tail fin of fishes and some other aquatic vertebrates, used for propulsion during locomotion.

caudate (ˈkɔːdeɪt) *or* **caudated** *adj.* having a tail or a tail-like appendage. [C17: from New Latin *caudātus,* from CAUDA] —**cauˈdation** *n.*

caudex (ˈkɔːdɛks) *n., pl.* **-dices** (-dɪˌsiːz) *or* **-dexes. 1.** the thickened persistent stem base of some herbaceous perennial plants. **2.** the woody stem of palms and tree ferns. [C19: from Latin]

caudillo (kɔːˈdiːljəʊ; *Spanish* kauˈðiʎo) *n., pl.* **-los** (-jəʊz; *Spanish* -ʎos). (in Spanish-speaking countries) a military or political leader. [Spanish, from Late Latin *capitellum,* diminutive of Latin *caput* head]

caudle (ˈkɔːdᵊl) *n.* a hot spiced wine drink made with gruel, formerly used medicinally. [C13: from Old Northern French *caudel,* from Medieval Latin *caldellum,* from Latin *calidus* warm]

caught (kɔːt) *vb.* the past tense and past participle of **catch.**

caul (kɔːl) *n. Anatomy.* **1.** a portion of the amniotic sac sometimes covering a child's head at birth. **2.** a large fold of peritoneum hanging from the stomach across the intestines; the large omentum. [C13: from Old French *cale,* back formation from *calotte* close-fitting cap, of Germanic origin]

cauld (kɔːld) *adj., n.* a Scot. word for **cold.**

cauldrife (ˈkɔːldrɪf) *adj. Scot.* **1.** susceptible to cold; chilly. **2.** lifeless. [C18: from CAULD + RIFE]

cauldron *or* **caldron** (ˈkɔːldrən) *n.* a large pot used for boiling, esp. one with handles. [C13: from earlier *cauderon,* from Anglo-French, from Latin *caldārium* hot bath, from *calidus* warm]

caulescent (kɔːˈlɛsᵊnt) *adj.* having a stem clearly visible above the ground. [C18: from Latin *caulis* stalk]

caulicle (ˈkɔːlɪkᵊl) *n. Botany.* a small stalk or stem. [C17: from Latin *cauliculus,* from *caulis* stem]

cauliflory (ˈkɔːlɪˌflɔːrɪ) *n. Botany.* the production of flowers on the trunk, branches, etc., of a woody plant, as opposed to the ends of the twigs. [C20: from Latin *caulis* stem + *-flory,* from *flōs* flower] —ˌ**cauliˈflorous** *adj.*

cauliflower (ˈkɒlɪˌflaʊə) *n.* **1.** a variety of cabbage, *Brassica oleracea botrytis,* having a large edible head of crowded white flowers on a very short thick stem. **2.** the flower head of this plant, used as a vegetable. [C16: from Italian *caoli fiori,* literally: cabbage flowers, from *cavolo* cabbage (from Latin *caulis*) + *fiore* flower (from Latin *flōs*)]

cauliflower cheese *n.* a dish of cauliflower with a cheese sauce, eaten hot.

cauliflower ear *n.* permanent swelling and distortion of the external ear as the result of ruptures of the blood vessels: usually caused by blows received in boxing. Also called: **boxer's ear.** Technical name: **aural haematoma.**

cauline (ˈkɔːlɪn, -laɪn) *adj.* relating to or growing from a plant stem. [C18: from New Latin *caulīnus,* from Latin *caulis* stem]

caulis (ˈkɔːlɪs) *n., pl.* **-les** (-liːz). *Rare.* the main stem of a plant. [C16: from Latin]

caulk *or* **calk** (kɔːk) *vb.* **1.** to stop up (cracks, crevices, etc.) with a filler. **2.** *Nautical.* to pack (the seams) between the planks of the bottom of (a vessel) with waterproof material to prevent leakage. [C15: from Old Northern French *cauquer* to press down, from Latin *calcāre* to trample, from *calx* heel] —ˈ**caulker** *or* ˈ**calker** *n.*

caus. *abbrev. for* causative.

causal (ˈkɔːzᵊl) *adj.* **1.** acting as or being a cause. **2.** stating, involving, or implying a cause: *the causal part of the argument.* **3.** *Philosophy.* (of a theory) explaining a phenomenon or analysing a concept in terms of some causal relation. —ˈ**causally** *adv.*

causalgia (kɔːˈzældʒɪə) *n. Pathol.* a burning sensation along the course of a peripheral nerve together with local changes in the appearance of the skin. [C19: from New Latin, from Greek *kausos* fever + -ALGIA]

causality (kɔːˈzælɪtɪ) *n., pl.* **-ties. 1. a.** the relationship of cause and effect. **b.** the principle that nothing can happen without being caused. **2.** causal agency or quality.

causation (kɔːˈzeɪʃən) *n.* **1.** the act or fact of causing; the production of an effect by a cause. **2.** the relationship of cause and effect. —**cauˈsational** *adj.*

causative (ˈkɔːzətɪv) *adj.* **1.** *Grammar.* relating to a form or class of verbs, such as *persuade,* that express causation. **2.** (*often postpositive* and foll. by *of*) producing an effect. ~*n.* **3.** the causative form or class of verbs. —ˈ**causatively** *adv.* —ˈ**causativeness** *n.*

cause (kɔːz) *n.* **1.** a person, thing, event, state, or action that produces an effect. **2.** grounds for action; motive; justification: *she had good cause to shout like that.* **3.** the ideals, etc., of a group or movement: *the Communist cause.* **4.** the welfare or interests of a person or group in a dispute: *they fought for the miners' cause.* **5.** a matter of widespread concern or importance: *the cause of public health.* **6. a.** a ground for legal action; matter giving rise to a lawsuit. **b.** the lawsuit itself. **7.** (in Aristotelian philosophy) any of four requirements for a thing's coming to be, namely material (material cause), its nature (formal cause), an agent (efficient cause), and a purpose (final cause). **8.** *Archaic.* a subject of debate or discussion. **9. make common cause with.** to join with (a person, group, etc.) for a common objective. ~*vb.* **10.** (*tr.*) to be the cause of; bring about; precipitate; be the reason for. [C13: from Latin *causa* cause, reason, motive] —ˈ**causable** *adj.* —ˌ**causaˈbility** *n.* —ˈ**causeless** *adj.* —ˈ**causer** *n.*

cause célèbre (ˈkɔːz səˈlɛbrə, -ˈlɛb; *French* koz selɛbrə) *n., pl.* **causes célèbres** (ˈkɔːz səˈlɛbrəz, -ˈlɛb; ˈkɔːzɪz səˈlɛbrə, -ˈlɛbz; *French* koz selɛbrə). a famous lawsuit, trial, or controversy. [C19: from French: famous case]

cause list *n. Brit.* a list of cases awaiting trial.

causerie (ˈkəʊzərɪ; *French* kozri) *n.* an informal talk or conversational piece of writing. [C19: from French, from *causer* to chat]

causeway (ˈkɔːzˌweɪ) *n.* **1.** a raised path or road crossing water, marshland, sand, etc. **2.** a paved footpath. [C15 *cauciwey* (from *cauci* + WAY); *cauci* paved road, from Medieval Latin (*via*) *calciāta, calciātus* paved with limestone, from Latin *calx* limestone]

causey (ˈkɔːzɪ) *n.* **1.** an archaic or dialect word for **causeway. 2.** *Scot.* a cobbled street. **3.** *Scot.* a cobblestone.

caustic (ˈkɔːstɪk) *adj.* **1.** capable of burning or corroding by chemical action: *caustic soda.* **2.** sarcastic; cutting: *a caustic reply.* **3.** of, relating to, or denoting light that is reflected or refracted by a curved surface. ~*n.* **4.** Also called: **caustic surface.** a surface that envelopes the light rays reflected or refracted by a curved surface. **5.** Also called: **caustic curve.** a curve formed by the intersection of a caustic surface with a plane. **6.** *Chem.* a caustic substance, esp. an alkali. [C14: from Latin *causticus,* from Greek *kaustikos,* from *kaiein* to burn] —ˈ**caustical** *adj.* —ˈ**caustically** *adv.* —ˈ**causticness** *or* **causticity** (kɔːˈstɪsɪtɪ) *n.*

caustic potash *n.* another name for **potassium hydroxide.**

caustic soda *n.* another name for **sodium hydroxide.**

cauterant (ˈkɔːtərənt) *adj.* **1.** caustic; cauterizing. ~*n.* **2.** another name for **cautery** (sense 2).

cauterize *or* **cauterise** (ˈkɔːtəˌraɪz) *vb.* (*tr.*) (esp. in the treatment of a wound) to burn or sear (body tissue) with a hot iron or caustic agent. [C14: from Old French *cauteriser,* from Late Latin *cautērizāre,* from *cautērium* branding iron, from Greek *kautērion,* from *kaiein* to burn] —ˌ**cauteriˈzation** *or* ˌ**cauteriˈsation** *n.*

cautery (ˈkɔːtərɪ) *n., pl.* **-teries. 1.** the coagulation of blood or destruction of body tissue by cauterizing. **2.** Also called: **cauterant.** an instrument or chemical agent for cauterizing. [C14: from Old French *cautère,* from Latin *cautērium;* see CAUTERIZE]

caution (ˈkɔːʃən) *n.* **1.** care, forethought, or prudence, esp. in the face of danger; wariness. **2.** something intended or serving as a warning; admonition. **3.** *Law, chiefly Brit.* a formal warning given to a person suspected or accused of an offence that his words will be taken down and may be used in evidence. **4.** a notice entered on the register of title to land that prevents a proprietor from disposing of his land without a notice to the person who entered the caution. **5.** *Informal.* an amusing or surprising person or thing: *she's a real caution.* ~*vb.* **6.** (*tr.*) to urge or warn (a person) to be careful. **7.** (*tr.*) *Law, chiefly Brit.* to give a caution to (a person). **8.** (*intr.*) to warn, urge, or advise: *he cautioned against optimism.* [C13: from Old French, from Latin *cautiō,* from *cavēre* to beware] —ˈ**cautioner** *n.*

cautionary (ˈkɔːʃənərɪ) *adj.* serving as a warning; intended to warn: *a cautionary tale.*

caution money *n. Chiefly Brit.* a sum of money deposited as security for good conduct, against possible debts, etc.

cautious (ˈkɔːʃəs) *adj.* showing or having caution; wary; prudent. —ˈ**cautiously** *adv.* —ˈ**cautiousness** *n.*

CAV *or* **Cur. adv. vult** *Law. abbrev. for* Curia advisari vult: used in English law to indicate that a court has decided to consider a case privately before giving judgment, as when time is needed to consider arguments or submissions made to it. Compare **avizandum.** [Medieval Latin: the court wishes to consider]

Cav. *or* **cav.** *abbrev. for* cavalry.

cavalcade (ˌkævəlˈkeɪd) *n.* **1.** a procession of people on horseback, in cars, etc. **2.** any procession: *a cavalcade of guests.* [C16: from French, from Italian *cavalcata,* from *cavalcare* to ride on horseback, from Late Latin *caballicāre,* from *caballus* horse]

cavalier (ˌkævəˈlɪə) *adj.* **1.** showing haughty disregard; offhand. ~*n.* **2.** a gallant or courtly gentleman, esp. one acting as a lady's escort. **3.** *Archaic.* a horseman, esp. one who is armed. [C16: from Italian *cavaliere,* from Old Provençal *cavalier,* from Late Latin *caballārius* rider, from *caballus* horse, of obscure origin] —ˌ**cavaˈlierly** *adv.*

Cavalier (ˌkævəˈlɪə) *n.* a supporter of Charles I during the English Civil War. Compare **Roundhead.**

cavalier King Charles spaniel *n.* See **King Charles spaniel.**

cavalla (kəˈvælə) *or* **cavally** *n., pl.* **-la, -las,** *or* **-lies.** any of various tropical carangid fishes, such as *Gnathanodon speciosus* (golden cavalla). [C19: from Spanish *caballa,* from Late Latin, feminine of *caballus* horse]

cavalry (ˈkævəlrɪ) *n., pl.* **-ries. 1.** (esp. formerly) the part of an army composed of mounted troops. **2.** the armoured element of a modern army. ~**3.** (*as modifier*): *a cavalry unit; a cavalry charge.* [C16: from French *cavallerie,* from Italian *cavalleria,* from *cavaliere* horseman; see CAVALIER] —ˈ**cavalryman** *n.*

cavalry twill *n.* a strong woollen twill fabric used for trousers, etc.

cavatina (ˌkævəˈtiːnə) *n., pl.* **-ne** (-nɪ). **1.** a solo song resembling a simple aria. **2.** an instrumental composition reminiscent of this. [C19: from Italian]

cave[1] (keɪv) *n.* **1.** an underground hollow with access from the ground surface or from the sea, often found in limestone areas and on rocky coastlines. **2.** *Brit. history.* a secession or a group seceding from a political party on some issue. See **Adullamite.** **3.** (*modifier*) living in caves. ~*vb.* **4.** (*tr.*) to hollow out. ~See also **cave in, caving.** [C13: from Old French, from Latin *cava,* plural of *cavum* cavity, from *cavus* hollow]

cave[2] (ˈkeɪvɪ) *Brit. school slang.* ~*n.* **1.** guard or lookout (esp. in the phrase **keep cave).** ~*sentence substitute.* **2.** watch out! [from Latin *cavē!* beware!]

caveat (ˈkeɪvɪˌæt, ˈkæv-) *n.* **1.** *Law.* a formal notice requesting the court or officer to refrain from taking some specified action without giving prior notice to the person lodging the caveat. **2.** a warning; caution. [C16: from Latin, literally: let him beware]

caveat emptor (ˈɛmptɔː) *n.* the principle that the buyer must bear the risk for the quality of goods purchased unless they are covered by the seller's warranty. [Latin: let the buyer beware]

caveator (ˈkeɪvɪˌeɪtə, ˈkæv-) *n. Law.* a person who enters a caveat.

cavefish (ˈkeɪvˌfɪʃ) *n., pl.* **-fish** *or* **-fishes.** any of various small freshwater cyprinodont fishes of the genera *Amblyopsis, Chologaster,* etc., living in subterranean and other waters in S North America. See also **blindfish.**

cave in *vb.* (*intr., adv.*) **1.** to collapse; subside. **2.** *Informal.* to yield completely, esp. under pressure. ~*n.* **cave-in.** **3.** the sudden collapse of a roof, piece of ground, etc., into a hollow beneath it; subsidence. **4.** the site of such a collapse, as at a mine or tunnel.

cavel (ˈkeɪvᵊl) *n. N.Z.* a drawing of lots among miners for an easy and profitable place at the coalface. [C19: from English dialect *cavel* to cast lots, apportion]

caveman (ˈkeɪvˌmæn) *n., pl.* **-men.** **1.** a man of the Palaeolithic age; cave dweller. **2.** *Informal and facetious.* a man who is primitive or brutal in behaviour, etc.

cavendish (ˈkævəndɪʃ) *n.* tobacco that has been sweetened and pressed into moulds to form bars. [C19: perhaps from the name of the first maker]

cavern (ˈkævᵊn) *n.* **1.** a cave, esp. when large and formed by underground water, or a large chamber in a cave. ~*vb.* (*tr.*) **2.** to shut in or as if in a cavern. **3.** to hollow out. [C14: from Old French *caverne,* from Latin *caverna,* from *cavus* hollow; see CAVE[1]]

cavernous (ˈkævənəs) *adj.* **1.** suggestive of a cavern in vastness, darkness, etc.: *cavernous hungry eyes.* **2.** filled with small cavities; porous. **3.** (of rocks) containing caverns or cavities. —ˈ**cavernously** *adv.*

cavesson (ˈkævɪsən) *n.* a kind of hard noseband, used (esp. formerly) in breaking a horse in. [C16: via French from Italian *cavezzone,* from *cavezza* halter, ultimately related to Latin *caput* head]

cavetto (kəˈvɛtəʊ; *Italian* kaˈvetto) *n., pl.* **-ti** (-tɪ; *Italian* -ti). *Architect.* a concave moulding, shaped to a quarter circle in cross section. [C17: from Italian, from *cavo* hollow, from Latin *cavus*]

caviar *or* **caviare** (ˈkævɪˌɑː, ˌkævɪˈɑː) *n.* **1.** the salted roe of sturgeon, esp. the beluga, usually served as an hors d'oeuvre. **2.** **caviar to the general.** something too good to appeal to popular taste. [C16: from earlier *cavery,* from Old Italian *caviari,* plural of *caviaro* caviar, from Turkish *havyār*]

cavicorn (ˈkævɪˌkɔːn) *adj.* (of sheep, goats, etc.) having hollow horns as distinct from the solid antlers of deer. [C19: from Latin *cavus* hollow + *cornū* horn]

cavie (ˈkeɪvɪ) *n. Scot.* a hen coop. [C18: via Dutch or Flemish *kavie,* from Latin *cavea* cavity]

cavil (ˈkævɪl) *vb.* **-ils, -illing, -illed** *or U.S.* **-ils, -iling, -iled.** **1.** (*intr.;* foll. by *at* or *about*) to raise annoying petty objections; quibble; carp. ~*n.* **2.** a captious trifling objection. [C16: from Old French *caviller,* from Latin *cavillārī* to jeer, from *cavilla* raillery] —ˈ**caviller** *n.* —ˈ**cavilling** *adj.*

caving (ˈkeɪvɪŋ) *n.* the sport of climbing in and exploring caves. —ˈ**caver** *n.*

cavitation (ˌkævɪˈteɪʃən) *n.* **1.** the formation and collapse of regions of low pressure in a flowing liquid. **2.** the formation of cavities in a structure.

cavity (ˈkævɪtɪ) *n., pl.* **-ties.** **1.** a hollow space; hole. **2.** *Dentistry.* a soft decayed area on a tooth. See **caries.** **3.** any empty or hollow space within the body: *the oral cavity.* **4.** *Electronics.* See **cavity resonator.** [C16: from French *cavité,* from Late Latin *cavitās,* from Latin *cavus* hollow]

cavity block *n.* a precast concrete block that contains a cavity or cavities.

cavity resonator *n. Electronics.* a conducting surface enclosing a space in which an oscillating electromagnetic field can be maintained, the dimensions of the cavity determining the resonant frequency of the oscillations. It is used in microwave devices, such as the klystron, for frequencies exceeding 300 megahertz. Also called: **resonant cavity, rhumbatron.**

cavity wall *n.* a wall that consists of two separate walls, joined by wall-ties, with an airspace between them.

cavo-relievo *or* **cavo-rilievo** (ˌkɑːvəʊrɪˈliːvəʊ, ˌkeɪ-) *n., pl.* **-vos** *or* **-vi** (-vɪ). a relief sculpture in which the highest point in the carving is below the level of the original surface. [Italian, literally: hollow relief]

cavort (kəˈvɔːt) *vb.* (*intr.*) to prance; caper. [C19: perhaps from CURVET] —**caˈvorter** *n.*

cavy (ˈkeɪvɪ) *n., pl.* **-vies.** any small South American hystricomorph rodent of the family *Caviidae,* esp. any of the genus *Cavia,* having a thickset body and very small tail. See also **guinea pig.** [C18: from New Latin *Cavia,* from Galibi *cabiai*]

caw (kɔː) *n.* **1.** the cry of a crow, rook, or raven. ~*vb.* **2.** (*intr.*) to make this cry. [C16: of imitative origin]

CAWU *abbrev. for* Clerical and Administrative Workers' Union.

Caxton (ˈkækstən) *n.* **1.** a book printed by William Caxton (?1422–91), English printer and translator. **2.** a style of type, imitating the Gothic, that Caxton used in his books.

cay (keɪ, kiː) *n.* a small low island or bank composed of sand and coral fragments, esp. in the Caribbean area. Also called: **key.** [C18: from Spanish *cayo,* probably from Old French *quai* QUAY]

cayenne pepper (keɪˈɛn) *n.* a very hot condiment, bright red in colour, made from the dried seeds and pods of various capsicums. Often shortened to **cayenne.** Also called: **red pepper.** [C18: ultimately from Tupi *quiynha*]

cayman *or* **caiman** (ˈkeɪmən) *n., pl.* **-mans.** any tropical American crocodilian of the genus *Caiman* and related genera, similar to alligators but with a more heavily armoured belly: family *Alligatoridae* (alligators, etc.). [C16: from Spanish *caimán,* from Carib *cayman,* probably of African origin]

Cayuga (keɪˈjuːgə, kaɪ-) *n.* **1.** (*pl.* **-gas** *or* **-ga**) a member of a North American Indian people (one of the Iroquois peoples) formerly living around Cayuga Lake, New York state. **2.** the language of this people, belonging to the Iroquoian family.

cayuse (ˈkaɪuːs) *n. Western U.S. and Canadian.* a small American Indian pony used by cowboys. [C19: from a Chinookan language]

cb *abbrev. for* centre of buoyancy (of a boat, etc.).

Cb *the chemical symbol for* columbium.

CB *abbrev. for:* **1.** Citizens' Band. **2.** Companion of the (Order of the) Bath (an English title). **3.** County Borough.

CBC *abbrev. for* Canadian Broadcasting Corporation.

CBD *or* **cbd** *abbrev. for:* **1.** cash before delivery. **2.** central business district.

CBE *abbrev. for* Commander of the (Order of the) British Empire.

CBI *abbrev. for* Confederation of British Industry.

CBR (of weapons or warfare) *abbrev. for* chemical, bacteriological, and radiation.

CBS *abbrev. for* Columbia Broadcasting System.

CBSO *abbrev. for* City of Birmingham Symphony Orchestra.

CBT *abbrev. for* computer-based training.

cc *or* **c.c.** *abbrev. for:* **1.** carbon copy *or* copies. **2.** cubic centimetre(s).

CC *abbrev. for:* **1.** City Council. **2.** County Council. **3.** Cricket Club.

cc. *abbrev. for* chapters.

CCD *Computer technol. abbrev. for* charged coupled device.

CCF (in Britain) *abbrev. for* Combined Cadet Force.

C clef *n. Music.* a symbol (𝄡), placed at the beginning of the staff, establishing middle C as being on its centre line. See **alto clef, soprano clef, tenor clef.**

CCTV *abbrev. for* closed-circuit television.

CCW *abbrev. for* Curriculum Council for Wales.

cd **1.** *abbrev. for* cash discount. ~**2.** *symbol for* candela.

Cd **1.** (in Britain) *abbrev. for* command (paper). ~**2.** *the chemical symbol for* cadmium.

CD *abbrev. for:* **1.** Civil Defence (Corps). **2.** compact disc. **3.** Corps Diplomatique (Diplomatic Corps). **4.** Conference on Disarmament: a United Nations standing conference, held in Geneva, to negotiate a global ban on chemical weapons.

c/d *Book-keeping. abbrev. for* carried down.

CDE *abbrev. for:* **1.** Conference on Confidence- and Security-Building and Disarmament in Europe. **2.** compact disc erasable: a compact disc that can be used to record and rerecord. Compare **CDR.**

cdf *Statistics. abbrev. for* cumulative distribution function.

Cdn *abbrev. for* Canadian.

CDN *international car registration for* Canada.

cDNA *abbrev. for* complementary DNA.

CD player *n.* a device for playing compact discs. In full: **compact-disc player.**

Cdr *Military. abbrev. for* Commander.

CDR *abbrev. for* compact disc recordable: a compact disc that can be used to record only once. Compare **CDE** (sense 2).

Cdre *abbrev. for* Commodore.

CD-ROM (-rɒm) *abbrev. for* compact disc read-only memory; a compact disc used with a computer system as a read-only optical disk.

CDT *abbrev. for:* **1.** *U.S. and Canadian.* Central Daylight Time. **2.** Craft, Design, and Technology: a subject on the GCSE syllabus, related to the National Curriculum.

CDU *abbrev. for* Christlich-Demokratische Union: a German (until 1990 West German) political party. [German: Christian Democratic Union]

CDV *abbrev. for:* **1.** CD-video. **2.** compact video disc.
CD-video *n.* a compact-disc player that, when connected to a television and hi-fi, produces high-quality stereo sound and synchronized pictures from a disc resembling a compact audio disc. In full: **compact-disc video.**
Ce *the chemical symbol for* cerium.
CE *abbrev. for:* **1.** chief engineer. **2.** Church of England. **3.** civil engineer. **4.** Common Entrance. **5.** Common Era.
ceanothus (ˌsiːəˈnəʊθəs) *n.* any shrub of the North American rhamnaceous genus *Ceanothus:* grown for their ornamental, often blue, flower clusters. [C19: New Latin, from Greek *keanōthos* a kind of thistle]
cease (siːs) *vb.* **1.** (when *tr.*, may take a gerund or an infinitive as object) to bring or come to an end; desist from; stop. ~*n.* **2.** **without cease.** without stopping; incessantly. [C14: from Old French *cesser,* from Latin *cessāre,* frequentative of *cēdere* to yield, CEDE]
cease-fire *Chiefly military.* ~*n.* **1.** a period of truce, esp. one that is temporary and a preliminary step to establishing a more permanent peace on agreed terms. ~*interj., n.* **2.** the order to stop firing.
ceaseless (ˈsiːslɪs) *adj.* without stop or pause; incessant. —**ˈceaselessly** *adv.*
cecity (ˈsiːsɪtɪ) *n.* a rare word for **blindness.** [C16: from Latin *caecitās,* from *caecus* blind]
cecropia moth (sɪˈkrəʊpɪə) *n.* a large North American saturniid moth, *Hyalophora* (or *Samia*) *cecropia,* with brightly coloured wings and feathery antennae. [C19: New Latin, from Latin *Cecropius* belonging to *Cecrops,* traditionally the first king of Attica, represented as half-human, half-dragon]
cecum (ˈsiːkəm) *n., pl.* **-ca** (-kə). *U.S.* a variant spelling of **caecum.** —**ˈcecal** *adj.*
cedar (ˈsiːdə) *n.* **1.** any Old World coniferous tree of the genus *Cedrus,* having spreading branches, needle-like evergreen leaves, and erect barrel-shaped cones: family *Pinaceae.* See also **cedar of Lebanon, deodar.** **2.** any of various other conifers, such as the red cedars and white cedars. **3.** the wood of any of these trees. **4.** any of certain other plants, such as the Spanish cedar. ~*adj.* **5.** made of the wood of a cedar tree. [C13: from Old French *cedre,* from Latin *cedrus,* from Greek *kedros*]
cedar of Lebanon (ˈlɛbənən) *n.* a cedar, *Cedrus libani,* of SW Asia with level spreading branches and fragrant wood.
cede (siːd) *vb.* **1.** (when *intr.,* often foll. by *to*) to transfer, make over, or surrender (something, esp. territory or legal rights): *the lands were ceded by treaty.* **2.** (*tr.*) to allow or concede (a point in an argument, etc.). [C17: from Latin *cēdere* to yield, give way] —**ˈceder** *n.*
cedi (ˈseɪdɪ) *n., pl.* **-di.** the standard monetary unit of Ghana, divided into 100 pesewa.
cedilla (sɪˈdɪlə) *n.* a character (¸) placed underneath a *c* before *a, o,* or *u,* esp. in French, Portuguese, or Catalan, denoting that it is to be pronounced (s), not (k). The same character is used in the scripts of other languages, as in Turkish under *s.* [C16: from Spanish: little *z,* from *ceda* zed, from Late Latin *zeta;* a small *z* was originally written after *c* in Spanish, to indicate a sibilant]
Ceefax (ˈsiːˌfæks) *n. Trademark.* the BBC Teletext service. See **Teletext.**
CEGB *Brit. abbrev. for* Central Electricity Generating Board.
ceiba (ˈseɪbə) *n.* **1.** any bombacaceous tropical tree of the genus *Ceiba,* such as the silk-cotton tree. **2.** silk cotton; kapok. [C19: from New Latin, from Spanish, of Arawak origin]
ceil (siːl) *vb.* **1.** (*tr.*) to line (a ceiling) with plaster, boarding, etc. **2.** (*tr.*) to provide with a ceiling. [C15 *celen,* perhaps back formation from CEILING]
ceilidh (ˈkeɪlɪ) *n.* (esp. in Scotland and Ireland) an informal social gathering with folk music, singing, dancing, and storytelling. [C19: from Gaelic]
ceiling (ˈsiːlɪŋ) *n.* **1.** the inner upper surface of a room. **2. a.** an upper limit, such as one set by regulation on prices or wages. **b.** (*as modifier*): *ceiling prices.* **3.** the upper altitude to which an aircraft can climb measured under specified conditions. See also **service ceiling, absolute ceiling.** **4.** *Meteorol.* the highest level in the atmosphere from which the earth's surface is visible at a particular time, usually the base of a cloud layer. **5.** a wooden or metal surface fixed to the interior frames of a vessel for rigidity. [C14: of uncertain origin]
ceilometer (siːˈlɒmɪtə) *n.* a device for determining the cloud ceiling, esp. by means of a reflected light beam. [C20: from CEILING + -METER]
cel *or* **cell** (sɛl) *n.* short for **celluloid** (senses 2b, c).
celadon (ˈsɛləˌdɒn) *n.* **1.** a type of porcelain having a greyish-green glaze: mainly Chinese. **2.** a pale greyish-green colour, sometimes somewhat yellow. [C18: from French, from the name of the shepherd hero of *L'Astrée* (1610), a romance by Honoré d'Urfé]
celandine (ˈsɛlənˌdaɪn) *n.* either of two unrelated plants, *Chelidonium majus* (see **greater celandine**) or *Ranunculus ficaria* (see **lesser celandine**). [C13: earlier *celydon,* from Latin *chelīdonia* (the plant), from *chelīdonius* of the swallow, from Greek *khelidōn* swallow; the plant's season was believed to parallel the migration of swallows]
-cele *n. combining form.* tumour or hernia: *hydrocele.* [from Greek *kēlē* tumour]
celeb (sɪˈlɛb) *n. Informal.* a celebrity.
celebrant (ˈsɛlɪbrənt) *n.* **1.** a person participating in a religious ceremony. **2.** *Christianity.* an officiating priest, esp. at the Eucharist.
celebrate (ˈsɛlɪˌbreɪt) *vb.* **1.** to rejoice in or have special festivities to mark (a happy day, event, etc.). **2.** (*tr.*) to observe (a birthday, anniversary, etc.): *she celebrates her ninetieth birthday next month.* **3.** (*tr.*) to perform (a solemn or religious ceremony), esp. to officiate at (Mass). **4.** (*tr.*) to praise publicly; proclaim. [C15: from Latin *celebrāre,* from *celeber* numerous, thronged, renowned] —ˌ**celeˈbration** *n.* —**ˈcelebrative** *adj.* —**ˈceleˌbrator** *n.* —**ˈceleˌbratory** *adj.*
celebrated (ˈsɛlɪˌbreɪtɪd) *adj.* (*usually prenominal*) famous: *a celebrated pianist; a celebrated trial.*
celebrity (sɪˈlɛbrɪtɪ) *n., pl.* **-ties.** **1.** a famous person: *a show-business celebrity.* **2.** fame or notoriety.
celeriac (sɪˈlɛrɪˌæk) *n.* a variety of celery, *Apium graveolens rapaceum,* with a large turnip-like root, used as a vegetable. [C18: from CELERY + *-ac,* of unexplained origin]
celerity (sɪˈlɛrɪtɪ) *n.* rapidity; swiftness; speed. [C15: from Old French *celerite,* from Latin *celeritās,* from *celer* swift]
celery (ˈsɛlərɪ) *n.* **1.** an umbelliferous Eurasian plant, *Apium graveolens dulce,* whose blanched leafstalks are used in salads or cooked as a vegetable. See also **celeriac.** **2. wild celery.** a related and similar plant, *Apium graveolens.* [C17: from French *céleri,* from Italian (Lombardy) dialect *selleri* (plural), from Greek *selinon* parsley]
celery pine *n.* a New Zealand gymnosperm tree, *Phyllocladus trichomanoides,* with celerylike shoots and useful wood: family *Phyllocladaceae.*
celesta (sɪˈlɛstə) *or* **celeste** (sɪˈlɛst) *n. Music.* a keyboard percussion instrument consisting of a set of steel plates of graduated length that are struck with key-operated hammers. The tone is an ethereal tinkling sound. Range: four octaves upwards from middle C. [C19: from French, Latinized variant of *céleste* heavenly]
celestial (sɪˈlɛstɪəl) *adj.* **1.** heavenly; divine; spiritual: *celestial peace.* **2.** of or relating to the sky: *celestial bodies.* [C14: from Medieval Latin *cēlestiālis,* from Latin *caelestis,* from *caelum* heaven] —**ceˈlestially** *adv.*
celestial equator *n.* the great circle lying on the celestial sphere the plane of which is perpendicular to the line joining the north and south celestial poles. Also called: **equinoctial, equinoctial circle.**
celestial globe *n.* a spherical model of the celestial sphere showing the relative positions of stars, constellations, etc.
celestial guidance *n.* the guidance of a spacecraft or missile by reference to the positions of one or more celestial bodies.
celestial horizon *n.* See **horizon** (sense 2b).
celestial latitude *n.* the angular distance of a celestial body north or south from the ecliptic. Sometimes shortened to **latitude.**
celestial longitude *n.* the angular distance measured eastwards from the vernal equinox to the intersection of the ecliptic with the great circle passing through a celestial body and the poles of the ecliptic. Sometimes shortened to **longitude.**
celestial mechanics *n.* the study of the motion of celestial bodies under the influence of gravitational fields.
celestial navigation *n.* navigation by observation of the positions of the stars. Also called: **astronavigation.**
celestial pole *n.* either of the two points at which the earth's axis, extended to infinity, would intersect the celestial sphere. Sometimes shortened to **pole.**
celestial sphere *n.* an imaginary sphere of infinitely large radius enclosing the universe so that all celestial bodies appear to be projected onto its surface.
celestite (ˈsɛlɪˌstaɪt) *or* **celestine** (ˈsɛlɪstɪn, -ˌstaɪn) *n.* a white, red, or blue mineral consisting of strontium sulphate in orthorhombic crystalline form: a source of strontium compounds. Formula: $SrSO_4$. [C19: from German *Zölestin,* from Latin *caelestis* CELESTIAL (referring to the blue colour) + -ITE[1]]
celiac (ˈsiːlɪˌæk) *adj. Anatomy.* the usual U.S. spelling of **coeliac.**
celibate (ˈsɛlɪbɪt) *n.* **1.** a person who is unmarried, esp. one who has taken a religious vow of chastity. ~*adj.* **2.** unmarried, esp. by vow. **3.** abstaining from sexual intercourse. [C17: from Latin *caelibātus,* from *caelebs* unmarried, of obscure origin] —**ˈcelibacy** *n.*
cell[1] (sɛl) *n.* **1.** a small simple room, as in a prison, convent, monastery, or asylum; cubicle. **2.** any small compartment: *the cells of a honeycomb.* **3.** *Biology.* the smallest unit of an organism that is able to function independently. It consists of a nucleus, containing the genetic material, surrounded by the cytoplasm in which are mitochondria, lysosomes, ribosomes, and other organelles. All cells are bounded by a cell membrane; plant cells have an outer cell wall in addition. **4.** *Biology.* any small cavity or area, such as the cavity containing pollen in an anther. **5.** a device for converting chemical energy into electrical energy, usually consisting of a container with two electrodes immersed in an electrolyte. See also **primary cell, secondary cell, dry cell, wet cell, fuel cell.** **6.** short for **electrolytic cell.** **7.** a small religious house dependent upon a larger one. **8.** a small group of persons operating as a nucleus of a larger political, religious, or other organization: *Communist cell.* **9.** *Maths.*

a small unit of volume in a mathematical coordinate system. **10.** *Zoology.* one of the areas on an insect wing bounded by veins. [C12: from Medieval Latin *cella* monk's cell, from Latin: room, storeroom; related to Latin *cēlāre* to hide] —'**cell-,like** *adj.*

cell[2] (sɛl) *n.* a variant spelling of **cel.**

cella ('sɛlə) *n., pl.* **-lae** (-liː). the inner room of a classical temple, esp. the room housing the statue of a deity. Also called: **naos.** [C17: from Latin: room, shrine; see CELL[1]]

cellar ('sɛlə) *n.* **1.** an underground room, rooms, or storey of a building, usually used for storage. Compare **basement. 2.** a place where wine is stored. **3.** a stock of bottled wines. ~*vb.* **4.** (*tr.*) to store in a cellar. [C13: from Anglo-French, from Latin *cellārium* food store, from *cella* CELLA]

cellarage ('sɛlərɪdʒ) *n.* **1.** an area of a cellar. **2.** a charge for storing goods in a cellar, etc.

cellarer ('sɛlərə) *n.* a monastic official responsible for food, drink, etc.

cellaret (ˌsɛlə'rɛt) *n.* a case, cabinet, or sideboard with compartments for holding wine bottles.

cell cycle *n.* the growth cycle of eukaryotic cells. It is divided into five stages, known as G_0, in which the cell is quiescent, G_1 and G_2, in which it increases in size, S, in which it duplicates its DNA, and M, in which it undergoes mitosis and divides.

cell division *n. Cytology.* the division of a cell into two new cells during growth or reproduction. See **amitosis, meiosis, mitosis.**

cell line *n. Biology.* a cell culture derived from a single cell and thus of invariable genetic make-up.

cell lineage *n. Biology.* the developmental history of a tissue from the time its constituent cells are initially produced to their full differentiation in the mature tissue.

cell membrane *n.* a very thin membrane, composed of lipids and protein, that surrounds the cytoplasm of a cell and controls the passage of substances into and out of the cell. Also called: **plasmalemma, plasma membrane.**

Cellnet ('sɛlˌnɛt) *n. Trademark.* a British Telecom car phone.

cello ('tʃɛləʊ) *n., pl.* **-los.** *Music.* a bowed stringed instrument of the violin family. Range: more than four octaves upwards from C below the bass staff. It has four strings, is held between the knees, and has an extendible metal spike at the lower end, which acts as a support. Full name: **violoncello.** —'**cellist** *n.*

cellobiose (ˌsɛləʊ'baɪəʊz) *or* **cellose** ('sɛləʊz) *n.* a disaccharide obtained by the hydrolysis of cellulose by cellulase. Formula: $C_{12}H_{22}O_{11}$. [C20: from CELLULOSE + BI-[1] + -OSE[2]]

celloidin (sə'lɔɪdɪn) *n.* a nitrocellulose compound derived from pyroxylin, used in a solution of alcohol and ether for embedding specimens before cutting sections for microscopy. [C20: from CELLULOSE + -OID + -IN]

Cellophane ('sɛləˌfeɪn) *n. Trademark.* a flexible thin transparent sheeting made from wood pulp and used as a moisture-proof wrapping. [C20: from CELLULOSE + -PHANE]

Cellosolve ('sɛləʊˌsɒlv) *n. Trademark.* an organic compound used as a solvent in the plastics industry; 2-ethoxyethan-1-ol. Formula: $C_2H_5OCH_2CH_2OH$.

cellphone ('sɛlˌfəʊn) *n.* a portable telephone operated by cellular radio. In full: **cellular telephone.**

cellular ('sɛljʊlə) *adj.* **1.** of, relating to, resembling, or composed of a cell or cells. **2.** having cells or small cavities; porous. **3.** divided into a network of cells. **4.** *Textiles.* woven with an open texture: *a cellular blanket.* —**cellularity** (ˌsɛljʊ'lærɪtɪ) *n.*

cellular radio *n.* radio communication based on a network of transmitters each serving a small area known as a 'cell': used in personal communications systems in which the mobile receiver switches frequencies automatically as it passes from one cell to another.

cellulase ('sɛljʊˌleɪz) *n.* any enzyme that converts cellulose to the disaccharide cellobiose. [C20: from CELLULOSE + -ASE]

cellule ('sɛljuːl) *n.* a very small cell. [C17: from Latin *cellula*, diminutive of *cella* CELL[1]]

cellulite ('sɛljʊˌlaɪt) *n.* a name sometimes given to subcutaneous fat alleged to resist dieting. [C20: from French, from *cellule* cell]

cellulitis (ˌsɛljʊ'laɪtɪs) *n.* inflammation of any of the tissues of the body, characterized by fever, pain, swelling, and redness of the affected area. [C19: from Latin *cellula* CELLULE + -ITIS]

celluloid ('sɛljʊˌlɔɪd) *n.* **1.** a flammable thermoplastic material consisting of cellulose nitrate mixed with a plasticizer, usually camphor: used in sheets, rods, and tubes for making a wide range of articles. **2. a.** a cellulose derivative used for coating film. **b.** one of the transparent sheets on which the constituent drawings of an animated film are prepared. **c.** a transparent sheet used as an overlay in artwork. **d.** cinema film.

cellulose ('sɛljʊˌləʊz, -ˌləʊs) *n.* a polysaccharide consisting of long unbranched chains of linked glucose units: the main constituent of plant cell walls and used in making paper, rayon, and film. [C18: from French *cellule* cell (see CELLULE) + -OSE[2]] —ˌ**cellu'losic** *adj., n.*

cellulose acetate *n.* nonflammable material made by acetylating cellulose: used in the manufacture of film, dopes, lacquers, and artificial fibres.

cellulose nitrate *n.* a compound made by treating cellulose with nitric and sulphuric acids, used in plastics, lacquers, and explosives: a nitrogen-containing ester of cellulose. Also called (not in chemical usage): **nitrocellulose.** See also **guncotton.**

cellulous ('sɛljʊləs) *adj. Rare.* consisting of cells; cellular.

cell wall *n.* the outer layer of a cell, esp. the structure in plant cells that consists of cellulose, lignin, etc., and gives mechanical support to the cell.

celom ('siːləm) *n.* a less frequent U.S. spelling of **coelom.**

celosia (sə'ləʊsɪə) *n.* See **cockscomb** (sense 2). [New Latin, from Greek *kēlos* dry, burnt (from the appearance of the flowers of some species)]

Celsius ('sɛlsɪəs) *adj.* denoting a measurement on the Celsius scale. Symbol: C [C18: named after Anders *Celsius* (1701–44), Swedish astronomer who invented it]

Celsius scale *n.* a scale of temperature in which 0° represents the melting point of ice and 100° represents the boiling point of water. See also **centigrade.** Compare **Fahrenheit scale.**

celt (sɛlt) *n. Archaeol.* a stone or metal axelike instrument with a bevelled edge. [C18: from Late Latin *celtes* chisel, of obscure origin]

Celt (kɛlt, sɛlt) *or* **Kelt** *n.* **1.** a person who speaks a Celtic language. **2.** a member of an Indo-European people who in pre-Roman times inhabited Britain, Gaul, Spain, and other parts of W and central Europe.

Celt. *abbrev. for* Celtic.

Celtiberian (ˌkɛltɪ'bɪərɪən, -taɪ-, ˌsɛl-) *n.* **1.** a member of a Celtic people (**Celtiberi**) who inhabited the Iberian peninsula during classical times. **2.** the extinct language of this people, possibly belonging to the Celtic branch of the Indo-European family, recorded in a number of inscriptions.

Celtic ('kɛltɪk, 'sɛl-) *or* **Keltic** *n.* **1.** a branch of the Indo-European family of languages that includes Gaelic, Welsh, and Breton, still spoken in parts of Scotland, Ireland, Wales, and Brittany. Modern Celtic is divided into the Brythonic (southern) and Goidelic (northern) groups. ~*adj.* **2.** of, relating to, or characteristic of the Celts or the Celtic languages. —'**Celtically** *or* '**Keltically** *adv.* —**Celticism** ('kɛltɪˌsɪzəm, 'sɛl-) *or* '**Kelti,cism** *n.* —'**Celticist,** '**Celtist** *or* '**Kelticist,** '**Keltist** *n.*

Celtic cross *n.* a Latin cross with a broad ring surrounding the point of intersection.

cembalo ('tʃɛmbələʊ) *n., pl.* **-li** (-lɪ) *or* **-los.** another word for **harpsichord.** [C19: shortened from CLAVICEMBALO] —'**cembalist** *n.*

cement (sɪ'mɛnt) *n.* **1.** a fine grey powder made of a mixture of calcined limestone and clay, used with water and sand to make mortar, or with water, sand, and aggregate, to make concrete. **2.** a binder, glue, or adhesive. **3.** something that unites or joins; bond. **4.** *Dentistry.* any of various materials used in filling teeth. **5.** mineral matter, such as silica and calcite, that binds together particles of rock, bones, etc., to form a solid mass of sedimentary rock. **6.** another word for **cementum.** ~*vb.* (*tr.*) **7.** to join, bind, or glue together with or as if with cement. **8.** to coat or cover with cement. [C13: from Old French *ciment*, from Latin *caementum* stone from the quarry, from *caedere* to hew] —**ce'menter** *n.*

cementation (ˌsiːmɛn'teɪʃən) *n.* **1.** the process of heating a solid with a powdered material to modify the properties of the solid, esp. the heating of wrought iron, surrounded with charcoal, to 750–900°C to produce steel. **2.** the process of cementing or being cemented. **3.** *Civil engineering.* the injection of cement grout into fissured rocks to make them watertight.

cementite (sɪ'mɛntaɪt) *n.* the hard brittle compound of iron and carbon that forms in carbon steels and some cast irons. Formula: Fe_3C.

cementum (sɪ'mɛntəm) *n.* a thin bonelike tissue that covers the dentine in the root of a tooth. [C19: New Latin, from Latin: CEMENT]

cemetery ('sɛmɪtrɪ) *n., pl.* **-teries.** a place where the dead are buried, esp. one not attached to a church. [C14: from Late Latin *coemētērium*, from Greek *koimētērion* room for sleeping, from *koiman* to put to sleep]

cen. *abbrev. for* central.

cenacle *or* **coenacle** ('sɛnəkᵊl) *n.* **1.** a supper room, esp. one on an upper floor. **2.** (*cap.*) the room in which the Last Supper took place. [C14: from Old French, from Late Latin *cēnāculum*, from *cēna* supper]

-cene *n. and adj. combining form.* denoting a recent geological period: *Miocene.* [from Greek *kainos* new]

CENELEC ('sɛnəˌlɛk) *n. acronym for* Commission Européenne de Normalisation Électrique: the EC standards organization for electrical goods. Also called: **CEN.**

cenesthesia (ˌsiːnɪs'θiːzɪə) *n. Psychol.* a variant spelling (esp. U.S.) of **coenaesthesia.**

CEng *abbrev. for* chartered engineer.

cenobite ('siːnəʊˌbaɪt) *n.* a variant spelling of **coenobite.**

cenogenesis (ˌsiːnəʊ'dʒɛnɪsɪs) *n.* a U.S. spelling of **caenogenesis.**

cenospecies ('siːnəˌspiːʃiːz) *n., pl.* **-species.** a species related to another by the ability to interbreed: *dogs and wolves are cenospecies.* [C20: from Greek *koinos* common + SPECIES]

cenotaph ('sɛnəˌtɑːf) *n.* a monument honouring a dead person or persons buried elsewhere. [C17: from Latin *cenotaphium*, from Greek *kenotaphion*, from *kenos* empty + *taphos* tomb] —ˌ**ceno'taphic** *adj.*

cenote (sɪ'nəʊteɪ) *n.* (esp. in the Yucatán peninsula) a natural well formed by the collapse of an overlying limestone crust: often used as a sacrificial site by the Mayas. [C19: via Mexican Spanish from Maya *conot*]

Cenozoic, Caenozoic (ˌsiːnəʊˈzəʊɪk), *or* **Cainozoic** *adj.* **1.** of, denoting, or relating to the most recent geological era, which began 70 000 000 years ago: characterized by the development and increase of the mammals. ~*n.* **2. the.** the Cenozoic era. [C19: from Greek *kainos* new, recent + *zōikos,* from *zōion* animal]

cense (sɛns) *vb.* (*tr.*) to burn incense near or before (an altar, shrine, etc.). [C14: from Old French *encenser;* see INCENSE[1]]

censer (ˈsɛnsə) *n.* a container for burning incense, esp. one swung at religious ceremonies. Also called: **thurible.**

censor (ˈsɛnsə) *n.* **1.** a person authorized to examine publications, theatrical presentations, films, letters, etc., in order to suppress in whole or part those considered obscene, politically unacceptable, etc. **2.** any person who controls or suppresses the behaviour of others, usually on moral grounds. **3.** (in republican Rome) either of two senior magistrates elected to keep the list of citizens up to date, control aspects of public finance, and supervise public morals. **4.** *Psychoanal.* the postulated factor responsible for regulating the translation of ideas and desires from the unconscious to the conscious mind. See also **superego.** ~*vb.* (*tr.*) **5.** to ban or cut portions of (a publication, film, letter, etc.). **6.** to act as a censor of (behaviour, etc.). [C16: from Latin, from *cēnsēre* to consider, assess] —ˈ**censorable** *adj.* —**censorial** (sɛnˈsɔːrɪəl) *adj.*

censorious (sɛnˈsɔːrɪəs) *adj.* harshly critical; fault-finding. —**cenˈsoriously** *adv.* —**cenˈsoriousness** *n.*

censorship (ˈsɛnsəˌʃɪp) *n.* **1.** a policy or programme of censoring. **2.** the act or system of censoring. **3.** *Psychoanal.* the activity of the mind in regulating impulses, etc., from the unconscious so that they are modified before reaching the conscious mind.

censurable (ˈsɛnʃərəbᵊl) *adj.* deserving censure, condemnation, or blame. —ˈ**censurableness** *or* ˌ**censuraˈbility** *n.* —ˈ**censurably** *adv.*

censure (ˈsɛnʃə) *n.* **1.** severe disapproval; harsh criticism. ~*vb.* **2.** to criticize (someone or something) severely; condemn. [C14: from Latin *cēnsūra,* from *cēnsēre* to consider, assess] —ˈ**censurer** *n.*

census (ˈsɛnsəs) *n., pl.* **-suses. 1.** an official periodic count of a population including such information as sex, age, occupation, etc. **2.** any offical count: *a traffic census.* **3.** (in ancient Rome) a registration of the population and a property evaluation for purposes of taxation. [C17: from Latin, from *cēnsēre* to assess] —ˈ**censual** *adj.*

cent (sɛnt) *n.* **1.** a monetary unit of Australia, Barbados, Botswana, Canada, Ethiopia, Guyana, Hong Kong, Kenya, Lesotho, Liberia, Malaysia, Mauritius, the Netherlands, New Zealand, Sierra Leone, Singapore, the Somali Republic, South Africa, Sri Lanka, Swaziland, Taiwan, Tanzania, Trinidad and Tobago, Uganda, the United States, and Western Samoa. It is worth one hundredth of their respective standard units. **2.** an interval of pitch between two frequencies f_2 and f_1 equal to 3986.31 log (f_2/f_1); one twelve-hundredth of the interval between two frequencies having the ratio 1:2 (an octave). [C16: from Latin *centēsimus* hundredth, from *centum* hundred]

cent. *abbrev. for:* **1.** centigrade. **2.** central. **3.** century.

cental (ˈsɛntᵊl) *n.* a unit of weight equal to 100 pounds (45.3 kilograms). [C19: from Latin *centum* hundred]

centaur (ˈsɛntɔː) *n. Greek myth.* one of a race of creatures with the head, arms, and torso of a man, and the lower body and legs of a horse. [C14: from Latin, from Greek *kentauros,* of unknown origin]

centaurea (ˌsɛntɔːˈrɪə, sɛnˈtɔːrɪə) *n.* any plant of the genus *Centaurea,* which includes the cornflower and knapweed. [C19: ultimately from Greek *Kentauros* the Centaur; see CENTAURY]

Centaurus (sɛnˈtɔːrəs) *n., Latin genitive* **Centauri** (sɛnˈtɔːraɪ). a conspicuous extensive constellation in the S hemisphere, close to the Southern Cross, that contains two first magnitude stars, Alpha Centauri and Beta Centauri, and the globular cluster Omega Centauri. Also called: **The Centaur.**

centaury (ˈsɛntɔːrɪ) *n., pl.* **-ries. 1.** any Eurasian plant of the genus *Centaurium,* esp. *C. erythraea,* having purplish-pink flowers and formerly believed to have medicinal properties: family *Gentianaceae.* **2.** any plant of the genus *Centaurea,* which includes the cornflower and knapweed: family *Compositae* (composites). [C14: ultimately from Greek *Kentauros* the Centaur; from the legend that Chiron the Centaur was responsible for divulging its healing properties]

centavo (sɛnˈtɑːvəʊ) *n., pl.* **-vos.** a monetary unit of Argentina, Bolivia, Brazil, Colombia, Cuba, the Dominican Republic, Ecuador, El Salvador, Guatemala, Honduras, Mexico, Nicaragua, Peru, the Philippines, and Portugal. It is worth one hundredth of their respective standard units. [Spanish: one hundredth part]

centenarian (ˌsɛntɪˈnɛərɪən) *n.* **1.** a person who is at least 100 years old. ~*adj.* **2.** being at least 100 years old. **3.** of or relating to a centenarian.

centenary (sɛnˈtiːnərɪ) *adj.* **1.** of or relating to a period of 100 years. **2.** occurring once every 100 years: *centenary celebrations.* ~*n., pl.* **-naries. 3.** a 100th anniversary or its celebration. [C17: from Latin *centēnārius* of a hundred, from *centēnī* a hundred each, from *centum* hundred]

centennial (sɛnˈtɛnɪəl) *adj.* **1.** relating to, lasting for, or completing a period of 100 years. **2.** occurring every 100 years. ~*n.* **3.** *U.S. and Canadian.* another name for **centenary.** [C18: from Latin *centum* hundred, on the model of BIENNIAL] —**cenˈtennially** *adv.*

center (ˈsɛntə) *n., vb.* the U.S. spelling of **centre.**

centering (ˈsɛntərɪŋ) *n.* a U.S. spelling of **centring.**

centesimal (sɛnˈtɛsɪməl) *n.* **1.** hundredth. ~*adj.* **2.** relating to division into hundredths. [C17: from Latin *centēsimus,* from *centum* hundred] —**cenˈtesimally** *adv.*

centesimo (sɛnˈtɛsɪˌməʊ) *n., pl.* **-mos.** a fractional monetary unit of Chile, Italy, Panama, and Uruguay. It is worth one hundredth of their respective standard units. [C19: from Spanish and Italian, from Latin *centēsimus* hundredth, from *centum* hundred]

centi- *or before a vowel* **cent-** *prefix.* **1.** denoting one hundredth: *centimetre.* Symbol: c **2.** *Rare.* denoting a hundred: *centipede.* [from French, from Latin *centum* hundred]

centiare (ˈsɛntɪˌɛə; *French* sɑ̃tjar) *or* **centare** (ˈsɛntɛə; *French* sɑ̃tar) *n.* a unit of area equal to one square metre. [French, from CENTI- + *are* from Latin *ārea;* see ARE[2], AREA]

centigrade (ˈsɛntɪˌgreɪd) *adj.* **1.** another name for **Celsius.** ~*n.* **2.** a unit of angle equal to one hundredth of a grade.

▷**Usage.** Although still used in meteorology, *centigrade,* when indicating the Celsius scale of temperature, is now usually avoided in other scientific contexts because of its possible confusion with the hundredth part of a grade.

centigram *or* **centigramme** (ˈsɛntɪˌgræm) *n.* one hundredth of a gram.

centile (ˈsɛntaɪl) *n.* another word for **percentile.**

centilitre *or U.S.* **centiliter** (ˈsɛntɪˌliːtə) *n.* one hundredth of a litre.

centillion (sɛnˈtɪljən) *n., pl.* **-lions** *or* **-lion. 1.** (in Britain and Germany) the number represented as one followed by 600 zeros (10^{600}). **2.** (in the U.S., Canada, and France) the number represented as one followed by 303 zeros (10^{303}).

centime (ˈsɒnˌtiːm; *French* sɑ̃tim) *n.* a monetary unit of Algeria, Belgium, Burundi, Cameroon, the Central African Republic, Chad, the Congo Republic, Dahomey, France, Gabon, Guinea, Haiti, the Ivory Coast, Liechtenstein, Luxembourg, Madagascar, Mali, Mauritania, Niger, Rwanda, Senegal, Switzerland, Tahiti, Togo, and Burkina-Faso. It is worth one hundredth of their respective standard units. [C18: from French, from Old French *centiesme* from Latin *centēsimus* hundredth, from *centum* hundred]

centimetre *or U.S.* **centimeter** (ˈsɛntɪˌmiːtə) *n.* one hundredth of a metre.

centimetre-gram-second *n.* See **cgs units.**

céntimo (ˈsɛntɪˌməʊ) *n., pl.* **-mos.** a monetary unit of Costa Rica, Paraguay, Spain, and Venezuela. It is worth one hundredth of their respective standard currency units. [from Spanish; see CENTIME]

centimorgan (ˈsɛntɪˌmɔːgən) *n. Genetics.* a unit of chromosome length, used in genetic mapping, equal to the length of chromosome over which crossing over occurs with 1 per cent frequency. [C20: named after Thomas Hunt *Morgan* (1866–1945), U.S. biologist]

centipede (ˈsɛntɪˌpiːd) *n.* any carnivorous arthropod of the genera *Lithobius, Scutigera,* etc., having a body of between 15 and 190 segments, each bearing one pair of legs: class *Chilopoda.* See also **myriapod.**

centipoise (ˈsɛntɪˌpɔɪz) *n.* one hundredth of a poise. 1 centipoise is equal to 0.001 newton second per square metre.

centner (ˈsɛntnə) *n.* **1.** Also called (esp. U.S.): **short hundredweight.** a unit of weight equivalent to 100 pounds (45.3 kilograms). **2.** (in some European countries) a unit of weight equivalent to 50 kilograms (110.23 pounds). **3.** a unit of weight equivalent to 100 kilograms. [C17: from German *Zentner,* ultimately from Latin *centēnārius* of a hundred; see CENTENARY]

cento (ˈsɛntəʊ) *n., pl.* **-tos.** a piece of writing, esp. a poem, composed of quotations from other authors. [C17: from Latin, literally: patchwork garment]

CENTO (ˈsɛntəʊ) *n. acronym for* Central Treaty Organization.

centra (ˈsɛntrə) *n.* a plural of **centrum.**

central (ˈsɛntrəl) *adj.* **1.** in, at, of, from, containing, or forming the centre of something: *the central street in a city; the central material of a golf ball.* **2.** main, principal, or chief; most important: *the central cause of a problem.* **3. a.** of or relating to the central nervous system. **b.** of or relating to the centrum of a vertebra. **4.** of, relating to, or denoting a vowel articulated with the tongue held in an intermediate position halfway between the positions for back and front vowels, as for the *a* of English *soda.* **5.** (of a force) directed from or towards a point. —ˈ**centrally** *adv.*

Central American *adj.* of or relating to Central America, an isthmus joining the continents of North and South America.

central angle *n.* an angle whose vertex is at the centre of a circle.

central bank *n.* a national bank that does business mainly with a government and with other banks: it regulates the volume and cost of credit.

Central European Time *n.* the standard time adopted by Western European countries one hour ahead of Greenwich Mean Time, corresponding to British Summer Time. Abbrev.: **CET.**

central heating *n.* a system for heating the rooms of a building by means of radiators or air vents connected by pipes or ducts to a central source of heat.

Central Intelligence Agency *n.* See **CIA.**

centralism ('sɛntrəˌlɪzəm) *n.* the principle or act of bringing something under central control; centralization. —'**centralist** *n., adj.* —ˌ**central'istic** *adj.*

centrality (sɛn'trælɪtɪ) *n., pl.* **-ties.** the state or condition of being central.

centralize *or* **centralise** ('sɛntrəˌlaɪz) *vb.* **1.** to draw or move (something) to or towards a centre. **2.** to bring or come under central control, esp. governmental control. —ˌ**centrali'zation** *or* ˌ**centrali'sation** *n.* —'**centralˌizer** *or* '**centralˌiser** *n.*

central limit theorem *n. Statistics.* the fundamental result that the sum (or mean) of independent identically distributed random variables with finite variance approaches a normally distributed random variable as their number increases, whence in particular if enough samples are repeatedly drawn from any population, the sum of the sample values can be thought of, approximately, as an outcome from a normally distributed random variable.

central locking *n.* a system by which all the doors of a motor vehicle can be locked simultaneously when the driver's door is locked.

central nervous system *n.* the mass of nerve tissue that controls and coordinates the activities of an animal. In vertebrates it consists of the brain and spinal cord. Abbrev.: **CNS.** Compare **autonomic nervous system.**

central processing unit *n.* the part of a computer that performs logical and arithmetical operations on the data as specified in the instructions. Abbrev.: **CPU.**

central reserve *or* **reservation** *n. Brit.* the strip, often covered with grass, that separates the two sides of a motorway or dual carriageway. U.S. and Austral. name: **median strip.** Canadian name: **median.**

Central Standard Time *n.* one of the standard times used in North America, based on the local time of the 90° meridian, six hours behind Greenwich Mean Time. Abbrev.: **CST.**

central sulcus *n.* a deep cleft in each hemisphere of the brain separating the frontal lobe from the parietal lobe.

central tendency *n. Statistics.* the tendency of the values of a random variable to cluster around the mean, median, and mode.

centre *or U.S.* **center** ('sɛntə) *n.* **1.** *Geom.* **a.** the midpoint of any line or figure, esp. the point within a circle or sphere that is equidistant from any point on the circumference or surface. **b.** the point within a body through which a specified force may be considered to act, such as the centre of gravity. **2.** the point, axis, or pivot about which a body rotates. **3.** a point, area, or part that is approximately in the middle of a larger area or volume. **4.** a place at which some specified activity is concentrated: *a shopping centre.* **5.** a person or thing that is a focus of interest. **6.** a place of activity or influence: *a centre of power.* **7.** a person, group, policy, or thing in the middle. **8.** (*usually cap.*) *Politics.* **a.** a political party or group favouring moderation, esp. the moderate members of a legislative assembly. **b.** (*as modifier*): *a Centre-Left alliance.* **9.** *Physiol.* any part of the central nervous system that regulates a specific function: *respiratory centre.* **10.** a bar with a conical point upon which a workpiece or part may be turned or ground. **11.** a punch mark or small conical hole in a part to be drilled, which enables the point of the drill to be located accurately. **12.** *Football, hockey, etc.* **a.** a player who plays in the middle of the forward line. **b.** the act or an instance of passing the ball from a wing to the middle of the field, court, etc. **13.** *Basketball.* **a.** the position of a player who jumps for the ball at the start of play. **b.** the player in this position. **14.** *Archery.* **a.** the ring around the bull's eye. **b.** a shot that hits this ring. ~*vb.* **15.** to move towards, mark, put, or be at a centre. **16.** (*tr.*) to focus or bring together: *to centre one's thoughts.* **17.** (*intr.*; often foll. by *on*) to have as a main point of view or theme: *the novel centred on crime.* **18.** (*tr.*) to adjust or locate (a workpiece or part) using a centre. **19.** (*intr.*; foll. by *on* or *round*) to have as a centre. **20.** (*tr.*) *Football, hockey, etc.* to pass (the ball) into the middle of the field or court. [C14: from Latin *centrum* the stationary point of a compass, from Greek *kentron* needle, from *kentein* to prick]

▷**Usage.** *To centre round* is considered illogical by many writers and speakers, who prefer the more precise phrase *to centre on.*

centre bit *n.* a drilling bit with a central projecting point and two side cutters.

centreboard ('sɛntəˌbɔːd) *n.* a supplementary keel for a sailing vessel, which may be adjusted by raising and lowering. Compare **daggerboard.**

centred dot *n. Printing.* **1.** Also called (esp. U.S. and Canadian): **bullet.** a heavy dot (·) used to draw attention to a particular paragraph. **2.** a dot placed at a central level in a line of type or writing.

centre-fire *adj.* **1.** (of a cartridge) having the primer in the centre of the base. **2.** (of a firearm) adapted for such cartridges. ~Compare **rim-fire.**

centrefold *or U.S.* **centerfold** ('sɛntəˌfəʊld) *n.* **1.** a large coloured illustration folded so that it forms the central spread of a magazine. **2.** a photograph of a nude or nearly nude woman in a magazine on such a spread.

centre forward *n. Soccer, hockey, etc.* the central forward in the attack.

centre half *or* **centre back** *n. Soccer.* a defender who plays in the middle of the defence.

centre of curvature *n.* the centre of a circle whose radius, the **radius of curvature,** is normal to the concave side of a curve at a given point.

centre of gravity *n.* the point through which the resultant of the gravitational forces on a body always acts.

centre of mass *n.* the point at which the mass of a system could be concentrated without affecting the behaviour of the system under the action of external forces.

centre of pressure *n.* **1.** *Physics.* the point in a body at which the resultant pressure acts when the body is immersed in a fluid. **2.** *Aeronautics.* the point at which the resultant aerodynamic forces intersect the chord line of the aerofoil.

centrepiece ('sɛntəˌpiːs) *n.* an object used as the centre of something, esp. for decoration.

centre punch *n.* a small steel tool with a conical tip used to punch a small indentation at the location of the centre of a hole to be drilled.

centre spread *n.* **1.** the pair of two facing pages in the middle of a magazine, newspaper, etc., often illustrated. **2.** a photograph of a nude or nearly nude woman in a magazine on such pages.

centre three-quarter *n. Rugby.* either of two middle players on the three-quarter line.

centrex ('sɛntrɛks) *n.* a telephone switching system that enables telephone calls to bypass the switchboard.

centri- *combining form.* a variant of **centro-.**

centric ('sɛntrɪk) *or* **centrical** *adj.* **1.** being central or having a centre. **2.** relating to or originating at a nerve centre. **3.** *Botany.* **a.** Also: **concentric.** (of vascular bundles) having one type of tissue completely surrounding the other. **b.** (of leaves, such as those of the onion) cylindrical. —'**centrically** *adv.* —**centricity** (sɛn'trɪsɪtɪ) *n.*

-centric *suffix forming adjectives.* having a centre as specified: *heliocentric.* [abstracted from ECCENTRIC, CONCENTRIC, etc.]

centrifugal (sɛn'trɪfjʊgᵊl, 'sɛntrɪˌfjuːgᵊl) *adj.* **1.** acting, moving, or tending to move away from a centre. Compare **centripetal.** **2.** of, concerned with, or operated by centrifugal force: *centrifugal pump.* **3.** *Botany.* (esp. of certain inflorescences) developing outwards from a centre. **4.** *Physiol.* another word for **efferent.** ~*n.* **5.** any device that uses centrifugal force for its action. **6.** the rotating perforated drum in a centrifuge. [C18: from New Latin *centrifugus,* from CENTRI- + Latin *fugere* to flee] —**cen'trifugally** *adv.*

centrifugal brake *n.* a safety mechanism on a hoist, crane, etc., that consists of revolving brake shoes that are driven outwards by centrifugal force into contact with a fixed brake drum when the rope drum revolves at excessive speed.

centrifugal clutch *n. Engineering.* an automatic clutch in which the friction surfaces are engaged by weighted levers acting under centrifugal force at a certain speed of rotation.

centrifugal force *n.* a fictitious force that can be thought of as acting outwards on any body that rotates or moves along a curved path.

centrifugal pump *n.* a pump having a high-speed rotating impeller whose blades throw the water outwards.

centrifuge ('sɛntrɪˌfjuːdʒ) *n.* **1.** any of various rotating machines that separate liquids from solids or dispersions of one liquid in another, by the action of centrifugal force. **2.** any of various rotating devices for subjecting human beings or animals to varying accelerations for experimental purposes. ~*vb.* **3.** (*tr.*) to subject to the action of a centrifuge. —**centrifugation** (ˌsɛntrɪfjʊ'geɪʃən) *n.*

centring ('sɛntrɪŋ) *or U.S.* **centering** *n.* a temporary structure, esp. one made of timber, used to support an arch during construction.

centriole ('sɛntrɪˌəʊl) *n.* either of two rodlike bodies in most animal cells that form the poles of the spindle during mitosis. [C19: from New Latin *centriolum,* diminutive of Latin *centrum* CENTRE]

centripetal (sɛn'trɪpɪtᵊl, 'sɛntrɪˌpiːtᵊl) *adj.* **1.** acting, moving, or tending to move towards a centre. Compare **centrifugal.** **2.** of, concerned with, or operated by centripetal force. **3.** *Botany.* (esp. of certain inflorescences) developing from the outside towards the centre. **4.** *Physiol.* another word for **afferent.** [C17: from New Latin *centripetus* seeking the centre; see CENTRI-, -PETAL] —**cen'tripetally** *adv.*

centripetal force *n.* a force that acts inwards on any body that rotates or moves along a curved path and is directed towards the centre of curvature of the path or the axis of rotation. Compare **centrifugal force.**

centrist ('sɛntrɪst) *n.* a person holding moderate political views. —'**centrism** *n.*

centro-, centri-, *or before a vowel* **centr-** *combining form.* denoting a centre: *centroclinal; centromere; centrosome; centrosphere; centrist.* [from Greek *kentron* CENTRE]

centrobaric (ˌsɛntrəʊ'bærɪk) *adj.* of or concerned with a centre of gravity. [C18: from Late Greek *kentrobarikos,* from Greek *kentron bareos* centre of gravity]

centroclinal (ˌsɛntrəʊˈklaɪnᵊl) *adj. Geology.* of, relating to, or designating a rock formation in which the strata slope down and in towards a central point or area.
centroid (ˈsɛntrɔɪd) *n.* **a.** the centre of mass of an object of uniform density, esp. of a geometric figure. **b.** the point in a set whose coordinates are the mean values of the coordinates of the other points in the set.
centrolecithal (ˌsɛntrəʊˈlɛsɪθəl) *adj. Zoology.* (of animal eggs) having a centrally located yolk.
centromere (ˈsɛntrəˌmɪə) *n.* the dense nonstaining region of a chromosome that attaches it to the spindle during mitosis. —**centromeric** (ˌsɛntrəˈmɛrɪk, -ˈmɪərɪk) *adj.*
centrosome (ˈsɛntrəˌsəʊm) *n.* a small protoplasmic body that surrounds the centriole. Also called: **centrosphere, astrosphere.** —**centrosomic** (ˌsɛntrəˈsɒmɪk) *adj.*
centrosphere (ˈsɛntrəˌsfɪə) *n.* **1.** the central part of the earth, below the crust. **2.** another name for **centrosome.**
centrum (ˈsɛntrəm) *n., pl.* **-trums** *or* **-tra** (-trə). the main part or body of a vertebra. [C19: from Latin: CENTRE]
centum (ˈsɛntəm) *adj.* denoting or belonging to the Indo-European languages in which original velar stops (*k*) were not palatalized, namely languages of the Hellenic, Italic, Celtic, Germanic, Anatolian, and Tocharian branches. Compare **satem.** [Latin: HUNDRED, chosen because the *c* represents the Indo-European *k*]
centuplicate *vb.* (sɛnˈtjuːplɪˌkeɪt). **1.** (*tr.*) to increase 100 times. ~*adj.* (sɛnˈtjuːplɪkɪt, -ˌkeɪt). **2.** increased a hundredfold. ~*n.* (sɛnˈtjuːplɪkɪt, -ˌkeɪt). **3.** one hundredfold. ~Also **centuple** (ˈsɛntjʊpᵊl). [C17: from Late Latin *centuplicāre,* from *centuplex* hundredfold, from Latin *centum* hundred + *-plex* -fold] —**cenˌtupliˈcation** *n.*
centurial (sɛnˈtjʊərɪəl) *adj.* **1.** of or relating to a Roman century. **2.** *Rare.* involving a period of 100 years.
centurion (sɛnˈtjʊərɪən) *n.* the officer commanding a Roman century. [C14: from Latin *centuriō,* from *centuria* CENTURY]
century (ˈsɛntʃərɪ) *n., pl.* **-ries. 1.** a period of 100 years. **2.** one of the successive periods of 100 years dated before or after an epoch or event, esp. the birth of Christ. **3. a.** a score or grouping of 100: *to score a century in cricket.* **b.** *Chiefly U.S.* (*as modifier*): *the basketball team passed the century mark in their last game.* **4.** (in ancient Rome) a unit of foot soldiers, originally 100 strong, later consisting of 60 to 80 men. See also **maniple. 5.** (in ancient Rome) a division of the people for purposes of voting. **6.** (*often cap.*) a style of type. [C16: from Latin *centuria,* from *centum* hundred]
century plant *n.* a tropical American agave, *Agave americana,* having large greyish leaves and greenish flowers on a tall fleshy stalk. It blooms only once in 10 to 30 years and was formerly thought to flower once in a century. Also called: **American aloe.**
ceorl (tʃɛəl) *n.* a freeman of the lowest class in Anglo-Saxon England. [Old English; see CHURL] —ˈ**ceorlish** *adj.*
cep (sɛp) *n.* an edible saprophytic basidiomycetous woodland fungus, *Boletus edulis,* with a brown shining cap covering white spore-bearing tubes and having a rich nutty flavour: family *Boletineae.* [C19: from French *cèpe,* from Gascon dialect *cep,* from Latin *cippus* stake]
cepaceous (sɪˈpeɪʃəs) *adj. Botany.* having an onion-like smell or taste. [from Latin *caepa* onion + -ACEOUS]
cephalad (ˈsɛfəˌlæd) *adv. Anatomy.* towards the head or anterior part. Compare **caudad.**
cephalalgia (ˌsɛfəˈlældʒɪə, -dʒə) *n.* a technical name for **headache.**
cephalic (sɪˈfælɪk) *adj.* **1.** of or relating to the head. **2.** situated in, on, or near the head.
-cephalic *or* **-cephalous** *adj. combining form.* indicating skull or head; -headed: *brachycephalic.* [from Greek *-kephalos*] —**-cephaly** *or* **-cephalism** *n. combining form.*
cephalic index *n.* the ratio of the greatest width of the human head to its greatest length, multiplied by 100.
cephalin (ˈsɛfəlɪn, ˈkɛf-) *or* **kephalin** (ˈkɛfəlɪn) *n.* a phospholipid, similar to lecithin, that occurs in the nerve tissue and brain. Systematic name: **phosphatidylethanolamine.**
cephalization *or* **cephalisation** (ˌsɛfəlaɪˈzeɪʃən) *n.* (in the evolution of animals) development of a head by the concentration of feeding and sensory organs and nervous tissue at the anterior end.
cephalo- *or before a vowel* **cephal-** *combining form.* indicating the head: *cephalopod.* [via Latin from Greek *kephalo-,* from *kephale* head]
cephalochordate (ˌsɛfələʊˈkɔːdeɪt) *n.* **1.** any chordate animal of the subphylum *Cephalochordata,* having a fishlike body and no vertebral column; a lancelet. ~*adj.* **2.** of, relating to, or belonging to the *Cephalochordata.*
cephalometer (ˌsɛfəˈlɒmɪtə) *n.* an instrument for positioning the human head for x-ray examination in cephalometry.
cephalometry (ˌsɛfəˈlɒmɪtrɪ) *n.* **1.** measurement of the dimensions of the human head by radiography: used mainly in orthodontics. **2.** measurement of the dimensions of the fetal head by radiography or ultrasound. —**cephalometric** (ˌsɛfələʊˈmɛtrɪk) *adj.*
cephalopod (ˈsɛfələˌpɒd) *n.* **1.** any marine mollusc of the class *Cephalopoda,* characterized by well-developed head and eyes and a ring of sucker-bearing tentacles. The group includes the octopuses, squids, cuttlefish, and pearly nautilus. ~*adj. also* **cephalopodic** *or* **cephalopodous** (ˌsɛfəˈlɒpədəs). **2.** of, relating to, or belonging to the *Cephalopoda.* —ˌ**cephaˈlopodan** *adj., n.*
cephalosporin (ˌsɛfələʊˈspɔːrɪn) *n.* any of a group of broad-spectrum antibiotics obtained from fungi of the genus *Cephalosporium.*
cephalothorax (ˌsɛfələʊˈθɔːræks) *n., pl.* **-raxes** *or* **-races** (-rəˌsiːz). the anterior part of many crustaceans and some other arthropods consisting of a united head and thorax. —**cephalothoracic** (ˌsɛfələʊθəˈræsɪk) *adj.*
-cephalus *n. combining form.* denoting a cephalic abnormality: *hydrocephalus.* [New Latin *-cephalus;* see -CEPHALIC]
Cepheid variable (ˈsiːfɪɪd) *n. Astronomy.* any of a class of variable stars with regular cycles of variations in luminosity (most ranging from three to fifty days). There is a relationship between the periods of variation and the absolute magnitudes, which is used for measuring the distance of such stars.
Cepheus (ˈsiːfjuːs) *n., Latin genitive* **Cephei** (ˈsiːfɪˌaɪ). a faint constellation in the N hemisphere near Cassiopeia and the Pole Star. See also **Cepheid variable.** [from Latin *Cēpheus* named after a Greek mythical king]
CER *abbrev. for* Closer Economic Relations: an intergovernment agreement between Australia and New Zealand.
ceraceous (sɪˈreɪʃəs) *adj.* waxlike or waxy. [C18: from Latin *cēra* wax]
ceramal (səˈreɪməl) *n.* another name for **cermet.** [C20: from CERAM(IC) + AL(LOY)]
ceramic (sɪˈræmɪk) *n.* **1.** a hard brittle material made by firing clay and similar substances. **2.** an object made from such a material. ~*adj.* **3.** of, relating to, or made from a ceramic: *this vase is ceramic.* **4.** of or relating to ceramics: *ceramic arts and crafts.* [C19: from Greek *keramikos,* from *keramos* potter's clay, pottery]
ceramic hob *n.* (on an electric cooker) a flat ceramic cooking surface having heating elements fitted on the underside, usually patterned to show the areas where heat is produced.
ceramic oxide *n.* a compound of oxygen with nonorganic material: recently discovered to act as a high-temperature superconductor.
ceramics (sɪˈræmɪks) *n.* (*functioning as sing.*) the art and techniques of producing articles of clay, porcelain, etc. —**ceramist** (ˈsɛrəmɪst) *or* **ceˈramicist** *n.*
cerargyrite (sɪˈrɑːdʒɪˌraɪt) *n.* a greyish-yellow or colourless soft secondary mineral consisting of silver chloride in cubic crystalline form: a source of silver. Formula: AgCl. Also called: **horn silver.** [C19: from Greek *keras* horn + *arguros* silver + -ITE[1]]
cerastes (səˈræstiːz) *n., pl.* **-tes.** any venomous snake of the genus *Cerastes,* esp. the horned viper. [C16: from Latin: horned serpent, from Greek *kerastēs* horned, from *keras* horn]
cerate (ˈsɪərɪt, -reɪt) *n.* a hard ointment or medicated paste consisting of lard or oil mixed with wax or resin. [C16: from Latin *cērātum,* from *cēra* wax]
cerated (ˈsɪəreɪtɪd) *adj.* **1.** (of certain birds, such as the falcon) having a cere. **2.** *Rare.* covered with wax.
cerato- *or before a vowel* **cerat-** *combining form.* **1.** denoting horn or a hornlike part: *ceratodus.* **2.** *Anatomy.* denoting the cornea. ~Also: **kerato-.** [from Greek *kerat-, keras* horn]
ceratodus (sɪˈrætədəs, ˌsɛrəˈtəʊdəs) *n., pl.* **-duses.** any of various extinct lungfish constituting the genus *Ceratodus,* common in Cretaceous and Triassic times. Compare **barramunda.** [C19: New Latin, from CERATO- + Greek *odous* tooth]
ceratoid (ˈsɛrəˌtɔɪd) *adj.* having the shape or texture of animal horn.
Cerberus (ˈsɜːbərəs) *n.* **a sop to Cerberus.** a bribe or something given to propitiate a potential source of danger or problems. [from *Cerberus,* the mythical dog that guarded the entrance to Hades] —**Cerberean** (səˈbɪərɪən) *adj.*
cercal (ˈsɜːkᵊl) *adj. Zoology.* **1.** of or relating to a tail. **2.** of or relating to the cerci.
cercaria (səˈkɛərɪə) *n., pl.* **-iae** (-ɪˌiː). one of the larval forms of trematode worms. It has a short forked tail and resembles an immature adult. [C19: New Latin, literally: tailed creature, from Greek *kerkos* tail] —**cerˈcarial** *adj.* —**cerˈcarian** *adj., n.*
cercis (ˈsɜːsɪs) *n.* any tree or shrub of the leguminous genus *Cercis,* which includes the redbud and Judas tree. [C19: New Latin, from Greek *kerkis* weaver's shuttle, Judas tree]
cercopithecoid (ˌsɜːkəʊpɪˈθiːkɔɪd) *adj.* **1.** of, relating to, or belonging to the primate superfamily *Cercopithecoidea* (Old World monkeys). ~*n. also* **cercopithecid** (ˌsɜːkəʊpɪˈθiːsɪd) **2.** an Old World monkey. [C19: from Latin *cercopithēcus* monkey with a tail (from Greek *kerkopithēkos,* from *kerkos* tail + *pithēkos* ape) + -OID]
cercus (ˈsɜːkəs) *n., pl.* **-ci** (-siː). one of a pair of sensory appendages at the tip of the abdomen of some insects and other arthropods. [C19: from New Latin, from Greek *kerkos* tail]
cere[1] (sɪə) *n.* a soft waxy swelling, containing the nostrils, at the base of the upper beak in such birds as the parrot. [C15: from Old French *cire* wax, from Latin *cēra*]
cere[2] (sɪə) *vb.* (*tr.*) to wrap (a corpse) in a cerecloth. [C15: from Latin *cērāre,* from *cēra* wax]
cereal (ˈsɪərɪəl) *n.* **1.** any grass that produces an edible grain, such as oat, rye, wheat, rice, maize, sorghum, and millet. **2.** the

grain produced by such a plant. **3.** any food made from this grain, esp. breakfast food. **4.** (*modifier*) of or relating to any of these plants or their products: *cereal farming*. [C19: from Latin *cereālis* concerning agriculture, of *Ceres*, the Roman goddess of agriculture]

cerebellar syndrome *n.* a disease of the cerebellum characterized by unsteady movements and mispronunciation of words. Also called: **Nonne's syndrome.**

cerebellum (ˌsɛrɪˈbɛləm) *n., pl.* **-lums** *or* **-la** (-lə). one of the major divisions of the vertebrate brain, situated in man above the medulla oblongata and beneath the cerebrum, whose function is coordination of voluntary movements and maintenance of bodily equilibrium. [C16: from Latin, diminutive of CEREBRUM] —ˌ**cereˈbellar** *adj.*

cerebral (ˈsɛrɪbrəl; *U.S. also* səˈriːbrəl) *adj.* **1.** of or relating to the cerebrum or to the entire brain. **2.** involving intelligence rather than emotions or instinct. **3.** *Phonetics.* another word for **cacuminal.** ~*n.* **4.** *Phonetics.* a consonant articulated in the manner of a cacuminal consonant. —ˈ**cerebrally** *adv.*

cerebral dominance *n.* the normal tendency for one half of the brain, usually the left cerebral hemisphere in right-handed people, to exercise more control over certain functions (e.g. handedness and language) than the other.

cerebral haemorrhage *n.* bleeding from an artery in the brain, which in severe cases causes a stroke.

cerebral hemisphere *n.* either half of the cerebrum.

cerebral palsy *n.* a nonprogressive impairment of muscular function and weakness of the limbs, caused by lack of oxygen to the brain before, during, or immediately after birth, brain injury during birth, or viral infection.

cerebrate (ˈsɛrɪˌbreɪt) *vb.* (*intr.*) *Usually facetious.* to use the mind; think; ponder; consider.

cerebration (ˌsɛrɪˈbreɪʃən) *n.* the act of thinking; consideration; thought. [C19: from Latin *cerebrum* brain]

cerebro- *or before a vowel* **cerebr-** *combining form.* indicating the brain: *cerebrospinal.* [from CEREBRUM]

cerebroside (ˈsɛrɪbrəʊˌsaɪd) *n. Biochem.* any glycolipid in which *N*-acyl sphingosine is combined with glucose or galactose: occurs in the myelin sheaths of nerves.

cerebrospinal (ˌsɛrɪbrəʊˈspaɪnᵊl) *adj.* of or relating to the brain and spinal cord.

cerebrospinal fluid *n.* the clear colourless fluid in the spaces inside and around the spinal cord and brain. Abbrev.: **CSF.**

cerebrospinal meningitis *or* **fever** *n.* an acute infectious form of meningitis caused by the bacterium *Neisseria meningitidis,* characterized by high fever, skin rash, delirium, stupor, and sometimes coma. Also called: **epidemic meningitis.**

cerebrotonia (ˌsɛrɪbrəʊˈtəʊnɪə) *n.* a personality type characterized by restraint, alertness, and an intellectual approach to life: said to be correlated with an ectomorph body type. Compare **somatotonia, viscerotonia.**

cerebrovascular (ˌsɛrɪbrəʊˈvæskjʊlə) *adj.* of or relating to the blood vessels and the blood supply of the brain.

cerebrovascular accident *or* **cerebral vascular accident** *n.* a sudden interruption of the blood supply to the brain caused by rupture of an artery in the brain (**cerebral haemorrhage**) or the blocking of a blood vessel, as by a clot of blood (**cerebral occlusion**). See **apoplexy, stroke** (sense 4).

cerebrum (ˈsɛrɪbrəm) *n., pl.* **-brums** *or* **-bra** (-brə). **1.** the anterior portion of the brain of vertebrates, consisting of two lateral hemispheres joined by a thick band of fibres: the dominant part of the brain in man, associated with intellectual function, emotion, and personality. See **telencephalon. 2.** the brain considered as a whole. **3.** the main neural bundle or ganglion of certain invertebrates. [C17: from Latin: the brain] —ˈ**cereˌbroid** *adj.* —**cerebric** (ˈsɛrɪbrɪk) *adj.*

cerecloth (ˈsɪəˌklɒθ) *n.* waxed waterproof cloth of a kind formerly used as a shroud. [C15: from earlier *cered cloth,* from Latin *cērāre* to wax; see CERE[2]]

cerement (ˈsɪəmənt) *n.* **1.** another name for **cerecloth. 2.** any burial clothes. [C17: from French *cirement,* from *cirer* to wax; see CERE[2]]

ceremonial (ˌsɛrɪˈməʊnɪəl) *adj.* **1.** involving or relating to ceremony or ritual. ~*n.* **2.** the observance of formality, esp. in etiquette. **3.** a plan for formal observances on a particular occasion; ritual. **4.** *Christianity.* **a.** the prescribed order of rites and ceremonies. **b.** a book containing this. —ˌ**cereˈmonialism** *n.* —ˌ**cereˈmonialist** *n.* —ˌ**cereˈmonially** *adv.*

ceremonious (ˌsɛrɪˈməʊnɪəs) *adj.* **1.** especially or excessively polite or formal. **2.** observing ceremony; involving formalities. —ˌ**cereˈmoniously** *adv.* —ˌ**cereˈmoniousness** *n.*

ceremony (ˈsɛrɪmənɪ) *n., pl.* **-nies. 1.** a formal act or ritual, often set by custom or tradition, performed in observation of an event or anniversary: *a ceremony commemorating Shakespeare's birth.* **2.** a religious rite or series of rites. **3.** a courteous gesture or act: *the ceremony of toasting the Queen.* **4.** ceremonial observances or gestures collectively: *the ceremony of a monarchy.* **5. stand on ceremony.** to insist on or act with excessive formality. **6. without ceremony.** in a casual or informal manner. [C14: from Medieval Latin *cērēmōnia,* from Latin *caerimōnia* what is sacred, a religious rite]

Cerenkov radiation (tʃɪˈrɛŋkɒf) *n.* See **Cherenkov radiation.**

ceresin (ˈsɛrɪsɪn) *n.* a white wax extracted from ozocerite. [C19: irregularly from Latin *cēra* wax]

cereus (ˈsɪərɪəs) *n.* **1.** any tropical American cactus of the genus *Cereus,* esp. *C. jamacaru* of N Brazil, which grows to a height of 13 metres (40 feet). **2.** any of several similar and related cacti, such as the night-blooming cereus. [C18: from New Latin, from Latin *cēreus* a wax taper, from *cēra* wax]

ceria (ˈsɪərɪə) *n.* another name (not in technical usage) for **ceric oxide.** [New Latin, from CERIUM]

ceric (ˈsɪərɪk) *adj.* of or containing cerium in the tetravalent state.

ceric oxide *n.* a white or yellow solid used in ceramics, enamels, and radiation shields. Formula: CeO_2. Also called: **cerium dioxide, ceria.**

ceriferous (sɪˈrɪfərəs) *adj. Biology.* producing or bearing wax.

cerise (səˈriːz, -ˈriːs) *n.* **a.** a moderate to dark red colour. **b.** (*as adj.*): *a cerise scarf.* [C19: from French: CHERRY]

cerium (ˈsɪərɪəm) *n.* a malleable ductile steel-grey element of the lanthanide series of metals, used in lighter flints and as a reducing agent in metallurgy. Symbol: Ce; atomic no.: 58; atomic wt.: 140.12; valency: 3 or 4; relative density: 6.77; melting pt.: 795°C; boiling pt.: 3468°C. [C19: New Latin, from *Ceres* (an asteroid) + -IUM]

cerium metals *pl. n.* the metals lanthanum, cerium, praseodymium, neodymium, promethium, and samarium, forming a subgroup of the lanthanides.

cermet (ˈsɜːmɪt) *n.* any of several materials consisting of a metal matrix with ceramic particles disseminated through it. They are hard and resistant to high temperatures. Also called: **ceramal.** [C20: from CER(AMIC) + MET(AL)]

cernuous (ˈsɜːnjʊəs) *adj. Botany.* (of some flowers or buds) drooping. [C17: from Latin *cernuus* leaning forwards, of obscure origin]

cero (ˈsɪərəʊ, ˈsɪrəʊ) *n., pl.* **-ro** *or* **-ros. 1.** a large spiny-finned food fish, *Scomberomorus regalis,* of warm American coastal regions of the Atlantic: family *Scombridae* (mackerels, tunnies, etc.). **2.** any similar or related fish. [C19: from Spanish: saw, sawfish, altered spelling of SIERRA]

cero- *combining form.* indicating the use of wax: *ceroplastic.* [from Greek *kēros* wax]

cerography (sɪəˈrɒgrəfɪ) *n.* the art of engraving on a waxed plate on which a printing surface is created by electrotyping. —**cerographic** (ˌsɪərəʊˈgræfɪk) *or* ˌ**ceroˈgraphical** *adj.* —**ceˈrographist** *n.*

ceroplastic (ˌsɪərəʊˈplæstɪk) *adj.* **1.** relating to wax modelling. **2.** modelled in wax.

ceroplastics (ˌsɪərəʊˈplæstɪks) *n.* (*functioning as sing.*) the art of wax modelling.

cerotic acid (sɪˈrɒtɪk) *n.* another name (not in technical usage) for **hexacosanoic acid.**

cerotype (ˈsɪərəˌtaɪp) *n.* a process for preparing a printing plate by engraving a wax-coated copper plate and then using this as a mould for an electrotype.

cerous (ˈsɪərəs) *adj.* of or containing cerium in the trivalent state. [C19: from CERIUM + -OUS]

cert (sɜːt) *n. Informal.* something that is a certainty, esp. a horse that is certain to win a race (esp. in the phrase **a dead cert**).

cert. *abbrev. for:* **1.** certificate. **2.** certification. **3.** certified.

certain (ˈsɜːtᵊn) *adj.* **1.** (*postpositive*) positive and confident about the truth of something; convinced: *I am certain that he wrote a book.* **2.** (*usually postpositive*) definitely known: *it is certain that they were on the bus.* **3.** (*usually postpositive*) sure; bound; destined: *he was certain to fail.* **4.** decided or settled upon; fixed: *the date is already certain for the invasion.* **5.** unfailing; reliable: *his judgment is certain.* **6.** moderate or minimum: *to a certain extent.* **7. make certain of.** to ensure (that one will get something); confirm. ~*adv.* **8. for certain.** definitely; without a doubt: *he will win for certain.* ~*determiner.* **9. a.** known but not specified or named: *certain people may doubt this.* **b.** (*as pronoun; functioning as pl.*): *certain of the members have not paid their subscriptions.* **10.** named but not known: *he had written to a certain Mrs Smith.* [C13: from Old French, from Latin *certus* sure, fixed, from *cernere* to discern, decide]

certainly (ˈsɜːtᵊnlɪ) *adv.* **1.** with certainty; without doubt: *he certainly rides very well.* ~*sentence substitute.* **2.** by all means; definitely: used in answer to questions.

certainty (ˈsɜːtᵊntɪ) *n., pl.* **-ties. 1.** the condition of being certain. **2.** something established as certain or inevitable. **3. for a certainty.** without doubt.

CertEd (in Britain) *abbrev. for* Certificate in Education.

certes (ˈsɜːtɪz) *adv. Archaic.* with certainty; truly. [C13: from Old French, ultimately from Latin *certus* CERTAIN]

certifiable (ˈsɜːtɪˌfaɪəbᵊl) *adj.* **1.** capable of being certified. **2.** fit to be certified as insane. —ˈ**certiˌfiably** *adv.*

certificate *n.* (səˈtɪfɪkɪt). **1.** an official document attesting the truth of the facts stated, as of birth, marital status, death, health, completion of an academic course, ability to practise a profession, etc. **2.** short for **share certificate.** ~*vb.* (səˈtɪfɪˌkeɪt). **3.** (*tr.*) to authorize by or present with an official document. [C15: from Old French *certificat,* from *certifier* CERTIFY] —**cerˈtificatory** *adj.*

certificate of incorporation *n. Company law.* a signed statement that a company is duly incorporated.

certificate of origin *n.* a document stating the name of the country that produced a specified shipment of goods: often required before importation of goods.
Certificate of Secondary Education *n.* See **CSE.**
certificate of unruliness *n.* (in Britain) the decision of a juvenile court that a young person on remand is too unmanageable for local-authority care and should be taken into custody.
certification (ˌsɜːtɪfɪˈkeɪʃən) *n.* **1.** the act of certifying or state of being certified. **2.** *Law.* a document attesting the truth of a fact or statement.
certified (ˈsɜːtɪˌfaɪd) *adj.* **1.** holding or guaranteed by a certificate. **2.** endorsed or guaranteed: *a certified cheque.* **3.** (of a person) declared legally insane.
certified accountant *n.* (in Britain) a member of the Chartered Association of Certified Accountants, who is authorized to audit company accounts. Compare **chartered accountant, certified public accountant.**
certified housing benefit *n. Social welfare.* (in Britain) a housing benefit paid by a local authority to persons on supplementary benefit who are certified as eligible by the Department of Health and Social Security. See also **housing benefit.**
certified public accountant *n.* (in the U.S.) a public accountant certified to have met state legal requirements. Compare **certified accountant.**
certify (ˈsɜːtɪˌfaɪ) *vb.* **-fies, -fying, -fied.** **1.** to confirm or attest (to), usually in writing: *the letter certified her age.* **2.** (*tr.*) to endorse or guarantee (that certain required standards have been met). **3.** to give reliable information or assurances: *he certified that it was Walter's handwriting.* **4.** (*tr.*) to declare legally insane. **5.** (*tr.*) *U.S. and Canadian.* (of a bank) to state in writing on (a cheque) that payment is guaranteed. [C14: from Old French *certifier,* from Medieval Latin *certificāre* to make certain, from Latin *certus* CERTAIN + *facere* to make] —ˈ**certiˌfier** *n.*
certiorari (ˌsɜːtɪɔːˈrɛəraɪ) *n. Law.* an order of a superior court directing that a record of proceedings in a lower court be sent up for review. See also **mandamus, prohibition.** [C15: from legal Latin: to be informed]
certitude (ˈsɜːtɪˌtjuːd) *n.* confidence; certainty. [C15: from Church Latin *certitūdō,* from Latin *certus* CERTAIN]
cerulean (sɪˈruːlɪən) *n.* **a.** a deep blue colour; azure. **b.** (*as adj.*): *a cerulean sea.* [C17: from Latin *caeruleus,* probably from *caelum* sky]
cerumen (sɪˈruːmɛn) *n.* the soft brownish-yellow wax secreted by glands in the auditory canal of the external ear. Nontechnical name: **earwax.** [C18: from New Latin, from Latin *cēra* wax + ALBUMEN] —**ceˈruminous** *adj.*
ceruse (səˈruːs) *n.* another name for **white lead** (sense 1). [C14: from Old French *céruse,* from Latin *cērussa,* perhaps ultimately from Greek *kēros* wax]
cerussite *or* **cerusite** (ˈsɪərəˌsaɪt) *n.* a usually white mineral, found in veins. It is a source of lead. Composition: lead carbonate. Formula: $PbCO_3$. Crystal structure: orthorhombic. Also called: **white lead ore.** [C19: from Latin *cērussa* (see CERUSE) + -ITE[1]]
cervelat (ˈsɜːvəˌlæt, -ˌlɑː) *n.* a smoked sausage made from pork and beef. [C17: via obsolete French from Italian *cervellata*]
cervical (ˈsɜːvɪkᵊl, səˈvaɪ-) *adj.* of or relating to the neck or cervix. [C17: from New Latin *cervīcālis,* from Latin *cervīx* neck]
cervical smear *n. Med.* a smear of cellular material taken from the neck (cervix) of the uterus for detection of cancer. Also called: **Pap test** *or* **smear.**
cervicitis (ˌsɜːvɪˈsaɪtɪs) *n.* inflammation of the neck of the uterus.
cervicum (ˈsɜːvɪkəm, səˈvaɪ-) *n. Zoology.* the flexible region between the prothorax and head in insects.
cervid (ˈsɜːvɪd) *n.* **1.** any ruminant mammal of the family *Cervidae,* including the deer, characterized by the presence of antlers. ~*adj.* **2.** of, relating to, or belonging to the *Cervidae.* [C19: from New Latin *Cervidae,* from Latin *cervus* deer]
cervine (ˈsɜːvaɪn) *adj.* **1.** resembling or relating to a deer. **2.** of a dark yellowish-brown colour. [C19: from Latin *cervīnus,* from *cervus* a deer]
cervix (ˈsɜːvɪks) *n., pl.* **cervixes** *or* **cervices** (səˈvaɪsiːz). **1.** the technical name for **neck. 2.** any necklike part of an organ, esp. the lower part of the uterus that extends into the vagina. [C18: from Latin]
Cesarean *or* **Cesarian** (sɪˈzɛərɪən) *adj. U.S.* variant spellings of **Caesarean.**
cesium (ˈsiːzɪəm) *n.* the usual U.S. spelling of **caesium.**
cespitose (ˈsɛspɪˌtəʊs) *adj.* a variant spelling (esp. U.S.) of **caespitose.** —ˈ**cespiˌtosely** *adv.*
cess[1] (sɛs) *n.* **1.** *Brit.* any of several special taxes, such as a land tax in Scotland. **2.** (formerly in Ireland) **a.** the obligation to provide the soldiers and household of the lord deputy with supplies at fixed prices. **b.** any military exaction. ~*vb.* **3.** (*tr.*) *Brit.* to tax or assess for taxation. **4.** (*tr.*) (formerly in Ireland) to impose (soldiers) upon a population, to be supported by them. [C16: short for ASSESSMENT]
cess[2] (sɛs) *n.* an Irish slang word for **luck** (esp. in the phrase **bad cess to you!**). [C19: probably from CESS[1] (sense 2)]
cess[3] (sɛs) *n.* short for **cesspool.**
cessation (sɛˈseɪʃən) *n.* a ceasing or stopping; discontinuance; pause: *temporary cessation of hostilities.* [C14: from Latin *cessātiō* a delaying, inactivity, from *cessāre* to be idle, desist from, from *cēdere* to yield, CEDE]
cesser (ˈsɛsə) *n. Law.* the coming to an end of a term interest or annuity.
cession (ˈsɛʃən) *n.* **1.** the act of ceding, esp. of ceding rights, property, or territory. **2.** something that is ceded, esp. land or territory. [C14: from Latin *cessiō,* from *cēdere* to yield]
cessionary (ˈsɛʃənərɪ) *n., pl.* **-aries.** *Law.* a person to whom something is transferred; assignee; grantee.
cesspool (ˈsɛsˌpuːl) *n.* **1.** Also called: ˈ**cessˌpit, sink, sump.** a covered cistern, etc., for collecting and storing sewage or waste water. **2.** a filthy or corrupt place: *a cesspool of iniquity.* [C17: changed (through influence of POOL[1]) from earlier *cesperalle,* from Old French *souspirail* vent, air, from *soupirer* to sigh; see SUSPIRE]
c'est la vie *French.* (sɛ la vi) that's life.
cestode (ˈsɛstəʊd) *n.* any parasitic flatworm of the class *Cestoda,* which includes the tapeworms. [C19: from New Latin *Cestoidea* ribbon-shaped creatures, from Latin *cestus* belt, girdle]
cestoid (ˈsɛstɔɪd) *adj.* (esp. of tapeworms and similar animals) ribbon-like in form.
cestus *or* **caestus** (ˈsɛstəs) *n., pl.* **-tus** *or* **-tuses.** (in classical Roman boxing) a pugilist's gauntlet of bull's hide loaded or studded with metal. [C18: from Latin *caestus,* probably from *caedere* to strike, slay]
cesura (sɪˈzjʊərə) *n., pl.* **-ras** *or* **-rae** (-riː). *Prosody.* a variant spelling of **caesura.** —**ceˈsural** *adj.*
CET *abbrev. for:* **1.** Central European Time. **2.** Common External Tariff.
cetacean (sɪˈteɪʃən) *adj. also* **cetaceous. 1.** of, relating to, or belonging to the *Cetacea,* an order of aquatic placental mammals having no hind limbs and a blowhole for breathing: includes toothed whales (dolphins, porpoises, etc.) and whalebone whales (rorquals, right whales, etc.). ~*n.* **2.** a whale. [C19: from New Latin *Cētācea,* ultimately from Latin *cētus* whale, from Greek *kētos*]
cetane (ˈsiːteɪn) *n.* a colourless insoluble liquid alkane hydrocarbon used in the determination of the cetane number of diesel fuel. Formula: $C_{16}H_{34}$. Also called: **hexadecane.** [C19: from Latin *cētus* whale + -ANE, so called because related compounds are found in sperm whale oil]
cetane number *n.* a measure of the quality of a diesel fuel expressed as the percentage of cetane in a mixture of cetane and 1-methylnapthalene of the same quality as the given fuel. Also called: **cetane rating.** Compare **octane number.**
cete (siːt) *n.* a group of badgers. [C15: perhaps from Latin *coetus* assembly, from *coīre* to come together]
ceteris paribus (ˈkɛtərɪs ˈpɑːrɪbʊs) other things being equal. [C17: Latin]
cetology (siːˈtɒlədʒɪ) *n.* the branch of zoology concerned with the study of whales (cetaceans). [C19: from Latin *cētus* whale] —**cetological** (ˌsiːtəˈlɒdʒɪkᵊl) *adj.* —**ceˈtologist** *n.*
cetrimide (ˈsɛtrɪˌmaɪd) *n.* a quaternary ammonium compound used as a detergent and, having powerful antiseptic properties, for sterilizing surgical instruments, cleaning wounds, etc.
Cetus (ˈsiːtəs) *n., Latin genitive* **Ceti** (ˈsiːtaɪ). a large constellation on the celestial equator near Pisces and Aquarius. It contains the variable star Mira Ceti. [Latin: whale]
Ceylonese (ˌsɛləˈniːz, ˌsiːlə-) *adj.* of or relating to Ceylon, island in the Indian Ocean consisting politically of Sri Lanka.
Ceylon moss (sɪˈlɒn) *n.* a red East Indian seaweed, *Gracilaria lichenoides,* from which agar is made.
cf *or* **CF** *abbrev. for* cost and freight. Also: **c & f.**
Cf *the chemical symbol for* californium.
CF *Chiefly Brit. abbrev. for* Chaplain to the Forces.
cf. *abbrev. for:* **1.** confer. [Latin: compare] **2.** (in bookbinding, etc.) calfskin.
c/f *Book-keeping. abbrev. for* carried forward.
CFC *abbrev. for* chlorofluorocarbon.
CFD *abbrev. for* computational fluid dynamics.
CFE *abbrev. for:* **1.** College of Further Education. **2.** Conventional Forces in Europe.
cfi *or* **CFI** *abbrev. for* cost, freight, and insurance (included in the price quoted). Also: **c.i.f.**
cg **1.** *abbrev. for* centre of gravity. ~**2.** *symbol for* centigram.
CG *abbrev. for:* **1.** captain general. **2.** coastguard. **3.** Coldstream Guards. **4.** consul general.
CGBR *abbrev. for* Central Government Borrowing Requirement.
CGM *Chiefly Brit. abbrev. for* Conspicuous Gallantry Medal.
CGS (in Britain) *abbrev. for* Chief of General Staff.
cgs units *pl. n.* a metric system of units based on the centimetre, gram, and second. For scientific and technical purposes these units have been replaced by SI units.
CGT *abbrev. for* capital gains tax.
ch *abbrev. for* custom house.
CH **1.** *abbrev. for* Companion of Honour (a Brit. title). ~**2.** *international car registration for* Switzerland. [from French *Confédération Helvétique*]
ch. *abbrev. for:* **1.** chain (unit of measure). **2.** chapter. **3.** *Chess.* check. **4.** chief. **5.** church.
chabazite (ˈkæbəˌzaɪt) *n.* a pink, white, or colourless zeolite mineral consisting of a hydrated silicate of calcium, sodium, potassium, and aluminium in hexagonal crystalline form. Formula: $(Ca,Na,K)Al_2Si_4O_{12}.6H_2O$. [C19: from French *chabazie* from Late Greek *khabazios,* erroneous for *khalazios* stone similar to a

hailstone, from Greek *khalazios* of hail, from *khalaza* hailstone + -ITE[1]]
Chablis ('ʃæblɪ; *French* ʃabli) *n.* (*sometimes not caps.*) a dry white burgundy wine made around Chablis, in central France.
cha-cha-cha (ˌtʃɑːtʃɑːˈtʃɑː) *or* **cha-cha** *n.* **1.** a modern ballroom dance from Latin America with small steps and swaying hip movements. **2.** a piece of music composed for this dance. *~vb.* (*intr.*) **3.** to perform this dance. [C20: from American (Cuban) Spanish]
chacma ('tʃækmə) *n.* a baboon, *Papio* (or *Chaeropithecus*) *ursinus*, having coarse greyish hair and occurring in southern and eastern Africa. [C19: from Hottentot]
chaconne (ʃəˈkɒn; *French* ʃakɔn) *n.* **1.** a musical form consisting of a set of continuous variations upon a ground bass. See also **passacaglia.** **2.** *Archaic.* a dance in slow triple time probably originating in Spain. [C17: from French, from Spanish *chacona*, probably imitative of the castanet accompaniment]
chacun à son goût *French.* (ʃakœ̃n a sõ gu) each to his own taste.
chad (tʃæd) *n.* the small pieces of cardboard or paper removed during the punching of holes in computer cards or paper tape. [C20: perhaps based on CHAFF[1]]
Chadic ('tʃædɪk) *n.* **1.** a subfamily of the Afro-Asiatic family of languages, spoken in an area west and south of Lake Chad in N central Africa, the chief member of which is Hausa. *~adj.* **2.** denoting, relating to, or belonging to this group of languages.
chador ('tʃʌdə) *n.* a variant spelling of **chuddar.**
chaeta ('kiːtə) *n., pl.* **-tae** (-tiː). any of the chitinous bristles on the body of such annelids as the earthworm and the lugworm: used in locomotion; a seta. [C19: New Latin, from Greek *khaitē* long hair]
chaetiferous (kiːˈtɪfərəs) *adj. Zoology.* having bristles.
chaetognath ('kiːtɒgˌnæθ) *n.* any small wormlike marine invertebrate of the phylum *Chaetognatha*, including the arrowworms, having a coelom and a ring of bristles around the mouth. [C19: New Latin *Chaetognatha*, literally: hair-jaw, from CHAETA + Greek *gnathos* jaw]
chaetopod ('kiːtəˌpɒd) *n.* any annelid worm of the classes *Oligochaeta* or *Polychaeta.* See **oligochaete, polychaete.** [C19: from New Latin *Chaetopoda*; see CHAETA, -POD]
chafe (tʃeɪf) *vb.* **1.** to make or become sore or worn by rubbing. **2.** (*tr.*) to warm (the hands, etc.) by rubbing. **3.** to irritate or be irritated or impatient: *he was chafed because he was not allowed out.* **4.** (*intr.*; often foll. by *on, against*, etc.) to cause friction; rub. **5. chafe at the bit.** See **champ**[1] (sense 3). *~n.* **6.** a soreness or irritation caused by friction. [C14: from Old French *chaufer* to warm, ultimately from Latin *calefacere*, from *calēre* to be warm + *facere* to make]
chafer ('tʃeɪfə) *n.* any of various scarabaeid beetles, such as the cockchafer and rose chafer. [Old English *ceafor*; related to Old Saxon *kevera*, Old High German *chevar*]
chaff[1] (tʃɑːf) *n.* **1.** the mass of husks, etc., separated from the seeds during threshing. **2.** finely cut straw and hay used to feed cattle. **3.** something of little worth; rubbish (esp. in the phrase **separate the wheat from the chaff**). **4.** the dry membranous bracts enclosing the flowers of certain composite plants. **5.** thin strips of metallic foil released into the earth's atmosphere to deflect radar signals and prevent detection. [Old English *ceaf*; related to Old High German *keva* husk] —**'chaffy** *adj.*
chaff[2] (tʃɑːf) *n.* **1.** light-hearted teasing or joking; banter. *~vb.* **2.** to tease good-naturedly; banter. [C19: probably slang variant of CHAFE, perhaps influenced by CHAFF[1]] —**'chaffer** *n.*
chaffer ('tʃæfə) *vb.* **1.** (*intr.*) to haggle or bargain. **2.** to chatter, talk, or say idly; bandy (words). **3.** (*tr.*) *Obsolete.* to deal in; barter. *~n.* **4.** haggling or bargaining. [C13 *chaffare*, from *chep* bargain + *fare* journey; see CHEAP, FARE] —**'chafferer** *n.*
chaffinch ('tʃæfɪntʃ) *n.* a common European finch, *Fringilla coelebs*, with black and white wings and, in the male, a reddish body and blue-grey head. [Old English *ceaffinc*, from *ceaf* CHAFF[1] + *finc* FINCH]
chafing dish ('tʃeɪfɪŋ) *n.* a vessel with a heating apparatus beneath it, for cooking or keeping food warm at the table.
Chagas' disease ('ʃɑːgəs) *n.* a form of trypanosomiasis found in South America, caused by the protozoan *Trypanosoma cruzi*, characterized by fever and, often, inflammation of the heart muscles. Also called: **(South) American trypanosomiasis.** Compare **sleeping sickness.** [C20: named after Carlos *Chagas* (1879–1934), Brazilian physician who first described it]
chagrin ('ʃægrɪn) *n.* **1.** a feeling of annoyance or mortification. *~vb.* (*tr.*) **2.** to embarrass and annoy; mortify. [C17: from French *chagrin, chagriner*, of unknown origin]
chain (tʃeɪn) *n.* **1.** a flexible length of metal links, used for confining, connecting, pulling, etc., or in jewellery. **2.** (*usually pl.*) anything that confines, fetters, or restrains: *the chains of poverty.* **3.** (*usually pl.*) Also called: **snow chains.** a set of metal links that fit over the tyre of a motor vehicle to increase traction and reduce skidding on an icy surface. **4. a.** a number of establishments such as hotels, shops, etc., having the same owner or management. **b.** (*as modifier*): *a chain store.* **5.** a series of related or connected facts, events, etc. **6.** (of reasoning) a sequence of arguments each of which takes the conclusion of the preceding as a premise. See (as an example) **sorites.** **7.** Also called: **Gunter's chain.** a unit of length equal to 22 yards. **8.** Also called: **engineer's chain.** a unit of length equal to 100 feet. **9.** *Austral. and N.Z.* **a.** the rail along which carcasses are moved in a slaughterhouse. **b.** a team of workers in a slaughterhouse. **10.** *Chem.* two or more atoms or groups bonded together so that the configuration of the resulting molecule, ion, or radical resembles a chain. See also **open chain, ring**[1] (sense 18). **11.** *Geography.* a series of natural features, esp. approximately parallel mountain ranges. **12. off the chain.** *Austral. and N.Z.* free from responsibility. *~vb.* **13.** *Surveying.* to measure with a chain or tape. **14.** (*tr.*; often foll. by *up*) to confine, tie, or make fast with or as if with a chain. **15.** short for **chain-stitch.** [C13: from Old French *chaine*, ultimately from Latin; see CATENA]
chain drive *n. Engineering.* a chain of links passing over sprockets that transmits rotation from one shaft to another.
chain gang *n. U.S.* a group of convicted prisoners chained together, usually while doing hard labour.
chain grate *n.* a type of mechanical stoker for a furnace, in which the grate consists of an endless chain that draws the solid fuel into the furnace as it rotates.
chain letter *n.* a letter, often with a request for and promise of money, that is sent to many people who add to or recopy it and send it on to others: illegal in many countries.
chain lightning *n.* another name for **forked lightning.**
chain mail *n.* another term for **mail**[2] (sense 1).
chainman ('tʃeɪnmən) *n., pl.* **-men.** *Surveying.* a person who does the chaining in a survey.
chainplate ('tʃeɪnˌpleɪt) *n.* a metal plate on the side of a vessel, to which the shrouds are attached.
chain printer *n.* a line printer in which the type is on a continuous chain, used to print computer output.
chain-react *vb.* (*intr.*) to undergo a chain reaction.
chain reaction *n.* **1.** a process in which a neutron colliding with an atomic nucleus causes fission and the ejection of one or more other neutrons, which induce other nuclei to split. **2.** a chemical reaction in which the product of one step is a reactant in the following step. **3.** a series of rapidly occurring events, each of which precipitates the next.
chain rule *n. Maths.* a theorem that may be used in the differentiation of the function of a function. It states that $du/dx = (du/dy)(dy/dx)$, where y is a function of x and u a function of y.
chain saw *n.* a motor-driven saw, usually portable, in which the cutting teeth form links in a continuous chain.
chain shot *n.* cannon shot comprising two balls or half balls joined by a chain, much used formerly, esp. in naval warfare to destroy rigging.
chain-smoke *vb.* to smoke (cigarettes, etc.) continually, esp. lighting one from the preceding one. —**chain smoker** *n.*
chain stitch *n.* **1.** an ornamental looped embroidery stitch resembling the links of a chain. *~vb.* **chain-stitch.** **2.** to sew (something) with this stitch.
chain store *n.* one of several retail enterprises under the same ownership and management. Also called: **multiple store.**
chain wheel *n. Engineering.* a toothed wheel that meshes with a roller chain to transmit motion.
chair (tʃɛə) *n.* **1.** a seat with a back on which one person sits, typically having four legs and often having arms. **2.** an official position of authority: *a chair on the board of directors.* **3.** the chairman of a debate or meeting: *the speaker addressed the chair.* **4.** a professorship: *the chair of German.* **5.** *Railways.* an iron or steel cradle bolted to a sleeper in which the rail sits and is locked in position. **6.** short for **sedan chair.** **7. in the chair.** chairing a debate or meeting. **8. take the chair.** to preside as chairman for a meeting, etc. **9. the chair.** an informal name for **electric chair.** *~vb.* (*tr.*) **10.** to preside over (a meeting). **11.** *Brit.* to carry aloft in a sitting position after a triumph or great achievement. **12.** to provide with a chair of office. **13.** to install in a chair. [C13: from Old French *chaiere*, from Latin *cathedra*, from Greek *kathedra*, from *kata-* down + *hedra* seat; compare CATHEDRAL]
chairborne ('tʃɛəˌbɔːn) *adj. Informal.* having an administrative or desk job rather than a more active one.
chairbound ('tʃɛəˌbaʊnd) *adj. Social welfare.* unable to walk; dependent on a wheelchair for mobility.
chair lift *n.* a series of chairs suspended from a power-driven cable for conveying people, esp. skiers, up a mountain.
chairman ('tʃɛəmən) *n., pl.* **-men.** **1.** Also called: **chairperson;** (*fem.*) **chairwoman.** a person who presides over a company's board of directors, a committee, a debate, an administrative department, etc. **2.** *Hist.* someone who carries a sedan chair. —**'chairmanˌship** *n.*
▷**Usage.** Some users object to the word *chairman* since they feel it is inappropriate and sexually discriminatory when applied to a woman. *Chairperson* has come to be widely used as an alternative to either *chairman* or *chairwoman*, since it has no gender bias. Other users, however, consider *chairperson* unacceptable on the grounds that it is unwieldy. Possible alternatives are the use of *chair*, accepting the pair *chairman/chairwoman*, or using *president.*
chairperson ('tʃɛəˌpɜːsᵊn) *n.* another word for **chairman** (sense 1).
▷**Usage.** See at **chairman.**
chaise (ʃeɪz) *n.* **1.** a light open horse-drawn carriage, esp. one with two wheels designed for two passengers. **2.** short for **post chaise** and **chaise longue.** **3.** a gold coin first issued in France

in the 14th century, depicting the king seated on a throne. [C18: from French, variant of Old French *chaiere* CHAIR]

chaise longue ('ʃeɪz 'lɒŋ; *French* ʃɛz lɔ̃g) *n., pl.* **chaise longues** *or* **chaises longues** ('ʃeɪz 'lɒŋ; *French* ʃɛz lɔ̃g). a long low chair for reclining, with a back and single armrest. [C19: from French: long chair]

chakra ('tʃækrə, 'tʃʌkrə) *n.* (in yoga) one of the major centres of spiritual power in the human body, reputed to be located along the spinal column. [C19: from Sanskrit *cakra* wheel, circle]

chalaza (kə'leɪzə) *n., pl.* **-zas** *or* **-zae** (-ziː). **1.** one of a pair of spiral threads of albumen holding the yolk of a bird's egg in position. **2.** the basal part of a plant ovule, where the integuments and nucellus are joined. [C18: New Latin, from Greek: hailstone] —**cha'lazal** *adj.*

chalazion (kə'leɪzɪən) *n.* a small cyst on the eyelid resulting from chronic inflammation of a meibomian gland. Also called: **meibomian cyst.** [C18: from Greek: a small CHALAZA]

chalcanthite (kæl'kænθaɪt) *n.* a blue secondary mineral consisting of hydrated copper sulphate in triclinic crystalline form. Formula: $CuSO_4.5H_2O$. [C19: via German from Latin *chalcanthum* copper sulphate solution, from Greek *khalkanthon,* from *khalkos* copper + *anthos* flower; see -ITE[1]]

chalcedony (kæl'sɛdənɪ) *n., pl.* **-nies.** a microcrystalline often greyish form of quartz with crystals arranged in parallel fibres: a gemstone. Formula: SiO_2. [C15: from Late Latin *chalcēdōnius,* from Greek *khalkēdōn* a precious stone (Revelation 21:19), perhaps named after *Khalkēdōn* Chalcedon, town in Asia Minor] —**chalcedonic** (ˌkælsɪ'dɒnɪk) *adj.*

chalcid *or* **chalcid fly** ('kælsɪd) *n.* any tiny hymenopterous insect of the family *Chalcididae* and related families, whose larvae are parasites of other insects. [C19: from New Latin *Chalcis* type genus, from Greek *khalkos* copper, referring to its metallic sheen]

chalco- *or before a vowel* **chalc-** *combining form.* indicating copper or a copper alloy: *chalcopyrite; chalcolithic.* [from Greek *khalkos* copper]

chalcocite ('kælkəˌsaɪt) *n.* a lead-grey or black mineral, found as a copper ore or in veins. It is a source of copper. Composition: copper sulphide. Formula: Cu_2S. Crystal structure: orthorhombic. [C19: changed from earlier *chalcosine,* from Greek *khalkos* copper + -ITE[1]]

chalcography (kæl'kɒgrəfɪ) *n.* the art of engraving on copper or brass. —**chal'cographer** *or* **chal'cographist** *n.* —**chalcographic** (ˌkælkə'græfɪk) *or* ˌ**chalco'graphical** *adj.*

chalcolithic (ˌkælkə'lɪθɪk) *adj. Archaeol.* of or relating to a period characterized by the use of both stone and bronze implements.

chalcopyrite (ˌkælkə'paɪraɪt, -'paɪə-) *n.* a widely distributed yellow mineral consisting of a sulphide of copper and iron in tetragonal crystalline form: the principal ore of copper. Formula: $CuFeS_2$. Also called: **copper pyrites.**

Chaldean *or* **Chaldaean** (kæl'diːən) *n.* **1.** a member of an ancient Semitic people who controlled S Babylonia from the late 8th to the late 7th century B.C. **2.** the dialect of Babylonian spoken by this people. **3.** *Rare.* an astrologer or soothsayer. ~*adj.* **4.** of or relating to the ancient Chaldeans or their language.

Chaldee (kæl'diː) *n.* **1.** a nontechnical term for **Biblical Aramaic,** once believed to be the language of the ancient Chaldeans. **2.** the actual language of the ancient Chaldeans. See also **Chaldean** (sense 2). **3.** an inhabitant of ancient Chaldea; a Chaldean. ~Also (for senses 1, 2): **Chaldaic** (kæl'deɪɪk).

chaldron ('tʃɔːldrən) *n.* a unit of capacity equal to 36 bushels. Formerly used in the U.S. for the measurement of solids, being equivalent to 1.268 cubic metres. Used in Britain for both solids and liquids, it is equivalent to 1.309 cubic metres. [C17: from Old French *chauderon* CAULDRON]

chalet ('ʃæleɪ; *French* ʃalɛ) *n.* **1.** a type of wooden house of Swiss origin, typically low, with wide projecting eaves. **2.** a similar house used esp. as a ski lodge, garden house, etc. [C19: from French (Swiss dialect)]

chalice ('tʃælɪs) *n.* **1.** *Poetic.* a drinking cup; goblet. **2.** *Christianity.* a gold or silver cup containing the wine at Mass. **3.** a cup-shaped flower. [C13: from Old French, from Latin *calix* cup; related to Greek *kalux* calyx]

chaliced ('tʃælɪst) *adj.* (of plants) having cup-shaped flowers.

chalicothere ('kælɪkəʊˌθɪə) *n.* any of various very large extinct Tertiary horselike perissodactyl mammals that had clawed feet but otherwise resembled titanotheres. [C19: from New Latin *Chalicotherium* type genus, from Greek *khalix* gravel + Greek *thērion* a little beast, from *thēr* wild animal]

chalk (tʃɔːk) *n.* **1.** a soft fine-grained white sedimentary rock consisting of nearly pure calcium carbonate, containing minute fossil fragments of marine organisms, usually without a cementing material. **2.** a piece of chalk or a substance like chalk, often coloured, used for writing and drawing on a blackboard. **3.** a line, mark, etc. made with chalk. **4.** *Billiards, etc.* a small cube of prepared chalk or similar substance for rubbing the tip of a cue. **5.** *Brit.* a score, tally, or record. **6. as alike** (*or* **different**) **as chalk and cheese.** *Informal.* totally different in essentials. **7. by a long chalk.** *Brit. informal.* by far. **8. can't tell** (*or* **doesn't know**) **chalk from cheese.** to be unable to judge or appreciate important differences. **9. not by a long chalk.** *Brit. informal.* by no means; not possibly. **10.** (*modifier*) made of chalk. ~*vb.* **11.** to draw or mark (something) with chalk. **12.** (*tr.*) to mark, rub, or whiten with or as if with chalk. **13.** (*intr.*) (of paint) to become chalky; powder. **14.** (*tr.*) to spread chalk on (land) as a fertilizer. ~See also **chalk out, chalk up.** [Old English *cealc,* from Latin *calx* limestone, from Greek *khalix* pebble] —'**chalkˌlike** *adj.* —'**chalky** *adj.* —'**chalkiness** *n.*

chalk and talk *n. Sometimes derogatory.* a formal method of teaching, in which the focal points are the blackboard and the teacher's voice, as contrasted with more informal child-centred activities.

chalkboard ('tʃɔːkˌbɔːd) *n.* a U.S. and Canadian word for **blackboard.**

chalkface ('tʃɔːkˌfeɪs) *n. Brit. informal.* **a.** the work or art of teaching in a school, esp. classroom teaching as distinct from organizational responsibilities (esp. in the phrase **at the chalkface**). **b.** (*as modifier*): *chalkface experience.*

chalk out *vb.* (*tr., adv.*) to outline (a plan, scheme, etc.); sketch.

chalkpit ('tʃɔːkˌpɪt) *n.* a quarry for chalk.

chalkstone ('tʃɔːkˌstəʊn) *n. Pathol.* another name for **tophus.**

chalk talk *n. U.S. and Canadian.* an informal lecture with pertinent points, explanatory diagrams, etc., shown on a blackboard.

chalk up *vb.* (*tr., adv.*) *Informal.* **1.** to score or register (something): *we chalked up 100 in the game.* **2.** to credit (money) to an account etc. (esp. in the phrase **chalk it up**).

challah *or* **hallah** ('hɑːlə; *Hebrew* xa'la) *n., pl.* **-lahs** *or* **-loth** (*Hebrew* -'lɔt). bread, usually in the form of a plaited loaf, traditionally eaten by Jews to celebrate the Sabbath. [from Hebrew *hallāh*]

challenge ('tʃælɪndʒ) *vb.* (*mainly tr.*) **1.** to invite or summon (someone to do something, esp. to take part in a contest). **2.** (*also intr.*) to call (something) into question; dispute. **3.** to make demands on; stimulate: *the job challenges his ingenuity.* **4.** to order (a person) to halt and be identified or to give a password. **5.** *Law.* to make formal objection to (a juror or jury). **6.** to lay claim to (attention, etc.). **7.** (*intr.*) *Hunting.* (of a hound) to cry out on first encountering the scent of a quarry. **8.** to inject (an experimental animal immunized with a test substance) with disease microorganisms to test for immunity to the disease. ~*n.* **9.** a call to engage in a fight, argument, or contest. **10.** a questioning of a statement or fact; a demand for justification or explanation. **11.** a demanding or stimulating situation, career, object, etc. **12.** a demand by a sentry, watchman, etc., for identification or a password. **13.** *U.S.* an assertion that a person is not entitled to vote or that a vote is invalid. **14.** *Law.* a formal objection to a person selected to serve on a jury (**challenge to the polls**) or to the whole body of jurors (**challenge to the array**). [C13: from Old French *chalenge,* from Latin *calumnia* CALUMNY] —'**challengeable** *adj.* —'**challenger** *n.*

challenging ('tʃælɪndʒɪŋ) *adj.* demanding or stimulating: *a challenging new job.*

challis ('ʃælɪ, -lɪs) *or* **challie** ('ʃælɪ) *n.* a lightweight plain-weave fabric of wool, cotton, etc., usually with a printed design. [C19: probably from a surname]

chalone ('kæləʊn) *n.* any internal secretion that inhibits a physiological process or function. [C20: from Greek *khalōn,* from *khalan* to slacken]

chalutz *or* ***halutz*** *Hebrew.* (xɑ'lʊts; *English* hɑː'lʊts) *n., pl.* ***-lutzim*** (-luː'tsiːm; *English* -'luːtsɪm). a member of an organization of immigrants to Israeli agricultural settlements. [literally: pioneer, fighter]

chalybeate (kə'lɪbɪɪt) *adj.* **1.** containing or impregnated with iron salts. ~*n.* **2.** any drug containing or tasting of iron. [C17: from New Latin *chalybēātus,* ultimately from *khalups* iron]

chalybite ('kælɪˌbaɪt) *n.* another name for **siderite** (sense 1).

cham (kæm) *n.* an archaic word for **khan**[1] (sense 1). [C16: from French, from Persian *khān;* see KHAN]

Cham (tʃæm) *n.* **1.** (*pl.* **Cham** *or* **Chams**) a member of a people of Indonesian stock living in Cambodia and central Vietnam. **2.** the language of this people, belonging to the Malayo-Polynesian family.

chamade (ʃə'mɑːd) *n. Military.* (formerly) a signal by drum or trumpet inviting an enemy to a parley. [C17: from French, from Portuguese *chamada,* from *chamar* to call, from Latin *clamāre*]

Chamaeleon (kə'miːlɪən) *n., Latin genitive* **Chamaeleontis** (kəˌmiːlɪ'ɒntɪs). a faint constellation lying between Volans and the South celestial pole.

chamaephyte ('kæməˌfaɪt) *n.* a plant whose buds are close to the ground. [C20: from Greek *khamai* on the ground + -PHYTE]

chamber ('tʃeɪmbə) *n.* **1.** a meeting hall, esp. one used for a legislative or judicial assembly. **2.** a reception room or audience room in an official residence, palace, etc. **3.** *Archaic or poetic.* a room in a private house, esp. a bedroom. **4. a.** a legislative, deliberative, judicial, or administrative assembly. **b.** any of the houses of a legislature. **5.** an enclosed space; compartment; cavity: *the smallest chamber in the caves.* **6.** the space between two gates of the locks of a canal, dry dock, etc. **7.** an enclosure for a cartridge in the cylinder of a revolver or for a shell in the breech of a cannon. **8.** *Obsolete.* a place where the money of a government, corporation, etc., was stored; treasury. **9.** short for **chamber pot. 10.** *N.Z.* the freezing room in an abattoir. **11.** (*modifier*) of, relating to, or suitable for chamber music: *a chamber concert.* ~*vb.* **12.** (*tr.*) to put in or provide with a chamber.

~See also **chambers.** [C13: from Old French *chambre,* from Late Latin *camera* room, Latin: vault, from Greek *kamara*]
chamber counsel *or* **counsellor** *n.* a counsel who advises in private and does not plead in court.
chambered nautilus *n.* another name for the **pearly nautilus.**
chamberhand ('tʃeɪmbəˌhænd) *n. N.Z.* a worker in the cold storage area of a slaughterhouse.
chamberlain ('tʃeɪmbəlɪn) *n.* **1.** an officer who manages the household of a king. **2.** the steward of a nobleman or landowner. **3.** the treasurer of a municipal corporation. [C13: from Old French *chamberlayn,* of Frankish origin; related to Old High German *chamarling* chamberlain, Latin *camera* CHAMBER] —'**chamberlainˌship** *n.*
chambermaid ('tʃeɪmbəˌmeɪd) *n.* a woman or girl employed to clean and tidy bedrooms, now chiefly in hotels.
chamber music *n.* music for performance by a small group of instrumentalists.
chamber of commerce *n.* (*sometimes caps.*) an organization composed mainly of local businessmen to promote, regulate, and protect their interests.
chamber of trade *n.* (*sometimes caps.*) a national organization representing local chambers of commerce.
chamber orchestra *n.* a small orchestra of about 25 players, used for the authentic performance of baroque and early classical music as well as modern music written specifically for a small orchestra.
chamber organ *n. Music.* a small compact organ used esp. for the authentic performance of preclassical music.
chamber pot *n.* a vessel for urine, used in bedrooms.
chambers ('tʃeɪmbəz) *pl. n.* **1.** a judge's room for hearing private cases not taken in open court. **2.** (in England) the set of rooms occupied by barristers where clients are interviewed (in London, mostly in the Inns of Court). **3.** *Brit. archaic.* a suite of rooms; apartments. **4.** (in the U.S.) the private office of a judge.
Chambertin (*French* ʃɑ̃bɛrtɛ̃) *n.* a dry red burgundy wine produced in Gevrey-Chambertin in E France.
chambray ('ʃæmbreɪ) *n.* a smooth light fabric of cotton, linen, etc., with white weft and a coloured warp. [C19: after *Cambrai;* see CAMBRIC]
chambré ('ʃɑ̃breɪ) *adj.* (of wine) at room temperature. [from French, from *chambrer* to bring (wine) to room temperature, from *chambre* room]
chameleon (kə'miːlɪən) *n.* **1.** any lizard of the family *Chamaeleontidae* of Africa and Madagascar, having long slender legs, a prehensile tail and tongue, and the ability to change colour. **2.** a changeable or fickle person. [C14: from Latin *chamaeleon,* from Greek *khamaileōn,* from *khamai* on the ground + *leōn* LION] —**chameleonic** (kəˌmiːlɪ'ɒnɪk) *adj.* —**cha'meleon-ˌlike** *adj.*
chametz *or* ***chometz*** *Hebrew.* (*Hebrew* xa'mɛtʒ; *Yiddish* 'xɒmətʒ) *n. Judaism.* leavened food which may not be eaten during Passover.
chamfer ('tʃæmfə) *n.* **1.** a narrow flat surface at the corner of a beam, post, etc., esp. one at an angle of 45°. Compare **bevel** (sense 1). ~*vb.* (*tr.*) **2.** to cut such a surface on (a beam, etc.). **3.** another word for **chase**[2] (sense 4). [C16: back formation from *chamfering,* from Old French *chamfrein,* from *chant* edge (see CANT[2]) + *fraindre* to break, from Latin *frangere*] —'**chamferer** *n.*
chamfron, chamfrain ('tʃæmfrən), *or* **chanfron** *n.* a piece of armour for a horse's head. [C14: from Old French *chanfrein,* from *chafresner* to harness, from *chief* head + *frener* to bridle]
chamois ('ʃæmɪ; *French* ʃamwa) *n., pl.* **-ois. 1.** ('ʃæmwɑː). a sure-footed goat antelope, *Rupicapra rupicapra,* inhabiting mountains of Europe and SW Asia, having vertical horns with backward-pointing tips. **2.** a soft suede leather formerly made from the hide of this animal, now obtained from the skins of sheep and goats. **3.** Also called: **chamois leather, shammy (leather), chammy (leather)** ('ʃæmɪ). a piece of such leather or similar material used for polishing, etc. **4.** ('ʃæmwɑː). a yellow to greyish-yellow colour. ~*vb.* (*tr.*) **5.** to dress (leather or skin) like chamois. **6.** to polish with a chamois. [C16: from Old French, from Late Latin *camox* of uncertain origin]
chamomile ('kæməˌmaɪl) *n.* a variant spelling of **camomile.**
champ[1] (tʃæmp) *vb.* **1.** to munch (food) noisily like a horse. **2.** (when *intr.,* often foll. by *on, at,* etc.) to bite (something) nervously or impatiently; gnaw. **3. champ** (*or* **chafe**) **at the bit.** *Informal.* to be impatient to start work, a journey, etc. ~*n.* **4.** the act or noise of champing. **5.** *Ulster dialect.* a dish of mashed potatoes and spring onions or leeks. [C16: probably of imitative origin] —'**champer** *n.*
champ[2] (tʃæmp) *n. Informal.* short for **champion** (sense 1).
champac *or* **champak** ('tʃæmpæk, 'tʃʌmpʌk) *n.* a magnoliaceous tree, *Michelia champaca,* of India and the East Indies. Its fragrant yellow flowers yield an oil used in perfumes and its wood is used for furniture. [C18: from Hindi *campak,* from Sanskrit *campaka,* of Dravidian origin]
champagne (ʃæm'peɪn) *n.* **1.** (*sometimes cap.*) a white sparkling wine produced around Reims and Epernay, France. **2.** (loosely) any effervescent white wine. **3. a.** a colour varying from a pale orange-yellow to a greyish-yellow. **b.** (*as adj.*): *a champagne carpet.*
champagne socialist *n.* a professed socialist who enjoys an extravagant lifestyle.
champaign (ʃæm'peɪn) *n.* **1.** Also called: **campagna.** an expanse of open level or gently undulating country. **2.** an obsolete word for **battlefield.** [C14: from Old French *champaigne,* from Late Latin *campānia;* see CAMPAIGN]
champers ('ʃæmpəz) *n.* a slang name for **champagne.**
champerty ('tʃæmpətɪ) *n., pl.* **-ties.** *Law.* (formerly) an illegal bargain between a party to litigation and an outsider whereby the latter agrees to pay for the action and thereby share in any proceeds recovered. See also **maintenance.** [C14: from Anglo-French *champartie,* from Old French *champart* share of produce, from *champ* field + *part* share (a feudal lord's)] —'**champertous** *adj.*
champignon (tʃæm'pɪnjən) *n.* any of various agaricaceous edible mushrooms, esp. *Marasmius oreades* (**fairy ring champignon**) and the meadow mushroom. [C16: from French, perhaps from Vulgar Latin *campīnus* (unattested) of the field, from Latin *campus* plain, field]
champion ('tʃæmpɪən) *n.* **1. a.** a person who has defeated all others in a competition: *a chess champion.* **b.** (*as modifier*): *a champion team.* **2. a.** a plant or animal that wins first place in a show, etc. **b.** (*as modifier*): *a champion marrow.* **3.** a person who defends a person or cause: *champion of the underprivileged.* **4.** (formerly) a warrior or knight who did battle for another, esp. a king or queen, to defend their rights or honour. ~*adj.* **5.** *Northern English dialect.* first rate; excellent. ~*adv.* **6.** *Northern English dialect.* very well; excellently. ~*vb.* (*tr.*) **7.** to support; defend: *we champion the cause of liberty.* [C13: from Old French, from Late Latin *campiō,* from Latin *campus* field, battlefield]
championship ('tʃæmpɪənˌʃɪp) *n.* **1.** (*sometimes pl.*) any of various contests held to determine a champion. **2.** the title or status of being a champion. **3.** support for or defence of a cause, person, etc.
champlevé *French.* (ʃɑ̃lve; *English* ˌʃæmplə'veɪ) *adj.* **1.** of or relating to a process of enamelling by which grooves are cut into a metal base and filled with enamel colours. ~*n.* **2.** an object enamelled by this process. [C19: from *champ* field (level surface) + *levé* raised]
Chanc. *abbrev. for:* **1.** Chancellor. **2.** Chancery.
chance (tʃɑːns) *n.* **1. a.** the unknown and unpredictable element that causes an event to result in a certain way rather than another, spoken of as a real force. **b.** (*as modifier*): *a chance meeting.* Related adj.: **fortuitous. 2.** fortune; luck; fate. **3.** an opportunity or occasion. **4.** a risk; gamble: *you take a chance with his driving.* **5.** the extent to which an event is likely to occur; probability. **6.** an unpredicted event, esp. a fortunate one: *that was quite a chance, finding him here.* **7.** *Archaic.* an unlucky event; mishap. **8. by chance. a.** accidentally: *he slipped by chance.* **b.** perhaps: *do you by chance have a room?* **9.** (**the**) **chances are ...** it is likely (that) .... **10. on the chance.** acting on the possibility; in case. **11. the main chance.** the opportunity for personal gain (esp. in the phrase **an eye to the main chance**). ~*vb.* **12.** (*tr.*) to risk; hazard: *I'll chance the worst happening.* **13.** to happen by chance; be the case by chance: *I chanced to catch sight of her as she passed.* **14. chance on** (*or* **upon**). to come upon by accident: *he chanced on the solution to his problem.* **15. chance one's arm.** to attempt to do something although the chance of success may be slight. [C13: from Old French *cheance,* from *cheoir* to fall, occur, from Latin *cadere*] —'**chanceful** *adj.* —'**chanceless** *adj.*
chancel ('tʃɑːnsəl) *n.* the part of a church containing the altar, sanctuary, and choir, usually separated from the nave and transepts by a screen. [C14: from Old French, from Latin *cancellī* (plural) lattice]
chancellery *or* **chancellory** ('tʃɑːnsələrɪ, -slərɪ) *n., pl.* **-leries** *or* **-lories. 1.** the building or room occupied by a chancellor's office. **2.** the position, rank, or office of a chancellor. **3.** *U.S.* **a.** the residence or office of an embassy or legation. **b.** the office of a consulate. **4.** *Brit.* another name for a diplomatic **chancery.** [C14: from Anglo-French *chancellerie,* from Old French *chancelier* CHANCELLOR]
chancellor ('tʃɑːnsələ, -slə) *n.* **1.** the head of the government in several European countries. **2.** *U.S.* the president of a university or, in some colleges, the chief administrative officer. **3.** *Brit. and Canadian.* the honorary head of a university. Compare **vice chancellor** (sense 1). **4.** *U.S.* (in some states) the presiding judge of a court of chancery or equity. **5.** *Brit.* the chief secretary of an embassy. **6.** *Christianity.* a clergyman acting as the law officer of a bishop. **7.** *Archaic.* the chief secretary of a prince, nobleman, etc. [C11: from Anglo-French *chanceler,* from Late Latin *cancellārius* porter, secretary, from Latin *cancellī* lattice; see CHANCEL] —'**chancellorˌship** *n.*
Chancellor of the Duchy of Lancaster *n. Brit.* a minister of the crown, nominally appointed as representative of the Queen as Duchess of Lancaster, but in practice chiefly employed on parliamentary work determined by the prime minister.
Chancellor of the Exchequer *n. Brit.* the cabinet minister responsible for finance.
chance-medley *n. Law.* a sudden quarrel in which one party kills another; unintentional but not blameless killing. [C15: from Anglo-French *chance medlee* mixed chance]

chancer ('tʃɑːnsə) *n. Slang.* an unscrupulous or dishonest opportunist who is prepared to try any dubious scheme for making money or furthering his own ends. [C19: from CHANCE + -ER[1]]

chancery ('tʃɑːnsərɪ) *n., pl.* **-ceries.** **1.** Also called: **Chancery Division.** (in England) the Lord Chancellor's court, now a division of the High Court of Justice. **2.** Also called: **court of chancery.** (in the U.S.) a court of equity. **3.** *Brit.* the political section or offices of an embassy or legation. **4.** another name for **chancellery.** **5.** a court of public records; archives. **6.** *Christianity.* a diocesan office under the supervision of a bishop's chancellor, having custody of archives, issuing official enactments, etc. **7. in chancery. a.** *Law.* (of a suit) pending in a court of equity. **b.** *Wrestling, boxing.* (of a competitor's head) locked under an opponent's arm. **c.** in an awkward or helpless situation. [C14: shortened from CHANCELLERY]

chancre ('ʃæŋkə) *n. Pathol.* a small hard nodular growth, which is the first diagnostic sign of acquired syphilis. [C16: from French, from Latin: CANCER] —'**chancrous** *adj.*

chancroid ('ʃæŋkrɔɪd) *n.* **1.** a soft venereal ulcer, esp. of the male genitals, caused by infection with the bacillus *Haemophilus ducreyi.* ~*adj.* **2.** relating to or resembling a chancroid or chancre. —**chan'croidal** *adj.*

chancy *or* **chancey** ('tʃɑːnsɪ) *adj.* **chancier, chanciest.** *Informal.* of uncertain outcome or temperament; risky. —'**chancily** *adv.* —'**chanciness** *n.*

chandelier (ˌʃændɪ'lɪə) *n.* an ornamental hanging light with branches and holders for several candles or bulbs. [C17: from French: candleholder, from Latin CANDELABRUM]

chandelle (ʃæn'dɛl; *French* ʃɑ̃dɛl) *n.* **1.** *Aeronautics.* an abrupt climbing turn almost to the point of stalling, in which an aircraft's momentum is used to increase its rate of climb. ~*vb.* **2.** (*intr.*) to carry out a chandelle. [French, literally: CANDLE]

chandler ('tʃɑːndlə) *n.* **1.** a dealer in a specified trade or merchandise: *corn chandler; ship's chandler.* **2.** a person who makes or sells candles. **3.** *Brit. obsolete.* a retailer of grocery provisions; shopkeeper. [C14: from Old French *chandelier* one who makes or deals in candles, from *chandelle* CANDLE]

chandlery ('tʃɑːndlərɪ) *n., pl.* **-dleries.** **1.** the business, warehouse, or merchandise of a chandler. **2.** a place where candles are kept.

Chandrasekhar limit (ˌtʃændrə'siːkə) *n. Astronomy.* the upper limit to the mass of a white dwarf, equal to 1.44 solar masses. A star having a mass above this limit will continue to collapse to form a neutron star. [C20: named after S. *Chandrasekhar* (born 1910), U.S. astronomer who calculated it]

change (tʃeɪndʒ) *vb.* **1.** to make or become different; alter. **2.** (*tr.*) to replace with or exchange for another: *to change one's name.* **3.** (sometimes foll. by *to* or *into*) to transform or convert or be transformed or converted. **4.** to give and receive (something) in return; interchange: *to change places with someone.* **5.** (*tr.*) to give or receive (money) in exchange for the equivalent sum in a smaller denomination or different currency. **6.** (*tr.*) to remove or replace the coverings of: *to change a baby.* **7.** (when *intr.*, may be foll. by *into* or *out of*) to put on other clothes. **8.** (*intr.*) (of the moon) to pass from one phase to the following one. **9.** to operate (the gear lever of a motor vehicle) in order to change the gear ratio: *to change gear.* **10.** to alight from (one bus, train, etc.) and board another. **11. change face.** to rotate the telescope of a surveying instrument through 180° horizontally and vertically, taking a second sighting of the same object in order to reduce error. **12. change feet.** *Informal.* to put on different shoes, boots, etc. **13. change front. a.** *Military.* to redeploy (a force in the field) so that its main weight of weapons points in another direction. **b.** to alter one's attitude, opinion, etc. **14. change hands.** to pass from one owner to another. **15. change one's mind.** to alter one's decision or opinion. **16. change one's tune.** to alter one's attitude or tone of speech. ~*n.* **17.** the act or fact of changing or being changed. **18.** a variation, deviation, or modification. **19.** the substitution of one thing for another; exchange. **20.** anything that is or may be substituted for something else. **21.** variety or novelty (esp. in the phrase **for a change**): *I want to go to France for a change.* **22.** a different or fresh set, esp. of clothes. **23.** money given or received in return for its equivalent in a larger denomination or in a different currency. **24.** the balance of money given or received when the amount tendered is larger than the amount due. **25.** coins of a small denomination regarded collectively. **26.** (*often cap.*) *Archaic.* a place where merchants meet to transact business; an exchange. **27.** the act of passing from one state or phase to another. **28.** the transition from one phase of the moon to the next. **29.** the order in which a peal of bells may be rung. **30.** *Sport.* short for **changeover** (sense 3b). **31.** *Slang.* desirable or useful information. **32.** *Obsolete.* fickleness or caprice. **33. change of heart.** a profound change of outlook, opinion, etc. **34. get no change out of (someone).** *Slang.* not to be successful in attempts to exploit or extract information from (someone). **35. ring the changes.** to vary the manner or performance of an action that is often repeated. ~See also **change down, changeover, change round, change up.** [C13: from Old French *changier,* from Latin *cambīre* to exchange, barter] —'**changeless** *adj.* —'**changelessly** *adv.* —'**changelessness** *n.* —'**changer** *n.*

changeable ('tʃeɪndʒəb^{ə}l) *adj.* **1.** able to change or be changed; fickle: *changeable weather.* **2.** varying in colour when viewed from different angles or in different lights. —ˌ**changea'bility** *or* '**changeableness** *n.* —'**changeably** *adv.*

change down *vb.* (*intr., adv.*) to select a lower gear when driving.

changeful ('tʃeɪndʒfʊl) *adj.* often changing; inconstant; variable. —'**changefully** *adv.* —'**changefulness** *n.*

changeling ('tʃeɪndʒlɪŋ) *n.* **1.** a child believed to have been exchanged by fairies for the parents' true child. **2.** *Archaic.* **a.** an idiot. **b.** a fickle or changeable person.

change of life *n.* a nontechnical name for **menopause.**

change of venue *n. Law.* the removal of a trial out of one jurisdiction into another.

changeover ('tʃeɪndʒˌəʊvə) *n.* **1.** an alteration or complete reversal from one method, system, or product to another: *a changeover to decimal currency.* **2.** a reversal of a situation, attitude, etc. **3.** *Sport.* **a.** the act of transferring to or being relieved by a team-mate in a relay race, as by handing over a baton, etc. **b.** Also called: **change, takeover.** the point in a relay race at which the transfer is made. **4.** *Sport, chiefly Brit.* the exchange of ends by two teams, esp. at half time. ~*vb.* **change over.** (*adv.*) **5.** to adopt (a completely different position or attitude): *the driver and navigator changed over after four hours.* **6.** (*intr.*) *Sport, chiefly Brit.* (of two teams) to exchange ends of a playing field, etc., as after half time.

change point *n. Surveying.* a point to which a foresight and backsight are taken in levelling; turning point.

change-ringing *n.* **1.** the art of bell-ringing in which a set of bells is rung in an established order which is then changed. **2.** variations on a topic or theme.

change round *vb.* (*adv.*) **1.** to place in or adopt a different or opposite position. ~*n.* **changeround.** **2.** the act of changing to a different position.

change up *vb.* (*intr., adv.*) to select a higher gear when driving.

channel[1] ('tʃæn^{ə}l) *n.* **1.** a broad strait connecting two areas of sea. **2.** the bed or course of a river, stream, or canal. **3.** a navigable course through a body of water. **4.** (*often pl.*) a means or agency of access, communication, etc.: *to go through official channels.* **5.** a course into which something can be directed or moved: *a new channel of thought.* **6.** *Electronics.* **a.** a band of radio frequencies assigned for a particular purpose, esp. the broadcasting of a television signal. **b.** a path for an electrical signal: *a stereo set has two channels.* **c.** a thin semiconductor layer between the source and drain of a field-effect transistor, the conductance of which is controlled by the gate voltage. **7.** a tubular or trough-shaped passage for fluids. **8.** a groove or flute, as in the shaft of a column. **9.** *Computer technol.* **a.** a path along which data can be transmitted between a central processing unit and one or more peripheral devices. **b.** one of the lines along the length of a paper tape on which information can be stored in the form of punched holes. **10.** short for **channel iron.** ~*vb.* **-nels, -nelling, -nelled** *or U.S.* **-nels, -neling, -neled.** **11.** to provide or be provided with a channel or channels; make or cut channels in (something). **12.** (*tr.*) to guide into or convey through a channel or channels: *information was channelled through to them.* **13.** to serve as a medium through whom the spirit of (a person of a former age) allegedly communicates with the living. **14.** (*tr.*) to form a groove or flute in (a column, etc.). [C13: from Old French *chanel,* from Latin *canālis* pipe, groove, conduit; see CANAL] —'**channeller** *n.*

channel[2] ('tʃæn^{ə}l) *n. Nautical.* a flat timber or metal ledge projecting from the hull of a vessel above the chainplates to increase the angle of the shrouds. [C18: variant of earlier *chainwale;* see CHAIN, WALE[1] (planking)]

channel captain *n. Marketing.* the most powerful member, and often the one that decides specifications, in a channel for distributing goods (which usually consists of a manufacturer, wholesaler, and retailer). The channel captain is usually the manufacturer but in the case of a chain store it may be the retailer.

channel iron *or* **bar** *n.* a rolled-steel bar with a U-shaped cross section. Sometimes shortened to **channel.**

channelize *or* **channelise** ('tʃænəlaɪz) *vb.* (*tr.*) to guide through or as if through a channel; provide a channel for.

chanson de geste *French.* (ʃɑ̃sɔ̃ də ʒɛst) *n.* one of a genre of Old French epic poems celebrating heroic deeds, the most famous of which is the *Chanson de Roland.* [literally: song of exploits]

chant (tʃɑːnt) *n.* **1.** a simple song or melody. **2.** a short simple melody in which several words or syllables are assigned to one note, as in the recitation of psalms. **3.** a psalm or canticle performed by using such a melody. **4.** a rhythmic or repetitious slogan, usually spoken or sung, as by sports supporters, etc. **5.** monotonous or singsong intonation in speech. ~*vb.* **6.** to sing or recite (a psalm, prayer, etc.) as a chant. **7.** to intone (a slogan) rhythmically or repetitiously. **8.** to speak or say monotonously as if intoning a chant. [C14: from Old French *chanter* to sing, from Latin *cantāre,* frequentative of *canere* to sing] —'**chantingly** *adv.*

chanter ('tʃɑːntə) *n.* **1.** a person who chants. **2.** the pipe on a set of bagpipes that is provided with finger holes and on which the melody is played.

chanterelle (ˌtʃæntə'rɛl) *n.* any saprophytic basidiomycetous fungus of the genus *Cantharellus,* esp. *C. cibarius,* having an edible yellow funnel-shaped mushroom: family *Cantharellaceae.* [C18:

from French, from New Latin *cantharella,* diminutive of Latin *cantharus* drinking vessel, from Greek *kantharos*]

chanteuse (*French* ʃɑ̃tøz) *n.* a female singer, esp. in a nightclub or cabaret. [French: singer]

chantey ('ʃæntɪ, 'tʃæn-) *n., pl.* **-teys.** the usual U.S. spelling of **shanty**².

chanticleer (ˌtʃæntɪ'klɪə) *or* **chantecler** (ˌtʃæntɪ'klɛə) *n.* a name for a cock, used esp. in fables. [C13: from Old French *Chantecler,* from *chanter cler* to sing clearly]

Chantilly (ʃæn'tɪlɪ; *French* ʃɑ̃tiji) *adj.* (*sometimes not cap.*) (of cream) lightly sweetened and whipped. [after *Chantilly,* a town in N France]

Chantilly lace *n.* (*sometimes not cap.*) a delicate ornamental lace.

chantry ('tʃɑːntrɪ) *n., pl.* **-tries.** *Christianity.* **1.** an endowment for the singing of Masses for the soul of the founder or others designated by him. **2.** a chapel or altar so endowed. **3.** (*as modifier*): *a chantry priest.* [C14: from Old French *chanterie,* from *chanter* to sing; see CHANT]

chanty ('ʃæntɪ, 'tʃæn-) *n., pl.* **-ties.** a variant of **shanty**².

Chanukah *or* **Hanukkah** ('hɑːnəkə, -nʊˌkɑː; *Hebrew* xanu'ka) *n.* the eight-day Jewish festival of lights beginning on the 25th of Kislev and commemorating the rededication of the temple by Judas Maccabaeus in 165 B.C. Also called: **Feast of Dedication, Feast of Lights.** [from Hebrew, literally: a dedication]

chaology (keɪ'ɒlədʒɪ) *n.* the study of chaos theory. —**cha'ologist** *n.*

chaos ('keɪɒs) *n.* **1.** complete disorder; utter confusion. **2.** (*usually cap.*) the disordered formless matter supposed to have existed before the ordered universe. **3.** an obsolete word for **abyss.** [C15: from Latin, from Greek *khaos;* compare CHASM, YAWN] —**chaotic** (keɪ'ɒtɪk) *adj.* —**cha'otically** *adv.*

chaos theory *n.* a theory, applied in various branches of science, that apparently random phenomena have underlying order.

chap¹ (tʃæp) *vb.* **chaps, chapping, chapped. 1.** (of the skin) to make or become raw and cracked, esp. by exposure to cold. **2.** *Scot.* (of a clock) to strike (the hour). **3.** *Scot.* to knock (at a door, window, etc.). ~*n.* **4.** (*usually pl.*) a cracked or sore patch on the skin caused by chapping. **5.** *Scot.* a knock. [C14: probably of Germanic origin; compare Middle Dutch, German *kappen* to chop off]

chap² (tʃæp) *n. Informal.* a man or boy; fellow. [C16 (in the sense: buyer): shortened from CHAPMAN]

chap³ (tʃɒp, tʃæp) *n.* a less common word for **chop**³.

chap. *abbrev. for:* **1.** chaplain. **2.** chapter.

chaparejos (ˌʃæpə'reɪəʊs; *Spanish* tʃapa'rexos) *or* **chaparajos** (ˌʃæpə'reɪəʊs; *Spanish* tʃapa'raxos) *pl. n.* another name for **chaps.** [from Mexican Spanish]

chaparral (ˌtʃæpə'ræl, ˌʃæp-) *n.* (in the southwestern U.S.) a dense growth of shrubs and trees, esp. evergreen oaks. [C19: from Spanish, from *chaparra* evergreen oak]

chaparral cock *n.* another name for **roadrunner.**

chaparral pea *n.* a thorny leguminous Californian shrub, *Pickeringia montana,* with reddish-purple showy flowers.

chapatti *or* **chapati** (tʃə'pætɪ, -'pʌtɪ, -'pɑːtɪ) *n., pl.* **-ti, -tis,** *or* **-ties.** (in Indian cookery) a flat coarse unleavened bread resembling a pancake. [from Hindi]

chapbook ('tʃæpˌbʊk) *n.* a book of popular ballads, stories, etc., formerly sold by chapmen or pedlars.

chape (tʃeɪp) *n.* **1.** a metal tip or trimming for a scabbard. **2.** the metal tongue of a buckle. [C14: from Old French: hood, metal cover, from Late Latin *cappa* CAP] —**'chapeless** *adj.*

chapeau ('ʃæpəʊ; *French* ʃapo) *n., pl.* **-peaux** (-pəʊ, -pəʊz; *French* -po) *or* **-peaus.** a hat. [C16: from French, from Late Latin *cappellus* hood, from *cappa* CAP]

chapel ('tʃæpᵊl) *n.* **1.** a place of Christian worship in a larger building, esp. a place set apart, with a separate altar, in a church or cathedral. **2.** a similar place of worship in or attached to a large house or institution, such as a college, hospital or prison. **3.** a church subordinate to a parish church. **4.** (in Britain) **a.** a Nonconformist place of worship. **b.** Nonconformist religious practices or doctrine. **c.** (*as adj.*): *he is chapel, but his wife is church.* Compare **church** (sense 8). **5. a.** the members of a trade union in a particular newspaper office, printing house, etc. **b.** a meeting of these members. **6.** a printing office. [C13: from Old French *chapele,* from Late Latin *cappella,* diminutive of *cappa* cloak (see CAP); originally denoting the sanctuary where the cloak of St Martin of Tours was kept as a relic]

chapel of ease *n.* a church built to accommodate those living at a distance from the parish church.

chaperon *or* **chaperone** ('ʃæpəˌrəʊn) *n.* **1.** (esp. formerly) an older or married woman who accompanies or supervises a young unmarried woman on social occasions. **2.** someone who accompanies and supervises a group, esp. of young people, usually when in public places. ~*vb.* **3.** to act as a chaperon to. [C14: from Old French, from *chape* hood, protective covering; see CAP] —**chaperonage** ('ʃæpərənɪdʒ) *n.*

chapess (tʃæp'ɛs) *n. Brit. informal.* a woman.

chapfallen ('tʃæpˌfɔːlən) *or* **chopfallen** *adj.* dejected; downhearted; crestfallen. [C16: from CHOPS + FALLEN]

chapiter ('tʃæpɪtə) *n. Architect.* another name for **capital**². [C15: from Old French *chapitre,* from Latin *capitellum* CAPITAL²]

chaplain ('tʃæplɪn) *n.* a Christian clergyman attached to a private chapel of a prominent person or institution or ministering to a military body, professional group, etc: *a military chaplain; a prison chaplain.* [C12: from Old French *chapelain,* from Late Latin *cappellānus,* from *cappella* CHAPEL] —**'chaplaincy, 'chaplainˌship,** *or* **'chaplainry** *n.*

chaplet ('tʃæplɪt) *n.* **1.** an ornamental wreath of flowers, beads, etc., worn on the head. **2.** a string of beads or something similar. **3.** *R.C. Church.* **a.** a string of prayer beads constituting one third of the rosary. **b.** the prayers counted on this string. **4.** a narrow convex moulding in the form of a string of beads; astragal. **5.** a metal support for the core in a casting mould, esp. for the core of a cylindrical pipe. [C14: from Old French *chapelet* garland of roses, from *chapel* hat; see CHAPEAU] —**'chapleted** *adj.*

Chaplinesque ('tʃæplɪn'ɛsk) *adj.* denoting or resembling the humorous style of Charlie Chaplin (1889–1977), British comedian.

chapman ('tʃæpmən) *n., pl.* **-men.** *Archaic.* a trader, esp. an itinerant pedlar. [Old English *cēapman,* from *cēap* buying and selling (see CHEAP)] —**'chapmanˌship** *n.*

chappal ('tʃʌpᵊl) *n.* one of a pair of sandals, usually of leather, worn in India. [from Hindi]

chappie ('tʃæpɪ) *n. Informal.* another word for **chap**².

chaps (tʃæps, ʃæps) *pl. n.* leather overalls without a seat, worn by cowboys. Also called: **chaparejos, chaparajos.** [C19: shortened from CHAPAREJOS]

chapstick ('tʃæpˌstɪk) *n. Chiefly U.S. and Canadian.* a cylinder of a substance for preventing or soothing chapped lips. [C20: from a trademark]

chaptalize *or* **chaptalise** ('tʃæptəˌlaɪz) *vb.* (*tr.*) to add sugar to (a fermenting wine) to increase the alcohol content. [C19: after J. A. *Chaptal* (1756–1832), French chemist who originated the process] —ˌ**chaptali'zation** *or* ˌ**chaptali'sation** *n.*

chapter ('tʃæptə) *n.* **1.** a division of a written work, esp. a narrative, usually titled or numbered. **2.** a sequence of events having a common attribute: *a chapter of disasters.* **3. chapter of accidents. a.** a series of misfortunes. **b.** the unforeseeable course of events. **4.** an episode or period in a life, history, etc. **5.** a numbered reference to that part of a Parliamentary session which relates to a specified Act of Parliament. **6.** a branch of some societies, clubs, etc., esp. of a secret society. **7.** the collective body or a meeting of the canons of a cathedral or collegiate church or of the members of a monastic or knightly order. Related adj.: **capitular. 8.** a general assembly of some organization. **9. chapter and verse.** exact authority for an action or statement. ~*vb.* **10.** (*tr.*) to divide into chapters. [C13: from Old French *chapitre,* from Latin *capitulum,* literally: little head, hence, section of writing, from *caput* head; in Medieval Latin: chapter of scripture or of a religious rule, a gathering for the reading of this, hence, assemblage of clergy]

chapterhouse ('tʃæptəˌhaʊs) *n.* **1.** the building attached to a cathedral, collegiate church, or religious house in which the chapter meets. **2.** *U.S.* the meeting place of a college fraternity or sorority.

char¹ (tʃɑː) *vb.* **chars, charring, charred. 1.** to burn or be burned partially, esp. so as to blacken the surface; scorch. **2.** (*tr.*) to reduce (wood) to charcoal by partial combustion. [C17: short for CHARCOAL]

char² *or* **charr** (tʃɑː) *n., pl.* **char, chars** *or* **charr, charrs.** any of various troutlike fishes of the genus *Salvelinus,* esp. *S. alpinus,* occurring in cold lakes and northern seas: family *Salmonidae* (salmon). [C17: of unknown origin]

char³ (tʃɑː) *n.* **1.** *Informal.* short for **charwoman.** ~*vb.* **chars, charring, charred. 2.** *Brit. informal.* to do housework, cleaning, etc., as a job. [C18: from Old English *cerr*]

char⁴ (tʃɑː) *n. Brit.* a slang word for **tea.** [from Chinese *ch'a*]

charabanc ('ʃærəˌbæŋ; *French* ʃarabɑ̃) *n. Brit.* a motor coach, esp. one used for sightseeing tours. [C19: from French *char-à-bancs,* wagon with seats]

characin ('kærəsɪn) *or* **characid** *n.* any small carnivorous freshwater cyprinoid fish of the family *Characidae,* of Central and South America and Africa. They are similar to the carps but more brightly coloured. [C19: from New Latin *Characinidae,* from *characinus,* from Greek *kharax* a fish, probably the sea bream]

character ('kærɪktə) *n.* **1.** the combination of traits and qualities distinguishing the individual nature of a person or thing. **2.** one such distinguishing quality; characteristic. **3.** moral force; integrity: *a man of character.* **4. a.** reputation, esp. a good reputation. **b.** (*as modifier*): *character assassination.* **5.** a summary or account of a person's qualities and achievements; testimonial: *my last employer gave me a good character.* **6.** capacity, position, or status: *he spoke in the character of a friend rather than a father.* **7.** a person represented in a play, film, story, etc.; role. **8.** an outstanding person: *one of the great characters of the century.* **9.** *Informal.* an odd, eccentric, or unusual person: *he's quite a character.* **10.** an informal word for **person:** *a shady character.* **11.** a symbol used in a writing system, such as a letter of the alphabet. **12.** Also called: **sort.** *Printing.* any single letter, numeral, punctuation mark, or symbol cast as a type. **13.** *Computer technol.* any letter, numeral, etc., which is a unit of information and can be represented uniquely by a binary pattern. **14.** a style of writing or printing. **15.** *Genetics.* any structure, function, attribute, etc., in an organism that is determined by a gene or group of genes. **16.** a short prose sketch of a distinctive type of person, usually representing a vice or virtue. **17. in** (*or* **out of**) **character.** typical (or not typical) of the apparent character of a person or thing. *~vb.* (*tr.*) **18.** to write, print, inscribe, or engrave. **19.** *Rare.* to portray or represent. [C14: from Latin: distinguishing mark, from Greek *kharaktēr* engraver's tool, from *kharassein* to engrave, stamp] —'**characterful** *adj.* —'**characterless** *adj.*

character actor *n.* an actor who specializes in playing odd or eccentric characters.

character armour *n. Psychol.* the defence an individual exhibits to others and to himself to disguise his underlying weaknesses.

character assassination *n.* the act of deliberately attempting to destroy a person's reputation by defamatory remarks.

character code *n. Computer technol.* a machine-readable code that identifies a specified character or a set of such codes.

characteristic (ˌkærɪktəˈrɪstɪk) *n.* **1.** a distinguishing quality, attribute, or trait. **2.** *Maths.* **a.** the integral part of a common logarithm, indicating the order of magnitude of the associated number: *the characteristic of 2.4771 is 2.* Compare **mantissa. b.** another name for **exponent** (sense 4), esp. in number representation in computing. *~adj.* **3.** indicative of a distinctive quality, etc.; typical. —ˌ**character'istically** *adv.*

characteristic curve *n. Photog.* a graph of the density of a particular photographic material plotted against the logarithm of the exposure producing this density.

characteristic function *n.* **1.** *Maths.* a function that assigns the value 1 to the members of a given set and the value 0 to its nonmembers. **2.** *Statistics.* a function derived from the probability distribution function that enables the distribution of the sum of given random variables to be analysed.

characterization *or* **characterisation** (ˌkærɪktəraɪˈzeɪʃən) *n.* **1.** description of character, traits, etc. **2.** the act of characterizing.

characterize *or* **characterise** (ˈkærɪktəˌraɪz) *vb.* (*tr.*) **1.** to be a characteristic of: *loneliness characterized the place.* **2.** to distinguish or mark as a characteristic. **3.** to describe or portray the character of. —'**characterˌizable** *or* '**characterˌisable** *adj.* —'**characterˌizer** *or* '**characterˌiser** *n.*

character printer *n. Computer technol.* an output device that prints one character at a time.

character recognition *n. Computer technol.* a magnetic or optical process used to detect the shape of individual characters printed or written on paper.

character sketch *n.* a brief description or portrayal of a person's character, qualities, etc.

character type *n. Psychol.* a cluster of personality traits commonly occurring together in an individual.

charactery (ˈkærɪktərɪ, -trɪ) *n., pl.* **-teries.** *Archaic.* **1.** the use of symbols to express thoughts. **2.** the group of symbols so used.

charade (ʃəˈrɑːd) *n.* **1.** an episode or act in the game of charades. **2.** *Chiefly Brit.* an absurd act; travesty.

charades (ʃəˈrɑːdz) *n.* (*functioning as sing.*) a parlour game in which one team acts out each syllable of a word, the other team having to guess the word. [C18: from French *charade* entertainment, from Provençal *charrado* chat, from *charra* chatter, of imitative origin]

charas (ˈtʃɑːrəs) *n.* another name for **hashish.** [C19: from Hindi]

charcoal (ˈtʃɑːˌkəʊl) *n.* **1.** a black amorphous form of carbon made by heating wood or other organic matter in the absence of air: used as a fuel, in smelting metal ores, in explosives, and as an absorbent. See **activated carbon. 2.** a stick or pencil of this for drawing. **3.** a drawing done in charcoal. **4.** short for **charcoal grey.** *~vb.* **5.** (*tr.*) to write, draw, or blacken with charcoal. [C14: from *char* (origin obscure) + COAL]

charcoal-burner *n.* (formerly) a person whose work was making charcoal by burning wood.

charcoal grey *n.* **a.** a very dark grey colour. **b.** (*as adj.*): *charcoal-grey trousers.*

chard (tʃɑːd) *n.* a variety of beet, *Beta vulgaris cicla,* with large succulent leaves and thick stalks, used as a vegetable. Also called: **Swiss chard, leaf beet, seakale beet.** [C17: probably from French *carde* edible leafstalk of the artichoke, but associated also with French *chardon* thistle, both ultimately from Latin *carduus* thistle; see CARDOON]

Chardonnay (ˌʃɑːdəˈneɪ) *n.* (*sometimes not cap.*) **1.** a white grape grown in the Burgundy region of France, Australia, California, New Zealand and elsewhere, used for making wine. **2.** any of various white wines made from this grape. [French]

charge (tʃɑːdʒ) *vb.* **1.** to set or demand (a price): *he charges too much for his services.* **2.** (*tr.*) to hold financially liable; enter a debit against. **3.** (*tr.*) to enter or record as an obligation against a person or his account. **4.** (*tr.*) to accuse or impute a fault to (a person, etc.), as formally in a court of law. **5.** (*tr.*) to command; place a burden upon or assign responsibility to: *I was charged to take the message to headquarters.* **6.** to make a rush at or sudden attack upon (a person or thing). **7.** (*tr.*) to fill (a receptacle) with the proper or appropriate quantity. **8.** (often foll. by *up*) to cause (an accumulator, capacitor, etc.) to take or store electricity or (of an accumulator) to have electricity fed into it. **9.** to fill or suffuse or to be filled or suffused with matter by dispersion, solution, or absorption: *to charge water with carbon dioxide.* **10.** (*tr.*) to fill or suffuse with feeling, emotion, etc.: *the atmosphere was charged with excitement.* **11.** (*tr.*) *Law.* (of a judge) to address (a jury) authoritatively. **12.** (*tr.*) to load (a firearm). **13.** (*tr.*) to aim (a weapon) in position ready for use. **14.** (*tr.*) *Heraldry.* to paint (a shield, banner, etc.) with a charge. **15.** (*intr.*) (of hunting dogs) to lie down at command. *~n.* **16.** a price charged for some article or service; cost. **17.** a financial liability, such as a tax. **18.** a debt or a book entry recording it. **19.** an accusation or allegation, such as a formal accusation of a crime in law. **20. a.** an onrush, attack, or assault. **b.** the call to such an attack in battle. **21.** custody or guardianship. **22.** a person or thing committed to someone's care. **23. a.** a cartridge or shell. **b.** the explosive required to discharge a firearm or other weapon. **c.** an amount of explosive material to be detonated at any one time. **24.** the quantity of anything that a receptacle is intended to hold. **25.** *Physics.* **a.** the attribute of matter responsible for all electrical phenomena, existing in two forms to which the signs negative and positive are arbitrarily assigned. **b.** a similar property of a body or system determined by the extent to which it contains an excess or deficiency of electrons. **c.** a quantity of electricity determined by the product of an electric current and the time for which it flows, measured in coulombs. **d.** the total amount of electricity stored in a capacitor. **e.** the total amount of electricity held in an accumulator, usually measured in ampere-hours. Symbol: q or Q **26.** a load or burden. **27.** a duty or responsibility; control. **28.** a command, injunction, or order. **29.** *Slang.* a thrill. **30.** *Law.* the address made by a judge to the jury at the conclusion of the evidence. **31.** *Heraldry.* a design, device, or image depicted on heraldic arms: *a charge of three lions.* **32.** the solid propellant used in rockets, sometimes including the inhibitor. **33. in charge.** in command. **34. in charge of. a.** having responsibility for. **b.** *U.S.* under the care of. [C13: from Old French *chargier* to load, from Late Latin *carricāre;* see CARRY]

chargeable (ˈtʃɑːdʒəbəl) *adj.* **1.** charged or liable to be charged. **2.** liable to result in a legal charge. —'**chargeableness** *or* ˌ**chargea'bility** *n.* —'**chargeably** *adv.*

charge account *n.* another term for **credit account.**

charge-cap (ˈtʃɑːdʒˌkæp) *vb.* (*tr.*) **-caps, -capping, -capped.** (in Britain) to impose on (a local authority) an upper limit on the community charge it may levy. —'**charge-ˌcapping** *n.*

charge card *n.* a card issued by a chain store, shop, or organization, that enables customers to obtain goods and services for which they pay at a later date.

charge carrier *n.* an electron, hole, or ion that transports the electric charge in an electric current.

charge-coupled device *n. Computer technol.* a coupled device for storing information by utilizing minute pockets of circulating electrical charge. Abbrev.: **CCD.**

chargé d'affaires (ˈʃɑːʒeɪ dæˈfɛə; *French* ʃarʒe dafɛr) *n., pl.* **chargés d'affaires** (ˈʃɑːʒeɪ, -ʒeɪz; *French* ʃarʒe). **1.** the temporary head of a diplomatic mission in the absence of the ambassador or minister. **2.** the head of a diplomatic mission of the lowest level. [C18: from French: (one) charged with affairs]

charge density *n.* the electric charge per unit volume of a medium or body or per unit area of a surface.

charge hand *n. Brit.* a workman whose grade of responsibility is just below that of a foreman.

charge nurse *n. Brit.* a nurse in charge of a ward in a hospital: the male equivalent of **sister.**

charge of quarters *n. U.S.* a member of the armed forces who handles administration in his unit, esp. after duty hours.

charger[1] (ˈtʃɑːdʒə) *n.* **1.** a person or thing that charges. **2.** a large strong horse formerly ridden into battle. **3.** a device for charging or recharging an accumulator.

charger[2] (ˈtʃɑːdʒə) *n. Antiques.* a large dish for serving at table or for display. [C14 *chargeour* something to bear a load, from *chargen* to CHARGE]

charge sheet *n. Brit.* a document on which a police officer enters details of the charge against a prisoner and the court in which he will appear.

charily (ˈtʃɛərɪlɪ) *adv.* **1.** cautiously; carefully. **2.** sparingly.

chariness (ˈtʃɛərɪnɪs) *n.* the state of being chary.

Chari-Nile (ˈtʃɑːrɪˈnaɪl) *n.* **1.** a group of languages of E Africa, now generally regarded as a branch of the Nilo-Saharan family, spoken in parts of the Sudan, Zaïre, Uganda, Kenya, Tanzania, and adjacent countries. *~adj.* **2.** relating to or belonging to this group of languages.

chariot (ˈtʃærɪət) *n.* **1.** a two-wheeled horse-drawn vehicle used in ancient Egypt, Greece, Rome, etc., in war, races, and processions. **2.** a light four-wheeled horse-drawn ceremonial carriage. **3.** *Poetic.* any stately vehicle. [C14: from Old French, augmentative of *char* CAR]

charioteer (ˌtʃærɪəˈtɪə) *n.* the driver of a chariot.

charisma (kəˈrɪzmə) *or* **charism** (ˈkærɪzəm) *n.* **1.** a special personal quality or power of an individual making him capable of influencing or inspiring large numbers of people. **2.** a quality inherent in a thing which inspires great enthusiasm and devotion. **3.** *Christianity.* a divinely bestowed power or talent. [C17: from Church Latin, from Greek *kharisma,* from *kharis* grace, favour] —**charismatic** (ˌkærɪzˈmætɪk) *adj.*

charismatic movement *n. Christianity.* any of various groups, within existing denominations, that emphasize communal prayer and the charismatic gifts of speaking in tongues, healing, etc.

charitable (ˈtʃærɪtəbᵊl) *adj.* **1.** generous in giving to the needy. **2.** kind or lenient in one's attitude towards others. **3.** concerned with or involving charity. —ˈ**charitableness** *n.* —ˈ**charitably** *adv.*

charity (ˈtʃærɪtɪ) *n., pl.* **-ties. 1. a.** the giving of help, money, food, etc., to those in need. **b.** (*as modifier*): *a charity show.* **2. a.** an institution or organization set up to provide help, money, etc., to those in need. **b.** (*as modifier*): *charity funds.* **3.** the help, money, etc., given to the needy; alms. **4.** a kindly and lenient attitude towards people. **5.** love of one's fellow men. [C13: from Old French *charite,* from Latin *cāritās* affection, love, from *cārus* dear]

charivari (ˌʃɑːrɪˈvɑːrɪ), **shivaree,** *or esp. U.S.* **chivaree** *n.* **1.** a discordant mock serenade to newlyweds, made with pans, kettles, etc. **2.** a confused noise; din. [C17: from French, from Late Latin *caribaria* headache, from Greek *karēbaria,* from *karē* head + *barus* heavy]

charkha *or* **charka** (ˈtʃɑːkə) *n.* (in India) a spinning wheel, esp. for cotton. [from Hindi]

charlady (ˈtʃɑːˌleɪdɪ) *n., pl.* **-dies.** another name for **charwoman.**

charlatan (ˈʃɑːlətᵊn) *n.* someone who professes knowledge or expertise, esp. in medicine, that he does not have; quack. [C17: from French, from Italian *ciarlatano,* from *ciarlare* to chatter] —ˈ**charlatanˌism** *or* ˈ**charlatanry** *n.* —ˌ**charlatanˈistic** *adj.*

Charles' law (tʃɑːlz) *n.* the principle that all gases expand equally for the same rise of temperature if they are held at constant pressure: also that the pressures of all gases increase equally for the same rise of temperature if they are held at constant volume. The law is now known to be only approximately true. Also called: **Gay-Lussac's law.** [C18: named after Jacques A. C. *Charles* (1746–1823), French physicist who first formulated it]

Charles's Wain (weɪn) *n.* another name for the **Plough.** [Old English *Carles wægn,* from *Carl* Charlemagne (?742–814 A.D.) + *wægn* WAIN]

charleston (ˈtʃɑːlstən) *n.* a fast rhythmic dance of the 1920s, characterized by kicking and by twisting of the legs from the knee down. [C20: named after *Charleston,* South Carolina]

charley horse (ˈtʃɑːlɪ) *n. U.S. and Canadian informal.* muscle stiffness or cramp following strenuous athletic exercise. [C19: of uncertain origin]

charlie (ˈtʃɑːlɪ) *n. Brit. informal.* a silly person; fool. [C20: shortened from *Charlie Hunt,* rhyming slang for CUNT]

Charlie[1] (ˈtʃɑːlɪ) *n. Communications.* a code word for the letter *c.*

Charlie[2] *or* **Charley** (ˈtʃɑːlɪ) *n. U.S. and Austral. military slang.* a member of the Vietcong or the Vietcong collectively: *Charlie hit us with rockets.* [shortened from *Victor Charlie,* communications code for *VC,* abbreviation of *Vietcong*]

Charlie[3] (ˈtʃɑːlɪ) *n. Slang.* cocaine.

charlock (ˈtʃɑːlɒk) *n.* **1.** Also called: **wild mustard.** a weedy cruciferous Eurasian plant, *Sinapsis arvensis* (or *Brassica kaber*), with hairy stems and foliage and yellow flowers. **2. white charlock.** Also called: **wild radish, runch** (rʌntʃ). a cruciferous plant, *Raphanus raphanistrum,* with yellow, mauve, or white flowers and podlike fruits. [Old English *cerlic,* of obscure origin]

charlotte (ˈʃɑːlət) *n.* **1.** a baked dessert served hot or cold, commonly made with fruit and layers or a casing of bread or cake crumbs, sponge cake, etc.: *apple charlotte.* **2.** short for **charlotte russe.** [C19: from French, from the name *Charlotte*]

charlotte russe (ruːs) *n.* a cold dessert made in a mould with sponge fingers enclosing a mixture of whipped cream, custard, etc. [French: Russian charlotte]

charm[1] (tʃɑːm) *n.* **1.** the quality of pleasing, fascinating, or attracting people. **2.** a pleasing or attractive feature. **3.** a small object worn or kept for supposed magical powers of protection; amulet; talisman. **4.** a trinket worn on a bracelet. **5.** a magic spell; enchantment. **6.** a formula or action used in casting such a spell. **7.** *Physics.* a property of certain elementary particles, used to explain some scattering experiments. **8. like a charm.** perfectly; successfully. *~vb.* **9.** to attract or fascinate; delight greatly. **10.** to cast a magic spell on. **11.** to protect, influence, or heal, supposedly by magic. **12.** (*tr.*) to influence or obtain by personal charm: *he charmed them into believing him.* [C13: from Old French *charme,* from Latin *carmen* song, incantation, from *canere* to sing]

charm[2] (tʃɑːm) *n. Southwest English dialect.* a loud noise, as of a number of people chattering or of birds singing. [C16: variant of CHIRM]

charmed (tʃɑːmd) *adj.* **1.** delighted or fascinated: *a charmed audience.* **2.** seemingly protected by a magic spell: *he bears a charmed life.* **3.** *Physics.* possessing charm: *a charmed quark.*

charmer (ˈtʃɑːmə) *n.* **1.** an attractive person. **2.** a person claiming or seeming to have magical powers.

Charmeuse (ʃɑːˈmuːz; *French* ʃarmøz) *n. Trademark.* a lightweight fabric with a satin-like finish.

charming (ˈtʃɑːmɪŋ) *adj.* delightful; pleasant; attractive. —ˈ**charmingly** *adv.*

charnel (ˈtʃɑːnᵊl) *n.* **1.** short for **charnel house.** *~adj.* **2.** ghastly; sepulchral; deathly. [C14: from Old French: burial place, from Latin *carnālis* fleshly, CARNAL]

charnel house *n.* (esp. formerly) a building or vault where corpses or bones are deposited.

Charollais *or* **Charolais** (ˈʃærəˌleɪ) *n.* a breed of large white beef cattle. [C19: from French: named after Monts du *Charollais,* E France]

charpoy (ˈtʃɑːpɔɪ) *or* **charpai** (ˈtʃɑːpaɪ) *n.* a bedstead of woven webbing or hemp stretched on a wooden frame on four legs, common in India. [C19: from Urdu *cārpāī*]

charqui (ˈtʃɑːkɪ) *n.* meat, esp. beef, cut into strips and dried. [C18: from Spanish, from Quechuan] —**charquid** (ˈtʃɑːkɪd) *adj.*

charr (tʃɑː) *n., pl.* **charr** *or* **charrs.** a variant spelling of **char** (the fish).

chart (tʃɑːt) *n.* **1.** a map designed to aid navigation by sea or air. **2.** an outline map, esp. one on which weather information is plotted. **3.** a sheet giving graphical, tabular, or diagrammatical information. **4.** another name for **graph** (sense 1). **5.** *Astrology.* another word for **horoscope** (sense 3). **6. the charts.** *Informal.* the lists produced weekly from various sources of the best-selling pop singles and albums. *~vb.* **7.** (*tr.*) to make a chart of. **8.** (*tr.*) to make a detailed plan of. **9.** (*tr.*) to plot or outline the course of. **10.** (*intr.*) *Pop music slang.* (of a record) to appear in the charts (sense 6). [C16: from Latin, from Greek *khartēs* papyrus, literally: something on which to make marks; related to Greek *kharattein* to engrave] —ˈ**chartable** *adj.*

charter (ˈtʃɑːtə) *n.* **1.** a formal document from the sovereign or state incorporating a city, bank, college, etc., and specifying its purposes and rights. **2.** (*sometimes cap.*) a formal document granting or demanding from the sovereign power of a state certain rights or liberties. **3.** a document issued by a society or an organization authorizing the establishment of a local branch or chapter. **4.** a special privilege or exemption. **5.** (*often cap.*) the fundamental principles of an organization; constitution: *the Charter of the United Nations.* **6. a.** the hire or lease of transportation. **b.** the agreement or contract regulating this. **c.** (*as modifier*): *a charter flight.* **7.** *Maritime law.* another word for **charter party.** *~vb.* (*tr.*) **8.** to lease or hire by charter party. **9.** to hire (a vehicle, etc.). **10.** to grant a charter of incorporation or liberties to (a group or person). [C13: from Old French *chartre,* from Latin *chartula* a little paper, from *charta* leaf of papyrus; see CHART] —ˈ**charterer** *n.*

charterage (ˈtʃɑːtərɪdʒ) *n. Rare.* **1.** the act or practice of chartering, esp. ships. **2.** a shipbroker's fee.

charter colony *n. American history.* a colony, such as Virginia or Massachusetts, created by royal charter under the control of an individual, trading company, etc., and exempt from interference by the Crown.

chartered accountant *n.* (in Britain) an accountant who has passed the professional examinations of the Institute of Chartered Accountants in England and Wales, the Institute of Chartered Accountants of Scotland, or the Institute of Chartered Accountants in Ireland. Abbrev.: **CA.**

chartered club *n. N.Z.* a private club licensed to serve alcohol to members.

chartered engineer *n.* (in Britain) an engineer who is registered with the Engineering Council as having the scientific and technical knowledge and practical experience to satisfy its professional requirements. Abbrev.: **CEng.**

chartered surveyor *n.* (in Britain) a member of the Royal Institution of Chartered Surveyors.

Charterhouse (ˈtʃɑːtəˌhaʊs) *n.* a Carthusian monastery. [C16: changed by folk etymology from Anglo-French *chartrouse,* after *Chartosse* (now Saint-Pierre-de-Chartreuse), village near Grenoble, France, the original home of the Carthusian order]

charter member *n.* an original or founder member of a society or organization.

charter party *n.* **1.** *Maritime law.* an agreement for the hire of all or part of a ship for a specified voyage or period of time. **2.** an individual or group that charters a ship, etc.

Chartism (ˈtʃɑːˌtɪzəm) *n. English history.* the principles of the reform movement in England from 1838 to 1848, which included manhood suffrage, payment of Members of Parliament, equal electoral districts, annual parliaments, voting by ballot, and the abolition of property qualifications for MPs. [named after the *People's Charter,* a document which stated their aims] —ˈ**Chartist** *n., adj.*

chartist (ˈtʃɑːtɪst) *n.* a stock market specialist who analyses and predicts market trends from graphs of recent price and volume movements of selected securities.

chartless (ˈtʃɑːtlɪs) *adj.* not mapped; uncharted.

chartography (kɑːˈtɒgrəfɪ) *n. Rare.* a variant spelling of **cartography.** —**charˈtographer** *n.* —**chartographic** (ˌkɑːtəˈgræfɪk) *or* ˌ**chartoˈgraphical** *adj.* —ˌ**chartoˈgraphically** *adv.*

chartreuse (ʃɑːˈtrɜːz; *French* ʃartrøz) *n.* **1.** either of two liqueurs, green or yellow, made from herbs and flowers. **2. a.** a colour varying from a clear yellowish-green to a strong greenish-yellow. **b.** (*as adj.*): *a chartreuse dress.* [C19: from French, after *La Grande Chartreuse,* monastery near Grenoble, France, where the liqueur is produced]

chartulary (ˈtʃɑːtjʊlərɪ) *n., pl.* **-laries.** a variant of **cartulary.**

charwoman (ˈtʃɑːˌwʊmən) *n., pl.* **-women.** *Brit.* a woman who is hired to clean, tidy, etc., in a house or office.

chary (ˈtʃɛərɪ) *adj.* **charier, chariest. 1.** wary; careful. **2.** choosy; finicky. **3.** shy. **4.** sparing; mean. [Old English *cearig;* related to *caru* CARE, Old High German *charag* sorrowful]

chase[1] (tʃeɪs) *vb.* **1.** to follow or run after (a person, animal, or goal) persistently or quickly. **2.** (*tr.*; often foll. by *out, away,* or *off*) to force to run (away); drive (out). **3.** (*tr.*) *Informal.* to court (a member of the opposite sex) in an unsubtle manner. **4.** (*tr.*; often foll. by *up*) *Informal.* to pursue persistently and energetically in order to obtain results, information, etc.: *chase up the builders and get a delivery date.* **5.** (*intr.*) *Informal.* to hurry; rush. ~*n.* **6.** the act of chasing; pursuit. **7.** any quarry that is pursued. **8.** *Brit.* an unenclosed area of land where wild animals are preserved to be hunted. **9.** *Brit.* the right to hunt a particular quarry over the land of others. **10. the chase.** the act or sport of hunting. **11.** short for **steeplechase.** **12.** *Real tennis.* a ball that bounces twice, requiring the point to be played again. **13. give chase.** to pursue (a person, animal, or thing) actively. [C13: from Old French *chacier,* from Vulgar Latin *captiāre* (unattested), from Latin *captāre* to pursue eagerly, from *capere* to take; see CATCH] —ˈ**chaseable** *adj.*

chase[2] (tʃeɪs) *n.* **1.** *Letterpress printing.* a rectangular steel or cast-iron frame into which metal type and blocks making up a page are locked for printing or plate-making. **2.** the part of a gun barrel from the front of the trunnions to the muzzle. **3.** a groove or channel, esp. one that is cut in a wall to take a pipe, cable, etc. ~*vb.* (*tr.*) **4.** Also: **chamfer.** to cut a groove, furrow, or flute in (a surface, column, etc.). [C17 (in the sense: frame for letterpress matter): probably from French *châsse* frame (in the sense: bore of a cannon, etc.): from Old French *chas* enclosure, from Late Latin *capsus* pen for animals; both from Latin *capsa* CASE[2]]

chase[3] (tʃeɪs) *vb.* (*tr.*) **1.** Also: **enchase.** to ornament (metal) by engraving or embossing. **2.** to form or finish (a screw thread) with a chaser. [C14: from Old French *enchasser* ENCHASE]

chaser[1] (ˈtʃeɪsə) *n.* **1.** a person or thing that chases. **2.** a drink drunk after another of a different kind, as beer after spirits. **3.** a cannon on a vessel situated either at the bow (**bow chaser**) or the stern (**stern chaser**) and used during pursuit by or of another vessel.

chaser[2] (ˈtʃeɪsə) *n.* **1.** a person who engraves. **2.** a lathe cutting tool for accurately finishing a screw thread, having a cutting edge consisting of several repetitions of the thread form.

chasm (ˈkæzəm) *n.* **1.** a deep cleft in the ground; abyss. **2.** a break in continuity; gap. **3.** a wide difference in interests, feelings, etc. [C17: from Latin *chasma,* from Greek *khasma;* related to Greek *khainein* to gape] —**chasmal** (ˈkæzməl) *or* ˈ**chasmic** *adj.*

chasmogamy (kæzˈmɒɡəmɪ) *adj. Botany.* the production of flowers that open, so as to expose the reproductive organs and allow cross-pollination. Compare **cleistogamy.** [C20: from New Latin (*flores*) *chasmogami* from Greek *khasma* CHASM + -GAMY] —**chasˈmogamous** *adj.*

chassé (ˈʃæseɪ) *n.* **1.** one of a series of gliding steps in ballet in which the same foot always leads. **2.** three consecutive dance steps, two fast and one slow, to four beats of music. ~*vb.* **-sés, -séing, -séd.** **3.** (*intr.*) to perform either of these steps. [C19: from French: a chasing]

chassepot (ˈʃæspəʊ; *French* ʃaspo) *n.* a breech-loading bolt-action rifle formerly used by the French Army. [C19: named after A. A. *Chassepot* (1833–1905), French gunsmith who invented it]

chasseur (ʃæˈsɜː; *French* ʃasœr) *n.* **1.** *French Army.* a member of a unit specially trained and equipped for swift deployment. **2.** (in some parts of Europe, esp. formerly) a uniformed attendant, esp. one in the livery of a huntsman. ~*adj.* **3.** (*often postpositive*) designating or cooked in a sauce consisting of white wine and mushrooms. [C18: from French: huntsman]

Chassidism, Chasidism, Hassidism, *or* **Hasidism** (ˈhæsɪdˌɪzəm) *n.* a Jewish religious movement founded in Poland about 1750, characterized by religious zeal and a spirit of prayer, joy, and charity. —**Chassidic, Chasidic, Hassidic,** *or* **Hasidic** (həˈsɪdɪk) *adj.*

chassis (ˈʃæsɪ) *n., pl.* **-sis** (-sɪz). **1.** the steel frame, wheels, engine, and mechanical parts of a motor vehicle, to which the body is attached. **2.** *Electronics.* a mounting for the circuit components of an electrical or electronic device, such as a radio or television. **3.** the landing gear of an aircraft. **4.** *Obsolete.* a wooden framework for a window, screen, etc. **5.** the frame on which a cannon carriage moves backwards and forwards. **6.** *Slang.* the body of a person, esp. a woman. [C17 (meaning: window frame): from French *châssis* frame, from Vulgar Latin *capsicum* (unattested), ultimately from Latin *capsa* CASE[2]]

chaste (tʃeɪst) *adj.* **1.** not having experienced sexual intercourse; virginal. **2.** abstaining from unlawful or immoral sexual intercourse. **3.** (of conduct, speech, etc.) pure; decent; modest. **4.** (of style or taste) free from embellishment; simple; restrained. [C13: from Old French, from Latin *castus* pure; compare CASTE] —ˈ**chastely** *adv.* —ˈ**chasteness** *n.*

chasten (ˈtʃeɪsᵊn) *vb.* (*tr.*) **1.** to bring to a state of submission; subdue; tame. **2.** to discipline or correct by punishment. **3.** to moderate; restrain; temper. [C16: from Old French *chastier,* from Latin *castigāre;* see CASTIGATE] —ˈ**chastener** *n.* —ˈ**chasteningly** *adv.*

chaste tree *n.* a small ornamental verbenaceous tree, *Vitex agnus-castus,* of S Europe and SW Asia, with spikes of pale blue flowers.

chastise (tʃæsˈtaɪz) *vb.* (*tr.*) **1.** to discipline or punish, esp. by beating. **2.** to scold severely. [C14 *chastisen,* irregularly from *chastien* to CHASTEN] —**chasˈtisable** *adj.* —**chastisement** (ˈtʃæstɪzmənt, tʃæsˈtaɪz-) *n.* —**chasˈtiser** *n.*

chastity (ˈtʃæstɪtɪ) *n.* **1.** the state of being chaste; purity. **2.** abstention from sexual intercourse; virginity or celibacy: *a vow of chastity.* [C13: from Old French *chasteté,* from Latin *castitās,* from *castus* CHASTE]

chastity belt *n.* a locking beltlike device with a loop designed to go between a woman's legs in order to prevent her from having sexual intercourse.

chasuble (ˈtʃæzjʊbᵊl) *n. Christianity.* a long sleeveless outer vestment worn by a priest when celebrating Mass. [C13: from French, from Late Latin *casubla* garment with a hood, apparently from *casula* cloak, literally: little house, from Latin *casa* cottage]

chat[1] (tʃæt) *n.* **1.** informal conversation or talk conducted in an easy familiar manner. **2.** any Old World songbird of the subfamily *Turdinae* (thrushes, etc.) having a harsh chattering cry. See also **stonechat, whinchat.** **3.** any of various North American warblers, such as *Icteria virens* (**yellow-breasted chat**). **4.** any of various Australian wrens (family *Muscicapidae*) of the genus *Ephthianura* and other genera. ~*vb.* **chats, chatting, chatted.** (*intr.*) **5.** to talk in an easy familiar way. ~See also **chat up.** [C16: short for CHATTER]

chat[2] (tʃæt) *n.* **1.** the catkin of the willow. **2.** the flower of the plantain. [C15: from French *chat* cat, referring to the furry appearance]

chateau *or* **château** (ˈʃætəʊ; *French* ʃɑto) *n., pl.* **-teaux** (-təʊ, -təʊz; *French* -to) *or* **-teaus.** **1.** a country house, castle, or manor house, esp. in France. **2.** (in Quebec) the residence of a seigneur or (formerly) a governor. **3.** (in the name of a wine) estate or vineyard. **4. chateau bottled.** (of wine) bottled on the estate where it was made. [C18: from French, from Old French *chastel,* from Latin *castellum* fortress, CASTLE]

Chateaubriand (*French* ʃɑtobrijɑ̃) *n.* a thick steak cut from the fillet of beef. [C19: named after F. R. *Chateaubriand* (1768–1848), French writer and statesman]

chateau wine *n.* a wine produced from any of certain vineyards in the Bordeaux region of France.

chatelain (ˈʃætᵊˌleɪn; *French* ʃɑtlɛ̃) *n.* the keeper or governor of a castle. [C16: from French, from Latin *castellānus* occupant of a CASTLE]

chatelaine (ˈʃætəˌleɪn; *French* ʃɑtlɛn) *n.* **1.** (esp. formerly) the mistress of a castle or fashionable household. **2.** a chain or clasp worn at the waist by women in the 16th to the 19th centuries, with handkerchief, keys, etc., attached. **3.** a decorative pendant worn on the lapel.

chatline (ˈtʃætˌlaɪn) *n.* a former telephone service enabling callers to join in general conversation with each other.

chatoyant (ʃəˈtɔɪənt) *adj.* **1.** having changeable lustre; twinkling. **2.** (of a gem, esp. a cabochon) displaying a band of light reflected off inclusions of other minerals. ~*n.* **3.** a gemstone with a changeable lustre, such as a **cat's eye.** [C18: from French, from *chatoyer* to gleam like a cat's eyes, from *chat* CAT] —**chaˈtoyancy** *n.*

chat show *n. Brit.* a television or radio show in which guests are interviewed informally. Also called: **talk show.**

chattel (ˈtʃætᵊl) *n.* **1.** (*often pl.*) *Property law.* **a. chattel personal.** an item of movable personal property, such as furniture, domestic animals, etc. **b. chattel real.** an interest in land less than a freehold, such as a lease. **2. goods and chattels.** personal property. [C13: from Old French *chatel* personal property, from Medieval Latin *capitāle* wealth; see CAPITAL[1]]

chattel house *n.* (esp. in Barbados) a movable wooden dwelling, usually set on a foundation of loose stones on rented land.

chattel mortgage *n. U.S. and Canadian.* a mortgage on movable personal property.

chatter (ˈtʃætə) *vb.* **1.** to speak (about unimportant matters) rapidly and incessantly; prattle. **2.** (*intr.*) (of birds, monkeys, etc.) to make rapid repetitive high-pitched noises resembling human speech. **3.** (*intr.*) (of the teeth) to click together rapidly through cold or fear. **4.** (*intr.*) to make rapid intermittent contact with a component, as in machining, causing irregular cutting. ~*n.* **5.** idle or foolish talk; gossip. **6.** the high-pitched repetitive noise made by a bird, monkey, etc. **7.** the rattling of objects, such as parts of a machine. **8.** the undulating pattern of marks in a machined surface from the vibration of the tool or workpiece. [C13: of imitative origin] —ˈ**chattery** *adj.*

chatterbox (ˈtʃætəˌbɒks) *n. Informal.* a person who talks constantly, esp. about trivial matters.

chatterer (ˈtʃætərə) *n.* **1.** someone or something that chatters. **2.** another name for **cotinga.**

chattering classes *n. Journalese, often derogatory.* (usually preceded by *the*) the educated sections of society, considered as enjoying discussion of political, social, and cultural issues.

chatter mark *n.* **1.** any of a series of grooves, pits, and scratches on the surface of a rock, usually made by the movement of a glacier. **2.** a mark or series of marks on a workpiece.

chatty (ˈtʃætɪ) *adj.* **-tier, -tiest.** **1.** full of trivial conversation; talkative. **2.** informal and friendly; gossipy: *a chatty letter.* —ˈ**chattily** *adv.* —ˈ**chattiness** *n.*

chat up *vb.* (*tr., adv.*) *Brit. informal.* **1.** to talk persuasively to (a person), esp. with an ulterior motive. **2.** to talk flirtatiously to (a person of the opposite sex), esp. with the intention of seducing him or her.

Chaucerian (tʃɔːˈsɪərɪən) *adj.* **1.** of, relating to, or characteristic of the writings of Geoffrey Chaucer (?1340–1400), English poet. ~*n.* **2.** an imitator of Chaucer, esp. one of a group of 15th-century Scottish writers who took him as a model. **3. a.** an admirer of Chaucer's works. **b.** a specialist in the study or teaching of Chaucer.

chaudfroid *French.* (ʃofrwa) *n.* a sweet or savoury jellied sauce used to coat cold meat, chicken, etc. [literally: hot-cold (because prepared as hot dish, but served cold)]

chauffer *or* **chaufer** (ˈtʃɔːfə) *n.* a small portable heater or stove. [C19: from French *chauffoir,* from *chauffer* to heat]

chauffeur (ˈʃəʊfə, ʃəʊˈfɜː) *n.* **1.** a person employed to drive a car. ~*vb.* **2.** to act as driver for (a person): *he chauffeured me to the stadium; he chauffeurs for the Duke.* [C20: from French, literally: stoker, from *chauffer* to heat] —**chauffeuse** (ʃəʊˈfɜːz) *fem. n.*

chaulmoogra (tʃɔːlˈmuːgrə) *n.* **1.** a tropical Asian tree, *Taraktogenos* (or *Hydnocarpus*) *kurzii:* family *Flacourtiaceae.* **2.** oil from the seed of this tree, used in treating leprosy. **3.** any of several similar or related trees. [from Bengali *cāulmugrā,* from *cāul* rice + *mugrā* hemp]

chaunt (tʃɔːnt) *n.* a less common variant of **chant.** —ˈ**chaunter** *n.*

chausses (ʃəʊs) *n.* (*functioning as sing.*) a tight-fitting medieval garment covering the feet and legs, usually made of chain mail. [C15: from Old French *chauces,* plural of *chauce* leg-covering, from Medieval Latin *calcea,* from Latin *calceus* shoe, from *calx* heel]

chautauqua (ʃəˈtɔːkwə) *n.* (in the U.S., formerly) a summer school or educational meeting held in the summer. [C19: named after *Chautauqua,* a lake in New York near which such a school was first held]

chauvinism (ˈʃəʊvɪˌnɪzəm) *n.* **1.** aggressive or fanatical patriotism; jingoism. **2.** enthusiastic devotion to a cause. **3.** smug irrational belief in the superiority of one's own race, party, sex, etc.: *male chauvinism.* [C19: from French *chauvinisme,* after Nicolas *Chauvin,* legendary French soldier under Napoleon, noted for his vociferous and unthinking patriotism] —ˈ**chauvinist** *n.* —ˌ**chauvinˈistic** *adj.* —ˌ**chauvinˈistically** *adv.*

chaw (tʃɔː) *Dialect.* ~*vb.* **1.** to chew (tobacco), esp. without swallowing it. ~*n.* **2.** something chewed, esp. a plug of tobacco. —ˈ**chawer** *n.*

chayote (tʃɑːˈjəʊteɪ, tʃaɪˈəʊtɪ) *n.* **1.** a tropical American cucurbitaceous climbing plant, *Sechium edule,* that has edible pear-shaped fruit enclosing a single enormous seed. **2.** the fruit of this plant, which is cooked and eaten as a vegetable. [from Spanish, from Nahuatl *chayotli*]

chazan, hazan, *or* ***hazzan*** *Hebrew.* (xaˈzan; *English* ˈhɑːzᵊn) *n., pl.* ***chazanim*** (xazaˈnim; *English* hɑːˈzɔːniːm) *or English* ***chazans.*** a person who leads synagogue services, esp. as a profession; cantor.

ChB *abbrev. for* Bachelor of Surgery. [Latin: *Chirurgiae Baccalaureus*]

ChE *abbrev. for* Chemical Engineer.

cheap (tʃiːp) *adj.* **1.** costing relatively little; inexpensive; good value. **2.** charging low prices: *a cheap hairdresser.* **3.** of poor quality; shoddy: *cheap furniture; cheap and nasty.* **4.** worth relatively little: *promises are cheap.* **5.** not worthy of respect; vulgar. **6.** ashamed; embarrassed: *to feel cheap.* **7.** stingy; miserly. **8.** *Informal.* mean; despicable: *a cheap liar.* **9. dirt cheap.** *Informal.* extremely inexpensive. ~*n.* **10. on the cheap.** *Brit. informal.* at a low cost. ~*adv.* **11.** at very little cost. [Old English *ceap* barter, bargain, price, property; related to Old Norse *kaup* bargain, Old High German *kouf* trade, Latin *caupō* innkeeper] —ˈ**cheapish** *adj.* —ˈ**cheaply** *adv.* —ˈ**cheapness** *n.*

cheapen (ˈtʃiːpᵊn) *vb.* **1.** to make or become lower in reputation, quality, etc.; degrade or be degraded. **2.** to make or become cheap or cheaper. —ˈ**cheapener** *n.*

cheap-jack *Informal.* ~*n.* **1.** a person who sells cheap and shoddy goods. ~*adj.* **2.** shoddy or inferior. [C19: from CHEAP + *Jack* (name used to typify a person)]

cheapo (ˈtʃiːpəʊ) *adj., n.* *Informal.* very cheap and possibly shoddy.

cheapskate (ˈtʃiːpˌskeɪt) *n. Informal.* a miserly person.

cheat (tʃiːt) *vb.* **1.** to deceive or practise deceit, esp. for one's own gain; trick or swindle (someone). **2.** (*intr.*) to obtain unfair advantage by trickery, as in a game of cards. **3.** (*tr.*) to escape or avoid (something unpleasant) by luck or cunning: *to cheat death.* **4.** (when *intr.,* usually foll. by *on*) *Informal.* to be sexually unfaithful to (one's wife, husband, or lover). ~*n.* **5.** a person who cheats. **6.** a deliberately dishonest transaction, esp. for gain; fraud. **7.** *Informal.* sham. **8.** *Law.* the obtaining of another's property by fraudulent means. **9.** the usual U.S. name for **ryebrome.** [C14: short for ESCHEAT] —ˈ**cheatable** *adj.* —ˈ**cheater** *n.* —ˈ**cheatingly** *adv.*

Chebyshev's inequality (ˈtʃɛbɪˌʃɒfs) *n. Statistics.* the fundamental theorem that the probability that a random variable differs from its mean by more than k standard deviations is less than or equal to $1/k^2$. [named after P. L. *Chebyshev* (1821–94), Russian mathematician]

Chechen (tʃɪˈtʃɛn) *n., pl.* **-chens** *or* **-chen.** a member of a people speaking a Circassian language and chiefly inhabiting the former ASSR of Checheno-Ingush, in S Russia.

check (tʃɛk) *vb.* **1.** to pause or cause to pause, esp. abruptly. **2.** (*tr.*) to restrain or control: *to check one's tears.* **3.** (*tr.*) to slow the growth or progress of; retard. **4.** (*tr.*) to rebuke or rebuff. **5.** (when *intr.,* often foll. by *on* or *up on*) to examine, investigate, or make an inquiry into (facts, a product, etc.) for accuracy, quality, or progress, esp. rapidly or informally. **6.** (*tr.*) *Chiefly U.S. and Canadian.* to mark off so as to indicate approval, correctness, or preference. Usual Brit. word: **tick. 7.** (*intr.;* often foll. by *with*) *Chiefly U.S. and Canadian.* to correspond or agree: *this report checks with the other.* **8.** (*tr.*) *Chiefly U.S., Canadian, and N.Z.* to leave in or accept for temporary custody. **9.** *Chess.* to place (an opponent's king) in check. **10.** (*tr.*) to mark with a pattern of squares or crossed lines. **11.** to crack or cause to crack. **12.** *Agriculture.* short for **checkrow. 13.** (*tr.*) *Ice hockey.* to impede (an opponent). **14.** (*intr.*) *Hunting.* (of hounds) to pause in the pursuit of quarry while relocating a lost scent. **15.** (*intr.;* foll. by *at*) *Falconry.* to change from one quarry to another while in flight. **16.** (*intr.*) to decline the option of opening the betting in a round of poker. **17. check the helm.** *Nautical.* to swing back the helm of a vessel to prevent it from turning too quickly or too far. ~*n.* **18.** a break in progress; stoppage. **19.** a restraint or rebuff. **20. a.** a person or thing that restrains, halts, etc. **b.** (*as modifier*): *a check line.* **21. a.** a control, esp. a rapid or informal one, designed to ensure accuracy, progress, etc. **b.** (*as modifier*): *a check list.* **22.** a means or standard to ensure against fraud or error. **23.** the U.S. word for **tick**[1]. **24.** the U.S. and Canadian spelling of **cheque. 25.** *U.S.* the bill in a restaurant. **26.** *Chiefly U.S. and Canadian.* a ticket or tag used to identify clothing or property deposited for custody. **27.** a pattern of squares or crossed lines. **28.** a single square in such a pattern. **29. a.** fabric with a pattern of squares or crossed lines. **b.** (*as modifier*): *a check suit.* **30.** *Chess.* the state or position of a king under direct attack, from which it must be moved or protected by another piece. **31.** a small crack, as one in veneer or one that occurs in timber during seasoning. **32.** part of the action of a piano that arrests the backward motion of a hammer after it has struck a string and holds it until the key is released. **33.** a chip or counter used in some card and gambling games. **34.** *Hunting.* a pause by the hounds in the pursuit of their quarry owing to loss of its scent. **35.** *Angling.* a ratchet fitted to a fishing reel to check the free running of the line. **36.** *Ice hockey.* the act of impeding an opponent with one's body or stick. **37. in check.** under control or restraint. ~*interj.* **38.** *Chess.* a call made to an opponent indicating that his king is in check. **39.** *Chiefly U.S. and Canadian.* an expression of agreement. ~See also **check in, check off, check out, checkup.** [C14: from Old French *eschec* a check at chess, hence, a pause (to verify something), via Arabic from Persian *shāh* the king! (in chess)] —ˈ**checkable** *adj.*

check digit *n. Computer technol.* a digit derived from and appended to a string of data digits, used to detect corruption of the data string during transmission or transcription.

checked (tʃɛkt) *adj.* **1.** having a pattern of small squares. **2.** *Phonetics.* (of a syllable) ending in a consonant.

checker[1] (ˈtʃɛkə) *n., vb.* **1.** the usual U.S. spelling of **chequer.** ~*n.* **2.** *Textiles.* a variant spelling of **chequer** (sense 2). **3.** the U.S. and Canadian name for **draughtsman** (sense 3). ~See also **checkers.**

checker[2] (ˈtʃɛkə) *n. Chiefly U.S. and Canadian.* **1.** a cashier, esp. in a supermarket. **2.** an attendant in a cloakroom, left-luggage office, etc.

checkerberry (ˈtʃɛkəbərɪ, -brɪ) *n., pl.* **-ries. 1.** the fruit of any of various plants, esp. the wintergreen (*Gaultheria procumbens*). **2.** any plant bearing this fruit.

checkerbloom (ˈtʃɛkəˌbluːm) *n.* a Californian malvaceous plant, *Sidalcea malvaeflora,* with pink or purple flowers.

checkerboard (ˈtʃɛkəˌbɔːd) *n.* the U.S. and Canadian name for a **draughtboard.**

checkers (ˈtʃɛkəz) *n.* (*functioning as sing.*) the U.S. and Canadian name for **draughts.**

check in *vb.* (*adv.*) **1.** (*intr.*) to record one's arrival, as at a hotel or for work; sign in or report. **2.** (*tr.*) to register the arrival of (passengers, etc.). ~*n.* **check-in. 3. a.** the formal registration of arrival, as at an airport or a hotel. **b.** (*as modifier*): *check-in time.* **4.** the place where one registers arrival at an airport, etc.

checking account *n.* the U.S. and Canadian name for **current account.**

check list *n.* a list of items, facts, names, etc., to be checked or referred to for comparison, identification, or verification.

checkmate (ˈtʃɛkˌmeɪt) *n.* **1.** *Chess.* **a.** the winning position in which an opponent's king is under attack and unable to escape. **b.** the move by which this position is achieved. **2.** utter defeat. ~*vb.* (*tr.*) **3.** *Chess.* to place (an opponent's king) in checkmate. **4.** to thwart or render powerless. ~*interj.* **5.** *Chess.* a call made when placing an opponent's king in checkmate. [C14: from Old French *eschec mat,* from Arabic *shāh māt,* the king is dead; see CHECK]

check off *vb.* (*tr., adv.*) **1.** to mark with a tick. **2.** to deduct (union contributions) directly from an employee's pay. ~*n.* **check-off. 3.** a procedure whereby an employer deducts union contributions directly from an employee's pay and pays the money to the union.

check out *vb.* (*adv.*) **1.** (*intr.*) to pay the bill and depart, esp. from a hotel. **2.** (*intr.*) to depart from a place; record one's departure from work. **3.** to investigate or prove to be in order after investigation: *the police checked out all the statements; their credentials checked out.* **4.** (*tr.*) *Informal.* to have a look at; inspect: *check out the wally in the pink shirt.* ~*n.* **checkout. 5. a.** the latest time for vacating a room in a hotel, etc. **b.** (*as modifier*): *checkout time.* **6.** a counter, esp. in a supermarket, where customers pay.

checkpoint ('tʃɛk,pɔɪnt) *n.* a place, as at a frontier or in a motor rally, where vehicles or travellers are stopped for official identification, inspection, etc.

checkrail ('tʃɛk,reɪl) *n. Brit.* another word for **guardrail** (sense 2).

checkrein ('tʃɛk,reɪn) *n.* the usual U.S. word for **bearing rein.**

checkroom ('tʃɛk,ruːm, -,rʊm) *n.* the U.S. and Canadian name for **left-luggage office.**

checkrow ('tʃɛk,rəʊ) *U.S. agriculture.* ~*n.* **1.** a row of plants, esp. corn, in which the spaces between adjacent plants are equal to those between adjacent rows to facilitate cultivation. ~*vb.* **2.** (*tr.*) to plant in checkrows.

checks and balances *pl. n. Government, chiefly U.S.* competition and mutual restraint among the various branches of government.

checkup ('tʃɛk,ʌp) *n.* **1.** an examination to see if something is in order. **2.** *Med.* a medical examination, esp. one taken at regular intervals to verify a normal state of health or discover a disease in its early stages. ~*vb.* **check up. 3.** (*intr., adv.* sometimes foll. by *on*) to investigate or make an inquiry into (a person's character, evidence, etc.), esp. when suspicions have been aroused.

check valve *n.* a valve that closes by fluid pressure to prevent return flow. Also called: **nonreturn valve.**

checky ('tʃɛkɪ) *adj.* (*usually postpositive*) *Heraldry.* having squares of alternating tinctures or furs; checked.

Cheddar ('tʃɛdə) *n.* (*sometimes not cap.*) any of several types of smooth hard yellow or whitish cheese. [C17: named after *Cheddar*, a village in Somerset in SW England, where it was originally made]

cheddite ('tʃɛdaɪt, 'ʃɛd-) *n.* an explosive made by mixing a powdered chlorate or perchlorate with a fatty substance, such as castor oil. [C20: from *Chedde* town in Savoy, France, where it was first made]

cheder or heder *Hebrew.* ('xɛdɛr; *English* 'heɪdə) *n., pl.* ***chadarim*** (xada'riːm) *or English* ***cheders. Judaism.*** **1.** (in Western countries) elementary religious education classes, usually outside normal school hours. **2.** more traditionally, a full-time elementary religious school. **3.** *Informal.* a place of corrective instruction; prison. [literally: room]

chee-chee ('tʃiː,tʃiː) *n.* a less common spelling of **chichi**[2].

cheek (tʃiːk) *n.* **1. a.** either side of the face, esp. that part below the eye. **b.** either side of the oral cavity; side of the mouth. **2.** *Informal.* impudence; effrontery. **3.** (*often pl.*) *Informal.* either side of the buttocks. **4.** (*often pl.*) a side of a door jamb. **5.** *Nautical.* one of the two fore-and-aft supports for the trestletrees on a mast of a sailing vessel, forming part of the hounds. **6.** one of the jaws of a vice. **7. cheek by jowl.** close together; intimately linked. **8. turn the other cheek.** to be submissive and refuse to retaliate even when provoked or treated badly. **9. with (one's) tongue in (one's) cheek.** See **tongue** (sense 20). ~*vb.* **10.** (*tr.*) *Informal.* to speak or behave disrespectfully to; act impudently towards. [Old English *ceace;* related to Middle Low German *kāke*, Dutch *kaak*] —**'cheekless** *adj.*

cheekbone ('tʃiːk,bəʊn) *n.* the nontechnical name for **zygomatic bone.**

cheekpiece ('tʃiːk,piːs) *n.* either of the two straps of a bridle that join the bit to the crownpiece.

cheek pouch *n.* a membranous pouch inside the mouth of many rodents and some other mammals: used for holding food.

cheeky ('tʃiːkɪ) *adj.* **cheekier, cheekiest.** disrespectful in speech or behaviour; impudent: *a cheeky child.* —**'cheekily** *adv.* —**'cheekiness** *n.*

cheep (tʃiːp) *n.* **1.** the short weak high-pitched cry of a young bird; chirp. ~*vb.* **2.** (*intr.*) (of young birds) to utter characteristic shrill sounds. —**'cheeper** *n.*

cheer (tʃɪə) *vb.* **1.** (usually foll. by *up*) to make or become happy or hopeful; comfort or be comforted. **2.** to applaud with shouts. **3.** (when *tr.*, sometimes foll. by *on*) to encourage (a team, person, etc.) with shouts, esp. in contests. ~*n.* **4.** a shout or cry of approval, encouragement, etc., often using such words as **hurrah!** or **rah! rah! rah! 5. three cheers.** three shouts of hurrah given in unison by a group to honour someone or celebrate something. **6.** happiness; good spirits. **7.** state of mind; spirits (archaic, except in the phrases **be of good cheer, with good cheer**). **8.** *Archaic.* provisions for a feast; fare. ~See also **cheers.** [C13 (in the sense: face, welcoming aspect): from Old French *chere,* from Late Latin *cara* face, from Greek *kara* head] —**'cheerer** *n.* —**'cheeringly** *adv.*

cheerful ('tʃɪəfʊl) *adj.* **1.** having a happy disposition; in good spirits. **2.** pleasantly bright; gladdening: *a cheerful room.* **3.** hearty; ungrudging; enthusiastic: *cheerful help.* —**'cheerfully** *adv.* —**'cheerfulness** *n.*

cheerio (,tʃɪərɪ'əʊ) *sentence substitute. Informal, chiefly Brit.* **1.** a farewell greeting. **2.** a drinking toast. ~*n.* **3.** *N.Z.* a type of small sausage.

cheerleader ('tʃɪə,liːdə) *n. U.S. and Canadian.* a person who leads a crowd in formal cheers, esp. at sports events.

cheerless ('tʃɪəlɪs) *adj.* dreary, gloomy, or pessimistic. —**'cheerlessly** *adv.* —**'cheerlessness** *n.*

cheerly ('tʃɪəlɪ) *adj., adv. Archaic or nautical.* cheerful or cheerfully.

cheers (tʃɪəz) *sentence substitute. Informal, chiefly Brit.* **1.** a drinking toast. **2.** goodbye! cheerio! **3.** thanks!

cheery ('tʃɪərɪ) *adj.* **cheerier, cheeriest.** showing or inspiring cheerfulness; gay. —**'cheerily** *adv.* —**'cheeriness** *n.*

cheese[1] (tʃiːz) *n.* **1.** the curd of milk separated from the whey and variously prepared as a food. **2.** a mass or complete cake of this substance. **3.** any of various substances of similar consistency, etc.: *lemon cheese.* **4.** *Slang.* an important person (esp. in the phrase **big cheese**). **5. as alike** (*or* **different**) **as chalk and cheese.** See **chalk** (sense 6). [Old English *cēse,* from Latin *cāseus* cheese; related to Old Saxon *kāsi*]

cheese[2] (tʃiːz) *vb. Slang.* **1.** (*tr.*) to stop; desist. **2. cheese it. a.** get away quick. **b.** be quiet! stop what you're doing! **3.** (*intr.*) *Prison slang.* to act in a grovelling manner. [C19: of unknown origin]

cheeseboard ('tʃiːz,bɔːd) *n.* a board from which cheese is served at a meal.

cheeseburger ('tʃiːz,bɜːgə) *n.* a hamburger cooked with a slice of cheese on top of it.

cheesecake ('tʃiːz,keɪk) *n.* **1.** a rich tart with a biscuit base, filled with a mixture of cream cheese, cream, sugar, and often sultanas, sometimes having a fruit topping. **2.** *Slang.* women displayed for their sex appeal, as in photographs in magazines, newspapers, or films. Compare **beefcake.**

cheesecloth ('tʃiːz,klɒθ) *n.* a loosely woven cotton cloth formerly used only for wrapping cheese.

cheese cutter *n.* **1.** a board with a wire attached for cutting cheese. **2.** *Nautical.* a keel that may be drawn up into the boat when not in use. **3.** a nautical peaked cap worn without a badge.

cheesed off *adj.* (*usually postpositive*) *Brit. slang.* bored, disgusted, or angry. [C20: from CHEESE[2]]

cheese-head *adj.* denoting or relating to a screw or bolt with a cylindrical slotted head.

cheese mite *n.* a white soft-bodied free-living mite, *Tyrophagus* (or *Tyroglyphus*) *longior*, sometimes found in decaying cheese.

cheesemonger ('tʃiːz,mʌŋgə) *n.* a person dealing in cheese, butter, etc.

cheeseparing ('tʃiːz,pɛərɪŋ) *adj.* **1.** penny-pinching; stingy. ~*n.* **2. a.** a paring of cheese rind. **b.** anything similarly worthless. **3.** stinginess.

cheese skipper *n.* a dipterous fly, *Piophila casei,* whose larvae feed on cheese and move by jumping: family *Piophilidae.*

cheese straw *n.* a long thin cheese-flavoured strip of pastry.

cheesewood ('tʃiːz,wʊd) *n. Austral.* the tough yellowish wood of Australian trees of the genus *Pittosporum:* family *Pittosporaceae.*

cheesy ('tʃiːzɪ) *adj.* **cheesier, cheesiest. 1.** like cheese in flavour, smell, or consistency. **2.** *Informal.* (of a smile) broad but possibly insincere: *a big cheesy grin.* —**'cheesiness** *n.*

cheetah *or* **chetah** ('tʃiːtə) *n.* a large feline mammal, *Acinonyx jubatus,* of Africa and SW Asia: the swiftest mammal, having very long legs, nonretractile claws, and a black-spotted light-brown coat. [C18: from Hindi *cītā,* from Sanskrit *citrakāya* tiger, from *citra* bright, speckled + *kāya* body]

chef (ʃɛf) *n.* a cook, esp. the principal cook in a restaurant. [C19: from French, from Old French *chief* head, CHIEF]

chef-d'oeuvre *French.* (ʃɛdœvrə) *n., pl.* ***chefs-d'oeuvre*** (ʃɛdœvrə). a masterpiece.

cheiro- *combining form.* a variant spelling of **chiro-.**

chela[1] ('kiːlə) *n., pl.* **lae** (-liː). a large pincer-like claw of such arthropods as the crab and scorpion. [C17: New Latin, from Greek *khēlē* claw] —**cheliferous** (kɪ'lɪfərəs) *adj.*

chela[2] ('tʃeɪlə) *n. Hinduism.* a disciple of a religious teacher. [C19: from Hindi *celā,* from Sanskrit *ceta* servant, slave] —**'chela,ship** *n.*

chelate ('kiːleɪt) *n.* **1.** *Chem.* a chemical compound whose molecules contain a closed ring of atoms of which one is a metal atom. ~*adj.* **2.** *Zoology.* of or possessing chelae. **3.** *Chem.* of or denoting a chelate. ~*vb.* **4.** (*intr.*) *Chem.* to form a chelate. [C20: from CHELA[1]] —**che'lation** *n.*

chelating agent *n.* a chemical compound that coordinates with a metal to form a chelate, often used to trap or remove heavy metal ions.

chelicera (kɪ'lɪsərə) *n., pl.* **-erae** (-ə,riː). one of a pair of appendages on the head of spiders and other arachnids: often modified as food-catching claws. [C19: from New Latin, from French *chélicère,* from *chél-* (see CHELA[1]) + *-cère* from Greek *keras* horn] —**che'liceral** *adj.*

chelicerate (kɪ'lɪsə,reɪt) *adj.* **1.** of, relating to, or belonging to the *Chelicerata,* a subphylum of arthropods, including arachnids and the horseshoe crab, in which the first pair of limbs are modified as chelicerae. ~*n.* **2.** any arthropod belonging to the *Chelicerata.*

cheliform ('kiːlɪ,fɔːm) *adj.* shaped like a chela; pincer-like.

Chellean ('ʃɛlɪən) *n., adj. Archaeol.* (*no longer in technical usage*) another word for **Abbevillian.** [C19: from French *chelléen,* from *Chelles,* France, where various items were found]

cheloid ('kiːlɔɪd) *n. Pathol.* a variant spelling of **keloid.** —**che'loidal** *adj.*

chelone (kə'ləʊnɪ) *n.* any plant of the hardy N American genus *Chelone,* grown for its white, rose, or purple flower spikes: family *Scrophulariaceae.* [New Latin, from Greek *chelōnē* a tortoise, from a fancied resemblance between a tortoise's head and the shape of the flower]

chelonian (kɪ'ləʊnɪən) *n.* **1.** any reptile of the order *Chelonia,* including the tortoises and turtles, in which most of the body is enclosed in a protective bony capsule. ~*adj.* **2.** of, relating to, or belonging to the *Chelonia.* [C19: from New Latin *Chelōnia,* from Greek *khelōnē* tortoise]

chelp (tʃɛlp) *vb.* (*intr.*) *Northern and Midland English dialect.* **1.** (esp. of women or children) to chatter or speak out of turn: *she's always chelping at the teacher.* **2.** (of birds) to squeak or chirp. [C19: perhaps from *ch*(*irp*) + (*y*)*elp*]

Chelsea bun ('tʃɛlsɪ) *n.* a rolled yeast currant bun decorated with sugar.

Chelsea Pensioner *n.* a resident of the Chelsea Royal Hospital in SW London, a home for old and invalid soldiers.

chem. *abbrev. for:* **1.** chemical. **2.** chemist. **3.** chemistry.

chem- *combining form.* variant of **chemo-** before a vowel.

chemautotroph (ˌkiːməʊ'ɔːtətrəʊf, ˌkɛm-) *n. Biology.* an organism, such as a bacterium, that obtains its energy from inorganic reactions using simple compounds, such as ammonia or carbon dioxide. —**chemautotrophic** (ˌkiːməʊˌɔːtə'trɒfɪk, ˌkɛm-) *adj.*

chemical ('kɛmɪkᵊl) *n.* **1.** any substance used in or resulting from a reaction involving changes to atoms or molecules. ~*adj.* **2.** of or used in chemistry: *chemical balance.* **3.** of, made from, or using chemicals: *chemical fertilizer.* —'**chemically** *adv.*

chemical bond *n.* a mutual attraction between two atoms resulting from a redistribution of their outer electrons. See also **covalent bond, electrovalent bond, coordinate bond.**

chemical engineering *n.* the branch of engineering concerned with the design, operation, maintenance, and manufacture of the plant and machinery used in industrial chemical processes. —**chemical engineer** *n.*

chemical equation *n.* a representation of a chemical reaction using symbols of the elements to indicate the amount of substance, usually in moles, of each reactant and product.

chemical machining *n.* the shaping of a metal part by controlled removal of unwanted metal by a flow of chemical solutions.

chemical potential *n.* a thermodynamic function of a substance in a system that is the partial differential of the Gibbs function of the system with respect to the number of moles of the substance. Symbol: μ

chemical reaction *n.* a process that involves changes in the structure and energy content of atoms, molecules, or ions but not their nuclei. Compare **nuclear reaction.**

chemical warfare *n.* warfare in which chemicals other than explosives are used as weapons, esp. warfare using asphyxiating or nerve gases, poisons, defoliants, etc.

chemico- *combining form.* chemical: *chemicophysical.*

chemiluminescence (ˌkɛmɪˌluːmɪ'nɛsəns) *n.* the phenomenon in which a chemical reaction leads to the emission of light without incandescence. —ˌ**chemiˌlumi'nescent** *adj.*

chemin de fer (ʃə'mæn də 'fɛə; *French* ʃəmɛ̃dfɛr) *n.* a gambling game, a variation of baccarat. [French: railway, referring to the fast tempo of the game]

chemiosmosis (ˌkɛmɪɒz'məʊsɪs) *n. Biochem.* the mechanism by which the synthesis and utilization of the biochemical energy source ATP is regulated: the energy generated by oxidative phosphorylation generates a proton gradient across the membrane of the mitochondrion that drives the enzymic resynthesis of ATP.

chemise (ʃə'miːz) *n.* **1.** an unwaisted loose-fitting dress hanging straight from the shoulders. **2.** a loose shirtlike undergarment. ~Also called: **shift.** [C14: from Old French: shirt, from Late Latin *camisa,* perhaps of Celtic origin]

chemisette (ˌʃɛmɪ'zɛt) *n.* an underbodice of lawn, lace, etc., worn to fill in a low-cut dress. [C19: from French, diminutive of CHEMISE]

chemism ('kɛmɪzəm) *n. Obsolete.* chemical action.

chemisorb (ˌkɛmɪ'sɔːb) *or* **chemosorb** *vb.* (*tr.*) to take up (a substance) by chemisorption.

chemisorption (ˌkɛmɪ'sɔːpʃən) *n.* an adsorption process in which an adsorbate is held on the surface of an adsorbent by chemical bonds.

chemist ('kɛmɪst) *n.* **1.** *Brit.* a shop selling medicines, cosmetics, etc. **2.** *Brit.* a qualified dispenser of prescribed medicines. **3.** a person studying, trained in, or engaged in chemistry. **4.** an obsolete word for **alchemist.** [C16: from earlier *chimist,* from New Latin *chimista,* shortened from Medieval Latin *alchimista* ALCHEMIST]

chemistry ('kɛmɪstrɪ) *n., pl.* **-tries.** **1.** the branch of physical science concerned with the composition, properties, and reactions of substances. See also **inorganic chemistry, organic chemistry, physical chemistry.** **2.** the composition, properties, and reactions of a particular substance. **3.** the nature and effects of any complex phenomenon: *the chemistry of humour.* **4.** *Informal.* a reaction, taken to be instinctual, between two persons (usually qualified by *good, bad,* etc.). [C17: from earlier *chimistrie,* from *chimist* CHEMIST]

chemmy ('ʃɛmɪ) *n. Cards.* short for **chemin de fer.**

chemo-, chemi-, *or before a vowel* **chem-** *combining form.* indicating that chemicals or chemical reactions are involved: *chemotherapy.* [New Latin, from Late Greek *khēmeia;* see ALCHEMY]

chemoattractant (ˌkɛməʊə'træktənt) *n.* a chemical substance that provokes chemotaxis, esp. one that causes a bacterium to move in the direction in which its concentration is increasing.

chemoheterotroph (ˌkiːməʊ'hɛtərəʊtrəʊf, ˌkɛm-) *n. Biology.* an organism that obtains its energy from the oxidation of organic compounds. —**chemoheterotrophic** (ˌkiːməʊˌhɛtərəʊ'trɒfɪk, ˌkɛm-) *adj.*

chemokinesis (ˌkɛməʊkaɪ'niːsɪs) *n. Immunol.* the random movement of cells, such as leucocytes, stimulated by substances in their environment.

chemonasty ('kɛməʊˌnæstɪ) *n. Botany.* the nastic movement of a plant in response to a chemical stimulus.

chemoprophylaxis (ˌkɛməʊˌprəʊfə'læksɪs, -ˌprɒfə-) *n.* the prevention of disease using chemical drugs. —ˌ**chemoˌprophy'lactic** *adj.*

chemoreceptor (ˌkɛməʊrɪ'sɛptə) *or* **chemoceptor** *n.* a sensory receptor in a biological cell membrane to which an external molecule binds to generate a smell or taste sensation.

chemosmosis (ˌkɛmɒz'məʊsɪs) *n.* a chemical reaction between two compounds after osmosis through an intervening semipermeable membrane. —**chemosmotic** (ˌkɛmɒz'mɒtɪk) *adj.*

chemosphere ('kɛməˌsfɪə) *n. Meteorol.* another name for **thermosphere.** —**chemospheric** (ˌkɛmə'sfɛrɪk) *adj.*

chemostat ('kiːməʊˌstæt, 'kɛm-) *n.* an apparatus for growing bacterial cultures at a constant rate by controlling the supply of nutrient medium.

chemosynthesis (ˌkɛməʊ'sɪnθɪsɪs) *n.* the formation of organic material by certain bacteria using energy derived from simple chemical reactions. —**chemosynthetic** (ˌkɛməʊsɪn'θɛtɪk) *adj.* —ˌ**chemosyn'thetically** *adv.*

chemotaxis (ˌkɛməʊ'tæksɪs) *n.* the movement of a microorganism or cell in response to a chemical stimulus. —ˌ**chemo'tactic** *adj.* —ˌ**chemo'tactically** *adv.*

chemotherapy (ˌkiːməʊ'θɛrəpɪ, kiːmə-) *n.* treatment of disease, esp. cancer, by means of chemical agents. Compare **radiotherapy.** —ˌ**chemo'therapist** *n.*

chemotropism (ˌkɛməʊ'trəʊˌpɪzəm) *n.* the growth response of an organism, esp. a plant, to a chemical stimulus. —**chemotropic** (ˌkɛməʊ'trɒpɪk) *adj.* —ˌ**chemo'tropically** *adv.*

chempaduk ('tʃɛmpəˌdʌk) *n.* **1.** an evergreen moraceous tree, *Artocarpus champeden* (or *A. integer*), of Malaysia, similar to the jackfruit. **2.** the fruit of this tree, edible when cooked, having yellow starchy flesh and a leathery rind. [from Malay]

chemurgy ('kɛmɜːdʒɪ) *n.* the branch of chemistry concerned with the industrial use of organic raw materials, esp. materials of agricultural origin. —**chem'urgic** *or* **chem'urgical** *adj.*

chenille (ʃə'niːl) *n.* **1.** a thick soft tufty silk or worsted velvet cord or yarn used in embroidery and for trimmings, etc. **2.** a fabric of such yarn. **3.** a rich and hard-wearing carpet of such fabric. [C18: from French, literally: hairy caterpillar, from Latin *canicula,* diminutive of *canis* dog]

chenopod ('kiːnəˌpɒd, 'kɛn-) *n.* any flowering plant of the family *Chenopodiaceae,* which includes the beet, mangel-wurzel, spinach, and goosefoot. [C16: from Greek *khēn* goose + *pous* foot] —**chenopodiaceous** (ˌkiːnəˌpəʊdɪ'eɪʃəs, ˌkɛn-) *adj.*

cheongsam ('tʃɔːŋ'sæm) *n.* a straight dress, usually of silk or cotton, with a stand-up collar and a slit in one side of the skirt, worn by Chinese women. [from Chinese (Cantonese), variant of Mandarin *ch'ang shan* long jacket]

cheque *or U.S.* **check** (tʃɛk) *n.* **1.** a bill of exchange drawn on a bank by the holder of a current account; payable on demand, if uncrossed, or into a bank account, if crossed. **2.** *Austral. and N.Z.* the total sum of money received for contract work or a crop. [C18: from CHECK, in the sense: a means of verification]

cheque account *n.* an account at a bank or a building society upon which cheques can be drawn.

chequebook *or U.S.* **checkbook** ('tʃɛkˌbʊk) *n.* a book containing detachable blank cheques and issued by a bank or building society to holders of cheque accounts.

chequebook journalism *n.* the practice of securing exclusive rights to material for newspaper stories by paying a high price for it, regardless of any moral implications such as paying people to boast of criminal or morally reprehensible activities.

cheque card *n.* a card issued by a bank or building society, guaranteeing payment of a customer's cheques up to a stated value.

chequer *or U.S.* **checker** ('tʃɛkə) *n.* **1.** any of the marbles, pegs, or other pieces used in the game of Chinese chequers. **2. a.** a pattern consisting of squares of different colours, textures, or materials. **b.** one of the squares in such a pattern. ~*vb.* (*tr.*) **3.** to make irregular in colour or character; variegate. **4.** to mark off with alternating squares of colour. ~See also **chequers.** [C13: chessboard, from Anglo-French *escheker,* from *eschec* CHECK]

chequerboard ('tʃɛkəˌbɔːd) *n.* another name for a **draughtboard.**

chequered *or esp. U.S.* **checkered** ('tʃɛkəd) *adj.* marked by fluctuations of fortune (esp. in the phrase **a chequered career**).

chequered flag *n.* the black-and-white checked flag traditionally shown to the winner and all finishers at the end of a motor race by a senior race official.

chequers ('tʃɛkəz) *n.* (*functioning as sing.*) another name for **draughts.**

Cheremiss *or* **Cheremis** (ˌtʃɛərəˈmɪs, -ˈmiːs; ˈtʃɛərəˌmɪs, -ˌmiːs) *n.* **1.** (*pl.* **-miss** *or* **-mis**) a member of an Ugrian people of the Volga region, esp. of the middle Volga basin in W central Russia. **2.** Also called: **Mari.** the language of this people, belonging to the Finno-Ugric family.

Cherenkov radiation *or* **Cerenkov radiation** (tʃɪˈrɛŋkɒf) *n.* the electromagnetic radiation produced when a charged particle moves through a medium at a greater velocity than the velocity of light in that medium. [C20: named after P. A. *Cherenkov* (born 1904), Soviet physicist]

cherish ('tʃɛrɪʃ) *vb.* (*tr.*) **1.** to feel or show great tenderness or care for; treasure. **2.** to cling fondly to (a hope, idea, etc.); nurse: *to cherish ambitions.* [C14: from Old French *cherir,* from *cher* dear, from Latin *cārus*] —'**cherishable** *adj.* —'**cherisher** *n.* —'**cherishingly** *adv.*

chernozem *or* **tschernosem** ('tʃɜːnəʊˌzɛm) *n.* a black soil, rich in humus and carbonates, in cool or temperate semiarid regions, as the grasslands of Russia. [from Russian, contraction of *chernaya zemlya* black earth]

Cherokee ('tʃɛrəˌkiː, ˌtʃɛrəˈkiː) *n.* **1.** (*pl.* **-kees** *or* **-kee**) a member of a North American Indian people formerly living in and around the Appalachian Mountains, now chiefly in Oklahoma; one of the Iroquois peoples. **2.** the language of this people, belonging to the Iroquoian family.

Cherokee rose *n.* an evergreen climbing Chinese rose, *Rosa laevigata,* that now grows wild in the southern U.S., having large white fragrant flowers.

cheroot (ʃəˈruːt) *n.* a cigar with both ends cut off squarely. [C17: from Tamil *curuttu* curl, roll]

cherry ('tʃɛrɪ) *n., pl.* **-ries. 1.** any of several trees of the rosaceous genus *Prunus,* such as *P. avium* (**sweet cherry**), having a small fleshy rounded fruit containing a hard stone. See also **bird cherry. 2.** the fruit or wood of any of these trees. **3.** any of various unrelated plants, such as the ground cherry and Jerusalem cherry. **4. a.** a bright red colour; cerise. **b.** (*as adj.*): *a cherry coat.* **5.** *Taboo slang.* virginity or the hymen as its symbol. **6.** (*modifier*) of or relating to the cherry fruit or wood: *cherry tart.* [C14: back formation from Old English *ciris* (mistakenly thought to be plural), ultimately from Late Latin *ceresia,* perhaps from Latin *cerasus* cherry tree, from Greek *kerasios*] —'**cherry-ˌlike** *adj.*

cherry brandy *n.* a red liqueur made of brandy flavoured with cherries.

cherry laurel *n.* a Eurasian rosaceous evergreen shrub, *Prunus laurocerasus,* having glossy aromatic leaves, white flowers, and purplish-black fruits.

cherry picker *n.* a hydraulic crane, esp. one mounted on a lorry, that has an elbow joint or telescopic arm supporting a basket-like platform enabling a person to service high power lines or to carry out similar operations above the ground.

cherry-pie *n.* a widely planted garden heliotrope, *Heliotropium peruvianum.*

cherry plum *n.* a small widely planted Asian rosaceous tree, *Prunus cerasifera,* with white flowers and red or yellow cherry-like fruit. Also called: **myrobalan.**

cherry tomato *n.* a miniature tomato not much bigger than a cherry.

chersonese ('kɜːsəˌniːs) *n.* **a.** a poetic or rhetorical word for **peninsula. b.** (*cap. when part of a name*): *Thracian Chersonese.* [C17: from Latin, from Greek *khersonēsos,* from *khersos* dry (land) + *nēsos* island]

chert (tʃɜːt) *n.* a microcrystalline form of silica usually occurring as bands or layers of pebbles in sedimentary rock. Formula: SiO_2. Varieties include flint, lyddite (Lydian stone). Also called: **hornstone.** [C17: of obscure origin] —'**cherty** *adj.*

cherub ('tʃɛrəb) *n., pl.* **cherubs** *or* **cherubim** ('tʃɛrəbɪm, -ʊbɪm). **1.** *Theol.* a member of the second order of angels, whose distinctive gift is knowledge, often represented as a winged child or winged head of a child. **2.** an innocent or sweet child. [Old English, from Hebrew *kĕrūbh*] —**cherubic** (tʃəˈruːbɪk) *or* **cheˈrubical** *adj.* —**cheˈrubically** *adv.*

chervil ('tʃɜːvɪl) *n.* **1.** an aromatic umbelliferous Eurasian plant, *Anthriscus cerefolium,* with small white flowers and aniseed-flavoured leaves used as herbs in soups and salads. **2. bur chervil.** a similar and related plant, *Anthriscus caucalis.* **3.** a related plant, *Chaerophyllum temulentum,* having a hairy purple-spotted stem. [Old English *cerfelle,* from Latin *caerephylla,* plural of *caerephyllum* chervil, from Greek *khairephullon,* from *khairein* to enjoy + *phullon* leaf]

chervonets (tʃəˈvɔːnɛts) *n.* (formerly) a Soviet monetary unit and gold coin worth ten roubles. [from Old Russian *červonyi,* from Old Polish *czerwony* golden, purple]

Ches. *abbrev. for* Cheshire.

Cheshire cheese ('tʃɛʃə) *n.* a mild-flavoured cheese with a crumbly texture, originally made in Cheshire, in NW England.

Cheshvan *or* **Heshvan** (xɛʃˈvan) *n.* (in the Jewish calendar) the eighth month of the year according to biblical reckoning and the second month of the civil year, usually falling within October and November. Also called: **Marcheshvan.** [from Hebrew]

chess[1] (tʃɛs) *n.* a game of skill for two players using a chessboard on which chessmen are moved. Initially each player has one king, one queen, two rooks, two bishops, two knights, and eight pawns, which have different types of moves according to kind. The object is to checkmate the opponent's king. [C13: from Old French *eschés,* plural of *eschec* check (at chess); see CHECK]

chess[2] (tʃɛs) *n. U.S.* a less common name for **rye-brome.** [C18: of unknown origin]

chess[3] (tʃɛs) *n., pl.* **chess** *or* **chesses.** a floorboard of the deck of a pontoon bridge. [C15 (in the sense: layer, tier): from Old French *chasse* frame, from Latin *capsa* box]

chessboard ('tʃɛsˌbɔːd) *n.* a square board divided into 64 squares of two alternating colours, used for playing chess or draughts.

chessel ('tʃɛsᵊl) *n.* a mould used in cheese-making. [C18: probably from CHEESE[1] + WELL[2]]

chessman ('tʃɛsˌmæn, -mən) *n., pl.* **-men.** any of the eight pieces and eight pawns used by each player in a game of chess. [C17: back formation from *chessmen,* from Middle English *chessemeyne* chess company, from *meynie, menye* company, body of men, from Old French *meyné*]

chesspiece ('tʃɛsˌpiːs) *n.* any of the eight pieces (excluding the pawns) used by each player in a game of chess.

chest (tʃɛst) *n.* **1. a.** the front part of the trunk from the neck to the belly. Related adj.: **pectoral. b.** (*as modifier*): *a chest cold.* **2. get (something) off one's chest.** *Informal.* to unburden oneself of troubles, worries, etc., by talking about them. **3.** a box, usually large and sturdy, used for storage or shipping: *a tea chest.* **4.** Also: **'chestful.** the quantity a chest holds. **5.** *Rare.* **a.** the place in which a public or charitable institution deposits its funds. **b.** the funds so deposited. **6.** a sealed container or reservoir for a gas: *a wind chest; a steam chest.* [Old English *cest,* from Latin *cista* wooden box, basket, from Greek *kistē* box] —'**chested** *adj.*

chesterfield ('tʃɛstəˌfiːld) *n.* **1.** a man's knee-length overcoat, usually with a fly front to conceal the buttons and having a velvet collar. **2.** a large tightly stuffed sofa, often upholstered in leather, with straight upholstered arms of the same height as the back. [C19: named after a 19th-century Earl of *Chesterfield*]

chestnut ('tʃɛsˌnʌt) *n.* **1.** any N temperate fagaceous tree of the genus *Castanea,* such as *C. sativa* (**sweet** or **Spanish chestnut**), which produce flowers in long catkins and nuts in a prickly bur. Compare **horse chestnut, water chestnut, dwarf chestnut. 2.** the edible nut of any of these trees. **3.** the hard wood of any of these trees, used in making furniture, etc. **4. a.** a reddish-brown to brown colour. **b.** (*as adj.*): *chestnut hair.* **5.** a horse of a yellow-brown or golden-brown colour. **6.** a small horny callus on the inner surface of a horse's leg. **7.** *Informal.* an old or stale joke. [C16: from earlier *chesten nut: chesten,* from Old French *chastaigne,* from Latin *castanea,* from Greek *kastanea*]

chest of drawers *n.* a piece of furniture consisting of a frame, often on short legs, containing a set of drawers.

chest of viols *n.* a set of viols of different sizes, usually six in number, used in consorts.

chest-on-chest *n.* another term for **tallboy.**

chest voice *or* **register** *n.* a voice of the lowest speaking or singing register. Compare **head voice.**

chesty ('tʃɛstɪ) *adj.* **chestier, chestiest.** *Informal.* **1.** *Brit.* suffering from or symptomatic of chest disease: *a chesty cough.* **2.** having a large well-developed chest or bosom. —'**chestiness** *n.*

chetah ('tʃiːtə) *n.* a variant spelling of **cheetah.**

Chetnik ('tʃɛtnɪk, tʃɛtˈniːk) *n.* a Serbian nationalist belonging to a group that fought against the Turks before World War I and engaged in guerrilla warfare during both World Wars. [from Serbian *četnik,* from *četa* troop]

cheval-de-frise (ʃəˌvældəˈfriːz) *n., pl.* **chevaux-de-frise** (ʃəˌvəʊdəˈfriːz). **1.** a portable barrier of spikes, etc., used to obstruct the passage of cavalry. **2.** a row of spikes or broken glass set as an obstacle on top of a wall. [C17: from French, literally: horse from Friesland (where it was first used)]

cheval glass (ʃəˈvæl) *n.* a full-length mirror mounted so as to swivel within a frame. [C19: from French *cheval* support (literally: horse)]

chevalier (ˌʃɛvəˈlɪə) *n.* **1.** a member of certain orders of merit, such as the French Legion of Honour. **2.** *French history.* **a.** a mounted soldier or knight, esp. a military cadet. **b.** the lowest title of rank in the old French nobility. **3.** an archaic word for **knight. 4.** a chivalrous man; gallant. [C14: from Old French, from Medieval Latin *caballārius* horseman, CAVALIER]

chevet (ʃəˈveɪ) *n.* a semicircular or polygonal east end of a church, esp. a French Gothic church, often with a number of attached apses. [C19: from French: pillow, from Latin *capitium,* from *caput* head]

Cheviot ('tʃiːvɪət, 'tʃɛv-) *n.* **1.** a large British breed of sheep reared for its wool. **2.** (*often not cap.*) a rough twill-weave woollen suiting fabric. [from the *Cheviot* Hills on the borders of England and Scotland]

chèvre ('ʃɛvrə) *n.* any cheese made from goats' milk. [C20: from French, literally: goat]

chevrette (ʃəˈvrɛt) *n.* **1.** the skin of a young goat. **2.** the leather made from this skin. [C18: from French: kid, from *chèvre* goat, from Latin *capra*]

chevron (ˈʃɛvrən) *n.* **1.** *Military.* a badge or insignia consisting of one or more V-shaped stripes to indicate a noncommissioned rank or length of service. **2.** *Heraldry.* an inverted V-shaped charge on a shield, one of the earliest ordinaries found in English arms. **3.** (*usually pl.*) a pattern of horizontal black and white V-shapes on a road sign indicating a sharp bend. **4.** any V-shaped pattern or device. **5.** Also called: **dancette.** an ornamental moulding having a zigzag pattern. [C14: from Old French, ultimately from Latin *caper* goat; compare Latin *capreoli* two pieces of wood forming rafters (literally: little goats)]

chevrotain (ˈʃɛvrəˌteɪn, -tɪn) *n.* any small timid ruminant artiodactyl mammal of the genera *Tragulus* and *Hyemoschus,* of S and SE Asia: family *Tragulidae.* They resemble rodents, and the males have long tusklike upper canines. Also called: **mouse deer.** [C18: from French, from Old French *chevrot* kid, from *chèvre* goat, from Latin *capra,* feminine of *caper* goat]

chevy (ˈtʃɛvɪ) *n., vb.* a variant of **chivy.**

chew (tʃuː) *vb.* **1.** to work the jaws and teeth in order to grind (food); masticate. **2.** to bite repeatedly: *she chewed her nails anxiously.* **3.** (*intr.*) to use chewing tobacco. **4. chew the fat** *or* **rag.** *Slang.* **a.** to argue over a point. **b.** to talk idly; gossip. ~*n.* **5.** the act of chewing. **6.** something that is chewed: *a chew of tobacco.* ~See also **chew out, chew over, chew up.** [Old English *ceowan;* related to Old High German *kiuwan,* Dutch *kauwen,* Latin *gingīva* a gum] —ˈ**chewable** *adj.* —ˈ**chewer** *n.*

Chewa (ˈtʃeɪwə) *n.* **1.** (*pl.* **-was** *or* **-wa**) a member of a Negro people of Malawi, E Zambia, and N Zimbabwe, in central Africa, related to the Bemba. **2.** the language of this people. See **Chichewa.**

chewie (ˈtʃuːɪ) *n. Austral. informal.* chewing gum.

chewing gum *n.* a preparation for chewing, usually made of flavoured and sweetened chicle or such substitutes as polyvinyl acetate.

chew out *vb.* (*tr., adv.*) *U.S. and Canadian informal.* to reprimand.

chew over *vb.* (*tr., adv.*) to consider carefully; ruminate on.

chew up *vb.* (*tr., adv.*) **1.** to damage or destroy (something) by or as by chewing or grinding. **2.** (*usually passive*) *Slang.* to cause (a person) to be nervous or worried: *he was all chewed up about the interview.*

chewy (ˈtʃuːɪ) *adj.* **chewier, chewiest.** of a consistency requiring chewing; somewhat firm and sticky.

Cheyenne (ʃaɪˈæn) *n.* **1.** (*pl.* **-enne** *or* **-ennes**) a member of a North American Indian people of the western Plains, now living chiefly in Montana and Oklahoma. **2.** the language of this people, belonging to the Algonquian family. [via Canadian French from Dakota *Shaiyena,* from *shaia* to speak incoherently, from *sha* red + *ya* to speak]

Cheyne-Stokes breathing (ˈtʃeɪnˈstəʊks) *n. Pathol.* alternating shallow and deep breathing, as in comatose patients. [C19: named after John *Cheyne* (1777–1836), Scottish physician, and William *Stokes* (1804–78), Irish physician]

chez *French.* (ʃe) *prep.* **1.** at the home of. **2.** with, among, or in the manner of.

chg. *Commerce, finance, etc. abbrev. for* charge.

chi[1] (kaɪ) *n.* the 22nd letter of the Greek alphabet (Χ, χ), a consonant, transliterated as *ch* or rarely *kh.*

chi[2] *or* **ch'i** (tʃiː) *or* **qi** *n.* (*sometimes cap.*) (in Oriental medicine, martial arts, etc.) vital energy believed to circulate round the body in currents. [Chinese, literally: energy]

chiack *or* **chyack** (ˈtʃaɪæk) *Austral. informal.* ~*vb.* (*tr.*) **1.** to tease or banter. ~*n.* **2.** good-humoured banter. [C19: from *chi-hike,* a shout or greeting]

Chian (ˈkaɪən) *adj.* **1.** of or relating to Chios, a Greek island off the Turkish coast. ~*n.* **2.** a native or inhabitant of Chios.

chianti (kɪˈæntɪ) *n.* (*sometimes cap.*) a dry red wine produced in the Chianti region of central Italy.

chiaroscuro (kɪˌɑːrəˈskʊərəʊ) *n., pl.* **-ros.** **1.** the artistic distribution of light and dark masses in a picture. **2.** monochrome painting using light and dark only, as in grisaille. [C17: from Italian, from *chiaro* CLEAR + *oscuro* OBSCURE] —**chiˌaroˈscurist** *n.* —**chiˌaroˈscurism** *n.*

chiasma (kaɪˈæzmə) *or* **chiasm** (ˈkaɪæzəm) *n., pl.* **-mas, -mata** (-mətə), *or* **-asms.** **1.** *Cytology.* the cross-shaped connection produced by the crossing over of pairing chromosomes during meiosis. **2.** *Anatomy.* the crossing over of two parts or structures, such as the fibres of the optic nerves in the brain. [C19: from Greek *khiasma* wooden crosspiece, from *khiazein* to mark with an X, from *khi* CHI] —**chiˈasmal** *or* **chiˈasmic** *adj.*

chiasmus (kaɪˈæzməs) *n., pl.* **-mi** (-maɪ). *Rhetoric.* reversal of the order of words in the second of two parallel phrases: *he came in triumph and in defeat departs.* [C19: from New Latin, from Greek *khiasmos* crisscross arrangement; see CHIASMA] —**chiastic** (kaɪˈæstɪk) *adj.*

chiastolite (kaɪˈæstəˌlaɪt) *n.* a variety of andalusite containing carbon impurities. Also called: **macle.** [C19: from German *Chiastolith,* from Greek *khiastos* crossed, marked with a chi + *lithos* stone]

Chibchan (ˈtʃɪbtʃən) *n.* **1.** a family of Indian languages found in Colombia and elsewhere in South America. ~*adj.* **2.** belonging or relating to this family of languages.

chibouk *or* **chibouque** (tʃɪˈbuːk) *n.* a Turkish tobacco pipe with an extremely long stem. [C19: from French *chibouque,* from Turkish *çubuk* pipe]

chic (ʃiːk, ʃɪk) *adj.* **1.** (esp. of fashionable clothes, women, etc.) stylish or elegant. ~*n.* **2.** stylishness, esp. in dress; modishness; fashionable good taste. [C19: from French, of uncertain origin] —ˈ**chicly** *adv.*

chicalote (ˌtʃiːkɑːˈləʊteɪ) *n.* a poppy, *Argemone platyceras,* of the southwestern U.S. and Mexico with prickly leaves and white or yellow flowers. [from Spanish, from Nahuatl *chicalotl*]

chicane (ʃɪˈkeɪn) *n.* **1.** a bridge or whist hand without trumps. **2.** *Motor racing.* a short section of sharp narrow bends formed by barriers placed on a motor-racing circuit to provide an additional test of driving skill. **3.** a less common word for **chicanery.** ~*vb.* **4.** (*tr.*) to deceive or trick by chicanery. **5.** (*tr.*) to quibble about; cavil over. **6.** (*intr.*) to use tricks or chicanery. [C17: from French *chicaner* to quibble, of obscure origin] —**chiˈcaner** *n.*

chicanery (ʃɪˈkeɪnərɪ) *n., pl.* **-eries.** **1.** verbal deception or trickery, esp. in legal quibbling; dishonest or sharp practice. **2.** a trick, deception, or quibble.

chicano (tʃɪˈkɑːnəʊ) *n., pl.* **-nos.** *U.S.* an American citizen of Mexican origin. [C20: from Spanish *mejicano* Mexican]

chiccory (ˈtʃɪkərɪ) *n., pl.* **-ries.** a variant spelling of **chicory.**

Chichewa (tʃɪˈtʃeɪwə) *n.* the language of the Chewa people of central Africa, widely used as a lingua franca in Malawi. It belongs to the Bantu group of the Niger-Congo family.

chichi[1] (ˈʃiːˌʃiː) *adj.* **1.** affectedly pretty or stylish. ~*n.* **2.** the quality of being affectedly pretty or stylish. [C20: from French]

chichi[2] (ˈtʃiːˌtʃiː) *n., pl.* **chichis.** (in India, formerly) **a.** a person of mixed British and Indian descent; Anglo-Indian. **b.** (*as modifier*): *a chichi accent.* ~Also (less common): **chee-chee.** [C18: perhaps from Hindi *chhī-chhī,* literally: dirt, or perhaps imitative of their supposed singsong speech]

chick (tʃɪk) *n.* **1.** the young of a bird, esp. of a domestic fowl. **2.** *Slang.* a girl or young woman, esp. an attractive one. **3.** a young child: used as a term of endearment. [C14: short for CHICKEN]

chickabiddy (ˈtʃɪkəˌbɪdɪ) *n., pl.* **-dies.** a term of endearment, esp. for a child. [C18: from CHICK + BIDDY[1]]

chickadee (ˈtʃɪkəˌdiː) *n.* any of various small North American songbirds of the genus *Parus,* such as *P. atricapillus* (**black-capped chickadee**), typically having grey-and-black plumage: family *Paridae* (titmice). [C19: imitative of its note]

chickaree (ˈtʃɪkəˌriː) *n.* another name for **American red squirrel** (see **squirrel** (sense 1)).

Chickasaw (ˈtʃɪkəˌsɔː) *n.* **1.** (*pl.* **-saws** *or* **-saw**) a member of a North American Indian people of N Mississippi. **2.** the language of this people, belonging to the Muskogean family and closely related to Choctaw.

chicken (ˈtʃɪkɪn) *n.* **1.** a domestic fowl bred for its flesh or eggs, esp. a young one. **2.** the flesh of such a bird used for food. **3.** any of various similar birds, such as a prairie chicken. **4.** *Slang.* a cowardly person. **5.** *Slang.* a young inexperienced person. **6.** *Informal.* any of various, often dangerous, games or challenges in which the object is to make one's opponent lose his nerve. **7. count one's chickens before they are hatched.** to be overoptimistic in acting on expectations which are not yet fulfilled. **8. no (spring) chicken.** *Slang.* no longer young: *she's no chicken.* ~*adj.* **9.** *Slang.* easily scared; cowardly; timid. [Old English *ciecen;* related to Old Norse *kjūklingr* gosling, Middle Low German *kūken* chicken]

chicken breast *n. Pathol.* another name for **pigeon breast.** —ˌ**chicken-ˈbreasted** *adj.*

chicken feed *n. Slang.* a trifling amount of money.

chicken-hearted *or* **chicken-livered** *adj.* easily frightened; cowardly. —ˌ**chicken-ˈheartedly** *adv.* —ˌ**chicken-ˈheartedness** *n.*

chicken louse *n.* a louse, *Menopon pallidum* (or *gallinae*); a parasite of poultry: order *Mallophaga* (bird lice).

chicken out *vb.* (*intr., adv.*) *Informal.* to fail to do something through fear or lack of conviction.

chickenpox (ˈtʃɪkɪnˌpɒks) *n.* a highly communicable viral disease most commonly affecting children, characterized by slight fever and the eruption of a rash.

chicken wire *n.* wire netting with a hexagonal mesh.

chickpea (ˈtʃɪkˌpiː) *n.* **1.** a bushy leguminous plant, *Cicer arietinum,* cultivated for its edible pealike seeds in the Mediterranean region, central Asia, and Africa. **2.** the seed of this plant. ~Also called: **garbanzo.** [C16 *ciche peasen,* from *ciche* (from French *chiche,* from Latin *cicer* chickpea) + *peasen;* see PEA]

chickweed (ˈtʃɪkˌwiːd) *n.* **1.** any of various caryophyllaceous plants of the genus *Stellaria,* esp. *S. media,* a common garden weed with small white flowers. **2. mouse-ear chickweed.** any of various similar and related plants of the genus *Cerastium.*

chicle (ˈtʃɪkᵊl) *n.* a gumlike substance obtained from the sapodilla; the main ingredient of chewing gum. Also called: **chicle gum.** [from Spanish, from Nahuatl *chictli*]

chico (ˈtʃiːkəʊ) *n., pl.* **-cos.** another name for **greasewood** (sense 1).

chicory ('tʃɪkərɪ) *n., pl.* **-ries.** 1. Also called: **succory.** a blue-flowered plant, *Cichorium intybus,* cultivated for its leaves, which are used in salads, and for its roots: family *Compositae* (composites). 2. the root of this plant, roasted, dried, and used as a coffee substitute. ~Compare **endive.** [C15: from Old French *chicorée,* from Latin *cichorium,* from Greek *kikhōrion*]

chide (tʃaɪd) *vb.* **chides, chiding, chided** *or* **chid; chided, chid** *or* **chidden.** 1. to rebuke or scold. 2. (*tr.*) to goad into action. [Old English *cīdan*] —'**chider** *n.* —'**chidingly** *adv.*

chief (tʃiːf) *n.* 1. the head, leader, or most important individual in a group or body of people. 2. another word for **chieftain** (sense 1). 3. *Heraldry.* the upper third of a shield. 4. **in chief.** primarily; especially. ~*adj.* 5. (*prenominal*) a. most important; principal. b. highest in rank or authority. ~*adv.* 6. *Archaic.* principally. [C13: from Old French, from Latin *caput* head]

chief justice *n.* 1. (in any of several Commonwealth countries) the judge presiding over a supreme court. 2. (in the U.S.) the presiding judge of a court composed of a number of members. ~See also **Lord Chief Justice.** —**chief justiceship** *n.*

chiefly ('tʃiːflɪ) *adv.* 1. especially or essentially; above all. 2. in general; mainly; mostly. ~*adj.* 3. of or relating to a chief or chieftain.

Chief of Staff *n.* 1. the senior staff officer under the commander of a major military formation or organization. 2. the senior officer of each service of the armed forces. Abbrevs.: **C of S, COS.**

chief petty officer *n.* the senior naval rank for personnel without commissioned or warrant rank. Abbrev.: **CPO.**

Chief Rabbi *n.* the chief religious minister of a national Jewish community.

chieftain ('tʃiːftən, -tɪn) *n.* 1. the head or leader of a tribe or clan. 2. the chief of a group of people. [C14: from Old French *chevetaine,* from Late Latin *capitāneus* commander; see CAPTAIN] —'**chieftaincy** *or* '**chieftain,ship** *n.*

chief technician *n.* a noncommissioned officer in the Royal Air Force junior to a flight sergeant.

chiel (tʃiːl) *n. Scot.* a young man; lad. [C14: a Scot. variant of CHILD]

chiffchaff ('tʃɪf,tʃæf) *n.* a common European warbler, *Phylloscopus collybita,* with a yellowish-brown plumage. [C18: imitative of its call]

chiffon (ʃɪ'fɒn, 'ʃɪfɒn) *n.* 1. a fine transparent or almost transparent plain-weave fabric of silk, nylon, etc. 2. (*often pl.*) *Now rare.* feminine finery. ~*adj.* 3. made of chiffon. 4. (of soufflés, pies, cakes, etc.) having a very light fluffy texture. [C18: from French, from *chiffe* rag; probably related to CHIP] —'**chiffony** *adj.*

chiffonier *or* **chiffonnier** (,ʃɪfə'nɪə) *n.* 1. a tall, elegant chest of drawers, originally intended for holding needlework. 2. a wide low open-fronted cabinet, sometimes fitted with two grille doors and shelves. [C19: from French, from *chiffon* rag; see CHIFFON]

chigetai (,tʃɪgɪ'taɪ) *n.* a variety of the Asiatic wild ass, *Equus hemionus,* of Mongolia. Also spelled: **dziggetai.** [from Mongolian *tchikhitei* long-eared, from *tchikhi* ear]

chigger ('tʃɪgə) *n.* 1. Also called: **chigoe, redbug.** *U.S. and Canadian.* the parasitic larva of any of various free-living mites of the family *Trombidiidae,* which causes intense itching of human skin. 2. another name for the **chigoe** (sense 1).

chignon ('ʃiːnjɒn; *French* ʃiɲɔ̃) *n.* an arrangement of long hair in a roll or knot at the back of the head. [C18: from French, from Old French *chaignon* link, from *chaine* CHAIN; influenced also by Old French *tignon* coil of hair, from *tigne,* moth, from Latin *tinea* moth] —'**chignoned** *adj.*

chigoe ('tʃɪgəʊ) *n.* 1. Also called: **chigger, jigger, sand flea.** a tropical flea, *Tunga penetrans,* the female of which lives on or burrows into the skin of its host, which includes man. 2. another name for **chigger** (sense 1). [C17: from Carib *chigo*]

Chihuahua (tʃɪ'wɑːwɑː, -wə) *n.* a breed of tiny dog originally from Mexico, having short smooth hair, large erect ears, and protruding eyes. [named after *Chihuahua,* state in N Mexico]

chilblain ('tʃɪl,bleɪn) *n. Pathol.* (*usually pl.*) an inflammation of the fingers, toes, or ears, caused by prolonged exposure to moisture and cold. [C16: from CHILL (n.) + BLAIN] —'**chil,blained** *adj.*

child (tʃaɪld) *n., pl.* **children.** 1. a. a boy or girl between birth and puberty. b. (*as modifier*): *child labour.* 2. a baby or infant. 3. an unborn baby. 4. **with child.** another term for **pregnant.** 5. a human offspring; a son or daughter. Related adj.: **filial.** 6. a childish or immature person. 7. a member of a family or tribe; descendant: *a child of Israel.* 8. a person or thing regarded as the product of an influence or environment: *a child of nature.* 9. *Midland and western English dialect.* a female infant. [Old English *cild;* related to Gothic *kilthei* womb, Sanskrit *jathara* belly, *jartu* womb] —'**childless** *adj.* —'**childlessness** *n.* —'**childly** *adj.*

child abuse *n.* physical, sexual, or emotional ill-treatment or neglect of a child by its parents or other adults responsible for its welfare. See also **nonaccidental injury.**

child-abuse register *n. Social welfare.* (in Britain) a list of children deemed to be at risk of abuse or injury from their parents or guardians, compiled and held by a local authority, area health authority, or NSPCC Special Unit. Also called: **NAI register.**

child-bearing *n.* a. the act or process of carrying and giving birth to a child. b. (*as modifier*): *of child-bearing age.*

childbed ('tʃaɪld,bɛd) *n.* a. (often preceded by *in*) the condition of giving birth to a child. b. (*as modifier*): *childbed fever.*

child benefit *n.* (in Britain and New Zealand) a regular government payment to the parents of children up to a certain age. Austral. equivalent: **child endowment.**

childbirth ('tʃaɪld,bɜːθ) *n.* the act of giving birth to a child.

childcare ('tʃaɪld,kɛə) *n. Brit.* 1. care provided for children without homes (or with a seriously disturbed home life) by a local authority. 2. care and supervision of children whose parents are working, provided by a childminder or local authority.

childe (tʃaɪld) *n. Archaic.* a young man of noble birth. [C13: variant of CHILD]

childermas ('tʃɪldə,mæs) *n. Archaic.* Holy Innocents Day, Dec. 28. [Old English *cylda-mæsse,* from *cildra,* genitive plural of CHILD, + *mæsse* MASS]

child guidance *n.* the counselling of emotionally disturbed children.

childhood ('tʃaɪldhʊd) *n.* the condition of being a child; the period of life before puberty.

childish ('tʃaɪldɪʃ) *adj.* 1. in the manner of, belonging to, or suitable to a child. 2. foolish or petty; puerile: *childish fears.* —'**childishly** *adv.* —'**childishness** *n.*

child labour *n.* the full-time employment of children below a minimum age laid down by statute.

childlike ('tʃaɪld,laɪk) *adj.* like or befitting a child, as in being innocent, trustful, etc. Compare **childish** (sense 2).

child minder *n.* a person who looks after children, esp. those whose parents are working.

children ('tʃɪldrən) *n.* the plural of **child.**

child's play *n. Informal.* something that is easy to do.

chile ('tʃɪlɪ) *n.* a variant spelling of **chilli.**

Chilean ('tʃɪlɪən) *adj.* 1. of or relating to Chile, a republic in South America, or its people ~*n* 2. a native or inhabitant of Chile.

Chile pine ('tʃɪlɪ) *n.* another name for the **monkey puzzle.**

Chile saltpetre *or* **nitre** *n.* a naturally occurring form of sodium nitrate: a soluble white or colourless mineral occurring in arid regions, esp. in Chile and Peru. Also called: **soda nitre.**

chiliad ('kɪlɪ,æd) *n.* 1. a group of one thousand. 2. one thousand years. [C16: from Greek *khilias,* from *khilioi* a thousand] —,**chili'adal** *or* ,**chili'adic** *adj.*

chiliasm ('kɪlɪ,æzəm) *n. Christian theol.* another term for **millenarianism** or the **millennium.** [C17: from Greek *khiliasmos,* from *khilioi* a thousand] —'**chili,ast** *n.* —,**chili'astic** *adj.*

chill (tʃɪl) *n.* 1. a moderate coldness. 2. a sensation of coldness resulting from a cold or damp environment, or from a sudden emotional reaction. 3. a feverish cold. 4. a check on enthusiasm or joy. 5. a metal plate placed in a sand mould to accelerate cooling and control local grain growth. 6. another name for **bloom**[1] (sense 9). ~*adj.* 7. another word for **chilly.** ~*vb.* 8. to make or become cold. 9. (*tr.*) to cool or freeze (food, drinks, etc.). 10. (*tr.*) a. to depress (enthusiasm, etc.). b. to discourage. 11. (*tr.*) to cool (a casting or metal object) rapidly in order to prevent the formation of large grains in the metal. [Old English *ciele;* related to *calan* to COOL, Latin *gelidus* icy] —'**chillingly** *adv.* —'**chillness** *n.*

chiller ('tʃɪlə) *n.* 1. *Informal.* short for **spine-chiller.** 2. *N.Z.* a refrigerated storage area for meat.

chilli ('tʃɪlɪ) *n., pl.* **chillies.** the small red hot-tasting pod of a type of capsicum used for flavouring sauces, pickles, etc. [C17: from Spanish *chile,* from Nahuatl *chilli*]

chilli con carne (kɒn 'kɑːnɪ) *n.* a highly seasoned Mexican dish of meat, onions, beans, and chilli powder. [from Spanish *chile con carne* chilli with meat]

chilli powder *n.* ground chilli blended with other spices.

chilli sauce *n.* a highly seasoned sauce made of tomatoes cooked with chilli and other spices and seasonings.

chill out *vb.* (*intr., adv.*) *Slang, chiefly U.S.* to relax.

chillum ('tʃɪləm) *n.* a short pipe, usually of clay, used esp. for smoking cannabis. [C18: from Hindi *cilam,* from Persian *chilam*]

chilly ('tʃɪlɪ) *adj.* **-lier, -liest.** 1. causing or feeling cool or moderately cold. 2. without warmth; unfriendly. 3. (of people) sensitive to cold. —'**chilliness** *n.*

chilly bin *n. N.Z. informal.* a portable insulated container with provision for packing food and drink in ice.

chilopod ('kaɪlə,pɒd) *n.* any arthropod of the class *Chilopoda,* which includes the centipedes. See also **myriapod.** [C19: from New Latin *Chilopoda,* from Greek *kheilos* lip + *pous* foot; referring to the modification of the first pair of legs into jawlike claws] —**chilopodan** (kaɪ'lɒpədən) *n., adj.* —**chi'lopodous** *adj.*

Chiltern Hundreds ('tʃɪltən 'hʌndrədz) *pl. n.* (in Britain) short for **Stewardship of the Chiltern Hundreds;** a nominal office that an MP applies for in order to resign his seat.

chimaera (kaɪ'mɪərə, kɪ-) *n.* 1. any tapering smooth-skinned cartilaginous deep-sea fish of the subclass *Holocephali* (or *Bradyodonti*), esp. any of the genus *Chimaera.* They have a skull in which the upper jaw is fused to the cranium. See also **rabbit-**

fish (sense 1). **2.** *Greek myth.* a variant spelling of **chimera** (sense 1).

chimb (tʃaɪm) *n.* a variant spelling of **chime**[2].

chime[1] (tʃaɪm) *n.* **1.** an individual bell or the sound it makes when struck. **2.** (*often pl.*) the machinery employed to sound a bell in this way. **3.** Also called: **bell.** a percussion instrument consisting of a set of vertical metal tubes of graduated length, suspended in a frame and struck with a hammer. **4.** a harmonious or ringing sound: *the chimes of children's laughter.* **5.** agreement; concord. ~*vb.* **6. a.** to sound (a bell) or (of a bell) to be sounded by a clapper or hammer. **b.** to produce (music or sounds) by chiming. **7.** (*tr.*) to indicate or show (time or the hours) by chiming. **8.** (*tr.*) to summon, announce, or welcome by ringing bells. **9.** (*intr.*; foll. by *with*) to agree or harmonize. **10.** to speak or recite in a musical or rhythmic manner. [C13: probably shortened from earlier *chymbe bell,* ultimately from Latin *cymbalum* CYMBAL] —**'chimer** *n.*

chime[2], **chimb** (tʃaɪm), *or* **chine** *n.* the projecting edge or rim of a cask or barrel. [Old English *cimb-;* related to Middle Low German *kimme* outer edge, Swedish *kimb*]

chime in *vb.* (*intr., adv.*) *Informal.* **1.** to join in or interrupt (a conversation), esp. repeatedly and unwelcomely. **2.** to voice agreement.

chimera *or* **chimaera** (kaɪ'mɪərə, kɪ-) *n.* **1.** (*often cap.*) *Greek myth.* a fire-breathing monster with the head of a lion, body of a goat, and tail of a serpent. **2.** a fabulous beast made up of parts taken from various animals. **3.** a wild and unrealistic dream or notion. **4.** *Biology.* an organism, esp. a cultivated plant, consisting of at least two genetically different kinds of tissue as a result of mutation, grafting, etc. [C16: from Latin *chimaera,* from Greek *khimaira* she-goat, from *khimaros* he-goat]

chimere (tʃɪ'mɪə, ʃɪ-), **chimer,** *or* **chimar** ('tʃɪmə, 'ʃɪm-) *n. Anglican Church.* a sleeveless red or black gown, part of a bishop's formal dress though not a vestment. [C14: perhaps from Medieval Latin *chimēra* (see CHIMERA) and related to Spanish *zamarra* sheepskin coat]

chimerical (kaɪ'mɛrɪkᵊl, kɪ-) *or* **chimeric** *adj.* **1.** wildly fanciful; imaginary. **2.** given to or indulging in fantasies. —**chi'merically** *adv.* —**chi'mericalness** *n.*

chimeric face *n.* a picture of a face made by joining the left and right halves of the faces of two separate people, shown esp. to patients who have a split brain in order to test the effects on separate hemispheres.

chimney ('tʃɪmnɪ) *n.* **1.** a vertical structure of brick, masonry, or steel that carries smoke or steam away from a fire, engine, etc. **2.** another name for **flue**[1] (sense 1). **3.** short for **chimney stack. 4.** an open-ended glass tube fitting around the flame of an oil or gas lamp in order to exclude draughts. **5.** *Brit.* a fireplace, esp. an old and large one. **6.** *Geology.* **a.** the part of a mineral deposit that consists of the most valuable ore. **b.** the vent of a volcano. **7.** *Mountaineering.* a vertical fissure large enough for a person's body to enter. **8.** anything resembling a chimney in shape or function. [C14: from Old French *cheminée,* from Late Latin *camīnāta,* from Latin *camīnus* furnace, from Greek *kaminos* fireplace, oven]

chimney breast *n.* the wall or walls that surround the base of a chimney or fireplace.

chimney corner *n.* a recess that contains a seat in a large open fireplace; inglenook.

chimneypiece ('tʃɪmnɪˌpiːs) *n.* another name (esp. Brit.) for **mantelpiece** (sense 1).

chimneypot ('tʃɪmnɪˌpɒt) *n.* a short pipe on the top of a chimney, which increases the draught and directs the smoke upwards.

chimney stack *n.* the part of a chimney that rises above the roof of a building.

chimney swallow *n.* **1.** another name for **common swallow** (see **swallow**[2]). **2.** a less common name for **chimney swift.**

chimney sweep *or* **sweeper** *n.* a person whose job is the cleaning out of soot from chimneys.

chimney swift *n.* a North American swift, *Chaetura pelagica,* that nests in chimneys and similar hollows.

chimp (tʃɪmp) *n. Informal.* short for **chimpanzee.**

chimpanzee (ˌtʃɪmpæn'ziː) *n.* a gregarious and intelligent anthropoid ape, *Pan troglodytes,* inhabiting forests in central W Africa. [C18: from Kongo dialect]

chin (tʃɪn) *n.* **1.** the protruding part of the lower jaw. **2.** the front part of the face below the lips. **3. keep one's chin up.** to keep cheerful under difficult circumstances. Sometimes shortened to **chin up! 4. take it on the chin.** *Informal.* to face squarely up to a defeat, adversity, etc. ~*vb.* **chins, chinning, chinned. 5.** *Gymnastics.* to raise one's chin to (a horizontal bar, etc.) when hanging by the arms. [Old English *cinn;* related to Old Norse *kinn,* Old High German *kinni,* Latin *gena* cheek, Old Irish *gin* mouth, Sanskrit *hanu*]

Chin. *abbrev. for:* **1.** China. **2.** Chinese.

china[1] ('tʃaɪnə) *n.* **1.** ceramic ware of a type originally from China. **2.** any porcelain or similar ware. **3.** cups, saucers, etc., collectively. **4.** (*modifier*) made of china. [C16 *chiny,* from Persian *chīnī*]

china[2] ('tʃaɪnə) *n. Brit. slang.* mate; pal (esp. in the phrase **my old china).** [C19: originally Cockney rhyming slang: *china plate, mate*]

China aster ('tʃəɪnə) *n.* a Chinese plant, *Callistephus chinensis,* widely cultivated for its aster-like flowers: family *Compositae* (composites).

china bark *n.* another name for **cinchona** (sense 2).

chinaberry ('tʃaɪnəbərɪ) *n., pl.* **-ries. 1.** Also called: **China tree, azedarach.** a spreading Asian meliaceous tree, *Melia azedarach,* widely grown in the U.S. for its ornamental white or purple flowers and beadlike yellow fruits. **2.** another name for **soapberry. 3.** the fruit of any of these trees.

china clay *or* **stone** *n.* another name for **kaolin.**

Chinagraph ('tʃaɪnəˌgrɑːf, -ˌgræf) *n. Trademark.* **a.** a coloured pencil used for writing on china, glass, etc. **b.** (*as modifier*): *a Chinagraph pencil.*

China ink *n.* another name for **Indian ink.**

Chinaman ('tʃaɪnəmən) *n., pl.* **-men. 1.** *Archaic or derogatory.* a native or inhabitant of China. **2.** (*often not cap.*) *Cricket.* a ball bowled by a left-handed bowler to a right-handed batsman that spins from off to leg.

China rose *n.* **1.** a rosaceous shrub, *Rosa chinensis* (or *R. indica*), with red, pink, or white fragrant flowers: the ancestor of many cultivated roses. **2.** a related dwarf plant, *Rosa semperflorens,* having crimson flowers. **3.** another name for **hibiscus.**

china stone *n.* **1.** a type of kaolinized granitic rock containing unaltered plagioclase. **2.** any of certain limestones having a very fine grain and smooth texture.

Chinatown ('tʃaɪnəˌtaʊn) *n.* a quarter of any city or town outside China with a predominantly Chinese population.

China tree *n.* another name for **chinaberry** (sense 1).

chinaware ('tʃaɪnəˌwɛə) *n.* **1.** articles made of china, esp. those made for domestic use. **2.** (*modifier*) made of china.

chin ball *n. N.Z.* a device fastened under the chin of a bull to mark cows he has mounted.

chincapin ('tʃɪŋkəpɪn) *n.* a variant spelling of **chinquapin.**

chinch (tʃɪntʃ) *n. Southern U.S.* another name for a **bedbug.** [C17: from Spanish *chinche,* from Latin *cīmex* bug]

chinch bug *n.* **1.** a black-and-white tropical American heteropterous insect, *Blissus leucopterus,* that is very destructive to grasses and cereals in the U.S.: family *Lygaeidae.* **2.** a related and similar European insect, *Ischnodemus sabuleti.*

chincherinchee (ˌtʃɪntʃərɪn'tʃiː, -'rɪntʃɪ) *n.* a bulbous South African liliaceous plant, *Ornithogalum thyrsoides,* having long spikes of white or yellow long-lasting flowers. [of unknown origin]

chinchilla (tʃɪn'tʃɪlə) *n.* **1.** a small gregarious hystricomorph rodent, *Chinchilla laniger,* inhabiting mountainous regions of South America: family *Chinchillidae.* It has a stocky body and is bred in captivity for its soft silvery grey fur. **2.** the highly valued fur of this animal. **3. mountain chinchilla.** Also called: **mountain viscacha.** any of several long-tailed rodents of the genus *Lagidium,* having coarse poor quality fur. **4.** a thick napped woollen cloth used for coats. [C17: from Spanish, perhaps from Aymara]

chin-chin *sentence substitute. Informal.* a greeting, farewell, or toast. [C18: from Chinese (Peking) *ch'ing-ch'ing* please-please]

chin cough *n.* another name for **whooping cough.** [C16: changed (through influence from CHINE[1] and CHIN) from earlier *chink-cough,* from CHINK[2] + COUGH]

Chindit ('tʃɪndɪt) *n.* a member of the Allied forces commanded by Orde Wingate (1903–44) fighting behind the Japanese lines in Burma (1943–45). [C20: from Burmese *chinthé* a fabulous lion a symbol of which was their badge; adoption of title perhaps influenced by *Chindwin,* a river in N Burma]

chine[1] (tʃaɪn) *n.* **1.** the backbone. **2.** the backbone of an animal with adjoining meat, cut for cooking. **3.** a ridge or crest of land. **4.** (in some boats) a corner-like intersection where the bottom meets the side. ~*vb.* **5.** (*tr.*) to cut (meat) along or across the backbone. [C14: from Old French *eschine,* of Germanic origin; compare Old High German *scina* needle, shinbone; see SHIN]

chine[2] (tʃaɪn) *n.* another word for **chime**[2].

chine[3] (tʃaɪn) *n. Southern English dialect.* a deep fissure in the wall of a cliff. [Old English *cīnan* to crack]

chiné ('ʃiːneɪ) *adj. Textiles.* having a mottled pattern. [C19: from French *chiner* to make in the Chinese fashion, from *Chine* China]

Chinee (tʃaɪ'niː) *n. Informal.* a Chinaman.

Chinese (tʃaɪ'niːz) *adj.* **1.** of, relating to, or characteristic of China, its people, or their languages. ~*n.* **2.** (*pl.* **-nese**) a native or inhabitant of China or a descendant of one. **3.** any of the languages of China belonging to the Sino-Tibetan family, sometimes regarded as dialects of one language. They share a single writing system that is not phonetic but ideographic. A phonetic system using the Roman alphabet was officially adopted by the Chinese government in 1966. See also **Mandarin Chinese, Pekingese, Cantonese.**

Chinese block *n.* a percussion instrument consisting of a hollow wooden block played with a drumstick.

Chinese cabbage *n.* **1.** Also called: **pe-tsai cabbage.** a Chinese plant, *Brassica pekinensis,* that is related to the cabbage and has crisp edible leaves growing in a loose cylindrical head. **2.** Also called: **pak-choi cabbage.** a similar and related plant, *Brassica chinensis.*

Chinese chequers *n.* (*functioning as sing.*) a board game played with marbles or pegs.

Chinese Chippendale *n.* **a.** a branch of Chippendale style in which Chinese styles and motifs are used. **b.** *(as modifier): a Chinese Chippendale cabinet.*
Chinese copy *n.* an exact copy of an original.
Chinese eddo *n.* another name for **taro.**
Chinese gooseberry *n.* another name for **kiwi fruit.**
Chinese ink *n.* another name for **Indian ink.**
Chinese lantern *n.* **1.** a collapsible lantern made of thin coloured paper. **2.** an Asian solanaceous plant, *Physalis franchetii,* cultivated for its attractive orange-red inflated calyx. See also **winter cherry.**
Chinese leaves *pl. n.* the edible leaves of a Chinese cabbage.
Chinese puzzle *n.* **1.** an intricate puzzle, esp. one consisting of boxes within boxes. **2.** a complicated problem.
Chinese red *n.* **a.** a bright red colour. **b.** *(as adj.): a Chinese-red bag.*
Chinese restaurant syndrome *n.* a group of symptoms such as dizziness, headache, and flushing thought to be caused in some people by consuming large amounts of monosodium glutamate, esp. as used in Chinese food.
Chinese sacred lily *n.* a Chinese amaryllidaceous plant, *Narcissus tazetta orientalis,* widely grown as a house plant for its fragrant yellow and white flowers. See also **polyanthus** (sense 2).
Chinese wall *n.* **1.** a notional barrier between the parts of a business, esp. between the market makers and brokers of a stock-exchange business, across which no information should pass to the detriment of clients. **2.** an insurmountable obstacle.
Chinese water deer *n.* a small Chinese or Korean deer, *Hydropotes inermis,* having tusks and no antlers: introduced into England and France.
Chinese water torture *n.* a form of torture in which water is made to drip onto a victim's forehead to drive him insane.
Chinese wax *or* **treewax** ('triːˌwæks) *n.* a yellowish wax secreted by an oriental scale insect, *Ceroplastes ceriferus,* and used commercially.
Chinese white *n.* white zinc oxide, formerly used in paints. Also called: **zinc white.**
Chinese windlass *n.* another name for **differential windlass.**
Chinese wood oil *n.* another name for **tung oil.**
Ching *or* **Ch'ing** (tʃɪŋ) *adj.* of, relating to, or designating the Manchu dynasty (1644–1912) of China.
chink[1] (tʃɪŋk) *n.* **1.** a small narrow opening, such as a fissure or crack. **2. chink in one's armour.** a small but fatal weakness. ~*vb.* **3.** *(tr.) Chiefly U.S. and Canadian.* to fill up or make cracks in. [C16: perhaps variant of earlier *chine,* from Old English *cine* crack; related to Middle Dutch *kene,* Danish *kin*] —'**chinky** *adj.*
chink[2] (tʃɪŋk) *vb.* **1.** to make or cause to make a light ringing sound, as by the striking of glasses or coins. ~*n.* **2.** such a sound. [C16: of imitative origin]
Chink (tʃɪŋk) *or* **Chinky** ('tʃɪŋkɪ) *n., pl.* **Chinks** *or* **Chinkies,** *adj.* a derogatory term for **Chinese.** [C20: probably from *Chinese,* influenced by CHINK[1] (referring to the characteristic shape of the Chinese eye)]
chinkapin ('tʃɪŋkəpɪn) *n.* a variant spelling of **chinquapin.**
chinless ('tʃɪnlɪs) *adj.* **1.** having a receding chin. **2.** weak or ineffectual.
chinless wonder *n. Brit. informal.* a person, esp. an upper-class one, lacking strength of character.
chino ('tʃiːnəʊ) *n., pl.* **-nos.** *U.S.* a durable cotton twill cloth. [C20: from American Spanish, of obscure origin]
Chino- *combining form.* of or relating to China. See also **Sino-.**
chinoiserie (ʃiːnˌwɑːzə'riː, -'wɑːzərɪ) *n.* **1.** a style of decorative or fine art based on imitations of Chinese motifs. **2.** an object or objects in this style. [French, from *chinois* CHINESE; see -ERY]
chinook (tʃɪ'nuːk, -'nʊk) *n.* **1.** Also called: **snow eater.** a warm dry southwesterly wind blowing down the eastern slopes of the Rocky Mountains. **2.** Also called: **wet chinook.** a warm moist wind blowing onto the Washington and Oregon coasts from the sea. [C19: from Salish *c'inuk*]
Chinook (tʃɪ'nuːk, -'nʊk) *n.* **1.** *(pl.* **-nook** *or* **-nooks)** a North American Indian people of the Pacific coast near the Columbia River. **2.** the language of this people, probably forming a separate branch of the Penutian phylum.
Chinook Jargon *n.* a pidgin language containing elements of North American Indian languages, English, and French: formerly used among fur traders and Indians on the NW coast of North America.
Chinook salmon *n.* a Pacific salmon, *Oncorhynchus tschawytscha,* valued as a food fish. Also called: **quinnat salmon, king salmon.**
chinos ('tʃiːnəʊz) *pl. n.* trousers made of chino.
chinquapin, chincapin, *or* **chinkapin** ('tʃɪŋkəpɪn) *n.* **1.** a dwarf chestnut tree, *Castanea pumila,* of the eastern U.S., yielding edible nuts. **2.** Also called: **giant chinquapin.** a large evergreen fagaceous tree, *Castanopsis chrysophylla,* of W North America. **3.** the nut of either of these trees. ~Compare **water chinquapin.** [C17: of Algonquian origin; compare Algonquian *chechinkamin* chestnut]
chintz (tʃɪnts) *n.* **1.** a printed, patterned cotton fabric, with glazed finish. **2.** a painted or stained Indian calico. [C17: from Hindi *chīnt,* from Sanskrit *citra* gaily-coloured]
chintzy ('tʃɪntsɪ) *adj.* **chintzier, chintziest. 1.** of, resembling, or covered with chintz. **2.** *Brit. informal.* typical of the decor associated with the use of chintz soft furnishings, as in a country cottage.
chinwag ('tʃɪnˌwæg) *n. Brit. informal.* a chat or gossipy conversation.
chionodoxa (kaɪˌɒnə'dɒksə) *n.* any plant of the liliaceous genus *Chionodoxa,* of S Europe and W Asia. See **glory-of-the-snow.** [C19: New Latin, from Greek *khiōn* snow + *doxa* glory]
chip (tʃɪp) *n.* **1.** a small piece removed by chopping, cutting, or breaking. **2.** a mark left after a small piece has been chopped, cut, or broken off something. **3.** (in some games) a counter used to represent money. **4.** a thin strip of potato fried in deep fat. **5.** the U.S. and Canadian name for **crisp** (sense 10). **6.** a small piece or thin slice of food. **7.** *Sport.* a shot, kick, etc., lofted into the air, esp. over an obstacle or an opposing player's head, and travelling only a short distance. **8.** *Electronics.* a tiny wafer of semiconductor material, such as silicon, processed to form a type of integrated circuit or component such as a transistor. **9.** a thin strip of wood or straw used for making woven hats, baskets, etc. **10.** *N.Z.* a container for soft fruit, made of thin sheets of wood; punnet. **11. chip off the old block.** *Informal.* a person who resembles one of his or her parents in behaviour. **12. have a chip on one's shoulder.** *Informal.* to be aggressively sensitive about a particular thing or bear a grudge. **13. have had one's chips.** *Brit. informal.* to be defeated, condemned to die, killed, etc. **14. when the chips are down.** *Informal.* at a time of crisis or testing. ~*vb.* **chips, chipping, chipped. 15.** to break small pieces from or become broken off in small pieces: *will the paint chip?* **16.** *(tr.)* to break or cut into small pieces: *to chip ice.* **17.** *(tr.)* to shape by chipping. **18.** *Sport.* to strike or kick (a ball) in a high arc. [Old English *cipp* (n.), *cippian* (vb.), of obscure origin] —'**chipper** *n.*
chip-based ('tʃɪpˌbeɪst) *adj.* (of electronic equipment or components) using or incorporating microchips.
chip basket *n.* **1.** a wire basket for holding potato chips, etc., while frying in deep fat. **2.** a basket made of thin strips of wood, used esp. for packing fruit.
chipboard ('tʃɪpˌbɔːd) *n.* a thin rigid sheet made of compressed wood chips bound with a synthetic resin.
chip heater *n. Austral. and N.Z.* a domestic water heater that burns chips of wood.
chip in *vb. (adv.) Informal.* **1.** to contribute (money, time, etc.) to a cause or fund. **2.** *(intr.)* to interpose a remark or interrupt with a remark.
chip log *n. Nautical.* a log for determining a vessel's speed, consisting of a wooden chip tossed overboard at the end of a line that is marked off in lengths of 47 feet 3 inches; the speed is calculated by counting the number of such intervals that pass overboard in a 28-second interval.
chipmunk ('tʃɪpˌmʌŋk) *n.* any burrowing sciurine rodent of the genera *Tamias* of E North America and *Eutamias* of W North America and Asia, typically having black-striped yellowish fur and cheek pouches for storing food. [C19: of Algonquian origin; compare Ojibwa *atchitamon* squirrel, literally: headfirst, referring to its method of descent from trees]
chipolata (ˌtʃɪpə'lɑːtə) *n. Chiefly Brit.* a small sausage in a narrow casing. [via French from Italian *cipollata* an onion-flavoured dish, from *cipolla* onion]
chip pan *n.* a deep pan for frying potato chips, etc.
Chippendale ('tʃɪpᵊnˌdeɪl) *adj.* (of furniture) designed by, made by, or in the style of Thomas Chippendale (?1718–79), British cabinet-maker, characterized by the use of Chinese and Gothic motifs, cabriole legs, and massive carving.
chipper[1] ('tʃɪpə) *adj. Informal.* **1.** cheerful; lively. **2.** smartly dressed.
chipper[2] ('tʃɪpər) *n. Irish informal.* a fish-and-chip shop.
Chippewa ('tʃɪpɪˌwɑː) *or* **Chippeway** ('tʃɪpɪˌweɪ) *n., pl.* **-was, -wa** *or* **-ways, -way.** another name for **Ojibwa.**
chipping ('tʃɪpɪŋ) *n.* another name for **chip** (sense 1).
chipping sparrow *n.* a common North American sparrow, *Spizella passerina,* having brown-and-grey plumage and a white eye stripe.
chippy[1] ('tʃɪpɪ) *n., pl.* **-pies. 1.** *Brit. informal.* a fish-and-chip shop. **2.** *Brit. and N.Z.* a slang word for **carpenter. 3.** *N.Z.* a potato crisp. [C19: from CHIP (n.)]
chippy[2] *or* **chippie** ('tʃɪpɪ) *n., pl.* **-pies.** an informal name for **chipmunk** or **chipping sparrow.**
chippy[3] *or* **chippie** ('tʃɪpɪ) *n., pl.* **-pies.** *Informal, chiefly U.S. and Canadian.* a promiscuous woman. [C19: perhaps from CHIP (n.)]
chippy[4] ('tʃɪpɪ) *adj.* **-pier, -piest.** *Canadian.* belligerent or touchy. [C19: from CHIP (n.), sense probably developing from: as dry as a chip of wood, hence irritable, touchy]
chip shot *n. Golf.* a short approach shot to the green, esp. one that is lofted.
chirality (kaɪ'rælɪtɪ) *n.* the configuration or handedness (left or right) of an asymmetric, optically active chemical compound. Also called: **dissymmetry.** [C19: from Greek *kheir* hand + -AL[1] + -ITY] —'**chiral** *adj.*
chirm (tʃɜːm) *n.* **1.** the chirping of birds. ~*vb.* **2.** *(intr.)* (esp. of a bird) to chirp. [Old English *cierm* noise; related to Old Saxon *karm*]
chiro- *or* **cheiro-** *combining form.* indicating the hand; of or by means of the hand: *chiromancy; chiropractic.* [via Latin from Greek *kheir* hand]

chirography (kaɪˈrɒgrəfɪ) *n.* another name for **calligraphy.** —**chiˈrographer** *n.* —**chirographic** (ˌkaɪrəˈgræfɪk) *or* **ˌchiroˈgraphical** *adj.*
chiromancy (ˈkaɪrəˌmænsɪ) *n.* another word for **palmistry.** —**ˈchiroˌmancer** *n.*
chironomid (kaɪˈrɒnəmɪd) *n.* **1.** a member of the *Chironomidae,* a family of nonbiting midges. ~*adj.* **2.** of or relating to this family. [C19: from New Latin *chironomus,* from Greek *kheironomos* a gesturer, from *kheir* hand + *nomos* manager + -ID[2]]
chiropody (kɪˈrɒpədɪ) *n.* the treatment of the feet, esp. the treatment of corns, verrucas, etc. —**chiˈropodist** *n.*
chiropractic (ˌkaɪrəˈpræktɪk) *n.* a system of treating bodily disorders by manipulation of the spine and other parts, based on the belief that the cause is the abnormal functioning of a nerve. [C20: from CHIRO- + *-practic,* from Greek *praktikos* effective, PRACTICAL] —**ˈchiroˌpractor** *n.*
chiropteran (kaɪˈrɒptərən) *adj.* **1.** of, relating to, or belonging to the *Chiroptera,* an order of placental mammals comprising the bats. ~*n.* **2.** Also called: **chiropter** (kaɪˈrɒptə). a bat.
chirp (tʃɜːp) *vb. (intr.)* **1.** (esp. of some birds and insects) to make a short high-pitched sound. **2.** to speak in a lively fashion. ~*n.* **3.** a chirping sound, esp. that made by a bird. [C15 (as *chirpinge,* gerund): of imitative origin] —**ˈchirper** *n.*
chirpy (ˈtʃɜːpɪ) *adj.* **chirpier, chirpiest.** *Informal* cheerful; lively. —**ˈchirpily** *adv.* —**ˈchirpiness** *n.*
chirr, chirre, *or* **churr** (tʃɜː) *vb.* **1.** *(intr.)* (esp. of certain insects, such as crickets) to make a shrill trilled sound. ~*n.* **2.** the sound of chirring. [C17: of imitative origin]
chirrup (ˈtʃɪrəp) *vb. (intr.)* **1.** (esp. of some birds) to chirp repeatedly. **2.** to make clucking sounds with the lips. ~*n.* **3.** such a sound. [C16: variant of CHIRP] —**ˈchirruper** *n.* —**ˈchirrupy** *adj.*
chirurgeon (kaɪˈrɜːdʒən) *n.* an archaic word for **surgeon.** [C13: from Old French *cirurgeon*] —**chiˈrurgery** *n.*
chisel (ˈtʃɪzᵊl) *n.* **1. a.** a hand tool for working wood, consisting of a flat steel blade with a cutting edge attached to a handle of wood, plastic, etc. It is either struck with a mallet or used by hand. **b.** a similar tool without a handle for working stone or metal. ~*vb.* **-els, -elling, -elled** *or U.S.* **-els, -eling, -eled. 2.** to carve (wood, stone, metal, etc.) or form (an engraving, statue, etc.) with or as with a chisel. **3.** *Slang.* to cheat or obtain by cheating. [C14: via Old French, from Vulgar Latin *cīsellus* (unattested), from Latin *caesus* cut, from *caedere* to cut]
chiselled *or U.S.* **chiseled** (ˈtʃɪzəld) *adj.* **1.** carved or formed with or as if with a chisel. **2.** clear-cut: *finely chiselled features.*
chiseller (ˈtʃɪzᵊlə) *n.* **1.** a person who uses a chisel. **2.** *Informal.* a cheat. **3.** *Dublin slang.* a child.
chi-square distribution (ˈkaɪˌskwɛə) *n. Statistics.* a continuous single-parameter distribution derived as a special case of the gamma distribution and used esp. to measure goodness of fit and to test hypotheses and obtain confidence intervals for the variance of a normally distributed variable.
chi-square test *n. Statistics.* a test derived from the chi-square distribution to compare the goodness of fit of theoretical and observed frequency distributions or to compare nominal data derived from unmatched groups of subjects.
chit[1] (tʃɪt) *n.* **1.** a voucher for a sum of money owed, esp. for food or drink. **2.** Also called: **chitty** (ˈtʃɪtɪ) *Chiefly Brit.* **a.** a note or memorandum. **b.** a requisition or receipt. [C18: from earlier *chitty,* from Hindi *cittha* note, from Sanskrit *citra* brightly-coloured]
chit[2] (tʃɪt) *n. Facetious or derogatory.* a pert, impudent, or self-confident girl or child. [C14 (in the sense: young of an animal, kitten): of obscure origin]
chital (ˈtʃiːtᵊl) *n.* another name for **axis**[2] (the deer). [from Hindi]
chitarrone (ˌkɪtɑːˈrəʊnɪ, ˌtʃɪt-) *n., pl.* **-ni** (-nɪ). a large lute with a double neck in common use during the baroque period, esp. in Italy. [Italian, from *chitarra,* from Greek *kithara* lyre]
chitchat (ˈtʃɪtˌtʃæt) *n.* **1.** talk of a gossipy nature. ~*vb.* **-chats, -chatting, -chatted. 2.** *(intr.)* to gossip.
chitin (ˈkaɪtɪn) *n.* a polysaccharide that is the principal component of the exoskeletons of arthropods and of the bodies of fungi. [C19: from French *chitine,* from Greek *khitōn* CHITON + -IN] —**ˈchitinous** *adj.* —**ˈchitinˌoid** *adj.*
chiton (ˈkaɪtᵊn, -tɒn) *n.* **1.** (in ancient Greece and Rome) a loose woollen tunic worn knee length by men and full length by women. **2.** Also called: **coat-of-mail shell.** any small primitive marine mollusc of the genus *Chiton* and related genera, having an elongated body covered with eight overlapping shell plates: class *Amphineura.* [C19: from Greek *khitōn* coat of mail, of Semitic origin; related to Hebrew *kethōnet*]
chitter (ˈtʃɪtə) *vb. (intr.)* **1.** *Chiefly U.S.* to twitter or chirp. **2.** a dialect word for **shiver**[1] or (of the teeth) **chatter.** [C14: of imitative origin]
chitterlings (ˈtʃɪtəlɪŋz), **chitlins** (ˈtʃɪtlɪnz), *or* **chitlings** (ˈtʃɪtlɪŋz) *pl. n. (sometimes sing.)* the intestines of a pig or other animal prepared as a dish. [C13: of uncertain origin; perhaps related to Middle High German *kutel*]
chiv (tʃɪv, ʃɪv) *or* **shiv** (ʃɪv) *Slang.* ~*n.* **1.** a knife. ~*vb.* **chivs, chivving, chivved** *or* **shivs, shivving, shivved. 2.** to stab (someone). [C17: perhaps from Romany *chiv* blade]
chivalrous (ˈʃɪvəlrəs) *adj.* **1.** gallant; courteous. **2.** involving chivalry. [C14: from Old French *chevalerous,* from CHEVALIER] —**ˈchivalrously** *adv.* —**ˈchivalrousness** *n.*
chivalry (ˈʃɪvəlrɪ) *n., pl.* **-ries. 1.** the combination of qualities expected of an ideal knight, esp. courage, honour, justice, and a readiness to help the weak. **2.** courteous behaviour, esp. towards women. **3.** the medieval system and principles of knighthood. **4.** knights, noblemen, etc., collectively. [C13: from Old French *chevalerie,* from CHEVALIER] —**ˈchivalric** *adj.*
chivaree (ˌʃɪvəˈriː, ˈʃɪvəˌriː) *n.* a U.S. spelling of **charivari.**
chive (tʃaɪv) *n.* a small Eurasian purple-flowered alliaceous plant, *Allium schoenoprasum,* whose long slender hollow leaves are used in cooking to flavour soups, stews, etc. Also called: **chives.** [C14: from Old French *cive,* ultimately from Latin *caepa* onion]
chivy, chivvy (ˈtʃɪvɪ), *or* **chevy** *Brit.* ~*vb.* **chivies, chivying, chivied, chivvies, chivvying, chivvied,** *or* **chevies, chevying, chevied. 1.** *(tr.)* to harass or nag. **2.** *(tr.)* to hunt. **3.** *(intr.)* to run about. ~*n., pl.* **chivies, chivvies,** *or* **chevies. 4.** a hunt. **5.** *Obsolete.* a hunting cry. [C19: variant of *chevy,* probably from *Chevy Chase,* title of a Scottish border ballad]
Chladni figure (ˈklɑːdnɪ) *n. Physics.* a pattern formed by fine powder placed on a vibrating surface, used to display the positions of nodes and antinodes. [C19: named after Ernst *Chladni* (1756–1827), German physicist]
chlamydate (ˈklæmɪˌdeɪt) *adj.* (of some molluscs) possessing a mantle. [C19: from Latin *chlamydātus* wearing a mantle, from Greek *khlamus* mantle]
chlamydeous (kləˈmɪdɪəs) *adj.* (of plants) relating to or possessing sepals and petals.
chlamydia (kləˈmɪdɪə) *n.* any virus-like bacterium of the genus *Chlamydia,* responsible for such diseases as trachoma, psittacosis, and some sexually transmitted diseases. [C20: New Latin, from Greek *khlamus* mantle + -IA]
chlamydospore (klæˈmɪdəˌspɔː) *n.* a thick-walled asexual spore of many fungi: capable of surviving adverse conditions.
chloanthite (kləʊˈænθaɪt) *n.* a form of nickel arsenide having commercial importance as a nickel ore. [C19: from Greek *khloanthēs* budding, sprouting + -ITE[1]]
chloasma (kləʊˈæzmə) *n., pl.* **chloasmata** (kləʊˈæzmətə) *Med.* the appearance on a person's skin, esp. of the face, of patches of darker colour: associated with hormonal changes caused by liver disease or the use of oral contraceptives. [C19: from New Latin, from Greek *khloasma* greenness]
chlor- *combining form.* a variant of **chloro-** before a vowel.
chloracne (klɔːˈræknɪ) *n.* a disfiguring skin disease that results from contact with or ingestion or inhalation of certain chlorinated aromatic hydrocarbons. [C20: from CHLORO- + ACNE]
chloral (ˈklɔːrəl) *n.* **1.** a colourless oily liquid with a pungent odour, made from chlorine and acetaldehyde and used in preparing chloral hydrate and DDT; trichloroacetaldehyde. **2.** short for **chloral hydrate.**
chloral hydrate *n.* a colourless crystalline soluble solid produced by the reaction of chloral with water and used as a sedative and hypnotic; 2,2,2-trichloro-1,1-ethanediol. Formula: $CCl_3CH(OH)_2$.
chlorambucil (klɔːˈræmbjʊsɪl) *n.* a drug derived from nitrogen mustard, administered orally in the treatment of leukaemia and other malignant diseases. Formula: $C_{14}H_{19}Cl_2NO_2$.
chloramine (ˈklɔːrəˌmiːn) *n.* **1.** an unstable colourless liquid with a pungent odour, made by the reaction of sodium hypochlorite and ammonia. Formula: NH_2Cl. **2.** any compound produced by replacing hydrogen atoms in an azo or amine group with chlorine atoms.
chloramphenicol (ˌklɔːræmˈfɛnɪˌkɒl) *n.* a broad-spectrum antibiotic used esp. in treating typhoid fever and rickettsial infections: obtained from the bacterium *Streptomyces venezuelae* or synthesized. Formula: $C_{11}H_{12}N_2O_5Cl_2$. [C20: from CHLORO- + AM(IDO)- + PHE(NO)- + NI(TRO)- + (GLY)COL]
chlorate (ˈklɔːˌreɪt, -rɪt) *n.* any salt of chloric acid, containing the monovalent ion ClO_3^-.
chlordane (ˈklɔːdeɪn) *or* **chlordan** (ˈklɔːdæn) *n.* a white insoluble toxic solid existing in several isomeric forms and usually used, as an insecticide, in the form of a brown impure liquid. Formula: $C_{10}H_6Cl_8$. [C20: from CHLORO- + (IN)D(ENE) + -ANE]
chlordiazepoxide (ˌklɔːdaɪˌeɪzɪˈpɒksaɪd) *n.* a chemical compound used as a tranquillizer and muscle relaxant and in the treatment of alcoholism. Formula: $C_{16}H_{14}ClN_3O$.
chlorella (klɔːˈrɛlə, klə-) *n.* any microscopic unicellular green alga of the genus *Chlorella:* some species are used in the preparation of human food. [C19: from New Latin, from CHLORO- + Latin *-ella,* diminutive suffix]
chlorenchyma (kləˈrɛŋkɪmə) *n.* plant tissue consisting of parenchyma cells that contain chlorophyll. [C19: from CHLOR(OPHYLL) + -ENCHYMA]
chlorhexidine (klɔːˈhɛksɪdiːn) *n.* an antiseptic compound used in skin cleansers, mouthwashes, etc. [C20: from CHLOR(O)- + HEX(ANE) + -I(DE) + (AM)INE]
chloric (ˈklɔːrɪk) *adj.* of or containing chlorine in the pentavalent state.
chloric acid *n.* a strong acid with a pungent smell, known only in solution and in the form of chlorate salts. Formula: $HClO_3$.
chloride (ˈklɔːraɪd) *n.* **1.** any salt of hydrochloric acid, containing the chloride ion Cl^-. **2.** any compound containing a chlorine

atom, such as methyl chloride (chloromethane), CH_3Cl. —**chloridic** (klə'rɪdɪk) *adj.*

chloride of lime *or* **chlorinated lime** *n.* another name for **bleaching powder.**

chlorinate ('klɔːrɪˌneɪt) *vb. (tr.)* **1.** to combine or treat (a substance) with chlorine. **2.** to disinfect (water) with chlorine. —ˌ**chlorin'ation** *n.* —'**chlorinˌator** *n.*

chlorine ('klɔːriːn) *or* **chlorin** ('klɔːrɪn) *n.* a toxic pungent greenish-yellow gas of the halogen group; the 15th most abundant element in the earth's crust, occurring only in the combined state, mainly in common salt: used in the manufacture of many organic chemicals, in water purification, and as a disinfectant and bleaching agent. Symbol: Cl; atomic no.: 17; atomic wt.: 35.453; valency: 1, 3, 5, or 7; density: 3.214 kg/m^3; melting pt.: –100.98°C; boiling pt.: –34.6°C. [C19 (coined by Sir Humphrey Davy (1778–1829)): from CHLORO- + -INE[2], referring to its colour]

chlorite[1] ('klɔːraɪt) *n.* any of a group of green soft secondary minerals consisting of the hydrated silicates of aluminium, iron, and magnesium in monoclinic crystalline form: common in metamorphic rocks. [C18: from Latin *chlōrītis* precious stone of a green colour, from Greek *khlōritis,* from *khlōros* greenish yellow] —**chloritic** (klɔː'rɪtɪk) *adj.*

chlorite[2] ('klɔːraɪt) *n.* any salt of chlorous acid, containing the monovalent ion ClO_2^-.

chloro- *or before a vowel* **chlor-** *combining form.* **1.** indicating the colour green: *chlorophyll.* **2.** chlorine: *chloroform.*

chloroacetic acid (ˌklɔːrəʊə'siːtɪk) *or* **chloracetic acid** (ˌklɔːrə'siːtɪk) *n.* **1.** a colourless crystalline soluble strong acid prepared by chlorinating acetic acid and used as an intermediate in the manufacture of many chemicals; monochloracetic acid. Formula: $CH_2ClCOOH$. **2.** either of two related compounds: **dichloracetic acid,** $CHCl_2COOH$, or **trichloracetic acid,** CCl_3COOH.

chlorobenzene (ˌklɔːrəʊ'bɛnziːn) *n.* a colourless volatile flammable insoluble liquid with an almond-like odour, made from chlorine and benzene and used as a solvent and in the preparation of many organic compounds, esp. phenol and DDT. Formula: C_6H_5Cl.

chlorofluorocarbon (ˌklɔːrəˌflʊərəʊ'kɑːbᵊn) *n. Chemistry.* any of various gaseous compounds of carbon, hydrogen, chlorine, and fluorine, used as refrigerants, aerosol propellants, solvents, and in foam: some cause a breakdown of ozone in the earth's atmosphere. Abbrev.: **CFC.**

chloroform ('klɔːrəˌfɔːm) *n.* a heavy volatile liquid with a sweet taste and odour, used as a solvent and cleansing agent and in refrigerants: formerly used as an inhalation anaesthetic. Systematic name: **trichloromethane.** Formula: $CHCl_3$. [C19: from CHLORO- + FORM(YL) (in an obsolete sense that applied to a CH radical)]

chlorohydrin (ˌklɔːrəʊ'haɪdrɪn) *n.* **1.** any of a class of organic compounds containing a hydroxyl group and a chlorine atom. **2.** a colourless unstable hygroscopic liquid that is used mainly as a solvent; 3-chloropropane-1,2-diol. Formula: $CH_2OHCHOHCH_2Cl$. [C20: from CHLORO- + HYDRO- + -IN]

Chloromycetin (ˌklɔːrəʊmaɪ'siːtɪn) *n. Trademark.* a brand of **chloramphenicol.**

chlorophyll *or U.S.* **chlorophyl** ('klɔːrəfɪl) *n.* the green pigment of plants, occurring in chloroplasts, that traps the energy of sunlight for photosynthesis and exists in several forms, the most abundant being **chlorophyll a** ($C_{55}H_{72}O_5N_4Mg$): used as a colouring agent in medicines or food **(E140).** —'**chloroˌphylloid** *adj.* —ˌ**chloro'phyllous** *adj.*

chlorophytum (ˌklɔːrə'faɪtəm) *n.* any plant of the genus *Chlorophytum,* esp. *C. elatum variegatum,* grown as a pot plant for its long narrow leaves with a light central stripe, and characterized by the production of offsets at the end of long scapes: family *Liliaceae.* Also called: **spider plant.** [New Latin, from Greek *chloros* green + *phyton* plant]

chloropicrin (ˌklɔːrəʊ'pɪkrɪn) *or* **chlorpicrin** (klɔː'pɪkrɪn) *n.* a colourless insoluble toxic lachrymatory liquid used as a pesticide and a tear gas; nitrotrichloromethane. Formula: CCl_3NO_2. [C20: from CHLORO- + PICRO- + -IN]

chloroplast ('klɔːrəʊˌplæst) *n.* a plastid containing chlorophyll and other pigments, occurring in plants that carry out photosynthesis. —ˌ**chloro'plastic** *adj.*

chloroprene ('klɔːrəʊˌpriːn) *n.* a colourless liquid derivative of butadiene that is used in making neoprene rubbers; 2-chloro-1,2-butadiene. Formula: $CH_2{:}CHCCl{:}CH_2$. [C20: from CHLORO- + (ISO)PRENE]

chloroquine ('klɔːrəʊˌkwiːn) *n.* a synthetic drug that is administered orally to treat malaria. Formula: $C_{18}H_{26}ClN_3$. [C20: from CHLORO- + QUIN(OLINE)]

chlorosis (klɔː'rəʊsɪs) *n.* **1.** Also called: **greensickness.** *Pathol.* a disorder, formerly common in adolescent girls, characterized by pale greenish-yellow skin, weakness, and palpitation and caused by insufficient iron in the body. **2.** *Botany.* a deficiency of chlorophyll in green plants caused by mineral deficiency, lack of light, disease, etc., the leaves appearing uncharacteristically pale. [C17: from CHLORO- + -OSIS] —**chlorotic** (klɔː'rɒtɪk) *adj.*

chlorothiazide (ˌklɔːrə'θaɪəˌzaɪd) *n.* a diuretic drug administered orally in the treatment of chronic heart and kidney disease and hypertension. Formula: $C_7H_6ClN_3O_4S_2$. [C20: from CHLORO- + THI(O)- + (DI)AZ(INE + DIOX)IDE]

chlorous ('klɔːrəs) *adj.* **1.** of or containing chlorine in the trivalent state. **2.** of or containing chlorous acid.

chlorous acid *n.* an unstable acid that is a strong oxidizing agent. Formula: $HClO_2$.

chlorpromazine (klɔː'prɒməˌziːn) *n.* a drug derived from phenothiazine, used as a sedative and tranquillizer, esp. in psychotic disorders. Formula: $C_{17}H_{19}ClN_2S$. [C20: from CHLORO- + PRO(PYL + A)M(INE) + AZINE]

chlorpropamide (klɔː'prəʊpəˌmaɪd) *n.* a drug that reduces blood glucose and is administered orally in the treatment of diabetes. Formula: $C_{10}H_{13}ClN_2O_3S$.

chlortetracycline (klɔːˌtɛtrə'saɪkliːn) *n.* an antibiotic used in treating many bacterial and rickettsial infections and some viral infections: obtained from the bacterium *Streptomyces aureofaciens.* Formula: $C_{22}H_{23}ClN_2O_8$.

chlorthalidone (klɔː'θælɪdəʊn) *n.* a diuretic used in the treatment of oedema, hypertension, and diabetes insipidus. [C20: from CHLOR(O)- + TH(IAZINE) + -AL[3] + -ID(E) + -ONE]

ChM *abbrev. for* Master of Surgery. [Latin *Chirurgiae Magister*]

chm. *abbrev. for:* **1.** Also: **chmn.** chairman. **2.** checkmate.

choanocyte ('kəʊənəˌsaɪt) *n.* any of the flagellated cells in sponges that maintain a flow of water through the body. A collar of protoplasm surrounds the base of the flagellum. Also called: **collar cell.** [C19: from Greek *khoanē* funnel (from *khein* to pour) + -CYTE]

chocaholic (ˌtʃɒkə'hɒlɪk) *n. Informal.* someone who is addicted to eating chocolate. [C20: from CHOC(OLATE) + -HOLIC]

choc-ice ('tʃɒkˌaɪs) *n.* an ice cream covered with a thin layer of chocolate.

chock (tʃɒk) *n.* **1.** a block or wedge of wood used to prevent the sliding or rolling of a heavy object. **2.** *Nautical.* **a.** a fairlead consisting of a ringlike device with an opening at the top through which a rope is placed. **b.** a cradle-like support for a boat, barrel, etc. **3.** *Mountaineering.* See **nut** (sense 10). ~*vb. (tr.)* **4.** (usually foll. by *up*) *Brit.* to cram full: *chocked up with newspapers.* **5.** to fit with or secure by a chock. **6.** to support (a boat, barrel, etc.) on chocks. ~*adv.* **7.** as closely or tightly as possible: *chock against the wall.* [C17: of uncertain origin; perhaps related to Old French *çoche* log; compare Provençal *soca* tree stump]

chock-a-block *adj., adv.* **1.** filled to capacity; in a crammed state. **2.** *Nautical.* with the blocks brought close together, as when a tackle is pulled as tight as possible.

chocker ('tʃɒkə) *adj.* **1.** *Austral. and N.Z. informal.* full up; packed. **2.** *Brit. slang.* irritated; fed up. [C20: from CHOCK-A-BLOCK]

chock-full, choke-full, *or* **chuck-full** *adj. (postpositive)* completely full. [C17 *choke-full;* see CHOKE, FULL]

chockstone ('tʃɒkˌstəʊn) *n. Mountaineering.* **1.** a stone securely jammed in a crack. It may vary in size from a pebble to a large boulder. **2.** another name for **chock** (sense 3).

choco *or* **chocko** ('tʃɒkəʊ) *n., pl.* **-os.** *Austral. slang.* (in World War II) **a.** a member of the citizen army; militiaman. **b.** a conscript. [C20: shortened from *chocolate soldier*]

chocolate ('tʃɒkəlɪt, 'tʃɒklɪt, -lət) *n.* **1.** a food preparation made from roasted ground cacao seeds, usually sweetened and flavoured. **2.** a drink or sweetmeat made from this. **3. a.** a moderate to deep brown colour. **b.** *(as adj.): a chocolate carpet.* [C17: from Spanish, from Aztec *xocolatl,* from *xococ* sour, bitter + *atl* water] —'**chocolaty** *adj.*

chocolate-box *n. (modifier) Informal.* sentimentally pretty or appealing.

choctaw ('tʃɒktɔː) *n. Ice skating.* a turn from the inside edge of one skate to the outside edge of the other or vice versa. [C19: after CHOCTAW]

Choctaw ('tʃɒktɔː) *n.* **1.** *(pl.* **-taws** *or* **-taw)** a member of a North American Indian people of Alabama. **2.** the language of this people, belonging to the Muskhogean family. [C18: from Choctaw *Chahta*]

Chogyal ('tʃɒgjɑːl) *n.* the title of the ruler of Sikkim in NE India.

choice (tʃɔɪs) *n.* **1.** the act or an instance of choosing or selecting. **2.** the opportunity or power of choosing. **3.** a person or thing chosen or that may be chosen: *he was a possible choice.* **4.** an alternative action or possibility: *what choice did I have?* **5.** a supply from which to select: *a poor choice of shoes.* ~*adj.* **6.** of superior quality; excellent: *choice wine.* [C13: from Old French *chois,* from *choisir* to CHOOSE] —'**choicely** *adv.* —'**choiceness** *n.*

choir (kwaɪə) *n.* **1.** an organized group of singers, esp. for singing in church services. **2. a.** the part of a cathedral, abbey, or church in front of the altar, lined on both sides with benches, and used by the choir and clergy. Compare **chancel. b.** *(as modifier): choir stalls.* **3.** a number of instruments of the same family playing together: *a brass choir.* **4.** Also called: **choir organ.** one of the manuals on an organ controlling a set of soft sweet-toned pipes. Compare **great** (sense 21), **swell** (sense 16). **5.** any of the nine orders of angels in medieval angelology. Archaic spelling: **quire.** [C13 *quer,* from Old French *cuer,* from Latin CHORUS] —'**choirˌlike** *adj.*

choirboy ('kwaɪəˌbɔɪ) *n.* one of a number of young boys who sing the treble part in a church choir.

choir loft *n.* a gallery in a cathedral, abbey, or church used by the choir.

choirmaster (ˈkwaɪəˌmɑːstə) *n.* a person who trains, leads, or conducts a choir.

choir school *n.* (in Britain) a school, esp. a preparatory school attached to a cathedral, college, etc., offering general education to boys whose singing ability is good.

choke (tʃəʊk) *vb.* **1.** (*tr.*) to hinder or stop the breathing of (a person or animal), esp. by constricting the windpipe or by asphyxiation. **2.** (*intr.*) to have trouble or fail in breathing, swallowing, or speaking. **3.** (*tr.*) to block or clog up (a passage, pipe, street, etc.). **4.** (*tr.*) to retard the growth or action of: *the weeds are choking my plants.* **5.** (*tr.*) to suppress (emotion): *she choked her anger.* **6.** (*intr.*) *Slang.* to die. **7.** (*tr.*) to enrich the petrol-air mixture by reducing the air supply to (a carburettor, petrol engine, etc.). **8.** (*intr.*) (esp. in sport) to be seized with tension and fail to perform well. ~*n.* **9.** the act or sound of choking. **10.** a device in the carburettor of a petrol engine that enriches the petrol-air mixture by reducing the air supply. **11.** any constriction or mechanism for reducing the flow of a fluid in a pipe, tube, etc. **12.** Also called: **choke coil.** *Electronics.* an inductor having a relatively high impedance, used to prevent the passage of high frequencies or to smooth the output of a rectifier. **13.** the inedible centre of the head of an artichoke. ~See also **choke back, choke up.** [Old English *ācēocian,* of Germanic origin; related to CHEEK] —ˈ**chokeable** *adj.* —ˈ**choky** *or* ˈ**chokey** *adj.*

choke back *or* **down** *vb.* (*tr., adv.*) to suppress (anger, tears, etc.).

chokeberry (ˈtʃəʊkbərɪ, -brɪ) *n., pl.* **-ries. 1.** any of various North American rosaceous shrubs of the genus *Aronia.* **2.** the red or purple bitter fruit of any of these shrubs.

chokebore (ˈtʃəʊkˌbɔː) *n.* **1.** a shotgun bore that becomes narrower towards the muzzle so that the shot is not scattered. **2.** a shotgun having such a bore.

choke chain *n.* a collar and lead for a dog so designed that if the dog drags on the lead the collar tightens round its neck.

chokecherry (ˈtʃəʊkˌtʃɛrɪ) *n., pl.* **-ries. 1.** any of several North American species of cherry, esp. *Prunus virginiana,* having very astringent dark red or black fruit. **2.** the fruit of any of these trees.

choke coil *n.* another name for **choke** (sense 12).

choked (tʃəʊkt) *adj. Brit. informal.* annoyed or disappointed.

chokedamp (ˈtʃəʊkˌdæmp) *n.* another word for **blackdamp.**

choke-full *adj.* a less common spelling of **chock-full.**

choker (ˈtʃəʊkə) *n.* **1.** a woman's high collar, popular esp. in the late 19th century. **2.** any neckband or necklace worn tightly around the throat. **3.** a high clerical collar; stock. **4.** a person or thing that chokes or strangles someone or something.

choke up *vb.* (*tr., adv.*) **1.** to block (a drain, pipe, etc.) completely. **2.** *Informal.* (*usually passive*) to overcome (a person) with emotion, esp. without due cause.

chokey *or* **choky** (ˈtʃəʊkɪ) *n. Brit.* a slang word for **prison.** [C17: from Anglo-Indian, from Hindi *caukī* a shed or lockup]

choko (ˈtʃəʊkəʊ) *n., pl.* **-kos.** the cucumber-like fruit of a tropical American cucurbitaceous vine, *Sechium edule:* eaten in the West Indies, Australia, and New Zealand. [C18: from a Brazilan Indian name]

cholagogue (ˈkɒləgɒg) *n.* a drug or other substance that promotes the flow of bile from the gall bladder into the duodenum. —ˌ**cholaˈgogic** *adj.*

cholangiography (kəˌlændʒɪˈɒgrəfɪ) *n.* radiographic examination of the bile ducts after the introduction into them of a contrast medium.

chole- *or before a vowel* **chol-** *combining form.* indicating bile or gall: *cholesterol.* [from Greek *kholē*]

cholecalciferol (ˌkəʊlɪkælˈsɪfəˌrɒl) *n.* a compound occurring naturally in fish-liver oils, used to treat rickets. Formula: $C_{27}H_{44}O$. Also called: **vitamin D₃.** See also **calciferol.**

cholecyst (ˈkɒlɪsɪst) *n. Rare.* another name for **gall bladder.**

cholecystectomy (ˌkɒlɪsɪˈstɛktəmɪ) *n., pl.* **-mies.** surgical removal of the gall bladder.

cholecystitis (ˌkɒlɪsɪsˈtaɪtɪs) *n.* inflammation of the gall bladder, due to bacterial infection or the presence of gallstones.

cholecystography (ˌkɒlɪsɪsˈtɒgrəfɪ) *n. Med.* radiography of the gall bladder after administration of a contrast medium.

cholecystokinin (ˌkɒlɪˌsɪstəˈkaɪnɪn) *n.* a hormone secreted by duodenal cells that stimulates the contraction of the gall bladder and secretion of pancreatic enzymes. Also called: **pancreozymin.**

cholent (ˈtʃɒlənt) *n. Judaism.* a meal usually consisting of a stew of meat, potatoes, and pulses prepared before the Sabbath on Friday and left to cook until eaten for Sabbath lunch.

choler (ˈkɒlə) *n.* **1.** anger or ill humour. **2.** *Archaic.* one of the four bodily humours; yellow bile. See **humour** (sense 8). **3.** *Obsolete.* biliousness. [C14: from Old French *colère,* from Medieval Latin *cholera,* from Latin: jaundice, CHOLERA]

cholera (ˈkɒlərə) *n.* an acute intestinal infection characterized by severe diarrhoea, cramp, etc.: caused by ingestion of water or food contaminated with the bacterium *Vibrio comma.* Also called: **Asiatic cholera, epidemic cholera, Indian cholera.** [C14: from Latin, from Greek *kholera* jaundice, from *kholē* bile] —ˈ**choleˌroid** *adj.*

choleric (ˈkɒlərɪk) *adj.* **1.** bad-tempered. **2.** bilious or causing biliousness. —ˈ**cholerically** *or* ˈ**cholericly** *adv.*

cholesterol (kəˈlɛstəˌrɒl) *n.* a sterol found in all animal tissues, blood, bile, and animal fats: a precursor of other body steroids. A high level of cholesterol in the blood is implicated in some cases of atherosclerosis, leading to heart disease. Former name: **cholesterin** (kəˈlɛstərɪn). Formula: $C_{27}H_{45}OH$. [C19: from CHOLE- + Greek *stereos* hard, solid, so called because first observed in gallstones]

cholesterolaemia *or U.S.* **cholesterolemia** (kəˌlɛstərəˈliːmɪə) *n.* the presence of abnormally high levels of cholesterol in the blood.

Chol Hamoed *Hebrew.* (*Hebrew* xol hɑˈmoed; *Yiddish* xaʊl həˈmaʊəd) *n. Judaism.* the middle days of the festivals of Passover and Sukkoth, on which necessary work is permitted. [literally: the weekdays of the festival]

choli (ˈkəʊlɪ) *n., pl.* **-lis.** a short-sleeved bodice, as worn by Indian women. [from Hindi]

cholic acid (ˈkəʊlɪk) *n.* a crystalline insoluble acid present in bile: used as an emulsifying agent and an intermediate in the synthesis of organic compounds. Formula: $C_{24}H_{40}O_5$. [C19: from Greek *kholikos;* see CHOLE-]

choline (ˈkəʊliːn, -ɪn, ˈkɒl-) *n.* a colourless viscous soluble alkaline substance present in animal tissues, esp. as a constituent of lecithin: used as a supplement to the diet of poultry and in medicine for preventing the accumulation of fat in the liver. Formula: $[(CH_3)_3NCH_2CH_2OH]^+ OH^-$. [C19: from CHOLE- + -INE², so called because of its action in the liver]

cholinergic (ˌkəʊlɪˈnɜːdʒɪk) *adj.* **1.** denoting nerve fibres that release acetylcholine when stimulated. **2.** of or relating to the type of chemical activity associated with acetylcholine and similar substances. [C20: from (ACETYL)CHOLIN(E) + Greek *ergon* work]

cholinesterase (ˌkəʊlɪˈnɛstəˌreɪs, ˌkɒl-) *n.* an enzyme that hydrolyses acetylcholine to choline and acetic acid.

cholla (ˈtʃəʊljɑː; *Spanish* ˈtʃoʎa) *n.* any of several spiny cacti of the genus *Opuntia* that grow in the southwestern U.S. and Mexico and have cylindrical stem segments. See also **prickly pear.** [Mexican Spanish, from Spanish: head, perhaps from Old French (dialect) *cholle* ball, of Germanic origin]

chollers (ˈtʃɒləz) *pl. n. Northeast English dialect.* the jowls or cheeks. [C18: perhaps from Old English *ceolur* throat. See JOWL²]

chometz *Hebrew.* (*Hebrew* xaˈmɛtʒ; *Yiddish* ˈxoməts) *n.* a variant spelling of **chametz.**

chomophyte (ˈkɒməʊˌfaɪt) *n.* any plant that grows on rocky ledges or in fissures and crevices.

chomp (tʃɒmp) *or* **chump** *vb.* **1.** to chew (food) noisily; champ. ~*n.* **2.** the act or sound of chewing in this manner. [variant of CHAMP¹]

chon (tʃəʊn) *n., pl.* **chon.** a Korean monetary unit worth one hundredth of a won.

chondral (ˈkɒndrəl) *adj.* of or relating to cartilage.

chondrify (ˈkɒndrɪˌfaɪ) *vb.* **-fies, -fying, -fied.** to become or convert into cartilage. —ˌ**chondrifiˈcation** *n.*

chondrin (ˈkɒndrɪn) *n.* a resilient translucent bluish-white substance that forms the matrix of cartilage.

chondriosome (ˈkɒndrɪəˌsəʊm) *n.* another name for **mitochondrion.** —ˌ**chondrioˈsomal** *adj.*

chondrite (ˈkɒndraɪt) *n.* a stony meteorite consisting mainly of silicate minerals in the form of chondrules. Compare **achondrite.** —**chondritic** (kɒnˈdrɪtɪk) *adj.*

chondro-, chondri-, *or before a vowel* **chondr-** *combining form.* **1.** indicating cartilage: *chondroma.* **2.** grain or granular: *chondrule.* [from Greek *khondros* grain, cartilage]

chondroma (kɒnˈdrəʊmə) *n., pl.* **-mas** *or* **-mata** (-mətə). *Pathol.* a benign cartilaginous growth or neoplasm. —**chonˈdromatous** *adj.*

chondroskeleton (ˈkɒndrəʊˌskɛlɪtən) *n.* the cartilaginous part of the skeleton of vertebrates.

chondrule (ˈkɒndruːl) *n.* one of the small spherical masses of mainly silicate minerals present in chondrites.

choo-choo (ˈtʃuːˌtʃuː) *n. Brit.* a child's name for a railway train. [C20: of imitative origin]

choof off (tʃʊf) *vb.* (*intr., adv.*) *Austral. slang.* to go away; make off.

chook (tʃʊk) *vb.* **1.** See **jook.** ~*n.* **2.** Also called: ˈ**chookie.** *Informal, chiefly Austral. and N.Z.* a hen or chicken.

choom (tʃʊm) *n.* (*often cap.*) *Austral. slang.* an Englishman.

choose (tʃuːz) *vb.* **chooses, choosing, chose, chosen. 1.** to select (a person, thing, course of action, etc.) from a number of alternatives. **2.** (*tr.; takes a clause as object or an infinitive*) to consider it desirable or proper: *I don't choose to read that book.* **3.** (*intr.*) to like; please: *you may stand if you choose.* **4. cannot choose but.** to be obliged to: *we cannot choose but vote for him.* **5. nothing** *or* **little to choose between.** (of two people or objects) almost equal. [Old English *ceosan;* related to Old Norse *kjōsa,* Old High German *kiosan*] —ˈ**chooser** *n.*

choosy (ˈtʃuːzɪ) *adj.* **choosier, choosiest.** *Informal.* particular in making a choice; difficult to please.

chop¹ (tʃɒp) *vb.* **chops, chopping, chopped. 1.** (often foll. by *down* or *off*) to cut (something) with a blow from an axe or other sharp tool. **2.** (*tr.*) to produce or make in this manner: *to chop firewood.* **3.** (*tr.;* often foll. by *up*) to cut into pieces. **4.** (*tr.*) *Brit.*

informal. to dispense with or reduce. **5.** (*intr.*) to move quickly or violently. **6.** *Tennis, cricket, etc.* to hit (a ball) sharply downwards. **7.** *Boxing, karate, etc.* to punch or strike (an opponent) with a short sharp blow. **8.** *West African.* an informal word for **eat.** ~*n.* **9.** a cutting blow. **10.** the act or an instance of chopping. **11.** a piece chopped off. **12.** a slice of mutton, lamb, or pork, generally including a rib. **13.** *Austral. and N.Z. slang.* a share (esp. in the phrase **get** *or* **hop in for one's chop**). **14.** *West African.* an informal word for **food. 15.** *Austral. and N.Z.* a competition of skill and speed in chopping logs. **16.** *Sport.* a sharp downward blow or stroke. **17. not much chop.** *Austral. and N.Z. informal.* not much good; poor. **18. the chop.** *Slang, chiefly Brit.* dismissal from employment. [C16: variant of CHAP[1]]

chop[2] (tʃɒp) *vb.* **chops, chopping, chopped. 1.** (*intr.*) to change direction suddenly; vacillate (esp. in the phrase **chop and change**). **2.** *Obsolete.* to barter. **3. chop logic.** to use excessively subtle or involved logic or argument. [Old English *ceapian* to barter; see CHEAP, CHAPMAN]

chop[3] (tʃɒp) *n.* a design stamped on goods as a trademark, esp. in the Far East. [C17: from Hindi *chhāp*]

chop chop *adv.* pidgin English for **quickly.** [C19: from Chinese dialect; related to Cantonese *kap kap*]

chopfallen (ˈtʃɒpˌfɔːlən) *adj.* a variant of **chapfallen.**

chophouse[1] (ˈtʃɒpˌhaʊs) *n.* a restaurant specializing in steaks, grills, chops, etc.

chophouse[2] (ˈtʃɒpˌhaʊs) *n.* (formerly) a customs house in China.

chopine (tʃɒˈpiːn) *or* **chopin** (ˈtʃɒpɪn) *n.* a sandal-like shoe on tall wooden or cork bases popular in the 18th century. [C16: from Old Spanish *chapín,* probably imitative of the sound made by the shoe when walking]

choplogic (ˈtʃɒpˌlɒdʒɪk) *n.* **a.** fallacious reasoning. **b.** (*as modifier*): *a choplogic speech.* [C16: from CHOP[2] + LOGIC]

chopper (ˈtʃɒpə) *n.* **1.** *Chiefly Brit.* a small hand axe. **2.** a butcher's cleaver. **3.** a person or thing that cuts or chops. **4.** an informal name for a **helicopter. 5.** *Chiefly Brit.* a slang name for **penis. 6.** a device for periodically interrupting an electric current or beam of radiation to produce a pulsed current or beam. See also **vibrator** (sense 2). **7.** a type of bicycle or motorcycle with very high handlebars and an elongated saddle. **8.** *Slang, chiefly U.S.* a sub-machine-gun.

choppers (ˈtʃɒpəz) *pl. n. Slang.* teeth, esp. false ones.

chopper tool *n.* a core tool of flint or stone, with a transverse cutting edge, characteristic of cultures in Asia and parts of the Middle East and Europe.

choppy (ˈtʃɒpɪ) *adj.* **-pier, -piest.** (of the sea, weather, etc.) fairly rough. —ˈ**choppily** *adv.* —ˈ**choppiness** *n.*

chops (tʃɒps) *pl. n.* **1.** the jaws or cheeks; jowls. **2.** the mouth. **3.** *Music slang.* **a.** embouchure. **b.** *Jazz.* skill. **4. lick one's chops.** *Informal.* to anticipate with pleasure. [C16: of uncertain origin]

chopsticks (ˈtʃɒpstɪks) *pl. n.* a pair of thin sticks, of ivory, wood, etc., used as eating utensils by the Chinese, Japanese, etc. [C17: from pidgin English, from *chop* quick, of Chinese dialect origin + STICK[1]]

chop suey (ˈsuːɪ) *n.* a Chinese-style dish originating in the U.S., consisting of meat or chicken, bean sprouts, etc., stewed and served with rice. [C19: from Chinese (Cantonese) *tsap sui* odds and ends]

choragus (kɔːˈreɪgəs) *n., pl.* **-gi** (-dʒaɪ) *or* **-guses. 1.** (in ancient Greek drama) **a.** the leader of a chorus. **b.** a sponsor of a chorus. **2.** a conductor of a festival. [C17: from Latin, from Greek *khoragos,* from *khoros* CHORUS + *agein* to lead] —**choragic** (kɔːˈrædʒɪk, -ˈreɪ-) *adj.*

choral *adj.* (ˈkɔːrəl). **1.** relating to, sung by, or designed for a chorus or choir. ~*n.* (kɒˈrɑːl). **2.** a variant spelling of **chorale.** —ˈ**chorally** *adv.*

chorale *or* **choral** (kɒˈrɑːl) *n.* **1.** a slow stately hymn tune, esp. of the Lutheran Church. **2.** *Chiefly U.S.* a choir or chorus. [C19: from German *Choralgesang,* translation of Latin *cantus chorālis* choral song]

chorale prelude *n.* a composition for organ using a chorale as a cantus firmus or as the basis for variations.

chord[1] (kɔːd) *n.* **1.** *Maths.* **a.** a straight line connecting two points on a curve or curved surface. **b.** the line segment lying between two points of intersection of a straight line and a curve or curved surface. **2.** *Engineering.* one of the principal members of a truss, esp. one that lies along the top or the bottom. **3.** *Anatomy.* a variant spelling of **cord. 4.** an emotional response, esp. one of sympathy: *the story struck the right chord.* **5.** an imaginary straight line joining the leading edge and the trailing edge of an aerofoil. **6.** *Archaic.* the string of a musical instrument. [C16: from Latin *chorda,* from Greek *khordē* gut, string; see CORD] —ˈ**chorded** *adj.*

chord[2] (kɔːd) *n.* **1.** the simultaneous sounding of a group of musical notes, usually three or more in number. See **concord** (sense 4), **discord** (sense 3). ~*vb.* **2.** (*tr.*) to provide (a melodic line) with chords. [C15: short for ACCORD; spelling influenced by CHORD[1]] —ˈ**chordal** *adj.*

chordate (ˈkɔːˌdeɪt) *n.* **1.** any animal of the phylum *Chordata,* including the vertebrates and protochordates, characterized by a notochord, dorsal tubular nerve cord, and pharyngeal gill slits. ~*adj.* **2.** of, relating to, or belonging to the *Chordata.* [C19: from Medieval Latin *chordata;* see CHORD[1] + -ATE[1]]

chording (ˈkɔːdɪŋ) *n. Music.* **1.** the distribution of chords throughout a piece of harmony. **2.** the intonation of a group of instruments or voices.

chordophone (ˈkɔːdəˌfəʊn) *n.* any musical instrument producing sounds through the vibration of strings, such as the piano, harp, violin, or guitar.

chord symbol *n. Music.* any of a series of letters and numerals, used as a shorthand indication of chords, esp. in jazz, folk, or pop music: *B7 indicates the dominant seventh chord in the key of E.*

chordwise (ˈkɔːdˌwaɪz) *adv.* **1.** in the direction of an aerofoil chord. ~*adj.* **2.** moving in this direction: *chordwise force.*

chore (tʃɔː) *n.* **1.** a small routine task, esp. a domestic one. **2.** an unpleasant task. [C19: variant of Middle English *chare;* related to CHAR[3]]

-chore *n. combining form.* (in botany) indicating a plant that is distributed by a certain means or agency: *anemochore.* [from Greek *khōrein* to move] —**-chorous** *or* **-choric** *adj. combining form.*

chorea (kɒˈrɪə) *n.* a disorder of the central nervous system characterized by uncontrollable irregular brief jerky movements. See **Huntington's chorea, Sydenham's chorea.** [C19: from New Latin, from Latin: dance, from Greek *khoreia,* from *khoros* dance; see CHORUS] —**choˈreal** *or* **choˈreic** *adj.*

choreo- *combining form.* indicating the art of dancing or ballet: *choreodrama; choreography.* [from Greek *khoreios,* from *khoros* dance]

choreodrama (ˌkɔːrɪəʊˈdrɑːmə) *n. Dancing.* dance drama performed by a group.

choreograph (ˈkɒrɪəˌgræf) *vb.* (*tr.*) to compose the steps and dances for (a piece of music or ballet).

choreography (ˌkɒrɪˈɒgrəfɪ) *or* **choregraphy** (kɒˈrɛgrəfɪ) *n.* **1.** the composition of dance steps and sequences for ballet and stage dancing. **2.** the steps and sequences of a ballet or dance. **3.** the notation representing such steps. **4.** the art of dancing. [C18: from Greek *khoreia* dance + -GRAPHY] —ˌ**choreˈographer** *or* **choˈregrapher** *n.* —**choreographic** (ˌkɒrɪəˈgræfɪk) *or* **choregraphic** (ˌkɒrəˈgræfɪk) *adj.* —ˌ**choreoˈgraphically** *or* ˌ**choreˈgraphically** *adv.*

choriamb (ˈkɒrɪˌæmb) *or* **choriambus** (ˌkɒrɪˈæmbəs) *n., pl.* **-ambs** *or* **-ambi** (-ˈæmbaɪ). *Prosody.* a metrical foot used in classical verse consisting of four syllables, two short ones between two long ones (–⏑⏑–). [C19: from Late Latin *choriambus,* from Greek *khoriambos,* from *khoreios* trochee, of a chorus, from *khoros* CHORUS] —ˌ**choriˈambic** *adj.*

choric (ˈkɒrɪk) *adj.* of, like, for, or in the manner of a chorus, esp. of singing, dancing, or the speaking of verse.

chorion (ˈkɔːrɪən) *n.* the outer of two membranes (see also **amnion**) that form a sac around the embryonic reptile, bird, or mammal: contributes to the placenta in mammals. [C16: from Greek *khorion* afterbirth] —ˌ**choriˈonic** *or* ˈ**chorial** *adj.*

chorionic gonadotrophin *n.* a hormone secreted by the chorionic villi of the placenta in mammals, esp. **human chorionic gonadotrophin.** It promotes the secretion of progesterone by the corpus luteum and its presence in the urine is an indication of pregnancy.

chorionic villus sampling *n.* a method of diagnosing genetic disorders early in pregnancy by the removal by catheter through the cervix or abdomen of a tiny sample of tissue from the chorionic villi. Abbrev.: **CVS.**

chorister (ˈkɒrɪstə) *n.* a singer in a choir, esp. a choirboy. [C14: from Medieval Latin *chorista*]

chorizo (tʃɔːˈriːzəʊ) *n., pl.* **-zos.** a kind of highly seasoned pork sausage of Spain or Mexico. [C19: Spanish]

C horizon *n.* the layer of a soil profile immediately below the B horizon and above the bedrock, composed of weathered rock little affected by soil-forming processes.

chorography (kɒˈrɒgrəfɪ) *n. Geography.* **1.** the technique of mapping regions. **2.** a description or map of a region, as opposed to a small area. [C16: via Latin from Greek *khōrographia,* from *khōros* place, country + -GRAPHY] —**choˈrographer** *n.* —**chorographic** (ˌkɒrəˈgræfɪk) *or* ˌ**choroˈgraphical** *adj.* —ˌ**choroˈgraphically** *adv*

choroid (ˈkɔːrɔɪd) *or* **chorioid** (ˈkɔːrɪˌɔɪd) *adj.* **1.** resembling the chorion, esp. in being vascular. ~*n.* **2.** the brownish vascular membrane of the eyeball between the sclera and the retina. [C18: from Greek *khoroeidēs,* erroneously for *khorioeidēs,* from CHORION]

choroid plexus *n.* a multilobed vascular membrane, projecting into the cerebral ventricles, that secretes cerebrospinal fluid.

chorology (kəˈrɒlədʒɪ) *n.* **1.** the study of the causal relations between geographical phenomena occurring within a particular region. **2.** the study of the spatial distribution of organisms. [C20: from German *Chorologie,* from Greek *choros* place + -LOGY] —**choˈrologist** *n.*

chortle (ˈtʃɔːtᵊl) *vb.* **1.** (*intr.*) to chuckle gleefully. ~*n.* **2.** a gleeful chuckle. [C19: coined (1871) by Lewis Carroll (1832–98) in *Through the Looking-glass;* probably a blend of CHUCKLE + SNORT] —ˈ**chortler** *n.*

chorus (ˈkɔːrəs) *n., pl.* **-ruses. 1.** a large choir of singers or a piece of music composed for such a choir. **2.** a body of singers or dancers who perform together, in contrast to principals or soloists. **3.** a section of a song in which a soloist is joined by a group of singers, esp. in a recurring refrain. **4.** an intermediate section of a pop song, blues, etc., as distinct from the verse. **5.** *Jazz.* any of a series of variations on a theme. **6.** (in ancient Greece) **a.** a lyric poem sung by a group of dancers, originally as a religious rite. **b.** an ode or series of odes sung by a group of actors. **7. a.** (in classical Greek drama) the actors who sang the chorus and commented on the action of the play. **b.** actors playing a similar role in any drama. **8. a.** (esp. in Elizabethan drama) the actor who spoke the prologue, etc. **b.** the part of the play spoken by this actor. **9.** a group of people or animals producing words or sounds simultaneously. **10.** any speech, song, or other form of utterance produced by a group of people or animals simultaneously: *a chorus of sighs; the dawn chorus.* **11. in chorus.** in unison. ~*vb.* **12.** to speak, sing, or utter (words, sounds, etc.) in unison. [C16: from Latin, from Greek *khoros*]

chorus girl *n.* a girl who dances or sings in the chorus of a musical comedy, revue, etc.

chorusmaster (ˈkɔːrəsˌmɑːstə) *n.* the conductor of a choir.

chorus pedal *n. Music.* an electronic device that creates the effect of more than one sound from a single source by combining a short delay with slight deviations in pitch.

chose[1] (tʃəʊz) *vb.* the past tense of **choose.**

chose[2] (ʃəʊz) *n. Law.* an article of personal property. [C17: from French: thing, from Latin *causa* cause, case, reason]

chosen (ˈtʃəʊzᵊn) *vb.* **1.** the past participle of **choose.** ~*adj.* **2.** selected or picked out, esp. for some special quality.

chosen people *pl. n.* any of various peoples believing themselves to be chosen by God, esp. the Jews.

chott (ʃɒt) *n.* a variant spelling of **shott.**

chou (ʃuː) *n., pl.* **choux** (ʃuː). **1.** a type of cabbage. **2.** a rosette. **3.** a round cream bun. [C18 (a bun): from French, from Latin *caulis* cabbage]

Chou (tʃəʊ) *or* **Zhou** *n.* the imperial dynasty of China from about 1126 to 255 B.C.

chough (tʃʌf) *n.* **1.** a large black passerine bird, *Pyrrhocorax pyrrhocorax,* of parts of Europe, Asia, and Africa, with a long downward-curving red bill: family *Corvidae* (crows). **2. alpine chough.** a smaller related bird, *Pyrrhocorax graculus,* with a shorter yellow bill. [C14: of uncertain origin; probably related to Old French *cauwe,* Old English *cēo*]

choux pastry (ʃuː) *n.* a very light pastry made with eggs, used for eclairs, etc. [partial translation of French *pâte choux* cabbage dough (from its round shape)]

chow (tʃaʊ) *n.* **1.** *Informal.* food. **2.** short for **chow-chow** (sense 1).

chow-chow *n.* **1.** a thick-coated breed of the spitz type of dog with a curled tail, originally from China. Often shortened to **chow.** **2.** a Chinese preserve of ginger, orange peel, etc. in syrup. **3.** a mixed vegetable pickle. [C19: from pidgin English, probably based on Mandarin Chinese *cha* miscellaneous]

chowder (ˈtʃaʊdə) *n. Chiefly U.S. and Canadian.* a thick soup or stew containing clams or fish. [C18: from French *chaudière* kettle, from Late Latin *caldāria;* see CAULDRON]

chow mein (meɪn) *n.* a Chinese-American dish, consisting of mushrooms, meat, shrimps, etc., served with fried noodles. [from Chinese (Cantonese), variant of Mandarin *ch'ao mien* fried noodles]

Chr. *abbrev. for:* **1.** Christ. **2.** Christian.

chrematistic (ˌkriːməˈtɪstɪk) *adj.* of, denoting, or relating to money-making. [C18: from Greek, from *khrēmatizein* to make money, from *khrēma* money] —ˌ**chremaˈtistics** *n.*

chresard (ˈkrɛsəd) *n.* the amount of water present in the soil that is available to plants. [C20: from Greek *khrēsis* use (from *khrēsthai* to use) + *ardein* to water]

chrestomathy (krɛsˈtɒməθɪ) *n., pl.* **-thies.** *Rare.* a collection of literary passages, used in the study of language. [C19: from Greek *khrēstomatheia,* from *khrēstos* useful + *mathein* to learn] —**chrestomathic** (ˌkrɛstəʊˈmæθɪk) *adj.*

chrism *or* **chrisom** (ˈkrɪzəm) *n.* a mixture of olive oil and balsam used for sacramental anointing in the Greek Orthodox and Roman Catholic Churches. [Old English *crisma,* from Medieval Latin, from Greek *khrisma* unction, from *khriein* to anoint] —**chrismal** (ˈkrɪzməl) *adj.*

chrismatory (ˈkrɪzmətərɪ, -trɪ) *n., pl.* **-ries.** *R.C. Church.* a small receptacle containing the three kinds of consecrated oil used in the sacraments.

chrisom (ˈkrɪzəm) *n.* **1.** *Christianity.* a white robe put on an infant at baptism and formerly used as a burial shroud if the infant died soon afterwards. **2.** *Archaic.* an infant wearing such a robe. **3.** a variant spelling of **chrism.**

Chrissie (ˈkrɪsɪ) *n. Chiefly Austral.* a slang name for **Christmas.**

Christ (kraɪst) *n.* **1.** Jesus of Nazareth (Jesus Christ), regarded by Christians as fulfilling Old Testament prophecies of the Messiah. **2.** the Messiah or anointed one of God as the subject of Old Testament prophecies. **3.** an image or picture of Christ. ~*interj.* **4.** *Taboo slang.* an oath expressing annoyance, surprise, etc. ~See also **Jesus.** [Old English *Crīst,* from Latin *Chrīstus,* from Greek *khristos* anointed one (from *khriein* to anoint), translating Hebrew *māshīah* MESSIAH] —ˈ**Christly** *adj.*

Christadelphian (ˌkrɪstəˈdɛlfɪən) *n.* **1.** a member of a Christian millenarian sect founded in the U.S. about 1848, holding that only the just will enter eternal life, that the wicked will be annihilated, and that the ignorant, the unconverted, and infants will not be raised from the dead. ~*adj.* **2.** of or relating to this body or its beliefs and practices. [C19: from Late Greek *khristadelphos,* from *khristos* CHRIST + *adelphos* brother]

christcross (ˈkrɪsˌkrɒs) *n. Archaic.* **1. a.** the mark of a cross formerly placed in front of the alphabet in hornbooks. **b.** the alphabet itself. **2.** a cross used in place of a signature by someone unable to sign his name.

christen (ˈkrɪsᵊn) *vb.* (*tr.*) **1.** to give a Christian name to in baptism as a sign of incorporation into a Christian Church. **2.** another word for **baptize.** **3.** to give a name to (anything), esp. with some ceremony. **4.** *Informal.* to use for the first time. [Old English *cristnian,* from *Crīst* CHRIST] —ˈ**christener** *n.*

Christendom (ˈkrɪsᵊndəm) *n.* **1.** the collective body of Christians throughout the world or throughout history. **2.** an obsolete word for **Christianity.**

christening (ˈkrɪsᵊnɪŋ) *n.* the Christian sacrament of baptism or the ceremony in which this is conferred.

Christhood (ˈkraɪsthʊd) *n.* the state of being the Christ, the anointed one of God.

Christian (ˈkrɪstʃən) *n.* **1. a.** a person who believes in and follows Jesus Christ. **b.** a member of a Christian Church or denomination. **2.** *Informal.* a person who possesses Christian virtues, esp. practical ones. ~*adj.* **3.** of, relating to, or derived from Jesus Christ, his teachings, example, or his followers. **4.** (*sometimes not cap.*) exhibiting kindness or goodness. —ˈ**christianly** *adj., adv.*

Christian Era *n.* the period beginning with the year of Christ's birth. Dates in this era are labelled A.D., those previous to it B.C. Also called: **Common Era.**

Christianity (ˌkrɪstɪˈænɪtɪ) *n.* **1.** the Christian religion. **2.** Christian beliefs, practices or attitudes. **3.** a less common word for **Christendom** (sense 1).

Christianize *or* **Christianise** (ˈkrɪstʃəˌnaɪz) *vb.* **1.** (*tr.*) to make Christian or convert to Christianity. **2.** (*tr.*) to imbue with Christian principles, spirit, or outlook. **3.** (*intr.*) *Rare.* to become Christian. —ˌ**Christianiˈzation** *or* ˌ**Christianiˈsation** *n.* —ˈ**Christianˌizer** *or* ˈ**Christianˌiser** *n.*

Christian name *n. Brit.* a personal name formally given to Christians at christening. The term is loosely used to mean any person's first name as distinct from his or her surname. Also called: **first name, forename,** (esp. U.S.) **given name.**

Christian Science *n.* the religious system and teaching of the Church of Christ, Scientist. It was founded in 1866 by Mary Baker Eddy (1821–1910), U.S. religious leader, and emphasizes spiritual healing and the unreality of matter. —**Christian Scientist** *n.*

Christlike (ˈkraɪstˌlaɪk) *adj.* resembling or showing the spirit of Jesus Christ. —ˈ**Christˌlikeness** *n.*

Christmas (ˈkrɪsməs) *n.* **1. a.** the annual commemoration by Christians of the birth of Jesus Christ on Dec. 25. **b.** Also called: **Christmas Day.** Dec. 25, observed as a day of secular celebrations when gifts and greetings are exchanged. **c.** (*as modifier*): *Christmas celebrations.* **2.** Also called: **Christmas Day.** (in England, Wales and Ireland) Dec. 25, one of the four quarter days. Compare **Lady Day, Midsummer Day, Michaelmas.** **3.** Also called: **Christmastide.** the season of Christmas extending from Dec. 24 (Christmas Eve) to Jan. 6 (the festival of the Epiphany or Twelfth Night). [Old English *Crīstes mæsse* MASS of CHRIST]

Christmas beetle *n.* any of various greenish-gold Australian scarab beetles of the genus *Anoplognathus,* which are common in summer.

Christmas box *n.* a tip or present given at Christmas, esp. to postmen, tradesmen, etc.

Christmas cactus *n.* a Brazilian cactus, *Schlumbergera* (formerly *Zygocactus*) *truncatus,* widely cultivated as an ornamental for its showy red flowers. Also called: **crab cactus, Easter cactus.**

Christmas card *n.* a greeting card sent at Christmas.

Christmas disease *n.* a relatively mild type of haemophilia, caused by lack of a protein (**Christmas factor**) implicated in the process of blood clotting. [C20: named after S. *Christmas,* the first patient suffering from the disease who was examined in detail]

Christmas Eve *n.* the evening or the whole day before Christmas Day.

Christmas pudding *n. Brit.* a rich steamed pudding containing suet, dried fruit, spices, brandy, etc., served at Christmas. Also called: **plum pudding.**

Christmas rose *n.* an evergreen ranunculaceous plant, *Helleborus niger,* of S Europe and W Asia, with white or pinkish winter-blooming flowers. Also called: **hellebore, winter rose.**

Christmas stocking *n.* a stocking hung up by children on Christmas Eve for Santa Claus to fill with presents.

Christmassy (ˈkrɪsməsɪ) *adj.* of, relating to, or suitable for Christmas.

Christmastide (ˈkrɪsməsˌtaɪd) *n.* another name for **Christmas** (sense 3).

Christmas tree *n.* **1.** an evergreen tree or an imitation of one, decorated as part of Christmas celebrations. **2.** Also called: **Christmas bush.** *Austral.* any of various trees or shrubs flowering at Christmas and used for decoration.

Christo- *combining form.* indicating or relating to Christ: *Christology.*
Christology (krɪ'stɒlədʒɪ, kraɪ-) *n.* the branch of theology concerned with the person, attributes, and deeds of Christ. —**Christological** (ˌkrɪstə'lɒdʒɪkᵊl) *adj.* —**Chris'tologist** *n.*
Christ's-thorn *n.* any of several plants of SW Asia, such as *Paliurus spina-christi* and the jujube, that have thorny stems and are popularly believed to have been used for Christ's Crown of Thorns.
Christy *or* **Christie** ('krɪstɪ) *n., pl.* **-ties.** *Skiing.* a turn in which the body is swung sharply round with the skis parallel, originating in Norway and used for stopping, slowing down, or changing direction quickly. [C20: shortened from *Christiania*, former name of Oslo]
chroma ('krəʊmə) *n.* **1.** the attribute of a colour that enables an observer to judge how much chromatic colour it contains irrespective of achromatic colour present. See also **saturation** (sense 4). **2.** (in colour television) the colour component in a composite coded signal. [C19: from Greek *khrōma* colour]
chromakey ('krəʊməˌkiː) *n.* (in colour television) a special effect in which a coloured background can be eliminated and a different background substituted. Also called: **colour separation overlay.**
chromate ('krəʊˌmeɪt) *n.* any salt or ester of chromic acid. Simple chromate salts contain the divalent ion, CrO_4^{2-}, and are orange.
chromatic (krə'mætɪk) *adj.* **1.** of, relating to, or characterized by a colour or colours. **2.** *Music.* **a.** involving the sharpening or flattening of notes or the use of such notes in chords and harmonic progressions. **b.** of or relating to the chromatic scale or an instrument capable of producing it: *a chromatic harmonica.* **c.** of or relating to chromaticism. Compare **diatonic.** [C17: from Greek *khrōmatikos*, from *khrōma* colour] —**chro'matically** *adv.* —**chro'maticism** *n.*
chromatic aberration *n.* a defect in a lens system in which different wavelengths of light are focused at different distances because they are refracted through different angles. It produces a blurred image with coloured fringes.
chromatic adaptation *n. Botany.* the alteration by plants of the proportions of their photosynthetic pigments in response to the intensity and colour of the available light, as shown by algae in the littoral zone, which change from green to red as the zone is descended.
chromatic colour *n. Physics.* a more formal term for **colour** (sense 2).
chromaticity (ˌkrəʊmə'tɪsɪtɪ) *n.* the quality of a colour or light with reference to its purity and its dominant wavelength.
chromaticity coordinates *pl. n. Physics.* three numbers used to specify a colour, each of which is equal to one of the three tristimulus values divided by the sum of these values. Symbols: *x, y, z*
chromaticity diagram *n. Physics.* a diagram in which values of two chromaticity coordinates are marked on a pair of rectangular axes, a point in the plane of these axes representing the chromaticity of any colour.
chromaticness (krəʊ'mætɪknɪs) *n. Physics.* the attribute of colour that involves both hue and saturation.
chromatics (krəʊ'mætɪks) *or* **chromatology** (ˌkrəʊmə'tɒlədʒɪ) *n.* (*functioning as sing.*) the science of colour. —**chromatist** ('krəʊmətɪst) *or* ˌ**chroma'tologist** *n.*
chromatic scale *n.* a twelve-note scale including all the semitones of the octave.
chromatid ('krəʊmətɪd) *n.* either of the two strands into which a chromosome divides during mitosis. They separate to form daughter chromosomes at anaphase.
chromatin ('krəʊmətɪn) *n. Cytology.* the part of the nucleus that consists of DNA, RNA, and proteins, forms the chromosomes, and stains with basic dyes. See also **euchromatin, heterochromatin.** —ˌ**chroma'tinic** *adj.* —'**chromaˌtoid** *adj.*
chromato- *or before a vowel* **chromat-** *combining form.* **1.** indicating colour or coloured: *chromatophore.* **2.** indicating chromatin: *chromatolysis.* [from Greek *khrōma, khrōmat-* colour]
chromatogram ('krəʊmətəˌgræm, krəʊ'mæt-) *n.* **1.** a column or strip of material containing constituents of a mixture separated by chromatography. **2.** a graph showing the quantity of a substance leaving a chromatography column as a function of time.
chromatography (ˌkrəʊmə'tɒgrəfɪ) *n.* the technique of separating and analysing the components of a mixture of liquids or gases by selective adsorption in, for example, a column of powder (**column chromatography**) or on a strip of paper (**paper chromatography**). See also **gas chromatography.** —ˌ**chroma'tographer** *n.* —**chromatographic** (ˌkrəʊmətə'græfɪk) *adj.* —ˌ**chromato'graphically** *adv.*
chromatology (ˌkrəʊmə'tɒlədʒɪ) *n.* another name for **chromatics.**
chromatolysis (ˌkrəʊmə'tɒlɪsɪs) *n. Cytology.* the dissolution of chromatin in injured cells.
chromatophore ('krəʊmətəˌfɔː) *n.* **1.** a cell in the skin of frogs, chameleons, etc., in which pigment is concentrated or dispersed, causing the animal to change colour. **2.** another name for **chromoplast.** —ˌ**chromato'phoric** *or* **chromatophorous** (ˌkrəʊmə'tɒfərəs) *adj.*
chrome (krəʊm) *n.* **1. a.** another word for **chromium,** esp. when present in a pigment or dye. **b.** (*as modifier*): *a chrome dye.* **2.** anything plated with chromium, such as fittings on a car body. **3.** a pigment or dye that contains chromium. ~*vb.* **4.** to plate or be plated with chromium, usually by electroplating. **5.** to treat or be treated with a chromium compound, as in dyeing or tanning. [C19: via French from Greek *khrōma* colour]
-chrome *n. and adj. combining form.* colour, coloured, or pigment: *monochrome.* [from Greek *khrōma* colour]
chrome alum *n.* a violet-red crystalline substance, used as a mordant in dyeing. Formula: $KCr(SO_4)_2.12H_2O$.
chrome dioxide *n.* another name for **chromium dioxide.**
chrome green *n.* **1.** any green pigment made by mixing lead chromate with Prussian blue. **2.** any green pigment containing chromic oxide.
chromel ('krəʊmɛl) *n.* a nickel-based alloy containing about 10 per cent chromium, used in heating elements. [C20: from CHRO(MIUM) + ME(TA)L]
chrome red *n.* any red pigment used in paints, consisting of a mixture of lead chromate and lead oxide; basic lead chromate.
chrome steel *n.* any of various hard rust-resistant steels containing chromium. Also called: **chromium steel.**
chrome tape *n.* magnetic recording tape coated with chrome dioxide.
chrome yellow *n.* any yellow pigment consisting of lead chromate mixed with lead sulphate.
chromic ('krəʊmɪk) *adj.* **1.** of or containing chromium in the trivalent state. **2.** of or derived from chromic acid.
chromic acid *n.* an unstable dibasic oxidizing acid known only in solution and in the form of chromate salts. Formula: H_2CrO_4.
chrominance ('krəʊmɪnəns) *n.* **1.** the quality of light that causes the sensation of colour. It is determined by comparison with a reference source of the same brightness and of known chromaticity. **2.** the information that defines the colour (hue and saturation) of a television image, but not the brightness. [C20: from CHROMO- + LUMINANCE]
chromite ('krəʊmaɪt) *n.* **1.** a brownish-black mineral consisting of a ferrous chromic oxide in cubic crystalline form, occurring principally in basic igneous rocks: the only commercial source of chromium and its compounds. Formula: $FeCr_2O_4$. **2.** a salt of chromous acid.
chromium ('krəʊmɪəm) *n.* a hard grey metallic element that takes a high polish, occurring principally in chromite: used in steel alloys and electroplating to increase hardness and corrosion-resistance. Symbol: Cr; atomic no.: 24; atomic wt.: 51.996; valency: 2, 3, or 6; relative density: 7.19; melting pt.: 1890°C; boiling pt.: 2482°C. [C19: from New Latin, from French: CHROME]
chromium dioxide *n.* a chemical compound used as a magnetic coating on cassette tapes; chromium(IV) oxide. Formula: CrO_2. Also called (*not in technical usage*) **chrome dioxide.**
chromium steel *n.* another name for **chrome steel.**
chromo ('krəʊməʊ) *n., pl.* **-mos.** short for **chromolithograph.**
chromo- *or before a vowel* **chrom-** *combining form.* **1.** indicating colour, coloured, or pigment: *chromogen.* **2.** indicating chromium: *chromyl.* [from Greek *khrōma* colour]
chromogen ('krəʊmədʒən) *n.* **1.** a compound that forms coloured compounds on oxidation. **2.** a substance that can be converted to a dye. **3.** a bacterium that produces a pigment.
chromogenic (ˌkrəʊmə'dʒɛnɪk) *adj.* **1.** producing colour. **2.** of or relating to a chromogen.
chromolithograph (ˌkrəʊməʊ'lɪθəˌgrɑːf, -ˌgræf) *n.* a picture produced by chromolithography.
chromolithography (ˌkrəʊməʊlɪ'θɒgrəfɪ) *n.* the process of making coloured prints by lithography. —ˌ**chromoli'thographer** *n.* —**chromolithographic** (ˌkrəʊməʊlɪθə'græfɪk) *adj.*
chromomere ('krəʊməˌmɪə) *n. Cytology.* any of the dense areas of chromatin along the length of a chromosome during the early stages of cell division.
chromonema (ˌkrəʊmə'niːmə) *n., pl.* **-mata** (-mətə). *Cytology.* **1.** the coiled mass of threads within a nucleus at cell division. **2.** a coiled chromatin thread within a single chromosome. [C20: from CHROMO- + Greek *nēma* thread, yarn] —ˌ**chromo'nemal, chromonematic** (ˌkrəʊməʊnɪ'mætɪk), *or* ˌ**chromo'nemic** *adj.*
chromophore ('krəʊməˌfɔː) *n.* a group of atoms in a chemical compound that are responsible for the colour of the compound. —ˌ**chromo'phoric** *or* ˌ**chromo'phorous** *adj.*
chromoplast ('krəʊməˌplæst) *n.* a coloured plastid in a plant cell, esp. one containing carotenoids.
chromoprotein (ˌkrəʊməʊ'prəʊtiːn) *n.* any of a group of conjugated proteins, such as haemoglobin, in which the protein is joined to a coloured group, usually a metallic porphyrin.
chromosome ('krəʊməˌsəʊm) *n.* any of the microscopic rod-shaped structures that appear in a cell nucleus during cell division, consisting of nucleoprotein arranged into units (genes) that are responsible for the transmission of hereditary characteristics. See also **homologous chromosomes.** —ˌ**chromo'somal** *adj.* —ˌ**chromo'somally** *adv.*
chromosome band *n.* any of the transverse bands that appear on a chromosome after staining. The banding pattern is unique to each type of chromosome, allowing characterization.
chromosome map *n.* a graphic representation of the positions of genes on chromosomes, obtained by observation of chromosome

bands or by determining the degree of linkage between genes. See also **genetic map.** —**chromosome mapping** *n.*

chromosome number *n.* the number of chromosomes present in each somatic cell, which is constant for any one species of plant or animal. In the reproductive cells this number is halved. See also **diploid** (sense 1), **haploid.**

chromosphere ('krəʊmə,sfɪə) *n.* a gaseous layer of the sun's atmosphere extending from the photosphere to the corona and visible during a total eclipse of the sun. —**chromospheric** (ˌkrəʊmə'sfɛrɪk) *adj.*

chromous ('krəʊməs) *adj.* of or containing chromium in the divalent state.

chromyl ('krəʊməl) *n.* (*modifier*) of, consisting of, or containing the divalent radical CrO_2.

chron. *or* **chronol.** *abbrev. for:* **1.** chronological. **2.** chronology.

Chron. *Bible. abbrev. for* Chronicles.

chronaxie *or* **chronaxy** ('krəʊnæksɪ) *n. Physiol.* the minimum time required for excitation of a nerve or muscle when the stimulus is double the minimum (threshold) necessary to elicit a basic response. Compare **rheobase.** [C20: from French, from CHRONO- + Greek *axia* worth, from *axios* worthy, of equal weight]

chronic ('krɒnɪk) *adj.* **1.** continuing for a long time; constantly recurring. **2.** (of a disease) developing slowly, or of long duration. Compare **acute** (sense 7). **3.** inveterate; habitual: *a chronic smoker.* **4.** *Informal.* **a.** very bad: *the play was chronic.* **b.** very serious: *he left her in a chronic condition.* [C15: from Latin *chronicus* relating to time, from Greek *khronikos,* from *khronos* time] —**'chronically** *adv.* —**chronicity** (krɒ'nɪsɪtɪ) *n.*

chronicle ('krɒnɪkᵊl) *n.* **1.** a record or register of events in chronological order. ~*vb.* **2.** (*tr.*) to record in or as if in a chronicle. [C14: from Anglo-French *cronicle,* via Latin *chronica* (pl.), from Greek *khronika* annals, from *khronikos* relating to time; see CHRONIC] —**'chronicler** *n.*

chronicle play *n.* a drama based on a historical subject.

chrono- *or before a vowel* **chron-** *combining form.* indicating time: *chronology; chronometer.* [from Greek *khronos* time]

chronobiology (ˌkrɒnəbaɪ'ɒlədʒɪ, ˌkrəʊnə-) *n.* the branch of biology concerned with the periodicity occurring in living organisms. See also **biological clock, circadian.**

chronogram ('krɒnə,græm, 'krəʊnə-) *n.* **1.** a phrase or inscription in which letters such as M, C, X, L and V can be read as Roman numerals giving a date. **2.** a record kept by a chronograph. —**chronogrammatic** (ˌkrɒnəʊgrə'mætɪk) *or* ˌ**chronogram'matical** *adj.* —ˌ**chronogram'matically** *adv.*

chronograph ('krɒnə,grɑːf, -,græf, 'krəʊnə-) *n.* an accurate instrument for recording small intervals of time. —**chronographer** (krə'nɒgrəfə) *n.* —**chronographic** (ˌkrɒnə'græfɪk) *adj.* —ˌ**chrono'graphically** *adv.*

chronological (ˌkrɒnə'lɒdʒɪkᵊl, ˌkrəʊ-) *or* **chronologic** *adj.* **1.** (esp. of a sequence of events) arranged in order of occurrence. **2.** relating to or in accordance with chronology. —ˌ**chrono'logically** *adv.*

chronology (krə'nɒlədʒɪ) *n., pl.* **-gies. 1.** the determination of the proper sequence of past events. **2.** the arrangement of dates, events, etc., in order of occurrence. **3.** a table or list of events arranged in order of occurrence. —**chro'nologist** *n.*

chronometer (krə'nɒmɪtə) *n.* a timepiece designed to be accurate in all conditions of temperature, pressure, etc., used esp. at sea. —**chronometric** (ˌkrɒnə'mɛtrɪk) *or* ˌ**chrono'metrical** *adj.* —ˌ**chrono'metrically** *adv.*

chronometry (krə'nɒmɪtrɪ) *n.* the science or technique of measuring time with extreme accuracy.

chronon ('krəʊnɒn) *n.* a unit of time equal to the time that a photon would take to traverse the diameter of an electron: about 10^{-24} seconds.

chronoscope ('krɒnə,skəʊp, 'krəʊnə-) *n.* an instrument that registers small intervals of time on a dial, cathode-ray tube, etc. —**chronoscopic** (ˌkrɒnə'skɒpɪk, ˌkrəʊnə-) *adj.* —ˌ**chrono'scopically** *adv.*

-chroous *or* **-chroic** *adj. combining form.* coloured in a specified way: *isochroous.* [from Greek *khrōs* skin, complexion, colour]

chrysalid ('krɪsəlɪd) *n.* **1.** another name for **chrysalis.** ~*adj. also* **chrysalidal** (krɪ'sælɪdᵊl). **2.** of or relating to a chrysalis.

chrysalis ('krɪsəlɪs) *n., pl.* **chrysalises** *or* **chrysalides** (krɪ'sælɪˌdiːz). **1.** the obtect pupa of a moth or butterfly. **2.** anything in the process of developing. [C17: from Latin *chrȳsallis,* from Greek *khrusallis,* from *khrusos* gold, of Semitic origin; compare Hebrew *harūz* gold]

chrysanthemum (krɪ'sænθəməm) *n.* **1.** any widely cultivated plant of the genus *Chrysanthemum,* esp. *C. morifolium* of China, having brightly coloured showy flower heads: family *Compositae* (composites). **2.** any other plant of the genus *Chrysanthemum,* such as oxeye daisy. [C16: from Latin: marigold, from Greek *khrusanthemon,* from *khrusos* gold + *anthemon* flower]

chrysarobin (ˌkrɪsə'rəʊbɪn) *n.* a tasteless odourless powder containing anthraquinone derivatives of araroba, formerly used medicinally to treat chronic skin conditions. [C20: from CHRYSO- (referring to its golden colour) + ARAROBA + -IN]

chryselephantine (ˌkrɪsɛlɪ'fæntɪn) *adj.* (of ancient Greek statues) made of or overlaid with gold and ivory. [C19: from Greek *khruselephantinos,* from *khrusos* gold + *elephas* ivory; see ELEPHANT]

chryso- *or before a vowel* **chrys-** *combining form.* indicating gold or the colour of gold: *chryselephantine; chrysolite.* [from Greek *khrusos* gold]

chrysoberyl ('krɪsə,bɛrɪl) *n.* a rare very hard greenish-yellow mineral consisting of beryllium aluminate in orthorhombic crystalline form and occurring in coarse granite: used as a gemstone in the form of cat's eye and alexandrite. Formula: $BeAl_2O_4$.

chrysolite ('krɪsə,laɪt) *n.* a brown or yellowish-green olivine consisting of magnesium iron silicate: used as a gemstone (see **peridot**). Formula: $(Mg,Fe)_2SiO_4$. —**chrysolitic** (ˌkrɪsə'lɪtɪk) *adj.*

chrysoprase ('krɪsə,preɪz) *n.* an apple-green variety of chalcedony: a gemstone. [C13 *crisopace,* from Old French, from Latin *chrȳsoprasus,* from Greek *khrusoprasos,* from CHRYSO- + *prason* leek]

chrysotile ('krɪsətɪl) *n.* a green, grey, or white fibrous mineral, a variety of serpentine, that is an important source of commercial asbestos. Formula: $Mg_3Si_2O_5(OH)_4$. [C20: from CHRYSO- + Greek *tilos* something plucked, shred, thread, from *tillein* to pluck]

chs. *abbrev. for* chapters.

chthonian ('θəʊnɪən) *or* **chthonic** ('θɒnɪk) *adj.* of or relating to the underworld. [C19: from Greek *khthonios* in or under the earth, from *khthōn* earth]

chub (tʃʌb) *n., pl.* **chub** *or* **chubs. 1.** a common European freshwater cyprinid game fish, *Leuciscus* (or *Squalius*) *cephalus,* having a cylindrical dark greenish body. **2.** any of various North American fishes, esp. certain whitefishes and minnows. [C15: of unknown origin]

Chubb (tʃʌb) *n. Trademark.* a type of patent lock containing a device that sets the bolt immovably if the lock is picked.

chubby ('tʃʌbɪ) *adj.* **-bier, -biest.** (esp. of the human form) plump and round. [C17: perhaps from CHUB, with reference to the plump shape of the fish] —**'chubbiness** *n.*

chuck¹ (tʃʌk) *vb.* (*mainly tr.*) **1.** *Informal.* to throw. **2.** to pat affectionately, esp. under the chin. **3.** (sometimes foll. by *in* or *up*) *Informal.* to give up; reject: *he chucked up his job; she chucked her boyfriend.* **4.** (*intr.*) (usually foll. by *up*) *Slang. chiefly U.S.* to vomit. **5. chuck off at.** *Austral. and N.Z.* to abuse. ~*n.* **6.** a throw or toss. **7.** a playful pat under the chin. **8. the chuck.** *Informal.* dismissal. ~See also **chuck in, chuck out.** [C16: of unknown origin]

chuck² (tʃʌk) *n.* **1.** Also called: **chuck steak.** a cut of beef extending from the neck to the shoulder blade. **2. a.** Also called: **three jaw chuck.** a device that holds a workpiece in a lathe or tool in a drill, having a number of adjustable jaws geared to move in unison to centralize the workpiece or tool. **b.** Also called: **four jaw chuck, independent jaw chuck.** a similar device having independently adjustable jaws for holding an unsymmetrical workpiece. [C17: variant of CHOCK]

chuck³ (tʃʌk) *vb.* **1.** (*intr.*) a less common word for **cluck** (sense 2). ~*n.* **2.** a clucking sound. **3.** *Archaic.* a term of endearment. [C14 *chukken* to cluck, of imitative origin]

chuck⁴ (tʃʌk) *n. Canadian W coast.* **1.** a large body of water. **2.** short for **saltchuck** (the sea). [C19: from Chinook Jargon, from Nootka *chauk*]

chuck-full *adj.* a less common spelling of **chock-full.**

chuckie ('tʃʌkɪ) *n. Scot. and N.Z.* a small stone. [probably from CHUCK¹]

chuck in *vb.* (*adv.*) *Informal.* **1.** (*tr.*) *Brit.* to abandon or give up: *chuck in a hopeless attempt.* **2.** (*intr.*) *Austral.* to contribute to the cost of something. ~*n.* **chuck-in. 3.** *Austral.* a contribution to the cost of something.

chuckle ('tʃʌkᵊl) *vb.* (*intr.*) **1.** to laugh softly or to oneself. **2.** (of animals, esp. hens) to make a clucking sound. ~*n.* **3.** a partly suppressed laugh. [C16: probably from CHUCK³] —**'chuckler** *n.* —**'chucklingly** *adv.*

chucklehead ('tʃʌkᵊl,hɛd) *n. Informal.* a stupid person; blockhead; dolt. —**'chuckle,headed** *adj.* —**'chuckle,headedness** *n.*

chuck out *vb.* (*tr., adv.;* often foll. by *of*) *Informal.* to eject forcibly (from); throw out (of): *he was chucked out of the lobby.*

chuck wagon *n.* a wagon carrying provisions and cooking utensils for men, such as cowboys, who work in the open. [C19: perhaps from CHUCK² (beef, food)]

chuckwalla ('tʃʌk,wɒlə) *n.* a lizard, *Sauromalus obesus,* that has an inflatable body and inhabits desert regions of the southwestern U.S.: family *Iguanidae* (iguanas). [from Mexican Spanish *chacahuala,* from Shoshonean *tcaxxwal*]

chuck-will's-widow *n.* a large North American nightjar, *Caprimulgus carolinensis,* similar to the whippoorwill.

chuddar, chudder, chuddah, *or* **chador** ('tʃʌdə) *n.* a large shawl or veil worn by Muslim or Hindu women that covers them from head to foot. [from Hindi *caddar,* from Persian *chaddar*]

chuddy ('tʃʌdɪ) *n. Austral. and N.Z. slang.* chewing gum.

chufa ('tʃuːfə) *n.* a sedge, *Cyperus esculentus,* of warm regions of the Old World, with nutlike edible tubers. [C19: from Old Spanish: a morsel, joke, from *chufar* to joke, from *chuflar* to deride, ultimately from Latin *sībilāre* to whistle]

chuff[1] (tʃʌf) *n.* **1.** a puffing sound of or as if of a steam engine. ~*vb.* **2.** (*intr.*) to move while emitting such sounds: *the train chuffed on its way.* [C20: of imitative origin]
chuff[2] (tʃʌf) *n. Dialect.* a boor; churl; sullen fellow. [C17: from obsolete *chuff* (n.) fat cheek, of obscure origin]
chuff[3] (tʃʌf) *vb.* (*tr.; usually passive*) *Brit. slang.* to please or delight: *he was chuffed by his pay rise.* [probably from *chuff* (adj.) pleased, happy (earlier: chubby), from C16 *chuff* (obsolete n.) a fat cheek, of unknown origin]
chuffy *or* **chuffie** ('tʃʌfɪ) *adj.* **-fier, -fiest. 1.** *Scot. or dialect.* plump or chubby. **2.** *Dialect.* surly.
chug (tʃʌg) *n.* **1.** a short dull sound, esp. one that is rapidly repeated, such as that made by an engine. ~*vb.* **chugs, chugging, chugged. 2.** (*intr.*) (of an engine, etc.) to operate while making such sounds. [C19: of imitative origin]
chukar (tʃʌ'kɑː) *n.* a common Indian partridge, *Alectoris chukar* (or *graeca*), having red legs and bill and a black-barred sandy plumage. [from Hindi *cakor,* from Sanskrit *cakora,* probably of imitative origin]
Chukchi *or* **Chukchee** ('tʃuktʃɪ) *n.* **1.** (*pl.* **-chi, -chis** *or* **-chee, -chees**) a member of a people of the Chukchi Peninsula in NE Siberia. **2.** the language of this people, related only to some of the smaller aboriginal languages of Siberia.
chukka boot *or* **chukka** ('tʃʌkə) *n.* an ankle-high boot made of suede or rubber and worn for playing polo. [C19: from CHUKKER]
chukker *or* **chukka** ('tʃʌkə) *n. Polo.* a period of continuous play, generally lasting 7½ minutes. [C20: from Hindi *cakkar,* from Sanskrit *cakra* wheel, circle]
chum[1] (tʃʌm) *n.* **1.** *Informal.* a close friend. ~*vb.* **chums, chumming, chummed. 2.** (*intr.;* usually foll. by *up with*) to be or become an intimate friend (of). **3.** (*tr.*) *Edinburgh dialect.* to accompany: *I'll chum you home.* [C17 (meaning: a person sharing rooms with another): probably shortened from *chamber fellow,* originally student slang (Oxford); compare CRONY]
chum[2] (tʃʌm) *n. Angling, chiefly U.S. and Canadian.* chopped fish, meal, etc., used as groundbait. [C19: origin uncertain]
chum[3] (tʃum) *n.* a Pacific salmon, *Oncorhynchus keta.* [from Chinook Jargon *tsum* spots, marks, from Chinook]
chumash *Hebrew.* (*Hebrew* xu'maʃ; *Yiddish* 'xuməʃ) *n. Judaism.* a printed book containing one of the Five Books of Moses. [literally: a fifth (part of the Torah)]
chummy ('tʃʌmɪ) *adj.* **-mier, -miest.** *Informal.* friendly. —'**chummily** *adv.* —'**chumminess** *n.*
chump[1] (tʃʌmp) *n.* **1.** *Informal.* a stupid person. **2.** a thick heavy block of wood. **3. a.** the thick blunt end of anything, esp. of a piece of meat. **b.** (*as modifier*): *a chump chop.* **4.** *Brit. slang.* the head (esp. in the phrase **off one's chump**). [C18: perhaps a blend of CHUNK and LUMP]
chump[2] (tʃʌmp) *vb.* a less common word for **chomp.**
chumping ('tʃʌmpɪŋ) *n. Yorkshire dialect.* collecting wood for bonfires on Guy Fawkes Day. [from CHUMP[1] (sense 2)]
chunder ('tʃʌndə) *Slang, chiefly Austral.* ~*vb.* (*intr.*) **1.** to vomit. ~*n.* **2.** vomit. [C20: of uncertain origin]
chunderous ('tʃʌndərəs) *adj. Austral. slang.* nauseating.
chunk (tʃʌŋk) *n.* **1.** a thick solid piece, as of meat, wood, etc. **2.** a considerable amount. [C17: variant of CHUCK[2]]
chunking ('tʃʌŋkɪŋ) *n. Psychol.* the grouping together of a number of items by the mind, after which they can be remembered as a single item, such as a word or a musical phrase.
chunky ('tʃʌŋkɪ) *adj.* **chunkier, chunkiest. 1.** thick and short. **2.** consisting of or containing thick pieces: *chunky dog food.* **3.** *Chiefly Brit.* (of clothes, esp. knitwear) made of thick bulky material. —'**chunkily** *adv.* —'**chunkiness** *n.*
chunter ('tʃʌntə) *vb.* (*intr.* often foll. by *on*) *Brit. informal.* to mutter or grumble incessantly in a meaningless fashion. [C16: probably of imitative origin]
chupatti *or* **chupatty** (tʃə'pætɪ, -'pʌtɪ, -'pɑːtɪ) *n., pl.* **-patti, -pattis, -patties.** variant spellings of **chapatti.**
chuppah *or* **huppah** ('hupə) *n. Judaism.* **1.** the canopy under which a marriage is performed. **2.** the wedding ceremony as distinct from the celebration. [from Hebrew]
church (tʃɜːtʃ) *n.* **1.** a building designed for public forms of worship, esp. Christian worship. **2.** an occasion of public worship. **3.** the clergy as distinguished from the laity. **4.** (*usually cap.*) institutionalized forms of religion as a political or social force: *conflict between Church and State.* **5.** (*usually cap.*) the collective body of all Christians. **6.** (*often cap.*) a particular Christian denomination or group of Christian believers. **7.** (*often cap.*) the Christian religion. **8.** (in Britain) the practices or doctrines of the Church of England and similar denominations. Compare **chapel** (sense 4b). Related adj.: **ecclesiastical.** ~*vb.* (*tr.*) **9.** *Church of England.* to bring (someone, esp. a woman after childbirth) to church for special ceremonies. **10.** *U.S.* to impose church discipline upon. [Old English *cirice,* from Late Greek *kurikon,* from Greek *kuriakon* (*dōma*) the Lord's (house), from *kuriakos* of the master, from *kurios* master, from *kuros* power]
churchgoer ('tʃɜːtʃ,gəʊə) *n.* **1.** a person who attends church regularly. **2.** an adherent of an established Church in contrast to a Nonconformist. —'**church,going** *n.*
church key *n. U.S.* a device with a triangular point at one end for making holes in the tops of cans.
churchly ('tʃɜːtʃlɪ) *adj.* appropriate to, associated with, or suggestive of church life and customs. —'**churchliness** *n.*
churchman ('tʃɜːtʃmən) *n., pl.* **-men. 1.** a clergyman. **2.** a male practising member of a church. —'**churchmanly** *adj.* —'**churchman,ship** *n.*
church mode *n. Music.* a less common name for **mode** (sense 3a).
Church of Christ, Scientist *n.* the official name for the **Christian Scientists.**
Church of England *n.* the reformed established state Church in England, Catholic in order and basic doctrine, with the Sovereign as its temporal head.
Church of Jesus Christ of Latter-Day Saints *n.* the official name for the Mormon Church.
Church of Rome *n.* another name for the **Roman Catholic Church.**
Church of Scotland *n.* the established church in Scotland, Calvinist in doctrine and Presbyterian in constitution.
church parade *n.* a parade by servicemen or members of a uniformed organization for the purposes of attending religious services.
Church Slavonic *or* **Slavic** *n.* Old Church Slavonic, esp. as preserved in the liturgical use of the Orthodox church.
church text *n.* a heavy typeface in Gothic style.
churchwarden (,tʃɜːtʃ'wɔːdᵊn) *n.* **1.** *Church of England, Episcopal Church.* one of two assistants of a parish priest who administer the secular affairs of the church. **2.** a long-stemmed tobacco pipe made of clay.
churchwoman ('tʃɜːtʃ,wumən) *n., pl.* **-women.** a female practising member of a church.
churchy ('tʃɜːtʃɪ) *adj.* **churchier, churchiest. 1.** like a church, church service, etc. **2.** excessively religious.
churchyard ('tʃɜːtʃ,jɑːd) *n.* the grounds surrounding a church, usually used as a graveyard.
churchyard beetle *n.* a blackish nocturnal ground beetle, *Blaps mucronata,* found in cellars and similar places.
churidars ('tʃuːrɪ,dɑːz) *pl. n.* long tight-fitting trousers, worn by Indian men and women. Also called: **churidar pyjamas.** [from Hindi]
churinga (tʃə'rɪŋgə) *n., pl.* **-ga** *or* **-gas.** a sacred amulet of the Australian Aborigines. [from a native Australian language]
churl (tʃɜːl) *n.* **1.** a surly ill-bred person. **2.** *Archaic.* a farm labourer. **3.** a variant spelling of **ceorl. 4.** *Archaic.* a miserly person. [Old English *ceorl;* related to Old Norse *karl,* Middle Low German *kerle,* Greek *gerōn* old man]
churlish ('tʃɜːlɪʃ) *adj.* **1.** rude or surly. **2.** of or relating to peasants. **3.** miserly. **4.** *Rare.* difficult to work or manage. —'**churlishly** *adv.* —'**churlishness** *n.*
churn (tʃɜːn) *n.* **1.** *Brit.* a large container for milk. **2.** a vessel or machine in which cream or whole milk is vigorously agitated to produce butter. **3.** any similar device. ~*vb.* **4. a.** to stir or agitate (milk or cream) in order to make butter. **b.** to make (butter) by this process. **5.** (sometimes foll. by *up*) to move or cause to move with agitation: *ideas churned in his head.* **6.** (of a bank, broker, etc.) to encourage an investor or policyholder to change investments, endowment policies, etc., to increase commissions at the client's expense. **7.** (of a government) to pay benefits to a wide category of people and claw it back by taxation from the well off. **8.** to promote the turnover of existing subscribers leasing, and new subscribers joining, a cable television system. [Old English *ciern;* related to Old Norse *kjarni,* Middle Low German *kerne* churn, German dialect *Kern* cream] —'**churner** *n.*
churning ('tʃɜːnɪŋ) *n.* **1.** the quantity of butter churned at any one time. **2.** the act, process, or effect of someone or something that churns.
churn out *vb.* (*tr., adv.*) *Informal.* **1.** to produce (something) at a rapid rate: *to churn out ideas.* **2.** to perform (something) mechanically: *to churn out a song.*
churr (tʃɜː) *vb., n.* a variant spelling of **chirr.**
churrigueresque (,tʃuərɪgə'rɛsk) *or* **churrigueresco** *adj.* of or relating to a style of baroque architecture of Spain in the late 17th and early 18th centuries. [C19: from Spanish *churriguresco* in the style of José *Churriguera* (1650–1725), Spanish architect and sculptor]
chute[1] (ʃuːt) *n.* **1.** an inclined channel or vertical passage down which water, parcels, coal, etc., may be dropped. **2.** a steep slope, used as a slide as for toboggans. **3.** a slide into a swimming pool. **4.** a narrow passageway through which animals file for branding, spraying, etc. **5.** a rapid or waterfall. [C19: from Old French *cheoite,* feminine past participle of *cheoir* to fall, from Latin *cadere;* in some senses, a variant spelling of SHOOT]
chute[2] (ʃuːt) *n., vb. Informal.* short for **parachute.** —'**chutist** *n.*
chutney ('tʃʌtnɪ) *n.* a pickle of Indian origin, made from fruit, vinegar, spices, sugar, etc.: *mango chutney.* [C19: from Hindi *catnī,* of uncertain origin]
chuttie *or* **chutty** ('tʃʌtɪ) *n., pl.* **-ties.** *Austral. informal.* chewing gum. [C20: perhaps from the phrase *chew it*]
chutzpah *or* **hutzpah** ('xutspə) *n. U.S. and Canadian informal.* shameless audacity; impudence. [C20: from Yiddish]
Chuvash (tʃu'vɑːʃ) *n.* **1.** (*pl.* **-vash** *or* **-vashes**) a member of a Mongoloid people of Russia, living chiefly in the middle Volga region. **2.** the language of this people, generally classed within the Turkic branch of the Altaic family.

chyack ('tʃaɪæk) *vb.* a variant spelling of **chiack.**
chyle (kaɪl) *n.* a milky fluid composed of lymph and emulsified fat globules, formed in the small intestine during digestion. [C17: from Late Latin *chȳlus,* from Greek *khulos* juice pressed from a plant; related to Greek *khein* to pour] —**chylaceous** (kaɪ'leɪʃəs) *or* '**chylous** *adj.*
chylomicron (ˌkaɪləʊ'maɪkrɒn) *n. Biochem.* a minute droplet of fat, found in blood and chyle, that is the form in which dietary fat is carried in these fluids.
chyme (kaɪm) *n.* the thick fluid mass of partially digested food that leaves the stomach. [C17: from Late Latin *chȳmus,* from Greek *khumos* juice; compare CHYLE] —'**chymous** *adj.*
chymosin ('kaɪməsɪn) *n.* another name for **rennin.** [C20: from CHYME + -OSE[2] + -IN]
chymotrypsin (ˌkaɪməʊ'trɪpsɪn) *n.* a powerful proteolytic enzyme secreted from the pancreas in the form of chymotrypsinogen, being converted to the active form by trypsin. [C20: from CHYME + TRYPSIN]
chymotrypsinogen (ˌkaɪməʊtrɪp'sɪnədʒɪn) *n.* the inactive precursor of chymotrypsin. [C20: from CHYMOTRYPSIN + -GEN]
chypre *French.* (ʃiprə) *n.* a perfume made from sandalwood. [literally: Cyprus, where it perhaps originated]
Ci *symbol for* curie.
CI 1. *abbrev. for* Channel Islands. ~2. *international car registration for* Ivory Coast.
CIA *abbrev. for* Central Intelligence Agency; a federal U.S. bureau created in 1947 to coordinate and conduct espionage and intelligence activities.
ciao *Italian.* (tʃau) *sentence substitute.* an informal word for **hello** or **goodbye.**
CIB (in New Zealand) *abbrev. for* Criminal Investigation Branch (of New Zealand police).
ciborium (sɪ'bɔːrɪəm) *n., pl.* **-ria** (-rɪə). *Christianity.* 1. a goblet-shaped lidded vessel used to hold consecrated wafers in Holy Communion. 2. a freestanding canopy fixed over an altar and supported by four pillars. [C17: from Medieval Latin, from Latin: drinking cup, from Greek *kibōrion* cup-shaped seed vessel of the Egyptian lotus, hence, a cup]
cicada (sɪ'kɑːdə) *or* **cicala** *n., pl.* **-das, -dae** (-diː) *or* **-las, -le** (-leɪ). any large broad insect of the homopterous family *Cicadidae,* most common in warm regions. Cicadas have membranous wings and the males produce a high-pitched drone by vibration of a pair of drumlike abdominal organs. [C19: from Latin]
cicala (sɪ'kɑːlə; *Italian* tʃi'kala) *n., pl.* **-las** *or* **-le** (-leɪ; *Italian* -le). another name for **cicada.** [C19: from Italian, from Latin: CICADA]
cicatricle ('sɪkəˌtrɪkᵊl) *n.* 1. *Zoology.* the blastoderm in the egg of a bird. 2. *Biology.* any small scar or mark. [C17: from Latin *cicātrīcula* a little scar, from CICATRIX]
cicatrix ('sɪkətrɪks) *n., pl.* **cicatrices** (ˌsɪkə'traɪsiːz). 1. the tissue that forms in a wound during healing; scar. 2. a scar on a plant indicating the former point of attachment of a part, esp. a leaf. [C17: from Latin: scar, of obscure origin] —**cicatricial** (ˌsɪkə'trɪʃəl) *adj.* —**cicatricose** (sɪ'kætrɪˌkəʊs, 'sɪkə-) *adj.*
cicatrize *or* **cicatrise** ('sɪkəˌtraɪz) *vb.* (of a wound or defect in tissue) to close or be closed by scar formation; heal. —ˌ**cica'trizant** *or* ˌ**cica'trisant** *adj.* —ˌ**cicatri'zation** *or* ˌ**cicatri'sation** *n.* —'**cicaˌtrizer** *or* '**cicaˌtriser** *n.*
cicely ('sɪsəlɪ) *n., pl.* **-lies.** short for **sweet cicely.** [C16: from Latin *seselis,* from Greek, of obscure origin; influenced in spelling by the English proper name *Cicely*]
cicero ('sɪsəˌrəʊ) *n., pl.* **-ros.** a measure for type that is somewhat larger than the pica. [C19: from its first being used in a 15th-century edition of *Cicero* (106–43 B.C.), Roman writer and orator]
cicerone (ˌsɪsə'rəʊnɪ, ˌtʃɪtʃ-) *n., pl.* **-nes** *or* **-ni** (-nɪ). a person who conducts and informs sightseers. [C18: from Italian: antiquarian scholar, guide, after *Cicero,* alluding to the eloquence and erudition of these men]
Ciceronian (ˌsɪsə'rəʊnɪən) *adj.* 1. of or resembling Cicero or his rhetorical style; eloquent. 2. (of literary style) characterized by the use of antithesis and long periods.
cichlid ('sɪklɪd) *n.* 1. any tropical freshwater percoid fish of the family *Cichlidae,* which includes the mouthbrooders. Cichlids are popular aquarium fishes. ~*adj.* 2. of, relating to, or belonging to the *Cichlidae.* [C19: from New Latin *Cichlidae,* ultimately from Greek *kikhlē* a sea fish] —'**cichloid** *adj.*
cicisbeo *Italian.* (tʃitʃiz'bɛːo) *n., pl.* **-bei** (-'bɛːi). the escort or lover of a married woman, esp. in 18th-century Italy. [C18: Italian, of uncertain origin]
CID (in Britain) *abbrev. for* Criminal Investigation Department; the detective division of a police force.
-cide *n. combining form.* 1. indicating a person or thing that kills: *insecticide.* 2. indicating a killing; murder: *homicide.* [from Latin *-cīda* (agent), *-cīdium* (act), from *caedere* to kill] —**-cidal** *adj. combining form.*
cider *or* **cyder** ('saɪdə) *n.* 1. Also called (U.S.): **hard cider.** an alcoholic drink made from the fermented juice of apples. 2. Also called: **sweet cider.** *U.S. and Canadian.* an unfermented drink made from apple juice. [C14: from Old French *cisdre,* via Medieval Latin, from Late Greek *sikera* strong drink, from Hebrew *shēkhār*]
ci-devant *French.* (sidəvɑ̃) *adj.* (esp. of an office-holder) former; recent. [literally: heretofore]
Cie *abbrev. for* compagnie. [French: company]
CIE *abbrev. for:* 1. Commission Internationale de l'Éclairage. [French: International Lighting Commission] 2. Companion of the Indian Empire. 3. (in the Irish Republic) Coras Iompair Eireann. [Irish Gaelic: Transport Organization of Ireland]
c.i.f. *or* **CIF** *abbrev. for* cost, insurance, and freight (included in the price quoted).
c.i.f.c.i. *abbrev. for* cost, insurance, freight, commission, and interest (included in the price quoted).
CIFE (in Britain) *abbrev. for* Colleges and Institutes for Further Education.
cig (sɪg) *or* **ciggy** ('sɪgɪ) *n., pl.* **cigs** *or* **ciggies.** *Informal.* a cigarette.
cigar (sɪ'gɑː) *n.* a cylindrical roll of cured tobacco leaves, for smoking. [C18: from Spanish *cigarro,* perhaps from Mayan *sicar* to smoke]
cigarette *or U.S. (sometimes)* **cigaret** (ˌsɪgə'rɛt) *n.* a short tightly rolled cylinder of tobacco, wrapped in thin paper and often having a filter tip, for smoking. Shortened forms: **cig, ciggy.** [C19: from French, literally: a little CIGAR]
cigarette card *n.* a small picture card, formerly given away with cigarettes, now collected as a hobby.
cigarette end *n.* the part of a cigarette that is held in the mouth and that remains unsmoked after it is finished.
cigarette holder *n.* a mouthpiece of wood, ivory, etc., used for holding a cigarette while it is smoked.
cigarette lighter *n.* See **lighter**[1].
cigarette paper *n.* a piece of thin paper rolled around tobacco to form a cigarette.
cigarillo (ˌsɪgə'rɪləʊ) *n., pl.* **-los.** a small cigar, often only slightly larger than a cigarette.
CIGS (in Britain, formerly) *abbrev. for* Chief of the Imperial General Staff.
cilia ('sɪlɪə) *n.* the plural of **cilium.**
ciliary ('sɪlɪərɪ) *adj.* 1. of or relating to cilia. 2. of or relating to the ciliary body.
ciliary body *n.* the part of the vascular tunic of the eye that connects the choroid with the iris.
ciliate ('sɪlɪɪt, -eɪt) *adj.* 1. Also: '**ciliˌated.** possessing or relating to cilia: *a ciliate epithelium.* 2. of or relating to protozoans of the subclass *Ciliata,* which have an outer layer of cilia. ~*n.* 3. a protozoan of the subclass *Ciliata.* —ˌ**cili'ation** *n.*
cilice ('sɪlɪs) *n.* a haircloth fabric or garment. [Old English *cilic,* from Latin *cilicium* shirt made of Cilician goats' hair, from Greek *kilikion,* from *Kilikia* Cilicia, an ancient region in present-day S Turkey]
ciliolate ('sɪlɪəlɪt, -ˌleɪt) *adj.* covered with minute hairs, as some plants. [C19: from New Latin *ciliolum,* diminutive of CILIUM]
cilium ('sɪlɪəm) *n., pl.* **cilia** ('sɪlɪə). 1. any of the short threads projecting from the surface of a cell, organism, etc., whose rhythmic beating causes movement of the organism or of the surrounding fluid. 2. the technical name for **eyelash.** [C18: New Latin, from Latin: (lower) eyelid, eyelash]
cill (sɪl) *n. Brit.* a variant spelling (used in the building industry) for **sill** (senses 1–4).
CIM *abbrev. for:* 1. computer input on microfilm. 2. computer integrated manufacture.
cimbalom *or* **cymbalom** ('tsɪmbələm) *n.* a type of dulcimer, esp. of Hungary. See **dulcimer** (sense 1). [C19: Hungarian, from Italian *cembalo;* see CEMBALO]
Ciment Fondu ('siːmɒŋ fɒn'duː; *French* simɑ̃ fɔ̃dy) *n. Trademark.* a type of quick-hardening refractory cement having a high alumina content. Also called: **aluminous cement.**
cimetidine (saɪ'mɛtɪdiːn) *n.* a drug used to suppress the formation of acid by the stomach and so to encourage the healing of gastric and duodenal ulcers. Formula: $C_{10}H_{16}$-N_6S.
cimex ('saɪmɛks) *n., pl.* **cimices** ('sɪmɪˌsiːz). any of the heteropterous insects of the genus *Cimex,* esp. the bedbug. [C16: from Latin: bug]
Cimmerian (sɪ'mɪərɪən) *adj.* (*sometimes not cap.*) very dark; gloomy. [after the *Cimmerians,* a mythological people who lived in a land of darkness at the edge of the world]
C in C *or* **C.-in-C.** *Military. abbrev. for* Commander in Chief.
cinch[1] (sɪntʃ) *n.* 1. *Slang.* an easy task. 2. *Slang.* a certainty. 3. a U.S. and Canadian name for **girth** (sense 3). 4. *U.S. informal.* a firm grip. ~*vb.* 5. (often foll. by *up*) *U.S. and Canadian.* to fasten a girth around (a horse). 6. (*tr.*) *Informal.* to make sure of. 7. (*tr.*) *Informal, chiefly U.S.* to get a firm grip on. [C19: from Spanish *cincha* saddle girth, from Latin *cingula* girdle, from *cingere* to encircle]
cinch[2] (sɪntʃ) *n.* a card game in which the five of trumps ranks highest. [C19: probably from CINCH[1]]
cinchona (sɪŋ'kəʊnə) *n.* 1. any tree or shrub of the South American rubiaceous genus *Cinchona,* esp. *C. calisaya,* having medicinal bark. 2. Also called: **cinchona bark, Peruvian bark, calisaya, china bark.** the dried bark of any of these trees, which yields quinine and other medicinal alkaloids. 3. any of the drugs derived from cinchona bark. [C18: New Latin, named after the Countess of *Chinchón* (1576–1639), vicereine of Peru] —**cinchonic** (sɪŋ'kɒnɪk) *adj.*
cinchonidine (sɪŋ'kɒnɪˌdiːn) *n.* an alkaloid that is a stereoisomer of cinchonine, with similar properties and uses.

cinchonine ('sɪŋkəˌniːn) *n.* an insoluble crystalline alkaloid isolated from cinchona bark and used as a substitute for quinine. Formula: $C_{19}H_{22}N_2O$.
cinchonism ('sɪŋkəˌnɪzəm) *n.* a condition resulting from an excessive dose of cinchona bark or its alkaloids, characterized chiefly by headache, ringing in the ears, and vomiting.
cinchonize *or* **cinchonise** ('sɪŋkəˌnaɪz) *vb.* (*tr.*) to treat (a patient) with cinchona or one of its alkaloids, esp. quinine. —ˌ**cinchoni'zation** *or* ˌ**cinchoni'sation** *n.*
cincture ('sɪŋktʃə) *n.* something that encircles or surrounds, esp. a belt, girdle, or border. [C16: from Latin *cinctūra*, from *cingere* to gird]
cinder ('sɪndə) *n.* **1.** a piece of incombustible material left after the combustion of coal, coke, etc.; clinker. **2.** a piece of charred material that burns without flames; ember. **3.** Also called: **sinter.** any solid waste from smelting or refining. **4.** (*pl.*) fragments of volcanic lava; scoriae. ~*vb.* **5.** (*tr.*) *Rare.* to burn to cinders. [Old English *sinder;* related to Old Norse *sindr,* Old High German *sintar,* Old Slavonic *sedra* stalactite] —'**cindery** *adj.*
cinder block *n.* the usual U.S. name for **breeze block.**
Cinderella (ˌsɪndə'rɛlə) *n.* **1.** a girl who achieves fame after being obscure. **2. a.** a poor, neglected, or unsuccessful person or thing. **b.** (*as modifier*): *a Cinderella service within the NHS.* **3.** (*modifier*) relating to dramatic success: *a Cinderella story.* [C19: after *Cinderella,* the heroine of a fairy tale who is aided by a fairy godmother]
cinder track *n.* a racetrack covered with fine cinders.
cine- *combining form.* indicating motion picture or cinema: *cine camera; cinephotography.*
cineaste ('sɪnɪˌæst) *n.* an enthusiast for films. [C20: French, from CINEMA + *-aste,* as *-ast* in *enthusiast*]
cine camera ('sɪnɪ) *n. Brit.* a camera in which a strip of film moves past the lens, usually to give 16 or 24 exposures per second, thus enabling moving pictures to be taken. U.S. and Canadian term: **movie camera.**
cine film *n. Brit.* photographic film, wound on a spool, usually 8, 16, or 35 millimetres wide, up to several hundred metres long, and having one or two lines of sprocket holes along its length enabling it to be used in a cine camera. U.S. and Canadian term: **movie film.**
cinema ('sɪnɪmə) *n.* **1.** *Chiefly Brit.* **a.** a place designed for the exhibition of films. **b.** (*as modifier*): *a cinema seat.* **2. the cinema. a.** the art or business of making films. **b.** films collectively. [C19 (earlier spelling: *kinema*): shortened from CINEMATOGRAPH] —**cinematic** (ˌsɪnɪ'mætɪk) *adj.* —ˌ**cine'matically** *adv.*
Cinemascope ('sɪnɪməˌskəʊp) *n. Trademark.* an anamorphic process of wide-screen film projection in which an image of approximately twice the usual width is squeezed into a 35mm frame and then screened by a projector having complementary lenses.
cinematheque (ˌsɪnɪmə'tɛk) *n.* a small intimate cinema. [C20: from French *cinémathèque* film library, from CINEMA + (*biblio*)*thèque* library]
cinematograph (ˌsɪnɪ'mætəˌgrɑːf, -ˌgræf) *Chiefly Brit.* ~*n.* **1.** a combined camera, printer, and projector. ~*vb.* **2.** to take pictures (of) with a film camera. [C19 (earlier spelling: *kinematograph*): from Greek *kinēmat-, kinēma* motion + -GRAPH] —**cinematographer** (ˌsɪnɪmə'tɒgrəfə) *n.* —**cinematographic** (ˌsɪnɪˌmætə'græfɪk) *adj.* —ˌ**cine**ˌ**mato'graphically** *adv.* —ˌ**cinema'tography** *n.*
cinéma vérité (*French* sinema verite) *n.* films characterized by subjects, actions, etc., that have the appearance of real life. [French, literally: cinema truth]
cineol ('sɪnɪˌɒl) *or* **cineole** ('sɪnɪˌəʊl) *n.* another name for **eucalyptol.** [C19: changed from New Latin *oleum cinae,* literally: oil of wormseed]
Cinerama (ˌsɪnə'rɑːmə) *n. Trademark.* wide-screen presentation of films using either three separate 35mm projectors or one 70mm projector to produce an image on a large deeply curved screen.
cineraria (ˌsɪnə'rɛərɪə) *n.* a plant, *Senecio cruentus,* of the Canary Islands, widely cultivated for its blue, purple, red, or variegated daisy-like flowers: family *Compositae* (composites). [C16: from New Latin, from Latin *cinerārius* of ashes, from *cinis* ashes; from its downy leaves]
cinerarium (ˌsɪnə'rɛərɪəm) *n., pl.* **-raria** (-'rɛərɪə). a place for keeping the ashes of the dead after cremation. [C19: from Latin, from *cinerārius* relating to ashes; see CINERARIA] —**cinerary** ('sɪnərərɪ) *adj.*
cinerator ('sɪnəˌreɪtə) *n.* another name (esp. U.S.) for **cremator** (sense 1). —ˌ**cine'ration** *n.*
cinereous (sɪ'nɪərɪəs) *or* **cineritious** (ˌsɪnə'rɪʃəs) *adj.* **1.** of a greyish colour. **2.** resembling or consisting of ashes. [C17: from Latin *cinereus,* from *cinis* ashes]
cinerin ('sɪnərɪn) *n.* either of two similar organic compounds found in pyrethrum and used as insecticides. Formulas: $C_{20}H_{28}O_3$ (**cinerin I**), $C_{21}H_{28}O_5$ (**cinerin II**). [C20: from Latin *ciner-, cinis* ashes + -IN]
cingulum ('sɪŋgjʊləm) *n., pl.* **-la** (-lə). *Anatomy.* a girdle-like part, such as the ridge round the base of a tooth or the band of fibres connecting parts of the cerebrum. [C19: from Latin: belt, from *cingere* to gird] —**cingulate** ('sɪŋgjʊlɪt, -ˌleɪt) *or* '**cingu**ˌ**lated** *adj.*
cinnabar ('sɪnəˌbɑː) *n.* **1.** a bright red or brownish-red mineral form of mercuric chloride (mercury(II) chloride), found close to areas of volcanic activity and hot springs. It is the main commercial source of mercury. Formula: HgS. Crystal structure: hexagonal. **2.** the red form of mercuric sulphide (mercury(II) sulphide), esp. when used as a pigment. **3.** a bright red to reddish-orange; vermilion. **4.** a large red-and-black European moth, *Callimorpha jacobaeae:* family *Arctiidae* (tiger moths, etc.). [C15: from Old French *cenobre,* from Latin *cinnābaris,* from Greek *kinnabari,* of Oriental origin]
cinnamic acid (sɪ'næmɪk) *n.* a white crystalline water-insoluble weak organic acid existing in two isomeric forms; 3-phenylpropenoic acid. The *trans-* form occurs naturally and its esters are used in perfumery. Formula: $C_6H_5CH{:}CHCOOH$. [C19: from CINNAM(ON) + -IC; from its being found in cinnamon oil]
cinnamon ('sɪnəmən) *n.* **1.** a tropical Asian lauraceous tree, *Cinnamomum zeylanicum,* having aromatic yellowish-brown bark. **2.** the spice obtained from the bark of this tree, used for flavouring food and drink. **3. Saigon cinnamon.** an E Asian lauraceous tree, *Cinnamomum loureirii,* the bark of which is used as a cordial and to relieve flatulence. **4.** any of several similar or related trees or their bark. See **cassia** (sense 2). **5.** a light yellowish brown. [C15: from Old French *cinnamome,* via Latin and Greek, from Hebrew *qinnamown*] —**cin'namic** *or* **cinnamonic** (ˌsɪnə'mɒnɪk) *adj.*
cinnamon bear *n.* a reddish-brown variety of the American black bear. See **black bear** (sense 1).
cinnamon sedge *n.* an angler's name for a small caddis fly, *Limnephilus lunatus,* having pale hind wings, that frequents sluggish water.
cinnamon stone *n.* another name for **hessonite.**
cinquain (sɪŋ'keɪn, 'sɪŋkeɪn) *n.* a stanza of five lines. [C18 (in the sense: a military company of five): from French *cinq* five, from Latin *quinque;* compare QUATRAIN]
cinque (sɪŋk) *n.* the number five in cards, dice, etc. [C14: from Old French *cinq* five]
cinquecento (ˌtʃɪŋkwɪ'tʃɛntəʊ) *n.* the 16th century, esp. in reference to Italian art, architecture, or literature. [C18: Italian, shortened from *milcinquecento* 1500] —ˌ**cinque'centist** *n.*
cinquefoil ('sɪŋkˌfɔɪl) *n.* **1.** any plant of the N temperate rosaceous genus *Potentilla,* typically having five-lobed compound leaves. **2.** an ornamental carving in the form of five arcs arranged in a circle and separated by cusps. **3.** *Heraldry.* a charge representing a five-petalled flower. [C13 *sink foil,* from Old French *cincfoille,* from Latin *quinquefolium* plant with five leaves, translating Greek *pentaphullon* from *pente* five + *phullon* leaf]
Cinzano (tʃɪn'zɑːnəʊ) *n. Trademark.* an Italian vermouth.
CIO *U.S. abbrev. for* Congress of Industrial Organizations. See also **AFL-CIO.**
cipher *or* **cypher** ('saɪfə) *n.* **1.** a method of secret writing using substitution or transposition of letters according to a key. **2.** a secret message. **3.** the key to a secret message. **4.** an obsolete name for **zero** (sense 1). **5.** any of the Arabic numerals (0, 1, 2, 3, etc., to 9) or the Arabic system of numbering as a whole. **6.** a person or thing of no importance; nonentity. **7.** a design consisting of interwoven letters; monogram. **8.** *Music.* a defect in an organ resulting in the continuous sounding of a pipe, the key of which has not been depressed. ~*vb.* **9.** to put (a message) into secret writing. **10.** (*intr.*) (of an organ pipe) to sound without having the appropriate key depressed. **11.** *Rare.* to perform (a calculation) arithmetically. [C14: from Old French *cifre* zero, from Medieval Latin *cifra,* from Arabic *sifr* zero, empty]
cipolin ('sɪpəlɪn) *n.* an Italian marble with alternating white and green streaks. [C18: from French, from Italian *cipollino* a little onion, from *cipolla* onion, from Late Latin *cēpulla,* diminutive of Latin *cēpa* onion; from its likeness to the layers of an onion]
cir. *or* **circ.** *abbrev. for:* **1.** (preceding a date) circa. **2.** circular. **3.** circulation. **4.** circumference.
circa ('sɜːkə) *prep.* (used with a date) at the approximate time of: *circa 1182* B.C. Abbrevs.: **c, ca.** [Latin: about; related to Latin *circus* circle, CIRCUS]
circadian (sɜː'keɪdɪən) *adj.* of or relating to biological processes that occur regularly at about 24-hour intervals, even in the absence of periodicity in the environment. See also **biological clock.** [C20: from Latin *circa* about + *diēs* day]
Circassian (sɜː'kæsɪən) *n.* **1.** a native of Circassia, a region on the Black Sea north of the Caucasus Mountains. **2.** a language or languages spoken in Circassia, belonging to the North-West Caucasian family. See also **Adygei, Kabardian.** ~*adj. also* **Circassic. 3.** relating to Circassia, its people, or language.
circinate ('sɜːsɪˌneɪt) *adj.* **1.** *Botany.* (of part of a plant, such as a young fern) coiled so that the tip is at the centre. **2.** *Anatomy.* resembling a ring or a circle. [C19: from Latin *circināre* to make round, from *circinus* pair of compasses, from *circus,* see CIRCUS] —'**circi**ˌ**nately** *adv.*
Circinus ('sɜːsɪnəs) *n., Latin genitive* **Circini** ('sɜːsɪˌnaɪ). a small faint constellation in the S hemisphere close to Centaurus and the Southern Cross. [C19: from Latin, a pair of compasses]

circle ('sɜːkᵊl) *n.* **1.** a closed plane curve every point of which is equidistant from a given fixed point, the centre. Equation: $(x-h)^2 + (y-k)^2 = r^2$ where *r* is the radius and (*h, k*) are the coordinates of the centre; area: πr^2; circumference: $2\pi r$. **2.** the figure enclosed by such a curve. **3.** *Theatre.* the section of seats above the main level of the auditorium, usually comprising the dress circle and the upper circle. **4.** something formed or arranged in the shape of a circle. **5.** a group of people sharing an interest, activity, upbringing, etc.; set: *golf circles; a family circle.* **6.** a domain or area of activity, interest, or influence. **7.** a circuit. **8.** a process or chain of events or parts that forms a connected whole; cycle. **9.** a parallel of latitude. See also **great circle, small circle. 10.** the ring of a circus. **11.** one of a number of Neolithic or Bronze Age rings of standing stones, such as Stonehenge in S England, found in Europe and thought to be associated with some form of ritual or astronomical measurement. **12.** *Hockey.* See **striking circle. 13.** a circular argument. See **vicious circle** (sense 2). **14. come full circle.** to arrive back at one's starting point. See also **vicious circle. 15. go** *or* **run round in circles.** to engage in energetic but fruitless activity. ~*vb.* **16.** to move in a circle (around): *we circled the city by car.* **17.** (*tr.*) to enclose in a circle; encircle. [C14: from Latin *circulus* a circular figure, from *circus* ring, circle] —'**circler** *n.*

circlet ('sɜːklɪt) *n.* a small circle or ring, esp. a circular ornament worn on the head. [C15: from Old French *cerclet* a little CIRCLE]

circlip ('sɜːˌklɪp) *n. Engineering.* a flat spring ring split at one point so that it can be sprung open, passed over a shaft or spindle, and allowed to close into a closely fitting annular recess to form a collar on the shaft. A similar design can be closed to pass into a bore and allowed to spring out into an annular recess to form a shoulder in the bore. Also called: **retaining ring.**

Circlorama (ˌsɜːkləˈrɑːmə) *n. Trademark.* a system of film projection in which a number of projectors and screens are employed to produce a picture that surrounds the viewer.

circs (sɜːks) *n. Brit. informal.* short for **circumstances** (see **circumstance** (sense 1)).

circuit ('sɜːkɪt) *n.* **1. a.** a complete route or course, esp. one that is curved or circular or that lies around an object. **b.** the area enclosed within such a route. **2.** the act of following such a route: *we made three circuits of the course.* **3. a.** a complete path through which an electric current can flow. **b.** (*as modifier*): *a circuit diagram.* **4. a.** a periodical journey around an area, as made by judges, salesmen, etc. **b.** the route traversed or places visited on such a journey. **c.** the persons making such a journey. **5.** an administrative division of the Methodist Church comprising a number of neighbouring churches. **6.** *English law.* one of six areas into which England is divided for the administration of justice. **7.** a number of theatres, cinemas, etc., under one management or in which the same film is shown or in which a company of performers plays in turn. **8.** *Sport.* **a.** a series of tournaments in which the same players regularly take part: *the international tennis circuit.* **b.** (usually preceded by *the*) the contestants who take part in such a series. **9.** *Chiefly Brit.* a motor racing track, usually of irregular shape. ~*vb.* **10.** to make or travel in a circuit around (something). [C14: from Latin *circuitus* a going around, from *circumīre,* from *circum* around + *īre* to go] —'**circuital** *adj.*

circuit binding *n.* a style of limp-leather binding, used esp. for Bibles and prayer books, in which the edges of the cover bend over to protect the edges of the pages.

circuit board *n.* short for **printed circuit board.** See **printed circuit.**

circuit breaker *n.* a device that under abnormal conditions, such as a short circuit, stops the flow of current in an electrical circuit. Sometimes shortened to **breaker.** Compare **fuse**[2] (sense 6).

circuit judge *n. Brit.* a judge presiding over a county court or crown court.

circuitous (səˈkjuːɪtəs) *adj.* indirect and lengthy; roundabout: *a circuitous route.* —**cirˈcuitously** *adv.* —**cirˈcuitousness** *n.*

circuit rider *n. U.S. and Canadian.* (formerly) a minister of religion who preached from place to place along an established circuit.

circuitry ('sɜːkɪtrɪ) *n.* **1.** the design of an electrical circuit. **2.** the system of circuits used in an electronic device.

circuit training *n.* a form of athletic training in which a number of exercises are performed in turn.

circuity (səˈkjuːɪtɪ) *n., pl.* **-ties.** (of speech, reasoning, etc.) a roundabout or devious quality.

circular ('sɜːkjʊlə) *adj.* **1.** of, involving, resembling, or shaped like a circle. **2.** circuitous. **3.** (of arguments) futile because the truth of the premises cannot be established independently of the conclusion. **4.** travelling or occurring in a cycle. **5.** (of letters, announcements, etc.) intended for general distribution. ~*n.* **6.** a printed or duplicated advertisement or notice for mass distribution. —**circularity** (ˌsɜːkjʊˈlærɪtɪ) *or* '**circularness** *n.* —'**circularly** *adv.*

circular breathing *n.* a technique for sustaining a phrase on a wind instrument, using the cheeks to force air out of the mouth while breathing in through the nose.

circular function *n.* another name for **trigonometric function** (sense 1).

circularize *or* **circularise** ('sɜːkjʊləˌraɪz) *vb.* (*tr.*) **1.** to distribute circulars to. **2.** to canvass or petition (people), as for support, votes, etc., by distributing letters, etc. **3.** to make circular. —ˌ**circulariˈzation** *or* ˌ**circulariˈsation** *n.* —'**circularˌizer** *or* '**circularˌiser** *n.*

circular measure *n.* the measurement of an angle in radians.

circular mil *n.* a unit of area of cross section of wire, equal to the area of a circle whose diameter is one thousandth of an inch. 1 circular mil is equal to 0.785×10^{-6} square inch or 0.2×10^{-9} square metre.

circular polarization *n.* a transformation of electromagnetic radiation (esp. light) to a form in which the vector representing the instantaneous intensity of the electric field describes a circle about the direction of propagation at any point in the path of the radiation.

circular saw *n.* a power-driven saw in which a circular disc with a toothed edge is rotated at high speed.

circular triangle *n.* a triangle in which each side is the arc of a circle.

circulate ('sɜːkjʊˌleɪt) *vb.* **1.** to send, go, or pass from place to place or person to person: *don't circulate the news.* **2.** to distribute or be distributed over a wide area. **3.** to move or cause to move through a circuit, system, etc., returning to the starting point: *blood circulates through the body.* **4.** to move in a circle: *the earth circulates around the sun.* [C15: from Latin *circulārī* to assemble in a circle, from *circulus* CIRCLE] —'**circuˌlative** *adj.* —'**circuˌlator** *n.* —'**circulatory** *adj.*

circulating decimal *n.* another name for **recurring decimal.**

circulating library *n.* **1.** another name (esp. U.S.) for **lending library. 2.** a small library circulated in turn to a group of schools or other institutions. **3.** a rare name for **subscription library.**

circulating medium *n. Finance.* currency serving as a medium of exchange.

circulation (ˌsɜːkjʊˈleɪʃən) *n.* **1.** the transport of oxygenated blood through the arteries to the capillaries, where it nourishes the tissues, and the return of oxygen-depleted blood through the veins to the heart, where the cycle is renewed. **2.** the flow of sap through a plant. **3.** any movement through a closed circuit. **4.** the spreading or transmission of something to a wider group of people or area. **5.** (of air and water) free movement within an area or volume. **6. a.** the distribution of newspapers, magazines, etc. **b.** the number of copies of an issue of such a publication that are distributed. **7.** *Library science.* **a.** a book loan, as from a library lending department. **b.** each loan transaction of a particular book. **c.** the total issue of library books over a specified period. **8.** a rare term for **circulating medium. 9. in circulation. a.** (of currency) serving as a medium of exchange. **b.** (of people) active in a social or business context.

circulatory system *n. Anatomy, zoology.* the system concerned with the transport of blood and lymph, consisting of the heart, blood vessels, lymph vessels, etc.

circum- *prefix.* around; surrounding; on all sides: *circumlocution; circumrotate.* [from Latin *circum* around, from *circus* circle]

circumambient (ˌsɜːkəmˈæmbɪənt) *adj.* surrounding. [C17: from Late Latin *circumambīre,* from CIRCUM- + *ambīre* to go round] —ˌ**circumˈambience** *or* ˌ**circumˈambiency** *n.*

circumambulate (ˌsɜːkəmˈæmbjʊˌleɪt) *vb.* **1.** to walk around (something). **2.** (*intr.*) to avoid the point. [C17: from Late Latin CIRCUM- + *ambulāre* to walk] —ˌ**circumˌambuˈlation** *n.* —ˌ**circumˈambuˌlator** *n.* —ˌ**circumˈambulatory** *adj.*

circumbendibus (ˌsɜːkəmˈbɛndɪbəs) *n. Humorous.* a circumlocution. [C17: coined from CIRCUM- + BEND[1], with a pseudo-Latin ending]

circumcise ('sɜːkəmˌsaɪz) *vb.* (*tr.*) **1.** to remove the foreskin of (a male). **2.** to incise surgically the skin over the clitoris of (a female). **3.** to remove the clitoris of (a female). **4.** to perform the religious rite of circumcision on (someone). [C13: from Latin *circumcīdere,* from CIRCUM- + *caedere* to cut] —'**circumˌciser** *n.*

circumcision (ˌsɜːkəmˈsɪʒən) *n.* **1. a.** surgical removal of the foreskin of males. **b.** surgical incision into the skin covering the clitoris in females. **c.** removal of the clitoris. **2.** the act of circumcision, performed as a religious rite by Jews and Muslims. **3.** *R.C. Church.* the festival celebrated on Jan. 1 in commemoration of the circumcision of Jesus.

circumference (səˈkʌmfərəns) *n.* **1.** the boundary of a specific area or geometric figure, esp. of a circle. **2.** the length of a closed geometric curve, esp. of a circle. The circumference of a circle is equal to the diameter multiplied by π. [C14: from Old French *circonference,* from Latin *circumferre* to carry around, from CIRCUM- + *ferre* to bear] —**circumferential** (səˌkʌmfəˈrɛnʃəl) *adj.* —**cirˌcumferˈentially** *adv.*

circumflex ('sɜːkəmˌflɛks) *n.* **1.** a mark (^) placed over a vowel to show that it is pronounced with rising and falling pitch, as in ancient Greek, as a long vowel rather than a short one, as in French, or with some other different quality. ~*adj.* **2.** (of certain nerves, arteries, or veins) bending or curving around. [C16: from Latin *circumflexus,* from *circumflectere* to bend around, from CIRCUM- + *flectere* to bend] —ˌ**circumˈflexion** *n.*

circumfluous (səˈkʌmflʊəs) *adj.* **1.** Also: **cirˈcumfluent.** flowing all around. **2.** surrounded by or as if by water. [C17: from

Latin *circumfluere* to flow around, from CIRCUM- + *fluere* to flow] —**cir'cumfluence** *n.*

circumfuse (ˌsɜːkəm'fjuːz) *vb.* (*tr.*) **1.** to pour or spread (a liquid, powder, etc.) around. **2.** to surround with a substance, such as a liquid. [C16: from Latin *circumfūsus,* from *circumfundere* to pour around, from CIRCUM- + *fundere* to pour] —**circumfusion** (ˌsɜːkəm'fjuːʒən) *n.*

circumlocution (ˌsɜːkəmlə'kjuːʃən) *n.* **1.** an indirect way of expressing something. **2.** an indirect expression. —**circumlocutory** (ˌsɜːkəm'lɒkjutərɪ, -trɪ) *adj.*

circumlunar (ˌsɜːkəm'luːnə) *adj.* around or revolving around the moon: *a circumlunar orbit.*

circumnavigate (ˌsɜːkəm'nævɪˌgeɪt) *vb.* (*tr.*) to sail or fly completely around. —ˌ**circum'navigable** *adj.* —ˌ**circumˌnavi'gation** *n.* —ˌ**circum'naviˌgator** *n.*

circumnutate (ˌsɜːkəm'njuːteɪt) *vb.* (*intr.*) (of the tip of a plant stem) to grow in an irregular curve, ellipse, or spiral. [C19: from CIRCUM- + *-nutate,* from Latin *nūtāre* to nod repeatedly, sway] —ˌ**circumnu'tation** *n.*

circumpolar (ˌsɜːkəm'pəulə) *adj.* **1.** (of a star or constellation) visible above the horizon at all times at a specified locality on the earth's surface. **2.** surrounding or located at or near either of the earth's poles.

circumscissile (ˌsɜːkəm'sɪsaɪl) *adj.* (of the dry dehiscent fruits of certain plants) opening completely by a transverse split. [C19: from CIRCUM- + Latin *scissilis* capable of splitting, from *scindere* to split]

circumscribe (ˌsɜːkəm'skraɪb, 'sɜːkəmˌskraɪb) *vb.* (*tr.*) **1.** to restrict within limits. **2.** to mark or set the bounds of. **3.** to draw a geometric construction around (another construction) so that the two are in contact but do not intersect. Compare **inscribe** (sense 4). **4.** to draw a line round. [C15: from Latin *circumscrībere,* from CIRCUM- + *scrībere* to write] —ˌ**circum'scribable** *adj.* —ˌ**circum'scriber** *n.*

circumscription (ˌsɜːkəm'skrɪpʃən) *n.* **1.** the act of circumscribing or the state of being circumscribed. **2.** something that limits or encloses. **3.** a circumscribed space. **4.** an inscription around a coin or medal. —ˌ**circum'scriptive** *adj.* —ˌ**circum'scriptively** *adv.*

circumsolar (ˌsɜːkəm'səulə) *adj.* surrounding or rotating around the sun.

circumspect ('sɜːkəmˌspɛkt) *adj.* cautious, prudent, or discreet. [C15: from Latin *circumspectus,* from CIRCUM- + *specere* to look] —ˌ**circum'spection** *n.* —ˌ**circum'spective** *adj.* —'**circumˌspectly** *adv.*

circumstance ('sɜːkəmstəns) *n.* **1.** (*usually pl.*) a condition of time, place, etc., that accompanies or influences an event or condition. **2.** an incident or occurrence, esp. a chance one. **3.** accessory information or detail. **4.** formal display or ceremony (archaic except in the phrase **pomp and circumstance**). **5.** **under** *or* **in no circumstances.** in no case; never. **6.** **under the circumstances.** because of conditions; this being the case. **7.** **in good** (*or* **bad**) **circumstances.** (of a person) in a good (or bad) financial situation. ~*vb.* (*tr.*) **8.** to place in a particular condition or situation. **9.** *Obsolete.* to give in detail. [C13: from Old French *circonstance,* from Latin *circumstantia,* from *circumstāre* to stand around, from CIRCUM- + *stāre* to stand]

circumstantial (ˌsɜːkəm'stænʃəl) *adj.* **1.** of or dependent on circumstances. **2.** fully detailed. **3.** incidental. —**circumstantiality** (ˌsɜːkəmˌstænʃɪ'ælɪtɪ) *n.* —ˌ**circum'stantially** *adv.*

circumstantial evidence *n.* indirect evidence that tends to establish a conclusion by inference. Compare **direct evidence.**

circumstantiate (ˌsɜːkəm'stænʃɪˌeɪt) *vb.* (*tr.*) to support by giving particulars. —ˌ**circumˌstanti'ation** *n.*

circumvallate (ˌsɜːkəm'væleɪt) *vb.* (*tr.*) to surround with a defensive fortification. [C19: from Latin *circumvallāre,* from CIRCUM- + *vallum* rampart] —ˌ**circumval'lation** *n.*

circumvent (ˌsɜːkəm'vɛnt) *vb.* (*tr.*) **1.** to evade or go around. **2.** to outwit. **3.** to encircle (an enemy) so as to intercept or capture. [C15: from Latin *circumvenīre,* from CIRCUM- + *venīre* to come] —ˌ**circum'venter** *or* ˌ**circum'ventor** *n.* —ˌ**circum'vention** *n.* —ˌ**circum'ventive** *adj.*

circumvolution (ˌsɜːkəmvə'luːʃən) *n.* **1.** the act of turning, winding, or folding around a central axis. **2.** a single complete turn, cycle, or fold. **3.** anything winding or sinuous. **4.** a roundabout course or procedure. [C15: from Medieval Latin *circumvolūtiō,* from Latin *circumvolvere,* from CIRCUM- + *volvere* to roll] —ˌ**circumvo'lutory** *adj.*

circus ('sɜːkəs) *n., pl.* **-cuses.** **1.** a travelling company of entertainers such as acrobats, clowns, trapeze artistes, and trained animals. **2.** a public performance given by such a company. **3.** an oval or circular arena, usually tented and surrounded by tiers of seats, in which such a performance is held. **4.** a travelling group of professional sportsmen: *a cricket circus.* **5.** (in ancient Rome) **a.** an open-air stadium, usually oval or oblong, for chariot races or public games. **b.** the games themselves. **6.** *Brit.* **a.** an open place, usually circular, in a town, where several streets converge. **b.** (*cap. when part of a name*): *Piccadilly Circus.* **7.** *Informal.* noisy or rowdy behaviour. **8.** *Informal.* a person or group of people whose behaviour is wild, disorganized, or (esp. unintentionally) comic. [C16: from Latin, from Greek *kirkos* ring]

ciré ('sɪəreɪ) *adj.* **1.** (of fabric) treated with a heat or wax process to make it smooth. ~*n.* **2.** such a surface on a fabric. **3.** a fabric having such a surface. [C20: French, from *cirer* to wax, from *cire,* from Latin *cēra* wax]

cire perdue *French.* (sir pɛrdy) *n.* a method of casting bronze, in which a mould is formed around a wax pattern, which is subsequently melted and drained away. [literally: lost wax]

cirque (sɜːk) *n.* **1.** Also called: **corrie, cwm.** a semicircular or crescent-shaped basin with steep sides and a gently sloping floor formed in mountainous regions by the erosive action of ice. **2.** *Archaeol.* an obsolete term for **circle** (sense 11). **3.** *Poetic.* a circle, circlet, or ring. [C17: from French, from Latin *circus* ring, circle, CIRCUS]

cirrate ('sɪreɪt), **cirrose,** *or* **cirrous** *adj. Biology.* bearing or resembling cirri. [C19: from Latin *cirrātus* curled, from CIRRUS]

cirrhosis (sɪ'rəusɪs) *n.* any of various chronic progressive diseases of the liver, characterized by death of liver cells, irreversible fibrosis, etc.: caused by inadequate diet, excessive alcohol, chronic infection, etc. Also called: **cirrhosis of the liver.** [C19: New Latin, from Greek *kirrhos* orange-coloured + -OSIS; referring to the appearance of the diseased liver] —**cir'rhosed** *adj.* —**cirrhotic** (sɪ'rɒtɪk) *adj.*

cirri ('sɪraɪ) *n.* the plural of **cirrus.**

cirripede ('sɪrɪˌpiːd) *or* **cirriped** ('sɪrɪˌpɛd) *n.* **1.** any marine crustacean of the subclass *Cirripedia,* including the barnacles, the adults of which are sessile or parasitic. ~*adj.* **2.** of, relating to, or belonging to the *Cirripedia.*

cirro- *or* **cirri-** *combining form.* indicating cirrus or cirri: *cirrocumulus; cirriped.*

cirrocumulus (ˌsɪrəu'kjuːmjuləs) *n., pl.* **-li** (-ˌlaɪ). *Meteorol.* a high cloud of ice crystals grouped into small separate globular masses, usually occurring above 6000 metres (20 000 feet). See also **mackerel sky.**

cirrose ('sɪrəus, sɪ'rəus) *or* **cirrous** ('sɪrəs) *adj.* **1.** *Biology.* another word for **cirrate. 2.** characteristic of cirrus clouds.

cirrostratus (ˌsɪrəu'strɑːtəs) *n., pl.* **-ti** (-taɪ). a uniform layer of cloud above about 6000 metres (20 000 feet). —ˌ**cirro'strative** *adj.*

cirrus ('sɪrəs) *n., pl.* **-ri** (-raɪ). **1.** *Meteorol.* a thin wispy fibrous cloud at high altitudes, composed of ice particles. **2.** a plant tendril or similar part. **3.** *Zoology.* **a.** a slender tentacle or filament in barnacles and other marine invertebrates. **b.** a hairlike structure in other animals, such as a filament on the appendage of an insect or a barbel of a fish. [C18: from Latin: curl, tuft, fringe]

cirsoid ('sɜːsɔɪd) *adj. Pathol.* resembling a varix. Also: **varicoid.** [C19: from Greek *kirsoeidēs,* from *kirsos* swollen vein + -OID]

cis- *prefix.* **1.** on this or the near side of: *cisalpine.* **2.** (often in italics) indicating that two groups of atoms in an unsaturated compound lie on the same side of a double bond: *cis*-butadiene. Compare **trans-** (sense 5). [from Latin]

cisalpine (sɪs'ælpaɪn) *adj.* **1.** on this (the southern) side of the Alps, as viewed from Rome. **2.** relating to a movement in the Roman Catholic Church to minimize the authority of the pope and to emphasize the independence of branches of the Church. Compare **ultramontane** (sense 2).

cisco ('sɪskəu) *n., pl.* **-coes** *or* **-cos.** any of various whitefish, esp. *Coregonus artedi* (also called **lake herring),** of cold deep lakes of North America. [C19: short for Canadian French *ciscoette,* from Ojibwa *pemitewiskawet* fish with oily flesh]

cislunar (sɪs'luːnə) *adj.* of or relating to the space between the earth and the moon. Compare **translunar.**

cismontane (sɪs'mɒnteɪn) *adj.* on this (the writer's or speaker's) side of the mountains, esp. the Alps. Compare **ultramontane** (sense 1). [C18: from Latin CIS- + *montānus* of the mountains, from *mōns* mountain]

cispadane ('sɪspəˌdeɪn, sɪs'peɪdeɪn) *adj.* on this (the southern) side of the River Po, as viewed from Rome. Compare **transpadane.** [from Latin CIS- + *Padānus* of the Po]

cisplatin (sɪs'plætɪn) *n.* a cytotoxic drug that acts by preventing DNA replication and hence cell divisions, used in the treatment of tumours of the ovary and testis. [C20: from CIS- + PLATIN(UM)]

cissing ('sɪsɪŋ) *n. Building trades.* the appearance of pinholes, craters, etc., in paintwork due to poor adhesion of the paint to the surface.

cissoid ('sɪsɔɪd) *n.* **1.** a geometric curve whose two branches meet in a cusp at the origin and are asymptotic to a line parallel to the *y*-axis. Its equation is $y^2(2a-x)=x^3$ where 2a is the distance between the *y*-axis and this line. ~*adj.* **2.** contained between the concave sides of two intersecting curves. Compare **sistroid.** [C17: from Greek *kissoeidēs,* literally: ivy-shaped, from *kissos* ivy]

cissus ('sɪsəs) *n.* any plant of the climbing genus *Cissus,* some species of which, esp. the kangaroo vine (*C. antarctica*) from Australia, are grown as greenhouse or house plants for their shiny green or mottled leaves: family *Vitaceae.* [New Latin, from Greek *kissos* ivy]

cissy ('sɪsɪ) *n.* a variant spelling of **sissy.**

cist[1] (sɪst) *n.* a wooden box for holding ritual objects used in ancient Rome and Greece. [C19: from Latin *cista* box, chest, basket, from Greek *kistē*]

cist[2] (sɪst) *or* **kist** *n. Archaeol.* a box-shaped burial chamber made from stone slabs or a hollowed tree trunk. [C19: from Welsh: chest, from Latin *cista* box; see CIST[1]]

cistaceous (sɪˈsteɪʃəs) *adj.* of, relating to, or belonging to the *Cistaceae,* a family of shrubby or herbaceous plants that includes the rockroses. [C19: from New Latin *Cistaceae,* from Greek *kistos* rockrose]

Cistercian (sɪˈstɜːʃən) *n.* **a.** a member of a Christian order of monks and nuns founded in 1098, which follows an especially strict form of the Benedictine rule. Also called: **White Monk. b.** (*as modifier*): *a Cistercian monk.* [C17: from French *Cistercien,* from Medieval Latin *Cisterciānus,* from *Cistercium* (modern *Cîteaux*), original home of the order]

cistern (ˈsɪstən) *n.* **1.** a tank for the storage of water, esp. on or within the roof of a house or connected to a WC. **2.** an underground reservoir for the storage of a liquid, esp. rainwater. **3.** *Anatomy.* another name for **cisterna.** [C13: from Old French *cisterne,* from Latin *cisterna* underground tank, from *cista* box] —**cisternal** (sɪˈstɜːnəl) *adj.*

cisterna (sɪˈstɜːnə) *n., pl.* **-nae** (-niː). a sac or partially closed space containing body fluid, esp. lymph or cerebrospinal fluid. [New Latin, from Latin; see CISTERN]

cis-trans test (ˈsɪsˈtrɑːnz) *n. Genetics.* a test to define the unit of genetic function, based on whether two mutations of the same character occur in a single chromosome (the cis position) or in different cistrons in each chromosome of a homologous pair (the trans position). [C20: see CIS-, TRANS-]

cistron (ˈsɪstrən) *n. Genetics.* the section of a chromosome that controls a single function; a functional gene. [C20: from *cis-trans;* see CIS-TRANS TEST]

cistus (ˈsɪstəs) *n.* any plant of the genus *Cistus.* See **rockrose.** [C16: New Latin, from Greek *kistos*]

cit. *abbrev. for:* **1.** citation. **2.** cited. **3.** citizen.

citadel (ˈsɪtədəl, -ˌdɛl) *n.* **1.** a stronghold within or close to a city. **2.** any strongly fortified building or place of safety; refuge. **3.** a specially strengthened part of the hull of a warship. **4.** (*often cap.*) the headquarters of the Salvation Army. [C16: from Old French *citadelle,* from Old Italian *cittadella* a little city, from *cittade* city, from Latin *cīvitās*]

citation (saɪˈteɪʃən) *n.* **1.** the quoting of a book or author in support of a fact. **2.** a passage or source cited for this purpose. **3.** a listing or recounting, as of facts. **4.** an official commendation or award, esp. for bravery or outstanding service, work, etc., usually in the form of a formal statement made in public. **5.** *Law.* **a.** an official summons to appear in court. **b.** the document containing such a summons. **6.** *Law.* the quoting of decided cases to serve as guidance to a court. —**citatory** (ˈsaɪtətərɪ, -trɪ) *adj.*

cite (saɪt) *vb.* (*tr.*) **1.** to quote or refer to (a passage, book, or author) in substantiation as an authority, proof, or example. **2.** to mention or commend (a soldier, etc.) for outstanding bravery or meritorious action. **3.** to summon to appear before a court of law. **4.** to enumerate: *he cited the king's virtues.* **5.** *Archaic.* to excite. [C15: from Old French *citer* to summon, from Latin *citāre* to rouse, from *citus* quick, from *ciēre* to excite] —ˈ**citable** *or* ˈ**citeable** *adj.* —ˈ**citer** *n.*

cithara (ˈsɪθərə) *or* **kithara** *n.* a stringed musical instrument of ancient Greece and elsewhere, similar to the lyre and played with a plectrum. [C18: from Greek *kithara*]

cither (ˈsɪθə) *or* **cithern** (ˈsɪθən) *n.* variants of **cittern.** [C17: from Latin *cithara,* from Greek *kithara* lyre]

citified *or* **cityfied** (ˈsɪtɪˌfaɪd) *adj. Often derogatory.* having the customs, manners, or dress of city people.

citify *or* **cityfy** (ˈsɪtɪˌfaɪ) *vb.* **-fies, -fying, -fied.** (*tr.*) **1.** to cause to conform to or adopt the customs, habits, or dress of city people. **2.** to make urban. —ˌ**citifiˈcation** *or* ˌ**cityfiˈcation** *n.*

citizen (ˈsɪtɪzən) *n.* **1.** a native registered or naturalized member of a state, nation, or other political community. Compare **alien. 2.** an inhabitant of a city or town. **3.** a native or inhabitant of any place. **4.** a civilian, as opposed to a soldier, public official, etc. [C14: from Anglo-French *citesein,* from Old French *citeien,* from *cité* CITY] —**citizeness** (ˈsɪtɪzənɪs, -ˌnɛs) *fem. n.* —ˈ**citizenly** *adj.*

citizenry (ˈsɪtɪzənrɪ) *n., pl.* **-ries.** citizens collectively.

Citizens' Band *n.* a range of radio frequencies assigned officially for use by the public for private communication. Abbrev.: **CB.**

citizenship (ˈsɪtɪzənˌʃɪp) *n.* **1.** the condition or status of a citizen, with its rights and duties. **2.** a person's conduct as a citizen: *an award for good citizenship.*

citole (ˈsɪtəʊl, sɪˈtəʊl) *n.* a rare word for **cittern.** [C14: from Old French, probably from Latin *cithara* CITHER]

citral (ˈsɪtrəl) *n.* a yellow volatile liquid with a lemon-like odour, found in oils of lemon grass, orange, and lemon and used in perfumery: a terpene aldehyde consisting of the *cis-* isomer (**citral-a** or **geranial**) and the *trans-* isomer (**citral-b** or **neral**). Formula: $(CH_3)_2C{:}CH(CH_2)_2C(CH_3){:}CHCHO$. [C19: from CITR(US) + -AL[3]]

citrate (ˈsɪtreɪt, -rɪt; ˈsaɪtreɪt) *n.* any salt or ester of citric acid. Salts of citric acid are used in beverages and pharmaceuticals. [C18: from CITR(US) + -ATE[1]]

citreous (ˈsɪtrɪəs) *adj.* of a greenish-yellow colour; citron.

citric (ˈsɪtrɪk) *adj.* of or derived from citrus fruits or citric acid.

citric acid *n.* a water-soluble weak tribasic acid found in many fruits, esp. citrus fruits, and used in pharmaceuticals and as a flavouring (**E330**). It is extracted from citrus fruits or made by fermenting molasses and is an intermediate in carbohydrate metabolism. Formula: $CH_2(COOH)C(OH)(COOH)CH_2COOH$.

citric acid cycle *n.* another name for **Krebs cycle.**

citriculture (ˈsɪtrɪˌkʌltʃə) *n.* the cultivation of citrus fruits. —ˌ**citriˈculturist** *n.*

citrin (ˈsɪtrɪn) *n.* another name for **vitamin P.**

citrine (ˈsɪtrɪn) *n.* **1.** a brownish-yellow variety of quartz: a gemstone; false topaz. **2.** the yellow colour of a lemon.

citron (ˈsɪtrən) *n.* **1.** a small Asian rutaceous tree, *Citrus medica,* having lemon-like fruit with a thick aromatic rind. See also **citron wood. 2.** the fruit of this tree. **3.** Also called: **citron melon.** a variety of watermelon, *Citrullus vulgaris citroides,* that has an inedible fruit with a hard rind. **4.** the rind of either of these fruits, candied and used for decoration and flavouring of foods. **5.** a greenish-yellow colour. [C16: from Old French, from Old Provençal, from Latin *citrus* citrus tree]

citronella (ˌsɪtrəˈnɛlə) *n.* **1.** Also called: **citronella grass.** a tropical Asian grass, *Cymbopogon* (or *Andropogon*) *nardus,* with bluish-green lemon-scented leaves. **2.** Also called: **citronella oil.** the yellow aromatic oil obtained from this grass, used in insect repellents, soaps, perfumes, etc. [C19: New Latin, from French *citronnelle* lemon balm, from *citron* lemon]

citronellal (ˌsɪtrəˈnɛlæl) *n.* a colourless slightly water-soluble liquid with a lemon-like odour, a terpene aldehyde found esp. in citronella and certain eucalyptus oils: used as a flavouring and in soaps and perfumes. Formula: $(CH_3)_2C{:}CH(CH_2)_2CH(CH_3)CH_2CHO$. Also called: **rhodinal.**

citron wood *n.* **1.** the wood of the citron tree. **2.** the wood of the sandarac.

citrulline (ˈsɪtrəˌliːn) *n.* an amino acid that occurs in watermelons and is an intermediate in the formation of urea. Formula: $NH_2CONH(CH_2)_3CHNH_2COOH$. [C20: from Medieval Latin *citrullus* a kind of watermelon, from Latin *citron,* referring to its colour]

citrus (ˈsɪtrəs) *n., pl.* **-ruses. 1.** any tree or shrub of the tropical and subtropical rutaceous genus *Citrus,* which includes the orange, lemon, lime, grapefruit, citron, and calamondin. ~*adj. also* **citrous. 2.** of, relating to, or belonging to the genus *Citrus* or to the fruits of plants of this genus. [C19: from Latin: citrus tree, sandarac tree; related to Greek *kedros* cedar]

cittern (ˈsɪtɜːn), **cither,** *or* **cithern** *n.* a medieval stringed instrument resembling a lute but having wire strings and a flat back. Compare **gittern.** [C16: perhaps a blend of CITHER + GITTERN]

city (ˈsɪtɪ) *n., pl.* **cities. 1.** any large town or populous place. **2.** (in Britain) a large town that has received this title from the Crown: usually the seat of a bishop. **3.** (in the U.S.) an incorporated urban centre with its own government and administration established by state charter. **4.** (in Canada) a similar urban municipality incorporated by the provincial government. **5.** an ancient Greek city-state; polis. **6.** the people of a city collectively. **7.** (*modifier*) in or characteristic of a city: *a city girl; city habits.* ~Related adjs.: **civic, urban, municipal.** [C13: from Old French *cité,* from Latin *cīvitās* citizenship, state, from *cīvis* citizen]

City (ˈsɪtɪ) *n.* **the.** the various financial institutions located in the City of London.

city blues *n.* (*functioning as sing.*) *Jazz.* another name for **urban blues.**

City Code *n.* (in Britain) short for **City Code on Takeovers and Mergers**: a code laid down in 1968 (later modified) to control takeover bids and mergers.

city desk *n.* **1.** *Brit.* the department of a newspaper office dealing with financial and commercial news. **2.** *U.S. and Canadian.* the department of a newspaper office dealing with local news.

city editor *n.* (on a newspaper) **1.** *Brit.* the editor in charge of financial and commercial news. **2.** *U.S. and Canadian.* the editor in charge of local news.

city father *n.* a person who is active or prominent in the public affairs of a city, such as an alderman.

city hall *n.* **1.** the building housing the administrative offices of a city or municipal government. **2.** *Chiefly U.S. and Canadian.* **a.** municipal government. **b.** the officials of a municipality collectively. **3.** *U.S. informal.* bureaucracy.

city manager *n.* (in the U.S.) an administrator hired by a municipal council to manage its affairs. See also **council-manager plan.**

City of God *n.* **1.** *Christianity.* heaven conceived of as the New Jerusalem. **2.** the Church in contrast to the world, as described by St Augustine (354–430 A.D.).

city planning *n.* the U.S. term for **town planning.** —**city planner** *n.*

cityscape (ˈsɪtɪskeɪp) *n.* an urban landscape; view of a city.

city slicker *n. Informal.* **1.** a person with the sophistication often attributed to city people. **2.** a smooth tricky untrustworthy person.

city-state *n.* a state consisting of a sovereign city and its dependencies. Among the most famous are the great independent cities of the ancient world, such as Athens, Sparta, Carthage, and Rome.

city technology college *n.* (in Britain) a type of senior secondary school specializing in technological subjects, set up in inner-city areas with funding from industry. Abbrev.: **CTC.**

civ. *abbrev. for:* 1. civil. 2. civilian.
civet ('sɪvɪt) *n.* 1. any catlike viverrine mammal of the genus *Viverra* and related genera, of Africa and S Asia, typically having blotched or spotted fur and secreting a powerfully smelling fluid from anal glands. 2. the yellowish fatty secretion of such an animal, used as a fixative in the manufacture of perfumes. 3. the fur of such an animal. 4. short for **palm civet.** [C16: from Old French *civette,* from Italian *zibetto,* from Arabic *zabād* civet perfume]
civic ('sɪvɪk) *adj.* of or relating to a city, citizens, or citizenship: *civic duties.* [C16: from Latin *cīvicus,* from *cīvis* citizen] —'**civically** *adv.*
civic centre *n. Brit.* the public buildings of a town, including recreational facilities and offices of local administration.
civics ('sɪvɪks) *n. (functioning as sing.)* 1. the study of the rights and responsibilities of citizenship. 2. *U.S. and Canadian.* the study of government and its workings.
civic university *n.* (in Britain) a university originally instituted as a higher education college serving a particular city.
civies ('sɪvɪz) *pl. n. Informal.* a variant spelling of **civvies.**
civil ('sɪvᵊl) *adj.* 1. of the ordinary life of citizens as distinguished from military, legal, or ecclesiastical affairs. 2. of or relating to the citizen as an individual: *civil rights.* 3. of or occurring within the state or between citizens: *civil strife.* 4. polite or courteous: *a civil manner.* 5. a less common word for **civic.** 6. of or in accordance with Roman law. 7. relating to the private rights of citizens. [C14: from Old French, from Latin *cīvīlis,* from *cīvis* citizen] —'**civilly** *adv.* —'**civilness** *n.*
civil day *n.* another name for **calendar day.** See **day** (sense 1).
civil death *n. Law.* (formerly) the loss of all civil rights because of a serious conviction. See also **attainder.**
civil defence *n.* the organizing of civilians to deal with enemy attacks.
civil disobedience *n.* a refusal to obey laws, pay taxes, etc.: a nonviolent means of protesting or of attempting to achieve political goals.
civil engineer *n.* a person qualified to design, construct, and maintain public works, such as roads, bridges, harbours, etc. —**civil engineering** *n.*
civilian (sɪ'vɪljən) *n.* **a.** a person whose primary occupation is civil or nonmilitary. **b.** *(as modifier): civilian life.* [C14 (originally: a practitioner of civil law): from *civile* (from the Latin phrase *jūs cīvīle* civil law) + -IAN]
civilianize *or* **civilianise** (sɪ'vɪljəˌnaɪz) *vb. (tr.)* to change the status of (an armed force, a base, etc.) from military to nonmilitary.
civility (sɪ'vɪlɪtɪ) *n., pl.* **-ties.** 1. politeness or courtesy, esp. when formal. 2. *(often pl.)* an act of politeness.
civilization *or* **civilisation** (ˌsɪvɪlaɪ'zeɪʃən) *n.* 1. a human society that has highly developed material and spiritual resources and a complex cultural, political, and legal organization; an advanced state in social development. 2. the peoples or nations collectively who have achieved such a state. 3. the total culture and way of life of a particular people, nation, region, or period: *classical civilization.* 4. the process of bringing or achieving civilization. 5. intellectual, cultural, and moral refinement. 6. cities or populated areas, as contrasted with sparsely inhabited areas, deserts, etc.
civilize *or* **civilise** ('sɪvɪˌlaɪz) *vb. (tr.)* 1. to bring out of savagery or barbarism into a state characteristic of civilization. 2. to refine, educate, or enlighten. —'**civiˌlizable** *or* '**civiˌlisable** *adj.* —'**civiˌlizer** *or* '**civiˌliser** *n.*
civilized *or* **civilised** ('sɪvɪˌlaɪzd) *adj.* 1. having a high state of culture and social development. 2. cultured; polite.
civil law *n.* 1. the law of a state relating to private and civilian affairs. 2. the body of law in force in ancient Rome, esp. the law applicable to private citizens. 3. any system of law based on the Roman system as distinguished from the common law and canon law. 4. the law of a state as distinguished from international law.
civil liberty *n.* the right of an individual to certain freedoms of speech and action.
civil list *n.* (in Britain) the annuities voted by Parliament for the support of the royal household and the royal family.
civil marriage *n. Law.* a marriage performed by some official other than a clergyman.
civil rights *pl. n.* 1. the personal rights of the individual citizen, in most countries upheld by law, as in the U.S. 2. *(modifier)* of, relating to, or promoting equality in social, economic, and political rights.
civil servant *n.* a member of the civil service.
civil service *n.* 1. the service responsible for the public administration of the government of a country. It excludes the legislative, judicial, and military branches. Members of the civil service have no official political allegiance and are not generally affected by changes of governments. 2. the members of the civil service collectively.
civil war *n.* war between parties, factions, or inhabitants of different regions within the same nation.
civil year *n.* another name for **calendar year.** See **year** (sense 1).
civism ('sɪvɪzəm) *n. Rare.* good citizenship. [C18: from French *civisme,* from Latin *cīvis* citizen]
civvy ('sɪvɪ) *n., pl.* **civvies** *or* **civies.** *Slang.* 1. a civilian. 2. *(pl.)* civilian dress as opposed to uniform. 3. **civvy street.** civilian life.
CJ *abbrev. for* Chief Justice.
CKD (in New Zealand) *abbrev. for* Completely Knocked Down: used of a car imported in parts, for local assembly.
cl *symbol for* centilitre.
Cl *the chemical symbol for* chlorine.
cl. *abbrev. for:* 1. class. 2. classification. 3. clerk. 4. cloth. 5. clergyman.
clabby-doo (ˌklæbɪ'duː) *n. Scot.* a variant of **clappy-doo.**
clachan (*Gaelic* 'klaxən; *English* 'klæ-) *n. Scot. and Irish dialect.* a small village; hamlet. [C15: from Scottish Gaelic: probably from *clach* stone]
clack (klæk) *vb.* 1. to make or cause to make a sound like that of two pieces of wood hitting each other. 2. *(intr.)* to jabber. 3. a less common word for **cluck.** ~*n.* 4. a short sharp sound. 5. a person or thing that produces this sound. 6. chatter. 7. Also called: **clack valve.** a simple nonreturn valve using either a hinged flap or a ball. [C13: probably from Old Norse *klaka* to twitter, of imitative origin] —'**clacker** *n.*
Clactonian (klæk'təʊnɪən) *n.* 1. one of the Lower Palaeolithic cultures found in England, characterized by the use of chopper tools. ~*adj.* 2. of, designating, or relating to this culture. [after *Clacton,* Essex, where the tools of this culture were first found]
clad[1] (klæd) *vb.* a past participle of **clothe.** [Old English *clāthode* clothed, from *clāthian* to CLOTHE]
clad[2] (klæd) *vb.* **clads, cladding, clad.** *(tr.)* to bond a metal to (another metal), esp. to form a protective coating. [C14 (in the obsolete sense: to clothe): special use of CLAD[1]]
Claddagh ring ('klædə) *n. Irish.* any of various elaborately designed rings, esp. one in the shape of two hands embracing a heart, given as a token of lasting affection. [from *Claddagh,* a small fishing village on the edge of Galway city]
cladding ('klædɪŋ) *n.* 1. the process of protecting one metal by bonding a second metal to its surface. 2. the protective coating so bonded to metal. 3. the material used for the outside facing of a building, etc.
clade (kleɪd) *n. Biology.* a group of organisms considered as having evolved from a common ancestor. [C20: from Greek *klādos* branch, shoot]
cladistics (klə'dɪstɪks) *n. (functioning as sing.) Biology.* a method of grouping animals by measurable likenesses or homologues. [C20: New Latin, from Greek *klādos* branch, shoot] —**cladism** ('klædɪzəm) *n.* —**cladist** ('klædɪst) *n.*
cladoceran (klə'dɒsərən) *n.* 1. any minute freshwater crustacean of the order *Cladocera,* which includes the water fleas. ~*adj.* 2. of, relating to, or belonging to the *Cladocera.* [C19: from New Latin *Cladocera,* from Greek *klados* shoot + *keras* horn]
cladode ('klædəʊd) *n. Botany.* a flattened stem resembling and functioning as a leaf, as in butcher's broom. Also called: **cladophyll, phylloclade.** [C19: from New Latin *cladōdium,* from Late Greek *kladōdēs* having many shoots]
cladogram ('kleɪdəʊˌgræm) *n. Biology.* a diagram illustrating the development of a clade by homologues. [C20: from CLADE + -O- + -GRAM]
cladophyll ('klædəfɪl) *n.* another name for **cladode.** [C19: from Greek *klados* branch + *phullon* leaf]
claes (klez) *pl. n.* a Scot. word for **clothes.**
claggy ('klægɪ) *adj.* **-gier, -giest.** *Chiefly dialect.* stickily clinging, as mud. [C16: from dialect *clag* to daub, clot, of unknown origin]
claim (kleɪm) *vb. (mainly tr.)* 1. to demand as being due or as one's property; assert one's title or right to: *he claimed the record.* 2. *(takes a clause as object or an infinitive)* to assert as a fact; maintain against denial: *he claimed to be telling the truth.* 3. to call for or need; deserve: *this problem claims our attention.* 4. to take: *the accident claimed four lives.* ~*n.* 5. an assertion of a right; a demand for something as due. 6. an assertion of something as true, real, or factual: *he made claims for his innocence.* 7. a right or just title to something; basis for demand: *a claim to fame.* 8. **lay claim to** *or* **stake a claim to.** to assert one's possession of or right to. 9. anything that is claimed, esp. in a formal or legal manner, such as a piece of land staked out by a miner. 10. **a.** a demand for payment in connection with an insurance policy, etc. **b.** the sum of money demanded. [C13: from Old French *claimer* to call, appeal, from Latin *clāmāre* to shout] —'**claimable** *adj.* —'**claimant** *or* '**claimer** *n.*
claiming race *n. U.S. and Canadian horse racing.* a race in which each owner declares beforehand the price at which his horse will be offered for sale after the race.
clairaudience (ˌklɛər'ɔːdɪəns) *n. Psychol.* the postulated ability to hear sounds beyond the range of normal hearing. Compare **clairvoyance.** [C19: from French *clair* clear + AUDIENCE, after CLAIRVOYANCE]
clair-obscure (ˌklɛərəb'skjʊə) *n.* another word for **chiaroscuro.** [C18: from French, literally: clear-obscure]
clairvoyance (klɛə'vɔɪəns) *n.* 1. the alleged power of perceiving things beyond the natural range of the senses. See also **extrasensory perception.** 2. keen intuitive understanding. [C19: from French: clear-seeing, from *clair* clear, from Latin *clārus* + *voyance,* from *voir* to see, from Latin *vidēre*]

clairvoyant (klɛəˈvɔɪənt) *adj.* **1.** of, possessing, or relating to clairvoyance. **2.** having great insight or second sight. ~*n.* **3.** a person claiming to have the power to foretell future events. —**clairˈvoyantly** *adv.*

clam[1] (klæm) *n.* **1.** any of various burrowing bivalve molluscs of the genera *Mya, Venus,* etc. Many species, such as the quahog and soft-shell clam, are edible and *Tridacna gigas* is the largest known bivalve, nearly 1.5 metres long. **2.** the edible flesh of such a mollusc. **3.** *Informal.* a reticent person. ~*vb.* **clams, clamming, clammed. 4.** (*intr.*) *Chiefly U.S.* to gather clams. ~See also **clam up.** [C16: from earlier *clamshell,* that is, shell that clamps; related to Old English *clamm* fetter, Old High German *klamma* constriction; see CLAMP[1]]

clam[2] (klæm) *vb.* **clams, clamming, clammed.** a variant of **clem.**

clamant (ˈkleɪmənt) *adj.* **1.** noisy. **2.** calling urgently. [C17: from Latin *clāmāns,* from *clāmāre* to shout]

clamatorial (ˌklæməˈtɔːrɪəl) *adj.* of or relating to the American flycatchers (family *Tyrannidae*). See **flycatcher** (sense 2). [C19: from New Latin *clāmātōres,* plural of Latin *clāmātor* one who shouts; see CLAMANT]

clambake (ˈklæmˌbeɪk) *n. U.S. and Canadian.* **1.** a picnic, often by the sea, at which clams, etc., are baked. **2.** an informal party.

clamber (ˈklæmbə) *vb.* **1.** (usually foll. by *up, over,* etc.) to climb (something) awkwardly, esp. by using both hands and feet. ~*n.* **2.** a climb performed in this manner. [C15: probably a variant of CLIMB] —ˈ**clamberer** *n.*

clammy (ˈklæmɪ) *adj.* **-mier, -miest. 1.** unpleasantly sticky; moist: *clammy hands.* **2.** (of the weather, atmosphere, etc.) close; humid. [C14: from Old English *clǣman* to smear; related to Old Norse *kleima,* Old High German *kleimen*] —ˈ**clammily** *adv.* —ˈ**clamminess** *n.*

clamour *or U.S.* **clamor** (ˈklæmə) *n.* **1.** a loud persistent outcry, as from a large number of people. **2.** a vehement expression of collective feeling or outrage: *a clamour against higher prices.* **3.** a loud and persistent noise: *the clamour of traffic.* ~*vb.* **4.** (*intr.;* often foll. by *for* or *against*) to make a loud noise or outcry; make a public demand. **5.** (*tr.*) to move, influence, or force by outcry: *the people clamoured him out of office.* [C14: from Old French *clamour,* from Latin *clāmor,* from *clāmāre* to cry out] —ˈ**clamourer** *or U.S.* ˈ**clamorer** *n.* —ˈ**clamorous** *adj.* —ˈ**clamorously** *adv.* —ˈ**clamorousness** *n.*

clamp[1] (klæmp) *n.* **1.** a mechanical device with movable jaws with which an object can be secured to a bench or with which two objects may be secured together. **2.** a means by which a fixed joint may be strengthened. **3.** *Nautical.* a horizontal beam fastened to the ribs for supporting the deck beams in a wooden vessel. ~*vb.* (*tr.*) **4.** to fix or fasten with or as if with a clamp. **5.** to immobilize (a car) by means of a wheel clamp. **6.** to inflict or impose forcefully: *they clamped a curfew on the town.* [C14: from Dutch or Low German *klamp;* related to Old English *clamm* bond, fetter, Old Norse *kleppr* lump]

clamp[2] (klæmp) *Brit. agriculture.* ~*n.* **1.** a mound formed out of a harvested root crop, covered with straw and earth to protect it from winter weather. **2.** a pile of bricks ready for processing in a furnace. ~*vb.* **3.** (*tr.*) to enclose (a harvested root crop) in a mound. [C16: from Middle Dutch *klamp* heap; related to CLUMP]

clamp down *vb.* (*intr., adv.;* often foll. by *on*) **1.** to behave repressively; attempt to suppress something regarded as undesirable. ~*n.* **clampdown. 2.** a sudden restrictive measure.

clamper (ˈklæmpə) *n.* a spiked metal frame fastened to the sole of a shoe to prevent slipping on ice.

clamshell (ˈklæmˌʃɛl) *n.* **1.** *U.S.* a dredging bucket that is hinged like the shell of a clam. **2.** *Aeronautics.* **a.** an aircraft cockpit canopy hinged at the front and rear. **b.** the hinged door of a cargo aircraft. **c.** another name for **eyelid** (sense 2).

clam up *vb.* (*intr., adv.*) *Informal.* to keep or become silent or withhold information.

clamworm (ˈklæmˌwɜːm) *n.* the U.S. name for the **ragworm.**

clan (klæn) *n.* **1.** a group of people interrelated by ancestry or marriage. **2.** a group of families with a common surname and a common ancestor, acknowledging the same leader, esp. among the Scots and the Irish. **3.** a group of people united by common characteristics, aims, or interests. [C14: from Scottish Gaelic *clann* family, descendants, from Latin *planta* sprout, PLANT]

clandestine (klænˈdɛstɪn) *adj.* secret and concealed, often for illicit reasons; furtive. [C16: from Latin *clandestīnus,* from *clam* secretly; related to Latin *celāre* to hide] —**clanˈdestinely** *adv.* —**clanˈdestineness** *n.*

clang (klæŋ) *vb.* **1.** to make or cause to make a loud resounding noise, as metal when struck. **2.** (*intr.*) to move or operate making such a sound: *the engine clanged on its way.* ~*n.* **3.** a resounding metallic noise. **4.** the harsh cry of certain birds. [C16: from Latin *clangere*]

clang association *n. Psychol.* the association made between two words because they sound similar; for example *cling* and *ring.*

clanger (ˈklæŋə) *n.* **1.** *Informal.* a conspicuous mistake (esp. in the phrase **drop a clanger**). **2.** something that clangs or causes a clang. [C20: from CLANG, referring to a mistake whose effects seem to clang]

clangour *or U.S.* **clangor** (ˈklæŋgə, ˈklæŋə) *n.* **1.** a loud resonant often-repeated noise. **2.** an uproar. ~*vb.* **3.** (*intr.*) to make or produce a loud resonant noise. [C16: from Latin *clangor* a noise, sound, from *clangere* to CLANG] —ˈ**clangorous** *adj.* —ˈ**clangorously** *adv.*

clank (klæŋk) *n.* **1.** an abrupt harsh metallic sound. ~*vb.* **2.** to make or cause to make such a sound. **3.** (*intr.*) to move or operate making such a sound. [C17: of imitative origin] —ˈ**clankingly** *adv.*

clannish (ˈklænɪʃ) *adj.* **1.** of or characteristic of a clan. **2.** tending to associate closely within a limited group to the exclusion of outsiders; cliquish. —ˈ**clannishly** *adv.* —ˈ**clannishness** *n.*

clansman (ˈklænzmən) *or* (*fem.*) **clanswoman** *n., pl.* **-men** *or* **-women.** a person belonging to a clan.

clap[1] (klæp) *vb.* **claps, clapping, clapped. 1.** to make or cause to make a sharp abrupt sound, as of two nonmetallic objects struck together. **2.** to applaud (someone or something) by striking the palms of the hands together sharply. **3.** (*tr.*) to strike (a person) lightly with an open hand, in greeting, encouragement, etc. **4.** (*tr.*) to place or put quickly or forcibly: *they clapped him into jail.* **5.** (of certain birds) to flap (the wings) noisily. **6.** (*tr.;* foll. by *up* or *together*) to contrive or put together hastily: *they soon clapped up a shed.* **7. clap eyes on.** *Informal.* to catch sight of. **8. clap hold of.** *Informal.* to grasp suddenly or forcibly. ~*n.* **9.** the sharp abrupt sound produced by striking the hands together. **10.** the act of clapping, esp. in applause: *he deserves a good clap.* **11.** a sudden sharp sound, esp. of thunder. **12.** a light blow. **13.** *Archaic.* a sudden action or mishap. [Old English *clæppan;* related to Old High German *klepfen,* Middle Dutch *klape* rattle, Dutch *klepel* clapper; all of imitative origin]

clap[2] (klæp) *n.* (usually preceded by *the*) a slang word for **gonorrhoea.** [C16: from Old French *clapoir* venereal sore, from *clapier* brothel, from Old Provençal, from *clap* heap of stones, of obscure origin]

clapboard (ˈklæpˌbɔːd, ˈklæbəd) *n.* **1. a.** a long thin timber board with one edge thicker than the other, used esp. in the U.S. and Canada in wood-frame construction by lapping each board over the one below. **b.** (*as modifier*): *a clapboard house.* ~*vb.* **2.** (*tr.*) to cover with such boards. [C16: partial translation of Low German *klappholt,* from *klappen* to crack + *holt* wood; related to Dutch *claphout;* see BOARD]

clap-net *n.* a net, used esp. by entomologists, that can be closed instantly by pulling a string.

clap on *vb.* (*tr.*) to don hastily: *they clapped on their armour.*

clapped out *adj.* (**clapped-out** *when prenominal*) *Informal.* **1.** *Brit., Austral., and N.Z.* (esp. of machinery) worn out; dilapidated. **2.** *Austral. and N.Z.* extremely tired; exhausted.

clapper (ˈklæpə) *n.* **1.** a person or thing that claps. **2.** a contrivance for producing a sound of clapping, as for scaring birds. **3.** Also called: **tongue.** a small piece of metal suspended within a bell that causes it to sound when made to strike against its side. **4.** a slang word for **tongue** (sense 1). **5. go (run, move) like the clappers.** *Brit. informal.* to move extremely fast.

clapperboard (ˈklæpəˌbɔːd) *n.* a pair of hinged boards clapped together during film shooting in order to aid in synchronizing sound and picture prints.

clapper bridge *n.* a primitive type of bridge in which planks or slabs of stone rest on piles of stones.

clapperclaw (ˈklæpəˌklɔː) *vb.* (*tr.*) *Archaic.* **1.** to claw or scratch with the hands and nails. **2.** to revile; abuse. [C16: perhaps from CLAPPER + CLAW] —ˈ**clapperˌclawer** *n.*

clappy-doo (ˌklæpɪˈduː) *or* **clabby-doo** *n. Scot.* a large black mussel. [C19: probably from Scottish Gaelic *clab* enormous mouth + *dubh* black]

claptrap (ˈklæpˌtræp) *n. Informal.* **1.** contrived but foolish talk. **2.** insincere and pretentious talk: *politicians' claptrap.* [C18 (in the sense: something contrived to elicit applause): from CLAP[1] + TRAP[1]]

claque (klæk) *n.* **1.** a group of people hired to applaud. **2.** a group of fawning admirers. [C19: from French, from *claquer* to clap, of imitative origin]

clarabella *or* **claribella** (ˌklærəˈbɛlə) *n.* an eight-foot flute stop on an organ. [C19: from Latin *clāra,* feminine of *clārus* clear + *bella,* feminine of *bellus* beautiful]

clarence (ˈklærəns) *n.* a closed four-wheeled horse-drawn carriage, having a glass front. [C19: named after the Duke of *Clarence* (1765–1837)]

clarendon (ˈklærəndən) *n. Printing.* a style of boldface roman type. [C20: named after the Clarendon Press at Oxford University]

claret (ˈklærət) *n.* **1.** *Chiefly Brit.* a red wine, esp. one from the Bordeaux district of SW France. **2. a.** a purplish-red colour. **b.** (*as adj.*): *a claret carpet.* [C14: from Old French (*vin*) *claret* clear (wine), from Medieval Latin *clārātum,* from *clārāre* to make clear, from Latin *clārus* CLEAR]

claret cup *n.* an iced drink made of claret, brandy, lemon, sugar, and sometimes sherry, Curaçao, etc.

clarify (ˈklærɪˌfaɪ) *vb.* **-fies, -fying, -fied. 1.** to make or become clear or easy to understand. **2.** to make or become free of impurities. **3.** to make (fat, butter, etc.) clear by heating, etc., or (of fat, etc.) to become clear as a result of such a process. [C14: from Old French *clarifier,* from Late Latin *clārificāre,* from Latin *clārus* clear + *facere* to make] —ˌ**clarifiˈcation** *n.* —ˈ**clariˌfier** *n.*

clarinet (ˌklærɪˈnɛt) *n. Music.* **1.** a keyed woodwind instrument with a cylindrical bore and a single reed. It is a transposing instrument, most commonly pitched in A or B flat. Obsolete name: **clarionet** (ˌklærɪəˈnɛt). **2.** an orchestral musician who plays the clarinet. [C18: from French *clarinette,* probably from Italian *clarinetto,* from *clarino* trumpet] —ˌ**clariˈnettist** *or* ˌ**clariˈnetist** *n.*

clarino (klæˈriːnəʊ) *Music.* ~*adj.* **1.** of or relating to a high passage for the trumpet in 18th-century music. ~*n., pl.* **-nos** *or* **-ni** (-nɪ). **2.** the high register of the trumpet. **3.** an organ stop similar to the high register of the trumpet. **4.** a trumpet or clarion.

clarion (ˈklærɪən) *n.* **1.** a four-foot reed stop of trumpet quality on an organ. **2.** an obsolete, high-pitched, small-bore trumpet. **3.** the sound of such an instrument or any similar sound. ~*adj.* **4.** (*prenominal*) clear and ringing; inspiring: *a clarion call to action.* ~*vb.* **5.** to proclaim loudly. [C14: from Medieval Latin *clāriō* trumpet, from Latin *clārus* clear]

clarity (ˈklærɪtɪ) *n.* **1.** clearness, as of expression. **2.** clearness, as of water. [C16: from Latin *clāritās,* from *clārus* CLEAR]

Clark cell (klɑːk) *n. Physics.* a cell having a mercury anode surrounded by a paste of mercuric sulphate and a zinc cathode in a saturated solution of zinc sulphate. Formerly used as a standard, its emf is 1.4345 volts. [C19: named after Hosiah *Clark* (died 1898), English scientist]

clarkia (ˈklɑːkɪə) *n.* any North American onagraceous plant of the genus *Clarkia:* cultivated for their red, purple, or pink flowers. [C19: New Latin, named after William *Clark* (1770–1838), U.S. explorer, who discovered it]

claro (ˈklɑːrəʊ) *n., pl.* **-ros** *or* **-roes.** a mild light-coloured cigar. [from Spanish: CLEAR]

clarsach (ˈklɑrsəx, ˈklɑːsək) *n.* the Celtic harp of Scotland and Ireland. [C15: *clareschaw,* from Scottish Gaelic *clarsach,* Irish Gaelic *cláirsach* harp]

clarts (klɑːts; *Scot.* klærts) *pl. n. Scot. and northern English dialect.* lumps of mud, esp. on shoes. [of unknown origin] —ˈ**clarty** *adj.*

clary (ˈklɛərɪ) *n., pl.* **claries.** any of several European plants of the genus *Salvia,* having aromatic leaves and blue flowers: family *Labiatae* (labiates). [C14: from earlier *sclarreye,* from Medieval Latin *sclareia,* of obscure origin]

-clase *n. combining form.* (in mineralogy) indicating a particular type of cleavage: *plagioclase.* [via French from Greek *klasis* a breaking, from *klan* to break]

clash (klæʃ) *vb.* **1.** to make or cause to make a loud harsh sound, esp. by striking together. **2.** (*intr.*) to be incompatible; conflict. **3.** (*intr.*) to engage together in conflict or contest. **4.** (*intr.*) (of dates or events) to coincide. **5.** (*intr.*) (of colours) to look ugly or inharmonious together. ~*n.* **6.** a loud harsh noise. **7.** a collision or conflict. **8.** *Scot.* gossip; tattle. [C16: of imitative origin] —ˈ**clasher** *n.* —ˈ**clashingly** *adv.*

clasp (klɑːsp) *n.* **1.** a fastening, such as a catch or hook, used for holding things together. **2.** a firm grasp, hold, or embrace. **3.** *Military.* a bar or insignia on a medal ribbon, to indicate either a second award or the battle, campaign, or reason for its award. ~*vb.* (*tr.*) **4.** to hold in a firm grasp. **5.** to grasp firmly with the hand. **6.** to fasten together with or as if with a clasp. [C14: of uncertain origin; compare Old English *clyppan* to embrace] —ˈ**clasper** *n.*

claspers (ˈklɑːspəz) *pl. n. Zoology.* **1.** a paired organ of male insects, used to clasp the female during copulation. **2.** a paired organ of male sharks and related fish, used to assist the transfer of spermatozoa into the body of the female during copulation.

clasp knife *n.* a large knife with one or more blades or other devices folding into the handle.

class (klɑːs) *n.* **1.** a collection or division of people or things sharing a common characteristic, attribute, quality, or property. **2.** a group of persons sharing a similar social position and certain economic, political, and cultural characteristics. **3.** (in Marxist theory) a group of persons sharing the same relationship to the means of production. **4. a.** the pattern of divisions that exist within a society on the basis of rank, economic status, etc. **b.** (*as modifier*): *the class struggle; class distinctions.* **5. a.** a group of pupils or students who are taught and study together. **b.** a meeting of a group of students for tuition. **6.** *U.S.* a group of students who graduated in a specified year: *the class of '53.* **7.** (*in combination and as modifier*) *Brit.* a grade of attainment in a university honours degree: *second-class honours.* **8.** one of several standards of accommodation in public transport. See also **first class, second class, third class. 9.** *Informal.* excellence or elegance, esp. in dress, design, or behaviour: *that girl's got class.* **10. a.** outstanding speed and stamina in a racehorse. **b.** (*as modifier*): *the class horse in the race.* **11.** *Biology.* any of the taxonomic groups into which a phylum is divided and which contains one or more orders. *Amphibia, Reptilia,* and *Mammalia* are three classes of phylum *Chordata.* **12.** *Maths, logic.* **a.** another name for **set**[2] (sense 3). **b. proper class.** a class which cannot itself be a member of other classes. **13. in a class by oneself** *or* **in a class of its own.** unequalled; unparalleled. ~*vb.* **14.** to have or assign a place within a group, grade, or class. [C17: from Latin *classis* class, rank, fleet; related to Latin *calāre* to summon] —ˈ**classable** *adj.* —ˈ**classer** *n.*

class. *abbrev. for:* **1.** classic(al). **2.** classification. **3.** classified.

class-A amplifier *n.* an electronic amplifier in which the output current flows for the whole of the input signal cycle.

class-B amplifier *n.* an electronic amplifier in which the output flows for half of the input signal cycle.

class-C amplifier *n.* an electronic amplifier in which the output current flows for less than half of the input cycle.

class-conscious *adj.* aware of belonging to a particular social rank or grade, esp. in being hostile or proud because of class distinctions. —ˌ**class-ˈconsciousness** *n.*

classic (ˈklæsɪk) *adj.* **1.** of the highest class, esp. in art or literature. **2.** serving as a standard or model of its kind; definitive. **3.** adhering to an established set of rules or principles in the arts or sciences: *a classic proof.* **4.** characterized by simplicity, balance, regularity, and purity of form; classical. **5.** of lasting interest or significance. **6.** continuously in fashion because of its simple and basic style: *a classic day dress.* ~*n.* **7.** an author, artist, or work of art of the highest excellence. **8.** a creation or work considered as definitive. **9.** *Horse racing.* **a.** any of the five principal races for three-year-old horses in Britain, namely the One Thousand Guineas, Two Thousand Guineas, Derby, Oaks, and Saint Leger. **b.** a race equivalent to any of these in other countries. ~See also **classics.** [C17: from Latin *classicus* of the first rank, from *classis* division, rank, CLASS]

▷**Usage.** The adjectives *classic* and *classical* can often be treated as synonyms, but there are two contexts in which they should be carefully distinguished. *Classic* is applied to that which is of the first rank, esp. in art and literature, as in: *Lewis Carroll's classic works for children. Classical* is used to refer to Greek and Roman culture.

classical (ˈklæsɪkᵊl) *adj.* **1.** of, relating to, or characteristic of the ancient Greeks and Romans or their civilization, esp. in the period of their ascendancy. **2.** designating, following, or influenced by the art or culture of ancient Greece or Rome: *classical architecture.* **3.** *Music.* **a.** of, relating to, or denoting any music or its period of composition marked by stability of form, intellectualism, and restraint. Compare **romantic** (sense 5). **b.** accepted as a standard: *the classical suite.* **c.** denoting serious art music in general. Compare **pop**[2]. **4.** *Music.* of or relating to a style of music composed, esp. at Vienna, during the late 18th and early 19th centuries. This period is marked by the establishment, esp. by Haydn and Mozart, of sonata form. **5.** denoting or relating to a style in any of the arts characterized by emotional restraint and conservatism: *a classical style of painting.* See **classicism** (sense 1). **6.** well versed in the art and literature of ancient Greece and Rome. **7.** (of an education) based on the humanities and the study of Latin and Greek. **8.** *Physics.* **a.** not involving the quantum theory or the theory of relativity: *classical mechanics.* **b.** obeying the laws of Newtonian mechanics or 19th-century physics: *a classical gas.* **9.** another word for **classic** (senses 2, 4). **10.** (of a logical or mathematical system) according with the law of excluded middle, so that every statement is known to be either true or false even if it is not known which. —ˌ**classiˈcality** *or* ˈ**classicalness** *n.* —ˈ**classically** *adv.*

▷**Usage.** See at **classic.**

classical college *n.* (in Quebec) a college offering a programme that emphasizes the classics and leads to university entrance.

classical conditioning *n. Psychol.* the alteration in responding that occurs when two stimuli are regularly paired in close succession: the response originally given to the second stimulus comes to be given to the first. See also **conditioned response.**

classical probability *n.* another name for **mathematical probability.**

Classical school *n.* economic theory based on the works of Adam Smith (1723–90) and David Ricardo (1772–1823), which explains the creation of wealth and advocates free trade.

classic blues *n.* (*functioning as sing. or pl.*) *Jazz.* a type of city blues performed by a female singer accompanied by a small group.

classicism (ˈklæsɪˌsɪzəm) *or* **classicalism** (ˈklæsɪkəˌlɪzəm) *n.* **1.** a style based on the study of Greek and Roman models, characterized by emotional restraint and regularity of form, associated esp. with the 18th century in Europe; the antithesis of romanticism. Compare **neoclassicism. 2.** knowledge or study of the culture of ancient Greece and Rome. **3. a.** a Greek or Latin form or expression. **b.** an expression in a modern language, such as English, that is modelled on a Greek or Latin form.

classicist (ˈklæsɪsɪst) *or* **classicalist** (ˈklæsɪkəlɪst) *n.* **1. a.** a student of ancient Latin and Greek. **b.** a person who advocates the study of ancient Latin and Greek. **2.** an adherent of classicism in literature or art. —ˌ**classiˈcistic** *adj.*

classicize *or* **classicise** (ˈklæsɪˌsaɪz) *vb.* **1.** (*tr.*) to make classic. **2.** (*intr.*) to imitate classical style.

classics (ˈklæsɪks) *pl. n.* **1. the.** a body of literature regarded as great or lasting, esp. that of ancient Greece or Rome. **2. the.** the ancient Greek and Latin languages. **3.** (*functioning as sing.*) ancient Greek and Roman culture considered as a subject for academic study.

classification (ˌklæsɪfɪˈkeɪʃən) *n.* **1.** systematic placement in categories. **2.** one of the divisions in a system of classifying. **3.** *Biology.* **a.** the placing of animals and plants in a series of increasingly specialized groups because of similarities in structure, origin, etc., that indicate a common relationship. The major groups are kingdom, phylum (in animals) or division (in plants), class, order, family, genus, and species. **b.** the study of the principles and practice of this process; taxonomy. **4.** *Government.* the designation of an item of information as being secret and not available to people outside a restricted group. [C18: from French; see CLASS, -IFY, -ATION] —ˌ**classifiˈcational** *adj.* —ˌ**classifiˈcatory** *adj.*

classification schedule *n. Library science.* the printed scheme of a system of classification.

classified (ˈklæsɪˌfaɪd) *adj.* **1.** arranged according to some system of classification. **2.** *Government.* (of information) not available to people outside a restricted group, esp. for reasons of national security. **3.** *U.S. and Canadian informal.* (of information) closely concealed or secret. **4.** (of advertisements in newspapers, etc.) arranged according to type. **5.** *Brit.* (of newspapers) containing sports results, esp. football results. **6.** (of British roads) having a number in the national road system. If the number is preceded by an M the road is a motorway, if by an A it is a first-class road, and if by a B it is a secondary road.

classify (ˈklæsɪˌfaɪ) *vb.* **-fies, -fying, -fied.** (*tr.*) **1.** to arrange or order by classes; categorize. **2.** *Government.* to declare (information, documents, etc.) of possible aid to an enemy and therefore not available to people outside a restricted group. [C18: back formation from CLASSIFICATION] —ˈ**classiˌfiable** *adj.* —ˈ**classiˌfier** *n.*

class interval *n. Statistics.* one of the intervals into which the range of a variable of a distribution is divided, esp. one of the divisions of the base line of a bar chart or histogram.

classis (ˈklæsɪs) *n., pl.* **classes** (ˈklæsiːz). (in some Reformed Churches) **1.** a governing body of elders or pastors. **2.** the district or group of local churches directed by such a body. [C16: from Latin; see CLASS]

classless (ˈklɑːslɪs) *adj.* **1.** not belonging to or forming a class. **2.** characterized by the absence of economic and social distinctions. —ˈ**classlessness** *n.*

class list *n.* (in Britain) a list categorizing students according to the class of honours they have obtained in their degree examination.

class mark *n.* **1.** *Statistics.* a value within a class interval, esp. its midpoint or the nearest integral value, used to represent the interval for computational convenience. **2.** Also called: **class number.** *Library science.* a symbol on a book or other publication indicating its subject field, shelf position, etc.

classmate (ˈklɑːsˌmeɪt) *n.* a friend or contemporary of the same class in a school, college, etc.

classroom (ˈklɑːsˌruːm, -ˌrʊm) *n.* a room in which classes are conducted, esp. in a school or college.

class struggle *n.* **the.** *Marxism.* the continual conflict between the capitalist and working classes for economic and political power. Also called: **class war.**

classy (ˈklɑːsɪ) *adj.* **classier, classiest.** *Slang.* elegant; stylish. —ˈ**classily** *adv.* —ˈ**classiness** *n.*

clastic (ˈklæstɪk) *adj.* **1.** (of sedimentary rock, etc.) composed of fragments of pre-existing rock that have been transported some distance from their points of origin. **2.** *Biology.* dividing into parts: *a clastic cell.* **3.** able to be dismantled for study or observation: *a clastic model of the brain.* [C19: from Greek *klastos* shattered, from *klan* to break]

clathrate (ˈklæθreɪt) *adj.* **1.** *Botany.* resembling a net or lattice. *~n.* **2.** *Chem.* a solid compound in which molecules of one substance are physically trapped in the crystal lattice of another. [C17: from Latin *clāthrāre* to provide with a lattice, from Greek *klēthra*, from *klaithron* a bar]

clatter (ˈklætə) *vb.* **1.** to make or cause to make a rattling noise, esp. as a result of movement. **2.** (*intr.*) to chatter. **3.** (*tr.*) *Scot. and northern English dialect.* to box the ears of. *~n.* **4.** a rattling sound or noise. **5.** a noisy commotion, such as one caused by loud chatter. [Old English *clatrung* clattering (gerund); related to Dutch *klateren* to rattle, German *klatschen* to smack, Norwegian *klattra* to knock] —ˈ**clatterer** *n.* —ˈ**clatteringly** *adv.* —ˈ**clattery** *adj.*

claudication (ˌklɔːdɪˈkeɪʃən) *n.* **1.** limping; lameness. **2.** *Pathol.* short for **intermittent claudication.** [C18: from Latin *claudicātiō*, from *claudicāre*, from *claudus* lame]

clause (klɔːz) *n.* **1.** *Grammar.* a group of words, consisting of a subject and a predicate including a finite verb, that does not necessarily constitute a sentence. See also **main clause, subordinate clause, coordinate clause.** **2.** a section of a legal document such as a contract, will, or draft statute. [C13: from Old French, from Medieval Latin *clausa* a closing (of a rhetorical period), back formation from Latin *clausula*, from *claudere* to close] —ˈ**clausal** *adj.*

claustral (ˈklɔːstrəl) *adj.* a less common variant of **cloistral.**

claustrophobia (ˌklɔːstrəˈfəʊbɪə, ˌklɒs-) *n.* an abnormal fear of being closed in or of being in a confined space. [C19: from *claustro-*, from Latin *claustrum* CLOISTER + -PHOBIA] —ˈ**claustroˌphobe** *n.* —ˌ**claustroˈphobic** *adj.* —ˌ**claustroˈphobically** *adv.*

clavate (ˈkleɪveɪt, -vɪt) *or* **claviform** *adj.* shaped like a club with the thicker end uppermost. [C19: from Latin *clāva* club] —ˈ**clavately** *adv.*

clave[1] (kleɪv, klɑːv) *n. Music.* one of a pair of hardwood sticks struck together to make a hollow sound. [C20: from American Spanish, from Latin *clavis* key]

clave[2] (kleɪv) *vb. Archaic.* a past tense of **cleave.**

clave[3] (kleɪv) *n. Zoology.* a clublike thickening at the upper end of an organ, esp. of the antenna of an insect. [C19: from Latin *clāva* club]

claver (ˈkleɪvə) *Scot.* *~vb.* (*intr.*) **1.** to talk idly; gossip. *~n.* **2.** (*often pl.*) idle talk; gossip. [C13: of uncertain origin]

clavicembalo (ˌklævɪˈtʃɛmbələʊ) *n., pl.* **-los.** another name for **harpsichord.** [C18: from Italian, from Medieval Latin *clāvis* key + *cymbalum* CYMBAL]

clavichord (ˈklævɪˌkɔːd) *n.* a keyboard instrument consisting of a number of thin wire strings struck from below by brass tangents. The instrument is noted for its delicate tones, since the tangents do not rebound from the string until the key is released. [C15: from Medieval Latin *clāvichordium*, from Latin *clāvis* key + *chorda* string, CHORD[1]] —ˈ**claviˌchordist** *n.*

clavicle (ˈklævɪkəl) *n.* **1.** either of the two bones connecting the shoulder blades with the upper part of the breastbone. Nontechnical name: **collarbone.** **2.** the corresponding structure in other vertebrates. [C17: from Medieval Latin *clāvicula*, from Latin *clāvis* key] —**clavicular** (kləˈvɪkjʊlə) *adj.* —**claviculate** (kləˈvɪkjʊˌleɪt) *adj.*

clavicorn (ˈklævɪˌkɔːn) *n.* **1.** any beetle of the group *Clavicornia*, including the ladybirds, characterized by club-shaped antennae. *~adj.* **2.** of, relating to, or belonging to the *Clavicornia.* [C19: from New Latin *Clavicornia*, from Latin *clāva* club + *cornū* horn]

clavier (kləˈvɪə, ˈklævɪə) *n.* **a.** any keyboard instrument. **b.** the keyboard itself. [C18: from French: keyboard, from Old French (in the sense: key bearer), from Latin *clāvis* key]

claviform (ˈklævɪˌfɔːm) *adj.* another word for **clavate.** [C19: from Latin *clāva* club]

claw (klɔː) *n.* **1.** a curved pointed horny process on the end of each digit in birds, some reptiles, and certain mammals. **2.** a corresponding structure in some invertebrates, such as the pincer of a crab. **3.** a part or member like a claw in function or appearance. **4.** *Botany.* the narrow basal part of certain petals and sepals. *~vb.* **5.** to scrape, tear, or dig (something or someone) with claws, etc. **6.** (*tr.*) to create by scratching as with claws: *to claw an opening.* [Old English *clawu*; related to Old High German *kluwi*, Sanskrit *glau-* ball, sphere] —ˈ**clawer** *n.* —ˈ**clawless** *adj.*

claw back *vb.* (*tr., adv.*) **1.** to get back (something) with difficulty. **2.** to recover (a sum of money), esp. by taxation or a penalty. *~n.* **clawback.** **3.** the recovery of a sum of money, esp. by taxation or a penalty. **4.** the sum so recovered.

claw hammer *n.* a hammer with a cleft at one end of the head for extracting nails. Also called: **carpenter's hammer.**

claw hatchet *n.* a hatchet with a claw at one end of its head for extracting nails.

claw off *vb.* (*adv., usually tr.*) *Nautical.* to avoid the dangers of (a lee shore or other hazard) by beating.

claw setting *n. Brit.* a jewellery setting with clawlike prongs. U.S. equivalent: **Tiffany setting.**

clay (kleɪ) *n.* **1.** a very fine-grained material that consists of hydrated aluminium silicate, quartz, and organic fragments and occurs as sedimentary rocks, soils, and other deposits. It becomes plastic when moist but hardens on heating and is used in the manufacture of bricks, cement, ceramics, etc. **2.** earth or mud in general. **3.** *Poetic.* the material of the human body. *~vb.* **4.** (*tr.*) to cover or mix with clay. [Old English *clǣg*; related to Old High German *klīa*, Norwegian *kli*, Latin *glūs* glue, Greek *gloios* sticky oil] —ˈ**clayey,** ˈ**clayish,** *or* ˈ**clayˌlike** *adj.*

claybank (ˈkleɪˌbæŋk) *n. U.S.* **a.** a dull brownish-orange colour. **b.** (*as adj.*): *a claybank horse.*

clay court *n.* a tennis court with a playing surface topped by a layer of crushed shale, brick, or stone.

clay mineral *n.* any of a group of minerals consisting of hydrated aluminium silicates: the major constituents of clays.

claymore (ˈkleɪˌmɔː; *Scot.* ˌkleˈmor) *n.* a large two-edged broadsword used formerly by Scottish Highlanders. [C18: from Gaelic *claidheamh mōr* great sword]

claypan (ˈkleɪˌpæn) *n.* a layer of stiff impervious clay situated just below the surface of the ground, which holds water after heavy rain.

clay pigeon *n.* **1.** a disc of baked clay hurled into the air from a machine as a target to be shot at. **2.** *U.S. slang.* a person in a defenceless position; sitting duck.

clay road *n. N.Z.* an unsealed and unmetalled road in a rural area.

claystone (ˈkleɪˌstəʊn) *n.* a compact very fine-grained rock consisting of consolidated clay particles.

claytonia (kleɪˈtəʊnɪə) *n.* any low-growing North American succulent portulacaceous plant of the genus *Claytonia.* [C18: named after John *Clayton* (1693–1773), American botanist]

-cle *suffix forming nouns.* indicating smallness: *cubicle; particle.* [via Old French from Latin *-culus.* See -CULE]

clean (kliːn) *adj.* **1.** without dirt or other impurities; unsoiled. **2.** without anything in it or on it: *a clean page.* **3.** without extraneous or foreign materials. **4.** without defect, difficulties, or problems: *a clean test flight.* **5. a.** (of a nuclear weapon) producing little or no radioactive fallout or contamination. **b.** uncontaminated. Compare **dirty** (sense 11). **6.** (of a wound, etc.) having no pus or other sign of infection. **7.** pure; morally sound. **8.** without objectionable language or obscenity: *a clean joke.* **9.** (of printer's proofs, etc.) relatively free from errors; easily readable: *clean copy.* **10.** thorough or complete: *a clean break.* **11.** dexterous or adroit: *a clean throw.* **12.** *Sport.* played fairly and without fouls. **13.** simple in design: *a ship's clean lines.* **14.** *Aeronautics.* causing little turbulence; streamlined. **15.** (of an aircraft) having no projections, such as rockets, flaps, etc., into the airstream. **16.** honourable or respectable. **17.** habitually neat. **18.** (esp. of a driving licence) showing or having no record of offences. **19.** *Slang.* **a.** innocent; not guilty. **b.** not carrying illegal drugs, weapons, etc. **20.** *Nautical.* (of a vessel) **a.** having its bottom clean. **b.** having a satisfactory bill of health. **21.** *Old Testament.* **a.** (of persons) free from ceremonial defilement. **b.** (of animals, birds, and fish) lawful to eat. **22.** *New Testament.* morally and spiritually pure. ~*vb.* **23.** to make or become free of dirt, filth, etc.: *the stove cleans easily.* **24.** (*tr.*) to remove in making clean: *to clean marks off the wall.* **25.** (*tr.*) to prepare (fish, poultry, etc.) for cooking: *to clean a chicken.* ~*adv.* **26.** in a clean way; cleanly. **27.** *Not standard.* (intensifier): *clean forgotten; clean dead.* **28. clean bowled.** *Cricket.* bowled by a ball that breaks the wicket without hitting the batsman or his bat. **29. come clean.** *Informal.* to make a revelation or confession. ~*n.* **30.** the act or an instance of cleaning: *he gave his shoes a clean.* **31. clean sweep.** See **sweep** (sense 33). ~See also **clean out, clean up.** [Old English *clǣne;* related to Old Frisian *klēne* small, neat, Old High German *kleini*] —'**cleanable** *adj.* —'**cleanness** *n.*

clean-cut *adj.* **1.** clearly outlined; neat: *clean-cut lines of a ship.* **2.** definite: *a clean-cut decision in boxing.*

cleaner ('kliːnə) *n.* **1.** a person, device, chemical agent, etc., that removes dirt, as from clothes or carpets. **2.** (*usually pl.*) a shop, etc. that provides a dry-cleaning service. **3. take (a person) to the cleaners.** *Informal.* to rob or defraud (a person) of all of his money.

clean-limbed *adj.* having well-proportioned limbs.

cleanly *adv.* ('kliːnlɪ). **1.** in a fair manner. **2.** easily or smoothly: *the screw went into the wood cleanly.* ~*adj.* ('klɛnlɪ), **-lier, -liest. 3.** habitually clean or neat. —**cleanlily** ('klɛnlɪlɪ) *adv.* —**cleanliness** ('klɛnlɪnɪs) *n.*

clean out *vb.* (*tr., adv.*) **1.** (foll. by *of* or *from*) to remove (something) (from or away from). **2.** *Slang.* to leave (someone) with no money: *gambling had cleaned him out.* **3.** *Informal.* to exhaust (stocks, goods, etc.) completely.

cleanse (klɛnz) *vb.* (*tr.*) **1.** to remove dirt, filth, etc., from. **2.** to remove guilt from. **3.** *Archaic.* to cure. [Old English *clǣnsian;* related to Middle Low German *klēnsen;* see CLEAN] —'**cleansable** *adj.*

cleanser ('klɛnzə) *n.* a cleansing agent, such as a detergent.

clean-shaven *adj.* (of men) having the facial hair shaved off.

cleanskin ('kliːnˌskɪn) *n. Austral.* **1.** an unbranded animal. **2.** *Slang.* a person without a criminal record.

clean up *vb.* (*adv.*) **1.** to rid (something) of dirt, filth, or other impurities. **2.** to make (someone or something) orderly or presentable. **3.** (*tr.*) to rid (a place) of undesirable people or conditions: *the campaign against vice had cleaned up the city.* **4.** (*intr.*) *Informal, chiefly U.S. and Canadian.* to make a great profit. ~*n.* **cleanup. 5. a.** the process of cleaning up or eliminating something. **b.** (*as modifier*): *a cleanup campaign.* **6.** *Informal, chiefly U.S.* a great profit.

clean wool *n.* wool that has been scoured to remove wax.

clear (klɪə) *adj.* **1.** free from darkness or obscurity; bright. **2.** (of weather) free from dullness or clouds. **3.** transparent: *clear water.* **4.** even and pure in tone or colour: *clear blue.* **5.** without discoloration, blemish, or defect: *a clear skin.* **6.** easy to see or hear; distinct. **7.** free from doubt or confusion: *his instructions are not clear.* **8.** (*postpositive*) certain in the mind; sure: *are you clear?* **9.** evident or obvious: *it is clear that he won't come now.* **10.** (of sounds or the voice) not harsh or hoarse. **11.** serene; calm. **12.** without qualification or limitation; complete: *a clear victory.* **13.** free of suspicion, guilt, or blame: *a clear conscience.* **14.** free of obstruction; open: *a clear passage.* **15.** free from debt or obligation. **16.** (of money, profits, etc.) without deduction; net. **17.** emptied of freight or cargo. **18.** (of timber) having a smooth, unblemished surface. **19.** Also: **in clear.** (of a message, etc.) not in code. **20.** Also: **light.** *Phonetics.* denoting an (l) in whose articulation the main part of the tongue is brought forward giving the sound of a front-vowel timbre. **21.** *Showjumping.* (of a round) ridden without any fences being knocked down or any points being lost. ~*adv.* **22.** in a clear or distinct manner. **23.** completely or utterly. **24.** (*postpositive;* often foll. by *of*) not in contact (with); free: *stand clear of the gates.* ~*n.* **25.** a clear space. **26.** another word for **clearance. 27. in the clear. a.** free of suspicion, guilt, or blame. **b.** *Sport.* able to receive a pass without being tackled. ~*vb.* **28.** to make or become free from darkness, obscurity, etc. **29.** (*intr.*) **a.** (of the weather) to become free from dullness, fog, rain, etc. **b.** (of mist, fog, etc.) to disappear. **30.** (*tr.*) to free from impurity or blemish. **31.** (*tr.*) to free from doubt or confusion: *to clear one's mind.* **32.** (*tr.*) to rid of objects, obstructions, etc. **33.** (*tr.*) to make or form (a path, way, etc.) by removing obstructions. **34.** (*tr.*) to free or remove (a person or thing) from something, such as suspicion, blame, or guilt. **35.** (*tr.*) to move or pass by or over without contact or involvement: *he cleared the wall easily.* **36.** (*tr.*) to rid (the throat) of phlegm or obstruction. **37.** (*tr.*) to make or gain (money) as profit. **38.** (*tr.;* often foll. by *off*) to discharge or settle (a debt). **39.** (*tr.*) to free (a debtor) from obligation. **40.** (*intr.*) (of a cheque) to pass through one's bank and be charged against one's account. **41.** *Banking.* to settle accounts by exchanging (commercial documents) in a clearing house. **42.** to permit (ships, aircraft, cargo, passengers, etc.) to unload, disembark, depart, etc., after fulfilling the customs and other requirements, or (of ships, etc.) to be permitted to unload, etc. **43.** to obtain or give (clearance). **44.** (*tr.*) to obtain clearance from. **45.** (*tr.*) to make microscope specimens transparent by immersion in a fluid such as xylene. **46.** (*tr.*) to permit (a person, company, etc.) to see or handle classified information. **47.** (*tr.*) *Military, etc.* **a.** to achieve transmission of (a signalled message) and acknowledgment of its receipt at its destination. **b.** to decode (a message, etc.). **48.** (*tr.*) *Sport.* to hit, kick, carry, or throw (the ball) out of the defence area. **49.** (*tr.*) *Computer technol.* to remove data from a storage device and replace it with particular characters that usually indicate zero. **50.** (*tr.*) *N.Z.* to remove (trees, scrub, etc.) from land. **51. clear the air.** See **air** (sense 10). **52. clear the decks.** to prepare for action, as by removing obstacles from a field of activity or combat. ~See also **clear away, clear off, clear out, clear up.** [C13 *clere,* from Old French *cler,* from Latin *clārus* clear, bright, brilliant, illustrious] —'**clearable** *adj.* —'**clearer** *n.* —'**clearly** *adv.* —'**clearness** *n.*

clearance ('klɪərəns) *n.* **1. a.** the process or an instance of clearing: *slum clearance.* **b.** (*as modifier*): *a clearance order.* **2.** space between two parts in motion or in relative motion. **3.** permission for an aircraft, ship, passengers, etc., to proceed. **4.** *Banking.* the exchange of commercial documents drawn on the members of a clearing house. **5. a.** the disposal of merchandise at reduced prices. **b.** (*as modifier*): *a clearance sale.* **6.** *Sport.* **a.** the act of hitting or kicking a ball out of the defensive area, as in football. **b.** an instance of this. **7.** the act of clearing an area of land of its inhabitants by mass eviction. **8.** *Dentistry.* the extraction of all of a person's teeth. **9.** a less common word for **clearing.**

clear away *vb.* (*adv.*) to remove (objects) from (the table) after a meal.

clearcole ('klɪəkəʊl) *n.* **1.** a type of size containing whiting. ~*vb.* **2.** (*tr.*) to paint (a wall) with this size. [C19: from French *claire colle* clear size]

clear-cut *adj.* (**clear cut** *when postpositive*). **1.** definite; not vague: *a clear-cut proposal.* **2.** clearly outlined.

clear-eyed *adj.* **1.** discerning; perceptive. **2.** having clear eyes or sharp vision.

clear-fell ('klɪəˌfɛl) *vb.* (*tr.*) to cut down all of the trees in (a wood, part of a wood, or throughout an area of land).

clear-headed *adj.* mentally alert; sensible; judicious. —ˌ**clear-'headedly** *adv.* —ˌ**clear-'headedness** *n.*

clearing ('klɪərɪŋ) *n.* an area with few or no trees or shrubs in wooded or overgrown land.

clearing bank *n.* (in Britain) any bank that makes use of the central clearing house in London for the transfer of credits and cheques between banks.

clearing house *n.* **1.** *Banking.* an institution where cheques and other commercial papers drawn on member banks are cancelled against each other so that only net balances are payable. **2.** a central agency for the collection and distribution of information or materials.

clearing sale *n. Austral.* the auction of plant, stock, and effects of a country property, esp. after the property has changed hands.

clear off *vb.* (*intr., adv.*) *Informal.* to go away: often used imperatively.

clear out *vb.* (*adv.*) **1.** (*intr.*) *Informal.* to go away: often used imperatively. **2.** (*tr.*) to remove and sort the contents of (a room, container, etc.). **3.** (*tr.*) *Slang.* to leave (someone) with no money. **4.** (*tr.*) *Slang.* to exhaust (stocks, goods, etc.) completely.

clear-sighted *adj.* **1.** involving accurate perception or judgment: *a clear-sighted compromise.* **2.** having clear vision. —ˌ**clear-'sightedly** *adv.* —ˌ**clear-'sightedness** *n.*

clearstory ('klɪəˌstɔːrɪ) *n.* a variant spelling of **clerestory.** —'**clearˌstoried** *adj.*

clear up *vb.* (*adv.*) **1.** (*tr.*) to explain or solve (a mystery, misunderstanding, etc.). **2.** to put (a place or thing that is disordered) in order. **3.** (*intr.*) (of the weather) to become brighter. ~*n.* **clear-up** ('klɪərˌʌp). **4.** the act or an instance of clearing up.

clearway ('klɪəˌweɪ) *n.* **1.** *Brit.* a stretch of road on which motorists may stop only in an emergency. **2.** an area at the end of a runway over which an aircraft taking off makes its initial climb: it is under the control of the airport.

clearwing *or* **clearwing moth** ('klɪəˌwɪŋ) *n.* any moth of the family *Sesiidae* (or *Aegeriidae*), characterized by the absence of scales from the greater part of the wings. They are day-flying and some, such as the **hornet clearwing** (*Sesia apiformis*), resemble wasps and other hymenopterans.

cleat (kliːt) *n.* **1.** a wedge-shaped block, usually of wood, attached to a structure to act as a support. **2.** a device consisting of two hornlike prongs projecting horizontally in opposite directions from a central base, used for securing lines on vessels, wharves, etc. **3.** a short length of angle iron used as a bracket. **4.** a piece of metal, leather, etc., attached to the sole of a shoe to prevent wear or slipping. **5.** a small triangular-shaped nail used in glazing. **6.** any of the main cleavage planes in a coal seam. ~*vb.* (*tr.*) **7.** to supply or support with a cleat or cleats. **8.** to secure (a line) on a cleat. [C14: of Germanic origin, compare Old High German *chlōz* clod, lump, Dutch *kloot* ball]

cleavage ('kliːvɪdʒ) *n.* **1.** *Informal.* the separation between a woman's breasts, esp. as revealed by a low-cut dress. **2.** a division or split. **3.** (of crystals) the act of splitting or the tendency to split along definite planes so as to yield smooth surfaces. **4.** Also called: **segmentation.** *Embryol.* (in animals) the repeated division of a fertilized ovum into a solid ball of cells (a morula), which later becomes hollow (a blastula). **5.** the breaking of a chemical bond in a molecule to give smaller molecules or radicals. **6.** *Geology.* the natural splitting of certain rocks, such as slates, into thin plates.

cleave[1] (kliːv) *vb.* **cleaves, cleaving; cleft, cleaved,** *or* **clove; cleft, cleaved,** *or* **cloven. 1.** to split or cause to split, esp. along a natural weakness. **2.** (*tr.*) to make by or as if by cutting: *to cleave a path.* **3.** (when *intr.*, foll. by *through*) to penetrate or traverse. [Old English *clēofan;* related to Old Norse *kljūfa,* Old High German *klioban,* Latin *glūbere* to peel] —'**cleavable** *adj.* —ˌ**cleava'bility** *n.*

cleave[2] (kliːv) *vb.* (*intr.;* foll. by *to*) to cling or adhere. [Old English *cleofian;* related to Old High German *klebēn* to stick]

cleaver ('kliːvə) *n.* a heavy knife or long-bladed hatchet, esp. one used by butchers.

cleavers ('kliːvəz) *n.* (*functioning as sing.*) a Eurasian rubiaceous plant, *Galium aparine,* having small white flowers and prickly stems and fruits. Also called: **goosegrass, hairif, sticky willie.** [Old English *clīfe;* related to *clīfan* to CLEAVE[2]]

cleck[1] (klɛk) *vb.* (*tr.*) *Scot.* **1.** (of birds) to hatch. **2.** to lay or hatch (a plot or scheme). [C15: from Old Norse *klekja*]

cleck[2] (klɛk) *South Wales dialect.* ~*vb.* **1.** (*intr.;* often foll. by *on*) to gossip (about); tell (on). ~*n.* **2.** (*often pl.*) a piece of gossip. [from Welsh, from *clecan* to gossip, and *clec* gossip] —'**clecky** *adj.*

cleek *or* **cleik** (kliːk) *n.* **1.** *Chiefly Scot.* a large hook, such as one used to land fish. **2.** *Golf.* (formerly) a club, a long-shafted iron (No. 1), used for long low shots. [C15: of uncertain origin]

clef (klɛf) *n.* one of several symbols placed on the left-hand side beginning of each stave indicating the pitch of the music written after it. See also **alto clef, bass clef, C clef, soprano clef, tenor clef, treble clef.** [C16: from French: key, clef, from Latin *clāvis;* related to Latin *claudere* to close]

cleft (klɛft) *vb.* **1.** the past tense and a past participle of **cleave**[1]. ~*n.* **2.** a fissure or crevice. **3.** an indentation or split in something, such as the chin, palate, etc. ~*adj.* **4.** split; divided. **5.** (of leaves) having one or more incisions reaching nearly to the midrib. [Old English *geclyft* (n.); related to Old High German *kluft* tongs, German *Kluft* gap, fissure; see CLEAVE[1]]

cleft palate *n.* a congenital crack or fissure in the midline of the hard palate, often associated with a harelip.

cleg (klɛg) *n.* another name for a **horsefly,** esp. one of the genus *Haematopota.* [C15: from Old Norse *kleggi*]

cleidoic egg (klaɪ'dəʊɪk) *n.* the egg of birds and insects, which is enclosed in a protective shell limiting the exchange of water, gases, etc. [C20: from Greek *kleidoun* to lock up, from *kleid-, kleis* key]

cleistogamy (klaɪ'stɒgəmɪ) *n.* self-pollination and fertilization of an unopened flower, as in the violet. Compare **chasmogamy.** —**cleis'togamous** *or* **cleistogamic** (ˌklaɪstə'gæmɪk) *adj.*

clem (klɛm) *or* **clam** *vb.* **clems, clemming, clemmed** *or* **clams, clamming, clammed.** (when *tr., usually passive*) *English dialect.* to be hungry or cause to be hungry. [C16: of Germanic origin; related to Dutch, German *klemmen* to pinch, cramp; compare Old English *beclemman* to shut in]

clematis ('klɛmətɪs, klə'meɪtɪs) *n.* any N temperate ranunculaceous climbing plant or erect shrub of the genus *Clematis,* having plumelike fruits. Many species are cultivated for their large colourful flowers. See also **traveller's joy.** [C16: from Latin, from Greek *klēmatis* climbing plant, brushwood, from *klēma* twig]

clemency ('klɛmənsɪ) *n., pl.* **-cies. 1.** mercy or leniency. **2.** mildness, esp. of the weather. [C15: from Latin *clēmentia,* from *clēmēns* gentle]

clement ('klɛmənt) *adj.* **1.** merciful. **2.** (of the weather) mild. [C15: from Latin *clēmēns* mild; probably related to Greek *klinein* to lean] —'**clemently** *adv.*

clementine ('klɛmənˌtiːn, -ˌtaɪn) *n.* a citrus fruit thought to be either a variety of tangerine or a hybrid between a tangerine and sweet orange. [C20: from French *clémentine,* perhaps from the female Christian name]

clench (klɛntʃ) *vb.* (*tr.*) **1.** to close or squeeze together (the teeth, a fist, etc.) tightly. **2.** to grasp or grip firmly. ~*n.* **3.** a firm grasp or grip. **4.** a device that grasps or grips, such as a clamp. ~*n., vb.* **5.** another word for **clinch.** [Old English *beclencan,* related to Old High German *klenken* to tie, Middle High German *klank* noose, Dutch *klinken* rivet]

cleome (klɪ'əʊmɪ) *n.* any herbaceous or shrubby plant of the mostly tropical capparidaceous genus *Cleome,* esp. *C. spinosa,* cultivated for their clusters of white or purplish flowers with long stamens. [C19: New Latin, of obscure origin]

cleopatra (ˌkliːə'pætrə, -'pɑː-) *n.* a yellow butterfly, *Gonepteryx cleopatra,* the male of which has its wings flushed with orange.

clepe (kliːp) *vb.* **clepes, cleping; cleped** (kliːpt, klɛpt), **clept, ycleped,** *or* **yclept.** (*tr.*) *Archaic.* to call by the name of. [Old English *cleopian;* related to Middle Low German *kleperen* to rattle]

clepsydra ('klɛpsɪdrə) *n., pl.* **-dras** *or* **-drae** (-ˌdriː). an ancient device for measuring time by the flow of water or mercury through a small aperture. Also called: **water clock.** [C17: from Latin, from Greek *klepsudra,* from *kleptein* to steal + *hudōr* water]

cleptomania (ˌklɛptəʊ'meɪnɪə, -'meɪnjə) *n.* a variant spelling of **kleptomania.** —ˌ**clepto'maniˌac** *n.*

clerestory *or* **clearstory** ('klɪəˌstɔːrɪ) *n., pl.* **-ries. 1.** a row of windows in the upper part of the wall of a church that divides the nave from the aisle, set above the aisle roof. **2.** the part of the wall in which these windows are set. Compare **blindstorey.** [C15: from CLEAR + STOREY] —'**cleređstoried** *or* '**clearˌstoried** *adj.*

clergy ('klɜːdʒɪ) *n., pl.* **-gies.** the collective body of men and women ordained as religious ministers, esp. of the Christian Church. [C13: from Old French *clergie,* from *clerc* ecclesiastic, CLERK]

clergyman ('klɜːdʒɪmən) *n., pl.* **-men.** a member of the clergy.

cleric ('klɛrɪk) *n.* a member of the clergy. [C17: from Church Latin *clēricus* priest, CLERK]

clerical ('klɛrɪkᵊl) *adj.* **1.** relating to or associated with the clergy: *clerical dress.* **2.** of or relating to office clerks or their work: *a clerical error.* **3.** supporting or advocating clericalism. —'**clerically** *adv.*

clerical collar *n.* a stiff white collar with no opening at the front that buttons at the back of the neck; the distinctive mark of the clergy in certain Churches. Informal name: **dog collar.**

clericalism ('klɛrɪkᵊˌlɪzəm) *n.* **1.** a policy of upholding the power of the clergy. **2.** the power of the clergy esp. when excessively strong. —'**clericalist** *n.*

clericals ('klɛrɪkᵊlz) *pl. n.* the distinctive dress of a clergyman.

clerihew ('klɛrɪˌhjuː) *n.* a form of comic or satiric verse, consisting of two couplets of metrically irregular lines, containing the name of a well-known person. [C20: named after Edmund *Clerihew* Bentley (1875–1956), British writer who invented it]

clerk (klɑːk; *U.S.* klɜːrk) *n.* **1.** a worker, esp. in an office, who keeps records, files, etc. **2. clerk to the justices.** (in England) a legally qualified person who sits in court with lay justices to advise them on points of law. **3.** an employee of a court, legislature, board, corporation, etc., who keeps records and accounts, etc.: *a town clerk.* **4.** Also called: **clerk of the House.** *Brit.* a senior official of the House of Commons. **5.** Also called: **clerk in holy orders.** a cleric. **6.** *U.S. and Canadian.* short for **salesclerk. 7.** Also called: **desk clerk.** *U.S. and Canadian.* a hotel receptionist. **8.** *Archaic.* a scholar. ~*vb.* **9.** (*intr.*) to serve as a clerk. [Old English *clerc,* from Church Latin *clēricus,* from Greek *klērikos* cleric, relating to the heritage (alluding to the Biblical Levites, whose inheritance was the Lord), from *klēros* heritage] —'**clerkdom** *n.* —'**clerkish** *adj.* —'**clerkship** *n.*

clerkess (klɑː'kɛs) *n.* a female office clerk.

clerkly ('klɑːklɪ) *adj.* **-lier, -liest. 1.** of or like a clerk. **2.** *Obsolete.* learned. ~*adv.* **3.** *Obsolete.* in the manner of a clerk. —'**clerkliness** *n.*

clerk of the works *n.* an employee who supervises building work in progress or the upkeep of existing buildings.

cleruchy ('klɛəˌruːkɪ) *n., pl.* **-chies.** (in the ancient world) a special type of Athenian colony, in which settlers (**cleruchs**) retained their Athenian citizenship and the community remained a political dependency of Athens. —**cleruchial** (klɪ'ruːkɪəl) *adj.*

cleveite ('kliːvaɪt) *n.* a crystalline variety of the mineral uranitite. [C19: named after P. T. *Cleve* (1840–1905), Swedish chemist; see -ITE[1]]

clever ('klɛvə) *adj.* **1.** displaying sharp intelligence or mental alertness. **2.** adroit or dexterous, esp. with the hands. **3.** smart in a superficial way. **4.** *Brit. informal.* sly; cunning. **5.** (*predicative; used with a negative*) *Dialect.* healthy; fit. [C13 *cliver* (in the sense: quick to seize, adroit), of uncertain origin] —'**cleverish** *adj.* —'**cleverly** *adv.* —'**cleverness** *n.*

clever-clever *adj. Informal.* clever in a showy manner; artful; overclever.

clever Dick *or* **cleverdick** ('klɛvəˌdɪk) *n. Informal.* a person considered to have an unwarrantably high opinion of his own ability or knowledge.

clevis ('klɛvɪs) *n.* the U-shaped component of a shackle for attaching a drawbar to a plough or similar implement. [C16: related to CLEAVE[1]]

clew (kluː) *n.* **1.** a ball of thread, yarn, or twine. **2.** *Nautical.* either of the lower corners of a square sail or the after lower corner of a fore-and-aft sail. **3.** (*usually pl.*) the rigging of a hammock. **4.** a rare variant of **clue.** ~*vb.* **5.** (*tr.*) to coil or roll into a ball. [Old English *cliewen* (vb.); related to Old High German *kliu* ball]

clew line *n. Nautical.* any of several lines fastened to the clews of a square sail and used for furling it.

clew up *vb.* (*adv.*) *Nautical.* to furl (a square sail) by gathering its clews up to the yard by means of clew lines.

clianthus (klɪˈænθəs) *n.* any Australian or New Zealand plant of the leguminous genus *Clianthus,* with ornamental clusters of slender scarlet flowers. [C19: New Latin, probably from Greek *klei-, kleos* glory + *anthos* flower]

cliché (ˈkliːʃeɪ) *n.* **1.** a word or expression that has lost much of its force through overexposure, as for example the phrase: *it's got to get worse before it gets better.* **2.** an idea, action, or habit that has become trite from overuse. **3.** *Printing, chiefly Brit.* a stereotype or electrotype plate. [C19: from French, from *clicher* to stereotype; imitative of the sound made by the matrix when it is dropped into molten metal] —ˈ**clichéd** *or* ˈ**cliché'd** *adj.*

click (klɪk) *n.* **1.** a short light often metallic sound. **2. a.** the locking member of a ratchet mechanism, such as a pawl or detent. **b.** the movement of such a mechanism between successive locking positions. **3.** *Phonetics.* any of various stop consonants, found in Khoisan and as borrowings in southern Bantu languages, that are produced by the suction of air into the mouth. ~*vb.* **4.** to make or cause to make a clicking sound: *to click one's heels.* **5.** (*intr.*) *Slang.* to be a great success: *that idea really clicked.* **6.** (*intr.*) *Informal.* to become suddenly clear: *it finally clicked when her name was mentioned.* **7.** (*intr.*) *Slang.* to go or fit together with ease: *they clicked from their first meeting.* [C17: of imitative origin] —ˈ**clicker** *n.*

click beetle *n.* any beetle of the family *Elateridae,* which have the ability to right themselves with a snapping movement when placed on their backs. Also called: **snapping beetle, skipjack.** See also **wireworm.**

clicker (ˈklɪkə) *n.* **1.** a person or thing that clicks. **2.** *Informal.* a foreman in a shoe factory or printing works.

client (ˈklaɪənt) *n.* **1.** a person, company, etc., that seeks the advice of a professional man or woman. **2.** a customer. **3.** a person who is registered with or receiving services or financial aid from a welfare agency. **4.** a person depending on another's patronage. [C14: from Latin *cliēns* retainer, dependant; related to Latin *clīnāre* to lean] —**cliental** (klaɪˈentᵊl) *adj.*

client-centred therapy *n. Psychol.* a form of psychotherapy in which the therapist makes no attempt to interpret what the patient says but encourages him to develop his own attitudes and insights, often by questioning him.

clientele (ˌkliːɒnˈtel) *or* **clientage** (ˈklaɪəntɪdʒ) *n.* customers or clients collectively. [C16: from Latin *clientēla,* from *cliēns* CLIENT]

Clifden nonpareil (ˈklɪftᵊn) *n.* a handsome nocturnal moth, *Catocala fraxini,* that is brown with bluish patches on the hindwings: related to the red underwing.

cliff (klɪf) *n.* a steep high rock face, esp. one that runs along the seashore and has the strata exposed. [Old English *clif;* related to Old Norse *kleif,* Middle Low German *klēf,* Dutch *klif;* see CLEAVE[2]] —ˈ**cliffy** *adj.*

cliffhanger (ˈklɪfˌhæŋə) *n.* **1. a.** a situation of imminent disaster usually occurring at the end of each episode of a serialized film. **b.** the serialized film itself. **2.** a situation that is dramatic or uncertain. —ˈ**cliffˌhanging** *adj.*

cliff swallow *n.* an American swallow, *Petrochelidon pyrrhonota,* that has a square-tipped tail and builds nests of mud on cliffs, walls, etc.

climacteric (klaɪˈmæktərɪk, ˌklaɪmækˈterɪk) *n.* **1.** a critical event or period. **2.** another name for **menopause. 3.** the period in the life of a man corresponding to the menopause, chiefly characterized by diminished sexual activity. **4.** *Botany.* the period during which certain fruits, such as apples, ripen, marked by a rise in the rate of respiration. ~*adj. also* **climacterical** (ˌklaɪmækˈterɪkᵊl). **5.** involving a crucial event or period. [C16: from Latin *clīmactēricus,* from Greek *klimaktērikos,* from *klimaktēr,* rung of a ladder from *klimax* ladder; see CLIMAX] —ˌ**climacˈterically** *adv.*

climactic (klaɪˈmæktɪk) *or* **climactical** *adj.* consisting of, involving, or causing a climax. —**cliˈmactically** *adv.*

climate (ˈklaɪmɪt) *n.* **1.** the long-term prevalent weather conditions of an area, determined by latitude, position relative to oceans or continents, altitude, etc. **2.** an area having a particular kind of climate. **3.** a prevailing trend or current of feeling: *the political climate.* [C14: from Late Latin *clima,* from Greek *klima* inclination, region; related to Greek *klinein* to lean] —**climatic** (klaɪˈmætɪk), **cliˈmatical,** *or* ˈ**climatal** *adj.* —**cliˈmatically** *adv.*

climatic zone *n.* any of the eight principal zones, roughly demarcated by lines of latitude, into which the earth can be divided on the basis of climate.

climatology (ˌklaɪməˈtɒlədʒɪ) *n.* the study of climates. —**climatologic** (ˌklaɪmətəˈlɒdʒɪk) *or* ˌ**climatoˈlogical** *adj.* —ˌ**climatoˈlogically** *adv.* —ˌ**climaˈtologist** *n.*

climax (ˈklaɪmæks) *n.* **1.** the most intense or highest point of an experience or of a series of events: *the party was the climax of the week.* **2.** a decisive moment in a dramatic or other work. **3.** a rhetorical device by which a series of sentences, clauses, or phrases are arranged in order of increasing intensity. **4.** *Ecology.* the stage in the development of a community during which it remains stable under the prevailing environmental conditions. **5.** Also called: **sexual climax.** (esp. in referring to women) another word for **orgasm.** ~*vb.* **6.** to reach or bring to a climax. [C16: from Late Latin, from Greek *klimax* ladder]

▷**Usage.** In formal English careful writers avoid the use of *climax* as a verb. The phrase *reach a climax* is preferred.

climb (klaɪm) *vb.* (*mainly intr.*) **1.** (*also tr.;* often foll. by *up*) to go up or ascend (stairs, a mountain, etc.). **2.** (often foll. by *along*) to progress with difficulty: *to climb along a ledge.* **3.** to rise to a higher point or intensity: *the temperature climbed.* **4.** to incline or slope upwards: *the road began to climb.* **5.** to ascend in social position. **6.** (of plants) to grow upwards by twining, using tendrils or suckers, etc. **7.** *Informal.* (foll. by *into*) to put (on) or get (into). **8.** to be a climber or mountaineer. ~*n.* **9.** the act or an instance of climbing. **10.** a place or thing to be climbed, esp. a route in mountaineering. [Old English *climban;* related to Old Norse *klembra* to squeeze, Old High German *climban* to clamber] —ˈ**climbable** *adj.*

climb down *vb.* (*intr., adv.*) **1.** to descend. **2.** (often foll. by *from*) to retreat (from an opinion, position, etc.). ~*n.* **climb-down. 3.** a retreat from an opinion, etc.

climber (ˈklaɪmə) *n.* **1.** a person or thing that climbs. **2.** a plant that lacks rigidity and grows upwards by twining, scrambling, or clinging with tendrils and suckers. **3.** *Chiefly Brit.* short for **social climber.**

climbing fish *or* **perch** *n.* an Asian labyrinth fish, *Anabas testudineus,* that resembles a perch and can travel over land on its spiny gill covers and pectoral fins.

climbing frame *n.* a structure of wood or metal tubing used by children for climbing.

climbing irons *pl. n.* spiked steel frames worn on the feet to assist in climbing trees, ice slopes, etc.

climbing wall *n. Mountaineering.* a specially constructed wall with recessed and projecting holds to give practice in rock climbing; a feature of many sports centres.

clime (klaɪm) *n. Poetic.* a region or its climate. [C16: from Late Latin *clima;* see CLIMATE]

clinandrium (klɪˈnændrɪəm) *n., pl.* **-dria** (-drɪə). *Botany.* a cavity in the upper part of the column of an orchid flower that contains the anthers. Also called: **androclinium.** [C19: from New Latin, literally: bed for stamen, from Greek *klinē* couch + *anēr* man + -IUM]

clinch (klɪntʃ) *vb.* **1.** (*tr.*) to secure (a driven nail) by bending the protruding point over. **2.** (*tr.*) to hold together in such a manner: *to clinch the corners of the frame.* **3.** (*tr.*) to settle (something, such as an argument, bargain, etc.) in a definite way. **4.** (*tr.*) *Nautical.* to fasten by means of a clinch. **5.** (*intr.*) to engage in a clinch, as in boxing or wrestling. ~*n.* **6.** the act of clinching. **7. a.** a nail with its point bent over. **b.** the part of such a nail, etc., that has been bent over. **8.** *Boxing, wrestling, etc.* an act or an instance in which one or both competitors hold on to the other to avoid punches, regain wind, etc. **9.** *Slang.* a lovers' embrace. **10.** *Nautical.* a loop or eye formed in a line by seizing the end to the standing part. ~Also (for senses 1, 2, 4, 7, 8, 10): **clench.** [C16: variant of CLENCH]

clincher (ˈklɪntʃə) *n.* **1.** *Informal.* something decisive, such as fact, score, etc. **2.** a person or thing that clinches.

cline (klaɪn) *n.* a continuous variation in form between members of a species having a wide variable geographical or ecological range. [C20: from Greek *klinein* to lean] —ˈ**clinal** *adj.* —ˈ**clinally** *adv.*

-cline *n. combining form.* indicating a slope: *anticline.* [back formation from INCLINE] —**-clinal** *adj. combining form.*

cling (klɪŋ) *vb.* **clings, clinging, clung.** (*intr.*) **1.** (often foll. by *to*) to hold fast or adhere closely (to something), as by gripping or sticking. **2.** (foll. by *together*) to remain in contact (with each other). **3.** to be or remain physically or emotionally close: *to cling to outmoded beliefs.* ~*n.* **4.** *Agriculture, chiefly U.S.* the tendency of cotton fibres in a sample to stick to each other. **5.** *Agriculture.* diarrhoea or scouring in animals. **6.** short for **clingstone.** [Old English *clingan;* related to CLENCH] —ˈ**clinger** *n.* —ˈ**clingingly** *adv.* —ˈ**clingy** *adj.* —ˈ**clinginess** *or* ˈ**clingingness** *n.*

clingfilm (ˈklɪŋˌfɪlm) *n.* a thin polythene material that clings closely to any surface around which it is placed: used for wrapping food.

clingfish (ˈklɪŋˌfɪʃ) *n., pl.* **-fish** *or* **-fishes.** any small marine teleost fish of the family *Gobiesocidae,* having a flattened elongated body with a sucking disc beneath the head for clinging to rocks, etc.

clinging vine *n. U.S. and Canadian informal.* a woman who displays excessive emotional dependence on a man.

clingstone (ˈklɪŋˌstəʊn) *n.* **a.** a fruit, such as certain peaches, in which the flesh tends to adhere to the stone. **b.** (*as modifier*): *a clingstone peach.* ~Compare **freestone** (sense 2).

clinic (ˈklɪnɪk) *n.* **1.** a place in which outpatients are given medical treatment or advice, often connected to a hospital. **2.** a similar place staffed by physicians or surgeons specializing in one or more specific areas: *eye clinic.* **3.** *Brit.* a private hospital or nursing home. **4.** the teaching of medicine to students at the bedside. **5.** *U.S.* a place where medical lectures are given. **6.** *U.S.* a clinical lecture. **7.** *Chiefly U.S. and Canadian.* a group or centre that offers advice or instruction: *a vocational clinic.* [C17: from Latin *clīnicus* one on a sickbed, from Greek, from *klinē* bed]

clinical ('klɪnɪkᵊl) *adj.* **1.** of or relating to a clinic. **2.** of or relating to the bedside of a patient, the course of his disease, or the observation and treatment of patients directly: *a clinical lecture; clinical medicine.* **3.** scientifically detached; strictly objective: *a clinical attitude to life.* **4.** plain, simple, and usually unattractive: *clinical furniture.* —'**clinically** *adv.* —'**clinicalness** *n.*

clinical psychology *n.* the branch of psychology that studies and treats mental illness and mental retardation.

clinical thermometer *n.* a finely calibrated thermometer for determining the temperature of the body, usually placed under the tongue or in the rectum.

clinician (klɪ'nɪʃən) *n.* a physician, psychiatrist, etc., who specializes in clinical work as opposed to one engaged in laboratory or experimental studies.

clink[1] (klɪŋk) *vb.* **1.** to make or cause to make a light and sharply ringing sound. **2.** (*intr.*) *Rare.* to rhyme. ~*n.* **3.** a light and sharply ringing sound. **4.** *Rare.* a rhyme. **5.** *Brit.* a pointed steel tool used for breaking up the surface of a road before it is repaired. [C14: perhaps from Middle Dutch *klinken;* related to Old Low German *chlanch,* German *Klang* sound]

clink[2] (klɪŋk) *n.* a slang word for **prison.** [C16: after *Clink,* name of a prison in Southwark, London]

clinker ('klɪŋkə) *n.* **1.** the ash and partially fused residues from a coal-fired furnace or fire. **2.** Also called: **clinker brick.** a hard brick used as a paving stone. **3.** a partially vitrified brick or mass of brick. **4.** *U.S. and Canadian slang.* a mistake or fault, esp. a wrong note in music. ~*vb.* **5.** (*intr.*) to form clinker during burning. [C17: from Dutch *klinker* a type of brick, from obsolete *klinckaerd,* literally: something that clinks (referring to the sound produced when one was struck), from *klinken* to CLINK[1]]

clinker-built *or* **clincher-built** *adj.* (of a boat or ship) having a hull constructed with each plank overlapping that below. Also called: **lapstrake.** Compare **carvel-built.** [C18 *clinker* a nailing together, probably from CLINCH]

clinkstone ('klɪŋk,stəʊn) *n.* a variety of phonolite that makes a metallic sound when struck.

clino- *or before a vowel* **clin-** *combining form.* indicating a slope or inclination: *clinometer.* [from New Latin, from Greek *klinein* to slant, lean]

clinometer (klaɪ'nɒmɪtə) *n.* an instrument used in surveying for measuring an angle of inclination. —**clinometric** (,klaɪnə'mɛtrɪk) *or* ,**clino'metrical** *adj.* —**cli'nometry** *n.*

clinopyroxene (,klaɪnəʊpaɪ'rɒksiːn) *n.* a member of the pyroxene group of minerals having a monoclinic crystal structure, such as augite, diopside, or jadeite.

clinostat ('klaɪnəʊ,stæt) *n.* an apparatus for studying tropisms in plants, usually a rotating disc to which the plant is attached so that it receives an equal stimulus on all sides.

clinquant ('klɪŋkənt) *adj.* **1.** glittering, esp. with tinsel. ~*n.* **2.** tinsel or imitation gold leaf. [C16: from French, from *clinquer* to clink, from Dutch *klinken,* of imitative origin]

clint (klɪnt) *n. Physical geography.* **1.** a section of a limestone pavement separated from adjacent sections by solution fissures. See **grike.** **2.** any small surface exposure of hard or flinty rock, as on a hillside or in a stream bed. [C12: from Danish and Swedish *klint,* from Old Swedish *klinter,* related to Icelandic *klettr* rock]

clintonia (klɪn'təʊnɪə) *n.* any temperate liliaceous plant of the genus *Clintonia,* having white, greenish-yellow, or purplish flowers, broad ribbed leaves, and blue berries. [C19: named after De Witt *Clinton* (1769–1828), U.S. politician and naturalist]

cliometrics (,klaɪəʊ'mɛtrɪks) *n.* (*functioning as sing.*) the study of economic history using statistics and computer analysis. [C20: from *Clio* (Greek Muse of history) + (ECONO)METRICS] —,**clio'metric** *or* ,**clio'metrical** *adj.* —**cliometrician** (,klaɪəʊmə'trɪʃən) *n.*

clip[1] (klɪp) *vb.* **clips, clipping, clipped.** (*mainly tr.*) **1.** (*also intr.*) to cut, snip, or trim with or as if with scissors or shears, esp. in order to shorten or remove a part. **2.** *Brit.* to punch (a hole) in something, esp. a ticket. **3.** to curtail or cut short. **4.** to move a short section from (a film, etc.). **5.** to shorten (a word). **6.** (*intr.*) to trot or move rapidly, esp. over a long distance: *a horse clipping along the road.* **7.** *Informal.* to strike with a sharp, often slanting, blow. **8.** *Slang.* to defraud or swindle, esp. by overcharging. **9. clip (someone's) wings. a.** to restrict (someone's) freedom. **b.** to thwart (someone's) ambition. ~*n.* **10.** the act or process of clipping. **11.** something clipped off. **12.** a short extract from a film, newspaper, etc. **13.** *Informal.* a sharp, often slanting, blow. **14.** *Informal.* speed: *a rapid clip.* **15.** *Austral. and N.Z.* the total quantity of wool shorn, as in one place, season, etc. **16.** another word for **clipped form.** [C12: from Old Norse *klippa* to cut; related to Low German *klippen*] —'**clippable** *adj.*

clip[2] (klɪp) *n.* **1.** any of various small implements used to hold loose articles together or to attach one article to another. **2.** an article of jewellery that can be clipped onto a dress, hat, etc. **3.** short for **paperclip** or **cartridge clip.** **4.** the pointed flange on a horseshoe that secures it to the front part of the hoof. **5.** *Archaic or dialect.* an embrace or hug. ~*vb.* **clips, clipping, clipped.** (*tr.*) **6.** to hold together tightly, as with a clip. **7.** *Archaic or dialect.* to embrace. [Old English *clyppan* to embrace; related to Old Frisian *kleppa,* Lithuanian *glebiu*]

clipboard ('klɪp,bɔːd) *n.* a portable writing board with a spring clip at the top for holding paper.

clip-clop *n.* the sound made by a horse's hooves.

clip-fed *adj.* (of an automatic firearm) loaded from a cartridge clip.

clip joint *n. Slang.* a place, such as a nightclub or restaurant, in which customers are overcharged.

clip on *vb.* **1.** (*tr.*) to attach by means of a clip. **2.** (*intr.*) to be attached by means of a clip: *this clips on here.* ~*adj.* **clip-on.** **3.** designed to be attached by means of a clip: *a clip-on bow tie.* ~*pl. n.* **clip-ons.** **4.** sunglasses designed to be clipped on to a person's spectacles.

clipped (klɪpt) *adj.* (of speech or tone of voice) abrupt, terse, and distinct.

clipped form *n.* a shortened form of a word, as for example *doc* for *doctor.*

clipper ('klɪpə) *n.* **1.** any fast sailing ship. **2.** a person or thing that cuts or clips. **3.** something, such as a horse or sled, that moves quickly. **4.** *Electronics.* another word for **limiter.**

clippers ('klɪpəz) *or* **clips** *pl. n.* **1.** a hand tool with two cutting blades for clipping fingernails, veneers, etc. **2.** a hairdresser's tool, operated either by hand or electrically, with one fixed and one reciprocating set of teeth for cutting short hair.

clippie ('klɪpɪ) *n. Brit. informal.* a bus conductress.

clipping ('klɪpɪŋ) *n.* **1.** something cut out or trimmed off, esp. an article from a newspaper; cutting. **2.** the distortion of an audio or visual signal in which the tops of peaks with a high amplitude are cut off, caused by, for example, overloading of amplifier circuits. ~*adj.* **3.** (*prenominal*) *Informal.* fast: *a clipping pace.*

clipshears ('klɪp,ʃiːrz) *or* **clipshear** ('klɪp,ʃiːr) *n.* a Scot. dialect name for an **earwig.** [from the resemblance of the forceps at the tip of its abdomen to shears]

clique (kliːk, klɪk) *n.* a small, exclusive group of friends or associates. [C18: from French, perhaps from Old French: latch, from *cliquer* to click; suggestive of the necessity to exclude nonmembers] —'**cliquey** *or* '**cliquy** *adj.* —'**cliquish** *adj.* —'**cliquishly** *adv.* —'**cliquishness** *n.*

clishmaclaver (,klɪʃmə'kleɪvə) *n. Scot.* idle talk; gossip. [C16: from *clish-clash,* reduplication of CLASH + CLAVER]

clitellum (klɪ'tɛləm) *n., pl.* **-la** (-lə). a thickened saddle-like region of epidermis in earthworms and leeches whose secretions bind copulating worms together and later form a cocoon around the eggs. [C19: from New Latin, from Latin *clitellae* (plural) packsaddle]

clitic ('klɪtɪk) *adj.* **1.** (of a word) incapable of being stressed, usually pronounced as if part of the word that follows or precedes it: for example, in French, *me, te,* and *le* are clitic pronouns. See also **proclitic, enclitic.** ~*n.* **2.** a clitic word. [C20: back formation from ENCLITIC and PROCLITIC]

clitoridectomy (,klɪtərɪ'dɛktəmɪ) *n.* surgical removal of the clitoris: a form of female circumcision, esp. practised as a religious or ethnic rite.

clitoris ('klɪtərɪs, 'klaɪ-) *n.* a part of the female genitalia consisting of a small elongated highly sensitive erectile organ at the front of the vulva: homologous with the penis. [C17: from New Latin, from Greek *kleitoris;* related to Greek *kleiein* to close] —'**clitoral** *adj.*

Cllr *abbrev. for* Councillor.

cloaca (kləʊ'eɪkə) *n., pl.* **-cae** (-kiː). **1.** a cavity in the pelvic region of most vertebrates, except higher mammals, and certain invertebrates, into which the alimentary canal and the genital and urinary ducts open. **2.** a sewer. [C18: from Latin: sewer; related to Greek *kluzein* to wash out] —**clo'acal** *adj.*

cloacitis (,kləʊə'saɪtɪs) *n. Vet. science.* inflammation of the cloaca in domestic fowl.

cloak (kləʊk) *n.* **1.** a wraplike outer garment fastened at the throat and falling straight from the shoulders. **2.** something that covers or conceals. ~*vb.* (*tr.*) **3.** to cover with or as if with a cloak. **4.** to hide or disguise. [C13: from Old French *cloque,* from Medieval Latin *clocca* cloak, bell; referring to the bell-like shape]

cloak-and-dagger *n.* (*modifier*) characteristic of or concerned with intrigue and espionage.

cloakroom ('kləʊk,ruːm, -,rʊm) *n.* **1.** a room in which hats, coats, luggage, etc., may be temporarily deposited. **2.** *Brit.* a euphemistic word for **lavatory.**

clobber[1] ('klɒbə) *vb.* (*tr.*) *Slang.* **1.** to beat or batter. **2.** to defeat utterly. **3.** to criticize severely. [C20: of unknown origin]

clobber[2] ('klɒbə) *n. Brit. slang.* personal belongings, such as clothes and accessories. [C19: of unknown origin]

clobber[3] ('klɒbə) *vb.* (*tr.*) to paint over existing decoration on (pottery). [C19 (originally in the sense: to patch up): of uncertain origin; perhaps related to CLOBBER[2]]

clobbering machine *n. N.Z. informal.* pressure to conform with accepted standards.

cloche (klɒʃ) *n.* **1.** a bell-shaped cover used to protect young plants. **2.** a woman's almost brimless close-fitting hat, typical of the 1920s and 1930s. [C19: from French: bell, from Medieval Latin *clocca*]

clock[1] (klɒk) *n.* **1.** a timepiece, usually free-standing, hanging, or built into a tower, having mechanically or electrically driven pointers that move constantly over a dial showing the numbers of the hours. Compare **digital clock, watch** (sense 7). **2.** any clocklike device for recording or measuring, such as a taximeter or pressure gauge. **3.** the downy head of a dandelion that has gone to seed. **4.** an electrical circuit which generates pulses at a predetermined rate and interval. **5.** *Computer technol.* an electronic pulse generator that transmits streams of regular pulses to which various parts of the computer and its operations are synchronized. **6.** short for **time clock. 7. around** *or* **round the clock.** all day and all night. **8.** (usually preceded by *the*) an informal word for **speedometer** or **mileometer. 9.** *Brit.* a slang word for **face. 10. against the clock. a.** under pressure, as to meet a deadline. **b.** (in certain sports, such as show jumping) timed by a stop clock: *the last round will be against the clock.* **11. put the clock back.** to regress. ~*vb.* **12.** (*tr.*) *Brit., Austral. and N.Z. slang.* to strike, esp. on the face or head. **13.** (*tr.*) *Brit. slang.* to see or notice. **14.** (*tr.*) to record time as with a stopwatch, esp. in the calculation of speed. **15.** *Electronics.* to feed a clock pulse to (a digital device) in order to cause it to switch to a new state. ~See also **atomic clock, biological clock, clock off, clock on, clock up.** [C14: from Middle Dutch *clocke* clock, from Medieval Latin *clocca* bell, ultimately of Celtic origin] —'**clocker** *n.* —'**clock,like** *adj.*

clock[2] (klɒk) *n.* an ornamental design either woven in or embroidered on the side of a stocking. [C16: from Middle Dutch *clocke,* from Medieval Latin *clocca* bell]

clock golf *n.* a putting game played on a circular area on a lawn.

clockmaker ('klɒk,meɪkə) *n.* a person who makes or mends clocks, watches, etc.

clock off *or* **out** *vb.* (*intr., adv.*) to depart from work, esp. when it involves registering the time of departure on a card.

clock on *or* **in** *vb.* (*intr., adv.*) to arrive at work, esp. when it involves registering the time of arrival on a card.

clock up *vb.* (*tr., adv.*) to record or register: *this car has clocked up 80 000 miles.*

clock-watcher *n.* an employee who checks the time in anticipation of a break or of the end of the working day.

clockwise ('klɒk,waɪz) *adv., adj.* in the direction that the hands of a clock rotate; from top to bottom towards the right when seen from the front.

clockwork ('klɒk,wɜːk) *n.* **1.** the mechanism of a clock. **2.** any similar mechanism, as in a wind-up toy. **3. like clockwork.** with complete regularity and precision.

clod (klɒd) *n.* **1.** a lump of earth or clay. **2.** earth, esp. when heavy or in hard lumps. **3.** Also called: **clodpole, clod poll, clodpate.** a dull or stupid person. **4.** a cut of beef taken from the shoulder. [Old English *clod-* (occurring in compound words) lump; related to CLOUD] —'**cloddy** *adj.* —'**cloddish** *adj.* —'**cloddishly** *adv.* —'**cloddishness** *n.*

clodhopper ('klɒd,hɒpə) *n. Informal.* **1.** a clumsy person; lout. **2.** (*usually pl.*) a large heavy shoe or boot. —'**clod,hopping** *adj.*

clog (klɒg) *vb.* **clogs, clogging, clogged. 1.** to obstruct or become obstructed with thick or sticky matter. **2.** (*tr.*) to encumber; hinder; impede. **3.** (*tr.*) to fasten a clog or impediment to (an animal, such as a horse). **4.** (*intr.*) to adhere or stick in a mass. **5.** *Slang.* (in soccer) to foul (an opponent). ~*n.* **6. a.** any of various wooden or wooden-soled shoes. **b.** (*as modifier*): *clog dance.* **7.** a heavy block, esp. of wood, fastened to the leg of a person or animal to impede motion. **8.** something that impedes motion or action; hindrance. [C14 (in the sense: block of wood): of unknown origin] —'**cloggy** *adj.* —'**clogginess** *n.*

cloisonné (klwɑː'zɒneɪ; *French* klwazɔne) *n.* **1. a.** a design made by filling in with coloured enamel an outline of flattened wire put on edge. **b.** the method of doing this. ~*adj.* **2.** of, relating to, or made by cloisonné. [C19: from French, from *cloisonner* to divide into compartments, from *cloison* partition, ultimately from Latin *claudere* to CLOSE[2]]

cloister ('klɔɪstə) *n.* **1.** a covered walk, usually around a quadrangle in a religious institution, having an open arcade or colonnade on the inside and a wall on the outside. **2.** (*sometimes pl.*) a place of religious seclusion, such as a monastery. **3.** life in a monastery or convent. ~*vb.* **4.** (*tr.*) to confine or seclude in or as if in a monastery. [C13: from Old French *cloistre,* from Medieval Latin *claustrum* monastic cell, from Latin: bolt, barrier, from *claudere* to close; influenced in form by Old French *cloison* partition] —'**cloister-,like** *adj.*

cloistered ('klɔɪstəd) *adj.* **1.** secluded or shut up from the world. **2.** living in a monastery or nunnery. **3.** (of a building, courtyard, etc.) having or provided with a cloister.

cloistral ('klɔɪstrəl) *or* **claustral** *adj.* of, like, or characteristic of a cloister.

clomb (kləʊm) *vb. Archaic.* a past tense and past participle of **climb.**

clomiphene ('kləʊmɪ,fiːn) *n.* a drug that stimulates the production of egg cells in the ovary: used to treat infertility in women.

clomp (klɒmp) *n., vb.* a less common word for **clump** (senses 2, 7).

clone (kləʊn) *n.* **1.** a group of organisms or cells of the same genetic constitution that are descended from a common ancestor by asexual reproduction, as by cuttings, grafting, etc., in plants. **2.** Also called: **gene clone.** a segment of DNA that has been isolated and replicated by laboratory manipulation: used to analyse genes and manufacture their products (proteins). **3.** *Informal.* a person or thing bearing a very close resemblance to another person or thing. ~*vb.* **4.** to produce or cause to produce a clone. **5.** *Informal.* to produce near copies (of a person or thing). [C20: from Greek *klōn* twig, shoot; related to *klan* to break] —'**clonal** *adj.* —'**clonally** *adv.*

clonk (klɒŋk) *vb.* **1.** (*intr.*) to make a loud dull thud. **2.** (*tr.*) *Informal.* to hit. ~*n.* **3.** a loud thudding sound. [C20: of imitative origin]

clonus ('kləʊnəs) *n.* a type of convulsion characterized by rapid contraction and relaxation of a muscle. [C19: from New Latin, from Greek *klonos* turmoil] —**clonic** ('klɒnɪk) *adj.* —**clonicity** (klɒ'nɪsɪtɪ) *n.*

clop (klɒp) *vb.* **clops, clopping, clopped. 1.** (*intr.*) to make or move along with a sound as of a horse's hooves striking the ground. ~*n.* **2.** a sound of this nature. [C20: of imitative origin]

cloqué ('klɒkeɪ) *n.* **a.** a fabric with an embossed surface. **b.** (*as modifier*): *a cloqué dress.* [from French, literally: blistered]

close[1] (kləʊs) *adj.* **1.** near in space or time; in proximity. **2.** having the parts near together; dense: *a close formation.* **3.** down or near to the surface; short: *a close haircut.* **4.** near in relationship: *a close relative.* **5.** intimate or confidential: *a close friend.* **6.** almost equal or even: *a close contest.* **7.** not deviating or varying greatly from a model or standard: *a close resemblance; a close translation.* **8.** careful, strict, or searching: *a close study.* **9.** (of a style of play in football, hockey, etc.) characterized by short passes. **10.** confined or enclosed. **11.** shut or shut tight. **12.** oppressive, heavy, or airless: *a close atmosphere.* **13.** strictly guarded: *a close prisoner.* **14.** neat or tight in fit: *a close cap.* **15.** secretive or reticent. **16.** miserly; not generous, esp. with money. **17.** (of money or credit) hard to obtain; scarce. **18.** restricted as to public admission or membership. **19.** hidden or secluded. **20.** Also: **closed.** restricted or prohibited as to the type of game or fish able to be taken. **21.** Also: **closed, narrow.** *Phonetics.* denoting a vowel pronounced with the lips relatively close together. ~*adv.* **22.** closely; tightly. **23.** near or in proximity. **24. close to the wind.** *Nautical.* sailing as nearly as possible towards the direction from which the wind is blowing. See also **wind**[1] (sense 26). [C13: from Old French *clos* close, enclosed, from Latin *clausus* shut up, from *claudere* to close] —'**closely** *adv.* —'**closeness** *n.*

close[2] (kləʊz) *vb.* **1.** to put or be put in such a position as to cover an opening; shut: *the door closed behind him.* **2.** (*tr.*) to bar, obstruct, or fill up (an entrance, a hole, etc.): *to close a road.* **3.** to bring the parts or edges of (a wound, etc.) together or (of a wound, etc.) to be brought together. **4.** (*intr.*; foll. by *on, over,* etc.) to take hold: *his hand closed over the money.* **5.** to bring or be brought to an end; terminate. **6.** to complete (an agreement, a deal, etc.) successfully or (of an agreement, deal, etc.) to be completed successfully. **7.** to cease or cause to cease to render service: *the shop closed at six.* **8.** (*intr.*) *Stock Exchange.* to have a value at the end of a day's trading, as specified: *steels closed two points down.* **9.** to complete an electrical circuit. **10.** (*tr.*) *Nautical.* to pass near. **11.** (*tr.*) *Archaic.* to enclose or shut in. **12. close one's eyes. a.** *Euphemistic.* to die. **b.** (often foll. by *to*) to ignore. ~*n.* **13.** the act of closing. **14.** the end or conclusion: *the close of the day.* **15.** a place of joining or meeting. **16.** (kləʊs). *Law.* private property, usually enclosed by a fence, hedge, or wall. **17.** (kləʊs). *Brit.* a courtyard or quadrangle enclosed by buildings or an entry leading to such a courtyard. **18.** (kləʊs). *Brit.* (*cap. when part of a street name*) a small quiet residential road: *Hillside Close.* **19.** *Brit.* a field. **20.** (kləʊs). the precincts of a cathedral or similar building. **21.** (kləʊs) *Scot.* the entry from the street to a tenement building. **22.** *Music.* another word for **cadence.** A perfect cadence is called a **full close,** an imperfect one a **half close. 23.** *Archaic or rare.* an encounter in battle; grapple. ~See also **close down, close in, close out, close-up, close with.** —**closer** ('kləʊzə) *n.*

close call (kləʊs) *n. U.S. and Canadian.* another expression for **close shave.**

close company (kləʊs) *n. Brit.* a company under the control of its directors or fewer than five independent participants. Also called: **closed company.**

closed (kləʊzd) *adj.* **1.** blocked against entry; shut. **2.** restricted; exclusive. **3.** not open to question or debate. **4.** (of a hunting season, etc.) close. **5.** *Maths.* **a.** (of a curve or surface) completely enclosing an area or volume. **b.** (of a set) having members that can be produced by a specific operation on other members of the same set: *the integers are a closed set under multiplication.* **6.** Also: **checked.** *Phonetics.* **a.** denoting a syllable that ends in a consonant. **b.** another word for **close**[1] (sense 21). **7.** not open to public entry or membership: *a closed society.*

closed book *n.* **1.** something deemed unknown or incapable of being understood. **2.** a matter that has been finally concluded and admits of no further consideration.

closed chain *n. Chem.* another name for **ring**[1] (sense 18).

closed circuit *n.* a complete electrical circuit through which current can flow when a voltage is applied. Compare **open circuit.**

closed-circuit television *n.* a television system in which signals are transmitted from the television camera to the receivers by cables or telephone links forming a closed circuit, as used in shops, hospitals, etc.

closed community *n. Ecology.* a plant community that does not allow for further colonization, all the available niches being occupied.

closed corporation *n. U.S.* a corporation the stock of which is owned by a small number of persons and is rarely traded on the open market. Also: **close corporation.**

closed cycle *n. Engineering.* a heat engine in which the working substance is continuously circulated and does not need replenishment.

closed-door *adj.* private; barred to members of the public: *a closed-door meeting.*

closed game *n. Chess.* a relatively complex game involving closed ranks and files and permitting only nontactical positional manoeuvring. Compare **open game.**

close down (kləʊz) *vb.* (*adv.*) **1.** to cease or cause to cease operations: *the shop closed down.* ~*n.* **close-down** (ˈkləʊzˌdaʊn). **2.** a closure or stoppage of operations, esp. in a factory. **3.** *Brit. radio, television.* the end of a period of broadcasting, esp. late at night.

closed primary *n. U.S. government.* a primary in which only members of a particular party may vote. Compare **open primary.**

closed scholarship *n.* a scholarship for which only certain people, such as those from a particular school or with a particular surname, are eligible.

closed sentence *n. Logic.* a formula that contains no free occurrence of any variable. Compare **open sentence.**

closed set *n. Maths.* **1.** a set that includes all the values obtained by application of a given operation to its members. **2.** a topological set containing all its own limit points. **3.** an interval on the real line including its end points, as [0, 1], the set of reals between and including 0 and 1.

closed shop *n.* an industrial establishment in which there exists a contract between a trade union and the employer permitting the employment of the union's members only. Compare **open shop** (sense 1), **union shop.**

close-fisted (ˌkləʊsˈfɪstɪd) *adj.* very careful with money; mean. —ˌ**close-ˈfistedness** *n.*

close-grained (ˌkləʊsˈgreɪnd) *adj.* (of wood) dense or compact in texture.

close harmony (kləʊs) *n.* a type of singing in which all the parts except the bass lie close together and are confined to the compass of a tenth.

close-hauled (ˌkləʊsˈhɔːld) *adj. Nautical.* with the sails flat, so as to sail as close to the wind as possible.

close in (kləʊz) *vb.* (*intr., adv.*) **1.** (of days) to become shorter with the approach of winter. **2.** (foll. by *on* or *upon*) to advance (on) so as to encircle or surround.

close-knit (ˌkləʊsˈnɪt) *adj.* closely united, esp. by social ties.

close-lipped (ˌkləʊsˈlɪpt) *or* **close-mouthed** (ˌkləʊsˈmaʊðd, -ˈmaʊθt) *adj.* not talking or revealing much.

close out (kləʊz) *vb.* (*adv.*) to terminate (a client's or other account) on which the margin is inadequate or exhausted, usually by sale of securities to realize cash.

close punctuation (kləʊs) *n.* punctuation in which many commas, full stops, etc., are used. Compare **open punctuation.**

close quarters (kləʊs) *pl. n.* **1.** a narrow cramped space or position. **2. at close quarters. a.** engaged in hand-to-hand combat. **b.** in close proximity; very near together.

close season (kləʊs) *or* **closed season** *n.* the period of the year when it is prohibited to kill certain game or fish.

close shave (kləʊs) *n. Informal.* a narrow escape.

close-stool (ˈkləʊs ˌstuːl) *n.* a wooden stool containing a covered chamber pot.

closet (ˈklɒzɪt) *n.* **1.** a small cupboard or recess. **2.** a small private room. **3.** short for **water closet. 4.** (*modifier*) *U.S. and Canadian.* private or secret. **5.** (*modifier*) *U.S. and Canadian.* suited or appropriate for use in private: *closet meditations.* **6.** (*modifier*) *U.S. and Canadian.* based on or devoted to theory; speculative: *a closet strategist.* ~*vb.* **-sets, -seting, -seted. 7.** (*tr.*) to shut up or confine in a small private room, esp. for conference or meditation. [C14: from Old French, from *clos* enclosure; see CLOSE[1]]

closet drama *n. Chiefly U.S.* **a.** drama suitable for reading rather than performing. **b.** a play of this kind.

closet queen *n. Informal.* a man who is homosexual but does not admit the fact.

close-up (ˈkləʊsˌʌp) *n.* **1.** a photograph or film or television shot taken at close range. **2.** a detailed or intimate view or examination: *a close-up of modern society.* ~*vb.* **close up** (kləʊz). (*adv.*) **3.** to shut entirely. **4.** (*intr.*) to draw together: *the ranks closed up.* **5.** (*intr.*) (of wounds) to heal completely.

close with (kləʊz) *vb.* (*intr., prep.*) to engage in battle with (an enemy).

closing time (ˈkləʊzɪŋ) *n.* the time at which pubs must legally stop selling alcoholic drinks.

clostridium (klɒˈstrɪdɪəm) *n., pl.* **-iums** *or* **-ia** (-ɪə). any anaerobic typically rod-shaped bacterium of the genus *Clostridium*, occurring in soil and the intestines of man and animals: family *Bacillaceae.* The genus includes the species causing botulism and tetanus. [C20: from New Latin, literally: small spindle, from Greek *klōstēr* spindle, from *klōthein* to spin; see -IUM] —**closˈtridial** *or* **closˈtridian** *adj.*

closure (ˈkləʊʒə) *n.* **1.** the act of closing or the state of being closed. **2.** an end or conclusion. **3.** something that closes or shuts, such as a cap or seal for a container. **4.** (in a deliberative body) a procedure by which debate may be halted and an immediate vote taken. See also **cloture, guillotine, gag rule. 5.** *Geology.* the vertical distance between the crest of an anticline and the lowest contour that surrounds it. **6.** *Phonetics.* the obstruction of the breath stream at some point along the vocal tract, such as the complete occlusion preliminary to the articulation of a stop. **7.** *Logic.* **a.** the closed sentence formed from a given open sentence by prefixing universal or existential quantifiers to bind all its free variables. **b.** the process of forming such a closed sentence. **8.** *Maths.* **a.** the smallest closed set containing a given set. **b.** the operation of forming such a set. **9.** *Psychol.* the tendency, first noted by Gestalt psychologists, to see an incomplete figure like a circle with a gap in it as more complete than it is. ~*vb.* **10.** (*tr.*) (in a deliberative body) to end (debate) by closure. [C14: from Old French, from Late Latin *clausūra* bar, from Latin *claudere* to close]

clot (klɒt) *n.* **1.** a soft thick lump or mass: *a clot of blood.* **2.** *Brit. informal.* a stupid person; fool. ~*vb.* **clots, clotting, clotted. 3.** to form or cause to form into a soft thick lump or lumps. [Old English *clott*, of Germanic origin; compare Middle Dutch *klotte* block, lump] —ˈ**clottish** *adj.*

cloth (klɒθ) *n., pl.* **cloths** (klɒθs, klɒðz). **1. a.** a fabric formed by weaving, felting or knitting wool, cotton, etc. **b.** (*as modifier*): *a cloth bag.* **2.** a piece of such fabric used for a particular purpose, as for a dishcloth. **3.** (usually preceded by *the*) **a.** the clothes worn by a clergyman. **b.** the clergy. **4.** *Obsolete.* clothing. **5.** *Nautical.* any of the panels of a sail. **6.** *Chiefly Brit.* a piece of coloured fabric, used on the stage as scenery. **7.** *West African.* a garment in a traditional non-European style. [Old English *clāth*; related to Old Frisian *klēth*, Middle High German *kleit* cloth, clothing]

clothbound (ˈklɒθˌbaʊnd) *adj.* (of a book) bound in stiff boards covered in cloth.

cloth cap *n. Brit.* **1.** Also called: **flat cap.** a flat woollen cap with a stiff peak. **2.** *Informal.* **a.** a symbol of working-class ethos or origin. **b.** (*as modifier*): *cloth-cap attitudes.*

clothe (kləʊð) *vb.* **clothes, clothing, clothed** *or* **clad.** (*tr.*) **1.** to dress or attire (a person). **2.** to provide with clothing or covering. **3.** to conceal or disguise. **4.** to endow or invest. [Old English *clāthian*, from *clāth* CLOTH; related to Old Norse *klætha*]

cloth-eared *adj. Informal.* **1.** deaf. **2.** insensitive.

clothes (kləʊðz) *pl. n.* **1. a.** articles of dress. **b.** (*as modifier*): *clothes brush.* **2.** *Chiefly Brit.* short for **bedclothes.** [Old English *clāthas*, plural of *clāth* CLOTH]

clotheshorse (ˈkləʊðzˌhɔːs) *n.* **1.** a frame on which to hang laundry for drying or airing. **2.** *Informal.* a dandy.

clothesline (ˈkləʊðzˌlaɪn) *n.* a piece of rope, cord, or wire on which clean washing is hung to dry or air.

clothes moth *n.* any of various tineid moths, esp. *Tineola bisselliella*, the larvae of which feed on wool or fur.

clothes peg *n.* a small wooden or plastic clip for attaching washing to a clothesline.

clothes pole *n.* **1.** a post to which a clothesline is attached. Also called: **clothes post. 2.** *Scot., U.S.* another term for **clothes prop.**

clothes-press *n.* a piece of furniture for storing clothes, usually containing wide drawers and a cabinet.

clothes prop *n.* a long wooden pole with a forked end, used to raise a line of washing to enable it to catch the breeze.

clothier (ˈkləʊðɪə) *n.* a person who makes, sells, or deals in clothes or cloth.

clothing (ˈkləʊðɪŋ) *n.* **1.** garments collectively. **2.** something that covers or clothes.

cloth of gold *n.* cloth woven from silk threads interspersed with gold.

clotted cream *n. Brit.* a thick cream made from scalded milk, esp. in SW England. Also called: **Devonshire cream.**

clotting factor *n.* any one of a group of substances, including factor VIII, the presence of which in the blood is essential for blood clotting to occur. Also called: **coagulation factor.**

cloture (ˈkləʊtʃə) *n.* **1.** closure in the U.S. Senate. ~*vb.* **2.** (*tr.*) to end (debate) in the U.S. Senate by cloture. [C19: from French *clôture*, from Old French CLOSURE]

cloud (klaʊd) *n.* **1.** a mass of water or ice particles visible in the sky, usually white or grey, from which rain or snow falls when the particles coagulate. See also **cirrus, cumulonimbus, cumulus, stratus. 2.** any collection of particles visible in the air, esp. of smoke or dust. **3.** a large number of insects or other small animals in flight. **4.** something that darkens, threatens, or carries gloom. **5.** *Jewellery.* a cloudlike blemish in a transparent stone. **6. in the clouds.** not in contact with reality. **7. under a cloud. a.** under reproach or suspicion. **b.** in a state of gloom or bad temper. **8. on cloud nine.** *Informal.* elated; very happy. ~*vb.* **9.** (when *intr.*, often foll. by *over* or *up*) to make or become cloudy, overcast, or indistinct. **10.** (*tr.*) to make obscure; darken. **11.** (*tr.*) to confuse or impair: *emotion clouded his judgment.* **12.** to make or become gloomy or depressed. **13.** (*tr.*) to place under or render liable to suspicion or disgrace. **14.** to render (liquids) milky or dull or (of liquids) to become milky or dull. **15.** to become or render mottled or variegated. [C13 (in the sense: a mass of vapour): from Old English *clūd* rock, hill; probably related to CLOD] —'**cloudless** *adj.* —'**cloudlessly** *adv.* —'**cloudlessness** *n.* —'**cloud,like** *adj.*

cloudberry ('klaʊdbərɪ, -brɪ) *n., pl.* **-ries.** a creeping Eurasian herbaceous rosaceous plant, *Rubus chamaemorus,* with white flowers and orange berry-like fruits (drupelets).

cloudburst ('klaʊd,bɜːst) *n.* a heavy downpour.

cloud chamber *n. Physics.* an apparatus for detecting high-energy particles by observing their tracks through a chamber containing a supersaturated vapour. Each particle ionizes molecules along its path and small droplets condense on them to produce a visible track. Also called: **Wilson cloud chamber.**

cloud-cuckoo-land *or* **cloudland** ('klaʊd,lænd) *n.* a realm of fantasy, dreams, or impractical notions.

clouded yellow *n.* See **yellow** (sense 6).

cloudlet ('klaʊdlɪt) *n.* a small cloud.

cloud rack *n.* a group of moving clouds.

cloudscape ('klaʊdskeɪp) *n.* **1.** a picturesque formation of clouds. **2.** a picture or photograph of such a formation.

cloudy ('klaʊdɪ) *adj.* **cloudier, cloudiest. 1.** covered with cloud or clouds. **2.** of or like a cloud or clouds. **3.** streaked or mottled like a cloud. **4.** opaque or muddy. **5.** obscure or unclear. **6.** troubled by gloom or depression: *his face had a cloudy expression.* —'**cloudily** *adv.* —'**cloudiness** *n.*

clough (klʌf) *n. Dialect.* a gorge or narrow ravine. [Old English *clōh*]

clout (klaʊt) *n.* **1.** *Informal.* a blow with the hand or a hard object. **2.** power or influence, esp. in politics. **3.** *Archery.* **a.** the target used in long-distance shooting. **b.** the centre of this target. **c.** a shot that hits the centre. **4.** Also called: **clout nail.** a short, flat-headed nail used esp. for attaching sheet metal to wood. **5.** *Brit. dialect.* **a.** a piece of cloth: *a dish clout.* **b.** a garment. **c.** a patch. *~vb.* (*tr.*) **6.** *Informal.* to give a hard blow to, esp. with the hand. **7.** to patch with a piece of cloth or leather. [Old English *clūt* piece of metal or cloth, *clūtian* to patch (C14: to strike with the hand); related to Dutch *kluit* a lump, and to CLOD] —'**clouter** *n.*

clove[1] (kləʊv) *n.* **1.** a tropical evergreen myrtaceous tree, *Eugenia aromatica,* native to the East Indies but cultivated elsewhere, esp. Zanzibar. **2.** the dried unopened flower buds of this tree, used as a pungent fragrant spice. [C14: from Old French *clou de girofle,* literally: nail of clove, *clou* from Latin *clāvus* nail + *girofle* clove tree]

clove[2] (kləʊv) *n.* any of the segments of a compound bulb that arise from the axils of the scales of a large bulb. [Old English *clufu* bulb; related to Old High German *klovolouh* garlic; see CLEAVE[1]]

clove[3] (kləʊv) *vb.* a past tense of **cleave**[1].

clove hitch *n.* a knot or hitch used for securing a rope to a spar, post, or larger rope.

cloven ('kləʊvᵊn) *vb.* **1.** a past participle of **cleave**[1]. *~adj.* **2.** split; cleft; divided.

cloven hoof *or* **foot** *n.* **1.** the divided hoof of a pig, goat, cow, deer, or related animal, which consists of the two middle digits of the foot. **2.** the mark or symbol of Satan. —,**cloven-'hoofed** *or* ,**cloven-'footed** *adj.*

clove oil *n.* a volatile pale-yellow aromatic oil obtained from clove flowers, formerly much used in confectionery, dentistry, and microscopy. Also called: **oil of cloves.**

clove pink *n.* another name for **carnation** (sense 1).

clover ('kləʊvə) *n.* **1.** any plant of the papilionaceous genus *Trifolium,* having trifoliate leaves and dense flower heads. Many species, such as red clover, white clover, and alsike, are grown as forage plants. **2.** any of various similar or related plants. **3. sweet clover.** another name for **melilot. 4. pin clover.** another name for **alfilaria. 5. in clover.** *Informal.* in a state of ease or luxury. [Old English *clāfre;* related to Old High German *klēo,* Middle Low German *klēver,* Dutch *klāver*]

cloverleaf ('kləʊvə,liːf) *n., pl.* **-leaves. 1.** an arrangement of connecting roads, resembling a four-leaf clover in form, that joins two intersecting main roads. **2.** (*modifier*) in the shape or pattern of a leaf of clover.

cloverleaf aerial *n.* a type of aerial, having three or four similar coplanar loops arranged symmetrically around an axis, to which in-phase signals are fed.

clovis point ('kləʊvɪs) *n.* a concave-based flint projectile dating from the 10th millennium B.C., found throughout most of Central and North America.

clown (klaʊn) *n.* **1.** a comic entertainer, usually grotesquely costumed and made up, appearing in the circus. **2.** any performer who elicits an amused response. **3.** someone who plays jokes or tricks. **4.** a person who acts in a comic or buffoon-like manner. **5.** a coarse clumsy rude person; boor. **6.** *Archaic.* a countryman or rustic. *~vb.* (*intr.*) **7.** to perform as a clown. **8.** to play jokes or tricks. **9.** to act foolishly. [C16: perhaps of Low German origin; compare Frisian *klönne,* Icelandic *klunni* clumsy fellow] —'**clownery** *n.* —'**clownish** *adj.* —'**clownishly** *adv.* —'**clownishness** *n.*

cloxacillin (,klɒksə'sɪlɪn) *n.* a semisynthetic penicillin used to treat staphylococcal infections due to penicillin-resistant organisms.

cloy (klɔɪ) *vb.* to make weary or cause weariness through an excess of something initially pleasurable or sweet. [C14 (originally: to nail, hence, to obstruct): from earlier *acloyen,* from Old French *encloer,* from Medieval Latin *inclavāre,* from Latin *clāvāre* to nail, from *clāvus* a nail] —**cloyedness** ('klɔɪɪdnɪs) *n.* —'**cloyingly** *adv.* —'**cloyingness** *n.*

cloze test (kləʊz) *n.* a test of the ability to comprehend text in which the reader has to supply the missing words that have been removed from the text at regular intervals. [altered from *close* to complete a pattern (in Gestalt theory)]

club (klʌb) *n.* **1.** a stout stick, usually with one end thicker than the other, esp. one used as a weapon. **2.** a stick or bat used to strike the ball in various sports, esp. golf. See **golf club. 3.** short for **Indian club. 4.** a group or association of people with common aims or interests: *a wine club.* **5. a.** the room, building, or facilities used by such a group. **b.** (*in combination*): *clubhouse.* **6.** a building in which elected, fee-paying members go to meet, dine, read, etc. **7.** a commercial establishment in which people can drink and dance; disco. See also **nightclub. 8.** *Chiefly Brit.* an organization, esp. in a shop, set up as a means of saving. **9.** *Brit.* an informal word for **friendly society. 10. a.** the black trefoil symbol on a playing card. **b.** a card with one or more of these symbols or (*when pl.*) the suit of cards so marked. **11.** *Nautical.* **a.** a spar used for extending the clew of a gaff topsail beyond the peak of the gaff. **b.** short for **club foot** (sense 3). **12. in the club.** *Brit. slang.* pregnant. **13. on the club.** *Brit. slang.* away from work due to sickness, esp. when receiving sickness benefit. *~vb.* **clubs, clubbing, clubbed. 14.** (*tr.*) to beat with or as if with a club. **15.** (often foll. by *together*) to gather or become gathered into a group. **16.** (often foll. by *together*) to unite or combine (resources, efforts, etc.) for a common purpose. **17.** (*tr.*) to use (a rifle or similar firearm) as a weapon by holding the barrel and hitting with the butt. **18.** (*intr.*) *Nautical.* to drift in a current, reducing speed by dragging anchor. [C13: from Old Norse *klubba,* related to Middle High German *klumpe* group of trees, CLUMP, Old English *clympre* lump of metal] —'**clubbing** *n.*

clubbable *or* **clubable** ('klʌbəbᵊl) *adj.* suitable to be a member of a club; sociable. —,**clubba'bility** *or* ,**cluba'bility** *n.*

clubber ('klʌbə) *n.* a person who regularly frequents nightclubs and similar establishments.

clubby ('klʌbɪ) *adj.* **-bier, -biest. 1.** sociable, esp. effusively so. **2.** exclusive or cliquish. —'**clubbily** *adv.*

club foot *n.* **1.** a congenital deformity of the foot, esp. one in which the foot is twisted so that most of the weight rests on the heel. Technical name: **talipes. 2.** a foot so deformed. **3.** *Nautical.* a boom attached to the foot of a jib. —,**club-'footed** *adj.*

club hand *n.* **1.** a deformity of the hand, analogous to club foot. **2.** a hand so deformed. —,**club-'handed** *adj.*

clubhaul ('klʌb,hɔːl) *vb. Nautical.* to force (a sailing vessel) onto a new tack, esp. in an emergency, by fastening a lee anchor to the lee quarter, dropping the anchor as the vessel comes about, and hauling in the anchor cable to swing the stern to windward.

clubhouse ('klʌb,haʊs) *n.* the premises of a sports or other club, esp. a golf club.

clubland ('klʌblənd) *n.* (in Britain) the area of London around St. James's, which contains most of the famous London clubs.

clubman ('klʌbmən) *or* (*fem.*) **clubwoman** *n., pl.* **-men** *or* **-women.** a person who is an enthusiastic member of a club or clubs.

club moss *n.* any mosslike pteridophyte plant of the order *Lycopodiales,* having erect or creeping stems covered with tiny overlapping leaves.

club root *n.* a disease of cabbages and related plants, caused by the fungus *Plasmodiophora brassicae,* in which the roots become thickened and distorted.

club sandwich *n. Chiefly U.S. and Canadian.* a sandwich consisting of three or more slices of toast or bread with a filling.

cluck (klʌk) *n.* **1.** the low clicking sound made by a hen or any similar sound. *~vb.* **2.** (*intr.*) (of a hen) to make a clicking sound. **3.** (*tr.*) to call or express (a feeling) by making a similar sound. [C17: of imitative origin]

clucky ('klʌkɪ) *adj. Austral. slang.* pregnant.

clue (kluː) *n.* **1.** something that helps to solve a problem or unravel a mystery. **2. not to have a clue. a.** to be completely baffled. **b.** to be completely ignorant or incompetent. *~vb.* **clues, cluing, clued. 3.** (*tr.;* usually foll. by *in* or *up*) to provide with helpful information. *~n., vb.* **4.** a variant spelling of **clew.** [C15: variant of CLEW]

clued-up *adj. Informal.* shrewd; well-informed.

clueless ('kluːlɪs) *adj. Slang.* helpless; stupid.

clumber spaniel ('klʌmbə) *n.* a type of thickset spaniel having a broad heavy head. Often shortened to **clumber.** [C19: named after *Clumber,* stately home of the Dukes of Newcastle where the breed was developed]

clump (klʌmp) *n.* **1.** a cluster, as of trees or plants. **2.** a dull heavy tread or any similar sound. **3.** an irregular mass: *a clump of hair or earth.* **4.** an inactive mass of microorganisms, esp. a mass of bacteria produced as a result of agglutination. **5.** an extra sole on a shoe. **6.** *Slang.* a blow. *~vb.* **7.** (*intr.*) to walk or tread heavily. **8.** to gather or be gathered into clumps, clusters, clots, etc. **9.** to cause (bacteria, blood cells, etc.) to collect together or (of bacteria, etc.) to collect together. **10.** (*tr.*) *Slang.* to punch (someone). [Old English *clympe;* related to Middle Dutch *klampe* heap of hay, Middle Low German *klampe* CLAMP[2],

Swedish *klimp* small lump] —ˈ**clumpy,** ˈ**clumpish,** *or* ˈ**clump-ˌlike** *adj.*

clumsy (ˈklʌmzɪ) *adj.* **-sier, -siest. 1.** lacking in skill or physical coordination. **2.** awkwardly constructed or contrived. [C16 (in obsolete sense: benumbed with cold; hence, awkward): perhaps from C13 dialect *clumse* to benumb, probably from Scandinavian; compare Swedish dialect *klumsig* numb] —ˈ**clumsily** *adv.* —ˈ**clumsiness** *n.*

clung (klʌŋ) *vb.* the past tense and past participle of **cling.**

clunk (klʌŋk) *n.* **1.** a blow or the sound of a blow. **2.** a dull metallic sound. **3.** a dull or stupid person. **4.** *Chiefly Scot.* **a.** the gurgling sound of a liquid. **b.** the sound of a cork being removed from a bottle. ~*vb.* **5.** to make or cause to make such a sound. [C19: of imitative origin]

Cluny lace (ˈkluːnɪ) *n.* a strong heavy silk and cotton bobbin lace made at Cluny in E central France or elsewhere.

clupeid (ˈkluːpɪɪd) *n.* **1.** any widely distributed soft-finned teleost fish of the family *Clupeidae,* typically having oily flesh, and including the herrings, sardines, shad, etc. ~*adj.* **2.** of, relating to, or belonging to the family *Clupeidae.* [C19: from New Latin *Clupeidae,* from Latin *clupea* small river fish]

clupeoid (ˈkluːpɪˌɔɪd) *adj.* **1.** of, relating to, or belonging to the *Isospondyli* (or *Clupeiformes*), a large order of soft-finned fishes, including the herrings, salmon, and tarpon. ~*n.* **2.** any fish belonging to the order *Isospondyli.* [C19: from Latin *clupea* small fish + -OID]

cluster (ˈklʌstə) *n.* **1.** a number of things growing, fastened, or occurring close together. **2.** a number of persons or things grouped together. **3.** *U.S. Military.* a metal insignia worn on a medal ribbon to indicate a second award or a higher class of a decoration or order. **4.** *Military.* **a.** a group of bombs dropped in one stick, esp. fragmentation and incendiary bombs. **b.** the basic unit of mines used in laying a minefield. **5.** *Astronomy.* an aggregation of stars or galaxies moving together through space. **6.** a group of two or more consecutive vowels or consonants. **7.** *Statistics.* a naturally occurring subgroup of a population used in stratified sampling. **8.** *Chem.* **a.** a chemical compound or molecule containing groups of metal atoms joined by metal-to-metal bonds. **b.** the group of linked metal atoms present. ~*vb.* **9.** to gather or be gathered in clusters. [Old English *clyster;* related to Low German *Kluster;* see CLOD, CLOT] —ˈ**clustered** *adj.* —ˈ**clusteringly** *adv.* —ˈ**clustery** *adj.*

cluster bomb *n.* a bomb that throws out a number of smaller bombs or antipersonnel projectiles when it explodes.

cluster fly *n.* a dipterous fly, *Pollenia rudis,* that tends to gather in large numbers in attics in the autumn: family *Calliphoridae.* The larvae are parasitic in earthworms.

clutch[1] (klʌtʃ) *vb.* **1.** (*tr.*) to seize with or as if with hands or claws. **2.** (*tr.*) to grasp or hold firmly. **3.** (*intr.;* usually foll. by *at*) to attempt to get hold or possession (of). ~*n.* **4.** a device that enables two revolving shafts to be joined or disconnected as required, esp. one that transmits the drive from the engine to the gearbox in a vehicle. **5.** a device for holding fast. **6.** a firm grasp. **7.** a hand, claw, or talon in the act of clutching: *in the clutches of a bear.* **8.** (*often pl.*) power or control: *in the clutches of the Mafia.* **9.** Also called: **clutch bag.** a handbag without handles. [Old English *clyccan;* related to Old Frisian *kletsie* spear, Swedish *klyka* clasp, fork]

clutch[2] (klʌtʃ) *n.* **1.** a hatch of eggs laid by a particular bird or laid in a single nest. **2.** a brood of chickens. **3.** *Informal.* a group, bunch, or cluster. ~*vb.* **4.** (*tr.*) to hatch (chickens). [C17 (Northern English dialect) *cletch,* from Old Norse *klekja* to hatch]

clutter (ˈklʌtə) *vb.* **1.** (*usually tr.;* often foll. by *up*) to strew or amass (objects) in a disorderly manner. **2.** (*intr.*) to move about in a bustling manner. **3.** (*intr.*) to chatter or babble. ~*n.* **4.** a disordered heap or mass of objects. **5.** a state of disorder. **6.** unwanted echoes that confuse the observation of signals on a radar screen. [C15 *clotter,* from *clotteren* to CLOT]

Clydesdale (ˈklaɪdzˌdeɪl) *n.* a heavy powerful breed of carthorse, originally from Scotland.

clype (klaɪp) *Scot.* ~*vb.* (*intr.*) **1.** to tell tales; be an informer. ~*n.* **2.** a person who tells tales. [C15: from Old English *clipian, cleopian;* see CLEPE]

clypeus (ˈklɪpɪəs) *n., pl.* **clypei** (ˈklɪpɪˌaɪ). a cuticular plate on the head of some insects between the labrum and the frons. [C19: from New Latin, from Latin *clipeus* round shield] —ˈ**clypeal** *adj.* —**clypeate** (ˈklɪpɪˌeɪt) *adj.*

clyster (ˈklɪstə) *n. Med.* a former name for **enema.** [C14: from Greek *klustēr,* from *kluzein* to rinse]

cm *symbol for* centimetre.

Cm *the chemical symbol for* curium.

Cmdr *Military. abbrev. for* Commander.

CMEA *abbrev. for* Council for Mutual Economic Assistance. See **Comecon.**

CMF *Austral. abbrev. for* Citizen Military Forces.

CMG *abbrev. for* Companion of St. Michael and St. George (a Brit. title).

cml *abbrev. for* commercial.

CMOS (ˈsiːmɒs) *adj. Computer technol. acronym for* complementary metal oxide silicon: *CMOS memory.*

CMV *abbrev. for* cytomegalovirus.

C/N, c/n, *or* **cn** *Commerce. abbrev. for* credit note.

CNAA (in Britain) *abbrev. for* the Council for National Academic Awards: a degree-awarding body separate from the universities.

CNAR *abbrev. for* compound net annual rate.

CND (in Britain) *abbrev. for* Campaign for Nuclear Disarmament.

cnemis (ˈniːmɪs) *n. Anatomy, zoology.* the shin or tibia. [from Geeek *knēmē* leg] —ˈ**cnemial** *adj.*

cnidarian (naɪˈdɛərɪən, knaɪ-) *n.* **1.** any coelenterate of the subphylum *Cnidaria,* which includes all coelenterates except the ctenophores. ~*adj.* **2.** of, relating to, or belonging to the *Cnidaria.* [C20: from New Latin *Cnidaria,* from Greek *knidē* nettle]

cnidoblast (ˈnaɪdəʊˌblɑːst, ˈknaɪ-) *n. Zoology.* any of the cells of a coelenterate that contain nematocysts. [C19: from New Latin *cnida,* from Greek *knidē* nettle + -BLAST]

CNS *abbrev. for* central nervous system.

Co *the chemical symbol for* cobalt.

CO *abbrev. for:* **1.** Commanding Officer. **2.** Commonwealth Office. **3.** conscientious objector. ~**4.** *U.S. zip code for* Colorado. ~**5.** *international car registration number for* Colombia.

Co. *or* **co.** *abbrev. for:* **1.** (*esp. in names of business organizations*) Company. **2. and co.** (kəʊ) *Informal.* and the rest of them: *Harold and co.*

Co. *abbrev. for* County.

co- *prefix.* **1.** together; joint or jointly; mutual or mutually: *coproduction.* **2.** indicating partnership or equality: *cofounder; copilot.* **3.** to the same or a similar degree: *coextend.* **4.** (in mathematics and astronomy) of the complement of an angle: *cosecant; codeclination.* [from Latin, reduced form of COM-]

c/o *abbrev. for:* **1.** care of. **2.** *Book-keeping.* carried over.

CoA *abbrev. for* coenzyme A.

coacervate (kəʊˈæsəvɪt, -ˌveɪt) *n.* either of two liquid phases that may separate from a hydrophilic sol, each containing a different concentration of a dispersed solid. [C17: from Latin *coacervāre* to heap up, from *acervus* a heap] —**coˌacerˈvation** *n.*

coach (kəʊtʃ) *n.* **1.** a vehicle for several passengers, used for transport over long distances, sightseeing, etc. **2.** a large four-wheeled enclosed carriage, usually horse-drawn. **3.** a railway carriage carrying passengers. **4.** a trainer or instructor: *a drama coach.* **5.** a tutor who prepares students for examinations. **6.** *Austral.* a tame bullock used as a decoy to attract wild cattle. ~*vb.* **7.** to give tuition or instruction to (a pupil). **8.** (*tr.*) to transport in a bus or coach. [C16: from French *coche,* from Hungarian *kocsi szekér* wagon of Kocs, village in Hungary where coaches were first made; in the sense: to teach, probably from the idea that the instructor carried his pupils] —ˈ**coacher** *n.*

coach bolt *n.* a large round-headed bolt used esp. to secure wood to masonry. Also called (chiefly U.S. and Canadian): **carriage bolt.**

coach box *n.* the seat of a coachman on a horse-drawn carriage or coach.

coach-built *adj.* (of a vehicle) having specially built bodywork. —ˈ**coach-ˌbuilder** *n.*

coach dog *n.* a former name for **Dalmatian.**

coach house *n.* **1.** a building in which a coach is kept. **2.** Also called: **coaching house, coaching inn.** *History.* an inn along a coaching route at which horses were changed.

coach line *n.* a decorative line on the bodywork of a motor vehicle. Also called: **carriage line.**

coachman (ˈkəʊtʃmən) *n., pl.* **-men. 1.** the driver of a coach or carriage. **2.** a fishing fly with white wings and a brown hackle.

coach screw *n.* a large screw with a square head used in timber work in buildings, etc.

coachwood (ˈkəʊtʃˌwʊd) *n.* an Australian tree, *Ceratopetalum apetalum,* yielding light aromatic wood used for furniture, turnery, etc.

coachwork (ˈkəʊtʃˌwɜːk) *n.* **1.** the design and manufacture of car bodies. **2.** the body of a car.

coaction[1] (kəʊˈækʃən) *n.* **1.** any relationship between organisms within a community. **2.** joint action. [C17: CO- + ACTION] —**coˈactive** *adj.* —**coˈactively** *adv.* —ˌ**coacˈtivity** *n.*

coaction[2] (kəʊˈækʃən) *n. Obsolete.* a force or compulsion, either to compel or restrain. [C14: from Late Latin *coāctiō,* from Latin *cōgere* to constrain, compel]

coadjutant (kəʊˈædʒətənt) *adj.* **1.** cooperating. ~*n.* **2.** a helper.

coadjutor (kəʊˈædʒʊtə) *n.* **1.** a bishop appointed as assistant to a diocesan bishop. **2.** *Rare.* an assistant. [C15: via Old French from Latin *co-* together + *adjūtor* helper, from *adjūtāre* to assist, from *juvāre* to help] —**coˈadjutress** *or* **coˈadjutrix** *fem. n.*

coadunate (kəʊˈædjʊnɪt, -ˌneɪt) *adj. Biology.* another word for **connate** (sense 3). [C19: from Late Latin *coadūnāre* to join together, from Latin *adūnāre* to join to, from *ūnus* one] —**coˌaduˈnation** *n.* —**coˈaduˌnative** *adj.*

coagulant (kəʊˈægjʊlənt) *or* **coagulator** (kəʊˈægjʊˌleɪtə) *n.* a substance that aids or produces coagulation.

coagulase (kəʊˈægjʊˌleɪz) *n.* any enzyme that causes coagulation of blood.

coagulate *vb.* (kəʊˈægjʊˌleɪt). **1.** to cause (a fluid, such as blood) to change into a soft semisolid mass or (of such a fluid) to change into such a mass; clot; curdle. **2.** *Chem.* to separate or cause to separate into distinct constituent phases. ~*n.* (kəʊˈægjʊlɪt, -ˌleɪt). **3.** the solid or semisolid substance produced by coagulation. [C16: from Latin *coāgulāre* to make (a liquid) curdle, from *coāgulum* rennet, from *cōgere* to drive together] —**coˈagulable** *adj.* —**coˌagulaˈbility** *n.* —**coˌaguˈlation** *n.* —**coagulative** (kəʊˈæɡjʊlətɪv) *adj.*

coagulation factor *n. Med.* another name for **clotting factor.**

coagulum (kəʊˈæɡjʊləm) *n., pl.* **-la** (-lə). any coagulated mass; clot; curd. [C17: from Latin: curdling agent; see COAGULATE]

coal (kəʊl) *n.* **1. a.** a compact black or dark-brown carbonaceous rock consisting of layers of partially decomposed vegetation deposited in the Carboniferous period: a fuel and a source of coke, coal gas, and coal tar. See also **anthracite, bituminous coal, lignite, peat**[1]. **b.** (*as modifier*): *coal cellar; coal merchant; coal mine; coal dust.* **2.** one or more lumps of coal. **3.** short for **charcoal. 4. coals to Newcastle.** something supplied where it is already plentiful. **5. haul (someone) over the coals.** to reprimand (someone). ~*vb.* **6.** to take in, provide with, or turn into coal. [Old English *col;* related to Old Norse *kol,* Old High German *kolo,* Old Irish *gūal*] —**ˈcoaly** *adj.*

coaler (ˈkəʊlə) *n.* **1.** a ship, train, etc., used to carry or supply coal. **2.** a person who sells or supplies coal.

coalesce (ˌkəʊəˈlɛs) *vb.* (*intr.*) to unite or come together in one body or mass; merge; fuse; blend. [C16: from Latin *coalēscere* from CO- + *alēscere* to increase, from *alere* to nourish] —**ˌcoaˈlescence** *n.* —**ˌcoaˈlescent** *adj.*

coalface (ˈkəʊlˌfeɪs) *n.* the exposed seam of coal in a mine.

coalfield (ˈkəʊlˌfiːld) *n.* an area rich in deposits of coal.

coalfish (ˈkəʊlˌfɪʃ) *n., pl.* **-fish** *or* **-fishes.** a dark-coloured gadoid food fish, *Pollachius virens,* occurring in northern seas. Also called (Brit.): **saithe, coley.**

coal gas *n.* a mixture of gases produced by the distillation of bituminous coal and used for heating and lighting: consists mainly of hydrogen, methane, and carbon monoxide.

coal heaver *n.* a workman who moves coal.

coal hole *n. Brit. informal.* a small coal cellar.

coalition (ˌkəʊəˈlɪʃən) *n.* **1. a.** an alliance or union between groups, factions, or parties, esp. for some temporary and specific reason. **b.** (*as modifier*): *a coalition government.* **2.** a fusion or merging into one body or mass. [C17: from Medieval Latin *coalitiō,* from Latin *coalēscere* to COALESCE] —**ˌcoaˈlitional** *adj.* —**ˌcoaˈlitionist** *or* **ˌcoaˈlitioner** *n.*

Coal Measures *pl. n.* **the.** a series of coal-bearing rocks formed in the upper Carboniferous period; the uppermost series of the Carboniferous system.

coal miner's lung *n.* an informal name for **anthracosis.**

coal oil *n.* **1.** *U.S. and Canadian.* petroleum or a refined product from petroleum, esp. kerosene. **2.** a crude oil produced, together with coal gas, during the distillation of bituminous coal.

Coalport (ˈkəʊlˌpɔːt) *n. Antiques.* a white translucent bone china having richly coloured moulded patterns, made in the 19th century at Coalport near Shrewsbury.

coal pot *n.* a cooking device using charcoal, consisting of a raised iron bowl and a central grid.

coal scuttle *n.* a domestic metal container for coal.

coal tar *n.* a black tar, produced by the distillation of bituminous coal, that can be further distilled to yield benzene, toluene, xylene, anthracene, phenol, etc.

coal-tar pitch *n.* a residue left by the distillation of coal tar: a mixture of hydrocarbons and finely divided carbon used as a binder for fuel briquettes, road surfaces, and carbon electrodes.

coal tit *n.* a small European songbird, *Parus ater,* having a black head with a white patch on the nape: family *Paridae* (tits).

coaming (ˈkəʊmɪŋ) *n.* a raised frame around the cockpit or hatchway of a vessel for keeping out water. [C17: of unknown origin]

coaptation (ˌkəʊæpˈteɪʃən) *n.* the joining or reuniting of two surfaces, esp. the ends of a broken bone or the edges of a wound. [C16: from Late Latin *coaptātiō* a meticulous joining together, from Latin *co-* together + *aptāre* to fit]

coarctate (kəʊˈɑːkteɪt) *adj.* **1.** (of a pupa) enclosed in a hard barrel-shaped case (puparium), as in the housefly. **2.** crowded or pressed together; constricted. ~*vb.* (*intr.*) **3.** *Pathol.* (esp. of the aorta) to become narrower; become constricted. —**ˌcoarcˈtation** *n.* [C15: from Latin *coarctāre,* to press together, from *artus* tight] —**ˌcoarcˈtation** *n.*

coarse (kɔːs) *adj.* **1.** rough in texture, structure, etc.; not fine: *coarse sand.* **2.** lacking refinement or taste; indelicate; vulgar: *coarse jokes.* **3.** of inferior quality; not pure or choice. **4.** (of a metal) not refined. **5.** (of a screw) having widely spaced threads. [C14: of unknown origin] —**ˈcoarsely** *adv.* —**ˈcoarseness** *n.*

coarse fish *n.* a freshwater fish that is not a member of the salmon family. Compare **game fish.** —**coarse fishing** *n.*

coarse-grained *adj.* **1.** having a large or coarse grain. **2.** (of a person) having a coarse nature; gross.

coarsen (ˈkɔːsᵊn) *vb.* to make or become coarse.

coast (kəʊst) *n.* **1. a.** the line or zone where the land meets the sea or some other large expanse of water. **b.** (*in combination*): *coastland.* Related adj.: **littoral. 2.** *Brit.* the seaside. **3.** *U.S.* **a.** a slope down which a sledge may slide. **b.** the act or an instance of sliding down a slope. **4.** *Obsolete.* borderland or frontier. **5. the coast is clear.** *Informal.* the obstacles or dangers are gone. ~*vb.* **6.** to move or cause to move by momentum or force of gravity. **7.** (*intr.*) to proceed without great effort: *to coast to victory.* **8.** to sail along (a coast). [C13: from Old French *coste* coast, slope, from Latin *costa* side, rib] —**ˈcoastal** *adj.* —**ˈcoastally** *adv.*

coaster (ˈkəʊstə) *n.* **1.** *Brit.* a vessel or trader engaged in coastal commerce. **2.** a small tray, sometimes on wheels, for holding a decanter, wine bottle, etc. **3.** a person or thing that coasts. **4.** a protective disc or mat for glasses or bottles. **5.** *U.S.* short for **roller coaster. 6.** *West African.* a European resident on the coast.

Coaster (ˈkəʊstə) *n. N.Z.* a person from the West Coast of the South Island, New Zealand.

coastguard (ˈkəʊstˌɡɑːd) *n.* **1.** a maritime force which aids shipping, saves lives at sea, prevents smuggling, etc. **2.** Also called: **coastguardsman.** a member of such a force.

coastline (ˈkəʊstˌlaɪn) *n.* the outline of a coast, esp. when seen from the sea, or the land adjacent to it.

coat (kəʊt) *n.* **1.** an outdoor garment with sleeves, covering the body from the shoulder to waist, knee, or foot. **2.** any similar garment, esp. one forming the top to a suit. **3.** a layer that covers or conceals a surface: *a coat of dust.* **4.** the hair, wool, or fur of an animal. **5.** *Rare.* the garb worn by members of a profession or group. **6.** short for **coat of arms. 7. on the coat.** *Austral.* **a.** in disfavour. **b.** (of a bet) not genuine. ~*vb.* **8.** (*tr.;* often foll. by *with*) to cover (with) a layer or covering. **9.** (*tr.*) to provide with a coat. [C16: from Old French *cote* of Germanic origin; compare Old Saxon *kotta,* Old High German *kozzo*]

coat armour *n. Heraldry.* **1.** coat of arms. **2.** an emblazoned surcoat.

coat dress *n.* **1.** a lightweight button-through garment that can be worn either as a dress or as a coat. **2.** formerly, a dress tailored and styled like a coat.

coated (ˈkəʊtɪd) *adj.* **1.** covered with an outer layer, film, etc. **2.** (of paper) having a coating of a mineral, esp. china clay, to provide a very smooth surface. **3.** (of textiles) having been given a plastic or other surface. **4.** *Photog., optics.* another word for **bloomed.**

coatee (kəʊˈtiː, ˈkəʊtiː) *n. Chiefly Brit.* a short coat, esp. for a baby.

coat hanger *n.* a curved piece of wood, wire, plastic, etc., fitted with a hook and used to hang up clothes.

coati (kəʊˈɑːtɪ), **coati-mondi,** *or* **coati-mundi** (kəʊˌɑːtɪˈmʌndɪ) *n., pl.* **-tis** *or* **-dis.** any omnivorous mammal of the genera *Nasua* and *Nasuella,* of Central and South America: family *Procyonidae,* order *Carnivora* (carnivores). They are related to but larger than the raccoons, having a long flexible snout and a brindled coat. [C17: from Portuguese *coati,* from Tupi, literally: belt-nosed, from *cua* belt + *tim* nose]

coating (ˈkəʊtɪŋ) *n.* **1.** a layer or film spread over a surface for protection or decoration. **2.** a heavy fabric suitable for coats. **3.** *Midland English dialect.* a severe rebuke; ticking-off.

coat of arms *n.* **1.** the heraldic bearings of a person, family, or corporation. **2.** a surcoat decorated with family or personal bearings.

coat of mail *n.* a protective garment made of linked metal rings (mail) or of overlapping metal plates; hauberk.

coat-of-mail shell *n.* another name for **chiton** (sense 2).

coat-tail *n.* the long tapering tails at the back of a man's tailed coat.

coauthor (kəʊˈɔːθə) *n.* **1.** a person who shares the writing of a book, article, etc., with another. ~*vb.* **2.** (*tr.*) to be the joint author of (a book, article, etc.).

coax[1] (kəʊks) *vb.* **1.** to seek to manipulate or persuade (someone) by tenderness, flattery, pleading, etc. **2.** (*tr.*) to obtain by persistent coaxing. **3.** (*tr.*) to work on or tend (something) carefully and patiently so as to make it function as one desires: *he coaxed the engine into starting.* **4.** (*tr.*) *Obsolete.* to caress. **5.** (*tr.*) *Obsolete.* to deceive. [C16: verb formed from obsolete noun *cokes* fool, of unknown origin] —**ˈcoaxer** *n.* —**ˈcoaxingly** *adv.*

coax[2] (ˈkəʊæks) *n.* short for **coaxial cable.**

coaxial (kəʊˈæksɪəl) *or* **coaxal** (kəʊˈæksᵊl) *adj.* **1.** having or mounted on a common axis. **2.** *Geometry.* (of a set of circles) having the same radical axis. **3.** *Electronics.* formed from, using, or connected to a coaxial cable.

coaxial cable *n.* a cable consisting of an inner insulated core of stranded or solid wire surrounded by an outer insulated flexible wire braid, used esp. as a transmission line for radio-frequency signals. Often shortened to **coax.**

cob[1] (kɒb) *n.* **1.** a male swan. **2.** a thickset type of riding and draught horse. **3.** short for **corncob, corncob pipe,** or **cobnut. 4.** *Brit.* another name for **hazel** (sense 1). **5.** a small rounded lump or heap of coal, ore, etc. **6.** *Brit. and N.Z.* a building material consisting of a mixture of clay and chopped straw. **7.** Also called: **cob loaf.** *Brit.* a round loaf of bread. ~*vb.* **cobs, cobbing, cobbed. 8.** (*tr.*) *Brit. informal.* to beat, esp. on the buttocks. [C15: of uncertain origin; probably related to Icelandic *kobbi* seal; see CUB]

cob[2] *or* **cobb** (kɒb) *n.* an archaic or dialect name for a **gull,** esp. the greater black-backed gull (*Larus marinus*). [C16: of Germanic origin; related to Dutch *kob, kobbe*]

cobaea (kəʊˈbiːə) *n.* any climbing shrub of the tropical American genus *Cobaea,* esp. *C. scandens,* grown for its large trumpet-shaped purple or white flowers: family *Polemoniaceae.* [named after Bernabé *Cobo* (1572–1659), Jesuit missionary and naturalist]

cobalt (ˈkəʊbɔːlt) *n.* a brittle hard silvery-white element that is a ferromagnetic metal: occurs principally in cobaltite and smaltite and is widely used in alloys. The radioisotope **cobalt-60,** with a half-life of 5.3 years, is used in radiotherapy and as a tracer. Symbol: Co; atomic no.: 27; atomic wt.: 58.933; valency: 2 or 3; relative density: 8.9; melting pt.: 1495°C; boiling pt.: 2870°C. [C17: German *Kobalt,* from Middle High German *kobolt* goblin; from the miners' belief that malicious goblins placed it in the silver ore]

cobalt bloom *n.* another name for **erythrite** (sense 1).

cobalt blue *n.* **1.** Also called: **Thénard's blue.** any greenish-blue pigment containing cobalt aluminate, usually made by heating cobaltous sulphate, aluminium oxide, and phosphoric acid together. **2. a.** a deep blue to greenish-blue colour. **b.** (*as adj.*): *a cobalt-blue car.*

cobalt bomb *n.* **1.** a cobalt-60 device used in radiotherapy. **2.** a nuclear weapon consisting of a hydrogen bomb encased in cobalt, which releases large quantities of radioactive cobalt-60 into the atmosphere.

cobaltic (kəʊˈbɔːltɪk) *adj.* of or containing cobalt, esp. in the trivalent state.

cobaltite (kəʊˈbɔːltaɪt, ˈkəʊbɔːlˌtaɪt) *or* **cobaltine** (ˈkəʊbɔːlˌtiːn, -tɪn) *n.* a rare silvery-white mineral consisting of cobalt arsenic sulphide in cubic crystalline form: a major ore of cobalt, used in ceramics. Formula: CoAsS.

cobaltous (kəʊˈbɔːltəs) *adj.* of or containing cobalt in the divalent state.

cobber (ˈkɒbə) *n. Austral., archaic. and N.Z.* a friend; mate: used as a term of address to males. [C19: from dialect *cob* to take a liking to someone]

cobble[1] (ˈkɒbᵊl) *n.* **1.** short for **cobblestone. 2.** *Geology.* a rock fragment, often rounded, with a diameter of 64–256 mm and thus smaller than a boulder but larger than a pebble. ~*vb.* **3.** (*tr.*) to pave (a road) with cobblestones. ~See also **cobbles.** [C15 (in *cobblestone*): from COB[1]]

cobble[2] (ˈkɒbᵊl) *vb.* (*tr.*) **1.** to make or mend (shoes). **2.** to put together clumsily. [C15: back formation from COBBLER[1]]

cobbler[1] (ˈkɒblə) *n.* **1.** a person who makes or mends shoes. **2.** *Austral. and N.Z. slang.* Also called: **snob.** a difficult sheep that struggles during shearing, often the last sheep to be shorn in the day. [C13 (as surname): of unknown origin]

cobbler[2] (ˈkɒblə) *n.* **1.** a sweetened iced drink, usually made from fruit and wine or liqueur. **2.** *Chiefly U.S.* a hot dessert made of fruit covered with a rich cakelike crust. [C19: (for sense 1) perhaps shortened from *cobbler's punch;* (for both senses) compare *cobble* (vb.)]

cobblers (ˈkɒbləz) *Brit. taboo slang.* ~*pl. n.* **1.** rubbish; nonsense: *a load of old cobblers.* **2.** another word for **testicles.** ~*interj.* **3.** an exclamation of strong disagreement. [C20: from rhyming slang *cobblers' awls* balls]

cobbler's pegs (pɛgz) *pl. n.* a common Australian weed, *Bidens pilosa,* with spiky peglike awns.

cobbler's wax *n.* a resin used for waxing thread.

cobbles (ˈkɒbᵊlz) *pl. n.* **1.** coal in small rounded lumps. **2.** cobblestones.

cobblestone (ˈkɒbᵊlˌstəʊn) *n.* a rounded stone used for paving. Sometimes shortened to **cobble.** Compare **sett.**

cobelligerent (ˌkəʊbɪˈlɪdʒərənt) *n.* a country fighting in a war on the side of another country.

cobia (ˈkəʊbɪə) *n.* a large dark-striped percoid game fish, *Rachycentron canadum,* of tropical and subtropical seas: family *Rachycentridae.* [of unknown origin]

coble (ˈkəʊbᵊl, ˈkɒbᵊl) *n. Scot. and northern English* a small single-masted flat-bottomed fishing boat. [C13: probably of Celtic origin; compare Welsh *ceubal* skiff]

cob money *n.* crude silver coins issued in the Spanish colonies of the New World from about 1600 until 1820.

cobnut (ˈkɒbˌnʌt) *or* **cob** *n.* other names for a **hazelnut.** [C16: from earlier *cobylle nut;* see COBBLE[1], NUT]

COBOL *or* **Cobol** (ˈkəʊˌbɒl) *n.* a high-level computer programming language designed for general commercial use. [C20: *co(mmon) b(usiness) o(riented) l(anguage)*]

cobra (ˈkəʊbrə) *n.* **1.** any highly venomous elapid snake of the genus *Naja,* such as *N. naja* (**Indian cobra**), of tropical Africa and Asia. When alarmed they spread the skin of the neck region into a hood. **2.** any related snake, such as the king cobra. [C19: from Portuguese *cobra* (*de capello*) snake (with a hood), from Latin *colubra* snake]

cobra de capello (diː kəˈpɛləʊ) *n., pl.* **cobras de capello.** a cobra, *Naja tripudians,* that has ringlike markings on the body and exists in many varieties in S and SE Asia.

coburg (ˈkəʊˌbɜːg) *n.* (*sometimes cap.*) a rounded loaf with a cross cut on the top. Also called: **coburg loaf.** [C19: apparently named in honour of Prince Albert (of *Saxe-Coburg-Gotha,* Queen Victoria's consort]

cobweb (ˈkɒbˌwɛb) *n.* **1.** a web spun by certain spiders, esp. those of the family *Theridiidae,* often found in the corners of disused rooms. **2.** a single thread of such a web. **3.** something like a cobweb, as in its flimsiness or ability to trap. [C14: *cob,* from *coppe,* from Old English (*ātor*)*coppe* spider; related to Middle Dutch *koppe* spider, Swedish (dialect) *etterkoppa*] —ˈ**cobˌwebbed** *adj.* —ˈ**cobˌwebby** *adj.*

cobwebs (ˈkɒbˌwɛbz) *pl. n.* **1.** mustiness, confusion, or obscurity. **2.** *Informal.* stickiness of the eyelids experienced upon first awakening.

coca (ˈkəʊkə) *n.* **1.** either of two shrubs, *Erythroxylon coca* or *E. truxiuense,* native to the Andes: family *Erythroxylaceae.* **2.** the dried leaves of these shrubs and related plants, which contain cocaine and are chewed by the peoples of the Andes for their stimulating effects. [C17: from Spanish, from Quechuan *kúka*]

Coca-Cola (ˌkəʊkəˈkəʊlə) *n.* **1.** *Trademark.* a carbonated soft drink flavoured with coca leaves, cola nuts, caramel, etc. **2.** (*modifier*) denoting the spread of American culture and values to other parts of the world: *Coca-Cola generation.*

cocaine *or* **cocain** (kəˈkeɪn) *n.* an addictive narcotic drug derived from coca leaves or synthesized, used medicinally as a topical anaesthetic. Formula: $C_{17}H_{21}NO_4$. [C19: from COCA + -INE[1]]

cocainism (kəʊˈkeɪˌnɪzəm, ˈkəʊkə-) *n.* habitual or excessive use of cocaine, resulting in impaired physical or mental abilities.

cocainize *or* **cocainise** (kəʊˈkeɪˌnaɪz, ˈkəʊkəˌnaɪz) *vb.* (*tr.*) to anaesthetize with cocaine. —ˌ**cocainiˈzation** *or* **coˌcainiˈsation** *n.*

cocci (ˈkɒksaɪ) *n.* the plural of **coccus.**

coccid (ˈkɒksɪd) *n.* any homopterous insect of the superfamily *Coccoidea,* esp. any of the family *Coccidae,* which includes the scale insects. [C19: from New Latin *Coccidae;* see COCCUS]

coccidioidomycosis (kɒkˌsɪdɪˌɔɪdəʊmaɪˈkəʊsɪs) *n.* a disease of the skin or viscera, esp. the lungs, caused by infection with the fungus *Coccidioides immitis.* [C20: from New Latin *Coccidioides* + -O- + MYCOSIS]

coccidiosis (kɒkˌsɪdɪˈəʊsɪs) *n.* any disease of domestic and other animals caused by parasitic protozoa of the order *Coccidia.* One species, *Isospora hominis,* occasionally infects humans. [C19: from New Latin; see COCCUS, -OSIS]

cocciferous (kɒkˈsɪfərəs) *adj.* (of plants) **1.** supporting the cochineal insect. **2.** *Obsolete.* bearing berries.

coccolith (ˈkɒkəlɪθ) *n.* any of the round calcareous plates in chalk formations: formed the outer layer of extinct unicellular plankton. [C19: New Latin, from Greek *kokkos* berry + *lithos* stone]

coccus (ˈkɒkəs) *n., pl.* **-ci** (-saɪ). **1.** any spherical or nearly spherical bacterium, such as a staphylococcus. Compare **bacillus** (sense 1), **spirillum** (sense 1). **2.** the part of a fruit that contains one seed and separates from the whole fruit at maturity. **3.** any of the scale insects of the genus *Coccus.* [C18: from New Latin, from Greek *kokkos* berry, grain] —ˈ**coccoid,** ˈ**coccal,** *or* **coccic** (ˈkɒksɪk) *adj.* —ˈ**coccous** *adj.*

coccyx (ˈkɒksɪks) *n., pl.* **coccyges** (kɒkˈsaɪdʒiːz). a small triangular bone at the end of the spinal column in man and some apes, representing a vestigial tail. [C17: from New Latin, from Greek *kokkux* cuckoo, of imitative origin; from the likeness of the bone to a cuckoo's beak] —**coccygeal** (kɒkˈsɪdʒɪəl) *adj.*

co-channel (ˈkəʊˌtʃænᵊl) *adj.* denoting or relating to a radio transmission that is on the same frequency channel as another: *co-channel interference.*

Cochin (ˈkəʊtʃɪn, ˈkɒtʃ-) *n.* a large breed of domestic fowl with dense plumage and feathered legs. [named after *Cochin,* India]

cochineal (ˌkɒtʃɪˈniːl, ˈkɒtʃɪˌniːl) *n.* **1.** Also called: **cochineal insect.** a Mexican homopterous insect, *Dactylopius coccus,* that feeds on cacti. **2.** a crimson substance obtained from the crushed bodies of these insects, used for colouring food and for dyeing. **3. a.** the colour of this dye. **b.** (*as adj.*): *cochineal shoes.* [C16: from Old Spanish *cochinilla,* from Latin *coccineus* scarlet-coloured, from *coccum* cochineal kermes, from Greek *kokkos* kermes berry]

cochlea (ˈkɒklɪə) *n., pl.* **-leae** (-lɪˌiː). the spiral tube, shaped like a snail's shell, that forms part of the internal ear, converting sound vibrations into nerve impulses. [C16: from Latin: snail, spiral, from Greek *kokhlias;* probably related to Greek *konkhē* CONCH] —ˈ**cochlear** *adj.*

cochleate (ˈkɒklɪˌeɪt, -lɪɪt) *or* **cochleated** *adj. Biology.* shaped like a snail's shell; spirally twisted.

cock[1] (kɒk) *n.* **1.** the male of the domestic fowl. **2. a.** any other male bird. **b.** the male of certain other animals, such as the lobster. **c.** (*as modifier*): *a cock sparrow.* **3.** short for **stopcock** or **weathercock. 4.** a taboo slang word for **penis. 5. a.** the hammer of a firearm. **b.** its position when the firearm is ready to be discharged. **6.** *Brit. informal.* a friend, mate, or fellow. **7.** a jaunty or significant tilting or turning upwards: *a cock of the head.* **8.** *Brit. informal.* nonsense. ~*vb.* **9.** (*tr.*) to set the firing pin, hammer, or breech block of (a firearm) so that a pull on the trigger will release it and thus fire the weapon. **10.** (*tr.*) to set the shutter mechanism of (a camera) so that the shutter can be tripped by pressing the shutter-release button. **11.** (*tr.;* sometimes foll. by *up*) to raise in an alert or jaunty manner. **12.** (*intr.*) to stick or stand up conspicuously. ~See also **cockup.** [Old English *cocc* (referring to the male fowl; the development of C15 sense spout, tap, and other transferred senses is not clear), ultimately of imitative origin; related to Old Norse *kokkr,* French *coq,* Late Latin *coccus*]

cock[2] (kɒk) *n.* **1.** a small, cone-shaped heap of hay, straw, etc. ~*vb.* **2.** (*tr.*) to stack (hay, straw, etc.) in such heaps. [C14 (in Old English, *cocc* is attested in place names): perhaps of Scandinavian origin; compare Norwegian *kok,* Danish dialect *kok*]

cockabully (kɒkəˈbʊlɪ) *n.* any of several small freshwater fish of New Zealand. [from Maori *kokopu*]

cockade (kɒ'keɪd) *n.* a feather or ribbon worn on military headwear. [C18: changed from earlier *cockard,* from French *cocarde,* feminine of *cocard* arrogant, strutting, from *coq* COCK[1]] —**cock'aded** *adj.*

cock-a-doodle-doo (ˌkɒkəˌduːdəl'duː) *interj.* an imitation or representation of a cock crowing.

cock-a-hoop *adj.* (*usually postpositive*) **1.** in very high spirits. **2.** boastful. **3.** askew; confused. [C16: perhaps from the phrase *to set the cock a hoop* to live prodigally, literally: to put a cock on a *hoop,* a full measure of grain]

cock-a-leekie (ˌkɒkə'liːkɪ) *n.* a variant of **cockieleekie.**

cockalorum (ˌkɒkə'lɔːrəm) *n.* **1.** a self-important little man. **2.** bragging talk; crowing. [C18: from COCK[1] + *-alorum,* a variant of Latin genitive plural ending *-orum;* perhaps intended to suggest: the cock of all cocks]

cock-and-bull story *n. Informal.* an obviously improbable story, esp. a boastful one or one used as an excuse.

cockatiel *or* **cockateel** (ˌkɒkə'tiːl) *n.* a crested Australian parrot, *Leptolophus hollandicus,* having a greyish-brown and yellow plumage. [C19: from Dutch *kaketielje,* from Portuguese *cacatilha* a little cockatoo, from *cacatua* COCKATOO]

cockatoo (ˌkɒkə'tuː, 'kɒkəˌtuː) *n., pl.* **-toos.** **1.** any of various parrots of the genus *Kakatoe* and related genera, such as *K. galerita* (**sulphur-crested cockatoo**), of Australia and New Guinea. They have an erectile crest and most of them are light-coloured. **2.** *Austral. and N.Z.* a small farmer or settler. **3.** *Austral. informal.* a lookout during some illegal activity. [C17: from Dutch *kaketoe,* from Malay *kakatua*]

cockatrice ('kɒkətrɪs, -ˌtraɪs) *n.* **1.** a legendary monster, part snake and part cock, that could kill with a glance. **2.** another name for **basilisk** (sense 1). [C14: from Old French *cocatris,* from Medieval Latin *cocatrix,* from Late Latin *calcātrix* trampler, tracker (translating Greek *ikhneumon* ICHNEUMON), from Latin *calcāre* to tread, from *calx* heel]

cockboat ('kɒkˌbəʊt) *or* **cockleboat** *n.* any small boat. [C15 *cokbote,* perhaps ultimately from Late Latin *caudica* dug-out canoe, from Latin *caudex* tree trunk]

cockchafer ('kɒkˌtʃeɪfə) *n.* any of various Old World scarabaeid beetles, esp. *Melolontha melolontha* of Europe, whose larvae feed on crops and grasses. Also called: **May beetle, May bug.** [C18: from COCK[1] + CHAFER]

cockcrow ('kɒkˌkrəʊ) *or* **cockcrowing** *n.* daybreak.

cocked hat *n.* **1.** a hat with opposing brims turned up and caught together in order to give two points (bicorn) or three points (tricorn). **2. knock into a cocked hat.** *Slang.* to outdo or defeat.

cocker[1] ('kɒkə) *n.* **1.** a devotee of cockfighting. **2.** short for **cocker spaniel.**

cocker[2] ('kɒkə) *vb.* **1.** (*tr.*) *Rare.* to pamper or spoil by indulgence. ~*n.* **2.** *Brit. informal.* a mate (esp. in the phrase **old cocker**). [C15: perhaps from COCK[1] with the sense: to make a cock (i.e. pet) of]

cockerel ('kɒkərəl, 'kɒkrəl) *n.* a young domestic cock, usually less than a year old. [C15: diminutive of COCK[1]]

cocker spaniel *n.* a small compact breed of spaniel having sleek silky fur, a domed head, and long fringed ears. [C19 *cocker,* from *cocking* hunting woodcocks]

cockeye ('kɒkˌaɪ) *n. Informal.* an eye affected with strabismus or one that squints.

cockeye bob *or* **cockeyed bob** *n. Austral. slang.* a sudden storm or cyclone.

cockeyed ('kɒkˌaɪd) *adj. Informal.* **1.** afflicted with cross-eye, squint, or any other visible abnormality of the eyes. **2.** appearing to be physically or logically abnormal, absurd, etc.; crooked; askew: *cockeyed ideas.* **3.** drunk.

cock feather *n. Archery.* the odd-coloured feather set on the shaft of an arrow at right angles to the nock. Compare **shaft feather.**

cockfight ('kɒkˌfaɪt) *n.* a fight between two gamecocks fitted with sharp metal spurs. —'**cockˌfighting** *n.*

cockhorse (ˌkɒk'hɔːs) *n.* another name for **rocking horse** or **hobbyhorse.**

cockieleekie, cockyleeky, *or* **cock-a-leekie** ('kɒkə'liːkɪ) *n. Scot.* a soup made from a fowl boiled with leeks.

cockiness ('kɒkɪnɪs) *n.* conceited self-assurance.

cockle[1] ('kɒkəl) *n.* **1.** any sand-burrowing bivalve mollusc of the family *Cardiidae,* esp. *Cardium edule* (**edible cockle**) of Europe, typically having a rounded shell with radiating ribs. **2.** any of certain similar or related molluscs. **3.** short for **cockleshell** (sense 1). **4.** a wrinkle or puckering, as in cloth or paper. **5.** a small furnace or stove. **6. cockles of one's heart.** one's deepest feelings (esp. in the phrase **warm the cockles of one's heart**). ~*vb.* **7.** to contract or cause to contract into wrinkles. [C14: from Old French *coquille* shell, from Latin *conchȳlium* shellfish, from Greek *konkhulion,* diminutive of *konkhule* mussel; see CONCH]

cockle[2] ('kɒkəl) *n.* any of several plants, esp. the corn cockle, that grow as weeds in cornfields.

cockleboat ('kɒkəlˌbəʊt) *n.* another word for **cockboat.**

cocklebur ('kɒkəlˌbɜː) *n.* **1.** any coarse weed of the genus *Xanthium,* having spiny burs: family *Compositae* (composites). **2.** the bur of any of these plants.

cockleshell ('kɒkəlˌʃɛl) *n.* **1.** the shell of the cockle. **2.** any of the valves of the shells of certain other bivalve molluscs, such as the scallop. **3.** any small light boat. **4.** a badge worn by pilgrims.

cockloft ('kɒkˌlɒft) *n.* a small loft, garret, or attic.

cockney ('kɒknɪ) *n.* **1.** (*often cap.*) a native of London, esp. of the working class born in the East End, speaking a characteristic dialect of English. Traditionally defined as someone born within the sound of the bells of St. Mary-le-Bow church. **2.** the urban dialect of London or its East End. **3.** *Austral.* a young snapper fish. ~*adj.* **4.** characteristic of cockneys or their dialect of English. [C14: from *cokeney,* literally: cock's egg, later applied contemptuously to townsmen, from *cokene,* genitive plural of *cok* COCK[1] + *ey* EGG] —'**cockneyish** *adj.*

cockneyfy *or* **cocknify** ('kɒknɪˌfaɪ) *vb.* **-fies, -fying, -fied.** (*tr.*) to cause (one's speech, manners, etc.) to fit the stereotyped idea of a cockney. —ˌ**cockneyfi'cation** *or* ˌ**cocknifi'cation** *n.*

cockneyism ('kɒknɪˌɪzəm) *n.* a characteristic of speech or custom peculiar to cockneys.

cock-of-the-rock *n.* either of two tropical South American birds, *Rupicola rupicola* or *R. peruviana,* having an erectile crest and (in the male) a brilliant red or orange plumage: family *Cotingidae* (cotingas).

cock of the walk *n. Informal.* a person who asserts himself in a strutting pompous way.

cockpit ('kɒkˌpɪt) *n.* **1.** the compartment in a small aircraft in which the pilot, crew, and sometimes the passengers sit. Compare **flight deck** (sense 1). **2.** the driver's compartment in a racing car. **3.** *Nautical.* **a.** an enclosed area towards the stern of a small vessel containing the wheel and tiller. **b.** (formerly) an apartment in a warship used as quarters for junior officers and as a first-aid station during combat. **4.** the site of numerous battles or campaigns. **5.** an enclosure used for cockfights.

cockroach ('kɒkˌrəʊtʃ) *n.* any insect of the suborder *Blattodea* (or *Blattaria*), such as *Blatta orientalis* (**oriental cockroach** or **black beetle**): order *Dictyoptera.* They have an oval flattened body with long antennae and biting mouthparts and are common household pests. See also **German cockroach, mantis.** [C17: from Spanish *cucaracha,* of obscure origin]

cockscomb *or* **coxcomb** ('kɒksˌkəʊm) *n.* **1.** the comb of a domestic cock. **2.** an amaranthaceous garden or pot plant, *Celosia cristata,* with yellow, crimson, or purple feathery plumelike flowers in a broad spike resembling the comb of a cock. **3.** any similar species of *Celosia.* **4.** *Informal.* a conceited dandy.

cocksfoot ('kɒksˌfʊt) *n., pl.* **-foots.** a perennial Eurasian grass, *Dactylis glomerata,* cultivated as a pasture grass in North America and South Africa.

cockshot ('kɒkˌʃɒt) *n.* another name for **cockshy.**

cockshy ('kɒkˌʃaɪ) *n., pl.* **-shies.** *Brit.* **1.** a target aimed at in throwing games. **2.** the throw itself. ~Often shortened to **shy.** [C18: from shying (throwing objects at) a cock, which was given as a prize to the person who hit it]

cockspur ('kɒkˌspɜː) *n.* **1.** a spur on the leg of a cock. **2.** an annual grass, *Echinochloa crus-galli,* widely distributed in tropical and warm temperate regions. **3.** a small thorny North American hawthorn tree, *Crataegus crus-galli.*

cocksure (ˌkɒk'ʃʊə, -'ʃɔː) *adj.* overconfident; arrogant. [C16: of uncertain origin] —ˌ**cock'surely** *adv.* —ˌ**cock'sureness** *n.*

cockswain ('kɒksən, -ˌsweɪn) *n.* a variant spelling of **coxswain.**

cocktail[1] ('kɒkˌteɪl) *n.* **1. a.** any mixed drink with a spirit base, usually drunk before meals. **b.** (*as modifier*): *the cocktail hour.* **2.** an appetizer of seafood, mixed fruits, etc. **3.** any combination of diverse elements, esp. one considered potent. **4.** (*modifier*) appropriate for formal occasions: *a cocktail dress.* [C19: of unknown origin]

cocktail[2] ('kɒkˌteɪl) *n.* **1.** a horse with a docked tail. **2.** an animal of unknown or mixed breeding. **3.** *Archaic.* a person of little breeding pretending to be a gentleman. [C19: originally *cocktailed* (adj.) having a tail like a cock's]

cocktail lounge *n.* a room in a hotel, restaurant, etc., where cocktails or other alcoholic drinks are served.

cocktail party phenomenon *n.* the ability to attend to and to understand what one person is saying when there are many people talking at once.

cocktail stick *n.* a small pointed stick used for holding cherries, olives, etc., in cocktails, and for serving snacks, such as small sausages.

cockup ('kɒkˌʌp) *n.* **1.** *Brit. slang.* something done badly. **2.** *Printing.* a letter rising above other letters in the line, esp. one of a large type size. ~*vb.* **cock up.** (*tr., adv.*) **3.** (of an animal) to raise (its ears), esp. in an alert manner. **4.** *Brit. slang.* to botch.

cocky[1] ('kɒkɪ) *adj.* **cockier, cockiest.** excessively proud of oneself. —'**cockily** *adv.*

cocky[2] ('kɒkɪ) *n., pl.* **cockies.** *Austral. informal.* **1.** short for **cockatoo** (sense 2). **2.** a farmer whose farm is regarded as small or of little account.

cockyleeky ('kɒkə'liːkɪ) *n.* a variant spelling of **cockieleekie.**

cocky's joy *n. Austral. slang.* golden syrup.

coco ('kəʊkəʊ) *n., pl.* **-cos.** short for **coconut** or **coconut palm.** [C16: from Portuguese *coco* grimace; from the likeness of the three holes of the nut to a face]

cocoa ('kəʊkəʊ) *or* **cacao** *n.* **1.** a powder made from cocoa beans after they have been roasted, ground, and freed from most of their fatty oil. **2.** a hot or cold drink made from cocoa and milk or water. **3. a.** a light to moderate brown colour. **b.** (*as adj.*): *cocoa paint.* [C18: altered from CACAO]

cocoa bean *n.* the seed of the cacao.

cocoa butter *n.* a yellowish-white waxy solid that is obtained from cocoa beans and used for confectionery, soap, etc.

coco de mer (də 'mɛə) *n.* **1.** a palm tree, *Lodoicea maldivica,* of the Seychelles, producing a large fruit containing a two-lobed edible nut. **2.** the nut of this palm. ~Also called: **double coconut.** [French: coconut of the sea]

coconut *or* **cocoanut** ('kəʊkəˌnʌt) *n.* **1.** the fruit of the coconut palm, consisting of a thick fibrous oval husk inside which is a thin hard shell enclosing edible white meat. The hollow centre is filled with a milky fluid (**coconut milk**). **2. a.** the meat of the coconut, often shredded and used in cakes, curries, etc. **b.** (*as modifier*): *coconut cake.* [C18: see COCO]

coconut butter *n.* a solid form of coconut oil.

coconut ice *n.* a sweetmeat made from desiccated coconut and sugar.

coconut matting *n.* a form of coarse matting made from the fibrous husk of the coconut.

coconut oil *n.* the fatty oil obtained from the meat of the coconut and used for making soap, cosmetics, etc.

coconut palm *n.* a tall palm tree, *Cocos nucifera,* widely planted throughout the tropics, having coconuts as fruits. Also called: **coco palm, coconut tree.**

coconut shy *n.* a fairground stall in which balls are thrown to knock coconuts off stands.

cocoon (kə'kuːn) *n.* **1. a.** a silky protective envelope secreted by silkworms and certain other insect larvae, in which the pupae develop. **b.** a similar covering for the eggs of the spider, earthworm, etc. **2.** a protective spray covering used as a seal on machinery. **3.** a cosy warm covering. ~*vb.* **4.** (*tr.*) to wrap in a cocoon. [C17: from French *cocon,* from Provençal *coucoun* eggshell, from *coco* shell, from Latin *coccum* kermes berry, from Greek *kokkos* grain, seed, berry; compare COCCUS]

cocopan ('kəʊkəʊˌpæn) *n.* (in South Africa) a small wagon running on narrow-gauge railway lines used in mines. Also called: **hopper.** [C20: from Zulu *'ngkumbana* short truck]

cocotte (kəʊ'kɒt, kə-; *French* kɔkɔt) *n.* **1.** a small fireproof dish in which individual portions of food are cooked and served. **2.** a prostitute or promiscuous woman. [C19: from French, from nursery word for a hen, feminine of *coq* COCK[1]]

cocoyam ('kəʊkəʊˌjæm) *n.* **1.** either of two food plants of West Africa, the taro or the yantia, both of which have edible underground stems. **2.** the underground stem of either of these plants. [C20: from COCOA + YAM]

cocuswood ('kəʊkəsˌwʊd) *n.* **1.** wood from the tropical American leguminous tree *Brya ebenus,* used for inlaying, turnery, musical instruments, etc. **2.** the source of this wood, an important timber tree in parts of the West Indies. ~Also called: **Jamaican ebony, West Indian ebony.**

cod[1] (kɒd) *n., pl.* **cod** *or* **cods. 1.** any of the gadoid food fishes of the genus *Gadus,* esp. *G. morhua* (or *G. callarias*), which occurs in the North Atlantic and has a long body with three rounded dorsal fins: family *Gadidae.* They are also a source of cod-liver oil. **2.** any other fish of the family *Gadidae* (see **gadid**). [C13: probably of Germanic origin; compare Old High German *cutte*]

cod[2] (kɒd) *n.* **1.** *Brit. and U.S. dialect.* a pod or husk. **2.** *Taboo.* an obsolete word for **scrotum. 3.** *Obsolete.* a bag or envelope. [Old English *codd* husk, bag; related to Old Norse *koddi,* Danish *kodde*]

cod[3] (kɒd) *vb.* **cods, codding, codded.** (*tr.*) **1.** *Brit. and Irish slang.* to make fun of; tease. **2.** *Brit. and Irish slang.* to play a trick on; fool. ~*n.* **3.** *Brit. and Irish slang.* a hoax or trick. **4.** *Irish slang.* a fraud; hoaxer: *he's an old cod.* ~*adj.* (*prenominal*) **5.** *Brit. slang.* mock; sham: *cod Latin.* [C19: perhaps from earlier *cod* a fool, perhaps shortened from CODGER]

cod[4] (kɒd) *n.* *Northern English dialect.* a fellow; chap: *he's a nice old cod.* [of unknown origin]

COD *abbrev. for:* **1.** cash on delivery. **2.** (in the U.S.) collect on delivery.

Cod. *or* **cod.** *abbrev. for* codex.

coda ('kəʊdə) *n.* **1.** *Music.* the final, sometimes inessential, part of a musical structure. **2.** a concluding part of a literary work, esp. a summary at the end of a novel of further developments in the lives of the characters. [C18: from Italian: tail, from Latin *cauda*]

cod-act *vb.* (*intr.*) *Irish informal.* to play tricks; fool. [from COD[3] + ACT]

codder[1] ('kɒdə) *n.* a cod fisherman or his boat.

codder[2] ('kɒdə) *n.* *Yorkshire dialect.* the leader of a team of workers on a press at a steelworks. [perhaps from COD[4]]

coddle ('kɒdᵊl) *vb.* (*tr.*) **1.** to treat with indulgence. **2.** to cook (something, esp. eggs) in water just below the boiling point. ~*n.* **3.** *Irish dialect.* stew made from ham and bacon scraps. [C16: of obscure origin; perhaps related to CAUDLE] —**'coddler** *n.*

code (kəʊd) *n.* **1.** a system of letters or symbols, and rules for their association by means of which information can be represented or communicated for reasons of secrecy, brevity, etc.: *binary code; Morse code.* See also **genetic code. 2.** a message in code. **3.** a symbol used in a code. **4.** a conventionalized set of principles, rules, or expectations: *a code of behaviour.* **5.** a system of letters or digits used for identification or selection purposes. ~*vb.* (*tr.*) **6.** to translate, transmit, or arrange into a code. [C14: from French, from Latin *cōdex* book, CODEX]

codec ('kəʊˌdɛk) *n.* *Electronics.* a set of equipment for coding and decoding signals. [C20: from CO(DE) + DEC(ODE)]

codeclination (ˌkəʊdɛklɪ'neɪʃən) *n.* another name for **polar distance.**

codeine ('kəʊdiːn) *n.* a white crystalline alkaloid prepared mainly from morphine and having a similar but milder action. It is used as an analgesic, a sedative, and to relieve coughing. Formula: $C_{18}H_{21}NO_3$. [C19: from Greek *kōdeia* head of a poppy, from *kōos* hollow place + -INE[2]]

Code Napoléon *French.* (kɔd napɔleɔ̃) *n.* the civil code of France, promulgated between 1804 and 1810, comprising the main body of French civil law. English name: **Napoleonic Code.**

cod end *n.* *Sea fishing.* the narrow end of a tapered trawl net. [from COD[2]]

coder ('kəʊdə) *n.* **1.** a person or thing that codes. **2.** *Electronics.* a device for transforming normal signals into a special coded form.

codetermination (ˌkəʊdɪtɜːmɪ'neɪʃən) *n.* joint participation of management and employees or employees' trade union representatives in some decisions.

codeword ('kəʊdˌwɜːd) *n.* (esp. in military use) a word used to identify a classified plan, operation, etc. Also: **codename.**

codex ('kəʊdɛks) *n., pl.* **codices** ('kəʊdɪˌsiːz, 'kɒdɪ-). **1.** a volume of manuscripts of an ancient text. **2.** *Obsolete.* a legal code. [C16: from Latin: tree trunk, wooden block, book]

codfish ('kɒdˌfɪʃ) *n., pl.* **-fish** *or* **-fishes.** a cod, esp. *Gadus morhua.*

codger ('kɒdʒə) *n.* *Informal.* a man, esp. an old or eccentric one: a term of affection or mild derision (often in the phrase **old codger**). [C18: probably variant of CADGER]

codices ('kəʊdɪˌsiːz, 'kɒdɪ-) *n.* the plural of **codex.**

codicil ('kɒdɪsɪl) *n.* **1.** *Law.* a supplement modifying a will or revoking some provision of it. **2.** an additional provision; appendix. [C15: from Late Latin *cōdicillus,* literally: a little book, diminutive of CODEX] —**codicillary** (ˌkɒdɪ'sɪlərɪ) *adj.*

codicology (ˌkəʊdɪ'kɒlədʒɪ) *n.* the study of manuscripts. [C20: via French from Latin *codic-,* CODEX + -LOGY] —**codicological** (ˌkəʊdɪkə'lɒdʒɪkᵊl) *adj.*

codification (ˌkəʊdɪfɪ'keɪʃən, ˌkɒ-) *n.* **1.** systematic organization of methods, rules, etc. **2.** *Law.* the collection into one body of the principles of a system of law.

codify ('kəʊdɪˌfaɪ, 'kɒ-) *vb.* **-fies, -fying, -fied.** (*tr.*) to organize or collect together (laws, rules, procedures, etc.) into a system or code. —**'codiˌfier** *n.*

codling[1] ('kɒdlɪŋ) *or* **codlin** ('kɒdlɪn) *n.* **1.** any of several varieties of long tapering apples used for cooking. **2.** any unripe apple. [C15 *querdlyng,* of uncertain origin]

codling[2] ('kɒdlɪŋ) *n.* a codfish, esp. a young one.

codling moth *or* **codlin moth** *n.* a tortricid moth, *Carpocapsa pomonella,* the larvae of which are a pest of apples.

codlins-and-cream *n.* an onagraceous plant, *Epilobium hirsutum,* native to Europe and Asia and introduced into North America, having purplish-red flowers and hairy stems and leaves. Also called: **hairy willowherb.**

cod-liver oil *n.* an oil extracted from the livers of cod and related fish, rich in vitamins A and D and used to treat deficiency of these vitamins.

codology (kɒd'ɒlədʒɪ) *n.* *Irish informal.* the art or practice of bluffing or deception.

codomain (ˌkəʊdəʊ'meɪn) *n.* *Maths.* another name for **range** (sense 8).

codon ('kəʊdɒn) *n.* *Genetics, biochem.* a unit that consists of three adjacent bases on a DNA molecule and that determines the position of a specific amino acid in a protein molecule during protein synthesis. [C20: from CODE + -ON]

codpiece ('kɒdˌpiːs) *n.* a bag covering the male genitals, attached to hose or breeches by laces, etc., worn in the 15th and 16th centuries. [C15: from COD[2] + PIECE]

co-driver *n.* one of two drivers who take turns to drive a car, esp. in a rally.

codswallop ('kɒdzˌwɒləp) *n.* *Brit. slang.* nonsense. [C20: of unknown origin]

co-ed (ˌkəʊ'ɛd) *adj.* **1.** coeducational. ~*n.* **2.** *U.S.* a female student in a coeducational college or university. **3.** *Brit.* a school or college providing coeducation.

coedit (kəʊ'ɛdɪt) *vb.* (*tr.*) to edit (a book, newspaper, etc.) jointly. —**co'editor** *n.*

coeducation (ˌkəʊɛdjʊ'keɪʃən) *n.* instruction in schools, colleges, etc., attended by both sexes. —ˌ**coedu'cational** *adj.* —ˌ**coedu'cationally** *adv.*

coefficient (ˌkəʊɪ'fɪʃənt) *n.* **1.** *Maths.* **a.** a numerical or constant factor in an algebraic term: *the coefficient of the term 3xyz is 3.* **b.** the product of all the factors of a term excluding one or more specified variables: *the coefficient of x in 3axyz is 3ayz.* **2.** *Physics.* a number that is the value of a given substance under specified conditions. [C17: from New Latin *coefficiēns,* from Latin *co-* together + *efficere* to EFFECT]

coefficient of expansion *n.* the amount of expansion (or contraction) per unit length of a material resulting from one degree change in temperature. Also called: **expansivity.**

coefficient of friction *n. Mechanical engineering.* the force required to move two sliding surfaces over each other, divided by the force holding them together. It is reduced once the motion has started.

coefficient of variation *n. Statistics.* a measure of the relative variation of distribution independent of the units of measurement; the standard deviation divided by the mean, sometimes expressed as a percentage.

coel- *prefix.* indicating a cavity within a body or a hollow organ or part: *coelacanth; coelenterate; coelenteron.* [New Latin, from Greek *koilos* hollow]

coelacanth ('siːlə,kænθ) *n.* a primitive marine bony fish of the genus *Latimeria* (subclass *Crossopterygii*), having fleshy limblike pectoral fins and occurring off the coast of E Africa: thought to be extinct until a living specimen was discovered in 1938. [C19: from New Latin *coelacanthus*, literally: hollow spine, from COEL- + Greek *akanthos* spine]

coelenterate (sɪ'lɛntə,reɪt, -rɪt) *n.* **1.** any invertebrates of the phylum *Coelenterata*, having a saclike body with a single opening (mouth), which occurs in polyp and medusa forms. The group includes the hydra, jellyfishes, sea anemones, and corals. *~adj.* **2.** of, relating to, or belonging to the *Coelenterata.* [C19: from New Latin *Coelenterata*, hollow-intestined (creatures); see COEL-, ENTERON] —**coelenteric** (,siːlɛn'tɛrɪk) *adj.*

coelenteron (sɪ'lɛntə,rɒn) *n., pl.* **-tera** (-tərə). the simple saclike body cavity of a coelenterate.

coeliac *or U.S.* **celiac** ('siːlɪ,æk) *adj.* of or relating to the abdomen. [C17: from Latin *coeliacus*, from Greek *koiliakos*, from *koilia* belly]

coeliac disease *n.* a chronic intestinal disorder of young children caused by sensitivity to the protein gliadin contained in the gluten of cereals, characterized by distention of the abdomen and frothy and pale foul-smelling stools.

coelom *or esp. U.S.* **celom** ('siːləʊm, -ləm) *n.* the body cavity of many multicellular animals, situated in the mesoderm and containing the digestive tract and other visceral organs. [C19: from Greek *koilōma* cavity, from *koilos* hollow; see COEL-] —**coelomic** *or esp. U.S.* **celomic** (sɪ'lɒmɪk) *adj.*

coelostat ('siːlə,stæt) *n.* an astronomical instrument consisting of a plane mirror mounted parallel to the earth's axis and rotated about this axis once every two days so that light from a celestial body, esp. the sun, is reflected onto a second mirror, which reflects the beam into a telescope. Compare **siderostat.** [C19: *coelo-*, from Latin *caelum* heaven, sky + -STAT]

coemption (kəʊ'ɛmpʃən) *n.* the buying up of the complete supply of a commodity. [C14: from Latin *coemptiōnem* a buying together]

coenacle ('sɛnək^əl) *n.* a variant spelling of **cenacle.**

coenesthesia, cenesthesia (,siːnɪs'θiːzɪə) *or* **coenesthesis, cenesthesis** (,siːnɪs'θiːsɪs) *n. Psychol.* general awareness of one's own body. —**coenesthetic** *or* **cenesthetic** (,siːnɪs'θɛtɪk) *adj.*

coeno- *or* (*before a vowel*) **coen-** *combining form.* common: *coenocyte.* [New Latin, from Greek *koinos* common]

coenobite *or* **cenobite** ('siːnəʊ,baɪt) *n.* a member of a religious order following a communal rule of life. Compare **eremite.** [C17: from Old French or ecclesiastical Latin, from Greek *koinobion* convent, from *koinos* common + *bios* life] —**coenobitic** (,siːnəʊ'bɪtɪk), ,**coeno'bitical** *or* ,**ceno'bitic,** ,**ceno'bitical** *adj.*

coenocyte ('siːnəʊ,saɪt) *n. Botany.* a mass of protoplasm containing many nuclei and enclosed by a cell wall: occurs in many fungi and some algae. —**coenocytic** (,siːnə'sɪtɪk) *adj.*

coenosarc ('siːnəʊ,sɑːk) *n.* a system of protoplasmic branches connecting the polyps of colonial organisms such as corals. [C19: from COENO- + Greek *sarx* flesh]

coenosteum (sɪ'nɒstɪəm) *n. Zoology.* the calcareous skeleton of a hydrocoral or a coral colony.

coenurus (siː'njʊərəs) *n., pl.* **-ri** (-raɪ). an encysted larval form of the tapeworm *Multiceps*, containing many encapsulated heads. In sheep it can cause the gid, and when eaten by dogs it develops into several adult forms. [C19: from New Latin, from COENO- + Greek *oura* tail, literally: common tail, referring to the single body with its many heads]

coenzyme (kəʊ'ɛnzaɪm) *n. Biochem.* a nonprotein organic molecule that forms a complex with certain enzymes and is essential for their activity. See also **apoenzyme.**

coenzyme A *n.* a constituent of biological cells that functions as the agent of acylation in metabolic reactions. Abbrev.: **CoA.**

coenzyme Q *n.* a quinone derivative, present in biological cells, that functions as an electron carrier in the electron transport chain. Also called: **ubiquinone.**

coequal (kəʊ'iːkwəl) *adj.* **1.** of the same size, rank, etc. *~n.* **2.** a person or thing equal with another. —**coequality** (,kəʊɪ'kwɒlɪtɪ) *or* **co'equalness** *n.* —**co'equally** *adv.*

coerce (kəʊ'ɜːs) *vb.* (*tr.*) to compel or restrain by force or authority without regard to individual wishes or desires. [C17: from Latin *coercēre* to confine, restrain, from *co-* together + *arcēre* to enclose] —**co'ercer** *n.* —**co'ercible** *adj.*

coercimeter (,kəʊɜː'sɪmɪtə) *n.* an instrument used for measurement of coercive force.

coercion (kəʊ'ɜːʃən) *n.* **1.** the act or power of coercing. **2.** government by force. —**co'ercionist** *n.* —**coercive** (kəʊ'ɜːsɪv) *adj.* —**co'ercively** *adv.* —**co'erciveness** *n.*

coercive force *n.* a measure of the magnetization of a ferromagnetic material as expressed by the external magnetic field strength necessary to demagnetize it. Measured in amperes per metre. Compare **coercivity.**

coercivity (,kəʊɜː'sɪvɪtɪ) *n.* the magnetic-field strength necessary to demagnetize a ferromagnetic material that is magnetized to saturation. It is measured in amperes per metre. Compare **coercive force.**

coessential (,kəʊɪ'sɛnʃəl) *adj. Christianity.* being one in essence or nature: a term applied to the three persons of the Trinity. —**coessentiality** (,kəʊɪ,sɛnʃɪ'ælɪtɪ) *or* ,**coes'sentialness** *n.* —,**coes'sentially** *adv.*

coetaneous (,kəʊɪ'teɪnɪəs) *adj. Rare.* of the same age or period. [C17: from Latin *coaetāneus*, from *co-* same + *aetās* age] —,**coe'taneously** *adv.* —,**coe'taneousness** *n.*

coeternal (,kəʊɪ'tɜːn^əl) *adj.* existing together eternally. —,**coe'ternally** *adv.*

coeternity (,kəʊɪ'tɜːnɪtɪ) *n.* existence for, from, or in eternity with another being.

coeval (kəʊ'iːv^əl) *adj.* **1.** of or belonging to the same age or generation. *~n.* **2.** a contemporary. [C17: from Late Latin *coaevus* from Latin *co-* + *aevum* age] —**coevality** (,kəʊɪ'vælɪtɪ) *n.* —**co'evally** *adv.*

coexecutor (,kəʊɪg'zɛkjʊtə) *n. Law.* a person acting jointly with another or others as executor. —,**coex'ecutrix** *fem. n.*

coexist (,kəʊɪg'zɪst) *vb.* (*intr.*) **1.** to exist together at the same time or in the same place. **2.** to exist together in peace. —,**coex'istence** *n.* —,**coex'istent** *adj.*

coextend (,kəʊɪk'stɛnd) *vb.* to extend or cause to extend equally in space or time. —,**coex'tension** *n.*

coextensive (,kəʊɪk'stɛnsɪv) *adj.* of the same limits or extent. —,**coex'tensively** *adv.*

cofactor ('kəʊ,fæktə) *n.* **1.** *Maths.* a number associated with an element in a determinant, equal to the determinant formed by removing the row and column in which the element appears from the given determinant. Also called: **signed minor.** See **minor.** **2.** *Biochem.* a nonprotein substance that forms a complex with certain enzymes and is essential for their activity. It may be a metal ion or a coenzyme.

C of C *abbrev. for* Chamber of Commerce.

C of E *abbrev. for* Church of England.

coff (kɒf) *vb.* **coffs, coffing, coffed** *or* **coft.** *Scot.* to buy; purchase. [C15: from the past participle of obsolete *copen* to buy, of Low German origin; compare German *kaufen* to buy]

coffee ('kɒfɪ) *n.* **1. a.** a drink consisting of an infusion of the roasted and ground or crushed seeds of the coffee tree. **b.** (*as modifier*): *coffee grounds.* **2.** Also called: **coffee beans.** the beanlike seeds of the coffee tree, used to make this beverage. **3.** short for **coffee tree. 4. a.** a medium to dark brown colour. **b.** (*as adj.*): *a coffee carpet.* [C16: from Italian *caffè*, from Turkish *kahve*, from Arabic *qahwah* coffee, wine]

coffee bag *n.* a small bag containing ground coffee beans, infused to make coffee.

coffee bar *n.* a café; snack bar.

coffee cup *n.* a cup from which coffee may be drunk, usually smaller than a teacup.

coffee house *n.* a place where coffee is served, esp. one that was a fashionable meeting place in 18th-century London.

coffee mill *n.* a machine for grinding roasted coffee beans.

coffee morning *n.* a social event (often held in order to raise money) at which coffee is served.

coffee nut *n.* **1.** the fruit of the Kentucky coffee tree. **2.** another name for **Kentucky coffee tree.**

coffeepot ('kɒfɪ,pɒt) *n.* a pot in which coffee is brewed or served.

coffee shop *n.* a shop where coffee is sold or drunk.

coffee table *n.* a low table, on which newspapers, etc., may be placed and coffee served.

coffee-table book *n.* a book designed to be looked at rather than read.

coffee tree *n.* **1.** any of several rubiaceous trees of the genus *Coffea*, esp. *C. arabica*, the seeds of which are used in the preparation of the beverage coffee. **2.** short for **Kentucky coffee tree.**

coffer ('kɒfə) *n.* **1.** a chest, esp. for storing valuables. **2.** (*usually pl.*) a store of money. **3.** Also called: **caisson, lacuna.** an ornamental sunken panel in a ceiling, dome, etc. **4.** a watertight box or chamber. **5.** short for **cofferdam.** *~vb.* (*tr.*) **6.** to store, as in a coffer. **7.** to decorate (a ceiling, dome, etc.) with coffers. [C13: from Old French *coffre*, from Latin *cophinus* basket, from Greek *kophinos*]

cofferdam ('kɒfə,dæm) *n.* **1.** a watertight structure that encloses an area under water, pumped dry to enable construction work to be carried out. **2.** (on a ship) a compartment separating two bulkheads or floors, as for insulation or to serve as a barrier against the escape of gas or oil. ~Often shortened to **coffer.**

coffin ('kɒfɪn) *n.* **1.** a box in which a corpse is buried or cremated. **2.** the part of a horse's foot that contains the coffin bone. **3.** Also called: **coffin block.** a frame for holding electrotype or stereotype printing plates. *~vb.* **4.** (*tr.*) to place in or as in a coffin. **5.** *Engineering.* another name for **flask** (sense 6). [C14: from Old French *cofin*, from Latin *cophinus* basket; see COFFER]

coffin bone *n.* the terminal phalangeal bone inside the hoof of the horse and similar animals.

coffin nail *n.* a slang term for **cigarette.**
coffle ('kɒfᵊl) *n.* (esp. formerly) a line of slaves, beasts, etc., fastened together. [C18: from Arabic *qāfilah* caravan]
C of I *abbrev. for* Church of Ireland.
C of S *abbrev. for:* **1.** Chief of Staff. **2.** Church of Scotland.
cog[1] (kɒg) *n.* **1.** any of the teeth or projections on the rim of a gearwheel. **2.** a gearwheel, esp. a small one. **3.** a person or thing playing a small part in a large organization or process. ~*vb.* **cogs, cogging, cogged.** **4.** (*tr.*) *Metallurgy.* to roll (cast-steel ingots) to convert them into blooms. [C13: of Scandinavian origin; compare Danish *kogge,* Swedish *kugge,* Norwegian *kug*]
cog[2] (kɒg) *vb.* **cogs, cogging, cogged.** *Slang.* to cheat in (a game, esp. dice), as by loading a dice. [C16: originally a dice-playing term, of unknown origin]
cog[3] (kɒg) *n.* **1.** a tenon that projects from the end of a timber beam for fitting into a mortise. ~*vb.* **cogs, cogging, cogged. 2.** (*tr.*) to join (pieces of wood) with cogs. [C19: of uncertain origin]
cog. *abbrev. for* cognate.
cogent ('kəʊdʒənt) *adj.* compelling belief or assent; forcefully convincing. [C17: from Latin *cōgent-, cōgēns,* driving together, from *cōgere,* from *co-* together + *agere* to drive] —'**cogency** *n.* —'**cogently** *adv.*
coggle ('kɒgᵊl) *vb.* (*intr.*) *Scot.* to wobble or rock; be unsteady. [of uncertain origin] —'**coggly** *adj.*
cogitable ('kɒdʒɪtəbᵊl) *adj. Rare.* conceivable.
cogitate ('kɒdʒɪˌteɪt) *vb.* to think deeply about (a problem, possibility, etc.); ponder. [C16: from Latin *cōgitāre,* from *co-* (intensive) + *agitāre* to turn over, AGITATE] —'**cogiˌtatingly** *adv.* —ˌ**cogi'tation** *n.* —'**cogiˌtator** *n.*
cogitative ('kɒdʒɪtətɪv) *adj.* **1.** capable of thinking. **2.** thoughtful. —'**cogitatively** *adv.* —'**cogitativeness** *n.*
cogito, ergo sum *Latin.* ('kɒgɪˌtəʊ 'ɜːgəʊ 'sʊm) I think, therefore I am; the basis of the philosophy of René Descartes (1596–1650).
Cognac ('kɒnjæk; *French* kɔɲak) *n.* (*sometimes not cap.*) a high-quality grape brandy, distilled in the district around Cognac in SW France.
cognate ('kɒgneɪt) *adj.* **1.** akin; related: *cognate languages.* **2.** related by blood or descended from a common maternal ancestor. Compare **agnate. 3. cognate object.** *Grammar.* a noun functioning as the object of a verb to which it is etymologically related, as in *think a thought* or *sing a song.* ~*n.* **4.** something that is cognate with something else. [C17: from Latin *cognātus,* from *co-* same + *gnātus* born, variant of *nātus,* past participle of *nāscī* to be born] —'**cognately** *adv.* —'**cognateness** *n.* —**cog'nation** *n.*
cognition (kɒg'nɪʃən) *n.* **1.** the mental act or process by which knowledge is acquired, including perception, intuition, and reasoning. **2.** the knowledge that results from such an act or process. [C15: from Latin *cognitiō,* from *cognōscere* from *co-* (intensive) + *nōscere* to learn; see KNOW] —**cog'nitional** *adj.* —**cognitive** ('kɒgnɪtɪv) *adj.*
cognitive dissonance *n. Psychol.* an uncomfortable mental state resulting from conflicting cognitions; usually resolved by changing some of the cognitions.
cognitive ethology *n.* a branch of ethology concerned with the influence of conscious awareness and intention on the behaviour of an animal.
cognitive map *n. Psychol.* a mental map of one's environment.
cognitive psychology *n.* the psychological study of higher mental processes, including thinking and perception.
cognitive science *n.* the scientific study of cognition, including elements of the traditional disciplines of philosophy, psychology, semantics, and linguistics, together with artificial intelligence and computer science.
cognitive therapy *n. Psychol.* a form of psychotherapy in which the patient is encouraged to change the way he sees the world and himself: used particularly to treat depression.
cognitivism ('kɒgnɪtɪˌvɪzəm) *n. Philosophy.* the meta-ethical thesis that moral judgments state facts and so are either true or false. Compare **emotivism, prescriptivism.** See also **naturalism** (sense 4), **non-naturalism.**
cognizable *or* **cognisable** ('kɒgnɪzəbᵊl, 'kɒnɪ-) *adj.* **1.** perceptible. **2.** *Law.* susceptible to the jurisdiction of a court. —'**cognizably** *or* '**cognisably** *adv.*
cognizance *or* **cognisance** ('kɒgnɪzəns, 'kɒnɪ-) *n.* **1.** knowledge; acknowledgment. **2. take cognizance of.** to take notice of; acknowledge, esp. officially. **3.** the range or scope of knowledge or perception. **4.** *Law.* **a.** the right of a court to hear and determine a cause or matter. **b.** knowledge of certain facts upon which the court must act without requiring proof. **c.** *Chiefly U.S.* confession. **5.** *Heraldry.* a distinguishing badge or bearing. [C14: from Old French *conoissance,* from *conoistre* to know, from Latin *cognōscere* to learn; see COGNITION]
cognizant *or* **cognisant** ('kɒgnɪzənt, 'kɒnɪ-) *adj.* (usually foll. by *of*) aware; having knowledge.
cognize *or* **cognise** ('kɒgnaɪz, kɒg'naɪz) *vb.* (*tr.*) to perceive, become aware of, or know.
cognomen (kɒg'nəʊmɛn) *n., pl.* **-nomens** *or* **-nomina** (-'nɒmɪnə, -'nəʊ-). (originally) an ancient Roman's third name or nickname, which later became his family name. See also **agnomen, nomen, praenomen.** [C19: from Latin: additional name, from *co-* together + *nōmen* name; influenced in form by *cognōscere* to learn] —**cognominal** (kɒg'nɒmɪnᵊl, -'nəʊ-) *adj.* —**cog'nominally** *adv.*
cognoscenti (ˌkɒnjəʊ'ʃɛntɪ, ˌkɒgnəʊ-) *or* **conoscenti** *pl. n., sing.* **-te** (-tiː). (*sometimes sing.*) people with informed appreciation of a particular field, esp. in the fine arts; connoisseurs. [C18: from obsolete Italian (modern *conoscente*), from Latin *cognōscere* to know, learn about]
cogon ('kəʊgəʊn) *n.* any of the coarse tropical grasses of the genus *Imperata,* esp. *I. cylindrica* and *I. exaltata* of the Philippines, which are used for thatching. [from Spanish *cogón,* from Tagalog *kugon*]
cog railway *or* **cogway** ('kɒgˌweɪ) *n. Chiefly U.S.* other terms for **rack railway.**
cogwheel ('kɒgˌwiːl) *n.* another name for **gearwheel.**
cohabit (kəʊ'hæbɪt) *vb.* (*intr.*) to live together as husband and wife, esp. without being married. [C16: via Late Latin, from Latin *co-* together + *habitāre* to live] —**co'habitant** *or* **co'habiter** *n.*
cohabitation (kəʊˌhæbɪ'teɪʃən) *n.* **1.** the state or condition of living together as husband and wife without being married. **2.** (of political parties) the state or condition of cooperating for specific purposes without forming a coalition.
coheir (kəʊ'ɛə) *n.* a person who inherits jointly with others. —**co'heiress** *fem. n.*
Cohen (kɒ'hɛn, kɔɪn) *n.* a variant spelling of **Kohen.**
cohere (kəʊ'hɪə) *vb.* (*intr.*) **1.** to hold or stick firmly together. **2.** to be connected logically; be consistent. **3.** *Physics.* to be held together by the action of molecular forces. [C16: from Latin *cohaerēre* from *co-* together + *haerēre* to cling, adhere]
coherence (kəʊ'hɪərəns) *or* **coherency** *n.* **1.** logical or natural connection or consistency. **2.** another word for **cohesion** (sense 1).
coherent (kəʊ'hɪərənt) *adj.* **1.** capable of logical and consistent speech, thought, etc. **2.** logical; consistent and orderly. **3.** cohering or sticking together. **4.** *Physics.* (of two or more waves) having the same frequency and the same phase or a fixed phase difference: *coherent light.* **5.** (of a system of units) consisting only of units the quotient or product of any two of which yield the unit of the resultant quantity. —**co'herently** *adv.*
coherer (kəʊ'hɪərə) *n. Physics.* an electrical component formerly used to detect radio waves, consisting of a tube containing loosely packed metal particles. The waves caused the particles to cohere, thereby changing the current through the circuit.
cohesion (kəʊ'hiːʒən) *n.* **1.** the act or state of cohering; tendency to unite. **2.** *Physics.* the force that holds together the atoms or molecules in a solid or liquid, as distinguished from adhesion. **3.** *Botany.* the fusion in some plants of flower parts, such as petals, that are usually separate. [C17: from Latin *cohaesus* stuck together, past participle of *cohaerēre* to COHERE]
cohesionless soil *n.* any free-running type of soil, such as sand or gravel, whose strength depends on friction between particles. Also called: **frictional soil.** Compare **cohesive soil.**
cohesive (kəʊ'hiːsɪv) *adj.* **1.** characterized by or causing cohesion. **2.** tending to cohere or stick together. —**co'hesively** *adv.* —**co'hesiveness** *n.*
cohesive soil *n.* sticky soil such as clay or clayey silt whose strength depends on the surface tension of capillary water. Compare **cohesionless soil.**
coho ('kəʊhəʊ) *n., pl.* **-ho** *or* **-hos.** a Pacific salmon, *Oncorhynchus kisutch.* Also called: **silver salmon.** [origin unknown; probably from an American Indian language]
cohobate ('kəʊhəʊˌbeɪt) *vb.* (*tr.*) *Pharmacol.* to redistil (a distillate), esp. by allowing it to mingle with the remaining matter. [C17: from New Latin *cohobāre,* perhaps from Arabic *ka'aba* to repeat an action]
cohort ('kəʊhɔːt) *n.* **1.** one of the ten units of between 300 and 600 men in an ancient Roman Legion. **2.** any band of warriors or associates: *the cohorts of Satan.* **3.** *Chiefly U.S.* an associate or follower. **4.** *Biology.* a taxonomic group that is a subdivision of a subclass (usually of mammals) or subfamily (of plants). **5.** *Statistics.* a group of people with a statistic in common, esp. having been born in the same year. [C15: from Latin *cohors* yard, company of soldiers; related to *hortus* garden]
cohosh ('kəʊhɒʃ, kəʊ'hɒʃ) *n.* any of several North American plants, such as the **blue cohosh** (*Caulophyllum thalictroides:* family *Leonticaceae*) and **black cohosh** (*Cimicifuga racemosa:* family *Ranunculaceae*). [C18: probably of Algonquian origin]
COHSE ('kəʊzɪ) *n.* (in Britain) *acronym for* Confederation of Health Service Employees.
cohune (kəʊ'huːn) *n.* a tropical American feather palm, *Attalea* (or *Orbignya*) *cohune,* whose large oily nuts yield an oil similar to coconut oil. Also called: **cohune palm.** See also **coquilla nut.** [C19: from American Spanish, from South American Indian *ókhún*]
COI (in Britain) *abbrev. for* Central Office of Information.
coif (kɔɪf) *n.* **1.** a close-fitting cap worn under a veil, worn in the Middle Ages by many women but now only by nuns. **2.** any similar cap, such as a leather cap worn under a chain-mail hood. **3.** (formerly in England) the white cap worn by a serjeant at law. **4.** a base for the elaborate women's headdresses of the 16th century. **5.** (kwɑːf) a less common word for **coiffure** (sense 1). ~*vb.* **coifs, coiffing, coiffed.** (*tr.*) **6.** to cover with or as if with

a coif. **7.** (kwɑːf). to arrange (the hair). [C14: from Old French *coiffe,* from Late Latin *cofea* helmet, cap, of obscure origin]

coiffeur (kwɑːˈfɜː; *French* kwafœr) *n.* a hairdresser. —**coiffeuse** (kwɑːˈfɜːz; *French* kwaføz) *fem. n.*

coiffure (kwɑːˈfjʊə; *French* kwafyr) *n.* **1.** a hairstyle. **2.** an obsolete word for **headdress.** *~vb.* **3.** (*tr.*) to dress or arrange (the hair).

coign *or* **coigne** (kɔɪn) *n.* variant spellings of **quoin.**

coign of vantage *n.* an advantageous position or stance for observation or action.

coil[1] (kɔɪl) *vb.* **1.** to wind or gather (ropes, hair, etc.) into loops or (of rope, hair, etc.) to be formed in such loops. **2.** (*intr.*) to move in a winding course. *~n.* **3.** something wound in a connected series of loops. **4.** a single loop of such a series. **5.** an arrangement of pipes in a spiral or loop, as in a condenser. **6.** an electrical conductor wound into the form of a spiral, sometimes with a soft iron core, to provide inductance or a magnetic field. See also **induction coil. 7.** an intrauterine contraceptive device in the shape of a coil. **8.** the transformer in a petrol engine that supplies the high voltage to the sparking plugs. [C16: from Old French *coillir* to collect together; see CULL] —ˈ**coiler** *n.*

coil[2] (kɔɪl) *n.* the troubles and activities of the world (in the Shakespearean phrase **this mortal coil**). [C16: of unknown origin]

coil spring *n.* a helical spring formed from wire.

coin (kɔɪn) *n.* **1.** a metal disc or piece used as money. **2.** metal currency, as opposed to securities, paper currency, etc. **3.** *Architect.* a variant spelling of **quoin. 4. pay (a person) back in (his) own coin.** to treat (a person) in the way that he has treated others. *~vb.* **5.** (*tr.*) to make or stamp (coins). **6.** (*tr.*) to make into a coin. **7.** (*tr.*) to fabricate or invent (words, etc.). **8.** (*tr.*) *Informal.* to make (money) rapidly (esp. in the phrase **coin it in**). **9. to coin a phrase.** said ironically after one uses a cliché. **10. the other side of the coin.** the opposite view of a matter. [C14: from Old French: stamping die, from Latin *cuneus* wedge] —ˈ**coinable** *adj.* —ˈ**coiner** *n.*

coinage (ˈkɔɪnɪdʒ) *n.* **1.** coins collectively. **2.** the act of striking coins. **3.** the currency of a country. **4.** the act of inventing something, esp. a word or phrase. **5.** a newly invented word, phrase, usage, etc.

coin box *n.* the part of a coin-operated machine into which coins are placed.

coincide (ˌkəʊɪnˈsaɪd) *vb.* (*intr.*) **1.** to occur or exist simultaneously. **2.** to be identical in nature, character, etc. **3.** to agree. [C18: from Medieval Latin *coincidere,* from Latin *co-* together + *incidere* to occur, befall, from *cadere* to fall]

coincidence (kəʊˈɪnsɪdəns) *n.* **1.** a chance occurrence of events remarkable either for being simultaneous or for apparently being connected. **2.** the fact, condition, or state of coinciding. **3.** (*modifier*) *Electronics.* of or relating to a circuit that produces an output pulse only when both its input terminals receive pulses within a specified interval: *coincidence gate.* Compare **anti-coincidence.**

coincident (kəʊˈɪnsɪdənt) *adj.* **1.** having the same position in space or time. **2.** (usually *postpositive* and foll. by *with*) in exact agreement; consonant.

coincidental (kəʊˌɪnsɪˈdentᵊl) *adj.* of or happening by a coincidence; fortuitous. —**coˌinciˈdentally** *adv.*

coin-op (ˈkɔɪnˌɒp) *n.* a launderette or other service installation in which the machines are operated by insertion of a coin.

coinsurance (ˌkəʊɪnˈʃʊərəns, -ˈʃɔː-) *n.* **1.** a method of insurance by which property is insured for a certain percentage of its value by a commercial insurance policy while the owner assumes liability for the remainder. **2.** joint insurance held by two or more persons.

coinsure (ˌkəʊɪnˈʃʊə, -ˈʃɔː) *vb.* **1.** (*intr.*) to take out coinsurance. **2.** to insure (property) jointly with another. —ˌ**coinˈsurer** *n.*

Cointreau (ˈkwɑːntrəʊ) *n. Trademark.* a colourless liqueur with orange flavouring.

coir (kɔɪə) *n.* the fibre prepared from the husk of the coconut, used in making rope and matting. [C16: from Malayalam *kāyar* rope, from *kāyaru* to be twisted]

coit (kɔɪt) *n. Austral. slang.* buttocks; backside. Also: **quoit.** [C20: perhaps a variant and special use of QUOIT, referring to roundness]

coitus (ˈkəʊɪtəs) *or* **coition** (kəʊˈɪʃən) *n.* technical terms for **sexual intercourse.** [C18 *coitus:* from Latin: a uniting, from *coīre* to meet, from *īre* to go] —ˈ**coital** *adj.*

coitus interruptus (ˌɪntəˈrʌptəs) *n.* the deliberate withdrawal of the penis from the vagina before ejaculation.

coitus reservatus (ˌrɛzəˈvɑːtəs) *n.* the deliberate delaying or avoidance of orgasm during intercourse.

cojones *Spanish.* (koˈxones) *pl. n.* **1.** testicles. **2.** manly courage.

coke[1] (kəʊk) *n.* **1.** a solid-fuel product containing about 80 per cent of carbon produced by distillation of coal to drive off its volatile constituents: used as a fuel and in metallurgy as a reducing agent for converting metal oxides into metals. **2.** any similar material, such as the layer formed in the cylinders of a car engine by incomplete combustion of the fuel. *~vb.* **3.** to become or convert into coke. [C17: probably a variant of C14 northern English dialect *colk* core, of obscure origin]

coke[2] (kəʊk) *n. Slang.* short for **cocaine.**

Coke (kəʊk) *n. Trademark.* short for **Coca-Cola.**

cokuloris (ˌkɒkəˈlɔːrɪs) *n. Films.* a palette with irregular holes, placed between lighting and camera to prevent glare. [C20: of unknown origin]

col (kɒl; *French* kɔl) *n.* **1.** the lowest point of a ridge connecting two mountain peaks, often constituting a pass. **2.** *Meteorol.* a pressure region between two anticyclones and two depressions, associated with variable weather. [C19: from French: neck, col, from Latin *collum* neck]

col. *abbrev. for:* **1.** colour(ed). **2.** column.

Col. *abbrev. for:* **1.** Colombia(n). **2.** Colonel. **3.** *Bible.* Colossians.

col-[1] *prefix.* a variant of **com-** before *l: collateral.*

col-[2] *prefix.* a variant of **colo-** before a vowel: *colectomy.*

cola[1] *or* **kola** (ˈkəʊlə) *n.* **1.** either of two tropical sterculiaceous trees, *Cola nitida* or *C. acuminata,* widely cultivated in tropical regions for their seeds (see **cola nut**). **2.** a sweet carbonated drink flavoured with cola nuts. [C18: from *kola,* probably variant of Mandingo *kolo* nut]

cola[2] (ˈkəʊlə) *n.* a plural of **colon**[1] (sense 3) or **colon**[2].

colander (ˈkɒləndə, ˈkʌl-) *or* **cullender** *n.* a pan with a perforated bottom for straining or rinsing foods. [C14 *colyndore,* probably from Old Provençal *colador,* via Medieval Latin, from Late Latin *cōlāre* to filter, from Latin *cōlum* sieve]

cola nut *n.* any of the seeds of the cola tree, which contain caffeine and theobromine and are used medicinally and in the manufacture of soft drinks.

colatitude (kəʊˈlætɪˌtjuːd) *n. Astronomy, navigation.* the complement of the celestial latitude.

colcannon (kəlˈkænən, ˈkɒlˌkænən) *n.* a dish, originating in Ireland, of potatoes and cabbage or other greens boiled and mashed together. [C18: from Irish Gaelic *cál ceannann,* literally: white-headed cabbage]

colchicine (ˈkɒltʃɪˌsiːn, -sɪn, ˈkɒlkɪ-) *n.* a pale-yellow crystalline alkaloid extracted from seeds or corms of the autumn crocus. It is used in the treatment of gout and to create polyploid plants by inhibiting chromosome separation during meiosis. Formula: $C_{22}H_{25}NO_6$. [C19: from COLCHICUM + -INE[2]]

colchicum (ˈkɒltʃɪkəm, ˈkɒlkɪ-) *n.* **1.** any Eurasian liliaceous plant of the genus *Colchicum,* such as the autumn crocus. **2.** the dried seeds or corms of the autumn crocus: a source of colchicine. [C16: from Latin, from Greek *kolkhikon,* from *kolkhikos* of Colchis, an ancient country on the Black Sea]

colcothar (ˈkɒlkəˌθɑː) *n.* a finely powdered form of ferric oxide produced by heating ferric sulphate and used as a pigment and as jewellers' rouge. Also called: **crocus.** [C17: from French *colcotar,* from Spanish *colcótar,* from Arabic dialect *qulquṭār*]

cold (kəʊld) *adj.* **1.** having relatively little warmth; of a rather low temperature: *cold weather; cold hands.* **2.** without sufficient or proper warmth: *this meal is cold.* **3.** lacking in affection, enthusiasm, or warmth of feeling: *a cold manner.* **4.** not affected by emotion; objective: *cold logic.* **5.** dead. **6.** sexually unresponsive or frigid. **7.** lacking in freshness: *a cold scent; cold news.* **8.** chilling to the spirit; depressing. **9.** (of a colour) having violet, blue, or green predominating; giving no sensation of warmth. **10.** *Metallurgy.* denoting or relating to a process in which work-hardening occurs as a result of the plastic deformation of a metal at too low a temperature for annealing to take place. **11.** (of a process) not involving heat, in contrast with traditional methods: *cold typesetting; cold technology.* **12.** *Informal.* (of a seeker) far from the object of a search. **13. cold comfort.** little or no comfort. **14. cold steel.** the use of bayonets, knives, etc., in combat. **15. from cold.** without advance notice; without giving preparatory information. **16. in cold blood.** showing no passion; deliberately; ruthlessly. **17. leave (someone) cold.** *Informal.* to fail to excite (someone): *the performance left me cold.* **18. throw** (*or* **pour**) **cold water on.** *Informal.* to be unenthusiastic about or discourage. *~n.* **19.** the absence of heat regarded as a positive force: *the cold took away our breath.* **20.** the sensation caused by loss or lack of heat. **21. (out) in the cold.** *Informal.* neglected; ignored. **22.** an acute viral infection of the upper respiratory passages characterized by discharge of watery mucus from the nose, sneezing, etc. **23. catch a cold.** *Slang.* to make a loss; lose one's investment. *~adv.* **24.** *Informal.* without preparation: *he played his part cold.* **25.** *Informal, chiefly U.S. and Canadian.* thoroughly; absolutely: *she turned him down cold.* [Old English *ceald;* related to Old Norse *kaldr,* Gothic *kalds,* Old High German *kalt;* see COOL] —ˈ**coldish** *adj.* —ˈ**coldly** *adv.* —ˈ**coldness** *n.*

cold-blooded *adj.* **1.** having or showing a lack of feeling or pity: *a cold-blooded killing.* **2.** *Informal.* particularly sensitive to cold. **3.** (of all animals except birds and mammals) having a body temperature that varies with that of the surroundings. Technical term: **poikilothermic.** —ˌ**cold-ˈbloodedly** *adv.* —ˌ**cold-ˈbloodedness** *n.*

cold call *n.* a call made by a salesman on a potential customer without making an appointment. —**cold calling** *n.*

cold cathode *n. Electronics.* a cathode from which electrons are emitted at an ambient temperature, due to a high potential gradient at the surface.

cold chisel *n.* a toughened steel chisel.

cold cream *n.* an emulsion of water and fat used cosmetically for softening and cleansing the skin.

cold cuts *pl. n.* cooked meats sliced and served cold.
cold-drawn *adj.* (of metal wire, bars, etc.) having been drawn unheated through a die to reduce dimensions, toughen, and improve surface finish.
cold duck *n.* an alcoholic beverage made from equal parts of burgundy and champagne.
cold feet *pl. n. Informal.* loss or lack of courage or confidence.
cold frame *n.* an unheated wooden frame with a glass top, used to protect young plants from the cold.
cold front *n. Meteorol.* **1.** the boundary line between a warm air mass and the cold air pushing it from beneath and behind as it moves. **2.** the line on the earth's surface where the cold front meets it. ~Compare **warm front.**
cold-hearted *adj.* lacking in feeling or warmth; unkind. —ˌ**cold-ˈheartedly** *adv.* —ˌ**cold-ˈheartedness** *n.*
coldie (ˈkəʊldɪ) *n. Austral. slang.* a cold can or bottle of beer.
cold light *n.* light emitted at low temperatures from a source that is not incandescent, as in fluorescence, phosphorescence, bioluminescence, or triboluminescence.
cold moulding *n.* the production of moulded articles from resins that polymerize chemically.
cold pack *n.* **1. a.** a method of lowering the body temperature by wrapping a person in a sheet soaked in cold water. **b.** the sheet so used. **2.** a tinning process in which raw food is packed in cans or jars and then heated.
cold-rolled *adj.* (of metal sheets, etc.) having been rolled without heating, producing a smooth surface finish.
cold rubber *n.* synthetic rubber made at low temperatures (about 5°C). It is stronger than that made at higher temperatures and is used for car tyres.
cold shoulder *Informal.* ~*n.* **1.** (often preceded by *the*) a show of indifference; a slight. ~*vb.* **cold-shoulder.** (*tr.*) **2.** to treat with indifference.
cold snap *n.* a sudden short spell of cold weather.
cold sore *n.* a cluster of blisters at the margin of the lips that sometimes accompanies the common cold, caused by a viral infection. Technical name: **herpes labialis.**
cold start *n. Computer technol.* the reloading of a program or operating system.
cold storage *n.* **1.** the storage of things in an artificially cooled place for preservation. **2.** *Informal.* a state of temporary suspension: *to put an idea into cold storage.*
cold sweat *n. Informal.* a bodily reaction to fear or nervousness, characterized by chill and moist skin.
cold turkey *n.* **1.** *Slang.* a method of curing drug addiction by abrupt withdrawal of all doses. **2.** the withdrawal symptoms, esp. nausea and shivering, brought on by this method.
cold war *n.* a state of political hostility and military tension between two countries or power blocs, involving propaganda, subversion, threats, economic sanctions, and other measures short of open warfare, esp. that between the American and Soviet blocs after World War II (the **Cold War**).
cold warrior *n.* a person who engages in or promotes a cold war.
cold wave *n.* **1.** *Meteorol.* a sudden spell of low temperatures over a wide area, often following the passage of a cold front. **2.** *Hairdressing.* a permanent wave made by chemical agents applied at normal temperatures.
cold-weld *vb.* (*tr.*) to join (two metal surfaces) without heat by forcing them together so that the oxide films are broken and adhesion occurs. —**cold welding** *n.*
cold work *n.* **1.** the craft of shaping metal without heat. ~*vb.* **cold-work.** (*tr.*) **2.** to shape (metal) in this way.
cole (kəʊl) *n.* any of various plants of the genus *Brassica,* such as the cabbage and rape. Also called: **colewort.** [Old English *cāl,* from Latin *caulis* plant stalk, cabbage]
colectomy (kəˈlɛktəmɪ) *n., pl.* **-mies.** surgical removal of part or all of the colon.
colemanite (ˈkəʊlməˌnaɪt) *n.* a colourless or white glassy mineral consisting of hydrated calcium borate in monoclinic crystalline form. It occurs with and is a source of borax. Formula: $Ca_2B_6O_{11}.5H_2O$. [C19: named after William T. *Coleman* (1824–93), American pioneer, owner of the mine in which it was discovered]
coleopter (ˌkɒlɪˈɒptə) *n. Aeronautics.* an aircraft that has an annular wing with the fuselage and engine on the centre line.
coleopteran (ˌkɒlɪˈɒptərən) *n. also* **coleopteron. 1.** any of the insects of the cosmopolitan order *Coleoptera,* in which the forewings are modified to form shell-like protective elytra. The order includes the beetles and weevils. ~*adj. also* **coleopterous. 2.** of, relating to, or belonging to the order *Coleoptera.* [C18: from New Latin *Coleoptera,* from Greek *koleoptera,* from *koleopteros* sheath-winged, from *koleon* sheath + *pteron* wing]
coleoptile (ˌkɒlɪˈɒptaɪl) *n.* a protective sheath around the plumule in grasses. [C19: from New Latin *coleoptilum,* from Greek *koleon* sheath + *ptilon* down, soft plumage]
coleorhiza (ˌkɒlɪəˈraɪzə) *n., pl.* **-zae** (-ziː). a protective sheath around the radicle in grasses. [C19: from New Latin, from Greek *koleon* sheath + *rhiza* root]
coleslaw (ˈkəʊlˌslɔː) *n.* a salad of shredded cabbage, mayonnaise, carrots, onions, etc. [C19: from Dutch *koolsla,* from *koolsalade,* literally: cabbage salad]
colestipol (kəˈlɛstɪˌpɒl) *n.* a drug that reduces the level of cholesterol in the blood: used, together with dietary restriction of cholesterol, to treat selected patients with hypercholesterolaemia and so prevent atherosclerosis.
coletit (ˈkəʊlˌtɪt) *n.* another name for **coal tit.**
coleus (ˈkəʊlɪəs) *n., pl.* **-uses.** any plant of the Old World genus *Coleus:* cultivated for their variegated leaves, typically marked with red, yellow, or white: family *Labiatae* (labiates). [C19: from New Latin, from Greek *koleos,* variant of *koleon* sheath; from the way in which the stamens are joined]
colewort (ˈkəʊlˌwɜːt) *n.* another name for **cole.**
coley (ˈkəʊlɪ, ˈkɒlɪ) *n. Brit.* any of various edible fishes, esp. the coalfish.
colic (ˈkɒlɪk) *n.* a condition characterized by acute spasmodic abdominal pain, esp. that caused by inflammation, distention, etc., of the gastrointestinal tract. [C15: from Old French *colique,* from Late Latin *cōlicus* ill with colic, from Greek *kōlon,* variant of *kolon* COLON[2]] —ˈ**colicky** *adj.*
colicroot (ˈkɒlɪkˌruːt) *n.* **1.** either of two North American liliaceous plants, *Aletris farinosa* or *A. aurea,* having tubular white or yellow flowers and a bitter root formerly used to relieve colic. **2.** any of various other plants formerly used to relieve colic.
colicweed (ˈkɒlɪkˌwiːd) *n.* any of several plants of the genera *Dicentra* or *Corydalis,* such as the squirrel corn and Dutchman's-breeches: family *Fumariaceae.*
coliform bacteria (ˈkɒlɪfɔːm) *pl. n.* a large group of bacteria that inhabit the intestinal tract of man and animals and may cause disease.
coliseum (ˌkɒlɪˈsɪəm) *or* **colosseum** *n.* a large building, such as a stadium or theatre, used for entertainments, sports, etc. [C18: from Medieval Latin *Colisseum,* variant of *Colosseum,* the amphitheatre in Rome]
colitis (kɒˈlaɪtɪs, kə-) *or* **colonitis** (ˌkɒləˈnaɪtɪs) *n.* inflammation of the colon. —**colitic** (kɒˈlɪtɪk) *adj.*
coll. *abbrev. for:* **1.** colleague. **2.** collection. **3.** collector. **4.** college. **5.** collegiate. **6.** colloquial.
collaborate (kəˈlæbəˌreɪt) *vb.* (*intr.*) **1.** (often foll. by *on, with,* etc.) to work with another or others on a joint project. **2.** to cooperate as a traitor, esp. with an enemy occupying one's own country. [C19: from Late Latin *collabōrāre,* from Latin *com-* together + *labōrāre* to work] —**colˌlaboˈration** *n.* —**colˈlaborative** *adj.* —**colˈlaboˌrator** *or* **colˌlaboˈrationist** *n.*
collage (kəˈlɑːʒ, kɒ-; *French* kɔlaʒ) *n.* **1.** an art form in which compositions are made out of pieces of paper, cloth, photographs, and other miscellaneous objects, juxtaposed and pasted on a dry ground. **2.** a composition made in this way. **3.** any collection of unrelated things. [C20: French, from *coller* to stick, from *colle* glue, from Greek *kolla*] —**colˈlagist** *n.*
collagen (ˈkɒlədʒən) *n.* a fibrous scleroprotein of connective tissue and bones that is rich in glycine and proline and yields gelatin on boiling. [C19: from Greek *kolla* glue + -GEN] —**collagenic** (ˌkɒləˈdʒɛnɪk) *or* **collagenous** (kəˈlædʒənəs) *adj.*
collapsar (kɒˈlæpsɑː) *n. Astronomy.* another name for **black hole.**
collapse (kəˈlæps) *vb.* **1.** (*intr.*) to fall down or cave in suddenly: *the whole building collapsed.* **2.** (*intr.*) to fail completely: *his story collapsed on investigation.* **3.** (*intr.*) to break down or fall down from lack of strength. **4.** to fold (furniture, etc.) compactly or (of furniture, etc.) to be designed to fold compactly. ~*n.* **5.** the act or instance of suddenly falling down, caving in, or crumbling. **6.** a sudden failure or breakdown. [C18: from Latin *collāpsus,* from *collābī* to fall in ruins, from *lābī* to fall] —**colˈlapsible** *or* **colˈlapsable** *adj.* —**colˌlapsiˈbility** *n.*
collar (ˈkɒlə) *n.* **1.** the part of a garment around the neck and shoulders, often detachable or folded over. **2.** any band, necklace, garland, etc., encircling the neck: *a collar of flowers.* **3.** a band or chain of leather, rope, or metal placed around an animal's neck to restrain, harness, or identify it. **4.** *Biology.* a marking or structure resembling a collar, such as that found around the necks of some birds or at the junction of a stem and a root. **5.** a section of a shaft or rod having a locally increased diameter to provide a bearing seat or a locating ring. **6.** a cut of meat, esp. bacon, taken from around the neck of an animal. **7.** **hot under the collar.** *Informal.* aroused with anger, annoyance, etc. ~*vb.* (*tr.*) **8.** to put a collar on; furnish with a collar. **9.** to seize by the collar. **10.** *Informal.* to seize; arrest; detain. [C13: from Latin *collāre* neckband, neck chain, collar, from *collum* neck]
collarbone (ˈkɒləˌbəʊn) *n.* the nontechnical name for **clavicle.**
collar cell *n.* another name for **choanocyte.**
collard (ˈkɒləd) *n.* **1.** a variety of the cabbage, *Brassica oleracea acephala,* having a crown of edible leaves. See also **kale. 2.** the leaves of this plant, eaten as a vegetable. [C18: variant of COLEWORT]
collared dove *n.* a European dove, *Streptopelia decaocto,* having a brownish-grey plumage with a black band on the back of the neck.
collarette (ˌkɒləˈrɛt) *n.* a woman's fur or lace collar.
collat. *abbrev. for* collateral.
collate (kɒˈleɪt, kə-) *vb.* (*tr.*) **1.** to examine and compare (texts, statements, etc.) in order to note points of agreement and disagreement. **2.** (in library work) to check the number and order of (the pages of a book). **3.** *Bookbinding.* **a.** to check the sequence of (the sections of a book) after gathering. **b.** a nontechnical word for **gather** (sense 9). **4.** (often foll. by *to*) *Christianity.*

to appoint (an incumbent) to a benefice. [C16: from Latin *collātus* brought together (past participle of *conferre* to gather), from *com-* together + *lātus,* past participle of *ferre* to bring]

collateral (kɒ'lætərəl, kə-) *n.* **1. a.** security pledged for the repayment of a loan. **b.** (*as modifier*): *a collateral loan.* **2.** a person, animal, or plant descended from the same ancestor as another but through a different line. ~*adj.* **3.** situated or running side by side. **4.** descended from a common ancestor but through different lines. **5.** serving to support or corroborate. **6.** aside from the main issue. **7.** uniting in tendency. [C14: from Medieval Latin *collaterālis,* from Latin *com-* together + *laterālis* of the side, from *latus* side] —**col'laterally** *adv.*

collateral damage *n. Military.* unintentional damage to civil property and civilian casualties, caused by military operations.

collation (kɒ'leɪʃən, kə-) *n.* **1.** the act or process of collating. **2.** a description of the technical features of a book. **3.** *R.C. Church.* a light meal permitted on fast days. **4.** any light informal meal. **5.** the appointment of a clergyman to a benefice.

collative (kɒ'leɪtɪv, 'kɒlə-) *adj.* **1.** involving collation. **2.** (of benefices) presented or held by collation.

collator (kɒ'leɪtə, kəʊ-; 'kɒleɪtə, 'kəʊ-) *n.* **1.** a person or machine that collates texts or manuscripts. **2.** *Computer technol.* a device for matching or checking punched cards in separate files and for merging two or more files sorted into the same ordered sequence.

colleague ('kɒliːg) *n.* a fellow worker or member of a staff, department, profession, etc. [C16: from French *collègue,* from Latin *collēga* one selected at the same time as another, from *com-* together + *lēgāre* to choose]

collect[1] (kə'lɛkt) *vb.* **1.** to gather together or be gathered together. **2.** to accumulate (stamps, books, etc.) as a hobby or for study. **3.** (*tr.*) to call for or receive payment of (taxes, dues, etc.). **4.** (*tr.*) to regain control of (oneself, one's emotions, etc.) as after a shock or surprise: *he collected his wits.* **5.** (*tr.*) to fetch: *collect your own post.* **6.** (*intr.;* sometimes foll. by *on*) *Slang.* to receive large sums of money, as from an investment: *he really collected when the will was read.* **7.** (*tr.*) *Austral. and N.Z. informal.* to collide with; be hit by. **8. collect on delivery.** the U.S. term for **cash on delivery.** ~*adv., adj.* **9.** *U.S.* (of telephone calls) on a reverse-charge basis. ~*n.* **10.** *Austral. informal.* a winning bet. [C16: from Latin *collēctus* collected, from *colligere* to gather together, from *com-* together + *legere* to gather]

collect[2] ('kɒlɛkt) *n. Christianity.* a short Church prayer generally preceding the lesson or epistle in Communion and other services. [C13: from Medieval Latin *collecta* (from the phrase *ōrātiō ad collēctam* prayer at the (people's) assembly), from Latin *colligere* to COLLECT[1]]

collectable *or* **collectible** (kə'lɛktəbᵊl) *adj.* **1.** (of antiques, objets d'art, etc.) of interest to a collector. ~*n.* **2.** any object regarded as being of interest to a collector.

collectanea (ˌkɒlɛk'teɪnɪə) *pl. n.* a collection of excerpts from one or more authors; miscellany; anthology. [C18: from Latin, from *collēctāneus* assembled, from *colligere* to COLLECT[1]]

collected (kə'lɛktɪd) *adj.* **1.** in full control of one's faculties; composed. **2.** assembled in totality or brought together into one volume or a set of volumes: *the collected works of Dickens.* **3.** (of a horse or a horse's pace) controlled so that movement is in short restricted steps: *a collected canter.* —**col'lectedly** *adv.* —**col'lectedness** *n.*

collection (kə'lɛkʃən) *n.* **1.** the act or process of collecting. **2.** a number of things collected or assembled together. **3.** something gathered into a mass or pile; accumulation: *a collection of rubbish.* **4.** a sum of money collected or solicited, as in church. **5.** removal, esp. regular removal of letters from a postbox. **6.** (*often pl.*) (at Oxford University) a college examination or an oral report by a tutor.

collective (kə'lɛktɪv) *adj.* **1.** formed or assembled by collection. **2.** forming a whole or aggregate. **3.** of, done by, or characteristic of individuals acting in cooperation. ~*n.* **4. a.** a cooperative enterprise or unit, such as a collective farm. **b.** the members of such a cooperative. **5.** short for **collective noun.** —**col'lectively** *adv.* —**col'lectiveness** *n.*

collective agreement *n.* a negotiated agreement, which is not enforceable at law, between an employer and employees' representatives, covering rates of pay or terms and conditions of employment, or both.

collective bargaining *n.* negotiation between one or more trade unions and one or more employers or an employers' organization on the incomes and working conditions of the employees.

collective farm *n.* (chiefly in Communist countries) a farm or group of farms managed and owned, through the state, by the community. Russian name: **kolkhoz.**

collective fruit *n.* another name for **multiple fruit.**

collective noun *n.* a noun that is singular in form but that refers to a group of people or things.

▷**Usage.** Collective nouns are usually used with singular verbs: *the family is on holiday; General Motors is mounting a big sales campaign.* In British usage, however, plural verbs are sometimes employed in this context, esp. where reference is being made to a collection of individual objects or persons rather than to the group as a unit: *the family are all on holiday.* Care should be taken that the same collective noun is not treated as both singular and plural in the same sentence: *the family is well and sends its best wishes* or *the family are all well and send their best wishes,* but not *the family is well and send their best wishes.*

collective ownership *n.* ownership by a group for the benefit of members of that group.

collective pitch lever *n.* a lever in a helicopter to change the angle of attack of all the rotor blades simultaneously, causing it to rise or descend. Compare **cyclic pitch lever.**

collective security *n.* a system of maintaining world peace and security by concerted action on the part of the nations of the world.

collective unconscious *n. Psychol.* (in Jungian psychological theory) a part of the unconscious mind incorporating patterns of memories, instincts, and experiences common to all mankind. These patterns are inherited, may be arranged into archetypes, and are observable through their effects on dreams, behaviour, etc.

collectivism (kə'lɛktɪˌvɪzəm) *n.* **1.** the principle of ownership of the means of production, by the state or the people. **2.** a social system based upon such a principle. —**col'lectivist** *n.* —**colˌlectiv'istic** *adj.*

collectivity (ˌkɒlɛk'tɪvɪtɪ) *n., pl.* **-ties.** **1.** the quality or state of being collective. **2.** a collective whole or aggregate. **3.** people regarded as a whole.

collectivize *or* **collectivise** (kə'lɛktɪˌvaɪz) *vb.* (*tr.*) to organize according to the principles of collectivism. —**colˌlectivi'zation** *or* **colˌlectivi'sation** *n.*

collector (kə'lɛktə) *n.* **1.** a person or thing that collects. **2.** a person employed to collect debts, rents, etc. **3.** the head of a district administration in India. **4.** a person who collects or amasses objects as a hobby. **5.** *Electronics.* the region in a transistor into which charge carriers flow from the base. —**col'lectorˌship** *n.*

collectorate (kə'lɛktərɪt) *n.* the office of a collector in India.

collector's item *or* **piece** *n.* a thing regarded as being exquisite or rare and thus worthy of the interest of one who collects such things.

colleen ('kɒliːn, kɒ'liːn) *n.* **1.** an Irish word for **girl.** **2.** an Irish girl. [C19: from Irish Gaelic *cailín* a girl, a young unmarried woman]

college ('kɒlɪdʒ) *n.* **1.** an institution of higher education; part of a university. **2.** a school or an institution providing specialized courses or teaching: *a college of music.* **3.** the building or buildings in which a college is housed. **4.** the staff and students of a college. **5.** an organized body of persons with specific rights and duties: *an electoral college.* **6.** a body of clerics living in community and supported by endowment. **7.** *Chiefly Brit.* an obsolete slang word for **prison.** [C14: from Latin *collēgium* company, society, band of associates, from *collēga;* see COLLEAGUE]

college of advanced technology *n. Brit.* (formerly) a college offering degree or equivalent courses in technology, with research facilities. In the mid-1960s these were granted university status. Abbrev.: **CAT.**

college of arms *n.* any of several institutions in Great Britain having a royal charter to deal with matters of heraldry, grant armorial bearings, record and trace genealogies, etc. Also called: **herald's college.**

College of Cardinals *n. R.C. Church.* the collective body of cardinals having the function of electing and advising the pope.

college of education *n. Brit.* a professional training college for teachers.

College of Justice *n.* the official name for the Scottish Court of Session; the supreme court of Scotland.

college pudding *n. Brit.* a baked or steamed suet pudding containing dried fruit and spice.

collegial (kə'liːdʒɪəl) *adj.* **1.** of or relating to a college. **2.** having authority or power shared among a number of people associated as colleagues. —**col'legially** *adv.*

collegian (kə'liːdʒɪən) *n.* a current member of a college; student.

collegiate (kə'liːdʒɪɪt) *adj.* **1.** Also: **collegial.** of or relating to a college or college students. **2.** (of a university) composed of various colleges of equal standing. ~*n.* **3.** *Canadian.* short for **collegiate institute.**

collegiate church *n.* **1.** *R.C. Church, Church of England.* a church that has an endowed chapter of canons and prebendaries attached to it but that is not a cathedral. **2.** *U.S. Protestantism.* one of a group of churches presided over by a body of pastors. **3.** *Scot. Protestantism.* a church served by two or more ministers. **4.** a large church endowed in the Middle Ages to become a school. **5.** a chapel either endowed by or connected with a college.

collegiate institute *n. Canadian.* (in certain provinces) a large secondary school meeting set requirements in terms of courses, facilities, and specialist staff.

collegium (kə'liːdʒɪəm) *n., pl.* **-giums** *or* **-gia** (-dʒɪə). **1.** (in the former Soviet Union) a board in charge of a department. **2.** another term for **College of Cardinals** or **Sacred College.** [Latin: COLLEGE]

col legno ('kɒl 'legnəʊ, 'leɪnjəʊ) *adv. Music.* to be played (on a stringed instrument) by striking the strings with the back of the bow. [Italian: with the wood]

collembolan (kə'lɛmbələn) *n.* **1.** any small primitive wingless insect of the order *Collembola,* which comprises the springtails. ~*adj.* **2.** of, relating to, or belonging to the *Collembola.* [C19:

from New Latin *Collembola,* from Greek *kolla* glue + *embolon* peg, wedge]

collenchyma (kəˈlɛŋkɪmə) *n.* a strengthening and supporting tissue in plants, consisting of elongated living cells whose walls are thickened with cellulose and pectins. [C19: New Latin, from Greek *kolla* glue + *enkhuma* infusion] —**collenchymatous** (ˌkɒlənˈkɪmətəs) *adj.*

Colles' fracture (ˈkɒlɪs) *n.* a fracture of the radius just above the wrist, with backward and outward displacement of the hand. [C19: named after Abraham *Colles* (died 1843), Irish surgeon]

collet (ˈkɒlɪt) *n.* **1.** (in a jewellery setting) a band or coronet-shaped claw that holds an individual stone. **2.** *Mechanical engineering.* an externally tapered sleeve made in two or more segments and used to grip a shaft passed through its centre when the sleeve is compressed by being inserted in a similarly tapered hole. **3.** *Horology.* a small metal collar that supports the inner end of the hairspring. ~*vb.* **4.** (*tr.*) *Jewellery.* to mount in a collet. [C16: from Old French: a little collar, from *col* neckband, neck, from Latin *collum* neck]

colleterial gland (ˌkɒlɪˈtɪərɪəl) *n. Zoology.* a paired accessory reproductive gland, present in most female insects, secreting a sticky substance that forms either the egg cases or the cement that binds the eggs to a surface. [C19: from New Latin *colleterium* glue-secreting organ, from Greek *kolla* glue + -AL[1]]

colliculus (kɒˈlɪkjʊləs) *n., pl.* **-li.** *Anatomy.* a small elevation, as on the surface of the optic lobe of the brain. [C19: New Latin]

collide (kəˈlaɪd) *vb.* (*intr.*) **1.** to crash together with a violent impact. **2.** to conflict in attitude, opinion, or desire; clash; disagree. [C17: from Latin *collīdere* to clash together, from *com-* together + *laedere* to strike, wound]

collider (kəˈlaɪdə) *n. Physics.* a particle accelerator in which beams of particles are made to collide.

collie (ˈkɒlɪ) *n.* any of several silky-coated breeds of dog developed for herding sheep and cattle. See **border collie, rough collie, bearded collie.** [C17: Scottish, probably from earlier *colie* black with coal dust, from *cole* COAL]

collier (ˈkɒlɪə) *n. Chiefly Brit.* **1.** a coal miner. **2. a.** a ship designed to transport coal. **b.** a member of its crew. [C14: from COAL + -IER]

colliery (ˈkɒljərɪ) *n., pl.* **-lieries.** *Chiefly Brit.* a coal mine.

colligate (ˈkɒlɪˌgeɪt) *vb.* (*tr.*) **1.** to connect or link together; tie; join. **2.** to relate (isolated facts, observations, etc.) by a general hypothesis. [C16: from Latin *colligāre* to fasten together, from *com-* together + *ligāre* to bind] —ˌ**colliˈgation** *n.*

colligative (kəˈlɪgətɪv) *adj.* (of a physical property of a substance) depending on the concentrations of atoms, ions, and molecules that are present rather than on their nature.

collimate (ˈkɒlɪˌmeɪt) *vb.* (*tr.*) **1.** to adjust the line of sight of (an optical instrument). **2.** to use a collimator on (a beam of radiation or particles). **3.** to make parallel or bring into line. [C17: from New Latin *collimāre,* erroneously for Latin *collīneāre* to aim, from *com-* (intensive) + *līneāre,* from *līnea* line] —ˌ**colliˈmation** *n.*

collimator (ˈkɒlɪˌmeɪtə) *n.* **1.** a small telescope attached to a larger optical instrument as an aid in fixing its line of sight. **2.** an optical system of lenses and slits producing a nondivergent beam of light, usually for use in spectroscopes. **3.** any device for limiting the size and angle of spread of a beam of radiation or particles.

collinear (kɒˈlɪnɪə) *adj.* **1.** lying on the same straight line. **2.** having a common line. —**collinearity** (ˌkɒlɪnɪˈærɪtɪ) *n.* —**colˈlinearly** *adv.*

collins (ˈkɒlɪnz) *n.* a tall fizzy iced drink made with gin, vodka, rum, etc., mixed with fruit juice, soda water, and sugar. [C20: probably after the proper name *Collins*]

collinsia (kəˈlɪnsɪə, -zɪə) *n.* a North American plant of the scrophulariaceous genus *Collinsia,* having blue, white, or purple flowers. [C19: New Latin, named after Zaccheus *Collins* (1764–1831), American botanist]

Collins Street Farmer *n. Austral. slang.* a businessman who invests in farms, land, etc. Also called: **Pitt Street Farmer.** [C20: after a principal business street in Melbourne]

collision (kəˈlɪʒən) *n.* **1.** a violent impact of moving objects; crash. **2.** the conflict of opposed ideas, wishes, attitudes, etc.: *a collision of interests.* **3.** *Physics.* an event in which two or more bodies or particles come together with a resulting exchange of energy and change of direction. [C15: from Late Latin *collīsiō* from Latin *collīdere* to COLLIDE]

collocate (ˈkɒləˌkeɪt) *vb.* (*tr.*) to group or place together in some system or order. [C16: from Latin *collocāre,* from *com-* together + *locāre* to place, from *locus* place]

collocation (ˌkɒləˈkeɪʃən) *n.* a grouping together of things in a certain order, as of the words in a sentence.

collocutor (ˈkɒləˌkjuːtə) *n.* a person who talks or engages in conversation with another.

collodion (kəˈləʊdɪən) *or* **collodium** (kəˈləʊdɪəm) *n.* a colourless or yellow syrupy liquid that consists of a solution of pyroxylin in ether and alcohol: used in medicine and in the manufacture of photographic plates, lacquers, etc. [C19: from New Latin *collōdium,* from Greek *kollōdēs* glutinous, from *kolla* glue]

collogue (kɒˈləʊg) *vb.* **collogues, colloguing, collogued.** (*intr.;* usually foll. by *with*) to confer confidentially; intrigue or conspire. [C16: perhaps from obsolete *colleague* (vb.) to be or act as a colleague, conspire, influenced by Latin *colloquī* to talk with; see COLLEAGUE]

colloid (ˈkɒlɔɪd) *n.* **1.** Also called: **colloidal solution** *or* **suspension.** a mixture having particles of one component, with diameters between 10^{-7} and 10^{-9} metre, suspended in a continuous phase of another component. The mixture has properties between those of a solution and a fine suspension. **2.** the solid suspended phase in such a mixture. **3.** *Obsolete.* a substance that in solution does not penetrate a semipermeable membrane. Compare **crystalloid** (sense 2). **4.** *Physiol.* a gelatinous substance of the thyroid follicles that holds the hormonal secretions of the thyroid gland. ~*adj.* **5.** *Pathol.* of or relating to the gluelike translucent material found in certain degenerating tissues. **6.** of, denoting, or having the character of a colloid. [C19: from Greek *kolla* glue + -OID] —**colˈloidal** *adj.* —**colloidality** (ˌkɒlɔɪˈdælɪtɪ) *n.*

collop (ˈkɒləp) *n. Dialect.* **1.** a slice of meat. **2.** a small piece of anything. [C14: of Scandinavian origin; compare Swedish *kalops* meat stew]

colloq. *abbrev. for* colloquial(ly).

colloquial (kəˈləʊkwɪəl) *adj.* **1.** of or relating to conversation. **2.** denoting or characterized by informal or conversational idiom or vocabulary. Compare **informal.** —**colˈloquially** *adv.* —**colˈloquialness** *n.*

colloquialism (kəˈləʊkwɪəˌlɪzəm) *n.* **1.** a word or phrase appropriate to conversation and other informal situations. **2.** the use of colloquial words and phrases.

colloquium (kəˈləʊkwɪəm) *n., pl.* **-quiums** *or* **-quia** (-kwɪə). **1.** an informal gathering for discussion. **2.** an academic seminar. [C17: from Latin: conversation, conference, COLLOQUY]

colloquy (ˈkɒləkwɪ) *n., pl.* **-quies. 1.** a formal conversation or conference. **2.** a literary work in dialogue form. **3.** an informal conference on religious or theological matters. [C16: from Latin *colloquium* from *colloquī* to talk with, from *com-* together + *loquī* to speak] —ˈ**colloquist** *n.*

collotype (ˈkɒləʊˌtaɪp) *n.* **1.** Also called: **photogelatin process.** a method of lithographic printing from a flat surface of hardened gelatin: used mainly for fine-detail reproduction in monochrome or colour. **2.** a print made using this process. [C19: from Greek *kolla* glue + TYPE] —**collotypic** (ˌkɒləˈtɪpɪk) *adj.*

collude (kəˈluːd) *vb.* (*intr.*) to conspire together, esp. in planning a fraud; connive. [C16: from Latin *collūdere,* literally: to play together, hence, conspire together, from *com-* together + *lūdere* to play] —**colˈluder** *n.*

collusion (kəˈluːʒən) *n.* **1.** secret agreement for a fraudulent purpose; connivance; conspiracy. **2.** a secret agreement between opponents at law in order to obtain a judicial decision for some wrongful or improper purpose. [C14: from Latin *collūsiō,* from *collūdere* to COLLUDE] —**colˈlusive** *adj.*

colluvium (kəˈluːvɪəm) *n., pl.* **-via** (-vɪə) *or* **-viums.** a mixture of rock fragments from the bases of cliffs. [Latin: collection of filth, from *colluere* to wash thoroughly, from *com-* (intensive) + *luere* to wash] —**colˈluvial** *adj.*

colly (ˈkɒlɪ) *Archaic or dialect.* ~*n., pl.* **-lies. 1.** soot or grime, such as coal dust. ~*adj.* **-lier, -liest. 2.** dirty; sooty. ~*vb.* **collies, collying, collied. 3.** (*tr.*) to begrime; besmirch. [C16: ultimately from Old English *col* COAL]

collyrium (kɒˈlɪrɪəm) *n., pl.* **-lyria** (-ˈlɪrɪə) *or* **-lyriums.** a technical name for **eyewash** (sense 1). [C16: from Latin, from Greek *kollurion* poultice, eye salve]

collywobbles (ˈkɒlɪˌwɒbᵊlz) *pl. n.* (usually preceded by *the*) *Slang.* **1.** an upset stomach. **2.** acute diarrhoea. **3.** an intense feeling of nervousness. [C19: probably from New Latin *cholera morbus* the disease cholera, influenced through folk etymology by COLIC and WOBBLE]

Colo. *abbrev. for* Colorado.

colo- *or before a vowel* **col-** *combining form.* indicating the colon: *colostomy; colotomy.*

coloboma (ˌkɒləˈbəʊmə) *n.* a structural defect of the eye, esp. in the choroid, retina, or iris. [C19: New Latin, from Greek *kolobōma* a part taken away in mutilation, from *kolobos* cut short]

colobus (ˈkɒləbəs) *n.* any leaf-eating arboreal Old World monkey of the genus *Colobus,* of W and central Africa, having a slender body, long silky fur, long tail, and reduced or absent thumbs. [C19: New Latin, from Greek *kolobos* cut short; referring to its thumb]

colocynth (ˈkɒləsɪnθ) *n.* **1.** a cucurbitaceous climbing plant, *Citrullus colocynthis,* of the Mediterranean region and Asia, having bitter-tasting fruit. **2.** the dried fruit pulp of this plant, used as a strong purgative. ~Also called: **bitter apple.** [C17: from Latin *colocynthis,* from Greek *kolokunthis,* from *kolokunthē* gourd, of obscure origin]

cologarithm (kəʊˈlɒgəˌrɪðəm) *n.* the logarithm of the reciprocal of a number; the negative value of the logarithm: *the cologarithm of 4 is log ¼.* Abbrev.: **colog.**

cologne (kəˈləʊn) *n.* a perfumed liquid or solid made of fragrant essential oils and alcohol. Also called: **Cologne water, eau de Cologne.** [C18: *Cologne water,* from *Cologne,* city in W Germany, where it was first manufactured (1709)]

Colombian (kəˈlɒmbɪən) *adj.* **1.** of or relating to Colombia, a republic in NW South America, or its people. ~*n.* **2.** a native or inhabitant of Colombia.

colon[1] ('kəʊlən) *n.* **1.** (*pl.* **-lons**) the punctuation mark : , usually preceding an explanation or an example of what has gone before, a list, or an extended quotation. **2.** (*pl.* **-lons**) this mark used for certain other purposes, such as expressions of time, as in *2:45 p.m.*, or when a ratio is given in figures, as in *5:3.* **3.** (*pl.* **-la** (-lə)) (in classical prosody) a part of a rhythmical period with two to six feet and one principal accent or ictus. [C16: from Latin, from Greek *kōlon* limb, hence part of a strophe, clause of a sentence]

colon[2] ('kəʊlən) *n., pl.* **-lons** *or* **-la** (-lə). the part of the large intestine between the caecum and the rectum. [C16: from Latin: large intestine, from Greek *kolon*]

colon[3] (kə'lɒn; *French* kɔlɔ̃) *n.* a colonial farmer or plantation owner, esp. in a French colony. [French: colonist, from Latin *colōnus,* from *colere* to till, inhabit]

colón (kəʊ'ləʊn; *Spanish* ko'lon) *n., pl.* **-lons** *or* **-lones** (*Spanish* -'lones). **1.** the standard monetary unit of Costa Rica in Central America, divided into 100 céntimos. **2.** the standard monetary unit of El Salvador in Central America, divided into 100 centavos. [C19: American Spanish, from Spanish, after Cristóbal *Colón* Christopher Columbus]

colonel ('kɜːnᵊl) *n.* an officer of land or air forces junior to a brigadier but senior to a lieutenant colonel. [C16: via Old French, from Old Italian *colonnello* column of soldiers, from *colonna* COLUMN] —'**colonelcy** *or* '**colonel,ship** *n.*

Colonel Blimp *n.* See **blimp**[2].

colonial (kə'ləʊnɪəl) *adj.* **1.** of, characteristic of, relating to, possessing, or inhabiting a colony or colonies. **2.** (*often cap.*) characteristic of or relating to the 13 British colonies that became the United States of America (1776). **3.** (*often cap.*) of or relating to the colonies of the British Empire. **4.** denoting, relating to, or having the style of Neoclassical architecture used in the British colonies in America in the 17th and 18th centuries. **5.** of or relating to the period of Australian history before Federation (1901). **6.** (of organisms such as corals and bryozoans) existing as a colony of polyps. **7.** (of animals and plants) having become established in a community in a new environment. ~*n.* **8.** a native of a colony. —**co'lonially** *adv.*

colonial experience *n. Austral.* experience of farming, etc., gained by a young Englishman in colonial Australia. —**colonial experiencer** *n.*

colonial goose *n. N.Z.* an old-fashioned name for stuffed roast mutton.

colonialism (kə'ləʊnɪə,lɪzəm) *n.* the policy and practice of a power in extending control over weaker peoples or areas. Also called: **imperialism.** —**co'lonialist** *n., adj.*

colonic (kə'lɒnɪk) *adj.* **1. a.** *Anatomy.* of or relating to the colon. **b.** *Med.* relating to irrigation of the colon for cleansing purposes. ~*n.* **2.** *Med.* irrigation of the colon by injecting large amounts of fluid high into the colon: *a high colonic.*

colonist ('kɒlənɪst) *n.* **1.** a person who settles or colonizes an area. **2.** an inhabitant or member of a colony.

colonitis (,kɒlə'naɪtɪs) *n. Pathol.* another word for **colitis.**

colonize *or* **colonise** ('kɒlə,naɪz) *vb.* **1.** to send colonists to or establish a colony in (an area). **2.** to settle in (an area) as colonists. **3.** (*tr.*) to transform (a community) into a colony. **4.** (of plants and animals) to become established in (a new environment). —'**colo,nizable** *or* '**colo,nisable** *adj.* —,**coloni'zation** *or* ,**coloni'sation** *n.* —'**colo,nizer** *or* '**colo,niser** *n.*

colonnade (,kɒlə'neɪd) *n.* **1.** a set of evenly-spaced columns. **2.** a row of regularly spaced trees. [C18: from French, from *colonne* COLUMN; on the model of Italian *colonnato,* from *colonna* column] —,**colon'naded** *adj.*

colonoscope (kə'lɒnə,skəʊp) *n.* an instrument for examining the colon, consisting of a flexible lighted tube that is inserted in the colon to look for abnormalities and to remove them or take tissue samples. [C20: from COLON[2] + -O- + -SCOPE] —**colonoscopy** (,kɒlən'ɒskəpɪ) *n.*

colony ('kɒlənɪ) *n., pl.* **-nies. 1.** a body of people who settle in a country distant from their homeland but maintain ties with it. **2.** the community formed by such settlers. **3.** a subject territory occupied by a settlement from the ruling state. **4. a.** a community of people who form a national, racial, or cultural minority: *an artists' colony; the American colony in London.* **b.** the area itself. **5.** *Zoology.* **a.** a group of the same type of animal or plant living or growing together. **b.** an interconnected group of polyps of a colonial organism. **6.** *Bacteriol.* a group of bacteria, fungi, etc., derived from one or a few spores, esp. when grown on a culture medium. [C16: from Latin *colōnia,* from *colere* to cultivate, inhabit]

colony-stimulating factor *n. Immunol.* any of a number of substances, secreted by the bone marrow, that cause stem cells to proliferate and differentiate, forming colonies of specific blood cells. Synthetic forms are being tested for their ability to reduce the toxic effects of chemotherapy. Abbrev.: **CSF.**

colophon ('kɒlə,fɒn, -fən) *n.* **1.** a publisher's emblem on a book. **2.** (formerly) an inscription at the end of a book showing the title, printer, date, etc. [C17: via Late Latin, from Greek *kolophōn* a finishing stroke]

colophony (kɒ'lɒfənɪ) *n.* another name for **rosin** (sense 1). [C14: from Latin *Colophōnia rēsina* resin from Colophon]

coloquintida (,kɒlə'kwɪntɪdə) *n.* another name for **colocynth.** [C14: from Medieval Latin, from *colocynthid-* COLOCYNTH]

color ('kʌlə) *n.* the U.S. spelling of **colour.** —'**colorable** *adj.* —'**colorer** *n.* —'**colorful** *adj.* —'**coloring** *n.* —'**colorist** *n.* —'**colorless** *adj.*

Colorado beetle (,kɒlə'rɑːdəʊ) *n.* a black-and-yellow beetle, *Leptinotarsa decemlineata,* that is a serious pest of potatoes, feeding on the leaves: family *Chrysomelidae.* Also called: **potato beetle.** [named after the U.S. state of *Colorado*]

Colorado ruby *n.* a fire-red form of garnet found in Colorado and other parts of North America.

Colorado topaz *n.* **1.** a tawny coloured form of topaz found in Colorado. **2.** quartz of a similar colour.

colorant ('kʌlərənt) *n.* any substance that imparts colour, such as a pigment, dye, or ink; colouring matter.

coloration (,kʌlə'reɪʃən) *n.* **1.** arrangement of colour and tones; colouring. **2.** the colouring or markings of insects, birds, etc. See also **apatetic, aposematic, cryptic. 3.** unwanted extraneous variations in the frequency response of a loudspeaker or listening environment.

coloratura (,kɒlərə'tʊərə) *or* **colorature** ('kɒlərə,tjʊə) *n. Music.* **1. a.** (in 18th- and 19th-century arias) a florid virtuoso passage. **b.** (*as modifier*): *a coloratura aria.* **2.** Also called: **coloratura soprano.** a lyric soprano who specializes in such music. [C19: from obsolete Italian, literally: colouring, from Latin *colōrāre* to COLOUR]

colorectal (,kəʊləʊ'rɛktᵊl) *adj.* of or relating to the colon and rectum.

colorific (,kʌlə'rɪfɪk) *adj.* producing, imparting, or relating to colour.

colorimeter (,kʌlə'rɪmɪtə) *n.* **1.** Also called: **tintometer.** an apparatus for determining the concentration of a solution of a coloured substance by comparing the intensity of its colour with that of a standard solution or with standard colour slides. **2.** any apparatus for measuring the quality of a colour by comparison with standard colours or combinations of colours. —**colorimetric** (,kʌlərɪ'mɛtrɪk) *or* ,**colori'metrical** *adj.* —,**colori'metrically** *adv.* —,**color'imetry** *n.*

colossal (kə'lɒsᵊl) *adj.* **1.** of immense size; huge; gigantic. **2.** (in figure sculpture) approximately twice life-size. Compare **heroic** (sense 7). **3.** Also: **giant.** *Architect.* of or relating to the order of columns and pilasters that extend more than one storey in a façade. —**co'lossally** *adv.*

colosseum (,kɒlə'sɪəm) *n.* a variant spelling of **coliseum.**

Colossian (kə'lɒʃən) *n.* **1.** a native or inhabitant of Colossae, an ancient city in the Asian part of present-day Turkey. **2.** *New Testament.* any of the Christians of Colossae to whom St. Paul's Epistle was addressed.

colossus (kə'lɒsəs) *n., pl.* **-si** (-saɪ) *or* **-suses.** something very large, esp. a statue. [C14: from Latin, from Greek *kolossos*]

colostomy (kə'lɒstəmɪ) *n., pl.* **-mies.** the surgical formation of an opening from the colon onto the surface of the body, which functions as an anus.

colostrum (kə'lɒstrəm) *n.* the thin milky secretion from the nipples that precedes and follows true lactation. It consists largely of serum and white blood cells. [C16: from Latin, of obscure origin] —**co'lostral** *adj.*

colotomy (kə'lɒtəmɪ) *n., pl.* **-mies.** a colonic incision.

colour *or U.S.* **color** ('kʌlə) *n.* **1. a.** an attribute of things that results from the light they reflect, transmit, or emit in so far as this light causes a visual sensation that depends on its wavelengths. **b.** the aspect of visual perception by which an observer recognizes this attribute. **c.** the quality of the light producing this aspect of visual perception. **d.** (*as modifier*): *colour vision.* **2.** Also called: **chromatic colour. a.** a colour, such as red or green, that possesses hue, as opposed to achromatic colours such as white or black. **b.** (*as modifier*): *a colour television; a colour film.* Compare **black-and-white** (sense 2). **3.** a substance, such as a dye, pigment, or paint, that imparts colour to something. **4. a.** the skin complexion of a person, esp. as determined by his race. **b.** (*as modifier*): *colour prejudice; colour problem.* **5.** the use of all the hues in painting as distinct from composition, form, and light and shade. **6.** the quantity and quality of ink used in a printing process. **7.** the distinctive tone of a musical sound; timbre. **8.** vividness, authenticity, or individuality: *period colour.* **9.** semblance or pretext (esp. in the phrases **take on a different colour, under colour of**). **10.** *U.S.* a precious mineral particle, esp. gold, found in auriferous gravel. **11.** *Physics.* one of three characteristics of quarks, designated red, blue, or green, but having only a remote formal relationship with the physical sensation. ~*vb.* **12.** to give or apply colour to (something). **13.** (*tr.*) to give a convincing or plausible appearance to (something, esp. to that which is spoken or recounted): *to colour an alibi.* **14.** (*tr.*) to influence or distort (something, esp. a report or opinion): *anger coloured her judgment.* **15.** (*intr.*; often foll. by *up*) to become red in the face, esp. when embarrassed or annoyed. **16.** (*intr.*) (esp. of ripening fruit) to change hue. ~See also **colours.** [C13 from Old French *colour* from Latin *color* tint, hue]

colourable ('kʌlərəbᵊl) *adj.* **1.** capable of being coloured. **2.** appearing to be true; plausible: *a colourable excuse.* **3.** pretended; feigned: *colourable affection.* —,**coloura'bility** *or* '**colourableness** *n.* —'**colourably** *adv.*

colour bar *n.* discrimination against people of a different race, esp. as practised by Whites against Blacks.

colour-blind *adj.* of or relating to any defect in the normal ability to distinguish certain colours. See **deuteranopia, protanopia, tritanopia.** —**colour blindness** *n.*
colour code *n.* a system of easily distinguishable colours, as for the identification of electrical wires or resistors.
colour contrast *n. Psychol.* the change in the appearance of a colour surrounded by another colour; for example, grey looks bluish if surrounded by yellow.
coloured ('kʌləd) *adj.* **1.** possessing colour. **2.** having a strong element of fiction or fantasy; distorted (esp. in the phrase **highly coloured**).
Coloured ('kʌləd) *n., pl.* **Coloureds** *or* **Coloured. 1.** an individual who is not a White, esp. a Negro. **2.** Also called: **Cape Coloured.** (in South Africa) a person of racially mixed parentage or descent. ~*adj.* **3.** designating or relating to a Coloured or Coloureds: *a Coloured gentleman.*
colourfast ('kʌlə,fɑːst) *adj.* (of a fabric) having a colour that does not run or change when washed or worn. —'**colour,fastness** *n.*
colour filter *n. Photog.* a thin layer of coloured gelatin, glass, etc., that transmits light of certain colours or wavelengths but considerably reduces the transmission of others.
colourful ('kʌləfʊl) *adj.* **1.** having intense colour or richly varied colours. **2.** vivid, rich, or distinctive in character. —'**colourfully** *adv.* —'**colourfulness** *n.*
colour guard *n.* a military guard in a parade, ceremony, etc., that carries and escorts the flag or regimental colours.
colour index *n.* **1.** *Astronomy.* the difference between the photographic magnitude and the visual magnitude of a star, indicating its colour and temperature. **2.** *Geology.* the sum of the dark or coloured minerals of a rock, expressed as a percentage of the total minerals. **3.** *Chem., physics.* a systematic arrangement of colours according to their hue, saturation, and brightness.
colouring ('kʌlərɪŋ) *n.* **1.** the process or art of applying colour. **2.** anything used to give colour, such as dye, paint, etc. **3.** appearance with regard to shade and colour. **4.** arrangements of colours and tones, as in the markings of birds and animals. **5.** the colour of a person's features or complexion. **6.** a false or misleading appearance.
colourist ('kʌlərɪst) *n.* **1.** a person who uses colour, esp. an artist. **2.** a person who colours photographs, esp. black-and-white ones. —,**colour'istic** *adj.*
colourize, colourise, *or U.S.* **colorize** ('kʌlə,raɪz) *vb.* (*tr.*) to add colour electronically to (an old black-and-white film). —,**colouri'zation, -i'sation** *or U.S.* ,**colori'zation** *n.*
colourless ('kʌləlɪs) *adj.* **1.** without colour. **2.** lacking in interest: *a colourless individual.* **3.** grey or pallid in tone or hue. **4.** without prejudice; neutral. —'**colourlessly** *adv.* —'**colourlessness** *n.*
colour line *n.* the social separation of racial groups within a community (esp. in the phrase **to cross the colour line**).
colourman ('kʌləmən) *n., pl.* **-men.** a person who deals in paints.
colour phase *n.* **1.** a seasonal change in the coloration of some animals. **2.** an abnormal variation in the coloration shown by a group of animals within a species.
colourpoint cat ('kʌlə,pɔɪnt) *n.* a Persian cat with the colouring of a Siamese. U.S. name: **Himalayan cat.**
colour-reversal *n.* (*modifier*) *Photog.* (of film or photographic paper) designed to produce a positive image directly from a positive subject.
colours ('kʌləz) *pl. n.* **1. a.** the flag that indicates nationality. **b.** *Military.* the ceremony of hoisting or lowering the colours. **2.** a pair of silk flags borne by a military unit, esp. British, comprising the **Queen's Colour** showing the unit's crest, and the **Regimental Colour** showing the crest and battle honours. **3.** true nature or character (esp. in the phrase **show one's colours**). **4.** a distinguishing badge or flag, as of an academic institution. **5.** *Sport, Brit.* a badge or other symbol denoting membership of a team, esp. at a school or college. **6.** *Informal.* a distinguishing embroidered patch denoting membership of a motorcycle gang. **7. nail one's colours to the mast.** to refuse to admit defeat.
colour scheme *n.* a planned combination or juxtaposition of colours, as in interior decorating.
colour separation overlay *n.* another term for **chromakey.**
colour sergeant *n.* a sergeant who carries the regimental, battalion, or national colours, as in a colour guard.
colour subcarrier ('sʌb,kærɪə) *n.* a component of a colour television signal on which is modulated the colour or chrominance information.
colour supplement *n. Brit.* an illustrated magazine accompanying a newspaper, esp. a Sunday newspaper.
colour temperature *n. Physics.* the temperature of a black-body radiator at which it would emit radiation of the same chromaticity as the light under consideration.
colourwash ('kʌlə,wɒʃ) *n.* **1.** a coloured distemper. ~*vb.* (*tr.*) **2.** to paint with colourwash.
colourway ('kʌlə,weɪ) *n.* one of several different combinations of colours in which a given pattern is printed on fabrics, wallpapers, etc.
coloury *or* **colory** ('kʌlərɪ) *adj.* possessing colour.
-colous *adj. combining form.* inhabiting or living on: *arenicolous.* [from Latin *-cola* inhabitant + -OUS; related to *colere* to inhabit]
colpitis (kɒl'paɪtɪs) *n. Pathol.* another name for **vaginitis.** [C19: from Greek *kolpos* bosom, womb, vagina + -ITIS]
colpo- *or before a vowel* **colp-** *combining form.* indicating the vagina: *colpitis; colpotomy.* [from Greek *kolpos* womb]
colporteur ('kɒl,pɔːtə; *French* kɔlpɔrtœr) *n.* a hawker of books, esp. bibles. [C18: from French, from *colporter,* probably from Old French *comporter* to carry (see COMPORT); influenced through folk etymology by *porter à col* to carry on one's neck] —'**col,portage** *n.*
colposcope ('kɒlpə,skəʊp) *n.* an instrument for examining the cervix, esp. for early signs of cancer. [C20: from COLPO- + -SCOPE]
colpotomy (kəl'pɒtəmɪ) *n.* a surgical incision into the wall of the vagina. [C20: from COLPO- + -TOMY]
colt (kəʊlt) *n.* **1.** a male horse or pony under the age of four. **2.** an awkward or inexperienced young person. **3.** *Sport.* **a.** a young and inexperienced player. **b.** a member of a junior team. [Old English *colt* young ass, of obscure origin; compare Swedish dialect *kult* young animal, boy]
Colt (kəʊlt) *n. Trademark.* a type of revolver. [C19: named after Samuel *Colt* (1814–62), American inventor]
colter ('kəʊltə) *n.* a variant spelling (esp. U.S.) of **coulter.**
coltish ('kəʊltɪʃ) *adj.* **1.** inexperienced; unruly. **2.** playful and lively. —'**coltishly** *adv.* —'**coltishness** *n.*
coltsfoot ('kəʊlts,fʊt) *n., pl.* **-foots.** a European plant, *Tussilago farfara,* with yellow daisy-like flowers and heart-shaped leaves: a common weed: family *Compositae* (composites).
colubrid ('kɒljʊbrɪd) *n.* **1.** any snake of the family *Colubridae,* including many harmless snakes, such as the grass snake and whip snakes, and some venomous types. ~*adj.* **2.** of, relating to, or belonging to the *Colubridae.* [C19: from New Latin *Colubridae,* from Latin *coluber* snake]
colubrine ('kɒljʊ,braɪn, -brɪn) *adj.* **1.** of or resembling a snake. **2.** of, relating to, or belonging to the *Colubrinae,* a subfamily of harmless colubrid snakes. [C16: from Latin *colubrīnus,* from *coluber* snake]
colugo (kə'luːgəʊ) *n., pl.* **-gos.** another name for **flying lemur.** [from a native word in Malaya]
Columba (kə'lʌmbə) *n., Latin genitive* **Columbae** (kə'lʌmbiː), as in *Alpha Columbae.* a small constellation in the S hemisphere south of Orion. [Latin, literally: dove]
columbarium (,kɒləm'bɛərɪəm) *n., pl.* **-ia** (-ɪə). **1.** another name for a **dovecote. 2.** a vault having niches for funeral urns. **3.** a hole in a wall into which a beam is inserted. [C18: from Latin, from *columba* dove]
Columbian (kə'lʌmbɪən) *adj.* **1.** of or relating to the United States. **2.** relating to Christopher Columbus (1451–1506), who discovered the New World (1492). ~*n.* **3.** a size of printers type, approximately equal to 16 point; two-line Brevier.
columbic (kə'lʌmbɪk) *adj.* another word for **niobic.**
columbine[1] ('kɒləm,baɪn) *n.* any plant of the ranunculaceous genus *Aquilegia,* having purple, blue, yellow, or red flowers with five spurred petals. Also called: **aquilegia.** [C13: from Medieval Latin *columbīna herba* dovelike plant, from Latin *columbīnus* dovelike, from the resemblance of the flower to a group of doves]
columbine[2] ('kɒləm,baɪn) *adj.* of, relating to, or resembling a dove. [C14: from Old French *colombin,* from Latin *columbīnus* dovelike, from *columba* dove]
Columbine ('kɒləm,baɪn) *n.* **1.** (originally) the character of a servant girl in commedia dell'arte. **2.** (later) the sweetheart of Harlequin in English pantomime.
columbite (kə'lʌmbaɪt) *n.* a black mineral consisting of a mixed niobium and tantalum oxide of iron and manganese in orthorhombic crystalline form: occurs in coarse granite, often with tantalite, and is an ore of niobium and tantalum. Formula: $(Fe,Mn)(Nb,Ta)_2O_6$. Also called: **niobite.** [C19: from COLUMBIUM + -ITE[1]]
columbium (kə'lʌmbɪəm) *n.* the former name of **niobium.** [C19: from New Latin, from *Columbia,* the United States of America]
columbous (kə'lʌmbəs) *adj.* another word for **niobous.**
Columbus Day (kə'lʌmbəs) *n.* Oct. 12, a legal holiday in most states of the U.S.: the date of Columbus' landing in the West Indies in 1492.
columella (,kɒljʊ'mɛlə) *n., pl.* **-lae** (-liː). **1.** the central part of plant or animal organs, as of the spore-producing body of some fungi and mosses. **2.** Also called: **columella auris** ('ɔːrɪs). a small rodlike bone in the middle ear of frogs, reptiles, and birds that transmits sound to the inner ear: homologous to the mammalian stapes. [C16: from Latin: diminutive of *columna* COLUMN] —,**colu'mellar** *adj.*
column ('kɒləm) *n.* **1.** an upright post or pillar usually having a cylindrical shaft, a base, and a capital. **2. a.** a form or structure in the shape of a column: *a column of air.* **b.** a monument. **3.** a row, line, or file, as of people in a queue. **4.** *Military.* a narrow formation in which individuals or units follow one behind the other. **5.** *Journalism.* **a.** any of two or more vertical sections of type on a printed page, esp. on a newspaper page. **b.** a regular article or feature in a paper: *the fashion column.* **6.** a vertical array of numbers or mathematical terms. **7.** *Botany.* a long structure in the flower of an orchid, consisting of the united stamens and style. **8.** *Anatomy, zoology.* any elongated structure, such as a tract of grey matter in the spinal cord or the stalk of a crinoid. [C15: from Latin *columna,* from *columen* top, peak;

related to Latin *collis* hill] —**columnar** (kəˈlʌmnə) *adj.* —ˈ**columned** *or* **columnated** (ˈkɒləmˌneɪtɪd) *adj.*

columniation (kəˌlʌmnɪˈeɪʃən) *n.* the arrangement of architectural columns.

column inch *n.* a unit of measurement for advertising space, one inch deep and one column wide.

columnist (ˈkɒləmɪst, -əmnɪst) *n.* a journalist who writes a regular feature in a newspaper: *a gossip columnist.*

colure (kəˈlʊə, ˈkəʊlʊə) *n.* either of two great circles on the celestial sphere, one of which passes through the celestial poles and the equinoxes and the other through the poles and the solstices. [C16: from Late Latin *colūrī* (plural), from Greek *kolourai* cut short, dock-tailed, from *kolos* docked + *oura* tail; so called because the view of the lower part is curtailed]

coly (ˈkəʊlɪ) *n., pl.* **-lies.** any of the arboreal birds of the genus *Colius,* family *Coliidae,* and order *Coliiformes,* of southern Africa. They have a soft hairlike plumage, crested head, and very long tail. Also called: **mousebird.** [C19: from New Latin *colius,* probably from Greek *kolios* woodpecker]

colza (ˈkɒlzə) *n.* another name for **rape**[2]. [C18: via French (Walloon) *kolzat* from Dutch *koolzaad,* from *kool* cabbage, COLE + *zaad* SEED]

colza oil *n.* the oil obtained from the seeds of the rape plant and used in making lubricants and synthetic rubber.

COM (kɒm) *n.* **a.** a process in which a computer output is converted direct to microfiche or film, esp. 35 or 16 millimetre film. **b.** (*as modifier*): *a COM machine.* [(*C*)*omputer* (*O*)*utput on* (*M*)*icrofilm*]

com. *abbrev. for:* **1.** comedy. **2.** comic. **3.** commerce. **4.** commercial. **5.** committee.

Com. *abbrev. for:* **1.** Commander. **2.** committee. **3.** Commodore. **4.** Communist.

com- *or* **con-** *prefix.* together; with; jointly: *commingle.* [from Latin *com-;* related to *cum* with. In compound words of Latin origin, *com-* becomes *col-* and *cor-* before *l* and *r, co-* before *gn, h,* and most vowels, and *con-* before consonants other than *b, p,* and *m.* Although its sense in compounds of Latin derivation is often obscured, it means: together, with, etc. (*combine, compile*); similar (*conform*); extremely, completely (*consecrate*)]

coma[1] (ˈkəʊmə) *n., pl.* **-mas.** a state of unconsciousness from which a person cannot be aroused, caused by injury to the head, rupture of cerebral blood vessels, narcotics, poisons, etc. [C17: from medical Latin, from Greek *kōma* heavy sleep; related to Greek *koitē* bed, perhaps to Middle Irish *cuma* grief]

coma[2] (ˈkəʊmə) *n., pl.* **-mae** (-miː). **1.** *Astronomy.* the luminous cloud surrounding the frozen solid nucleus in the head of a comet, formed by vaporization of part of the nucleus when the comet is close to the sun. **2.** *Botany.* **a.** a tuft of hairs attached to the seed coat of some seeds. **b.** the terminal crown of leaves of palms and moss stems. **3.** *Optics.* a type of lens defect characterized by the formation of a diffuse pear-shaped image from a point object. [C17: from Latin: hair of the head, from Greek *komē*] —ˈ**comal** *adj.*

Coma Berenices (ˈkəʊmə ˌberɪˈnaɪsiːz) *n., Latin genitive* **Comae Berenices** (ˈkəʊmiː). a faint constellation in the N hemisphere between Ursa Major and Boötes containing the **Coma Cluster,** a cluster of approximately 10 000 galaxies, at a mean distance of 220 million light years. [from Latin, literally: Berenice's hair, named after *Berenice* (died 221 B.C.), consort of Ptolemy III]

Comanche (kəˈmæntʃɪ) *n.* **1.** (*pl.* **-ches** *or* **-che**) a member of a North American Indian people, formerly ranging from the River Platte in the central U.S. to the Mexican border, now living in Oklahoma. **2.** the language of this people, belonging to the Shoshonean subfamily of the Uto-Aztecan family.

Comanchean (kəˈmæntʃɪən) (in North America) ~*adj.* **1.** of or relating to the early part of the Cretaceous system and period. ~*n.* **2.** the strata and time corresponding to the early Cretaceous.

comate (ˈkəʊmeɪt) *adj. Botany.* **1.** having tufts of hair; hairy. **2.** having or relating to a coma. [C17: from Latin *comātus,* from *coma* hair]

comatose (ˈkəʊməˌtəʊs, -ˌtəʊz) *adj.* **1.** in a state of coma. **2.** torpid; lethargic. —ˈ**comaˌtosely** *adv.*

comatulid (kəˈmætjʊlɪd) *or* **comatula** *n., pl.* **-lids** *or* **-lae** (-liː). any of a group of crinoid echinoderms, including the feather stars, in which the adults are free-swimming. [C19: from New Latin *Comatulidae,* from *Comatula* type genus, from Latin *comātus* hairy]

comb (kəʊm) *n.* **1.** a toothed device of metal, plastic, wood, etc., used for disentangling or arranging hair. **2.** a tool or machine that separates, cleans, and straightens wool, cotton, etc. **3.** *Austral. and N.Z.* the fixed cutter on a sheep-shearing machine. **4.** anything resembling a toothed comb in form or function. **5.** the fleshy deeply serrated outgrowth on the top of the heads of certain birds, esp. the domestic fowl. **6.** anything resembling the comb of a bird. **7.** a currycomb. **8.** a honeycomb. **9.** the row of fused cilia in a ctenophore. **10. go over** (*or* **through**) **with a fine-tooth(ed) comb.** to examine very thoroughly. ~*vb.* **11.** (*tr.*) to use a comb on. **12.** (when *tr.,* often foll. by *through*) to search or inspect with great care: *the police combed the woods.* ~See also **comb out.** [Old English *camb;* related to Old Norse *kambr,* Old High German *camb*]

comb. *abbrev. for* combining.

combat *n.* (ˈkɒmbæt, -bət, ˈkʌm-). **1.** a fight, conflict, or struggle. **2. a.** an action fought between two military forces. **b.** (*as modifier*): *a combat jacket.* **3. single combat.** a fight between two individuals; duel. **4. close** *or* **hand-to-hand combat.** fighting at close quarters. ~*vb.* (kəmˈbæt; ˈkɒmbæt, ˈkʌm-). **-bats, -bating, -bated.** **5.** (*tr.*) to fight or defy. **6.** (*intr.;* often foll. by *with* or *against*) to struggle or strive (against); be in conflict (with): *to combat against disease.* [C16: from French, from Old French *combattre,* from Vulgar Latin *combattere* (unattested), from Latin *com-* with + *battuere* to beat, hit] —**com**ˈ**batable** *adj.* —**com**ˈ**bater** *n.*

combatant (ˈkɒmbətᵊnt, ˈkʌm-) *n.* **1.** a person or group engaged in or prepared for a fight, struggle, or dispute. ~*adj.* **2.** engaged in or ready for combat.

combat fatigue *n.* another term for **battle fatigue.**

combative (ˈkɒmbətɪv, ˈkʌm-) *adj.* eager or ready to fight, argue, etc.; aggressive. —ˈ**combatively** *adv.* —ˈ**combativeness** *n.*

combe *or* **comb** (kuːm) *n.* variant spellings of **coomb.**

comber (ˈkəʊmə) *n.* **1.** a person, tool, or machine that combs wool, flax, etc. **2.** a long curling wave; roller.

combination (ˌkɒmbɪˈneɪʃən) *n.* **1.** the act of combining or state of being combined. **2.** a union of separate parts, qualities, etc. **3.** an alliance of people or parties; group having a common purpose. **4. a.** the set of numbers that opens a combination lock. **b.** the mechanism of this type of lock. **5.** *Brit.* a motorcycle with a sidecar attached. **6.** *Maths.* **a.** an arrangement of the numbers, terms, etc., of a set into specified groups without regard to order in the group: *the combinations of a, b, and c, taken two at a time, are ab, bc, ac.* **b.** a group formed in this way. The number of combinations of *n* objects taken *r* at a time is $n!/[(n-r)!r!]$. Symbol: ${}_nC_r$. Compare **permutation** (sense 1). **7.** the chemical reaction of two or more compounds, usually to form one other compound. **8.** *Chess.* a tactical manoeuvre involving a sequence of moves and more than one piece. ~See also **combinations.** —ˌ**combi**ˈ**national** *adj.*

combination lock *n.* a type of lock that can only be opened when a set of dials releasing the tumblers of the lock are turned to show a specific sequence of numbers.

combination room *n. Brit.* (at Cambridge University) a common room.

combinations (ˌkɒmbɪˈneɪʃənz) *pl. n. Brit.* a one-piece woollen undergarment with long sleeves and legs. Often shortened to **combs** *or* **coms.** U.S. and Canadian term: **union suit.**

combination tone *n.* another term for **resultant tone.**

combinative (ˈkɒmbɪˌneɪtɪv, -nətɪv), **combinatorial** (ˌkɒmbɪnəˈtɔːrɪəl), *or* **combinatory** (ˈkɒmbɪnətərɪ, -trɪ) *adj.* **1.** resulting from being, tending to be, or able to be joined or mixed together. **2.** *Linguistics.* (of a sound change) occurring only in specific contexts or as a result of some other factor, such as change of stress within a word. Compare **isolative** (sense 1).

combinatorial analysis *n.* the branch of mathematics concerned with the theory of enumeration, or combinations and permutations, in order to solve problems about the possibility of constructing arrangements of objects which satisfy specified conditions. Also called: **combinatorics** (ˌkɒmbɪnəˈtɔːrɪks).

combine *vb.* (kəmˈbaɪn). **1.** to integrate or cause to be integrated; join together. **2.** to unite or cause to unite to form a chemical compound. **3.** *Agriculture.* to harvest (crops) with a combine harvester. ~*n.* (ˈkɒmbaɪn). **4.** *Agriculture.* short for **combine harvester.** **5.** an association of enterprises, esp. in order to gain a monopoly of a market. **6.** an association of business corporations, political parties, sporting clubs, etc., for a common purpose. [C15: from Late Latin *combīnāre,* from Latin *com-* together + *bīnī* two by two] —**com**ˈ**binable** *adj.* —**com**ˌ**bina**ˈ**bility** *n.* —**com**ˈ**biner** *n.*

combine harvester (ˈkɒmbaɪn) *n.* a machine that simultaneously cuts, threshes, and cleans a standing crop of grain.

combings (ˈkəʊmɪŋz) *pl. n.* **1.** the loose hair, wool, etc., removed by combing, esp. that of animals. **2.** the unwanted loose short fibres removed in combing cotton, etc.

combining form *n.* a linguistic element that occurs only as part of a compound word, such as *anthropo-* in *anthropology* and *anthropomorph.*

comb jelly *n.* another name for a **ctenophore.**

combo (ˈkɒmbəʊ) *n., pl.* **-bos.** **1.** a small group of musicians, esp. of jazz musicians. **2.** *Informal.* any combination. **3.** *Austral. slang.* a white man who lives with an Aboriginal woman.

comb out *vb.* (*tr., adv.*) **1.** to remove (tangles or knots) from (the hair) with a comb. **2.** to isolate and remove for a purpose. **3.** to survey carefully; examine systematically. ~*n.* **comb-out.** **4.** an act of combing out.

combust (kəmˈbʌst) *adj.* **1.** *Astrology.* (of a star or planet) invisible for a period between 24 and 30 days each year due to its proximity to the sun. ~*vb.* **2.** *Chem.* to burn.

combustible (kəmˈbʌstəbᵊl) *adj.* **1.** capable of igniting and burning. **2.** easily annoyed; excitable. ~*n.* **3.** a combustible substance. —**com**ˌ**busti**ˈ**bility** *or* **com**ˈ**bustibleness** *n.* —**com**ˈ**bustibly** *adv.*

combustion (kəmˈbʌstʃən) *n.* **1.** the process of burning. **2.** any process in which a substance reacts with oxygen to produce a significant rise in temperature and the emission of light. **3.** a chemical process in which two compounds, such as sodium and chlorine, react together to produce heat and light. **4.** a process in which a compound reacts slowly with oxygen to produce little heat and no light. [C15: from Old French, from Latin *combūrere* to burn up, from *com-* (intensive) + *ūrere* to burn] —**com'bustive** *n., adj.*

combustion chamber *n.* an enclosed space in which combustion takes place, such as the space above the piston in the cylinder head of an internal-combustion engine or the chambers in a gas turbine or rocket engine in which fuel and oxidant burn.

combustor (kəm'bʌstə) *n.* the combustion system of a jet engine or ramjet, comprising the combustion chamber, the fuel injection apparatus, and the igniter.

comdg *Military. abbrev. for* commanding.

Comdr *Military. abbrev. for* Commander.

Comdt *Military. abbrev. for* Commandant.

come (kʌm) *vb.* **comes, coming, came, come.** (*mainly intr.*) **1.** to move towards a specified person or place: *come to my desk.* **2.** to arrive by movement or by making progress. **3.** to become perceptible: *light came into the sky.* **4.** to occur in the course of time: *Christmas comes but once a year.* **5.** to exist or occur at a specific point in a series: *your turn comes next.* **6.** to happen as a result: *no good will come of this.* **7.** to originate or be derived: *good may come of evil.* **8.** to occur to the mind: *the truth suddenly came to me.* **9.** to extend or reach: *she comes up to my shoulder.* **10.** to be produced or offered: *that dress comes in red only.* **11.** to arrive at or be brought into a particular state or condition: *you will soon come to grief; the new timetable comes into effect on Monday.* **12.** (foll. by *from*) to be or have been a resident or native (of): *I come from London.* **13.** to become: *your wishes will come true.* **14.** (*tr.; takes an infinitive*) to be given awareness: *I came to realize its enormous value.* **15.** (of grain) to germinate. **16.** *Taboo slang.* to have an orgasm. **17.** (*tr.*) *Brit. informal.* to play the part of: *don't come the fine gentleman with me.* **18.** (*tr.*) *Brit. informal.* to cause or produce: *don't come that nonsense again.* **19.** (*subjunctive use*) when (a specified time or event has arrived or begun): *she'll be sixteen come Sunday; come the revolution, you'll be the first to go.* **20. as...as they come.** the most characteristic example of a class or type. **21. come again?** *Informal.* what did you say? **22. come and.** (*imperative or dependent imperative*) to move towards a particular person or thing or accompany a person with some specified purpose: *come and see what I've found.* **23. come clean.** *Informal.* to make a revelation or confession. **24. come good.** *Informal.* to recover and perform well after a bad start or setback. **25. come it.** *Slang.* **a.** to pretend; act a part. **b.** to exaggerate. **c.** (often foll. by *over*) to try to impose (upon). **d.** to divulge a secret; inform the police. **26. come to light.** to be revealed. **27. come to light with.** *Austral. and N.Z. informal.* to find or produce. **28. come to pass.** *Archaic.* to take place. **29. how come?** *Informal.* what is the reason that? ~*interj.* **30.** an exclamation expressing annoyance, irritation, etc.: *come now! come come!* ~See also **come about, come across, come along, come at, come away, comeback, come between, come by, comedown, come forward, come in, come into, come of, come off, come on, come out, come over, come round, come through, come to, come up, come upon.** [Old English *cuman;* related to Old Norse *koma,* Gothic *qiman,* Old High German *queman* to come, Sanskrit *gámati* he goes]

come about *vb.* (*intr., adv.*) **1.** to take place; happen. **2.** *Nautical.* to change tacks.

come across *vb.* (*intr.*) **1.** (*prep.*) to meet or find by accident. **2.** (*adv.*) (of a person or his words) to communicate the intended meaning or impression. **3.** (often foll. by *with*) to provide what is expected.

come-all-ye (kə'mɔːljə, -jiː) *n.* a street ballad or folk song. [C19: from the common opening words *come all ye (young maidens, loyal heroes, etc.) ...*]

come along *vb.* **1.** (*intr., adv.*) to progress: *how's your French coming along?* **2. come along! a.** hurry up! **b.** make an effort!

come at *vb.* (*intr., prep.*) **1.** to discover or reach (facts, the truth, etc.). **2.** to attack (a person): *he came at me with an axe.* **3.** *Austral. slang.* to agree to do (something). **4.** (*usually used with a negative*) *Austral. slang.* to stomach, tolerate: *I couldn't come at it.* **5.** *Austral. slang.* to presume; impose: *what are you coming at?*

come-at-able *adj.* an informal expression for **accessible.**

come away *vb.* (*intr., adv.*) **1.** to become detached. **2.** (foll. by *with*) to leave (with).

comeback ('kʌm,bæk) *n. Informal.* **1.** a return to a former position, status, etc. **2.** a return or response, esp. recriminatory. **3.** a quick reply; retort. **4.** *Austral.* a sheep that is three-quarters merino and one-quarter crossbred. **5.** *Austral.* the fleece obtained from this sheep. ~*vb.* **come back.** (*intr., adv.*) **6.** to return. **7.** to become fashionable again. **8.** to reply after a period of consideration: *I'll come back to you on that next week.* **9.** *U.S. and Canadian.* to argue back; retort. **10. come back to (someone).** (of something forgotten) to return to (someone's) memory.

come between *vb.* (*intr., prep.*) to cause the estrangement or separation of (two people): *nothing could come between the two lovers.*

come by *vb.* (*intr., prep.*) to find or obtain (a thing), esp. accidentally: *do you ever come by any old books?*

Comecon ('kɒmɪ,kɒn) *n.* an association of Soviet-oriented Communist nations, founded in 1949 to coordinate economic development, etc. Also: **CMEA.** [C20: *Co(uncil for) M(utual) Econ(omic Assistance)*]

comedian (kə'miːdɪən) *n.* **1.** an entertainer who specializes in jokes, comic skits, etc. **2.** an actor in comedy. **3.** an amusing or entertaining person: sometimes used ironically.

comedic (kə'miːdɪk) *adj.* of or relating to comedy.

comedienne (kə,miːdɪ'ɛn) *n.* a female comedian.

comedo ('kɒmɪ,dəʊ) *n., pl.* **comedos** *or* **comedones** (,kɒmɪ'dəʊniːz). *Pathol.* the technical name for **blackhead.** [C19: from New Latin, from Latin: glutton, from *comedere* to eat up, from *com-* (intensive) + *edere* to eat]

comedown ('kʌm,daʊn) *n.* **1.** a decline in position, status, or prosperity. **2.** *Informal.* a disappointment. **3.** *Slang.* a depressed or unexcited state. ~*vb.* **come down.** (*intr., adv.*) **4.** to come to a place regarded as lower. **5.** to lose status, wealth, etc. (esp. in the phrase **to come down in the world**). **6.** to reach a decision: *the report came down in favour of a pay increase.* **7.** (often foll. by *to*) to be handed down or acquired by tradition or inheritance. **8.** *Brit.* to leave college or university. **9.** (foll. by *with*) to succumb (to illness or disease). **10.** (foll. by *on*) to rebuke or criticize harshly. **11.** (foll. by *to*) to amount in essence (to): *it comes down to two choices.* **12.** *Slang.* to lose the effects of a drug and return to a normal or more normal state. **13.** *Austral. informal.* (of a river) to flow in flood.

comedy ('kɒmɪdɪ) *n., pl.* **-dies.** **1.** a dramatic or other work of light and amusing character. **2.** the genre of drama represented by works of this type. **3.** (in classical literature) a play in which the main characters and motive triumph over adversity. **4.** the humorous aspect of life or of events. **5.** an amusing event or sequence of events. **6.** humour or comic style: *the comedy of Chaplin.* [C14: from Old French *comédie,* from Latin *cōmoedia,* from Greek *kōmōidia,* from *kōmos* village festival + *aeidein* to sing]

comedy of manners *n.* **1.** a comedy dealing with the way of life and foibles of a social group. **2.** the genre represented by works of this type.

come forward *vb.* (*intr., adv.*) **1.** to offer one's services; volunteer. **2.** to present oneself.

come-hither *adj.* (*usually prenominal*) *Informal.* alluring; seductive: *a come-hither look.*

come in *vb.* (*intr., mainly adv.*) **1.** to enter, used in the imperative when admitting a person. **2.** to prove to be: *it came in useful.* **3.** to become fashionable or seasonable. **4.** *Cricket.* to begin an innings. **5.** *Athletics, horse racing, etc.* to finish a race (in a certain position). **6.** (of a politician or political party) to win an election. **7.** *Radio, television.* to be received: *news is coming in of a big fire in Glasgow.* **8.** (of money) to be received as income. **9.** to play a role; advance one's interests: *where do I come in?* **10.** (foll. by *for*) to be the object of: *the Chancellor came in for a lot of criticism in the Commons.* **11. this is where we came in.** we are at the same point now as when we began.

come into *vb.* (*intr., prep.*) **1.** to enter. **2.** to inherit. **3. come into one's own.** to become fulfilled: *she really came into her own when she got divorced.*

comely ('kʌmlɪ) *adj.* **-lier, -liest.** **1.** good-looking; attractive. **2.** *Archaic.* suitable; fitting. [Old English *cȳmlīc* beautiful; related to Old High German *cūmi* frail, Middle High German *komlīche* suitably] —'**comeliness** *n.*

come of *vb.* (*intr., prep.*) **1.** to be descended from. **2.** to result from: *nothing came of his experiments.*

come off *vb.* (*intr., mainly adv.*) **1.** (*also prep.*) to fall (from), losing one's balance. **2.** to become detached or be capable of being detached. **3.** (*prep.*) to be removed from (a price, tax, etc.): *will anything come off income tax in the budget?* **4.** (*copula*) to emerge from or as if from a trial or contest: *he came off the winner.* **5.** *Informal.* to take place or happen. **6.** *Informal.* to have the intended effect; succeed: *his jokes did not come off.* **7.** *Taboo slang.* to have an orgasm. **8. come off it!** *Informal.* stop trying to fool me!

come on ~*vb.* (*intr., mainly adv.*) **1.** (of power, a water supply, etc.) to become available; start running or functioning. **2.** to make or show progress; develop: *my plants are coming on nicely.* **3.** to advance, esp. in battle. **4.** to begin: *she felt a cold coming on; a new bowler has come on.* **5.** *Theatre.* to make an entrance on stage. **6.** to be considered, esp. in a court of law. **7.** (*prep.*) See **come upon.** **8. come on! a.** hurry up! **b.** cheer up! pull yourself together! **c.** make an effort! **d.** don't exaggerate! stick to the facts! **9.** to attempt to give a specified impression: *he came on like a hard man.* **10. come on strong.** to make a forceful or exaggerated impression. ~*n.* **come-on.** **11.** *Informal.* anything that serves as a lure or enticement.

come out *vb.* (*intr., adv.*) **1.** to be made public or revealed: *the news of her death came out last week.* **2.** to make a debut in society or on stage. **3.** Also: **come out of the closet.** to declare openly that one is a homosexual. **4.** *Chiefly Brit.* to go on strike. **5.** to declare oneself: *the government came out in favour of scrapping the project.* **6.** to be shown visibly or clearly: *you came out very well in the photos.* **7.** to yield a satisfactory solution: *these sums just won't come out.* **8.** to be published: *the paper comes out on Fridays.* **9.** (foll. by *in*) to become covered with: *you're coming* *out in spots.* **10.** (foll. by *with*) to speak or declare openly: *you can rely on him to come out with the facts.*

come over *vb.* (*intr.*) **1.** (*adv.*) (of a person or his words) to communicate the intended meaning or impression: *he came over very well.* **2.** (*adv.*) to change allegiances: *some people came over to our side in the war.* **3.** *Informal.* to undergo or feel a particular sensation: *I came over funny.* ~*n.* **comeover. 4.** (in the Isle of Man) a person who has come over from the mainland of Britain to settle.

comer ('kʌmə) *n.* **1.** (*in combination*) a person who comes: *all-comers; newcomers.* **2.** *Informal.* a potential success.

come round *or* **around** *vb.* (*intr., adv.*) **1.** to be restored to life or consciousness. **2.** to change or modify one's mind or opinion.

comestible (kə'mɛstɪbᵊl) *n.* **1.** (*usually pl.*) food. ~*adj.* **2.** a rare word for **edible.** [C15: from Late Latin *comestibilis,* from *comedere* to eat up; see COMEDO]

comet ('kɒmɪt) *n.* a celestial body that travels around the sun, usually in a highly elliptical orbit: thought to consist of a solid frozen nucleus part of which vaporizes on approaching the sun to form a gaseous luminous coma and a long luminous tail. [C13: from Old French *comète,* from Latin *comēta,* from Greek *komētēs* long-haired, from *komē* hair] —'**cometary** *or* **cometic** (kɒ'mɛtɪk) *adj.*

come through *vb.* (*intr.*) **1.** (*adv.*) to emerge successfully. **2.** (*prep.*) to survive (an illness, setback, etc.).

come to *vb.* (*intr.*) **1.** (*adv.* or *prep. and reflexive*) to regain consciousness or return to one's normal state. **2.** (*adv.*) *Nautical.* to slow a vessel or bring her to a stop. **3.** (*prep.*) to amount to (a sum of money): *your bill comes to four pounds.* **4.** (*prep.*) to arrive at (a certain state): *what is the world coming to?*

come up *vb.* (*intr., adv.*) **1.** to come to a place regarded as higher. **2.** (of the sun) to rise. **3.** to begin: *a wind came up.* **4.** to be regurgitated or vomited. **5.** to present itself or be discussed: *that question will come up again.* **6.** *Brit.* to begin a term, esp. one's first term, at a college or university. **7.** to appear from out of the ground: *my beans have come up early this year.* **8.** *Informal.* to win: *have your premium bonds ever come up?* **9.** **come up against.** to be faced with; come into conflict or competition with. **10. come up to.** to equal or meet a standard: *that just doesn't come up to scratch.* **11. come up with.** to produce or find: *she always comes up with the right answer.*

come upon *vb.* (*intr., prep.*) to meet or encounter unexpectedly: *I came upon an old friend in the street today.*

comeuppance (ˌkʌm'ʌpəns) *n. Informal.* just retribution. [C19: from *come up* (in the sense: to appear before a judge or court for judgment)]

comfit ('kʌmfɪt, 'kɒm-) *n.* a sugar-coated sweet containing a nut or seed. [C15: from Old French, from Latin *confectum* something prepared, from *conficere* to produce; see CONFECT]

comfort ('kʌmfət) *n.* **1.** a state of ease or well-being. **2.** relief from affliction, grief, etc. **3.** a person, thing, or event that brings solace or ease. **4.** *Obsolete.* support. **5.** (*usually pl.*) something that affords physical ease and relaxation. ~*vb.* (*tr.*) **6.** to ease the pain of; soothe; cheer. **7.** to bring physical ease to. [C13: from Old French *confort,* from Late Latin *confortāre* to strengthen very much, from Latin *con-* (intensive) + *fortis* strong] —'**comforting** *adj.* —'**comfortingly** *adv.* —'**comfortless** *adj.* —'**comfortlessly** *adv.* —'**comfortlessness** *n.*

comfortable ('kʌmftəbᵊl, 'kʌmfətəbᵊl) *adj.* **1.** giving comfort or physical relief. **2.** at ease. **3.** free from affliction or pain. **4.** (of a person or situation) relaxing. **5.** *Informal.* having adequate income. **6.** *Informal.* (of income) adequate to provide comfort. —'**comfortableness** *n.* —'**comfortably** *adv.*

comforter ('kʌmfətə) *n.* **1.** a person or thing that comforts. **2.** *Chiefly Brit.* a woollen scarf. **3.** a baby's dummy. **4.** *U.S.* a quilted bed covering.

Comforter ('kʌmfətə) *n. Christianity.* an epithet of the Holy Spirit. [C14: translation of Latin *consolātor,* representing Greek *paraklētos;* see PARACLETE]

comfort station *n. U.S.* a public lavatory and rest room.

comfrey ('kʌmfrɪ) *n.* any hairy Eurasian boraginaceous plant of the genus *Symphytum,* having blue, purplish-pink, or white flowers. [C15: from Old French *cunfirie,* from Latin *conferva* water plant; see CONFERVA]

comfy ('kʌmfɪ) *adj.* **-fier, -fiest.** *Informal.* short for **comfortable.**

comic ('kɒmɪk) *adj.* **1.** of, relating to, characterized by, or characteristic of comedy. **2.** (*prenominal*) acting in, writing, or composing comedy: *a comic writer.* **3.** humorous; funny. ~*n.* **4.** a person who is comic, esp. a comic actor; comedian. **5.** a book or magazine containing comic strips. **6.** (*usually pl.*) *Chiefly U.S. and Canadian.* comic strips in newspapers, etc. [C16: from Latin *cōmicus,* from Greek *kōmikos* relating to COMEDY]

comical ('kɒmɪkᵊl) *adj.* **1.** causing laughter. **2.** ludicrous; laughable. —'**comically** *adv.* —'**comicalness** *n.*

comic opera *n.* a play largely set to music, employing comic effects or situations. See also **opéra bouffe, opera buffa.**

comic strip *n.* a sequence of drawings in a newspaper, magazine, etc., relating a humorous story or an adventure. Also called: **strip cartoon.**

coming ('kʌmɪŋ) *adj.* **1.** (*prenominal*) (of time, events, etc.) approaching or next: *this coming Thursday.* **2.** promising (esp. in the phrase **up and coming**). **3.** of future importance: *this is the coming thing.* **4. coming up!** *Informal.* an expression used to announce that a meal is about to be served. **5. have it coming to one.** *Informal.* to deserve what one is about to suffer. **6. not know whether one is coming or going.** to be totally confused. ~*n.* **7.** arrival or approach. **8.** (*often cap.*) the return of Christ in glory. See also **Second Coming.**

comitia (kə'mɪʃɪə) *n.* an ancient Roman assembly that elected officials and exercised judicial and legislative authority. [C17: from Latin *comitium* assembly, from *com-* together + *īre* to go] —**comitial** (kə'mɪʃəl) *adj.*

comity ('kɒmɪtɪ) *n., pl.* **-ties. 1.** mutual civility; courtesy. **2.** short for **comity of nations. 3.** the policy whereby one religious denomination refrains from proselytizing the members of another. [C16: from Latin *cōmitās,* from *cōmis* affable, obliging, of uncertain origin]

comity of nations *n.* the friendly recognition accorded by one nation to the laws and usages of another.

comm. *abbrev. for:* **1.** commerce. **2.** commercial. **3.** committee. **4.** commonwealth.

comma ('kɒmə) *n.* **1.** the punctuation mark , indicating a slight pause in the spoken sentence and used where there is a listing of items or to separate a nonrestrictive clause or phrase from a main clause. **2.** *Music.* a minute interval. **3.** short for **comma butterfly.** [C16: from Latin, from Greek *komma* clause, from *koptein* to cut]

comma bacillus *n.* a comma-shaped bacterium, *Vibrio comma,* that causes cholera in man: family *Spirillaceae.*

comma butterfly *n.* an orange-brown European vanessid butterfly, *Polygonia c-album,* with a white comma-shaped mark on the underside of each hind wing.

command (kə'mɑːnd) *vb.* **1.** (when *tr., may take a clause as object or an infinitive*) to order, require, or compel. **2.** to have or be in control or authority over (a person, situation, etc.). **3.** (*tr.*) to have knowledge or use of: *he commands the language.* **4.** (*tr.*) to receive as due or because of merit: *his nature commands respect.* **5.** to dominate (a view, etc.) as from a height. ~*n.* **6.** an order; mandate. **7.** the act of commanding. **8.** the power or right to command. **9.** the exercise of the power to command. **10.** ability or knowledge; control: *a command of French.* **11.** *Chiefly military.* the jurisdiction of a commander. **12.** a military unit or units commanding a specific area or function, as in the RAF. **13.** *Brit.* **a.** an invitation from the monarch. **b.** (*as modifier*): *a command performance.* **14.** *Computer technol.* another name for **instruction** (sense 3). [C13: from Old French *commander,* from Latin *com-* (intensive) + *mandāre* to entrust, enjoin, command]

commandant ('kɒmənˌdænt, -ˌdɑːnt) *n.* an officer commanding a place, group, or establishment.

command economy *n.* an economy in which business activities and the allocation of resources are determined by government order rather than market forces. Also called: **planned economy.**

commandeer (ˌkɒmən'dɪə) *vb.* (*tr.*) **1.** to seize for public or military use. **2.** to seize arbitrarily. [C19: from Afrikaans *kommandeer,* from French *commander* to COMMAND]

commander (kə'mɑːndə) *n.* **1.** an officer in command of a military formation or operation. **2.** a naval commissioned rank junior to captain but senior to lieutenant commander. **3.** the second in command of larger British warships. **4.** someone who holds authority. **5.** a high-ranking member of some knightly or fraternal orders. **6.** an officer responsible for a district of the Metropolitan Police in London. **7.** *History.* the administrator of a house, priory, or landed estate of a medieval religious order. —**com'manderˌship** *n.*

commander in chief *n., pl.* **commanders in chief. 1.** the officer holding supreme command of the forces in an area or operation. **2.** the officer holding command of a major subdivision of one military service.

command guidance *n.* a method of controlling a missile during flight by transmitting information to it.

commanding (kə'mɑːndɪŋ) *adj.* (*usually prenominal*) **1.** being in command. **2.** having the air of authority: *a commanding voice.* **3.** (of a position, situation, etc.) exerting control. **4.** (of a height, viewpoint, etc.) overlooking; advantageous. —**com'mandingly** *adv.*

commanding officer *n.* an officer in command of a military unit.

command language *n. Computer technol.* the language used to access a computer system.

commandment (kə'mɑːndmənt) *n.* **1.** a divine command, esp. one of the Ten Commandments of the Old Testament. **2.** *Literary.* any command.

command module *n.* the cone-shaped module used as the living quarters in an Apollo spacecraft and functioning as the splash-down vehicle.

commando (kə'mɑːndəʊ) *n., pl.* **-dos** *or* **-does. 1. a.** an amphibious military unit trained for raiding. **b.** a member of such a unit. **2.** the basic unit of the Royal Marine Corps. **3.** (originally) an armed force raised by Boers during the Boer War. **4.** (*modifier*) denoting or relating to a commando or force of commandos: *a commando raid; a commando unit.* [C19: from Afrikaans *kommando,* from Dutch *commando* command, from French *commander* to COMMAND]

commando operation *n. Surgery.* a major operation for treatment of cancer of the head and neck, involving removal of many facial structures and subsequent surgical reconstruction.

command paper *n.* (in Britain) a government document that is presented to Parliament, in theory by royal command. See also **green paper, white paper.**

command performance *n.* a performance of a play, opera, etc., at the request of a ruler or of royalty.

command post *n. Military.* the position from which a unit commander and his staff exercise command.

commeasure (kə'mɛʒə) *vb. (tr.)* to coincide with in degree, extent, quality, etc. —**com'measurable** *adj.*

commedia dell'arte (*Italian* kom'meːdia del'larte) *n.* a form of popular comedy developed in Italy during the 16th to 18th centuries, with stock characters such as Punchinello, Harlequin, and Columbine, in situations improvised from a plot outline. [Italian, literally: comedy of art]

comme il faut *French.* (kɔm il fo) correct or correctly.

commemorate (kə'mɛmə,reɪt) *vb. (tr.)* to honour or keep alive the memory of. [C16: from Latin *commemorāre* be mindful of, from *com-* (intensive) + *memorāre* to remind, from *memor* mindful] —**com'memorative** *or* **com'memoratory** *adj.* —**com'memoratively** *adv.* —**com'memo,rator** *n.*

commemoration (kə,mɛmə'reɪʃən) *n.* **1.** the act or an instance of commemorating. **2.** a ceremony or service in memory of a person or event. —**com,memo'rational** *adj.*

commence (kə'mɛns) *vb.* to start or begin; come or cause to come into being, operation, etc. [C14: from Old French *comencer,* from Vulgar Latin *cominitiāre* (unattested), from Latin *com-* (intensive) + *initiāre* to begin, from *initium* a beginning] —**com'mencer** *n.*

commencement (kə'mɛnsmənt) *n.* **1.** the beginning; start. **2. a.** *U.S. and Canadian.* a ceremony for the presentation of awards at secondary schools. **b.** *U.S.* a ceremony for the conferment of academic degrees.

commend (kə'mɛnd) *vb. (tr.)* **1.** to present or represent as being worthy of regard, confidence, kindness, etc.; recommend. **2.** to give in charge; entrust. **3.** to express a good opinion of; praise. **4.** to give the regards of: *commend me to your aunt.* [C14: from Latin *commendāre* to commit to someone's care, from *com-* (intensive) + *mandāre* to entrust] —**com'mendable** *adj.* —**com'mendableness** *n.* —**com'mendably** *adv.* —**com'mendatory** *adj.*

commendam (kə'mɛndæm) *n.* **1.** the temporary holding of an ecclesiastical benefice. **2.** a benefice so held. [C16: from Medieval Latin phrase *dare in commendam* to give in trust, from *commenda* trust, back formation from Latin *commendāre* to entrust, COMMEND]

commendation (,kɒmɛn'deɪʃən) *n.* **1.** the act or an instance of commending; praise. **2.** *U.S.* an award. **3.** *(often pl.) Archaic.* a greeting.

commensal (kə'mɛnsəl) *adj.* **1.** (of two different species of plant or animal) living in close association without being interdependent. **2.** *Rare.* of or relating to eating together, esp. at the same table: *commensal pleasures.* ~*n.* **3.** a commensal plant or animal. **4.** *Rare.* a companion at table. [C14: from Medieval Latin *commensālis,* from Latin *com-* together + *mensa* table] —**com'mensalism** *n.* —**commensality** (,kɒmɛn'sælɪtɪ) *n.* —**com'mensally** *adv.*

commensurable (kə'mɛnsərəbəl, -ʃə-) *adj.* **1.** *Maths.* **a.** having a common factor. **b.** having units of the same dimensions and being related by whole numbers: *hours and minutes are commensurable.* **2.** well-proportioned; proportionate. —**com,mensura'bility** *n.* —**com'mensurably** *adv.*

commensurate (kə'mɛnsərɪt, -ʃə-) *adj.* **1.** having the same extent or duration. **2.** corresponding in degree, amount, or size; proportionate. **3.** able to be measured by a common standard; commensurable. [C17: from Late Latin *commēnsūrātus,* from Latin *com-* same + *mēnsurāre* to MEASURE] —**com'mensurately** *adv.* —**com'mensurateness** *n.* —**commensuration** (kə,mɛnsə'reɪʃən, -ʃə-) *n.*

comment ('kɒmɛnt) *n.* **1.** a remark, criticism, or observation. **2.** talk or gossip. **3.** a note explaining or criticizing a passage in a text. **4.** explanatory or critical matter added to a text. ~*vb.* **5.** (when *intr.,* often foll. by *on;* when *tr.,* takes a clause as object) to remark or express an opinion. **6.** *(intr.)* to write notes explaining or criticizing a text. [C15: from Latin *commentum* invention, from *comminiscī* to contrive, related to *mens* mind] —**'commenter** *n.*

commentary ('kɒməntərɪ, -trɪ) *n., pl.* **-taries. 1.** an explanatory series of notes or comments. **2.** a spoken accompaniment to a broadcast, film, etc., esp. of a sporting event. **3.** an explanatory essay or treatise on a text. **4.** *(usually pl.)* a personal record of events or facts: *the commentaries of Caesar.* —**commentarial** (,kɒmən'tɛərɪəl) *adj.*

commentate ('kɒmən,teɪt) *vb.* **1.** *(intr.)* to serve as a commentator. **2.** *(tr.) U.S.* to make a commentary on (a text, event, etc.).

▷**Usage.** The verb *commentate,* derived from *commentator,* is sometimes used as a synonym for *comment on* or *provide a commentary for.* It is not yet fully accepted as standard, though widespread in sports reporting and journalism.

commentator ('kɒmən,teɪtə) *n.* **1.** a person who provides a spoken commentary for a broadcast, film, etc., esp. of a sporting event. **2.** a person who writes notes on a text, event, etc.

commerce ('kɒmɜːs) *n.* **1.** the activity embracing all forms of the purchase and sale of goods and services. **2.** social relations and exchange, esp. of opinions, attitudes, etc. **3.** *Archaic.* sexual intercourse. [C16: from Latin *commercium* trade, from *commercārī,* from *mercārī* to trade, from *merx* merchandise]

commercial (kə'mɜːʃəl) *adj.* **1.** of, connected with, or engaged in commerce; mercantile. **2.** sponsored or paid for by an advertiser: *commercial television.* **3.** having profit as the main aim: *commercial music.* **4.** (of goods, chemicals, etc.) of unrefined quality or presentation and produced in bulk for use in industry. ~*n.* **5.** a commercially sponsored advertisement on radio or television. —**commerciality** (kə,mɜːʃɪ'ælɪtɪ) *n.* —**com'mercially** *adv.*

commercial art *n.* graphic art for commercial uses such as advertising, packaging, etc. —**commercial artist** *n.*

commercial bank *n.* a bank primarily engaged in making short-term loans from funds deposited in current accounts.

commercial break *n.* an interruption in a radio or television programme for the broadcasting of advertisements.

commercial college *n.* a college providing tuition in commercial skills, such as shorthand and book-keeping.

commercialism (kə'mɜːʃə,lɪzəm) *n.* **1.** the spirit, principles, or procedure of commerce. **2.** exclusive or inappropriate emphasis on profit. —**com'mercialist** *n.* —**com,mercial'istic** *adj.*

commercialize *or* **commercialise** (kə'mɜːʃə,laɪz) *vb. (tr.)* **1.** to make commercial in aim, methods, or character. **2.** to exploit for profit, esp. at the expense of quality. —**com,mercialí'zation** *or* **com,mercialí'sation** *n.*

commercial paper *n. Chiefly U.S.* a short-term negotiable document, such as a bill of exchange, promissory note, etc., calling for the transference of a specified sum of money at a designated date.

commercial traveller *n.* another name for a **travelling salesman.**

commercial vehicle *n.* a vehicle for carrying goods or (less commonly) passengers.

commère ('kɒmɛə; *French* kɔmɛr) *n.* a female compere. [French, literally: godmother, from COM- + *mère* mother; see COMPERE]

commie *or* **commy** ('kɒmɪ) *n., pl.* **-mies,** *adj. Informal and derogatory.* short for **communist.**

commination (,kɒmɪ'neɪʃən) *n.* **1.** the act or an instance of threatening punishment or vengeance. **2.** *Church of England.* a recital of prayers, including a list of God's judgments against sinners, in the office for Ash Wednesday. [C15: from Latin *comminātiō,* from *comminārī* to menace, from *com-* (intensive) + *minārī* to threaten] —**comminatory** ('kɒmɪnətərɪ, -trɪ) *adj.*

commingle (kɒ'mɪŋgᵊl) *vb.* to mix or be mixed; blend.

comminute ('kɒmɪ,njuːt) *vb.* **1.** to break (a bone) into several small fragments. **2.** to divide (property) into small lots. **3.** *(tr.)* to pulverize. [C17: from Latin *comminuere,* from *com-* (intensive) + *minuere* to reduce; related to MINOR] —**,commi'nution** *n.*

comminuted fracture *n.* a fracture in which the bone is splintered or fragmented.

commis ('kɒmɪs, 'kɒmɪ) *n., pl.* **-mis. 1.** an agent or deputy. **2.** an apprentice waiter or chef. [C16 (meaning: deputy): from French, from *commettre* to employ, COMMIT]

commiserate (kə'mɪzə,reɪt) *vb.* (when *intr.,* usually foll. by *with*) to feel or express sympathy or compassion (for). [C17: from Latin *commiserārī,* from *com-* together + *miserārī* to bewail, pity, from *miser* wretched] —**com'miserable** *adj.* —**com,miser'ation** *n.* —**com'miserative** *adj.* —**com'miseratively** *adv.* —**com'miser,ator** *n.*

commissaire (,kɒmɪ'sɛə) *n.* (in professional cycle racing) a referee who travels in an open-topped car with the riders to witness any infringement of the rules. [from French: see COMMISSARY]

commissar ('kɒmɪ,sɑː, ,kɒmɪ'sɑː) *n.* (in the former Soviet Union) **1.** Also called: **political commissar.** an official of the Communist Party responsible for political education, esp. in a military unit. **2.** Also called: **People's Commissar.** (before 1946) the head of a government department. [C20: from Russian *kommissar,* from German, from Medieval Latin *commissārius* COMMISSARY]

commissariat (,kɒmɪ'sɛərɪət) *n.* **1.** (in the former Soviet Union) a government department before 1946. **2. a.** a military department in charge of food supplies, equipment, etc. **b.** the offices of such a department. **3.** food supplies. [C17: from New Latin *commissāriātus,* from Medieval Latin *commissārius* COMMISSARY]

commissary ('kɒmɪsərɪ) *n., pl.* **-saries. 1.** *U.S.* a shop supplying food or equipment, as in a military camp. **2.** *U.S. army.* an officer responsible for supplies and food. **3.** *U.S.* a snack bar or restaurant in a film studio. **4.** a representative or deputy, esp. an official representative of a bishop. [C14: from Medieval Latin *commissārius* official in charge, from Latin *committere* to entrust, COMMIT] —**commissarial** (,kɒmɪ'sɛərɪəl) *adj.* —**'commissary,ship** *n.*

commission (kə'mɪʃən) *n.* **1.** a duty or task committed to a person or group to perform. **2.** authority to undertake or perform certain duties or functions. **3.** a document granting such authority. 4. *Military.* **a.** a document conferring a rank on an officer. **b.** the rank or authority thereby granted. **5.** a group of people charged with certain duties: *a commission of inquiry.* **6.** a government agency or board empowered to exercise administrative, judicial, or legislative authority. **7. a.** the authority given to a person or organization to act as an agent to a principal in commercial transactions. **b.** the fee allotted to an agent for services rendered. **8.** the state of being charged with specific duties or responsibilities. **9.** the act of committing a sin, crime, etc. **10.** something, esp. a sin, crime, etc., that is committed. **11.** good working condition or (esp. of a ship) active service (esp. in the phrases **in** *or* **into commission, out of commission**). **12.** *U.S.* the head of a department of municipal government. ~*vb.* **13.** (*tr.*) to grant authority to; charge with a duty or task. **14.** (*tr.*) *Military.* to confer a rank on or authorize an action by. **15.** (*tr.*) to equip and test (a ship) for active service. **16.** to make or become operative or operable: *the plant is due to commission next year.* **17.** (*tr.*) to place an order for (something): *to commission a portrait.* [C14: from Old French, from Latin *commissiō* a bringing together, from *committere* to COMMIT] —**com'missional** *or* **com'missionary** *adj.*

commissionaire (kəˌmɪʃəˈnɛə) *n. Chiefly Brit.* a uniformed doorman at a hotel, theatre, etc. [C18: from French, from COMMISSION]

commissioned officer *n.* a military officer holding a commission, such as Second Lieutenant in the British Army, Acting Sub-Lieutenant in the Royal Navy, Pilot Officer in the Royal Air Force, and officers of all ranks senior to these.

commissioner (kəˈmɪʃənə) *n.* **1.** a person authorized to perform certain tasks or endowed with certain powers. **2.** *Government.* **a.** any of several types of civil servant. **b.** an ombudsman. **3.** a member of a commission. —**com'missioner,ship** *n.*

commissioner for oaths *n.* a solicitor authorized to authenticate oaths on sworn statements.

commission plan *n.* (in the U.S.) a system of municipal government that combines legislative and executive authority in a commission of five or six elected members.

commissure (ˈkɒmɪˌsjʊə) *n.* **1.** a band of tissue linking two parts or organs, such as the nervous tissue connecting the right and left sides of the brain in vertebrates. **2.** any of various joints between parts, as between the carpels, leaf lobes, etc., of a plant. [C15: from Latin *commissūra* a joining together, from *committere* COMMIT] —**commissural** (kəˈmɪsjʊrəl, ˌkɒmɪˈsjʊərəl) *adj.*

commit (kəˈmɪt) *vb.* **-mits, -mitting, -mitted.** (*tr.*) **1.** to hand over, as for safekeeping; charge; entrust: *to commit a child to the care of its aunt.* **2. commit to memory.** to learn by heart; memorize. **3.** to confine officially or take into custody: *to commit someone to prison.* **4.** (*usually passive*) to pledge or align (oneself), as to a particular cause, action, or attitude: *a committed radical.* **5.** to order (forces) into action. **6.** to perform (a crime, error, etc.); do; perpetrate. **7.** to surrender, esp. for destruction: *she committed the letter to the fire.* **8.** to refer (a bill, etc.) to a committee of a legislature. [C14: from Latin *committere* to join, from *com-* together + *mittere* to put, send] —**com'mittable** *adj.* —**com'mitter** *n.*

commitment (kəˈmɪtmənt) *n.* **1.** the act of committing or pledging. **2.** the state of being committed or pledged. **3.** an obligation, promise, etc. that restricts one's freedom of action. **4.** the referral of a bill to a committee or legislature. **5.** Also called (esp. formerly): **mittimus.** *Law.* a written order of a court directing that a person be imprisoned. **6.** the official consignment of a person to a mental hospital or prison. **7.** commission or perpetration, esp. of a crime. **8.** a future financial obligation or contingent liability. ~Also called (esp. for senses 5 and 6): **committal** (kəˈmɪtᵊl).

committee *n.* **1.** (kəˈmɪtɪ). a group of people chosen or appointed to perform a specified service or function. **2.** (ˌkɒmɪˈtiː). (formerly) a person to whom the care of a mentally incompetent person or his property was entrusted by a court. See also **receiver** (sense 2). [C15: from *committen* to entrust + -EE]

committeeman (kəˈmɪtɪmən, -ˌmæn) *n., pl.* **-men.** *Chiefly U.S.* a member of one or more committees. —**com'mittee,woman** *fem. n.*

commix (kɒˈmɪks) *vb.* a rare word for **mix.** [C15: back formation from *commixt* mixed together; see MIX] —**com'mixture** *n.*

commo (ˈkɒməʊ) *n., pl.* **-mos,** *adj. Austral. slang.* short for **communist.**

commode (kəˈməʊd) *n.* **1.** a piece of furniture, usually highly ornamented, containing drawers or shelves. **2.** a bedside table with a cabinet below for a chamber pot or washbasin. **3.** a movable piece of furniture, sometimes in the form of a chair, with a hinged flap concealing a chamber pot. **4.** a woman's high-tiered headdress of lace, worn in the late 17th century. [C17: from French, from Latin *commodus* COMMODIOUS]

commodious (kəˈməʊdɪəs) *adj.* **1.** (of buildings, rooms, etc.) large and roomy; spacious. **2.** *Archaic.* suitable; convenient. [C15: from Medieval Latin *commodiōsus,* from Latin *commodus* convenient, from *com-* with + *modus* measure] —**com'modiously** *adv.* —**com'modiousness** *n.*

commodity (kəˈmɒdɪtɪ) *n., pl.* **-ties.** **1.** an article of commerce. **2.** something of use, advantage, or profit. **3.** *Economics.* an exchangeable unit of economic wealth, esp. a primary product or raw material. **4.** *Obsolete.* **a.** a quantity of goods. **b.** convenience or expediency. [C14: from Old French *commodité,* from Latin *commoditās* suitability, benefit; see COMMODIOUS]

commodore (ˈkɒməˌdɔː) *n.* **1.** *Brit.* a naval rank junior to rear admiral and senior to captain. **2.** the senior captain of a shipping line. **3.** the officer in command of a convoy of merchant ships. **4.** the titular head of a yacht or boat club. [C17: probably from Dutch *commandeur,* from French, from Old French *commander* to COMMAND]

common (ˈkɒmən) *adj.* **1.** belonging to or shared by two or more people: *common property.* **2.** belonging to or shared by members of one or more nations or communities; public: *a common culture.* **3.** of ordinary standard; average: *common decency.* **4.** prevailing; widespread: *common opinion.* **5.** widely known or frequently encountered; ordinary: *a common brand of soap.* **6.** widely known and notorious: *a common nuisance.* **7.** *Derogatory.* considered by the speaker to be low-class, vulgar, or coarse: *a common accent.* **8.** (*prenominal*) having no special distinction, rank, or status: *the common man.* **9.** *Maths.* **a.** having a specified relationship with a group of numbers or quantities: *common denominator.* **b.** (of a tangent) tangential to two or more circles. **10.** *Prosody.* (of a syllable) able to be long or short, or (in nonquantitative verse) stressed or unstressed. **11.** *Grammar.* (in certain languages) denoting or belonging to a gender of nouns, esp. one that includes both masculine and feminine referents: *Latin* sacerdos *is common.* **12.** *Anatomy.* **a.** having branches: *the common carotid artery.* **b.** serving more than one function: *the common bile duct.* **13.** *Christianity.* of or relating to the common of the Mass or divine office. **14. common or garden.** *Informal.* ordinary; unexceptional. ~*n.* **15.** (*sometimes pl.*) a tract of open public land, esp. one now used as a recreation area. **16.** *Law.* the right to go onto someone else's property and remove natural products, as by pasturing cattle or fishing (esp. in the phrase **right of common**). **17.** *Christianity.* **a.** a form of the proper of the Mass used on festivals that have no special proper of their own. **b.** the ordinary of the Mass. **18.** *Archaic.* the ordinary people; the public, esp. those undistinguished by rank or title. **19. in common.** mutually held or used with another or others. ~See also **commons.** [C13: from Old French *commun,* from Latin *commūnis* general, universal] —**'commonness** *n.*

commonable (ˈkɒmənəbᵊl) *adj.* **1.** (of land) held in common. **2.** *English history.* (esp. of sheep and cattle) entitled to be pastured on common land.

commonage (ˈkɒmənɪdʒ) *n.* **1.** *Chiefly law.* **a.** the use of something, esp. a pasture, in common with others. **b.** the right to such use. **2.** the state of being held in common. **3.** something held in common, such as land. **4.** another word for **commonalty** (sense 1).

commonality (ˌkɒməˈnælɪtɪ) *n., pl.* **-ties.** **1.** the fact of being common to more than one individual; commonness. **2.** another word for **commonalty** (sense 1).

commonalty (ˈkɒmənəltɪ) *n., pl.* **-ties.** **1.** the ordinary people as distinct from those with authority, rank, or title, esp. when considered as a political and social unit or estate of the realm. Compare **third estate.** **2.** the members of an incorporated society. [C13: from Old French *comunalte,* from *comunal* communal]

common carrier *n.* a person or firm engaged in the business of transporting goods or passengers.

common chord *n. Music.* a chord consisting of the keynote, a major or minor third, and a perfect fifth: *the notes G, B, and D form the common chord of G major.*

common cold *n.* a mild viral infection of the upper respiratory tract, characterized by sneezing, coughing, watery eyes, nasal congestion, etc.

common denominator *n.* **1.** an integer exactly divisible by each denominator of a group of fractions: 1/3, 1/4, and 1/6 have a common denominator of 12. **2.** a belief, attribute, etc., held in common by members of a class or group.

common divisor *n.* another name for **common factor.**

Common Entrance *n.* (in Britain) an entrance examination for a public school, usually taken at the age of 13.

commoner (ˈkɒmənə) *n.* **1.** a person who does not belong to the nobility. **2.** a person who has a right in or over common land jointly with another or others. **3.** *Brit.* a student at a university or other institution who is not on a scholarship.

Common Era *n.* another name for **Christian Era.**

common factor *n.* a number or quantity that is a factor of each member of a group of numbers or quantities: *5 is a common factor of 15 and 20.* Also called: **common divisor.**

common fee *n.* (in Australia) the agreed usual charge for any medical service, which determines the amount of reimbursement under the federal health scheme.

common fraction *n.* another name for **simple fraction.**

common good *n.* the part of the property of a Scottish burgh, in the form of land or funds, that is at the disposal of the community.

common ground *n.* an agreed basis, accepted by both or all parties, for identifying issues in an argument.

common knowledge *n.* something widely or generally known.

common law *n.* **1.** the body of law based on judicial decisions and custom, as distinct from statute law. **2.** the law of a state that is of general application, as distinct from regional customs. **3.** (*modifier*) of or denoting a marriage that is deemed to exist

after a man and a woman have cohabited for a number of years: *common-law marriage; common-law wife.*
common logarithm *n.* a logarithm to the base ten. Usually written $\log_{10}$ or log Compare **natural logarithm.** See also **base**[1] (sense 15b).
commonly ('kɒmənlı) *adv.* **1.** usually; ordinarily: *he was commonly known as Joe.* **2.** *Derogatory.* in a coarse or vulgar way: *she dresses commonly.*
Common Market *n.* **the.** another name for **European Community.**
common measure *n.* **1.** another term for **common time.** **2.** the usual stanza form of a ballad, consisting of four iambic lines rhyming a b c b or a b a b.
common metre *n.* a stanza form, used esp. for hymns, consisting of four lines, two of eight syllables alternating with two of six.
common multiple *n.* an integer or polynomial that is a multiple of each integer or polynomial in a group: *20 is a common multiple of 2, 4, 5, 10.*
common noun *n. Grammar.* a noun that refers to each member of a whole class sharing the features connoted by the noun, as for example *planet, orange,* and *drum.* Compare **proper noun.**
commonplace ('kɒmən,pleıs) *adj.* **1.** ordinary; everyday: *commonplace duties.* **2.** dull and obvious; trite: *commonplace prose.* ~*n.* **3.** something dull and trite, esp. a remark; platitude; truism. **4.** a passage in a book marked for inclusion in a commonplace book, etc. **5.** an ordinary or common thing. [C16: translation of Latin *locus commūnis* argument of wide application, translation of Greek *koinos topos*] —'**common,placeness** *n.*
commonplace book *n.* a notebook in which quotations, poems, remarks, etc., that catch the owner's attention are entered.
common prayer *n.* the liturgy of public services of the Church of England, esp. Morning and Evening Prayer.
common room *n. Chiefly Brit.* a sitting room in schools, colleges, etc., for the relaxation of students or staff.
commons ('kɒmənz) *n.* **1.** *(functioning as pl.)* people not of noble birth viewed as forming a political order. **2.** *(functioning as pl.)* the lower classes as contrasted to the ruling classes of society; the commonalty. **3.** *(functioning as sing.) Brit.* a building or hall for dining, recreational purposes, etc., usually attached to a college, etc. **4.** *(usually functioning as pl.) Brit.* food or rations (esp. in the phrase **short commons).**
Commons ('kɒmənz) *n.* **the.** See **House of Commons.**
common seal *n.* the official seal of a corporate body.
common sense *n.* **1.** plain ordinary good judgment; sound practical sense. ~*adj.* **common-sense;** *also* **common-sensical.** **2.** inspired by or displaying sound practical sense.
common stock *n.* the U.S. name for **ordinary shares.**
common time *n. Music.* a time signature indicating four crotchet beats to the bar; four-four time. Symbol: **C**
commonweal ('kɒmən,wi:l) *n. Archaic.* **1.** the good of the community. **2.** another name for **commonwealth.**
commonwealth ('kɒmən,wɛlθ) *n.* **1.** the people of a state or nation viewed politically; body politic. **2.** a state or nation in which the people possess sovereignty; republic. **3.** the body politic organized for the general good. **4.** a group of persons united by some common interest. **5.** *Obsolete.* the general good; public welfare.
Commonwealth ('kɒmən,wɛlθ) *n.* **the.** **1.** Official name: **the Commonwealth of Nations.** an association of sovereign states that are or at some time have been ruled by Britain. All member states recognize the reigning British sovereign as **Head of the Commonwealth.** **2. a.** the republic that existed in Britain from 1649 to 1660. **b.** the part of this period up to 1653, when Cromwell became Protector. **3.** the official designation of Australia, four states of the U.S. (Kentucky, Massachusetts, Pennsylvania, and Virginia), and Puerto Rico.
commotion (kə'məʊʃən) *n.* **1.** violent and turbulent disturbance; upheaval. **2.** political insurrection; disorder. **3.** a confused noise; din. [C15: from Latin *commōtiō,* from *commovēre* to throw into disorder, from *com-* (intensive) + *movēre* to MOVE] —**com'motional** *adj.*
commove (kə'mu:v) *vb. (tr.) Rare.* **1.** to disturb; stir up. **2.** to agitate or excite emotionally.
communal ('kɒmjʊn°l) *adj.* **1.** belonging or relating to a community as a whole. **2.** relating to different groups within a society: *communal strife.* **3.** of or relating to a commune or a religious community. —**communality** (,kɒmjʊ'nælıtı) *n.* —'**communally** *adv.*
communalism ('kɒmjʊnə,lızəm) *n.* **1.** a system or theory of government in which the state is seen as a loose federation of self-governing communities. **2.** an electoral system in which ethnic groups vote separately for their own representatives. **3.** loyalty to the interests of one's own ethnic group rather than to society as a whole. **4.** the practice or advocacy of communal living or ownership. —'**communalist** *n.* —,**communal'istic** *adj.*
communalize *or* **communalise** ('kɒmjʊnə,laız) *vb. (tr.)* to render (something) the property of a commune or community. —,**communali'zation** *or* ,**communali'sation** *n.* —'**communal,izer** *or* '**communal,iser** *n.*
communard ('kɒmjʊ,nɑ:d) *n.* a member of a commune.
Communard ('kɒmjʊ,nɑ:d) *n.* any person who participated in or supported the Paris Commune formed after the Franco-Prussian War in 1871. [C19: from French]
commune[1] *vb.* (kə'mju:n). *(intr.;* usually foll. by *with)* **1.** to talk or converse intimately. **2.** to experience strong emotion or spiritual feelings (for): *to commune with nature.* ~*n.* ('kɒmju:n). **3.** intimate conversation; exchange of thoughts; communion. [C13: from Old French *comuner* to hold in common, from *comun* COMMON]
commune[2] (kə'mju:n) *vb. (intr.) Christianity, chiefly U.S.* to partake of Communion. [C16: back formation from COMMUNION]
commune[3] ('kɒmju:n) *n.* **1.** a group of families or individuals living together and sharing possessions and responsibilities. **2.** any small group of people having common interests or responsibilities. **3.** the smallest administrative unit in Belgium, France, Italy, and Switzerland, governed by a mayor and council. **4.** the government or inhabitants of a commune. **5.** a medieval town enjoying a large degree of autonomy. [C18: from French, from Medieval Latin *commūnia,* from Latin: things held in common, from [C18: from French, from Medieval Latin *commūnia,* from Latin: things held in common, from *commūnis* COMMON]
communicable (kə'mju:nıkəb°l) *adj.* **1.** capable of being communicated. **2.** (of a disease or its causative agent) capable of being passed on readily. —**com,munica'bility** *or* **com'municableness** *n.* —**com'municably** *adv.*
communicant (kə'mju:nıkənt) *n.* **1.** *Christianity.* a person who receives Communion. **2.** a person who communicates or informs. ~*adj.* **3.** communicating.
communicate (kə'mju:nı,keıt) *vb.* **1.** to impart (knowledge) or exchange (thoughts, feelings, or ideas) by speech, writing, gestures, etc. **2.** *(tr.;* usually foll. by *to)* to allow (a feeling, emotion, etc.) to be sensed (by), willingly or unwillingly; transmit (to): *the dog communicated his fear to the other animals.* **3.** *(intr.)* to have a sympathetic mutual understanding. **4.** *(intr.;* usually foll. by *with)* to make or have a connecting passage or route; connect: *the kitchen communicates with the dining room.* **5.** *(tr.)* to transmit (a disease); infect. **6.** *(intr.) Christianity.* to receive or administer Communion. [C16: from Latin *commūnicāre* to share, from *commūnis* COMMON] —**com'muni,cator** *n.* —**com'municatory** *adj.*
communication (kə,mju:nı'keıʃən) *n.* **1.** the act or an instance of communicating; the imparting or exchange of information, ideas, or feelings. **2.** something communicated, such as a message, letter, or telephone call. **3. a.** *(usually pl.; sometimes functioning as sing.)* the study of ways in which human beings communicate, including speech, gesture, telecommunication systems, publishing and broadcasting media, etc. **b.** *(as modifier): communication theory.* **4.** a connecting route, passage, or link. **5.** *(pl.) Military.* the system of routes and facilities by which forces, supplies, etc., are moved up to or within an area of operations.
communication cord *n. Brit.* a cord or chain in a train which may be pulled by a passenger to stop the train in an emergency.
communication interface *n.* an electronic circuit, usually designed to a specific standard, that enables one machine to telecommunicate with another machine.
communications satellite *n.* an artificial satellite used to relay radio, television, and telephone signals around the earth's surface. A **passive satellite** merely reflects transmissions from its surface. An **active satellite** receives and retransmits signals. See also **Syncom.**
communicative (kə'mju:nıkətıv) *adj.* **1.** inclined or able to communicate readily; talkative. **2.** of or relating to communication. —**com'municatively** *adv.* —**com'municativeness** *n.*
communion (kə'mju:njən) *n.* **1.** an exchange of thoughts, emotions, etc. **2.** possession or sharing in common; participation. **3.** (foll. by *with)* strong emotional or spiritual feelings (for): *communion with nature.* **4.** a religious group or denomination having a common body of beliefs, doctrines, and practices. **5.** the spiritual union held by Christians to exist between individual Christians and Christ, their Church, or their fellow Christians. [C14: from Latin *commūniō* general participation, from *commūnis* COMMON] —**com'munional** *adj.* —**com'munionally** *adv.*
Communion (kə'mju:njən) *n. Christianity.* **1.** the act of participating in the Eucharist. **2.** the celebration of the Eucharist, esp. the part of the service during which the consecrated elements are received. **3. a.** the consecrated elements of the Eucharist. **b.** *(as modifier): Communion cup.* ~Also called: **Holy Communion.**
communion of saints *n. Christianity.* the spiritual fellowship of all true Christians, living and dead.
communiqué (kə'mju:nı,keı) *n.* an official communication or announcement, esp. to the press or public. [C19: from French, from *communiquer* to COMMUNICATE]
communism ('kɒmjʊ,nızəm) *n.* **1.** advocacy of a classless society in which private ownership has been abolished and the means of production and subsistence belong to the community. **2.** any social, economic, or political movement or doctrine aimed at achieving such a society. **3.** *(usually cap.)* a political movement based upon the writings of Karl Marx (1818–83) that considers history in terms of class conflict and revolutionary struggle, resulting eventually in the victory of the proletariat and the

establishment of a socialist order based on public ownership of the means of production. See also **Marxism, Marxism-Leninism, socialism.** **4.** (*usually cap.*) a social order or system of government established by a ruling Communist Party, esp. in the former Soviet Union. **5.** (*often cap.*) *Chiefly U.S.* any leftist political activity or thought, esp. when considered to be subversive. **6.** communal living; communalism. [C19: from French *communisme,* from *commun* COMMON]

communist ('kɒmjʊnɪst) *n.* **1.** a supporter of any form of communism. **2.** (*often cap.*) a supporter of Communism or a Communist movement or state. **3.** (*often cap.*) a member of a Communist party. **4.** a person who practises communal living; communalist. **5.** another name for **Communard.** ~*adj.* **6.** of, characterized by, favouring, or relating to communism; communistic.

communistic (ˌkɒmjʊ'nɪstɪk) *adj.* of, characteristic of, or relating to communism. —ˌ**commu'nistically** *adv.*

communitarian (kəˌmjuːnɪ'tɛərɪən) *n.* **1.** a member of a communist community. **2.** an advocate of communalism.

community (kə'mjuːnɪtɪ) *n., pl.* **-ties. 1. a.** the people living in one locality. **b.** the locality in which they live. **c.** (*as modifier*): *community spirit.* **2.** a group of people having cultural, religious, ethnic, or other characteristics in common: *the Protestant community.* **3.** a group of nations having certain interests in common. **4.** the public in general; society. **5.** common ownership or participation. **6.** similarity or agreement: *community of interests.* **7.** (in Wales since 1974 and Scotland since 1975) the smallest unit of local government; a subdivision of a district. **8.** *Ecology.* a group of interdependent plants and animals inhabiting the same region and interacting with each other through food and other relationships. [C14: from Latin *commūnitās,* from *commūnis* COMMON]

community aerial *or* **antenna** *n.* a television or radio receiving aerial from which received signals are distributed by cable to the local community.

community association *n.* (in Britain) an organization of people and groups working for the common good of a neighbourhood, usually operating under a written constitution registered with the Charity Commissioners.

community care *n. Social welfare.* **1.** help available to persons living in their own homes, rather than services provided in residential institutions. **2.** the policy of transferring responsibility for people in need from large, often isolated, state institutions to their relatives and local welfare agencies.

community centre *n.* a building used by members of a community for social gatherings, educational activities, etc.

community charge *n.* (in Britain) a flat-rate charge paid by each adult in a community to their local authority in place of rates. Also called: **poll tax.**

community chest *n. U.S.* a fund raised by voluntary contribution for local welfare activities.

community college *n.* **1.** *Brit.* another term for **village college.** **2.** *Chiefly U.S. and Canadian.* a nonresidential college offering two-year courses of study. **3.** *N.Z.* an adult education college with trade classes.

community council *n.* (in Scotland and Wales) an independent voluntary local body set up to attend to local interests and organize community activities.

community education *n.* the provision of a wide range of educational and special interest courses and activities by a local authority.

community home *n.* (in Britain) **1.** a home provided by a local authority for children who cannot remain with parents or relatives, or be placed with foster parents. **2.** a boarding school for young offenders. Former name: **approved school.** Formal name: **community home with education on the premises.** Abbrev.: **CHE.**

community policing *n.* the assigning of the same one or two policemen to a particular area so that they become familiar with the residents and the residents with them, as a way of reducing crime.

community relations *pl. n.* **1.** the particular state of affairs in an area where potentially conflicting ethnic, religious, cultural, political, or linguistic groups live together: *community relations in this neighbourhood were strained before the riots.* **2. a.** social engineering or mediating work with conflicting groups: *he spent ten years in community relations.* **b.** (*as modifier*): *a community-relations officer.*

community school *n. Brit.* a school offering some nonacademic activities related to life in a particular community and often serving as a community centre.

community service *n.* **1.** voluntary work, intended to be for the common good, usually done as part of an organized scheme. **2.** See **community-service order.**

community-service order *n.* (in Britain) a court order requiring an offender over seventeen years old to do unpaid socially beneficial work under supervision instead of going to prison.

community singing *n.* singing, esp. of hymns, by a large gathering of people.

communize *or* **communise** ('kɒmjʊˌnaɪz) *vb.* (*tr.*) (*sometimes cap.*) **1.** to make (property) public; nationalize. **2.** to make (a person or country) communist. —ˌ**communi'zation** *or* ˌ**communi'sation** *n.*

commutable (kə'mjuːtəbᵊl) *adj.* **1.** *Law.* (of a punishment) capable of being reduced in severity. **2.** able to be exchanged. —**comˌmuta'bility** *or* **com'mutableness** *n.*

commutate ('kɒmjʊˌteɪt) *vb.* (*tr.*) **1.** to reverse the direction of (an electric current). **2.** to convert (an alternating current) into a direct current.

commutation (ˌkɒmjʊ'teɪʃən) *n.* **1.** a substitution or exchange. **2. a.** the replacement of one method of payment by another. **b.** the payment substituted. **3.** the reduction in severity of a penalty imposed by law. **4.** the process of commutating an electric current. **5.** *U.S.* the travelling done by a commuter.

commutation ticket *n.* a U.S. name for **season ticket.**

commutative (kə'mjuːtətɪv, 'kɒmjʊˌteɪtɪv) *adj.* **1.** relating to or involving substitution. **2.** *Maths, logic.* **a.** (of an operator) giving the same result irrespective of the order of the arguments; thus disjunction and addition are commutative but implication and subtraction are not. **b.** relating to this property: *the commutative law of addition.* —**com'mutatively** *adv.*

commutator ('kɒmjʊˌteɪtə) *n.* **1.** a device used to reverse the direction of flow of an electric current. **2.** the segmented metal cylinder or disc mounted on the armature shaft of an electric motor, generator, etc., used to make electrical contact with the rotating coils and ensure unidirectional current flow.

commute (kə'mjuːt) *vb.* **1.** (*intr.*) to travel some distance regularly between one's home and one's place of work. **2.** (*tr.*) to substitute; exchange. **3.** (*tr.*) *Law.* to reduce (a sentence) to one less severe. **4.** to pay (an annuity) at one time, esp. with a discount, instead of in instalments. **5.** (*tr.*) to transform; change: *to commute base metal into gold.* **6.** (*intr.*) to act as or be a substitute. **7.** (*intr.*) to make a substitution; change. [C17: from Latin *commūtāre* to replace, from *com-* mutually + *mūtāre* to change] —**com'mutable** *adj.* —**com'mutableness** *or* **comˌmuta'bility** *n.*

commuter (kə'mjuːtə) *n.* **a.** a person who travels to work over an appreciable distance, usually from the suburbs to the centre of a city. **b.** (*as modifier*): *the commuter belt.*

comodo *or* **commodo** (kə'məʊdəʊ) *adj., adv. Music.* (to be performed) at a convenient relaxed speed. [Italian: comfortable, from Latin *commodus,* convenient; see COMMODIOUS]

comose ('kəʊməʊs, kəʊ'məʊs) *adj. Botany.* another word for **comate.** [C18: from Latin *comōsus* hairy, from *coma* long hair; see COMA[2]]

comp (kɒmp) *Informal.* ~*n.* **1.** a compositor. **2.** an accompanist. **3.** an accompaniment. **4.** a competition. ~*vb.* **5.** (*intr.*) to work as a compositor in the printing industry. **6.** to play an accompaniment (to).

comp. *abbrev. for:* **1.** companion. **2.** comparative. **3.** compare. **4.** compiled. **5.** compiler. **6.** complete. **7.** composer. **8.** composition. **9.** compositor. **10.** compound. **11.** comprehensive. **12.** comprising.

compact[1] *adj.* (kəm'pækt). **1.** closely packed together; dense. **2.** neatly fitted into a restricted space. **3.** concise; brief. **4.** well constructed; solid; firm. **5.** (foll. by *of*) composed or made up (of). **6.** *Maths, logic.* (of a relation) having the property that for any pair of elements such that *a* is related to *b,* there is some element *c* such that *a* is related to *c* and *c* to *b,* as *less than* on the rational numbers. **7.** *U.S. and Canadian.* (of a car) small and economical. ~*vb.* (kəm'pækt). (*tr.*) **8.** to pack or join closely together; compress; condense. **9.** (foll. by *of*) to create or form by pressing together: *sediment compacted of three types of clay.* **10.** *Metallurgy.* to compress (a metal powder) to form a stable product suitable for sintering. ~*n.* ('kɒmpækt). **11.** a small flat case containing a mirror, face powder, etc., designed to be carried in a woman's handbag. **12.** *U.S. and Canadian.* a comparatively small and economical car. **13.** *Metallurgy.* a mass of metal prepared for sintering by cold-pressing a metal powder. [C16: from Latin *compactus,* from *compingere* to put together, from *com-* together + *pangere* to fasten] —**com'pacter** *n.* —**com'paction** *n.* —**com'pactly** *adv.* —**com'pactness** *n.*

compact[2] ('kɒmpækt) *n.* an official contract or agreement. [C16: from Latin *compactum,* from *compacīscī* to agree, from *com-* together + *pacīscī* to contract; see PACT]

compact camera ('kɒmpækt) *n.* a simple 35 mm snapshot camera not having interchangeable lenses or through-the-lens focusing but sometimes having automatic focusing, exposure, and winding. Sometimes shortened to **compact.**

compact disc ('kɒmpækt) *n.* a small digital audio disc on which sound is recorded as a series of metallic pits enclosed in PVC, played at 250 revolutions per minute and read by an optical laser system. Also called: **compact audio disc.** Abbrevs.: **CD, CAD.**

compact disc player *n.* a machine with a laser beam for playing compact discs.

compactify (kəm'pæktɪˌfaɪ) *vb.* **-fies, -fying, -fied.** to make or become compact; esp. of higher dimensions in space–time, to become tightly curved so as to be unobservable under normal circumstances. —**com'pactifiˌcation** *n.*

compact video disc *n.* a compact laser disc that plays both pictures and sound. Abbrev.: **CDV.**

compadre (kɒm'pɑːdreɪ, kəm-) *n. Southwestern U.S.* a masculine friend. [from Spanish: godfather, from Medieval Latin *compater,* from Latin *com-* with + *pater* father]

compages (kəm'peɪdʒiːz) *n.* (*functioning as sing.*) a structure or framework. [C17: from Latin, from *com-* together + *pag-*, from *pangĕre* to fasten]
compander (kəm'pændə) *n.* a system for improving the signal-to-noise ratio of a signal at a transmitter or recorder by first compressing the volume range of the signal and then restoring it to its original amplitude level at the receiving or reproducing apparatus. [C20: from COM(PRESSOR) + (EX)PANDER]
companion[1] (kəm'pænjən) *n.* **1.** a person who is an associate of another or others; comrade. **2.** (esp. formerly) an employee, usually a woman, who provides company for an employer, esp. an elderly woman. **3. a.** one of a pair; match. **b.** (*as modifier*): *a companion volume.* **4.** a guidebook or handbook. **5.** a member of the lowest rank of any of certain orders of knighthood. **6.** *Astronomy.* the fainter of the two components of a double star. ~*vb.* **7.** (*tr.*) to accompany or be a companion to. [C13: from Late Latin *compāniō*, literally: one who eats bread with another, from Latin *com-* with + *pānis* bread] —**com'panionless** *adj.*
companion[2] (kəm'pænjən) *n. Nautical.* **a.** a raised frame on an upper deck with windows to give light to the deck below. **b.** (*as modifier*): *a companion ladder.* [C18: from Dutch *kompanje* quarterdeck, from Old French *compagne*, from Old Italian *compagna* pantry, perhaps ultimately from Latin *pānis* bread]
companionable (kəm'pænjənəbᵊl) *adj.* suited to be a companion; sociable. —**com'panionableness** *or* **com,paniona'bility** *n.* —**com'panionably** *adv.*
companionate (kəm'pænjənɪt) *adj.* **1.** resembling, appropriate to, or acting as a companion. **2.** harmoniously suited.
companion set *n.* a set of fire irons on a stand.
companionship (kəm'pænjən,ʃɪp) *n.* the relationship of friends or companions; fellowship.
companionway (kəm'pænjən,weɪ) *n.* a stairway or ladder leading from one deck to another in a boat or ship.
company ('kʌmpənɪ) *n., pl.* **-nies. 1.** a number of people gathered together; assembly. **2.** the fact of being with someone; companionship: *I enjoy her company.* **3.** a social visitor or visitors; guest or guests. **4.** a business enterprise. **5.** the members of an enterprise not specifically mentioned in the enterprise's title. Abbrevs.: **Co., co. 6.** a group of actors, usually including business and technical personnel. **7.** a small unit of troops, usually comprising two or more platoons. **8.** the officers and crew of a ship. **9.** a unit of Girl Guides. **10.** *English history.* a medieval guild. **11. keep** *or* **bear company. a.** to accompany (someone). **b.** (esp. of lovers) to associate with each other; spend time together. **12. part company. a.** to end a friendship or association, esp. as a result of a quarrel; separate. **b.** (foll. by *with*) to leave; go away (from); be separated (from). ~*vb.* **-nies, -nying, -nied. 13.** *Archaic.* to keep company or associate (with someone). [C13: from Old French *compaignie*, from *compain* companion, fellow, from Late Latin *compāniō*; see COMPANION[1]]
company doctor *n.* **1.** a businessman or accountant who specializes in turning ailing companies into profitable enterprises. **2.** a physician employed by a company to look after its staff and to advise on health matters.
company man *n.* an employee who puts allegiance to the company for which he works above personal opinion or friendship.
company secretary *n. Brit.* an officer of an incorporated company who has certain legal obligations.
company sergeant major *n. Military.* the senior Warrant Officer II in a British or Commonwealth regiment or battalion, responsible under the company second in command for all aspects of duty and discipline of the NCOs and men in that subunit. Abbrev.: **CSM.** Compare **regimental sergeant major.** See also **warrant officer.**
company union *n. Chiefly U.S. and Canadian.* an unaffiliated union of workers usually restricted to a single business enterprise.
compar. *abbrev. for* comparative.
comparable ('kɒmpərəbᵊl) *adj.* **1.** worthy of comparison. **2.** able to be compared (with). —,**compara'bility** *or* **'comparableness** *n.* —**'comparably** *adv.*
comparative (kəm'pærətɪv) *adj.* **1.** denoting or involving comparison: *comparative literature.* **2.** judged by comparison; relative: *a comparative loss of prestige.* **3.** *Grammar.* denoting the form of an adjective that indicates that the quality denoted is possessed to a greater extent. In English the comparative form of an adjective is usually marked by the suffix *-er* or the word *more.* Compare **positive** (sense 10), **superlative** (sense 2). ~*n.* **4.** the comparative form of an adjective. —**com'paratively** *adv.* —**com'parativeness** *n.*
comparative judgment *n. Psychol.* any judgment about whether there is a difference between two or more stimuli. Compare **absolute judgment.**
comparative psychology *n.* the study of the similarities and differences in the behaviour of different species.
comparator (kəm'pærətə) *n.* **1.** any instrument used to measure a property of a system by comparing it with a standard system. **2.** an electric circuit that compares two signals and gives an indication of the extent of their dissimilarity.
compare (kəm'pɛə) *vb.* **1.** (*tr.*; foll. by *to*) to regard or represent as analogous or similar; liken: *the general has been compared to Napoleon.* **2.** (*tr.*) to examine in order to observe resemblances or differences: *to compare rum and gin.* **3.** (*intr.*; usually foll. by *with*) to be of the same or similar quality or value: *gin compares with rum in alcoholic content.* **4.** (*intr.*) to bear a specified relation of quality or value when examined: *this car compares badly with the other.* **5.** (*tr.*) *Grammar.* to give the positive, comparative, and superlative forms of (an adjective). **6.** (*intr.*) *Archaic.* to compete or vie. **7. compare notes.** to exchange opinions. ~*n.* **8.** comparison or analogy (esp. in the phrase **beyond compare**). [C15: from Old French *comparer*, from Latin *comparāre* to couple together, match, from *compar* equal to one another, from *com-* together + *par* equal; see PAR] —**com'parer** *n.*
comparison (kəm'pærɪsᵊn) *n.* **1.** the act or process of comparing. **2.** the state of being compared. **3.** comparable quality or qualities; likeness: *there was no comparison between them.* **4.** a rhetorical device involving comparison, such as a simile. **5.** Also called: **degrees of comparison.** *Grammar.* the listing of the positive, comparative, and superlative forms of an adjective or adverb. **6. bear** *or* **stand comparison (with).** to be sufficiently similar in class or range to be compared with (something else), esp. favourably.
compartment (kəm'pɑːtmənt) *n.* **1.** one of the sections into which an area, esp. an enclosed space, is divided or partitioned. **2.** any separate part or section: *a compartment of the mind.* **3.** a small storage space; locker. [C16: from French *compartiment*, ultimately from Late Latin *compartīrī* to share, from Latin *com-* with + *partīrī* to apportion, from *pars* PART] —**compartmental** (,kɒmpɑːt'mɛntᵊl) *adj.* —,**compart'mentally** *adv.*
compartmentalize *or* **compartmentalise** (,kɒmpɑːt'mɛntᵊ,laɪz) *vb.* (*usually tr.*) to put or divide into (compartments, categories, etc.), esp. to an excessive degree. —,**compart,mentali'zation** *or* ,**compart,mentali'sation** *n.*
compass ('kʌmpəs) *n.* **1.** an instrument for finding direction, usually having a magnetized needle swinging freely on a pivot, which points to magnetic north. **2.** (*often pl.*) Also called: **pair of compasses.** an instrument used for drawing circles, measuring distances, etc., that consists of two arms, joined at one end, one arm of which serves as a pivot or stationary reference point, while the other is extended or describes a circle. **3.** limits or range: *within the compass of education.* **4.** *Music.* the interval between the lowest and highest note attainable by a voice or musical instrument. **5.** *Archaic.* a circular course. ~*vb.* (*tr.*) **6.** to encircle or surround; hem in. **7.** to comprehend or grasp mentally. **8.** to achieve; attain; accomplish. **9.** *Obsolete.* to plot. [C13: from Old French *compas*, from *compasser* to measure, from Vulgar Latin *compassāre* (unattested) to pace out, ultimately from Latin *passus* step] —**'compassable** *adj.*
compass card *n.* a compass in the form of a card that rotates so that "0°" or "North" points to magnetic north.
compassion (kəm'pæʃən) *n.* a feeling of distress and pity for the suffering or misfortune of another, often including the desire to alleviate it. [C14: from Old French, from Late Latin *compassiō* fellow feeling, from *compatī* to suffer with, from Latin *com-* with + *patī* to bear, suffer]
compassionate (kəm'pæʃənət) *adj.* **1.** showing or having compassion. **2. compassionate leave.** leave granted, esp. to a serviceman, on the grounds of bereavement, family illness, etc. —**com'passionately** *adv.* —**com'passionateness** *n.*
compass plant *n.* **1.** Also called: **rosinweed.** a tall plant, *Silphium laciniatum*, of central North America, that has yellow flowers and lower leaves that tend to align themselves at right angles to the strongest light, esp. in a north-south plane: family *Compositae* (composites). **2.** any of several similar plants.
compass rose *n.* a circle or decorative device printed on a map or chart showing the points of the compass measured from true north and usually magnetic north.
compass saw *n.* a hand saw with a narrow tapered blade for making a curved cut.
compass window *n. Architect.* a bay window having a semicircular shape.
compatible (kəm'pætəbᵊl) *adj.* **1.** (usually foll. by *with*) able to exist together harmoniously. **2.** (usually foll. by *with*) consistent or congruous: *her deeds were not compatible with her ideology.* **3.** (of plants) **a.** capable of forming successful grafts. **b.** capable of self-fertilization. **4.** (of pieces of machinery, computer equipment, etc.) capable of being used together without special modification or adaptation. [C15: from Medieval Latin *compatibilis*, from Late Latin *compatī* to be in sympathy with; see COMPASSION] —**com,pati'bility** *or* **com'patibleness** *n.* —**com'patibly** *adv.*
compatriot (kəm'pætrɪət) *n.* a fellow countryman. [C17: from French *compatriote*, from Late Latin *compatriōta*; see PATRIOT] —**com,patri'otic** *adj.* —**com'patriotism** *n.*
compeer ('kɒmpɪə) *n.* **1.** a person of equal rank, status, or ability; peer. **2.** a companion or comrade. [C13: from Old French *comper*, from Medieval Latin *compater* godfather; see COMPADRE]
compel (kəm'pɛl) *vb.* **-pels, -pelling, -pelled.** (*tr.*) **1.** to cause (someone) by force (to be or do something). **2.** to obtain by force; exact: *to compel obedience.* **3.** to overpower or subdue. **4.** *Archaic.* to herd or drive together. [C14: from Latin *compellere* to drive together, from *com-* together + *pellere* to drive] —**com'pellable** *adj.* —**com'pellably** *adv.* —**com'peller** *n.*

compellation (ˌkɒmpɛˈleɪʃən) *n.* a rare word for **appellation.** [C17: from Latin *compellātiō,* from *compellāre* to accost, from *appellāre* to call]

compelling (kəmˈpɛlɪŋ) *adj.* arousing or denoting strong interest, esp. admiring interest.

compendious (kəmˈpɛndɪəs) *adj.* containing or stating the essentials of a subject in a concise form; succinct. —**comˈpendiously** *adv.* —**comˈpendiousness** *n.*

compendium (kəmˈpɛndɪəm) *n., pl.* **-diums** *or* **-dia** (-dɪə). **1.** *Brit.* a book containing a collection of useful hints. **2.** *Brit.* a selection, esp. of different games or other objects in one container. **3.** a concise but comprehensive summary of a larger work. [C16: from Latin: a saving, literally: something weighed, from *pendere* to weigh]

compensable (kəmˈpɛnsəbᵊl) *adj. Chiefly U.S.* entitled to compensation or capable of being compensated.

compensate (ˈkɒmpɛnˌseɪt) *vb.* **1.** to make amends to (someone), esp. for loss or injury. **2.** (*tr.*) to serve as compensation or damages for (injury, loss, etc.). **3.** to offset or counterbalance the effects of (a force, weight, movement, etc.) so as to nullify the effects of an undesirable influence and produce equilibrium. **4.** (*intr.*) to attempt to conceal or offset one's shortcomings by the exaggerated exhibition of qualities regarded as desirable. [C17: from Latin *compēnsāre,* from *pensāre,* from *pendere* to weigh] —**compensatory** (ˈkɒmpɛnˌseɪtərɪ; kəmˈpɛnsətərɪ, -trɪ) *or* **compensative** (ˈkɒmpɛnˌseɪtɪv, kəmˈpɛnsə-) *adj.* —**ˈcompenˌsator** *n.*

compensated semiconductor *n. Physics.* a semiconductor in which donors and acceptors are related in such a way that their opposing electrical effects are partially cancelled.

compensation (ˌkɒmpɛnˈseɪʃən) *n.* **1.** the act or process of making amends for something. **2.** something given as reparation for loss, injury, etc.; indemnity. **3.** the automatic movements made by the body to maintain balance. **4.** the attempt to conceal or offset one's shortcomings by the exaggerated exhibition of qualities regarded as desirable. **5.** *Biology.* abnormal growth and increase in size in one organ in response to the removal or inactivation of another. —ˌ**compenˈsational** *adj.*

compensation order *n.* (in Britain) the requirement of a court that an offender pay compensation for injury, loss, or damage resulting from an offence, either in preference to or as well as a fine.

compensation point *n. Botany.* the concentration of atmospheric carbon dioxide at which the rate of carbon dioxide uptake by a photosynthesizing plant is exactly balanced by its rate of carbon dioxide release in respiration.

compensatory finance *n.* another name for **deficit financing.**

compere (ˈkɒmpɛə) *Brit.* ~*n.* **1.** a master of ceremonies who introduces cabaret, television acts, etc. ~*vb.* **2.** to act as a compere (for). [C20: from French, literally: godfather; see COMPEER, COMPADRE]

compete (kəmˈpiːt) *vb.* (*intr.;* often foll. by *with*) to contend (against) for profit, an award, athletic supremacy, etc.; engage in a contest (with). [C17: from Late Latin *competere* to strive together, from Latin: to meet, come together, agree, from *com-* together + *petere* to seek]

competence (ˈkɒmpɪtəns) *n.* **1.** the condition of being capable; ability. **2.** a sufficient income to live on. **3.** the state of being legally competent or qualified. **4.** *Embryol.* the ability of embryonic tissues to react to external conditions in a way that influences subsequent development. **5.** *Linguistics.* (in transformational grammar) the form of the human language faculty, independent of its psychological embodiment in actual human beings. Compare **performance** (sense 7), **langue, parole** (sense 5).

competency (ˈkɒmpɪtənsɪ) *n., pl.* **-cies. 1.** *Law.* capacity to testify in a court of law; eligibility to be sworn. **2.** a less common word for **competence** (senses 1, 2).

competent (ˈkɒmpɪtənt) *adj.* **1.** having sufficient skill, knowledge, etc.; capable. **2.** suitable or sufficient for the purpose: *a competent answer.* **3.** *Law.* (of a witness) having legal capacity; qualified to testify, etc. **4.** (*postpositive;* foll. by *to*) belonging as a right; appropriate. [C14: from Latin *competēns,* from *competere* to be competent; see COMPETE] —**ˈcompetently** *adv.* —**ˈcompetentness** *n.*

competition (ˌkɒmpɪˈtɪʃən) *n.* **1.** the act of competing; rivalry. **2.** a contest in which a winner is selected from among two or more entrants. **3.** a series of games, sports events, etc. **4.** the opposition offered by a competitor or competitors. **5.** a competitor or competitors offering opposition. **6.** *Ecology.* the struggle between individuals of the same or different species for food, space, light, etc., when these are inadequate to supply the needs of all.

competitive (kəmˈpɛtɪtɪv) *adj.* **1.** involving or determined by rivalry: *competitive sports.* **2.** sufficiently low in price or high in quality to be successful against commercial rivals. **3.** relating to or characterized by an urge to compete: *a competitive personality.* —**comˈpetitively** *adv.* —**comˈpetitiveness** *n.*

competitive exclusion *n. Ecology.* the dominance of one species over another when both are competing for the same resources, etc.

competitor (kəmˈpɛtɪtə) *n.* a person, group, team, firm, etc., that vies or competes; rival.

compilation (ˌkɒmpɪˈleɪʃən) *n.* **1.** something collected or compiled, such as a list, report, etc. **2.** the act or process of collecting or compiling.

compilation film *n.* film from an archive used in a film or documentary to give a feeling of the relevant period.

compile (kəmˈpaɪl) *vb.* (*tr.*) **1.** to make or compose from other materials or sources: *to compile a list of names.* **2.** to collect or gather for a book, hobby, etc. **3.** *Computer technol.* to create (a set of machine instructions) from a high-level programming language, using a compiler. [C14: from Latin *compīlāre* to pile together, plunder, from *com-* together + *pīlāre* to thrust down, pack]

compiler (kəmˈpaɪlə) *n.* **1.** a person who collects or compiles something. **2.** a computer program by which a high-level programming language, such as COBOL or FORTRAN, is converted into machine language that can be acted upon by a computer. Compare **assembler.**

complacency (kəmˈpleɪsənsɪ) *or* **complacence** *n., pl.* **-cencies** *or* **-cences. 1.** a feeling of satisfaction, esp. extreme self-satisfaction; smugness. **2.** an obsolete word for **complaisance.**

complacent (kəmˈpleɪsᵊnt) *adj.* **1.** pleased or satisfied, esp. extremely self-satisfied. **2.** an obsolete word for **complaisant.** [C17: from Latin *complacēns* very pleasing, from *complacēre* to be most agreeable to, from *com-* (intensive) + *placēre* to please] —**comˈplacently** *adv.*

complain (kəmˈpleɪn) *vb.* (*intr.*) **1.** to express resentment, displeasure, etc., esp. habitually; grumble. **2.** (foll. by *of*) to state the presence of pain, illness, etc., esp. in the hope of sympathy: *she complained of a headache.* [C14: from Old French *complaindre,* from Vulgar Latin *complangere* (unattested), from Latin *com-* (intensive) + *plangere* to bewail] —**comˈplainer** *n.* —**comˈplainingly** *adv.*

complainant (kəmˈpleɪnənt) *n. Law.* a person who makes a complaint, usually before justices; plaintiff.

complaint (kəmˈpleɪnt) *n.* **1.** the act of complaining; an expression of grievance. **2.** a cause for complaining; grievance. **3.** a mild ailment. **4.** *English law.* a statement by which a civil proceeding in a magistrates' court is commenced.

complaisance (kəmˈpleɪzəns) *n.* **1.** deference to the wishes of others; willing compliance. **2.** an act of willing compliance.

complaisant (kəmˈpleɪzᵊnt) *adj.* showing a desire to comply or oblige; polite. [C17: from French *complaire,* from Latin *complacēre* to please greatly; compare COMPLACENT] —**comˈplaisantly** *adv.*

complanate (kəmˈpleɪneɪt) *adj. Botany.* having a flattened or compressed aspect.

compleat (kəmˈpliːt) *adj.* an archaic spelling of **complete,** used in the titles of handbooks, in imitation of *The Compleat Angler* by Izaak Walton (1593–1683), English writer.

complect (kəmˈplɛkt) *vb.* (*tr.*) *Archaic.* to interweave or entwine. [C16: from Latin *complectī;* see COMPLEX]

complected (kəmˈplɛktɪd) *adj.* (*in combination*) a U.S. dialect word for **complexioned.**

complement *n.* (ˈkɒmplɪmənt). **1.** a person or thing that completes something. **2.** one of two parts that make up a whole or complete each other. **3.** a complete amount, number, etc. (often in the phrase **full complement**). **4.** the officers and crew needed to man a ship. **5.** *Grammar.* **a.** a noun phrase that follows a copula or similar verb, as for example *an idiot* in the sentence *He is an idiot.* **b.** a clause that serves as the subject or direct object of a verb or the direct object of a preposition, as for example *that he would be early* in the sentence *I hoped that he would be early.* **6.** *Maths.* the angle that when added to a specified angle produces a right angle. **7.** *Logic, maths.* the class of all things, or of all members of a given universe of discourse, that are not members of a given set. **8.** *Music.* the inverted form of an interval that, when added to the interval, completes the octave: *the sixth is the complement of the third.* **9.** *Immunol.* a group of proteins in the blood serum that, when activated by antibodies, causes destruction of alien cells, such as bacteria. ~*vb.* (ˈkɒmplɪˌmɛnt). **10.** (*tr.*) to add to, make complete, or form a complement to. [C14: from Latin *complēmentum,* from *complēre* to fill up, from *com-* (intensive) + *plēre* to fill]

complementarity (ˌkɒmplɪmənˈtærɪtɪ) *n., pl.* **-ties. 1.** a state or system that involves complementary components. **2.** *Physics.* the principle that the complete description of a phenomenon in microphysics requires the use of two distinct theories that are complementary to each other. See also **duality** (sense 2).

complementary (ˌkɒmplɪˈmɛntərɪ, -trɪ) *or* **complemental** *adj.* **1.** acting as or forming a complement; completing. **2.** forming a satisfactory or balanced whole. **3.** forming a mathematical complement: *sine and cosine are complementary functions.* **4.** *Maths, logic.* (of a pair of sets, functions, etc.) mutually exclusive and exhaustive, each being the complement of the other. **5.** (of genes) producing an effect in association with other genes. **6.** involving or using the treatments and techniques of complementary medicine. —ˌ**compleˈmentarily** *or* ˌ**compleˈmentally** *adv.* —ˌ**compleˈmentariness** *n.*

complementary angle *n.* either of two angles whose sum is 90°. Compare **supplementary angle.**

complementary colour *n.* one of any pair of colours, such as yellow and blue, that give white or grey when mixed in the correct proportions.

complementary DNA *n.* a form of DNA artificially synthesized from a messenger RNA template and used in genetic engineering to produce gene clones. Abbrev.: **cDNA.**

complementary gene *n.* one of a pair of genes, each from different loci, that together are required for the expression of a certain characteristic.

complementary medicine *n.* another name for **alternative medicine.**

complementary wavelength *n. Physics.* the wavelength of monochromatic light that could be mixed in suitable proportions with a given coloured light so as to produce some specified achromatic light.

complementation (ˌkɒmplɪmɛnˈteɪʃən) *n.* **1.** the act or process of forming a complement. **2.** *Genetics.* the combination of two homologous chromosomes, each with a different recessive mutant gene, in a single cell to produce a normal phenotype. The deficiency of one homologue is supplied by the normal allele of the other.

complement fixation test *n. Med.* a serological test for detecting the presence of a specific antibody or antigen, used in the diagnosis of syphilis, etc.

complementizer (ˈkɒmplɪmənˌtaɪzə) *n. Generative grammar.* a word or morpheme that serves to introduce a complement clause or a reduced form of such a clause, as *that* in *I wish that he would leave.*

complete (kəmˈpliːt) *adj.* **1.** having every necessary part or element; entire. **2.** ended; finished. **3.** (*prenominal*) thorough; absolute: *he is a complete rogue.* **4.** perfect in quality or kind: *he is a complete scholar.* **5.** (of a logical system) constituted such that a contradiction arises on the addition of any proposition that cannot be deduced from the axioms of the system. Compare **consistent** (sense 4). **6.** (of flowers) having sepals, petals, stamens, and carpels. **7.** *Archaic.* expert or skilled; accomplished. *~vb.* (*tr.*) **8.** to make whole or perfect. **9.** to end; finish. **10.** (in land law) to pay any outstanding balance on a contract for the conveyance of land in exchange for the title deeds, so that the ownership of the land changes hands. **11.** *American football.* (of an offensive player) to catch a forward pass successfully. [C14: from Latin *complētus,* past participle of *complēre* to fill up; see COMPLEMENT] **—comˈpletely** *adv.* **—comˈpleteness** *n.* **—comˈpleter** *n.* **—comˈpletion** *n.* **—comˈpletive** *adj.*

complex (ˈkɒmplɛks) *adj.* **1.** made up of various interconnected parts; composite. **2.** (of thoughts, writing, etc.) intricate or involved. **3.** *Grammar.* **a.** (of a word) containing at least one bound form. **b.** (of a noun phrase) containing both a lexical noun and an embedded clause, as for example the italicized parts of the following sentence: I didn't know *the man who served me.* **c.** (of a sentence) formed by subordination of one clause to another. **4.** *Maths.* **a.** of or involving one or more complex numbers. **b.** consisting of a real and an imaginary part, either of which can be zero. *~n.* **5.** a whole made up of interconnected or related parts: *a building complex.* **6.** *Psychoanal.* a group of emotional ideas or impulses that have been banished from the conscious mind but that continue to influence a person's behaviour. **7.** *Informal.* an obsession or excessive fear: *he's got a complex about cats.* **8.** Also called: **coordination compound.** a chemical compound in which molecules, groups, or ions are attached to a central metal atom, esp. a transition metal atom, by coordinate bonds. **9.** any chemical compound in which one molecule is linked to another by a coordinate bond. [C17: from Latin *complexus,* from *complectī* to entwine, from *com-* together + *plectere* to braid] **—ˈcomplexly** *adv.* **—ˈcomplexness** *n.*

complex conjugate *n. Maths.* the complex number whose imaginary part is the negation of that of a given complex number, the real parts of both numbers being equal: *a* – i*b is the complex conjugate of a* + i*b.*

complex fraction *n. Maths.* a fraction in which the numerator or denominator or both contain fractions. Also called: **compound fraction.**

complexion (kəmˈplɛkʃən) *n.* **1.** the colour and general appearance of a person's skin, esp. of the face. **2.** aspect, character, or nature: *the general complexion of a nation's finances.* **3.** *Obsolete.* **a.** the temperament of a person. **b.** the temperature and general appearance of the body. [C14: from medical Latin *complexiō* one's bodily characteristics, from Latin: a combination, from *complectī* to embrace; see COMPLEX] **—comˈplexional** *adj.*

complexioned (kəmˈplɛkʃənd) *adj.* (*in combination*) of a specified complexion: *light-complexioned.*

complexity (kəmˈplɛksɪtɪ) *n., pl.* **-ties.** **1.** the state or quality of being intricate or complex. **2.** something intricate or complex; complication.

complex number *n.* any number of the form $a + bi$, where a and b are real numbers and $i = \sqrt{-1}$. Complex numbers include real and imaginary numbers.

complexometric titration (kəmˌplɛksəʊˈmɛtrɪk) *n. Chem.* a titration in which a complex is formed, usually by the use of a chelating agent, such as EDTA, the end point being marked by a sharp decrease in the concentration of metal ions.

complexone (kəmˈplɛksəʊn) *n. Chem.* any chelating agent, such as EDTA, used for the analytical determination of metals.

complex salt *n.* a salt that contains one or more complex ions. Compare **double salt.**

complex sentence *n. Grammar.* a sentence containing at least one main clause and one subordinate clause.

complex wave *n. Physics.* a waveform consisting of a fundamental frequency with superimposed harmonics.

compliance (kəmˈplaɪəns) *or* **compliancy** *n.* **1.** the act of complying; acquiescence. **2.** a disposition to yield to or comply with others. **3.** a measure of the ability of a mechanical system to respond to an applied vibrating force, expressed as the reciprocal of the system's stiffness. Symbol: *C*

compliance officer *n.* a specialist, usually a lawyer, employed by a financial group operating in a variety of fields and for multiple clients to ensure that no conflict of interest arises and that all obligations and regulations are complied with.

compliant (kəmˈplaɪənt) *or* **compliable** *adj.* complying, obliging, or yielding. **—comˈpliantly** *or* **comˈpliably** *adv.* **—comˈpliantness** *or* **comˈpliableness** *n.*

complicacy (ˈkɒmplɪkəsɪ) *n., pl.* **-cies.** a less common word for **complexity.**

complicate *vb.* (ˈkɒmplɪˌkeɪt). **1.** to make or become complex. *~adj.* (ˈkɒmplɪkɪt). **2.** *Biology.* folded on itself: *a complicate leaf.* **3.** a less common word for **complicated.** [C17: from Latin *complicāre* to fold together, from *plicāre* to fold]

complicated (ˈkɒmplɪˌkeɪtɪd) *adj.* made up of intricate parts or aspects that are difficult to understand or analyse. **—ˈcompliˌcatedly** *adv.* **—ˈcompliˌcatedness** *n.*

complication (ˌkɒmplɪˈkeɪʃən) *n.* **1.** a condition, event, etc., that is complex or confused. **2.** the act or process of complicating. **3.** a situation, event, or condition that complicates or frustrates: *her coming was a serious complication.* **4.** a disease or disorder arising as a consequence of another disease.

complice (ˈkɒmplɪs, ˈkʌm-) *n. Obsolete.* an associate or accomplice. [C15: from Old French, from Late Latin *complex* partner, associate, from Latin *complicāre* to fold together; see COMPLICATE]

complicity (kəmˈplɪsɪtɪ) *n., pl.* **-ties.** **1.** the fact or condition of being an accomplice, esp. in a criminal act. **2.** a less common word for **complexity.**

compliment *n.* (ˈkɒmplɪmənt). **1.** a remark or act expressing respect, admiration, etc. **2.** (*usually pl.*) a greeting of respect or regard. **3.** *Archaic.* a gift or gratuity; tip. *~vb.* (ˈkɒmplɪˌmɛnt). (*tr.*) **4.** to express admiration of; congratulate or commend. **5.** to express or show respect or regard for, esp. by a gift. ~Compare **complement.** [C17: from French, from Italian *complimento,* from Spanish *cumplimiento,* from *cumplir* to complete, do what is fitting, be polite]

complimentary (ˌkɒmplɪˈmɛntərɪ, -trɪ) *adj.* **1.** conveying, containing, or resembling a compliment. **2.** expressing praise; flattering. **3.** given free, esp. as a courtesy or for publicity purposes. **—ˌcompliˈmentarily** *adv.*

compline (ˈkɒmplɪn, -plaɪn) *or* **complin** (ˈkɒmplɪn) *n. R.C. Church.* the last of the seven canonical hours of the divine office. [C13: from Old French *complie,* from Medieval Latin *hōra complēta,* literally: the completed hour, from Latin *complēre* to fill up, COMPLETE]

complot *Archaic.* *~n.* (ˈkɒmplɒt). **1.** a plot or conspiracy. *~vb.* (kəmˈplɒt), **-plots, -plotting, -plotted.** **2.** to plot together; conspire. [C16: from Old French, of unknown origin] **—comˈplotter** *n.*

comply (kəmˈplaɪ) *vb.* **-plies, -plying, -plied.** (*intr.*) **1.** (usually foll. by *with*) to act in accordance with rules, wishes, etc.; be obedient (to). **2.** *Obsolete.* to be obedient or complaisant. [C17: from Italian *complire,* from Spanish *cumplir* to complete; see COMPLIMENT] **—comˈplier** *n.*

compo (ˈkɒmpəʊ) *n., pl.* **-pos.** **1.** a mixture of materials, such as mortar, plaster, etc. **2.** *Austral. and N.Z. informal.* compensation, esp. for injury or loss of work. *~adj.* **3.** *Military.* intended to last for several days: *compo rations; a compo pack.* [short for *composition, compensation, composite*]

component (kəmˈpəʊnənt) *n.* **1.** a constituent part or aspect of something more complex: *a component of a car.* **2.** Also called: **element.** any electrical device, such as a resistor, that has distinct electrical characteristics and that may be connected to other electrical devices to form a circuit. **3.** *Maths.* **a.** one of a set of two or more vectors whose resultant is a given vector. **b.** the projection of this given vector onto a specified line. **4.** one of the minimum number of chemically distinct constituents necessary to describe fully the composition of each phase in a system. See **phase rule.** *~adj.* **5.** forming or functioning as a part or aspect; constituent. [C17: from Latin *compōnere* to put together, from *pōnere* to place, put] **—componential** (ˌkɒmpəˈnɛnʃəl) *adj.*

compony (kəmˈpəʊnɪ) *or* **componé** (kəmˈpəʊneɪ) *adj.* (*usually postpositive*) *Heraldry.* made up of alternating metal and colour, colour and fur, or fur and metal. [C16: from Old French *componé,* from *copon* piece, COUPON]

comport (kəmˈpɔːt) *vb.* **1.** (*tr.*) to conduct or bear (oneself) in a specified way. **2.** (*intr.*; foll. by *with*) to agree (with); correspond (to). [C16: from Latin *comportāre* to bear, collect, from *com-* together + *portāre* to carry]

comportment (kəmˈpɔːtmənt) *n.* conduct; bearing.

compose (kəmˈpəʊz) *vb.* (*mainly tr.*) **1.** to put together or make up by combining; put in proper order. **2.** to be the component elements of. **3.** to produce or create (a musical or literary work).

4. (*intr.*) to write music. **5.** to calm (someone, esp. oneself); make quiet. **6.** to adjust or settle (a quarrel, etc.). **7.** to order the elements of (a painting, sculpture, etc.); design. **8.** *Printing.* to set up (type). [C15: from Old French *composer,* from Latin *compōnere* to put in place; see COMPONENT]

composed (kəmˈpəʊzd) *adj.* (of people) calm; tranquil; serene. —**composedly** (kəmˈpəʊzɪdlɪ) *adv.* —**comˈposedness** *n.*

composer (kəmˈpəʊzə) *n.* **1.** a person who composes music. **2.** a person or machine that composes anything, esp. type for printing.

composing room *n.* the room in a printing establishment in which type is set.

composing stick *n. Printing.* a metal holder of adjustable width in which a compositor sets a line of type at a time by hand; now rarely used.

composite (ˈkɒmpəzɪt) *adj.* **1.** composed of separate parts; compound. **2.** of, relating to, or belonging to the plant family *Compositae.* **3.** *Maths.* capable of being factorized: *a composite function.* **4.** (*sometimes cap.*) denoting or relating to one of the five classical orders of architecture: characterized by a combination of the Ionic and Corinthian styles. See also **Doric, Tuscan.** ~*n.* **5.** something composed of separate parts; compound. **6.** any plant of the family *Compositae,* typically having flower heads composed of ray flowers (e.g. dandelion), disc flowers (e.g. thistle), or both (e.g. daisy). **7.** a material, such as reinforced concrete, made of two or more distinct materials. **8.** a proposal that has been composited. ~*vb.* (ˈkɒmpəˌzaɪt) (*tr.*) **9.** to merge related motions from local branches of (a political party, trade union, etc.) so as to produce a manageable number of proposals for discussion at national level. [C16: from Latin *compositus* well arranged, from *compōnere* to collect, arrange; see COMPONENT] —ˈ**compositely** *adv.* —ˈ**compositeness** *n.*

composite colour signal *n.* a colour television signal in which luminance and two chrominance components are encoded into a single signal.

composite number *n.* an integer that can be factorized into two or more other integers. Compare **prime number.**

composite photograph *n.* a photograph formed by superimposing two or more separate photographs.

composite school *n. Canadian.* a secondary school offering both academic and nonacademic courses.

composition (ˌkɒmpəˈzɪʃən) *n.* **1.** the act of putting together or making up by combining parts or ingredients. **2.** something formed in this manner or the resulting state or quality; a mixture. **3.** the parts of which something is composed or made up; constitution. **4.** a work of music, art, or literature. **5.** the harmonious arrangement of the parts of a work of art in relation to each other and to the whole. **6.** a piece of writing undertaken as an academic exercise in grammatically acceptable writing; an essay. **7.** *Printing.* the act or technique of setting up type. **8.** *Linguistics.* the formation of compound words. **9.** *Logic.* the fallacy of inferring that the properties of the part are also true of the whole, as *every member of the team has won a prize, so the team will win a prize.* **10. a.** a settlement by mutual consent, esp. a legal agreement whereby the creditors agree to accept partial payment of a debt in full settlement. **b.** the sum so agreed. **11.** *Chem.* the nature and proportions of the elements comprising a chemical compound. [C14: from Old French, from Latin *compositus;* see COMPOSITE, -ION] —ˌ**compoˈsitional** *adj.*

composition of forces *n.* the combination of two or more forces into a single equivalent force (the resultant).

compositor (kəmˈpɒzɪtə) *n. Printing.* a person who sets and corrects type and generally assembles plating and other matter. Sometimes shortened to **comp.** —**compositorial** (kəmˌpɒzɪˈtɔːrɪəl) *adj.*

compos mentis *Latin.* (ˈkɒmpəs ˈmɛntɪs) *adj.* (*postpositive*) of sound mind; sane.

compossible (kɒmˈpɒsɪbᵊl) *adj. Rare.* possible in coexistence with something else.

compost (ˈkɒmpɒst) *n.* **1.** a mixture of organic residues such as decomposed vegetation, manure, etc., used as a fertilizer. **2.** a mixture, as of sand, peat, and charcoal, in which plants are grown, esp. in pots. **3.** *Rare.* a compound or mixture. ~*vb.* (*tr.*) **4.** to make (vegetable matter) into compost. **5.** to fertilize with compost. [C14: from Old French *compost,* from Latin *compositus* put together; see COMPOSITE]

composure (kəmˈpəʊʒə) *n.* calmness, esp. of the mind; tranquillity; serenity.

compotation (ˌkɒmpəˈteɪʃən) *n. Rare.* the act of drinking together in a company. [C16: from Latin *compōtātiō,* translation of Greek SYMPOSIUM] —ˈ**compoˌtator** *n.*

compote (ˈkɒmpəʊt; *French* kɔ̃pɔt) *n.* a dish of fruit stewed with sugar or in a syrup and served hot or cold. [C17: from French *composte,* from Latin *composita,* feminine of *compositus* put in place; see COMPOSITE]

compound[1] *n.* (ˈkɒmpaʊnd). **1.** a substance that contains atoms of two or more chemical elements held together by chemical bonds. **2.** any combination of two or more parts, aspects, etc. **3.** a word formed from two existing words or combining forms. ~*vb.* (kəmˈpaʊnd). (*mainly tr.*) **4.** to mix or combine so as to create a compound or other product. **5.** to make by combining parts, elements, aspects, etc.: *to compound a new plastic.* **6.** to intensify by an added element: *his anxiety was compounded by her crying.* **7.** *Finance.* to calculate or pay (interest) on both the principal and its accrued interest. **8.** (*also intr.*) to come to an agreement in (a quarrel, dispute, etc.). **9.** (*also intr.*) to settle (a debt, promise, etc.) for less than what is owed; compromise. **10.** *Law.* to agree not to prosecute in return for a consideration: *to compound a crime.* **11.** *Electrical engineering.* to place duplex windings on the field coil of (a motor or generator), one acting as a shunt, the other being in series with the main circuit, thus making the machine self-regulating. ~*adj.* (ˈkɒmpaʊnd). **12.** composed of or created by the combination of two or more parts, elements, etc. **13.** (of a word) consisting of elements that are also words or productive combining forms. **14.** (of a sentence) formed by coordination of two or more sentences. **15.** (of a verb or the tense, mood, etc., of a verb) formed by using an auxiliary verb in addition to the main verb: *the future in English is a compound tense involving the use of such auxiliary verbs as "shall" and "will."* **16.** *Music.* **a.** denoting a time in which the number of beats per bar is a multiple of three: *six-four is an example of compound time.* **b.** (of an interval) greater than an octave. **17.** *Zoology.* another word for **colonial** (sense 6). **18.** (of a steam engine, turbine, etc.) having multiple stages in which the steam or working fluid from one stage is used in a subsequent stage. **19.** (of a piston engine) having a supercharger powered by a turbine in the exhaust stream. [C14: from earlier *compounen,* from Old French *compondre* to collect, set in order, from Latin *compōnere*] —**comˈpoundable** *adj.* —**comˈpounder** *n.*

compound[2] (ˈkɒmpaʊnd) *n.* **1.** (esp. in South Africa) an enclosure, esp. on the mines, containing the living quarters for Black workers. **2.** any similar enclosure, such as a camp for prisoners of war. **3.** (formerly in India, China, etc.) the enclosure in which a European's house or factory stood. [C17: by folk etymology (influenced by COMPOUND[1]) from Malay *kampong* village]

compound engine *n.* **1.** a steam engine in which the steam is expanded in more than one stage, first in a high-pressure cylinder and then in one or more low-pressure cylinders. **2.** a reciprocating engine in which the exhaust gases are expanded in a turbine to drive a supercharger.

compound eye *n.* the convex eye of insects and some crustaceans, consisting of numerous separate light-sensitive units (ommatidia). See also **ocellus.**

compound fault *n. Geology.* a series of closely spaced faults.

compound flower *n.* a flower head made up of many small flowers appearing as a single bloom, as in the daisy.

compound fraction *n.* another name for **complex fraction.**

compound fracture *n.* a fracture in which the broken bone either pierces the skin or communicates with an open wound.

compound interest *n.* interest calculated on both the principal and its accrued interest. Compare **simple interest.**

compound leaf *n.* a leaf consisting of two or more leaflets borne on the same leafstalk.

compound lens *n.* another term for **lens** (sense 2).

compound microscope *n.* an instrument for magnifying small objects, consisting of a lens of short focal length for forming an image that is further magnified by a second lens of longer focal length. Compare **simple microscope.**

compound number *n.* a quantity expressed in two or more different but related units: *3 hours 10 seconds is a compound number.*

compound sentence *n.* a sentence containing at least two coordinate clauses.

compound time *n.* See **compound** (sense 16).

comprador *or* **compradore** (ˌkɒmprəˈdɔː) *n.* (formerly in China and some other Asian countries) a native agent of a foreign enterprise. [C17: from Portuguese: buyer, from Late Latin *comparātor,* from Latin *comparāre* to purchase, from *parāre* to prepare]

comprehend (ˌkɒmprɪˈhɛnd) *vb.* **1.** to perceive or understand. **2.** (*tr.*) to comprise or embrace; include. [C14: from Latin *comprehendere,* from *prehendere* to seize]

comprehensible (ˌkɒmprɪˈhɛnsəbᵊl) *adj.* capable of being comprehended. —ˌ**compreˌhensiˈbility** *or* ˌ**compreˈhensibleness** *n.* —ˌ**compreˈhensibly** *adv.*

comprehension (ˌkɒmprɪˈhɛnʃən) *n.* **1.** the act or capacity of understanding. **2.** the state of including or comprising something; comprehensiveness. **3.** *Logic, obsolete.* the attributes implied by a given concept or term; connotation.

comprehensive (ˌkɒmprɪˈhɛnsɪv) *adj.* **1.** of broad scope or content; including all or much. **2.** (of a car insurance policy) providing protection against most risks, including third-party liability, fire, theft, and damage. **3.** having the ability to understand. **4.** of, relating to, or being a comprehensive school. ~*n.* **5.** short for **comprehensive school.** —ˌ**compreˈhensively** *adv.* —ˌ**compreˈhensiveness** *n.*

comprehensive school *n.* **1.** *Chiefly Brit.* a secondary school for children of all abilities from the same district. **2.** *Canadian.* another name for **composite school.**

compress *vb.* (kəmˈprɛs). **1.** (*tr.*) to squeeze together or compact into less space; condense. ~*n.* (ˈkɒmprɛs). **2.** a wet or dry cloth or gauze pad with or without medication, applied firmly to some part of the body to relieve discomfort, reduce fever, drain a wound, etc. **3.** a machine for packing material, esp. cotton, under pressure. [C14: from Late Latin *compressāre,* from Latin *comprimere,* from *premere* to press] —**com'pressible** *adj.* —**com'pressibleness** *n.* —**com'pressibly** *adv.*

compressed (kəm'prɛst) *adj.* **1.** squeezed together or condensed. **2.** (of the form of flatfishes, certain plant parts, etc.) flattened laterally along the whole length.

compressed air *n.* air at a higher pressure than atmospheric pressure: used esp. as a source of power for machines.

compressibility (kəm,prɛsɪ'bɪlɪtɪ) *n.* **1.** the ability to be compressed. **2.** *Physics.* the reciprocal of the bulk modulus; the ratio of volume strain to stress at constant temperature. Symbol: *k*

compression (kəm'prɛʃən) *n.* **1.** Also called: **compressure** (kəm'prɛʃə). the act of compressing or the condition of being compressed. **2.** an increase in pressure of the charge in an engine or compressor obtained by reducing its volume.

compression-ignition engine *n.* a type of internal-combustion engine, such as a diesel, in which ignition occurs as a result of the rise in temperature caused by compression of the mixture in the cylinder.

compression ratio *n.* the ratio of the volume enclosed by the cylinder of an internal-combustion engine at the beginning of the compression stroke to the volume enclosed at the end of it.

compressive (kəm'prɛsɪv) *adj.* compressing or having the power or capacity to compress. —**com'pressively** *adv.*

compressor (kəm'prɛsə) *n.* **1.** any reciprocating or rotating device that compresses a gas. **2.** the part of a gas turbine that compresses the air before it enters the combustion chambers. **3.** any muscle that causes compression of any part or structure. **4.** a medical instrument for holding down a part of the body. **5.** an electronic device for reducing the variation in signal amplitude in a transmission system. Compare **expander, compander.**

comprise (kəm'praɪz) *vb.* (*tr.*) **1.** to include; contain. **2.** to constitute the whole of; consist of: *her singing comprised the entertainment.* [C15: from French *compris* included, understood, from *comprendre* to COMPREHEND] —**com'prisable** *adj.* —**com'prisal** *n.*

compromise ('kɒmprə,maɪz) *n.* **1.** settlement of a dispute by concessions on both or all sides. **2.** the terms of such a settlement. **3.** something midway between two or more different things. **4.** an exposure of one's good name, reputation, etc., to injury. ~*vb.* **5.** to settle (a dispute) by making concessions. **6.** (*tr.*) to expose (a person or persons) to disrepute. **7.** (*tr.*) to prejudice unfavourably; weaken: *his behaviour compromised his chances.* **8.** (*tr.*) *Obsolete.* to pledge mutually. [C15: from Old French *compromis,* from Latin *comprōmissum* mutual agreement to accept the decision of an arbiter, from *comprōmittere,* from *prōmittere* to promise] —**'compro,miser** *n.* —**'compro,misingly** *adv.*

compte rendu *French.* (kɔ̃t rɑ̃dy) *n., pl.* ***comptes rendus*** (kɔ̃t rɑ̃dy). **1.** a short review or notice, esp. of a book. **2.** a statement of account. [literally: account rendered]

Comptometer (kɒmp'tɒmɪtə) *n. Trademark.* a high-speed calculating machine.

Compton effect ('kɒmptən) *n.* a phenomenon in which a collision between a photon and a particle results in an increase in the kinetic energy of the particle and a corresponding increase in the wavelength of the photon. [C20: named after A. H. *Compton* (1892–1962), U.S. physicist]

comptroller (kən'trəʊlə) *n.* a variant spelling of **controller** (sense 2), esp. as a title of any of various financial executives. —**comp'troller,ship** *n.*

compulsion (kəm'pʌlʃən) *n.* **1.** the act of compelling or the state of being compelled. **2.** something that compels. **3.** *Psychiatry.* an inner drive that causes a person to perform actions, often of a trivial and repetitive nature, against his will. See also **obsession.** [C15: from Old French, from Latin *compellere* to COMPEL]

compulsive (kəm'pʌlsɪv) *adj.* **1.** relating to or involving compulsion. ~*n.* **2.** *Psychiatry.* an individual who is subject to a psychological compulsion. —**com'pulsively** *adv.* —**com'pulsiveness** *n.*

compulsory (kəm'pʌlsərɪ) *adj.* **1.** required by regulations or laws; obligatory: *compulsory education.* **2.** involving or employing compulsion; compelling; necessary; essential. —**com'pulsorily** *adv.* —**com'pulsoriness** *n.*

compulsory purchase *n.* purchase of a house or other property by a local authority or government department for public use or to make way for development, regardless of whether or not the owner wishes to sell.

compunction (kəm'pʌŋkʃən) *n.* a feeling of remorse, guilt, or regret. [C14: from Church Latin *compunctiō,* from Latin *compungere* to sting, from *com-* (intensive) + *pungere* to puncture; see POINT] —**com'punctious** *adj.* —**com'punctiously** *adv.*

compurgation (,kɒmpɜː'geɪʃən) *n. Law.* (formerly) a method of trial whereby a defendant might be acquitted if a sufficient number of persons swore to his innocence. [C17: from Medieval Latin *compurgātiō,* from Latin *compurgāre* to purify entirely, from *com-* (intensive) + *purgāre* to PURGE] —**'compur,gator** *n.* —**com'purgatory** *or* **com,purga'torial** *adj.*

computation (,kɒmpjʊ'teɪʃən) *n.* a calculation involving numbers or quantities. —,**compu'tational** *adj.*

computational fluid dynamics *n.* (*functioning as sing.*) the prediction of the effects of fluid motion past objects by numerical methods rather than model experiments.

compute (kəm'pjuːt) *vb.* **1.** to calculate (an answer, result, etc.), often with the aid of a computer. ~*n.* **2.** calculation; computation (esp. in the phrase **beyond compute**). [C17: from Latin *computāre,* from *putāre* to think] —**com'putable** *adj.* —**com,puta'bility** *n.*

computed tomography *n. Med.* another name (esp. U.S.) for **computerized tomography.**

computer (kəm'pjuːtə) *n.* **1. a.** a device, usually electronic, that processes data according to a set of instructions. The **digital computer** stores data in discrete units and performs arithmetical and logical operations at very high speed. The **analog computer** has no memory and is slower than the digital computer but has a continuous rather than a discrete input. The **hybrid computer** combines some of the advantages of digital and analog computers. **b.** (*as modifier*): *computer technology.* **2.** a person who computes or calculates.

computer-aided design *n.* the use of computer techniques in designing products, esp. involving the use of computer graphics. Abbrev.: **CAD.**

computer-aided engineering *n.* the use of computers to automate manufacturing processes. Abbrev.: **CAE.**

computer architecture *n.* the structure, behaviour, and design of computers.

computerate (kəm'pjuːtərɪt) *adj.* able to use computers. [C20: COMPUTER + -ATE[1], by analogy with *literate*]

computer conferencing *n.* the conduct of meetings by the use of computer-based telecommunications.

computer dating *n.* a meeting between a man and a woman arranged by an agency that claims to match its clients by a computer.

computer game *n.* any of various games, recorded on cassette for use in a home computer, that are played by manipulating a joystick or the keys on the keyboard of a computer in response to the graphics on the screen.

computer graphics *n.* (*functioning as sing.*) the use of a computer to produce and manipulate pictorial images on a video screen, as in animation techniques or the production of audiovisual aids.

computerize *or* **computerise** (kəm'pjuːtə,raɪz) *vb.* **1.** (*tr.*) to cause (certain operations) to be performed by a computer, esp. as a replacement for human labour. **2.** (*intr.*) to install a computer. **3.** (*tr.*) to control or perform (operations within a system) by means of a computer. **4.** (*tr.*) to process or store (information) by means of or in a computer. —**com,puteri'zation** *or* **com,puteri'sation** *n.*

computerized tomography *n. Med.* a radiological technique that produces images of cross sections through a patient's body. Also called (esp. U.S.): **computed tomography.** Abbrev.: **CT.** See also **CT scanner.**

computer language *n.* another term for **programming language.**

computer literate *adj.* able to use computers. —**computer literacy** *n.*

computer science *n.* the study of computers and their application.

computer typesetting *n.* a system for the high-speed composition of type by a device driven by punched paper tape or magnetic tape that has been processed by a computer. Also called: **automatic typesetting.**

Comr *abbrev. for* Commissioner.

comrade ('kɒmreɪd, -rɪd) *n.* **1.** an associate or companion. **2.** a fellow member of a political party, esp. a fellow Communist or socialist. [C16: from French *camarade,* from Spanish *camarada* group of soldiers sharing a billet, from *cámara* room, from Latin; see CAMERA, CHAMBER] —**'comradely** *adj.* —**'comrade,ship** *n.*

comsat ('kɒmsæt) *n.* short for **communications satellite.**

comstockery ('kʌm,stɒkərɪ, 'kɒm-) *n. U.S.* immoderate censorship on grounds of immorality. [C20: coined (1905) by George Bernard Shaw (1856–1950) after Anthony *Comstock* (1844–1915), U.S. moral crusader, who founded the Society for the Suppression of Vice]

Com. Ver. *abbrev. for* Common Version (of the Bible).

con[1] (kɒn) *Informal.* ~*n.* **1. a.** short for **confidence trick. b.** (*as modifier*): *con man.* ~*vb.* **cons, conning, conned. 2.** (*tr.*) to swindle or defraud. [C19: from CONFIDENCE]

con[2] (kɒn) *n.* (*usually pl.*) **1.** an argument or vote against a proposal, motion, etc. **2.** a person who argues or votes against a proposal, motion, etc. ~Compare **pro**[1]. See also **pros and cons.** [from Latin *contrā* against, opposed to]

con[3] (kɒn) *n. Slang.* short for **convict.**

con[4] *or* (*esp. U.S.*) **conn** (kɒn) *Nautical.* ~*vb.* **cons** *or* **conns, conning, conned. 1.** (*tr.*) to direct the steering of (a vessel). ~*n.* **2.** the place where a person who cons a vessel is stationed. [C17 *cun,* from earlier *condien* to guide, from Old French *conduire,* from Latin *condūcere;* see CONDUCT]

con[5] (kɒn) *vb.* **cons, conning, conned.** (*tr.*) *Archaic.* to study attentively or learn (esp. in the phrase **con by rote**). [C15: variant of CAN[1] in the sense: to come to know]

con[6] (kɒn) *prep. Music.* with. [Italian]

con. *abbrev. for:* **1.** concerto. **2.** conclusion. **3.** connection. **4.** consolidated. **5.** continued. **6.** contra. [Latin: against]

Con. *abbrev. for:* **1.** Conformist. **2.** Conservative. **3.** Consul.

con- *prefix.* a variant of **com-.**

conacre (kʌ'neːkər) *n. Irish.* farming land let for a season or for eleven months. [C19: from CORN[1] + ACRE]
con amore (kɒn æ'mɔːrɪ) *adj., adv. Music.* (to be performed) lovingly. [C19: from Italian: with love]
conation (kəʊ'neɪʃən) *n.* the element in psychological processes that tends towards activity or change and appears as desire, volition, and striving. [C19: from Latin *cōnātiō* an attempting, from *cōnārī* to try] —**co'national** *adj.*
conative ('kɒnətɪv, 'kəʊ-) *adj.* **1.** *Grammar.* denoting an aspect of verbs in some languages used to indicate the effort of the agent in performing the activity described by the verb. **2.** of or relating to conation.
conatus (kəʊ'neɪtəs) *n., pl.* **-tus.** **1.** an effort or striving of natural impulse. **2.** (esp. in the philosophy of Spinoza (1632–77)) the tendency of all things to persist in their own being. [C17: from Latin: effort, from *cōnārī* to try]
con brio (kɒn 'briːəʊ) *adj., adv. Music.* (to be performed) with liveliness or spirit, as in the phrase **allegro con brio.** [Italian: with energy]
conc. *abbrev. for:* **1.** concentrate. **2.** concentrated. **3.** concentration. **4.** concerning. **5.** concerto.
concatenate (kɒn'kætɪˌneɪt) *vb.* **1.** (*tr.*) to link or join together, esp. in a chain or series. *~adj.* **2.** linked or joined together. [C16: from Late Latin *concatēnāre* from Latin *com-* together + *catēna* CHAIN]
concatenation (kɒnˌkætɪ'neɪʃən) *n.* **1.** a series of interconnected events, concepts, etc. **2.** the act of linking together or the state of being joined. **3.** *Logic.* a function that forms a single string of symbols from two given strings by placing the second after the first.
concave ('kɒnkeɪv, kɒn'keɪv) *adj.* **1.** curving inwards. **2.** *Physics.* having one or two surfaces curved or ground in the shape of a section of the interior of a sphere, paraboloid, etc.: *a concave lens.* **3.** *Maths.* (of a polygon) containing an interior angle greater than 180°. **4.** an obsolete word for **hollow.** *~vb.* **5.** (*tr.*) to make concave. ~Compare **convex.** [C15: from Latin *concavus* arched, from *cavus* hollow] —'**concavely** *adv.* —'**concaveness** *n.*
concavity (kɒn'kævɪtɪ) *n., pl.* **-ties.** **1.** the state or quality of being concave. **2.** a concave surface or thing; cavity.
concavo-concave (kɒnˌkeɪvəʊkɒn'keɪv) *adj.* (esp. of a lens) having both sides concave; biconcave.
concavo-convex *adj.* **1.** having one side concave and the other side convex. **2.** (of a lens) having a concave face with greater curvature than the convex face. Compare **convexo-concave** (sense 2).
conceal (kən'siːl) *vb.* (*tr.*) **1.** to keep from discovery; hide. **2.** to keep secret. [C14: from Old French *conceler,* from Latin *concēlāre,* from *com-* (intensive) + *cēlāre* to hide] —**con'cealable** *adj.* —**con'cealer** *n.* —**con'cealment** *n.*
concede (kən'siːd) *vb.* **1.** (when *tr., may take a clause as object*) to admit or acknowledge (something) as true or correct. **2.** to yield or allow (something, such as a right). **3.** (*tr.*) to admit as certain in outcome: *to concede an election.* [C17: from Latin *concēdere,* from *cēdere* to give way, CEDE] —**con'cededly** *adv.* —**con'ceder** *n.*
conceit (kən'siːt) *n.* **1.** a high, often exaggerated, opinion of oneself or one's accomplishments; vanity. **2.** *Literary.* an elaborate image or far-fetched comparison, esp. as used by the English Metaphysical poets. **3.** *Archaic.* **a.** a witty expression. **b.** fancy; imagination. **c.** an idea. **4.** *Obsolete.* a small ornament. *~vb.* (*tr.*) **5.** *Northern English dialect.* to like or be able to bear (something, such as food or drink). **6.** *Obsolete.* to think or imagine. [C14: from CONCEIVE]
conceited (kən'siːtɪd) *adj.* **1.** having a high or exaggerated opinion of oneself or one's accomplishments. **2.** *Archaic.* fanciful. **3.** *Obsolete.* witty or intelligent. —**con'ceitedly** *adv.* —**con'ceitedness** *n.*
conceivable (kən'siːvəb[ə]l) *adj.* capable of being understood, believed, or imagined; possible. —**conˌceiva'bility** *or* **con'ceivableness** *n.* —**con'ceivably** *adv.*
conceive (kən'siːv) *vb.* **1.** (when *intr.,* foll. by *of;* when *tr., often takes a clause as object*) to have an idea (of); imagine; think. **2.** (*tr.; takes a clause as object or an infinitive*) to hold as an opinion; believe. **3.** (*tr.*) to develop or form, esp. in the mind: *she conceived a passion for music.* **4.** to become pregnant with (young). **5.** (*tr.*) *Rare.* to express in words. [C13: from Old French *conceivre,* from Latin *concipere* to take in, from *capere* to take] —**con'ceiver** *n.*
concelebrate (kən'sɛlɪˌbreɪt) *vb. Christianity.* to celebrate (the Eucharist or Mass) jointly with one or more other priests. [C16: from Latin *concelebrāre*] —**conˌcele'bration** *n.*
concent (kən'sɛnt) *n. Archaic.* a concord, as of sounds, voices, etc. [C16: from Latin *concentus* harmonious sounds, from *concinere* to sing together, from *canere* to sing]
concentrate ('kɒnsənˌtreɪt) *vb.* **1.** to come or cause to come to a single purpose or aim: *to concentrate one's hopes on winning.* **2.** to make or become denser or purer by the removal of certain elements, esp. the solvent of a solution. **3.** (*tr.*) to remove rock or sand from (an ore) to make it purer. **4.** (*intr.;* often foll. by *on*) to bring one's faculties to bear (on); think intensely (about). *~n.* **5.** a concentrated material or solution: *tomato concentrate.* [C17: back formation from CONCENTRATION, ultimately from Latin *com-* same + *centrum* CENTRE] —'**concenˌtrator** *n.*
concentration (ˌkɒnsən'treɪʃən) *n.* **1.** intense mental application; complete attention. **2.** the act or process of concentrating. **3.** something that is concentrated. **4.** the strength of a solution, esp. the amount of dissolved substance in a given volume of solvent, usually expressed in moles per cubic metre or cubic decimetre (litre). Symbol: *c* **5.** the process of increasing the concentration of a solution. **6.** *Military.* **a.** the act of bringing together military forces. **b.** the application of fire from a number of weapons against a target. **7.** *Economics.* the degree to which the output or employment in an industry is accounted for by only a few firms. **8.** another name (esp. U.S.) for **Pelmanism.**
concentration camp *n.* a guarded prison camp in which nonmilitary prisoners are held, esp. one of those in Nazi Germany in which millions were exterminated.
concentrative ('kɒnsənˌtreɪtɪv) *adj.* tending to concentrate; characterized by concentration. —'**concenˌtratively** *adv.* —'**concenˌtrativeness** *n.*
concentre (kɒn'sɛntə) *vb.* to converge or cause to converge on a common centre; concentrate. [C16: from French *concentrer;* see CONCENTRATE]
concentric (kən'sɛntrɪk) *adj.* having a common centre: *concentric circles.* Compare **eccentric** (sense 3). [C14: from Medieval Latin *concentricus,* from Latin *com-* same + *centrum* CENTRE] —**con'centrically** *adv.* —**concentricity** (ˌkɒnsən'trɪsɪtɪ) *n.*
concept ('kɒnsɛpt) *n.* **1.** an idea, esp. an abstract idea: *the concepts of biology.* **2.** *Philosophy.* a general idea or notion that corresponds to some class of entities and that consists of the characteristic or essential features of the class. **3.** *Philosophy.* **a.** the conjunction of all the characteristic features of something. **b.** a theoretical construct within some theory. **c.** a directly intuited object of thought. **d.** the meaning of a predicate. [C16: from Latin *conceptum* something received or conceived, from *concipere* to take in, CONCEIVE]
conceptacle (kən'sɛptək[ə]l) *n.* a flask-shaped cavity containing the reproductive organs in some algae and fungi. [C17: from Latin *conceptāculum* receptacle, from *concipere* to receive, CONCEIVE]
conception (kən'sɛpʃən) *n.* **1.** something conceived; notion, idea, design, or plan. **2.** the description under which someone considers something: *her conception of freedom is wrong.* **3.** the fertilization of an ovum by a sperm in the Fallopian tube followed by implantation in the womb. **4.** origin or beginning: *from its conception the plan was a failure.* **5.** the act or power of forming notions; invention. [C13: from Latin *conceptiō,* from *concipere* to CONCEIVE] —**con'ceptional** *or* **con'ceptive** *adj.*
conceptual (kən'sɛptjʊəl) *adj.* **1.** relating to or concerned with concepts; abstract. **2.** concerned with the definitions or relations of the concepts of some field of enquiry rather than with the facts. —**con'ceptually** *adv.*
conceptualism (kən'sɛptjʊəˌlɪzəm) *n.* **1.** the philosophical theory that the application of general words to a variety of objects reflects the existence of some mental entity through which the application is mediated and which constitutes the meaning of the term. Compare **nominalism, realism, Platonism.** **2.** the philosophical view that there is no reality independent of our conception of it, or (as in Kantian philosophy) that the intellect is not a merely passive recipient of experience but rather imposes a structure on it. —**con'ceptualist** *n.* —**conˌceptual'istic** *adj.*
conceptualize *or* **conceptualise** (kən'sɛptjʊəˌlaɪz) *vb.* to form (a concept or concepts) out of observations, experience, data, etc. —**conˌceptuali'zation** *or* **conˌceptuali'sation** *n.*
concern (kən'sɜːn) *vb.* (*tr.*) **1.** to relate to; be of importance or interest to; affect. **2.** (usually foll. by *with* or *in*) to involve or interest (oneself): *he concerns himself with other people's affairs.* *~n.* **3.** something that affects or is of importance to a person; affair; business. **4.** regard for or interest in a person or a thing: *he felt a strong concern for her.* **5.** anxiety, worry, or solicitude. **6.** important bearing or relation: *his news has great concern for us.* **7.** a commercial company or enterprise. **8.** *Informal.* a material thing, esp. one of which one has a low opinion. [C15: from Late Latin *concernere* to mingle together, from Latin *com-* together + *cernere* to sift, distinguish]
concerned (kən'sɜːnd) *adj.* **1.** (*postpositive*) interested, guilty, involved, or appropriate: *I shall find the boy concerned and punish him.* **2.** worried, troubled, or solicitous. —**concernedly** (kən'sɜːnɪdlɪ) *adv.* —**con'cernedness** *n.*
concerning (kən'sɜːnɪŋ) *prep.* **1.** about; regarding; on the subject of. *~adj.* **2.** worrying or troublesome.
concernment (kən'sɜːnmənt) *n.* **1.** *Rare.* affair or business; concern. **2.** *Archaic.* a matter of importance.
concert *n.* ('kɒnsɜːt, -sət). **1. a.** a performance of music by players or singers that does not involve theatrical staging. Compare **recital** (sense 1). **b.** (*as modifier*): *a concert version of an opera.* **2.** agreement in design, plan, or action. **3. in concert. a.** acting in a co-ordinated fashion with a common purpose. **b.** (of musicians, esp. rock musicians) performing live. *~vb.* (kən'sɜːt). **4.** to arrange or contrive (a plan) by mutual agreement. [C16: from French *concerter* to bring into agreement, from Italian *concertare,* from Late Latin *concertāre* to work together, from Latin: to dispute, debate, from *certāre* to contend]
concertante (ˌkɒntʃə'tæntɪ) *Music.* *~adj.* **1.** characterized by contrasting alternating tutti and solo passages. *~n., pl.* **-ti** (-tɪ).

2. a composition characterized by such contrasts. [C18: from Italian, from *concertare* to perform a concert, from *concerto* CONCERT]

concerted (kən'sɜːtɪd) *adj.* 1. mutually contrived, planned, or arranged; combined (esp. in the phrases **concerted action, concerted effort**). 2. *Music.* arranged in parts for a group of singers or players. —**con'certedly** *adv.*

concertgoer ('kɒnsəːtˌɡəʊə) *n.* a person who attends concerts of music.

concert grand *n.* a full-size grand piano, usually around 7 feet in length. Compare **baby grand, boudoir grand.**

concertina (ˌkɒnsə'tiːnə) *n.* 1. a small hexagonal musical instrument of the reed organ family in which metallic reeds are vibrated by air from a set of bellows operated by the player's hands. Notes are produced by pressing buttons. ~*vb.* **-nas, -naing, -naed.** 2. (*intr.*) to collapse or fold up like a concertina. [C19: CONCERT + *-ina*] —ˌ**concer'tinist** *n.*

concertino (ˌkɒntʃə'tiːnəʊ) *n., pl.* **-ni** (-nɪ). 1. the small group of soloists in a concerto grosso. Compare **ripieno.** 2. a short concerto. [C19: from Italian: a little CONCERTO]

concertize *or* **concertise** ('kɒnsəˌtaɪz) *vb.* (*intr.*) (esp. of a soloist or conductor) to give concerts.

concertmaster ('kɒnsətˌmɑːstə) *n.* a U.S. and Canadian word for **leader** (of an orchestra).

concerto (kən'tʃɛətəʊ) *n., pl.* **-tos** *or* **-ti** (-tɪ). 1. a composition for an orchestra and one or more soloists. The classical concerto usually consisted of three movements. See also **sonata** (sense 1), **symphony** (sense 1). 2. another word for **ripieno.** [C18: from Italian: CONCERT]

concerto grosso ('ɡrɒsəʊ) *n., pl.* **concerti grossi** ('ɡrɒsɪ) *or* **concerto grossos.** a composition for an orchestra and a group of soloists, chiefly of the baroque period. [Italian, literally: big concerto]

concert overture *n.* See **overture** (sense 1c).

concert party *n.* 1. a musical entertainment popular in the early 20th century, esp. one at a British seaside resort. 2. *Stock Exchange, informal.* a group of individuals or companies who secretly agree to purchase shares separately in a particular company, which they plan to amalgamate later into a single holding: a malpractice that is illegal in some countries.

concert pitch *n.* 1. the frequency of 440 hertz assigned to the A above middle C. See **pitch**[1] (sense 27b), **international pitch.** 2. *Informal.* a state of extreme readiness.

concertstück (kən'sɜːtˌʃtuːk) *n. Music.* 1. a composition in concerto style but shorter than a full concerto. 2. (loosely) a piece suitable for concert performance. [from German *Konzertstück* a concertino]

concert tuning *n. Music.* the standard tuning for a guitar: E A D G B E.

concession (kən'sɛʃən) *n.* 1. the act of yielding or conceding, as to a demand or argument. 2. something conceded. 3. *Brit.* a reduction in the usual price of a ticket granted to a special group of customers: *a student concession.* 4. any grant of rights, land, or property by a government, local authority, corporation, or individual. 5. the right, esp. an exclusive right, to market a particular product in a given area. 6. *U.S. and Canadian.* **a.** the right to maintain a subsidiary business on a lessor's premises. **b.** the premises so granted or the business so maintained. **c.** a free rental period for such premises. 7. *Canadian.* (chiefly in Ontario and Quebec) **a.** a land subdivision in a township survey. **b.** another name for a **concession road.** [C16: from Latin *concēssiō* an allowing, from *concēdere* to CONCEDE] —**con'cessible** *adj.*

concessionaire (kənˌsɛʃə'nɛə), **concessioner** (kən'sɛʃənə), or **concessionary** *n.* someone who holds or operates a concession.

concessionary (kən'sɛʃənərɪ) *adj.* 1. of, granted, or obtained by a concession. ~*n., pl.* **-aries.** 2. another word for **concessionaire.**

concession road *n. Canadian.* (esp. in Ontario) one of a series of roads separating concessions in a township.

concessive (kən'sɛsɪv) *adj.* 1. implying or involving concession; tending to concede. 2. *Grammar.* a conjunction, preposition, phrase, or clause describing a state of affairs that might have been expected to rule out what is described in the main clause but in fact does not: *"Although" in the sentence "Although they had been warned, they refused to take care" is a concessive conjunction.* [C18: from Late Latin *concēssīvus,* from Latin *concēdere* to CONCEDE]

conch (kɒŋk, kɒntʃ) *n., pl.* **conchs** (kɒŋks) *or* **conches** ('kɒntʃɪz). 1. any of various tropical marine gastropod molluscs of the genus *Strombus* and related genera, esp. *S. gigas* (giant conch), characterized by a large brightly coloured spiral shell. 2. the shell of such a mollusc, used as a trumpet. 3. *Architect.* another name for **concha** (sense 2). [C16: from Latin *concha,* from Greek *konkhē* shellfish]

concha ('kɒŋkə) *n., pl.* **-chae** (-kiː). 1. any bodily organ or part resembling a shell in shape, such as the external ear. 2. Also called: **conch.** *Architect.* the half dome of an apse. —'**conchal** *adj.*

conchie *or* **conchy** ('kɒntʃɪ) *n., pl.* **-chies.** *Informal.* short for **conscientious objector.**

conchiferous (kɒŋ'kɪfərəs) *adj.* 1. (esp. of molluscs) having or producing a shell. 2. (of rocks) containing shells.

conchiolin (kɒŋ'kaɪəlɪn) *n.* a fibrous insoluble protein that forms the basic structure of the shells of molluscs. Formula: $C_{30}H_{48}O_{11}N_9$. [C19: from CONCH; see -IN]

conchoid ('kɒŋkɔɪd) *n. Geometry.* a plane curve consisting of two branches situated about a line to which they are asymptotic, so that a line from a fixed point (the pole) intersecting both branches is of constant length between asymptote and either branch. Equation: $(x - a)^2(x^2 + y^2) = b^2x^2$ where a is the distance between the pole and a vertical asymptote and b is the length of the constant segment.

conchoidal (kɒŋ'kɔɪdᵊl) *adj.* 1. (of the fracture of minerals and rocks) having smooth shell-shaped convex and concave surfaces. 2. (of minerals and rocks, such as flint) having such a fracture. —**con'choidally** *adv.*

conchology (kɒŋ'kɒlədʒɪ) *n.* the study and collection of mollusc shells. —**conchological** (ˌkɒŋkə'lɒdʒɪkᵊl) *adj.* —**con'chologist** *n.*

concierge (ˌkɒnsɪ'ɛəʒ; *French* kɔ̃sjɛrʒ) *n.* (esp. in France) a caretaker of a block of flats, hotel, etc., esp. one who lives on the premises. [C17: from French, ultimately from Latin *conservus,* from *servus* slave]

conciliar (kən'sɪlɪə) *adj.* of, from, or by means of a council, esp. an ecclesiastical one. —**con'ciliarly** *adv.*

conciliate (kən'sɪlɪˌeɪt) *vb.* (*tr.*) 1. to overcome the hostility of; placate; win over. 2. to win or gain (favour, regard, etc.), esp. by making friendly overtures. 3. *Archaic.* to make compatible; reconcile. [C16: from Latin *conciliāre* to bring together, from *concilium* COUNCIL] —**con'ciliable** *adj.* —**con'ciliˌator** *n.*

conciliation (kənˌsɪlɪ'eɪʃən) *n.* the act or process of conciliating, esp. the involvement of a third party in an industrial dispute to assist the parties in reaching a settlement.

conciliatory (kən'sɪljətərɪ, -trɪ) *or* **conciliative** (kən'sɪljətɪv) *adj.* intended to placate or reconcile. —**con'ciliatorily** *adv.* —**con'ciliatoriness** *n.*

concinnity (kən'sɪnɪtɪ) *n., pl.* **-ties.** a harmonious arrangement of parts, esp. in literary works, speeches, etc. [C16: from Latin *concinnitās* a skilful combining of various things, from *concinnāre* to adjust, of obscure origin] —**con'cinnous** *adj.*

concise (kən'saɪs) *adj.* expressing much in few words; brief and to the point. [C16: from Latin *concīsus* cut up, cut short, from *concīdere* to cut to pieces, from *caedere* to cut, strike down] —**con'cisely** *adv.* —**con'ciseness** *n.*

concision (kən'sɪʒən) *n.* 1. the quality of being concise; brevity; terseness. 2. *Archaic.* a cutting apart or off; severing; division.

conclave ('kɒnkleɪv, 'kɒŋ-) *n.* 1. a confidential or secret meeting. 2. *R.C. Church.* **a.** the closed apartments where the college of cardinals elects a new pope. **b.** a meeting of the college of cardinals for this purpose. [C14: from Medieval Latin *conclāve,* from Latin: cage, place that may be locked, from *clāvis* key] —'**conclavist** *n.*

conclude (kən'kluːd) *vb.* (*mainly tr.*) 1. (*also intr.*) to come or cause to come to an end or conclusion. 2. (*takes a clause as object*) to decide by reasoning; deduce: *the judge concluded that the witness had told the truth.* 3. to arrange finally; settle: *to conclude a treaty; it was concluded that he should go.* 4. *Obsolete.* to confine. [C14: from Latin *conclūdere* to enclose, end, from *claudere* to close] —**con'cluder** *n.*

conclusion (kən'kluːʒən) *n.* 1. end or termination. 2. the last main division of a speech, lecture, essay, etc. 3. the outcome or result of an act, process, event, etc. (esp. in the phrase **a foregone conclusion**). 4. a final decision or judgment; resolution (esp. in the phrase **come to a conclusion**). 5. *Logic.* **a.** a statement that purports to follow from another or others (the **premises**) by means of an argument. **b.** a statement that does validly follow from given premises. 6. *Law.* **a.** an admission or statement binding on the party making it; estoppel. **b.** the close of a pleading or of a conveyance. 7. **in conclusion.** lastly; to sum up. 8. **jump to conclusions.** to come to a conclusion prematurely, without sufficient thought or on incomplete evidence. 9. **try conclusions with.** *Archaic.* to engage in competition with (someone). [C14: via Old French from Latin; see CONCLUDE, -ION]

conclusive (kən'kluːsɪv) *adj.* 1. putting an end to doubt; decisive; final. 2. approaching or involving an end or conclusion. —**con'clusively** *adv.* —**con'clusiveness** *n.*

concoct (kən'kɒkt) *vb.* (*tr.*) 1. to make by combining different ingredients. 2. to invent; make up; contrive. [C16: from Latin *concoctus* cooked together, from *concoquere,* from *coquere* to cook] —**con'cocter** *or* **con'coctor** *n.* —**con'coctive** *adj.*

concoction (kən'kɒkʃən) *n.* 1. the act or process of concocting. 2. something concocted. 3. an untruth; lie.

concomitance (kən'kɒmɪtəns) *n.* 1. existence or occurrence together or in connection with another. 2. a thing that exists in connection with another. 3. *Christian theol.* the doctrine that the body and blood of Christ are present in the Eucharist.

concomitant (kən'kɒmɪtənt) *adj.* 1. existing or occurring together; associative. ~*n.* 2. a concomitant act, person, etc. [C17: from Late Latin *concomitārī* to accompany, from *com-* with + *comes* companion, fellow] —**con'comitantly** *adv.*

concord ('kɒnkɔːd, 'kɒŋ-) *n.* 1. agreement or harmony between people or nations; amity. 2. a treaty establishing peaceful relations between nations. 3. agreement or harmony between things, ideas, etc. 4. *Music.* a combination of musical notes, esp.

one containing a series of consonant intervals. Compare **discord** (sense 3). **5.** *Grammar.* another word for **agreement** (sense 6). [C13: from Old French *concorde,* from Latin *concordia,* from *concors* of the same mind, harmonious, from *com-* same + *cors* heart]

concordance (kən'kɔːdᵊns) *n.* **1.** a state or condition of agreement or harmony. **2.** a book that indexes the principal words in a literary work, often with the immediate context and an account of the meaning. **3.** an index produced by computer or machine, alphabetically listing every word in a text. **4.** an alphabetical list of subjects or topics.

concordant (kən'kɔːdᵊnt) *adj.* being in agreement: harmonious. —**con'cordantly** *adv.*

concordat (kɒn'kɔːdæt) *n.* a pact or treaty, esp. one between the Vatican and another state concerning the interests of religion in that state. [C17: via French, from Medieval Latin *concordātum,* from Latin: something agreed, from *concordāre* to be of one mind; see CONCORD]

Concorde ('kɒnkɔːd, 'kɒŋ-) *n.* the first commercial supersonic airliner. Of Anglo-French construction, it is capable of over 2160 km per hr (1200 mph).

Concord grape ('kɒŋkəd, 'kɒnkɔːd) *n.* a variety of grape with purple-black fruit covered with a bluish bloom. [C19: discovered at *Concord,* Massachusetts]

concours d'élégance *French.* (kɔ̃kur delegɑ̃s) *n.* a parade of cars or other vehicles, prizes being awarded to the most elegant, best designed, or best turned-out.

concourse ('kɒnkɔːs, 'kɒŋ-) *n.* **1.** a crowd; throng. **2.** a coming together; confluence: *a concourse of events.* **3.** a large open space for the gathering of people in a public place. **4.** *Chiefly U.S.* a ground for sports, racing, athletics, etc. [C14: from Old French *concours,* ultimately from Latin *concurrere* to run together, from *currere* to run]

concrescence (kən'krɛsəns) *n. Biology.* a growing together of initially separate parts or organs. [C17: from Latin *concrēscentia,* from *concrēscere* to grow together, from *crēscere* to grow; see CRESCENT] —**con'crescent** *adj.*

concrete ('kɒnkriːt) *n.* **1. a.** a construction material made of a mixture of cement, sand, stone, and water that hardens to a stonelike mass. **b.** (*as modifier*): *a concrete slab.* **2.** *Physics.* a mass formed by the coalescence of separate particles. ~*adj.* **3.** relating to a particular instance or object; specific as opposed to general: *a concrete example.* **4. a.** relating to or characteristic of things capable of being perceived by the senses, as opposed to abstractions. **b.** (*as n.*): *the concrete.* **5.** formed by the coalescence of particles; condensed; solid. ~*vb.* **6.** (*tr.*) to construct in or cover with concrete. **7.** (kən'kriːt). to become or cause to become solid; coalesce. [C14: from Latin *concrētus* grown together, hardened, from *concrēscere;* see CONCRESCENCE] —**'concretely** *adv.* —**'concreteness** *n.* —**con'cretive** *adj.* —**con'cretively** *adv.*

concrete music *n.* music consisting of an electronically modified montage of tape-recorded sounds.

concrete noun *n.* a noun that refers to a material object. Compare **abstract noun.**

concrete number *n.* a number referring to a particular object or objects, as in *three dogs, ten men.*

concrete poetry *n.* poetry in which the visual form of the poem is used to convey meaning.

concretion (kən'kriːʃən) *n.* **1.** the act or process of coming or growing together; coalescence. **2.** a solid or solidified mass. **3.** something made real, tangible, or specific. **4.** any of various rounded or irregular mineral masses that are different in composition from the sedimentary rock that surrounds them. **5.** *Pathol.* another word for **calculus.** —**con'cretionary** *adj.*

concretize *or* **concretise** ('kɒnkrɪˌtaɪz, 'kɒŋ-) *vb.* (*tr.*) to render concrete; make real or specific; give tangible form to. —**ˌconcreti'zation** *or* **ˌconcreti'sation** *n.*

concubinage (kɒn'kjuːbɪnɪdʒ) *n.* **1.** cohabitation without legal marriage. **2.** the state of living as a concubine.

concubine ('kɒŋkjʊˌbaɪn, 'kɒn-) *n.* **1.** (in polygamous societies) a secondary wife, usually of lower social rank. **2.** a woman who cohabits with a man. [C13: from Old French, from Latin *concubīna,* from *concumbere* to lie together, from *cubare* to lie] —**concubinary** (kɒŋ'kjʊbɪnərɪ) *n., adj.*

concupiscence (kən'kjuːpɪsəns) *n.* strong desire, esp. sexual desire. [C14: from Church Latin *concupiscentia,* from Latin *concupiscere* to covet ardently, from *cupere* to wish, desire] —**con'cupiscent** *adj.*

concur (kən'kɜː) *vb.* **-curs, -curring, -curred.** (*intr.*) **1.** to agree; be of the same mind; be in accord. **2.** to combine, act together, or cooperate. **3.** to occur simultaneously; coincide. **4.** *Rare.* to converge. [C15: from Latin *concurrere* to run together, from *currere* to run] —**con'curringly** *adv.*

concurrence (kən'kʌrəns) *n.* **1.** the act of concurring. **2.** agreement in opinion; accord; assent. **3.** cooperation or combination. **4.** simultaneous occurrence; coincidence. **5.** *Geometry.* a point at which three or more lines intersect. **6.** *Rare.* rivalry or competition. ~Also (for senses 1–4): **concurrency.**

concurrent (kən'kʌrənt) *adj.* **1.** taking place at the same time or in the same location. **2.** cooperating. **3.** meeting at, approaching, or having a common point: *concurrent lines.* **4.** having equal authority or jurisdiction. **5.** in accordance or agreement; harmonious. ~*n.* **6.** something joint or contributory; a concurrent circumstance or cause. **7.** *Archaic.* a competitor or rival. —**con'currently** *adv.*

concurrent processing *n.* the ability of a computer to process two or more programs in parallel.

concuss (kən'kʌs) *vb.* (*tr.*) **1.** to injure (the brain) by a violent blow, fall, etc. **2.** to shake violently; agitate; disturb. [C16: from Latin *concussus* violently shaken, from *concutere* to disturb greatly, from *quatere* to shake]

concussion (kən'kʌʃən) *n.* **1.** a jarring of the brain, caused by a blow or a fall, usually resulting in loss of consciousness. **2.** any violent shaking; jarring. —**con'cussive** *adj.*

condemn (kən'dɛm) *vb.* (*tr.*) **1.** to express strong disapproval of; censure. **2.** to pronounce judicial sentence on. **3.** to demonstrate the guilt of: *his secretive behaviour condemned him.* **4.** to judge or pronounce unfit for use: *that food has been condemned.* **5.** to compel or force into a particular state or activity: *his disposition condemned him to boredom.* [C13: from Old French *condempner,* from Latin *condemnāre,* from *damnāre* to condemn; see DAMN] —**condemnable** (kən'dɛməbᵊl) *adj.* —**con'demnably** *adv.* —**ˌcondem'nation** *n.* —**condemnatory** (ˌkɒndɛm'neɪtərɪ, kən'dɛmnətərɪ, -trɪ) *adj.* —**con'demner** *n.* —**con'demningly** *adv.*

condemned cell *n.* a prison cell in which a person condemned to death awaits execution.

condensate (kən'dɛnseɪt) *n.* a substance formed by condensation, such as a liquid from a vapour.

condensation (ˌkɒndɛn'seɪʃən) *n.* **1.** the act or process of condensing, or the state of being condensed. **2.** anything that has condensed from a vapour, esp. on a window. **3.** *Chem.* a type of reaction in which two organic molecules combine to form a larger molecule as well as a simple molecule such as water, methanol, etc. **4.** anything that has been shortened, esp. an abridged version of a book. **5.** *Psychoanal.* **a.** the fusion of two or more ideas, etc., into one symbol, occurring esp. in dreams. **b.** the reduction of many experiences into one word or action, as in a phobia. —**ˌconden'sational** *adj.*

condensation trail *n.* another name for **vapour trail.**

condense (kən'dɛns) *vb.* **1.** (*tr.*) to increase the density of; compress. **2.** to reduce or be reduced in volume or size; make or become more compact. **3.** to change or cause to change from a gaseous to a liquid or solid state. **4.** *Chem.* to undergo or cause to undergo condensation. [C15: from Latin *condēnsāre,* from *dēnsāre* to make thick, from *dēnsus* DENSE] —**con'densable** *or* **con'densible** *adj.* —**conˌdensa'bility** *or* **conˌdensi'bility** *n.*

condensed (kən'dɛnst) *adj.* **1.** (of printers' type) narrower than usual for a particular height. Compare **expanded** (sense 1). **2.** *Botany.* designating an inflorescence in which the flowers are crowded together and are almost or completely sessile. **3.** *Chem.* designating a polycyclic ring system in a molecule in which two rings share two or more common atoms, as in naphthalene.

condensed matter *n.* solids and liquids.

condensed milk *n.* milk reduced by evaporation to a thick concentration, with sugar added. Compare **evaporated milk.**

condenser (kən'dɛnsə) *n.* **1. a.** an apparatus for reducing gases to their liquid or solid form by the abstraction of heat. **b.** a device for abstracting heat, as in a refrigeration unit. **2.** a lens that concentrates light into a small area. **3.** another name for **capacitor.** **4.** a person or device that condenses.

condescend (ˌkɒndɪ'sɛnd) *vb.* (*intr.*) **1.** to act graciously towards another or others regarded as being on a lower level; behave patronizingly. **2.** to do something that one regards as below one's dignity. [C14: from Church Latin *condēscendere* to stoop, condescend, from Latin *dēscendere* to DESCEND]

condescendence (ˌkɒndɪ'sɛndəns) *n.* **1.** *Scots Law.* a statement of facts presented by the plaintiff in a cause. **2.** a less common word for **condescension.**

condescending (ˌkɒndɪ'sɛndɪŋ) *adj.* showing or implying condescension by stooping to the level of one's inferiors, esp. in a patronizing way. —**ˌconde'scendingly** *adv.*

condescension (ˌkɒndɪ'sɛnʃən) *n.* the act or an instance of behaving in a patronizing way.

condign (kən'daɪn) *adj.* (esp. of a punishment) fitting; deserved. [C15: from Old French *condigne,* from Latin *condignus,* from *dignus* worthy] —**con'dignly** *adv.*

condiment ('kɒndɪmənt) *n.* any spice or sauce such as salt, pepper, mustard, etc. [C15: from Latin *condīmentum* seasoning, from *condīre* to pickle]

condition (kən'dɪʃən) *n.* **1.** a particular state of being or existence; situation with respect to circumstances: *the human condition.* **2.** something that limits or restricts something else; a qualification: *you may enter only under certain conditions.* **3.** (*pl.*) external or existing circumstances: *conditions were right for a takeover.* **4.** state of health or physical fitness, esp. good health (esp. in the phrases **in condition, out of condition**). **5.** an ailment or physical disability: *a heart condition.* **6.** something indispensable to the existence of something else: *your happiness is a condition of mine.* **7.** something required as part of an agreement or pact; terms: *the conditions of the lease are set out.* **8.** *Law.* **a.** a declaration or provision in a will, contract, etc., that makes some right or liability contingent upon the happening of some event. **b.** the event itself. **9.** *Logic.* a statement whose truth is either required for the truth of a given statement (a

necessary condition) or sufficient to guarantee the truth of the given statement (a **sufficient condition**). See **sufficient** (sense 2), **necessary** (sense 3e). **10.** *Maths, logic.* a presupposition, esp. a restriction on the domain of quantification, indispensable to the proof of a theorem and stated as part of it. **11.** *Statistics.* short for **experimental condition. 12.** rank, status, or position in life. **13. on** (*or* **upon**) **condition that.** (*conj.*) provided that. *~vb.* (*mainly tr.*) **14.** *Psychol.* **a.** to alter the response of (a person or animal) to a particular stimulus or situation. **b.** to establish a conditioned response in (a person or animal). **15.** to put into a fit condition or state. **16.** to improve the condition of (one's hair) by use of special cosmetics. **17.** to accustom or inure. **18.** to subject to a condition. **19.** (*intr.*) *Archaic.* to make conditions. [C14: from Latin *conditiō,* from *condīcere* to discuss, agree together, from *con-* together + *dīcere* to say]

conditional (kən'dɪʃənᵊl) *adj.* **1.** depending on other factors; not certain. **2.** *Grammar.* (of a clause, conjunction, form of a verb, or whole sentence) expressing a condition on which something else is contingent: *"If he comes" is a conditional clause in the sentence "If he comes I shall go".* **3. a.** (of an equation or inequality) true for only certain values of the variable: $x^2 - 1 = x + 1$ is a conditional equation, only true for $x = 2$ or -1. **b.** (of an infinite series) convergent, but becoming divergent when the absolute values of the terms are considered. **4.** Also: **hypothetical.** *Logic.* (of a proposition) consisting of two component propositions associated by the words *if...then* so that the proposition is false only when the antecedent is true and the consequent false. Usually written: $p \to q$ or $p \supset q$, where p is the antecedent, q the consequent, and $\to$ or $\supset$ symbolizes *implies.* *~n.* **5.** *Grammar.* **a.** a conditional form of a verb. **b.** a conditional clause or sentence. **6.** *Logic.* a conditional proposition. **—con͵dition'ality** *n.* **—con'ditionally** *adv.*

conditional access *n.* the encryption of television programme transmissions so that only authorized subscribers with suitable decoding apparatus may have access to them.

conditionalization *or* **conditionalisation** (kən͵dɪʃənᵊlaɪ'zeɪʃən) *n. Logic.* the derivation from an argument of a conditional statement with the conjunction of the premises as antecedent and the conclusion as consequent. If the argument is valid conditionalization yields a truth.

conditional probability *n. Statistics.* the probability of one event, *A,* occurring given that another, *B,* is already known to have occurred: written *P*(*A*/*B*) and equal to *P*(*A and B*)/*P*(*B*).

condition code register *n. Computer technol.* a hardware register used for storing the current values of the condition codes.

condition codes *pl. n.* a set of single bits that indicate specific conditions within a computer. The values of the condition codes are often determined by the outcome of a prior software operation and their principal use is to govern choices between alternative instruction sequences.

conditioned (kən'dɪʃənd) *adj.* **1.** *Psychol.* of or denoting a response that has been learned. Compare **unconditioned. 2.** (foll. by *to*) accustomed; inured; prepared by training.

conditioned response *n. Psychol.* a response that is transferred from the second to the first of a pair of stimuli. See **classical conditioning.** A well-known Pavlovian example is salivation by a dog when it hears a bell ring, because food has always been presented when the bell has been rung previously. Also called (esp. formerly): **conditioned reflex.** See also **unconditioned response.**

conditioned stimulus *n. Psychol.* a stimulus to which an organism has learned to make a response by classical conditioning. Compare **unconditioned stimulus.**

conditioned suppression *n. Psychol.* the reduction in the frequency of a learned response, e.g. pressing a bar for water, that occurs when a stimulus previously associated with pain is present.

conditioner (kən'dɪʃənə) *n.* **1.** a person or thing that conditions. **2.** a substance, esp. a cosmetic, applied to something to improve its condition: *hair conditioner.*

conditioning (kən'dɪʃənɪŋ) *n.* **1.** *Psychol.* the learning process by which the behaviour of an organism becomes dependent on an event occurring in its environment. See also **classical conditioning, instrumental learning.** *~adj.* **2.** (of a shampoo, cosmetic, etc.) intended to improve the condition of something: *a conditioning rinse.*

condo ('kɒndəʊ) *n., pl.* **-dos.** *U.S. and Canadian informal.* a condominium building or apartment.

condole (kən'dəʊl) *vb.* (*intr.;* foll. by *with*) to express sympathy with someone in grief, pain, etc. [C16: from Church Latin *condolēre* to suffer pain (with another), from Latin *com-* together + *dolēre* to grieve, feel pain] **—con'dolatory** *adj.* **—con'doler** *n.* **—con'dolingly** *adv.*

condolence (kən'dəʊləns) *or* **condolement** *n.* (*often pl.*) an expression of sympathy with someone in grief, etc.

con dolore (kɒn dɒ'lɔːrɪ) *adj., adv. Music.* (to be performed) in a sad manner. [Italian: with sorrow]

condom ('kɒndəm) *n.* a sheathlike covering of thin rubber worn on the penis during sexual intercourse to prevent conception or infection. [C18: of unknown origin]

condominium (͵kɒndə'mɪnɪəm) *n., pl.* **-ums. 1.** joint rule or sovereignty. **2.** a country ruled by two or more foreign powers. **3.** *U.S. and Canadian.* **a.** an apartment building in which each apartment is individually wholly owned and the common areas are jointly owned. **b.** the title under which an apartment in such a building is owned. Sometimes shortened to **condo.** Compare **cooperative** (sense 5). [C18: from New Latin, from Latin *com-* together + *dominium* ownership; see DOMINION]

condone (kən'dəʊn) *vb.* (*tr.*) **1.** to overlook or forgive (an offence). **2.** *Law.* (esp. of a spouse) to pardon or overlook (an offence, usually adultery). [C19: from Latin *condōnāre* to remit a debt, from *com-* (intensive) + *dōnāre* to DONATE] **—con'donable** *adj.* **—condonation** (͵kɒndəʊ'neɪʃən) *n.* **—con'doner** *n.*

condor ('kɒndɔː) *n.* either of two very large rare New World vultures, *Vultur gryphus* (**Andean condor**), which has black plumage with white around the neck, and *Gymnogyps californianus* (**California condor**), which is similar but nearly extinct. [C17: from Spanish *cóndor,* from Quechuan *kuntur*]

condottiere (͵kɒndɒ'tjɛərɪ) *n., pl.* **-ri** (-riː). a commander or soldier in a professional mercenary company in Europe from the 13th to the 16th centuries. [C18: from Italian, from *condotto* leadership, from *condurre* to lead, from Latin *condūcere;* see CONDUCT]

conduce (kən'djuːs) *vb.* (*intr.;* foll. by *to*) to lead or contribute (to a result). [C15: from Latin *condūcere* to lead together, from *com-* together + *dūcere* to lead] **—con'ducer** *n.* **—con'ducible** *adj.* **—con'ducingly** *adv.*

conducive (kən'djuːsɪv) *adj.* (when *postpositive,* foll. by *to*) contributing, leading, or tending. **—con'duciveness** *n.*

conduct *n.* ('kɒndʌkt). **1.** the manner in which a person behaves; behaviour. **2.** the way of managing a business, affair, etc.; handling. **3.** *Rare.* the act of guiding or leading. **4.** *Rare.* a guide or leader. *~vb.* (kən'dʌkt). **5.** (*tr.*) to accompany and guide (people, a party, etc.) (esp. in the phrase **conducted tour**). **6.** (*tr.*) to lead or direct (affairs, business, etc.); control. **7.** (*tr.*) to do or carry out: *conduct a survey.* **8.** (*tr.*) to behave or manage (oneself): *the child conducted himself well.* **9.** Also (esp. U.S.): **direct.** to control or guide (an orchestra, choir, etc.) by the movements of the hands or a baton. **10.** to transmit (heat, electricity, etc.): *metals conduct heat.* [C15: from Medieval Latin *conductus* escorted, from Latin: drawn together, from *condūcere* to CONDUCE] **—con'ductible** *adj.* **—con͵ducti'bility** *n.*

conductance (kən'dʌktəns) *n.* the ability of a system to conduct electricity, measured by the ratio of the current flowing through the system to the potential difference across it; the reciprocal of resistance. It is measured in reciprocal ohms, mhos, or siemens. Symbol: G

conducting tissue *n. Botany.* another name for **vascular tissue.**

conductiometric titration (kən͵dʌktɪəʊ'mɛtrɪk) *n. Chem.* a titration technique in which the end-point is determined by measuring the conductance of the solution.

conduction (kən'dʌkʃən) *n.* **1.** the transfer of heat or electricity through a medium. **2.** the transmission of an electrical or chemical impulse along a nerve fibre. **3.** the act of conveying or conducting, as through a pipe. **4.** *Physics.* another name for **conductivity** (sense 1). **—con'ductional** *adj.*

conduction band *n.* See **energy band.**

conductive (kən'dʌktɪv) *adj.* of, denoting, or having the property of conduction. **—con'ductively** *adv.*

conductive education *n.* an educational system, developed in Hungary by András Petö, in which teachers (**conductors**) teach children and adults with motor disorders to function independently, by guiding them to attain their own goals in their own way.

conductivity (͵kɒndʌk'tɪvɪtɪ) *n., pl.* **-ties. 1.** Also called: **conduction.** the property of transmitting heat, electricity, or sound. **2.** a measure of the ability of a substance to conduct electricity; the reciprocal of resistivity. Symbol: κ Formerly called: **specific conductance. 3.** See **thermal conductivity.**

conductivity water *n.* water that has a conductivity of less than 0.043×10^{-6} S cm^{-1}.

conductor (kən'dʌktə) *n.* **1.** an official on a bus who collects fares, checks tickets, etc. **2.** Also called: (esp. U.S.): **director.** a person who conducts an orchestra, choir, etc. **3.** a person who leads or guides. **4.** *U.S. and Canadian.* a railway official in charge of a train. **5.** a substance, body, or system that conducts electricity, heat, etc. **6.** See **lightning conductor. —con'ductor͵ship** *n.* **—conductress** (kən'dʌktrɪs) *fem. n.*

conduit ('kɒndɪt, -djʊɪt) *n.* **1.** a pipe or channel for carrying a fluid. **2.** a rigid tube or duct for carrying and protecting electrical wires or cables. **3.** *Botany.* a water-transporting element in a plant; a xylem vessel or a tracheid. **4.** a rare word for **fountain.** [C14: from Old French, from Medieval Latin *conductus* channel, aqueduct, from Latin *condūcere* to lead, CONDUCE]

conduplicate (kɒn'djuːplɪkɪt) *adj. Botany.* folded lengthways on itself: *conduplicate leaves in the bud.* [C18: from Latin *conduplicāre* to double; see DUPLICATE] **—con͵dupli'cation** *n.*

condyle ('kɒndɪl) *n.* the rounded projection on the articulating end of a bone, such as the ball portion of a ball-and-socket joint. [C17: from Latin *condylus* knuckle, joint, from Greek *kondulos*] **—'condylar** *adj.*

condyloid ('kɒndɪ͵lɔɪd) *adj.* of or resembling a condyle.

condyloma (͵kɒndɪ'ləʊmə) *n., pl.* **-mas** *or* **-mata** (-mətə). a wartlike tumour of the skin near the anus or genital organs, esp. as a result of syphilis. [C17: from New Latin, from Greek *kondulōma,* from *kondulos* CONDYLE + -OMA] —**condylomatous** (ˌkɒndɪˈlɒmətəs, -ˈləʊ-) *adj.*

cone (kəʊn) *n.* **1. a.** a geometric solid consisting of a plane base bounded by a closed curve, usually a circle or an ellipse, every point of which is joined to a fixed point, the vertex, lying outside the plane of the base. A **right circular cone** has a vertex perpendicularly above or below the centre of a circular base. Volume of a cone: $1/3\pi r^2h$, where r is the radius of the base and h is the height of the cone. **b.** a geometric surface formed by a line rotating about the vertex and connecting the peripheries of two closed plane bases, usually circular or elliptical, above and below the vertex. See also **conic section.** **2.** anything that tapers from a circular section to a point, such as a wafer shell used to contain ice cream. **3. a.** the reproductive body of conifers and related plants, made up of overlapping scales, esp. the mature **female cone,** whose scales each bear a seed. **b.** a similar structure in horsetails, club mosses, etc. Technical name: **strobilus. 4.** a small cone-shaped bollard used as a temporary traffic marker on roads. **5.** Also called: **retinal cone.** any one of the cone-shaped cells in the retina of the eye, sensitive to colour and bright light. ~*vb.* **6.** (*tr.*) to shape like a cone or part of a cone. [C16: from Latin *cōnus,* from Greek *kōnus* pine cone, geometrical cone]

coneflower (ˈkəʊnˌflaʊə) *n.* any North American plant of the genera *Rudbeckia, Ratibida,* and *Echinacea,* which have rayed flowers with a conelike centre: family *Compositae* (composites). See also **black-eyed Susan.**

cone off *vb.* (*tr., adv.*) *Brit.* to close (one carriageway of a motorway) by placing warning cones across it.

cone shell *n.* any of various tropical marine gastropod molluscs of the genus *Conus* and related genera, having a smooth conical shell. Sometimes shortened to **cone.**

con espressione (*Italian* kɒn ˌespresˈsjone) *adj., adv. Music.* (to be performed) with feeling; expressively. [Italian, literally: with expression]

Conestoga wagon (ˌkɒnɪˈstəʊgə) *n. U.S. and Canadian.* a large heavy horse-drawn covered wagon used in the 19th century. [C19: after *Conestoga,* Pennsylvania, where it was first made]

coney (ˈkəʊnɪ) *n.* a variant spelling of **cony.**

conf. *abbrev. for:* **1.** *confer* [Latin: compare] **2.** conference. **3.** confessor.

confab (ˈkɒnfæb) *Informal.* ~*n.* **1.** a conversation or chat. ~*vb.* **-fabs, -fabbing, -fabbed. 2.** (*intr.*) to converse.

confabulate (kənˈfæbjʊˌleɪt) *vb.* (*intr.*) **1.** to talk together; converse; chat. **2.** *Psychiatry.* to replace the gaps left by a disorder of the memory with imaginary remembered experiences consistently believed to be true. See also **paramnesia.** [C17: from Latin *confābulārī,* from *fābulārī* to talk, from *fābula* a story; see FABLE] —**conˌfabuˈlation** *n.* —**conˈfabuˌlator** *n.* —**conˈfabulatory** *adj.*

confect (kənˈfɛkt) *vb.* (*tr.*) **1.** to prepare by combining ingredients. **2.** to make; construct. [C16: from Latin *confectus* prepared, from *conficere* to accomplish, from *com-* (intensive) + *facere* to make]

confection (kənˈfɛkʃən) *n.* **1.** the act or process of compounding or mixing. **2.** any sweet preparation of fruit, nuts, etc., such as a preserve or a sweet. **3.** *Old-fashioned.* an elaborate article of clothing, esp. for women. **4.** *Informal.* anything regarded as overelaborate or frivolous: *the play was merely an ingenious confection.* **5.** a medicinal drug sweetened with sugar, honey, etc. [C14: from Old French, from Latin *confectiō* a preparing, from *conficere* to produce; see CONFECT]

confectionary (kənˈfɛkʃənərɪ) *n., pl.* **-aries. 1.** a place where confections are kept or made. **2.** a rare word for **confection.** ~*adj.* **3.** of or characteristic of confections.

confectioner (kənˈfɛkʃənə) *n.* a person who makes or sells sweets or confections.

confectioners' sugar *n.* the U.S. term for **icing sugar.**

confectionery (kənˈfɛkʃənərɪ) *n., pl.* **-eries. 1.** sweets and other confections collectively. **2.** the art or business of a confectioner.

Confed. *abbrev. for:* **1.** Confederate. **2.** Confederation.

confederacy (kənˈfɛdərəsɪ, -ˈfɛdrəsɪ) *n., pl.* **-cies. 1.** a union or combination of peoples, states, etc.; alliance; league. **2.** a combination of groups or individuals for unlawful purposes. [C14: from Anglo-French *confederacie,* from Late Latin *confoederātiō* agreement, CONFEDERATION]

confederate *n.* (kənˈfɛdərɪt, -ˈfɛdrɪt). **1.** a nation, state, or individual that is part of a confederacy. **2.** someone who is part of a conspiracy; accomplice. ~*adj.* (kənˈfɛdərɪt, -ˈfɛdrɪt). **3.** united in a confederacy; allied. ~*vb.* (kənˈfɛdəˌreɪt). **4.** to form into or become part of a confederacy. [C14: from Late Latin *confoederātus,* from *confoederāre* to unite by a league, from Latin *com-* together + *foedus* treaty]

Confederate (kənˈfɛdərɪt, -ˈfɛdrɪt) *adj.* **1.** of, supporting, or relating to the Confederate States of America, the 11 Southern states that seceded from the Union in 1861, precipitating the Civil War (1861–65) with the North. ~*n.* **2.** a supporter of the Confederate States of America.

confederation (kənˌfɛdəˈreɪʃən) *n.* **1.** the act or process of confederating or the state of being confederated. **2.** a loose alliance of political units. The union of the Swiss cantons is the oldest surviving confederation. Compare **federation. 3.** (esp. in Canada) another name for a **federation.** —**conˌfederˈationˌism** *n.* —**conˌfederˈationist** *n.* —**conˈfederative** *adj.*

confer (kənˈfɜː) *vb.* **-fers, -ferring, -ferred. 1.** (*tr.;* foll. by *on* or *upon*) to grant or bestow (an honour, gift, etc.). **2.** (*intr.*) to hold or take part in a conference or consult together. **3.** (*tr.*) an obsolete word for **compare.** [C16: from Latin *conferre* to gather together, compare, from *com-* together + *ferre* to bring] —**conˈferment** *or* **conˈferral** *n.* —**conˈferrable** *adj.* —**conˈferrer** *n.*

conferee *or* **conferree** (ˌkɒnfɜːˈriː) *n.* **1.** a person who takes part in a conference. **2.** a person on whom an honour or gift is conferred.

conference (ˈkɒnfərəns, -frəns) *n.* **1.** a meeting for consultation, exchange of information, or discussion, esp. one with a formal agenda. **2.** a formal meeting of two or more states, political groups, etc., esp. to discuss differences or formulate common policy. **3.** an assembly of the clergy or of clergy and laity of any of certain Protestant Christian Churches acting as representatives of their denomination: *the Methodist conference.* **4.** *Sport, U.S. and Canadian.* a league of clubs or teams. **5.** *Rare.* an act of bestowal. [C16: from Medieval Latin *conferentia,* from Latin *conferre* to bring together; see CONFER] —**conferential** (ˌkɒnfəˈrɛnʃəl) *adj.*

conference call *n.* a special telephone facility by which three or more people using conventional or cellular phones can be linked up to speak to one another.

Conference pear (ˈkɒnfərəns, -frəns) *n.* a variety of pear that has sweet and juicy fruit.

conferencing (ˈkɒnfərənsɪŋ) *n.* the practice of holding a conference, esp. by means of a telephone service (audioconferencing) or a telephone service also using television equipment (videoconferencing).

conferva (kɒnˈfɜːvə) *n., pl.* **-vae** (-viː) *or* **-vas.** any of various threadlike green algae, esp. any of the genus *Tribonema,* typically occurring in fresh water. [C18: from Latin: a water plant, from *confervēre* to grow together, heal, literally: to seethe, from *fervēre* to boil; named with reference to its reputed healing properties] —**conˈferval** *adj.* —**conˈfervoid** *n., adj.*

confess (kənˈfɛs) *vb.* (when *tr., may take a clause as object*) **1.** (when *intr.,* often foll. by *to*) to make an acknowledgment or admission (of faults, misdeeds, crimes, etc.). **2.** (*tr.*) to admit or grant to be true; concede. **3.** *Christianity, chiefly R.C. Church.* to declare (one's sins) to God or to a priest as his representative, so as to obtain pardon and absolution. **4.** (*tr.*) *Archaic.* to acknowledge one's belief or faith in; declare allegiance to. [C14: from Old French *confesser,* from Late Latin *confessāre,* from Latin *confessus* confessed, from *confitērī* to admit, from *fatērī* to acknowledge; related to Latin *fārī* to speak] —**conˈfessable** *adj.*

confessant (kənˈfɛsᵊnt) *n. Christianity, chiefly R.C. Church.* a person who makes a confession.

confessedly (kənˈfɛsɪdlɪ) *adv.* (*sentence modifier*) by admission or confession; avowedly.

confession (kənˈfɛʃən) *n.* **1.** the act of confessing. **2.** something confessed. **3.** an acknowledgment or declaration, esp. of one's faults, misdeeds, or crimes. **4.** *Christianity, chiefly R.C. Church.* the act of a penitent accusing himself of his sins. **5. confession of faith.** a formal public avowal of religious beliefs. **6.** a religious denomination or sect united by a common system of beliefs. —**conˈfessionary** *adj.*

confessional (kənˈfɛʃənᵊl) *adj.* **1.** of, like, or suited to a confession. ~*n.* **2.** *Christianity, chiefly R.C. Church.* a small stall, usually enclosed and divided by a screen or curtain, where a priest hears confessions. **3.** a book of penitential prayers.

confessor (kənˈfɛsə) *n.* **1.** *Christianity, chiefly R.C. Church.* a priest who hears confessions and sometimes acts as a spiritual counsellor. **2.** *History.* a person who bears witness to his Christian religious faith by the holiness of his life, esp. in resisting threats or danger, but does not suffer martyrdom. **3.** a person who makes a confession.

confetti (kənˈfɛtɪ) *n.* small pieces of coloured paper thrown on festive occasions, esp. at the bride and groom at weddings. [C19: from Italian, plural of *confetto,* originally, a bonbon; see COMFIT]

confidant *or* (*fem.*) **confidante** (ˌkɒnfɪˈdænt, ˈkɒnfɪˌdænt) *n.* a person to whom private matters are confided. [C17: from French *confident,* from Italian *confidente,* n. use of adj.: trustworthy, from Latin *confīdens* CONFIDENT]

confide (kənˈfaɪd) *vb.* **1.** (usually foll. by *in;* when *tr., may take a clause as object*) to disclose (secret or personal matters) in confidence (to); reveal in private (to). **2.** (*intr.;* foll. by *in*) to have complete trust. **3.** (*tr.*) to entrust into another's keeping. [C15: from Latin *confīdere,* from *fīdere* to trust; related to Latin *foedus* treaty] —**conˈfider** *n.*

confidence (ˈkɒnfɪdəns) *n.* **1.** a feeling of trust in a person or thing: *I have confidence in his abilities.* **2.** belief in one's own abilities; self-assurance. **3.** trust or a trustful relationship: *take me into your confidence.* **4.** something confided or entrusted; secret. **5. in confidence.** as a secret.

confidence interval *n. Statistics.* an interval of values bounded by **confidence limits** within which the true value of a population parameter is stated to lie with a specified probability.

confidence level *n. Statistics.* a measure of the reliability of a result. A confidence level of 95 per cent or 0.95 means that there is a probability of at least 95 per cent that the result is reliable. Compare **significance** (sense 4).

confidence man *or* **trickster** *n.* another name for **con man.**

confidence trick *or U.S. and Canadian* **confidence game** *n.* a swindle involving money, goods, etc., in which the victim's trust is won by the swindler. Informal shortened forms: **con trick,** *U.S. and Canadian* **con game.**

confident ('kɒnfɪdənt) *adj.* **1.** (*postpositive;* foll. by *of*) having or showing confidence or certainty; sure: *confident of success.* **2.** sure of oneself; bold. **3.** presumptuous; excessively bold. [C16: from Latin *confīdens* trusting, having self-confidence, from *confīdere* to have complete trust in; see CONFIDE] —'**confidently** *adv.*

confidential (ˌkɒnfɪ'dɛnʃəl) *adj.* **1.** spoken, written, or given in confidence; secret; private. **2.** entrusted with another's confidence or secret affairs: *a confidential secretary.* **3.** suggestive of or denoting intimacy: *a confidential approach.* —ˌ**confiˌdenti'ality** *or* ˌ**confi'dentialness** *n.* —ˌ**confi'dentially** *adv.*

confiding (kən'faɪdɪŋ) *adj.* unsuspicious; trustful. —**con'fidingly** *adv.* —**con'fidingness** *n.*

configuration (kənˌfɪgjʊ'reɪʃən) *n.* **1.** the arrangement of the parts of something. **2.** the external form or outline achieved by such an arrangement. **3.** *Physics, chem.* **a.** Also called: **conformation.** the shape of a molecule as determined by the arrangement of its atoms. **b.** the structure of an atom or molecule as determined by the arrangement of its electrons and nucleons. **4.** *Psychol.* the unit or pattern in perception studied by Gestalt psychologists. **5.** *Computer technol.* the particular choice of hardware items and their interconnection that make up a particular computer system. [C16: from Late Latin *configūrātiō* a similar formation, from *configūrāre* to model on something, from *figūrāre* to shape, fashion] —**conˌfigu'rational** *or* **con'figurative** *adj.* —**conˌfigu'rationally** *adv.*

confine *vb.* (kən'faɪn). (*tr.*) **1.** to keep or close within bounds; limit; restrict. **2.** to keep shut in; restrict the free movement of: *arthritis confined him to bed.* ~*n.* ('kɒnfaɪn). **3.** (*often pl.*) a limit; boundary. [C16: from Medieval Latin *confīnāre* from Latin *confīnis* adjacent, from *fīnis* end, boundary] —**con'finable** *or* **con'fineable** *adj.* —'**confineless** *adj.* —**con'finer** *n.*

confined (kən'faɪnd) *adj.* **1.** enclosed or restricted; limited. **2.** in childbed; undergoing childbirth. —**confinedly** (kən'faɪnɪdlɪ) *adv.* —**con'finedness** *n.*

confinement (kən'faɪnmənt) *n.* **1.** the act of confining or the state of being confined. **2.** the period from the onset of labour to the birth of a child. **3.** *Physics.* another name for **containment** (sense 3).

confirm (kən'fɜːm) *vb.* (*tr.*) **1.** (*may take a clause as object*) to prove to be true or valid; corroborate; verify. **2.** (*may take a clause as object*) to assert for a second or further time, so as to make more definite: *he confirmed that he would appear in court.* **3.** to strengthen or make more firm: *his story confirmed my doubts.* **4.** to make valid by a formal act or agreement; ratify. **5.** to administer the rite of confirmation to. [C13: from Old French *confermer,* from Latin *confirmāre,* from *firmus* FIRM[1]] —**con'firmable** *adj.* —**con'firmatory** *or* **con'firmative** *adj.* —**con'firmer** *n.*

confirmand ('kɒnfəˌmænd) *n.* a candidate for confirmation.

confirmation (ˌkɒnfə'meɪʃən) *n.* **1.** the act of confirming. **2.** something that confirms; verification. **3.** a rite in several Christian churches that confirms a baptized person in his faith and admits him to full participation in the church. **4.** (in the philosophy of science) the relationship between an observation and the theory which it supposedly renders more probable. Compare **hypothetico-deductive.**

confirmed (kən'fɜːmd) *adj.* **1.** (*prenominal*) long-established in a habit, way of life, etc.: *a confirmed bachelor.* **2.** having received the rite of confirmation. **3.** (of a disease) another word for **chronic.** —**confirmedly** (kən'fɜːmɪdlɪ) *adv.* —**confirmedness** (kən'fɜːmɪdnɪs, -'fɜːmd-) *n.*

confiscable (kən'fɪskəbᵊl) *adj.* subject or liable to confiscation or seizure.

confiscate ('kɒnfɪˌskeɪt) *vb.* (*tr.*) **1.** to seize (property), esp. for public use and esp. by way of a penalty. ~*adj.* **2.** seized or confiscated; forfeit. **3.** having lost or been deprived of property through confiscation. [C16: from Latin *confiscāre* to seize for the public treasury, from *fiscus* basket, treasury] —ˌ**confis'cation** *n.* —'**confisˌcator** *n.* —**confiscatory** (kən'fɪskətərɪ, -trɪ) *adj.*

Confiteor (kən'fɪtɪˌɔː) *n. R.C. Church.* a prayer consisting of a general confession of sinfulness and an entreaty for forgiveness. [C13: from Latin: I confess; from the beginning of the Latin prayer of confession]

confiture ('kɒnfɪˌtjʊə) *n.* a confection, preserve of fruit, etc. [C19: from French, from Old French *confire* to prepare, from Latin *conficere* to produce; see CONFECT]

conflagrant (kən'fleɪgrənt) *adj. Rare.* burning fiercely.

conflagration (ˌkɒnflə'greɪʃən) *n.* a large destructive fire. [C16: from Latin *conflagrātiō,* from *conflagrāre* to be burnt up, from *com-* (intensive) + *flagrāre* to burn; related to Latin *fulgur* lightning] —'**conflaˌgrative** *adj.*

conflate (kən'fleɪt) *vb.* (*tr.*) to combine or blend (two things, esp. two versions of a text) so as to form a whole. [C16: from Latin *conflāre* to blow together, from *flāre* to blow] —**con'flation** *n.*

conflict *n.* ('kɒnflɪkt). **1.** a struggle or clash between opposing forces; battle. **2.** a state of opposition between ideas, interests, etc.; disagreement or controversy. **3.** a clash, as between two appointments made for the same time. **4.** *Psychol.* opposition between two simultaneous but incompatible wishes or drives, sometimes leading to a state of emotional tension and thought to be responsible for neuroses. ~*vb.* (kən'flɪkt). (*intr.*) **5.** to come into opposition; clash. **6.** to fight. [C15: from Latin *conflictus,* from *conflīgere* to combat, from *flīgere* to strike] —**con'fliction** *n.* —**con'flictive** *or* **con'flictory** *adj.*

conflicting (kən'flɪktɪŋ) *adj.* clashing; contradictory: *conflicting rumours.* —**con'flictingly** *adv.*

confluence ('kɒnflʊəns) *or* **conflux** ('kɒnflʌks) *n.* **1.** a merging or flowing together, esp. of rivers. **2.** a gathering together, esp. of people.

confluent ('kɒnflʊənt) *adj.* **1.** flowing together or merging. ~*n.* **2.** a stream that flows into another, usually of approximately equal size. [C17: from Latin *confluēns,* from *confluere* to flow together, from *fluere* to flow]

confocal (kɒn'fəʊkᵊl) *adj.* having a common focus or common foci: *confocal ellipses.*

confocal microscope *n.* a light microscope with an optical system designed to reject background from matter outside the focal plane and therefore allowing images of different sections of a specimen to be obtained.

conform (kən'fɔːm) *vb.* **1.** (*intr.;* usually foll. by *to*) to comply in actions, behaviour, etc., with accepted standards or norms. **2.** (*intr.;* usually foll. by *with*) to be in accordance; fit in: *he conforms with my idea of a teacher.* **3.** to make or become similar in character or form. **4.** (*intr.*) to comply with the practices of an established church, esp. the Church of England. **5.** (*tr.*) to bring (oneself, ideas, etc.) into harmony or agreement. [C14: from Old French *conformer,* from Latin *confirmāre* to establish, strengthen, from *firmāre* to make firm, from *firmus* FIRM[1]] —**con'former** *n.* —**con'formingly** *adv.*

conformable (kən'fɔːməbᵊl) *adj.* **1.** corresponding in character; similar. **2.** obedient; submissive. **3.** (foll. by *to*) in agreement or harmony (with); consistent (with). **4.** (of rock strata) lying in a parallel arrangement so that their original relative positions have remained undisturbed. **5.** *Maths.* (of two matrices) related so that the number of columns in one is equal to the number of rows in the other. —**conˌforma'bility** *or* **con'formableness** *n.* —**con'formably** *adv.*

conformal (kən'fɔːməl) *adj.* **1.** *Maths.* **a.** (of a transformation) preserving the angles of the depicted surface. **b.** (of a parameter) relating to such a transformation. **2.** Also called: **orthomorphic.** (of a map projection) maintaining true shape over a small area and scale in every direction. [C17: from Late Latin *conformālis* having the same shape, from Latin *com-* same + *forma* shape]

conformation (ˌkɒnfɔː'meɪʃən) *n.* **1.** the general shape or outline of an object; configuration. **2.** the arrangement of the parts of an object. **3.** the act or state of conforming. **4.** *Chem.* **a.** another name for **configuration** (sense 3a). **b.** one of the configurations of a molecule that can easily change its shape and can consequently exist in equilibrium with molecules of different configuration. —ˌ**confor'mational** *adj.*

conformational analysis *n. Chem.* the study of the spatial arrangement of atoms or groups of atoms in a molecule and the way in which this influences chemical behaviour.

conformist (kən'fɔːmɪst) *n.* **1.** a person who adopts the attitudes, behaviour, dress, etc. of the group to which he belongs. **2.** a person who complies with the practices of an established church, esp. the Church of England. ~*adj.* **3.** of a conforming nature or character.

conformity (kən'fɔːmɪtɪ) *or* **conformance** *n., pl.* **-ities** *or* **-ances. 1.** compliance in actions, behaviour, etc., with certain accepted standards or norms. **2.** correspondence or likeness in form or appearance; congruity; agreement. **3.** compliance with the practices of an established church.

confound (kən'faʊnd) *vb.* (*tr.*) **1.** to astound or perplex; bewilder. **2.** to mix up; confuse. **3.** to treat mistakenly as similar to or identical with (one or more other things). **4.** (kɒn'faʊnd) to curse or damn (usually as an expletive in the phrase **confound it!**). **5.** to contradict or refute (an argument, etc.). **6.** to rout or defeat (an enemy). **7.** *Archaic.* to put to shame; abash. **8.** *Obsolete.* to waste. [C13: from Old French *confondre,* from Latin *confundere* to mingle, pour together, from *fundere* to pour] —**con'foundable** *adj.* —**con'founder** *n.*

confounded (kən'faʊndɪd) *adj.* **1.** bewildered; confused. **2.** (*prenominal*) *Informal.* execrable; damned. —**con'foundedly** *adv.* —**con'foundedness** *n.*

confraternity (ˌkɒnfrə'tɜːnɪtɪ) *n., pl.* **-ties.** a group of men united for some particular purpose, esp. Christian laymen organized for religious or charitable service; brotherhood. [C15: from Medieval Latin *confrāternitās;* see CONFRÈRE, FRATERNITY] —ˌ**confra'ternal** *adj.*

confrère ('kɒnfrɛə) *n.* a fellow member of a profession, fraternity, etc. [C15: from Old French, from Medieval Latin *confrāter* fellow member, from Latin *frāter* brother]

confront (kən'frʌnt) *vb.* (*tr.*) **1.** (usually foll. by *with*) to present or face (with something), esp. in order to accuse or criticize. **2.** to face boldly; oppose in hostility. **3.** to be face to face with; be in front of. **4.** to bring together for comparison. [C16: from Medieval Latin *confrontārī* to stand face to face with, from *frons* forehead] —**con'fronter** *n.*

confrontation (ˌkɒnfrʌn'teɪʃən) *or Archaic* **confrontment** (kɒn'frʌntmənt) *n.* **1.** the act or an instance of confronting. **2.** a situation of mutual hostility between two powers or nations without open warfare. **3.** a state of conflict between two antagonistic forces, creeds, ideas, etc. —ˌ**confron'tational** *adj.*

Confucian (kən'fjuːʃən) *adj.* **1.** of or relating to the doctrines of Confucius (551–479 B.C.), Chinese philosopher. ~*n.* **2.** a follower of Confucius.

Confucianism (kən'fjuːʃəˌnɪzəm) *n.* the ethical system of Confucius, emphasizing moral order, the humanity and virtue of China's ancient rulers, and gentlemanly education. —**Con'fucianist** *n.*

con fuoco (kɒn fuː'əʊkəʊ) *adj., adv. Music.* (to be performed) in a fiery manner. [Italian: with fire]

confuse (kən'fjuːz) *vb.* (*tr.*) **1.** to bewilder; perplex. **2.** to mix up (things, ideas, etc.); jumble. **3.** to make unclear: *he confused his talk with irrelevant details.* **4.** to fail to recognize the difference between; mistake (one thing) for another. **5.** to disconcert; embarrass. **6.** to cause to become disordered: *the enemy ranks were confused by gas.* [C18: back formation from *confused,* from Latin *confūsus* mingled together, from *confundere* to pour together; see CONFOUND] —**con'fusable** *adj.* —**conˌfusa'bility** *n.* —**con'fused** *adj.* —**confusedly** (kən'fjuːzɪdlɪ, -'fjuːzd-) *adv.* —**con'fusedness** *n.* —**con'fusing** *adj.* —**con'fusingly** *adv.*

confused elderly *adj. Social welfare.* **a.** old and no longer having mental abilities sufficient for independent living. **b.** (*as collective n.;* preceded by *the*): *the confused elderly.*

confusion (kən'fjuːʒən) *n.* **1.** the act of confusing or the state of being confused. **2.** disorder; jumble. **3.** bewilderment; perplexity. **4.** lack of clarity; indistinctness. **5.** embarrassment; abashment. —**con'fusional** *adj.*

confute (kən'fjuːt) *vb.* (*tr.*) **1.** to prove (a person or thing) wrong, invalid, or mistaken; disprove. **2.** *Obsolete.* to put an end to. [C16: from Latin *confūtāre* to check, silence] —**con'futable** *adj.* —**confutation** (ˌkɒnfjʊ'teɪʃən) *n.* —**con'futative** *adj.* —**con'futer** *n.*

cong. *abbrev. for:* **1.** *Pharmacol.* congius. [Latin: gallon] **2.** congregation.

Cong. *abbrev. for:* **1.** Congregational. **2.** Congress. **3.** Congressional.

conga ('kɒŋgə) *n.* **1.** a Latin American dance of three steps and a kick to each bar, usually performed by a number of people in single file. **2.** Also called: **conga drum.** a large tubular bass drum, used chiefly in Latin American and funk music and played with the hands. ~*vb.* **-gas, -gaing, -gaed. 3.** (*intr.*) to perform this dance. [C20: from American Spanish, feminine of *congo* belonging to the *Congo,* republic in central Africa]

congé ('kɒnʒeɪ) *n.* **1.** permission to depart or dismissal, esp. when formal. **2.** a farewell. **3.** *Architect.* a concave moulding. See also **cavetto.** [C16: from Old French *congié,* from Latin *commeātus* leave of absence, from *meātus* movement, from *meāre* to go, pass]

congeal (kən'dʒiːl) *vb.* **1.** to change or cause to change from a soft or fluid state to a firm or solid state. **2.** to form or cause to form into a coagulated mass; curdle; jell. **3.** (*intr.*) (of ideas) to take shape or become fixed in form. [C14: from Old French *congeler,* from Latin *congelāre,* from *com-* together + *gelāre* to freeze] —**con'gealable** *adj.* —**con'gealer** *n.* —**con'gealment** *n.*

congelation (ˌkɒndʒɪ'leɪʃən) *n.* **1.** the process of congealing. **2.** something formed by this process.

congener (kən'dʒiːnə, 'kɒndʒɪnə) *n.* a member of a class, group, or other category, esp. any animal of a specified genus. [C18: from Latin, from *com-* same + *genus* kind]

congeneric (ˌkɒndʒɪ'nɛrɪk) *or* **congenerous** (kɒn'dʒɛnərəs) *adj.* belonging to the same group, esp. (of animals or plants) belonging to the same genus.

congenial (kən'dʒiːnjəl, -nɪəl) *adj.* **1.** friendly, pleasant, or agreeable: *a congenial atmosphere to work in.* **2.** having a similar disposition, tastes, etc.; compatible; sympathetic. [C17: from CON- (same) + GENIAL] —**congeniality** (kənˌdʒiːnɪ'ælɪtɪ) *or* **con'genialness** *n.* —**con'genially** *adv.*

congenic (kən'dʒɛnɪk) *adj. Genetics.* (of inbred animal cells) genetically identical except for a single gene locus.

congenital (kən'dʒɛnɪtᵊl) *adj.* **1.** denoting or relating to any nonhereditary condition, esp. an abnormal condition, existing at birth: *congenital blindness.* **2.** *Informal.* complete, as if from birth: *a congenital idiot.* [C18: from Latin *congenitus* born together with, from *genitus* born, from *gignere* to bear, beget] —**con'genitally** *adv.* —**con'genitalness** *n.*

conger ('kɒŋgə) *n.* any large marine eel of the family *Congridae,* esp. *Conger conger,* occurring in temperate and tropical coastal waters. [C14: from Old French *congre,* from Latin *conger,* from Greek *gongros* sea eel]

congeries (kɒn'dʒɪəriːz) *n.* (*functioning as sing. or pl.*) a collection of objects or ideas; mass; heap. [C17: from Latin, from *congerere* to pile up, from *gerere* to carry]

congest (kən'dʒɛst) *vb.* **1.** to crowd or become crowded to excess; overfill. **2.** to overload or clog (an organ or part) with blood or (of an organ or part) to become overloaded or clogged with blood. **3.** (*tr.; usually passive*) to block (the nose) with mucus. [C16: from Latin *congestus* pressed together, from *congerere* to assemble; see CONGERIES] —**con'gested** *adj.* —**con'gestible** *adj.* —**con'gestion** *n.* —**con'gestive** *adj.*

congius ('kɒndʒɪəs) *n., pl.* **-gii** (-dʒɪˌaɪ). **1.** *Pharmacol.* a unit of liquid measure equal to 1 Imperial gallon. **2.** an ancient Roman unit of liquid measure equal to about 0.7 Imperial gallon or 0.84 U.S. gallon. [C14: from Latin, probably from Greek *konkhos* liquid measure, CONCH]

conglobate ('kɒngləʊˌbeɪt) *vb.* **1.** to form into a globe or ball. ~*adj.* **2.** a rare word for **globular.** [C17: from Latin *conglobāre* to gather into a ball, from *globāre* to make round, from *globus* a sphere] —ˌ**conglo'bation** *n.*

conglomerate *n.* (kən'glɒmərɪt). **1.** a thing composed of heterogeneous elements; mass. **2.** any coarse-grained sedimentary rock consisting of rounded fragments of rock embedded in a finer matrix. Compare **agglomerate** (sense 3). **3.** a large corporation consisting of a group of companies dealing in widely diversified goods, services, etc. ~*vb.* (kən'glɒməˌreɪt). **4.** to form into a cluster or mass. ~*adj.* (kən'glɒmərɪt). **5.** made up of heterogeneous elements; massed. **6.** (of sedimentary rocks) consisting of rounded fragments within a finer matrix. [C16: from Latin *conglomerāre* to roll up, from *glomerāre* to wind into a ball, from *glomus* ball of thread]

conglomeration (kənˌglɒmə'reɪʃən) *n.* **1.** a conglomerate mass. **2.** a mass of miscellaneous things. **3.** the act of conglomerating or the state of being conglomerated.

conglutinant (kən'gluːtɪnənt) *adj.* (of the edges of a wound or fracture) promoting union; adhesive.

conglutinate (kən'gluːtɪˌneɪt) *vb.* **1.** to cause (the edges of a wound or fracture) to join during the process of healing or (of the edges of a wound or fracture) to join during this process. **2.** to stick or become stuck together. [C16: from Latin *conglūtināre* to glue together, from *glūtināre* to glue, from *glūten* GLUE] —**conˌgluti'nation** *n.* —**con'glutinative** *adj.*

congo eel *or* **snake** ('kɒŋgəʊ) *n.* an aquatic salamander, *Amphiuma means,* having an eel-like body with gill slits and rudimentary limbs and inhabiting still muddy waters in the southern U.S.: family *Amphiumidae.* [named after the *Congo* in W Africa]

Congolese (ˌkɒŋgə'liːz) *adj.* **1.** of or relating to the People's Republic of the Congo, in W central Africa. ~*n.* (*pl.* **-lese**) **2.** a native or inhabitant of this republic.

Congo red *n.* a brownish-red soluble powder, used as a dye, a diagnostic indicator, a biological stain, and a chemical indicator. Formula: $C_{32}H_{22}N_6O_6S_2Na_2$.

congou ('kɒŋguː) *or* **congo** ('kɒŋgəʊ) *n.* a kind of black tea from China. [C18: from Chinese (Amoy) *kong hu tē* tea prepared with care]

congrats (kən'græts) *or* (*Chiefly Brit.*) **congratters** (kən'grætəz) *pl. n., sentence substitute.* informal shortened forms of **congratulations.**

congratulate (kən'grætjʊˌleɪt) *vb.* (*tr.*) **1.** (usually foll. by *on*) to communicate pleasure, approval, or praise to (a person or persons); compliment. **2.** (often foll. by *on*) to consider (oneself) clever or fortunate (as a result of): *she congratulated herself on her tact.* **3.** *Obsolete.* to greet; salute. [C16: from Latin *congrātulārī,* from *grātulārī* to rejoice, from *grātus* pleasing] —**conˌgratu'lation** *n.* —**con'gratuˌlator** *n.* —**con'gratulatory** *or* **con'gratulative** *adj.*

congratulations (kənˌgrætjʊ'leɪʃənz) *pl. n., sentence substitute.* expressions of pleasure or joy; felicitations.

congregant ('kɒŋgrɪgənt) *n.* a member of a congregation, esp. a Jewish congregation.

congregate *vb.* ('kɒŋgrɪˌgeɪt). **1.** to collect together in a body or crowd; assemble. ~*adj.* ('kɒŋgrɪgɪt, -ˌgeɪt). **2.** collected together; assembled. **3.** relating to collecting; collective. [C15: from Latin *congregāre* to collect into a flock, from *grex* flock] —'**congreˌgative** *adj.* —'**congreˌgativeness** *n.* —'**congreˌgator** *n.*

congregation (ˌkɒŋgrɪ'geɪʃən) *n.* **1.** a group of persons gathered for worship, prayer, etc., esp. in a church or chapel. **2.** the act of congregating or collecting together. **3.** a group of people, objects, etc., collected together; assemblage. **4.** the group of persons habitually attending a given church, chapel, etc. **5.** *R.C. Church.* **a.** a society of persons who follow a common rule of life but who are bound only by simple vows. **b.** an administrative subdivision of the papal curia. **c.** an administrative committee of bishops for arranging the business of a general council. **6.** *Chiefly Brit.* an assembly of senior members of a university.

congregational (ˌkɒŋgrɪ'geɪʃənᵊl) *adj.* **1.** of or relating to a congregation. **2.** (*usually cap.*) of, relating to, or denoting the Congregational Church, its members, or its beliefs. —ˌ**congre'gationally** *adv.*

Congregational Church *n.* any evangelical Protestant Christian Church that is governed according to the principles of Congregationalism. In 1972 the majority of churches in the Congregational Church in England and Wales voted to become part of the United Reformed Church.

Congregationalism (ˌkɒŋgrɪ'geɪʃənəˌlɪzəm) *n.* a system of Christian doctrines and ecclesiastical government in which each congregation is self-governing and maintains bonds of faith with similar local congregations. —ˌ**Congre'gationalist** *adj., n.*

congress ('kɒŋgrɛs) *n.* **1.** a meeting or conference, esp. of representatives of a number of sovereign states. **2.** a national legislative assembly. **3.** a society or association. **4.** sexual intercourse. [C16: from Latin *congressus* from *congredī* to meet with, from *com-* together + *gradī* to walk, step]

Congress (ˈkɒŋgrɛs) *n.* **1.** the bicameral federal legislature of the U.S., consisting of the House of Representatives and the Senate. **2.** this body during any two-year term. —**Conˈgressional** *adj.*

congressional (kənˈgrɛʃənᵊl) *adj.* of or relating to a congress. —**conˈgressionalist** *n.* —**conˈgressionally** *adv.*

Congressional district *n.* (in the U.S.) an electoral division of a state, entitled to send one member to the U.S. House of Representatives.

Congressional Medal of Honor *n.* See **Medal of Honor.**

Congressman (ˈkɒŋgrɛsmən) *or (fem.)* **Congresswoman** *n., pl.* **-men** *or* **-women.** (in the U.S.) a member of Congress, esp. of the House of Representatives.

congruence (ˈkɒŋgrʊəns) *or* **congruency** *n.* **1.** the quality or state of corresponding, agreeing, or being congruent. **2.** *Maths.* the relationship between two integers, *x* and *y*, such that their difference, with respect to another integer called the modulus, *n*, is a multiple of the modulus. Usually written $x \equiv y \pmod{n}$, as in $25 \equiv 11 \pmod 7$.

congruent (ˈkɒŋgrʊənt) *adj.* **1.** agreeing; corresponding; congruous. **2.** having identical shapes so that all parts correspond: *congruent triangles.* Compare **similar** (sense 2). **3.** of or concerning two integers related by a congruence. [C15: from Latin *congruere* to meet together, agree] —ˈ**congruently** *adv.*

congruous (ˈkɒŋgrʊəs) *adj.* **1.** corresponding or agreeing. **2.** suitable; appropriate. [C16: from Latin *congruus* suitable, harmonious; see CONGRUENT] —**congruity** (kənˈgruːɪtɪ) *or* ˈ**congruousness** *n.* —ˈ**congruously** *adv.*

conic (ˈkɒnɪk) *adj. also* **conical. 1. a.** having the shape of a cone. **b.** of or relating to a cone. ~*n.* **2.** another name for **conic section.** ~See also **conics.** [C16: from New Latin, from Greek *kōnikos,* from *kōnus* CONE] —ˈ**conically** *adv.*

conic projection *or* **conical projection** *n.* a map projection on which the earth is shown as projected onto a cone with its apex over one of the poles and with parallels of latitude radiating from this apex.

conics (ˈkɒnɪks) *n. (functioning as sing.)* the branch of geometry concerned with the parabola, ellipse, and hyperbola.

conic section *n.* one of a group of curves formed by the intersection of a plane and a right circular cone. It is either a circle, ellipse, parabola, or hyperbola, depending on the eccentricity, *e*, which is constant for a particular curve: $e = 0$ for a circle; $e < 1$ for an ellipse; $e = 1$ for a parabola; $e > 1$ for a hyperbola. Often shortened to **conic.**

conidiophore (kəʊˈnɪdɪəˌfɔː) *n.* a simple or branched hypha that bears spores (conidia) in such fungi as *Penicillium.* [C19: from CONIDIUM + -PHORE] —**conidiophorous** (kəʊˌnɪdɪˈɒfərəs, kə-) *adj.*

conidium (kəʊˈnɪdɪəm) *n., pl.* **-nidia** (-ˈnɪdɪə). an asexual spore formed at the tip of a specialized hypha (conidiophore) in fungi such as *Penicillium.* [C19: from New Latin, from Greek *konis* dust + -IUM] —**coˈnidial** *or* **coˈnidian** *adj.*

conifer (ˈkəʊnɪfə, ˈkɒn-) *n.* any gymnosperm tree or shrub of the group *Coniferae,* typically bearing cones and evergreen leaves. The group includes the pines, spruces, firs, larches, yews, junipers, cedars, cypresses, and sequoias. [C19: from Latin, from *cōnus* CONE + *ferre* to bear]

coniferous (kəˈnɪfərəs, kɒ-) *adj.* of, relating to, or belonging to the plant group *Coniferae.* See **conifer.**

coniine (ˈkəʊnɪˌiːn, -nɪɪn, -niːn), **conin** (ˈkəʊnɪn), *or* **conine** (ˈkəʊniːn, -nɪn) *n.* a colourless poisonous soluble liquid alkaloid found in hemlock; 2-propylpiperidine. Formula: $C_5H_{10}NC_3H_7$. Also called: **cicutine** (ˈsɪkjʊtiːn), **conicine** (ˈkəʊnɪsiːn). [C19: from CONIUM + -INE[2]]

coniology (ˌkəʊnɪˈɒlədʒɪ) *n.* a variant spelling of **koniology.**

conium (ˈkəʊnɪəm) *n.* **1.** either of the two N temperate plants of the umbelliferous genus *Conium,* esp. hemlock. **2.** an extract of either of these plants, used to treat spasmodic disorders. [C19: from Late Latin: hemlock, from Greek *kōneion;* perhaps related to Greek *kōnos* CONE]

conj. *abbrev. for:* **1.** *Grammar.* conjugation, conjunction, *or* conjunctive. **2.** *Astronomy.* conjunction.

conjectural (kənˈdʒɛktʃərəl) *adj.* involving or inclined to conjecture. —**conˈjecturally** *adv.*

conjecture (kənˈdʒɛktʃə) *n.* **1.** the formation of conclusions from incomplete evidence; guess. **2.** the inference or conclusion so formed. **3.** *Obsolete.* interpretation of occult signs. ~*vb.* **4.** to infer or arrive at (an opinion, conclusion, etc.) from incomplete evidence. [C14: from Latin *conjectūra* an assembling of facts, from *conjicere* to throw together, from *jacere* to throw] —**conˈjecturable** *adj.* —**conˈjecturably** *adv.* —**conˈjecturer** *n.*

conjoin (kənˈdʒɔɪn) *vb.* to join or become joined. [C14: from Old French *conjoindre,* from Latin *conjungere,* from *jungere* to JOIN] —**conˈjoiner** *n.*

conjoint (kənˈdʒɔɪnt) *adj.* united, joint, or associated. —**conˈjointly** *adv.*

conjugal (ˈkɒndʒʊgᵊl) *adj.* of or relating to marriage or the relationship between husband and wife: *conjugal rights.* [C16: from Latin *conjugālis,* from *conjunx* wife or husband, from *conjungere* to unite; see CONJOIN] —**conjugality** (ˌkɒndʒʊˈgælɪtɪ) *n.* —ˈ**conjugally** *adv.*

conjugant (ˈkɒndʒʊgənt) *n.* either of a pair of organisms or gametes undergoing conjugation.

conjugate *vb.* (ˈkɒndʒʊˌgeɪt). **1.** *(tr.) Grammar.* to inflect (a verb) systematically; state or set out the conjugation of (a verb). **2.** *(intr.)* (of a verb) to undergo inflection according to a specific set of rules. **3.** *(tr.)* to join (two or more substances) together, esp. in such a way that the resulting substance may easily be turned back into its original components. **4.** *(intr.) Biology.* to undergo conjugation. **5.** *(tr.) Obsolete.* to join together, esp. in marriage. **6.** *(intr.) Rare.* to have sexual intercourse. ~*adj.* (ˈkɒndʒʊgɪt, -ˌgeɪt). **7.** joined together in pairs; coupled. **8.** *Maths.* **a.** (of two angles) having a sum of 360°. **b.** (of two complex numbers) differing only in the sign of the imaginary part as $4 + 3i$ and $4 - 3i$. **c.** (of two algebraic numbers) being roots of the same irreducible algebraic equation with rational coefficients: *$3 \pm 2\sqrt{2}$ are conjugate algebraic numbers, being roots of $x^2 - 6x + 1$.* **d.** (of two elements of a determinant) interchanged when the rows and columns are interchanged. **e.** (of two arcs) forming a complete circle or other closed curved figure. **9.** *Chem.* of, denoting, or concerning the state of equilibrium in which two liquids can exist as two separate phases that are both solutions. The liquid that is the solute in one phase is the solvent in the other. **10.** another word for **conjugated. 11.** *Chem.* (of acids and bases) related by loss or gain of a proton: *Cl^- is the conjugate base of HCl; HCl is the conjugate acid of Cl^-.* **12.** *Physics.* (of points connected with a lens) having the property that an object placed at one point will produce an image at the other point. **13.** (of a compound leaf) having one pair of leaflets. **14.** (of words) cognate; related in origin. ~*n.* (ˈkɒndʒʊgɪt). **15.** one of a pair or set of conjugate substances, values, quantities, words, etc. [C15: from Latin *conjugāre* to join together, from *com-* together + *jugāre* to marry, connect, from *jugum* a yoke] —ˈ**conjugable** *adj.* —ˈ**conjugately** *adv.* —ˈ**conjugateness** *n.* —ˈ**conjuˌgative** *adj.* —ˈ**conjuˌgator** *n.*

conjugated (ˈkɒndʒʊˌgeɪtɪd) *adj.* **1.** *Chem.* **a.** (of a molecule, compound, or substance) containing two or more double bonds alternating with single bonds. **b.** (of a double bond) separated from another double bond by one single bond. **2.** *Chem.* formed by the union of two compounds: *a conjugated protein.* ~Also: **conjugate.**

conjugated protein *n.* a biochemical compound consisting of a sequence of amino acids making up a simple protein to which another nonprotein group (a prosthetic group), such as a carbohydrate or lipid group, is attached.

conjugation (ˌkɒndʒʊˈgeɪʃən) *n.* **1.** *Grammar.* **a.** inflection of a verb for person, number, tense, voice, mood, etc. **b.** the complete set of the inflections of a given verb. **2.** a joining, union, or conjunction. **3.** a type of sexual reproduction in ciliate protozoans involving the temporary union of two individuals and the subsequent migration and fusion of the gametic nuclei. **4.** the union of gametes, esp. isogametes, as in some algae and fungi. **5.** the pairing of chromosomes in the early phase of a meiotic division. **6.** *Chem.* the existence of alternating double or triple bonds in a chemical compound, with consequent electron delocalization over part of the molecule. —ˌ**conjuˈgational** *adj.* —ˌ**conjuˈgationally** *adv.*

conjunct *adj.* (kənˈdʒʌŋkt, ˈkɒndʒʌŋkt). **1.** joined; united. **2.** *Music.* relating to or denoting two adjacent degrees of a scale. ~*n.* **3.** *Logic.* one of the propositions or formulas in a conjunction. [C15: from Latin *conjunctus,* from *conjugere* to unite; see CONJOIN] —**conˈjunctly** *adv.*

conjunction (kənˈdʒʌŋkʃən) *n.* **1.** the act of joining together; combination; union. **2.** simultaneous occurrence of events; coincidence. **3.** any word or group of words, other than a relative pronoun, that connects words, phrases, or clauses; for example *and* and *while.* Abbrev.: **conj.** See also **coordinating conjunction, subordinating conjunction. 4.** *Astronomy.* **a.** the position of a planet or the moon when it is in line with the sun as seen from the earth. The inner planets are in **inferior conjunction** when the planet is between the earth and the sun and in **superior conjunction** when the sun lies between the earth and the planet. Compare **opposition** (sense 8a). **b.** the apparent proximity or coincidence of two celestial bodies on the celestial sphere. **5.** *Astrology.* an exact aspect of 0° between two planets, etc., an orb of 8° being allowed. Compare **opposition** (sense 9) and **square** (sense 9). **6.** *Logic.* **a.** the operator that forms a compound sentence from two given sentences, and corresponds to the English *and.* **b.** a sentence so formed. Usually written $p\&q$, $p \wedge q$, or $p.q.$, where p,q are the component sentences, it is true only when both these are true. **c.** the relation between such sentences. —**conˈjunctional** *adj.* —**conˈjunctionally** *adv.*

conjunction-reduction *n. Transformational grammar.* a rule that reduces coordinate sentences, applied, for example, to convert *John lives in Ireland and Brian lives in Ireland* into *John and Brian live in Ireland.*

conjunctiva (ˌkɒndʒʌŋkˈtaɪvə) *n., pl.* **-vas** *or* **-vae** (-viː). the delicate mucous membrane that covers the eyeball and the under surface of the eyelid. [C16: from New Latin *membrāna conjunctīva* the conjunctive membrane, from Late Latin *conjunctīvus* CONJUNCTIVE] —ˌ**conjuncˈtival** *adj.*

conjunctive (kənˈdʒʌŋktɪv) *adj.* **1.** joining; connective. **2.** joined. **3.** of or relating to conjunctions or their use. **4.** *Logic.* relating to, characterized by, or containing a conjunction. ~*n.*

5. a less common word for **conjunction** (sense 3). [C15: from Late Latin *conjunctīvus*, from Latin *conjungere* to CONJOIN] —**con'junctively** *adv.*

conjunctive eye movement *n.* any movement of both eyes in the same direction.

conjunctivitis (kənˌdʒʌŋktɪ'vaɪtɪs) *n.* inflammation of the conjunctiva.

conjuncture (kən'dʒʌŋktʃə) *n.* **1.** a combination of events, esp. a critical one. **2.** *Rare.* a union; conjunction. —**con'junctural** *adj.*

conjuration (ˌkɒndʒʊ'reɪʃən) *n.* **1.** a magic spell; incantation. **2.** a less common word for **conjuring.** **3.** *Archaic.* supplication; entreaty.

conjure ('kʌndʒə) *vb.* **1.** (*intr.*) to practise conjuring or be a conjurer. **2.** (*intr.*) to call upon supposed supernatural forces by spells and incantations. **3.** (kən'dʒʊə). (*tr.*) to appeal earnestly or strongly to: *I conjure you to help me.* **4. a name to conjure with. a.** a person thought to have great power or influence. **b.** any name that excites the imagination. [C13: from Old French *conjurer* to plot, from Latin *conjūrāre* to swear together, form a conspiracy, from *jūrāre* to swear]

conjurer *or* **conjuror** ('kʌndʒərə) *n.* **1.** a person who practises conjuring, esp. for people's entertainment. **2.** a person who practises magic; sorcerer.

conjure up *vb.* (*tr., adv.*) **1.** to present to the mind; evoke or imagine: *he conjured up a picture of his childhood.* **2.** to call up or command (a spirit or devil) by an incantation.

conjuring ('kʌndʒərɪŋ) *n.* **1.** the performance of tricks that appear to defy natural laws. ~*adj.* **2.** denoting or relating to such tricks or entertainment.

conk (kɒŋk) *Slang.* ~*vb.* **1.** to strike (someone) a blow, esp. on the head or nose. ~*n.* **2.** a punch or blow, esp. on the head or nose. **3.** the head or (esp. Brit. and N.Z.) the nose. [C19: probably changed from CONCH]

conker ('kɒŋkə) *n.* an informal name for **horse chestnut** (sense 2).

conkers ('kɒŋkəz) *n.* (*functioning as sing.*) *Brit.* a game in which a player swings a horse chestnut (conker), threaded onto a string, against that of another player to try to break it. [C19: from dialect *conker* snail shell, originally used in the game]

conk out *vb.* (*intr., adv.*) *Informal.* **1.** (of machines, cars, etc.) to fail suddenly. **2.** to tire suddenly or collapse, as from exhaustion. [C20: of uncertain origin]

con man *n. Informal.* **1.** a person who swindles another by means of a confidence trick. **2.** a plausible character. ~More formal term: **confidence man.**

con moto (kɒn 'məʊtəʊ) *adj., adv. Music.* (to be performed) in a brisk or lively manner. [Italian, literally: with movement]

conn (kɒn) *vb., n.* a variant spelling (esp. U.S.) of **con**[4].

Conn. *abbrev. for* Connecticut.

connate ('kɒneɪt) *adj.* **1.** existing in a person or thing from birth; congenital or innate. **2.** allied or associated in nature or origin; cognate: *connate qualities.* **3.** Also called: **coadunate.** *Biology.* (of similar parts or organs) closely joined or united together by growth. **4.** *Geology.* (of fluids) produced or originating at the same time as the rocks surrounding them: *connate water.* [C17: from Late Latin *connātus* born at the same time, from Latin *nātus*, from *nāscī* to be born] —'**connately** *adv.* —'**connateness** *n.*

connatural (kə'nætʃərəl) *adj.* **1.** having a similar nature or origin. **2.** congenital or innate; connate. —**con'naturally** *adv.*

connect (kə'nɛkt) *vb.* **1.** to link or be linked together; join; fasten. **2.** (*tr.*) to relate or associate: *I connect him with my childhood.* **3.** (*tr.*) to establish telephone communications with or between. **4.** (*intr.*) to be meaningful or meaningfully related. **5.** (*intr.*) (of two public vehicles, such as trains or buses) to have the arrival of one timed to occur just before the departure of the other, for the convenient transfer of passengers. **6.** (*intr.*) *Informal.* to hit, punch, kick, etc., solidly. **7.** (*intr.*) *U.S. and Canadian informal.* to be successful. **8.** (*intr.*) *Slang.* to find a source of drugs, esp. illegal drugs. [C17: from Latin *connectere* to bind together, from *nectere* to bind, tie] —**con'nectible** *or* **con'nectable** *adj.* —**con'nector** *or* **con'necter** *n.*

connected (kə'nɛktɪd) *adj.* **1.** joined or linked together. **2.** (of speech) coherent and intelligible. **3.** *Logic, maths.* (of a relation) such that either it or its converse holds between any two members of its domain. —**con'nectedly** *adv.*

connecting rod *n.* **1.** a rod or bar for transmitting motion, esp. one that connects a rotating part to a reciprocating part. **2.** such a rod that connects the piston to the crankshaft in an internal-combustion engine or reciprocating pump. See also **big end, little end.** **3.** a similar rod that connects the crosshead of a steam engine to the crank. ~Often shortened to **con rod.**

connection *or* **connexion** (kə'nɛkʃən) *n.* **1.** the act or state of connecting; union. **2.** something that connects, joins, or relates; link or bond. **3.** a relationship or association. **4.** logical sequence in thought or expression; coherence. **5.** the relation of a word or phrase to its context: *in this connection the word has no political significance.* **6.** (*often pl.*) an acquaintance, esp. one who is influential or has prestige. **7.** a relative, esp. if distant and related by marriage. **8. a.** an opportunity to transfer from one train, bus, aircraft, ship, etc., to another. **b.** the vehicle, aircraft, etc., scheduled to provide such an opportunity. **9.** (*pl.*) *N.Z.* the persons owning or controlling a racehorse. **10.** a link, usually a wire or metallic strip, between two components in an electric circuit. **11.** a communications link between two points, esp. by telephone. **12.** *Slang.* a supplier of illegal drugs, such as heroin. **13.** *Rare.* sexual intercourse. **14.** *Rare.* a small sect or religious group united by a body of distinct beliefs or practices. —**con'nectional** *or* **con'nexional** *adj.*

connectionism (kə'nɛkʃənɪzəm) *n. Psychol.* the theory that the connections between brain cells mediate thought and govern behaviour.

connective (kə'nɛktɪv) *adj.* **1.** serving to connect or capable of connecting. ~*n.* **2.** a thing that connects. **3.** *Grammar, logic.* **a.** a less common word for **conjunction** (sense 3). **b.** any word that connects phrases, clauses, or individual words. **c.** a symbol used in a formal language in the construction of compound sentences from simpler sentences, corresponding to terms such as *or, and, not,* etc., in ordinary speech. **4.** *Botany.* the tissue of a stamen that connects the two lobes of the anther. **5.** *Anatomy.* a nerve-fibre bundle connecting two nerve centres. —**con'nectively** *adv.* —**connectivity** (ˌkɒnɛk'tɪvɪtɪ) *n.*

connective tissue *n.* an animal tissue developed from the embryonic mesoderm that consists of collagen or elastic fibres, fibroblasts, fatty cells, etc., within a jelly-like matrix. It supports organs, fills the spaces between them, and forms tendons and ligaments.

conning tower ('kɒnɪŋ) *n.* **1.** Also called: **sail.** a superstructure of a submarine, used as the bridge when the vessel is on the surface. **2.** the armoured pilot house of a warship. [C19: see CON[4]]

conniption (kə'nɪpʃən) *n.* (*often pl.*) *U.S. and Canadian slang.* a fit of rage or tantrums. [C19: arbitrary pseudo-Latin coinage]

connivance (kə'naɪvəns) *n.* **1.** the act or fact of conniving. **2.** *Law.* the tacit encouragement of or assent to another's wrongdoing, esp. (formerly) of the petitioner in a divorce suit to the respondent's adultery.

connive (kə'naɪv) *vb.* (*intr.*) **1.** to plot together, esp. secretly; conspire. **2.** (foll. by *at*) *Law.* to give assent or encouragement (to the commission of a wrong). [C17: from French *conniver*, from Latin *connīvēre* to blink, hence, leave uncensured; *-nīvēre* related to *nictāre* to wink] —**con'niver** *n.* —**con'nivingly** *adv.*

connivent (kə'naɪvənt) *adj.* (of parts of plants and animals) touching without being fused, as some petals, insect wings, etc. [C17: from Latin *connīvēns*, from *connīvēre* to shut the eyes, CONNIVE] —**con'nivently** *adv.*

connoisseur (ˌkɒnɪ'sɜː) *n.* a person with special knowledge or appreciation of a field, esp. in the arts. [C18: from French, from Old French *conoiseor*, from *connoistre* to know, from Latin *cognōscere*] —ˌ**connois'seurship** *n.*

connotation (ˌkɒnə'teɪʃən) *n.* **1.** an association or idea suggested by a word or phrase; implication. **2.** the act or fact of connoting. **3.** *Logic.* another name for **intension** (sense 1). —**connotative** ('kɒnəˌteɪtɪv, kə'nəʊtə-) *or* **con'notive** *adj.* —'**connoˌtatively** *or* **con'notively** *adv.*

connote (kɒ'nəʊt) *vb.* (*tr.; often takes a clause as object*) **1.** (of a word, phrase, etc.) to imply or suggest (associations or ideas) other than the literal meaning: *the word "maiden" connotes modesty.* **2.** to involve as a consequence or condition. [C17: from Medieval Latin *connotāre*, from *notāre* to mark, make a note, from *nota* mark, sign, note]

connubial (kə'njuːbɪəl) *adj.* of or relating to marriage; conjugal: *connubial bliss.* [C17: from Latin *cōnūbiālis* from *cōnūbium* marriage, from *com-* together + *nūbere* to marry] —**conˌnubi'ality** *n.* —**con'nubially** *adv.*

conodont ('kəʊnədɒnt, 'kɒn-) *n.* any of various small Palaeozoic toothlike fossils derived from an extinct unknown animal. [C19: from Greek *kōnos* CONE + -ODONT]

conoid ('kəʊnɔɪd) *n.* **1.** a geometric surface formed by rotating a parabola, ellipse, or hyperbola about one axis. ~*adj. also* **conoidal** (kəʊ'nɔɪdᵊl). **2.** conical, cone-shaped. [C17: from Greek *kōnoeidēs*, from *kōnos* CONE] —**co'noidally** *adv.*

conoscenti (ˌkɒnəʊ'ʃɛntɪ) *pl. n., sing.* **-te** (-tiː). a variant spelling of **cognoscenti.**

conquer ('kɒŋkə) *vb.* **1.** to overcome (an enemy, army, etc.); defeat. **2.** to overcome (an obstacle, feeling, desire, etc.); surmount. **3.** (*tr.*) to gain possession or control of by or as if by force or war; win. **4.** (*tr.*) to gain the love, sympathy, etc., of (someone) by seduction or force of personality. [C13: from Old French *conquerre*, from Vulgar Latin *conquērere* (unattested) to obtain, from Latin *conquīrere* to search for, collect, from *quaerere* to seek] —'**conquerable** *adj.* —'**conquerableness** *n.* —'**conquering** *adj.* —'**conqueror** *n.*

conquest ('kɒnkwɛst, 'kɒŋ-) *n.* **1.** the act or an instance of conquering or the state of having been conquered; victory. **2.** a person, thing, etc., that has been conquered or won. **3.** the act or art of gaining a person's compliance, love, etc., by seduction or force of personality. **4.** a person, whose compliance, love, etc., has been won over by seduction or force of personality. [C13: from Old French *conqueste*, from Vulgar Latin *conquēsta* (unattested), from Latin *conquīsīta*, feminine past participle of *conquīrere* to seek out, procure; see CONQUER]

conquian ('kɒŋkɪən) *n.* another word for **cooncan.**

conquistador (kɒn'kwɪstəˌdɔː; *Spanish* konkista'ðor) *n., pl.* **-dors** *or* **-dores** (*Spanish* -'ðores). an adventurer or conqueror, esp.

one of the Spanish conquerors of the New World in the 16th century. [C19: from Spanish, from *conquistar* to conquer; see CONQUEST]

con rod *n.* short for **connecting rod.**

cons. *abbrev. for:* **1.** consecrated. **2.** consigned. **3.** consignment. **4.** consolidated. **5.** consonant. **6.** constitutional. **7.** construction. **8.** consulting.

Cons. *or* **cons.** *abbrev. for:* **1.** Conservative. **2.** Constitution. **3.** Consul.

consanguinity (ˌkɒnsæŋˈgwɪnɪtɪ) *n.* **1.** relationship by blood; kinship. **2.** close affinity or connection. **3.** *Geology.* (of rocks) similarity of origin, as shown by common mineral and chemical compositions and often texture. [C14: see CON-, SANGUINE] —ˌ**consanˈguineous** *or* **conˈsanguine** *adj.* —ˌ**consanˈguineously** *adv.*

conscience (ˈkɒnʃəns) *n.* **1. a.** the sense of right and wrong that governs a person's thoughts and actions. **b.** regulation of one's actions in conformity to this sense. **c.** a supposed universal faculty of moral insight. **2.** conscientiousness; diligence. **3.** a feeling of guilt or anxiety: *he has a conscience about his unkind action.* **4.** *Obsolete.* consciousness. **5. in (all) conscience. a.** with regard to truth and justice. **b.** certainly. **6. on one's conscience.** causing feelings of guilt or remorse. [C13: from Old French, from Latin *conscientia* knowledge, consciousness, from *conscīre* to know; see CONSCIOUS] —ˈ**conscienceless** *adj.*

conscience clause *n.* a clause in a law or contract exempting persons with moral scruples.

conscience money *n.* money paid voluntarily to compensate for dishonesty, esp. money paid voluntarily for taxes formerly evaded.

conscience-stricken *adj.* feeling anxious or guilty. Also: **conscience-smitten.**

conscientious (ˌkɒnʃɪˈɛnʃəs) *adj.* **1.** involving or taking great care; painstaking; diligent. **2.** governed by or done according to conscience. —ˌ**consciˈentiously** *adv.* —ˌ**consciˈentiousness** *n.*

conscientious objector *n.* a person who refuses to serve in the armed forces on the grounds of conscience.

conscionable (ˈkɒnʃənəbᵊl) *adj. Obsolete.* acceptable to one's conscience. [C16: from *conscions,* obsolete form of CONSCIENCE] —ˈ**conscionableness** *n.* —ˈ**conscionably** *adv.*

conscious (ˈkɒnʃəs) *adj.* **1. a.** alert and awake; not sleeping or comatose. **b.** aware of one's surroundings, one's own thoughts and motivations, etc. **2. a.** aware of and giving value or emphasis to a particular fact or phenomenon: *I am conscious of your great kindness to me.* **b.** (*in combination*): *clothes-conscious.* **3.** done with full awareness; deliberate: *a conscious effort; conscious rudeness.* **4. a.** denoting or relating to a part of the human mind that is aware of a person's self, environment, and mental activity and that to a certain extent determines his choices of action. **b.** (*as n.*): *the conscious is only a small part of the mind.* ~Compare **unconscious.** [C17: from Latin *conscius* sharing knowledge, from *com-* with + *scīre* to know] —ˈ**consciously** *adv.* —ˈ**consciousness** *n.*

consciousness raising *n.* **a.** the process of developing awareness in a person or group of a situation regarded as wrong or unjust, with the aim of producing active participation in changing it. **b.** (*as modifier*): *a consciousness-raising group.*

conscript *n.* (ˈkɒnskrɪpt). **1. a.** a person who is enrolled for compulsory military service. **b.** (*as modifier*): *a conscript army.* ~*vb.* (kənˈskrɪpt). **2.** (*tr.*) to enrol (youths, civilians, etc.) for compulsory military service. [C15: from Latin *conscrīptus,* past participle of *conscrībere* to write together in a list, enrol, from *scrībere* to write]

conscript fathers *pl. n. Literary.* august legislators, esp. Roman senators.

conscription (kənˈskrɪpʃən) *n.* compulsory military service.

consecrate (ˈkɒnsɪˌkreɪt) *vb.* (*tr.*) **1.** to make or declare sacred or holy; sanctify. **2.** to dedicate (one's life, time, etc.) to a specific purpose. **3.** to ordain (a bishop). **4.** *Christianity.* to sanctify (bread and wine) for the Eucharist to be received as the body and blood of Christ. **5.** to cause to be respected or revered; venerate: *time has consecrated this custom.* ~*adj.* **6.** *Archaic.* consecrated. [C15: from Latin *consecrāre,* from *com-* (intensive) + *sacrāre* to devote, from *sacer* sacred] —ˌ**conseˈcration** *n.* —ˈ**conseˌcrator** *n.* —**consecratory** (ˌkɒnsɪˈkreɪtərɪ) *or* ˈ**conseˌcrative** *adj.*

Consecration (ˌkɒnsɪˈkreɪʃən) *n. R.C. Church.* the part of the Mass after the sermon during which the bread and wine are believed to change into the Body and Blood of Christ.

consecution (ˌkɒnsɪˈkjuːʃən) *n.* **1.** a sequence or succession of events or things. **2.** a logical sequence of deductions; inference. [C16: from Latin *consecūtiō,* from *consequī* to follow up, pursue]

consecutive (kənˈsɛkjʊtɪv) *adj.* **1.** (of a narrative, account, etc.) following chronological sequence. **2.** following one another without interruption; successive. **3.** characterized by logical sequence. **4.** *Music.* another word for **parallel** (sense 3). **5.** *Grammar.* expressing consequence or result: *consecutive clauses.* [C17: from French *consécutif,* from Latin *consecūtus* having followed, from *consequī* to pursue] —**conˈsecutively** *adv.* —**conˈsecutiveness** *n.*

consensual (kənˈsɛnsjʊəl) *adj.* **1.** *Law.* (of a contract, agreement, etc.) existing by consent. **2.** (of certain reflex actions of a part of the body) responding to stimulation of another part. —**conˈsensually** *adv.*

consensus (kənˈsɛnsəs) *n.* general or widespread agreement (esp. in the phrase **consensus of opinion**). [C19: from Latin, from *consentīre* to feel together, agree; see CONSENT]

▷**Usage.** Since *consensus* refers to a collective opinion, the words *of opinion* in the phrase *consensus of opinion* are redundant and are therefore avoided in careful usage.

consensus sequence *n. Biochem.* a DNA sequence common to different organisms and having a similar function in each.

consent (kənˈsɛnt) *vb.* **1.** to give assent or permission (to do something); agree; accede. **2.** (*intr.*) *Obsolete.* to be in accord; agree in opinion, feelings, etc. ~*n.* **3.** acquiescence to or acceptance of something done or planned by another; permission. **4.** accordance or harmony in opinion; agreement (esp. in the phrase **with one consent**). **5. age of consent.** the lowest age at which the law recognizes the right of a person, esp. a girl, to consent to sexual intercourse. [C13: from Old French *consentir,* from Latin *consentīre* to feel together, agree, from *sentīre* to feel] —**conˈsenter** *n.* —**conˈsenting** *adj.*

consentaneous (ˌkɒnsɛnˈteɪnɪəs) *adj. Rare.* **1.** (foll. by *to*) accordant or consistent (with). **2.** done by general consent. [C17: from Latin *consentāneus,* from *consentīre* to CONSENT] —ˌ**consenˈtaneously** *adv.* —**consentaneity** (kənˌsɛntəˈniːɪtɪ) *or* ˌ**consenˈtaneousness** *n.*

consentient (kənˈsɛnʃənt) *adj.* being in agreement; united in opinion. —**conˈsentience** *n.*

consenting adult *n. Brit.* a male person over the age of twenty-one, who may legally engage in homosexual behaviour in private.

consequence (ˈkɒnsɪkwəns) *n.* **1.** a result or effect of some previous occurrence. **2.** an unpleasant result (esp. in the phrase **take the consequences**). **3.** significance or importance: *it's of no consequence; a man of consequence.* **4.** *Logic.* **a.** a conclusion reached by reasoning. **b.** the conclusion of an argument. **c.** the relations between the conclusion and the premises of a valid argument. **5.** the relation between an effect and its cause. **6. in consequence.** as a result.

consequences (ˈkɒnsɪkwənsɪz) *pl. n.* (*functioning as sing.*) *Brit.* a game in which each player writes down a part of a story, folds over the paper, and passes it on to another player who continues the story. After several stages, the resulting (nonsensical) stories are read out.

consequent (ˈkɒnsɪkwənt) *adj.* **1.** following as an effect or result. **2.** following as a logical conclusion or by rational argument. **3.** (of a river) flowing in the direction of the original slope of the land or dip of the strata. ~*n.* **4.** something that follows something else, esp. as a result. **5.** *Logic.* the resultant clause in a conditional sentence. **6. affirming the consequent.** *Logic.* the fallacy of inferring the antecedent of a conditional sentence, given the truth of the conditional and its consequent, as *if John is six feet tall, he's more than five feet: he's more than five feet so he's six feet.* **7.** an obsolete term for **denominator** (sense 1). [C15: from Latin *consequēns* following closely, from *consequī* to pursue]

▷**Usage.** See at **consequential.**

consequential (ˌkɒnsɪˈkwɛnʃəl) *adj.* **1.** important or significant. **2.** self-important; conceited. **3.** following as a consequence; resultant, esp. indirectly: *consequential loss.* —ˌ**conseˌquentiˈality** *or* ˌ**conseˈquentialness** *n.* —ˌ**conseˈquentially** *adv.*

▷**Usage.** Although both *consequential* and *consequent* can refer to that which follows as a result, *consequent* is more frequently used in this sense in modern English: *the new measures were put into effect, and the consequent protest led to the dismissal of those responsible.*

consequentialism (ˌkɒnsɪˈkwɛnʃəˌlɪzəm) *n. Ethics.* the doctrine that an action is right or wrong according as its consequences are good or bad.

consequently (ˈkɒnsɪkwəntlɪ) *adv., sentence connector.* as a result or effect; therefore; hence.

conservancy (kənˈsɜːvənsɪ) *n., pl.* **-cies. 1.** (in Britain) a court or commission with jurisdiction over a river, port, area of countryside, etc. **2.** another word for **conservation** (sense 2).

conservation (ˌkɒnsəˈveɪʃən) *n.* **1.** the act or an instance of conserving or keeping from change, loss, injury, etc. **2. a.** protection, preservation, and careful management of natural resources and of the environment. **b.** (*as modifier*): *a conservation area.* —ˌ**conserˈvational** *adj.*

conservationist (ˌkɒnsəˈveɪʃənɪst) *n.* a person who advocates or strongly promotes preservation and careful management of natural resources and of the environment.

conservation of charge *n.* the principle that the total charge of any isolated system is constant and independent of changes that take place within the system.

conservation of energy *n.* the principle that the total energy of any isolated system is constant and independent of any changes occurring within the system.

conservation of mass *n.* the principle that the total mass of any isolated system is constant and is independent of any chemical and physical changes taking place within the system.

conservation of momentum *n.* the principle that the total linear or angular momentum in any isolated system is constant, provided that no external force is applied.

conservation of parity *n.* the principle that the parity of the total wave function describing a system of elementary particles is conserved. In fact it is not conserved in weak interactions.

conservatism (kən'sɜːvəˌtɪzəm) *n.* **1.** opposition to change and innovation. **2.** a political philosophy advocating the preservation of the best of the established order in society and opposing radical change.

Conservatism (kən'sɜːvəˌtɪzəm) *n.* (in Britain, Canada, etc.) **1.** the form of conservatism advocated by the Conservative Party. **2.** the policies, doctrines, or practices of the Conservative Party.

conservative (kən'sɜːvətɪv) *adj.* **1.** favouring the preservation of established customs, values, etc., and opposing innovation. **2.** of, characteristic of, or relating to conservatism. **3.** tending to be moderate or cautious: *a conservative estimate.* **4.** conventional in style or type: *a conservative suit.* **5.** *Med.* (of treatment) designed to alleviate symptoms. Compare **radical** (sense 4). **6.** *Physics.* (of a field of force, system, etc.) doing work by moving an object or particle but being independent of the path along which the object or particle is displaced: *electrostatic fields of force are conservative.* ~*n.* **7.** a person who is reluctant to change or consider new ideas; conformist. **8.** a supporter or advocate of conservatism. ~*adj., n.* **9.** a less common word for **preservative.** —**con'servatively** *adv.* —**con'servativeness** *n.*

Conservative (kən'sɜːvətɪv) ~*adj.* **1.** (in Britain) of, supporting, or relating to the Conservative Party, the major right-wing party, which advocates a mixed economy and free enterprise. **2.** of, supporting, or relating to various right-wing political parties in other countries. ~*n.* **3.** a supporter or member of a Conservative Party.

Conservative Judaism *n.* a movement reacting against the radicalism of Reform Judaism, rejecting extreme change and advocating moderate relaxations of traditional Jewish law, by an extension of the process by which its adherents claim traditional orthodox Judaism evolved. Compare **Orthodox Judaism, Reform Judaism.**

conservatoire (kən'sɜːvəˌtwɑː) *n.* an institution or school for instruction in music. Also called: **conservatory.** [C18: from French: CONSERVATORY]

conservator ('kɒnsəˌveɪtə, kən'sɜːvə-) *n.* a person who conserves or keeps safe; custodian, guardian, or protector.

conservatorium (kənˌsɜːvə'tɔːrɪəm) *n. Austral.* the usual term for **conservatoire.**

conservatory (kən'sɜːvətrɪ) *n., pl.* **-tories. 1.** a greenhouse, esp. one attached to a house. **2.** another word for **conservatoire.** ~*adj.* **3.** preservative.

conserve *vb.* (kən'sɜːv). (*tr.*) **1.** to keep or protect from harm, decay, loss, etc. **2.** to preserve (a foodstuff, esp. fruit) with sugar. ~*n.* ('kɒnsɜːv, kən'sɜːv). **3.** a preparation of fruit in sugar, similar to jam but usually containing whole pieces of fruit. [(vb.) C14: from Latin *conservāre* to keep safe, from *servāre* to save, protect; (n.) C14: from Medieval Latin *conserva,* from Latin *conservāre*] —**con'servable** *adj.* —**con'server** *n.*

consider (kən'sɪdə) *vb.* (*mainly tr.*) **1.** (*also intr.*) to think carefully about or ponder on (a problem, decision, etc.); contemplate. **2.** (*may take a clause as object*) to judge, deem, or have as an opinion: *I consider him a fool.* **3.** to have regard for; respect: *consider your mother's feelings.* **4.** to look at; regard: *he considered her face.* **5.** (*may take a clause as object*) to bear in mind as possible or acceptable: *when buying a car consider this make.* **6.** to describe or discuss: *in this programme we consider the traffic problem.* **7.** (*may take a clause as object*) to keep in mind and make allowances (for): *consider his childhood.* [C14: from Latin *consīderāre* to inspect closely, literally: to observe the stars, from *sīdus* star] —**con'siderer** *n.*

considerable (kən'sɪdərəb[ə]l) *adj.* **1.** large enough to reckon with: *a considerable quantity.* **2.** a lot of; much: *he had considerable courage.* **3.** worthy of respect: *a considerable man in the scientific world.* —**con'siderably** *adv.*

considerate (kən'sɪdərɪt) *adj.* **1.** thoughtful towards other people; kind. **2.** *Rare.* carefully thought out; considered. —**con'siderately** *adv.* —**con'siderateness** *n.*

consideration (kənˌsɪdə'reɪʃən) *n.* **1.** the act or an instance of considering; deliberation; contemplation. **2. take into consideration.** to bear in mind; consider. **3. under consideration.** being currently discussed or deliberated. **4.** a fact or circumstance to be taken into account when making a judgment or decision. **5. on no consideration.** for no reason whatsoever; never. **6.** thoughtfulness for other people; kindness. **7.** payment for a service; recompense; fee. **8.** thought resulting from deliberation; opinion. **9.** *Law.* the promise, object, etc., given by one party to persuade another to enter into a contract. **10.** estimation; esteem. **11. in consideration of. a.** because of. **b.** in return for.

considered (kən'sɪdəd) *adj.* **1.** presented or thought out with care: *a considered opinion.* **2.** (*qualified by a preceding adverb*) esteemed: *highly considered.*

considering (kən'sɪdərɪŋ) *prep.* **1.** in view of. ~*adv.* **2.** *Informal.* all in all; taking into account the circumstances: *it's not bad considering.* ~*conj.* **3.** (*subordinating*) in view of the fact that.

consign (kən'saɪn) *vb.* (*mainly tr.*) **1.** to hand over or give into the care or charge of another; entrust. **2.** to commit irrevocably: *he consigned the papers to the flames.* **3.** to commit for admittance: *to consign someone to jail.* **4.** to address or deliver (goods) for sale, disposal, etc.: *it was consigned to his London address.* **5.** (*intr.*) *Obsolete.* to assent; agree. [C15: from Old French *consigner,* from Latin *consignāre* to put one's seal to, sign, from *signum* mark, SIGN] —**con'signable** *adj.* —**ˌconsign'ation** *n.*

consignee (ˌkɒnsaɪ'niː) *n.* a person, agent, organization, etc., to which merchandise is consigned.

consignment (kən'saɪnmənt) *n.* **1.** the act of consigning; commitment. **2.** a shipment of goods consigned. **3. on consignment.** for payment by the consignee after sale: *he made the last shipment on consignment.*

consignor (kən'saɪnə, ˌkɒnsaɪ'nɔː) *or* **consigner** (kən'saɪnə) *n.* a person, enterprise, etc., that consigns goods.

consist (kən'sɪst) *vb.* (*intr.*) **1.** (foll. by *of* or *in*) to be composed (of); be formed (of): *syrup consists of sugar and water.* **2.** (foll. by *in* or *of*) to have its existence (in); lie (in); be expressed (by): *his religion consists only in going to church.* **3.** to be compatible or consistent; accord. [C16: from Latin *consistere* to halt, stand firm, from *sistere* to stand, cause to stand; related to *stāre* to STAND]

consistency (kən'sɪstənsɪ) *or* **consistence** *n., pl.* **-encies** *or* **-ences. 1.** agreement or accordance with facts, form, or characteristics previously shown or stated. **2.** agreement or harmony between parts of something complex; compatibility. **3.** degree of viscosity or firmness. **4.** the state or quality of holding or sticking together and retaining shape. **5.** conformity with previous attitudes, behaviour, practice, etc.

consistent (kən'sɪstənt) *adj.* **1.** showing consistency; not self-contradictory. **2.** (*postpositive;* foll. by *with*) in agreement or harmony; accordant. **3.** steady; even: *consistent growth.* **4.** *Maths.* (of two or more equations) satisfied by at least one common set of values of the variables: $x + y = 4$ *and* $x - y = 2$ *are consistent.* **5.** *Logic.* **a.** (of a set of statements) capable of all being true at the same time or under the same interpretation. **b.** (of a formal system) not permitting the deduction of a contradiction from the axioms. Compare **complete** (sense 5). **6.** *Obsolete.* stuck together; cohering. —**con'sistently** *adv.*

consistory (kən'sɪstərɪ) *n., pl.* **-ries. 1.** *Church of England.* **a.** the court of a diocese (other than Canterbury) administering ecclesiastical law. **b.** the area in a church where the consistory meets. **2.** *R.C. Church.* an assembly of the cardinals and the pope. **3.** (in certain Reformed Churches) the governing body of a local congregation or church. **4.** *Archaic.* a council or assembly. [C14: from Old French *consistorie,* from Medieval Latin *consistōrium* ecclesiastical tribunal, ultimately from Latin *consistere* to stand still] —**consistorial** (ˌkɒnsɪ'stɔːrɪəl) *or* **ˌconsis'torian** *adj.*

consociate *vb.* (kən'səʊʃɪˌeɪt). **1.** to enter into or bring into friendly association. ~*adj.* (kən'səʊʃɪɪt, -ˌeɪt). **2.** associated or united. ~*n.* (kən'səʊʃɪɪt, -ˌeɪt). **3.** an associate or partner. [C16: from Latin *consociāre,* from *socius* partner] —**conˌsoci'ation** *n.*

consocies (kən'səʊʃiːz) *n., pl.* **-cies.** *Ecology.* a natural community with a single dominant species. [C20: from CONSOCIATE + SPECIES]

consolation (ˌkɒnsə'leɪʃən) *n.* **1.** the act of consoling or state of being consoled; solace. **2.** a person or thing that is a source of comfort in a time of suffering, grief, disappointment, etc. —**consolatory** (kən'sɒlətərɪ, -trɪ) *adj.*

consolation prize *n.* a prize given to console a loser of a game.

console[1] (kən'səʊl) *vb.* to serve as a source of comfort to (someone) in disappointment, loss, sadness, etc. [C17: from Latin *consōlārī,* from *sōlārī* to comfort; see SOLACE] —**con'solable** *adj.* —**con'soler** *n.* —**con'solingly** *adv.*

console[2] ('kɒnsəʊl) *n.* **1.** an ornamental bracket, esp. one used to support a wall fixture, bust, etc. **2.** the part of an organ comprising the manuals, pedals, stops, etc. **3.** a desk or table on which the controls of an electronic system are mounted. **4.** a cabinet for a television, gramophone, etc., designed to stand on the floor. **5.** See **console table.** [C18: from French, shortened from Old French *consolateur* one that provides support, hence, supporting bracket, from Latin *consōlātor* a comforter; see CONSOLE[1]]

console table ('kɒnsəʊl) *n.* a table with one or more curved legs of bracket-like construction, designed to stand against a wall.

consolidate (kən'sɒlɪˌdeɪt) *vb.* **1.** to form or cause to form into a solid mass or whole; unite or be united. **2.** to make or become stronger or more stable. **3.** *Military.* to strengthen or improve one's control over (a situation, force, newly captured area, etc.). [C16: from Latin *consolidare* to make firm, from *solidus* strong, SOLID] —**con'soliˌdator** *n.*

consolidated fund *n. Brit.* a fund into which tax revenue is paid in order to meet standing charges, esp. interest payments on the national debt.

consolidation (kənˌsɒlɪ'deɪʃən) *n.* **1.** the act of consolidating or state of being consolidated. **2.** something that is consolidated or integrated. **3.** *Law.* **a.** the combining of two or more actions at law. **b.** the combination of a number of Acts of Parliament into one codifying statute. **4.** *Geology.* the process, including compression and cementation, by which a loose deposit is transformed into a hard rock. **5.** *Psychol.* the process in the brain that makes the memory for an event enduring; the process is thought to continue for some time after the event. —**con'soliˌdative** *adj.*

consols ('kɒnsɒlz, kən'sɒlz) *pl. n.* irredeemable British government securities carrying annual interest rates of two and a half or four per cent. Also called: **bank annuities.** [short for *consolidated stock*]

consolute ('kɒnsəˌluːt) *adj.* **1.** (of two or more liquids) mutually soluble in all proportions. **2.** (of a substance) soluble in each of two conjugate liquids. **3.** of or concerned with the particular state in which two partially miscible liquids become totally miscible. [C20: from Late Latin *consolūtus,* from Latin *con-* together + *solvere* to dissolve]

consommé (kən'sɒmeɪ, 'kɒnsɒˌmeɪ; *French* kɔ̃sɔme) *n.* a clear soup made from meat or chicken stock. [C19: from French, from *consommer* to finish, use up, from Latin *consummāre;* so called because all the goodness of the meat goes into the liquid]

consonance ('kɒnsənəns) *or* **consonancy** *n., pl.* **-nances** *or* **-nancies. 1.** agreement, harmony, or accord. **2.** *Prosody.* similarity between consonants, but not between vowels, as between the *s* and *t* sounds in *sweet silent thought.* Compare **assonance** (sense 1). **3.** *Music.* **a.** an aesthetically pleasing sensation or perception associated with the interval of the octave, the perfect fourth and fifth, the major and minor third and sixth, and chords based on these intervals. Compare **dissonance** (sense 3). **b.** an interval or chord producing this sensation.

consonant ('kɒnsənənt) *n.* **1.** a speech sound or letter of the alphabet other than a vowel; a stop, fricative, or continuant. ~*adj.* **2.** (*postpositive;* foll. by *with* or *to*) consistent; in agreement. **3.** harmonious in tone or sound. **4.** *Music.* characterized by the presence of a consonance. **5.** being or relating to a consonant. [C14: from Latin *consonāns,* from *consonāre* to sound at the same time, be in harmony, from *sonāre* to sound] —**'consonantly** *adv.*

consonantal (ˌkɒnsə'næntᵊl) *adj.* **1.** relating to, functioning as, or constituting a consonant, such as the semivowel *w* in English *work.* **2.** consisting of or characterized by consonants: *a consonantal cluster.* —ˌ**conso'nantally** *adv.*

con sordino *adv. Music.* See **sordino** (sense 3).

consort *vb.* (kən'sɔːt). **1.** (*intr.;* usually foll. by *with*) to keep company (with undesirable people); associate. **2.** (*intr.*) to agree or harmonize. **3.** (*tr.*) *Rare.* to combine or unite. ~*n.* ('kɒnsɔːt). **4.** (esp. formerly) **a.** a small group of instruments, either of the same type, such as viols, (a **whole consort**) or of different types (a **broken consort**). **b.** (*as modifier*): *consort music.* **5.** the husband or wife of a reigning monarch. **6.** a partner or companion, esp. a husband or wife. **7.** a ship that escorts another. **8.** *Obsolete.* **a.** companionship or association. **b.** agreement or accord. [C15: from Old French, from Latin *consors* sharer, partner, from *sors* lot, fate, portion] —**con'sortable** *adj.* —**con'sorter** *n.*

consortium (kən'sɔːtɪəm) *n., pl.* **-tia** (-tɪə). **1.** an association of financiers, companies, etc., esp. one formed for a particular purpose. **2.** *Law.* the right of husband or wife to the company, assistance, and affection of the other. [C19: from Latin: community of goods, partnership; see CONSORT] —**con'sortial** *adj.*

conspecific (ˌkɒnspɪ'sɪfɪk) *adj.* (of animals or plants) belonging to the same species.

conspectus (kən'spɛktəs) *n.* **1.** an overall view; survey. **2.** a summary; résumé. [C19: from Latin: a viewing, from *conspicere* to observe, from *specere* to look]

conspicuous (kən'spɪkjʊəs) *adj.* **1.** clearly visible; obvious or showy. **2.** attracting attention because of a striking quality or feature: *conspicuous stupidity.* [C16: from Latin *conspicuus,* from *conspicere* to perceive; see CONSPECTUS] —**con'spicuously** *adv.* —**con'spicuousness** *n.*

conspicuous consumption *n.* spending in a lavish or ostentatious way, esp. to impress others with one's wealth.

conspiracy (kən'spɪrəsɪ) *n., pl.* **-cies. 1.** a secret plan or agreement to carry out an illegal or harmful act, esp. with political motivation; plot. **2.** the act of making such plans in secret. —**con'spirator** *n.* —**conspiratorial** (kənˌspɪrə'tɔːrɪəl) *or* **con'spiratory** *adj.* —**conˌspira'torially** *adv.*

conspire (kən'spaɪə) *vb.* (when *intr.,* sometimes foll. by *against*) **1.** to plan or agree on (a crime or harmful act) together in secret. **2.** (*intr.*) to act together towards some end as if by design: *the elements conspired to spoil our picnic.* [C14: from Old French *conspirer,* from Latin *conspīrāre* to plot together, literally: to breathe together, from *spīrāre* to breathe] —**con'spirer** *n.* —**con'spiringly** *adv.*

con spirito (kɒn 'spɪrɪtəʊ) *adj., adv. Music.* (to be performed) in a spirited or lively manner (also in the phrases **allegro con spirito, presto con spirito**). [Italian: with spirit]

const. *abbrev. for:* **1.** constant. **2.** constitution.

constable ('kʌnstəbᵊl, 'kɒn-) *n.* **1.** (in Britain, Australia, Canada, New Zealand, etc.) a police officer of the lowest rank. **2.** any of various officers of the peace, esp. one who arrests offenders, serves writs, etc. **3.** the keeper or governor of a royal castle or fortress. **4.** (in medieval Europe) the chief military officer and functionary of a royal household, esp. in France and England. **5.** an officer of a hundred in medieval England, originally responsible for raising the military levy but later assigned other administrative duties. [C13: from Old French, from Late Latin *comes stabulī* officer in charge of the stable, from Latin *comes* comrade + *stabulum* dwelling, stable; see also COUNT^2] —**'constableˌship** *n.*

constabulary (kən'stæbjʊlərɪ) *Chiefly Brit.* ~*n., pl.* **-laries. 1.** the police force of a town or district. ~*adj.* **2.** of or relating to constables, constabularies, or their duties.

constancy ('kɒnstənsɪ) *n.* **1.** the quality of having a resolute mind, purpose, or affection; steadfastness. **2.** freedom from change or variation; stability. **3.** *Psychol.* the perceptual phenomenon in which attributes of an object appear to remain the same in a variety of different presentations, e.g., a given object looks roughly the same size regardless of its distance from the observer. **4.** *Ecology.* the frequency of occurrence of a particular species in sample plots from a plant community.

constant ('kɒnstənt) *adj.* **1.** fixed and invariable; unchanging. **2.** continual or continuous; incessant: *constant interruptions.* **3.** resolute in mind, purpose, or affection; loyal. ~*n.* **4.** something that is permanent or unchanging. **5.** a specific quantity that is always invariable: *the velocity of light is a constant.* **6. a.** *Maths.* a symbol representing an unspecified number that remains invariable throughout a particular series of operations. **b.** *Physics.* a theoretical or experimental quantity or property that is considered invariable throughout a particular series of calculations or experiments. **7.** See **logical constant.** [C14: from Old French, from Latin *constāns* standing firm, from *constāre* to be steadfast, from *stāre* to stand] —**'constantly** *adv.*

constantan ('kɒnstənˌtæn) *n.* an alloy of copper (60 per cent) and nickel (40 per cent). It has a high resistivity that does not vary significantly with temperature and is used in resistors and, with copper, in thermocouples. [C20: formed from CONSTANT]

Constantia (kɒn'stænʃə) *n.* any of several red or white wines produced around Constantia, a district of the Cape Peninsula of South Africa.

constatation (ˌkɒnstə'teɪʃən) *n.* **1.** the process of verification. **2.** a statement or assertion. [C20: from French, from *constater* to verify, from Latin *constat* it is certain; see CONSTANT]

constellate ('kɒnstɪˌleɪt) *vb.* to form into clusters in or as if in constellations.

constellation (ˌkɒnstɪ'leɪʃən) *n.* **1. a.** any of the 88 groups of stars as seen from the earth and the solar system, many of which were named by the ancient Greeks after animals, objects, or mythological persons. **b.** an area on the celestial sphere containing such a group. **2.** a gathering of brilliant or famous people or things. **3.** *Psychoanal.* a group of ideas felt to be related. [C14: from Late Latin *constellātiō,* from Latin *com-* together + *stella* star] —ˌ**constel'lational** *adj.* —**constellatory** (kən'stɛlətərɪ, -trɪ) *adj.*

consternate ('kɒnstəˌneɪt) *vb.* (*tr.; usually passive*) to fill with anxiety, dismay, dread, or confusion. [C17: from Latin *consternāre,* from *sternere* to lay low, spread out]

consternation (ˌkɒnstə'neɪʃən) *n.* a feeling of anxiety, dismay, dread, or confusion.

constipate ('kɒnstɪˌpeɪt) *vb.* (*tr.*) to cause constipation in. [C16: from Latin *constīpāre* to press closely together, from *stīpāre* to crowd together] —**'constiˌpated** *adj.*

constipation (ˌkɒnstɪ'peɪʃən) *n.* infrequent or difficult evacuation of the bowels, with hard faeces, caused by functional or organic disorders or improper diet.

constituency (kən'stɪtjʊənsɪ) *n., pl.* **-cies. 1.** the whole body of voters who elect one representative to a legislature or all the residents represented by one deputy. **2. a.** a district that sends one representative to a legislature. **b.** (*as modifier*): *constituency organization.*

constituent (kən'stɪtjʊənt) *adj.* (*prenominal*) **1.** forming part of a whole; component. **2.** having the power to frame a constitution or to constitute a government (esp. in the phrases **constituent assembly, constituent power**). **3.** *Becoming rare.* electing or having the power to elect. ~*n.* **4.** a component part; ingredient. **5.** a resident of a constituency, esp. one entitled to vote. **6.** *Chiefly law.* a person who appoints another to act for him, as by power of attorney. **7.** *Linguistics.* a word, phrase, or clause forming a part of a larger construction. Compare **immediate constituent, ultimate constituent.** [C17: from Latin *constituēns* setting up, from *constituere* to establish, CONSTITUTE] —**con'stituently** *adv.*

constitute ('kɒnstɪˌtjuːt) *vb.* (*tr.*) **1.** to make up; form; compose: *the people who constitute a jury.* **2.** to appoint to an office or function: *a legally constituted officer.* **3.** to set up (a school or other institution) formally; found. **4.** *Law.* to give legal form to (a court, assembly, etc.). **5.** *Law, obsolete.* to set up or enact (a law). [C15: from Latin *constituere,* from *com-* (intensive) + *statuere* to place] —**'constiˌtuter** *or* **'constiˌtutor** *n.*

constitution (ˌkɒnstɪ'tjuːʃən) *n.* **1.** the act of constituting or state of being constituted. **2.** the way in which a thing is composed; physical make-up; structure. **3.** the fundamental political principles on which a state is governed, esp. when considered as embodying the rights of the subjects of that state. **4.** (*often cap.*) (in certain countries, esp. Australia and the U.S.) a statute embodying such principles. **5.** a person's state of health. **6.** a person's disposition of mind; temperament.

constitutional (ˌkɒnstɪ'tjuːʃənᵊl) *adj.* **1.** denoting, characteristic of, or relating to a constitution. **2.** authorized by or subject to a constitution. **3.** of or inherent in the physical make-up or basic nature of a person or thing: *a constitutional weakness.* **4.** beneficial to one's physical wellbeing. ~*n.* **5.** a regular walk taken for the benefit of one's health. —ˌ**consti'tutionally** *adv.*

constitutionalism (ˌkɒnstɪˈtjuːʃənəˌlɪzəm) *n.* **1.** the principles, spirit, or system of government in accord with a constitution, esp. a written constitution. **2.** adherence to or advocacy of such a system or such principles. —ˌ**constiˈtutionalist** *n.*
constitutionality (ˌkɒnstɪˌtjuːʃəˈnælɪtɪ) *n.* the quality or state of being in accord with a constitution.
constitutional monarchy *n.* a monarchy governed according to a constitution that limits and defines the powers of the sovereign. Also called: **limited monarchy.**
constitutional psychology *n.* a school of thought postulating that the personality of an individual is dependent on the type of his physique (somatotype).
constitutional strike *n.* a stoppage of work by the workforce of an organization, with the approval of the trade union concerned, in accordance with the dispute procedure laid down in a collective agreement between the parties.
constitutive (ˈkɒnstɪˌtjuːtɪv) *adj.* **1.** having power to enact, appoint, or establish. **2.** *Chem.* (of a physical property) determined by the arrangement of atoms in a molecule rather than by their nature. **3.** *Biochem.* (of an enzyme) formed continuously, irrespective of the cell's needs. **4.** another word for **constituent** (sense 1). —ˈ**constiˌtutively** *adv.*
constr. *abbrev. for* construction.
constrain (kənˈstreɪn) *vb.* (*tr.*) **1.** to compel or force, esp. by persuasion, circumstances, etc.; oblige. **2.** to restrain by or as if by force; confine. [C14: from Old French *constreindre,* from Latin *constringere* to bind together, from *stringere* to bind] —**conˈstrainer** *n.*
constrained (kənˈstreɪnd) *adj.* embarrassed, unnatural, or forced: *a constrained smile.* —**constrainedly** (kənˈstreɪnɪdlɪ) *adv.*
constraint (kənˈstreɪnt) *n.* **1.** compulsion, force, or restraint. **2.** repression or control of natural feelings or impulses. **3.** a forced unnatural manner; inhibition. **4.** something that serves to constrain; restrictive condition: *social constraints kept him silent.* **5.** *Linguistics.* any very general restriction on a sentence formation rule.
constrict (kənˈstrɪkt) *vb.* (*tr.*) **1.** to make smaller or narrower, esp. by contracting at one place. **2.** to hold in or inhibit; limit. [C18: from Latin *constrictus* compressed, from *constringere* to tie up together; see CONSTRAIN]
constriction (kənˈstrɪkʃən) *n.* **1.** a feeling of tightness in some part of the body, such as the chest. **2.** the act of constricting or condition of being constricted. **3.** something that is constricted. **4.** *Genetics.* a localized narrow region of a chromosome, esp. at the centromere. —**conˈstrictive** *adj.* —**conˈstrictively** *adv.* —**conˈstrictiveness** *n.*
constrictor (kənˈstrɪktə) *n.* **1.** any of various very large nonvenomous snakes, such as the pythons, boas, and anaconda, that coil around and squeeze their prey to kill it. **2.** any muscle that constricts or narrows a canal or passage; sphincter. **3.** a person or thing that constricts.
constringe (kənˈstrɪndʒ) *vb.* (*tr.*) *Rare.* to shrink or contract. [C17: from Latin *constringere* to bind together; see CONSTRAIN] —**conˈstringency** *n.* —**conˈstringent** *adj.*
constringence (kənˈstrɪndʒəns) *n. Physics.* inverse of the dispersive power of a medium.
construct *vb.* (kənˈstrʌkt). (*tr.*) **1.** to put together substances or parts, esp. systematically, in order to make or build (a building, bridge, etc.); assemble. **2.** to compose or frame mentally (an argument, sentence, etc.). **3.** *Geometry.* to draw (a line, angle, or figure) so that certain requirements are satisfied. ~*n.* (ˈkɒnstrʌkt). **4.** something formulated or built systematically. **5.** a complex idea resulting from a synthesis of simpler ideas. **6.** *Psychol.* a model devised on the basis of observation, designed to relate what is observed to some theoretical framework. [C17: from Latin *constructus* piled up, from *construere* to heap together, build, from *struere* to arrange, erect] —**conˈstructible** *adj.* —**conˈstructor** *or* **conˈstructer** *n.*
construction (kənˈstrʌkʃən) *n.* **1.** the process or act of constructing or manner in which a thing is constructed. **2.** the thing constructed; a structure. **3. a.** the business or work of building dwellings, offices, etc. **b.** (*as modifier*): *a construction site.* **4.** an interpretation or explanation of a law, text, action, etc.: *they put a sympathetic construction on her behaviour.* **5.** *Grammar.* a group of words that together make up one of the constituents into which a sentence may be analysed; a phrase or clause. **6.** *Geometry.* a drawing of a line, angle, or figure satisfying certain conditions, used in solving a problem or proving a theorem. **7.** an abstract work of art in three dimensions or relief. See also **constructivism** (sense 1). —**conˈstructional** *adj.* —**conˈstructionally** *adv.*
constructionist (kənˈstrʌkʃənɪst) *n. U.S.* a person who interprets constitutional law in a certain way, esp. strictly.
constructive (kənˈstrʌktɪv) *adj.* **1.** serving to build or improve; positive: *constructive criticism.* **2.** *Law.* deduced by inference or construction; not expressed but inferred. **3.** *Law.* having an implied legal effect: *constructive notice.* **4.** another word for **structural.** —**conˈstructively** *adv.* —**conˈstructiveness** *n.*
constructive dismissal *n.* a course of action taken by an employer that is detrimental to an employee and designed to leave the employee with no option but to resign.
constructivism (kənˈstrʌktɪˌvɪzəm) *n.* **1.** a movement in abstract art evolved in Russia after World War I, which explored the use of movement and machine-age materials in sculpture and had considerable influence on modern art and architecture. **2.** *Philosophy.* the theory that mathematical entities do not exist independently of our construction of them. Compare **intuitionism** (sense 4), **finitism.** —**conˈstructivist** *adj., n.*
construe (kənˈstruː) *vb.* **-strues, -struing, -strued.** (*mainly tr.*) **1.** to interpret the meaning of (something): *you can construe that in different ways.* **2.** (*may take a clause as object*) to discover by inference; deduce. **3.** to analyse the grammatical structure of; parse (esp. a Latin or Greek text as a preliminary to translation). **4.** to combine (words) syntactically. **5.** (*also intr.*) *Old-fashioned.* to translate literally, esp. aloud as an academic exercise. ~*n.* **6.** *Old-fashioned.* something that is construed, such as a piece of translation. [C14: from Latin *construere* to pile up; see CONSTRUCT] —**conˈstruable** *adj.* —**conˌstruaˈbility** *n.* —**conˈstruer** *n.*
consubstantial (ˌkɒnsəbˈstænʃəl) *adj. Christian theol.* (esp. of the three persons of the Trinity) regarded as identical in substance or essence though different in aspect. [C15: from Church Latin *consubstāntiālis,* from Latin COM- + *substantia* SUBSTANCE] —ˌ**consubˌstantiˈality** *n.* —ˌ**consubˈstantially** *adv.*
consubstantiate (ˌkɒnsəbˈstænʃɪˌeɪt) *vb.* (*intr.*) *Christian theol.* (of the Eucharistic bread and wine and Christ's body and blood) to undergo consubstantiation.
consubstantiation (ˌkɒnsəbˌstænʃɪˈeɪʃən) *n. Christian theol.* (in the belief of High-Church Anglicans) **1.** the doctrine that after the consecration of the Eucharist the substance of the body and blood of Christ coexists within the substance of the consecrated bread and wine. **2.** the mystical process by which this is believed to take place during consecration. ~Compare **transubstantiation.**
consuetude (ˈkɒnswɪˌtjuːd) *n.* an established custom or usage, esp. one having legal force. [C14: from Latin *consuētūdō,* from *consuēscere* to accustom, from CON- + *suēscere* to be wont] —ˌ**consueˈtudinary** *adj.*
consul (ˈkɒnsᵊl) *n.* **1.** an official appointed by a sovereign state to protect its commercial interests and aid its citizens in a foreign city. **2.** (in ancient Rome) either of two annually elected magistrates who jointly exercised the highest authority in the republic. **3.** (in France from 1799 to 1804) any of the three chief magistrates of the First Republic. [C14: from Latin, from *consulere* to CONSULT] —**consular** (ˈkɒnsjʊlə) *adj.* —ˈ**consulˌship** *n.*
consular agent *n.* a consul of one of the lower grades.
consulate (ˈkɒnsjʊlɪt) *n.* **1.** the business premises or residence of a consul. **2.** government by consuls. **3.** the office or period of office of a consul or consuls. **4.** (*often cap.*) **a.** the government of France by the three consuls from 1799 to 1804. **b.** this period of French history. **5.** (*often cap.*) **a.** the consular government of the Roman republic. **b.** the office or rank of a Roman consul.
consul general *n., pl.* **consuls general.** a consul of the highest grade, usually stationed in a city of considerable commercial importance.
consult (kənˈsʌlt) *vb.* **1.** (when *intr.,* often foll. by *with*) to ask advice from (someone); confer with (someone). **2.** (*tr.*) to refer to for information: *to consult a map.* **3.** (*tr.*) to have regard for (a person's feelings, interests, etc.) in making decisions or plans; consider. **4.** (*intr.*) to make oneself available to give professional advice, esp. at scheduled times and for a fee. [C17: from French *consulter,* from Latin *consultāre* to reflect, take counsel, from *consulere* to consult] —**conˈsultable** *adj.* —**conˈsulter** *or* **conˈsultor** *n.*
consultant (kənˈsʌltᵊnt) *n.* **1. a.** a physician, esp. a specialist, who is asked to confirm a diagnosis. **b.** a physician or surgeon holding the highest appointment in a particular branch of medicine or surgery in a hospital. **2.** a specialist who gives expert advice or information. **3.** a person who asks advice in a consultation. —**conˈsultancy** *n.*
consultation (ˌkɒnsᵊlˈteɪʃən) *n.* **1.** the act or procedure of consulting. **2.** a conference for discussion or the seeking of advice, esp. from doctors or lawyers.
consultative (kənˈsʌltətɪv), **consultatory** (kənˈsʌltətərɪ, -trɪ), *or* **consultive** *adj.* available for, relating to, or involving consultation; advisory. —**conˈsultatively** *adv.*
consulting (kənˈsʌltɪŋ) *adj.* (*prenominal*) acting in an advisory capacity on professional matters: *a consulting engineer.*
consulting room *n.* a room in which a doctor, esp. a general practitioner, sees his patients.
consumable (kənˈsjuːməbᵊl) *adj.* **1.** capable of being consumed. ~*n.* **2.** (*usually pl.*) goods intended to be bought and used; consumer goods.
consume (kənˈsjuːm) *vb.* **1.** (*tr.*) to eat or drink. **2.** (*tr.; often passive*) to engross or obsess. **3.** (*tr.*) to use up; expend: *my car consumes little oil.* **4.** to destroy or be destroyed by burning, decomposition, etc.: *fire consumed the forest.* **5.** (*tr.*) to waste or squander: *the time consumed on that project was excessive.* **6.** (*passive*) to waste away. [C14: from Latin *consūmere* to devour, from *com-* (intensive) + *sūmere* to take up, from *emere* to take, purchase] —**conˈsuming** *adj.* —**conˈsumingly** *adv.*
consumedly (kənˈsjuːmɪdlɪ) *adv. Old-fashioned.* (intensifier): *a consumedly fascinating performance.*

consumer (kən'sjuːmə) *n.* **1.** a person who purchases goods and services for his own personal needs. Compare **producer** (sense 5). **2.** a person or thing that consumes. **3.** (*usually pl.*) *Ecology.* an organism, esp. an animal, within a community that feeds upon plants or other animals. See also **decomposer, producer** (sense 7).

consumer durable *n.* a manufactured product that has a relatively long useful life, such as a car or a television.

consumer goods *pl. n.* goods that satisfy personal needs rather than those required for the production of other goods or services. Compare **capital goods.**

consumerism (kən'sjuːmə,rɪzəm) *n.* **1.** protection of the interests of consumers. **2.** advocacy of a high rate of consumption and spending as a basis for a sound economy. —**con'sumerist** *n., adj.*

consummate *vb.* ('kɒnsə,meɪt). **1.** (*tr.*) to bring to completion or perfection; fulfil. **2.** (*tr.*) to complete (a marriage) legally by sexual intercourse. ~*adj.* (kən'sʌmɪt, 'kɒnsəmɪt). **3.** accomplished or supremely skilled: *a consummate artist.* **4.** (*prenominal*) (intensifier): *a consummate fool.* [C15: from Latin *consummāre* to complete, from *summus* highest, utmost] —**con'summately** *adv.* —,**consum'mation** *n.* —'**consum,mative** *or* **con'summatory** *adj.* —'**consum,mator** *n.*

consummatory behaviour (kən'sʌmətərɪ) *n. Psychol.* any behaviour that leads directly to the satisfaction of an innate drive, e.g. eating or drinking.

consumption (kən'sʌmpʃən) *n.* **1.** the act of consuming or the state of being consumed, esp. by eating, burning, etc. **2.** *Economics.* expenditure on goods and services for final personal use. **3.** the quantity consumed. **4.** *Pathol.* a condition characterized by a wasting away of the tissues of the body, esp. as seen in tuberculosis of the lungs. [C14: from Latin *consumptiō* a wasting, from *consūmere* to CONSUME]

consumptive (kən'sʌmptɪv) *adj.* **1.** causing consumption; wasteful; destructive. **2.** *Pathol.* relating to or affected with consumption, esp. tuberculosis of the lungs. ~*n.* **3.** *Pathol.* a person who suffers from consumption. —**con'sumptively** *adv.* —**con'sumptiveness** *n.*

cont. *abbrev. for:* **1.** containing. **2.** contents. **3.** continent(al). **4.** continued.

contact *n.* ('kɒntækt). **1.** the act or state of touching physically. **2.** the state or fact of close association or communication (esp. in the phrases **in contact, make contact**). **3. a.** a junction of two or more electrical conductors. **b.** the part of the conductors that makes the junction. **c.** the part of an electrical device to which such connections are made. **4.** an acquaintance, esp. one who might be useful in business, as a means of introduction, etc. **5.** any person who has been exposed to a contagious disease. **6.** *Photog.* See **contact print.** **7.** (*usually pl.*) an informal name for **contact lens.** **8.** (*modifier*) of or relating to irritation or inflammation of the skin caused by touching the causative agent: *contact dermatitis.* **9.** (*modifier*) denoting an insecticide or herbicide that kills on contact, rather than after ingestion or absorption. **10.** (*modifier*) of or maintaining contact. **11.** (*modifier*) requiring or involving (physical) contact: *the contact sport of boxing.* ~*vb.* ('kɒntækt, kən'tækt). **12.** (when *intr.*, often foll. by *with*) to put, come, or be in association, touch, or communication. ~*interj.* **13.** *Aeronautics.* (formerly) a call made by the pilot to indicate that an aircraft's ignition is switched on and that the engine is ready for starting by swinging the propeller. [C17: from Latin *contactus,* from *contingere* to touch on all sides, pollute, from *tangere* to touch] —**contactual** (kɒn'tæktjʊəl) *adj.* —**con'tactually** *adv.*

contactable (kɒn'tæktəbᵊl) *adj.* able to be communicated with: *the manager is not contactable at the moment.*

contact flight *n.* **1.** a flight in which the pilot remains in sight of land or water. **2.** air navigation by observation of prominent landmarks, beacons, etc.

contact lens *n.* a thin convex lens, usually of plastic, placed directly on the surface of the eye to correct defects of vision.

contact man *n.* an intermediary or go-between.

contactor (kɒn'tæktə) *n.* a type of switch for repeatedly opening and closing an electric circuit. Its operation can be mechanical, electromagnetic, or pneumatic.

contact print *n.* a photographic print made by exposing the printing paper through a negative placed directly onto it.

contagion (kən'teɪdʒən) *n.* **1.** the transmission of disease from one person to another by direct or indirect contact. **2.** a contagious disease. **3.** another name for **contagium.** **4.** a corrupting or harmful influence that tends to spread; pollutant. **5.** the spreading of an emotional or mental state among a number of people: *the contagion of mirth.* [C14: from Latin *contāgiō* a touching, infection, from *contingere*; see CONTACT]

contagious (kən'teɪdʒəs) *adj.* **1.** (of a disease) capable of being passed on by direct contact with a diseased individual or by handling clothing, etc., contaminated with the causative agent. Compare **infectious.** **2.** (of an organism) harbouring or spreading the causative agent of a transmissible disease. **3.** causing or likely to cause the same reaction or emotion in several people; catching; infectious: *her laughter was contagious.* —**con'tagiously** *adv.* —**con'tagiousness** *n.*

contagious abortion *n.* another name for **brucellosis.**

contagium (kən'teɪdʒɪəm) *n., pl.* **-gia** (-dʒɪə). *Pathol.* the specific virus or other direct cause of any infectious disease. [C17: from Latin, variant of *contāgiō* CONTAGION]

contain (kən'teɪn) *vb.* (*tr.*) **1.** to hold or be capable of holding or including within a fixed limit or area: *this contains five pints.* **2.** to keep (one's feelings, behaviour, etc.) within bounds; restrain. **3.** to consist of; comprise: *the book contains three different sections.* **4.** *Military.* to prevent (enemy forces) from operating beyond a certain level or area. **5.** to be a multiple of, leaving no remainder: *6 contains 2 and 3.* [C13: from Old French *contenir,* from Latin *continēre,* from *com-* together + *tenēre* to hold] —**con'tainable** *adj.*

container (kən'teɪnə) *n.* **1.** an object used for or capable of holding, esp. for transport or storage, such as a carton, box, etc. **2. a.** a large cargo-carrying standard-sized container that can be loaded from one mode of transport to another. **b.** (*as modifier*): *a container port; a container ship.*

containerize *or* **containerise** (kən'teɪnə,raɪz) *vb.* (*tr.*) **1.** to convey (cargo) in standard-sized containers. **2.** to adapt (a port or transportation system) to the use of standard-sized containers. —**con,taineri'zation** *or* **con,taineri'sation** *n.*

containment (kən'teɪnmənt) *n.* **1.** the act or condition of containing, esp. of restraining the ideological or political power of a hostile country or the operations of a hostile military force. **2.** (from 1947 to the mid-1970s) a principle of U.S. foreign policy that seeks to prevent the expansion of Communist power. **3.** Also called: **confinement.** *Physics.* the process of preventing the plasma in a controlled thermonuclear reaction from reaching the walls of the reaction vessel, usually by confining it within a configuration of magnetic fields. See **magnetic bottle.**

contaminate *vb.* (kən'tæmɪ,neɪt). (*tr.*) **1.** to make impure, esp. by touching or mixing; pollute. **2.** to make radioactive by the addition of radioactive material. ~*adj.* (kən'tæmɪnɪt, -,neɪt). **3.** *Archaic.* contaminated. [C15: from Latin *contamināre* to defile; related to Latin *contingere* to touch] —**con'taminable** *adj.* —**con'taminant** *n.* —**con'taminative** *adj.* —**con'tami,nator** *n.*

contamination (kən,tæmɪ'neɪʃən) *n.* **1.** the act or process of contaminating or the state of being contaminated. **2.** something that contaminates. **3.** *Linguistics.* the process by which one word or phrase is altered because of mistaken associations with another word or phrase; for example, the substitution of *irregardless* for *regardless* by association with such words as *irrespective.*

contango (kən'tæŋgəʊ) *n., pl.* **-gos.** **1.** (formerly, on the London Stock Exchange) postponement of payment for and delivery of stock from one account day to the next. **2.** the fee paid for such a postponement. ~Also called: **carry-over, continuation.** Compare **backwardation.** ~*vb.* **-goes, -going, -goed.** (*tr.*) **3.** to arrange such a postponement of payment (for): *my brokers will contango these shares.* [C19: apparently an arbitrary coinage based on CONTINUE]

contd *abbrev. for* continued.

conte *French.* (kɔ̃t) *n.* a tale or short story, esp. of adventure.

conté ('kɒnteɪ; *French* kɔ̃te) *n.* a hard crayon used by artists, etc., made of clay and graphite and often coloured a reddish-brown. Also called: **conté-crayon.** [C19: named after N.J. *Conté,* 18th-century French chemist]

contemn (kən'tɛm) *vb.* (*tr.*) *Formal.* to treat or regard with contempt; scorn. [C15: from Latin *contemnere,* from *temnere* to slight] —**contemner** (kən'tɛmnə, -'tɛmə) *n.* —**contemnible** (kən'tɛmnɪbᵊl) *adj.* —**con'temnibly** *adv.*

contemp. *abbrev. for* contemporary.

contemplate ('kɒntɛm,pleɪt, -təm-) *vb.* (*mainly tr.*) **1.** to think about intently and at length; consider calmly. **2.** (*intr.*) to think intently and at length, esp. for spiritual reasons; meditate. **3.** to look at thoughtfully; observe pensively. **4.** to have in mind as a possibility: *to contemplate changing jobs.* [C16: from Latin *contemplāre,* from *templum* TEMPLE[1]] —'**contem,plator** *n.*

contemplation (,kɒntɛm'pleɪʃən, -təm-) *n.* **1.** thoughtful or long consideration or observation. **2.** spiritual meditation esp. (in Christian religious practice) concentration of the mind and soul upon God. Compare **meditation.** **3.** purpose or intention.

contemplative ('kɒntɛm,pleɪtɪv, -təm-; kən'tɛmplə-) *adj.* **1.** denoting, concerned with, or inclined to contemplation; meditative. ~*n.* **2.** a person dedicated to religious contemplation or to a way of life conducive to this. —'**contem,platively** *adv.* —'**contem,plativeness** *n.*

contemporaneous (kən,tɛmpə'reɪnɪəs) *adj.* existing, beginning, or occurring in the same period of time. —**contemporaneity** (kən,tɛmpərə'niːɪtɪ) *or* **con,tempo'raneousness** *n.* —**con,tempo'raneously** *adv.*

contemporary (kən'tɛmprərɪ) *adj.* **1.** belonging to the same age; living or occurring in the same period of time. **2.** existing or occurring at the present time. **3.** conforming to modern or current ideas in style, fashion, design, etc. **4.** having approximately the same age as one another. ~*n., pl.* **-raries.** **5.** a person living at the same time or of approximately the same age as another. **6.** something that is contemporary. **7.** *Journalism.* a rival newspaper. [C17: from Medieval Latin *contemporārius,* from Latin *com-* together + *temporārius* relating to time, from *tempus* time] —**con'temporarily** *adv.* —**con'temporariness** *n.*

▷**Usage.** *Contemporary* is most acceptable when used to mean of the same period, in a sentence like *it is useful to compare Shakespeare's plays with those of contemporary* (that is, other Elizabethan) *playwrights.* The word is, however, often used to mean modern or up-to-date in contexts such as *the furniture was of a contemporary design.* The second use should be avoided where ambiguity is likely to arise, as in *a production of* Othello *in contemporary dress. Modern dress* or *Elizabethan dress* should be used in such contexts to avoid ambiguity.

contemporize *or* **contemporise** (kənˈtɛmpəˌraɪz) *vb.* to be or make contemporary; synchronize.

contempt (kənˈtɛmpt) *n.* **1.** the attitude or feeling of a person towards a person or thing that he considers worthless or despicable; scorn. **2.** the state of being scorned; disgrace (esp. in the phrase **hold in contempt**). **3.** wilful disregard of or disrespect for the authority of a court of law or legislative body: *contempt of court.* [C14: from Latin *contemptus* a despising, from *contemnere* to CONTEMN]

contemptible (kənˈtɛmptəbᵊl) *adj.* deserving or worthy of contempt; despicable. —**conˌtemptiˈbility** *or* **conˈtemptibleness** *n.* —**conˈtemptibly** *adv.*

contemptuous (kənˈtɛmptjʊəs) *adj.* (when *predicative,* often foll. by *of*) showing or feeling contempt; disdainful. —**conˈtemptuously** *adv.* —**conˈtemptuousness** *n.*

contend (kənˈtɛnd) *vb.* **1.** (*intr.;* often foll. by *with*) to struggle in rivalry, battle, etc.; vie. **2.** to argue earnestly; debate. **3.** (*tr.; may take a clause as object*) to assert or maintain. [C15: from Latin *contendere* to strive, from *com-* with + *tendere* to stretch, aim] —**conˈtender** *n.* —**conˈtendingly** *adv.*

content[1] (ˈkɒntɛnt) *n.* **1.** (*often pl.*) everything that is inside a container: *the contents of a box.* **2.** (*usually pl.*) **a.** the chapters or divisions of a book. **b.** a list, printed at the front of a book, of chapters or divisions together with the number of the first page of each. **3.** the meaning or significance of a poem, painting, or other work of art, as distinguished from its style or form. **4.** all that is contained or dealt with in a discussion, piece of writing, etc.; substance. **5.** the capacity or size of a thing. **6.** the proportion of a substance contained in an alloy, mixture, etc.: *the lead content of petrol.* [C15: from Latin *contentus* contained, from *continēre* to CONTAIN]

content[2] (kənˈtɛnt) *adj.* (*postpositive*) **1.** mentally or emotionally satisfied with things as they are. **2.** assenting to or willing to accept circumstances, a proposed course of action, etc. ~*vb.* **3.** (*tr.*) to make (oneself or another person) content or satisfied: *to content oneself with property.* ~*n.* **4.** peace of mind; mental or emotional satisfaction. ~*interj.* **5.** *Brit.* (in the House of Lords) a formal expression of assent, as opposed to the expression **not content.** [C14: from Old French, from Latin *contentus* contented, that is, having restrained desires, from *continēre* to restrain] —**conˈtently** *adv.* —**conˈtentment** *n.*

content-addressable storage *n. Computer technol.* another name for **associative storage.**

contented (kənˈtɛntɪd) *adj.* accepting one's situation or life with equanimity and satisfaction. —**conˈtentedly** *adv.* —**conˈtentedness** *n.*

contention (kənˈtɛnʃən) *n.* **1.** a struggling between opponents; competition. **2.** dispute in an argument (esp. in the phrase **bone of contention**). **3.** a point asserted in argument. [C14: from Latin *contentiō* exertion, from *contendere* to CONTEND]

contentious (kənˈtɛnʃəs) *adj.* **1.** tending to argue or quarrel. **2.** causing or characterized by dispute; controversial. **3.** *Law.* relating to a cause or legal business that is contested, esp. a probate matter. —**conˈtentiously** *adv.* —**conˈtentiousness** *n.*

content word (ˈkɒntɛnt) *n.* a word to which an independent meaning can be given by reference to a world outside any sentence in which the word may occur. Compare **function word, lexical meaning.**

conterminous (kənˈtɜːmɪnəs), **conterminal,** *or* **coterminous** (kəʊˈtɜːmɪnəs) *adj.* **1.** enclosed within a common boundary. **2.** meeting at the ends; without a break or interruption. [C17: from Latin *conterminus,* from CON- + *terminus* end, boundary] —**conˈterminously, conˈterminally,** *or* **coˈterminously** *adv.*

contest *n.* (ˈkɒntɛst). **1.** a formal game or match in which two or more people, teams, etc., compete and attempt to win. **2.** a struggle for victory between opposing forces or interests. ~*vb.* (kənˈtɛst). **3.** (*tr.*) to try to disprove; call in question. **4.** (when *intr.,* foll. by *with* or *against*) to fight, dispute, or contend (with): *contest an election.* [C16: from Latin *contestārī* to introduce a lawsuit, from *testis* witness] —**conˈtestable** *adj.* —**conˈtestableness** *or* **conˌtestaˈbility** *n.* —**conˈtestably** *adv.* —**ˌcontesˈtation** *n.* —**conˈtester** *n.* —**conˈtestingly** *adv.*

contestant (kənˈtɛstənt) *n.* a person who takes part in a contest; competitor.

context (ˈkɒntɛkst) *n.* **1.** the parts of a piece of writing, speech, etc., that precede and follow a word or passage and contribute to its full meaning: *it is unfair to quote out of context.* **2.** the conditions and circumstances that are relevant to an event, fact, etc. [C15: from Latin *contextus* a putting together, from *contexere* to interweave, from *com-* together + *texere* to weave, braid]

contextual (kənˈtɛkstjʊəl) *adj.* relating to, dependent on, or using context: *contextual criticism of a book.* —**conˈtextually** *adv.*

contextualize *or* **contextualise** (kənˈtɛkstjʊəˌlaɪz) *vb.* (*tr.*) to state the social, grammatical, or other context of; put into context.

contexture (kənˈtɛkstʃə) *n.* **1.** the fact, process, or manner of weaving or of being woven together. **2.** the arrangement of assembled parts; structure. **3.** an interwoven structure; fabric. —**conˈtextural** *adj.*

contiguous (kənˈtɪgjʊəs) *adj.* **1.** touching along the side or boundary; in contact. **2.** physically adjacent; neighbouring. **3.** preceding or following in time. [C17: from Latin *contiguus,* from *contingere* to touch; see CONTACT] —**contiguity** (ˌkɒntɪˈgjuːɪtɪ) *or* **conˈtiguousness** *n.* —**conˈtiguously** *adv.*

continent[1] (ˈkɒntɪnənt) *n.* **1.** one of the earth's large land masses (Asia, Australia, Africa, Europe, North and South America, and Antarctica). **2.** that part of the earth's crust that rises above the oceans and is composed of sialic rocks. Including the continental shelves, the continents occupy 30 per cent of the earth's surface. **3.** *Obsolete.* **a.** mainland as opposed to islands. **b.** a continuous extent of land. [C16: from the Latin phrase *terra continens* continuous land, from *continēre;* see CONTAIN] —**continental** (ˌkɒntɪˈnɛntᵊl) *adj.* —ˌ**contiˈnentally** *adv.*

continent[2] (ˈkɒntɪnənt) *adj.* **1.** able to control urination and defecation. **2.** exercising self-restraint, esp. from sexual activity; chaste. [C14: from Latin *continent-,* present participle of *continēre;* see CONTAIN] —**ˈcontinence** *or* **ˈcontinency** *n.* —**ˈcontinently** *adv.*

Continent (ˈkɒntɪnənt) *n.* **the.** the mainland of Europe as distinguished from the British Isles.

Continental (ˌkɒntɪˈnɛntᵊl) *adj.* **1.** of or characteristic of Europe, excluding the British Isles. ~*n.* **2.** (*sometimes not cap.*) an inhabitant of Europe, excluding the British Isles. **3.** *U.S. History.* a currency note issued by the Continental Congress (1774–89). —ˌ**Contiˈnentalˌism** *n.* —ˌ**Contiˈnentalist** *n.*

continental breakfast *n.* a light breakfast of coffee and rolls.

continental climate *n.* a climate characterized by hot summers, cold winters, and little rainfall, typical of the interior of a continent.

continental crust *n. Geology.* that part of the earth's crust that underlies the continents and continental shelves.

continental divide *n.* the watershed of a continent, esp. (*often caps.*) the principal watershed of North America, formed by the Rocky Mountains.

continental drift *n. Geology.* the theory that the earth's continents move gradually over the surface of the planet on a substratum of magma. The present-day configuration of the continents is thought to be the result of the fragmentation of a single landmass, Pangaea, that existed 200 million years ago. See also **plate tectonics.**

continental quilt *n. Brit.* a quilt, stuffed with down or a synthetic material and containing pockets of air, used as a bed cover in place of the top sheet and blankets. Also called: **duvet,** (Austral.) **doona.**

continental shelf *n.* the sea bed surrounding a continent at depths of up to about 200 metres (100 fathoms), at the edge of which the **continental slope** drops steeply to the ocean floor.

contingence (kənˈtɪndʒəns) *n.* **1.** the state of touching or being in contact. **2.** another word for **contingency.**

contingency (kənˈtɪndʒənsɪ) *n., pl.* **-cies.** **1. a.** a possible but not very likely future event or condition; eventuality. **b.** (*as modifier*): *a contingency plan.* **2.** something dependent on a possible future event. **3.** a fact, event, etc., incidental to or dependent on something else. **4.** (in systemic grammar) **a.** modification of the meaning of a main clause by use of a bound clause introduced by a binder such as *if, when, though,* or *since.* Compare **adding** (sense 3). **b.** (*as modifier*): *a contingency clause.* **5.** *Logic.* **a.** the state of being contingent. **b.** a contingent statement. **6.** dependence on chance; uncertainty. **7.** *Statistics.* **a.** the degree of association between theoretical and observed common frequencies of two graded or classified variables. It is measured by the chi-square test. **b.** (*as modifier*): *a contingency table; the contingency coefficient.*

contingency table *n. Statistics.* an array having the frequency of occurrence of certain events in each of a number of samples.

contingent (kənˈtɪndʒənt) *adj.* **1.** (when *postpositive,* often foll. by *on* or *upon*) dependent on events, conditions, etc., not yet known; conditional. **2.** *Logic.* (of a proposition) true under certain conditions, false under others; not necessary. **3.** (in systemic grammar) denoting contingency (sense 4). **4.** *Metaphysics.* (of some being) existing only as a matter of fact; not necessarily existing. **5.** happening by chance or without known cause; accidental. **6.** that may or may not happen; uncertain. ~*n.* **7.** a part of a military force, parade, etc. **8.** a representative group distinguished by common origin, interests, etc., that is part of a larger group or gathering. **9.** a possible or chance occurrence. [C14: from Latin *contingere* to touch, fall to one's lot, befall; see also CONTACT] —**conˈtingently** *adv.*

continual (kənˈtɪnjʊəl) *adj.* **1.** recurring frequently, esp. at regular intervals. **2.** occurring without interruption; continuous in time. [C14: from Old French *continuel,* from Latin *continuus* uninterrupted, from *continēre* to hold together, CONTAIN] —**conˌtinuˈality** *or* **conˈtinualness** *n.* —**conˈtinually** *adv.*

continuance (kənˈtɪnjʊəns) *n.* **1.** the act or state of continuing. **2.** the duration of an action, condition, etc. **3.** *U.S.* the postponement or adjournment of a legal proceeding.

continuant (kənˈtɪnjʊənt) *Phonetics.* ~*n.* **1.** a speech sound, such as (l), (r), (f), or (s), in which the closure of the vocal tract is incomplete, allowing the continuous passage of the breath. ~*adj.* 2. relating to or denoting a continuant.

continuation (kənˌtɪnjʊˈeɪʃən) *n.* 1. a part or thing added, esp. to a book or play, that serves to continue or extend; sequel. 2. a renewal of an interrupted action, process, etc.; resumption. 3. the act or fact of continuing without interruption; prolongation. 4. another word for **contango** (senses 1, 2).

continuative (kənˈtɪnjʊətɪv) *adj.* 1. serving or tending to continue. 2. *Grammar.* a. (of any word, phrase, or clause) expressing continuation. b. (of verbs) another word for **progressive** (sense 8). ~*n.* 3. a continuative word, phrase, or clause. —**conˈtinuatively** *adv.*

continuator (kənˈtɪnjʊˌeɪtə) *n.* a person who continues something, esp. the work of someone else.

continue (kənˈtɪnjuː) *vb.* **-ues, -uing, -ued.** 1. (when *tr.*, *may take an infinitive*) to remain or cause to remain in a particular condition, capacity, or place. 2. (when *tr.*, *may take an infinitive*) to carry on uninterruptedly (a course of action); persist in (something): *he continued running.* 3. (when *tr.*, *may take an infinitive*) to resume after an interruption: *we'll continue after lunch.* 4. to draw out or be drawn out; prolong or be prolonged: *continue the chord until it meets the tangent.* 5. (*tr.*) *Law, chiefly Scots.* to postpone or adjourn (legal proceedings). [C14: from Old French *continuer*, from Latin *continuāre* to join together, from *continuus* CONTINUOUS] —**conˈtinuable** *adj.* —**conˈtinuer** *n.* —**conˈtinuingly** *adv.*

continued fraction *n.* a number plus a fraction whose denominator contains a number and a fraction whose denominator contains a number and a fraction, and so on.

continuity (ˌkɒntɪˈnjuːɪtɪ) *n., pl.* **-ties.** 1. logical sequence, cohesion, or connection. 2. a continuous or connected whole. 3. the comprehensive script or scenario of detail and movement in a film or broadcast. 4. the continuous projection of a film, using automatic rewind.

continuity girl *or* **man** *n.* a girl or man whose job is to ensure continuity and consistency, esp. in matters of dress, make-up, etc., in successive shots of a film, esp. when these shots are filmed on different days.

continuity studio *n.* a small studio and control room where linking announcements, etc., are made to give continuity to a television or radio broadcast channel.

continuo (kənˈtɪnjʊˌəʊ) *n., pl.* **-os.** 1. *Music.* a. a shortened form of **basso continuo** (see **thorough bass**). b. (*as modifier*): *a continuo accompaniment.* 2. the thorough-bass part as played on a keyboard instrument, often supported by a cello, bassoon, etc. [Italian, literally: continuous]

continuous (kənˈtɪnjʊəs) *adj.* 1. prolonged without interruption; unceasing: *a continuous noise.* 2. in an unbroken series or pattern. 3. *Maths.* (of a function or curve) changing gradually in value as the variable changes in value. At any value $x = a$ of the continuous function $f(x)$, $\lim_{x\to a} f(x) = f(a)$. At every value a of the independent variable, the difference between $f(x)$ and $f(a)$ approaches zero as x approaches a when f is a continuous function. Compare **discontinuous** (sense 2). See also **limit** (sense 5). 4. *Statistics.* (of a variable) having a continuum of possible values so that its distribution requires integration rather than summation to determine its cumulative probability. Compare **discrete** (sense 3). 5. *Grammar.* another word for **progressive** (sense 8). [C17: from Latin *continuus*, from *continēre* to hold together, CONTAIN] —**conˈtinuously** *adv.* —**conˈtinuousness** *n.*

continuous assessment *n.* the assessment of a pupil's progress throughout a course of study rather than exclusively by examination at the end of it.

continuous creation *n.* 1. the theory that matter is being created continuously in the universe. See **steady-state theory.** 2. the theory that animate matter is being continuously created from inanimate matter.

continuous spectrum *n.* a spectrum that contains or appears to contain all wavelengths over a wide portion of its range. The emission spectrum of incandescent solids is continuous; spectra consisting of a large number of lines may appear continuous.

continuous stationery *n. Computer technol.* paper that is perforated between pages and folded concertina fashion, used in dot-matrix, line, and daisywheel printers.

continuous waves *pl. n.* radio waves generated as a continuous train of oscillations having a constant frequency and amplitude. Abbrev: **CW.**

continuum (kənˈtɪnjʊəm) *n., pl.* **-tinua** (-ˈtɪnjʊə) *or* **-tinuums.** 1. a continuous series or whole, no part of which is perceptibly different from the adjacent parts. 2. *Maths.* a set of elements between any two of which a third element can always be inserted: *a continuum of real numbers.* [C17: from Latin, neuter of *continuus* CONTINUOUS]

conto (ˈkɒntəʊ; *Portuguese* ˈkõtu) *n., pl.* **-tos** (-təʊz; *Portuguese* -tuʃ). 1. a Portuguese monetary unit worth 1000 escudos. 2. an unofficial Brazilian monetary unit worth 1000 cruzeiros. [C17: from Portuguese, from Late Latin *computus* calculation, from *computāre* to reckon, COMPUTE; see COUNT[1]]

contort (kənˈtɔːt) *vb.* to twist or bend severely out of place or shape, esp. in a strained manner. [C15: from Latin *contortus* intricate, obscure, from *contorquēre* to whirl around, from *torquēre* to twist, wrench] —**conˈtortive** *adj.*

contorted (kənˈtɔːtɪd) *adj.* 1. twisted out of shape. 2. (esp. of petals and sepals in a bud) twisted so that they overlap on one side. —**conˈtortedly** *adv.* —**conˈtortedness** *n.*

contortion (kənˈtɔːʃən) *n.* 1. the act or process of contorting or the state of being contorted. 2. a twisted shape or position. 3. something twisted or out of the ordinary in character, meaning, etc: *mental contortions.* —**conˈtortional** *adj.* —**conˈtortioned** *adj.*

contortionist (kənˈtɔːʃənɪst) *n.* 1. a performer who contorts his body for the entertainment of others. 2. a person who twists or warps meaning or thoughts: *a verbal contortionist.* —**conˌtorˈtionˈistic** *adj.*

contour (ˈkɒntʊə) *n.* 1. the outline of a mass of land, figure, or body; a defining line. 2. a. See **contour line.** b. (*as modifier*): *a contour map.* 3. (*often pl.*) the shape or surface, esp. of a curving form: *the contours of her body were full and round.* 4. (*modifier*) shaped to fit the form of something: *a contour chair.* ~*vb.* (*tr.*) 5. to shape so as to form the contour of something. 6. to mark contour lines on. 7. to construct (a road, railway, etc.) to follow the outline of the land. [C17: from French, from Italian *contorno*, from *contornare* to sketch, from *tornare* to TURN]

contour feather *n.* any of the feathers that cover the body of an adult bird, apart from the wings and tail, and determine its shape.

contour interval *n.* the difference in altitude represented by the space between two contour lines on a map.

contour line *n.* a line on a map or chart joining points of equal height or depth. Often shortened to **contour.**

contour ploughing *n.* ploughing following the contours of the land, to minimize the effects of erosion.

contr. *abbrev. for:* 1. contraction. 2. contralto.

contra- *prefix.* 1. against; contrary; opposing; contrasting: *contraceptive; contradistinction.* 2. (in music) pitched below: *contrabass.* [from Latin, from *contrā* against]

contraband (ˈkɒntrəˌbænd) *n.* 1. a. goods that are prohibited by law from being exported or imported. b. illegally imported or exported goods. 2. illegal traffic in such goods; smuggling. 3. Also called: **contraband of war.** *International law.* goods that a neutral country may not supply to a belligerent. 4. (during the American Civil War) a Black slave captured by the Union forces or one who escaped to the Union lines. ~*adj.* 5. (of goods) a. forbidden by law from being imported or exported. b. illegally imported or exported. [C16: from Spanish *contrabanda*, from Italian *contrabando* (modern *contrabbando*), from Medieval Latin *contrabannum*, from CONTRA- + *bannum* ban, of Germanic origin] —ˈ**contraˌbandist** *n.*

contrabass (ˌkɒntrəˈbeɪs) *n.* 1. a member of any of various families of musical instruments that is lower in pitch than the bass. 2. another name for **double bass.** ~*adj.* 3. of or denoting the instrument of a family that is lower than the bass. —**contrabassist** (ˌkɒntrəˈbeɪsɪst, -ˈbæs-) *n.*

contrabassoon (ˌkɒntrəbəˈsuːn) *n.* the largest instrument in the oboe family, pitched an octave below the bassoon; double bassoon. —ˌ**contrabasˈsoonist** *n.*

contraception (ˌkɒntrəˈsɛpʃən) *n.* the intentional prevention of conception by artificial or natural means. Artificial methods in common use include preventing the sperm from reaching the ovum (using condoms, diaphragms, etc.), inhibiting ovulation (using oral contraceptive pills), preventing implantation (using intrauterine devices), killing the sperm (using spermicides), and preventing the sperm from entering the seminal fluid (by vasectomy). Natural methods include the rhythm method and coitus interruptus. Compare **birth control, family planning.** [C19: from CONTRA- + CONCEPTION]

contraceptive (ˌkɒntrəˈsɛptɪv) *adj.* 1. relating to or used for contraception; able or tending to prevent impregnation. ~*n.* 2. any device that prevents or tends to prevent conception.

contract *vb.* (kənˈtrækt). 1. to make or become smaller, narrower, shorter, etc.: *metals contract as the temperature is reduced.* 2. (ˈkɒntrækt). (when *intr.*, sometimes foll. by *for*; when *tr.*, *may take an infinitive*) to enter into an agreement with (a person, company, etc.) to deliver (goods or services) or to do (something) on mutually agreed and binding terms, often in writing. 3. to draw or be drawn together; coalesce or cause to coalesce. 4. (*tr.*) to acquire, incur, or become affected by (a disease, liability, debt, etc.). 5. (*tr.*) to shorten (a word or phrase) by the omission of letters or syllables, usually indicated in writing by an apostrophe. 6. *Phonetics.* to unite (two vowels) or (of two vowels) to be united within a word or at a word boundary so that a new long vowel or diphthong is formed. 7. (*tr.*) to wrinkle or draw together (the brow or a muscle). 8. (*tr.*) to arrange (a marriage) for; betroth. ~*n.* (ˈkɒntrækt). 9. a formal agreement between two or more parties. 10. a document that states the terms of such an agreement. 11. the branch of law treating of contracts. 12. marriage considered as a formal agreement. 13. See **contract bridge.** 14. *Bridge.* a. (in the bidding sequence before play) the highest bid, which determines trumps and the number of tricks one side must try to make. b. the number and suit of these tricks. 15. *Slang.* a. a criminal agreement to kill a particular person in return for an agreed sum of money. b. (*as modifier*): *a contract killing.* [C16: from Latin *contractus* agreement, something drawn up, from *contrahere* to draw together, from *trahere* to draw] —**conˈtractible** *adj.* —**conˈtractibly** *adv.*

contract bridge ('kɒntrækt) *n.* the most common variety of bridge, in which the declarer receives points counting towards game and rubber only for tricks he bids as well as makes, any overtricks receiving bonus points. Compare **auction bridge.**

contractile (kən'træktaɪl) *adj.* having the power to contract or to cause contraction. —**contractility** (ˌkɒntræk'tɪlɪtɪ) *n.*

contraction (kən'trækʃən) *n.* **1.** an instance of contracting or the state of being contracted. **2.** *Physiol.* any normal shortening or tensing of an organ or part, esp. of a muscle, e.g. during childbirth. **3.** *Pathol.* any abnormal tightening or shrinking of an organ or part. **4.** a shortening of a word or group of words, often marked in written English by an apostrophe: *I've come* for *I have come.* —**con'tractive** *adj.* —**con'tractively** *adv.* —**con'tractiveness** *n.*

contract of employment *n.* a written agreement between an employer and an employee, that, taken together with the rights of each under statute and common law, determines the employment relations between them.

contractor ('kɒntræktə, kən'træk-) *n.* **1.** a person or firm that contracts to supply materials or labour, esp. for building. **2.** something that contracts, esp. a muscle. **3.** *Law.* a person who is a party to a contract. **4.** the declarer in bridge.

contract out *vb.* (*intr., adv.*) *Brit.* to agree not to participate in something, esp. the state pension scheme.

contractual (kən'træktjʊəl) *adj.* of the nature of or assured by a contract. —**con'tractually** *adv.*

contracture (kən'trækʃə) *n.* a disorder in which a skeletal muscle is permanently tightened (contracted), most often caused by spasm or paralysis of the antagonist muscle that maintains normal muscle tension.

contradance ('kɒntrəˌdɑːns) *n.* a variant spelling of **contredanse.**

contradict (ˌkɒntrə'dɪkt) *vb.* **1.** (*tr.*) to affirm the opposite of (a proposition, statement, etc.). **2.** (*tr.*) to declare (a proposition, statement, etc.) to be false or incorrect; deny. **3.** (*intr.*) to be argumentative or contrary. **4.** (*tr.*) to be inconsistent with (a proposition, theory, etc.): *the facts contradicted his theory.* **5.** (*intr.*) (of two or more facts, principles, etc.) to be at variance; be in contradiction. [C16: from Latin *contrādīcere,* from CONTRA- + *dīcere* to speak, say] —ˌ**contra'dictable** *adj.* —ˌ**contra'dicter** *or* ˌ**contra'dictor** *n.* —ˌ**contra'dictive** *or* ˌ**contra'dictious** *adj.* —ˌ**contra'dictively** *or* ˌ**contra'dictiously** *adv.* —ˌ**contra'dictiveness** *or* ˌ**contra'dictiousness** *n.*

contradiction (ˌkɒntrə'dɪkʃən) *n.* **1.** the act of going against; opposition; denial. **2.** a declaration of the opposite or contrary. **3.** a statement that is at variance with itself (often in the phrase **a contradiction in terms**). **4.** conflict or inconsistency, as between events, qualities, etc. **5.** a person or thing containing conflicting qualities. **6.** *Logic.* a statement that is false under all circumstances; necessary falsehood.

contradictory (ˌkɒntrə'dɪktərɪ) *adj.* **1.** inconsistent; incompatible. **2.** given to argument and contention: *a contradictory person.* **3.** *Logic.* (of a pair of statements) unable both to be true or both to be false under the same circumstances. Compare **contrary** (sense 5), **subcontrary** (sense 1). ~*n., pl.* **-ries. 4.** *Logic.* a statement that cannot be true when a given statement is true or false when it is false. —ˌ**contra'dictorily** *adv.* —ˌ**contra'dictoriness** *n.*

contradistinction (ˌkɒntrədɪ'stɪŋkʃən) *n.* a distinction made by contrasting different qualities. —ˌ**contradis'tinctive** *adj.* —ˌ**contradis'tinctively** *adv.*

contradistinguish (ˌkɒntrədɪ'stɪŋgwɪʃ) *vb.* (*tr.*) to differentiate by means of contrasting or opposing qualities.

contraflow ('kɒntrəˌfləʊ) *n. Brit.* two-way traffic on one carriageway of a motorway, esp. to allow maintenance work to be carried out or an accident to be cleared.

contrail ('kɒntreɪl) *n.* another name for **vapour trail.** [C20: from CON(DENSATION) + TRAIL]

contraindicate (ˌkɒntrə'ɪndɪˌkeɪt) *vb.* (*tr.; usually passive*) *Med.* to advise against or indicate the possible danger of (a drug, treatment, etc.). —ˌ**contra'indicant** *n.* —ˌ**contraˌindi'cation** *n.*

contralateral (ˌkɒntrə'lætərəl) *adj. Anatomy, zoology.* relating to or denoting the opposite side of a body, structure, etc.

contralto (kən'træltəʊ, -'trɑːl-) *n., pl.* **-tos** *or* **-ti** (-tɪ). **1.** the lowest female voice, usually having a range of approximately from F a fifth below middle C to D a ninth above it. In the context of a choir often shortened to **alto. 2.** a singer with such a voice. ~*adj.* **3.** of or denoting a contralto: *the contralto part.* [C18: from Italian; see CONTRA-, ALTO]

contraposition (ˌkɒntrəpə'zɪʃən) *n.* **1.** the act of placing opposite or against, esp. in contrast or antithesis. **2.** *Logic.* the derivation of the contrapositive of a given categorial proposition.

contrapositive (ˌkɒntrə'pɒzɪtɪv) *adj.* **1.** placed opposite or against. ~*n.* **2.** *Logic.* **a.** a conditional statement derived from another by negating and interchanging antecedent and consequent. **b.** a categorial proposition obtained from another, esp. validly, by any of a number of operations including negation, transferring the terms, changing their quality, and also possibly weakening from universal to particular.

contrapposto (ˌkɒntrə'pɒstəʊ) *n., pl.* **-tos.** (in the visual arts) a curving or asymmetrical arrangement of the human figure with the shoulders, hips, and legs in different planes. [C20: from Italian, from the past participle of *contrapporre,* from Latin *contra* CONTRA- + *pōnere* to place]

contraption (kən'træpʃən) *n. Informal, often facetious or derogatory.* a device or contrivance, esp. one considered strange, unnecessarily intricate, or improvised. [C19: perhaps from CON(TRIVANCE) + TRAP[1] + (INVEN)TION]

contrapuntal (ˌkɒntrə'pʌntᵊl) *adj. Music.* characterized by counterpoint. [C19: from Italian *contrappunto* COUNTERPOINT + -AL[1]] —ˌ**contra'puntally** *adv.*

contrapuntist (ˌkɒntrə'pʌntɪst) *or* **contrapuntalist** *n. Music.* a composer skilled in counterpoint.

contrariety (ˌkɒntrə'raɪətɪ) *n., pl.* **-ties. 1.** opposition between one thing and another; disagreement. **2.** an instance of such opposition; inconsistency; discrepancy. **3.** *Logic.* the relationship between two contraries.

contrarily *adv.* **1.** (kən'trɛərɪlɪ). in a perverse or obstinate manner. **2.** ('kɒntrərɪlɪ). on the other hand; from the opposite point of view. **3.** ('kɒntrərɪlɪ). in an opposite, adverse, or unexpected way.

contrarious (kən'trɛərɪəs) *adj. Rare.* **1.** (of people or animals) perverse or obstinate. **2.** (of conditions) unfavourable. —**con'trariously** *adv.* —**con'trariousness** *n.*

contrariwise ('kɒntrərɪˌwaɪz) *adv.* **1.** from a contrasting point of view; on the other hand. **2.** in the reverse way or direction. **3.** (kən'trɛərɪˌwaɪz). in a contrary manner.

contrary ('kɒntrərɪ) *adj.* **1.** opposed in nature, position, etc.: *contrary ideas.* **2.** (kən'trɛərɪ). perverse; obstinate. **3.** (esp. of wind) adverse; unfavourable. **4.** (of plant parts) situated at right angles to each other. **5.** *Logic.* (of a pair of propositions) related so that they cannot both be true at once, although they may both be false together. Compare **subcontrary** (sense 1), **contradictory** (sense 3). ~*n., pl.* **-ries. 6.** the exact opposite (esp. in the phrase **to the contrary). 7. on the contrary.** quite the reverse; not at all. **8.** either of two exactly opposite objects, facts, or qualities. **9.** *Logic.* a statement that cannot be true when a given statement is true. ~*adv.* (usually foll. by *to*) **10.** in an opposite or unexpected way: *contrary to usual belief.* **11.** in conflict (with) or contravention (of): *contrary to nature.* [C14: from Latin *contrārius* opposite, from *contrā* against] —**con'trariness** *n.*

contrast *vb.* (kən'trɑːst). **1.** (often foll. by *with*) to distinguish or be distinguished by comparison of unlike or opposite qualities. ~*n.* ('kɒntrɑːst). **2.** distinction or emphasis of difference by comparison of opposite or dissimilar things, qualities, etc. (esp. in the phrases **by contrast, in contrast to** *or* **with). 3.** a person or thing showing notable differences when compared with another. **4.** (in painting) the effect of the juxtaposition of different colours, tones, etc. **5. a.** (of a photographic emulsion) the degree of density measured against exposure used. **b.** the extent to which adjacent areas of an optical image, esp. on a television screen or in a photographic negative or print, differ in brightness. **6.** *Psychol.* the phenomenon that when two different but related stimuli are presented close together in space and/or time they are perceived as being more different than they really are. [C16: (n.): via French from Italian, from *contrastare* (vb.), from Latin *contra-* against + *stare* to stand] —**con'trastable** *adj.* —**con'trastably** *adv.* —**con'trasting** *adj.* —**con'trastive** *adj.* —**con'trastively** *adv.*

contrast medium *n. Med.* a radiopaque substance, such as barium sulphate, used to increase the contrast of an image in radiography.

contrasty (kən'trɑːstɪ) *adj.* (of a photograph or subject) having sharp gradations in tone, esp. between light and dark areas.

contrasuggestible (ˌkɒntrəsə'dʒɛstɪbᵊl) *adj. Psychol.* responding or tending to respond to a suggestion by doing or believing the opposite. —ˌ**contrasugˌgesti'bility** *n.* —ˌ**contrasug'gestion** *n.*

contravallation (ˌkɒntrəvə'leɪʃən) *n.* fortifications built by besiegers around the place besieged. [C17: from CONTRA- + Latin *vallātiō* entrenchment; compare French *contrevallation*]

contravene (ˌkɒntrə'viːn) *vb.* (*tr.*) **1.** to come into conflict with or infringe (rules, laws, etc.). **2.** to dispute or contradict (a statement, proposition, etc.). [C16: from Late Latin *contrāvenīre,* from Latin CONTRA- + *venīre* to come] —ˌ**contra'vener** *n.* —**contravention** (ˌkɒntrə'vɛnʃən) *n.*

contrayerva (ˌkɒntrə'jɜːvə) *n.* the root of any of several tropical American moraceous plants of the genus *Dorstenia,* esp. *D. contrayerva,* used as a stimulant and tonic. [C17: from Spanish *contrayerba,* from CONTRA- + *yerba* grass, (poisonous) plant, from Latin *herba;* referring to the belief that it was an antidote to poisons]

contredanse *or* **contradance** ('kɒntrəˌdɑːns) *n.* **1.** a courtly Continental version of the English country dance, similar to the quadrille. **2.** music written for or in the rhythm of this dance. [C19: from French, changed from English *country dance; country* altered to French *contre* (opposite) by folk etymology (because the dancers face each other)]

contre-jour ('kɒntrəˌʒʊə) *n. Photog.* **a.** the technique of taking photographs into the light, with the light source behind the subject. **b.** (*as modifier*): *a contre-jour shot.* [C20: from French, literally: against day(light)]

contretemps ('kɒntrəˌtɑːn; *French* kɔ̃trətɑ̃) *n., pl.* **-temps. 1.** an awkward or difficult situation or mishap. **2.** *Fencing.* a feint made with the purpose of producing a counterthrust from one's opponent. **3.** a small disagreement that is rather embarrassing. [C17: from French, from *contre* against + *temps* time, from Latin *tempus*]

contrib. *abbrev. for:* **1.** contribution. **2.** contributor.

contribute (kən'trɪbjuːt) *vb.* (often foll. by *to*) **1.** to give (support, money, etc.) for a common purpose or fund. **2.** to supply (ideas, opinions, etc.) as part of a debate or discussion. **3.** (*intr.*) to be partly instrumental (in) or responsible (for): *drink contributed to the accident.* **4.** to write (articles) for a publication. [C16: from Latin *contribuere* to collect, from *tribuere* to grant, bestow] **—con'tributable** *adj.* **—con'tributive** *adj.* **—con'tributively** *adv.* **—con'tributiveness** *n.*

contribution (ˌkɒntrɪ'bjuːʃən) *n.* **1.** the act of contributing. **2.** something contributed, such as money or ideas. **3.** an article, story, etc., contributed to a newspaper or other publication. **4.** *Insurance.* a portion of the total liability incumbent on each of two or more companies for a risk with respect to which all of them have issued policies. **5.** *Archaic.* a levy, esp. towards the cost of a war.

contributor (kən'trɪbjʊtə) *n.* **1.** a person who contributes, esp. one who writes for a newspaper or one who makes a donation to a cause, etc. **2.** something that is a factor in or is partly responsible for something: *alcohol was a contributor to his death.*

contributory (kən'trɪbjʊtərɪ, -trɪ) *adj.* **1.** (often foll. by *to*) sharing in or being partly responsible (for the cause of something): *a contributory factor.* **2.** giving or donating to a common purpose or fund. **3.** of, relating to, or designating an insurance or pension scheme in which the premiums are paid partly by the employer and partly by the employees who benefit from it. **4.** liable or subject to a tax or levy. *~n., pl.* **-ries. 5.** a person or thing that contributes. **6.** *Company law.* a member or former member of a company liable to contribute to the assets on the winding-up of the company.

contributory negligence *n. Law.* failure by an injured person to have taken proper precautions to prevent an accident.

con trick *n. Informal.* a shortened form of **confidence trick.**

contrite (kən'traɪt, 'kɒntraɪt) *adj.* **1.** full of guilt or regret; remorseful. **2.** arising from a sense of shame or guilt: *contrite promises.* **3.** *Theol.* remorseful for past sin and resolved to avoid future sin. [C14: from Latin *contrītus* worn out, from *conterere* to bruise, from *terere* to grind] **—con'tritely** *adv.* **—con'triteness** *n.*

contrition (kən'trɪʃən) *n.* **1.** deeply felt remorse; penitence. **2.** *Christianity.* detestation of past sins and a resolve to make amends, either from love of God (**perfect contrition**) or from hope of heaven (**imperfect contrition**).

contrivance (kən'traɪvəns) *n.* **1.** something contrived, esp. an ingenious device; contraption. **2.** the act or faculty of devising or adapting; inventive skill or ability. **3.** an artificial rather than natural selection or arrangement of details, parts, etc. **4.** an elaborate or deceitful plan or expedient; stratagem.

contrive (kən'traɪv) *vb.* **1.** (*tr.*) to manage (something or to do something), esp. by means of a trick; engineer: *he contrived to make them meet.* **2.** (*tr.*) to think up or adapt ingeniously or elaborately: *he contrived a new mast for the boat.* **3.** to plot or scheme (treachery, evil, etc.). [C14: from Old French *controver,* from Late Latin *contropāre* to represent by figures of speech, compare, from Latin *com-* together + *tropus* figure of speech, TROPE] **—con'trivable** *adj.* **—con'triver** *n.*

contrived (kən'traɪvd) *adj.* obviously planned, artificial, or lacking in spontaneity; forced; unnatural.

control (kən'trəʊl) *vb.* **-trols, -trolling, -trolled.** (*tr.*) **1.** to command, direct, or rule: *to control a country.* **2.** to check, limit, curb, or regulate; restrain: *to control one's emotions; to control a fire.* **3.** to regulate or operate (a machine). **4.** to verify (a scientific experiment) by conducting a parallel experiment in which the variable being investigated is held constant or is compared with a standard. **5. a.** to regulate (financial affairs). **b.** to examine and verify (financial accounts). *~n.* **6.** power to direct or determine: *under control; out of control.* **7.** a means of regulation or restraint; curb; check: *a frontier control.* **8.** (*often pl.*) a device or mechanism for operating a car, aircraft, etc. **9.** a standard of comparison used in a statistical analysis or scientific experiment. **10. a.** a device that regulates the operation of a machine. A **dynamic control** is one that incorporates a governor so that it responds to the output of the machine it regulates. **b.** (*as modifier*): *control panel; control room.* **11.** *Spiritualism.* an agency believed to assist the medium in a séance. **12.** Also called: **control mark.** a letter, or letter and number, printed on a sheet of postage stamps, indicating authenticity, date, and series of issue. **13.** one of a number of checkpoints on a car rally, orienteering course, etc., where competitors check in and their time, performance, etc., is recorded. [C15: from Old French *conteroller* to regulate, from *contrerolle* duplicate register, system of checking, from *contre-* COUNTER- + *rolle* ROLL] **—con'trollable** *adj.* **—conˌtrolla'bility** *or* **con'trollableness** *n.* **—con'trollably** *adv.*

control account *n. Accounting.* an account to which are posted the debit and credit totals of other accounts, usually in preparation of financial statements.

control chart *n. Statistics.* a chart on which observed values of a variable are plotted, usually against the expected value of the variable and its allowable deviation, so that excessive variations in the quality, quantity, etc., of the variable can be detected.

control column *n.* a lever or pillar, usually fitted with a handwheel, used to control the movements of an aircraft. Also called: **control stick, joy stick.**

control commands *pl. n.* keyed instructions conveyed to a computer by using the control key in conjunction with the standard keys.

control experiment *n.* an experiment designed to check or correct the results of another experiment by removing the variable or variables operating in that other experiment. The comparison obtained is an indication or measurement of the effect of the variables concerned.

control grid *n. Electronics.* another name for **grid** (sense 5), esp. in a tetrode or pentode.

control group *n.* any group used as a control in a statistical experiment, esp. a group of patients who receive either a placebo or a standard drug during an investigation of the effects of another drug on other patients.

control key *n.* a key on the keyboard of a computer that is used in conjunction with the standard keys in order to initiate a specific function, such as editing.

controller (kən'trəʊlə) *n.* **1.** a person who directs, regulates, or restrains. **2.** Also called: **comptroller.** a business executive or government officer who is responsible for financial planning, control, etc. **3.** the equipment concerned with controlling the operation of an electrical device. **—con'trollerˌship** *n.*

controlling interest *n.* a quantity of shares in a business that is sufficient to ensure control over its direction.

control rod *n.* one of a number of rods or tubes containing a neutron absorber, such as boron, that can be inserted into or retracted from the core of a nuclear reactor in order to control its rate of reaction.

control stick *n.* the lever by which a pilot controls the lateral and longitudinal movements of an aircraft. Also called: **control column, joy stick.**

control surface *n.* a movable surface, such as a rudder, elevator, aileron, etc., that controls an aircraft or rocket.

control tower *n.* a tower at an airport from which air traffic is controlled.

controversy ('kɒntrəˌvɜːsɪ, kən'trɒvəsɪ) *n., pl.* **-sies.** dispute, argument, or debate, esp. one concerning a matter about which there is strong disagreement and esp. one carried on in public or in the press. [C14: from Latin *contrōversia,* from *contrōversus* turned in an opposite direction, from CONTRA- + *vertere* to turn] **—controversial** (ˌkɒntrə'vɜːʃəl) *adj.* **—ˌcontro'versialˌism** *n.* **—ˌcontro'versialist** *n.* **—ˌcontro'versially** *adv.*

controvert ('kɒntrəˌvɜːt, ˌkɒntrə'vɜːt) *vb.* (*tr.*) **1.** to deny, refute, or oppose (some argument or opinion). **2.** to argue or wrangle about. [C17: from Latin *contrōversus;* see CONTROVERSY] **—'controˌverter** *n.* **—ˌcontro'vertible** *adj.* **—ˌcontro'vertibly** *adv.*

contumacious (ˌkɒntjʊ'meɪʃəs) *adj.* stubbornly resistant to authority; wilfully obstinate. **—ˌcontu'maciously** *adv.* **—ˌcontu'maciousness** *n.*

contumacy ('kɒntjʊməsɪ) *n., pl.* **-cies. 1.** obstinate and wilful rebelliousness or resistance to authority; insubordination; disobedience. **2.** the wilful refusal of a person to appear before a court or to comply with a court order. [C14: from Latin *contumācia,* from *contumāx* obstinate; related to *tumēre* to swell, be proud]

contumely ('kɒntjʊmɪlɪ) *n., pl.* **-lies. 1.** scornful or insulting language or behaviour. **2.** a humiliating or scornful insult. [C14: from Latin *contumēlia* invective, from *tumēre* to swell, as with wrath] **—contumelious** (ˌkɒntjʊ'miːlɪəs) *adj.* **—ˌcontu'meliously** *adv.* **—ˌcontu'meliousness** *n.*

contuse (kən'tjuːz) *vb.* (*tr.*) to injure (the body) without breaking the skin; bruise. [C15: from Latin *contūsus* bruised, from *contundere* to grind, from *tundere* to beat, batter] **—con'tusive** *adj.*

contusion (kən'tjuːʒən) *n.* an injury in which the skin is not broken; bruise. **—con'tusioned** *adj.*

conundrum (kə'nʌndrəm) *n.* **1.** a riddle, esp. one whose answer makes a play on words. **2.** a puzzling question or problem. [C16: of unknown origin]

conurbation (ˌkɒnɜː'beɪʃən) *n.* a large densely populated urban sprawl formed by the growth and coalescence of individual towns or cities. [C20: from CON- + *-urbation,* from Latin *urbs* city; see URBAN]

conure ('kɒnjʊə) *n.* any of various small American parrots of the genus *Aratinga* and related genera. [C19: from New Latin *conurus,* from Greek *kōnos* CONE + *oura* tail]

conus ('kəʊnəs) *n., pl.* **-ni.** *Anatomy, zoology.* any of several cone-shaped structures, such as the conus medullaris, the lower end of the spinal cord.

convalesce (ˌkɒnvə'lɛs) *vb.* (*intr.*) to recover from illness, injury, or the aftereffects of a surgical operation, esp. by resting. [C15: from Latin *convalēscere,* from *com-* (intensive) + *valēscere* to grow strong, from *valēre* to be strong]

convalescence (ˌkɒnvə'lɛsəns) *n.* **1.** gradual return to health after illness, injury, or an operation, esp. through rest. **2.** the period during which such recovery occurs. **—ˌconva'lescent** *n., adj.* **—ˌconva'lescently** *adv.*

convection (kənˈvɛkʃən) *n.* **1.** the process of heat or mass transfer through a fluid, caused by movement of molecules from cool regions to warmer regions of lower density. **2.** *Meteorol.* the process by which masses of relatively warm air are raised into the atmosphere, often cooling and forming clouds, with compensatory downward movements of cooler air. **3.** *Geology.* the slow circulation of subcrustal material, thought to be the mechanism by which tectonic plates are moved. [C19: from Late Latin *convectiō* a bringing together, from Latin *convehere* to bring together, gather, from *vehere* to bear, carry] —**conˈvectional** *adj.* —**conˈvective** *adj.*

convector (kənˈvɛktə) *n.* a space-heating device from which heat is transferred to the surrounding air by convection.

convenance *French.* (kõvnɑ̃s) *n.* suitable behaviour; propriety. [from *convenir* to be suitable, from Latin *convenīre;* see CONVENE]

convene (kənˈviːn) *vb.* **1.** to gather, call together, or summon, esp. for a formal meeting. **2.** (*tr.*) to order to appear before a court of law, judge, tribunal, etc. [C15: from Latin *convenīre* to assemble, from *venīre* to come]

convener *or* **convenor** (kənˈviːnə) *n.* **1.** a person who convenes or chairs a meeting, committee, etc., esp. one who is specifically elected to do so: *a convener of shop stewards.* **2.** the chairman and civic head of certain Scottish councils, esp. of a regional or islands council. Compare **provost** (sense 3).

convenience (kənˈviːnɪəns) *n.* **1.** the state or quality of being suitable or opportune: *the convenience of the hour.* **2.** a convenient time or situation. **3. at your convenience.** at a time suitable to you. **4. at your earliest convenience.** *Formal.* as soon as possible. **5.** usefulness, comfort, or facility. **6.** an object that is particularly useful, esp. a labour-saving device. **7.** *Euphemistic, chiefly Brit.* a lavatory, esp. a public one. **8. make a convenience of.** to take advantage of; impose upon.

convenience food *n.* food that needs little preparation and can be used at any time.

convenience store *n.* a shop that has long opening hours, caters to local tastes, and is conveniently situated.

convenient (kənˈviːnɪənt) *adj.* **1.** suitable for one's purpose or needs; opportune. **2.** easy to use. **3.** close by or easily accessible; handy. [C14: from Latin *conveniēns* appropriate, fitting, from *convenīre* to come together, be in accord with, from *venīre* to come] —**conˈveniently** *adv.*

convent (ˈkɒnvənt) *n.* **1.** a building inhabited by a religious community, usually of nuns. **2.** the religious community inhabiting such a building. **3.** Also called: **convent school.** a school in which the teachers are nuns. [C13: from Old French *covent,* from Latin *conventus* meeting, from *convenīre* to come together; see CONVENE]

conventicle (kənˈvɛntɪkəl) *n.* **1.** a secret or unauthorized assembly for worship. **2.** a small meeting house or chapel for a religious assembly, esp. of Nonconformists or Dissenters. [C14: from Latin *conventiculum* a meeting, from *conventus;* see CONVENT] —**conˈventicler** *n.*

convention (kənˈvɛnʃən) *n.* **1. a.** a large formal assembly of a group with common interests, such as a political party or trade union. **b.** the persons attending such an assembly. **2.** *U.S. politics.* an assembly of delegates of one party to select candidates for office. **3.** *Diplomacy.* an international agreement second only to a treaty in formality: *a telecommunications convention.* **4.** any agreement, compact, or contract. **5.** the most widely accepted or established view of what is thought to be proper behaviour, good taste, etc. **6.** an accepted rule, usage, etc.: *a convention used by printers.* **7.** *Bridge.* Also called: **conventional.** a bid or play not to be taken at its face value, which one's partner can interpret according to a prearranged bidding system. [C15: from Latin *conventiō* an assembling, agreeing]

conventional (kənˈvɛnʃənəl) *adj.* **1.** following the accepted customs and proprieties, esp. in a way that lacks originality: *conventional habits.* **2.** established by accepted usage or general agreement. **3.** of or relating to a convention or assembly. **4.** *Law.* based upon the agreement or consent of parties. **5.** *Arts.* represented in a simplified or generalized way; conventionalized. **6.** (of weapons, warfare, etc.) not nuclear. ~*n.* **7.** *Bridge.* another word for **convention** (sense 7). —**conˈventionally** *adv.*

conventionalism (kənˈvɛnʃənəˌlɪzəm) *n.* **1.** advocacy of or conformity to that which is established. **2.** something conventional. **3.** *Philosophy.* a theory that moral principles are not enshrined in the nature of things but merely reflect customary practice. **4.** *Philosophy.* the theory that meaning is a matter of convention and thus that scientific laws merely reflect such general linguistic agreement. —**conˈventionalist** *n.*

conventionality (kənˌvɛnʃəˈnælɪtɪ) *n., pl.* **-ties. 1.** the quality or characteristic of being conventional, esp. in behaviour, thinking, etc. **2.** (*often pl.*) something conventional, esp. a normal or accepted rule of behaviour; propriety.

conventionalize *or* **conventionalise** (kənˈvɛnʃənəˌlaɪz) *vb.* (*tr.*) **1.** to make conventional. **2.** to simplify or stylize (a design, decorative device, etc.). —**conˌventionaliˈzation** *or* **conˌventionaliˈsation** *n.*

conventual (kənˈvɛntjʊəl) *adj.* **1.** of, belonging to, or characteristic of a convent. ~*n.* **2.** a member of a convent. —**conˈventually** *adv.*

converge (kənˈvɜːdʒ) *vb.* **1.** to move or cause to move towards the same point. **2.** to meet or cause to meet; join. **3.** (*intr.*) (of opinions, effects, etc.) to tend towards a common conclusion or result. **4.** (*intr.*) *Maths.* (of an infinite series) to approach a finite limit as the number of terms increases. **5.** (*intr.*) (of animals and plants during evolutionary development) to undergo convergence. [C17: from Late Latin *convergere,* from Latin *com-* together + *vergere* to incline]

convergence (kənˈvɜːdʒəns) *n.* **1.** Also called: **conˈvergency.** the act, degree, or a point of converging. **2.** concurrence of opinions, results, etc. **3.** *Maths.* the property or manner of approaching a finite limit, esp. of an infinite series: *conditional convergence.* **4.** the combining of different forms of electronic technology, such as data processing and word processing converging into information processing. **5.** Also called: **convergent evolution.** the evolutionary development of a superficial resemblance between unrelated animals that occupy a similar environment, as in the evolution of wings in birds and bats. **6.** *Meteorol.* an accumulation of air in a region that has a greater inflow than outflow of air, often giving rise to vertical air currents. See also **Intertropical Convergence Zone. 7.** the turning of the eyes inwards in order to fixate an object nearer than that previously being fixated. Compare **divergence** (sense 6).

convergence zone *n.* *Geology.* a zone where tectonic plates collide, typified by earthquakes, mountain formation, and volcanic activity.

convergent (kənˈvɜːdʒənt) *adj.* **1.** (of two or more lines, paths, etc.) moving towards or meeting at some common point. **2.** (of forces, ideas, etc.) tending towards the same result; merging. **3.** *Maths.* (of an infinite series) having a finite limit.

convergent thinking *n.* *Psychol.* analytical, usually deductive, thinking in which ideas are examined for their logical validity or in which a set of rules is followed, e.g. in arithmetic.

conversable (kənˈvɜːsəbəl) *adj.* **1.** easy or pleasant to talk to. **2.** able or inclined to talk. —**conˈversableness** *n.* —**conˈversably** *adv.*

conversant (kənˈvɜːsənt) *adj.* (*usually postpositive* and foll. by *with*) experienced (in), familiar (with), or acquainted (with). —**conˈversance** *or* **conˈversancy** *n.* —**conˈversantly** *adv.*

conversation (ˌkɒnvəˈseɪʃən) *n.* **1.** the interchange through speech of information, ideas, etc.; spoken communication. **2. make conversation.** to talk in an artificial way.

conversational (ˌkɒnvəˈseɪʃənəl) *adj.* **1.** of, using, or in the manner of conversation. **2.** inclined to or skilled in conversation; conversable. —ˌ**converˈsationally** *adv.*

conversational implicature *n.* *Logic, philosophy.* another term for **implicature.**

conversationalist (ˌkɒnvəˈseɪʃənəlɪst) *or* **conversationist** *n.* a person who enjoys or excels in conversation.

conversation piece *n.* **1.** something, esp. an unusual object, that provokes conversation. **2.** (esp. in 18th-century Britain) a group portrait in a landscape or domestic setting. **3.** a play emphasizing dialogue.

conversazione *Italian.* (konversatˈtsjone; *English* ˌkɒnvəˌsætsɪˈəʊnɪ) *n., pl.* **-zioni** (*Italian* -ˈtsjoni) *or* **-ziones** (*English* -tsɪˈəʊniːz). a social gathering for discussion of the arts, literature, etc. [C18: literally: conversation]

converse[1] *vb.* (kənˈvɜːs). (*intr.;* often foll. by *with*) **1.** to engage in conversation (with). **2.** to commune spiritually (with). **3.** *Obsolete.* **a.** to associate; consort. **b.** to have sexual intercourse. ~*n.* (ˈkɒnvɜːs). **4.** conversation (often in the phrase **hold converse with**). **5.** *Obsolete.* **a.** fellowship or acquaintance. **b.** sexual intercourse. [C16: from Old French *converser,* from Latin *conversārī* to keep company with, from *conversāre* to turn constantly, from *vertere* to turn] —**conˈverser** *n.*

converse[2] (ˈkɒnvɜːs) *adj.* **1.** (*prenominal*) reversed; opposite; contrary. ~*n.* **2.** something that is opposite or contrary. **3.** *Logic.* **a.** a categorical proposition obtained from another by the transposition of subject and predicate, as *all bald men are bad* from *all bad men are bald.* **b.** a proposition so derived, possibly by weakening a universal proposition to the corresponding particular, as *some socialists are rich* from *all rich men are socialists.* **4.** *Logic, maths.* a relation that holds between two relata only when a given relation holds between them in reverse order: thus *father of* is the converse of *son of.* [C16: from Latin *conversus* turned around; see CONVERSE[1]] —**conˈversely** *adv.*

conversion (kənˈvɜːʃən) *n.* **1. a.** a change or adaptation in form, character, or function. **b.** something changed in one of these respects. **2.** a change to another attitude or belief, as in a change of religion. **3.** *Maths.* a change in the units or form of a number or expression: *the conversion of miles to kilometres involves multiplying by 1.61.* **4.** *Logic.* a form of inference by which one proposition is obtained as the converse of another proposition. **5.** *Law.* **a.** unauthorized dealing with or the assumption of rights of ownership to another's personal property. **b.** the changing of real property into personalty or personalty into realty. **6.** *Rugby.* a score made after a try by kicking the ball over the crossbar from a place kick. **7.** *Physics.* a change of fertile material to fissile material in a reactor. **8. a.** an alteration to a car engine to improve its performance. **b.** (*as modifier*): *a conversion kit.* **9.** material alteration to the structure or fittings of a building undergoing a change in function or legal status. **10.** *N.Z.* the unauthorized appropriation of a motor vehicle. [C14: from

Latin *conversiō* a turning around; see CONVERT] —**con'version-al** *or* **con'versionary** *adj.*

conversion hysteria *n.* a form of neurosis in which severe physical symptoms like blindness or paralysis appear with no apparent physical cause.

convert *vb.* (kən'vɜːt). (*mainly tr.*) **1.** to change or adapt the form, character, or function of; transform. **2.** to cause (someone) to change in opinion, belief, etc. **3.** to change (a person or his way of life, etc.) for the better. **4.** (*intr.*) to admit of being changed (into): *the table converts into a tray.* **5.** (*also intr.*) to change or be changed into another chemical compound or physical state: *to convert water into ice.* **6.** *Law.* **a.** to assume unlawful proprietary rights over (personal property). **b.** to change (property) from realty into personalty or vice versa. **7.** (*also intr.*) *Rugby.* to make a conversion after (a try). **8.** *Logic.* to transpose the subject and predicate of (a proposition) by conversion. **9.** to change (a value or measurement) from one system of units to another. **10.** to exchange (a security or bond) for something of equivalent value. ~*n.* ('kɒnvɜːt). **11.** a person who has been converted to another belief, religion, etc. [C13: from Old French *convertir,* from Latin *convertere* to turn around, alter, transform, from *vertere* to turn] —**con'vertive** *adj.*

converter *or* **convertor** (kən'vɜːtə) *n.* **1.** a person or thing that converts. **2.** *Physics.* **a.** a device for converting alternating current to direct current or vice versa. **b.** a device for converting a signal from one frequency to another. **3.** a vessel in which molten metal is refined, using a blast of air or oxygen. See also **Bessemer converter, L-D converter. 4.** short for **converter reactor. 5.** *Computer technol.* a device for converting one form of coded information to another, such as an analogue-to-digital converter.

converter reactor *n.* a nuclear reactor for converting one fuel into another, esp. one that transforms fertile material into fissionable material. Compare **breeder reactor.**

convertible (kən'vɜːtəb^{ə}l) *adj.* **1.** capable of being converted. **2.** (of a car) having a folding or removable roof. **3.** *Finance.* **a.** a bond or debenture that can be converted to ordinary or preference shares on a fixed date at a fixed price. **b.** (of a paper currency) exchangeable on demand for precious metal to an equivalent value. ~*n.* **4.** a car with a folding or removable roof. —**con,verti'bility** *or* **con'vertibleness** *n.* —**con'vertibly** *adv.*

convertiplane, convertaplane, *or* **convertoplane** (kən'vɜːtə,pleɪn) *n.* an aircraft that can land and take off vertically by temporarily directing its propulsive thrust downwards.

convertite ('kɒnvə,taɪt) *n. Archaic.* a convert, esp. a reformed prostitute.

convex ('kɒnvɛks, kɒn'vɛks) *adj.* **1.** curving or bulging outwards. **2.** *Physics.* having one or two surfaces curved or ground in the shape of a section of the exterior of a sphere, paraboloid, ellipsoid, etc.: *a convex lens.* **3.** *Maths.* (of a polygon) containing no interior angle greater than 180°. ~*vb.* **4.** (*tr.*) to make convex. ~Compare **concave.** [C16: from Latin *convexus* vaulted, rounded] —**'convexly** *adv.*

convexity (kən'vɛksɪtɪ) *n., pl.* **-ties. 1.** the state or quality of being convex. **2.** a convex surface, object, etc.; bulge.

convexo-concave (kən,vɛksəʊkɒn'keɪv) *adj.* **1.** having one side convex and the other side concave. **2.** (of a lens) having a convex face with greater curvature than the concave face. Compare **concavo-convex** (sense 2).

convexo-convex *adj.* (esp. of a lens) having both sides convex; biconvex.

convey (kən'veɪ) *vb.* (*tr.*) **1.** to take, carry, or transport from one place to another. **2.** to communicate (a message, information, etc.). **3.** (of a channel, path, etc.) to conduct, transmit, or transfer. **4.** *Law.* to transmit or transfer (the title to property). **5.** *Archaic.* to steal. [C13: from Old French *conveier,* from Medieval Latin *conviāre* to escort, from Latin *com-* with + *via* way] —**con'veyable** *adj.*

conveyance (kən'veɪəns) *n.* **1.** the act of conveying. **2.** a means of transport. **3.** *Law.* **a.** a transfer of the legal title to property. **b.** the document effecting such a transfer. —**con'veyancer** *n.* —**con'veyancing** *n.*

conveyor *or* **conveyer** (kən'veɪə) *n.* **1.** a person or thing that conveys. **2.** short for **conveyor belt.**

conveyor belt *n.* a flexible endless strip of fabric or linked plates driven by rollers and used to transport objects, esp. in a factory.

convict *vb.* (kən'vɪkt). (*tr.*) **1.** to pronounce (someone) guilty of an offence. ~*n.* ('kɒnvɪkt). **2.** a person found guilty of an offence against the law, esp. one who is sentenced to imprisonment. **3.** a person serving a prison sentence. ~*adj.* (kən'vɪkt). **4.** *Obsolete.* convicted. [C14: from Latin *convictus* convicted of crime, from *convincere* to prove guilty, CONVINCE] —**con'victable** *or* **con'victible** *adj.*

conviction (kən'vɪkʃən) *n.* **1.** the state or appearance of being convinced. **2.** a fixed or firmly held belief, opinion, etc. **3.** the act of convincing. **4.** the act or an instance of convicting or the state of being convicted. **5. carry conviction.** to be convincing. —**con'victional** *adj.*

convictive (kən'vɪktɪv) *adj.* able or serving to convince or convict. —**con'victively** *adv.*

convince (kən'vɪns) *vb.* (*tr.*) **1.** (*may take a clause as object*) to make (someone) agree, understand, or realize the truth or validity of something; persuade. **2.** *Obsolete.* **a.** to overcome. **b.** to prove guilty. [C16: from Latin *convincere* to demonstrate incontrovertibly, from *com-* (intensive) + *vincere* to overcome, conquer] —**con'vincement** *n.* —**con'vincer** *n.* —**con'vincible** *adj.*

convincing (kən'vɪnsɪŋ) *adj.* **1.** credible or plausible. **2.** *Chiefly law.* persuading by evidence or argument. —**con'vincingly** *adv.* —**con'vincingness** *n.*

convivial (kən'vɪvɪəl) *adj.* sociable; jovial or festive: *a convivial atmosphere.* [C17: from Late Latin *convīviālis* pertaining to a feast, from Latin *convīvium,* a living together, banquet, from *vīvere* to live] —**con'vivialist** *n.* —**con,vivi'ality** *n.* —**con'vivially** *adv.*

convocation (,kɒnvə'keɪʃən) *n.* **1.** a large formal assembly, esp. one specifically convened. **2.** the act of convoking or state of being convoked. **3.** *Church of England.* either of the synods of the provinces of Canterbury or York. **4.** *Episcopal Church.* **a.** an assembly of the clergy and part of the laity of a diocese. **b.** a district represented at such an assembly. **5.** (*sometimes cap.*) (in some British universities) a legislative assembly composed mainly of graduates. **6.** (in India) a degree-awarding ceremony. **7.** (in Australia and New Zealand) the graduate membership of a university. —,**convo'cational** *adj.* —**'convo,cator** *n.*

convoke (kən'vəʊk) *vb.* (*tr.*) to call (a meeting, assembly, etc.) together; summon. [C16: from Latin *convocāre,* from *vocāre* to call] —**convocative** (kən'vɒkətɪv) *adj.* —**con'voker** *n.*

convolute ('kɒnvə,luːt) *vb.* (*tr.*) **1.** to form into a twisted, coiled, or rolled shape. ~*adj.* **2.** *Botany.* rolled longitudinally upon itself: *a convolute petal.* **3.** another word for **convoluted** (sense 2). [C18: from Latin *convolūtus* rolled up, from *convolvere* to roll together, from *volvere* to turn] —**'convo,lutely** *adv.*

convoluted ('kɒnvə,luːtɪd) *adj.* **1.** (esp. of meaning, style, etc.) difficult to comprehend; involved. **2.** wound together; coiled. —**'convo,lutedly** *adv.* —**'convo,lutedness** *n.*

convolution (,kɒnvə'luːʃən) *n.* **1.** a twisting together; a turn, twist, or coil. **2.** an intricate, involved, or confused matter or condition. **3.** Also called: **gyrus.** any of the numerous convex folds or ridges of the surface of the brain. —,**convo'lutional** *or* ,**convo'lutionary** *adj.*

convolve (kən'vɒlv) *vb.* to wind or roll together; coil; twist. [C16: from Latin *convolvere;* see CONVOLUTE]

convolvulaceous (kən,vɒlvjʊ'leɪʃəs) *adj.* of, relating to, or belonging to the *Convolvulaceae,* a family of plants having trumpet-shaped flowers and typically a climbing, twining, or prostrate habit: includes bindweed, morning-glory, and sweet potato.

convolvulus (kən'vɒlvjʊləs) *n., pl.* **-luses** *or* **-li** (-,laɪ). any typically twining herbaceous convolvulaceous plant of the genus *Convolvulus,* having funnel-shaped flowers and triangular leaves. See also **bindweed.** [C16: from Latin: bindweed; see CONVOLUTE]

convoy ('kɒnvɔɪ) *n.* **1.** a group of merchant ships with an escort of warships. **2.** a group of land vehicles assembled to travel together. **3.** the act of travelling or escorting by convoy (esp. in the phrase **in convoy**). ~*vb.* **4.** (*tr.*) to escort while in transit. [C14: from Old French *convoier* to CONVEY]

convulsant (kən'vʌlsənt) *adj.* **1.** producing convulsions. ~*n.* **2.** a drug that produces convulsions. [C19: from French, from *convulser* to CONVULSE]

convulse (kən'vʌls) *vb.* **1.** (*tr.*) to shake or agitate violently. **2.** (*tr.*) to cause (muscles) to undergo violent spasms or contractions. **3.** (*intr.; often foll. by with*) *Informal.* to shake or be overcome (with violent emotion, esp. laughter). [C17: from Latin *convulsus,* from *convellere* to tear up, from *vellere* to pluck, pull] —**con'vulsive** *adj.* —**con'vulsively** *adv.* —**con'vulsiveness** *n.*

convulsion (kən'vʌlʃən) *n.* **1.** a violent involuntary contraction of a muscle or muscles. **2.** a violent upheaval, disturbance, or agitation, esp. a social one. **3.** (*usually pl.*) *Informal.* uncontrollable laughter: *I was in convulsions.* —**con'vulsionary** *adj.*

cony *or* **coney** ('kəʊnɪ) *n., pl.* **-nies** *or* **-neys. 1.** a rabbit or fur made from the skin of a rabbit. **2.** (in the Bible) another name for the **hyrax,** esp. the Syrian rock hyrax. **3.** another name for the **pika. 4.** *Archaic.* a fool or dupe. [C13: back formation from *conies,* from Old French *conis,* plural of *conil,* from Latin *cunīculus* rabbit]

coo (kuː) *vb.* **coos, cooing, cooed. 1.** (*intr.*) (of doves, pigeons, etc.) to make a characteristic soft throaty call. **2.** (*tr.*) to speak in a soft murmur. **3.** (*intr.*) to murmur lovingly (esp. in the phrase **bill and coo**). ~*n.* **4.** the sound of cooing. ~*interj.* **5.** *Brit. slang.* an exclamation of surprise, awe, etc. —**'cooer** *n.* —**'cooingly** *adv.*

cooee *or* **cooey** ('kuːiː) *interj.* **1.** a call used to attract attention, esp. (originally) a long loud high-pitched call on two notes used in the Australian bush. ~*vb.* **cooees, cooeeing, cooeed** *or* **cooeys, cooeying, cooeyed. 2.** (*intr.*) to utter this call. ~*n.* **3.** *Austral. and N.Z. informal.* calling distance (esp. in the phrase **within (a) cooee (of)**). [C19: from a native Australian language]

cook (kʊk) *vb.* **1.** to prepare (food) by the action of heat, as by boiling, baking, etc., or (of food) to become ready for eating through such a process. Related adj.: **culinary. 2.** to subject or be subjected to the action of intense heat: *the town cooked in the sun.* **3.** (*tr.*) *Slang.* to alter or falsify (something, esp. figures, accounts, etc.): *to cook the books.* **4.** (*tr.*) *Slang.* to spoil or ruin (something). **5.** (*intr.*) *Slang.* to happen (esp. in the phrase **what's cooking?**). **6.** (*tr.*) *Slang.* to prepare (any of several drugs) by heating. **7.** (*intr.*) *Music slang.* to play vigorously: *the band was cooking.* **8. cook someone's goose.** *Informal.* **a.** to spoil a person's plans. **b.** to bring about someone's ruin, downfall, etc. ~*n.* **9.** a person who prepares food for eating, esp. as an occupation. ~See also **cook up.** [Old English *cōc* (n.), from Latin *coquus* a cook, from *coquere* to cook] —'**cookable** *adj.*

cook-chill *n.* a method of food preparation used by caterers, in which cooked dishes are chilled rapidly and reheated as required.

cooker ('kʊkə) *n.* **1.** an apparatus, usually of metal and heated by gas, electricity, oil, or solid fuel, for cooking food; stove. **2.** *Brit.* any large sour apple used in cooking.

cookery ('kʊkərɪ) *n.* **1.** the art, study, or practice of cooking. **2.** *U.S.* a place for cooking. **3.** *Canadian.* a cookhouse at a mining or lumber camp.

cookery book *or* **cookbook** ('kʊkˌbʊk) *n.* a book containing recipes and instructions for cooking.

cook-general *n., pl.* **cooks-general.** *Brit.* (formerly, esp. in the 1920s and '30s) a domestic servant who did cooking and housework.

cookhouse ('kʊkˌhaʊs) *n.* a place for cooking, esp. a camp kitchen.

cookie *or* **cooky** ('kʊkɪ) *n., pl.* **-ies.** **1.** the U.S. and Canadian word for **biscuit.** **2.** a Scot. word for **bun.** **3.** *Informal.* a person: *smart cookie.* **4. that's the way the cookie crumbles.** *Informal.* matters are inevitably or unalterably so. [C18: from Dutch *koekje*, diminutive of *koek* cake]

Cook Island Maori (kʊk) *n. N.Z.* a dialect of Maori spoken in the Cook Islands in the SW Pacific.

cookout ('kʊkˌaʊt) *n. U.S. and Canadian.* a party where a meal is cooked and eaten out of doors.

cook shop *n.* **1.** *Brit.* a shop that sells cookery equipment. **2.** *U.S.* a restaurant.

Cook's tour *n. Informal.* a rapid but extensive tour or survey of anything. [C19: after Thomas *Cook* (1808–92), British travel agent]

cook up *vb.* (*tr., adv.*) **1.** *Informal.* to concoct or invent (a story, alibi, etc.). **2.** to prepare (a meal), esp. quickly. **3.** *Slang.* to prepare (a drug) for use by heating, as by dissolving heroin in a spoon. ~*n.* **cook-up.** **4.** (in the Caribbean) a dish consisting of mixed meats, rice, shrimps, and sometimes vegetables.

cool (kuːl) *adj.* **1.** moderately cold: *a cool day.* **2.** comfortably free of heat: *a cool room.* **3.** producing a pleasant feeling of coldness: *a cool shirt.* **4.** able to conceal emotion; calm: *a cool head.* **5.** lacking in enthusiasm, affection, cordiality, etc.: *a cool welcome.* **6.** calmly audacious or impudent. **7.** *Informal.* (esp. of numbers, sums of money, etc.) without exaggeration; actual: *a cool ten thousand.* **8.** (of a colour) having violet, blue, or green predominating; cold. **9.** (of jazz) characteristic of the late 1940s and early 1950s, economical and rhythmically relaxed. **10.** *Informal.* sophisticated or elegant, esp. in an unruffled way. **11.** *Informal, chiefly U.S. and Canadian.* excellent; marvellous. ~*adv.* **12.** *Not standard.* in a cool manner; coolly. ~*n.* **13.** coolness: *the cool of the evening.* **14.** *Slang.* calmness; composure (esp. in the phrases **keep** *or* **lose one's cool**). **15.** *Slang.* unruffled elegance or sophistication. ~*vb.* **16.** (usually foll. by *down* or *off*) to make or become cooler. **17.** (usually foll. by *down* or *off*) to lessen the intensity of (anger or excitement) or (of anger or excitement) to become less intense; calm down. **18. cool it.** (*usually imperative*) *Slang.* to calm down; take it easy. **19. cool one's heels.** to wait or be kept waiting. ~See also **cool out.** [Old English *cōl*; related to Old Norse *kōlna*, Old High German *kuoli*; see COLD, CHILL] —'**coolingly** *adv.* —'**coolingness** *n.* —'**coolish** *adj.* —'**coolly** *adv.* —'**coolness** *n.*

coolabah *or* **coolibah** ('kuːləˌbɑː) *n.* an Australian myrtaceous tree, *Eucalyptus microtheca*, that grows along rivers and has smooth bark and long narrow leaves. [from a native Australian language]

coolamon ('kuːləmɒn) *n. Austral.* a shallow dish of wood or bark, used for carrying water. [C19: from a native Australian language]

coolant ('kuːlənt) *n.* **1.** a fluid used to cool a system or to transfer heat from one part of it to another. **2.** a liquid, such as an emulsion of oil, water, and soft soap, used to lubricate and cool the workpiece and cutting tool during machining.

cool bag *or* **box** *n.* an insulated container used to keep food cool on picnics, to carry frozen food, etc.

cool drink *n. S. African.* any soft drink.

cooler ('kuːlə) *n.* **1.** a container, vessel, or apparatus for cooling, such as a heat exchanger. **2.** a slang word for **prison.** **3.** a drink consisting of wine, fruit juice, and carbonated water.

Cooley's anaemia ('kuːlɪz) *n.* another name for **thalassaemia.** [named after Thomas B. *Cooley* (1871–1945), U.S. paediatrician who reported on it in children in the Mediterranean area]

Coolgardie safe (kuːl'gɑːdɪ) *n.* a cupboard with wetted hessian walls for keeping food cool: used esp. in Australia. Sometimes shortened to **Coolgardie.** [named after *Coolgardie*, Western Australia, perhaps because of resemblance to COOL and GUARD]

coolie *or* **cooly** ('kuːlɪ) *n., pl.* **-ies.** **1.** a cheaply hired unskilled Oriental labourer. **2.** *Derogatory.* an Indian living in South Africa. [C17: from Hindi *kulī*, probably of Dravidian origin; related to Tamil *kūli* hire, hireling]

cooling-off period *n.* **1.** a period during which the contending sides to a dispute reconsider their options before taking further action. **2.** a period, often 14 days, that begins when a sale contract or life-assurance policy is received by a member of the public, during which the contract or policy can be cancelled without loss.

cooling tower *n.* a tall hollow structure in which steam is condensed or water that is used as a coolant in some industrial process is allowed to cool for reuse by trickling down a surface.

cool out *vb.* (*intr., adv.*) *Caribbean.* to relax and cool down.

coolth (kuːlθ) *n.* coolness. [C16: originally dialect, from COOL + -TH[1]]

coom *or* **coomb** (kuːm) *n. Dialect, chiefly Scot. and northern English.* waste material, such as dust from coal, grease from axles, etc. [C16 (meaning: soot): probably a variant of CULM[1]]

coomb, combe, coombe, *or* **comb** (kuːm) *n.* **1.** *Chiefly southern English* a short valley or deep hollow, esp. in chalk areas. **2.** *Chiefly northern English* another name for a **cirque.** [Old English *cumb* (in place names), perhaps of Celtic origin; compare Old French *combe* small valley, also probably of Celtic origin]

coon (kuːn) *n.* **1.** *Informal.* short for **raccoon.** **2.** *Derogatory slang.* a Negro or Australian Aborigine.

cooncan ('kuːnˌkæn) *or* **conquian** *n.* a card game for two players, similar to rummy. [C19: from (Mexican) Spanish *con quién* with whom?, apparently with reference to the forming and declaring of sequences and sets of cards]

coonhound ('kuːnˌhaʊnd) *n.* another name for **raccoon dog** (sense 2).

coon's age *n. U.S. slang.* a long time.

coonskin ('kuːnˌskɪn) *n.* **1.** the pelt of a raccoon. **2.** a raccoon cap with the tail hanging at the back. **3.** *U.S.* an overcoat made of raccoon.

coontie ('kuːntɪ) *n.* **1.** an evergreen plant, *Zamia floridana* of S Florida, related to the cycads and having large dark green leathery leaves: family *Zamiaceae.* **2.** a starch derived from the underground stems of this plant. [C19: from Seminole *kunti* flour from this plant]

coop[1] (kuːp) *n.* **1.** a cage or small enclosure for poultry or small animals. **2.** a small narrow place of confinement, esp. a prison cell. **3.** a wicker basket for catching fish. ~*vb.* **4.** (*tr.*; often foll. by *up* or *in*) to confine in a restricted area. [C15: probably from Middle Low German *kūpe* basket, tub; related to Latin *cūpa* cask, vat]

coop[2] *or* **co-op** ('kəʊˌɒp) *n.* a cooperative, cooperative society, or shop run by a cooperative society.

coop. *or* **co-op.** *abbrev. for* cooperative.

cooper ('kuːpə) *n.* **1.** Also called: **hooper.** a person skilled in making and repairing barrels, casks, etc. ~*vb.* **2.** (*tr.*) to make or mend (barrels, casks, etc.). **3.** (*intr.*) to work as a cooper. [C13: from Middle Dutch *cūper* or Middle Low German *kūper*; see COOP[1]]

cooperage ('kuːpərɪdʒ) *n.* **1.** Also called: **coopery.** the craft, place of work, or products of a cooper. **2.** the labour fee charged by a cooper.

cooperate *or* **co-operate** (kəʊ'ɒpəˌreɪt) *vb.* (*intr.*) **1.** to work or act together. **2.** to be of assistance or be willing to assist. **3.** *Economics.* (of firms, workers, consumers, etc.) to engage in economic cooperation. [C17: from Late Latin *cooperārī* to work with, combine, from Latin *operārī* to work] —**co'operˌator** *or* **co-'operˌator** *n.*

cooperation *or* **co-operation** (kəʊˌɒpə'reɪʃən) *n.* **1.** joint operation or action. **2.** assistance or willingness to assist. **3.** *Economics.* the combination of consumers, workers, farmers, etc., in activities usually embracing production, distribution, or trade. **4.** *Ecology.* beneficial but inessential interaction between two species in a community. —**coˌoper'ationist** *or* **co-ˌoper'ationist** *n.*

cooperative *or* **co-operative** (kəʊ'ɒpərətɪv, -'ɒprə-) *adj.* **1.** willing to cooperate; helpful. **2.** acting in conjunction with others; cooperating. **3. a.** (of an enterprise, farm, etc.) owned collectively and managed for joint economic benefit. **b.** (of an economy or economic activity) based on collective ownership and cooperative use of the means of production and distribution. ~*n.* **4.** a cooperative organization. **5.** Also called: **cooperative apartment.** *U.S.* a block of flats belonging to a corporation in which shares are owned in proportion to the relative value of the flat occupied. Sometimes shortened to **coop.** Compare **condominium** (sense 3). —**co'operatively** *or* **co-'operatively** *adv.* —**co'operativeness** *or* **co-'operativeness** *n.*

cooperative bank *n.* a U.S. name for **building society.**

cooperative farm *n.* **1.** a farm that is run in cooperation with others in the purchasing and using of machinery, stock, etc., and in the marketing of produce through its own institutions (**farmers' cooperatives**). **2.** a farm that is owned by a cooperative society. **3.** a farm run on a communal basis, such as a kibbutz. **4.** another name for **collective farm.**

cooperative society *n.* a commercial enterprise owned and managed by and for the benefit of customers or workers. Often shortened to **coop, co-op.**

cooperativity (kəʊˌɒpərə'tɪvɪtɪ) *n. Biochem., chem.* an interaction between structural units within a molecule or between molecules in an assemblage that enables the system to respond more sharply to an external change than would isolated units.

Cooper pair (ˈkuːpə) *n. Physics.* a pair of weakly bound electrons responsible for the transfer of charge in a superconducting material. [C20: named after Leon Neil *Cooper* (born 1930), U.S. physicist]

Cooper's hawk *n.* a small North American hawk, *Accipiter cooperii,* having a bluish-grey back and wings and a reddish-brown breast. [C19: named after William *Cooper* (died 1864), American naturalist]

coopery (ˈkuːpərɪ) *n., pl.* **-eries.** another word for **cooperage** (sense 1).

coopt *or* **co-opt** (kəʊˈɒpt) *vb. (tr.)* **1.** to add (someone) to a committee, board, etc., by the agreement of the existing members. **2.** to appoint summarily; commandeer. [C17: from Latin *cooptāre* to elect, from *optāre* to choose] —**coˈoption, co-ˈoption** *or* **ˌcoopˈtation, ˌco-opˈtation** *n.* —**coˈoptative** *or* **co-ˈoptative** *adj.*

Coopworth (ˈkuːpˌwɜːθ) *n.* a New Zealand breed of sheep derived from the Romney Marsh.

coordinal *or* **co-ordinal** (kəʊˈɔːdɪnᵊl) *adj.* (of animals or plants) belonging to the same order.

coordinate *or* **co-ordinate** *vb.* (kəʊˈɔːdɪˌneɪt). **1.** *(tr.)* to organize or integrate (diverse elements) in a harmonious operation. **2.** to place (things) in the same class or order, or (of things) to be placed in the same class or order. **3.** *(intr.)* to work together, esp. harmoniously. **4.** *(intr.)* to take or be in the form of a harmonious order. **5.** *Chem.* to form or cause to form a coordinate bond. ~*n.* (kəʊˈɔːdɪnɪt, -ˌneɪt) **6.** *Maths.* any of a set of numbers that defines the location of a point in space with reference to a system of axes. See **Cartesian coordinates, polar coordinates. 7.** a person or thing equal in rank, type, etc. ~*adj.* (kəʊˈɔːdɪnɪt, -ˌneɪt). **8.** of, concerned with, or involving coordination. **9.** of the same rank, type, etc. **10.** of or involving the use of coordinates: *coordinate geometry.* ~See also **coordinates.** —**coˈordinately** *or* **co-ˈordinately** *adv.* —**coˈordinateness** *or* **co-ˈordinateness** *n.* —**coˈordinative** *or* **co-ˈordinative** *adj.* —**coˈordiˌnator** *or* **co-ˈordiˌnator** *n.*

coordinate bond *n.* a type of covalent chemical bond in which both the shared electrons are provided by one of the atoms. Also called: **dative bond, semipolar bond.**

coordinate clause *n.* one of two or more clauses in a sentence having the same status and introduced by coordinating conjunctions. Compare **subordinate clause.**

coordinate geometry *n.* another term for **analytical geometry.**

coordinates (kəʊˈɔːdɪnɪts, -ˌneɪts) *pl. n.* clothes of matching or harmonious colours and design, suitable for wearing together. Compare **separates.**

coordinating conjunction *n.* a conjunction that introduces coordinate clauses, such as *and, but,* and *or.* Compare **subordinating conjunction.**

coordination *or* **co-ordination** (kəʊˌɔːdɪˈneɪʃən) *n.* balanced and effective interaction of movement, actions, etc. [C17: from Late Latin *coordinātiō,* from Latin *ordinātiō* an arranging; see ORDINATE]

coordination compound *n.* another name for **complex** (sense 8).

coordination number *n. Chem.* the number of coordinated species surrounding the central atom in a complex or crystal.

coorie (ˈkuːrɪ) *vb. (intr.) Scot.* a variant spelling of **courie.**

coot (kuːt) *n.* **1.** any aquatic bird of the genus *Fulica,* esp. *F. atra* of Europe and Asia, having lobed toes, dark plumage, and a white bill with a frontal shield: family *Rallidae* (rails, crakes, etc.). **2.** a foolish person, esp. an old man (often in the phrase **old coot**). [C14: probably from Low German; compare Dutch *koet*]

cootch *or* **cwtch** (kutʃ) *South Wales dialect.* ~*n.* **1.** a hiding place. **2.** a room, shed, etc., used for storage: *a coal cootch.* ~*vb.* **3.** *(tr.)* to hide. **4.** (often foll. by *up*) to cuddle or be cuddled. **5.** *(tr.)* to clasp (someone or something) to oneself. [from French *couche* COUCH, probably influenced by Welsh *cwt* hut]

cootie (ˈkuːtɪ) *n. U.S. and N.Z.* a slang name for the **body louse.** See **louse** (sense 1). Also called (N.Z.) **kutu.** [C20: perhaps from Malay or Maori *kutu* louse]

cop[1] (kɒp) *Slang.* ~*n.* **1.** another name for **policeman. 2.** *Brit.* an arrest (esp. in the phrase **a fair cop**). **3.** an instance of plagiarism. ~*vb.* **cops, copping, copped.** *(tr.)* **4.** to seize or catch. **5.** to steal. **6.** to buy, steal, or otherwise obtain (illegal drugs). Compare **score** (sense 26). **7.** to suffer (a punishment): *you'll cop a clout if you do that!* Also in the phrase **cop it. 8. cop it sweet.** *Austral. slang.* to accept a penalty without complaint. ~See also **cop out.** [C18: (vb.) perhaps from obsolete *cap* to arrest, from Old French *caper* to seize; sense 1, back formation from COPPER[2]]

cop[2] (kɒp) *n.* **1.** a conical roll of thread wound on a spindle. **2.** *Now chiefly dialect.* the top or crest, as of a hill. [Old English *cop, copp* top, summit, of uncertain origin; perhaps related to Old English *copp* CUP]

cop[3] (kɒp) *n. Brit. slang.* (*usually used with a negative*) worth or value: *that work is not much cop.* [C19: n. use of COP[1] (in the sense: to catch, hence something caught, something of value)]

COP (in New Zealand) *abbrev. for* Certificate of Proficiency: a pass in a university subject.

copacetic, copasetic *or* **copesetic, copesettic** (ˌkəʊpəˈsɛtɪk) *adj. U.S. and Canadian slang.* very good; excellent; completely satisfactory. [C20: of unknown origin]

copaiba (kəʊˈpaɪbə) *or* **copaiva** (kəʊˈpaɪvə) *n.* a transparent yellowish viscous oleoresin obtained from certain tropical South American trees of the caesalpiniaceous genus *Copaifera:* used in varnishes and ointments. Also called: **copaiba balsam, copaiba resin.** [C18: via Spanish via Portuguese from Tupi]

copal (ˈkəʊpᵊl, -pæl) *n.* a hard aromatic resin, yellow, orange, or red in colour, obtained from various tropical trees and used in making varnishes and lacquers. [C16: from Spanish, from Nahuatl *copalli* resin]

copalm (ˈkəʊˌpɑːm) *n.* **1.** the aromatic brown resin obtained from the sweet gum tree. **2.** another name for the **sweet gum.** [C19: from Louisiana French, from Mexican Spanish *copalme;* see COPAL, PALMATE]

coparcenary (kəʊˈpɑːsənərɪ) *or* **coparceny** (kəʊˈpɑːsɪnɪ) *n. Law.* a form of joint ownership of property, esp. joint heirship. Also called: **parcenary.**

coparcener (kəʊˈpɑːsɪnə) *n. Law.* a person who inherits an estate as coheir with others. Also called: **parcener.**

copartner (kəʊˈpɑːtnə) *n.* a partner or associate, esp. an equal partner in business.

copartnership (kəʊˈpɑːtnəʃɪp) *n.* **1.** a partnership or association between two equals, esp. in a business enterprise. **2.** a form of industrial democracy in which the employees of an organization are partners in the company and share in part of its profits.

cope[1] (kəʊp) *vb.* **1.** *(intr.;* foll. by *with)* to contend (against). **2.** *(intr.)* to deal successfully with or handle a situation; manage: *she coped well with the problem.* **3.** *(tr.) Archaic.* **a.** to deal with. **b.** to meet in battle. [C14: from Old French *coper* to strike, cut, from *coup* blow; see COUP[1]]

cope[2] (kəʊp) *n.* **1.** a large ceremonial cloak worn at solemn liturgical functions by priests of certain Christian sects. **2.** any covering shaped like a cope. ~*vb.* **3.** *(tr.)* to dress (someone) in a cope. [Old English *cāp,* from Medieval Latin *cāpa,* from Late Latin *cappa* hooded cloak; see CAP]

cope[3] (kəʊp) *vb. (tr.)* **1.** to provide (a wall) with a coping. **2.** to join (two moulded timber members). ~*n.* **3.** another name for **coping.** [C17: probably from French *couper* to cut; see COPE[1]]

copeck (ˈkəʊpɛk) *n.* a variant spelling of **kopeck.**

Copenhagen blue *n.* **a.** a greyish-blue colour. **b.** *(as adj.): Copenhagen-blue markings.*

Copenhagen interpretation *n.* an interpretation of quantum mechanics developed by Niels Bohr and his colleagues at the University of Copenhagen in Denmark, based on the concept of wave–particle duality and the idea that the observation influences the result of an experiment.

copepod (ˈkəʊpɪˌpɒd) *n.* **1.** any minute free-living or parasitic crustacean of the subclass *Copepoda* of marine and fresh waters: an important constituent of plankton. ~*adj.* **2.** of, relating to, or belonging to the *Copepoda.* [C19: from New Latin *Copepoda,* from Greek *kōpē* oar + *pous* foot]

coper (ˈkəʊpə) *n.* a horse-dealer. [C17 (a dealer, chapman): from dialect *cope* to buy, barter, from Low German; related to Dutch *koopen* to buy]

Copernican system (kəˈpɜːnɪkən) *n.* the theory published in 1543 by the Polish astronomer Nicolaus Copernicus (1473–1543), which stated that the earth and the planets rotated around the sun and which opposed the Ptolemaic system.

copestone (ˈkəʊpˌstəʊn) *n.* **1.** Also called: **coping stone.** a stone used to form a coping. **2.** Also called: **capstone.** the stone at the top of a building, wall, etc.

copier (ˈkɒpɪə) *n.* **1.** a person or device that copies. **2.** another word for **copyist.**

copilot (ˈkəʊˌpaɪlət) *n.* a second or relief pilot of an aircraft.

coping (ˈkəʊpɪŋ) *n.* the sloping top course of a wall, usually made of masonry or brick. Also called: **cope.**

coping saw *n.* a handsaw with a U-shaped frame used for cutting curves in a material too thick for a fret saw.

coping stone *n.* another word for **copestone** (sense 1).

copious (ˈkəʊpɪəs) *adj.* **1.** abundant; extensive in quantity. **2.** having or providing an abundant supply. **3.** full of words, ideas, etc.; profuse. [C14: from Latin *cōpiōsus* well supplied, from *cōpia* abundance, from *ops* wealth] —**ˈcopiously** *adv.* —**ˈcopiousness** *n.*

copita (*Spanish* koˈpita; *English* kəˈpiːtə) *n.* **1.** a tulip-shaped sherry glass. **2.** a glass of sherry. [diminutive of *copa* cup]

coplanar (kəʊˈpleɪnə) *adj.* lying in the same plane: *coplanar lines.* —**ˌcoplaˈnarity** *n.*

copolymer (kəʊˈpɒlɪmə) *n.* a chemical compound of high molecular weight formed by uniting the molecules of two or more different compounds (monomers). Compare **polymer, oligomer.**

copolymerize *or* **copolymerise** (kəʊˈpɒlɪməˌraɪz) *vb.* to react (two compounds) together to produce a copolymer. —**coˌpolymeriˈzation** *or* **coˌpolymeriˈsation** *n.*

cop out *Slang.* ~*vb.* **1.** *(intr., adv.)* to fail to assume responsibility or to commit oneself. ~*n.* **cop-out. 2.** an instance of avoiding responsibility or commitment. **3.** a person who acts in this way. [C20: probably from COP[1]]

copper[1] (ˈkɒpə) *n.* **1. a.** a malleable ductile reddish metallic element occurring as the free metal, copper glance, and copper pyrites: used as an electrical and thermal conductor and in such alloys as brass and bronze. Symbol: Cu; atomic no.: 29; atomic wt.: 63.54; valency: 1 or 2; relative density: 8.96; melting pt.: 1083°C; boiling pt.: 2595°C. Related adjs.: **cupric, cuprous.** Related prefix: **cupro-.** **b.** (*as modifier*): *a copper coin.* **2. a.** the reddish-brown colour of copper. **b.** (*as adj.*): *copper hair.* **3.** *Informal.* any copper or bronze coin. **4.** *Chiefly Brit.* a large vessel, formerly of copper, used for boiling or washing. **5.** any of various small widely distributed butterflies of the genera *Lycaena, Heodes,* etc., typically having reddish-brown wings: family *Lycaenidae.* ~*vb.* **6.** (*tr.*) to coat or cover with copper. [Old English *coper,* from Latin *Cyprium aes* Cyprian metal, from Greek *Kupris* Cyprus]

copper[2] ('kɒpə) *n.* a slang word for **policeman.** Often shortened to **cop.** [C19: from COP[1] (vb.) + -ER[1]]

copperas ('kɒpərəs) *n.* a less common name for **ferrous sulphate.** [C14: *coperose,* via Old French from Medieval Latin *cuperosa,* perhaps originally in the phrase *aqua cuprosa* copper water]

copper beech *n.* a cultivated variety of European beech that has reddish leaves.

copper-bottomed *adj.* reliable, esp. financially reliable. [from the former practice of coating the bottoms of ships with copper to prevent the timbers rotting]

copper-fasten *vb.* (*tr.*) *Irish.* to make (a bargain or agreement) binding.

copperhead ('kɒpə,hɛd) *n.* **1.** a venomous reddish-brown snake, *Agkistrodon contortrix,* of the eastern U.S.: family *Crotalidae* (pit vipers). **2.** a venomous reddish-brown Australian elapid snake, *Denisonia superba.* **3.** *U.S. informal.* a Yankee supporter of the South during the Civil War.

copperplate ('kɒpə,pleɪt) *n.* **1.** a polished copper plate on which a design has been etched or engraved. **2.** a print taken from such a plate. **3.** a fine handwriting based upon that used on copperplate engravings.

copper pyrites ('paɪraɪts) *n.* (*functioning as sing.*) another name for **chalcopyrite.**

coppersmith ('kɒpə,smɪθ) *n.* **1.** a person who works copper or copper alloys. **2.** an Asian barbet (a bird), *Megalaima haemacephala,* the call of which has a ringing metallic note.

copper sulphate *n.* a copper salt found naturally as chalcanthite and made by the action of sulphuric acid on copper oxide. It usually exists as blue crystals of the pentahydrate that form a white anhydrous powder when heated: used as a mordant, in electroplating, and in plant sprays. Formula: $CuSO_4$.

coppice ('kɒpɪs) *n.* **1.** a thicket or dense growth of small trees or bushes, esp. one regularly trimmed back to stumps so that a continual supply of small poles and firewood is obtained. ~*vb.* **2.** (*tr.*) to trim back (trees or bushes) to form a coppice. **3.** (*intr.*) to form a coppice. [C14: from Old French *copeiz,* from *couper* to cut] —'**coppiced** *adj.* —'**coppicing** *n.*

copra ('kɒprə) *n.* the dried, oil-yielding kernel of the coconut. [C16: from Portuguese, from Malayalam *koppara,* probably from Hindi *khoprā* coconut]

copro- *or before a vowel* **copr-** *combining form.* indicating dung or obscenity: *coprology.* [from Greek *kopros* dung]

coprolalia (,kɒprə'leɪlɪə) *n.* obsessive use of obscene or foul language.

coprolite ('kɒprə,laɪt) *n.* any of various rounded stony nodules thought to be the fossilized faeces of Mesozoic reptiles. —**coprolitic** (,kɒprə'lɪtɪk) *adj.*

coprology (kɒp'rɒlədʒɪ) *n.* preoccupation with excrement. Also called: **scatology.**

coprophagous (kɒ'prɒfəgəs) *adj.* (esp. of certain beetles) feeding on dung. —**cop'rophagy** *n.*

coprophilia (,kɒprəʊ'fɪlɪə) *n.* an abnormal interest in faeces and their evacuation.

coprophilous (kə'prɒfɪləs) or **coprophilic** (,kɒprəʊ'fɪlɪk) *adj.* growing in or on dung.

coprosma (kə'prɒzmə) *n.* any shrub of the Australasian rubiaceous genus *Coprosma:* sometimes planted for ornament. [C19: New Latin, from Greek *kopros* excrement + *osmē* smell]

coprozoic (,kɒprəʊ'zəʊɪk) *adj.* (of animals) living in dung.

copse (kɒps) *n.* another word for **coppice** (sense 1). [C16: by shortening from COPPICE]

Copt (kɒpt) *n.* **1.** a member of the Coptic Church. **2.** an Egyptian descended from the ancient Egyptians. [C17: from Arabic *qubt* Copts, from Coptic *kyptios* Egyptian, from Greek *Aiguptios,* from *Aiguptos* Egypt]

copter *or* **'copter** ('kɒptə) *n. Informal.* short for **helicopter.**

Coptic ('kɒptɪk) *n.* **1.** an Afro-Asiatic language, written in the Greek alphabet but descended from ancient Egyptian. It was extinct as a spoken language by about 1600 A.D. but survives in the Coptic Church. ~*adj.* **2.** of or relating to this language. **3.** of or relating to the Copts.

Coptic Church *n.* the ancient Christian Church of Egypt.

copula ('kɒpjʊlə) *n., pl.* **-las** *or* **-lae** (-,liː). **1.** a verb, such as *be, seem,* or *taste,* that is used merely to identify or link the subject with the complement of a sentence. Copulas may serve to link nouns (or pronouns), as in *he became king,* nouns (or pronouns) and adjectival complements, as in *sugar tastes sweet,* or nouns (or pronouns) and adverbial complements, as in *John is in jail.* **2.** anything that serves as a link. **3.** *Logic.* the often unexpressed link between the subject and predicate terms of a categorial proposition, as *are* in *all men are mortal.* [C17: from Latin: bond, connection, from *co-* together + *apere* to fasten] —'**copular** *adj.*

copulate ('kɒpjʊ,leɪt) *vb.* (*intr.*) to perform sexual intercourse. [C17: from Latin *copulāre* to join together; see COPULA] —,**copu'lation** *n.* —'**copulatory** *adj.*

copulative ('kɒpjʊlətɪv) *adj.* **1.** serving to join or unite. **2.** of or characteristic of copulation. **3.** *Grammar.* (of a verb) having the nature of a copula. —'**copulatively** *adv.*

copy ('kɒpɪ) *n., pl.* **copies. 1.** an imitation or reproduction of an original. **2.** a single specimen of something that occurs in a multiple edition, such as a book, article, etc. **3. a.** matter to be reproduced in print. **b.** written matter or text as distinct from graphic material in books, newspapers, etc. **4.** the words used to present a promotional message in an advertisement. **5.** *Journalism, informal.* suitable material for an article or story: *disasters are always good copy.* **6.** *Archaic.* a model to be copied, esp. an example of penmanship. ~*vb.* **copies, copying, copied. 7.** (when *tr.,* often foll. by *out*) to make a copy or reproduction of (an original). **8.** (*tr.*) to imitate as a model. **9.** (*intr.*) to imitate unfairly. [C14: from Medieval Latin *cōpia* an imitation, something copied, from Latin: abundance, riches; see COPIOUS]

copybook ('kɒpɪ,bʊk) *n.* **1.** a book of specimens, esp. of penmanship, for imitation. **2.** *Chiefly U.S.* a book for or containing documents. **3. blot one's copybook.** *Informal.* to spoil one's reputation by making a mistake, offending against social customs, etc. **4.** (*modifier*) trite or unoriginal: *copybook sentiments.*

copycat ('kɒpɪ,kæt) *n. Informal.* **a.** a person, esp. a child, who imitates or copies another. **b.** (*as modifier*): *copycat murders.*

copy desk *n. Journalism.* a desk where copy is edited.

copy-edit *vb. Journalism, etc.* to prepare (copy) for printing by styling, correcting, etc. —**copy editor** *n.*

copygraph ('kɒpɪ,grɑːf, -,græf) *n.* another name for **hectograph.**

copyhold ('kɒpɪ,həʊld) *n. Law.* (formerly) **a.** a tenure less than freehold of land in England evidenced by a copy of the Court roll. **b.** land held in this way.

copyholder ('kɒpɪ,həʊldə) *n.* **1.** *Printing.* one who reads aloud from the copy as the proof corrector follows the reading in the proof. **2.** *Printing.* a device that holds copy in place for the compositor. **3.** *Law.* (formerly) a person who held land by copyhold tenure.

copyist ('kɒpɪɪst) *n.* **1.** a person who makes written copies; transcriber. **2.** a person who imitates or copies.

copyread ('kɒpɪ,riːd) *vb.* **-reads, -reading, -read.** *U.S.* to subedit.

copyreader ('kɒpɪ,riːdə) *n. U.S.* a person who edits and prepares newspaper copy for publication; subeditor.

copyright ('kɒpɪ,raɪt) *n.* **1.** the exclusive right to produce copies and to control an original literary, musical, or artistic work, granted by law for a specified number of years (in Britain, usually 50 years from the death of the author, composer, etc.). Symbol: © ~*adj.* **2.** (of a work, etc.) subject to or controlled by copyright. ~*vb.* **3.** (*tr.*) to take out a copyright on. —'**copy,rightable** *adj.* —'**copy,righter** *n.*

copyright deposit library *n.* one of six libraries legally entitled to receive a gratis copy of every book published in the United Kingdom: the British Library, Bodleian, Cambridge University, Trinity College in Dublin, Scottish National Library, and National Library of Wales.

copy taster *n.* a person who selects or approves text for publication, esp. in a periodical.

copy typist *n.* a typist whose job is to type from written or typed drafts rather than dictation.

copywriter ('kɒpɪ,raɪtə) *n.* a person employed to write advertising copy. —'**copy,writng** *n.*

coq au vin *French.* (kɔk o vɛ̃) *n.* chicken stewed with red wine, onions, etc. [literally: cock with wine]

coquelicot ('kəʊklɪ,kəʊ) *n.* another name for **corn poppy.** [C18: from French: crow of a cock, from its resemblance to a cock's comb]

coquet (kəʊ'kɛt, kɒ-) *vb.* **-quets, -quetting, -quetted.** (*intr.*) **1.** to behave flirtatiously. **2.** to dally or trifle. [C17: from French: a gallant, literally: a little cock, from *coq* cock]

coquetry ('kəʊkɪtrɪ, 'kɒk-) *n., pl.* **-ries.** flirtation.

coquette (kəʊ'kɛt, kɒ'kɛt) *n.* **1.** a woman who flirts. **2.** any hummingbird of the genus *Lophornis,* esp. the crested Brazilian species *L. magnifica.* [C17: from French, feminine of COQUET] —**co'quettish** *adj.* —**co'quettishly** *adv.* —**co'quettishness** *n.*

coquilla nut (kɒ'kiːljə) *n.* the nut of a South American palm tree, *Attalea funifera,* having a hard brown shell used for carving. See also **cohune.** [C19: from Portuguese *coquilho,* diminutive of *côco* coconut; see COCO]

coquille (*French* kɔkij) *n.* **1.** any dish, esp. seafood, served in a scallop shell: *Coquilles St. Jacques.* **2.** a scallop shell, or dish resembling a shell. **3.** *Fencing.* a bell-shaped hand guard on a foil. [French, literally: shell, from Latin *conchylium* mussel; see COCKLE[1]]

coquimbite (kɒ'kɪmbaɪt) *n. Mineralogy.* hydrated ferric sulphate found in certain rocks and in volcanic fumaroles. [C19: from *Coquimbo,* Chilean province where it was originally found, + -ITE[1]]

coquina (kɒ'kiːnə) *n.* a soft limestone containing shells, corals, etc., that occurs in parts of the U.S. [C19: from Spanish: shellfish, probably from *concha* shell, CONCH]

coquito (kɒ'kiːtəʊ) *n., pl.* **-tos.** a Chilean palm tree, *Jubaea spectabilis,* yielding edible nuts and a syrup. [C19: from Spanish: a little coco palm, from *coco* coco palm]

cor (kɔː) *interj. Brit. slang.* an exclamation of surprise, amazement, or admiration. [C20: corruption of *God*]

cor. *abbrev. for:* **1.** corner. **2.** cornet. **3.** coroner.

Cor. *Bible. abbrev. for* Corinthians.

coraciiform (ˌkɒrə'saɪɪˌfɔːm) *adj.* of, relating to, or belonging to the *Coraciiformes,* an order of birds including the kingfishers, bee-eaters, hoopoes, and hornbills. [C20: from New Latin *Coracias* name of genus, from Greek *korakias* a chough + -I- + -FORM; related to Greek *korax* raven]

coracle ('kɒrək^{ə}l) *n.* a small roundish boat made of waterproofed hides stretched over a wicker frame. [C16: from Welsh *corwgl;* related to Irish *curach* boat]

coracoid ('kɒrəˌkɔɪd) *n.* a paired ventral bone of the pectoral girdle in vertebrates. In mammals it is reduced to a peg (the **coracoid process**) on the scapula. [C18: from New Latin *coracoīdēs,* from Greek *korakoeidēs* like a raven, curved like a raven's beak, from *korax* raven]

coral ('kɒrəl) *n.* **1.** any marine mostly colonial coelenterate of the class *Anthozoa* having a calcareous, horny, or soft skeleton. See also **stony coral, sea fan. 2. a.** the calcareous or horny material forming the skeleton of certain of these animals. **b.** (*as modifier*): *a coral reef.* See also **red coral. 3. a.** a rocklike aggregation of certain of these animals or their skeletons, forming an island or reef. **b.** (*as modifier*): *a coral island.* **4. a.** an object made of coral, esp. a piece of jewellery. **b.** (*as modifier*): *a coral necklace.* **5. a.** a deep-pink to yellowish-pink colour. **b.** (*as adj.*): *coral lipstick.* **6.** the roe of a lobster or crab, which becomes pink when cooked. [C14: from Old French, from Latin *corāllium,* from Greek *korallion,* probably of Semitic origin]

coral fern *n. Austral.* a scrambling fern of the genus *Gleichenia,* having repeatedly forked fronds.

coralline ('kɒrəˌlaɪn) *adj.* **1.** Also: **coralloid.** of, relating to, or resembling coral. **2.** of the colour of coral. ~*n.* **3.** any of various red algae impregnated with calcium carbonate, esp. any of the genus *Corallina.* **4.** any of various animals that resemble coral, such as certain sponges. [C16: from Late Latin *corallīnus* coral red, from Latin *corāllium* CORAL]

corallite ('kɒrəlaɪt) *n.* the skeleton of a coral polyp.

coralloid ('kɒrəlɔɪd) *adj.* of or resembling coral.

coral reef *n.* a marine ridge or reef consisting of coral and other organic material consolidated into limestone.

coralroot ('kɒrəlˌruːt) *n.* any N temperate leafless orchid of the genus *Corallorhiza,* with small yellow-green or purple flowers and branched roots resembling coral.

coral snake *n.* **1.** any venomous elapid snake of the genus *Micrurus* and related genera, of tropical and subtropical America, marked with red, black, yellow, and white transverse bands. **2.** any of various other brightly coloured elapid snakes of Africa and SE Asia.

coral tree *n. Austral.* any of various thorny trees of the papilionaceous genus *Erythrina,* having bright red flowers and reddish shiny seeds.

coram populo Latin. ('kɔːræm 'pɒpʊˌləʊ) *adv.* in the presence of the people; publicly.

cor anglais ('kɔːr 'ɑːŋgleɪ) *n., pl.* **cors anglais** ('kɔːz 'ɑːŋgleɪ). *Music.* a woodwind instrument, the alto of the oboe family. It is a transposing instrument in F. Range: two and a half octaves upwards from E on the third space of the bass staff. Also called: **English horn.** [C19: from French: English horn]

coranto (kɒ'ræntəʊ) *n., pl.* **-tos.** a variant of **courante.**

corban ('kɔːb^{ə}n; *Hebrew* kɔr'ban) *n.* **1.** *Old Testament.* a gift to God. **2.** *New Testament, Judaism.* the Temple treasury or a consecration or gift to it (Matthew 27:6; Mark 7:11). [C14: from Late Latin, from Greek *korban,* from Hebrew *qorbān* offering, literally: a drawing near]

corbeil *or* **corbeille** ('kɔːb^{ə}l; *French* kɔrbɛj) *n. Architect.* a carved ornament in the form of a basket of fruit, flowers, etc. [C18: from French *corbeille* basket, from Late Latin *corbicula* a little basket, from Latin *corbis* basket]

corbel ('kɔːb^{ə}l) *Architect.* ~*n.* **1.** Also called: **truss.** a bracket, usually of stone or brick. ~*vb.* **-bels, -belling, -belled** *or U.S.* **-bels, -beling, -beled. 2.** (*tr.*) to lay (a stone or brick) so that it forms a corbel. [C15: from Old French, literally: a little raven, from Medieval Latin *corvellus,* from Latin *corvus* raven]

corbelling *or U.S.* **corbeling** ('kɔːbəlɪŋ) *n.* a set of corbels stepped outwards, one above another.

corbel out *or* **off** *vb.* (*tr., adv.*) to support on corbels.

corbicula (kɔː'bɪkjʊlə) *n., pl.* **-lae** (-ˌliː). the technical name for **pollen basket.** [C19: from Late Latin, diminutive of Latin *corbis* basket]

corbie ('kɔːbɪ; *Scot.* 'kɔrbɪ) *n.* a Scot. name for **raven** or **crow**[1]. [C15: from Old French *corbin,* from Latin *corvīnus* CORVINE]

corbie gable *n. Architect.* a gable having corbie-steps.

corbie-step *or* **corbel step** *n. Architect.* any of a set of steps on the top of a gable. Also called: **crow step.**

cor blimey ('kɔː 'blaɪmɪ) *or* **gorblimey** *interj. Brit. slang.* an exclamation of surprise or annoyance. [C20: corruption of *God blind me*]

cord (kɔːd) *n.* **1.** string or thin rope made of several twisted strands. **2.** a length of woven or twisted strands of silk, etc., sewn on clothing or used as a belt. **3.** a ribbed fabric, esp. corduroy. **4.** any influence that binds or restrains. **5.** the U.S. and Canadian name for **flex** (sense 1). **6.** *Anatomy.* any part resembling a string or rope: *the spinal cord.* **7.** a unit of volume for measuring cut wood, equal to 128 cubic feet. ~*vb.* (*tr.*) **8.** to bind or furnish with a cord or cords. **9.** to stack (wood) in cords. [C13: from Old French *corde,* from Latin *chorda* cord, from Greek *khordē;* see CHORD[1]] —'**corder** *n.* —'**cordˌlike** *adj.*

cordage ('kɔːdɪdʒ) *n.* **1.** *Nautical.* the lines and rigging of a vessel. **2.** an amount of wood measured in cords.

cordate ('kɔːdeɪt) *adj.* heart-shaped: *a cordate leaf; cordate shells.* —'**cordately** *adv.*

corded ('kɔːdɪd) *adj.* **1.** bound or fastened with cord. **2.** (of a fabric) ribbed. **3.** (of muscles) standing out like cords.

Cordelier (ˌkɔːdɪ'lɪə) *n. R.C. Church.* a Franciscan friar of the order of the Friars Minor. [C19: from Old French *cordelle,* literally: a little cord, from the knotted cord girdles that they wear]

cord grass *n.* a coarse perennial grass of the genus *Spartina,* characteristically growing in mud or marsh. Also called: **rice grass.**

cordial ('kɔːdɪəl) *adj.* **1.** warm and friendly: *a cordial greeting.* **2.** giving heart; stimulating. ~*n.* **3.** a drink with a fruit base, usually sold in concentrated form and diluted with water before being drunk: *lime cordial.* **4.** another word for **liqueur.** [C14: from Medieval Latin *cordiālis,* from Latin *cor* heart] —'**cordially** *adv.* —'**cordialness** *n.*

cordiality (ˌkɔːdɪ'ælɪtɪ) *n., pl.* **-ties.** warmth of feeling.

cordierite ('kɔːdɪəˌraɪt) *n.* a grey or violet-blue dichroic mineral that consists of magnesium aluminium iron silicate in orthorhombic crystalline form and is found in metamorphic rocks. Formula: $(MgFe_2)Al_4Si_5O_{18}$. Also called: **dichroite, iolite.** [C19: named after Pierre L. A. *Cordier* (1777–1861), French geologist who described it]

cordiform ('kɔːdɪˌfɔːm) *adj.* heart-shaped. [C19: from Latin *cor* heart]

cordillera (ˌkɔːdɪl'jɛərə) *n.* a series of parallel ranges of mountains, esp. in the northwestern U.S. [C18: from Spanish, from *cordilla,* literally: a little cord, from *cuerda* mountain range, CORD] —ˌ**cordil'leran** *adj.*

cordite ('kɔːdaɪt) *n.* any of various explosive materials used for propelling bullets, shells, etc., containing cellulose nitrate, sometimes mixed with nitroglycerin, plasticizers, and stabilizers. [C19: from CORD + -ITE[1], referring to its stringy appearance]

cordless ('kɔːdlɪs) *adj.* (of an electrical device) operated by an internal battery so that no connection to mains supply or other apparatus is needed.

cordless telephone *n.* a portable battery-powered telephone with a short-range radio link to a fixed base unit.

cordoba ('kɔːdəbə) *n.* the standard monetary unit of Nicaragua, divided into 100 centavos. [Spanish *córdoba,* named in honour of Francisco Fernández de *Córdoba* (died 1518), Spanish explorer]

cordon ('kɔːd^{ə}n) *n.* **1.** a chain of police, soldiers, ships, etc., stationed around an area. **2.** a ribbon worn as insignia of honour or rank. **3.** a cord or ribbon worn as an ornament or fastening. **4.** Also called: **string course, belt course, table.** *Architect.* an ornamental projecting band or continuous moulding along a wall. **5.** *Horticulture.* a form of fruit tree consisting of a single stem bearing fruiting spurs, produced by cutting back all lateral branches. ~*vb.* **6.** (*tr.;* often foll. by *off*) to put or form a cordon (around); close (off). [C16: from Old French, literally: a little cord, from *corde* string, CORD]

cordon bleu (*French* kɔrdɔ̃ blø) *n.* **1.** *French history.* **a.** the sky-blue ribbon worn by members of the highest order of knighthood under the Bourbon monarchy (1589–1793, 1815–30). **b.** a knight entitled to wear the cordon bleu. **2.** any very high distinction. ~*adj.* **3.** of or denoting food prepared to a very high standard. [French, literally: blue ribbon]

cordon sanitaire *French.* (kɔrdɔ̃ sanitɛr) *n.* **1.** a guarded line serving to cut off an infected area. **2.** a line of buffer states, esp. when protecting a nation from infiltration or attack. [C19: literally: sanitary line]

cordovan ('kɔːdəv^{ə}n) *n.* a fine leather now made principally from horsehide, isolated from the skin layers above and below it and tanned. [C16: from Spanish *cordobán* (n.), from *cordobán* (adj.) of *Córdoba,* city in S Spain]

Cordovan ('kɔːdəv^{ə}n) *n.* **1.** a native or inhabitant of Córdoba, Spain. ~*adj.* **2.** of or relating to Córdoba, Spain.

cords (kɔːdz) *pl. n.* trousers, esp. jeans, made of corduroy.

corduroy ('kɔːdəˌrɔɪ, ˌkɔːdə'rɔɪ) *n.* **a.** a heavy cotton pile fabric with lengthways ribs. **b.** (*as modifier*): *a corduroy coat.* ~See also **corduroys.** [C18: perhaps from the proper name *Corderoy*]

corduroy road *n.* a road across swampy ground, made of logs laid transversely.

corduroys (ˌkɔːdə'rɔɪz, 'kɔːdəˌrɔɪz) *pl. n.* trousers or breeches of corduroy.

cordwain (ˈkɔːdˌweɪn) *n.* an archaic name for **cordovan.** [C12 *cordewan,* from Old French *cordoan,* from Old Spanish *cordovan* CORDOVAN]

cordwainer (ˈkɔːdˌweɪnə) *n. Archaic.* a shoemaker or worker in cordovan leather. —ˈ**cordˌwainery** *n.*

cordwood (ˈkɔːdˌwʊd) *n.* wood that has been cut into lengths of four feet so that it can be stacked in cords.

core (kɔː) *n.* **1.** the central part of certain fleshy fruits, such as the apple or pear, consisting of the seeds and supporting parts. **2. a.** the central, innermost, or most essential part of something: *the core of the argument.* **b.** (*as modifier*): *the core meaning.* **3.** a piece of magnetic material, such as soft iron, placed inside the windings of an electromagnet or transformer to intensify and direct the magnetic field. **4.** *Geology.* the central part of the earth, beneath the mantle, consisting mainly of iron and nickel. **5.** a cylindrical sample of rock, soil, etc., obtained by the use of a hollow drill. **6.** shaped body of material (in metal casting usually of sand) supported inside a mould to form a cavity of predetermined shape in the finished casting. **7.** *Physics.* the region of a nuclear reactor in which the reaction takes place. **8.** a layer of wood serving as a backing for a veneer. **9.** *Computer technol.* **a.** a ferrite ring used in a computer memory to store one bit of information. **b.** the whole memory of a computer when made up of a number of such rings. **c.** (*as modifier*): *core memory.* **10.** *Archaeol.* a lump of stone or flint from which flakes or blades have been removed. **11.** *Physics.* the nucleus together with all complete electron shells of an atom. ~*vb.* **12.** (*tr.*) to remove the core from (fruit). [C14: of uncertain origin] —ˈ**coreless** *adj.*

CORE (kɔː) *n.* (in the U.S.) *acronym for* Congress of Racial Equality.

coreferential (ˌkəʊrɛfəˈrɛnʃəl) *adj. Philosophy.* (of more than one linguistic expression) designating the same individual or class.

coreligionist (ˌkəʊrɪˈlɪdʒənɪst) *n.* an adherent of the same religion as another.

corella (kəˈrɛlə) *n.* any of certain white Australian cockatoos of the genus *Kakatoe.* [C19: probably from native Australian *carall*]

coreopsis (ˌkɒrɪˈɒpsɪs) *n.* any plant of the genus *Coreopsis,* of America and tropical Africa, cultivated for their yellow, brown, or yellow-and-red daisy-like flowers: family *Compositae* (composites). Also called: **calliopsis.** Compare **caryopsis.** [C18: from New Latin, from Greek *koris* bedbug + -OPSIS; so called from the appearance of the seed]

co-respondent (ˌkəʊrɪˈspɒndənt) *n. Law.* a person cited in divorce proceedings, alleged to have committed adultery with the respondent. —ˌ**co-reˈspondency** *n.*

co-respondent shoes *pl. n.* men's two-coloured shoes, usually black and white or brown and white. Also called: **co-respondents.**

core store *n.* a computer memory made up of a matrix of cores.

core subjects *pl. n. Brit. education.* three foundation subjects (English, mathematics, and science) that are compulsory throughout each key stage in the National Curriculum.

core time *n.* See **flexitime.**

corf (kɔːf) *n., pl.* **corves.** *Brit.* a wagon or basket used formerly in mines. [C14: from Middle Dutch *corf* or Middle Low German *korf,* probably from Latin *corbis* basket]

Corfam (ˈkɔːfæm) *n. Trademark.* a synthetic water-repellent material used as a substitute for shoe leather.

corgi (ˈkɔːgɪ) *n.* either of two long-bodied short-legged sturdy breeds of dog, the Cardigan and the Pembroke. Also called: **Welsh corgi.** [C20: from Welsh, from *cor* dwarf + *ci* dog]

coriaceous (ˌkɒrɪˈeɪʃəs) *or* **corious** *adj.* of or resembling leather. [C17: from Late Latin *coriāceus* from *corium* leather]

coriander (ˌkɒrɪˈændə) *n.* **1.** a European umbelliferous plant, *Coriandrum sativum,* widely cultivated for its aromatic seeds. **2.** the dried ripe seeds of this plant collectively, used in flavouring food, etc. [C14: from Old French *coriandre,* from Latin *coriandrum,* from Greek *koriannon,* of uncertain origin]

Corinthian (kəˈrɪnθɪən) *adj.* **1.** of, characteristic of, or relating to Corinth, a Greek port in the NE Peloponnese. **2.** of, denoting, or relating to one of the five classical orders of architecture: characterized by a bell-shaped capital having carved ornaments based on acanthus leaves. See also **Ionic, Doric, Composite, Tuscan.** **3.** given to luxury; dissolute. **4.** ornate and elaborate. ~*n.* **5.** a native or inhabitant of Corinth. **6.** an amateur sportsman. **7.** *Rare.* a man about town, esp. one who is dissolute.

Coriolis force (ˌkɒrɪˈəʊlɪs) *n.* a hypothetical force postulated to explain a deflection in the path of a body moving relative to the earth when observed from the earth. The deflection (**Coriolis effect**) is due to the earth's rotation and is to the left in the S hemisphere and to the right in the N hemisphere. [C19: named after Gaspard G. *Coriolis* (1792–1843), French civil engineer]

corious (ˈkɒrɪəs) *adj.* a variant of **coriaceous.**

corium (ˈkɔːrɪəm) *n., pl.* **-ria** (-rɪə). **1.** Also called: **derma, dermis.** the deep inner layer of the skin, beneath the epidermis, containing connective tissue, blood vessels, and fat. **2.** *Entomol.* the leathery basal part of the forewing of hemipterous insects. [C19: from Latin: rind, skin, leather]

corixid (kəˈrɪksɪd) *n.* **1.** any heteropterous water bug of the vegetarian family *Corixidae,* typified by *Corixa punctata,* common in sluggish waters. The forelegs have become modified and are used in stridulation, as by the **water singer** (*Micronecta poweri*). See also **water boatman.** ~*adj.* **2.** of or relating to the Corixidae. [from New Latin *corixa,* from Greek *koris* bedbug]

cork (kɔːk) *n.* **1.** the thick light porous outer bark of the cork oak, used widely as an insulator and for stoppers for bottles, casks, etc. **2.** a piece of cork or other material used as a stopper. **3.** an angling float. **4.** Also called: **phellem.** *Botany.* a protective layer of dead impermeable cells on the outside of the stems and roots of woody plants, produced by the outer layer of the cork cambium. ~*vb.* (*tr.*) **5.** to stop up (a bottle, cask, etc.) with or as if with a cork; fit with a cork. **6.** (often foll. by *up*) to restrain: *to cork up the emotions.* **7.** to black (the face, hands, etc.) with burnt cork. [C14: probably from Arabic *qurq,* from Latin *cortex* bark, especially of the cork oak] —ˈ**corkˌlike** *adj.*

corkage (ˈkɔːkɪdʒ) *n.* a charge made at a restaurant for serving wine, etc., bought off the premises.

corkboard (ˈkɔːkˌbɔːd) *n.* a thin slab made of granules of cork, used as a floor or wall finish and as an insulator.

cork cambium *n.* a layer of meristematic cells in the cortex of the stems and roots of woody plants, the outside of which gives rise to cork cells and the inside to secondary cortical cells (phelloderm). Also called: **phellogen.**

corked (kɔːkt) *adj.* **1.** Also: ˈ**corky.** (of a wine) tainted through having a cork containing excess tannin. **2.** (*postpositive*) *Brit.* a slang word for **drunk.**

corker (ˈkɔːkə) *n.* **1.** *Slang.* **a.** something or somebody striking or outstanding: *that was a corker of a joke.* **b.** an irrefutable remark that puts an end to discussion. **2.** a person or machine that inserts corks.

corking (ˈkɔːkɪŋ) *adj.* (*prenominal*) *Brit. slang.* excellent.

cork oak *n.* an evergreen Mediterranean oak tree, *Quercus suber,* with a porous outer bark from which cork is obtained. Also called: **cork tree.**

Corkonian (kɔːˈkəʊnɪən, kərˈkɔːnɪən) *n.* a native or inhabitant of the city of Cork in S Ireland.

corkscrew (ˈkɔːkˌskruː) *n.* **1.** a device for drawing corks from bottles, typically consisting of a pointed metal spiral attached to a handle or screw mechanism. **2.** *Boxing slang.* a blow that ends with a twist of the fist, esp. one intended to cut the opponent. **3.** (*modifier*) resembling a corkscrew in shape. ~*vb.* **4.** to move or cause to move in a spiral or zigzag course.

cork-tipped (ˈkɔːkˌtɪpt) *adj.* (of a cigarette) having a filter of cork or some material resembling cork.

corkwing (ˈkɔːkˌwɪŋ) *n.* a greenish or bluish European fish of the wrasse family, *Ctenolabrus melops.* [of uncertain origin]

corkwood (ˈkɔːkˌwʊd) *n.* **1.** a small tree, *Leitneria floridana,* of the southeastern U.S., having very lightweight porous wood: family *Leitneriaceae.* **2.** any other tree with light porous wood. **3.** the wood of any of these trees.

corm (kɔːm) *n.* an organ of vegetative reproduction in plants such as the crocus, consisting of a globular stem base swollen with food and surrounded by papery scale leaves. Compare **bulb** (sense 1). [C19: from New Latin *cormus,* from Greek *kormos* tree trunk from which the branches have been lopped] —ˈ**cormous** *adj.*

cormel (ˈkɔːməl) *n.* a new small corm arising from the base of a fully developed one.

cormophyte (ˈkɔːməˌfaɪt) *n.* any of the *Cormophyta,* a major division (now obsolete) of plants having a stem, root, and leaves: includes the mosses, ferns, and seed plants. [C19: from Greek *kormos* tree trunk + -PHYTE] —**cormophytic** (ˌkɔːməˈfɪtɪk) *adj.*

cormorant (ˈkɔːmərənt) *n.* any aquatic bird of the family *Phalacrocoracidae,* of coastal and inland waters, having a dark plumage, a long neck and body, and a slender hooked beak: order *Pelecaniformes* (pelicans, etc.). [C13: from Old French *cormareng,* from *corp* raven, from Latin *corvus* + *-mareng* of the sea, from Latin *mare* sea]

corn[1] (kɔːn) *n.* **1.** *Brit.* **a.** any of various cereal plants, esp. the predominant crop of a region, such as wheat in England and oats in Scotland and Ireland. **b.** the seeds of such plants, esp. after harvesting. **c.** a single seed of such plants; a grain. **2.** the usual U.S., Canadian, Austral., and N.Z. name for **maize.** See also **sweet corn** (sense 1), **popcorn** (sense 1). **3. a.** the plants producing these kinds of grain considered as a growing crop: *spring corn.* **b.** (*in combination*): *a cornfield.* **4.** short for **corn whisky.** **5.** *Slang.* an idea, song, etc., regarded as banal or sentimental. **6.** *Archaic or dialect.* any hard particle or grain. ~*vb.* (*tr.*) **7.** to feed (animals) with corn, esp. oats. **8. a.** to preserve in brine. **b.** to salt. **9.** to plant corn on. [Old English *corn;* related to Old Norse, Old High German *corn,* Gothic *kaúrn,* Latin *grānum,* Sanskrit *jīrṇá* fragile]

corn[2] (kɔːn) *n.* **1.** a hardening or thickening of the skin, esp. of the toes, caused by pressure or friction. **2. tread on (someone's) corns.** *Brit. informal.* to offend or hurt (someone) by touching on a sensitive subject or encroaching on his privileges. [C15: from Old French *corne* horn, from Latin *cornū*]

cornaceous (kɔːˈneɪʃəs) *adj.* of, relating to, or belonging to the *Cornaceae,* a family of temperate plants, mostly trees and shrubs, including dogwood, cornel, and spotted laurel (see **laurel** (sense 5)). [C19: from New Latin *Cornaceae,* from *Cornus* genus name, from Latin: CORNEL]

cornball (ˈkɔːnˌbɔːl) *Chiefly U.S.* ~*n.* **1.** a person given to mawkish or unsophisticated behaviour. ~*adj.* **2.** another word for corny. [C20: from *corn ball* a sweet consisting of a ball of popcorn and molasses]

corn borer *n.* the larva of the pyralid moth *Pyrausta nubilalis,* native to S and Central Europe: in E North America a serious pest of maize.

corn bread *n. Chiefly U.S.* a kind of bread made from maize meal. Also called: **Indian bread.**

corn bunting *n.* a heavily built European songbird, *Emberiza calandra,* with a streaked brown plumage: family *Emberizidae* (buntings).

corncob ('kɔːnˌkɒb) *n.* **1.** the core of an ear of maize, to which kernels are attached. **2.** short for **corncob pipe.**

corncob pipe *n.* a pipe made from a dried corncob.

corncockle ('kɔːnˌkɒkᵊl) *n.* a European caryophyllaceous plant, *Agrostemma githago,* that has reddish-purple flowers and grows in cornfields and by roadsides.

corncrake ('kɔːnˌkreɪk) *n.* a common Eurasian rail, *Crex crex,* of fields and meadows, with a buff speckled plumage and reddish wings.

corncrib ('kɔːnˌkrɪb) *n. Chiefly U.S. and Canadian.* a ventilated building for the storage of unhusked maize.

corn dolly *n.* a decorative figure made by plaiting straw.

cornea ('kɔːnɪə) *n., pl.* **-neas** (-nɪəz) *or* **-neae** (-nɪˌiː). the convex transparent membrane that forms the anterior covering of the eyeball and is continuous with the sclera. [C14: from Medieval Latin *cornea tēla* horny web, from Latin *cornū* HORN] —**'corneal** *adj.*

corn earworm *n. U.S.* the larva of the noctuid moth *Heliothis armigera,* which feeds on maize and many other crop plants. See also **bollworm.**

corned (kɔːnd) *adj.* (esp. of beef) cooked and then preserved or pickled in salt or brine, now often canned.

cornel ('kɔːnᵊl) *n.* any cornaceous plant of the genus *Cornus,* such as the dogwood and dwarf cornel. [C16: probably from Middle Low German *kornelle,* from Old French *cornelle,* from Vulgar Latin *cornicula* (unattested), from Latin *cornum* cornel cherry, from *cornus* cornel tree]

cornelian (kɔːˈniːlɪən) *n.* a variant spelling of **carnelian.**

corneous ('kɔːnɪəs) *adj.* horny; hornlike. [C17: from Latin *corneus* horny, from *cornū* HORN]

corner ('kɔːnə) *n.* **1.** the place, position, or angle formed by the meeting of two converging lines or surfaces. **2.** a projecting angle of a solid object or figure. **3.** the place where two streets meet. **4.** any small, secluded, secret, or private place. **5.** a dangerous or awkward position, esp. from which escape is difficult: *a tight corner.* **6.** any part, region or place, esp. a remote place. **7.** something used to protect or mark a corner, as of the hard cover of a book. **8.** *Commerce.* a monopoly over the supply of a commodity so that its market price can be controlled. **9.** *Soccer, hockey, etc.* a free kick or shot from the corner of the field, taken against a defending team when the ball goes out of play over their goal line after last touching one of their players. **10.** either of two opposite angles of a boxing ring in which the opponents take their rests. **11.** *Mountaineering.* a junction between two rock faces forming an angle of between 60° and 120°. U.S. name: **dihedral. 12. cut corners.** to do something in the easiest and shortest way, esp. at the expense of high standards. **13. (just) round the corner.** close at hand. **14. turn the corner.** to pass the critical point (in an illness, etc.). **15.** (*modifier*) located on a corner: *a corner shop.* **16.** (*modifier*) suitable or designed for a corner: *a corner table.* **17.** *Logic.* either of a pair of symbols used in the same way as ordinary quotation marks to indicate quasi quotation. See **quasi-quotation.** ~*vb.* **18.** (*tr.*) to manoeuvre (a person or animal) into a position from which escape is difficult or impossible: *finally they cornered the fox.* **19.** (*tr.*) to furnish or provide with corners. **20.** (*tr.*) to place in or move into a corner. **21.** (*tr.*) **a.** to acquire enough of (a commodity) to attain control of the market. **b.** Also: **engross.** to attain control of (a market) in such a manner. Compare **forestall** (sense 3). **22.** (*intr.*) (of vehicles, etc.) to turn a corner. **23.** (*intr.*) *U.S.* to be situated on a corner. **24.** (*intr.*) (in soccer, etc.) to take a corner. [C13: from Old French *corniere,* from Latin *cornū* point, extremity, HORN]

cornerback ('kɔːnəˌbæk) *n. American football.* a defensive back.

cornerstone ('kɔːnəˌstəʊn) *n.* **1.** a stone at the corner of a wall, uniting two intersecting walls; quoin. **2.** a stone placed at the corner of a building during a ceremony to mark the start of construction. **3.** a person or thing of prime importance; basis: *the cornerstone of the whole argument.*

cornerwise ('kɔːnəˌwaɪz) *or* **cornerways** ('kɔːnəˌweɪz) *adv., adj.* with a corner in front; diagonally.

cornet ('kɔːnɪt) *n.* **1.** Also called: **cornet à pistons** ('kɔːnɪt ə 'pɪstənz; *French* kɔrnɛ a pistɔ̃). a three-valved brass instrument of the trumpet family. Written range: about two and a half octaves upwards from E below middle C. It is a transposing instrument in B flat or A. **2.** a person who plays the cornet. **3.** a variant spelling of **cornett. 4.** a cone-shaped paper container for sweets, etc. **5.** *Brit.* a cone-shaped wafer container for ice cream. **6.** (formerly) the lowest rank of commissioned cavalry officer in the British army. **7.** *S. African.* short for **field cornet. 8.** a starched and wired muslin or lace cap worn by women from the 12th to the 15th centuries. **9.** the large white headdress of some nuns. [C14: from Old French, from *corn,* from Latin *cornū* HORN]

cornetcy ('kɔːnɪtsɪ) *n., pl.* **-cies.** *Obsolete.* the commission or rank of a cornet.

cornetist *or* **cornettist** (kɔːˈnɛtɪst) *n.* a person who plays the cornet.

cornett (kɔːˈnɛt) *or* **cornet** *n.* a musical instrument consisting of a straight or curved tube of wood or ivory having finger holes like a recorder and a cup-shaped mouthpiece like a trumpet. [from Old French *cornet* a little horn, from *corn* horn, from Latin *cornū*]

corn exchange *n.* a building where corn is bought and sold.

corn factor *n.* a person who deals in corn.

cornfield ('kɔːnˌfiːld) *n.* a field planted with cereal crops.

cornflakes ('kɔːnˌfleɪks) *pl. n.* a breakfast cereal made from toasted maize, eaten with milk, sugar, etc.

cornflour ('kɔːnˌflaʊə) *n.* a fine starchy maize flour, used esp. for thickening sauces. U.S. and Canadian name: **cornstarch.**

cornflower ('kɔːnˌflaʊə) *n.* a Eurasian herbaceous plant, *Centaurea cyanus,* with blue, purple, pink, or white flowers, formerly a common weed in cornfields: family *Compositae* (composites). Also called: **bluebottle.** See also **bachelor's-buttons.**

cornhusk ('kɔːnˌhʌsk) *n. U.S. and Canadian.* the outer protective covering of an ear of maize; the chaff.

cornice ('kɔːnɪs) *n.* **1.** *Architect.* **a.** the top projecting mouldings of an entablature. **b.** a continuous horizontal projecting course or moulding at the top of a wall, building, etc. **2.** an overhanging ledge of snow formed by the wind on the edge of a mountain ridge, cliff, or corrie. ~*vb.* **3.** (*tr.*) *Architect.* to furnish or decorate with or as if with a cornice. [C16: from Old French, from Italian, perhaps from Latin *cornix* crow, but influenced also by Latin *corōnis* decorative flourish used by scribes, from Greek *korōnis,* from *korōnē* curved object, CROWN]

corniche ('kɔːnɪʃ) *n.* a coastal road, esp. one built into the face of a cliff. [C19: from *corniche road,* originally the coastal road between Nice, in SE France, and Monte Carlo, in Monaco; see CORNICE]

corniculate (kɔːˈnɪkjʊˌleɪt, -lɪt) *adj.* **1.** having horns or hornlike projections. **2.** relating to or resembling a horn. [C17: from Latin *corniculātus* horned, from *corniculum* a little horn, from *cornū* HORN]

Cornish ('kɔːnɪʃ) *adj.* **1.** of, relating to, or characteristic of Cornwall, a county of SW England, its inhabitants, their former language, or their present-day dialect of English. ~*n.* **2.** a former language of Cornwall, belonging to the S Celtic branch of the Indo-European family and closely related to Breton: extinct by 1800. **3. the.** (*functioning as pl.*) the natives or inhabitants of Cornwall. —**'Cornishman** *n.*

Cornish pasty ('pæstɪ) *n. Cookery.* a pastry case with a filling of meat and vegetables.

Cornish split *n.* another term for **Devonshire split.**

corn lily *n.* any of several South African iridaceous plants of the genus *Ixia,* which have coloured lily-like flowers.

corn marigold *n.* an annual plant, *Chrysanthemum segetum,* with yellow daisy-like flower heads: a common weed of cultivated land: family *Compositae* (composites).

corn meal *n.* meal made from maize. Also called: **Indian meal.**

corn oil *n.* an oil prepared from maize, used in cooking and in making soaps, lubricants, etc.

corn on the cob *n.* a cob of maize, boiled and eaten as a vegetable.

corn-picker *n. Chiefly U.S. and Canadian.* a machine for removing ears of maize from the standing stalks, often also equipped to separate the corn from the husk and shell.

corn pone *n. Southern U.S.* corn bread, esp. a plain type made with water. Sometimes shortened to **pone.**

corn poppy *n.* a poppy, *Papaver rhoeas,* that has bright red flowers and grows in cornfields. Since World War I it has been the symbol of fallen soldiers. Also called: **coquelicot, Flanders poppy, field poppy.**

corn rose *n. Brit., archaic.* any of several red-flowered weeds of cornfields, such as the corn poppy.

corn row (rəʊ) *n.* a Black, originally African, hair-style in which the hair is plaited in close parallel rows, resembling furrows in a ploughed field.

corn salad *n.* any valerianaceous plant of the genus *Valerianella,* esp. the European species *V. locusta,* which often grows in cornfields and whose leaves are sometimes used in salads. Also called: **lamb's lettuce.**

corn shock *n.* a stack or bundle of bound or unbound corn piled upright for curing or drying.

corn shuck *n. U.S. and Canadian.* the husk of an ear of maize.

corn silk *n. U.S. and Canadian.* the silky tuft of styles and stigmas at the tip of an ear of maize, formerly used as a diuretic.

corn smut *n.* **1.** an ascomycetous parasitic fungus, *Ustilago zeae,* that causes gall-like deformations on maize grain. **2.** the condition produced by this fungus.

corn snow *n. Skiing, U.S. and Canadian.* granular snow formed by alternate freezing and thawing.

cornstalk ('kɔːnˌstɔːk) *n.* **1.** a stalk or stem of corn. **2.** *Austral. slang.* **a.** (*often cap.*) a native Australian. **b.** a tall thin man.

cornstarch ('kɔːnˌstɑːtʃ) *n.* the U.S. and Canadian name for **cornflour.**

cornstone (ˈkɔːnˌstəʊn) *n.* a mottled green and red limestone.
corn syrup *n. U.S. and Canadian.* syrup prepared from maize.
cornu (ˈkɔːnjuː) *n., pl.* **-nua** (-njʊə). *Anatomy.* a part or structure resembling a horn or having a hornlike pattern, such as a cross section of the grey matter of the spinal cord. [C17: from Latin: a horn] —ˈ**cornual** *adj.*
cornucopia (ˌkɔːnjʊˈkəʊpɪə) *n.* **1.** a representation of the mythical horn of Amalthea, the goat that suckled Zeus, in painting, sculpture, etc., overflowing with fruit, vegetables, etc.; horn of plenty. **2.** a great abundance; overflowing supply. **3.** a horn-shaped container. [C16: from Late Latin, from Latin *cornū cōpiae* horn of plenty] —ˌ**cornuˈcopian** *adj.*
cornute (kɔːˈnjuːt) *or* **cornuted** *adj. Biology.* having or resembling cornua; hornlike: *the cornute process of a bone.* [C17: from Latin *cornūtus* horned, from *cornū* HORN]
corn whisky *n.* whisky made from maize.
corny (ˈkɔːnɪ) *adj.* **cornier, corniest.** *Slang.* **1.** trite or banal. **2.** sentimental or mawkish. **3.** abounding in corn. [C16 (C20 in the sense rustic, banal): from CORN[1] +-Y[1]]
corody *or* **corrody** (ˈkɒrədɪ) *n., pl.* **-dies.** *History.* **1.** (originally) the right of a lord to receive free quarters from his vassal. **2.** an allowance for maintenance. [C15: from Medieval Latin *corrōdium* something provided, from Old French *corroyer* to provide, of Germanic origin]
corol. *or* **coroll.** *abbrev. for* corollary.
corolla (kəˈrɒlə) *n.* the petals of a flower collectively, forming an inner floral envelope. Compare **calyx.**
corollaceous (ˌkɒrəˈleɪʃəs) *adj.* of, relating to, resembling, or having a corolla.
corollary (kəˈrɒlərɪ) *n., pl.* **-laries.** **1.** a proposition that follows directly from the proof of another proposition. **2.** an obvious deduction. **3.** a natural consequence or result. *~adj.* **4.** consequent or resultant. [C14: from Latin *corollārium* money paid for a garland, from Latin *corolla* garland, from *corōna* CROWN]
corona (kəˈrəʊnə) *n., pl.* **-nas** *or* **-nae** (-niː). **1.** a circle of light around a luminous body, usually the moon. **2.** Also called: **aureole.** the outermost region of the sun's atmosphere, visible as a faint halo during a solar eclipse. **3.** *Architect.* the flat vertical face of a cornice just above the soffit. **4.** something resembling a corona or halo. **5.** a circular chandelier suspended from the roof of a church. **6.** *Botany.* **a.** the trumpet-shaped part of the corolla of daffodils and similar plants; the crown. **b.** a crown of leafy outgrowths from inside the petals of some flowers. **7.** *Anatomy.* a crownlike structure, such as the top of the head. **8.** *Zoology.* the head or upper surface of an animal, such as the body of an echinoid or the disc and arms of a crinoid. **9.** a long cigar with blunt ends. **10.** *Physics.* short for **corona discharge.** [C16: from Latin: crown, from Greek *korōne* anything curved; related to Greek *korōnis* wreath, *korax* crow, Latin *curvus* curved]
Corona Australis (ɒˈstreɪlɪs) *n., Latin genitive* **Coronae Australis** (kəˈrəʊniː). a small faint constellation in the S hemisphere between Ara and Pavo. [literally: Southern crown]
Corona Borealis (ˌbɔːrɪˈeɪlɪs) *n., Latin genitive* **Coronae Borealis** (kəˈrəʊniː). a small compact constellation in the N hemisphere lying between Boötes and Hercules. [literally: Northern crown]
coronach (ˈkɒrənəx, -nək) *n. Scot. or Irish.* a dirge or lamentation for the dead. [C16: from Scottish Gaelic *corranach;* related to Irish *rānadh* a crying]
corona discharge *n.* an electrical discharge appearing on and around the surface of a charged conductor, caused by ionization of the surrounding gas. Also called: **corona.** See also **Saint Elmo's fire.**
coronagraph *or* **coronograph** (kəˈrəʊnəˌgrɑːf, -ˌgræf) *n.* an optical instrument used to simulate an eclipse of the sun so that the faint solar corona can be studied.
coronal *n.* (ˈkɒrənᵊl). **1.** *Poetic.* a circlet for the head; crown. **2.** a wreath or garland. **3.** *Anatomy.* short for **coronal suture.** *~adj.* (kəˈrəʊnᵊl). **4.** of or relating to a corona or coronal. **5.** *Phonetics.* a less common word for **retroflex.** [C16: from Late Latin *corōnālis* belonging to a CROWN]
coronal suture *n.* the serrated line across the skull between the frontal bone and the parietal bones.
coronary (ˈkɒrənərɪ) *adj.* **1.** *Anatomy.* designating blood vessels, nerves, ligaments, etc., that encircle a part or structure. *~n., pl.* **-naries.** **2.** short for **coronary thrombosis.** [C17: from Latin *corōnārius* belonging to a wreath or crown; see CORONA]
coronary artery *n.* either of two arteries branching from the aorta and supplying blood to the heart.
coronary bypass *n.* the surgical bypass of a narrowed or blocked coronary artery by grafting a section of a healthy blood vessel taken from another part of the patient's body.
coronary heart disease *n.* any heart disorder caused by disease of the coronary arteries.
coronary insufficiency *n.* inadequate circulation of blood through the coronary arteries, characterized by attacks of angina pectoris.
coronary thrombosis *n.* a condition of interrupted blood flow to the heart due to a blood clot in a coronary artery, usually as a consequence of atherosclerosis: characterized by intense pain. Sometimes shortened to: **coronary.** Compare **myocardial infarction.**
coronation (ˌkɒrəˈneɪʃən) *n.* the act or ceremony of crowning a monarch. [C14: from Old French, from *coroner* to crown, from Latin *corōnāre*]
coroner (ˈkɒrənə) *n.* a public official responsible for the investigation of violent, sudden, or suspicious deaths. The investigation (**coroner's inquest**) is held in the presence of a jury (**coroner's jury**). See also **procurator fiscal.** Compare **medical examiner.** [C14: from Anglo-French *corouner* officer in charge of the pleas of the Crown, from Old French *corone* CROWN] —ˈ**coronerˌship** *n.*
coronet (ˈkɒrənɪt) *n.* **1.** any small crown, esp. one worn by princes or peers as a mark of rank. **2.** a woman's jewelled circlet for the head. **3.** the margin between the skin of a horse's pastern and the horn of the hoof. **4.** the knob at the base of a deer's antler. **5.** *Heraldry.* a support for a crest shaped like a crown. [C15: from Old French *coronete* a little crown, from *corone* CROWN]
coroneted (ˌkɒrəˈnɛtɪd) *adj.* **1.** wearing a coronet. **2.** belonging to the peerage.
co-routine (ˈkəʊruːˌtiːn) *n. Computer technol.* a section of a computer program similar to but differing from a subroutine in that it can be left and re-entered at any point.
corozo (kəˈrəʊzəʊ) *n., pl.* **-zos.** a tropical American palm, *Corozo oleifera,* whose seeds yield a useful oil. [C18: via Spanish from an Indian name]
corp. *abbrev. for:* **1.** corporation. **2.** corporal.
corpora (ˈkɔːpərə) *n.* the plural of **corpus.**
corporal[1] (ˈkɔːpərəl, -prəl) *adj.* **1.** of or relating to the body; bodily. **2.** an obsolete word for **corporeal.** [C14: from Latin *corporālis* of the body, from *corpus* body] —ˌ**corpoˈrality** *n.* —ˈ**corporally** *adv.*
corporal[2] (ˈkɔːpərəl, -prəl) *n.* **1.** a noncommissioned officer junior to a sergeant in the army, air force, or marines. **2.** (in the Royal Navy) a petty officer who assists the master-at-arms. [C16: from Old French, via Italian, from Latin *caput* head; perhaps also influenced in Old French by *corps* body (of men)] —ˈ**corporalˌship** *n.*
corporal[3] (ˈkɔːpərəl, -prəl) *or* **corporale** (ˌkɔːpəˈreɪlɪ) *n.* a white linen cloth on which the bread and wine are placed during the Eucharist. [C14: from Medieval Latin *corporāle pallium* eucharistic altar cloth, from Latin *corporālis* belonging to the body, from *corpus* body (of Christ)]
Corporal of Horse *n.* a noncommissioned rank in the British Household Cavalry above that of sergeant and below that of staff sergeant.
corporal punishment *n.* punishment of a physical nature, such as caning, flogging, or beating.
corporate (ˈkɔːpərɪt, -prɪt) *adj.* **1.** forming a corporation; incorporated. **2.** of or belonging to a corporation or corporations: *corporate finance.* **3.** of or belonging to a united group; joint. [C15: from Latin *corporātus* made into a body, from *corporāre,* from *corpus* body] —ˈ**corporately** *adv.*
corporate identity *or* **image** *n.* the way an organization is presented to or perceived by its members and the public.
corporate raider *n. Finance.* a person or organization that acquires a substantial holding of the shares of a company in order to take it over or to force its management to act in a desired way.
corporate venturing *n. Finance.* the provision of venture capital by one company for another in order to obtain information about the company requiring capital or as a step towards acquiring it.
corporation (ˌkɔːpəˈreɪʃən) *n.* **1.** a group of people authorized by law to act as an individual and having its own powers, duties, and liabilities. **2.** Also called: **municipal corporation.** the municipal authorities of a city or town. **3.** a group of people acting as one body. **4.** See **public corporation.** **5.** *Informal.* a large paunch or belly.
corporation tax *n.* a British tax on the profits of a company or other incorporated body.
corporatism (ˈkɔːpərɪtɪzəm, -prɪtɪzəm) *n.* the organization of a state on a corporative basis. —ˈ**corporatist** *n., adj.*
corporative (ˈkɔːpərətɪv, -prətɪv) *adj.* **1.** of or characteristic of a corporation. **2.** (of a state) organized into and governed by corporations of individuals involved in any given profession, industry, etc.
corporator (ˈkɔːpəˌreɪtə) *n.* a member of a corporation.
corporeal (kɔːˈpɔːrɪəl) *adj.* **1.** of the nature of the physical body; not spiritual. **2.** of a material nature; physical. [C17: from Latin *corporeus,* from *corpus* body] —**corˌporeˈality** *or* **corˈporealness** *n.* —**corˈporeally** *adv.*
corporeity (ˌkɔːpəˈriːɪtɪ) *n.* bodily or material nature or substance; physical existence; corporeality.
corposant (ˈkɔːpəˌzænt) *n.* another name for **Saint Elmo's fire.** [C17: from Portuguese *corpo-santo,* literally: holy body, from Latin *corpus sanctum*]
corps (kɔː) *n., pl.* **corps** (kɔːz). **1.** a military formation that comprises two or more divisions and additional support arms. **2.** a military body with a specific function: *intelligence corps; medical corps.* **3.** a body of people associated together: *the diplomatic corps.* [C18: from French, from Latin *corpus* body]
corps de ballet (ˈkɔː də ˈbæleɪ; *French* kɔr də balɛ) *n.* the members of a ballet company who dance together in a group.
corps diplomatique (ˌdɪpləʊmæˈtiːk) *n.* another name for **diplomatic corps.** Abbrev.: **CD.**

corpse (kɔːps) *n.* **1.** a dead body, esp. of a human being; cadaver. ~*vb.* **2.** *Theatre slang.* to laugh or cause to laugh involuntarily or inopportunely while on stage. [C14: from Old French *corps* body, from Latin *corpus* body]

corpsman ('kɔːmən) *n., pl.* **-men.** *U.S. military.* a medical orderly or stretcher-bearer.

corpulent ('kɔːpjʊlənt) *adj.* physically bulky; fat. [C14: from Latin *corpulentus* fleshy] —'**corpulence** *or* '**corpulency** *n.* —'**corpulently** *adv.*

cor pulmonale (kɔː pʌlmə'nɑːlɪ) *n.* pulmonary heart disease: a serious heart condition in which there is enlargement and failure of the right ventricle resulting from lung disease. [New Latin]

corpus ('kɔːpəs) *n., pl.* **-pora** (-pərə). **1.** a collection or body of writings, esp. by a single author or on a specific topic: *the corpus of Dickens' works.* **2.** the main body, section, or substance of something. **3.** *Anatomy.* **a.** any distinct mass or body. **b.** the main part of an organ or structure. **4.** *Linguistics.* a body of data, esp. the finite collection of grammatical sentences of a language that a linguistic theory seeks to describe by means of an algorithm. **5.** a capital or principal sum, as contrasted with a derived income. **6.** *Obsolete.* a human or animal body, esp. a dead one. [C14: from Latin: body]

corpus callosum (kə'ləʊsəm) *n., pl.* **corpora callosa** (kə'ləʊsə). the band of white fibres that connects the cerebral hemispheres in mammals. [New Latin, literally: callous body]

corpus cavernosum (ˌkævə'nəʊsəm) *n., pl.* **corpora cavernosa.** either of two masses of erectile tissue in the penis of mammals. [New Latin, literally: cavernous body]

Corpus Christi ('krɪstɪ) *n. Chiefly R.C. Church.* a festival in honour of the Eucharist, observed on the Thursday after Trinity Sunday. [C14: from Latin: body of Christ]

corpuscle ('kɔːpʌsᵊl) *n.* **1.** any cell or similar minute body that is suspended in a fluid, esp. any of the **red blood corpuscles** (see **erythrocyte**) or **white blood corpuscles** (see **leucocyte**). **2.** *Anatomy.* the encapsulated ending of a sensory nerve. **3.** *Physics.* a discrete particle such as an electron, photon, ion, or atom. **4.** Also called: **corpuscule** (kɔː'pʌskjuːl). any minute particle. [C17: from Latin *corpusculum* a little body, from *corpus* body] —**corpuscular** (kɔː'pʌskjʊlə) *adj.*

corpuscular theory *n.* the theory, originally proposed by Isaac Newton (1642–1727), and revived with the development of the quantum theory, that light consists of a stream of particles. See **photon.** Compare **wave theory.**

corpus delicti (dɪ'lɪktaɪ) *n. Law.* the body of facts that constitute an offence. [New Latin, literally: the body of the crime]

corpus juris ('dʒʊərɪs) *n.* a body of law, esp. the laws of a nation or state. [from Late Latin, literally: a body of law]

corpus luteum ('luːtɪəm) *n., pl.* **corpora lutea** ('luːtɪə). a yellow glandular mass of tissue that forms in a Graafian follicle following release of an ovum. It secretes progesterone, a hormone necessary to maintain pregnancy. [New Latin, literally: yellow body]

corpus luteum hormone *n.* another name for **progesterone.**

corpus spongiosum (ˌspʌndʒɪ'əʊsəm) *n.* a mass of tissue that, with the corpora cavernosa, forms the erectile tissue of the penis of mammals. [New Latin, literally: spongy body]

corpus striatum (straɪ'eɪtəm) *n., pl.* **corpora striata** (straɪ'eɪtə). a striped mass of white and grey matter situated in front of the thalamus in each cerebral hemisphere. [New Latin, literally: striated body]

corpus vile ('kɔːpəs 'vaɪlɪ) *n., pl.* **corpora vilia** ('kɔːpərə 'vɪlɪə) *Latin.* a person or thing fit only to be the object of an experiment. [literally: worthless body]

corr. *abbrev. for:* **1.** correct. **2.** corrected. **3.** correction. **4.** correspondence. **5.** correspondent. **6.** corresponding.

corrade (kɒ'reɪd) *vb.* (of rivers, streams, etc.) to erode (land) by the abrasive action of rock particles. [C17: from Latin *corrādere* to scrape together, from *rādere* to scrape]

corral (kɒ'rɑːl) *n.* **1.** *Chiefly U.S. and Canadian.* an enclosure for confining cattle or horses. **2.** *Chiefly U.S.* (formerly) a defensive enclosure formed by a ring of covered wagons. ~*vb.* **-rals, -ralling, -ralled.** (*tr.*) *U.S. and Canadian.* **3.** to drive into and confine in or as in a corral. **4.** *Informal.* to capture. [C16: from Spanish, from Vulgar Latin *currāle* (unattested) area for vehicles, from Latin *currus* wagon, from *currere* to run]

corrasion (kə'reɪʒən) *n.* erosion of a rock surface by rock fragments transported over it by water, wind, or ice. Compare **abrasion** (sense 3), **attrition** (sense 4). —**corrasive** (kə'reɪsɪv) *adj.*

correa ('kɒrɪə, kə'riːə) *n.* an Australian evergreen shrub of the genus *Correa*, with large showy tubular flowers. [C19: after Jose Francesco *Correa* da Serra (1750–1823), Portuguese botanist]

correct (kə'rɛkt) *vb.* (*tr.*) **1.** to make free from errors. **2.** to indicate the errors in. **3.** to rebuke or punish in order to set right or improve: *to correct a child; to stand corrected.* **4.** to counteract or rectify (a malfunction, ailment, etc.): *these glasses will correct your sight.* **5.** to adjust or make conform, esp. to a standard. ~*adj.* **6.** free from error; true; accurate: *the correct version.* **7.** in conformity with accepted standards: *correct behaviour.* [C14: from Latin *corrigere* to make straight, put in order, from *com-* (intensive) + *regere* to rule] —**cor'rectable** *or* **cor'rectible** *adj.* —**cor'rectly** *adv.* —**cor'rectness** *n.* —**cor'rector** *n.*

correction (kə'rɛkʃən) *n.* **1.** the act or process of correcting. **2.** something offered or substituted for an error; an improvement. **3.** the act or process of punishing; reproof. **4.** a number or quantity added to or subtracted from a scientific or mathematical calculation or observation to increase its accuracy. —**cor'rectional** *adj.*

correctitude (kə'rɛktɪˌtjuːd) *n.* the quality of correctness, esp. conscious correctness in behaviour.

corrective (kə'rɛktɪv) *adj.* **1.** tending or intended to correct. ~*n.* **2.** something that tends or is intended to correct. —**cor'rectively** *adv.*

correl. *abbrev. for* correlative.

correlate ('kɒrɪˌleɪt) *vb.* **1.** to place or be placed in a mutual, complementary, or reciprocal relationship. **2.** (*tr.*) to establish or show a correlation. ~*adj.* **3.** having a mutual, complementary, or reciprocal relationship. ~*n.* **4.** either of two things mutually or reciprocally related. —'**correˌlatable** *adj.*

correlation (ˌkɒrɪ'leɪʃən) *n.* **1.** a mutual or reciprocal relationship between two or more things. **2.** the act or process of correlating or the state of being correlated. **3.** *Statistics.* the extent of correspondence between the ordering of two variables. Correlation is positive or direct when two variables move in the same direction and negative or inverse when they move in opposite directions. [C16: from Medieval Latin *correlātiō*, from *com-* together + *relātiō*, RELATION] —ˌ**corre'lational** *adj.*

correlation coefficient *n. Statistics.* a statistic measuring the degree of correlation between two variables as by dividing their covariance by the square root of the product of their variances. The closer the correlation coefficient is to 1 or −1 the greater the correlation; if it is random, the coefficient is zero. See also **Pearson's correlation coefficient, Spearman's rank-order coefficient.**

correlative (kɒ'rɛlətɪv) *adj.* **1.** in mutual, complementary, or reciprocal relationship; corresponding. **2.** denoting words, usually conjunctions, occurring together though not adjacently in certain grammatical constructions, as for example *neither* and *nor* in such sentences as *he neither ate nor drank.* ~*n.* **3.** either of two things that are correlative. **4.** a correlative word. —**cor'relatively** *adv.* —**cor'relativeness** *or* **corˌrela'tivity** *n.*

correspond (ˌkɒrɪ'spɒnd) *vb.* (*intr.*) **1.** (usually foll. by *with* or *to*) to conform, be in agreement, or be consistent or compatible (with); tally (with). **2.** (usually foll. by *to*) to be similar or analogous in character or function. **3.** (usually foll. by *with*) to communicate by letter. [C16: from Medieval Latin *correspondēre*, from Latin *respondēre* to RESPOND] —ˌ**corre'spondingly** *adv.*

▷**Usage.** See at **similar.**

correspondence (ˌkɒrɪ'spɒndəns) *n.* **1.** the act or condition of agreeing or corresponding. **2.** similarity or analogy. **3.** agreement or conformity. **4. a.** communication by the exchange of letters. **b.** the letters so exchanged.

correspondence column *n.* a section of a newspaper or magazine in which are printed readers' letters to the editor.

correspondence school *n.* an educational institution that offers tuition (**correspondence courses**) by post.

correspondent (ˌkɒrɪ'spɒndənt) *n.* **1.** a person who communicates by letter or by letters. **2.** a person employed by a newspaper, etc., to report on a special subject or to send reports from a foreign country. **3.** a person or firm that has regular business relations with another, esp. one in a different part of the country or abroad. **4.** something that corresponds to another. ~*adj.* **5.** similar or analogous.

corrida (ko'rriða) *n.* the Spanish word for **bullfight.** [Spanish, from the phrase *corrida de toros*, literally: a running of bulls, from *correr* to run, from Latin *currere*]

corridor ('kɒrɪˌdɔː) *n.* **1.** a hallway or passage connecting parts of a building. **2.** a strip of land or airspace that affords access, either from a landlocked country to the sea (such as the **Polish corridor,** 1919-39, which divided Germany) or from a state to an exclave (such as the **Berlin corridor,** 1945–90, which passed through East Germany). **3.** a passageway connecting the compartments of a railway coach. **4. corridors of power.** the higher echelons of government, the Civil Service, etc., considered as the location of power and influence. **5.** a flight path that affords safe access for intruding aircraft. **6.** the path that a spacecraft must follow when re-entering the atmosphere, above which lift is insufficient and below which heating effects are excessive. [C16: from Old French, from Old Italian *corridore*, literally: place for running, from *correre* to run, from Latin *currere*]

corrie ('kɒrɪ) *n.* **1.** (in Scotland) a circular hollow on a hillside. **2.** *Geology.* another name for **cirque** (sense 1). [C18: from Gaelic *coire* cauldron, kettle]

Corriedale ('kɒrɪˌdeɪl) *n.* a breed of sheep reared for both wool and meat, originally developed in New Zealand.

corrie-fisted (ˌkɒrɪ'fɪstɪd) *adj. Scot. dialect.* left-handed. [C20: from earlier *car, ker* left hand or side, from Gaelic *cearr* left or wrong hand]

corrigendum (ˌkɒrɪ'dʒɛndəm) *n., pl.* **-da** (-də). **1.** an error to be corrected. **2.** (*sometimes pl.*) Also called: **erratum.** a slip of paper inserted into a book after printing, listing errors and corrections. [C19: from Latin: that which is to be corrected, from *corrigere* to CORRECT]

corrigible ('kɒrɪdʒɪbəl) *adj.* **1.** capable of being corrected. **2.** submissive or submitting to correction. [C15: from Old French, from Medieval Latin *corrigibilis,* from Latin *corrigere* to set right, CORRECT] —ˌ**corrigi'bility** *n.* —'**corrigibly** *adv.*
corrival (kə'raɪvəl) *n., vb.* a rare word for **rival.** [C16: from Old French, from Late Latin *corrīvālis,* from Latin *com-* together, mutually + *rīvālis* RIVAL] —**cor'rivalry** *n.*
corroborant (kə'rɒbərənt) *Archaic.* ~*adj.* **1.** serving to corroborate. **2.** strengthening. ~*n.* **3.** something that strengthens; tonic.
corroborate *vb.* (kə'rɒbəˌreɪt). **1.** (*tr.*) to confirm or support (facts, opinions, etc.), esp. by providing fresh evidence: *the witness corroborated the accused's statement.* ~*adj.* (kə'rɒbərɪt). *Archaic.* **2.** serving to corroborate a fact, an opinion, etc. **3.** (of a fact) corroborated. [C16: from Latin *corrōborāre* to invigorate, from *rōborāre* to make strong, from *rōbur* strength, literally: oak] —**corˌrobo'ration** *n.* —**corroborative** (kə'rɒbərətɪv) *or* **corˌrobo'ratory** *adj.* —**cor'roboratively** *adv.* —**cor'roboˌrator** *n.*
corroboree (kə'rɒbərɪ) *n. Austral.* **1.** a native assembly of sacred, festive, or warlike character. **2.** any noisy gathering. [C19: from a native Australian language]
corrode (kə'rəʊd) *vb.* **1.** to eat away or be eaten away, esp. by chemical action as in the oxidation or rusting of a metal. **2.** (*tr.*) to destroy gradually; consume: *his jealousy corroded his happiness.* [C14: from Latin *corrōdere* to gnaw to pieces, from *rōdere* to gnaw; see RODENT, RAT] —**cor'rodant** *or* **cor'rodent** *n.* —**cor'roder** *n.* —**cor'rodible** *adj.* —**corˌrodi'bility** *n.*
corrody ('kɒrədɪ) *n., pl.* **-dies.** a variant spelling of **corody.**
corrosion (kə'rəʊʒən) *n.* **1.** a process in which a solid, esp. a metal, is eaten away and changed by a chemical action, as in the oxidation of iron in the presence of water by an electrolytic process. **2.** slow deterioration by being eaten or worn away. **3.** the condition produced by or the product of corrosion.
corrosive (kə'rəʊsɪv) *adj.* **1.** (esp. of acids or alkalis) capable of destroying solid materials. **2.** tending to eat away or consume. **3.** cutting; sarcastic: *a corrosive remark.* ~*n.* **4.** a corrosive substance, such as a strong acid or alkali. —**cor'rosively** *adv.* —**cor'rosiveness** *n.*
corrosive sublimate *n.* another name for **mercuric chloride.**
corrugate *vb.* ('kɒrʊˌgeɪt). **1.** (*usually tr.*) to fold or be folded into alternate furrows and ridges. ~*adj.* ('kɒrʊgɪt, -ˌgeɪt). **2.** folded into furrows and ridges; wrinkled. [C18: from Latin *corrūgāre,* from *rūga* a wrinkle] —ˌ**corru'gation** *n.*
corrugated iron *n.* a thin structural sheet made of iron or steel, formed with alternating ridges and troughs.
corrugated paper *n.* a packaging material made from layers of heavy paper, the top layer of which is grooved and ridged.
corrugator ('kɒrʊˌgeɪtə) *n.* a muscle whose contraction causes wrinkling of the brow.
corrupt (kə'rʌpt) *adj.* **1.** lacking in integrity; open to or involving bribery or other dishonest practices: *a corrupt official; corrupt practices in an election.* **2.** morally depraved. **3.** putrid or rotten. **4.** contaminated; unclean. **5.** (of a text or manuscript) made meaningless or different in meaning from the original by scribal errors or alterations. **6.** (of computer programs or data) containing errors. ~*vb.* **7.** to become or cause to become dishonest or disloyal. **8.** to debase or become debased morally; deprave. **9.** (*tr.*) to infect or contaminate; taint. **10.** (*tr.*) to cause to become rotten. **11.** (*tr.*) to alter (a text, manuscript, etc.) from the original. **12.** (*tr.*) *Computer technol.* to introduce errors into (data or a program). [C14: from Latin *corruptus* spoiled, from *corrumpere* to ruin, literally: break to pieces, from *rumpere* to break] —**cor'rupter** *or* **cor'ruptor** *n.* —**cor'ruptive** *adj.* —**cor'ruptively** *adv.* —**cor'ruptly** *adv.* —**cor'ruptness** *n.*
corruptible (kə'rʌptəbəl) *adj.* susceptible to corruption; capable of being corrupted. —**corˌrupti'bility** *or* **cor'ruptibleness** *n.* —**cor'ruptibly** *adv.*
corruption (kə'rʌpʃən) *n.* **1.** the act of corrupting or state of being corrupt. **2.** moral perversion; depravity. **3.** dishonesty, esp. bribery. **4.** putrefaction or decay. **5.** alteration, as of a manuscript. **6.** an altered form of a word. —**cor'ruptionist** *n.*
corsac ('kɔːsæk) *n.* a fox, *Vulpes corsac,* of central Asia. [C19: from a Turkic language]
corsage (kɔː'sɑːʒ) *n.* **1.** a flower or small bunch of flowers worn pinned to the lapel, bosom, etc., or sometimes carried by women. **2.** the bodice of a dress. [C15: from Old French, from *cors* body, from Latin *corpus*]
corsair ('kɔːsɛə) *n.* **1.** a pirate. **2.** a privateer, esp. of the Barbary Coast of N Africa. [C15: from Old French *corsaire* pirate, from Medieval Latin *cursārius,* from Latin *cursus* a running, COURSE]
corse (kɔːs) *n.* an archaic word for **corpse.**
corselet ('kɔːslɪt) *n.* **1.** Also spelt: **corslet.** a piece of armour for the top part of the body. **2.** a one-piece foundation garment, usually combining a brassiere and a corset. [C15: from Old French, from *cors* bodice of a garment, from Latin *corpus* body]
corset ('kɔːsɪt) *n.* **1. a.** a stiffened, elasticated, or laced foundation garment, worn esp. by women, that usually extends from below the chest to the hips, providing support for the spine and stomach and shaping the figure. **b.** a similar garment worn because of injury, weakness, etc., by either sex. **2.** *Informal.* a restriction or limitation, esp. government control of bank lending. **3.** a stiffened outer bodice worn by either sex, esp. in the 16th century. ~*vb.* **4.** (*tr.*) to dress or enclose in, or as in, a corset. [C14: from Old French, literally: a little bodice; see CORSELET]
corsetière (ˌkɔːsɛtɪ'ɛə, kɔːˌsɛt-) *or* (*masc.*) **corsetier** (ˌkɔːsɪ'tɪə) *n.* a person who makes and fits corsets.
corsetry ('kɔːsɪtrɪ) *n.* **1.** the making of or dealing in corsets. **2.** corsets considered collectively.
Corsican ('kɔːsɪkən) *adj.* of or relating to Corsica, an island in the Mediterranean west of N Italy. ~*n.* **2.** a native or inhabitant of Corsica.
cortege *or* **cortège** (kɔː'teɪʒ) *n.* **1.** a formal procession, esp. a funeral procession. **2.** a train of attendants; retinue. [C17: from French, from Italian *corteggio,* from *corteggiare* to attend, from *corte* COURT]
Cortes ('kɔːtɛz; *Spanish* 'kortes) *n.* the national assembly of Spain and (until 1910) Portugal. [C17: from Spanish, literally: courts, plural of *corte* court, from Latin *cohors* COHORT]
cortex ('kɔːtɛks) *n., pl.* **-tices** (-tɪˌsiːz). **1.** *Anatomy.* the outer layer of any organ or part, such as the grey matter in the brain that covers the cerebrum (**cerebral cortex**) or the outer part of the kidney (**renal cortex**). **2.** *Botany.* **a.** the unspecialized tissue in plant stems and roots between the vascular bundles and the epidermis. **b.** the outer layer of a part such as the bark of a stem. [C17: from Latin: bark, outer layer] —**cortical** ('kɔːtɪkəl) *adj.* —'**cortically** *adv.*
corticate ('kɔːtɪkɪt, -ˌkeɪt) *or* **corticated** *adj.* (of plants, seeds, etc.) having a bark, husk, or rind. [C19: from Latin *corticātus* covered with bark] —ˌ**corti'cation** *n.*
cortico- *or before a vowel* **cortic-** *combining form.* indicating the cortex: *corticotrophin.*
corticolous (kɔː'tɪkələs) *adj. Biology.* living or growing on the surface of bark.
corticosteroid (ˌkɔːtɪkəʊ'stɪərɔɪd) *or* **corticoid** *n.* **1.** any steroid hormone produced by the adrenal cortex that affects carbohydrate, protein, and electrolyte metabolism, gonad function, and immune response. **2.** any similar synthetic substance, used in treating inflammatory and allergic diseases. ~See **glucocorticoid, mineralocorticoid.**
corticosterone (ˌkɔːtɪ'kɒstəˌrəʊn) *n.* a glucocorticoid hormone secreted by the adrenal cortex. Formula: $C_{21}H_{30}O_4$. See also **corticosteroid.** [C20: from CORTICO- + STER(OL) + -ONE]
corticotrophic (ˌkɔːtɪkəʊ'trəʊfɪk) *or* **corticotropic** (ˌkɔːtɪkəʊ'trɒpɪk) *adj.* stimulating the adrenal cortex; adrenocorticotrophic.
corticotrophin (ˌkɔːtɪkəʊ'trəʊfɪn) *n.* another name for **adrenocorticotrophic hormone.** See **ACTH.**
cortisol ('kɔːtɪˌsɒl) *n.* another name for **hydrocortisone.** [C20: from CORTIS(ONE) + -OL[2]]
cortisone ('kɔːtɪˌsəʊn, -ˌzəʊn) *n.* a glucocorticoid hormone, the synthetic form of which has been used in treating rheumatoid arthritis, allergic and skin diseases, leukaemia, etc.; 17-hydroxy-11-dehydrocorticosterone. Formula: $C_{21}H_{28}O_5$. [C20: shortened from CORTICOSTERONE]
corundum (kə'rʌndəm) *n.* a grey, blue, green, red, yellow, or brown mineral, found in metamorphosed shales and limestones, in veins, and in some igneous rocks. It is used as an abrasive and as gemstone; the red variety is ruby, the blue is sapphire. Composition: aluminium oxide. Formula: Al_2O_3. Crystal structure: hexagonal (rhombohedral). [C18: from Tamil *kuruntam;* related to Sanskrit *kuruvinda* ruby]
coruscate ('kɒrəˌskeɪt) *vb.* (*intr.*) to emit flashes of light; sparkle. [C18: from Latin *coruscāre* to flash, vibrate]
coruscation (ˌkɒrə'skeɪʃən) *n.* **1.** a gleam or flash of light. **2.** a sudden or striking display of brilliance, wit, etc.
corvée ('kɔːveɪ) *n.* **1.** *European history.* a day's unpaid labour owed by a feudal vassal to his lord. **2.** the practice or an instance of forced labour. [C14: from Old French, from Late Latin *corrogāta* contribution, from Latin *corrogāre* to collect, from *rogāre* to ask]
corves (kɔːvz) *n.* the plural of **corf.**
corvette (kɔː'vɛt) *n.* a lightly armed escort warship. [C17: from Old French, perhaps from Middle Dutch *corf* basket, small ship, from Latin *corbis* basket]
corvine ('kɔːvaɪn) *adj.* **1.** of, relating to, or resembling a crow. **2.** of, relating to, or belonging to the passerine bird family *Corvidae,* which includes the crows, raven, rook, jackdaw, magpies, and jays. [C17: from Latin *corvīnus* raven-like, from *corvus* a raven]
Corvus ('kɔːvəs) *n., Latin genitive* **Corvi** ('kɔːvaɪ). a small quadrilateral-shaped constellation in the S hemisphere, lying between Virgo and Hydra. [Latin: raven]
corydalis (kə'rɪdəlɪs) *n.* any erect or climbing plant of the N temperate genus *Corydalis,* having finely-lobed leaves and spurred yellow or pinkish flowers: family *Fumariaceae.* Also called: **fumitory.** [C19: from New Latin, from Greek *korudallis* variant of *korudos* crested lark, from *korus* helmet, crest; alluding to the appearance of the flowers]
Corydon ('kɒrɪdən, -ˌdɒn) *n.* (in pastoral literature) a shepherd or rustic: used as a proper name.
corymb ('kɒrɪmb, -rɪm) *n.* an inflorescence in the form of a flat-topped flower cluster with the oldest flowers at the periphery. This type of raceme occurs in the candytuft. [C18: from

Latin *corymbus,* from Greek *korumbos* cluster] —ˈ**corymbed** *adj.* —**coˈrymbose** *or* **coˈrymbous** *adj.* —**coˈrymbosely** *adv.*
coryphaeus (ˌkɒrɪˈfiːəs) *n., pl.* **-phaei** (-ˈfiːaɪ). **1.** (in ancient Greek drama) the leader of the chorus. **2.** *Archaic or literary.* a leader of a group. [C17: from Latin, from Greek *koruphaios* leader, from *koruphē* summit]
coryphée (ˌkɒrɪˈfeɪ) *n.* a leading dancer of a corps de ballet. [C19: from French, from Latin *coryphaeus* CORYPHAEUS]
coryza (kəˈraɪzə) *n.* acute inflammation of the mucous membrane of the nose, with discharge of mucus; a head cold. [C17: from Late Latin: catarrh, from Greek *koruza*]
cos[1] *or* **cos lettuce** (kɒs) *n.* a variety of lettuce with a long slender head and crisp leaves. Compare **cabbage lettuce.** Usual U.S. and Canadian name: **romaine.** [C17: named after *Kos,* the Aegean island of its origin]
cos[2] (kɒz) *abbrev. for* cosine.
COS *abbrev. for* Chief of Staff.
Cos. *or* **cos.** *abbrev. for:* **1.** Companies. **2.** Counties.
c.o.s. *or* **COS** *abbrev. for* cash on shipment.
cosec (ˈkəʊsɛk) *abbrev. for* cosecant.
cosecant (kəʊˈsiːkənt) *n.* (of an angle) a trigonometric function that in a right-angled triangle is the ratio of the length of the hypotenuse to that of the opposite side; the reciprocal of sine. Abbrev.: **cosec.**
cosech (ˈkəʊsɛtʃ, -sɛk) *n.* hyperbolic cosecant; a hyperbolic function that is the reciprocal of sinh.
coseismal (kəʊˈsaɪzməl) *or* **coseismic** *adj.* **1.** of or designating points at which earthquake waves are felt at the same time. **2.** (of a line on a map) connecting such points. ~*n.* **3.** such a line on a map.
coset (ˈkəʊˌsɛt) *n. Maths.* a set that when added to another set produces a specified larger set.
cosh[1] (kɒʃ) *Brit.* ~*n.* **1.** a blunt weapon, often made of hard rubber; bludgeon. **2.** an attack with such a weapon. ~*vb.* (*tr.*) **3.** to hit with such a weapon, esp. on the head. [C19: from Romany *kosh,* from *koshter* skewer, stick]
cosh[2] (kɒʃ, ˈkɒsˈeɪtʃ) *n.* hyperbolic cosine; a hyperbolic function, $\cosh z = \frac{1}{2}(e^z + e^{-z})$, related to cosine by the expression $\cosh iz = \cos z$, where $i = \sqrt{-1}$. [C19: from COS(INE) + H(YPERBOLIC)]
cosher (ˈkɒʃə) *vb. Irish.* **1.** (*tr.*) to pamper or coddle. **2.** (*intr.*) to live or be entertained at the expense of another.
cosignatory (kəʊˈsɪgnətərɪ, -trɪ) *n., pl.* **-ries.** **1.** a person, country, etc., that signs a document jointly with others. ~*adj.* **2.** signing jointly with another or others.
cosine (ˈkəʊˌsaɪn) *n.* (of an angle) **1.** a trigonometric function that in a right-angled triangle is the ratio of the length of the adjacent side to that of the hypotenuse; the sine of the complement. **2.** a function that in a circle centred at the origin of a Cartesian coordinate system is the ratio of the abscissa of a point on the circumference to the radius of the circle. ~Abbrev.: **cos.** [C17: from New Latin *cosinus;* see CO-, SINE[1]]
COSLA (ˈkɒzlə) *n. acronym for* Convention of Scottish Local Authorities.
cosmetic (kɒzˈmɛtɪk) *n.* **1.** any preparation applied to the body, esp. the face, with the intention of beautifying it. ~*adj.* **2.** serving or designed to beautify the body, esp. the face. **3.** having no other function than to beautify: *cosmetic illustrations in a book.* [C17: from Greek *kosmētikos,* from *kosmein* to arrange, from *kosmos* order] —**cosˈmetically** *adv.* —**cosˌmetiˈcology** *n.*
cosmetician (ˌkɒzmɪˈtɪʃən) *n.* a person who makes, sells, or applies cosmetics.
cosmetic surgery *n.* surgery performed to improve the appearance, rather than for medical reasons.
cosmic (ˈkɒzmɪk) *adj.* **1.** of or relating to the whole universe: *cosmic laws.* **2.** occurring or originating in outer space, esp. as opposed to the vicinity of the earth, the solar system, or the local galaxy: *cosmic rays.* **3.** immeasurably extended in space or time; vast. **4.** *Rare.* harmonious. —ˈ**cosmically** *adv.*
cosmic dust *n.* fine particles of solid matter occurring throughout interstellar space and often collecting into clouds of extremely low density. See also **nebula** (sense 1).
cosmic rays *pl. n.* radiation consisting of atomic nuclei, esp. protons, of very high energy that reach the earth from outer space. Also called: **cosmic radiation.**
cosmic string *n.* any of a number of linear defects in space–time postulated in certain theories of cosmology to exist in the universe as a consequence of the big bang.
cosmine (ˈkɒzmiːn) *or* **cosmin** *n. Zoology.* a substance resembling dentine, forming the outer layer of cosmoid scales. [C20: from Greek *kosmos* arrangement + -INE[1]]
cosmo- *or before a vowel* **cosm-** *combining form.* indicating the world or universe: *cosmology; cosmonaut; cosmography.* [from Greek: COSMOS]
cosmodrome (ˈkɒzməˌdrəʊm) *n.* a site, esp. one in the former Soviet Union, from which spacecraft are launched.
cosmogony (kɒzˈmɒgənɪ) *n., pl.* **-nies.** **1.** the study of the origin and development of the universe or of a particular system in the universe, such as the solar system. **2.** a theory of such an origin or evolution. [C17: from Greek *kosmogonia,* from COSMO- + *gonos* creation] —**cosˈmogonal** *adj.* —**cosmogonic** (ˌkɒzməˈgɒnɪk) *or* ˌ**cosmoˈgonical** *adj.* —**cosˈmogonist** *n.*
cosmography (kɒzˈmɒgrəfɪ) *n.* **1.** a representation of the world or the universe. **2.** the science dealing with the whole order of nature. —**cosˈmographer** *or* **cosˈmographist** *n.* —**cosmographic** (ˌkɒzməˈgræfɪk) *or* ˌ**cosmoˈgraphical** *adj.* —ˌ**cosmoˈgraphically** *adv.*
cosmoid (ˈkɒzmɔɪd) *adj.* (of the scales of coelacanths and lungfish) consisting of two inner bony layers and an outer layer of cosmine. [C20: from COSM(INE) + -OID]
cosmological argument *n. Philosophy.* one of the arguments that purport to prove the existence of God from empirical facts about the universe, esp. the argument to the existence of a first cause. Compare **ontological argument** (sense 1), **teleological argument.**
cosmological principle *n. Astronomy.* the theory that the universe is uniform, homogenous, and isotropic, and therefore appears the same from any position.
cosmology (kɒzˈmɒlədʒɪ) *n.* **1.** the philosophical study of the origin and nature of the universe. **2.** the branch of astronomy concerned with the evolution and structure of the universe. **3.** a particular account of the origin or structure of the universe: *Ptolemaic cosmology.* —**cosmological** (ˌkɒzməˈlɒdʒɪkəl) *or* ˌ**cosmoˈlogic** *adj.* —ˌ**cosmoˈlogically** *adv.* —**cosˈmologist** *n.*
cosmonaut (ˈkɒzməˌnɔːt) *n.* an astronaut, esp. one from the former Soviet Union. [C20: from Russian *kosmonavt,* from COSMO- + Greek *nautēs* sailor]
cosmopolis (kɒzˈmɒpəlɪs) *n.* an international city. [C19: see COSMO-, POLIS[1]]
cosmopolitan (ˌkɒzməˈpɒlɪtən) *n.* **1.** a person who has lived and travelled in many countries, esp. one who is free of national prejudices. ~*adj.* **2.** having interest in or familiar with many parts of the world. **3.** sophisticated or urbane. **4.** composed of people or elements from all parts of the world or from many different spheres. **5.** (of plants or animals) widely distributed. [C17: from French, ultimately from Greek *kosmopolitēs,* from *kosmo-* COSMO- + *politēs* citizen] —ˌ**cosmoˈpolitanism** *n.*
cosmopolite (kɒzˈmɒpəˌlaɪt) *n.* **1.** a less common word for **cosmopolitan** (sense 1). **2.** an animal or plant that occurs in most parts of the world. —**cosˈmopolitˌism** *n.*
cosmos (ˈkɒzmɒs) *n.* **1.** the world or universe considered as an ordered system. **2.** any ordered system. **3.** harmony; order. **4.** (*pl.* **-mos** *or* **-moses**) any tropical American plant of the genus *Cosmos,* cultivated as garden plants for their brightly coloured flowers: family *Compositae* (composites). [C17: from Greek *kosmos* order, world, universe]
Cosmos (ˈkɒzmɒs) *n. Astronautics.* any of various types of Soviet satellite, including Cosmos 1 (launched 1962) and nearly 2000 subsequent satellites.
Cosmotron (ˈkɒzməˌtrɒn) *n.* a large synchrotron for accelerating protons to high energies (of the order of 1 GeV). [C20: from COSM(IC RAY) + -TRON]
coss (kɒs) *n.* another name for **kos.**
Cossack (ˈkɒsæk) *n.* **1.** (formerly) any of the free warrior-peasants of chiefly East Slavonic descent who lived in communes, esp. in the Ukraine, and served as cavalry under the tsars. ~*adj.* **2.** of, relating to, or characteristic of the Cossacks: *a Cossack dance.* [C16: from Russian *kazak* vagabond, of Turkic origin]
cossack hat *n.* a warm brimless hat of fur or sheepskin.
cosset (ˈkɒsɪt) *vb.* (*tr.*) **-sets, -seting, -seted.** **1.** to pamper; coddle; pet. ~*n.* **2.** any pet animal, esp. a lamb. [C16: of unknown origin]
cossie (ˈkɒzɪ) *n. Chiefly Austral.* an informal name for a swimming costume.
cost (kɒst) *n.* **1.** the price paid or required for acquiring, producing, or maintaining something, usually measured in money, time, or energy; expense or expenditure; outlay. **2.** suffering or sacrifice; loss; penalty: *count the cost to your health; I know to my cost.* **3. a.** the amount paid for a commodity by its seller: *to sell at cost.* **b.** (*as modifier*): *the cost price.* **4.** (*pl.*) *Law.* the expenses of judicial proceedings. **5. at any cost** *or* **at all costs.** regardless of cost or sacrifice involved. **6. at the cost of.** at the expense of losing. ~*vb.* **costs, costing, cost.** **7.** (*tr.*) to be obtained or obtainable in exchange for (money or something equivalent); be priced at: *the ride cost one pound.* **8.** to cause or require the expenditure, loss, or sacrifice (of): *the accident cost him dearly.* **9.** to estimate the cost of (a product, process, etc.) for the purposes of pricing, budgeting, control, etc. [C13: from Old French (n.), from *coster* to cost, from Latin *constāre* to stand at, cost, from *stāre* to stand] —ˈ**costless** *adj.*
costa (ˈkɒstə) *n., pl.* **-tae** (-tiː). **1.** the technical name for **rib**[1] (sense 1). **2.** a riblike part, such as the midrib of a plant leaf. [C19: from Latin: rib, side, wall] —ˈ**costal** *adj.*
cost accounting *n.* the recording and controlling of all the expenditures of an enterprise in order to facilitate control of separate activities. Also called: **management accounting.** —**cost accountant** *n.*
co-star *n.* **1.** an actor who shares star billing with another. ~*vb.* **-stars, -starring, -starred.** **2.** (*intr.;* often foll. by *with*) to share star billing (with another actor). **3.** (*tr.*) to present as sharing top billing: *the film co-starred Mae West and W. C. Fields.*
costard (ˈkʌstəd) *n.* **1.** an English variety of apple tree. **2.** the large ribbed apple of this tree. **3.** *Archaic, humorous.* a slang word for **head.** [C14: from Anglo-Norman, from Old French *coste* rib]

Costa Rican ('kɒstə 'riːkən) *adj.* of or relating to Costa Rica, a republic in Central America. ~*n.* **2.** a native or inhabitant of Costa Rica.
costate ('kɒsteɪt) *adj.* **1.** *Anatomy.* having ribs. **2.** (of leaves) having veins or ridges, esp. parallel ones. [C19: from Late Latin *costātus,* from Latin *costa* rib]
cost-benefit *adj.* denoting or relating to a method of assessing a project that takes into account its costs and its benefits to society as well as the revenue it generates: *a cost-benefit analysis; the project was assessed on a cost-benefit basis.*
cost centre *n.* a unit, such as a department of a company, to which costs may be allocated for cost accounting purposes.
cost-effective *adj.* providing adequate financial return in relation to outlay. —**cost-effectiveness** *n.*
costermonger ('kɒstə,mʌŋgə) *or* **coster** *n. Brit., rare.* a person who sells fruit, vegetables, etc., from a barrow. [C16: *coster-,* from COSTARD + MONGER]
costive ('kɒstɪv) *adj.* **1.** having constipation; constipated. **2.** sluggish. **3.** niggardly. [C14: from Old French *costivé,* from Latin *constipātus;* see CONSTIPATE] —'**costively** *adv.* —'**costiveness** *n.*
costly ('kɒstlɪ) *adj.* **-lier, -liest. 1.** of great price or value; expensive. **2.** entailing great loss or sacrifice: *a costly victory.* **3.** splendid; lavish. —'**costliness** *n.*
costmary ('kɒst,mɛərɪ) *n., pl.* **-maries.** a herbaceous plant, *Chrysanthemum balsamita,* native to Asia. Its fragrant leaves were used as a seasoning and to flavour ale: family *Compositae* (composites). Also called: **alecost.** [C15 *costmarie,* from *coste* costmary, from Latin *costum* (from Greek *kostos*) + *Marie* (the Virgin) Mary]
cost of living *n.* **1. a.** the basic cost of the food, clothing, shelter, and fuel necessary to maintain life, esp. at a standard of living regarded as basic or minimal. **b.** (*as modifier*): *the cost-of-living index.* **2.** the average expenditure of a person or family in a given period.
costotomy (kɒ'stɒtəmɪ) *n., pl.* **-mies.** surgical incision into a rib.
cost-plus *n.* **a.** a method of establishing a selling price in which an agreed percentage is added to the cost price to cover profit. **b.** (*as modifier*): *cost-plus pricing.*
cost-push inflation *n.* See **inflation.**
costrel ('kɒstrəl) *n. Obsolete.* a flask, usually of earthenware or leather. [C14: from Old French *costerel,* from *coste* side, rib, from Latin *costa*]
cost rent *n.* (in Britain) the rent of a dwelling calculated on the cost of providing and maintaining the property without allowing for a profit.
costume ('kɒstjuːm) *n.* **1.** a complete style of dressing, including all the clothes, accessories, etc., worn at one time, as in a particular country or period; dress: *national costume.* **2.** *Old-fashioned.* a woman's suit. **3.** a set of clothes, esp. unusual or period clothes, worn in a play by an actor or at a fancy dress ball: *a jester's costume.* **4.** short for **swimming costume.** ~*vb.* (*tr.*) **5.** to furnish the costumes for (a show, film, etc.). **6.** to dress (someone) in a costume. [C18: from French, from Italian: dress, habit, CUSTOM]
costume jewellery *n.* jewellery that is decorative but has little intrinsic value.
costume piece *n.* any theatrical production, film, television presentation, etc., in which the performers wear the costumes of a former age. Also called: **costume drama.**
costumier (kɒ'stjuːmɪə) *or* **costumer** (kɒ'stjuːmə) *n.* a person or firm that makes or supplies theatrical or fancy costumes.
cosy *or U.S.* **cozy** ('kəʊzɪ) *adj.* **-sier, -siest** *or U.S.* **-zier, -ziest. 1.** warm and snug. **2.** intimate; friendly. **3.** convenient, esp. for devious purposes: *a cosy deal.* ~*n., pl.* **-sies** *or U.S.* **-zies. 4.** a cover for keeping things warm: *egg cosy.* [C18: from Scots, of unknown origin] —'**cosily** *or U.S.* '**cozily** *adv.* —'**cosiness** *or U.S.* '**coziness** *n.*
cosy along *vb.* **-sies, -sying, -sied.** (*tr., adv.*) to reassure (someone), esp. with false assurances.
cosy up *or U.S.* **cozy up** *vb.* (*intr.,* often foll. by *to*) *Chiefly U.S. and Canadian.* **1.** to seek to become intimate or to ingratiate oneself (with someone). **2.** to draw close to (somebody or something) for warmth or for affection; snuggle up.
cot[1] (kɒt) *n.* **1.** a child's boxlike bed, usually incorporating vertical bars. **2.** a collapsible or portable bed. **3.** a light bedstead. **4.** *Nautical.* a hammock-like bed with a stiff frame. [C17: from Hindi *khāt* bedstead, from Sanskrit *khátvā,* of Dravidian origin; related to Tamil *kattil* bedstead]
cot[2] (kɒt) *n.* **1.** *Literary or archaic.* a small cottage. **2.** Also called: **cote. a.** a small shelter, esp. one for pigeons, sheep, etc. **b.** (*in combination*): *dovecot.* **3.** another name for **fingerstall.** [Old English *cot;* related to Old Norse *kot* little hut, Middle Low German *cot*]
cot[3] (kɒt) *abbrev. for* cotangent.
cotan ('kəʊ,tæn) *abbrev. for* cotangent.
cotangent (kəʊ'tændʒənt) *n.* (of an angle) a trigonometric function that in a right-angled triangle is the ratio of the length of the adjacent side to that of the opposite side; the reciprocal of tangent. Abbrevs.: **cot, cotan, ctn.** —**cotangential** (,kəʊtæn'dʒɛnʃəl) *adj.*
cot case *n.* **1.** *Austral., humorous.* a person who is incapacitated by drink. **2.** *Chiefly N.Z.* a person confined to bed through illness.
cot death *n.* the unexplained sudden death of an infant during sleep. Technical name: **sudden infant death syndrome.** Also called (U.S. and Canadian): **crib death.**
cote[1] (kəʊt) *or* **cot** *n.* **1. a.** a small shelter for pigeons, sheep, etc. **b.** (*in combination*): *dovecote.* **2.** *Dialect, chiefly Brit.* a small cottage. [Old English *cote;* related to Low German *Kote;* see COT[2]]
cote[2] (kəʊt) *vb.* (*tr.*) *Archaic.* to pass by, outstrip, or surpass. [C16: perhaps from Old French *costoier* to run alongside, from *coste* side; see COAST]
cotemporary (kəʊ'tɛmpərərɪ) *adj.* a variant of **contemporary.**
cotenant (kəʊ'tɛnənt) *n.* a person who holds property jointly or in common with others. —**co'tenancy** *n.*
coterie ('kəʊtərɪ) *n.* a small exclusive group of friends or people with common interests; clique. [C18: from French, from Old French: association of tenants, from *cotier* (unattested) cottager, from Medieval Latin *cotārius* COTTER[2]; see COT[2]]
coterminous (kəʊ'tɜːmɪnəs) *or* **conterminous** *adj.* **1.** having a common boundary; bordering; contiguous. **2.** coextensive or coincident in range, time, scope, etc.
coth (kɒθ) *n.* hyperbolic cotangent; a hyperbolic function that is the ratio of cosh to sinh, being the reciprocal of tanh. [C20: from COT(ANGENT) + H(YPERBOLIC)]
cothurnus (kəʊ'θɜːnəs) *or* **cothurn** ('kəʊθɜːn, kəʊ'θɜːn) *n., pl.* **-thurni** (-'θɜːnaɪ) *or* **-thurns.** the buskin worn in ancient Greek tragedy. [C18: from Latin, from Greek *kothornos*]
cotidal (kəʊ'taɪdᵊl) *adj.* (of a line on a tidal chart) joining points at which high tide occurs simultaneously.
cotillion *or* **cotillon** (kə'tɪljən, kəʊ-) *n.* **1.** a French formation dance of the 18th century. **2.** *U.S.* a quadrille. **3.** *U.S.* a complicated dance with frequent changes of partners. **4.** *U.S. and Canadian.* a formal ball, esp. one at which debutantes are presented. [C18: from French *cotillon* dance, from Old French: petticoat, from *cote* COAT]
cotinga (kə'tɪŋgə) *n.* any tropical American passerine bird of the family *Cotingidae,* such as the umbrella bird and the cock-of-the-rock, having a broad slightly hooked bill. Also called: **chatterer.**
cotoneaster (kə,təʊnɪ'æstə) *n.* any Old World shrub of the rosaceous genus *Cotoneaster:* cultivated for their small ornamental white or pinkish flowers and red or black berries. [C18: from New Latin, from Latin *cotōneum* QUINCE]
cotquean ('kɒt,kwiːn) *n. Archaic.* **1.** a coarse woman. **2.** a man who does housework. [C16: see COT[2], QUEAN]
cotransport (kəʊ'træns,pɔːt) *n. Biochem.* the transport of one solute across a membrane from a region of low concentration of another solute to a region of high concentration of that solute. See **active transport.**
co-trimoxazole (,kəʊtrɪ'mɒksəzəʊl) *n.* an antibiotic consisting of a mixture of trimethoprim (an antiseptic) and sulphamethoxazole (a sulpha drug): used esp. to treat infections of the urinary tract.
Cotswold ('kɒts,wəʊld, -wəld) *n.* a breed of sheep with long wool that originated in the Cotswold hills in SW England.
cotta ('kɒtə) *n. R.C. Church.* a short form of surplice. [C19: from Italian: tunic, from Medieval Latin; see COAT]
cottage ('kɒtɪdʒ) *n.* **1.** a small simple house, esp. in a rural area. **2.** *U.S. and Canadian.* a small house in the country or at a resort, used for holiday purposes. **3.** *U.S.* one of several housing units, as at a hospital, for accommodating people in groups. **4.** *Slang.* a public lavatory. [C14: from COT[2]]
cottage cheese *n.* a mild loose soft white cheese made from skimmed milk curds.
cottage flat *n. Brit.* any of the flats in a two-storey house that is divided into four flats, two on each floor.
cottage hospital *n. Brit.* a small rural hospital.
cottage industry *n.* an industry in which employees work in their own homes, often using their own equipment.
cottage loaf *n. Brit.* a loaf consisting of two round pieces, the smaller of which sits on top of the larger.
cottage piano *n.* a small upright piano.
cottage pie *n. Brit.* another term for **shepherd's pie.**
cottager ('kɒtɪdʒə) *n.* **1.** a person who lives in a cottage. **2.** a rural labourer. **3.** *Chiefly Canadian.* a person holidaying in a cottage, esp. an owner and seasonal resident of a cottage in a resort area. **4.** *History.* another name for **cotter**[2].
cottaging ('kɒtɪdʒɪŋ) *n. Brit.* homosexual activity between men in a public lavatory. [C20: from COTTAGE (sense 4)]
cotter[1] ('kɒtə) *Machinery.* ~*n.* **1.** any part, such as a pin, wedge, key, etc., that is used to secure two other parts so that relative motion between them is prevented. **2.** short for **cotter pin.** ~*vb.* **3.** (*tr.*) to secure (two parts) with a cotter. [C14: shortened from *cotterel,* of unknown origin]
cotter[2] ('kɒtə) *n.* **1.** Also called: **cottier.** *English history.* a villein in late Anglo-Saxon and early Norman times occupying a cottage and land in return for labour. **2.** Also called: **cottar.** a peasant occupying a cottage and land in the Scottish Highlands under the same tenure as an Irish cottier. ~See also **cottier** (sense 2), **cottager** (sense 1). [C14: from Medieval Latin *cotārius,* from Middle English *cote* COT[2]]

cotter pin *n. Machinery.* **1.** a split pin secured, after passing through holes in the parts to be attached, by spreading the ends. **2.** a tapered pin threaded at the smaller end and secured by a nut after insertion.
cottid ('kɒtɪd) *n.* any fish of the scorpaenoid family *Cottidae,* typically possessing a large head, tapering body, and spiny fins, including the pogge, sea scorpion, bullhead, father lasher, and cottus. [from New Latin *Cottidae,* from *cottus,* from Greek *kottos,* the name of an unidentified river fish]
cottier ('kɒtɪə) *n.* **1.** another name for **cotter**[2] (sense 1). **2.** (in Ireland) a peasant farming a smallholding under **cottier tenure** (the holding of not more than half an acre at a rent of not more than five pounds a year). **3.** another name for **cottager** (sense 1). [C14: from Old French *cotier;* see COTE[1], COTERIE]
cotton ('kɒtᵊn) *n.* **1.** any of various herbaceous plants and shrubs of the malvaceous genus *Gossypium,* such as **sea-island cotton,** cultivated in warm climates for the fibre surrounding the seeds and the oil within the seeds. **2.** the soft white downy fibre of these plants: used to manufacture textiles. **3.** cotton plants collectively, as a cultivated crop. **4. a.** a cloth or thread made from cotton fibres. **b.** (*as modifier*): *a cotton dress.* **5.** any substance, such as kapok (**silk cotton**), resembling cotton but obtained from other plants. ~See also **cotton on, cotton to.** [C14: from Old French *coton,* from Arabic dialect *qutun,* from Arabic *qutn*] —'**cottony** *adj.*
cottonade (ˌkɒtᵊ'neɪd) *n.* a coarse fabric of cotton or mixed fibres, used for work clothes, etc. [C19: from French *cotonnade,* from *coton* COTTON + -ADE]
cotton belt *n.* a belt of land in the southeastern U.S. that specializes in the production of cotton.
cotton bush *n. Austral.* any of various downy chenopodiaceous shrubs, esp. *Kochia aphylla,* which is used to feed livestock.
cotton cake *n.* cottonseed meal compressed into nuts or cubes of various sizes for feeding to animals.
cotton candy *n.* the U.S. and Canadian name for **candyfloss.**
cotton flannel *n.* a plain-weave or twill-weave fabric with nap on one side only. Also called: **Canton flannel.**
cotton grass *n.* any of various N temperate and arctic grasslike bog plants of the cyperaceous genus *Eriophorum,* whose clusters of long silky hairs resemble cotton tufts. Also called: **bog cotton.**
cottonmouth ('kɒtᵊnˌmaʊθ) *n.* another name for the **water moccasin.**
cotton on *vb.* (*intr., adv.;* often foll. by *to*) *Informal.* **1.** to perceive the meaning (of). **2.** to make use (of).
cotton picker *n.* **1.** a machine for harvesting cotton fibre. **2.** a person who picks ripe cotton fibre from the plants.
cotton-picking *adj. U.S. and Canadian slang.* (intensifier qualifying something undesirable): *you cotton-picking layabout!*
cotton sedge *n. Canadian.* another name for **cotton grass.**
cottonseed ('kɒtᵊnˌsiːd) *n., pl.* **-seeds** *or* **-seed.** the seed of the cotton plant: a source of oil and fodder.
cottonseed meal *n.* the residue of cottonseed kernels from which oil has been extracted, used as fodder or fertilizer.
cottonseed oil *n.* a yellowish or dark red oil with a nutlike smell, extracted or expelled from cottonseed, used in cooking and in the manufacture of paints, soaps, etc.
cotton stainer *n.* any of various heteropterous insects of the genus *Dysdercus:* serious pests of cotton, piercing and staining the cotton bolls: family *Pyrrhocoridae.*
cottontail ('kɒtᵊnˌteɪl) *n.* any of several common rabbits of the genus *Sylvilagus,* such as *S. floridanus* (**eastern cottontail**), of American woodlands.
cotton to *vb.* (*intr., prep.*) *U.S. and Canadian informal.* **1.** to become friendly with. **2.** to approve of.
cotton waste *n.* refuse cotton yarn, esp. when used as a cleaning material.
cottonweed ('kɒtᵊnˌwiːd) *n.* **1.** a downy perennial plant, *Otanthus maritimus,* of European coastal regions, having small yellow flowers surrounded by large hairy bracts: family *Compositae* (composites). **2.** any of various similar plants.
cottonwood ('kɒtᵊnˌwʊd) *n.* any of several North American poplars, esp. *Populus deltoides,* whose seeds are covered with cottony hairs.
cotton wool *n.* **1.** Also called: **purified cotton.** *Chiefly Brit.* bleached and sterilized cotton from which the gross impurities, such as the seeds and waxy matter, have been removed: used for surgical dressings, tampons, etc. Usual U.S. term: **absorbent cotton. 2.** cotton in the natural state. **3.** *Brit. informal.* **a.** a state of pampered comfort and protection. **b.** (*as modifier*): *a cotton-wool existence.*
cottony-cushion scale *n.* a small scale insect, *Icerya purchasi,* that is a serious pest of citrus trees in California: it is controlled by introducing an Australian ladybird, *Rodolia cardinalis,* into affected areas.
cottus ('kɒtəs) *n.* a scorpaenoid fish of the family *Cottidae;* the type genus, having four yellowish knobs on top of its head. See also **cottid.**
cotyledon (ˌkɒtɪ'liːdᵊn) *n.* **1.** a simple embryonic leaf in seed-bearing plants, which, in some species, forms the first green leaf after germination. **2.** a tuft of villi on the mammalian placenta. [C16: from Latin: a plant, navelwort, from Greek *kotulēdōn,* from *kotulē* cup, hollow] —ˌ**coty'ledonous** *or* ˌ**coty'ledoˌnoid** *adj.* —ˌ**coty'ledonal** *adj.* —ˌ**coty'ledonary** *adj.*
cotyloid ('kɒtɪˌlɔɪd) *or* **cotyloidal** *Anatomy.* ~*adj.* **1. a.** shaped like a cup. **b.** of or relating to the acetabulum. ~*n.* **2.** a small bone forming part of the acetabular cavity in some mammals. [C18: from Greek *kotuloeidēs* cup-shaped, from *kotulē* a cup]
cotype ('kəʊˌtaɪp) *n. Biology.* an additional type specimen from the same brood as the original type specimen.
coucal ('kuːkæl, -kᵊl) *n.* any ground-living bird of the genus *Centropus,* of Africa, S Asia, and Australia, having long strong legs: family *Cuculidae* (cuckoos). [C19: from French, perhaps from *couc(ou)* cuckoo + *al(ouette)* lark]
couch (kaʊtʃ) *n.* **1.** a piece of upholstered furniture, usually having a back and armrests, for seating more than one person. **2.** a bed, esp. one used in the daytime by the patients of a doctor or a psychoanalyst. **3.** a frame upon which barley is malted. **4.** a priming layer of paint or varnish, esp. in a painting. **5.** *Papermaking.* **a.** a board on which sheets of handmade paper are dried by pressing. **b.** a felt blanket onto which sheets of partly dried paper are transferred for further drying. **c.** a roll on a papermaking machine from which the wet web of paper on the wire is transferred to the next section. **6.** *Archaic.* the lair of a wild animal. ~*vb.* **7.** (*tr.*) to express in a particular style of language: *couched in an archaic style.* **8.** (when *tr., usually reflexive or passive*) to lie down or cause to lie down for or as for sleep. **9.** (*intr.*) *Archaic.* to crouch or kneel. **10.** (*intr.*) *Archaic.* to lie in ambush; lurk. **11.** (*tr.*) to spread (barley) on a frame for malting. **12.** (*intr.*) (of decomposing leaves) to lie in a heap or bed. **13.** (*tr.*) to embroider or depict by couching. **14.** (*tr.*) to lift (sheets of handmade paper) onto the board on which they will be dried. **15.** (*tr.*) *Surgery.* to remove (a cataract) by downward displacement of the lens of the eye. **16.** (*tr.*) *Archaic.* to lower (a lance) into a horizontal position. [C14: from Old French *couche* a bed, lair, from *coucher* to lay down, from Latin *collocāre* to arrange, from *locāre* to place; see LOCATE] —'**coucher** *n.*
couchant ('kaʊtʃənt) *adj.* (*usually postpositive*) *Heraldry.* in a lying position: *a lion couchant.* [C15: from French: lying, from Old French *coucher* to lay down; see COUCH]
couchette (kuː'ʃɛt) *n.* a bed or berth in a railway carriage, esp. one converted from seats. [C20: from French, diminutive of *couche* bed]
couch grass (kaʊtʃ, kuːtʃ) *n.* a grass, *Agropyron repens,* with a yellowish-white creeping underground stem by which it spreads quickly: a troublesome weed. Sometimes shortened to **couch.** Also called: **scutch grass, twitch grass, quitch grass.**
couching ('kaʊtʃɪŋ) *n.* **a.** a method of embroidery in which the thread is caught down at intervals by another thread passed through the material from beneath. **b.** a pattern or work done by this method.
couch potato *n. Slang.* a lazy person whose recreation consists chiefly of watching television and videos.
cou-cou ('kuːkuː, 'kʊkuː) *n.* a preparation of boiled corn meal and okras stirred to a stiff consistency with a **cou-cou stick:** eaten in the West Indies. [of uncertain origin]
coudé (kuː'deɪ) *adj.* (of a reflecting telescope) having plane mirrors positioned to reflect light from the primary mirror along the axis onto a photographic plate or spectroscope. [French, literally: bent in the shape of an elbow, from *coude* an elbow]
cougar ('kuːgə) *n.* another name for **puma.** [C18: from French *couguar,* from Portuguese *cuguardo,* from Tupi *suasuarana,* literally: deerlike, from *suasú* deer + *rana* similar to]
cough (kɒf) *vb.* **1.** (*intr.*) to expel air abruptly and explosively through the partially closed vocal chords. **2.** (*intr.*) to make a sound similar to this. **3.** (*tr.*) to utter or express with a cough or coughs. ~*n.* **4.** an act, instance, or sound of coughing. **5.** a condition of the lungs or throat that causes frequent coughing. [Old English *cohhetten;* related to Middle Dutch *kochen,* Middle High German *kūchen* to wheeze; probably of imitative origin] —'**cougher** *n.*
cough drop *n.* a lozenge to relieve a cough.
cough mixture *n.* any medicine that relieves coughing.
cough up *vb.* (*adv.*) **1.** *Informal.* to surrender (money, information, etc.), esp. reluctantly. **2.** (*tr.*) to bring into the mouth or eject (phlegm, food, etc.) by coughing.
could (kʊd) *vb.* (takes an infinitive without *to* or an implied infinitive) used as an auxiliary: **1.** to make the past tense of **can**[1]. **2.** to make the subjunctive mood of **can**[1], esp. used in polite requests or in conditional sentences: *could I see you tonight? she'd telephone if she could.* **3.** to indicate suggestion of a course of action: *you could take the car tomorrow if it's raining.* **4.** (often foll. by *well*) to indicate a possibility: *he could well be a spy.* [Old English *cūthe;* influenced by WOULD, SHOULD; see CAN[1]]
couldn't ('kʊdᵊnt) *contraction of* could not.
couldst (kʊdst) *vb. Archaic.* the form of **could** used with the pronoun *thou* or its relative form.
coulee ('kuːleɪ, -lɪ) *n.* **1. a.** a flow of molten lava. **b.** such lava when solidified. **2.** *Western U.S. and Canadian.* a steep-sided ravine formed by heavy rain or melting snow. **3.** a small intermittent stream in such a ravine. [C19: from Canadian French *coulée* a flow, from French, from *couler* to flow, from Latin *cōlāre* to sift, purify; see COLANDER]
coulibiaca (ˌkuːlɪ'bjɑːkə) *n.* a variant spelling of **koulibiaca.**

coulisse (kuːˈliːs) *n.* **1.** Also called: **cullis.** a timber member grooved to take a sliding panel, such as a sluicegate, portcullis, or stage flat. **2. a.** a flat piece of scenery situated in the wings of a theatre; wing flat. **b.** a space between wing flats. **3.** part of the Paris Bourse where unofficial securities are traded. Compare **parquet** (sense 4). [C19: from French: groove, from Old French *couleïce* PORTCULLIS]

couloir (ˈkuːlwɑː; *French* kulwar) *n.* a deep gully on a mountain side, esp. in the French Alps. [C19: from French: corridor, from *couler* to pour; see COULEE]

coulomb (ˈkuːlɒm) *n.* the derived SI unit of electric charge; the quantity of electricity transported in one second by a current of 1 ampere. Symbol: C [C19: named after C. A. de *Coulomb* (1736–1806), French physicist]

Coulomb field *n.* the electrostatic field around an electrically charged body or particle. The interaction between two such fields produces **Coulomb force.**

Coulomb's law *n.* the principle that the force of attraction or repulsion between two point electric charges is directly proportional to the product of the charges and inversely proportional to the square of the distance between them. The law also holds for magnetic poles.

coulometer (kuːˈlɒmɪtə) *or* **coulombmeter** (ˈkuːlɒmˌmiːtə) *n.* an electrolytic cell for measuring the magnitude of an electric charge by determining the total amount of decomposition resulting from the passage of the charge through the cell. Also called: **voltameter.** [C19: from COULOMB + METER] —**coulometric** (ˌkuːləˈmɛtrɪk) *adj.* —**couˈlometry** *n.*

coulter (ˈkəʊltə) *n.* a blade or sharp-edged disc attached to a plough so that it cuts through the soil vertically in advance of the ploughshare. Also (esp. U.S.): **colter.** [Old English *culter,* from Latin: ploughshare, knife]

coumarin *or* **cumarin** (ˈkuːmərɪn) *n.* a white vanilla-scented crystalline ester, used in perfumes and flavourings and as an anticoagulant. Formula: $C_9H_6O_2$. [C19: from French *coumarine,* from *coumarou* tonka-bean tree, from Spanish *cumarú,* from Tupi] —**ˈcoumaric** *or* **ˈcumaric** *adj.*

coumarone (ˈkuːməˌrəʊn) *n.* another name for **benzofuran.** [C19: from COUMAR(IN) + -ONE]

council (ˈkaʊnsəl) *n.* **1.** an assembly of people meeting for discussion, consultation, etc.: *an emergency council.* **2.** a body of people elected or appointed to serve in an administrative, legislative, or advisory capacity: *a student council.* **3.** *Brit.* (*sometimes cap.; often preceded by the*) the local governing authority of a town, county, etc. **4.** a meeting or the deliberation of a council. **5.** (*modifier*) of, relating to, provided for, or used by a local council: *a council chamber; council offices.* **6.** (*modifier*) *Brit.* provided by a local council, esp. (of housing) at a subsidized rent: *a council house; a council estate.* **7.** *Austral.* an administrative or legislative assembly, esp. the upper house of a state parliament in Australia. **8.** *Christianity.* an assembly of bishops, theologians, and other representatives of several churches or dioceses, convened for regulating matters of doctrine or discipline. [C12: from Old French *concile,* from Latin *concilium* assembly, from *com-* together + *calāre* to call; influenced also by Latin *consilium* advice, COUNSEL]

councillor *or U.S.* **councilor** (ˈkaʊnsələ) *n.* a member of a council. —**ˈcouncillorˌship** *or U.S.* **ˈcouncilorˌship** *n.*

councilman (ˈkaʊnsəlmən) *n., pl.* **-men.** *Chiefly U.S.* a member of a council, esp. of a town or city; councillor.

council-manager plan *n.* (in the U.S.) a system of local government with an elected legislative council and an appointed administrative manager. See also **city manager.**

council of war *n.* **1.** an assembly of military leaders in wartime. **2.** an emergency meeting to formulate a plan.

councilor (ˈkaʊnsələ) *n.* **1.** a variant U.S. spelling of **councillor. 2.** an archaic spelling of **counsellor.** —**ˈcouncilorˌship** *n.*

council school *n. Brit.* (esp. formerly) any school maintained by the state.

counsel (ˈkaʊnsəl) *n.* **1.** advice or guidance on conduct, behaviour, etc. **2.** discussion, esp. on future procedure; consultation: *to take counsel with a friend.* **3.** a person whose advice or guidance is or has been sought. **4.** a barrister or group of barristers engaged in conducting cases in court and advising on legal matters: *counsel for the prosecution.* **5.** a policy or plan. **6.** *Christianity.* any of the **counsels of perfection** or **evangelical counsels,** namely poverty, chastity, and obedience. **7. counsel of perfection.** excellent but unrealizable advice. **8.** private opinions or plans (esp. in the phrase **keep one's own counsel**). **9.** *Archaic.* wisdom; prudence. ~*vb.* **-sels, -selling, -selled** *or U.S.* **-sels, -seling, -seled. 10.** (*tr.*) to give advice or guidance to. **11.** (*tr.; often takes a clause as object*) to recommend the acceptance of (a plan, idea, etc.); urge. **12.** (*intr.*) *Archaic.* to take counsel; consult. [C13: from Old French *counseil,* from Latin *consilium* deliberating body; related to CONSUL, CONSULT] —**ˈcounsellable** *or U.S.* **ˈcounselable** *adj.*

counselling *or U.S.* **counseling** (ˈkaʊnsəlɪŋ) *n.* systematic guidance offered by social workers, doctors, etc., in which a person's problems are discussed and advice is given.

counsellor *or U.S.* **counselor** (ˈkaʊnsələ) *n.* **1.** a person who gives counsel; adviser. **2.** a person, such as a social worker, who is involved in counselling. **3.** Also called: **counselor-at-law.** *U.S.* a lawyer, esp. one who conducts cases in court; attorney. **4.** a senior British diplomatic officer. **5.** a U.S. diplomatic officer ranking just below an ambassador or minister. **6.** a person who advises students or others on personal problems or academic and occupational choice. —**ˈcounsellorˌship** *or U.S.* **ˈcounselorˌship** *n.*

count[1] (kaʊnt) *vb.* **1.** to add up or check (each unit in a collection) in order to ascertain the sum; enumerate: *count your change.* **2.** (*tr.*) to recite numbers in ascending order up to and including. **3.** (*tr.; often foll. by in*) to take into account or include: *we must count him in.* **4. not counting.** excluding. **5.** (*tr.*) to believe to be; consider; think; deem: *count yourself lucky.* **6.** (*intr.*) to recite or list numbers in ascending order either in units or groups: *to count in tens.* **7.** (*intr.*) to have value, importance, or influence: *this picture counts as a rarity.* **8.** (*intr.; often foll. by for*) to have a certain specified value or importance: *the job counts for a lot.* **9.** (*intr.*) *Music.* to keep time by counting beats. ~*n.* **10.** the act of counting or reckoning. **11.** the number reached by counting; sum. **12.** *Law.* a paragraph in an indictment containing a distinct and separate charge. **13.** *Physics.* the total number of photons or ionized particles detected by a counter. **14. keep count.** to keep a record of items, events, etc. **15. lose count.** to fail to keep an accurate record of items, events, etc. **16.** *Boxing, wrestling.* the act of telling off a number of seconds by the referee, as when a boxer has been knocked down or a wrestler pinned by his opponent. **17. out for the count.** *Boxing.* knocked out and unable to continue after a count of ten by the referee. **18. take the count.** *Boxing.* to be unable to continue after a count of ten. **19.** *Archaic.* notice; regard; account. ~See also **count against, countdown, count on, count out.** [C14: from Anglo-French *counter,* from Old French *conter,* from Latin *computāre* to calculate, COMPUTE]

count[2] (kaʊnt) *n.* **1.** a nobleman in any of various European countries having a rank corresponding to that of a British earl. **2.** any of various officials in the late Roman Empire and under various Germanic kings in the early Middle Ages. [C16: from Old French *conte,* from Late Latin *comes* occupant of a state office, from Latin: overseer, associate, literally: one who goes with, from COM- with + *īre* to go] —**ˈcountˌship** *n.*

countable (ˈkaʊntəbᵊl) *adj.* **1.** capable of being counted. **2.** *Maths., logic.* able to be counted using the natural numbers; finite or denumerable. **3.** *Linguistics.* denoting a count noun.

count against *vb.* (*intr., prep.*) to have influence to the disadvantage of: *your bad timekeeping will count against you.*

countdown (ˈkaʊntˌdaʊn) *n.* **1.** the act of counting backwards to time a critical operation exactly, such as the launching of a rocket or the detonation of explosives. ~*vb.* **count down.** (*intr., adv.*) **2.** to count numbers backwards towards zero, esp. in timing such a critical operation.

countenance (ˈkaʊntɪnəns) *n.* **1.** the face, esp. when considered as expressing a person's character or mood: *a pleasant countenance.* **2.** support or encouragement; sanction. **3.** composure; self-control (esp. in the phrases **keep** *or* **lose one's countenance; out of countenance**). ~*vb.* (*tr.*) **4.** to support or encourage; sanction. **5.** to tolerate; endure. [C13: from Old French *contenance* mien, behaviour, from Latin *continentia* restraint, control; see CONTAIN] —**ˈcountenancer** *n.*

counter[1] (ˈkaʊntə) *n.* **1.** a horizontal surface, as in a shop or bank, over which business is transacted. **2.** (in some cafeterias) a long table on which food is served to customers. **3. a.** a small flat disc of wood, metal, or plastic, used in various board games. **b.** a similar disc or token used as an imitation coin. **4.** a person or thing that may be used or manipulated. **5.** a skating figure consisting of three circles. **6. under the counter. (under-the-counter** when prenominal) (of the sale of goods, esp. goods in short supply) clandestine, surreptitious, or illegal; not in an open manner. **7. over the counter. (over-the-counter** when prenominal) (of security transactions) through a broker rather than on a stock exchange. [C14: from Old French *comptouer,* ultimately from Latin *computāre* to COMPUTE]

counter[2] (ˈkaʊntə) *n.* **1.** a person who counts. **2.** an apparatus that records the number of occurrences of events. **3.** any instrument for detecting or counting ionizing particles or photons. See **Geiger counter, scintillation counter, crystal counter. 4.** *Electronics.* another name for **scaler** (sense 2). [C14: from Old French *conteor,* from Latin *computātor;* see COUNT[1]]

counter[3] (ˈkaʊntə) *adv.* **1.** in a contrary direction or manner. **2.** in a wrong or reverse direction. **3. run counter to.** to have a contrary effect or action to. ~*adj.* **4.** opposing; opposite; contrary. ~*n.* **5.** something that is contrary or opposite to some other thing. **6.** an act, effect, or force that opposes another. **7.** a return attack, such as a blow in boxing. **8.** *Fencing.* a parry in which the foils move in a circular fashion. **9.** the portion of the stern of a boat or ship that overhangs the water aft of the rudder. **10.** Also called: **void.** *Printing.* the inside area of a typeface that is not type high, such as the centre of an "o", and therefore does not print. **11.** the part of a horse's breast under the neck and between the shoulders. **12.** a piece of leather forming the back of a shoe. ~*vb.* **13.** to say or do (something) in retaliation or response. **14.** (*tr.*) to move, act, or perform in a manner or direction opposite to (a person or thing). **15.** to return the attack of (an opponent). [C15: from Old French *contre,* from Latin *contrā* against]

counter- *prefix.* 1. against; opposite; contrary: *counterattack.* 2. complementary; corresponding: *counterfoil.* 3. duplicate or substitute: *counterfeit.* [via Norman French from Latin *contrā* against, opposite; see CONTRA-]

counteract (ˌkaʊntərˈækt) *vb.* (*tr.*) to oppose, neutralize, or mitigate the effects of by contrary action; check. —ˌ**counterˈaction** *n.* —ˌ**counterˈactive** *adj.* —ˌ**counterˈactively** *adv.*

counterattack (ˈkaʊntərəˌtæk) *n.* 1. an attack in response to an attack. ~*vb.* 2. to make a counterattack (against).

counterattraction (ˈkaʊntərəˌtrækʃən) *n.* a rival attraction.

counterbalance *n.* (ˈkaʊntəˌbæləns). 1. a weight or force that balances or offsets another. ~*vb.* (ˌkaʊntəˈbæləns). (*tr.*) 2. to act as a counterbalance. ~Also: **counterpoise.**

counterblast (ˈkaʊntəˌblɑːst) *n.* 1. an aggressive response to a verbal attack. 2. a blast that counteracts another.

counterchange (ˌkaʊntəˈtʃeɪndʒ) *vb.* (*tr.*) 1. to change parts, qualities, etc. 2. *Poetic.* to chequer, as with contrasting colours.

countercharge (ˈkaʊntəˌtʃɑːdʒ) *n.* 1. a charge brought by an accused person against the accuser. 2. *Military.* a retaliatory charge. ~*vb.* 3. (*tr.*) to make a countercharge against.

countercheck *n.* (ˈkaʊntəˌtʃɛk). 1. a check or restraint, esp. one that acts in opposition to another. 2. a restraint that reinforces another restraint. 3. a double check, as for accuracy. ~*vb.* (ˌkaʊntəˈtʃɛk). (*tr.*) 4. to oppose by counteraction. 5. to control or restrain by a second check. 6. to double-check.

counterclaim (ˈkaʊntəˌkleɪm) *Chiefly law.* ~*n.* 1. a claim set up in opposition to another, esp. by the defendant in a civil action against the plaintiff. ~*vb.* 2. to set up (a claim) in opposition to another claim. —ˌ**counterˈclaimant** *n.*

counterclockwise (ˌkaʊntəˈklɒkˌwaɪz) *or* **contraclockwise** *adv., adj.* the U.S. and Canadian equivalent of **anticlockwise.**

counterconditioning (ˌkəʊntərkənˈdɪʃənɪŋ) *n.* *Psychol.* the conditioning of a response that is incompatible with some previously learned response; for example, in psychotherapy an anxious person might be taught relaxation, which is incompatible with anxiety.

counterculture (ˈkaʊntəˌkʌltʃə) *n.* an alternative culture, deliberately at variance with the social norm.

counterespionage (ˌkaʊntərˈɛspɪəˌnɑːʒ) *n.* activities designed to detect and counteract enemy espionage.

counterexample (ˈkaʊntərɪgˌzɑːmpᵊl) *n.* an example or fact that is inconsistent with a hypothesis and may be used in argument against it.

counterfactual (ˌkaʊntəˈfæktʃʊəl) *Logic.* ~*adj.* 1. expressing what has not happened but could, would, or might under differing conditions. ~*n.* 2. a conditional statement in which the first clause is a past tense subjunctive statement expressing something contrary to fact, as in: *if she had hurried she would have caught the bus.*

counterfeit (ˈkaʊntəfɪt) *adj.* 1. made in imitation of something genuine with the intent to deceive or defraud; forged. 2. simulated; sham: *counterfeit affection.* ~*n.* 3. an imitation designed to deceive or defraud. 4. *Archaic.* an impostor; cheat. 5. *Archaic.* a portrait. ~*vb.* 6. (*tr.*) to make a fraudulent imitation of. 7. (*intr.*) to make counterfeits. 8. to feign; simulate. 9. (*tr.*) to imitate; copy. [C13: from Old French *contrefait,* from *contrefaire* to copy, from *contre-* COUNTER- + *faire* to make, from Latin *facere*] —ˈ**counterfeiter** *n.*

counterfoil (ˈkaʊntəˌfɔɪl) *n.* *Brit.* the part of a cheque, postal order, receipt, etc., detached and retained as a record of the transaction. Also called (esp. U.S. and Canadian): **stub.**

counterfort (ˈkaʊntəˌfɔːt) *n.* *Civil engineering.* a strengthening buttress at right angles to a retaining wall, bonded to it to provide stability. [from a partial translation of French *contrefort,* from *contre* counter + *fort* strength; see FORT]

counterglow (ˈkaʊntəˌgləʊ) *n.* another name for **gegenschein.**

counterinsurgency (ˌkaʊntərɪnˈsɜːdʒənsɪ) *n.* action taken by a government to counter the activities of rebels, guerrillas, etc.

counterintelligence (ˌkaʊntərɪnˈtɛlɪdʒəns) *n.* 1. activities designed to frustrate enemy espionage. 2. intelligence collected about enemy espionage.

counterirritant (ˌkaʊntərˈɪrɪtᵊnt) *n.* 1. an agent that causes a superficial irritation of the skin and thereby relieves inflammation of deep structures. ~*adj.* 2. producing a counterirritation. —ˌ**counterˌirriˈtation** *n.*

counter jumper *n.* *Old-fashioned derogatory.* a sales assistant in a shop.

countermand *vb.* (ˌkaʊntəˈmɑːnd). (*tr.*) 1. to revoke or cancel (a command, order, etc.). 2. to order (forces, etc.) to return or retreat; recall. ~*n.* (ˈkaʊntəˌmɑːnd). 3. a command revoking another. [C15: from Old French *contremander,* from *contre-* COUNTER- + *mander* to command, from Latin *mandāre;* see MANDATE]

countermarch (ˈkaʊntəˌmɑːtʃ) *vb.* 1. *Chiefly military.* a. to march or cause to march back along the same route. b. to change the order of soldiers during a march. ~*n.* 2. the act or instance of countermarching. 3. a reversal of method, conduct, etc.

countermeasure (ˈkaʊntəˌmɛʒə) *n.* action taken to oppose, neutralize, or retaliate against some other action.

countermine *n.* (ˈkaʊntəˌmaɪn). 1. *Military.* a tunnel dug to defeat similar activities by an enemy. 2. a plot to frustrate another plot. ~*vb.* (ˌkaʊntəˈmaɪn). 3. to frustrate by countermeasures. 4. *Military.* to take measures to defeat the underground operations of (an enemy). 5. *Military.* to destroy enemy mines in (an area) with mines of one's own.

countermove (ˈkaʊntəˌmuːv) *n.* 1. an opposing move. ~*vb.* 2. to make or do (something) as an opposing move. —ˈ**counterˌmovement** *n.*

counteroffensive (ˈkaʊntərəˌfɛnsɪv) *n.* a series of attacks by a defending force against an attacking enemy.

counteroffer (ˈkaʊntərˌɒfə) *n.* a response to a bid in which a seller amends his original offer, making it more favourable to the buyer.

counterpane (ˈkaʊntəˌpeɪn) *n.* another word for **bedspread.** [C17: from obsolete *counterpoint* (influenced by *pane* coverlet), changed from Old French *coutepointe* quilt, from Medieval Latin *culcita puncta* quilted mattress]

counterpart (ˈkaʊntəˌpɑːt) *n.* 1. a person or thing identical to or closely resembling another. 2. one of two parts that complement or correspond to each other. 3. a person acting opposite another in a play. 4. a duplicate, esp. of a legal document; copy.

counterplot (ˈkaʊntəˌplɒt) *n.* 1. a plot designed to frustrate another plot. ~*vb.* **-plots, -plotting, -plotted.** 2. (*tr.*) to oppose with a counterplot. 3. (*intr.*) to devise or carry out a counterplot.

counterpoint (ˈkaʊntəˌpɔɪnt) *n.* 1. the technique involving the simultaneous sounding of two or more parts or melodies. 2. a melody or part combined with another melody or part. See also **descant** (sense 1). 3. the musical texture resulting from the simultaneous sounding of two or more melodies or parts. 4. **strict counterpoint.** the application of the rules of counterpoint as an academic exercise. 5. a contrasting or interacting element, theme, or item; foil. 6. *Prosody.* the use of a stress or stresses at variance with the regular metrical stress. ~*vb.* 7. (*tr.*) to set in contrast. ~Related adj.: **contrapuntal.** [C15: from Old French *contrepoint,* from *contre-* COUNTER- + *point* dot, note in musical notation, that is, an accompaniment set against the notes of a melody]

counterpoise (ˈkaʊntəˌpɔɪz) *n.* 1. a force, influence, etc., that counterbalances another. 2. a state of balance; equilibrium. 3. a weight that balances another. 4. a radial array of metallic wires, rods, or tubes arranged horizontally around the base of a vertical aerial to increase its transmitting efficiency. ~*vb.* (*tr.*) 5. to oppose with something of equal effect, weight, or force; offset. 6. to bring into equilibrium. 7. *Archaic.* to consider (one thing) carefully in relation to another.

counterpoise bridge *n.* another name for **bascule bridge** (see **bascule** (sense 1)).

counterproductive (ˌkaʊntəprəˈdʌktɪv) *adj.* tending to hinder or act against the achievement of an aim.

counterproof (ˈkaʊntəˌpruːf) *n.* *Printing.* a reverse impression of a newly printed proof of an engraving made by laying it while wet upon plain paper and passing it through the press.

counterproposal (ˈkaʊntəprəˌpəʊzᵊl) *n.* a proposal offered as an alternative to a previous proposal.

counterpunch (ˈkaʊntəˌpʌntʃ) *Boxing.* ~*vb.* (*intr.*) 1. to punch an attacking opponent; return an attack. ~*n.* 2. a return punch.

Counter-Reformation (ˌkaʊntəˌrɛfəˈmeɪʃən) *n.* the reform movement of the Roman Catholic Church in the 16th and early 17th centuries considered as a reaction to the Protestant Reformation.

counter-revolution (ˌkaʊntəˌrɛvəˈluːʃən) *n.* a revolution opposed to a previous revolution and aimed at reversing its effects. —ˌ**counter-ˌrevoˈlutionist** *n.*

counter-revolutionary (ˌkaʊntəˌrɛvəˈluːʃənərɪ, -nrɪ) *n., pl.* **-aries.** 1. a person opposed to revolution. 2. a person who opposes a specific revolution or revolutionary government. ~*adj.* 3. characterized by opposition to a revolution or revolutions in general.

counterscarp (ˈkaʊntəˌskɑːp) *n.* *Fortifications.* the outer side of the ditch of a fort. Compare **escarp** (sense 1).

countershading (ˌkaʊntəˈʃeɪdɪŋ) *n.* (in the coloration of certain animals) a pattern, serving as camouflage, in which dark colours occur on parts of the body exposed to the light and pale colours on parts in the shade.

countershaft (ˈkaʊntəˌʃɑːft) *n.* an intermediate shaft that is driven by, but rotates in the opposite direction to, a main shaft, esp. in a gear train.

countersign *vb.* (ˈkaʊntəˌsaɪn, ˌkaʊntəˈsaɪn). 1. (*tr.*) to sign (a document already signed by another). ~*n.* (ˈkaʊntəˌsaɪn). 2. Also called: **countersignature.** the signature so written. 3. a secret sign given in response to another sign. 4. *Chiefly military.* a password.

countersink (ˈkaʊntəˌsɪŋk) *vb.* **-sinks, -sinking, -sank, -sunk.** (*tr.*) 1. to enlarge the upper part of (a hole) in timber, metal, etc., so that the head of a bolt or screw can be sunk below the surface. 2. to drive (a screw) or sink (a bolt) into such an enlarged hole. ~*n.* 3. Also called: **countersink bit.** a tool for countersinking. 4. a countersunk depression or hole.

counterspy (ˈkaʊntəˌspaɪ) *n., pl.* **-spies.** a spy working against or investigating enemy espionage.

counterstain (ˈkaʊntəˌsteɪn) *vb.* *Microscopy.* 1. to apply two or more stains in sequence to (a specimen to be examined), each of which colours a different tissue. 2. (*tr.; usually passive*) to apply (one of a series of stains) to a specimen to be examined: *haematoxylin is counterstained with eosin.*

countersubject ('kaʊntəˌsʌbdʒɪkt) *n. Music.* (in a fugue) the theme in one voice that accompanies the statement of the subject in another.

countertenor (ˌkaʊntə'tɛnə) *n.* **1.** an adult male voice with an alto range. **2.** a singer with such a voice.

counterterrorism (ˌkaʊntə'tɛrəˌrɪzəm) *n.* an act or acts of terrorism committed in revenge or retaliation for a previous terrorist act. —ˌ**counter'terrorist** *adj.*

countertype ('kaʊntəˌtaɪp) *n.* **1.** an opposite type. **2.** a corresponding type.

countervail (ˌkaʊntə'veɪl, 'kaʊntəˌveɪl) *vb.* **1.** (when *intr.*, usually foll. by *against*) to act or act against with equal power or force. **2.** (*tr.*) to make up for; compensate; offset. [C14: from Old French *contrevaloir,* from Latin *contrā valēre,* from *contrā* against + *valēre* to be strong]

countervailing duty *n.* an extra import duty imposed by a country on certain imports, esp. to prevent dumping or to counteract subsidies in the exporting country.

counterweigh (ˌkaʊntə'weɪ) *vb.* another word for **counterbalance.**

counterweight ('kaʊntəˌweɪt) *n.* a counterbalancing weight, influence, or force. —'**counterˌweighted** *adj.*

counterword ('kaʊntəˌwɜːd) *n.* a word widely used in a sense much looser than its original meaning, such as *tremendous* or *awful.*

counterwork ('kaʊntəˌwɜːk) *n.* **1.** work done in opposition to other work. **2.** defensive fortifications put up against attack. —'**counterˌworker** *n.*

countess ('kaʊntɪs) *n.* **1.** the wife or widow of a count or earl. **2.** a woman of the rank of count or earl.

counting house *n. Rare, chiefly Brit.* a room or building used by the accountants of a business.

countless ('kaʊntlɪs) *adj.* innumerable; myriad.

count noun *n. Linguistics, logic.* a noun that can be qualified by the indefinite article, and may be used in the plural, as *telephone* and *thing* but not *airs and graces* or *bravery.* Compare **mass noun, sortal.**

count on *vb.* (*intr., prep.*) to rely or depend on.

count out *vb.* (*tr., adv.*) **1.** *Informal.* to leave out; exclude: *count me out!* **2.** (of a boxing referee) to judge (a floored boxer) to have failed to recover within the specified time. See **count**[1] (sense 15). **3.** to count (something) aloud.

count palatine *n., pl.* **counts palatine.** *History.* **1.** (in the Holy Roman Empire) **a.** originally an official who administered the king's domains or his justice. **b.** later, a count who exercised royal authority in his own domains. **2.** (in England and Ireland) an earl or other lord of a county palatine. **3.** (in the late Roman Empire) a palace official who exercised judicial authority.

countrified *or* **countryfied** ('kʌntrɪˌfaɪd) *adj.* in the style, manners, etc., of the country; rural.

country ('kʌntrɪ) *n., pl.* **-tries. 1.** a territory distinguished by its people, culture, language, geography, etc. **2.** an area of land distinguished by its political autonomy; state. **3.** the people of a territory or state: *the whole country rebelled.* **4.** an area associated with a particular person: *Burns country.* **5. a.** the part of the land that is away from cities or industrial areas; rural districts. **b.** (*as modifier*): *country cottage.* **c.** (*in combination*): *a countryman.* Related adj.: **pastoral, rural. 6.** short for **country music. 7.** *Archaic.* a particular locality or district. **8. up country.** away from the coast or the capital. **9.** one's native land or nation of citizenship. **10.** (usually preceded by *the*) *Brit. informal.* the outlying area or area furthest from the finish of a sports ground or racecourse. **11.** (*modifier*) rough; uncouth; rustic: *country manners.* **12. across country.** not keeping to roads, etc. **13. go** *or* **appeal to the country.** *Chiefly Brit.* to dissolve Parliament and hold an election. **14. unknown country.** an unfamiliar topic, place, matter, etc. [C13: from Old French *contrée,* from Medieval Latin *contrāta,* literally: that which lies opposite, from Latin *contrā* opposite]

country and western *n.* **1.** another name for **country music. 2.** a fusion of cowboy songs and Appalachian music. **3.** (*as modifier*): *country-and-western music.* ~Abbrev.: **C & W.**

country blues *n.* (*sometimes functioning as sing.*) acoustic folk blues with a guitar accompaniment. Compare **urban blues.**

country club *n.* a club in the country, having sporting and social facilities.

country code *n.* a code of good practice recommended to those who use the countryside for recreational purposes.

country cousin *n.* an unsophisticated person from the country, esp. one regarded as an object of amusement.

country dance *n.* a type of folk dance in which couples are arranged in sets and perform a series of movements, esp. facing one another in a line. —**country dancing** *n.*

country gentleman *n.* a rich man with an estate in the country.

country house *n.* a large house in the country, esp. a mansion belonging to a wealthy family.

countryman ('kʌntrɪmən) *n., pl.* **-men. 1.** a person who lives in the country. **2.** a person from a particular country or from one's own country (esp. in the phrase **fellow countryman**). —'**countryˌwoman** *fem. n.*

country music *n.* a type of 20th-century popular music based on White folk music of the southeastern U.S. Sometimes shortened to **country.**

country park *n. Brit.* an area of countryside, usually not less than 10 hectares, set aside for public recreation.

country rock[1] *n.* the rock surrounding a mineral vein or igneous intrusion.

country rock[2] *n.* a style of rock music influenced by country and western.

country seat *n.* a large estate or property in the country.

countryside ('kʌntrɪˌsaɪd) *n.* a rural area or its population.

county ('kaʊntɪ) *n., pl.* **-ties. 1. a.** any of the administrative subdivisions of certain states, esp. any of the 52 units into which England and Wales, except for seven major conurbations, have been divided for purposes of local government since April 1, 1974. See also **metropolitan county. b.** (*as modifier*): *county cricket.* **2.** *N.Z.* an electoral division in a rural area. **3.** *Obsolete.* the lands under the jurisdiction of a count or earl. ~*adj.* **4.** *Brit. informal.* having the characteristics and habits of the inhabitants of country houses and estates, esp. an upper-class accent and an interest in horses, dogs, etc. [C14: from Old French *conté* land belonging to a count, from Late Latin *comitātus* office of a count, from *comes* COUNT[2]]

county borough *n.* **1.** (in England and Wales from 1888 to 1974) a borough administered independently of the county around it. **2.** (in the Republic of Ireland) any of the four largest boroughs, governed independently of the administrative county around it by an elected council that constitutes an all-purpose authority.

county court *n.* (in England) a local court exercising limited jurisdiction in civil matters.

county palatine *n., pl.* **counties palatine. 1.** the lands of a count palatine. **2.** (in England and Ireland) a county in which the earl or other lord exercised many royal powers, esp. judicial authority.

county seat *n. Chiefly U.S.* another term for **county town.**

county town *n.* the town in which a county's affairs are or were administered.

coup[1] (kuː) *n.* **1.** a brilliant and successful stroke or action. **2.** short for **coup d'état.** [C18: from French: blow, from Latin *colaphus* blow with the fist, from Greek *kolaphos*]

coup[2] *or* **cowp** (kaʊp) *Scot.* ~*vb.* **1.** to turn or fall over. ~*n.* **2.** a rubbish tip. [C15: perhaps identical with obsolete *cope* to strike; see COPE[1]]

coup[3] (kaʊp) *vb. Scot.* to barter; traffic; deal. [C14: from Old Norse *kaupa* to buy]

coup de foudre *French.* (ku də fudrə) *n., pl.* ***coups de foudre*** (ku də fudrə). a sudden and amazing action or event. [literally: lightning flash]

coup de grâce *French.* (ku də grɑs) *n., pl.* ***coups de grâce*** (ku də grɑs). **1.** a mortal or finishing blow, esp. one delivered as an act of mercy to a sufferer. **2.** a final or decisive stroke. [literally: blow of mercy]

coup de main *French.* (ku də mɛ̃) *n., pl.* ***coups de main*** (ku də mɛ̃). *Chiefly military.* an attack that achieves complete surprise. [literally: blow with the hand]

coup d'état ('kuː deɪ'tɑː; *French* ku deta) *n., pl.* **coups d'état** ('kuːz deɪ'tɑː; *French* ku deta). a sudden violent or illegal seizure of government. [French, literally: stroke of state]

coup de théâtre *French.* (ku də teɑtrə) *n., pl.* ***coups de théâtre*** (ku də teɑtrə). **1.** a dramatic turn of events, esp. in a play. **2.** a sensational device of stagecraft. **3.** a stage success. [literally: stroke of the theatre]

coup d'oeil *French.* (ku dœj) *n., pl.* ***coups d'oeil*** (ku dœj). a quick glance. [literally: stroke of the eye]

coupe (kuːp) *n.* **1.** a dessert of fruit and ice cream, usually served in a glass goblet. **2.** a dish or stemmed glass bowl designed for this dessert. [C19: from French: goblet, CUP]

coupé ('kuːpeɪ) *n.* **1.** Also called: **fixed-head coupé.** a four-seater car with a fixed roof, a sloping back, and usually two doors. Compare **drophead coupé. 2.** a four-wheeled horse-drawn carriage with two seats inside and one outside for the driver. **3.** an end compartment in a European railway carriage with seats on one side only. [C19: from French, short for *carosse coupé,* literally: cut-off carriage, from *couper* to cut, from *coup* blow, stroke]

couple ('kʌpᵊl) *n.* **1.** two people who regularly associate with each other or live together: *an engaged couple.* **2.** (*functioning as sing. or pl.*) two people considered as a pair, for or as if for dancing, games, etc. **3.** *Chiefly hunting or coursing.* **a.** a pair of collars joined by a leash, used to attach hounds to one another. **b.** two hounds joined in this way. **c.** the unit of reckoning for hounds in a pack: *twenty and a half couple.* **4.** a pair of equal and opposite parallel forces that have a tendency to produce rotation with a turning moment equal to the product of either force and the perpendicular distance between them. **5.** *Physics.* **a.** two dissimilar metals, alloys, or semiconductors in electrical contact, across which a voltage develops. See **thermocouple. b.** Also called: **galvanic couple.** two dissimilar metals or alloys in electrical contact that when immersed in an electrolyte act as the electrodes of an electrolytic cell. **6.** a connector or link between two members, such as a tie connecting a pair of rafters in a roof. **7. a couple of.** (*functioning as sing. or pl.*) **a.** a combination of two; a pair of: *a couple of men.* **b.** *Informal.* a small number of; a few: *a couple of days.* ~*pron.* **8.** (usually preceded by *a; functioning as sing. or pl.*) two; a pair: *give him a couple.* ~*vb.* **9.** (*tr.*) to connect (two things) together or to connect (one thing) to (another): *to couple railway carriages.* **10.**

(*tr.*) to do (two things) simultaneously or alternately: *he couples studying with teaching.* **11.** to form or be formed into a pair or pairs. **12.** to associate, put, or connect together: *history is coupled with sociology.* **13.** to link (two circuits) by electromagnetic induction. **14.** (*intr.*) to have sexual intercourse. **15.** to join or be joined in marriage; marry. **16.** (*tr.*) to attach (two hounds to each other). [C13: from Old French: a pair, from Latin *cōpula* a bond; see COPULA]

coupledom ('kʌpᵊldəm) *n.* the state of living as a couple, esp. when regarded as being interested in each other to the exclusion of the outside world.

coupler ('kʌplə) *n.* **1.** a link or rod transmitting power between two rotating mechanisms or a rotating part and a reciprocating part. **2.** *Music.* a device on an organ or harpsichord connecting two keys, two manuals, etc., so that both may be played at once. **3.** *Electronics.* a device, such as a transformer, used to couple two or more electrical circuits. **4.** a U.S. and Canadian word for **coupling** (sense 2).

couplet ('kʌplɪt) *n.* two successive lines of verse, usually rhymed and of the same metre. [C16: from French, literally: a little pair; see COUPLE]

coupling ('kʌplɪŋ) *n.* **1.** a mechanical device that connects two things. **2.** a device for connecting railway cars or trucks together. **3.** the part of the body of a horse, dog, or other quadruped that lies between the forequarters and the hindquarters. **4.** *Electronics.* the act or process of linking two or more circuits so that power can be transferred between them usually by mutual induction, as in a transformer, or by means of a capacitor or inductor common to both circuits. See also **direct coupling.** **5.** *Physics.* an interaction between different properties of a system, such as a group of atoms or nuclei, or between two or more systems. **6.** *Genetics.* the occurrence of two specified nonallelic genes from the same parent on the same chromosome.

coupon ('ku:pɒn) *n.* **1. a.** a detachable part of a ticket or advertisement entitling the holder to a discount, free gift, etc. **b.** a detachable slip usable as a commercial order form. **c.** a voucher given away with certain goods, a certain number of which are exchangeable for goods offered by the manufacturers. **2.** one of a number of detachable certificates attached to a bond, esp. a bearer bond, the surrender of which entitles the bearer to receive interest payments. **3.** one of several detachable cards used for making hire-purchase payments. **4.** a ticket issued to facilitate rationing. **5.** *Brit.* a detachable entry form for any of certain competitions, esp. football pools. [C19: from French, from Old French *colpon* piece cut off, from *colper* to cut, variant of *couper;* see COPE[1]]

courage ('kʌrɪdʒ) *n.* **1.** the power or quality of dealing with or facing danger, fear, pain, etc. **2. the courage of one's convictions.** the confidence to act in accordance with one's beliefs. **3. take one's courage in both hands.** to nerve oneself to perform an action. **4.** *Obsolete.* mind; disposition; spirit. [C13: from Old French *corage,* from *cuer* heart, from Latin *cor*]

courageous (kə'reɪdʒəs) *adj.* possessing or expressing courage. —**cou'rageously** *adv.* —**cou'rageousness** *n.*

courante (ku'rɑ:nt) *n. Music.* **1.** an old dance in quick triple time **2.** a movement of a (mostly) 16th- to 18th-century suite based on this. ~Also called (esp. for the dance): **coranto.** [C16: from French, literally: running, feminine of *courant,* present participle of *courir* to run, from Latin *currere*]

courbaril ('kuəbərɪl) *n.* a tropical American leguminous tree, *Hymenaea courbaril.* Its wood is a useful timber and its gum is a source of copal. Also called: **West Indian locust**. [C18: from a native American name]

coureur de bois (*French* kurœr də bwa) *n., pl.* **coureurs de bois** (kurœr də bwa). *Canadian history.* a French Canadian woodsman or Métis who traded with Indians for furs. [Canadian French: trapper (literally: wood-runner)]

courgette (kuə'ʒɛt) *n.* a small variety of vegetable marrow, cooked and eaten as a vegetable. U.S., Canadian, and Austral. name: **zucchini.** [from French, diminutive of *courge* marrow, gourd]

courie *or* **coorie** ('ku:rɪ) *vb.* (*intr.*) *Scot.* (often foll. by *doun*) to nestle or snuggle. [C19: from *coor* a Scot. word for COWER]

courier ('kuərɪə) *n.* **1.** a special messenger, esp. one carrying diplomatic correspondence. **2.** a person who makes arrangements for or accompanies a group of travellers on a journey or tour. [C16: from Old French *courrier,* from Old Latin *corriere,* from *correre* to run, from Latin *currere*]

courlan ('kuələn) *n.* another name for **limpkin.** [C19: from French, variant of *courliri,* from Galibi *kurliri*]

course (kɔ:s) *n.* **1.** a continuous progression from one point to the next in time or space; onward movement: *the course of his life.* **2.** a route or direction followed: *they kept on a southerly course.* **3. a.** the path or channel along which something moves: *the course of a river.* **b.** (*in combination*): *a watercourse.* **4.** an area or stretch of land or water on which a sport is played or a race is run: *a golf course.* **5.** a period of time; duration: *in the course of the next hour.* **6.** the usual order of and time required for a sequence of events; regular procedure: *the illness ran its course.* **7.** a mode of conduct or action: *if you follow that course, you will fail.* **8.** a connected series of events, actions, etc. **9. a.** a prescribed number of lessons, lectures, etc., in an educational curriculum. **b.** the material covered in such a curriculum. **10.** a prescribed regimen to be followed for a specific period of time: *a course of treatment.* **11.** a part of a meal served at one time: *the fish course.* **12.** a continuous, usually horizontal, layer of building material, such as a row of bricks, tiles, etc. **13.** *Nautical.* any of the sails on the lowest yards of a square-rigged ship. **14.** *Knitting.* the horizontal rows of stitches. Compare **wale**[1] (sense 2b.). **15.** (in medieval Europe) a charge by knights in a tournament. **16. a.** a hunt by hounds relying on sight rather than scent. **b.** a match in which two greyhounds compete in chasing a hare. **17.** the part or function assigned to an individual bell in a set of changes. **18.** *Archaic.* a running race. **19. as a matter of course.** as a natural or normal consequence, mode of action, or event. **20. the course of nature.** the ordinary course of events. **21. in course of.** in the process of: *the ship was in course of construction.* **22. in due course.** at some future time, esp. the natural or appropriate time. **23. of course. a.** (*adv.*) as expected; naturally. **b.** (*sentence substitute*) certainly; definitely. **24. run** (*or* **take**) **its course.** (of something) to complete its development or action. ~*vb.* **25.** (*intr.*) to run, race, or flow, esp. swiftly and without interruption. **26.** to cause (hounds) to hunt by sight rather than scent or (of hounds) to hunt (a quarry) thus. **27.** (*tr.*) to run through or over; traverse. **28.** (*intr.*) to take a direction; proceed on a course. ~See also **courses.** [C13: from Old French *cours,* from Latin *cursus* a running, from *currere* to run]

courser[1] ('kɔ:sə) *n.* **1.** a person who courses hounds or dogs, esp. greyhounds. **2.** a hound or dog trained for coursing.

courser[2] ('kɔ:sə) *n. Literary.* a swift horse; steed. [C13: from Old French *coursier,* from *cours* COURSE]

courser[3] ('kɔ:sə) *n.* a terrestrial plover-like shore bird, such as *Cursorius cursor* (cream-coloured courser), of the subfamily *Cursoriinae* of desert and semidesert regions of the Old World: family *Glareolidae,* order *Charadriiformes.* [C18: from Latin *cursōrius* suited for running, from *cursus* COURSE]

courses ('kɔ:sɪz) *pl. n.* (*sometimes sing.*) *Physiol.* another word for **menses.**

coursework ('kɔ:sˌwɜ:k) *n.* written or oral work completed by a student within a given period, which is assessed as part of an educational course.

coursing ('kɔ:sɪŋ) *n.* **1.** hunting with hounds or dogs that follow their quarry by sight. **2.** a sport in which hounds are matched against one another in pairs for the hunting of hares by sight.

court (kɔ:t) *n.* **1.** an area of ground wholly or partly surrounded by walls or buildings. **2.** *Brit.* (*cap. when part of a name*) **a.** a block of flats: *Selwyn Court.* **b.** a mansion or country house. **c.** a short street, sometimes closed at one end. **3.** a space inside a building, sometimes surrounded with galleries. **4. a.** the residence, retinues, or household of a sovereign or nobleman. **b.** (*as modifier*): *a court ball.* **5.** a sovereign or prince and his retinue, advisers, etc. **6.** any formal assembly, reception, etc., held by a sovereign or nobleman with his courtiers. **7.** homage, flattering attention, or amorous approaches (esp. in the phrase **pay court to someone**). **8.** *Law.* **a.** a tribunal having power to adjudicate in civil, criminal, military, or ecclesiastical matters. **b.** the regular sitting of such a judicial tribunal. **c.** the room or building in which such a tribunal sits. **9. a.** a marked outdoor or enclosed area used for any of various ball games, such as tennis, squash, etc. **b.** a marked section of such an area: *the service court.* **10. a.** the board of directors or council of a corporation, company, etc. **b.** *Chiefly Brit.* the supreme council of some universities. **11.** a branch of any of several friendly societies. **12. go to court.** to take legal action. **13. hold court.** to preside over admirers, attendants, etc. **14. out of court. a.** without a trial or legal case: *the case was settled out of court.* **b.** too unimportant for consideration. **c.** *Brit.* so as to ridicule completely (in the phrase **laugh out of court**). **15. the ball is in your court.** you are obliged to make the next move. ~*vb.* **16.** to attempt to gain the love of (somene); woo. **17.** (*tr.*) to pay attention to (someone) in order to gain favour. **18.** (*tr.*) to try to obtain (fame, honour, etc.). **19.** (*tr.*) to invite, usually foolishly, as by taking risks: *to court disaster.* **20.** *Old-fashioned.* to be conducting a serious emotional relationship usually leading to marriage. [C12: from Old French, from Latin *cohors* COHORT]

court-bouillon ('kuət'bu:jɒn; *French* kurbujɔ̃) *n.* a stock made from root vegetables, water, and wine or vinegar, used primarily for poaching fish. [from French, from *court* short, from Latin *curtus* + *bouillon* broth, from *bouillir* to BOIL[1]]

court card *n.* (in a pack of playing cards) a king, queen, or jack of any suit. U.S. equivalent: **face card.** [C17: altered from earlier *coat-card,* from the decorative coats worn by the figures depicted]

court circular *n.* (in countries having a monarchy) a daily report of the activities, engagements, etc., of the sovereign, published in a national newspaper.

court cupboard *n.* a wooden stand with two or three tiers, used in the 16th and 17th centuries to display pewter, silver, etc.

court dress *n.* the formal clothing worn at court.

Courtelle (kɔ:'tɛl) *n. Trademark.* a synthetic acrylic fibre resembling wool.

courteous ('kɜ:tɪəs) *adj.* polite and considerate in manner. [C13 *corteis,* literally: with courtly manners, from Old French; see COURT] —'**courteously** *adv.* —'**courteousness** *n.*

courtesan *or* **courtezan** (ˌkɔːtɪˈzæn) *n.* (esp. formerly) a prostitute, or the mistress of a man of rank. [C16: from Old French *courtisane,* from Italian *cortigiana* female courtier, from *cortigiano* courtier, from *corte* COURT]

courtesy (ˈkɜːtɪsɪ) *n., pl.* **-sies.** **1.** politeness; good manners. **2.** a courteous gesture or remark. **3.** favour or consent (esp. in the phrase **by courtesy of**). **4.** common consent as opposed to right (esp. in the phrase **by courtesy**). See also **courtesy title.** **5.** (ˈkɜːtsɪ). an archaic spelling of **curtsy.** [C13 *curteisie,* from Old French, from *corteis* COURTEOUS]

courtesy light *n.* the interior light in a motor vehicle.

courtesy title *n.* any of several titles having no legal significance, such as those borne by the children of peers.

court hand *n.* a style of handwriting formerly used in English law courts.

courthouse (ˈkɔːtˌhaʊs) *n.* a public building in which courts of law are held.

courtier (ˈkɔːtɪə) *n.* **1.** an attendant at a court. **2.** a person who seeks favour in an ingratiating manner. [C13: from Anglo-French *courteour* (unattested), from Old French *corteier* to attend at court]

court-leet *n.* the full name for **leet**[1] (sense 1).

courtly (ˈkɔːtlɪ) *adj.* **-lier, -liest.** **1.** of or suitable for a royal court. **2.** refined in manner. **3.** ingratiating. —ˈ**courtliness** *n.*

courtly love *n.* a tradition represented in Western European literature between the 12th and the 14th centuries, idealizing love between a knight and a revered (usually married) lady.

court martial *n., pl.* **court martials** *or* **courts martial.** **1.** a military court that tries persons subject to military law. ~*vb.* **court-martial, -tials, -tialling, -tialled** *or U.S.* **-tials, -tialing, -tialed.** **2.** (*tr.*) to try by court martial.

Court of Appeal *n.* a branch of the Supreme Court of Judicature that hears appeals from the High Court in both criminal and civil matters and from the county and crown courts.

court of first instance *n.* a court in which legal proceedings are begun or first heard.

court of honour *n.* a military court that is instituted to investigate matters involving personal honour.

court of inquiry *n.* **1.** *Brit.* a group of people appointed to investigate the causes of a disaster, accident, etc. **2.** a military court set up to inquire into a military matter.

Court of Session *n.* the supreme civil court in Scotland.

Court of St James's *n.* the official name of the royal court of Britain.

court plaster *n.* a plaster, composed of isinglass on silk, formerly used to cover superficial wounds. [C18: so called because formerly used by court ladies for beauty spots]

court roll *n. History.* the register of land holdings, etc., of a manorial court.

courtroom (ˈkɔːtˌruːm, -ˌrʊm) *n.* a room in which the sittings of a law court are held.

courtship (ˈkɔːtʃɪp) *n.* **1.** the act, period, or art of seeking the love of someone with intent to marry. **2.** the seeking or soliciting of favours. **3.** *Obsolete.* courtly behaviour.

court shoe *n.* a low-cut shoe for women, having no laces or straps.

court tennis *n.* the U.S. term for **real tennis.**

courtyard (ˈkɔːtˌjɑːd) *n.* an open area of ground surrounded by walls or buildings; court.

couscous (ˈkuːskuːs) *n.* a spicy dish, originating from North Africa, consisting of steamed semolina served with a meat stew. [C17: via French from Arabic *kouskous,* from *kaskasa* to pound until fine]

cousin (ˈkʌzᵊn) *n.* **1.** Also called: **first cousin, cousin-german, full cousin.** the child of one's aunt or uncle. **2.** a relative who has descended from one of one's common ancestors. A person's **second cousin** is the child of one of his parents' first cousins. A person's **third cousin** is the child of one of his parents' second cousins. A **first cousin once removed** (or loosely **second cousin**) is the child of one's first cousin. **3.** a member of a group related by race, ancestry, interests, etc.: *our Australian cousins.* **4.** a title used by a sovereign when addressing another sovereign or a nobleman. [C13: from Old French *cosin,* from Latin *consōbrīnus* cousin, from *sōbrīnus* cousin on the mother's side; related to *soror* sister] —ˈ**cousinˌhood** *or* ˈ**cousinˌship** *n.* —ˈ**cousinly** *adj., adv.*

couteau (kuːˈtəʊ) *n., pl.* **-teaux** (-ˈtəʊz). a large two-edged knife used formerly as a weapon. [C17: from Old French *coutel,* from Latin *cultellus* a little knife, from *culter* knife, ploughshare]

couth (kuːθ) *adj.* **1.** *Facetious.* refined. **2.** *Archaic.* familiar; known. [Old English *cūth* known, past participle of *cunnan* to know; sense 1, back formation from UNCOUTH]

couthie *or* **couthy** (ˈkuːθɪ) *adj. Scot.* **1.** sociable; friendly; congenial. **2.** comfortable; snug. **3.** plain; homely; unsophisticated: *a couthie saying.* [C13: see COUTH, UNCOUTH]

couture (kuːˈtʊə; *French* kutyr) *n.* high fashion designing and dressmaking. [from French: sewing, dressmaking, from Old French *cousture* seam, from Latin *consuere* to stitch together, from *suere* to sew]

couturier (kuːˈtʊərɪˌeɪ; *French* kutyrje) *n.* a person who designs, makes, and sells fashion clothes for women. [from French: dressmaker; see COUTURE] —**couturière** (kuːˌtʊːrɪˈɛə; *French* kutyrjɛr) *fem. n.*

couvade (kuːˈvɑːd; *French* kuvad) *n. Anthropol.* a custom in certain cultures of treating the husband of a woman giving birth as if he were bearing the child. [C19: from French, from *couver* to hatch, from Latin *cubāre* to lie down]

couvert (kuˈvɛə) *n.* another word for **cover** (sense 32). [C18: from French]

COV *abbrev. for:* **1.** *Statistics.* covariance. **2.** *Genetics.* crossover value.

covalency (kəʊˈveɪlənsɪ) *or U.S.* **covalence** *n.* **1.** the formation and nature of covalent bonds. **2.** the number of covalent bonds that a particular atom can make with other atoms in forming a molecule. —**coˈvalent** *adj.* —**coˈvalently** *adv.*

covalent bond *n.* a type of chemical bond involving the sharing of electrons between atoms in a molecule, esp. the sharing of a pair of electrons by two adjacent atoms.

covariance (kəʊˈvɛərɪəns) *n. Statistics.* a measure of the association between two random variables, equal to the expected value of the product of the deviations from the mean of the two variables, and estimated by the sum of products of deviations from the sample mean for associated values of the two variables, divided by the number of sample points. Written as: *Cov (X, Y).*

cove[1] (kəʊv) *n.* **1.** a small bay or inlet, usually between rocky headlands. **2.** a narrow cavern formed in the sides of cliffs, mountains, etc., usually by erosion. **3.** a sheltered place. **4.** Also called: **coving.** *Architect.* a concave curved surface between the wall and ceiling of a room. ~*vb.* **5.** (*tr.*) to form an architectural cove in. [Old English *cofa;* related to Old Norse *kofi,* Old High German *kubisi* tent]

cove[2] (kəʊv) *n. Slang, Brit. old-fashioned and Austral.* a fellow; chap. [C16: probably from Romany *kova* thing, person]

coven (ˈkʌvᵊn) *n.* **1.** a meeting of witches. **2.** a company of 13 witches. [C16: probably from Old French *covin* group, ultimately from Latin *convenīre* to come together; compare CONVENT]

covenant (ˈkʌvənənt) *n.* **1.** a binding agreement; contract. **2.** *Law.* **a.** an agreement in writing under seal, as to pay a stated annual sum to a charity. **b.** a particular clause in such an agreement, esp. in a lease. **3.** (in early English law) an action in which damages were sought for breach of a sealed agreement. **4.** *Bible.* God's promise to the Israelites and their commitment to worship him alone. ~*vb.* **5.** to agree to a covenant (concerning). [C13: from Old French, from *covenir* to agree, from Latin *convenīre* to come together, make an agreement; see CONVENE] —**covenantal** (ˌkʌvəˈnæntᵊl) *adj.* —ˌ**coveˈnantally** *adv.*

Covenant (ˈkʌvənənt) *n. Scottish history.* any of the bonds entered into by Scottish Presbyterians to defend their religion, esp. one in 1638 (**National Covenant**) and one of 1643 (**Solemn League and Covenant**).

covenantee (ˌkʌvənənˈtiː) *n.* the person to whom the promise in a covenant is made.

Covenanter (ˈkʌvənəntə, ˌkʌvəˈnæntə) *n.* a person upholding the National Covenant of 1638 or the Solemn League and Covenant of 1643 between Scotland and England to establish and defend Presbyterianism.

covenantor *or* **covenanter** (ˈkʌvənəntə) *n.* a party who makes a promise and who is to perform the obligation expressed in a covenant.

Coventry (ˈkɒvəntrɪ) **send to Coventry.** to ostracize or ignore. [after *Coventry,* a city in central England]

cover (ˈkʌvə) *vb.* (*mainly tr.*) **1.** to place or spread something over so as to protect or conceal. **2.** to provide with a covering; clothe. **3.** to put a garment, esp. a hat, on (the body or head). **4.** to extend over or lie thickly on the surface of; spread: *snow covered the fields.* **5.** to bring upon (oneself); invest (oneself) as if with a covering: *covered with shame.* **6.** (sometimes foll. by *up*) to act as a screen or concealment for; hide from view. **7.** *Military.* to protect (an individual, formation, or place) by taking up a position from which fire may be returned if those being protected are fired upon. **8.** (*also intr.,* often foll. by *for*) to assume responsibility for (a person or thing): *to cover for a colleague in his absence.* **9.** (*intr.;* foll. by *for* or *up for*) to provide an alibi (for). **10.** to have as one's territory: *this salesman covers your area.* **11.** to travel over: *to cover three miles a day.* **12.** (*tr.*) to have or place in the aim and within the range of (a firearm). **13.** to include or deal with: *his talk covered all aspects of the subject.* **14.** (of an asset or income) to be sufficient to meet (a liability or expense). **15.** **a.** to insure against loss, risk, etc. **b.** to provide for (loss, risk, etc.) by insurance. **16.** (*also intr.*) *Finance.* to purchase (securities, etc.) in order to meet contracts, esp. short sales. **17.** to deposit (an equivalent stake) in a bet or wager. **18.** (*also intr.*) to play a card higher in rank than (one played beforehand by another player). **19.** to act as reporter or photographer on (a news event, etc.) for a newspaper or magazine: *to cover sports events.* **20.** *Sport.* to guard or protect (an opponent, teammate, or area). **21.** *Music.* to record a cover version of. **22.** (of a male animal, esp. a horse) to copulate with (a female animal). **23.** (of a bird) to brood (eggs). ~*n.* **24.** anything that covers, spreads over, protects, or conceals. **25.** woods or bushes providing shelter or a habitat for wild creatures. **26.** **a.** a blanket used on a bed for warmth. **b.** another word for **bedspread.** **27.** *Finance.* liquid assets, reserves, or guaranteed income sufficient to discharge a liability, meet an expenditure, etc. **28.** a pretext, disguise, or false identity: *the thief sold brushes as a cover.* **29.**

Insurance. another word for **coverage** (sense 3). **30.** an envelope or package for sending through the post: *under plain cover.* **31.** *Philately.* **a.** an entire envelope that has been postmarked. **b. on cover.** (of a postage stamp) kept in this form by collectors. **32. a.** an individual table setting, esp. in a restaurant. **b.** (*as modifier*): *a cover charge.* **33.** *Sport.* the guarding or protection of an opponent, team-mate, or area. **34.** Also called: **cover version.** a version by a different artist of a previously recorded musical item. **35.** *Cricket.* **a.** (*often pl.*) the area more or less at right angles to the pitch on the off side and usually about halfway to the boundary: *to field in the covers.* **b.** (*as modifier*): *a cover drive by a batsman.* **c.** Also called: **cover point.** a fielder in such a position. **36.** *Ecology.* the percentage of the ground surface covered by a given species of plant. **37. break cover.** (esp. of game animals) to come out from a shelter or hiding place. **38. take cover.** to make for a place of safety or shelter. **39. under cover.** protected, concealed, or in secret: *under cover of night.* ~See also **cover-up.** [C13: from Old French *covrir,* from Latin *cooperīre* to cover completely, from *operīre* to cover over] —'**coverable** *adj.* —'**coverer** *n.* —'**coverless** *adj.*

coverage ('kʌvərɪdʒ) *n.* **1.** the amount or extent to which something is covered. **2.** *Journalism.* the amount and quality of reporting or analysis given to a particular subject or event. **3.** the extent of the protection provided by insurance. **4.** *Finance.* **a.** the value of liquid assets reserved to meet liabilities. **b.** the ratio of liquid assets to specific liabilities. **c.** the ratio of total net profit to distributed profit in a company. **5.** the section of the public reached by a medium of communication.

coverall ('kʌvər,ɔːl) *n.* **1.** a thing that covers something entirely. **2.** (*usually pl.*) protective outer garments for the body.

cover crop *n.* a crop planted between main crops to prevent leaching or soil erosion or to provide green manure.

covered wagon *n. U.S. and Canadian.* a large horse-drawn wagon with an arched canvas top, used formerly for prairie travel.

cover girl *n.* a girl, esp. a glamorous one, whose picture appears on the cover of a newspaper or magazine.

cover glass *n.* a thin square of mounted glass used to protect a photographic slide.

covering ('kʌvərɪŋ) *n.* another word for **cover** (sense 24).

covering letter *n.* an accompanying letter sent as an explanation, introduction, or record.

coverlet ('kʌvəlɪt) *n.* another word for **bedspread.**

Coverley ('kʌvəlɪ) *n.* See **Sir Roger de Coverley.**

cover note *n. Brit.* a certificate issued by an insurance company stating that a policy is operative: used as a temporary measure between the commencement of cover and the issue of the policy.

cover point *n. Cricket.* **a.** a fielding position in the covers. **b.** a fielder in this position.

covers ('kəuvɜːs) *abbrev. for* coversed sine.

coversed sine ('kəuvɜːst) *n.* a trigonometric function equal to one minus the sine of the specified angle. Abbrev.: **covers.**

cover-shoulder *n.* a type of blouse worn in Ghana.

cover slip *n.* a very thin piece of glass placed over a specimen on a glass slide that is to be examined under a microscope.

covert ('kʌvət) *adj.* **1.** concealed or secret: *covert jealousy.* **2.** *Archaic.* sheltered; protected. **3.** *Law.* See **feme covert.** Compare **discovert.** ~*n.* **4.** a shelter or disguise. **5.** a thicket or woodland providing shelter for game. **6.** short for **covert cloth. 7.** *Ornithol.* any of the small feathers on the wings and tail of a bird that surround the bases of the larger feathers. **8.** a flock of coots. [C14: from Old French: covered, from *covrir* to COVER] —'**covertly** *adv.* —'**covertness** *n.*

covert cloth *n.* a twill-weave cotton or worsted suiting fabric. Sometimes shortened to **covert.**

covert coat *n. Brit.* a short topcoat worn for hunting.

coverture ('kʌvətʃə) *n.* **1.** *Law.* the condition or status of a married woman considered as being under the protection and influence of her husband. **2.** *Rare.* shelter, concealment, or disguise. [C13: from Old French, from *covert* covered; see COVERT]

cover-up *n.* **1.** concealment or attempted concealment of a mistake, crime, etc. ~*vb.* **cover up.** (*adv.*) **2.** (*tr.*) to cover completely. **3.** (when *intr.*, often foll. by *for*) to attempt to conceal (a mistake or crime): *she tried to cover up for her friend.* **4.** (*intr.*) *Boxing.* to defend the body and head with the arms.

cover version *n.* another name for **cover** (sense 34).

cove stripe *n. Nautical.* a decorative stripe painted along the sheer strake of a vessel, esp. of a sailing boat.

covet ('kʌvɪt) *vb.* (*tr.*) **-vets, -veting, -veted.** to wish, long, or crave for (something, esp. the property of another person). [C13: from Old French *coveitier,* from *coveitié* eager desire, ultimately from Latin *cupiditās* CUPIDITY] —'**covetable** *adj.* —'**coveter** *n.*

covetous ('kʌvɪtəs) *adj.* (*usually postpositive* and foll. by *of*) jealously eager for the possession of something (esp. the property of another person). —'**covetously** *adv.* —'**covetousness** *n.*

covey ('kʌvɪ) *n.* **1.** a small flock of grouse or partridge. **2.** a small group, as of people. [C14: from Old French *covee,* from *cover* to sit on, hatch; see COUVADE]

covin ('kʌvɪn) *n. Law.* a conspiracy between two or more persons to act to the detriment or injury of another. [C14: from Old French; see COVEN, CONVENE]

cow[1] (kaʊ) *n.* **1.** the mature female of any species of cattle, esp. domesticated cattle. **2.** the mature female of various other mammals, such as the elephant, whale, and seal. **3.** (*not in technical use*) any domestic species of cattle. **4.** *Informal.* a disagreeable woman. **5.** *Austral. and N.Z. slang.* something objectionable (esp. in the phrase **a fair cow). 6. till the cows come home.** *Informal.* for a very long time; effectively for ever. [Old English *cū*; related to Old Norse *kýr,* Old High German *kuo,* Latin *bōs,* Greek *boūs,* Sanskrit *gāūs*]

cow[2] (kaʊ) *vb.* (*tr.*) to frighten or overawe, as with threats. [C17: from Old Norse *kūga* to oppress, related to Norwegian *kue,* Swedish *kuva*]

cowage *or* **cowhage** ('kaʊɪdʒ) *n.* **1.** a tropical climbing leguminous plant, *Stizolobium* (or *Mucuna*) *pruriens,* whose bristly pods cause severe itching and stinging. **2.** the pods of this plant or the stinging hairs covering them. [C17: from Hindi *kavāch,* of obscure origin]

cowal ('kaʊəl) *n. Austral.* a shallow lake or swampy depression supporting vegetation. [from a native Australian language]

coward ('kaʊəd) *n.* a person who shrinks from or avoids danger, pain, or difficulty. [C13: from Old French *cuard,* from *coue* tail, from Latin *cauda;* perhaps suggestive of a frightened animal with its tail between its legs]

cowardice ('kaʊədɪs) *n.* lack of courage in facing danger, pain, or difficulty.

cowardly ('kaʊədlɪ) *adj.* of or characteristic of a coward; lacking courage. —'**cowardliness** *n.*

cow bail *n.* See **bail**[3] (sense 3).

cowbane ('kaʊ,beɪn) *n.* **1.** Also called: **water hemlock.** any of several N temperate poisonous umbelliferous marsh plants of the genus *Cicuta,* esp. *C. virosa,* having clusters of small white flowers. **2.** a similar and related plant, *Oxypolis rigidior* of the southeastern and central U.S. **3.** any umbelliferous plant reputed to be poisonous to cattle.

cowbell ('kaʊ,bɛl) *n.* **1.** a bell hung around a cow's neck so that the cow can be easily located. **2.** a metal percussion instrument usually mounted on the bass drum or hand-held and struck with a drumstick. **3.** *U.S.* another name for **bladder campion.**

cowberry ('kaʊbərɪ, -brɪ) *n., pl.* **-ries. 1.** a creeping ericaceous evergreen shrub, *Vaccinium vitis-idaea,* of N temperate and arctic regions, with pink or red flowers and edible slightly acid berries. **2.** the berry of this plant. ~Also called: **red whortleberry.**

cowbind ('kaʊ,baɪnd) *n.* any of various bryony plants, esp. the white bryony.

cowbird ('kaʊ,bɜːd) *n.* any of various American orioles of the genera *Molothrus, Tangavius,* etc., esp. *M. ater* (common or brown-headed cowbird). They have a dark plumage and short bill.

cowboy ('kaʊ,bɔɪ) *n.* **1.** Also called: '**cow,hand.** a hired man who herds and tends cattle, usually on horseback, esp. in the western U.S. **2.** a conventional character of Wild West folklore, films, etc., esp. one involved in fighting Indians. **3.** *Informal.* **a.** a person who is an irresponsible or unscrupulous operator in business. **b.** (*as modifier*): *cowboy contractors; cowboy shop steward.* **4.** *Austral.* a boy who tends cattle. —'**cow,girl** *fem. n.*

cowcatcher ('kaʊ,kætʃə) *n. U.S. and Canadian.* a metal frame on the front of a locomotive to clear the track of animals or other obstructions.

cow cocky *n., pl.* **cow cockies.** *Austral. and N.Z.* a one-man dairy farmer.

cower ('kaʊə) *vb.* (*intr.*) to crouch or cringe, as in fear. [C13: from Middle Low German *kūren* to lie in wait; related to Swedish *kura* to lie in wait, Danish *kure* to squat]

cowfeteria (,kaʊfɪ'tɪərɪə) *n. N.Z. informal.* a calf feeder with multiple teats. [from a blend of *cow* and *cafeteria*]

cowfish ('kaʊ,fɪʃ) *n., pl.* **-fish** *or* **-fishes. 1.** any trunkfish, such as *Lactophrys quadricornis,* having hornlike spines over the eyes. **2.** (loosely) any of various large aquatic animals, such as a sea cow.

Cow Gum *n. Trademark.* a colourless adhesive based on a natural rubber solution.

cowherb ('kaʊ,hɜːb) *n.* a European caryophyllaceous plant, *Saponaria vaccaria,* having clusters of pink flowers: a weed in the U.S. See also **soapwort.**

cowherd ('kaʊ,hɜːd) *n.* a person employed to tend cattle.

cowhide ('kaʊ,haɪd) *n.* **1.** the hide of a cow. **2.** the leather made from such a hide. ~Also called: **cowskin.**

Cowichan sweater ('kaʊɪtʃən) *n. Canadian.* a heavy sweater of grey, unbleached wool with symbolic designs that were originally black-and-white but are now sometimes coloured: knitted originally by Cowichan Indians in British Columbia. Also called: **Indian sweater, siwash, siwash sweater.**

cowitch ('kaʊ,ɪtʃ) *n.* another name for **cowage.** [C17: alteration of COWAGE by folk etymology]

cowk (kaʊk) *vb.* (*intr.*) *Northeast Scot. dialect.* to retch or feel nauseated. [of obscure origin]

cowl (kaʊl) *n.* **1.** a hood, esp. a loose one. **2.** the hooded habit of a monk. **3.** a cover fitted to a chimney to increase ventilation and prevent draughts. **4.** the part of a car body that supports the windscreen and the bonnet. **5.** *Aeronautics.* another word for **cowling.** ~*vb.* (*tr.*) **6.** to cover or provide with a cowl. **7.** to make a monk of. [Old English *cugele,* from Late Latin *cuculla* cowl, from Latin *cucullus* covering, cap, hood]

cowlick ('kaʊˌlɪk) *n.* a tuft of hair over the forehead.

cowling ('kaʊlɪŋ) *n.* a streamlined metal covering, esp. one fitted around an aircraft engine. Also called: **cowl.** Compare **fairing**[1].

cowl neckline *n.* a neckline of women's clothes loosely folded over and sometimes resembling a folded hood.

cowman ('kaʊmən) *n., pl.* **-men.** **1.** *Brit.* another name for **cowherd.** **2.** *U.S. and Canadian.* a man who owns cattle; rancher.

co-worker *n.* a fellow worker; associate.

cow parsley *n.* a common Eurasian umbelliferous hedgerow plant, *Anthriscus sylvestris,* having umbrella-shaped clusters of white flowers. Also called: **keck.**

cow parsnip *n.* any tall coarse umbelliferous plant of the genus *Heracleum,* such as *H. sphondylium* of Europe and Asia, having thick stems and flattened clusters of white or purple flowers. Also called: **hogweed, keck.**

cowpat ('kaʊˌpæt) *n.* a single dropping of cow dung.

cowpea ('kaʊˌpiː) *n.* **1.** a leguminous tropical climbing plant, *Vigna sinensis,* producing long pods containing edible pealike seeds: grown for animal fodder and sometimes as human food. **2.** Also called: **black-eyed pea.** the seed of this plant.

Cowper's glands ('kuːpəz) *pl. n.* two small yellowish glands near the prostate that secrete a mucous substance into the urethra during sexual stimulation in males. Compare **Bartholin's glands.** [C18: named after William *Cowper* (1666–1709), English anatomist who discovered them]

cow pillow *n.* (in India) a large cylindrical pillow stuffed with cotton and used for reclining rather than sleeping.

cow pony *n.* a horse used by cowboys when herding.

cowpox ('kaʊˌpɒks) *n.* a contagious viral disease of cows characterized by vesicles on the skin, esp. on the teats and udder. Inoculation of humans with this virus provides temporary immunity to smallpox.

cowpuncher ('kaʊˌpʌntʃə) *or* **cowpoke** ('kaʊˌpəʊk) *n. U.S. and Canadian.* informal words for **cowboy.**

cowrie *or* **cowry** ('kaʊrɪ) *n., pl.* **-ries.** **1.** any marine gastropod mollusc of the mostly tropical family *Cypraeidae,* having a glossy brightly marked shell with an elongated opening. **2.** the shell of any of these molluscs, esp. the shell of *Cypraea moneta* (**money cowry**), used as money in parts of Africa and S Asia. [C17: from Hindi *kaurī,* from Sanskrit *kaparda,* of Dravidian origin; related to Tamil *kōtu* shell]

cow shark *n.* any large primitive shark, esp. *Hexanchus griseum,* of the family *Hexanchidae* of warm and temperate waters. Also called: **six-gilled shark.**

cowskin ('kaʊˌskɪn) *n.* another word for **cowhide.**

cowslip ('kaʊˌslɪp) *n.* **1.** Also called: **paigle.** a primrose, *Primula veris,* native to temperate regions of the Old World, having fragrant yellow flowers. **2.** *U.S. and Canadian.* another name for **marsh marigold.** [Old English *cūslyppe;* see COW[1], SLIP[3]]

cow tree *n.* a South American moraceous tree, *Brosimum galactodendron,* producing latex used as a substitute for milk.

cox (kɒks) *n.* **1.** a coxswain, esp. of a racing eight or four. ~*vb.* **2.** to act as coxswain of (a boat). —'**coxless** *adj.*

coxa ('kɒksə) *n., pl.* **coxae** ('kɒksiː). **1.** a technical name for the hipbone or hip joint. **2.** the basal segment of the leg of an insect. [C18: from Latin: hip] —'**coxal** *adj.*

coxalgia (kɒk'sældʒɪə) *n.* **1.** pain in the hip joint. **2.** disease of the hip joint causing pain. [C19: from COXA + -ALGIA] —**cox'algic** *adj.*

coxcomb ('kɒksˌkəʊm) *n.* **1.** a variant spelling of **cockscomb.** **2.** *Archaic.* a foppish man. **3.** *Obsolete.* the cap, resembling a cock's comb, worn by a jester.

coxcombry ('kɒksˌkəʊmrɪ) *n., pl.* **-ries.** conceited arrogance or foppishness.

Coxsackie virus (kʊk'sɑːkɪ) *n.* any of various viruses that occur in the intestinal tract of man and cause diseases, some of which resemble poliomyelitis. [C20: after *Coxsackie,* a town in New York state, where the virus was first found]

Cox's Orange Pippin ('pɪpɪn) *n.* a variety of eating apple with sweet flesh and a red-tinged green skin. Often shortened to **Cox.** [C19: named after R. *Cox,* its English propagator]

coxswain ('kɒksən, -ˌsweɪn) *n.* the helmsman of a lifeboat, racing shell, etc. Also called: **cockswain.** [C15: from *cock* a ship's boat + SWAIN]

coy (kɔɪ) *adj.* **1.** (usually of a woman) affectedly demure, esp. in a playful or provocative manner. **2.** shy; modest. **3.** evasive, esp. in an annoying way. [C14: from Old French *coi* reserved, from Latin *quiētus* QUIET] —'**coyish** *adj.* —'**coyly** *adv.* —'**coyness** *n.*

Coy. *Military. abbrev. for* company.

coyote ('kɔɪəʊt, kɔɪ'əʊt, kɔɪ'əʊtɪ) *n., pl.* **-otes** *or* **-ote.** **1.** Also called: **prairie wolf.** a predatory canine mammal, *Canis latrans,* related to but smaller than the wolf, roaming the deserts and prairies of North America. **2.** (in American Indian legends of the West) a trickster and culture hero represented as a man or as an animal. [C19: from Mexican Spanish, from Nahuatl *coyotl*]

coyotillo (ˌkəʊjəʊ'tiːljəʊ) *n., pl.* **-los.** a thorny poisonous rhamnaceous shrub, *Karwinskia humboldtiana* of Mexico and the southwestern U.S., the berries of which cause paralysis. [Mexican Spanish, literally: a little COYOTE]

coypu ('kɔɪpuː) *n., pl.* **-pus** *or* **-pu.** **1.** an aquatic South American hystricomorph rodent, *Myocastor coypus,* introduced into Europe: family *Capromyidae.* It resembles a small beaver with a ratlike tail and is bred in captivity for its soft grey underfur. **2.** the fur of this animal. ~Also called: **nutria.** [C18: from American Spanish *coipú,* from Araucanian *kóypu*]

coz (kʌz) *n.* an archaic word for **cousin:** used chiefly as a term of address.

cozen ('kʌzᵊn) *vb.* to cheat or trick (someone). [C16: cant term perhaps related to COUSIN] —'**cozenage** *n.* —'**cozener** *n.*

cozy ('kəʊzɪ) *adj.* **-zier, -ziest.** *n.* the usual U.S. spelling of **cosy.** —'**cozily** *adv.* —'**coziness** *n.*

cp *abbrev. for:* **1.** candlepower. **2.** chemically pure.

CP *abbrev. for:* **1.** Canadian Press. **2.** *Military.* Command Post. **3.** Common Prayer. **4.** Communist Party. **5.** (in Britain) Community Programme. **6.** (in Australia) Country Party. **7.** Court of Probate.

cp. *abbrev. for* compare

CPA (in the U.S.) *abbrev. for* certified public accountant.

CPAG (in Britain) *abbrev. for* Child Poverty Action Group.

cpd *Zoology, botany, chem. abbrev. for* compound.

cpi *abbrev. for* characters per inch.

CPI *abbrev. for* consumer price index.

Cpl *abbrev. for* Corporal.

CP/M *n.* an operating system widely used on microcomputers to enable a wide range of software from many suppliers to be run on them.

CPO *abbrev. for* Chief Petty Officer.

CPR *abbrev. for* cardiopulmonary resuscitation.

cps *abbrev. for:* **1.** *Physics.* cycles per second. **2.** *Computer technol.* characters per second.

CPS (in England and Wales) *abbrev for.* Crown Prosecution Service.

CPSA (in Britain) *abbrev. for* Civil and Public Services Association.

CPSU *abbrev. for* Communist Party of the Soviet Union.

CPU *Computer technol. abbrev. for* central processing unit.

CPVE (in Britain) *abbrev. for* Certificate of Pre-vocational Education: a certificate awarded for completion of a broad-based course of study offered as a less advanced alternative to traditional school-leaving qualifications.

CQ **1.** *Telegraphy, telephony.* a symbol transmitted by an amateur radio operator requesting two-way communication with any other amateur radio operator listening. **2.** *Military. abbrev. for* charge of quarters.

CQSW (in Britain) *abbrev. for* Certificate of Qualification in Social Work.

Cr **1.** *abbrev. for* Councillor. **2.** *the chemical symbol for* chromium.

CR *abbrev. for:* **1.** Community of the Resurrection. **2.** Costa Rica. ~**3.** *international car registration for* Costa Rica.

cr. *abbrev. for:* **1.** credit. **2.** creditor.

crab[1] (kræb) *n.* **1.** any chiefly marine decapod crustacean of the genus *Cancer* and related genera (section *Brachyura*), having a broad flattened carapace covering the cephalothorax, beneath which is folded the abdomen. The first pair of limbs are modified as pincers. See also **fiddler crab, soft-shell crab, pea crab, oyster crab.** **2.** any of various similar or related arthropods, such as the hermit crab and horseshoe crab. **3.** short for **crab louse.** **4.** a manoeuvre in which an aircraft flies slightly into the crosswind to compensate for drift. **5.** a mechanical lifting device, esp. the travelling hoist of a gantry crane. **6.** *Wrestling.* See **Boston crab.** **7.** **catch a crab.** *Rowing.* to make a stroke in which the oar either misses the water or digs too deeply, causing the rower to fall backwards. ~*vb.* **crabs, crabbing, crabbed.** **8.** (*intr.*) to hunt or catch crabs. **9.** (*tr.*) to fly (an aircraft) slightly into a crosswind to compensate for drift. **10.** (*intr.*) *Nautical.* to move forwards with a slight sideways motion, as to overcome an offsetting current. **11.** (*intr.*) to move sideways. ~See also **crabs.** [Old English *crabba;* related to Old Norse *krabbi,* Old High German *krebiz* crab, Dutch *krabben* to scratch]

crab[2] (kræb) *Informal.* ~*vb.* **crabs, crabbing, crabbed.** **1.** (*intr.*) to find fault; grumble. **2.** (*tr.*) *Chiefly U.S.* to spoil (esp. in the phrase **crab someone's act**). ~*n.* **3.** an irritable person. **4.** **draw the crabs.** *Austral.* to attract unwelcome attention. [C16: probably back formation from CRABBED]

crab[3] (kræb) *n.* short for **crab apple.** [C15: perhaps of Scandinavian origin; compare Swedish *skrabbe* crab apple]

Crab (kræb) *n.* **the.** the constellation Cancer, the fourth sign of the zodiac.

crab apple *n.* **1.** any of several rosaceous trees of the genus *Malus* that have white, pink, or red flowers and small sour apple-like fruits. **2.** the fruit of any of these trees, used to make jam.

crabbed ('kræbɪd) *adj.* **1.** surly; irritable; perverse. **2.** (esp. of handwriting) cramped and hard to decipher. **3.** *Rare.* abstruse. [C13: probably from CRAB[1] (from its wayward gait), influenced by CRAB (APPLE) (from its tartness)] —'**crabbedly** *adv.* —'**crabbedness** *n.*

crabber ('kræbə) *n.* **1.** a crab fisherman. **2.** a boat used for crab-fishing.

crabby ('kræbɪ) *adj.* **-bier, -biest.** bad-tempered.

crab canon *n. Music.* a canon in which the imitating voice repeats the notes of the theme in reverse order. Also called **retrograde canon, canon cancrizans.** [from the mistaken medieval notion that crabs move backwards]

crab grass *n.* any of several coarse weedy grasses of the genus *Digitaria,* which grow in warm regions and tend to displace other grasses in lawns.

crab louse *n.* a parasitic louse, *Pthirus* (or *Phthirus*) *pubis,* that infests the pubic region in man.

crabs (kræbz) *n.* (*sometimes functioning as sing.*) the lowest throw in a game of chance, esp. two aces in dice. [plural of CRAB[1]]

crabstick ('kræbˌstɪk) *n.* **1.** a stick, cane, or cudgel made of crab-apple wood. **2.** *Informal.* a bad-tempered person.

crabwise ('kræbˌwaɪz) *adj., adv.* (of motion) sideways; like a crab.

crabwood ('kræbˌwʊd) *n.* **1.** a tropical American meliaceous tree, *Carapa guianensis.* **2.** the wood of this tree, used for construction.

CRAC *abbrev. for* Careers Research and Advisory Centre.

crack (kræk) *vb.* **1.** to break or cause to break without complete separation of the parts: *the vase was cracked but unbroken.* **2.** to break or cause to break with a sudden sharp sound; snap: *to crack a nut.* **3.** to make or cause to make a sudden sharp sound: *to crack a whip.* **4.** to cause (the voice) to change tone or become harsh or (of the voice) to change tone, esp. to a higher register; break. **5.** *Informal.* to fail or cause to fail. **6.** to yield or cause to yield: *to crack under torture.* **7.** (*tr.*) to hit with a forceful or resounding blow. **8.** (*tr.*) to break into or force open: *to crack a safe.* **9.** (*tr.*) to solve or decipher (a code, problem, etc.). **10.** (*tr.*) *Informal.* to tell (a joke, etc.). **11.** to break (a molecule) into smaller molecules or radicals by the action of heat, as in the distillation of petroleum. **12.** (*tr.*) to open (esp. a bottle) for drinking: *let's crack another bottle.* **13.** (*intr.*) *Scot., northern English dialect.* to chat; gossip. **14.** (*tr.*) *Informal.* to achieve (esp. in the phrase **crack it**). **15.** (*tr.*) *Austral. informal.* to find or catch: *to crack a wave in surfing.* **16. crack a smile.** *Informal.* to break into a smile. **17. crack hardy** *or* **hearty.** *Austral. and N.Z. informal.* to disguise one's discomfort, etc.; put on a bold front. ~*n.* **18.** a sudden sharp noise. **19.** a break or fracture without complete separation of the two parts: *a crack in the window.* **20.** a narrow opening or fissure. **21.** *Informal.* a resounding blow. **22.** a physical or mental defect; flaw. **23.** a moment or specific instant: *the crack of day.* **24.** a broken or cracked tone of voice, as a boy's during puberty. **25.** (often foll. by *at*) *Informal.* an attempt; opportunity to try: *he had a crack at the problem.* **26.** *Slang.* a gibe; wisecrack; joke. **27.** *Slang.* a person that excels. **28.** *Scot., northern English dialect.* a talk; chat. **29.** *Slang.* a processed form of cocaine hydrochloride used as a stimulant. It is highly addictive. **30.** *Informal, chiefly Irish.* fun; informal entertainment; *the crack was great in here last night.* **31.** *Obsolete slang.* a burglar or burglary. **32. crack of dawn. a.** the very instant that the sun rises. **b.** very early in the morning. **33. a fair crack of the whip.** *Informal.* a fair chance or opportunity. **34. crack of doom.** doomsday; the end of the world; the Day of Judgment. ~*adj.* **35.** (*prenominal*) *Slang.* first-class; excellent: *a crack shot.* ~See also **crack down, crack up.** [Old English *cracian;* related to Old High German *krahhōn,* Dutch *kraken,* Sanskrit *gárjati* he roars]

crackbrain ('krækˌbreɪn) *n.* a person who is insane.

crackbrained ('krækˌbreɪnd) *adj.* insane, idiotic, or crazy.

crack down *vb.* (*intr., adv.;* often foll. by *on*) **1.** to take severe measures (against); become stricter (with). ~*n.* **crackdown. 2.** severe or repressive measures.

cracked (krækt) *adj.* **1.** damaged by cracking. **2.** *Informal.* crazy.

cracker ('krækə) *n.* **1.** a decorated cardboard tube that emits a bang when pulled apart, releasing a toy, a joke, or a paper hat. **2.** short for **firecracker. 3.** a thin crisp biscuit, usually unsweetened. **4.** a person or thing that cracks. **5.** *U.S.* another word for **poor White. 6.** *Brit. slang.* a thing or person of notable qualities or abilities. **7. not worth a cracker.** *Austral. and N.Z. informal.* worthless; useless.

cracker-barrel *adj. U.S.* rural; rustic; homespun: *a cracker-barrel philosopher.*

crackerjack ('krækəˌdʒæk) *Informal.* ~*adj.* **1.** excellent. ~*n.* **2.** a person or thing of exceptional quality or ability. [C20: changed from CRACK (first-class) + JACK (man)]

crackers ('krækəz) *adj.* (*postpositive*) *Brit.* a slang word for **insane.**

cracket ('krækɪt) *n. Dialect.* **1.** a low stool, often one with three legs. **2.** a box for a miner to kneel on when working a low seam. [variant of CRICKET[3]]

crackhead ('krækˌhɛd) *n. Slang.* a person addicted to the drug crack.

cracking ('krækɪŋ) *adj.* **1.** (*prenominal*) *Informal.* fast; vigorous (esp. in the phrase **a cracking pace**). **2. get cracking.** *Informal.* to start doing something quickly or do something with increased speed. ~*adv., adj.* **3.** *Brit. informal.* first-class; excellent: *a cracking good match.* ~*n.* **4.** the process in which molecules are cracked, esp. the oil-refining process in which heavy oils are broken down into hydrocarbons of lower molecular weight by heat or catalysis. See also **catalytic cracker.**

crackjaw ('krækˌdʒɔː) *Informal.* ~*adj.* **1.** difficult to pronounce. ~*n.* **2.** a word or phrase that is difficult to pronounce.

crackle ('kræk[ə]l) *vb.* **1.** to make or cause to make a series of slight sharp noises, as of paper being crushed or of a wood fire burning. **2.** (*tr.*) to decorate (porcelain or pottery) by causing a fine network of cracks to appear in the glaze. **3.** (*intr.*) to abound in vivacity or energy. ~*n.* **4.** the act or sound of crackling. **5.** intentional crazing in the glaze of a piece of porcelain or pottery. **6.** Also called: **'crackleˌware.** porcelain or pottery so decorated.

crackling ('kræklɪŋ) *n.* the crisp browned skin of roast pork.

cracknel ('krækn[ə]l) *n.* **1.** a type of hard plain biscuit. **2.** (*often pl.*) *U.S. and Canadian.* crisply fried bits of fat pork. [C15: perhaps from Old French *craquelin,* from Middle Dutch *krākelinc,* from *krāken* to CRACK]

crackpot ('krækˌpɒt) *Informal.* ~*n.* **1.** an eccentric person; crank. ~*adj.* **2.** (*usually prenominal*) eccentric; crazy.

cracksman ('kræksmən) *n., pl.* **-men.** *Slang.* a burglar, esp. a safe-breaker.

crack up *vb.* (*adv.*) **1.** (*intr.*) to break into pieces. **2.** (*intr.*) *Informal.* to undergo a physical or mental breakdown. **3.** (*tr.*) *Informal.* to present or report, esp. in glowing terms: *it's not all it's cracked up to be.* ~*n.* **crackup. 4.** *Informal.* a physical or mental breakdown.

crack willow *n.* **1.** a species of commonly grown willow, *Salix fragilis,* with branches that snap easily. **2.** any of various related willows.

-cracy *n. combining form.* indicating a type of government or rule: *plutocracy; mobocracy.* See also **-crat.** [from Greek *-kratia,* from *kratos* power]

cradle ('kreɪd[ə]l) *n.* **1.** a baby's bed with enclosed sides, often with a hood and rockers. **2.** a place where something originates or is nurtured during its early life: *the cradle of civilization.* **3.** the earliest period of life: *they knew each other from the cradle.* **4.** a frame, rest, or trolley made to support or transport a piece of equipment, aircraft, ship, etc. **5.** a platform, cage, or trolley, in which workmen are suspended on the side of a building or ship. **6.** the part of a telephone on which the handset rests when not in use. **7.** another name for **creeper** (sense 5). **8.** *Agriculture.* **a.** a framework of several wooden fingers attached to a scythe to gather the grain into bunches as it is cut. **b.** a scythe equipped with such a cradle; cradle scythe. **c.** a collar of wooden fingers that prevents a horse or cow from turning its head and biting itself. **9.** Also called: **rocker.** a boxlike apparatus for washing rocks, sand, etc., containing gold or gem stones. **10.** *Engraving.* a tool that produces the pitted surface of a copper mezzotint plate before the design is engraved upon it. **11.** a framework used to prevent the bedclothes from touching a sensitive part of an injured person. **12. from the cradle to the grave.** throughout life. **13. rob the cradle.** *Informal.* to take for a lover, husband, or wife a person much younger than oneself. ~*vb.* **14.** (*tr.*) to rock or place in or as if in a cradle; hold tenderly. **15.** (*tr.*) to nurture in or bring up from infancy. **16.** (*tr.*) to replace (the handset of a telephone) on the cradle. **17.** to reap (grain) with a cradle scythe. **18.** (*tr.*) to wash (soil bearing gold, etc.) in a cradle. **19.** *Lacrosse.* to keep (the ball) in the net of the stick, esp. while running with it. **20.** (*intr.*) *Rare.* to lie in a cradle. [Old English *cradol;* related to Old High German *kratto* basket] —**'cradler** *n.*

cradle snatcher *n. Informal.* another name for **baby snatcher** (sense 2).

cradlesong ('kreɪd[ə]lˌsɒŋ) *n.* another word for **lullaby.**

cradling ('kreɪdlɪŋ) *n. Architect.* a framework of iron or wood, esp. as used in the construction of a ceiling.

craft (krɑːft) *n.* **1.** skill or ability, esp. in handiwork. **2.** skill in deception and trickery; guile; cunning. **3.** an occupation or trade requiring special skill, esp. manual dexterity. **4. a.** the members of such a trade, regarded collectively. **b.** (*as modifier*): *a craft guild.* **5.** a single vessel, aircraft, or spacecraft. **6.** (*functioning as pl.*) ships, boats, aircraft, or spacecraft collectively. ~*vb.* **7.** (*tr.*) to make or fashion with skill, esp. by hand. [Old English *cræft* skill, strength; related to Old Norse *kraptr* power, skill, Old High German *kraft*]

craft apprenticeship *n.* a period of training for a skilled trade in industry, such as for a plumber or electrician.

craftsman ('krɑːftsmən) *n., pl.* **-men. 1.** a member of a skilled trade; someone who practises a craft; artisan. **2.** Also called: (*fem.*) **craftswoman.** an artist skilled in the techniques of an art or craft. —**'craftsmanly** *adj.* —**'craftsmanˌship** *n.*

craft union *n.* a labour organization membership of which is restricted to workers in a specified trade or craft. Compare **industrial union.**

crafty ('krɑːftɪ) *adj.* **craftier, craftiest. 1.** skilled in deception; shrewd; cunning. **2.** *Archaic.* skilful. —**'craftily** *adv.* —**'craftiness** *n.*

crag (kræg) *n.* a steep rugged rock or peak. [C13: of Celtic origin; related to Old Welsh *creik* rock]

Crag (kræg) *n.* a formation of shelly sandstone in E England, deposited during the Pliocene and Pleistocene epochs.

craggy ('krægɪ) *or U.S.* **cragged** ('krægɪd) *adj.* **-gier, -giest. 1.** having many crags. **2.** (of the face) rugged; rocklike. —**'craggily** *adv.* —**'cragginess** *n.*

cragsman ('krægzmən) *n., pl.* **-men.** a rock climber.

craig (kreg, kreɪg) *n.* a Scot. word for **crag.**

crake (kreɪk) *n. Zoology.* any of several rails that occur in the Old World, such as the corncrake and the spotted crake. [C14: from Old Norse *krāka* crow or *krākr* raven, of imitative origin]

cram (kræm) *vb.* **crams, cramming, crammed.** **1.** (*tr.*) to force (people, material, etc.) into (a room, container, etc.) with more than it can hold; stuff. **2.** to eat or cause to eat more than necessary. **3.** *Informal.* to study or cause to study (facts, etc.), esp. for an examination, by hastily memorizing. ~*n.* **4.** the act or condition of cramming. **5.** a crush. [Old English *crammian;* related to Old Norse *kremja* to press]

crambo (ˈkræmbəʊ) *n.* a word game in which one team says a rhyme or rhyming line for a word or line given by the other team. [C17: from earlier *crambe,* probably from Latin *crambē repetīta* cabbage repeated, hence an old story, a rhyming game, from Greek *krambē*]

cram-full *adj.* stuffed full.

crammer (ˈkræmə) *n.* a person or school that prepares pupils for an examination, esp. pupils who have already failed that examination.

cramoisy *or* **cramoisie** (ˈkræmɔɪzɪ, -əzɪ) *Archaic.* ~*adj.* **1.** of a crimson colour. ~*n.* **2.** crimson cloth. [C15: from Old French *cramoisi,* from Arabic *qirmizī* red obtained from kermes; see CRIMSON, KERMES]

cramp[1] (kræmp) *n.* **1.** a painful involuntary contraction of a muscle, typically caused by overexertion, heat, or chill. **2.** temporary partial paralysis of a muscle group: *writer's cramp.* **3.** (*usually pl. in the U.S. and Canada*) severe abdominal pain. ~*vb.* **4.** (*tr.*) to affect with or as if with a cramp. [C14: from Old French *crampe,* of Germanic origin; compare Old High German *krampho*]

cramp[2] (kræmp) *n.* **1.** Also called: **cramp iron.** a strip of metal with its ends bent at right angles, used to bind masonry. **2.** a device for holding pieces of wood while they are glued; clamp. **3.** something that confines or restricts. **4.** a confined state or position. ~*vb.* (*tr.*) **5.** to secure or hold with a cramp. **6.** to confine, hamper, or restrict. **7. cramp (someone's) style.** *Informal.* to prevent (a person) from using his abilities or acting freely and confidently. [C15: from Middle Dutch *crampe* cramp, hook, of Germanic origin; compare Old High German *khramph* bent; see CRAMP[1]]

cramp ball *n.* a hard round blackish ascomycetous fungus, *Daldinia concentrica,* characteristically found on the bark of ash trees and formerly carried to ward off cramp. The specific name refers to the concentric rings revealed if the fungus is sliced.

cramped (kræmpt) *adj.* **1.** closed in; restricted. **2.** (esp. of handwriting) small and irregular; difficult to read.

cramper (ˈkræmpə) *n. Curling.* a spiked metal plate used as a brace for the feet in throwing the stone.

crampon (ˈkræmpən) *n.* **1.** one of a pair of pivoted steel levers used to lift heavy objects; grappling iron. **2.** (*often pl.*) one of a pair of frames each with 10 or 12 metal spikes, strapped to boots for climbing or walking on ice or snow. ~*vb.* **3.** to climb using crampons. [C15: from French, from Middle Dutch *crampe* hook; see CRAMP[2]]

cran (kræn) *n.* a unit of capacity used for measuring fresh herring, equal to 37.5 gallons. [C18: of uncertain origin]

cranage (ˈkreɪnɪdʒ) *n.* **1.** the use of a crane. **2.** a fee charged for such use.

cranberry (ˈkrænbərɪ, -brɪ) *n., pl.* **-ries.** **1.** any of several trailing ericaceous shrubs of the genus *Vaccinium,* such as the European *V. oxycoccus,* that bear sour edible red berries. **2.** the berry of this plant, used to make sauce or jelly. [C17: from Low German *kraanbere,* from *kraan* CRANE + *bere* BERRY]

cranberry bush *or* **tree** *n.* a North American caprifoliaceous shrub or small tree, *Viburnum trilobum,* producing acid red fruit.

crane (kreɪn) *n.* **1.** any large long-necked long-legged wading bird of the family *Gruidae,* inhabiting marshes and plains in most parts of the world except South America, New Zealand, and Indonesia: order *Gruiformes.* See also **demoiselle** (sense 1), **whooping crane.** **2.** (*not in ornithological use*) any similar bird, such as a heron. **3.** a device for lifting and moving heavy objects, typically consisting of a pivoted boom rotating about a vertical axis with lifting gear suspended from the end of the boom. See also **gantry.** **4.** *Films.* a large trolley carrying a boom, on the end of which is mounted a camera. ~*vb.* **5.** (*tr.*) to lift or move (an object) by or as if by a crane. **6.** to stretch out (esp. the neck), as to see over other people's heads. **7.** (*intr.*) (of a horse) to pull up short before a jump. [Old English *cran;* related to Middle High German *krane,* Latin *grūs,* Greek *géranos*]

crane fly *n.* any dipterous fly of the family *Tipulidae,* having long legs, slender wings, and a narrow body. Also called (Brit.): **daddy-longlegs.**

cranesbill (ˈkreɪnz,bɪl) *n.* any of various plants of the genus *Geranium,* having pink or purple flowers and long slender beaked fruits: family *Geraniaceae.* See also **herb Robert, storksbill.**

cranial (ˈkreɪnɪəl) *adj.* of or relating to the skull. —ˈ**cranially** *adv.*

cranial index *n.* the ratio of the greatest length to the greatest width of the cranium, multiplied by 100: used in comparative anthropology. Compare **cephalic index.**

cranial nerve *n.* any of the 12 paired nerves that have their origin in the brain and reach the periphery through natural openings in the skull.

craniate (ˈkreɪnɪɪt, -ˌeɪt) *adj.* **1.** having a skull or cranium. ~*adj., n.* **2.** another word for **vertebrate.**

cranio- *or before a vowel* **crani-** *combining form.* indicating the cranium or cranial: *craniotomy.*

craniology (ˌkreɪnɪˈɒlədʒɪ) *n.* the branch of science concerned with the shape and size of the human skull, esp. with reference to variations between different races. —**craniological** (ˌkreɪnɪəˈlɒdʒɪkᵊl) *adj.* —ˌ**cranioˈlogically** *adv.* —ˌ**craniˈologist** *n.*

craniometer (ˌkreɪnɪˈɒmɪtə) *n.* an instrument for measuring the cranium or skull.

craniometry (ˌkreɪnɪˈɒmɪtrɪ) *n.* the study and measurement of skulls. —**craniometric** (ˌkreɪnɪəˈmɛtrɪk) *or* ˌ**cranioˈmetrical** *adj.* —ˌ**cranioˈmetrically** *adv.* —ˌ**craniˈometrist** *n.*

craniotomy (ˌkreɪnɪˈɒtəmɪ) *n., pl.* **-mies.** **1.** surgical incision into the skull, esp. to expose the brain for neurosurgery. **2.** surgical crushing of a fetal skull to extract a dead fetus.

cranium (ˈkreɪnɪəm) *n., pl.* **-niums** *or* **-nia** (-nɪə). **1.** the skull of a vertebrate. **2.** the part of the skull that encloses the brain. Nontechnical name: **brainpan.** [C16: from Medieval Latin *crānium* skull, from Greek *kranion*]

crank[1] (kræŋk) *n.* **1.** a device for communicating motion or for converting reciprocating motion into rotary motion or vice versa, consisting of an arm projecting from a shaft, often with a second member attached to it parallel to the shaft. **2.** Also called: **crank handle, starting handle.** a handle incorporating a crank, used to start an engine or motor. **3.** *Informal.* **a.** an eccentric or odd person, esp. someone who stubbornly maintains unusual views. **b.** *U.S. and Canadian.* a bad-tempered person. **4.** *Rare.* a clever turn of speech (esp. in the phrase **quips and cranks**). **5.** *Archaic.* a bend or turn. ~*vb.* **6.** (*tr.*) to rotate (a shaft) by means of a crank. **7.** (*tr.*) to start (an engine, motor, etc.) by means of a crank handle. **8.** (*tr.*) to bend, twist, or make into the shape of a crank. **9.** (*intr.*) *Obsolete.* to twist or wind. ~See also **crank up.** [Old English *cranc;* related to Middle Low German *krunke* wrinkle, Dutch *krinkel* CRINKLE]

crank[2] (kræŋk) *or* **cranky** *adj.* (of a sailing vessel) easily keeled over by the wind; tender. [C17: of uncertain origin; perhaps related to CRANK[1]]

crankcase (ˈkræŋk,keɪs) *n.* the metal housing that encloses the crankshaft, connecting rods, etc., in an internal-combustion engine, reciprocating pump, etc.

crankpin (ˈkræŋk,pɪn) *n.* a short cylindrical bearing surface fitted between two arms of a crank and set parallel to the main shaft of the crankshaft.

crankshaft (ˈkræŋk,ʃɑːft) *n.* a shaft having one or more cranks, esp. the main shaft of an internal-combustion engine to which the connecting rods are attached.

crank up *vb.* (*intr., adv.*) *Slang.* to inject a narcotic drug.

cranky[1] (ˈkræŋkɪ) *adj.* **crankier, crankiest.** **1.** *Informal.* eccentric. **2.** *U.S., Canadian, and Irish informal.* fussy and bad-tempered. **3.** shaky; out of order. **4.** full of bends and turns. **5.** *Dialect.* unwell. —ˈ**crankily** *adv.* —ˈ**crankiness** *n.*

cranky[2] (ˈkræŋkɪ) *adj.* **crankier, crankiest.** *Nautical.* another word for **crank**[2].

crannog (ˈkrænəg) *or* **crannoge** (ˈkrænədʒ) *n.* an ancient Celtic lake or bog dwelling dating from the late Bronze Age to the 16th century A.D., often fortified and used as a refuge. [C19: from Irish Gaelic *crannóg,* from Old Irish *crann* tree]

cranny (ˈkrænɪ) *n., pl.* **-nies.** a narrow opening, as in a wall or rock face; chink; crevice (esp. in the phrase **every nook and cranny**). [C15: from Old French *cran* notch, fissure; compare CRENEL] —ˈ**crannied** *adj.*

crap[1] (kræp) *n.* **1.** a losing throw in the game of craps. **2.** another name for **craps.** [C20: back formation from CRAPS]

crap[2] (kræp) *Slang* ~*n.* **1.** nonsense. **2.** rubbish. **3.** a taboo word for **faeces.** ~*vb.* **craps, crapping, crapped.** **4.** (*intr.*) a taboo word for **defecate.** [C15 *crappe* chaff, from Middle Dutch, probably from *crappen* to break off]

crapaud (ˈkræpəʊ, ˈkrɑː-) *n. Caribbean.* a frog or toad. [from French: toad]

crape (kreɪp) *n.* **1.** a variant spelling of **crepe.** **2.** crepe, esp. when used for mourning clothes. **3.** a band of black crepe worn in mourning. —ˈ**crapy** *adj.*

crape myrtle *or* **crepe myrtle** *n.* an oriental lythraceous shrub, *Lagerstroemia indica,* cultivated in warm climates for its pink, red, or white flowers.

crap out *vb.* (*intr., adv.*) **1.** *U.S. slang.* to make a losing throw in craps. **2.** *U.S. slang.* to fail; withdraw. **3.** *U.S. slang.* to rest. **4.** *Slang.* to fail to do or attempt something through fear.

crappie (ˈkræpɪ) *n., pl.* **-pies.** either of two North American freshwater percoid food and game fishes, *Pomoxis nigromaculatus* (**black crappie**) or *P. annularis* (**white crappie**): family *Centrarchidae* (sunfishes, etc.). [C19: from Canadian French *crapet*]

craps (kræps) *n.* (*usually functioning as sing.*) **1.** a gambling game using two dice, in which a player wins the bet if 7 or 11 is thrown first, and loses if 2, 3, or 12 is thrown. **2. shoot craps.** to play this game. [C19: probably from *crabs* lowest throw at dice, plural of CRAB[1]]

crapshooter ('kræpˌʃuːtə) *n. U.S.* a person who plays the game of craps.
crapulent ('kræpjʊlənt) *or* **crapulous** ('kræpjʊləs) *adj.* **1.** given to or resulting from intemperance. **2.** suffering from intemperance; drunken. [C18: from Late Latin *crāpulentus* drunk, from Latin *crāpula,* from Greek *kraipalē* drunkenness, headache resulting therefrom] —'**crapulence** *n.* —'**crapulently** *or* '**crapulously** *adv.* —'**crapulousness** *n.*
craquelure ('krækəlʊə) *n.* a network of fine cracks on old paintings caused by the deterioration of pigment or varnish. [C20: from French, from *craqueler* to crackle, from *craquer* to crack, of imitative origin]
crash[1] (kræʃ) *vb.* **1.** to make or cause to make a loud noise as of solid objects smashing or clattering. **2.** to fall or cause to fall with force, breaking in pieces with a loud noise as of solid objects smashing. **3.** (*intr.*) to break or smash in pieces with a loud noise. **4.** (*intr.*) to collapse or fail suddenly: *this business is sure to crash.* **5.** to cause (an aircraft) to hit land or water violently resulting in severe damage or (of an aircraft) to hit land or water in this way. **6.** to cause (a car, etc.) to collide with another car or other object or (of two or more cars) to be involved in a collision. **7.** to move or cause to move violently or noisily: *to crash through a barrier.* **8.** *Brit. informal.* short for **gate-crash.** **9.** (*intr.*) (of a computer system or program) to fail suddenly and completely because of a malfunction. **10.** (*intr.*) *Slang.* another term for **crash out.** ~*n.* **11.** an act or instance of breaking and falling to pieces. **12.** a sudden loud noise: *the crash of thunder.* **13.** a collision, as between vehicles. **14.** a sudden descent of an aircraft as a result of which it hits land or water. **15.** the sudden collapse of a business, stock exchange, etc., esp. one causing further financial failure. **16.** (*modifier*) **a.** requiring or using intensive effort and all possible resources in order to accomplish something quickly: *a crash programme.* **b.** sudden or vigorous: *a crash halt; a crash tackle.* ~See also **crash out.** [C14: probably from *crasen* to smash, shatter + *dasshen* to strike violently, DASH; see CRAZE] —'**crasher** *n.*
crash[2] (kræʃ) *n.* a coarse cotton or linen cloth used for towelling, curtains, etc. [C19: from Russian *krashenina* coloured linen]
crash barrier *n.* a barrier erected along the centre of a motorway, around a racetrack, etc., for safety purposes.
crash dive *n.* **1.** a sudden steep dive from the surface by a submarine. ~*vb.* **crash-dive. 2.** (usually of an aircraft) to descend steeply and rapidly, before hitting the ground. **3.** to perform or cause to perform a crash dive.
crash helmet *n.* a padded helmet worn for motorcycling, flying, bobsleighing, etc., to protect the head in a crash.
crashing ('kræʃɪŋ) *adj.* (*prenominal*) *Informal.* (intensifier) (esp. in the phrase **a crashing bore).**
crash-land *vb.* to land (an aircraft) in an emergency causing some damage to it or (of an aircraft) to land in this way. —'**crash-ˌlanding** *n.*
crash out *vb.* (*intr., adv.*) *Slang.* **1. a.** to go to sleep. **b.** to spend the night (in a place): *we crashed out at John's place.* **2.** to pass out.
crash pad *n. Slang.* a place to sleep or live temporarily.
crash-test *vb.* (*tr.*) to test (a new product) for safety and reliability by finding out its breaking point under pressure, heat, etc.
crashworthiness ('kræʃˌwɜːðɪnɪs) *n.* the ability of a vehicle structure to withstand a crash. —'**crashˌworthy** *adj.*
crasis ('kreɪsɪs) *n., pl.* **-ses** (-siːz). the fusion or contraction of two adjacent vowels into one. Also called: **syneresis.** [C17: from Greek *krasis* a mingling, from *kerannunai* to mix]
crass (kræs) *adj.* **1.** stupid; gross. **2.** *Rare.* thick or coarse. [C16: from Latin *crassus* thick, dense, gross] —'**crassly** *adv.* —'**crassness** *or* '**crassiˌtude** *n.*
crassulacean acid metabolism (ˌkræsjʊ'leɪʃən) *n.* the full name for **CAM** (sense 2).
crassulaceous (ˌkræsjʊ'leɪʃəs) *adj.* of, relating to, or belonging to the *Crassulaceae,* a family of herbaceous or shrubby flowering plants with fleshy succulent leaves, including the houseleeks and stonecrops. [C19: from New Latin *Crassula* name of genus, from Medieval Latin: stonecrop, from Latin *crassus* thick]
-crat *n. combining form.* indicating a person who takes part in or is a member of a form of government or class: *democrat; technocrat.* See also **-cracy.** [from Greek *-kratēs,* from *-kratia* -CRACY] —**-cratic** *or* **-cratical** *adj. combining form.*
cratch (krætʃ) *n.* a rack for holding fodder for cattle, etc. [C14: from Old French: CRÈCHE]
crate (kreɪt) *n.* **1.** a fairly large container, usually made of wooden slats or wickerwork, used for packing, storing, or transporting goods. **2.** *Slang.* an old car, aeroplane, etc. ~*vb.* **3.** (*tr.*) to pack or place in a crate. [C16: from Latin *crātis* wickerwork, hurdle] —'**crater** *n.* —'**crateful** *n.*
crater ('kreɪtə) *n.* **1.** the bowl-shaped opening at the top or side of a volcano or top of a geyser through which lava and gases are emitted. **2.** a similarly shaped depression formed by the impact of a meteorite or exploding bomb. **3.** any of the tens of thousands of roughly circular or polygonal walled formations covering the surface of the moon and some other planets, formed probably either by volcanic action or by the impact of meteorites. They can have a diameter of up to 240 kilometres (150 miles) and a depth of 8900 metres (29 000 feet). **4.** a pit in an otherwise smooth surface. **5.** a large open bowl with two handles, used for mixing wines, esp. in ancient Greece. ~*vb.* **6.** to make or form craters in (a surface, such as the ground). [C17: from Latin: mixing bowl, crater, from Greek *kratēr,* from *kerannunai* to mix] —'**craterless** *adj.* —'**crater-ˌlike** *adj.* —'**craterous** *adj.*
Crater ('kreɪtə) *n., Latin genitive* **Crateris** ('kreɪtərɪs). a small faint constellation in the S hemisphere lying between Virgo and Hydra.
craton ('kreɪtᵊn) *n. Geology.* a large stable part of the earth's crust or lithosphere that has not been deformed significantly for many millions, possibly even hundreds of millions, of years. See **shield** (sense 7). [C20: from Greek *kratos* strength] —**cratonic** (krə'tɒnɪk) *adj.*
cratur ('kretər) *n. Irish and Scot.* **1. the.** whisky or whiskey: *a drop of the cratur.* **2.** a person. [from CREATURE]
craunch (krɔːntʃ) *vb.* a dialect word for **crunch.** —'**craunchable** *adj.* —'**craunchy** *adj.* —'**craunchiness** *n.*
cravat (krə'væt) *n.* a scarf of silk or fine wool, worn round the neck, esp. by men. [C17: from French *cravate,* from Serbo-Croatian *Hrvat* Croat; so called because worn by Croats in the French army during the Thirty Years' War]
crave (kreɪv) *vb.* **1.** (when *intr.,* foll. by *for* or *after*) to desire intensely; long (for). **2.** (*tr.*) to need greatly or urgently. **3.** (*tr.*) to beg or plead for. [Old English *crafian;* related to Old Norse *krefja* to demand, *krǣfr* strong; see CRAFT] —'**craver** *n.*
craven ('kreɪvᵊn) *adj.* **1.** cowardly; mean-spirited. ~*n.* **2.** a coward. [C13 *cravant,* probably from Old French *crevant* bursting, from *crever* to burst, die, from Latin *crepāre* to burst, crack] —'**cravenly** *adv.* —'**cravenness** *n.*
craving ('kreɪvɪŋ) *n.* an intense desire or longing.
craw (krɔː) *n.* **1.** a less common word for **crop** (sense 6). **2.** the stomach of an animal. **3. stick in one's craw** *or* **throat.** *Informal.* to be difficult, or against one's conscience, for one to accept, utter, or believe. [C14: related to Middle High German *krage,* Middle Dutch *crāghe* neck, Icelandic *kragi* collar]
crawfish ('krɔːˌfɪʃ) *n., pl.* **-fish** *or* **-fishes.** a variant (esp. U.S.) of **crayfish** (esp. sense 2).
crawl[1] (krɔːl) *vb.* (*intr.*) **1.** to move slowly, either by dragging the body along the ground or on the hands and knees. **2.** to proceed or move along very slowly or laboriously: *the traffic crawled along the road.* **3.** to act or behave in a servile manner; fawn; cringe. **4.** to be or feel as if overrun by something unpleasant, esp. crawling creatures: *the pile of refuse crawled with insects.* **5.** (of insects, worms, snakes, etc.) to move with the body close to the ground. **6.** to swim the crawl. ~*n.* **7.** a slow creeping pace or motion. **8.** Also called: **Australian crawl, front crawl.** *Swimming.* a stroke in which the feet are kicked like paddles while the arms reach forward and pull back through the water. [C14: probably from Old Norse *krafla* to creep; compare Swedish *kravla,* Middle Low German *krabbelen* to crawl, Old Norse *krabbi* CRAB[1]] —'**crawlingly** *adv.*
crawl[2] (krɔːl) *n.* an enclosure in shallow, coastal water for fish, lobsters, etc. [C17: from Dutch *kraal* KRAAL]
crawler ('krɔːlə) *n.* **1.** *Slang.* a servile flatterer. **2.** a person or animal that crawls. **3.** *U.S.* an informal name for an **earthworm. 4.** (*pl.*) a baby's overalls; rompers.
crawler lane *n.* a lane on an uphill section of a motorway reserved for slow vehicles.
crawling ('krɔːlɪŋ) *n.* a defect in freshly applied paint or varnish characterized by bare patches and ridging.
crawling peg *n.* a method of stabilizing exchange rates, prices, etc., by maintaining a fixed level for a specified period or until the rate or price has persisted at an upper or lower limit for a specified period and then permitting a predetermined incremental rise or fall.
crawly ('krɔːlɪ) *adj.* **crawlier, crawliest.** *Informal.* feeling or causing a sensation like creatures crawling on one's skin.
craw-thumper *n. Irish informal.* an ostentatiously pious person. [C18: in the sense: breast-beater, from CRAW]
cray (kreɪ) *n. Austral. and N.Z. informal.* a crayfish.
crayfish ('kreɪˌfɪʃ) *or esp. U.S.* **crawfish** *n., pl.* **-fish** *or* **-fishes. 1.** any freshwater decapod crustacean of the genera *Astacus* and *Cambarus,* resembling a small lobster. **2.** any of various similar crustaceans, esp. the spiny lobster. [C14: *cray,* by folk etymology, from Old French *crevice* crab, from Old High German *krebiz* + FISH]
crayon ('kreɪən, -ɒn) *n.* **1.** a small stick or pencil of charcoal, wax, clay, or chalk mixed with coloured pigment. **2.** a drawing made with crayons. ~*vb.* **3.** to draw or colour with crayons. [C17: from French, from *craie,* from Latin *crēta* chalk] —'**crayonist** *n.*
craythur *n. Irish.* **1.** ('kreːθər) **the.** a variant of **cratur** (sense 1). **2.** ('kreːtʃər) a variant of **cratur** (sense 2). [from Irish Gaelic *Créatur* creature]
craze (kreɪz) *n.* **1.** a short-lived current fashion. **2.** a wild or exaggerated enthusiasm: *a craze for chestnuts.* **3.** mental disturbance; insanity. ~*vb.* **4.** to make or become mad. **5.** *Ceramics, metallurgy.* to develop or cause to develop a fine network of cracks. **6.** (*tr.*) *Brit. dialect or obsolete.* to break. **7.** (*tr.*) *Archaic.* to weaken. [C14 (in the sense: to break, shatter): probably of Scandinavian origin; compare Swedish *krasa* to shatter, ultimately of imitative origin]

crazed (kreɪzd) *adj.* **1.** driven insane. **2.** (of porcelain or pottery) having a fine network of cracks in the glaze.
crazy (ˈkreɪzɪ) *adj.* **-zier, -ziest. 1.** *Informal.* insane. **2.** fantastic; strange; ridiculous: *a crazy dream.* **3.** (*postpositive;* foll. by *about* or *over*) *Informal.* extremely fond (of). **4.** *Slang.* very good or excellent. **5.** *Archaic.* likely to collapse; rickety. —ˈ**crazily** *adv.* —ˈ**craziness** *n.*
crazy bone *n.* the U.S. name for **funny bone.**
crazy paving *n. Brit.* a form of paving, as for a path, made of slabs of stone of irregular shape fitted together.
crazy quilt *n.* a patchwork quilt made from assorted pieces of material of irregular shape, size, and colour.
CRE (in Britain) *abbrev. for* Commission for Racial Equality.
creak (kriːk) *vb.* **1.** to make or cause to make a harsh squeaking sound. **2.** (*intr.*) to make such sounds while moving: *the old car creaked along.* ~*n.* **3.** a harsh squeaking sound. [C14: variant of CROAK, of imitative origin] —ˈ**creaky** *adj.* —ˈ**creakily** *adv.* —ˈ**creakiness** *n.* —ˈ**creakingly** *adv.*
cream (kriːm) *n.* **1. a.** the fatty part of milk, which rises to the top if the milk is allowed to stand. **b.** (*as modifier*): *cream buns.* **2.** anything resembling cream in consistency: *shoe cream; beauty cream.* **3.** the best one or most essential part of something; pick: *the cream of the bunch; the cream of the joke.* **4.** a soup containing cream or milk: *cream of chicken soup.* **5.** any of various dishes, cakes, biscuits, etc., resembling or containing cream. **6.** a confection made of fondant or soft fudge, often covered in chocolate. **7. cream sherry.** a full-bodied sweet sherry. **8. a.** a yellowish-white colour. **b.** (*as adj.*): *cream wallpaper.* ~*vb.* **9.** (*tr.*) to skim or otherwise separate the cream from (milk). **10.** (*tr.*) to beat (foodstuffs, esp. butter and sugar) to a light creamy consistency. **11.** (*intr.*) to form cream. **12.** (*tr.*) to add or apply cream or any creamlike substance to: *to cream one's face; to cream coffee.* **13.** (*tr.;* sometimes foll. by *off*) to take away the best part of. **14.** (*tr.*) to prepare or cook (vegetables, chicken, etc.) with cream or milk. **15.** to allow (milk) to form a layer of cream on its surface or (of milk) to form such a layer. **16.** (*tr.*) *Slang, chiefly U.S. and Canadian.* to beat thoroughly. **17.** (*intr.*) *Taboo slang.* (of men) to ejaculate, as during orgasm. [C14: from Old French *cresme,* from Late Latin *crāmum* cream, of Celtic origin; influenced by Church Latin *chrisma* unction, CHRISM] —ˈ**creamˌlike** *adj.*
cream cheese *n.* a smooth soft white cheese made from soured cream or milk.
cream cracker *n. Brit.* a crisp unsweetened biscuit, often eaten with cheese.
creamcups (ˈkriːmˌkʌps) *n.* (*functioning as sing. or pl.*) a Californian papaveraceous plant, *Platystemon californicus,* with small cream-coloured or yellow flowers on long flower stalks.
creamer (ˈkriːmə) *n.* **1.** a vessel or device for separating cream from milk. **2.** a powdered substitute for cream, used in coffee. **3.** *Chiefly U.S. and Canadian.* a small jug or pitcher for serving cream.
creamery (ˈkriːmərɪ) *n., pl.* **-eries. 1.** an establishment where milk and cream are made into butter and cheese. **2.** a place where dairy products are sold. **3.** a place where milk is left to stand until the cream rises to the top.
creamlaid (ˈkriːmˌleɪd) *adj.* (of laid paper) cream-coloured and of a ribbed appearance.
cream of tartar *n.* another name for **potassium hydrogen tartrate,** esp. when used in baking powders.
cream puff *n.* **1.** a shell of light pastry with a custard or cream filling. **2.** *Informal.* an effeminate man.
cream sauce *n.* a white sauce made from cream, butter, etc.
cream soda *n.* a carbonated soft drink flavoured with vanilla.
cream tea *n.* afternoon tea including bread or scones served with clotted cream and jam.
creamware (ˈkriːmˌwɛə) *n.* a type of earthenware with a deep cream body developed about 1720 and widely produced. See also **Queensware.**
creamwove (ˈkriːmˌwəʊv) *adj.* (of wove paper) cream-coloured and even-surfaced.
creamy (ˈkriːmɪ) *adj.* **creamier, creamiest. 1.** resembling cream in colour, taste, or consistency. **2.** containing cream. —ˈ**creamily** *adv.* —ˈ**creaminess** *n.*
crease[1] (kriːs) *n.* **1.** a line or mark produced by folding, pressing, or wrinkling. **2.** a wrinkle or furrow, esp. on the face. **3.** *Cricket.* any three lines near each wicket marking positions for the bowler or batsman. See also **bowling crease, popping crease, return crease. 4.** *Ice hockey.* the small rectangular area in front of each goal cage. **5.** Also called: **goal crease.** *Lacrosse.* the circular area surrounding the goal. ~*vb.* **6.** to make or become wrinkled or furrowed. **7.** (*tr.*) to graze with a bullet, causing superficial injury. **8.** (often foll. by *up*) *Slang.* to be or cause to be greatly amused. [C15: from earlier *crēst;* probably related to Old French *cresté* wrinkled] —ˈ**creaseless** *adj.* —ˈ**creaser** *n.* —ˈ**creasy** *adj.*
crease[2] (kriːs) *n.* a rare spelling of **kris.**
crease-resistant *adj.* (of a fabric, garment, etc.) designed to remain uncreased when subjected to wear or use.
create (kriːˈeɪt) *vb.* **1.** (*tr.*) to cause to come into existence. **2.** (*tr.*) to invest with a new honour, office, or title; appoint. **3.** (*tr.*) to be the cause of: *these circumstances created the revolution.* **4.** (*tr.*) to act (a role) in the first production of a play. **5.** (*intr.*) to be engaged in creative work. **6.** (*intr.*) *Brit. slang.* to make a fuss or uproar. [C14 *creat* created, from Latin *creātus,* from *creāre* to produce, make] —**creˈatable** *adj.*
creatine (ˈkriːəˌtiːn, -tɪn) *or* **creatin** (ˈkriːətɪn) *n.* an important metabolite involved in many biochemical reactions and present in many types of living cells. [C19: *creat-* from Greek *kreas* flesh + -INE[2]]
creatinine (kriːˈætəˌniːn) *n.* an anhydride of creatine that is abundant in muscle and excreted in the urine. [C19: from German *Kreatinin,* from *Kreatin* CREATINE + *-in* -INE[2]]
creation (kriːˈeɪʃən) *n.* **1.** the act or process of creating. **2.** the fact of being created or produced. **3.** something that has been brought into existence or created, esp. a product of human intelligence or imagination. **4.** the whole universe, including the world and all the things in it. **5.** an unusual or striking garment or hat. —**creˈational** *adj.*
Creation (kriːˈeɪʃən) *n. Theol.* **1.** (often preceded by *the*) God's act of bringing the universe into being. **2.** the universe as thus brought into being by God.
creationism (kriːˈeɪʃəˌnɪzəm) *n.* **1.** the belief that God brings individual human souls into existence at conception or birth. Compare **traducianism. 2.** the doctrine that ascribes the origins of all things to God's acts of creation rather than to evolution. —**creˈationist** *n.* —**creˌationˈistic** *adj.*
creative (kriːˈeɪtɪv) *adj.* **1.** having the ability or power to create. **2.** characterized by originality of thought or inventiveness; having or showing imagination: *a creative mind.* **3.** designed to or tending to stimulate the imagination or invention: *creative toys.* —**creˈatively** *adv.* —**creˈativeness** *n.* —ˌ**creaˈtivity** *n.*
creator (kriːˈeɪtə) *n.* a person or thing that creates; originator. —**creˈatorˌship** *n.* —**creˈatress** *or* **creˈatrix** *fem. n.*
Creator (kriːˈeɪtə) *n.* (usually preceded by *the*) an epithet of God.
creature (ˈkriːtʃə) *n.* **1.** a living being, esp. an animal. **2.** something that has been created, whether animate or inanimate: *a creature of the imagination.* **3.** a human being; person: used as a term of scorn, pity, or endearment. **4.** a person who is dependent upon another; tool or puppet. [C13: from Church Latin *creātūra,* from Latin *creāre* to create] —ˈ**creatural** *or* ˈ**creaturely** *adj.* —ˈ**creatureliness** *n.*
creature comforts *pl. n.* material things or luxuries that help to provide for one's bodily comfort.
crèche (krɛʃ, kreɪʃ; *French* krɛʃ) *n.* **1.** *Chiefly Brit.* a day nursery for very young children. **2.** a tableau of Christ's Nativity. **3.** a foundling home or hospital. [C19: from Old French: manger, crib, ultimately of Germanic origin; compare Old High German *kripja* crib]
credence (ˈkriːdᵊns) *n.* **1.** acceptance or belief, esp. with regard to the truth of the evidence of others: *I cannot give credence to his account.* **2.** something supporting a claim to belief; recommendation; credential (esp. in the phrase **letters of credence**). **3.** short for **credence table.** [C14: from Medieval Latin *crēdentia* trust, credit, from Latin *crēdere* to believe]
credence table *n.* **1.** a small sideboard, originally one at which food was tasted for poison before serving. **2.** *Christianity.* a small table or ledge on which the bread, wine, etc., are placed before being consecrated in the Eucharist.
credendum (krɪˈdɛndəm) *n., pl.* **-da** (-də). (*often pl.*) *Christianity.* an article of faith. [Latin: a thing to be believed, from *crēdere* to believe]
credent (ˈkriːdᵊnt) *adj. Obsolete.* believing or believable. [C17: from Latin *crēdēns* believing]
credential (krɪˈdɛnʃəl) *n.* **1.** something that entitles a person to confidence, authority, etc. **2.** (*pl.*) a letter or certificate giving evidence of the bearer's identity or competence. ~*adj.* **3.** entitling one to confidence, authority, etc. [C16: from Medieval Latin *crēdentia* credit, trust; see CREDENCE] —**creˈdentialed** *adj.*
credenza (krɪˈdɛnzə) *n.* another name for **credence table.** [Italian: see CREDENCE]
credibility gap *n.* a disparity between claims or statements made and the evident facts of the situation or circumstances to which they relate.
credible (ˈkrɛdɪbᵊl) *adj.* **1.** capable of being believed. **2.** trustworthy. [C14: from Latin *crēdibilis,* from Latin *crēdere* to believe] —**credibleness** *or* ˌ**crediˈbility** *n.* —ˈ**credibly** *adv.*
credit (ˈkrɛdɪt) *n.* **1.** commendation or approval, as for an act or quality: *she was given credit for her work.* **2.** a person or thing serving as a source of good influence, repute, ability, etc.: *a credit to the team.* **3.** the quality of being believable or trustworthy: *that statement had credit.* **4.** influence or reputation coming from the approval or good opinion of others: *he acquired credit within the community.* **5.** belief in the truth, reliability, quality, etc., of someone or something: *I would give credit to that philosophy.* **6.** a sum of money or equivalent purchasing power, as at a shop, available for a person's use. **7. a.** the positive balance in a person's bank account. **b.** the sum of money that a bank makes available to a client in excess of any deposit. **8. a.** the practice of permitting a buyer to receive goods or services before payment. **b.** the time permitted for paying for such goods or services. **9.** reputation for solvency and commercial or financial probity, inducing confidence among creditors. **10.** *Accounting.* **a.** acknowledgment of an income, liability, or capital item by entry on the right-hand side of an account. **b.** the right-hand

side of an account. **c.** an entry on this side. **d.** the total of such entries. **e.** (*as modifier*): *credit entries*. Compare **debit** (sense 1). **11.** *Education*. **a.** a distinction awarded to an examination candidate obtaining good marks. **b.** a section of an examination syllabus satisfactorily completed, as in higher and professional education. **12. letter of credit.** an order authorizing a named person to draw money from correspondents of the issuer. **13. on credit.** with payment to be made at a future date. ~*vb.* (*tr.*) **-dits, -diting, -dited**. **14.** (foll. by *with*) to ascribe (to); give credit (for): *they credited him with the discovery*. **15.** to accept as true; believe. **16.** to do credit to. **17.** *Accounting*. **a.** to enter (an item) as a credit in an account. **b.** to acknowledge (a payer) by making such an entry. Compare **debit** (sense 2). **18.** to award a credit to (a student). ~See also **credits.** [C16: from Old French *crédit*, from Italian *credito*, from Latin *crēditum* loan, from *crēdere* to believe] —**'creditless** *adj.*

creditable ('krɛdɪtəbᵊl) *adj.* **1.** deserving credit, honour, etc.; praiseworthy. **2.** *Obsolete*. credible. —**'creditableness** *or* **ˌcredita'bility** *n.* —**'creditably** *adv.*

credit account *n.* *Brit.* a credit system by means of which customers may obtain goods and services before payment. Also called: **charge account.**

credit card *n.* a card issued by banks, businesses, etc., enabling the holder to obtain goods and services on credit.

credit line *n.* **1.** an acknowledgment of origin or authorship, as in a newspaper or film. **2.** Also called: **line of credit.** *U.S. and Canadian*. the maximum credit that a customer is allowed.

creditor ('krɛdɪtə) *n.* a person or commercial enterprise to whom money is owed. Compare **debtor.**

credit rating *n.* an evaluation of the creditworthiness of an individual or business enterprise.

credit-reference agency *n.* an agency, other than a bank, that specializes in providing credit ratings of people or organizations.

credits ('krɛdɪts) *pl. n.* a list of those responsible for the production of a film or television programme.

credit squeeze *n.* the control of credit facilities as an instrument of economic policy, associated with restrictions on bank loans and overdrafts, raised interest rates, etc.

credit standing *n.* reputation for discharging financial obligations.

credit transfer *n.* a method of settling a debt by transferring money through a bank or post office, esp. for those who do not have cheque accounts.

credit union *n.* a cooperative association whose members can obtain low-interest loans out of their combined savings.

creditworthy ('krɛdɪtˌwɜːðɪ) *adj.* (of an individual or business enterprise) adjudged as meriting credit on the basis of such factors as earning power, previous record of debt repayment, etc. —**'creditˌworthiness** *n.*

credo ('kriːdəʊ, 'kreɪ-) *n., pl.* **-dos.** any formal or authorized statement of beliefs, principles, or opinions.

Credo ('kriːdəʊ, 'kreɪ-) *n., pl.* **-dos. 1.** the Apostles' Creed or the Nicene Creed. **2.** a musical setting of the Creed. [C12: from Latin, literally: I believe; first word of the Apostles' and Nicene Creeds]

credulity (krɪ'djuːlɪtɪ) *n.* disposition to believe something on little evidence; gullibility.

credulous ('krɛdjʊləs) *adj.* **1.** tending to believe something on little evidence. **2.** arising from or characterized by credulity: *credulous beliefs*. [C16: from Latin *crēdulus*, from *crēdere* to believe] —**'credulously** *adv.* —**'credulousness** *n.*

cree (kriː) *n.* *South Wales and southwest English dialect*. temporary immunity from the rules of a game: said by children. [of unknown origin]

Cree (kriː) *n.* **1.** (*pl.* **Cree** *or* **Crees**) a member of a North American Indian people living in the Canadian provinces of Ontario, Saskatchewan, and Manitoba. **2.** the language of this people, belonging to the Algonquian family. **3.** a syllabic writing system of this and certain other languages. [from first syllable of Canadian French *Christianaux*, probably based on Ojibwa *Kenistenoag* (tribal name)]

creed (kriːd) *n.* **1.** a concise, formal statement of the essential articles of Christian belief, such as the Apostles' Creed or the Nicene Creed. **2.** any statement or system of beliefs or principles. [Old English *crēda*, from Latin *crēdo* I believe] —**'creedal** *or* **'credal** *adj.*

creek (kriːk) *n.* **1.** *Chiefly Brit.* a narrow inlet or bay, esp. of the sea. **2.** *U.S., Canadian, Austral., and N.Z.* a small stream or tributary. **3. up the creek.** *Slang*. in trouble; in a difficult position. [C13: from Old Norse *kriki* nook; related to Middle Dutch *krēke* creek, inlet]

Creek (kriːk) *n.* **1.** (*pl.* **Creek** *or* **Creeks**) a member of a confederacy of North American Indian peoples formerly living in the U.S. states of Georgia and Alabama, now chiefly in Oklahoma. **2.** any of the languages of these peoples, belonging to the Muskhogean family.

creel (kriːl) *n.* **1.** a wickerwork basket, esp. one used to hold fish. **2.** a wickerwork trap for catching lobsters, etc. **3.** the framework on a spinning machine that holds the bobbins. **4.** *West Yorkshire dialect*. a wooden frame suspended from a ceiling, used for drying clothes. [C15: from Scottish, of obscure origin]

creep (kriːp) *vb.* **creeps, creeping, crept.** (*intr.*) **1.** to crawl with the body near to or touching the ground. **2.** to move slowly, quietly, or cautiously. **3.** to act in a servile way; fawn; cringe. **4.** to move or slip out of place, as from pressure or wear. **5.** (of plants) to grow along the ground or over rocks, producing roots, suckers, or tendrils at intervals. **6.** (of a body or substance) to become permanently deformed as a result of an applied stress, often when combined with heating. **7.** to develop gradually: *creeping unrest*. **8.** to have the sensation of something crawling over the skin. **9.** (of metals) to undergo slow plastic deformation. ~*n.* **10.** the act of creeping or a creeping movement. **11.** *Slang*. a person considered to be obnoxious or servile. **12.** the continuous permanent deformation of a body or substance as a result of stress or heat. **13.** *Geology*. the gradual downwards movement of loose rock material, soil, etc., on a slope. **14.** a slow relative movement of two adjacent parts, structural components, etc. **15.** slow plastic deformation of metals. ~See also **creeps.** [Old English *crēopan*; related to Old Frisian *kriāpa*, Old Norse *krjūpa*, Middle Low German *krūpen*]

creeper ('kriːpə) *n.* **1.** a person or animal that creeps. **2.** a plant, such as the ivy or periwinkle, that grows by creeping. **3.** the U.S. and Canadian name for the **tree creeper. 4.** a hooked instrument for dragging deep water. **5.** Also called: **cradle.** a flat board or framework mounted on casters, used to lie on when working under cars. **6.** Also called: **daisycutter.** *Cricket*. a bowled ball that keeps low or travels along the ground. **7.** either of a pair of low iron supports for logs in a hearth. **8.** *Informal*. a shoe with a soft sole.

creepie ('kriːpɪ, 'krɪp-) *n.* *Chiefly Scot.* a low stool.

creeping bent grass *n.* a grass, *Agrostris palustris*, grown as a pasture grass in Europe and North America: roots readily from the stem.

creeping Jennie ('dʒɛnɪ) *or U.S. and Canadian* **creeping Charlie** *n.* other names for **moneywort.**

creeping Jesus *n.* *Derogatory slang*. **1.** an obsequious or servile person. **2.** a hypocritically religious person.

creeping thistle *n.* a weedy Eurasian thistle, *Cirsium arvense*, common as a fast-spreading weed in the U.S. U.S. and Canadian name: **Canada thistle.**

creeps (kriːps) *pl. n.* (preceded by *the*) *Informal*. a feeling of fear, repulsion, disgust, etc.

creepy ('kriːpɪ) *adj.* **creepier, creepiest. 1.** *Informal*. having or causing a sensation of repulsion, horror, or fear, as of creatures crawling on the skin. **2.** creeping; slow-moving. —**'creepily** *adv.* —**'creepiness** *n.*

creepy-crawly *Brit. informal.* ~*n., pl.* **-crawlies. 1.** a small crawling creature. ~*adj.* **2.** feeling or causing a sensation as of creatures crawling on one's skin.

creese (kriːs) *n.* a rare spelling of **kris.**

cremate (krɪ'meɪt) *vb.* (*tr.*) to burn up (something, esp. a corpse) and reduce to ash. [C19: from Latin *cremāre*] —**cre'mation** *n.* —**cre'mationism** *n.* —**cre'mationist** *n.*

cremator (krɪ'meɪtə) *n.* **1.** Also called (esp. U.S.): **cinerator.** *Brit.* a furnace for cremating corpses. **2.** a person who operates such a furnace.

crematorium (ˌkrɛmə'tɔːrɪəm) *n., pl.* **-riums** *or* **-ria** (-rɪə). *Brit.* a building in which corpses are cremated.

crematory ('krɛmətərɪ, -trɪ) *adj.* **1.** of or relating to cremation or crematoriums. ~*n., pl.* **-ries. 2.** another word (esp. U.S.) for **crematorium.**

crème (krɛm, kriːm, kreɪm) *n.* **1.** cream. **2.** any of various sweet liqueurs: *crème de moka*. ~*adj.* **3.** (of a liqueur) rich and sweet.

crème brûlée *French.* (krɛm bryle) *n.* a cream or custard dessert covered with caramelized sugar. [literally, burnt cream]

crème caramel *n.* a dessert made of eggs, sugar, milk, etc., topped with caramel. Also called: **caramel cream.**

crème de cacao ('krɛm də kɑː'kɑːəʊ, 'kəʊkəʊ; 'kriːm, 'kreɪm) *n.* a sweet liqueur with a chocolate flavour. [French, literally: cream of cacao]

crème de la crème *French.* (krɛm də la krɛm) *n.* the very best. [literally: cream of the cream]

crème de menthe ('krɛm də 'mɛnθ, 'mɪnt; 'kriːm, 'kreɪm) *n.* a liqueur flavoured with peppermint, usually bright green in colour. [French, literally: cream of mint]

crème fraîche ('krɛm 'frɛʃ) *n.* thickened and slightly fermented cream. [French, literally: fresh cream]

crenate ('kriːneɪt) *or* **crenated** *adj.* having a scalloped margin, as certain leaves. [C18: from New Latin *crēnātus*, from Medieval Latin, probably from Late Latin *crēna* a notch] —**'crenately** *adv.*

crenation (krɪ'neɪʃən) *or* **crenature** ('krɛnəˌtjʊə, 'kriː-) *n.* **1.** any of the rounded teeth or the notches between them on a crenate structure. **2.** a crenate formation or condition.

crenel ('krɛnᵊl) *or* **crenelle** (krɪ'nɛl) *n.* **1.** any of a set of openings formed in the top of a wall or parapet and having slanting sides, as in a battlement. **2.** another name for **crenation.** [C15: from Old French, literally: a little notch, from *cren* notch, from Late Latin *crēna*]

crenellate *or U.S.* **crenelate** ('krɛnɪˌleɪt) *vb.* (*tr.*) **1.** to supply with battlements. **2.** to form square indentations in (a moulding, etc.). [C19: from Old French *creneler*, from CRENEL] —**'crenelˌlated** *or U.S.* **'crenelˌated** *adj.* —**ˌcrenel'lation** *or U.S.* **ˌcrenel'ation** *n.*

crenulate ('krɛnjʊˌleɪt, -lɪt) *or* **crenulated** *adj.* having a margin very finely notched with rounded projections, as certain leaves.

[C18: from New Latin *crēnulātus,* from *crēnula,* literally: a little notch; see CRENEL]

crenulation (ˌkrɛnjʊˈleɪʃən) *n.* **1.** any of the teeth or notches of a crenulate structure. **2.** a crenulate formation.

creodont (ˈkriːəˌdɒnt) *n.* any of a group of extinct Tertiary mammals some of which are thought to have been the ancestors of modern carnivores: order *Carnivora.* [C19: from New Latin *Creodonta,* from Greek *kreas* flesh + *odōn* tooth]

creole (ˈkriːəʊl) *n.* **1.** a language that has its origin in extended contact between two language communities, one of which is generally European. It incorporates features from each and constitutes the mother tongue of a community. Compare **pidgin.** ~*adj.* **2.** denoting, relating to, or characteristic of creole. **3.** (of a sauce or dish) containing or cooked with tomatoes, green peppers, onions, etc. [C17: via French and Spanish probably from Portuguese *crioulo* slave born in one's household, person of European ancestry born in the colonies, probably from *criar* to bring up, from Latin *creāre* to CREATE]

Creole (ˈkriːəʊl) *n.* **1.** (*sometimes not cap.*) (in the West Indies and Latin America) **a.** a native-born person of European, esp. Spanish, ancestry. **b.** a native-born person of mixed European and Negro ancestry who speaks a French or Spanish creole. **c.** a native-born Negro as distinguished from one brought from Africa. **2.** (in Louisiana and other Gulf States of the U.S.) a native-born person of French ancestry. **3.** the creolized French spoken in Louisiana, esp. in New Orleans. ~*adj.* **4.** of, relating to, or characteristic of any of these peoples.

creolized *or* **creolised** (ˈkriːəˌlaɪzd) *adj.* (of a language) incorporating a considerable range of features from one or more unrelated languages, as the result of contact between language communities.

creophagous (krɪˈɒfəgəs) *adj.* flesh-eating or carnivorous. [C19: from Greek *kreophagos,* from *kreas* flesh + *-phagein* to consume] —**creophagy** (krɪˈɒfədʒɪ) *n.*

creosol (ˈkriːəˌsɒl) *n.* a colourless or pale yellow insoluble oily liquid with a smoky odour and a burning taste; 2-methoxy-4-methylphenol: an active principle of creosote. Formula: $CH_3O(CH_3)C_6H_3OH$. [C19: from CREOS(OTE) + -OL[1]]

creosote (ˈkrɪəˌsəʊt) *n.* **1.** a colourless or pale yellow liquid mixture with a burning taste and penetrating odour distilled from wood tar, esp. from beechwood, contains creosol and other phenols, and is used as an antiseptic. **2.** Also called: **coal-tar creosote.** a thick dark liquid mixture prepared from coal tar, containing phenols: used as a preservative for wood. ~*vb.* **3.** to treat (wood) with creosote. [C19: from Greek *kreas* flesh + *sōtēr* preserver, from *sōzein* to keep safe] —**creosotic** (ˌkrɪəˈsɒtɪk) *adj.*

creosote bush *n.* a shrub, *Larrea* (or *Covillea*) *tridentata* of the western U.S. and Mexico, that has resinous leaves with an odour resembling creosote: family *Zygophyllaceae.* Also called: **greasewood.**

crepe *or* **crape** (kreɪp) *n.* **1. a.** a light cotton, silk, or other fabric with a fine ridged or crinkled surface. **b.** (*as modifier*): *a crepe dress.* **2.** a black armband originally made of this, worn as a sign of mourning. **3.** a very thin pancake, often rolled or folded around a filling. **4.** short for **crepe paper** or **crepe rubber.** ~*vb.* **5.** (*tr.*) to cover or drape with crepe. [C19: from French *crêpe,* from Latin *crispus* curled, uneven, wrinkled]

crepe de Chine (kreɪp də ʃiːn) *n.* **a.** a very thin crepe of silk or a similar light fabric. **b.** (*as modifier*): *a crepe-de-Chine blouse.* [C19: from French: Chinese crepe]

crepe hair *n.* artificial hair, usually plaited and made of wool or vegetable fibre, used in theatrical make-up.

crepe paper *n.* thin crinkled coloured paper, resembling crepe and used for decorations.

creperie (ˈkrɛpərɪ, ˈkreɪp-) *n.* an eating establishment that specializes in pancakes; pancake house.

crepe rubber *n.* **1.** a type of crude natural rubber in the form of colourless or pale yellow crinkled sheets, prepared by pressing bleached coagulated latex through corrugated rollers: used for the soles of shoes and in making certain surgical and medical goods. Sometimes shortened to **crepe.** Compare **smoked rubber.** **2.** a similar synthetic rubber.

crêpe suzette (kreɪp suːˈzɛt) *n., pl.* **crêpes suzettes.** (*sometimes pl.*) an orange-flavoured pancake flambéed in a liqueur or brandy.

crepitate (ˈkrɛpɪˌteɪt) *vb.* (*intr.*) to make a rattling or crackling sound; rattle or crackle. [C17: from Latin *crepitāre*] —ˈ**crepitant** *adj.*

crepitation (ˌkrɛpɪˈteɪʃən) *n.* **1.** the act of crepitating. **2.** *Zoology.* the sudden expulsion of an acrid fluid by some beetles as a means of self-defence. **3.** another name for **crepitus.**

crepitus (ˈkrɛpɪtəs) *n.* **1.** a crackling chest sound heard in pneumonia and other lung diseases. **2.** the grating sound of two ends of a broken bone rubbing together. ~Also called: **crepitation.** [C19: from Latin, from *crepāre* to crack, creak]

crept (krɛpt) *vb.* the past tense and past participle of **creep.**

crepuscular (krɪˈpʌskjʊlə) *adj.* **1.** of or like twilight; dim. **2.** (of certain insects, birds, and other animals) active at twilight or just before dawn. [C17: from Latin *crepusculum* dusk, from *creper* dark]

crepy *or* **crepey** (ˈkreɪpɪ) *adj.* (esp. of the skin) having a dry wrinkled appearance like crepe.

Cres. *abbrev. for* Crescent.

crescendo (krɪˈʃɛndəʊ) *n., pl.* **-dos** *or* **-di** (-dɪ). **1.** *Music.* **a.** a gradual increase in loudness or the musical direction or symbol indicating this. Abbrev.: **cresc.** Symbol: $<$ (written over the music affected). **b.** (*as modifier*): *a crescendo passage.* **2.** any similar gradual increase in loudness: *the cheers reached a crescendo.* ~*vb.* **-does, -doing, -doed.** **3.** (*intr.*) to increase in loudness or force. ~*adv.* **4.** with a crescendo. [C18: from Italian, literally: increasing, from *crescere* to grow, from Latin]

crescent (ˈkrɛsᵊnt, -zᵊnt) *n.* **1.** the biconcave shape of the moon in its first or last quarters. **2.** any shape or object resembling this. **3.** *Chiefly Brit.* **a.** a crescent-shaped street, often lined with houses of the same style. **b.** (*cap. when part of a name*): *Pelham Crescent.* **4.** *Heraldry.* a crescent moon, used as the cadency mark of a second son. **5.** (*often cap.* and preceded by *the*) **a.** the emblem of Islam or Turkey. **b.** Islamic or Turkish power. ~*adj.* **6.** *Archaic or poetic.* increasing or growing. [C14: from Latin *crescēns* increasing, from *crescere* to grow] —**crescentic** (krəˈsɛntɪk) *adj.*

cresol (ˈkriːsɒl) *n.* an aromatic compound derived from phenol, existing in three isomeric forms: found in coal tar and creosote and used in making synthetic resins and as an antiseptic and disinfectant; hydroxytoluene. Formula: $C_6H_4(CH_3)OH$. Also called: **cresylic acid.** Systematic name: **methylphenol.**

cress (krɛs) *n.* any of various cruciferous plants of the genera *Lepidum, Cardamine, Arabis,* etc., having pungent-tasting leaves often used in salads and as a garnish. See also **watercress, garden cress.** [Old English *cressa;* related to Old High German *cresso* cress, *kresan* to crawl]

cresset (ˈkrɛsɪt) *n. History.* a metal basket mounted on a pole in which oil or pitch was burned for illumination. [C14: from Old French *craisset,* from *craisse* GREASE]

crest (krɛst) *n.* **1.** a tuft or growth of feathers, fur, or skin along the top of the heads of some birds, reptiles, and other animals. **2.** something resembling or suggesting this. **3.** the top, highest point, or highest stage of something. **4.** a ridge on the neck of a horse, dog, lion, etc. **5.** the mane or hair growing from this ridge. **6.** an ornamental piece, such as a plume, on top of a helmet. **7.** *Heraldry.* a symbol of a family or office, usually representing a beast or bird, borne in addition to a coat of arms and used in medieval times to decorate the helmet. **8.** a ridge along the top of a roof, wall, etc. **9.** a ridge along the surface of a bone. **10.** Also called: **cresting.** *Archery.* identifying rings painted around an arrow shaft. ~*vb.* **11.** (*intr.*) to come or rise to a high point. **12.** (*tr.*) to lie at the top of; cap. **13.** (*tr.*) to go to or reach the top of (a hill, wave, etc.). [C14: from Old French *creste,* from Latin *crista*] —ˈ**crested** *adj.* —ˈ**crestless** *adj.*

crested dog's-tail *n.* a common wiry perennial grass, *Cynosurus cristatus,* of meadows and pasture. [C19: named from the fancied resemblance between its one-sided flower spike and a dog's feathery tail]

crested tit *n.* a small European songbird, *Parus cristatus,* that has a greyish-brown plumage with a prominent speckled black-and-white crest: family *Paridae* (tits).

crestfallen (ˈkrɛstˌfɔːlən) *adj.* dejected, depressed, or disheartened. —ˈ**crestˌfallenly** *adv.*

cresting (ˈkrɛstɪŋ) *n.* **1.** an ornamental ridge along the top of a roof, wall, etc. **2.** *Furniture.* a shaped decorative toprail or horizontal carved ornament surmounting a chair, mirror, etc.

cresylic (krɪˈsɪlɪk) *adj.* of, concerned with, or containing creosote or cresol. [C19: from CRE(O)S(OTE) + -YL + -IC]

cretaceous (krɪˈteɪʃəs) *adj.* consisting of or resembling chalk. [C17: from Latin *crētāceus,* from *crēta,* literally: Cretan earth, that is, chalk] —**creˈtaceously** *adv.*

Cretaceous (krɪˈteɪʃəs) *adj.* **1.** of, denoting, or formed in the last period of the Mesozoic era, between the Jurassic and Tertiary periods, lasting 65 million years during which chalk deposits were formed and flowering plants first appeared. ~*n.* **2. the.** the Cretaceous period or rock system.

Cretan (ˈkriːtən) *adj.* **1.** of or relating to Crete, a Greek island in the E Mediterranean. ~*n.* **2.** a native or inhabitant of Crete.

cretic (ˈkriːtɪk) *n. Prosody.* a metrical foot consisting of three syllables, the first long, the second short, and the third long (¯˘¯). Also called: **amphimacer.** Compare **amphibrach.** [C16: from Latin *crēticus* consisting of the amphimacer, literally: Cretan, from Greek *krētikos,* from *Krētē* Crete]

cretin (ˈkrɛtɪn) *n.* **1.** a person afflicted with cretinism: a mentally retarded dwarf with wide-set eyes, a broad flat nose, and protruding tongue. **2.** a person considered to be extremely stupid. [C18: from French *crétin,* from Swiss French *crestin,* from Latin *Chrīstiānus* CHRISTIAN, alluding to the humanity of such people, despite their handicaps] —ˈ**cretinˌoid** *adj.* —ˈ**cretinous** *adj.*

cretinism (ˈkrɛtɪˌnɪzəm) *n.* a condition arising from a deficiency of thyroid hormone, present from birth, characterized by dwarfism and mental retardation. See also **myxoedema.**

cretonne (krɛˈtɒn, ˈkrɛtɒn) *n.* **a.** a heavy cotton or linen fabric with a printed design, used for furnishing. **b.** (*as modifier*): *cretonne chair covers.* [C19: from French, from *Creton* Norman village where it originated]

Creutzfeldt-Jakob disease (ˈkrɔɪtsfɛlt ˈjɑːkɒp) *n. Pathol.* a fatal slow-developing virus disease that affects the central nervous system, characterized by mental deterioration and loss of coordination of the limbs. [C20: named after Hans G. *Creutzfeldt* (1885–1964) and Alfons *Jakob* (1884–1931), German physicians]

crevasse (krɪˈvæs) *n.* **1.** a deep crack or fissure, esp. in the ice of a glacier. **2.** *U.S.* a break in a river embankment. ~*vb.* **3.** (*tr.*) *U.S.* to make a break or fissure in (a dyke, wall, etc.). [C19: from French: CREVICE]

crevice (ˈkrevɪs) *n.* a narrow fissure or crack; split; cleft. [C14: from Old French *crevace,* from *crever* to burst, from Latin *crepāre* to crack]

crew[1] (kruː) *n.* (*sometimes functioning as pl.*) **1.** the men who man a ship, boat, aircraft, etc. **2.** *Nautical.* a group of people assigned to a particular job or type of work. **3.** *Informal.* a gang, company, or crowd. **4.** *Archaic.* a band of armed men. ~*vb.* **5.** to serve on (a ship) as a member of the crew. [C15 *crue* (military) reinforcement, from Old French *creue* augmentation, from Old French *creistre* to increase, from Latin *crescere*]

crew[2] (kruː) *vb.* a past tense of **crow**[2].

crew cut *n.* a closely cropped haircut for men, originating in the U.S. [C20: from the style of haircut worn by the boat crews at Harvard and Yale Universities]

crewel (ˈkruːɪl) *n.* a loosely twisted worsted yarn, used in fancy work and embroidery. [C15: of unknown origin] —ˈ**crewelist** *n.* —ˈ**crewel,work** *n.*

crew neck *n.* a plain round neckline in sweaters. —ˈ**crew-,neck** *or* ˈ**crew-,necked** *adj.*

crib (krɪb) *n.* **1.** a child's bed with slatted wooden sides; cot. **2.** a cattle stall or pen. **3.** a fodder rack or manger. **4.** a bin or granary for storing grain, etc. **5.** a small crude cottage or room. **6.** *N.Z.* a weekend cottage: term is South Island usage only. **7.** any small confined space. **8.** *Informal.* a brothel. **9.** a wicker basket. **10.** a representation of the manger in which the infant Jesus was laid at birth. **11.** *Informal.* a theft, esp. of another's writing or thoughts. **12.** Also called (esp. U.S.): **pony.** *Informal, chiefly Brit.* a translation of a foreign text or a list of answers used by students, often illicitly, as an aid in lessons, examinations, etc. **13.** short for **cribbage. 14.** *Cribbage.* the discard pile. **15.** Also called: **cribwork.** a framework of heavy timbers laid in layers at right angles to one another, used in the construction of foundations, mines, etc. **16.** a storage area for floating logs contained by booms. **17.** *Austral. and N.Z.* food, esp. a light meal. ~*vb.* **cribs, cribbing, cribbed. 18.** (*tr.*) to put or enclose in or as if in a crib; furnish with a crib. **19.** (*tr.*) *Informal.* to steal (another's writings or thoughts). **20.** (*intr.*) *Informal.* to copy either from a crib or from someone else during a lesson or examination. **21.** (*tr.*) to line (a construction hole) with timber beams, logs, or planks. **22.** (*intr.*) *Informal.* to grumble. [Old English *cribb;* related to Old Saxon *kribbia,* Old High German *krippa;* compare Middle High German *krēbe* basket] —ˈ**cribber** *n.*

cribbage (ˈkrɪbɪdʒ) *n.* a game of cards for two to four, in which players try to win a set number of points before their opponents. Often shortened to **crib.** [C17: of uncertain origin]

cribbage board *n.* a board, with pegs and holes, used for scoring at cribbage.

crib-biting *n.* a harmful habit of horses in which the animal leans on the manger or seizes it with the teeth and swallows a gulp of air. —ˈ**crib-,biter** *n.*

crib death *n.* the U.S. and Canadian term for **cot death.**

cribellum (krɪˈbɛləm) *n., pl.* **-la** (-lə). a sievelike spinning organ in certain spiders that occurs between the spinnerets. [C19: New Latin, from Late Latin *cribellum,* diminutive of Latin *cribrum* a sieve]

cribriform (ˈkrɪbrɪ,fɔːm) *or* **cribrous** (ˈkrɪbrəs) *or* **cribrose** (ˈkraɪ,brəʊs) *adj. Anatomy, botany.* pierced with holes; sievelike. [C18: from New Latin *crībriformis,* from Latin *crībrum* a sieve + -FORM]

crib-wall *n. N.Z.* a supporting wall constructed by laying cribs at right angles to each other, as in cribwork.

cribwork (ˈkrɪb,wɜːk) *n.* another name for **crib** (sense 15).

crick[1] (krɪk) *Informal.* ~*n.* **1.** a painful muscle spasm or cramp, esp. in the neck or back. ~*vb.* **2.** (*tr.*) to cause a crick in (the neck, back, etc.). [C15: of uncertain origin]

crick[2] (krɪk) *n. U.S. and Canadian.* a dialect word for **creek** (sense 2).

cricket[1] (ˈkrɪkɪt) *n.* **1.** any insect of the orthopterous family *Gryllidae,* having long antennae and, in the males, the ability to produce a chirping sound (stridulation) by rubbing together the leathery forewings. **2.** any of various related insects, such as the mole cricket. [C14: from Old French *criquet,* from *criquer* to creak, of imitative origin]

cricket[2] (ˈkrɪkɪt) *n.* **1. a.** a game played by two teams of eleven players on a field with a wicket at either end of a 22-yard pitch, the object being for one side to score runs by hitting a hard leather-covered ball with a bat while the other side tries to dismiss them by bowling, catching, running them out, etc. **b.** (*as modifier*): *a cricket bat.* **2. not cricket.** *Informal.* not fair play. ~*vb.* (*intr.*) **3.** to play cricket. [C16: from Old French *criquet* goal post, wicket, of uncertain origin] —ˈ**cricketer** *n.*

cricket[3] (ˈkrɪkɪt) *n.* a small low stool. [C17: of unknown origin]

cricoid (ˈkraɪkɔɪd) *adj.* **1.** of or relating to the ring-shaped lowermost cartilage of the larynx. ~*n.* **2.** this cartilage. [C18: from New Latin *cricoīdes,* from Greek *krikoeidēs* ring-shaped, from *krikos* ring]

cri de coeur (kriː də kɜː) *n., pl.* **cris de coeur.** a cry from the heart; heartfelt or sincere appeal. [C20: altered from French *cri du coeur*]

crier (ˈkraɪə) *n.* **1.** a person or animal that cries. **2.** (formerly) an official who made public announcements, esp. in a town or court. **3.** a person who shouts advertisements about the goods he is selling.

crikey (ˈkraɪkɪ) *interj. Slang.* an expression of surprise. [C19: euphemistic for *Christ!*]

crim (krɪm) *n., adj. Austral. and N.Z. slang.* short for **criminal.**

crim. *abbrev. for* criminal.

crim. con. *Law. abbrev. for* criminal conversation.

crime (kraɪm) *n.* **1.** an act or omission prohibited and punished by law. **2. a.** unlawful acts in general: *a wave of crime.* **b.** (*as modifier*): *crime wave.* **3.** an evil act. **4.** *Informal.* something to be regretted: *it is a crime that he died young.* [C14: from Old French, from Latin *crīmen* verdict, accusation, crime]

Crimean (kraɪˈmɪən) *adj.* of or relating to Crimea, a peninsula in S Ukraine.

crime passionnel (*French* krim pasjɔnɛl) *n., pl.* **crimes passionnels.** a crime committed from passion, esp. sexual passion. Also called: **crime of passion.** [from French]

crime sheet *n. Mil.* a record of an individual's offences against regulations.

criminal (ˈkrɪmɪnᵊl) *n.* **1.** a person charged with and convicted of crime. **2.** a person who commits crimes for a living. ~*adj.* **3.** of, involving, or guilty of crime. **4.** (*prenominal*) of or relating to crime or its punishment: *criminal court; criminal lawyer.* **5.** *Informal.* senseless or deplorable: *a criminal waste of money.* [C15: from Late Latin *crīminālis;* see CRIME, -AL[1]] —ˈ**criminally** *adv.*

criminal conversation *n.* **1.** (formerly) a common law action brought by a husband by which he claimed damages against an adulterer. **2.** another term for **adultery.**

criminality (,krɪmɪˈnælɪtɪ) *n., pl.* **-ties. 1.** the state or quality of being criminal. **2.** (*often pl.*) *Now rare.* a criminal act or practice.

criminalize *or* **criminalise** (ˈkrɪmɪnə,laɪz) to declare (an action or activity) criminal. —,**criminaliˈzation** *or* ,**criminaliˈsation** *n.*

criminal law *n.* the body of law dealing with the constitution of offences and the punishment of offenders.

criminate (ˈkrɪmɪ,neɪt) *vb.* (*tr.*) *Rare.* **1.** to charge with a crime; accuse. **2.** to condemn or censure (an action, event, etc.). **3.** short for **incriminate.** [C17: from Latin *crīminārī* to accuse] —,**crimiˈnation** *n.* —ˈ**criminative** *or* **criminatory** (ˈkrɪmɪnətərɪ, -trɪ) *adj.* —ˈ**crimi,nator** *n.*

criminology (,krɪmɪˈnɒlədʒɪ) *n.* the scientific study of crime, criminal behaviour, law enforcement, etc. See also **penology.** [C19: from Latin *crimin-* CRIME, -LOGY] —**criminological** (,krɪmɪnəˈlɒdʒɪkᵊl) *or* ,**criminoˈlogic** *adj.* —,**criminoˈlogically** *adv.* —,**crimiˈnologist** *n.*

crimmer (ˈkrɪmə) *n.* a variant spelling of **krimmer.**

crimp[1] (krɪmp) *vb.* (*tr.*) **1.** to fold or press into ridges. **2.** to fold and pinch together (something, such as the edges of two pieces of metal). **3.** to curl or wave (the hair) tightly, esp. with curling tongs. **4.** to decorate (the edge of pastry) by pinching with the fingers to give a fluted effect. **5.** to gash (fish or meat) with a knife to make the flesh firmer and crisper when cooked. **6.** to bend or mould (leather) into shape, as for shoes. **7.** *Metallurgy.* to bend the edges of (a metal plate) before forming into a cylinder. **8.** *U.S. informal.* to hinder. ~*n.* **9.** the act or result of folding or pressing together or into ridges. **10.** a tight wave or curl in the hair. **11.** a crease or fold in a metal sheet for rigidity or to make a lapped joint. **12.** the natural wave of wool fibres. [Old English *crympan;* related to *crump* bent, Old Norse *kreppa* to contract, Old High German *crumpf,* Old Swedish *crumb* crooked; see CRAMP] —ˈ**crimper** *n.* —ˈ**crimpy** *adj.*

crimp[2] (krɪmp) *n.* **1.** (formerly) a person who swindled or pressganged men into naval or military service. ~*vb.* **2.** to recruit by coercion or under false pretences. [C17: of unknown origin]

crimple (ˈkrɪmpᵊl) *vb.* to crumple, wrinkle, or curl.

Crimplene (ˈkrɪmpliːn) *n. Trademark.* a synthetic material similar to Terylene, characterized by its crease-resistance.

crimson (ˈkrɪmzən) *n.* **1. a.** a deep or vivid red colour. **b.** (*as adj.*): *a crimson rose.* ~*vb.* **2.** to make or become crimson. **3.** (*intr.*) to blush. [C14: from Old Spanish *cremesin,* from Arabic *qirmizi* red of the kermes, from *qirmiz* KERMES] —ˈ**crimsonness** *n.*

cringe (krɪndʒ) *vb.* (*intr.*) **1.** to shrink or flinch, esp. in fear or servility. **2.** to behave in a servile or timid way. **3.** *Informal.* **a.** to wince in embarrassment or distaste. **b.** to experience a sudden feeling of embarrassment or distaste. ~*n.* **4.** the act of cringing. **5. the cultural cringe.** *Austral.* subservience to overseas cultural standards. [Old English *cringan* to yield in battle; related to Old Norse *krangr* weak, Middle High German *krenken* to weaken] —ˈ**cringer** *n.* —ˈ**cringingly** *adv.*

cringe-making *adj. Brit. informal.* causing feelings of acute embarrassment or distaste.

cringle (ˈkrɪŋgᵊl) *n.* an eye at the edge of a sail, usually formed from a thimble or grommet. [C17: from Low German *Kringel* small RING; see CRANK, CRINKLE]

crinite[1] (ˈkraɪnaɪt) *adj. Biology.* covered with soft hairs or tufts. [C16: from Latin *crīnītus* hairy, from *crīnis* hair]

crinite[2] (ˈkraɪnaɪt, ˈkrɪn-) *n.* short for **encrinite.** [C19: from Greek *krinon* lily + -ITE[1]]
crinkle (ˈkrɪŋkəl) *vb.* **1.** to form or cause to form wrinkles, twists, or folds. **2.** to make or cause to make a rustling noise. *~n.* **3.** a wrinkle, twist, or fold. **4.** a rustling noise. [Old English *crincan* to bend, give way; related to Middle Dutch *krinkelen* to crinkle, Middle High German *krank* weak, ill, *krenken* to weaken]
crinkleroot (ˈkrɪŋkəlˌruːt) *n.* any of several species of the toothwort *Dentaria,* esp. *D. diphylla* of E North America, which has a fleshy pungent rhizome and clusters of white or pinkish flowers: family *Cruciferae* (crucifers).
crinkly (ˈkrɪŋklɪ) *adj.* **1.** wrinkled; crinkled. *~n., pl.* **-lies. 2.** *Slang.* an old person.
crinkum-crankum (ˈkrɪŋkəmˈkræŋkəm) *n.* a fanciful name for any object that is full of twists and turns. [C18: coinage based on CRANK[1]]
crinoid (ˈkraɪnɔɪd, ˈkrɪn-) *n.* **1.** any primitive echinoderm of the class *Crinoidea,* having delicate feathery arms radiating from a central disc. The group includes the free-swimming feather stars, the sessile sea lilies, and many stemmed fossil forms. *~adj.* **2.** of, relating to, or belonging to the *Crinoidea.* **3.** shaped like a lily. [C19: from Greek *krinoeidēs* lily-like] —**criˈnoidal** *adj.*
crinoline (ˈkrɪnəlɪn) *n.* **1.** a stiff fabric, originally of horsehair and linen used in lining garments. **2.** a petticoat stiffened with this, worn to distend skirts, esp. in the mid-19th century. **3.** a framework of steel hoops worn for the same purpose. [C19: from French, from Italian *crinolino,* from *crino* horsehair, from Latin *crīnis* hair + *lino* flax, from Latin *līnum*]
crinum (ˈkraɪnəm) *n.* any plant of the mostly tropical amaryllidaceous genus *Crinum,* having straplike leaves and clusters of lily-like flowers. Also called: **crinum lily.** [Latin: lily, from Greek *krinon*]
criollo (kriːˈəʊləʊ; *Spanish* ˈkrjoʎo) *n., pl.* **-los** (-ləʊz; *Spanish* -ʎos). **1.** a native or inhabitant of Latin America of European descent, esp. of Spanish descent. **2. a.** any of various South American breeds of domestic animal. **b.** (*as modifier*): *a criollo pony.* **3.** a high-quality variety of cocoa. *~adj.* **4.** of, relating to, or characteristic of a criollo or criollos. [Spanish: native; see CREOLE]
crios (krɪs) *n. Irish.* a multicoloured woven woollen belt traditionally worn by men in the Aran Islands. [Irish Gaelic]
cripes (kraɪps) *interj. Slang.* an expression of surprise. [C20: euphemistic for *Christ!*]
cripple (ˈkrɪpəl) *n.* **1.** a person who is lame. **2.** a person who is or seems disabled or deficient in some way: *a mental cripple.* **3.** *U.S. dialect.* a dense thicket, usually in marshy land. *~vb.* **4.** (*tr.*) to make a cripple of; disable. [Old English *crypel;* related to *crēopan* to CREEP, Old Frisian *kreppel* a cripple, Middle Low German *kröpel*] —ˈ**crippler** *n.*
crippling (ˈkrɪplɪŋ) *adj.* very damaging or injurious. —ˈ**crippling̃ly** *adv.*
crisis (ˈkraɪsɪs) *n., pl.* **-ses** (-siːz). **1.** a crucial stage or turning point in the course of something, esp. in a sequence of events or a disease. **2.** an unstable period, esp. one of extreme trouble or danger in politics, economics, etc. **3.** *Pathol.* a sudden change, for better or worse, in the course of a disease. [C15: from Latin: decision, from Greek *krisis,* from *krinein* to decide]
crisp (krɪsp) *adj.* **1.** dry and brittle. **2.** fresh and firm: *crisp lettuce.* **3.** invigorating or bracing: *a crisp breeze.* **4.** clear; sharp: *crisp reasoning.* **5.** lively or stimulating: *crisp conversation.* **6.** clean and orderly; neat: *a crisp appearance.* **7.** concise and pithy; terse: *a crisp reply.* **8.** wrinkled or curly: *crisp hair.* *~vb.* **9.** to make or become crisp. *~n.* **10.** *Brit.* a very thin slice of potato fried and eaten cold as a snack. **11.** something that is crisp. [Old English, from Latin *crispus* curled, uneven, wrinkled] —ˈ**crisply** *adv.* —ˈ**crispness** *n.*
crispate (ˈkrɪspeɪt, -pɪt), **crispated,** *or* **crisped** *adj.* having a curled or waved appearance. [C19: from Latin *crispāre* to curl]
crispation (krɪˈspeɪʃən) *n.* **1.** the act of curling or state of being curled. **2.** any slight muscular spasm or contraction that gives a creeping sensation. **3.** a slight undulation, such as a ripple on the surface of water.
crispbread (ˈkrɪspˌbrɛd) *n.* a thin dry biscuit made of wheat or rye.
crisper (ˈkrɪspə) *n.* a compartment in a refrigerator for storing salads, vegetables, etc., in order to keep them fresh.
crispy (ˈkrɪspɪ) *adj.* **crispier, crispiest. 1.** crisp. **2.** having waves or curls. —ˈ**crispily** *adv.* —ˈ**crispiness** *n.*
crisscross (ˈkrɪsˌkrɒs) *vb.* **1.** to move or cause to move in a crosswise pattern. **2.** to mark with or consist of a pattern of crossing lines. *~adj.* **3.** (esp. of a number of lines) crossing one another in different directions. *~n.* **4.** a pattern made of crossing lines. **5.** a U.S. term for **noughts and crosses.** *~adv.* **6.** in a crosswise manner or pattern.
crissum (ˈkrɪsəm) *n., pl.* **-sa** (-sə). the area or feathers surrounding the cloaca of a bird. [C19: from New Latin, from Latin *crissāre* to move the haunches] —ˈ**crissal** *adj.*
crista (ˈkrɪstə) *n., pl.* **-tae** (-tiː). *Biology.* a structure resembling a ridge or crest, as on the inner membrane of a mitochondrion. [C20: from Latin: CREST]
cristate (ˈkrɪsteɪt) *or* **cristated** *adj.* **1.** having a crest. **2.** forming a crest. [C17: from Latin *cristātus,* from *crista* CREST]
cristobalite (krɪsˈtəʊbəˌlaɪt) *n.* a white microcrystalline mineral consisting of silica and occurring in volcanic rocks. Formula: SiO_2. [C19: from German, named after Cerro San *Cristóbal,* Mexico, where it was discovered]
crit. *abbrev. for:* **1.** *Med.* critical. **2.** criticism.
criterion (kraɪˈtɪərɪən) *n., pl.* **-ria** (-rɪə) *or* **-rions. 1.** a standard by which something can be judged or decided. **2.** *Philosophy.* a defining characteristic of something. [C17: from Greek *kritērion* from *kritēs* judge, from *krinein* to decide]
▷**Usage.** *Criteria,* the plural of *criterion,* is not acceptable as a singular noun in careful written and spoken English: *this criterion is not valid; these criteria are not valid.*
critic (ˈkrɪtɪk) *n.* **1.** a person who judges something. **2.** a professional judge of art, music, literature, etc. **3.** a person who often finds fault and criticizes. [C16: from Latin *criticus,* from Greek *kritikos* capable of judging, from *kritēs* judge; see CRITERION]
critical (ˈkrɪtɪkəl) *adj.* **1.** containing or making severe or negative judgments. **2.** containing careful or analytical evaluations: *a critical dissertation.* **3.** of or involving a critic or criticism. **4.** of or forming a crisis; crucial; decisive: *a critical operation.* **5.** urgently needed: *critical medical supplies.* **6.** *Physics.* of, denoting, or concerned with a state in which the properties of a system undergo an abrupt change: *a critical temperature.* **7. go critical.** (of a nuclear power station or reactor) to reach a state in which a nuclear-fission chain reaction becomes self-sustaining. —ˈ**critically** *adv.* —ˈ**criticalness** *n.*
critical angle *n.* **1.** the smallest possible angle of incidence for which light rays are totally reflected at an interface between substances of different refractive index. **2.** another name for **stalling angle.**
critical apparatus *n.* the variant readings, footnotes, etc. found in a scholarly work or a critical edition of a text. Also called: **apparatus criticus.**
critical constants *pl. n.* the physical constants that express the properties of a substance in its critical state. See **critical pressure, critical temperature.**
critical damping *n. Physics.* the minimum amount of viscous damping that results in a displaced system returning to its original position without oscillation. Symbol: C_c
criticality (ˌkrɪtɪˈkælɪtɪ) *n.* **1.** the state of being critical. **2.** *Physics.* the condition in a nuclear reactor when the fissionable material can sustain a chain reaction by itself.
critical mass *n.* the minimum mass of fissionable material that can sustain a nuclear chain reaction.
critical path analysis *n.* a technique for planning complex projects by analysing alternative systems with reference to the critical path, which is the sequence of stages requiring the longest time. Compare **programme evaluation and review technique.**
critical period *n. Psychol.* a period in a lifetime during which a specific stage of development usually occurs. If it fails to do so, it cannot readily occur afterwards.
critical point *n.* **1.** *Physics.* **a.** the point on a phase diagram that represents the critical state of a substance. **b.** another name for **critical state. 2.** *Maths.* the U.S. name for **stationary point.**
critical pressure *n.* the pressure of a gas or the saturated vapour pressure of a substance in its critical state.
critical region *n.* that part of a statistical distribution in which the probability of a given hypothesis is less than the chosen significance level, so that the hypothesis would be rejected.
critical state *n.* the state of a substance in which two of its phases have the same temperature, pressure, and volume. Also called: **critical point.**
critical temperature *n.* the temperature of a substance in its critical state. A gas can only be liquefied by pressure alone at temperatures below its critical temperature.
critical volume *n.* the volume occupied by one mole or unit mass of a substance in its critical state.
criticism (ˈkrɪtɪˌsɪzəm) *n.* **1.** the act or an instance of making an unfavourable or severe judgment, comment, etc. **2.** the analysis or evaluation of a work of art, literature, etc. **3.** the occupation of a critic. **4.** a work that sets out to evaluate or analyse. **5.** Also called: **textual criticism.** the investigation of a particular text, with related material, in order to establish an authentic text.
criticize *or* **criticise** (ˈkrɪtɪˌsaɪz) *vb.* **1.** to judge (something) with disapproval; censure. **2.** to evaluate or analyse (something). —ˈ**critiˌcizable** *or* ˈ**critiˌcisable** *adj.* —ˈ**critiˌcizer** *or* ˈ**critiˌciser** *n.* —ˈ**critiˌcizingly** *or* ˈ**critiˌcisingly** *adv.*
critique (krɪˈtiːk) *n.* **1.** a critical essay or commentary, esp. on artistic work. **2.** the act or art of criticizing. [C17: from French, from Greek *kritikē,* from *kritikos* able to discern]
critter (ˈkrɪtə) *n. U.S. and Canadian.* a dialect word for **creature.**
CRO *abbrev. for:* **1.** cathode-ray oscilloscope. **2.** (in Britain) Community Relations Officer. **3.** Criminal Records Office.
croak (krəʊk) *vb.* **1.** (*intr.*) (of frogs, crows, etc.) to make a low, hoarse cry. **2.** to utter (something) in this manner, esp. when exhausted: *he croaked out the news.* **3.** (*intr.*) to grumble or be pessimistic. **4.** *Slang.* **a.** (*intr.*) to die. **b.** (*tr.*) to kill. *~n.* **5.** a low hoarse utterance or sound. [Old English *crācettan;* related to Old Norse *krāka* a crow; see CREAK] —ˈ**croaky** *adj.* —ˈ**croakily** *adv.* —ˈ**croakiness** *n.*

croaker ('krəʊkə) *n.* **1.** an animal, bird, etc., that croaks. **2.** any of various mainly tropical marine sciaenid fishes, such as *Umbrina roncador* (**yellowfin croaker**), that utter croaking noises. **3.** a grumbling person.

Croat ('krəʊæt) *n.* **1. a.** a native or inhabitant of the republic of Croatia, formerly part of Yugoslavia. **b.** a speaker of Croatian, esp. one in regions bordering on Croatia. *~n., adj.* **2.** another word for **Croatian.**

Croatian (krəʊ'eɪʃən) *adj.* **1.** of, relating to, or characteristic of Croatia, its people, or their dialect of Serbo-Croatian. *~n.* **2.** the dialect of Serbo-Croatian spoken in Croatia. **3. a.** a native or inhabitant of Croatia. **b.** a speaker of the Croatian dialect, esp. one in regions bordering on Croatia.

crocein ('krəʊsɪɪn) *n.* any one of a group of red or orange acid azo dyes. [C20: from Latin *croceus* yellow + -IN]

crochet ('krəʊʃeɪ, -ʃɪ) *vb.* **-chets** (-ʃeɪz, -ʃɪz), **-cheting** (-ʃeɪɪŋ, -ʃɪɪŋ), **-cheted** (-ʃeɪd, -ʃɪd). **1.** to make (a piece of needlework, a garment, etc.) by looping and intertwining thread with a hooked needle (**crochet hook**). *~n.* **2.** work made by crocheting. **3.** *Architect.* another name for **crocket. 4.** *Zoology.* a hooklike structure of insect larvae that aids locomotion. [C19: from French *crochet,* diminutive of *croc* hook, probably of Scandinavian origin] —'**crocheter** *n.*

crocidolite (krəʊ'sɪdəˌlaɪt) *n.* a blue fibrous amphibole mineral consisting of sodium iron silicate: a variety of asbestos used in cement products and pressure piping. [C19: from Greek *krokis* nap on woollen cloth + -LITE]

crock[1] (krɒk) *n.* **1.** an earthen pot, jar, etc. **2.** a piece of broken earthenware. [Old English *crocc* pot; related to Old Norse *krukka* jug, Middle Low German *krūke* pot]

crock[2] (krɒk) *n.* **1.** *Slang, chiefly Brit.* a person or thing, such as a car, that is old or decrepit (esp. in the phrase **old crock). 2.** an old broken-down horse or ewe. *~vb.* **3.** *Slang, chiefly Brit.* to become or cause to become weak or disabled. [C15: originally Scottish; related to Norwegian *krake* unhealthy animal, Dutch *kraak* decrepit person or animal]

crock[3] (krɒk) *n.* **1.** *Dialect, chiefly Brit.* soot or smut. **2.** colour that rubs off fabric. *~vb.* **3.** (*tr.*) *Dialect, chiefly Brit.* to soil with or as if with soot. **4.** (*intr.*) (of a dyed fabric) to release colour when rubbed, as a result of imperfect dyeing. [C17: probably from CROCK[1]]

crocked (krɒkt) *adj. Slang.* **1.** *Brit.* injured. **2.** *U.S. and Canadian.* drunk.

crockery ('krɒkərɪ) *n.* china dishes, earthen vessels, etc., collectively.

crocket ('krɒkɪt) *n.* a carved ornament in the form of a curled leaf or cusp, used in Gothic architecture. Also called: **crochet.** [C17: from Anglo-French *croket* a little hook, from *croc* hook, of Scandinavian origin]

crocodile ('krɒkəˌdaɪl) *n.* **1.** any large tropical reptile, such as *C. niloticus* (**African crocodile**), of the family *Crocodylidae:* order *Crocodilia* (crocodilians). They have a broad head, tapering snout, massive jaws, and a thick outer covering of bony plates. **2.** any other reptile of the order *Crocodilia;* a crocodilian. **3. a.** leather made from the skin of any of these animals. **b.** (*as modifier*): *crocodile shoes.* **4.** *Brit. informal.* a line of schoolchildren walking two by two. [C13: via Old French, from Latin *crocodīlus,* from Greek *krokodeilos* lizard, ultimately from *krokē* pebble + *drilos* worm; referring to its fondness for basking on shingle]

crocodile bird *n.* an African courser, *Pluvianus aegyptius,* that lives close to rivers and is thought to feed on insects parasitic on crocodiles.

crocodile clip *n.* a clasp with serrated interlocking edges used for making electrical connections.

crocodile tears *pl. n.* an insincere show of grief; false tears. [from the belief that crocodiles wept over their prey to allure further victims]

crocodilian (ˌkrɒkə'dɪlɪən) *n.* **1.** any large predatory reptile of the order *Crocodilia,* which includes the crocodiles, alligators, and caymans. They live in or near water and have a long broad snout, powerful jaws, a four-chambered heart, and socketed teeth. *~adj.* **2.** of, relating to, or belonging to the *Crocodilia.* **3.** of, relating to, or resembling a crocodile.

crocoite ('krəʊkəʊˌaɪt) *or* **crocoisite** (krəʊ'kəʊɪˌsaɪt, 'krəʊkwəˌsaɪt) *n.* a rare orange secondary mineral consisting of lead chromate in monoclinic crystalline form. Formula: $PbCrO_4$. Also called: **red-lead ore.** [C19: from Greek *krokoeis* saffron-coloured, golden + -ITE[1]]

crocosmia (krə'kɒzmɪə) *n.* any plant of the cormous S. African genus *Crocosmia,* including the plant known to gardeners as montbretia, a cross between *C. anrea* and *C. pottsii,* with graceful orange or yellow flowers: family *Iridaceae.* [New Latin, from Greek *krokos* saffron + *osmē* smell, from the odour of the dried flowers when wetted]

crocus ('krəʊkəs) *n., pl.* **-cuses. 1.** any plant of the iridaceous genus *Crocus,* widely cultivated in gardens, having white, yellow, or purple flowers. See also **autumn crocus. 2.** another name for **jeweller's rouge.** *~adj.* **3.** of a saffron yellow colour. [C17: from New Latin, from Latin *crocus,* from Greek *krokos* saffron, of Semitic origin]

Croesus ('kriːsəs) *n.* a very rich man. [named after a king (died ?546 B.C.) of Lydia, in Asia Minor, noted for his great wealth]

croft (krɒft) *n. Brit.* **1.** a small enclosed plot of land, adjoining a house, worked by the occupier and his family, esp. in Scotland. **2.** *Lancashire dialect.* a patch of wasteland, formerly one used for bleaching fabric in the sun. [Old English *croft;* related to Middle Dutch *krocht* hill, field, Old English *creopan* to CREEP]

crofter ('krɒftə) *n. Brit.* an owner or tenant of a small farm, esp. in Scotland or northern England.

crofting ('krɒftɪŋ) *n. Brit.* the system or occupation of working land in crofts.

Crohn's disease (krəʊnz) *n.* inflammation, thickening, and ulceration of any of various parts of the intestine, esp. the ileum. Also called: **regional enteritis.** [C20: named after B. B. *Crohn* (1884–1983), U.S. physician]

croissant ('krwʌsɒŋ; *French* krwasɑ̃) *n.* a flaky crescent-shaped bread roll made of a yeast dough similar to puff pastry. [French, literally: crescent]

Croix de Guerre *French.* (krwa də gɛr) *n.* a French military decoration awarded for gallantry in battle: established 1915. [literally: cross of war]

Cro-Magnon man ('krəʊ'mænjɒn, -'mægnɒn) *n.* an early type of modern man, *Homo sapiens,* who lived in Europe during late Palaeolithic times, having tall stature, long head, and a relatively large cranial capacity. [C19: named after the cave in the Dordogne, France, where the remains were first found]

crombec ('krɒmbɛk) *n.* any African Old World warbler of the genus *Sylvietta,* having colourful plumage. [C19: via French from Dutch *krom* crooked + *bek* BEAK[1]]

cromlech ('krɒmlɛk) *n.* **1.** a circle of prehistoric standing stones. **2.** (no longer in technical usage) a megalithic chamber tomb or dolmen. [C17: from Welsh, from *crom,* feminine of *crwm* bent, arched + *llech* flat stone]

Cromwellian (krɒm'wɛlɪən) *adj.* **1.** of, relating to, or characteristic of Oliver Cromwell (1599–1658), English general and statesman. *~n.* **2.** a supporter of Oliver Cromwell.

Cromwell Current ('krɒmwɛl, -wəl) *n.* an equatorial Pacific current, flowing eastward from the Hawaiian Islands to the Galápagos Islands. [C20: named after T. *Cromwell* (1922–58), U.S. oceanographer]

crone (krəʊn) *n.* a witchlike old woman. [C14: from Old Northern French *carogne* carrion, ultimately from Latin *caro* flesh]

cronk (krɒŋk) *adj. Austral.* unfit; unsound. [C19: compare CRANK[2]]

crony ('krəʊnɪ) *n., pl.* **-nies.** a friend or companion. [C17: student slang (Cambridge), from Greek *khronios* of long duration, from *khronos* time]

crook (krʊk) *n.* **1.** a curved or hooked thing. **2.** a staff with a hooked end, such as a bishop's crosier or shepherd's staff. **3.** a turn or curve; bend. **4.** *Informal.* a dishonest person, esp. a swindler or thief. **5.** the act or an instance of crooking or bending. **6.** Also called: **shank.** a piece of tubing added to a brass instrument in order to obtain a lower harmonic series. *~vb.* **7.** to bend or curve or cause to bend or curve. *~adj.* **8.** *Austral. and N.Z. slang.* **a.** ill. **b.** of poor quality. **c.** unpleasant; bad. **9. go (off) crook.** *Austral. and N.Z. slang.* to lose one's temper. **10. go crook at** *or* **on.** *Austral. and N.Z. slang.* to rebuke or upbraid. [C12: from Old Norse *krokr* hook; related to Swedish *krok,* Danish *krog* hook, Old High German *krācho* hooked tool]

crookback ('krʊkˌbæk) *n.* a rare word for **hunchback.** —'**crookˌbacked** *adj.*

crooked ('krʊkɪd) *adj.* **1.** bent, angled or winding. **2.** set at an angle; not straight. **3.** deformed or contorted. **4.** *Informal.* dishonest or illegal. **5. crooked on.** (*also* krʊkt) *Austral. informal.* hostile or averse to. —'**crookedly** *adv.* —'**crookedness** *n.*

Crookes lens (krʊks) *n.* a type of lens, used in sunglasses, that is made from glass containing cerium. It reduces the transmission of ultraviolet radiation. [named after Sir William *Crookes* (1832–1919), British chemist and physicist]

Crookes radiometer *n. Physics.* a type of radiometer consisting of an evacuated glass bulb containing a set of lightweight vanes, each blackened on one side. The vanes are mounted on a vertical axis and revolve when light, or other radiant energy, falls on them.

Crookes space *n.* a dark region that occurs near the cathode in some low-pressure gas-discharge tubes. Also called: **Crookes dark space.**

Crookes tube *n.* a type of cathode-ray tube in which the electrons are produced by a glow discharge in a low-pressure gas.

croon (kruːn) *vb.* **1.** to sing or speak in a soft low tone. **2.** *Scot. and northern English dialect.* to lament or wail. *~n.* **3.** a soft low singing or humming. [C14: via Middle Dutch *crōnen* to groan; compare Old High German *chrōnan* to chatter, Latin *gingrīre* to cackle (of geese)] —'**crooner** *n.*

crop (krɒp) *n.* **1.** the produce of cultivated plants, esp. cereals, vegetables, and fruit. **2. a.** the amount of such produce in any particular season. **b.** the yield of some other farm produce: *the lamb crop.* **3.** a group of products, thoughts, people, etc., appearing at one time or in one season: *a crop of new publications.* **4.** the stock of a thonged whip. **5.** short for **riding crop. 6. a.** a pouchlike expanded part of the oesophagus of birds, in which food is stored or partially digested before passing on to the gizzard. **b.** a similar structure in insects, earthworms, and other invertebrates. **7.** the entire tanned hide of an animal. **8.** a short cropped hairstyle. See also **Eton crop.** **9.** a notch in or a piece cut out of the ear of an animal. **10.** the act of cropping. ~*vb.* **crops, cropping, cropped.** (*mainly tr.*) **11.** to cut (hair, grass, etc.) very short. **12.** to cut and collect (mature produce) from the land or plant on which it has been grown. **13.** to clip part of (the ear or ears) of (an animal), esp. as a means of identification. **14.** (*also intr.*) to cause (land) to bear or (of land) to bear or yield a crop: *the land cropped well.* **15.** (of herbivorous animals) to graze on (grass or similar vegetation). **16.** *Photog.* to cut off or mask unwanted edges or areas of (a negative or print). ~See also **crop out, crop up.** [Old English *cropp;* related to Old Norse *kroppr* rump, body, Old High German *kropf* goitre, Norwegian *kröypa* to bend]

crop-dusting *n.* the spreading of fungicide, etc. on crops in the form of dust, often from an aircraft.

crop-eared *adj.* having the ears or hair cut short.

crop out *vb.* (*intr., adv.*) (of a formation of rock strata) to appear or be exposed at the surface of the ground; outcrop.

cropper ('krɒpə) *n.* **1.** a person who cultivates or harvests a crop. **2. a.** a cutting machine for removing the heads from castings and ingots. **b.** a guillotine for cutting lengths of bar or strip. **3.** a machine for shearing the nap from cloth. **4.** a plant or breed of plant that will produce a certain kind of crop under specified conditions: *a poor cropper on light land.* **5.** (*often cap.*) a variety of domestic pigeon with a puffed-out crop. **6. come a cropper.** *Informal.* **a.** to fall heavily. **b.** to fail completely.

crop rotation *n.* the system of growing a sequence of different crops on the same ground so as to maintain or increase its fertility.

crop up *vb.* (*intr., adv.*) *Informal.* to occur or appear, esp. unexpectedly.

croquet ('krəʊkeɪ, -kɪ) *n.* **1.** a game for two to four players who hit a wooden ball through iron hoops with mallets in order to hit a peg. **2.** the act of croqueting. ~*vb.* **-quets** (-keɪz, -kɪz), **-queting** (-keɪɪŋ, -kɪɪŋ), **-queted** (-keɪd, -kɪd). **3.** to drive away (another player's ball) by hitting one's own ball when the two are in contact. [C19: perhaps from French dialect, variant of CROCHET (little hook)]

croquette (krəʊ'kɛt, krɒ-) *n.* a savoury cake of minced meat, fish, etc., fried in breadcrumbs. [C18: from French, from *croquer* to crunch, of imitative origin]

crore (krɔː) *n.* (in Indian English) ten million. [C17: from Hindi *karōr,* from Prakrit *krodi*]

crosier *or* **crozier** ('krəʊʒə) *n.* **1.** a staff surmounted by a crook or cross, carried by bishops as a symbol of pastoral office. **2.** the tip of a young plant, esp. a fern frond, that is coiled into a hook. [C14: from Old French *crossier* staff bearer, from *crosse* pastoral staff, literally: hooked stick, of Germanic origin]

cross (krɒs) *n.* **1.** a structure or symbol consisting essentially of two intersecting lines or pieces at right angles to one another. **2.** a wooden structure used as a means of execution, consisting of an upright post with a transverse piece to which people were nailed or tied. **3.** a representation of the Cross used as an emblem of Christianity or as a reminder of Christ's death. **4.** any mark or shape consisting of two intersecting lines, esp. such a symbol (×) used as a signature, point of intersection, error mark, etc. **5.** a sign representing the Cross made either by tracing a figure in the air or by touching the forehead, breast, and either shoulder in turn. **6.** any conventional variation of the Christian symbol, used emblematically, decoratively, or heraldically, such as a Maltese, tau, or Greek cross. **7.** *Heraldry.* any of several charges in which one line crosses or joins another at right angles. **8.** a cruciform emblem awarded to indicate membership of an order or as a decoration for distinguished service. **9.** (*sometimes cap.*) Christianity or Christendom, esp. as contrasted with non-Christian religions: *Cross and Crescent.* **10.** the place in a town or village where a cross has been set up. **11.** a pipe fitting, in the form of a cross, for connecting four pipes. **12.** *Biology.* **a.** the process of crossing; hybridization. **b.** an individual produced as a result of this process. **13.** a mixture of two qualities or types: *he's a cross between a dictator and a saint.* **14.** an opposition, hindrance, or misfortune; affliction (esp. in the phrase **bear one's cross).** **15.** *Slang.* a match or game in which the outcome has been rigged. **16.** *Slang.* a fraud or swindle. **17.** *Boxing.* a straight punch delivered from the side, esp. with the right hand. **18.** *Football.* the act or an instance of kicking or passing the ball from a wing to the middle of the field. **19. on the cross. a.** diagonally. **b.** *Slang.* dishonestly. ~*vb.* **20.** (sometimes foll. by *over*) to move or go across (something); traverse or intersect: *we crossed the road.* **21. a.** to meet and pass: *the two trains crossed.* **b.** (of each of two letters in the post) to be dispatched before receipt of the other. **22.** (*tr.;* usually foll. by *out, off,* or *through*) to cancel with a cross or with lines; delete. **23.** (*tr.*) to place or put in a form resembling a cross: *to cross one's legs.* **24.** (*tr.*) to mark with a cross or crosses. **25.** (*tr.*) *Brit.* to draw two parallel lines across the face of (a cheque) and so make it payable only into a bank account. **26.** (*tr.*) **a.** to trace the form of the Cross, usually with the thumb or index finger upon (someone or something) in token of blessing. **b.** to make the sign of the Cross upon (oneself). **27.** (*intr.*) (of telephone lines) to interfere with each other so that three or perhaps four callers are connected together at one time. **28.** to cause fertilization between (plants or animals of different breeds, races, varieties, etc.). **29.** (*tr.*) to oppose the wishes or plans of; thwart: *his opponent crosses him at every turn.* **30.** *Football.* to kick or pass (the ball) from a wing to the middle of the field. **31.** (*tr.*) *Nautical.* to set (the yard of a square sail) athwartships. **32. cross a bridge when one comes to it.** to deal with matters, problems, etc., as they arise; not to anticipate difficulties. **33. cross one's fingers.** to fold one finger across another in the hope of bringing good luck: *keep your fingers crossed.* **34. cross one's heart.** to promise or pledge, esp. by making the sign of a cross over one's heart. **35. cross one's mind.** to occur to one briefly or suddenly. **36. cross someone's palm.** to give someone money. **37. cross the path (of).** to meet or thwart (someone). **38. cross swords.** to argue or fight. ~*adj.* **39.** angry; ill-humoured; vexed. **40.** lying or placed across; transverse: *a cross timber.* **41.** involving interchange; reciprocal. **42.** contrary or unfavourable. **43.** another word for **crossbred** (sense 1). **44.** a Brit. slang word for **dishonest.** [Old English *cros,* from Old Irish *cross* (unattested), from Latin *crux;* see CRUX] —'**crosser** *n.* —'**crossly** *adv.* —'**crossness** *n.*

Cross (krɒs) *n.* **the. 1.** the cross on which Jesus Christ was crucified. **2.** the Crucifixion of Jesus.

cross- *combining form.* **1.** indicating action from one individual, group, etc., to another: *cross-cultural; cross-fertilize; cross-refer.* **2.** indicating movement, position, etc., across something (sometimes implying interference, opposition, or contrary action): *crosscurrent; crosstalk.* **3.** indicating a crosslike figure or intersection: *crossbones.* [from CROSS (in various senses)]

crossandra (krɒ'sɑːndrə) *n.* any shrub of the free-flowering mostly African genus *Crossandra,* grown in greenhouses for their large yellow, lilac, or orange flowers: family *Acanthaceae.* [New Latin, from Greek *krossos* fringed + *andros,* genitive of *anēr* man, male (from the fringed anthers)]

cross assembler *n.* an assembler that runs on a computer other than the one for which it assembles programs.

crossbar ('krɒs,bɑː) *n.* **1.** a horizontal bar, line, stripe, etc. **2.** a horizontal beam across a pair of goal posts. **3.** a horizontal bar mounted on vertical posts used in athletics or show-jumping. **4.** the horizontal bar on a man's bicycle that joins the handlebar and saddle supports.

crossbeam ('krɒs,biːm) *n.* a beam that spans from one support to another.

cross bedding *n. Geology.* layering within one or more beds in a series of rock strata that does not run parallel to the plane of stratification. Also called: **false bedding.**

cross-bench *n.* (*usually pl.*) *Brit.* a seat in Parliament occupied by a neutral or independent member. —'**cross-,bencher** *n.*

crossbill ('krɒs,bɪl) *n.* any of various widely distributed finches of the genus *Loxia,* such as *L. curvirostra,* that occur in coniferous woods and have a bill with crossed mandible tips for feeding on conifer seeds.

crossbones ('krɒs,bəʊnz) *pl. n.* See **skull and crossbones.**

crossbow ('krɒs,bəʊ) *n.* a type of medieval bow fixed transversely on a wooden stock grooved to direct a square-headed arrow (quarrel). —'**cross,bowman** *n.*

crossbred ('krɒs,brɛd) *adj.* **1.** (of plants or animals) produced as a result of crossbreeding. ~*n.* **2.** a crossbred plant or animal, esp. an animal resulting from a cross between two pure breeds. Compare **grade** (sense 9), **purebred** (sense 2).

crossbreed ('krɒs,briːd) *vb.* **-breeds, -breeding, -bred. 1.** Also: **interbreed.** to breed (animals or plants) using parents of different races, varieties, breeds, etc. ~*n.* **2.** the offspring produced by such a breeding.

cross-buttock *n.* a wrestling throw in which the hips are used as a fulcrum to throw an opponent.

crosscheck (,krɒs'tʃɛk) *vb.* **1.** to verify (a fact, report, etc.) by considering conflicting opinions or consulting other sources. **2.** (in ice hockey) to check illegally, as by chopping at an opponent's arms or stick. ~*n.* **3.** the act or an instance of crosschecking.

cross colour *n.* distortion in a colour television receiver in which high-frequency luminance detail is interpreted as colour information and reproduced as flashes of spurious colour.

cross-correlation *n. Statistics.* the correlation between two sequences of random variables in a time series.

cross-country *adj., adv.* **1.** by way of fields, woods, etc., as opposed to roads: *cross-country running.* **2.** across a country: *a cross-country railway.* ~*n.* **3.** a long race held over open ground.

cross-cultural *adj.* involving or bridging the differences between cultures.

crosscurrent ('krɒs,kʌrənt) *n.* **1.** a current in a river or sea flowing across another current. **2.** a conflicting tendency moving counter to the usual trend.

cross-curricular *adj. Brit. education.* denoting or relating to an approach to a topic that includes contributions from several different disciplines and viewpoints.

crosscut ('krɒs,kʌt) *adj.* **1.** cut at right angles or obliquely to the major axis. ~*n.* **2.** a transverse cut or course. **3.** a less common word for **short cut. 4.** *Mining.* a tunnel through a vein of ore or from the shaft to a vein. ~*vb.* **-cuts, -cutting, -cut. 5.** to cut across. **6.** Also: **intercut.** *Films.* to link (two sequences or two shots) so that they appear to be taking place at the same time.

crosscut file *n.* a file having two intersecting rows of teeth.

crosscut saw *n.* a saw for cutting timber across the grain.

cross-dating *n. Archaeol.* a method of dating objects, remains, etc., by comparison and correlation with other sites and levels.

cross-dressing *n.* **1.** transvestism. See **transvestite.** **2.** the wearing of clothes normally associated with the opposite sex as a fashion.

crosse (krɒs) *n.* a light staff with a triangular frame to which a network is attached, used in playing lacrosse. [French, from Old French *croce* CROSIER]

cross-examine *vb.* (*tr.*) **1.** *Law.* to examine (a witness for the opposing side), as in attempting to discredit his testimony. Compare **examine-in-chief.** **2.** to examine closely or relentlessly. —ˈ**cross-ex,amiˈnation** *n.* —ˈ**cross-exˈaminer** *n.*

cross-eye *n.* a turning inwards towards the nose of one or both eyes, caused by abnormal alignment. See also **strabismus.** —ˈ**cross-,eyed** *adj.*

cross-fade *vb. Radio, television.* to fade in (one sound or picture source) as another is being faded out.

cross-fertilization *n.* **1.** fertilization by the fusion of male and female gametes from different individuals of the same species. Compare **self-fertilization.** **2.** (*not in technical use*) cross-pollination. —ˈ**cross-ˈfertile** *adj.*

cross-fertilize *vb.* to subject or be subjected to cross-fertilization.

crossfire (ˈkrɒs,faɪə) *n.* **1.** *Military, etc.* converging fire from one or more positions. **2.** a lively exchange of ideas, opinions, etc.

cross-garnet *n.* a hinge with a long horizontal strap fixed to the face of a door and a short vertical leaf fixed to the door frame.

cross-grained *adj.* **1.** (of timber) having the fibres arranged irregularly or in a direction that deviates from the axis of the piece. **2.** perverse, cantankerous, or stubborn.

cross hairs *pl. n.* two fine mutually perpendicular lines or wires that cross in the focal plane of a theodolite, gunsight, or other optical instrument and are used to define the line of sight. Also called: **cross wires.**

crosshatch (ˈkrɒs,hætʃ) *vb. Drawing.* to shade or hatch (forms, figures, etc.) with two or more sets of parallel lines that cross one another. —ˈ**cross,hatching** *n.*

crosshead (ˈkrɒs,hɛd) *n.* **1.** *Printing.* a subsection or paragraph heading printed within the body of the text. **2.** a block or beam, usually restrained by sliding bearings in a reciprocating mechanism, esp. the junction piece between the piston rod and connecting rod of an engine. **3.** *Nautical.* a bar fixed across the top of the rudder post to which the tiller is attached. **4.** a block, rod, or beam fixed at the head of any part of a mechanism.

cross-index *n.* **1.** a note or notes referring the reader to other material. ~*vb.* **2.** (*intr.*) (of a note in a book) to refer to related material. **3.** to provide or be provided with cross-indexes.

crossing (ˈkrɒsɪŋ) *n.* **1.** the place where one thing crosses another. **2.** a place, often shown by markings, lights, or poles, where a street, railway, etc., may be crossed. **3.** the intersection of the nave and transept in a church. **4.** the act or instance of travelling across something, esp. the sea. **5.** the act or process of crossbreeding.

crossing over *n. Biology.* the interchange of sections between pairing homologous chromosomes during the diplotene stage of meiosis. It results in the rearrangement of genes and produces variation in the inherited characteristics of the offspring. See also **linkage** (sense 4).

crossjack (ˈkrɒs,dʒæk; *Nautical* ˈkrɔːdʒɪk, ˈkrɒdʒ-) *n. Nautical.* a square sail on a ship's mizzenmast.

cross-legged (ˈkrɒsˈlɛgɪd, -ˈlɛgd) *adj.* standing or sitting with one leg crossed over the other.

crosslet *or* **cross crosslet** (ˈkrɒslɪt) *n. Heraldry.* a cross having a smaller cross near the end of each arm. [C16 *croslet* a little CROSS]

cross-link *or* **cross-linkage** *n.* a chemical bond, atom, or group of atoms that connects two adjacent chains of atoms in a large molecule such as a polymer or protein.

cross-match *n. Immunology.* to test the compatibility of (a donor's and recipient's blood) by checking that the red cells of each do not agglutinate in the other's serum.

cross-nodal *adj.* having to do with interaction between the senses.

cross of Lorraine *n.* a cross with two horizontal bars above and below the midpoint of the vertical bar, the lower longer than the upper.

Cross of Valour *n.* the highest Canadian award for bravery. Abbrev.: **CV.**

crossopterygian (krɒ,sɒptəˈrɪdʒɪən) *n.* **1.** any bony fish of the subclass *Crossopterygii*, having fleshy limblike pectoral fins. The group, now mostly extinct, contains the ancestors of the amphibians. See also **coelacanth.** ~*adj.* **2.** of, relating to, or belonging to the *Crossopterygii*. [C19: from New Latin *Crossopterygiī*, from Greek *krossoi* fringe, tassels + *pterugion* a little wing, from *pterux* wing]

crossover (ˈkrɒs,əʊvə) *n.* **1.** a place at which a crossing is made. **2.** *Genetics.* **a.** another term for **crossing over.** **b.** a chromosomal structure or character resulting from crossing over. **3.** *Railways.* a point of transfer between two main lines. **4.** short for **crossover network.** ~*adj.* **5.** (of music, fashion, art, etc.) combining two distinct styles. **6.** (of a singer, musician, etc.) having become popular outside the musical category in which he or she first became known.

crossover network *n.* an electronic network in a loudspeaker system that separates the signal into two or more frequency bands, the lower frequencies being fed to a woofer, the higher frequencies to a tweeter.

crossover value *n. Genetics.* the percentage of offspring showing recombination among the total offspring of a given cross. It indicates the amount of crossing over that has occurred and therefore the relative positions of the genes on the chromosomes. Abbrev.: **COV.**

crosspatch (ˈkrɒs,pætʃ) *n. Informal.* a peevish bad-tempered person. [C18: from CROSS + obsolete *patch* fool]

crosspiece (ˈkrɒs,piːs) *n.* a transverse beam, joist, etc.

cross-ply *adj.* (of a motor tyre) having the fabric cords in the outer casing running diagonally to stiffen the sidewalls. Compare **radial-ply.**

cross-pollinate *vb.* to subject or be subjected to cross-pollination.

cross-pollination *n.* the transfer of pollen from the anthers of one flower to the stigma of another flower by the action of wind, insects, etc. Compare **self-pollination.**

cross press *n.* a fall in wrestling using the weight of the body to pin an opponent's shoulders to the floor.

cross product *n. Maths.* **1.** another name for **vector product.** **2.** another name for **Cartesian product.**

cross protection *n. Botany.* the protection against a viral infection given to a plant by its prior inoculation with a related but milder virus.

cross-purpose *n.* **1.** a contrary aim or purpose. **2. at cross-purposes.** conflicting; opposed; disagreeing.

cross-question *vb.* (*tr.*) **1.** to cross-examine. ~*n.* **2.** a question asked in cross-examination. —ˈ**cross-ˈquestioning** *n.*

cross-refer *vb.* to refer from one part of something, esp. a book, to another.

cross-reference *n.* **1.** a reference within a text to another part of the text. ~*vb.* **2.** to cross-refer.

cross relation *n.* another term (esp. U.S.) for **false relation.**

crossroad (ˈkrɒs,rəʊd) *n. U.S. and Canadian.* **1.** a road that crosses another road. **2.** Also called: ˈ**cross,way.** a road that crosses from one main road to another.

crossroads (ˈkrɒs,rəʊdz) *n.* (*functioning as sing.*) **1.** an area or the point at which two or more roads cross each other. **2.** the point at which an important choice has to be made (esp. in the phrase **at the crossroads**).

Crossroads care attendant scheme *n. Social welfare.* (in Britain) a service providing paid attendants for disabled people who need continuous supervision. [so named because the idea arose out of criticism of the plight of a disabled character in the TV serial *Crossroads*]

crossruff (ˈkrɒs,rʌf) *Bridge, whist.* ~*n.* **1.** the alternate trumping of each other's leads by two partners, or by declarer and dummy. ~*vb.* **2.** (*intr.*) to trump alternately in two hands of a partnership.

cross section *n.* **1.** *Maths.* a plane surface formed by cutting across a solid, esp. perpendicular to its longest axis. **2.** a section cut off in this way. **3.** the act of cutting anything in this way. **4.** a random selection or sample, esp. one regarded as representative: *a cross section of the public.* **5.** *Surveying.* a vertical section of a line of ground at right angles to a survey line. **6.** *Physics.* a measure of the probability that a collision process will result in a particular reaction. It is expressed by the effective area that one participant presents as a target for the other. —ˈ**cross-ˈsectional** *adj.*

cross-slide *n.* the part of a lathe or planing machine on which the tool post is mounted and across which it slides at right angles to the bed of the lathe.

cross-stitch *n.* **1.** an embroidery stitch made by two stitches forming a cross. **2.** embroidery worked with this stitch. ~*vb.* **3.** to embroider (a piece of needlework) with cross-stitch.

crosstalk (ˈkrɒs,tɔːk) *n.* **1.** unwanted signals in one channel of a communications system as a result of a transfer of energy from one or more other channels. **2.** *Brit.* rapid or witty talk or conversation.

cross-town *adj. U.S. and Canadian.* going across or following a route across a town: *a cross-town bus.*

cross training *n.* training in two or more sports to improve performance, esp. on one's main sport.

crosstree (ˈkrɒs,triː) *n. Nautical.* either of a pair of wooden or metal braces on the head of a mast to support the topmast, etc.

cross vine *n.* a woody bignoniaceous vine, *Bignonia capreolata*, of the southeastern U.S., having large trumpet-shaped reddish flowers.

crosswalk (ˈkrɒs,wɔːk) *n.* the U.S. and Canadian name for **pedestrian crossing.**

crosswind (ˈkrɒs,wɪnd) *n.* a wind that blows at right angles to the direction of travel.

cross wires *pl. n.* another name for **cross hairs.**

crosswise (ˈkrɒs,waɪz) *or* **crossways** (ˈkrɒs,weɪz) *adj., adv.* **1.** across; transversely. **2.** in the shape of a cross.

crossword puzzle (ˈkrɒs,wɜːd) *n.* a puzzle in which the solver guesses words suggested by numbered clues and writes them into corresponding boxes in a grid to form a vertical and horizontal pattern. Sometimes shortened to **crossword.**

crosswort ('krɒsˌwɜːt) *n.* a herbaceous perennial Eurasian rubiaceous plant, *Galium cruciata,* with pale yellow flowers and whorls of hairy leaves. Also called: **mugwort.**

crotal *or* **crottle** ('krɒtᵊl) *n. Scot.* any of various lichens used in dyeing wool, esp. for the manufacture of tweeds. [Gaelic *crotal*]

crotch (krɒtʃ) *n.* **1.** Also called (Brit.): **crutch. a.** the angle formed by the inner sides of the legs where they join the human trunk. **b.** the human external genitals or the genital area. **c.** the corresponding part of a pair of trousers, pants, etc. **2.** a forked region formed by the junction of two members. **3.** a forked pole or stick. [C16: probably variant of CRUTCH] —**crotched** (krɒtʃt) *adj.*

crotchet ('krɒtʃɪt) *n.* **1.** *Music.* a note having the time value of a quarter of a semibreve. Usual U.S. and Canadian name: **quarter note. 2.** a small hook or hooklike device. **3.** a perverse notion. **4.** *Zoology.* a small notched or hooked process, as in an insect. [C14: from Old French *crochet,* literally: little hook, from *croche* hook; see CROCKET]

crotchety ('krɒtʃɪtɪ) *adj.* **1.** *Informal.* cross; irritable; contrary. **2.** full of crotchets. —'**crotchetiness** *n.*

croton ('krəʊtᵊn) *n.* **1.** any shrub or tree of the chiefly tropical euphorbiaceous genus *Croton,* esp. *C. tiglium,* the seeds of which yield croton oil. **2.** any of various tropical plants of the related genus *Codiaeum,* esp. *C. variegatum pictum,* a house plant with variegated foliage. [C18: from New Latin, from Greek *krotōn* tick, castor-oil plant (whose berries resemble ticks)]

Croton bug ('krəʊtᵊn) *n. U.S.* another name for the **German cockroach.** [C19: named after the *Croton* river, whose water was piped to New York City in 1842]

crotonic acid (krəʊ'tɒnɪk) *n.* a colourless crystalline insoluble unsaturated carboxylic acid produced by oxidation of crotonaldehyde and used in organic synthesis; *trans*-2-butenoic acid. Formula: $CH_3CH{:}CHCOOH$.

croton oil *n.* a yellowish-brown oil obtained from the plant *Croton tiglium,* formerly used as a drastic purgative. See also **croton** (sense 1).

crottle ('krɒtᵊl) *n.* a variant spelling of **crotal.**

crouch (kraʊtʃ) *vb.* **1.** (*intr.*) to bend low with the limbs pulled up close together, esp. (of an animal) in readiness to pounce. **2.** (*intr.*) to cringe, as in humility or fear. **3.** (*tr.*) to bend (parts of the body), as in humility or fear. ~*n.* **4.** the act of stooping or bending. [C14: perhaps from Old French *crochir* to become bent like a hook, from *croche* hook]

croup[1] (kruːp) *n.* a throat condition, occurring usually in children, characterized by a hoarse cough and laboured breathing, resulting from inflammation and partial obstruction of the larynx. [C16 *croup* to cry hoarsely, probably of imitative origin] —'**croupous** *or* '**croupy** *adj.*

croup[2] *or* **croupe** (kruːp) *n.* the hindquarters of a quadruped, esp. a horse. [C13: from Old French *croupe;* related to German *Kruppe*]

croup[3] (kruːp) *vb.* (*intr.*) *Scot. and northern English dialect.* to squat on one's haunches; crouch. Also: '**croupy, croupy down.** [extended verbal use of CROUP[2]]

croupier ('kruːpɪə; *French* krupje) *n.* a person who deals cards, collects bets, etc., at a gaming table. [C18: literally: one who rides behind another, from French *croupe* CROUP[2]]

crouse (kruːs) *adj. Scot. and northern English dialect.* lively, confident, or saucy. [C14 (Scottish and Northern) English: from Middle Low German *krūs* twisted, curled, confused]

croute (kruːt) *n.* a small round of toasted bread on which a savoury mixture is served. [from French *croûte* CRUST]

crouton ('kruːtɒn) *n.* a small piece of fried or toasted bread, usually served in soup. [French: diminutive of *croûte* CRUST]

crow[1] (krəʊ) *n.* **1.** any large gregarious songbird of the genus *Corvus,* esp. *C. corone* (**carrion crow**) of Europe and Asia: family *Corvidae.* Other species are the raven, rook, and jackdaw and all have a heavy bill, glossy black plumage, and rounded wings. Related adj.: **corvine. 2.** any of various other corvine birds, such as the jay, magpie, and nutcracker. **3.** any of various similar birds of other families. **4.** *Austral. slang.* an old or ugly woman. **5.** short for **crowbar. 6. as the crow flies.** as directly as possible. **7. draw the crow.** *Austral.* to get the worst of any allocation. **8. eat crow.** *U.S. and Canadian informal.* to be forced to do something humiliating. **9. stone the crows.** (*interj.*) *Brit. and Austral. slang.* an expression of surprise, dismay, etc. [Old English *crāwa;* related to Old Norse *krāka,* Old High German *krāia,* Dutch *kraai*]

crow[2] (krəʊ) *vb.* (*intr.*) **1.** (past tense **crowed** *or* **crew**) to utter a shrill squawking sound, as a cock. **2.** (often foll. by *over*) to boast one's superiority. **3.** (esp. of babies) to utter cries of pleasure. ~*n.* **4.** the act or an instance of crowing. [Old English *crāwan;* related to Old High German *krāen,* Dutch *kraaien*] —'**crower** *n.* —'**crowingly** *adv.*

Crow (krəʊ) *n.* **1.** (*pl.* **Crows** *or* **Crow**) a member of a North American Indian people living in E Montana in the western U.S. **2.** the language of this people, belonging to the Siouan family.

crowbar ('krəʊˌbɑː) *n.* a heavy iron lever with one pointed end, and one forged into a wedge shape.

crowberry ('krəʊbərɪ, -brɪ) *n., pl.* **-ries. 1.** a low-growing N temperate evergreen shrub, *Empetrum nigrum,* with small purplish flowers and black berry-like fruit: family *Empetraceae.* **2.** any of several similar or related plants. **3.** the fruit of any of these plants.

crow-bill *n.* a type of forceps used to extract bullets, etc., from wounds.

crow blackbird *n.* another name for **grackle.**

crowboot ('krəʊˌbuːt) *n.* a type of Eskimo boot made of fur and leather.

crowd[1] (kraʊd) *n.* **1.** a large number of things or people gathered or considered together. **2.** a particular group of people, esp. considered as a social or business set: *the crowd from the office.* **3. a.** (preceded by *the*) the common people; the masses. **b.** (*as modifier*): *crowd ideas.* ~*vb.* **4.** (*intr.*) to gather together in large numbers; throng. **5.** (*tr.*) to press together into a confined space. **6.** (*tr.*) to fill to excess; fill by pushing into. **7.** (*tr.*) *Informal.* to urge or harass by urging. **8. crowd on sail.** *Nautical.* to hoist as much sail as possible. **9. follow the crowd.** to conform with the majority. [Old English *crūdan;* related to Middle Low German *krūden* to molest, Middle Dutch *crūden* to push, Norwegian *kryda* to swarm] —'**crowded** *adj.* —'**crowdedly** *adv.* —'**crowdedness** *n.* —'**crowder** *n.*

crowd[2] (kraʊd) *n. Music.* an ancient bowed stringed instrument; crwth. [C13: from Welsh *crwth*]

crowdie ('kraʊdɪ) *n. Scot.* **1.** a porridge of meal and water; brose. **2.** a cheese-like dish made by straining the whey from soured milk and beating up the remaining curd with salt. [C17: of unknown origin]

crowd puller *n. Informal.* a person, object, event, etc., that attracts a large audience.

crowfoot ('krəʊˌfʊt) *n., pl.* **-foots. 1.** any of several plants of the genus *Ranunculus,* such as *R. sceleratus* and *R. aquatilis* (**water crowfoot**) that have yellow or white flowers and divided leaves resembling the foot of a crow. See also **buttercup. 2.** any of various other plants that have leaves or other parts resembling a bird's foot. **3.** *pl.* **feet.** *Nautical.* a bridle-like arrangement of lines rove through a wooden block or attached to a ring for supporting an awning from above. **4.** *pl.* **feet.** *Military.* another name for **caltrop.**

crown (kraʊn) *n.* **1.** an ornamental headdress denoting sovereignty, usually made of gold embedded with precious stones. **2.** a wreath or garland for the head, awarded as a sign of victory, success, honour, etc. **3.** (*sometimes cap.*) monarchy or kingship. **4.** an award, distinction, or title, given as an honour to reward merit, victory, etc. **5.** anything resembling or symbolizing a crown, such as a sergeant major's badge or a heraldic bearing. **6. a.** *History.* a coin worth 25 pence (five shillings). **b.** any of several continental coins, such as the krona or krone, with a name meaning *crown.* **7.** the top or summit of something, esp. of a rounded object: *crown of a hill; crown of the head.* **8.** the centre part of a road, esp. when it is cambered. **9.** *Botany.* **a.** the leaves and upper branches of a tree. **b.** the junction of root and stem, usually at the level of the ground. **c.** another name for **corona** (sense 6). **10.** *Zoology.* **a.** the cup and arms of a crinoid, as distinct from the stem. **b.** the crest of a bird. **11.** the outstanding quality, achievement, state, etc.: *the crown of his achievements.* **12. a.** the enamel-covered part of a tooth above the gum. **b. artificial crown.** a substitute crown, usually of gold, porcelain, or acrylic resin, fitted over a decayed or broken tooth. **13.** the part of a cut gem above the girdle. **14.** *Horology.* a knurled knob for winding a watch. **15.** the part of an anchor where the arms are joined to the shank. **16.** the highest part of an arch or vault. **17.** a standard size of printing paper, 15 by 20 inches. ~*vb.* (*tr.*) **18.** to put a crown on the head of, symbolically vesting with royal title, powers, etc. **19.** to place a crown, wreath, garland, etc., on the head of. **20.** to place something on or over the head or top of: *he crowned the pie with cream.* **21.** to confer a title, dignity, or reward upon: *he crowned her best cook.* **22.** to form the summit or topmost part of: *the steeple crowned the tower.* **23.** to cap or put the finishing touch to a series of events: *to crown it all it rained, too.* **24.** *Draughts.* to promote (a draught) to a king by placing another draught on top of it, as after reaching the end of the board. **25.** to attach a crown to (a tooth). **26.** *Slang.* to hit over the head. [C12: from Old French *corone,* from Latin *corōna* wreath, crown, from Greek *korōnē* crown, something curved] —'**crownless** *adj.*

Crown (kraʊn) *n.* (*sometimes not cap.;* usually preceded by *the*) **1.** the sovereignty or realm of a monarch. **2. a.** the government of a constitutional monarchy. **b.** (*as modifier*): *Crown property.*

Crown Agent *n.* **1.** a member of a board appointed by the Minister for Overseas Development to provide financial, commercial, and professional services for a number of overseas governments and international bodies. **2.** *Scot.* (*not caps.*) a solicitor dealing with criminal prosecutions.

crown and anchor *n.* a game played with dice marked with crowns and anchors.

Crown attorney *n. Canadian.* a lawyer who acts for the Crown, esp. as prosecutor in a criminal court.

crown cap *n. Brit.* an airtight metal seal crimped on the top of most bottled beers, ciders, mineral waters, etc.

crown colony *n.* a British colony whose administration and legislature is controlled by the Crown.

crown court *n. English law.* a court of criminal jurisdiction holding sessions in towns throughout England and Wales at which circuit judges hear and determine cases.

Crown Derby *n.* a type of porcelain manufactured at Derby in central England from 1784–1848, marked with a crown.
crowned head *n.* a monarch: *the crowned heads of Europe.*
crowner ('kraʊnə) *n.* a promotional label consisting of a shaped printed piece of card or paper attached to a product on display.
crown ether *n. Chem.* a type of cyclic ether consisting of a ring of carbon and oxygen atoms, with two carbon atoms between each oxygen atom.
crown glass *n.* **1.** another name for **optical crown. 2.** an old form of window glass made by blowing a globe and spinning it until it forms a flat disc.
crown graft *n. Horticulture.* a type of graft in which the scion is inserted at the crown of the stock.
crown green *n.* a type of bowling green in which the sides are lower than the middle.
crown imperial *n.* a liliaceous garden plant, *Fritillaria imperialis,* with a cluster of leaves and orange bell-shaped flowers at the top of the stem.
crowning ('kraʊnɪŋ) *n. Obstetrics.* the stage of labour when the infant's head is passing through the vaginal opening.
crown jewels *pl. n.* the jewellery, including the regalia, used by a sovereign on a state occasion.
crownland ('kraʊnˌlænd) *n.* a large administrative division of the former empire of Austria-Hungary.
crown land *n.* **1.** (in the United Kingdom) land belonging to the Crown. **2.** public land in some dominions of the Commonwealth.
crown lens *n.* a lens made of optical crown, esp. the optical-crown part of a compound achromatic lens.
crown-of-thorns *n.* **1.** a starfish, *Acanthaster planci,* that has a spiny test and feeds on living coral in coral reefs. **2.** Also called: **Christ's thorn.** a thorny euphorbiaceous Madagascan shrub, *Euphorbia splendens,* cultivated as a hedging shrub or pot plant, having flowers with scarlet bracts.
crownpiece ('kraʊnˌpiːs) *n.* **1.** the piece forming or fitting the top of something. **2.** the strap of a bridle that goes over a horse's head behind the ears.
crown prince *n.* the male heir to a sovereign throne.
crown princess *n.* **1.** the wife of a crown prince. **2.** the female heir to a sovereign throne.
Crown Prosecution Service *n.* (in England and Wales) an independent prosecuting body, established in 1986, that decides whether cases brought by the police should go to the courts: headed by the Director of Public Prosecutions. Compare **procurator fiscal.** Abbrev.: **CPS.**
Crown prosecutor *n. Canadian.* another name for **Crown attorney.**
crown roast *n.* a roast consisting of ribs of lamb or pork arranged in a crown shape.
crown saw *n.* a hollow cylinder with cutting teeth forming a rotary saw for trepanning.
crown vetch *n.* a trailing papilionaceous European plant, *Coronilla varia,* with clusters of white or pink flowers: cultivated in North America as a border plant. Also called (U.S.): **axseed** ('æksiːd).
crown wheel *n.* **1.** *Horology.* the wheel next to the winding knob that has one set of teeth at right angles to the other. **2.** the larger of the two gears in a bevel gear.
crownwork ('kraʊnˌwɜːk) *n.* **1. a.** the manufacture of artificial crowns for teeth. **b.** such an artificial crown or crowns. **2.** *Fortifications.* a covering or protective outwork.
crow's-foot *n., pl.* **-feet. 1.** (*often pl.*) a wrinkle at the outer corner of the eye. **2.** an embroidery stitch with three points, used esp. as a finishing at the end of a seam. **3.** a system of diverging short ropes to distribute the pull of a single rope, used esp. in balloon and airship riggings.
crow's-nest *n.* a lookout platform high up on a ship's mast.
crow step *n.* another term for **corbie-step.**
croze (krəʊz) *n.* **1.** the recess cut at the end of a barrel or cask to receive the head. **2.** a tool for cutting this recess. [C17: probably from Old French *crues* a hollow]
crozier ('krəʊʒə) *n.* a variant spelling of **crosier.**
CRP (in India) *abbrev. for* Central Reserve Police.
CRT *abbrev. for:* **1.** cathode-ray tube. **2.** (in Britain) composite rate tax: a system of paying interest to savers by which a rate of tax for a period, such as one financial year, is determined in advance, and interest is paid net of tax which is deducted at source.
cru (kruː; *French* kry) *n. Winemaking.* (in France) a vineyard, group of vineyards, or wine-producing region. [from French: production, from *crû,* past participle of *croître* to grow]
cruces ('kruːsiːz) *n.* a plural of **crux.**
crucial ('kruːʃəl) *adj.* **1.** involving a final or supremely important decision or event; decisive; critical. **2.** *Informal.* very important. **3.** *Slang.* very good. [C18: from French, from Latin *crux* CROSS] —'**crucially** *adv.*
crucian ('kruːʃən) *n.* a European cyprinid fish, *Carassius carassius,* with a dark-green back, a golden-yellow undersurface, and reddish dorsal and tail fins: an aquarium fish. [C18: from Low German *Karusse*]
cruciate ('kruːʃɪɪt, -ˌeɪt) *adj.* shaped or arranged like a cross: *cruciate petals.* [C17: from New Latin *cruciātus,* from Latin *crux* cross] —'**cruciately** *adv.*
crucible ('kruːsɪbᵊl) *n.* **1.** a vessel in which substances are heated to high temperatures. **2.** the hearth at the bottom of a metallurgical furnace in which the metal collects. **3.** a severe trial or test. [C15 *corusible,* from Medieval Latin *crūcibulum* night lamp, crucible, of uncertain origin]
crucible steel *n.* a high-quality steel made by melting wrought iron, charcoal, and other additives in a crucible.
crucifer ('kruːsɪfə) *n.* **1.** any plant of the family *Cruciferae,* having a corolla of four petals arranged like a cross and a fruit called a siliqua. The family includes the brassicas, mustard, cress, and wallflower. **2.** a person who carries a cross. [C16: from Late Latin, from Latin *crux* cross + *ferre* to carry]
cruciferous (kruːˈsɪfərəs) *adj.* of, relating to, or belonging to the plant family *Cruciferae.* See **crucifer** (sense 1).
crucifix ('kruːsɪfɪks) *n.* a cross or image of a cross with a figure of Christ upon it. [C13: from Church Latin *crucifixus* the crucified Christ, from *crucifīgere* to CRUCIFY]
crucifixion (ˌkruːsɪˈfɪkʃən) *n.* a method of putting to death by nailing or binding to a cross, normally by the hands and feet, which was widespread in the ancient world.
Crucifixion (ˌkruːsɪˈfɪkʃən) *n.* **1.** (usually preceded by *the*) the crucifying of Christ at Calvary, regarded by Christians as the culminating redemptive act of his ministry. **2.** a picture or representation of this.
cruciform ('kruːsɪˌfɔːm) *adj.* **1.** shaped like a cross. ~*n.* **2.** a geometric curve, shaped like a cross, that has four similar branches asymptotic to two mutually perpendicular pairs of lines. Equation: $x^2y^2 - a^2x^2 - a^2y^2 = 0$, where $x = y = \pm a$ are the four lines. [C17: from Latin *crux* cross + -FORM] —'**cruciˌformly** *adv.*
crucify ('kruːsɪˌfaɪ) *vb.* **-fies, -fying, -fied.** (*tr.*) **1.** to put to death by crucifixion. **2.** *Slang.* to defeat, ridicule, etc., totally: *the critics crucified his performance.* **3.** to treat very cruelly; torment. **4.** to subdue (passion, lust, etc.); mortify. [C13: from Old French *crucifier,* from Late Latin *crucifīgere* to crucify, to fasten to a cross, from Latin *crux* cross + *fīgere* to fasten] —'**cruciˌfier** *n.*
cruck (krʌk) *n.* one of a pair of curved wooden timbers supporting the end of the roof in certain types of building. [C19: variant of CROOK (*n.*)]
crud (krʌd) *Slang.* ~*n.* **1.** a sticky substance, esp. when dirty and encrusted. **2.** an undesirable residue from a process, esp. one inside a nuclear reactor. **3.** something or someone that is worthless, disgusting, or contemptible. **4.** (sometimes preceded by *the*) a disease; rot. ~*interj.* **5.** an expression of disgust, disappointment, etc. [C14: earlier form of CURD] —'**cruddy** *adj.*
crude (kruːd) *adj.* **1.** lacking taste, tact, or refinement; vulgar: *a crude joke.* **2.** in a natural or unrefined state. **3.** lacking care, knowledge, or skill: *a crude sketch.* **4.** (*prenominal*) stark; blunt: *the crude facts.* **5.** (of statistical data) unclassified or unanalysed. **6.** *Archaic.* unripe. ~*n.* **7.** short for **crude oil.** [C14: from Latin *crūdus* bloody, raw; related to Latin *cruor* blood] —'**crudely** *adv.* —'**crudity** *or* '**crudeness** *n.*
crude oil *n.* petroleum before it has been refined.
cruel ('kruːəl) *adj.* **1.** causing or inflicting pain without pity: *a cruel teacher.* **2.** causing pain or suffering: *a cruel accident.* [C13: from Old French, from Latin *crūdēlis,* from *crūdus* raw, bloody] —'**cruelly** *adv.* —'**cruelness** *n.*
cruelty ('kruːəltɪ) *n., pl.* **-ties. 1.** deliberate infliction of pain or suffering. **2.** the quality or characteristic of being cruel. **3.** a cruel action. **4.** *Law.* conduct that causes danger to life or limb or a threat to bodily or mental health, on proof of which a decree of divorce may be granted.
cruelty-free *adj.* (of a cosmetic or other product) developed without being tested on animals.
cruet ('kruːɪt) *n.* **1.** a small container for holding pepper, salt, vinegar, oil, etc., at table. **2.** a set of such containers, esp. on a stand. **3.** *Christianity.* either of a pair of small containers for the wine and water used in the Eucharist. [C13: from Anglo-French, diminutive of Old French *crue* flask, of Germanic origin; compare Old Saxon *krūka,* Old English *crūce* pot]
cruise (kruːz) *vb.* **1.** (*intr.*) to make a trip by sea in a liner for pleasure, usually calling at a number of ports. **2.** to sail or travel over (a body of water) for pleasure in a yacht, cruiser, etc. **3.** (*intr.*) to search for enemy vessels in a warship. **4.** (*intr.*) (of a vehicle, aircraft, or vessel) to travel at a moderate and efficient speed. **5.** (*intr.*) *Informal.* to search the streets or other public places for a sexual partner. ~*n.* **6.** an act or instance of cruising, esp. a trip by sea. [C17: from Dutch *kruisen* to cross, from *cruis* CROSS; related to French *croiser* to cross, cruise, Spanish *cruzar,* German *kreuzen*]
cruise control *n.* a system in a road vehicle that automatically maintains a selected speed until cancelled.
cruise missile *n.* an air-breathing low-flying subsonic missile that is continuously powered and guided throughout its flight and carries a warhead.
cruiser ('kruːzə) *n.* **1.** a high-speed, long-range warship of medium displacement, armed with medium calibre weapons or missiles. **2.** Also called: **cabin cruiser.** a pleasure boat, esp. one that is power-driven and has a cabin. **3.** any person or thing that cruises. **4.** *Boxing.* short for **cruiserweight** (see **light heavyweight**).

cruiserweight ('kruːzəˌweɪt) *n. Boxing.* another term (esp. Brit.) for **light heavyweight.**
cruiseway ('kruːzˌweɪ) *n.* a canal used for recreational purposes.
cruizie, cruzie, *or* **crusie** ('kruːzɪ) *n. Scot.* an oil lamp. [C18: perhaps from *cruset* crucible, from French *creuset*]
cruller *or* **kruller** ('krʌlə) *n. U.S. and Canadian.* a light sweet ring-shaped cake, fried in deep fat. [C19: from Dutch *krulle,* from *krullen* to CURL]
crumb (krʌm) *n.* **1.** a small fragment of bread, cake, or other baked foods. **2.** a small piece or bit: *crumbs of information.* **3.** the soft inner part of bread. **4.** *Slang.* a contemptible person. ~*vb.* **5.** (*tr.*) to prepare or cover (food) with breadcrumbs. **6.** to break into small fragments. ~*adj.* **7.** (esp. of pie crusts) made with a mixture of biscuit crumbs, sugar, etc. [Old English *cruma;* related to Middle Dutch *krome,* Middle High German *krūme,* Latin *grūmus* heap of earth] —'**crumber** *n.*
crumble ('krʌmbᵊl) *vb.* **1.** to break or be broken into crumbs or fragments. **2.** (*intr.*) to fall apart or away: *his resolution crumbled.* ~*n.* **3.** *Brit.* a baked pudding consisting of a crumbly mixture of flour, fat, and sugar over stewed fruit: *apple crumble.* [C16: variant of *crimble,* of Germanic origin; compare Low German *krömeln,* Dutch *kruimelen*]
crumbly ('krʌmblɪ) *adj.* **-blier, -bliest.** easily crumbled or crumbling. —'**crumbliness** *n.*
crumbs (krʌmz) *interj. Slang.* an expression of dismay or surprise. [C20: euphemistic for *Christ!*]
crumby ('krʌmɪ) *adj.* **crumbier, crumbiest. 1.** full of or littered with crumbs. **2.** soft, like the inside of bread. **3.** a variant spelling of **crummy**[1].
crumhorn *or* **krummhorn** ('krʌmˌhɔːn) *n.* a medieval woodwind instrument of bass pitch, consisting of an almost cylindrical tube curving upwards and blown through a double reed covered by a pierced cap. [C17 *cromorne, krumhorn,* from German *Krummhorn:* curved horn]
crummy[1] ('krʌmɪ) *adj.* **-mier, -miest.** *Slang.* **1.** of little value; inferior; contemptible. **2.** unwell or depressed: *to feel crummy.* [C19: variant spelling of CRUMBY]
crummy[2] ('krʌmɪ) *n., pl.* **-mies.** *Canadian.* a lorry that carries loggers to work from their camp. [probably originally meaning: makeshift camp, from CRUMMY[1]]
crump (krʌmp) *vb.* **1.** (*intr.*) to thud or explode with a loud dull sound. **2.** (*tr.*) to bombard with heavy shells. ~*n.* **3.** a crunching, thudding, or exploding noise. [C17: of imitative origin]
crumpet ('krʌmpɪt) *n. Chiefly Brit.* **1.** a light soft yeast cake full of small holes on the top side, eaten toasted and buttered. **2.** (in Scotland) a fairly thick sweetened cake made of batter. **3.** *Slang.* women collectively. **4. a piece of crumpet.** *Slang.* a sexually desirable woman. **5. not worth a crumpet.** *Austral. slang.* utterly worthless. [C17: of uncertain origin]
crumple ('krʌmpᵊl) *vb.* **1.** (when *intr.,* often foll. by *up*) to collapse or cause to collapse: *his courage crumpled.* **2.** (when *tr.,* often foll. by *up*) to crush or cause to be crushed so as to form wrinkles or creases. **3.** (*intr.*) to shrink; shrivel. ~*n.* **4.** a loose crease or wrinkle. [C16: from obsolete *crump* to bend; related to Old High German *krimpfan* to wrinkle, Old Norse *kreppa* to contract] —'**crumply** *adj.*
crunch (krʌntʃ) *vb.* **1.** to bite or chew (crisp foods) with a crushing or crackling sound. **2.** to make or cause to make a crisp or brittle sound: *the snow crunched beneath his feet.* ~*n.* **3.** the sound or act of crunching. **4. the crunch.** *Informal.* the critical moment or situation. ~*adj.* **5.** *Informal.* critical; decisive: *crunch time.* ~Also: **craunch.** [C19: changed (through influence of MUNCH) from earlier *craunch,* of imitative origin] —'**crunchable** *adj.* —'**crunchy** *adj.* —'**crunchily** *adv.* —'**crunchiness** *n.*
crunchie ('krʌntʃɪ) *n. S. African derogatory slang.* another name for an **Afrikaner.**
crunode ('kruːnəʊd) *n.* a point at which two branches of a curve intersect, each branch having a distinct tangent; node. [C19: *cru-* from Latin *crux* cross + NODE]
cruor (kruɔː) *n., pl.* **cruores** ('kruɔːriːz). *Med.* a blood clot.
crupper ('krʌpə) *n.* **1.** a strap from the back of a saddle that passes under the horse's tail to prevent the saddle from slipping forwards. **2.** the part of the horse's rump behind the saddle. [C13: from Old French *crupiere,* from *crupe* CROUP[2]]
crura ('krʊərə) *n.* the plural of **crus.**
crural ('krʊərəl) *adj.* of or relating to the leg or thigh. [C16: from Latin *crūrālis,* from *crūs* leg, shin]
crus (krʌs) *n., pl.* **crura** ('krʊərə). **1.** *Anatomy.* the leg, esp. from the knee to the foot. **2.** (*usually pl.*) leglike parts or structures. [C17: from Latin: leg]
crusade (kruː'seɪd) *n.* **1.** (*often cap.*) any of the military expeditions undertaken in the 11th, 12th, and 13th centuries by the Christian powers of Europe to recapture the Holy Land from the Muslims. **2.** (formerly) any holy war undertaken on behalf of a religious cause. **3.** a vigorous and dedicated action or movement in favour of a cause. ~*vb.* (*intr.*) **4.** to campaign vigorously for something. **5.** to go on a crusade. [C16: from earlier *croisade,* from Old French *crois* cross, from Latin *crux;* influenced also by Spanish *cruzada,* from *cruzar* to take up the cross] —**cru'sader** *n.*
crusado (kruː'seɪdəʊ) *or* **cruzado** (kruː'zeɪdəʊ; *Portuguese* kru'zɑːdu) *n., pl.* **-does** *or* **-dos** (-dəʊz; *Portuguese* -duʃ). a former gold or silver coin of Portugal bearing on its reverse the figure of a cross. [C16: literally, marked with a cross, from *cruzar* to bear a cross; see CRUSADE]
cruse (kruːz) *n.* a small earthenware container used, esp. formerly, for liquids. [Old English *crūse;* related to Middle High German *krūse,* Dutch *kroes* jug]
crush (krʌʃ) *vb.* (*mainly tr.*) **1.** to press, mash, or squeeze so as to injure, break, crease, etc. **2.** to break or grind (rock, ore, etc.) into small particles. **3.** to put down or subdue, esp. by force: *to crush a rebellion.* **4.** to extract (juice, water, etc.) by pressing: *to crush the juice from a lemon.* **5.** to oppress harshly. **6.** to hug or clasp tightly: *he crushed her to him.* **7.** to defeat or humiliate utterly, as in argument or by a cruel remark. **8.** (*intr.*) to crowd; throng. **9.** (*intr.*) to become injured, broken, or distorted by pressure. ~*n.* **10.** a dense crowd, esp. at a social occasion. **11.** the act of crushing; pressure. **12.** a drink or pulp prepared by or as if by crushing fruit: *orange crush.* **13.** *Informal.* **a.** an infatuation: *she had a crush on him.* **b.** the person with whom one is infatuated. [C14: from Old French *croissir,* of Germanic origin; compare Gothic *kriustan* to gnash; see CRUNCH] —'**crushable** *adj.* —ˌ**crusha'bility** *n.* —'**crusher** *n.*
crush bar *n.* a bar at a theatre for serving drinks during the intervals of a play.
crush barrier *n.* a barrier erected to separate sections of large crowds in order to prevent crushing.
crusie ('kruːzɪ) *n.* a variant spelling of **cruizie.**
crust (krʌst) *n.* **1. a.** the hard outer part of bread. **b.** a piece of bread consisting mainly of this. **2.** the baked shell of a pie, tart, etc. **3.** any hard or stiff outer covering or surface: *a crust of ice.* **4.** the solid outer shell of the earth, with an average thickness of 30–35 km in continental regions and 5 km beneath the oceans, forming the upper part of the lithosphere and lying immediately above the mantle, from which it is separated by the Mohorovičić discontinuity. See also **sial, sima. 5.** the dry covering of a skin sore or lesion; scab. **6.** a layer of acid potassium tartrate deposited by some wine, esp. port, on the inside of the bottle. **7.** the hard outer layer of such organisms as lichens and crustaceans. **8.** *Slang.* impertinence. **9.** *Brit., Austral., and N.Z. slang.* a living (esp. in the phrase **earn a crust**). ~*vb.* **10.** to cover with or acquire a crust. **11.** to form or be formed into a crust. [C14: from Latin *crūsta* hard surface, rind, shell]
crustacean (krʌ'steɪʃən) *n.* **1.** any arthropod of the mainly aquatic class *Crustacea,* typically having a carapace hardened with lime and including the lobsters, crabs, shrimps, woodlice, barnacles, copepods, and water fleas. ~*adj. also* **crustaceous. 2.** of, relating to, or belonging to the *Crustacea.* [C19: from New Latin *crūstāceus* hard-shelled, from Latin *crūsta* shell, CRUST]
crustaceous (krʌ'steɪʃəs) *adj.* **1.** forming, resembling, or possessing a surrounding crust or shell. **2.** *Zoology.* another word for **crustacean** (sense 2).
crustal ('krʌstᵊl) *adj.* of or relating to the earth's crust.
crustose ('krʌstəʊs) *adj. Biology.* having a crustlike appearance: *crustose lichens.*
crusty ('krʌstɪ) *adj.* **crustier, crustiest. 1.** having or characterized by a crust, esp. having a thick crust. **2.** having a rude or harsh character or exterior; surly; curt: *a crusty remark.* —'**crustily** *adv.* —'**crustiness** *n.*
crutch (krʌtʃ) *n.* **1.** a long staff of wood or metal having a rest for the armpit, for supporting the weight of the body. **2.** something that supports, helps, or sustains: *a crutch to the economy.* **3.** *Brit.* another word for **crotch** (sense 1). **4.** *Nautical.* **a.** a forked support for a boom or oar, etc. **b.** a brace for reinforcing the frames at the stern of a wooden vessel. ~*vb.* **5.** (*tr.*) to support or sustain (a person or thing) as with a crutch. **6.** *Austral. and N.Z. slang.* to clip (wool) from the hindquarters of a sheep. [Old English *crycc;* related to Old High German *krucka,* Old Norse *krykkja;* see CROSIER, CROOK]
crutchings ('krʌtʃɪŋz) *pl. n. Austral. and N.Z.* the wool clipped from a sheep's hindquarters.
crux (krʌks) *n., pl.* **cruxes** *or* **cruces** ('kruːsiːz). **1.** a vital or decisive stage, point, etc. (often in the phrase **the crux of the matter**). **2.** a baffling problem or difficulty. **3.** *Mountaineering.* the most difficult and often decisive part of a climb or pitch. **4.** a rare word for **cross.** [C18: from Latin: cross]
Crux (krʌks) *n., Latin genitive* **Crucis** ('kruːsɪs). the more formal name for the **Southern Cross.**
crux ansata (æn'seɪtə) *n., pl.* **cruces ansatae** (æn'seɪtiː). another term for **ankh.** [New Latin, literally: cross with a handle]
cruzado (kruː'zeɪdəʊ; *Portuguese* kru'zɑːdu) *n., pl.* **-does** *or* **-dos** (-dəʊz; *Portuguese* -duʃ). **1.** the former standard monetary unit of Brazil, divided into 100 centavos. **2.** another name for **crusado.** [C16: literally marked with a cross, from *cruzar* to bear a cross; see CRUSADE]
cruzeiro (kruː'zæərəʊ; *Portuguese* kru'zeiru) *n., pl.* **-ros** (-rəʊz; *Portuguese* -ruʃ). the standard monetary unit of Brazil. [Portuguese: from *cruz* CROSS]
cruzie ('kruːzɪ) *n.* a variant spelling of **cruizie.**
crwth (kruːθ) *n.* an ancient stringed instrument of Celtic origin similar to the cithara but bowed in later types. [Welsh; compare Middle Irish *crott* harp]
cry (kraɪ) *vb.* **cries, crying, cried. 1.** (*intr.*) to utter inarticulate sounds, esp. when weeping; sob. **2.** (*intr.*) to shed tears; weep. **3.** (*intr.;* usually foll. by *out*) to scream or shout in pain, terror,

etc. **4.** (*tr.; often foll. by out*) to utter or shout (words of appeal, exclamation, fear, etc.). **5.** (*intr.; often foll. by out*) (of animals, birds, etc.) to utter loud characteristic sounds. **6.** (*tr.*) to hawk or sell by public announcement: *to cry newspapers*. **7.** to announce (something) publicly or in the streets. **8.** (*intr.; foll. by for*) to clamour or beg. **9.** *Scot.* to call. **10. cry for the moon.** to desire the unattainable. **11. cry one's eyes** *or* **heart out.** to weep bitterly. **12. cry quits** (*or* **mercy**). to give up a task, fight, etc. ~*n., pl.* **cries. 13.** the act or sound of crying; a shout, exclamation, scream, or wail. **14.** the characteristic utterance of an animal or bird: *the cry of gulls*. **15.** *Scot.* a call. **16.** *Archaic.* an oral announcement, esp. one made by town criers. **17.** a fit of weeping. **18.** *Hunting.* the baying of a pack of hounds hunting their quarry by scent. **19.** a pack of hounds. **20. a far cry. a.** a long way. **b.** something very different. **21. in full cry.** (esp. of a pack of hounds) in hot pursuit of a quarry. ~See also **cry down, cry off, cry out, cry up.** [C13: from Old French *crier*, from Latin *quirītāre* to call for help]

crybaby ('kraɪˌbeɪbɪ) *n., pl.* **-bies.** a person, esp. a child, given to frequent crying or complaint.

cry down *vb.* (*tr., adv.*) **1.** to belittle; disparage. **2.** to silence by making a greater noise: *to cry down opposition*.

crying ('kraɪɪŋ) *adj.* (*prenominal*) notorious; lamentable (esp. in the phrase **crying shame**).

cryo- *combining form.* indicating low temperature; frost, cold, or freezing: *cryogenics; cryosurgery*. [from Greek *kruos* icy cold, frost]

cryobiology (ˌkraɪəʊbaɪ'ɒlədʒɪ) *n.* the branch of biology concerned with the study of the effects of very low temperatures on organisms. —ˌ**cryobi'ologist** *n.*

cryocable (ˌkraɪəʊ'keɪbᵊl) *n.* a highly conducting electrical cable cooled with a refrigerant such as liquid nitrogen.

cry off *vb.* (*intr.*) *Informal.* to withdraw from or cancel (an agreement or arrangement).

cryogen ('kraɪədʒən) *n.* a substance used to produce low temperatures; a freezing mixture.

cryogenics (ˌkraɪə'dʒɛnɪks) *n.* (*functioning as sing.*) the branch of physics concerned with the production of very low temperatures and the phenomena occurring at these temperatures. —ˌ**cryo'genic** *adj.*

cryoglobulin (ˌkraɪəʊ'glɒbjʊlɪn) *n. Med.* an abnormal immunoglobulin, present in the blood in certain diseases, that precipitates below about 10°C, obstructing small blood vessels in the fingers and toes.

cryohydrate (ˌkraɪəʊ'haɪdreɪt) *n.* a crystalline substance containing water and a salt in definite proportions: a eutectic crystallizing below the freezing point of water.

cryolite ('kraɪəˌlaɪt) *n.* a white or colourless mineral consisting of a fluoride of sodium and aluminium in monoclinic crystalline form: used in the production of aluminium, glass, and enamel. Formula: Na_3AlF_6.

cryometer (kraɪ'ɒmɪtə) *n.* a thermometer for measuring low temperatures. —**cry'ometry** *n.*

cryonics (kraɪ'ɒnɪks) *n.* (*functioning as sing.*) the practice of freezing a human corpse in the hope of restoring it to life in the future.

cryophilic (ˌkraɪə'fɪlɪk) *adj. Biology.* able to thrive at low temperatures.

cryophyte ('kraɪəˌfaɪt) *n.* a plant, esp. an alga or moss, that grows on snow or ice.

cryoplankton (ˌkraɪəʊ'plæŋktən) *n.* minute organisms, esp. algae, living in ice, snow, or icy water.

cryoprecipitate (ˌkraɪəʊprɪ'sɪpɪteɪt) *n.* a precipitate obtained by controlled thawing of a previously frozen substance. Factor VIII, for treating haemophilia, is often obtained as a cryoprecipitate from frozen blood.

cryoscope ('kraɪəˌskəʊp) *n.* any instrument used to determine the freezing point of a substance.

cryoscopy (kraɪ'ɒskəpɪ) *n., pl.* **-pies.** the determination of freezing points, esp. for the determination of molecular weights by measuring the lowering of the freezing point of a solvent when a known quantity of solute is added. —**cryoscopic** (ˌkraɪə'skɒpɪk) *adj.*

cryostat ('kraɪəˌstæt) *n.* an apparatus for maintaining a constant low temperature or a vessel in which a substance is stored at a low temperature.

cryosurgery (ˌkraɪəʊ'sɜːdʒərɪ) *n.* surgery involving the local destruction of tissues by quick freezing for therapeutic benefit.

cryotherapy (ˌkraɪəʊ'θɛrəpɪ) *or* **crymotherapy** (ˌkraɪməʊ'θɛrəpɪ) *n.* medical treatment in which all or part of the body is subjected to cold temperatures, as by means of ice packs.

cryotron ('kraɪəˌtrɒn) *n.* a miniature switch working at the temperature of liquid helium and depending for its action on the production and destruction of superconducting properties in the conductor.

cry out *vb.* (*intr., adv.*) **1.** to scream or shout aloud, esp. in pain, terror, etc. **2.** (often foll. by *for*) *Informal.* to demand in an obvious manner: *our inner cities are crying out for redevelopment*. **3. for crying out loud.** *Informal.* an exclamation of anger, impatience, or dismay.

crypt (krɪpt) *n.* **1.** a cellar, vault, or underground chamber, esp. beneath a church, where it is often used as a chapel, burial place, etc. **2.** *Anatomy.* any pitlike recess or depression. [C18: from Latin *crypta*, from Greek *kruptē* vault, secret place, from *kruptos* hidden, from *kruptein* to hide] —'**cryptal** *adj.*

cryptaesthesia *or U.S.* **cryptesthesia** (ˌkrɪptəs'θiːzɪə) *n. Psychol.* another term for **extrasensory perception.**

cryptanalysis (ˌkrɪptə'nælɪsɪs) *n.* the study of codes and ciphers; cryptography. [C20: from CRYPTOGRAPH + ANALYSIS] —**cryptanalytic** (ˌkrɪptænə'lɪtɪk) *adj.* —**crypt'analyst** *n.*

cryptic ('krɪptɪk) *or* **cryptical** *adj.* **1.** hidden; secret; occult. **2.** (esp. of comments, sayings, etc.) esoteric or obscure in meaning. **3.** (of the coloration of animals) tending to conceal by disguising or camouflaging the shape. [C17: from Late Latin *crypticus*, from Greek *kruptikos*, from *kruptos* concealed; see CRYPT] —'**cryptically** *adv.*

crypto- *or before a vowel* **crypt-** *combining form.* secret, hidden, or concealed: *cryptography; crypto-fascist*. [New Latin, from Greek *kruptos* hidden, from *kruptein* to hide]

cryptobiosis (ˌkrɪptəʊbaɪ'əʊsɪs) *n. Zoology.* a temporary state in an animal in which metabolic activity is absent or undetectable.

cryptoclastic (ˌkrɪptəʊ'klæstɪk) *adj.* (of minerals and rocks) composed of microscopic fragments.

cryptocrystalline (ˌkrɪptəʊ'krɪstəlaɪn) *adj.* (of rocks) composed of crystals that can be distinguished individually only by the use of a polarizing microscope.

cryptogam ('krɪptəʊˌgæm) *n.* (in former classification schemes) any plant that does not produce seeds, including algae, fungi, mosses, and ferns. Compare **phanerogam.** [C19: from New Latin *Cryptogamia*, from CRYPTO- + Greek *gamos* marriage] —ˌ**crypto'gamic** *or* **cryptogamous** (krɪp'tɒgəməs) *adj.*

cryptogenic (ˌkrɪptəʊ'dʒɛnɪk) *adj.* (esp. of diseases) of unknown or obscure origin.

cryptograph ('krɪptəʊˌgræf, -ˌgrɑːf) *n.* **1.** something written in code or cipher. **2.** a code using secret symbols (**cryptograms**). **3.** a device for translating text into cipher, or vice versa.

cryptography (krɪp'tɒgrəfɪ) *or* **cryptology** (krɪp'tɒlədʒɪ) *n.* the science or study of analysing and deciphering codes, ciphers, etc.; cryptanalysis. —**cryp'tographer, cryp'tographist,** *or* **cryp'tologist** *n.* —**cryptographic** (ˌkrɪptə'græfɪk) *or* ˌ**crypto'graphical** *adj.* —ˌ**crypto'graphically** *adv.*

cryptomeria (ˌkrɪptəʊ'mɪərɪə) *n.* a coniferous tree, *Cryptomeria japonica*, of China and Japan, with curved needle-like leaves and small round cones: family *Taxodiaceae*. [C19: from New Latin, from CRYPTO- + Greek *meros* part; so called because the seeds are hidden by scales]

cryptometer (krɪp'tɒmɪtə) *n.* an instrument used to determine the opacity of pigments and paints.

cryptophyte ('krɪptəˌfaɪt) *n.* any perennial plant that bears its buds below the soil or water surface. —**cryptophytic** (ˌkrɪptə'fɪtɪk) *adj.*

cryptorchid (krɪp'tɔːkɪd) *n.* **1.** an animal or human in which the testes fail to descend into the scrotum. ~*adj.* **2.** denoting or relating to such an individual. [from CRYPTO- + *orchid*, from Greek *orkhis* testicle] —**cryp'torchidˌism** *n.*

cryptozoic (ˌkrɪptəʊ'zəʊɪk) *adj.* (of animals) living in dark places, such as holes, caves, and beneath stones.

Cryptozoic (ˌkrɪptəʊ'zəʊɪk) *adj.* **1.** of or relating to that part of geological time represented by rocks in which the evidence of life is slight and the life forms are primitive; pre-Phanerozoic. ~*n.* **2. the.** the Cryptozoic era. ~See also **Precambrian.** Compare **Phanerozoic.**

cryptozoite (ˌkrɪptəʊ'zəʊaɪt) *n.* a malarial parasite at the stage of development in its host before it enters the red blood cells.

cryst. *abbrev. for:* **1.** crystalline. **2.** Also: **crystall.** crystallography.

crystal ('krɪstᵊl) *n.* **1.** a piece of solid substance, such as quartz, with a regular shape in which plane faces intersect at definite angles, due to the regular internal structure of its atoms, ions, or molecules. **2.** a single grain of a crystalline substance. **3.** anything resembling a crystal, such as a piece of cut glass. **4. a.** a highly transparent and brilliant type of glass, often used in cut-glass tableware, ornaments, etc. **b.** (*as modifier*): *a crystal chandelier*. **5.** something made of or resembling crystal. **6.** crystal glass articles collectively. **7.** *Electronics.* **a.** a crystalline element used in certain electronic devices as a detector, oscillator, transducer, etc. **b.** (*as modifier*): *crystal pick-up; crystal detector*. **8.** a transparent cover for the face of a watch, usually of glass or plastic. **9.** (*modifier*) of or relating to a crystal or the regular atomic arrangement of crystals: *crystal structure; crystal lattice*. ~*adj.* **10.** resembling crystal; transparent: *crystal water*. [Old English *cristalla*, from Latin *crystallum*, from Greek *krustallos* ice, crystal, from *krustainein* to freeze]

crystal ball *n.* the glass globe used in crystal gazing.

crystal class *n. Crystallog.* any of 32 possible types of crystals, classified according to their rotational symmetry about axes through a point. Also called: **point group.**

crystal counter *n.* an instrument for detecting and measuring the intensity of high-energy radiation, in which particles collide with a crystal and momentarily increase its conductivity.

crystal detector *n. Electronics.* a demodulator, used esp. in early radio receivers, consisting of a thin metal wire in point contact with a semiconductor crystal.

crystal form *n. Crystallog.* a symmetrical set of planes in space, associated with a crystal, having the same symmetry as the crystal class. Compare **crystal habit.**

crystal gazing *n.* **1.** the act of staring into a crystal globe (**crystal ball**) supposedly in order to arouse visual perceptions of the future, etc. **2.** the act of trying to foresee or predict something. —**crystal gazer** *n.*
crystal habit *n. Crystallog.* the external shape of a crystal. Compare **crystal form.**
crystal lattice *n.* the regular array of points about which the atoms, ions, or molecules composing a crystal are centred.
crystalline ('krɪstəˌlaɪn) *adj.* **1.** having the characteristics or structure of crystals. **2.** consisting of or containing crystals. **3.** made of or like crystal; transparent; clear. —**crystallinity** (ˌkrɪstə'lɪnɪtɪ) *n.*
crystalline lens *n.* a biconvex transparent elastic structure in the eye situated behind the iris, serving to focus images on the retina.
crystallite ('krɪstəˌlaɪt) *n.* any of the minute rudimentary or imperfect crystals occurring in many glassy rocks. —**crystallitic** (ˌkrɪstə'lɪtɪk) *adj.*
crystallize, crystalize *or* **crystallise, crystalise** ('krɪstəˌlaɪz) *vb.* **1.** to form or cause to form crystals; assume or cause to assume a crystalline form or structure. **2.** to coat or become coated with sugar: *crystallized fruit.* **3.** to give a definite form or expression to (an idea, argument, etc.) or (of an idea, argument, etc.) to assume a recognizable or definite form. —'**crystalˌlizable, 'crystalˌizable** *or* **'crystalˌlisable, 'crystalˌisable** *adj.* —ˌ**crystalˌliza'bility, ˌcrystalˌiza'bility** *or* ˌ**crystalˌlisa'bility, ˌcrystalˌisa'bility** *n.* —ˌ**crystalli'zation, ˌcrystali'zation** *or* ˌ**crystalli'sation, ˌcrystali'sation** *n.* —'**crystalˌlizer, 'crystalˌizer** *or* **'crystalˌliser, 'crystalˌiser** *n.*
crystallo- *or before a vowel* **crystall-** *combining form.* crystal: *crystallography.*
crystallography (ˌkrɪstə'lɒgrəfɪ) *n.* the science concerned with the formation, properties, and structure of crystals. —ˌ**crystal'lographer** *n.* —**crystallographic** (ˌkrɪstələʊ'græfɪk) *adj.* —ˌ**crystallo'graphically** *adv.*
crystalloid ('krɪstəˌlɔɪd) *adj.* **1.** resembling or having the appearance or properties of a crystal or crystalloid. ~*n.* **2.** a substance that in solution can pass through a semipermeable membrane. Compare **colloid** (sense 3). **3.** *Botany.* any of numerous crystals of protein occurring in certain seeds and other storage organs. —ˌ**crystal'loidal** *adj.*
crystal microphone *n.* a microphone that uses a piezoelectric crystal to convert sound energy into electrical energy.
crystal nucleus *n. Chem.* the tiny crystal that forms at the onset of crystallization.
crystal pick-up *n.* a record-player pick-up in which the current is generated by the deformation of a piezoelectric crystal caused by the movements of the stylus.
crystal set *n.* an early form of radio receiver having a crystal detector to demodulate the radio signals but no amplifier, therefore requiring earphones.
crystal system *n. Crystallog.* any of six, or sometimes seven, classifications of crystals depending on their symmetry. The classes are cubic, tetragonal, hexagonal, orthorhombic, monoclinic, and triclinic. Sometimes an additional system, trigonal, is distinguished, although this is usually included in the hexagonal system. See also **crystal class.**
crystal violet *n.* another name for **gentian violet.**
cry up *vb.* (*tr., adv.*) to praise highly; extol.
Cs *the chemical symbol for* caesium.
CS *abbrev. for:* **1.** Also: **cs.** capital stock. **2.** chartered surveyor. **3.** Christian Science. **4.** Christian Scientist. **5.** Civil Service. **6.** Also: **cs.** Court of Session. ~ **7.** *international car registration for* Czechoslovakia.
cs. *abbrev. for* case.
CSB *abbrev. for* chemical stimulation of the brain.
CSBM *abbrev. for* Confidence- and Security-Building Measures (to improve military transparency and predictability in Europe).
csc *abbrev. for* cosecant.
CSC *abbrev. for* Civil Service Commission.
CSCE *abbrev. for* Conference for Security and Cooperation in Europe.
csch *n.* a U.S. form of **cosech.**
CSE (in Britain) *abbrev. for* Certificate of Secondary Education; a series of examinations the first grade of pass of which is an equivalent to a GCE O level.
CSEU *abbrev. for* Confederation of Shipbuilding and Engineering Unions.
CSF *abbrev. for:* **1.** *Physiol.* cerebrospinal fluid. **2.** *Immunol.* colony-stimulating factor.
CS gas *n.* a gas causing tears, salivation, and painful breathing, used in civil disturbances; *ortho*-chlorobenzal malononitrile. Formula: $C_6H_4ClCH{:}C(CN)_2$. [C20: from the surname initials of its U.S. inventors, Ben Carson and Roger Staughton]
CSIRO (in Australia) *abbrev. for* Commonwealth Scientific and Industrial Research Organization.
CSM (in Britain) *abbrev. for* Company Sergeant-Major.
C-spanner *n.* a sickle-shaped spanner having a projection at the end of the curve, used for turning large narrow nuts that have an indentation into which the projection on the spanner fits.
CSR (in Australia) *abbrev. for* Colonial Sugar Refining Company.
CSS (in Britain) *abbrev. for* Certificate in Social Service.
CST *abbrev. for* Central Standard Time.
CSU (in Britain) *abbrev. for* Civil Service Union.
CSV *abbrev. for* Community Service Volunteer.
CSYS (in Scotland) *abbrev. for* Certificate of Sixth Year Studies.
ct *abbrev. for:* **1.** cent. **2.** court.
CT *abbrev. for:* **1.** central time. **2.** Connecticut. **3.** computerized tomography (see also **CT scanner**).
ct. *abbrev. for* certificate.
CTC (in Britain) *abbrev. for* city technology college.
ctenidium (tɪ'nɪdɪəm) *n., pl.* **-ia** (-ɪə). one of the comblike respiratory gills of molluscs. [C19: New Latin, from Greek *ktenidion,* diminutive of *kteis* comb]
ctenoid ('tiːnɔɪd, 'tɛn-) *adj. Biology.* toothed like a comb, as the scales of perches. [C19: from Greek *ktenoeidēs,* from *kteis* comb + *-oeidēs* -OID]
ctenophore ('tɛnəˌfɔː, 'tiːnə-) *n.* any marine invertebrate of the phylum *Ctenophora,* including the sea gooseberry and Venus's-girdle, whose body bears eight rows of fused cilia, for locomotion. Also called: **comb jelly.** [C19: from New Latin *ctenophorus,* from Greek *kteno-, kteis* comb + -PHORE] —**ctenophoran** (tɪ'nɒfərən) *adj., n.*
ctn *abbrev. for* cotangent.
CTO *Philately. abbrev. for* cancelled to order (of postage stamps); postmarked in sheets for private sale.
CTR *abbrev. for* Control Traffic Zone: an area established about an aerodrome or airport to afford protection to aircraft entering or leaving the terminal area.
ctr. *abbrev. for* centre.
cts *abbrev. for* cents.
cts. *abbrev. for* certificates.
CT scanner *n.* computerized tomography scanner: an X-ray machine that can produce stereographic images. Former name: **CAT scanner.**
CTV *abbrev. for* Canadian Television Network Limited.
Cu *the chemical symbol for* copper. [from Late Latin *cuprum*]
cu. *abbrev. for* cubic.
cub (kʌb) *n.* **1.** the young of certain animals, such as the lion, bear, etc. **2.** a young or inexperienced person. ~*vb.* **cubs, cubbing, cubbed. 3.** to give birth to (cubs). [C16: perhaps from Old Norse *kubbi* young seal; see COB[1]] —'**cubbish** *adj.* —'**cubbishly** *adv.*
Cub (kʌb) *n.* short for **Cub Scout.**
cubage ('kjuːbɪdʒ) *n.* another word for **cubature** (sense 2).
Cuba libre ('kjuːbə 'liːbrə) *n. Chiefly U.S.* a drink of rum, cola, lime juice, and ice. [Spanish, literally: free Cuba, a toast during the Cuban War of Independence]
Cuban ('kjuːbən) *adj.* **1.** of or relating to Cuba, a republic and the largest island in the West Indies. ~*n.* **2.** a native or inhabitant of Cuba.
cubane ('kjuːbeɪn) *n.* a type of hydrocarbon formed by eight CH groups, each of which is situated at the corner of a cube. Formula: C_8H_8. [C20: from CUBE[1] +-ANE]
Cuban heel *n.* a moderately high heel for a shoe or boot.
cubature ('kjuːbətʃə) *n.* **1.** the determination of the cubic contents of something. **2.** Also called: **cubage.** cubic contents. [C17: from CUBE[1] + *-ature,* on the model of *quadrature*]
cubbyhole ('kʌbɪˌhəʊl) *n.* **1.** a small enclosed space or room. **2.** any small compartment, such as a pigeonhole. ~Often shortened to **cubby** ('kʌbɪ). [C19: from dialect *cub* cattle pen; see COVE[1]]
cube[1] (kjuːb) *n.* **1.** a solid having six plane square faces in which the angle between two adjacent sides is a right angle. **2.** the product of three equal factors: the cube of 2 is $2 \times 2 \times 2$ (usually written 2^3). **3.** something in the form of a cube: *a bath cube.* ~*vb.* **4.** to raise (a number or quantity) to the third power. **5.** (*tr.*) to measure the cubic contents of. **6.** (*tr.*) to make, shape, or cut (something, esp. food) into cubes. [C16: from Latin *cubus* die, cube, from Greek *kubos*] —'**cuber** *n.*
cube[2] ('kjuːbeɪ) *n.* **1.** any of various tropical American plants, esp. any of the leguminous genus *Lonchocarpus,* the roots of which yield rotenone. **2.** an extract from the roots of these plants: a fish poison and insecticide. [American Spanish *cubé,* of unknown origin]
cubeb ('kjuːbɛb) *n.* **1.** a SE Asian treelike piperaceous woody climbing plant, *Piper cubeba,* with brownish berries. **2.** the unripe spicy fruit of this plant, dried and used as a stimulant and diuretic and sometimes smoked in cigarettes. [C14: from Old French *cubebe,* from Medieval Latin *cubēba,* from Arabic *kubābah*]
cube root *n.* the number or quantity whose cube is a given number or quantity: 2 is the cube root of 8 (usually written $\sqrt[3]{8}$ or $8^{1/3}$).
cubic ('kjuːbɪk) *adj.* **1.** having the shape of a cube. **2. a.** having three dimensions. **b.** denoting or relating to a linear measure that is raised to the third power: *a cubic metre.* Abbrevs.: **cu., c. 3.** *Maths.* of, relating to, or containing a variable to the third power or a term in which the sum of the exponents of the variables is three. **4.** Also: **isometric, regular.** *Crystallog.* relating to or belonging to the crystal system characterized by three equal perpendicular axes. The unit cell of cubic crystals is a cube with a lattice point at each corner (**simple cubic**) and one in the cube's centre (**body-centred cubic**), or a lattice point at each corner and one at the centre of each face (**face-centred cubic**).

~*n.* 5. *Maths.* **a.** a cubic equation, such as $x^3 + x + 2 = 0$. **b.** a cubic term or expression.
cubical ('kju:bɪkᵊl) *adj.* 1. of or related to volume: *cubical expansion.* 2. shaped like a cube. 3. of or involving the third power. —'**cubically** *adv.* —'**cubicalness** *n.*
cubicle ('kju:bɪkᵊl) *n.* a partially or totally enclosed section of a room, as in a dormitory. [C15: from Latin *cubiculum,* from *cubāre* to lie down, lie asleep]
cubic measure *n.* a system of units for the measurement of volumes, based on the cubic inch, the cubic centimetre, etc.
cubiculum (kju:'bɪkjʊləm) *n., pl.* **-la** (-lə). an underground burial chamber in Imperial Rome, such as those found in the catacombs. [C19: from Latin: CUBICLE]
cubiform ('kju:bɪ,fɔ:m) *adj.* having the shape of a cube.
cubism ('kju:bɪzəm) *n.* (*often cap.*) a French school of painting, collage, relief, and sculpture, initiated in about 1907, which amalgamated viewpoints of natural forms into a multifaceted surface of geometrical planes. —'**cubist** *adj., n.* —**cu'bistic** *adj.* —**cu'bistically** *adv.*
cubit ('kju:bɪt) *n.* an ancient measure of length based on the length of the forearm. [C14: from Latin *cubitum* elbow, cubit]
cubital ('kju:bɪtᵊl) *adj.* of or relating to the forearm.
cuboid ('kju:bɔɪd) *adj.* also **cuboidal** (kju:'bɔɪdᵊl). 1. shaped like a cube; cubic. 2. of or denoting the cuboid bone. ~*n.* 3. the cubelike bone of the foot; the outer distal bone of the tarsus. 4. *Maths.* a geometric solid whose six faces are rectangles; rectangular parallelepiped.
Cu-bop ('kju:,bɒp) *n. Jazz.* music of the 1940s in which Cuban rhythms are combined with bop. Compare **Afro-Cuban.**
cub reporter *n.* a trainee reporter on a newspaper.
Cub Scout *or* **Cub** *n.* a member of the junior branch of the Scout Association.
cucking stool ('kʌkɪŋ) *n. History.* a stool to which suspected witches, scolds, etc., were tied and pelted or ducked into water as a punishment. Compare **ducking stool.** [C13 *cucking stol,* literally: defecating chair, from *cukken* to defecate; compare Old Norse *kúkr* excrement]
cuckold ('kʌkəld) *n.* 1. a man whose wife has committed adultery, often regarded as an object of scorn. ~*vb.* 2. (*tr.*) to make a cuckold of. [C13 *cukeweld,* from Old French *cucuault,* from *cucu* CUCKOO; perhaps an allusion to the parasitic cuckoos that lay their eggs in the nests of other birds] —'**cuckoldry** *n.*
cuckoo ('kʊku:) *n., pl.* **-oos.** 1. any bird of the family *Cuculidae,* having pointed wings, a long tail, and zygodactyl feet: order *Cuculiformes.* Many species, including the **European cuckoo** (*Cuculus canorus*), lay their eggs in the nests of other birds and have a two-note call. 2. *Informal.* an insane or foolish person. ~*adj.* 3. *Informal.* insane or foolish. ~*interj.* 4. an imitation or representation of the call of a cuckoo. ~*vb.* **-oos, -ooing, -ooed.** 5. (*tr.*) to repeat over and over. 6. (*intr.*) to make the sound imitated by the word *cuckoo.* [C13: from Old French *cucu,* of imitative origin; related to German *kuckuck,* Latin *cucūlus,* Greek *kokkux*]
cuckoo bee *n.* any of several species of parasitic or inquiline bee the queen of which lays her eggs in the nest of the bumblebee or other species, sometimes killing the host queen, leaving her eggs to be raised by the workers of the nest.
cuckoo clock *n.* a clock in which a mechanical cuckoo pops out with a sound like a cuckoo's call when the clock strikes.
cuckooflower ('kʊku:,flaʊə) *n.* another name for **lady's-smock** and **ragged robin.**
cuckoopint ('kʊku:,paɪnt) *n.* a European aroid plant, *Arum maculatum,* with arrow-shaped leaves, a spathe marked with purple, a pale purple spadix, and scarlet berries. Also called: **lords-and-ladies.**
cuckoo shrike *n.* any Old World tropical songbird of the family *Campephagidae,* typically having a strong notched bill, long rounded tail, and pointed wings. See also **minivet.**
cuckoo spit *n.* a white frothy mass on the stems and leaves of many plants, produced by froghopper larvae (**cuckoo spit insects**) which feed on the plant juices. Also called: **frog spit.**
cuculiform (kjʊ'kju:lɪ,fɔ:m) *adj.* of, relating to, or belonging to the order *Cuculiformes,* which includes the cuckoos. [from Latin *cucūlus* cuckoo + -FORM]
cucullate ('kju:kə,leɪt, -lɪt) *adj.* shaped like a hood or having a hoodlike part: *cucullate sepals.* [C18: from Late Latin *cucullātus,* from Latin *cucullus* hood, cap] —'**cucul,lately** *adv.*
cucumber ('kju:,kʌmbə) *n.* 1. a creeping cucurbitaceous plant, *Cucumis sativus,* cultivated in many forms for its edible fruit. Compare **squirting cucumber.** 2. the cylindrical fruit of this plant, which has hard thin green rind and white crisp flesh. 3. any of various similar or related plants or their fruits. 4. **cool as a cucumber.** very calm; self-possessed. [C14: from Latin *cucumis,* of unknown origin]
cucumber tree *n.* 1. any of several American trees or shrubs of the genus *Magnolia,* esp. *M. acuminata,* of E and central North America, having cup-shaped greenish flowers and cucumber-shaped fruits. 2. an E Asian tree, *Averrhoa bilimbi,* with edible fruits resembling small cucumbers: family *Averrhoaceae.* See also **carambola.**
cucurbit (kju:'kɜ:bɪt) *n.* any creeping flowering plant of the mainly tropical and subtropical family *Cucurbitaceae,* which includes the pumpkin, cucumber, squashes, and gourds. [C14: from Old French, from Latin *cucurbita* gourd, cup] —**cu,curbi'taceous** *adj.*
cud (kʌd) *n.* 1. partially digested food regurgitated from the first stomach of cattle and other ruminants to the mouth for a second chewing. 2. **chew the cud.** to reflect or think over something. [Old English *cudu,* from *cwidu* what has been chewed; related to Old Norse *kvātha* resin (for chewing), Old High German *quiti* glue, Sanskrit *jatu* rubber]
cudbear ('kʌd,bɛə) *n.* another name for **orchil.** [C18: whimsical alteration of *Cuthbert,* the Christian name of Dr Gordon, 18th-century Scot who patented the dye. See CUDDY[2]]
cuddle ('kʌdᵊl) *vb.* 1. to hold (another person or thing) close or (of two people, etc.) to hold each other close, as for affection, comfort, or warmth; embrace; hug. 2. (*intr.*; foll. by *up*) to curl or snuggle up into a comfortable or warm position. ~*n.* 3. a close embrace, esp. when prolonged. [C18: of uncertain origin] —'**cuddlesome** *adj.* —'**cuddly** *adj.*
cuddy[1] ('kʌdɪ) *n., pl.* **-dies.** 1. a small cabin in a boat. 2. a small room, cupboard, etc. [C17: perhaps from Dutch *kajute;* compare Old French *cahute*]
cuddy[2] *or* **cuddie** ('kʌdɪ) *n., pl.* **-dies.** *Dialect, chiefly Scot.* 1. a donkey or horse. 2. a stupid fellow; fool. [C18: probably from *Cuddy,* nickname for *Cuthbert*]
cuddy[3] ('kʌdɪ) *n.* a young coalfish. [C18: of unknown origin]
cudgel ('kʌdʒəl) *n.* 1. a short stout stick used as a weapon. 2. **take up the cudgels.** (often foll. by *for* or *on behalf of*) to join in a dispute, esp. to defend oneself or another. ~*vb.* **-els, -elling, -elled** *or U.S.* **-els, -eling, -eled.** 3. (*tr.*) to strike with a cudgel or similar weapon. 4. **cudgel one's brains.** to think hard about a problem. [Old English *cycgel;* related to Middle Dutch *koghele* stick with knob] —'**cudgeller** *n.*
cudgerie ('kʌdʒərɪ) *n. Austral.* 1. a large tropical rutaceous tree, *Flindersia schottina,* having light-coloured wood. 2. Also called: **pink poplar.** an anacardiaceous rainforest tree, *Euroschinus falcatus.*
cudweed ('kʌd,wi:d) *n.* 1. any of various temperate woolly plants of the genus *Gnaphalium,* having clusters of whitish or yellow button-like flowers: family *Compositae* (composites). 2. any of several similar and related plants of the genus *Filago,* esp. *F. germanica.*
cue[1] (kju:) *n.* 1. **a.** (in the theatre, films, music, etc.) anything spoken or done that serves as a signal to an actor, musician, etc., to follow with specific lines or action. **b. on cue.** at the right moment. 2. a signal or reminder to do something. 3. *Psychol.* the part of any sensory pattern that is identified as the signal for a response. 4. the part, function, or action assigned to or expected of a person. ~*vb.* **cues, cueing, cued.** 5. (*tr.*) to give a cue or cues to (an actor). 6. (usually foll. by *in* or *into*) to signal (to something or somebody) at a specific moment in a musical or dramatic performance: *to cue in a flourish of trumpets.* 7. (*tr.*) to give information or a reminder to (someone). 8. (*intr.*) to signal the commencement of filming, as with the word "Action!" [C16: probably from name of the letter *q,* used in an actor's script to represent Latin *quando* when]
cue[2] (kju:) *n.* 1. *Billiards, etc.* a long tapered shaft with a leather tip, used to drive the balls. 2. hair caught at the back forming a tail or braid. 3. *U.S.* a variant spelling of **queue.** ~*vb.* **cues, cueing, cued.** 4. to drive (a ball) with a cue. 5. (*tr.*) to twist or tie (the hair) into a cue. [C18: variant of QUEUE]
cue ball *n. Billiards, etc.* the ball struck by the cue, as distinguished from the object balls.
cue bid *n. Contract bridge.* a bid in a suit made to show an ace or a void in that suit.
cueing ('kju:ɪŋ) *n.* another name for **foldback.**
cuesta ('kwɛstə) *n.* a long low ridge with a steep scarp slope and a gentle back slope, formed by the differential erosion of strata of differing hardness. [Spanish: shoulder, from Latin *costa* side, rib]
cuff[1] (kʌf) *n.* 1. the part of a sleeve nearest the hand, sometimes turned back and decorative. 2. the part of a gauntlet or glove that extends past the wrist. 3. the U.S., Canadian, and Australian name for **turn-up** (sense 5). 4. **off the cuff.** *Informal.* improvised; extemporary. ~See also **cuffs.** [C14 *cuffe* glove, of obscure origin]
cuff[2] (kʌf) *vb.* 1. (*tr.*) to strike with an open hand. ~*n.* 2. a blow of this kind. [C16: of obscure origin]
cuff link *n.* one of a pair of linked buttons, used to join the buttonholes on the cuffs of a shirt.
cuffs (kʌfs) *pl. n. Informal.* short for **handcuffs.**
Cufic ('ku:fɪk, 'kju:-) *n., adj.* a variant spelling of **Kufic.**
cui bono *Latin.* (kwi: 'bəʊnəʊ) for whose benefit? for what purpose?
cuirass (kwɪ'ræs) *n.* 1. a piece of armour, of leather or metal covering the chest and back. 2. a hard outer protective covering of some animals, consisting of shell, plate, or scales. 3. any similar protective covering, as on a ship. ~*vb.* 4. (*tr.*) to equip with a cuirass. [C15: from French *cuirasse,* from Late Latin *coriacea,* from *coriaceus* made of leather, from Latin *corium* leather]
cuirassier (,kwɪrə'sɪə) *n.* a mounted soldier, esp. of the 16th century, who wore a cuirass.

cuir-bouilli (ˌkwɪəbuːˈjiː) *n.* a type of leather hardened by soaking in wax, used for armour before the 14th century. [French, literally: boiled leather]

Cuisenaire rod (ˌkwɪzəˈnɛə) *n. Trademark.* one of a set of rods of various colours and lengths representing different numbers, used to teach arithmetic to young children. [C20: named after Emil-Georges *Cuisenaire* (?1891–1976), Belgian educationalist]

cuisine (kwɪˈziːn) *n.* **1.** a style or manner of cooking: *French cuisine.* **2.** the food prepared by a restaurant, household, etc. [C18: from French, literally: kitchen, from Late Latin *coquīna,* from Latin *coquere* to cook]

cuisine minceur *French* (kɥizin mɛ̃sœr) *n.* a style of cooking, originating in France, that limits the use of starch, sugar, butter, and cream traditionally used in French cookery. [literally: slimness cooking]

cuisse (kwɪs) *or* **cuish** (kwɪʃ) *n.* a piece of armour for the thigh. [C15: back formation from *cuisses* (plural), from Old French *cuisseaux* thigh guards, from *cuisse* thigh, from Latin *coxa* hipbone]

culch *or* **cultch** (kʌltʃ) *n.* **1.** a mass of broken stones, shells, and gravel that forms the basis of an oyster bed. **2.** the oyster spawn attached to such a structure. **3.** *Dialect.* refuse; rubbish. [C17: perhaps ultimately from Old French *culche* bed, COUCH]

culchie (ˈkʌltʃiː) *n. Irish informal.* a rough labouring countryman. [of unknown origin]

cul-de-sac (ˈkʌldəˌsæk, ˈkʊl-) *n., pl.* **culs-de-sac** *or* **cul-de-sacs.** **1.** a road with one end blocked off; dead end. **2.** an inescapable position. **3.** any tube-shaped bodily cavity or pouch closed at one end, such as the caecum. [C18: from French, literally: bottom of the bag]

-cule *suffix forming nouns.* indicating smallness: *animalcule.* [from Latin *-culus,* diminutive suffix; compare -CLE]

culet (ˈkjuːlɪt) *n.* **1.** *Jewellery.* the flat face at the bottom of a gem. **2.** either of the plates of armour worn at the small of the back. [C17: from obsolete French, diminutive of *cul,* from Latin *cūlus* bottom]

culex (ˈkjuːlɛks) *n., pl.* **-lices** (-lɪˌsiːz). any mosquito of the genus *Culex,* such as *C. pipiens,* the common mosquito. [C15: from Latin: midge, gnat; related to Old Irish *cuil* gnat]

culicid (kjuːˈlɪsɪd) *n.* **1.** any dipterous insect of the family *Culicidae,* which comprises the mosquitos. ~*adj.* **2.** of, relating to, or belonging to the *Culicidae.* [C19: from New Latin *Culicidae,* from Latin *culex* gnat, CULEX]

culinary (ˈkʌlɪnərɪ) *adj.* of, relating to, or used in the kitchen or in cookery. [C17: from Latin *culīnārius,* from *culīna* kitchen] —ˈ**culinarily** *adv.*

cull (kʌl) *vb. (tr.)* **1.** to choose or gather the best or required examples. **2.** to take out (an animal, esp. an inferior one) from a herd. **3.** to reduce the size of (a herd or flock) by killing a proportion of its members. **4.** to gather (flowers, fruit, etc.). ~*n.* **5.** the act or product of culling. **6.** an inferior animal taken from a herd or group. [C15: from Old French *coillir* to pick, from Latin *colligere;* see COLLECT[1]]

cullender (ˈkʌlɪndə) *n.* a variant of **colander.**

culler (kʌlə) *n.* **1.** a person employed to cull animals. **2.** *Austral. and N.Z.* an animal, esp. a sheep, designated for culling. **3.** *Austral and N.Z.* a person employed by the government to destroy deer in overpopulated bush country.

cullet (ˈkʌlɪt) *n.* waste glass for melting down to be reused. [C17: perhaps variant of COLLET (literally: little neck, referring to the glass neck of newly blown bottles, etc.)]

cullis (ˈkʌlɪs) *n.* **1.** a gutter in or at the eaves of a roof. **2.** another word for **coulisse** (sense 1). [C19: from French *coulisse* channel, groove; see COULISSE]

cully (ˈkʌlɪ) *n., pl.* **-lies.** *Slang.* pal; mate. [C17: of unknown origin]

culm[1] (kʌlm) *n. Mining.* **1.** coal-mine waste. **2.** inferior anthracite. [C14: probably related to COAL]

culm[2] (kʌlm) *n.* the hollow jointed stem of a grass or sedge. [C17: from Latin *culmus* stalk; see HAULM]

Culm *or* **Culm Measures** *n.* a formation consisting mainly of shales and sandstone deposited during the Carboniferous period in parts of Europe. [C19: from CULM[1]]

culmiferous (kʌlˈmɪfərəs) *adj.* (of grasses) having a hollow jointed stem.

culminant (ˈkʌlmɪnənt) *adj.* highest or culminating.

culminate (ˈkʌlmɪˌneɪt) *vb.* **1.** (when *intr.,* usually foll. by *in*) to end or cause to end, esp. to reach or bring to a final or climactic stage. **2.** *(intr.)* (of a celestial body) to cross the meridian of the observer. [C17: from Late Latin *culmināre* to reach the highest point, from Latin *culmen* top]

culmination (ˌkʌlmɪˈneɪʃən) *n.* **1.** the final, highest, or decisive point. **2.** the act of culminating. **3.** *Astronomy.* the highest or lowest altitude attained by a heavenly body as it crosses the meridian.

culottes (kjuːˈlɒts) *pl. n.* women's flared trousers cut to look like a skirt. [C20: from French, literally: breeches, from *cul* bottom; see CULET]

culpa (ˈkʊlpɑː) *n., pl.* **-pae** (-piː). **1.** *Civil law.* an act of neglect. **2.** a fault; sin; guilt. [Latin: fault]

culpable (ˈkʌlpəbᵊl) *adj.* deserving censure; blameworthy. [C14: from Old French *coupable,* from Latin *culpābilis,* from *culpāre* to blame, from *culpa* fault] —ˌ**culpaˈbility** *or* ˈ**culpableness** *n.* —ˈ**culpably** *adv.*

culpable homicide *n. Scots Law.* manslaughter.

culprit (ˈkʌlprɪt) *n.* **1.** *Law.* a person awaiting trial, esp. one who has pleaded not guilty. **2.** the person responsible for a particular offence, misdeed, etc. [C17: from Anglo-French *cul-,* short for *culpable* guilty + *prit* ready, indicating that the prosecution was ready to prove the guilt of the one charged]

cult (kʌlt) *n.* **1.** a specific system of religious worship, esp. with reference to its rites and deity. **2.** a sect devoted to such a system. **3.** a quasi-religious organization using devious psychological techniques to gain and control adherents. **4.** *Sociol.* a group having an exclusive ideology and ritual practices centred on sacred symbols, esp. one characterized by lack of organizational structure. **5.** intense interest in and devotion to a person, idea, or activity: *the cult of yoga.* **6.** the person, idea, etc., arousing such devotion. **7. a.** something regarded as fashionable or significant by a particular group. **b.** *(as modifier): a cult show.* **8.** *(modifier)* of, relating to, or characteristic of a cult or cults: *a cult figure.* [C17: from Latin *cultus* cultivation, refinement, from *colere* to till] —ˈ**cultic** *adj.* —ˈ**cultism** *n.* —ˈ**cultist** *n.*

cultch (kʌltʃ) *n.* a variant spelling of **culch.**

cultigen (ˈkʌltɪdʒən) *n.* a species of plant that is known only as a cultivated form and did not originate from a wild type. [C20: from CULTI(VATED) + -GEN]

cultivable (ˈkʌltɪvəbᵊl) *or* **cultivatable** (ˈkʌltɪˌveɪtəbᵊl) *adj.* (of land) capable of being cultivated. [C17: from French, from Old French *cultiver* to CULTIVATE] —ˌ**cultivaˈbility** *n.*

cultivar (ˈkʌltɪˌvɑː) *n.* a variety of a plant that was produced from a natural species and is maintained by cultivation. [C20: from CULTI(VATED) + VAR(IETY)]

cultivate (ˈkʌltɪˌveɪt) *vb. (tr.)* **1.** to till and prepare (land or soil) for the growth of crops. **2.** to plant, tend, harvest, or improve (plants) by labour and skill. **3.** to break up (land or soil) with a cultivator or hoe. **4.** to improve or foster (the mind, body, etc.) as by study, education, or labour. **5.** to give special attention to: *to cultivate a friendship; to cultivate a hobby.* **6.** to give or bring culture to (a person, society, etc.); civilize. [C17: from Medieval Latin *cultivāre* to till, from Old French *cultiver,* from Medieval Latin *cultīvus* cultivable, from Latin *cultus* cultivated, from *colere* to till, toil over]

cultivated (ˈkʌltɪˌveɪtɪd) *adj.* **1.** cultured, refined, or educated. **2.** (of land or soil) **a.** subjected to tillage or cultivation. **b.** tilled and broken up. **3.** (of plants) specially bred or improved by cultivation.

cultivation (ˌkʌltɪˈveɪʃən) *n.* **1.** *Agriculture.* **a.** the planting, tending, improving, or harvesting of crops or plants. **b.** the preparation of ground to promote their growth. **2.** development, esp. through education, training, etc. **3.** culture or sophistication, esp. social refinement.

cultivator (ˈkʌltɪˌveɪtə) *n.* **1.** a farm implement equipped with shovels, blades, etc., used to break up soil and remove weeds. **2.** a person or thing that cultivates. **3.** a person who grows, tends, or improves plants or crops.

cultrate (ˈkʌltreɪt) *or* **cultrated** *adj.* shaped like a knife blade: *cultrate leaves.* [C19: from Latin *cultrātus,* from *culter* knife]

cultural (ˈkʌltʃərəl) *adj.* **1.** of or relating to artistic or social pursuits or events considered to be valuable or enlightened. **2.** of or relating to a culture or civilization. **3.** (of certain varieties of plant) obtained by specialized breeding. —ˈ**culturally** *adv.*

cultural anthropology *n.* the branch of anthropology dealing with cultural as opposed to biological and racial features. —**cultural anthropologist** *n.*

cultural lag *or* **culture lag** *n.* the difference in the rate of change between two parts of a culture.

culture (ˈkʌltʃə) *n.* **1.** the total of the inherited ideas, beliefs, values, and knowledge, which constitute the shared bases of social action. **2.** the total range of activities and ideas of a group of people with shared traditions, which are transmitted and reinforced by members of the group: *the Mayan culture.* **3.** a particular civilization at a particular period. **4.** the artistic and social pursuits, expression, and tastes valued by a society or class, as in the arts, manners, dress, etc. **5.** the enlightenment or refinement resulting from these pursuits. **6.** the cultivation of plants, esp. by scientific methods designed to improve stock or to produce new ones. **7.** *Stockbreeding.* the rearing and breeding of animals, esp. with a view to improving the strain. **8.** the act or practice of tilling or cultivating the soil. **9.** *Biology.* **a.** the experimental growth of microorganisms, such as bacteria and fungi, in a nutrient substance (see **culture medium**), usually under controlled conditions. **b.** a group of microorganisms grown in this way. ~*vb. (tr.)* **10.** to cultivate (plants or animals). **11.** to grow (microorganisms) in a culture medium. [C15: from Old French, from Latin *cultūra* a cultivating, from *colere* to till; see CULT] —ˈ**culturist** *n.* —ˈ**cultureless** *adj.*

cultured (ˈkʌltʃəd) *adj.* **1.** showing or having good taste, manners, upbringing, and education. **2.** artificially grown or synthesized: *cultured pearls.*

cultured pearl *n.* a pearl induced to grow in the shell of an oyster or clam, by the insertion of a small object around which layers of nacre are deposited.

culture-free test *n.* a test (usually for intelligence) that does not put anyone taking it at a disadvantage, for instance, as regards material or cultural background.
culture medium *n.* a nutritive substance, such as an agar gel, in which cultures of bacteria and fungi are grown.
culture shock *n. Sociol.* the feelings of isolation, rejection, etc., experienced when one culture is brought into sudden contact with another, as when a primitive tribe is confronted by modern civilization.
culture vulture *n. Informal.* a person considered to be excessively, and often pretentiously, interested in the arts.
cultus ('kʌltəs) *n., pl.* **-tuses** *or* **-ti** (-taɪ). *Chiefly R.C. Church.* another word for **cult** (sense 1). [C17: from Latin: a toiling over something, refinement, CULT]
culver ('kʌlvə) *n.* an archaic or poetic name for **pigeon**[1] or **dove.** [Old English *culfre,* from Latin *columbula* a little dove, from *columba* dove]
culverin ('kʌlvərɪn) *n.* **1.** a long-range medium to heavy cannon used during the 15th, 16th, and 17th centuries. **2.** a medieval musket. [C15: from Old French *coulevrine,* from *couleuvre,* from Latin *coluber* serpent]
Culver's root *or* **physic** ('kʌlvəz) *n.* **1.** a tall North American scrophulariaceous plant, *Veronicastrum virginicum,* having spikes of small white or purple flowers. **2.** the dried roots of this plant, formerly used as a cathartic and emetic. [C19: named after a Dr *Culver,* 18th-century American physician]
culvert ('kʌlvət) *n.* **1.** a drain or covered channel that crosses under a road, railway, etc. **2.** a channel for an electric cable. [C18: of unknown origin]
cum (kʌm) *prep.* used between two nouns to designate an object of a combined nature: *a kitchen-cum-dining room.* [Latin: with, together with, along with]
cumacean (kjʊ'meɪʃ[ə]n) *n.* **1.** any small malacostracan marine crustacean of the *Cumacea* family, mostly dwelling on the sea bed but sometimes found among the plankton. ~*adj.* **2.** of, relating to, or belonging to the *Cumacea.* [C19: from New Latin *cuma,* from Greek *kuma* (see CYMA) + -EAN]
cumber ('kʌmbə) *vb. (tr.)* **1.** to obstruct or hinder. **2.** *Obsolete.* to inconvenience. ~*n.* **3.** a hindrance or burden. [C13: probably from Old French *combrer* to impede, prevent, from *combre* barrier; see ENCUMBER] —'**cumberer** *n.*
cumbersome ('kʌmbəsəm) *or* **cumbrous** ('kʌmbrəs) *adj.* **1.** awkward because of size, weight, or shape: *cumbersome baggage.* **2.** difficult because of extent or complexity: *cumbersome accounts.* [C14: *cumber,* short for ENCUMBER + -SOME[1]] —'**cumbersomely** *or* '**cumbrously** *adv.* —'**cumbersomeness** *or* '**cumbrousness** *n.*
cumbrance ('kʌmbrəns) *n.* **1.** a burden, obstacle, or hindrance. **2.** trouble or bother.
Cumbrian ('kʌmbrɪən) *adj.* **1.** of or relating to Cumbria, a county of NW England that includes the Lake District mountain area. ~*n.* **2.** a native or inhabitant of Cumbria.
cum dividend *adv.* (of shares, etc.) with the right to current dividend. Compare **ex dividend.** [*cum,* from Latin: with]
cum grano salis *Latin.* (kʊm 'grɑːnəʊ 'sɑːlɪs) *adv.* with a grain of salt; not too literally.
cumin *or* **cummin** ('kʌmɪn) *n.* **1.** an umbelliferous Mediterranean plant, *Cuminum cyminum,* with finely divided leaves and small white or pink flowers. **2.** the aromatic seeds (collectively) of this plant, used as a condiment and a flavouring. [C12: from Old French, from Latin *cumīnum,* from Greek *kuminon,* of Semitic origin; compare Hebrew *kammōn*]
cum laude (kʌm 'lɔːdɪ, kʊm 'laʊdeɪ) *adv. Chiefly U.S.* with praise: the lowest of three designations for above-average achievement in examinations. [Latin]
cummerbund *or* **kummerbund** ('kʌməˌbʌnd) *n.* a wide sash, worn with a dinner jacket. [C17: from Hindi *kamarband,* from Persian, from *kamar* loins, waist + *band* band]
cum new *adv., adj.* (of shares, etc.) with the right to take up any scrip issue or rights issue. Compare **ex new.**
cumquat ('kʌmkwɒt) *n.* a variant spelling of **kumquat.**
cumshaw ('kʌmʃɔː) *n.* (used, esp. formerly, by beggars in Chinese ports) a present or tip. [C19: from pidgin English, from Chinese (Amoy) *kam siā,* from Mandarin *kan hsieh* grateful thanks]
cumulate *vb.* ('kjuːmjʊˌleɪt). **1.** to accumulate. **2.** *(tr.)* to combine (two or more sequences) into one. ~*adj.* ('kjuːmjʊlɪt, -ˌleɪt). **3.** heaped up. [C16: from Latin *cumulāre* from *cumulus* heap] —'**cumulately** *adv.* —ˌ**cumu'lation** *n.*
cumulative ('kjuːmjʊlətɪv) *adj.* **1.** growing in quantity, strength, or effect by successive additions or gradual steps: *cumulative pollution.* **2.** gained by or resulting from a gradual building up: *cumulative benefits.* **3.** *Finance.* **a.** (of preference shares) entitling the holder to receive any arrears of dividend before any dividend is distributed to ordinary shareholders. **b.** (of dividends or interest) intended to be accumulated if not paid when due. **4.** *Statistics.* **a.** (of a frequency) including all values of a variable either below or above a specified value. **b.** (of error) tending to increase as the sample size is increased. —'**cumulatively** *adv.* —'**cumulativeness** *n.*
cumulative distribution function *n. Statistics.* a function defined on the sample space of a distribution and taking as its value at each point the probability that the random variable has that value or less. The function $F(x) = P(X \leq x)$ where X is the random variable, which is the sum or integral of the probability density function of the distribution. Sometimes shortened to **distribution function.**
cumulative evidence *n. Law.* additional evidence reinforcing testimony previously given.
cumulative voting *n.* a system of voting in which each elector has as many votes as there are candidates in his constituency. Votes may all be cast for one candidate or distributed among several.
cumulet ('kjuːmjʊlɪt) *n.* *(sometimes cap.)* a variety of domestic fancy pigeon, pure white or white with light red markings. [C19: from CUMULUS]
cumuliform ('kjuːmjʊlɪˌfɔːm) *adj.* resembling a cumulus cloud.
cumulonimbus (ˌkjuːmjʊləʊ'nɪmbəs) *n., pl.* **-bi** (-baɪ) *or* **-buses.** *Meteorol.* a cumulus cloud of great vertical extent, the top often forming an anvil shape and the bottom being dark coloured, indicating rain or hail: associated with thunderstorms.
cumulostratus (ˌkjuːmjʊləʊ'streɪtəs) *n., pl.* **-ti** (-taɪ). *Meteorol.* another name for **stratocumulus.**
cumulous ('kjuːmjʊləs) *adj.* resembling or consisting of cumulus clouds.
cumulus ('kjuːmjʊləs) *n., pl.* **-li** (-ˌlaɪ). **1.** a bulbous or billowing white or dark grey cloud associated with rising air currents. Compare **cirrus** (sense 1), **stratus.** **2.** *Histology.* the mass of cells surrounding a recently ovulated egg cell in a Graafian follicle. [C17: from Latin: mass]
cunctation (kʌŋk'teɪʃən) *n. Rare.* delay. [C16: from Latin *cunctātiō* a hesitation, from *cunctārī* to delay] —**cunctative** ('kʌŋktətɪv) *adj.* —**cunc'tator** *n.*
cuneal ('kjuːnɪəl) *adj.* wedge-shaped; cuneiform. [C16: from New Latin *cuneālis,* from *cuneus* wedge]
cuneate ('kjuːnɪɪt, -ˌeɪt) *adj.* wedge-shaped: cuneate leaves are attached at the narrow end. [C19: from Latin *cuneāre* to make wedge-shaped, from *cuneus* a wedge] —'**cuneately** *adv.*
cuneiform ('kjuːnɪˌfɔːm) *adj.* **1.** Also: **cuneal.** wedge-shaped. **2.** of, relating to, or denoting the wedge-shaped characters employed in the writing of several ancient languages of Mesopotamia and Persia, esp. Sumerian, Babylonian, etc. **3.** of or relating to a tablet in which this script is employed. **4.** of or relating to any of the three tarsal bones. ~*n.* **5.** cuneiform characters or writing. **6.** any one of the three tarsal bones. [C17: probably from Old French *cunéiforme,* from Latin *cuneus* wedge]
cunjevoi ('kʌndʒɪˌvɔɪ) *n. Austral.* **1.** an aroid plant, *Alocasia macrorrhiza,* of tropical Asia and Australia, cultivated for its edible rhizome. **2.** a sea squirt. [C19: from a native Australian language]
cunnilingus (ˌkʌnɪ'lɪŋgəs) *or* **cunnilinctus** (ˌkʌnɪ'lɪŋktəs) *n.* a sexual activity in which the female genitalia are stimulated by the partner's lips and tongue. Compare **fellatio.** [C19: from New Latin, from Latin *cunnus* vulva + *lingere* to lick]
cunning ('kʌnɪŋ) *adj.* **1.** crafty and shrewd, esp. in deception; sly: *cunning as a fox.* **2.** made with or showing skill or cleverness; ingenious. ~*n.* **3.** craftiness, esp. in deceiving; slyness. **4.** cleverness, skill, or ingenuity. [Old English *cunnende;* related to *cunnan* to know (see CAN[1]), *cunnian* to test, experience, Old Norse *kunna* to know] —'**cunningly** *adv.* —'**cunningness** *n.*
cunt (kʌnt) *n. Taboo.* **1.** the female genitals. **2.** *Offensive slang.* a woman considered sexually. **3.** *Offensive slang.* a mean or obnoxious person. [C13: of Germanic origin; related to Old Norse *kunta,* Middle Low German *kunte*]
cup (kʌp) *n.* **1.** a small open container, usually having one handle, used for drinking from. **2.** the contents of such a container: *that cup was too sweet.* **3.** Also called: **teacup, cupful.** a unit of capacity used in cooking equal to approximately half a pint, 8 fluid ounces, or about one quarter of a litre. **4.** something resembling a cup in shape or function, such as the flower base of some plants of the rose family or a cuplike bodily organ. **5.** either of two cup-shaped parts of a brassiere, designed to support the breasts. **6.** a cup-shaped trophy awarded as a prize. **7.** *Brit.* **a.** a sporting contest in which a cup is awarded to the winner. **b.** *(as modifier): a cup competition.* **8.** a mixed drink with one ingredient as a base, usually served from a bowl: *claret cup.* **9.** *Golf.* the hole or metal container in the hole on a green. **10.** the chalice or the consecrated wine used in the Eucharist. **11.** one's lot in life. **12. in one's cups.** drunk. **13. one's cup of tea.** *Informal.* one's chosen or preferred thing, task, company, etc.: *she's not my cup of tea.* ~*vb.* **cups, cupping, cupped.** *(tr.)* **14.** to form (something, such as the hands) into the shape of a cup. **15.** to put into or as if into a cup. **16.** to draw blood to the surface of the body of (a person) by using a cupping glass. [Old English *cuppe,* from Late Latin *cuppa* cup, alteration of Latin *cūpa* cask] —'**cup**ˌ**like** *adj.*
cupbearer ('kʌpˌbɛərə) *n.* an attendant who fills and serves wine cups, as in a royal household.
cupboard ('kʌbəd) *n.* a piece of furniture or a recessed area of a room, with a door concealing storage space.
cupboard love *n.* a show of love inspired only by some selfish or greedy motive.
cupcake ('kʌpˌkeɪk) *n.* a small cake baked in a cup-shaped foil or paper case.
cupel ('kjuːp[ə]l, kjʊ'pɛl) *n.* **1.** a refractory pot in which gold or silver is refined. **2.** a small porous bowl made of bone ash in which gold and silver are recovered from a lead button during

assaying. ~*vb.* **-pels, -pelling, -pelled** *or U.S.* **-pels, -peling, -peled. 3.** (*tr.*) to refine (gold or silver) by means of cupellation. [C17: from French *coupelle,* diminutive of *coupe* CUP] —'**cupeller** *n.*

cupellation (ˌkjuːpɪ'leɪʃən) *n.* **1.** the process of recovering precious metals from lead by melting the alloy in a cupel and oxidizing the lead by means of an air blast. **2.** the manufacture of lead oxide by melting and oxidizing lead.

Cup Final *n.* **1.** (often preceded by *the*) the annual final of the FA Cup soccer competition, played at Wembley or the Scottish Cup played at Hampden. **2.** (*often not cap.*) the final of any cup competition.

cupid ('kjuːpɪd) *n.* a figure of a winged boy with a bow and arrow representing Cupid, the Roman god of love, esp. in Baroque art. [C14: from Latin *Cupīdō,* from *cupīdō* desire, from *cupidus* desirous; see CUPIDITY]

cupidity (kjuː'pɪdɪtɪ) *n.* strong desire, esp. for possessions or money; greed. [C15: from Latin *cupiditās,* from *cupidus* eagerly desiring, from *cupere* to long for]

Cupid's bow *n.* a shape of the upper lip considered to resemble Cupid's double-curved bow.

cupid's dart *n.* another name for **catananche.**

cupola ('kjuːpələ) *n.* **1.** a roof or ceiling in the form of a dome. **2.** a small structure, usually domed, on the top of a roof or dome. **3.** a protective dome for a gun on a warship. **4.** a vertical air-blown coke-fired cylindrical furnace in which metals, esp. iron, are remelted for casting. [C16: from Italian, from Late Latin *cūpula* a small cask, from Latin *cūpa* tub] —**cupolated** ('kjuːpəˌleɪtɪd) *adj.*

cuppa *or* **cupper** ('kʌpə) *n. Brit. informal.* a cup of tea.

cupped (kʌpt) *adj.* hollowed like a cup; concave.

cupping ('kʌpɪŋ) *n. Med.* the process of applying a cupping glass to the skin.

cupping glass *n. Med.* a glass vessel from which air can be removed by suction or heat to create a partial vacuum: formerly used in drawing blood to the surface of the skin for slow blood-letting. Also called: **artificial leech.**

cupreous ('kjuːprɪəs) *adj.* **1.** of, consisting of, containing, or resembling copper; coppery. **2.** of the reddish-brown colour of copper. [C17: from Late Latin *cupreus,* from *cuprum* COPPER[1]]

cupressus (kjʊ'prɛsəs) *n.* any tree of the genus *Cupressus.* See **cypress**[1].

cupric ('kjuːprɪk) *adj.* of or containing copper in the divalent state. [C18: from Late Latin *cuprum* copper]

cupriferous (kjuː'prɪfərəs) *adj.* (of a substance such as an ore) containing or yielding copper.

cuprite ('kjuːpraɪt) *n.* a red secondary mineral consisting of cuprous oxide in cubic crystalline form: a source of copper. Formula: Cu_2O.

cupro-, cupri-, *or before a vowel* **cupr-** *combining form.* indicating copper: *cupronickel; cuprite.* [from Latin *cuprum*]

cupronickel (ˌkjuːprəʊ'nɪkᵊl) *n.* any ductile corrosion-resistant copper alloy containing up to 40 per cent nickel: used in condenser tubes, turbine blades, etc.

cuprous ('kjuːprəs) *adj.* of or containing copper in the monovalent state.

cuprum ('kjuːprəm) *n.* an obsolete name for **copper.** [Latin: COPPER[1]]

cup tie *n. Sport.* an eliminating match or round between two teams in a cup competition.

cup-tied *adj. Sport.* **1.** (of a team) unable to play another fixture because of involvement in a cup tie. **2.** (of a player) unable to play in a cup tie because of some disallowance.

cupula ('kʌpjʊlə) *n., pl.* **-lai** (-lɪ). *Anatomy, zoology.* a dome-shaped structure, esp. the sensory structure within the semicircular canals of the ear.

cupulate ('kjuːpjʊˌleɪt) *or* **cupular** ('kjuːpjʊlə) *adj.* **1.** shaped like a small cup. **2.** (of plants or animals) having cupules.

cupule ('kjuːpjuːl) *n. Biology.* a cup-shaped part or structure, such as the cup around the base of an acorn. [C19: from Late Latin *cūpula;* see CUPOLA]

cur (kɜː) *n.* **1.** any vicious dog, esp. a mongrel. **2.** a despicable or cowardly person. [C13: shortened from *kurdogge;* probably related to Old Norse *kurra* to growl]

cur. *abbrev. for* currency.

curable ('kjʊərəbᵊl) *adj.* capable of being cured. —ˌ**cura'bility** *or* '**curableness** *n.* —'**curably** *adv.*

Curaçao (ˌkjʊərə'səʊ) *n.* an orange-flavoured liqueur originally made on the Caribbean island of Curaçao.

curacy ('kjʊərəsɪ) *n., pl.* **-cies.** the office or position of curate.

Cur. adv. vult *abbrev.* See **CAV.**

curagh *Gaelic.* ('kʌrəx; 'kʌrə) *n.* a variant spelling of **currach.**

curare *or* **curari** (kjʊ'rɑːrɪ) *n.* **1.** black resin obtained from certain tropical South American trees, acting on the motor nerves to cause muscular paralysis: used medicinally as a muscle relaxant and by South American Indians as an arrow poison. **2.** any of various trees of the genera *Chondrodendron* and *Strychnos* from which this resin is obtained. [C18: from Portuguese and Spanish, from Carib *kurarī*]

curarine ('kjʊərəˌriːn) *n.* an alkaloid extracted from curare, used as a muscle relaxant in surgery. Formula: $C_{19}H_{26}ON_2$.

curarize *or* **curarise** ('kjʊərəˌraɪz) *vb.* (*tr.*) to paralyse or treat with curare. —ˌ**curari'zation** *or* ˌ**curari'sation** *n.*

curassow ('kjʊərəˌsəʊ) *n.* any gallinaceous ground-nesting bird of the family *Cracidae,* of S North, Central, and South America. Curassows have long legs and tails and, typically, a distinctive crest of curled feathers. See also **guan.** [C17: anglicized variant of Curaçao island]

curate ('kjʊərɪt) *n.* **1.** a clergyman appointed to assist a parish priest. **2.** a clergyman who has the charge of a parish (**curate-in-charge**). **3.** *Irish.* an assistant barman. [C14: from Medieval Latin *cūrātus,* from *cūra* spiritual oversight, CURE]

curate's egg *n.* something that is bad but may be euphemistically described as being only partly so. [C20: simile derived from a cartoon in *Punch* (November, 1895) in which a timid curate, who has been served a bad egg while breakfasting with his bishop, says that parts of the egg are excellent]

curative ('kjʊərətɪv) *adj.* **1.** able or tending to cure. ~*n.* **2.** anything able to heal or cure. —'**curatively** *adv.* —'**curativeness** *n.*

curator (kjʊə'reɪtə) *n.* **1.** the administrative head of a museum, art gallery, or similar institution. **2.** *Law, chiefly Scot.* a guardian of a minor. [C14: from Latin: one who cares, from *cūrāre* to care for, from *cūra* care] —**curatorial** (ˌkjʊərə'tɔːrɪəl) *adj.* —**cu'ratorˌship** *n.*

curb (kɜːb) *n.* **1.** something that restrains or holds back. **2.** any enclosing framework, such as a wall of stones around the top of a well. **3. a.** Also called: **curb bit.** a horse's bit with an attached chain or strap, which checks the horse. **b.** Also called: **curb chain.** the chain or strap itself. **4.** a hard swelling on the hock of a horse. ~*vb.* (*tr.*) **5.** to control with or as if with a curb; restrain. ~See also **kerb.** [C15: from Old French *courbe* curved piece of wood or metal, from Latin *curvus* curved]

curbing ('kɜːbɪŋ) *n.* the U.S. spelling of **kerbing.**

curb roof *n.* a roof having two or more slopes on each side of the ridge. See also **mansard** (sense 1), **gambrel roof** (sense 2).

curbstone ('kɜːbˌstəʊn) *n.* the U.S. spelling of **kerbstone.**

curch (kɜːtʃ) *n.* a woman's plain cap or kerchief. Also called: **curchef.** [C15: probably back formation from *courcheis* (plural), from Old French *couvrechies,* plural of *couvrechef* KERCHIEF]

curculio (kɜː'kjuːlɪˌəʊ) *n., pl.* **-lios.** any of various American weevils, esp. *Conotrachelus nenuphar* (**plum curculio**), a pest of fruit trees. [C18: from Latin: grain weevil]

curcuma ('kɜːkjʊmə) *n.* any tropical Asian tuberous plant of the genus *Curcuma,* such as *C. longa,* which is the source of turmeric, and *C. zedoaria,* which is the source of zedoary: family *Zingiberaceae.* [C17: from New Latin, from Arabic *kurkum* turmeric]

curd (kɜːd) *n.* **1.** (*often pl.*) a substance formed from the coagulation of milk by acid or rennet, used in making cheese or eaten as a food. **2.** something similar in consistency. ~*vb.* **3.** to turn into or become curd. [C15: from earlier *crud,* of unknown origin] —'**curdy** *adj.* —'**curdiness** *n.*

curd cheese *n.* a mild white cheese made from skimmed milk curds, smoother and fattier than cottage cheese.

curdle ('kɜːdᵊl) *vb.* **1.** to turn or cause to turn into curd. **2. curdle someone's blood.** to fill someone with fear. [C16 (*crudled,* past participle): from CURD] —'**curdler** *n.*

cure (kjʊə) *vb.* **1.** (*tr.*) to get rid of (an ailment, fault, or problem); heal. **2.** (*tr.*) to restore to health or good condition. **3.** (*intr.*) to bring about a cure. **4.** (*tr.*) to preserve (meat, fish, etc.) by salting, smoking, etc. **5.** (*tr.*) **a.** to treat or finish (a substance) by chemical or physical means. **b.** to vulcanize (rubber). **6.** (*tr.*) to assist the hardening of (concrete, mortar, etc.) by keeping it moist. ~*n.* **7.** a return to health, esp. after specific treatment. **8.** any course of medical therapy, esp. one proved effective in combating a disease. **9.** a means of restoring health or improving a condition, situation, etc. **10.** the spiritual and pastoral charge of a parish: *the cure of souls.* **11.** a process or method of preserving meat, fish, etc., by salting, pickling, or smoking. [(n.) C13: from Old French, from Latin *cūra* care; in ecclesiastical sense, from Medieval Latin *cūra* spiritual charge; (vb.) C14: from Old French *curer,* from Latin *cūrāre* to attend to, heal, from *cūra* care] —'**cureless** *adj.* —'**curer** *n.*

curé ('kjʊəreɪ) *n.* a parish priest in France. [French, from Medieval Latin *cūrātus;* see CURATE]

cure-all *n.* something reputed to cure all ailments.

curet *or* **curette** (kjʊə'rɛt) *n.* **1.** a surgical instrument for removing dead tissue, growths, etc., from the walls of certain body cavities. ~*vb.* **-rets** *or* **-rettes, -retting, -retted. 2.** (*tr.*) to scrape or clean with such an instrument. [C18: from French *curette,* from *curer* to heal, make clean; see CURE]

curettage (ˌkjʊərɪ'tɑːʒ, kjʊə'rɛtɪdʒ) *or* **curettement** (kjʊə'rɛtmənt) *n.* the process of using a curet. See also **D and C.**

curfew ('kɜːfjuː) *n.* **1.** an official regulation setting restrictions on movement, esp. after a specific time at night. **2.** the time set as a deadline by such a regulation. **3.** (in medieval Europe) **a.** the ringing of a bell to prompt people to extinguish fires and lights. **b.** the time at which the curfew bell was rung. **c.** the bell itself. [C13: from Old French *cuevrefeu,* literally: cover the fire]

curia ('kjʊərɪə) *n., pl.* **-riae** (-rɪˌiː). **1.** (*sometimes cap.*) the papal court and government of the Roman Catholic Church. **2.** (in ancient Rome) **a.** any of the ten subdivisions of the Latin, Sabine, or Etruscan tribes. **b.** a meeting place of such a subdivision. **c.** the senate house of Rome. **d.** the senate of an Italian town under Roman administration. **3.** (in the Middle Ages) a court held in the king's name. [C16: from Latin, from Old Latin *coviria* (unattested), from CO- + *vir* man] —'**curial** *adj.*

curie ('kjʊərɪ, -riː) *n.* a unit of radioactivity equal to 3.7×10^{10} disintegrations per second. Symbol: Ci [C20: named after Pierre *Curie* (1859–1906), French physicist and chemist]

Curie point *or* **temperature** *n.* the temperature above which a ferromagnetic substance loses its ferromagnetism and becomes paramagnetic. [C20: named after Pierre *Curie*]

Curie's law *n.* the principle that the magnetic susceptibility of a paramagnetic substance is inversely proportional to its thermodynamic temperature. See also **Curie-Weiss law.**

Curie-Weiss law (-vaɪs) *n.* the principle that the magnetic susceptibility of a paramagnetic substance is inversely proportional to the difference between its temperature and its Curie point. [C20: named after Pierre *Curie* and Pierre-Ernest *Weiss* (died 1940), French physicist]

curio ('kjʊərɪˌəʊ) *n., pl.* **-rios.** a small article valued as a collector's item, esp. something fascinating or unusual. [C19: shortened from CURIOSITY]

curiosa (ˌkjʊərɪ'əʊsə) *n.* (*functioning as pl.*) **1.** curiosities. **2.** books on strange subjects, esp. erotica. [New Latin: from Latin *cūriōsus* CURIOUS]

curiosity (ˌkjʊərɪ'ɒsɪtɪ) *n., pl.* **-ties. 1.** an eager desire to know; inquisitiveness. **2. a.** the quality of being curious; strangeness. **b.** (*as modifier*): *the ring had curiosity value only.* **3.** something strange or fascinating. **4.** a rare or strange object; curio. **5.** *Obsolete.* fastidiousness.

curious ('kjʊərɪəs) *adj.* **1.** eager to learn; inquisitive. **2.** over inquisitive; prying. **3.** interesting because of oddness or novelty; strange; unexpected. **4.** *Rare.* (of workmanship, etc.) highly detailed, intricate, or subtle. **5.** *Obsolete.* fastidious or hard to please. [C14: from Latin *cūriōsus* taking pains over something, from *cūra* care] —'**curiously** *adv.* —'**curiousness** *n.*

curium ('kjʊərɪəm) *n.* a silvery-white metallic transuranic element artificially produced from plutonium. Symbol: Cm; atomic no.: 96; half-life of most stable isotope, ^{247}Cm: 1.6 x 10^7 years; valency: 3; relative density: 13.51 (calculated); melting pt.: 1340°C (approx.). [C20: New Latin, named after Marie *Curie* (1867–1934), Polish-born French physicist and chemist, and her husband Pierre (1859–1906)]

curl (kɜːl) *vb.* **1.** (*intr.*) (esp. of hair) to grow into curves or ringlets. **2.** (*tr.*; sometimes foll. by *up*) to twist or roll (something, esp. hair) into coils or ringlets. **3.** (often foll. by *up*) to become or cause to become spiral-shaped or curved; coil: *the heat made the leaves curl up.* **4.** (*intr.*) to move in a curving or twisting manner. **5.** (*intr.*) to play the game of curling. **6. curl one's lip.** to show contempt, as by raising a corner of the lip. ~*n.* **7.** a curve or coil of hair. **8.** a curved or spiral shape or mark, as in wood. **9.** the act of curling or state of being curled. **10.** any of various plant diseases characterized by curling of the leaves. **11.** Also called: **rotation.** *Maths.* a vector quantity associated with a vector field that is the vector product of the operator ∇ and a vector function ***A***, where $\nabla = \boldsymbol{i}\partial/\partial x + \boldsymbol{j}\partial/\partial y + \boldsymbol{k}\partial/\partial z$, ***i***, ***j***, and ***k*** being unit vectors. Usually written curl ***A***, rot ***A***. Compare **divergence** (sense 4), **gradient** (sense 4). ~See also **curl up.** [C14: probably from Middle Dutch *crullen* to curl; related to Middle High German *krol* curly, Middle Low German *krūs* curly]

curled paperwork *n.* another name for **rolled paperwork.**

curler ('kɜːlə) *n.* **1.** any of various pins, clasps, or rollers used to curl or wave hair. **2.** a person or thing that curls. **3.** a person who plays curling.

curlew ('kɜːljuː) *n.* any large shore bird of the genus *Numenius*, such as *N. arquata* of Europe and Asia: family *Scolopacidae* (sandpipers, etc.), order *Charadriiformes.* They have a long downward-curving bill and occur in northern and arctic regions. Compare **stone curlew.** [C14: from Old French *corlieu*, perhaps of imitative origin]

curlew sandpiper *n.* a common Eurasian sandpiper, *Calidris ferruginea*, having a brick-red breeding plumage and a greyish winter plumage.

curli ('kɜːlɪ) *pl. n. Bacteriol.* curled hairlike processes on the surface of the bacterium *Escherichia coli* by means of which the bacterium adheres to and infects wounds. [C20: from *curl(ed)* (PIL)I]

curlicue ('kɜːlɪˌkjuː) *n.* an intricate ornamental curl or twist. [C19: from CURLY + CUE[2]]

curling ('kɜːlɪŋ) *n.* a game played on ice, esp. in Scotland, in which heavy stones with handles (**curling stones**) are slid towards a target (**tee**).

curling tongs *pl. n.* a metal scissor-like device that is heated, so that strands of hair may be twined around it in order to form curls. Also called: **curling iron, curling irons, curling pins.**

curlpaper ('kɜːlˌpeɪpə) *n.* a strip of paper used to roll up and set a section of hair, usually wetted, into a curl.

curl up *vb.* (*adv.*) **1.** (*intr.*) to adopt a reclining position with the legs close to the body and the back rounded. **2.** to become or cause to become spiral-shaped or curved. **3.** (*intr.*) to retire to a quiet cosy setting: *to curl up with a good novel.* **4.** *Brit. informal.* to be or cause to be embarrassed or disgusted: (esp. in **curl up and die**).

curly ('kɜːlɪ) *adj.* **curlier, curliest. 1.** tending to curl; curling. **2.** having curls. **3.** (of timber) having irregular curves or waves in the grain. **4.** *Austral. and N.Z.* difficult to counter or answer: *a curly question.* —'**curliness** *n.*

curmudgeon (kɜː'mʌdʒən) *n.* a surly or miserly person. [C16: of unknown origin] —**cur'mudgeonly** *adj.*

currach, curagh, *or* ***curragh*** *Gaelic.* ('kʌrəx, 'kʌrə) *n.* a Scot. or Irish name for **coracle.** [C15: from Irish Gaelic *currach*; compare CORACLE]

currajong ('kʌrəˌdʒɒŋ) *n.* a variant spelling of **kurrajong.**

currant ('kʌrənt) *n.* **1.** a small dried seedless grape of the Mediterranean region, used in cooking. **2.** any of several mainly N temperate shrubs of the genus *Ribes*, esp. *R. rubrum* (redcurrant) and *R. nigrum* (blackcurrant): family *Grossulariaceae.* See also **gooseberry** (sense 1). **3.** the small acid fruit of any of these plants. [C16: shortened from *rayson of Corannte* raisin of Corinth]

currant bun *n.* **1.** *Brit.* a sweet bun containing currants. **2.** *Scot.* another name for **black bun.**

currawong ('kʌrəˌwɒŋ) *n.* any Australian crowlike songbird of the genus *Strepera*, having black, grey, and white plumage: family *Cracticidae.* Also called: **bell magpie.** [from a native Australian name]

currency ('kʌrənsɪ) *n., pl.* **-cies. 1.** a metal or paper medium of exchange that is in current use in a particular country. **2.** general acceptance or circulation; prevalence: *the currency of ideas.* **3.** the period of time during which something is valid, accepted, or in force. **4.** the act of being passed from person to person. **5.** *Austral.* (formerly) the local medium of exchange, esp. in the colonies, as distinct from sterling. **6.** *Austral. slang.* (formerly) the native-born Australians, as distinct from the British immigrants. [C17: from Medieval Latin *currentia*, literally: a flowing, from Latin *currere* to run, flow]

currency note *n.* another name for **treasury note** (sense b).

current ('kʌrənt) *adj.* **1.** of the immediate present; in progress: *current events.* **2.** most recent; up-to-date: *the current issue of a magazine.* **3.** commonly known, practised, or accepted; widespread: *a current rumour.* **4.** circulating and valid at present: *current coins.* ~*n.* **5.** (esp. of water or air) a steady usually natural flow. **6.** a mass of air, body of water, etc., that has a steady flow in a particular direction. **7.** the rate of flow of such a mass. **8.** Also called: **electric current.** *Physics.* **a.** a flow of electric charge through a conductor. **b.** the rate of flow of this charge. It is usually measured in amperes. Symbol: *I* **9.** a general trend or drift: *currents of opinion.* [C13: from Old French *corant*, literally: running, from *corre* to run, from Latin *currere*] —'**currently** *adv.* —'**currentness** *n.*

current account *n.* **1.** an account at a bank or building society against which cheques may be drawn at any time. U.S. and Canadian name: **checking account. 2.** *Economics.* that part of the balance of payments composed of the balance of trade and the invisible balance. Compare **capital account** (sense 1).

current assets *pl. n.* cash and operating assets that are convertible into cash within a year. Also called: **floating assets.** Compare **fixed assets.**

current-cost accounting *n.* a method of accounting that values assets at their current replacement cost rather than their original cost. It is often used in times of high inflation.

current density *n.* the ratio of the electric current flowing at a particular point in a conductor to the cross-sectional area of the conductor taken perpendicular to the current flow at that point. It is measured in amperes per square metre. Symbol: J

current efficiency *n. Physics.* the ratio of the actual mass of a substance liberated from an electrolyte by the passage of current to the theoretical mass liberated according to Faraday's law.

current expenses *pl. n.* noncapital and usually recurrent expenditures necessary for the operation of a business.

current liabilities *pl. n.* business liabilities maturing within a year.

curricle ('kʌrɪkᵊl) *n.* a two-wheeled open carriage drawn by two horses side by side. [C18: from Latin *curriculum* from *currus* chariot, from *currere* to run]

curriculum (kə'rɪkjʊləm) *n., pl.* **-la** (-lə) *or* **-lums. 1.** a course of study in one subject at a school or college. **2.** a list of all the courses of study offered by a school or college. **3.** any programme or plan of activities. [C19: from Latin: course, from *currere* to run] —**cur'ricular** *adj.*

curriculum vitae ('viːtaɪ, 'vaɪtiː) *n., pl.* **curricula vitae.** an outline of a person's educational and professional history, usually prepared for job applications. Abbrev.: **CV.** [Latin, literally: the course of one's life]

currier ('kʌrɪə) *n.* **1.** *Rare.* a person who grooms horses. **2.** a person who curries leather. [C14: from Old French *corier*, from Latin *coriārius* a tanner, from *corium* leather]

curriery ('kʌrɪərɪ) *n., pl.* **-eries.** the trade, work, or place of occupation of a leather currier.

currish ('kɜːrɪʃ) *adj.* of or like a cur; rude or bad-tempered. —'**currishly** *adv.* —'**currishness** *n.*

curry[1] ('kʌrɪ) *n., pl.* **-ries. 1.** a spicy dish of oriental, esp. Indian, origin that is made in many ways but usually consists of meat or fish prepared in a hot piquant sauce. **2.** curry seasoning or sauce. **3. give someone curry.** *Austral. slang.* to assault (a person) verbally or physically. ~*vb.* **-ries, -rying, -ried. 4.** (*tr.*)

to prepare (food) with curry powder or sauce. [C16: from Tamil *kari* sauce, relish]

curry[2] ('kʌrɪ) *vb.* **-ries, -rying, -ried.** (*tr.*) **1.** to beat vigorously, as in order to clean. **2.** to dress and finish (leather) after it has been tanned to make it strong, flexible, and waterproof. **3.** to groom (a horse). **4. curry favour.** to ingratiate oneself, esp. with superiors. [C13: from Old French *correer* to make ready, from Vulgar Latin *conrēdāre* (unattested), from *rēdāre* (unattested) to provide, of Germanic origin]

currycomb ('kʌrɪˌkəʊm) *n.* a square comb consisting of rows of small teeth, used for grooming horses.

curry powder *n.* a mixture of finely ground pungent spices, such as turmeric, cumin, coriander, ginger, etc., used in making curries.

curry puff *n.* (in Malaysia) a type of pie or pasty consisting of a pastry case containing curried meat and vegetables.

curse (kɜːs) *n.* **1.** a profane or obscene expression of anger, disgust, surprise, etc.; oath. **2.** an appeal to a supernatural power for harm to come to a specific person, group, etc. **3.** harm resulting from an appeal to a supernatural power: *to be under a curse.* **4.** something that brings or causes great trouble or harm. **5.** a saying, charm, effigy, etc., used to invoke a curse. **6.** an ecclesiastical censure of excommunication. **7.** (preceded by *the*) *Informal.* menstruation or a menstrual period. ~*vb.* **curses, cursing, cursed** *or* (*Archaic*) **curst. 8.** (*intr.*) to utter obscenities or oaths. **9.** (*tr.*) to abuse (someone) with obscenities or oaths. **10.** (*tr.*) to invoke supernatural powers to bring harm to (someone or something). **11.** (*tr.*) to bring harm upon. **12.** (*tr.*) another word for **excommunicate.** [Old English *cursian* to curse, from *curs* a curse] —'**curser** *n.*

cursed ('kɜːsɪd, kɜːst) *or* **curst** *adj.* **1.** under a curse. **2.** deserving to be cursed; detestable; hateful. **3.** *Archaic or dialect.* bad-tempered. —'**cursedly** *adv.* —'**cursedness** *n.*

curses ('kɜːsɪz) *interj. Often facetious.* an expression of disappointment or dismay.

cursive ('kɜːsɪv) *adj.* **1.** of or relating to handwriting in which letters are formed and joined in a rapid flowing style. **2.** *Printing.* of or relating to typefaces that resemble handwriting. ~*n.* **3.** a cursive letter or printing type. **4.** a manuscript written in cursive letters. [C18: from Medieval Latin *cursīvus*, running, ultimately from Latin *currere* to run] —'**cursively** *adv.*

cursor ('kɜːsə) *n.* **1.** the sliding part of a measuring instrument, esp. a transparent sliding square on a slide rule. **2.** any of various devices, typically a movable point of light, that identify a specific position on a visual display unit.

cursorial (kɜː'sɔːrɪəl) *adj. Zoology.* adapted for running: *a cursorial skeleton; cursorial birds.*

cursory ('kɜːsərɪ) *adj.* hasty and usually superficial; quick: *a cursory check.* [C17: from Late Latin *cursōrius* of running, from Latin *cursus* a course, from *currere* to run] —'**cursorily** *adv.* —'**cursoriness** *n.*

curst (kɜːst) *vb.* **1.** *Archaic.* a past tense and past participle of **curse.** ~*adj.* **2.** a variant of **cursed.**

curt (kɜːt) *adj.* **1.** rudely blunt and brief; abrupt: *a curt reply.* **2.** short or concise. [C17: from Latin *curtus* cut short, mutilated] —'**curtly** *adv.* —'**curtness** *n.*

curtail (kɜː'teɪl) *vb.* (*tr.*) to cut short; abridge. [C16: changed (through influence of TAIL[1]) from obsolete *curtal* to dock; see CURTAL] —**cur'tailer** *n.* —**cur'tailment** *n.*

curtail step ('kɜːteɪl) *n.* the step or steps at the foot of a flight of stairs, widened at one or both ends and terminated with a scroll.

curtain ('kɜːtᵊn) *n.* **1.** a piece of material that can be drawn across an opening or window, to shut out light or to provide privacy. **2.** a barrier to vision, access, or communication: *a curtain of secrecy.* **3.** a hanging cloth or similar barrier for concealing all or part of a theatre stage from the audience. **4.** (often preceded by *the*) the end of a scene of a play, opera, etc., marked by the fall or closing of the curtain. **5.** the rise or opening of the curtain at the start of a performance. ~*vb.* **6.** (*tr.*; sometimes foll. by *off*) to shut off or conceal with or as if with a curtain. **7.** (*tr.*) to provide (a window, etc.) with curtains. ~See also **curtains.** [C13: from Old French *courtine*, from Late Latin *cortīna* enclosed place, curtain, probably from Latin *cohors* courtyard]

curtain call *n.* the appearance of performers at the end of a theatrical performance to acknowledge applause.

curtain lecture *n.* a scolding or rebuke given in private, esp. by a wife to her husband. [alluding to the curtained beds where such rebukes were once given]

curtain-raiser *n.* **1.** *Theatre.* a short dramatic piece presented before the main play. **2.** any preliminary event: *the debate was a curtain-raiser to the election.*

curtains ('kɜːtᵊnz) *pl. n. Informal.* death or ruin; the end: *if the enemy see us it will be curtains for us.*

curtain speech *n.* **1.** a talk given in front of the curtain after a stage performance, often by the author or an actor. **2.** the final speech of an act or a play.

curtain wall *n.* **1.** a non-load-bearing external wall attached to a framed structure, often one that is prefabricated. **2.** a low wall outside the outer wall of a castle, serving as a first line of defence.

curtal ('kɜːtᵊl) *Obsolete.* ~*adj.* **1.** cut short. **2.** (of friars) wearing a short frock. ~*n.* **3.** an animal whose tail has been docked. **4.** something that is cut short. [C16: from Old French *courtault* animal whose tail has been docked, from *court* short, from Latin *curtus;* see CURT]

curtal axe *n.* an obsolete term for **cutlass.** [C16: alteration by folk etymology of Old French *coutelas* CUTLASS; see CURTAL]

curtana (kɜː'tɑːnə) *n.* the unpointed sword carried before an English sovereign at a coronation as an emblem of mercy. [C15: from Anglo-Latin, from Old French *cortain*, the name of the legendary hero Roland's sword, which was broken at the point, ultimately from Latin *curtus* short]

curtate ('kɜːteɪt) *adj.* shortened. [C17: from Late Latin *curtāre* to shorten, from Latin *curtus* cut short; see CURT]

curtilage ('kɜːtɪlɪdʒ) *n.* the enclosed area of land adjacent to a dwelling house. [C14: from Old French *cortillage*, from *cortil* a little yard, from *cort* COURT]

curtsy *or* **curtsey** ('kɜːtsɪ) *n., pl.* **-sies** *or* **-seys. 1.** a formal gesture of greeting and respect made by women in which the knees are bent, the head slightly bowed, and the skirt held outwards. ~*vb.* **-sies, -sying, -sied** *or* **-seys, -seying, -seyed. 2.** (*intr.*) to make a curtsy. [C16: variant of COURTESY]

curule ('kjʊəruːl) *adj.* (in ancient Rome) of the highest rank, esp. one entitled to use a curule chair. [C16: from Latin *curūlis* of a chariot, from *currus* chariot, from *currere* to run]

curule chair *n.* an upholstered folding seat with curved legs used by the highest civil officials of ancient Rome.

curvaceous (kɜː'veɪʃəs) *adj. Informal.* (of a woman) having a well-rounded body. —**cur'vaceously** *adv.*

curvature ('kɜːvətʃə) *n.* **1.** something curved or a curved part of a thing. **2.** any normal or abnormal curving of a bodily part: *curvature of the spine.* **3.** *Geometry.* the change in inclination of a tangent to a curve over unit length of arc. For a circle or sphere it is the reciprocal of the radius. See also **radius of curvature, centre of curvature. 4.** the act of curving or the state or degree of being curved or bent.

curve (kɜːv) *n.* **1.** a continuously bending line that has no straight parts. **2.** something that curves or is curved, such as a bend in a road or the contour of a woman's body. **3.** the act or extent of curving; curvature. **4.** *Maths.* **a.** a system of points whose coordinates satisfy a given equation; a locus of points. **b.** the graph of a function with one independent variable. **5.** a line representing data, esp. statistical data, on a graph: *an unemployment curve.* **6.** short for **French curve.** ~*vb.* **7.** to take or cause to take the shape or path of a curve; bend. ~Related adj.: **sinuous.** [C15: from Latin *curvāre* to bend, from *curvus* crooked] —**curvedly** ('kɜːvɪdlɪ) *adv.* —'**curvedness** *n.* —'**curvy** *adj.*

curvet (kɜː'vɛt) *n.* **1.** *Dressage.* a low leap with all four feet off the ground. ~*vb.* **-vets, -vetting, -vetted** *or* **-vets, -veting, -veted. 2.** *Dressage.* to make or cause to make such a leap. **3.** (*intr.*) to prance or frisk about. [C16: from Old Italian *corvetta*, from Old French *courbette*, from *courber* to bend, from Latin *curvāre*]

curvilinear (ˌkɜːvɪ'lɪnɪə) *or* **curvilineal** *adj.* **1.** consisting of, bounded by, or characterized by a curved line. **2.** along a curved line: *curvilinear motion.* **3.** *Maths.* (of a set of coordinates) determined by or determining a system of three orthogonal surfaces. —ˌ**curviˌline'arity** *n.* —ˌ**curvi'linearly** *adv.*

cuscus ('kʌskʌs) *n., pl.* **-cuses.** any of several large nocturnal phalangers of the genus *Phalanger*, of N Australia, New Guinea, and adjacent islands, having dense fur, prehensile tails, large eyes, and a yellow nose. [C17: New Latin, probably from a native name in New Guinea]

cusec ('kjuːsɛk) *n.* a unit of flow equal to 1 cubic foot per second. 1 cusec is equivalent to 0.028 317 cubic metre per second. [C20: from *cu(bic foot per) sec(ond)*]

cushat ('kʌʃət) *n.* another name for **wood pigeon.** [Old English *cūscote;* perhaps related to *sceōtan* to shoot]

cushie-doo (ˌkʊʃɪ'duː) *n.* a Scot. name for a **wood pigeon.** Often shortened to **cushie.** [from CUSHAT + DOO]

Cushing's disease *or* **syndrome** ('kʊʃɪŋz) *n.* a rare condition caused by excess corticosteroid hormones in the body, characterized chiefly by obesity of the trunk and face, high blood pressure, fatigue, and loss of calcium from the bones. [C20: named after H. W. *Cushing* (1869–1939), U.S. neurosurgeon]

cushion ('kʊʃən) *n.* **1.** a bag made of cloth, leather, plastic, etc., filled with feathers, air, or other yielding substance, used for sitting on, leaning against, etc. **2.** something resembling a cushion in function or appearance, esp. one to support or pad or to absorb shock. **3.** the resilient felt-covered rim of a billiard table. **4.** another name for **pillow** (sense 2). **5.** short for **air cushion. 6.** a capital, used in Byzantine, Romanesque, and Norman architecture, in the form of a bowl with a square top. ~*vb.* (*tr.*) **7.** to place on or as on a cushion. **8.** to provide with cushions. **9.** to protect, esp. against hardship or change. **10. a.** to check the motion of (a mechanism) gently, esp. by the compression of trapped fluid in a cylinder. **b.** to provide with a means of absorbing shock. [from Latin *culcita* mattress] —'**cushiony** *adj.*

cushion plant *n.* a type of low-growing plant having many closely spaced short upright shoots, typical of alpine and arctic habitats.

Cushitic (kʊ'ʃɪtɪk) *n.* **1.** a group of languages of Somalia, Ethiopia, NE Kenya, and adjacent regions: a subfamily within the Afro-Asiatic family of languages. ~*adj.* **2.** denoting, relating to, or belonging to this group of languages.

cushy ('kʊʃɪ) *adj.* **cushier, cushiest.** *Informal.* easy; comfortable: *a cushy job.* [C20: from Hindi *khush* pleasant, from Persian *khōsh*]
cusk (kʌsk) *n., pl.* **cusks** *or* **cusk.** the usual U.S. and Canadian name for the **torsk.** [C17: probably alteration of *tusk* of Scandinavian origin; compare Old Norse *thorskr* codfish]
CUSO ('kjuːsəʊ) *n. acronym for* Canadian University Services Overseas.
cusp (kʌsp) *n.* **1.** any of the small elevations on the grinding or chewing surface of a tooth. **2.** any of the triangular flaps of a heart valve. **3.** a point or pointed end. **4.** Also called: **spinode.** *Geom.* a point at which two arcs of a curve intersect and at which the two tangents are coincident. **5.** *Architect.* a carving at the meeting place of two arcs. **6.** *Astronomy.* either of the points of a crescent moon or of a satellite or inferior planet in a similar phase. **7.** *Astrology.* any division between houses or signs of the zodiac. [C16: from Latin *cuspis* point, pointed end]
cuspate ('kʌspɪt, -peɪt), **cuspated,** *or* **cusped** (kʌspt) *adj.* **1.** having a cusp or cusps. **2.** shaped like a cusp; cusplike.
cuspid ('kʌspɪd) *n.* a tooth having one point; canine tooth.
cuspidate ('kʌspɪˌdeɪt), **cuspidated,** *or* **cuspidal** ('kʌspɪdᵊl) *adj.* **1.** having a cusp or cusps. **2.** (esp. of leaves) narrowing to a point. [C17: from Latin *cuspidāre* to make pointed, from *cuspis* a point]
cuspidation (ˌkʌspɪ'deɪʃən) *n. Architect.* decoration using cusps.
cuspidor ('kʌspɪˌdɔː) *n.* another word (esp. U.S.) for **spittoon.** [C18: from Portuguese, from *cuspir* to spit, from Latin *conspuere,* from *spuere* to spit]
cuss (kʌs) *Informal.* ~*n.* **1.** a curse; oath. **2.** a person or animal, esp. an annoying one. ~*vb.* **3.** another word for **curse** (senses 8, 9).
cussed ('kʌsɪd) *adj. Informal.* **1.** another word for **cursed. 2.** obstinate. **3.** annoying: *a cussed nuisance.* —**'cussedly** *adv.* —**'cussedness** *n.*
custard ('kʌstəd) *n.* **1.** a baked sweetened mixture of eggs and milk. **2.** a sauce made of milk and sugar thickened with cornflour. [C15: alteration of Middle English *crustade* kind of pie, probably from Old Provençal *croustado,* from *crosta* CRUST]
custard apple *n.* **1.** a West Indian tree, *Annona reticulata:* family *Annonaceae.* **2.** the large heart-shaped fruit of this tree, which has a fleshy edible pulp. **3.** any of several related trees or fruits, esp. the papaw and sweetsop. ~Also called (for senses 1, 2): **bullock's heart.**
custard pie *n.* **a.** a flat, open pie filled with real or artificial custard, as thrown in slapstick comedy. **b.** (*as modifier*): *custard-pie humour.*
custard powder *n.* a powder containing cornflour, sugar, etc., for thickening milk to make a yellow sauce. (See **custard** sense 2).
custodian (kʌ'stəʊdɪən) *n.* **1.** a person who has custody, as of a prisoner, ward, etc. **2.** a guardian or keeper, as of an art collection, etc.
custodianship (kʌ'stəʊdɪənʃɪp) *n.* **1.** the condition of being a custodian. **2.** (in Britain) a legal basis for the care of children under the Children's Act 1975, midway between fostering and adoption, devised for children settled in long-term foster care or living permanently with relatives or a step-parent.
custody ('kʌstədɪ) *n., pl.* **-dies. 1.** the act of keeping safe or guarding, esp. the right of guardianship of a minor. **2.** the state of being held by the police; arrest (esp. in the phrases **in custody, take into custody**). [C15: from Latin *custōdia,* from *custōs* guard, defender] —**custodial** (kʌ'stəʊdɪəl) *adj.*
custom ('kʌstəm) *n.* **1.** a usual or habitual practice; typical mode of behaviour. **2.** the long-established habits or traditions of a society collectively; convention: *custom dictates good manners.* **3. a.** a practice which by long-established usage has come to have the force of law. **b.** such practices collectively (esp. in the phrase **custom and practice**). **4.** habitual patronage, esp. of a shop or business. **5.** the customers of a shop or business collectively. **6.** (in feudal Europe) a tribute paid by a vassal to his lord. ~*adj.* **7.** made to the specifications of an individual customer (often in the combinations **custom-built, custom-made**). **8.** specializing in goods so made. ~See also **customs.** [C12: from Old French *costume,* from Latin *consuētūdō,* from *consuēscere* to grow accustomed to, from *suēscere* to be used to]
customable ('kʌstəməbᵊl) *adj.* subject to customs.
customary ('kʌstəmərɪ, -təmrɪ) *adj.* **1.** in accordance with custom or habitual practice; usual; habitual. **2.** *Law.* **a.** founded upon long continued practices and usage rather than law. **b.** (of land, esp. a feudal estate) held by custom. ~*n., pl.* **-aries. 3. a.** a statement in writing of customary laws and practices. **b.** a body of such laws and customs. —**'customarily** *adv.* —**'customariness** *n.*
custom-built *adj.* (of cars, houses, etc.) made according to the specifications of an individual buyer.
customer ('kʌstəmə) *n.* **1.** a person who buys. **2.** *Informal.* a person with whom one has dealings: *a queer customer.*
custom house *or* **customs house** *n.* a government office, esp. at a port, where customs are collected and ships cleared for entry.
customize *or* **customise** ('kʌstəˌmaɪz) *vb.* (*tr.*) to make (something) according to a customer's individual requirements.
custom-made *adj.* (of suits, dresses, etc.) made according to the specifications of an individual buyer.
customs ('kʌstəmz) *n.* (*functioning as sing. or pl.*) **1.** duty on imports or exports. **2.** the government department responsible for the collection of these duties. **3.** the part of a port, airport, frontier station, etc., where baggage and freight are examined for dutiable goods and contraband. **4.** the procedure for examining baggage and freight, paying duty, etc. **5.** (*as modifier*): *customs officer.*
customs union *n.* an association of nations which promotes free trade within the union and establishes common tariffs on trade with nonmember nations.
custos ('kʌstɒs) *n., pl.* **custodes** (kʌ'stəʊdiːz). a superior in the Franciscan religious order. Also called (in England): **guardian.** [C15: from Latin: keeper, guard]
custumal ('kʌstjʊməl) *n., adj.* another word for **customary** (senses 2, 3). [C16: from Medieval Latin *custumālis* relating to CUSTOM]
cut (kʌt) *vb.* **cuts, cutting, cut. 1.** to open up or incise (a person or thing) with a sharp edge or instrument; gash. **2.** (of a sharp instrument) to penetrate or incise (a person or thing). **3.** to divide or be divided with or as if with a sharp instrument: *cut a slice of bread.* **4.** (*intr.*) to use a sharp-edged instrument or an instrument that cuts. **5.** (*tr.*) to trim or prune by or as if by clipping: *to cut hair.* **6.** (*tr.*) to reap or mow (a crop, grass, etc.). **7.** (*tr.*) to geld or castrate. **8.** (*tr.;* sometimes foll. by *out*) to make, form, or shape by cutting: *to cut a suit.* **9.** (*tr.*) to hollow or dig out; excavate: *to cut a tunnel through the mountain.* **10.** to strike (an object) sharply. **11.** (*tr.*) *Sport.* to hit (a ball) with a downward slicing stroke so as to impart spin or cause it to fall short. **12.** *Cricket.* to hit (the ball) to the off side, usually between cover and third man, with a roughly horizontal bat. **13.** to hurt or wound the feelings of (a person), esp. by malicious speech or action. **14.** (*tr.*) *Informal.* to refuse to recognize; snub. **15.** (*tr.*) *Informal.* to absent oneself from (an activity, location, etc.), esp. without permission or in haste: *to cut class.* **16.** (*tr.*) to abridge, shorten, or edit by excising a part or parts. **17.** (*tr.;* often foll. by *down*) to lower, reduce, or curtail: *to cut losses.* **18.** (*tr.*) to dilute or weaken: *to cut whisky with water.* **19.** (*tr.*) to dissolve or break up: *to cut fat.* **20.** (when *intr.,* foll. by *across* or *through*) to cross or traverse: *the footpath cuts through the field.* **21.** (*intr.*) to make a sharp or sudden change in direction; veer. **22.** to grow (teeth) through the gums or (of teeth) to appear through the gums. **23.** (*intr.*) *Films.* **a.** to call a halt to a shooting sequence. **b.** (foll. by *to*) to move quickly to another scene. **24.** *Films.* to edit (film). **25.** (*tr.*) to switch off (a light, car engine, etc.). **26.** (*tr.*) (of a performer, recording company, etc.) to make (a record or tape of a song, concert, performance, etc.). **27.** *Cards.* **a.** to divide (the pack) at random into two parts after shuffling. **b.** (*intr.*) to pick cards from a spread pack to decide dealer, partners, etc. **28.** (*tr.*) to remove (material) from an object by means of a chisel, lathe, etc. **29.** (*tr.*) (of a tool) to bite into (an object). **30.** (*intr.*) (of a horse) to injure the leg just above the hoof by a blow from the opposite foot. **31. cut a caper** *or* **capers. a.** to skip or jump playfully. **b.** to act or behave playfully; frolic. **32. cut both ways. a.** to have both good and bad effects. **b.** to affect both sides of something, as two parties in an argument, etc. **33. cut a dash.** to behave or dress showily or strikingly; make a stylish impression. **34. cut (a person) dead.** *Informal.* to ignore (a person) completely. **35. cut a (good, poor,** etc.) **figure.** to appear or behave in a specified manner. **36. cut and run.** *Informal.* to make a rapid escape. **37. cut it fine.** *Informal.* to allow little margin of time, space, etc. **38. cut corners.** to do something in the easiest or shortest way, esp. at the expense of high standards: *we could finish this project early only if we cut corners.* **39. cut loose.** to free or become freed from restraint, custody, anchorage, etc. **40. cut no ice.** *Informal.* to fail to make an impression. **41. cut one's teeth on.** *Informal.* **a.** to use at an early age or stage. **b.** to practise on. ~*adj.* **42.** detached, divided, or separated by cutting. **43.** *Botany.* incised or divided: *cut leaves.* **44.** made, shaped, or fashioned by cutting. **45.** reduced or diminished by or as if by cutting: *cut prices.* **46.** gelded or castrated. **47.** weakened or diluted. **48.** *Brit.* a slang word for **drunk. 49.** hurt; resentful. **50. cut and dried.** *Informal.* settled or arranged in advance. **51. cut lunch.** *Austral. and N.Z.* a sandwich lunch carried from home to work, school, etc. ~*n.* **52.** the act of cutting. **53.** a stroke or incision made by cutting; gash. **54.** a piece or part cut off, esp. a section of food cut from the whole: *a cut of meat.* **55.** the edge of anything cut or sliced. **56.** a passage, channel, path, etc., cut or hollowed out. **57.** an omission or deletion, esp. in a text, film, or play. **58.** a reduction in price, salary, etc. **59.** a decrease in government finance in a particular department or area, usually leading to a reduction of services, staff numbers, etc. **60.** short for **power cut. 61.** *Chiefly U.S. and Canadian.* a quantity of timber cut during a specific time or operation. **62.** *Informal.* a portion or share. **63.** *Informal.* a straw, slip of paper, etc., used in drawing lots. **64.** the manner or style in which a thing, esp. a garment, is cut; fashion. **65. a.** *Irish informal.* a person's general appearance: *I didn't like the cut of him.* **b.** *Irish derogatory.* a dirty or untidy condition: *look at the cut of your shoes.* **66.** a direct route; short cut. **67.** the U.S. name for **block** (sense 17). **68.** *Sport.* the spin of a cut ball. **69.** *Cricket.* a stroke made with the bat in a roughly horizontal position. **70.** *Films.* an immediate transition from one shot to the next, brought about by splicing the two shots

together. **71.** *Informal.* an individual piece of music on a record; track. **72.** words or an action that hurt another person's feelings. **73.** a refusal to recognize an acquaintance; snub. **74.** *Informal, chiefly U.S.* an unauthorized absence, esp. from a school class. **75.** *Chem.* a fraction obtained in distillation, as in oil refining. **76.** the metal removed in a single pass of a machine tool. **77. a.** the shape of the teeth of a file. **b.** their coarseness or fineness. **78.** *Brit.* a stretch of water, esp. a canal. **79. a cut above.** *Informal.* superior (to); better (than). ~See also **cut across, cut along, cutback, cut down, cut in, cut off, cut out, cut up.** [C13: probably of Scandinavian origin; compare Norwegian *kutte* to cut, Icelandic *kuti* small knife]

cut across *vb.* (*prep.*) **1.** (*intr.*) to be contrary to ordinary procedure or limitations: *opinion on the Common Market still cuts clean across party lines.* **2.** to cross or traverse, making a shorter route: *she cut across the field quickly.*

cut along *vb.* (*intr., adv.*) *Brit. informal.* to hurry off.

cut-and-cover *adj.* designating a method of constructing a tunnel by excavating a cutting to the required depth and then backfilling the excavation over the tunnel roof.

cut and paste *n.* a technique used in word processing by which a section of text can be moved within a document.

cut and thrust *n.* **1.** *Fencing.* using both the blade and the point of a sword. **2.** (in argument, debate, etc.) a lively and spirited exchange of ideas or opinions.

cutaneous (kjuːˈteɪnɪəs) *adj.* of, relating to, or affecting the skin. [C16: from New Latin *cutāneus,* from Latin *cutis* skin; see HIDE²] —**cuˈtaneously** *adv.*

cutaway (ˈkʌtəˌweɪ) *n.* **1.** a man's coat cut diagonally from the front waist to the back of the knees. **2. a.** a drawing or model of a machine, engine, etc., in which part of the casing is omitted to reveal the workings. **b.** (*as modifier*): *a cutaway model.* **3.** *Films, television.* a shot separate from the main action of a scene, to emphasize something or to show simultaneous events.

cutback (ˈkʌtˌbæk) *n.* **1.** a decrease or reduction. **2.** another word (esp. U.S.) for **flashback.** ~*vb.* **cut back** (*adv.*) **3.** (*tr.*) to shorten by cutting off the end; prune. **4.** (when *intr.*, foll. by *on*) to reduce or make a reduction (in). **5.** (*intr.*) *Chiefly U.S* (in films) to show an event that took place earlier in the narrative; flash back.

cutch (kʌtʃ) *n.* another name for **catechu.**

cutcherry *or* **cutchery** (ˈkʌtʃərɪ) *n., pl.* **-cherries** *or* **-cheries.** (formerly in India) government offices and law courts collectively. [C17: from Hindi *Kachahrī*]

cut down *vb.* (*adv.*) **1.** (*tr.*) to fell. **2.** (when *intr.*, often foll. by *on*) to reduce or make a reduction (in): *to cut down on drink.* **3.** (*tr.*) to remake (an old garment) in order to make a smaller one. **4.** (*tr.*) to kill: *he was cut down in battle.* **5. cut (a person) down to size.** to reduce in importance or decrease the conceit of.

cute (kjuːt) *adj.* **1.** appealing or attractive, esp. in a pretty way. **2.** *Informal, chiefly U.S. and Canadian.* affecting cleverness or prettiness. **3.** clever; shrewd. [C18 (in the sense: clever): shortened from ACUTE] —**ˈcutely** *adv.* —**ˈcuteness** *n.*

cut glass *n.* **1. a.** glass, esp. bowls, vases, etc., decorated by facet-cutting or grinding. **b.** (*as modifier*): *a cut-glass vase.* **2.** (*modifier*) (of an accent) upper-class; refined.

cuticle (ˈkjuːtɪkᵊl) *n.* **1.** dead skin, esp. that round the base of a fingernail or toenail. **2.** another name for **epidermis. 3.** any covering layer or membrane. **4.** the protective layer, containing cutin, that covers the epidermis of higher plants. **5.** the hard protective layer covering the epidermis of many invertebrates. [C17: from Latin *cutīcula* diminutive of *cutis* skin] —**cuticular** (kjuːˈtɪkjʊlə) *adj.*

cuticula (kjuːˈtɪkjʊlə) *n., pl.* **-lae** (-liː). *Anatomy.* cuticle. [C18: from Latin; see CUTICLE]

cutie *or* **cutey** (ˈkjuːtɪ) *n. Slang.* a person regarded as appealing or attractive, esp. a girl or woman.

cut in *vb.* (*adv.*) **1.** (*intr.*; often foll. by *on*) Also: **cut into.** to break in or interrupt. **2.** (*intr.*) to interrupt a dancing couple to dance with one of them. **3.** (*intr.*) (of a driver, motor vehicle, etc.) to draw in front of another vehicle leaving too little space. **4.** (*tr.*) *Informal.* to allow to have a share. **5.** (*intr.*) to take the place of a person in a card game. ~*n.* **cut-in. 6.** *Films.* a separate shot or scene inserted at a relevant point.

cutin (ˈkjuːtɪn) *n.* a waxy waterproof substance, consisting of derivatives of fatty acids, that is the main constituent of the plant cuticle. [C19: from Latin *cutis* skin + -IN]

cutinize *or* **cutinise** (ˈkjuːtɪˌnaɪz) *vb.* to become or cause to become covered or impregnated with cutin. —ˌ**cutiniˈzation** *or* ˌ**cutiniˈsation** *n.*

cutis (ˈkjuːtɪs) *n., pl.* **-tes** (-tiːz) *or* **-tises.** *Anatomy.* a technical name for the **skin.** [C17: from Latin: skin]

cutlass (ˈkʌtləs) *n.* a curved, one-edged sword formerly used by sailors. [C16: from French *coutelas,* from *coutel* knife, from Latin *cultellus* a small knife, from *culter* knife; see COULTER]

cutlass fish *n. U.S.* another name for the **hairtail** (the fish).

cutler (ˈkʌtlə) *n.* a person who makes or sells cutlery. [C14: from French *coutelier,* ultimately from Latin *culter* knife; see CUTLASS]

cutlery (ˈkʌtlərɪ) *n.* **1.** implements used for eating, such as knives, forks, and spoons. **2.** instruments used for cutting. **3.** the art or business of a cutler.

cutlet (ˈkʌtlɪt) *n.* **1.** a piece of meat taken esp. from the best end of neck of lamb, pork, etc. **2.** a flat croquette of minced chicken, lobster, etc. [C18: from Old French *costelette,* literally: a little rib, from *coste* rib, from Latin *costa*]

cut off *vb.* (*tr., adv.*) **1.** to remove by cutting. **2.** to intercept or interrupt something, esp. a telephone conversation. **3.** to discontinue the supply of: *to cut off the water.* **4.** to bring to an end. **5.** to deprive of rights; disinherit: *she was cut off without a penny.* **6.** to sever or separate: *she was cut off from her family.* **7.** to occupy a position so as to prevent or obstruct (a retreat or escape). ~*n.* **cutoff. 8. a.** the act of cutting off; limit or termination. **b.** (*as modifier*): *the cutoff point.* **9.** *Chiefly U.S.* a route or way that is shorter than the usual one; short cut. **10.** a device to terminate the flow of a fluid in a pipe or duct. **11.** the remnant of metal, plastic, etc., left after parts have been machined or trimmed. **12.** *Electronics.* **a.** the value of voltage, frequency, etc., below or above which an electronic device cannot function efficiently. **b.** (*as modifier*): *cutoff voltage.* **13.** a channel cutting across the neck of a meander, which leaves an oxbow lake. **14.** another name for **oxbow** (the lake).

cut out *vb.* (*adv.*) **1.** (*tr.*) to delete or remove. **2.** (*tr.*) to shape or form by cutting: *to cut out a dress.* **3.** (*tr.*; *usually passive*) to suit or equip for: *you're not cut out for this job.* **4.** (*intr.*) (of an engine, etc.) to cease to operate suddenly. **5.** (*tr.*) *Printing.* to remove the background from a photograph or drawing to make the outline of the subject stand out. **6.** (*intr.*) (of an electrical device) to switch off, usually automatically. **7.** (*tr.*) *Informal.* to oust and supplant (a rival). **8.** (*intr.*) (of a person) to be excluded from a card game. **9.** (*tr.*) *Informal.* to cease doing something, esp. something undesirable (esp. in the phrase **cut it out**). **10.** (*tr.*) *Soccer.* to intercept (a pass). **11.** (*tr.*) to separate (cattle) from a herd. **12.** (*intr.*) *Austral. and N.Z.* to end or finish: *the road cuts out at the creek.* **13. have one's work cut out.** to have as much work as one can manage. ~*n.* **cutout. 14.** something that has been or is intended to be cut out from something else. **15.** a photograph or drawing from which the background has been cut away. **16.** a device that switches off or interrupts an electric circuit, esp. a switch acting as a safety device. **17.** an impressed stamp cut out from an envelope for collecting purposes. **18.** *Austral. slang.* the end of shearing.

cut-price *or esp. U.S.* **cut-rate** *adj.* **1.** available at prices or rates below the standard price or rate. **2.** (*prenominal*) offering goods or services at prices below the standard price: *a cut-price shop.*

cutpurse (ˈkʌtˌpɜːs) *n.* an archaic word for **pickpocket.**

CUTS (kʌts) *n. acronym for* Computer Users' Tape System.

cut sheet feed *n. Computer technol.* the automatic movement of single sheets of paper through the platen of the printer.

cut string *n.* another name for **bridgeboard.**

cutter (ˈkʌtə) *n.* **1.** a person or thing that cuts, esp. a person who cuts cloth for clothing. **2.** a sailing boat with its mast stepped further aft so as to have a larger foretriangle than that of a sloop. **3.** a ship's boat, powered by oars or sail, for carrying passengers or light cargo. **4.** a small lightly armed boat, as used in the enforcement of customs regulations. **5.** a pig weighing between 68 and 82 kg, from which fillets and larger joints are cut.

cutthroat (ˈkʌtˌθrəʊt) *n.* **1.** a person who cuts throats; murderer. **2.** Also called: **cutthroat razor.** *Brit.* a razor with a long blade that usually folds into the handle. U.S. name: **straight razor.** ~*adj.* **3.** bloodthirsty or murderous; cruel. **4.** fierce or relentless in competition: *cutthroat prices.* **5.** (of some games) played by three people: *cutthroat poker.*

cutting (ˈkʌtɪŋ) *n.* **1.** a piece cut off from the main part of something. **2.** *Horticulture.* **a.** a method of vegetative propagation in which a part of a plant, such as a stem or leaf, is induced to form its own roots. **b.** a part separated for this purpose. **3.** Also called (esp. U.S. and Canadian): **clipping.** an article, photograph, etc., cut from a newspaper or other publication. **4.** the editing process by which a film is cut and made. **5.** an excavation in a piece of high land for a road, railway, etc., enabling it to remain at approximately the same level. **6.** *Irish informal.* sharp-wittedness: *there is no cutting in him.* **7.** (*modifier*) designed for or adapted to cutting; edged; sharp: *a cutting tool.* ~*adj.* **8.** keen; piercing: *a cutting wind.* **9.** tending to hurt the feelings: *a cutting remark.* —**ˈcuttingly** *adv.*

cutting compound *n. Engineering.* a mixture, such as oil, water, and soap, used for cooling drills and other cutting tools.

cutting edge *n.* the leading position in any field; forefront: *on the cutting edge of space technology.*

cutting grass *n.* a W African name for **cane rat** (sense 1).

cuttle (ˈkʌtᵊl) *n.* **1.** short for **cuttlefish** or **cuttlebone. 2. little cuttle.** a small cuttlefish, *Sepiola atlantica,* often found on beaches. [Old English *cudele;* related to Old High German *kiot* bag, Norwegian dialect *kaule* cuttle, Old English *codd* bag]

cuttlebone (ˈkʌtᵊlˌbəʊn) *n.* the internal calcareous shell of the cuttlefish, used as a mineral supplement to the diet of cage-birds and as a polishing agent.

cuttlefish (ˈkʌtᵊlˌfɪʃ) *n., pl.* **-fish** *or* **-fishes.** any cephalopod mollusc of the genus *Sepia* and related genera, which occur near the bottom of inshore waters and have a broad flattened body: order *Decapoda* (decapods). Sometimes shortened to **cuttle.** See also **squid.**

cutty (ˈkʌtɪ) *Scot. and northern English dialect.* ~*adj.* **1.** short or cut short. ~*n., pl.* **-ties. 2.** something cut short, such as a spoon or short-stemmed tobacco pipe. **3.** an immoral girl or woman (in Scotland used as a general term of abuse for a woman). **4.** a short thickset girl. [C18 (Scottish and northern English): from CUT (vb.)]

cutty grass *n.* a species of sedge, *Cyperus ustulatus,* of New Zealand with sharp leaves.

cutty stool *n.* (formerly in Scotland) the church seat on which an unchaste person sat while being harangued by the minister.

cut up *vb.* (*tr., adv.*) **1.** to cut into pieces. **2.** to inflict injuries on. **3.** (*usually passive*) *Informal.* to affect the feelings of deeply. **4.** *Informal.* to subject to severe criticism. **5. cut up rough.** *Brit. informal.* to become angry or bad-tempered. ~*n.* **cut-up** **6.** *Informal, chiefly U.S.* a joker or prankster.

cut-up technique *n.* a technique of writing involving cutting up lines or pages of prose and rearranging these fragments, popularized by the novelist William Burroughs.

cutwater ('kʌt,wɔːtə) *n.* the forward part of the stem of a vessel, which cuts through the water.

cutwork ('kʌt,wɜːk) *n.* openwork embroidery in which the pattern is cut away from the background.

cutworm ('kʌt,wɜːm) *n.* the caterpillar of various noctuid moths, esp. those of the genus *Argrotis,* which is a pest of young crop plants in North America.

cuvée (kuː'veɪ) *n.* an individual batch or blend of wine. [C19: from French, literally: put in a cask, from *cuve* cask]

cuvette (kjuː'vɛt) *n.* a shallow dish or vessel for holding liquid. [C17: from French, diminutive of *cuve* cask, from Latin *cupa*]

CV *abbrev. for:* **1.** curriculum vitae. **2.** (in Canada) Cross of Valour.

CVA *abbrev. for* cerebrovascular accident.

CVO *abbrev. for* Commander of the Royal Victorian Order.

CVS *abbrev. for:* **1.** (in Britain) Council of Voluntary Service. **2.** chorionic villus sampling.

CW **1.** *Radio. abbrev. for* continuous waves. ~*n.* **2. a.** an informal term for **Morse code. b.** (*as modifier*): *his CW speed is 30 words per minute.* **3.** *abbrev. for* chemical weapons and chemical warfare.

CWA (in Australia) *abbrev. for* Country Women's Association.

Cwlth *abbrev. for* Commonwealth.

cwm (kuːm) *n.* **1.** (in Wales) a valley. **2.** *Geology.* another name for **cirque** (sense 1).

c.w.o. *or* **CWO** *abbrev. for* cash with order.

CWS *abbrev. for* Cooperative Wholesale Society.

cwt *abbrev. for* hundredweight. [*c,* from the Latin numeral *C* one hundred (*centum*)]

CY *international car registration for* Cyprus.

-cy *suffix.* **1.** (*forming nouns from adjectives ending in -t, -tic, -te, and -nt*) indicating state, quality, or condition: *plutocracy; lunacy; intimacy; infancy.* **2.** (*forming abstract nouns from other nouns*) rank or office: *captaincy.* [via Old French from Latin *-cia, -tia,* Greek *-kia, -tia,* abstract noun suffixes]

cyan ('saɪæn, 'saɪən) *n.* **1.** a highly saturated green-blue that is the complementary colour of red and forms, with magenta and yellow, a set of primary colours. ~*adj.* **2.** of this colour: *a cyan filter.* [C19: from Greek *kuanos* dark blue]

cyan- *combining form.* a variant of **cyano-** before a vowel: *cyanamide; cyanide.*

cyanamide (saɪ'ænə,maɪd, -mɪd) *or* **cyanamid** (saɪ'ænəmɪd) *n.* **1.** Also called: **cyanogenamide** (,saɪənəʊ'dʒɛnə,maɪd, -mɪd). a white or colourless crystalline soluble weak dibasic acid, which can be hydrolysed to urea. Formula: H_2NCN. **2.** a salt or ester of cyanamide. **3.** short for **calcium cyanamide.**

cyanate ('saɪə,neɪt) *n.* any salt or ester of cyanic acid, containing the ion ^-OCN or the group -OCN.

cyanic (saɪ'ænɪk) *adj. Rare.* having a blue or bluish colour.

cyanic acid *n.* a colourless poisonous volatile liquid acid that hydrolyses readily to ammonia and carbon dioxide. Formula: HOCN. Compare **isocyanic acid, fulminic acid.**

cyanide ('saɪə,naɪd) *or* **cyanid** ('saɪənɪd) *n.* **1.** any salt of hydrocyanic acid. Cyanides contain the ion CN^- and are extremely poisonous. **2.** another name (not in technical usage) for **nitrile.** —,**cyani'dation** *n.*

cyanide process *n.* a process for recovering gold and silver from ores by treatment with a weak solution of sodium cyanide. Also called: **cyaniding.**

cyanine ('saɪə,niːn) *or* **cyanin** ('saɪənɪn) *n.* **1.** a blue dye used to extend the sensitivity of photographic emulsions to colours other than blue and ultraviolet. **2.** any of a class of chemically related dyes, used for the same purpose.

cyanite ('saɪə,naɪt) *n.* a grey, green, or blue mineral consisting of aluminium silicate in triclinic crystalline form. It occurs in metamorphic rocks and is used as a refractory. Formula: Al_2SiO_5. —**cyanitic** (,saɪə'nɪtɪk) *adj.*

cyano- *or before a vowel* **cyan-** *combining form.* **1.** blue or dark blue: *cyanotype.* **2.** indicating cyanogen: *cyanohydrin.* **3.** indicating cyanide. [from Greek *kuanos* (adj.) dark blue, (n.) dark blue enamel, lapis lazuli]

cyanobacteria (,saɪənəʊbæk'tɪərɪə) *pl. n., sing.* **-rium** (-rɪəm). a group of bacteria containing a blue photosynthetic pigment and formerly regarded as algae; blue-green algae.

cyanocobalamin (,saɪənəʊkəʊ'bæləmɪn) *n.* a complex red crystalline compound, containing cyanide and cobalt and occurring in liver: lack of it in the tissues leads to pernicious anaemia. Formula: $C_{63}H_{88}O_{14}N_{14}PCo$. Also called: **vitamin B_{12}.** [C20: from CYANO- + COBAL(T) + (VIT)AMIN]

cyanogen (saɪ'ænədʒɪn) *n.* an extremely poisonous colourless flammable gas with an almond-like odour: has been used in chemical warfare. Formula: $(CN)_2$. [C19: from French *cyanogène;* see CYANO-, -GEN; so named because it is one of the constituents of Prussian blue]

cyanogenesis (,saɪənəʊ'dʒɛnɪsɪs) *n. Botany.* the release by certain plants, such as cherry laurel, of hydrogen cyanide, esp. after wounding or invasion by pathogens.

cyanohydrin (,saɪənəʊ'haɪdrɪn) *n.* any of a class of organic compounds containing a cyanide group and a hydroxyl group bound to the same carbon atom.

cyanophyte (saɪ'ænəfaɪt) *n.* a former name for a blue-green alga. See **blue-green algae.**

cyanosis (,saɪə'nəʊsɪs) *n. Pathol.* a bluish-purple discoloration of skin and mucous membranes usually resulting from a deficiency of oxygen in the blood. —**cyanotic** (,saɪə'nɒtɪk) *adj.*

cyanotype (saɪ'ænə,taɪp) *n.* another name for **blueprint** (sense 1).

cybernate ('saɪbə,neɪt) *vb.* to control (a manufacturing process) with a servomechanism or (of a process) to be controlled by a servomechanism. [C20: from CYBER(NETICS) + -ATE[1]] —,**cyber'nation** *n.*

cybernetics (,saɪbə'nɛtɪks) *n.* (*functioning as sing.*) the branch of science concerned with control systems in electronic and mechanical devices and the extent to which useful comparisons can be made between man-made and biological systems. See also **feedback** (sense 1). [C20: from Greek *kubernētēs* steersman, from *kubernan* to steer, control] —,**cyber'netic** *adj.* —,**cyber'neticist** *n.*

cyberphobia (,saɪbə'fəʊbɪə) *n.* an irrational fear of computers. [C20: from CYBER(NETICS) + -PHOBIA] —,**cyber'phobic** *adj.*

cyberpunk ('saɪbə,pʌŋk) *n.* **1.** a genre of science fiction that features rebellious computer hackers and is set in a dystopian society integrated by computer networks. **2.** a writer of cyberpunk. [C20: from CYBER(NETICS) + PUNK[1] (sense 1)]

cycad ('saɪkæd) *n.* any tropical or subtropical gymnosperm plant of the order *Cycadales,* having an unbranched stem with fernlike leaves crowded at the top. See also **sago palm** (sense 2). [C19: from New Latin *Cycas* name of genus, from Greek *kukas,* scribe's error for *koïkas,* from *koïx* a kind of palm, probably of Egyptian origin] —,**cyca'daceous** *adj.*

cyclamate ('saɪklə,meɪt, 'sɪklə,meɪt) *n.* a salt or ester of cyclamic acid. Certain of the salts have a very sweet taste and were formerly used as food additives and sugar substitutes. [C20: *cycl(ohexyl-sulph)amate*]

cyclamen ('sɪkləmən, -,mɛn) *n.* **1.** any Old World plant of the primulaceous genus *Cyclamen,* having nodding white, pink, or red flowers, with reflexed petals. See also **sowbread.** ~*adj.* **2.** of a dark reddish-purple colour. [C16: from Medieval Latin, from Latin *cyclamīnos,* from Greek *kuklaminos,* probably from *kuklos* circle, referring to the bulb-like roots]

cycle ('saɪk[ə]l) *n.* **1.** a recurring period of time in which certain events or phenomena occur and reach completion or repeat themselves in a regular sequence. **2.** a completed series of events that follows or is followed by another series of similar events occurring in the same sequence. **3.** the time taken or needed for one such series. **4.** a vast period of time; age; aeon. **5.** a group of poems or prose narratives forming a continuous story about a central figure or event: *the Arthurian cycle.* **6.** a series of miracle plays: *the Chester cycle.* **7.** a group or sequence of songs (see **song cycle**). **8.** short for **bicycle, tricycle, motorcycle,** etc. **9.** *Astronomy.* the orbit of a celestial body. **10.** a recurrent series of events or processes in plants and animals: *a life cycle; a growth cycle.* **11.** *Physics.* a continuous change or a sequence of changes in the state of a system that leads to the restoration of the system to its original state after a finite period of time. **12.** one of a series of repeated changes in the magnitude of a periodically varying quantity, such as current or voltage. **13.** *Computer technol.* **a.** a set of operations that can be both treated and repeated as a unit. **b.** the time required to complete a set of operations. **c.** one oscillation of the regular voltage waveform used to synchronize processes in a digital computer. **14.** (in generative grammar) the set of cyclic rules. ~*vb.* **15.** (*tr.*) to process through a cycle or system. **16.** (*intr.*) to move in or pass through cycles. **17.** to travel by or ride a bicycle or tricycle. [C14: from Late Latin *cyclus,* from Greek *kuklos* cycle, circle, ring, wheel; see WHEEL]

cycle of erosion *n.* the hypothetical sequence of modifications to the earth's surface by erosion, from the original uplift of the land to the ultimate low plain, usually divided into the youthful, mature, and old stages.

cyclic ('saɪklɪk, 'sɪklɪk) *or* **cyclical** ('saɪklɪk[ə]l, 'sɪklɪk[ə]l) *adj.* **1.** recurring or revolving in cycles. **2.** (of an organic compound) containing a closed saturated or unsaturated ring of atoms. See also **heterocyclic** and **homocyclic.** **3.** *Botany.* **a.** arranged in whorls: *cyclic petals.* **b.** having parts arranged in this way: *cyclic flowers.* **4.** *Music.* of or relating to a musical form consisting of several movements sharing thematic material. **5.** *Geometry.* (of a polygon) having vertices that lie on a circle. **6.** (in generative grammar) denoting one of a set of transformational rules all of which must apply to a clause before any one of them applies to any clause in which the first clause is embedded. —'**cyclically** *adv.*

cyclical unemployment *n.* unemployment caused by fluctuations in the level of economic activity inherent in trade cycles.
cyclic AMP *n.* cyclic adenosine monophosphate: a constituent of biological cells, responsible for triggering processes that are dependent on hormones.
cyclic pitch lever *n.* a lever in a helicopter to change the angle of attack of individual rotor blades, causing the helicopter to move forwards, backwards, or sideways. Compare **collective pitch lever.**
cycling shorts *pl. n.* tight-fitting shorts reaching partway to the knee for cycling, sport, etc.
cyclist ('saɪklɪst) *or U.S.* **cycler** *n.* a person who rides or travels by bicycle, motorcycle, etc.
cyclo- *or before a vowel* **cycl-** *combining form.* **1.** indicating a circle or ring: *cyclotron.* **2.** denoting a cyclic compound: *cyclohexane.* [from Greek *kuklos* CYCLE]
cycloalkane (ˌsaɪkləʊ'ælkeɪn) *n.* any saturated hydrocarbon similar to an alkane but having a cyclic molecular structure and the general formula C_nH_{2n}. Also called: **cycloparaffin.**
cyclo-cross *n.* **a.** a form of cycle race held over rough ground. **b.** this sport.
cyclogiro ('saɪkləʊˌdʒaɪrəʊ) *n. Aeronautics.* an aircraft lifted and propelled by pivoted blades rotating parallel to roughly horizontal transverse axes.
cyclograph ('saɪkləʊˌgrɑːf, -ˌgræf) *n.* another name for **arcograph.**
cyclohexane (ˌsaɪkləʊ'hɛkseɪn, ˌsɪk-) *n.* a colourless insoluble flammable liquid cycloalkane with a pungent odour, made by hydrogenation of benzene and used as a paint remover and solvent. Formula: C_6H_{12}.
cyclohexanone (ˌsaɪkləʊ'hɛksəˌnəʊn) *n.* a colourless liquid used as a solvent for cellulose lacquers. Formula: $C_6H_{10}O$.
cycloid ('saɪklɔɪd) *adj.* **1.** resembling a circle. **2.** (of fish scales) rounded, thin, and smooth-edged, as those of the salmon. **3.** *Psychiatry.* (of a type of personality) characterized by exaggerated swings of mood between elation and depression. See also **cyclothymia.** *~n.* **4.** *Geometry.* the curve described by a point on the circumference of a circle as the circle rolls along a straight line. Compare **trochoid** (sense 1). **5.** a fish that has cycloid scales. —**cy'cloidal** *adj.* —**cy'cloidally** *adv.*
cyclometer (saɪ'klɒmɪtə) *n.* a device that records the number of revolutions made by a wheel and hence the distance travelled. —**cy'clometry** *n.*
cyclone ('saɪkləʊn) *n.* **1.** another name for **depression** (sense 6). **2.** a violent tropical storm; hurricane. *~adj.* **3.** *Austral. and N.Z.* (of fencing) made of interlaced wire and metal. [C19: from Greek *kuklōn* a turning around, from *kukloein* to revolve, from *kuklos* wheel] —**cyclonic** (saɪ'klɒnɪk), **cy'clonical,** *or* **'cyclonal** *adj.* —**cy'clonically** *adv.*
cyclonite ('saɪkləˌnaɪt) *n.* a white crystalline insoluble explosive prepared by the action of nitric acid on hexamethylenetetramine; cyclotrimethylenetrinitramine: used in bombs and shells. Formula: $C_3H_6N_6O_6$. [C20: from CYCLO- + (*trimethylene-tri*)*nit*(*ramin*)*e*]
cycloparaffin (ˌsaɪkləʊ'pærəfɪn, ˌsɪk-) *n.* another name for **cycloalkane.**
Cyclopean (ˌsaɪkləʊ'piːən, saɪ'kləʊpɪən) *adj.* **1.** of, relating to, or resembling the Cyclops, a mythical one-eyed giant, esp. in being enormous. **2.** denoting, relating to, or having the kind of masonry used in preclassical Greek architecture, characterized by large dry undressed blocks of stone.
cyclopedia *or* **cyclopaedia** (ˌsaɪkləʊ'piːdɪə) *n.* a less common word for **encyclopedia.** —ˌ**cyclo'pedic** *or* ˌ**cyclo'paedic** *adj.* —ˌ**cyclo'pedist** *or* ˌ**cyclo'paedist** *n.*
cyclopentadiene (ˌsaɪkləʊˌpɛntə'daɪiːn) *n.* a colourless liquid unsaturated cyclic hydrocarbon obtained in the cracking of petroleum hydrocarbons and the distillation of coal tar: used in the manufacture of plastics and insecticides. Formula: C_5H_6.
cyclopentane (ˌsaɪkləʊ'pɛnteɪn, ˌsɪk-) *n.* a colourless insoluble cycloalkane found in petroleum and used mainly as a solvent. Formula: C_5H_{10}.
cyclophosphamide (ˌsaɪkləʊ'fɒsfəˌmaɪd) *n.* an alkylating agent used in the treatment of leukaemia and lymphoma. [C20: from CYCLO- + PHOSPH(ORUS) + AMIDE]
cycloplegia (ˌsaɪkləʊ'pliːdʒɪə, ˌsɪk-) *n.* paralysis of the muscles that adjust the shape of the lens of the eye, resulting in loss of ability to focus. —ˌ**cyclo'plegic** *adj.*
cyclopropane (ˌsaɪkləʊ'prəʊpeɪn, ˌsɪk-) *n.* a colourless flammable gaseous hydrocarbon, used in medicine as an anaesthetic; trimethylene. It is a cycloalkane with molecules containing rings of three carbon atoms. Formula: C_3H_6; boiling pt.: –34°C.
cyclops ('saɪklɒps) *n., pl.* **cyclops** *or* **cyclopes** (saɪ'kləʊpiːz). any copepod of the genus *Cyclops,* characterized by having one eye. [named after the *Cyclops* of Greek mythology, a one-eyed giant, from Greek *Kuklōps*, literally: round eye, from *kuklos* circle + *ōps* eye]
cyclorama (ˌsaɪkləʊ'rɑːmə) *n.* **1.** Also called: **panorama.** a large picture, such as a battle scene, on the interior wall of a cylindrical room, designed to appear in natural perspective to a spectator in the centre. **2.** *Theatre.* **a.** a curtain or wall curving along the back of a stage, usually painted to represent the sky and serving to enhance certain lighting effects. **b.** any set of curtains that enclose the back and sides of a stage setting. [C19: CYCLO- + Greek *horama* view, sight, on the model of *panorama*] —**cycloramic** (ˌsaɪkləʊ'ræmɪk) *adj.*
cyclosis (saɪ'kləʊsɪs) *n., pl.* **-ses** (-siːz). *Biology.* the circulation of cytoplasm or cell organelles, such as food vacuoles in some protozoans. [C19: from Greek *kuklōsis* an encircling, from *kukloun* to surround, from *kuklos* circle]
cyclosporin-A (ˌsaɪkləʊ'spɔːrɪn) *n.* a drug extracted from a fungus and used in transplant surgery to suppress the body's immune mechanisms, and so prevent rejection of an organ.
cyclostome ('saɪkləˌstəʊm, 'sɪk-) *n.* **1.** any primitive aquatic jawless vertebrate of the class *Cyclostomata,* such as the lamprey and hagfish, having a round sucking mouth and pouchlike gills. *~adj.* **2.** of, relating to, or belonging to the class *Cyclostomata.* ~Also: **marsipobranch.** —**cyclostomate** (saɪ'klɒstəmɪt, -ˌmeɪt) *or* **cyclostomatous** (ˌsaɪkləʊ'stɒmətəs, -'stəʊmə-, ˌsɪk-) *adj.*
cyclostyle ('saɪkləˌstaɪl) *n.* **1.** a kind of pen with a small toothed wheel, used for cutting minute holes in a specially prepared stencil. Copies of the design so formed can be printed on a duplicator by forcing ink through the holes. **2.** an office duplicator using a stencil prepared in this way. *~vb.* **3.** (*tr.*) to print on a duplicator using such a stencil. —'**cycloˌstyled** *adj.*
cyclothymia (ˌsaɪkləʊ'θaɪmɪə, ˌsɪk-) *n. Psychiatry.* a condition characterized by periodical swings of mood between excitement and depression, activity and inactivity. See also **manic-depressive.** —ˌ**cyclo'thymic** *or* ˌ**cyclo'thymiˌac** *adj., n.*
cyclotron ('saɪkləˌtrɒn) *n.* a type of particle accelerator in which the particles spiral inside two D-shaped hollow metal electrodes under the effect of a strong vertical magnetic field, gaining energy by a high-frequency voltage applied between these electrodes.
cyder ('saɪdə) *n.* a variant spelling (esp. Brit.) of **cider.**
cyesis (saɪ'iːsɪs) *n., pl.* **-ses** (-siːz). *Med.* the technical name for **pregnancy.** [from Greek *kuēsis*]
cygnet ('sɪgnɪt) *n.* a young swan. [C15 *sygnett,* from Old French *cygne* swan, from Latin *cygnus,* from Greek *kuknos*]
Cygnus ('sɪgnəs) *n., Latin genitive* **Cygni** ('sɪgnaɪ). a constellation in the N hemisphere lying between Pegasus and Draco in the Milky Way. The constellation contains the expanding supernova remnant, the **Cygnus Loop.** It may also contain a black hole. [Latin: swan; see CYGNET]
cyl. *abbrev. for:* **1.** cylinder. **2.** cylindrical.
cylinder ('sɪlɪndə) *n.* **1.** a solid consisting of two parallel planes bounded by identical closed curves, usually circles, that are interconnected at every point by a set of parallel lines, usually perpendicular to the planes. Volume: *base area* × *length.* **2.** a surface formed by a line moving round a closed plane curve at a fixed angle to it. **3.** any object shaped like a cylinder. **4.** the chamber in a reciprocating internal-combustion engine, pump, or compressor within which the piston moves. See also **cylinder block.** **5.** the rotating mechanism of a revolver, situated behind the barrel and containing cartridge chambers. **6.** *Printing.* any of the rotating drums on a printing press. **7.** Also called: **cylinder seal.** a cylindrical seal of stone, clay, or precious stone decorated with linear designs, found in the Middle East and Balkans: dating from about 6000 B.C. **8.** Also called: **hot-water cylinder.** *Brit.* a vertical cylindrical tank for storing hot water, esp. an insulated one made of copper used in a domestic hot-water system. *~vb.* **9.** (*tr.*) to provide (a system) with cylinders. [C16: from Latin *cylindrus,* from Greek *kulindros* a roller, from *kulindein* to roll] —'**cylinder-ˌlike** *adj.*
cylinder barrel *n. Engineering.* the metal casting containing a cylinder of a reciprocating internal-combustion engine.
cylinder block *n.* the metal casting containing the cylinders and cooling channels or fins of a reciprocating internal-combustion engine. Sometimes shortened to **block.**
cylinder head *n.* the detachable metal casting that fits onto the top of a cylinder block. In an engine it contains part of the combustion chamber and in an overhead-valve four-stroke engine it houses the valves and their operating mechanisms. Sometimes shortened to **head.**
cylinder press *n. Printing.* another name for **flat-bed press.**
cylindrical (sɪ'lɪndrɪkəl) *or* **cylindric** *adj.* of, shaped like, or characteristic of a cylinder. —**cyˌlindri'cality** *or* **cy'lindricalness** *n.* —**cy'lindrically** *adv.*
cylindrical coordinates *pl. n.* three coordinates defining the location of a point in three-dimensional space in terms of its polar coordinates (r, θ) in one plane, usually the (x, y) plane, and its perpendicular distance, z, measured from this plane.
cylindroid ('sɪlɪnˌdrɔɪd) *n.* **1.** a cylinder with an elliptical cross section. *~adj.* **2.** resembling a cylinder.
cylix ('saɪlɪks, 'sɪl-) *n., pl.* **-lices** (-lɪˌsiːz). a variant of **kylix.**
cyma ('saɪmə) *n., pl.* **-mae** (-miː) *or* **-mas.** **1.** either of two mouldings having a double curve, part concave and part convex. **Cyma recta** has the convex part nearer the wall and **cyma reversa** has the concave part nearer the wall. **2.** *Botany.* a variant of **cyme.** [C16: from New Latin, from Greek *kuma* something swollen, from *kuein* to be pregnant]
cymar (sɪ'mɑː) *n.* a woman's short fur-trimmed jacket, popular in the 17th and 18th centuries. [C17: variant of *simar,* from French *simarre,* perhaps ultimately from Basque *zamar* sheepskin]

cymatium (sɪˈmeɪtɪəm, -ʃɪəm) *n., pl.* **-tia** (-tɪə, -ʃɪə). *Architect.* the top moulding of a classical cornice or entablature. [C16: see CYMA]

cymbal (ˈsɪmbᵊl) *n.* a percussion instrument of indefinite pitch consisting of a thin circular piece of brass, which vibrates when clashed together with another cymbal or struck with a stick. [Old English *cymbala,* from Medieval Latin, from Latin *cymbalum,* from Greek *kumbalon,* from *kumbē* something hollow] —ˈ**cymbaler,** ˌ**cymbalˈeer,** *or* ˈ**cymbalist** *n.* —ˈ**cymbalˌlike** *adj.*

cymbalo (ˈsɪmbəˌləʊ) *n., pl.* **-los.** another name for **dulcimer.** [from Italian; see CYMBAL]

cyme (saɪm) *n.* an inflorescence in which the first flower is the terminal bud of the main stem and subsequent flowers develop as terminal buds of lateral stems. [C18: from Latin *cȳma* cabbage sprout, from Greek *kuma* anything swollen; see CYMA] —**cymiferous** (saɪˈmɪfərəs) *adj.*

cymene (ˈsaɪmiːn) *n.* a colourless insoluble liquid with an aromatic odour that exists in three isomeric forms; methylpropylbenzene: used as solvents and for making synthetic resins. The *para-* isomer is present in several essential oils. Formula: $CH_3C_6H_4CH(CH_3)_2$. [C19: *cym-* from Greek *kuminon* CUMIN + -ENE]

cymogene (ˈsaɪməˌdʒiːn) *n. U.S.* a mixture of volatile flammable hydrocarbons, mainly butane, obtained in the distillation of petroleum. [C19: from CYMENE + -GENE]

cymograph (ˈsaɪməˌgrɑːf, -ˌgræf) *n.* **1.** a variant of **kymograph. 2.** an instrument for tracing the outline of an architectural moulding. —**cymographic** (ˌsaɪməˈgræfɪk) *adj.*

cymoid (ˈsaɪmɔɪd) *adj. Architect., botany.* resembling a cyme or cyma.

cymophane (ˈsaɪməˌfeɪn) *n.* a yellow or green opalescent variety of chrysoberyl. [C19: from Greek *kuma* wave, undulation + -PHANE]

cymose (ˈsaɪməʊs, -məʊz, saɪˈməʊs) *adj.* having the characteristics of a cyme. —ˈ**cymosely** *adv.*

Cymric *or* **Kymric** (ˈkɪmrɪk) *n.* **1.** the Welsh language. **2.** the Brythonic group of Celtic languages. *~adj.* **3.** of or relating to the Cymry, any of their languages, Wales, or the Welsh.

Cymry *or* **Kymry** (ˈkɪmrɪ) *n.* **the.** (*functioning as pl.*) **1.** the Brythonic branch of the Celtic people, comprising the present-day Welsh, Cornish, and Bretons. See **Brythonic. 2.** the Welsh people. [Welsh: the Welsh]

cynghanedd (kʌŋˈhanɛð) *n.* a complex system of rhyme and alliteration used in Welsh verse. [from Welsh]

cynic (ˈsɪnɪk) *n.* **1.** a person who believes the worst about people or the outcome of events. *~adj.* **2.** a less common word for **cynical. 3.** *Astronomy.* of or relating to Sirius, the Dog Star. [C16: via Latin from Greek *Kunikos,* from *kuōn* dog]

Cynic (ˈsɪnɪk) *n.* a member of a sect in ancient Athens that scorned worldly things and held that self-control was the key to the only good.

cynical (ˈsɪnɪkᵊl) *adj.* **1.** distrustful or contemptuous of virtue, esp. selflessness in others; believing the worst of others, esp. that all acts are selfish. **2.** sarcastic; mocking. **3.** showing contempt for accepted standards of behaviour, esp. of honesty or morality: *the politician betrayed his promises in a cynical way.* —ˈ**cynically** *adv.* —ˈ**cynicalness** *n.*

cynicism (ˈsɪnɪˌsɪzəm) *n.* **1.** the attitude or beliefs of a cynic. **2.** a cynical action, remark, idea, etc.

Cynicism (ˈsɪnɪˌsɪzəm) *n.* the doctrines of the Cynics.

cynopodous (saɪˈnɒpədəs) *adj.* (of some mammals, such as dogs) having claws that do not retract. [from New Latin, from Greek *kuōn* dog + -PODOUS]

cynosure (ˈsɪnəˌzjʊə, -ʃʊə) *n.* **1.** a person or thing that attracts notice, esp. because of its brilliance or beauty. **2.** something that serves as a guide. [C16: from Latin *Cynosūra* the constellation of Ursa Minor, from Greek *Kunosoura,* from *kuōn* dog + *oura* tail] —ˌ**cynoˈsural** *adj.*

cyperaceous (ˌsaɪpəˈreɪʃəs) *adj.* of, relating to, or belonging to the *Cyperaceae,* a family of grasslike flowering plants with solid triangular stems, including the sedges, bulrush, cotton grass, and certain rushes. Some are grown as water plants or as ornamental grasses; and *Cyperus papyrus* is the papyrus plant. Compare **juncaceous.** [C19: from New Latin *Cypērus* type genus, from Latin *cypēros* a kind of rush, from Greek *kupeiros* marsh plant, probably of Semitic origin]

cypher (ˈsaɪfə) *n., vb.* a variant spelling of **cipher.**

cy pres (siː preɪ) *n. Law.* the doctrine that the intention of a donor or testator should be carried out as closely as practicable when literal compliance is impossible. [C15: from Anglo-French, literally: as near (as possible, etc.)]

cypress[1] (ˈsaɪprəs) *n.* **1.** any coniferous tree of the N temperate genus *Cupressus,* having dark green scalelike leaves and rounded cones: family *Cupressaceae.* **2.** any of several similar and related trees, such as the widely cultivated *Chamaecyparis lawsoniana* (**Lawson's cypress**), of the western U.S. **3.** any of various other coniferous trees, esp. the swamp cypress. **4.** the wood of any of these trees. [Old English *cypresse,* from Latin *cyparissus,* from Greek *kuparissos;* related to Latin *cupressus*]

cypress[2] *or* **cyprus** (ˈsaɪprəs) *n.* a fabric, esp. a fine silk, lawn, or crepelike material, often black and worn as mourning. [C14 *cyprus* from the island of *Cyprus*]

cypress pine *n.* any coniferous tree of the Australian genus *Callitrus,* having leaves in whorls and yielding valuable timber: family *Cupressaceae.*

cypress vine *n.* a tropical American convolvulaceous climbing plant, *Quamoclit pennata,* having finely divided compound leaves and scarlet or white tubular flowers.

Cyprian (ˈsɪprɪən) *adj.* **1.** of or relating to Cyprus, an island in the E Mediterranean. **2.** of or resembling the ancient orgiastic worship of Aphrodite, Greek goddess of love, on Cyprus. *~n.* **3.** (*often not cap.*) *Obsolete.* a licentious person, esp. a prostitute or dancer. *~n., adj.* **4.** another word for **Cypriot.**

cyprinid (sɪˈpraɪnɪd, ˈsɪprɪnɪd) *n.* **1.** any teleost fish of the mainly freshwater family *Cyprinidae,* typically having toothless jaws and cycloid scales and including such food and game fishes as the carp, tench, roach, rudd, and dace. *~adj.* **2.** of, relating to, or belonging to the *Cyprinidae.* **3.** resembling a carp; cyprinoid. [C19: from New Latin *Cyprīnidae,* from Latin *cyprīnus* carp, from Greek *kuprinos*]

cyprinodont (sɪˈprɪnəˌdɒnt, sɪˈpraɪ-) *n.* **1.** any small tropical or subtropical soft-finned fish of the mostly marine family *Cyprinodontidae,* resembling carp but having toothed jaws. The group includes the guppy, killifish, swordtail, and topminnow. *~adj.* **2.** of, relating to, or belonging to the *Cyprinodontidae.* [C19: from Latin *cyprīnus* carp (see CYPRINID) + -ODONT]

cyprinoid (ˈsɪprɪˌnɔɪd, sɪˈpraɪnɔɪd) *adj.* **1.** of, relating to, or belonging to the *Cyprinoidea,* a large suborder of teleost fishes including the cyprinids, characins, electric eels, and loaches. **2.** of, relating to, or resembling the carp. *~n.* **3.** any fish belonging to the *Cyprinoidea.* [C19: from Latin *cyprīnus* carp]

Cypriot (ˈsɪprɪət) *or* **Cypriote** (ˈsɪprɪˌəʊt) *n.* **1.** a native, citizen, or inhabitant of Cyprus, an island in the E Mediterranean. **2.** the dialect of Ancient or Modern Greek spoken in Cyprus. *~adj.* **3.** denoting or relating to Cyprus, its inhabitants, or dialects.

cypripedium (ˌsɪprɪˈpiːdɪəm) *n.* **1.** any orchid of the genus *Cypripedium,* having large flowers with an inflated pouchlike lip. See also **lady's-slipper. 2.** any cultivated tropical orchid of the genus *Paphiopedilum,* having yellow, green, or brownish-purple waxy flowers. [C18: from New Latin, from Latin *Cypria* the Cyprian, that is, Venus + *pēs* foot (that is, Venus' slipper)]

cypsela (ˈsɪpsɪlə) *n., pl.* **-lae** (-ˌliː). the dry one-seeded fruit of the daisy and related plants, which resembles an achene but is surrounded by a calyx sheath. [C19: from New Latin, from Greek *kupselē* chest, hollow vessel]

Cyrenaic (ˌsaɪrəˈneɪɪk, ˌsɪrə-) *adj.* **1.** of or relating to the ancient Greek city of Cyrene, in N Africa. **2.** of or relating to the philosophical school founded in Cyrene, which held pleasure to be the highest good. *~n.* **3.** an inhabitant of Cyrene. **4.** a follower of the Cyrenaic school of philosophy.

Cyrillic (sɪˈrɪlɪk) *adj.* **1.** denoting or relating to the alphabet derived from that of the Greeks, supposedly by Saint Cyril (?827–869 A.D.), for the writing of Slavonic languages: now used primarily for Russian, Bulgarian, and the Serbian dialect of Serbo-Croatian. *~n.* **2.** this alphabet.

cyst (sɪst) *n.* **1.** *Pathol.* any abnormal membranous sac or blisterlike pouch containing fluid or semisolid material. **2.** *Anat.* any normal sac or vesicle in the body. **3.** a thick-walled protective membrane enclosing a cell, larva, or organism. [C18: from New Latin *cystis,* from Greek *kustis* pouch, bag, bladder]

-cyst *n. combining form.* indicating a bladder or sac: *otocyst.* [from Greek *kustis* bladder]

cystectomy (sɪˈstɛktəmɪ) *n., pl.* **-mies. 1.** surgical removal of the gall bladder or of part of the urinary bladder. **2.** surgical removal of any abnormal cyst.

cysteine (ˈsɪstɪˌiːn, -ɪn) *n.* a sulphur-containing amino acid, present in proteins, that oxidizes on exposure to air to form cystine. Formula: $HSCH_2CH(NH_2)COOH$. [C19: variant of CYSTINE] —ˌ**cysteˈinic** *adj.*

cystic (ˈsɪstɪk) *adj.* **1.** of, relating to, or resembling a cyst. **2.** having or enclosed within a cyst; encysted. **3.** relating to the gall bladder or urinary bladder.

cysticercoid (ˌsɪstɪˈsɜːkɔɪd) *n.* the larva of any of certain tapeworms, which resembles a cysticercus but has a smaller bladder.

cysticercus (ˌsɪstɪˈsɜːkəs) *n., pl.* **-ci** (-saɪ). an encysted larval form of many tapeworms, consisting of a head (scolex) inverted in a fluid-filled bladder. See also **hydatid** (sense 1), **coenurus.** [C19: from New Latin, from Greek *kustis* pouch, bladder + *kerkos* tail]

cystic fibrosis *n.* a congenital disease of the exocrine glands, usually affecting young children, characterized by chronic infection of the respiratory tract and by pancreatic insufficiency.

cystine (ˈsɪstiːn, -tɪn) *n.* a sulphur-containing amino acid present in proteins: yields two molecules of cysteine on reduction. Formula: $HOOCCH(NH_2)CH_2SSCH_2CH(NH_2)COOH$. [C19: see CYSTO- (bladder), -INE[2]; named from its being discovered in a type of urinary calculus]

cystitis (sɪˈstaɪtɪs) *n.* inflammation of the urinary bladder.

cysto- *or before a vowel* **cyst-** *combining form.* indicating a cyst or bladder: *cystocarp; cystoscope.*

cystocarp (ˈsɪstəˌkɑːp) *n.* a reproductive body in red algae, developed after fertilization and consisting of filaments bearing carpospores. —ˌ**cystoˈcarpic** *adj.*

cystocele (ˈsɪstəˌsiːl) *n. Pathol.* a hernia of the urinary bladder, esp. one protruding into the vagina.

cystogenous (sɪs'tɒdʒɪnəs) *adj. Biology.* forming or secreting cysts.

cystography (sɪs'tɒgrəfɪ) *n.* radiography of the urinary bladder using a contrast medium.

cystoid ('sɪstɔɪd) *adj.* **1.** resembling a cyst or bladder. ~*n.* **2.** a tissue mass, such as a tumour, that resembles a cyst but lacks an outer membrane.

cystolith ('sɪstəlɪθ) *n.* **1.** a knoblike deposit of calcium carbonate in the epidermal cells of such plants as the stinging nettle. **2.** *Pathol.* a urinary calculus.

cystoscope ('sɪstəˌskəʊp) *n.* a slender tubular medical instrument for examining the interior of the urethra and urinary bladder. —**cystoscopic** (ˌsɪstə'skɒpɪk) *adj.* —**cystoscopy** (sɪs'tɒskəpɪ) *n.*

cystotomy (sɪ'stɒtəmɪ) *n., pl.* **-mies. 1.** surgical incision into the gall bladder or urinary bladder. **2.** surgical incision into the capsule of the lens of the eye.

cytaster (saɪ'tæstə, 'saɪtæs-) *n. Cytology.* another word for **aster** (sense 3). [C19: from CYTO- + ASTER]

-cyte *n. combining form.* indicating a cell: *spermatocyte.* [from New Latin *-cyta,* from Greek *kutos* container, body, hollow vessel]

cytidine ('sɪtɪˌdaɪn) *n. Biochem.* a nucleoside formed by the condensation of cytosine and ribose. [C20: from CYTO- + -IDE + -INE[2]]

cytidylic acid (ˌsɪtɪ'dɪlɪk) *n.* a nucleotide consisting of cytosine, ribose or deoxyribose, and a phosphate group. It is a constituent of DNA or RNA. Also called: **cytidine monophosphate.**

cyto- *combining form.* indicating a cell: *cytolysis; cytoplasm.* [from Greek *kutos* vessel, container; related to *kuein* to contain]

cytochemistry (ˌsaɪtəʊ'kɛmɪstrɪ) *n.* the chemistry of living cells. —ˌ**cyto'chemical** *adj.*

cytochrome ('saɪtəʊˌkrəʊm) *n.* any of a group of naturally occurring compounds, consisting of iron, a protein, and a porphyrin, that are important in cell oxidation-reduction reactions.

cytochrome reductase *n.* another name for **flavoprotein.**

cytogenesis (ˌsaɪtəʊ'dʒɛnɪsɪs) *or* **cytogeny** (saɪ'tɒdʒənɪ) *n.* the origin and development of plant and animal cells.

cytogenetics (ˌsaɪtəʊdʒɪ'nɛtɪks) *n.* (*functioning as sing.*) the branch of genetics that correlates the structure of chromosomes with heredity and variation. —ˌ**cytoge'netic** *adj.* —ˌ**cyto-ge'netically** *adv.*

cytokinesis (ˌsaɪtəʊkɪ'niːsɪs, -kaɪ-) *n.* division of the cytoplasm of a cell, occurring at the end of mitosis or meiosis.

cytokinin (ˌsaɪtəʊ'kaɪnɪn) *n.* any of a group of plant hormones.

cytology (saɪ'tɒlədʒɪ) *n.* **1.** the study of plant and animal cells, including their structure, function, and formation. **2.** the detailed structure of a tissue, as revealed by microscopic examination. —**cytological** (ˌsaɪtə'lɒdʒɪkᵊl) *adj.* —ˌ**cyto'logically** *adv.* —**cy'tologist** *n.*

cytolysin (saɪ'tɒlɪsɪn) *n.* a substance that can partially or completely destroy animal cells.

cytolysis (saɪ'tɒlɪsɪs) *n. Cytology.* the dissolution of cells, esp. by the destruction of their membranes. —**cytolytic** (ˌsaɪtə'lɪtɪk) *adj.*

cytomegalovirus (ˌsaɪtəʊ'mɛgələʊˌvaɪrəs) *n.* a virus, related to the herpes viruses, that may cause serious disease in patients whose immune systems are compromised and the birth of handicapped children to pregnant women infected with it. Abbrev.: **CMV.**

cytoplasm ('saɪtəʊˌplæzəm) *n.* the protoplasm of a cell contained within the cell membrane but excluding the nucleus: contains organelles, vesicles, and other inclusions. —ˌ**cyto'plasmic** *adj.*

cytoplast ('saɪtəʊˌplɑːst, -ˌplæst) *n.* the intact cytoplasm of a single cell. —**cytoplastic** (ˌsaɪtəʊ'plæstɪk) *adj.*

cytosine ('saɪtəsɪn) *n.* a white crystalline pyrimidine occurring in nucleic acids; 6-amino-2-hydroxy pyrimidine. Formula: $C_4H_5N_3O$. See also **DNA, RNA.** [C19: from CYTO- + -OSE[2] + -INE[2]]

cytoskeleton (ˌsaɪtəʊ'skɛlɪtən) *n.* a network of fibrous proteins that governs the shape and movement of a biological cell.

cytosol ('saɪtəʊˌsɒl) *n.* the solution of proteins and metabolites inside a biological cell, in which the organelles are suspended.

cytotaxis (ˌsaɪtəʊ'tæksɪs) *n. Biology.* movement of cells due to external stimulation.

cytotaxonomy (ˌsaɪtəʊtæk'sɒnəmɪ) *n.* classification of organisms based on cell structure, esp. the number, shape, etc., of the chromosomes. —ˌ**cytoˌtaxo'nomic** *adj.* —ˌ**cytotax'onomist** *n.*

cytotoxic (ˌsaɪtəʊ'tɒksɪk) *adj.* poisonous to living cells: denoting certain drugs used in the treatment of leukaemia and other cancers. —**cytotoxicity** (ˌsaɪtəʊ'tɒksɪsɪtɪ) *n.*

cytotoxin (ˌsaɪtəʊ'tɒksɪn) *n.* any substance that is poisonous to living cells.

czar (zɑː) *n.* a variant spelling (esp. U.S.) of **tsar.** —'**czardom** *n.*

czardas ('tʃɑːdæʃ) *n.* **1.** a Hungarian national dance of alternating slow and fast sections. **2.** a piece of music composed for or in the rhythm of this dance. [from Hungarian *csárdás*]

czarevitch ('zɑːrɪvɪtʃ) *n.* a variant spelling (esp. U.S.) of **tsarevitch.**

czarevna (zɑː'rɛvnə) *n.* a variant spelling (esp. U.S.) of **tsarevna.**

czarina (zɑː'riːnə) *or* **czaritza** (zɑː'rɪtsə) *n.* variant spellings (esp. U.S.) of **tsarina** or **tsaritsa.**

czarism ('zɑːrɪzəm) *n.* a variant spelling (esp. U.S.) of **tsarism.**

czarist ('zɑːrɪst) *adj., n.* a variant spelling (esp. U.S.) of **tsarist.**

Czech (tʃɛk) *adj.* **1. a.** of, relating to, or characteristic of Bohemia and Moravia in Czechoslovakia, their people, or their language. **b.** (loosely) of, relating to, or characteristic of Czechoslovakia, a republic in central Europe, or its people. ~*n.* **2.** one of the two official languages of Czechoslovakia, belonging to the West Slavonic branch of the Indo-European family. Czech and Slovak are closely related and mutually intelligible. **3. a.** a native or inhabitant of Bohemia or Moravia. **b.** (loosely) a native, inhabitant, or citizen of Czechoslovakia. [C19: from Polish, from Czech *Čech*]

Czechoslovak (ˌtʃɛkəʊ'sləʊvæk) *or* **Czechoslovakian** (ˌtʃɛkəʊsləʊ'vækɪən) *adj.* **1.** of, relating to, or characteristic of Czechoslovakia, its peoples, or their languages. ~*n.* **2.** (loosely) either of the two mutually intelligible languages of Czechoslovakia; Czech or Slovak.

d *symbol for:* **1.** *Physics.* density or relative density. **2.** *Maths.* a small increment in a given variable or function: used to indicate a derivative of one variable with respect to another, as in dy/dx. **3.** *Chess.* See **algebraic notation.**

D *symbol for:* **1.** *Music.* **a.** a note having a frequency of 293.66 hertz (**D above middle C**) or this value multiplied or divided by any power of 2; the second note of the scale of C major. **b.** a key, string, or pipe producing this note. **c.** the major or minor key having this note as its tonic. **2.** *Chem.* deuterium. **3.** *Maths.* the first derivative of a function, as in $D(x^3 + x^2) = 3x^2 + 2x$. **4.** *Physics.* dispersion. **5.** *Aeronautics.* drag. **6. a.** a semiskilled or unskilled manual worker, or a trainee or apprentice to a skilled worker. **b.** (as modifier): *D worker.* ~See also **occupation groupings.** ~ **7.** *the Roman numeral for* 500. See **Roman numerals.** ~ **8.** *international car registration for* Germany. [from German *Deutschland*]

2,4-D *n.* a synthetic auxin widely used as a weedkiller; 2,4-dichlorophenoxyacetic acid.

d. *abbrev. for:* **1.** date. **2.** (in animal pedigrees) dam. **3.** daughter. **4.** day. **5.** degree. **6.** delete. **7.** *Brit. currency before decimalization.* penny *or* pennies. [Latin *denarius* or *denarii*] **8.** depart(s). **9.** diameter. **10.** died. **11.** dinar(s). **12.** dollar(s). **13.** dose. **14.** drachma(s).

D. *abbrev. for:* **1.** *U.S. politics.* Democrat(ic). **2.** *Government.* Department. **3.** Deus. [Latin: God] **4.** dinar(s). **5.** *Optics.* diopter. **6.** Director. **7.** Dominus. [Latin: Lord] **8.** Don (a Spanish title). **9.** Duchess. **10.** Duke. **11.** Dutch.

'd *contraction of* would *or* had: *I'd; you'd.*

DA *abbrev. for:* **1.** (in the U.S.) District Attorney. **2.** Diploma of Art. **3.** duck's arse (hairstyle).

D/A *or* **d.a.** *abbrev. for:* **1.** deposit account. **2.** *Commerce.* documents against acceptance.

dab[1] (dæb) *vb.* **dabs, dabbing, dabbed.** **1.** to touch or pat lightly and quickly: *he dabbed the spilt coffee with the cloth.* **2.** (*tr.*) to daub with short tapping strokes: *to dab the wall with paint.* **3.** (*tr.*) to apply (paint, cream, etc.) with short tapping strokes. ~*n.* **4.** a small amount, esp. of something soft or moist: *a dab of ink.* **5.** a small light stroke or tap, as with the hand. **6.** (*often pl.*) *Chiefly Brit.* a slang word for **fingerprint.** [C14: of imitative origin]

dab[2] (dæb) *n.* **1.** a small common European brown flatfish, *Limanda limanda,* covered with rough toothed scales: family *Pleuronectidae:* a food fish. **2.** (*often pl.*) any of various other small flatfish, esp. flounders. ~Compare **sand dab.** [C15: from Anglo-French *dabbe,* of uncertain origin]

dab[3] (dæb) *n. Brit. informal.* See **dab hand.** [C17: perhaps from DAB[1] (vb.)]

dabber ('dæbə) *n.* a pad used by printers and engravers for applying ink, etc., by hand.

dabble ('dæbᵊl) *vb.* **1.** to dip, move, or splash (the fingers, feet, etc.) in a liquid. **2.** (*intr.;* usually foll. by *in, with,* or *at*) to deal (with) or work (at) frivolously or superficially; play (at). **3.** (*tr.*) to daub, mottle, splash, or smear: *his face was dabbled with paint.* [C16: probably from Dutch *dabbelen;* see DAB[1]] —**'dabbler** *n.*

dabchick ('dæb,tʃɪk) *n.* any of several small grebes of the genera *Podiceps* and *Podilymbus,* such as *Podiceps ruficollis* of the Old World. [C16: probably from Old English *dop* to dive + CHICK; see DEEP, DIP]

dab hand *n. Brit. informal.* a person who is particularly skilled at something; expert: *a dab hand at chess.*

dabster ('dæbstə) *n.* **1.** *Brit.* a dialect word for **dab hand.** **2.** *U.S. informal.* an incompetent or amateurish worker; bungler. [C18: from DAB[1] + -STER]

da capo (dɑː 'kɑːpəʊ) *adj., adv. Music.* to be repeated (in whole or part) from the beginning. Abbrev.: **DC.** See also **fine**[3]. [C18: from Italian, literally: from the head]

dace (deɪs) *n., pl.* **dace** *or* **daces.** **1.** a European freshwater cyprinid fish, *Leuciscus leuciscus,* with a slender bluish-green body. **2.** any of various similar fishes. [C15: from Old French *dars* DART, probably referring to its swiftness]

dacha *or* **datcha** ('dætʃə) *n.* a country house or cottage in Russia. [from Russian: a giving, gift]

dachshund ('dæks,hʊnd; *German* 'dakshʊnt) *n.* a long-bodied short-legged breed of dog. [C19: from German, from *Dachs* badger + *Hund* dog, HOUND]

dacoit (də'kɔɪt) *n.* (in India and Burma) a member of a gang of armed robbers. [C19: from Hindi *dakait,* from *dākā* robbery]

dacoity (də'kɔɪtɪ) *n., pl.* **-coities.** (in India and Burma) robbery by an armed gang.

Dacron ('deɪkrɒn, 'dæk-) *n.* the U.S. name (trademark) for **Terylene.**

dactyl ('dæktɪl) *n.* **1.** Also called: **dactylic.** *Prosody.* a metrical foot of three syllables, one long followed by two short (-⏑⏑). Compare **bacchius.** **2.** *Zoology.* any digit of a vertebrate. [C14: via Latin from Greek *daktulos* finger, dactyl, comparing the finger's three joints to the three syllables]

dactylic (dæk'tɪlɪk) *adj.* **1.** of, relating to, or having a dactyl: *dactylic verse.* ~*n.* **2.** a variant of **dactyl** (sense 1). —**dac'tylically** *adv.*

dactylo- *or before a vowel* **dactyl-** *combining form.* finger or toe: *dactylogram.* [from Greek *daktulos* finger]

dactylogram (dæk'tɪlə,græm) *n. Chiefly U.S.* a technical term for **fingerprint.**

dactylography (,dæktɪ'lɒgrəfɪ) *n. Chiefly U.S.* the scientific study of fingerprints for purposes of identification. —**,dacty'lographer** *n.* —**dactylographic** (dæk,tɪlə'græfɪk) *adj.*

dactylology (,dæktɪ'lɒlədʒɪ) *n., pl.* **-gies.** the method of using manual sign language, as in communicating with the deaf.

dad (dæd) *n.* an informal word for **father.** [C16: childish word; compare Greek *tata,* Sanskrit *tatas*]

Dada ('dɑːdɑː) *or* **Dadaism** ('dɑːdɑː,ɪzəm) *n.* a nihilistic artistic movement of the early 20th century in W Europe and the U.S., founded on principles of irrationality, incongruity, and irreverence towards accepted aesthetic criteria. [C20: from French, from a children's word for hobbyhorse, the name being arbitrarily chosen] —**'Dadaist** *n., adj.* —**,Dada'istic** *adj.* —**,Dada'istically** *adv.*

Dad and Dave (dæd ən deɪv) *n. Austral.* stereotypes of the unsophisticated rural dweller before World War II. [from characters in the stories of Steale Rudd (1868–1935), Australian author]

daddy ('dædɪ) *n., pl.* **-dies.** **1.** an informal word for **father.** **2.** **the daddy.** *Slang, chiefly U.S., Canadian, and Austral.* the supreme or finest example: *the daddy of them all.*

daddy-longlegs *n.* **1.** *Brit.* an informal name for a **crane fly.** **2.** *U.S. and Canadian.* an informal name for **harvestman** (sense 2).

dado ('deɪdəʊ) *n., pl.* **-does** *or* **-dos.** **1.** the lower part of an interior wall that is decorated differently from the upper part. **2.** *Architect.* the part of a pedestal between the base and the cornice. ~*vb.* **3.** (*tr.*) to provide with a dado. [C17: from Italian: die, die-shaped pedestal, perhaps from Arabic *dad* game]

dae (de) *vb.* a Scot. word for **do**[1].

daedal *or* **dedal** ('diːdᵊl) *adj. Literary.* skilful or intricate. [C16: via Latin from Greek *daidalos*]

daemon ('diːmən) *or* **daimon** *n.* **1.** a demigod. **2.** the guardian spirit of a place or person. **3.** a variant spelling of **demon** (sense 3). —**daemonic** (diː'mɒnɪk) *adj.*

daff[1] (dæf) *n. Informal.* short for **daffodil.**

daff[2] (dɑːf) *vb.* (*intr.*) *Chiefly Scot.* to frolic; play the fool. [C16: from obsolete *daff* fool, of uncertain origin]

daffodil ('dæfədɪl) *n.* **1.** Also called: **Lent lily.** a widely cultivated Eurasian amaryllidaceous plant, *Narcissus pseudonarcissus,* having spring-blooming yellow nodding flowers. **2.** any other plant of the genus *Narcissus.* **3. a.** a brilliant yellow colour. **b.** (*as adj.*): *daffodil paint.* **4.** a daffodil, or a representation of one, as a national emblem of Wales. [C14: perhaps from Dutch *de affodil* the asphodel, from Medieval Latin *affodillus,* variant of Latin *asphodelus* ASPHODEL]

daffy ('dæfɪ) *adj.* **daffier, daffiest.** *Informal.* another word for **daft** (senses 1, 2). [C19: from obsolete *daff* fool; see DAFT]

daft (dɑːft) *adj. Chiefly Brit.* **1.** *Informal.* foolish, simple, or stupid. **2.** a slang word for **insane.** **3.** *Informal.* (*postpositive;* foll. by *about*) extremely fond (of). **4.** *Slang.* frivolous; giddy. [Old English *gedæfte* gentle, foolish; related to Middle Low German *ondaft* incapable] —**'daftly** *adv.* —**'daftness** *n.*

dag[1] (dæg) *n.* **1.** short for **daglock.** ~*vb.* **dags, dagging, dagged.** **2.** to cut the daglock away from (a sheep). [C18: of obscure origin] —**'dagger** *n.*

dag[2] (dæg) *n.* **1.** *Austral. informal.* a character; eccentric. **2.** *Austral. informal.* a person who is untidily dressed. **3.** *Austral. informal.* a conventional person. **4.** *N.Z. informal.* a person with a good sense of humour. [back formation from DAGGY]

dagga ('daxə, 'dɑːgə) *n.* hemp smoked as a narcotic. [C19: from Afrikaans, from Hottentot *dagab*]

dagger ('dægə) *n.* **1.** a short stabbing weapon with a pointed blade. **2.** Also called: **obelisk.** a character (†) used in printing to indicate a cross reference, esp. to a footnote. **3.** **at daggers drawn.** in a state of open hostility. **4.** **look daggers.** to glare with hostility; scowl. ~*vb.* (*tr.*) **5.** to mark with a dagger. **6.** *Archaic.* to stab with a dagger. [C14: of uncertain origin]

daggerboard ('dægə,bɔːd) *n.* a light bladelike board inserted into the water through a slot in the keel of a boat to reduce keeling and leeway. Compare **centreboard.**

daggy ('dægɪ) *adj. Austral. and N.Z. informal.* untidy; dishevelled. [from DAG[1]]

daglock ('dæɡˌlɒk) *n.* a dung-caked lock of wool around the hindquarters of a sheep. [C17: see DAG[1], LOCK[2]]
dago ('deɪɡəʊ) *n., pl.* **-gos** *or* **-goes.** *Derogatory.* a member of a Latin race, esp. a Spaniard or Portuguese. [C19: alteration of *Diego,* a common Spanish name]
dagoba ('dɑːɡəbə) *n.* a dome-shaped shrine containing relics of the Buddha or a Buddhist saint. [C19: from Sinhalese *dāgoba,* from Sanskrit *dhātugarbha* containing relics]
daguerreotype (də'ɡerəʊˌtaɪp) *n.* **1.** one of the earliest photographic processes, in which the image was produced on iodine-sensitized silver and developed in mercury vapour. **2.** a photograph formed by this process. [C19: named after Louis *Daguerre* (1789–1851), French inventor] —**da'guerreoˌtyper** *or* **da'guerreoˌtypist** *n.* —**da'guerreoˌtypy** *n.*
dah (dɑː) *n.* the long sound used in combination with the short sound *dit,* in the spoken representation of Morse and other telegraphic codes. Compare **dash**[1] (sense 14).
dahabeah, dahabeeyah, *or* **dahabiah** (ˌdɑːhə'biːə) *n.* a houseboat used on the Nile. [from Arabic *dhahabīyah,* literally: the golden one (that is, gilded barge)]
dahlia ('deɪljə) *n.* **1.** any herbaceous perennial plant of the Mexican genus *Dahlia,* having showy flowers and tuberous roots, esp. any horticultural variety derived from *D. pinnata:* family *Compositae* (composites). **2.** the flower or root of any of these plants. [C19: named after Anders *Dahl,* 18th-century Swedish botanist; see -IA]
Dáil Éireann ('daːl 'eːrɪn) *or* **Dáil** *n.* (in the Republic of Ireland) the lower chamber of parliament. See also **Oireachtas.** [from Irish *dáil* assembly (from Old Irish *dāl*) + *Éireann* of Eire]
dailies ('deɪlɪz) *pl. n. Films.* another word for **rushes.**
daily ('deɪlɪ) *adj.* **1.** of or occurring every day or every weekday: *a daily paper.* **2. earn one's daily bread.** to earn one's living. **3. the daily round.** the usual activities of one's day. ~*n., pl.* **-lies. 4.** a daily publication, esp. a newspaper. **5.** Also called: **daily help.** *Brit.* another name for a **charwoman.** ~*adv.* **6.** every day. **7.** constantly; often. [Old English *dæglīc;* see DAY, -LY[1]]
daily double *n. Horse racing.* a single bet on the winners of two named races in any one day's racing.
daimon ('daɪmɒn) *n.* a variant of **daemon** or **demon** (sense 3). —**dai'monic** *adj.*
daimyo *or* **daimio** ('daɪmjəʊ) *n., pl.* **-myo, -myos** *or* **-mio, -mios.** (in Japan) one of the territorial magnates who dominated much of the country from about the 10th to the 19th century. [from Japanese, from Ancient Chinese *d'âi miäng* great name]
dainty ('deɪntɪ) *adj.* **-tier, -tiest. 1.** delicate or elegant: *a dainty teacup.* **2.** pleasing to the taste; choice; delicious: *a dainty morsel.* **3.** refined, esp. excessively genteel; fastidious. ~*n., pl.* **-ties. 4.** a choice piece of food, esp. a small cake or sweet; delicacy. [C13: from Old French *deintié,* from Latin *dignitās* DIGNITY] —**'daintily** *adv.* —**'daintiness** *n.*
daiquiri ('daɪkɪrɪ, 'dæk-) *n., pl.* **-ris.** *Chiefly U.S. and Canadian.* an iced drink containing rum, lime juice, and syrup or sugar. [C20: named after *Daiquiri,* rum-producing town in Cuba]
dairy ('dɛərɪ) *n., pl.* **dairies. 1.** a company that supplies milk and milk products. **2.** a shop that sells provisions, esp. milk and milk products. **3.** a room or building where milk and cream are stored or made into butter and cheese. **4. a.** (*modifier*) of or relating to the production of milk and milk products: *dairy cattle.* **b.** (*in combination*): *a dairymaid; a dairyman.* **5.** (*modifier*) containing milk or milk products: *dairy produce.* **6.** *Judaism.* See also **milchik.** [C13 *daierie,* from Old English *dǣge* servant girl, one who kneads bread; see DOUGH, LADY]
dairy factory *n. N.Z.* a factory making butter, cheese, lactose, etc. from milk collected from surrounding farming areas.
dairying ('dɛərɪɪŋ) *n.* the business of producing, processing, and selling dairy products.
dairymaid ('dɛərɪˌmeɪd) *n.* (esp. formerly) a girl or woman who works in a dairy, esp. one who milks cows and makes butter and cheese on a farm.
dairyman ('dɛərɪmən) *n., pl.* **-men.** a man who works in a dairy or deals in dairy products.
dais ('deɪɪs, deɪs) *n.* a raised platform, usually at one end of a hall, used by speakers, etc. [C13: from Old French *deis,* from Latin *discus:* DISCUS]
daisy ('deɪzɪ) *n., pl.* **-sies. 1.** a small low-growing European plant, *Bellis perennis,* having a rosette of leaves and flower heads of yellow central disc flowers and pinkish-white outer ray flowers: family *Compositae* (composites). **2.** Also called: **oxeye daisy, marguerite, moon daisy.** a Eurasian composite plant, *Chrysanthemum leucanthemum,* having flower heads with a yellow centre and white outer rays. **3.** any of various other composite plants having conspicuous ray flowers, such as the Michaelmas daisy and Shasta daisy. **4.** *Slang.* an excellent person or thing. **5. pushing up the daisies.** dead and buried. [Old English *dægesēge* day's eye] —**'daisied** *adj.*
daisy bush *n.* any of various shrubs of the genus *Olearia,* of Australia and New Zealand, with daisy-like flowers: family *Compositae* (composites).
daisy chain *n.* a garland made, esp. by children, by threading daisies together through each other's stalks.
daisycutter ('deɪzɪˌkʌtə) *n. Cricket.* a ball bowled so that it rolls along the ground towards the batsman.
daisywheel ('deɪzɪˌwiːl) *n. Computer technol.* a component of a computer printer in the shape of a wheel with many spokes that prints characters using a disk with characters around the circumference as the print element. Also called: **printwheel.**
dak (dɑːk) *or* **dawk** (dɔːk) *n.* (in India, formerly) **a.** a system of mail delivery or passenger transport by relays of bearers or horses stationed at intervals along a route. **b.** (*as modifier*): *dak bearers.* [C18: from Hindi *dāk,* from Sanskrit *drāk* quickly]
Dak. *abbrev. for* Dakota.
dak bungalow *n.* (in India, formerly) a house where travellers on a dak route could be accommodated.
Dakin's solution ('deɪkɪnz) *n.* a dilute solution containing sodium hypochlorite and boric acid, used as an antiseptic in the treatment of wounds. [C20: named after Henry D. *Dakin* (1880–1952), British chemist]
dal[1] (dɑːl) *n.* **1.** split grain, a common foodstuff in India; pulse. **2.** a variant spelling of **dhal.**
dal[2] *symbol for* decalitre(s).
Dalai Lama ('dælaɪ 'lɑːmə) *n.* (until 1959) the chief lama and ruler of Tibet. [from Mongolian *dalai* ocean; see LAMA]
dalasi (də'lɑːsɪ) *n.* the standard monetary unit of The Gambia, divided into 100 butats. [from a Gambian native name]
dale (deɪl) *n.* an open valley, usually in an area of low hills. [Old English *dæl;* related to Old Frisian *del,* Old Norse *dalr,* Old High German *tal* valley]
Dalek ('dɑːlɛk) *n.* any of a set of fictional robot-like creations that are aggressive, mobile, and produce rasping staccato speech. [C20: from a children's television series, *Dr Who*]
d'Alembert's principle (ˌdælɑːm'bɛəz) *n. Physics.* the principle that for a moving body the external forces are in equilibrium with the inertial forces; a generalization of Newton's third law of motion. [C18: named after Jean Le Rond *d'Alembert* (1717–83), French mathematician]
dalesman ('deɪlzmən) *n., pl.* **-men.** a person living in a dale, esp. in the dales of N England.
daleth *or* **daled** ('dɑːlɪd; *Hebrew* 'dalɛt) *n.* the fourth letter of the Hebrew alphabet (ד), transliterated as *d* or, when final, *dh.* [Hebrew]
dalgyte ('dælɡaɪt) *n. Austral.* another name for **bilby.**
dalliance ('dælɪəns) *n.* **1.** waste of time in frivolous action or in dawdling. **2.** an archaic word for **flirtation.**
dally ('dælɪ) *vb.* **-lies, -lying, -lied.** (*intr.*) **1.** to waste time idly; dawdle. **2.** (usually foll. by *with*) to deal frivolously or lightly with; trifle; toy: *to dally with someone's affections.* [C14: from Anglo-French *dalier* to gossip, of uncertain origin] —**'dallier** *n.*
Dally ('dælɪ) *n., pl.* **-lies.** *Austral. and N.Z. informal.* (in the 19th century) an immigrant from Yugoslavia. [short for DALMATIAN]
Dalmatian (dæl'meɪʃən) *n.* **1.** Also called (esp. formerly): **carriage dog, coach dog.** a large breed of dog having a short smooth white coat with black or (in liver-spotted dalmatians) brown spots. **2.** a native or inhabitant of Dalmatia, a region of Croatia. ~*adj.* **3.** of or relating to Dalmatia or its inhabitants.
dalmatic (dæl'mætɪk) *n.* **1.** a wide-sleeved tunic-like vestment open at the sides, worn by deacons and bishops. **2.** a similar robe worn by a king at his coronation. [C15: from Late Latin *dalmatica* (*vestis*) Dalmatian (robe) (originally made of Dalmatian wool)]
dal segno ('dæl 'sɛnjəʊ) *adj., adv. Music.* (of a piece of music) to be repeated from the point marked with a sign to the word *fine.* Abbrev.: **DS.** See also **fine**[3]. [Italian, literally: from the sign]
dalton ('dɔːltən) *n.* another name for **atomic mass unit.** [C20: named after John *Dalton* (1766–1844), British chemist and physicist]
daltonism ('dɔːltəˌnɪzəm) *n.* colour blindness, esp. the confusion of red and green. [C19: from French *daltonisme,* after John *Dalton*] —**daltonic** (dɔːl'tɒnɪk) *adj.*
Dalton plan *or* **system** ('dɔːltən) *n.* a system devised to encourage pupils to learn and develop at their own speed, using libraries and other sources to complete long assignments. [C20: named after *Dalton,* Massachusetts, where the plan was used in schools]
Dalton's atomic theory *n. Chem.* the theory that matter consists of indivisible particles called atoms and that atoms of a given element are all identical and can neither be created nor destroyed. Compounds are formed by combination of atoms in simple ratios to give compound atoms (molecules). The theory was the basis of modern chemistry. [C19: named after John *Dalton*]
Dalton's law *n.* the principle that the pressure exerted by a mixture of gases in a fixed volume is equal to the sum of the pressures that each gas would exert if it occupied the whole volume. Also called: **Dalton's law of partial pressures.** [C19: named after John *Dalton*]
dam[1] (dæm) *n.* **1.** a barrier of concrete, earth, etc., built across a river to create a body of water, as for a domestic water supply. **2.** a reservoir of water created by such a barrier. **3.** something that resembles or functions as a dam. ~*vb.* **dams, damming, dammed. 4.** (*tr.;* often foll. by *up*) to obstruct or restrict by or as if by a dam. [C12: probably from Middle Low German; compare Old Icelandic *damma* to block up]
dam[2] (dæm) *n.* the female parent of an animal, esp. of domestic livestock. [C13: variant of DAME]

dam[3] (dæm) *interj., adv., adj.* a variant spelling of **damn** (senses 1–4); often used in combination, as in **damfool, damme, dammit.**

dam[4] *symbol for* decametre(s).

damage (ˈdæmɪdʒ) *n.* **1.** injury or harm impairing the function or condition of a person or thing. **2.** loss of something desirable. **3.** *Informal.* cost; expense (esp. in the phrase **what's the damage?**). ~*vb.* **4.** (*tr.*) to cause damage to. **5.** (*intr.*) to suffer damage. [C14: from Old French, from Latin *damnum* injury, loss, fine] —ˈ**damageable** *adj.* —ˌ**damageaˈbility** *n.* —ˈ**damager** *n.* —ˈ**damaging** *adj.* —ˈ**damagingly** *adv.*

damages (ˈdæmɪdʒɪz) *pl. n. Law.* money to be paid as compensation to a person for injury, loss, etc.

daman (ˈdæmən) *n.* a rare name for the **hyrax**, esp. the Syrian rock hyrax. See also **cony** (sense 2). [from Arabic *damān Isrā ʼīl* sheep of Israel]

damar (ˈdæmə) *n.* a variant spelling of **dammar.**

Damara (dəˈmɑːrə) *n.* **1.** (*pl.* **-ras** *or* **-ra**) Also called: **Bergdama.** a member of a Negroid people of South West Africa. **2.** the language of this people, a dialect of Nama.

damascene (ˈdæməˌsiːn, ˌdæməˈsiːn) *vb.* **1.** (*tr.*) to ornament (metal, esp. steel) by etching or by inlaying other metals, usually gold or silver. ~*n.* **2.** a design or article produced by this process. ~*adj.* **3.** of or relating to this process. [C14: from Latin *damascēnus* of Damascus (capital of Syria)]

Damascene (ˈdæməˌsiːn, ˌdæməˈsiːn) *adj.* **1.** of or relating to Damascus, capital of Syria. ~*n.* **2.** a native or inhabitant of Damascus. **3.** a variety of domestic fancy pigeon with silvery plumage.

Damascus steel (dəˈmɑːskəs, -ˈmæs-) *or* **damask steel** *n. History.* a hard flexible steel with wavy markings caused by forging the metal in strips: used for sword blades.

damask (ˈdæməsk) *n.* **1. a.** a reversible fabric, usually silk or linen, with a pattern woven into it. It is used for table linen, curtains, etc. **b.** table linen made from this. **c.** (*as modifier*): *a damask tablecloth.* **2.** short for **Damascus steel. 3.** the wavy markings on such steel. **4. a.** the greyish-pink colour of the damask rose. **b.** (*as adj.*): *damask wallpaper.* ~*vb.* **5.** (*tr.*) another word for **damascene** (sense 1). [C14: from Medieval Latin *damascus,* from Damascus, where this fabric was originally made]

damask rose *n.* a rose, *Rosa damascena,* native to Asia and cultivated for its pink or red fragrant flowers, which are used to make the perfume attar. [C16: from Medieval Latin *rosa damascēna* rose of Damascus]

dame (deɪm) *n.* **1.** (formerly) a woman of rank or dignity; lady. **2.** a nun who has taken the vows of her order, esp. a Benedictine. **3.** *Archaic, chiefly Brit.* a matronly or elderly woman. **4.** *Slang, chiefly U.S. and Canadian.* a woman. **5.** Also called: **pantomime dame.** *Brit.* the role of a comic old woman in a pantomime, usually played by a man. [C13: from Old French, from Latin *domina* lady, mistress of a household]

Dame (deɪm) *n.* (in Britain) **1.** the title of a woman who has been awarded the Order of the British Empire or any of certain other orders of chivalry. **2.** the legal title of the wife or widow of a knight or baronet, placed before her name: *Dame Judith.* Compare **Lady.**

dame school *n.* (formerly) a small school, often in a village, usually run by an elderly woman in her own home to teach young children to read and write.

dame's violet, dame's rocket, *or* **damewort** (ˈdeɪmˌwɜːt) *n.* a Eurasian cruciferous hairy perennial plant, *Hesperis matronalis,* cultivated in gardens for its mauve or white fragrant flowers.

dammar, damar, *or* **dammer** (ˈdæmə) *n.* any of various resins obtained from SE Asian trees, esp. of the genera *Agathis* (conifers) and *Shorea* (family *Dipterocarpaceae*): used for varnishes, lacquers, bases for oil paints, etc. [C17: from Malay *damar* resin]

dammit (ˈdæmɪt) *interj.* a contracted form of *damn it.*

damn (dæm) *interj.* **1.** *Slang.* an exclamation of annoyance (often in exclamatory phrases such as **damn it! damn you!** etc.). **2.** *Informal.* an exclamation of surprise or pleasure (esp. in the exclamatory phrase **damn me!**). ~*adj.* **3.** (*prenominal*) *Slang.* deserving damnation; detestable. ~*adv., adj.* (*prenominal*) **4.** *Slang.* (intensifier): *damn fool; a damn good pianist.* ~*adv.* **5. damn all.** *Slang.* absolutely nothing. ~*vb.* (*mainly tr.*) **6.** to condemn as bad, worthless, etc. **7.** to curse. **8.** to condemn to eternal damnation. **9.** (*often passive*) to doom to ruin; cause to fail: *the venture was damned from the start.* **10.** (*also intr.*) to prove (someone) guilty: *damning evidence.* **11.** to swear (at) using the word *damn.* **12. as near as damn it.** *Brit. informal.* as near as possible; very near. **13. damn with faint praise.** to praise so unenthusiastically that the effect is condemnation. ~*n.* **14.** *Slang.* something of negligible value; jot (esp. in the phrase **not worth a damn**). **15. not give a damn.** *Informal.* to be unconcerned; not care. [C13: from Old French *dampner,* from Latin *damnāre* to injure, condemn, from *damnum* loss, injury, penalty]

damnable (ˈdæmnəbᵊl) *adj.* **1.** execrable; detestable. **2.** liable to or deserving damnation. —ˈ**damnableness** *or* ˌ**damnaˈbility** *n.* —ˈ**damnably** *adv.*

damnation (dæmˈneɪʃən) *n.* **1.** the act of damning or state of being damned. **2.** a cause or instance of being damned. ~*interj.* **3.** an exclamation of anger, disappointment, etc.

damnatory (ˈdæmnətərɪ, -trɪ) *adj.* threatening or occasioning condemnation.

damned (dæmd) *adj.* **1. a.** condemned to hell. **b.** (*as n.*): *the damned.* ~*adv., adj. Slang.* **2.** (intensifier): *a damned good try; a damned liar; I should damned well think so!* **3.** used to indicate amazement, disavowal, or refusal (in such phrases as **I'll be damned** *and* **damned if I care**).

damnedest (ˈdæmdɪst) *n. Informal.* utmost; best (esp. in the phrases **do** or **try one's damnedest**).

damnify (ˈdæmnɪˌfaɪ) *vb.* **-fies, -fying, -fied.** (*tr.*) *Law.* to cause loss or damage to (a person); injure. [C16: from Old French *damnifier,* ultimately from Latin *damnum* harm, + *facere* to make] —ˌ**damnifiˈcation** *n.*

damoiselle, damosel, *or* **damozel** (ˌdæməˈzɛl) *n.* archaic variants of **damsel.**

damp (dæmp) *adj.* **1.** slightly wet, as from dew, steam, etc. **2.** *Archaic.* dejected. ~*n.* **3.** slight wetness; moisture; humidity. **4.** rank air or poisonous gas, esp. in a mine. See also **firedamp. 5.** a discouragement; damper. **6.** *Archaic.* dejection. ~*vb.* (*tr.*) **7.** to make slightly wet. **8.** (often foll. by *down*) to stifle or deaden: *to damp one's ardour.* **9.** (often foll. by *down*) to reduce the flow of air to (a fire) to make it burn more slowly or to extinguish it. **10.** *Physics.* to reduce the amplitude of (an oscillation or wave). **11.** *Music.* to muffle (the sound of an instrument). ~See also **damp off.** [C14: from Middle Low German *damp* steam; related to Old High German *demphen* to cause to steam] —ˈ**dampish** *adj.* —ˈ**damply** *adv.* —ˈ**dampness** *n.*

dampcourse (ˈdæmpˌkɔːs) *n.* a horizontal layer of impervious material in a brick wall, fairly close to the ground, to stop moisture rising. Also called: **damp-proof course.**

dampen (ˈdæmpən) *vb.* **1.** to make or become damp. **2.** (*tr.*) to stifle; deaden. —ˈ**dampener** *n.*

damper (ˈdæmpə) *n.* **1.** a person, event, or circumstance that depresses or discourages. **2. put a damper on.** to produce a depressing or inhibiting effect on. **3.** a movable plate to regulate the draught in a stove or furnace flue. **4.** a device to reduce electronic, mechanical, acoustic, or aerodynamic oscillations in a system. **5.** *Music.* the pad in a piano or harpsichord that deadens the vibration of each string as its key is released. **6.** *Chiefly Austral. and N.Z.* any of various unleavened loaves and scones, typically cooked on an open fire.

damping (ˈdæmpɪŋ) *n.* **1.** moistening or wetting. **2.** stifling, as of spirits. **3.** *Electronics.* the introduction of resistance into a resonant circuit with the result that the sharpness of response at the peak of a frequency is reduced. **4.** *Engineering.* any method of dispersing energy in a vibrating system.

damping off *n.* any of various diseases of plants, esp. the collapse and death of seedlings caused by the parasitic fungus *Pythium debaryanum* and related fungi in conditions of excessive moisture.

damp off *vb.* (*intr., adv.*) (of plants, seedlings, shoots, etc.) to be affected by damping off.

damp-proof *vb. Building trades.* **1.** to protect against the incursion of damp by adding a dampcourse or by coating with a moisture-resistant preparation. ~*adj.* **2.** protected against damp or causing protection against damp: *a damp-proof course.*

damsel (ˈdæmzᵊl) *n. Archaic or poetic.* a young unmarried woman; maiden. [C13: from Old French *damoisele,* from Vulgar Latin *domnicella* (unattested) young lady, from Latin *domina* mistress; see DAME]

damsel bug *n.* any of various bugs of the carnivorous family *Nabiidae,* related to the bedbugs but feeding on other insects. The larvae of some species mimic and associate with ants.

damselfish (ˈdæmzᵊlˌfɪʃ) *n., pl.* **-fish** *or* **-fishes.** any small tropical percoid fish of the family *Pomacentridae,* having a brightly coloured deep compressed body. See also **anemone fish.**

damselfly (ˈdæmzᵊlˌflaɪ) *n., pl.* **-flies.** any insect of the suborder *Zygoptera,* similar to but smaller than dragonflies and usually resting with the wings closed over the back: order *Odonata.*

damson (ˈdæmzən) *n.* **1.** a small rosaceous tree, *Prunus domestica instititia* (or *P. instititia*), cultivated for its blue-black edible plumlike fruit and probably derived from the bullace. See also **plum**[1] (sense 1). **2.** the fruit of this tree. [C14: from Latin *prūnum Damascēnum* Damascus plum]

damson cheese *n.* thick damson jam.

dan[1] (dæn) *n.* a small buoy used as a marker at sea. Also called: **dan buoy.** [C17: of unknown origin]

dan[2] (dæn) *n. Judo, karate.* **1.** any one of the 10 black-belt grades of proficiency. **2.** a competitor entitled to dan grading. ~Compare **kyu.** [Japanese]

Dan (dæn) *n.* an archaic title of honour, equivalent to *Master* or *Sir: Dan Chaucer.*

Dan. *abbrev. for:* **1.** *Bible.* Daniel. **2.** Danish.

dance (dɑːns) *vb.* **1.** (*intr.*) to move the feet and body rhythmically, esp. in time to music. **2.** (*tr.*) to perform (a particular dance). **3.** (*intr.*) to skip or leap, as in joy, etc. **4.** to move or cause to move in a light rhythmical way. **5. dance attendance on (someone).** to attend (someone) solicitously or obsequiously. ~*n.* **6.** a series of rhythmical steps and movements, usually in time to music. **7.** an act of dancing. **8. a.** a social meeting arranged for dancing; ball. **b.** (*as modifier*): *a dance hall.* **9.** a piece of music in the rhythm of a particular dance form, such as a waltz. **10.** dancelike movements made by some insects and birds, esp. as part of a behaviour pattern. **11. lead (someone) a dance.** *Brit. informal.* to cause (someone) continued worry and exasperation; play up. [C13: from Old French *dancier*] —'**danceable** *adj.* —'**dancer** *n.* —'**dancing** *n., adj.*

dance of death *n.* a pictorial, literary, or musical representation, current esp. in the Middle Ages, of a dance in which living people, in order of social precedence, are led off to their graves, by a personification of death. Also called (French): **danse macabre.**

dancette (dɑːn'sɛt) *n.* another name for **chevron** (sense 5).

dancing girl *n.* a professional female dancer who dances to entertain customers at a club, theatre, etc.

D and C *n. Med.* dilation and curettage; a therapeutic or diagnostic procedure in obstetrics and gynaecology involving dilation of the cervix and curettage of the cavity of the uterus, as for abortion.

dandelion ('dændɪˌlaɪən) *n.* **1.** a plant, *Taraxacum officinale,* native to Europe and Asia and naturalized as a weed in North America, having yellow rayed flowers and deeply notched basal leaves, which are used for salad or wine: family *Compositae* (composites). **2.** any of several similar related plants. [C15: from Old French *dent de lion,* literally: tooth of a lion, referring to its leaves]

dander[1] ('dændə) *n.* **1.** small particles or scales of hair or feathers. **2. get one's** (*or* **someone's**) **dander up.** *Informal.* to become or cause to become annoyed or angry. [C19: changed from DANDRUFF]

dander[2] ('dændə; *Scot.* 'dændər) *Scot. and northern English dialect.* ~*n.* **1.** a stroll. ~*vb.* **2.** (*intr.*) to stroll. [C19: of unknown origin]

Dandie Dinmont ('dændɪ 'dɪnmɒnt) *n.* a breed of small terrier with a long coat and drooping ears. Also called: **Dandie Dinmont terrier.** [C19: named after a character who owned two terriers in *Guy Mannering* (1815), a novel by Sir Walter Scott (1771–1832), Scottish writer]

dandify ('dændɪˌfaɪ) *vb.* **-fies, -fying, -fied.** (*tr.*) to dress like or cause to resemble a dandy. —ˌ**dandifi'cation** *n.*

dandiprat ('dændɪˌpræt) *n.* **1.** a small English coin minted in the 16th century. **2.** *Archaic.* **a.** a small boy. **b.** an insignificant person. [C16: of unknown origin]

dandle ('dænd^əl) *vb.* (*tr.*) **1.** to move (a young child, etc.) up and down (on the knee or in the arms). **2.** to pet; fondle. [C16: of uncertain origin] —'**dandler** *n.*

dandruff ('dændrəf) *n.* loose scales of dry dead skin shed from the scalp. Also called (now rarely): **dandriff.** [C16 *dand-,* of unknown origin + *-ruff,* probably from Middle English *roufe* scab, from Old Norse *hrūfa*] —'**dandruffy** *adj.*

dandy[1] ('dændɪ) *n., pl.* **-dies. 1.** a man greatly concerned with smartness of dress; beau. **2.** a yawl or ketch. ~*adj.* **-dier, -diest. 3.** *Informal.* very good or fine. [C18: perhaps short for *jack-a-dandy*] —'**dandily** *adv.* —'**dandyish** *adj.* —'**dandyism** *n.*

dandy[2] ('dændɪ) *n.* another name for **dengue.**

dandy-brush *n.* a stiff brush used for grooming a horse.

dandy roll *or* **roller** *n.* a light roller used in the manufacture of certain papers to produce watermarks.

Dane (deɪn) *n.* **1.** a native, citizen, or inhabitant of Denmark. **2.** any of the Vikings who invaded England from the late 8th to the 11th century A.D..

Danegeld ('deɪnˌgɛld) *or* **Danegelt** ('deɪnˌgɛlt) *n.* the tax first levied in the late 9th century in Anglo-Saxon England to provide protection money for or to finance forces to oppose Viking invaders. [C11: from *Dan* Dane + *geld* tribute; see YIELD]

danewort ('deɪnˌwɜːt) *n.* a caprifoliaceous shrub, *Sambucus ebulus,* native to Europe and Asia and having serrated leaves and white flowers. See also **elder**[2].

dang (dæŋ) *interj., adv., adj.* a euphemistic word for **damn** (senses 1–4).

danger ('deɪndʒə) *n.* **1.** the state of being vulnerable to injury, loss, or evil; risk. **2.** a person or thing that may cause injury, pain, etc. **3.** *Obsolete.* power. **4. in danger of.** liable to. **5. on the danger list.** critically ill in hospital. [C13 *daunger* power, hence power to inflict injury, from Old French *dongier* (from Latin *dominium* ownership) blended with Old French *dam* injury, from Latin *damnum*] —'**dangerless** *adj.*

danger money *n.* extra money paid to compensate for the risks involved in certain dangerous jobs.

dangerous ('deɪndʒərəs) *adj.* causing danger; perilous. —'**dangerously** *adv.* —'**dangerousness** *n.*

dangle ('dæŋg^əl) *vb.* **1.** to hang or cause to hang freely: *his legs dangled over the wall.* **2.** (*tr.*) to display as an enticement: *the hope of a legacy was dangled before her.* ~*n.* **3.** the act of dangling or something that dangles. [C16: perhaps from Danish *dangle,* probably of imitative origin] —'**dangler** *n.* —'**danglingly** *adv.*

dangling participle *n. Grammar.* another name (esp. U.S. and Canadian) for **misplaced modifier.**

Dani ('dɑːnɪ) *n.* **1.** (*pl.* **Dani** ('dɑːnɪ)). a member of a New Guinea people living in the central highlands of West Irian. **2.** the language of this people, probably related to other languages of New Guinea.

Daniel ('dænjəl) *n.* (often preceded by *a*) a wise upright person. [referring to *Daniel* in the Apocryphal *Book of Susanna*]

Daniell cell ('dænjəl) *n. Physics.* a type of cell having a zinc anode in dilute sulphuric acid separated by a porous barrier from a copper cathode in copper sulphate solution. It has an emf of 1.1 volts. [C19: named after John *Daniell* (1790–1845), British scientist]

danio ('deɪnɪˌəʊ) *n., pl.* **-os.** any brightly coloured tropical freshwater cyprinid fish of the genus *Danio* and related genera: popular aquarium fishes. [C19: from New Latin, of obscure origin]

Danish ('deɪnɪʃ) *adj.* **1.** of, relating to, or characteristic of Denmark, its people, or their language. ~*n.* **2.** the official language of Denmark, belonging to the North Germanic branch of the Indo-European family.

Danish blue *n.* a strong-tasting white cheese with blue veins.

Danish loaf *n. Brit.* a large white loaf with a centre split having the top crust dusted with flour, esp. one baked on the sole of the oven.

Danish pastry *n.* a rich puff pastry filled with apple, almond paste, icing, etc.

dank (dæŋk) *adj.* (esp. of cellars, caves, etc.) unpleasantly damp and chilly. [C14: probably of Scandinavian origin; compare Swedish *dank* marshy spot] —'**dankly** *adv.* —'**dankness** *n.*

danny ('dænɪ) *or* **donny** *n., pl.* **-nies.** *Dialect.* the hand (used esp. when addressing children). [probably from *dandy,* childish pronunciation of HAND]

Dano-Norwegian (ˌdeɪnəʊnɔː'wiːdʒən) *n.* another name for **Bokmål.**

danse macabre *French.* (dɑ̃s makɑbrə) *n.* another name for **dance of death.**

danseur *French.* (dɑ̃sœr) *or* (*fem.*) ***danseuse*** (dɑ̃søz) *n.* a ballet dancer.

Dantean ('dæntɪən, dæn'tiːən) *or* **Dantesque** (dæn'tɛsk) *adj.* relating to or in the style of Dante Alighieri (1265–1321), Italian poet.

danthonia (dæn'θəʊnɪə) *n.* any of various grasses of Australia and New Zealand having narrow leaves and small terminal panicles of densely crowded florets. [named after E. *Danthoine,* French botanist]

Danzig ('dænsɪg) *n.* a rare variety of domestic fancy pigeon originating in the area of Danzig (Gdańsk), Poland.

dap[1] (dæp) *vb.* **daps, dapping, dapped. 1.** *Angling.* to fish with a natural or artificial fly on a floss silk line so that the wind makes the fly bob on and off the surface of the water. **2.** (*intr.*) (as of a bird) to dip lightly into water. **3.** to bounce or cause to bounce. [C17: of imitative origin]

dap[2] (dæp) *n. Southwest Brit. dialect.* another word for **plimsoll.** [C20: probably special use of DAP[1] (in the sense: to bounce, skip)]

DAP *Computer technol. abbrev. for* distributed array processor.

daphne ('dæfnɪ) *n.* any shrub of the Eurasian thymelaeaceous genus *Daphne,* such as the mezereon and spurge laurel: ornamentals with shiny evergreen leaves and clusters of small bell-shaped flowers. See also **laurel** (sense 4). [via Latin from Greek: laurel]

daphnia ('dæfnɪə) *n.* any water flea of the genus *Daphnia,* having a rounded body enclosed in a transparent shell and bearing branched swimming antennae. [C19: from New Latin, probably from *Daphne,* nymph in Greek mythology]

dapper ('dæpə) *adj.* **1.** neat and spruce in dress and bearing; trim. **2.** small and nimble. [C15: from Middle Dutch: active, nimble] —'**dapperly** *adv.* —'**dapperness** *n.*

dapple ('dæp^əl) *vb.* **1.** to mark or become marked with spots or patches of a different colour; mottle. ~*n.* **2.** mottled or spotted markings. **3.** a dappled horse, etc. ~*adj.* **4.** marked with dapples or spots. [C14: of unknown origin]

dapple-grey *n.* a horse with a grey coat having spots of darker colour.

dapsone ('dæpˌsəʊn) *n.* an antibiotic drug used to treat leprosy and certain types of dermatitis. Formula: $C_{12}H_{12}N_2O_2S$. [C20: from *d(i)a(minodi)p(henyl) s(ulph)one*]

DAR *abbrev. for* Daughters of the American Revolution.

daraf ('dæræf) *n. Physics.* a unit of elastance equal to a reciprocal farad. [C20: reverse spelling of FARAD]

darbies ('dɑːbɪz) *pl. n. Brit.* a slang term for **handcuffs.** [C16: perhaps from the phrase *Father Derby's* or *Father Darby's bonds,* a rigid agreement between a usurer and his client]

Darby and Joan ('dɑːbɪ; dʒəʊn) *n.* **1.** an ideal elderly married couple living in domestic harmony. **2. Darby and Joan Club.** a club for elderly people. [C18: a couple in an 18th-century English ballad]

darcy ('dɑːsɪ) *n. Geology.* a unit expressing the permeability coefficient of rock. Symbol: D [named after Henri-Philibert-Gaspard *Darcy* (1803–58), French hydraulic engineer]

Dard (dɑːd) *n.* a member of any of the Indo-European peoples speaking a Dardic language.

Dardan ('dɑːd^ən) *or* **Dardanian** (dɑː'deɪnɪən) *n.* another name for a **Trojan.**

Dardic ('dɑːdɪk) *adj.* **1.** belonging or relating to a group of languages spoken in Kashmir, N Pakistan, and E Afghanistan, regarded as a subbranch of the Indic branch of the Indo-European family but showing certain Iranian characteristics. ~*n.* **2.** this group of languages.

dare (dɛə) *vb.* **1.** (*tr.*) to challenge (a person to do something) as proof of courage. **2.** (can take an infinitive with or without *to*) to be courageous enough to try (to do something): *she dares to* *dress differently from the others; you wouldn't dare!* **3.** (*tr.*) *Rare.* to oppose without fear; defy. **4. I dare say.** Also: **I daresay. a.** (it is) quite possible (that). **b.** probably: used as sentence substitute. ~*n.* **5.** a challenge to do something as proof of courage. **6.** something done in response to such a challenge. [Old English *durran;* related to Old High German *turran* to venture] —ˈ**darer** *n.*

▷**Usage.** When used negatively or interrogatively and not followed by an infinitive with *to, dare* does not add *-s: he dare not; dare she come?*

daredevil (ˈdɛəˌdɛvᵊl) *n.* **1.** a recklessly bold person. ~*adj.* **2.** reckless; daring; bold. —ˈ**dareˌdevilry** *or* ˈ**dareˌdeviltry** *n.*

darg (dɑːg) *n.* **1.** *Scot. and northern English dialect.* a day's work. **2.** *Austral.* a specified amount of work; job. [C15: formed by syncope from *day-work*]

dargah *or* **durgah** (ˈdɜːgɑː) *n.* the tomb of a Muslim saint; a Muslim shrine. [Persian]

daric (ˈdærɪk) *n.* a gold coin of ancient Persia. Compare **siglos.** [C16: from Greek *Dareikos,* probably after Darius I of Persia]

daring (ˈdɛərɪŋ) *adj.* **1.** bold or adventurous; reckless. ~*n.* **2.** courage in taking risks; boldness. —ˈ**daringly** *adv.*

dariole (ˈdærɪˌəʊl) *n.* **1.** Also called: **dariole mould.** a small cup-shaped mould used for making individual sweet or savoury dishes. **2.** a dish prepared in such a mould. [C14: from Old French]

Darjeeling (dɑːˈdʒiːlɪŋ) *n.* a high-quality black tea grown in the mountains around Darjeeling, a town in NE India.

dark (dɑːk) *adj.* **1.** having little or no light: *a dark street.* **2.** (of a colour) reflecting or transmitting little light: *dark brown.* Compare **light**[1] (sense 28), **medium** (sense 2). **3. a.** (of complexion, hair colour, etc.) not fair or blond; swarthy; brunette. **b.** (*in combination*): *dark-eyed.* **4.** gloomy or dismal. **5.** sinister; evil: *a dark purpose.* **6.** sullen or angry: *a dark scowl.* **7.** ignorant or unenlightened: *a dark period in our history.* **8.** secret or mysterious: *keep it dark.* **9.** *Phonetics.* denoting an (1) pronounced with a velar articulation giving back vowel resonance. In English, *l* is usually dark when final or preconsonantal. Compare **light**[1] (sense 29). ~*n.* **10.** absence of light; darkness. **11.** night or nightfall. **12.** a dark place, patch, or shadow. **13.** a state of ignorance (esp. in the phrase **in the dark**). ~*vb.* **14.** an archaic word for **darken.** [Old English *deorc;* related to Old High German *terchennen* to hide] —ˈ**darkish** *adj.* —ˈ**darkly** *adv.* —ˈ**darkness** *n.*

Dark Ages *pl. n.* **the.** *European history.* **1.** the period from about the late 5th century A.D. to about 1000 A.D., once considered an unenlightened period. **2.** (occasionally) the whole medieval period.

dark current *n.* the residual current produced by a photoelectric device when not illuminated.

darken (ˈdɑːkən) *vb.* **1.** to make or become dark or darker. **2.** to make or become gloomy, angry, or sad: *his mood darkened.* **3. darken (someone's) door.** (*usually used with a negative*) to visit someone: *never darken my door again!* —ˈ**darkener** *n.*

dark-field illumination *n.* illumination of the field of a microscope from the side so that the specimen is viewed against a dark background.

dark-field microscope *n.* another name for an **ultramicroscope.**

dark glasses *pl. n.* spectacles with lenses tinted to reduce transmitted light.

dark horse *n.* **1.** a competitor in a race or contest about whom little is known; an unknown. **2.** a person who reveals little about himself or his activities, esp. one who has unexpected talents or abilities. **3.** *U.S. politics.* a candidate who is unexpectedly nominated or elected.

dark lantern *n.* a lantern having a sliding shutter or panel to dim or hide the light.

darkle (ˈdɑːkᵊl) *vb. Archaic or literary.* **1.** to grow dark; darken. **2.** (*intr.*) to appear dark or indistinct. [C19: back formation from DARKLING]

darkling (ˈdɑːklɪŋ) *Poetic.* ~*adv., adj.* **1.** in the dark or night. ~*adj.* **2.** darkening or almost dark; obscure. [C15: from DARK + -LING[2]]

dark matter *n.* *Astronomy.* matter known to make up a substantial part of the mass of the universe, but not detectable by its absorption or emission of electromagnetic radiation.

dark nebula *n.* a type of nebula that is observed by its blocking of radiation from other sources. See **nebula.**

dark reaction *n. Botany.* the stage of photosynthesis involving the reduction of carbon dioxide and the dissociation of water, using chemical energy stored in ATP: does not require the presence of light. Compare **light reaction.**

darkroom (ˈdɑːkˌruːm, -ˌrʊm) *n.* a room in which photographs are processed in darkness or safe light.

darksome (ˈdɑːksəm) *adj. Literary.* dark or darkish.

dark star *n.* an invisible star known to exist only from observation of its radio, infrared, or other spectrum or of its gravitational effect, such as an invisible component of a binary or multiple star.

darky, darkie, *or* **darkey** (ˈdɑːkɪ) *n., pl.* **darkies** *or* **darkeys.** *Informal.* **1.** an offensive word for a Negro. **2.** *Austral.* an offensive word for an Aborigine.

darling (ˈdɑːlɪŋ) *n.* **1.** a person very much loved: often used as a term of address. **2.** a favourite: *the teacher's darling.* ~*adj.* (*prenominal*) **3.** beloved. **4.** much admired; pleasing: *a darling hat.* [Old English *dēorling;* see DEAR, -LING[1]]

darn[1] (dɑːn) *vb.* **1.** to mend (a hole or a garment) with a series of crossing or interwoven stitches. ~*n.* **2.** a patch of darned work on a garment. **3.** the process or act of darning. [C16: probably from French (Channel Islands dialect) *darner;* compare Welsh, Breton *darn* piece] —ˈ**darner** *n.* —ˈ**darning** *n.*

darn[2] (dɑːn) *interj., adj., adv., n.* a euphemistic word for **damn** (senses 1–4, 15).

darned (dɑːnd) *adv., adj. Slang.* **1.** (intensifier): *this darned car won't start; a darned good shot.* ~*adj.* **2.** another word for **damned** (senses 2, 3).

darnel (ˈdɑːnᵊl) *n.* any of several grasses of the genus *Lolium,* esp. *L. temulentum,* that grow as weeds in grain fields in Europe and Asia. [C14: probably related to French (Walloon dialect) *darnelle,* of obscure origin]

darning egg *or* **mushroom** *n.* a rounded piece of wood or plastic used in darning to support the fabric around the hole.

darning needle *n.* **1.** a long needle with a large eye used for darning. **2.** *U.S. and Canadian.* a dialect name for a **dragonfly.**

darogha (dɑːˈrəʊgɑː) *n.* (in India and Pakistan) **1.** a manager. **2.** an inspector. [Urdu]

dart (dɑːt) *n.* **1.** a small narrow pointed missile that is thrown or shot, as in the game of darts. **2.** a sudden quick movement. **3.** *Zoology.* a slender pointed structure, as in snails for aiding copulation or in nematodes for penetrating the host's tissues. **4.** a tapered tuck made in dressmaking. ~*vb.* **5.** to move or throw swiftly and suddenly; shoot: *she darted across the room.* ~See also **darts.** [C14: from Old French, of Germanic origin; related to Old English *daroth* spear, Old High German *tart* dart] —ˈ**darting** *adj.* —ˈ**dartingly** *adv.*

dartboard (ˈdɑːtˌbɔːd) *n.* a circular piece of wood, cork, etc., used as the target in the game of darts. It is divided into numbered sectors with central inner and outer bull's-eyes.

darter (ˈdɑːtə) *n.* **1.** Also called: **anhinga, snakebird.** any aquatic bird of the genus *Anhinga* and family *Anhingidae,* of tropical and subtropical inland waters, having a long slender neck and bill: order *Pelecaniformes* (pelicans, cormorants, etc.). **2.** any small brightly coloured North American freshwater fish of the genus *Etheostoma* and related genera: family *Percidae* (perches).

Dartmoor (ˈdɑːtˌmʊə) *n.* **1.** a small strong breed of pony, originally from Dartmoor, a moorland plateau in SW England. **2.** a hardy coarse-wooled breed of sheep originally from Dartmoor.

darts (dɑːts) *n.* (*functioning as sing.*) any of various competitive games in which darts are thrown at a dartboard.

Darwinian (dɑːˈwɪnɪən) *adj.* **1.** of or relating to Charles Darwin (1809–82), British naturalist, or to Darwinism. ~*n.* **2.** a person who accepts, supports, or uses this theory.

Darwinism (ˈdɑːwɪˌnɪzəm) *or* **Darwinian theory** *n.* the theory of the origin of animal and plant species by evolution through a process of natural selection. Compare **Lamarckism.** See also **Neo-Darwinism.** —ˈ**Darwinist** *or* ˈ**Darwinite** *n., adj.* —ˌ**Darwinˈistic** *adj.*

Darwin's finches (ˈdɑːwɪnz) *pl. n.* the finches of the subfamily *Geospizinae* of the Galapagos Islands, showing great variation in bill structure and feeding habits: provided Darwin with evidence to support his theory of evolution.

dash[1] (dæʃ) *vb.* (*mainly tr.*) **1.** to hurl; crash: *he dashed the cup to the floor; the waves dashed against the rocks.* **2.** to mix: *white paint dashed with blue.* **3.** (*intr.*) to move hastily or recklessly; rush: *he dashed to her rescue.* **4.** (usually foll. by *off* or *down*) to write (down) or finish (off) hastily. **5.** to destroy; frustrate: *his hopes were dashed.* **6.** to daunt (someone); cast down; discourage: *he was dashed by her refusal.* ~*n.* **7.** a sudden quick movement; dart. **8.** a small admixture: *coffee with a dash of cream.* **9.** a violent stroke or blow. **10.** the sound of splashing or smashing: *the dash of the waves.* **11.** panache; style: *he rides with dash.* **12. cut a dash.** See **cut** (sense 33). **13.** the punctuation mark —, used singly in place of a colon, esp. to indicate a sudden change of subject or grammatical anacoluthon, or in pairs to enclose a parenthetical remark. **14.** the symbol (–) used, in combination with the symbol *dot* (•), in the written representation of Morse and other telegraphic codes. Compare **dah. 15.** *Athletics.* another word (esp. U.S. and Canadian) for **sprint. 16.** *Informal.* short for **dashboard.** [Middle English *dasche, dasse*]

dash[2] (dæʃ) *interj.* *Informal.* a euphemistic word for **damn** (senses 1, 2).

dash[3] (dæʃ) *W. African.* ~*n.* **1.** a gift, commission, tip, or bribe. ~*vb.* **2.** to give (a dash) to someone. [C16: perhaps from Fanti]

dashboard (ˈdæʃˌbɔːd) *n.* **1.** Also called (Brit.): **fascia.** the instrument panel in a car, boat, or aircraft. Sometimes shortened to **dash. 2.** *Obsolete.* a board at the side of a carriage or boat to protect against splashing.

dasheen (dæˈʃiːn) *n.* another name for **taro.** [C19: perhaps changed from French *(chou) de Chine* (cabbage) of China]

dasher (ˈdæʃə) *n.* the plunger in a churn, often with paddles attached.

dashiki (dɑːˈʃiːkɪ) *n.* a large loose-fitting buttonless upper garment worn esp. by Negroes in the U.S., Africa, and the Caribbean. [C20: of W African origin]
dashing (ˈdæʃɪŋ) *adj.* **1.** spirited; lively: *a dashing young man.* **2.** stylish; showy: *a dashing hat.* —ˈ**dashingly** *adv.*
dashpot (ˈdæʃˌpɒt) *n.* a device for damping vibrations; the vibrating part is attached to a piston moving in a liquid-filled cylinder. [C20: from DASH[1] + POT]
Dassehra (ˈdæsɛræ) *n.* an annual Hindu festival celebrated on the 10th lunar day of Navaratri; images of the goddess Durga are immersed in water.
dassie (ˈdæsɪ) *n.* another name for a **hyrax,** esp. the rock hyrax. [C19: from Afrikaans]
dastard (ˈdæstəd) *n. Archaic.* a contemptible sneaking coward. [C15 (in the sense: dullard): probably from Old Norse *dæstr* exhausted, out of breath]
dastardly (ˈdæstədlɪ) *adj.* mean and cowardly. —ˈ**dastardliness** *n.*
dasypaedal (ˌdæsɪˈpiːdᵊl) *adj.* (of the young of some species of birds after hatching) having a covering of down. [from Greek *dasus* shaggy + *pais, paid-* child]
dasyure (ˈdæsɪˌjʊə) *n.* any small carnivorous marsupial, such as *Dasyurus quoll* (**eastern dasyure**), of the subfamily *Dasyurinae,* of Australia, New Guinea, and adjacent islands. See also **Tasmanian devil.** [C19: from New Latin *Dasyūrus,* from Greek *dasus* shaggy + *oura* tail; see DENSE]
DAT *abbrev. for* digital audio tape.
dat. *abbrev. for* dative.
data (ˈdeɪtə, ˈdɑːtə) *n.* **1.** a series of observations, measurements, or facts; information. **2.** Also called: **information.** *Computer technol.* the information operated on by a computer program. [C17: from Latin, literally: (things) given, from *dare* to give]
▷**Usage.** Although now generally used as a singular noun, *data* is properly a plural.
data bank *n.* a store of a large amount of information, esp. in a form that can be handled by a computer.
database (ˈdeɪtəˌbeɪs) *n.* a systematized collection of data that can be accessed immediately and manipulated by a data-processing system for a specific purpose.
database management *n.* the maintenance of information stored in a computer system.
data capture *n.* any process for converting information into a form that can be handled by a computer.
data dictionary *n. Computer technol.* an index of data held in a data base and used to assist in the access to data. Also called: **data directory.**
data disk *n.* a disk used to store information for computer processing.
data diskette *n.* a flexible disk used to store information for computer processing.
dataflow architecture (ˈdeɪtəˌfləʊ, ˈdɑːtə-) *n.* a means of arranging computer data processing in which operations are governed by the data present and the processing it requires rather than by a prewritten program that awaits data to be processed.
data pen *n.* a device for reading or scanning magnetically coded data on labels, packets, etc.
data processing *n.* **a.** a sequence of operations performed on data, esp. by a computer, in order to extract information, reorder files, etc. **b.** (*as modifier*): *a data-processing centre.* See also **automatic data processing.**
data protection *n.* (in Britain) safeguards for individuals relating to personal data stored on a computer.
datary (ˈdeɪtərɪ) *n., pl.* **-ries.** *R.C. Church.* the head of the **dataria** (deɪˈtɛərɪə), the papal office that assesses candidates for benefices reserved to the Holy See. [C16: from Medieval Latin *datārius* (unattested) official who dated papal letters, from Late Latin *data* DATE[1]]
data set *n. Computer technol.* another name for **file**[1] (sense 7).
data structure *n.* an organized form, such as an array list or string, in which connected data items are held in a computer.
datcha (ˈdætʃə) *n.* a variant spelling of **dacha.**
date[1] (deɪt) *n.* **1.** a specified day of the month: *today's date is October 27.* **2.** the particular day or year of an event: *the date of the Norman Conquest was 1066.* **3.** (*pl.*) the years of a person's birth and death or of the beginning and end of an event or period. **4.** an inscription on a coin, letter, etc., stating when it was made or written. **5. a.** an appointment for a particular time, esp. with a person of the opposite sex: *she has a dinner date.* **b.** the person with whom the appointment is made. **6.** the present moment; now (esp. in the phrases **to date, up to date**). ~*vb.* **7.** (*tr.*) to mark (a letter, coin, etc.) with the day, month, or year. **8.** (*tr.*) to assign a date of occurrence or creation to. **9.** (*intr.*; foll. by *from* or *back to*) to have originated (at a specified time): *his decline dates from last summer.* **10.** (*tr.*) to reveal the age of: *that dress dates her.* **11.** to make or become old-fashioned: *some good films hardly date at all.* **12.** *Informal, chiefly U.S. and Canadian.* **a.** to be a boyfriend or girlfriend of (someone of the opposite sex). **b.** to accompany (a member of the opposite sex) on a date. [C14: from Old French, from Latin *dare* to give, as in the phrase *epistula data Romae* letter handed over at Rome] —ˈ**datable** *or* ˈ**dateable** *adj.* —ˈ**dateless** *adj.*
▷**Usage.** See at **year.**
date[2] (deɪt) *n.* **1.** the fruit of the date palm, having sweet edible flesh and a single large woody seed. **2.** short for **date palm.** [C13: from Old French, from Latin, from Greek *daktulos* finger]
dated (ˈdeɪtɪd) *adj.* **1.** unfashionable; outmoded. **2.** (of a security) having a fixed date for redemption.
Datel (ˈdeɪˌtɛl) *n. Trademark.* a British Telecom service providing for the direct transmission of data from one computer to another. [C20: from DA(TA) + TEL(EX)]
dateless (ˈdeɪtlɪs) *adj.* **1.** likely to remain fashionable, relevant, or interesting regardless of age; timeless. **2.** having no date or limit.
dateline (ˈdeɪtˌlaɪn) *n. Journalism.* the date and location of a story, placed at the top of an article.
date line *n.* (*often caps.*) short for **International Date Line.**
date palm *n.* a tall feather palm, *Phoenix dactylifera,* native to Syria but grown in other tropical regions for its sweet edible fruit (dates).
date stamp *n.* **1.** an adjustable rubber stamp for recording the date. **2.** an inked impression made by this.
dating (ˈdeɪtɪŋ) *n.* any of several techniques, such as radioactive dating, dendochronology, or varve dating, for establishing the age of rocks, palaeontological or archaeological specimens, etc.
dating agency *n.* an agency that provides introductions to people seeking a companion with similar interests.
dative (ˈdeɪtɪv) *Grammar.* ~*adj.* **1.** denoting a case of nouns, pronouns, and adjectives used to express the indirect object, to identify the recipients, and for other purposes. ~*n.* **2. a.** the dative case. **b.** a word or speech element in this case. [C15: from Latin *datīvus,* from *dare* to give; translation of Greek *dotikos*] —**datival** (deɪˈtaɪvᵊl) *adj.* —ˈ**datively** *adv.*
dative bond *n. Chem.* another name for **coordinate bond.**
dato (ˈdɑːtəʊ) *n., pl.* **-tos.** the chief of any of certain Muslim tribes in the Philippine Islands. [C19: from Spanish, ultimately from Malay *dato'* grandfather]
datolite (ˈdætəˌlaɪt) *n.* a colourless mineral consisting of a hydrated silicate of calcium and boron in monoclinic crystalline form, occurring in cavities in igneous rocks. Formula: $CaBSiO_4(OH)$. [C19: *dato-* from Greek *dateisthai* to divide + -LITE]
Datuk (dæˈtʊk) *n.* (in Malaysia) a title denoting membership of a high order of chivalry. [from Malay *datu* chief] —**Datin** (dæˈtiːn) *fem. n.*
datum (ˈdeɪtəm, ˈdɑːtəm) *n., pl.* **-ta** (-tə). **1.** a single piece of information; fact. **2.** a proposition taken for granted as unquestionable often in order to construct some theoretical framework upon it; a given. See also **sense datum.** [C17: from Latin: something given; see DATA]
datum plane, level, *or* **line** *n. Surveying.* the horizontal plane from which heights and depths are calculated.
datura (dəˈtjʊərə) *n.* any of various chiefly Indian solanaceous plants of the genus *Datura,* such as the moonflower and thorn apple, having large trumpet-shaped flowers, prickly pods, and narcotic properties. [C16: from New Latin, from Hindi *dhatūra* jimson weed, from Sanskrit *dhattūra*]
DATV *abbrev. for* digitally assisted television: a technique in which special digital signals are transmitted with an analogue picture signal to assist the receiver to display the picture to the best advantage.
daub (dɔːb) *vb.* **1.** (*tr.*) to smear or spread (paint, mud, etc.), esp. carelessly. **2.** (*tr.*) to cover or coat (with paint, plaster, etc.) carelessly. **3.** to paint (a picture) clumsily or badly. ~*n.* **4.** an unskilful or crude painting. **5.** something daubed on, esp. as a wall covering. See also **wattle and daub.** **6.** a smear (of paint, mud, etc.) **7.** the act of daubing. [C14: from Old French *dauber* to paint, whitewash, from Latin *dealbāre,* from *albāre* to whiten, from *albus* white] —ˈ**dauber** *n.* —ˈ**dauby** *adj.*
daube (dəʊb) *n.* a braised meat stew. [from French]
daubery (ˈdɔːbərɪ) *n.* **1.** the act or an instance of daubing. **2.** an unskilful painting.
daud (dɔːd, dɒd) *n. Scot.* a lump or chunk of something. [C18: from earlier *dad* to strike, of unknown origin]
daughter (ˈdɔːtə) *n.* **1.** a female offspring; a girl or woman in relation to her parents. **2.** a female descendant. **3.** a female from a certain country, etc., or one closely connected with a certain environment, etc.: *a daughter of the church.* **4.** (*often cap.*) *Archaic.* a form of address for a girl or woman. ~(*modifier*) **5.** *Biology.* denoting a cell or unicellular organism produced by the division of one of its own kind. **6.** *Physics.* (of a nuclide) formed from another nuclide by radioactive decay. [Old English *dohtor;* related to Old High German *tohter* daughter, Greek *thugatēr,* Sanskrit *duhitā*] —ˈ**daughterhood** *n.* —ˈ**daughterless** *adj.* —ˈ**daughter-ˌlike** *adj.* —ˈ**daughterliness** *n.* —ˈ**daughterly** *adj.*
daughter-in-law *n., pl.* **daughters-in-law.** the wife of one's son.
daunt (dɔːnt) *vb.* (*tr.*; *often passive*) **1.** to intimidate. **2.** to dishearten. [C13: from Old French *danter,* changed from *donter* to conquer, from Latin *domitāre* to tame] —ˈ**daunter** *n.* —ˈ**daunting** *adj.* —ˈ**dauntingly** *adv.*
dauntless (ˈdɔːntlɪs) *adj.* bold; fearless; intrepid. —ˈ**dauntlessly** *adv.* —ˈ**dauntlessness** *n.*
dauphin (ˈdɔːfɪn; *French* dofɛ̃) *n.* (from 1349–1830) the title of the direct heir to the French throne; the eldest son of the king of

France. [C15: from Old French: originally a family name; adopted as a title by the Counts of Vienne and later by the French crown princes]

dauphine (ˈdɔːfiːn; *French* dofin) *or* **dauphiness** (ˈdɔːfɪnɪs) *n. French history.* the wife of a dauphin.

daur (dɔːr) *vb.* a Scot. word for **dare.**

daven (ˈdɑvən) *vb. (intr.) Judaism.* **1.** to pray. **2.** to lead prayers. [from Yiddish]

davenport (ˈdævənˌpɔːt) *n.* **1.** *Chiefly Brit.* a tall narrow desk with a slanted writing surface and drawers at the side. **2.** *U.S. and Canadian.* a large sofa, esp. one convertible into a bed. [C19: sense 1 said to be named after Captain *Davenport* who commissioned the first ones]

Davis Cup (ˈdeɪvɪs) *n.* **1.** an annual international lawn tennis championship for men's teams. **2.** the trophy awarded for this. [C20: after Dwight F. *Davis* (1879–1945), American civic leader who donated the cup]

davit (ˈdævɪt, ˈdeɪ-) *n.* a cranelike device, usually one of a pair, fitted with a tackle for suspending or lowering equipment, esp. a lifeboat. [C14: from Anglo-French *daviot,* diminutive of *Davi* David]

Davy Jones (ˈdeɪvɪ ˈdʒəʊnz) *n.* **1.** Also called: **Davy Jones's locker.** the ocean's bottom, esp. when regarded as the grave of those lost or buried at sea. **2.** the spirit or devil of the sea. [C18: of unknown origin]

Davy lamp *n.* See **safety lamp.** [C19: named after Sir Humphrey *Davy* (1778–1829), British chemist who invented it]

daw (dɔː) *n.* an archaic, dialect, or poetic name for a **jackdaw.** [C15: related to Old High German *taha*]

dawdle (ˈdɔːdᵊl) *vb.* **1.** *(intr.)* to be slow or lag behind. **2.** (when *tr.*, often foll. by *away*) to waste (time); trifle. [C17: of uncertain origin] —ˈ**dawdler** *n.* —ˈ**dawdlingly** *adv.*

dawk (dɔːk) *n.* a variant spelling of **dak.**

dawn (dɔːn) *n.* **1.** daybreak; sunrise. Related adj.: **auroral. 2.** the sky when light first appears in the morning. **3.** the beginning of something. ~*vb. (intr.)* **4.** to begin to grow light after the night. **5.** to begin to develop, appear, or expand. **6.** (usually foll. by *on* or *upon*) to begin to become apparent (to). [Old English *dagian* to dawn; see DAY] —ˈ**dawnˌlike** *adj.*

dawn chorus *n.* the singing of large numbers of birds at dawn.

dawney (ˈdɑːniː) *adj. Irish.* (of a person) dull or slow; listless. [of unknown origin]

dawn raid *n. Stock Exchange.* an unexpected attempt to acquire a substantial proportion of a company's shares at the start of a day's trading as a preliminary to a takeover bid.

dawn redwood *n.* a deciduous conifer, *Metasequoia glyptostroboides,* native to China but planted in other regions as an ornamental tree: family *Taxodiaceae.* Until recently it was thought to be extinct.

day (deɪ) *n.* **1.** Also called: **civil day.** the period of time, the **calendar day,** of 24 hours duration reckoned from one midnight to the next. **2.** the period of light between sunrise and sunset, as distinguished from the night. **3.** the part of a day occupied with regular activity, esp. work: *he took a day off.* **4.** *(sometimes pl.)* a period or point in time: *he was a good singer in his day; in days gone by; any day now.* **5.** the period of time, the **sidereal day,** during which the earth makes one complete revolution on its axis relative to a particular star. The **mean sidereal day** lasts 23 hours 56 minutes 4.1 seconds of the mean solar day. **6.** the period of time, the **solar day,** during which the earth makes one complete revolution on its axis relative to the sun. The **mean solar day** is the average length of the apparent solar day and is some four minutes (3 minutes 56.5 seconds of sidereal time) longer than the sidereal day. **7.** the period of time taken by a specified planet to make one complete rotation on its axis: *the Martian day.* **8.** *(often cap.)* a day designated for a special observance, esp. a holiday: *Christmas Day.* **9. all in a day's work.** part of one's normal activity; no trouble. **10. at the end of the day.** in the final reckoning. **11. day of rest.** the Sabbath; Sunday. **12. end one's days.** to pass the end of one's life. **13. every dog has his day.** one's luck will come. **14. in this day and age.** nowadays. **15. it's early days.** it's too early to tell how things will turn out. **16. late in the day. a.** very late (in a particular situation). **b.** too late. **17. that will be the day. a.** I look forward to that. **b.** that is most unlikely to happen. **18.** a time of success, recognition, power, etc.: *his day will soon come.* **19.** a struggle or issue at hand: *the day is lost.* **20. a.** the ground surface over a mine. **b.** *(as modifier): the day level.* **21. from day to day.** without thinking of the future. **22. call it a day.** to stop work or other activity. **23. day after day.** without respite; relentlessly. **24. day by day.** gradually or progressively; daily: *he weakened day by day.* **25. day in, day out.** every day and all day long. **26. from Day I** *or* **Day One.** from the very beginning. **27. one of these days.** at some future time. **28.** *(modifier)* of, relating to, or occurring in the day: *the day shift.* ~Related adj.: **diurnal.** See also **days.** [Old English *dæg;* related to Old High German *tag,* Old Norse *dagr*]

Dayak (ˈdaɪæk) *n., pl.* **-aks** *or* **-ak.** a variant spelling of **Dyak.**

dayan (dɑˈjɑn, ˈdɑjən) *n. Judaism.* a senior rabbi, esp. one who sits in a religious court. [from Hebrew, literally: judge]

day bed *n.* a narrow bed, with a head piece and sometimes a foot piece and back, on which to recline during the day.

day blindness *n.* a nontechnical name for **hemeralopia.**

daybook (ˈdeɪˌbʊk) *n. Book-keeping.* a book in which the transactions of each day are recorded as they occur.

dayboy (ˈdeɪˌbɔɪ) *n. Brit.* a boy who attends a boarding school daily, but returns home each evening.

daybreak (ˈdeɪˌbreɪk) *n.* the time in the morning when light first appears; dawn; sunrise.

daycare (ˈdeɪˌkɛə) *n. Social welfare.* **1.** *Brit.* occupation, treatment, or supervision during the working day for people who might be at risk if left on their own, or whose usual carers need daytime relief. **2.** *Brit.* welfare services provided by a local authority, health service, or voluntary body during the day. Compare **residential care. 3.** *N.Z.* short for **daycare centre.**

daycare centre *n.* another name (esp. U.S. and N.Z.) for **day nursery.**

daycentre (ˈdeɪˌsɛntə) *or* **day centre** *n. Social welfare.* (in Britain) **1.** a building used for daycare or other welfare services. See also **drop-in centre. 2.** the enterprise itself, including staff, users, and organization.

day-clean *n. Caribbean and West African informal.* the time after first dawn when the sun begins to shine; clear daybreak.

daydream (ˈdeɪˌdriːm) *n.* **1.** a pleasant dreamlike fantasy indulged in while awake; idle reverie. **2.** a pleasant scheme or wish that is unlikely to be fulfilled; pipe dream. ~*vb.* **3.** *(intr.)* to have daydreams; indulge in idle fantasy. —ˈ**dayˌdreamer** *n.* —ˈ**dayˌdreamy** *adj.*

dayflower (ˈdeɪˌflaʊə) *n.* any of various tropical and subtropical plants of the genus *Commelina,* having jointed creeping stems, narrow pointed leaves, and blue or purplish flowers which wilt quickly: family *Commelinaceae.*

dayfly (ˈdeɪˌflaɪ) *n., pl.* **-flies.** another name for a **mayfly.**

Day-Glo *n. Trademark.* **a.** a brand of fluorescent colouring materials, as of paint. **b.** *(as modifier): Day-Glo colours.*

day hospital *n. Brit.* part of a hospital that offers therapeutic services, where patients usually attend all day but go home or to a hospital ward at night.

day labourer *n.* an unskilled worker hired and paid by the day.

daylight (ˈdeɪˌlaɪt) *n.* **1. a.** light from the sun. **b.** *(as modifier): daylight film.* **2.** the period when it is light; daytime. **3.** daybreak. **4. see daylight. a.** to understand something previously obscure. **b.** to realize that the end of a difficult task is approaching. ~See also **daylights.**

daylight lamp *n. Physics.* a lamp whose light has a range of wavelengths similar to that of natural sunlight.

daylight robbery *n. Informal.* blatant overcharging.

daylights (ˈdeɪˌlaɪts) *pl. n.* consciousness or wits (esp. in the phrases **scare, knock,** or **beat the (living) daylights out of someone**).

daylight-saving time *n.* time set usually one hour ahead of the local standard time, widely adopted in the summer to provide extra daylight in the evening. Also called (in the U.S.): **daylight time.** See also **British Summer Time.**

day lily *n.* **1.** any widely cultivated Eurasian liliaceous plant of the genus *Hemerocallis,* having large yellow, orange, or red lily-like flowers, which typically last for only one day and are immediately succeeded by others. **2.** the flower of any of these plants.

daylong (ˈdeɪˌlɒŋ) *adj., adv.* lasting the entire day; all day.

day name *n. W African.* a name indicating a person's day of birth.

day-neutral *adj.* (of plants) having an ability to mature and bloom that is not affected by day length.

day nursery *n. Social welfare, Brit. and N.Z.* an establishment offering daycare to preschool children, enabling their parents to work full time or have extended relief if child care is a problem. Also called (N.Z.): **daycare centre.**

Day of Atonement *n.* another name for **Yom Kippur.**

Day of Judgment *n.* another name for **Judgment Day.**

day of reckoning *n.* a time when the effects of one's past mistakes or misdeeds catch up with one.

day release *n. Brit.* a system whereby workers are released for part-time education without loss of pay.

day return *n.* a reduced fare for a journey (by train, etc.) travelling both ways in one day.

day room *n.* a communal living room in a residential institution such as a hospital.

days (deɪz) *adv. Informal.* during the day, esp. regularly: *he works days.*

day school *n.* **1.** a private school taking day students only. Compare **boarding school. 2.** a school giving instruction during the daytime. Compare **night school.**

day shift *n.* **1.** a group of workers who work a shift during the daytime in an industry or occupation where a night shift or a back shift is also worked. **2.** the period worked. ~See also **back shift.**

Days of Awe *pl. n. Judaism.* another name for **High Holidays.** [a literal translation of YAMIM NORA'IM]

days of grace *pl. n.* days permitted by custom for payment of a promissory note, bill of exchange, etc., after it falls due.

dayspring (ˈdeɪˌsprɪŋ) *n.* a poetic word for **dawn.**

daystar (ˈdeɪˌstɑː) *n.* **1.** a poetic word for the **sun. 2.** another word for the **morning star.**

daytime (ˈdeɪˌtaɪm) *n.* the time between dawn and dusk; the day as distinct from evening or night.

day-to-day *adj.* routine; everyday: *day-to-day chores.*
day trip *n.* a journey made to and from a place within one day. —'**day-ˌtripper** *n.*
daze (deɪz) *vb.* (*tr.*) **1.** to stun or stupefy, esp. by a blow or shock. **2.** to bewilder, amaze, or dazzle. ~*n.* **3.** a state of stunned confusion or shock (esp. in the phrase **in a daze**). [C14: from Old Norse *dasa-*, as in *dasast* to grow weary] —**dazedly** ('deɪzɪdlɪ) *adv.*
dazzle ('dæzᵊl) *vb.* **1.** (*usually tr.*) to blind or be blinded partially and temporarily by sudden excessive light. **2.** to amaze, as with brilliance: *she was dazzled by his wit; she dazzles in this film.* ~*n.* **3.** bright light that dazzles. **4.** bewilderment caused by glamour, brilliance, etc.: *the dazzle of fame.* [C15: from DAZE] —'**dazzling** *adj.* —'**dazzlingly** *adv.*
dB *or* **db** *symbol for* decibel *or* decibels.
DBE *abbrev. for* Dame Commander of the Order of the British Empire (a Brit. title).
Dbh *or* **DBH** *Forestry. abbrev. for* diameter at breast height.
DBib *abbrev. for* Douay Bible.
DBMS *abbrev. for* database management system.
DBS *abbrev. for:* **1.** direct broadcasting by satellite. **2.** direct broadcasting satellite.
dbx *or* **DBX** *n. Trademark. Electronics.* a noise-reduction system that works as a compander across the full frequency spectrum.
DC *abbrev. for:* **1.** *Music.* da capo. **2.** direct current. Compare **AC.** **3.** district commissioner. **4.** Also: **D.C.** District of Columbia.
DCB *abbrev. for* Dame Commander of the Order of the Bath (a Brit. title).
DCF *Account. abbrev. for* discounted cash flow.
DCL *abbrev. for* Doctor of Civil Law.
DCM *Brit. military. abbrev. for* Distinguished Conduct Medal.
DCMG *abbrev. for* Dame Commander of the Order of St Michael and St George (a Brit. title).
DCVO *abbrev. for* Dame Commander of the Royal Victorian Order (a Brit. title).
DD *abbrev. for* Doctor of Divinity.
D-day *n.* **1.** the day, June 6, 1944, on which the Allied invasion of Europe began. **2.** the day on which any large-scale operation is planned to start. [C20: from *D(ay)-day;* compare H-HOUR]
DDR *abbrev. for* Deutsche Demokratische Republik (the former East Germany; GDR).
DDS *abbrev. for:* **1.** Dewey Decimal System. **2.** Doctor of Dental Surgery.
DDSc *abbrev. for* Doctor of Dental Science.
DDT *n.* dichlorodiphenyltrichloroethane; a colourless odourless substance used as an insecticide. It is toxic to animals and is known to accumulate in the tissues. It is now banned in the UK.
de, De *or before a vowel* **d', D'** (də) of; from: occurring as part of some personal names and originally indicating place of origin: *Simon de Montfort; D'Arcy; de la Mare.* [from Latin *dē;* see DE-]
DE *abbrev. for:* **1.** (in Britain) Department of Employment. **2.** Delaware.
de- *prefix forming verbs and verbal derivatives.* **1.** removal of or from something specified: *deforest; dethrone.* **2.** reversal of something: *decode; decompose; desegregate.* **3.** departure from: *decamp.* [from Latin, from *dē* (prep.) from, away from, out of, etc. In compound words of Latin origin, *de-* also means away, away from (*decease*); down (*degrade*); reversal (*detect*); removal (*defoliate*); and is used intensively (*devote*) and pejoratively (*detest*)]
deacon ('diːkən) *n. Christianity.* **1.** (in the Roman Catholic and other episcopal churches) an ordained minister ranking immediately below a priest. **2.** (in Protestant churches) a lay official appointed or elected to assist the minister, esp. in secular affairs. **3.** *Scot.* the president of an incorporated trade or body of craftsmen in a burgh. [Old English, ultimately from Greek *diakonos* servant] —'**deaconˌship** *n.*
deaconess ('diːkənɪs) *n. Christianity.* (in the early church and in some modern Churches) a female member of the laity with duties similar to those of a deacon.
deaconry ('diːkənrɪ) *n., pl.* **-ries.** **1.** the office or status of a deacon. **2.** deacons collectively.
deactivate (diː'æktɪˌveɪt) *vb.* **1.** (*tr.*) to make (a bomb, etc.) harmless or inoperative. **2.** (*intr.*) to become less radioactive. **3.** (*tr.*) *U.S.* to end the active status of (a military unit). **4.** *Chem.* to return or cause to return from an activated state to a normal or ground state. —**deˌacti'vation** *n.* —**de'actiˌvator** *n.*
dead (dɛd) *adj.* **1. a.** no longer alive. **b.** (*as n.*): *the dead.* **2.** not endowed with life; inanimate. **3.** no longer in use, valid, effective, or relevant: *a dead issue; a dead language.* **4.** unresponsive or unaware; insensible: *he is dead to my strongest pleas.* **5.** lacking in freshness, interest, or vitality: *a dead handshake.* **6.** devoid of physical sensation; numb: *his gums were dead from the anaesthetic.* **7.** resembling death; deathlike: *a dead sleep.* **8.** no longer burning or hot: *dead coals.* **9.** (of flowers or foliage) withered; faded. **10.** (*prenominal*) (intensifier): *a dead stop; a dead loss.* **11.** *Informal.* very tired. **12.** *Electronics.* **a.** drained of electric charge; discharged: *the battery was dead.* **b.** not connected to a source of potential difference or electric charge. **13.** lacking acoustic reverberation: *a dead sound; a dead surface.* **14.** *Sport.* (of a ball, etc.) out of play. **15.** unerring; accurate; precise (esp. in the phrase **a dead shot**). **16.** lacking resilience or bounce: *a dead ball.* **17.** *Printing.* **a.** (of type) set but no longer needed for use. Compare **standing** (sense 7). **b.** (of copy) already composed. **18.** not yielding a return; idle: *dead capital.* **19.** *Informal.* certain to suffer a terrible fate; doomed: *you're dead if your mother catches you at that.* **20.** (of colours) not glossy or bright; lacklustre. **21.** stagnant: *dead air.* **22.** *Military.* shielded from view, as by a geographic feature or environmental condition: *a dead zone; dead space.* **23. dead as a doornail.** *Informal.* completely dead. **24. dead from the neck up.** *Informal.* stupid or unintelligent. **25. dead to the world.** *Informal.* unaware of one's surroundings, esp. fast asleep or very drunk. **26. leave for dead.** *Informal.* to outdistance by far. **27. wouldn't be seen dead (in, at,** etc.). *Informal.* to refuse to wear, to go (to), etc. ~*n.* **28.** a period during which coldness, darkness, or some other quality associated with death is at its most intense: *the dead of winter.* ~*adv.* **29.** (intensifier): *dead easy; stop dead; dead level.* **30. dead on.** exactly right. [Old English *dēad;* related to Old High German *tōt,* Old Norse *dauthr;* see DIE[1]] —'**deadness** *n.*
dead-and-alive *adj. Brit.* (of a place, activity, or person) dull; uninteresting.
dead-ball line *n. Rugby.* a line not more than 22 metres behind the goal line at each end of the field beyond which the ball is out of play.
deadbeat ('dɛdˌbiːt) *n.* **1.** *Informal, chiefly U.S. and Canadian.* a lazy or socially undesirable person. **2.** a high grade escapement used in pendulum clocks. **3.** (*modifier*) (of a clock escapement) having a beat without any recoil. **4.** (*modifier*) *Physics.* **a.** (of a system) returning to an equilibrium position with little or no oscillation. **b.** (of an instrument or indicator) indicating a true reading without oscillation.
dead beat *adj. Informal.* tired out; exhausted.
deadboy ('dɛdˌbɔɪ) *n.* See **deadman** (sense 2).
dead-cat bounce *n. Stock exchange informal.* a temporary recovery in prices following a substantial fall as a result of speculators buying stocks they have already sold rather than as a result of a genuine reversal of the downward trend.
dead centre *n.* **1.** the exact top (**top dead centre**) or bottom (**bottom dead centre**) of the piston stroke in a reciprocating engine or pump. **2.** a nonrotating pointed rod mounted in the tailstock or headstock of a lathe to support a workpiece. ~Also called: **dead point.**
dead duck *n. Slang.* a person or thing doomed to death, failure, etc., esp. because of a mistake or misjudgment.
deaden ('dɛdᵊn) *vb.* **1.** to make or become less sensitive, intense, lively, etc; damp or be damped down; dull. **2.** (*tr.*) to make acoustically less resonant: *he deadened the room with heavy curtains.* —'**deadener** *n.* —'**deadening** *adj.*
dead end *n.* **1.** another name for **cul-de-sac.** **2.** a situation in which further progress is impossible. **3.** (*as modifier*): *a dead-end street; a dead-end job.*
deadeye ('dɛdˌaɪ) *n.* **1.** *Nautical.* either of a pair of disclike wooden blocks, supported by straps in grooves around them, between which a line is rove so as to draw them together to tighten a shroud. Compare **bull's-eye** (sense 9). **2.** *Informal, chiefly U.S.* an expert marksman.
deadfall ('dɛdˌfɔːl) *n.* a type of trap, used esp. for catching large animals, in which a heavy weight falls to crush the prey. Also called: **downfall.**
dead fingers *n.* (*functioning as sing.*) *Med.* a disease of users of pneumatic drills, characterized by anaesthesia of the fingertips and cyanosis.
dead finish *n. Austral.* **1.** *Informal.* the last straw; the extreme of tolerance. **2.** any of various trees or shrubs, esp. *Acacia tetragonophylla,* of Australia, that form impenetrable thickets.
dead hand *n.* **1.** an oppressive or discouraging influence or factor: *the dead hand of centralized control.* **2.** *Law.* a less common word for **mortmain.**
deadhead ('dɛdˌhɛd) *n.* **1.** a dull unenterprising person. **2.** a person who uses a free ticket, as for a train, the theatre, etc. **3.** *U.S. and Canadian.* a train, etc., travelling empty. ~*vb.* **4.** (*tr.*) to cut off withered flowers from (a plant). **5.** (*intr.*) *U.S. and Canadian.* to drive an empty bus, train, etc.
dead heat *n.* **a.** a race or contest in which two or more participants tie for first place. **b.** a tie between two or more contestants in any position.
dead key *n.* a key on the keyboard of a typewriter which does not automatically advance the carriage when depressed.
dead leg *n. Informal.* temporary loss of sensation in the leg, caused by a blow to a muscle.
dead letter *n.* **1.** a letter that cannot be delivered or returned because it lacks adequate directions. **2.** a law or ordinance that is no longer enforced but has not been formally repealed. **3.** *Informal.* anything considered as gone, forgotten, or no longer worthy of consideration.
dead letter box *or* **drop** *n.* a place where messages and other material can be left and collected secretly without the sender and the recipient meeting.
deadlight ('dɛdˌlaɪt) *n.* **1.** *Nautical.* **a.** a bull's-eye let into the deck or hull of a vessel to admit light to a cabin. **b.** a shutter of wood or metal for sealing off a porthole or cabin window. **2.** a skylight designed not to be opened.
deadline ('dɛdˌlaɪn) *n.* a time limit for any activity.

dead load *n.* the intrinsic invariable weight of a structure, such as a bridge. Also called: **dead weight.** Compare **live load.**

deadlock ('dɛd,lɒk) *n.* **1.** a state of affairs in which further action between two opposing forces is impossible; stalemate. **2.** a tie between opposite sides in a contest. **3.** a lock having a bolt that can be opened only with a key. ~*vb.* **4.** to bring or come to a deadlock.

dead loss *n.* **1.** *Informal.* a person, thing, or situation that is completely useless or unprofitable. **2.** a complete loss for which no compensation is received.

deadly ('dɛdlɪ) *adj.* **-lier, -liest. 1.** likely to cause death: *deadly poison; deadly combat.* **2.** *Informal.* extremely boring. ~*adv., adj.* **3.** like death in appearance or certainty: *deadly pale; a deadly sleep.* —'**deadliness** *n.*

deadly nightshade *n.* a poisonous Eurasian solanaceous plant, *Atropa belladonna,* having dull purple bell-shaped flowers and small very poisonous black berries. Also called: **belladonna, dwale.**

deadly sins *pl. n. Theol.* the sins of pride, covetousness, lust, envy, gluttony, anger, and sloth.

deadman ('dɛd,mæn) *n., pl.* **-men. 1.** *Civil engineering.* a heavy plate, wall, or block buried in the ground that acts as an anchor for a retaining wall, sheet pile, etc., by a tie connecting the two. **2.** *Mountaineering.* a metal plate with a wire loop attached for thrusting into firm snow to serve as a belay point, a smaller version being known as a **deadboy.**

dead man's fingers *n. (functioning as sing.)* a soft coral, *Alcyonium digitatum,* with long finger-like polyps.

dead man's handle *or* **pedal** *n.* a safety switch on a piece of machinery, such as a train, that allows operation only while depressed by the operator.

dead march *n.* a piece of solemn funeral music played to accompany a procession, esp. at military funerals.

dead marine *n. Austral. and N.Z. informal.* an empty beer bottle.

dead-nettle *n.* any Eurasian plant of the genus *Lamium,* such as *L. alba* (white dead-nettle), having leaves resembling nettles but lacking stinging hairs: family *Labiatae* (labiates).

deadpan ('dɛd,pæn) *adj., adv.* with a deliberately emotionless face or manner: *deadpan humour.*

dead point *n.* another name for **dead centre.**

dead reckoning *n.* a method of establishing one's position using the distance and direction travelled rather than astronomical observations.

dead set *adv.* **1.** absolutely: *he is dead set against going to Spain.* ~*n.* **2.** the motionless position of a dog when pointing with its muzzle towards game. ~*adj.* **3.** (of a hunting dog) in this position. ~*interj.* **4.** *Austral. slang.* an expression of affirmation: *dead set, I worked from dawn to dusk.*

dead-smooth file *n. Engineering.* the smoothest grade of file commonly used.

dead stock *n.* farm equipment. Compare **livestock.**

dead time *n. Electronics.* the interval of time immediately following a stimulus, during which an electrical device, component, etc., is insensitive to a further stimulus.

dead weight *n.* **1.** a heavy weight or load. **2.** an oppressive burden; encumbrance. **3.** the difference between the loaded and the unloaded weights of a ship. **4.** another name for **dead load. 5.** (in shipping) freight chargeable by weight rather than by bulk.

deadwood ('dɛd,wʊd) *n.* **1.** dead trees or branches. **2.** *Informal.* a useless person; encumbrance. **3.** *Nautical.* a filler piece between the keel and the stern of a wooden vessel.

deaf (dɛf) *adj.* **1. a.** partially or totally unable to hear. **b.** (*as collective n.;* preceded by *the*): *the deaf.* ~See also **tone-deaf. 2.** refusing to heed: *deaf to the cries of the hungry.* [Old English *dēaf;* related to Old Norse *daufr*] —'**deafly** *adv.* —'**deafness** *n.*

deaf aid *n.* another name for **hearing aid.**

deaf-and-dumb *Offensive.* ~*adj.* **1.** unable to hear or speak. ~*n.* **2.** a deaf-mute person.

deafen ('dɛfᵊn) *vb.* (*tr.*) to make deaf, esp. momentarily, as by a loud noise. —'**deafeningly** *adv.*

deaf-mute *n.* **1.** a person who is unable to hear or speak. See also **mute**[1] (sense 7), **mutism** (sense 2b). ~*adj.* **2.** unable to hear or speak. [C19: translation of French *sourd-muet*] —'**deaf,muteness** *or* '**deaf-,mutism** *n.*

deaf without speech *adj.* **a.** (usually of a prelingually deaf person) able to utter sounds but not speak. **b.** (*as collective n.;* preceded by *the*): *the deaf without speech.*

deal[1] (diːl) *vb.* **deals, dealing, dealt** (dɛlt). **1.** (*intr.*) (foll. by *in*) to engage (in) commercially: *to deal in upholstery.* **2.** (often foll. by *out*) to apportion (something, such as cards) to a number of people; distribute. **3.** (*tr.*) to give (a blow) to (someone); inflict. **4.** (*intr.*) *Slang.* to sell any illegal drug. ~*n.* **5.** *Informal.* a bargain, transaction, or agreement. **6.** a particular type of treatment received, esp. as the result of an agreement: *a fair deal.* **7.** an indefinite amount, extent, or degree (esp. in the phrases **good** *or* **great deal**). **8.** *Cards.* **a.** the process of distributing the cards. **b.** a player's turn to do this. **c.** a single round in a card game. **9.** See **big deal.** ~See also **deal with.** [Old English *dǣlan,* from *dǣl* a part; compare Old High German *teil* a part, Old Norse *deild* a share]

deal[2] (diːl) *n.* **1.** a plank of softwood timber, such as fir or pine, or such planks collectively. **2.** the sawn wood of various coniferous trees, such as that from the Scots pine (**red deal**) or from the Norway Spruce (**white deal**). ~*adj.* **3.** of fir or pine. [C14: from Middle Low German *dele* plank; see THILL]

dealate ('diːeɪ,leɪt, -lɪt) *or* **dealated** ('diːeɪ,leɪtɪd) *adj.* (of ants and other insects) having lost their wings, esp. by biting or rubbing them off after mating. —**,dea'lation** *n.*

dealer ('diːlə) *n.* **1.** a person or firm engaged in commercial purchase and sale; trader: *a car dealer.* **2.** *Cards.* the person who distributes the cards. **3.** *Slang.* a person who sells illegal drugs. —'**dealer,ship** *n.*

dealfish ('diːl,fɪʃ) *n., pl.* **-fish** *or* **-fishes.** any soft-finned deep-sea teleost fish of the genus *Trachipterus,* esp. *T. arcticus,* related to the ribbonfishes and having a very long tapelike body and a fan-shaped tail fin.

dealings ('diːlɪŋz) *pl. n.* (*sometimes sing.*) transactions or business relations.

dealt (dɛlt) *vb.* the past tense and past participle of **deal**[1].

deal with *vb.* (*tr., adv.*) **1.** to take action on: *to deal with each problem in turn.* **2.** to punish: *the headmaster will deal with the culprit.* **3.** to treat or be concerned with: *the book deals with medieval architecture.* **4.** to conduct oneself (towards others), esp. with regard to fairness: *he can be relied on to deal fairly with everyone.* **5.** to do business with: *the firm deals with many overseas suppliers.*

deaminate (diː'æmɪ,neɪt) *or* **deaminize, deaminise** *vb.* (*tr.*) to remove one or more amino groups from (a molecule). —**de,ami'nation, de,amini'zation,** *or* **de,amini'sation** *n.*

dean (diːn) *n.* **1.** the chief administrative official of a college or university faculty. **2.** (at Oxford and Cambridge universities) a college fellow with responsibility for undergraduate discipline. **3.** *Chiefly Church of England.* the head of a chapter of canons and administrator of a cathedral or collegiate church. **4.** *R.C. Church.* the cardinal bishop senior by consecration and head of the college of cardinals. Related adj.: **decanal.** See also **rural dean.** [C14: from Old French *deien,* from Late Latin *decānus* one set over ten persons, from Latin *decem* ten] —'**dean,ship** *n.*

deanery ('diːnərɪ) *n., pl.* **-eries. 1.** the office or residence of dean. **2.** the group of parishes presided over by a rural dean.

de-anglicization *or* **de-anglicisation** *n.* (in Ireland) the elimination of English influence, language, customs, etc.

Dean of Faculty *n.* the president of the Faculty of Advocates in Scotland.

dean of guild *n.* the titular head of the guild or merchant company in a Scots burgh, who formerly exercised jurisdiction over all building in the burgh in the **Dean of Guild Court.**

dear (dɪə) *adj.* **1.** beloved; precious. **2.** used in conventional forms of address preceding a title or name, as in *Dear Sir* or *my dear Mr Smith.* **3.** (*postpositive;* foll. by *to*) important; close: *a wish dear to her heart.* **4. a.** highly priced. **b.** charging high prices. **5.** appealing or pretty: *what a dear little ring!* **6. for dear life.** urgently or with extreme vigour or desperation. ~*interj.* **7.** used in exclamations of surprise or dismay, such as *Oh dear!* and *dear me!* ~*n.* **8.** (*often used in direct address*) someone regarded with affection and tenderness; darling. ~*adv.* **9.** dearly: *his errors have cost him dear.* [Old English *dēore;* related to Old Norse *dȳrr*] —'**dearness** *n.*

Dear John letter *n. Informal.* a letter from a girl breaking off a love affair.

dearly ('dɪəlɪ) *adv.* **1.** very much: *I would dearly like you to go.* **2.** affectionately. **3.** at a great cost.

dearth (dɜːθ) *n.* an inadequate amount, esp. of food; scarcity. [C13 *derthe,* from *dēr* DEAR]

deary *or* **dearie** ('dɪərɪ) *n.* **1.** (*pl.* **dearies**) *Informal.* a term of affection: now often sarcastic or facetious. **2. deary** *or* **dearie me!** an exclamation of surprise or dismay.

deasil ('diːzᵊl, 'diːʃᵊl) *Scot.* ~*adv.* **1.** in the direction of the apparent course of the sun; clockwise. ~*n.* **2.** motion in this direction. ~Compare **withershins.** [C18: Scot. Gaelic *deiseil*]

death (dɛθ) *n.* **1.** the permanent end of all functions of life in an organism or some of its cellular components. **2.** an instance of this: *his death ended an era.* **3.** a murder or killing: *he had five deaths on his conscience.* **4.** termination or destruction: *the death of colonialism.* **5.** a state of affairs or an experience considered as terrible as death: *your constant nagging will be the death of me.* **6.** a cause or source of death. **7.** (*usually cap.*) a personification of death, usually a skeleton or an old man holding a scythe. **8. to death** *or* **to the death.** until dead: *bleed to death; a fight to the death.* **9. at death's door.** likely to die soon. **10. catch one's death (of cold).** *Informal.* to contract a severe cold. **11. do to death. a.** to kill. **b.** to overuse (a joke, etc.) so that it no longer has any effect. **12. in at the death. a.** present when an animal that is being hunted is caught and killed. **b.** present at the finish or climax. **13. like death warmed up.** *Informal.* very ill. **14. like grim death.** as if afraid of one's life. **15. put to death.** to kill deliberately or execute. ~Related adjs.: **fatal, lethal, mortal.** [Old English *dēath;* related to Old High German *tōd* death, Gothic *dauthus*]

death adder *n.* a venomous Australian elapid snake, *Acanthophis antarcticus,* resembling an adder.

deathbed ('dɛθ,bɛd) *n.* **1. a.** the bed in which a person is about to die. **b.** (*as modifier*): *a deathbed conversion.* **2. on one's deathbed.** about to die.

deathblow ('dɛθ,bləʊ) *n.* a thing or event that destroys life or hope, esp. suddenly.

death camp *n.* a concentration camp in which the conditions are so brutal that few prisoners survive, or one to which prisoners are sent for execution.
death cap *or* **angel** *n.* a poisonous woodland saprophytic basidiomycetous fungus, *Amanita phalloides,* differing from the edible mushroom (*Agaricus*) in its white gills (pinkish-brown in *Agaricus*) and the presence of a volva. See also **amanita.**
death cell *n.* a prison cell for criminals sentenced to death.
death certificate *n.* a legal document issued by a qualified medical practitioner certifying the death of a person and stating the cause if known.
death-dealing *adj.* fatal; lethal.
death duty *n.* a tax on property inheritances: in Britain, replaced in 1975 by capital transfer tax and since 1986 by inheritance tax. Also called: **estate duty.**
death grant *n.* (in the British National Insurance scheme) a grant payable to a relative, executor, etc., after the death of a person.
death knell *or* **bell** *n.* **1.** something that heralds death or destruction. **2.** a bell rung to announce a death.
deathless ('dɛθlɪs) *adj.* immortal, esp. because of greatness; everlasting. —'**deathlessly** *adv.* —'**deathlessness** *n.*
deathly ('dɛθlɪ) *adj.* **1.** deadly. **2.** resembling death: *a deathly quiet.* —'**deathliness** *n.*
death mask *n.* a cast of a person's face taken shortly after death. Compare **life mask.**
death penalty *n.* (often preceded by *the*) capital punishment.
death rate *n.* the ratio of deaths in a specified area, group, etc., to the population of that area, group, etc. Also called (esp. U.S.): **mortality rate.**
death rattle *n.* a low-pitched gurgling sound sometimes made by a dying person, caused by air passing through an accumulation of mucus in the trachea.
death ray *n.* an imaginary ray capable of killing.
death row *or* **house** *n. U.S.* the part of a prison where those sentenced to death are confined.
death seat *n. U.S. and Austral. slang.* the seat beside the driver of a vehicle.
death's-head *n.* a human skull or a representation of one.
death's-head moth *n.* a European hawk moth, *Acherontia atropos,* having markings resembling a human skull on its upper thorax.
deathtrap ('dɛθˌtræp) *n.* a building, vehicle, etc., that is considered very unsafe.
death warrant *n.* **1.** the official authorization for carrying out a sentence of death. **2. sign one's (own) death warrant.** to cause one's own destruction.
deathwatch ('dɛθˌwɒtʃ) *n.* **1.** a vigil held beside a dying or dead person. **2. deathwatch beetle.** a beetle, *Xestobium rufovillosum,* whose woodboring larvae are a serious pest. The adult produces a rapid tapping sound with its head that was once popularly supposed to presage death. See also **anobiid.**
death wish *n.* (in Freudian psychology) the desire for self-annihilation. See also **Thanatos.**
deave (diːv) *vb.* (*tr.*) *Scot.* **1.** to deafen. **2.** to bewilder or weary (a person) with noise. [Old English *dēafian*]
deb (dɛb) *n. Informal.* short for **debutante.**
deb. *abbrev. for* debenture.
debacle (deɪ'bɑːkᵊl, dɪ-) *n.* **1.** a sudden disastrous collapse or defeat, esp. one involving a disorderly retreat; rout. **2.** the breaking up of ice in a river during spring or summer, often causing flooding. **3.** a violent rush of water carrying along debris. [C19: from French *débâcle,* from Old French *desbacler* to unbolt, ultimately from Latin *baculum* rod, staff]
debag (diː'bæg) *vb.* **-bags, -bagging, -bagged.** (*tr.*) *Brit. slang.* to remove the trousers from (someone) by force.
debar (dɪ'bɑː) *vb.* **-bars, -barring, -barred.** (*tr.*; usually foll. by *from*) to exclude from a place, a right, etc.; bar. —**de'barment** *n.*
debark[1] (dɪ'bɑːk) *vb.* a less common word for **disembark.** [C17: from French *débarquer,* from *dé-* DIS-[1] + *barque* BARQUE] —**debarkation** (ˌdiːbɑː'keɪʃən) *n.*
debark[2] (diː'bɑːk) *vb.* (*tr.*) to remove the bark from (a tree).
debase (dɪ'beɪs) *vb.* (*tr.*) to lower in quality, character, or value, as by adding cheaper metal to coins; adulterate. [C16: see DE-, BASE[2]] —**debasedness** (dɪ'beɪsɪdnɪs) *n.* —**de'basement** *n.* —**de'baser** *n.* —**de'basingly** *adv.*
debatable *or* **debateable** (dɪ'beɪtəbᵊl) *adj.* **1.** open to question; disputable. **2.** *Law.* in dispute, as land or territory to which two parties lay claim.
debate (dɪ'beɪt) *n.* **1.** a formal discussion, as in a legislative body, in which opposing arguments are put forward. **2.** discussion or dispute. **3.** the formal presentation and opposition of a specific motion, followed by a vote. ~*vb.* **4.** to discuss (a motion), esp. in a formal assembly. **5.** to deliberate upon (something): *he debated with himself whether to go.* [C13: from Old French *debatre* to discuss, argue, from Latin *battuere*] —**de'bater** *n.*
debauch (dɪ'bɔːtʃ) *vb.* **1.** (when *tr., usually passive*) to lead into a life of depraved self-indulgence. **2.** (*tr.*) to seduce (a woman). ~*n.* **3.** an instance or period of extreme dissipation. [C16: from Old French *desbaucher* to corrupt, literally: to shape (timber) roughly, from *bauch* beam, of Germanic origin] —**debauchedly** (dɪ'bɔːtʃɪdlɪ) *adv.* —**de'bauchedness** *n.* —**de'baucher** *n.* —**de'bauchery** *or* **de'bauchment** *n.*
debauchee (ˌdɛbɔː'tʃiː, -ɔː'ʃiː) *n.* a man who leads a life of reckless drinking, promiscuity, and self-indulgence.
debe ('dɛbɛ) *n. E African.* a tin. [C20: from Swahili]
debenture (dɪ'bɛntʃə) *n.* **1.** Also called: **debenture bond.** a long-term bond, bearing fixed interest and usually unsecured, issued by a company or governmental agency. **2.** a certificate acknowledging the debt of a stated sum of money to a specified person. **3.** a customs certificate providing for a refund of excise or import duty. [C15: from Latin phrase *dēbentur mihi* there are owed to me, from *dēbēre* to owe] —**de'bentured** *adj.*
debilitate (dɪ'bɪlɪˌteɪt) *vb.* (*tr.*) to make feeble; weaken. [C16: from Latin *dēbilitāre,* from *dēbilis* weak] —**deˌbili'tation** *n.* —**de'bilitative** *adj.*
debility (dɪ'bɪlɪtɪ) *n., pl.* **-ties.** weakness or infirmity.
debit ('dɛbɪt) *Accounting.* ~*n.* **1. a.** acknowledgment of a sum owing by entry on the left side of an account. **b.** the left side of an account. **c.** an entry on this side. **d.** the total of such entries. **e.** (*as modifier*): *a debit balance.* Compare **credit** (sense 10). ~*vb.* **-its, -iting, -ited. 2.** (*tr.*) **a.** to record (an item) as a debit in an account. **b.** to charge (a person or his account) with a debt. Compare **credit** (sense 17). [C15: from Latin *dēbitum* DEBT]
debit card *n.* an embossed plastic card issued by a bank or building society to enable its customers to pay for goods or services by inserting it into a computer-controlled device at the place of sale, which is connected through the telephone network to the bank or building society. It may also function as a credit card or cash card.
debonair *or* **debonnaire** (ˌdɛbə'nɛə) *adj.* (esp. of a man or his manner) **1.** suave and refined. **2.** carefree; gay. **3.** courteous and cheerful; affable. [C13: from Old French *debonaire,* from *de bon aire* having a good disposition] —ˌ**debo'nairly** *adv.* —ˌ**debo'nairness** *n.*
debouch (dɪ'baʊtʃ) *vb.* **1.** (*intr.*) (esp. of troops) to move into a more open space, as from a narrow or concealed place. **2.** (*intr.*) (of a river, glacier, etc.) to flow from a valley into a larger area or body. ~*n.* **3.** Also called: **débouché** (*French* debuʃe). *Fortifications.* an outlet or passage, as for the exit of troops. [C18: from French *déboucher,* from *dé-* DIS-[1] + *bouche* mouth, from Latin *bucca* cheek]
debouchment (dɪ'baʊtʃmənt) *n.* **1.** the act or an instance of debouching. **2.** Also called: **debouchure** (ˌdeɪbuː'ʃʊə). an outlet, mouth, or opening.
Debrett (də'brɛt) *n.* a list of the British aristocracy. In full: **Debrett's Peerage.** [C19: after J. *Debrett* (c. 1750–1822), London publisher who first issued it]
débridement (dɪ'briːdmənt, deɪ-) *n.* the surgical removal of dead tissue or cellular debris from the surface of a wound. [C19: from French, from Old French *desbrider* to unbridle, from *des-* DE- + *bride* BRIDLE]
debrief (diː'briːf) *vb.* (of a soldier, astronaut, diplomat, etc.) to make or (of his superiors) to elicit a report after a mission or event. Compare **brief** (sense 13).
debris *or* **débris** ('deɪbrɪ, 'dɛbrɪ) *n.* **1.** fragments or remnants of something destroyed or broken; rubble. **2.** a collection of loose material derived from rocks, or an accumulation of animal or vegetable matter. [C18: from French, from obsolete *debrisier* to break into pieces, from *bruisier* to shatter, of Celtic origin]
debris bug *n.* a bug of the family *Cimicidae* found where vegetable debris accumulates and feeding on small arthropods like springtails: related to the bedbugs.
de Broglie waves (də 'brəʊglɪ) *pl. n. Physics.* the set of waves that represent the behaviour of an elementary particle, or some atoms and molecules, under certain conditions. The **de Broglie wavelength,** λ, is given by $\lambda = h/mv$, where h is the Planck constant, m the mass, and v the velocity of the particle. Also called: **matter waves.** [C20: named after Louis Victor *de Broglie* (1892–1987), French physicist]
debt (dɛt) *n.* **1.** something that is owed, such as money, goods, or services. **2. bad debt.** a debt that has little or no prospect of being paid. **3.** an obligation to pay or perform something; liability. **4.** the state of owing something, esp. money, or of being under an obligation (esp. in the phrases **in debt, in (someone's) debt**). [C13: from Old French *dette,* from Latin *dēbitum,* from *dēbēre* to owe, from DE- + *habēre* to have; English spelling influenced by the Latin etymon] —'**debtless** *adj.*
debt of honour *n.* a debt that is morally but not legally binding, such as one contracted in gambling.
debtor ('dɛtə) *n.* a person or commercial enterprise that owes a financial obligation. Compare **creditor.**
debt swap *n.* See **swap** (sense 4).
debud (diː'bʌd) *vb.* **-buds, -budding, -budded.** another word for **disbud.**
debug (diː'bʌg) *Informal.* ~*vb.* **-bugs, -bugging, -bugged.** (*tr.*) **1.** to locate and remove concealed microphones from (a room, etc.). **2.** to locate and remove defects in (a device, system, plan, etc.). **3.** to remove insects from. ~*n.* **4. a.** something, esp. a computer program, that locates and removes defects in (a device, system, etc.) **b.** (*as modifier*): *a debug program.* [C20: from DE- + BUG[1]]
debunk (diː'bʌŋk) *vb.* (*tr.*) *Informal.* to expose the pretensions or falseness of, esp. by ridicule. [C20: from DE- + BUNK[2]] —**de'bunker** *n.*

deburr (diːˈbɜː) *vb.* (*tr.*) **1.** to remove burrs from (a workpiece). **2.** *Textiles.* to remove dirt and debris from (raw wool).

debus (diːˈbʌs) *vb.* **debuses, debusing, debused** *or* **debusses, debussing, debussed.** to unload (goods) or (esp. of troops) to alight from a bus.

debut (ˈdeɪbjuː, ˈdɛbjuː) *n.* **1. a.** the first public appearance of an actor, musician, etc., or the first public presentation of a show. **b.** (*as modifier*): *debut album.* **2.** the presentation of a debutante. ~*vb.* (*intr.*) **3.** to make a debut. [C18: from French *début,* from Old French *desbuter* to play first (hence: make one's first appearance), from *des-* DE- + *but* goal, target; see BUTT[2]]

debutante (ˈdɛbjʊˌtɑːnt, -ˌtænt) *n.* **1.** a young woman of upper-class background who is presented to society, usually at a formal ball. **2.** a girl or young woman regarded as being upper-class, wealthy, and of a frivolous or snobbish social set. [C19: from French, from *débuter* to lead off in a game, make one's first appearance; see DEBUT]

dec. *abbrev. for:* **1.** deceased. **2.** declaration. **3.** declension. **4.** declination. **5.** decrease. **6.** *Music.* decrescendo.

Dec. *abbrev. for* December.

deca-, deka- *or before a vowel* **dec-, dek-** *prefix.* denoting ten: *decagon.* In conjunction with scientific units the symbol **da** is used. [from Greek *deka*]

decade (ˈdɛkeɪd, dɪˈkeɪd) *n.* **1.** a period of ten consecutive years. **2.** a group or series of ten. [C15: from Old French, from Late Latin *decad-, decas,* from Greek *dekas,* from *deka* ten] —**deˈcadal** *adj.*

decadence (ˈdɛkədəns) *or* **decadency** *n.* **1.** deterioration, esp. of morality or culture; decay; degeneration. **2.** the state reached through such a process. [C16: from French, from Medieval Latin *dēcadentia,* literally: a falling away; see DECAY]

decadent (ˈdɛkədənt) *adj.* **1.** characterized by decay or decline, as in being self-indulgent or morally corrupt. **2.** belonging to a period of decline in artistic standards. ~*n.* **3.** a decadent person. **4.** (*often cap.*) one of a group of French and English writers of the late 19th century whose works were characterized by refinement of style and a tendency toward the artificial and abnormal. —ˈ**decadently** *adv.*

decaffeinate (dɪˈkæfɪˌneɪt) *vb.* (*tr.*) to remove all or part of the caffeine from (coffee, tea, etc.).

decagon (ˈdɛkəˌgɒn) *n.* a polygon having ten sides. —**decagonal** (dɪˈkægənᵊl) *adj.* —**deˈcagonally** *adv.*

decahedron (ˌdɛkəˈhiːdrən) *n.* a solid figure having ten plane faces. See also **polyhedron.** —ˌ**decaˈhedral** *adj.*

decal (dɪˈkæl, ˈdiːkæl) *n.* **1.** short for **decalcomania.** ~*vb.* **2.** to transfer (a design) by decalcomania.

decalcify (diːˈkælsɪˌfaɪ) *vb.* **-fies, -fying, -fied.** (*tr.*) to remove calcium or lime from (bones, teeth, etc.). —**decalcification** (diːˌkælsɪfɪˈkeɪʃən) *n.* —**deˈcalciˌfier** *n.*

decalcomania (dɪˌkælkəˈmeɪnɪə) *n.* **1.** the art or process of transferring a design from prepared paper onto another surface, such as china, glass or paper. **2.** a design so transferred. [C19: from French *décalcomanie,* from *décalquer* to transfer by tracing, from *dé-* DE- + *calquer* to trace + *-manie* -MANIA]

decalescence (ˌdiːkəˈlɛsᵊns) *n.* the absorption of heat when a metal is heated through a particular temperature range, caused by a change in internal crystal structure. [C19: from Late Latin *dēcalescere* to become warm, from Latin DE- + *calescere,* from *calēre* to be warm] —ˌ**decaˈlescent** *adj.*

decalitre *or U.S.* **decaliter** (ˈdɛkəˌliːtə) *n.* ten litres. One decalitre is equal to about 2.2 imperial gallons. Symbol: **dal**

decametre *or U.S.* **decameter** (ˈdɛkəˌmiːtə) *n.* ten metres. Symbol: **dam**

decamp (dɪˈkæmp) *vb.* (*intr.*) **1.** to leave a camp; break camp. **2.** to depart secretly or suddenly; abscond. —**deˈcampment** *n.*

decanal (dɪˈkeɪnᵊl) *adj.* **1.** of or relating to a dean or deanery. **2.** (of part of a choir) on the same side of a cathedral, etc., as the dean; on the S side of the choir. ~Compare **cantorial.** [C18: from Medieval Latin *decānālis, decānus* DEAN] —**deˈcanally** *or* **decanically** (dɪˈkænɪkəlɪ) *adv.*

decane (ˈdɛkeɪn) *n.* a liquid alkane hydrocarbon existing in several isomeric forms. Formula: $C_{10}H_{22}$. [C19: from DECA- + -ANE]

decanedioic acid (ˌdɛkeɪndaɪˈəʊɪk) *n.* a white crystalline carboxylic acid obtained by heating castor oil with sodium hydroxide, used in the manufacture of polyester resins and rubbers and plasticizers. Formula: $HOOC(CH_2)_8COOH$. Also called: **sebacic acid.**

decani (dɪˈkeɪnaɪ) *adj., adv. Music.* to be sung by the decanal side of a choir. Compare **cantoris.** [Latin: genitive of *decānus*]

decanoic acid (ˌdɛkəˈnəʊɪk) *n.* a white crystalline insoluble carboxylic acid with an unpleasant odour, used in perfumes and for making fruit flavours. Formula: $C_9H_{19}COOH$. Also called: **capric acid.**

decant (dɪˈkænt) *vb.* **1.** to pour (a liquid, such as wine) from one container to another, esp. without disturbing any sediment. **2.** (*tr.*) to rehouse (people) while their homes are being rebuilt or refurbished. [C17: from Medieval Latin *dēcanthāre,* from *canthus* spout, rim; see CANTHUS]

decanter (dɪˈkæntə) *n.* a stoppered bottle, usually of glass, into which a drink, such as wine, is poured for serving.

decapitate (dɪˈkæpɪˌteɪt) *vb.* (*tr.*) to behead. [C17: from Late Latin *dēcapitāre,* from Latin DE- + *caput* head] —**deˌcapiˈtation** *n.* —**deˈcapiˌtator** *n.*

decapod (ˈdɛkəˌpɒd) *n.* **1.** any crustacean of the mostly marine order *Decapoda,* having five pairs of walking limbs: includes the crabs, lobsters, shrimps, prawns, and crayfish. **2.** any cephalopod mollusc of the order *Decapoda,* having a ring of eight short tentacles and two longer ones: includes the squids and cuttlefish. ~*adj.* **3.** of, relating to, or belonging to either of these orders. **4.** (of any other animal) having ten limbs. —**decapodal** (dɪˈkæpədᵊl), **deˈcapodan,** *or* **deˈcapodous** *adj.*

decapsulate (diːˈkæpsjʊˌleɪt) *vb.* (*tr.*) *Med.* to remove a capsule from (a part or organ, esp. the kidney). —**deˌcapsuˈlation** *n.*

decarbonate (diːˈkɑːbəˌneɪt) *vb.* (*tr.*) to remove carbon dioxide from (a solution, substance, etc.). —**deˌcarbonˈation** *n.* —**deˈcarbonˌator** *n.*

decarbonize *or* **decarbonise** (diːˈkɑːbəˌnaɪz) *vb.* (*tr.*) to remove carbon from (the walls of the combustion chamber of an internal-combustion engine). Also: **decoke, decarburize.** —**deˌcarboniˈzation** *or* **deˌcarboniˈsation** *n.* —**deˈcarbonˌizer** *or* **deˈcarbonˌiser** *n.*

decarboxylase (ˌdiːkɑːˈbɒksɪˌleɪs) *n.* an enzyme that catalyses the removal of carbon dioxide from a compound.

decarboxylation (ˌdiːkɑːˌbɒksəˈleɪʃən) *n.* the removal or loss of a carboxyl group from an organic compound.

decarburize *or* **decarburise** (diːˈkɑːbjʊˌraɪz) *vb.* another word for **decarbonize.** —**deˌcarburiˈzation, deˌcarburiˈsation,** *or* **deˌcarbuˈration** *n.*

decare (ˈdɛkɛə, dɛˈkɛə) *n.* ten ares or 1000 square metres. [C19: from French *décare;* see DECA-, ARE[2]]

decastyle (ˈdɛkəˌstaɪl) *n. Architect.* a portico consisting of ten columns.

decasyllable (ˈdɛkəˌsɪləbᵊl) *n.* a word or line of verse consisting of ten syllables. —**decasyllabic** (ˌdɛkəsɪˈlæbɪk) *adj.*

decathlon (dɪˈkæθlɒn) *n.* an athletic contest for men in which each athlete competes in ten different events. Compare **pentathlon.** [C20: from DECA- + Greek *athlon* contest, prize; see ATHLETE] —**deˈcathlete** *n.*

decay (dɪˈkeɪ) *vb.* **1.** to decline or cause to decline gradually in health, prosperity, excellence, etc.; deteriorate; waste away. **2.** to rot or cause to rot as a result of bacterial, fungal, or chemical action; decompose. **3.** (*intr.*) Also: **disintegrate.** *Physics.* **a.** (of an atomic nucleus) to undergo radioactive disintegration. **b.** (of an elementary particle) to transform into two or more different elementary particles. **4.** (*intr.*) *Physics.* (of a stored charge, magnetic flux, etc.) to decrease gradually when the source of energy has been removed. ~*n.* **5.** the process of decline, as in health, mentality, beauty, etc. **6.** the state brought about by this process. **7.** decomposition, as of vegetable matter. **8.** rotten or decayed matter: *the dentist drilled out the decay.* **9.** *Physics.* **a.** See **radioactive decay. b.** a spontaneous transformation of an elementary particle into two or more different particles. **10.** *Physics.* a gradual decrease of a stored charge, magnetic flux, current, etc., when the source of energy has been removed. See also **time constant. 11.** *Music.* the fading away of a note. [C15: from Old Northern French *decaïr,* from Late Latin *dēcadere,* literally: to fall away, from Latin *cadere* to fall] —**deˈcayable** *adj.*

decd *abbrev. for* deceased.

decease (dɪˈsiːs) *n.* **1.** a more formal word for **death.** ~*vb.* **2.** (*intr.*) a more formal word for **die**[1]. [C14 (n.): from Old French *deces,* from Latin *dēcēdere* to depart]

deceased (dɪˈsiːst) *adj.* **a.** a more formal word for **dead** (sense 1). **b.** (*as n.*): *the deceased.*

decedent (dɪˈsiːdᵊnt) *n. Law, chiefly U.S.* a deceased person. [C16: from Latin *dēcēdēns* departing; see DECEASE]

deceit (dɪˈsiːt) *n.* **1.** the act or practice of deceiving. **2.** a statement, act, or device intended to mislead; fraud; trick. **3.** a tendency to deceive. [C13: from Old French *deceite,* from *deceivre* to DECEIVE]

deceitful (dɪˈsiːtfʊl) *adj.* full of deceit. —**deˈceitfully** *adv.* —**deˈceitfulness** *n.*

deceive (dɪˈsiːv) *vb.* (*tr.*) **1.** to mislead by deliberate misrepresentation or lies. **2.** to delude (oneself). **3.** to be unfaithful to (one's sexual partner). **4.** *Archaic.* to disappoint: *his hopes were deceived.* [C13: from Old French *deceivre,* from Latin *dēcipere* to ensnare, cheat, from *capere* to take] —**deˈceivable** *adj.* —**deˈceivably** *adv.* —**deˈceivableness** *or* **deˌceivaˈbility** *n.* —**deˈceiver** *n.* —**deˈceiving** *n., adj.* —**deˈceivingly** *adv.*

decelerate (diːˈsɛləˌreɪt) *vb.* to slow down or cause to slow down. [C19: from DE- + ACCELERATE] —**deˌcelerˈation** *n.* —**deˈcelerˌator** *n.*

decelerometer (dɪˌsɛləˈrɒmɪtə) *n.* an instrument for measuring deceleration.

December (dɪˈsɛmbə) *n.* the twelfth and last month of the year, consisting of 31 days. [C13: from Old French *decembre,* from Latin *december* the tenth month (the Roman year began with March), from *decem* ten]

decemvir (dɪˈsɛmvə) *n., pl.* **-virs** *or* **-viri** (-vɪˌriː). **1.** (in ancient Rome) a member of a board of ten magistrates, esp. either of the two commissions established in 451 and 450 B.C. to revise the laws. **2.** a member of any governing body composed of ten men. [C17: from Latin, from *decem* ten + *virī* men] —**deˈcemviral** *adj.*

decemvirate (dɪˈsɛmvɪrɪt, -ˌreɪt) *n.* **1.** a board of decemvirs. **2.** the rule or rank of decemvirs.

decenary *or* **decennary** (dɪ'sɛnərɪ) *adj. History.* of or relating to a tithing. [C13: from Medieval Latin *decēna* a tithing, from *decem* ten]

decencies ('diːsᵊnsɪz) *pl. n.* **1. the.** those things that are considered necessary for a decent life. **2.** another word for **proprieties.**

decency ('diːsᵊnsɪ) *n., pl.* **-cies. 1.** conformity to the prevailing standards of propriety, morality, modesty, etc. **2.** the quality of being decent.

decennial (dɪ'sɛnɪəl) *adj.* **1.** lasting for ten years. **2.** occurring every ten years. ~*n.* **3.** a tenth anniversary or its celebration. —**de'cennially** *adv.*

decennium (dɪ'sɛnɪəm) *or* **decennary** (dɪ'sɛnərɪ) *n., pl.* **-niums, -nia** (-nɪə), *or* **-naries.** a less common word for **decade.** [C17: from Latin, from *decem* ten + *annus* year]

decent ('diːsᵊnt) *adj.* **1.** polite or respectable: *a decent family.* **2.** proper and suitable; fitting: *a decent burial.* **3.** conforming to conventions of sexual behaviour; not indecent. **4.** free of oaths, blasphemy, etc.: *decent language.* **5.** good or adequate: *a decent wage.* **6.** *Informal.* kind; generous: *he was pretty decent to me.* **7.** *Informal.* sufficiently clothed to be seen by other people: *are you decent?* [C16: from Latin *decēns* suitable, from *decēre* to be fitting] —**'decently** *adv.* —**'decentness** *n.*

decentralize *or* **decentralise** (diː'sɛntrəˌlaɪz) *vb.* **1.** to reorganize (a government, industry, etc.) into smaller more autonomous units. **2.** to disperse (a concentration, as of industry or population). —**de'centralist** *n., adj.* —**deˌcentrali'zation** *or* **deˌcentrali'sation** *n.*

decentralized processing *n. Computer technol.* the use of word processing or data processing units in stand-alone or localized situations.

deception (dɪ'sɛpʃən) *n.* **1.** the act of deceiving or the state of being deceived. **2.** something that deceives; trick.

deceptive (dɪ'sɛptɪv) *adj.* **1.** likely or designed to deceive; misleading: *appearances can be deceptive.* **2.** *Music.* (of a cadence) another word for **interrupted** (sense 3). —**de'ceptively** *adv.* —**de'ceptiveness** *n.*

decerebrate *vb.* (diː'sɛrɪˌbreɪt). **1.** (*tr.*) to remove the brain or a large section of the brain or to cut the spinal cord at the level of the brain stem of (a person or animal). ~*n.* (diː'sɛrɪbrɪt). **2.** a decerebrated individual. [C19: from DE- + CEREBRO- + -ATE[1]] —**deˌcere'bration** *n.*

decern (dɪ'sɜːn) *vb.* (*tr.*) **1.** *Scots Law.* to decree or adjudge. **2.** an archaic spelling of **discern.** [C15: from Old French *decerner,* from Latin *dēcernere* to judge, from *cernere* to discern]

deci- *prefix.* denoting one tenth; 10^{-1}: *decimetre.* Symbol: d [from French *déci-*, from Latin *decimus* tenth]

deciare ('dɛsɪˌɛə) *n.* one tenth of an are or 10 square metres. [C19: from French *déciare;* see DECI-, ARE[2]]

decibel ('dɛsɪˌbɛl) *n.* **1.** a unit for comparing two currents, voltages, or power levels, equal to one tenth of a bel. **2.** a similar unit for measuring the intensity of a sound. It is equal to ten times the logarithm to the base ten of the ratio of the intensity of the sound to be measured to the intensity of some reference sound, usually the lowest audible note of the same frequency. Abbrev.: **dB.** See also **perceived noise decibel.**

decidable (dɪ'saɪdəbᵊl) *adj.* **1.** able to be decided. **2.** *Logic.* (of a formal theory) having the property that it is possible by a mechanistic procedure to determine whether or not any well-formed formula is a theorem.

decide (dɪ'saɪd) *vb.* **1.** (*may take a clause or an infinitive as object;* when *intr.,* sometimes foll. by *on* or *about*) to reach a decision: *decide what you want; he decided to go.* **2.** (*tr.*) to cause (a person) to reach a decision: *the weather decided me against going.* **3.** (*tr.*) to determine or settle (a contest or question): *he decided his future plans.* **4.** (*tr.*) to influence decisively the outcome of (a contest or question): *Borg's stamina decided the match.* **5.** (*intr.;* foll. by *for* or *against*) to pronounce a formal verdict. [C14: from Old French *decider,* from Latin *dēcīdere,* literally: to cut off, from *caedere* to cut]

decided (dɪ'saɪdɪd) *adj.* (*prenominal*) **1.** unmistakable: *a decided improvement.* **2.** determined; resolute: *a girl of decided character.* —**de'cidedly** *adv.* —**de'cidedness** *n.*

decider (dɪ'saɪdə) *n.* the point, goal, game, etc., that determines who wins a match or championship.

decidua (dɪ'sɪdjʊə) *n., pl.* **-ciduas** *or* **-ciduae** (-'sɪdjʊˌiː). the specialized mucous membrane that lines the uterus of some mammals during pregnancy: is shed, with the placenta, at parturition. [C18: from New Latin, from Latin *dēciduus* falling down; see DECIDUOUS] —**de'cidual** *or* **de'ciduate** *adj.*

deciduous (dɪ'sɪdjʊəs) *adj.* **1.** (of trees and shrubs) shedding all leaves annually at the end of the growing season. Compare **evergreen** (sense 1). **2.** (of antlers, wings, teeth, etc.) being shed at the end of a period of growth. **3.** *Rare.* impermanent; transitory. Compare **evergreen** (sense 2). [C17: from Latin *dēciduus* falling off, from *dēcidere* to fall down, from *cadere* to fall] —**de'ciduously** *adv.* —**de'ciduousness** *n.*

decile ('dɛsɪl, -aɪl) *n. Statistics.* one of nine actual or notional values of a variable dividing its distribution into ten groups with equal frequencies: the ninth decile is the value below which 90% of the population lie. See also **percentile.** [C17: from DECA- + -ILE]

decilitre *or U.S.* **deciliter** ('dɛsɪˌliːtə) *n.* one tenth of a litre. Symbol: **dl**

decillion (dɪ'sɪljən) *n.* **1.** (in Britain, France, and Germany) the number represented as one followed by 60 zeros (10^{60}). **2.** (in the U.S. and Canada) the number represented as one followed by 33 zeros (10^{33}). [C19: from Latin *decem* ten + *-illion* as in *million*] —**de'cillionth** *adj.*

decimal ('dɛsɪməl) *n.* **1.** Also called: **decimal fraction.** a fraction that has a denominator of a power of ten, the power depending on or deciding the decimal place. It is indicated by a decimal point to the left of the numerator, the denominator being omitted. Zeros are inserted between the point and the numerator, if necessary, to obtain the correct decimal place. **2.** any number used in the decimal system. ~*adj.* **3. a.** relating to or using powers of ten. **b.** of the base ten. **4.** (*prenominal*) expressed as a decimal. [C17: from Medieval Latin *decimālis* of tithes, from Latin *decima* a tenth, from *decem* ten] —**'decimally** *adv.*

decimal classification *n.* another term for **Dewey Decimal System.**

decimal currency *n.* a system of currency in which the monetary units are parts or powers of ten.

decimal fraction *n.* another name for **decimal** (sense 1).

decimalize *or* **decimalise** ('dɛsɪməˌlaɪz) *vb.* to change (a system, number, etc.) to the decimal system: *Britain has decimalized her currency.* —**ˌdecimali'zation** *or* **ˌdecimali'sation** *n.*

decimal place *n.* **1.** the position of a digit after the decimal point, each successive position to the right having a denominator of an increased power of ten: *in 0.025, 5 is in the third decimal place.* **2.** the number of digits to the right of the decimal point: *3.142 is a number given to three decimal places.* Compare **significant figures** (sense 2).

decimal point *n.* a full stop or a raised full stop placed between the integral and fractional parts of a number in the decimal system.

▷**Usage.** Conventions relating to the use of the decimal point are confused. The IX General Conference on Weights and Measures resolved in 1948 that the decimal point should be a point on the line or a comma, but not a centre dot. It also resolved that figures could be grouped in threes about the decimal point, but that no point or comma should be used for this purpose. These conventions are adopted in this dictionary. However, the Decimal Currency Board recommended that for sums of money the centre dot should be used as the decimal point and that the comma should be used as the thousand marker. Moreover, in some countries the position is reversed, the comma being used as the decimal point and the dot as the thousand marker.

decimal system *n.* **1.** the number system in general use, having a base of ten, in which numbers are expressed by combinations of the ten digits 0 to 9. **2.** a system of measurement, such as the metric system, in which the multiple and submultiple units are related to a basic unit by powers of ten.

decimate ('dɛsɪˌmeɪt) *vb.* (*tr.*) **1.** to destroy or kill a large proportion of: *a plague decimated the population.* **2.** (esp. in the ancient Roman army) to kill every tenth man of (a mutinous section). [C17: from Latin *decimāre,* from *decimus* tenth, from *decem* ten] —**ˌdeci'mation** *n.* —**'deciˌmator** *n.*

decimetre *or U.S.* **decimeter** ('dɛsɪˌmiːtə) *n.* one tenth of a metre. Symbol: **dm** —**decimetric** (ˌdɛsɪ'mɛtrɪk) *adj.*

decipher (dɪ'saɪfə) *vb.* (*tr.*) **1.** to determine the meaning of (something obscure or illegible). **2.** to convert from code into plain text; decode. —**de'cipherable** *adj.* —**deˌciphera'bility** *n.* —**de'cipherer** *n.* —**de'cipherment** *n.*

decision (dɪ'sɪʒən) *n.* **1.** a judgment, conclusion, or resolution reached or given; verdict. **2.** the act of making up one's mind. **3.** firmness of purpose or character; determination. [C15: from Old French, from Latin *dēcīsiō,* literally: a cutting off; see DECIDE] —**de'cisional** *adj.*

decision support system *n.* a system in which one or more computers and computer programs assist in decision-making by providing information.

decision table *n.* a table within a computer program that specifies the actions to be taken when certain conditions arise.

decision theory *n. Statistics.* the study of strategies for decision making under conditions of uncertainty in such a way as to maximize the expected utility. See also **game theory.**

decisive (dɪ'saɪsɪv) *adj.* **1.** influential; conclusive: *a decisive argument.* **2.** characterized by the ability to make decisions, esp. quickly; resolute. —**de'cisively** *adv.* —**de'cisiveness** *n.*

deck (dɛk) *n.* **1.** *Nautical.* any of various platforms built into a vessel: *a promenade deck; the poop deck.* **2.** a similar floor or platform, as in a bus. **3. a.** the horizontal platform that supports the turntable and pick-up of a record player. **b.** See **tape deck.** **4.** *Chiefly U.S.* a pack of playing cards. **5.** Also called: **pack.** *Computer technol.* a collection of punched cards relevant to a particular program. **6. clear the decks.** *Informal.* to prepare for action, as by removing obstacles from a field of activity or combat. **7. hit the deck.** *Informal.* **a.** to fall to the floor or ground, esp. in order to avoid injury. **b.** to prepare for action. **c.** to get out of bed. ~*vb.* (*tr.*) **8.** (often foll. by *out*) to dress or decorate. **9.** to build a deck on (a vessel). ~See also **deck over.** [C15: from Middle Dutch *dec* a covering; related to THATCH] —**'decker** *n.*

deck-access *adj.* (of a block of flats) having a continuous inset balcony at each level onto which the front door of each flat on that level opens.

deck beam *n. Nautical.* a stiffening deck member supported at its extremities by knee connections to frames or bulkheads.

deck bridge *n. Civil engineering.* a bridge with an upper horizontal beam that carries the roadway.

deck chair *n.* a folding chair for use out of doors, consisting of a wooden frame suspending a length of canvas.

deck crane *n. Nautical.* a deck-mounted crane used for loading and unloading cargo.

deck department *n.* the part of a ship's crew, from the captain down, concerned with running the ship but not with heavy machinery or catering.

-decker *adj.* (*in combination*): having a certain specified number of levels or layers: *a double-decker bus.*

deck hand *n.* **1.** a seaman assigned various duties, such as mooring and cargo handling, on the deck of a ship. **2.** (in Britain) a seaman over 17 years of age who has seen sea duty for at least one year. **3.** a helper aboard a yacht.

deckhouse ('dɛk,haus) *n.* a houselike cabin on the deck of a ship.

deckle *or* **deckel** ('dɛkᵊl) *n.* **1.** a frame used to contain pulp on the mould in the making of handmade paper. **2.** Also called: **deckle strap.** a strap on each edge of the moving web of paper on a paper-making machine that fixes the width of the paper. **3.** See **deckle edge.** [C19: from German *Deckel* lid, from *decken* to cover]

deckle edge *n.* **1.** the rough edge of handmade paper, caused by pulp seeping between the mould and the deckle: often left as ornamentation in fine books and writing papers. **2.** a trimmed edge imitating this. —**'deckle-'edged** *adj.*

deck officer *n.* a ship's officer who is part of the deck crew.

deck over *vb.* (*tr.*) to complete the construction of the upper deck between the bulwarks of (a vessel).

deck tennis *n.* a game played on board ship in which a quoit is tossed to and fro across a high net on a small court resembling a tennis court.

decl. *Grammar. abbrev. for* declension.

declaim (dɪ'kleɪm) *vb.* **1.** to make (a speech, statement, etc.) loudly and in a rhetorical manner. **2.** to speak lines from (a play, poem, etc.) with studied eloquence; recite. **3.** (*intr.*; foll. by *against*) to protest (against) loudly and publicly. [C14: from Latin *dēclāmāre*, from *clāmāre* to call out] —**de'claimer** *n.*

declamation (,dɛklə'meɪʃən) *n.* **1.** a rhetorical or emotional speech, made esp. in order to protest or condemn; tirade. **2.** a speech, verse, etc., that is or can be spoken. **3.** the act or art of declaiming. **4.** *Music.* the artistry or technique involved in singing recitative passages.

declamatory (dɪ'klæmətərɪ, -trɪ) *adj.* **1.** relating to or having the characteristics of a declamation. **2.** merely rhetorical; empty and bombastic. —**de'clamatorily** *adv.*

declarant (dɪ'klɛərənt) *n. Chiefly law.* a person who makes a declaration.

declaration (,dɛklə'reɪʃən) *n.* **1.** an explicit or emphatic statement. **2.** a formal statement or announcement; proclamation. **3.** the act of declaring. **4.** the ruling of a judge or court on a question of law, esp. in the chancery division of the High Court. **5.** *Law.* an unsworn statement of a witness admissible in evidence under certain conditions. See also **statutory declaration. 6.** *Cricket.* the voluntary closure of an innings before all ten wickets have fallen. **7.** *Contract bridge.* the final contract. **8.** a statement or inventory of goods, etc., submitted for tax assessment: *a customs declaration.* **9.** *Cards.* an announcement of points made after taking a trick, as in bezique.

declarative (dɪ'klærətɪv) *adj.* making or having the nature of a declaration. —**de'claratively** *adv.*

declarator (dɪ'klærətə) *n. Scots Law.* an action seeking to have some right, status, etc., judicially ascertained.

declaratory (dɪ'klærətərɪ, -trɪ) *adj.* **1.** another word for **declarative. 2.** *Law.* **a.** (of a statute) stating the existing law on a particular subject; explanatory. **b.** (of a decree or judgment) stating the rights of the parties without specifying the action to be taken. —**de'claratorily** *adv.*

declare (dɪ'klɛə) *vb.* (*mainly tr.*) **1.** (*may take a clause as object*) to make clearly known or announce officially: *to declare one's interests; war was declared.* **2.** to state officially that (a person, fact, etc.) is as specified: *he declared him fit.* **3.** (*may take a clause as object*) to state emphatically; assert. **4.** to show, reveal, or manifest: *the heavens declare the glory of God.* **5.** (*intr.*; often foll. by *for* or *against*) to make known one's choice or opinion. **6.** to make a complete statement of (dutiable goods, etc.). **7.** (*also intr.*) *Cards.* **a.** to display (a card or series of cards) on the table so as to add to one's score. **b.** to decide (the trump suit) by making the winning bid. **8.** (*intr.*) *Cricket.* to close an innings voluntarily before all ten wickets have fallen. **9.** to authorize the payment of (a dividend) from corporate net profit. [C14: from Latin *dēclārāre* to make clear, from *clārus* bright, clear] —**de'clarable** *adj.*

declarer (dɪ'klɛərə) *n.* **1.** a person who declares. **2.** *Bridge.* the player who, as first bidder of the suit of the final contract, plays both hands of the partnership.

declass (diː'klɑːs) *vb.* (*tr.*) to lower in social status or position; degrade.

déclassé (*French* deklɑse) *adj.* having lost social standing or status. [C19: from French *déclasser* to DECLASS] —**déclassée** *fem. adj.*

declassify (diː'klæsɪ,faɪ) *vb.* **-fies, -fying, -fied.** (*tr.*) to release (a document or information) from the security list. —**de'classi,fiable** *adj.* —**de,classifi'cation** *n.*

declension (dɪ'klɛnʃən) *n.* **1.** *Grammar.* **a.** inflection of nouns, pronouns, or adjectives for case, number, and gender. **b.** the complete set of the inflections of such a word: *"puella" is a first-declension noun in Latin.* **2.** a decline or deviation from a standard, belief, etc. **3.** a downward slope or bend. [C15: from Latin *dēclīnātiō*, literally: a bending aside, hence variation, inflection; see DECLINE] —**de'clensional** *adj.* —**de'clensionally** *adv.*

declinate ('dɛklɪ,neɪt, -nɪt) *adj.* (esp. of plant parts) descending from the horizontal in a curve; drooping.

declination (,dɛklɪ'neɪʃən) *n.* **1.** *Astronomy.* the angular distance in degrees of a star, planet, etc., from the celestial equator measured north (positive) or south (negative) along the great circle passing through the celestial poles and the body. Symbol: δ. Compare **right ascension. 2.** See **magnetic declination. 3.** a refusal, esp. a courteous or formal one. —**,decli'national** *adj.*

decline (dɪ'klaɪn) *vb.* **1.** to refuse to do or accept (something), esp. politely. **2.** (*intr.*) to grow smaller; diminish: *demand has declined over the years.* **3.** to slope or cause to slope downwards. **4.** (*intr.*) to deteriorate gradually, as in quality, health, or character. **5.** *Grammar.* to state or list the inflections of (a noun, adjective, or pronoun), or (of a noun, adjective, or pronoun) to be inflected for number, case, or gender. Compare **conjugate** (sense 1). ~*n.* **6.** gradual deterioration or loss. **7.** a movement downward or towards something smaller; diminution. **8.** a downward slope; declivity. **9.** *Archaic.* any slowly progressive disease, such as tuberculosis. [C14: from Old French *decliner* to inflect, turn away, sink, from Latin *dēclīnāre* to bend away, inflect grammatically] —**de'clinable** *adj.* —**de'cliner** *n.*

declinometer (,dɛklɪ'nɒmɪtə) *n.* an instrument for measuring magnetic declination.

declivity (dɪ'klɪvɪtɪ) *n., pl.* **-ties.** a downward slope, esp. of the ground. Compare **acclivity.** [C17: from Latin *dēclīvitās*, from DE- + *clīvus* a slope, hill] —**de'clivitous** *adj.*

declutch (dɪ'klʌtʃ) *vb.* (*intr.*) to disengage the clutch of a motor vehicle.

decoct (dɪ'kɒkt) *vb.* to extract (the essence or active principle) from (a medicinal or similar substance) by boiling. [C15: see DECOCTION]

decoction (dɪ'kɒkʃən) *n.* **1.** *Pharmacol.* the extraction of the water-soluble substances of a drug or medicinal plants by boiling. **2.** the essence or liquor resulting from this. [C14: from Old French, from Late Latin *dēcoctiō*, from *dēcoquere* to boil down, from *coquere* to COOK]

decode (diː'kəʊd) *vb.* **1.** to convert (a message, text, etc.) from code into ordinary language. **2.** *Computer technol.* to convert (coded characters) from one form to another, as from binary-coded decimals to decimal numbers. Compare **encode** (sense 2). **3.** *Electronics.* to convert (a coded electrical signal) into normal analogue components. **4.** to analyse and understand the construction of words and phrases, esp. in a foreign language. —**de'coder** *n.*

decoke (diː'kəʊk) *vb.* (*tr.*) another word for **decarbonize.**

decollate (dɪ'kɒleɪt, 'dɛkə,leɪt, ,diːkə'leɪt) *vb.* **1.** to separate (continuous stationery, etc.) into individual forms. **2.** an archaic word for **decapitate.** [C16: from Latin *dēcollāre* to behead, from DE- + *collum* neck] —**,decol'lation** *n.* —**'decol,lator** *n.*

décolletage (,deɪkɒl'tɑːʒ; *French* dekɔltaʒ) *n.* a low-cut neckline or a woman's garment with a low neck. [C19: from French; see DÉCOLLETÉ]

décolleté (deɪ'kɒlteɪ; *French* dekɔlte) *adj.* **1.** (of a woman's garment) low-cut. **2.** wearing a low-cut garment. [C19: from French *décolleter* to cut out the neck (of a dress), from *collet* collar]

decolonize *or* **decolonise** (diː'kɒlə,naɪz) *vb.* (*tr.*) to grant independence to (a colony). —**de,coloni'zation** *or* **de,coloni'sation** *n.*

decolorant (diː'kʌlərənt) *adj.* **1.** able to decolour or bleach. ~*n.* **2.** a substance that decolours.

decolour (diː'kʌlə), **decolorize,** *or* **decolorise** *vb.* (*tr.*) to deprive of colour, as by bleaching. —**de,color'ation** *n.* —**de,colori'zation** *or* **de,colori'sation** *n.*

decommission (,diːkə'mɪʃən) *vb.* (*tr.*) **1.** to dismantle (an industrial plant or a nuclear reactor that is no longer required for use) to an extent such that it can be safely abandoned. **2.** to remove (a warship or military aircraft) from service.

decompensation (diː,kɒmpɛn'seɪʃən) *n. Pathol.* inability of an organ, esp. the heart, to maintain its function due to overload caused by a disease.

decompose (,diːkəm'pəʊz) *vb.* **1.** to break down (organic matter) or (of organic matter) to be broken down into constituent elements by bacterial or fungal action; rot. **2.** *Chem.* to break down or cause to break down into simpler chemical compounds. **3.** to break up or separate into constituent parts. **4.** (*tr.*) *Maths.* to express in terms of a number of independent simpler components, as a set as a canonical union of disjoint subsets, or a vector

into orthogonal components. —ˌdecomˈposable *adj.* —ˌdecomˌposaˈbility *n.* —decomposition (ˌdiːkɒmpəˈzɪʃən) *n.*
decomposer (ˌdiːkəmˈpəʊzə) *n. Ecology.* any organism in a community, such as a bacterium or fungus, that breaks down dead tissue into its constituent parts. See also **consumer** (sense 3), **producer** (sense 7).
decompound (ˌdiːkəmˈpaʊnd) *adj.* **1.** (of a compound leaf) having leaflets consisting of several distinct parts. **2.** made up of one or more compounds. ~*vb.* **3.** a less common word for **decompose. 4.** *Obsolete.* to mix with or form from one or more compounds.
decompress (ˌdiːkəmˈprɛs) *vb.* **1.** to relieve (a substance) of pressure or (of a substance) to be relieved of pressure. **2.** to return (a diver, caisson worker, etc.) to a condition of normal atmospheric pressure from a condition of increased pressure or (of a diver, etc.) to be returned to such a condition. —ˌ**decomˈpression** *n.* —ˌ**decomˈpressive** *adj.*
decompression chamber *n.* a chamber in which the pressure of air can be varied slowly for returning people from abnormal pressures to atmospheric pressure without inducing decompression sickness.
decompression sickness *or* **illness** *n.* a disorder characterized by severe pain in muscles and joints, cramp, and difficulty in breathing, caused by a sudden and sustained decrease in air pressure. Also called: **caisson disease, aeroembolism.** Nontechnical name: **the bends.**
decongestant (ˌdiːkənˈdʒɛstənt) *adj.* **1.** relieving congestion, esp. nasal congestion. ~*n.* **2.** a decongestant drug.
deconsecrate (diːˈkɒnsɪˌkreɪt) *vb.* (*tr.*) to transfer (a church) to secular use. —**deˌconseˈcration** *n.*
deconstruct (ˌdiːkənˈstrʌkt) *vb.* (*tr.*) **1.** to apply the theories of deconstruction to (a text, film, etc.). **2.** to expose or dismantle the existing structure in (a system, organization, etc.).
deconstruction (ˌdiːkənˈstrʌkʃən) *n.* a technique of literary analysis that regards meaning as resulting from the differences between words rather than their reference to the things they stand for. Different meanings are discovered by taking apart the structure of the language used and exposing the assumption that words have a fixed reference point beyond themselves.
decontaminate (ˌdiːkənˈtæmɪˌneɪt) *vb.* (*tr.*) to render (an area, building, object, etc.) harmless by the removal, distribution, or neutralization of poisons, radioactivity, etc. —ˌ**deconˈtaminant** *n.* —ˌ**deconˌtamiˈnation** *n.* —ˌ**deconˈtaminative** *adj.* —ˌ**deconˈtamiˌnator** *n.*
decontrol (ˌdiːkənˈtrəʊl) *vb.* **-trols, -trolling, -trolled.** (*tr.*) to free of restraints or controls, esp. government controls: *to decontrol prices.*
décor *or* **decor** (ˈdeɪkɔː) *n.* **1.** a style or scheme of interior decoration, furnishings, etc., as in a room or house. **2.** stage decoration; scenery. [C19: from French, from *décorer* to DECORATE]
decorate (ˈdɛkəˌreɪt) *vb.* **1.** (*tr.*) to make more attractive by adding ornament, colour, etc. **2.** to paint or wallpaper (a room, house, etc.). **3.** (*tr.*) to confer a mark of distinction, esp. a military medal, upon. **4.** (*tr.*) to evaporate a metal film onto (a crystal) in order to display dislocations in structure. [C16: from Latin *decorāre,* from *decus* adornment; see DECENT]
Decorated style *or* **architecture** *n.* a 14th-century style of English architecture characterized by the ogee arch, geometrical tracery, and floral decoration.
decoration (ˌdɛkəˈreɪʃən) *n.* **1.** an addition that renders something more attractive or ornate; adornment. **2.** the act, process, or art of decorating. **3.** a medal, badge, etc., conferred as a mark of honour.
decorative (ˈdɛkərətɪv, ˈdɛkrətɪv) *adj.* serving to decorate or adorn; ornamental. —ˈ**decoratively** *adv.* —ˈ**decorativeness** *n.*
decorator (ˈdɛkəˌreɪtə) *n.* **1.** *Brit.* a person whose profession is the painting and wallpapering of buildings. **2.** a person who decorates. **3.** See **interior decorator** (sense 1).
decorous (ˈdɛkərəs) *adj.* characterized by propriety in manners, conduct, etc. [C17: from Latin *decōrus,* from *decor* elegance] —ˈ**decorously** *adv.* —ˈ**decorousness** *n.*
decorticate (diːˈkɔːtɪˌkeɪt) *vb.* **1.** (*tr.*) to remove the bark or some other outer layer from. **2.** *Surgery.* to remove the cortex of (an organ or part). [C17: from Latin *dēcorticāre,* from DE- + *-corticāre,* from *cortex* bark] —**deˌcortiˈcation** *n.* —**deˈcortiˌcator** *n.*
decorum (dɪˈkɔːrəm) *n.* **1.** propriety, esp. in behaviour or conduct. **2.** a requirement of correct behaviour in polite society. [C16: from Latin: propriety]
decoupage (ˌdeɪkuːˈpɑːʒ) *n.* **1.** the art or process of decorating a surface with shapes or illustrations cut from paper, card, etc. **2.** anything produced by this technique. [C20: from French, from *découper* to cut out, from DE- + *couper* to cut]
decouple (ˌdiːˈkʌpᵊl) *vb.* (*tr.*) to separate (joined or coupled subsystems) thereby enabling them to exist and operate separately.
decoupling (diːˈkʌplɪŋ) *n. Electronics.* the reduction or avoidance of undesired distortion or oscillations in a circuit, caused by unwanted common coupling between two or more circuits.
decoy *n.* (ˈdiːkɔɪ, dɪˈkɔɪ). **1.** a person or thing used to beguile or lead someone into danger; lure. **2.** *Military.* something designed to deceive an enemy or divert his attention. **3.** a bird or animal, or an image of one, used to lure game into a trap or within shooting range. **4.** an enclosed space or large trap, often with a wide funnelled entrance, into which game can be lured for capture. ~*vb.* (dɪˈkɔɪ). **5.** to lure or be lured by or as if by means of a decoy. [C17: probably from Dutch *de kooi,* literally: the cage, from Latin *cavea* CAGE] —**deˈcoyer** *n.*
decrease *vb.* (dɪˈkriːs). **1.** to diminish or cause to diminish in size, number, strength, etc. ~*n.* (ˈdiːkriːs, dɪˈkriːs). **2.** the act or process of diminishing; reduction. **3.** the amount by which something has been diminished. [C14: from Old French *descreistre,* from Latin *dēcrescere* to grow less, from DE- + *crescere* to grow] —**deˈcreasingly** *adv.*
decree (dɪˈkriː) *n.* **1.** an edict, law, etc., made by someone in authority. **2.** an order or judgment of a court made after hearing a suit, esp. in matrimonial proceedings. See **decree nisi, decree absolute.** ~*vb.* **decrees, decreeing, decreed. 3.** to order, adjudge, or ordain by decree. [C14: from Old French *decre,* from Latin *dēcrētum* ordinance, from *dēcrētus* decided, past participle of *dēcernere* to determine; see DECERN] —**deˈcreeable** *adj.* —**deˈcreer** *n.*
decree absolute *n.* the final decree in divorce proceedings, which leaves the parties free to remarry. Compare **decree nisi.**
decree nisi (ˈnaɪsaɪ) *n.* a provisional decree, esp. in divorce proceedings, which will later be made absolute unless cause is shown why it should not. Compare **decree absolute.**
decreet (dɪˈkriːt) *n. Scots Law.* the final judgment or sentence of a court. [C14 *decret:* from Old French, from Latin *dēcrētum* DECREE]
decrement (ˈdɛkrɪmənt) *n.* **1.** the act of decreasing; diminution. **2.** *Maths.* a negative increment. **3.** *Physics.* a measure of the damping of an oscillator, expressed by the ratio of the amplitude of a cycle to its amplitude after one period. [C17: from Latin *dēcrēmentum,* from *dēcrescere* to DECREASE]
decrepit (dɪˈkrɛpɪt) *adj.* **1.** enfeebled by old age; infirm. **2.** broken down or worn out by hard or long use; dilapidated. [C15: from Latin *dēcrepitus,* from *crepāre* to creak] —**deˈcrepitly** *adv.* —**deˈcrepiˌtude** *n.*
decrepitate (dɪˈkrɛpɪˌteɪt) *vb.* **1.** (*tr.*) to heat (a substance, such as a salt) until it emits a crackling sound or until this sound stops. **2.** (*intr.*) (esp. of a salt) to crackle, as while being heated. [C17: from New Latin *dēcrepitāre,* from Latin *crepitāre* to crackle, from *crepāre* to creak] —**deˌcrepiˈtation** *n.*
decresc. *Music. abbrev. for* decrescendo.
decrescendo (ˌdiːkrɪˈʃɛndəʊ) *n., adj.* another word for **diminuendo.** [Italian, from *decrescere* to DECREASE]
decrescent (dɪˈkrɛsənt) *adj.* (esp. of the moon) decreasing; waning. [C17: from Latin *dēcrescēns* growing less; see DECREASE] —**deˈcrescence** *n.*
decretal (dɪˈkriːtᵊl) *n.* **1.** *R.C. Church.* a papal edict on doctrine or church law. ~*adj.* **2.** of or relating to a decretal or a decree. [C15: from Old French, from Late Latin *dēcrētālis;* see DECREE] —**deˈcretalist** *n.*
decriminalize *or* **decriminalise** (diːˈkrɪmənᵊˌlaɪz) *vb.* (*tr.*) to remove (an action) from the legal category of criminal offence: *to decriminalize the possession of marijuana.* —ˌ**decriminaliˈzation** *or* ˌ**decriminaliˈsation** *n.*
decry (dɪˈkraɪ) *vb.* **-cries, -crying, -cried.** (*tr.*) **1.** to express open disapproval of; disparage. **2.** to depreciate by proclamation: *to decry obsolete coinage.* [C17: from Old French *descrier,* from *des-* DIS-[1] + *crier* to CRY] —**deˈcrial** *n.* —**deˈcrier** *n.*
decrypt (diːˈkrɪpt) *vb.* (*tr.*) **1.** to decode (a message) with or without previous knowledge of its key. **2.** to make intelligible (a television or other signal) that has been deliberately distorted for transmission. [C20: from DE- + *crypt,* as in CRYPTIC] —**deˈcrypted** *adj.* —**deˈcryption** *n.*
decubitus (dɪˈkjuːbɪtəs) *n. Med.* the posture adopted when lying down. [C19: Latin, past participle of *decumbere* to lie down] —**deˈcubital** *adj.*
decubitus ulcer *n.* a chronic ulcer of the skin and underlying tissues caused by prolonged pressure on the body surface of bedridden patients. Nontechnical names: **bedsore, pressure sore.**
decumbent (dɪˈkʌmbənt) *adj.* **1.** lying down or lying flat. **2.** *Botany.* (of certain stems) lying flat with the tip growing upwards. [C17: from Latin *dēcumbēns,* present participle of *dēcumbere* to lie down] —**deˈcumbence** *or* **deˈcumbency** *n.* —**deˈcumbently** *adv.*
decuple (ˈdɛkjʊpᵊl) *vb.* **1.** (*tr.*) to increase by ten times. ~*n.* **2.** an amount ten times as large as a given reference. ~*adj.* **3.** increasing tenfold. [C15: from Old French, from Late Latin *decuplus* tenfold, from Latin *decem* ten]
decurion (dɪˈkjʊərɪən) *n.* (in the Roman Empire) **1.** a local councillor. **2.** the commander of a troop of ten cavalrymen. [C14: from Latin *decuriō,* from *decuria* company of ten, from *decem* ten]
decurrent (dɪˈkʌrənt) *adj. Botany.* extending down the stem, esp. (of a leaf) having the base of the blade extending down the stem as two wings. [C15: from Latin *dēcurrere* to run down, from *currere* to run] —**deˈcurrently** *adv.*
decurved (diːˈkɜːvd) *adj.* bent or curved downwards: *a decurved bill; decurved petals.*
decury (ˈdɛkjʊərɪ) *n., pl.* **-ries.** (in ancient Rome) a body of ten men. [C16: from Latin *decuria;* see DECURION]

decussate *vb.* (dɪˈkʌseɪt). **1.** to cross or cause to cross in the form of the letter X; intersect. *~adj.* (dɪˈkʌseɪt, dɪˈkʌsɪt). **2.** in the form of the letter X; crossed; intersected. **3.** *Botany.* (esp. of leaves) arranged in opposite pairs, with each pair at right angles to the one above and below it. [C17: from Latin *decussāre,* from *decussis* the number ten, from *decem* ten] —**deˈcussately** *adv.* —ˌ**decusˈsation** *n.*

dedal (ˈdiːdᵊl) *adj.* a variant spelling (esp. U.S.) of **daedal.**

dedans *French.* (dədɑ̃) *n. Real Tennis.* the open gallery at the server's end of the court. [literally: interior]

dedicate (ˈdɛdɪˌkeɪt) *vb.* (*tr.*) **1.** (often foll. by *to*) to devote (oneself, one's time, etc.) wholly to a special purpose or cause; commit wholeheartedly or unreservedly. **2.** (foll. by *to*) to address or inscribe (a book, artistic performance, etc.) to a person, cause, etc. as a token of affection or respect. **3.** (foll. by *to*) to request or play (a record) on radio for another person as a greeting. **4.** to assign or allocate to a particular project, function, etc. **5.** to set apart for a deity or for sacred uses; consecrate. *~adj.* **6.** an archaic word for **dedicated.** [C15: from Latin *dēdicāre* to announce, from *dicāre* to make known, variant of *dīcere* to say] —ˌ**dedicaˈtee** *n.* —ˈ**dediˌcator** *n.* —**dedicatory** (ˈdɛdɪˌkeɪtərɪ, ˈdɛdɪkətərɪ, -trɪ) *or* ˈ**dediˌcative** *adj.*

dedicated (ˈdɛdɪˌkeɪtɪd) *adj.* **1.** devoted to a particular purpose or cause: *a dedicated man.* **2.** assigned or allocated to a particular project, function, etc.: *a dedicated transmission line; dedicated parking space.* **3.** *Computer technol.* designed to fulfil one function: *a dedicated microprocessor.*

dedication (ˌdɛdɪˈkeɪʃən) *n.* **1.** the act of dedicating or the state of being dedicated. **2.** an inscription or announcement prefixed to a book, piece of music, etc., dedicating it to a person or thing. **3.** complete and wholehearted devotion, esp. to a career, ideal, etc. **4.** a ceremony in which something, such as a church, is dedicated. —ˌ**dediˈcational** *adj.*

de dicto *Latin.* (ˈdeɪˈdɪktəʊ) *adj. Logic, philosophy.* relating to the expression of a belief, possibility, etc., rather than to the individuals mentioned, as in *the number of the planets is the number of satellites of the sun,* the truth of which is independent of what number that is. Compare **de re.** See also **Electra paradox.** [literally: about the saying]

dedifferentiation (diːˌdɪfəˌrɛnʃɪˈeɪʃən) *n.* the reversion of the cells of differentiated tissue to a less specialized form.

deduce (dɪˈdjuːs) *vb.* (*tr.*) **1.** (*may take a clause as object*) to reach (a conclusion about something) by reasoning; conclude (that); infer. **2.** *Archaic.* to trace the origin, course, or derivation of. [C15: from Latin *dēdūcere* to lead away, derive, from DE- + *dūcere* to lead] —**deˈducible** *adj.* —**deˌduciˈbility** *or* **deˈducibleness** *n.*

deduct (dɪˈdʌkt) *vb.* (*tr.*) to take away or subtract (a number, quantity, part, etc.): *income tax is deducted from one's wages.* [C15: from Latin *dēductus,* past participle of *dēdūcere* to DEDUCE]

deductible (dɪˈdʌktɪbᵊl) *adj.* **1.** capable of being deducted. **2.** *U.S. and Canadian.* short for **tax-deductible.** *~n.* **3.** *Insurance.* the U.S. and Canadian name for **excess** (sense 6). —**deˌductiˈbility** *n.*

deduction (dɪˈdʌkʃən) *n.* **1.** the act or process of deducting or subtracting. **2.** something, esp. a sum of money, that is or may be deducted. **3. a.** the process of reasoning typical of mathematics and logic, whose conclusions follow necessarily from their premises. **b.** an argument of this type. **c.** the conclusion of such an argument. **4.** *Logic.* **a.** a systematic method of deriving conclusions that cannot be false when the premises are true, esp. one amenable to formalization and study by the science of logic. **b.** an argument of this type. Compare **induction** (sense 4).

deduction theorem *n. Logic.* the property of many formal systems that the conditional derived from a valid argument by taking the conjunction of the premises as antecedent and the conclusion as consequent is true.

deductive (dɪˈdʌktɪv) *adj.* of or relating to deduction: *deductive reasoning.* —**deˈductively** *adv.*

dee (diː) *vb.* a Scot. word for **die**[1].

deed (diːd) *n.* **1.** something that is done or performed; act. **2.** a notable achievement; feat; exploit. **3.** action or performance, as opposed to words. **4.** *Law.* a formal legal document signed, witnessed, and delivered to effect a conveyance or transfer of property or to create a legal obligation or contract. *~vb.* **5.** (*tr.*) *U.S. and Canadian.* to convey or transfer (property) by deed. [Old English *dēd;* related to Old High German *tāt,* Gothic *gadeths;* see DO[1]]

deed box *n.* a lockable metal box for storing documents.

deed poll *n. Law.* a deed made by one party only, esp. one by which a person changes his name.

deejay (ˈdiːˌdʒeɪ) *n.* an informal name for **disc jockey.** [C20: from the initials DJ]

deek (diːk) *vb.* (*tr.; imperative*) *Edinburgh and Northumbrian dialect.* to look at: *deek that!* [perhaps of Romany origin]

deem (diːm) *vb.* (*tr.*) to judge or consider: *I do not deem him worthy of this honour.* [Old English *dēman;* related to Old High German *tuomen* to judge, Gothic *domjan;* see DOOM]

de-emphasize *or* **de-emphasise** (diːˈɛmfəˌsaɪz) *vb.* (*tr.*) to remove emphasis from.

deemster (ˈdiːmstə) *n.* the title of one of the two justices in the Isle of Man. Also called: **dempster.** —ˈ**deemsterˌship** *n.*

de-energize *or* **de-energise** (diːˈɛnədʒaɪz) *vb.* (*tr.*) *Electrical engineering.* to disconnect (an electrical circuit) from its source. —**de-ˌenergiˈzation** *or* **de-ˌenergiˈsation** *n.*

deep (diːp) *adj.* **1.** extending or situated relatively far down from a surface: *a deep pool.* **2.** extending or situated relatively far inwards, backwards, or sideways: *a deep border of trees.* **3.** *Cricket.* relatively far from the pitch: *the deep field; deep third man.* **4. a.** (*postpositive*) of a specified dimension downwards, inwards, or backwards: *six feet deep.* **b.** (*in combination*): *a six-foot-deep trench.* **5.** coming from or penetrating to a great depth: *a deep breath.* **6.** difficult to understand or penetrate; abstruse. **7.** learned or intellectually demanding: *a deep discussion.* **8.** of great intensity; extreme: *deep happiness; deep trouble.* **9.** (*postpositive;* foll. by *in*) absorbed or enveloped (by); engrossed or immersed (in): *deep in study; deep in debt.* **10.** very cunning or crafty; devious: *a deep plot.* **11.** mysterious or obscure: *a deep secret.* **12.** (of a colour) having an intense or dark hue. **13.** low in pitch or tone: *a deep voice.* **14. go off the deep end.** *Informal.* **a.** to lose one's temper; react angrily. **b.** *Chiefly U.S.* to act rashly. **15. in deep water.** in a tricky position or in trouble. **16. throw (someone) in at the deep end.** See **end** (sense 27). *~n.* **17.** any deep place on land or under water, esp. below 6000 metres (3000 fathoms). **18. the deep. a.** a poetic term for the **ocean. b.** *Cricket.* the area of the field relatively far from the pitch. **19.** the most profound, intense, or central part: *the deep of winter.* **20.** a vast extent, as of space or time. **21.** *Nautical.* one of the intervals on a sounding lead, one fathom apart. *~adv.* **22.** far on in time; late: *they worked deep into the night.* **23.** profoundly or intensely. **24. deep down.** *Informal.* in reality, esp. as opposed to appearance: *she is a very kind person deep down.* **25. deep in the past.** long ago. [Old English *dēop;* related to Old High German *tiof* deep, Old Norse *djupr*] —ˈ**deeply** *adv.* —ˈ**deepness** *n.*

deep-discount bond *n.* a fixed-interest security that pays little or no interest but is issued at a substantial discount to its redemption value, thus largely substituting capital gain for income.

deep-dish pie *n. Chiefly U.S. and Canadian.* a pie baked in a deep dish and having only a top crust.

deep-dyed *adj. Usually derogatory.* thoroughgoing; absolute; complete.

deepen (ˈdiːpᵊn) *vb.* to make or become deep, deeper, or more intense. —ˈ**deepener** *n.*

deepfreeze (ˌdiːpˈfriːz) *n.* **1.** a type of refrigerator in which food, etc., is stored for long periods at temperatures below freezing. **2.** storage in or as if in a deepfreeze. **3.** *Informal.* a state of suspended activity. *~vb.* **deep-freeze, -freezes, -froze** *or* **-freezed, -frozen** *or* **-freezed. 4.** (*tr.*) to freeze or keep in or as if in a deepfreeze.

deep-fry *vb.* **-fries, -frying, -fried.** to cook (fish, potatoes, etc.) in sufficient hot fat to cover the food entirely.

deep kiss *n.* another name for **French kiss.**

deep-laid *adj.* (of a plot or plan) carefully worked out and kept secret.

deep-litter *n.* (*modifier*) *Poultry farming.* **1.** denoting a system in which a number of hens are housed in one covered enclosure, within which they can move about freely, on a layer of straw or wood shavings several centimetres deep: *deep-litter system.* **2.** kept in or produced by the deep-litter method: *deep-litter eggs.*

deep-rooted *or* **deep-seated** *adj.* (of ideas, beliefs, prejudices, etc.) firmly fixed, implanted, or held; ingrained.

deep-sea *n.* (*modifier*) of, found in, or characteristic of the deep parts of the sea: *deep-sea fishing.*

deep-set *adj.* (of the eyes) deeply set into the face.

deep-six *vb.* (*tr.*) *U.S. slang.* to dispose of (something, such as documents) completely; destroy. [C20: from *six feet deep,* the traditional depth for a grave]

deep space *n.* any region of outer space beyond the system of the earth and moon.

deep structure *n. Generative grammar.* a representation of a sentence at a level where logical or grammatical relations are made explicit, before transformational rules have been applied. Compare **surface structure.**

deep therapy *n.* radiotherapy with very penetrating short-wave radiation.

deer (dɪə) *n., pl.* **deer** *or* **deers. 1.** any ruminant artiodactyl mammal of the family *Cervidae,* including reindeer, elk, muntjacs, and roe deer, typically having antlers in the male. Related adj.: **cervine. 2.** (in N Canada) another name for **caribou.** [Old English *dēor* beast; related to Old High German *tior* wild beast, Old Norse *dȳr*]

deergrass (ˈdɪəˌgrɑːs) *n.* a perennial cyperaceous plant, *Trichophorum caespitosum,* that grows in dense tufts in peat bogs of temperate regions.

deerhound (ˈdɪəˌhaʊnd) *n.* a very large rough-coated breed of dog of the greyhound type.

deer lick *n.* a naturally or artificially salty area of ground where deer come to lick the salt.

deer mouse *n.* any of various mice of the genus *Peromyscus,* esp. *P. maniculatus,* of North and Central America, having brownish fur with white underparts: family *Cricetidae.* See also **white-footed mouse.** [so named because of its agility]

deerskin (ˈdɪəˌskɪn) *n.* **a.** the hide of a deer. **b.** (*as modifier*): *a deerskin jacket.*

deerstalker (ˈdɪəˌstɔːkə) *n.* **1.** Also called: **stalker.** a person who stalks deer, esp. in order to shoot them. **2.** a hat, peaked in front and behind, with earflaps usually turned up and tied together on the top. —ˈ**deerˌstalking** *adj., n.*

de-escalate (diːˈɛskəˌleɪt) *vb.* to reduce the level or intensity of (a crisis, etc.). —**de-ˌescaˈlation** *n.*

def (dɛf) *adj. Slang.* (esp. of hip-hop) very good. [C20: perhaps from *definitive*]

def. *abbrev. for:* **1.** defective. **2.** defence. **3.** defendant. **4.** deferred. **5.** definite. **6.** definition.

deface (dɪˈfeɪs) *vb.* (*tr.*) to spoil or mar the surface, legibility, or appearance of; disfigure. —**deˈfaceable** *adj.* —**deˈfacement** *n.* —**deˈfacer** *n.*

de facto (deɪ ˈfæktəʊ) *adv.* **1.** in fact. ~*adj.* **2.** existing in fact, whether legally recognized or not: *a de facto regime.* Compare **de jure.** ~*n., pl.* **-tos. 3.** *Austral. and N.Z.* a de facto husband or wife. [C17: Latin]

defaecate (ˈdɛfɪˌkeɪt) *vb.* a variant spelling of **defecate.**

defalcate (ˈdiːfælˌkeɪt) *vb.* (*intr.*) *Law.* to misuse or misappropriate property or funds entrusted to one. [C15: from Medieval Latin *dēfalcāre* to cut off, from Latin DE- + *falx* sickle] —ˌ**defalˈcation** *n.* —ˈ**defalˌcator** *n.*

defamation (ˌdɛfəˈmeɪʃən) *n.* **1.** *Law.* the injuring of a person's good name or reputation. Compare **libel, slander. 2.** the act of defaming or state of being defamed.

defamatory (dɪˈfæmətərɪ, -trɪ) *adj.* injurious to someone's name or reputation. —**deˈfamatorily** *adv.*

defame (dɪˈfeɪm) *vb.* (*tr.*) **1.** to attack the good name or reputation of; slander; libel. **2.** *Archaic.* to indict or accuse. [C14: from Old French *defamer,* from Latin *dēfāmāre,* from *diffāmāre* to spread by unfavourable report, from *fāma* FAME] —**deˈfamer** *n.*

default (dɪˈfɔːlt) *n.* **1.** a failure to act, esp. a failure to meet a financial obligation or to appear in a court of law at a time specified. **2.** absence: *he lost the chess game by default.* **3. in default of.** through or in the lack or absence of. **4. judgment by default.** *Law.* a judgment in the plaintiff's favour when the defendant fails to plead or to appear. **5.** lack, want, or need. **6.** (*also* ˈdiːfɔːlt). *Computer technol.* **a.** the preset selection of an option offered by a system, which will always be followed except when explicitly altered. **b.** (*as modifier*): *default setting.* ~*vb.* **7.** (*intr.;* often foll. by *on* or *in*) to fail to make payment when due. **8.** (*intr.*) to fail to fulfil or perform an obligation, engagement, etc: *to default in a sporting contest.* **9.** *Law.* to lose (a case) by failure to appear in court. [C13: from Old French *defaute,* from *defaillir* to fail, from Vulgar Latin *dēfallīre* (unattested) to be lacking]

defaulter (dɪˈfɔːltə) *n.* **1.** a person who defaults. **2.** *Chiefly Brit.* a person, esp. a soldier, who has broken the disciplinary code of his service.

defeasance (dɪˈfiːzᵊns) *n. Chiefly law.* **1.** the act or process of rendering null and void; annulment. **2. a.** a condition, the fulfilment of which renders a deed void. **b.** the document containing such a condition. [C14: from Old French, from *desfaire* to DEFEAT]

defeasible (dɪˈfiːzəbᵊl) *adj.* **1.** *Law.* (of an estate or interest in land) capable of being defeated or rendered void. **2.** *Philosophy.* (of a judgment, opinion, etc.) having a presupposition in its favour but open to revision if countervailing evidence becomes known. Compare **incorrigible** (sense 3). —**deˈfeasibleness** *or* **deˌfeasiˈbility** *n.*

defeat (dɪˈfiːt) *vb.* (*tr.*) **1.** to overcome in a contest or competition; win a victory over. **2.** to thwart or frustrate: *this accident has defeated all his hopes of winning.* **3.** *Law.* to render null and void; annul. ~*n.* **4.** the act of defeating or state of being defeated. **5.** an instance of defeat. **6.** overthrow or destruction. **7.** *Law.* an annulment. [C14: from Old French *desfait,* from *desfaire* to undo, ruin, from *des-* DIS-[1] + *faire* to do, from Latin *facere*] —**deˈfeater** *n.*

defeatism (dɪˈfiːtɪzəm) *n.* a ready acceptance or expectation of defeat. —**deˈfeatist** *n., adj.*

defecate *or* **defaecate** (ˈdɛfɪˌkeɪt) *vb.* **1.** (*intr.*) to discharge waste from the body through the anus. **2.** (*tr.*) to clarify or remove impurities from (a solution, esp. of sugar). [C16: from Latin *dēfaecāre* to cleanse from dregs, from DE- + *faex* sediment, dregs] —ˌ**defeˈcation** *or* ˌ**defaeˈcation** *n.* —ˈ**defeˌcator** *or* ˈ**defaeˌcator** *n.*

defect *n.* (dɪˈfɛkt, ˈdiːfɛkt). **1.** a lack of something necessary for completeness or perfection; shortcoming; deficiency. **2.** an imperfection, failing, or blemish. **3.** *Crystallog.* a local deviation from regularity in the crystal lattice of a solid. See also **point defect, dislocation** (sense 3). ~*vb.* (dɪˈfɛkt). **4.** (*intr.*) to desert one's country, cause, allegiance, etc., esp. in order to join the opposing forces. [C15: from Latin *dēfectus,* from *dēficere* to forsake, fail; see DEFICIENT] —**deˈfector** *n.*

defection (dɪˈfɛkʃən) *n.* **1.** the act or an instance of defecting. **2.** abandonment of duty, allegiance, principles, etc.; backsliding. **3.** another word for **defect** (senses 1, 2).

defective (dɪˈfɛktɪv) *adj.* **1.** having a defect or flaw; imperfect; faulty. **2.** (of a person) below the usual standard or level, esp. in intelligence. **3.** *Grammar.* (of a word) lacking the full range of inflections characteristic of its form class, as for example *must,* which has no past tense. —**deˈfectively** *adv.* —**deˈfectiveness** *n.*

defence *or U.S.* **defense** (dɪˈfɛns) *n.* **1.** resistance against danger, attack, or harm; protection. **2.** a person or thing that provides such resistance. **3.** a plea, essay, speech, etc., in support of something; vindication; justification. **4. a.** a country's military measures or resources. **b.** (*as modifier*): *defence spending.* **5.** *Law.* a defendant's denial of the truth of the allegations or charge against him. **6.** *Law.* the defendant and his legal advisers collectively. Compare **prosecution. 7.** *Sport.* **a.** the action of protecting oneself, one's goal, or one's allotted part of the playing area against an opponent's attacks. **b.** the method of doing this. **c.** (usually preceded by *the*) the players in a team whose function is to do this. **8.** *American football.* (usually preceded by *the*) **a.** the team that does not have possession of the ball. **b.** the members of a team that play in such circumstances. **9.** *Psychoanal.* See **defence mechanism. 10.** (*pl.*) fortifications. [C13: from Old French, from Late Latin *dēfensum,* past participle of *dēfendere* to DEFEND] —**deˈfenceless** *or U.S.* **deˈfenseless** *adj.* —**deˈfencelessly** *or U.S.* **deˈfenselessly** *adv.* —**deˈfencelessness** *or U.S.* **deˈfenselessness** *n.*

defence in depth *n. Military.* the act or practice of positioning successive mutually supporting lines of defence in a given area.

defence mechanism *n.* **1.** *Psychoanal.* a usually unconscious mental process designed to reduce the anxiety, shame, etc., associated with instinctive desires. **2.** *Physiol.* the protective response of the body against disease organisms.

defend (dɪˈfɛnd) *vb.* **1.** to protect (a person, place, etc.) from harm or danger; ward off an attack on. **2.** (*tr.*) to support in the face of criticism, esp. by argument or evidence. **3.** to represent (a defendant) in court in a civil or criminal action. **4.** *Sport.* to guard or protect (oneself, one's goal, etc.) against attack. **5.** (*tr.*) to protect (a championship or title) against a challenge. [C13: from Old French *defendre,* from Latin *dēfendere* to ward off, from DE- + *-fendere* to strike] —**deˈfendable** *adj.* —**deˈfender** *n.*

defendant (dɪˈfɛndənt) *n.* **1.** a person against whom an action or claim is brought in a court of law. Compare **plaintiff.** ~*adj.* **2.** making a defence; defending.

defenestration (diːˌfɛnɪˈstreɪʃən) *n.* the act of throwing someone out of a window. [C17: from New Latin *dēfenestrātiō,* from Latin DE- + *fenestra* window]

defensible (dɪˈfɛnsɪbᵊl) *adj.* capable of being defended, as in war, an argument, etc. —**deˌfensiˈbility** *or* **deˈfensibleness** *n.* —**deˈfensibly** *adv.*

defensive (dɪˈfɛnsɪv) *adj.* **1.** intended, suitable, or done for defence, as opposed to offence. **2.** rejecting criticisms of oneself or covering up one's failings. ~*n.* **3.** a position of defence. **4. on the defensive.** in an attitude or position of defence, as in being ready to reject criticism. —**deˈfensively** *adv.* —**deˈfensiveness** *n.*

defensive medicine *n.* the practice by a doctor of ordering extensive tests in order to minimize liability if accused of negligence.

defer[1] (dɪˈfɜː) *vb.* **-fers, -ferring, -ferred.** (*tr.*) to delay or cause to be delayed until a future time; postpone. [C14: from Old French *differer* to be different, postpone; see DIFFER] —**deˈferrable** *or* **deˈferable** *adj.* —**deˈferrer** *n.*

defer[2] (dɪˈfɜː) *vb.* **-fers, -ferring, -ferred.** (*intr.;* foll. by *to*) to yield (to) or comply (with) the wishes or judgments of another. [C15: from Latin *dēferre,* literally: to bear down, from DE- + *ferre* to bear]

deference (ˈdɛfərəns) *n.* **1.** submission to or compliance with the will, wishes, etc., of another. **2.** courteous regard; respect. [C17: from French *déférence;* see DEFER[2]]

deferent[1] (ˈdɛfərənt) *adj.* another word for **deferential.**

deferent[2] (ˈdɛfərənt) *adj.* **1.** (esp. of a bodily nerve, vessel, or duct) conveying an impulse, fluid, etc., outwards, down, or away; efferent. ~*n.* **2.** *Astronomy.* (in the Ptolemaic system) a circle centred on the earth around which the centre of the epicycle was thought to move. [C17: from Latin *dēferre; see* DEFER[2]]

deferential (ˌdɛfəˈrɛnʃəl) *adj.* marked by or showing deference or respect; respectful. —ˌ**deferˈentially** *adv.*

deferment (dɪˈfɜːmənt) *or* **deferral** (dɪˈfɜːrəl) *n.* the act of deferring or putting off until another time; postponement.

deferred (dɪˈfɜːd) *adj.* **1.** withheld over a certain period; postponed: *a deferred payment.* **2.** (of shares) ranking behind other types of shares for dividend.

deferred annuity *n.* an annuity that commences not less than one year after the final purchase premium. Compare **immediate annuity.**

deferred sentence *n. Law.* a sentence that is postponed for a specific period to allow a court to examine the conduct of the offender during the deferment. Compare **suspended sentence.**

defervescence (ˌdɛfəˈvɛsəns) *n. Med.* **1.** the abatement of a fever. **2.** the period during which this occurs.

defiance (dɪˈfaɪəns) *n.* **1.** open or bold resistance to or disregard for authority, opposition, or power. **2.** a challenging attitude or behaviour; challenge.

defiant (dɪˈfaɪənt) *adj.* marked by resistance or bold opposition, as to authority; challenging. —**deˈfiantly** *adv.*

defibrillation (dɪˌfaɪbrɪˈleɪʃən, -fɪb-) *n. Med.* the application of an electric current to the heart to restore normal rhythmical contractions after a heart attack caused by fibrillation.

defibrillator (dɪˈfaɪbrɪˌleɪtə, -ˈfɪb-) *n. Med.* an apparatus for stopping fibrillation of the heart by application of an electric current to the chest wall or directly to the heart.

deficiency (dɪˈfɪʃənsɪ) *n., pl.* **-cies.** **1.** the state or quality of being deficient. **2.** a lack or insufficiency; shortage. **3.** another word for **deficit.** **4.** *Biology.* the absence of a gene or a region of a chromosome normally present.

deficiency disease *n.* **1.** *Med.* any condition, such as pellagra, beriberi, or scurvy, produced by a lack of vitamins or other essential substances. Compare **avitaminosis.** **2.** *Botany.* any disease caused by lack of essential minerals.

deficient (dɪˈfɪʃənt) *adj.* **1.** lacking some essential; incomplete; defective. **2.** inadequate in quantity or supply; insufficient. [C16: from Latin *dēficiēns* lacking, from *dēficere* to fall short; see DEFECT] —**deˈficiently** *adv.*

deficit (ˈdɛfɪsɪt, dɪˈfɪsɪt) *n.* **1.** the amount by which an actual sum is lower than that expected or required. **2. a.** an excess of liabilities over assets. **b.** an excess of expenditures over revenues during a certain period. **c.** an excess of payments over receipts on the balance of payments. [C18: from Latin, literally: there is lacking, from *dēficere* to be lacking]

deficit financing *n.* government spending in excess of revenues so that a budget deficit is incurred, which is financed by borrowing: recommended by Keynesian economists in order to increase economic activity and reduce unemployment. Also called: **compensatory finance, pump priming.**

de fide *Latin.* (diː ˈfaɪdɪ) *adj. R.C. Church.* (of a doctrine) belonging to the essentials of the faith, esp. by virtue of a papal ruling. [literally: from faith]

defilade (ˌdɛfɪˈleɪd) *Military fortifications.* ~*n.* **1.** protection provided by obstacles against enemy crossfire from the rear, or observation. **2.** the disposition of defensive fortifications to produce this protection. ~*vb.* (*tr.*) **3.** to provide protection for by defilade. [C19: see DE-, ENFILADE]

defile[1] (dɪˈfaɪl) *vb.* (*tr.*) **1.** to make foul or dirty; pollute. **2.** to tarnish or sully the brightness of; taint; corrupt. **3.** to damage or sully (someone's good name, reputation, etc.). **4.** to make unfit for ceremonial use; desecrate. **5.** to violate the chastity of. [C14: from earlier *defoilen* (influenced by *filen* to FILE[3]), from Old French *defouler* to trample underfoot, abuse, from DE- + *fouler* to tread upon; see FULL[2]] —**deˈfilement** *n.* —**deˈfiler** *n.*

defile[2] (ˈdiːfaɪl, dɪˈfaɪl) *n.* **1.** a narrow pass or gorge, esp. one between two mountains. **2.** a single file of soldiers, etc. ~*vb.* **3.** *Chiefly military.* to march or cause to march in single file. [C17: from French *défilé*, from *défiler* to file off, from *filer* to march in a column, from Old French: to spin, from *fil* thread, from Latin *fīlum*]

define (dɪˈfaɪn) *vb.* (*tr.*) **1.** to state precisely the meaning of (words, terms, etc.). **2.** to describe the nature, properties, or essential qualities of. **3.** to determine the boundary or extent of. **4.** (*often passive*) to delineate the form or outline of: *the shape of the tree was clearly defined by the light behind it.* **5.** to fix with precision; specify. [C14: from Old French *definer* to determine, from Latin *dēfīnīre* to set bounds to, from *fīnīre* to FINISH] —**deˈfinable** *adj.* —**deˌfinaˈbility** *n.* —**deˈfinably** *adv.* —**deˈfiner** *n.*

definiendum (dɪˌfɪnɪˈɛndəm) *n., pl.* **-da** (-də). something to be defined, esp. the term or phrase to be accounted for in a dictionary entry. Compare **definiens.** [Latin]

definiens (dɪˈfɪnɪənz) *n., pl.* **definientia** (dɪˌfɪnɪˈɛnʃə). the word or words used to define or give an account of the meaning of another word, as in a dictionary entry. Compare **definiendum.** [Latin: defining]

definite (ˈdɛfɪnɪt) *adj.* **1.** clearly defined; exact; explicit. **2.** having precise limits or boundaries. **3.** known for certain; sure: *it is definite that they have won.* **4.** *Botany.* **a.** denoting a type of growth in which the main stem ends in a flower, as in a cymose inflorescence; determinate. **b.** (esp. of flower parts) limited or fixed in number in a given species. [C15: from Latin *dēfīnītus* limited, distinct; see DEFINE] —ˈ**definiteness** *n.* —**definitude** (dɪˈfɪnɪˌtjuːd) *n.*

▷**Usage.** *Definite* and *definitive* should be carefully distinguished. *Definite* indicates precision and firmness, as in *a definite decision. Definitive* includes these senses but also indicates conclusiveness. *A definite answer* indicates a clear and firm answer to a particular question; *a definitive answer* implies an authoritative resolution of a complex question.

definite article *n. Grammar.* a determiner that expresses specificity of reference, such as *the* in English. Compare **indefinite article.**

definite description *n.* **1.** a description that is modified by the definite article or a possessive, such as *the woman in white* or *Rosemary's baby.* **2.** a similar plural expression, such as *the kings of Scotland.*

definite integral *n. Maths.* **a.** the evaluation of the indefinite integral between two limits, representing the area between the given function and the *x*-axis between these two values of *x*. **b.** the expression for that function, $\int_a^b f(x)\mathrm{d}x$, where $f(x)$ is the given function and $x = a$ and $x = b$ are the limits of integration. Where $F(x) = \int f(x)\mathrm{d}x$, the indefinite integral, $\int_a^b f(x)\mathrm{d}x = F(b)-F(a)$.

definitely (ˈdɛfɪnɪtlɪ) *adv.* **1.** in a definite manner. **2.** (*sentence modifier*) certainly: *he said he was coming, definitely.* ~*sentence substitute.* **3.** unquestionably: used to confirm an assumption by a questioner.

definition (ˌdɛfɪˈnɪʃən) *n.* **1.** a formal and concise statement of the meaning of a word, phrase, etc. **2.** the act of defining a word, phrase, etc. **3.** specification of the essential properties of something, or of the criteria which uniquely identify it. **4.** the act of making clear or definite. **5.** the state or condition of being clearly defined or definite. **6.** a measure of the clarity of an optical, photographic, or television image as characterized by its sharpness and contrast. —ˌ**defiˈnitional** *adj.*

definitive (dɪˈfɪnɪtɪv) *adj.* **1.** serving to decide or settle finally; conclusive. **2.** most reliable, complete, or authoritative: *the definitive reading of a text.* **3.** serving to define or outline. **4.** *Zoology.* fully developed; complete: *the definitive form of a parasite.* **5. a.** (of postage stamps) permanently on sale. **b.** (*as n.*) a definitive postage stamp. ~*n.* **6.** *Grammar.* a word indicating specificity of reference, such as the definite article or a demonstrative adjective or pronoun. —**deˈfinitively** *adv.* —**deˈfinitiveness** *n.*

▷**Usage.** See at **definite.**

deflagrate (ˈdɛfləˌgreɪt, ˈdiː-) *vb.* to burn or cause to burn with great heat and light. [C18: from Latin *dēflagrāre*, from DE- + *flagrāre* to burn] —ˌ**deflaˈgration** *n.*

deflate (dɪˈfleɪt) *vb.* **1.** to collapse or cause to collapse through the release of gas. **2.** (*tr.*) to take away the self-esteem or conceit from. **3.** *Economics.* to cause deflation of (an economy, the money supply, etc.). [C19: from DE- + (IN)FLATE] —**deˈflator** *n.*

deflation (dɪˈfleɪʃən) *n.* **1.** the act of deflating or state of being deflated. **2.** *Economics.* a reduction in the level of total spending and economic activity resulting in lower levels of output, employment, investment, trade, profits, and prices. Compare **disinflation.** **3.** the removal of loose rock material, sand, and dust by the wind. —**deˈflationary** *adj.* —**deˈflationist** *n., adj.*

deflationary gap *n. Economics.* a situation in which total spending in an economy is insufficient to buy all the output that can be produced with full employment.

deflect (dɪˈflɛkt) *vb.* to turn or cause to turn aside from a course; swerve. [C17: from Latin *dēflectere*, from *flectere* to bend] —**deˈflector** *n.*

deflection *or* **deflexion** (dɪˈflɛkʃən) *n.* **1.** the act of deflecting or the state of being deflected. **2.** the amount of deviation. **3.** the change in direction of a light beam as it crosses a boundary between two media with different refractive indexes. **4.** a deviation of the indicator of a measuring instrument from its zero position. **5.** the movement of a structure or structural member when subjected to a load. —**deˈflective** *adj.*

deflexed (dɪˈflɛkst, ˈdiːflɛkst) *adj.* (of leaves, petals, etc.) bent sharply outwards and downwards.

deflocculate (dɪˈflɒkjʊˌleɪt) *vb.* (*tr.*) **1.** to disperse, forming a colloid or suspension. **2.** to prevent flocculation of (a colloid or suspension). —**deˌflocculˈlation** *n.* —**deˈflocculˌlant** *n.*

defloration (ˌdiːflɔːˈreɪʃən) *n.* the act of deflowering. [C15: from Late Latin *dēflōrātiō*; see DE-, FLOWER]

deflower (diːˈflaʊə) *vb.* (*tr.*) **1.** to deprive of virginity, esp. by rupturing the hymen through sexual intercourse. **2.** to despoil of beauty, innocence, etc.; mar; violate. **3.** to rob or despoil of flowers. —**deˈflowerer** *n.*

defoliant (diːˈfəʊlɪənt) *n.* a chemical sprayed or dusted onto trees to cause their leaves to fall, esp. to remove cover from an enemy in warfare.

defoliate *vb.* (diːˈfəʊlɪˌeɪt). **1.** to deprive (a plant) of its leaves, as by the use of a herbicide, or (of a plant) to shed its leaves. ~*adj.* (diːˈfəʊlɪɪt). **2.** (of a plant) having shed its leaves. [C18: from Medieval Latin *dēfoliāre*, from Latin DE- + *folium* leaf] —**deˌfoliˈation** *n.* —**deˈfoliˌator** *n.*

deforce (dɪˈfɔːs) *vb.* (*tr.*) *Property law.* **1.** to withhold (property, esp. land) wrongfully or by force from the rightful owner. **2.** to eject or keep forcibly from possession of property. [C13: from Anglo-French, from *deforcer*] —**deˈforcement** *n.*

deforest (diːˈfɒrɪst) *vb.* (*tr.*) to clear of trees. Also: **disforest.** —**deˌforesˈtation** *n.* —**deˈforester** *n.*

deform (dɪˈfɔːm) *vb.* **1.** to make or become misshapen or distorted. **2.** (*tr.*) to mar the beauty of; disfigure. **3.** (*tr.*) to subject or be subjected to a stress that causes a change of dimensions. [C15: from Latin *dēformāre*, from DE- + *forma* shape, beauty] —**deˈformable** *adj.* —**deˌformaˈbility** *n.* —**deˈformer** *n.*

deformation (ˌdiːfɔːˈmeɪʃən) *n.* **1.** the act of deforming; distortion. **2.** the result of deforming; a change in form, esp. for the worse. **3.** a change in the dimensions of an object resulting from a stress.

deformed (dɪˈfɔːmd) *adj.* **1.** disfigured or misshapen. **2.** morally perverted; warped. —**deformedly** (dɪˈfɔːmɪdlɪ) *adv.* —**deˈformedness** *n.*

deformity (dɪˈfɔːmɪtɪ) *n., pl.* **-ties.** **1.** a deformed condition; disfigurement. **2.** *Pathol.* an acquired or congenital distortion of an organ or part. **3.** a deformed person or thing. **4.** a defect, esp. of the mind or morals; depravity.

defraud (dɪˈfrɔːd) *vb.* (*tr.*) to take away or withhold money, rights, property, etc., from (a person) by fraud; cheat; swindle. —**defraudation** (ˌdiːfrɔːˈdeɪʃən) *or* **deˈfraudment** *n.* —**deˈfrauder** *n.*

defray (dɪˈfreɪ) *vb.* (*tr.*) to furnish or provide money for (costs, expenses, etc.); pay. [C16: from Old French *deffroier* to pay expenses, from *de-* DIS-[1] + *frai* expenditure, originally: cost incurred through breaking something, from Latin *frangere* to break] —**de'frayable** *adj.* —**de'frayal** *or* **de'frayment** *n.* —**de'frayer** *n.*

defrock (diː'frɒk) *vb.* (*tr.*) to deprive (a person in holy orders) of ecclesiastical status; unfrock.

defrost (diː'frɒst) *vb.* **1.** to make or become free of frost or ice. **2.** to thaw, esp. through removal from a refrigerator.

defroster (diː'frɒstə) *n.* a device by which the de-icing process of a refrigerator is accelerated, usually by circulating the refrigerant without the expansion process.

deft (dɛft) *adj.* quick and neat in movement; nimble; dexterous. [C13 (in the sense: gentle): see DAFT] —**'deftly** *adv.* —**'deftness** *n.*

defunct (dɪ'fʌŋkt) *adj.* **1.** no longer living; dead or extinct. **2.** no longer operative or valid. [C16: from Latin *dēfungī* to discharge (one's obligations), die; see DE-, FUNCTION] —**de'functive** *adj.* —**de'functness** *n.*

defuse *or U.S.* (*sometimes*) **defuze** (diː'fjuːz) *vb.* (*tr.*) **1.** to remove the triggering device of (a bomb, etc.). **2.** to remove the cause of tension from (a crisis, etc.).

defy (dɪ'faɪ) *vb.* **-fies, -fying, -fied.** (*tr.*) **1.** to resist (a powerful person, authority, etc.) openly and boldly. **2.** to elude, esp. in a baffling way: *his actions defy explanation.* **3.** *Formal.* to challenge or provoke (someone to do something judged to be impossible); dare: *I defy you to climb that cliff.* **4.** *Archaic.* to invite to do battle or combat. [C14: from Old French *desfier,* from *des-* DE- + *fier* to trust, from Latin *fīdere*] —**de'fier** *n.*

deg. *abbrev. for* degree.

dégagé *French.* (degaʒe) *adj.* **1.** unconstrained in manner; casual; relaxed. **2.** uninvolved; detached.

degas (diː'gæs) *vb.* **-gases** *or* **-gasses, -gassing, -gassed. 1.** (*tr.*) to remove gas from (a container, vacuum tube, liquid, adsorbent, etc.). **2.** (*intr.*) to lose adsorbed or absorbed gas by desorption. —**de'gasser** *n.*

degauss (diː'gaʊs, -'gɔːs) *vb.* (*tr.*) **1.** to neutralize the magnetic field of a ship's hull (as a protection against magnetic mines) using equipment producing an opposing magnetic field. **2.** another word for **demagnetize.**

degearing (diː'gɪərɪŋ) *n. Finance.* the process in which a company replaces some or all of its fixed-interest loan stock with ordinary shares.

degeneracy (dɪ'dʒɛnərəsɪ) *n., pl.* **-cies. 1.** the act or state of being degenerate. **2.** the process of becoming degenerate. **3.** *Physics.* the number of degenerate quantum states of a particular orbital, degree of freedom, etc.

degenerate *vb.* (dɪ'dʒɛnəˌreɪt). (*intr.*) **1.** to become degenerate. **2.** *Biology.* (of organisms or their parts) to become less specialized or functionally useless. ~*adj.* (dɪ'dʒɛnərɪt). **3.** having declined or deteriorated to a lower mental, moral, or physical level; debased; degraded; corrupt. **4.** *Physics.* **a.** (of the constituents of a system) having the same energy but different wave functions. **b.** (of a semiconductor) containing a similar number of electrons in the conduction band to the number of electrons in the conduction band of metals. **c.** (of a resonant device) having two or more modes of equal frequency. **5.** (of a code) containing symbols that represent more than one letter, figure, etc. **6.** (of a plant or animal) having undergone degeneration. ~*n.* (dɪ'dʒɛnərɪt). **7.** a degenerate person. [C15: from Latin *dēgenerāre,* from *dēgener* departing from its kind, ignoble, from DE- + *genus* origin, race] —**de'generately** *adv.* —**de'generateness** *n.* —**de'generative** *adj.*

degenerate matter *n. Astrophysics.* the highly compressed state of a star's matter when its atoms virtually touch in the final stage of its evolution into a white dwarf.

degeneration (dɪˌdʒɛnə'reɪʃən) *n.* **1.** the process of degenerating. **2.** the state of being degenerate. **3.** *Biology.* the loss of specialization, function, or structure by organisms and their parts, as in the development of vestigial organs. **4. a.** impairment or loss of the function and structure of cells or tissues, as by disease or injury, often leading to death (necrosis) of the involved part. **b.** the resulting condition. **5.** *Electronics.* negative feedback of a signal.

degenerative joint disease *n.* another name for **osteoarthritis.**

deglutinate (diː'gluːtɪˌneɪt) *vb.* (*tr.*) to extract the gluten from (a cereal, esp. wheat). [C17: from Latin *dēglūtināre* to unglue, from DE- + *glūtināre,* from *glūten* GLUE] —**deˌgluti'nation** *n.*

deglutition (ˌdiːgluː'tɪʃən) *n.* the act of swallowing. [C17: from French *déglutition,* from Late Latin *dēglūtīre* to swallow down, from DE- + *glutīre* to swallow]

degradable (dɪ'greɪdəbᵊl) *adj.* **1.** (of waste products, packaging materials, etc.) capable of being decomposed chemically or biologically. See also **biodegradable. 2.** capable of being degraded. —**deˌgrada'bility** *n.*

degradation (ˌdɛgrə'deɪʃən) *n.* **1.** the act of degrading or the state of being degraded. **2.** a state of degeneration, squalor, or poverty. **3.** some act, constraint, etc., that is degrading. **4.** the wearing down of the surface of rocks, cliffs, etc., by erosion, weathering, or some other process. **5.** *Chem.* a breakdown of a molecule into atoms or smaller molecules. **6.** *Physics.* an irreversible process in which the energy available to do work is decreased. **7.** *R.C. Church.* the permanent unfrocking of a priest.

degrade (dɪ'greɪd) *vb.* **1.** (*tr.*) to reduce in worth, character, etc.; disgrace; dishonour. **2.** (diː'greɪd). (*tr.*) to reduce in rank, status, or degree; remove from office; demote. **3.** (*tr.*) to reduce in strength, quality, intensity, etc. **4.** to reduce or be reduced by erosion or down-cutting, as a land surface or bed of a river. Compare **aggrade. 5.** *Chem.* to decompose or be decomposed into atoms or smaller molecules. [C14: from Late Latin *dēgradāre,* from Latin DE- + *gradus* rank, degree] —**de'grader** *n.*

degrading (dɪ'greɪdɪŋ) *adj.* causing humiliation; debasing. —**de'gradingly** *adv.* —**de'gradingness** *n.*

degrease (diː'griːs) *vb.* (*tr.*) to remove grease from.

degree (dɪ'griː) *n.* **1.** a stage in a scale of relative amount or intensity: *a high degree of competence.* **2.** an academic award conferred by a university or college on successful completion of a course or as an honorary distinction (**honorary degree**). **3.** any of three categories of seriousness of a burn. See **burn**[1] (sense 21). **4.** (in the U.S.) any of the categories into which a crime is divided according to its seriousness: *first-degree murder.* **5.** *Genealogy.* a step in a line of descent, used as a measure of the closeness of a blood relationship. **6.** *Grammar.* any of the forms of an adjective used to indicate relative amount or intensity: in English they are *positive, comparative,* and *superlative.* **7.** *Music.* any note of a diatonic scale relative to the other notes in that scale: *D is the second degree of the scale of C major.* **8.** a unit of temperature on a specified scale: *the normal body temperature of man is 36.8 degrees centigrade.* Symbol: °. See also **Celsius scale, Fahrenheit scale. 9.** a measure of angle equal to one three-hundred-and-sixtieth of the angle traced by one complete revolution of a line about one of its ends. Symbol: °. See also **minute**[1] (sense 2), **second**[2] (sense 2). Compare **radian. 10. a.** a unit of latitude or longitude, divided into 60 minutes, used to define points on the earth's surface or on the celestial sphere. **b.** a point or line defined by units of latitude and/or longitude. Symbol: °. **11.** a unit on any of several scales of measurement, as for alcohol content or specific gravity. Symbol: °. **12.** *Maths.* **a.** the highest power or the sum of the powers of any term in a polynomial or by itself: $x^4 + x + 3$ *and* xyz^2 *are of the fourth degree.* **b.** the greatest power of the highest order derivative in a differential equation. **13.** *Obsolete.* a step; rung. **14.** *Archaic.* a stage in social status or rank. **15. by degrees.** little by little; gradually. **16. to a degree.** somewhat; rather. **17. degrees of frost.** See **frost** (sense 3). [C13: from Old French *degre,* from Latin DE- + *gradus* step, GRADE] —**de'greeless** *adj.*

degree day *n.* a day on which university degrees are conferred.

degree-day *n.* a unit used in estimating fuel requirements in heating buildings. It is equal to a fall of temperature of 1 degree below the mean outside temperature (usually taken as 18°C) for one day.

degree of freedom *n.* **1.** *Physics.* one of the minimum number of parameters necessary to describe a state or property of a system. **2.** one of the independent components of motion (translation, vibration, and rotation) of an atom or molecule. **3.** *Chem.* one of a number of intensive properties that can be independently varied without changing the number of phases in a system. See also **phase rule. 4.** *Statistics.* one of the independent unrestricted random variables constituting a statistic.

degression (dɪ'grɛʃən) *n.* **1.** a decrease by stages. **2.** a gradual decrease in the tax rate on amounts below a specified sum. [C15: from Medieval Latin *dēgressiō* descent, from Latin *dēgredī* to go down, from DE- + *gradī* to take steps, go]

degust (dɪ'gʌst) *or* **degustate** (dɪ'gʌsteɪt) *vb.* (*tr.*) *Rare.* to taste, esp. with care or relish; savour. [C17: from Latin *dēgustāre,* from *gustāre,* from *gustus* a tasting, taste] —**degustation** (ˌdiːgʌ'steɪʃən) *n.*

dehisce (dɪ'hɪs) *vb.* (*intr.*) (of fruits, anthers, etc.) to burst open spontaneously, releasing seeds, pollen, etc. [C17: from Latin *dēhiscere* to split open, from DE- + *hiscere* to yawn, gape]

dehiscent (dɪ'hɪsənt) *adj.* (of fruits, anthers, etc.) opening spontaneously to release seeds or pollen. —**de'hiscence** *n.*

dehorn (diː'hɔːn) *vb.* (*tr.*) **1.** to remove or prevent the growth of the horns of (cattle, sheep, or goats). **2.** to cut back (the larger limbs of a tree) drastically. —**de'horner** *n.*

dehumanize *or* **dehumanise** (diː'hjuːməˌnaɪz) *vb.* (*tr.*) **1.** to deprive of human qualities. **2.** to render mechanical, artificial, or routine. —**deˌhumani'zation** *or* **deˌhumani'sation** *n.*

dehumidifier (ˌdiːhjuː'mɪdɪˌfaɪə) *n.* a device for reducing the moisture content of the atmosphere.

dehumidify (ˌdiːhjuː'mɪdɪˌfaɪ) *vb.* **-fies, -fying, -fied.** (*tr.*) to remove water from (something, esp. the air). —ˌ**dehuˌmidifi'cation** *n.*

dehydrate (diː'haɪdreɪt, ˌdiːhaɪ'dreɪt) *vb.* **1.** to lose or cause to lose water; make or become anhydrous. **2.** to lose or cause to lose hydrogen atoms and oxygen atoms in the proportions in which they occur in water, as in a chemical reaction. **3.** to lose or deprive of water, as the body or tissues. —ˌ**dehy'dration** *n.* —**de'hydrator** *n.*

dehydrogenase (diː'haɪdrədʒəˌneɪz) *n.* an enzyme, such as any of the respiratory enzymes, that activates oxidation-reduction reactions by transferring hydrogen from substrate to acceptor.

dehydrogenate (diːˈhaɪdrədʒəˌneɪt), **dehydrogenize,** *or* **dehydrogenise** (diːˈhaɪdrədʒəˌnaɪz) *vb.* (*tr.*) to remove hydrogen from. —**deˌhydrogeˈnation, deˌhydrogeniˈzation,** *or* **deˌhydrogeniˈsation** *n.*

dehydroretinol (diːˌhaɪdrəʊˈrɛtɪnɒl) *n.* another name for **vitamin** A_2.

dehypnotize *or* **dehypnotise** (diːˈhɪpnəˌtaɪz) *vb.* (*tr.*) to bring out of the hypnotic state. —**deˌhypnotiˈzation** *or* **deˌhypnotiˈsation** *n.*

de-ice (diːˈaɪs) *vb.* to free or be freed of ice.

de-icer (diːˈaɪsə) *n.* **1.** a mechanical or thermal device designed to melt or stop the formation of ice on an aircraft, usually fitted to the aerofoil surfaces. Compare **anti-icer. 2.** a chemical or other substance used for this purpose, esp. an aerosol that can be sprayed on car windscreens to remove ice or frost.

deicide (ˈdiːɪˌsaɪd) *n.* **1.** the act of killing a god. **2.** a person who kills a god. [C17: from ecclesiastical Latin *deicida,* from Latin *deus* god; see -CIDE] —ˌ**deiˈcidal** *adj.*

deictic (ˈdaɪktɪk) *adj.* **1.** *Logic.* proving by direct argument. Compare **elenctic. 2.** another word for **indexical** (sense 2). [C17: from Greek *deiktikos* concerning proof, from *deiknunai* to show] —ˈ**deictically** *adv.*

deid (diːd) *adj.* a Scot. word for **dead.**

deif (diːf) *adj.* a Scot. word for **deaf.**

deific (diːˈɪfɪk, deɪ-) *adj.* **1.** making divine or exalting to the position of a god. **2.** divine or godlike.

deification (ˌdiːɪfɪˈkeɪʃən, ˌdeɪ-) *n.* **1.** the act or process of exalting to the position of a god. **2.** the state or condition of being deified.

deiform (ˈdiːɪˌfɔːm) *adj.* having the form or appearance of a god; sacred or divine.

deify (ˈdiːɪˌfaɪ, ˈdeɪɪ-) *vb.* **-fies, -fying, -fied.** (*tr.*) **1.** to exalt to the position of a god or personify as a god. **2.** to accord divine honour or worship to. **3.** to exalt in an extreme way; idealize. [C14: from Old French *deifier,* from Late Latin *deificāre,* from Latin *deus* god + *facere* to make] —ˈ**deiˌfier** *n.*

deign (deɪn) *vb.* **1.** (*intr.*) to think it fit or worthy of oneself (to do something); condescend: *he will not deign to speak to us.* **2.** (*tr.*) *Archaic.* to vouchsafe: *he deigned no reply.* [C13: from Old French *deignier,* from Latin *dignārī* to consider worthy, from *dignus* worthy]

Dei gratia *Latin.* (ˈdiːɪ ˈgreɪʃɪə, ˈdeɪɪ ˈgrɑːtɪə) *adv.* by the grace of God.

deil (diːl) *n.* a Scot. word for **devil.**

deindex (diːˈɪndɛks) *vb.* (*tr.*) to cause to become no longer index-linked.

deindividuation (diːˌɪndɪvɪdjʊˈeɪʃən) *n. Psychol.* the loss of a person's sense of individuality and personal responsibility.

deindustrialization *or* **deindustrialisation** (ˌdiːɪnˌdʌstrɪəlaɪˈzeɪʃən) *n.* the decline in importance of manufacturing industry in the economy of a nation or area. —ˌ**deinˈdustrialˌize** *or* ˌ**deinˈdustrialˌise** *vb.*

de-ionize *or* **de-ionise** (diːˈaɪəˌnaɪz) *vb.* (*tr.*) to remove ions from (water, etc.), esp. by ion exchange. —**deˌioniˈzation** *or* **deˌioniˈsation** *n.*

deipnosophist (daɪpˈnɒsəfɪst) *n. Rare.* a person who is a master of dinner-table conversation. [C17: from Greek *deipnosophistai,* title of a Greek work by Athenaeus (3rd century), describing learned discussions at a banquet, from *deipnon* meal + *sophistai* wise men; see SOPHIST]

deism (ˈdiːɪzəm, ˈdeɪ-) *n.* belief in the existence of God based solely on natural reason, without reference to revelation. Compare **theism.** [C17: from French *déisme,* from Latin *deus* god] —ˈ**deist** *n., adj.* —**deˈistic** *or* **deˈistical** *adj.* —**deˈistically** *adv.*

deity (ˈdiːɪtɪ, ˈdeɪ-) *n., pl.* **-ties. 1.** a god or goddess. **2.** the state of being divine; godhead. **3.** the rank, status, or position of a god. **4.** the nature or character of God. [C14: from Old French, from Late Latin *deitās,* from Latin *deus* god]

Deity (ˈdiːɪtɪ, ˈdeɪ-) *n.* **the.** the Supreme Being; God.

deixis (ˈdaɪksɪs) *n. Grammar.* the use or reference of a deictic word. [C20: from Greek, from *deiknunai* to show]

déjà vu (ˈdeɪʒæ ˈvuː; *French* deʒa vy) *n.* the experience of perceiving a new situation as if it had occurred before. It is sometimes associated with exhaustion or certain types of mental disorder. [literally: already seen]

deject (dɪˈdʒɛkt) *vb.* **1.** (*tr.*) to have a depressing effect on; dispirit; dishearten. ~*adj.* **2.** *Archaic.* downcast; dejected. [C15: from Latin *dēicere* to cast down, from DE- + *iacere* to throw]

dejecta (dɪˈdʒɛktə) *pl. n.* waste products excreted through the anus; faeces. [C19: New Latin: things cast down; see DEJECT]

dejected (dɪˈdʒɛktɪd) *adj.* miserable; despondent; downhearted. —**deˈjectedly** *adv.* —**deˈjectedness** *n.*

dejection (dɪˈdʒɛkʃən) *n.* **1.** lowness of spirits; depression; melancholy. **2. a.** faecal matter evacuated from the bowels; excrement. **b.** the act of defecating; defecation.

de jure (deɪ ˈdʒʊəreɪ) *adv.* according to law; by right; legally. Compare **de facto.** [Latin]

deka- *or* **dek-** *combining form.* variants of **deca-.**

dekko (ˈdɛkəʊ) *n., pl.* **-kos.** *Brit. slang.* a look; glance; view (esp. in the phrase **take a dekko (at)**). [C19: from Hindi *dekho!* look! from *dekhnā* to see]

del (dɛl) *n. Maths.* the differential operator $\boldsymbol{i}(\partial/\partial x) + \boldsymbol{j}(\partial/\partial y) + \boldsymbol{k}(\partial/\partial z)$, where ***i, j,*** and ***k*** are unit vectors in the *x, y,* and *z* directions. Symbol: ∇. Also called: **nabla.**

del. *abbrev. for* delegate.

Del. *abbrev. for* Delaware.

delaine (dəˈleɪn) *n.* a sheer wool or wool and cotton fabric. [C19: from French *mousseline de laine* muslin of wool]

delaminate (diːˈlæmɪˌneɪt) *vb.* to divide or cause to divide into thin layers. —**deˌlamiˈnation** *n.*

delate (dɪˈleɪt) *vb.* (*tr.*) **1.** (formerly) to bring a charge against; denounce; impeach. **2.** *Rare.* to report (an offence, etc.). **3.** *Obsolete.* to make known or public. [C16: from Latin *dēlātus,* from *dēferre* to bring down, report, indict, from DE- + *ferre* to bear] —**deˈlation** *n.* —**deˈlator** *n.*

Delaware[1] (ˈdɛləˌwɛə) *n.* **1.** (*pl.* **-wares** *or* **-ware**) a member of a North American Indian people formerly living near the Delaware River, in the northeastern U.S. **2.** the language of this people, belonging to the Algonquian family.

Delaware[2] (ˈdɛləˌwɛə) *n.* an American variety of grape that has sweet light red fruit.

delay (dɪˈleɪ) *vb.* **1.** (*tr.*) to put off to a later time; defer. **2.** (*tr.*) to slow up, hinder, or cause to be late; detain. **3.** (*intr.*) to be irresolute or put off doing something; procrastinate. **4.** (*intr.*) to linger; dawdle. ~*n.* **5.** the act or an instance of delaying or being delayed. **6.** the interval between one event and another; lull; interlude. [C13: from Old French *delaier,* from *des-* off + *laier,* variant of *laissier* to leave, from Latin *laxāre* to loosen, from *laxus* slack, LAX] —**deˈlayer** *n.*

delayed action *or* **delay action** *n.* **a.** a device for operating a mechanism, such as a camera shutter, a short time after setting. **b.** (*as modifier*): *a delayed-action fuse.*

delayed drop *n. Aeronautics.* a parachute descent with the opening of the parachute delayed, usually for a predetermined period.

delayed neutron *n.* a neutron produced in a nuclear reactor by the breakdown of a fission product and released a short time after neutrons produced in the primary process.

delayed opening *n. Aeronautics.* the automatic opening of a parachute after a predetermined delay to allow the parachutist to reach a particular height.

delayering (diːˈleɪərɪŋ) *n.* the process of pruning the administrative structure of a large organization by reducing the number of tiers in its hierarchy.

delaying action *n.* a measure or measures taken to gain time, as when weaker military forces harass the advance of a superior enemy without coming to a pitched battle.

delay line *n.* a device in which a known delay time is introduced in the transmission of a signal. An **acoustic delay line** delays a sound wave by circulating it through a liquid or solid medium.

del credere agent (dɛl ˈkreɪdərɪ) *n.* an agent who, in addition to obtaining orders, guarantees that the buyer will pay for the goods. [C18: from Italian: of trust]

dele (ˈdiːlɪ) *n., pl.* **deles. 1.** a sign (₰) indicating that typeset matter is to be deleted. Compare **stet.** ~*vb.* **deles, deleing, deled. 2.** (*tr.*) to mark (matter to be deleted) with a dele. [C18: from Latin: delete (imperative), from *dēlēre* to destroy, obliterate; see DELETE]

delectable (dɪˈlɛktəbᵊl) *adj.* highly enjoyable, esp. pleasing to the taste; delightful. [C14: from Latin *dēlectābilis,* from *dēlectāre* to DELIGHT] —**deˈlectableness** *or* **deˌlectaˈbility** *n.* —**deˈlectably** *adv.*

delectation (ˌdiːlɛkˈteɪʃən) *n.* pleasure; enjoyment.

delegacy (ˈdɛlɪgəsɪ) *n., pl.* **-cies. 1.** a less common word for **delegation** (senses 1, 2). **2. a.** an elected standing committee at some British universities. **b.** a department or institute of a university: *a delegacy of Education.*

delegate *n.* (ˈdɛlɪˌgeɪt, -gɪt). **1.** a person chosen or elected to act for or represent another or others, esp. at a conference or meeting. **2.** *U.S. government.* a representative of a territory in the U.S. House of Representatives. ~*vb.* (ˈdɛlɪˌgeɪt). **3.** to give or commit (duties, powers, etc.) to another as agent or representative; depute. **4.** (*tr.*) to send, authorize, or elect (a person) as agent or representative. **5.** (*tr.*) *Chiefly U.S.* to assign (a person owing a debt to oneself) to one's creditor in substitution for oneself. [C14: from Latin *dēlēgāre* to send on a mission, from *lēgāre* to send, depute; see LEGATE] —**delegable** (ˈdɛlɪgəbᵊl) *adj.*

delegation (ˌdɛlɪˈgeɪʃən) *n.* **1.** a person or group chosen to represent another or others. **2.** the act of delegating or state of being delegated. **3.** *U.S. politics.* all the members of Congress from one state.

delete (dɪˈliːt) *vb.* (*tr.*) to remove (something printed or written); erase; cancel; strike out. [C17: from Latin *dēlēre* to destroy, obliterate]

deleterious (ˌdɛlɪˈtɪərɪəs) *adj.* harmful; injurious; hurtful. [C17: from New Latin *dēlētērius,* from Greek *dēlētērios* injurious, destructive, from *dēleisthai* to hurt] —ˌ**deleˈteriously** *adv.* —ˌ**deleˈteriousness** *n.*

deletion (dɪˈliːʃən) *n.* **1.** the act of deleting or fact of being deleted. **2.** a deleted passage, word, etc., in a piece of text. **3.** the loss or absence of a section of a chromosome.

Delft (dɛlft) *n.* **1.** Also called: ˈ**delftware.** tin-glazed earthenware made in Delft, a town in the SW Netherlands, since the 17th century, typically having blue decoration on a white ground. **2.** a similar earthenware made in England.

deli (ˈdɛlɪ) *n., pl.* **delis.** an informal word for **delicatessen.**

Delian (ˈdiːlɪən) *n.* **1.** a native or inhabitant of Delos, a Greek island in the SW Aegean Sea. *~adj.* **2.** of or relating to Delos. **3.** of or relating to Frederick Delius (1862–1934), British composer.

deliberate *adj.* (dɪˈlɪbərɪt). **1.** carefully thought out in advance; planned; studied; intentional: *a deliberate insult.* **2.** careful or unhurried in speech or action: *a deliberate pace.* *~vb.* (dɪˈlɪbəˌreɪt). **3.** to consider (something) deeply; ponder; think over. [C15: from Latin *dēlīberāre* to consider well, from *lībrāre* to weigh, from *lībra* scales] —**deˈliberately** *adv.* —**deˈliberateness** *n.* —**deˈliberˌator** *n.*

deliberation (dɪˌlɪbəˈreɪʃən) *n.* **1.** thoughtful, careful, or lengthy consideration. **2.** (*often pl.*) formal discussion and debate, as of a committee, jury, etc. **3.** care, thoughtfulness, or absence of hurry, esp. in movement or speech.

deliberative (dɪˈlɪbərətɪv) *adj.* **1.** involved in, organized for, or having the function of deliberating: *a deliberative assembly.* **2.** characterized by or resulting from deliberation: *a deliberative conclusion.* —**deˈliberatively** *adv.* —**deˈliberativeness** *n.*

delicacy (ˈdɛlɪkəsɪ) *n., pl.* **-cies. 1.** fine or subtle quality, character, construction, etc.: *delicacy of craftsmanship.* **2.** fragile, soft, or graceful beauty. **3.** something that is considered choice to eat, such as caviar. **4.** fragile construction or constitution; frailty. **5.** refinement of feeling, manner, or appreciation: *the delicacy of the orchestra's playing.* **6.** fussy or squeamish refinement, esp. in matters of taste, propriety, etc. **7.** need for tactful or sensitive handling. **8.** accuracy or sensitivity of response or operation, as of an instrument. **9.** (in systemic grammar) the level of detail at which a linguistic description is made; the degree of fine distinction in a linguistic description. **10.** *Obsolete.* gratification, luxury, or voluptuousness.

delicate (ˈdɛlɪkɪt) *adj.* **1.** exquisite, fine, or subtle in quality, character, construction, etc. **2.** having a soft or fragile beauty. **3.** (of colour, tone, taste, etc.) pleasantly subtle, soft, or faint. **4.** easily damaged or injured; lacking robustness, esp. in health; fragile. **5.** precise, skilled, or sensitive in action or operation: *a delicate mechanism.* **6.** requiring tact and diplomacy. **7.** sensitive in feeling or manner; showing regard for the feelings of others. **8.** excessively refined; squeamish. *~n.* **9.** *Archaic.* a delicacy; dainty. [C14: from Latin *dēlicātus* affording pleasure, from *dēliciae* (pl.) delight, pleasure; see DELICIOUS] —**ˈdelicately** *adv.* —**ˈdelicateness** *n.*

delicatessen (ˌdɛlɪkəˈtɛsᵊn) *n.* **1.** various foods, esp. unusual or imported foods, already cooked or prepared. **2.** a shop selling these foods. [C19: from German *Delikatessen*, literally: delicacies, pl. of *Delikatesse* a delicacy, from French *délicatesse*]

delicious (dɪˈlɪʃəs) *adj.* **1.** very appealing to the senses, esp. to the taste or smell. **2.** extremely enjoyable or entertaining: *a delicious joke.* [C13: from Old French, from Late Latin *dēliciōsus*, from Latin *dēliciae* delights, charms, from *dēlicere* to entice; see DELIGHT] —**deˈliciously** *adv.* —**deˈliciousness** *n.*

delict (dɪˈlɪkt, ˈdiːlɪkt) *n.* **1.** *Law, chiefly Scots.* a wrongful act for which the person injured has the right to a civil remedy. See also **tort. 2.** *Roman law.* a civil wrong redressable by compensation or punitive damages. [C16: from Latin *dēlictum* a fault, crime, from *dēlinquere* to fail, do wrong; see DELINQUENCY]

delight (dɪˈlaɪt) *vb.* **1.** (*tr.*) to please greatly. **2.** (*intr.*; foll. by *in*) to take great pleasure (in). *~n.* **3.** extreme pleasure or satisfaction; joy. **4.** something that causes this: *music was always his delight.* [C13: from Old French *delit*, from *deleitier* to please, from Latin *dēlectāre*, from *dēlicere* to allure, from DE- + *lacere* to entice; see DELICIOUS; English spelling influenced by *light*] —**deˈlighter** *n.*

delighted (dɪˈlaɪtɪd) *adj.* **1.** (often foll. by an infinitive) extremely pleased (to do something): *I'm delighted to hear it!* *~sentence substitute.* **2.** I should be delighted to! —**deˈlightedly** *adv.* —**deˈlightedness** *n.*

delightful (dɪˈlaɪtful) *adj.* giving great delight; very pleasing, beautiful, charming, etc. —**deˈlightfully** *adv.* —**deˈlightfulness** *n.*

Delilah (dɪˈlaɪlə) *n.* a voluptuous and treacherous woman; temptress. [from Samson's Philistine mistress, who betrayed him (Judges 16:4–22)]

delimit (diːˈlɪmɪt) *or* **delimitate** *vb.* (*tr.*) to mark or prescribe the limits or boundaries of; demarcate. —**deˌlimiˈtation** *n.* —**deˈlimitative** *adj.*

delineate (dɪˈlɪnɪˌeɪt) *vb.* (*tr.*) **1.** to trace the shape or outline of; sketch. **2.** to represent pictorially, as by making a chart or diagram; depict. **3.** to portray in words, esp. with detail and precision; describe. [C16: from Latin *dēlīneāre* to sketch out, from *līnea* LINE[1]] —**deˈlineable** *adj.* —**deˌlineˈation** *n.* —**deˈlineative** *adj.*

delineator (dɪˈlɪnɪˌeɪtə) *n.* a tailor's pattern, adjustable for different sizes.

delinquency (dɪˈlɪŋkwənsɪ) *n., pl.* **-cies. 1.** an offence or misdeed, usually of a minor nature, esp. one committed by a young person. See **juvenile delinquency. 2.** failure or negligence in duty or obligation; dereliction. **3.** a delinquent nature or delinquent behaviour. [C17: from Late Latin *dēlinquentia* a fault, offence, from Latin *dēlinquere* to transgress, from DE- + *linquere* to forsake]

delinquent (dɪˈlɪŋkwənt) *n.* **1.** someone, esp. a young person, guilty of delinquency. See **juvenile delinquent. 2.** *Archaic.* a person who fails in an obligation or duty. *~adj.* **3.** guilty of an offence or misdeed, esp. one of a minor nature. **4.** failing in or neglectful of duty or obligation. [C17: from Latin *dēlinquēns* offending; see DELINQUENCY] —**deˈlinquently** *adv.*

deliquesce (ˌdɛlɪˈkwɛs) *vb.* (*intr.*) **1.** (esp. of certain salts) to dissolve gradually in water absorbed from the air. **2.** (of a plant stem) to form many branches. [C18: from Latin *dēliquēscere* to melt away, become liquid, from DE- + *liquēscere* to melt, from *liquēre* to be liquid]

deliquescence (ˌdɛlɪˈkwɛsᵊns) *n.* **1.** the process of deliquescing. **2.** a solution formed when a solid or liquid deliquesces. —**ˌdeliˈquescent** *adj.*

delirious (dɪˈlɪrɪəs) *adj.* **1.** affected with delirium. **2.** wildly excited, esp. with joy or enthusiasm. —**deˈliriously** *adv.* —**deˈliriousness** *n.*

delirium (dɪˈlɪrɪəm) *n., pl.* **-liriums, -liria** (-ˈlɪrɪə). **1.** a state of excitement and mental confusion, often accompanied by hallucinations, caused by high fever, poisoning, brain injury, etc. **2.** violent excitement or emotion; frenzy. [C16: from Latin: madness, from *dēlīrāre*, literally: to swerve from a furrow, hence be crazy, from DE- + *līra* ridge, furrow] —**deˈliriant** *adj.*

delirium tremens (ˈtrɛmɛnz, ˈtriː-) *n.* a severe psychotic condition occurring in some persons with chronic alcoholism, characterized by delirium, tremor, anxiety, and vivid hallucinations. Abbrevs.: **DT's** (informal), **dt.** [C19: New Latin, literally: trembling delirium]

delitescence (ˌdɛlɪˈtɛsᵊns) *n.* the sudden disappearance of a lesion or of the signs and symptoms of a disease. [C18: from Latin *dēlitēscens*, present participle of *dēlitēscere* to lurk, from *latēscere* to become hidden, from *latēre* to be hidden; see LATENT] —**ˌdeliˈtescent** *adj.*

deliver (dɪˈlɪvə) *vb.* (*mainly tr.*) **1.** to carry (goods, etc.) to a destination, esp. to carry and distribute (goods, mail, etc.) to several places: *to deliver letters; our local butcher delivers.* **2.** (often foll. by *over* or *up*) to hand over, transfer, or surrender. **3.** (often foll. by *from*) to release or rescue (from captivity, harm, corruption, etc.). **4.** (*also intr.*) **a.** to aid in the birth of (offspring). **b.** to give birth to (offspring). **c.** (usually foll. by *of*) to aid or assist (a female) in the birth (of offspring). **d.** (*passive*; foll. by *of*) to give birth (to offspring). **5.** to utter or present (a speech, oration, idea, etc.). **6.** short for **deliver the goods:** see sense 11, below. **7.** to utter (an exclamation, noise, etc.): *to deliver a cry of exultation.* **8.** to discharge or release (something, such as a blow or shot) suddenly. **9.** *Chiefly U.S.* to cause (voters, constituencies, etc.) to support a given candidate, cause, etc.: *can you deliver the Bronx?* **10. deliver oneself of.** to speak with deliberation or at length: *to deliver oneself of a speech.* **11. deliver the goods.** *Informal.* to produce or perform something promised or expected. [C13: from Old French *delivrer*, from Late Latin *dēlīberāre* to set free, from Latin DE- + *līberāre* to free] —**deˈliverable** *adj.* —**deˌliveraˈbility** *n.* —**deˈliverer** *n.*

deliverance (dɪˈlɪvərəns) *n.* **1.** a formal pronouncement or expression of opinion. **2.** rescue from moral corruption or evil; salvation. **3.** another word for **delivery** (senses 3–5).

delivery (dɪˈlɪvərɪ) *n., pl.* **-eries. 1. a.** the act of delivering or distributing goods, mail, etc. **b.** something that is delivered. **c.** (*as modifier*): *a delivery service.* **2.** the act of giving birth to a child: *she had an easy delivery.* **3.** manner or style of utterance, esp. in public speaking or recitation: *the chairman had a clear delivery.* **4.** the act of giving or transferring or the state of being given or transferred. **5.** the act of rescuing or state of being rescued; liberation. **6.** *Sport.* **a.** the act or manner of bowling or throwing a ball. **b.** the ball so delivered: *a fast delivery.* **7.** an actual or symbolic handing over of property, a deed, etc. **8.** the discharge rate of a compressor or pump.

delivery van *n.* a small van used esp. for delivery rounds. U.S. and Canadian name: **panel truck.**

dell (dɛl) *n.* a small, esp. wooded hollow. [Old English; related to Middle Low German *delle* valley; compare DALE]

delocalize *or* **delocalise** (diːˈləʊkᵊˌlaɪz) *vb.* (*tr.*) **1.** to remove from the usual locality. **2.** to free from local influences. —**deˌlocaliˈzation** *or* **deˌlocaliˈsation** *n.*

delouse (diːˈlaʊs, -ˈlaʊz) *vb.* (*tr.*) to rid (a person or animal) of lice as a sanitary measure.

Delphic (ˈdɛlfɪk) *or* **Delphian** *adj.* **1.** of or relating to the ancient Greek city of Delphi or its oracle or temple. **2.** obscure or ambiguous.

delphinium (dɛlˈfɪnɪəm) *n., pl.* **-iums** *or* **-ia** (-ɪə). any ranunculaceous plant of the genus *Delphinium:* many varieties are cultivated as garden plants for their spikes of blue, pink, or white spurred flowers. See also **larkspur.** [C17: New Latin, from Greek *delphinion* larkspur, from *delphis* DOLPHIN, referring to the shape of the nectary]

Delphinus (dɛlˈfaɪnəs) *n., Latin genitive* **Delphini** (dɛlˈfaɪnaɪ). a small constellation in the N hemisphere, between Pegasus and Sagitta. [C17: from Latin: DOLPHIN]

Delsarte system (ˈdɛlsɑːt) *n.* a method of teaching drama and dancing based on the exercises of Alexandre Delsarte (1811–71), famous teacher at the Paris Conservatoire.

delta (ˈdɛltə) *n.* **1.** the fourth letter in the Greek alphabet (Δ or δ), a consonant transliterated as *d.* **2.** an object resembling a capital delta in shape. **3.** (*cap. when part of name*) the flat alluvial area at the mouth of some rivers where the mainstream splits up into several distributaries: *the Mississippi Delta.* **4.** *Maths.* a finite increment in a variable. [C16: via Latin from Greek, of Semitic origin; compare Hebrew *dāleth*] —**deltaic** (dɛlˈteɪɪk) *or* ˈ**deltic** *adj.*

Delta (ˈdɛltə) *n.* **1.** (*foll. by the genitive case of a specified constellation*) usually the fourth brightest star in a constellation. **2.** any of a group of U.S. launch vehicles used to put unmanned satellites into orbit. **3.** *Communications.* a code word for the letter *d.*

delta connection *n.* a connection used in a three-phase electrical system in which three elements in series form a triangle, the supply being input and output at the three junctions. Compare **star connection.**

delta iron *n.* an allotrope of iron that exists between 1400°C and the melting point of iron and has the same structure as alpha iron.

delta particle *n. Physics.* a very short-lived hyperon.

delta ray *n.* a particle, esp. an electron, ejected from matter by ionizing radiation.

delta rhythm *or* **wave** *n. Physiol.* the normal electrical activity of the cerebral cortex during deep sleep, occurring at a frequency of 1 to 4 hertz and detectable with an electroencephalograph. See also **brain wave.**

delta stock *n.* any of the fourth rank of active securities on the Stock Exchange. Market makers need not display prices of these securities continuously and any prices displayed are taken only as an indication rather than an offer to buy or sell.

delta wing *n.* a triangular sweptback aircraft wing.

deltiology (ˌdɛltɪˈɒlədʒɪ) *n.* the collection and study of picture postcards. [C20: from Greek *deltion,* diminutive of *deltos* a writing tablet + -LOGY] —ˌ**deltiˈologist** *n.*

deltoid (ˈdɛltɔɪd) *n.* **1.** the thick muscle forming the rounded contour of the outer edge of the shoulder and acting to raise the arm. ~*adj.* **2.** shaped like a Greek capital delta, Δ; triangular. [C18: from Greek *deltoeidēs* triangular, from DELTA]

delude (dɪˈluːd) *vb.* (*tr.*) **1.** to deceive the mind or judgment of; mislead; beguile. **2.** *Rare.* to frustrate (hopes, expectations, etc.). [C15: from Latin *dēlūdere* to mock, play false, from DE- + *lūdere* to play] —**deˈludable** *adj.* —**deˈluder** *n.* —**deˈludingly** *adv.*

deluge (ˈdɛljuːdʒ) *n.* **1.** a great flood of water. **2.** torrential rain; downpour. **3.** an overwhelming rush or number: *a deluge of requests.* ~*vb.* (*tr.*) **4.** to flood, as with water; soak, swamp, or drown. **5.** to overwhelm or overrun; inundate. [C14: from Old French, from Latin *dīluvium* a washing away, flood, from *dīluere* to wash away, drench, from *di-* DIS-[1] + *-luere,* from *lavere* to wash]

delusion (dɪˈluːʒən) *n.* **1.** a mistaken or misleading opinion, idea, belief, etc.: *he has delusions of grandeur.* **2.** *Psychiatry.* a belief held in the face of evidence to the contrary, that is resistant to all reason. See also **illusion, hallucination.** **3.** the act of deluding or state of being deluded. —**deˈlusional** *adj.* —**deˈlusive** *adj.* —**deˈlusively** *adv.* —**deˈlusiveness** *n.* —**delusory** (dɪˈluːsərɪ) *adj.*

de luxe (də ˈlʌks, ˈlʊks) *adj.* **1.** (esp. of products, articles for sale, etc.) rich, elegant, or sumptuous; superior in quality, number of accessories, etc.: *the de luxe model of a car.* ~*adv.* **2.** *Chiefly U.S.* in a luxurious manner. [C19: from French, literally: of luxury]

delve (dɛlv) *vb.* (*mainly intr.;* often foll. by *in* or *into*) **1.** to inquire or research deeply or intensively (for information, etc.): *he delved in the Bible for quotations.* **2.** to search or rummage (in a drawer, the pockets, etc.). **3.** (esp. of an animal) to dig or burrow deeply (into the ground, etc.). **4.** (*also tr.*) *Archaic or dialect.* to dig or turn up (earth, a garden, etc.), as with a spade. [Old English *delfan;* related to Old High German *telban* to dig, Russian *dolbit* to hollow out with a chisel] —ˈ**delver** *n.*

Dem. *U.S. abbrev. for* Democrat(ic).

demagnetize *or* **demagnetise** (diːˈmægnəˌtaɪz) *vb.* to lose magnetic properties or remove magnetic properties from. Also: **degauss.** —**deˌmagnetiˈzation** *or* **deˌmagnetiˈsation** *n.* —**deˈmagnetˌizer** *or* **deˈmagnetˌiser** *n.*

demagogic (ˌdɛməˈgɒgɪk) *or* **demagogical** *adj.* of, characteristic of, relating to, or resembling a demagogue. —ˌ**demaˈgogically** *adv.*

demagogue *or U.S.* (*sometimes*) **demagog** (ˈdɛməˌgɒg) *n.* **1.** a political agitator who appeals with crude oratory to the prejudice and passions of the mob. **2.** (esp. in the ancient world) any popular political leader or orator. [C17: from Greek *dēmagōgos* people's leader, from *dēmos* people + *agein* to lead]

demagoguery (ˌdɛməˈgɒgərɪ) *or* **demagoguism** (ˈdɛməˌgɒgɪzəm) *n.* the methods, practices, or rhetoric of a demagogue.

demagogy (ˈdɛməˌgɒgɪ) *n., pl.* **-gogies.** **1.** demagoguery. **2.** rule by a demagogue or by demagogues. **3.** a group of demagogues.

de-man *vb.* (*tr.*) **-mans, -manning, -manned.** *Brit.* to reduce the workforce of (a plant, industry, etc.).

demand (dɪˈmɑːnd) *vb.* (*tr.; may take a clause as object or an infinitive*) **1.** to request peremptorily or urgently. **2.** to require or need as just, urgent, etc.: *the situation demands attention.* **3.** to claim as a right; exact: *his parents demanded obedience of him.* **4.** *Law.* to make a formal legal claim to (property, esp. realty). ~*n.* **5.** an urgent or peremptory requirement or request. **6.** something that requires special effort or sacrifice: *a demand on one's time.* **7.** the act of demanding something or the thing demanded: *the kidnappers' demand was a million pounds.* **8.** an insistent question or query. **9.** *Economics.* **a.** willingness and ability to purchase goods and services. **b.** the amount of a commodity that consumers are willing and able to purchase at a specified price. Compare **supply**[1] (sense 9). **10.** *Law.* a formal legal claim, esp. to real property. **11. in demand.** sought after; popular. **12. on demand.** as soon as requested: *a draft payable on demand.* [C13: from Anglo-French *demaunder,* from Medieval Latin *dēmandāre,* from Latin: to commit to, from DE- + *mandāre* to command, entrust; see MANDATE] —**deˈmandable** *adj.* —**deˈmander** *n.*

demandant (dɪˈmɑːndənt) *n. Law.* (formerly) the plaintiff in an action relating to real property. [C14: from Old French, from *demander* to DEMAND]

demand bill *or* **draft** *n.* a bill of exchange that is payable on demand. Also called: **sight bill.**

demand deposit *n.* a bank deposit from which withdrawals may be made without notice. Compare **time deposit.**

demanding (dɪˈmɑːndɪŋ) *adj.* requiring great patience, skill, etc.: *a demanding job.* —**deˈmandingly** *adv.*

demand loan *n.* another name for **call loan.**

demand management *n. Economics.* the regulation of total spending in an economy to required levels, attempted by a government esp. in order to avoid unemployment or inflation: a measure advocated by Keynesian economists.

demand note *n.* a promissory note payable on demand.

demand-pull inflation *n.* See **inflation** (sense 2).

demantoid (dɪˈmæntɔɪd) *n.* a bright green variety of andradite garnet. [C19: from German, from obsolete *Demant* diamond, from Old French *diamant* + -OID]

demarcate (ˈdiːmɑːˌkeɪt) *vb.* (*tr.*) **1.** to mark, fix, or draw the boundaries, limits, etc., of. **2.** to separate or distinguish between (areas with unclear boundaries). —ˈ**demarˌcator** *n.*

demarcation *or* **demarkation** (ˌdiːmɑːˈkeɪʃən) *n.* **1.** the act of establishing limits or boundaries. **2.** a limit or boundary. **3. a.** a strict separation of the kinds of work performed by members of different trade unions. **b.** (*as modifier*): *demarcation dispute.* **4.** separation or distinction (often in the phrase **line of demarcation**). [C18: Latinized version of Spanish *demarcación,* from *demarcar* to appoint the boundaries of, from *marcar* to mark, from Italian *marcare,* of Germanic origin; see MARK[1]]

démarche *French.* (demarʃ) *n.* **1.** a move, step, or manoeuvre, esp. in diplomatic affairs. **2.** a representation or statement of views, complaints, etc., to a public authority. [C17: literally: walk, gait, from Old French *demarcher* to tread, trample; see DE-, MARCH[1]]

dematerialize *or* **dematerialise** (diːməˈtɪərɪəˌlaɪz) *vb.* (*intr.*) **1.** to cease to have material existence, as in science fiction or spiritualism. **2.** to disappear without trace; vanish. —**demaˌterialiˈzation** *or* **demaˌterialiˈsation** *n.*

deme (diːm) *n.* **1. a.** (in preclassical Greece) the territory inhabited by a tribe. **b.** (in ancient Attica) a geographical unit of local government. **2.** *Biology.* a group of individuals within a species that possess particular characteristics of cytology, genetics, etc. [C19: from Greek *dēmos* district in local government, the populace]

demean[1] (dɪˈmiːn) *vb.* (*tr.*) to lower (oneself) in dignity, status, or character; humble; debase. [C17: see DE-, MEAN[2]; on the model of *debase*]

demean[2] (dɪˈmiːn) *vb.* (*tr.*) *Rare.* to behave or conduct (oneself) in a specified way. [C13: from Old French *demener,* from DE- + *mener* to lead, drive, from Latin *mināre* to drive (animals), from *minārī* to use threats]

demeanour *or U.S.* **demeanor** (dɪˈmiːnə) *n.* **1.** the way a person behaves towards others; conduct. **2.** bearing, appearance, or mien. [C15: see DEMEAN[2]]

dement (dɪˈmɛnt) *vb.* **1.** (*intr.*) to deteriorate mentally, esp. because of old age. **2.** (*tr.*) *Rare.* to drive mad; make insane. [C16: from Late Latin *dēmentāre* to drive mad, from Latin DE- + *mēns* mind]

demented (dɪˈmɛntɪd) *adj.* mad; insane. —**deˈmentedly** *adv.* —**deˈmentedness** *n.*

dementia (dɪˈmɛnʃə, -ʃɪə) *n.* a state of serious emotional and mental deterioration, of organic or functional origin. [C19: from Latin: madness; see DEMENT]

dementia praecox (ˈpriːkɒks) *n.* a former name for **schizophrenia.** [C19: New Latin, literally: premature dementia]

demerara (ˌdɛməˈrɛərə, -ˈrɑːrə) *n.* **1.** brown crystallized cane sugar from the West Indies and nearby countries. **2.** a highly flavoured rum used mainly for blending purposes. [C19: named after *Demerara,* a region of Guyana]

demerger (diːˈmɜːdʒə) *n.* the separation of two or more companies which have previously been merged. —**deˈmerge** *vb.*

demerit (diːˈmɛrɪt, ˈdiːˌmɛrɪt) *n.* **1.** something, esp. conduct, that deserves censure. **2.** *U.S. and Canadian.* a mark given against a person for failure or misconduct, esp. in schools or the armed forces. **3.** a fault or disadvantage. [C14 (originally: worth, desert, later specialized to mean: something worthy of blame): from Latin *dēmerērī* to deserve] —**deˌmeriˈtorious** *adj.* —**deˌmeriˈtoriously** *adv.*

demersal (dɪ'mɜːsᵊl) *adj.* living or occurring in deep water or on the bottom of a sea or lake: *demersal fish.* [C19: from Latin *dēmersus* submerged (from *dēmergere* to plunge into, from *mergere* to dip) + -AL[1]]

demesne (dɪ'meɪn, -'miːn) *n.* **1.** land, esp. surrounding a house or manor, retained by the owner for his own use. **2.** *Property law.* the possession and use of one's own property or land. **3.** the territory ruled by a state or a sovereign; realm; domain. **4.** a region or district; domain. [C14: from Old French *demeine;* see DOMAIN]

demi- *prefix.* **1.** half: *demirelief.* Compare **hemi-, semi-** (sense 1). **2.** of less than full size, status, or rank: *demigod.* [via French from Medieval Latin *dīmedius,* from Latin *dīmidius* half, from *dis-* apart + *medius* middle]

demibastion (ˌdɛmɪ'bæstɪən) *n. Fortifications.* half a bastion, having only one flank, at right angles to the wall.

demicanton (ˌdɛmɪ'kæntɒn, -kæn'tɒn) *n.* either of the two parts of certain Swiss cantons.

demigod ('dɛmɪˌgɒd) *n.* **1. a.** a mythological being who is part mortal, part god. **b.** a lesser deity. **2.** a person with outstanding or godlike attributes. [C16: translation of Latin *sēmideus*] —**'demiˌgoddess** *fem. n.*

demijohn ('dɛmɪˌdʒɒn) *n.* a large bottle with a short narrow neck, often with small handles at the neck and encased in wickerwork. [C18: probably by folk etymology from French *dame-jeanne,* from *dame* lady + *Jeanne* Jane]

demilitarize *or* **demilitarise** (diː'mɪlɪtəˌraɪz) *vb. (tr.)* **1.** to remove and prohibit any military presence or function in (an area): *demilitarized zone.* **2.** to free of military character, purpose, etc.: *11 regiments were demilitarized.* —**deˌmilitari'zation** *or* **deˌmilitari'sation** *n.*

demilune ('dɛmɪˌluːn, -ˌljuːn) *n.* **1.** *Fortifications.* an outwork in front of a fort, shaped like a crescent moon. **2.** a crescent-shaped object or formation; half-moon. [C18: from French, literally: half-moon]

demimondaine (ˌdɛmɪ'mɒndeɪn; *French* dəmimɔ̃dɛn) *n.* a woman of the demimonde. [C19: from French]

demimonde (ˌdɛmɪ'mɒnd; *French* dəmimɔ̃d) *n.* **1.** (esp. in the 19th century) those women considered to be outside respectable society, esp. on account of sexual promiscuity. **2.** any social group considered to be not wholly respectable. [C19: from French, literally: half-world]

demineralize *or* **demineralise** (diː'mɪnərəˌlaɪz) *vb. (tr.)* to remove dissolved salts from (a liquid, esp. water). —**deˌminerali'zation** *or* **deˌminerali'sation** *n.*

demi-pension *French.* (dəmipɑ̃sjɔ̃) *n.* another name for **half board.**

demirelief (ˌdɛmɪrɪ'liːf) *n.* a less common term for **mezzo-relievo.**

demirep ('dɛmɪˌrɛp) *n. Rare.* a woman of bad repute, esp. a prostitute. [C18: from DEMI- + REP(UTATION)]

demise (dɪ'maɪz) *n.* **1.** failure or termination: *the demise of one's hopes.* **2.** a euphemistic or formal word for **death. 3.** *Property law.* **a.** a transfer of an estate by lease. **b.** the passing or transfer of an estate on the death of the owner. **4.** the immediate transfer of sovereignty to a successor upon the death, abdication, etc., of a ruler (esp. in the phrase **demise of the crown**). ~*vb.* **5.** to transfer or be transferred by inheritance, will, or succession. **6.** *(tr.) Property law.* to transfer (an estate, etc.) for a limited period; lease. **7.** *(tr.)* to transfer (sovereignty, a title, etc.) by or as if by the death, deposition, etc., of a ruler. [C16: from Old French, feminine of *demis* dismissed, from *demettre* to send away, from Latin *dīmittere;* see DISMISS] —**de'misable** *adj.*

demisemiquaver ('dɛmɪˌsɛmɪˌkweɪvə) *n. Music.* a note having the time value of one thirty-second of a semibreve. Usual U.S. and Canadian name: **thirty-second note.**

demission (dɪ'mɪʃən) *n. Rare.* relinquishment of or abdication from an office, responsibility, etc. [C16: from Anglo-French *dimissioun,* from Latin *dīmissiō* a dismissing; see DISMISS]

demist (diː'mɪst) *vb.* to free or become free of condensation through evaporation produced by a heater and/or blower. —**de'mister** *n.*

demit (dɪ'mɪt) *vb.* **-mits, -mitting, -mitted.** *Archaic, chiefly Scot.* **1.** to resign (an office, position, etc.). **2.** *(tr.)* to dismiss. [C16: from Latin *dīmittere* to send forth, discharge, renounce, from DI-[2] + *mittere* to send]

demitasse ('dɛmɪˌtæs; *French* dəmitɑs) *n.* a small cup used to serve coffee, esp. after a meal. [C19: French, literally: half-cup]

demiurge ('dɛmɪˌɜːdʒ, 'diː-) *n.* **1. a.** (in the philosophy of Plato) the creator of the universe. **b.** (in Gnostic and some other philosophies) the creator of the universe, supernatural but subordinate to the Supreme Being. **2.** (in ancient Greece) a magistrate with varying powers found in any of several states. [C17: from Church Latin *dēmiūrgus,* from Greek *dēmiourgos* skilled workman, literally: one who works for the people, from *dēmos* people + *ergon* work] —**ˌdemi'urgeous, ˌdemi'urgic,** *or* **ˌdemi'urgical** *adj.* —**ˌdemi'urgically** *adv.*

demivierge ('dɛmɪˌvjɛəʒ) *n.* a woman who engages in promiscuous sexual activity but retains her virginity. [C20: French, literally: half-virgin]

demivolt *or* **demivolte** ('dɛmɪˌvɒlt) *n. Dressage.* a half turn on the hind legs.

demo ('dɛməʊ) *n., pl.* **-os.** *Informal.* **1.** short for **demonstration** (sense 4). **2.** a demonstration record or tape, used for audition purposes. **3.** *U.S.* short for **demonstrator** (sense 3).

demo- *or before a vowel* **dem-** *combining form.* indicating people or population: *demography.* [from Greek *dēmos*]

demob (diː'mɒb) *Brit. informal.* ~*vb.* **-mobs, -mobbing, -mobbed. 1.** short for **demobilize.** ~*n.* **2. a.** short for **demobilization. b.** *(as modifier): a demob suit.* **3.** a soldier who has been demobilized.

demobilize *or* **demobilise** (diː'məʊbɪˌlaɪz) *vb.* to disband, as troops, etc. —**deˌmobili'zation** *or* **deˌmobili'sation** *n.*

democracy (dɪ'mɒkrəsɪ) *n., pl.* **-cies. 1.** government by the people or their elected representatives. **2.** a political or social unit governed ultimately by all its members. **3.** the practice or spirit of social equality. **4.** a social condition of classlessness and equality. **5.** the common people, esp. as a political force. [C16: from French *démocratie,* from Late Latin *dēmocratia,* from Greek *dēmokratia* government by the people; see DEMO-, -CRACY]

democrat ('dɛməˌkræt) *n.* **1.** an advocate of democracy; adherent of democratic principles. **2.** a member or supporter of a democratic party or movement.

Democrat ('dɛməˌkræt) *n.* (in the U.S.) a member or supporter of the Democratic Party, the older of the two major political parties. Compare **Liberal Democrat, social democrat** (sense 2). —**ˌDemo'cratic** *adj.*

democratic (ˌdɛmə'krætɪk) *adj.* **1.** of, characterized by, derived from, or relating to the principles of democracy. **2.** upholding or favouring democracy or the interests of the common people. **3.** popular with or for the benefit of all: *democratic sports.* —**ˌdemo'cratically** *adv.*

democratic centralism *n.* the Leninist principle that policy should be decided centrally by officials, who are nominally democratically elected.

democratize *or* **democratise** (dɪ'mɒkrəˌtaɪz) *vb. (tr.)* to make democratic. —**deˌmocrati'zation** *or* **deˌmocrati'sation** *n.*

démodé *French.* (demɔde) *adj.* out of fashion; outmoded. [French, from *dé-* out of + *mode* style, fashion]

demodulate (diː'mɒdjʊˌleɪt) *vb.* to carry out demodulation on (a wave or signal). —**de'moduˌlator** *n.*

demodulation (ˌdiːmɒdjʊ'leɪʃən) *n. Electronics.* the act or process by which an output wave or signal is obtained having the characteristics of the original modulating wave or signal; the reverse of modulation.

demographics (ˌdɛmə'græfɪks, ˌdiːmə-) *pl. n.* data resulting from the science of demography; population statistics.

demographic timebomb *n. Chiefly Brit.* a predicted shortage of school-leavers and consequently of available workers, caused by an earlier drop in the birth rate, resulting in an older workforce.

demography (dɪ'mɒgrəfɪ) *n.* the scientific study of human populations, esp. with reference to their size, structure, and distribution. [C19: from French *démographie,* from Greek *dēmos* the populace; see -GRAPHY] —**de'mographer** *or* **de'mographist** *n.* —**demographic** (ˌdɛmə'græfɪk, ˌdiːmə-) *or* **ˌdemo'graphical** *adj.* —**ˌdemo'graphically** *adv.*

demoiselle (dəmwɑː'zɛl) *n.* **1.** Also called: **demoiselle crane, Numidian crane.** a small crane, *Anthropoides virgo,* of central Asia, N Africa, and SE Europe, having grey plumage with long black breast feathers and white ear tufts. **2.** a less common name for a **damselfly. 3.** another name for **damselfish. 4.** a literary word for **damsel.** [C16: from French: young woman; see DAMSEL]

demolish (dɪ'mɒlɪʃ) *vb. (tr.)* **1.** to tear down or break up (buildings, etc.). **2.** to destroy; put an end to (an argument, etc.). **3.** *Facetious.* to eat up: *she demolished the whole cake!* [C16: from French *démolir,* from Latin *dēmōlīrī* to throw down, destroy, from DE- + *mōlīrī* to strive, toil, construct, from *mōles* mass, bulk] —**de'molisher** *n.* —**de'molishment** *n.*

demolition (ˌdɛmə'lɪʃən, ˌdiː-) *n.* **1.** the act of demolishing or state of being demolished. **2.** *Chiefly military.* **a.** destruction by explosives. **b.** *(as modifier): a demolition charge.* —**ˌdemo'litionist** *n., adj.*

demolitions (ˌdɛmə'lɪʃənz, ˌdiː-) *pl. n. Chiefly military.* **a.** explosives, as when used to blow up bridges, etc. **b.** *(as modifier): a demolitions expert.*

demon ('diːmən) *n.* **1.** an evil spirit or devil. **2.** a person, habit, obsession, etc., thought of as evil, cruel, or persistently tormenting. **3.** Also called: **daemon, daimon.** an attendant or ministering spirit; genius: *the demon of inspiration.* **4. a.** a person who is extremely skilful in, energetic at, or devoted to a given activity, esp. a sport: *a demon at cycling.* **b.** *(as modifier): a demon cyclist.* **5.** a variant spelling of **daemon** (sense 1). **6.** *Austral. and N.Z. informal.* a detective or policeman. [C15: from Latin *daemōn* evil spirit, spirit, from Greek *daimōn* spirit, deity, fate; see DAEMON]

demonetarize *or* **demonetarise** (diː'mʌnətəraɪz) *vb. (tr.)* another word for **demonetize** (sense 1). —**deˌmonetari'zation** *or* **deˌmonetari'sation** *n.*

demonetize *or* **demonetise** (diː'mʌnɪˌtaɪz) *vb. (tr.)* **1.** to deprive (a metal) of its capacity as a monetary standard. **2.** to withdraw from use as currency. —**deˌmoneti'zation** *or* **deˌmoneti'sation** *n.*

demoniac (dɪ'məʊnɪˌæk) *adj. also* **demoniacal** (ˌdiːmə'naɪəkᵊl). **1.** of, like, or suggestive of a demon; demonic. **2.** suggesting inner possession or inspiration: *the demoniac fire of genius.* **3.** frantic; frenzied; feverish: *demoniac activity.* ~*n.* **4.** a person possessed by an evil spirit or demon. —ˌ**demoˈniacally** *adv.*

demonic (dɪˈmɒnɪk) *adj.* **1.** of, relating to, or characteristic of a demon; fiendish. **2.** inspired or possessed by a demon, or seemingly so: *demonic laughter.* —**deˈmonically** *adv.*

demonism (ˈdiːməˌnɪzəm) *n.* **1. a.** belief in the existence and power of demons. **b.** worship of demons. **2.** another word for **demonology.** —ˈ**demonist** *n.*

demonize *or* **demonise** (ˈdiːməˌnaɪz) *vb.* (*tr.*) **1.** to make into or like a demon. **2.** to subject to demonic influence.

demonolater (ˌdiːməˈnɒlətə) *n.* a person who worships demons. [C19: back formation from DEMONOLATRY]

demonolatry (ˌdiːməˈnɒlətrɪ) *n.* the worship of demons. [C17: see DEMON, -LATRY]

demonology (ˌdiːməˈnɒlədʒɪ) *n.* the study of demons or demonic beliefs. Also called: **demonism.** —**demonological** (ˌdiːmənəˈlɒdʒɪkᵊl) *adj.* —ˌ**demonˈologist** *n.*

demonstrable (ˈdɛmənstrəbᵊl, dɪˈmɒn-) *adj.* able to be demonstrated or proved. —ˌ**demonstraˈbility** *or* ˈ**demonstrableness** *n.* —**demonstrably** (ˈdɛmənstrəblɪ, dɪˈmɒn-) *adv.*

demonstrate (ˈdɛmənˌstreɪt) *vb.* **1.** (*tr.*) to show, manifest, or prove, esp. by reasoning, evidence, etc.: *it is easy to demonstrate the truth of this proposition.* **2.** (*tr.*) to evince; reveal the existence of: *the scheme later demonstrated a fatal flaw.* **3.** (*tr.*) to explain or illustrate by experiment, example, etc. **4.** (*tr.*) to display, operate, and explain the workings of (a machine, product, etc.). **5.** (*intr.*) to manifest support, protest, etc., by public parades or rallies. **6.** (*intr.*) to be employed as a demonstrator of machinery, etc. **7.** (*intr.*) *Military.* to make a show of force, esp. in order to deceive one's enemy. [C16: from Latin *dēmonstrāre* to point out, from *monstrāre* to show]

demonstration (ˌdɛmənˈstreɪʃən) *n.* **1.** the act of demonstrating. **2.** proof or evidence leading to proof. **3.** an explanation, display, illustration, or experiment showing how something works. **4.** a manifestation of grievances, support, or protest by public rallies, parades, etc. **5.** a manifestation of emotion. **6.** a show of military force or preparedness. **7.** *Maths.* a logical presentation of the assumptions and equations used in solving a problem or proving a theorem. —ˌ**demonˈstrational** *adj.* —ˌ**demonˈstrationist** *n.*

demonstration model *n.* a nearly new product, such as a car or washing machine, that has been used only to demonstrate its performance by a dealer and is offered for sale at a discount.

demonstrative (dɪˈmɒnstrətɪv) *adj.* **1.** tending to manifest or express one's feelings easily or unreservedly. **2.** (*postpositive;* foll. by *of*) serving as proof; indicative. **3.** involving or characterized by demonstration: *a demonstrative lecture.* **4.** conclusive; indubitable: *demonstrative arguments.* **5.** *Grammar.* denoting or belonging to a class of determiners used to point out the individual referent or referents intended, such as *this, that, these,* and *those.* Compare **interrogative, relative.** ~*n.* **6.** *Grammar.* a demonstrative word or construction. —**deˈmonstratively** *adv.* —**deˈmonstrativeness** *n.*

demonstrator (ˈdɛmənˌstreɪtə) *n.* **1.** a person who demonstrates equipment, machines, products, etc. **2.** a person who takes part in a public demonstration. **3.** *U.S.* a piece of merchandise, such as a car that one test-drives, used to display merits or performance to prospective buyers.

demoralize *or* **demoralise** (dɪˈmɒrəˌlaɪz) *vb.* (*tr.*) **1.** to undermine the morale of; dishearten: *he was demoralized by his defeat.* **2.** to debase morally; corrupt. **3.** to throw into confusion. —**deˌmoraliˈzation** *or* **deˌmoraliˈsation** *n.* —**deˈmoralˌizer** *or* **deˈmoralˌiser** *n.*

De Morgan's laws (də ˈmɔːgənz) *pl. n.* (in formal logic and set theory) the principles that conjunction and disjunction, or union and intersection, are dual. Thus the negation of *P & Q* is equivalent to *not-P* or *not-Q.* [named after Augustus *De Morgan* (1806–71), British mathematician]

demos (ˈdiːmɒs) *n.* **1.** the people of a nation regarded as a political unit. **2.** *Rare.* the common people; masses. [C19: from Greek: the populace; see DEME]

demote (dɪˈməʊt) *vb.* (*tr.*) to lower in rank or position; relegate. [C19: from DE- + (PRO)MOTE] —**deˈmotion** *n.*

demotic (dɪˈmɒtɪk) *adj.* **1.** of or relating to the common people; popular. **2.** of or relating to a simplified form of hieroglyphics used in ancient Egypt by the ordinary literate class outside the priesthood. Compare **hieratic.** ~*n.* **3.** the demotic script of ancient Egypt. [C19: from Greek *dēmotikos* of the people, from *dēmotēs* a man of the people, commoner; see DEMOS] —**deˈmotist** *n.*

Demotic (dɪˈmɒtɪk) *n.* **1.** the spoken form of Modern Greek, now increasingly used in literature. Compare **Katharevusa.** ~*adj.* **2.** denoting or relating to this.

demount (diːˈmaʊnt) *vb.* (*tr.*) to remove (a motor, gun, etc.) from its mounting or setting. —**deˈmountable** *adj.*

dempster (ˈdɛmpstə) *n.* a variant spelling of **deemster.**

demulcent (dɪˈmʌlsᵊnt) *adj.* **1.** soothing; mollifying. ~*n.* **2.** a drug or agent that soothes the irritation of inflamed or injured skin surfaces. [C18: from Latin *dēmulcēre* to caress soothingly, from DE- + *mulcēre* to stroke]

demulsify (diːˈmʌlsɪˌfaɪ) *vb.* **-fies, -fying, -fied.** to undergo or cause to undergo a process in which an emulsion is permanently broken down into its constituents. [C20: from DE- + EMULSIFY] —**deˌmulsifiˈcation** *n.* —**deˈmulsiˌfier** *n.*

demur (dɪˈmɜː) *vb.* **-murs, -murring, -murred.** (*intr.*) **1.** to raise objections or show reluctance; object. **2.** *Law.* to raise an objection by entering a demurrer. **3.** *Archaic.* to hesitate; delay. ~*n. also* **demurral** (dɪˈmʌrəl). **4.** the act of demurring. **5.** an objection raised. **6.** *Archaic.* hesitation. [C13: from Old French *demorer,* from Latin *dēmorārī* to loiter, linger, from *morārī* to delay, from *mora* a delay] —**deˈmurrable** *adj.*

demure (dɪˈmjʊə) *adj.* **1.** sedate; decorous; reserved. **2.** affectedly modest or prim; coy. [C14: perhaps from Old French *demorer* to delay, linger; perhaps influenced by *meur* ripe, MATURE] —**deˈmurely** *adv.* —**deˈmureness** *n.*

demurrage (dɪˈmʌrɪdʒ) *n.* **1.** the delaying of a ship, railway wagon, etc., caused by the charterer's failure to load, unload, etc., before the time of scheduled departure. **2.** the extra charge required as compensation for such delay. **3.** a fee charged by the Bank of England for changing bullion into notes. [C17: from Old French *demorage, demourage;* see DEMUR]

demurrer (dɪˈmʌrə) *n.* **1.** *Law.* a pleading that admits an opponent's point but denies that it is a relevant or valid argument. **2.** any objection raised.

demy (dɪˈmaɪ) *n., pl.* **-mies.** **1. a.** a size of printing paper, 17½ by 22½ inches (444.5 × 571.5 mm). **b.** a size of writing paper, 15½ by 20 inches (Brit.) (393.7 × 508 mm) or 16 by 21 inches (U.S.) (406.4 × 533.4 mm). **2.** either one of two book sizes, 8½ by 5½ inches (**demy octavo**) or (chiefly Brit.) 11¾ by 8⅝ inches (**demy quarto**). [C16: see DEMI-]

demystify (diːˈmɪstɪˌfaɪ) *vb.* **-fies, -fying, -fied.** (*tr.*) to remove the mystery from; make clear. —**deˌmystifiˈcation** *n.*

demythologize *or* **demythologise** (ˌdiːmɪˈθɒləˌdʒaɪz) *vb.* (*tr.*) **1.** to eliminate all mythical elements from (a piece of writing, esp. the Bible) so as to arrive at an essential meaning. **2.** to restate (a message, esp. a religious one) in rational terms. —ˌ**demyˌthologiˈzation** *or* ˌ**demyˌthologiˈsation** *n.*

den (dɛn) *n.* **1.** the habitat or retreat of a lion or similar wild animal; lair. **2.** a small or secluded room in a home, often used for carrying on a hobby. **3.** a squalid or wretched room or retreat. **4.** a site or haunt: *a den of vice.* **5.** *Scot.* a small wooded valley; dingle. **6.** *Scot. and northern English dialect.* a place of sanctuary in certain catching games; home or base. ~*vb.* **dens, denning, denned.** **7.** (*intr.*) to live in or as if in a den. [Old English *denn;* related to Old High German *tenni* threshing floor, early Dutch *denne* low ground, den, cave]

Den. *abbrev. for* Denmark.

denarius (dɪˈnɛərɪəs) *n., pl.* **-narii** (-ˈnɛərɪˌaɪ). **1.** a silver coin of ancient Rome, often called a penny in translation. **2.** a gold coin worth 25 silver denarii. [C16: from Latin: coin originally equal to ten asses, from *dēnārius* (adj.) containing ten, from *dēnī* ten each, from *decem* ten]

denary (ˈdiːnərɪ) *adj.* **1.** calculated by tens; based on ten; decimal. **2.** containing ten parts; tenfold. [C16: from Latin *dēnārius* containing ten; see DENARIUS]

denationalize *or* **denationalise** (diːˈnæʃənᵊˌlaɪz) *vb.* **1.** to return or transfer (an industry, etc.) from public to private ownership. **2.** to deprive (an individual, people, institution, etc.) of national character or nationality. —**deˌnationaliˈzation** *or* **deˌnationaliˈsation** *n.*

denaturalize *or* **denaturalise** (diːˈnætʃrəˌlaɪz) *vb.* (*tr.*) **1.** to deprive of nationality. **2.** to make unnatural. —**deˌnaturaliˈzation** *or* **deˌnaturaliˈsation** *n.*

denature (diːˈneɪtʃə) *or* **denaturize, denaturise** (diːˈneɪtʃəˌraɪz) *vb.* (*tr.*) **1.** to change the nature of. **2.** to change (a protein) by chemical or physical means, such as the action of acid or heat, to cause loss of solubility, biological activity, etc. **3.** to render (something, such as ethanol) unfit for consumption by adding nauseous substances. **4.** to render (fissile material) unfit for use in nuclear weapons by addition of an isotope. —**deˈnaturant** *n.* —**deˌnaturˈation** *n.*

denatured alcohol *n. Chem.* ethanol rendered unfit for human consumption by the addition of a noxious substance, as in methylated spirits.

denazify (diːˈnɑːtsɪˌfaɪ) *vb.* **-fies, -fying, -fied.** (*tr.*) to free or declare (people, institutions, etc.) freed from Nazi influence or ideology. —**deˌnazifiˈcation** *n.*

dendriform (ˈdɛndrɪˌfɔːm) *adj.* branching or treelike in appearance.

dendrite (ˈdɛndraɪt) *n.* **1.** Also called: **dendron.** any of the short branched threadlike extensions of a nerve cell, which conduct impulses towards the cell body. **2.** a branching mosslike crystalline structure in some rocks and minerals. **3.** a crystal that has branched during growth and has a treelike form. [C18: from Greek *dendritēs* relating to a tree] —**dendritic** (dɛnˈdrɪtɪk) *or* **denˈdritical** *adj.* —**denˈdritically** *adv.*

dendro-, dendri-, *or before a vowel* **dendr-** *combining form.* tree: *dendrochronology; dendrite.* [New Latin, from Greek, from *dendron* tree]

dendrochronology (ˌdɛndrəʊkrəˈnɒlədʒɪ) *n.* the study of the annual rings of trees, used esp. to date past events. —**dendrochronological** (ˌdɛndrəʊˌkrɒnᵊˈlɒdʒɪkᵊl) *adj.* —ˌ**dendrochroˈnologist** *n.*

dendrogram (ˈdɛndrəʊˌgræm) *n.* any branching diagram, such as a cladogram, showing the interconnections between things.

dendroid ('dɛndrɔɪd) *or* **dendroidal** (dɛn'drɔɪdᵊl) *adj.* **1.** freely branching; arborescent; treelike. **2.** (esp. of tree ferns) having a tall trunklike stem. [C19: from Greek *dendroeidēs* like a tree]

dendrology (dɛn'drɒlədʒɪ) *n.* the branch of botany that is concerned with the natural history of trees and shrubs. —**dendrological** (ˌdɛndrə'lɒdʒɪkᵊl), ˌ**dendro'logic,** *or* **den'drologous** *adj.* —**den'drologist** *n.*

dendron ('dɛndrɒn) *n.* another name for **dendrite** (sense 1).

dene[1] *or* **dean** (diːn) *n. Brit.* a valley, esp. one that is narrow and wooded. [Old English *denu* valley; see DEN]

dene[2] *or* **dean** (diːn) *n. Dialect, chiefly southern English.* a sandy stretch of land or dune near the sea. [C13: probably related to Old English *dūn* hill; see DOWN[3]]

Dene ('dɛnɪ, 'dɛneɪ) *pl. n.* the North American Indian peoples of the Northwest Territories in Canada. The official body representing them is called the Dene Nation. [via French *déné,* from Athapason *dene* people]

Deneb ('dɛnɛb) *n.* the brightest star in the constellation Cygnus and one of the brightest but remotest stars in the night sky. Visual magnitude: 1.3; spectral type: A2. [C19: from Arabic *dhanab* a tail]

Denebola (dɪ'nɛbələ) *n.* the second brightest star in the constellation Leo. Visual magnitude: 2.2; spectral type: A2. [from Arabic *dhanab al-(asad)* tail of the (lion)]

denegation (ˌdɛnɪ'geɪʃən) *n.* a denial, contradiction, or refusal. [C17: from Late Latin *dēnegātiō,* from Latin *dēnegāre* to deny, refuse, from *negāre* to deny]

dene hole *n.* a hole or shaft excavated in the chalk of southern England or northern France, of uncertain origin and purpose. [of uncertain origin: perhaps from DENE[1]]

denervate ('dɛnəˌveɪt) *vb.* (*tr.*) to deprive (a tissue or organ) of its nerve supply. —ˌ**dener'vation** *n.*

DEng. *abbrev. for* Doctor of Engineering.

dengue ('dɛŋgɪ) *or* **dandy** ('dændɪ) *n.* an acute viral disease transmitted by mosquitoes, characterized by headache, fever, pains in the joints, and skin rash. Also called: **breakbone fever.** [C19: from Spanish, probably of African origin; compare Swahili *kidinga*]

deniable (dɪ'naɪəbᵊl) *adj.* able to be denied; questionable. —**de'niably** *adv.*

denial (dɪ'naɪəl) *n.* **1.** a refusal to agree or comply with a statement; contradiction. **2.** the rejection of the truth of a proposition, doctrine, etc.: *a denial of God's existence.* **3.** a negative reply; rejection of a request. **4.** a refusal to acknowledge; renunciation; disavowal: *a denial of one's leader.* **5.** a psychological process in which painful truths are forced out of an individual's consciousness. See also **defence mechanism.** **6.** abstinence; self-denial.

denier[1] *n.* **1.** ('dɛnɪˌeɪ, 'dɛnjə). a unit of weight used to measure the fineness of silk and man-made fibres, esp. when woven into women's tights, etc. It is equal to 1 gram per 9000 metres. **2.** (də'njeɪ, -'nɪə). any of several former European coins of various denominations. [C15: from Old French: coin, from Latin *dēnārius* DENARIUS]

denier[2] (dɪ'naɪə) *n.* a person who denies.

denigrate ('dɛnɪˌgreɪt) *vb.* **1.** (*tr.*) to belittle or disparage the character of; defame. **2.** a rare word for **blacken.** [C16: from Latin *dēnigrāre* to make very black, defame, from *nigrāre* to blacken, from *niger* black] —ˌ**deni'gration** *n.* —'**deniˌgrator** *n.*

denim ('dɛnɪm) *n. Textiles.* **1.** **a.** a hard-wearing twill-weave cotton fabric used for trousers, work clothes, etc. **b.** (*as modifier*): *a denim jacket.* **2.** **a.** a similar lighter fabric used in upholstery. **b.** (*as modifier*): *denim cushion covers.* [C17: from French *(serge) de Nîmes* (serge) of Nîmes, a city in S France]

denims ('dɛnɪmz) *pl. n.* jeans or overalls made of denim.

denitrate (diː'naɪtreɪt) *vb.* to undergo or cause to undergo a process in which a compound loses a nitro or nitrate group, nitrogen dioxide, or nitric acid. —ˌ**deni'tration** *n.*

denitrify (diː'naɪtrɪˌfaɪ) *vb.* **-fies, -fying, -fied.** to undergo or cause to undergo loss or removal of nitrogen compounds or nitrogen. —**deˌnitrifi'cation** *n.*

denizen ('dɛnɪzən) *n.* **1.** an inhabitant; occupant; resident. **2.** *Brit.* an individual permanently resident in a foreign country where he enjoys certain rights of citizenship. **3.** a plant or animal established in a place to which it is not native. **4.** a naturalized foreign word. ~*vb.* **5.** (*tr.*) to make a denizen. [C15: from Anglo-French *denisein,* from Old French *denzein,* from *denz* within, from Latin *de intus* from within]

denom. *abbrev. for* (religious) denomination.

denominate *vb.* (dɪ'nɒmɪˌneɪt). **1.** (*tr.*) to give a specific name to; designate. ~*adj.* (dɪ'nɒmɪnɪt, -ˌneɪt). **2.** *Maths.* (of a number) representing a multiple of a unit of measurement: *4 is the denominate number in 4 miles.* [C16: from DE- + Latin *nōmināre* to call by name; see NOMINATE] —**de'nominable** *adj.*

denomination (dɪˌnɒmɪ'neɪʃən) *n.* **1.** a group having a distinctive interpretation of a religious faith and usually its own organization. **2.** a grade or unit in a series of designations of value, weight, measure, etc.: *coins of this denomination are being withdrawn.* **3.** a name given to a class or group; classification. **4.** the act of giving a name. **5.** a name; designation. [C15: from Latin *dēnōminātiō* a calling by name; see DENOMINATE] —**deˌnomi'national** *adj.* —**deˌnomi'nationally** *adv.*

denominationalism (dɪˌnɒmɪ'neɪʃənᵊˌlɪzəm) *n.* **1.** adherence to particular principles, esp. to the tenets of a religious denomination; sectarianism. **2.** the tendency to divide or cause to divide into sects or denominations. **3.** division into denominations. —**deˌnomi'nationalist** *n., adj.*

denominative (dɪ'nɒmɪnətɪv) *adj.* **1.** giving or constituting a name; naming. **2.** *Grammar.* **a.** (of a word other than a noun) formed from or having the same form as a noun. **b.** (*as n.*): *the verb "to mushroom" is a denominative.* —**de'nominatively** *adv.*

denominator (dɪ'nɒmɪˌneɪtə) *n.* **1.** the divisor of a fraction, as 8 in ⅞. Compare **numerator** (sense 1). **2.** *Archaic.* a person or thing that denominates or designates.

denotation (ˌdiːnəʊ'teɪʃən) *n.* **1.** the act or process of denoting; indication. **2.** a particular meaning, esp. one given explicitly rather than by suggestion. **3.** **a.** something designated or referred to. See **referent.** Compare **connotation.** **b.** another name for **extension** (sense 11).

denotative (dɪ'nəʊtətɪv) *adj.* **1.** able to denote; designative. **2.** explicit; overt. —**de'notatively** *adv.*

denote (dɪ'nəʊt) *vb.* (*tr.; may take a clause as object*) **1.** to be a sign, symbol, or symptom of; indicate or designate. **2.** (of words, phrases, expressions, etc.) to have as a literal or obvious meaning. [C16: from Latin *dēnotāre* to mark, from *notāre* to mark, NOTE] —**de'notable** *adj.* —**de'notement** *n.*

denouement (deɪ'nuːmɒn) *or* **dénouement** (*French* denumɑ̃) *n.* **1.** **a.** the final clarification or resolution of a plot in a play or other work. **b.** the point at which this occurs. **2.** final outcome; solution. [C18: from French, literally: an untying, from *dénouer* to untie, from Old French *desnoer,* from *des-* DE- + *noer* to tie, knot, from Latin *nōdāre,* from *nōdus* a knot; see NODE]

denounce (dɪ'naʊns) *vb.* (*tr.*) **1.** to deplore or condemn openly or vehemently. **2.** to give information against; accuse. **3.** to announce formally the termination of (a treaty, etc.). **4.** *Obsolete.* **a.** to announce (something evil). **b.** to portend. [C13: from Old French *denoncier* to proclaim, from Latin *dēnuntiāre* to make an official proclamation, threaten, from DE- + *nuntiāre* to announce] —**de'nouncement** *n.* —**de'nouncer** *n.*

de novo *Latin.* (diː 'nəʊvəʊ) *adv.* from the beginning; anew.

dense (dɛns) *adj.* **1.** thickly crowded or closely set: *a dense crowd.* **2.** thick; impenetrable: *a dense fog.* **3.** *Physics.* having a high density. **4.** stupid; dull; obtuse. **5.** (of a photographic negative) having many dark or exposed areas. **6.** (of an optical glass, colour, etc.) transmitting little or no light. [C15: from Latin *densus* thick; related to Greek *dasus* thickly covered with hair or leaves] —'**densely** *adv.* —'**denseness** *n.*

densimeter (dɛn'sɪmɪtə) *n. Physics.* any instrument for measuring density. —**densimetric** (ˌdɛnsɪ'mɛtrɪk) *adj.* —**den'simetry** *n.*

densitometer (ˌdɛnsɪ'tɒmɪtə) *n.* an instrument for measuring the optical density of a material by directing a beam of light onto the specimen and measuring its transmission or reflection. —**densitometric** (ˌdɛnsɪtə'mɛtrɪk) *adj.* —ˌ**densi'tometry** *n.*

density ('dɛnsɪtɪ) *n., pl.* **-ties.** **1.** the degree to which something is filled, crowded, or occupied: *high density of building in towns.* **2.** obtuseness; stupidity. **3.** a measure of the compactness of a substance, expressed as its mass per unit volume. It is measured in kilograms per cubic metre or pounds per cubic foot. Symbol: ρ See also **relative density.** **4.** a measure of a physical quantity per unit of length, area, or volume. See **charge density, current density.** **5.** *Physics, photog.* See **transmission density, reflection density.**

density function *n. Statistics.* short for **probability density function.**

dent[1] (dɛnt) *n.* **1.** a hollow or dip in a surface, as one made by pressure or a blow. **2.** an appreciable effect, esp. of lessening: *a dent in our resources.* ~*vb.* **3.** to impress or be impressed with a dent or dents. [C13 (in the sense: a stroke, blow): variant of DINT]

dent[2] (dɛnt) *n.* **1.** a toothlike protuberance, esp. the tooth of a sprocket or gearwheel. **2.** *Textiles.* the space between two wires in a loom through which a warp thread is drawn. [C16: from French: tooth]

dent. *abbrev. for:* **1.** dental. **2.** dentistry.

dental ('dɛntᵊl) *adj.* **1.** of or relating to the teeth. **2.** of or relating to dentistry. **3.** *Phonetics.* **a.** pronounced or articulated with the tip of the tongue touching the backs of the upper teeth, as for *t* in French *tout.* **b.** (esp. in the phonology of some languages, such as English) another word for **alveolar.** ~*n.* **4.** *Phonetics.* a dental consonant. [C16: from Medieval Latin *dentālis,* from Latin *dens* tooth]

dental clinic *n. N.Z.* a school clinic in which minor dental work is carried out by dental nurses.

dental floss *n.* a soft usually flattened often waxed thread for cleaning the teeth and the spaces between them.

dental hygiene *n.* the maintenance of the teeth and gums in healthy condition, esp. by proper brushing, the removal of plaque, etc. Also called: **oral hygiene.**

dental hygienist *n.* a dentist's assistant skilled in dental hygiene. Also called: **oral hygienist.**

dentalium (dɛn'teɪlɪəm) *n., pl.* **-liums** *or* **-lia** (-lɪə). any scaphopod mollusc of the genus *Dentalium.* See **tusk shell.** [C19: New Latin, from Medieval Latin *dentālis* DENTAL]

dental nurse *n.* **1.** a dentist's assistant, esp. one who passes instruments, mixes fillings, etc. **2.** *N.Z.* a nurse trained to do fillings and carry out other minor dental work on schoolchildren.
dental plaque *n.* a filmy deposit on the surface of a tooth consisting of a mixture of mucus, bacteria, food, etc. Also called: **bacterial plaque.**
dental surgeon *n.* another name for **dentist.**
dentate ('dɛnteɪt) *adj.* **1.** having teeth or toothlike processes. **2.** (of leaves) having a toothed margin. [C19: from Latin *dentātus*] —'**dentately** *adv.*
dentation (dɛn'teɪʃən) *n.* **1.** the state or condition of being dentate. **2.** an angular projection or series of projections, as on the margin of a leaf.
dentex ('dɛntɛks) *n.* a large active predatory sparid fish, *Dentex dentex*, of Mediterranean and E Atlantic waters, having long sharp teeth and powerful jaws. [C19: from Latin *dentix, dentex* from *dens* tooth]
denti- *or before a vowel* **dent-** *combining form.* indicating a tooth: *dentiform; dentine.* [from Latin *dēns, dent-*]
denticle ('dɛntɪkᵊl) *n.* a small tooth or toothlike part, such as any of the placoid scales of sharks. [C14: from Latin *denticulus*]
denticulate (dɛn'tɪkjʊlɪt, -ˌleɪt) *adj.* **1.** *Biology.* very finely toothed: *denticulate leaves.* **2.** having denticles. **3.** *Architect.* having dentils. [C17: from Latin *denticulātus* having small teeth] —**den'ticulately** *adv.*
denticulation (dɛnˌtɪkjʊ'leɪʃən) *n.* **1.** a denticulate structure. **2.** a less common word for **denticle.**
dentiform ('dɛntɪˌfɔːm) *adj.* shaped like a tooth.
dentifrice ('dɛntɪfrɪs) *n.* any substance, esp. paste or powder, for use in cleaning the teeth. [C16: from Latin *dentifricium* tooth powder, from *dent-, dens* tooth + *fricāre* to rub]
dentil ('dɛntɪl) *n.* one of a set of small square or rectangular blocks evenly spaced to form an ornamental row, usually under a classical cornice on a building, piece of furniture, etc. [C17: from French, from obsolete *dentille* a little tooth, from *dent* tooth]
dentilabial (ˌdɛntɪ'leɪbɪəl) *adj.* another word for **labiodental.**
dentilingual (ˌdɛntɪ'lɪŋgwəl) *adj.* **1.** *Phonetics.* pronounced or articulated with the tongue touching the upper teeth. ~*n.* **2.** a consonant so pronounced.
dentine ('dɛntiːn) *or* **dentin** ('dɛntɪn) *n.* the calcified tissue surrounding the pulp cavity of a tooth and comprising the bulk of the tooth. [C19: from DENTI- + -IN] —'**dentinal** *adj.*
dentist ('dɛntɪst) *n.* a person qualified to practise dentistry. [C18: from French *dentiste,* from *dent* tooth]
dentistry ('dɛntɪstrɪ) *n.* the branch of medical science concerned with the diagnosis and treatment of diseases and disorders of the teeth and gums.
dentition (dɛn'tɪʃən) *n.* **1.** the arrangement, type, and number of the teeth in a particular species. Man has a **primary dentition** of deciduous teeth and a **secondary dentition** of permanent teeth. **2.** teething or the time or process of teething. [C17: from Latin *dentītiō* a teething]
dentoid ('dɛntɔɪd) *adj.* resembling a tooth.
denture ('dɛntʃə) *n.* (*usually pl.*) **1.** Also called: **dental plate, false teeth.** a partial or full set of artificial teeth. **2.** *Rare.* a set of natural teeth. [C19: from French, from *dent* tooth + -URE]
denuclearize *or* **denuclearise** (dɪ'njuːklɪəˌraɪz) *vb.* (*tr.*) to deprive (a country, state, etc.) of nuclear weapons. —**deˌnucleari'zation** *or* **deˌnucleari'sation** *n.*
denudate ('dɛnjʊˌdeɪt, dɪ'njuːdeɪt) *vb.* **1.** a less common word for **denude.** ~*adj.* **2.** denuded; bare.
denude (dɪ'njuːd) *vb.* (*tr.*) **1.** to divest of covering; make bare; uncover; strip. **2.** to expose (rock) by the erosion of the layers above. [C16: from Latin *dēnūdāre;* see NUDE] —**denudation** (ˌdɛnjʊ'deɪʃən, ˌdiː-) *n.* —**de'nuder** *n.*
denumerable (dɪ'njuːmərəbᵊl) *adj. Maths.* capable of being put into a one-to-one correspondence with the positive integers; countable. —**de'numerably** *adv.*
denunciate (dɪ'nʌnsɪˌeɪt) *vb.* (*tr.*) to condemn; denounce. [C16: from Latin *dēnuntiāre;* see DENOUNCE] —**de'nunciˌator** *n.* —**de'nunciatory** *adj.*
denunciation (dɪˌnʌnsɪ'eɪʃən) *n.* **1.** open condemnation; censure; denouncing. **2.** *Law, obsolete.* a charge or accusation of crime made by an individual before a public prosecutor or tribunal. **3.** a formal announcement of the termination of a treaty. **4.** *Archaic.* an announcement in the form of an impending threat or warning.
Denver boot ('dɛnvə) *n.* another name for **wheel clamp.** [C20: from *Denver*, Colorado, where the device was first used]
deny (dɪ'naɪ) *vb.* **-nies, -nying, -nied.** (*tr.*) **1.** to declare (an assertion, statement, etc.) to be untrue: *he denied that he had killed her.* **2.** to reject as false; refuse to accept or believe. **3.** to withhold; refuse to give. **4.** to refuse to fulfil the requests or expectations of: *it is hard to deny a child.* **5.** to refuse to acknowledge or recognize; disown; disavow: *the baron denied his wicked son.* **6.** to refuse (oneself) things desired. [C13: from Old French *denier,* from Latin *dēnegāre,* from *negāre*]
deoch-an-doruis ('djɒxən'dɒrɪs, dɒx-) *n. Scot.* a parting drink or stirrup cup. Also: **doch-an-doris.** [Scottish Gaelic: drink at the door]
deodand ('diːəʊˌdænd) *n. English law.* (formerly) a thing that had caused a person's death and was forfeited to the crown for a charitable purpose: abolished 1862. [C16: from Anglo-French *deodande,* from Medieval Latin *deōdandum,* from Latin *Deō dandum* (something) to be given to God, from *deus* god + *dare* to give]
deodar ('diːəʊˌdɑː) *n.* **1.** a Himalayan cedar, *Cedrus deodara,* with drooping branches. **2.** the durable fragrant highly valued wood of this tree. [C19: from Hindi *deodār,* from Sanskrit *devadāru,* literally: wood of the gods, from *deva* god + *dāru* wood]
deodorant (diː'əʊdərənt) *n.* **1. a.** a substance applied to the body to suppress or mask the odour of perspiration or other body odours. **b.** (*as modifier*): *a deodorant spray.* Compare **antiperspirant.** **2.** any substance for destroying or masking odours, such as liquid sprayed into the air.
deodorize *or* **deodorise** (diː'əʊdəˌraɪz) *vb.* (*tr.*) to remove, disguise, or absorb the odour of, esp. when unpleasant. —**deˌodori'zation** *or* **deˌodori'sation** *n.* —**de'odorˌizer** *or* **de'odorˌiser** *n.*
Deo gratias *Latin.* ('deɪəʊ 'grɑːtɪəs) thanks be to God. Abbrev.: **DG.**
deontic (diː'ɒntɪk) *adj. Logic.* **a.** of or relating to such ethical concepts as obligation and permissibility. **b.** designating the branch of modal logic that deals with the formalization of these concepts. [C19: from Greek *deon* duty, from impersonal *dei* it behoves, it is binding]
deontological (dɪˌɒntə'lɒdʒɪkᵊl) *adj. Philosophy.* (of an ethical theory) regarding obligation as deriving from reason or as residing primarily in certain specific rules of conduct rather than in the maximization of some good.
deontology (ˌdiːɒn'tɒlədʒɪ) *n.* the branch of ethics dealing with duty, moral obligation, and moral commitment. [C19: from Greek *deon* duty (see DEONTIC) + -LOGY] —ˌ**deon'tologist** *n.*
Deo volente *Latin.* ('deɪəʊ vɒ'lɛntɪ) God willing. Abbrev.: **DV.**
deoxidize *or* **deoxidise** (diː'ɒksɪˌdaɪz) *vb.* **1.** (*tr.*) **a.** to remove oxygen atoms from (a compound, molecule, etc.). **b.** another word for **deoxygenate.** **2.** another word for **reduce** (sense 11). —**deˌoxidi'zation** *or* **deˌoxidi'sation** *n.* —**de'oxiˌdizer** *or* **de'oxiˌdiser** *n.*
deoxy- *or* **desoxy-** *combining form.* indicating the presence of less oxygen than in a specified related compound: *deoxyribonucleic acid.*
deoxycorticosterone (diːˌɒksɪˌkɔːtɪkəʊ'stɪərəʊn) *or* **deoxycortone** (diːˌɒksɪ'kɔːtəʊn) *n.* a corticosteroid hormone important in maintaining sodium and water balance in the body.
deoxygenate (diː'ɒksɪdʒɪˌneɪt) *or* **deoxygenize, deoxygenise** (diː'ɒksɪdʒɪˌnaɪz) *vb.* (*tr.*) to remove oxygen from (water, air, etc.). —**deˌoxygen'ation** *n.*
deoxyribonuclease (diːˌɒksɪˌraɪbəʊ'njuːklɪeɪz) *n.* the full name for **DNAase.**
deoxyribonucleic acid (diːˌɒksɪˌraɪbəʊnjuː'kleɪɪk) *or* **desoxyribonucleic acid** *n.* the full name for **DNA.**
deoxyribose (diːˌɒksɪ'raɪbəʊs, -bəʊz) *or* **desoxyribose** (dɛsˌɒksɪ'raɪbəʊs, -bəʊz) *n.* a pentose sugar obtained by the hydrolysis of DNA. Formula: $C_5H_{10}O_4$.
dep. *abbrev. for:* **1.** departs. **2.** departure. **3.** deponent. **4.** deposed. **5.** deposit. **6.** depot. **7.** deputy.
depart (dɪ'pɑːt) *vb.* (*mainly intr.*) **1.** to go away; leave. **2.** to start out; set forth. **3.** (usually foll. by *from*) to deviate; differ; vary: *to depart from normal procedure.* **4.** (*tr.*) to quit (archaic, except in the phrase **depart this life).** [C13: from Old French *departir,* from DE- + *partir* to go away, divide, from Latin *partīrī* to divide, distribute, from *pars* a part]
departed (dɪ'pɑːtɪd) *adj. Euphemistic.* **a.** dead; deceased. **b.** (*as sing. or collective n.;* preceded by *the*): *the departed.*
department (dɪ'pɑːtmənt) *n.* **1.** a specialized division of a large concern, such as a business, store, or university: *the geography department.* **2.** a major subdivision or branch of the administration of a government. **3.** a branch or subdivision of learning: *physics is a department of science.* **4.** a territorial and administrative division in several countries, such as France. **5.** *Informal.* a specialized sphere of knowledge, skill, or activity: *wine-making is my wife's department.* [C18: from French *département,* from *départir* to divide; see DEPART] —**departmental** (ˌdiːpɑːt'mɛntᵊl) *adj.* —ˌ**depart'mentally** *adv.*
departmentalism (ˌdiːpɑːt'mɛntəˌlɪzəm) *n.* division into departments, esp. when resulting in impaired efficiency.
departmentalize *or* **departmentalise** (ˌdiːpɑːt'mɛntəˌlaɪz) *vb.* (*tr.*) to organize into departments, esp. excessively. —ˌ**departˌmentali'zation** *or* ˌ**departˌmentali'sation** *n.*
department store *n.* a large shop divided into departments selling a great many kinds of goods.
departure (dɪ'pɑːtʃə) *n.* **1.** the act or an instance of departing. **2.** a deviation or variation from previous custom; divergence. **3.** a project, course of action, venture, etc.: *selling is a new departure for him.* **4.** *Nautical.* **a.** the net distance travelled due east or west by a vessel. **b.** Also called: **point of departure.** the latitude and longitude of the point from which a vessel calculates dead reckoning. **5.** a euphemistic word for **death.**
depasture (diː'pɑːstʃə) *vb.* **1.** to graze or denude by grazing (a pasture, esp. a meadow specially grown for the purpose). **2.** (*tr.*) to pasture (cattle or sheep).
depend (dɪ'pɛnd) *vb.* (*intr.*) **1.** (foll. by *on* or *upon*) to put trust (in); rely (on); be sure (of). **2.** (usually foll. by *on* or *upon;* often with *it* as subject) to be influenced or determined (by); be resultant (from): *whether you come or not depends on what father says; it all depends on you.* **3.** (foll. by *on* or *upon*) to rely (on) for

income, support, etc. **4.** (foll. by *from*) *Rare.* to hang down; be suspended. **5.** to be undecided or pending. [C15: from Old French *dependre,* from Latin *dēpendēre* to hang from, from DE- + *pendēre* to hang]

dependable (dɪˈpɛndəbᵊl) *adj.* able to be depended on; reliable; trustworthy. —**deˌpendaˈbility** *or* **deˈpendableness** *n.* —**deˈpendably** *adv.*

dependant (dɪˈpɛndənt) *n.* a person who depends on another person, organization, etc., for support, aid, or sustenance, esp. financial support.

dependence *or U.S. (sometimes)* **dependance** (dɪˈpɛndəns) *n.* **1.** the state or fact of being dependent, esp. for support or help. **2.** reliance; trust; confidence. **3.** *Rare.* an object or person relied upon.

dependency *or U.S. (sometimes)* **dependancy** (dɪˈpɛndənsɪ) *n., pl.* **-cies.** **1.** a territory subject to a state on which it does not border. **2.** a dependent or subordinate person or thing. **3.** *Psychol.* overreliance by a person on another person or on a drug, etc. **4.** another word for **dependence.**

dependent *or U.S. (sometimes)* **dependant** (dɪˈpɛndənt) *adj.* **1.** depending on a person or thing for aid, support, life, etc. **2.** (*postpositive;* foll. by *on* or *upon*) influenced or conditioned (by); contingent (on). **3.** subordinate; subject: *a dependent prince.* **4.** *Obsolete.* hanging down. **5.** *Maths.* **a.** (of a variable) having a value depending on that assumed by a related independent variable. **b.** (of a linear equation) having every solution as a solution of one or more given linear equations. ~*n.* **6.** *Grammar.* an element in a phrase or clause that is not the governor. **7.** a variant spelling (esp. U.S.) of **dependant.** —**deˈpendently** *adv.*

dependent clause *n. Grammar.* another term for **subordinate clause.**

dependent variable *n.* **1.** a variable in a mathematical equation or statement whose value depends on that taken on by the independent variable: *in "y = f(x)", "y" is the dependent variable.* **2.** *Psychol., statistics.* the variable measured by the experimenter. It is controlled by the value of the independent variable, of which it is an index.

depersonalization *or* **depersonalisation** (dɪˌpɜːsnᵊlaɪˈzeɪʃən) *n.* **1.** the act or an instance of depersonalizing. **2.** *Psychiatry.* an abnormal state of consciousness in which the subject feels unreal and detached from himself and the world.

depersonalize *or* **depersonalise** (dɪˈpɜːsnᵊˌlaɪz) *vb.* (*tr.*) **1.** to deprive (a person, organization, system, etc.) of individual or personal qualities; render impersonal. **2.** to cause (someone) to lose his sense of personal identity. [C19: from DE- + PERSONAL + -IZE]

depict (dɪˈpɪkt) *vb.* (*tr.*) **1.** to represent by or as by drawing, sculpture, painting, etc.; delineate; portray. **2.** to represent in words; describe. [C17: from Latin *dēpingere,* from *pingere* to paint] —**deˈpicter** *or* **deˈpictor** *n.* —**deˈpiction** *n.* —**deˈpictive** *adj.*

depicture (dɪˈpɪktʃə) *vb.* a less common word for **depict.**

depilate (ˈdɛpɪˌleɪt) *vb.* (*tr.*) to remove the hair from. [C16: from Latin *dēpilāre,* from *pilāre* to make bald, from *pilus* hair] —ˌ**depiˈlation** *n.* —ˈ**depiˌlator** *n.*

depilatory (dɪˈpɪlətərɪ, -trɪ) *adj.* **1.** able or serving to remove hair. ~*n., pl.* **-ries.** **2.** a chemical that is used to remove hair from the body.

deplane (diːˈpleɪn) *vb.* (*intr.*) *Chiefly U.S. and Canadian.* to disembark from an aeroplane. [C20: from DE- + PLANE[1]]

deplete (dɪˈpliːt) *vb.* (*tr.*) **1.** to use up (supplies, money, energy, etc.); reduce or exhaust. **2.** to empty entirely or partially. **3.** *Med.* to empty or reduce the fluid contents of (an organ or vessel). [C19: from Latin *dēplēre* to empty out, from DE- + *plēre* to fill] —**deˈpletable** *adj.* —**deˈpletion** *n.* —**deˈpletive** *or* **deˈpletory** *adj.*

depleted uranium *n. Chem.* uranium containing a smaller proportion of the isotope uranium–235 than is present in the natural form of uranium.

depletion layer *n. Electronics.* a region at the interface between dissimilar zones of conductivity in a semiconductor, in which there are few charge carriers.

deplorable (dɪˈplɔːrəbᵊl) *adj.* **1.** lamentable: *a deplorable lack of taste.* **2.** worthy of censure or reproach; very bad: *deplorable behaviour.* —**deˈplorableness** *or* **deˌploraˈbility** *n.* —**deˈplorably** *adv.*

deplore (dɪˈplɔː) *vb.* (*tr.*) **1.** to express or feel sorrow about; lament; regret. **2.** to express or feel strong disapproval of; censure. [C16: from Old French *deplorer,* from Latin *dēplōrāre* to weep bitterly, from *plōrāre* to weep, lament] —**deˈplorer** *n.* —**deˈploringly** *adv.*

deploy (dɪˈplɔɪ) *vb. Chiefly military.* **1.** to adopt or cause to adopt a battle formation, esp. from a narrow front formation. **2.** (*tr.*) to redistribute (forces) to or within a given area. [C18: from French *déployer,* from Latin *displicāre* to unfold; see DISPLAY] —**deˈployment** *n.*

deplume (diːˈpluːm) *vb.* (*tr.*) **1.** to deprive of feathers; pluck. **2.** to deprive of honour, position, wealth, etc. —ˌ**depluˈmation** *n.*

depolarize *or* **depolarise** (diːˈpəʊləˌraɪz) *vb.* to undergo or cause to undergo a loss of polarity or polarization. —**deˌpolariˈzation** *or* **deˌpolariˈsation** *n.* —**deˈpolarˌizer** *or* **deˈpolarˌiser** *n.*

depoliticize *or* **depoliticise** (ˌdiːpəˈlɪtɪˌsaɪz) *vb.* (*tr.*) to deprive of a political nature; render apolitical: *two years on the committee totally depoliticized him.*

depolymerize *or* **depolymerise** (diːˈpɒlɪməˌraɪz) *vb.* to break (a polymer) into constituent monomers or (of a polymer) to decompose in this way. —**deˌpolymeriˈzation** *or* **deˌpolymeriˈsation** *n.*

depone (dɪˈpəʊn) *vb. Law, chiefly Scots.* to declare (something) under oath; testify; depose. [C16: from Latin *dēpōnere* to put down, from DE- + *pōnere* to put, place]

deponent (dɪˈpəʊnənt) *adj.* **1.** *Grammar.* (of a verb, esp. in Latin) having the inflectional endings of a passive verb but the meaning of an active verb. ~*n.* **2.** *Grammar.* a deponent verb. **3.** *Law.* **a.** a person who makes an affidavit. **b.** a person, esp. a witness, who makes a deposition. [C16: from Latin *dēpōnēns* putting aside, putting down, from *dēpōnere* to put down, DEPONE]

depopulate (dɪˈpɒpjʊˌleɪt) *vb.* to be or cause to be reduced in population. —**deˌpopuˈlation** *n.*

deport (dɪˈpɔːt) *vb.* (*tr.*) **1.** to remove (an alien) forcibly from a country; expel. **2.** to carry (an inhabitant) forcibly away from his homeland; transport; exile; banish. **3.** to conduct, hold, or behave (oneself) in a specified manner. [C15: from French *déporter,* from Latin *dēportāre* to carry away, banish, from DE- + *portāre* to carry] —**deˈportable** *adj.*

deportation (ˌdiːpɔːˈteɪʃən) *n.* **1.** the act of expelling an alien from a country; expulsion. **2.** the act of transporting someone from his country; banishment.

deportee (ˌdiːpɔːˈtiː) *n.* a person deported or awaiting deportation.

deportment (dɪˈpɔːtmənt) *n.* the manner in which a person behaves, esp. in physical bearing: *military deportment.* [C17: from French *déportement,* from Old French *deporter* to conduct (oneself); see DEPORT]

deposal (dɪˈpəʊzᵊl) *n.* another word for **deposition** (sense 2).

depose (dɪˈpəʊz) *vb.* **1.** (*tr.*) to remove from an office or position, esp. one of power or rank. **2.** *Law.* to testify or give (evidence, etc.) on oath, esp. when taken down in writing; make a deposition. [C13: from Old French *deposer* to put away, put down, from Late Latin *dēpōnere* to depose from office, from Latin: to put aside; see DEPONE] —**deˈposable** *adj.* —**deˈposer** *n.*

deposit (dɪˈpɒzɪt) *vb.* (*tr.*) **1.** to put or set down, esp. carefully or in a proper place; place. **2.** to entrust for safekeeping; consign. **3.** to place (money) in a bank or similar institution in order to earn interest or for safekeeping. **4.** to give (money) in part payment or as security. **5.** to lay down naturally; cause to settle: *the river deposits silt.* ~*n.* **6. a.** an instance of entrusting money or valuables to a bank or similar institution. **b.** the money or valuables so entrusted. **7.** money given in part payment or as security, as when goods are bought on hire-purchase. See also **down payment.** **8.** a consideration, esp. money, given temporarily as security against loss of or damage to something borrowed or hired. **9.** an accumulation of sediments, mineral ores, coal, etc. **10.** any deposited material, such as a sediment or a precipitate that has settled out of solution. **11.** a coating produced on a surface, esp. a layer of metal formed by electrolysis. **12.** a depository or storehouse. **13. on deposit.** payable as the first instalment, as when buying on hire-purchase. [C17: from Medieval Latin *dēpositāre,* from Latin *dēpositus* put down]

deposit account *n. Brit.* a bank account that earns interest and usually requires notice of withdrawal.

depositary (dɪˈpɒzɪtərɪ, -trɪ) *n., pl.* **-taries.** **1.** a person or group to whom something is entrusted for safety or preservation. **2.** a variant spelling of **depository** (sense 1).

deposition (ˌdɛpəˈzɪʃən, ˌdiːpə-) *n.* **1.** *Law.* **a.** the giving of testimony on oath. **b.** the testimony so given. **c.** the sworn statement of a witness used in court in his absence. **2.** the act or instance of deposing. **3.** the act or an instance of depositing. **4.** something that is deposited; deposit. [C14: from Late Latin *dēpositiō* a laying down, disposal, burying, testimony]

Deposition (ˌdɛpəˈzɪʃən, ˌdiːpə-) *n.* the taking down of Christ's body from the Cross or a representation of this.

depositor (dɪˈpɒzɪtə) *n.* a person who places or has money on deposit in a bank or similar organization.

depository (dɪˈpɒzɪtərɪ, -trɪ) *n., pl.* **-ries.** **1.** a store, such as a warehouse, for furniture, valuables, etc.; repository. **2.** a variant spelling of **depositary** (sense 1). [C17 (in the sense: place of a deposit): from Medieval Latin *dēpositōrium;* C18 (in the sense: depositary): see DEPOSIT, -ORY[1]]

depot (ˈdɛpəʊ) *n.* **1.** a storehouse or warehouse. **2.** *Military.* **a.** a store for supplies. **b.** a training and holding centre for recruits and replacements. **3.** *Chiefly Brit.* a building used for the storage and servicing of buses or railway engines. **4.** *U.S. and Canadian.* **a.** a bus or railway station. **b.** (*as modifier*): *a depot manager.* [C18: from French *dépôt,* from Latin *dēpositum* a deposit, trust]

deprave (dɪˈpreɪv) *vb.* (*tr.*) **1.** to make morally bad; corrupt; vitiate. **2.** *Obsolete.* to defame; slander. [C14: from Latin *dēprāvāre* to distort, corrupt, from DE- + *prāvus* crooked] —**depravation** (ˌdɛprəˈveɪʃən) *n.* —**deˈpraver** *n.*

depraved (dɪˈpreɪvd) *adj.* morally bad or debased; corrupt; perverted. —**depravedness** (dɪˈpreɪvɪdnɪs) *n.*

depravity (dɪˈprævɪtɪ) *n., pl.* **-ties.** the state or an instance of moral corruption.

deprecate (ˈdɛprɪˌkeɪt) *vb.* (*tr.*) **1.** to express disapproval of; protest against. **2.** to depreciate (a person, someone's character, etc.); belittle. **3.** *Archaic.* to try to ward off by prayer. [C17: from Latin *dēprecārī* to avert, ward off by entreaty, from DE- + *precārī* to PRAY] —ˈ**depreˌcating** *adj.* —ˈ**depreˌcatingly** *adv.* —ˌ**depreˈcation** *n.* —ˈ**deprecative** *adj.* —ˈ**deprecatively** *adv.* —ˈ**depreˌcator** *n.*

deprecatory (ˈdɛprɪkətərɪ) *adj.* **1.** expressing disapproval; protesting. **2.** expressing apology; apologetic. —ˈ**deprecatorily** *adv.*

depreciable (dɪˈpriːʃəbᵊl) *adj.* **1.** *U.S.* able to be depreciated for tax deduction. **2.** liable to depreciation.

depreciate (dɪˈpriːʃɪˌeɪt) *vb.* **1.** to reduce or decline in value or price. **2.** (*tr.*) to lessen the value of by derision, criticism, etc.; disparage. [C15: from Late Latin *dēpretiāre* to lower the price of, from Latin DE- + *pretium* PRICE] —**deˈpreciˌatingly** *adv.* —**deˈpreciˌator** *n.* —**depreciatory** (dɪˈpriːʃɪətərɪ, -trɪ) *or* **deˈpreciative** *adj.*

depreciation (dɪˌpriːʃɪˈeɪʃən) *n.* **1.** *Accounting.* **a.** the reduction in value of a fixed asset due to use, obsolescence, etc. **b.** the amount deducted from gross profit to allow for such reduction in value. **2.** *Accounting.* a modified amount permitted for purposes of tax deduction. **3.** the act or an instance of depreciating or belittling; disparagement. **4.** a decrease in the exchange value of currency against gold or other currencies brought about by excess supply of that currency under conditions of fluctuating exchange rates. Compare **devaluation** (sense 1).

depredate (ˈdɛprɪˌdeɪt) *vb.* (*tr.*) *Rare.* to plunder or destroy; pillage. [C17: from Late Latin *dēpraedārī* to ravage, from Latin DE- + *praeda* booty; see PREY] —ˈ**depreˌdator** *n.* —**depredatory** (ˈdɛprɪˌdeɪtərɪ, dɪˈprɛdɪtərɪ, -trɪ) *adj.*

depredation (ˌdɛprɪˈdeɪʃən) *n.* the act or an instance of plundering; robbery; pillage.

depress (dɪˈprɛs) *vb.* (*tr.*) **1.** to lower in spirits; make gloomy; deject. **2.** to weaken or lower the force, vigour, or energy of. **3.** to lower prices of (securities or a security market). **4.** to press or push down. **5.** to lower the pitch of (a musical sound). **6.** *Obsolete.* to suppress or subjugate. [C14: from Old French *depresser,* from Latin *dēprimere* from DE- + *premere* to PRESS[1]] —**deˈpressible** *adj.* —**deˈpressing** *adj.* —**deˈpressingly** *adv.*

depressant (dɪˈprɛsᵊnt) *adj.* **1.** *Med.* able to diminish or reduce nervous or functional activity. **2.** causing gloom or dejection; depressing. ~*n.* **3.** a depressant drug.

depressed (dɪˈprɛst) *adj.* **1.** low in spirits; downcast; despondent. **2.** lower than the surrounding surface. **3.** pressed down or flattened. **4.** Also: **distressed.** characterized by relative economic hardship, such as unemployment: *a depressed area.* **5.** lowered in force, intensity, or amount. **6.** (of plant parts) flattened as though pressed from above. **7.** *Zoology.* flattened from top to bottom: *the depressed bill of the spoonbill.*

depression (dɪˈprɛʃən) *n.* **1.** the act of depressing or state of being depressed. **2.** a depressed or sunken place or area. **3.** a mental disorder characterized by extreme gloom, feelings of inadequacy, and inability to concentrate. **4.** *Pathol.* an abnormal lowering of the rate of any physiological activity or function, such as respiration. **5.** an economic condition characterized by substantial and protracted unemployment, low output and investment, etc.; slump. **6.** Also called: **cyclone, low.** *Meteorol.* a body of moving air below normal atmospheric pressure, which often brings rain. **7.** (esp. in surveying and astronomy) the angular distance of an object, celestial body, etc., below the horizontal plane through the point of observation. Compare **elevation** (sense 11).

Depression (dɪˈprɛʃən) *n.* (usually preceded by *the*) the worldwide economic depression of the early 1930s, when there was mass unemployment. Also called: the **Great Depression,** the **Slump.**

depressive (dɪˈprɛsɪv) *adj.* **1.** tending to depress; causing depression. **2.** *Psychol.* tending to be subject to periods of depression. See also **manic-depressive.** —**deˈpressively** *adv.* —**deˈpressiveness** *n.*

depressomotor (dɪˌprɛsəʊˈməʊtə) *adj.* **1.** *Physiol.* retarding motor activity. ~*n.* **2.** a depressomotor drug.

depressor (dɪˈprɛsə) *n.* **1.** a person or thing that depresses. **2.** any muscle that draws down a part. **3.** any surgical or medical instrument used to press down or aside an organ or part: *a tongue depressor.* **4.** Also called: **depressor nerve.** any nerve that when stimulated produces a fall in blood pressure by dilating the arteries or lowering the heartbeat.

depressurize *or* **depressurise** (dɪˈprɛʃəˌraɪz) *vb.* (*tr.*) to reduce the pressure of a gas inside (a container or enclosed space), as in an aircraft cabin. —**deˌpressuriˈzation** *or* **deˌpressuriˈsation** *n.*

deprive (dɪˈpraɪv) *vb.* (*tr.*) **1.** (foll. by *of*) to prevent from possessing or enjoying; dispossess (of). **2.** *Archaic.* to remove from rank or office; depose; demote. [C14: from Old French *depriver,* from Medieval Latin *dēprīvāre,* from Latin DE- + *prīvāre* to deprive of, rob; see PRIVATE] —**deˈprivable** *adj.* —**deˈprival** *n.* —**deprivation** (ˌdɛprɪˈveɪʃən) *n.* —**deˈpriver** *n.*

deprived (dɪˈpraɪvd) *adj.* lacking adequate food, shelter, education, etc.: *deprived inner-city areas.*

de profundis *Latin.* (deɪ prɒˈfʊndɪs) *adv.* out of the depths of misery or dejection.

depside (ˈdɛpsaɪd, -sɪd) *n.* any ester formed by the condensation of the carboxyl group of one phenolic carboxylic acid with the hydroxyl group of another, found in plant cells. [C20: *deps-,* from Greek *depsein* to knead + -IDE]

dept *abbrev. for* department.

depth (dɛpθ) *n.* **1.** the extent, measurement, or distance downwards, backwards, or inwards. **2.** the quality of being deep; deepness. **3.** intensity or profundity of emotion or feeling. **4.** profundity of moral character; penetration; sagacity; integrity. **5.** complexity or abstruseness, as of thought or objects of thought. **6.** intensity, as of silence, colour, etc. **7.** lowness of pitch. **8.** *Nautical.* the distance from the top of a ship's keel to the top of a particular deck. **9.** (*often pl.*) a deep, far, inner, or remote part, such as an inaccessible region of a country. **10.** (*often pl.*) the deepest, most intense, or most severe part: *the depths of winter.* **11.** (*usually pl.*) a low moral state; demoralization: *how could you sink to such depths?* **12.** (*often pl.*) a vast space or abyss. **13. beyond** *or* **out of one's depth. a.** in water deeper than one is tall. **b.** beyond the range of one's competence or understanding. **14. in depth.** thoroughly or comprehensively. See also **in-depth.** [C14: from *dep* DEEP + -TH[1]]

depth charge *or* **bomb** *n.* a bomb used to attack submarines that explodes at a pre-set depth of water.

depth gauge *n.* a device attached to a drill bit to prevent the hole from exceeding a predetermined depth.

depth of field *n.* the range of distance in front of and behind an object focused by an optical instrument, such as a camera or microscope, within which other objects will also appear clear and sharply defined in the resulting image. Compare **depth of focus.**

depth of focus *n.* the amount by which the distance between the camera lens and the film can be altered without the resulting image appearing blurred. Compare **depth of field.**

depth psychology *n. Psychol.* the study of unconscious motives and attitudes.

depurate (ˈdɛpjʊˌreɪt) *vb.* **1.** to cleanse or purify or to be cleansed or purified. **2.** to promote the elimination of waste products from (the body). [C17: from Medieval Latin *dēpūrāre,* from Latin DE- + *pūrāre* to purify; see PURE] —ˌ**depuˈration** *n.* —ˈ**depuˌrator** *n.*

depurative (ˈdɛpjʊˌreɪtɪv, -rətɪv) *adj.* **1.** used for or capable of depurating; purifying; purgative. ~*n.* **2.** a depurative substance or agent.

deputation (ˌdɛpjʊˈteɪʃən) *n.* **1.** the act of appointing a person or body of people to represent or act on behalf of others. **2.** a person or, more often, a body of people so appointed; delegation.

depute *vb.* (dɪˈpjuːt) (*tr.*) **1.** to appoint as an agent, substitute, or representative. **2.** to assign or transfer (authority, duties, etc.) to a deputy; delegate. ~*n.* (ˈdɛpjuːt). **3.** *Scot.* **a.** a deputy. **b.** (*as modifier; usually postpositive*): *sheriff depute.* [C15: from Old French *deputer,* from Late Latin *dēputāre* to assign, allot, from Latin DE- + *putāre* to think, consider]

deputize *or* **deputise** (ˈdɛpjʊˌtaɪz) *vb.* to appoint or act as deputy.

deputy (ˈdɛpjʊtɪ) *n., pl.* **-ties. 1. a.** a person appointed to act on behalf of or represent another. **b.** (*as modifier*): *the deputy chairman.* **2.** a member of the legislative assembly or of the lower chamber of the legislature in various countries, such as France. **3.** *Brit. mining.* another word for **fireman** (sense 4). [C16: from Old French *depute,* from *deputer* to appoint; see DEPUTE]

deputy minister *n.* (in Canada) the senior civil servant in a government department.

der. *abbrev. for:* **1.** derivation. **2.** derivative.

deracinate (dɪˈræsɪˌneɪt) *vb.* (*tr.*) **1.** to pull up by or as if by the roots; uproot; extirpate. **2.** to remove, as from a natural environment. [C16: from Old French *desraciner,* from *des-* DIS-[1] + *racine* root, from Late Latin *rādīcīna* a little root, from Latin *rādīx* a root] —**deˌraciˈnation** *n.*

deraign *or* **darraign** (dəˈreɪn) *vb.* (*tr.*) *Obsolete.* **1.** *Law.* to contest (a claim, suit, etc.). **2.** to arrange (soldiers) for battle. [C13: from Old French *deraisnier* to defend, from Vulgar Latin *ratiōnāre* (unattested) to REASON] —**deˈraignment** *or* **darˈraignment** *n.*

derail (dɪˈreɪl) *vb.* **1.** to go or cause to go off the rails, as a train, tram, etc. ~*n.* **2.** Also called: **deˈrailer.** *Chiefly U.S.* a device designed to make rolling stock or locomotives leave the rails to avoid a collision or accident. —**deˈrailment** *n.*

derailleur (dəˈreɪljə) *n.* a mechanism for changing gear on bicycles, consisting of a device that lifts the driving chain from one sprocket wheel to another of different size. [French *dérailleur* derailer]

derange (dɪˈreɪndʒ) *vb.* (*tr.*) **1.** to disturb the order or arrangement of; throw into disorder; disarrange. **2.** to disturb the action or operation of. **3.** to make insane; drive mad. [C18: from Old French *desrengier,* from *des-* DIS-[1] + *reng* row, order]

derangement (dɪˈreɪndʒmənt) *n.* **1.** the act of deranging or state of being deranged. **2.** disorder or confusion. **3.** *Psychiatry.* a mental disorder or serious mental disturbance.

derate (diːˈreɪt) *vb.* (*tr.*) *Brit.* to assess the value of (some types of property, such as agricultural land) at a lower rate than others for local taxation. —**deˈrating** *n.*

deration (diːˈræʃən) *vb.* (*tr.*) to end rationing of (food, petrol, etc.).

derby (ˈdɜːrbɪ) *n., pl.* **-bies.** the U.S. and Canadian name for **bowler**[2].

Derby[1] ('dɑːbɪ; *U.S.* 'dɜːrbɪ) *n.* **1. the.** an annual horse race run at Epsom Downs, Surrey, since 1780: one of the English flat-racing classics. **2.** any of various other horse races. **3. local Derby.** a football match between two teams from the same area. [C18: named after the twelfth Earl of *Derby* (died 1834), who founded the horse race at Epsom Downs in 1780]

Derby[2] ('dɑːbɪ) *n.* **1.** a firm-textured pale-coloured type of cheese from Derbyshire, a county in central England. **2. sage Derby.** a green-and-white Derby cheese flavoured with sage.

de re *Latin.* ('deɪ 'reɪ) *adj. Logic, philosophy.* (of a belief, possibility, etc.) relating to the individual rather than to an expression, as the necessity of *the number of wonders of the world is prime* since that number, seven, is necessarily prime. Compare **de dicto.** [literally: about the thing]

derecognize *or* **derecognise** (diː'rɛkəgˌnaɪz) *vb.* (*tr.*) **1.** to cease to recognize a trade union as having special negotiating rights within a company or industry. **2.** to advise (a trade union) of such action. —ˌ**derecog'nition** *n.*

deregister (diː'rɛdʒɪstə) *vb.* to remove (oneself, a car, etc.) from a register. —ˌ**deregis'tration** *n.*

deregulate (diː'regjʊˌleɪt) *vb.* (*tr.*) to remove regulations or controls from. —**deˌregu'lation** *n.* —**de'regulator** *n.* —**de'regulatory** *adj.*

derelict ('dɛrɪlɪkt) *adj.* **1.** deserted or abandoned, as by an owner, occupant, etc. **2.** falling into ruins; neglected; dilapidated. **3.** neglectful of duty or obligation; remiss. ~*n.* **4.** a person abandoned or neglected by society; a social outcast or vagrant. **5.** property deserted or abandoned by an owner, occupant, etc. **6.** a vessel abandoned at sea. **7.** a person who is neglectful of duty or obligation. [C17: from Latin *dērelictus* forsaken, from *dērelinquere* to abandon, from DE- + *relinquere* to leave]

dereliction (ˌdɛrɪ'lɪkʃən) *n.* **1.** deliberate, conscious, or wilful neglect (esp. in the phrase **dereliction of duty**). **2.** the act of abandoning or deserting or the state of being abandoned or deserted. **3.** *Law.* **a.** accretion of dry land gained by the gradual receding of the sea or by a river changing its course. **b.** the land thus left.

derequisition (diːˌrɛkwɪ'zɪʃən) *vb.* (*tr.*) to release from military to civilian use.

derestrict (ˌdiːrɪ'strɪkt) *vb.* (*tr.*) to render or leave free from restriction, esp. a road from speed limits. —ˌ**dere'striction** *n.*

deride (dɪ'raɪd) *vb.* (*tr.*) to speak of or treat with contempt, mockery, or ridicule; scoff or jeer at. [C16: from Latin *dērīdēre* to laugh to scorn, from DE- + *rīdēre* to laugh, smile] —**de'rider** *n.* —**de'ridingly** *adv.*

de rigueur *French.* (də rigœr; *English* də rɪ'gɜː) *adj.* required by etiquette or fashion. [literally: of strictness]

derisible (dɪ'rɪzɪbᵊl) *adj.* subject to or deserving of derision; ridiculous.

derision (dɪ'rɪʒən) *n.* **1.** the act of deriding; mockery; scorn. **2.** an object of mockery or scorn. [C15: from Late Latin *dērīsiō*, from Latin *dērīsus*; see DERIDE]

derisive (dɪ'raɪsɪv, -zɪv) *adj.* showing or characterized by derision; mocking; scornful. —**de'risively** *adv.* —**de'risiveness** *n.*

derisory (dɪ'raɪsərɪ, -zərɪ) *adj.* **1.** subject to or worthy of derision, esp. because of being ridiculously small or inadequate. **2.** another word for **derisive.**

deriv. *abbrev. for:* **1.** derivation. **2.** derivative. **3.** derived.

derivation (ˌdɛrɪ'veɪʃən) *n.* **1.** the act of deriving or state of being derived. **2.** the source, origin, or descent of something, such as a word. **3.** something derived; a derivative. **4. a.** the process of deducing a mathematical theorem, formula, etc., as a necessary consequence of a set of accepted statements. **b.** this sequence of statements. **c.** the operation of finding a derivative. —ˌ**deri'vational** *adj.*

derivative (dɪ'rɪvətɪv) *adj.* **1.** resulting from derivation; derived. **2.** based on or making use of other sources; not original or primary. **3.** copied from others, esp. slavishly; plagiaristic. ~*n.* **4.** a term, idea, etc., that is based on or derived from another in the same class. **5.** a word derived from another word. **6.** *Chem.* a compound that is formed from, or can be regarded as formed from, a structurally related compound: *chloroform is a derivative of methane.* **7.** *Maths.* **a.** Also called: **differential coefficient, first derivative.** the change of a function, f(x), with respect to an infinitesimally small change in the independent variable, x; the limit of $[f(a + \Delta x) - f(a)]/\Delta x$, at $x = a$, as the increment, Δx, tends to 0. Symbol: $df(x)/dx$, $f'(x)$, $Df(x)$: the derivative of x^n is nx^{n-1}. **b.** the rate of change of one quantity with respect to another: *velocity is the derivative of distance with respect to time.* **8.** *Psychoanal.* an activity that represents the expression of hidden impulses and desires by channelling them into socially acceptable forms. —**de'rivatively** *adv.*

derive (dɪ'raɪv) *vb.* **1.** (usually foll. by *from*) to draw or be drawn (from) in source or origin; trace or be traced. **2.** (*tr.*) to obtain by reasoning; deduce; infer. **3.** (*tr.*) to trace the source or development of. **4.** (usually foll. by *from*) to produce or be produced (from) by a chemical reaction. **5.** *Maths.* to obtain (a function) by differentiation. [C14: from Old French *deriver* to spring from, from Latin *dērīvāre* draw off, from DE- + *rīvus* a stream] —**de'rivable** *adj.* —**de'river** *n.*

derived fossil *n.* a fossil eroded from a sediment and redeposited in a younger sediment.

derived unit *n.* a unit of measurement obtained by multiplication or division of the base units of a system without the introduction of numerical factors.

-derm *n. combining form.* indicating skin: *endoderm.* [via French from Greek *derma* skin]

derma[1] ('dɜːmə) *n.* another name for **corium.** Also: **derm** (dɜːm). [C18: New Latin, from Greek: skin, from *derein* to skin]

derma[2] ('dɜːmə) *n.* beef or fowl intestine used as a casing for certain dishes, esp. kishke. [from Yiddish *derme,* plural of *darm* intestine, from Old High German *daram;* related to Old English *thearm* gut, Old Norse *tharmr*]

dermal ('dɜːməl) *adj.* of or relating to the skin.

dermapteran (dɜː'mæptərən) *n.* **1.** any insect of the order *Dermaptera,* the earwigs. ~*adj.* **2.** of, relating to, or belonging to this order. [C19: from Greek *derma* (see DERMA[1]) + *pteron* wing]

dermatitis (ˌdɜːmə'taɪtɪs) *n.* inflammation of the skin.

dermato-, derma- *or before a vowel* **dermat-, derm-** *combining form.* indicating skin: *dermatology; dermatome; dermal; dermatitis.* [from Greek *derma* skin]

dermatogen (də'mætədʒən, 'dɜːməˌtəʊdʒən) *n. Botany.* a meristem at the apex of stems and roots that gives rise to the epidermis.

dermatoglyphics (ˌdɜːmətəʊ'glɪfɪks) *pl. n.* **1.** the lines forming a skin pattern, esp. on the palms of the hands and soles of the feet. **2.** (*functioning as sing.*) the study of such skin patterns. [C20: from DERMATO- + Greek *gluphē* a carving; see GLYPH]

dermatoid ('dɜːməˌtɔɪd) *adj.* resembling skin.

dermatology (ˌdɜːmə'tɒlədʒɪ) *n.* the branch of medicine concerned with the skin and its diseases. —**dermatological** (ˌdɜːmətə'lɒdʒɪkᵊl) *adj.* —ˌ**derma'tologist** *n.*

dermatome ('dɜːməˌtəʊm) *n.* **1.** a surgical instrument for cutting thin slices of skin, esp. for grafting. **2.** the area of skin supplied by nerve fibres from a single posterior spinal root. **3.** *Embryol.* the part of a somite in a vertebrate embryo that gives rise to the dermis. —**dermatomic** (ˌdɜːmə'tɒmɪk) *adj.*

dermatophyte ('dɜːmətəʊˌfaɪt) *n.* any parasitic fungus that affects the skin. —**dermatophytic** (ˌdɜːmətəʊ'fɪtɪk) *adj.*

dermatophytosis (ˌdɜːmətəʊfaɪ'təʊsɪs) *n.* a fungal infection of the skin, esp. the feet. See **athlete's foot.**

dermatoplasty ('dɜːmətəʊˌplæstɪ) *n.* any surgical operation on the skin, esp. skin grafting. —ˌ**dermato'plastic** *adj.*

dermatosis (ˌdɜːmə'təʊsɪs) *n., pl.* **-toses** (-'təʊsiːz). any skin disease.

dermestid (ˌdɜː'mɛstɪd) *n.* any beetle of the family *Dermestidae,* whose members are destructive at both larval and adult stages to a wide range of stored organic materials such as wool, fur, feathers, and meat. They include the bacon (*or* larder), cabinet, carpet, leather, and museum beetles. [C19: from New Latin *dermestida,* from Greek *dermēstēs,* from *derma* skin + *esthiein* to eat]

dermis ('dɜːmɪs) *n.* another name for **corium.** [C19: New Latin, from EPIDERMIS] —'**dermic** *adj.*

dermoid ('dɜːmɔɪd) *adj.* **1.** of or resembling skin. ~*n.* **2.** a congenital cystic tumour whose walls are lined with epithelium.

dernier cri *French.* (dɛrnje kri) *n.* **le** (lə). the latest fashion; the last word. [literally: last cry]

dero ('dɛrəʊ) *n., pl.* **deros.** *Austral. slang.* **1.** a tramp or derelict. **2.** *Often humorous.* a person. [C20: shortened from DERELICT]

derogate *vb.* ('dɛrəˌgeɪt). **1.** (*intr.;* foll. by *from*) to cause to seem inferior or be in disrepute; detract. **2.** (*intr.;* foll. by *from*) to deviate in standard or quality; degenerate. **3.** (*tr.*) to cause to seem inferior, etc.; disparage. **4.** (*tr.*) to curtail the application of (a law or regulation). ~*adj.* ('dɛrəgɪt, -ˌgeɪt). **5.** *Archaic.* debased or degraded. [C15: from Latin *dērogāre* to repeal some part of a law, modify it, from DE- + *rogāre* to ask, propose a law] —'**derogately** *adv.* —ˌ**dero'gation** *n.* —**derogative** (dɪ'rɒgətɪv) *adj.* —**de'rogatively** *adv.*

derogatory (dɪ'rɒgətərɪ, -trɪ) *adj.* tending or intended to detract, disparage, or belittle; intentionally offensive. —**de'rogatorily** *adv.* —**de'rogatoriness** *n.*

derrick ('dɛrɪk) *n.* **1.** a simple crane having lifting tackle slung from a boom. **2.** the framework erected over an oil well to enable drill tubes to be raised and lowered. ~*vb.* **3.** to raise or lower the jib of (a crane). [C17 (in the sense: gallows): from *Derrick,* name of a celebrated hangman at Tyburn]

derrière (ˌdɛrɪ'ɛə; *French* dɛrjɛr) *n.* a euphemistic word for **buttocks.** [C18: literally: behind (prep.), from Old French *deriere,* from Latin *dē retrō* from the back]

derring-do ('dɛrɪŋ'duː) *n. Archaic or literary.* a daring spirit or deed; boldness or bold action. [C16: from Middle English *durring don* daring to do, from *durren* to dare + *don* to do]

derringer *or* **deringer** ('dɛrɪndʒə) *n.* a short-barrelled pocket pistol of large calibre. [C19: named after Henry *Deringer,* American gunsmith who invented it]

derris ('dɛrɪs) *n.* any East Indian leguminous woody climbing plant of the genus *Derris,* esp. *D. elliptica,* whose roots yield the compound rotenone. [C19: New Latin, from Greek: covering, leather, from *deros* skin, hide, from *derein* to skin]

derry[1] ('dɛrɪ) *n., pl.* **-ries.** *Austral. and N.Z.* **1.** dislike or prejudice. **2. have a derry on.** to have a prejudice or grudge against. [C19: probably from *derry down,* a refrain in some folk songs, alluding to the phrase *have a down on;* see DOWN[1]]

derry[2] ('dɛrɪ) *n., pl.* **-ries.** *Slang.* a derelict house, esp. one used by tramps, drug addicts, etc. [C20: shortened from DERELICT]
derv (dɜːv) *n.* a Brit. name for **diesel oil** when used for road transport. [C20: from *d(iesel) e(ngine) r(oad) v(ehicle)*]
dervish ('dɜːvɪʃ) *n.* a member of any of various Muslim orders of ascetics, some of which (**whirling dervishes**) are noted for a frenzied, ecstatic, whirling dance. [C16: from Turkish: beggar, from Persian *darvīsh* mendicant monk] —'**dervish-ˌlike** *adj.*
DES (in Britain) *abbrev. for* Department of Education and Science.
desalinate (diː'sælɪˌneɪt) *or* **desalinize, desalinise** *vb.* (*tr.*) to remove the salt from (esp. from sea water). Also: **desalt** (diː'sɔːlt).
desalination (diːˌsælɪ'neɪʃən) *or* **desalinization, desalinisation** *n.* the process of removing salt, esp. from sea water so that it can be used for drinking or irrigation.
desaturation (diːˌsætʃə'reɪʃən) *n. Physics.* the addition of white light to a pure colour to produce a paler less saturated colour.
desc. *abbrev. for* descendant.
descant *n.* ('dɛskænt, 'dɪs-). **1.** Also called: **discant.** a decorative counterpoint added above a basic melody. **2.** a comment, criticism, or discourse. ~*adj.* ('dɛskænt, 'dɪs-) **3.** Also: **discant.** of or pertaining to the highest member in common use of a family of musical instruments: *a descant recorder.* ~*vb.* (dɛs'kænt, dɪs-). (*intr.*) **4.** Also: **discant.** (often foll. by *on* or *upon*) to compose or perform a descant (for a piece of music). **5.** (often foll. by *on* or *upon*) to discourse at length or make varied comments. **6.** *Archaic.* to sing sweetly or melodiously. [C14: from Old Northern French, from Medieval Latin *discanthus,* from Latin DIS-[1] + *cantus* song; see CHANT] —**des'canter** *n.*
descend (dɪ'sɛnd) *vb.* (*mainly intr.*) **1.** (*also tr.*) to move, pass, or go down (a hill, slope, staircase, etc.) **2.** (of a hill, slope, or path) to lead or extend down; slope; incline. **3.** to move to a lower level, pitch, etc.; fall. **4.** (often foll. by *from*) to be connected by a blood relationship (to a dead or extinct individual, race, species, etc.). **5.** to be passed on by parents or ancestors; be inherited. **6.** to sink or come down in morals or behaviour; lower oneself. **7.** (often foll. by *on* or *upon*) to arrive or attack in a sudden or overwhelming way: *their relatives descended upon them last week.* **8.** (of the sun, moon, etc.) to move towards the horizon. [C13: from Old French *descendre,* from Latin *dēscendere,* from DE- + *scandere* to climb; see SCAN] —**des'cendable** *adj.*
descendant (dɪ'sɛndənt) *n.* **1.** a person, animal, or plant when described as descended from an individual, race, species, etc. **2.** something that derives or is descended from an earlier form. ~*adj.* **3.** a variant spelling of **descendent.**
Descendant (dɪ'sɛndənt) *n. Astrology.* the point on the ecliptic lying directly opposite the Ascendant.
descendent (dɪ'sɛndənt) *adj.* **1.** coming or going downwards; descending. **2.** deriving by descent, as from an ancestor.
descender (dɪ'sɛndə) *n.* **1.** a person or thing that descends. **2.** *Printing.* the portion of a letter, such as j, p, or y, below the level of the base of an x or n.
descendeur *French.* (dɛsɑ̃dœr) *n. Mountaineering.* a shaped metal piece through which the rope can be fed: used to control the rate of descent in abseiling. Also called: **descender.** [C20]
descendible *or* **descendable** (dɪ'sɛndəbᵊl) *adj. Law.* capable of being inherited.
descent (dɪ'sɛnt) *n.* **1.** the act of descending. **2.** a downward slope or inclination. **3.** a passage, path, or way leading downwards. **4.** derivation from an ancestor or ancestral group; lineage. **5.** (in genealogy) a generation in a particular lineage. **6.** a decline or degeneration. **7.** a movement or passage in degree or state from higher to lower. **8.** (often foll. by *on*) a sudden and overwhelming arrival or attack. **9.** *Property law.* (formerly) the transmission of real property to the heir on an intestacy.
deschool (ˌdiː'skuːl) *vb.* (*tr.*) to separate education from the institution of school and operate through the pupil's life experience as opposed to a set curriculum.
descramble (diː'skræmbᵊl) *vb.* to restore (a scrambled signal) to an intelligible form, esp. automatically by the use of electronic devices. —ˌ**de'scrambler** *n.*
describe (dɪ'skraɪb) *vb.* (*tr.*) **1.** to give an account or representation of in words. **2.** to pronounce or label: *he has been described as a genius.* **3.** to draw a line or figure, such as a circle. [C15: from Latin *dēscrībere* to copy off, write out, delineate, from DE- + *scrībere* to write] —**de'scribable** *adj.* —**de'scriber** *n.*
description (dɪ'skrɪpʃən) *n.* **1.** a statement or account that describes; representation in words. **2.** the act, process, or technique of describing. **3.** sort, kind, or variety: *reptiles of every description.* **4.** *Geometry.* the act of drawing a line or figure, such as an arc. **5.** *Philosophy.* a noun phrase containing a predicate that may replace a name as the subject of a sentence.
descriptive (dɪ'skrɪptɪv) *adj.* **1.** characterized by or containing description; serving to describe. **2.** *Grammar.* (of an adjective) serving to describe the referent of the noun modified, as for example the adjective *brown* as contrasted with *my* and *former.* **3.** relating to or based upon description or classification rather than explanation or prescription: *descriptive linguistics.* —**de'scriptively** *adv.* —**de'scriptiveness** *n.*
descriptive geometry *n.* the study of the projection of three-dimensional figures onto a plane surface.
descriptive linguistics *n.* (*functioning as sing.*) the study of the description of the internal phonological, grammatical, and semantic structures of languages at given points in time without reference to their histories or to one another. Also called: **synchronic linguistics.** Compare **historical linguistics.**
descriptive metaphysics *n.* (*functioning as sing.*) the philosophical study of the structure of how we think about the world.
descriptive notation *n. Chess.* a method of denoting the squares on the chessboard in which each player names the files from the pieces that stand on them at the opening and numbers the ranks away from himself. Compare **algebraic notation.**
descriptive statistics *n.* (*functioning as sing.*) the use of statistics to describe a set of known data in a clear and concise manner, as in terms of its mean and variance, or diagramatically, as by a histogram. Compare **statistical inference.**
descriptivism (dɪ'skrɪptɪˌvɪzəm) *n. Ethics.* the theory that moral utterances have a truth value. Compare **prescriptivism, emotivism.** —**de'scriptiˌvist** *adj.*
descry (dɪ'skraɪ) *vb.* **-scries, -scrying, -scried.** (*tr.*) **1.** to discern or make out; catch sight of. **2.** to discover by looking carefully; detect. [C14: from Old French *descrier* to proclaim, DECRY] —**de'scrier** *n.*
desecrate ('dɛsɪˌkreɪt) *vb.* (*tr.*) **1.** to violate or outrage the sacred character of (an object or place) by destructive, blasphemous, or sacrilegious action. **2.** to remove the consecration from (a person, object, building, etc.); deconsecrate. [C17: from DE- + CONSECRATE] —'**deseˌcrator** *or* '**deseˌcrater** *n.* —ˌ**dese'cration** *n.*
desegregate (diː'sɛgrɪˌgeɪt) *vb.* to end racial segregation in (a school or other public institution). —ˌ**desegre'gation** *n.* —ˌ**desegre'gationist** *n., adj.*
deselect (ˌdiːsɪ'lɛkt) *vb.* (*tr.*) **1.** *Brit. Politics.* (of a constituency organization) to refuse to select (an existing MP) for re-election. **2.** *U.S.* to discharge (a trainee) during the period of training. —ˌ**dese'lection** *n.*
desensitize *or* **desensitise** (diː'sɛnsɪˌtaɪz) *vb.* (*tr.*) **1.** to render insensitive or less sensitive: *the patient was desensitized to the allergen; to desensitize photographic film.* **2.** *Psychol.* to decrease the abnormal fear in (a person) of a situation or object, by exposing him to it either in reality or in his imagination. —**deˌsensiti'zation** *or* **deˌsensiti'sation** *n.* —**de'sensiˌtizer** *or* **de'sensiˌtiser** *n.*
desert[1] ('dɛzət) *n.* **1.** a region that is devoid or almost devoid of vegetation, esp. because of low rainfall. **2.** an uncultivated uninhabited region. **3.** a place which lacks some desirable feature or quality: *a cultural desert.* **4.** (*modifier*) of, relating to, or like a desert; infertile or desolate. [C13: from Old French, from Church Latin *dēsertum,* from Latin *dēserere* to abandon, literally: to sever one's links with, from DE- + *serere* to bind together]
desert[2] (dɪ'zɜːt) *vb.* **1.** (*tr.*) to leave or abandon (a person, place, etc.) without intending to return, esp. in violation of a duty, promise, or obligation. **2.** *Military.* to abscond from (a post or duty) with no intention of returning. **3.** (*tr.*) to fail (someone) in time of need: *his good humour temporarily deserted him.* [C15: from French *déserter,* from Late Latin *dēsertāre,* from Latin *dēserere* to forsake; see DESERT[1]] —**de'serter** *n.*
desert[3] (dɪ'zɜːt) *n.* **1.** (*often pl.*) something that is deserved or merited; just reward or punishment. **2.** the state of deserving a reward or punishment. **3.** virtue or merit. [C13: from Old French *deserte,* from *deservir* to DESERVE]
desert boots *pl. n.* ankle-high suede boots with laces and soft soles, worn informally by men and women.
desert cooler *n.* (in India) a cooling device in which air is driven by an electric fan through wet grass.
desertification (dɪˌzɜːtɪfɪ'keɪʃən) *n.* a process by which fertile land turns into barren land or desert.
desertion (dɪ'zɜːʃən) *n.* **1.** the act of deserting or abandoning or the state of being deserted or abandoned. **2.** *Law.* wilful abandonment, esp. of one's spouse or children, without consent and in breach of obligations.
desert island *n.* a small remote tropical island.
desert lynx *n.* another name for **caracal.**
desert oak *n.* a tree, *Casuarina decaisneana,* of Central and NW Australia, the timber of which is resistant to termite attack.
desert pea *n.* an Australian trailing leguminous plant, *Clianthus formosus,* with scarlet flowers.
desert rat *n.* **1.** a jerboa, *Jaculus orientalis,* inhabiting the deserts of N Africa. **2.** *Brit. informal.* a soldier who served in North Africa with the British 7th Armoured Division in 1941–42.
desert soil *n.* a type of soil developed in arid climates, characterized by a lack of leaching and small humus content.
deserve (dɪ'zɜːv) *vb.* **1.** (*tr.*) to be entitled to or worthy of; merit. **2.** (*intr.*; foll. by *of*) *Obsolete.* to be worthy. [C13: from Old French *deservir,* from Latin *dēservīre* to serve devotedly, from DE- + *servīre* to SERVE] —**de'served** *adj.* —**deservedness** (dɪ'zɜːvɪdnɪs) *n.* —**de'server** *n.*
deservedly (dɪ'zɜːvɪdlɪ) *adv.* according to merit; justly.
deserving (dɪ'zɜːvɪŋ) *adj.* **1.** (often *postpositive* and foll. by *of*) worthy, esp. of praise or reward. ~*n.* **2.** *Rare.* a merit or demerit; desert. —**de'servingly** *adv.* —**de'servingness** *n.*
desexualize *or* **desexualise** (diː'sɛksjʊəˌlaɪz) *vb.* (*tr.*) to deprive of sexual characteristics by the surgical removal of the testicles

or ovaries; castrate or spay. Often shortened to **desex** (di:'sɛks). —**deˌsexualiˈzation** *or* **deˌsexualiˈsation** *n.*

deshabille (ˌdeɪzæ'bi:l) *n.* a variant of **dishabille.**

desiccant ('dɛsɪkənt) *adj.* **1.** desiccating or drying. ~*n.* **2.** a substance, such as calcium oxide, that absorbs water and is used to remove moisture; a drying agent. [C17: from Latin *dēsiccāns* drying up; see DESICCATE]

desiccate ('dɛsɪˌkeɪt) *vb.* **1.** (*tr.*) to remove most of the water from (a substance or material); dehydrate. **2.** (*tr.*) to preserve (food) by removing moisture; dry. **3.** (*intr.*) to become dried up. [C16: from Latin *dēsiccāre* to dry up, from DE- + *siccāre* to dry, from *siccus* dry] —ˌ**desicˈcation** *n.* —ˈ**desiccative** *adj.*

desiccated ('dɛsɪˌkeɪtɪd) *adj.* **1.** dehydrated and powdered: *desiccated coconut.* **2.** lacking in spirit or animation.

desiccator ('dɛsɪˌkeɪtə) *n.* **1.** any apparatus for drying milk, fruit, etc. **2.** an airtight box or jar containing a desiccant, used to dry chemicals and protect them from the water vapour in the atmosphere.

desiderata (dɪˌzɪdə'rɑ:tə) *n.* the plural of **desideratum.**

desiderate (dɪ'zɪdəˌreɪt) *vb.* (*tr.*) to feel the lack of or need for; long for; miss. [C17: from Latin *dēsīderāre,* from DE- + *sīdus* star; see DESIRE] —**deˌsiderˈation** *n.*

desiderative (dɪ'zɪdərətɪv) *adj.* **1.** feeling or expressing desire. **2.** (in certain languages, of a verb) related in form to another verb and expressing the subject's desire or intention to perform the act denoted by the other verb. ~*n.* **3.** a desiderative verb.

desideratum (dɪˌzɪdə'rɑ:təm) *n., pl.* **-ta** (-tə). something lacked and wanted. [C17: from Latin; see DESIDERATE]

design (dɪ'zaɪn) *vb.* **1.** to work out the structure or form of (something), as by making a sketch, outline, pattern, or plans. **2.** to plan and make (something) artistically or skilfully. **3.** (*tr.*) to form or conceive in the mind; invent. **4.** (*tr.*) to intend, as for a specific purpose; plan. **5.** (*tr.*) *Obsolete.* to mark out or designate. ~*n.* **6.** a plan, sketch, or preliminary drawing. **7.** the arrangement or pattern of elements or features of an artistic or decorative work: *the design of the desk is Chippendale.* **8.** a finished artistic or decorative creation. **9.** the art of designing. **10.** a plan, scheme, or project. **11.** an end aimed at or planned for; intention; purpose. **12.** (*often pl.;* often foll. by *on* or *against*) a plot or hostile scheme, often to gain possession of (something) by illegitimate means. **13.** a coherent or purposeful pattern, as opposed to chaos: *God's design appears in nature.* **14. argument from design.** *Philosophy.* another name for **teleological argument.** [C16: from Latin *dēsignāre* to mark out, describe, from DE- + *signāre* to mark, from *signum* a mark, SIGN] —**deˈsignable** *adj.*

designate *vb.* ('dɛzɪgˌneɪt). (*tr.*) **1.** to indicate or specify. **2.** to give a name to; style; entitle. **3.** to select or name for an office or duty; appoint. ~*adj.* ('dɛzɪgnɪt, -ˌneɪt). **4.** (*immediately postpositive*) appointed, but not yet in office: *a minister designate.* [C15: from Latin *dēsignātus* marked out, defined; see DESIGN] —ˈ**desigˌnative** *or* **designatory** (ˌdɛzɪg'neɪtərɪ) *adj.* —ˈ**desigˌnator** *n.*

designated *adj. Logic.* (of a truth value) corresponding to truth in a two-valued logic, or having one of the analogous values in a many-valued logic.

designated employment *n.* (in Britain) any of certain kinds of jobs reserved for handicapped workers under the Disabled Persons (Employment) Act 1944.

designation (ˌdɛzɪg'neɪʃən) *n.* **1.** something that designates, such as a name or distinctive mark. **2.** the act of designating or the fact of being designated.

designedly (dɪ'zaɪnɪdlɪ) *adv.* by intention or design; on purpose.

designer (dɪ'zaɪnə) *n.* **1.** a person who devises and executes designs, as for works of art, clothes, machines, etc. **2.** (*modifier*) designed by and bearing the label or signature of a well-known fashion designer: *designer jeans.* **3.** (*modifier*) (of things, ideas, etc.) having an appearance of fashionable trendiness: *designer pop songs; designer stubble.* **4.** (*modifier*) (of cells, chemicals, etc.) designed (or produced) to perform a specific function or combat a specific problem: *designer insecticide.* **5.** a person who devises plots or schemes; intriguer.

designer drug *n.* **1.** *Med.* a synthetic antibiotic designed to be effective against a particular bacterium. **2.** any of various narcotic or hallucinogenic substances manufactured illegally from a range of chemicals.

designing (dɪ'zaɪnɪŋ) *adj.* artful and scheming; conniving; crafty. —**deˈsigningly** *adv.*

desinence ('dɛsɪnəns) *n. Grammar.* an ending or termination, esp. an inflectional ending of a word. [C16: from French *désinence,* from Latin *dēsinēns* ending, from *dēsinere* to leave off, from DE- + *sinere* to leave, permit] —ˈ**desinent** *or* **desinential** (ˌdɛsɪ'nɛnʃəl) *adj.*

desirable (dɪ'zaɪərəbᵊl) *adj.* **1.** worthy of desire or recommendation: *a desirable residence.* **2.** arousing desire, esp. sexual desire; attractive. ~*n.* **3.** a person or thing that is the object of desire. —**deˌsiraˈbility** *or* **deˈsirableness** *n.* —**deˈsirably** *adv.*

desire (dɪ'zaɪə) *vb.* (*tr.*) **1.** to wish or long for; crave; want. **2.** to express a wish or make a request for; ask for. ~*n.* **3.** a wish or longing; craving. **4.** an expressed wish; request. **5.** sexual appetite; lust. **6.** a person or thing that is desired. [C13: from Old French *desirer,* from Latin *dēsīderāre* to desire earnestly; see DESIDERATE] —**deˈsirer** *n.*

desirous (dɪ'zaɪərəs) *adj.* (usually *postpositive* and foll. by *of*) having or expressing desire (for); having a wish or longing (for). —**deˈsirously** *adv.* —**deˈsirousness** *n.*

desist (dɪ'zɪst) *vb.* (*intr.;* often foll. by *from*) to cease, as from an action; stop or abstain. [C15: from Old French *desister,* from Latin *dēsistere* to leave off, stand apart, from DE- + *sistere* to stand, halt] —**deˈsistance** *or* **deˈsistence** *n.*

desk (dɛsk) *n.* **1.** a piece of furniture with a writing surface and usually drawers or other compartments. **2.** a service counter or table in a public building, such as a hotel: *information desk.* **3.** a support, lectern, or book rest for the book from which services are read in a church. **4.** the editorial section of a newspaper, etc., responsible for a particular subject: *the news desk.* **5. a.** a music stand shared by two orchestral players. **b.** these two players. **6.** (*modifier*) **a.** made for use at a desk: *a desk calendar.* **b.** done at a desk: *a desk job.* [C14: from Medieval Latin *desca* table, from Latin *discus* disc, dish]

desk-bound *adj.* engaged in or involving sedentary work, as at an office desk.

desk clerk *n. U.S. and Canadian.* a hotel receptionist. Also called: **clerk.**

deskill (di:'skɪl) *vb.* (*tr.*) **1.** to mechanize or computerize (a job or process) to such an extent that little human skill is required to do it. **2.** to cause (skilled persons or a labour force) to work at a job that does not utilize their skills.

desktop ('dɛskˌtɒp) *n.* (*modifier*) denoting a computer system, esp. for word processing, that is small enough to use at a desk.

desktop publishing *n.* a means of publishing reports, advertising, etc., to near-typeset quality using a desktop computer and a laser printer. Abbrev.: **DTP.**

desman ('dɛsmən) *n., pl.* **-mans.** either of two molelike amphibious mammals, *Desmana moschata* (**Russian desman**) or *Galemys pyrenaicus* (**Pyrenean desman**), having dense fur and webbed feet: family *Talpidae,* order *Insectivora* (insectivores). [C18: from Swedish *desmansråtta,* from *desman* musk (of Germanic origin) + *råtta* rat]

desmid ('dɛsmɪd) *n.* any freshwater green alga of the mainly unicellular family *Desmidiaceae,* typically constricted into two symmetrical halves. [C19: from New Latin *Desmidium* (genus name), from Greek *desmos* bond, from *dein* to bind] —**desˈmidian** *adj.*

desmoid ('dɛsmɔɪd) *adj.* **1.** *Anatomy.* resembling a tendon or ligament. ~*n.* **2.** *Pathol.* a very firm tumour of connective tissue. [C19: from Greek *desmos* band + -OID; see DESMID]

desmosome ('dɛsməˌsəʊm) *n. Cytology.* an attachment between adjacent cells.

desolate *adj.* ('dɛsəlɪt). **1.** uninhabited; deserted. **2.** made uninhabitable; laid waste; devastated. **3.** without friends, hope, or encouragement; forlorn, wretched, or abandoned. **4.** gloomy or dismal; depressing. ~*vb.* ('dɛsəˌleɪt). (*tr.*) **5.** to deprive of inhabitants; depopulate. **6.** to make barren or lay waste; devastate. **7.** to make wretched or forlorn. **8.** to forsake or abandon. [C14: from Latin *dēsōlāre* to leave alone, from DE- + *sōlāre* to make lonely, lay waste, from *sōlus* alone] —ˈ**desoˌlater** *or* ˈ**desoˌlator** *n.* —ˈ**desolately** *adv.* —ˈ**desolateness** *n.*

desolation (ˌdɛsə'leɪʃən) *n.* **1.** the act of desolating or the state of being desolated; ruin or devastation. **2.** solitary misery; wretchedness. **3.** a desolate region; barren waste.

desorb (dɪ'sɔ:b, -'zɔ:b) *vb. Chem.* to change from an adsorbed state on a surface to a gaseous or liquid state.

desorption (dɪ'sɔ:pʃən, -'zɔ:p-) *n.* the action or process of desorbing.

desoxy- *combining form.* a variant of **deoxy-.**

despair (dɪ'spɛə) *vb.* **1.** (*intr.;* often foll. by *of*) to lose or give up hope: *I despair of his coming.* **2.** (*tr.*) *Obsolete.* to give up hope of; lose hope in. ~*n.* **3.** total loss of hope. **4.** a person or thing that causes hopelessness or for which there is no hope. [C14: from Old French *despoir* hopelessness, from *desperer* to despair, from Latin *dēspērāre,* from DE- + *spērāre* to hope]

despairing (dɪ'spɛərɪŋ) *adj.* marked by or resulting from despair; hopeless or desperate. —**desˈpairingly** *adv.*

despatch (dɪ'spætʃ) *vb.* (*tr.*) a less common spelling of **dispatch.** —**desˈpatcher** *n.*

desperado (ˌdɛspə'rɑ:dəʊ) *n., pl.* **-does** *or* **-dos.** a reckless or desperate person, esp. one ready to commit any violent illegal act. [C17: probably pseudo-Spanish variant of obsolete *desperate* (n.) a reckless character]

desperate ('dɛspərɪt, -prɪt) *adj.* **1.** careless of danger, as from despair; utterly reckless. **2.** (of an act) reckless; risky. **3.** used or undertaken in desperation or as a last resort: *desperate measures.* **4.** critical; very grave: *in desperate need.* **5.** (often *postpositive* and foll. by *for*) in distress and having a great need or desire. **6.** moved by or showing despair or hopelessness; despairing. [C15: from Latin *dēspērāre* to have no hope; see DESPAIR] —ˈ**desperately** *adv.* —ˈ**desperateness** *n.*

desperation (ˌdɛspə'reɪʃən) *n.* **1.** desperate recklessness. **2.** the act of despairing or the state of being desperate.

despicable ('dɛspɪkəbᵊl, dɪ'spɪk-) *adj.* worthy of being despised; contemptible; mean. [C16: from Late Latin *dēspicābilis,* from *dēspicārī* to disdain; compare DESPISE] —ˌ**despicaˈbility** *or* ˈ**despicableness** *n.* —ˈ**despicably** *adv.*

despise (dɪˈspaɪz) *vb.* (*tr.*) to look down on with contempt; scorn: *he despises flattery.* [C13: from Old French *despire,* from Latin *dēspicere* to look down, from DE- + *specere* to look] —**deˈspiser** *n.*
despite (dɪˈspaɪt) *prep.* **1.** in spite of; undeterred by. ~*n.* **2.** *Archaic.* contempt; insult. **3. in despite of.** (*prep.*) *Rare.* in spite of. ~*vb.* **4.** (*tr.*) an archaic word for **spite.** [C13: from Old French *despit,* from Latin *dēspectus* contempt; see DESPISE]
despiteful (dɪˈspaɪtfʊl) *or* **despiteous** (dɪˈspɪtɪəs) *adj.* an archaic word for **spiteful.** —**deˈspitefully** *adv.* —**deˈspitefulness** *n.*
despoil (dɪˈspɔɪl) *vb.* (*tr.*) to strip or deprive by force; plunder; rob; loot. [C13: from Old French *despoillier,* from Latin *dēspoliāre,* from DE- + *spoliāre* to rob (esp. of clothing); see SPOIL] —**deˈspoiler** *n.* —**deˈspoilment** *n.*
despoliation (dɪˌspəʊlɪˈeɪʃən) *n.* **1.** the act of despoiling; plunder or pillage. **2.** the state of being despoiled.
despond *vb.* **1.** (*intr.*) (dɪˈspɒnd). to lose heart or hope; become disheartened; despair. ~*n.* **2.** (ˈdɛspɒnd, dɪˈspɒnd). an archaic word for **despondency.** [C17: from Latin *dēspondēre* to promise, make over to, yield, lose heart, from DE- + *spondēre* to promise] —**deˈspondingly** *adv.*
despondent (dɪˈspɒndənt) *adj.* downcast or disheartened; lacking hope or courage; dejected. —**deˈspondence** *n.* —**deˈspondency** *n.* —**deˈspondently** *adv.*
despot (ˈdɛspɒt) *n.* **1.** an absolute or tyrannical ruler; autocrat or tyrant. **2.** any person in power who acts tyrannically. **3.** a title borne by numerous persons of rank in the later Roman, Byzantine, and Ottoman Empires: *the despot of Servia.* [C16: from Medieval Latin *despota,* from Greek *despotēs* lord, master; related to Latin *domus* house] —**despotic** (dɛsˈpɒtɪk) *or* **desˈpotical** *adj.* —**desˈpotically** *adv.*
despotism (ˈdɛspəˌtɪzəm) *n.* **1.** the rule of a despot; arbitrary, absolute, or tyrannical government. **2.** arbitrary or tyrannical authority or behaviour.
despumate (dɪˈspjuːmeɪt, ˈdɛspjʊˌmeɪt) *vb.* **1.** (*tr.*) to clarify or purify (a liquid) by skimming a scum from its surface. **2.** (*intr.*) (of a liquid) to form a scum or froth. [C17: from Latin *dēspūmāre* to skim off, from DE- + *spūma* foam, froth] —ˌ**despuˈmation** *n.*
desquamate (ˈdɛskwəˌmeɪt) *vb.* (*intr.*) (esp. of the skin in certain diseases) to peel or come off in scales. [C18: from Latin *dēsquāmāre* to scale off, from DE- + *squāma* a scale] —ˌ**desquaˈmation** *n.*
des res (dɛz rɛz) *n.* (in estate agents' jargon) a desirable residence.
dessert (dɪˈzɜːt) *n.* **1.** the sweet, usually last course of a meal. **2.** *Chiefly Brit.* (esp. formerly) fruit, dates, nuts, etc., served at the end of a meal. [C17: from French, from *desservir* to clear a table, from *des-* DIS-[1] + *servir* to SERVE]
dessertspoon (dɪˈzɜːtˌspuːn) *n.* a spoon intermediate in size between a tablespoon and a teaspoon.
dessiatine (ˈdɛsjəˌtiːn) *n.* a Russian unit of area equal to approximately 2.7 acres or 10 800 square metres. [C18: from Russian *desyatina,* literally: tithe, from *desyat* ten]
destabilize *or* **destabilise** (diːˈsteɪbɪˌlaɪz) *vb.* (*tr.*) to undermine or subvert (a government, economy, etc.) so as to cause unrest or collapse. —ˌ**destabiliˈzation** *or* ˌ**destabiliˈsation** *n.*
de-Stalinization *or* **de-Stalinisation** (diːˌstɑːlɪnaɪˈzeɪʃən) *n.* the elimination of the influence of Joseph Stalin (1879–1953), Soviet statesman.
destination (ˌdɛstɪˈneɪʃən) *n.* **1.** the predetermined end of a journey or voyage. **2.** the ultimate end or purpose for which something is created or a person is destined. **3.** *Rare.* the act of destining or predetermining.
destine (ˈdɛstɪn) *vb.* (*tr.*) to set apart or appoint (for a certain purpose or person, or to do something); intend; design. [C14: from Old French *destiner,* from Latin *dēstināre* to appoint, from DE- + *-stināre,* from *stāre* to stand]
destined (ˈdɛstɪnd) *adj.* (*postpositive*) **1.** foreordained or certain; meant: *he is destined to be famous.* **2.** (usually foll. by *for*) heading (towards a specific destination); directed: *a letter destined for Europe.*
destiny (ˈdɛstɪnɪ) *n., pl.* **-nies. 1.** the future destined for a person or thing; fate; fortune; lot. **2.** the predetermined or inevitable course of events. **3.** the ultimate power or agency that predetermines the course of events. [C14: from Old French *destinee,* from *destiner* to DESTINE]
destitute (ˈdɛstɪˌtjuːt) *adj.* **1.** lacking the means of subsistence; totally impoverished. **2.** (*postpositive;* foll. by *of*) completely lacking; deprived or bereft (of): *destitute of words.* **3.** *Obsolete.* abandoned or deserted. [C14: from Latin *dēstitūtus* forsaken, from *dēstituere* to leave alone, from *statuere* to place] —ˈ**destiˌtuteness** *n.*
destitution (ˌdɛstɪˈtjuːʃən) *n.* **1.** the state of being destitute; utter poverty. **2.** *Rare.* lack or deficiency.
destrier (ˈdɛstrɪə) *n.* an archaic word for **warhorse** (sense 1). [C13: from Old French, from *destre* right hand, from Latin *dextra;* from the fact that a squire led a knight's horse with his right hand]
destroy (dɪˈstrɔɪ) *vb.* (*mainly tr.*) **1.** to ruin; spoil; render useless. **2.** to tear down or demolish; break up; raze. **3.** to put an end to; do away with; extinguish. **4.** to kill or annihilate. **5.** to crush, subdue, or defeat. **6.** (*intr.*) to be destructive or cause destruction. [C13: from Old French *destruire,* from Latin *dēstruere* to pull down, from DE- + *struere* to pile up, build] —**deˈstroyable** *adj.*
destroyer (dɪˈstrɔɪə) *n.* **1.** a small fast lightly armoured but heavily armed warship. **2.** a person or thing that destroys.
destroyer escort *n.* a lightly armed warship smaller than a destroyer, designed to escort fleets or convoys.
destroying angel *n.* a white slender very poisonous basidiomycetous toadstool, *Amanita virosa,* having a pronounced volva, frilled, shaggy stalk, and sickly smell.
destruct (dɪˈstrʌkt) *vb.* **1.** to destroy (one's own missile or rocket) for safety. **2.** (*intr.*) (of a missile or rocket) to be destroyed, for safety, by those controlling it; self-destruct. ~*n.* **3.** the act of destructing. ~*adj.* **4.** designed to be capable of destroying itself or the object, system, or installation containing it: *destruct mechanism.*
destructible (dɪˈstrʌktəbᵊl) *adj.* capable of being or liable to be destroyed. —**deˌstructiˈbility** *n.*
destruction (dɪˈstrʌkʃən) *n.* **1.** the act of destroying or state of being destroyed; demolition. **2.** a cause of ruin or means of destroying. [C14: from Latin *dēstructiō* a pulling down; see DESTROY]
destructionist (dɪˈstrʌkʃənɪst) *n.* a person who believes in destruction, esp. of social institutions.
destructive (dɪˈstrʌktɪv) *adj.* **1.** (often *postpositive* and foll. by *of* or *to*) causing or tending to cause the destruction (of). **2.** intended to disprove or discredit, esp. without positive suggestions or help; negative: *destructive criticism.* Compare **constructive** (sense 1). —**deˈstructively** *adv.* —**deˈstructiveness** *or* **destructivity** (ˌdiːstrʌkˈtɪvɪtɪ) *n.*
destructive distillation *n.* the decomposition of a complex substance, such as wood or coal, by heating it in the absence of air and collecting the volatile products.
destructor (dɪˈstrʌktə) *n.* **1.** a furnace or incinerator for the disposal of refuse, esp. one that uses the resulting heat to generate power. **2.** a device used to blow up a dangerously defective missile or rocket after launching.
desuetude (dɪˈsjuːɪˌtjuːd, ˈdɛswɪtjuːd) *n.* the condition of not being in use or practice; disuse: *those ceremonies had fallen into desuetude.* [C15: from Latin *dēsuētūdō,* from *dēsuescere* to lay aside a habit, from DE- + *suescere* to grow accustomed]
desulphurize *or* **desulphurise** (diːˈsʌlfjʊˌraɪz) *vb.* to free or become free from sulphur. —**deˌsulphuriˈzation** *or* **deˌsulphuriˈsation** *n.* —**deˈsulphurˌizer** *or* **deˈsulphurˌiser** *n.*
desultory (ˈdɛsəltərɪ, -trɪ) *adj.* **1.** passing or jumping from one thing to another, esp. in a fitful way; unmethodical; disconnected. **2.** occurring in a random or incidental way; haphazard: *a desultory thought.* [C16: from Latin *dēsultōrius,* relating to one who vaults or jumps, hence superficial, from *dēsilīre* to jump down, from DE- + *salīre* to jump] —ˈ**desultorily** *adv.* —ˈ**desultoriness** *n.*
DET *abbrev. for* diethyltryptamine, a hallucinogenic drug.
detach (dɪˈtætʃ) *vb.* (*tr.*) **1.** to disengage and separate or remove, as by pulling; unfasten; disconnect. **2.** *Military.* to separate (a small unit) from a larger, esp. for a special assignment. [C17: from Old French *destachier,* from *des-* DIS-[1] + *attachier* to ATTACH] —**deˈtachable** *adj.* —**deˌtachaˈbility** *n.* —**deˈtacher** *n.*
detached (dɪˈtætʃt) *adj.* **1.** disconnected or standing apart; not attached: *a detached house.* **2.** having or showing no bias or emotional involvement; disinterested. **3.** *Social welfare.* working at the clients' normal location rather than from an office; not dependent on premises for providing a service: *a detached youth worker.* Compare **outreach** (sense 7). **4.** *Ophthalmol.* (of the retina) separated from the choroid layer of the eyeball to which it is normally attached, resulting in loss of vision in the affected part.
detachment (dɪˈtætʃmənt) *n.* **1.** indifference to other people or to one's surroundings; aloofness. **2.** freedom from self-interest or bias; disinterest. **3.** the act of disengaging or separating something. **4.** the condition of being disengaged or separated; disconnection. **5.** *Military.* **a.** the separation of a small unit from its main body, esp. of ships or troops. **b.** the unit so detached. **6.** *Logic.* the rule whereby the consequent of a true conditional statement, given the truth of its antecedent, may be asserted on its own. See also **modus ponens.**
detail (ˈdiːteɪl) *n.* **1.** an item or smaller part that is considered separately; particular. **2.** an item or circumstance that is insignificant or unimportant: *passengers' comfort was regarded as a detail.* **3.** treatment of or attention to items or particulars: *this essay includes too much detail.* **4.** items collectively; particulars. **5.** a small or accessory section or element in a painting, building, statue, etc., esp. when considered in isolation. **6.** *Military.* **a.** the act of assigning personnel for a specific duty, esp. a fatigue. **b.** the personnel selected. **c.** the duty or assignment. **7. go into detail.** to include all or most particulars. **8. in detail.** including all or most particulars or items thoroughly. ~*vb.* (*tr.*) **9.** to list or relate fully. **10.** *Military.* to select (personnel) for a specific duty. **11.** to decorate or elaborate (carving, etc.) with fine delicate drawing or designs. [C17: from French *détail,* from Old French *detailler* to cut in pieces, from *de-* DIS-[1] + *tailler* to cut; see TAILOR]
detail drawing *n.* a separate large-scale drawing of a small part or section of a building, machine, etc.

detailed ('diːteɪld) *adj.* having many details or giving careful attention to details.

detain (dɪ'teɪn) *vb.* (*tr.*) **1.** to delay; hold back; stop. **2.** to confine or hold in custody; restrain. **3.** *Archaic.* to retain or withhold. [C15: from Old French *detenir,* from Latin *dētinēre* to hold off, keep back, from DE- + *tenēre* to hold] —**de'tainable** *adj.* —**detainee** (ˌdiːteɪ'niː) *n.* —**de'tainment** *n.*

detainer (dɪ'teɪnə) *n. Law.* **1.** the wrongful withholding of the property of another person. **2. a.** the detention of a person in custody. **b.** a writ authorizing the further detention of a person already in custody. [C17: from Anglo-French *detener* (n.), from *detener* to DETAIN]

detect (dɪ'tɛkt) *vb.* (*tr.*) **1.** to perceive or notice: *to detect a note of sarcasm.* **2.** to discover the existence or presence of (esp. something likely to elude observation): *to detect alcohol in the blood.* **3.** to extract information from (an electromagnetic wave). **4.** *Obsolete.* to reveal or expose (a crime, criminal, etc.). [C15: from Latin *dētectus* uncovered, from *dētegere* to uncover, from DE- + *tegere* to cover] —**de'tectable** *or* **de'tectible** *adj.* —**de'tecter** *n.*

detection (dɪ'tɛkʃən) *n.* **1.** the act of discovering or the fact of being discovered: *detection of crime.* **2.** the act or process of extracting information, esp. at audio or video frequencies, from an electromagnetic wave. See also **demodulation.**

detective (dɪ'tɛktɪv) *n.* **1. a.** a police officer who investigates crimes. **b.** See **private detective. c.** (*as modifier*): *a detective story.* ~*adj.* **2.** used in or serving for detection. **3.** serving to detect.

detector (dɪ'tɛktə) *n.* **1.** a person or thing that detects. **2.** any mechanical sensing device. **3.** *Electronics.* a device used in the detection of radio signals.

detent (dɪ'tɛnt) *n.* the locking piece of a mechanism, often spring-loaded to check the movement of a wheel in one direction only. See also **pawl.** [C17: from Old French *destente,* a loosening, trigger: see DÉTENTE]

détente (deɪ'tɑːnt; *French* detɑ̃t) *n.* the relaxing or easing of tension, esp. between nations. [French, literally: a loosening, from Old French *destendre* to release, from *tendre* to stretch]

detention (dɪ'tɛnʃən) *n.* **1.** the act of detaining or state of being detained. **2. a.** custody or confinement, esp. of a suspect awaiting trial. **b.** (*as modifier*): *a detention order.* **3.** a form of punishment in which a pupil is detained after school. **4.** the withholding of something belonging to or claimed by another. [C16: from Latin *dētentiō* a keeping back; see DETAIN]

detention centre *n.* a place where young persons may be detained for short periods by order of a court.

deter (dɪ'tɜː) *vb.* **-ters, -terring, -terred.** (*tr.*) to discourage (from acting) or prevent (from occurring), usually by instilling fear, doubt, or anxiety. [C16: from Latin *dēterrēre,* from DE- + *terrēre* to frighten] —**de'terment** *n.*

deterge (dɪ'tɜːdʒ) *vb.* (*tr.*) to wash or wipe away; cleanse: *to deterge a wound.* [C17: from Latin *dētergēre* to wipe away, from DE- + *tergēre* to wipe]

detergency (dɪ'tɜːdʒənsɪ) *or* **detergence** *n.* cleansing power.

detergent (dɪ'tɜːdʒənt) *n.* **1.** a cleansing agent, esp. a surface-active chemical such as an alkyl sulphonate, widely used in industry, laundering, shampoos, etc. ~*adj. also* **detersive** (dɪ'tɜːsɪv). **2.** having cleansing power. [C17: from Latin *dētergēns* wiping off; see DETERGE]

deteriorate (dɪ'tɪərɪəˌreɪt) *vb.* **1.** to make or become worse or lower in quality, value, character, etc.; depreciate. **2.** (*intr.*) to wear away or disintegrate. [C16: from Late Latin *dēteriōrāre,* from Latin *dēterior* worse] —**deˌterio'ration** *n.* —**de'teriorative** *adj.*

determinable (dɪ'tɜːmɪnəbᵊl) *adj.* **1.** able to be decided, fixed, or found out. **2.** *Law.* liable to termination under certain conditions; terminable. —**de'terminably** *adv.*

determinant (dɪ'tɜːmɪnənt) *adj.* **1.** serving to determine or affect. ~*n.* **2.** a factor, circumstance, etc., that influences or determines. **3.** *Maths.* a square array of elements that represents the sum of certain products of these elements, used to solve simultaneous equations, in vector studies, etc. Compare **matrix** (sense 9).

determinate (dɪ'tɜːmɪnɪt) *adj.* **1.** definitely limited, defined, or fixed; distinct. **2.** a less common word for **determined. 3. a.** able to be predicted or deduced. **b.** (of an effect) obeying the law of causality. **4.** *Botany.* (of an inflorescence) having the main and branch stems ending in flowers; cymose. **5.** (of a structure, stress, etc.) able to be fully analysed or determined. —**de'terminately** *adv.* —**de'terminateness** *n.*

determination (dɪˌtɜːmɪ'neɪʃən) *n.* **1.** the act or an instance of making a decision. **2.** the condition of being determined; resoluteness. **3.** the act or an instance of ending an argument by the opinion or decision of an authority. **4.** the act or an instance of fixing or settling the quality, limit, position, etc., of something. **5.** a decision or opinion reached, rendered, or settled upon. **6.** a resolute movement towards some object or end. **7.** *Law.* the termination of an estate or interest. **8.** *Law.* the decision reached by a court of justice on a disputed matter. **9.** *Logic.* **a.** the process of qualifying or limiting a proposition or concept. **b.** the qualifications or limitations used in this process. **10.** the condition of embryonic tissues of being able to develop into only one particular tissue or organ in the adult.

determinative (dɪ'tɜːmɪnətɪv) *adj.* **1.** able to or serving to settle or determine; deciding. ~*n.* **2.** a factor, circumstance, etc., that settles or determines. **3.** *Grammar.* a less common word for **determiner. 4.** (in a logographic writing system) a logogram that bears a separate meaning, from which compounds and inflected forms are built up. —**de'terminatively** *adv.* —**de'terminativeness** *n.*

determine (dɪ'tɜːmɪn) *vb.* **1.** to settle or decide (an argument, question, etc.) conclusively, as by referring to an authority. **2.** (*tr.*) to ascertain or conclude, esp. after observation or consideration. **3.** (*tr.*) to shape or influence; give direction to: *experience often determines ability.* **4.** (*tr.*) to fix in scope, extent, variety, etc.: *the river determined the edge of the property.* **5.** to make or cause to make a decision: *he determined never to marry.* **6.** (*tr.*) *Logic.* to define or limit (a notion) by adding or requiring certain features or characteristics. **7.** (*tr.*) *Geom.* to fix or specify the position, form, or configuration of: *two points determine a line.* **8.** *Chiefly law.* to come or bring to an end, as an estate or interest in land. **9.** (*tr.*) to decide (a legal action or dispute). [C14: from Old French *determiner,* from Latin *dēterminãre* to set boundaries to, from DE- + *terminãre* to limit; see TERMINATE]

determined (dɪ'tɜːmɪnd) *adj.* of unwavering mind; resolute; firm. —**de'terminedly** *adv.* —**de'terminedness** *n.*

determiner (dɪ'tɜːmɪnə) *n.* **1.** a word, such as a number, article, personal pronoun, that determines (limits) the meaning of a noun phrase, e.g. *their* in 'their black cat'. **2.** a person or thing that determines.

determinism (dɪ'tɜːmɪˌnɪzəm) *n.* the philosophical doctrine that all events including human actions and choices are fully determined by preceding events and states of affairs, and so that freedom of choice is illusory. Also called: **necessitarianism.** Compare **free will** (sense 1b). —**de'terminist** *n., adj.* —**deˌtermin'istic** *adj.*

deterrent (dɪ'tɛrənt) *n.* **1.** something that deters. **2.** a weapon or combination of weapons, esp. nuclear, held by one state, etc., to deter attack by another. ~*adj.* **3.** tending or used to deter; restraining. [C19: from Latin *dēterrēns* hindering; see DETER] —**de'terrence** *n.*

detest (dɪ'tɛst) *vb.* (*tr.*) to dislike intensely; loathe. [C16: from Latin *dētestārī* to curse (while invoking a god as witness), from DE- + *testārī* to bear witness, from *testis* a witness] —**de'tester** *n.*

detestable (dɪ'tɛstəbᵊl) *adj.* being or deserving to be abhorred or detested; abominable; odious. —**deˌtesta'bility** *or* **de'testableness** *n.* —**de'testably** *adv.*

detestation (ˌdiːtɛs'teɪʃən) *n.* **1.** intense hatred; abhorrence. **2.** a person or thing that is detested.

dethrone (dɪ'θrəʊn) *vb.* (*tr.*) to remove from a throne or deprive of any high position or title; depose: *the champion was dethroned by a young boxer.* —**de'thronement** *n.* —**de'throner** *n.*

detinue ('dɛtɪˌnjuː) *n. Law.* an action brought by a plaintiff to recover goods wrongfully detained. [C15: from Old French *detenue,* from *detenir* to DETAIN]

detonate ('dɛtəˌneɪt) *vb.* to cause (a bomb, mine, etc.) to explode or (of a bomb, mine, etc.) to explode; set off or be set off. [C18: from Latin *dētonāre* to thunder down, from DE- + *tonāre* to THUNDER]

detonation (ˌdɛtə'neɪʃən) *n.* **1.** an explosion or the act of exploding. **2.** the spontaneous combustion in an internal-combustion engine of part of the mixture before it has been reached by the flame front, causing the engine to knock. **3.** *Physics.* rapid combustion, esp. that occurring within a shock wave. —'**detoˌnative** *adj.*

detonator ('dɛtəˌneɪtə) *n.* **1.** a small amount of explosive, as in a percussion cap, used to initiate a larger explosion. **2.** a device, such as an electrical generator, used to set off an explosion from a distance. **3.** a substance or object that explodes or is capable of exploding.

detour ('diːtʊə) *n.* **1.** a deviation from a direct, usually shorter route or course of action. ~*vb.* **2.** to deviate or cause to deviate from a direct route or course of action. [C18: from French *détour,* from Old French *destorner* to divert, turn away, from *des-* DE- + *torner* to TURN]

detoxicate (diː'tɒksɪˌkeɪt) *vb.* (*tr.*) **1.** to rid (a patient) of a poison or its effects. **2.** to counteract (a poison). [C19: DE- + *-toxicate,* from Latin *toxicum* poison; see TOXIC] —**de'toxicant** *adj., n.* —**deˌtoxi'cation** *n.*

detoxification centre *n.* a place that specializes in the treatment of alcoholism or drug addiction.

detoxify (diː'tɒksɪˌfaɪ) *vb.* **-fies, -fying, -fied.** (*tr.*) to remove poison from; detoxicate. —**deˌtoxcifi'cation** *n.*

detract (dɪ'trækt) *vb.* **1.** (when *intr.,* usually foll. by *from*) to take away a part (of); diminish: *her anger detracts from her beauty.* **2.** (*tr.*) to distract or divert. **3.** (*tr.*) *Obsolete.* to belittle or disparage. [C15: from Latin *dētractus* drawn away, from *dētrahere* to pull away, disparage, from DE- + *trahere* to drag] —**de'tractingly** *adv.* —**de'tractive** *or* **de'tractory** *adj.* —**de'tractively** *adv.* —**de'tractor** *n.*

detraction (dɪ'trækʃən) *n.* **1.** a person, thing, circumstance, etc., that detracts. **2.** the act of discrediting or detracting from another's reputation, esp. by slander; disparagement.

detrain (diː'treɪn) *vb.* to leave or cause to leave a railway train, as passengers, etc. —**de'trainment** *n.*

detribalize *or* **detribalise** (diːˈtraɪbəˌlaɪz) *vb.* (*tr.*) **1.** to cause members of a tribe to lose their characteristic customs or social, religious, or other organizational features. **2.** to cause tribal people to adopt urban ways of life. —**deˌtribaliˈzation** *or* **deˌtribaliˈsation** *n.*

detriment (ˈdɛtrɪmənt) *n.* **1.** disadvantage or damage; harm; loss. **2.** a cause of disadvantage or damage. [C15: from Latin *dētrīmentum*, a rubbing off, hence damage, from *dēterere* to rub away, from DE- + *terere* to rub]

detrimental (ˌdɛtrɪˈmɛntᵊl) *adj.* (when *postpositive*, foll. by *to*) harmful; injurious; prejudicial: *smoking can be detrimental to health.* —ˌ**detriˈmentally** *adv.*

detrition (dɪˈtrɪʃən) *n.* the act of rubbing or wearing away by friction. [C17: from Medieval Latin *dētrītiō*, from Latin *dētrītus* worn away; see DETRIMENT]

detritovore (dɪˈtraɪtəˌvɔː) *n. Ecology.* any organism that feeds on detritus.

detritus (dɪˈtraɪtəs) *n.* **1.** a loose mass of stones, silt, etc., worn away from rocks. **2.** an accumulation of disintegrated material or debris. **3.** the organic debris formed from the decay of organisms. [C18: from French *détritus*, from Latin *dētrītus* a rubbing away; see DETRIMENT] —**deˈtrital** *adj.*

de trop *French.* (də tro) *adj.* (*postpositive*) not wanted; in the way; superfluous. [literally: of too much]

detrude (dɪˈtruːd) *vb.* (*tr.*) to force down or thrust away or out. [C16: from Latin *dētrūdere* to push away, from DE- + *trūdere* to thrust] —**detrusion** (dɪˈtruːʒən) *n.*

detruncate (diːˈtrʌŋkeɪt) *vb.* (*tr.*) another word for **truncate.** —ˌ**detrunˈcation** *n.*

detumescence (ˌdiːtjʊˈmɛsəns) *n.* the subsidence of a swelling, esp. the return of a swollen organ, such as the penis, to the flaccid state. [C17: from Latin *dētumescere* to cease swelling, from DE- + *tumescere*, from *tumēre* to swell]

deuce[1] (djuːs) *n.* **1. a.** a playing card or dice with two pips or spots; two. **b.** a throw of two in dice. **2.** *Tennis, table tennis, etc.* a tied score (in tennis 40-all) that requires one player to gain two successive points to win the game. [C15: from Old French *deus* two, from Latin *duos*, accusative masculine of *duo* two]

deuce[2] (djuːs) *Informal.* ~*interj.* **1.** an expression of annoyance or frustration. ~*n.* **2. the deuce.** (intensifier): used in such phrases as **what the deuce, where the deuce,** etc. [C17: probably special use of DEUCE[1] (in the sense: lowest throw at dice)]

deuced (ˈdjuːsɪd, djuːst) *Brit. informal.* ~*adj.* **1.** (intensifier, usually qualifying something undesirable) damned; confounded: *he's a deuced idiot.* ~*adv.* **2.** (intensifier): *deuced good luck.* —ˈ**deucedly** *adv.*

Deus *Latin.* (ˈdeɪʊs) *n.* God. [related to Greek *Zeus*]

deus ex machina *Latin.* (ˈdeɪʊs ɛks ˈmækɪnə) *n.* **1.** (in ancient Greek and Roman drama) a god introduced into a play to resolve the plot. **2.** any unlikely or artificial device serving this purpose. [literally: god out of a machine, translating Greek *theos ek mēkhanēs*]

Deut. *Bible. abbrev. for* Deuteronomy.

deuteragonist (ˌdjuːtəˈrægənɪst) *n.* (in ancient Greek drama) the character next in importance to the protagonist, esp. the antagonist. [C19: from Greek *deuteragōnistēs*, from DEUTERO- + *agōnistēs* contestant, actor]

deuteranopia (ˌdjuːtərəˈnəʊpɪə) *n.* a form of colour blindness in which there is a tendency to confuse blues and greens, and greens and reds, and in which sensitivity to green is reduced. [C20: New Latin, from DEUTERO- (referring to the theory in which green is the second primary colour) + AN- + Greek *-ops* eye] —**deuteranopic** (ˌdjuːtərəˈnɒpɪk) *adj.*

deuterate (ˈdjuːtəˌreɪt) *vb.* to treat or combine with deuterium.

deuteride (ˈdjuːtəˌraɪd) *n.* a compound of deuterium with some other element. It is analogous to a hydride.

deuterium (djuːˈtɪərɪəm) *n.* a stable isotope of hydrogen, occurring in natural hydrogen (156 parts per million) and in heavy water: used as a tracer in chemistry and biology. Symbol: D or ^{2}H; atomic no.: 1; atomic wt.: 2.014; boiling pt.: –249.7°C. [C20: New Latin; see DEUTERO-, -IUM; from the fact that it is the second heaviest hydrogen isotope]

deuterium oxide *n.* another name for **heavy water.**

deutero-, deuto- *or before a vowel* **deuter-, deut-** *combining form.* **1.** second or secondary: *deuterogamy; deuterium.* **2.** (in chemistry) indicating the presence of deuterium. [from Greek *deuteros* second]

deuterogamy (ˌdjuːtəˈrɒgəmɪ) *n.* another word for **digamy.** —ˌ**deuterˈogamist** *n.*

deuteron (ˈdjuːtəˌrɒn) *n.* the nucleus of a deuterium atom, consisting of one proton and one neutron.

deuterotoky (ˌdjuːtəˈrɒtəkɪ) *n. Biology.* parthenogenesis in which both males and females are produced. [from DEUTERO- + *-toky* from Greek *tokos* bringing forth]

deutoplasm (ˈdjuːtəˌplæzəm) *or* **deuteroplasm** (ˈdjuːtərəʊˌplæzəm) *n.* nutritive material in a cell, esp. the yolk in a developing ovum. —ˌ**deutoˈplasmic** *or* ˌ**deutoˈplastic** *adj.*

Deutschmark (ˈdɔɪtʃˌmɑːk) *or* **Deutsche Mark** (ˈdɔɪtʃə) *n.* the standard monetary unit of Germany divided into 100 pfennigs; formerly the standard monetary unit of West Germany. Abbrev.: **DM.**

deutzia (ˈdjuːtsɪə) *n.* any saxifragaceous shrub of the genus *Deutzia:* cultivated for their clusters of white or pink spring-blooming flowers. [C19: New Latin, named after Jean *Deutz*, 18th-century Dutch patron of botany]

deva (ˈdeɪvə) *n.* (in Hinduism and Buddhism) a divine being or god. [C19: from Sanskrit: god]

devaluation (diːˌvæljuːˈeɪʃən) *n.* **1.** a decrease in the exchange value of a currency against gold or other currencies, brought about by a government. Compare **depreciation** (sense 4). **2.** a reduction in value, status, importance, etc.

devalue (diːˈvæljuː) *or* **devaluate** (diːˈvæljuːˌeɪt) *vb.* **-values, -valuing, -valued** *or* **-valuates, -valuating, -valuated. 1.** to reduce (a currency) or (of a currency) be reduced in exchange value. **2.** (*tr.*) to reduce the value or worth of (something).

Devanagari (ˌdeɪvəˈnɑːgərɪ) *n.* a syllabic script in which Sanskrit, Hindi, and other modern languages of India are written. [C18: from Sanskrit: alphabet of the gods, from *deva* god + *nagari* an Indian alphabet]

devastate (ˈdɛvəˌsteɪt) *vb.* (*tr.*) **1.** to lay waste or make desolate; ravage; destroy. **2.** to confound or overwhelm, as with grief or shock. [C17: from Latin *dēvastāre*, from DE- + *vastāre* to ravage; related to *vastus* waste, empty] —ˌ**devasˈtation** *n.* —ˈ**devasˌtative** *adj.* —ˈ**devasˌtator** *n.*

devastating (ˈdɛvəˌsteɪtɪŋ) *adj.* extremely effective in a destructive way: *a devastating war; a devastating report on urban deprivation.* —ˈ**devasˌtatingly** *adv.*

develop (dɪˈvɛləp) *vb.* **1.** to come or bring to a later or more advanced or expanded stage; grow or cause to grow gradually. **2.** (*tr.*) to elaborate or work out in detail. **3.** to disclose or unfold (thoughts, a plot, etc.) gradually or (of thoughts, etc.) to be gradually disclosed or unfolded. **4.** to come or bring into existence; generate or be generated: *he developed a new faith in God.* **5.** (*intr.*; often foll. by *from*) to follow as a result (of); ensue (from): *a row developed following the chairman's remarks.* **6.** (*tr.*) to contract (a disease or illness). **7.** (*tr.*) to improve the value or change the use of (land), as by building. **8.** (*tr.*) to exploit or make available the natural resources of (a country or region). **9.** (*tr.*) *Photog.* **a.** to treat (film, plate, or paper previously exposed to light, or the latent image in such material) with chemical solutions in order to produce a visible image. **b.** to process (photographic material) in order to produce negatives and prints. **10.** *Biology.* to progress or cause to progress from simple to complex stages in the growth of an individual or the evolution of a species. **11.** (*tr.*) to elaborate upon (a musical theme) by varying the melody, key, etc. **12.** (*tr.*) *Maths.* to expand (a function or expression) in the form of a series. **13.** (*tr.*) *Geometry.* to project or roll out (a surface) onto a plane without stretching or shrinking any element. **14.** *Chess.* to bring (a piece) into play from its initial position on the back rank. **15.** (*tr.*) *Obsolete.* to disclose or reveal. [C19: from Old French *desveloper* to unwrap, from *des-* DIS-[1] + *veloper* to wrap; see ENVELOP] —**deˈvelopable** *adj.*

developer (dɪˈvɛləpə) *n.* **1.** a person or thing that develops something, esp. a person who develops property. **2.** *Photog.* a solution of a chemical reducing agent that converts the latent image recorded in the emulsion of a film or paper into a visible image.

developing agent *n.* another name for **developer** (sense 2).

developing country *n.* a nonindustrialized poor country that is seeking to develop its resources by industrialization.

development (dɪˈvɛləpmənt) *n.* **1.** the act or process of growing, progressing, or developing. **2.** the product or result of developing. **3.** a fact, event, or happening, esp. one that changes a situation. **4.** an area or tract of land that has been developed. **5.** Also called: **development section.** the section of a movement, usually in sonata form, in which the basic musical themes are developed. **6.** *Chess.* **a.** the process of developing pieces. **b.** the manner in which they are developed. **c.** the position of the pieces in the early part of a game with reference to their attacking potential or defensive efficiency. —**deˌvelopˈmental** *adj.* —**deˌvelopˈmentally** *adv.*

developmental disorder *n. Psychiatry.* any condition, such as autism or dyslexia, that appears in childhood and is characterized by delay in the development of one or more psychological functions, such as language skill.

development area *n.* (in Britain) an area suffering from high unemployment and economic depression, because of the decline of its main industries, that is given government help to establish new industries.

development education *n. Brit.* an area of study that aims to give pupils an understanding of their involvement in world affairs.

development system *n.* a computer system, including hardware and software, that is specifically designed to aid in the development of software and interfaces.

development well *n.* (in the oil industry) a well drilled for the production of oil or gas from a field already proven by appraisal drilling to be suitable for exploitation.

devest (dɪˈvɛst) *vb.* (*tr.*) a rare variant spelling of **divest.**

deviance (ˈdiːvɪəns) *n.* **1.** Also called: **deviancy.** the act or state of being deviant. **2.** *Statistics.* a measure of the degree of fit of a statistical model compared to that of a more complete model.

deviant (ˈdiːvɪənt) *adj.* **1.** deviating, as from what is considered acceptable behaviour. ~*n.* **2.** a person whose behaviour, esp. sexual behaviour, deviates from what is considered to be acceptable.

deviate *vb.* (ˈdiːvɪˌeɪt). **1.** (*usually intr.*) to differ or diverge or cause to differ or diverge, as in belief or thought. **2.** (*usually* *intr.*) to turn aside or cause to turn aside; diverge or cause to diverge. **3.** (*intr.*) *Psychol.* to depart from an accepted standard or convention. ~*n.*, *adj.* (ˈdiːvɪɪt). **4.** another word for **deviant.** [C17: from Late Latin *dēviāre* to turn aside from the direct road, from DE- + *via* road] —ˈ**devi̦ator** *n.* —ˈ**deviatory** *adj.*

deviation (ˌdiːvɪˈeɪʃən) *n.* **1.** an act or result of deviating. **2.** *Statistics.* the difference between an observed value in a series of such values and their arithmetic mean. **3.** the error of a compass due to local magnetic disturbances.

deviationism (ˌdiːvɪˈeɪʃəˌnɪzəm) *n.* ideological deviation (esp. from orthodox Communism). —ˌ**deviˈationist** *n.*, *adj.*

device (dɪˈvaɪs) *n.* **1.** a machine or tool used for a specific task; contrivance. **2.** *Euphemistic.* a bomb. **3.** a plan or plot, esp. a clever or evil one; scheme; trick. **4.** any ornamental pattern or picture, as in embroidery. **5.** computer hardware that is designed for a specific function. **6.** a written, printed, or painted design or figure, used as a heraldic sign, emblem, trademark, etc. **7.** a particular pattern of words, figures of speech, etc., used in literature to produce an effect on the reader. **8.** *Archaic.* the act or process of planning or devising. **9. leave (someone) to his own devices.** to leave (someone) alone to do as he wishes. [C13: from Old French *devis* purpose, contrivance and *devise* difference, intention, from *deviser* to divide, control; see DEVISE]

devil (ˈdɛvᵊl) *n.* **1.** *Theol.* (*often cap.*) the chief spirit of evil and enemy of God, often represented as the ruler of hell and often depicted as a human figure with horns, cloven hoofs, and tail. **2.** *Theol.* one of the subordinate evil spirits of traditional Jewish and Christian belief. **3.** a person or animal regarded as cruel, wicked, or ill-natured. **4.** a person or animal regarded as unfortunate or wretched: *that poor devil was ill for months.* **5.** a person or animal regarded as clever, daring, mischievous, or energetic. **6.** *Informal.* something difficult or annoying. **7.** *Christian Science.* the opposite of truth; an error, lie, or false belief in sin, sickness, and death. **8.** (in Malaysia) a ghost. **9.** a portable furnace or brazier, esp. one used in road-making or one used by plumbers. Compare **salamander** (sense 7). **10.** any of various mechanical devices, such as a machine for making wooden screws or a rag-tearing machine. **11.** See **printer's devil.** **12.** *Law.* (in England) a junior barrister who does work for another in order to gain experience, usually for a half fee. **13.** *Meteorology.* a small whirlwind in arid areas that raises dust or sand in a column. **14. between the devil and the deep blue sea.** between equally undesirable alternatives. **15. devil of a.** *Informal.* (intensifier): *a devil of a fine horse.* **16. give the devil his due.** to acknowledge the talent or the success of an opponent or unpleasant person. **17. go to the devil. a.** to fail or become dissipated. **b.** (*interj.*) used to express annoyance with the person causing it. **18. like the devil.** with great speed, determination, etc. **19. play the devil with.** *Informal.* to make much worse; upset considerably: *the damp plays the devil with my rheumatism.* **20. raise the devil. a.** to cause a commotion. **b.** to make a great protest. **21. talk** (*or* **speak**) **of the devil!** (*interj.*) used when an absent person who has been the subject of conversation appears. **22. the devil!** (intensifier): **a.** used in such phrases as **what the devil, where the devil,** etc. **b.** an exclamation of anger, surprise, disgust, etc. **23. the devil's own.** a very difficult or problematic (thing). **24. (let) the devil take the hindmost.** look after oneself and leave others to their fate. **25. the devil to pay.** problems or trouble to be faced as a consequence of an action. **26. the very devil.** something very difficult or awkward. ~*vb.* **-ils, -illing, -illed** *or U.S.* **-ils, -iling, -iled.** **27.** (*tr.*) to prepare (esp. meat, poultry, or fish) by coating with a highly flavoured spiced paste or mixture of condiments before cooking. **28.** (*tr.*) to tear (rags) with a devil. **29.** (*intr.*) to serve as a printer's devil. **30.** (*intr.*) *Chiefly Brit.* to do hackwork, esp. for a lawyer or author; perform arduous tasks, often without pay or recognition of one's services. **31.** (*tr.*) *U.S. informal.* to harass, vex, torment, etc. [Old English *dēofol*, from Latin *diabolus*, from Greek *diabolos* enemy, accuser, slanderer, from *diaballein*, literally: to throw across, hence, to slander]

devilfish (ˈdɛvᵊlˌfɪʃ) *n.*, *pl.* **-fish** *or* **-fishes.** **1.** Also called: **devil ray.** another name for **manta** (the fish). **2.** another name for **octopus.**

devilish (ˈdɛvəlɪʃ, ˈdɛvlɪʃ) *adj.* **1.** of, resembling, or befitting a devil; diabolic; fiendish. ~*adv.*, *adj. Informal.* **2.** (intensifier): *devilish good food; this devilish heat.* —ˈ**devilishly** *adv.* —ˈ**devilishness** *n.*

devil-may-care *adj.* careless or reckless; happy-go-lucky: *a devil-may-care attitude.*

devilment (ˈdɛvᵊlmənt) *n.* devilish or mischievous conduct.

devilry (ˈdɛvᵊlrɪ) *or* **deviltry** *n.*, *pl.* **-ries** *or* **-tries.** **1.** reckless or malicious fun or mischief. **2.** wickedness or cruelty. **3.** black magic or other forms of diabolism. [C18: from French *diablerie*, from *diable* DEVIL]

devil's advocate *n.* **1.** a person who advocates an opposing or unpopular view, often for the sake of argument. **2.** *R.C. Church.* the official appointed to put the case against the beatification or canonization of a candidate. Technical name: **promotor fidei** (prəʊˈməʊtɔː fɪˈdeiː). [translation of New Latin *advocātus diabolī*]

devil's bit *n.* short for **devil's bit scabious** (see **scabious**[2] (sense 3)).

devil's coach-horse *n.* a large black rove beetle, *Ocypus olens*, with large jaws and ferocious habits.

devil's darning needle *n.* a popular name for a **dragonfly.**

devil's food cake *n. Chiefly U.S. and Canadian.* a rich chocolate cake.

devils-on-horseback *n.* (*functioning as sing. or pl.*) a savoury of prunes wrapped in bacon slices and served on toast.

devious (ˈdiːvɪəs) *adj.* **1.** not sincere or candid; deceitful; underhand. **2.** (of a route or course of action) rambling; indirect; roundabout. **3.** going astray from a proper or accepted way; erring. [C16: from Latin *dēvius* lying to one side of the road, from DE- + *via* road] —ˈ**deviously** *adv.* —ˈ**deviousness** *n.*

devisable (dɪˈvaɪzəbᵊl) *adj.* **1.** *Law.* (of property, esp. realty) capable of being transferred by will. **2.** able to be invented, contrived, or devised.

devisal (dɪˈvaɪzᵊl) *n.* the act of inventing, contriving, or devising; contrivance.

devise (dɪˈvaɪz) *vb.* **1.** to work out, contrive, or plan (something) in one's mind. **2.** (*tr.*) *Law.* to dispose of (property, esp. real property) by will. **3.** (*tr.*) *Obsolete.* to imagine or guess. ~*n. Law.* **4. a.** a disposition of property by will. **b.** the property so transmitted. Compare **bequeath** (sense 1). **5.** a will or clause in a will disposing of real property. Compare **bequest** (sense 2). [C15: from Old French *deviser* to divide, apportion, intend, from Latin *dīvidere* to DIVIDE] —**deˈviser** *n.*

devisee (dɪvaɪˈziː, ˌdɛvɪ-) *n. Property law.* a person to whom property, esp. realty, is devised by will. Compare **legatee.**

devisor (dɪˈvaɪzə) *n. Property law.* a person who devises property, esp. realty, by will.

devitalize *or* **devitalise** (diːˈvaɪtəˌlaɪz) *vb.* (*tr.*) to lower or destroy the vitality of; make weak or lifeless: *the war devitalized the economy.* —**deˌvitaliˈzation** *or* **deˌvitaliˈsation** *n.*

devitrify (diːˈvɪtrɪˌfaɪ) *vb.* **-fies, -fying, -fied.** **1.** to change from a vitreous state to a crystalline state. **2.** to lose or cause to lose the properties of a glass and become brittle and opaque. —**deˌvitrifiˈcation** *n.*

devoice (diːˈvɔɪs) *or* **devocalize, devocalise** (diːˈvəʊkəˌlaɪz) *vb.* (*tr.*) *Phonetics.* to make (a voiced speech sound) voiceless.

devoid (dɪˈvɔɪd) *adj.* (*postpositive;* foll. by *of*) destitute or void (of); free (from). [C15: originally past participle of *devoid* (*vb.*) to remove, from Old French *devoidier*, from *de-* DE- + *voider* to VOID]

devoirs (dəˈvwɑː; *French* dəvwar) *pl. n.* (*sometimes sing.*) compliments or respects; courteous attentions. [C13: from Old French: duty, from *devoir* to be obliged to, owe, from Latin *dēbēre;* see DEBT]

devolution (ˌdiːvəˈluːʃən) *n.* **1.** the act, fact, or result of devolving. **2.** a passing onwards or downwards from one stage to another. **3.** another word for **degeneration** (sense 3). **4.** a transfer or allocation of authority, esp. from a central government to regional governments or particular interests. [C16: from Medieval Latin *dēvolūtiō* a rolling down, from Latin *dēvolvere* to roll down, sink into; see DEVOLVE] —ˌ**devoˈlutionary** *adj.* —ˌ**devoˈlutionist** *n.*, *adj.*

devolve (dɪˈvɒlv) *vb.* **1.** (foll. by *on, upon, to,* etc.) to pass or cause to pass to a successor or substitute, as duties, power, etc. **2.** (*intr.* foll. by *on* or *upon*) *Law.* (of an estate, etc.) to pass to another by operation of law, esp. on intestacy or bankruptcy. **3.** (*intr.;* foll. by *on* or *upon*) to depend (on): *your argument devolves on how you interpret this clause.* **4.** *Archaic.* to roll down or cause to roll down. [C15: from Latin *dēvolvere* to roll down, fall into, from DE- + *volvere* to roll] —**deˈvolvement** *n.*

devon (ˈdɛvən) *n. Austral.* a bland processed meat in sausage form, eaten cold in slices. [named after *Devon*]

Devon (ˈdɛvᵊn) *n.* a breed of large red cattle originally from the county of Devon, in SW England.

Devonian (dəˈvəʊnɪən) *adj.* **1.** of, denoting, or formed in the fourth period of the Palaeozoic era, between the Silurian and Carboniferous periods, lasting for 50 million years during which amphibians first appeared. **2.** of or relating to Devon. ~*n.* **3. the.** the Devonian period or rock system.

Devon minnow *n. Angling.* a spinning lure intended to imitate the swimming motion of a minnow. Often shortened to **Devon.**

Devonshire cream (ˈdɛvᵊnʃə) *n.* another name for **clotted cream.**

Devonshire split *n.* a kind of yeast bun split open and served with whipped cream or butter and jam. Also called: **Cornish split, split.**

devote (dɪˈvəʊt) *vb.* (*tr.*) **1.** to apply or dedicate (oneself, time, money, etc.) to some pursuit, cause, etc. **2.** *Obsolete.* to curse or doom. [C16: from Latin *dēvōtus* devoted, solemnly promised, from *dēvovēre* to vow; see DE-, VOW] —**deˈvotement** *n.*

devoted (dɪˈvəʊtɪd) *adj.* **1.** feeling or demonstrating loyalty or devotion; ardent; devout. **2.** (*postpositive;* foll. by *to*) set apart, dedicated, or consecrated. —**deˈvotedly** *adv.* —**deˈvotedness** *n.*

devotee (ˌdɛvəˈtiː) *n.* **1.** a person ardently enthusiastic about or devoted to something, such as a sport or pastime. **2.** a zealous follower of a religion.

devotion (dɪˈvəʊʃən) *n.* **1.** (often foll. by *to*) strong attachment (to) or affection (for a cause, person, etc.) marked by dedicated loyalty. **2.** religious zeal; piety. **3.** (*often pl.*) religious observance or prayers.

devotional (dɪˈvəʊʃənᵊl) *adj.* **1.** relating to, characterized by, or conducive to devotion. ~*n.* **2.** (*often pl.*) a short religious or prayer service. —**deˌvotionˈality** *or* **deˈvotionalness** *n.* —**deˈvotionally** *adv.*

devour (dɪˈvaʊə) *vb.* (*tr.*) **1.** to swallow or eat up greedily or voraciously. **2.** to waste or destroy; consume: *the flames devoured the curtains.* **3.** to consume greedily or avidly with the senses or mind: *he devoured the manuscripts.* **4.** to engulf or absorb: *the flood devoured the land.* [C14: from Old French *devourer,* from Latin *dēvorāre* to gulp down, from DE- + *vorāre* to consume greedily; see VORACIOUS] —**deˈvourer** *n.* —**deˈvouring** *adj.* —**deˈvouringly** *adv.*

devout (dɪˈvaʊt) *adj.* **1.** deeply religious; reverent. **2.** sincere; earnest; heartfelt: *a devout confession.* [C13: from Old French *devot,* from Late Latin *dēvōtus,* from Latin: faithful; see DEVOTE] —**deˈvoutly** *adv.* —**deˈvoutness** *n.*

dew (djuː) *n.* **1. a.** drops of water condensed on a cool surface, esp. at night, from vapour in the air. **b.** (*in combination*): *dewdrop.* **2.** something like or suggestive of this, esp. in freshness: *the dew of youth.* **3.** small drops of moisture, such as tears. ~*vb.* **4.** (*tr.*) *Poetic.* to moisten with or as with dew. [Old English *dēaw;* related to Old High German *tou* dew, Old Norse *dögg*]

dewan *or* **diwan** (dɪˈwɑːn) *n.* (formerly in India) the chief minister or finance minister of a state ruled by an Indian prince. [C17: from Hindi *dīwān,* from Persian *dēvan* register, book of accounts; see DIVAN]

Dewar flask (ˈdjuːə) *n.* a type of vacuum flask, esp. one used in scientific experiments to keep liquid air, helium, etc.; Thermos. [C20: named after Sir James *Dewar* (1842–1923), British chemist and physicist]

dewberry (ˈdjuːbərɪ, -brɪ) *n., pl.* **-ries. 1.** any trailing bramble, such as *Rubus hispidus* of North America and *R. caesius* of Europe and NW Asia, having blue-black fruits. **2.** the fruit of any such plant.

dewclaw (ˈdjuːˌklɔː) *n.* **1.** a nonfunctional claw in dogs; the rudimentary first digit. **2.** an analogous rudimentary hoof in deer, goats, etc. —**ˈdewˌclawed** *adj.*

dewdrop (ˈdjuːˌdrɒp) *n.* **1.** a drop of dew. **2.** *Brit. euphemistic.* a drop of mucus on the end of one's nose.

Dewey Decimal System (ˈdjuːɪ) *n.* a frequently used system of library book classification and arrangement with ten main subject classes. Also called: **decimal classification.** Abbrev.: **DDS.** [C19: named after Melvil *Dewey* (1851–1931), U.S. educator who invented the system]

dewlap (ˈdjuːˌlæp) *n.* **1.** a loose fold of skin hanging from beneath the throat in cattle, dogs, etc. **2.** loose skin on an elderly person's throat. [C14 *dewlappe,* from DEW (probably changed by folk etymology from an earlier form of different meaning) + LAP[1] (from Old English *læppa* hanging flap), perhaps of Scandinavian origin; compare Danish *doglæp*] —**ˈdewˌlapped** *adj.*

DEW line (djuː) *n. acronym for* distant early warning line, a network of radar stations situated mainly in Arctic regions to give early warning of aircraft or missile attack on North America.

dew point *n.* the temperature at which water vapour in the air becomes saturated and dew begins to form.

dew pond *n.* a shallow pond, usually man-made, that is kept supplied with water by dew and condensation.

dew-worm *n.* any large earthworm that is found on the ground at night and is used as fishing bait.

dewy (ˈdjuːɪ) *adj.* **dewier, dewiest. 1.** moist with or as with dew: *a dewy complexion.* **2.** of or resembling dew. **3.** *Poetic.* suggesting, falling, or refreshing like dew: *dewy sleep.* —**ˈdewily** *adv.* —**ˈdewiness** *n.*

dewy-eyed *adj.* naive, innocent, or trusting, esp. in a romantic or childlike way.

Dexedrine (ˈdɛksɪˌdriːn) *n.* a trademark for **dextroamphetamine.**

dexiotropic (ˌdɛksɪəʊˈtrɒpɪk) *adj. Embryol.* (of cleavage) spiral; twisting in a spiral fashion from left to right.

dexter[1] (ˈdɛkstə) *adj.* **1.** *Archaic.* of or located on the right side. **2.** (*usually postpositive*) *Heraldry.* of, on, or starting from the right side of a shield from the bearer's point of view and therefore on the spectator's left. **3.** *Archaic.* favourable, auspicious, or propitious. ~Compare **sinister.** [C16: from Latin; compare Greek *dexios* on the right hand]

dexter[2] (ˈdɛkstə) *n.* a small breed of red or black cattle, originally from Ireland. [C19: perhaps from the surname of the original breeder]

dexterity (dɛkˈstɛrɪtɪ) *n.* **1.** physical, esp. manual, skill or nimbleness. **2.** mental skill or adroitness: cleverness. **3.** *Rare.* the characteristic of being right-handed. [C16: from Latin *dexteritās* aptness, readiness, prosperity; see DEXTER[1]]

dexterous *or* **dextrous** (ˈdɛkstrəs) *adj.* **1.** possessing or done with dexterity. **2.** a rare word for **right-handed.** —**ˈdexterously** *or* **ˈdextrously** *adv.* —**ˈdexterousness** *or* **ˈdextrousness** *n.*

dextral (ˈdɛkstrəl) *adj.* **1.** of, relating to, or located on the right side, esp. of the body; right-hand. **2.** of or relating to a person who prefers to use his right foot, hand, or eye; right-handed. **3.** (of the shells of certain gastropod molluscs) coiling in an anticlockwise direction from the apex; dextrorse. ~Compare **sinistral.** —**dextrality** (dɛkˈstrælɪtɪ) *n.* —**ˈdextrally** *adv.*

dextran (ˈdɛkstrən) *n. Biochem.* a polysaccharide produced by the action of bacteria on sucrose: used as a substitute for plasma in blood transfusions. [C19: from DEXTRO- + -AN]

dextrin (ˈdɛkstrɪn) *or* **dextrine** (ˈdɛkstrɪn, -triːn) *n.* any of a group of sticky substances that are intermediate products in the conversion of starch to maltose: used as thickening agents in foods and as gums. [C19: from French *dextrine;* see DEXTRO-, -IN]

dextro (ˈdɛkstrəʊ) *adj.* short for **dextrorotatory.**

dextro- *or before a vowel* **dextr-** *combining form.* **1.** on or towards the right: *dextrorotation.* **2.** (in chemistry) indicating a dextrorotatory compound: *dextroglucose.* [from Latin, from *dexter* on the right side]

dextroamphetamine (ˌdɛkstrəʊæmˈfɛtəˌmiːn, -mɪn) *n.* a dextrorotatory amphetamine, used in medicine.

dextrocardia (ˌdɛkstrəʊˈkɑːdɪə) *n. Med.* the abnormal location of the heart in the right side of the chest.

dextroglucose (ˌdɛkstrəʊˈgluːkəʊz, -kəʊs) *n.* another name for **dextrose.**

dextrogyrate (ˌdɛkstrəʊˈdʒaɪrɪt, -ˌreɪt) *or* **dextrogyre** (ˈdɛkstrəʊˌdʒaɪə) *adj.* having dextrorotation.

dextrorotation (ˌdɛkstrəʊrəʊˈteɪʃən) *n.* a rotation to the right; clockwise rotation, esp. of the plane of polarization of plane-polarized light passing through a crystal, liquid, or solution, as seen by an observer facing the oncoming light. Compare **laevorotation.** —**dextrorotatory** (ˌdɛkstrəʊˈrəʊtətərɪ, -trɪ) *or* **ˌdextroˈrotary** *adj.*

dextrorse (ˈdɛkstrɔːs, dɛkˈstrɔːs) *or* **dextrorsal** (dɛkˈstrɔːsᵊl) *adj.* (of some climbing plants) growing upwards in a spiral from left to right or anticlockwise. Compare **sinistrorse.** [C19: from Latin *dextrorsum* towards the right, from DEXTRO- + *vorsus* turned, variant of *versus,* from *vertere* to turn] —**ˈdextrorsely** *adv.*

dextrose (ˈdɛkstrəʊz, -trəʊs) *n.* a white soluble sweet-tasting crystalline solid that is the dextrorotatory isomer of glucose, occurring widely in fruit, honey, and in the blood and tissue of animals. Formula: $C_6H_{12}O_6$. Also called: **grape sugar, dextroglucose.**

dextrous (ˈdɛkstrəs) *adj.* a variant spelling of **dexterous.** —**ˈdextrously** *adv.* —**ˈdextrousness** *n.*

dey (deɪ) *n.* **1.** the title given to commanders or (from 1710) governors of the Janissaries of Algiers (1671–1830). **2.** a title applied by Western writers to various other Ottoman governors, such as the bey of Tunis. [C17: from French, from Turkish *dayi,* literally: maternal uncle, hence title given to an older person]

DF *abbrev. for* Defender of the Faith.

D/F *or* **DF** *Telecomm. abbrev. for:* **1.** direction finder. **2.** direction finding.

DFC *abbrev. for* Distinguished Flying Cross.

DFM *abbrev. for* Distinguished Flying Medal.

dg *symbol for* decigram.

DG *abbrev. for:* **1.** Deo gratias. **2.** director-general.

DH (in Britain) *abbrev. for* Department of Health.

DHA (in Britain) *abbrev. for* District Health Authority.

dhak (dɑːk, dɔːk) *n.* a tropical Asian leguminous tree, *Butea frondosa,* that has bright red flowers and yields a red resin, used as an astringent. [C19: from Hindi]

dhal, dal, *or* **dholl** (dɑːl) *n.* **1.** a tropical African and Asian leguminous shrub, *Cajanus cajan,* cultivated in tropical regions for its nutritious pealike seeds. **2.** the seed of this shrub. ~Also called: **pigeon pea.** [C17: from Hindi *dāl* split pulse, from Sanskrit *dal* to split]

dharma (ˈdɑːmə) *n.* **1.** *Hinduism.* social custom regarded as a religious and moral duty. **2.** *Hinduism.* **a.** the essential principle of the cosmos; natural law. **b.** conduct that conforms with this. **3.** *Buddhism.* ideal truth as set forth in the teaching of Buddha. [Sanskrit: habit, usage, law, from *dhārayati* he holds]

dharna *or* **dhurna** (ˈdʌnə, ˈdɑː-) *n.* (in India) a method of obtaining justice, as the payment of a debt, by sitting, fasting, at the door of the person from whom reparation is sought. [C18: from Hindi, literally: a placing]

dhobi (ˈdəʊbɪ) *n., pl.* **-bis.** (in India, Malaya, East Africa, etc., esp. formerly) a washerman. [C19: from Hindi, from *dhōb* washing; related to Sanskrit *dhāvaka* washerman]

dhobi itch *n.* a fungal disease of the skin: a type of ringworm chiefly affecting the groin. Also called: **tinea cruris.**

dhole (dəʊl) *n.* a fierce canine mammal, *Cuon alpinus,* of the forests of central and SE Asia, having a reddish-brown coat and rounded ears: hunts in packs. [C19: of uncertain origin]

dholl (dɑːl) *n.* a variant spelling of **dhal.**

dhoti (ˈdəʊtɪ), **dhooti, dhootie,** *or* **dhuti** (ˈduːtɪ) *n., pl.* **-tis.** a long loincloth worn by men in India. [C17: from Hindi]

dhow (daʊ) *n.* a lateen-rigged coastal Arab sailing vessel with one or two masts. [C19: from Arabic *dāwa*]

DHSS (formerly in Britain) *abbrev. for* Department of Health and Social Security.

Di *the chemical symbol for* didymium.

DI *abbrev. for* Donor Insemination.

di. *or* **dia.** *abbrev. for* diameter.

di-[1] *prefix.* **1.** twice; two; double: *dicotyledon.* **2. a.** containing two specified atoms or groups of atoms: *dimethyl ether; carbon dioxide.* **b.** a nontechnical equivalent of **bi-**[1] (sense 5). [via Latin from Greek, from *dis* twice, double, related to *duo* two. Compare BI-[1]]

di-[2] *combining form.* variant of **dia-** before a vowel: *diopter.*
dia- *or* **di-** *prefix.* **1.** through, throughout, or during: *diachronic.* **2.** across: *diactinic.* **3.** apart: *diacritic.* **4.** (in botany) at right angles: *diatropism.* **5.** in opposite or different directions: *diamagnetism.* [from Greek *dia* through, between, across, by]
diabase ('daɪəˌbeɪs) *n.* **1.** *Brit.* an altered dolerite. **2.** *U.S.* another name for **dolerite.** [C19: from French, from Greek *diabasis* a crossing over, from *diabainein* to cross over, from DIA- + *bainein* to go] —ˌ**dia'basic** *adj.*
diabetes (ˌdaɪə'biːtɪs, -tiːz) *n.* any of various disorders, esp. diabetes mellitus, characterized by excretion of an abnormally large amount of urine. [C16: from Latin: siphon, from Greek, literally: a passing through (referring to the excessive urination), from *diabainein* to pass through, cross over; see DIABASE]
diabetes insipidus (ɪn'sɪpɪdəs) *n.* a disorder of the pituitary gland causing excessive thirst and excretion of large quantities of dilute urine. [C18: New Latin, literally: insipid diabetes]
diabetes mellitus (mə'laɪtəs) *n.* a disorder of carbohydrate metabolism characterized by excessive thirst and excretion of abnormally large quantities of urine containing an excess of sugar, caused by a deficiency of insulin. [C18: New Latin, literally: honey-sweet diabetes]
diabetic (ˌdaɪə'bɛtɪk) *adj.* **1.** of, relating to, or having diabetes. **2.** for the use of diabetics: *diabetic chocolate.* ~*n.* **3.** a person who has diabetes.
diablerie (dɪ'ɑːblərɪ; *French* djɑbləri) *n.* **1.** magic or witchcraft connected with devils. **2.** demonic lore or esoteric knowledge of devils. **3.** the domain of devils. **4.** devilry; mischief. [C18: from Old French, from *diable* devil, from Latin *diabolus;* see DEVIL]
diabolic (ˌdaɪə'bɒlɪk) *adj.* **1.** of, relating to, or proceeding from the devil; satanic. **2.** befitting a devil; extremely cruel or wicked; fiendish. **3.** very difficult or unpleasant. [C14: from Late Latin *diabolicus,* from Greek *diabolikos,* from *diabolos* DEVIL] —ˌ**dia'bolically** *adv.* —ˌ**dia'bolicalness** *n.*
diabolical (ˌdaɪə'bɒlɪkəl) *adj. Informal.* **1.** excruciatingly bad; outrageous. **2.** (intensifier): *a diabolical liberty.* —ˌ**dia'bolically** *adv.* —ˌ**dia'bolicalness** *n.*
diabolism (daɪ'æbəˌlɪzəm) *n.* **1. a.** activities designed to enlist the aid of devils, esp. in witchcraft or sorcery. **b.** worship of devils or beliefs and teachings concerning them. **c.** the nature of devils. **2.** character or conduct that is devilish or fiendish; devilry. —**di'abolist** *n.*
diabolize *or* **diabolise** (daɪ'æbəˌlaɪz) *vb.* (*tr.*) **1. a.** to make (someone or something) diabolical. **b.** to subject to the influence of devils. **2.** to portray as diabolical.
diabolo (dɪ'æbəˌləʊ) *n., pl.* **-los.** **1.** a game in which one throws and catches a spinning top on a cord fastened to two sticks held in the hands. **2.** the top used in this game.
diacaustic (ˌdaɪə'kɔːstɪk, -'kɒs-) *adj.* **1.** (of a caustic curve or surface) formed by refracted light rays. ~*n.* **2.** a diacaustic curve or surface. ~Compare **catacaustic.**
diacetylmorphine (daɪˌæsətɪl'mɔːfiːn) *n.* another name for **heroin.**
diachronic (ˌdaɪə'krɒnɪk) *adj.* of, relating to, or studying the development of a phenomenon through time; historical: *diachronic linguistics.* Compare **synchronic.** [C19: from DIA- + Greek *khronos* time]
diachronism (daɪ'ækrəˌnɪzəm) *n. Geology.* the passage of a geological formation across time planes, as occurs when a marine sediment laid down by an advancing sea is noticeably younger in the direction of advancement. —**di'achronous** *adj.*
diacid (daɪ'æsɪd) *adj.* **1.** another word for **diacidic.** **2.** (of a salt or acid) containing two acidic hydrogen atoms: *NaH_2PO_4 is a diacid salt of phosphoric acid.* ~*n.* **3.** an acid or salt that contains two acidic hydrogen atoms.
diacidic (ˌdaɪə'sɪdɪk) *adj.* (of a base, such as calcium hydroxide $Ca(OH)_2$) capable of neutralizing two protons with one of its molecules. Also: **diacid.** Compare **dibasic.**
diaconal (daɪ'ækənəl) *adj.* of or associated with a deacon or the diaconate. [C17: from Late Latin *diācōnālis,* from *diāconus* DEACON]
diaconate (daɪ'ækənɪt, -ˌneɪt) *n.* the office, sacramental status, or period of office of a deacon. [C17: from Late Latin *diācōnātus;* see DEACON]
diacritic (ˌdaɪə'krɪtɪk) *n.* **1.** Also called: **diacritical mark.** a sign placed above or below a character or letter to indicate that it has a different phonetic value, is stressed, or for some other reason. ~*adj.* **2.** another word for **diacritical.** [C17: from Greek *diakritikos* serving to distinguish, from *diakrinein,* from DIA- + *krinein* to separate]
diacritical (ˌdaɪə'krɪtɪkəl) *adj.* **1.** of or relating to a diacritic. **2.** showing up a distinction. —ˌ**dia'critically** *adv.*
diactinic (ˌdaɪæk'tɪnɪk) *adj. Physics.* able to transmit photochemically active radiation. —**di'actinism** *n.*
diadelphous (ˌdaɪə'dɛlfəs) *adj.* **1.** (of stamens) having united filaments so that they are arranged in two groups. **2.** (of flowers) having diadelphous stamens. [C19: from DI-[1] + Greek *adelphos* brother]
diadem ('daɪəˌdɛm) *n.* **1.** a royal crown, esp. a light jewelled circlet. **2.** royal dignity or power. ~*vb.* **3.** (*tr.*) to adorn or crown with or as with a diadem. [C13: from Latin *diadēma,* from Greek: fillet, royal headdress, from *diadein* to bind around, from DIA- + *dein* to bind]
diadem spider *n.* a common Eurasian spider, *Araneus diadematus,* that constructs orb webs: family *Argiopidae.*
diadochy (daɪ'ædəʊkɪ) *n. Geology.* the replacement of one element in a crystal by another. [C20: from Greek *diadochē* succession]
diadromous (daɪ'ædrəməs) *adj.* **1.** *Botany.* of or possessing a leaf venation in the shape of a fan. **2.** (of some fishes) migrating between fresh and salt water. See also **anadromous, catadromous.**
diaeresis *or* **dieresis** (daɪ'ɛrɪsɪs) *n., pl.* **-ses** (-ˌsiːz). **1.** the mark ¨, in writing placed over the second of two adjacent vowels to indicate that it is to be pronounced separately rather than forming a diphthong with the first, as in some spellings of *coöperate, naïve,* etc. **2.** this mark used for any other purpose, such as to indicate that a special pronunciation is appropriate to a particular vowel. Compare **umlaut.** **3.** a pause in a line of verse occurring when the end of a foot coincides with the end of a word. [C17: from Latin *diaresis,* from Greek *diairesis* a division, from *diairein,* from DIA- + *hairein* to take; compare HERESY] —**diaeretic** *or* **dieretic** (ˌdaɪə'rɛtɪk) *adj.*
diag. *abbrev. for* diagram.
diagenesis (ˌdaɪə'dʒɛnɪsɪs) *n.* **1.** the sum of the physical, chemical, and biological changes that take place in sediments before they become consolidated into rocks, excluding weathering and metamorphic changes. **2.** *Chem.* recrystallization of a solid to form large crystal grains from smaller ones. —**diagenetic** (ˌdaɪədʒə'nɛtɪk) *adj.*
diageotropism (ˌdaɪədʒɪ'ɒtrəˌpɪzəm) *n.* a diatropic response of plant parts, such as rhizomes, to the stimulus of gravity. —**diageotropic** (ˌdaɪəˌdʒiːəʊ'trɒpɪk) *adj.*
diagnose ('daɪəgˌnəʊz) *vb.* **1.** to determine or distinguish by diagnosis. **2.** (*tr.*) to examine (a person or thing), as for a disease. —ˌ**diag'nosable** *adj.*
diagnosis (ˌdaɪəg'nəʊsɪs) *n., pl.* **-ses** (-siːz). **1. a.** the identification of diseases from the examination of symptoms. **b.** an opinion or conclusion so reached. **2. a.** thorough analysis of facts or problems in order to gain understanding and aid future planning. **b.** an opinion or conclusion reached through such analysis. **3.** a detailed description of an organism, esp. a plant, for the purpose of classification. [C17: New Latin, from Greek: a distinguishing, from *diagignōskein* to distinguish, from *gignōskein* to perceive, KNOW]
diagnostic (ˌdaɪəg'nɒstɪk) *adj.* **1.** of, relating to, or of value in diagnosis. ~*n.* **2.** *Med.* any symptom that provides evidence for making a specific diagnosis. **3.** a diagnosis. —ˌ**diag'nostically** *adv.*
diagnostician (ˌdaɪəgnɒs'tɪʃən) *n.* a specialist or expert in making diagnoses.
diagnostics (ˌdaɪəg'nɒstɪks) *n.* (*functioning as sing.*) the art or practice of diagnosis, esp. of diseases.
diagonal (daɪ'ægənəl) *adj.* **1.** *Maths.* connecting any two vertices that in a polygon are not adjacent and in a polyhedron are not in the same face. **2.** slanting; oblique. **3.** marked with slanting lines or patterns. ~*n.* **4.** *Maths.* a diagonal line or plane. **5.** *Chess.* any oblique row of squares of the same colour. **6.** cloth marked or woven with slanting lines or patterns. **7.** something put, set, or drawn obliquely. **8.** another name for **solidus** (sense 1). **9.** one front leg and the hind leg on the opposite side of a horse, which are on the ground together when the horse is trotting. [C16: from Latin *diagōnālis,* from Greek *diagōnios,* from DIA- + *gōnia* angle] —**di'agonally** *adv.*
diagonal process *n. Maths, logic.* a form of argument in which a new member of a set is constructed from a list of its known members by making the *n*th term of the new member differ from the *n*th term of the *n*th member. The new member is thus different from every member of the list.
diagram ('daɪəˌgræm) *n.* **1.** a sketch, outline, or plan demonstrating the form or workings of something. **2.** *Maths.* a pictorial representation of a quantity or of a relationship: *a Venn diagram.* ~*vb.* **-grams, -gramming, -grammed** *or U.S.* **-grams, -graming, -gramed.** **3.** to show in or as if in a diagram. [C17: from Latin *diagramma,* from Greek, from *diagraphein,* from *graphein* to write] —**diagrammatic** (ˌdaɪəgrə'mætɪk) *adj.* —ˌ**diagram'matically** *adv.*
diagraph ('daɪəˌgrɑːf, -ˌgræf) *n.* **1.** a device for enlarging or reducing maps, plans, etc. **2.** a protractor and scale used in drawing. [C19: from French *diagraphe,* from Greek *diagraphein* to represent with lines; see DIAGRAM]
diakinesis (ˌdaɪəkɪ'niːsɪs, -kaɪ-) *n.* the final stage of the prophase of meiosis, during which homologous chromosomes start to separate after crossing over. [C20: from DIA- + Greek *kinēsis* movement]
dial ('daɪəl, daɪl) *n.* **1.** the face of a watch, clock, chronometer, sundial, etc., marked with divisions representing units of time. **2.** the circular graduated disc of various measuring instruments. **3. a.** the control on a radio or television set used to change the station or channel. **b.** the panel on a radio on which the frequency, wavelength, or station is indicated by means of a pointer. **4.** a numbered disc on a telephone that is rotated a set distance for each digit of a number being called. **5.** a miner's compass for surveying in a mine. **6.** *Brit.* a slang word for **face**

(sense 1). ~*vb.* **dials, dialling, dialled** *or U.S.* **dials, dialing, dialed.** 7. to establish or try to establish a telephone connection with (a subscriber or his number) by operating the dial on a telephone. 8. (*tr.*) to indicate, measure, or operate with a dial. [C14: from Medieval Latin *diālis* daily, from Latin *diēs* day] —'**dialler** *n.*

dial. *abbrev. for* dialect(al).

dialect ('daɪəˌlɛkt) *n.* **a.** a form of a language spoken in a particular geographical area or by members of a particular social class or occupational group, distinguished by its vocabulary, grammar, and pronunciation. **b.** a form of a language that is considered inferior: *the farmer spoke dialect and was despised by the merchants.* **c.** (*as modifier*): *a dialect word.* [C16: from Latin *dialectus,* from Greek *dialektos* speech, dialect, discourse, from *dialegesthai* to converse, from *legein* to talk, speak] —ˌ**dia'lectal** *adj.*

dialect atlas *n.* another term for **linguistic atlas.**

dialect geography *n.* another term for **linguistic geography.** —**dialect geographer** *n.*

dialectic (ˌdaɪə'lɛktɪk) *n.* 1. disputation or debate, esp. intended to resolve differences between two views rather than to establish one of them as true. 2. *Philosophy.* **a.** the conversational Socratic method of argument. **b.** (in Platonism) the highest study, that of the Forms. 3. (in Kantian theory) the exposure of the contradictions implicit in applying empirical concepts beyond the limits of experience. 4. *Philosophy.* the process of reconciliation of contradiction either of beliefs or in historical processes. See also **Hegelian dialectic, dialectical materialism.** ~*adj.* 5. of or relating to logical disputation. [C17: from Latin *dialectica,* from Greek *dialektikē* (*tekhnē*) (the art) of argument; see DIALECT] —ˌ**dialec'tician** *n.*

dialectical (ˌdaɪə'lɛktɪkᵊl) *adj.* of or relating to dialectic or dialectics. —ˌ**dia'lectically** *adv.*

dialectical materialism *n.* the economic, political, and philosophical system of Karl Marx (1818–83) and Friedrich Engels (1820–95) that combines traditional materialism and Hegelian dialectic. —**dialectical materialist** *n.*

dialectics (ˌdaɪə'lɛktɪks) *n.* (*functioning as pl. or* (*sometimes*) *sing.*) 1. the study of reasoning or of argumentative methodology. 2. a particular methodology or system; a logic. 3. the application of the Hegelian dialectic or the rationale of dialectical materialism.

dialectology (ˌdaɪəlɛk'tɒlədʒɪ) *n.* the study of dialects and dialectal variations. —**dialectological** (ˌdaɪəˌlɛktə'lɒdʒɪkᵊl) *adj.* —ˌ**diaˌlecto'logically** *adv.* —ˌ**dialec'tologist** *n.*

dial gauge *n.* another name for an **indicator** (sense 6).

diallage ('daɪəlɪdʒ) *n.* a green or brownish-black variety of the mineral augite in the form of layers of platelike crystals. [C19: from Greek *diallagē* interchange]

dialling code *n.* a sequence of numbers which are dialled for connection with another exchange before an individual subscriber's telephone number is dialled.

dialling tone *or U.S. and Canadian* **dial tone** *n.* a continuous sound, either purring or high-pitched, heard over a telephone indicating that a number can be dialled. Compare **ringing tone, engaged tone.**

dialogism (daɪ'æləˌdʒɪzəm) *n.* 1. *Logic.* a deduction with one premise and a disjunctive conclusion. 2. *Rhetoric.* a discussion in an imaginary dialogue or discourse.

dialogist (daɪ'ælədʒɪst) *n.* a person who writes or takes part in a dialogue. —ˌ**dialo'gistic** *or* ˌ**dialo'gistical** *adj.*

dialogize *or* **dialogise** (daɪ'æləˌdʒaɪz) *vb.* (*intr.*) to carry on a dialogue.

dialogue *or U.S.* (*often*) **dialog** ('daɪəˌlɒg) *n.* 1. conversation between two or more people. 2. an exchange of opinions on a particular subject; discussion. 3. the lines spoken by characters in drama or fiction. 4. a particular passage of conversation in a literary or dramatic work. 5. a literary composition in the form of a dialogue. 6. a political discussion between representatives of two nations or groups. ~*vb. Rare.* 7. (*tr.*) to put into the form of a dialogue. 8. (*intr.*) to take part in a dialogue; converse. [C13: from Old French *dialoge,* from Latin *dialogus,* from Greek *dialogos,* from *dialegesthai* to converse; see DIALECT] —**dialogic** (ˌdaɪə'lɒdʒɪk) *adj.* —'**diaˌloguer** *n.*

dialyse *or U.S.* **dialyze** ('daɪəˌlaɪz) *vb.* (*tr.*) to separate by dialysis. —'**diaˌlysable** *or U.S.* '**diaˌlyzable** *adj.* —ˌ**diaˌlysa'bility** *or U.S.* ˌ**diaˌlyza'bility** *n.* —ˌ**dialy'sation** *or U.S.* ˌ**dialy'zation** *n.*

dialyser *or U.S.* **dialyzer** ('daɪəˌlaɪzə) *n.* a machine that performs dialysis, esp. one that removes impurities from the blood of patients with malfunctioning kidneys; kidney machine.

dialysis (daɪ'ælɪsɪs) *n., pl.* **-ses** (-ˌsiːz). 1. the separation of small molecules from large molecules and colloids in a solution by the selective diffusion of the small molecules through a semipermeable membrane. 2. *Med.* See **haemodialysis.** [C16: from Late Latin: a separation, from Greek *dialusis* a dissolution, from *dialuein* to tear apart, dissolve, from *luein* to loosen] —**dialytic** (ˌdaɪə'lɪtɪk) *adj.* —ˌ**dia'lytically** *adv.*

diam. *abbrev. for* diameter.

diamagnet ('daɪəˌmægnɪt) *n.* a substance exhibiting diamagnetism.

diamagnetic (ˌdaɪəmæg'nɛtɪk) *adj.* of, exhibiting, or concerned with diamagnetism. —ˌ**diamag'netically** *adv.*

diamagnetism (ˌdaɪə'mægnɪˌtɪzəm) *n.* the phenomenon exhibited by substances that have a relative permeability less than unity and a negative susceptibility. It is caused by the orbital motion of electrons in the atoms of the material and is unaffected by temperature. Compare **ferromagnetism, paramagnetism.**

diamanté (ˌdaɪə'mæntɪ, ˌdɪə-) *adj.* 1. decorated with glittering ornaments, such as artificial jewels or sequins. ~*n.* 2. a fabric so covered. [C20: from French, from *diamanter* to adorn with diamonds, from *diamant* DIAMOND]

diamantine (ˌdaɪə'mæntaɪn) *adj.* of or resembling diamonds. [C17: from French *diamantin,* from *diamant* DIAMOND]

diameter (daɪ'æmɪtə) *n.* 1. **a.** a straight line connecting the centre of a geometric figure, esp. a circle or sphere, with two points on the perimeter or surface. **b.** the length of such a line. 2. the thickness of something, esp. with circular cross section. [C14: from Medieval Latin *diametrus,* variant of Latin *diametros,* from Greek: diameter, diagonal, from DIA- + *metron* measure]

diametral (daɪ'æmɪtrəl) *adj.* 1. located on or forming a diameter: *diametral plane.* 2. a less common word for **diametric.** —**di'ametrally** *adv.*

diametric (ˌdaɪə'mɛtrɪk) *or* **diametrical** *adj.* 1. Also: **diametral.** of, related to, or along a diameter. 2. completely opposed.

diametrically (ˌdaɪə'mɛtrɪkəlɪ) *adv.* completely; utterly (esp. in the phrase **diametrically opposed).**

diamine ('daɪəˌmiːn, -mɪn; ˌdaɪə'miːn) *n.* any chemical compound containing two amino groups in its molecules.

diamond ('daɪəmənd) *n.* 1. **a.** a colourless exceptionally hard mineral (but often tinted yellow, orange, blue, brown, or black by impurities), found in certain igneous rocks (esp. the kimberlites of South Africa). It is used as a gemstone, as an abrasive, and on the working edges of cutting tools. Composition: carbon. Formula: C. Crystal structure: cubic. **b.** (*as modifier*): *a diamond ring.* 2. *Geometry.* **a.** a figure having four sides of equal length forming two acute angles and two obtuse angles; rhombus. **b.** (*modifier*) rhombic. 3. **a.** a red lozenge-shaped symbol on a playing card. **b.** a card with one or more of these symbols or (*when pl.*) the suit of cards so marked. 4. *Baseball.* **a.** the whole playing field. **b.** the square formed by the four bases. 5. (formerly) a size of printer's type approximately equal to 4½ point. 6. **black diamond.** a figurative name for **coal.** 7. **diamond cut diamond.** an encounter between two equally able people. 8. **rough diamond. a.** an unpolished diamond. **b.** a person of fine character who lacks refinement and polish. ~*vb.* 9. (*tr.*) to decorate with or as with diamonds. [C13: from Old French *diamant,* from Medieval Latin *diamas,* modification of Latin *adamas* the hardest iron or steel, diamond; see ADAMANT] —'**diamond-ˌlike** *adj.*

diamond anniversary *n.* a 60th, or occasionally 75th, anniversary.

diamondback ('daɪəmənd,bæk) *n.* 1. Also called: **diamondback terrapin** *or* **turtle.** any edible North American terrapin of the genus *Malaclemys,* esp. *M. terrapin,* occurring in brackish and tidal waters and having diamond-shaped markings on the shell: family *Emydidae.* 2. a large North American rattlesnake, *Crotalus adamanteus,* having cream-and-grey diamond-shaped markings.

diamond bird *n.* any small insectivorous Australian songbird of the genus *Pardalotus,* having a diamond-patterned plumage. Also called: **pardalote.**

diamond jubilee *n.* the celebration of a 60th, or occasionally 75th, anniversary.

diamond point *n.* a diamond-tipped engraving tool.

diamond snake *n.* a python, *Morelia argus,* of Australia and New Guinea, with yellow diamond-shaped markings.

diamond wedding *n.* the 60th, or occasionally the 75th, anniversary of a marriage.

diamond willow *n. Canadian.* wood that may come from any species of willow and has a diamond pattern in the grain, used for making walking sticks, table lamps, etc.

diamorphine (ˌdaɪə'mɔːfiːn) *n.* a technical name for **heroin.**

diandrous (daɪ'ændrəs) *adj.* (of some flowers or flowering plants) having two stamens.

dianoetic (ˌdaɪənəʊ'ɛtɪk) *adj.* of or relating to thought, esp. to discursive reasoning rather than intuition. Compare **discursive** (sense 2). [C17: from Greek *dianoētikos,* from *dianoia* the thinking process, an opinion, from DIA- + *noein* to think]

dianoia (ˌdaɪə'nɔɪə) *n. Philosophy.* 1. perception and experience regarded as lower modes of knowledge. Compare **noesis.** 2. the faculty of discursive reasoning. [from Greek; see DIANOETIC]

dianthus (daɪ'ænθəs) *n., pl.* **-thuses.** any Eurasian caryophyllaceous plant of the widely cultivated genus *Dianthus,* such as the carnation, pink, and sweet william. [C19: New Latin, from Greek DI-[1] + *anthos* flower]

diapason (ˌdaɪə'peɪzᵊn, -'peɪsᵊn) *n. Music.* 1. either of two stops (**open** and **stopped diapason**) usually found throughout the compass of a pipe organ that give it its characteristic tone colour. 2. the compass of an instrument or voice. 3. (chiefly in French usage) **a.** a standard pitch used for tuning, esp. the now largely obsolete one of A above middle C = 435 hertz, known as **diapason normal** (*French* djapazɔ̃ nɔrmal). **b.** a tuning fork or pitch pipe. 4. (in classical Greece) an octave. [C14: from Latin: the whole octave, from Greek: (*hē*) *dia pasōn* (*khordōn sumphōnia*) (con-

cord) through all (the notes), from *dia* through + *pas* all] —**dia'pasonal** *or* **diapasonic** (ˌdaɪəpeɪˈzɒnɪk, -ˈsɒn-) *adj.*
diapause (ˈdaɪəˌpɔːz) *n.* a period of suspended development and growth accompanied by decreased metabolism in insects and some other animals. It is correlated with seasonal changes. [C19: from Greek *diapausis* pause, from *diapauein* to pause, bring to an end, from DIA- + *pauein* to stop]
diapedesis (ˌdaɪəpəˈdiːsɪs) *n.* the passage of blood cells through the unruptured wall of a blood vessel into the surrounding tissues. [C17: New Latin, from Greek: a leaping through, from *diapēdan* to spring through, from DIA- + *pēdan* to leap] —**diapedetic** (ˌdaɪəpəˈdɛtɪk) *adj.*
diapente (ˌdaɪəˈpɛntɪ) *n. Music.* (in classical Greece) the interval of a perfect fifth. [C14: from Latin, from Greek *dia pente khordōn sumphōnia* concord through five notes, from *dia* through + *pente* five]
diaper (ˈdaɪəpə) *n.* **1.** the U.S. and Canadian word for **nappy**[1]. **2. a.** a woven pattern on fabric consisting of a small repeating design, esp. diamonds. **b.** fabric having such a pattern. **c.** such a pattern, used as decoration. ~*vb.* **3.** (*tr.*) to decorate with such a pattern. [C14: from Old French *diaspre,* from Medieval Latin *diasprus* made of diaper, from Medieval Greek *diaspros* pure white, from DIA- + *aspros* white, shining]
diaphanous (daɪˈæfənəs) *adj.* (usually of fabrics such as silk) fine and translucent. [C17: from Medieval Latin *diaphanus,* from Greek *diaphanēs* transparent, from *diaphainein* to show through, from DIA- + *phainein* to show] —**di'aphanously** *adv.* —**di'aphanousness** *or* **diaphaneity** (ˌdaɪəfəˈniːɪtɪ) *n.*
diaphone (ˈdaɪəˌfəʊn) *n.* **1. a.** the set of all realizations of a given phoneme in a language. **b.** one of any number of corresponding sounds in different dialects of a language. **2.** a foghorn that emits a two-toned signal. [C20: from DIA(LECT) + PHONE[2]]
diaphony (daɪˈæfənɪ) *n. Music.* **1.** a style of two-part polyphonic singing; organum or a freer form resembling it. **2.** (in classical Greece) another word for **dissonance** (sense 3). Compare **symphony** (sense 5a). [C17: from Late Latin *diaphōnia,* from Greek, from *diaphōnos* discordant, from DIA- + *phōnē* sound] —**diaphonic** (ˌdaɪəˈfɒnɪk) *adj.*
diaphoresis (ˌdaɪəfəˈriːsɪs) *n.* **1.** a technical name for **perspiration. 2.** perceptible and excessive perspiration; sweat. [C17: via Late Latin from Greek, from *diaphorein* to disperse by perspiration, from DIA- + *phorein* to carry, variant of *pherein*]
diaphoretic (ˌdaɪəfəˈrɛtɪk) *adj.* **1.** relating to or causing perspiration or sweat. ~*n.* **2.** a diaphoretic drug or agent.
diaphototropism (ˌdaɪəfəʊtəʊˈtrəʊpɪzəm) *n.* growth of a plant or plant part in a direction transverse to that of the light. [C20: from Greek, from DIA- + PHOTOTROPIC] —**diaphototropic** (ˌdaɪəfəʊtəʊˈtrɒpɪk) *adj.*
diaphragm (ˈdaɪəˌfræm) *n.* **1.** *Anatomy.* any separating membrane, esp. the dome-shaped muscular partition that separates the abdominal and thoracic cavities in mammals. **2.** a circular rubber or plastic contraceptive membrane placed over the mouth of the uterine cervix before copulation to prevent entrance of sperm. **3.** any thin dividing membrane. **4.** Also called: **stop.** a disc with a fixed or adjustable aperture to control the amount of light or other radiation entering an optical instrument, such as a camera. **5.** a thin disc that vibrates when receiving or producing sound waves, used to convert sound signals to electrical signals or vice versa in telephones, etc. **6.** *Chem.* **a.** a porous plate or cylinder dividing an electrolytic cell, used to permit the passage of ions and prevent the mixing of products formed at the electrodes. **b.** a semipermeable membrane used to separate two solutions in osmosis. **7.** *Botany.* a transverse plate of cells that occurs in the stems of certain aquatic plants. [C17: from Late Latin *diaphragma,* from Greek, from DIA- + *phragma* fence] —**diaphragmatic** (ˌdaɪəfrægˈmætɪk) *adj.* —ˌ**diaphrag'matically** *adv.*
diaphysis (daɪˈæfɪsɪs) *n., pl.* **-ses** (-ˌsiːz). the shaft of a long bone. Compare **epiphysis.** [C19: New Latin, from Greek *diaphusis,* from *diaphuesthai* to grow between, from DIA- + *phuein* to produce] —**diaphysial** (ˌdaɪəˈfɪzɪəl) *adj.*
diapir (ˈdaɪəˌpɪə) *n. Geology.* an anticlinal fold in which the brittle overlying rock has been pierced by material, such as salt, from beneath. [C20: from Greek *diapeirainein* to make holes through, pierce]
diapophysis (ˌdaɪəˈpɒfɪsɪs) *n., pl.* **-ses** (-ˌsiːz). *Anatomy.* the upper or articular surface of a transverse vertebral process. [C19: New Latin, from DI-[2] + APOPHYSIS] —**diapophysial** (ˌdaɪæpəˈfɪzɪəl) *adj.*
diapositive (ˌdaɪəˈpɒzɪtɪv) *n.* a positive transparency; slide.
diarch (ˈdaɪɑːk) *adj. Botany.* (of a vascular bundle) having two strands of xylem. [C19: from Greek DI-[1] + *archē* beginning, origin]
diarchy *or* **dyarchy** (ˈdaɪɑːkɪ) *n., pl.* **-chies.** government by two states, individuals, etc. —**di'archic, di'archical, di'archal,** *or* **dy'archic, dy'archical, dy'archal** *adj.*
diarist (ˈdaɪərɪst) *n.* a person who keeps or writes a diary, esp. one that is subsequently published.
diarrhoea *or esp. U.S.* **diarrhea** (ˌdaɪəˈrɪə) *n.* frequent and copious discharge of abnormally liquid faeces. [C16: from Late Latin, from Greek *diarrhoia,* from *diarrhein* to flow through, from DIA- + *rhein* to flow] —ˌ**diar'rhoeal,** ˌ**diar'rhoeic** *or esp. U.S.* ˌ**diar'rheal,** ˌ**diar'rheic** *adj.*
diarthrosis (ˌdaɪɑːˈθrəʊsɪs) *n., pl.* **-ses** (-siːz). *Anatomy.* any freely movable joint, such as the shoulder and hip joints. [C16: New Latin, from DI-[2] + Greek *arthrōsis,* from *arthroun* to fasten by a joint, from *arthron* joint] —ˌ**diar'throdial** *adj.*
diary (ˈdaɪərɪ) *n., pl.* **-ries. 1.** a personal record of daily events, appointments, observations, etc. **2.** a book for keeping such a record. [C16: from Latin *diārium* daily allocation of food or money, journal, from *diēs* day]
diascope (ˈdaɪəˌskəʊp) *n.* an optical projector used to display transparencies.
Diaspora (daɪˈæspərə) *n.* **1. a.** the dispersion of the Jews after the Babylonian and Roman conquests of ancient Palestine. **b.** the Jewish communities outside Israel. **c.** the Jews living outside Israel. **d.** the extent of Jewish settlement outside Israel. **2.** (in the New Testament) the body of Christians living outside Palestine. **3.** (*often not cap.*) a dispersion or spreading, as of people originally belonging to one nation or having a common culture. [C19: from Greek: a scattering, from *diaspeirein* to disperse, from DIA- + *speirein* to scatter, sow; see SPORE]
diaspore (ˈdaɪəˌspɔː) *n.* **1.** a white, yellowish, or grey mineral consisting of hydrated aluminium oxide in orthorhombic crystalline form, found in bauxite and corundum. Formula: $Al_2O_3.H_2O$. **2.** any propagative part of a plant, esp. one that is easily dispersed, such as a spore. [C19: from Greek *diaspora* a scattering, dispersion; see DIASPORA: so named from its dispersion and crackling when highly heated]
diastalsis (ˌdaɪəˈstælsɪs) *n., pl.* **-ses** (-siːz). *Physiol.* a downward wave of contraction occurring in the intestine during digestion. See also **peristalsis.** [C20: New Latin, from DIA- + (PERI)STALSIS] —ˌ**dia'staltic** *adj.*
diastase (ˈdaɪəˌsteɪs, -ˌsteɪz) *n.* any of a group of enzymes that hydrolyse starch to maltose. They are present in germinated barley and in the pancreas. See also **amylase.** [C19: from French, from Greek *diastasis* a separation; see DIASTASIS] —ˌ**dia'stasic** *adj.*
diastasis (daɪˈæstəsɪs) *n., pl.* **-ses** (-ˌsiːz). **1.** *Pathol.* **a.** the separation of an epiphysis from the long bone to which it is normally attached without fracture of the bone. **b.** the separation of any two parts normally joined. **2.** *Physiol.* the last part of the diastolic phase of the heartbeat. [C18: New Latin, from Greek: a separation, from *diistanai* to separate, from DIA- + *histanai* to place, make stand] —**diastatic** (ˌdaɪəˈstætɪk) *adj.*
diastema (ˌdaɪəˈstiːmə) *n., pl.* **-mata** (-mətə). **1.** an abnormal space, fissure, or cleft in a bodily organ or part. **2.** a gap between the teeth. [C19: New Latin, from Greek: gap, from *diistanai* to separate; see DIASTASIS]
diaster (daɪˈæstə) *n. Cytology.* the stage in cell division at which the chromosomes are in two groups at the poles of the spindle before forming daughter nuclei. [C19: from DI-[1] + Greek *astēr* star] —**di'astral** *adj.*
diastereoisomer (ˌdaɪəˌstɛrɪəʊˈaɪsəmə) *n. Chem.* a type of isomer that differs in the spatial arrangement of atoms in the molecule, but is not a mirror image; a stereoisomer that is not an enantiomer.
diastole (daɪˈæstəlɪ) *n.* the dilation of the chambers of the heart that follows each contraction, during which they refill with blood. Compare **systole.** [C16: via Late Latin from Greek: an expansion, from *diastellein* to expand, from DIA- + *stellein* to place, bring together, make ready] —**diastolic** (ˌdaɪəˈstɒlɪk) *adj.*
diastrophism (daɪˈæstrəˌfɪzəm) *n.* the process of movement and deformation of the earth's crust that gives rise to large-scale features such as continents, ocean basins, and mountains. See also **orogeny, epeirogeny.** [C19: from Greek *diastrophē* a twisting; see DIA-, STROPHE] —**diastrophic** (ˌdaɪəˈstrɒfɪk) *adj.*
diastyle (ˈdaɪəˌstaɪl) *Architect.* ~*adj.* **1.** having columns about three diameters apart. ~*n.* **2.** a diastyle building. [C16: via Latin from Greek *diastȳlos* having spaced pillars]
diatessaron (ˌdaɪəˈtɛsəˌrɒn) *n.* **1.** *Music.* (in classical Greece) the interval of a perfect fourth. **2.** a conflation of the four Gospels into a single continuous narrative. [C14: from Late Latin, from Greek *dia tessarōn khordōn sumphōnia* concord through four notes, from *dia* through + *tessares* four]
diathermancy (ˌdaɪəˈθɜːmənsɪ) *n., pl.* **-cies.** the property of transmitting infrared radiation. [C19: from French *diathermansie,* from DIA- + Greek *thermansis* heating, from *thermainein* to heat, from *thermos* hot] —ˌ**dia'thermanous** *adj.*
diathermic (ˌdaɪəˈθɜːmɪk) *adj.* **1.** of or relating to diathermy. **2.** able to conduct heat; passing heat freely.
diathermy (ˈdaɪəˌθɜːmɪ) *or* **diathermia** (ˌdaɪəˈθɜːmɪə) *n.* local heating of the body tissues with an electric current for medical or surgical purposes. [C20: from New Latin *diathermia,* from DIA- + Greek *thermē* heat]
diathesis (daɪˈæθɪsɪs) *n., pl.* **-ses** (-ˌsiːz). a hereditary or acquired susceptibility of the body to one or more diseases. [C17: New Latin, from Greek: propensity, from *diatithenai* to dispose, from DIA- + *tithenai* to place] —**diathetic** (ˌdaɪəˈθɛtɪk) *adj.*
diatom (ˈdaɪətəm, -ˌtɒm) *n.* any microscopic unicellular alga of the class *Bacillariophyceae,* occurring in marine or fresh water singly or in colonies, each cell having a cell wall made of two halves and impregnated with silica. See also **diatomite.** [C19: from New Latin *Diatoma* (genus name), from Greek *diatomos* cut

in two, from *diatemnein* to cut through, from DIA- + *temnein* to cut]
diatomaceous (ˌdaɪətəˈmeɪʃəs) *adj.* of, relating to, consisting of, or containing diatoms or their fossil remains.
diatomaceous earth *n.* an unconsolidated form of diatomite. Also called: **kieselguhr.**
diatomic (ˌdaɪəˈtɒmɪk) *adj.* (of a compound or molecule) **a.** containing two atoms. **b.** containing two characteristic groups or atoms: *ethylene glycol is a diatomic alcohol.* —**diatomicity** (ˌdaɪætəˈmɪsɪtɪ) *n.*
diatomite (daɪˈætəˌmaɪt) *n.* a soft very fine-grained whitish rock consisting of the siliceous remains of diatoms deposited in small ponds or lakes. It is used as an absorbent, filtering medium, insulator, filler, etc. See also **diatomaceous earth.**
diatonic (ˌdaɪəˈtɒnɪk) *adj.* **1.** of, relating to, or based upon any scale of five tones and two semitones produced by playing the white keys of a keyboard instrument, esp. the natural major or minor scales forming the basis of the key system in Western music. Compare **chromatic** (sense 2). **2.** not involving the sharpening or flattening of the notes of the major or minor scale nor the use of such notes as modified by accidentals. [C16: from Late Latin *diatonicus,* from Greek *diatonikos,* from *diatonos* extending, from *diateinein* to stretch out, from DIA- + *teinein* to stretch] —ˌ**diaˈtonically** *adv.* —**diatonicism** (ˌdaɪəˈtɒnɪˌsɪzəm) *n.*
diatribe (ˈdaɪəˌtraɪb) *n.* a bitter or violent criticism or attack; denunciation. [C16: from Latin *diatriba* learned debate, from Greek *diatribē* discourse, pastime, from *diatribein* to while away, from DIA- + *tribein* to rub]
diatropism (daɪˈætrəˌpɪzəm) *n.* a response of plants or parts of plants to an external stimulus by growing at right angles to the direction of the stimulus. —**diatropic** (ˌdaɪəˈtrɒpɪk) *adj.*
diazepam (daɪˈeɪzəˌpæm) *n.* a chemical compound used as a tranquillizer and muscle relaxant. Formula: $C_{16}H_{13}ClN_2O$. [C20: from DI-[1] + AZO- + EP(OXIDE) + *-am*]
diazine (ˈdaɪəˌziːn; daɪˈæziːn, -ɪn) *or* **diazin** (ˈdaɪəzɪn, daɪˈæzɪn) *n.* any organic compound whose molecules contain a hexagonal ring of four carbon atoms and two nitrogen atoms, esp. any of three isomers with the formula $C_4N_2H_4$. See also **pyrimidine.**
diazo (daɪˈeɪzəʊ) *adj.* **1.** of, consisting of, or containing the divalent group, =N:N, or the divalent group, -N:N-: *diazo compound.* See also **azo. 2.** Also: **dyeline.** of or relating to the reproduction of documents using the bleaching action of ultraviolet radiation on diazonium salts. ~*n., pl.* **-os** *or* **-oes. 3.** a document produced by this method.
diazole (daɪˈeɪzəʊl) *n.* any organic compound whose molecules contain a pentagonal ring of three carbon atoms and two nitrogen atoms, esp. imidazole (**1,3–diazole**) or pyrazole (**1,1–diazole**).
diazomethane (daɪˌeɪzəʊˈmiːθeɪn) *n.* a yellow odourless explosive gas, used as a methylating agent. Formula: CH_2:N:N.
diazonium (ˌdaɪəˈzəʊnɪəm) *n.* (*modifier*) of, consisting of, or containing the group, Ar-N:N-, where Ar is an aryl group: *diazonium group or radical; a diazonium compound.* [C19: DIAZO + (AMM)ONIUM]
diazonium salt *n.* any of a class of compounds with the general formula $[ArN:N]^-M^+$, where Ar is an aryl group and M is a metal atom; made by the action of nitrous acid on aromatic amines and used in dyeing.
diazotize *or* **diazotise** (daɪˈeɪzəˌtaɪz) *vb.* (*tr.*) to cause (an aryl amine) to react with nitrous acid to produce a diazonium salt. —**diˌazotiˈzation** *or* **diˌazotiˈsation** *n.*
dib (dɪb) *vb.* **dibs, dibbing, dibbed.** (*intr.*) to fish by allowing the bait to bob and dip on the surface. [C17: perhaps alteration of DAB[1]]
dibasic (daɪˈbeɪsɪk) *adj.* **1.** (of an acid, such as sulphuric acid, H_2SO_4) containing two acidic hydrogen atoms. Compare **diacidic. 2.** (of a salt) derived by replacing two acidic hydrogen atoms: *dibasic sodium phosphate,* Na_2HPO_4. —**dibasicity** (ˌdaɪbeɪˈsɪsɪtɪ) *n.*
dibble[1] (ˈdɪbᵊl) *n.* **1.** Also called (esp. Brit.): **dibber** (ˈdɪbə). a small hand tool used to make holes in the ground for planting or transplanting bulbs, seeds, or roots. ~*vb.* **2.** to make a hole in (the ground) with a dibble. **3.** to plant (bulbs, seeds, etc.) with a dibble. [C15: of obscure origin] —ˈ**dibbler** *n.*
dibble[2] (ˈdɪbᵊl) *vb.* (*intr.*) **1.** a variant of **dib. 2.** a less common word for **dabble.**
dibbuk (ˈdɪbək; *Hebrew* diˈbuk) *n., pl.* **-buks** *or* **-bukkim** (*Hebrew* -buˈkim). a variant spelling of **dybbuk.**
dibranchiate (daɪˈbræŋkɪɪt, -ˌeɪt) *adj.* **1.** of, relating to, or belonging to the *Dibranchiata,* a group or former order of cephalopod molluscs, including the octopuses, squids, and cuttlefish, having two gills. ~*n.* **2.** any dibranchiate mollusc.
dibromide (daɪˈbrəʊmaɪd) *n.* any chemical compound that contains two bromine atoms per molecule.
dibs (dɪbz) *pl. n.* **1.** another word for **jacks. 2.** a slang word for **money. 3.** (foll. by *on*) *Informal.* rights (to) or claims (on): used mainly by children. [C18: shortened from *dibstones* children's game played with knucklebones or pebbles, probably from *dib* to tap, dip, variant of DAB[1]]
dicarboxylic acid (daɪˌkɑːbɒkˈsɪlɪk) *n.* any carboxylic acid that contains two carboxyl groups per molecule.
dicast (ˈdɪkæst) *n.* (in ancient Athens) a juror in the popular courts chosen by lot from a list of citizens. [C19: from Greek *dikastēs,* from *dikazein* to judge, from *dikē* right, judgment, order] —**diˈcastic** *adj.*
dice (daɪs) *pl. n.* **1.** cubes of wood, plastic, etc., each of whose sides has a different number of spots (1 to 6), used in games of chance and in gambling to give random numbers. **2.** (*functioning as sing.*) Also called: **die.** one of these cubes. **3.** small cubes as of vegetables, chopped meat, etc. **4. no dice.** *Slang, chiefly U.S. and Canadian.* an expression of refusal or rejection. ~*vb.* **5.** to cut (food, etc.) into small cubes. **6.** (*intr.*) to gamble with or play at a game involving dice. **7.** (*intr.*) to take a chance or risk (esp. in the phrase **dice with death**). **8.** (*tr.*) *Austral. informal.* to abandon or reject. **9.** (*tr.*) to decorate or mark with dicelike shapes. [C14: plural of DIE[2]] —ˈ**dicer** *n.*
dicentra (daɪˈsɛntrə) *n.* any Asian or North American plant of the genus *Dicentra,* such as bleeding heart and Dutchman's-breeches, having finely divided leaves and ornamental clusters of drooping flowers: family *Fumariaceae.* [C19: New Latin, from Greek *dikentros* having two sharp points, from DI-[1] + *kentron* sharp point, from *kentein* to prick; see CENTRE]
dicephalous (daɪˈsɛfələs) *adj.* having two heads. —**diˈcephalism** *n.*
dicey (ˈdaɪsɪ) *adj.* **dicier, diciest.** *Informal, chiefly Brit.* difficult or dangerous; risky; tricky.
dichasium (daɪˈkeɪzɪəm) *n., pl.* **-sia** (-zɪə). a cymose inflorescence in which each branch bearing a flower gives rise to two other flowering branches, as in the stitchwort. Compare **monochasium.** [C19: New Latin, from Greek *dikhasis* a dividing, from *dikhazein* to divide in two, from *dikha* in two] —**diˈchasial** *adj.* —**diˈchasially** *adv.*
dichlamydeous (ˌdaɪkləˈmɪdɪəs) *adj.* (of a flower) having a corolla and calyx. [C19: from Greek, from DI-[1] + *khlamus* a cloak + -EOUS]
dichloride (daɪˈklɔːraɪd) *n.* a compound in which two atoms of chlorine are combined with another atom or group. Also called: **bichloride.**
dichlorodifluoromethane (daɪˌklɔːrəʊdaɪˌflʊərəʊˈmiːθeɪn) *n.* a colourless nonflammable gas easily liquefied by pressure: used as a propellant in aerosols and fire extinguishers and as a refrigerant. Formula: CCl_2F_2. See also **Freon.**
dichlorodiphenyltrichloroethane (daɪˌklɔːrəʊdaɪˌfiːnaɪltraɪˌklɔːrəʊˈiːθeɪn, -nɪl-; -ˌfɛn-) *n.* the full name for **DDT.**
dichloromethane (dɑɪˌklɔːrəʊˈmiːθeɪn) *n.* a noxious colourless liquid widely used as a solvent, e.g. in paint strippers. Formula: CH_2Cl_2. Traditional name: **methylene dichloride.**
dicho- *or before a vowel* **dich-** *combining form.* in two parts; in pairs: *dichotomy.* [from Greek *dikho-,* from *dikha* in two]
dichogamy (daɪˈkɒgəmɪ) *n.* the maturation of male and female parts of a flower at different times, preventing self-pollination. Compare **homogamy** (sense 2). —**diˈchogamous** *or* **dichogamic** (ˌdaɪkəʊˈgæmɪk) *adj.*
dichoptic (daɪˈkɒptɪk) *adj. Zoology.* having the eyes distinctly separate.
dichotic (daɪˈkɒtɪk) *adj.* relating to or involving the stimulation of each ear simultaneously by different sounds. [DICHO- + -IC]
dichotomize *or* **dichotomise** (daɪˈkɒtəˌmaɪz) *vb.* to divide or become divided into two parts or classifications. —**diˈchotomist** *n.* —**diˌchotomiˈzation** *or* **diˌchotomiˈsation** *n.*
dichotomy (daɪˈkɒtəmɪ) *n., pl.* **-mies. 1.** division into two parts or classifications, esp. when they are sharply distinguished or opposed: *the dichotomy between eastern and western cultures.* **2.** *Logic.* the division of a class into two mutually exclusive subclasses: *the dichotomy of married and single people.* **3.** *Botany.* a simple method of branching by repeated division into two equal parts. **4.** the phase of the moon, Venus, or Mercury when half of the disc is visible. [C17: from Greek *dichotomia;* see DICHO-, -TOMY] —**diˈchotomous** *or* **dichotomic** (ˌdaɪkəʊˈtɒmɪk) *adj.* —**diˈchotomously** *adv.*
dichroic (daɪˈkrəʊɪk) *or* **dichroitic** (ˌdaɪkrəʊˈɪtɪk) *adj.* **1.** (of a solution or uniaxial crystal) exhibiting dichroism. **2.** another word for **dichromatic.** [C19: from Greek *dikhroos* having two colours, from DI-[1] + *khrōs* colour]
dichroic filter *n.* an optical colour filter operating on the principle of wave interference between closely spaced reflecting surfaces, rather than by colour absorption.
dichroism (ˈdaɪkrəʊˌɪzəm) *n.* **1.** Also called: **dichromaticism.** a property of a uniaxial crystal, such as tourmaline, of showing a perceptible difference in colour when viewed along two different axes in transmitted white light. See also **pleochroism. 2.** a property of certain solutions as a result of which the wavelength (colour) of the light transmitted depends on the concentration of the solution and the length of the path of the light within the solution.
dichroite (ˈdaɪkrəʊˌaɪt) *n.* another name for **cordierite.** [C19: from Greek *dikhroos* two-coloured + -ITE[1]]
dichromate (daɪˈkrəʊmeɪt) *n.* any salt or ester of dichromic acid. Dichromate salts contain the ion $Cr_2O_7^{2-}$ Also called: **bichromate.**
dichromatic (ˌdaɪkrəʊˈmætɪk) *adj.* **1.** Also: **dichroic.** having or consisting of only two colours. **2.** (of animal species) having two different colour varieties that are independent of sex and age. **3.** able to perceive only two (instead of three) primary

colours and the mixes of these colours. —**dichromatism** (daɪˈkrəʊməˌtɪzəm) *n.*

dichromaticism (ˌdaɪkrəʊˈmætɪˌsɪzəm) *n.* another name for **dichroism** (sense 1).

dichromic (daɪˈkrəʊmɪk) *adj.* of or involving only two colours; dichromatic.

dichromic acid *n.* an unstable dibasic oxidizing acid known only in solution and in the form of dichromate salts. Formula: $H_2Cr_2O_7$.

dichroscope (ˈdaɪkrəˌskəʊp) *n.* an instrument used for investigating the dichroism of solutions or crystals. Also called: **diˈchroiˌscope, diˈchrooˌscope.** [C19: from Greek *dikhroos* two-coloured + -SCOPE] —**dichroscopic** (ˌdaɪkrəˈskɒpɪk), **ˌdichroiˈscopic,** *or* **ˌdichrooˈscopic** *adj.*

dick[1] (dɪk) *n. Chiefly U.S.* a slang word for **detective.** [C20: by shortening and alteration from DETECTIVE; probably influenced by proper name *Dick*]

dick[2] (dɪk) *n. Slang.* **1.** *Brit.* a fellow or person. **2. clever dick.** *Brit.* a person who is obnoxiously opinionated or self-satisfied; know-all. **3.** a taboo word for **penis.** [C16 (meaning: fellow): from the name *Dick,* familiar form of *Richard,* applied generally (like *Jack*) to any fellow, lad, etc.; hence, C19: penis]

dickens (ˈdɪkɪnz) *n. Informal.* a euphemistic word for **devil** (used as intensifier in the interrogative phrase **what the dickens**). [C16: from the name *Dickens*]

Dickensian (dɪˈkɛnzɪən) *adj.* **1.** of the British novelist Charles Dickens (1812–70) or his works. **2.** resembling or suggestive of conditions described in Dickens' novels, esp.: **a.** squalid and poverty-stricken: *working conditions were truly Dickensian.* **b.** characterized by jollity and conviviality: *a Dickensian scene round the Christmas tree.* **3.** grotesquely comic, as some of the characters of Dickens.

dicker (ˈdɪkə) *vb.* **1.** to trade (goods) by bargaining; barter. **2.** (*intr.*) to negotiate a political deal. ~*n.* **3. a.** a petty bargain or barter. **b.** the item or items bargained or bartered. **4.** a political deal or bargain. [C12: ultimately from Latin *decuria* DECURY; related to Middle Low German *dēker* lot of ten hides]

dickhead (ˈdɪkˌhɛd) *n. Slang.* a stupid or despicable man or boy. [C20: from DICK[2] (in the sense: penis) + HEAD]

Dick test (dɪk) *n.* a skin test for determining whether a person is immune or susceptible to scarlet fever. [C20: named after George F. *Dick* (1881–1967), U.S. physician who devised it]

dicky[1] *or* **dickey** (ˈdɪkɪ) *n., pl.* **dickies** *or* **dickeys. 1.** a woman's false blouse front, worn to fill in the neck of a jacket or low-cut dress. **2.** a man's false shirt front, esp. one worn with full evening dress. **3.** Also called: **dicky bow.** *Brit.* a bow tie. **4.** *Chiefly Brit.* an informal name for **donkey,** esp. a male one. **5.** Also called: **ˈdickyˌbird, ˈdickeyˌbird.** a child's word for a **bird,** esp. a small one. **6.** a folding outside seat at the rear of some early cars. U.S. and Canadian name: **rumble seat.** [C18 (in the senses: donkey, shirt front): from *Dickey,* diminutive of *Dick* (name); the relationship of the various senses is obscure]

dicky[2] *or* **dickey** (ˈdɪkɪ) *adj.* **dickier, dickiest.** *Brit. informal.* in bad condition; shaky, unsteady, or unreliable: *I feel a bit dicky today.* [C18: perhaps from the name *Dick* in the phrase *as queer as Dick's hatband* feeling ill]

diclinous (ˈdaɪklɪnəs, daɪˈklaɪ-) *adj.* (of flowers and flowering plants) unisexual. Compare **monoclinous.** —**ˈdiclinism** *n.* —**dicliny** (ˈdaɪklɪnɪ, daɪˈklaɪ-) *n.*

dicotyledon (daɪˌkɒtɪˈliːdᵊn, ˌdaɪkɒt-) *n.* any flowering plant of the group *Dicotyledonae,* having two embryonic seed leaves and leaves with netlike veins. The group includes many herbaceous plants and most families of trees and shrubs. Often shortened to **dicot.** Compare **monocotyledon.** —**ˌdicotyˈledonous** *adj.*

dicrotic (daɪˈkrɒtɪk) *or* **dicrotal** (ˈdaɪkrətᵊl) *adj. Physiol.* having or relating to a double pulse for each heartbeat. [C19: from Greek *dikrotos* double-beating, from DI-[1] + *krotein* to beat] —**dicrotism** (ˈdaɪkrəˌtɪzəm) *n.*

dict. *abbrev. for:* **1.** dictation. **2.** dictator. **3.** dictionary.

dicta (ˈdɪktə) *n.* a plural of **dictum.**

Dictaphone (ˈdɪktəˌfəʊn) *n. Trademark.* a tape recorder designed for recording dictation and later reproducing it for typing.

dictate *vb.* (dɪkˈteɪt). **1.** to say (messages, letters, speeches, etc.) aloud for mechanical recording or verbatim transcription by another person. **2.** (*tr.*) to prescribe (commands) authoritatively. **3.** (*intr.*) to act in a tyrannical manner; seek to impose one's will on others. ~*n.* (ˈdɪkteɪt). **4.** an authoritative command. **5.** a guiding principle or rule: *the dictates of reason.* [C17: from Latin *dictāre* to say repeatedly, order, from *dīcere* to say]

dictation (dɪkˈteɪʃən) *n.* **1.** the act of dictating material to be recorded or taken down in writing. **2.** the material dictated. **3.** authoritative commands or the act of giving them. —**dicˈtational** *adj.*

dictation test *n. Austral.* a language test formerly used by the Australian government to disqualify unwelcome immigrants.

dictator (dɪkˈteɪtə) *n.* **1. a.** a ruler who is not effectively restricted by a constitution, laws, recognized opposition, etc. **b.** an absolute, esp. tyrannical, ruler. **2.** (in ancient Rome) a person appointed during a crisis to exercise supreme authority. **3.** a person who makes pronouncements, as on conduct, fashion, etc., which are regarded as authoritative. **4.** a person who behaves in an authoritarian or tyrannical manner. —**dictatress** (dɪkˈteɪtrɪs) *or* **dictatrix** (ˈdɪktətrɪks) *fem. n.*

dictatorial (ˌdɪktəˈtɔːrɪəl) *adj.* **1.** of or characteristic of a dictator. **2.** tending to dictate; tyrannical; overbearing. —**ˌdictaˈtorially** *adv.* —**ˌdictaˈtorialness** *n.*

dictatorship (dɪkˈteɪtəˌʃɪp) *n.* **1.** the rank, office, or period of rule of a dictator. **2.** government by a dictator or dictators. **3.** a country ruled by a dictator or dictators. **4.** absolute or supreme power or authority.

diction (ˈdɪkʃən) *n.* **1.** the choice and use of words in writing or speech. **2.** the manner of uttering or enunciating words and sounds; elocution. [C15: from Latin *dictiō* a saying, mode of expression, from *dīcere* to speak, say]

dictionary (ˈdɪkʃənərɪ, -ʃənrɪ) *n., pl.* **-aries. 1. a.** a reference book that consists of an alphabetical list of words with their meanings and parts of speech, and often a guide to accepted pronunciation and syllabification, irregular inflections of words, derived words of different parts of speech, and etymologies. **b.** a similar reference book giving equivalent words in two or more languages. Such dictionaries often consist of two or more parts, in each of which the alphabetical list is given in a different language: *a German-English dictionary.* **c.** (*as modifier*): *a dictionary definition.* See also **glossary, lexicon, thesaurus. 2.** a reference book listing words or terms of a particular subject or activity, giving information about their meanings and other attributes: *a dictionary of gardening.* **3.** a collection of information or examples with the entries alphabetically arranged: *a dictionary of quotations.* [C16: from Medieval Latin *dictiōnārium* collection of words, from Late Latin *dictiō* word; see DICTION]

dictionary catalogue *n.* a catalogue of the authors, titles and subjects of books in one alphabetical sequence.

Dictograph (ˈdɪktəˌgrɑːf, -ˌgræf) *n. Trademark.* a telephonic instrument for secretly monitoring or recording conversations by means of a small, sensitive, and often concealed microphone.

dictum (ˈdɪktəm) *n., pl.* **-tums** *or* **-ta** (-tə). **1.** a formal or authoritative statement or assertion; pronouncement. **2.** a popular saying or maxim. **3.** *Law.* See **obiter dictum.** [C16: from Latin, from *dīcere* to say]

dictyopteran (ˌdɪktɪˈɒptərən) *n.* any insect of the order *Dictyoptera,* which comprises the cockroaches and mantises. [New Latin, from Greek *diktuon* a net, from *dikein* to cast + *pteron* a wing]

dicyclic (daɪˈsaɪklɪk) *adj.* **1.** *Botany.* having the perianth arranged in two whorls; having separate petals and sepals. **2.** *Chem.* (of a molecule) containing only two rings of atoms.

dicynodont (daɪˈsɪnəˌdɒnt) *n.* any of various extinct Triassic mammal-like reptiles having a single pair of tusklike teeth. [C19: from Greek, from DI-[1] + *kuōn* dog + -ODONT]

did (dɪd) *vb.* the past tense of **do**[1].

didactic (dɪˈdæktɪk) *adj.* **1.** intended to instruct, esp. excessively. **2.** morally instructive; improving. **3.** (of works of art or literature) containing a political or moral message to which aesthetic considerations are subordinated. [C17: from Greek *didaktikos* skilled in teaching, from *didaskein* to teach] —**diˈdactically** *adv.* —**diˈdacticism** *n.*

didactics (dɪˈdæktɪks) *n.* (*functioning as sing.*) the art or science of teaching.

didactyl (daɪˈdæktɪl) *adj.* (esp. of many marsupials) having the hind toes separate. —**diˈdactylism** *n.*

diddle[1] (ˈdɪdᵊl) *vb. Informal.* **1.** (*tr.*) to cheat or swindle. **2.** (*intr.*) an obsolete word for **dawdle.** [C19: back formation from Jeremy *Diddler,* a scrounger in J. Kenney's farce *Raising the Wind* (1803)] —**ˈdiddler** *n.*

diddle[2] (ˈdɪdᵊl) *vb. Dialect.* to jerk (an object) up and down or back and forth; shake rapidly. [C17: probably variant of *doderen* to tremble, totter; see DODDER[1]]

diddy (ˈdɪdɪ) *n., pl.* **-dies.** *Dialect.* a female breast or nipple. [C18: from *titty,* diminutive of TIT[2]]

didgeridoo (ˌdɪdʒərɪˈduː) *n. Music.* a deep-toned native Australian wind instrument made from a long section of thick bamboo pipe. [C20: imitative of its sound]

didicoy, diddicoy (ˈdɪdɪˌkɔɪ), *or* **didakai** (ˈdɪdəˌkaɪ) *n., pl.* **-coys** *or* **-kais.** (in Britain) one of a group of caravan-dwelling roadside people, who live like Gypsies but are not true Romanies. [C19: from Romany]

didn't (ˈdɪdᵊnt) *contraction of* did not.

dido (ˈdaɪdəʊ) *n., pl.* **-dos** *or* **-does.** (*usually pl.*) *Informal.* an antic; prank; trick. [C19: originally U.S.: of uncertain origin]

didst (dɪdst) *vb. Archaic.* (used with the pronoun *thou* or its relative equivalent) a form of the past tense of **do**[1].

didymium (daɪˈdɪmɪəm, dɪ-) *n.* **1.** a mixture of the metallic rare earths neodymium and praseodymium, once thought to be an element. **2.** a mixture of rare earths and their oxides used in colouring glass. [C19: from New Latin, from Greek *didumos* twin + -IUM]

didymous (ˈdɪdɪməs) *adj. Biology.* in pairs or in two parts. [C18: from Greek *didumos* twin, from *duo* two]

didynamous (daɪˈdɪnəməs) *adj.* (of plants) having four stamens arranged in two pairs of unequal length, as in the foxglove. [C18: from New Latin *Didynamia* name of former class, from DI-[1] + Greek *dunamis* power, referring to the greater strength of the two long stamens]

die[1] (daɪ) *vb.* **dies, dying, died.** (*mainly intr.*) **1.** (of an organism or its cells, organs, etc.) to cease all biological activity permanently: *she died of pneumonia.* **2.** (of something inanimate) to cease to exist; come to an end: *the memory of her will never die.* **3.** (often foll. by *away, down,* or *out*) to lose strength, power, or energy, esp. by degrees. **4.** (often foll. by *away* or *down*) to become calm or quiet; subside: *the noise slowly died down.* **5.** to stop functioning: *the engine died.* **6.** to languish or pine, as with love, longing, etc. **7.** (usually foll. by *of*) *Informal.* to be nearly overcome (with laughter, boredom, etc.). **8.** *Theol.* to lack spiritual life within the soul, thus separating it from God and leading to eternal punishment. **9.** (*tr.*) to undergo or suffer (a death of a specified kind) (esp. in phrases such as **die a saintly death**). **10.** (foll. by *to*) to become indifferent or apathetic (to): *to die to the world.* **11. never say die.** *Informal.* never give up. **12. die hard.** to cease to exist after resistance or a struggle: *old habits die hard.* **13. die in harness.** to die while still working or active, prior to retirement. **14. be dying.** (foll. by *for* or an infinitive) to be eager or desperate (for something or to do something): *I'm dying to see the new house.* ~See also **dieback, die down, die out.** [Old English *dīegan,* probably of Scandinavian origin; compare Old Norse *deyja,* Old High German *touwen*]

die[2] (daɪ) *n.* **1. a.** a shaped block of metal or other hard material used to cut or form metal in a drop forge, press, or similar device. **b.** a tool of metal, silicon carbide, or other hard material with a conical hole through which wires, rods, or tubes are drawn to reduce their diameter. **2.** an internally-threaded tool for cutting external threads. Compare **tap**[2] (sense 6). **3.** a casting mould giving accurate dimensions and a good surface to the object cast. See also **die-cast. 4.** *Architect.* the dado of a pedestal, usually cubic. **5.** another name for **dice** (sense 2). **6. as straight as a die.** perfectly honest. **7. the die is cast.** the decision that commits a person irrevocably to an action has been taken. [C13 *dee,* from Old French *de,* perhaps from Vulgar Latin *datum* (unattested) a piece in games, n. use of past participle of Latin *dare* to play]

dieback ('daɪˌbæk) *n.* **1.** a disease of trees and shrubs characterized by death of the young shoots, which spreads to the larger branches: caused by injury to the roots or attack by bacteria or fungi. **2.** any similar condition of herbaceous plants. ~*vb.* **die back. 3.** (*intr., adv.*) (of plants) to suffer from dieback.

die-cast *vb.* **-casts, -casting, -cast.** (*tr.*) to shape or form (a metal or plastic object) by introducing molten metal or plastic into a reusable mould, esp. under pressure, by gravity, or by centrifugal force. —**'die-ˌcasting** *n.*

diecious (daɪ'iːʃəs) *adj.* a variant spelling of **dioecious.** —**di'eciously** *adv.*

die down *vb.* (*intr., adv.*) **1.** (of some perennial plants) to wither and die above ground, leaving only the root alive during the winter. **2.** to lose strength or power, esp. by degrees. **3.** to become calm or quiet.

dièdre *French.* (djɛdrə) *n. Mountaineering.* a large shallow groove or corner in a rock face. [C20: dihedral]

dieffenbachia (ˌdiːfᵊn'bækɪə) *n.* any plant of the tropical American evergreen perennial genus *Dieffenbachia,* some species of which are grown as pot plants for their handsome variegated foliage. The plants are poisonous and the sap is extremely acrid: family *Araceae.* [named after Ernst *Dieffenbach* (died 1855), German horticulturist]

die-hard *n.* **1.** a person who resists change or who holds onto an untenable position or outdated attitude. **2.** (*modifier*) obstinately resistant to change. —**'die-ˌhardism** *n.*

dieldrin ('diːldrɪn) *n.* a crystalline insoluble substance, consisting of a chlorinated derivative of naphthalene: a contact insecticide the use of which is now restricted as it accumulates in the tissues of animals. Formula: $C_{12}H_8OCl_6$. [C20: from DIEL(S-AL)D(E)R (REACTION) + -IN]

dielectric (ˌdaɪɪ'lɛktrɪk) *n.* **1.** a substance or medium that can sustain an electric field. **2.** a substance or body of very low electrical conductivity; insulator. ~*adj.* **3.** of, concerned with, or having the properties of a dielectric. [from DIA- + ELECTRIC] —**ˌdie'lectrically** *adv.*

dielectric constant *n.* another name for **relative permittivity.**

dielectric heating *n.* a technique in which an insulator is heated by the application of a high-frequency electric field.

dielectric lens *n. Physics.* a lens constructed of a material that converges or diverges a beam of electromagnetic radiation of radio frequency.

Diels-Alder reaction ('diːlz'ɔːldə) *n. Chem.* a type of chemical reaction in which one organic compound containing conjugated double bonds adds to another containing an ethylenic bond to form a product containing a ring. [C20: named after Otto *Diels* (1876–1954) and Kurt *Alder* (1902–58), German chemists]

diencephalon (ˌdaɪen'sɛfəˌlɒn) *n.* the part of the brain that includes the basal ganglia, thalamus, hypothalamus, and associated areas. —**diencephalic** (ˌdaɪɛnsɪ'fælɪk) *adj.*

diene ('daɪiːn) *n. Chem.* a hydrocarbon that contains two carbon-to-carbon double bonds in its molecules.

-diene *n. combining form.* denoting an organic compound containing two double bonds between carbon atoms: *butadiene.* [from DI-[1] + -ENE]

die out *or* **off** *vb.* (*intr., adv.*) **1.** (of a family, race, etc.) to die one after another until few or none are left. **2.** to become extinct, esp. after a period of gradual decline.

dieresis (daɪ'ɛrɪsɪs) *n., pl.* **-ses** (-ˌsiːz) a variant spelling of **diaeresis.** —**dieretic** (ˌdaɪə'rɛtɪk) *adj.*

diesel ('diːzᵊl) *n.* **1.** See **diesel engine. 2.** a ship, locomotive, lorry, etc., driven by a diesel engine. **3.** *Informal.* short for **diesel oil** (*or* **fuel**). [C19: named after Rudolf *Diesel* (1858–1913), German engineer]

diesel cycle *n.* a four-stroke cycle in which combustion takes place at constant pressure and heat is rejected at constant volume. Compare **Otto cycle.**

diesel-electric *n.* **1.** a locomotive fitted with a diesel engine driving an electric generator that feeds electric traction motors. ~*adj.* **2.** of or relating to such a locomotive or system.

diesel engine *or* **motor** *n.* a type of internal-combustion engine in which atomized fuel oil is sprayed into the cylinder and ignited by compression alone.

diesel-hydraulic *n.* **1.** a locomotive driven by a diesel engine through hydraulic transmission and torque converters. ~*adj.* **2.** of or relating to such a locomotive or system.

diesel oil *or* **fuel** *n.* a fuel obtained from petroleum distillation that is used in diesel engines. It has a relatively low ignition temperature (540°C) and is ignited by the heat of compression. Also called (Brit.): **derv.** See also **cetane number.**

Dies Irae *Latin.* ('diːeɪz 'ɪəraɪ) *n.* **1.** *Christianity.* a famous Latin hymn of the 13th century, describing the Last Judgment. It is used in the Mass for the dead. **2.** a musical setting of this hymn, usually part of a setting of the Requiem. [literally: day of wrath]

diesis ('daɪɪsɪs) *n., pl.* **-ses** (-ˌsiːz). **1.** *Printing.* another name for **double dagger. 2.** *Music.* **a.** (in ancient Greek theory) any interval smaller than a whole tone, esp. a semitone in the Pythagorean scale. **b.** (in modern theory) the discrepancy of pitch in just intonation between an octave and either a succession of four ascending minor thirds (**great diesis**), or a succession of three ascending major thirds (**minor diesis**). [C16: via Latin from Greek: a quarter tone, literally: a sending through, from *diienai;* the double dagger was originally used in musical notation]

dies non ('daɪiːz nɒn) *n. Law.* a day on which no legal business may be transacted. Also called: **dies non juridicus** (dʒʊ'rɪdɪkəs). Compare **juridical days.** [C19: shortened from Latin phrase *diēs nōn jūridicus* literally: day which is not juridical, that is, not reserved for legal affairs]

diestock ('daɪˌstɒk) *n.* the device holding the dies used to cut an external screw thread.

diestrus (daɪ'iːstrəs) *n.* the U.S. spelling of **dioestrus.**

diet[1] ('daɪət) *n.* **1. a.** a specific allowance or selection of food, esp. prescribed to control weight or in disorders in which certain foods are contraindicated: *a salt-free diet; a 900-calorie diet.* **b.** (*as modifier*): *a diet bread.* **2.** the food and drink that a person or animal regularly consumes: *a diet of nuts and water.* **3.** regular activities or occupations. ~*vb.* **4.** (*usually intr.*) to follow or cause to follow a dietary regimen. [C13: from Old French *diete,* from Latin *diaeta,* from Greek *diaita* mode of living, from *diaitan* to direct one's own life] —**'dieter** *n.*

diet[2] ('daɪət) *n.* **1.** (*sometimes cap.*) a legislative assembly in various countries, such as Japan. **2.** (*sometimes cap.*) Also called: **Reichstag.** the assembly of the estates of the Holy Roman Empire. **3.** *Scots Law.* **a.** the date fixed by a court for hearing a case. **b.** a single session of a court. [C15: from Medieval Latin *diēta* public meeting, probably from Latin *diaeta* DIET[1] but associated with Latin *diēs* day]

dietary ('daɪətərɪ, -trɪ) *adj.* **1.** of or relating to a diet. ~*n., pl.* **-taries. 2.** a regulated diet. **3.** a system of dieting.

dietary fibre *n.* fibrous substances in fruits and vegetables, such as the structural polymers of cell walls, consumption of which aids digestion and is believed to help prevent certain diseases. Also called: **roughage.**

dietetic (ˌdaɪɪ'tɛtɪk) *or* **dietetical** *adj.* **1.** denoting or relating to diet or the regulation of food intake. **2.** prepared for special dietary requirements. —**ˌdie'tetically** *adv.*

dietetics (ˌdaɪɪ'tɛtɪks) *n.* (*functioning as sing.*) the scientific study and regulation of food intake and preparation.

diethylene glycol (daɪ'ɛθɪˌliːn 'glaɪkɒl) *n.* a colourless soluble liquid used as an antifreeze and solvent. Formula: $(C_2H_4OH)_2O$.

diethyl ether (daɪ'ɛθɪl) *n.* a formal name for **ether** (sense 1).

diethylstilboestrol (daɪˌɛθɪlstɪl'bɛstrɒl, -ˌiːθaɪl-) *n.* another name for **stilboestrol.**

dietitian *or* **dietician** (ˌdaɪɪ'tɪʃən) *n.* a person who specializes in dietetics.

Dieu et mon droit *French.* (djø e mɔ̃ drwa) God and my right: motto of the Royal Arms of Great Britain.

diff. *abbrev. for:* **1.** difference. **2.** different.

differ ('dɪfə) *vb.* (*intr.*) **1.** (often foll. by *from*) to be dissimilar in quality, nature, or degree (to); vary (from). **2.** (often foll. by *from* or *with*) to be at variance (with); disagree (with). **3.** *Dialect.* to quarrel or dispute. **4. agree to differ.** to end an argument amicably while maintaining differences of opinion. [C14: from Latin *differre,* literally: to bear off in different directions, hence scatter, put off, be different, from *dis-* apart + *ferre* to bear]

difference (ˈdɪfərəns, ˈdɪfrəns) *n.* **1.** the state or quality of being unlike. **2.** a specific instance of being unlike. **3.** a distinguishing mark or feature. **4.** a significant change in a situation: *the difference in her is amazing.* **5.** a disagreement or argument: *he had a difference with his wife.* **6.** a degree of distinctness, as between two people or things. **7. a.** the result of the subtraction of one number, quantity, etc., from another. **b.** the single number that when added to the subtrahend gives the minuend; remainder. **8.** *Logic.* another name for **differentia. 9.** *Maths.* (of two sets) **a.** the set of members of the first that are not members of the second. Symbol: A – B **b. symmetric difference.** the set of members of one but not both of the given sets. Often symbolized: A ⊕ B **10.** *Heraldry.* an addition to the arms of a family to represent a younger branch. **11. make a difference. a.** to have an effect. **b.** to treat differently. **12. split the difference. a.** to settle a dispute by a compromise. **b.** to divide a remainder equally. **13. with a difference.** with some peculiarly distinguishing quality, good or bad. *~vb.* (*tr.*) **14.** *Rare.* to distinguish. **15.** *Heraldry.* to add a charge to (arms) to differentiate a branch of a family.

difference threshold *n. Psychol.* the minimum difference between two stimuli that is just detectable by a person.

different (ˈdɪfərənt, ˈdɪfrənt) *adj.* **1.** partly or completely unlike. **2.** not identical or the same; other: *he wears a different tie every day.* **3.** out of the ordinary; unusual. —ˈ**differently** *adv.* —ˈ**differentness** *n.*

▷**Usage.** The constructions *different from, different to,* and *different than* are all found in the works of writers of English during the past. Nowadays, however, the most widely acceptable preposition to use after *different* is *from. Different to,* while not uncommon in British English, is considered by many careful writers and speakers to be incorrect, or less acceptable. *Different than* is a standard construction in American English, and has the advantage of conciseness when a clause or phrase follows, as in *this result is only slightly different than in the U.S.* As, however, this idiom is not regarded as totally acceptable in British usage, it is preferable either to use *different from: this result is only slightly different from that obtained in the U.S.* or to rephrase the sentence: *this result differs only slightly from that in the U.S.*

differentia (ˌdɪfəˈrɛnʃɪə) *n., pl.* **-tiae** (-ʃɪˌiː). *Logic.* a feature by which two subclasses of the same class of named objects can be distinguished. Also called: **difference.** [C19: from Latin: diversity, DIFFERENCE]

differentiable (ˌdɪfəˈrɛnʃɪəbᵊl) *adj.* **1.** capable of being differentiated. **2.** *Maths.* possessing a derivative. —ˌ**differˌentiaˈbility** *n.*

differential (ˌdɪfəˈrɛnʃəl) *adj.* **1.** of, relating to, or using a difference. **2.** constituting a difference; distinguishing. **3.** *Maths.* of, containing, or involving one or more derivatives or differentials. **4.** *Physics, engineering.* relating to, operating on, or based on the difference between two opposing effects, motions, forces, etc.: *differential amplifier.* *~n.* **5.** a factor that differentiates between two comparable things. **6.** *Maths.* **a.** an increment in a given function, expressed as the product of the derivative of that function and the corresponding increment in the independent variable. **b.** an increment in a given function of two or more variables, $f(x_1, x_2, \dots x_n)$, expressed as the sum of the products of each partial derivative and the increment in the corresponding variable. **7.** an epicyclic gear train that permits two shafts to rotate at different speeds while being driven by a third shaft. See also **differential gear. 8.** *Chiefly Brit.* the difference between rates of pay for different types of labour, esp. when forming a pay structure within an industry. **9.** (in commerce) a difference in rates, esp. between comparable labour services or transportation routes. —ˌ**differˈentially** *adv.*

differential calculus *n.* the branch of calculus concerned with the study, evaluation, and use of derivatives and differentials. Compare **integral calculus.**

differential coefficient *n. Maths.* another name for **derivative.**

differential equation *n.* an equation containing differentials or derivatives of a function of one independent variable. A **partial differential equation** results from a function of more than one variable.

differential gear *n.* the epicyclic gear mounted in the driving axle of a road vehicle that permits one driving wheel to rotate faster than the other, as when cornering.

differential operator *n.* the mathematical operator del ∇, used in vector analysis, where $\nabla = \mathbf{i}\partial/\partial x + \mathbf{j}\partial/\partial y + \mathbf{k}\partial/\partial z$, ***i, j,*** and ***k*** being unit vectors and $\partial/\partial x$, $\partial/\partial y$, and $\partial/\partial z$ the partial derivatives of a function in *x, y,* and *z.*

differential windlass *n.* a windlass employing the velocity ratio incurred in unwinding from a small drum while winding onto a larger drum rotating at a common speed. Also called: **Chinese windlass.**

differentiate (ˌdɪfəˈrɛnʃɪˌeɪt) *vb.* **1.** (*tr.*) to serve to distinguish between. **2.** (when *intr.*, often foll. by *between*) to perceive, show, or make a difference (in or between); discriminate. **3.** (*intr.*) to become dissimilar or distinct. **4.** *Maths.* to perform a differentiation on (a quantity, expression, etc.). **5.** (*intr.*) (of unspecialized cells, etc.) to change during development to more specialized forms. —ˌ**differˈentiˌator** *n.*

differentiation (ˌdɪfəˌrɛnʃɪˈeɪʃən) *n.* **1.** the act, process, or result of differentiating. **2.** *Maths.* an operation used in calculus in which the derivative of a function or variable is determined; the inverse of **integration** (sense 6). **3.** any process in which a mixture of materials separates out partially or completely into its constituent parts, as in the cooling and solidification of a magma into two or more different rock types or in the gradual separation of an originally homogeneous earth into crust, mantle, and core.

difficult (ˈdɪfɪkᵊlt) *adj.* **1.** not easy to do; requiring effort: *a difficult job.* **2.** not easy to understand or solve; intricate: *a difficult problem.* **3.** hard to deal with; troublesome: *a difficult child.* **4.** not easily convinced, pleased, or satisfied. **5.** full of hardships or trials: *difficult times ahead.* [C14: back formation from DIFFICULTY] —ˈ**difficultly** *adv.*

difficulty (ˈdɪfɪkᵊltɪ) *n., pl.* **-ties. 1.** the state or quality of being difficult. **2.** a task, problem, etc., that is hard to deal with. **3.** (*often pl.*) a troublesome or embarrassing situation, esp. a financial one. **4.** a dispute or disagreement. **5.** (*often pl.*) an objection or obstacle: *he always makes difficulties.* **6.** a trouble or source of trouble; worry. **7.** lack of ease; awkwardness: *he could run only with difficulty.* [C14: from Latin *difficultās,* from *difficilis* difficult, from *dis-* not + *facilis* easy, FACILE]

diffident (ˈdɪfɪdənt) *adj.* lacking self-confidence; timid; shy. [C15: from Latin *diffīdere* to distrust, from *dis-* not + *fīdere* to trust] —ˈ**diffidence** *n.* —ˈ**diffidently** *adv.*

diffract (dɪˈfrækt) *vb.* to undergo or cause to undergo diffraction: *to diffract light; the light diffracts at a slit.* —**difˈfractive** *adj.* —**difˈfractively** *adv.* —**difˈfractiveness** *n.*

diffraction (dɪˈfrækʃən) *n.* **1.** *Physics.* a deviation in the direction of a wave at the edge of an obstacle in its path. **2.** any phenomenon caused by diffraction and interference of light, such as the formation of light and dark fringes by the passage of light through a small aperture. **3.** deflection of sound waves caused by an obstacle or by nonhomogeneity of a medium. [C17: from New Latin *diffractiō* a breaking to pieces, from Latin *diffringere* to shatter, from *dis-* apart + *frangere* to break]

diffraction grating *n.* a glass plate or a mirror with a large number of equidistant parallel lines or grooves on its surface. It causes diffraction of transmitted or reflected light, ultraviolet radiation, or x-rays.

diffraction pattern *n. Physics.* the distinctive pattern of light and dark fringes, rings, etc., formed by diffraction.

diffractometer (ˌdɪfrækˈtɒmɪtə) *n. Physics.* an instrument used in studying diffraction, as in the determination of crystal structure by diffraction of x-rays.

diffuse *vb.* (dɪˈfjuːz). **1.** to spread or cause to spread in all directions. **2.** to undergo or cause to undergo diffusion. **3.** to scatter or cause to scatter; disseminate; disperse. *~adj.* (dɪˈfjuːs). **4.** spread out over a wide area. **5.** lacking conciseness. **6.** (esp. of some creeping stems) spreading loosely over a large area. **7.** characterized by or exhibiting diffusion: *diffuse light; diffuse reflection.* **8.** *Botany.* (of plant growth) occurring throughout a tissue. [C15: from Latin *diffūsus* spread abroad, from *diffundere* to pour forth, from *dis-* away + *fundere* to pour] —**diffusely** (dɪˈfjuːslɪ) *adv.* —**difˈfuseness** *n.* —**diffusible** (dɪˈfjuːzəbᵊl) *adj.* —**difˌfusiˈbility** *or* **difˈfusibleness** *n.*

diffused junction *n.* a semiconductor junction formed by diffusing acceptor or donor impurity atoms into semiconductor material to form regions of p-type or n-type conductivity. See also **photolithography** (sense 2). Compare **alloyed junction.**

diffuser *or* **diffusor** (dɪˈfjuːzə) *n.* **1.** a person or thing that diffuses. **2.** a part of a lighting fixture consisting of a translucent or frosted covering or of a rough reflector: used to scatter the light and prevent glare. **3.** a cone, wedge, or baffle placed in front of the diaphragm of a loudspeaker to diffuse the sound waves. **4.** a duct, esp. in a wind tunnel or jet engine, that widens gradually in the direction of flow to reduce the speed and increase the pressure of the air or fluid. **5.** *Photog.* a light-scattering medium, such as a screen of fine fabric, placed in the path of a source of light to reduce the sharpness of shadows and thus soften the lighting. **6.** a perforated plate or similar device for distributing compressed air in the aeration of sewage.

diffusion (dɪˈfjuːʒən) *n.* **1.** the act or process of diffusing or being diffused; dispersion. **2.** verbosity. **3.** *Physics.* **a.** the random thermal motion of atoms, molecules, clusters of atoms, etc., in gases, liquids, and some solids. **b.** the transfer of atoms or molecules by their random motion from one part of a medium to another. **4.** *Physics.* the transmission or reflection of electromagnetic radiation, esp. light, in which the radiation is scattered in many directions and not directly reflected or refracted; scattering. **5.** Also called: **diffusivity.** *Physics.* the degree to which the directions of propagation of reverberant sound waves differ from point to point in an enclosure. **6.** *Anthropol.* the transmission of social institutions, skills, and myths from one culture to another.

diffusion coefficient *or* **constant** *n.* the rate at which a diffusing substance is transported between opposite faces of a unit cube of a system when there is unit concentration difference between them. Symbol: *D* Also called: **diffusivity.**

diffusion line *or* **range** *n.* a range of ready-to-wear clothes by a well-known designer, made in less expensive fabrics than the main collection.

diffusive (dɪˈfjuːsɪv) *adj.* characterized by diffusion. —**difˈfusively** *adv.* —**difˈfusiveness** *n.*

diffusivity (ˌdɪfjuːˈsɪvɪtɪ) *n.* **1.** a measure of the ability of a substance to transmit a difference in temperature; expressed as the thermal conductivity divided by the product of specific heat capacity and density. **2.** *Physics.* **a.** the ability of a substance to permit or undergo diffusion. **b.** another name for **diffusion coefficient.** **3.** another name for **diffusion** (sense 5).

dig (dɪg) *vb.* **digs, digging, dug.** **1.** (when *tr.*, often foll. by *up*) to cut into, break up, and turn over or remove (earth, soil, etc.), esp. with a spade. **2.** to form or excavate (a hole, tunnel, passage, etc.) by digging, usually with an implement or (of animals) with feet, claws, etc.: *to dig a tunnel.* **3.** (often foll. by *through*) to make or force (one's way), esp. by removing obstructions: *he dug his way through the crowd.* **4.** (*tr.*; often foll. by *out* or *up*) to obtain by digging: *to dig potatoes; to dig up treasure.* **5.** (*tr.*; often foll. by *out* or *up*) to find or discover by effort or searching: *to dig out unexpected facts.* **6.** (*tr.*; foll. by *in* or *into*) to thrust or jab (a sharp instrument, weapon, etc.); poke: *he dug his spurs into the horse's side.* **7.** (*tr.*; foll. by *in* or *into*) to mix (compost, etc.) with soil by digging. **8.** (*tr.*) *Informal.* to like, understand, or appreciate. **9.** (*intr.*) *U.S. slang.* to work hard, esp. for an examination. **10.** (*intr.*) *Brit. informal.* to have lodgings: *I dig in South London.* ~*n.* **11.** the act of digging. **12.** a thrust or poke, esp. in the ribs. **13.** a cutting or sarcastic remark. **14.** *Informal.* an archaeological excavation. ~See also **dig in, digs.** [C13 *diggen,* of uncertain origin]

Dig (dɪg) *n. N.Z. informal.* short for **Digger** (sense 1).

dig. *abbrev. for* digest (book or summary).

digamma (daɪˈgæmə) *n.* a letter of the Greek alphabet (Ϝ) that became obsolete before the classical period of the language. It represented a semivowel like English *W* and was used as a numeral in later stages of written Greek, and passed into the Roman alphabet as *F.* [C17: via Latin from Greek, from DI-[1] + GAMMA; from its shape, which suggests one gamma upon another]

digamy (ˈdɪgəmɪ) *n., pl.* **-mies.** a second marriage contracted after the termination of the first by death or divorce. Also called: **deuterogamy.** Compare **bigamy.** [C17: from Late Latin *digamia,* from Greek, from DI-[1] + *gamos* marriage] —ˈ**digamist** *n.* —ˈ**digamous** *adj.*

digastric (daɪˈgæstrɪk) *adj.* **1.** (of certain muscles) having two fleshy portions joined by a tendon. ~*n.* **2.** a muscle of the mandible that assists in lowering the lower jaw. [C17: from New Latin *digastricus* (with two bellies), from DI-[1] + *gastricus* gastric, from Greek *gastēr* belly]

digenesis (daɪˈdʒɛnɪsɪs) *n. Zoology.* another name for **alternation of generations.**

digenetic (ˌdaɪdʒɪˈnɛtɪk) *adj. Zoology.* **1.** of or relating to digenesis. **2.** (of parasites) having two hosts.

digest *vb.* (dɪˈdʒɛst, daɪ-). **1.** to subject (food) to a process of digestion. **2.** (*tr.*) to assimilate mentally. **3.** *Chem.* to soften or disintegrate or be softened or disintegrated by the action of heat, moisture, or chemicals; decompose. **4.** (*tr.*) to arrange in a methodical or systematic order; classify. **5.** (*tr.*) to reduce to a summary. **6.** (*tr.*) *Archaic.* to tolerate. ~*n.* (ˈdaɪdʒɛst). **7.** a comprehensive and systematic compilation of information or material, often condensed. **8.** a magazine, periodical, etc., that summarizes news of current events. **9.** a compilation of rules of law based on decided cases. [C14: from Late Latin *dīgesta* writings grouped under various heads, from Latin *dīgerere* to divide, from *di-* apart + *gerere* to bear]

digestant (dɪˈdʒɛstənt, daɪ-) *n.* a substance, such as hydrochloric acid or a bile salt, that promotes or aids digestion, esp. one used therapeutically.

digester (dɪˈdʒɛstə, daɪ-) *n.* **1.** *Chem.* an apparatus or vessel, such as an autoclave, in which digestion is carried out. **2.** a less common word for **digestant.** **3.** a person or thing that digests.

digestible (dɪˈdʒɛstəbᵊl, daɪ-) *adj.* capable of being digested or easy to digest. —**diˌgestiˈbility** *or* **diˈgestibleness** *n.* —**diˈgestibly** *adv.*

digestif *French.* (diʒɛstif) *n.* something, esp. a drink, taken as an aid to digestion, either before or after a meal.

digestion (dɪˈdʒɛstʃən, daɪ-) *n.* **1.** the act or process in living organisms of breaking down ingested food material into easily absorbed and assimilated substances by the action of enzymes and other agents. **2.** mental assimilation, esp. of ideas. **3.** *Bacteriol.* the decomposition of sewage by the action of bacteria. **4.** *Chem.* the treatment of material with heat, solvents, chemicals, etc., to cause softening or decomposition. [C14: from Old French, from Latin *dīgestiō* a dissolving, digestion] —**diˈgestional** *adj.*

digestive (dɪˈdʒɛstɪv, daɪ-) *or* **digestant** (daɪˈdʒɛstənt) *adj.* **1.** relating to, aiding, or subjecting to digestion: *a digestive enzyme.* ~*n.* **2.** a less common word for **digestant.** **3.** short for **digestive biscuit.** —**diˈgestively** *adv.*

digestive biscuit *n.* a round semisweet biscuit made from wholemeal flour.

digged (dɪgd) *vb. Archaic.* a past tense of **dig.**

digger (ˈdɪgə) *n.* **1.** a person, animal, or machine that digs. **2.** a miner, esp. one who digs for gold. **3.** a tool or part of a machine used for excavation, esp. a mechanical digger fitted with a head for digging trenches.

Digger (ˈdɪgə) *n.* **1.** (*sometimes not cap.*) *Slang.* **a.** an Australian or New Zealander, esp. a soldier: often used as a term of address. **b.** (*as modifier*): *a Digger accent.* **2.** one of a number of tribes of America whose diet was largely composed of roots dug out of the ground.

digger wasp *n.* any solitary wasp of the families *Sphecidae* and *Pamphilidae* that digs nest holes in the ground, rotten wood, or a hollow stem and stocks them with live insects for the larvae.

diggings (ˈdɪgɪŋz) *pl. n.* **1.** (*functioning as pl.*) material that has been dug out. **2.** (*functioning as sing. or pl.*) a place where mining, esp. gold mining, has taken place. **3.** (*functioning as pl.*) *Brit. informal.* a less common name for **digs.**

dight (daɪt) *vb.* **dights, dighting, dight** *or* **dighted.** (*tr.*) *Archaic.* to adorn or equip, as for battle. [Old English *dihtan* to compose, from Latin *dictāre* to DICTATE]

dig in *vb.* (*adv.*) **1.** *Military.* to provide (a defensive position) by digging foxholes, trenches, etc. **2.** *Informal.* to entrench (oneself) firmly. **3.** (*intr.*) *Informal.* to defend or maintain a position firmly, as in an argument. **4.** (*intr.*) *Informal.* to begin vigorously to eat: *don't wait, just dig in.* **5. dig one's heels in.** *Informal.* to refuse stubbornly to move or be persuaded.

digit (ˈdɪdʒɪt) *n.* **1.** a finger or toe. **2.** Also called: **figure.** any of the ten Arabic numerals from 0 to 9. **3.** another name for **finger** (sense 4). **4.** *Astronomy.* one twelfth of the diameter of the sun or moon, used to express the magnitude of an eclipse. [C15: from Latin *digitus* toe, finger]

digital (ˈdɪdʒɪtᵊl) *adj.* **1.** of, relating to, resembling, or possessing a digit or digits. **2.** performed with the fingers. **3.** representing data as a series of numerical values. **4.** displaying information as numbers rather than by a pointer moving over a dial: *a digital voltmeter; digital read-out.* **5.** *Electronics.* responding to discrete values of input voltage and producing discrete output voltage levels, as in a logic circuit: *digital circuit.* **6.** a less common word for **digitate.** ~*n.* **7.** *Music.* one of the keys on the manuals of an organ or on a piano, harpsichord, etc. —ˈ**digitally** *adv.*

digital audio tape *n.* magnetic tape on which sound is recorded digitally, giving high-fidelity reproduction. Abbrev.: **DAT.**

digital clock *or* **watch** *n.* a clock or watch in which the hours, minutes, and sometimes seconds are indicated by digits, rather than by hands on a dial. Compare **analogue clock.**

digital computer *n.* an electronic computer in which the input is discrete rather than continuous, consisting of combinations of numbers, letters, and other characters written in an appropriate programming language and represented internally in binary notation. Compare **analog computer.**

digitalin (ˌdɪdʒɪˈteɪlɪn) *n.* a poisonous amorphous white glycoside extracted from digitalis leaves and used in treating heart disease. Formula: $C_{36}H_{56}O_{14}$. [C19: from DIGITAL(IS) + -IN]

digitalis (ˌdɪdʒɪˈteɪlɪs) *n.* **1.** any Eurasian scrophulariaceous plants of the genus *Digitalis,* such as the foxglove, having bell-shaped flowers and a basal rosette of leaves. **2.** a drug prepared from the dried leaves or seeds of the foxglove: a mixture of glycosides used medicinally as a heart stimulant. [C17: from New Latin, from Latin: relating to a finger (referring to the corollas of the flower); based on German *Fingerhut* foxglove, literally: finger-hat]

digitalism (ˈdɪdʒɪtəˌlɪzəm) *n.* a serious condition resulting from digitalis poisoning, characterized by nausea, vomiting, and a disturbance in heart rhythm or rate.

digitalize *or* **digitalise** (ˈdɪdʒɪtəˌlaɪz) *vb.* (*tr.*) to administer digitoxin or digoxin to (a patient) for the treatment of certain heart disorders. —ˌ**digitaliˈzation** *or* ˌ**digitaliˈsation** *n.*

digital mapping *n.* a method of preparing maps in which the data is stored in a computer for ease of access and updating. —**digital map** *n.*

digital recording *n.* a sound recording process that converts audio or analogue signals into a series of pulses that correspond to the voltage level. These can be stored on tape or on any other memory system.

digitate (ˈdɪdʒɪˌteɪt) *or* **digitated** *adj.* **1.** (of compound leaves) having the leaflets in the form of a spread hand. **2.** (of animals) having digits or corresponding parts. —ˈ**digiˌtately** *adv.* —ˌ**digiˈtation** *n.*

digitiform (ˈdɪdʒɪtɪˌfɔːm) *adj.* shaped like a finger.

digitigrade (ˈdɪdʒɪtɪˌgreɪd) *adj.* **1.** (of dogs, cats, horses, etc.) walking so that only the toes touch the ground. ~*n.* **2.** a digitigrade animal.

digitize *or* **digitise** (ˈdɪdʒɪˌtaɪz) *vb.* (*tr.*) to transcribe (data) into a digital form so that it can be directly processed by a computer. —ˌ**digitiˈzation** *or* ˌ**digitiˈsation** *n.* —ˈ**digiˌtizer** *or* ˈ**digiˌtiser** *n.*

digitoxin (ˌdɪdʒɪˈtɒksɪn) *n.* a white toxic bitter-tasting glycoside, extracted from digitalis leaves and used in the treatment of heart failure. Formula: $C_{41}H_{64}O_{13}$. [from DIGI(TALIS) + TOXIN]

digitron (ˈdɪdʒɪˌtrɒn) *n. Electronics.* a type of tube, for displaying information, having a common anode and several cathodes shaped in the form of characters, which can be lit by a glow discharge. Also called: **Nixie tube.** [C20: from DIGIT + -TRON]

digitule (ˈdɪdʒɪtjuːl) *n. Zoology.* any small finger-like process.

diglossia (daɪˈglɒsɪə) *n. Linguistics.* the existence in a language of a high, or socially prestigious, and a low, or everyday, form, as German and Swiss German in Switzerland. [C20: New Latin, via French, from Greek *diglōssos* speaking two languages: see DIGLOT]

diglot (ˈdaɪglɒt) *adj.* **1.** a less common word for **bilingual.** ~*n.* **2.** a bilingual book. [C19: from Greek (Attic) *diglōttos,* from DI-[1] + *glōtta* tongue] —**diˈglottic** *adj.*

dignified (ˈdɪgnɪˌfaɪd) *adj.* characterized by dignity of manner or appearance; stately; noble. —**ˈdigniˌfiedly** *adv.* —**ˈdigniˌfiedness** *n.*

dignify (ˈdɪgnɪˌfaɪ) *vb.* **-fies, -fying, -fied.** (*tr.*) **1.** to invest with honour or dignity; ennoble. **2.** to add distinction to: *the meeting was dignified by the minister.* **3.** to add a semblance of dignity to, esp. by the use of a pretentious name or title: *she dignifies every plant with its Latin name.* [C15: from Old French *dignifier,* from Late Latin *dignificāre,* from Latin *dignus* worthy + *facere* to make]

dignitary (ˈdɪgnɪtərɪ, -trɪ) *n., pl.* **-taries.** a person of high official position or rank, esp. in government or the church.

dignity (ˈdɪgnɪtɪ) *n., pl.* **-ties.** **1.** a formal, stately, or grave bearing: *he entered the room with great dignity.* **2.** the state or quality of being worthy of honour: *the dignity of manual labour.* **3.** relative importance; rank: *he is next in dignity to the mayor.* **4.** sense of self-importance (often in the phrases **stand** (or **be**) **on one's dignity, beneath one's dignity**). **5.** high rank, esp. in government or the church. **6.** a person of high rank or such persons collectively. [C13: from Old French *dignite,* from Latin *dignitās* merit, from *dignus* worthy]

digonal (daɪˈgəʊnəl) *adj. Maths.* of or relating to a symmetry operation in which the original figure is reconstructed after a 180° turn about an axis.

digoneutic (ˌdaɪgəˈnjuːtɪk) *adj. Zoology.* producing offspring twice yearly. [C19: from DI-[1] + Greek *gonein* to beget] —**ˌdigoˈneutism** *n.*

digoxin (daɪˈdʒɒksɪn) *n.* a glycoside extracted from digitalis leaves and used in the treatment of heart failure.

digraph (ˈdaɪgrɑːf, -græf) *n.* a combination of two letters or characters used to represent a single speech sound such as *gh* in English *tough.* Compare **ligature** (sense 5), **diphthong.** —**digraphic** (daɪˈgræfɪk) *adj.*

digress (daɪˈgrɛs) *vb.* (*intr.*) **1.** to depart from the main subject in speech or writing. **2.** to wander from one's path or main direction. [C16: from Latin *dīgressus* turned aside, from *dīgredī,* from *dis-* apart + *gradī* to go] —**diˈgresser** *n.*

digression (daɪˈgrɛʃən) *n.* an act or instance of digressing from a main subject in speech or writing. —**diˈgressional** *adj.*

digressive (daɪˈgrɛsɪv) *adj.* characterized by digression or tending to digress. —**diˈgressively** *adv.* —**diˈgressiveness** *n.*

digs (dɪgz) *pl. n. Brit. informal.* lodgings. [C19: shortened from DIGGINGS, perhaps referring to where one *digs* or works, but see also DIG IN]

dihedral (daɪˈhiːdrəl) *adj.* **1.** having or formed by two intersecting planes; two-sided: *a dihedral angle.* ~*n.* **2.** Also called: **dihedron, dihedral angle.** the figure formed by two intersecting planes. **3.** the U.S. name for **corner** (sense 11). **4.** the upward inclination of an aircraft wing in relation to the lateral axis. Compare **anhedral.**

dihedron (daɪˈhiːdrən) *n.* another name for **dihedral** (sense 2).

dihybrid (daɪˈhaɪbrɪd) *n. Genetics.* the offspring of two individuals that differ with respect to two pairs of genes; an individual heterozygous for two pairs of genes. —**diˈhybridism** *n.*

dihydric (daɪˈhaɪdrɪk) *adj.* (of an alcohol) containing two hydroxyl groups per molecule.

dik-dik (ˈdɪkˌdɪk) *n.* any small antelope of the genus *Madoqua,* inhabiting semiarid regions of Africa, having an elongated muzzle and, in the male, small stout horns. [C19: an East African name, probably of imitative origin]

dike (daɪk) *n., vb.* a variant spelling of **dyke.**

dikkop (ˈdɪkəp) *n.* a South African name for **stone curlew.** [from Afrikaans, from *dik* thick + *kop* head]

diktat (ˈdɪktɑːt) *n.* **1.** decree or settlement imposed, esp. by a ruler or a victorious nation. **2.** a dogmatic statement. [German: dictation, from Latin *dictātum,* from *dictāre* to DICTATE]

dilapidate (dɪˈlæpɪˌdeɪt) *vb.* to fall or cause to fall into ruin or decay. [C16: from Latin *dīlapidāre* to scatter, waste, from *dis-* apart + *lapidāre* to stone, throw stones, from *lapis* stone]

dilapidated (dɪˈlæpɪˌdeɪtɪd) *adj.* falling to pieces or in a state of disrepair; shabby.

dilapidation (dɪˌlæpɪˈdeɪʃən) *n.* **1.** the state of being or becoming dilapidated. **2.** (*often pl.*) *Property law.* **a.** the state of disrepair of premises at the end of a tenancy due to neglect. **b.** the extent of repairs necessary to such premises. —**diˈlapiˌdator** *n.*

dilatancy (daɪˈleɪtənsɪ, dɪ-) *n.* a phenomenon caused by the nature of the stacking or fitting together of particles or granules in a heterogeneous system, such as the solidification of certain sols under pressure, and the thixotropy of certain gels.

dilatant (daɪˈleɪtᵊnt, dɪ-) *adj.* **1.** tending to dilate; dilating. **2.** *Physics.* of, concerned with, or exhibiting dilatancy. ~*n.* **3.** something, such as a catheter, that causes dilation.

dilate (daɪˈleɪt, dɪ-) *vb.* **1.** to expand or cause to expand; make or become wider or larger: *the pupil of the eye dilates in the dark.* **2.** (*intr.*; often foll. by *on* or *upon*) to speak or write at length; expand or enlarge. [C14: from Latin *dīlātāre* to spread out, amplify, from *dis-* apart + *lātus* wide] —**diˈlatable** *adj.* —**diˌlataˈbility** *or* **diˈlatableness** *n.* —**diˈlation** *or* **dilatation** (ˌdaɪləˈteɪʃən, ˌdɪ-) *n.* —**ˌdilaˈtational** *adj.* —**dilative** (daɪˈleɪtɪv, dɪ-) *adj.*

dilatometer (ˌdɪləˈtɒmɪtə) *n.* any instrument for measuring changes in dimension: often a glass bulb fitted with a long stopper through which a capillary tube runs, used for measuring volume changes of liquids. —**dilatometric** (ˌdɪlətəˈmɛtrɪk) *adj.* —**ˌdilatoˈmetrically** *adv.* —**ˌdilaˈtometry** *n.*

dilator, dilater (daɪˈleɪtə, dɪ-), *or* **dilatator** (ˌdaɪləˈteɪtə, ˌdɪ-) *n.* **1.** something that dilates an object, esp. a surgical instrument for dilating a bodily cavity. **2.** a muscle that expands an orifice or dilates an organ.

dilatory (ˈdɪlətərɪ, -trɪ) *adj.* **1.** tending or inclined to delay or waste time. **2.** intended or designed to waste time or defer action. [C15: from Late Latin *dīlātōrius* inclined to delay, from *differre* to postpone; see DIFFER] —**ˈdilatorily** *adv.* —**ˈdilatoriness** *n.*

dildo *or* **dildoe** (ˈdɪldəʊ) *n., pl.* **-dos** *or* **-does.** an object used as a substitute for an erect penis. [C17: of unknown origin]

dilemma (dɪˈlɛmə, daɪ-) *n.* **1.** a situation necessitating a choice between two equal, esp. equally undesirable, alternatives. **2.** a problem that seems incapable of a solution. **3.** *Logic.* a form of argument one of whose premises is the conjunction of two conditional statements and the other of which affirms the disjunction of their antecedents, and whose conclusion is the disjunction of their consequents. Its form is *if p then q and if r then s; either p or r so either q or s.* **4. on the horns of a dilemma. a.** faced with the choice between two equally unpalatable alternatives. **b.** in an awkward situation. [C16: via Latin from Greek, from DI-[1] + *lēmma* assumption, proposition, from *lambanein* to take, grasp] —**dilemmatic** (ˌdɪlɪˈmætɪk, ˌdaɪlɪ-) *or* **dilˈemmic** *adj.*

dilettante (ˌdɪlɪˈtɑːntɪ) *n., pl.* **-tantes** *or* **-tanti** (-ˈtɑːntɪ). **1.** a person whose interest in a subject is superficial rather than professional. **2.** a person who loves the arts. ~*adj.* **3.** of or characteristic of a dilettante. [C18: from Italian, from *dilettare* to delight, from Latin *dēlectāre*] —**ˌdiletˈtantish** *or* **ˌdiletˈtanteish** *adj.* —**ˌdiletˈtantism** *or* **ˌdiletˈtanteism** *n.*

diligence[1] (ˈdɪlɪdʒəns) *n.* **1.** steady and careful application. **2.** proper attention or care. **3.** *Law.* the degree of care required in a given situation. [C14: from Latin *dīligentia* care, attentiveness]

diligence[2] (ˈdɪlɪdʒəns; *French* diliʒɑ̃s) *n. History.* a stagecoach. [C18: from French, shortened from *carosse de diligence,* literally: coach of speed]

diligent (ˈdɪlɪdʒənt) *adj.* **1.** careful and persevering in carrying out tasks or duties. **2.** carried out with care and perseverance: *diligent work.* [C14: from Old French, from Latin *dīligere* to value, from *dis-* apart + *legere* to read] —**ˈdiligently** *adv.*

dill (dɪl) *n.* **1.** an umbelliferous aromatic Eurasian plant, *Anethum graveolens,* with finely dissected leaves and umbrella-shaped clusters of yellow flowers. **2.** the leaves or seedlike fruits of this plant, used for flavouring in pickles, soups, etc., and in medicine. **3.** *Slang, chiefly Austral. and N.Z.* a fool; idiot. [Old English *dile;* related to Old High German *tilli*] —**ˈdilly** *adj.*

dill pickle *n.* a pickled cucumber flavoured with dill.

dilly (ˈdɪlɪ) *n., pl.* **-lies.** *Slang, chiefly U.S. and Canadian.* a person or thing that is remarkable. [C20: perhaps from girl's proper name *Dilly*]

dilly bag *n. Austral.* a small bag, esp. one made of plaited grass, etc., often used for carrying food. Sometimes shortened to **dilly.** [from native Australian *dilly* small bag or basket]

dilly-dally (ˌdɪlɪˈdælɪ) *vb.* **-lies, -lying, -lied.** (*intr.*) *Informal.* to loiter or vacillate. [C17: by reduplication from DALLY]

diluent (ˈdɪljʊənt) *adj.* **1.** causing dilution or serving to dilute. ~*n.* **2.** a substance used for or causing dilution. [C18: from Latin *dīluēns* dissolving; see DILUTE]

dilute (daɪˈluːt) *vb.* **1.** to make or become less concentrated, esp. by adding water or a thinner. **2.** to make or become weaker in force, effect, etc.: *he diluted his story.* ~*adj.* **3.** *Chem.* **a.** (of a solution, suspension, mixture, etc.) having a low concentration or a concentration that has been reduced by admixture. **b.** (of a substance) present in solution, esp. a weak solution in water: *dilute acetic acid.* [C16: from Latin *dīluere,* from *dis-* apart + *-luere,* from *lavāre* to wash] —**ˌdiluˈtee** *n.* —**diˈluter** *n.*

dilution (daɪˈluːʃən) *n.* **1.** the act of diluting or state of being diluted. **2.** a diluted solution.

diluvial (daɪˈluːvɪəl, dɪ-) *or* **diluvian** *adj.* **1.** of or connected with a deluge, esp. with the great Flood described in the book of Genesis. **2.** of or relating to diluvium. [C17: from Late Latin *dīluviālis;* see DILUVIUM]

diluvialism (daɪˈluːvɪəlɪzm) *n.* the theory, generally abandoned in the mid-19th century, that the earth's surface was shaped by the biblical flood.

diluvium (daɪˈluːvɪəm, dɪ-) *n., pl.* **-via** (-vɪə). *Geology.* a former name for **drift** (sense 12). [C19: from Latin: flood, from *dīluere* to wash away; see DILUTE]

dim (dɪm) *adj.* **dimmer, dimmest.** **1.** badly illuminated: *a dim room.* **2.** not clearly seen; indistinct; faint: *a dim shape.* **3.** having weak or indistinct vision: *eyes dim with tears.* **4.** lacking in understanding; mentally dull. **5.** not clear in the mind; obscure: *a dim memory.* **6.** lacking in brilliance, brightness, or lustre: *a dim colour.* **7.** tending to be unfavourable; gloomy or disapproving (esp. in the phrase **take a dim view**). ~*vb.* **dims, dimming, dimmed.** **8.** to become or cause to become dim. **9.** (*tr.*) to cause to seem less bright, as by comparison. **10.** the U.S.

and Canadian word for **dip** (sense 5). [Old English *dimm;* related to Old Norse *dimmr* gloomy, dark] —**'dimly** *adv.* —**'dimness** *n.*

dim. *abbrev. for:* **1.** dimension. **2.** Also: **dimin.** *Music.* diminuendo. **3.** Also: **dimin.** diminutive.

dime (daɪm) *n.* **1.** a coin of the U.S. and Canada, worth one tenth of a dollar or ten cents. **2. a dime a dozen.** very cheap or common. [C14: from Old French *disme,* from Latin *decimus* tenth, from *decem* ten]

dimenhydrinate (ˌdaɪmɛnˈhaɪdrɪˌneɪt) *n.* a white slightly soluble bitter-tasting crystalline substance, used as an antihistamine and for the prevention of nausea, esp. in travel sickness. Formula: $C_{24}H_{28}ClN_5O_3$. [from *dime(thyl* + AMI)N(E) + *(diphen)hydr(am)in(e)* + -ATE[1]]

dime novel *n. U.S.* (formerly) a cheap melodramatic novel, usually in paperback. Also called (esp. Brit.): **penny-dreadful.**

dimension (dɪˈmɛnʃən) *n.* **1.** (*often pl.*) a measurement of the size of something in a particular direction, such as the length, width, height, or diameter. **2.** (*often pl.*) scope; size; extent: *a problem of enormous dimensions.* **3.** aspect: *a new dimension to politics.* **4.** *Maths.* the number of coordinates required to locate a point in space. **5.** *Physics.* **a.** the product or the quotient of the fundamental physical quantities (such as mass, length, or time) raised to the appropriate power in a derived physical quantity: *the dimensions of velocity are length divided by time.* **b.** the power to which such a fundamental quantity has to be raised in a derived quantity. ~*vb.* **6.** (*tr.*) *Chiefly U.S.* **a.** to shape or cut to specified dimensions. **b.** to mark with specified dimensions. [C14: from Old French, from Latin *dīmensiō* an extent, from *dīmētīrī* to measure out, from *mētīrī*] —**diˈmensional** *adj.* —**diˌmensionˈality** *n.* —**diˈmensionally** *adv.* —**diˈmensionless** *adj.*

dimer (ˈdaɪmə) *n. Chem.* **a.** a molecule composed of two identical simpler molecules (monomers). **b.** a compound consisting of dimers.

dimercaprol (ˌdaɪməˈkæprɒl) *n.* a colourless oily liquid with an offensive smell, used as an antidote to lewisite and similar toxic substances. Formula: $CH_2(SH)CH(SH)CH_2OH$. Also called: **BAL.** [C20: by shortening and altering from *dimercaptopropanol*]

dimerize *or* **-ise** (ˈdaɪməˌraɪz) *vb.* to react or cause to react to form a dimer. —ˌ**dimeriˈzation** *or* **-iˈsation** *n.*

dimerous (ˈdɪmərəs) *adj.* **1.** consisting of or divided into two segments, as the tarsi of some insects. **2.** (of flowers) having their floral parts arranged in whorls of two. [C19: from New Latin *dimerus,* from Greek *dimerēs,* from DI-[1] + *meros* part] —**ˈdimerism** *n.*

dimeter (ˈdɪmɪtə) *n. Prosody.* a line of verse consisting of two metrical feet or a verse written in this metre.

dimethylformamide (daɪˌmiːθaɪlˈfɔːməˌmaɪd, -ˌmɛθɪ-) *n.* a colourless liquid widely used as a solvent and sometimes as a catalyst. Formula: $(CH_3)_2NCHO$. Abbrev.: **DMF.**

dimethylsulphoxide (daɪˌmiːθaɪlsʌlˈfɒksaɪd, -ˌmɛθɪl-) *n.* a colourless odourless liquid substance used as a solvent and in medicine as an agent to improve the penetration of drugs applied to the skin. Formula: $(CH_3)_2SO$. Abbrev.: **DMSO.**

dimetric (daɪˈmɛtrɪk) *adj. Crystallog.* another word for **tetragonal.**

dimidiate *adj.* (dɪˈmɪdɪɪt). **1.** divided in halves. **2.** *Biology.* having one of two sides or parts more developed than the other: *dimidiate antlers.* ~*vb.* (dɪˈmɪdɪˌeɪt). (*tr.*) **3.** *Rare.* to divide in half. **4.** *Heraldry.* to halve (two bearings) so that they can be represented on the same shield. [C17: from Latin *dīmidiāre* to halve, from *dīmidius* half, from *dis-* apart + *medius* middle] —**diˌmidiˈation** *n.*

diminish (dɪˈmɪnɪʃ) *vb.* **1.** to make or become smaller, fewer, or less. **2.** (*tr.*) *Architect.* to cause (a column, etc.) to taper. **3.** (*tr.*) *Music.* to decrease (a minor or perfect interval) by a semitone. **4.** to belittle or be belittled; reduce in authority, status, etc.; depreciate. [C15: blend of *diminuen* to lessen (from Latin *dēminuere* to make smaller, from *minuere* to reduce) + archaic *minish* to lessen] —**diˈminishable** *adj.* —**diˈminishingly** *adv.* —**diˈminishment** *n.*

diminished (dɪˈmɪnɪʃt) *adj.* **1.** reduced or lessened; made smaller. **2.** *Music.* denoting any minor or perfect interval reduced by a semitone. **3.** *Music.* denoting a triad consisting of the root plus a minor third and a diminished fifth. **4.** *Music.* (*postpositive*) (esp. in jazz or pop music) denoting a diminished seventh chord having as its root the note specified: *B diminished.*

diminished responsibility *n. Law.* a plea under which proof of mental derangement is submitted as demonstrating lack of premeditation and therefore criminal responsibility.

diminished seventh chord *n.* a chord often used in an enharmonic modulation and very common in modern music, esp. jazz and pop music, consisting of a diminished triad with an added diminished seventh above the root. Often shortened to **diminished seventh.**

diminishing returns *pl. n. Economics.* **1.** progressively smaller rises in output resulting from the increased application of a variable input, such as labour, to a fixed quantity, as of capital or land. **2.** the increase in the average cost of production that may arise beyond a certain point as a result of increasing the overall scale of production.

diminuendo (dɪˌmɪnjuˈɛndəʊ) *Music.* ~*n., pl.* **-dos. 1. a.** a gradual decrease in loudness or the musical direction indicating this. Abbrev.: **dim.** Symbol: $>$ (written over the music affected). **b.** a musical passage affected by a diminuendo. ~*adj.* **2.** gradually decreasing in loudness. **3.** with a diminuendo. ~Also: **decrescendo.** [C18: from Italian, from *diminuire* to DIMINISH]

diminution (ˌdɪmɪˈnjuːʃən) *n.* **1.** reduction; decrease. **2.** *Music.* the presentation of the subject of a fugue, etc., in which the note values are reduced in length. Compare **augmentation** (sense 3). [C14: from Latin *dēminūtiō;* see DIMINISH]

diminutive (dɪˈmɪnjʊtɪv) *adj.* **1.** very small; tiny. **2.** *Grammar.* **a.** denoting an affix added to a word to convey the meaning *small* or *unimportant* or to express affection, as for example, the suffix *-ette* in French. **b.** denoting a word formed by the addition of a diminutive affix. ~*n.* **3.** *Grammar.* a diminutive word or affix. **4.** a tiny person or thing. ~Compare (for senses 2, 3) **augmentative.** —**diminutival** (dɪˌmɪnjʊˈtaɪvᵊl) *adj.* —**diˈminutively** *adv.* —**diˈminutiveness** *n.*

dimissory (dɪˈmɪsərɪ) *adj.* **1.** granting permission to be ordained: *a bishop's dimissory letter.* **2.** granting permission to depart.

dimity (ˈdɪmɪtɪ) *n., pl.* **-ties. a.** a light strong cotton fabric with woven stripes or squares. **b.** (*as modifier*): *a dimity bonnet.* [C15: from Medieval Latin *dimitum,* from Greek *dimiton,* from DI-[1] + *mitos* thread of the warp]

dimmer (ˈdɪmə) *n.* **1.** a device, such as a rheostat, for varying the current through an electric light and thus changing the illumination. **2.** (*often pl.*) *U.S.* **a.** a dipped headlight on a road vehicle. **b.** a parking light on a car.

dimorph (ˈdaɪmɔːf) *n.* either of two forms of a substance that exhibits dimorphism.

dimorphism (daɪˈmɔːfɪzəm) *n.* **1.** the occurrence within a plant of two distinct forms of any part, such as the leaves of some aquatic plants. **2.** the occurrence in an animal species of two distinct types of individual. **3.** a property of certain substances that enables them to exist in two distinct crystalline forms. —**diˈmorphic** *or* **diˈmorphous** *adj.*

dimple (ˈdɪmpᵊl) *n.* **1.** a small natural dent or crease in the flesh, esp. on the cheeks or chin. **2.** any slight depression in a surface. **3.** a bubble or dent in glass. ~*vb.* **4.** to make or become dimpled. **5.** (*intr.*) to produce dimples by smiling. [C13 *dympull;* compare Old English *dyppan* to dip, German *Tümpel* pool] —**ˈdimply** *adj.*

dim sum (ˈdɪm ˈsʌm) *n.* a Chinese appetizer of steamed dumplings containing various fillings. [Cantonese]

dimwit (ˈdɪmˌwɪt) *n. Informal.* a stupid or silly person. —ˌ**dimˈwitted** *adj.* —ˌ**dimˈwittedly** *adv.* —ˌ**dimˈwittedness** *n.*

din[1] (dɪn) *n.* **1.** a loud discordant confused noise. ~*vb.* **dins, dinning, dinned. 2.** (*tr.;* usually foll. by *into*) to instil (into a person) by constant repetition. **3.** (*tr.*) to subject to a din. **4.** (*intr.*) to make a din. [Old English *dynn;* compare Old Norse *dynr,* Old High German *tuni*]

din[2] (dɪn) *n. Judaism.* **1.** a particular religious law; the halacha about something. **2.** the ruling of a Beth Din or religious court. [from Hebrew, literally: judgment]

DIN (dɪn) *n.* **1.** a logarithmic expression of the speed of a photographic film, plate, etc., given as $-10\log_{10}E$, where E is the exposure of a point 0.1 density units above the fog level; high-speed films have high numbers. Compare **ASA/BS, ISO rating. 2.** a system of standard plugs, sockets, and cables used for interconnecting domestic audio and video equipment. [C20: from German *D(eutsche) I(ndustrie) N(ormen)* German Industry Standard]

Din. *abbrev. for* dinar.

dinar (ˈdiːnɑː) *n.* **1.** the standard monetary unit of the following countries. Algeria: divided into 100 centimes. Iraq: divided into 1000 fils. Jordan: divided into 1000 fils. Kuwait: divided into 1000 fils. Libya: divided into 100 piastres. Yemen: divided into 1000 fils. Tunisia: divided into 1000 milliemes. Yugoslavia: divided into 100 paras. Abbrev.: **Din., D., d. 2.** an Iranian monetary unit worth one hundredth of a rial. **3.** a coin, esp. one of gold, formerly used in the Middle East. [C17: from Arabic, from Late Greek *dēnarion,* from Latin *dēnārius* DENARIUS]

dine (daɪn) *vb.* **1.** (*intr.*) to eat dinner. **2.** (*intr.;* often foll. by *on, off,* or *upon*) to make one's meal (of): *the guests dined upon roast beef.* **3.** (*tr.*) *Informal.* to entertain to dinner (esp. in the phrase **to wine and dine someone**). [C13: from Old French *disner,* contracted from Vulgar Latin *disjējūnāre* (unattested) to cease fasting, from *dis-* not + Late Latin *jējūnāre* to fast; see JEJUNE]

dine out *vb.* (*intr., adv.*) **1.** to dine away from home, esp. in a restaurant. **2.** (foll. by *on*) to have dinner at the expense of someone else mainly for the sake of one's knowledge or conversation about (a subject or story).

diner (ˈdaɪnə) *n.* **1.** a person eating a meal, esp. in a restaurant. **2.** *Chiefly U.S. and Canadian.* a small cheap restaurant, often at the roadside. **3.** a fashionable bar, or a section of one, where food is served.

dineric (dɪˈnɛrɪk) *adj.* of or concerned with the interface between two immiscible liquids. [C20: from DI-[1] + Late Greek *nēron* water + -IC]

dinette (daɪˈnɛt) *n.* an alcove or small area for use as a dining room.

ding[1] (dɪŋ) *vb.* **1.** to ring or cause to ring, esp. with tedious repetition. **2.** (*tr.*) another word for **din**[1] (sense 2). **3.** (*tr.*) *Austral. slang.* to abandon (an enterprise). ~*n.* **4.** an imitation or representation of the sound of a bell. **5.** *Austral. slang, derogatory.* an Italian or Greek immigrant. **6.** *Austral. slang.* a party (the social event). [C13: probably of imitative origin, but influenced by DIN[1] + RING[2]; compare Old Swedish *diunga* to beat]

ding[2] (dɪŋ) *vb. Scot.* **1.** to strike; dash down. **2.** to surpass. [Middle English *dingen*]

Ding an sich (dɪŋ æn sɪk; *German* dɪŋ an zɪç) *n. Philosophy.* the thing in itself.

dingbat (ˈdɪŋˌbæt) *n. U.S. slang.* **1.** any unnamed object, esp. one used as a missile. **2.** a crazy or stupid person. [C19: of unknown origin]

dingbats (ˈdɪŋˌbæts) *Austral. and N.Z. slang.* ~*pl. n.* **1. the.** delirium tremens. **2. give someone the dingbats.** to make someone nervous. ~*adj.* **3.** crazy or stupid.

ding-dong *n.* **1.** the sound of a bell or bells, esp. two bells tuned a fourth or fifth apart. **2.** an imitation or representation of the sound of a bell. **3. a.** a violent exchange of blows or words. **b.** (*as modifier*): *a ding-dong battle.* ~*adj.* **4.** sounding or ringing repeatedly. [C16: of imitative origin; see DING[1]]

dinge[1] (dɪndʒ) *n.* dinginess. [C19: back formation from DINGY]

dinge[2] (dɪndʒ) *U.S. derogatory slang.* ~*n.* **1.** a Negro. ~*adj.* **2.** of or relating to Negroes.

dinge[3] (dɪndʒ) *English dialect and Irish.* ~*vb.* (*tr.*) **1.** to make a dent in (something). ~*n.* **2.** a dent. [of unknown origin]

dinges (ˈdɪŋəs) *n. S. African informal.* a jocular word for something whose name is unknown or forgotten; thingumabob. [from Afrikaans, from *ding* thing]

dinghy (ˈdɪŋɪ) *n., pl.* **-ghies.** any small boat, powered by sail, oars, or outboard motor. Also (esp. formerly): **dingy, dingey.** [C19: from Hindi or Bengali *dingi* a little boat, from *dingā* boat]

dingle (ˈdɪŋgᵊl) *n.* a small wooded dell. [C13: of uncertain origin]

dingo (ˈdɪŋgəʊ) *n., pl.* **-goes.** **1.** a wild dog, *Canis dingo,* of Australia, having a yellowish-brown coat and resembling a wolf. **2.** *Austral. slang.* a cheat or coward. ~*vb.* **-goes, -going, -goed.** (*intr.*) *Austral. slang.* **3. a.** to act in a cowardly manner. **b.** to drop out of something. **4.** (foll. by *on*) to let (someone) down. [C18: native Australian name]

dingy (ˈdɪndʒɪ) *adj.* **-gier, -giest.** **1.** lacking light or brightness; drab. **2.** dirty; discoloured. [C18: perhaps from an earlier dialect word related to Old English *dynge* dung] —ˈ**dingily** *adv.* —ˈ**dinginess** *n.*

dining car *n.* a railway coach in which meals are served at tables. Also called: **restaurant car.**

dining room *n.* a room where meals are eaten.

dinitrobenzene (daɪˌnaɪtrəʊˈbɛnziːn, -bɛnˈziːn) *n.* a yellow crystalline compound existing in three isomeric forms, obtained by reaction of benzene with nitric and sulphuric acids. The *meta*-form is used in the manufacture of dyes and plastics. Formula: $C_6H_4(NO_2)_2$.

dinitrogen tetroxide (daɪˈnaɪtrədʒən) *n.* a colourless gaseous substance that exists in equilibrium with nitrogen dioxide. As the temperature is reduced the proportion of the tetroxide increases. Formula: N_2O_4.

dink (dɪŋk) *adj.* **1.** *Scot. and northern English dialect.* neat or neatly dressed. ~*vb.* **2.** *Austral. and N.Z., chiefly children's slang.* **a.** (*tr.*) to carry a second person on (a horse, bicycle, etc.). **b.** (*intr.*) (of two people) to travel together on a horse, bicycle, etc. [C16: of unknown origin]

Dinka (ˈdɪŋkə) *n.* **1.** (*pl.* **-kas** *or* **-ka**) a member of a Nilotic people of the S Sudan, noted for their height, which often reaches seven feet tall: chiefly herdsmen. **2.** the language of this people, belonging to the Nilotic group of the Nilo-Saharan family. [from Dinka *jieng* people]

dinkie (ˈdɪŋkɪ) *n.* **1.** an affluent married childless person. ~*adj.* **2.** designed for or appealing to dinkies. [C20: from *d(ouble) i(ncome) n(o) k(ids)* + -IE]

dinkum (ˈdɪŋkəm) *adj. Austral. and N.Z. informal.* **1.** genuine or right (usually preceded by *fair* and used esp. as an interjection): *a fair dinkum offer.* **2. dinkum oil.** the truth. [C19: from English dialect: work, of unknown origin]

dinky (ˈdɪŋkɪ) *adj.* **dinkier, dinkiest.** *Informal.* **1.** *Brit.* small and neat; dainty. **2.** *U.S.* inconsequential; insignificant. [C18 (in the sense: dainty): from DINK]

dinky-di (ˈdɪŋkɪˈdaɪ) *adj. Austral. informal.* typical: *dinky-di Pom idleness.* [C20: variant of DINKUM]

dinna (ˈdɪnə) *vb. Scot.* do not.

dinner (ˈdɪnə) *n.* **1.** a meal taken in the evening. **2.** a meal taken at midday, esp. when it is the main meal of the day; lunch. **3. a.** a formal evening meal, as of a club, society, etc. **b.** a public banquet in honour of someone or something. **4.** a complete meal at a fixed price in a restaurant; table d'hôte. **5.** (*modifier*) of, relating to, or used at dinner: *dinner plate; dinner table; dinner hour.* **6. do like a dinner.** (*usually passive*) *Austral. informal.* to do for, overpower, or outdo. [C13: from Old French *disner;* see DINE]

dinner-dance *n.* a formal dinner followed by dancing.

dinner jacket *n.* a man's semiformal evening jacket without tails, usually black with a silk facing over the collar and lapels. Abbrevs.: **DJ, dj.** U.S. and Canadian name: **tuxedo.**

dinner lady *n. Brit.* a female cook or canteen worker in a school.

dinner service *n.* a set of matching plates, dishes, etc., suitable for serving a meal to a certain number of people.

dinoceras (daɪˈnɒsərəs) *n.* another name for a **uintathere.** [C19: New Latin, from Greek *deinos* fearful + *keras* horn]

dinoflagellate (ˌdaɪnəʊˈflædʒɪlɪt, -ˌleɪt) *n.* **1.** any of a group of unicellular biflagellate aquatic organisms forming a constituent of plankton: can be regarded as an order of protozoans (*Dinoflagellata*) or a class of algae (*Dinophyceae*). ~*adj.* **2.** of or relating to dinoflagellates. [C19: from New Latin *Dinoflagellata,* from Greek *dinos* whirling + FLAGELLUM + -ATE[1]]

dinosaur (ˈdaɪnəˌsɔː) *n.* **1.** any extinct terrestrial reptile of the orders *Saurischia* and *Ornithischia,* many of which were of gigantic size and abundant in the Mesozoic era. See also **saurischian, ornithischian.** Compare **pterosaur, plesiosaur.** **2.** a person or thing that is considered to be out of date. [C19: from New Latin *dinosaurus,* from Greek *deinos* fearful + *sauros* lizard] —ˌ**dinoˈsaurian** *adj.*

dinothere (ˈdaɪnəˌθɪə) *n.* any extinct late Tertiary elephant-like mammal of the genus *Dinotherium* (or *Deinotherium*), having a down-turned jaw with tusks curving downwards and backwards. [C19: from New Latin *dinotherium,* from Greek *deinos* fearful + *thērion,* diminutive of *thēr* beast]

dint (dɪnt) *n.* **1. by dint of.** by means or use of: *by dint of hard work.* **2.** *Archaic.* a blow or a mark made by a blow. ~*vb.* **3.** (*tr.*) to mark with dints. ~*n., vb.* **4.** a variant of **dent**[1]. [Old English *dynt;* related to Old Norse *dyttr* blow] —ˈ**dintless** *adj.*

dioc. *abbrev. for:* **1.** diocesan. **2.** diocese.

diocesan (daɪˈɒsɪsᵊn) *adj.* **1.** of or relating to a diocese. ~*n.* **2.** the bishop of a diocese.

diocese (ˈdaɪəsɪs) *n.* the district under the jurisdiction of a bishop. [C14: from Old French, from Late Latin *diocēsis,* from Greek *dioikēsis* administration, from *dioikein* to manage a household, from *oikos* house]

diode (ˈdaɪəʊd) *n.* **1.** a semiconductor device containing one p-n junction, used in circuits for converting alternating current to direct current. More formal name: **semiconductor diode.** **2.** the earliest and simplest type of electronic valve having two electrodes, an anode and a cathode, between which a current can flow only in one direction. It was formerly widely used as a rectifier and detector but has now been replaced in most electrical circuits by the more efficient and reliable semiconductor diode. [C20: from DI-[1] + -ODE[2]]

dioecious, diecious (daɪˈiːʃəs), *or* **dioicous** (daɪˈɔɪkəs) *adj.* (of some plants) having the male and female reproductive organs in separate flowers on separate plants. Compare **monoecious.** [C18: from New Latin *Dioecia* name of class, from DI-[1] + Greek *oikia* house, dwelling] —**diˈoeciously, diˈeciously,** *or* **diˈoicously** *adv.* —**diˈoeciousness, diˈeciousness,** *or* **diˈoicousness** *n.*

dioestrus *or U.S.* **diestrus** (daɪˈiːstrəs) *n.* a period of sexual inactivity between periods of oestrus in animals that have several oestrous cycles in one breeding season.

diol (ˈdaɪɒl) *n. Chem.* any of a class of alcohols that have two hydroxyl groups in each molecule. Also called: **glycol, dihydric alcohol.** [from DI-[1] + (ALCOH)OL]

Dionysia (ˌdaɪəˈnɪzɪə) *n.* (in ancient Greece) festivals of Dionysus, god of wine, fruitfulness, and vegetation: a source of Athenian drama.

Dionysiac (ˌdaɪəˈnɪzɪˌæk) *adj.* **1.** of or relating to Dionysus or his worship. **2.** a less common word for **Dionysian.**

Dionysian (ˌdaɪəˈnɪzɪən) *adj.* **1.** of or relating to Dionysus. **2.** (*sometimes not cap.*) (in Nietzchean philosophy) of or relating to the set of creative qualities that encompasses spontaneity, irrationality, the rejection of discipline, etc. **3.** (*often not cap.*) wild or orgiastic. ~Compare (for senses 2, 3) **Apollonian.**

Diophantine equation (ˌdaɪəʊˈfæntaɪn) *n.* (in number theory) an equation in more than one variable and with integral coefficients, for which integral solutions are sought. [named after *Diophantus,* 3rd-century A.D. Greek mathematician]

diopside (daɪˈɒpsaɪd, -sɪd) *n.* a colourless or pale-green pyroxene mineral consisting of calcium magnesium silicate in monoclinic crystalline form: used as a gemstone. Formula: $CaMgSi_2O_6$. [C19: from DI-[2] + Greek *opsis* sight, appearance + -IDE]

dioptase (daɪˈɒpteɪs, -teɪz) *n.* a green glassy mineral consisting of hydrated copper silicate in hexagonal crystalline form. Formula: H_2CuSiO_4. [C19: from French, from Greek *dia-* through + *optos* visible]

dioptometer (ˌdaɪɒpˈtɒmɪtə) *n.* an instrument for measuring ocular refraction. [from DI-[2] + OPT(IC) + -METER] —ˌ**diopˈtometry** *n.*

dioptre *or U.S.* **diopter** (daɪˈɒptə) *n.* a unit for measuring the refractive power of a lens: the reciprocal of the focal length of the lens expressed in metres. [C16: from Latin *dioptra* optical instrument, from Greek, from *dia-* through + *opsesthai* to see] —**diˈoptral** *adj.*

dioptric (daɪˈɒptrɪk) *or* **dioptrical** *adj.* **1.** of or concerned with dioptrics. **2.** of or denoting refraction or refracted light. —**diˈoptrically** *adv.*

dioptrics (daɪˈɒptrɪks) *n.* (*functioning as sing.*) the branch of geometrical optics concerned with the formation of images by lenses. [C20: from DIOPTRE + -ICS]

diorama (ˌdaɪəˈrɑːmə) *n.* **1.** a miniature three-dimensional scene, in which models of figures are seen against a background.

2. a picture made up of illuminated translucent curtains, viewed through an aperture. 3. a museum display, as of an animal, of a specimen in its natural setting. 4. *Films.* a scene produced by the rearrangement of lighting effects. [C19: from French, from Greek *dia-* through + Greek *horama* view, from *horan* to see] —**dioramic** (ˌdaɪəˈræmɪk) *adj.*

diorite (ˈdaɪəˌraɪt) *n.* a dark coarse-grained igneous plutonic rock consisting of plagioclase feldspar and ferromagnesian minerals such as hornblende. [C19: from French, from Greek *diorizein* to distinguish (from *dia-* apart + *horizein* to define) + -ITE[1]] —**dioritic** (ˌdaɪəˈrɪtɪk) *adj.*

dioxan (daɪˈɒksən) *or* **dioxane** (daɪˈɒkseɪn) *n.* a colourless insoluble toxic liquid made by heating ethanediol with sulphuric acid; 1,4-diethylene dioxide: used as a solvent, esp. for waxes and cellulose acetate resins. Formula: $(CH_2)_2O(CH_2)_2O$.

dioxide (daɪˈɒksaɪd) *n.* 1. any oxide containing two oxygen atoms per molecule, both of which are bonded to an atom of another element. 2. another name for a **peroxide** (sense 4).

dioxin (daɪˈɒksɪn) *n.* any of a number of mostly poisonous chemical by-products of the manufacture of certain herbicides and bactericides, esp. the extremely toxic 2,3,7,8 tetrachlorodibenzo-para-dioxin.

dip (dɪp) *vb.* **dips, dipping, dipped.** 1. to plunge or be plunged quickly or briefly into a liquid, esp. to wet or coat. 2. (*intr.*) to undergo a slight decline, esp. temporarily: *sales dipped in November.* 3. (*intr.*) to slope downwards: *the land dips towards the river.* 4. (*intr.*) to sink or appear to sink quickly: *the sun dipped below the horizon.* 5. (*tr.*) to switch (car headlights) from the main to the lower beam. U.S. and Canadian word: **dim.** 6. (*tr.*) **a.** to immerse (poultry, sheep, etc.) briefly in a liquid chemical to rid them of or prevent infestation by insects, etc. **b.** to immerse (grain, vegetables, or wood) in a preservative liquid. 7. (*tr.*) to stain or dye by immersing in a liquid. 8. (*tr.*) to baptize (someone) by immersion. 9. (*tr.*) to plate or galvanize (a metal, etc.) by immersion in an electrolyte or electrolytic cell. 10. (*tr.*) to scoop up a liquid or something from a liquid in the hands or in a container. 11. to lower or be lowered briefly: *she dipped her knee in a curtsy.* 12. (*tr.*) to make (a candle) by plunging the wick into melted wax. 13. (*intr.*) to plunge a container, the hands, etc., into something, esp. to obtain or retrieve an object: *he dipped in his pocket for money.* 14. (*intr.*; foll. by *in* or *into*) to dabble (in); play (at): *he dipped into black magic.* 15. (*intr.*) (of an aircraft) to drop suddenly and then regain height. 16. (*intr.*) (of a rock stratum or mineral vein) to slope downwards from the horizontal. 17. (*intr.*; often foll. by *for*) (in children's games) to select (a leader, etc.) by reciting any of various rhymes. ~*n.* 18. the act of dipping or state of being dipped. 19. a brief swim in water. 20. **a.** any liquid chemical preparation in which poultry, sheep, etc. are dipped. **b.** any liquid preservative into which objects, esp. of wood, are dipped. 21. a preparation of dyeing agents into which fabric is immersed. 22. a depression, esp. in a landscape. 23. something taken up by dipping. 24. a container used for dipping; dipper. 25. a momentary sinking down. 26. the angle of slope of rock strata, fault planes, etc., from the horizontal plane. 27. Also called: **angle of dip, magnetic dip, inclination.** the angle between the direction of the earth's magnetic field and the plane of the horizon; the angle that a magnetic needle free to swing in a vertical plane makes with the horizontal. 28. a creamy mixture into which pieces of food are dipped before being eaten. 29. *Surveying.* the angular distance of the horizon below the plane of observation. 30. a candle made by plunging a wick repeatedly into wax. 31. a momentary loss of altitude when flying. 32. (in gymnastics) a chinning exercise on the parallel bars. 33. a slang word for **pickpocket.** ~See also **dip into, dip out.** [Old English *dyppan;* related to Old High German *tupfen* to wash, German *taufen* to baptize; see DEEP]

dip. *or* **Dip.** *abbrev. for* diploma.

DipAD (in Britain) *abbrev. for* Diploma in Art and Design.

dip-and-scarp *adj.* (of topography) characterized by alternating steeper scarp slopes and gentler dip slopes.

DipChemEng *abbrev. for* Diploma in Chemical Engineering.

dip circle *n.* an instrument for measuring dip, consisting of a dip needle with a vertical circular scale of angles. Also called: **inclinometer.**

DipCom *abbrev. for* Diploma of Commerce.

DipEd (in Britain) *abbrev. for* Diploma in Education.

dipeptide (daɪˈpɛptaɪd) *n.* a compound consisting of two linked amino acids. See **peptide.**

dipetalous (daɪˈpɛtələs) *adj.* another word for **bipetalous.**

dip fault *n. Geology.* a fault that runs perpendicular to the strike of the affected rocks (i.e. parallel to the plane of the angle of dip of the rocks).

diphase (ˈdaɪˌfeɪz) *or* **diphasic** *adj. Physics.* of, having, or concerned with two phases.

diphasic (daɪˈfeɪzɪk) *adj.* 1. *Zoology.* (of parasites) having a free active stage in the life cycle. 2. *Physics.* another word for **diphase.**

diphenyl (daɪˈfiːnaɪl, -nɪl; -ˈfɛnɪl) *n.* another name for **biphenyl.**

diphenylamine (daɪˌfiːnaɪləˈmiːn, -ˈæmɪn; -nɪl-; -ˌfɛn-) *n.* a colourless insoluble crystalline derivative of benzene, used in the manufacture of dyes, as a stabilizer in plastics, etc. Formula: $(C_6H_5)_2NH$.

diphenylhydantoin sodium (daɪˌfiːnaɪlhaɪˈdæntəʊɪn, -nɪl-, -ˌfɛn-) *n.* a white soluble bitter-tasting powder used as an anticonvulsant in the treatment of epilepsy. Formula: $C_{15}H_{11}N_2O_2Na$.

diphosgene (daɪˈfɒzdʒiːn) *n.* an oily liquid with an extremely poisonous vapour, made by treating methanol with phosgene and chlorinating the product: has been used in chemical warfare. Formula: $ClCOOCCl_3$.

diphtheria (dɪpˈθɪərɪə, dɪf-) *n.* an acute contagious disease caused by the bacillus *Corynebacterium diphtheriae,* producing fever, severe prostration, and difficulty in breathing and swallowing as the result of swelling of the throat and formation of a false membrane. [C19: New Latin, from French *diphthérie,* from Greek *diphthera* leather; from the nature of the membrane] —**diphˈtherial, diphtheritic** (ˌdɪpθəˈrɪtɪk, dɪf-), *or* **diphtheric** (dɪpˈθɛrɪk, dɪf-) *adj.* —**ˈdiphtheˌroid** *adj.*

diphthong (ˈdɪfθɒŋ, ˈdɪp-) *n.* 1. a vowel sound, occupying a single syllable, during the articulation of which the tongue moves from one position to another, causing a continual change in vowel quality, as in the pronunciation of *a* in English *late,* during which the tongue moves from the position of (e) towards (ɪ). 2. a digraph or ligature representing a composite vowel such as this, as *ae* in *Caesar.* [C15: from Late Latin *diphthongus,* from Greek *diphthongos,* from DI-[1] + *phthongos* sound] —**diphˈthongal** *adj.*

diphthongize *or* **diphthongise** (ˈdɪfθɒŋˌaɪz, -ˌgaɪz; ˈdɪp-) *vb.* (*often passive*) to make (a simple vowel) into a diphthong. —ˌ**diphthongiˈzation** *or* ˌ**diphthongiˈsation** *n.*

diphycercal (ˌdɪfɪˈsɜːkəl) *adj. Ichthyol.* of or possessing a symmetrical or pointed tail with the vertebral column extending to the tip, as in primitive fishes. [C19: from Greek *diphuēs* twofold (from DI-[1] + *phuē* growth) + *kerkos* tail]

diphyletic (ˌdaɪfaɪˈlɛtɪk) *adj.* relating to or characterized by descent from two ancestral groups of animals or plants.

diphyllous (daɪˈfɪləs) *adj.* (of certain plants) having two leaves.

diphyodont (ˈdɪfɪəʊˌdɒnt) *adj.* having two successive sets of teeth, as mammals (including man). Compare **polyphyodont.** [C19: from Greek *diphuēs* double (see DIPHYCERCAL) + -ODONT]

dip into *vb.* (*intr., prep.*) 1. to draw (upon): *he dipped into his savings.* 2. to read (passages) at random or cursorily in (a book, newspaper, etc.).

dipl. *abbrev. for:* 1. diplomat(ic). 2. Also: **Dip., dip.** diploma.

diplegia (daɪˈpliːdʒə) *n.* paralysis of corresponding parts on both sides of the body; bilateral paralysis. —**diˈplegic** *adj.*

diplex (ˈdaɪplɛks) *adj.* permitting the transmission or reception of two signals simultaneously in the same direction over a radio or telecommunications channel. Compare **duplex** (sense 5), **simplex** (sense 1). [C19: DI-[1] + Latin *-plex* -FOLD, on the model of *duplex*] —ˈ**diplexer** *n.*

diplo- *or before a vowel* **dipl-** *combining form.* double: *diplococcus.* [from Greek, from *diploos,* from DI-[1] + *-ploos* -fold]

diplobiont (ˌdɪpləʊˈbaɪɒnt) *n. Biology.* an organism that has both haploid and diploid individuals in its life cycle. —ˌ**diplobiˈontic** *adj.*

diploblastic (ˌdɪpləʊˈblæstɪk) *adj.* (of jellyfish, corals, and other coelenterates) having a body developed from only two germ layers (ectoderm and endoderm). Compare **triploblastic.**

diplocardiac (ˌdɪpləʊˈkɑːdɪˌæk) *adj.* (of birds and mammals) having a four-chambered heart, which enables two separate circulations and prevents mixing of the arterial and venous blood.

diplococcus (ˌdɪpləʊˈkɒkəs) *n., pl.* **-cocci** (-ˈkɒksaɪ). any of various spherical Gram-positive bacteria that occur in pairs, esp. any of the genus *Diplococcus,* such as *D. pneumoniae,* which causes pneumonia: family *Lactobacillaceae.* —ˌ**diploˈcoccal** *or* **diplococcic** (ˌdɪpləʊˈkɒksɪk, -ˈkɒkɪk) *adj.*

diplodocus (dɪˈplɒdəkəs, ˌdɪpləʊˈdəʊkəs) *n., pl.* **-cuses.** any herbivorous quadrupedal late Jurassic dinosaur of the genus *Diplodocus,* characterized by a very long neck and tail and a total body length of 27 metres: suborder *Sauropoda* (sauropods). [C19: from New Latin, from DIPLO- + Greek *dokos* beam]

diploë (ˈdɪpləʊˌiː) *n. Anatomy.* the spongy bone separating the two layers of compact bone of the skull. [C17: via New Latin, from Greek: a fold, from *diploos* double]

diploid (ˈdɪplɔɪd) *adj.* 1. *Biology.* (of cells or organisms) having paired homologous chromosomes so that twice the haploid number is present. 2. double or twofold. ~*n. Biology.* 3. a diploid cell or organism. —**dipˈloidic** *adj.* —ˈ**diploidy** *n.*

diploma (dɪˈpləʊmə) *n.* 1. a document conferring a qualification, recording success in examinations or successful completion of a course of study. 2. an official document that confers an honour or privilege. [C17: from Latin: official letter or document, literally: letter folded double, from Greek; see DIPLO-]

diplomacy (dɪˈpləʊməsɪ) *n., pl.* **-cies.** 1. the conduct of the relations of one state with another by peaceful means. 2. skill in the management of international relations. 3. tact, skill, or cunning in dealing with people. [C18: from French *diplomatie,* from *diplomatique* DIPLOMATIC]

diplomat (ˈdɪpləˌmæt) *n.* 1. an official, such as an ambassador or first secretary, engaged in diplomacy. 2. a person who deals with people tactfully or skilfully.

diplomate (ˈdɪpləˌmeɪt) *n.* any person who has been granted a diploma, esp. a physician certified as a specialist.

diplomatic (ˌdɪpləˈmætɪk) *adj.* 1. of or relating to diplomacy or diplomats. 2. skilled in negotiating, esp. between states or people. **3.** tactful in dealing with people. **4.** of or relating to diplomatics. [C18: from French *diplomatique* concerning the documents of diplomacy, from New Latin *diplōmaticus;* see DIPLOMA] —ˌ**diploˈmatically** *adv.*

diplomatic bag *n.* a container or bag in which official mail is sent, free from customs inspection, to and from an embassy or consulate.

diplomatic corps *or* **body** *n.* the entire body of diplomats accredited to a given state.

diplomatic immunity *n.* the immunity from local jurisdiction and exemption from taxation in the country to which they are accredited afforded to diplomats.

diplomatics (ˌdɪpləˈmætɪks) *n.* (*functioning as sing.*) **1.** the critical study of historical documents. **2.** a less common word for **diplomacy.**

diplomatic service *n.* the government institution of a country that provides diplomats to represent that country abroad.

diplomatist (dɪˈpləʊmətɪst) *n.* a less common word for **diplomat.**

diplonema (ˌdɪpləʊˈniːmə) *n. Biology.* the stage during meiosis at which the chromosomes are distinctly doubled.

diplont (ˈdɪplɒnt) *n.* an animal or plant that has the diploid number of chromosomes in its somatic cells. [C20: DIPLO- + Greek *ōn* being, from *einai* to be] —**dipˈlontic** *adj.*

diplopia (dɪˈpləʊpɪə) *n.* a visual defect in which a single object is seen in duplicate; double vision. It can be caused by incorrect fixation or by an abnormality in the visual system. [C19: New Latin, from DIPLO- + Greek *ōps* eye] —**diplopic** (dɪˈplɒpɪk) *adj.*

diplopod (ˈdɪpləˌpɒd) *n.* any arthropod of the class *Diplopoda,* which includes the millipedes.

diplosis (dɪˈpləʊsɪs) *n. Biology.* the doubling of the haploid number of chromosomes that occurs during fusion of gametes to form a diploid zygote. [C20: from Greek *diplōsis* doubling, from *diploun* to double, from *diploos* double]

diplostemonous (ˌdɪpləʊˈstiːmənəs, -ˈstɛm-) *adj.* (of plants) having twice as many stamens as petals, esp. with the stamens arranged in two whorls. [C19: from New Latin *diplostemonus* (unattested), from DIPLO- + *-stemonus* relating to a STAMEN]

diplotene (ˈdɪpləʊˌtiːn) *n.* the fourth stage of the prophase of meiosis, during which the chromosomes of each bivalent separate, usually with the interchange of genetic material. See also **chiasma** (sense 1), **crossing over.** [C20: from DIPLO- + Greek *tainia* band]

diplozoic (ˌdɪpləˈzəʊɪk) *adj.* (of certain animals) bilaterally symmetrical.

DipMet *abbrev. for* Diploma in Metallurgy.

dip needle *n.* a magnetized needle pivoted through its centre of gravity able to rotate freely in a vertical plane, used to determine the inclination of the earth's magnetic field. See also **dip circle.**

dipnoan (dɪpˈnəʊən) *adj.* **1.** of, relating to, or belonging to the *Dipnoi,* a subclass of bony fishes comprising the lungfishes. ~*n.* **2.** any lungfish. [C19: from New Latin *Dipnoi,* from Greek *dipnoos,* double-breathing, from DI-[1] + *pnoē* breathing, air, from *pnein* to breathe]

dipody (ˈdɪpədɪ) *n., pl.* **-dies.** *Prosody.* a metrical unit consisting of two feet. [C19: from Late Latin *dipodia,* from Greek DI-[1] + *pous* foot]

dipole (ˈdaɪˌpəʊl) *n.* **1.** two electric charges or magnetic poles that have equal magnitudes but opposite signs and are separated by a small distance. **2.** a molecule in which the centre of positive charge does not coincide with the centre of negative charge. **3.** Also called: **dipole aerial.** a directional radio or television aerial consisting of two equal lengths of metal wire or rods, with a connecting wire fixed between them in the form of a T. —**diˈpolar** *adj.*

dipole moment *n. Chem.* a measure of the polarity in a chemical bond or molecule, equal to the product of one charge and the distance between the charges. Symbol: μ

dip out *vb.* (*intr., adv.*) **1.** (often foll. by *on*) *Austral. informal.* to fail to take part (in) or advantage (of). **2.** *N.Z.* to fail; miss out: *he dipped out in the examination.*

dipper (ˈdɪpə) *n.* **1.** a ladle used for dipping. **2.** Also called: **water ouzel.** any aquatic songbird of the genus *Cinclus* and family *Cinclidae,* esp. *C. cinclus.* They inhabit fast-flowing streams and resemble large wrens. **3.** a person or thing that dips, such as the mechanism for directing car headlights downwards. **4.** a small metal cup clipped onto a painter's palette for holding diluent or medium. **5.** *Archaic.* an Anabaptist. ~See also **big dipper.**

dippy (ˈdɪpɪ) *adj.* **-pier, -piest.** *Slang.* odd, eccentric, or crazy. [C20: of unknown origin]

dipropellant (ˌdaɪprəˈpɛlənt) *n.* another name for **bipropellant.**

diprotodont (daɪˈprəʊtəʊˌdɒnt) *n.* any marsupial of the group or suborder *Diprotodontia,* including kangaroos, phalangers, and wombats, having fewer than three upper incisor teeth on each side of the jaw. Compare **polyprotodont.** [C19: from Greek from DI-[1] + PROTO- + -ODONT]

dip-slip fault *n. Geology.* a fault on which the movement is along the dip of the fault.

dipsomania (ˌdɪpsəʊˈmeɪnɪə) *n.* a compulsive desire to drink alcoholic beverages. [C19: New Latin, from Greek *dipsa* thirst + -MANIA]

dipsomaniac (ˌdɪpsəʊˈmeɪnɪˌæk) *n.* **1.** any person who has an uncontrollable and recurring urge to drink alcohol. Shortened form: **dipso.** ~*adj.* **2.** relating to or affected with dipsomania. —**dipsomaniacal** (ˌdɪpsəʊməˈnaɪəkəl) *adj.*

dipstick (ˈdɪpˌstɪk) *n.* a graduated rod or strip dipped into a container to indicate the fluid level.

dip switch *n.* a device for dipping car headlights.

dipteral (ˈdɪptərəl) *adj. Architect.* having a double row of columns.

dipteran (ˈdɪptərən) *or* **dipteron** (ˈdɪptəˌrɒn) *n.* **1.** any dipterous insect. ~*adj.* **2.** another word for **dipterous** (sense 1).

dipterocarpaceous (ˌdɪptərəʊkɑːˈpeɪʃəs) *adj.* of, relating to, or belonging to the *Dipterocarpaceae,* a family of trees chiefly native to Malaysia, having two-winged fruits. Many species yield useful timber and resins. [C19: via New Latin from Greek *dipteros* two-winged + *karpos* fruit]

dipterous (ˈdɪptərəs) *adj.* **1.** Also: **dipteran.** of, relating to, or belonging to the *Diptera,* a large order of insects having a single pair of wings and sucking or piercing mouthparts. The group includes flies, mosquitoes, craneflies, and midges. **2.** *Botany.* having two winglike parts: *a dipterous seed.* [C18: from New Latin, from Greek *dipteros,* from *di-* two + *pteros* wing]

diptych (ˈdɪptɪk) *n.* **1.** a pair of hinged wooden tablets with waxed surfaces for writing. **2.** a painting or carving on two panels, usually hinged like a book. [C17: from Greek *diptukhos* folded together, from DI-[1] + *ptukhos* fold; compare TRIPTYCH]

dir. *abbrev. for* director.

Dirac constant *n.* a constant used in quantum mechanics equal to the Planck constant divided by 2π. It has a value of $1.0544 \pm 0.0003 \times 10^{-34}$ joule seconds. Symbol: $\hbar$ Also called: **crossed-h, h-bar.** [C20: named after P. A. M. *Dirac* (1902–84), British physicist]

dire (daɪə) *adj.* (*usually prenominal*) **1.** Also: **direful.** disastrous; fearful. **2.** desperate; urgent: *a dire need.* **3.** foreboding disaster; ominous: *a dire warning.* [C16: from Latin *dīrus* ominous, fearful; related to Greek *deos* fear] —ˈ**direly** *adv.* —ˈ**direness** *n.*

direct (dɪˈrɛkt, daɪ-) *vb.* (*mainly tr.*) **1.** to regulate, conduct, or control the affairs of. **2.** (*also intr.*) to give commands or orders with authority to (a person or group): *he directed them to go away.* **3.** to tell or show (someone) the way to a place. **4.** to aim, point, or cause to move towards a goal. **5.** to address (a letter, parcel, etc.). **6.** to address (remarks, words, etc.): *to direct comments at someone.* **7.** (*also intr.*) to provide guidance to (actors, cameramen, etc.) in the rehearsal of a play or the filming of a motion picture. **8.** (*also intr.*) **a.** to conduct (a piece of music or musicians), usually while performing oneself. **b.** another word (esp. U.S.) for **conduct** (sense 9). ~*adj.* **9.** without delay or evasion; straightforward: *a direct approach.* **10.** without turning aside; uninterrupted; shortest; straight: *a direct route.* **11.** without intervening persons or agencies; immediate: *a direct link.* **12.** honest; frank; candid: *a direct answer.* **13.** (*usually prenominal*) precise; exact: *a direct quotation.* **14.** diametrical: *the direct opposite.* **15.** in an unbroken line of descent, as from father to son over succeeding generations: *a direct descendant.* **16.** (of government, decisions, etc.) by or from the electorate rather than through representatives. **17.** *Logic, maths.* (of a proof) progressing from the premises to the conclusion, rather than eliminating the possibility of the falsehood of the conclusion. Compare **indirect proof.** **18.** *Astronomy.* moving from west to east on the celestial sphere. Compare **retrograde** (sense 4a.). **19. a.** of or relating to direct current. **b.** (of a secondary induced current) having the same direction as the primary current. **20.** *Music.* **a.** (of motion) in the same direction. See **motion** (sense 9). **b.** (of an interval or chord) in root position; not inverted. ~*adv.* **21.** directly; straight: *he went direct to the office.* [C14: from Latin *dīrectus,* from *dīrigere* to guide, from *dis-* apart + *regere* to rule] —**diˈrectness** *n.*

direct access *n.* a method of reading data from a computer file without reading through the file from the beginning as on a disk or drum. Also called: **random access.** Compare **sequential access.**

direct action *n.* action such as strikes or civil disobedience, employed by organized labour or other groups to obtain demands from an employer, government, etc.

direct coupling *n. Electronics.* conductive coupling between electronic circuits, as opposed to inductive or capacitative coupling. See also **coupling** (sense 4). —**direct coupled** *adj.*

direct current *n.* a continuous electric current that flows in one direction only, without substantial variation in magnitude. Abbrev.: **DC.** Compare **alternating current.**

direct debit *n.* an order given to a bank or building society by a holder of an account, instructing it to pay to a specified person or organization any sum demanded by that person or organization. Compare **standing order.**

direct distance dialing *n.* the U.S. and Canadian equivalent of **subscriber trunk dialling.**

direct dye *n.* any of a number of dyes that can be applied without the use of a mordant. They are usually azo dyes applied to cotton or rayon from a liquid bath containing an electrolyte such as sodium sulphate.

directed (dɪˈrɛktɪd, daɪ-) *adj. Maths.* (of a number, line, or angle) having either a positive or negative sign to distinguish measurement in one direction or orientation from that in the opposite direction or orientation.

direct evidence *n. Law.* evidence, usually the testimony of a witness, directly relating to the fact in dispute. Compare **circumstantial evidence.**
direct-grant school *n.* (in Britain, formerly) a school financed by endowment, fees, and a state grant conditional upon admittance of a percentage of nonpaying pupils nominated by the local education authority.
direct injection *n.* See **solid injection.**
direct input *n.* a device, such as a keyboard, used to insert data directly into a computerized system.
direction (dɪˈrɛkʃən, daɪ-) *n.* **1.** the act of directing or the state of being directed. **2.** management, control, or guidance. **3.** the work of a stage or film director. **4.** the course or line along which a person or thing moves, points, or lies. **5.** the course along which a ship, aircraft, etc., is travelling, expressed as the angle between true or magnetic north and an imaginary line through the main fore-and-aft axis of the vessel. **6.** the place towards which a person or thing is directed. **7.** a line of action; course. **8.** the name and address on a letter, parcel, etc. **9.** *Music.* the process of conducting an orchestra, choir, etc. **10.** *Music.* an instruction in the form of a word or symbol heading or occurring in the body of a passage, movement, or piece to indicate tempo, dynamics, mood, etc. **11.** (*modifier*) *Maths.* **a.** (of an angle) being any one of the three angles that a line in space makes with the three positive directions of the coordinate axes. Usually given as α, β, and γ with respect to the x-, y-, and z- axes. **b.** (of a cosine) being the cosine of any of the direction angles. ~See also **directions.**
directional (dɪˈrɛkʃənᵊl, daɪ-) *adj.* **1.** of or relating to a spatial direction. **2.** *Electronics.* **a.** having or relating to an increased sensitivity to radio waves, sound waves, nuclear particles, etc., coming from a particular direction. **b.** (of an aerial) transmitting or receiving radio waves more effectively in some directions than in others. **3.** *Physics, electronics.* **a.** concentrated in, following, or producing motion in a particular direction. **b.** indicating direction. —**diˌrectionˈality** *n.*
directional drilling *n.* a method of drilling for oil in which the well is not drilled vertically, as when a number of wells are to be drilled from a single platform to reach different areas of an oil field. Also called: **deviated drilling.**
direction finder *n.* a highly directional aerial system that can be used to determine the direction of incoming radio signals, used esp. as a navigation aid. Abbrevs.: **D/F** or **DF** —**direction finding** *n.*
directions (dɪˈrɛkʃənz, daɪ-) *pl. n.* (*sometimes sing.*) instructions for doing something or for reaching a place.
directive (dɪˈrɛktɪv, daɪ-) *n.* **1.** an instruction; order. ~*adj.* **2.** tending to direct; directing. **3.** indicating direction.
direct labour *n. Commerce.* **1.** work that is an essential part of a production process or the provision of a service. Compare **indirect labour. 2.** *Brit.* workers who are part of an employer's own labour force rather than hired through a contractor, such as building workers employed by a local authority.
direct lighting *n. Electrical engineering.* a lighting system in which a large proportion (at least 90 per cent) of the light is directed downwards.
directly (dɪˈrɛktlɪ, daɪ-) *adv.* **1.** in a direct manner. **2.** at once; without delay. **3.** (foll. by *before* or *after*) immediately; just. ~*conj.* **4.** (*subordinating*) as soon as: *we left directly the money arrived.*
direct-mail shot *n. Marketing.* the posting of unsolicited sales literature to potential customers' homes or business addresses.
direct marketing *n.* selling goods directly to consumers rather than through retailers, usually by mail order, direct-mail shot, newspaper advertising, door-to-door selling, or telephone selling. Also called: **direct selling.**
direct memory access *n.* a process in which data may be moved directly to or from the main memory of a computer system by operations not under the control of the central processing unit. Abbrev.: **DMA.**
direct method *n.* a method of teaching a foreign language with minimal use of the pupil's native language and of formal grammar.
direct object *n. Grammar.* a noun, pronoun, or noun phrase whose referent receives the direct action of a verb. For example, *a book* is the direct object in the sentence *They bought Anne a book.* Compare **indirect object.**
Directoire *French.* (dirɛktwar) *adj.* **1.** of, in, or relating to a decorative style of the end of the 18th century in France, during the rule of the Directory; a form of neoclassicism. **2.** characteristic of women's dress of this period, typically an almost transparent dress with the waistline under the bust.
director (dɪˈrɛktə, daɪ-) *n.* **1.** a person or thing that directs, controls, or regulates. **2.** a member of the governing board of a business concern who may or may not have an executive function. **3.** a person who directs the affairs of an institution, trust, educational programme, etc. **4.** the person responsible for the artistic and technical aspects of making a film or television programme. Compare **producer** (sense 4). **5.** *Music.* another word (esp. U.S.) for **conductor** (sense 2). —ˌ**direcˈtorial** *adj.* —ˌ**direcˈtorially** *adv.* —**diˈrectorˌship** *n.* —**diˈrectress** *fem. n.*
directorate (dɪˈrɛktərɪt, daɪ-) *n.* **1.** a board of directors. **2.** Also: **diˈrectorˌship.** the position of director.
director-general *n., pl.* **directors-general.** the head of a large organization such as the CBI or BBC.
Director of Public Prosecutions *n.* (in Britain) an official who, as head of the Crown Prosecution Service, is responsible for conducting all criminal prosecutions initiated by the police. Abbrev.: **DPP.**
directory (dɪˈrɛktərɪ, -trɪ; daɪ-) *n., pl.* **-ries. 1.** a book, arranged alphabetically or classified by trade listing names, addresses, telephone numbers, etc., of individuals or firms. **2.** a book or manual giving directions. **3.** a book containing the rules to be observed in the forms of worship used in churches. **4.** a less common word for **directorate** (sense 2). **5.** *Computer technol.* an area of a disk, Winchester disk, or floppy disk that contains the names and locations of files currently held on that disk. ~*adj.* **6.** directing.
direct primary *n. U.S. government.* a primary in which voters directly select the candidates who will run for office.
direct question *n.* a question asked in direct speech, such as *Why did you come?* Compare **indirect question.**
direct-reading *adj.* (of an instrument) calibrated so that a given quantity to be measured can be read directly off the scale without the need of a multiplying constant.
directrix (dɪˈrɛktrɪks, daɪ-) *n.* **1.** *Geometry.* a fixed reference line, situated on the convex side of a conic section, that is used when defining or calculating its eccentricity. **2.** a directress. [C17: New Latin, feminine of DIRECTOR]
direct selling *n.* another name for **direct marketing.**
direct speech *or esp. U.S.* **direct discourse** *n.* the reporting of what someone has said or written by quoting his exact words.
direct tax *n.* a tax paid by the person or organization on which it is levied. Compare **indirect tax.**
dirge (dɜːdʒ) *n.* **1.** a chant of lamentation for the dead. **2.** the funeral service in its solemn or sung forms. **3.** any mourning song or melody. [C13: changed from Latin *dīrige* direct (imperative), opening word of the Latin antiphon used in the office of the dead] —ˈ**dirgeful** *adj.*
dirham (ˈdɪəræm) *n.* **1.** the standard monetary unit of Morocco, divided into 100 francs. **2.** the standard monetary unit of the United Arab Emirates, divided into 10 dinars and 1000 fils. **3. a.** a Kuwaiti monetary unit worth one tenth of a dinar and 100 fils. **b.** a Tunisian monetary unit worth one tenth of a dinar and 100 millimes. **c.** a Qatari monetary unit worth one hundredth of a riyal. **4.** any of various silver coins minted in North African countries at different periods. [C18: from Arabic, from Latin: DRACHMA]
dirigible (dɪˈrɪdʒɪbᵊl) *adj.* **1.** able to be steered or directed. ~*n.* **2.** another name for **airship.** [C16: from Latin *dīrigere* to DIRECT] —ˌ**dirigiˈbility** *n.*
dirigisme (diːriːˈʒiːzəm) *n.* control by the state of economic and social matters. [C20: from French] —**dirigˈiste** *adj.*
diriment (ˈdɪrɪmənt) *adj.* **1.** (of an impediment to marriage in canon law) totally invalidating. **2.** *Rare.* nullifying. [C19: from Latin *dirimēns* separating, from Latin *dirimere* to part, from DIS-[1] + *emere* to obtain]
dirk (dɜːk) *n.* **1.** a dagger esp. as formerly worn by Scottish Highlanders. ~*vb.* (*tr.*) **2.** to stab with a dirk. [C16: from Scottish *durk*, perhaps from German *dolch* dagger]
dirndl (ˈdɜːndᵊl) *n.* **1.** a woman's dress with a full gathered skirt and fitted bodice; originating from Tyrolean peasant wear. **2.** a gathered skirt of this kind. [German (Bavarian and Austrian): shortened from *Dirndlkleid*, from *Dirndl* little girl + *Kleid* dress]
dirt (dɜːt) *n.* **1.** any unclean substance, such as mud, dust, excrement, etc.; filth. **2.** loose earth; soil. **3. a.** packed earth, gravel, cinders, etc., used to make a racetrack. **b.** (*as modifier*): *a dirt track.* **4.** *Mining.* the gravel or soil from which minerals are extracted. **5.** a person or thing regarded as worthless. **6.** obscene or indecent speech or writing. **7.** moral corruption. **8. do (someone) dirt.** *Slang.* to do something vicious to (someone). **9. eat dirt.** *Slang.* to accept insult without complaining. **10. treat someone like dirt.** to have no respect or consideration for someone. [C13: from Old Norse *drit* excrement; related to Middle Dutch *drēte*]
dirt-cheap *adj., adv. Informal.* at an extremely low price.
dirt road *n.* an unsealed country road.
dirty (ˈdɜːtɪ) *adj.* **dirtier, dirtiest. 1.** covered or marked with dirt; filthy. **2. a.** obscene; salacious: *dirty books.* **b.** sexually clandestine: *a dirty weekend.* **3.** causing one to become grimy: *a dirty job.* **4.** (of a colour) not clear and bright; impure. **5.** unfair; dishonest; unscrupulous; unsporting. **6.** mean; nasty: *a dirty cheat.* **7.** scandalous; unkind: *a dirty rumour.* **8.** revealing dislike or anger: *a dirty look.* **9.** (of weather) rainy or squally; stormy. **10.** (of an aircraft) having projections into the airstream, such as lowered flaps. **11.** (of a nuclear weapon) producing a large quantity of radioactive fallout or contamination. Compare **clean** (sense 5). **12. be dirty on.** *Austral. slang.* to be offended by or be hostile towards. **13. dirty dog.** a despicable person. **14. dirty linen.** *Informal.* intimate secrets, esp. those that might give rise to gossip. **15. dirty work.** unpleasant or illicit activity. **16. do the dirty on.** *Brit. informal.* to behave meanly or unkindly towards. ~*vb.* **dirties, dirtying, dirtied.**

17. to make or become dirty; stain; soil. —'**dirtily** *adv.* —'**dirtiness** *n.*

dirty trick *n.* **1.** a malicious and contemptible action. **2.** (*pl.*) **a.** underhand activity and machinations in political or governmental affairs. **b.** (*as modifier*): *dirty-tricks operation.*

dis-[1] *prefix.* **1.** indicating reversal: *disconnect; disembark.* **2.** indicating negation, lack, or deprivation: *dissimilar; distrust; disgrace.* **3.** indicating removal or release: *disembowel; disburden.* **4.** expressing intensive force: *dissever.* [from Latin *dis-* apart; in some cases, via Old French *des-*. In compound words of Latin origin, *dis-* becomes *dif-* before *f* and *di-* before some consonants]

dis-[2] *combining form.* variant of **di-**[1] before *s*: *dissyllable.*

disability (ˌdɪsəˈbɪlɪtɪ) *n., pl.* **-ties. 1.** the condition of being unable to perform a task or function because of a physical or mental impairment. **2.** something that disables; handicap. **3.** lack of necessary intelligence, strength, etc. **4.** an incapacity in the eyes of the law to enter into certain transactions.

disability clause *n.* (in life assurance policies) a clause enabling a policyholder to cease payment of premiums without loss of coverage and often to receive a pension or indemnity if he becomes permanently disabled.

disable (dɪsˈeɪbᵊl) *vb. (tr.)* **1.** to make ineffective, unfit, or incapable, as by crippling. **2.** to make or pronounce legally incapable. —**disˈablement** *n.*

disabled (dɪˈseɪbᵊld) *adj.* **a.** lacking one or more physical powers, such as the ability to walk or to coordinate one's movements, as from the effects of a disease or accident, or through mental impairment. **b.** (*as collective n.;* preceded by *the*): *the disabled.*

disablement benefit *n.* (in the National Insurance scheme) a weekly payment to a person disabled at work.

disabuse (ˌdɪsəˈbjuːz) *vb. (tr.;* usually foll. by *of*) to rid (oneself, another person, etc.) of a mistaken or misguided idea; set right. —ˌ**disaˈbusal** *n.*

disaccharide (daɪˈsækəˌraɪd, -rɪd) *or* **disaccharid** *n.* any of a class of sugars, such as maltose, lactose, and sucrose, having two linked monosaccharide units per molecule.

disaccord (ˌdɪsəˈkɔːd) *n.* **1.** lack of agreement or harmony. ~*vb.* **2.** (*intr.*) to be out of agreement; disagree.

disaccredit (ˌdɪsəˈkrɛdɪt) *vb. (tr.)* to take away the authorization or credentials of.

disaccustom (ˌdɪsəˈkʌstəm) *vb. (tr.;* usually foll. by *to*) to cause to lose a habit.

disadvantage (ˌdɪsədˈvɑːntɪdʒ) *n.* **1.** an unfavourable circumstance, state of affairs, thing, person, etc. **2.** injury, loss, or detriment. **3.** an unfavourable condition or situation (esp. in the phrase **at a disadvantage**). ~*vb.* **4.** (*tr.*) to put at a disadvantage; handicap.

disadvantaged (ˌdɪsədˈvɑːntɪdʒd) *adj.* socially or economically deprived or discriminated against.

disadvantageous (dɪsˌædvənˈteɪdʒəs, ˌdɪsæd-) *adj.* unfavourable; detrimental. —**disˌadvanˈtageously** *adv.* —**disˌadvanˈtageousness** *n.*

disaffect (ˌdɪsəˈfɛkt) *vb. (tr.; often passive)* to cause to lose loyalty or affection; alienate. —ˌ**disafˈfectedly** *adv.* —ˌ**disafˈfectedness** *n.* —ˌ**disafˈfection** *n.*

disaffiliate (ˌdɪsəˈfɪlɪˌeɪt) *vb.* to sever an affiliation (with); dissociate. —ˌ**disafˌfiliˈation** *n.*

disaffirm (ˌdɪsəˈfɜːm) *vb. (tr.)* **1.** to deny or contradict (a statement). **2.** *Law.* **a.** to annul or reverse (a decision). **b.** to repudiate obligations. —ˌ**disafˈfirmance** *or* **disaffirmation** (ˌdɪsæfəˈmeɪʃən) *n.*

disafforest (ˌdɪsəˈfɒrɪst) *vb. (tr.)* **1.** *English law.* to reduce (land) from the status of a forest to the state of ordinary ground. **2.** to remove forests from (land). —ˌ**disafˌforesˈtation** *or* ˌ**disafˈforestment** *n.*

disagree (ˌdɪsəˈgriː) *vb.* **-grees, -greeing, -greed.** (*intr.;* often foll. by *with*) **1.** to dissent in opinion (from another person) or dispute (about an idea, fact, etc.). **2.** to fail to correspond; conflict. **3.** to be unacceptable (to) or unfavourable (for); be incompatible (with): *curry disagrees with me.* **4.** to be opposed (to) in principle.

disagreeable (ˌdɪsəˈgrɪəbᵊl) *adj.* **1.** not likable, esp. offensive, bad-tempered, or disobliging: *disagreeable remarks.* **2.** not to one's liking; unpleasant: *a disagreeable task.* —ˌ**disaˈgreeableness** *or* ˌ**disaˌgreeaˈbility** *n.* —ˌ**disaˈgreeably** *adv.*

disagreement (ˌdɪsəˈgriːmənt) *n.* **1.** refusal or failure to agree. **2.** a failure to correspond. **3.** an argument or dispute.

disallow (ˌdɪsəˈlaʊ) *vb. (tr.)* **1.** to reject as untrue or invalid. **2.** to cancel. —ˌ**disalˈlowable** *adj.* —ˌ**disalˈlowance** *n.*

disambiguate (ˌdɪsæmˈbɪgjʊˌeɪt) *vb. (tr.)* to make (an ambiguous expression) unambiguous.

disannul (ˌdɪsəˈnʌl) *vb.* **-nuls, -nulling, -nulled.** (*tr.*) *Chiefly law.* to cancel; make void. —ˌ**disanˈnulment** *n.*

disappear (ˌdɪsəˈpɪə) *vb.* **1.** (*intr.*) to cease to be visible; vanish. **2.** (*intr.*) to go away or become lost, esp. secretly or without explanation. **3.** (*intr.*) to cease to exist, have effect, or be known; become extinct or lost: *the pain has disappeared.* **4.** (*tr.*) (esp. in South and Central America) to arrest secretly and presumably imprison or kill (a member of an opposing political group). —ˌ**disapˈpearance** *n.*

disapplication (ˌdɪsæplɪˈkeɪʃən) *n. Brit. Education.* a provision for exempting schools or individuals from the requirements of the National Curriculum in special circumstances.

disappoint (ˌdɪsəˈpɔɪnt) *vb. (tr.)* **1.** to fail to meet the expectations, hopes, desires, or standards of; let down. **2.** to prevent the fulfilment of (a plan, intention, etc.); frustrate; thwart. [C15 (originally meaning: to remove from office): from Old French *desapointier;* see DIS-[1], APPOINT] —ˌ**disapˈpointing** *adj.* —ˌ**disapˈpointingly** *adv.*

disappointed (ˌdɪsəˈpɔɪntɪd) *adj.* saddened by the failure of an expectation, etc. —ˌ**disapˈpointedly** *adv.*

disappointment (ˌdɪsəˈpɔɪntmənt) *n.* **1.** the act of disappointing or the state of being disappointed. **2.** a person, thing, or state of affairs that disappoints.

disapprobation (ˌdɪsæprəʊˈbeɪʃən) *n.* moral or social disapproval.

disapproval (ˌdɪsəˈpruːvᵊl) *n.* the act or a state or feeling of disapproving; censure; condemnation.

disapprove (ˌdɪsəˈpruːv) *vb.* **1.** (*intr.;* often foll. by *of*) to consider wrong, bad, etc. **2.** (*tr.*) to withhold approval from. —ˌ**disapˈproving** *adj.* —ˌ**disapˈprovingly** *adv.*

disarm (dɪsˈɑːm) *vb.* **1.** (*tr.*) to remove defensive or offensive capability from (a country, army, etc.). **2.** (*tr.*) to deprive of weapons. **3.** (*tr.*) to win the confidence or affection of. **4.** (*intr.*) (of a nation, etc.) to decrease the size and capability of one's armed forces. **5.** (*intr.*) to lay down weapons. —**disˈarmer** *n.*

disarmament (dɪsˈɑːməmənt) *n.* **1.** the reduction of offensive or defensive fighting capability, as by a nation. **2.** the act of disarming or the state of being disarmed.

disarming (dɪsˈɑːmɪŋ) *adj.* tending to neutralize or counteract hostility, suspicion, etc. —**disˈarmingly** *adv.*

disarrange (ˌdɪsəˈreɪndʒ) *vb. (tr.)* to throw into disorder. —ˌ**disarˈrangement** *n.*

disarray (ˌdɪsəˈreɪ) *n.* **1.** confusion, dismay, and lack of discipline. **2.** (esp. of clothing) disorderliness; untidiness. ~*vb. (tr.)* **3.** to throw into confusion. **4.** *Archaic.* to undress.

disarticulate (ˌdɪsɑːˈtɪkjʊˌleɪt) *vb.* to separate or cause to separate at the joints, esp. those of bones. —ˌ**disarˌticuˈlation** *n.* —ˌ**disarˈticuˌlator** *n.*

disassemble (ˌdɪsəˈsɛmbᵊl) *vb. (tr.)* to take apart (a piece of machinery, etc.); dismantle. —ˌ**disasˈsembly** *n.*

disassembler (ˌdɪsəˈsɛmblə) *n. Computer technol.* a computer program that translates machine code into assembly language.

disassociate (ˌdɪsəˈsəʊʃɪˌeɪt) *vb.* a less common word for **dissociate.** —ˌ**disasˌsociˈation** *n.*

disaster (dɪˈzɑːstə) *n.* **1.** an occurrence that causes great distress or destruction. **2.** a thing, project, etc., that fails or has been ruined. [C16 (originally in the sense: malevolent astral influence): from Italian *disastro,* from *dis-* (pejorative) + *astro* star, from Latin *astrum,* from Greek *astron*] —**disˈastrous** *adj.*

disavow (ˌdɪsəˈvaʊ) *vb. (tr.)* to deny knowledge of, connection with, or responsibility for. —ˌ**disaˈvowal** *n.* —ˌ**disaˈvowedly** *adv.* —ˌ**disaˈvower** *n.*

disband (dɪsˈbænd) *vb.* to cease to function or cause to stop functioning, as a unit, group, etc. —**disˈbandment** *n.*

disbar (dɪsˈbɑː) *vb.* **-bars, -barring, -barred.** (*tr.*) *Law.* to deprive of the status of barrister; expel from the Bar. —**disˈbarment** *n.*

disbelief (ˌdɪsbɪˈliːf) *n.* refusal or reluctance to believe.

disbelieve (ˌdɪsbɪˈliːv) *vb.* **1.** (*tr.*) to reject as false or lying; refuse to accept as true or truthful. **2.** (*intr.;* usually foll. by *in*) to have no faith (in): *disbelieve in God.* —ˌ**disbeˈliever** *n.* —ˌ**disbeˈlieving** *adj.* —ˌ**disbeˈlievingly** *adv.*

disbranch (dɪsˈbrɑːntʃ) *vb. (tr.)* to remove or cut a branch or branches from (a tree).

disbud (dɪsˈbʌd) *or* **debud** (diːˈbʌd) *vb.* **-buds, -budding, -budded. 1.** to remove superfluous buds, flowers, or shoots from (a plant, esp. a fruit tree). **2.** *Vet. science.* to remove the horn buds of (calves, lambs, and kids).

disburden (dɪsˈbɜːdᵊn) *vb.* **1.** to remove a load from (a person or animal). **2.** (*tr.*) to relieve (oneself, one's mind, etc.) of a distressing worry or oppressive thought. —**disˈburdenment** *n.*

disburse (dɪsˈbɜːs) *vb. (tr.)* to pay out. [C16: from Old French *desborser,* from *des-* DIS-[1] + *borser* to obtain money, from *borse* bag, from Late Latin *bursa*] —**disˈbursable** *adj.* —**disˈbursement** *n.* —**disˈburser** *n.*

disc *or* (*now esp. U.S.*) **disk** (dɪsk) *n.* **1.** a flat circular plate. **2.** something resembling or appearing to resemble this: *the sun's disc.* **3.** another word for (gramophone) **record. 4.** *Anatomy.* any approximately circular flat structure in the body, esp. an intervertebral disc. **5. a.** the flat receptacle of composite flowers, such as the daisy. **b.** (*as modifier*): *a disc flower.* **6.** the middle part of the lip of an orchid. **7. a.** Also called: **parking disc.** a marker or device for display in a parked vehicle showing the time of arrival or the latest permitted time of departure or both. **b.** (*as modifier*): *a disc zone; disc parking.* **8.** *Computer technol.* a variant spelling of **disk** (sense 2). ~*vb.* **9.** to work (land) with a disc harrow. [C18: from Latin *discus,* from Greek *diskos* quoit]

disc. *abbrev. for:* **1.** discount. **2.** discovered.

discal (ˈdɪskᵊl) *adj. Biology, zoology.* relating to or resembling a disc; disclike: *discal cells.*

discalced (dɪsˈkælst) *adj.* barefooted: used to denote friars and nuns who wear sandals. [C17: from Latin *discalceātus,* from DIS-[1] + *calceātus* shod, from *calceāre* to provide with shoes, from *calceus* shoe, from *calx* heel]
discant *n.* (ˈdɪskænt), *vb.* (dɪsˈkænt). a variant of **descant** (senses 1, 3, 4). —**disˈcanter** *n.*
discard *vb.* (dɪsˈkɑːd). **1.** (*tr.*) to get rid of as useless or undesirable. **2.** *Cards.* to throw out (a card or cards) from one's hand. **3.** *Cards.* to play (a card not of the suit led nor a trump) when unable to follow suit. ~*n.* (ˈdɪskɑːd). **4.** a person or thing that has been cast aside. **5.** *Cards.* a discarded card. **6.** the act of discarding. —**disˈcarder** *n.*
disc brake *n.* a type of brake in which two calliper-operated pads rub against a flat disc attached to the wheel hub when the brake is applied.
disc camera *n.* a type of small compact camera in which the film is on a disc (**disc film**) instead of a spool.
discern (dɪˈsɜːn) *vb.* **1.** (*tr.*) to recognize or perceive clearly. **2.** to recognize or perceive (differences). [C14: from Old French *discerner,* from Latin *discernere* to divide, from DIS-[1] (apart) + *cernere* to separate] —**disˈcerner** *n.*
discernible *or (rarely)* **discernable** (dɪˈsɜːnəbᵊl) *adj.* able to be discerned; perceptible. —**disˈcernibly** *or (rarely)* **disˈcernably** *adv.*
discerning (dɪˈsɜːnɪŋ) *adj.* having or showing good taste or judgment; discriminating. —**disˈcerningly** *adv.*
discernment (dɪˈsɜːnmənt) *n.* keen perception or judgment.
disc flower *or* **floret** *n.* any of the small tubular flowers at the centre of the flower head of certain composite plants, such as the daisy. Compare **ray flower.**
discharge *vb.* (dɪsˈtʃɑːdʒ). **1.** (*tr.*) to release or allow to go: *the hospital discharged the patient.* **2.** (*tr.*) to dismiss from or relieve of duty, office, employment, etc. **3.** to fire or be fired, as a gun. **4.** to pour forth or cause to pour forth: *the boil discharges pus.* **5.** (*tr.*) to remove (the cargo) from (a boat, etc.); unload. **6.** (*tr.*) to perform (the duties of) or meet (the demands of an office, obligation, etc.): *he discharged his responsibilities as mayor.* **7.** (*tr.*) to relieve oneself of (a responsibility, debt, etc.). **8.** (*intr.*) *Physics.* **a.** to lose or remove electric charge. **b.** to form an arc, spark, or corona in a gas. **c.** to take or supply electrical current from a cell or battery. **9.** (*tr.*) *Law.* to release (a prisoner from custody, etc.). **10.** (*tr.*) to remove dye from (a fabric), as by bleaching. **11.** (*intr.*) (of a dye or colour) to blur or run. **12.** (*tr.*) *Architect.* **a.** to spread (weight) evenly over a supporting member. **b.** to relieve a member of (excess weight) by distribution of pressure. ~*n.* (ˈdɪstʃɑːdʒ, dɪsˈtʃɑːdʒ). **13.** a person or thing that is discharged. **14. a.** dismissal or release from an office, job, institution, etc. **b.** the document certifying such release. **15.** the fulfilment of an obligation or release from a responsibility or liability. **16.** the act of removing a load, as of cargo. **17.** a pouring forth of a fluid; emission. **18. a.** the act of firing a projectile. **b.** the volley, bullet, missile, etc., fired. **19.** *Law.* **a.** a release, as of a person held under legal restraint. **b.** an annulment, as of a court order. **20.** *Physics.* **a.** the act or process of removing or losing charge or of equalizing a potential difference. **b.** a transient or continuous conduction of electricity through a gas by the formation and movement of electrons and ions in an applied electric field. —**disˈchargeable** *adj.* —**disˈcharger** *n.*
discharge tube *n. Electronics.* an electrical device in which current flow is by electrons and ions in an ionized gas, as in a fluorescent light or neon tube.
disc harrow *n.* a harrow with sharp-edged slightly concave discs mounted on horizontal shafts and used to cut clods or debris on the surface of the soil or to cover seed after planting.
disciple (dɪˈsaɪpᵊl) *n.* **1.** a follower of the doctrines of a teacher or a school of thought. **2.** one of the personal followers of Christ (including his 12 apostles) during his earthly life. [Old English *discipul,* from Latin *discipulus* pupil, from *discere* to learn] —**disˈcipleˌship** *n.* —**discipular** (dɪˈsɪpjʊlə) *adj.*
Disciples of Christ *pl. n.* a Christian denomination founded in the U.S. in 1809.
disciplinant (ˈdɪsɪˌplɪnənt) *n.* (*often cap.*) *R.C. Church.* a person belonging to a former order of flagellants in Spain.
disciplinarian (ˌdɪsɪplɪˈnɛərɪən) *n.* **1.** a person who imposes or advocates discipline. ~*adj.* **2.** a less common word for **disciplinary.**
disciplinary (ˈdɪsɪˌplɪnərɪ) *or* **disciplinarian** *adj.* **1.** of, promoting, or used for discipline; corrective. **2.** relating to a branch of learning: *criticism that crosses disciplinary boundaries.*
discipline (ˈdɪsɪplɪn) *n.* **1.** training or conditions imposed for the improvement of physical powers, self-control, etc. **2.** systematic training in obedience to regulations and authority. **3.** the state of improved behaviour, etc., resulting from such training or conditions. **4.** punishment or chastisement. **5.** a system of rules for behaviour, methods of practice, etc. **6.** a branch of learning or instruction. **7.** the laws governing members of a Church. **8.** a scourge of knotted cords. ~*vb.* (*tr.*) **9.** to improve or attempt to improve the behaviour, orderliness, etc., of by training, conditions, or rules. **10.** to punish or correct. [C13: from Latin *disciplīna* teaching, from *discipulus* DISCIPLE] —ˈ**disciˌplinable** *adj.* —**disciplinal** (ˌdɪsɪˈplaɪnᵊl, ˈdɪsɪplɪnᵊl) *adj.* —ˈ**disciˌpliner** *n.*
discission (dɪsˈsɪʒən) *n. Med.* surgical incision, esp. of a cataract.

disc jockey *n.* a person who announces and plays recorded music, esp. pop music, on a radio programme, etc. Abbrevs.: **DJ, dj.**
disclaim (dɪsˈkleɪm) *vb.* **1.** (*tr.*) to deny or renounce (any claim, connection, etc.). **2.** (*tr.*) to deny the validity or authority of. **3.** *Law.* to renounce or repudiate (a legal claim or right). —**disclamation** (ˌdɪskləˈmeɪʃən) *n.*
disclaimer (dɪsˈkleɪmə) *n.* a repudiation or denial.
disclimax (dɪsˈklaɪmæks) *n. Ecology.* a climax community resulting from the activities of man or domestic animals in climatic and other conditions that would otherwise support a different type of community.
disclose (dɪsˈkləʊz) *vb.* (*tr.*) **1.** to make (information) known. **2.** to allow to be seen; lay bare. —**disˈcloser** *n.*
disclosing agent *n. Dentistry.* a vegetable dye, administered as a liquid or in tablet form (**disclosing tablet**), that stains plaque, making it readily apparent on the teeth.
disclosure (dɪsˈkləʊʒə) *n.* **1.** something that is disclosed. **2.** the act of disclosing; revelation.
disco (ˈdɪskəʊ) *n., pl.* **-cos.** **1. a.** an occasion at which typically young people dance to amplified pop records, usually compered by a disc jockey and featuring special lighting effects. **b.** (*as modifier*): *disco dancing.* **2.** a nightclub or other public place where such dances take place. **3.** mobile equipment, usually accompanied by a disc jockey who operates it, for providing music for a disco. **4. a.** a type of dance music designed to be played in discos, with a solid thump on each beat. **b.** (*as modifier*): *a disco record.*
discobolus *or* **discobolos** (dɪsˈkɒbələs) *n., pl.* **-li** (-ˌlaɪ). **1.** (in classical Greece) a discus thrower. **2.** a statue of a discus thrower. [C18: from Latin, from Greek *diskobolos,* from *diskos* DISCUS + *-bolos,* from *ballein* to throw]
discography (dɪsˈkɒgrəfɪ) *n.* **1.** a classified reference list of gramophone records. **2.** another word for **discology.** —**disˈcographer** *n.*
discoid (ˈdɪskɔɪd) *adj. also* **discoidal** (dɪsˈkɔɪdᵊl). **1.** like a disc. **2.** (of a composite flower such as the tansy) consisting of disc flowers only. ~*n.* **3.** a disclike object.
discology (dɪsˈkɒlədʒɪ) *n.* the study of gramophone records. —**disˈcologist** *n.*
discolour *or U.S.* **discolor** (dɪsˈkʌlə) *vb.* to change or cause to change in colour; fade or stain. —**disˌcolorˈation** *or* **disˌcolourˈation** *n.* —**disˈcolourment** *or U.S.* **disˈcolorment** *n.*
discombobulate (ˌdɪskəmˈbɒbjʊˌleɪt) *vb.* (*tr.*) *Informal, chiefly U.S. and Canadian.* to throw into confusion. [C20: probably a whimsical alteration of DISCOMPOSE or DISCOMFIT]
discomfit (dɪsˈkʌmfɪt) *vb.* (*tr.*) **1.** to make uneasy, confused, or embarrassed. **2.** to frustrate the plans or purpose of. **3.** *Archaic.* to defeat in battle. [C14: from Old French *desconfire* to destroy, from *des-* (indicating reversal) + *confire* to make, from Latin *conficere* to produce; see CONFECT] —**disˈcomfiter** *n.* —**disˈcomfiture** *n.*
discomfort (dɪsˈkʌmfət) *n.* **1.** an inconvenience, distress, or mild pain. **2.** something that disturbs or deprives of ease. ~*vb.* **3.** (*tr.*) to make uncomfortable or uneasy.
discomfortable (dɪsˈkʌmfətəbᵊl, -ˈkʌmftə-) *adj. Archaic.* tending to deprive of mental or physical ease or comfort.
discommend (ˌdɪskəˈmɛnd) *vb.* (*tr.*) **1.** *Rare.* to express disapproval of. **2.** *Obsolete.* to bring into disfavour. —ˌ**discomˈmendable** *adj.* —**disˌcommenˈdation** *n.*
discommode (ˌdɪskəˈməʊd) *vb.* (*tr.*) to cause inconvenience or annoyance to; disturb. —ˌ**discomˈmodious** *adj.* —ˌ**discomˈmodiously** *adv.*
discommodity (ˌdɪskəˈmɒdɪtɪ) *n., pl.* **-ties.** **1.** *Economics.* a commodity without utility. **2.** *Archaic.* the state or a source of inconvenience.
discommon (dɪsˈkɒmən) *vb.* (*tr.*) *Law.* to deprive (land) of the character and status of common, as by enclosure.
discompose (ˌdɪskəmˈpəʊz) *vb.* (*tr.*) **1.** to disturb the composure of; disconcert. **2.** *Now rare.* to disarrange. —ˌ**discomˈposedly** *adv.* —ˌ**discomˈposingly** *adv.* —ˌ**discomˈposure** *n.*
disconcert (ˌdɪskənˈsɜːt) *vb.* (*tr.*) **1.** to disturb the composure of. **2.** to frustrate or upset. —ˌ**disconˈcerting** *adj.* —ˌ**disconˈcertingly** *adv.* —ˌ**disconˈcertion** *or* ˌ**disconˈcertment** *n.*
disconcerted (ˌdɪskənˈsɜːtɪd) *adj.* perturbed, embarrassed, or confused. —ˌ**disconˈcertedly** *adv.* —ˌ**disconˈcertedness** *n.*
disconfirm (ˌdɪskənˈfɜːm) *vb.* (*tr.*) (of a fact or argument) to suggest that a hypothesis is wrong or ill-formulated. —ˌ**disconfirˈmation** *n.*
disconformity (ˌdɪskənˈfɔːmɪtɪ) *n., pl.* **-ties.** **1.** lack of conformity; discrepancy. **2.** the junction between two parallel series of stratified rocks, representing a considerable period of erosion of the much older underlying rocks before the more recent ones were deposited.
disconnect (ˌdɪskəˈnɛkt) *vb.* (*tr.*) to undo or break the connection of or between (something, such as a plug and a socket). —ˌ**disconˈnecter** *n.* —ˌ**disconˈnection** *or* ˌ**disconˈnexion** *n.* —ˌ**disconˈnective** *adj.*
disconnected (ˌdɪskəˈnɛktɪd) *adj.* **1.** not rationally connected; confused or incoherent. **2.** not connected or joined. —ˌ**disconˈnectedly** *adv.* —ˌ**disconˈnectedness** *n.*
disconsider (ˌdɪskənˈsɪdə) *vb.* (*tr.*) *Archaic.* to discredit. —ˌ**disconˌsiderˈation** *n.*

disconsolate (dɪsˈkɒnsəlɪt) *adj.* **1.** sad beyond comfort; inconsolable. **2.** disappointed; dejected. [C14: from Medieval Latin *disconsōlātus,* from DIS-[1] + *consōlātus* comforted; see CONSOLE[1]] —**disˈconsolately** *adv.* —**disˈconsolateness** *or* **disˌconsoˈlation** *n.*
discontent (ˌdɪskənˈtɛnt) *n.* **1.** Also called: **ˌdisconˈtentment.** lack of contentment, as with one's condition or lot in life. **2.** a discontented person. ~*adj.* **3.** dissatisfied. ~*vb.* **4.** (*tr.*) to make dissatisfied. —**ˌdisconˈtented** *adj.* —**ˌdisconˈtentedly** *adv.* —**ˌdisconˈtentedness** *n.*
discontinue (ˌdɪskənˈtɪnjuː) *vb.* **-ues, -uing, -ued. 1.** to come or bring to an end; interrupt or be interrupted; stop. **2.** (*tr.*) *Law.* to terminate or abandon (an action, suit, etc.). —**ˌdisconˈtinuance** *n.* —**ˌdisconˌtinuˈation** *n.* —**ˌdisconˈtinuer** *n.*
discontinuity (dɪsˌkɒntɪˈnjuːɪtɪ) *n., pl.* **-ties. 1.** lack of rational connection or cohesion. **2.** a break or interruption. **3.** *Maths.* **a.** the property of being discontinuous. **b.** the point or the value of the variable at which a curve or function becomes discontinuous. **4.** *Geology.* **a.** a zone within the earth where a sudden change in physical properties, such as the velocity of earthquake waves, occurs. Such a zone marks the boundary between the different layers of the earth, as between the core and mantle. See also **Mohorovičić discontinuity. b.** a surface separating rocks that are not continuous with each other.
discontinuous (ˌdɪskənˈtɪnjʊəs) *adj.* **1.** characterized by interruptions or breaks; intermittent. **2.** *Maths.* (of a function or curve) changing suddenly in value for one or more values of the variable or at one or more points. Compare **continuous** (sense 3). —**ˌdisconˈtinuously** *adv.* —**ˌdisconˈtinuousness** *n.*
discophile (ˈdɪskəˌfaɪl) *or* **discophil** (ˈdɪskəfɪl) *n.* a collector or connoisseur of gramophone records.
discord *n.* (ˈdɪskɔːd). **1.** lack of agreement of harmony; strife. **2.** harsh confused mingling of sounds. **3.** a combination of musical notes containing one or more dissonant intervals. See **dissonance** (sense 3), **concord** (sense 4). ~*vb.* (dɪsˈkɔːd). **4.** (*intr.*) to disagree; clash. [C13: from Old French *descort,* from *descorder* to disagree, from Latin *discordāre,* from *discors* at variance, from DIS-[1] + *cor* heart]
discordance (dɪsˈkɔːdᵊns) *or* **discordancy** *n.* **1.** *Geology.* an arrangement of rock strata in which the older underlying ones dip at a different angle from the younger overlying ones; unconformity. **2.** lack of agreement or consonance. **3.** variants of **discord.**
discordant (dɪsˈkɔːdᵊnt) *adj.* **1.** at variance; disagreeing. **2.** harsh in sound; inharmonious. —**disˈcordantly** *adv.*
discotheque (ˈdɪskəˌtɛk) *n.* the full name of **disco.** [C20: from French *discothèque,* from Greek *diskos* disc + -O- + Greek *thēkē* case]
discount *vb.* (dɪsˈkaʊnt, ˈdɪskaʊnt). (*mainly tr.*) **1.** to leave out of account as being unreliable, prejudiced, or irrelevant. **2.** to anticipate and make allowance for, often so as to diminish the effect of. **3. a.** to deduct (a specified amount or percentage) from the usual price, cost, etc. **b.** to reduce (the regular price, cost, etc.) by a stated percentage or amount. **4.** to sell or offer for sale at a reduced price. **5.** to buy or sell (a bill of exchange, etc.) before maturity, with a deduction for interest determined by the time to maturity and also by risk. **6.** (*also intr.*) to loan money on (a negotiable instrument that is not immediately payable) with a deduction for interest determined by risk and time to maturity. ~*n.* (ˈdɪskaʊnt). **7.** a deduction from the full amount of a price or debt, as in return for prompt payment or to a special group of customers. See also **cash discount, trade discount. 8.** Also called: **discount rate. a.** the amount of interest deducted in the purchase or sale of or the loan of money on unmatured negotiable instruments. **b.** the rate of interest deducted. **9. a.** (in the issue of shares) a percentage deducted from the par value to give a reduced amount payable by subscribers. **b.** the amount by which the par value of something, esp. shares, exceeds its market value. Compare **premium** (sense 3). **10.** the act or an instance of discounting a negotiable instrument. **11. at a discount. a.** below the regular price. **b.** (of share values) below par. **c.** held in low regard; not sought after or valued. **12.** (*modifier*) offering or selling at reduced prices: *a discount shop.* —**disˈcountable** *adj.* —**ˈdiscounter** *n.*
discounted cash flow *n. Account.* a technique for appraising an investment that takes into account the different values of future returns according to when they will be received. Abbrev.: **DCF.**
discountenance (dɪsˈkaʊntɪnəns) *vb.* (*tr.*) **1.** to make ashamed or confused. **2.** to disapprove of. ~*n.* **3.** disapproval.
discount house *n.* **1.** *Chiefly Brit.* a financial organization engaged in discounting bills of exchange, etc. on a large scale primarily by borrowing call money from commercial banks. **2.** *Chiefly U.S.* another name for **discount store.**
discount market *n.* the part of the money market consisting of banks, discount houses, and brokers on which bills are discounted.
discount store *n.* a shop where goods are sold at a low price.
discourage (dɪsˈkʌrɪdʒ) *vb.* (*tr.*) **1.** to deprive of the will to persist in something. **2.** to inhibit; prevent: *this solution discourages rust.* **3.** to oppose by expressing disapproval. —**disˈcouragement** *n.* —**disˈcourager** *n.* —**disˈcouragingly** *adv.*
discourse *n.* (ˈdɪskɔːs, dɪsˈkɔːs). **1.** verbal communication; talk; conversation. **2.** a formal treatment of a subject in speech or writing, such as a sermon or dissertation. **3.** a unit of text used by linguists for the analysis of linguistic phenomena that range over more than one sentence. **4.** *Archaic.* the ability to reason or the reasoning process. ~*vb.* (dɪsˈkɔːs). **5.** (*intr.; often foll. by on or upon*) to speak or write (about) formally and extensively. **6.** (*intr.*) to hold a discussion. **7.** (*tr.*) *Archaic.* to give forth (music). [C14: from Medieval Latin *discursus* argument, from Latin: a running to and fro, from *discurrere* to run different ways, from DIS-[1] + *currere* to run] —**disˈcourser** *n.*
discourteous (dɪsˈkɜːtɪəs) *adj.* showing bad manners; impolite; rude. —**disˈcourteously** *adv.* —**disˈcourteousness** *n.*
discourtesy (dɪsˈkɜːtɪsɪ) *n., pl.* **-sies. 1.** bad manners; rudeness. **2.** a rude remark or act.
discover (dɪˈskʌvə) *vb.* (*tr.; may take a clause as object*) **1.** to be the first to find or find out about: *Fleming discovered penicillin.* **2.** to learn about or encounter for the first time; realize: *she discovered the pleasures of wine.* **3.** to find after study or search: *I discovered a leak in the tank.* **4.** to reveal or make known. —**disˈcoverable** *adj.* —**disˈcoverer** *n.*
discovered check *n. Chess.* check given by moving a man that has been masking a potential check from a bishop, rook, or queen.
discovert (dɪsˈkʌvət) *adj. Law.* (of a woman) not under the protection of a husband; being a widow, spinster, or divorcée. [C14: from Old French *descovert,* past participle of *descouvrir* to DISCOVER] —**disˈcoverture** *n.*
discovery (dɪˈskʌvərɪ) *n., pl.* **-eries. 1.** the act, process, or an instance of discovering. **2.** a person, place, or thing that has been discovered. **3.** *Law.* the compulsory disclosure by a party to an action of relevant documents in his possession.
disc plough *n.* a plough that cuts by means of revolving steel discs.
discredit (dɪsˈkrɛdɪt) *vb.* (*tr.*) **1.** to damage the reputation of. **2.** to cause to be disbelieved or distrusted. **3.** to reject as untrue or of questionable accuracy. ~*n.* **4.** a person, thing, or state of affairs that causes disgrace. **5.** damage to a reputation. **6.** lack of belief or confidence.
discreditable (dɪsˈkrɛdɪtəbᵊl) *adj.* tending to bring discredit; shameful or unworthy. —**disˈcreditably** *adv.*
discreet (dɪˈskriːt) *adj.* careful to avoid social embarrassment or distress, esp. by keeping confidences secret; tactful. [C14: from Old French *discret,* from Medieval Latin *discrētus,* from Latin *discernere* to DISCERN] —**disˈcreetly** *adv.* —**disˈcreetness** *n.*
discrepancy (dɪˈskrɛpənsɪ) *n., pl.* **-cies.** a conflict or variation, as between facts, figures, or claims.
discrepant (dɪˈskrɛpənt) *adj.* inconsistent; conflicting; at variance. [C15: from Latin *discrepāns,* from *discrepāre* to differ in sound, from DIS-[1] + *crepāre* to be noisy] —**disˈcrepantly** *adv.*
discrete (dɪsˈkriːt) *adj.* **1.** separate or distinct in form or concept. **2.** consisting of distinct or separate parts. **3.** *Statistics.* **a.** (of a variable) having consecutive values that are not infinitesimally close, so that its analysis requires summation rather than integration. **b.** (of a distribution) relating to a discrete variable. Compare **continuous** (sense 4). [C14: from Latin *discrētus* separated, set apart; see DISCREET] —**disˈcretely** *adv.* —**disˈcreteness** *n.*
discretion (dɪˈskrɛʃən) *n.* **1.** the quality of behaving or speaking in such a way as to avoid social embarrassment or distress. **2.** freedom or authority to make judgments and to act as one sees fit (esp. in the phrases **at one's own discretion, at the discretion of**). **3. age** *or* **years of discretion.** the age at which a person is considered to be able to manage his own affairs.
discretionary (dɪˈskrɛʃənərɪ, -ənrɪ) *or* **discretional** *adj.* having or using the ability to decide at one's own discretion: *discretionary powers.* —**disˈcretionarily** *or* **disˈcretionally** *adv.*
discretionary trust *n.* a trust in which the beneficiaries' shares are not fixed by the settler in the trust deed but are left to the discretion of other persons, often the trustees.
discriminant (dɪˈskrɪmɪnənt) *n.* an algebraic expression related to the coefficients of a polynomial equation whose value gives information about the roots of the polynomial: $b^2 - 4ac$ *is the discriminant of* $ax^2 + bx + c = 0$.
discriminate *vb.* (dɪˈskrɪmɪˌneɪt). **1.** (*intr.;* usu. foll. by *in favour of* or *against*) to single out a particular person, group, etc., for special favour or, esp., disfavour, often because of a characteristic such as race, colour, sex, intelligence, etc. **2.** (when *intr.,* foll. by *between* or *among*) to recognize or understand the difference (between); distinguish: *to discriminate right and wrong; to discriminate between right and wrong.* **3.** (*intr.*) to constitute or mark a difference. **4.** (*intr.*) to be discerning in matters of taste. ~*adj.* (dɪˈskrɪmɪnɪt). **5.** showing or marked by discrimination. [C17: from Latin *discrīmināre* to divide, from *discrīmen* a separation, from *discernere* to DISCERN] —**disˈcriminately** *adv.* —**disˈcrimiˌnator** *n.*
discriminating (dɪˈskrɪmɪˌneɪtɪŋ) *adj.* **1.** able to see fine distinctions and differences. **2.** discerning in matters of taste. **3.** (of a tariff, import duty, etc.) levied at differential rates in order to favour or discourage imports or exports. —**disˈcrimiˌnatingly** *adv.*
discrimination (dɪˌskrɪmɪˈneɪʃən) *n.* **1.** unfair treatment of a person, racial group, minority, etc.; action based on prejudice. **2.** subtle appreciation in matters of taste. **3.** the ability to see fine distinctions and differences. **4.** *Electronics.* the selection of a signal having a particular frequency, amplitude, phase, etc.,

caused by the elimination of other signals by means of a discriminator. —**dis,crimi'national** *adj.*

discrimination learning *n. Psychol.* a learning process in which an organism learns to react differently to different stimuli. Compare **generalization** (sense 3).

discriminator (dɪ'skrɪmɪˌneɪtə) *n.* **1.** an electronic circuit that converts a frequency or phase modulation into an amplitude modulation for subsequent demodulation. **2.** an electronic circuit that has an output voltage only when the amplitude of the input pulses exceeds a predetermined value.

discriminatory (dɪ'skrɪmɪnətərɪ, -trɪ) *or* **discriminative** (dɪ'skrɪmɪnətɪv) *adj.* **1.** based on or showing prejudice; biased. **2.** capable of making fine distinctions. **3.** (of a statistical test) unbiased. —**dis'criminatorily** *or* **dis'criminatively** *adv.*

discursive (dɪ'skɜːsɪv) *adj.* **1.** passing from one topic to another, usually in an unmethodical way; digressive. **2.** *Philosophy.* of or relating to knowledge obtained by reason and argument rather than intuition. Compare **dianoetic.** [C16: from Medieval Latin *discursīvus,* from Late Latin *discursus* DISCOURSE] —**dis'cursively** *adv.* —**dis'cursiveness** *n.*

discus ('dɪskəs) *n., pl.* **discuses** *or* **disci** ('dɪskaɪ). **1.** (originally) a circular stone or plate used in throwing competitions by the ancient Greeks. **2.** *Field sports.* **a.** a similar disc-shaped object with a heavy middle thrown by athletes. **b.** (*as modifier*): *a discus thrower.* **3.** (preceded by *the*) the event or sport of throwing the discus. **4.** a South American cichlid fish, *Symphysodon discus,* that has a compressed coloured body and is a popular aquarium fish. [C17: from Latin, from Greek *diskos* from *dikein* to throw]

discuss (dɪ'skʌs) *vb.* (*tr.*) **1.** to have a conversation about; consider by talking over; debate. **2.** to treat (a subject) in speech or writing: *the first three volumes discuss basic principles.* **3.** *Facetious, rare.* to eat or drink with enthusiasm. [C14: from Late Latin *discussus* examined, from *discutere* to investigate, from Latin: to dash to pieces, from DIS-[1] + *quatere* to shake, strike] —**dis'cussant** *or* **dis'cusser** *n.* —**dis'cussible** *or* **dis'cussable** *adj.*

discussion (dɪ'skʌʃən) *n.* the examination or consideration of a matter in speech or writing. —**dis'cussional** *adj.*

disc wheel *n.* a road wheel of a motor vehicle that has a round pressed disc in place of spokes. Compare **wire wheel.**

disdain (dɪs'deɪn) *n.* **1.** a feeling or show of superiority and dislike; contempt; scorn. ~*vb.* **2.** (*tr.; may take an infinitive*) to refuse or reject with disdain. [C13 *dedeyne,* from Old French *desdeign,* from *desdeigner* to reject as unworthy, from Latin *dēdignārī;* see DIS-[1], DEIGN]

disdainful (dɪs'deɪnfʊl) *adj.* showing or feeling disdain. —**dis'dainfully** *adv.* —**dis'dainfulness** *n.*

disease (dɪ'ziːz) *n.* **1.** any impairment of normal physiological function affecting all or part of an organism, esp. a specific pathological change caused by infection, stress, etc., producing characteristic symptoms; illness or sickness in general. **2.** a corresponding condition in plants. **3.** any situation or condition likened to this: *the disease of materialism.* [C14: from Old French *desaise;* see DIS-[1], EASE]

diseased (dɪ'ziːzd) *adj.* having or affected with disease.

diseconomy (ˌdɪsɪ'kɒnəmɪ) *n. Economics.* disadvantage, such as lower efficiency or higher average costs, resulting from the scale on which an enterprise produces goods or services.

disembark (ˌdɪsɪm'bɑːk) *vb.* to land or cause to land from a ship, aircraft, etc.: *several passengers disembarked; we will disembark the passengers.* —**disembarkation** (dɪsˌɛmbɑː'keɪʃən) *or* ˌ**disem'barkment** *n.*

disembarrass (ˌdɪsɪm'bærəs) *vb.* (*tr.*) **1.** to free from embarrassment, entanglement, etc. **2.** to relieve or rid of something burdensome. —ˌ**disem'barrassment** *n.*

disembodied (ˌdɪsɪm'bɒdɪd) *adj.* **1.** lacking a body or freed from the body; incorporeal. **2.** lacking in substance, solidity, or any firm relation to reality.

disembody (ˌdɪsɪm'bɒdɪ) *vb.* **-bodies, -bodying, -bodied.** (*tr.*) to free from the body or from physical form. —ˌ**disem'bodiment** *n.*

disembogue (ˌdɪsɪm'bəʊg) *vb.* **-bogues, -boguing, -bogued.** **1.** (of a river, stream, etc.) to discharge (water) at the mouth. **2.** (*intr.*) to flow out. [C16: from Spanish *desembocar,* from *des-* DIS-[1] + *embocar* put into the mouth, from *em-* in + *boca* mouth, from Latin *bucca* cheek] —ˌ**disem'boguement** *n.*

disembowel (ˌdɪsɪm'baʊəl) *vb.* **-els, -elling, -elled** *or U.S.* **-els, -eling, -eled.** (*tr.*) to remove the entrails of. —ˌ**disem'bowelment** *n.*

disembroil (ˌdɪsɪm'brɔɪl) *vb.* (*tr.*) to free from entanglement or a confused situation.

disenable (ˌdɪsɪ'neɪbᵊl) *vb.* (*tr.*) to cause to become incapable; prevent. —ˌ**disen'ablement** *n.*

disenchant (ˌdɪsɪn'tʃɑːnt) *vb.* (*tr.*) to free from or as if from an enchantment; disillusion. —ˌ**disen'chanter** *n.* —ˌ**disen'chantingly** *adv.* —ˌ**disen'chantment** *n.*

disencumber (ˌdɪsɪn'kʌmbə) *vb.* (*tr.*) to free from encumbrances. —ˌ**disen'cumberment** *n.*

disendow (ˌdɪsɪn'daʊ) *vb.* (*tr.*) to take away an endowment from. —ˌ**disen'dower** *n.* —ˌ**disen'dowment** *n.*

disenfranchise (ˌdɪsɪn'fræntʃaɪz) *vb.* another word for **disfranchise.** —**disenfranchisement** (ˌdɪsɪn'fræntʃɪzmənt) *n.*

disengage (ˌdɪsɪn'geɪdʒ) *vb.* **1.** to release or become released from a connection, obligation, etc.: *press the clutch to disengage the gears.* **2.** *Military.* to withdraw (forces) from close action. **3.** *Fencing.* to move (one's blade) from one side of an opponent's blade to another in a circular motion to bring the blade into an open line of attack.

disengagement (ˌdɪsɪn'geɪdʒmənt) *n.* **1.** the act or process of disengaging or the state of being disengaged. **2.** leisure; ease. —ˌ**disen'gaged** *adj.*

disentail (ˌdɪsɪn'teɪl) *Property law.* ~*vb.* **1.** to free (an estate) from entail. ~*n.* **2.** the act of disentailing; disentailment. —ˌ**disen'tailment** *n.*

disentangle (ˌdɪsɪn'tæŋgᵊl) *vb.* **1.** to release or become free from entanglement or confusion. **2.** (*tr.*) to unravel or work out. —ˌ**disen'tanglement** *n.*

disenthral *or U.S.* **disenthrall** (ˌdɪsɪn'θrɔːl) *vb.* **-thrals, -thralling, -thralled** *or U.S.* **-thralls, -thralling, -thralled.** (*tr.*) to set free. —ˌ**disen'thralment** *or U.S.* ˌ**disen'thrallment** *n.*

disentitle (ˌdɪsɪn'taɪtᵊl) *vb.* (*tr.*) to deprive of a title, right, or claim.

disentomb (ˌdɪsɪn'tuːm) *vb.* (*tr.*) to disinter; unearth.

disentwine (ˌdɪsɪn'twaɪn) *vb.* to become or cause to become untwined; unwind.

disepalous (daɪ'sɛpələs) *adj.* (of flowers or plants) having two sepals.

disequilibrium (ˌdɪsiːkwɪ'lɪbrɪəm) *n.* a loss or absence of equilibrium, esp. in an economy.

disestablish (ˌdɪsɪ'stæblɪʃ) *vb.* (*tr.*) to deprive (a church, custom, institution, etc.) of established status. —ˌ**dises'tablishment** *n.*

disesteem (ˌdɪsɪ'stiːm) *vb.* **1.** (*tr.*) to think little of. ~*n.* **2.** lack of esteem.

diseuse (*French* dizøz) *n.* (esp. formerly) an actress who presents dramatic recitals, usually sung accompanied by music. Male counterpart: **diseur** (*French* dizœr). [C19: from French, feminine of *diseur* speaker, from *dire* to speak, from Latin *dīcere*]

disfavour *or U.S.* **disfavor** (dɪs'feɪvə) *n.* **1.** disapproval or dislike. **2.** the state of being disapproved of or disliked. **3.** an unkind act. ~*vb.* **4.** (*tr.*) to regard or treat with disapproval or dislike.

disfeature (dɪs'fiːtʃə) *vb.* (*tr.*) to mar the features or appearance of; deface. —**dis'featurement** *n.*

disfigure (dɪs'fɪgə) *vb.* (*tr.*) **1.** to spoil the appearance or shape of; deface. **2.** to mar the effect or quality of. —**dis'figurer** *n.*

disfigurement (dɪs'fɪgəmənt) *or* **disfiguration** *n.* **1.** something that disfigures. **2.** the act of disfiguring or the state of being disfigured.

disforest (dɪs'fɒrɪst) *vb.* (*tr.*) **1.** another word for **deforest. 2.** *English law.* a less common word for **disafforest.** —**dis,fores'tation** *n.*

disfranchise (dɪs'fræntʃaɪz) *or* **disenfranchise** *vb.* (*tr.*) **1.** to deprive (a person) of the right to vote or other rights of citizenship. **2.** to deprive (a place) of the right to send representatives to an elected body. **3.** to deprive (a business concern, etc.) of some privilege or right. **4.** to deprive (a person, place, etc.) of any franchise or right. —**disfranchisement** (dɪs'fræntʃɪzmənt) *or* ˌ**disen'franchisement** *n.*

disfrock (dɪs'frɒk) *vb.* another word for **unfrock.**

disgorge (dɪs'gɔːdʒ) *vb.* **1.** to throw out (swallowed food, etc.) from the throat or stomach; vomit. **2.** to discharge or empty of (contents). **3.** (*tr.*) to yield up unwillingly or under pressure. **4.** (*tr.*) *Angling.* to remove (a hook) from the mouth or throat of (a fish). —**dis'gorgement** *n.*

disgorger (dɪs'gɔːdʒə) *n. Angling.* a thin notched metal implement for removing hooks from a fish.

disgrace (dɪs'greɪs) *n.* **1.** a condition of shame, loss of reputation, or dishonour. **2.** a shameful person, thing, or state of affairs. **3.** exclusion from confidence or trust: *he is in disgrace with his father.* ~*vb.* (*tr.*) **4.** to bring shame upon; be a discredit to. **5.** to treat or cause to be treated with disfavour. —**dis'gracer** *n.*

disgraceful (dɪs'greɪsfʊl) *adj.* shameful; scandalous. —**dis'gracefully** *adv.* —**dis'gracefulness** *n.*

disgruntle (dɪs'grʌntᵊl) *vb.* (*tr.*) to make sulky or discontented. [C17: DIS-[1] + obsolete *gruntle* to complain; see GRUNT] —**dis'gruntled** *adj.* —**dis'gruntlement** *n.*

disguise (dɪs'gaɪz) *vb.* **1.** to modify the appearance or manner in order to conceal the identity of (oneself, someone, or something). **2.** (*tr.*) to misrepresent in order to obscure the actual nature or meaning: *to disguise the facts.* ~*n.* **3.** a mask, costume, or manner that disguises. **4.** the act of disguising or the state of being disguised. [C14: from Old French *desguisier,* from *des-* DIS-[1] + *guise* manner; see GUISE] —**dis'guisable** *adj.* —**dis'guised** *adj.* —**disguisedly** (dɪs'gaɪzɪdlɪ) *adv.* —**dis'guiser** *n.*

disgust (dɪs'gʌst) *vb.* (*tr.*) **1.** to sicken or fill with loathing. **2.** to offend the moral sense, principles, or taste of. ~*n.* **3.** a great loathing or distaste aroused by someone or something. **4. in disgust.** as a result of disgust. [C16: from Old French *desgouster,* from *des-* DIS-[1] + *gouster* to taste, from *goust* taste, from Latin *gustus*] —**dis'gustedly** *adv.* —**dis'gustedness** *n.*

disgusting (dɪs'gʌstɪŋ) *adj.* loathsome; repugnant. Also (rare): **dis'gustful.** —**dis'gustingly** *adv.*

dish (dɪʃ) *n.* **1.** a container used for holding or serving food, esp. an open shallow container of pottery, glass, etc. **2.** the food that is served or contained in a dish. **3.** a particular article or preparation of food: *a local fish dish.* **4.** Also called: **ˈdishful.** the amount contained in a dish. **5.** something resembling a dish, esp. in shape. **6.** a concavity or depression. **7.** short for **dish aerial** or **satellite dish aerial. 8.** *Informal.* an attractive person. **9.** *Informal.* something that one particularly enjoys or excels in. ~*vb. (tr.)* **10.** to put into a dish. **11.** to make hollow or concave. **12.** *Brit. informal.* to ruin or spoil: *he dished his chances of getting the job.* ~See also **dish out, dish up.** [Old English *disc,* from Latin *discus* quoit, see DISC] —**ˈdishˌlike** *adj.*
dishabille (ˌdɪsæˈbiːl) *or* **deshabille** *n.* **1.** the state of being partly or carelessly dressed. **2.** *Archaic.* clothes worn in such a state. [C17: from French *déshabillé* undressed, from *dés-* DIS-[1] + *habiller* to dress; see HABILIMENT]
dish aerial *n.* **1.** a microwave aerial, used esp. in radar, radio telescopes, and satellite broadcasting, consisting of a parabolic reflector. Formal name: **parabolic aerial.** Often shortened to **dish. 2.** short for **satellite dish aerial.** ~Also called: **dish antenna.**
disharmony (dɪsˈhɑːmənɪ) *n., pl.* **-nies. 1.** lack of accord or harmony. **2.** a situation, circumstance, etc., that is inharmonious. —**disharmonious** (ˌdɪshɑːˈməʊnɪəs) *adj.* —ˌ**disharˈmoniously** *adv.*
dishcloth (ˈdɪʃˌklɒθ) *n.* a cloth or rag for washing or drying dishes. Also called (dialect): **dishclout** (ˈdɪʃˌkluːt).
dishcloth gourd *n.* **1.** any of several tropical climbing plants of the cucurbitaceous genus *Luffa,* esp. *L. cylindrica,* which is cultivated for ornament and for the fibrous interior of its fruits (see **loofah**). **2.** the fruit of any of these plants. ~Also called: **vegetable sponge.**
dishearten (dɪsˈhɑːtᵊn) *vb. (tr.)* to weaken or destroy the hope, courage, enthusiasm, etc., of. —**disˈhearteningly** *adv.* —**disˈheartenment** *n.*
dished (dɪʃt) *adj.* **1.** shaped like a dish; concave. **2.** (of a pair of road wheels) arranged so that they are closer to one another at the bottom than at the top. **3.** *Informal.* exhausted or defeated.
dishevel (dɪˈʃɛvᵊl) *vb.* **-els, -elling, -elled** *or U.S.* **-els, -eling, -eled.** to disarrange (the hair or clothes) of (someone). [C15: back formation from DISHEVELLED] —**diˈshevelment** *n.*
dishevelled (dɪˈʃɛvᵊld) *adj.* **1.** (esp. of hair) hanging loosely. **2.** (of general appearance) unkempt; untidy. [C15 *dischevelee,* from Old French *deschevelé,* from *des-* DIS-[1] + *chevel* hair, from Latin *capillus*]
dishonest (dɪsˈɒnɪst) *adj.* not honest or fair; deceiving or fraudulent. —**disˈhonestly** *adv.*
dishonesty (dɪsˈɒnɪstɪ) *n., pl.* **-ties. 1.** lack of honesty or fairness; deceit. **2.** a deceiving act or statement; fraud.
dishonour *or U.S.* **dishonor** (dɪsˈɒnə) *vb. (tr.)* **1.** to treat with disrespect. **2.** to fail or refuse to pay (a cheque, bill of exchange, etc.). **3.** to cause the disgrace of (a woman) by seduction or rape. ~*n.* **4.** a lack of honour or respect. **5.** a state of shame or disgrace. **6.** a person or thing that causes a loss of honour: *he was a dishonour to his family.* **7.** an insult; affront: *we did him a dishonour by not including him.* **8.** refusal or failure to accept or pay a commercial paper. —**disˈhonourer** *or U.S.* **disˈhonorer** *n.*
dishonourable *or U.S.* **dishonorable** (dɪsˈɒnərəbᵊl, -ˈɒnrəbᵊl) *adj.* **1.** characterized by or causing dishonour or discredit. **2.** having little or no integrity; unprincipled. —**disˈhonourableness** *or U.S.* **disˈhonorableness** *n.* —**disˈhonourably** *or U.S.* **disˈhonorably** *adv.*
dish out *vb. Informal.* **1.** *(tr., adv.)* to distribute. **2. dish it out.** to inflict punishment: *he can't take it, but he can sure dish it out.*
dishpan (ˈdɪʃˌpæn) *n. Chiefly U.S. and Canadian.* a large pan for washing dishes, pots, etc.
dishtowel (ˈdɪʃˌtaʊəl) *n.* another name (esp. U.S. and Canadian) for a **tea towel.**
dish up *vb. (adv.)* **1.** to serve (a meal, food, etc.). **2.** *(tr.) Informal.* to prepare or present, esp. in an attractive manner.
dishwasher (ˈdɪʃˌwɒʃə) *n.* **1.** an electrically operated machine for washing, rinsing, and drying dishes, cutlery, etc. **2.** a person who washes dishes, etc.
dishwater (ˈdɪʃˌwɔːtə) *n.* **1.** water in which dishes and kitchen utensils are or have been washed. **2.** something resembling this: *that was dishwater, not coffee.*
dishy (ˈdɪʃɪ) *adj.* **dishier, dishiest.** *Informal, chiefly Brit.* good-looking or attractive.
disillusion (ˌdɪsɪˈluːʒən) *vb.* **1.** *(tr.)* to destroy the ideals, illusions, or false ideas of. ~*n. also* **disillusionment. 2.** the act of disillusioning or the state of being disillusioned. —**disillusive** (ˌdɪsɪˈluːsɪv) *adj.*
disincentive (ˌdɪsɪnˈsɛntɪv) *n.* **1.** something that acts as a deterrent. ~*adj.* **2.** acting as a deterrent: *a disincentive effect on productivity.*
disincline (ˌdɪsɪnˈklaɪn) *vb.* to make or be unwilling, reluctant, or averse. —**disinclination** (ˌdɪsɪnklɪˈneɪʃən) *n.*
disinfect (ˌdɪsɪnˈfɛkt) *vb. (tr.)* to rid of microorganisms potentially harmful to man, esp. by chemical means. —ˌ**disinˈfection** *n.* —ˌ**disinˈfector** *n.*
disinfectant (ˌdɪsɪnˈfɛktənt) *n.* an agent that destroys or inhibits the activity of microorganisms that cause disease.
disinfest (ˌdɪsɪnˈfɛst) *vb. (tr.)* to rid of vermin. —**disˌinfesˈtation** *n.*
disinflation (ˌdɪsɪnˈfleɪʃən) *n. Economics.* a reduction or stabilization of the general price level intended to improve the balance of payments without incurring reductions in output, employment, and investment. Compare **deflation** (sense 2).
disinformation (ˌdɪsɪnfəˈmeɪʃən) *n.* false information intended to deceive or mislead.
disingenuous (ˌdɪsɪnˈdʒɛnjʊəs) *adj.* not sincere; lacking candour. —ˌ**disinˈgenuously** *adv.* —ˌ**disinˈgenuousness** *n.*
disinherit (ˌdɪsɪnˈhɛrɪt) *vb. (tr.)* **1.** *Law.* to deprive (an heir or next of kin) of inheritance or right to inherit. **2.** to deprive of a right or heritage. —ˌ**disinˈheritance** *n.*
disintegrate (dɪsˈɪntɪˌgreɪt) *vb.* **1.** to break or be broken into fragments or constituent parts; shatter. **2.** to lose or cause to lose cohesion or unity. **3.** *(intr.)* to lose judgment or control; deteriorate. **4.** *Physics.* **a.** to induce or undergo nuclear fission, as by bombardment with fast particles. **b.** another word for **decay** (sense 3). —**disˈintegrable** *adj.* —**disˌinteˈgration** *n.* —**disˈintegrative** *adj.* —**disˈinteˌgrator** *n.*
disinter (ˌdɪsɪnˈtɜː) *vb.* **-ters, -terring, -terred.** *(tr.)* **1.** to remove or dig up; exhume. **2.** to bring (a secret, hidden facts, etc.) to light; expose. —ˌ**disinˈterment** *n.*
disinterest (dɪsˈɪntrɪst, -tərɪst) *n.* **1.** freedom from bias or involvement. **2.** lack of interest; indifference. ~*vb.* **3.** *(tr.)* to free from concern for personal interests.
disinterested (dɪsˈɪntrɪstɪd, -tərɪs-) *adj.* free from bias or partiality; objective. —**disˈinterestedly** *adv.* —**disˈinterestedness** *n.*
▷**Usage.** In spoken and sometimes written English, *disinterested* (impartial) is used where *uninterested* (showing or feeling lack of interest) is meant. Careful writers and speakers avoid this confusion: *a disinterested judge; he was uninterested in public reaction.*
disintermediation (dɪsˌɪntəˌmiːdɪˈeɪʃən) *n. Finance.* the elimination of such financial intermediaries as banks and brokers in transactions between principals, often as a result of deregulation and the use of computers.
disinvest (dɪsɪnˈvɛst) *vb. Economics.* **1.** (usually foll. by *in*) to remove investment (from). **2.** *(intr.)* to reduce the capital stock of an economy or enterprise, as by not replacing obsolete machinery. —ˌ**disinˈvestment** *n.*
disject (dɪsˈdʒɛkt) *vb. (tr.)* to break apart; scatter. [C16: from Latin *disjectus,* from *disjicere* to scatter, from DIS-[1] + *jacere* to throw]
disjecta membra *Latin.* (dɪsˈdʒɛktə ˈmɛmbrə) *pl. n.* scattered fragments, esp. parts taken from a writing or writings.
disjoin (dɪsˈdʒɔɪn) *vb.* to disconnect or become disconnected; separate. —**disˈjoinable** *adj.*
disjoint (dɪsˈdʒɔɪnt) *vb.* **1.** to take apart or come apart at the joints. **2.** *(tr.)* to disunite or disjoin. **3.** to dislocate or become dislocated. **4.** *(tr.; usually passive)* to end the unity, sequence, or coherence of. ~*adj.* **5.** *Maths.* (of two sets) having no members in common. **6.** *Obsolete.* disjointed.
disjointed (dɪsˈdʒɔɪntɪd) *adj.* **1.** having no coherence; disconnected. **2.** separated at the joint. **3.** dislocated. —**disˈjointedly** *adv.* —**disˈjointedness** *n.*
disjunct *adj.* (dɪsˈdʒʌŋkt). **1.** not united or joined. **2.** (of certain insects) having deep constrictions between the head, thorax, and abdomen. **3.** *Music.* denoting two notes the interval between which is greater than a second. ~*n.* (ˈdɪsdʒʌŋkt). **4.** *Logic.* one of the propositions or formulas in a disjunction.
disjunction (dɪsˈdʒʌŋkʃən) *n.* **1.** Also called: **disˈjuncture.** the act of disconnecting or the state of being disconnected; separation. **2.** *Cytology.* the separation of the chromosomes of each homologous pair during the anaphase of meiosis. **3.** *Logic.* **a.** the operator that forms a compound sentence from two given sentences and corresponds to the English *or.* **b.** a sentence so formed. Usually written $p \vee q$ where *p, q* are the component sentences, it is true (inclusive sense) whenever either or both of the latter are true; the exclusive disjunction, for which there is no symbol, is true when either but not both disjuncts is. **c.** the relation between such sentences.
disjunctive (dɪsˈdʒʌŋktɪv) *adj.* **1.** serving to disconnect or separate. **2.** *Grammar.* **a.** denoting a word, esp. a conjunction, that serves to express opposition or contrast: *but* in the sentence *She was poor but she was honest.* **b.** denoting an inflection of pronouns in some languages that is used alone or after a preposition, such as *moi* in French. **3.** Also: **alternative.** *Logic.* relating to, characterized by, or containing disjunction. ~*n.* **4.** *Grammar.* **a.** a disjunctive word, esp. a conjunction. **b.** a disjunctive pronoun. **5.** *Logic.* a disjunctive proposition; disjunction. —**disˈjunctively** *adv.*
disk (dɪsk) *n.* **1.** a variant spelling (esp. U.S. and Canadian) of **disc. 2.** Also called: **disk pack, magnetic disk.** *Computer technol.* a direct-access storage device consisting of a stack of plates coated with a magnetic layer, the whole assembly rotating rapidly as a single unit. Each surface has a read-write head that can move radially to read or write data on concentric tracks. Compare **drum**[1] (sense 9).
disk crash *n. Computer technol.* the failure of a disk storage system, usually resulting from the read/write head touching the moving disk surface and causing mechanical damage.

disk drive *n. Computer technol.* the unit that controls the mechanism for handling a diskette.
diskette (dɪsˈkɛt) *n. Computer technol.* another name for **floppy disk.**
disk operating system *n.* an operating system used on a computer system with one or more disk drives. Often shortened to: **DOS.**
disk pack *n. Computer technol.* another name for **disk** (sense 2).
dislike (dɪsˈlaɪk) *vb.* **1.** (*tr.*) to consider unpleasant or disagreeable. ~*n.* **2.** a feeling of aversion or antipathy. —**disˈlikable** *or* **disˈlikeable** *adj.*
dislimn (dɪsˈlɪm) *vb.* (*tr.*) *Poetic.* to efface.
dislocate (ˈdɪsləˌkeɪt) *vb.* (*tr.*) **1.** to disrupt or shift out of place or position. **2.** to displace (an organ or part) from its normal position, esp. a bone from its joint.
dislocation (ˌdɪsləˈkeɪʃən) *n.* **1.** the act of displacing or the state of being displaced; disruption. **2.** (esp. of the bones in a joint) the state or condition of being dislocated. **3.** a line, plane, or region in which there is a discontinuity in the regularity of a crystal lattice. **4.** *Geology.* a less common word for **fault** (sense 6).
dislodge (dɪsˈlɒdʒ) *vb.* to remove from or leave a lodging place, hiding place, or previously fixed position. —**disˈlodgment** *or* **disˈlodgement** *n.*
disloyal (dɪsˈlɔɪəl) *adj.* not loyal or faithful; deserting one's allegiance or duty. —**disˈloyally** *adv.*
disloyalty (dɪsˈlɔɪəltɪ) *n., pl.* **-ties.** the condition or an instance of being unfaithful or disloyal.
dismal (ˈdɪzməl) *adj.* **1.** causing gloom or depression. **2.** causing dismay or terror. **3.** *Rare.* calamitous. [C13: from *dismal* (n.) list of 24 unlucky days in the year, from Medieval Latin *diēs malī* bad days, from Latin *diēs* day + *malus* bad] —ˈ**dismally** *adv.* —ˈ**dismalness** *n.*
dismal science *n.* **the.** a name for economics coined by the British historian Thomas Carlyle (1795–1881).
dismantle (dɪsˈmæntᵊl) *vb.* (*tr.*) **1.** to take apart. **2.** to demolish or raze. **3.** to strip of covering. [C17: from Old French *desmanteler* to remove a cloak from; see MANTLE] —**disˈmantlement** *n.* —**disˈmantler** *n.*
dismast (dɪsˈmɑːst) *vb.* (*tr.*) to break off the mast or masts of (a sailing vessel). —**disˈmastment** *n.*
dismay (dɪsˈmeɪ) *vb.* (*tr.*) **1.** to fill with apprehension or alarm. **2.** to fill with depression or discouragement. ~*n.* **3.** consternation or agitation. [C13: from Old French *desmaiier* (unattested), from *des-* DIS-[1] + *esmayer* to frighten, ultimately of Germanic origin; see MAY[1]] —**disˈmaying** *adj.*
dismember (dɪsˈmɛmbə) *vb.* (*tr.*) **1.** to remove the limbs or members of. **2.** to cut to pieces. **3.** to divide or partition (something, such as an empire). —**disˈmemberer** *n.* —**disˈmemberment** *n.*
dismiss (dɪsˈmɪs) *vb.* (*tr.*) **1.** to remove or discharge from employment or service. **2.** to send away or allow to go or disperse. **3.** to dispel from one's mind; discard; reject. **4.** to cease to consider (a subject): *they dismissed the problem.* **5.** to decline further hearing to (a claim or action): *the judge dismissed the case.* **6.** *Cricket.* to bowl out a side for a particular number of runs. ~*sentence substitute.* **7.** *Military.* an order to end an activity or give permission to disperse. [C15: from Medieval Latin *dismissus* sent away, variant of Latin *dīmissus,* from *dīmittere,* from *dī-* DIS-[1] + *mittere* to send] —**disˈmissible** *adj.* —**disˈmissive** *adj.*
dismissal (dɪsˈmɪsᵊl) *n.* **1.** an official notice of discharge from employment or service. **2.** the act of dismissing or the condition of being dismissed.
dismount (dɪsˈmaʊnt) *vb.* **1.** to get off a horse, bicycle, etc. **2.** (*tr.*) to disassemble or remove from a mounting. ~*n.* **3.** the act of dismounting. —**disˈmountable** *adj.*
Disneyesque (ˌdɪznɪˈɛsk) *adj.* resembling or in the style of the cartoon characters created by Walt Disney (1901–66), U.S. film producer.
disobedience (ˌdɪsəˈbiːdɪəns) *n.* lack of obedience.
disobedient (ˌdɪsəˈbiːdɪənt) *adj.* not obedient; neglecting or refusing to obey. —ˌ**disoˈbediently** *adv.*
disobey (ˌdɪsəˈbeɪ) *vb.* to neglect or refuse to obey (someone, an order, etc.). —ˌ**disoˈbeyer** *n.*
disoblige (ˌdɪsəˈblaɪdʒ) *vb.* (*tr.*) **1.** to disregard the desires of. **2.** to slight; insult. **3.** *Informal.* to cause trouble or inconvenience to. —ˌ**disoˈbliging** *adj.* —ˌ**disoˈbligingly** *adv.* —ˌ**disoˈbligingness** *n.*
disomic (daɪˈsəʊmɪk) *adj. Genetics.* having an extra chromosome in the haploid state that is homologous to an existing chromosome in this set. —**diˈsomy** *n.*
disoperation (dɪsˌɒpəˈreɪʃən) *n. Ecology.* a relationship between two organisms in a community that is harmful to both.
disorder (dɪsˈɔːdə) *n.* **1.** a lack of order; disarray; confusion. **2.** a disturbance of public order or peace. **3.** an upset of health; ailment. **4.** a deviation from the normal system or order. ~*vb.* (*tr.*) **5.** to upset the order of; disarrange; muddle. **6.** to disturb the health or mind of.
disorderly (dɪsˈɔːdəlɪ) *adj.* **1.** untidy; irregular. **2.** uncontrolled; unruly. **3.** *Law.* violating public peace or order. ~*adv.* **4.** in an irregular or confused manner. —**disˈorderliness** *n.*
disorderly conduct *n. Law.* any of various minor offences tending to cause a disturbance of the peace.
disorderly house *n. Law.* an establishment in which unruly behaviour habitually occurs, esp. a brothel or a gaming house.
disorganize *or* **disorganise** (dɪsˈɔːgəˌnaɪz) *vb.* (*tr.*) to disrupt or destroy the arrangement, system, or unity of. —**disˌorganiˈzation** *or* **disˌorganiˈsation** *n.* —**disˈorganˌizer** *or* **disˈorganˌiser** *n.*
disorientate (dɪsˈɔːrɪɛnˌteɪt) *or* **disorient** *vb.* (*tr.*) **1.** to cause (someone) to lose his bearings. **2.** to perplex; confuse. —**disˌorienˈtation** *n.*
disown (dɪsˈəʊn) *vb.* (*tr.*) to deny any connection with; refuse to acknowledge. —**disˈowner** *n.* —**disˈownment** *n.*
disparage (dɪˈspærɪdʒ) *vb.* (*tr.*) **1.** to speak contemptuously of; belittle. **2.** to damage the reputation of. [C14: from Old French *desparagier,* from *des-* DIS-[1] + *parage* equality, from Latin *par* equal] —**disˈparagement** *n.* —**disˈparager** *n.* —**disˈparaging** *adj.* —**disˈparagingly** *adv.*
disparate (ˈdɪspərɪt) *adj.* **1.** utterly different or distinct in kind. ~*n.* **2.** (*pl.*) unlike things or people. [C16: from Latin *disparāre* to divide, from DIS-[1] + *parāre* to prepare; also influenced by Latin *dispar* unequal] —ˈ**disparately** *adv.* —ˈ**disparateness** *n.*
disparity (dɪˈspærɪtɪ) *n., pl.* **-ties.** **1.** inequality or difference, as in age, rank, wages, etc. **2.** dissimilarity.
dispassion (dɪsˈpæʃən) *n.* detachment; objectivity.
dispassionate (dɪsˈpæʃənɪt) *adj.* devoid of or uninfluenced by emotion or prejudice; objective; impartial. —**disˈpassionately** *adv.* —**disˈpassionateness** *n.*
dispatch *or* **despatch** (dɪˈspætʃ) *vb.* (*tr.*) **1.** to send off promptly, as to a destination or to perform a task. **2.** to discharge or complete (a task, duty, etc.) promptly. **3.** *Informal.* to eat up quickly. **4.** to murder or execute. ~*n.* **5.** the act of sending off a letter, messenger, etc. **6.** prompt action or speed (often in the phrase **with dispatch**). **7.** an official communication or report, sent in haste. **8.** *Journalism.* a report sent to a newspaper, etc., by a correspondent. **9.** murder or execution. [C16: from Italian *dispacciare,* from Provençal *despachar,* from Old French *despeechier* to set free, from *des-* DIS-[1] + *-peechier,* ultimately from Latin *pedica* a fetter] —**disˈpatcher** *n.*
dispatch box *n.* a case or box used to hold valuables, documents, etc.
dispatch case *n.* a case used for carrying papers, documents, books, etc., usually flat and stiff.
dispatch rider *n.* a horseman or motorcyclist who carries dispatches.
dispel (dɪˈspɛl) *vb.* **-pels, -pelling, -pelled.** (*tr.*) to disperse or drive away. [C17: from Latin *dispellere,* from DIS-[1] + *pellere* to drive] —**disˈpeller** *n.*
dispend (dɪˈspɛnd) *vb.* (*tr.*) *Obsolete.* to spend. [C14: from Old French *despendre,* from Latin *dispendere* to distribute; see DISPENSE]
dispensable (dɪˈspɛnsəbᵊl) *adj.* **1.** not essential; expendable. **2.** capable of being distributed. **3.** (of a law, vow, etc.) able to be relaxed. —**disˌpensaˈbility** *or* **disˈpensableness** *n.*
dispensary (dɪˈspɛnsərɪ, -srɪ) *n., pl.* **-ries.** a place where medicine and medical supplies are dispensed.
dispensation (ˌdɪspɛnˈseɪʃən) *n.* **1.** the act of distributing or dispensing. **2.** something distributed or dispensed. **3.** a system or plan of administering or dispensing. **4.** *Chiefly R.C. Church.* **a.** permission to dispense with an obligation of church law. **b.** the document authorizing such permission. **5.** any exemption from a rule or obligation. **6.** *Christianity.* **a.** the ordering of life and events by God. **b.** a divine decree affecting an individual or group. **c.** a religious system or code of prescriptions for life and conduct regarded as of divine origin. —ˌ**dispenˈsational** *adj.*
dispensatory (dɪˈspɛnsətərɪ, -trɪ) *n., pl.* **-ries.** **1.** a book listing the composition, preparation, and application of various drugs. ~*adj.* **2.** of or involving dispensation.
dispense (dɪˈspɛns) *vb.* **1.** (*tr.*) to give out or distribute in portions. **2.** (*tr.*) to prepare and distribute (medicine), esp. on prescription. **3.** (*tr.*) to administer (the law, etc.). **4.** (*intr.;* foll. by *with*) to do away (with) or manage (without). **5.** to grant a dispensation to (someone) from (some obligation of church law). **6.** to exempt or excuse from a rule or obligation. [C14: from Medieval Latin *dispensāre* to pardon, from Latin *dispendere* to weigh out, from DIS-[1] + *pendere* to weigh]
dispenser (dɪˈspɛnsə) *n.* **1.** a device, such as a vending machine, that automatically dispenses a single item or a measured quantity. **2.** a person or thing that dispenses.
dispensing optician *n.* See **optician.**
dispermous (daɪˈspɜːməs) *adj.* (of flowering plants) producing or having two seeds. [C18: from DI-[1] + Greek *sperma* seed]
dispersal (dɪˈspɜːsᵊl) *n.* **1.** another word for **dispersion** (sense 1). **2.** the spread of animals, plants, or seeds to new areas.
dispersal prison *n.* a prison organized and equipped to accommodate a proportion of the most dangerous and highest security risk prisoners.
dispersant (dɪsˈpɜːsənt) *n.* a liquid or gas used to disperse small particles or droplets, as in an aerosol.
disperse (dɪˈspɜːs) *vb.* **1.** to scatter; distribute over a wide area. **2.** to dissipate or cause to dissipate. **3.** to leave or cause to leave a gathering, often in a random manner. **4.** to separate or be separated by dispersion. **5.** (*tr.*) to diffuse or spread (news,

information, etc.). **6.** to separate (particles) throughout a solid, liquid, or gas, as in the formation of a suspension or colloid. ~*adj.* **7.** of or consisting of the particles in a colloid or suspension: *disperse phase.* [C14: from Latin *dispĕrsus* scattered, from *dispergere* to scatter widely, from DI-[2] + *spargere* to strew] —**dis'persedly** (dɪˈspɜːsɪdlɪ) *adv.* —**dis'perser** *n.*

dispersion (dɪˈspɜːʃən) *n.* **1.** the act of dispersing or the condition of being dispersed. **2.** *Physics.* **a.** the separation of electromagnetic radiation into constituents of different wavelengths. **b.** a measure of the ability of a substance to separate by refraction, expressed by the first differential of the refractive index with respect to wavelength at a given value of wavelength. Symbol: *D* **3.** *Statistics.* the degree to which values of a frequency distribution are scattered around some central point, usually the arithmetic mean or median. **4.** *Chem.* a system containing particles dispersed in a solid, liquid, or gas. **5.** *Military.* the pattern of fire from a weapon system. **6.** the deviation of a rocket from its prescribed path. **7.** *Ecology.* the distribution pattern of an animal or a plant population.

Dispersion (dɪˈspɜːʃən) *n.* **the.** another name for the **Diaspora.**

dispersion hardening *n.* the strengthening of an alloy as a result of the presence of fine particles in the lattice.

dispersive (dɪˈspɜːsɪv) *adj.* tending or serving to disperse. —**dis'persively** *adv.* —**dis'persiveness** *n.*

dispersive medium *n. Physics.* a substance in which waves of different frequencies travel at different speeds.

dispersoid (dɪˈspɜːsɔɪd) *n. Chem.* a system, such as a colloid or suspension, in which one phase is dispersed in another.

dispirit (dɪˈspɪrɪt) *vb.* (*tr.*) to lower the spirit or enthusiasm of; make downhearted or depressed; discourage. —**dis'pirited** *adj.* —**dis'piritedly** *adv.* —**dis'piritedness** *n.* —**dis'piriting** *adj.* —**dis'piritingly** *adv.*

displace (dɪsˈpleɪs) *vb.* (*tr.*) **1.** to move from the usual or correct location. **2.** to remove from office or employment. **3.** to occupy the place of; replace; supplant. **4.** to force (someone) to leave home or country, as during a war. **5.** *Chem.* to replace (an atom or group in a chemical compound) by another atom or group. **6.** *Physics.* to cause a displacement of (a quantity of liquid, usually water of a specified type and density). —**dis'placeable** *adj.* —**dis'placer** *n.*

displaced person *n.* a person forced from his home or country, esp. by war or revolution. Abbrev.: **DP.**

displacement (dɪsˈpleɪsmənt) *n.* **1.** the act of displacing or the condition of being displaced. **2.** the weight or volume displaced by a floating or submerged body in a fluid. **3.** *Chem.* another name for **substitution. 4.** the volume displaced by the piston of a reciprocating pump or engine. **5.** *Psychoanal.* the transferring of emotional feelings from their original object to one that disguises their real nature. **6.** *Geology.* the distance any point on one side of a fault plane has moved in relation to a corresponding point on the opposite side. **7.** *Astronomy.* an apparent change in position of a body, such as a star. **8.** *Maths.* the distance measured in a particular direction from a reference point. Symbol: *s*

displacement activity *n.* **1.** *Psychol.* behaviour that occurs typically when there is a conflict between motives and that has no relevance to either motive: e.g. head scratching. **2.** *Zoology.* the substitution of a pattern of animal behaviour that is different from behaviour relevant to the situation: e.g. preening at an apparently inappropriate time.

displacement ton *n.* the full name for **ton**[1] (sense 6).

displant (dɪsˈplɑːnt) *vb.* (*tr.*) *Obsolete.* **1.** to displace. **2.** to transplant (a plant).

display (dɪˈspleɪ) *vb.* **1.** (*tr.*) to show or make visible. **2.** (*tr.*) to disclose or make evident; reveal: *to display anger.* **3.** (*tr.*) to flaunt in an ostentatious way: *to display military might.* **4.** (*tr.*) to spread or open out; unfurl or unfold. **5.** (*tr.*) to give prominence to (headings, captions, etc.) by the use of certain typefaces. **6.** (*intr.*) *Zoology.* to engage in a display. ~*n.* **7.** the act of exhibiting or displaying; show: *a display of fear.* **8.** something exhibited or displayed. **9.** an ostentatious or pretentious exhibition: *a display of his accomplishments.* **10. a.** an arrangement of certain typefaces to give prominence to headings, captions, etc. **b.** printed matter that is eye-catching. **11.** *Electronics.* **a.** a device capable of representing information visually, as on a cathode-ray tube screen. **b.** the information so presented. **12.** *Zoology.* a pattern of behaviour in birds, fishes, etc., by which the animal attracts attention while it is courting the female, defending its territory, etc. **13.** (*modifier*) relating to or using typefaces that give prominence to the words they are used to set. [C14: from Anglo-French *despleier* to unfold, from Late Latin *displicāre* to scatter, from DIS-[1] + *plicāre* to fold] —**dis'player** *n.*

displease (dɪsˈpliːz) *vb.* to annoy, offend, or cause displeasure to (someone). —**dis'pleasing** *adj.* —**dis'pleasingly** *adv.*

displeasure (dɪsˈplɛʒə) *n.* **1.** the condition of being displeased. **2.** *Archaic.* **a.** pain. **b.** an act or cause of offence. ~*vb.* **3.** an archaic word for **displease.**

displode (dɪsˈpləʊd) *vb.* an obsolete word for **explode.** [C17: from Latin *displōdere from* DIS-[1] + *plaudere* to clap]

disport (dɪˈspɔːt) *vb.* **1.** (*tr.*) to indulge (oneself) in pleasure. **2.** (*intr.*) to frolic or gambol. ~*n.* **3.** *Archaic.* amusement. [C14: from Anglo-French *desporter,* from *des-* DIS-[1] + *porter* to carry]

disposable (dɪˈspəʊzəbəl) *adj.* **1.** designed for disposal after use: *disposable cups.* **2.** available for use if needed: *disposable assets.* ~*n.* **3.** something, such as a baby's nappy, that is designed for disposal. **4.** (*pl.*) short for **disposable goods.** —**dis,posa'bility** *or* **dis'posableness** *n.*

disposable goods *pl. n.* consumer goods that are used up a short time after purchase, including perishables, newspapers, clothes, etc. Compare **durable goods.** Also called: **disposables.**

disposable income *n.* **1.** the money a person has available to spend after paying taxes, pension contributions, etc. **2.** the total amount of money that the individuals in a community, country, etc., have available to buy consumer goods.

disposal (dɪˈspəʊzəl) *n.* **1.** the act or means of getting rid of something. **2.** placement or arrangement in a particular order. **3.** a specific method of tending to matters, as in business. **4.** the act or process of transferring something to or providing something for another. **5.** the power or opportunity to make use of someone or something (esp. in the phrase **at one's disposal**). **6.** a means of destroying waste products, as by grinding into particles. ~Also (for senses 2–5): **disposition.**

dispose (dɪˈspəʊz) *vb.* **1.** (*intr.;* foll. by *of*) **a.** to deal with or settle. **b.** to give, sell, or transfer to another. **c.** to throw out or away. **d.** to consume, esp. hurriedly. **e.** to kill. **2.** to arrange or settle (matters) by placing into correct or final condition: *man proposes, God disposes.* **3.** (*tr.*) to make willing or receptive. **4.** (*tr.*) to adjust or place in a certain order or position. **5.** (*tr.;* often foll. by *to*) to accustom or condition. ~*n.* **6.** an obsolete word for **disposal** or **disposition.** [C14: from Old French *disposer,* from Latin *dispōnere* to set in different places, arrange, from DIS-[1] + *pōnere* to place] —**dis'poser** *n.*

disposed (dɪˈspəʊzd) *adj.* **a.** having an inclination as specified (towards something). **b.** (*in combination*): *well-disposed.*

disposition (ˌdɪspəˈzɪʃən) *n.* **1.** a person's usual temperament or frame of mind. **2.** a natural or acquired tendency, inclination, or habit in a person or thing. **3.** another word for **disposal** (senses 2–5). **4.** *Philosophy, logic.* a property that consists not in the present state of an object, but in its propensity to change in a certain way under certain conditions, such as brittleness which consists in the propensity to break when struck. Compare **occurrent. 5.** *Archaic.* manner of placing or arranging. —ˌ**dispo'sitional** *adj.*

dispossess (ˌdɪspəˈzɛs) *vb.* (*tr.*) to take away possession of something, esp. property; expel. —ˌ**dispos'session** *n.* —ˌ**dispos'sessor** *n.* —ˌ**dispos'sessory** *adj.*

disposure (dɪˈspəʊʒə) *n.* a rare word for **disposal** or **disposition.**

dispraise (dɪsˈpreɪz) *vb.* **1.** (*tr.*) to express disapproval or condemnation of. ~*n.* **2.** the disapproval, etc., expressed. —**dis'praiser** *n.* —**dis'praisingly** *adv.*

disprize (dɪsˈpraɪz) *vb.* (*tr.*) *Archaic.* to scorn; disdain.

disproof (dɪsˈpruːf) *n.* **1.** facts that disprove something. **2.** the act of disproving.

disproportion (ˌdɪsprəˈpɔːʃən) *n.* **1.** lack of proportion or equality. **2.** an instance of disparity or inequality. ~*vb.* **3.** (*tr.*) to cause to become exaggerated or unequal. —ˌ**dispro'portionable** *adj.* —ˌ**dispro'portionableness** *n.* —ˌ**dispro'portionably** *adv.*

disproportionate *adj.* (ˌdɪsprəˈpɔːʃənɪt). **1.** out of proportion; unequal. ~*vb.* (ˌdɪsprəˈpɔːʃəˌneɪt). **2.** *Chem.* to undergo or cause to undergo disproportionation. —ˌ**dispro'portionately** *adv.* —ˌ**dispro'portionateness** *n.*

disproportionation (ˌdɪsprəˌpɔːʃəˈneɪʃən) *n.* a reaction between two identical molecules in which one is reduced and the other oxidized.

disprove (dɪsˈpruːv) *vb.* (*tr.*) to show (an assertion, claim, etc.) to be incorrect. —**dis'provable** *adj.* —**dis'proval** *n.*

disputable (dɪˈspjuːtəbəl, ˈdɪspjʊtə-) *adj.* capable of being argued; debatable. —**dis,puta'bility** *or* **dis'putableness** *n.* —**dis'putably** *adv.*

disputant (dɪˈspjuːtənt, ˈdɪspjʊtənt) *n.* **1.** a person who argues; contestant. ~*adj.* **2.** engaged in argument.

disputation (ˌdɪspjʊˈteɪʃən) *n.* **1.** the act or an instance of arguing. **2.** a formal academic debate on a thesis. **3.** an obsolete word for **conversation.**

disputatious (ˌdɪspjʊˈteɪʃəs) *or* **disputative** (dɪˈspjuːtətɪv) *adj.* inclined to argument. —ˌ**dispu'tatiously** *or* **dis'putatively** *adv.* —ˌ**dispu'tatiousness** *or* **dis'putativeness** *n.*

dispute *vb.* (dɪˈspjuːt). **1.** to argue, debate, or quarrel about (something). **2.** (*tr.; may take a clause as object*) to doubt the validity, etc., of. **3.** (*tr.*) to seek to win; contest for. **4.** (*tr.*) to struggle against; resist. ~*n.* (dɪˈspjuːt, ˈdɪspjuːt). **5.** an argument or quarrel. **6.** *Rare.* a fight. [C13: from Late Latin *disputāre* to contend verbally, from Latin: to discuss, from DIS-[1] + *putāre* to think] —**dis'puter** *n.*

disqualify (dɪsˈkwɒlɪˌfaɪ) *vb.* **-fies, -fying, -fied.** (*tr.*) **1.** to make unfit or unqualified. **2.** to make ineligible, as for entry to an examination. **3.** to debar (a player or team) from a sporting contest. **4.** to divest or deprive of rights, powers, or privileges: *disqualified from driving.* —**dis'quali,fiable** *adj.* —**dis,qualifi'cation** *n.* —**dis'quali,fier** *n.*

disquiet (dɪsˈkwaɪət) *n.* **1.** a feeling or condition of anxiety or uneasiness. ~*vb.* **2.** (*tr.*) to make anxious or upset. ~*adj.* **3.** *Archaic.* uneasy or anxious. —**dis'quietedly** *or* **dis'quietly**

adv. —**dis'quietedness** *or* **dis'quietness** *n.* —**dis'quieting** *adj.* —**dis'quietingly** *adv.*
disquietude (dɪs'kwaɪɪˌtjuːd) *n.* a feeling or state of anxiety or uneasiness.
disquisition (ˌdɪskwɪ'zɪʃən) *n.* a formal written or oral examination of a subject. [C17: from Latin *disquīsītiō*, from *disquīrere* to make an investigation, from DIS-[1] + *quaerere* to seek] —ˌ**disqui'sitional** *adj.*
disrate (dɪs'reɪt) *vb.* (*tr.*) *Naval.* to punish (an officer) by lowering him in rank.
disregard (ˌdɪsrɪ'gɑːd) *vb.* (*tr.*) **1.** to give little or no attention to; ignore. **2.** to treat as unworthy of consideration or respect. ~*n.* **3.** lack of attention or respect. **4.** (*often pl.*) *Social welfare.* capital or income which is not counted in calculating the amount payable to a claimant for a means-tested benefit. —ˌ**disre'garder** *n.* —ˌ**disre'gardful** *adj.* —ˌ**disre'gardfully** *adv.* —ˌ**disre'gardfulness** *n.*
disrelish (dɪs'rɛlɪʃ) *vb.* **1.** (*tr.*) to have a feeling of aversion for; dislike. ~*n.* **2.** such a feeling.
disremember (ˌdɪsrɪ'mɛmbə) *vb. Informal, chiefly U.S.* to fail to recall (someone or something).
disrepair (ˌdɪsrɪ'pɛə) *n.* the condition of being worn out or in poor working order; a condition requiring repairs.
disreputable (dɪs'rɛpjʊtəbᵊl) *adj.* **1.** having or causing a lack of repute. **2.** disordered in appearance. —**dis**ˌ**reputa'bility** *or* **dis'reputableness** *n.* —**dis'reputably** *adv.*
disrepute (ˌdɪsrɪ'pjuːt) *n.* a loss or lack of credit or repute.
disrespect (ˌdɪsrɪ'spɛkt) *n.* **1.** contempt; rudeness. ~*vb.* **2.** (*tr.*) to show lack of respect for. —ˌ**disre'spectful** *adj.* —ˌ**disre'spectfully** *adv.* —ˌ**disre'spectfulness** *n.*
disrespectable (ˌdɪsrɪ'spɛktəbᵊl) *adj.* unworthy of respect; not respectable. —ˌ**disre**ˌ**specta'bility** *n.*
disrobe (dɪs'rəʊb) *vb.* **1.** to remove the clothing of (a person) or (of a person) to undress. **2.** (*tr.*) to divest of authority, etc. —**dis'robement** *n.* —**dis'rober** *n.*
disrupt (dɪs'rʌpt) *vb.* **1.** (*tr.*) to throw into turmoil or disorder. **2.** (*tr.*) to interrupt the progress of (a movement, meeting, etc.). **3.** to break or split (something) apart. [C17: from Latin *disruptus* burst asunder, from *dīrumpere* to dash to pieces, from DIS-[1] + *rumpere* to burst] —**dis'rupter** *or* **dis'ruptor** *n.* —**dis'ruption** *n.*
disruptive (dɪs'rʌptɪv) *adj.* involving, causing, or tending to cause disruption. —**dis'ruptively** *adv.*
disruptive discharge *n.* a sudden large increase in current through an insulating medium resulting from failure of the medium to withstand an applied electric field.
dissatisfied (dɪs'sætɪsˌfaɪd) *adj.* having or showing dissatisfaction; discontented. —**dis'satis**ˌ**fiedly** *adv.*
dissatisfy (dɪs'sætɪsˌfaɪ) *vb.* **-fies, -fying, -fied.** (*tr.*) to fail to satisfy; disappoint. —ˌ**dissatis'faction** *n.* —ˌ**dissatis'factory** *adj.*
dissect (dɪ'sɛkt, daɪ-) *vb.* **1.** to cut open and examine the structure of (a dead animal or plant). **2.** (*tr.*) to examine critically and minutely. [C17: from Latin *dissecāre*, from DIS-[1] + *secāre* to cut] —**dis'sectible** *adj.* —**dis'section** *n.* —**dis'sector** *n.*
dissected (dɪ'sɛktɪd, daɪ-) *adj.* **1.** *Botany.* in the form of narrow lobes or segments: *dissected leaves.* **2.** *Geology.* (of plains) cut by erosion into hills and valleys, esp. following tectonic movements.
disseise *or* **disseize** (dɪs'siːz) *vb.* (*tr.*) *Property law.* to deprive of seisin; wrongfully dispossess of a freehold interest in land. [C14: from Anglo-Norman *desseisir*, from DIS-[1] + SEIZE] —**dis'seisor** *or* **dis'seizor** *n.*
disseisin *or* **disseizin** (dɪs'siːzɪn) *n.* the act of disseising or state of being disseised. [C14: from Old French *dessaisine*; see DIS-[1], SEISIN]
disselboom ('dɪsəlˌbʊəm) *n. S. African.* the pole or single shaft of a wagon or cart. [from Afrikaans *dissel* shaft + *boom* beam]
dissemble (dɪ'sɛmbᵊl) *vb.* **1.** to conceal (one's real motives, emotions, etc.) by pretence. **2.** (*tr.*) to pretend; simulate. **3.** *Obsolete.* to ignore. [C15: from earlier *dissimulen*, from Latin *dissimulāre*; probably influenced by obsolete *semble* to resemble] —**dis'semblance** *n.* —**dis'sembler** *n.* —**dis'sembling** *n., adj.* —**dis'semblingly** *adv.*
disseminate (dɪ'sɛmɪˌneɪt) *vb.* (*tr.*) to distribute or scatter about; diffuse. [C17: from Latin *dissēmināre*, from DIS-[1] + *sēmināre* to sow, from *sēmen* seed] —**dis**ˌ**semi'nation** *n.* —**dis'seminative** *adj.* —**dis'semi**ˌ**nator** *n.*
disseminated sclerosis *n.* another name for **multiple sclerosis.**
disseminule (dɪ'sɛmɪˌnjuːl) *n.* any propagative part of a plant, such as a seed or spore, that helps to spread the species. [C20: from DISSEMINATE + -ULE]
dissension (dɪ'sɛnʃən) *n.* disagreement, esp. when leading to a quarrel. [C13: from Latin *dissēnsiō*, from *dissentīre* to dissent]
dissent (dɪ'sɛnt) *vb.* (*intr.*) **1.** to have a disagreement or withhold assent. **2.** *Christianity.* to refuse to conform to the doctrines, beliefs, or practices of an established church, and to adhere to a different system of beliefs and practices. ~*n.* **3.** a difference of opinion. **4.** *Christianity.* separation from an established church; Nonconformism. **5.** the voicing of a minority opinion in announcing the decision on a case at law; dissenting judgment. [C16: from Latin *dissentīre* to disagree, from DIS-[1] + *sentīre* to perceive, feel] —**dis'senter** *n.* —**dis'senting** *adj.* —**dis'sentingly** *adv.*
Dissenter (dɪ'sɛntə) *n. Christianity, chiefly Brit.* a Nonconformist or a person who refuses to conform to the established church.
dissentient (dɪ'sɛnʃənt) *adj.* **1.** dissenting, esp. from the opinion of the majority. ~*n.* **2.** a dissenter. —**dis'sentience** *or* **dis'sentiency** *n.* —**dis'sentiently** *adv.*
dissentious (dɪ'sɛnʃəs) *adj.* argumentative.
dissepiment (dɪ'sɛpɪmənt) *n. Biology.* a dividing partition or membrane, such as that between the chambers of a syncarpous ovary. [C18: from Late Latin *dissaepīmentum*, from DIS-[1] + *saepīmentum* hedge, from *saepīre* to enclose] —**dis**ˌ**sepi'mental** *adj.*
dissertate ('dɪsəˌteɪt) *vb.* (*intr.*) *Rare.* to give or make a dissertation. [C18: from Latin *dissertāre* to debate, from *disserere* to examine, from DIS-[1] + *serere* to arrange] —'**disser**ˌ**tator** *n.*
dissertation (ˌdɪsə'teɪʃən) *n.* **1.** a written thesis, often based on original research, usually required for a higher degree. **2.** a formal discourse. —ˌ**disser'tational** *adj.* —ˌ**disser'tationist** *n.*
disserve (dɪs'sɜːv) *vb.* (*tr.*) *Archaic.* to do a disservice to.
disservice (dɪs'sɜːvɪs) *n.* an ill turn; wrong; injury, esp. when trying to help. —**dis'serviceable** *adj.*
dissever (dɪ'sɛvə) *vb.* **1.** to break off or become broken off. **2.** (*tr.*) to divide up into parts. [C13: from Old French *dessevrer*, from Late Latin DIS-[1] + *sēparāre* to SEPARATE] —**dis'severance, dis'severment,** *or* **dis**ˌ**sever'ation** *n.*
dissident ('dɪsɪdənt) *adj.* **1.** disagreeing; dissenting. ~*n.* **2.** a person who disagrees, esp. one who disagrees with the government. [C16: from Latin *dissidēre* to be remote from, from DIS-[1] + *sedēre* to sit] —'**dissidence** *n.* —'**dissidently** *adv.*
dissimilar (dɪ'sɪmɪlə) *adj.* not alike; not similar; different. —**dis'similarly** *adv.*
dissimilarity (ˌdɪsɪmɪ'lærɪtɪ) *n., pl.* **-ties.** **1.** difference; unlikeness. **2.** a point or instance of difference.
dissimilate (dɪ'sɪmɪˌleɪt) *vb.* **1.** to make or become dissimilar. **2.** (usually foll. by *to*) *Phonetics.* to change or displace (a consonant) or (of a consonant) to be changed to or displaced by (another consonant) so that its manner of articulation becomes less similar to a speech sound in the same word. Thus (r) in the final syllable of French *marbre* is dissimilated to (l) in its English form *marble.* [C19: from DIS-[1] + ASSIMILATE] —**dis'similative** *adj.* —**dis'similatory** *adj.*
dissimilation (ˌdɪsɪmɪ'leɪʃən) *n.* **1.** the act or an instance of making dissimilar. **2.** *Phonetics.* the alteration or omission of a consonant as a result of being dissimilated. **3.** *Biology.* a less common word for **catabolism.**
dissimilitude (ˌdɪsɪ'mɪlɪˌtjuːd) *n.* **1.** dissimilarity; difference. **2.** a point of difference.
dissimulate (dɪ'sɪmjʊˌleɪt) *vb.* to conceal (one's real feelings) by pretence. —**dis**ˌ**simu'lation** *n.* —**dis'simulative** *adj.* —**dis'simu**ˌ**lator** *n.*
dissipate ('dɪsɪˌpeɪt) *vb.* **1.** to exhaust or be exhausted by dispersion. **2.** (*tr.*) to scatter or break up. **3.** (*intr.*) to indulge in the pursuit of pleasure. [C15: from Latin *dissipāre* to disperse, from DIS-[1] + *supāre* to throw] —'**dissi**ˌ**pater** *or* '**dissi**ˌ**pator** *n.* —'**dissi**ˌ**pative** *adj.*
dissipated ('dɪsɪˌpeɪtɪd) *adj.* **1.** indulging without restraint in the pursuit of pleasure; debauched. **2.** wasted, scattered, or exhausted. —'**dissi**ˌ**patedly** *adv.* —'**dissi**ˌ**patedness** *n.*
dissipation (ˌdɪsɪ'peɪʃən) *n.* **1.** the act of dissipating or condition of being dissipated. **2.** unrestrained indulgence in physical pleasures, esp. alcohol. **3.** excessive expenditure; wastefulness. **4.** amusement; diversion.
dissociable (dɪ'səʊʃɪəbᵊl, -ʃə-) *adj.* **1.** able to be dissociated; distinguishable. **2.** incongruous; irreconcilable. **3.** (dɪ'səʊʃəbᵊl). Also: **dis'social.** a less common word for **unsociable.** —**dis**ˌ**socia'bility** *or* **dis'sociableness** *n.* —**dis'sociably** *adv.*
dissociate (dɪ'səʊʃɪˌeɪt, -sɪ-) *vb.* **1.** to break or cause to break the association between (people, organizations, etc.). **2.** (*tr.*) to regard or treat as separate or unconnected. **3.** to undergo or subject to dissociation. —**dis'sociative** *adj.*
dissociation (dɪˌsəʊsɪ'eɪʃən, -ʃɪ-) *n.* **1.** the act of dissociating or the state of being dissociated. **2.** *Chem.* **a.** a reversible chemical change of the molecules of a single compound into two or more other molecules, atoms, ions, or radicals. **b.** any decomposition of the molecules of a single compound into two or more other compounds, atoms, ions, or radicals. **3.** separation of molecules or atoms that occurs when a liquid or solid changes to a gas. **4.** *Psychiatry.* the separation of a group of mental processes or ideas from the rest of the personality, so that they lead an independent existence, as in cases of multiple personality.
dissociative hysteria *n. Psychol.* an emotional disorder characterized by fugue states or multiple personality.
dissoluble (dɪ'sɒljʊbᵊl) *adj.* a less common word for **soluble.** [C16: from Latin *dissolūbilis*, from *dissolvere* to DISSOLVE] —**dis**ˌ**solu'bility** *or* **dis'solubleness** *n.*
dissolute ('dɪsəˌluːt) *adj.* given to dissipation; debauched. [C14: from Latin *dissolūtus* loose, from *dissolvere* to DISSOLVE] —'**disso**ˌ**lutely** *adv.* —'**disso**ˌ**luteness** *n.*
dissolution (ˌdɪsə'luːʃən) *n.* **1.** the resolution or separation into component parts; disintegration. **2.** destruction by breaking up and dispersing. **3.** the termination of a meeting or assembly,

such as Parliament. **4.** the termination of a formal or legal relationship, such as a business enterprise, marriage, etc. **5.** the state of being dissolute; dissipation. **6.** the act or process of dissolving. —ˈ**dissoˌlutive** *adj.*

dissolve (dɪˈzɒlv) *vb.* **1.** to go or cause to go into solution: *salt dissolves in water; water dissolves sugar.* **2.** to become or cause to become liquid; melt. **3.** to disintegrate or disperse. **4.** to come or bring to an end. **5.** to dismiss (a meeting, parliament, etc.) or (of a meeting, etc.) to be dismissed. **6.** to collapse or cause to collapse emotionally: *to dissolve into tears.* **7.** to lose or cause to lose distinctness or clarity. **8.** (*tr.*) to terminate legally, as a marriage, etc. **9.** (*intr.*) *Films, television.* to fade out one scene and replace with another to make two scenes merge imperceptibly (**fast dissolve**) or slowly overlap (**slow dissolve**) over a period of about three or four seconds. ~*n.* **10.** *Films, television.* a scene filmed or televised by dissolving. [C14: from Latin *dissolvere* to make loose, from DIS-[1] + *solvere* to release] —**disˈsolvable** *adj.* —**disˌsolvaˈbility** *or* **disˈsolvableness** *n.* —**disˈsolver** *n.*

dissolvent (dɪˈzɒlvənt) *n.* **1.** a rare word for **solvent** (sense 3). ~*adj.* **2.** able to dissolve.

dissonance (ˈdɪsənəns) *or* **dissonancy** *n.* **1.** a discordant combination of sounds. **2.** lack of agreement or consistency. **3.** *Music.* **a.** a sensation commonly associated with all intervals of the second and seventh, all diminished and augmented intervals, and all chords based on these intervals. Compare **consonance** (sense 3). **b.** an interval or chord of this kind.

dissonant (ˈdɪsənənt) *adj.* **1.** discordant; cacophonous. **2.** incongruous or discrepant. **3.** *Music.* characterized by dissonance. [C15: from Latin *dissonāre* to be discordant, from DIS-[1] + *sonāre* to sound] —ˈ**dissonantly** *adv.*

dissuade (dɪˈsweɪd) *vb.* (*tr.*) **1.** (often foll. by *from*) to deter (someone) by persuasion from a course of action, policy, etc. **2.** to advise against (an action, etc.). [C15: from Latin *dissuādēre,* from DIS-[1] + *suādēre* to persuade] —**disˈsuadable** *adj.* —**disˈsuader** *n.* —**disˈsuasion** *n.* —**disˈsuasive** *adj.* —**disˈsuasively** *adv.* —**disˈsuasiveness** *n.*

dissyllable (dɪˈsɪləbᵊl, ˈdɪsˌsɪl-, ˈdaɪsɪl-) *or* **disyllable** (ˈdaɪsɪləbᵊl, dɪˈsɪl-) *n. Grammar.* a word of two syllables. —**dissyllabic** (ˌdɪsɪˈlæbɪk, ˌdɪssɪ-, ˌdaɪ-) *or* **disyllabic** (ˌdaɪsɪˈlæbɪk, ˌdɪ-) *adj.*

dissymmetry (dɪˈsɪmɪtrɪ, dɪsˈsɪm-) *n., pl.* **-tries. 1.** lack of symmetry. **2.** the relationship between two objects when one is the mirror image of the other. **3.** another name for **chirality.** —**dissymmetric** (ˌdɪsɪˈmɛtrɪk, ˌdɪssɪ-) *or* ˌ**dissymˈmetrical** *adj.* —ˌ**dissymˈmetrically** *adv.*

dist. *abbrev. for:* **1.** distant. **2.** distinguish(ed). **3.** district.

distaff (ˈdɪstɑːf) *n.* **1.** the rod on which wool, flax, etc., is wound preparatory to spinning. **2.** *Figurative.* women's work. [Old English *distæf,* from *dis-* bunch of flax + *stæf* STAFF[1]; see DIZEN]

distaff side *n.* the female side or branch of a family. Compare **spear side.**

distal (ˈdɪstᵊl) *adj. Anatomy.* (of a muscle, bone, limb, etc.) situated farthest from the centre, median line, or point of attachment or origin. Compare **proximal.** [C19: from DISTANT + -AL[1]] —ˈ**distally** *adv.*

distance (ˈdɪstəns) *n.* **1.** the intervening space between two points or things. **2.** the length of this gap. **3.** the state of being apart in space; remoteness. **4.** an interval between two points in time. **5.** the extent of progress; advance. **6.** a distant place or time: *he lives at a distance from his work.* **7.** a separation or remoteness in relationship; disparity. **8. keep one's distance.** to maintain a proper or discreet reserve in respect of another person. **9.** *Geom.* **a.** the length of the shortest line segment joining two points. **b.** the length along a straight line or curve. **10.** (preceded by *the*) the most distant or a faraway part of the visible scene or landscape. **11.** *Horse racing.* **a.** *Brit.* a point on a racecourse 240 yards from the winning post. **b.** *Brit.* any interval of more than 20 lengths between any two finishers in a race. **c.** *U.S.* the part of a racecourse that a horse must reach in any heat before the winner passes the finishing line in order to qualify for later heats. **12. go the distance. a.** *Boxing.* to complete a bout without being knocked out. **b.** to be able to complete an assigned task or responsibility. **13.** the distant parts of a picture, such as a landscape. **14. middle distance. a.** (in a picture) halfway between the foreground and the horizon. **b.** (in a natural situation) halfway between the observer and the horizon. **15.** (*modifier*) *Athletics.* relating to or denoting the longer races, usually those longer than a mile: *a distance runner.* ~*vb.* (*tr.*) **16.** to hold or place at a distance. **17.** to separate (oneself) mentally or emotionally from something. **18.** to outdo; outstrip.

distance learning *n.* a teaching system consisting of video, audio, and written material designed for a person to use in studying a subject at home.

distant (ˈdɪstənt) *adj.* **1.** far away or apart in space or time. **2.** (*postpositive*) separated in space or time by a specified distance. **3.** apart in relevance, association, or relationship: *a distant cousin.* **4.** coming from or going to a faraway place: *a distant journey.* **5.** remote in manner; aloof. **6.** abstracted; absent: *a distant look.* [C14: from Latin *distāre* to be distant, from DIS-[1] + *stāre* to stand] —ˈ**distantly** *adv.* —ˈ**distantness** *n.*

distant early warning *n.* a U.S. radar detection system to warn of missile attack. See also **DEW line.**

distaste (dɪsˈteɪst) *n.* **1.** (often foll. by *for*) an absence of pleasure (in); dislike (of); aversion (to): *to look at someone with distaste.* ~*vb.* **2.** (*tr.*) an archaic word for **dislike.**

distasteful (dɪsˈteɪstful) *adj.* unpleasant or offensive. —**disˈtastefully** *adv.* —**disˈtastefulness** *n.*

distemper[1] (dɪsˈtɛmpə) *n.* **1.** any of various infectious diseases of animals, esp. **canine distemper,** a highly contagious viral disease of dogs, characterized initially by high fever and a discharge from the nose and eyes. See also **hard pad, strangles. 2.** *Archaic.* **a.** a disease or disorder. **b.** disturbance. **c.** discontent. ~*vb.* **3.** (*tr.*) *Archaic.* to disturb. [C14: from Late Latin *distemperāre* to derange the health of, from Latin DIS-[1] + *temperāre* to mix in correct proportions]

distemper[2] (dɪsˈtɛmpə) *n.* **1.** a technique of painting in which the pigments are mixed with water, glue, size, etc., used for poster, mural, and scene painting. **2.** the paint used in this technique or any of various water-based paints, including, in Britain, whitewash. ~*vb.* **3.** (*tr.*) to mix (pigments) with water and size. **4.** to paint (something) with distemper. [C14: from Medieval Latin *distemperāre* to soak, from Latin DIS-[1] + *temperāre* to mingle]

distend (dɪˈstɛnd) *vb.* **1.** to expand or be expanded by or as if by pressure from within; swell; inflate. **2.** (*tr.*) to stretch out or extend. **3.** (*tr.*) to magnify in importance; exaggerate. [C14: from Latin *distendere,* from DIS-[1] + *tendere* to stretch] —**disˈtender** *n.* —**disˈtensible** *adj.* —**disˌtensiˈbility** *n.* —**disˈtension** *or* **disˈtention** *n.*

distich (ˈdɪstɪk) *n. Prosody.* a unit of two verse lines, usually a couplet. [C16: from Greek *distikhos* having two lines, from DI-[1] + *stikhos* STICH] —ˈ**distichal** *adj.*

distichous (ˈdɪstɪkəs) *adj.* (of leaves) arranged in two vertical rows on opposite sides of the stem. —ˈ**distichously** *adv.*

distil *or U.S.* **distill** (dɪsˈtɪl) *vb.* **-tils** *or* **-tills, -tilling, -tilled. 1.** to subject to or undergo distillation. See also **rectify** (sense 2). **2.** (sometimes foll. by *out* or *off*) to purify, separate, or concentrate, or be purified, separated, or concentrated by distillation. **3.** to obtain or be obtained by distillation: *to distil whisky.* **4.** to exude or give off (a substance) in drops or small quantities. **5.** (*tr.*) to extract the essence of as if by distillation. [C14: from Latin *dēstillāre* to distil, from DE- + *stillāre* to drip] —**disˈtillable** *adj.*

distillate (ˈdɪstɪlɪt, -ˌleɪt) *n.* **1.** Also called: **distillation.** the product of distillation. **2.** a concentrated essence.

distillation (ˌdɪstɪˈleɪʃən) *or* **distillment** *n.* **1.** the act, process, or product of distilling. **2.** the process of evaporating or boiling a liquid and condensing its vapour. **3.** purification or separation of mixture by using different evaporation rates or boiling points of their components. See also **fractional distillation. 4.** the process of obtaining the essence or an extract of a substance, usually by heating it in a solvent. **5.** another name for **distillate** (sense 1). **6.** a concentrated essence. —**disˈtillatory** *adj.*

distiller (dɪˈstɪlə) *n.* a person or organization that distils, esp. a company that makes spirits.

distillery (dɪˈstɪlərɪ) *n., pl.* **-eries.** a place where alcoholic drinks, etc., are made by distillation.

distinct (dɪˈstɪŋkt) *adj.* **1.** easily sensed or understood; clear; precise. **2.** (when postpositive, foll. by *from*) not the same (as); separate (from); distinguished (from). **3.** not alike; different. **4.** sharp; clear. **5.** recognizable; definite: *a distinct improvement.* **6.** explicit; unequivocal. **7.** *Maths, logic.* (of a pair of entities) not numerically identical. **8.** *Botany.* (of parts of a plant) not joined together; separate. [C14: from Latin *distinctus,* from *distinguere* to DISTINGUISH] —**disˈtinctly** *adv.* —**disˈtinctness** *n.*

distinction (dɪˈstɪŋkʃən) *n.* **1.** the act or an instance of distinguishing or differentiating. **2.** a distinguishing feature. **3.** the state of being different or distinguishable. **4.** special honour, recognition, or fame. **5.** excellence of character; distinctive qualities: *a man of distinction.* **6.** distinguished appearance. **7.** a symbol of honour or rank.

distinctive (dɪˈstɪŋktɪv) *adj.* **1.** serving or tending to distinguish. **2.** denoting one of a set of minimal features of a phoneme in a given language that serve to distinguish it from other phonemes. The distinctive features of /p/ in English are that it is voiceless, bilabial, non-nasal, and plosive; /b/ is voiced, bilabial, non-nasal, and plosive: the two differ by the distinctive feature of voice. —**disˈtinctively** *adv.* —**disˈtinctiveness** *n.*

distinctiveness ratio *n. Statistics.* the ratio of the relative frequency of some event in a given sample to that in the general population or another relevant sample.

distingué *French.* (distɛ̃ge) *adj.* distinguished or noble.

distinguish (dɪˈstɪŋgwɪʃ) *vb.* (*mainly tr.*) **1.** (when *intr.,* foll. by *between* or *among*) to make, show, or recognize a difference or differences (between or among); differentiate (between). **2.** to be a distinctive feature of; characterize. **3.** to make out; perceive. **4.** to mark for a special honour or title. **5.** to make (oneself) noteworthy: *he distinguished himself by his cowardice.* **6.** to classify; categorize: *we distinguished three species.* [C16: from Latin *distinguere* to separate, discriminate] —**disˈtinguishable** *adj.* —**disˈtinguishably** *adv.* —**disˈtinguisher** *n.* —**disˈtinguishing** *adj.* —**disˈtinguishingly** *adv.*

distinguished (dɪˈstɪŋgwɪʃt) *adj.* **1.** noble or dignified in appearance or behaviour. **2.** eminent; famous; celebrated.

distort (dɪˈstɔːt) *vb.* (*tr.*) **1.** (*often passive*) to twist or pull out of shape; make bent or misshapen; contort; deform. **2.** to alter or misrepresent (facts, motives, etc.). **3.** *Electronics.* to reproduce or amplify (a signal) inaccurately, changing the shape of the waveform. [C16: from Latin *distortus* misshapen, from *distorquēre* to turn different ways, from DIS-[1] + *torquēre* to twist] —**disˈtorted** *adj.* —**disˈtortedly** *adv.* —**disˈtortedness** *n.* —**disˈtorter** *n.* —**disˈtortive** *adj.*

distortion (dɪˈstɔːʃən) *n.* **1.** the act or an instance of distorting or the state of being distorted. **2.** something that is distorted. **3.** an aberration of a lens or optical system in which the magnification varies with the lateral distance from the axis. **4.** *Electronics.* **a.** an undesired change in the shape of an electrical wave or signal. **b.** the result of such a change in waveform, esp. a loss of clarity in radio reception or sound reproduction. **5.** *Psychol.* a change in perception so that it does not correspond to reality. **6.** *Psychoanal.* the disguising of the meaning of unconscious thoughts so that they may appear in consciousness, e.g. in dreams. —**disˈtortional** *adj.*

distr. *abbrev. for:* **1.** distribution. **2.** distributor.

distract (dɪˈstrækt) *vb.* (*tr.*) **1.** (*often passive*) to draw the attention of (a person) away from something. **2.** to divide or confuse the attention of (a person). **3.** to amuse or entertain. **4.** to trouble greatly. **5.** to make mad. [C14: from Latin *distractus* perplexed, from *distrahere* to pull in different directions, from DIS-[1] + *trahere* to drag] —**disˈtracter** *n.* —**disˈtractible** *adj.* —**disˌtractiˈbility** *n.* —**disˈtracting** *adj.* —**disˈtractingly** *adv.* —**disˈtractive** *adj.* —**disˈtractively** *adv.*

distracted (dɪˈstræktɪd) *adj.* **1.** bewildered; confused. **2.** mad. —**disˈtractedly** *adv.* —**disˈtractedness** *n.*

distraction (dɪˈstrækʃən) *n.* **1.** the act or an instance of distracting or the state of being distracted. **2.** something that serves as a diversion or entertainment. **3.** an interruption; an obstacle to concentration. **4.** mental turmoil or madness.

distrain (dɪˈstreɪn) *vb. Law.* to seize (personal property) by way of distress. [C13: from Old French *destreindre,* from Latin *distringere* to impede, from DIS-[1] + *stringere* to draw tight] —**disˈtrainable** *adj.* —**disˈtrainment** *n.* —**disˈtrainor** *or* **disˈtrainer** *n.*

distrainee (ˌdɪstreɪˈniː) *n. Law.* a person whose property has been seized by way of distraint.

distraint (dɪˈstreɪnt) *n. Law.* the act or process of distraining; distress.

distrait (dɪˈstreɪ; *French* distrɛ) *adj.* absent-minded; abstracted. [C18: from French, from *distraire* to DISTRACT]

distraught (dɪˈstrɔːt) *adj.* **1.** distracted or agitated. **2.** *Rare.* mad. [C14: changed from obsolete *distract* through influence of obsolete *straught,* past participle of STRETCH]

distress (dɪˈstrɛs) *vb.* (*tr.*) **1.** to cause mental pain to; upset badly. **2.** (*usually passive*) to subject to financial or other trouble. **3.** to damage (esp. furniture), as by scratching or denting it, in order to make it appear older than it is. **4.** *Law.* a less common word for **distrain. 5.** *Archaic.* to compel. ~*n.* **6.** mental pain; anguish. **7.** the act of distressing or the state of being distressed. **8.** physical or financial trouble. **9. in distress.** (of a ship, aircraft, etc.) in dire need of help. **10.** *Law.* **a.** the seizure and holding of property as security for payment of or in satisfaction of a debt, claim, etc.; distraint. **b.** the property thus seized. **c.** *U.S.* (*as modifier*): *distress merchandise.* [C13: from Old French *destresse* distress, via Vulgar Latin, from Latin *districtus* divided in mind; see DISTRAIN] —**disˈtressful** *adj.* —**disˈtressfully** *adv.* —**disˈtressfulness** *n.* —**disˈtressing** *adj., n.* —**disˈtressingly** *adv.*

distressed (dɪˈstrɛst) *adj.* **1.** much troubled; upset; afflicted. **2.** in financial straits; poor. **3.** (of furniture, fabric, etc.) having signs of ageing artificially applied. **4.** *Economics.* another word for **depressed** (sense 4).

distress merchandise *n. U.S.* goods sold at reduced prices in order to pay overdue debts, etc.

distress signal *n.* a signal by radio, Very light, etc. from a ship or other vessel in need of immediate assistance.

distributary (dɪˈstrɪbjʊtərɪ, -trɪ) *n., pl.* **-taries.** one of several outlet streams draining a river, esp. on a delta.

distribute (dɪˈstrɪbjuːt) *vb.* (*tr.*) **1.** to give out in shares; dispense. **2.** to hand out or deliver: *to distribute handbills.* **3.** (*often passive*) to spread throughout a space or area: *gulls are distributed along the west coast.* **4.** (*often passive*) to divide into classes or categories; classify: *these books are distributed in four main categories.* **5.** *Printing.* to return (used type) to the correct positions in the type case. **6.** *Logic.* to incorporate in a distributed term of a categorial proposition. **7.** *Maths, logic.* to expand an expression containing two operators in such a way that the precedence of the operators is changed; for example, distributing multiplication over addition in $a(b + c)$ yields $ab + ac$. **8.** *Obsolete.* to dispense (justice). [C15: from Latin *distribuere* from DIS-[1] + *tribuere* to give] —**disˈtributable** *adj.*

distributed array processor *n.* a type of computer system that uses a coordinated array of separate processors applied to a single problem. Abbrev.: **DAP.**

distributed logic *n.* a computer system in which remote terminals and electronic devices, distributed throughout the system, supplement the main computer by doing some of the computing or decision making.

distributed practice *n. Psychol.* learning with reasonably long intervals between separate occasions of learning. Compare **massed practice.**

distributed systems *pl. n.* two or more computers linked by telecommunication, each of which can perform independently.

distributed term *n. Logic.* a term applying equally to every member of the class it designates, as *doctors* in *no doctors are overworked.*

distributee (dɪˌstrɪbjuˈtiː) *n. Law, chiefly U.S.* a person entitled to share in the estate of an intestate.

distribution (ˌdɪstrɪˈbjuːʃən) *n.* **1.** the act of distributing or the state or manner of being distributed. **2.** a thing or portion distributed. **3.** arrangement or location. **4.** *Commerce.* the process of physically satisfying the demand for goods and services. **5.** *Economics.* the division of the total income of a community among its members, esp. between labour incomes (wages and salaries) and property incomes (rents, interest, and dividends). **6.** *Statistics.* the set of possible values of a random variable, or points in a sample space, considered in terms of new theoretical or observed frequency: *a normal distribution.* **7.** *Law.* the apportioning of the estate of a deceased intestate among the persons entitled to share in it. **8.** *Law.* the lawful division of the assets of a bankrupt among his creditors. **9.** *Finance.* **a.** the division of part of a company's profit as a dividend to its shareholders. **b.** the amount paid by dividend in a particular distribution. **10.** *Engineering.* the way in which the fuel-air mixture is supplied to each cylinder of a multicylinder internal-combustion engine. —ˌ**distriˈbutional** *adj.*

distribution channel *n. Marketing.* the network of organizations, including manufacturers, wholesalers, and retailers, that distributes goods or services to consumers.

distribution function *n.* short for **cumulative distribution function.**

distributive (dɪˈstrɪbjʊtɪv) *adj.* **1.** characterized by or relating to distribution. **2.** *Grammar.* referring separately to the individual people or items in a group, as the words *each* and *every.* ~*n.* **3.** *Grammar.* a distributive word. —**disˈtributively** *adv.* —**disˈtributiveness** *n.*

distributive bargaining *n. Industrial relations.* a negotiation process aimed at reaching a compromise agreement over how resources may be allocated between the parties.

distributive law *n. Maths, logic.* a theorem asserting that one operator can validly be distributed over another. See **distribute** (sense 7).

distributor *or* **distributer** (dɪˈstrɪbjʊtə) *n.* **1.** a person or thing that distributes. **2.** a wholesaler or middleman engaged in the distribution of a category of goods, esp. to retailers in a specific area. **3.** the device in a petrol engine that distributes the high-tension voltage to the sparking plugs in the sequence of the firing order.

district (ˈdɪstrɪkt) *n.* **1. a.** an area of land marked off for administrative or other purposes. **b.** (*as modifier*): *district nurse.* **2.** a locality separated by geographical attributes; region. **3.** any subdivision of any territory, region, etc. **4.** (in England and Wales) any of the subdivisions of the nonmetropolitan counties that elects a council responsible for local planning, housing, rates, etc. See also **metropolitan district. 5.** (in Scotland until 1975) a landward division of a county. **6.** (in Scotland after 1975) any of the subdivisions of the regions that elect a council responsible for environmental health services, housing, etc. **7.** any of the 26 areas into which Northern Ireland has been divided since 1973. Elected district councils are responsible for environmental health services etc. ~*vb.* **8.** (*tr.*) to divide into districts. [C17: from Medieval Latin *districtus* area of jurisdiction, from Latin *distringere* to stretch out; see DISTRAIN]

district attorney *n.* (in the U.S.) the state prosecuting officer in a specified judicial district.

district court *n.* **1.** (in Scotland) a court of summary jurisdiction held by a stipendiary magistrate or one or more justices of the peace to deal with minor criminal offences. **2.** (in the U.S.) **a.** a federal trial court serving a federal judicial district. **b.** (in some states) a court having general jurisdiction in a state judicial district. **3.** (in Australia and New Zealand) a court lower than a high court. Former name: **magistrates' court.**

district court judge *n. Austral. and N.Z.* a judge presiding over a lower court. Former name: **magistrate.**

district high school *n. N.Z.* a school in a rural area that includes primary and post-primary classes.

district nurse *n.* (in Britain) a nurse employed within the National Health Service to attend patients in a particular area, usually by visiting them in their own homes.

distringas (dɪsˈtrɪŋgæs) *n. Law.* (formerly) a writ directing a sheriff to distrain. [from Latin: you shall distrain (the opening word of the writ)]

distrix (ˈdɪstrɪks) *n. Med.* the splitting of the ends of hairs. [from Greek DIS-[2] + *thrix* hair]

distrust (dɪsˈtrʌst) *vb.* **1.** to regard as untrustworthy or dishonest. ~*n.* **2.** suspicion; doubt. —**disˈtruster** *n.* —**disˈtrustful** *adj.* —**disˈtrustfully** *adv.* —**disˈtrustfulness** *n.*

disturb (dɪˈstɜːb) *vb.* (*tr.*) **1.** to intrude on; interrupt. **2.** to destroy or interrupt the quietness or peace of. **3.** to disarrange; muddle. **4.** (*often passive*) to upset or agitate; trouble: *I am disturbed at your bad news.* **5.** to inconvenience; put out: *don't* *disturb yourself on my account.* [C13: from Latin *disturbāre,* from DIS-[1] + *turbāre* to confuse] —**dis'turber** *n.* —**dis'turbing** *adj.* —**dis'turbingly** *adv.*

disturbance (dɪ'stɜːbəns) *n.* **1.** the act of disturbing or the state of being disturbed. **2.** an interruption or intrusion. **3.** an unruly outburst or tumult. **4.** *Law.* an interference with another's rights. **5.** *Geology.* a minor movement of the earth causing a small earthquake. **6.** *Meteorol.* a small depression. **7.** *Psychiatry.* a mental or emotional disorder.

disturbed (dɪ'stɜːbd) *adj. Psychiatry.* emotionally upset, troubled, or maladjusted.

disulfiram (ˌdaɪsʌl'fɪərəm) *n.* a drug used in the treatment of alcoholism that acts by inducing nausea and vomiting following ingestion of alcohol. [C20: from tetraethylthi*uram disulfi*de]

disulphate (daɪ'sʌlfeɪt) *n.* another name for **pyrosulphate.**

disulphide (daɪ'sʌlfaɪd) *n.* any chemical compound containing two sulphur atoms per molecule. Also called (not in technical usage): **bisulphide.**

disulphuric acid (ˌdaɪsʌl'fjʊərɪk) *n.* another name for **pyrosulphuric acid.**

disunite (ˌdɪsjuː'naɪt) *vb.* **1.** to separate or become separate; disrupt. **2.** (*tr.*) to set at variance; estrange. —**dis'union** *n.* —ˌ**disu'niter** *n.*

disunity (dɪs'juːnɪtɪ) *n., pl.* **-ties.** dissension or disagreement.

disuse (dɪs'juːs) *n.* the condition of being unused; neglect (often in the phrases **in** *or* **into disuse**).

disused (dɪs'juːzd) *adj.* no longer used: *a disused mine.*

disyllable ('daɪsɪləbᵊl, dɪ'sɪl-) *n.* a variant of **dissyllable.** —**disyllabic** (ˌdaɪsɪ'læbɪk, ˌdɪ-) *adj.*

dit (dɪt) *n.* the short sound used, in combination with the long sound *dah,* in the spoken representation of Morse and other telegraphic codes. Compare **dot**[1] (sense 6).

dita ('diːtə) *n.* an apocynaceous shrub, *Alstonia scholaris,* of tropical Africa and Asia, having large shiny whorled leaves and medicinal bark. [C19: from Tagalog]

ditch (dɪtʃ) *n.* **1.** a narrow channel dug in the earth, usually used for drainage, irrigation, or as a boundary marker. **2.** any small, natural waterway. **3.** *Irish.* a bank made of earth excavated from and placed alongside a drain or stream. **4.** *Informal.* either of the gutters at the side of a tenpin bowling lane. **5. last ditch.** a last resort or place of last defence. ~*vb.* **6.** to make a ditch or ditches in (a piece of ground). **7.** (*intr.*) to edge with a ditch. **8.** *Slang.* to crash or be crashed, esp. deliberately, as to avoid more unpleasant circumstances: *he had to ditch the car.* **9.** (*tr.*) *Slang.* to abandon or discard: *to ditch a girlfriend.* **10.** *Slang.* to land (an aircraft) on water in an emergency. **11.** (*tr.*) *U.S. slang.* to evade: *to ditch the police.* [Old English *dīc;* related to Old Saxon *dīk,* Old Norse *dīki,* Middle High German *tīch* dyke, pond, Latin *fīgere* to stick, see DYKE] —'**ditcher** *n.* —'**ditchless** *adj.*

ditchwater ('dɪtʃˌwɔːtə) *n.* **1.** stagnant water. **2. (as) dull as ditchwater.** extremely uninspiring.

ditheism ('daɪθiːˌɪzəm) *n. Theol.* **1.** the belief in two equal gods. **2.** the belief that two equal principles reign over the world, one good and one evil. —'**ditheist** *n.* —ˌ**dithe'istic** *adj.*

dither ('dɪðə) *vb.* (*intr.*) **1.** *Chiefly Brit.* to be uncertain or indecisive. **2.** *Chiefly U.S.* to be in an agitated state. **3.** to tremble, as with cold. ~*n.* **4.** *Chiefly Brit.* a state of indecision. **5.** a state of agitation. [C17: variant of C14 (northern English dialect) *didder,* of uncertain origin] —'**ditherer** *n.* —'**dithery** *adj.*

dithionite (daɪ'θaɪəˌnaɪt) *n.* any salt of dithionous acid. Also called: **hyposulphite, hydrosulphite.**

dithionous acid (daɪ'θaɪənəs) *n.* an unstable dibasic acid known only in solution and in the form of dithionite salts. It is a powerful reducing agent. Formula: $H_2S_2O_4$. Also called: **hyposulphurous acid, hydrosulphurous acid.** [from DI-[1] + *thion-,* from Greek *theion* sulphur + -OUS]

dithyramb ('dɪθɪˌræm, -ˌræmb) *n.* **1.** (in ancient Greece) a passionate choral hymn in honour of Dionysus, god of wine, revelry, and of the drama; the forerunner of Greek drama. **2.** any utterance or a piece of writing that resembles this. [C17: from Latin *dīthyrambus,* from Greek *dithurambos;* related to *iambos* IAMB]

dithyrambic (ˌdɪθɪ'ræmbɪk) *adj.* **1.** *Prosody.* of or relating to a dithyramb. **2.** passionately eloquent. —ˌ**dithy'rambically** *adv.*

dittander (dɪ'tændə, 'dɪtᵊn-) *n.* a cruciferous plant, *Lepidium latifolium,* of coastal regions of Europe, N Africa, and SW Asia, with clusters of small white flowers.

dittany ('dɪtənɪ) *n., pl.* **-nies.** **1.** an aromatic Cretan plant, *Origanum dictamnus,* with pink drooping flowers: formerly credited with great medicinal properties: family *Labiatae* (labiates). **2.** Also called: **stone mint.** a North American labiate plant, *Cunila origanoides,* with clusters of purplish flowers. **3.** another name for **gas plant.** [C14: from Old French *ditan,* from Latin *dictamnus,* from Greek *diktamnon,* perhaps from *Diktē,* mountain in Crete]

ditto ('dɪtəʊ) *n., pl.* **-tos.** **1.** the aforementioned; the above; the same. Used in accounts, lists, etc., to avoid repetition and symbolized by two small marks („) known as **ditto marks,** placed under the thing repeated. Abbrev.: **do.** **2.** *Informal.* **a.** a duplicate. **b.** (*as modifier*): *a ditto copy.* ~*adv.* **3.** in the same way. ~ **4.** *sentence substitute. Informal.* used to avoid repeating or to confirm agreement with an immediately preceding sentence. ~*vb.* **-tos, -toing, -toed.** **5.** (*tr.*) to copy; repeat. [C17: from Italian (Tuscan dialect), variant of *detto* said, from *dicere* to say, from Latin]

dittography (dɪ'tɒgrəfɪ) *n., pl.* **-phies.** **1.** the unintentional repetition of letters or words. **2.** a passage of manuscript demonstrating dittography. —**dittographic** (ˌdɪtə'græfɪk) *adj.*

ditty ('dɪtɪ) *n., pl.* **-ties.** a short simple song or poem. [C13: from Old French *ditie* poem, from *ditier* to compose, from Latin *dictāre* DICTATE]

ditty bag *n.* a sailor's cloth bag for personal belongings or tools. A box used for these purposes is termed a **ditty box.** [C19: perhaps from obsolete *dutty* calico, from Hindi *dhōtī* loincloth, DHOTI]

diuresis (ˌdaɪjʊ'riːsɪs) *n.* excretion of an unusually large quantity of urine. [C17: from New Latin, from Greek *diourein* to urinate]

diuretic (ˌdaɪjʊ'rɛtɪk) *adj.* **1.** acting to increase the flow of urine. ~*n.* **2.** a drug or agent that increases the flow of urine. —ˌ**diu'retically** *adv.* —ˌ**diu'reticalness** *n.*

diurnal (daɪ'ɜːnᵊl) *adj.* **1.** happening during the day or daily. **2.** (of flowers) open during the day and closed at night. **3.** (of animals) active during the day. ~Compare **nocturnal.** ~*n.* **4.** a service book containing all the canonical hours except matins. [C15: from Late Latin *diurnālis,* from Latin *diurnus,* from *diēs* day] —**di'urnally** *adv.*

diurnal parallax *n.* See **parallax** (sense 2).

div[1] (dɪv) *n. Maths.* short for **divergence** (sense 4).

div[2] (dɪv) *n. Prison slang.* a stupid or foolish person. [C20: probably shortened and changed from DEVIANT]

div. *abbrev. for:* **1.** divide(d). **2.** dividend. **3.** division. **4.** divorce(d).

diva ('diːvə) *n., pl.* **-vas** *or* **-ve** (-vɪ). a highly distinguished female singer; prima donna. [C19: via Italian from Latin: a goddess, from *dīvus* DIVINE]

divagate ('daɪvəˌgeɪt) *vb.* (*intr.*) *Rare.* to digress or wander. [C16: from Latin DI-[2] + *vagārī* to wander] —ˌ**diva'gation** *n.*

divalent (daɪ'veɪlənt, 'daɪˌveɪ-) *adj. Chem.* **1.** having a valency of two. **2.** having two valencies. ~Also: **bivalent.** —**di'valency** *n.*

divan (dɪ'væn) *n.* **1. a.** a backless sofa or couch, designed to be set against a wall. **b.** a bed resembling such a couch. **2.** (esp. formerly) a room for smoking and drinking, as in a coffee shop. **3. a.** a Muslim law court, council chamber, or counting house. **b.** a Muslim council of state. **4.** a collection of poems. **5.** (in Muslim law) an account book. ~Also called (for senses 2–5): **diwan.** [C16: from Turkish *dīvān,* from Persian *dīwān*]

divaricate *vb.* (daɪ'værɪˌkeɪt). **1.** (*intr.*) (esp. of branches) to diverge at a wide angle. ~*adj.* (daɪ'værɪkɪt, -ˌkeɪt). **2.** branching widely; forked. [C17: from Latin *dīvāricāre* to stretch apart, from DI-[2] + *vāricāre* to stand astride] —**di'varicately** *adv.* —**di'variˌcatingly** *adv.* —**diˌvari'cation** *n.*

divaricator (daɪ'værɪˌkeɪtə) *n. Zoology.* a muscle in brachiopods that controls the opening of the shell.

dive (daɪv) *vb.* **dives, diving, dived** *or U.S.* **dove, dived.** (*mainly intr.*) **1.** to plunge headfirst into water. **2.** (of a submarine, swimmer, etc.) to submerge under water. **3.** (*also tr.*) to fly (an aircraft) in a steep nose-down descending path, or (of an aircraft) to fly in such a path. **4.** to rush, go, or reach quickly, as in a headlong plunge: *he dived for the ball.* **5.** (*also tr.;* foll. by *in* or *into*) to dip or put (one's hand) quickly or forcefully (into): *to dive into one's pocket.* **6.** (usually foll. by *in* or *into*) to involve oneself (in something), as in eating food. ~*n.* **7.** a headlong plunge into water, esp. one of several formalized movements executed as a sport. **8.** an act or instance of diving. **9.** a steep nose-down descent of an aircraft. **10.** *Slang.* a disreputable or seedy bar or club. **11.** *Boxing slang.* the act of a boxer pretending to be knocked down or out: *he took a dive in the fourth round.* [Old English *dȳfan;* related to Old Norse *dȳfa* to dip, Frisian *dīvi;* see DEEP, DIP]

dive-bomb *vb.* (*tr.*) to bomb (a target) using or in the manner of a dive bomber.

dive bomber *n.* a military aircraft designed to release its bombs on a target during a steep dive.

dive brake *n.* **1.** a flap or spoiler extended from the wings of a ground-attack aircraft for controlling a dive. **2.** another name for **air brake.**

Divehi ('dɪvɛɪ) *n.* the language of the Maldive Islands in the Indian Ocean, belonging to the Indic branch of the Indo-European family.

diver ('daɪvə) *n.* **1.** a person or thing that dives. **2.** a person who works or explores underwater. **3.** any aquatic bird of the genus *Gavia,* family *Gaviidae,* and order *Gaviiformes* of northern oceans, having a straight pointed bill, small wings, and a long body: noted for swiftness and skill in swimming and diving. U.S. and Canadian name: **loon.** **4.** any of various other diving birds.

diverge (daɪ'vɜːdʒ) *vb.* **1.** to separate or cause to separate and go in different directions from a point. **2.** (*intr.*) to be at variance; differ: *our opinions diverge.* **3.** (*intr.*) to deviate from a prescribed course. **4.** (*intr.*) *Maths.* (of a series) to have no limit. [C17: from Medieval Latin *dīvergere,* from Latin DI-[2] + *vergere* to turn]

divergence (daɪ'vɜːdʒəns) *n.* **1.** the act or result of diverging or the amount by which something diverges. **2.** the condition of being divergent. **3.** *Meteorol.* the outflowing of airstreams from a particular area, caused by expanding air. **4.** *Maths.* **a.** the scalar product of the operator, ∇, and a vector function, $\boldsymbol{A}$, where $\nabla = \boldsymbol{i}\partial/\partial x + \boldsymbol{j}\partial/\partial y + \boldsymbol{k}\partial/\partial z$, and $\boldsymbol{i}, \boldsymbol{j}$, and $\boldsymbol{k}$ are unit vectors. Usually written: div **A**, $\nabla\boldsymbol{A}$, or $\nabla.\boldsymbol{A}$. Compare **curl** (sense 11), **gradient** (sense 4). **b.** the property of being divergent. **5.** the spreading of a stream of electrons as a result of their mutual electrostatic repulsion. **6.** the turning of the eyes outwards in order to fixate an object farther away than that previously being fixated. Compare **convergence** (sense 7). **7.** Also called: **divergent evolution.** the evolutionary development of structures or organisms that differ from each other in form and function but have evolved from the same basic structure or organism. Compare **convergence** (sense 5). ~Also called (for senses 1, 2): **divergency.**

divergent (daɪˈvɜːdʒənt) *adj.* **1.** diverging or causing divergence. **2.** *Maths.* (of a series) having no limit; not convergent. **3.** *Botany.* (of plant organs) farther apart at their tops than at their bases. **—diˈvergently** *adv.*

divergent thinking *n. Psychol.* thinking in an unusual and unstereotyped way, e.g. to generate several possible solutions to a problem. Compare **convergent thinking.**

divers (ˈdaɪvəz) *determiner. Archaic or literary.* **a.** various; sundry; some. **b.** (*as pronoun; functioning as pl.*): *divers of them.* [C13: from Old French, from Latin *dīversus* turned in different directions; see DIVERT]

diverse (daɪˈvɜːs, ˈdaɪvɜːs) *adj.* **1.** having variety; assorted. **2.** distinct in kind. [C13: from Latin *dīversus;* see DIVERS] **—diˈversely** *adv.* **—diˈverseness** *n.*

diversification (daɪˌvɜːsɪfɪˈkeɪʃən) *n.* **1.** *Commerce.* the practice of varying products, operations, etc., in order to spread risk, expand, exploit spare capacity, etc. **2.** (in regional planning policies) the attempt to provide regions with an adequate variety of industries. **3.** the act of diversifying.

diversiform (daɪˈvɜːsɪˌfɔːm) *adj.* having various forms.

diversify (daɪˈvɜːsɪˌfaɪ) *vb.* **-fies, -fying, -fied. 1.** (*tr.*) to create different forms of; variegate; vary. **2.** (of an enterprise) to vary (products, operations, etc.) in order to spread risk, expand, etc. **3.** to distribute (investments) among several securities in order to spread risk. [C15: from Old French *diversifier,* from Medieval Latin *dīversificāre,* from Latin *dīversus* DIVERSE + *facere* to make] **—diˈversiˌfiable** *adj.* **—diˌversiˌfiaˈbility** *n.* **—diˈversiˌfier** *n.*

diversion (daɪˈvɜːʃən) *n.* **1.** the act of diverting from a specified course. **2.** *Chiefly Brit.* an official detour used by traffic when a main route is closed. **3.** something that distracts from business, etc.; amusement. **4.** *Military.* a feint attack designed to draw an enemy away from the main attack. **—diˈversional** *or* **diˈversionary** *adj.*

diversity (daɪˈvɜːsɪtɪ) *n.* **1.** the state or quality of being different or varied. **2.** a point of difference. **3.** *Logic.* the relation that holds between two entities when and only when they are not identical; the property of being numerically distinct.

divert (daɪˈvɜːt) *vb.* **1.** to turn (a person or thing) aside from a course; deflect. **2.** (*tr.*) to entertain; amuse. **3.** (*tr.*) to distract the attention of. [C15: from French *divertir,* from Latin *dīvertere* to turn aside, from DI-[2] + *vertere* to turn] **—diˈverter** *n.* **—diˈvertible** *adj.* **—diˈverting** *adj.* **—diˈvertingly** *adv.* **—diˈvertive** *adj.*

diverticulitis (ˌdaɪvəˌtɪkjʊˈlaɪtɪs) *n.* inflammation of one or more diverticula, esp. of the colon.

diverticulosis (ˌdaɪvəˌtɪkjʊˈləʊsɪs) *n. Pathol.* the presence of several diverticula, esp. in the intestines. [from New Latin, from DIVERTICULUM + -OSIS]

diverticulum (ˌdaɪvəˈtɪkjʊləm) *n., pl.* **-la** (-lə). any sac or pouch formed by herniation of the wall of a tubular organ or part, esp. the intestines. [C16: from New Latin, from Latin *dēverticulum* by-path, from *dēvertere* to turn aside, from *vertere* to turn] **—ˌdiverˈticular** *adj.*

divertimento (dɪˌvɜːtɪˈmɛntəʊ) *n., pl.* **-ti** (-tɪ). **1.** a piece of entertaining music in several movements, often scored for a mixed ensemble and having no fixed form. **2.** an episode in a fugue. ~See also **divertissement.** [C18: from Italian]

divertissement (dɪˈvɜːtɪsmənt; *French* divɛrtismɑ̃) *n.* **1.** a brief entertainment or diversion, usually between the acts of a play. **2.** *Music.* **a.** a fantasia on popular melodies; potpourri. **b.** a piece or pieces written to be played during the intervals in a play, opera, etc. **c.** another word for **divertimento.** [C18: from French: entertainment]

Dives (ˈdaɪviːz) *n.* a very rich man. [after the prosperous subject of a parable (Luke 16:19–31)]

divest (daɪˈvɛst) *vb.* (*tr.;* usually foll. by *of*) **1.** to strip (of clothes): *to divest oneself of one's coat.* **2.** to deprive or dispossess. **3.** *Property law.* to take away an estate or interest in property vested (in a person). [C17: changed from earlier DEVEST] **—diˈvestible** *adj.* **—divestiture** (daɪˈvɛstɪtʃə), **divesture** (daɪˈvɛstʃə), *or* **diˈvestment** *n.*

divi (ˈdɪvɪ) *n.* an alternative spelling of **divvy.**

divide (dɪˈvaɪd) *vb.* **1.** to separate or be separated into parts or groups; split up; part. **2.** to share or be shared out in parts; distribute. **3.** to diverge or cause to diverge in opinion or aim: *the issue divided the management.* **4.** (*tr.*) to keep apart or be a boundary between: *the Rio Grande divides Mexico from the United States.* **5.** (*intr.*) (in Parliament and similar legislatures) to vote by separating into two groups. **6.** to categorize; classify. **7.** to calculate the quotient of (one number or quantity) and (another number or quantity) by division: *to divide 50 by 10; to divide 10 into 50; to divide by 10.* **8.** (*intr.*) to diverge: *the roads divide.* **9.** (*tr.*) to mark increments of (length, angle, etc.) as by use of an engraving machine. ~*n.* **10.** *Chiefly U.S. and Canadian.* an area of relatively high ground separating drainage basins; watershed. See also **continental divide. 11.** a division; split. [C14: from Latin *dīvidere* to force apart, from DI-[2] + *vid-* separate, from the source of *viduus* bereaved, *vidua* WIDOW] **—diˈvidable** *adj.*

divided (dɪˈvaɪdɪd) *adj.* **1.** *Botany.* another word for **dissected** (sense 1). **2.** split; not united. **—diˈvidedly** *adv.* **—diˈvidedness** *n.*

divided highway *n.* the U.S. and Canadian term for **dual carriageway.**

dividend (ˈdɪvɪˌdɛnd) *n.* **1.** *Finance.* **a.** a distribution from the net profits of a company to its shareholders. **b.** a pro-rata portion of this distribution received by a shareholder. **2.** the share of a cooperative society's surplus allocated at the end of a period to members. **3.** *Insurance.* a sum of money distributed from a company's net profits to the holders of certain policies. **4.** something extra; bonus. **5.** a number or quantity to be divided by another number or quantity. Compare **divisor. 6.** *Law.* the proportion of an insolvent estate payable to the creditors. [C15: from Latin *dīvidendum* what is to be divided; see DIVIDE]

dividend cover *n.* the number of times that a company's dividends to shareholders could be paid out of its annual profits after tax, used as an indication of the probability that dividends will be maintained in subsequent years.

divider (dɪˈvaɪdə) *n.* **1.** Also called: **room divider.** a screen or piece of furniture placed so as to divide a room into separate areas. **2.** a person or thing that divides. **3.** *Electronics.* an electrical circuit with an output that is a well-defined fraction of a given input: *a voltage divider.*

dividers (dɪˈvaɪdəz) *pl. n.* a type of compass with two pointed arms, used for measuring lines or dividing them.

divi-divi (ˌdɪvɪˈdɪvɪ) *n., pl.* **-divis** *or* **-divi. 1.** a tropical American caesalpiniaceous tree, *Caesalpinia coriaria.* **2.** the pods of this plant, which yield a substance used in tanning leather. [C19: from Spanish, of Cariban origin]

divination (ˌdɪvɪˈneɪʃən) *n.* **1.** the art, practice, or gift of discerning or discovering future events or unknown things, as though by supernatural powers. **2.** a prophecy. **3.** a presentiment or guess. **—divinatory** (dɪˈvɪnətərɪ, -trɪ) *adj.*

divine (dɪˈvaɪn) *adj.* **1.** of, relating to, or characterizing God or a deity. **2.** godlike. **3.** of, relating to, or associated with religion or worship: *the divine liturgy.* **4.** of supreme excellence or worth. **5.** *Informal.* splendid; perfect. ~*n.* **6.** (*often cap.;* preceded by *the*) another term for **God. 7.** a priest, esp. one learned in theology. ~*vb.* **8.** to perceive or understand (something) by intuition or insight. **9.** to conjecture (something); guess. **10.** to discern (a hidden or future reality) as though by supernatural power. **11.** (*tr.*) to search for (underground supplies of water, metal, etc.) using a divining rod. [C14: from Latin *dīvīnus,* from *dīvus* a god; related to *deus* a god] **—diˈvinable** *adj.* **—diˈvinely** *adv.* **—diˈvineness** *n.* **—diˈviner** *n.*

divine office *n.* (*sometimes caps.*) the canonical prayers (in the Roman Catholic Church those of the breviary) recited daily by priests, those in religious orders, etc.

divine right of kings *n. History.* the concept that the right to rule derives from God and that kings are answerable for their actions to God alone.

divine service *n.* a service of the Christian church, esp. one at which no sacrament is given.

diving beetle *n.* any of the aquatic predatory beetles of the widely distributed family *Dytiscidae,* characterized by flattened hindlegs adapted for swimming and diving.

diving bell *n.* an early diving submersible having an open bottom and being supplied with compressed air.

diving board *n.* a platform or springboard from which swimmers may dive.

diving duck *n.* any of various ducks, such as the pochard, scaup, redhead, and canvasback, that inhabit bays, estuaries, lakes, etc., and can dive and swim beneath the surface of the water.

diving suit *or* **dress** *n.* a waterproof suit used by divers, having a heavy detachable helmet and an air supply.

divining rod *n.* a rod, usually a forked hazel twig, said to move or dip when held over ground in which water, metal, etc., is to be found. Also called: **dowsing rod.**

divinity (dɪˈvɪnɪtɪ) *n., pl.* **-ties. 1.** the nature of a deity or the state of being divine. **2.** a god or other divine being. **3.** (*often cap.;* preceded by *the*) another term for **God. 4.** another word for **theology.**

divinize *or* **divinise** (ˈdɪvɪˌnaɪz) *vb.* (*tr.*) to make divine; deify. **—ˌdiviniˈzation** *or* **ˌdiviniˈsation** *n.*

divisibility (dɪˌvɪzɪˈbɪlɪtɪ) *n.* the capacity of a dividend to be exactly divided by a given number.

divisible (dɪˈvɪzəbᵊl) *adj.* capable of being divided, usually with no remainder. **—diˈvisibleness** *n.* **—diˈvisibly** *adv.*

division (dɪˈvɪʒən) *n.* **1.** the act of dividing or state of being divided. **2.** the act of sharing out; distribution. **3.** something that divides or keeps apart, such as a boundary. **4.** one of the parts, groups, etc., into which something is divided. **5.** a part of a government, business, country, etc., that has been made into a unit for administrative, political, or other reasons. **6.** a formal vote in Parliament or a similar legislative body. **7.** a difference of opinion, esp. one that causes separation. **8.** (in sports) a section, category, or class organized according to age, weight, skill, etc. **9.** a mathematical operation, the inverse of multiplication, in which the quotient of two numbers or quantities is calculated. Usually written: $a \div b$, $^a/_b$, a/b. **10. a.** *Army.* a major formation, larger than a regiment or brigade but smaller than a corps, containing the necessary arms to sustain independent combat. **b.** *Navy.* a group of ships of similar type or a tactical unit of naval aircraft. **c.** *Air Force.* an organization normally comprising two or more wings with required support units. **11.** (*pl.*) *Navy.* the assembly of all crew members for the captain's inspection. **12.** *Biology.* a major taxonomic division of the plant kingdom that contains one or more classes and corresponds to a phylum. **13.** *Horticulture.* any type of propagation in plants in which a new plant grows from a separated part of the original. **14.** *Logic.* the fallacy of inferring that the properties of the whole are also true of the parts, as *Britain is in debt, so John Smith is in debt.* **15.** (esp. in 17th-century English music) the art of breaking up a melody into quick phrases, esp. over a ground bass. [C14: from Latin *dīvīsiō,* from *dīvidere* to DIVIDE] —**diˈvisional** *or* **diˈvisionary** *adj.* —**diˈvisionally** *adv.*

divisionism (dɪˈvɪʒəˌnɪzəm) *n.* the pointillism of the French painter Georges Seurat (1859–91) and his followers. —**diˈvisionist** *n., adj.*

division of labour *n.* a system of organizing the manufacture of an article in a series of separate specialized operations, each of which is carried out by a different worker or group of workers.

division sign *n.* the symbol ÷, placed between the dividend and the divisor to indicate division, as in 12 ÷ 6 = 2.

divisive (dɪˈvaɪsɪv) *adj.* **1.** causing or tending to cause disagreement or dissension. **2.** *Archaic.* having the quality of distinguishing. —**diˈvisively** *adv.* —**diˈvisiveness** *n.*

divisor (dɪˈvaɪzə) *n.* **1.** a number or quantity to be divided into another number or quantity (the dividend). **2.** a number that is a factor of another number.

divorce (dɪˈvɔːs) *n.* **1.** the dissolution of a marriage by judgment of a court or by accepted custom. **2.** a judicial decree declaring a marriage to be dissolved. **3.** a separation, esp. one that is total or complete. ~*vb.* **4.** to separate or be separated by divorce; give or obtain a divorce (to a couple or from one's spouse). **5.** (*tr.*) to remove or separate, esp. completely. [C14: from Old French, from Latin *dīvortium* from *dīvertere* to separate; see DIVERT] —**diˈvorceable** *adj.* —**diˈvorcer** *n.* —**diˈvorcive** *adj.*

divorcée (dɪvɔːˈsiː) *or* (*masc.*) **divorcé** (dɪˈvɔːseɪ) *n.* a person who has been divorced.

divorcement (dɪˈvɔːsmənt) *n.* a less common word for **divorce.**

divot (ˈdɪvət) *n.* a piece of turf dug out of a grass surface, esp. by a golf club or by horses' hooves. [C16: from Scottish, of obscure origin]

divulgate (dɪˈvʌlgeɪt) *vb.* (*tr.*) *Archaic.* to make publicly known. [C16: from Latin *dīvulgāre;* see DIVULGE] —**diˈvulgator** *or* **diˈvulgater** *n.* —ˌ**divulˈgation** *n.*

divulge (daɪˈvʌldʒ) *vb.* (*tr.; may take a clause as object*) to make known (something private or secret); disclose. [C15: from Latin *dīvulgāre,* from DI-[2] + *vulgāre* to spread among the people, from *vulgus* the common people] —**diˈvulgence** *or* **diˈvulgement** *n.* —**diˈvulger** *n.*

divulsion (daɪˈvʌlʃən) *n.* a tearing or pulling apart. [C17: from Latin *dīvulsiō,* from *dīvulsus* torn apart, from *dīvellere* to rend, from DI-[2] + *vellere* to pull] —**diˈvulsive** *adj.*

divvy (ˈdɪvɪ) *Informal.* ~*n., pl.* **-vies. 1.** *Brit.* short for **dividend,** esp. (formerly) one paid by a cooperative society. **2.** *U.S. and Canadian.* a share; portion. ~*vb.* **-vies, -vying, -vied. 3.** (*tr.;* usually foll. by *up*) to divide and share.

Diwali (dɪˈwɑːlɪ) *n.* a major Hindu religious festival, honouring Lakshmi, the goddess of wealth. Held over the New Year according to the Vikrama calendar, it is marked by feasting, gifts, and the lighting of lamps.

diwan (dɪˈwɑːn) *n.* a variant of **dewan** or **divan** (senses 2–5).

dixie (ˈdɪksɪ) *n.* **1.** *Chiefly military.* a large metal pot for cooking, brewing tea, etc. **2.** a mess tin. [C19: from Hindi *degcī,* diminutive of *degcā* pot]

Dixie (ˈdɪksɪ) *n.* **1.** a song adopted as a marching tune by the Confederate (southern) states during the American Civil War. ~*adj.* **2.** of, relating to, or characteristic of the southern states of the U.S. [C19: perhaps from the nickname of New Orleans (Louisiana), from *dixie* a ten-dollar bill printed there, from French *dix* ten]

Dixieland (ˈdɪksɪˌlænd) *n.* **1.** a form of jazz that originated in New Orleans, becoming popular esp. with White musicians in the second decade of the 20th century. **2.** a revival of this style in the 1950s.

DIY *or* **d.i.y.** (in Britain) *abbrev. for* do-it-yourself.

dizen (ˈdaɪzən) *vb.* an archaic word for **bedizen.** [C16: from Middle Dutch *dīsen* to dress a distaff with flax; see DISTAFF] —ˈ**dizenment** *n.*

dizzy (ˈdɪzɪ) *adj.* **-zier, -ziest. 1.** affected with a whirling or reeling sensation; giddy. **2.** mentally confused or bewildered. **3.** causing or tending to cause vertigo or bewilderment. **4.** *Informal.* foolish or flighty. ~*vb.* **-zies, -zying, -zied. 5.** (*tr.*) to make dizzy. [Old English *dysig* silly; related to Old High German *tusīg* weak, Old Norse *dos* quiet] —ˈ**dizzily** *adv.* —ˈ**dizziness** *n.*

DJ *or* **d.j.** *abbrev. for:* **1.** disc jockey. **2.** dinner jacket.

djebel (ˈdʒɛbəl) *n.* a variant spelling of **jebel.**

djinni *or* **djinny** (dʒɪˈniː, ˈdʒɪnɪ) *n., pl.* **djinn** (dʒɪn). variant spellings of **jinni.**

dk *abbrev. for:* **1.** dark. **2.** deck. **3.** dock.

DK *international car registration for* Denmark.

dl *symbol for* decilitre(s).

D/L *abbrev. for* demand loan.

DLitt *or* **DLit** *abbrev. for:* **1.** Doctor of Letters. **2.** Doctor of Literature. [Latin *Doctor Litterarum*]

DLP (formerly) *abbrev. for* Democratic Labor Party (of Australia).

dlr *abbrev. for* dealer.

dlvy *abbrev. for* delivery.

dm *symbol for* decimetre.

DM *abbrev. for* Deutschmark.

DMA *Computer technol. abbrev. for* direct memory access.

DMAC *abbrev. for* duobinary multiplexed analogue component: a transmission coding system using duobinary techniques for the digital sound and data components of colour television using satellite broadcasting.

D-mark *or* **D-Mark** *n.* short for **Deutschmark.**

DMF *abbrev. for* dimethylformamide.

DMS (in Britain) *abbrev. for* Diploma in Management Studies.

DMSO *abbrev. for* dimethylsulphoxide.

DMT *abbrev. for* dimethyltryptamine, a hallucinogenic drug.

DMus *abbrev. for* Doctor of Music.

DMZ *abbrev. for* demilitarized zone.

DNA *n.* deoxyribonucleic acid; a nucleic acid that is the main constituent of the chromosomes of all organisms (except some viruses). The DNA molecule consists of two polynucleotide chains in the form of a double helix, containing phosphate and the sugar deoxyribose and linked by hydrogen bonds between the complementary bases adenine and thymine or cytosine and guanine. DNA is self-replicating, plays a central role in protein synthesis, and is responsible for the transmission of hereditary characteristics from parents to offspring. See also **genetic code.**

DNAase (ˌdiːɛnˈeɪeɪz) *or* **DNase** (ˌdiːɛnˈeɪz) *n.* deoxyribonuclease; any of a number of enzymes that hydrolyse DNA. See **endonuclease, exonuclease.**

D-notice *n. Brit.* an official notice sent to newspapers, prohibiting the publication of certain security information. [C20: from their administrative classification letter]

DNS (in Britain) *abbrev. for* Department for National Savings.

do[1] (duː; *unstressed* dʊ, də) *vb.* **does, doing, did, done. 1.** to perform or complete (a deed or action): *to do a portrait; the work is done.* **2.** (often *intr.;* foll. by *for*) to serve the needs of; be suitable for (a person, situation, etc.); suffice: *there isn't much food, but it'll do for the two of us.* **3.** (*tr.*) to arrange or fix: *you should do the garden now.* **4.** (*tr.*) to prepare or provide; serve: *this restaurant doesn't do lunch on Sundays.* **5.** (*tr.*) to make tidy, elegant, ready, etc., as by arranging or adorning: *to do one's hair.* **6.** (*tr.*) to improve (esp. in the phrase **do something to** *or* **for**). **7.** (*tr.*) to find an answer to (a problem or puzzle). **8.** (*tr.*) to translate or adapt the form or language of: *the book was done into a play.* **9.** (*intr.*) to conduct oneself: *do as you please.* **10.** (*intr.*) to fare or manage: *how are you doing these days?* **11.** (*tr.*) to cause or produce: *complaints do nothing to help.* **12.** (*tr.*) to give or render: *your portrait doesn't do you justice; do me a favour.* **13.** (*tr.*) to work at, esp. as a course of study or a profession: *he is doing chemistry; what do you do for a living?* **14.** (*tr.*) to perform (a play, etc.); act: *they are doing "Hamlet" next week.* **15.** (*tr.*) to travel at a specified speed, esp. as a maximum: *this car will do 120 mph.* **16.** (*tr.*) to travel or traverse (a distance): *we did 15 miles on our walk.* **17.** (takes an infinitive without *to*) used as an auxiliary before the subject of an interrogative sentence as a way of forming a question: *do you agree? when did John go out?* **18.** (takes an infinitive without *to*) used as an auxiliary to intensify positive statements and commands: *I do like your new house; do hurry!* **19.** (takes an infinitive without *to*) used as an auxiliary before a negative adverb to form negative statements or commands: *he does not like cheese; do not leave me here alone!* **20.** (takes an infinitive without *to*) used as an auxiliary in inverted constructions: *little did he realize that; only rarely does he come in before ten o'clock.* **21.** used as an auxiliary to replace an earlier verb or verb phrase to avoid repetition: *he likes you as much as I do.* **22.** (*tr.*) *Informal.* to visit or explore as a sightseer or tourist: *to do Westminster Abbey.* **23.** (*tr.*) to wear out; exhaust. **24.** (*intr.*) to happen (esp. in the phrase **nothing doing**). **25.** (*tr.*) *Slang.* to serve (a period of time) as a prison sentence: *he's doing three years for burglary; he's doing time.* **26.** (*tr.*) *Informal.* to cheat or swindle. **27.** (*tr.*) *Slang.* to rob: *they did three shops last night.* **28.** (*tr.*) *Slang.* **a.** to arrest. **b.** to convict of a crime. **29.** (*tr.*) *Austral. slang.* to lose or spend (money) completely. **30.** (*tr.*) *Slang, chiefly Brit.* to treat violently; assault. **31.** (*tr.*) *U.S. slang.* to take or use (a drug). **32.** (*tr.*) *Taboo slang.* (of a male) to have sexual intercourse with. **33. do (a).** *Informal.* act like; imitate: *he's a good mimic—he can do all his friends well.* **34. do or die.** to make a final or supreme effort. **35. how do you do?** a conventional formula when being introduced. **36. make do.**

to manage with whatever is available. ~*n., pl.* **dos** *or* **do's.** **37.** *Slang.* an act or instance of cheating or swindling. **38.** *Informal, chiefly Brit. and N.Z.* a formal or festive gathering; party. **39.** **do's and don'ts.** *Informal.* those things that should or should not be done; rules. ~See also **do away with, do by, do down, do for, do in, done, do out, do over, do up, do with, do without.** [Old English *dōn;* related to Old Frisian *duān,* Old High German *tuon,* Latin *abdere* to put away, Greek *tithenai* to place; see DEED, DOOM]

do[2] (dəʊ) *n., pl.* **dos.** a variant spelling of **doh.**

DO *abbrev. for:* **1.** Doctor of Optometry. **2.** Doctor of Osteopathy.

do. *abbrev. for* ditto.

D/O *or* **d.o.** *Commerce. abbrev. for* delivery order.

DOA *abbrev. for* dead on arrival.

doab ('dəʊɑːb) *n.* the alluvial land between two converging rivers. [C20: from Persian *dōāb,* from *dō* two + *āb* water]

doable ('duːəbᵊl) *adj.* capable of being done; practical.

doat (dəʊt) *vb. (intr.)* a variant (now rare) spelling of **dote.**

do away with *vb. (intr., adv. + prep.)* **1.** to kill or destroy. **2.** to discard or abolish.

dobber-in (ˌdɒbər'ɪn) *n. Austral. slang.* an informant or traitor. Sometimes shortened to **dobber.**

dobbin ('dɒbɪn) *n.* **1.** a name for a horse, esp. a workhorse, often used in children's tales, etc. **2.** *N.Z.* a trolley for moving loose wool in a woolshed or shearing shed. [C16: from *Robin,* pet form of *Robert*]

dobby ('dɒbɪ) *n., pl.* **-bies.** an attachment to a loom, used in weaving small figures. [C17: perhaps from *Dobby,* pet form of *Robert*]

Dobell's solution ('dəʊbəlz) *n.* a solution of sodium borate, sodium bicarbonate, phenol, and glycerol, used as an astringent or antiseptic wash for the throat and nose. [C19: named after Horace B. *Dobell* (1828–1917), British physician]

Doberman pinscher ('dəʊbəmən 'pɪnʃə) *or* **Doberman** *n.* a fairly large slender but muscular breed of dog, originally from Germany, with a glossy black-and-tan coat, a short tail, and erect ears. Also spelt **Dobermann.** [C19: probably named after L. *Dobermann,* 19th-century German dog breeder who bred it + *Pinscher,* a type of terrier, perhaps after *Pinzgau,* district in Austria]

dob in *vb.* **dobs, dobbing, dobbed.** *(adv.) Austral. and N.Z. slang.* **1.** *(tr.)* to inform against or report, esp. to the police. **2.** to contribute to a fund for a specific purpose.

dobla ('dəʊblɑː) *n.* a medieval Spanish gold coin, probably worth 20 maravedis. [Spanish, from Latin *dupla,* feminine of *duplus* twofold, DOUBLE]

doblón (də'bləʊn; *Spanish* do'βlon) *n.* a variant spelling of **doubloon.** [Spanish; see DOUBLOON]

dobra ('dəʊbrə) *n.* the standard monetary unit of São Tomé e Principe, off the coast of W Africa.

Dobro ('dəʊbrəʊ) *n., pl.* **-bros.** *Trademark.* an acoustic guitar having a metal resonator built into the body.

dobsonfly ('dɒbsᵊnˌflaɪ) *n., pl.* **-flies.** *U.S. and Canadian.* a large North American neuropterous insect, *Corydalis cornutus:* the male has elongated horn-like mouthparts and the larva (a **hellgrammite** or **dobson**) is used as bait by anglers: suborder *Megaloptera.*

do by *vb. (intr., prep.)* to treat in the manner specified: *employers do well by hard working employees.*

doc (dɒk) *n. Informal.* short for **doctor,** esp. a medical doctor: often used as a term of address.

doc. *abbrev. for* document.

docent (dəʊ'sɛnt; *German* do'tsɛnt) *n.* (in the U.S.) a lecturer in some colleges or universities. [C19: from German *Dozent,* from Latin *docēns* from *docēre* to teach] —'**docent,ship** *n.*

Docetism ('dəʊsɪˌtɪzəm) *n.* (in the early Christian Church) a heresy that the humanity of Christ, his sufferings, and his death were apparent rather than real. [C19: from Medieval Latin *Docētae,* from Greek *Dokētai,* from *dokein* to seem]

DOCG *abbrev. for* Denominazione di Origine Controllata Garantita: used of wines. [Italian, literally: name of origin guaranteed controlled]

doch-an-doris ('dɒxən'dɒrɪs) *n.* a variant spelling of **deoch-an-doruis.**

docile ('dəʊsaɪl) *adj.* **1.** easy to manage, control, or discipline; submissive. **2.** *Rare.* ready to learn; easy to teach. [C15: from Latin *docilis* easily taught, from *docēre* to teach] —'**docilely** *adv.* —**docility** (dəʊ'sɪlɪtɪ) *n.*

dock[1] (dɒk) *n.* **1.** a wharf or pier. **2.** a space between two wharves or piers for the mooring of ships. **3.** an area of water that can accommodate a ship and can be closed off to allow regulation of the water level. **4.** short for **dry dock.** **5.** **in** *or* **into dock.** *Brit. informal.* **a.** (of people) in hospital. **b.** (of cars, etc.) in a repair shop. **6.** short for **scene dock.** **7.** *Chiefly U.S. and Canadian.* a platform from which lorries, goods trains, etc., are loaded and unloaded. ~*vb.* **8.** to moor (a vessel) at a dock or (of a vessel) to be moored at a dock. **9.** to put (a vessel) into a dry dock for repairs or (of a vessel) to come into a dry dock. **10.** (of two spacecraft) to link together in space or link together (two spacecraft) in space. [C14: from Middle Dutch *docke;* perhaps related to Latin *ducere* to lead]

dock[2] (dɒk) *n.* **1.** the bony part of the tail of an animal, esp. a dog or sheep. **2.** the part of an animal's tail left after the major part of it has been cut off. ~*vb. (tr.)* **3.** to remove (the tail or part of the tail) of (an animal) by cutting through the bone: *to dock a tail; to dock a horse.* **4.** to deduct (an amount) from (a person's wages, pension, etc.): *they docked a third of his wages.* [C14: *dok,* of uncertain origin]

dock[3] (dɒk) *n.* an enclosed space in a court of law where the accused sits or stands during his trial. [C16: from Flemish *dok* sty]

dock[4] (dɒk) *n.* **1.** any of various temperate weedy plants of the polygonaceous genus *Rumex,* having greenish or reddish flowers and typically broad leaves. **2.** any of several similar or related plants. [Old English *docce;* related to Middle Dutch, Old Danish *docke,* Gaelic *dogha*]

dockage[1] ('dɒkɪdʒ) *n.* **1.** a charge levied upon a vessel for using a dock. **2.** facilities for docking vessels. **3.** the practice of docking vessels.

dockage[2] ('dɒkɪdʒ) *n.* **1.** a deduction, as from a price or wages. **2.** *Agriculture.* the seeds of weeds and other waste material in commercial seeds, removable by normal cleaning methods.

docken ('dɒkᵊn) *n. Chiefly Scot.* **1.** another name for **dock**[4]. **2.** something of no value or importance: *not worth a docken.* [C14 *doken,* from Old English *doccan,* pl. of *docce* DOCK[4]]

docker[1] ('dɒkə) *n. Brit.* a man employed in the loading or unloading of ships. U.S. and Canadian equivalent: **longshoreman.** See also **stevedore.**

docker[2] ('dɒkə) *n.* a person or thing that docks something, such as the tail of a horse.

docket ('dɒkɪt) *n.* **1.** *Chiefly Brit.* a piece of paper accompanying or referring to a package or other delivery, stating contents, delivery instructions, etc., sometimes serving as a receipt. **2.** *Law.* **a.** an official summary of the proceedings in a court of justice. **b.** a register containing such a summary. **3.** *Brit.* **a.** a customs certificate declaring that duty has been paid. **b.** a certificate giving particulars of a shipment and allowing its holder to obtain a delivery order. **4.** a summary of contents, as in a document. **5.** *U.S.* a list of things to be done. **6.** *U.S. law.* **a.** a list of cases awaiting trial. **b.** the names of the parties to pending litigation. ~*vb. (tr.)* **7.** to fix a docket to (a package, etc.). **8.** *Law.* **a.** to make a summary of (a document, judgment, etc.). **b.** to abstract and enter in a book or register. **9.** to endorse (a document, etc.) with a summary. [C15: of unknown origin]

dockland ('dɒkˌlænd) *n.* the area around the docks.

dockyard ('dɒkˌjɑːd) *n.* a naval establishment with docks, workshops, etc., for the building, fitting out, and repair of vessels.

Doc Martens (dɒk 'mɑːtənz) *pl. n. Trademark.* a brand of lace-up boots with thick lightweight resistant soles. In full: **Doctor Martens.**

doco ('dɒkəʊ) *n., pl.* **docos.** *Austral. informal.* short for **documentary.**

doctor ('dɒktə) *n.* **1.** a person licensed to practise medicine. **2.** a person who has been awarded a higher academic degree in any field of knowledge. **3.** *Chiefly U.S. and Canadian.* a person licensed to practise dentistry or veterinary medicine. **4.** *(often cap.)* Also called: **Doctor of the Church.** a title given to any of several of the leading Fathers or theologians in the history of the Christian Church down to the late Middle Ages whose teachings have greatly influenced orthodox Christian thought. **5.** *Angling.* any of various gaudy artificial flies. **6.** *Informal.* a person who mends or repairs things. **7.** *Slang.* a cook on a ship or at a camp. **8.** *Archaic.* a man, esp. a teacher, of learning. **9.** a device used for local repair of electroplated surfaces, consisting of an anode of the plating material embedded in an absorbent material containing the solution. **10.** (in a paper-making machine) a blade that is set to scrape the roller in order to regulate the thickness of pulp or ink on it. **11.** **go for the doctor.** *Austral. slang.* to make a great effort or move very fast, esp. in a horse race. **12.** **what the doctor ordered.** something needed or desired. **13.** **you're the doctor.** you are to make the decision. ~*vb.* **14.** *(tr.)* **a.** to give medical treatment to. **b.** to prescribe for (a disease or disorder). **15.** *(intr.) Informal.* to practise medicine: *he doctored in Easter Island for six years.* **16.** *(tr.)* to repair or mend, esp. in a makeshift manner. **17.** *(tr.)* to make different in order to deceive, tamper with, falsify, or adulterate. **18.** *(tr.)* to adapt for a desired end, effect, etc. **19.** *(tr.)* to castrate (a cat, dog, etc.). [C14: from Latin: teacher, from *docēre* to teach] —'**doctoral** *or* **doctorial** (dɒk'tɔːrɪəl) *adj.*

doctorate ('dɒktərɪt, -trɪt) *n.* the highest academic degree in any field of knowledge. Also called: **doctor's degree.**

Doctor of Philosophy *n.* a doctorate awarded for original research in any subject except law, medicine, or theology. Abbrevs.: **PhD, DPhil.**

doctrinaire (ˌdɒktrɪ'nɛə) *adj.* **1.** stubbornly insistent on the observation of the niceties of a theory, esp. without regard to practicality, suitability, etc. **2.** theoretical; impractical. ~*n.* **3.** a person who stubbornly attempts to apply a theory without regard to practical difficulties. —ˌ**doctri'nairism** *or* ˌ**doctri'narism** *n.* —ˌ**doctri'narian** *n.*

doctrine ('dɒktrɪn) *n.* **1.** a creed or body of teachings of a religious, political, or philosophical group presented for acceptance or belief; dogma. **2.** a principle or body of principles that is taught or advocated. [C14: from Old French, from Latin *doctrīna* teaching, from *doctor* see DOCTOR] —**doctrinal** (dɒk'traɪnᵊl) *adj.* —**doctrinality** (ˌdɒktrɪ'nælɪtɪ) *n.* —**doc'trinally** *adv.* —**'doctrinism** *n.* —**'doctrinist** *n.*

doctrine of descent *n.* the theory that animals and plants arose by descent from previously existing organisms; theory of evolution.

docudrama ('dɒkjʊˌdrɑːmə) *n.* a film or television programme based on true events, presented in a dramatized form.

document *n.* ('dɒkjʊmənt). **1.** a piece of paper, booklet, etc., providing information, esp. of an official or legal nature. **2.** *Archaic.* evidence; proof. ~*vb.* ('dɒkjʊˌmɛnt). (*tr.*) **3.** to record or report in detail, as in the press, on television, etc.: *the trial was well documented by the media.* **4.** to support (statements in a book) with citations, references, etc. **5.** to support (a claim, etc.) with evidence or proof. **6.** to furnish (a vessel) with official documents specifying its ownership, registration, weight, dimensions, and function. [C15: from Latin *documentum* a lesson, from *docēre* to teach]

documentary (ˌdɒkjʊ'mɛntərɪ, -trɪ) *adj.* **1.** Also: **documental.** consisting of, derived from, or relating to documents. **2.** presenting factual material with little or no fictional additions: *the book gives a documentary account of the massacre.* ~*n., pl.* **-ries. 3.** a factual film or television programme about an event, person, etc., presenting the facts with little or no fiction. —ˌ**docu'mentarily** *adv.*

documentation (ˌdɒkjʊmɛn'teɪʃən) *n.* **1.** the act of supplying with or using documents or references. **2.** the documents or references supplied. **3.** the furnishing and use of documentary evidence, as in a court of law. **4.** *Computer technol.* the written comments, graphical illustrations, flowcharts, manuals, etc., supplied with a program or software system.

document reader *n. Computer technol.* a device that reads and inputs into a computer marks and characters on a special form, as by optical or magnetic character recognition.

DOD (in the U.S.) *abbrev. for* Department of Defense.

dodder[1] ('dɒdə) *vb.* (*intr.*) **1.** to move unsteadily; totter. **2.** to shake or tremble, as from age. [C17: variant of earlier *dadder;* related to Norwegian *dudra* to tremble] —**'dodderer** *n.* —**'doddery** *adj.*

dodder[2] ('dɒdə) *n.* any rootless parasitic plant of the convolvulaceous genus *Cuscuta,* lacking chlorophyll and having slender twining stems with suckers for drawing nourishment from the host plant, scalelike leaves, and whitish flowers. [C13: of Germanic origin; related to Middle Dutch, Middle Low German *dodder,* Middle High German *toter*]

doddering ('dɒdərɪŋ) *adj.* shaky, feeble, or infirm, esp. from old age.

doddle ('dɒdᵊl) *n. Brit. informal.* something easily accomplished.

dodeca- *n. combining form.* indicating twelve: *dodecagon; dodecahedron; dodecaphonic.* [from Greek *dōdeka* twelve]

dodecagon (dəʊ'dɛkəˌgɒn) *n.* a polygon having twelve sides. —**dodecagonal** (ˌdəʊdɛ'kægənᵊl) *adj.*

dodecahedron (ˌdəʊdɛkə'hiːdrən) *n.* a solid figure having twelve plane faces. A **regular dodecahedron** has regular pentagons as faces. See also **polyhedron.** —ˌ**dodeca'hedral** *adj.*

dodecanoic acid (ˌdəʊdɛkə'nəʊɪk) *n.* a crystalline fatty acid found as glycerides in many vegetable oils: used in making soaps, insecticides, and synthetic resins. Formula: $CH_3(CH_2)_{10}COOH$. Also called: **lauric acid.** [C20: from *dodecane* (see DODECA-, -ANE)]

dodecaphonic (ˌdəʊdɛkə'fɒnɪk) *adj.* of or relating to the twelve-tone system of serial music. —ˌ**dodeca'phonism** *n.* —ˌ**dodeca'phonist** *n.* —ˌ**dodeca'phony** *n.*

dodecasyllable (ˌdəʊdɛkə'sɪləbᵊl) *n. Prosody.* a line of twelve syllables.

dodge (dɒdʒ) *vb.* **1.** to avoid or attempt to avoid (a blow, discovery, etc.), as by moving suddenly. **2.** to evade (questions, etc.) by cleverness or trickery. **3.** (*intr.*) *Change-ringing.* to make a bell change places with its neighbour when sounding in successive changes. **4.** (*tr.*) *Photog.* to lighten or darken (selected areas on a print) by manipulating the light from an enlarger. ~*n.* **5.** a plan or expedient contrived to deceive. **6.** a sudden evasive or hiding movement. **7.** a clever contrivance. **8.** *Change-ringing.* the act of dodging. [C16: of unknown origin]

dodge ball *n.* a game in which the players form a circle and try to hit opponents in the circle with a large ball.

Dodgem ('dɒdʒəm) *n. Trademark.* another name for **bumper car.**

dodger ('dɒdʒə) *n.* **1.** a person who evades or shirks. **2.** a shifty dishonest person. **3.** a canvas shelter, mounted on a ship's bridge or over the companionway of a sailing yacht to protect the helmsman from bad weather. **4.** *U.S. and Austral.* a handbill. **5.** *Dialect and Austral.* food, esp. bread.

dodgy ('dɒdʒɪ) *adj.* **dodgier, dodgiest.** *Brit., Austral., and N.Z. informal.* **1.** risky, difficult, or dangerous. **2.** uncertain or unreliable; tricky.

dodo ('dəʊdəʊ) *n., pl.* **dodos** *or* **dodoes. 1.** any flightless bird, esp. *Raphus cucullatus,* of the recently extinct family *Raphidae* of Mauritius and adjacent islands: order *Columbiformes* (pigeons, etc.). They had a hooked bill, short stout legs, and greyish plumage. See also **ratite. 2.** *Informal.* an intensely conservative or reactionary person who is unaware of changing fashions, ideas, etc. **3.** (**as**) **dead as a dodo.** (of a person or thing) irretrievably defunct or out of date. [C17: from Portuguese *doudo,* from *duodo* stupid] —**'dodoism** *n.*

do down *vb.* (*tr., adv.*) **1.** to belittle or humiliate. **2.** to deceive or cheat.

doe (dəʊ) *n., pl.* **does** *or* **doe.** the female of the deer, hare, rabbit, and certain other animals. [Old English *dā;* related to Old English *dēon* to suck, Sanskrit *dhēnā* cow]

Doe (dəʊ) *n. Law.* (formerly) the name of the fictitious plaintiff in an action of ejectment.

DOE (in Britain) *abbrev. for* Department of the Environment.

doek (dʊk) *n. S. African informal.* a square of cloth worn mainly by African women to cover the head, esp. to indicate married status. [C18: from Afrikaans: cloth]

doer ('duːə) *n.* **1.** a person or thing that does something or acts in a specified manner: *a doer of good.* **2.** an active or energetic person. **3.** a thriving animal, esp. a horse.

does (dʌz) *vb.* (used with a singular noun or the pronouns *he, she,* or *it*) a form of the present tense (indicative mood) of **do**[1].

doeskin ('dəʊˌskɪn) *n.* **1.** the skin of a deer, lamb, or sheep. **2.** a very supple leather made from this skin and used esp. for gloves. **3.** a heavy smooth satin-weave or twill-weave cloth. **4.** (*modifier*) made of doeskin.

doff (dɒf) *vb.* (*tr.*) **1.** to take off or lift (one's hat) in salutation. **2.** to remove (clothing). [Old English *dōn of;* see DO[1], OFF; compare DON[1]] —**'doffer** *n.*

do for *vb.* (*prep.*) *Informal.* **1.** (*tr.*) to convict of a crime or offence: *they did him for manslaughter.* **2.** (*intr.*) to cause the ruin, death, or defeat of: *the last punch did for him.* **3.** (*intr.*) to do housework for. **4. do well for oneself.** to thrive or succeed.

dog (dɒg) *n.* **1. a.** a domesticated canine mammal, *Canis familiaris,* occurring in many breeds that show a great variety in size and form. **b.** (*as modifier*): *dog biscuit.* **2. a.** any other carnivore of the family *Canidae,* such as the dingo and coyote. **b.** (*as modifier*): *the dog family.* **3. a.** the male of animals of the dog family. **b.** (*as modifier*): *a dog fox.* **4.** (*modifier*) **a.** spurious, inferior, or useless: *dog Latin.* **b.** (*in combination*): *dogberry.* **5.** a mechanical device for gripping or holding, esp. one of the axial slots by which gear wheels or shafts are engaged to transmit torque. **6.** *Informal.* a fellow; chap: *you lucky dog.* **7.** *Informal.* a man or boy regarded as unpleasant, contemptible, or wretched. **8.** *Slang.* an unattractive or boring girl or woman. **9.** *U.S. and Canadian informal.* something unsatisfactory or inferior. **10.** *Austral. slang, offensive.* a police informer. **11.** short for **firedog. 12.** any of various atmospheric phenomena. See **fogdog, seadog, sundog. 13. a dog's chance.** no chance at all. **14. a dog's dinner** *or* **breakfast.** *Informal.* something that is messy or bungled. **15. a dog's life.** a wretched existence. **16. dog eat dog.** ruthless competition or self-interest. **17. like a dog's dinner.** *Informal.* dressed smartly or ostentatiously. **18. put on the dog.** *U.S. and Canadian informal.* to behave pretentiously or ostentatiously. **19. dog tied up.** *Austral. slang.* an unpaid bill, esp. at a public house. ~*vb.* **dogs, dogging, dogged.** (*tr.*) **20.** to pursue or follow after like a dog. **21.** to trouble; plague: *to be dogged by ill health.* **22.** to chase with a dog or dogs. **23.** to grip, hold, or secure by a mechanical device. ~*adv.* **24.** (usually in combination) thoroughly; utterly: *dog-tired.* ~See also **dogs.** [Old English *docga,* of obscure origin] —**'dogˌlike** *adj.*

dogbane ('dɒgˌbeɪn) *n.* any of several North American apocynaceous plants of the genus *Apocynum,* esp. *A. androsaemifolium,* having bell-shaped white or pink flowers: thought to be poisonous to dogs.

dogberry[1] ('dɒgˌbɛrɪ, -bərɪ, -brɪ) *n., pl.* **-ries. 1.** any of certain plants that have berry-like fruits, such as the European dogwood or the bearberry. **2.** the fruit of any of these plants.

dogberry[2] ('dɒgˌbɛrɪ, -bərɪ, -brɪ) *n., pl.* **-ries.** (*sometimes cap.*) a foolish, meddling, and usually old official. [after *Dogberry,* character in Shakespeare's *Much Ado about Nothing* (1598)] —**'dogberryˌism** *n.*

dog biscuit *n.* a hard biscuit for dogs.

dog box *n.* **1.** *Austral. informal.* a compartment in a railway carriage with no corridor. **2.** *N.Z. informal.* disgrace; disfavour (in the phrase **in the dog box**).

dogcart ('dɒgˌkɑːt) *n.* a light horse-drawn two-wheeled vehicle: originally, one containing a box or section for transporting gun dogs.

dog-catcher *n. Now chiefly U.S. and Canadian.* a local official whose job is to catch and impound stray dogs, cats, etc.

dog collar *n.* **1.** a collar for a dog. **2.** an informal name for a **clerical collar. 3.** *Informal.* a tight-fitting necklace.

dog days *pl. n.* **1.** the hot period of the summer reckoned in ancient times from the heliacal rising of Sirius (the Dog Star). **2.** a period marked by inactivity. [C16: translation of Late Latin *diēs caniculārēs,* translation of Greek *hēmerai kunades*]

doge (dəʊdʒ) *n.* (formerly) the chief magistrate in the republics of Venice (until 1797) and Genoa (until 1805). [C16: via French from Italian (Venetian dialect), from Latin *dux* leader] —**'dogeship** *n.*

dog-ear *vb.* **1.** (*tr.*) to fold down the corner of (a page). ~*n. also* **dog's-ear. 2.** a folded-down corner of a page.

dog-eared *adj.* **1.** having dog-ears. **2.** shabby or worn.

dog-end *n.* an informal name for **cigarette end.**

dog fennel *n.* 1. another name for **mayweed.** 2. a weedy plant, *Eupatorium capillifolium,* of the southeastern U.S., having divided leaves and greenish rayless flower heads: family *Compositae* (composites).
dogfight ('dɒg,faɪt) *n.* 1. close quarters combat between fighter aircraft. 2. any rough violent fight.
dogfish ('dɒg,fɪʃ) *n., pl.* **-fish** *or* **-fishes.** 1. any of several small spotted European sharks, esp. *Scyliorhinus caniculus* (**lesser spotted dogfish**): family *Scyliorhinidae.* 2. any small shark of the family *Squalidae,* esp. *Squalus acanthias* (**spiny dogfish**), typically having a spine on each dorsal fin. 3. any small smooth-skinned shark of the family *Triakidae,* esp. *Mustelus canis* (**smooth dogfish** or **smooth hound**). 4. a less common name for the **bowfin.**
dogged ('dɒgɪd) *adj.* obstinately determined; wilful or tenacious. —'**doggedly** *adv.* —'**doggedness** *n.*
dogger[1] ('dɒgə) *n.* a Dutch fishing vessel with two masts. [C14: probably from Middle Dutch *dogge* trawler]
dogger[2] ('dɒgə) *n.* a large concretion of consolidated material occurring in certain sedimentary rocks. [C17: of uncertain origin]
dogger[3] ('dɒgə) *n. Austral.* a hunter of dingoes. [C20: from DOG (see sense 2a) + -ER[1]]
Dogger ('dɒgə) *n. Geology.* a formation of mid-Jurassic rocks in N England.
doggerel ('dɒgərəl) *or* **dogrel** ('dɒgrəl) *n.* 1. **a.** comic verse, usually irregular in measure. **b.** (*as modifier*): *a doggerel rhythm.* 2. nonsense; drivel. [C14 *dogerel* worthless, perhaps from *dogge* DOG]
doggery ('dɒgərɪ) *n., pl.* **-geries.** 1. surly behaviour. 2. dogs collectively. 3. a mob.
doggish ('dɒgɪʃ) *adj.* 1. of or like a dog. 2. surly; snappish. —'**doggishly** *adv.* —'**doggishness** *n.*
doggo ('dɒgəʊ) *adv. Brit. informal.* in hiding and keeping quiet (esp. in the phrase **lie doggo**). [C19: probably from DOG]
doggone ('dɒgɒn) *U.S. and Canadian informal.* ~*interj.* 1. an exclamation of annoyance, disappointment, etc. ~*adj.* (*prenominal*), *adv.* 2. Also: **doggoned.** another word for **damn** (senses 3, 4). [C19: euphemism for *God damn*]
doggy *or* **doggie** ('dɒgɪ) *n., pl.* **-gies.** 1. a children's word for a dog. ~*adj.* 2. of, like, or relating to a dog. 3. fond of dogs.
doggy bag *n.* a bag into which leftovers from a meal may be put and taken away, supposedly for the diner's dog.
doggy paddle *or* **doggie paddle** *n.* 1. a swimming stroke in which the swimmer lies on his front, paddles his hands in imitation of a swimming dog, and beats his legs up and down. ~*vb.* **doggy-paddle** *or* **doggie-paddle.** 2. (*intr.*) to swim using the doggy paddle. Also called: **dog paddle.**
dog handler *n.* a member of the police force, security organization, etc., who works in collaboration with a specially trained dog.
doghouse ('dɒg,haʊs) *n.* 1. the U.S. and Canadian name for **kennel**[1]. 2. *Informal.* disfavour (in the phrase **in the doghouse**).
dogie, dogy, *or* **dogey** ('dəʊgɪ) *n., pl.* **-gies** *or* **-geys.** *Western U.S. and Canadian.* a motherless calf. [C19: from *dough-guts,* because they were fed on flour and water paste]
dog in the manger *n.* **a.** a person who prevents others from using something he has no use for. **b.** (*as modifier*): *a dog-in-the-manger attitude.*
dog Latin *n.* spurious or incorrect Latin.
dogleg ('dɒg,lɛg) *n.* 1. **a.** a sharp bend or angle. **b.** something with a sharp bend. ~*vb.* **-legs, -legging, -legged.** 2. (*intr.*) to go off at an angle. ~*adj.* 3. of or with the shape of a dogleg. —**doglegged** (,dɒg'lɛgɪd, 'dɒg,lɛgd) *adj.*
dogleg fence *n. Austral.* a fence made of sloping poles supported by forked uprights.
dogma ('dɒgmə) *n., pl.* **-mas** *or* **-mata** (-mətə). 1. a religious doctrine or system of doctrines proclaimed by ecclesiastical authority as true. 2. a belief, principle, or doctrine or a code of beliefs, principles, or doctrines: *Marxist dogma.* [C17: via Latin from Greek: opinion, belief, from *dokein* to seem good]
dogman ('dɒgmən) *n., pl.* **-men** *Austral.* a person who directs the operation of a crane whilst riding on an object being lifted by it.
dogmatic (dɒg'mætɪk) *or* **dogmatical** *adj.* 1. **a.** (of a statement, opinion, etc.) forcibly asserted as if authoritative and unchallengeable. **b.** (of a person) prone to making such statements. 2. of, relating to, or constituting dogma: *dogmatic writings.* 3. based on assumption rather than on empirical observation. —**dog'matically** *adv.*
dogmatics (dɒg'mætɪks) *n.* (*functioning as sing.*) the study of religious dogmas and doctrines. Also called: **dogmatic** (*or* **doctrinal**) **theology.**
dogmatist ('dɒgmətɪst) *n.* 1. a dogmatic person. 2. a person who formulates dogmas.
dogmatize *or* **dogmatise** ('dɒgmə,taɪz) *vb.* to say or state (something) in a dogmatic manner. —'**dogmatism** *n.* —,**dogmati'zation** *or* ,**dogmati'sation** *n.* —'**dogma,tizer** *or* '**dogma,tiser** *n.*
do-gooder *n. Informal, usually disparaging.* a well-intentioned person, esp. a naive or impractical one. —,**do-'goodery** *n.* —,**do-'gooding** *n., adj.*
dog paddle *n.* another name for **doggy paddle.**
dog rose *n.* a prickly wild rose, *Rosa canina,* that is native to Europe and has pink or white delicate scentless flowers. [translation of the Latin name, from Greek; from the belief that its root was effective against the bite of a mad dog]
dogs (dɒgz) *pl. n.* 1. **the.** *Brit. informal.* greyhound racing. 2. *Slang.* the feet. 3. *Marketing informal.* goods with a low market share, which are unlikely to yield substantial profits. 4. **go to the dogs.** *Informal.* to go to ruin physically or morally. 5. **let sleeping dogs lie.** to leave things undisturbed.
dogsbody ('dɒgz,bɒdɪ) *n., pl.* **-bodies.** 1. *Informal.* a person who carries out menial tasks for others; drudge. ~*vb.* **-bodies, -bodying, -bodied.** 2. (*intr.*) to act as a dogsbody.
dog's disease *n. Austral. informal.* influenza.
dogsled ('dɒg,slɛd) *n. Chiefly U.S. and Canadian.* a sleigh drawn by dogs. Also called: **dog sledge** (Brit.), **dog sleigh.**
dog's mercury *n.* a hairy somewhat poisonous euphorbiaceous perennial of the spurge family, *Mercurialis perennis,* having broad lanceolate toothed leaves and small greenish flowers like catkins: often creeping to carpet shady woodlands.
dog's-tail *n.* any of several grasses of the genus *Cynosurus,* esp. *C. cristatus* (crested dog's-tail), that are native to Europe and have flowers clustered in a dense narrow spike.
Dog Star *n.* **the.** another name for **Sirius.**
dog's-tongue *n.* another name for **hound's-tongue.**
dog's-tooth check *or* **dog-tooth check** *n.* other names for **hound's-tooth check.**
dog tag *n. U.S. slang.* a military personal-identification disc.
dog-tired *adj.* (*usually postpositive*) *Informal.* exhausted.
dogtooth ('dɒg,tuːθ) *n., pl.* **-teeth.** 1. another name for a **canine** (sense 3). 2. *Architect.* a carved ornament in the form of four leaflike projections radiating from a raised centre, used in England in the 13th century.
dogtooth violet *n.* a name for various plants of the liliaceous genus *Erythronium,* esp. the North American *E. americanum,* with yellow nodding flowers, or the European *E. dens-canis,* with purple flowers. Also called: **adders-tongue, fawn lily.**
dog train *n. Canadian.* a sleigh drawn by a team of dogs.
dogtrot ('dɒg,trɒt) *n.* a gently paced trot.
dog tucker *n. N.Z.* the meat of a sheep killed on a farm and used as dog food.
dogvane ('dɒg,veɪn) *n. Nautical.* a light windvane consisting of a feather or a piece of cloth or yarn mounted on the side of a vessel. Also called: **telltale.**
dog violet *n.* a violet, *Viola canina,* that grows in Europe and N Asia and has blue yellow-spurred flowers.
dogwatch ('dɒg,wɒtʃ) *n.* 1. either of two two-hour watches aboard ship, from four to six p.m. or from six to eight p.m. 2. *N.Z.* a shift from midnight to six a.m. in a mine.
dogwood ('dɒg,wʊd) *n.* any of various cornaceous trees or shrubs of the genus *Cornus,* esp. *C. sanguinea,* a European shrub with clusters of small white flowers and black berries: the shoots are red in winter.
dogy ('dəʊgɪ) *n., pl.* **-gies.** a variant spelling of **dogie.**
doh (dəʊ) *n., pl.* **dohs.** 1. *Music.* (in tonic sol-fa) the first degree of any major scale. 2. **up to high doh.** *Informal, chiefly Scot.* extremely excited or keyed up. [C18: from Italian; see GAMUT]
doily, doyley, *or* **doyly** ('dɔɪlɪ) *n., pl.* **-lies** *or* **-leys.** a decorative mat of lace or lacelike paper, etc., laid on or under plates. [C18: named after *Doily,* a London draper]
do in *vb.* (*tr., adv.*) *Slang.* 1. to murder or kill. 2. to exhaust.
doing ('duːɪŋ) *n.* 1. an action or the performance of an action: *whose doing is this?* 2. *Informal.* a beating or castigation.
doings ('duːɪŋz) *pl. n.* 1. deeds, actions or events. 2. *Brit. and N.Z. informal.* anything of which the name is not known, or euphemistically left unsaid, etc.: *have you got the doings for starting the car?*
doit (dɔɪt) *n.* 1. a former small copper coin of the Netherlands. 2. a trifle. [C16: from Middle Dutch *duit*]
doited ('dɔɪtɪd) *or* **doitit** ('dɔɪtɪt) *adj. Scot.* foolish or childish, as from senility. [C15: probably from *doten* to DOTE]
do-it-yourself *n.* **a.** the hobby or process of constructing and repairing things oneself. **b.** (*as modifier*): *a do-it-yourself kit.*
dojo ('dəʊdʒəʊ) *n., pl.* **-jos.** a room or mat for the practice of judo. [C20: from Japanese]
dol (dɒl) *n.* a unit of pain intensity, as measured by dolorimetry. [C20: by shortening, from Latin *dolor* pain]
dol. *abbrev. for:* 1. *Music.* dolce. 2. (*pl.* **dols.**) dollar.
dolabriform (dəʊ'læbrɪ,fɔːm) *or* **dolabrate** (dəʊ'læbreɪt) *adj. Botany.* shaped like a hatchet or axe head. [C18: from Latin *dolābra* pickaxe]
Dolby ('dɒlbɪ) *n. Trademark.* any of various specialized electronic circuits, esp. those used for noise reduction in tape recorders by functioning as companders on high-frequency signals. [named after R. *Dolby* (born 1933), its U.S. inventor]
dolce ('dɒltʃɪ; *Italian* 'doltʃe) *adj., adv. Music.* (to be performed) gently and sweetly. [Italian: sweet]
dolce far niente *Italian.* ('doltʃe far 'njɛnte) *n.* pleasant idleness. [literally: sweet doing nothing]
dolce vita ('dɒltʃɪ 'viːtə; *Italian* 'doltʃe 'vita) *n.* a life of luxury. [Italian, literally: sweet life]
doldrums ('dɒldrəmz) *n.* **the.** 1. a depressed or bored state of mind. 2. a state of inactivity or stagnation. 3. **a.** a belt of light winds or calms along the equator. **b.** the weather conditions

experienced in this belt, formerly a hazard to sailing vessels. [C19: probably from Old English *dol* DULL, influenced by TANTRUM]

dole[1] (dəʊl) *n.* **1.** a small portion or share, as of money or food, given to a poor person. **2.** the act of giving or distributing such portions. **3.** (usually preceded by *the*) *Brit. informal.* money received from the state while out of work. **4. on the dole.** *Brit. informal.* receiving such money. **5.** *Archaic.* fate. ~*vb.* **6.** (*tr.*; usually foll. by *out*) to distribute, esp. in small portions. [Old English *dāl* share; related to Old Saxon *dēl*, Old Norse *deild*, Gothic *dails*, Old High German *teil*; see DEAL[1]]

dole[2] (dəʊl) *n. Archaic.* grief or mourning. [C13: from Old French, from Late Latin *dolus*, from Latin *dolēre* to lament]

dole bludger *n. Austral. slang, offensive.* a person who draws unemployment benefit without making any attempt to find work.

doleful ('dəʊlfʊl) *adj.* dreary; mournful. Archaic word: **dolesome** ('dəʊlsəm). —'**dolefully** *adv.* —'**dolefulness** *n.*

dolente (dɒ'lɛntɪ) *adj., adv. Music.* (to be performed) in a sorrowful manner.

dolerite ('dɒləˌraɪt) *n.* **1.** a dark basic igneous rock consisting of plagioclase feldspar and a pyroxene, such as augite; a coarse-grained basalt. **2.** any dark igneous rock whose composition cannot be determined with the naked eye. [C19: from French *dolérite*, from Greek *doleros* deceitful; so called because of the difficulty of determining its composition] —**doleritic** (ˌdɒlə'rɪtɪk) *adj.*

dolichocephalic (ˌdɒlɪkəʊsɪ'fælɪk) *or* **dolichocephalous** (ˌdɒlɪkəʊ'sɛfələs) *adj.* **1.** having a head much longer than it is broad, esp. one with a cephalic index under 75. ~*n.* **2.** an individual with such a head. ~Compare **brachycephalic, mesocephalic.** —ˌ**dolicho'cephalism** *or* ˌ**dolicho'cephaly** *n.*

dolichosaurus (ˌdɒlɪkəʊ'sɔːrəs) *n.* any of various extinct Cretaceous aquatic reptiles that had long necks and bodies and well-developed limbs. [C20: from Greek, from *dolikhos* long + -SAUR]

doline *or* **dolina** (də'liːnə) *n.* a shallow usually funnel-shaped depression of the ground surface formed by solution in limestone regions. [C20: from Russian *dolina*, valley, plain; related to DALE]

doll (dɒl) *n.* **1.** a small model or dummy of a human being, used as a toy. **2.** *Slang.* a pretty girl or woman of little intelligence: sometimes used as a term of address. [C16: probably from *Doll*, pet name for *Dorothy*] —'**dollish** *adj.* —'**dollishly** *adv.* —'**dollishness** *n.*

dollar ('dɒlə) *n.* **1.** the standard monetary unit of the U.S. and its dependencies, divided into 100 cents. **2.** the standard monetary unit, comprising 100 cents, of the following countries: Australia, the Bahamas, Barbados (and other E Caribbean islands), Belize, Bermuda, British Honduras, Canada, the Cayman Islands, the Fiji Islands, Guyana, Hong Kong, Jamaica, Liberia, Malaysia, Singapore, Brunei, New Zealand, Taiwan (**New Taiwan dollar**), Trinidad and Tobago, and Zimbabwe. **3.** *Brit informal.* (formerly) five shillings or a coin of this value. [C16: from Low German *daler*, from German *Taler*, *Thaler*, short for *Joachimsthaler* coin made from metal mined in *Joachimsthal* Jachymov, town in Czechoslovakia]

dollarbird ('dɒləˌbɜːd) *n.* a bird, *Eurystomus orientalis*, of S and SE Asia and Australia, with a round white spot on each wing: family *Coraciidae* (rollers), order *Coraciiformes*.

dollar diplomacy *n. Chiefly U.S.* **1.** a foreign policy that encourages and protects capital investment and commercial and financial involvement abroad. **2.** use of financial power as a diplomatic weapon.

dollarfish ('dɒləˌfɪʃ) *n., pl.* **-fish** *or* **-fishes.** any of various fishes that have a rounded compressed silvery body, esp. the moonfishes or the American butterfish.

dollop ('dɒləp) *Informal.* ~*n.* **1.** a semisolid lump. **2.** a large serving, esp. of food. ~*vb.* **3.** (*tr.*; foll. by *out*) to serve out (food). [C16: of unknown origin]

doll up *vb.* (*tr., adv.*) *Slang.* to adorn or dress (oneself or another, esp. a child) in a stylish or showy manner.

dolly ('dɒlɪ) *n., pl.* **-lies.** **1.** a child's word for a **doll.** **2.** *Films, television.* a wheeled support on which a camera may be mounted. **3.** a cup-shaped anvil held against the head of a rivet while the other end is being hammered. **4.** a shaped block of lead used to hammer dents out of sheet metal. **5.** a distance piece placed between the head of a pile and the pile-driver to form an extension to the length of the pile. **6.** *Cricket.* **a.** a simple catch. **b.** See **dolly drop.** **7.** Also called: **dolly bird.** *Slang, chiefly Brit.* an attractive and fashionable girl, esp. one who is considered to be unintelligent. ~*vb.* **-lies, -lying, -lied.** **8.** *Films, television.* to wheel (a camera) backwards or forwards on a dolly.

dolly drop *n. Cricket.* a full toss bowled in a slow high arc.

dolly mixture *n.* **1.** a mixture of tiny coloured sweets. **2.** one of these.

Dolly Varden ('dɒlɪ 'vɑːdᵊn) *n.* **1.** a woman's large-brimmed hat trimmed with flowers. **2.** a red-spotted trout, *Salvelinus malma*, occurring in lakes in W North America. [C19: from the name of a character in Dickens' *Barnaby Rudge* (1841)]

dolma ('dɒlmə, -mɑː) *n., pl.* **dolmas, dolmades** (dɒl'mɑːdiːz). a vine leaf stuffed with a filling of meat and rice. [C19: Turkish *dolma* literally something filled]

dolman ('dɒlmən) *n., pl.* **-mans.** **1.** a long Turkish outer robe. **2.** Also called: **dolman jacket.** a hussar's jacket worn slung over the shoulder. **3.** a woman's cloak with voluminous capelike sleeves. [C16: via French from German *Dolman*, from Turkish *dolaman* a winding round, from *dolamak* to wind]

dolman sleeve *n.* a sleeve that is very wide at the armhole and tapers to a tight wrist.

dolmen ('dɒlmɛn) *n.* **1.** (in British archaeology) a Neolithic stone formation, consisting of a horizontal stone supported by several vertical stones, and thought to be a tomb. **2.** (in French archaeology) any megalithic tomb. [C19: from French, probably from Old Breton *tol* table, from Latin *tăbula* board + Breton *mĕn* stone, of Celtic origin; see TABLE]

dolomite ('dɒləˌmaɪt) *n.* **1.** a white mineral often tinted by impurities, found in sedimentary rocks and veins. It is used in the manufacture of cement and as a building stone (marble). Composition: calcium magnesium carbonate. Formula: $CaMg(CO_3)_2$. Crystal structure: hexagonal (rhombohedral). **2.** a sedimentary rock resembling limestone but consisting principally of the mineral dolomite. It is an important source of magnesium and its compounds, and is used as a building material and refractory. [C18: named after Déodat de *Dolomieu* (1750–1801), French mineralogist] —**dolomitic** (ˌdɒlə'mɪtɪk) *adj.*

dolorimetry (ˌdɒlə'rɪmɪtrɪ) *n.* a technique for measuring the level of pain perception by applying heat to the skin.

doloroso (ˌdɒlə'rəʊsəʊ) *adj., adv. Music.* (to be performed) in a sorrowful manner. [Italian: dolorous]

dolorous ('dɒlərəs) *adj.* causing or involving pain or sorrow. —'**dolorously** *adv.* —'**dolorousness** *n.*

dolos ('dɒlɒs) *n., pl.* **-osse.** *S. African.* a knucklebone of a sheep, buck, etc., used esp. by diviners. [from Afrikaans, possibly from *dollen* play + *os* ox or from *dobbel* dice + *os* ox]

dolostone ('dɒləˌstəʊn) *n.* rock composed of the mineral dolerite.

dolour *or U.S.* **dolor** ('dɒlə) *n. Poetic.* grief or sorrow. [C14: from Latin, from *dolēre* to grieve]

dolphin ('dɒlfɪn) *n.* **1.** any of various marine cetacean mammals of the family *Delphinidae*, esp. *Delphinus delphis*, that are typically smaller than whales and larger than porpoises and have a beaklike snout. **2. river dolphin.** any freshwater cetacean of the family *Platanistidae*, inhabiting rivers of North and South America and S Asia. They are smaller than marine dolphins and have a longer narrower snout. **3.** Also called: **dorado.** either of two large marine percoid fishes, *Coryphaena hippurus* or *C. equisetis*, that resemble the cetacean dolphins and have an iridescent coloration. **4.** *Nautical.* a post or buoy for mooring a vessel. [C13: from Old French *dauphin*, via Latin, from Greek *delphin-*, *delphis*]

dolphinarium (ˌdɒlfɪ'nɛərɪəm) *n.* a pool or aquarium for dolphins, esp. one in which they give public displays.

dolphin striker *n. Nautical.* a short vertical strut between the bowsprit and a rope or cable (martingale) from the end of the jib boom to the stem or bows, used for maintaining tension and preventing upward movement of the jib boom. Also called: **martingale boom, martingale.**

dolt (dəʊlt) *n.* a slow-witted or stupid person; [C16: probably related to Old English *dol* stupid; see DULL] —'**doltish** *adj.* —'**doltishly** *adv.* —'**doltishness** *n.*

dom (dɒm) *n.* **1.** (*sometimes cap.*) *R.C. Church.* a title given to Benedictine, Carthusian, and Cistercian monks and to certain of the canons regular. **2.** (formerly in Portugal and Brazil) a title borne by royalty, princes of the Church, and nobles. [C18 (monastic title): from Latin *dominus* lord]

DOM *abbrev. for:* **1.** Deo Optimo Maximo [Latin: to God, the best, the Greatest] **2.** Dirty Old Man. ~ **3.** *international car registration for* Dominican Republic.

dom. *abbrev. for:* **1.** domain. **2.** domestic.

Dom. *R.C. Church. abbrev. for* Dominican.

-dom *suffix forming nouns.* **1.** state or condition: *freedom; martyrdom.* **2.** rank or office: *earldom.* **3.** domain: *kingdom; Christendom.* **4.** a collection of persons: *officialdom.* [Old English *-dōm*]

domain (də'meɪn) *n.* **1.** land governed by a ruler or government. **2.** land owned by one person or family. **3.** a field or scope of knowledge or activity. **4.** a region having specific characteristics or containing certain types of plants or animals. **5.** *Austral. and N.Z.* a park or recreation reserve maintained by a public authority, often the government. **6.** *Law.* the absolute ownership and right to dispose of land. See also **demesne, eminent domain.** **7.** *Maths.* **a.** the set of values of the independent variable of a function for which the functional value exists: *the domain of sin x is all real numbers.* Compare **range** (sense 8). **b.** any open set containing at least one point. **8.** *Logic.* another term for **universe of discourse** (esp. in the phrase **domain of quantification**). **9.** *Philosophy.* range of significance (esp. in the phrase **domain of definition**). **10.** Also called: **magnetic domain.** *Physics.* one of the regions in a ferromagnetic solid in which all the atoms have their magnetic moments aligned in the same direction. [C17: from French *domaine*, from Latin *dominium* property, from *dominus* lord]

domatium (dɒ'meɪʃɪəm) *n., pl.* **-tia.** *Botany.* a plant cavity inhabited by commensal insects or mites.

dome (dəʊm) *n.* **1.** a hemispherical roof or vault or a structure of similar form. **2.** something shaped like this. **3.** *Crystallog.* a crystal form in which two planes intersect along an edge parallel to a lateral axis. **4.** a slang word for the **head.** **5.** *Geology.* another name for **pericline** (sense 2). ~*vb.* (*tr.*) **6.** to cover with or as if with a dome. **7.** to shape like a dome. [C16: from French, from Italian *duomo* cathedral, from Latin *domus* house] —'**dome,like** *adj.* —**domical** ('dəʊmɪkəl, 'dɒm-) *adj.*

dome fastener *n.* the usual Canadian name for **press stud.**

domesday ('duːmz,deɪ) *n.* a variant spelling of **doomsday.**

domestic (də'mɛstɪk) *adj.* **1.** of or involving the home or family. **2.** enjoying or accustomed to home or family life. **3.** (of an animal) bred or kept by man as a pet or for purposes such as the supply of food. **4.** of, produced in, or involving one's own country or a specific country: *domestic and foreign affairs.* ~*n.* **5.** a household servant. [C16: from Old French *domestique,* from Latin *domesticus* belonging to the house, from *domus* house] —**do'mestically** *adv.*

domesticate (də'mɛstɪ,keɪt) *or U.S.* (*sometimes*) **domesticize** (də'mɛstɪ,saɪz) *vb.* (*tr.*) **1.** to bring or keep (wild animals or plants) under control or cultivation. **2.** to accustom to home life. **3.** to adapt to an environment: *to domesticate foreign trees.* —**do'mesticable** *adj.* —**do,mesti'cation** *n.* —**do'mesticative** *adj.* —**do'mesti,cator** *n.*

domestic court *n.* (in England) a magistrates' court for domestic proceedings, such as matrimonial, guardianship, custodianship, affiliation, or adoption disputes.

domestic fowl *n.* a domesticated gallinaceous bird thought to be descended from the red jungle fowl (*Gallus gallus*) and occurring in many varieties. Often shortened to **fowl.**

domesticity (,dəʊmɛ'stɪsɪtɪ) *n., pl.* **-ties.** **1.** home life. **2.** devotion to or familiarity with home life. **3.** (*usually pl.*) a domestic duty, matter, or condition.

domestic science *n.* the study of cooking, needlework, and other subjects concerned with household skills.

domicile ('dɒmɪ,saɪl) *or* **domicil** ('dɒmɪsɪl) *n.* **1.** a dwelling place. **2.** a permanent legal residence. **3.** *Commerce, Brit.* the place where a bill of exchange is to be paid. ~*vb. also* **domiciliate** (,dɒmɪ'sɪlɪ,eɪt). **4.** to establish or be established in a dwelling place. [C15: from Latin *domicilium,* from *domus* house] —**domiciliary** (,dɒmɪ'sɪlɪərɪ) *adj.*

domiciliary care *or* **services** *n. Social welfare.* services, such as meals-on-wheels, health visiting, and home help, provided by a welfare agency for people in their own homes.

dominance ('dɒmɪnəns) *n.* control; ascendancy.

dominant ('dɒmɪnənt) *adj.* **1.** having primary control, authority, or influence; governing; ruling. **2.** predominant or primary: *the dominant topic of the day.* **3.** occupying a commanding position. **4.** *Genetics.* **a.** (of a gene) producing the same phenotype in the organism whether its allele is identical or dissimilar. **b.** (of a character) controlled by such a gene. Compare **recessive** (sense 2). **5.** *Music.* of or relating to the fifth degree of a scale. **6.** *Ecology.* (of a plant or animal species within a community) more prevalent than any other species and determining the appearance and composition of the community. ~*n.* **7.** *Genetics.* **a.** a dominant gene or character. **b.** an organism having such a gene or character. **8.** *Music.* **a.** the fifth degree of a scale and the second in importance after the tonic. **b.** a key or chord based on this. **9.** *Ecology.* a dominant plant or animal in a community. —'**dominantly** *adv.*

dominant hemisphere *n.* See **cerebral dominance.**

dominant seventh chord *n.* a chord consisting of the dominant and the major third, perfect fifth, and minor seventh above it. Its most natural resolution is to a chord on the tonic.

dominant tenement *n. Property law.* the land or tenement with the benefit of an easement over land belonging to another. Compare **servient tenement.**

dominant wavelength *n. Physics.* the wavelength of monochromatic light that would give the same visual sensation if combined in a suitable proportion with an achromatic light. See also **complementary wavelength.**

dominate ('dɒmɪ,neɪt) *vb.* **1.** to control, rule, or govern (someone or something). **2.** to tower above (surroundings, etc.); overlook. **3.** (*tr.; usually passive*) to predominate in (something or someone). [C17: from Latin *dominārī* to be lord over, from *dominus* lord] —'**domi,nating** *adj.* —'**domi,natingly** *adv.* —'**dominative** *adj.* —'**domi,nator** *n.*

domination (,dɒmɪ'neɪʃən) *n.* **1.** the act of dominating or state of being dominated. **2.** authority; rule; control.

dominations (,dɒmɪ'neɪʃənz) *pl. n.* (*sometimes cap.*) the fourth order of medieval angelology. Also called: **dominions.**

dominatrix (,dɒmɪ'neɪtrɪks) *n., pl.* **dominatrices** (,dɒmɪnə'traɪsiːz). **1.** a woman who is the dominant sexual partner in a sadomasochistic relationship. **2.** a dominant woman. [C16: from Latin, fem. of *dominātor,* from *dominārī* to be lord over]

dominee ('duːmɪnɪ, 'dʊə-) *n.* (in South Africa) a minister in any of the Afrikaner Churches. Also called: **predikant.** [from Afrikaans, from Dutch; compare DOMINIE]

domineer (,dɒmɪ'nɪə) *vb.* (*intr.;* often foll. by *over*) to act with arrogance or tyranny; behave imperiously. [C16: from Dutch *domineren,* from French *dominer* to DOMINATE] —,**domi'neering** *adj.* —,**domi'neeringly** *adv.* —,**domi'neeringness** *n.*

dominical (də'mɪnɪkəl) *adj.* **1.** of, relating to, or emanating from Jesus Christ as Lord. **2.** of or relating to Sunday as the Lord's Day. [C15: from Late Latin *dominicālis,* from Latin *dominus* lord]

dominical letter *n. Christianity.* any one of the letters A to G as used to denote Sundays in a given year in order to determine the church calendar.

Dominican[1] (də'mɪnɪkən) *n.* **1. a.** a member of an order of preaching friars founded by the Spanish priest Saint Dominic (?1170–1221) in 1215; a Blackfriar. **b.** a nun of one of the orders founded under the patronage of Saint Dominic. ~*adj.* **2.** of or relating to Saint Dominic or the Dominican order.

Dominican[2] (də'mɪnɪkən) *adj.* **1.** of or relating to the Dominican Republic or Dominica, both in the West Indies. ~*n.* **2.** a native or inhabitant of the Dominican Republic or Dominica.

dominie ('dɒmɪnɪ) *n.* **1.** a Scot. word for **schoolmaster.** **2.** a minister or clergyman: also used as a term of address. [C17: from Latin *dominē,* vocative case of *dominus* lord]

dominion (də'mɪnjən) *n.* **1.** rule; authority. **2.** the land governed by one ruler or government. **3.** sphere of influence; area of control. **4.** a name formerly applied to self-governing divisions of the British Empire. **5.** (*cap.*) **the.** New Zealand. **6.** *Law.* a less common word for **dominium.** [C15: from Old French, from Latin *dominium* ownership, from *dominus* master]

Dominion Day *n.* the former name for **Canada Day.**

dominions (də'mɪnjənz) *pl. n.* (*often cap.*) another term for **dominations.**

dominium (də'mɪnɪəm) *or* (*rarely*) **dominion** *n. Property law.* the ownership or right to possession of property, esp. realty. [C19: from Latin: property, ownership; see DOMINION]

domino[1] ('dɒmɪ,nəʊ) *n., pl.* **-noes.** **1.** a small rectangular block used in dominoes, divided on one side into two equal areas, each of which is either blank or marked with from one to six dots. **2.** (*modifier*) exhibiting the domino effect: *a domino pattern of takeovers.* ~See also **dominoes.** [C19: from French, from Italian, perhaps from *domino!* master, said by the winner]

domino[2] ('dɒmɪ,nəʊ) *n., pl.* **-noes** *or* **-nos.** **1.** a large hooded cloak worn with an eye mask at a masquerade. **2.** the eye mask worn with such a cloak. [C18: from French or Italian, probably from Latin *dominus* lord, master]

domino effect *n.* a series of similar or related events occurring as a direct and inevitable result of one initial event. [C20: alluding to a row of dominoes, each standing on end, all of which fall when one is pushed: originally used with reference to possible Communist takeovers of countries in SE Asia]

dominoes ('dɒmɪ,nəʊz) *n.* (*functioning as sing.*) any of several games in which matching halves of dominoes are laid together.

Dominus *Latin.* ('dɒmɪnʊs) *n.* God or Christ.

domkop ('dɒm,kɒp) *n. S. African slang.* an idiot; thickhead. [Afrikaans]

don[1] (dɒn) *vb.* **dons, donning, donned.** (*tr.*) to put on (clothing). [C14: from DO[1] + ON; compare DOFF]

don[2] (dɒn) *n.* **1.** *Brit.* a member of the teaching staff at a university or college, esp. at Oxford or Cambridge. **2.** a Spanish gentleman or nobleman. **3.** *Archaic.* a person of rank. **4.** *Austral. and N.Z. informal.* an expert: *he's a don at public speaking.* [C17: ultimately from Latin *dominus* lord]

Don (dɒn; *Spanish* don) *n.* a Spanish title equivalent to *Mr*: placed before a name to indicate respect. [C16: via Spanish, from Latin *dominus* lord; see DON[2]]

Dona (*Portuguese* 'dõnə) *n.* a Portuguese title of address equivalent to *Mrs* or *Madam*: placed before a name to indicate respect. [C19: from Latin *domina* lady, feminine of *dominus* master]

Doña ('dɒnjə; *Spanish* 'doɲa) *n.* a Spanish title of address equivalent to *Mrs* or *Madam*: placed before a name to indicate respect. [C17: via Spanish, from Latin *domina;* see DONA]

donah ('dəʊnə) *n. Austral. informal.* (in the 19th century) a girlfriend. [from Spanish *doña* or Portuguese *dona,* from Latin *domina* lady]

donate (dəʊ'neɪt) *vb.* to give (money, time, etc.), esp. to a charity. —**do'nator** *n.*

donation (dəʊ'neɪʃən) *n.* **1.** the act of giving, esp. to a charity. **2.** a contribution. [C15: from Latin *dōnātiō* a presenting, from *dōnāre* to give, from *dōnum* gift]

Donatist ('dəʊnətɪst) *n.* a member of a schismatic heretical Christian sect originating in N Africa in 311 A.D., that maintained that it alone constituted the true church. [C15: from Late Latin *Dōnātista* a follower of *Dōnātus,* bishop of Carthage] —'**Dona,tism** *n.*

donative ('dəʊnətɪv) *n.* **1.** a gift or donation. **2.** a benefice capable of being conferred as a gift. ~*adj.* **3.** of or like a donation. **4.** being or relating to a benefice. [C15: from Latin *dōnātīvum* donation made to soldiers by a Roman emperor, from *dōnāre* to present]

done (dʌn) *vb.* **1.** the past participle of **do**[1]. **2. be** *or* **have done with.** to end relations with. **3. have done.** to be completely finished: *have you done?* **4. that's done it. a.** an exclamation of frustration when something is ruined. **b.** an exclamation when something is completed. ~*interj.* **5.** an expression of agreement, as on the settlement of a bargain between two parties. ~*adj.* **6.** completed; finished. **7.** cooked enough: *done to a turn.* **8.** used up: *they had to surrender when the ammunition was done.* **9.** socially proper or acceptable: *that isn't done in higher circles.* **10.** *Informal.* cheated; tricked. **11. done for.** *Informal.* **a.** dead

or almost dead. **b.** in serious difficulty. **12. done in** *or* **up.** *Informal.* physically exhausted.
donee (dəʊ'niː) *n. Law.* **1.** a person who receives a gift. **2.** a person to whom a power of appointment is given. [C16: from DON(OR) + -EE]
doner kebab ('dɒnə) *n.* a fast-food dish comprising grilled meat and salad served in pitta bread with chilli sauce.
dong[1] (dɒŋ) *n.* **1.** the deep reverberating sound of a large bell. **2.** *Austral. and N.Z. informal.* a heavy blow. **3.** a slang word for **penis.** ~*vb.* **4.** (*intr.*) (of a bell) to make a deep reverberating sound. **5.** (*tr.*) *Austral. and N.Z. informal.* to strike or punch. [C16: of imitative origin]
dong[2] (dɒŋ) *n.* the standard monetary unit of Vietnam. [from Vietnamese]
donga[1] ('dɒŋgə) *n. S. African, Austral., and N.Z.* a steep-sided gully created by soil erosion. [C19: from Afrikaans, of Zulu origin]
donga[2] ('dɒŋgə) *n.* (in Papua New Guinean) a house or shelter.
dongle ('dɒŋgᵊl) *n. Computer technol.* an electronic device that accompanies a software item to prevent the unauthorized copying of programs.
donjon ('dʌndʒən, 'dɒn-) *n.* the heavily fortified central tower or keep of a medieval castle. Also called: **dungeon.** [C14: archaic variant of *dungeon*]
Don Juan ('dɒn 'dʒuːən; *Spanish* don xwan) *n.* a successful seducer of women. [after a legendary Spanish nobleman and philanderer]
donkey ('dɒŋkɪ) *n.* **1.** Also called: **ass.** a long-eared domesticated member of the horse family (*Equidae*), descended from the African wild ass (*Equus asinus*). **2.** a stupid or stubborn person. **3. talk the hind leg(s) off a donkey.** to talk endlessly. [C18: perhaps from *dun* dark + *-key,* as in *monkey*]
donkey derby *n.* a race in which contestants ride donkeys, esp. at a rural fête.
donkey engine *n.* a small auxiliary engine, such as one used for pumping water into the boilers of a steamship.
donkey jacket *n.* a hip-length jacket usually made of a thick navy fabric with a waterproof panel across the shoulders.
donkey-lick *vb. Austral. slang.* to defeat decisively.
donkey's years *n. Informal.* a long time.
donkey vote *n. Austral.* a vote on a preferential ballot on which the voter's order of preference follows the order in which the candidates are listed.
donkey-work *n.* **1.** groundwork. **2.** drudgery.
donko ('dɒŋkəʊ) *n., pl.* **-kos.** *N.Z. informal.* a tearoom or cafeteria in a factory, wharf area, etc.
Donna ('dɒnə; *Italian* 'dɔnna) *n.* an Italian title of address equivalent to *Madam,* indicating respect. [C17: from Italian, from Latin *domina* lady, feminine of *dominus* lord, master]
donnée *or* ***donné*** *French.* (dɔne) *n.* **1.** a subject or theme. **2.** a basic assumption or fact. [literally: (a) given]
donnert ('dɒnərt), **donnard,** *or* **donnered** ('dɒnərd) *adj. Scot.* stunned. [C18: from Scottish dialect *donner* to astound, perhaps from Dutch *donderen* to thunder, from Middle Dutch *donder* thunder]
donnish ('dɒnɪʃ) *adj.* of or resembling a university don. —'**donnishly** *adv.* —'**donnishness** *n.*
donny ('dɒnɪ) *n.* a variant of **danny.**
donnybrook ('dɒnɪˌbrʊk) *n.* a rowdy brawl. [C19: after *Donnybrook Fair,* an annual event until 1855 near Dublin]
donor ('dəʊnə) *n.* **1.** a person who makes a donation. **2.** *Med.* any person who voluntarily gives blood, skin, etc., for use in the treatment of another person. **3.** *Law.* **a.** a person who makes a gift of property. **b.** a person who bestows upon another a power of appointment over property. **4.** the atom supplying both electrons in a coordinate bond. **5.** an impurity, such as antimony or arsenic, that is added to a semiconductor material in order to increase its n-type conductivity by contributing free electrons. Compare **acceptor** (sense 2). [C15: from Old French *doneur,* from Latin *dōnātor,* from *dōnāre* to give] —'**donor**ˌ**ship** *n.*
donor card *n.* a card carried by a person to show that the bodily organs specified on it may be used for transplants after the person's death.
Don Quixote ('dɒn kiː'həʊtiː, 'kwɪksət; *Spanish* don ki'xote) *n.* an impractical idealist. [after the hero of Cervantes' *Don Quixote de la Mancha* (1605)]
don't (dəʊnt) *contraction of* do not.
▷**Usage.** The use of *don't* for *doesn't* (*he don't care*) is not generally acceptable either in written or spoken English.
don't know *n.* a person who has not reached a definite opinion on a subject, esp. as a response to a questionnaire.
donut ('dəʊnʌt) *n.* a variant spelling (esp. U.S.) of **doughnut.**
doo (duː) *n.* a Scot. word for **dove** or **pigeon**[1].
doodah ('duːdɑː) *or U.S. and Canadian* **doodad** ('duːdæd) *n. Informal.* **1.** an unnamed thing, esp. an object the name of which is unknown or forgotten. **2. all of a doodah.** excited; agitated. [C20: of uncertain origin]
doodle ('duːdᵊl) *Informal.* ~*vb.* **1.** to scribble or draw aimlessly. **2.** to play or improvise idly. **3.** (*intr.;* often foll. by *away*) *U.S.* to dawdle or waste time. ~*n.* **4.** a shape, picture, etc., drawn aimlessly. [C20: perhaps from C17 *doodle* a foolish person, but influenced in meaning by DAWDLE; compare Low German *dudeltopf* simpleton] —'**doodler** *n.*
doodlebug ('duːdᵊlˌbʌg) *n.* **1.** another name for the **V-1.** **2.** a diviner's rod. **3.** a U.S. name for an **antlion** (the larva). **4.** *U.S.* any of certain insect larvae that resemble the antlion. [C20: probably from DOODLE + BUG[1]]
dook[1] *or* **douk**[1] (dʊk) *n. Scot.* a wooden plug driven into a wall to hold a nail, screw, etc. [of unknown origin]
dook[2] *or* **douk**[2] (dʊk) *Scot.* ~*vb.* **1.** to dip or plunge. **2.** to bathe. ~*n.* **3.** an instance of dipping, plunging, or bathing. [a Scot. form of DUCK[2]]
dooket ('duːkɪt, 'dʊkɪt) *n. Scot.* **1.** a dovecote. **2.** a small closet or cupboard.
doolally (duː'lælɪ) *adj. Slang.* out of one's mind; crazy. [C19: originally military slang, from *Deolali,* a town near Bombay, India]
doolan ('duːlən) *n. N.Z. informal.* a Roman Catholic. [probably from the Irish surname *Doolan*]
doom (duːm) *n.* **1.** death or a terrible fate. **2.** a judgment or decision. **3.** (*sometimes cap.*) another term for the **Last Judgment.** ~*vb.* **4.** (*tr.*) to destine or condemn to death or a terrible fate. [Old English *dōm;* related to Old Norse *dōmr* judgment, Gothic *dōms* sentence, Old High German *tuom* condition, Greek *thomos* crowd, Sanskrit *dhāman* custom; see DO[1], DEEM, DEED, -DOM]
doom-laden *adj.* conveying a sense of disaster and tragedy.
doom palm *n.* a variant spelling of **doum palm.**
doomsday *or* **domesday** ('duːmzˌdeɪ) *n.* **1.** (*sometimes cap.*) the day on which the Last Judgment will occur. **2.** any day of reckoning. **3.** (*modifier*) characterized by predictions of disaster: *doomsday scenario.* [Old English *dōmes dæg* Judgment Day; related to Old Norse *domsdagr*]
doomster ('duːmstə) *n. Informal.* **1.** a person habitually given to predictions of impending disaster or doom. **2.** *Archaic.* a judge.
doomwatch ('duːmˌwɒtʃ) *n.* **1.** surveillance of the environment to warn of and prevent harm to it from human factors such as pollution or overpopulation. **2.** a watching for or prediction of impending disaster. —'**doomwatcher** *n.*
doomy ('duːmɪ) *adj. Informal.* **1.** despondent or pessimistic. **2.** depressing, frightening, or chilling.
doon *or* **doun** (duːn) *prep., adv., adj.* a Scot. word for **down**[1].
doona ('duːnə) *n.* the Austral. name for **continental quilt.** [from a trademark]
door (dɔː) *n.* **1. a.** a hinged or sliding panel for closing the entrance to a room, cupboard, etc. **b.** (*in combination*): *doorbell; doorknob.* **2.** a doorway or entrance to a room or building. **3.** a means of access or escape: *a door to success.* **4. lay at someone's door.** to lay (the blame or responsibility) on someone. **5. out of doors.** in or into the open air. **6. show someone the door.** to order someone to leave. ~See also **next door.** [Old English *duru;* related to Old Frisian *dure,* Old Norse *dyrr,* Old High German *turi,* Latin *forēs,* Greek *thura*]
do-or-die *adj.* (*prenominal*) of or involving a determined and sometimes reckless effort to succeed.
doorframe ('dɔːˌfreɪm) *n.* a frame that supports a door. Also called: '**door**ˌ**case.**
door furniture *n.* locks, handles, etc., designed for use on doors.
doorjamb ('dɔːˌdʒæm) *n.* one of the two vertical members forming the sides of a doorframe. Also called: **doorpost.**
doorkeeper ('dɔːˌkiːpə) *n.* **1.** a person attending or guarding a door or gateway. **2.** *R.C. Church.* (formerly) the lowest grade of holy orders.
doorknock ('dɔːnɒk) *n. Austral.* a fund-raising campaign for charity conducted by seeking donations from door to door.
doorman ('dɔːˌmæn, -mən) *n., pl.* **-men.** a man employed to attend the doors of certain buildings.
doormat ('dɔːˌmæt) *n.* **1.** a mat, placed at the entrance to a building, for wiping dirt from shoes. **2.** *Informal.* a person who offers little resistance to ill-treatment by others.
doornail ('dɔːˌneɪl) *n.* **(as) dead as a doornail.** dead beyond any doubt.
doorpost ('dɔːˌpəʊst) *n.* another name for **doorjamb.**
doorsill ('dɔːˌsɪl) *n.* a horizontal member of wood, stone, etc., forming the bottom of a doorframe.
doorstep ('dɔːˌstɛp) *n.* **1.** a step in front of a door. **2. on one's doorstep.** very close or accessible. **3.** *Informal.* a thick slice of bread. ~*vb.* **-steps, -stepping, -stepped.** (*tr.*) **4.** to canvass (a district) or interview (a member of the public) by or in the course of door-to-door visiting.
doorstop ('dɔːˌstɒp) *n.* **1.** a heavy object, wedge, or other device which prevents an open door from moving. **2.** a projecting piece of rubber, etc., fixed to the floor to stop a door from striking a wall.
door to door *adj.* (**door-to-door** *when prenominal*), *adv.* **1.** (of selling, canvassing, etc.) from one house to the next. **2.** (of journeys, deliveries, etc.) direct.
doorway ('dɔːˌweɪ) *n.* **1.** an opening into a building, room, etc., esp. one that has a door. **2.** a means of access or escape: *a doorway to freedom.*
dooryard ('dɔːˌjɑːd) *n. U.S. and Canadian.* a yard in front of the front or back door of a house.
do out *vb.* (*tr., adv.*) *Informal.* **1.** to make tidy or clean; redecorate. **2.** (foll. by *of*) to deprive (a person) of by swindling or cheating.

do over *vb. (tr., adv.)* **1.** *Informal.* to renovate or redecorate. **2.** *Brit., Austral., and N.Z. slang.* to beat up; thrash.
doo-wop ('du:ˌwɒp) *n.* rhythm-and-blues harmony vocalizing developed by unaccompanied street-corner groups in the U.S. in the 1950s. [C20: of imitative origin]
dopa ('dəʊpə) *n.* See **L-dopa.**
dopamine ('dɒpəmɪn) *n.* a chemical found in the brain that acts as a neurotransmitter and is an intermediate compound in the synthesis of noradrenaline. Formula: $(HO)_2C_6(CH_2)_2NH_2$. [from *d(ihydr)o(xy)p(henylethyl)amine*]
dopant ('dəʊpənt) *n.* an element or compound used to dope a semiconductor. [C20: see DOPE, -ANT]
dope (dəʊp) *n.* **1.** any of a number of preparations made by dissolving cellulose derivatives in a volatile solvent, applied to fabric in order to improve strength, tautness, etc. **2.** an additive used to improve the properties of something, such as an antiknock compound added to petrol. **3.** a thick liquid, such as a lubricant, applied to a surface. **4.** a combustible absorbent material, such as sawdust or wood pulp, used to hold the nitroglycerin in dynamite. **5.** *Slang.* **a.** any illegal drug, usually cannabis. **b.** *(as modifier): a dope fiend.* **6.** a drug administered to a racehorse or greyhound to affect its performance. **7.** *Informal.* a person considered to be stupid or slow-witted. **8.** *Informal.* news or facts, esp. confidential information. **9.** *U.S. and Canadian informal.* a photographic developing solution. ~*vb.* *(tr.)* **10.** *Electronics.* to add impurities to (a semiconductor) in order to produce or modify its properties. **11.** to apply or add dope to. **12.** to administer a drug to (oneself or another). **13.** *(intr.)* to take dope. [C19: from Dutch *doop* sauce, from *doopen* to DIP]
dope out *vb. (tr., adv.) U.S. slang.* to devise, solve, or contrive: *to dope out a floor plan.*
dope sheet *n. Horse racing slang.* a publication giving information on horses running in races.
dopester ('dəʊpstə) *n. U.S. and Canadian slang.* a person who makes predictions, esp. in sport or politics.
dopey *or* **dopy** ('dəʊpɪ) *adj.* **dopier, dopiest.** **1.** *Slang.* silly. **2.** *Informal.* half-asleep or in a state of semiconsciousness, as when under the influence of a drug. —'**dopily** *adv.* —'**dopiness** *n.*
doppelgänger ('dɒpᵊlˌgɛŋə; *German* 'dɔpəlˌgɛŋər) *n. Legend.* a ghostly duplicate of a living person. [from German *Doppelgänger,* literally: double-goer]
Dopper ('dɒpə) *n.* (in South Africa) a member of the most conservative Afrikaner Church, which practises a strict Calvinism. [C19: from Afrikaans, of unknown origin]
Doppler effect ('dɒplə) *n.* a phenomenon, observed for sound waves and electromagnetic radiation, characterized by a change in the apparent frequency of a wave as a result of relative motion between the observer and the source. Also called: **Doppler shift.** [C19: named after C. J. *Doppler* (1803–53), Austrian physicist]
dor (dɔ:) *n.* any European dung beetle of the genus *Geotrupes* and related genera, esp. *G. stercorarius,* having a droning flight. [Old English *dora* bumblebee; related to Middle Low German *dorte* DRONE[1]]
dorado (də'rɑ:dəʊ) *n.* **1.** another name for **dolphin** (sense 3). **2.** a S. American river fish of the genus *Salminus* that resembles a salmon.
Dorado (də'rɑ:dəʊ) *n., Latin genitive* **Doradus** (də'rɑ:dəs). a constellation in the S hemisphere lying between Reticulum and Pictor and containing part of the Large Magellanic Cloud. [C17: from Spanish, from *dorar* to gild, from Latin DE- + *-aurāre,* from *aurum* gold]
Dorian ('dɔ:rɪən) *n.* **1.** a member of a Hellenic people who invaded Greece around 1100 B.C., overthrew the Mycenaean civilization, and settled chiefly in the Peloponnese peninsula in S Greece. ~*adj.* **2.** of or relating to this people or their dialect of Ancient Greek; Doric. **3.** *Music.* of or relating to a mode represented by the ascending natural diatonic scale from D to D. See also **Hypo-.**
Doric ('dɒrɪk) *adj.* **1.** of or relating to the Dorians, esp. the Spartans, or their dialect of Ancient Greek. **2.** of, denoting, or relating to one of the five classical orders of architecture: characterized by a column having no base, a heavy fluted shaft, and a capital consisting of an ovolo moulding beneath a square abacus. See also **Ionic, composite** (sense 4), **Corinthian, Tuscan.** **3.** *(sometimes not cap.)* rustic. ~*n.* **4.** one of four chief dialects of Ancient Greek, spoken chiefly in the Peloponnese. **5.** any rural dialect of English, esp. a Scots one. Compare **Aeolic, Arcadic, Ionic.** See also **Attic** (sense 3).
dork (dɔ:k) *n. Slang.* **1.** a stupid or incompetent person. **2.** *U.S.* a penis. [C20: of unknown origin] —'**dorky** *adj.*
Dorking ('dɔ:kɪŋ) *n.* a heavy breed of domestic fowl. [C19: after *Dorking,* town in Surrey]
dorm (dɔ:m) *n. Informal.* short for **dormitory.**
dormant ('dɔ:mənt) *adj.* **1.** quiet and inactive, as during sleep. **2.** latent or inoperative. **3.** (of a volcano) neither extinct nor erupting. **4.** *Biology.* alive but in a resting torpid condition with suspended growth and reduced metabolism. **5.** *(usually postpositive) Heraldry.* (of a beast) in a sleeping position. ~Compare **active, passive.** [C14: from Old French *dormant,* from *dormir* to sleep, from Latin *dormīre*] —'**dormancy** *n.*
dormer ('dɔ:mə) *n.* a construction with a gable roof and a window at its outer end that projects from a sloping roof. Also called: **dormer window.** [C16: from Old French *dormoir,* from Latin *dormītōrium* DORMITORY]
dormie *or* **dormy** ('dɔ:mɪ) *adj. Golf.* (of a player or side) as many holes ahead of an opponent as there are still to play: *dormie three.* [C19: of unknown origin]
Dormition of the Blessed Virgin *n.* another name for **Feast of the Assumption:** see **Assumption.**
dormitory ('dɔ:mɪtərɪ, -trɪ) *n., pl.* **-ries.** **1.** a large room, esp. at a school or institution, containing several beds. **2.** *U.S.* a building, esp. at a college or camp, providing living and sleeping accommodation. **3.** *(modifier) Brit.* denoting or relating to an area from which most of the residents commute to work (esp. in the phrase **dormitory suburb**). ~Often shortened (for senses 1, 2) to **dorm.** [C15: from Latin *dormītōrium,* from *dormīre* to sleep]
Dormobile ('dɔ:məʊˌbi:l) *n. Trademark.* a vanlike vehicle specially equipped for living in while travelling.
dormouse ('dɔ:ˌmaʊs) *n., pl.* **-mice.** any small Old World rodent of the family *Gliridae,* esp. the Eurasian *Muscardinus avellanarius,* resembling a mouse with a furry tail. [C15: *dor-,* perhaps from Old French *dormir* to sleep, from Latin *dormīre* + MOUSE]
dornick[1] ('dɔ:nɪk) *or* **dorneck** *n.* a heavy damask cloth, formerly used for vestments, curtains, etc. [C15: from *Doornik* Tournai in Belgium where it was first manufactured]
dornick[2] ('dɔ:nɪk) *n. U.S.* a small stone or pebble. [C15: probably from Irish Gaelic *dornōg,* from *dorn* hand]
doronicum (də'rɒnɪkəm) *n.* any plant of the Eurasian and N African genus *Doronicum,* such as leopard's-bane, having yellow daisy-like flower heads: family *Compositae* (composites). [C17: New Latin, from Arabic *dorūnaj*]
Dorothy Dixer (ˌdɒrəθɪ 'dɪksə) *n. Austral. informal.* a parliamentary question asked by a member of the government so that the minister may give a prepared answer. [from pen name *Dorothy Dix* of U.S. journalist Elizabeth Meriwether (1870–1951), who wrote a column replying to correspondents' problems]
dorp (dɔ:p) *n. Archaic except in S. Africa.* a small town or village. [C16: from Dutch: village; related to THORP]
dorsad ('dɔ:sæd) *adj. Anatomy.* towards the back or dorsal aspect. [C19: from Latin *dorsum* back + *ad* to, towards]
dorsal ('dɔ:sᵊl) *adj.* **1.** *Anatomy, zoology.* relating to the back or spinal part of the body. Compare **ventral** (sense 1). **2.** *Botany.* of, relating to, or situated on the side of an organ that is directed away from the axis. **3.** articulated with the back of the tongue, as the (k) sound in English *coot.* [C15: from Medieval Latin *dorsālis,* from Latin *dorsum* back] —'**dorsally** *adv.*
dorsal fin *n.* any unpaired median fin on the backs of fishes and some other aquatic vertebrates: maintains balance during locomotion.
Dorset Down ('dɔ:sɪt) *n.* a breed of stocky sheep having a broad head, dark face, and a dense fleece, originating from Dorset in SW England: kept for lamb production.
Dorset Horn *n.* a breed of horned sheep with dense fine-textured wool, originating from Dorset.
dorsiferous (dɔ:'sɪfərəs) *adj. Botany, zoology, rare.* bearing or carrying (young, spores, etc.) on the back or dorsal surface.
dorsiflexion (ˌdɔ:sɪ'flɛkʃən) *n. Med.* the bending back of a part, esp. the hand or foot or their digits.
dorsigrade ('dɔ:sɪˌgreɪd) *adj.* (of animals such as certain armadillos) walking on the backs of the toes. [C19: from Latin, from *dorsum* back + -GRADE]
dorsiventral (ˌdɔ:sɪ'vɛntrəl) *adj.* **1.** (of leaves and similar flat parts) having distinct upper and lower faces. **2.** a variant spelling of **dorsoventral.** —**dorsiventrality** (ˌdɔ:sɪvɛn'trælɪtɪ) *n.* —ˌ**dorsi'ventrally** *adv.*
dorso-, dorsi-, *or before a vowel* **dors-** *combining form.* indicating dorsum or dorsal: *dorsoventral.*
dorsoventral (ˌdɔ:səʊ'vɛntrəl) *adj.* **1.** relating to both the dorsal and ventral sides; extending from the back to the belly. **2.** *Botany.* a variant spelling of **dorsiventral.** —ˌ**dorso'ventrally** *adv.*
dorsum ('dɔ:səm) *n., pl.* **-sa** (-sə). *Anatomy.* **1.** a technical name for the **back.** **2.** any analogous surface: *the dorsum of the hand.* [C18: from Latin: back]
dorty ('dɔ:tɪ) *adj.* **dortier, dortiest.** *Scot.* haughty, or sullen. [C17: from Scottish *dort* peevishness] —'**dortiness** *n.*
dory[1] ('dɔ:rɪ) *n., pl.* **-ries.** **1.** any spiny-finned marine teleost food fish of the family *Zeidae,* esp. the John Dory, having a deep compressed body. **2.** another name for **walleye** (the fish). [C14: from French *dorée* gilded, from *dorer* to gild, from Late Latin *deaurāre,* ultimately from Latin *aurum* gold]
dory[2] ('dɔ:rɪ) *n., pl.* **-ries.** *U.S. and Canadian.* a flat-bottomed boat with a high bow and stern. [C18: from Mosquito (an American Indian language of Honduras and Nicaragua) *dóri* dugout]
DOS (dɒs) *n. Computer technol. Trademark. acronym for* disk-operating system, often prefixed, as in MS-DOS and PC-DOS; a computer operating system.
dos-à-dos (ˌdəʊsɪ'dəʊ; *French* dozado) *n.* **1.** a seat on which the users sit back to back. **2.** an alternative spelling of **do-si-do.** [literally: back to back]
dosage ('dəʊsɪdʒ) *n.* **1.** the administration of a drug or agent in prescribed amounts. **2.** the optimum therapeutic dose and opti-

mum interval between doses. **3.** another name for **dose** (senses 3, 4).

dose (dəʊs) *n.* **1.** *Med.* a specific quantity of a therapeutic drug or agent taken at any one time or at specified intervals. **2.** *Informal.* something unpleasant to experience: *a dose of influenza.* **3.** Also called: **dosage.** the total energy of ionizing radiation absorbed by unit mass of material, esp. of living tissue; usually measured in grays (SI unit) or rads. **4.** Also called: **dosage.** a small amount of syrup added to wine, esp. sparkling wine, when the sediment is removed and the bottle is corked. **5.** *Slang.* a venereal infection, esp. gonorrhoea. **6. like a dose of salts.** very quickly indeed. ~*vb.* (*tr.*) **7.** to administer a dose or doses to (someone). **8.** *Med.* to prescribe (a therapeutic drug or agent) in appropriate quantities. **9.** (often foll. by *up*) to give (someone, esp. oneself) drugs, medicine, etc., esp. in large quantities. **10.** to add syrup to (wine) during bottling. [C15: from French, from Late Latin *dosis,* from Greek: a giving, from *didonai* to give] —'**doser** *n.*

dose equivalent *n.* a quantity that expresses the probability that exposure to ionizing radiation will cause biological effects. It is usually obtained by multiplying the dose by the quality factor of the radiation, but other factors may be considered. It is measured in sieverts (SI unit) or rems.

dosh (dɒʃ) *n. Brit. and Austral.* a slang word for **money.** [C20: of unknown origin]

do-si-do (ˌdəʊsɪ'dəʊ) *n.* **1.** a square-dance figure in which dancers pass each other with right shoulders close or touching and circle back to back. ~*sentence substitute.* **2.** a call instructing dancers to perform such a figure. ~Also: **dos-à-dos.** [C20: from DOS-À-DOS]

dosimeter (dəʊ'sɪmiːtə) *or* **dosemeter** ('dəʊsˌmiːtə) *n.* an instrument for measuring the dose of x-rays or other radiation absorbed by matter or the intensity of a source of radiation. —**dosimetric** (ˌdəʊsɪ'mɛtrɪk) *adj.* —**dosimetrician** (ˌdəʊsɪmə'trɪʃən) *or* **do'simetrist** *n.* —**do'simetry** *n.*

dosing strip *n.* (in New Zealand) an area set aside for treating dogs suspected of having hydatid disease.

doss (dɒs) *Brit. slang.* ~*vb.* **1.** (*intr.;* often foll. by *down*) to sleep, esp. in a dosshouse. ~*n.* **2.** a bed, esp. in a dosshouse. **3.** a slang word for **sleep.** **4.** short for **dosshouse.** [C18: of uncertain origin]

dossal *or* **dossel** ('dɒsᵊl) *n.* **1.** an ornamental hanging, placed at the back of an altar or at the sides of a chancel. **2.** Also called: **dosser.** *Archaic.* an ornamental covering for the back of a chair. [C17: from Medieval Latin *dossāle,* neuter of *dossālis,* variant of *dorsālis* DORSAL]

dosser¹ ('dɒsə) *n.* **1.** *Rare.* a bag or basket for carrying objects on the back. **2.** another word for **dossal** (sense 2). [C14: from Old French *dossier,* from Medieval Latin *dorsārium,* from Latin *dorsum* back]

dosser² ('dɒsə) *n.* **1.** *Brit. slang.* a person who sleeps in dosshouses. **2.** *Brit. slang.* another word for **dosshouse.** **3.** *Dublin dialect.* a lazy person; idler.

dosshouse ('dɒsˌhaʊs) *n. Brit. slang.* a cheap lodging house, esp. one used by tramps. U.S. name: **flophouse.**

dossier ('dɒsɪˌeɪ, -sɪə; *French* dosje) *n.* a collection of papers containing information on a particular subject or person. [C19: from French: a file with a label on the back, from *dos* back, from Latin *dorsum*]

dost (dʌst) *vb. Archaic or dialect.* (used with the pronoun *thou* or its relative equivalent) a singular form of the present tense (indicative mood) of **do**¹.

dot¹ (dɒt) *n.* **1.** a small round mark made with or as with a pen, etc.; spot; speck; point. **2.** anything resembling a dot; a small amount: *a dot of paint.* **3.** the mark (˙) that appears above the main stem of the letters *i, j.* **4.** *Music.* **a.** the symbol (•) placed after a note or rest to increase its time value by half. **b.** this symbol written above or below a note indicating that it must be played or sung staccato. **5.** *Maths., logic.* **a.** the symbol (.) indicating multiplication or logical conjunction. **b.** a decimal point. **6.** the symbol (•) used, in combination with the symbol for *dash* (—), in the written representation of Morse and other telegraphic codes. Compare **dit.** **7. the year dot.** *Informal.* as long ago as can be remembered. **8. on the dot.** at exactly the arranged time. ~*vb.* **dots, dotting, dotted.** **9.** (*tr.*) to mark or form with a dot: *to dot a letter; a dotted crotchet.* **10.** (*tr.*) to scatter or intersperse (with dots or something resembling dots): *bushes dotting the plain.* **11.** (*intr.*) to make a dot or dots. **12. dot one's i's and cross one's t's.** to pay meticulous attention to detail. [Old English *dott* head of a boil; related to Old High German *tutta* nipple, Norwegian *dott,* Dutch *dott* lump] —'**dotter** *n.*

dot² (dɒt) *n. Civil law.* a woman's dowry. [C19: from French, from Latin *dōs;* related to *dōtāre* to endow, *dāre* to give] —**dotal** ('dəʊtᵊl) *adj.*

dotage ('dəʊtɪdʒ) *n.* **1.** feebleness of mind, esp. as a result of old age. **2.** foolish infatuation. [C14: from DOTE + -AGE]

dotard ('dəʊtəd) *n.* a person who is weak-minded, esp. through senility. [C14: from DOTE + -ARD] —'**dotardly** *adj.*

dotation (dəʊ'teɪʃən) *n. Law.* the act of giving a dowry; endowment. [C14: from Latin *dōtātiō,* from *dōtāre* to endow]

dote *or (now rarely)* **doat** (dəʊt) *vb.* (*intr.*) **1.** (foll. by *on* or *upon*) to love to an excessive or foolish degree. **2.** to be foolish or weak-minded, esp. as a result of old age. [C13: related to Middle Dutch *doten* to be silly, Norwegian *dudra* to shake] —'**doter** *or (now rarely)* '**doater** *n.*

doth (dʌθ) *vb. Archaic or dialect.* (used with the pronouns *he, she,* or *it* or with a noun) a singular form of the present tense of **do**¹.

dot-matrix printer *n. Computer technol.* a printer in which each character is produced by a subset of an array of needles at the printhead.

dot product *n.* another name for **scalar product.**

dotted ('dɒtɪd) *adj.* **1.** having dots, esp. a pattern of dots. **2.** *Music.* **a.** (of a note) increased to one and a half times its original time value. See **dot**¹ (sense 4). **b.** (of a musical rhythm) characterized by dotted notes. Compare **double-dotted.** See also **notes inégales.** **3. sign on the dotted line.** to agree formally, esp. by signing one's name on a document.

dotterel *or* **dottrel** ('dɒtrəl) *n.* **1.** a rare Eurasian plover, *Eudromias morinellus,* with reddish-brown underparts and white bands around the head and neck. **2.** *Austral.* any similar and related bird, esp. of the genus *Charadrius.* **3.** *Dialect.* a person who is foolish or easily duped. [C15 *dotrelle;* see DOTE]

dottle *or* **dottel** ('dɒtᵊl) *n.* the plug of tobacco left in a pipe after smoking. [C15: diminutive of *dot* lump; see DOT¹]

dotty ('dɒtɪ) *adj.* **-tier, -tiest.** **1.** *Slang, chiefly Brit.* feeble-minded; slightly crazy. **2.** *Brit. slang.* (foll. by *about*) extremely fond (of) **3.** marked with dots. [C19: from DOT¹: sense development of 1 from meaning of "unsteady on one's feet"] —'**dottily** *adv.* —'**dottiness** *n.*

Douay Bible *or* **Version** ('duːeɪ) *n.* an English translation of the Bible from the Latin Vulgate text completed by Roman Catholic scholars at Douai in N France in 1610.

double ('dʌbᵊl) *adj.* (*usually prenominal*) **1.** as much again in size, strength, number, etc.: *a double portion.* **2.** composed of two equal or similar parts; in a pair; twofold: *a double egg cup.* **3.** designed for two users: *a double room.* **4.** folded in two; composed of two layers: *double paper.* **5.** stooping; bent over. **6.** having two aspects or existing in two different ways; ambiguous: *a double meaning.* **7.** false, deceitful, or hypocritical: *a double life.* **8.** (of flowers) having more than the normal number of petals. **9.** *Maths.* **a.** (of a root) being one of two equal roots of a polynomial equation. **b.** (of an integral) having an integrand containing two independent variables requiring two integrations, in each of which one variable is kept constant. **10.** *Music.* **a.** (of an instrument) sounding an octave lower than the pitch indicated by the notation: *a double bass.* **b.** (of time) duple, usually accompanied by the direction *alla breve.* ~*adv.* **11.** twice over; twofold. **12.** two together; two at a time (esp. in the phrase **see double**). ~*n.* **13.** twice the number, amount, size, etc. **14.** a double measure of spirits, such as whisky or brandy. **15.** a duplicate or counterpart, esp. a person who closely resembles another; understudy. **16.** a wraith or ghostly apparition that is the exact counterpart of a living person; doppelgänger. **17.** a sharp turn, esp. a return on one's own tracks. **18.** an evasive shift or artifice; trick. **19.** an actor who plays two parts in one play. **20.** *Bridge.* a call that increases certain scoring points if the last preceding bid becomes the contract. **21.** *Billiards, etc.* a strike in which the object ball is struck so as to make it rebound against the cushion to an opposite pocket. **22.** a bet on two horses in different races in which any winnings from the horse in the first race are placed on the horse in the later race. **23.** (*often cap.*) *Chiefly R.C. Church.* one of the higher-ranking feasts on which the antiphons are recited both before and after the psalms. **24.** *Music.* an ornamented variation in 16th and 17th century music. **25.** Also called: **double time.** a pace of twice the normal marching speed. **26.** *Tennis.* See **double fault.** **27. a.** the narrow outermost ring on a dartboard. **b.** a hit on this ring. **28.** *Printing.* another word for **doublet** (sense 5). **29. at** *or* **on the double.** **a.** at twice normal marching speed. **b.** quickly or immediately. ~*vb.* **30.** to make or become twice as much. **31.** to bend or fold (material, a bandage, etc.). **32.** (*tr.;* sometimes foll. by *up*) to clench (a fist). **33.** (*tr.;* often foll. by *together* or *up*) to join or couple: *he doubled up the team.* **34.** (*tr.*) to repeat exactly; copy. **35.** (*intr.*) to play two parts or serve two roles. **36.** (*intr.*) to turn sharply; follow a winding course. **37.** *Nautical.* to sail around (a headland or other point). **38.** *Music.* **a.** to duplicate (a voice or instrumental part) either in unison or at the octave above or below it. **b.** (*intr.;* usually foll. by *on*) to be capable of performing (upon an instrument additional to one's normal one): *the third trumpeter doubles on cornet.* **39.** *Bridge.* to make a call that will double certain scoring points if the preceding bid becomes the contract. **40.** *Billiards, etc.* to cause (a ball) to rebound or (of a ball) to rebound from a cushion across or up or down the table. **41.** *Chess.* **a.** to cause two pawns of the same colour to be on the same file. **b.** to place both rooks of the same colour on the same rank or the same file. **42.** (*intr.;* foll. by *for*) to act as substitute (for an actor or actress). **43.** (*intr.*) to go or march at twice the normal speed. ~See also **double back, doubles, double up.** [C13: from Old French, from Latin *duplus* twofold, from *duo* two + *-plus* -FOLD] —'**doubleness** *n.* —'**doubler** *n.*

double-acting *adj.* **1.** (of a reciprocating engine or pump) having a piston or pistons that are pressurized alternately on opposite sides. Compare **single-acting.** **2.** (of a hinge, door, etc.) having complementary actions in opposed directions.

double agent *n.* a spy employed by two mutually antagonistic countries, companies, etc.
double-aspect theory *n. Philosophy.* a monistic theory that holds that mind and body are not distinct substances but merely different aspects of a single substance.
double back *vb.* (*intr., adv.*) to go back in the opposite direction (esp. in the phrase **to double back on one's tracks**).
double-bank *vb. Austral. and N.Z. informal.* to carry a second person on (a horse, bicycle, etc.). Also: **dub.**
double bar *n. Music.* a symbol, consisting of two ordinary bar lines or a single heavy one, that marks the end of a composition or a section within it.
double-barrelled *or U.S.* **double-barreled** *adj.* **1.** (of a gun) having two barrels. **2.** extremely forceful or vehement. **3.** *Brit.* (of surnames) having hyphenated parts. **4.** serving two purposes; ambiguous: *a double-barrelled remark.*
double bass (beɪs) *n.* **1.** Also called (U.S.): **bass viol.** a stringed instrument, the largest and lowest member of the violin family. Range: almost three octaves upwards from E in the space between the fourth and fifth leger lines below the bass staff. It is normally bowed in classical music, but it is very common in a jazz or dance band, where it is practically always played pizzicato. Informal name: **bass fiddle.** ~*adj.* **double-bass. 2.** of or relating to an instrument whose pitch lies below that regarded as the bass; contrabass.
double bassoon *n. Music.* the lowest and largest instrument in the oboe class; contrabassoon.
double bill *n.* a programme or event with two main items.
double bind *n.* a situation of conflict from which there is no escape; unresolvable dilemma.
double-blind *adj.* of or relating to an experiment to discover reactions to certain commodities, drugs, etc., in which neither the experimenters nor the subjects know the particulars of the test items during the experiments. Compare **single-blind.**
double boiler *n.* the U.S. and Canadian name for **double saucepan.**
double bond *n.* a type of chemical bond consisting of two covalent bonds linking two atoms in a molecule.
double-breasted *adj.* (of a garment) having overlapping fronts such as to give a double thickness of cloth.
double bridle *n.* a bridle with four reins coming from a bit with two rings on each side.
double-check *vb.* **1.** to check twice or again; verify. ~*n.* **double check. 2.** a second examination or verification. **3.** *Chess.* a simultaneous check from two pieces brought about by moving one piece to give check and thereby revealing a second check from another piece.
double chin *n.* a fold of fat under the chin. —ˌ**double-ˈchinned** *adj.*
double concerto *n.* a concerto for two solo instruments.
double cream *n.* thick cream with a high fat-content.
double cross *n.* a technique for producing hybrid stock, esp. seed for cereal crops, by crossing the hybrids between two different pairs of inbred lines.
double-cross *vb.* **1.** (*tr.*) to cheat or betray. ~*n.* **2.** the act or an instance of double-crossing; betrayal. —ˈ**double-ˈcrosser** *n.*
double dagger *n.* a character (‡) used in printing to indicate a cross reference, esp. to a footnote. Also called: **diesis, double obelisk.**
double-dealing *n.* **a.** action characterized by treachery or deceit. **b.** (*as modifier*): *double-dealing treachery.* —ˈ**double-ˈdealer** *n.*
double-decker *n.* **1.** *Chiefly Brit.* a bus with two passenger decks. **2.** *Informal, chiefly U.S., Canadian, and N.Z.* **a.** a thing or structure having two decks, layers, etc. **b.** (*as modifier*): *a double-decker sandwich.*
double-declutch *vb.* (*intr.*) *Brit.* to change to a lower gear in a motor vehicle by first placing the gear lever into the neutral position before engaging the desired gear, at the same time releasing the clutch pedal and increasing the engine speed. U.S. term: **double-clutch.**
double decomposition *n.* a chemical reaction between two compounds that results in the interchange of one part of each to form two different compounds, as in $AgNO_3 + KI \rightarrow AgI + KNO_3$. Also called: **metathesis.**
double density *n. Computer technol.* a disk with more than the normal capacity for storage.
double digging *n. Brit.* a method of digging ground in a series of trenches two spits deep, transferring the soil from the bottom spit of one trench to the top spit of the preceding one.
double-dotted *adj. Music.* **1.** (of a note) increased to one and three quarters of its original time value by the addition of two dots. **2.** (of a rhythm) characterized by pairs of notes in which the first one, lengthened by two dots, makes up seven eighths of the time value of the pair.
double drummer *n. Austral. informal.* a type of cicada.
double-dumped *adj. N.Z.* (of a wool bale) compressed, with two bales occupying the volume-equivalent of one ordinary bale.
double Dutch *n. Brit. informal.* incomprehensible talk; gibberish.
double-dyed *adj.* **1.** confirmed; inveterate: *a double-dyed villain.* **2.** dyed twice.
double eagle *n.* a former U.S. gold coin, having a nominal value of 20 dollars.
double-edged *adj.* **1.** acting in two ways; having a dual effect: *a double-edged law.* **2.** (of a remark, argument, etc.) having two possible interpretations, esp. applicable both for and against or being really malicious though apparently innocuous. **3.** (of a sword, knife, etc.) having a cutting edge on either side of the blade.
double entendre (ˈdʌbəl ɑːnˈtɑːndrə, -ˈtɑːnd; *French* dubl ɑ̃tɑ̃drə) *n.* **1.** a word, phrase, etc., that can be interpreted in two ways, esp. one having one meaning that is indelicate. **2.** the type of humour that depends upon such ambiguity. [C17: from obsolete French: double meaning]
double entry *n.* **a.** a book-keeping system in which any commercial transaction is entered as a debit in one account and as a credit in another. Compare **single entry. b.** (*as modifier*): *double-entry book-keeping.*
double exposure *n.* **1.** the act or process of recording two superimposed images on a photographic medium, usually done intentionally to produce a special effect. **2.** the photograph resulting from such an act.
double-faced *adj.* **1.** (of textiles) having a finished nap on each side; reversible. **2.** insincere or deceitful.
double fault *Tennis.* ~*n.* **1.** the serving of two faults in succession, thereby losing a point. ~*vb.* **double-fault. 2.** (*intr.*) to serve a double fault.
double feature *n. Films.* a programme showing two full-length films. Informal name (U.S.): **twin bill.**
double first *n. Brit.* a first-class honours degree in two subjects.
double flat *n.* **1.** *Music.* **a.** an accidental that lowers the pitch of the following note two semitones. Usual symbol: 𝄫 **b.** a note affected by this accidental. ~*adj.* **double-flat. 2.** (*postpositive*) denoting a note of a given letter name lowered in pitch by two semitones.
double glazing *n.* **1.** two panes of glass in a window, fitted to reduce the transmission of heat, sound, etc. **2.** the fitting of glass in such a manner.
double Gloucester *n.* a type of smooth orange-red cheese of mild flavour.
double-header *n.* **1.** a train drawn by two locomotives coupled together to provide extra power. **2.** Also called: **twin bill.** *Sport, U.S. and Canadian.* two games played consecutively by the same teams or by two different teams. **3.** *Austral. and N.Z. informal.* a coin with the impression of a head on each side. **4.** *Austral. informal.* a double ice-cream cone.
double-helical gear *n.* another name for **herringbone gear.**
double helix *n. Biochem.* the form of the molecular structure of DNA, consisting of two helical polynucleotide chains linked by hydrogen bonds and coiled around the same axis.
double-hung *adj.* (of a window) having two vertical sashes, the upper one sliding in grooves outside those of the lower.
double indemnity *n. U.S. and Canadian.* (in life assurance policies) a clause providing for the payment of double the policy's face value in the event of the policyholder's accidental death.
double jeopardy *n. Chiefly U.S.* the act of prosecuting a defendant a second time for an offence for which he has already been tried.
double-jointed *adj.* having unusually flexible joints permitting an abnormal degree of motion of the parts.
double knit *n.* **a.** a knitted material made on two sets of needles that produce a double thickness joined with interlocking stitches. **b.** (*as modifier*): *a double-knit fabric.*
double knitting *n.* **a.** a widely used medium thickness of knitting wool. **b.** (*as modifier*): *double-knitting wool.*
double-minded *adj. Rare.* undecided; vacillating. —ˌ**double-ˈmindedness** *n.*
double negation *n. Logic.* the principle that a statement is equivalent to the denial of its negation, as *it is not the case that John is not here* meaning *John is here.*
double negative *n.* a syntactic construction, often considered ungrammatical in standard Modern English, in which two negatives are used where one is needed, as in *I wouldn't never have believed it.*
▷**Usage.** There are two contexts where double negatives are found. An adjective with negative force is often used with a negative in order to express a nuance of meaning somewhere between the positive and the negative: *he was a not infrequent visitor; it is not an uncommon sight.* Two negatives are also found together where they reinforce each other rather than conflict: *he never went back, not even to collect his belongings.* These two uses of what is technically a double negative are acceptable. A third case, illustrated by *I shouldn't wonder if it didn't rain today,* has the force of a weak positive statement (*I expect it to rain today*) and is common in informal English.
double obelisk *n.* another name for **double dagger.**
double or quits *n.* a game, throw, toss, etc., to decide whether the stake due is to be doubled or cancelled.
double-park *vb.* to park (a car or other vehicle) alongside or directly opposite another already parked by the roadside, thereby causing an obstruction.
double play *n. Baseball.* a play in which two runners are put out.
double pneumonia *n.* pneumonia affecting both lungs.

double printing *n. Photog.* the exposure of the same positive photographic emulsion to two or more negatives, resulting in the superimposition of multiple images after development.
double-quick *adj.* 1. very quick; rapid. ~*adv.* 2. in a very quick or rapid manner.
double-reed *adj.* relating to or denoting a wind instrument in which the sounds are produced by air passing over two reeds that vibrate against each other.
double refraction *n.* the splitting of a ray of unpolarized light into two unequally refracted rays polarized in mutually perpendicular planes. Also called: **birefringence.**
doubles ('dʌbᵊlz) *n.* (*functioning as pl.*) **a.** a game between two pairs of players, as in tennis, badminton, etc. **b.** (*as modifier*): *a doubles player.*
double salt *n.* a solid solution of two simple salts formed by crystallizing a solution of the two salts. Compare **complex salt.**
double saucepan *n. Brit.* a cooking utensil consisting of two saucepans, one fitting inside the other. The bottom saucepan contains water that, while boiling, gently heats food in the upper pan. U.S. and Canadian name: **double boiler.**
double scull *n. Rowing.* a racing shell in which two scullers sit one behind the other and pull two oars each. Compare **pair-oar.**
double sharp *n.* 1. *Music.* **a.** an accidental that raises the pitch of the following note by two semitones. Usual symbol: × **b.** a note affected by this accidental. ~*adj.* 2. (*immediately postpositive*) denoting a note of a given letter name raised in pitch by two semitones.
double-space *vb.* to type (copy) with a full space between lines.
double spread *n. Printing.* two facing pages of a publication treated as a single unit.
double standard *n.* a set of principles that allows greater freedom to one person or group than to another.
double star *n.* two stars, appearing close together when viewed through a telescope; either physically associated (see **binary star**) or not associated (**optical double star**).
double-stop *vb.* **-stops, -stopping, -stopped.** to play (two notes or parts) simultaneously on a violin or related instrument by drawing the bow over two strings.
double-system sound recording *n. Films.* a system in which picture and sound are taken simultaneously and the sound is recorded separately on magnetic tape.
doublet ('dʌblɪt) *n.* 1. (formerly) a man's close-fitting jacket, with or without sleeves (esp. in the phrase **doublet and hose.**) 2. **a.** a pair of similar things, esp. two words deriving ultimately from the same source, for example *reason* and *ratio* or *fragile* and *frail.* **b.** one of such a pair. 3. *Jewellery.* a false gem made by welding a thin layer of a gemstone onto a coloured glass base or by fusing two small stones together to make a larger one. 4. *Physics.* **a.** a multiplet that has two members. **b.** a closely spaced pair of related spectral lines. 5. Also called: **double.** *Printing.* the unintentional repetition of lines, words, or letters when composing. 6. (*pl.*) two dice each showing the same number of spots on one throw. 7. *Physics.* two simple lenses designed to be used together, the optical distortion in one being balanced by that in the other. [C14: from Old French, from DOUBLE]
double tackle *n.* a lifting or pulling tackle in which a rope is passed around the twin pulleys of a pair of pulley blocks in sequence.
double take *n.* (esp. in comedy) a delayed reaction by a person to a remark, situation, etc.
double talk *n.* 1. rapid speech with a mixture of nonsense syllables and real words; gibberish. 2. empty, deceptive, or ambiguous talk, esp. by politicians.
doublethink ('dʌbᵊlˌθɪŋk) *n.* deliberate, perverse, or unconscious acceptance or promulgation of conflicting facts, principles, etc.
double time *n.* 1. a doubled wage rate, paid for working on public holidays, etc. 2. *Music.* **a.** a time twice as fast as an earlier section. **b.** two beats per bar. 3. *U.S. Army.* **a.** a fast march of 180 paces to the minute. **b.** a slow running pace, keeping in step. ~*vb.* **double-time.** 4. to move or cause to move in double time.
doubleton ('dʌbᵊltən) *n. Bridge, etc.* an original holding of two cards only in a suit.
double-tongue *vb.* **-tongues, -tonguing, -tongued.** *Music.* to play (fast staccato passages) on a wind instrument by rapid obstruction and uncovering of the air passage through the lips with the tongue. Compare **single-tongue, triple-tongue.** —**double tonguing** *n.*
double-tongued *adj.* deceitful or hypocritical in speech.
double top *n. Darts.* a score of double 20.
doubletree ('dʌbᵊlˌtriː) *n.* a horizontal pivoted bar on a vehicle to the ends of which swingletrees are attached for harnessing two horses side by side.
double up *vb.* (*adv.*) 1. to bend or cause to bend in two: *he doubled up with the pain.* 2. (*intr.*) to share a room or bed designed for one person, family, etc. 3. (*intr.*) *Brit.* to use the winnings from one bet as the stake for another. U.S. and Canadian term: **parlay.**
doubloon (dʌ'bluːn) *or* **doblón** *n.* 1. a former Spanish gold coin. 2. (*pl.*) *Slang.* money. [C17: from Spanish *doblón,* from DOBLA]
doublure (də'bluə; *French* dublyr) *n.* a decorative lining of vellum or leather, etc., on the inside of a book cover. [C19: from French: lining, from Old French *doubler* to make double]
doubly ('dʌblɪ) *adv.* 1. to or in a double degree, quantity, or measure: *doubly careful.* 2. in two ways: *doubly wrong.*
doubt (daʊt) *n.* 1. uncertainty about the truth, fact, or existence of something (esp. in the phrases **in doubt, without doubt, beyond a shadow of doubt,** etc.). 2. (*often pl.*) lack of belief in or conviction about something: *all his doubts about the project disappeared.* 3. an unresolved difficulty, point, etc. 4. *Philosophy.* the methodical device, esp. in the philosophy of Descartes, of identifying certain knowledge as the residue after rejecting any proposition which might, however improbably, be false. 5. *Obsolete.* fear. 6. **give (someone) the benefit of the doubt.** to presume (someone suspected of guilt) innocent; judge leniently. 7. **no doubt.** almost certainly. ~*vb.* 8. (*tr.; may take a clause as object*) to be inclined to disbelieve: *I doubt we are late.* 9. (*tr.*) to distrust or be suspicious of: *he doubted their motives.* 10. (*intr.*) to feel uncertainty or be undecided. 11. (*tr.; may take a clause as object*) *Scot.* to be inclined to believe. 12. (*tr.*) *Archaic.* to fear. 13. **I wouldn't doubt (someone).** *Irish.* I would expect nothing else from (someone). [C13: from Old French *douter,* from Latin *dubitāre*] —'**doubtable** *adj.* —'**doubtably** *adv.* —'**doubter** *n.* —'**doubtingly** *adv.*
▷**Usage.** Where a clause follows *doubt* in a positive statement, the conjunction may be *whether, that,* or *if.* *Whether* (*I doubt whether he is there*) is universally accepted; *that* (*I doubt that he is there*) is less widely accepted and *if* (*I doubt if he is there*) is usually restricted to informal contexts. In negative statements, *doubt* is followed by *that: I do not doubt that he is telling the truth.* In such sentences, *but* (*I do not doubt but that he is telling the truth*) is redundant.
doubtful ('daʊtfʊl) *adj.* 1. unlikely; improbable. 2. characterized by or causing doubt; uncertain: *a doubtful answer.* 3. unsettled; unresolved. 4. of questionable reputation or morality. 5. having reservations or misgivings. —'**doubtfully** *adv.* —'**doubtfulness** *n.*
doubting Thomas ('tɒməs) *n.* a person who insists on proof before he will believe anything; sceptic. [after *Thomas* (the apostle), who did not believe that Jesus had been resurrected until he had proof]
doubtless ('daʊtlɪs) *adv. also* **doubtlessly.** *sentence substitute or sentence modifier.* 1. certainly. 2. probably. ~*adj.* 3. certain; assured. —'**doubtlessness** *n.*
douc (duːk) *n.* an Old World monkey, *Pygathrix nemaeus,* of SE Asia, with a bright yellow face surrounded by tufts of reddish-brown fur, a white tail, and white hindquarters: one of the langurs. [C18: from French, from the native name]
douce (duːs) *adj. Scot. and northern English dialect.* quiet; sober; sedate. [C14: from Old French, feminine of *dous,* from Latin *dulcis* sweet] —'**doucely** *adv.*
douceur (duː'sɜː; *French* dusœr) *n.* 1. a gratuity, tip, or bribe. 2. sweetness. [C17: from French, from Late Latin *dulcor,* from Latin *dulcis* sweet]
douche (duːʃ) *n.* 1. a stream of water or air directed onto the body surface or into a body cavity, for cleansing or medical purposes. 2. the application of such a stream of water or air. 3. an instrument, such as a special syringe, for applying a douche. ~*vb.* 4. to cleanse or treat or be cleansed or treated by means of a douche. [C18: from French, from Italian *doccia,* pipe; related to Latin *ductus* DUCT]
dough (dəʊ) *n.* 1. a thick mixture of flour or meal and water or milk, used for making bread, pastry, etc. 2. any similar pasty mass. 3. a slang word for **money.** [Old English *dāg;* related to Old Norse *deig,* Gothic *daigs,* Old High German *teig* dough, Sanskrit *degdhi* he daubs; see DAIRY, DUFF[1], LADY]
doughboy ('dəʊˌbɔɪ) *n.* 1. *U.S. informal.* an infantryman, esp. in World War I. 2. dough that is boiled or steamed as a dumpling.
doughnut *or* (*esp. U.S.*) **donut** ('dəʊnʌt) *n.* 1. a small cake of sweetened dough, often ring-shaped or spherical with a jam or cream filling, cooked in hot fat. 2. anything shaped like a ring, such as the reaction vessel of a thermonuclear reactor. ~*vb.* **-nuts, -nutting, -nutted.** 3. (*tr.*) *Informal.* (of Members of Parliament) to surround (a speaker) during the televising of Parliament to give the impression that the chamber is crowded or the speaker is well supported.
doughty ('daʊtɪ) *adj.* **-tier, -tiest.** hardy; resolute. [Old English *dohtig;* related to Old High German *toht* worth, Middle Dutch *duchtich* strong, Greek *tukhē* luck] —'**doughtily** *adv.* —'**doughtiness** *n.*
doughy ('dəʊɪ) *adj.* **doughier, doughiest.** resembling dough in consistency, colour, etc.; soft, pallid, or flabby.
Douglas fir, spruce, *or* **hemlock** ('dʌgləs) *n.* a North American pyramidal coniferous tree, *Pseudotsuga menziesii,* widely planted for ornament and for timber, having needle-like leaves and hanging cones: family *Pinaceae.* Also called: **Oregon fir, Oregon pine.** [C19: named after David *Douglas* (1798–1834), Scottish botanist]
Douglas scale *n.* an international scale of sea disturbance and swell ranging from 0 to 9 with one figure for disturbance and one for swell. [C20: named after Sir Henry *Douglas* (1876–1939), former director of the British Naval Meteorological Service]
douk (dʊk) *n.* a variant spelling of **dook**[1] and **dook**[2].
Doukhobor *or* **Dukhobor** ('duːkəʊˌbɔː) *n.* a member of a Russian sect of Christians that originated in the 18th century. In the late 19th century a large minority emigrated to W Canada, where

most Doukhobors now live. [from Russian *dukhoborcy* spirit wrestler, from *dukh* spirit + *borcy* wrestler]

douma *Russian.* ('du:mə) *n.* a variant spelling of **duma.**

doum palm *or* **doom palm** (du:m) *n.* an Egyptian palm tree, *Hyphaene thebaica,* with a divided trunk and edible apple-sized fruits. [C19 *doum,* via French from Arabic *dawm*]

doun (du:n) *prep., adv., adj.* a variant spelling of **doon.**

do up *vb.* (*adv.; mainly tr.*) **1.** to wrap and make into a bundle: *to do up a parcel.* **2.** to cause the downfall of (a person). **3.** to beautify or adorn. **4.** (*also intr.*) to fasten or be fastened: *this skirt does up at the back.* **5.** *Informal.* to renovate or redecorate. **6.** *Slang.* to assault.

dour (dʊə) *adj.* **1.** sullen. **2.** hard or obstinate. [C14: probably from Latin *dūrus* hard] —'**dourly** *adv.* —'**dourness** *n.*

doura ('dʊərə) *n.* a variant of **durra.**

dourine ('dʊəri:n) *n.* an infectious disease of horses characterized by swollen glands, inflamed genitals, and paralysis of the hindquarters, caused by the protozoan *Trypanosoma equiperdum* contracted during copulation. [C19: from French, from Arabic *darina* to be dirty, scabby]

douroucouli (ˌdu:ru:'ku:lɪ) *n.* a nocturnal omnivorous New World monkey, *Aotus trivirgatus,* of Central and South America, with large eyes, thick fur, and a round head with pale and dark markings. [from a South American Indian name]

douse[1] *or* **dowse** (daʊs) *vb.* **1.** to plunge or be plunged into water or some other liquid; duck. **2.** (*tr.*) to drench with water, esp. in order to wash or clean. **3.** (*tr.*) to put out (a light, candle, etc.). ~*n.* **4.** an immersion. [C16: perhaps related to obsolete *douse* to strike, of obscure origin] —'**douser** *or* '**dowser** *n.*

douse[2] (daʊs) *vb.* (*tr.*) **1.** *Nautical.* to lower (sail) quickly. **2.** *Archaic.* to take off (clothes, esp. a hat). **3.** *Archaic.* to strike or beat. ~*n.* **4.** *Archaic.* a blow. [C16: of uncertain origin; perhaps related to DOUSE[1]]

douzepers ('du:zˌpɛəz) *pl. n. French history.* the 12 great peers of the realm, seen as the symbolic heirs of Emperor Charlemagne's 12 chosen peers. [C13: from Old French *douze pers;* see DOZEN, PEER[1]]

DOVAP ('dəʊˌvæp) *n.* a tracking system for determining the position and velocity of spacecraft, missiles, etc., based on the Doppler effect. [C20: from *Do(ppler) v(elocity) a(nd) p(osition)*]

dove[1] (dʌv) *n.* **1.** any of various birds of the family *Columbidae,* having a heavy body, small head, short legs, and long pointed wings: order *Columbiformes.* They are typically smaller than pigeons. **2.** *Politics.* a person opposed to war. Compare **hawk**[1] (sense 3). **3.** a gentle or innocent person: used as a term of endearment. **4. a.** a greyish-brown colour. **b.** (*as adj.*): *dove walls.* [Old English *dūfe* (unattested except as a feminine proper name); related to Old Saxon *dūbva,* Old High German *tūba*] —'**doveˌlike** *adj.* —'**dovish** *adj.*

dove[2] (dəʊv) *vb. Chiefly U.S.* a past tense of **dive.**

Dove (dʌv) *n. Christianity.* **the.** a manifestation of the Holy Spirit (John 1:32).

dovecote ('dʌvˌkəʊt) *or* **dovecot** ('dʌvˌkɒt) *n.* a structure for housing pigeons, often raised on a pole or set on a wall, containing compartments for the birds to roost and lay eggs.

dovekie *or* **dovekey** ('dʌvkɪ) *n.* another name for the **little auk** (see **auk**). [C19: Scottish diminutive of DOVE[1]]

dove prion *n.* a common petrel, *Pachyptila desolata,* of the southern seas, having a bluish back and white underparts. Also called: **Antarctic prion,** (N.Z. informal) **blue billy.**

Dover's powder ('dəʊvəz) *n.* a preparation of opium and ipecac, formerly used to relieve pain, induce sweating, and check spasms. [C19: named after Thomas *Dover* (1660–1742), English physician]

dovetail ('dʌvˌteɪl) *n.* **1.** a wedge-shaped tenon. **2.** Also called: **dovetail joint.** a joint containing such tenons. ~*vb.* **3.** (*tr.*) to join by means of dovetails. **4.** to fit or cause to fit together closely or neatly: *he dovetailed his arguments to the desired conclusion.*

dovetail saw *n. Building trades.* a saw similar to a tenon saw but of smaller size.

dow (daʊ, dəʊ) *vb.* **dows, dowing, dowed** *or* **dought.** (*intr.*) *Scot. and northern English dialect.* **1.** to be able. **2.** to do well. [Old English *dugan* (unattested) to be worthy; see DOUGHTY]

dowable ('daʊəbᵊl) *adj. Law.* **1.** capable of being endowed. **2.** (of a person, esp. a widow) entitled to dower.

dowager ('daʊədʒə) *n.* **1. a.** a widow possessing property or a title obtained from her husband. **b.** (*as modifier*): *the dowager duchess.* **2.** a wealthy or dignified elderly woman. [C16: from Old French *douagiere,* from *douage* DOWER]

dowdy ('daʊdɪ) *adj.* **-dier, -diest. 1.** (esp. of a woman's dress) drab, unflattering, and old-fashioned. ~*n., pl.* **-dies. 2.** a dowdy woman. [C14: *dowd* slut, of unknown origin] —'**dowdily** *adv.* —'**dowdiness** *n.* —'**dowdyish** *adj.*

dowel ('daʊəl) *n.* a wooden or metal peg that fits into two corresponding holes to join two adjacent parts. Also called: **dowel pin.** [C14: from Middle Low German *dövel* plug, from Old High German *tubili;* related to Greek *thuphos* wedge]

doweling *or* **dowelling** ('daʊlɪŋ, -əlɪŋ) *n. Carpentry, cabinetmaking.* **1.** the joining of two pieces of wood or other material by using dowels. **2.** wood or other material in a long thin rod for cutting up into dowels.

dower ('daʊə) *n.* **1.** the life interest in a part of her husband's estate allotted to a widow by law. **2.** an archaic word for **dowry** (sense 1). **3.** a natural gift or talent. ~*vb.* **4.** (*tr.*) to endow. [C14: from Old French *douaire,* from Medieval Latin *dōtārium,* from Latin *dōs* gift] —'**dowerless** *adj.*

dower house *n.* a house set apart for the use of a widow, often on her deceased husband's estate.

dowie, dowy ('daʊɪ, 'dəʊɪ), *or* **dowly** ('daʊlɪ, 'dəʊlɪ) *adj.* **-wier, -wiest.** *Scot. and northern English dialect.* dull, melancholy, or dismal. [C16: variant of *dolly,* probably from *dol* DULL]

dowitcher ('daʊɪtʃə) *n.* either of two snipelike shore birds, *Limnodromus griseus* or *L. scolopaceus,* of arctic and subarctic North America: family *Scolopacidae* (sandpipers, etc.), order *Charadriiformes.* [C19: of Iroquoian origin]

do with *vb.* **1. could** *or* **can do with.** to find useful; benefit from: *she could do with a good night's sleep.* **2. have to do with.** to be involved in or connected with: *his illness has a lot to do with his failing the exam.* **3. to do with.** concerning; related to. **4. what...do with. a.** to put or place: *what did you do with my coat?* **b.** to handle or treat: *what are we going to do with these hooligans?* **c.** to fill one's time usefully: *she didn't know what to do with herself when the project was finished.*

do without *vb.* (*intr.*) **1.** to forgo; manage without: *I can't do without cigarettes.* **2.** (*prep.*) not to require (uncalled-for comments or advice): *we can do without your criticisms thank you.*

Dow-Jones average ('daʊ'dʒəʊnz) *n. U.S.* a daily index of stock-exchange prices based on the average price of a selected number of securities. [C20: named after Charles H. *Dow* (died 1902) and Edward D. *Jones* (died 1920), American financial statisticians]

down[1] (daʊn) *prep.* **1.** used to indicate movement from a higher to a lower position: *they went down the mountain.* **2.** at a lower or further level or position on, in, or along: *he ran down the street.* ~*adv.* **3.** downwards; at or to a lower level or position: *don't fall down.* **4.** (*particle*) used with many verbs when the result of the verb's action is to lower or destroy its object: *pull down; knock down; bring down.* **5.** (*particle*) used with several verbs to indicate intensity or completion: *calm down.* **6.** immediately: *cash down.* **7.** on paper: *write this down.* **8.** arranged; scheduled: *the meeting is down for next week.* **9.** in a helpless position: *they had him down on the ground.* **10. a.** away from a more important place: *down from London.* **b.** away from a more northerly place: *down from Scotland.* **c.** (of a member of some British universities) away from the university; on vacation. **d.** in a particular part of a country: *down south.* **11.** *Nautical.* (of a helm) having the rudder to windward. **12.** reduced to a state of lack or want: *down to the last pound.* **13.** lacking a specified amount: *at the end of the day the cashier was ten pounds down.* **14.** lower in price: *bacon is down.* **15.** including all intermediate terms, grades, people, etc.: *from managing director down to tea-lady.* **16.** from an earlier to a later time: *the heirloom was handed down.* **17.** to a finer or more concentrated state: *to grind down; boil down.* **18.** *Sport.* being a specified number of points, goals, etc. behind another competitor, team, etc.: *six goals down.* **19.** (of a person) being inactive, owing to illness: *down with flu.* **20.** (*functioning as imperative*) (to dogs): *down Rover!* **21.** (*functioning as imperative*) **down with.** wanting the end of somebody or something: *down with the king!* **22. get down on something.** *Austral. and N.Z.* to procure something, esp. in advance of needs or in anticipation of someone else. ~*adj.* **23.** (*postpositive*) depressed or miserable. **24.** (*prenominal*) of or relating to a train or trains from a more important place or one regarded as higher: *the down line.* **25.** (*postpositive*) (of a device, machine, etc., esp. a computer) temporarily out of action. **26.** made in cash: *a down payment.* ~*vb.* **27.** (*tr.*) to knock, push or pull down. **28.** (*intr.*) to go or come down. **29.** (*tr.*) *Informal.* to drink, esp. quickly: *he downed three gins.* **30.** (*tr.*) to bring (someone) down, esp. by tackling. ~*n.* **31.** *American football.* one of a maximum of four consecutive attempts by one team to advance the ball a total of at least ten yards. **32.** a descent; downward movement. **33.** a lowering or a poor period (esp. in the phrase **ups and downs**). **34. have a down on.** *Informal.* to bear ill will towards (someone or something). [Old English *dūne,* short for *adūne,* variant of *of dūne,* literally: from the hill, from *of,* OFF + *dūn* hill; see DOWN[3]]

down[2] (daʊn) *n.* **1.** the soft fine feathers with free barbs that cover the body of a bird and prevent loss of heat. In the adult they lie beneath and between the contour feathers. **2.** another name for **eiderdown** (sense 1). **3.** *Botany.* a fine coating of soft hairs, as on certain leaves, fruits, and seeds. **4.** any growth or coating of soft fine hair, such as that on the human face. [C14: of Scandinavian origin; related to Old Norse *dūnn*]

down[3] (daʊn) *n. Archaic.* a hill, esp. a sand dune. ~See also **downs** (sense 1). [Old English *dūn;* related to Old Frisian *dūne,* Old Saxon *dūna* hill, Old Irish *dūn* fortress, Greek *this* sandbank; see DUNE, TOWN]

Down (daʊn) *n.* any of various lowland breeds of sheep, typically of stocky build and having dense close wool, originating from various parts of southern England, such as Oxford, Hampshire, etc. See also **Dorset Down.**

down-and-out *adj.* **1.** without any means of livelihood; impoverished and, often, socially outcast. ~*n.* **2.** a person who is destitute and, often, homeless; a social outcast or derelict.

downbeat ('daʊnˌbi:t) *n.* **1.** *Music.* the first beat of a bar or the downward gesture of a conductor's baton indicating this. Com-

pare **upbeat.** ~*adj.* 2. *Informal.* depressed; gloomy. 3. *Informal.* relaxed; unemphatic.
down-bow ('daʊnˌbəʊ) *n.* a downward stroke of the bow from its nut to its tip across a stringed instrument. Compare **up-bow.**
downburst ('daʊnˌbɜːst) *n.* a very high-speed downward movement of turbulent air in a limited area for a short time. Near the ground it spreads out from its centre with high horizontal velocities. Also called: **microburst.**
downcast ('daʊnˌkɑːst) *adj.* 1. dejected. 2. (esp. of the eyes) directed downwards. ~*n.* 3. *Mining.* a ventilation shaft. 4. *Geology.* another word for **downthrow.**
downcome ('daʊnˌkʌm) *n.* 1. *Archaic.* downfall. 2. another name for **downcomer.**
downcomer ('daʊnˌkʌmə) *n.* a pipe that connects a cistern to a W.C., wash basin, etc. Also called: **downcome.**
downdraught ('daʊnˌdrɑːft) *n.* the large-scale downward movement of air in the lee of large objects, mountains, etc.
downer ('daʊnə) *n. Slang.* 1. Also called: **down.** a barbiturate, tranquillizer, or narcotic. Compare **upper.** 2. a depressing experience. 3. a state of depression: *he's on a downer today.*
downfall ('daʊnˌfɔːl) *n.* 1. a sudden loss of position, health, or reputation. 2. a fall of rain, snow, etc., esp. a sudden heavy one. 3. another word for **deadfall.**
downfallen ('daʊnˌfɔːlən) *adj.* 1. (of a building, etc.) decrepit. 2. *Chiefly U.S.* (of a person) ruined; fallen.
downgrade ('daʊnˌgreɪd) *vb.* (*tr.*) 1. to reduce in importance, esteem, or value, esp. to demote (a person) to a poorer job. 2. to speak of disparagingly. ~*n.* 3. *Chiefly U.S. and Canadian.* a downward slope, esp. in a road. 4. **on the downgrade.** waning in importance, popularity, health, etc.
downhaul ('daʊnˌhɔːl) *n. Nautical.* a line for hauling down a sail or for increasing the tension at its luff.
downhearted (ˌdaʊn'hɑːtɪd) *adj.* discouraged; dejected. —ˌ**down'heartedly** *adv.* —ˌ**down'heartedness** *n.*
downhill ('daʊn'hɪl) *adj.* 1. going or sloping down. ~*adv.* 2. towards the bottom of a hill; downwards. 3. **go downhill.** *Informal.* to decline; deteriorate. ~*n.* 4. the downward slope of a hill; descent. 5. a competitive event in which skiers are timed in a downhill run.
downhole ('daʊnˌhəʊl) *adj.* (in the oil industry) denoting any piece of equipment that is used in the well itself.
downhome (ˌdaʊn'həʊm) *adj. Slang, chiefly U.S.* of, relating to, or reminiscent of rural life, esp. in the southern U.S.; unsophisticated; homely.
Downing Street ('daʊnɪŋ) *n. Informal.* the prime minister of Great Britain or the British Government. [after the street in W central London, containing official residences of the prime minister and the chancellor of the exchequer, named after Sir George *Downing* (1623–84), English statesman]
download ('daʊnˌləʊd) *vb.* (*tr.*) 1. to copy or transfer (data or a program) from one computer's memory to that of another, esp. in a network of computers. 2. to broadcast specialist programmes, for such groups as doctors, outside normal broadcasting hours. These programmes are often recorded on video tapes and viewed at leisure.
down-market *adj.* relating to commercial products, services, etc., that are cheap, have little prestige, or are poor in quality.
down payment *n.* the deposit paid on an item purchased on hire-purchase, mortgage, etc.
downpipe ('daʊnˌpaɪp) *n. Brit. and N.Z.* a pipe for carrying rainwater from a roof gutter to the ground or to a drain. Also called: **rainwater pipe, drainpipe.** Usual U.S. and Canadian name: **downspout.**
downplay ('daʊnˌpleɪ) *vb.* (*tr.*) to play down; make little of.
downpour ('daʊnˌpɔː) *n.* a heavy continuous fall of rain.
downrange ('daʊn'reɪndʒ) *adj., adv.* in the direction of the intended flight path of a rocket or missile.
downright ('daʊnˌraɪt) *adj.* 1. frank or straightforward; blunt: *downright speech.* 2. *Archaic.* directed or pointing straight down. ~*adv., adj.* (*prenominal*) 3. (intensifier): *a downright certainty; downright rude.* —'**downˌrightly** *adv.* —'**downˌrightness** *n.*
downs (daʊnz) *pl. n.* 1. Also called: **downland.** rolling upland, esp. in the chalk areas of S Britain, characterized by lack of trees and used mainly as pasture. 2. *Austral. and N.Z.* a flat grassy area, not necessarily of uplands.
downside ('daʊnˌsaɪd) *n.* the disadvantageous aspect of a situation: *the downside of twentieth-century living.*
downspout ('daʊnˌspaʊt) *n.* a U.S. and Canadian name for **downpipe.**
Down's syndrome (daʊnz) *n.* a. *Pathol.* a chromosomal abnormality resulting in a flat face and nose, short stubby fingers, a vertical fold of skin at the inner edge of the eye, and mental retardation. Former name: **mongolism.** b. (*as modifier*): *a Down's syndrome baby.* [C19: after John *Langdon-Down* (1828–96), British physician]
downstage ('daʊn'steɪdʒ) *Theatre.* ~*adv.* 1. at or towards the front of the stage. ~*adj.* 2. of or relating to the front of the stage. ~*n.* 3. the front half of the stage.
downstairs ('daʊn'stɛəz) *adv.* 1. down the stairs; to or on a lower floor. ~*n.* 2. a. a lower or ground floor. b. (*as modifier*): *a downstairs room.* 3. *Brit. informal.* the servants of a household collectively. Compare **upstairs** (sense 6).
downstate ('daʊnˌsteɪt) *U.S.* ~*adj.* 1. in, or relating to the part of the state away from large cities, esp. the southern part. ~*adv.* 2. towards the southern part of a state. ~*n.* 3. the southern part of a state.
downstream ('daʊn'striːm) *adv., adj.* 1. in or towards the lower part of a stream; with the current. 2. (in the oil industry) of or for the refining, distribution, or marketing of oil or its derived products. Compare **upstream** (sense 2).
downswing ('daʊnˌswɪŋ) *n.* 1. Also called: **downturn.** a statistical downward trend in business activity, the death rate, etc. 2. *Golf.* the downward movement or line of a club when striking the ball.
downthrow ('daʊnˌθrəʊ) *n.* 1. the state of throwing down or being thrown down. 2. *Geology.* the sinking of rocks on one side of a fault plane.
downtime *n. Commerce.* time during which a machine or plant is not working because it is incapable of production, as when under repair: the term is sometimes used to include all nonproductive time. Compare **idle time.**
down-to-earth *adj.* sensible; practical; realistic.
downtown ('daʊn'taʊn) *U.S., Canadian, and N.Z.* ~*n.* 1. the central or lower part of a city, esp. the main commercial area. ~*adv.* 2. towards, to, or into this area. ~*adj.* 3. of, relating to, or situated in the downtown area: *downtown Manhattan.* —'**down'towner** *n.*
downtrodden ('daʊnˌtrɒdᵊn) *or* **downtrod** *adj.* 1. subjugated; oppressed. 2. trodden down; trampled.
downturn ('daʊnˌtɜːn) *n.* another term for **downswing** (sense 1).
down under *Informal.* ~*n.* 1. Australia or New Zealand. ~*adv.* 2. in or to Australia or New Zealand.
downward ('daʊnwəd) *adj.* 1. descending from a higher to a lower level, condition, position, etc. 2. descending from a beginning. ~*adv.* 3. a variant of **downwards.** —'**downwardly** *adv.* —'**downwardness** *n.*
downward mobility *n. Sociol.* the movement of an individual, social group, or class to a lower status. Compare **upward mobility.** See also **horizontal mobility, vertical mobility.**
downwards ('daʊnwədz) *or* **downward** *adv.* 1. from a higher to a lower place, level, etc. 2. from an earlier time or source to a later: *from the Tudors downwards.*
downwash ('daʊnˌwɒʃ) *n.* the downward deflection of an airflow, esp. one caused by an aircraft wing.
downwind ('daʊn'wɪnd) *adv., adj.* 1. in the same direction towards which the wind is blowing; with the wind from behind. 2. towards or on the side away from the wind; leeward.
downy ('daʊnɪ) *adj.* **downier, downiest.** 1. covered with soft fine hair or feathers. 2. light, soft, and fluffy. 3. made from or filled with down. 4. resembling downs; undulating. 5. *Brit. slang.* sharp-witted; knowing. —'**downiness** *n.*
downy mildew *n.* 1. a serious plant disease, characterized by yellowish patches on the undersurface of the leaves, caused by the parasitic fungi of the family *Peronosporaceae,* such as *Peronospora destructor:* affects onions, cauliflower, lettuce, etc. 2. any of the fungi causing this disease. ~Compare **powdery mildew.**
dowry ('daʊərɪ) *n., pl.* **-ries.** 1. the money or property brought by a woman to her husband at marriage. 2. (esp. formerly) a gift made by a man to his bride or her parents. 3. *Christianity.* a sum of money required on entering certain orders of nuns. 4. a natural talent or gift. 5. *Obsolete.* a widow's dower. [C14: from Anglo-French *douarie,* from Medieval Latin *dōtārium;* see DOWER]
dowsabel ('duːsəˌbɛl, 'daʊs-) *n.* an obsolete word for **sweetheart.** [C16: from Latin *Dulcibella* feminine given name, from *dulcis* sweet + *bellus* beautiful]
dowse[1] (daʊs) *vb., n.* a variant spelling of **douse**[1]. —'**dowser** *n.*
dowse[2] (daʊz) *vb.* (*intr.*) to search for underground water, minerals, etc., using a divining rod; divine. [C17: of unknown origin] —'**dowser** *n.*
dowsing rod ('daʊzɪŋ) *n.* another name for **divining rod.**
doxastic (dɒks'æstɪk) *adj. Logic.* 1. of or relating to belief. 2. denoting the branch of modal logic that studies the concept of belief. [C18: from Greek *doxastikos* having an opinion, ultimately from *doxazein* to conjecture]
doxographer (ˌdɒks'ɒgrəfə) *n. Rare.* a person who collects the opinions and conjectures of ancient Greek philosophers. [C19: from New Latin *doxographus,* from Greek *doxa* opinion, conjecture + *graphos* writer] —ˌ**doxo'graphic** *adj.* —ˌ**dox'ography** *n.*
doxology (dɒk'sɒlədʒɪ) *n., pl.* **-gies.** a hymn, verse, or form of words in Christian liturgy glorifying God. [C17: from Medieval Latin *doxologia,* from Greek, from *doxologos* uttering praise, from *doxa* praise; see -LOGY] —**doxological** (ˌdɒksə'lɒdʒɪkᵊl) *adj.* —ˌ**doxo'logically** *adv.*
doxy[1] *or* **doxie** ('dɒksɪ) *n., pl.* **doxies.** opinion or doctrine, esp. concerning religious matters. [C18: independent use of *-doxy* as in *orthodoxy, heterodoxy*]
doxy[2] ('dɒksɪ) *n., pl.* **doxies.** *Archaic slang.* a prostitute or mistress. [C16: probably from Middle Flemish *docke* doll; compare Middle Dutch *docke* doll]
doyen ('dɔɪən; *French* dwayɛ̃) *n.* the senior member of a group, profession, or society. [C17: from French, from Late Latin

decānus leader of a group of ten; see DEAN] —**doyenne** (dɔɪˈɛn; *French* dwajɛn) *fem. n.*
doyley (ˈdɔɪlɪ) *n.* a variant spelling of **doily.**
doz. *abbrev. for* dozen.
doze (dəʊz) *vb. (intr.)* **1.** to sleep lightly or intermittently. **2.** (often foll. by *off*) to fall into a light sleep. *~n.* **3.** a short sleep. [C17: probably from Old Norse *dūs* lull; related to Danish *döse* to drowse, Swedish dialect *dusa* slumber] —**ˈdozer** *n.*
dozed (dozd, dəʊzd) *adj. Chiefly Irish.* (of timber or rubber) rotten or decayed. [C18: probably from DOZE]
dozen (ˈdʌzᵊn) *determiner.* **1.** (preceded by *a* or a numeral) **a.** twelve or a group of twelve: *a dozen eggs; two dozen oranges.* **b.** *(as pronoun; functioning as sing. or pl.): give me a dozen; there are at least a dozen who haven't arrived yet.* *~n., pl.* **dozens** *or* **dozen. 2. daily dozen.** *Brit.* regular physical exercises. **3. by the dozen.** in large quantities. **4.** See **baker's dozen. 5. talk nineteen to the dozen.** to talk without stopping. ~See also **dozens.** [C13: from Old French *douzaine,* from *douze* twelve, from Latin *duodecim,* from *duo* two + *decem* ten] —**ˈdozenth** *adj.*
dozens (ˈdʌzᵊnz) *pl. n.* (usually foll. by *of*) *Informal.* a lot: *I've got dozens of things to do.*
dozer (ˈdəʊzə) *n. Brit.* short for **bulldozer.**
dozy (ˈdəʊzɪ) *adj.* **dozier, doziest. 1.** drowsy. **2.** *Brit. informal.* stupid. **3.** *Chiefly U.S., Austral., and N.Z.* (of timber) rotten, soft in the middle. —**ˈdozily** *adv.* —**ˈdoziness** *n.*
DP *abbrev. for:* **1.** data processing. **2.** displaced person.
D/P *Commerce. abbrev. for* documents against presentation.
DPH *abbrev. for* Diploma in Public Health.
DPhil, *or* **DPh** *abbrev. for* Doctor of Philosophy. Also: **PhD.**
dpi *abbrev. for* dots per inch: a measure of the resolution of a typesetting machine, computer screen, etc.
DPM *abbrev. for* Diploma in Psychological Medicine.
DPN *n. Biochem.* diphosphopyridine nucleotide; the former name for **NAD.**
DPNH *n. Biochem.* the reduced form of DPN; the former name for **NADH.**
DPP (in Britain) *abbrev. for* Director of Public Prosecutions.
dpt *abbrev. for* department.
DPW *abbrev. for* Department of Public Works.
dr *abbrev. for:* **1.** debtor. **2.** Also: **dr.** dram. **3.** drawer.
Dr *abbrev. for:* **1.** Doctor. **2.** (in street names) Drive.
DR *abbrev. for* **dry riser.**
dr. *abbrev. for:* **1.** debit. **2.** Also: **dr** dram. **3.** drachma.
drab[1] (dræb) *adj.* **drabber, drabbest. 1.** dull; dingy; shabby. **2.** cheerless; dreary: *a drab evening.* **3.** of the colour drab. *~n.* **4.** a light olive-brown colour. **5.** a fabric of a dull grey or brown colour. [C16: from Old French *drap* cloth, from Late Latin *drappus,* perhaps of Celtic origin] —**ˈdrably** *adv.* —**ˈdrabness** *n.*
drab[2] (dræb) *Archaic.* *~n.* **1.** a slatternly woman. **2.** a whore. *~vb.* **drabs, drabbing, drabbed. 3.** *(intr.)* to consort with prostitutes. [C16: of Celtic origin; compare Scottish Gaelic *drabag*]
drabbet (ˈdræbɪt) *n. Brit.* a yellowish-brown fabric of coarse linen. [C19: see DRAB[1]]
drabble (ˈdræbᵊl) *vb.* to make or become wet or dirty. [C14: from Low German *drabbelen* to paddle in mud; related to DRAB[2]]
dracaena (drəˈsiːnə) *n.* **1.** any tropical liliaceous plant of the genus *Dracaena:* some species are cultivated as house plants for their decorative foliage. See also **dragon tree. 2.** any of several similar plants of the related genus *Cordyline.* [C19: from New Latin, from Latin: she-dragon, from Greek *drakaina,* feminine of *drakōn* DRAGON]
drachm (dræm) *n.* **1.** Also called: **fluid dram.** *Brit.* one eighth of a fluid ounce. **2.** *U.S.* another name for **dram** (sense 2). **3.** another name for **drachma.** [C14: learned variant of DRAM]
drachma (ˈdrækmə) *n., pl.* **-mas** *or* **-mae** (-miː). **1.** the standard monetary unit of Greece, divided into 100 lepta. **2.** *U.S.* another name for **dram** (sense 2). **3.** a silver coin of ancient Greece. **4.** a unit of weight in ancient Greece. [C16: from Latin, from Greek *drakhmē* a handful, from *drassesthai* to seize]
drack *or* **drac** (dræk) *adj. Austral. slang.* (esp. of a woman) unattractive. [perhaps from *Dracula's* daughter]
Draco (ˈdreɪkəʊ) *n., Latin genitive* **Draconis** (dreɪˈkəʊnɪs). a faint extensive constellation twisting around the N celestial pole and lying between Ursa Major and Cepheus. [from Latin, from Greek *drakōn* DRAGON]
draco lizard (ˈdreɪkəʊ) *n.* another name for **flying lizard.**
dracone (ˈdrækəʊn) *n.* a large flexible cylindrical container towed by a ship, used for transporting liquids. [C20: from Latin: DRAGON]
Draconian (dreɪˈkəʊnɪən) *or* **Draconic** (dreɪˈkɒnɪk) *adj. (sometimes not cap.)* **1.** of or relating to Draco, 7th-century B.C. Athenian statesman, or his code of laws that prescribed death for almost every offence. **2.** harsh. —**Draˈconianism** *n.* —**Draˈconically** *adv.*
draconic (dreɪˈkɒnɪk) *adj.* of, like, or relating to a dragon. [C17: from Latin *dracō* DRAGON] —**draˈconically** *adv.*
draff (dræf) *n.* the residue of husks after fermentation of the grain used in brewing, used as a food for cattle. [C13: from Old Norse *draf;* related to Old High German *trebir,* Russian *drob* fragment; see DRIVEL] —**ˈdraffy** *adj.*
draft (drɑːft) *n.* **1.** a plan, sketch, or drawing of something. **2.** a preliminary outline of a book, speech, etc. **3.** another word for **bill of exchange. 4.** a demand or drain on something. **5.** the divergent duct leading from a water turbine to its tailrace. **6.** *U.S.* selection for compulsory military service. **7.** detachment of military personnel from one unit to another. **8.** *Commerce.* an allowance on merchandise sold by weight. **9.** a line or narrow border that is chiselled on the surface of a stone to serve as a guide for levelling it. **10.** *Austral. and N.Z.* a group of livestock separated from the rest of the herd or flock. *~vb. (tr.)* **11.** to draw up an outline or sketch for something: *to draft a speech.* **12.** to prepare a plan or design of. **13.** to detach (military personnel) from one unit to another. **14.** *U.S.* to select for compulsory military service. **15.** to chisel a draft on (stone, etc.). **16.** *Austral. and N.Z.* **a.** to select (cattle or sheep) from a herd or flock. **b.** to select (farm stock) for sale. *~n., vb.* **17.** the usual U.S. spelling of **draught** (senses 1–8, 11). [C16: variant of DRAUGHT] —**ˈdrafter** *n.*
draft board *n. U.S.* a tribunal responsible for the selection of personnel liable for compulsory military service.
draft dodger *n. U.S.* one who evades compulsory military service.
draftee (drɑːfˈtiː) *n. U.S.* a conscript.
draftsman (ˈdrɑːftsmən) *n., pl.* **-men.** the usual U.S. spelling of **draughtsman** (senses 1, 2). —**ˈdraftsmanship** *n.*
drafty (ˈdrɑːftɪ) *adj.* **draftier, draftiest.** the usual U.S. spelling of **draughty.** —**ˈdraftily** *adv.* —**ˈdraftiness** *n.*
drag (dræg) *vb.* **drags, dragging, dragged. 1.** to pull or be pulled with force, esp. along the ground or other surface. **2.** *(tr.;* often foll. by *away* or *from)* to persuade to come away (from something attractive or interesting): *he couldn't drag himself away from the shop.* **3.** to trail or cause to trail on the ground. **4.** *(tr.)* to move (oneself, one's feet, etc.) with effort or difficulty: *he drags himself out of bed at dawn.* **5.** to linger behind. **6.** (often foll. by *on* or *out*) to prolong or be prolonged tediously or unnecessarily: *his talk dragged on for hours.* **7.** *(tr.;* foll. by *out)* to pass (time) in discomfort, poverty, unhappiness, etc.: *he dragged out his few remaining years.* **8.** (when *intr.,* usually foll. by *for*) to search (the bed of a river, canal, etc.) with a dragnet or hook: *they dragged the river for the body.* **9.** *(tr.* foll. by *out* or *from)* to crush (clods) or level (a soil surface) by use of a drag. **10.** (of hounds) to follow (a fox or its trail) to the place where it has been lying. **11.** *(intr.) Slang.* to draw (on a cigarette, pipe, etc.). **12. drag anchor.** (of a vessel) to move away from its mooring because the anchor has failed to hold. **13. drag one's feet** *or* **heels.** *Informal.* to act with deliberate slowness. **14. drag (someone's) name in the mud.** to disgrace or defame (someone). *~n.* **15.** the act of dragging or the state of being dragged. **16.** an implement, such as a dragnet, dredge, etc., used for dragging. **17.** Also called: **drag harrow.** a type of harrow consisting of heavy beams, often with spikes inserted, used to crush clods, level soil, or prepare seedbeds. **18.** a sporting coach with seats inside and out, usually drawn by four horses. **19.** a braking or retarding device, such as a metal piece fitted to the underside of the wheel of a horse-drawn vehicle. **20.** a person or thing that slows up progress. **21.** slow progress or movement. **22.** *Aeronautics.* the resistance to the motion of a body passing through a fluid, esp. through air: applied to an aircraft in flight, it is the component of the resultant aerodynamic force measured parallel to the direction of air flow. **23.** the trail of scent left by a fox or other animal hunted with hounds. **24.** an artificial trail of a strong-smelling substance, sometimes including aniseed, drawn over the ground for hounds to follow. **25.** See **drag hunt. 26.** *Angling.* unnatural movement imparted to a fly, esp. a dry fly, by tension on the angler's line. **27.** *Informal.* a person or thing that is very tedious; bore: *exams are a drag.* **28.** *Slang.* a car. **29.** short for **drag race. 30.** *Slang.* **a.** women's clothes worn by a man, usually by a transvestite (esp. in the phrase **in drag**). **b.** *(as modifier): a drag club; drag show.* **c.** clothes collectively. **31.** *Informal.* a draw on a cigarette, pipe, etc. **32.** *U.S. slang.* influence or persuasive power. **33.** *Chiefly U.S. slang.* a street or road. ~See also **drag down, drag in, drag out of, drag up.** [Old English *dragan* to DRAW; related to Swedish *dragga*]
drag down *vb. (tr., adv.)* to depress or demoralize: *the flu really dragged her down.*
dragée (dræˈʒeɪ) *n.* **1.** a sweet made of a nut, fruit, etc., coated with a hard sugar icing. **2.** a tiny beadlike sweet used for decorating cakes, etc. **3.** a medicinal pill coated with sugar to disguise the taste. [C19: from French; see DREDGE[2]]
draggle (ˈdrægᵊl) *vb.* **1.** to make or become wet or dirty by trailing on the ground; bedraggle. **2.** *(intr.)* to lag; dawdle. [C16: probably frequentative of DRAG]
draggletailed (ˈdrægᵊlˌteɪld) *adj. Archaic.* (esp. of a woman) bedraggled; besmirched.
draggy (ˈdrægɪ) *adj.* **-gier, -giest.** *Slang.* **1.** slow or boring: *a draggy party.* **2.** dull and listless.
draghound (ˈdrægˌhaʊnd) *n.* a hound used to follow an artificial trail of scent in a drag hunt.
drag hunt *n.* **1.** a hunt in which hounds follow an artificial trail of scent. **2.** a club that organizes such hunts. *~vb.* **drag-hunt. 3.** to follow draghounds, esp. on horseback, or cause (draghounds) to follow an artificial trail of scent.
drag in *vb. (tr., adv.)* to introduce or mention (a topic, name, etc.) with slight or no pretext.

dragline (ˈdræɡˌlaɪn) *n.* **1.** another word for **dragrope** (sense 2). **2.** Also called: **dragline crane, dragline excavator.** a power shovel that operates by being dragged by cables at the end of an arm or jib: used for quarrying, opencast mining, etc.

drag link *n.* a link for conveying motion between cranks on parallel shafts that are slightly offset. It is used in cars to connect the steering gear to the steering arm.

dragnet (ˈdræɡˌnɛt) *n.* **1.** a heavy or weighted net used to scour the bottom of a pond, river, etc., as when searching for something. **2.** any system of coordinated efforts by police forces to track down wanted persons.

dragoman (ˈdræɡəʊmən) *n., pl.* **-mans** *or* **-men.** (in some Middle Eastern countries, esp. formerly) a professional interpreter or guide. [C14: from French, from Italian *dragomano,* from Medieval Greek *dragoumanos,* from Arabic *targumān* an interpreter, from Aramaic *tūrgemānā,* of Akkadian origin]

dragon (ˈdræɡən) *n.* **1.** a mythical monster usually represented as breathing fire and having a scaly reptilian body, wings, claws, and a long tail. **2.** *Informal.* a fierce or intractable person, esp. a woman. **3.** any of various very large lizards, esp. the Komodo dragon. **4.** *Archaic.* a large snake. **5.** any of various North American aroid plants, esp. the green dragon. **6.** *Christianity.* a manifestation of Satan or an attendant devil. **7.** a yacht of the International Dragon Class, 8.88m long (29.2 feet), used in racing. **8. chase the dragon.** *Slang.* to smoke opium or heroin. [C13: from Old French, from Latin *dracō,* from Greek *drakōn;* related to *drakos* eye] —ˈ**dragoness** *fem. n.* —ˈ**dragonish** *adj.*

dragonet (ˈdræɡənɪt) *n.* any small spiny-finned fish of the family *Callionymidae,* having a flat head and a slender tapering brightly coloured body and living at the bottom of shallow seas. [C14 (meaning: small dragon): from French; applied to fish C18]

dragonfly (ˈdræɡənˌflaɪ) *n., pl.* **-flies. 1.** any predatory insect of the suborder *Anisoptera,* having a large head and eyes, a long slender body, two pairs of iridescent wings that are outspread at rest, and aquatic larvae: order *Odonata.* See also **damselfly. 2.** any other insect of the order *Odonata.*

dragonhead (ˈdræɡənˌhɛd) *or* **dragon's-head** *n.* **1.** any plant of the genus *Dracocephalum,* of Europe, Asia, and North America, having dense spikes of white or bluish flowers: family *Labiatae* (labiates). **2.** any North American plant of the related genus *Physostegia,* having pink or purplish flowers.

dragonnade (ˌdræɡəˈneɪd) *n.* **1.** *History.* the persecution of French Huguenots during the reign (1643–1715) of Louis XIV by dragoons quartered in their villages and homes. **2.** subjection by military force. ~*vb.* **3.** (*tr.*) to subject to persecution by military troops. [C18: from French, from *dragon* DRAGOON]

dragonroot (ˈdræɡənˌruːt) *n.* **1.** a North American aroid plant, *Arisaema dracontium,* having a greenish spathe and a long pointed spadix. **2.** the tuberous root of this plant, formerly used in medicine.

dragon's blood *n.* **1.** a red resinous substance obtained from the fruit of a Malaysian palm, *Daemonorops* (or *Calamus*) *draco:* formerly used medicinally and now used in varnishes and lacquers. **2.** any of several similar resins obtained from other trees, esp. from the dragon tree.

dragon's teeth *pl. n.* **1.** *Informal.* concrete antitank obstacles protruding from the ground in rows: used in World War II. **2. sow dragon's teeth.** to take some action that is intended to prevent strife or trouble but that actually brings it about. [sense 2 from the story of Cadmus in Greek mythology, who sowed a dragon's teeth from which sprang soldiers who fought each other until few remained]

dragon tree *n.* a liliaceous tree, *Dracaena draco,* of the Canary Islands, having clusters of sword-shaped leaves at the tips of its branches: a source of dragon's blood.

dragoon (drəˈɡuːn) *n.* **1.** (originally) a mounted infantryman armed with a carbine. **2.** (*sometimes cap.*) a domestic fancy pigeon. **3. a.** a type of cavalryman. **b.** (*pl.; cap. when part of a name*)*: the Royal Dragoons.* ~*vb.* (*tr.*) **4.** to coerce; force: *he was dragooned into admitting it.* **5.** to persecute by military force. [C17: from French *dragon* (special use of DRAGON), soldier armed with a carbine, perhaps suggesting that a carbine, like a dragon, breathed forth fire] —**dra**ˈ**goonage** *n.*

drag out of *vb.* (*tr., adv. +prep.*) to obtain or extract (a confession, statement, etc.), esp. by force: *we dragged the name out of him.* Also: **drag from.**

drag race *n.* a type of motor race in which specially built or modified cars or motorcycles are timed over a measured course. —**drag racer** *n.* —**drag racing** *n.*

dragrope (ˈdræɡˌrəʊp) *n.* **1.** a rope used to drag military equipment, esp. artillery. **2.** Also called: **dragline, guide rope.** a rope trailing from a balloon or airship for mooring or braking purposes.

drag sail *n.* another term for **sea anchor.**

dragster (ˈdræɡstə) *n.* a car specially built or modified for drag racing.

drag up *vb.* (*tr., adv.*) *Informal.* **1.** to rear (a child) poorly and in an undisciplined manner. **2.** to introduce or revive (an unpleasant fact or story).

drail (dreɪl) *Angling.* ~*n.* **1.** a weighted hook used in trolling. ~*vb.* **2.** (*intr.*) to fish with a drail. [C16: apparently from TRAIL, influenced by DRAW]

drain (dreɪn) *n.* **1.** a pipe or channel that carries off water, sewage, etc. **2.** an instance or cause of continuous diminution in resources or energy; depletion. **3.** *Surgery.* a device, such as a tube, for insertion into a wound, incision, or bodily cavity to drain off pus, etc. **4.** *Electronics.* the electrode region in a field-effect transistor into which majority carriers flow from the interelectrode conductivity channel. **5. down the drain.** wasted. ~*vb.* **6.** (*tr.;* often foll. by *off*) to draw off or remove (liquid) from: *to drain water from vegetables; to drain vegetables.* **7.** (*intr.;* often foll. by *away*) to flow (away) or filter (off). **8.** (*intr.*) to dry or be emptied as a result of liquid running off or flowing away: *leave the dishes to drain.* **9.** (*tr.*) to drink the entire contents of (a glass, cup, etc.). **10.** (*tr.*) to consume or make constant demands on (resources, energy, etc.); exhaust; sap. **11.** (*intr.*) to disappear or leave, esp. gradually: *the colour drained from his face.* **12.** (*tr.*) (of a river, etc.) to carry off the surface water from (an area). **13.** (*intr.*) (of an area) to discharge its surface water into rivers, streams, etc. [Old English *drēahnian;* related to Old Norse *drangr* dry wood; see DRY] —ˈ**drainable** *adj.* —ˈ**drainer** *n.*

drainage (ˈdreɪnɪdʒ) *n.* **1.** the process or a method of draining. **2.** a system of watercourses or drains. **3.** liquid, sewage, etc., that is drained away.

drainage basin *or* **area** *n.* another name for **catchment area.**

draining board *n.* a sloping grooved surface at the side of a sink, used for draining washed dishes, etc. Also called: **drainer.**

drainpipe (ˈdreɪnˌpaɪp) *n.* a pipe for carrying off rainwater, sewage, etc.; downpipe.

drainpipes (ˈdreɪnˌpaɪps) *pl. n.* trousers with very narrow legs.

drain rod *n.* one of a series of flexible rods with threaded ends that screw together and can be pushed to and fro in a drain to clear a blockage.

drake[1] (dreɪk) *n.* the male of any duck. [C13: perhaps from Low German; compare Middle Dutch *andrake,* Old High German *antrahho*]

drake[2] (dreɪk) *n.* **1.** *Angling.* an artificial fly resembling a mayfly. **2.** *History.* a small cannon. **3.** an obsolete word for **dragon.** [Old English *draca,* ultimately from Latin *dracō* DRAGON]

Dralon (ˈdreɪlɒn) *n. Trademark.* an acrylic fibre fabric used esp. for upholstery.

dram (dræm) *n.* **1.** one sixteenth of an ounce (avoirdupois). 1 dram is equivalent to 0.0018 kilogram. **2.** Also called: **drachm, drachma.** *U.S.* one eighth of an apothecaries' ounce; 60 grains. 1 dram is equivalent to 0.0039 kilogram. **3.** a small amount of an alcoholic drink, esp. a spirit; tot. [C15: from Old French *dragme,* from Late Latin *dragma,* from Greek *drakhmē;* see DRACHMA]

DRAM *or* **D-RAM** (ˈdiːræm) *acronym for* dynamic random access memory: **a.** a widely used type of random access memory. See **RAM**[1]. **b.** a chip containing such a memory.

drama (ˈdrɑːmə) *n.* **1.** a work to be performed by actors on stage, radio, or television; play. **2.** the genre of literature represented by works intended for the stage. **3.** the art of the writing and production of plays. **4.** a situation or sequence of events that is highly emotional, tragic, or turbulent. [C17: from Late Latin: a play, from Greek: something performed, from *drān* to do]

Dramamine (ˈdræməˌmiːn) *n.* a trademark for **dimenhydrinate.**

dramatic (drəˈmætɪk) *adj.* **1.** of or relating to drama. **2.** like a drama in suddenness, emotional impact, etc. **3.** striking; effective. **4.** acting or performed in a flamboyant way. **5.** *Music.* (of a voice) powerful and marked by histrionic quality. —**dra**ˈ**matically** *adv.*

dramatic irony *n. Theatre.* the irony occurring when the implications of a situation, speech, etc., are understood by the audience but not by the characters in the play.

dramatics (drəˈmætɪks) *n.* **1.** (*functioning as sing. or pl.*) **a.** the art of acting or producing plays. **b.** dramatic productions. **2.** (*usually functioning as pl.*) histrionic behaviour.

dramatis personae (ˈdrɑːmətɪs pəˈsəʊnaɪ) *pl. n.* (*often functioning as sing.*) **1.** the characters or a list of characters in a play or story. **2.** the main personalities in any situation or event. [C18: from New Latin]

dramatist (ˈdræmətɪst) *n.* a writer of plays; playwright.

dramatization *or* **dramatisation** (ˌdræmətaɪˈzeɪʃən) *n.* **1.** the reconstruction of an event, novel, story, etc. in a form suitable for dramatic presentation. **2.** the art or act of dramatizing.

dramatize *or* **dramatise** (ˈdræməˌtaɪz) *vb.* **1.** (*tr.*) to put into dramatic form. **2.** to express or represent (something) in a dramatic or exaggerated way: *he dramatizes his illness.* —ˈ**dramaˌtizable** *or* ˈ**dramaˌtisable** *adj.* —ˈ**dramaˌtizer** *or* ˈ**dramaˌtiser** *n.*

dramaturge (ˈdræməˌtɜːdʒ) *n.* **1.** Also called: **dramaturgist.** a dramatist, esp. one associated with a particular company or theatre. **2.** Also called: **dramaturg.** a literary adviser on the staff of a theatre, film corporation, etc., whose responsibilities may include selection and editing of texts, liaison with authors, preparation of printed programmes, and public relations work. [C19: probably from French, from Greek *dramatourgos* playwright, from DRAMA + *ergon* work]

dramaturgy (ˈdræməˌtɜːdʒɪ) *n.* the art and technique of the theatre; dramatics. —ˌ**drama**ˈ**turgic** *or* ˌ**drama**ˈ**turgical** *adj.* —ˌ**drama**ˈ**turgically** *adv.*

Drambuie (dræmˈbjuːɪ) *n. Trademark.* a liqueur based on Scotch whisky and made exclusively in Scotland from a recipe dating from the 18th century.

drank (dræŋk) *vb.* the past tense of **drink.**

drap (dræp) *n., vb.* a Scot. word for **drop.**

drape (dreɪp) *vb.* **1.** (*tr.*) to hang or cover with flexible material or fabric, usually in folds; adorn. **2.** to hang or arrange or be hung or arranged, esp. in folds. **3.** (*tr.*) to place casually and loosely; hang: *she draped her arm over the back of the chair.* ~*n.* **4.** (*often pl.*) a cloth or hanging that covers something in folds; drapery. **5.** the way in which fabric hangs. ~See also **drapes.** [C15: from Old French *draper,* from *drap* piece of cloth; see DRAB[1]] —ˈ**drapable** *or* ˈ**drapeable** *adj.*

draper (ˈdreɪpə) *n.* **1.** *Brit.* a dealer in fabrics and sewing materials. **2.** *Archaic.* a maker of cloth.

drapery (ˈdreɪpərɪ) *n., pl.* **-peries.** **1.** fabric or clothing arranged and draped. **2.** (*often pl.*) curtains or hangings that drape. **3.** *Brit.* the occupation or shop of a draper. **4.** fabrics and cloth collectively. —ˈ**draperied** *adj.*

drapes (dreɪps) *or* **draperies** (ˈdreɪpərɪz) *pl. n. Chiefly U.S. and Canadian.* curtains, esp. ones of heavy fabric.

drappie (ˈdræpɪ) *n. Scot.* a little drop, esp. a small amount of spirits.

drastic (ˈdræstɪk) *adj.* extreme or forceful; severe. [C17: from Greek *drastikos,* from *dran* to do, act] —ˈ**drastically** *adv.*

drat (dræt) *interj. Slang.* an exclamation of annoyance (also in the phrases **drat it! drat you!** etc.). [C19: probably alteration of *God rot*]

dratted (ˈdrætɪd) *adj.* (*prenominal*) *Informal.* wretched; annoying.

draught *or U.S.* **draft** (drɑːft) *n.* **1.** a current of air, esp. one intruding into an enclosed space. **2. a.** the act of pulling a load, as by a vehicle or animal. **b.** (*as modifier*): *a draught horse.* **3.** the load or quantity drawn. **4.** a portion of liquid to be drunk, esp. a dose of medicine. **5.** the act or an instance of drinking; a gulp or swallow. **6.** the act or process of drawing air, smoke, etc., into the lungs. **7.** the amount of air, smoke, etc., inhaled in one breath. **8. a.** beer, wine, etc., stored in bulk, esp. in a cask, as opposed to being bottled. **b.** (*as modifier*): *draught beer.* **c. on draught.** drawn from a cask or keg. **9.** Also called: **draughtsman.** any one of the 12 flat thick discs used by each player in the game of draughts. U.S. and Canadian equivalent: **checker.** **10.** the depth of a loaded vessel in the water, taken from the level of the waterline to the lowest point of the hull. **11. feel the draught.** to be short of money. Usual U.S. spelling **draft.** ~See also **draughts.** [C14: probably from Old Norse *drahtr,* of Germanic origin; related to DRAW] —ˈ**draughter** *or U.S.* ˈ**drafter** *n.*

draughtboard (ˈdrɑːftˌbɔːd) *n.* a square board divided into 64 squares of alternating colours, used for playing draughts or chess.

draughts (drɑːfts) *n.* (*functioning as sing.*) a game for two players using a draughtboard and 12 draughtsmen each. The object is to jump over and capture the opponent's pieces. U.S. and Canadian name: **checkers.** [C14: plural of DRAUGHT (in obsolete sense: a chess move)]

draughtsman *or U.S.* **draftsman** (ˈdrɑːftsmən) *n., pl.* **-men.** **1.** a person who practises or is qualified in mechanical drawing, employed to prepare detailed scale drawings of machinery, buildings, devices, etc. **2.** Also called (*fem.*): ˈ**draughtsˌwoman.** a person skilled in drawing. **3.** *Brit.* any of the 12 flat thick discs used by each player in the game of draughts. U.S. and Canadian equivalent: **checker.** —ˈ**draughtsmanˌship** *or U.S.* ˈ**draftsmanˌship** *n.*

draughty *or U.S.* **drafty** (ˈdrɑːftɪ) *adj.* **draughtier, draughtiest** *or U.S.* **draftier, draftiest.** characterized by or exposed to draughts of air. —ˈ**draughtily** *or U.S.* ˈ**draftily** *adv.* —ˈ**draughtiness** *or U.S.* ˈ**draftiness** *n.*

Dravidian (drəˈvɪdɪən) *n.* **1.** a family of languages spoken in S and central India and Sri Lanka, including Tamil, Malayalam, Telugu, Kannada, and Gondi. **2.** a member of one of the aboriginal races of India, pushed south by the Indo-Europeans and now mixed with them. ~*adj.* **3.** denoting, belonging to, or relating to this family of languages or these peoples.

draw (drɔː) *vb.* **draws, drawing, drew, drawn.** **1.** to cause (a person or thing) to move towards or away by pulling. **2.** to bring, take, or pull (something) out, as from a drawer, holster, etc. **3.** (*tr.*) to extract or pull or take out: *to draw teeth; to draw a card from a pack.* **4.** (*tr.; often foll. by off*) to take (liquid) out of a cask, keg, tank, etc., by means of a tap. **5.** (*intr.*) to move, go, or proceed, esp. in a specified direction: *to draw alongside.* **6.** (*tr.*) to attract or elicit: *to draw a crowd; draw attention.* **7.** (*tr.*) to cause to flow: *to draw blood.* **8.** to depict or sketch (a form, figure, picture, etc.) in lines, as with a pencil or pen, esp. without the use of colour; delineate. **9.** (*tr.*) to make, formulate, or derive: *to draw conclusions, comparisons, parallels.* **10.** (*tr.*) to write (a legal document) in proper form. **11.** (*tr.; sometimes foll. by in*) to suck or take in (air, liquid, etc.): *to draw a breath.* **12.** (*intr.*) to induce or allow a draught to carry off air, smoke, etc.: *the flue draws well.* **13.** (*tr.*) to take or receive from a source: *to draw money from the bank.* **14.** (*tr.*) to earn: *draw interest.* **15.** (*tr.*) *Finance.* to write out (a bill of exchange or promissory note): *to draw a cheque.* **16.** (*tr.*) to choose at random: *to draw lots.* **17.** (*tr.*) to reduce the diameter of (a wire or metal rod) by pulling it through a die. **18.** (*tr.*) to shape (a sheet of metal or glass) by rolling, by pulling it through a die or by stretching. **19.** *Archery.* to bend (a bow) by pulling the string. **20.** to steep (tea) or (of tea) to steep in boiling water. **21.** (*tr.*) to disembowel: *draw a chicken.* **22.** (*tr.*) to cause (pus, blood, etc.) to discharge from an abscess or wound. **23.** (*intr.*) (of two teams, contestants, etc.) to finish a game with an equal number of points, goals, etc.; tie. **24.** (*tr.*) *Bridge, whist.* to keep leading a suit in order to force out (all outstanding cards). **25. draw trumps.** *Bridge, whist.* to play the trump suit until the opponents have none left. **26.** (*tr.*) *Billiards.* to cause (the cue ball) to spin back after a direct impact with another ball by applying backspin when making the stroke. **27.** (*tr.*) to search (a place) in order to find wild animals, game, etc., for hunting. **28.** *Golf.* to drive (the ball) too far to the left. **29.** (*tr.*) *Curling.* to deliver (the stone) gently. **30.** (*tr.*) *Nautical.* (of a vessel) to require (a certain depth) in which to float. **31. draw (a) blank.** to get no results from something. **32. draw and quarter.** to disembowel and dismember (a person) after hanging. **33. draw stumps.** *Cricket.* to close play, as by pulling out the stumps. **34. draw the line (at).** See **line**[1] (sense 51). **35. draw the short straw.** See **short straw.** **36. draw the shot.** *Bowls.* to deliver the bowl in such a way that it approaches the jack. ~*n.* **37.** the act of drawing. **38.** *U.S.* a sum of money advanced to finance anticipated expenses. **39.** an event, occasion, act, etc., that attracts a large audience. **40.** a raffle or lottery. **41.** something taken or chosen at random, as a ticket in a raffle or lottery. **42.** a contest or game ending in a tie. **43.** *U.S. and Canadian.* a small natural drainage way or gully. **44.** a defect found in metal castings due to the contraction of the metal on solidification. ~See also **drawback, draw in, draw off, draw on, draw out, draw up.** [Old English *dragan;* related to Old Norse *draga;* Old Frisian *draga,* Old Saxon *dragan,* Old High German *tragan* to carry] —ˈ**drawable** *adj.*

drawback (ˈdrɔːˌbæk) *n.* **1.** a disadvantage or hindrance. **2.** a refund of customs or excise duty paid on goods that are being exported or used in the production of manufactured exports. ~*vb.* **draw back.** (*intr., adv.;* often foll. by *from*) **3.** to retreat; move backwards. **4.** to turn aside from an undertaking.

drawbar (ˈdrɔːˌbɑː) *n.* a strong metal bar on a tractor, locomotive, etc., bearing a hook or link and pin to attach a trailer, wagon, etc.

drawbridge (ˈdrɔːˌbrɪdʒ) *n.* a bridge that may be raised to prevent access or to enable vessels to pass.

drawee (drɔːˈiː) *n.* the person or organization on which a cheque or other order for payment is drawn.

drawer (ˈdrɔːə) *n.* **1.** a person or thing that draws, esp. a draughtsman. **2.** a person who draws a cheque. **3.** a person who draws up a commercial paper. **4.** *Archaic.* a person who draws beer, etc., in a bar. **5.** (drɔː). a boxlike container in a chest, table, etc., made for sliding in and out.

drawers (drɔːz) *pl. n.* a legged undergarment for either sex, worn below the waist. Also called: **underdrawers.**

draw-gate *n.* the valve that controls a sluice.

draw gear *n. Brit.* an apparatus for coupling railway cars.

draw in *vb.* (*intr., adv.*) **1.** (of hours of daylight) to become shorter. **2.** (of a train) to arrive at a station.

drawing (ˈdrɔːɪŋ) *n.* **1.** a picture or plan made by means of lines on a surface, esp. one made with a pencil or pen without the use of colour. **2.** a sketch, plan, or outline. **3.** the art of making drawings; draughtsmanship.

drawing account *n. U.S.* an account out of which an employee, partner, or salesman may make withdrawals to meet expenses or as advances against expected income.

drawing board *n.* **1.** a smooth flat rectangular board on which paper, canvas, etc., is placed for making drawings. **2. back to the drawing board.** return to an earlier stage in an enterprise because a planned undertaking has failed.

drawing card *n. U.S. and Canadian theatre.* a performer, act, etc., certain to attract a large audience.

drawing pin *n. Brit.* a short tack with a broad smooth head for fastening papers to a drawing board, etc. U.S. and Canadian name: **thumbtack.**

drawing room *n.* **1.** a room where visitors are received and entertained; living room; sitting room. **2.** *Archaic.* a ceremonial or formal reception, esp. at court.

drawknife (ˈdrɔːˌnaɪf) *or* **drawshave** *n., pl.* **-knives** *or* **-shaves.** a woodcutting tool with two handles at right angles to the blade, used to shave wood. U.S. name: **spokeshave.**

drawl (drɔːl) *vb.* **1.** to speak or utter (words) slowly, esp. prolonging the vowel sounds. ~*n.* **2.** the way of speech of someone who drawls. [C16: probably frequentative of DRAW] —ˈ**drawler** *n.* —ˈ**drawling** *adj.* —ˈ**drawly** *adj.*

drawn (drɔːn) *adj.* haggard, tired, or tense in appearance.

drawn butter *n.* melted butter often with seasonings.

drawn work *n.* ornamental needlework done by drawing threads out of the fabric and using the remaining threads to form lacelike patterns. Also called: **drawn-thread work.**

draw off *vb.* (*adv.*) **1.** (*tr.*) to cause (a liquid) to flow from something. **2.** to withdraw (troops).

draw on *vb.* **1.** (*intr., prep.*) to use or exploit (a source, fund, etc.): *to draw on one's experience.* **2.** (*intr., adv.*) to come near: *the time for his interview drew on.* **3.** (*tr., prep.*) to withdraw (money) from (an account). **4.** (*tr., adv.*) to put on (clothes). **5.** (*tr., adv.*)

to lead further; entice or encourage: *the prospect of nearing his goal drew him on.*

draw out *vb. (adv.)* **1.** to extend or cause to be extended: *he drew out his stay.* **2.** *(tr.)* to cause (a person) to talk freely: *she's been quiet all evening—see if you can draw her out.* **3.** *(tr.; foll. by of)* Also: **draw from.** to elicit (information) (from): *he managed to draw out of his son where he had been.* **4.** *(tr.)* to withdraw (money) as from a bank account or a business. **5.** *(intr.)* (of hours of daylight) to become longer. **6.** *(intr.)* (of a train) to leave a station. **7.** *(tr.)* to extend (troops) in line; lead from camp. **8.** *(intr.)* (of troops) to proceed from camp.

drawplate ('drɔːˌpleɪt) *n.* a plate having conical holes through which wire is drawn to reduce its diameter.

drawstring ('drɔːˌstrɪŋ) *n.* **a.** a cord, ribbon, etc., run through a hem around an opening, as on the bottom of a sleeve or at the mouth of a bag, so that when it is pulled tighter, the opening closes. **b.** *(as modifier): a drawstring neckline.*

drawtube ('drɔːˌtjuːb) *n.* a tube, such as one of the component tubes of a telescope, fitting coaxially within another tube through which it can slide.

draw up *vb. (adv.)* **1.** to come or cause to come to a halt. **2.** *(tr.)* **a.** to prepare a draft of (a legal document). **b.** to formulate and write out in appropriate form: *to draw up a contract.* **3.** *(used reflexively)* to straighten oneself. **4.** to form or arrange (a body of soldiers, etc.) in order or formation.

dray[1] (dreɪ) *n.* **1. a.** a low cart without fixed sides, used for carrying heavy loads. **b.** *(in combination): a drayman.* **2.** any other vehicle or sledge used to carry a heavy load. [Old English *drǣge* dragnet; related to Old Norse *draga* load of timber carried on horseback and trailing on the ground; see DRAW]

dray[2] (dreɪ) *n.* a variant spelling of **drey.**

drayhorse ('dreɪˌhɔːs) *n.* a large powerful horse used for drawing a dray.

dread (drɛd) *vb. (tr.)* **1.** to anticipate with apprehension or terror. **2.** to fear greatly. **3.** *Archaic.* to be in awe of. ~*n.* **4.** great fear; horror. **5.** an object of terror. **6.** *Slang.* a Rastafarian. **7.** *Archaic.* deep reverence. ~*adj.* **8.** *Literary.* awesome; awe-inspiring. [Old English *ondrǣdan;* related to Old Saxon *antdrādan,* Old High German *intrātan*]

dreadful ('drɛdfʊl) *adj.* **1.** extremely disagreeable, shocking, or bad: *what a dreadful play.* **2.** (intensifier): *this is a dreadful waste of time.* **3.** causing dread; terrifying. **4.** *Archaic.* inspiring awe. —'**dreadfulness** *n.*

dreadfully ('drɛdfʊlɪ) *adv.* **1.** in a shocking, or disagreeable manner. **2.** (intensifier): *you're dreadfully kind.*

dreadlocks ('drɛdˌlɒks) *pl. n.* hair worn in the Rastafarian style of long matted or tightly curled strands.

dreadnought *or* **dreadnaught** ('drɛdˌnɔːt) *n.* **1.** a battleship armed with heavy guns of uniform calibre. **2.** an overcoat made of heavy cloth. **3.** *Slang.* a heavyweight boxer. **4.** a person who fears nothing.

dream (driːm) *n.* **1. a.** mental activity, usually in the form of an imagined series of events, occurring during certain phases of sleep. **b.** *(as modifier): a dream sequence.* **c.** *(in combination): dreamland.* **2. a.** a sequence of imaginative thoughts indulged in while awake; daydream; fantasy. **b.** *(as modifier): a dream world.* **3.** a person or thing seen or occurring in a dream. **4.** a cherished hope; ambition; aspiration. **5.** a vain hope. **6.** a person or thing that is as pleasant, or seemingly unreal as a dream. **7. go like a dream.** to move, develop, or work very well. ~*vb.* **dreams, dreaming, dreamt** (drɛmt) *or* **dreamed. 8.** *(may take a clause as object)* to undergo or experience (a dream or dreams). **9.** *(intr.)* to indulge in daydreams. **10.** *(intr.)* to suffer delusions; be unrealistic: *you're dreaming if you think you can win.* **11.** (when *intr.,* foll. by *of* or *about*) to have an image (of) or fantasy (about) in or as if in a dream. **12.** *(intr.; foll. by of)* to consider the possibility (of): *I wouldn't dream of troubling you.* ~See also **dream up.** ~*adj.* **13.** too good to be true; ideal: *dream kitchen.* [Old English *drēam* song; related to Old High German *troum,* Old Norse *draumr,* Greek *thrulos* noise] —'**dreamful** *adj.* —'**dreamfully** *adv.* —'**dreaming** *n., adj.* —'**dreamingly** *adv.* —'**dreamless** *adj.* —'**dreamlessly** *adv.* —'**dreamlessness** *n.* —'**dreamˌlike** *adj.*

dreamboat ('driːmˌbəʊt) *n. Old-fashioned slang.* an exceptionally attractive person or thing, esp. a person of the opposite sex.

dreamer ('driːmə) *n.* **1.** a person who dreams habitually. **2.** a person who lives in or escapes to a world of fantasy or illusion; escapist. **3.** *Archaic.* a prophet; visionary.

dreamland ('driːmlænd) *n.* a utopia existing only in dreams or the imagination.

dreamt (drɛmt) *vb.* a past tense and past participle of **dream.**

dream time *n.* **1.** another name for **alcheringa. 2.** *Austral. informal.* any remote period, out of touch with the actualities of the present.

dream up *vb. (tr., adv.)* to invent by ingenuity and imagination: *to dream up an excuse for leaving.*

dreamy ('driːmɪ) *adj.* **dreamier, dreamiest. 1.** vague or impractical. **2.** resembling a dream in quality. **3.** relaxing; gentle: *dreamy music.* **4.** *Informal.* wonderful. **5.** having dreams, esp. daydreams. —'**dreamily** *adv.* —'**dreaminess** *n.*

dreary ('drɪərɪ) *adj.* **drearier, dreariest. 1.** sad or dull; dismal. **2.** wearying; boring. **3.** *Archaic.* miserable. ~Also (literary): **drear.** [Old English *drēorig* gory; related to Old High German *trūreg* sad] —'**drearily** *adv.* —'**dreariness** *n.*

dreck (drɛk) *n. Slang, chiefly U.S.* rubbish; trash. [from Yiddish *drek* filth, dregs] —'**drecky** *adj.*

dredge[1] (drɛdʒ) *n.* **1.** Also called: **dredger.** a machine, in the form of a bucket ladder, grab, or suction device, used to remove material from a riverbed, channel, etc. **2.** another name for **dredger**[1] (sense 1). ~*vb.* **3.** to remove (material) from a riverbed, channel, etc., by means of a dredge. **4.** *(tr.)* to search for (a submerged object) with or as if with a dredge; drag. [C16: perhaps ultimately from Old English *dragan* to DRAW; see DRAG]

dredge[2] (drɛdʒ) *vb.* to sprinkle or coat (food) with flour, sugar, etc. [C16: from Old French *dragie,* perhaps from Latin *tragēmata* spices, from Greek]

dredger[1] ('drɛdʒə) *n.* **1.** Also called: **dredge.** a vessel used for dredging, often bargelike and usually equipped with retractable steel piles that are driven into the bottom for stability. **2.** another name for **dredge**[1] (sense 1).

dredger[2] ('drɛdʒə) *n.* a container with a perforated top for sprinkling flour, sugar, etc.

dredge up *vb. (tr., adv.)* **1.** to bring to notice, esp. with considerable effort and from an obscure, remote, or unlikely source: *to dredge up worthless ideas.* **2.** to raise with or as if with a dredge: *they dredged up the corpse from the lake.*

dree (driː) *Scot., literary.* ~*vb.* **drees, dreeing, dreed. 1.** *(tr.)* to endure. **2. dree one's weird.** to endure one's fate. ~*adj.* **3.** another word for **dreich.** [Old English *drēogan;* related to Old Norse *drȳgja* to perpetrate]

dreg (drɛg) *n.* a small quantity: *not a dreg of pity.* See also **dregs.** [see DREGS]

dreggy ('drɛgɪ) *adj.* **-gier, -giest.** like or full of dregs.

D region *or* **layer** *n.* the lowest region of the ionosphere, extending from a height of about 60 kilometres to about 90 kilometres: contains a low concentration of free electrons and reflects low-frequency radio waves. See also **ionosphere.**

dregs (drɛgz) *pl. n.* **1.** solid particles that tend to settle at the bottom of some liquids, such as wine or coffee. **2.** residue or remains. **3.** *Brit. slang.* a despicable person. [C14 *dreg,* from Old Norse *dregg;* compare Icelandic *dreggjar* dregs, Latin *fracēs* oil dregs]

dreich *or* **dreigh** (driːx) *adj. Scot. dialect.* dreary. [Middle English *dreig, drih* enduring, from Old English *drēog* (unattested); see DREE]

dreikanter ('draɪkæntə) *n.* a pebble, common in desert areas, typically having three curved faces shaped by wind-blown sand. [C20: from German: three-edged thing]

drench (drɛntʃ) *vb. (tr.)* **1.** to make completely wet; soak. **2.** to give liquid medicine to (an animal), esp. by force. ~*n.* **3.** the act or an instance of drenching. **4.** a dose of liquid medicine given to an animal. [Old English *drencan* to cause to drink; related to Old High German *trenken*] —'**drencher** *n.* —'**drenching** *n., adj.*

drepanid ('drɛpənɪd) *n.* any moth of the superfamily *Drepanoidae* (family *Drepanidae*): it comprises the hook-tip moths.

Dresden ('drɛzdᵊn) *n.* **1.** Also called: **Dresden china.** porcelain ware, esp. delicate and elegantly decorative objects and figures of high quality, made at Meissen, near Dresden in SE Germany, since 1710. ~*adj.* **2.** relating to, designating, or made of Dresden china.

dress (drɛs) *vb.* **1.** to put clothes on (oneself or another); attire. **2.** *(intr.)* **a.** to change one's clothes. **b.** to wear formal or evening clothes. **3.** *(tr.)* to provide (someone) with clothing; clothe. **4.** *(tr.)* to arrange merchandise in (a shop window) for effective display. **5.** *(tr.)* to comb out or arrange (the hair) into position. **6.** *(tr.)* to apply protective or therapeutic covering to (a wound, sore, etc.). **7.** *(tr.)* to prepare (food, esp. fowl and fish) for cooking or serving by cleaning, trimming, gutting, etc. **8.** *(tr.)* to put a finish on (the surface of stone, metal, etc.). **9.** *(tr.)* to till and cultivate (land), esp. by applying manure, compost, or fertilizer. **10.** *(tr.)* to prune and trim (trees, bushes, etc.). **11.** *(tr.)* to groom (an animal, esp. a horse). **12.** *(tr.)* to convert (tanned hides) into leather. **13.** *(tr.)* to spay or neuter (an animal). **14.** *Angling.* to tie (a fly). **15.** *Military.* to bring (troops) into line or (of troops) to come into line (esp. in the phrase **dress ranks). 16. dress ship.** *Nautical.* to decorate a vessel by displaying all signal flags on lines run from the bow to the stern over the mast trucks. ~*n.* **17.** a one-piece garment for a woman, consisting of a skirt and bodice. **18.** complete style of clothing; costume: *formal dress; military dress.* **19.** *(modifier)* suitable or required for a formal occasion: *a dress shirt.* **20.** the outer covering or appearance, esp. of living things: *trees in their spring dress of leaves.* ~See also **dress down, dress up.** [C14: from Old French *drecier,* ultimately from Latin *dīrigere* to DIRECT]

dressage ('drɛsɑːʒ) *n* **1.** the method of training a horse to perform manoeuvres in response to the rider's body signals. **2.** the manoeuvres performed by a horse trained in this method. [French: preparation, from Old French *dresser* to prepare; see DRESS]

dress circle *n.* a tier of seats in a theatre or other auditorium, usually the first gallery above the ground floor.

dress coat *n.* a man's formal tailcoat with a cutaway skirt.

dress down *vb. (tr., adv.) Informal.* to reprimand severely or scold (a person).

dresser[1] ('drɛsə) *n.* **1.** a set of shelves, usually also with cupboards or drawers, for storing or displaying dishes, etc. **2.** *U.S.* a chest of drawers for storing clothing in a bedroom or dressing room, often having a mirror on the top. [C14 *dressour,* from Old French *dreceore,* from *drecier* to arrange; see DRESS]
dresser[2] ('drɛsə) *n.* **1.** a person who dresses in a specified way: *a fashionable dresser.* **2.** *Theatre.* a person employed to assist actors in putting on and taking off their costumes. **3.** a tool used for dressing stone or other materials. **4.** *Brit.* a person who assists a surgeon during operations. **5.** *Brit.* See **window-dresser.**
dress form *n.* an adjustable dummy used in dressmaking that can be made to conform to a person's figure.
dressing ('drɛsɪŋ) *n.* **1.** a sauce for food, esp. for salad. **2.** the U.S. and Canadian name for **stuffing** (sense 2). **3.** a covering for a wound, sore, etc. **4.** manure or artificial fertilizer spread on land. **5.** size used for stiffening textiles. **6.** the processes in the conversion of certain rough tanned hides into leather ready for use. ~See also **dressings.**
dressing case *n.* (esp. formerly) a box or case fitted with all the toilet articles necessary for dressing oneself, arranging one's hair, etc.
dressing-down *n. Informal.* a severe scolding or thrashing.
dressing gown *n.* a full robe worn before dressing or for lounging.
dressing room *n.* **1.** *Theatre.* a room backstage for an actor to change clothing and to make up. **2.** any room used for changing clothes, such as one at a sports ground or off a bedroom.
dressings ('drɛsɪŋz) *pl. n.* dressed stonework, mouldings, and carved ornaments used to form quoins, keystones, sills, and similar features.
dressing station *n. Military.* a first-aid post close to a combat area.
dressing table *n.* a piece of bedroom furniture with a mirror and a set of drawers for clothes, cosmetics, etc.
dressmaker ('drɛs,meɪkə) *n.* a person whose occupation is making clothes, esp. for women. —'**dress,making** *n.*
dress parade *n. Military.* a formal parade of sufficient ceremonial importance for the wearing of dress uniform.
dress rehearsal *n.* **1.** the last complete rehearsal of a play or other work, using costumes, scenery, lighting, etc., as for the first night. **2.** any full-scale practice.
dress shield *n.* a fabric pad worn under the armpits or attached to the armhole of a garment to prevent sweat from showing on or staining the clothing.
dress shirt *n.* a man's shirt, usually white, worn as part of formal evening dress, usually having a stiffened or decorative front.
dress suit *n.* a man's evening suit, esp. tails.
dress uniform *n. Military.* formal ceremonial uniform.
dress up *vb. (adv.)* **1.** to attire (oneself or another) in one's best clothes. **2.** to put fancy dress, disguise, etc., on (oneself or another), as in children's games: *let's dress up as ghosts!* **3.** *(tr.)* to improve the appearance or impression of: *it's no good trying to dress up the facts.*
dressy ('drɛsɪ) *adj.* **dressier, dressiest. 1.** (of clothes) elegant. **2.** (of persons) dressing stylishly. **3.** over-elegant. —'**dressily** *adv.* —'**dressiness** *n.*
drew (druː) *vb.* the past tense of **draw.**
drey *or* **dray** (dreɪ) *n.* a squirrel's nest. [C17: of unknown origin]
dribble ('drɪbᵊl) *vb.* **1.** *(usually intr.)* to flow or allow to flow in a thin stream or drops; trickle. **2.** *(intr.)* to allow saliva to trickle from the mouth. **3.** (in soccer, basketball, hockey, etc.) to propel (the ball) by repeatedly tapping it with the hand, foot, or stick. ~*n.* **4.** a small quantity of liquid falling in drops or flowing in a thin stream. **5.** a small quantity or supply. **6.** an act or instance of dribbling. [C16: frequentative of *drib,* variant of DRIP] —'**dribbler** *n.* —'**dribbly** *adj.*
driblet *or* **dribblet** ('drɪblɪt) *n.* a small quantity or amount, as of liquid. [C17: from obsolete *drib* to fall bit by bit + -LET]
dribs and drabs (drɪbz) *pl. n.* small sporadic amounts.
dried (draɪd) *vb.* the past tense and past participle of **dry.**
drier[1] ('draɪə) *adj.* a comparative of **dry.**
drier[2] ('draɪə) *n.* a variant spelling of **dryer**[1].
driest ('draɪɪst) *adj.* a superlative of **dry.**
drift (drɪft) *vb. (mainly intr.)* **1.** *(also tr.)* to be carried along by or as if by currents of air or water or (of a current) to carry (a vessel, etc.) along. **2.** to move aimlessly from place to place or from one activity to another. **3.** to wander or move gradually away from a fixed course or point; stray. **4.** *(also tr.)* (of snow, sand, etc.) to accumulate in heaps or banks or to drive (snow, sand, etc.) into heaps or banks. ~*n.* **5.** something piled up by the wind or current, such as a snowdrift. **6.** tendency, trend, meaning, or purport: *the drift of the argument.* **7.** a state of indecision or inaction. **8.** the extent to which a vessel, aircraft, projectile, etc. is driven off its course by adverse winds, tide, or current. **9.** a general tendency of surface ocean water to flow in the direction of the prevailing winds: *North Atlantic Drift.* **10.** a driving movement, force, or influence; impulse. **11.** a controlled four-wheel skid, used by racing drivers to take bends at high speed. **12.** a loose unstratified deposit of sand, gravel, etc., esp. one transported and deposited by a glacier or ice sheet. **13.** a horizontal passage in a mine that follows the mineral vein. **14.** something, esp. a group of animals, driven along by human or natural agencies: *a drift of cattle.* **15.** Also called: **driftpin.** a tapering steel tool driven into holes to enlarge or align them before bolting or riveting. **16.** an uncontrolled slow change in some operating characteristic of a piece of equipment, esp. an electronic circuit or component. **17.** *Linguistics.* gradual change in a language, esp. in so far as this is influenced by the internal structure of the language rather than by contact with other languages. **18.** *S. African.* a ford. **19.** *Engineering.* a copper or brass bar used as a punch. [C13: from Old Norse: snowdrift; related to Old High German *trift* pasturage] —'**drifty** *adj.*
driftage ('drɪftɪdʒ) *n.* **1.** the act of drifting. **2.** matter carried along or deposited by drifting. **3.** the amount by which an aircraft or vessel has drifted from its intended course.
drift anchor *n.* another term for **sea anchor.**
drifter ('drɪftə) *n.* **1.** a person or thing that drifts. **2.** a person who moves aimlessly from place to place, usually without a regular job. **3.** a boat used for drift-net fishing. **4.** *Nautical.* a large jib of thin material used in light breezes.
drift ice *n.* masses of ice floating in the open sea.
drift net *n.* a large fishing net supported by floats or attached to a drifter that is allowed to drift with the tide or current.
drift transistor *n.* a transistor in which the impurity concentration in the base increases from the collector-base junction to the emitter-base junction, producing a resistivity gradient that greatly increases its high-frequency response.
drift tube *n. Physics.* a hollow cylindrical electrode to which a radio-frequency voltage is applied in a linear accelerator.
driftwood ('drɪft,wʊd) *n.* wood floating on or washed ashore by the sea or other body of water.
drill[1] (drɪl) *n.* **1.** a rotating tool that is inserted into a drilling machine or tool for boring cylindrical holes. **2.** a hand tool, either manually or electrically operated, for drilling holes. **3.** *Military.* **a.** training in procedures or movements, as for ceremonial parades or the use of weapons. **b.** *(as modifier)*: *drill hall.* **4.** strict and often repetitious training or exercises used as a method of teaching. **5.** *Informal.* correct procedure or routine. **6.** a marine gastropod mollusc, *Urosalpinx cinera,* closely related to the whelk, that preys on oysters. ~*vb.* **7.** to pierce, bore, or cut (a hole) in (material) with or as if with a drill: *to drill a hole; to drill metal.* **8.** to instruct or be instructed in military procedures or movements. **9.** *(tr.)* to teach by rigorous exercises or training. **10.** *(tr.) Informal.* to hit (a ball) in a straight line at great speed. **11.** *(tr.) Informal.* to riddle with bullets. [C17: from Middle Dutch *drillen;* related to Old High German *drāen* to turn] —'**drillable** *adj.* —'**driller** *n.*
drill[2] (drɪl) *n.* **1.** a machine for planting seeds in rows or depositing fertilizer. **2.** a small furrow in which seeds are sown. **3.** a row of seeds planted using a drill. ~*vb.* **4.** to plant (seeds) by means of a drill. [C18: of uncertain origin; compare German *Rille* furrow] —'**driller** *n.*
drill[3] (drɪl) *or* **drilling** *n.* a hard-wearing twill-weave cotton cloth, used for uniforms, etc. [C18: variant of German *Drillich,* from Latin *trilīx,* from TRI- + *līcium* thread]
drill[4] (drɪl) *n.* an Old World monkey, *Mandrillus leucophaeus,* of W Africa, related to the mandrill but smaller and less brightly coloured. [C17: from a West African word; compare MANDRILL]
drilling mud *n.* a mixture of clays, water, and chemicals pumped down the drill string while an oil well is being drilled to lubricate the mechanism, carry away rock cuttings, and maintain pressure so that oil or gas does not escape.
drilling platform *n.* a structure, either fixed to the sea bed or mobile, which supports the machinery and equipment (**drilling rig**), together with the stores, required for digging an offshore oil well.
drilling rig *n.* **1.** the full name for **rig** (sense 6). **2.** a mobile drilling platform used for exploratory offshore drilling.
drillmaster ('drɪl,mɑːstə) *n.* **1.** Also called: **drill sergeant.** a military drill instructor. **2.** a person who instructs in a strict manner.
drill press *n.* a machine tool for boring holes, having a fixed stand and work table with facilities for lowering the rotating tool to the workpiece.
drillstock ('drɪl,stɒk) *n.* the part of a machine tool that holds the shank of a drill or bit; chuck.
drill string *or* **pipe** *n.* (in the oil industry) a pipe made of lengths of steel tubing that is attached to the drilling tool and rotates during drilling to form a bore.
drily ('draɪlɪ) *adv.* a variant spelling of **dryly.**
drink (drɪŋk) *vb.* **drinks, drinking, drank** (dræŋk), **drunk** (drʌŋk). **1.** to swallow (a liquid); imbibe. **2.** *(tr.)* to take in or soak up (liquid); absorb: *this plant drinks a lot of water.* **3.** *(tr.;* usually foll. by *in)* to pay close attention (to); be fascinated (by): *he drank in the speaker's every word.* **4.** *(tr.)* to bring (oneself into a certain condition) by consuming alcohol. **5.** *(tr.;* often foll. by *away)* to dispose of or ruin by excessive expenditure on alcohol: *he drank away his fortune.* **6.** *(intr.)* to consume alcohol, esp. to excess. **7.** (when *intr.,* foll. by *to)* to drink (a toast) in celebration, honour, or hope (of). **8. drink (someone) under the table.** to be able to drink more intoxicating beverage than (someone). **9. drink the health of.** to salute or celebrate with a toast. **10. drink with the flies.** *Austral. informal.* to drink alone. ~*n.* **11.** liquid suitable for drinking; any beverage. **12.**

alcohol or its habitual or excessive consumption. **13.** an amount or portion of liquid for drinking; draught. **14. the drink.** *Informal.* the sea. [Old English *drincan;* related to Old Frisian *drinka,* Gothic *drigkan,* Old High German *trinkan*] —**'drinkable** *adj.*

drink-driving *n.* (*modifier*) of or relating to driving a car after drinking alcohol: *drink-driving offences; drink-driving campaign.*

drinker ('drɪŋkə) *n.* **1.** a person who drinks, esp. a person who drinks alcohol habitually. **2.** short for **drinker moth.**

drinker moth *n.* a large yellowish-brown bombycid eggar moth, *Philudoria potatoria,* having a stout hairy body, the larvae of which drink dew and feed on grasses. Also called: **drinker.**

drinking fountain *n.* a device for providing a flow or jet of drinking water, usually in public places.

drinking-up time *n.* (in Britain) a short time allowed for finishing drinks before closing time in a public house.

drinking water *n.* water reserved or suitable for drinking.

drip (drɪp) *vb.* **drips, dripping, dripped. 1.** to fall or let fall in drops. ~*n.* **2.** the formation and falling of drops of liquid. **3.** the sound made by falling drops. **4.** *Architect.* a projection at the front lower edge of a sill or cornice designed to throw water clear of the wall below. **5.** *Informal.* an inane, insipid person. **6.** *Med.* **a.** the usually intravenous drop-by-drop administration of a therapeutic solution, as of salt or sugar. **b.** the solution administered. [Old English *dryppan,* from *dropa* DROP]

drip-dry *adj.* **1.** designating clothing or a fabric that will dry relatively free of creases if hung up when wet. ~*vb.* **-dries, -drying, -dried. 2.** to dry or become dry thus.

drip-feed *n.* **1.** another name for **drip** (sense 6). ~*vb.* (*tr.*) **drip feed. 2.** to administer a solution (to someone) by means of a drip-feed. **3.** *Informal.* to fund (a new company) in stages rather than by injecting a large sum at its inception.

dripping ('drɪpɪŋ) *n.* **1.** the fat that exudes from meat while it is being roasted or fried, used for basting or as shortening, etc. **2.** (*often pl.*) liquid that falls in drops. ~*adv.* **3.** (intensifier): *dripping wet.*

dripping pan *or* **drip pan** *n.* a shallow pan placed under roasting meat to catch the dripping.

drippy ('drɪpɪ) *adj.* **-pier, -piest. 1.** *Informal.* mawkish, insipid, or inane. **2.** tending to drip.

dripstone ('drɪpˌstəʊn) *n.* **1.** the form of calcium carbonate existing in stalactites or stalagmites. **2.** Also called: **label, hood mould.** *Architect.* a drip made of stone.

drisheen (drɪ'ʃiːn) *n. Irish.* a pudding made of sheep's intestines filled with meal and sheep's blood. [C20: from Irish Gaelic *drisín* an animal's intestines]

drive (draɪv) *vb.* **drives, driving, drove** (drəʊv), **driven** ('drɪvᵊn). **1.** to push, propel, or be pushed or propelled. **2.** to control and guide the movement of (a vehicle, draught animal, etc.): *to drive a car.* **3.** (*tr.*) to compel or urge to work or act, esp. excessively. **4.** (*tr.*) to goad or force into a specified attitude or state: *work drove him to despair.* **5.** (*tr.*) to cause (an object) to make or form (a hole, crack, etc.): *his blow drove a hole in the wall.* **6.** to move or cause to move rapidly by striking or throwing with force. **7.** *Sport.* to hit (a ball) very hard and straight, as (in cricket) with the bat swinging more or less vertically. **8.** *Golf.* to strike (the ball) with a driver, as in teeing off. **9.** (*tr.*) **a.** to chase (game) from cover into more open ground. **b.** to search (an area) for game. **10.** to transport or be transported in a driven vehicle. **11.** (*intr.*) to rush or dash violently, esp. against an obstacle or solid object: *the waves drove against the rock.* **12.** (*tr.*) to carry through or transact with vigour (esp. in the phrase **drive a hard bargain**). **13.** (*tr.*) to force (a component) into or out of its location by means of blows or a press. **14.** (*tr.*) *Mining.* to excavate horizontally. **15.** (*tr.*) *N.Z.* to fell (a tree or trees) by the impact of another felled tree. **16. drive home. a.** to cause to penetrate to the fullest extent. **b.** to make clear by special emphasis. ~*n.* **17.** the act of driving. **18.** a trip or journey in a driven vehicle. **19. a.** a road for vehicles, esp. a private road leading to a house. **b.** (*cap. when part of a street name*): *Woodland Drive.* **20.** vigorous or urgent pressure, as in business. **21.** a united effort, esp. directed towards a common goal: *a charity drive.* **22.** *Brit.* a large gathering of persons to play cards, etc. See **beetle drive, whist drive. 23.** energy, ambition, or initiative. **24.** *Psychol.* a motive or interest, such as sex, hunger, or ambition, that actuates an organism to attain a goal. **25.** a sustained and powerful military offensive. **26. a.** the means by which force, torque, motion, or power is transmitted in a mechanism: *fluid drive.* **b.** (*as modifier*): *a drive shaft.* **27.** *Sport.* a hard straight shot or stroke. **28.** a search for and chasing of game towards waiting guns. **29.** *n. Electronics.* the signal applied to the input of an amplifier. [Old English *drīfan;* related to Old Frisian *drīva,* Old Norse *drīfa,* Gothic *dreiban,* Old High German *trīban*] —**'drivable** *or* **'driveable** *adj.* —ˌ**driva'bility** *or* ˌ**drivea'bility** *n.*

drive at *vb.* (*intr., prep.*) *Informal.* to intend or mean: *what are you driving at?*

drive-in *n. Chiefly U.S. and Canadian.* **a.** a cinema designed to be used by patrons seated in their cars. **b.** (*modifier*) a public facility or service designed for use in such a manner: *a drive-in restaurant; a drive-in bank.*

drivel ('drɪvᵊl) *vb.* **-els, -elling, -elled** *or U.S.* **-els, -eling, -eled. 1.** to allow (saliva) to flow from the mouth; dribble. **2.** (*intr.*) to speak foolishly or childishly. **3.** *Archaic.* to flow or trickle: *a wound drivelling blood.* ~*n.* **4.** foolish or senseless talk. **5.** saliva flowing from the mouth; slaver. [Old English *dreflian* to slaver; see DRAFF] —**'driveller** *n.*

driven ('drɪvᵊn) *vb.* the past participle of **drive.**

driver ('draɪvə) *n.* **1.** a person who drives a vehicle. **2. in the driver's seat.** in a position of control. **3.** a person who drives animals. **4.** a mechanical component that exerts a force on another to produce motion. **5.** *Golf.* a club, a No. 1 wood, with a large head and deep face for tee shots. **6.** *Electronics.* a circuit whose output provides the input of another circuit. **7.** *Computer technol.* a computer program that controls a device. —**'driverless** *adj.*

driver ant *n.* any of various tropical African predatory ants of the subfamily *Dorylinae,* which live in temporary nests and travel in vast hordes preying on other animals. See also **army ant.**

drive shaft *n.* another name for **propeller shaft.**

driveway ('draɪvˌweɪ) *n.* a private road for vehicles, often connecting a house or garage with a public road; drive.

driving ('draɪvɪŋ) *adj.* **1.** having or moving with force and violence: *driving rain.* **2.** forceful or energetic. **3.** relating to the controlling of a motor vehicle in motion: *driving test.*

driving chain *n. Engineering.* a roller chain that transmits power from one toothed wheel to another. Also called: **drive chain.**

driving licence *n.* an official document or certificate authorizing a person to drive a motor vehicle.

driving wheel *n.* **1.** a wheel, esp. a gear wheel, that causes other wheels to rotate. **2.** any wheel of a vehicle that transforms torque into a tractive force.

drizzle ('drɪzᵊl) *n.* **1.** very light rain, specifically consisting of droplets less than 0.5 mm in diameter. ~*vb.* **2.** (*intr.*) to rain lightly. **3.** (*tr.*) to moisten with tiny droplets. [Old English *drēosan* to fall; related to Old Saxon *driosan,* Gothic *driusan,* Norwegian *drjōsa*] —**'drizzly** *adj.*

drogue (drəʊg) *n.* **1.** any funnel-like device, esp. one of canvas, used as a sea anchor. **2. a.** a small parachute released behind a jet aircraft to reduce its landing speed. **b.** a small parachute released before a heavier main parachute during the landing of a spacecraft. **3.** a device towed behind an aircraft as a target for firing practice. **4.** a funnel-shaped device on the end of the refuelling hose of a tanker aircraft, to assist stability and the location of the probe of the receiving aircraft. **5.** another name for **windsock.** [C18: probably based ultimately on Old English *dragan* to DRAW]

droit (drɔɪt; *French* drwa) *n., pl.* **droits** (drɔɪts; *French* drwa). a legal or moral right or claim; due. [C15: from French: legal right, from Medieval Latin *dīrēctum* law, from Latin: a straight line; see DIRECT]

droit du seigneur (*French* drwa dy sɛɲœr) *n.* in feudal times, the right of a lord to have sexual intercourse with a vassal's bride on her wedding night. [from French, literally: the right of the lord]

droll (drəʊl) *adj.* amusing in a quaint or odd manner; comical. [C17: from French *drôle* scamp, from Middle Dutch: imp] —**'drollness** *n.* —**'drolly** *adv.*

drollery ('drəʊlərɪ) *n., pl.* **-eries. 1.** humour; comedy. **2.** *Rare.* a droll act, story, or remark.

-drome *n. combining form.* **1.** a course, racecourse: *hippodrome.* **2.** a large place for a special purpose: *aerodrome.* [via Latin from Greek *dromos* race, course]

dromedary ('drʌmədərɪ, -drɪ, 'drɒm-) *n., pl.* **-daries. 1.** a type of Arabian camel bred for racing and riding, having a single hump and long slender legs. **2.** another name for **Arabian camel.** [C14: from Late Latin *dromedārius* (*camēlus*), from Greek *dromas* running]

dromond ('drɒmənd, 'drʌm-) *or* **dromon** ('drɒmən, 'drʌm-) *n.* a large swift sailing vessel of the 12th to 15th centuries. [C13: from Anglo-French *dromund,* ultimately from Late Greek *dromōn* light swift ship, from *dromos* a running]

-dromous *adj. combining form.* moving or running: *anadromous; catadromous.* [via New Latin from Greek *-dromos,* from *dromos* a running]

drone[1] (drəʊn) *n.* **1.** a male bee in a colony of social bees, whose sole function is to mate with the queen. **2.** *Brit.* a person who lives off the work of others. **3.** a pilotless radio-controlled aircraft. [Old English *drān;* related to Old High German *treno* drone, Gothic *drunjus* noise, Greek *tenthrēnē* wasp; see DRONE[2]] —**'dronish** *adj.*

drone[2] (drəʊn) *vb.* **1.** (*intr.*) to make a monotonous low dull sound; buzz or hum. **2.** (when *intr.,* often foll. by *on*) to utter (words) in a monotonous tone, esp. to talk without stopping. ~*n.* **3.** a monotonous low dull sound. **4.** *Music.* **a.** a sustained bass note or chord of unvarying pitch accompanying a melody. **b.** (*as modifier*): *a drone bass.* **5.** *Music.* one of the single-reed pipes in a set of bagpipes, used for accompanying the melody played on the chanter. **6.** a person who speaks in a low monotonous tone. [C16: related to DRONE[1] and Middle Dutch *drōnen,* German *dröhnen*] —**'droning** *adj.* —**'droningly** *adv.*

drongo ('drɒŋgəʊ) *n., pl.* **-gos. 1.** Also called: **drongo shrike.** any insectivorous songbird of the family *Dicruridae,* of the Old World tropics, having a glossy black plumage, a forked tail, and a stout bill. **2.** *Austral. and N.Z. slang.* a slow-witted person. [C19: from Malagasy]

droob (druːb) *n. Austral. slang.* a pathetic person. [C20: of unknown origin]

drook (drʊk) *vb. (tr.) Scot.* a variant spelling of **drouk.**

drookit (ˈdrʊkɪt) *adj. Scot.* a variant spelling of **droukit.**

drool (druːl) *vb.* **1.** *(intr.;* often foll. by *over)* to show excessive enthusiasm (for) or pleasure (in); gloat (over). *~vb., n.* **2.** another word for **drivel** (senses 1, 2, 5). [C19: probably alteration of DRIVEL]

droop (druːp) *vb.* **1.** to sag or allow to sag, as from weakness or exhaustion; hang down; sink. **2.** *(intr.)* to be overcome by weariness; languish; flag. **3.** *(intr.)* to lose courage; become dejected. *~n.* **4.** the act or state of drooping. [C13: from Old Norse *drūpa;* see DROP] —ˈ**drooping** *adj.* —ˈ**droopingly** *adv.* —ˈ**droopy** *adj.* —ˈ**droopily** *adv.* —ˈ**droopiness** *n.*

drop (drɒp) *n.* **1.** a small quantity of liquid that forms or falls in a spherical or pear-shaped mass; globule. **2.** a very small quantity of liquid. **3.** a very small quantity of anything. **4.** something resembling a drop in shape or size, such as a decorative pendant or small sweet. **5.** the act or an instance of falling; descent. **6.** a decrease in amount or value; slump: *a drop in prices.* **7.** the vertical distance that anything may fall. **8.** a steep or sheer incline or slope. **9.** short for **fruit drop. 10.** the act of unloading troops, equipment, or supplies by parachute. **11.** (in cable television) a short spur from a trunk cable that feeds signals to an individual house. **12.** *Theatre.* See **drop curtain. 13.** another word for **trap door** or **gallows. 14.** *Chiefly U.S. and Canadian.* a slot or aperture through which an object can be dropped to fall into a receptacle. **15.** *Nautical.* the midships height of a sail bent to a fixed yard. Compare **hoist** (sense 6a). **16.** *Austral. cricket slang.* a fall of the wicket: *he came in at first drop.* **17.** See **drop shot. 18. a drop in the bucket** (*or* **in the ocean**). an amount very small in relation to what is needed or desired. **19. at the drop of a hat.** without hesitation or delay. **20. have had a drop too much.** to be drunk. **21. have the drop on (someone).** *U.S. and N.Z.* to have the advantage over (someone). *~vb.* **drops, dropping, dropped. 22.** (of liquids) to fall or allow to fall in globules. **23.** to fall or allow to fall vertically. **24.** *(tr.)* to allow to fall by letting go of. **25.** to sink or fall or cause to sink or fall to the ground, as from a blow, wound, shot, weariness, etc. **26.** *(intr.;* foll. by *back, behind,* etc.) to fall, move, or go in a specified manner, direction, etc. **27.** *(intr.;* foll. by *in, by,* etc.) *Informal.* to pay a casual visit (to). **28.** to decrease or cause to decrease in amount or value: *the cost of living never drops.* **29.** to sink or cause to sink to a lower position, as on a scale. **30.** to make or become less in strength, volume, etc. **31.** *(intr.)* to sink or decline in health or condition. **32.** *(intr.;* sometimes foll. by *into)* to pass easily into a state or condition: *to drop into a habit.* **33.** *(intr.)* to move along gently as with a current of water or air. **34.** *(tr.)* to allow to pass casually in conversation: *to drop a hint.* **35.** *(tr.)* to leave out (a word or letter). **36.** *(tr.)* to set down or unload (passengers or goods). **37.** *(tr.)* to send or post: *drop me a line.* **38.** *(tr.)* to discontinue; terminate: *let's drop the matter.* **39.** *(tr.)* to cease to associate or have to do with. **40.** *(tr.) Slang, chiefly U.S.* to cease to employ: *he was dropped from his job.* **41.** *(tr.;* sometimes foll. by *in, off,* etc.) *Informal.* to leave or deposit, esp. at a specified place. **42.** (of animals) to give birth to (offspring). **43.** *Slang, chiefly U.S. and Canadian.* to lose (money), esp. when gambling. **44.** *(tr.)* to lengthen (a hem, etc.). **45.** *(tr.)* to unload (troops, equipment, or supplies) by parachute. **46.** *(tr.) Nautical.* to leave behind; sail out of sight of. **47.** *(tr.) Sport.* to omit (a player) from a team. **48.** *(tr.)* to lose (a score, game, or contest): *the champion dropped his first service game.* **49.** *(tr.) Golf, basketball, etc.* to hit or throw (a ball) into a goal: *he dropped a 30 foot putt.* **50.** *(tr.)* to hit (a ball) with a drop shot. **51. drop astern.** *Nautical.* to fall back to the stern (of another vessel). **52.** *(tr.) Motor-racing slang.* to spin (the car) and (usually) crash out of the race. **53.** *(tr.) Slang.* to swallow (a drug, esp. a barbiturate or LSD). **54. drop dead!** *Slang.* an exclamation of contempt. *~n., vb.* **55.** *Rugby.* short for **drop kick** or **drop-kick.** ~See also **drop away, drop off, dropout, drops.** [Old English *dropian;* related to Old High German *triofan* to DRIP]

drop away *vb. (intr., adv.)* to fall or go away gradually.

drop cannon *n. Billiards.* a shot in which the first object ball joins or gathers with the cue ball and the other object ball, esp. at the top of the table.

drop curtain *n. Theatre.* a curtain that is suspended from the flies and can be raised and lowered onto the stage. Also called: **drop cloth, drop.**

drop forge *n.* **1.** Also called: **drop hammer.** a device for forging metal between two dies, one of which is fixed, the other acting by gravity or by steam or hydraulic pressure. *~vb.* **drop-forge.** *(tr.)* **2.** to forge (metal) into (a component) by the use of a drop forge.

drop goal *n. Rugby.* a goal scored with a drop kick during the run of play.

drop hammer *n.* another name for **drop forge.**

drophead coupé *n. Brit.* a two-door four-seater car with a folding roof and a sloping back.

drop-in centre *n. Social welfare.* (in Britain) a daycentre run by the social services or a charity that clients may attend on an informal basis.

drop kick *n.* **1.** a kick in certain sports such as rugby, in which the ball is dropped and kicked as it bounces from the ground. Compare **punt**[2], **place kick. 2.** a wrestling attack, illegal in amateur wrestling, in which a wrestler leaps in the air and kicks his opponent in the face or body with both feet. *~vb.* **drop-kick. 3.** to kick (a ball, etc.) using a drop kick. **4.** to kick (an opponent in wrestling) by the use of a drop kick.

drop leaf *n.* **a.** a hinged flap on a table that can be raised and supported by a bracket or additional pivoted leg to extend the surface. **b.** *(as modifier): a drop-leaf table.*

droplet (ˈdrɒplɪt) *n.* a tiny drop.

droplight (ˈdrɒpˌlaɪt) *n.* an electric light that may be raised or lowered by means of a pulley or other mechanism.

drop lock *n. Finance.* a variable-rate bank loan used on international markets that is automatically replaced by a fixed-rate long-term bond if the long-term interest rates fall to a specified level; it thus combines the advantages of a bank loan with those of a bond.

drop off *vb. (adv.)* **1.** *(intr.)* to grow smaller or less; decline. **2.** *(tr.)* to allow to alight; set down. **3.** *(intr.) Informal.* to fall asleep. *~n.* **drop-off. 4.** a steep or vertical descent. **5.** a sharp decrease.

dropout (ˈdrɒpˌaʊt) *n.* **1.** a student who fails to complete a school or college course. **2.** a person who rejects conventional society. **3. drop-out.** *Rugby.* a drop kick taken by the defending team to restart play, as after a touchdown. **4. drop-out.** *Electronics.* a momentary loss of signal in a magnetic recording medium as a result of an imperfection in its magnetic coating. *~vb.* **drop out.** *(intr., adv.;* often foll. by *of)* **5.** to abandon or withdraw from (a school, social group, job, etc.).

dropper (ˈdrɒpə) *n.* **1.** a small tube having a rubber bulb at one end for drawing up and dispensing drops of liquid. **2.** a person or thing that drops. **3.** *Angling.* a short length of monofilament by which a fly is attached to the main trace or leader above the tail fly. **4.** *Austral. and N.Z.* a batten attached to the top wire of a fence to keep the wires apart.

droppings (ˈdrɒpɪŋz) *pl. n.* the dung of certain animals, such as rabbits, sheep, and birds.

drops (drɒps) *pl. n.* any liquid medication applied by means of a dropper.

drop scone *n.* a flat spongy cake made by dropping a spoonful of batter on a griddle. Also called: **girdlecake, griddlecake, Scotch pancake,** (Scot.) **pancake.**

drop shipment *n.* a consignment invoiced to a wholesaler or other middleman but sent directly to the retailer by a manufacturer.

drop shot *n.* **1.** *Tennis, squash, etc.* a softly-played return that drops abruptly after clearing the net, intended to give an opponent no chance of reaching the ball and usually achieved by imparting backspin. **2.** a type of shot made by permitting molten metal to percolate through a sieve and then dropping it into a tank of water.

dropsonde (ˈdrɒpsɒnd) *n. Meteorol.* a radiosonde dropped by parachute. [C20: DROP + (RADIO)SONDE]

dropsy (ˈdrɒpsɪ) *n.* **1.** *Pathol.* a condition characterized by an accumulation of watery fluid in the tissues or in a body cavity. **2.** *Slang.* a tip or bribe. [C13: shortened from *ydropesie,* from Latin *hydrōpisis,* from Greek *hudrōps,* from *hudōr* water] —**dropsical** (ˈdrɒpsɪkᵊl) *or* ˈ**dropsied** *adj.* —ˈ**dropsically** *adv.*

drop tank *n.* an external aircraft tank, usually containing fuel, that can be detached and dropped in flight.

dropwort (ˈdrɒpˌwɜːt) *n.* **1.** a Eurasian rosaceous plant, *Filipendula vulgaris,* with finely divided leaves and clusters of white or reddish flowers. See also **meadowsweet** (sense 1). **2. water dropwort.** any of several umbelliferous marsh plants of the genus *Oenanthe,* esp. *O. fistulosa,* with umbrella-shaped clusters of white flowers.

droshky (ˈdrɒʃkɪ) *or* **drosky** (ˈdrɒskɪ) *n., pl.* **-kies.** an open four-wheeled horse-drawn passenger carriage, formerly used in Russia. [C19: from Russian *drozhki,* diminutive of *drogi* a wagon, from *droga* shaft]

drosometer (drɒˈsɒmɪtə) *n.* an instrument that measures the amount of dew deposited. [C19: from Greek *drosos* dew + -METER]

drosophila (drɒˈsɒfɪlə) *n., pl.* **-las** *or* **-lae** (-ˌliː). any small dipterous fly of the genus *Drosophila,* esp. *D. melanogaster,* a species widely used in laboratory genetics studies: family *Drosophilidae.* They feed on plant sap, decaying fruit, etc. Also called: **fruit fly, vinegar fly.** [C19: New Latin, from Greek *drosos* dew, water + *-phila;* see -PHILE]

dross (drɒs) *n.* **1.** the scum formed, usually by oxidation, on the surfaces of molten metals. **2.** worthless matter; waste. [Old English *drōs* dregs; related to Old High German *truosana*] —ˈ**drossy** *adj.* —ˈ**drossiness** *n.*

drought (draʊt) *n.* **1.** a prolonged period of scanty rainfall. **2.** a prolonged shortage. **3.** an archaic or dialect word for **thirst.** Archaic and Scot. form: **drouth** (druːθ). [Old English *drūgoth;* related to Dutch *droogte;* see DRY] —ˈ**droughty** *adj.*

drouk *or* **drook** (drʊk) *vb. (tr.) Scot.* to drench; soak. [C16: of uncertain origin; compare Old Norse *drukna* to be drowned]

droukit *or* **drookit** (ˈdrʊkɪt) *adj. Scot.* drenched; soaked. [from DROUK]

drouthy (ˈdrʊθɪ) *adj. Scot.* thirsty or dry.

drove[1] (drəʊv) *vb.* the past tense of **drive.**

drove[2] (drəʊv) *n.* **1.** a herd of livestock being driven together. **2.** (*often pl.*) a moving crowd of people. **3.** a narrow irrigation channel. **4.** Also called: **drove chisel.** a chisel with a broad edge used for dressing stone. ~*vb.* **5. a.** (*tr.*) to drive (a group of livestock), usually for a considerable distance. **b.** (*intr.*) to be employed as a drover. **6.** to work (a stone surface) with a drove. [Old English *drāf* herd; related to Middle Low German *drēfwech* cattle pasture; see DRIVE, DRIFT]

drover (ˈdrəʊvə) *n.* a person whose occupation is the driving of sheep or cattle, esp. to and from market.

drown (draʊn) *vb.* **1.** to die or kill by immersion in liquid. **2.** (*tr.*) to destroy or get rid of as if by submerging: *he drowned his sorrows in drink.* **3.** (*tr.*) to drench thoroughly; inundate; flood. **4.** (*tr.;* sometimes foll. by *out*) to render (a sound) inaudible by making a loud noise. [C13: probably from Old English *druncnian;* related to Old Norse *drukna* to be drowned] —ˈ**drowner** *n.*

drowse (draʊz) *vb.* **1.** to be or cause to be sleepy, dull, or sluggish. ~*n.* **2.** the state of being drowsy. [C16: probably from Old English *drūsian* to sink; related to *drēosan* to fall]

drowsy (ˈdraʊzɪ) *adj.* **drowsier, drowsiest. 1.** heavy with sleepiness; sleepy. **2.** inducing sleep; soporific. **3.** sluggish or lethargic; dull. —ˈ**drowsily** *adv.* —ˈ**drowsiness** *n.*

drub (drʌb) *vb.* **drubs, drubbing, drubbed.** (*tr.*) **1.** to beat as with a stick; cudgel; club. **2.** to defeat utterly, as in a contest. **3.** to drum or stamp (the feet). **4.** to instil with force or repetition: *the master drubbed Latin into the boys.* ~*n.* **5.** a blow, as from a stick. [C17: probably from Arabic *dáraba* to beat] —ˈ**drubber** *n.*

drudge (drʌdʒ) *n.* **1.** a person, such as a servant, who works hard at wearisome menial tasks. ~*vb.* **2.** (*intr.*) to toil at such tasks. [C16: perhaps from *druggen* to toil] —ˈ**drudger** *n.* —ˈ**drudgingly** *adv.*

drudgery (ˈdrʌdʒərɪ) *n., pl.* **-eries.** hard, menial, and monotonous work.

drug (drʌg) *n.* **1.** any synthetic or natural chemical substance used in the treatment, prevention, or diagnosis of disease. Related adj.: **pharmaceutical. 2.** a chemical substance, esp. a narcotic, taken for the pleasant effects it produces. **3. drug on the market.** a commodity available in excess of the demands of the market. ~*vb.* **drugs, drugging, drugged.** (*tr.*) **4.** to mix a drug with (food, drink, etc.). **5.** to administer a drug to. **6.** to stupefy or poison with or as if with a drug. [C14: from Old French *drogue,* probably of Germanic origin] —ˈ**druggy** *adj.*

drug addict *n.* any person who is abnormally dependent on narcotic drugs. See **addiction.**

drugget (ˈdrʌgɪt) *n.* a coarse fabric used as a protective floor-covering, etc. [C16: from French *droguet* useless fabric, from *drogue* trash]

druggie (ˈdrʌgɪ) *n. Informal.* a drug addict.

druggist (ˈdrʌgɪst) *n.* a U.S. and Canadian term for a **pharmacist.**

drugstore (ˈdrʌgˌstɔː) *n. U.S. and Canadian.* a shop where medical prescriptions are made up and a wide variety of goods and usually light meals are sold.

druid (ˈdruːɪd) *n.* (*sometimes cap.*) **1.** a member of an ancient order of priests in Gaul, Britain, and Ireland in the pre-Christian era. **2.** a member of any of several modern movements attempting to revive druidism. [C16: from Latin *druides* of Gaulish origin; compare Old Irish *druid* wizards] —**druidess** (ˈdruːɪdɪs) *n. fem.* —**druˈidic** *or* **druˈidical** *adj.* —ˈ**druidˌism** *n.*

drum[1] (drʌm) *n.* **1.** *Music.* a percussion instrument sounded by striking a membrane stretched across the opening of a hollow cylinder or hemisphere. **2. beat the drum for.** *Informal.* to attempt to arouse interest in. **3.** the sound produced by a drum or any similar sound. **4.** an object that resembles a drum in shape, such as a large spool or a cylindrical container. **5.** *Architect.* **a.** one of a number of cylindrical blocks of stone used to construct the shaft of a column. **b.** the wall or structure supporting a dome or cupola. **6.** short for **eardrum. 7.** Also called: **drumfish.** any of various North American marine and freshwater sciaenid fishes, such as *Equetus pulcher* (**striped drum**), that utter a drumming sound. **8.** a type of hollow rotor for steam turbines or axial compressors. **9.** *Computer technol.* a rotating cylindrical device on which data may be stored for later retrieval: now mostly superseded by disks. See **disk** (sense 2). **10.** *Archaic.* a drummer. **11.** *Austral. slang.* a brothel. **12. not to run a drum.** *Austral. slang.* (of a racehorse) to fail to perform as tipped. **13. the drum.** *Austral. informal.* the necessary information (esp. in the phrase **give (someone) the drum).** ~*vb.* **drums, drumming, drummed. 14.** to play (music) on or as if on a drum. **15.** to beat or tap (the fingers) rhythmically or regularly. **16.** (*intr.*) (of birds) to produce a rhythmical sound, as by beating the bill against a tree, branch, etc. **17.** (*tr.;* sometimes foll. by *up*) to summon or call by drumming. **18.** (*tr.*) to instil by constant repetition: *to drum an idea into someone's head.* ~See also **drum out, drum up.** [C16: probably from Middle Dutch *tromme,* of imitative origin]

drum[2] (drʌm) *n. Scot., Irish.* a narrow ridge or hill. [C18: from Scottish Gaelic *druim*]

drumbeat (ˈdrʌmˌbiːt) *n.* the sound made by beating a drum.

drum brake *n.* a type of brake used on the wheels of vehicles, consisting of two pivoted shoes that rub against the inside walls of the brake drum when the brake is applied.

drumfire (ˈdrʌmˌfaɪə) *n.* heavy, rapid, and continuous gunfire, the sound of which resembles rapid drumbeats.

drumfish (ˈdrʌmˌfɪʃ) *n., pl.* **-fish** *or* **-fishes.** another name for **drum**[1] (sense 7).

drumhead (ˈdrʌmˌhɛd) *n.* **1.** *Music.* the part of a drum that is actually struck with a stick or the hand. **2.** the head of a capstan, pierced with holes for the capstan bars. **3.** another name for **eardrum.**

drumhead court-martial *n.* a military court convened to hear urgent charges of offences committed in action. [C19: from the use of a drumhead as a table around which the court-martial was held]

drumlin (ˈdrʌmlɪn) *n.* a streamlined mound of glacial drift, rounded or elongated in the direction of the original flow of ice. [C19: from Irish Gaelic *druim* ridge + *-lin* -LING[1]]

drum machine *n.* a synthesizer specially programmed to reproduce the sound of drums and other percussion instruments in variable rhythms and combinations selected by the musician; the resulting beat is produced continually until stopped or changed.

drum major *n.* the noncommissioned officer, usually of warrant officer's rank, who is appointed to command the corps of drums of a military band and who is in command of both the drums and the band when paraded together.

drum majorette *n. Chiefly U.S.* a girl who marches at the head of a procession, twirling a baton.

drummer (ˈdrʌmə) *n.* **1.** a person who plays a drum or set of drums. **2.** *Chiefly U.S.* a salesman, esp. a travelling salesman. **3.** *Austral. and N.Z. slang.* the slowest shearer in a team.

drum out *vb.* (*tr., adv.;* usually foll. by *of*) **a.** to expel from a club, association, etc. **b.** (formerly) to dismiss from military service to the beat of a drum.

drumstick (ˈdrʌmˌstɪk) *n.* **1.** a stick used for playing a drum. **2.** the lower joint of the leg of a cooked fowl.

drum up *vb.* (*tr., adv.*) to evoke or obtain (support, business, etc.) by solicitation or canvassing.

drunk (drʌŋk) *adj.* **1.** intoxicated with alcohol to the extent of losing control over normal physical and mental functions. **2.** overwhelmed by strong influence or emotion: *drunk with power.* ~*n.* **3.** a person who is drunk or drinks habitually to excess. **4.** *Informal.* a drinking bout.

drunkard (ˈdrʌŋkəd) *n.* a person who is frequently or habitually drunk.

drunken (ˈdrʌŋkən) *adj.* **1.** intoxicated with or as if with alcohol. **2.** frequently or habitually drunk. **3.** (*prenominal*) caused by or relating to alcoholic intoxication: *a drunken brawl.* —ˈ**drunkenly** *adv.* —ˈ**drunkenness** *n.*

drunkometer (drʌŋˈkɒmɪtə) *n.* the usual U.S. name for **Breathalyzer.**

drupe (druːp) *n.* an indehiscent fruit consisting of outer epicarp, fleshy or fibrous mesocarp, and stony endocarp enclosing a single seed. It occurs in the peach, plum, and cherry. [C18: from Latin *druppa* wrinkled overripe olive, from Greek: olive] —**drupaceous** (druːˈpeɪʃəs) *adj.*

drupelet (ˈdruːplɪt) *or* **drupel** (ˈdruːpᵊl) *n.* a small drupe, usually one of a number forming a compound fruit.

druse (druːz) *n.* **1.** an aggregate of small crystals within a cavity, esp. those lining a cavity in a rock or mineral. **2.** *Botany.* a globular mass of calcium oxalate crystals formed around an organic core, found in some plant cells. [C19: from German, from Old High German *druos* bump]

Druse *or* **Druze** (druːz) *n.* a member of a religious sect in Syria, Lebanon, and Israel, having certain characteristics in common with the Muslims. [C18: from Arabic *Durūz* the Druses, after *Ismail al-Darazi* Ismail the tailor, 11th-century Muslim leader who founded the sect] —ˈ**Drusean,** ˈ**Drusian** *or* ˈ**Druzean,** ˈ**Druzian** *adj.*

dry (draɪ) *adj.* **drier, driest** *or* **dryer, dryest. 1.** lacking moisture; not damp or wet. **2.** having little or no rainfall. **3.** not in or under water: *dry land.* **4.** having the water drained away or evaporated: *a dry river.* **5.** not providing milk: *a dry cow.* **6.** (of the eyes) free from tears. **7. a.** *Informal.* in need of a drink; thirsty. **b.** causing thirst: *dry work.* **8.** eaten without butter, jam, etc.: *dry toast.* **9.** (of a wine, cider, etc.) not sweet. **10.** *Pathol.* not accompanied by or producing a mucous or watery discharge: *a dry cough.* **11.** consisting of solid as opposed to liquid substances or commodities. **12.** without adornment; plain: *dry facts.* **13.** lacking interest or stimulation: *a dry book.* **14.** lacking warmth or emotion; cold: *a dry greeting.* **15.** (of wit or humour) shrewd and keen in an impersonal, sarcastic, or laconic way. **16.** opposed to or prohibiting the sale of alcoholic liquor for human consumption: *a dry area.* **17.** *N.Z.* (of a ewe) without a lamb after the mating season. **18.** *Electronics.* (of a soldered electrical joint) imperfect because the solder has not adhered to the metal, thus reducing conductance. ~*vb.* **dries, drying, dried. 19.** (when *intr.,* often foll. by *off*) to make or become dry or free from moisture. **20.** (*tr.*) to preserve (meat, vegetables, fruit, etc.) by removing the moisture. ~*n., pl.* **drys** *or* **dries. 21.** *Brit. informal.* a Conservative politician who is considered to be a hard-liner. Compare **wet** (sense 10). **22. the dry.** *Austral. informal.* the dry season. **23.** *U.S. and Canadian.* an informal word for **prohibitionist.** ~See also **dry out, dry**

up. [Old English *drȳge*; related to Old High German *truckan*, Old Norse *draugr* dry wood] —ˈ**dryable** *adj.* —ˈ**dryness** *n.*

dryad (ˈdraɪəd, -æd) *n., pl.* **-ads** *or* **-ades** (-əˌdiːz). *Greek myth.* a nymph or divinity of the woods. [C14: from Latin *Dryas*, from Greek *Druas*, from *drus* tree] —**dryadic** (draɪˈædɪk) *adj.*

dry battery *n.* an electric battery consisting of two or more dry cells.

dry-blowing *n. Austral.* **1.** *Mining.* the use of the wind for separating gold from ore. **2.** *Informal.* any tedious activity.

dry-bone ore *n.* a mining term for **smithsonite.**

dry-bulb thermometer *n.* an ordinary thermometer used alongside a wet-bulb thermometer to obtain relative humidity. See also **psychrometer.**

dry cell *n.* a primary cell in which the electrolyte is in the form of a paste or is treated in some way to prevent it from spilling. Compare **wet cell.**

dry-clean *vb. (tr.)* to clean (clothing, fabrics, etc.) with a solvent other than water, such as trichloroethylene. —ˌ**dry-**ˈ**cleaner** *n.* —ˌ**dry-**ˈ**cleaning** *n.*

dry distillation *n.* another name for **destructive distillation.**

dry dock *n.* **1.** a basin-like structure that is large enough to admit a ship and that can be pumped dry for work on the ship's bottom. ~*vb.* **dry-dock.** **2.** to put (a ship) into a dry dock, or (of a ship) to go into a dry dock.

dryer[1] (ˈdraɪə) *n.* **1.** a person or thing that dries. **2.** an apparatus for removing moisture by forced draught, heating, or centrifuging. **3.** any of certain chemicals added to oils such as linseed oil in order to accelerate their drying when used as bases in paints, etc.

dryer[2] (ˈdraɪə) *adj.* a variant spelling of **drier**[1].

dry farming *n.* a system of growing crops in arid or semiarid regions without artificial irrigation, by reducing evaporation and by special methods of tillage. —**dry farmer** *n.*

dry fly *n. Angling.* **a.** an artificial fly designed and prepared to be floated or skimmed on the surface of the water. **b.** (*as modifier*): *dry-fly fishing.* ~Compare **wet fly.**

dry hole *n.* (in the oil industry) a well that is drilled but does not produce oil or gas in commercially worthwhile amounts.

dry ice *n.* solid carbon dioxide, which sublimes at −78.5°C: used as a refrigerant. Also called: **carbon dioxide snow.**

drying (ˈdraɪɪŋ) *n.* **1.** the action or process of making or becoming dry. **2.** Also called (not now in technical usage): **seasoning.** the processing of timber until it has a moisture content suitable for the purposes for which it is to be used. ~*adj.* **3.** causing dryness: *a drying wind.*

drying oil *n.* one of a number of animal or vegetable oils, such as linseed oil, that harden by oxidation on exposure to air: used as a base for some paints and varnishes.

dry kiln *n.* an oven in which cut timber is dried and seasoned.

dry law *n. Chiefly U.S.* a law prohibiting the sale of alcoholic beverages.

dryly *or* **drily** (ˈdraɪlɪ) *adv.* in a dry manner.

dry martini *n.* a cocktail of between four and ten parts gin to one part dry vermouth.

dry measure *n.* a unit or a system of units for measuring dry goods, such as fruit, grains, etc.

dry nurse *n.* **1.** a nurse who cares for a child without suckling it. Compare **wet nurse.** ~*vb.* **dry-nurse.** **2.** to care for (a baby or young child) without suckling.

dryopithecine (ˌdraɪəʊˈpɪθəˌsiːn) *n.* any extinct Old World ape of the genus *Dryopithecus*, common in Miocene and Pliocene times: thought to be the ancestors of modern apes. [C20: from New Latin *Dryopithēcus*, from Greek *drus* tree + *pithēkos* ape]

dry out *vb. (adv.)* **1.** to make or become dry. **2.** to undergo or cause to undergo treatment for alcoholism or drug addiction.

dry point *n.* **1.** a technique of intaglio engraving with a hard steel needle, without acid, on a copper plate. **2.** the sharp steel needle used in this process. **3.** an engraving or print produced by this method.

dry riser *n.* a vertical pipe, not containing water, having connections on different floors of a building for a fireman's hose to be attached. A fire tender can be connected at the lowest level of the pipe to make water rise under pressure within the pipe. Abbrev.: **DR.**

dry rot *n.* **1.** crumbling and drying of timber, bulbs, potatoes, or fruit, caused by saprophytic basidiomycetous fungi. **2.** any fungus causing this decay, esp. of the genus *Merulius.* **3.** moral degeneration or corrupt practices, esp. when previously unsuspected.

dry run *n.* **1.** *Military.* practice in weapon firing without live ammunition. **2.** *Informal.* a trial or practice, esp. in simulated conditions; rehearsal.

dry-salt *vb.* to preserve (food) by treating with salt and removing moisture.

drysalter (ˈdraɪˌsɔːltə) *n. Obsolete.* a dealer in certain chemical products, such as dyestuffs and gums, and in dried, tinned, or salted foods and edible oils.

Drysdale (ˈdraɪzdeɪl) *n.* a New Zealand breed of sheep with hair growing among its wool: bred for its coat which is used in making carpets.

dry steam *n.* steam that does not contain droplets of water.

dry-stone *adj.* (of a wall) made without mortar.

dry up *vb. (adv.)* **1.** *(intr.)* to become barren or unproductive; fail: *in middle age his inspiration dried up.* **2.** to dry (dishes, cutlery, etc.) with a tea towel after they have been washed. **3.** *(intr.) Informal.* to stop talking or speaking: *when I got on the stage I just dried up; dry up!*

dry valley *n.* a valley originally produced by running water but now waterless.

DS *or* **ds** *Music. abbrev. for* dal segno.

DSc *abbrev. for* Doctor of Science.

DSC *Military. abbrev. for* Distinguished Service Cross.

DSIR (in New Zealand) *abbrev. for* Department of Scientific and Industrial Research.

DSM *Military. abbrev. for* Distinguished Service Medal.

DSO *Brit. military. abbrev. for* Distinguished Service Order.

dsp *abbrev. for* decessit sine prole. [Latin: died without issue]

DSS (in Britain) *abbrev. for*: **1.** Director of Social Services. **2.** Department of Social Security.

DST *abbrev. for* Daylight Saving Time.

DSW (in New Zealand) *abbrev. for* Department of Social Welfare.

DTI (in Britain) *abbrev. for* Department of Trade and Industry.

DTL *Electronics. abbrev. for* diode transistor logic: a stage in the development of electronic logic circuits.

DTP *abbrev. for* desktop publishing.

DT's *Informal. abbrev. for* delirium tremens.

Du. *abbrev. for:* **1.** Duke. **2.** Dutch.

duad (ˈdjuːæd) *n.* a rare word for **pair.** [C17: from Greek *duas* two, a pair]

dual (ˈdjuːəl) *adj.* **1.** relating to or denoting two. **2.** twofold; double. **3.** (in the grammar of Old English, Ancient Greek, and certain other languages) denoting a form of a word indicating that exactly two referents are being referred to. **4.** *Maths, logic.* (of structures or expressions) having the property that the interchange of certain pairs of terms, and usually the distribution of negation, yields equivalent structures or expressions. ~*n.* **5.** *Grammar.* **a.** the dual number. **b.** a dual form of a word. [C17: from Latin *duālis* concerning two, from *duo* two] —ˈ**dually** *adv.*

Duala (duˈɑːlə, -lɑː) *n.* **1.** (*pl.* **-la** *or* **-las**) a member of a Negroid people of W Africa living chiefly in Cameroon. **2.** the language of this people, belonging to the Bantu group of the Niger-Congo family.

dual carriageway *n. Brit.* a road on which traffic travelling in opposite directions is separated by a central strip of turf, etc. U.S. and Canadian name: **divided highway.**

dualism (ˈdjuːəˌlɪzəm) *n.* **1.** the state of being twofold or double. **2.** *Philosophy.* the doctrine, as opposed to idealism and materialism, that reality consists of two basic types of substance usually taken to be mind and matter or two basic types of entity, mental and physical. Compare **monism.** **3. a.** the theory that the universe has been ruled from its origins by two conflicting powers, one good and one evil, both existing as equally ultimate first causes. **b.** the theory that there are two personalities, one human and one divine, in Christ. —ˈ**dualist** *n.* —**dual**ˈ**istic** *adj.* —ˌ**dual**ˈ**istically** *adv.*

duality (djuːˈælɪtɪ) *n., pl.* **-ties.** **1.** the state or quality of being two or in two parts; dichotomy. **2.** *Physics.* the principle that in microphysics wave theory and corpuscular theory are complementary. The propagation of electromagnetic radiation is analysed using wave theory but its interaction with matter is described in terms of photons. The condition of particles such as electrons, neutrons, and atoms is described in terms of de Broglie waves. **3.** *Geometry.* the interchangeability of the roles of the point and the plane in statements and theorems in projective geometry.

dual-purpose *adj.* having or serving two functions.

dub[1] (dʌb) *vb.* **dubs, dubbing, dubbed.** **1.** *(tr.)* to invest (a person) with knighthood by the ritual of tapping on the shoulder with a sword. **2.** *(tr.)* to invest with a title, name, or nickname. **3.** *(tr.)* to dress (leather) by rubbing. **4.** *Angling.* to dress (a fly). ~*n.* **5.** the sound of a drum. [Old English *dubbian*; related to Old Norse *dubba* to dub a knight, Old High German *tubili* plug, peg]

dub[2] (dʌb) *vb.* **dubs, dubbing, dubbed.** *Films, television.* **1.** to alter the soundtrack of (an old recording, film, etc.). **2.** *(tr.)* to substitute for the soundtrack of (a film) a new soundtrack, esp. in a different language. **3.** *(tr.)* to provide (a film or tape) with a soundtrack. **4.** *(tr.)* to alter (a taped soundtrack) by removing some parts and exaggerating others. ~*n.* **5.** *Films.* the new sounds added. **6. a.** *Music.* a style of record production associated with reggae, involving the removal or exaggeration of instrumental parts, extensive use of echo, etc. **b.** (*as modifier*): *a dub mix.* [C20: shortened from DOUBLE]

dub[3] (dʌb) *vb.* **dubs, dubbing, dubbed.** *Austral. and N.Z. informal.* short for **double-bank.**

dub[4] (dʌb) *U.S. and Canadian informal.* ~*n.* **1.** a clumsy or awkward person or player. ~*vb.* **dubs, dubbing, dubbed.** **2.** to bungle (a shot), as in golf. [C19: of uncertain origin]

dub[5] (dʌb) *n. Scot. and northern English dialect.* a pool of water; puddle. [C16: Scottish dialect *dubbe*; related to Middle Low German *dobbe*]

dub[6] (dʌb) *vb.* **dubs, dubbing, dubbed.** *(intr.;* foll. by *in, up,* or *out) Slang.* to contribute to the cost of (something); pay. [C19: of obscure origin]

dubbin ('dʌbɪn) *or* **dubbing** *n. Brit.* a greasy mixture of tallow and oil applied to leather to soften it and make it waterproof. [C18: from *dub* to dress leather; see DUB[1]]
dubbing[1] ('dʌbɪŋ) *n. Films.* **1.** the replacement of a soundtrack in one language by one in another language. **2.** the combination of several soundtracks into a single track. **3.** the addition of a soundtrack to a film or broadcast.
dubbing[2] ('dʌbɪŋ) *n.* **1.** *Angling.* hair or fur spun on waxed silk and added to the body of an artificial fly to give it shape. **2.** a variant of **dubbin**.
dubbo ('dʌbəʊ) *Austral. slang.* ~*adj.* **1.** stupid ~*n.,pl.* **-bos. 2.** a stupid person. [of uncertain origin]
dubiety (djuː'baɪɪtɪ) *or* **dubiosity** (ˌdjuːbɪ'ɒsɪtɪ) *n., pl.* **-ties. 1.** the state of being doubtful. **2.** a doubtful matter. [C18: from Late Latin *dubietās*, from Latin *dubius* DUBIOUS]
dubious ('djuːbɪəs) *adj.* **1.** marked by or causing doubt: *a dubious reply.* **2.** unsettled in mind; uncertain; doubtful. **3.** of doubtful quality; untrustworthy: *a dubious reputation.* **4.** not certain in outcome. [C16: from Latin *dubius* wavering] —'**dubiously** *adv.* —'**dubiousness** *n.*
dubitable ('djuːbɪtəbᵊl) *adj.* open to doubt. [C17: from Latin *dubitāre* to DOUBT] —'**dubitably** *adv.*
dubitation (ˌdjuːbɪ'teɪʃən) *n.* another word for **doubt.**
Dublin Bay prawn ('dʌblɪn) *n.* a large prawn usually used in a dish of scampi.
Dubliner ('dʌblɪnə) *n.* a native or inhabitant of Dublin, the capital of the Republic of Ireland.
dubonnet (djuː'bɒneɪ) *n.* **a.** a dark purplish-red colour. **b.** (*as adj.*): *a dubonnet coat.* [from DUBONNET]
Dubonnet (djuː'bɒneɪ) *n. Trademark.* a sweet usually red apéritif wine flavoured with quinine and cinchona.
ducal ('djuːkᵊl) *adj.* of or relating to a duke or duchy. [C16: from French, from Late Latin *ducālis* of a leader, from *dux* leader] —'**ducally** *adv.*
ducat ('dʌkət) *n.* **1.** any of various former European gold or silver coins, esp. those used in Italy or the Netherlands. **2.** (*often pl.*) any coin or money. [C14: from Old French, from Old Italian *ducato* coin stamped with the doge's image, from *duca* doge, from Latin *dux* leader]
duce ('duːtʃɪ; *Italian* 'duːtʃe) *n.* leader. [C20: from Italian, from Latin *dux*]
Duchenne dystrophy (duː'ʃɛn) *or* **Duchenne muscular dystrophy** *n.* the most common form of muscular dystrophy, usually affecting only boys. Abbrev.: **DMD.** [named after Guillaume *Duchenne* (1806–75), French neurologist]
duchess ('dʌtʃɪs) *n.* **1.** the wife or widow of a duke. **2.** a woman who holds the rank of duke in her own right. ~*vb.* **3.** *Austral. informal.* to overwhelm with flattering attention. [C14: from Old French *duchesse*, feminine of *duc* DUKE]
duchy ('dʌtʃɪ) *n., pl.* **duchies.** the territory of a duke or duchess; dukedom. [C14: from Old French *duche*, from *duc* DUKE]
duck[1] (dʌk) *n., pl.* **ducks** *or* **duck. 1.** any of various small aquatic birds of the family *Anatidae*, typically having short legs, webbed feet, and a broad blunt bill: order *Anseriformes*. **2.** the flesh of this bird, used as food. **3.** the female of such a bird, as opposed to the male (drake). **4.** any other bird of the family *Anatidae*, including geese, and swans. **5.** Also: **ducks.** *Brit. informal.* dear or darling: used as a term of endearment or of general address. See also **ducky. 6.** *Informal.* a person, esp. one regarded as odd or endearing. **7.** *Cricket.* a score of nothing by a batsman. **8. like water off a duck's back.** *Informal.* without effect. **9. take to something like a duck to water.** *Informal.* to become adept at or attracted to something very quickly. [Old English *dūce* duck, diver; related to DUCK[2]]
duck[2] (dʌk) *vb.* **1.** to move (the head or body) quickly downwards or away, esp. so as to escape observation or evade a blow. **2.** to submerge or plunge suddenly and often briefly under water. **3.** (when *intr.*, often foll. by *out*) *Informal.* to dodge or escape (a person, duty, etc.). **4.** (*intr.*) *Bridge.* to play a low card when possessing a higher one rather than try to win a trick. ~*n.* **5.** the act or an instance of ducking. [C14: related to Old High German *tūhhan* to dive, Middle Dutch *dūken*] —'**ducker** *n.*
duck[3] (dʌk) *n.* a heavy cotton fabric of plain weave, used for clothing, tents, etc. See also **ducks.** [C17: from Middle Dutch *doek*; related to Old High German *tuoh* cloth]
duck[4] (dʌk) *n.* an amphibious vehicle used in World War II. [C20: from code name DUKW]
duck-billed platypus *n.* an amphibious egg-laying mammal, *Ornithorhynchus anatinus*, of E Australia, having dense fur, a broad bill and tail, and webbed feet: family *Ornithorhynchidae*. Sometimes shortened to **duckbill, platypus.** See also **monotreme.**
duckboard ('dʌkˌbɔːd) *n.* a board or boards laid so as to form a floor or path over wet or muddy ground.
duck-egg blue *n.* **a.** a pale greenish-blue colour. **b.** (*as adj.*): *duck-egg blue walls.*
duckfoot quote ('dʌkfʊt) *n. Printing.* a chevron-shaped quotation mark (« or ») used on the Continent of Europe.
duck hawk *n.* a variety of peregrine falcon, *Falco peregrinus anatum*, occurring in North America.
ducking stool *n. History.* a chair or stool used for the punishment of offenders by plunging them into water.
duckling ('dʌklɪŋ) *n.* a young duck.
ducks (dʌks) *pl. n.* clothing made of duck, esp. white trousers for sports.
ducks and drakes *n.* (*functioning as sing.*) **1.** a game in which a flat stone is bounced across the surface of water. **2. make ducks and drakes of** *or* **play (at) ducks and drakes with.** to use recklessly; squander or waste.
duck's arse *n.* a hairstyle in which the hair is swept back to a point at the nape of the neck, resembling a duck's tail. Also called: **DA.**
duck shove *vb. Austral. and N.Z. informal.* to evade responsibility. —**duck shover** *n.* —**duck shoving** *n.*
duck soup *n. U.S. slang.* something that is easy to do.
duckweed ('dʌkˌwiːd) *n.* any of various small stemless aquatic plants of the family *Lemnaceae*, esp. any of the genus *Lemna*, that have rounded leaves and occur floating on still water in temperate regions.
ducky *or* **duckie** ('dʌkɪ) *Informal.* ~*n., pl.* **duckies. 1.** *Brit.* darling or dear: used as a term of endearment among women, but now often used in imitation of the supposed usage of homosexual men. ~*adj.* **2.** delightful; fine.
duct (dʌkt) *n.* **1.** a tube, pipe, or canal by means of which a substance, esp. a fluid or gas, is conveyed. **2.** any bodily passage, esp. one conveying secretions or excretions. **3.** a narrow tubular cavity in plants, often containing resin or some other substance. **4.** Also called: **conduit.** a channel or pipe carrying electric cable or wires. **5.** a passage through which air can flow, as in air conditioning. **6.** the ink reservoir in a printing press. [C17: from Latin *ductus* a leading (in Medieval Latin: aqueduct), from *dūcere* to lead] —'**ductless** *adj.*
ductile ('dʌktaɪl) *adj.* **1.** (of a metal, such as gold or copper) able to sustain large deformations without fracture and able to be hammered into sheets or drawn out into wires. **2.** able to be moulded; pliant; plastic. **3.** easily led or influenced; tractable. [C14: from Old French, from Latin *ductilis*, from *dūcere* to lead] —'**ductilely** *adv.* —**ductility** (dʌk'tɪlɪtɪ) *or* '**ductileness** *n.*
ductless gland *n. Anatomy.* See **endocrine gland.**
ductule ('dʌktjuːl) *n. Anatomy, zoology.* a small duct.
dud (dʌd) *Informal.* ~*n.* **1.** a person or thing that proves ineffectual or a failure. **2.** a shell, etc., that fails to explode. **3.** (*pl.*) *Old-fashioned.* clothes or other personal belongings. ~*adj.* **4.** failing in its purpose or function: *a dud cheque.* [C15 (in the sense: an article of clothing, a thing, used disparagingly): of unknown origin]
dude (djuːd) *n. Informal.* **1.** *Western U.S. and Canadian.* a city dweller, esp. one holidaying on a ranch. **2.** *U.S. and Canadian.* a dandy. **3.** *U.S. and Canadian.* any person. [C19: of unknown origin] —'**dudish** *adj.* —'**dudishly** *adv.*
dudeen (duː'diːn) *n.* a clay pipe with a short stem. [C19: from Irish *dūidīn* a little pipe, from *dūd* pipe]
dude ranch *n. U.S. and Canadian.* a ranch used as a holiday resort offering activities such as riding and camping.
dudgeon[1] ('dʌdʒən) *n.* anger or resentment (archaic, except in the phrase **in high dudgeon**). [C16: of unknown origin]
dudgeon[2] ('dʌdʒən) *n.* **1.** *Obsolete.* a wood used in making the handles of knives, daggers, etc. **2.** *Archaic.* a dagger, knife, etc., with a dudgeon hilt. [C15: from Anglo-Norman *digeon*, of obscure origin]
due (djuː) *adj.* **1.** (*postpositive*) immediately payable. **2.** (*postpositive*) owed as a debt, irrespective of any date for payment. **3.** requisite; fitting; proper. **4.** (*prenominal*) adequate or sufficient; enough. **5.** (*postpositive*) expected or appointed to be present or arrive: *the train is now due.* **6. due to.** attributable to or caused by. ~*n.* **7.** something that is owed, required, or due. **8. give (a person) his due.** to give or allow what is deserved or right. ~*adv.* **9.** directly or exactly; straight: *a course due west.* ~See also **dues.** [C13: from Old French *deu*, from *devoir* to owe, from Latin *dēbēre*; see DEBT, DEBIT]
▷**Usage.** There is considerable controversy over the use of *due to* as a compound preposition equivalent to *because of.* Careful users of English prefer *because of* or *owing to*, at least in formal contexts, and restrict *due* to its adjectival function. There is no dispute about the postpositive adjectival use of *due to* to mean *caused by* (*the error was due to carelessness*), but *owing to* is not ordinarily used in this way.
due bill *n. Chiefly U.S.* a document acknowledging indebtedness, exchangeable for goods or services.
duel ('djuːəl) *n.* **1.** a prearranged combat with deadly weapons between two people following a formal procedure in the presence of seconds and traditionally fought until one party was wounded or killed, usually to settle a quarrel involving a point of honour. **2.** a contest or conflict between two persons or parties. ~*vb.* **duels, duelling, duelled** *or U.S.* **duels, dueling, dueled.** (*intr.*) **3.** to fight in a duel. **4.** to contest closely. [C15: from Medieval Latin *duellum*, from Latin, poetical variant of *bellum* war; associated by folk etymology with Latin *duo* two] —'**dueller** *or* '**duellist** *n.*
duello (djuː'ɛləʊ) *n., pl.* **-los. 1.** the art of duelling. **2.** the code of rules for duelling. [C16: from Italian; see DUEL]
duenna (djuː'ɛnə) *n.* (in Spain and Portugal, etc.) an elderly woman retained by a family to act as governess and chaperon to young girls. [C17: from Spanish *dueña*, from Latin *domina* lady, feminine of *dominus* master]

due process of law *n.* the administration of justice in accordance with established rules and principles.

dues (dju:z) *pl. n. (sometimes sing.)* charges, as for membership of a club or organization; fees: *trade-union dues.*

duet (dju:ˈɛt) *n.* **1.** Also called (esp. for instrumental compositions): **duo.** a musical composition for two performers or voices. **2.** an action or activity performed by a pair of closely connected individuals. [C18: from Italian *duetto* a little duet, from *duo* duet, from Latin: two] —**duˈettist** *n.*

duff[1] (dʌf) *n.* **1.** a thick flour pudding, often flavoured with currants, citron, etc., and boiled in a cloth bag: *plum duff.* **2. up the duff.** *Slang, chiefly Austral.* pregnant. [C19: Northern English variant of DOUGH]

duff[2] (dʌf) *vb. (tr.)* **1.** *Slang.* to change the appearance of or give a false appearance to (old or stolen goods); fake. **2.** *Austral. slang* to steal (cattle), altering the brand. **3.** Also: **sclaff.** *Golf, informal.* to bungle (a shot) by hitting the ground behind the ball. ~*adj.* **4.** *Brit. informal.* bad or useless, as by not working out or operating correctly; dud: *a duff idea; a duff engine.* ~See also **duff up.** [C19: probably back formation from DUFFER]

duff[3] (dʌf) *n. Slang.* the rump or buttocks. [C20: special use of DUFF[1]]

duffel *or* **duffle** (ˈdʌfᵊl) *n.* **1.** a heavy woollen cloth with a thick nap. **2.** *Chiefly U.S. and Canadian.* equipment or supplies, esp. those of a camper. [C17: after *Duffel,* Belgian town]

duffel bag *n.* a cylindrical drawstring canvas bag, originally used esp. by sailors for carrying personal articles.

duffel coat *n.* a knee-length or short wool coat, usually with a hood and fastened with toggles.

duffer (ˈdʌfə) *n.* **1.** *Informal.* a dull or incompetent person. **2.** *Slang.* something worthless. **3.** *Dialect.* a peddler or hawker. **4.** *Austral. slang.* **a.** a mine that proves unproductive. **b.** a person who steals cattle. [C19: of uncertain origin]

duff up *vb. (tr., adv.) Brit. slang.* to beat or thrash (a person) severely.

dug[1] (dʌg) *vb.* the past tense and past participle of **dig.**

dug[2] (dʌg) *n.* **1.** the nipple, teat, udder, or breast of a female mammal. **2.** a human breast, esp. when old and withered. [C16: of Scandinavian origin; compare Danish *dægge* to coddle, Gothic *daddjan* to give suck]

dug[3] (dʌg) *n.* a Scot. word for **dog.**

dugite (ˈdu:gaɪt) *n.* a medium-sized venomous snake, *Pseudonaja affinis,* of Central and W Australia, having a small head and slender olive-coloured body with black specks.

dugong (ˈdu:gɒŋ) *n.* a whalelike sirenian mammal, *Dugong dugon,* occurring in shallow tropical waters from E Africa to Australia: family *Dugongidae.* [C19: from Malay *duyong*]

dugout (ˈdʌgˌaʊt) *n.* **1.** a canoe made by hollowing out a log. **2.** *Military.* a covered excavation dug to provide shelter. **3.** *Slang.* a retired officer, former civil servant, etc., recalled to employment. **4.** (at a sports ground) the covered bench where managers, trainers, etc. sit and players wait when not on the field.

duiker *or* **duyker** (ˈdaɪkə) *n., pl.* **-kers** *or* **-ker.** **1.** Also called: **duikerbok** (ˈdaɪkəbɒk). any small antelope of the genera *Cephalophus* and *Sylvicapra,* occurring throughout Africa south of the Sahara, having short straight backward-pointing horns, pointed hooves, and an arched back. **2.** *S. African.* any of several cormorants, esp. the long-tailed shag (*Phalacrocorax africanus*). [C18: via Afrikaans from Dutch *duiker* diver, from *duiken* to dive; see DUCK[2]]

duka (ˈdu:ka) *n. E African.* a shop; store. [C20: from Swahili]

duke (dju:k) *n.* **1.** a nobleman of high rank: in the British Isles standing above the other grades of the nobility. **2.** the prince or ruler of a small principality or duchy. [C12: from Old French *duc,* from Latin *dux* leader]

dukedom (ˈdju:kdəm) *n.* **1.** another name for a **duchy.** **2.** the title, rank, or position of a duke.

dukes (dju:ks) *pl. n. Slang.* the fists. [C19: from *Duke of Yorks* rhyming slang for *forks* (fingers)]

Dukhobor (ˈdu:kəʊˌbɔ:) *pl. n.* a variant spelling of **Doukhobor.**

dulcet (ˈdʌlsɪt) *adj.* (of a sound) soothing or pleasant; sweet. [C14: from Latin *dulcis* sweet] —ˈ**dulcetly** *adv.* —ˈ**dulcetness** *n.*

dulciana (ˌdʌlsɪˈɑ:nə) *n.* a sweet-toned organ stop, controlling metal pipes of narrow scale. [C18: from Latin *dulcis* sweet]

dulcify (ˈdʌlsɪˌfaɪ) *vb.* **-fies, -fying, -fied.** *(tr.)* **1.** *Rare.* to make pleasant or agreeable. **2.** a rare word for **sweeten.** [C16: from Late Latin *dulcificāre,* from Latin *dulcis* sweet + *facere* to make] —ˌ**dulcifiˈcation** *n.*

dulcimer (ˈdʌlsɪmə) *n. Music.* **1.** a tuned percussion instrument consisting of a set of strings of graduated length stretched over a sounding board and struck with a pair of hammers. **2.** an instrument used in U.S. folk music, consisting of an elliptical body, a fretted fingerboard, and usually three strings plucked with a goose quill. [C15: from Old French *doulcemer,* from Old Italian *dolcimelo,* from *dolce* sweet, from Latin *dulcis* + *-melo,* perhaps from Greek *melos* song]

dulcinea (ˌdʌlsɪˈnɪə) *n.* a man's sweetheart. [C18: from the name of DON QUIXOTE's mistress *Dulcinea* del Toboso; from Spanish *dulce* sweet]

dulia (ˈdju:lɪə) *n.* the veneration accorded to saints in the Roman Catholic and Eastern Churches, as contrasted with hyperdulia and latria. [C17: from Medieval Latin: service, from Greek *douleia* slavery, from *doulos* slave]

dull (dʌl) *adj.* **1.** slow to think or understand; stupid. **2.** lacking in interest. **3.** lacking in perception or the ability to respond; insensitive. **4.** lacking sharpness; blunt. **5.** not acute, intense, or piercing. **6.** (of weather) not bright or clear; cloudy. **7.** not active, busy, or brisk. **8.** lacking in spirit or animation; listless. **9.** (of colour) lacking brilliance or brightness; sombre. **10.** not loud or clear; muffled. **11.** *Med.* (of sound elicited by percussion, esp. of the chest) not resonant. ~*vb.* **12.** to make or become dull. [Old English *dol;* related to Old Norse *dul* conceit, Old High German *tol* foolish, Greek *tholeros* confused] —ˈ**dullish** *adj.* —ˈ**dullness** *or* ˈ**dulness** *n.* —ˈ**dully** *adv.*

dullard (ˈdʌləd) *n.* a dull or stupid person.

dullsville (ˈdʌlzvɪl) *n. Slang.* **1.** a thing, place, or activity that is boring or dull. **2.** the state of being bored.

dulosis (dju:ˈləʊsɪs) *n.* a practice of some ants, in which one species forces members of a different species to do the work of the colony. Also called: **helotism.** [C20: from Greek: enslavement, from *doulos* slave] —**dulotic** (dju:ˈlɒtɪk) *adj.*

dulse (dʌls) *n.* any of several seaweeds, esp. *Rhodymenia palmata,* that occur on rocks and have large red edible fronds. [C17: from Old Irish *duilesc* seaweed]

duly (ˈdju:lɪ) *adv.* **1.** in a proper or fitting manner. **2.** at the proper time; punctually. [C14: see DUE, -LY[2]]

duma *or* ***douma*** *Russian.* (ˈdu:mə) *n. Russian history.* **1.** *(usually cap.)* the elective legislative assembly established in 1905: overthrown by the Bolsheviks in 1917. **2.** (before 1917) any official assembly or council. [C20: from *duma* thought, of Germanic origin; related to Gothic *dōms* judgment]

dumb (dʌm) *adj.* **1.** lacking the power to speak, either because of defects in the vocal organs or because of hereditary deafness; mute. **2.** lacking the power of human speech: *dumb animals.* **3.** temporarily lacking or bereft of the power to speak: *struck dumb.* **4.** refraining from speech; uncommunicative. **5.** producing no sound; silent: *a dumb piano.* **6.** made, done, or performed without speech. **7.** *Informal.* **a.** slow to understand; dim-witted. **b.** foolish; stupid. [Old English; related to Old Norse *dumbr,* Gothic *dumbs,* Old High German *tump*] —ˈ**dumbly** *adv.* —ˈ**dumbness** *n.*

dumb ague *n.* an irregular form of malarial fever (ague) lacking the typically symptomatic chill.

dumbbell (ˈdʌmˌbɛl) *n.* **1.** *Gymnastics, etc.* an exercising weight consisting of a single bar with a heavy ball or disc at either end. **2.** *Dog training.* a small wooden object shaped like this used for the dog to retrieve. **3.** *Slang, chiefly U.S. and Canadian.* a fool.

dumb-cane *n.* a West Indian aroid plant, *Dieffenbachia seguine,* chewing the stem of which induces speechlessness by paralysing the throat muscles.

dumbfound *or* **dumfound** (dʌmˈfaʊnd) *vb. (tr.)* to strike dumb with astonishment; amaze. [C17: from DUMB + (CON)FOUND]

dumb show *n.* **1.** a part of a play acted in pantomime, popular in early English drama. **2.** meaningful gestures; mime.

dumbstruck (ˈdʌmˌstrʌk) *or* **dumbstricken** (ˈdʌmˌstrɪkᵊn) *adj.* temporarily deprived of speech through shock or surprise.

dumbwaiter (ˈdʌmˌweɪtə) *n.* **1.** *Brit.* **a.** a stand placed near a dining table to hold food. **b.** a revolving circular tray placed on a table to hold food. U.S. and Canadian name: **lazy Susan.** **2.** a lift for carrying food, rubbish, etc., between floors.

dumdum (ˈdʌmˌdʌm) *n.* a soft-nosed or hollow-nosed small-arms bullet that expands on impact and inflicts extensive laceration. Also called: **dumdum bullet.** [C19: named after *Dum-Dum,* town near Calcutta where these bullets were made]

dummy (ˈdʌmɪ) *n., pl.* **-mies.** **1.** a figure representing the human form, used for displaying clothes, in a ventriloquist's act, as a target, etc. **2. a.** a copy or imitation of an object, often lacking some essential feature of the original. **b.** *(as modifier): a dummy drawer.* **3.** *Slang.* a stupid person; fool. **4.** *Derogatory, slang.* a person without the power of speech; mute. **5.** *Informal.* a person who says or does nothing. **6. a.** a person who appears to act for himself while acting on behalf of another. **b.** *(as modifier): a dummy buyer.* **7.** *Military.* a weighted round without explosives, used in drill and training. **8.** *Bridge.* **a.** the hand exposed on the table by the declarer's partner and played by the declarer. **b.** the declarer's partner. **9. a.** a prototype of a proposed book, indicating the general appearance and dimensions of the finished product. **b.** a designer's layout of a page indicating the positions for illustrations, etc. **10.** a feigned pass or move in a sport such as football or rugby. **11.** *Brit.* a rubber teat for babies to suck or bite on. U.S. and Canadian equivalent: **pacifier.** **12.** *(modifier)* counterfeit; sham. **13.** *(modifier)* (of a card game) played with one hand exposed or unplayed. ~*vb.* **-mies, -mying, -mied.** **14.** to prepare a dummy of (a proposed book, page, etc.). **15.** Also: **sell (someone) a dummy.** *Sport.* to use a dummy pass in order to trick (an opponent). [C16: see DUMB, -Y[3]]

dummy head *n.* a model of the human head with a microphone in each ear intended to receive sound in binaural and surround sound reproduction and transmission.

dummy load *n.* a resistive component that absorbs all the output power of an electrical generator or radio transmitter in order to simulate working conditions for test purposes.

dummy run *n.* a practice or rehearsal; trial run.

dummy variable *n.* a variable or constant appearing in a mathematical expression that can be replaced by any arbitrary variable or constant, not occurring in the expression, without affecting the value of the whole.

dumortierite (djuːˈmɔːtɪəˌraɪt) *n.* a hard fibrous blue or green mineral consisting of hydrated aluminium borosilicate. Formula: $Al_8BSi_3O_{19}(OH)$. [C19: named after Eugène *Dumortier*, 19th-century French palaeontologist who discovered it]

dump[1] (dʌmp) *vb.* **1.** to drop, fall, or let fall heavily or in a mass. **2.** (*tr.*) to empty (objects or material) out of a container. **3.** to unload, empty, or make empty (a container), as by tilting or overturning. **4.** (*tr.*) *Informal.* to dispose of. **5.** (*tr.*) to dispose of (waste, esp. radioactive nuclear waste) in the sea or on land. **6.** *Commerce.* **a.** to market (goods) in bulk and at low prices. **b.** to offer for sale large quantities of (goods) on foreign markets at low prices in order to maintain a high price in the home market and obtain a share of the foreign markets. **7.** (*tr.*) to store (supplies, arms, etc.) temporarily. **8.** (*tr.*) *Surfing.* (of a wave) to hurl a swimmer or surfer down. **9.** (*tr.*) *Austral. and N.Z.* to compact (bales of wool) by hydraulic pressure. **10.** (*tr.*) *Computer technol.* to record (the contents of part or all of the memory) on a storage device, such as magnetic tape, at a series of points during a computer run. ~*n.* **11. a.** a place or area where waste materials are dumped. **b.** (*in combination*): *rubbish dump.* **12.** a pile or accumulation of rubbish. **13.** the act of dumping. **14.** *Informal.* a dirty or unkempt place. **15.** *Military.* a place where weapons, supplies, etc., are stored. [C14: probably of Scandinavian origin; compare Norwegian *dumpa* to fall suddenly, Middle Low German *dumpeln* to duck] —ˈ**dumper** *n.*

dump[2] (dʌmp) *n.* *Obsolete.* a mournful song; lament. [C16: see DAMP]

dumpling (ˈdʌmplɪŋ) *n.* **1.** a small ball of dough cooked and served with stew. **2.** a pudding consisting of a round pastry case filled with fruit: *apple dumpling.* **3.** *Informal.* a short plump person. [C16: *dump-*, perhaps variant of LUMP[1] + -LING[1]]

dump orbit *n.* an earth orbit into which communications satellites may be moved at the end of their operational lives, where there is no risk of their interference or collision with working satellites in the normal orbits. Also called: **graveyard orbit.**

dumps (dʌmps) *pl. n. Informal.* a state of melancholy or depression (esp. in the phrase **down in the dumps**). [C16: probably from Middle Dutch *domp* haze, mist; see DAMP]

dump truck *or* **dumper-truck** *n.* a small truck used on building sites, having a load-bearing container at the front that can be tipped up to unload the contents.

dumpy[1] (ˈdʌmpɪ) *adj.* **dumpier, dumpiest.** short and plump; squat. [C18: perhaps related to DUMPLING] —ˈ**dumpily** *adv.* —ˈ**dumpiness** *n.*

dumpy[2] (ˈdʌmpɪ) *or* **dumpish** (ˈdʌmpɪʃ) *adj. Rare.* in low spirits; depressed; morose. [C17: from C16 *dump;* see DUMPS]

dumpy level *n. Surveying.* a levelling instrument consisting of a horizontal telescope with various rotational arrangements and a spirit level.

dun[1] (dʌn) *vb.* **duns, dunning, dunned.** **1.** (*tr.*) to press or importune (a debtor) for the payment of a debt. ~*n.* **2.** a person, esp. a hired agent, who importunes another for the payment of a debt. **3.** a demand for payment, esp. one in writing. [C17: of unknown origin]

dun[2] (dʌn) *n.* **1.** a brownish-grey colour. **2.** a horse of this colour. **3.** *Angling.* **a.** an immature adult mayfly (the subimago), esp. one of the genus *Ephemera.* **b.** an artificial fly imitating this or a similar fly. ~*adj.* **dunner, dunnest.** **4.** of a dun colour. **5.** dark and gloomy. [Old English *dunn;* related to Old Norse *dunna* wild duck, Middle Irish *doun* dark; see DUSK]

Duncan Phyfe *or* **Fife** (ˈdʌŋkən ˈfaɪf) *n.* (*modifier*) *U.S. furniture.* of or in the manner of Duncan Phyfe (?1768–1854), U.S. cabinetmaker, esp. in that which followed the Sheraton and Directoire styles.

dunce (dʌns) *n.* a person who is stupid or slow to learn. [C16: from *Dunses* or *Dunsmen,* term of ridicule applied to the followers of John *Duns* Scotus (?1265–1308), Scottish theologian, especially by 16th-century humanists] —ˈ**dunce**ˌ**like** *adj.*

dunce cap *or* **dunce's cap** *n.* a conical paper hat, formerly placed on the head of a dull child at school.

Dundee cake (dʌnˈdiː) *n. Chiefly Brit.* a fairly rich fruit cake decorated with almonds, originally made in Dundee in E Scotland.

dunderhead (ˈdʌndəˌhɛd) *n.* a stupid or slow-witted person; dunce. Also called: **dunderpate.** [C17: probably from Dutch *donder* thunder + HEAD; compare BLOCKHEAD] —ˈ**dunder**ˌ**headed** *adj.* —ˈ**dunder**ˌ**headedness** *n.*

dune (djuːn) *n.* a mound or ridge of drifted sand, occurring on the sea coast and in deserts. [C18: via Old French from Middle Dutch *dūne;* see DOWN[3]]

dung (dʌŋ) *n.* **1. a.** excrement, esp. of animals; manure. **b.** (*as modifier*): *dung cart.* **2.** something filthy. ~*vb.* **3.** (*tr.*) to cover (ground) with manure. [Old English: prison; related to Old High German *tunc* cellar roofed with dung, Old Norse *dyngja* manure heap] —ˈ**dungy** *adj.*

dungaree (ˌdʌŋgəˈriː) *n.* **1.** a coarse cotton fabric used chiefly for work clothes, etc. **2.** (*pl.*) **a.** a suit of workman's overalls made of this material consisting of trousers with a bib attached. **b.** a casual garment resembling this, usually worn by women or children. **3.** *U.S.* trousers. [C17: from Hindi *dungrī,* after *Dungrī,* district of Bombay, where this fabric originated]

dungas (ˈdʌŋgəz) *pl. n. Austral. informal.* short for **dungarees.**

dung beetle *or* **chafer** *n.* any of the various beetles of the family *Scarabaeidae* and related families that feed on or breed in dung.

dungeon (ˈdʌndʒən) *n.* **1.** a close prison cell, often underground. **2.** a variant of **donjon.** [C14: from Old French *donjon;* related to Latin *dominus* master]

dung fly *n.* any of various muscid flies of the subfamily *Cordilurinae,* such as the predatory **yellow dung fly** (*Scatophaga stercoraria*), that frequents cowpats to feed and lay its eggs.

dunghill (ˈdʌŋˌhɪl) *n.* **1.** a heap of dung. **2.** a foul place, condition, or person.

dunite (ˈdʌnaɪt) *n.* an ultrabasic igneous rock consisting mainly of olivine. [C19: named after Dun Mountain, a mountain in New Zealand where it is abundant]

duniwassal (ˈduːnɪˌwɑːsəl) *n.* (in Scotland) a minor nobleman. [C16: from Gaelic *duine* man +*uasal* noble]

dunk (dʌŋk) *vb.* **1.** to dip (bread, etc.) in tea, soup, etc., before eating. **2.** to submerge or be submerged in liquid. [C20: from Pennsylvania Dutch, from Middle High German *dunken,* from Old High German *dunkōn;* see DUCK[2], TINGE] —ˈ**dunker** *n.*

Dunker (ˈdʌŋkə) *or* **Dunkard** (ˈdʌŋkəd) *n.* a member of the German Baptist Brethren. [C18: from German *Tunker* ducker]

dunlin (ˈdʌnlɪn) *n.* a small sandpiper, *Calidris* (or *Erolia*) *alpina,* of northern and arctic regions, having a brown back and black breast in summer. Also called: **red-backed sandpiper.** [C16: DUN[2] + -LING[1]]

dunnage (ˈdʌnɪdʒ) *n.* loose material used for packing cargo. [C14: of uncertain origin]

dunnakin (ˈdʌnəkɪn) *n. Dialect.* a lavatory. Also called: **dunny.** [of obscure origin; but perhaps related to DUNG]

dunnite (ˈdʌnaɪt) *n.* an explosive containing ammonium picrate. [C20: named after Colonel B. W. *Dunn* (1860–1936), American army officer who invented it]

dunno (dʌˈnəʊ, dʊ-, də-) *Slang. contraction of* (I) do not know.

dunnock (ˈdʌnək) *n.* another name for **hedge sparrow.** [C15: from DUN[2] + -OCK]

dunny (ˈdʌnɪ) *n., pl.* **-nies.** **1.** *Scot. dialect.* a cellar or basement. **2.** *Dialect.* another word for **dunnakin.** **3.** *Austral. and N.Z. informal.* **a.** a lavatory. **b.** (*as modifier*): *a dunny roll; a dunny seat.* [C20: of obscure origin; but see DUNNAKIN]

dunt (dʌnt, dʊnt) *Scot. and northern English dialect.* ~*n.* **1.** a blow; thump. **2.** the injury caused by such a blow. ~*vb.* **3.** to strike or hit. [C15: perhaps variant of DINT]

duo (ˈdjuːəʊ) *n., pl.* **duos** *or* **dui** (ˈdjuːiː). **1.** *Music.* **a.** a pair of performers. **b.** another word for **duet.** **2.** a pair of actors, entertainers, etc. **3.** *Informal.* a pair of closely connected individuals. [C16: via Italian from Latin: two]

duo- *combining form.* indicating two: *duotone.* [from Latin]

duobinary (ˌdjuːəʊˈbaɪnərɪ) *adj.* denoting a communications system for coding digital data in which three data bands are used, 0, +1, –1. Compare **binary notation.**

duodecimal (ˌdjuːəʊˈdɛsɪməl) *adj.* **1.** relating to twelve or twelfths. ~*n.* **2.** a twelfth. **3.** one of the numbers used in a duodecimal number system. —ˌ**duo**ˈ**decimally** *adv.*

duodecimo (ˌdjuːəʊˈdɛsɪˌməʊ) *n., pl.* **-mos.** **1.** a book size resulting from folding a sheet of paper into twelve leaves. Also called: **twelvemo.** Often written: **12mo, 12°.** **2.** a book of this size. [C17: from Latin phrase *in duodecimō* in twelfth, from *duodecim* twelve]

duodenary (ˌdjuːəˈdiːnərɪ) *adj.* of or relating to the number 12; duodecimal. [C17: from Latin *duodēnārius* containing twelve]

duodenitis (ˌdjuːəʊdɪˈnaɪtɪs) *n.* inflammation of the duodenum.

duodenum (ˌdjuːəʊˈdiːnəm) *n., pl.* **-na** (-nə) *or* **-nums.** the first part of the small intestine, between the stomach and the jejunum. [C14: from Medieval Latin, shortened from *intestinum duodenum digitorum* intestine of twelve fingers' length, from Latin *duodēnī* twelve each] —ˌ**duo**ˈ**denal** *adj.*

duologue *or U.S.* (*sometimes*) **duolog** (ˈdjuːəˌlɒg) *n.* **1.** a part or all of a play in which the speaking roles are limited to two actors. **2.** a less common word for **dialogue.**

duopoly (djʊˈɒpəlɪ) *n.* a situation in which control of a commodity or service in a particular market is vested in just two producers or suppliers. —**duopolistic** (djʊɒˌpəˈlɪstɪk) *adj.*

duotone (ˈdjuːəˌtəʊn) *n. Printing.* **1.** a process for producing halftone illustrations using two shades of a single colour or black and a colour. **2.** a picture produced by this process.

dup (dʌp) *vb.* **dups, dupping, dupped.** (*tr.*) *Archaic or dialect.* to open. [C16: contraction of DO[1] + UP]

dup. *abbrev. for* duplicate.

dupatta (dʊˈpʌtə) *n.* a scarf worn in India.

dupe (djuːp) *n.* **1.** a person who is easily deceived. **2.** a person who unwittingly serves as the tool of another person or power. ~*vb.* **3.** (*tr.*) to deceive, esp. by trickery; make a dupe or tool of; cheat; fool. [C17: from French, from Old French *duppe,* contraction of *de huppe* of (a) hoopoe (from Latin *upupa*); from the bird's reputation for extreme stupidity] —ˈ**dupable** *adj.* —ˌ**dupa**ˈ**bility** *n.* —ˈ**duper** *n.* —ˈ**dupery** *n.*

dupion (ˈdjuːpɪən, -ˈpiːɒn) *n.* a silk fabric made from the threads of double cocoons. [C19: from French *doupion,* from Italian *doppione* double]

duple ('djuːpᵊl) *adj.* **1.** a less common word for **double.** **2.** *Music.* (of time or music) having two beats in a bar. [C16: from Latin *duplus* twofold, double]
duplet ('djuːplɪt) *n.* **1.** a pair of electrons shared between two atoms in a covalent bond. **2.** *Music.* a group of two notes played in the time of three.
duple time *n.* musical time with two beats in each bar.
duplex ('djuːplɛks) *n.* **1.** *U.S. and Canadian.* a duplex apartment or house. **2.** a double-stranded region in a nucleic acid molecule. ~*adj.* **3.** having two parts. **4.** *Machinery.* having pairs of components of independent but identical function. **5.** permitting the transmission of simultaneous signals in both directions in a radio, telecommunications, or computer channel. Compare **diplex, simplex** (sense 1). [C19: from Latin: twofold, from *duo* two + *-plex* -FOLD] —**du'plexity** *n.*
duplex apartment *n. U.S. and Canadian.* an apartment on two floors.
duplex chain *n. Engineering.* a roller chain having two sets of rollers linked together, used for heavy-duty applications.
duplex house *n. U.S. and Canadian.* a house divided into two separate dwellings. Also called: **semidetached.**
duplicate *adj.* ('djuːplɪkɪt). **1.** copied exactly from an original. **2.** identical. **3.** existing as a pair or in pairs; twofold. ~*n.* ('djuːplɪkɪt). **4.** an exact copy; double. **5.** something additional or supplementary of the same kind. **6.** two exact copies (esp. in the phrase **in duplicate**). ~*vb.* ('djuːplɪˌkeɪt). **7.** (*tr.*) to make a replica of. **8.** (*tr.*) to do or make again. **9.** (*tr.*) to make in a pair; make double. **10.** (*intr.*) *Biology.* to reproduce by dividing into two identical parts: *the chromosomes duplicated in mitosis.* [C15: from Latin *duplicāre* to double, from *duo* two + *plicāre* to fold] —**duplicable** ('djuːplɪkəbᵊl) *adj.* —ˌ**duplica'bility** *n.* —'**duplicately** *adv.* —'**duplicative** *adj.*
duplicate bridge *n.* a form of contract bridge, esp. at clubs and in competitions, in which the hands are kept as dealt and played by different players. The partners with the highest average score are the winners. Also called: **board bridge.** Compare **rubber bridge.**
duplication (ˌdjuːplɪ'keɪʃən) *n.* **1.** the act of duplicating or the state of being duplicated. **2.** a copy; duplicate. **3.** *Genetics.* a mutation in which there are two or more copies of a gene or of a segment of a chromosome.
duplicator ('djuːplɪˌkeɪtə) *n.* an apparatus for making replicas of an original, such as a machine using a stencil wrapped on an ink-loaded drum.
duplicident (djuː'plɪsɪdənt) *adj.* (of certain animals, such as rabbits) having two pairs of incisors in the upper jaw.
duplicity (djuː'plɪsɪtɪ) *n., pl.* **-ties.** deception; double-dealing. [C15: from Old French *duplicite,* from Late Latin *duplicitās* a being double, from Latin DUPLEX] —**du'plicitous** *adj.*
dupondius (djuː'pɒndɪəs) *n., pl.* **-dii** (-dɪˌaɪ). a brass coin of ancient Rome worth half a sesterce. [from Latin, from *duo* two + *pondus* weight]
duppy ('dʌpɪ) *n., pl.* **-pies.** *Caribbean.* a spirit or ghost. [C18: probably of African origin]
Dur. *abbrev. for* Durham.
durable ('djʊərəbᵊl) *adj.* long-lasting; enduring: *a durable fabric.* [C14: from Old French, from Latin *dūrābilis,* from *dūrāre* to last; see ENDURE] —ˌ**dura'bility** *or* '**durableness** *n.* —'**durably** *adv.*
durable goods *pl. n.* goods, such as most producer goods and some consumer goods, that require infrequent replacement. Compare **disposable goods, perishables.** Also called: **durables.**
durable press *n.* **a.** another term for **permanent press.** **b.** (*as modifier*): *durable-press skirts.*
dural ('djʊərəl) *adj.* relating to or affecting the dura mater.
Duralumin (djʊ'ræljʊmɪn) *n. Trademark.* a light strong aluminium alloy containing 3.5–4.5 per cent of copper with small quantities of silicon, magnesium, and manganese; used in aircraft manufacture.
dura mater ('djʊərə 'meɪtə) *n.* the outermost and toughest of the three membranes (see **meninges**) covering the brain and spinal cord. Often shortened to **dura.** [C15: from Medieval Latin, hard mother]
duramen (djʊ'reɪmɛn) *n.* another name for **heartwood.** [C19: from Latin: hardness, from *dūrāre* to harden]
durance ('djʊərəns) *n. Archaic or literary.* **1.** imprisonment. **2.** duration. [C15: from Old French, from *durer* to last, from Latin *dūrāre*]
duration (djʊ'reɪʃən) *n.* the length of time that something lasts or continues. [C14: from Medieval Latin *dūrātiō,* from Latin *dūrāre* to last] —**du'rational** *adj.*
durative ('djʊərətɪv) *Grammar.* ~*adj.* **1.** denoting an aspect of verbs that includes the imperfective and the progressive. ~*n.* **2. a.** the durative aspect of a verb. **b.** a verb in this aspect.
durbar ('dɜːbɑː, ˌdɜː'bɑː) *n.* **a.** (formerly) the court of a native ruler or a governor in India and British Colonial West Africa. **b.** a levee at such a court. [C17: from Hindi *darbār* court, from Persian, from *dar* door + *bār* entry, audience]
duress (djʊ'rɛs, djʊə-) *n.* **1.** compulsion by use of force or threat; constraint; coercion (often in the phrase **under duress**). **2.** *Law.* the illegal exercise of coercion. **3.** confinement; imprisonment. [C14: from Old French *duresse,* from Latin *dūritia* hardness, from *dūrus* hard]
Durex ('djʊərɛks) *n., pl.* **-rex.** *Trademark.* **1.** a brand of condom. **2.** *Austral.* a brand of adhesive tape.
durgah ('dɜːgɑː) *n.* a variant spelling of **dargah.**
Durga Puja (ˌdʊəgæ 'puːdʒə) *n.* another name for **Navaratri.** [from Sanskrit, *Durga* (Hindu goddess) and *puja* worship]
Durham ('dʌrəm) *n.* a variety of shorthorn cattle originating from Durham in NE England. See **shorthorn.**
durian *or* **durion** ('djʊərɪən) *n.* **1.** a SE Asian bombacaceous tree, *Durio zibethinus,* having edible oval fruits with a hard spiny rind. **2.** the fruit of this tree, which has an offensive smell but a pleasant taste: supposedly an aphrodisiac. [C16: from Malay, from *duri* thorn]
duricrust ('djʊərɪˌkrʌst) *n.* a hard crust formed by the precipitation of minerals from water on or in soil from semiarid regions.
during ('djʊərɪŋ) *prep.* **1.** concurrently with (some other activity): *kindly don't sleep during my lectures!* **2.** within the limit of (a period of time): *during the day.* [C14: from *duren* to last, ultimately from Latin *dūrāre* to last]
durmast *or* **durmast oak** ('dɜːˌmɑːst) *n.* **1.** Also called: **sessile oak.** a large Eurasian oak tree, *Quercus petraea,* with lobed leaves and sessile acorns. Compare **pedunculate oak.** **2.** the heavy elastic wood of this tree, used in building and cabinetwork. [C18: probably alteration of *dun mast;* see DUN[2], MAST[2]]
durn (dɜːn) *interj., adj., adv., n.* a U.S. variant of **darn**[2].
duro ('dʊərəʊ) *n., pl.* **-ros.** the silver peso of Spain or Spanish America. [from Spanish, shortened from *peso duro* hard peso, ultimately from Latin *dūrus* hard]
Duroc ('djʊərɒk) *n.* an American breed of red lard pig. [C19: from *Duroc,* name of a stallion owned by the man who developed this breed]
durra ('dʌrə), **doura,** *or* **dourah** ('dʊərə) *n.* an Old World variety of sorghum, *Sorghum vulgare durra,* with erect hairy flower spikes and round seeds: cultivated for grain and fodder. Also called: **Guinea corn, Indian millet.** [C18: from Arabic *dhurah* grain]
durrie ('dʌrɪ) *n.* a cotton carpet made in India, often in rectangular pieces fringed at the ends: sometimes used as a sofa cover, wall hanging, etc. [from Hindi *darī*]
durry ('dʌrɪ) *n., pl.* **-ries.** *Austral. slang.* a cigarette. [from DURRIE]
durst (dɜːst) *vb.* a past tense of **dare.**
durum *or* **durum wheat** ('djʊərəm) *n.* a variety of wheat, *Triticum durum,* with a high gluten content, cultivated mainly in the Mediterranean region, and used chiefly to make pastas. [C20: short for New Latin *trīticum dūrum,* literally: hard wheat]
durzi ('dɜːzɪ) *n.* an Indian tailor. [C19: from Hindi, from Persian *darzi* from *darz* sewing]
dusk (dʌsk) *n.* **1.** twilight or the darker part of twilight. **2.** *Poetic.* gloom; shade. ~*adj.* **3.** *Poetic.* shady; gloomy. ~*vb.* **4.** *Poetic.* to make or become dark. [Old English *dox;* related to Old Saxon *dosan* brown, Old High German *tusin* yellow, Norwegian *dusmen* misty, Latin *fuscus* dark brown]
dusky ('dʌskɪ) *adj.* **duskier, duskiest.** **1.** dark in colour; swarthy or dark-skinned. **2.** dim. —'**duskily** *adv.* —'**duskiness** *n.*
dust (dʌst) *n.* **1.** dry fine powdery material, such as particles of dirt, earth or pollen. **2.** a cloud of such fine particles. **3.** the powdery particles to which something is thought to be reduced by death, decay, or disintegration. **4. a.** the mortal body of man. **b.** the corpse of a dead person. **5.** the earth; ground. **6.** *Informal.* a disturbance; fuss (esp. in the phrases **kick up a dust, raise a dust**). **7.** something of little or no worth. **8.** *Informal.* (in mining parlance) silicosis or any similar respiratory disease. **9.** short for **gold dust.** **10.** ashes or household refuse. **11. bite the dust. a.** to suffer complete defeat. **b.** to die. **12. dust and ashes.** something that is very disappointing. **13. shake the dust off one's feet.** to depart angrily or contemptuously. **14. throw dust in the eyes of.** to confuse or mislead. ~*vb.* **15.** (*tr.*) to sprinkle or cover (something) with (dust or some other powdery substance): *to dust a cake with sugar; to dust sugar onto a cake.* **16.** to remove dust by wiping, sweeping, or brushing. **17.** *Archaic.* to make or become dirty with dust. ~See also **dust down, dust-up.** [Old English *dūst;* related to Danish *dyst* flour dust, Middle Dutch *dūst* dust, meal dust, Old High German *tunst* storm] —'**dustless** *adj.*
dust-bath *n.* the action of a bird of driving dust into its feathers, which may dislodge parasites.
dustbin ('dʌstˌbɪn) *n.* a large, usually cylindrical container for rubbish, esp. one used by a household. U.S. and Canadian names: **garbage can, trash can.**
dust bowl *n.* a semiarid area in which the surface soil is exposed to wind erosion and dust storms occur.
dustcart ('dʌstˌkɑːt) *n.* a road vehicle for collecting domestic refuse. U.S. and Canadian name: **garbage truck.**
dust coat *n. Brit.* a loose lightweight coat worn for early open motor-car riding. U.S. name: **duster.**
dust cover *n.* **1.** another name for **dustsheet.** **2.** another name for **dust jacket.** **3.** a perspex cover for the turntable of a record player.
dust devil *n.* a strong miniature whirlwind that whips up dust, litter, leaves, etc., into the air.

dust down *vb. (tr., adv.).* **1.** to remove dust from by brushing or wiping. **2.** to reprimand severely. —**dusting down** *n.*
duster ('dʌstə) *n.* **1.** a cloth used for dusting furniture, etc. U.S. name: **dust cloth. 2.** a machine for blowing out dust over trees or crops. **3.** a person or thing that dusts.
duster coat *n.* a woman's loose summer coat with wide sleeves and no buttons, popular in the mid-20th century.
dust explosion *n.* an explosion caused by the ignition of an inflammable dust, such as flour or sawdust, in the air.
dusting-powder *n.* fine powder (such as talcum powder) used to absorb moisture, etc.
dust jacket *or* **cover** *n.* a removable paper cover used to protect a bound book. Also called: **book jacket, jacket.**
dustman ('dʌstmən) *n., pl.* **-men.** *Brit.* a man whose job is to collect domestic refuse.
dustpan ('dʌstˌpæn) *n.* a short-handled hooded shovel into which dust is swept from floors, etc.
dustsheet ('dʌstˌʃiːt) *n. Brit.* a large cloth or sheet used for covering furniture to protect it from dust. Also called: **dust cover.**
dust shot *n.* the smallest size of shot for a shotgun.
dust storm *n.* a windstorm that whips up clouds of dust.
dust-up *Informal.* ~*n.* **1.** a quarrel, fight, or argument. ~*vb.* **dust up. 2.** *(tr., adv.)* to attack or assault (someone).
dusty ('dʌstɪ) *adj.* **dustier, dustiest. 1.** covered with or involving dust. **2.** like dust in appearance or colour. **3.** (of a colour) tinged with grey; pale: *dusty pink.* **4. give** *(or* **get) a dusty answer.** to give *(or* get) an unhelpful or bad-tempered reply. **5. not so dusty.** *Informal.* not too bad; fairly well: often in response to the greeting *how are you?* —'**dustily** *adv.* —'**dustiness** *n.*
dusty miller *n.* **1.** Also called: **snow-in-summer.** a caryophyllaceous plant, *Cerastium tomentosum,* of SE Europe and Asia, having white flowers and downy stems and leaves: cultivated as a rock plant. **2.** a plant, *Artemisia stelleriana,* of NE Asia and E North America, having small yellow flower heads and downy stems and leaves: family *Compositae* (composites). **3.** any of various other downy plants, such as the rose campion.
dutch (dʌtʃ) *n. Cockney slang.* wife. [C19: short for *duchess*]
Dutch (dʌtʃ) *n.* **1.** the language of the Netherlands, belonging to the West Germanic branch of the Indo-European family and quite closely related to German and English. See also **Flemish, Afrikaans. 2. the Dutch.** *(functioning as pl.)* the natives, citizens, or inhabitants of the Netherlands. **3.** See **Pennsylvania Dutch. 4.** See **double Dutch. 5. in Dutch.** *Slang.* in trouble. ~*adj.* **6.** of, relating to, or characteristic of the Netherlands, its inhabitants, or their language. ~*adv.* **7. go Dutch.** *Informal.* to share expenses equally.
Dutch auction *n.* an auction in which the price is lowered by stages until a buyer is found.
Dutch barn *n. Brit.* a farm building consisting of a steel frame and a curved roof.
Dutch cap *n.* **1.** a woman's lace cap with triangular flaps, characteristic of Dutch national dress. **2.** a contraceptive device for women. See **diaphragm** (sense 2).
Dutch cheese *n.* any of various small round hard cheeses of the Netherlands, esp. Edam and Gouda.
Dutch courage *n.* **1.** false courage gained from drinking alcohol. **2.** alcoholic drink.
Dutch disease *n.* the deindustrialization of an economy as a result of the discovery of a natural resource, as that which occurred in Holland with the exploitation of North Sea Oil, which raised the value of the Dutch currency, making its exports uncompetitive and causing its industry to decline.
Dutch doll *n.* a jointed wooden doll.
Dutch door *n.* the U.S. and Canadian name for **stable door.**
Dutch elm *n.* a widely planted hybrid elm tree, *Ulmus hollandica,* with spreading branches and a short trunk.
Dutch elm disease *n.* a disease of elm trees caused by the fungus *Ceratocystis ulmi* and characterized by withering of the foliage and stems and eventual death of the tree.
Dutch gold *n.* another name for **Dutch metal.**
Dutch hoe *n.* a type of hoe in which the head consists of a two-edged cross-blade attached to two prongs or of a single pressing of this shape.
Dutchman ('dʌtʃmən) *n., pl.* **-men. 1.** a native, citizen, or inhabitant of the Netherlands. **2.** a piece of wood, metal, etc., used to repair or patch faulty workmanship.
Dutchman's-breeches *n. (functioning as sing.)* a North American plant, *Dicentra cucullaria,* with finely divided basal leaves and pink flowers: family *Fumariaceae.* Also called: **colicweed.**
Dutchman's-pipe *n.* a woody climbing plant, *Aristolochia sipho,* of the eastern U.S., cultivated for its greenish-brown mottled flowers, which are shaped like a curved pipe: family *Aristolochiaceae.*
Dutch mattress *n.* another name for **mattress** (sense 2).
Dutch medicine *n. S. African.* patent medicine, esp. made of herbs.
Dutch metal *or* **gold** *n.* a substitute for gold leaf, consisting of thin sheets of copper that have been turned yellow by exposure to the fumes of molten zinc.
Dutch oven *n.* **1.** an iron or earthenware container with a cover used for stews, etc. **2.** a metal box, open in front, for cooking in front of an open fire.
Dutch Reformed Church *n.* any of the three Calvinist Churches to which most Afrikaans-speaking South Africans belong.
Dutch rise *n. N.Z.* an increase in wages that is of no benefit to the recipient.
Dutch rush *n. (sometimes not cap.)* a horsetail, *Equisetum hyemale,* whose siliceous stems have been used for polishing and scouring pots and pans. Also called: **scouring rush.**
Dutch treat *n. Informal.* an entertainment, meal, etc., where each person pays for himself.
Dutch uncle *n. Informal.* a person who criticizes or reproves frankly and severely.
Dutch wife *n.* a long hard bolster used, esp. in the tropics, to support one's uppermost knee when sleeping on one's side.
duteous ('djuːtɪəs) *adj. Formal or archaic.* dutiful; obedient. —'**duteously** *adv.* —'**duteousness** *n.*
dutiable ('djuːtɪəbᵊl) *adj.* (of goods) liable to duty. —ˌ**dutia'bility** *n.*
dutiful ('djuːtɪfʊl) *adj.* **1.** exhibiting or having a sense of duty. **2.** characterized by or resulting from a sense of duty: *a dutiful answer.* —'**dutifully** *adv.* —'**dutifulness** *n.*
duty ('djuːtɪ) *n., pl.* **-ties. 1.** a task or action that a person is bound to perform for moral or legal reasons. **2.** respect or obedience due to a superior, older persons, etc.: *filial duty.* **3.** the force that binds one morally or legally to one's obligations. **4.** a government tax, esp. on imports. **5.** *Brit.* **a.** the quantity of work for which a machine is designed. **b.** a measure of the efficiency of a machine. **6.** the quantity of water necessary to irrigate an area of land to grow a particular crop. **7. a.** a job or service allocated. **b.** *(as modifier): duty rota.* **8. do duty for.** to act as a substitute for. **9. on** *(or* **off) duty.** at *(or* not at) work. [C13: from Anglo-French *dueté,* from Old French *deu* DUE]
duty-bound *adj.* morally obliged as a matter of duty.
duty-free *adj., adv.* with exemption from customs or excise duties.
duty-free shop *n.* a shop, esp. one at a port or on board a ship, that sells perfume, tobacco, etc., at duty-free prices.
duty officer *n.* an officer (in the armed forces, police, etc.) on duty at a particular time.
duumvir (djuː'ʌmvə) *n., pl.* **-virs** *or* **-viri** (-vɪˌriː). **1.** *Roman history.* one of two coequal magistrates or officers. **2.** either of two men who exercise a joint authority. [C16: from Latin, from *duo* two + *vir* man]
duumvirate (djuː'ʌmvɪrɪt) *n.* the office of or government by duumvirs.
duvet ('duːveɪ) *n.* **1.** another name for **continental quilt. 2.** Also called: **duvet jacket.** a down-filled jacket used esp. by mountaineers. [C18: from French, from earlier *dumet,* from Old French *dum* DOWN[2]]
duvetyn, duvetine, *or* **duvetyne** ('djuːvəˌtiːn) *n.* a soft napped velvety fabric of cotton, silk, wool, or rayon. [C20: from French *duvetine,* from *duvet* down + -INE[1]]
dux (dʌks) *n.* (in Scottish and certain other schools) the top pupil in a class or school. [Latin: leader]
duyker ('daɪkə) *n.* a variant spelling of **duiker.**
DV *abbrev. for:* **1.** Deo volente. [Latin: God willing] **2.** Douay Version (of the Bible).
dvandva ('dvɑːndvɑː) *n.* **1.** a class of compound words consisting of two elements having a coordinate relationship as if connected by *and.* **2.** a compound word of this type, such as *Austro-Hungarian, tragicomic.* [from Sanskrit *dvamdva* a pair, from the reduplication of *dva* TWO]
DVM *abbrev. for* Doctor of Veterinary Medicine.
D/W *abbrev. for* dock warrant.
dwaal (dwɑːl) *n. S. African.* a state of befuddlement; daze. [Afrikaans]
dwale (dweɪl) *n.* another name for **deadly nightshade.** [C14: perhaps of Scandinavian origin]
dwam (dwɑːm) *or* **dwaum** (dwɔːm) *Scot.* ~*n.* **1.** a stupor or daydream (esp. in the phrase **in a dwam**). ~*vb. (intr.)* to faint or fall ill. [Old English *dwolma* confusion]
dwang (dwæŋ) *n. Scot. and N.Z.* another name for **nogging** (sense 1). [C19: Scot.; compare Dutch *dwang* force, Middle Low German *dwanc*]
dwarf (dwɔːf) *n., pl.* **dwarfs** *or* **dwarves** (dwɔːvz). **1.** an abnormally undersized person, esp. one with a large head and short arms and legs. Compare **midget. 2. a.** an animal or plant much below the average height for the species. **b.** *(as modifier): a dwarf tree.* **3.** (in folklore) a small ugly manlike creature, often possessing magical powers. **4.** *Astronomy.* short for **dwarf star.** ~*vb.* **5.** to become or cause to become comparatively small in size, importance, etc. **6.** *(tr.)* to stunt the growth of. [Old English *dweorg;* related to Old Norse *dvergr,* Old High German *twerc*] —'**dwarfish** *adj.* —'**dwarfishly** *adv.* —'**dwarfishness** *n.*
dwarf bean *n.* another name for **French bean.**
dwarf chestnut *n.* **1.** the edible nut of the chinquapin tree. **2.** another name for **chinquapin** (sense 1).
dwarf cornel *n.* an arctic and subarctic cornaceous plant, *Chamaepericlymenum suecicum* (or *Cornus suecica),* having small purple flowers surrounded by petal-like bracts.
dwarfism ('dwɔːfɪzəm) *n.* the condition of being a dwarf.

dwarf male *n.* a male animal that is much smaller, and often internally simpler, than its female counterpart. Dwarf males are commonly carried by the female, as in certain species of angler fish.

dwarf mallow *n.* a European malvaceous plant, *Malva neglecta* (or *M. rotundifolia*), having rounded leaves and small pinkish-white flowers.

dwarf star *n.* any of a class of faint stars lying in the main sequence of the Hertzsprung-Russell diagram and having a very high density and small diameter compared to the much brighter class of stars, **giant stars.** Both types belong to the same spectral classes (G, K, and M). Sometimes shortened to **dwarf.** See **red dwarf, white dwarf.**

dwell (dwɛl) *vb.* **dwells, dwelling, dwelt** (dwɛlt) *or* **dwelled.** (*intr.*) **1.** *Formal, literary.* to live as a permanent resident. **2.** to live (in a specified state): *to dwell in poverty.* ~*n.* **3.** a regular pause in the operation of a machine. **4.** a flat or constant-radius portion on a linear or rotary cam. [Old English *dwellan* to seduce, get lost; related to Old Saxon *bidwellian* to prevent, Old Norse *dvelja,* Old High German *twellen* to prevent] —**'dweller** *n.*

dwelling ('dwɛlɪŋ) *n. Formal, literary.* a place of residence.

dwell on *or* **upon** *vb.* (*intr., prep.*) to think, speak, or write at length: *he dwells on his misfortunes.*

dwelt (dwɛlt) *vb.* a past tense of **dwell.**

dwindle ('dwɪndᵊl) *vb.* to grow or cause to grow less in size, intensity, or number; diminish or shrink gradually. [C16: from Old English *dwīnan* to waste away; related to Old Norse *dvīna* to pine away]

dwt *abbrev. for:* **1.** deadweight tonnage. **2.** Also **dwt.** *Obsolete.* pennyweight. [*d*, from Latin *denarius* penny]

DX *Telegraphy, telephony.* **1.** *symbol for* long distance. **2.** (of a radio station) indicating that it is far away.

Dy *the chemical symbol for* dysprosium.

dyad ('daɪæd) *n.* **1.** *Maths.* an operator that is the unspecified product of two vectors. It can operate on a vector to produce either a scalar or vector product. **2.** an atom or group that has a valency of two. **3.** a group of two; couple. [C17: from Late Latin *dyas,* from Greek *duas* two, a pair]

dyadic (daɪ'ædɪk) *adj.* **1.** of or relating to a dyad. **2.** relating to or based on two; twofold. **3.** *Logic, maths.* (of a relation, predicate, etc.) relating two terms; binary. Compare **monadic, polyadic.** ~*n.* **4.** *Maths.* the sum of two or more dyads.

Dyak *or* **Dayak** ('daɪæk) *n., pl.* **-aks** *or* **-ak.** a member of a Malaysian people of the interior of the island of Borneo: noted for their long houses. [from Malay *Dayak* upcountry, from *darat* land]

dyarchy ('daɪɑːkɪ) *n., pl.* **-chies.** a variant spelling of **diarchy.** —**dy'archic, dy'archical,** *or* **dy'archal** *adj.*

dybbuk ('dɪbək; *Hebrew* di'buk) *n., pl.* **-buks** *or* **-bukkim** (*Hebrew* -bu'kim). *Judaism.* (in the folklore of the cabala) the soul of a dead sinner that has transmigrated into the body of a living person. [from Yiddish *dibbūk* devil, from Hebrew *dibbūq;* related to *dābhaq* to hang on, cling]

dye (daɪ) *n.* **1.** a staining or colouring substance, such as a natural or synthetic pigment. **2.** a liquid that contains a colouring material and can be used to stain fabrics, skins, etc. **3.** the colour or shade produced by dyeing. ~*vb.* **dyes, dyeing, dyed. 4.** (*tr.*) to impart a colour or stain to (something, such as fabric or hair) by or as if by the application of a dye. [Old English *dēagian,* from *dēag* a dye; related to Old High German *tugōn* to change, Lettish *dūkans* dark] —**'dyable** *or* **'dyeable** *adj.* —**'dyer** *n.*

dyed-in-the-wool *adj.* **1.** extreme or unchanging in attitude, opinion, etc. **2.** (of a fabric) made of dyed yarn.

dyeing ('daɪɪŋ) *n.* the process or industry of colouring yarns, fabric, etc.

dyeline ('daɪˌlaɪn) *adj.* another word for **diazo** (sense 2).

dyer's-greenweed *or esp. U.S.* **dyer's-broom** *n.* a small Eurasian papilionaceous shrub, *Genista tinctoria,* whose yellow flowers yield a yellow dye, formerly mixed with woad to produce the colour Kendal green. Also called: **woadwaxen, woodwaxen.**

dyer's rocket *n.* a Eurasian resedaceous plant, *Reseda luteola,* with a spike of yellowish-green flowers and long narrow leaves: formerly cultivated as the source of a yellow dye, used with woad to make Lincoln green. Also called: **weld.**

dyer's-weed *n.* any of several plants that yield a dye, such as woad, dyer's rocket, and dyer's-greenweed.

dyestuff ('daɪˌstʌf) *n.* a substance that can be used as a dye or from which a dye can be obtained.

dyewood ('daɪˌwʊd) *n.* any wood, such as brazil, from which dyes and pigments can be obtained.

dying ('daɪɪŋ) *vb.* **1.** the present participle of **die**[1]. ~*adj.* **2.** relating to or occurring at the moment of death: *a dying wish.*

dyke[1] *or* **dike** (daɪk) *n.* **1.** an embankment constructed to prevent flooding, keep out the sea, or confine a river to a particular course. **2.** a ditch or watercourse. **3.** a bank made of earth excavated for and placed alongside a ditch. **4.** *Scot.* a wall, esp. a dry-stone wall. **5.** a barrier or obstruction. **6.** a vertical or near-vertical wall-like body of igneous rock intruded into cracks in older rock. **7.** *Austral. and N.Z. informal.* **a.** a lavatory. **b.** (*as modifier*): *a dyke roll.* ~*vb.* **8.** *Civil engineering.* an embankment or wall built to confine a river to a particular course. **9.** (*tr.*) to protect, enclose, or drain (land) with a dyke. [C13: modification of Old English *dic* ditch; compare Old Norse *dīki* ditch]

dyke[2] *or* **dike** (daɪk) *n. Slang.* a lesbian. [C20: of unknown origin]

dynameter (daɪ'næmɪtə) *n.* an instrument for determining the magnifying power of telescopes.

dynamic (daɪ'næmɪk) *adj.* **1.** of or concerned with energy or forces that produce motion, as opposed to *static.* **2.** of or concerned with dynamics. **3.** Also: **dynamical.** characterized by force of personality, ambition, energy, new ideas, etc. **4.** *Music.* of, relating to, or indicating dynamics: *dynamic marks.* **5.** *Computer technol.* (of a memory) needing its contents to be refreshed periodically. Compare **static** (sense 8). [C19: from French *dynamique,* from Greek *dunamikos* powerful, from *dunamis* power, from *dunasthai* to be able] —**dy'namically** *adv.*

dynamic psychology *n. Psychol.* any system of psychology that emphasizes the interaction between different motives, emotions, and drives.

dynamic range *n.* the range of signal amplitudes over which an electronic communications channel can operate within acceptable limits of distortion. The range is determined by system noise at the lower end and by the onset of overload at the upper end.

dynamics (daɪ'næmɪks) *n.* **1.** (*functioning as sing.*) the branch of mechanics concerned with the forces that change or produce the motions of bodies. Compare **statics, kinematics. 2.** (*functioning as sing.*) the branch of mechanics that includes statics and kinetics. See **statics, kinetics. 3.** (*functioning as sing.*) the branch of any science concerned with forces. **4.** those forces that produce change in any field or system. **5.** *Music.* **a.** the various degrees of loudness called for in performance. **b.** Also called: **dynamic marks, dynamic markings.** directions and symbols used to indicate degrees of loudness.

dynamism ('daɪnəˌmɪzəm) *n.* **1.** *Philosophy.* any one of several theories that attempt to explain phenomena in terms of an immanent force or energy. Compare **mechanism** (sense 5), **vitalism. 2.** the forcefulness of an energetic personality. —**'dynamist** *n.* —**ˌdyna'mistic** *adj.*

dynamite ('daɪnəˌmaɪt) *n.* **1.** an explosive consisting of nitroglycerin or ammonium nitrate mixed with kieselguhr, sawdust, or wood pulp. **2.** *Informal.* a spectacular or potentially dangerous person or thing. ~*vb.* **3.** (*tr.*) to mine or blow up with dynamite. [C19 (coined by Alfred Nobel (1833–96), inventor of the explosive): from DYNAMO- + -ITE[1]] —**'dynaˌmiter** *n.*

dynamo ('daɪnəˌməʊ) *n., pl.* **-mos. 1.** a device for converting mechanical energy into electrical energy, esp. one that produces direct current. Compare **generator** (sense 1). **2.** *Informal.* an energetic hard-working person. [C19: short for *dynamoelectric machine*]

dynamo- *or sometimes before a vowel* **dynam-** *combining form.* indicating power: *dynamoelectric; dynamite.* [from Greek, from *dunamis* power]

dynamoelectric (ˌdaɪnəməʊɪ'lɛktrɪk) *or* **dynamoelectrical** *adj.* of or concerned with the interconversion of mechanical and electrical energy.

dynamometer (ˌdaɪnə'mɒmɪtə) *n.* any of a number of instruments for measuring power or force.

dynamometry (ˌdaɪnə'mɒmɪtrɪ) *n.* **1.** the science of power measurement. **2.** the manufacture and use of dynamometers. —**dynamometric** (ˌdaɪnəməʊ'mɛtrɪk) *or* **ˌdynamo'metrical** *adj.*

dynamotor ('daɪnəˌməʊtə) *n.* an electrical machine having a single magnetic field and two independent armature windings of which one acts as a motor and the other a generator: used to convert direct current from an accumulator into alternating current.

dynast ('dɪnəst, -æst) *n.* a ruler, esp. a hereditary one. [C17: from Latin *dynastēs,* from Greek *dunastēs,* from *dunasthai* to be powerful]

dynasty ('dɪnəstɪ) *n., pl.* **-ties. 1.** a sequence of hereditary rulers: *an Egyptian dynasty.* **2.** any sequence of powerful leaders of the same family: *the Kennedy dynasty.* [C15: via Late Latin from Greek *dunasteia,* from *dunastēs* DYNAST] —**dynastic** (dɪ'næstɪk) *or* **dy'nastical** *adj.* —**dy'nastically** *adv.*

dynatron oscillator ('daɪnəˌtrɒn) *n. Electronics.* an oscillator containing a tetrode in which the screen grid is more positive than the anode, causing the anode current to decrease as its voltage increases. [C20: from DYNA(MO)- + -TRON]

dyne (daɪn) *n.* the cgs unit of force; the force that imparts an acceleration of 1 centimetre per second per second to a mass of 1 gram. 1 dyne is equivalent to 10^{-5} newton or 7.233×10^{-5} poundal. [C19: from French, from Greek *dunamis* power, force]

dynode ('daɪnəʊd) *n.* an electrode onto which a beam of electrons can fall, causing the emission of a greater number of electrons by secondary emission. They are used in photomultipliers to amplify the signal.

dys- *prefix.* **1.** diseased, abnormal, or faulty: *dysentery; dyslexia.* **2.** difficult or painful: *dysuria.* **3.** unfavourable or bad: *dyslogistic.* [via Latin from Greek *dus-*]

dysarthria (dɪs'ɑːθrɪə) *n.* imperfect articulation of speech caused by damage to the nervous system. [from DYS- + *arthria* from Greek *arthron* articulation]

dyscrasia (dɪs'kreɪzɪə) *n. Obsolete.* any abnormal physiological condition, esp. of the blood. [C19: New Latin, from Medieval

Latin: an imbalance of humours, from Greek, from DYS- + *-krasia,* from *krasis* a mixing]

dysentery ('dɪsᵊntrɪ) *n.* infection of the intestine with bacteria or amoebae, marked chiefly by severe diarrhoea with the passage of mucus and blood. [C14: via Latin from Greek *dusenteria,* from *dusentera,* literally: bad bowels, from DYS- + *enteron* intestine] —**dysenteric** (ˌdɪsᵊn'tɛrɪk) *adj.*

dysfunction (dɪs'fʌŋkʃən) *n. Med.* any disturbance or abnormality in the function of an organ or part. —ˌ**dys'functional** *adj.*

dysgenic (dɪs'dʒɛnɪk) *adj.* **1.** of, relating to, or contributing to a degeneration or deterioration in the fitness and quality of a race or strain. **2.** of or relating to dysgenics.

dysgenics (dɪs'dʒɛnɪks) *n.* (*functioning as sing.*) the study of factors capable of reducing the quality of a race or strain, esp. the human race. Also called: **cacogenics.**

dysgraphia (dɪs'græfɪə) *n.* inability to write correctly, caused by disease of part of the brain.

dyskinesia (dɪskɪ'niːzɪə) *n.* involuntary repetitive movements, such as those occurring in chorea. [DYS- + *-kinesia* from Greek *kinesis* movement]

dyslalia (dɪs'leɪlɪə) *n.* defective speech characteristic of those affected by aphasia.

dyslexia (dɪs'lɛksɪə) *n.* impaired ability to read, not caused by low intelligence. Nontechnical name: **word blindness.** [C19: New Latin, from DYS- + *-lexia,* from *legein* to speak] —**dyslectic** (dɪs'lɛktɪk) *adj., n.* —**dys'lexic** *adj.*

dyslogistic (ˌdɪslə'dʒɪstɪk) *adj. Rare.* disapproving. [C19: from DYS- + *-logistic,* as in *eulogistic*] —ˌ**dyslo'gistically** *adv.*

dysmenorrhoea *or esp. U.S.* **dysmenorrhea** (ˌdɪsmɛnə'rɪə, dɪsˌmɛn-) *n.* abnormally difficult or painful menstruation. —ˌ**dysmenor'rhoeal** *or esp. U.S.* ˌ**dysmenor'rheal** *adj.*

dysmorphophobia (dɪsˌmɔːfəʊ'fəʊbɪə) *n.* an obsessive fear that one's body, or any part of it, is repulsive or may become so.

dyspepsia (dɪs'pɛpsɪə) *or* **dyspepsy** (dɪs'pɛpsɪ) *n.* indigestion or upset stomach. [C18: from Latin, from Greek *duspepsia,* from DYS- + *pepsis* digestion]

dyspeptic (dɪs'pɛptɪk) *adj. also* **dyspeptical. 1.** relating to or suffering from dyspepsia. **2.** irritable. ~*n.* **3.** a person suffering from dyspepsia. —**dys'peptically** *adv.*

dysphagia (dɪs'feɪdʒɪə) *n.* difficulty in swallowing, caused by obstruction or spasm of the oesophagus. [C18: New Latin, from DYS- + Greek *-phagos;* see PHAGO-] —**dysphagic** (dɪs'fædʒɪk) *adj.*

dysphasia (dɪs'feɪzɪə) *n.* impaired coordination of speech caused by a brain lesion. [see DYS- + -PHASIA] —**dys'phasic** *adj., n.*

dysphemism ('dɪsfɪˌmɪzəm) *n.* **1.** substitution of a derogatory or offensive word or phrase for an innocuous one. **2.** the word or phrase so substituted. [C19: DYS- + EUPHEMISM] —**dysphe'mistic** *adj.*

dysphonia (dɪs'fəʊnɪə) *n.* any impairment in the ability to speak normally, as from spasm or strain of the vocal cords. [C18: New Latin, from Greek: harshness of sound, from DYS- + *-phōnia* -PHONY] —**dysphonic** (dɪs'fɒnɪk) *adj.*

dysphoria (dɪs'fɔːrɪə) *n.* a feeling of being ill at ease. [C20: New Latin, from Greek DYS- + *-phoria,* from *pherein* to bear] —**dysphoric** (dɪs'fɒrɪk) *adj.*

dysplasia (dɪs'pleɪzɪə) *n.* abnormal development of an organ or part of the body, including congenital absence. [C20: New Latin, from DYS- + *-plasia,* from Greek *plasis* a moulding] —**dysplastic** (dɪs'plæstɪk) *adj.*

dyspnoea *or U.S.* **dyspnea** (dɪsp'niːə) *n.* difficulty in breathing or in catching the breath. Compare **eupnoea.** [C17: via Latin from Greek *duspnoia,* from DYS- + *pnoē* breath, from *pnein* to breathe] —**dysp'noeal, dysp'noeic** *or U.S.* **dysp'neal, dysp'neic** *adj.*

dyspraxia (dɪs'præksɪə) *n. Pathol.* an impairment in the control of the motor system. [DYS- + PRAX(IS) + -IA]

dysprosium (dɪs'prəʊsɪəm) *n.* a soft silvery-white metallic element of the lanthanide series: used in laser materials and as a neutron absorber in nuclear control rods. Symbol: Dy; atomic no.: 66; atomic wt.: 162.50; valency: 3; relative density: 8.56; melting pt.: 1407°C; boiling pt.: 2335°C. [C20: New Latin, from Greek *dusprositos* difficult to get near + -IUM]

dyssynergia (dɪsɪ'nɜːdʒɪə) *n.* muscular incoordination caused by a brain disorder. [from DYS- + Greek *synergia* cooperation]

dystaxia (dɪs'tæksɪə) *n. Pathol.* lack of muscular coordination resulting in shaky limb movements and unsteady gait. [from DYS- + Greek *-taxia,* from *tassein* to put in order]

dysteleology (ˌdɪstelɪ'ɒlədʒɪ, -tiːlɪ-) *n. Philosophy.* the denial of purpose in life. Compare **teleology.** —**dysˌteleo'logical** *adj.* —ˌ**dystele'ologist** *n.*

dysthymia (dɪs'θaɪmɪə) *n. Psychiatry.* **1.** the characteristics of the neurotic and introverted, including anxiety, depression, and compulsive behaviour. **2.** *Obsolete.* a relatively mild depression. [C19: New Latin, from Greek *dusthumia,* from DYS- + *thumos* mind] —**dys'thymic** *adj.*

dystocia (dɪs'təʊʃə) *n. Med.* abnormal, slow, or difficult childbirth, usually because of disordered or ineffective contractions of the uterus. [New Latin, from Greek, from *dus-* (see DYS-) + *tokos* childbirth + -IA] —**dys'tocial** *adj.*

dystonia (dɪs'təʊnɪə) *n.* a neurological disorder, caused by disease of the basal ganglia, in which the muscles of the trunk, shoulders, and neck go into spasm, so that the head and limbs are held in unnatural positions. [from DYS- + *-tonia* from Greek *tonos* tension, from *teinen* to stretch]

dystopia (dɪs'təʊpɪə) *n.* an imaginary place where everything is as bad as it can be. [C19 (coined by the philosopher J. S. Mill): from DYS- + UTOPIA] —**dys'topian** *adj., n.*

dystrophin ('dɪstrəfɪn) *n.* a protein, the absence of which is believed to cause muscular dystrophy.

dystrophy ('dɪstrəfɪ) *or* **dystrophia** (dɪ'strəʊfɪə) *n.* **1.** any of various bodily disorders, characterized by wasting of tissues. See also **muscular dystrophy. 2.** *Ecology.* a condition of lake water when it is too acidic and poor in oxygen to support life, resulting from excessive humus content. [C19: New Latin *dystrophia,* from DYS- + Greek *trophē* food] —**dystrophic** (dɪs'trɒfɪk) *adj.*

dysuria (dɪs'jʊərɪə) *n.* difficult or painful urination. [C14: via Latin from Greek *dusouria,* from DYS- + -URIA] —**dys'uric** *adj.*

dytiscid (dɪ'tɪsɪd, daɪ-) *n.* **1.** any carnivorous aquatic beetle of the family *Dytiscidae,* having large flattened back legs used for swimming. ~*adj.* **2.** of, relating to, or belonging to the *Dytiscidae.* [C19: from New Latin *Dytiscus* genus name, changed from Greek *dutikos* able to dive, from *duein* to dive]

Dyula (diː'uːlə, 'djuːlə) *n.* **1.** (*pl.* **-la** *or* **-las**) a member of a negroid people of W Africa, living chiefly in the rain forests of Côte d'Ivoire, where they farm rice, etc. **2.** the language of this people, belonging to the Mande branch of the Niger-Congo family.

DZ *international car registration for* Algeria. [from Arabic *Djazïr*]

dz. *abbrev. for* dozen.

dziggetai ('dʒɪgɪˌtaɪ) *n.* a variant of **chigetai.**

dzo (zəʊ) *n., pl.* **dzos** *or* **dzo.** a variant spelling of **zo.**

Dzongka ('zɒŋkə) *n.* the official language of Bhutan in central Asia: a dialect of Tibetan.

e *or* **E** (iː) *n., pl.* **e's, E's,** *or* **Es.** **1.** the fifth letter and second vowel of the modern English alphabet. **2.** any of several speech sounds represented by this letter, in English as in *he, bet,* or *below.*

e *symbol for:* **1.** *Maths.* a transcendental number, fundamental to mathematics, that is the limit of $(1 + 1/n)^n$ as n increases to infinity: used as the base of natural logarithms. Approximate value: 2.718 282...; relation to π: $e^{\pi i} = -1$, where $i = \sqrt{-1}$. **2.** electron. **3.** *Chess.* See **algebraic notation.**

E *symbol for:* **1.** earth. **2.** East. **3.** English. **4.** Egypt(ian). **5.** exa-. **6.** *Music.* **a.** a note having a frequency of 329.63 hertz (**E above middle C**) or this value multiplied or divided by any power of 2; the third note of the scale of C major. **b.** a key, string, or pipe producing this note. **c.** the major or minor key having this note as its tonic. **7.** *Physics.* **a.** energy. **b.** electric field strength. **c.** electromotive force. **d.** Young's modulus (of elasticity). **8.** *Logic.* a universal negative categorical proposition, such as *no pigs can fly:* often symbolized as **SeP.** Compare **A, I, O.** [from Latin *(n)e(go)* I deny] **9. a.** a person without a regular income, or who is dependent on the state on a long-term basis because of unemployment, sickness, old age, etc. **b.** (*as modifier*): *E worker.* ~See also **occupation groupings.** ~ **10.** international car registration for Spain. [from Spanish *España*]

e. *abbrev. for:* **1.** engineer(ing). **2.** *Telephony.* Erlang.

E. *abbrev. for* Earl.

e- *prefix forming verbs and verbal derivatives.* **1.** out: *eviscerate; egest.* **2.** away: *elapse; elongate.* **3.** outside: *evaginate.* **4.** completely: *evaporate.* **5.** without: *ebracteate.* [from Latin *ē-* away; related to EX-[1]]

E- *prefix.* used with numbers indicating a standardized system within the European Economic Community, as of recognized food additives or standard pack sizes. See also **E number.**

ea. *abbrev. for* each.

each (iːtʃ) *determiner.* **1. a.** every (one) of two or more considered individually: *each day; each person.* **b.** (*as pronoun*): *each gave according to his ability.* ~*adv.* **2.** for, to, or from each one; apiece: *four apples each.* [Old English *ǣlc;* related to Old High German *ēogilīh,* Old Frisian *ellik,* Dutch *elk*]

each other *pron.* used when the action, attribution, etc., is reciprocal: *furious with each other.*

▷**Usage.** *Each other* and *one another* are interchangeable in modern British usage, despite recommendations by some authorities that the meaning of the former be restricted to each of two and the latter to each of three or more.

each way *adj., adv. Horse racing etc., chiefly Brit.* (of a bet) made on the same runner or contestant to win or come second or third in a race. Also: **both ways.** U.S. term: **across-the-board.**

EACSO (iːˈɑːksəʊ) *n. acronym for* East African Common Services Organization.

eager[1] (ˈiːgə) *adj.* **1.** (*postpositive;* often foll. by *to* or *for*) impatiently desirous (of); anxious or avid (for): *he was eager to see her departure.* **2.** characterized by or feeling expectancy or great desire: *an eager look.* **3.** *Archaic.* tart or biting; sharp. [C13: from Old French *egre,* from Latin *acer* sharp, keen] —ˈ**eagerly** *adv.* —ˈ**eagerness** *n.*

eager[2] (ˈeɪgə) *n.* a variant spelling of **eagre.**

eager beaver *n. Informal.* a person who displays conspicuous diligence, esp. one who volunteers for extra work.

eagle (ˈiːgᵊl) *n.* **1.** any of various birds of prey of the genera *Aquila, Harpia,* etc. (see **golden eagle, harpy eagle**), having large broad wings and strong soaring flight: family *Accipitridae* (hawks, etc.). See also **sea eagle.** Related adj.: **aquiline.** **2.** a representation of an eagle used as an emblem, etc., esp. representing power: *the Roman eagle.* **3.** a standard, seal, etc., bearing the figure of an eagle. **4.** *Golf.* a score of two strokes under par for a hole. **5.** a former U.S. gold coin worth ten dollars: withdrawn from circulation in 1934. **6.** the shoulder insignia worn by a U.S. full colonel or equivalent rank. [C14: from Old French *aigle,* from Old Provençal *aigla,* from Latin *aquila,* perhaps from *aquilus* dark]

eagle-eyed *adj.* having keen or piercing eyesight.

eagle-hawk *n.* **1.** Also called: **wedge-tailed eagle.** a large aggressive Australian eagle, *Aquila audax.* ~*vb.* (*intr.*) **2.** *Austral. slang.* to pluck wool from a sheep's dead body.

eagle owl *n.* a large owl, *Bubo bubo,* of Europe and Asia. It has brownish speckled plumage and large ear tufts.

eagle ray *n.* any of various rays of the family *Myliobatidae,* related to the stingrays but having narrower pectoral fins and a projecting snout with heavily browed eyes.

eaglestone (ˈiːgᵊlˌstəʊn) *n.* a hollow oval nodule of clay ironstone, formerly thought to have magical properties.

eaglet (ˈiːglɪt) *n.* a young eagle.

eaglewood (ˈiːgᵊlˌwʊd) *n.* **1.** an Asian thymelaeaceous tree, *Aquilaria agallocha,* having fragrant wood that yields a resin used as a perfume. **2.** the wood of this tree. ~Also called: **aloes, aloes wood, agalloch, lignaloes.**

eagre *or* **eager** (ˈeɪgə) *n.* a tidal bore, esp. of the Humber or Severn estuaries. [C17: perhaps from Old English *ēagor* flood; compare Old English *ēa* river, water]

EAK *international car registration for* East Africa Kenya.

ealdorman (ˈɔːldəmən) *n., pl.* **-men.** an official of Anglo-Saxon England, appointed by the king, who was responsible for law, order, and justice in his shire and for leading his local fyrd in battle. [Old English *ealdor* lord + MAN]

EAM *n.* (in World War II) the leftist resistance in German-occupied Greece. [C20: from Modern Greek *Ethniko Apeleutherotiko Metopo* National Liberation Front]

-ean *suffix forming adjectives.* a variant of **-an:** *Caesarean.*

E & OE *abbrev. for* errors and omissions excepted.

ear[1] (ɪə) *n.* **1.** the organ of hearing and balance in higher vertebrates and of balance only in fishes. In man and other mammals it consists of three parts (see **external ear, middle ear, internal ear**). Related adj.: **aural.** **2.** the outermost cartilaginous part of the ear (pinna) in mammals, esp. man. **3.** the sense of hearing. **4.** sensitivity to musical sounds, poetic diction, etc.: *he has an ear for music.* **5.** attention, esp. favourable attention; consideration; heed (esp. in the phrases **give ear to, lend an ear**). **6.** an object resembling the external ear in shape or position, such as a handle on a jug. **7.** Also called (esp. Brit.): **earpiece.** a display box at the head of a newspaper page, esp. the front page, for advertisements, etc. **8. all ears.** very attentive; listening carefully. **9. by ear.** without reading from written music. **10. fall on deaf ears.** to be ignored or pass unnoticed. **11. have hard ears.** *Caribbean.* to be stubbornly disobedient. **12. a flea in one's ear.** *Informal.* a sharp rebuke. **13. have the ear of.** to be in a position to influence: *he has the ear of the president.* **14. head over ears.** tumultuously; with a powerful and confusing effect: *head over ears in love.* **15. in one ear and out the other.** heard but unheeded. **16. keep** (*or* **have**) **one's ear to the ground.** to be or try to be well informed about current trends and opinions. **17. make a pig's ear of.** *Informal.* to ruin disastrously. **18. one's ears are burning.** one is aware of being the topic of another's conversation. **19. out on one's ear.** *Informal.* dismissed unceremoniously. **20. play by ear. a.** to act according to the demands of a situation rather than to a plan; improvise. **b.** to perform a musical piece on an instrument without written music. **21. prick up one's ears.** to start to listen attentively; become interested. **22. set by the ears.** to cause disagreement or commotion. **23. a thick ear.** *Informal.* a blow on the ear delivered as punishment, in anger, etc. **24. turn a deaf ear.** to be deliberately unresponsive. **25. up to one's ears.** *Informal.* deeply involved, as in work or debt. **26. wet behind the ears.** *Informal.* inexperienced; naive; immature. [Old English *ēare;* related to Old Norse *eyra,* Old High German *ōra,* Gothic *ausō,* Greek *ous,* Latin *auris*] —ˈ**earless** *adj.* —ˈ**earˌlike** *adj.*

ear[2] (ɪə) *n.* **1.** the part of a cereal plant, such as wheat or barley, that contains the seeds, grains, or kernels. ~*vb.* **2.** (*intr.*) (of cereal plants) to develop such parts. [Old English *ēar;* related to Old High German *ahar,* Old Norse *ax,* Gothic *ahs* ear, Latin *acus* chaff, Greek *akros* pointed]

earache (ˈɪərˌeɪk) *n.* pain in the middle or inner ear. Technical name: **otalgia.** Compare **otitis.**

earbash (ˈɪəˌbæʃ) *vb.* (*intr.*) *Austral. and N.Z. slang.* to talk incessantly. —ˈ**earˌbasher** *n.* —ˈ**earˌbashing** *n.*

eardrop (ˈɪəˌdrɒp) *n.* a pendant earring.

eardrops (ˈɪəˌdrɒps) *pl. n.* liquid medication for inserting into the external ear.

eardrum (ˈɪəˌdrʌm) *n.* the nontechnical name for **tympanic membrane.**

eared (ɪəd) *adj.* **a.** having an ear or ears. **b.** (*in combination*): *long-eared; two-eared.*

eared seal *n.* any seal of the pinniped family *Otariidae,* typically having visible earflaps and conspicuous hind limbs that can be used for locomotion on land. Compare **earless seal.**

earflap (ˈɪəˌflæp) *n.* **1.** Also called: **earlap.** either of two pieces of fabric or fur attached to a cap, which can be let down to keep the ears warm. **2.** *Zoology.* a small flap of skin forming the pinna of such animals as seals.

earful (ˈɪəfʊl) *n. Informal.* **1.** something heard or overheard. **2.** a rebuke or scolding, esp. a lengthy or severe one.

earing (ˈɪərɪŋ) *n. Nautical.* a line fastened to a corner of a sail for reefing. [C17: from EAR[1] + -ING[1] or perhaps RING[1]]

earl (ɜːl) *n.* **1.** (in the British Isles) a nobleman ranking below a marquess and above a viscount. Female equivalent: **countess.**

2. (in Anglo-Saxon England) a royal governor of any of the large divisions of the kingdom, such as Wessex. [Old English *eorl;* related to Old Norse *jarl* chieftain, Old Saxon *erl* man]

earlap ('ɪəˌlæp) *n.* 1. another word for **earflap** (sense 1). 2. *Rare.* a. the external ear. b. the ear lobe. [C16: from EAR[1] + LAP[1]]

earldom ('ɜːldəm) *n.* 1. the rank, title, or dignity of an earl or countess. 2. the lands of an earl or countess.

earless seal *n.* any seal of the pinniped family *Phocidae,* typically having rudimentary hind limbs, no external earflaps, and a body covering of hair with no underfur. Also called: **hair seal.** Compare **eared seal.**

Earl Marshal *n.* an officer of the English peerage who presides over the College of Heralds and organizes royal processions and other important ceremonies.

ear lobe *n.* the fleshy lower part of the external ear.

early ('ɜːlɪ) *adj.* **-lier, -liest,** *adv.* 1. before the expected or usual time. 2. occurring in or characteristic of the first part of a period or sequence. 3. occurring in or characteristic of a period far back in time. 4. occurring in the near future. **5. at the earliest.** not before the time or date mentioned. **6. early days.** a. too soon to tell how things will turn out. b. *Austral. and N.Z.* during the 19th-century pioneering period in Australia and New Zealand. [Old English *ǣrlīce,* from *ǣr* ERE + *-līce* -LY[2]; related to Old Norse *arliga*] —'**earliness** *n.*

early bird *n. Informal.* a person who rises early or arrives in good time.

Early Bird *n.* one of a number of communications satellites, the first of which was launched in 1965 into a stationary orbit and provided telephone channels between Europe and the U.S. See also **Intelsat.**

Early Christian *adj.* denoting or relating to the style of architecture that started in Italy in the 3rd century A.D. and spread through the Roman empire until the 5th century.

early closing *n. Brit.* 1. a. the shutting of most of the shops in a town one afternoon each week. b. (*as adj.*): *early-closing day.* 2. the day on which this happens: *Thursday is early closing in Aylesbury.*

Early English *n.* a style of architecture used in England in the 12th and 13th centuries, characterized by lancet arches, narrow openings, and plate tracery.

early music *n.* 1. music of the Middle Ages and Renaissance, sometimes also including music of the baroque and early classical periods. ~(*modifier*) **early-music** 2. of or denoting an approach to musical performance emphasizing the use of period instruments and historically researched scores and playing techniques: *the early-music movement.*

early purple orchid *n.* a Eurasian orchid, *Orchis mascula,* with purplish-crimson flowers and stems marked with blackish-purple spots.

early warning *n.* advance notice of some impending event or development.

early warning system *n.* a network of radar and communications units intended to detect at the earliest possible moment an attack by enemy aircraft or missiles.

earmark ('ɪəˌmɑːk) *vb.* (*tr.*) 1. to set aside or mark out for a specific purpose. 2. to make an identification mark on the ear of (a domestic animal). ~*n.* 3. a mark of identification on the ear of a domestic animal. 4. any distinguishing mark or characteristic.

earmuff ('ɪəˌmʌf) *n.* one of a pair of pads of fur or cloth, joined by a headband, for keeping the ears warm.

earn (ɜːn) *vb.* 1. to gain or be paid (money or other payment) in return for work or service. 2. (*tr.*) to acquire, merit, or deserve through behaviour or action: *he has earned a name for duplicity.* 3. (*tr.*) (of securities, investments, etc.) to gain (interest, return, profit, etc.). [Old English *earnian;* related to Old High German *arnēn* to reap, Old Saxon *asna* salary, tithe] —'**earner** *n.*

earned income *n.* income derived from paid employment and comprising mainly wages and salaries.

earnest[1] ('ɜːnɪst) *adj.* 1. serious in mind or intention: *an earnest student.* 2. showing or characterized by sincerity of intention: *an earnest promise.* 3. demanding or receiving serious attention. ~*n.* **4. in earnest.** with serious or sincere intentions. [Old English *eornost;* related to Old High German *ernust* seriousness, Old Norse *ern* energetic, efficient, Gothic *arniba* secure] —'**earnestly** *adv.* —'**earnestness** *n.*

earnest[2] ('ɜːnɪst) *n.* 1. a part or portion of something given in advance as a guarantee of the remainder. 2. Also called: **earnest money.** *Contract law.* something given, usually a nominal sum of money, to confirm a contract. 3. any token of something to follow; pledge; assurance. [C13: from Old French *erres* pledges, plural of *erre* earnest money, from Latin *arrha,* shortened from *arrabō* pledge, from Greek *arrabon,* from Hebrew *'ērābhōn* pledge, from *'ārabh* he pledged]

earnings ('ɜːnɪŋz) *pl. n.* 1. money or other payment earned. 2. a. the profits of an enterprise. b. an individual's investment income.

EAROM ('ɪərɒm) *n. Computer technol. acronym for* electrically alterable read only memory.

earphone ('ɪəˌfəʊn) *n.* a device for converting electric currents into sound waves, held close to or inserted into the ear.

earpiece ('ɪəˌpiːs) *n.* the earphone in a telephone receiver.

ear piercing *n.* 1. the making of a hole in the lobe of an ear, using a sterilized needle, so that an earring may be worn fastened in the hole. ~*adj.* **ear-piercing.** 2. so loud or shrill as to hurt the ears.

earplug ('ɪəˌplʌg) *n.* a small piece of soft material, such as wax, placed in the ear to keep out noise or water.

earring ('ɪəˌrɪŋ) *n.* an ornament for the ear, usually clipped onto the lobe or fastened through a hole pierced in the lobe.

ear shell *n.* another name for the **abalone.**

earshot ('ɪəˌʃɒt) *n.* the range or distance within which sound may be heard (esp. in the phrases **within earshot, out of earshot**).

ear-splitting *adj.* so loud or shrill as to hurt the ears.

earth (ɜːθ) *n.* 1. (*sometimes cap.*) the third planet from the sun, the only planet on which life is known to exist. It is not quite spherical, being flattened at the poles, and consists of three geological zones, the core, mantle, and thin outer crust. The surface, covered with large areas of water, is enveloped by an atmosphere principally of nitrogen (78 per cent), oxygen (21 per cent), and some water vapour. The age is estimated at over four thousand million years. Distance from sun: 149.6 million kilometres; equatorial diameter: 12 756 km; mass: 5.976×10^{24} kg; sidereal period of axial rotation: 23 hours 56 minutes 4 seconds; sidereal period of revolution: 365.256 days. Related adjs.: **terrestrial, telluric.** 2. the inhabitants of this planet: *the whole earth rejoiced.* 3. the dry surface of this planet as distinguished from sea or sky; land; ground. 4. the loose soft material that makes up a large part of the surface of the ground and consists of disintegrated rock particles, mould, clay, etc.; soil. 5. worldly or temporal matters as opposed to the concerns of the spirit. 6. the hole in which a burrowing animal, esp. a fox, lives. 7. *Chem.* See **rare earth, alkaline earth.** 8. a. a connection between an electrical circuit or device and the earth, which is at zero potential. b. a terminal to which this connection is made. U.S. and Canadian equivalent: **ground.** 9. Also called: **earth colour.** any of various brown pigments composed chiefly of iron oxides. **10.** (*modifier*) *Astrology.* of or relating to a group of three signs of the zodiac, Taurus, Virgo, and Capricorn. Compare **air** (sense 18), **fire** (sense 24), **water** (sense 12). **11. cost the earth.** *Informal.* to be very expensive. **12. come back** *or* **down to earth.** to return to reality from a fantasy or daydream. **13. on earth.** used as an intensifier in such phrases as **what on earth, who on earth,** etc. **14. run to earth.** a. to hunt (an animal, esp. a fox) to its earth and trap it there. b. to find (someone) after searching. ~*vb.* **15.** (*intr.*) (of a hunted fox) to go to ground. **16.** (*tr.*) to connect (a circuit, device, etc.) to earth. ~See also **earth up.** [Old English *eorthe;* related to Old Norse *jorth,* Old High German *ertha,* Gothic *airtha,* Greek *erā*]

earthborn ('ɜːθˌbɔːn) *adj. Chiefly poetic.* 1. of earthly origin. 2. human; mortal.

earthbound ('ɜːθˌbaʊnd) *adj.* 1. confined to the earth. 2. lacking in imagination; pedestrian or dull. 3. moving or heading towards the earth.

earth closet *n.* a type of lavatory in which earth is used to cover excreta.

earthen ('ɜːθən) *adj.* (*prenominal*) 1. made of baked clay: *an earthen pot.* 2. made of earth.

earthenware ('ɜːθənˌwɛə) *n.* a. vessels, etc., made of baked clay. b. (*as adj.*): *an earthenware pot.*

earth inductor compass *n.* a compass that depends on the current induced in a coil revolving in the earth's magnetic field. Also called: **inductor compass.**

earthlight ('ɜːθˌlaɪt) *n.* another name for **earthshine.**

earthling ('ɜːθlɪŋ) *n.* (esp. in poetry or science fiction) an inhabitant of the earth; human being. [C16: from EARTH + LING[1]]

earthly ('ɜːθlɪ) *adj.* **-lier, -liest.** 1. of or characteristic of the earth as opposed to heaven; material or materialistic; worldly. 2. (*usually used with a negative*) *Informal.* conceivable or possible; feasible (in such phrases as **not an earthly (chance),** etc.). —'**earthliness** *n.*

earthman ('ɜːθˌmæn) *n., pl.* **-men.** (esp. in science fiction) an inhabitant or native of the earth.

earth mother *n.* 1. (in various mythologies) a. a female goddess considered as the source of fertility and life. b. the earth personified. 2. *Informal.* a sensual or fecund woman.

earthnut ('ɜːθˌnʌt) *n.* 1. Also called: **pignut.** a perennial umbelliferous plant, *Conopodium majus,* of Europe and Asia, having edible dark brown tubers. 2. any of various plants having an edible root, tuber, underground pod, or similar part, such as the peanut or truffle.

earth pillar *n.* a landform consisting of a column of clay or earth capped and protected from erosion by a boulder.

earthquake ('ɜːθˌkweɪk) *n.* a sudden release of energy in the earth's crust or upper mantle, usually caused by movement along a fault plane or by volcanic activity and resulting in the generation of seismic waves which can be destructive. Related adj.: **seismic.**

earth return *n.* the return path for an electrical circuit made by connections to earth at each end.

earthrise ('ɜːθˌraɪz) *n.* the rising of the earth above the lunar horizon, as seen from the moon or a spacecraft.

earth science *n.* any of various sciences, such as geology, geography, and geomorphology, that are concerned with the structure, age, and other aspects of the earth.

earthshaking ('ɜːθˌʃeɪkɪŋ) *adj. Informal.* of enormous importance or consequence; momentous.

earthshine ('ɜːθˌʃaɪn) *or* **earthlight** *n.* the ashen light reflected from the earth, which illuminates the new moon when it is not receiving light directly from the sun.

earthstar ('ɜːθˌstɑː) *n.* any of various basidiomycetous saprophytic woodland fungi of the genus *Geastrum,* whose brown onion-shaped reproductive body splits into a star shape to release the spores.

earth up *vb.* (*tr., adv.*) to cover (part of a plant, esp. the stem) with soil in order to protect from frost, light, etc.

earthward ('ɜːθwəd) *adj.* **1.** directed towards the earth. ~*adv.* **2.** a variant of **earthwards.**

earthwards ('ɜːθwədz) *or* **earthward** *adv.* towards the earth.

earth wax *n.* another name for **ozocerite.**

earthwork ('ɜːθˌwɜːk) *n.* **1.** excavation of earth, as in engineering construction. **2.** a fortification made of earth.

earthworm ('ɜːθˌwɜːm) *n.* **1.** any of numerous oligochaete worms of the genera *Lumbricus, Allolobophora, Eisenia,* etc., which burrow in the soil and help aerate and break up the ground. **2.** *Archaic.* a grovelling person.

earthy ('ɜːθɪ) *adj.* **earthier, earthiest. 1.** of, composed of, or characteristic of earth. **2.** robust, lusty, or uninhibited. **3.** unrefined, coarse, or crude. **4.** an archaic word for **worldly** (sense 1). **5.** *Electrical engineering.* on the earthed side of an electrical circuit, but not necessarily with a direct current connection to earth. —'**earthily** *adv.* —'**earthiness** *n.*

ear trumpet *n.* a trumpet-shaped instrument that amplifies sounds and is held to the ear: an old form of hearing aid.

earwax ('ɪəˌwæks) *n.* the nontechnical name for **cerumen.**

earwig ('ɪəˌwɪg) *n.* **1.** any of various insects of the order *Dermaptera,* esp. *Forficula auricularia* (**common European earwig**), which typically have an elongated body with small leathery forewings, semicircular membranous hindwings, and curved forceps at the tip of the abdomen. ~*vb.* **-wigs, -wigging, -wigged. 2.** to eavesdrop. **3.** (*tr.*) *Archaic.* to attempt to influence (a person) by private insinuation. [Old English *ēarwicga,* from *ēare* EAR[1] + *wicga* beetle, insect; probably from a superstition that the insect crept into human ears]

earwigging ('ɪəˌwɪgɪŋ) *n. Informal.* a scolding or harangue: *I'll give him an earwigging about that.*

EAS *Aeronautics. abbrev. for* equivalent air speed.

ease (iːz) *n.* **1.** freedom from discomfort, worry, or anxiety. **2.** lack of difficulty, labour, or awkwardness; facility. **3.** rest, leisure, or relaxation. **4.** freedom from poverty or financial embarrassment; affluence: *a life of ease.* **5.** lack of restraint, embarrassment, or stiffness: *his ease of manner disarmed us.* **6. at ease. a.** *Military.* (of a standing soldier, etc.) in a relaxed position with the feet apart rather than at attention. **b.** a command to adopt such a position. **c.** in a relaxed attitude or frame of mind. ~*vb.* **7.** to make or become less burdensome. **8.** (*tr.*) to relieve (a person) of worry or care; comfort. **9.** (*tr.*) to make comfortable or give rest to. **10.** (*tr.*) to make less difficult; facilitate. **11.** to move or cause to move into, out of, etc., with careful manipulation: *to ease a car into a narrow space.* **12.** (when *intr.,* often foll. by *off* or *up*) to lessen or cause to lessen in severity, pressure, tension, or strain; slacken, loosen, or abate. **13. ease oneself** *or* **ease nature.** *Archaic, euphemistic.* to urinate or defecate. **14. ease the helm.** *Nautical.* to relieve the pressure on the rudder of a vessel, esp. by bringing the bow into the wind. [C13: from Old French *aise* ease, opportunity, from Latin *adjacēns* neighbouring (area); see ADJACENT] —'**easer** *n.*

easeful ('iːzfʊl) *adj.* characterized by or bringing ease; peaceful; tranquil. —'**easefully** *adv.* —'**easefulness** *n.*

easel ('iːzᵊl) *n.* a frame, usually in the form of an upright tripod, used for supporting or displaying an artist's canvas, blackboard, etc. [C17: from Dutch *ezel* ASS[1]; related to Gothic *asilus,* German *Esel,* Latin *asinus* ass]

easement ('iːzmənt) *n.* **1.** *Property law.* the right enjoyed by a landowner of making limited use of his neighbour's land, as by crossing it to reach his own property. **2.** the act of easing or something that brings ease.

easily ('iːzɪlɪ) *adv.* **1.** with ease; without difficulty or exertion. **2.** by far; beyond question; undoubtedly: *he is easily the best in the contest.* **3.** probably; almost certainly: *he may easily come first.*

▷**Usage.** See at **easy.**

easiness ('iːzɪnɪs) *n.* **1.** the quality or condition of being easy to accomplish, do, obtain, etc. **2.** ease or relaxation of manner; nonchalance.

east (iːst) *n.* **1.** one of the four cardinal points of the compass, 90° clockwise from north and 180° from west. **2.** the direction along a parallel towards the sunrise, at 90° to north; the direction of the earth's rotation. **3. the east.** (*often cap.*) any area lying in or towards the east. Related adj.: **oriental. 4.** *Cards.* (*usually cap.*) the player or position at the table corresponding to east on the compass. ~*adj.* **5.** situated in, moving towards, or facing the east. **6.** (esp. of the wind) from the east. ~*adv.* **7.** in, to, or towards the east. **8.** *Archaic.* (of the wind) from the east. ~Symbol: E [Old English *ēast;* related to Old High German *ōstar* to the east, Old Norse *austr,* Latin *aurora* dawn, Greek *eōs,* Sanskrit *usās* dawn, morning]

East (iːst) *n.* **the. 1.** the continent of Asia regarded as culturally distinct from Europe and the West; the Orient. **2.** (formerly) the countries under Communist rule, lying mainly in the E hemisphere. Compare **West** (sense 2). **3. a.** of or denoting the eastern part of a specified country, area, etc. **b.** (*as part of a name*): *East Sussex.* —'**Eastern** *adj.*

eastbound ('iːstˌbaʊnd) *adj.* going or leading towards the east.

east by north *n.* **1.** one point on the compass north of east, 78° 45′ clockwise from north. ~*adj., adv.* **2.** in, from, or towards this direction.

east by south *n.* **1.** one point on the compass south of east, 101° 15′ clockwise from north. ~*adj., adv.* **2.** in, from, or towards this direction.

east coast fever *n.* a disease of cattle, endemic in east and central Africa, caused by a parasite, *Theileria parva,* that is carried by ticks.

Easter ('iːstə) *n.* **1.** a festival of the Christian Church commemorating the Resurrection of Christ: falls on the Sunday following the first full moon after the vernal equinox. **2.** Also called: **Easter Sunday, Easter Day.** the day on which this festival is celebrated. **3.** the period between Good Friday and Easter Monday. Related adj.: **Paschal.** [Old English *ēastre,* after a Germanic goddess *Eostre;* related to Old High German *ōstarūn* Easter, Old Norse *austr* to the EAST, Old Slavonic *ustru* like summer]

Easter cactus *n.* another name for **Christmas cactus.**

Easter egg *n.* an egg given to children at Easter, usually a chocolate egg or a hen's egg with its shell painted.

Easter-ledges *n.* **1.** (*functioning as sing.*) another name for **bistort** (sense 1). **2. Easter-ledge pudding.** *Northern English dialect.* a pudding made from the young leaves of the bistort.

Easter lily *n.* any of various lilies, esp. *Lilium longiflorum,* that have large showy white flowers.

easterly ('iːstəlɪ) *adj.* **1.** of, relating to, or situated in the east. ~*adv., adj.* **2.** towards or in the direction of the east. **3.** from the east: *an easterly wind.* ~*n., pl.* **-lies. 4.** a wind from the east.

eastern ('iːstən) *adj.* **1.** situated in or towards the east. **2.** facing or moving towards the east.

Eastern Church *n.* **1.** any of the Christian Churches of the former Byzantine Empire. **2.** any Church owing allegiance to the Orthodox Church and in communion with the Greek patriarchal see of Constantinople. **3.** any Church, including Uniat Churches, having Eastern forms of liturgy and institutions.

Easterner ('iːstənə) *n.* (*sometimes not cap.*) a native or inhabitant of the east of any specified region, esp. of the Orient or of the eastern states of the U.S.

eastern hemisphere *n.* (*often caps.*) **1.** that half of the globe containing Europe, Asia, Africa, and Australia, lying east of the Greenwich meridian. **2.** the lands in this, esp. Asia.

easternmost ('iːstənˌməʊst) *adj.* situated or occurring farthest east.

Eastern Orthodox Church *n.* another name for the **Orthodox Church.**

Eastern rite *n.* the rite and liturgy of an Eastern Church or of a Uniat Church.

Eastern Standard Time *n.* one of the standard times used in North America, five hours behind Greenwich Mean Time. Abbrev.: **EST.**

Easter term *n.* the term at the Inns of Court following the Hilary term.

Eastertide ('iːstəˌtaɪd) *n.* the Easter season.

East Germanic *n.* a subbranch of the Germanic languages: now extinct. The only member of which records survive is Gothic.

East Indian *n.* **1.** *Caribbean.* an immigrant to the West Indies who is of Indian origin; an Asian West Indian. ~*adj.* **2.** *U.S. and Canadian.* of, relating to, or originating in the East Indies.

easting ('iːstɪŋ) *n.* **1.** *Nautical.* the net distance eastwards made by a vessel moving towards the east. **2.** *Cartography.* **a.** the distance eastwards of a point from a given meridian indicated by the first half of a map grid reference. **b.** a longitudinal grid line. Compare **northing** (sense 3).

east-northeast *n.* **1.** the point on the compass or the direction midway between northeast and east, 67° 30′ clockwise from north. ~*adj., adv.* **2.** in, from, or towards this direction. ~Symbol: ENE

east-southeast *n.* **1.** the point on the compass or the direction midway between east and southeast, 112° 30′ clockwise from north. ~*adj., adv.* **2.** in, from, or towards this direction. ~Symbol: ESE

eastward ('iːstwəd) *adj.* **1.** situated or directed towards the east. ~*adv.* **2.** a variant of **eastwards.** ~*n.* **3.** the eastward part, direction, etc. —'**eastwardly** *adv., adj.*

eastwards ('iːstwədz) *or* **eastward** *adv.* towards the east.

easy ('iːzɪ) *adj.* **easier, easiest. 1.** not requiring much labour or effort; not difficult; simple: *an easy job.* **2.** free from pain, care, or anxiety: *easy in one's mind.* **3.** not harsh or restricting; lenient: *easy laws.* **4.** tolerant and undemanding; easy-going: *an easy disposition.* **5.** readily influenced or persuaded; pliant: *she was an easy victim of his wiles.* **6.** not tight or constricting; loose: *an easy fit.* **7.** not strained or extreme; moderate; gentle: *an easy pace; an easy ascent.* **8.** *Economics.* **a.** readily obtainable. **b.** (of a market) characterized by low demand or excess supply with prices tending to fall. Compare **tight** (sense 10). **9.** *Informal.* ready to fall in with any suggestion made; not predisposed: *he is easy about what to do.* **10.** *Slang.* sexually available. **11. easy**

on the eye. *Informal.* pleasant to look at; attractive, esp. sexually. **12. woman of easy virtue.** a sexually available woman, esp. a prostitute. ~*adv.* **13.** *Informal.* in any easy or relaxed manner. **14. easy does it.** *Informal.* go slowly and carefully; be careful. **15. go easy.** (*usually imperative;* often foll. by *on*) to exercise moderation. **16. stand easy.** *Military.* a command to soldiers standing at ease that they may relax further. **17. take it easy. a.** to avoid stress or undue hurry. **b.** to remain calm; not become agitated or angry. ~*vb.* **easies, easying, easied. 18.** (*usually imperative*) Also: **easy-oar.** to stop rowing. [C12: from Old French *aisié,* past participle of *aisier* to relieve, EASE]

▷**Usage.** *Easy* is not used as an adverb by careful speakers and writers except in certain set phrases: *to take it easy; easy does it.* Where a fixed expression is not involved, the usual adverbial form of *easy* is preferred: *this polish goes on more easily* (not *easier) than the other.*

easy-care *adj.* (esp. of a fabric or garment) hardwearing, practical, and requiring no special treatment during washing, cleaning, etc.

easy chair *n.* a comfortable upholstered armchair.

easy game *or* **easy mark** *n. Informal.* a person who is easily deceived or taken advantage of.

easy-going ('iːzɪ'gəʊɪŋ) *adj.* **1.** relaxed in manner or attitude; inclined to be excessively tolerant. **2.** moving at a comfortable pace: *an easy-going horse.*

easy meat *n. Informal.* **1.** someone easily seduced or deceived. **2.** something easy to get or do.

easy money *n.* **1.** money made with little effort, sometimes dishonestly. **2.** *Commerce.* money that can be borrowed at a low interest rate.

Easy Street n. (*sometimes not caps.*) *Informal.* a state of financial security.

eat (iːt) *vb.* **eats, eating, ate, eaten. 1.** to take into the mouth and swallow (food, etc.), esp. after biting and chewing. **2.** (*tr.;* often foll. by *away* or *up*) to destroy as if by eating: *the damp had eaten away the woodwork.* **3.** (often foll. by *into*) to use up or waste: *taxes ate into his inheritance.* **4.** (often foll. by *into* or *through*) to make (a hole, passage, etc.) by eating or gnawing: *rats ate through the floor.* **5.** to take or have (a meal or meals): *we always eat at six.* **6.** (*tr.*) to include as part of one's diet: *he doesn't eat fish.* **7.** (*tr.*) *Informal.* to cause to worry; make anxious: *what's eating you?* **8.** (*tr.*) *Taboo slang.* to perform cunnilingus or fellatio upon. **9. I'll eat my hat if.** *Informal.* to be greatly surprised if (something happens that proves one wrong). **10. eat one's heart out.** to brood or pine with grief or longing. **11. eat one's words.** to take back something said; recant; retract. **12. eat out of (someone's) hand.** to be entirely obedient to (someone). **13. eat (someone) out of house and home.** to ruin (someone, esp. one's parent or one's host) by consuming all his food. ~See also **eat out, eats, eat up.** [Old English *etan;* related to Gothic *itan,* Old High German *ezzan,* Latin *edere,* Greek *edein,* Sanskrit *admi*] —'**eater** *n.*

eatable ('iːtəbᵊl) *adj.* fit or suitable for eating; edible.

eatables ('iːtəbᵊlz) *pl. n.* (*sometimes sing.*) food.

eatage ('iːtɪdʒ) *n. Northern English dialect.* grazing rights.

eaten ('iːtᵊn) *vb.* the past participle of **eat.**

eatery ('iːtərɪ) *n., pl.* **-eries** (-ərɪz) *Informal.* a restaurant or eating house.

eating ('iːtɪŋ) *n.* **1.** food, esp. in relation to its quality or taste: *this fruit makes excellent eating.* ~*adj.* **2.** relating to or suitable for eating, esp. uncooked: *eating pears.* **3.** relating to or for eating: *an eating house.*

eat out *vb.* (*intr., adv.*) to eat away from home, esp. in a restaurant.

eats (iːts) *pl. n. Informal.* articles of food; provisions.

eat up *vb.* (*adv., mainly tr.*) **1.** (*also intr.*) to eat or consume entirely: often used as an exhortation to children. **2.** *Informal.* to listen to with enthusiasm or appreciation: *the audience ate up the speaker's every word.* **3.** (*often passive*) *Informal.* to affect grossly: *she was eaten up by jealousy.* **4.** *Informal.* to travel (a distance) quickly: *we just ate up the miles.*

EAU *international car registration for* East Africa Uganda.

eau de Cologne (əʊ də kə'ləʊn) *n.* See **cologne.** [French, literally: water of Cologne]

eau de Javelle (əʊ də ʒæ'vɛl, ʒə-; *French* od ʒavɛl) *n.* another name for **Javel water.**

eau de nil (əʊ də niːl) *n., adj.* **a.** a pale yellowish-green colour. **b.** (*as adj.*): *eau-de-nil walls.* [French, literally: water of (the) Nile]

eau de vie (əʊ də viː; *French* od vi) *n.* brandy or other spirits. [French, literally: water of life]

eaves (iːvz) *pl. n.* the edge of a roof that projects beyond the wall. [Old English *efes;* related to Gothic *ubizwa* porch, Greek *hupsos* height]

eavesdrop ('iːvz,drɒp) *vb.* **-drops, -dropping, -dropped.** (*intr.*) to listen secretly to the private conversation of others. [C17: back formation from earlier *evesdropper,* from Old English *yfesdrype* water dripping from the eaves; see EAVES, DROP; compare Old Norse *upsardropi*] —'**eaves,dropper** *n.*

ebb (ɛb) *vb.* (*intr.*) **1.** (of tide water) to flow back or recede. Compare **flow** (sense 9). **2.** to fall away or decline. ~*n.* **3. a.** the flowing back of the tide from high to low water or the period in which this takes place. **b.** (*as modifier*): *the ebb tide.* Compare **flood** (sense 3). **4. at a low ebb.** in a state or period of weakness, lack of vigour, or decline. [Old English *ebba;* related to Old Norse *efja* river bend, Gothic *ibuks* moving backwards, Old High German *ippihōn* to roll backwards, Middle Dutch *ebbe* ebb]

EBCDIC ('ɛpsɪ,dɪk) *n. acronym for* extended binary-coded decimal-interchange code: a computer code for representing alphanumeric characters.

E-boat *n.* (in World War II) a fast German boat carrying guns and torpedoes. [from *enemy* boat]

ebon ('ɛbᵊn) *n., adj.* a poetic word for **ebony.** [C14: from Latin *hebenus;* see EBONY]

ebonite ('ɛbə,naɪt) *n.* another name for **vulcanite.**

ebonize *or* **ebonise** ('ɛbə,naɪz) *vb.* (*tr.*) to stain or otherwise finish in imitation of ebony.

ebony ('ɛbənɪ) *n., pl.* **-onies. 1.** any of various tropical and subtropical trees of the genus *Diospyros,* esp. *D. ebenum* of S India, that have hard dark wood: family *Ebenaceae.* See also **persimmon. 2.** the wood of such a tree, much used for cabinet-work. **3. a.** a black colour, sometimes with a dark olive tinge. **b.** (*as adj.*): *an ebony skin.* [C16 *hebeny,* from Late Latin *ebeninus* from Greek *ebeninos,* from *ebenos* ebony, of Egyptian origin]

Ebor. ('iːbɔː) *abbrev. for* Eboracensis. [Latin: (Archbishop) of York]

ebracteate (ɪ'bræktɪ,eɪt, -tɪɪt) *adj.* (of plants) having no bracts. [C19: from New Latin *ebracteātus;* see E-, BRACTEATE]

EBU *abbrev. for* European Broadcasting Union.

ebullient (ɪ'bʌljənt, ɪ'bʊl-) *adj.* **1.** overflowing with enthusiasm or excitement; exuberant. **2.** boiling. [C16: from Latin *ēbullīre* to bubble forth, be boisterous, from *bullīre* to BOIL[1]] —**e'bullience** *or* **e'bulliency** *n.* —**e'bulliently** *adv.*

ebulliometer (ɪ,bʌlɪ'ɒmɪtə) *n. Physics.* a device used to determine the boiling point of a solution. —**e,bulli'ometry** *n.*

ebullioscopy (ɪ,bʌlɪ'ɒskəpɪ, ɪ,bʊl-) *n. Chem.* a technique for finding molecular weights of substances by measuring the extent to which they change the boiling point of a solvent. [C19: from *ebullioscope,* from Latin *ebullire* to boil over + -SCOPE] —**ebullioscopic** (ɪ,bʌlɪə'skɒpɪk, ɪ,bʊl-) *adj.* —**e,bullio'scopically** *adv.*

ebullition (,ɛbə'lɪʃən) *n.* **1.** the process of boiling. **2.** a sudden outburst, as of intense emotion. [C16: from Late Latin *ēbullītiō;* see EBULLIENT]

eburnation (,iːbə'neɪʃən, ,ɛb-) *n.* a degenerative condition of bone or cartilage characterized by unusual hardness. [C19: from Latin *eburnus* of ivory, from *ebur* ivory]

EBV *abbrev. for* Epstein-Barr virus.

EC *abbrev. for:* **1.** European Community. **2.** (in London postal code) East Central. ~ **3.** *international car registration for* Ecuador.

ec- *combining form.* out from; away from: *ecbolic; eccentric; ecdysis.* [from Greek *ek* (before a vowel *ex*) out of, away from; see EX-[1]]

ecad ('iːkæd) *n.* an organism whose form has been affected by its environment. [C20: from EC(OLOGY) + -AD[1]]

ecarinate (iː'kærɪnɪt) *adj. Biology.* having no carina or keel. [E- + CARINATE]

écarté (eɪ'kɑːteɪ; *French* ekarte) *n.* **1.** a card game for two, played with 32 cards and king high. **2.** *Ballet.* **a.** a body position in which one arm and the same leg are extended at the side of the body. **b.** (*as adj.*): *the écarté position.* [C19: from French, from *écarter* to discard, from *carte* CARD[1]]

ecbolic (ɛk'bɒlɪk) *adj.* **1.** hastening labour or abortion. ~*n.* **2.** a drug or agent that hastens labour or abortion. [C18: from Greek *ekbolē* a throwing out, from *ekballein* to throw out, from *ballein* to throw]

Ecce Homo ('ɛkeɪ 'həʊməʊ, 'ɛksɪ) *n.* a picture or sculpture of Christ crowned with thorns. [Latin: behold the man, the words of Pontius Pilate to his accusers (John 19:5)]

eccentric (ɪk'sɛntrɪk) *adj.* **1.** deviating or departing from convention, esp. in a bizarre manner; irregular or odd. **2.** situated away from the centre or the axis. **3.** not having a common centre: *eccentric circles.* Compare **concentric. 4.** not precisely circular. ~*n.* **5.** a person who deviates from normal forms of behaviour esp. in a bizarre manner. **6.** a device for converting rotary motion to reciprocating motion. [C16: from Medieval Latin *eccentricus,* from Greek *ekkentros* out of centre, from *ek-* EX-[1] + *kentron* centre] —**ec'centrically** *adv.*

eccentricity (,ɛksɛn'trɪsɪtɪ) *n., pl.* **-ties. 1.** unconventional or irregular behaviour. **2.** deviation from a circular path or orbit. **3.** a measure of the elongation of an elliptical orbit, esp. of a planet or satellite: the distance between the foci divided by the length of the major axis. **4.** *Geometry.* a number that expresses the shape of a conic section: the ratio of the distance of a point on the curve from a fixed point (the focus) to the distance of the point from a fixed line (the directrix). **5.** the degree of displacement of the geometric centre of a part from the true centre, esp. of the axis of rotation of a wheel.

ecchymosis (,ɛkɪ'məʊsɪs) *n., pl.* **-ses** (-siːz). discoloration of the skin through bruising. [C16: from New Latin, from Greek *ekkhumōsis,* from *ekkhumousthai* to pour out, from *khumos* juice] —**ecchymosed** ('ɛkɪ,məʊzd, -,məʊst) *or* **ecchymotic** (,ɛkɪ'mɒtɪk) *adj.*

eccl. *or* **eccles.** *abbrev. for* ecclesiastic(al).

Eccles. *or* **Eccl.** *Bible. abbrev. for* Ecclesiastes.
Eccles cake (ˈɛkᵊlz) *n. Brit.* a pastry with a filling of dried fruit. [named after *Eccles,* town in NW England]
ecclesia (ɪˈkliːzɪə) *n., pl.* **-siae** (-zɪˌiː). **1.** (in formal Church usage) a congregation. **2.** the assembly of citizens of an ancient Greek state. [C16: from Medieval Latin, from Late Greek *ekklēsia* assembly, from *ekklētos* called, from *ekkalein* to call out, from *kalein* to call]
ecclesiast. *abbrev. for* ecclesiastical.
ecclesiastic (ɪˌkliːzɪˈæstɪk) *n.* **1.** a clergyman or other person in holy orders. *~adj.* **2.** of or associated with the Christian Church or clergy.
ecclesiastical (ɪˌkliːzɪˈæstɪkᵊl) *adj.* of or relating to the Christian Church. —**ecˌclesiˈastically** *adv.*
ecclesiasticism (ɪˌkliːzɪˈæstɪˌsɪzəm) *n.* exaggerated attachment to the practices or principles of the Christian Church.
ecclesiolatry (ɪˌkliːzɪˈɒlətrɪ) *n.* obsessional devotion to ecclesiastical traditions. —**ecˌclesiˈolater** *n.*
ecclesiology (ɪˌkliːzɪˈɒlədʒɪ) *n.* **1.** the study of the Christian Church. **2.** the study of Church architecture and decoration. —**ecclesiological** (ɪˌkliːzɪəˈlɒdʒɪkᵊl) *adj.* —**ecˌclesioˈlogically** *adv.* —**ecˌclesiˈologist** *n.*
Ecclus. *Bible. abbrev. for* Ecclesiasticus.
eccremocarpus (ˌɛkrəməˈkɑːpəs) *n.* any plant of the evergreen climbing genus *Eccremocarpus,* esp. *E. scaber,* grown for its decorative pinnate foliage and bright orange-red bell flowers: family *Bignoniaceae.* [New Latin, from Greek *ekkremēs* suspended + *karpos* fruit]
eccrine (ˈɛkrɪn) *adj.* of or denoting glands that secrete externally, esp. the numerous sweat glands on the human body. Compare **apocrine.** [from Greek *ekkrinein* to secrete, from *ek-* EC- + *krinein* to separate]
eccrinology (ˌɛkrɪˈnɒlədʒɪ) *n.* the branch of medical science concerned with secretions of the eccrine glands.
ecdemic (ɛkˈdɛmɪk) *adj.* not indigenous or endemic; foreign: *an ecdemic disease.*
ecdysiast (ɛkˈdɪzɪˌæst) *n.* a facetious word for **stripper** (sense 1). [C20: (coined by H. L. Mencken) from ECDYSIS + *-ast,* variant of -IST]
ecdysis (ˈɛkdɪsɪs) *n., pl.* **-ses** (-ˌsiːz). the periodic shedding of the cuticle in insects and other arthropods or the outer epidermal layer in reptiles. See also **ecdysone.** [C19: New Latin, from Greek *ekdusis,* from *ekduein* to strip, from *ek-* EX-[1] + *duein* to put on] —**ecˈdysial** *adj.*
ecdysone (ɛkˈdaɪˌsəʊn) *n.* a hormone secreted by the prothoracic gland of insects that controls ecdysis and stimulates metamorphosis. [C20: from German *ecdyson,* from Greek *ekdusis;* see ECDYSIS]
ecesis (ɪˈsiːsɪs) *n.* the establishment of a plant in a new environment. [C20: from Greek *oikēsis* a dwelling in, from *oikein* to inhabit; related to *oikos* a house]
ECG *abbrev. for:* **1.** electrocardiogram. **2.** electrocardiograph.
echard (ˈɛkɑːd) *n.* water that is present in the soil but cannot be absorbed or otherwise utilized by plants. [C20: from Greek *ekhein* to hold back + *ardein* to water]
echelon (ˈɛʃəˌlɒn) *n.* **1.** a level of command, responsibility, etc. (esp. in the phrase **the upper echelons**). **2.** *Military.* **a.** a formation in which units follow one another but are offset sufficiently to allow each unit a line of fire ahead. **b.** a group formed in this way. **3.** *Physics.* a type of diffraction grating consisting of a series of plates of equal thickness arranged stepwise with a constant offset. *~vb.* **4.** to assemble in echelon. [C18: from French *échelon,* literally: rung of a ladder, from Old French *eschiele* ladder, from Latin *scāla;* see SCALE[3]]
echeveria (ˌɛtʃɪˈvɪərɪə) *n.* any of various tropical American crassulaceous plants of the genus *Echeveria,* cultivated for their colourful foliage. [named after M. *Echeveri,* 19th-century Mexican botanical artist]
echidna (ɪˈkɪdnə) *n., pl.* **-nas** *or* **-nae** (-niː). any of the spine-covered monotreme mammals of the genera *Tachyglossus* of Australia and *Zaglossus* of New Guinea: family *Tachyglossidae.* They have a long snout and claws for hunting ants and termites. Also called: **spiny anteater.** [C19: from New Latin, from Latin: viper, from Greek *ekhidna*]
echinate (ˈɛkɪˌneɪt) *or* **echinated** *adj. Biology.* covered with spines, bristles, or bristle-like outgrowths.
echino- *or before a vowel* **echin-** *combining form* indicating spiny or prickly: *echinoderm.* [from New Latin, via Latin from Greek *ekhinos* sea urchin, hedgehog]
echinococcus (ɪˌkaɪnəˈkɒkəs) *n.* any of the tapeworms constituting the genus *Echinococcus,* the larvae of which are parasitic in man and domestic animals.
echinoderm (ɪˈkaɪnəʊˌdɜːm) *n.* any of the marine invertebrate animals constituting the phylum *Echinodermata,* characterized by tube feet, a calcite body-covering (test), and a five-part symmetrical body. The group includes the starfish, sea urchins, and sea cucumbers. —**eˌchinoˈdermal** *or* **eˌchinoˈdermatous** *adj.*
echinoid (ɪˈkaɪnɔɪd, ˈɛkə-) *n.* **1.** any of the echinoderms constituting the class *Echinoidea,* typically having a rigid ovoid body. The class includes the sea urchins and sand dollars. *~adj.* **2.** of or belonging to this class.
echinus (ɪˈkaɪnəs) *n., pl.* **-ni** (-naɪ). **1.** *Architect.* an ovolo moulding between the shaft and the abacus of a Doric column. **2.** any of the sea urchins of the genus *Echinus,* such as *E. esculentus* (**edible sea urchin**) of the Mediterranean. [C14: from Latin, from Greek *ekhinos*]
echium (ˈɛkɪəm) *n.* any plant of the Mediterranean genus *Echium* whose bell-shaped flowers are borne on single-sided spikes in a wide variety of colours; *E. vulgare* is viper's bugloss: family *Boraginaceae.* [New Latin, from Greek *echion,* from *echis* viper, from its use as an antidote to a viper bite]
echo (ˈɛkəʊ) *n., pl.* **-oes.** **1. a.** the reflection of sound or other radiation by a reflecting medium, esp. a solid object. **b.** the sound so reflected. **2.** a repetition or imitation, esp. an unoriginal reproduction of another's opinions. **3.** something that evokes memories, esp. of a particular style or era. **4.** (*sometimes pl.*) an effect that continues after the original cause has disappeared; repercussion: *the echoes of the French Revolution.* **5.** a person who copies another, esp. one who obsequiously agrees with another's opinions. **6. a.** the signal reflected by a radar target. **b.** the trace produced by such a signal on a radar screen. **7.** the repetition of certain sounds or syllables in a verse line. **8.** the quiet repetition of a musical phrase. **9.** Also called: **echo organ** *or* **echo stop.** a manual or stop on an organ that controls a set of quiet pipes that give the illusion of sounding at a distance. **10.** an electronic effect in recorded music that adds vibration or resonance. *~vb.* **-oes, -oing, -oed.** **11.** to resound or cause to resound with an echo: *the cave echoed their shouts.* **12.** (*intr.*) (of sounds) to repeat or resound by echoes; reverberate. **13.** (*tr.*) (of persons) to repeat (words, opinions, etc.), in imitation, agreement, or flattery. **14.** (*tr.*) (of things) to resemble or imitate (another style, earlier model, etc.). **15.** (*tr.*) (of a computer) to display (a character) on the screen of a visual display unit as a response to receiving that character from a keyboard entry. [C14: via Latin from Greek *ēkhō;* related to Greek *ēkhē* sound] —**ˈechoing** *adj.* —**ˈecholess** *adj.* —**ˈechoˌlike** *adj.*
Echo[1] (ˈɛkəʊ) *n.* either of two U.S. passive communications satellites, the first of which was launched in 1960.
Echo[2] (ˈɛkəʊ) *n. Communications.* code word for the letter *e.*
echocardiography (ˌɛkəʊkɑːdɪˈɒgrəfɪ) *n.* examination of the heart using ultrasound techniques.
echo chamber *n.* a room with walls that reflect sound. It is used to make acoustic measurements and as a source of reverberant sound to be mixed with direct sound for recording or broadcasting. Also called: **reverberation chamber.**
echography (ɛˈkɒgrəfɪ) *n.* medical examination of the internal structures of the body by means of ultrasound.
echoic (ɛˈkəʊɪk) *adj.* **1.** characteristic of or resembling an echo. **2.** onomatopoeic; imitative.
echoic memory *n. Psychol.* the ability to recapture the exact impression of a sound for a few seconds after the sound has finished. Compare **iconic memory.**
echoism (ˈɛkəʊˌɪzəm) *n.* **1.** onomatopoeia as a source of word formation. **2.** phonetic assimilation of one vowel to the vowel in the preceding syllable.
echolalia (ˌɛkəʊˈleɪlɪə) *n. Psychiatry.* the tendency to repeat mechanically words just spoken by another person: can occur in cases of brain damage, mental retardation, and schizophrenia. [C19: from New Latin, from ECHO + Greek *lalia* talk, chatter, from *lalein* to chatter] —**echolalic** (ˌɛkəʊˈlælɪk) *adj.*
echolocation (ˌɛkəʊləʊˈkeɪʃən) *n.* determination of the position of an object by measuring the time taken for an echo to return from it and its direction.
echo plate *n.* (in sound recording or broadcasting) an electromechanical device for producing echo and reverbation effects.
echopraxia (ˌɛkəʊˈpræksɪə) *or* **echopraxis** *n.* the involuntary imitation of the actions of others.
echo sounder *n.* a navigation and position-finding device that determines depth by measuring the time taken for a pulse of high-frequency sound to reach the sea bed or a submerged object and for the echo to return. —**echo sounding** *n.*
echovirus (ˈɛkəʊˌvaɪrəs) *or* **ECHO virus** *n.* any of a group of viruses that can cause symptoms of mild meningitis, the common cold, or infections of the intestinal and respiratory tracts. [C20: from the initials of *Enteric Cytopathic Human Orphan* ("orphan" because originally believed to be unrelated to any disease) + VIRUS]
echt *German.* (ɛçt; *English* ɛkt) *adj.* real; genuine; authentic.
éclair (eɪˈklɛə, ɪˈklɛə) *n.* a finger-shaped cake of choux pastry, usually filled with cream and covered with chocolate. [C19: from French, literally: lightning (probably so called because it does not last long), from *éclairer,* from Latin *clārāre* to make bright, from *clārus* bright]
eclampsia (ɪˈklæmpsɪə) *n. Pathol.* a toxic condition of unknown cause that sometimes develops in the last three months of pregnancy, characterized by high blood pressure, abnormal weight gain and convulsions. Compare **pre-eclampsia.** [C19: from New Latin, from Greek *eklampsis* a shining forth, from *eklampein,* from *lampein* to shine] —**ecˈlamptic** *adj.*
éclat (eɪˈklɑː; *French* ekla) *n.* **1.** brilliant or conspicuous success, effect, etc. **2.** showy display; ostentation. **3.** social distinction. **4.** approval; acclaim; applause. [C17: from French, from *éclater* to burst; related to Old French *esclater* to splinter, perhaps of Germanic origin; compare SLIT]

eclectic (ɪˈklɛktɪk, ɛˈklɛk-) *adj.* **1.** (in art, philosophy, etc.) selecting what seems best from various styles, doctrines, ideas, methods, etc. **2.** composed of elements drawn from a variety of sources, styles, etc. ~*n.* **3.** a person who favours an eclectic approach, esp. in art or philosophy. [C17: from Greek *eklektikos,* from *eklegein* to select, from *legein* to gather] —**ecˈlectically** *adv.*

eclecticism (ɪˈklɛktɪˌsɪzəm, ɛˈklɛk-) *n.* **1.** an eclectic system or method. **2.** the use or advocacy of such a system.

eclipse (ɪˈklɪps) *n.* **1.** the total or partial obscuring of one celestial body by another. A **solar eclipse** occurs when the moon passes between the sun and the earth; a **lunar eclipse** when the earth passes between the sun and the moon. See also **total eclipse, partial eclipse, annular eclipse.** Compare **occultation. 2.** the period of time during which such a phenomenon occurs. **3.** any dimming or obstruction of light. **4.** a loss of importance, power, fame, etc., esp. through overshadowing by another. ~*vb.* (*tr.*) **5.** to cause an eclipse of. **6.** to cast a shadow upon; darken; obscure. **7.** to overshadow or surpass in importance, power, etc. [C13: back formation from Old English *eclypsis,* from Latin *eclīpsis,* from Greek *ekleipsis* a forsaking, from *ekleipein* to abandon, from *leipein* to leave] —**eˈclipser** *n.*

eclipse plumage *n.* seasonal plumage that occurs in certain birds after the breeding plumage and before the winter plumage: is characterized by dull coloration.

eclipsing binary *or* **variable** *n.* a binary star whose orbital plane lies in or near the line of sight so that one component is regularly eclipsed by its companion. See also **variable star.**

eclipsis (ɪˈklɪpsɪs) *n. Linguistics.* **1.** a rare word for **ellipsis** (sense 1). **2.** (in Gaelic) phonetic change of an initial consonant under the influence of a preceding word. Unvoiced plosives become voiced, while voiced plosives are changed to nasals.

ecliptic (ɪˈklɪptɪk) *n.* **1.** *Astronomy.* **a.** the great circle on the celestial sphere representing the apparent annual path of the sun relative to the stars. It is inclined at 23.45° to the celestial equator. The **poles of the ecliptic** lie on the celestial sphere due north and south of the plane of the ecliptic. **b.** (*as modifier*): *the ecliptic plane.* **2.** an equivalent great circle, opposite points of which pass through the Tropics of Cancer and Capricorn, on the terrestrial globe. ~*adj.* **3.** of or relating to an eclipse. —**eˈcliptically** *adv.*

eclogite (ˈɛkləˌdʒaɪt) *n.* a rare coarse-grained basic rock consisting of large bright red garnets in a greenish mixture of pyroxene, quartz, feldspar, etc. Its origin is thought to be intermediate between igneous and metamorphic. [C19: from Greek *eklogē* a selection]

eclogue (ˈɛklɒg) *n.* a pastoral or idyllic poem, usually in the form of a conversation or soliloquy. [C15: from Latin *ecloga* short poem, collection of extracts, from Greek *eklogē* selection, from *eklegein* to select; see ECLECTIC]

eclosion (ɪˈkləʊʒən) *n.* the emergence of an insect larva from the egg or an adult from the pupal case. [C19: from French *éclosion,* from *éclore* to hatch, ultimately from Latin *exclūdere* to shut out, EXCLUDE]

eco (ˈiːkəʊ) *n.* **a.** short for **ecology. b.** (*as modifier*): *an eco group.*

eco- *combining form.* denoting ecology or ecological: *ecocide; ecosphere.*

ecocide (ˈiːkəˌsaɪd, ˈɛkə-) *n.* total destruction of an area of the natural environment, esp. by human agency.

ecol. *abbrev. for:* **1.** ecological. **2.** ecology.

ecological (ˌiːkəˈlɒdʒɪkᵊl) *adj.* **1.** of or relating to ecology. **2.** (of a practice, policy, product, etc.) tending to benefit or cause minimal damage to the environment. —ˌ**ecoˈlogically** *adv.*

ecology (ɪˈkɒlədʒɪ) *n.* **1.** the study of the relationships between living organisms and their environment. **2.** the set of relationships of a particular organism with its environment. **3. human ecology.** the study of the relationships between human groups and their physical environment. ~Also called (for senses 1, 2): **bionomics.** [C19: from German *Ökologie,* from Greek *oikos* house (hence, environment)] —**eˈcologist** *n.*

econ. *abbrev. for:* **1.** economical. **2.** economics. **3.** economy.

econometrics (ɪˌkɒnəˈmɛtrɪks) *n.* (*functioning as sing.*) the application of mathematical and statistical techniques to economic problems and theories. —**eˌconoˈmetric** *or* **eˌconoˈmetrical** *adj.* —**econometrician** (ɪˌkɒnəməˈtrɪʃən) *or* **eˌconoˈmetrist** *n.*

economic (ˌiːkəˈnɒmɪk, ˌɛkə-) *adj.* **1.** of or relating to an economy, economics, or finance: *economic development; economic theories.* **2.** *Brit.* capable of being produced, operated, etc., for profit; profitable: *the firm is barely economic.* **3.** concerning or affecting material resources or welfare: *economic pests.* **4.** concerned with or relating to the necessities of life; utilitarian. **5.** a variant of **economical. 6.** *Informal.* inexpensive; cheap.

economical (ˌiːkəˈnɒmɪkᵊl, ˌɛkə-) *adj.* **1.** using the minimum required; not wasteful of time, effort, resources, etc.: *an economical car; an economical style.* **2.** frugal; thrifty: *she was economical by nature.* **3.** a variant of **economic** (senses 1–4).

economically (ˌiːkəˈnɒmɪkəlɪ, ˌɛkə-) *adv.* **1.** with economy or thrift; without waste. **2.** with regard to the economy of a person, country, etc.

economic determinism *n.* a doctrine that states that all cultural, social, political, and intellectual activities are a product of the economic organization of society.

economic geography *n.* the study of the geographical distribution of economic resources and their use.

economic geology *n.* the study of how geological deposits can be used as economic resources.

economic indicator *n.* a statistical measure representing an economic variable: *the retail price index is an economic indicator of the actual level of prices.*

economic rent *n.* **1.** *Economics.* a payment to a factor of production (land, labour, or capital) in excess of that needed to keep it in its present use. **2.** (in Britain) the rent of a dwelling based on recouping the costs of providing it plus a profit sufficient to motivate the landlord to let it.

economics (ˌiːkəˈnɒmɪks, ˌɛkə-) *n.* **1.** (*functioning as sing.*) the social science concerned with the production and consumption of goods and services and the analysis of the commercial activities of a society. See also **macroeconomics, microeconomics. 2.** (*pl.*) financial aspects: *the economics of the project are very doubtful.*

economic zone *n.* another term for **exclusive economic zone.**

economism (ɪˈkɒnəˌmɪzəm) *n.* **1. a.** a political theory that regards economics as the main factor in society, ignoring or reducing to simplistic economic terms other factors such as culture, nationality, etc. **b.** the belief that the main aim of a political group, trade union, etc., is to improve the material living standards of its members. **2.** (*often cap.*) (in Tsarist Russia) a political belief that the sole concern of the working classes should be with improving their living conditions and not with political reforms.

economist (ɪˈkɒnəmɪst) *n.* **1.** a specialist in economics. **2.** *Archaic.* a person who advocates or practises frugality.

economize *or* **economise** (ɪˈkɒnəˌmaɪz) *vb.* (often foll. by *on*) to limit or reduce (expense, waste, etc.). —**eˌconomiˈzation** *or* **eˌconomiˈsation** *n.*

economizer *or* **economiser** (ɪˈkɒnəˌmaɪzə) *n.* **1.** a device that uses the waste heat from a boiler flue to preheat the feed water. **2.** a person or thing that economizes.

Economo's disease (ɪˈkɒnəməʊz) *n. Pathol.* another name for **sleeping sickness** (sense 2). [C20: named after K. von *Economo* (1876–1931), Austrian neurologist]

economy (ɪˈkɒnəmɪ) *n., pl.* **-mies. 1.** careful management of resources to avoid unnecessary expenditure or waste; thrift. **2.** a means or instance of this; saving. **3.** sparing, restrained, or efficient use, esp. to achieve the maximum effect for the minimum effort: *economy of language.* **4. a.** the complex of human activities concerned with the production, distribution, and consumption of goods and services. **b.** a particular type or branch of such production, distribution, and consumption: *a socialist economy; an agricultural economy.* **5.** the management of the resources, finances, income, and expenditure of a community, business enterprise, etc. **6. a.** a class of travel in aircraft, providing less luxurious accommodation than first class at a lower fare. **b.** (*as modifier*): *economy class.* **7.** (*modifier*) offering or purporting to offer a larger quantity for a lower price: *economy pack.* **8.** the orderly interplay between the parts of a system or structure: *the economy of nature.* **9.** *Philosophy.* the principle that, of two competing theories, the one with less ontological presupposition is to be preferred. **10.** *Archaic.* the management of household affairs; domestic economy. [C16: via Latin from Greek *oikonomia* domestic management, from *oikos* house + *-nomia,* from *nemein* to manage]

economy of scale *n. Economics.* a fall in average costs resulting from an increase in the scale of production.

ecophysiology (ˌiːkəʊˌfɪzɪˈɒlədʒɪ) *n.* the study of the ways in which organisms are adapted to their environment.

écorché (ˌeɪkɔːˈʃeɪ) *n.* an anatomical figure without the skin, so that the muscular structure is visible. [C19: French, literally: skinned]

ecospecies (ˈiːkəʊˌspiːʃiːz, -ˌspiːsiːz; ˈɛkəʊ-) *n. Ecology.* a species of plant or animal that can be divided into several ecotypes. [C20: from ECO(LOGY) + SPECIES] —**ecospecific** (ˌiːkəʊspɪˈsɪfɪk, ˌɛkəʊ-) *adj.*

ecosphere (ˈiːkəʊˌsfɪə, ˈɛkəʊ-) *n.* the parts of the universe, esp. on the earth, in which life can exist.

écossaise (ˌeɪkɒˈseɪz; *French* ekɔsɛz) *n.* **1.** a lively dance in two-four time. **2.** the tune for such a dance. [C19: French, literally: Scottish (dance)]

ecosystem (ˈiːkəʊˌsɪstəm, ˈɛkəʊ-) *n. Ecology.* a system involving the interactions between a community and its non-living environment. [C20: from ECO(LOGY) + SYSTEM]

ecotone (ˈiːkəˌtəʊn, ˈɛkə-) *n.* the zone between two major ecological communities. [C20: from ECO(LOGY) + *-tone,* from Greek *tonos* tension, TONE] —ˈ**ecoˌtonal** *adj.*

ecotype (ˈiːkəˌtaɪp, ˈɛkə-) *n. Ecology.* a group of organisms within a species that are adapted to different environmental conditions and therefore differ from one another in structure and physiology. —**ecotypic** (ˌiːkəˈtɪpɪk, ˌɛkə-) *adj.* —ˌ**ecoˈtypically** *adv.*

ECOWAS (ɛˈkəʊəs) *n. acronym for* Economic Community of West African States; an economic association established in 1975 among Benin, Burkina-Faso (then called Upper Volta), The Gambia, Ghana, Guinea, Guinea-Bissau, Ivory Coast, Liberia, Mali, Mauritania, Niger, Nigeria, Senegal, Sierra Leone, and Togo.

écraseur (ˌeɪkrɑːˈzɜː) *n.* a surgical device consisting of a heavy wire loop placed around a part to be removed and tightened until it cuts through. [C19: from French, from *écraser* to crush]
ecru (ˈɛkruː, ˈeɪkruː) *n.* **1.** a greyish-yellow to a light greyish colour; the colour of unbleached linen. ~*adj.* **2.** of the colour ecru. [C19: from French, from *é-* (intensive) + *cru* raw, from Latin *crūdus;* see CRUDE]
ECS *abbrev. for* European Communications Satellite.
ECSC *abbrev. for* European Coal and Steel Community.
ecstasy (ˈɛkstəsɪ) *n., pl.* **-sies. 1.** (*often pl.*) a state of exalted delight, joy, etc.; rapture. **2.** intense emotion of any kind: *an ecstasy of rage.* **3.** *Psychol.* overpowering emotion characterized by loss of self-control and sometimes a temporary loss of consciousness: often associated with orgasm, religious mysticism, and the use of certain drugs. **4.** *Archaic.* a state of prophetic inspiration, esp. of poetic rapture. **5.** *Slang.* 3,4-methylenedioxymethamphetamine: a powerful drug that acts as a stimulant and can produce hallucinations. [C14: from Old French *extasie,* via Medieval Latin from Greek *ekstasis* displacement, trance, from *existanai* to displace, from *ex-* out + *histanai* to cause to stand]
ecstatic (ɛkˈstætɪk) *adj.* **1.** in a trancelike state of great rapture or delight. **2.** showing or feeling great enthusiasm: *ecstatic applause.* ~*n.* **3.** a person who has periods of intense trancelike joy. —**ecˈstatically** *adv.*
ecstatics (ɛkˈstætɪks) *pl. n.* fits of delight or rapture.
ECT *abbrev. for* electroconvulsive therapy.
ectasia (ɛkˈteɪzɪə) *or* **ectasis** (ɛkˈtəsɪs) *n. Pathol.* the distension or dilation of any part of the body. —**ecˈtatic** *adj.*
ecthyma (ˈɛkθɪmə) *n. Pathol.* a local inflammation of the skin characterized by flat ulcerating pustules. [C19: from New Latin, from Greek *ekthuma* pustule, from *ekthuein* to break out, from *ek-* out + *thuein* to seethe]
ecto- *combining form.* indicating outer, outside, external: *ectoplasm.* [from Greek *ektos* outside, from *ek, ex* out]
ectoblast (ˈɛktəʊˌblæst) *n.* another name for **ectoderm** or **epiblast.** —ˌ**ectoˈblastic** *adj.*
ectocrine (ˈɛktəʊˌkriːn, -krɪn) *n.* a substance that is released by an organism into the external environment and influences the development, behaviour, etc., of members of the same or different species. [C20: from ECTO- + *-crine,* as in *endocrine*]
ectoderm (ˈɛktəʊˌdɜːm) *or* **exoderm** *n.* the outer germ layer of an animal embryo, which gives rise to epidermis and nervous tissue. See also **mesoderm** and **endoderm.** —ˌ**ectoˈdermal** *or* ˌ**ectoˈdermic** *adj.*
ectoenzyme (ˌɛktəʊˈɛnzaɪm) *n.* any of a group of enzymes secreted from the cells in which they are produced into the surrounding medium; extracellular enzyme. Also called: **exoenzyme.**
ectogenesis (ˌɛktəʊˈdʒɛnəsɪs) *n.* the growth of an organism outside the body in which it would normally be found, such as the growth of an embryo outside the mother's body or the growth of bacteria outside the body of a host. —ˌ**ectogeˈnetic,** ˌ**ectoˈgenic,** *or* **ectogenous** (ɛkˈtɒdʒɪnəs) *adj.* —ˌ**ectoˈgenically** *adv.*
ectomere (ˈɛktəʊˌmɪə) *n. Embryol.* any of the blastomeres that later develop into ectoderm. —**ectomeric** (ˌɛktəʊˈmɛrɪk) *adj.*
ectomorph (ˈɛktəʊˌmɔːf) *n.* a person with a thin body build: said to be correlated with cerebrotonia. Compare **endomorph, mesomorph.** —ˌ**ectoˈmorphic** *adj.* —ˈ**ectoˌmorphy** *n.*
-ectomy *n. combining form.* indicating surgical excision of a part: *appendectomy.* [from New Latin *-ectomia,* from Greek *ek-* out + -TOMY]
ectoparasite (ˌɛktəʊˈpærəˌsaɪt) *n.* a parasite, such as the flea, that lives on the outer surface of its host. Also called: **exoparasite.** —**ectoparasitic** (ˌɛktəʊˌpærəˈsɪtɪk) *adj.*
ectophyte (ˈɛktəʊˌfaɪt) *n.* a parasitic plant that lives on the surface of its host. —**ectophytic** (ˌɛktəʊˈfɪtɪk) *adj.*
ectopia (ɛkˈtəʊpɪə) *n. Med.* congenital displacement or abnormal positioning of an organ or part. [C19: from New Latin, from Greek *ektopos* out of position, from *ek-* out of + *topos* place] —**ectopic** (ɛkˈtɒpɪk) *adj.*
ectopic pregnancy *n. Pathol.* the abnormal development of a fertilized egg outside the cavity of the uterus, usually within a Fallopian tube.
ectoplasm (ˈɛktəʊˌplæzəm) *n.* **1.** *Cytology.* the outer layer of cytoplasm that differs in many cells from the inner cytoplasm (see **endoplasm**) in being a clear gel. **2.** *Spiritualism.* the substance supposedly emanating from the body of a medium during trances. —ˌ**ectoˈplasmic** *adj.*
ectoproct (ˈɛktəʊˌprɒkt) *n., adj.* another word for **bryozoan.** [from ECTO- + *-proct,* from Greek *prōktos* rectum]
ectosarc (ˈɛktəʊˌsɑːk) *n. Zoology.* the ectoplasm of an amoeba or any other protozoan. [C19: ECTO- + *-sarc,* from Greek *sarx* flesh] —ˌ**ectoˈsarcous** *adj.*
ectotrophic (ˌɛktəʊˈtrɒfɪk) *adj. Botany.* denoting a type of mycorrhiza in which the fungus forms a layer on the outside of the roots of the plant. Compare **endotrophic.**
ectype (ˈɛkˌtaɪp) *n.* **1.** a copy as distinguished from a prototype. **2.** *Architect.* a cast embossed or in relief. [C17: from Greek *ektupos* worked in relief, from *ek-* out of + *tupos* mould; see TYPE] —**ectypal** (ˈɛktɪpᵊl) *adj.*
écu (eɪˈkjuː; *French* eky) *n.* **1.** any of various former French gold or silver coins. **2.** a small shield. [C18: from Old French *escu,* from Latin *scūtum* shield]
ECU (ˈeɪkjuː *or sometimes* ˈiːˈsiːˈjuː) *n. acronym for* European Currency Unit: a unit of currency based on the composite value of several different currencies in the European Community and functioning both as the reserve asset and accounting unit of the European Monetary System.
Ecua. *abbrev. for* Ecuador.
Ecuadorian *or* **Ecuadoran** (ˌɛkwəˈdɔːrɪən -ran) *adj.* **1.** of or relating to the South American republic of Ecuador or its people, customs, etc. ~*n.* **2.** a native or inhabitant of Ecuador.
ecumenical, oecumenical (ˌiːkjʊˈmɛnɪkᵊl, ˌɛk-) *or* **ecumenic, oecumenic** *adj.* **1.** of or relating to the Christian Church throughout the world, esp. with regard to its unity. **2. a.** tending to promote unity among Churches. **b.** of or relating to the international movement initiated among non-Catholic Churches in 1910 aimed at Christian unity: embodied, since 1937, in the World Council of Churches. **3.** *Rare.* universal; general; worldwide. [C16: via Late Latin from Greek *oikoumenikos,* from *oikein* to inhabit, from *oikos* house] —ˌ**ecuˈmenically** *or* ˌ**oecuˈmenically** *adv.*
ecumenical council *n.* an assembly of bishops and other ecclesiastics representative of the Christian Church throughout the world. Roman Catholic canon law states that an ecumenical council must be convened by the pope.
ecumenicism (ˌiːkjʊˈmɛnɪˌsɪzəm, ˌɛk-) *or* **ecumenicalism** *n.* the aim of unity among all Christian churches throughout the world.
écurie (*French* ekyri) *n.* a team of motor-racing cars. [C20: French, literally: a stable]
eczema (ˈɛksɪmə) *n. Pathol.* a skin inflammation with lesions that scale, crust, or ooze a serous fluid, often accompanied by intense itching or burning. [C18: from New Latin, from Greek *ekzema,* from *ek-* out + *zein* to boil; see YEAST] —**eczematous** (ɛkˈsɛmətəs) *adj.*
ed. *abbrev. for:* **1.** edited. **2.** (*pl.* **eds.**) edition. **3.** (*pl.* **eds.**) editor. **4.** education.
-ed[1] *suffix.* forming the past tense of most English verbs. [Old English *-de, -ede, -ode, -ade*]
-ed[2] *suffix.* forming the past participle of most English verbs. [Old English *-ed, -od, -ad*]
-ed[3] *suffix forming adjectives from nouns.* possessing or having the characteristics of: *salaried; red-blooded.* [Old English *-ede*]
edacious (ɪˈdeɪʃəs) *adj. Chiefly humorous.* devoted to eating; voracious; greedy. [C19: from Latin *edāx* voracious, from *edere* to eat] —**eˈdaciously** *adv.* —**edacity** (ɪˈdæsɪtɪ) *or* **eˈdaciousness** *n.*
Edam (ˈiːdæm) *n.* a hard round mild-tasting Dutch cheese, yellow in colour with a red outside covering. [named after *Edam,* town in NW Netherlands]
edaphic (ɪˈdæfɪk) *adj.* of or relating to the physical and chemical conditions of the soil, esp. in relation to the plant and animal life it supports. Compare **biotic** (sense 2). [C20: from Greek *edaphos* bottom, soil] —**eˈdaphically** *adv.*
EDC *abbrev. for* European Defence Community.
eddo *or* **Chinese eddo** (ˈɛdəʊ) *n., pl.* **eddoes.** other names for **taro.**
eddy (ˈɛdɪ) *n., pl.* **-dies. 1.** a movement in a stream of air, water, or other fluid in which the current doubles back on itself causing a miniature whirlwind or whirlpool. **2.** a deviation from or disturbance in the main trend of thought, life, etc., esp. one that is relatively unimportant. ~*vb.* **-dies, -dying, -died. 3.** to move or cause to move against the main current. [C15: probably of Scandinavian origin; compare Old Norse *itha;* related to Old English *ed-* again, back, Old High German *it-*]
eddy current *n.* an electric current induced in a massive conductor, such as the core of an electromagnet, transformer, etc., by an alternating magnetic field. Also called: **Foucault current.**
edelweiss (ˈeɪdᵊlˌvaɪs) *n.* a small alpine flowering plant, *Leontopodium alpinum,* having white woolly oblong leaves and a tuft of attractive floral leaves surrounding the flowers: family *Compositae* (composites). [C19: German, literally: noble white]
edema (ɪˈdiːmə) *n., pl.* **-mata** (-mətə). the usual U.S. spelling of **oedema.** —**edematous** (ɪˈdɛmətəs) *or* **eˈdemaˌtose** *adj.*
Eden (ˈiːdᵊn) *n.* **1.** a delightful place, region, dwelling, etc.; paradise. **2.** a state of great delight, happiness, or contentment; bliss. [C14: from the biblical Garden of *Eden,* from Late Latin, from Hebrew *'ēdhen* place of pleasure] —**Edenic** (iːˈdɛnɪk) *adj.*
edentate (iːˈdɛnteɪt) *n.* **1.** any of the placental mammals that constitute the order *Edentata,* which inhabit tropical regions of Central and South America. The order includes anteaters, sloths, and armadillos. ~*adj.* **2.** of, relating to, or belonging to the order *Edentata.* [C19: from Latin *ēdentātus* lacking teeth, from *ēdentāre* to render toothless, from *e-* out + *dēns* tooth]
edentulous (iːˈdɛntjʊləs) *or* **edentulate** (iːˈdɛntjʊlɪt) *adj.* having no teeth.
edge (ɛdʒ) *n.* **1.** the border, brim, or margin of a surface, object, etc. **2.** a brink or verge: *the edge of a cliff; the edge of a breakthrough.* **3.** a line along which two faces or surfaces of a solid meet. **4.** the sharp cutting side of a blade. **5.** keenness, sharpness, or urgency: *the walk gave an edge to his appetite.* **6.** force, effectiveness, or incisiveness: *the performance lacked edge.* **7.** *Dialect.* **a.** a cliff, ridge, or hillside. **b.** (*cap.*) (in place names):

Hade Edge. **8. have the edge on** *or* **over.** to have a slight advantage or superiority (over). **9. on edge. a.** nervously irritable; tense. **b.** nervously excited or eager. **10. set (someone's) teeth on edge.** to make (someone) acutely irritated or uncomfortable. ~*vb.* **11.** (*tr.*) to provide an edge or border for. **12.** (*tr.*) to shape or trim (the edge or border of something), as with a knife or scissors: *to edge a pie.* **13.** to push (one's way, someone, something, etc.) gradually, esp. edgeways. **14.** (*tr.*) *Cricket.* to hit (a bowled ball) with the edge of the bat. **15.** (*tr.*) to tilt (a ski) sideways so that one edge digs into the snow. **16.** (*tr.*) to sharpen (a knife, etc.). [Old English *ecg;* related to Old Norse *egg,* Old High German *ecka* edge, Latin *aciēs* sharpness, Greek *akis* point] —**'edgeless** *adj.* —**'edger** *n.*

edge tool *n.* a tool with one or more cutting edges.

edgeways ('ɛdʒ,weɪz) *or esp. U.S. and Canadian.* **edgewise** ('ɛdʒ,waɪz) *adv.* **1.** with the edge forwards or uppermost: *they carried the piano in edgeways.* **2.** on, by, with, or towards the edge: *he held it edgeways.* **3. get a word in edgeways.** (*usually used with a negative*) to succeed in interrupting a conversation in which someone else is talking incessantly.

edging ('ɛdʒɪŋ) *n.* **1.** anything placed along an edge to finish it, esp. as an ornament, fringe, or border on clothing or along a path in a garden. **2.** the act of making an edge. ~*adj.* **3.** relating to or used for making an edge: *edging shears.*

edgy ('ɛdʒɪ) *adj.* **-ier, -iest. 1.** (*usually postpositive*) nervous, irritable, tense, or anxious. **2.** (of paintings, drawings, etc.) excessively defined. —**'edgily** *adv.* —**'edginess** *n.*

edh (ɛð) *or* **eth** *n.* a character of the runic alphabet (ð) used to represent the voiced dental fricative as in *then, mother, bathe.* It is used in modern phonetic transcription for the same purpose. Compare **theta** (sense 2), **thorn** (sense 5).

edible ('ɛdɪbᵊl) *adj.* fit to be eaten; eatable. [C17: from Late Latin *edibilis,* from Latin *edere* to eat] —**,edi'bility** *or* **'edibleness** *n.*

edibles ('ɛdɪbᵊlz) *pl. n.* articles fit to eat; food.

edict ('iːdɪkt) *n.* **1.** a decree, order, or ordinance issued by a sovereign, state, or any other holder of authority. **2.** any formal or authoritative command, proclamation, etc. [C15: from Latin *ēdictum,* from *ēdīcere* to declare] —**e'dictal** *adj.* —**e'dictally** *adv.*

edification (,ɛdɪfɪ'keɪʃən) *n.* **1.** improvement, instruction, or enlightenment, esp. when morally or spiritually uplifting. **2.** the act of edifying or state of being edified. —**,edifi'catory** *adj.*

edifice ('ɛdɪfɪs) *n.* **1.** a building, esp. a large or imposing one. **2.** a complex or elaborate institution or organization. [C14: from Old French, from Latin *aedificium,* from *aedificāre* to build; see EDIFY] —**edificial** (,ɛdɪ'fɪʃəl) *adj.*

edify ('ɛdɪ,faɪ) *vb.* **-fies, -fying, -fied.** (*tr.*) to improve the morality, intellect, etc., of, esp. by instruction. [C14: from Old French *edifier,* from Latin *aedificāre* to construct, from *aedēs* a dwelling, temple + *facere* to make] —**'edi,fier** *n.* —**'edi,fying** *adj.* —**'edi,fyingly** *adv.*

edile ('iːdaɪl) *n.* a variant spelling of **aedile.**

edit ('ɛdɪt) *vb.* (*tr.*) **1.** to prepare (text) for publication by checking and improving its accuracy, clarity, etc. **2.** to be in charge of (a publication, esp. a periodical): *he edits the local newspaper.* **3.** to prepare (a film, tape, etc.) by rearrangement, selection, or rejection of previously filmed or taped material. **4.** (often foll. by *out*) to remove (incorrect or unwanted matter), as from a manuscript or film. ~*n.* **5.** *Informal.* an act of editing: *give the book a final edit.* [C18: back formation from EDITOR]

edit. *abbrev. for:* **1.** edited. **2.** edition. **3.** editor.

edition (ɪ'dɪʃən) *n.* **1.** *Printing.* **a.** the entire number of copies of a book, newspaper, or other publication printed at one time from a single setting of type. **b.** a single copy from this number: *a first edition; the evening edition.* **2.** one of a number of printings of a book or other publication, issued at separate times with alterations, amendments, etc. Compare **impression** (sense 6). **3. a.** an issue of a work identified by its format: *a leather-bound edition of Shakespeare.* **b.** an issue of a work identified by its editor or publisher: *the Oxford edition of Shakespeare.* [C16: from Latin *ēditiō* a bringing forth, publishing, from *ēdere* to give out; see EDITOR]

editio princeps (ɪ'dɪʃɪəʊ 'prɪnsɛps) *n., pl.* **editiones principes** (ɪ,dɪʃɪ'əʊniːz 'prɪnsɪ,piːz). *Latin.* the first printed edition of a work.

editor ('ɛdɪtə) *n.* **1.** a person who edits written material for publication. **2.** a person in overall charge of the editing and often the policy of a newspaper or periodical. **3.** a person in charge of one section of a newspaper or periodical: *the sports editor.* **4.** *Films.* **a.** a person who makes a selection and arrangement of individual shots in order to construct the flowing sequence of images for a film. **b.** a device for editing film, including a viewer and a splicer. **5.** *Television, radio.* a person in overall control of a programme that consists of various items, such as a news or magazine style programme. **6.** a computer program that facilitates the deletion or insertion of data to information already stored in a computer. [C17: from Late Latin: producer, exhibitor, from *ēdere* to give out, publish, from *ē-* out + *dāre* to give] —**'editor,ship** *n.*

editorial (,ɛdɪ'tɔːrɪəl) *adj.* **1.** of or relating to editing or editors. **2.** of, relating to, or expressed in an editorial. **3.** of or relating to the content of a publication rather than its commercial aspects. ~*n.* **4.** an article in a newspaper, etc., expressing the opinion of the editor or the publishers. —**,edi'torialist** *n.* —**,edi'torially** *adv.*

editorialize *or* **editorialise** (,ɛdɪ'tɔːrɪə,laɪz) *vb.* (*intr.*) **1.** to express an opinion in or as in an editorial. **2.** to insert one's personal opinions into an otherwise objective account. —**,edi,toriali'zation** *or* **,edi,toriali'sation** *n.* —**,edi'torial,izer** *or* **,edi'torial,iser** *n.*

editor in chief *n.* the controlling editor of a publication.

EDM *Surveying. abbrev. for* electronic distance measurement.

Edo ('ɛdəʊ) *n.* **1.** (*pl.* **Edo** *or* **Edos**) a member of a Negroid people of SW Nigeria around Benin, noted for their 16th-century bronze sculptures. **2.** Also called: **Bini.** the language of this people, belonging to the Kwa branch of the Niger-Congo family.

Edomite ('iːdə,maɪt) *n.* **1.** an inhabitant of the ancient kingdom of Edom, situated between the Dead Sea and the Gulf of Aqaba, whose people were hostile to the Israelites in Old Testament times. **2.** the ancient Semitic language of this people, closely related to Hebrew. —**'Edom,itish** *or* **Edomitic** (,iːdə'mɪtɪk) *adj.*

EDP *or* **edp** *abbrev. for* electronic data processing.

EDT (in the U.S. and Canada) *abbrev. for* Eastern Daylight Time.

EDTA *n.* ethylenediaminetetra-acetic acid; a colourless crystalline slightly soluble organic compound used in inorganic chemistry and biochemistry. It is a powerful chelating agent used to stabilize bleach in detergents. Formula: $[(HOOCCH_2)_2NCH_2]_2$.

educ. *abbrev. for:* **1.** educated. **2.** education(al).

educable ('ɛdjʊkəbᵊl) *or* **educatable** ('ɛdjʊ,keɪtəbᵊl) *adj.* capable of being trained or educated; able to learn. —**,educa'bility** *or* **,edu,cata'bility** *n.*

educate ('ɛdjʊ,keɪt) *vb.* (*mainly tr.*) **1.** (*also intr.*) to impart knowledge by formal instruction to (a pupil); teach. **2.** to provide schooling for (children): *I have educated my children at the best schools.* **3.** to improve or develop (a person, judgment, taste, skills, etc.). **4.** to train for some particular purpose or occupation. [C15: from Latin *ēducāre* to rear, educate, from *dūcere* to lead]

educated ('ɛdjʊ,keɪtɪd) *adj.* **1.** having an education, esp. a good one. **2.** displaying culture, taste, and knowledge; cultivated. **3.** (*prenominal*) based on experience or information (esp. in the phrase **an educated guess**).

education (,ɛdjʊ'keɪʃən) *n.* **1.** the act or process of acquiring knowledge, esp. systematically during childhood and adolescence. **2.** the knowledge or training acquired by this process: *his education has been invaluable to him.* **3.** the act or process of imparting knowledge, esp. at a school, college, or university: *education is my profession.* **4.** the theory of teaching and learning: *a course in education.* **5.** a particular kind of instruction or training: *a university education; consumer education.*

educational (,ɛdjʊ'keɪʃənᵊl) *adj.* **1.** providing knowledge; instructive or informative: *an educational toy.* **2.** of or relating to education. —**,edu'cationally** *adv.*

educationalist (,ɛdjʊ'keɪʃənəlɪst) *or* **educationist** *n.* a specialist in educational theory or administration.

educational psychology *n.* the study of methods of training and teaching and their effectiveness, and of the problems experienced in learning formal material; in particular, the study of how to help people, esp. school children, with learning problems to overcome their difficulties.

Educational Welfare Officer *n.* (in Britain) a local education authority worker whose job it is to find out whether difficulties outside school are contributing to a child's classroom problems or irregular attendance and who may intervene to help the child to benefit more from schooling. Former names: **school attendance officer, truancy officer.**

educative ('ɛdjʊkətɪv) *adj.* producing or resulting in education: *an educative experience.*

educator ('ɛdjʊ,keɪtə) *n.* **1.** a person who educates; teacher. **2.** a specialist in education; educationalist.

educatory ('ɛdjʊkətərɪ, -trɪ; ,ɛdjʊ'keɪtərɪ, -trɪ) *adj.* educative or educational: *an educatory procedure.*

educe (ɪ'djuːs) *vb.* (*tr.*) *Rare.* **1.** to evolve or develop, esp. from a latent or potential state. **2.** to draw out or elicit (information, solutions, etc.). [C15: from Latin *ēdūcere* to draw out, from *ē-* out + *dūcere* to lead] —**e'ducible** *adj.* —**eductive** (ɪ'dʌktɪv) *adj.*

educt ('iːdʌkt) *n.* a substance separated from another substance without chemical change. Compare **product** (sense 4). [C18: from Latin *ēductus;* see EDUCE]

eduction (ɪ'dʌkʃən) *n.* **1.** something educed. **2.** the act or process of educing. **3.** the exhaust stroke of a steam or internal-combustion engine. Compare **induction.** [C17: from Latin *ēductiō,* from *ēdūcere* to EDUCE]

edulcorate (ɪ'dʌlkə,reɪt) *vb.* (*tr.*) to free from soluble impurities by washing. [C17: from Medieval Latin *ēdulcorāre,* from Late Latin *dulcor* sweetness] —**e,dulco'ration** *n.*

Edwardian (ɛd'wɔːdɪən) *adj.* denoting, relating to, or having the style of life, architecture, dress, etc., current in Britain during the reign (1901–10) of Edward VII. —**Ed'wardianism** *n.*

ee (iː) *n., pl.* **een** (iːn) a Scot. word for **eye**[1].

EE *abbrev. for:* **1.** Early English. **2.** electrical engineer(ing). **3.** (in New Zealand) ewe equivalent.

e.e. *abbrev. for* errors excepted.

-ee *suffix forming nouns.* **1.** indicating a person who is the recipient of an action (as opposed, esp. in legal terminology, to the agent, indicated by *-or* or *-er*): *assignee; grantee; lessee.* **2.**

indicating a person in a specified state or condition: *absentee; employee.* **3.** indicating a diminutive form of something: *bootee.* [via Old French *-e, -ee,* past participial endings, from Latin *-ātus, -āta* -ATE[1]]

EE & MP *abbrev. for* Envoy Extraordinary and Minister Plenipotentiary.

EEC *abbrev. for* European Economic Community (now called European Community).

EEG *abbrev. for:* **1.** electroencephalogram. **2.** electroencephalograph.

eel (iːl) *n.* **1.** any teleost fish of the order *Apodes* (or *Anguilliformes*), such as the European freshwater species *Anguilla anguilla,* having a long snakelike body, a smooth slimy skin, and reduced fins. **2.** any of various other animals with a long body and smooth skin, such as the mud eel and the electric eel. **3.** an evasive or untrustworthy person. [Old English *ǣl;* related to Old Frisian *ēl,* Old Norse *āll,* Old High German *āl*] —**'eel-ˌlike** *adj.* —**'eely** *adj.*

eelgrass ('iːlˌgrɑːs) *n.* **1.** any of several perennial submerged marine plants of the genus *Zostera,* esp. *Z. marina,* having grasslike leaves: family *Zosteraceae.* **2.** another name for **tape grass.**

eelpout ('iːlˌpaʊt) *n.* **1.** any marine eel-like blennioid fish of the family *Zoarcidae,* such as *Zoarces viviparus* (**viviparous eelpout** or blenny). **2.** another name for **burbot.** [Old English *ǣlepūte;* related to Middle Dutch *aalpuit*]

eelworm ('iːlˌwɜːm) *n.* any of various nematode worms, esp. the wheatworm and the vinegar eel.

e'en (iːn) *adv., n. Poetic or archaic.* a contraction of **even**[2] or **evening.**

e'er (ɛə) *adv. Poetic or archaic.* a contraction of **ever.**

-eer *or* **-ier** *suffix.* **1.** (*forming nouns*) indicating a person who is concerned with or who does something specified: *auctioneer; engineer; profiteer; mutineer.* **2.** (*forming verbs*) to be concerned with something specified: *electioneer.* [from Old French *-ier,* from Latin *-arius* -ARY]

eerie ('ɪərɪ) *adj.* **eerier, eeriest.** (esp. of places, an atmosphere, etc.) mysteriously or uncannily frightening or disturbing; weird; ghostly. [C13: originally Scottish and Northern English, probably from Old English *earg* cowardly, miserable] —**'eerily** *adv.* —**'eeriness** *n.*

EETPU (in Britain) *abbrev. for* Electrical, Electronic, Telecommunications, and Plumbing Union.

eff (ɛf) *vb.* **1.** euphemism for **fuck** (esp. in the phrase **eff off**). **2. eff and blind.** *Slang.* to use obscene language. —**'effing** *n., adj.*

effable ('ɛfəb^əl) *adj. Archaic.* capable of being expressed in words. [C17: from Old French, from Late Latin *effābilis,* from Latin *effārī,* from *ex-* out + *fārī* to speak]

efface (ɪ'feɪs) *vb.* (*tr.*) **1.** to obliterate or make dim: *to efface a memory.* **2.** to make (oneself) inconspicuous or humble through modesty, cowardice, or obsequiousness. **3.** to rub out (a line, drawing, etc.); erase. [C15: from French *effacer,* literally: to obliterate the face; see FACE] —**ef'faceable** *adj.* —**ef'facement** *n.* —**ef'facer** *n.*

effect (ɪ'fɛkt) *n.* **1.** something that is produced by a cause or agent; result. **2.** power or ability to influence or produce a result; efficacy: *with no effect.* **3.** the condition of being operative (esp. in the phrases **in** or **into effect**): *the law comes into effect at midnight.* **4. take effect.** to become operative or begin to produce results. **5.** basic meaning or purpose (esp. in the phrase **to that effect**). **6.** an impression, usually one that is artificial or contrived (esp. in the phrase **for effect**). **7.** a scientific phenomenon: *the Doppler effect.* **8. in effect. a.** in fact; actually. **b.** for all practical purposes. **9.** the overall impression or result: *the effect of a painting.* ~*vb.* **10.** (*tr.*) to cause to occur; bring about; accomplish. ~See also **effects.** [C14: from Latin *effectus* a performing, tendency, from *efficere* to accomplish, from *facere* to do] —**ef'fecter** *n.* —**ef'fectible** *adj.*

effective (ɪ'fɛktɪv) *adj.* **1.** productive of or capable of producing a result. **2.** in effect; operative: *effective from midnight.* **3.** producing a striking impression; impressive: *an effective entrance.* **4.** (*prenominal*) actual rather than theoretical; real: *the effective income after deductions.* **5.** (of a military force, etc.) equipped and prepared for action. **6.** *Physics.* (of an alternating quantity) having a value that is the square root of the mean of the squares of the magnitude measured at each instant over a defined period of time, usually one cycle. ~*n.* **7.** a serviceman who is equipped and prepared for action. —**ef'fectively** *adv.* —**ef'fectiveness** *n.*

effector *or* **effecter** (ɪ'fɛktə) *n. Physiol.* a nerve ending that terminates in a muscle or gland and provides neural stimulation causing contraction or secretion.

effects (ɪ'fɛkts) *pl. n.* **1.** Also called: **personal effects.** personal property or belongings. **2.** lighting, sounds, etc., to accompany and enhance a stage, film, or broadcast production.

effectual (ɪ'fɛktjʊəl) *adj.* **1.** capable of or successful in producing an intended result; effective. **2.** (of documents, agreements, etc.) having legal force. —**efˌfectu'ality** *or* **ef'fectualness** *n.*

effectually (ɪ'fɛktjʊəlɪ) *adv.* **1.** with the intended effect; thoroughly. **2.** to all practical purposes; in effect.

effectuate (ɪ'fɛktjʊˌeɪt) *vb.* (*tr.*) to cause to happen; effect; accomplish. —**efˌfectu'ation** *n.*

effeminate (ɪ'fɛmɪnɪt) *adj.* **1.** (of a man or boy) displaying characteristics regarded as typical of a woman; not manly. **2.** lacking firmness or vigour: *an effeminate piece of writing.* [C14: from Latin *effēmināre* to make into a woman, from *fēmina* woman] —**ef'feminacy** *or* **ef'feminateness** *n.* —**ef'feminately** *adv.*

effendi (ɛ'fɛndɪ) *n., pl.* **-dis.** **1.** (in the Ottoman Empire) a title of respect used to address men of learning or social standing. **2.** (in Turkey since 1934) the oral title of address equivalent to *Mr.* [C17: from Turkish *efendi* master, from Modern Greek *aphentēs,* from Greek *authentēs* lord, doer; see AUTHENTIC]

efferent ('ɛfərənt) *adj.* carrying or conducting outwards from a part or an organ of the body, esp. from the brain or spinal cord. Compare **afferent.** [C19: from Latin *efferre* to bear off, from *ferre* to bear] —**'efference** *n.* —**'efferently** *adv.*

effervesce (ˌɛfə'vɛs) *vb.* (*intr.*) **1.** (of a liquid) to give off bubbles of gas. **2.** (of a gas) to issue in bubbles from a liquid. **3.** to exhibit great excitement, vivacity, etc. [C18: from Latin *effervescere* to foam up, from *fervescere* to begin to boil, from *fervēre* to boil, ferment] —**ˌeffer'vescible** *adj.*

effervescent (ˌɛfə'vɛs^ənt) *adj.* **1.** (of a liquid) giving off bubbles of gas; bubbling. **2.** high-spirited; vivacious. —**ˌeffer'vescence** *n.* —**ˌeffer'vescently** *adv.* —**ˌeffer'vescingly** *adv.*

effete (ɪ'fiːt) *adj.* **1.** weak, ineffectual, or decadent as a result of overrefinement: *an effete academic.* **2.** exhausted of vitality or strength; worn out; spent. **3.** (of animals or plants) no longer capable of reproduction. [C17: from Latin *effētus* having produced young, hence, exhausted by bearing, from *fētus* having brought forth; see FETUS] —**ef'fetely** *adv.* —**ef'feteness** *n.*

efficacious (ˌɛfɪ'keɪʃəs) *adj.* capable of or successful in producing an intended result; effective as a means, remedy, etc. [C16: from Latin *efficāx* powerful, efficient, from *efficere* to achieve; see EFFECT] —**ˌeffi'caciously** *adv.* —**efficacy** ('ɛfɪkəsɪ) *or* **ˌeffi'caciousness** *n.*

efficiency (ɪ'fɪʃənsɪ) *n., pl.* **-cies.** **1.** the quality or state of being efficient; competence; effectiveness. **2.** the ratio of the useful work done by a machine, engine, device, etc., to the energy supplied to it, often expressed as a percentage. See also **thermal efficiency.**

efficiency apartment *n. U.S.* a small flat or bedsitter.

efficient (ɪ'fɪʃənt) *adj.* **1.** functioning or producing effectively and with the least waste of effort; competent. **2.** *Philosophy.* producing a direct effect; causative. [C14: from Latin *efficiēns* effecting] —**ef'ficiently** *adv.*

efficient cause *n. Philosophy.* that which produces an effect by a causal process. Compare **final cause.** See also **cause** (sense 7).

effigy ('ɛfɪdʒɪ) *n., pl.* **-gies.** **1.** a portrait of a person, esp. as a monument or architectural decoration. **2.** a crude representation of someone, used as a focus for contempt or ridicule and often hung up or burnt in public (often in the phrases **burn** or **hang in effigy**). [C18: from Latin *effigiēs,* from *effingere* to form, portray, from *fingere* to shape] —**effigial** (ɪ'fɪdʒɪəl) *adj.*

effleurage (ˌɛflɜː'rɑːʒ) *n. Med.* a light stroking movement used in massage. [C19: from French]

effloresce (ˌɛflɔː'rɛs) *vb.* (*intr.*) **1.** to burst forth into or as if into flower; bloom. **2.** to become powdery by loss of water or crystallization. **3.** to become encrusted with powder or crystals as a result of chemical change or the evaporation of a solution. [C18: from Latin *efflōrēscere* to blossom, from *flōrēscere,* from *flōs* flower]

efflorescence (ˌɛflɔː'rɛs^əns) *n.* **1.** a bursting forth or flowering. **2.** *Chem., geology.* **a.** the process of efflorescing. **b.** the powdery substance formed as a result of this process, esp. on the surface of rocks. **3.** any skin rash or eruption. —**ˌefflo'rescent** *adj.*

effluence ('ɛflʊəns) *or* **efflux** ('ɛflʌks) *n.* **1.** the act or process of flowing out. **2.** something that flows out.

effluent ('ɛflʊənt) *n.* **1.** liquid discharged as waste, as from an industrial plant or sewage works. **2.** radioactive waste released from a nuclear power station. **3.** a stream that flows out of another body of water. **4.** something that flows out or forth. ~*adj.* **5.** flowing out or forth. [C18: from Latin *effluere* to run forth, from *fluere* to flow]

effluvium (ɛ'fluːvɪəm) *n., pl.* **-via** (-vɪə) *or* **-viums.** an unpleasant smell or exhalation, as of gaseous waste or decaying matter. [C17: from Latin: a flowing out; see EFFLUENT] —**ef'fluvial** *adj.*

effort ('ɛfət) *n.* **1.** physical or mental exertion, usually considerable when unqualified: *the rock was moved with effort.* **2.** a determined attempt: *our effort to save him failed.* **3.** achievement; creation: *a great literary effort.* **4.** *Physics.* an applied force acting against inertia. [C15: from Old French *esfort,* from *esforcier* to force, ultimately from Latin *fortis* strong; see FORCE] —**'effortful** *adj.*

effort bargain *n.* a bargain in which the reward to an employee is based on the effort that the employee puts in.

effortless ('ɛfətlɪs) *adj.* **1.** requiring or involving little effort; easy. **2.** *Archaic.* making little effort; passive. —**'effortlessly** *adv.* —**'effortlessness** *n.*

effrontery (ɪ'frʌntərɪ) *n., pl.* **-ies.** shameless or insolent boldness; impudent presumption; audacity; temerity. [C18: from French *effronterie,* from Old French *esfront* barefaced, shameless, from Late Latin *effrons,* literally: putting forth one's forehead; see FRONT]

effulgent (ɪ'fʌldʒənt) *adj.* radiant; brilliant. [C18: from Latin *effulgēre* to shine forth, from *fulgēre* to shine] —**ef'fulgence** *n.* —**ef'fulgently** *adv.*

effuse *vb.* (ɪ'fjuːz). **1.** to pour or flow out. **2.** to spread out; diffuse. **3.** *(intr.)* to talk profusely, esp. in an excited manner. **4.** to cause (a gas) to flow or (of a gas) to flow under pressure. *~adj.* (ɪ'fjuːs). **5.** *Botany.* (esp. of an inflorescence) spreading out loosely. [C16: from Latin *effūsus* poured out, from *effundere* to shed, from *fundere* to pour]

effusiometer (ɪˌfjuːzɪ'ɒmɪtə) *n. Physics.* an apparatus for determining rates of effusion of gases, usually used for measuring molecular weights.

effusion (ɪ'fjuːʒən) *n.* **1.** an unrestrained outpouring in speech or words. **2.** the act or process of being poured out. **3.** something that is poured out. **4.** the flow of a gas through a small aperture under pressure, esp. when the density is such that the mean distance between molecules is large compared to the diameter of the aperture. **5.** *Med.* **a.** the escape of blood or other fluid into a body cavity or tissue. **b.** the fluid that has escaped.

effusive (ɪ'fjuːsɪv) *adj.* **1.** extravagantly demonstrative of emotion; gushing. **2.** (of rock) formed by the solidification of magma. **—ef'fusively** *adv.* **—ef'fusiveness** *n.*

Efik ('ɛfɪk) *n.* **1.** *(pl.* **Efiks** *or* **Efik)** a member of a subgroup of the Ibibio people of SE Nigeria. **2.** the language spoken by this people, variously classified as belonging to the Benue-Congo or Kwa divisions of the Niger-Congo family.

EFIS *Aeronautics. abbrev. for* electronic flight information systems.

EFL *abbrev. for* English as a Foreign Language.

eft[1] (ɛft) *n.* **1.** a dialect or archaic name for a **newt. 2.** any of certain terrestrial newts, such as *Diemictylus viridescens* (**red eft**) of eastern North America. [Old English *efeta*]

eft[2] (ɛft) *adv. Archaic.* **a.** again. **b.** afterwards. [Old English; see AFT, AFTER]

EFTA ('ɛftə) *n. acronym for* European Free Trade Association; established in 1960 to eliminate trade tariffs on industrial products; comprised Britain, Denmark, Norway, Sweden, Switzerland, Austria, and Portugal. Finland became an associate member in 1961 and Iceland joined in 1970. Britain (1972), Denmark (1972), and Portugal (1986) left EFTA to join the European Community.

EFTPOS ('ɛftpɒs) *acronym for* electronic funds transfer at point of sale.

EFTS *Computer technol. abbrev. for* electronic funds transfer system.

eftsoons (ɛft'suːnz) *adv. Archaic.* **1.** soon afterwards. **2.** repeatedly. [Old English *eft sōna,* literally: afterwards soon]

Eg. *abbrev. for:* **1.** Egypt(ian). **2.** Egyptology.

e.g. eg, *or* **eg.** *abbrevs. for* exempli gratia. [Latin: for example]

egad (ɪ'gæd, iː'gæd) *interj. Archaic.* a mild oath or expression of surprise. [C17: probably variant of *Ah God!*]

egalitarian (ɪˌgælɪ'tɛərɪən) *adj.* **1.** of, relating to, or upholding the doctrine of the equality of mankind and the desirability of political, social, and economic equality. *~n.* **2.** an adherent of egalitarian principles. [C19: alteration of *equalitarian,* through influence of French *égal* EQUAL] **—eˌgali'tarianˌism** *n.*

Egeria (ɪ'dʒɪərɪə) *n.* a female adviser. [C17: name of the mythical adviser of Numa Pompilius, king of Rome]

egest (iː'dʒɛst) *vb. (tr.)* to excrete (waste material). [C17: from Latin *ēgerere* to carry out, from *gerere* to carry] **—e'gestion** *n.* **—e'gestive** *adj.*

egesta (iː'dʒɛstə) *pl. n.* anything egested, as waste material from the body; excrement. [C18: from Latin, literally: (things) carried out; see EGEST]

egg[1] (ɛg) *n.* **1.** the oval or round reproductive body laid by the females of birds, reptiles, fishes, insects, and some other animals, consisting of a developing embryo, its food store, and sometimes jelly or albumen, all surrounded by an outer shell or membrane. **2.** Also called: **egg cell.** any female gamete; ovum. **3.** the egg of the domestic hen used as food. **4.** something resembling an egg, esp. in shape or in being in an early stage of development. **5. good** (*or* **bad) egg.** *Old-fashioned informal.* **a.** a good (or bad) person. **b.** an exclamation of delight (or dismay). **6. lay an egg.** *Slang, chiefly U.S. and Canadian.* **a.** to make a joke or give a performance, etc., that fails completely. **b.** (of a joke, performance, etc.) to fail completely; flop. **7. put** *or* **have all one's eggs in one basket.** to stake everything on a single venture. **8. teach one's grandmother to suck eggs.** to presume to teach someone something that he knows already. **9. with egg on one's face.** *Informal.* made to look ridiculous. *~vb. (tr.)* **10.** to dip (food) in beaten egg before cooking. **11.** *U.S. informal.* to throw eggs at. [C14: from Old Norse *egg;* related to Old English *ǣg,* Old High German *ei*]

egg[2] (ɛg) *vb. (tr.;* usually foll. by *on)* to urge or incite, esp. to daring or foolish acts. [Old English *eggian,* from Old Norse *eggja* to urge; related to Old English *ecg* EDGE, Middle Low German *eggen* to harrow]

egg and dart, egg and tongue, *or* **egg and anchor** *n.* (in architecture and cabinetwork) **a.** an ornamental moulding in which a half egg shape alternates with a dart, tongue, or anchor shape. **b.** *(as modifier): egg-and-dart moulding.*

egg-and-spoon race *n.* a race in which runners carry an egg balanced in a spoon.

eggbeater ('ɛgˌbiːtə) *n.* **1.** Also called: **'eggˌwhisk.** a kitchen utensil for beating eggs, whipping cream, etc.; whisk. **2.** *Chiefly U.S. and Canadian.* an informal name for **helicopter.**

egg cup *n.* a small cuplike container, used for holding a boiled egg while it is being eaten.

egger *or* **eggar** ('ɛgə) *n.* any of various widely distributed moths of the family *Lasiocampidae,* such as *Lasiocampa quercus* (**oak egger**) of Europe, having brown bodies and wings. [C18: from EGG, from the egg-shaped cocoon]

egghead ('ɛgˌhɛd) *n. Informal.* an intellectual; highbrow.

eggler ('ɛglə) *n. Archaic or dialect.* an egg dealer: sometimes itinerant.

eggnog (ˌɛg'nɒg) *n.* a drink that can be served hot or cold, made of eggs, milk, sugar, spice, and brandy, rum, or other spirit. Also called: **egg flip.** [C19: from EGG[1] + NOG[1]]

eggplant ('ɛgˌplɑːnt) *n.* another name (esp. U.S. and Canadian) for **aubergine** (sense 1).

egg roll *n.* a Chinese-American dish consisting of egg dough filled with a minced mixture of pork, bamboo shoots, onions, etc., and browned in deep fat.

eggs Benedict *n.* a dish consisting of toast, covered with a slice of ham, poached egg, and hollandaise sauce.

eggshell ('ɛgˌʃɛl) *n.* **1.** the hard porous protective outer layer of a bird's egg, consisting of calcite and protein. **2.** a yellowish-white colour. **3.** a type of paper with a slightly rough finish. **4.** *(modifier)* (of paint) having a very slight sheen. *~adj.* **5.** of a yellowish-white colour.

eggshell porcelain *or* **china** *n.* a type of very thin translucent porcelain originally made in China.

egg slice *n.* a spatula for removing omelettes, fried eggs, etc., from a pan.

egg spoon *n.* a small spoon for eating a boiled egg.

egg timer *n.* a device, typically a miniature hourglass, for timing the boiling of an egg.

egg tooth *n.* (in embryo birds and reptiles) a temporary tooth or (in birds) projection of the beak used for piercing the eggshell.

egg white *n.* the white of an egg; albumen.

egis ('iːdʒɪs) *n.* a rare spelling of **aegis.**

eglandular (iː'glændjʊlə) *adj.* having no glands. [E- + GLANDULAR]

eglantine ('ɛglənˌtaɪn) *n.* another name for **sweetbrier.** [C14: from Old French *aiglent,* ultimately from Latin *acus* needle, from *acer* sharp, keen]

EGM *abbrev. for* extraordinary general meeting.

ego ('iːgəʊ, 'ɛgəʊ) *n., pl.* **egos. 1.** the self of an individual person; the conscious subject. **2.** *Psychoanal.* the conscious mind, based on perception of the environment from birth onwards: responsible for modifying the antisocial instincts of the id and itself modified by the conscience (superego). **3.** one's image of oneself; morale: *to boost one's ego.* **4.** egotism; conceit. [C19: from Latin: I]

egocentric (ˌiːgəʊ'sɛntrɪk, ˌɛg-) *adj.* **1.** regarding everything only in relation to oneself; self-centred; selfish. **2.** *Philosophy.* pertaining to a theory in which everything is considered in relation to the self: *an egocentric universe. ~n.* **3.** a self-centred person; egotist. **—ˌegocen'tricity** *n.*

egocentrism (ˌiːgəʊ'sɛntrɪzəm, ˌɛgəʊ-) *n.* **1.** the condition or fact of being egocentric. **2.** *Psychol.* a stage in a child's development characterized by lack of awareness that other people's points of view differ from his own.

ego ideal *n. Psychoanal.* an internal ideal of personal perfection that represents what one wants to be rather than what one ought to be and is derived from one's early relationship with one's parents. See also **superego.**

egoism ('iːgəʊˌɪzəm, 'ɛg-) *n.* **1.** concern for one's own interests and welfare. **2.** *Ethics.* the theory that the pursuit of one's own welfare is the highest good. Compare **altruism. 3.** self-centredness; egotism.

egoist ('iːgəʊɪst, 'ɛg-) *n.* **1.** a person who is preoccupied with his own interests; a selfish person. **2.** a conceited person; egotist. **3.** *Ethics.* a person who lives by the values of egoism. **—ˌego'istic** *or* **ˌego'istical** *adj.* **—ˌego'istically** *adv.*

egomania (ˌiːgəʊ'meɪnɪə, ˌɛg-) *n. Psychiatry.* **1.** obsessive love for oneself and regard for one's own needs. **2.** any action dictated by this point of view. **—ˌego'maniˌac** *n.* **—egomaniacal** (ˌiːgəʊmə'naɪkəl, ˌɛg-) *adj.*

egotism ('iːgəˌtɪzəm, 'ɛgə-) *n.* **1.** an inflated sense of self-importance or superiority; self-centredness. **2.** excessive reference to oneself. [C18: from Latin *ego* I + -ISM]

egotist ('iːgətɪst, 'ɛg-) *n.* **1.** a conceited boastful person. **2.** a self-interested person; egoist. **—ˌego'tistic** *or* **ˌego'tistical** *adj.* **—ˌego'tistically** *adv.*

ego trip *Informal. ~n.* **1.** something undertaken to boost or draw attention to a person's own image or appraisal of himself. *~vb.* **ego-trip, -trips, -tripping, -tripped.** *(intr.)* **2.** to act in this way.

egregious (ɪ'griːdʒəs, -dʒɪəs) *adj.* **1.** outstandingly bad; flagrant: *an egregious lie.* **2.** *Archaic.* distinguished; eminent. [C16: from Latin *ēgregius* outstanding (literally: standing out from the herd), from *ē-* out + *grex* flock, herd] **—e'gregiously** *adv.* **—e'gregiousness** *n.*

egress *n.* ('iːgrɛs). **1.** Also called: **egression.** the act of going or coming out; emergence. **2.** a way out, such as a path; exit. **3.** the right or permission to go out or depart. **4.** *Astronomy.* another name for **emersion** (sense 2). *~vb.* (ɪ'grɛs). *(intr.)* **5.**

to go forth; issue. [C16: from Latin *ēgredī* to come forth, depart, from *gradī* to move, step]

egret ('iːgrɪt) *n.* any of various wading birds of the genera *Egretta, Hydranassa,* etc., that are similar to herons but usually have a white plumage and, in the breeding season, long feathery plumes (see **aigrette**): family *Ardeidae,* order *Ciconiiformes.* [C15: from Old French *aigrette,* from Old Provençal *aigreta,* from *aigron* heron, of Germanic origin; compare Old High German *heigaro* HERON]

Egypt. *abbrev. for* Egyptian.

Egyptian (ɪ'dʒɪpʃən) *adj.* **1.** of, relating to, or characteristic of the republic of Egypt, in NE Africa, its inhabitants, or their dialect of Arabic. **2.** of, relating to, or characteristic of the ancient Egyptians, their language, or culture. **3.** (of type) having square slab serifs. **4.** *Archaic.* of or relating to the Gypsies. ~*n.* **5.** a native or inhabitant of Egypt. **6.** a member of an indigenous non-Semitic people who established an advanced civilization in Egypt that flourished from the late fourth millennium B.C. **7.** the extinct language of the ancient Egyptians, belonging to the Afro-Asiatic family of languages. It is recorded in hieroglyphic inscriptions, the earliest of which date from before 3000 B.C. It was extinct by the fourth century A.D. See also **Coptic.** **8.** a large size of drawing paper. **9.** an archaic name for a **Gypsy.**

Egyptian jasper *n.* a type of jasper, generally with zones of colour, found in desert regions of Egypt.

Egyptology (ˌiːdʒɪp'tɒlədʒɪ) *n.* the study of the archaeology and language of ancient Egypt. —**Egyptological** (ɪˌdʒɪptə'lɒdʒɪkᵊl) *adj.* —ˌ**Egyp'tologist** *n.*

eh (eɪ) *interj.* an exclamation used to express questioning surprise or to seek the repetition or confirmation of a statement or question: *Eh? What did you say?*

EHF *abbrev. for* extremely high frequency.

EHO (in Britain) *abbrev. for* Environmental Health Officer.

EI *abbrev. for:* **1.** East Indian. **2.** East Indies.

eider *or* **eider duck** ('aɪdə) *n.* any of several sea ducks of the genus *Somateria,* esp. *S. mollissima,* and related genera, which occur in the N hemisphere. The male has black and white plumage, and the female is the source of eiderdown. [C18: from Old Norse *æthr;* related to Swedish *ejder,* Dutch, German *Eider*]

eiderdown ('aɪdəˌdaʊn) *n.* **1.** the breast down of the female eider duck, with which it lines the nest, used for stuffing pillows, quilts, etc. **2.** a thick warm cover for a bed, made of two layers of material enclosing a soft filling. **3.** *U.S.* a warm cotton fabric having a woollen nap.

eidetic (aɪ'dɛtɪk) *adj. Psychol.* **1.** (of visual, or sometimes auditory, images) exceptionally vivid and allowing detailed recall of something previously perceived: thought to be common in children. **2.** relating to or subject to such imagery. [C20: from Greek *eidētikos,* from *eidos* shape, form] —**ei'detically** *adv.*

eidolon (aɪ'dəʊlɒn) *n., pl.* **-la** (-lə) *or* **-lons.** **1.** an unsubstantial image; apparition; phantom. **2.** an ideal or idealized figure. [C19: from Greek: phantom, IDOL]

Eid-ul-Adha ('iːd ʊl ˌɑːdə) *n.* an annual Muslim festival marking the end of the pilgrimage to Mecca. Animals are sacrificed and their meat shared among the poor. [from Arabic, *id ul adha* festival of sacrifice]

Eid-ul-Fitr ('iːd ʊl ˌfiːtə) *n.* an annual Muslim festival marking the end of Ramadan, involving the exchange of gifts and a festive meal. [from Arabic, *id ul fitr* festival of fast-breaking]

eigen- *n. combining form.* characteristic; proper: *eigenvalue.* [from German, literally: own]

eigenfrequency ('aɪgənˌfriːkwənsɪ) *n., pl.* **-cies.** *Physics.* a resonance frequency of a system.

eigenfunction ('aɪgənˌfʌŋkʃən) *n. Maths, physics.* a function satisfying a differential equation, esp. an allowed function for a system in wave mechanics.

eigentone ('aɪgənˌtəʊn) *n.* a characteristic acoustic resonance frequency of a system.

eigenvalue ('aɪgənˌvæljuː) *n. Maths, physics.* one of the particular values of a certain parameter for which a differential equation has an eigenfunction. In wave mechanics an eigenvalue is equivalent to the energy of a quantum state of a system.

eight (eɪt) *n.* **1.** the cardinal number that is the sum of one and seven and the product of two and four. See also **number** (sense 1). **2.** a numeral, 8, VIII, etc., representing this number. **3.** *Music.* the numeral 8 used as the lower figure in a time signature to indicate that the beat is measured in quavers. **4.** the amount or quantity that is one greater than seven. **5.** something represented by, or consisting of eight units, such as a playing card with eight symbols on it. **6.** *Rowing.* **a.** a racing shell propelled by eight oarsmen. **b.** the crew of such a shell. **7.** Also called: **eight o'clock.** eight hours after noon or midnight. **8. have one over the eight.** *Slang.* to be drunk. **9.** See **figure of eight.** ~*determiner.* **10. a.** amounting to eight. **b.** (*as pronoun*): *I could only find eight.* ~Related prefixes: **octa-, octo-.** [Old English *eahta;* related to Old High German *ahto,* Old Norse *ātta,* Old Irish *ocht,* Latin *octō,* Greek *okto,* Sanskrit *astau*]

eight ball *n. U.S. and Canadian.* **1.** (in pool) the black ball, marked with the number eight. **2. behind the eight ball.** in a difficult situation; snookered.

eighteen ('eɪ'tiːn) *n.* **1.** the cardinal number that is the sum of ten and eight and the product of two and nine. See also **number** (sense 1). **2.** a numeral, 18, XVIII, etc., representing this number. **3.** the amount or quantity that is eight more than ten. **4.** something represented by, representing, or consisting of 18 units. **5.** (*functioning as sing. or pl.*) a team of 18 players in Australian Rules football. ~*determiner.* **6. a.** amounting to eighteen: *eighteen weeks.* **b.** (*as pronoun*): *eighteen of them knew.* [Old English *eahtatēne;* related to Old Norse *attjan,* Old High German *ahtozehan*]

eighteenmo ('eɪ'tiːnməʊ) *n., pl.* **-mos.** **1.** Also called: **octodecimo.** a book size resulting from folding a sheet of paper into 18 leaves or 36 pages. Often written: **18mo, 18°.** **2.** a book of this size.

eighteenth ('eɪ'tiːnθ) *adj.* **1.** (*usually prenominal*) **a.** coming after the seventeenth in numbering or counting order, position, time, etc.; being the ordinal number of *eighteen:* often written 18th. **b.** (*as n.*): *come on the eighteenth.* ~*n.* **2. a.** one of 18 approximately equal parts of something. **b.** (*as modifier*): *an eighteenth part.* **3.** the fraction that is equal to one divided by 18 (1/18).

eightfold ('eɪtˌfəʊld) *adj.* **1.** equal to or having eight times as many or as much. **2.** composed of eight parts. ~*adv.* **3.** by or up to eight times as much.

eighth (eɪtθ) *adj.* **1.** (*usually prenominal*) **a.** coming after the seventh and before the ninth in numbering or counting order, position, time, etc.; being the ordinal number of *eight:* often written 8th. **b.** (*as n.*): *the eighth in line.* ~*n.* **2. a.** one of eight equal or nearly equal parts of an object, quantity, measurement, etc. **b.** (*as modifier*): *an eighth part.* **3.** the fraction equal to one divided by eight (1/8). **4.** another word for **octave.** ~*adv.* **5.** Also: '**eighthly.** after the seventh person, position, event, etc.

eighth note *n.* the usual U.S. and Canadian name for **quaver** (sense 4).

eightieth ('eɪtɪɪθ) *adj.* **1.** (*usually prenominal*) **a.** being the ordinal number of *eighty* in numbering or counting order, position, time, etc.: often written 80th. **b.** (*as n.*): *the eightieth in succession.* ~*n.* **2. a.** one of 80 approximately equal parts of something. **b.** (*as modifier*): *an eightieth part.* **3.** the fraction equal to one divided by 80 (1/80).

eightsome reel ('eɪtsəm) *n.* a Scottish dance for eight people.

eightvo ('eɪtvəʊ) *n., pl.* **-vos.** *Bookbinding.* another word for **octavo.**

eighty ('eɪtɪ) *n., pl.* **-ies.** **1.** the cardinal number that is the product of ten and eight. See also **number** (sense 1). **2.** a numeral, 80, LXXX, etc., representing this number. **3.** (*pl.*) the numbers 80-89, esp. the 80th to the 89th year of a person's life or of a particular century. **4.** the amount or quantity that is eight times as big as ten. **5.** something represented by, representing, or consisting of 80 units. ~*determiner.* **6. a.** amounting to eighty: *eighty pages of nonsense.* **b.** (*as pronoun*): *eighty are expected.* [Old English *eahtatig;* related to Old Frisian *achtig,* Old High German *ahtozug*]

eikon ('aɪkɒn) *n.* a variant spelling of **icon.**

einkorn ('aɪnˌkɔːn) *n.* a variety of wheat, *Triticum monococcum,* of Greece and SW Asia, having pale red kernels, and cultivated in hilly regions as grain for horses. [C20: from German, literally: one kernel]

Einsteinian (aɪn'staɪnɪən) *adj.* of or relating to the works of Albert Einstein (1879–1955), German-born U.S. physicist and mathematician.

einsteinium (aɪn'staɪnɪəm) *n.* a metallic transuranic element artificially produced from plutonium. Symbol: Es; atomic no.: 99; half-life of most stable isotope, ^{254}Es: 276 days. [C20: New Latin, named after Albert *Einstein*]

Einstein shift ('aɪnstaɪn) *n. Astronomy.* a small displacement towards the red in the spectra, caused by the interaction between the radiation and the gravitational field of a massive body, such as the sun.

Einstein's law *n.* **1.** the principle that mass (m) and energy (E) are equivalent according to the equation $E = mc^2$, where c is the velocity of light. **2.** the principle that the maximum energy of a photoelectron is $h\nu - \Phi$, where ν is the frequency of the incident radiation, h is the Planck constant, and Φ is the work function.

eirenic (aɪ'riːnɪk) *adj.* a variant spelling of **irenic.**

eirenicon *or* **irenicon** (aɪ'riːnɪˌkɒn) *n.* a proposition that attempts to harmonize conflicting viewpoints. [C19: from Greek, from *eirēnikos* of or concerning peace, from *eirēnē* peace]

EIS *abbrev. for* Educational Institute of Scotland.

eisegesis (ˌaɪsə'dʒiːsɪs) *n., pl.* **-ses** (-siːz). the interpretation of a text, esp. a biblical text, using one's own ideas. Compare **exegesis.** [C19: from Greek *eis* into, in + *-egesis,* as in EXEGESIS]

eisteddfod (aɪ'stɛdfəd; *Welsh* aɪ'stɛðvɔd) *n., pl.* **-fods** *or* **-fodau** (*Welsh* aɪˌstɛð'vɒdaɪ). any of a number of annual festivals in Wales, esp. the **Royal National Eisteddfod,** in which competitions are held in music, poetry, drama, and the fine arts. [C19: from Welsh, literally: session, from *eistedd* to sit (from *sedd* seat) + *-fod,* from *bod* to be] —ˌ**eistedd'fodic** *adj.*

either ('aɪðə, 'iːðə) *determiner.* **1. a.** one or the other (of two): *either coat will do.* **b.** (*as pronoun*): *either is acceptable.* **2.** both one and the other: *there were ladies at either end of the table.* ~*conj.* **3.** (*coordinating*) used preceding two or more possibilities joined by "*or*": *you may have either cheese or a sweet.* ~*adv.* (*sentence modifier*) **4.** (*used with a negative*) used to indicate that the clause immediately preceding is a partial reiteration of a previous clause: *John isn't a liar, but he isn't exactly honest either.* [Old English *ǣgther,* short for *ǣghwæther* each of two; related to Old Frisian *ēider,* Old High German *ēogihweder;* see EACH, WHETHER]

▷**Usage.** *Either* is followed by a singular verb in good usage: *either is good; either of these books is useful.* Careful writers and speakers are cautious in using *either* to mean *both* or *each* because of the possible ambiguity, as in the following sentence: *a ship could be moored on either side of the channel.* Agreement between the verb and its subject in *either...or...* constructions follows the pattern given for *neither...nor...* See at **neither.**

either-or *adj.* presenting an unavoidable need to choose between two alternatives: *an either-or situation.*

ejaculate *vb.* (ɪˈdʒækjʊˌleɪt). **1.** to eject or discharge (semen) in orgasm. **2.** (*tr.*) to utter abruptly; blurt out. ~*n.* (ɪˈdʒækjʊlɪt). **3.** another word for **semen.** [C16: from Latin *ējaculārī* to hurl out, from *jaculum* javelin, from *jacere* to throw] —**eˈjacuˌlator** *n.*

ejaculation (ɪˌdʒækjʊˈleɪʃən) *n.* **1.** an abrupt emphatic utterance or exclamation. **2.** a discharge of semen. —**eˈjaculatory** *or* **eˈjaculative** *adj.*

ejaculatio praecox (ɪˌdʒækjʊˈleɪʃɪəʊ ˈpriːkɒks) *n.* premature ejaculation during sexual intercourse. [Latin]

eject (ɪˈdʒɛkt) *vb.* **1.** (*tr.*) to drive or force out; expel or emit. **2.** (*tr.*) to compel (a person) to leave; evict; dispossess. **3.** (*tr.*) to dismiss, as from office. **4.** (*intr.*) to leave an aircraft rapidly, using an ejection seat or capsule. **5.** (*tr.*) *Psychiatry.* to attribute (one's own motivations and characteristics) to others. [C15: from Latin *ejicere,* from *jacere* to throw] —**eˈjection** *n.*

ejecta (ɪˈdʒɛktə) *pl. n.* matter thrown out by an erupting volcano. [C19: Latin, literally: (things) ejected; see EJECT]

ejection seat *or* **ejector seat** *n.* a seat, esp. as fitted to military aircraft, that is fired by a cartridge or rocket to eject the occupant from the aircraft in an emergency.

ejective (ɪˈdʒɛktɪv) *adj.* **1.** relating to or causing ejection. **2.** *Phonetics.* (of a plosive or fricative consonant, as in some African languages) pronounced with a glottal stop. ~*n.* **3.** *Phonetics.* an ejective consonant. —**eˈjectively** *adv.*

ejectment (ɪˈdʒɛktmənt) *n.* **1.** *Property law.* (formerly) an action brought by a wrongfully dispossessed owner seeking to recover possession of his land. **2.** the act of ejecting or state of being ejected; dispossession.

ejector (ɪˈdʒɛktə) *n.* **1.** a person or thing that ejects. **2.** the mechanism in a firearm that ejects the empty cartridge or shell after firing.

eke[1] (iːk) *vb.* (*tr.*) *Archaic.* to increase, enlarge, or lengthen. [Old English *eacan;* related to Old Norse *auka* to increase, Latin *augēre* to increase]

eke[2] (iːk) *sentence connector. Archaic.* also; moreover. [Old English *eac;* related to Old Norse, Gothic *auk* also, Old High German *ouh,* Latin *autem* but, *aut* or]

eke out *vb.* (*tr., adv.*) **1.** to make (a supply) last, esp. by frugal use: *they eked out what little food was left.* **2.** to support (existence) with difficulty and effort. **3.** to add to (something insufficient), esp. with effort: *to eke out an income with evening work.*

ekistics (ɪˈkɪstɪks) *n.* (*functioning as sing.*) the science or study of human settlements. [C20: from Greek *oikistikos* of or concerning settlements, from *oikizein* to settle (a colony), from *oikos* a house] —**eˈkistic** *or* **eˈkistical** *adj.* —ˌ**ekisˈtician** *n.*

ekpwele (ɛkˈpweɪleɪ) *or* **ekuele** (eɪˈkweɪleɪ) *n., pl.* **-le** (-leɪ). since 1973, the standard monetary unit of Equatorial Guinea. [from the native name in Equatorial Guinea]

el (ɛl) *n. U.S. informal.* a shortened form of **elevated railway** *or* **railroad.**

elaborate *adj.* (ɪˈlæbərɪt). **1.** planned or executed with care and exactness; detailed. **2.** marked by complexity, ornateness, or detail. ~*vb.* (ɪˈlæbəˌreɪt). **3.** (*intr.;* usually foll. by *on* or *upon*) to add information or detail (to an account); expand (upon). **4.** (*tr.*) to work out in detail; develop. **5.** (*tr.*) to make more complicated or ornate. **6.** (*tr.*) to produce by careful labour; create. **7.** (*tr.*) *Physiol.* to change (food or simple substances) into more complex substances for use in the body. [C16: from Latin *ēlabōrāre* to take pains, from *labōrāre* to toil] —**eˈlaborately** *adv.* —**eˈlaborateness** *n.* —**eˌlaboˈration** *n.* —**elaborative** (ɪˈlæbərətɪv) *adj.* —**eˈlaboˌrator** *n.*

elaeoptene (ˌɛlɪˈɒptiːn) *n.* a variant spelling of **eleoptene.**

Elamite (ˈiːləˌmaɪt) *n.* **1.** an inhabitant of the ancient kingdom of Elam, east of the River Tigris. **2.** Also called: **Elamitic, Susian.** the extinct language of this people, of no known relationship, recorded in cuneiform inscriptions dating from the 25th to the 4th centuries B.C. ~*adj.* **3.** of or relating to Elam, its people, or their language.

élan (eɪˈlɑːn, eɪˈlæn; *French* elɑ̃) *n.* a combination of style and vigour: *he performed the concerto with élan.* [C19: from French, from *élancer* to throw forth, ultimately from Latin *lancea* LANCE]

eland (ˈiːlənd) *n.* **1.** a large spiral-horned antelope, *Taurotragus oryx,* inhabiting bushland in eastern and southern Africa. It has a dewlap and a hump on the shoulders and is light brown with vertical white stripes. **2. giant eland.** a similar but larger animal, *T. derbianus,* living in wooded areas of central and W Africa. [C18: via Afrikaans from Dutch *eland* elk; related to Old Slavonic *jeleni* stag, Greek *ellos* fawn]

élan vital *French.* (elɑ̃ vital) *n.* a creative principle held by Henri Bergson to be present in all organisms and responsible for evolution. Compare **Bergsonism.** [literally: vital impetus]

elapid (ˈɛləpɪd) *n.* **1.** any venomous snake of the mostly tropical family *Elapidae,* having fixed poison fangs at the front of the upper jaw and including the cobras, coral snakes, and mambas. ~*adj.* **2.** of, relating to, or belonging to the *Elapidae.* [C19: from New Latin *Elapidae,* from Medieval Greek *elaps, elops* a fish, sea serpent; perhaps related to Greek *lepis* scale]

elapse (ɪˈlæps) *vb.* (*intr.*) (of time) to pass by. [C17: from Latin *ēlābī* to slip away, from *lābī* to slip, glide]

elasmobranch (ɪˈlæsməˌbræŋk, ɪˈlæz-) *n.* **1.** any cartilaginous fish of the subclass *Elasmobranchii* (or *Selachii*), which includes the sharks, rays, dogfish, and skates. ~*adj.* **2.** of, relating to, or belonging to the *Elasmobranchii.* ~Also called: **selachian.** [C19: from New Latin *elasmobranchii,* from Greek *elasmos* metal plate + *brankhia* gills]

elasmosaur (ɪˈlæzməˌsɔː) *n.* a very long-necked extinct marine reptile: a type of plesiosaur. [C19: from Greek *elasmos* metal plate + *sauros* lizard]

elastance (ɪˈlæstəns) *n. Physics.* the reciprocal of capacitance. It is measured in reciprocal farads (darafs). [C19: from ELASTIC + -ANCE]

elastase (ɪˈlæsteɪs) *n.* an enzyme that digests elastin.

elastic (ɪˈlæstɪk) *adj.* **1.** (of a body or material) capable of returning to its original shape after compression, expansion, stretching, or other deformation. **2.** capable of adapting to change: *an elastic schedule.* **3.** quick to recover from fatigue, dejection, etc.; buoyant. **4.** springy or resilient: *an elastic walk.* **5.** (of gases) capable of expanding spontaneously. **6.** *Physics.* (of collisions) involving no overall change in translational kinetic energy. **7.** made of elastic. ~*n.* **8.** tape, cord, or fabric containing interwoven strands of flexible rubber or similar substance allowing it to stretch and return to its original shape. **9.** *Chiefly U.S. and Canadian.* something made of elastic, such as a garter or a rubber band. [C17: from New Latin *elasticus* impulsive, from Greek *elastikos,* from *elaunein* to beat, drive] —**eˈlastically** *adv.*

elasticate (ɪˈlæstɪˌkeɪt) *vb.* (*tr.*) to insert elastic sections or thread into (a fabric or garment): *an elasticated waistband.* —**eˌlastiˈcation** *n.*

elastic band *n.* another name for **rubber band.**

elasticity (ɪlæˈstɪsɪtɪ, ˌiːlæ-) *n.* **1.** the property of a body or substance that enables it to resume its original shape or size when a distorting force is removed. See also **elastic limit. 2.** the state or quality of being elastic; flexibility or buoyancy. **3.** a measure of the sensitivity of demand for goods or services to changes in price or other marketing variables, such as advertising.

elasticize *or* **elasticise** (ɪˈlæstɪˌsaɪz) *vb.* (*tr.*) **1.** to make elastic. **2.** another word for **elasticate.**

elastic limit *n.* the greatest stress that can be applied to a material without causing permanent deformation.

elastic modulus *n.* another name for **modulus of elasticity.**

elastic rebound *n. Geology.* a theory of earthquakes that envisages gradual deformation of the fault zone without fault slippage until friction is overcome, when the fault suddenly slips to produce the earthquake.

elastin (ɪˈlæstɪn) *n. Biochem.* a fibrous scleroprotein constituting the major part of elastic tissue, such as the walls of arteries. [C19: from ELASTIC + -IN]

elastivity (ɪlæˈstɪvɪtɪ) *n. Physics.* a measure of the resistance of a substance to an electric field; the reciprocal of the permittivity of a dielectric.

elastomer (ɪˈlæstəmə) *n.* any material, such as natural or synthetic rubber, that is able to resume its original shape when a deforming force is removed. [C20: from ELASTIC + -MER] —**elastomeric** (ɪˌlæstəˈmɛrɪk) *adj.*

Elastoplast (ɪˈlæstəˌplɑːst) *n. Trademark.* a gauze surgical dressing backed by adhesive tape.

elate (ɪˈleɪt) *vb.* (*tr.*) to fill with high spirits, exhilaration, pride or optimism. [C16: from Latin *ēlāt-* stem of past participle of *efferre* to bear away, from *ferre* to carry] —**eˈlated** *adj.* —**eˈlatedly** *adv.* —**eˈlatedness** *n.*

elater (ˈɛlətə) *n.* **1.** an elaterid beetle. **2.** *Botany.* a spirally thickened filament, occurring in liverwort capsules and horsetails, thought to aid dispersal of spores. [C17: via New Latin from Greek: driver, from *elaunein* to beat, drive; compare ELASTIC]

elaterid (ɪˈlætərɪd) *n.* **1.** any of the beetles constituting the widely distributed family *Elateridae* (click beetles). The group includes the wireworms and certain fireflies. ~*adj.* **2.** of, relating to, or belonging to the family *Elateridae.* [C19: from New Latin *Elateridae,* from ELATER]

elaterin (ɪˈlætərɪn) *n.* a white crystalline substance found in elaterium, used as a purgative. [C19: from ELATERIUM + -IN]

elaterite (ɪˈlætəˌraɪt) *n.* a dark brown naturally occurring bitumen resembling rubber. [C19: from ELATER + -ITE[1]]

elaterium (ˌɛləˈtɪərɪəm) *n.* a greenish sediment prepared from the juice of the squirting cucumber, used as a purgative. [C16: from Latin, from Greek *elatērion* squirting cucumber, from *elatērios* purgative, from *elaunein* to drive]

elation (ɪˈleɪʃən) *n.* joyfulness or exaltation of spirit, as from success, pleasure, or relief; high spirits.

elative (ˈiːlətɪv) *adj.* **1.** (in the grammar of Finnish and other languages) denoting a case of nouns expressing a relation of motion or direction, usually translated by the English prepositions *out of* or *away from.* Compare **illative** (sense 3). ~*n.* **2.** **a.** the elative case. **b.** an elative word or speech element. [C19: from Latin *ēlātus,* past participle of *efferre* to carry out; see ELATE]

E layer *n.* another name for **E region.**

elbow (ˈɛlbəʊ) *n.* **1.** the joint between the upper arm and the forearm, formed by the junction of the radius and ulna with the humerus. **2.** the corresponding joint or bone of birds or mammals. **3.** the part of a garment that covers the elbow. **4.** something resembling an elbow, such as a sharp bend in a road or river. **5. at one's elbow.** within easy reach. **6. out at elbow(s).** ragged or impoverished. **7. up to the elbows with** *or* **in.** busily occupied with; deeply immersed in. ~*vb.* **8.** to make (one's way) by shoving, jostling, etc. **9.** (*tr.*) to knock or shove with or as if with the elbow. **10.** (*tr.*) to reject; dismiss (esp. in the phrases **give** *or* **get the elbow**). [Old English *elnboga;* see ELL[2], BOW[2]; related to Old Norse *olbogi,* Old High German *elinbogo*]

elbow grease *n. Facetious.* vigorous physical labour, esp. hard rubbing.

elbowroom (ˈɛlbəʊˌruːm, -ˌrʊm) *n.* sufficient scope to move or function.

eld (ɛld) *n. Archaic.* **1.** old age. **2.** olden days; antiquity. [Old English *eldu;* related to Old Norse *elli;* see OLD]

elder[1] (ˈɛldə) *adj.* **1.** born earlier; senior. Compare **older. 2.** (in piquet and similar card games) denoting or relating to the nondealer (the **elder hand**), who has certain advantages in the play. **3.** *Archaic.* **a.** prior in rank, position, or office. **b.** of a previous time; former. ~*n.* **4.** an older person; one's senior. **5.** *Anthropol.* a senior member of a tribe who has influence or authority. **6.** (in certain Protestant Churches) a lay office having teaching, pastoral, or administrative functions. **7.** another word for **presbyter.** [Old English *eldra,* comparative of *eald* OLD; related to Old Norse *ellri,* Old High German *altiro,* Gothic *althiza*] —**ˈelderˌship** *n.*

elder[2] (ˈɛldə) *n.* **1.** Also called: **elderberry.** any of various caprifoliaceous shrubs or small trees of the genus *Sambucus,* having clusters of small white flowers and red, purple, or black berry-like fruits. **2.** any of various unrelated plants, such as box elder and marsh elder. ~Compare **alder.** [Old English *ellern;* related to Old Norse *elrir,* Old High German *erlīn,* Old Slavonic *jelīcha,* Latin *alnus*]

elderberry (ˈɛldəˌbɛrɪ) *n., pl.* **-ries. 1.** the berry-like fruit of the elder, used for making wines, jellies, etc. **2.** another name for **elder**[2] (sense 1).

Elder Brethren *pl. n.* the senior members of the governing body of Trinity House.

elderly (ˈɛldəlɪ) *adj.* (of people) **a.** quite old; past middle age. **b.** (*as collective n.* preceded by *the*): *the elderly.* —**ˈelderliness** *n.*

elder statesman *n.* an old, experienced, and eminent person, esp. a politician, whose advice is often sought.

eldest (ˈɛldɪst) *adj.* being the oldest, esp. the oldest surviving child of the same parents. [Old English *eldesta,* superlative of *eald* OLD]

ELDO (ˈɛldəʊ) *n. acronym for* European Launcher Development Organization.

El Dorado (ɛl dɒˈrɑːdəʊ; *Spanish* el doˈraðo) *n.* **1.** a fabled city in South America, rich in treasure and sought by Spanish explorers in the 16th century. **2.** Also: **ˌeldoˈrado.** any place of great riches or fabulous opportunity. [C16: from Spanish, literally: the gilded (place)]

eldritch *or* **eldrich** (ˈɛldrɪtʃ) *adj. Poetic, Scot.* unearthly; weird. [C16: perhaps from Old English *ælf* ELF + *rīce* realm; see RICH]

Eleatic (ˌɛlɪˈætɪk) *adj.* **1.** denoting or relating to a school of philosophy founded in Elea in Greece in the 6th century B.C. It held that one pure immutable Being is the only object of knowledge and that information obtained by the senses is illusory. ~*n.* **2.** a follower of this school. —**Eleaticism** (ˌɛlɪˈætɪˌsɪzəm) *n.*

elecampane (ˌɛlɪkæmˈpeɪn) *n.* a perennial flowering plant, *Inula helenium,* of Europe, Asia, and North America having large hairy leaves and narrow yellow petals: family *Compositae* (composites). [C16: from Medieval Latin *enula campāna,* from *enula* (from Greek *helenion*) + *campānus* of the field]

elect (ɪˈlɛkt) *vb.* **1.** (*tr.*) to choose (someone) to be (a representative or a public official) by voting: *they elected him Mayor.* **2.** to select; choose: *to elect to die rather than surrender.* **3.** (*tr.*) (of God) to select or predestine for the grace of salvation. ~*adj.* **4.** (*immediately postpositive*) voted into office but not yet installed: *the president elect.* **5. a.** chosen or choice; selected or elite. **b.** (*as collective n.* preceded by *the*): *the elect.* **6.** *Christianity.* **a.** selected or predestined by God to receive salvation; chosen. **b.** (*as collective n.* preceded by *the*): *the elect.* [C15: from Latin *ēligere* to select, from *legere* to choose] —**eˈlectable** *adj.*

elect. *or* **elec.** *abbrev. for:* **1.** electric(al). **2.** electricity.

election (ɪˈlɛkʃən) *n.* **1.** the selection by vote of a person or persons from among candidates for a position, esp. a political office. **2.** a public vote on an official proposition. **3.** the act or an instance of choosing. **4.** *Christianity.* **a.** the doctrine of Calvin that God chooses certain individuals for salvation without reference to their faith or works. **b.** the doctrine of Arminius and others that God chooses for salvation those who, by grace, persevere in faith and works.

electioneer (ɪˌlɛkʃəˈnɪə) *vb.* (*intr.*) **1.** to be active in a political election or campaign. ~*n.* **2.** a person who engages in this activity. —**eˌlectionˈeering** *n., adj.*

elective (ɪˈlɛktɪv) *adj.* **1.** of or based on selection by vote: *elective procedure.* **2.** selected by vote: *an elective official.* **3.** having the power to elect. **4.** open to choice; optional: *an elective course of study.* ~*n.* **5.** an optional course or hospital placement undertaken by a medical student. —**eˈlectively** *adv.* —**electivity** (ˌiːlɛkˈtɪvɪtɪ) *or* **eˈlectiveness** *n.*

elector (ɪˈlɛktə) *n.* **1.** someone who is eligible to vote in the election of a government. **2.** (*often cap.*) a member of the U.S. electoral college. **3.** (*often cap.*) (in the Holy Roman Empire) any of the German princes entitled to take part in the election of a new emperor. —**eˈlectorˌship** *n.*

electoral (ɪˈlɛktərəl) *adj.* relating to or consisting of electors. —**eˈlectorally** *adv.*

electoral college *n.* **1.** (*often caps.*) *U.S.* a body of electors chosen by the voters who formally elect the president and vice president. **2.** any body of electors.

electorate (ɪˈlɛktərɪt) *n.* **1.** the body of all qualified voters. **2.** the rank, position, or territory of an elector of the Holy Roman Empire. **3.** *Austral. and N.Z.* the area represented by a Member of Parliament. **4.** *Austral. and N.Z.* the voters in a constituency.

Electra complex (ɪˈlɛktrə) *n. Psychoanal.* the sexual attachment of a female child to her father. See also **penis envy.** [C20: named after *Electra,* a character in Greek mythology who incites her brother Orestes to kill their mother, the murderess of their father]

Electra paradox *n. Logic.* the supposed paradox that one may know something to be true of an object under one description but not another, as when Electra knew that Orestes was her brother but not that the man before her was her brother although he was Orestes. This shows the predicate "knows" to be intensional, that Electra's knowledge here is de dicto, and that the statement of it yields an opaque context. See also **de dicto.**

electret (ɪˈlɛktrət) *n.* a permanently polarized dielectric material; its electric field is similar to the magnetic field of a permanent magnet. [C20: from *electr(icity + magn)et*]

electric (ɪˈlɛktrɪk) *adj.* **1.** of, derived from, produced by, producing, transmitting, or powered by electricity: *electric current; an electric cord; an electric blanket; an electric fence; an electric fire.* **2.** (of a musical instrument) amplified electronically: *an electric guitar; an electric mandolin.* **3.** very tense or exciting; emotionally charged: *an electric atmosphere.* ~*n.* **4.** *Informal.* an electric train, car, etc. **5.** *Brit. informal.* electricity or electrical power. **6.** (*pl.*) an electric circuit or electric appliances. [C17: from New Latin *electricus* amber-like (because friction causes amber to become charged), from Latin *ēlectrum* amber, from Greek *ēlektron,* of obscure origin]

▷**Usage.** See at **electronic.**

electrical (ɪˈlɛktrɪkᵊl) *adj.* of, relating to, or concerned with electricity. —**eˈlectrically** *adv.*

▷**Usage.** See at **electronic.**

electrical engineering *n.* the branch of engineering concerned with the practical applications of electricity. —**electrical engineer** *n.*

electric-arc furnace *n.* another name for **arc furnace.**

electric-arc welding *n.* another name for **arc welding.**

electric blanket *n.* a blanket that contains an electric heating element, used to warm a bed.

electric blue *n., adj.* **a.** a strong metallic blue colour. **b.** (*as adj.*): *an electric-blue evening dress.*

electric chair *n.* (in the U.S.) **a.** an electrified chair for executing criminals. **b.** (usually preceded by *the*) execution by this method.

electric charge *n.* another name for **charge** (sense 25).

electric circuit *n. Physics.* another name for **circuit** (sense 3a).

electric constant *n.* the permittivity of free space, which has the value 8.854 185 × 10^{-12} farad per metre. Symbol: ε_0 Also called: **absolute permittivity.**

electric current *n.* another name for **current** (sense 8).

electric discharge *n. Physics.* another name for **discharge** (sense 20b).

electric-discharge lamp *n.* another name for **fluorescent lamp.**

electric displacement *n. Physics.* the charge per unit area displaced across a layer of conductor in an electric field. Symbol: *D* Also called: **electric flux density.**

electric eel *n.* an eel-like freshwater cyprinoid fish, *Electrophorus electricus,* of N South America, having electric organs in the body: family *Electrophoridae.*

electric eye *n.* another name for **photocell.**

electric field *n.* a field of force surrounding a charged particle within which another charged particle experiences a force. Compare **magnetic field.**

electric field strength *n.* the strength or intensity of an electric field at any point, usually measured in volts per metre. Symbol: *E*

electric fire *n.* a device that provides heat for a room from an incandescent electric element.

electric flux *n.* the amount of electricity displaced across a given area in a dielectric. Symbol: Ψ

electric flux density *n.* another name for **electric displacement.**
electric furnace *n.* any furnace in which the heat is provided by an electric current.
electric guitar *n.* an electrically amplified guitar, used mainly in pop music. Compare **acoustic guitar.**
electric hare *n.* (in greyhound racing) a model of a hare, mounted on an electrified rail, which the dogs chase.
electrician (ɪlɛk'trɪʃən, ˌiːlɛk-) *n.* a person whose occupation is the installation, maintenance, and repair of electrical devices.
electricity (ɪlɛk'trɪsɪtɪ, ˌiːlɛk-) *n.* **1.** any phenomenon associated with stationary or moving electrons, ions, or other charged particles. **2.** the science concerned with electricity. **3.** an electric current or charge: *a motor powered by electricity.* **4.** emotional tension or excitement, esp. between or among people.
electric motor *n.* a device that converts electrical energy to mechanical torque.
electric needle *n.* a surgical instrument for cutting tissue by the application of a high-frequency current.
electric organ *n.* **1.** *Music.* **a.** a pipe organ operated by electrical means. **b.** another name for **electronic organ. 2.** *Zoology.* a small group of modified muscle cells on the body of certain fishes, such as the electric eel, that gives an electric shock to any animal touching them.
electric potential *n.* **a.** the work required to transfer a unit positive electric charge from an infinite distance to a given point. **b.** the potential difference between the point and some other reference point. Symbol: *V* or ϕ Sometimes shortened to **potential.**
electric ray *n.* any ray of the order *Torpediniformes,* of tropical and temperate seas, having a flat rounded body with an electric organ in each of the fins, close to the head.
electric shock *n.* the physiological reaction, characterized by pain and muscular spasm, to the passage of an electric current through the body. It can affect the respiratory system and heart rhythm. Sometimes shortened to **shock.**
electric storm *n.* a violent atmospheric disturbance in which the air is highly charged with static electricity, causing a storm. Compare **thunderstorm.**
electric strength *n.* the maximum voltage sustainable by an insulating material, after which it loses its insulating properties.
electric susceptibility *n.* another name for **susceptibility** (sense 4a).
electrify (ɪ'lɛktrɪˌfaɪ) *vb.* **-fies, -fying, -fied.** (*tr.*) **1.** to adapt or equip (a system, device, etc.) for operation by electrical power. **2.** to charge with or subject to electricity. **3.** to startle or excite intensely; shock or thrill. —**e'lectriˌfiable** *adj.* —**eˌlectrifi'cation** *n.* —**e'lectriˌfier** *n.*
electro (ɪ'lɛktrəʊ) *n., pl.* **-tros.** short for **electroplate** or **electrotype.**
electro- *or sometimes before a vowel* **electr-** *combining form.* **1.** electric or electrically: *electrocardiograph; electrocute.* **2.** electrolytic: *electroanalysis.* [from New Latin, from Latin *ēlectrum* amber, from Greek *ēlektron*]
electroacoustic (ɪˌlɛktrəʊə'kuːstɪk) *adj.* another word for **acoustoelectronic.**
electroanalysis (ɪˌlɛktrəʊə'nælɪsɪs) *n.* chemical analysis by electrolysis or electrodeposition. —**electroanalytic** (ɪˌlɛktrəʊˌænə'lɪtɪk) *or* **eˌlectroˌana'lytical** *adj.*
electrocardiogram (ɪˌlɛktrəʊ'kɑːdɪəʊˌgræm) *n.* a tracing of the electric currents that initiate the heartbeat, used to diagnose possible heart disorders. Abbrev.: **ECG.**
electrocardiograph (ɪˌlɛktrəʊ'kɑːdɪəʊˌgrɑːf, -ˌgræf) *n.* an instrument that is used for recording the electrical activity of the heart. Abbrev.: **ECG.** —**eˌlectroˌcardio'graphic** *adj.* —**eˌlectroˌcardio'graphically** *adv.* —**electrocardiography** (ɪˌlɛktrəʊˌkɑːdɪ'ɒgrəfɪ) *n.*
electrochemical equivalent *n.* the mass of an element liberated from its ions or converted into them by one coulomb of electric charge.
electrochemical series *n.* another name for **electromotive series.**
electrochemistry (ɪˌlɛktrəʊ'kɛmɪstrɪ) *n.* the branch of chemistry concerned with the study of electric cells and electrolysis. —**electrochemical** (ɪˌlɛktrəʊ'kɛmɪkᵊl) *adj.* —**eˌlectro'chemically** *adv.* —**eˌlectro'chemist** *n.*
electrochromatography (ɪˌlɛktrəʊkrəʊmə'tɒgrəfɪ) *n.* chromatography effected by the influence of an applied electric field. —**eˌlectrochro'matic** *adj.*
electroconvulsive therapy (ɪˌlɛktrəʊkən'vʌlsɪv) *n. Med.* the treatment of certain psychotic conditions by passing an electric current through the brain to induce coma or convulsions. Abbrev.: **ECT.** Also called: **electroshock therapy.** See also **shock therapy.**
electrocorticogram (ɪˌlɛktrəʊ'kɔːtɪkəʊˌgræm) *n.* a record of brain waves obtained by placing electrodes directly on the surface of the exposed cerebral cortex. Compare **electroencephalogram, electroencephalograph.**
electrocute (ɪ'lɛktrəˌkjuːt) *vb.* (*tr.*) **1.** to kill as a result of an electric shock. **2.** *U.S.* to execute in the electric chair. [C19: from ELECTRO- + (exe)cute] —**eˌlectro'cution** *n.*
electrocyte (ɪ'lɛktrəʊˌsaɪt) *n. Zoology.* a specialized muscle or nerve cell that generates electricity, as found in an electric organ.
electrode (ɪ'lɛktrəʊd) *n.* **1.** a conductor through which an electric current enters or leaves an electrolyte, an electric arc, or an electronic valve or tube. **2.** an element in a semiconducting device that emits, collects, or controls the movement of electrons or holes.
electrode efficiency *n. Chem.* the ratio of the amount of metal deposited in an electrolytic cell to that theoretically deposited according to Faraday's laws.
electrodeposit (ɪˌlɛktrəʊdɪ'pɒzɪt) *vb.* **1.** (*tr.*) to deposit (a metal) by electrolysis. ~*n.* **2.** the deposit so formed. —**electrodeposition** (ɪˌlɛktrəʊˌdɛpə'zɪʃən) *n.*
electrode potential *n. Chem.* the potential difference developed when an electrode of an element is placed in a solution containing ions of that element.
electrodialysis (ɪˌlɛktrəʊdaɪ'ælɪsɪs) *n.* dialysis in which electrolytes are removed from a colloidal solution by a potential difference between two electrodes separated by one or more membranes.
electrodynamic (ɪˌlɛktrəʊdaɪ'næmɪk) *adj.* **1.** operated by an electromotive force between current-carrying coils: *an electrodynamic wattmeter.* **2.** of or relating to electrodynamics.
electrodynamics (ɪˌlɛktrəʊdaɪ'næmɪks) *n.* (*functioning as sing.*) the branch of physics concerned with the interactions between electrical and mechanical forces.
electrodynamometer (ɪˌlɛktrəʊˌdaɪnə'mɒmɪtə) *n.* an instrument that uses the interaction of the magnetic fields of two coils to measure electric current, voltage, or power.
electroencephalogram (ɪˌlɛktrəʊɛn'sɛfələˌgræm) *n. Med.* the tracing obtained from an electroencephalograph. Abbrev.: **EEG.**
electroencephalograph (ɪˌlɛktrəʊɛn'sɛfələˌgrɑːf, -ˌgræf) *n.* an instrument for recording the electrical activity of the brain, usually by means of electrodes placed on the scalp: used to diagnose tumours of the brain, to study brain waves, etc. Abbrev.: **EEG.** See also **brain wave.** —**eˌlectroenˌcephalo'graphic** *adj.* —**eˌlectroenˌcephalo'graphically** *adv.* —**electroencephalography** (ɪˌlɛktrəʊɛnˌsɛfə'lɒgrəfɪ) *n.*
electroendosmosis (ɪˌlɛktrəʊˌɛndɒz'məʊsɪs, -dɒs-) *n.* another name for **electro-osmosis.**
electrofluor (ɪ'lɛktrəʊˌfluːɔː) *n. Physics.* a transparent material that stores electrical energy and subsequently releases it as light. [C20: from ELECTRO- + FLUOR(ESCENCE)]
electroform (ɪ'lɛktrəˌfɔːm) *vb.* to form (a metallic object) by electrolytic deposition on a mould or matrix.
electrogen (ɪ'lɛktrəʊˌdʒɛn) *n.* a molecule that emits electrons when it is illuminated. —**eˌlectro'genic** *adj.*
electrograph (ɪ'lɛktrəʊˌgrɑːf, -ˌgræf) *n.* **1.** an apparatus for engraving metal printing cylinders, esp. in gravure printing. **2.** the equipment used for the electrical transmission of pictures. **3. a.** a recording electrometer. **b.** a graph produced by this instrument. **4.** a visual record of the surface composition of a metal, obtained by placing an electrolyte-soaked paper over the metal and passing a current through the paper to an electrode on the other side. —**electrographic** (ɪˌlɛktrəʊ'græfɪk) *adj.* —**eˌlectro'graphically** *adv.* —**electrography** (ɪlɛk'trɒgrəfɪ, ˌiːlɛk-) *n.*
electrojet (ɪ'lɛktrəʊˌdʒɛt) *n.* a narrow belt of fast-moving ions in the ionosphere, under the influence of the earth's magnetic field, causing auroral displays.
electrokinetic (ɪˌlɛktrəʊkɪ'nɛtɪk, -kaɪ-) *adj.* of or relating to the motion of charged particles and its effects.
electrokinetics (ɪˌlɛktrəʊkɪ'nɛtɪks, -kaɪ-) *n.* (*functioning as sing.*) the branch of physics concerned with the motion of charged particles.
electroluminescence (ɪˌlɛktrəʊˌluːmɪ'nɛsᵊns) *n. Physics.* **a.** the emission of light by a phosphor when activated by an alternating field or by a gas when activated by an electric discharge. **b.** the light emitted by this process. —**eˌlectroˌlumi'nescent** *adj.*
electrolyse *or U.S.* **electrolyze** (ɪ'lɛktrəʊˌlaɪz) *vb.* (*tr.*) **1.** to decompose (a chemical compound) by electrolysis. **2.** to destroy (living tissue, such as hair roots) by electrolysis. [C19: back formation from ELECTROLYSIS on pattern of *analyse*] —**eˌlectroly'sation** *or U.S.* **eˌlectroly'zation** *n.* —**e'lectroˌlyser** *or U.S.* **e'lectroˌlyzer** *n.*
electrolysis (ɪlɛk'trɒlɪsɪs) *n.* **1.** the conduction of electricity by a solution or melt, esp. the use of this process to induce chemical changes. **2.** the destruction of living tissue, such as hair roots, by an electric current, usually for cosmetic reasons. [C19: from ELECTRO- + -LYSIS]
electrolyte (ɪ'lɛktrəʊˌlaɪt) *n.* **1.** a solution or molten substance that conducts electricity. **2. a.** a chemical compound that dissociates in solution into ions. **b.** any of the ions themselves.
electrolytic (ɪˌlɛktrəʊ'lɪtɪk) *adj.* **1.** *Physics.* **a.** of, concerned with, or produced by electrolysis or electrodeposition. **b.** of, relating to, or containing an electrolyte. ~*n.* **2.** *Electronics.* Also called: **electrolytic capacitor.** a small capacitor consisting of two electrodes separated by an electrolyte. —**eˌlectro'lytically** *adv.*
electrolytic cell *n.* any device in which electrolysis occurs. Sometimes shortened to **cell.**
electrolytic gas *n.* a mixture of two parts of hydrogen and one part of oxygen by volume, formed by the electrolysis of water.

electromagnet (ɪˌlɛktrəʊˈmæɡnɪt) *n.* a magnet consisting of an iron or steel core wound with a coil of wire, through which a current is passed.

electromagnetic (ɪˌlɛktrəʊmæɡˈnɛtɪk) *adj.* **1.** of, containing, or operated by an electromagnet: *an electromagnetic pump.* **2.** of, relating to, or consisting of electromagnetism: *electromagnetic moment.* **3.** of or relating to electromagnetic radiation: *the electromagnetic spectrum.* —**eˌlectromagˈnetically** *adv.*

electromagnetic field *n.* a field of force equivalent to an electric field and a magnetic field at right angles to each other and to the direction of propagation.

electromagnetic interaction *or* **force** *n. Physics.* an interaction between charged particles arising from their electric and magnetic fields; its strength is about 100 times weaker than the strong interaction. See **interaction** (sense 2), **electroweak interaction.**

electromagnetic moment *n.* a measure of the magnetic strength of a magnet or current-carrying coil, expressed as the torque produced when the magnet or coil is set with its axis perpendicular to unit magnetic flux density. It is measured in ampere metres squared. Symbol: m Also called: **magnetic moment.** Compare **magnetic dipole moment.**

electromagnetic pump *n.* a device for pumping liquid metals by placing a pipe between the poles of an electromagnet and passing a current through the liquid metal.

electromagnetic radiation *n.* radiation consisting of an electric and magnetic field at right angles to each other and to the direction of propagation. It requires no supporting medium and travels through empty space at 2.9979×10^8 metres per second. See also **photon.**

electromagnetics (ɪˌlɛktrəʊmæɡˈnɛtɪks) *n.* (*functioning as sing.*) *Physics.* another name for **electromagnetism** (sense 2).

electromagnetic spectrum *n.* the complete range of electromagnetic radiation from the longest radio waves (wavelength 10^5 metres) to the shortest gamma radiation (wavelength 10^{-13} metre).

electromagnetic unit *n.* any unit that belongs to a system of electrical cgs units in which the magnetic constant is given the value of unity and is taken as a pure number. Abbrevs.: **EMU, e.m.u.** Compare **electrostatic unit.**

electromagnetic wave *n.* a wave of energy propagated in an electromagnetic field. See also **electromagnetic radiation.**

electromagnetism (ɪˌlɛktrəʊˈmæɡnɪˌtɪzəm) *n.* **1.** magnetism produced by an electric current. **2.** Also called: **electromagnetics.** the branch of physics concerned with magnetism produced by electric currents and with the interaction of electric and magnetic fields.

electromechanical (ɪˌlɛktrəʊmɪˈkænɪkᵊl) *adj.* of, relating to, or concerning an electrically operated mechanical device. —**eˌlectromeˈchanically** *adv.*

electromerism (ɪˌlɛktrəʊˈmɛrɪzəm) *n. Chem.* a type of tautomerism in which the isomers (**electromers**) differ in the distribution of charge in their molecules. [C20: from ELECTRO- + (iso)merism]

electrometallurgy (ɪˌlɛktrəʊmɪˈtælədʒɪ, -ˈmɛtəˌlɜːdʒɪ) *n.* metallurgy involving the use of electric-arc furnaces, electrolysis, and other electrical operations. —**eˌlectroˌmetalˈlurgical** *adj.* —**eˌlectrometˈallurgist** *n.*

electrometer (ɪlɛkˈtrɒmɪtə, ˌiːlɛk-) *n.* an instrument for detecting or determining the magnitude of a potential difference or charge by the electrostatic forces between charged bodies. —**electrometric** (ɪˌlɛktrəʊˈmɛtrɪk) *or* **eˌlectroˈmetrical** *adj.* —**eˌlectroˈmetrically** *adv.* —**elecˈtrometry** *n.*

electromotive (ɪˌlɛktrəʊˈməʊtɪv) *adj.* of, concerned with, producing, or tending to produce an electric current.

electromotive force *n. Physics.* **a.** a source of energy that can cause a current to flow in an electrical circuit or device. **b.** the rate at which energy is drawn from this source when unit current flows through the circuit or device, measured in volts. Abbrevs.: **emf, EMF.** Symbol: *E* Compare **potential difference.**

electromotive series *n. Chem.* a series of the metals, together with hydrogen, ranged in the order of their electrode potentials.

electromyography (ɪˌlɛktrəʊmaɪˈɒɡrəfɪ) *n. Med.* a technique for recording the electrical activity of muscles: used in the diagnosis of nerve and muscle disorders.

electron (ɪˈlɛktrɒn) *n.* a stable elementary particle present in all atoms, orbiting the nucleus in numbers equal to the atomic number of the element; a lepton with a negative charge of 1.6022×10^{-19} coulomb, a rest mass of 9.1096×10^{-31} kilogram, a radius of 2.818×10^{-15} metre, and a spin of ½. [C19: from ELECTRO- + -ON]

electron affinity *n.* a measure of the ability of an atom or molecule to form a negative ion, expressed as the energy released when an electron is attached. Symbol: *A*

electron capture *n. Physics.* the transformation of an atomic nucleus in which an electron from the atom is spontaneously absorbed into the nucleus. A proton is changed into a neutron, thereby reducing the atomic number by one. A neutrino is emitted. The process may be detected by the consequent emission of the characteristic x-rays of the resultant element. Former name: **K-capture.**

electronegative (ɪˌlɛktrəʊˈnɛɡətɪv) *adj.* **1.** having a negative electric charge. **2.** (of an atom, group, molecule, etc.) tending to gain or attract electrons and form negative ions or polarized bonds. Compare **electropositive.**

electronegativity (ɪˌlɛktrəʊˌnɛɡəˈtɪvɪtɪ) *n.* **1.** the state of being electronegative. **2.** a measure of the ability of a specified atom to attract electrons in a molecule.

electron gun *n.* a heated cathode with an associated system of electrodes and coils for producing and focusing a beam of electrons, used esp. in cathode-ray tubes.

electronic (ɪlɛkˈtrɒnɪk, ˌiːlɛk-) *adj.* **1.** of, concerned with, using, or operated by devices, such as transistors or valves, in which electrons are conducted through a semiconductor, free space, or gas. **2.** of or concerned with electronics. **3.** of or concerned with electrons or an electron: *an electronic energy level in a molecule.* **4.** making use of electronic systems, such as computerized banking transactions: *electronic shopping.* —**elecˈtronically** *adv.*

▷**Usage.** *Electronic* is used to refer to equipment, such as television sets, computers, etc., in which the current is controlled by transistors, valves, and similar components and also to the components themselves. *Electrical* is used in a more general sense, often to refer to the use of electricity as a whole as opposed to other forms of energy: *electrical engineering; an electrical appliance. Electric,* in many cases used interchangeably with *electrical,* is often restricted to the description of particular devices or to concepts relating to the flow of current: *electric fire; electric charge.*

electronic configuration *n. Chem.* the arrangement of electrons in the orbitals of an atom or molecule.

electronic countermeasures *n. Military.* (in electronic warfare) actions intended to interfere with an enemy's use of electromagnetic radiation equipment.

electronic data processing *n.* data processing largely performed by electronic equipment, such as computers. Abbrevs.: **EDP, edp.** Compare **automatic data processing.**

electronic editing *n. Radio, television.* editing of a sound or vision tape recording by electronic rerecording rather than by physical cutting.

electronic file cabinet *n. Computer technol.* a device, controlled by software, for the storage and retrieval of information.

electronic flash *n. Photog.* an electronic device for producing a very bright flash of light by means of an electric discharge in a gas-filled tube.

electronic flight information systems *pl. n.* (in an aircraft) the computer-operated visual displays on the flight deck, showing information about the aircraft's state and performance in flight.

electronic funds transfer at point of sale *n.* a system for debiting a retail sale direct to the customer's bank, building-society, or credit-card account by means of a computer link using the telephone network. The customer inserts his debit card or credit card, with a personal identification number, into the computer at the point of sale. Acronym: **EFTPOS.**

electronic game *n.* any of various small hand-held computerized games, usually battery operated, having a small screen on which graphics are displayed and buttons to operate the game.

electronic graphics *pl. n.* (on television) the production of graphic designs and text by electronic means.

electronic ignition *n.* any system that uses an electronic circuit to supply the voltage to the sparking plugs of an internal-combustion engine.

electronic keyboard *n.* a typewriter keyboard used to operate an electronic device such as a computer, word processor, etc.

electronic mail *n.* the transmission and distribution of information, facsimiles of documents, etc., from one computer terminal to another. Abbrev.: **E-mail.**

electronic mailbox *n.* a device used to store electronic mail.

electronic music *n.* a form of music consisting of sounds produced by oscillating electric currents either controlled from an instrument panel or keyboard or prerecorded on magnetic tape.

electronic office *n.* integrated computer systems designed to handle office work.

electronic organ *n. Music.* an electrophonic instrument played by means of a keyboard, in which sounds are produced and amplified by any of various electronic or electrical means. See also **synthesizer.**

electronic point of sale *n.* a computerized system for recording sales in retail shops, using a laser scanner at the cash till to read bar codes on the packages of the items sold. The retailer's stock record is automatically adjusted and the customer receives an itemized bill. Acronym: **EPOS.**

electronic publishing *n.* the publication of information on magnetic tape, disks, etc., so that it can be accessed by a computer.

electronics (ɪlɛkˈtrɒnɪks, ˌiːlɛk-) *n.* **1.** (*functioning as sing.*) the science and technology concerned with the development, behaviour, and applications of electronic devices and circuits. **2.** (*functioning as pl.*) the circuits and devices of a piece of electronic equipment: *the electronics of a television set.*

electronic surveillance *n.* **1.** the use of such electronic devices as television monitors, video cameras, etc., to prevent burglary, shop lifting, break-ins, etc. **2.** monitoring events, conversations, etc., at a distance by electronic means, esp. by such covert means as wire tapping or bugging.

electronic tag *n.* another name for **tag**[1] (sense 2).

electronic transfer of funds *n.* the transfer of money from one bank or building-society account to another by means of a computer link using the telephone network. Abbrev.: **ETF.**

electronic warfare *n.* the military use of electronics to prevent or reduce an enemy's effective use and to protect friendly use of electromagnetic radiation equipment.

electron lens *n.* a system, such as an arrangement of electrodes or magnets, that produces a field for focusing a beam of electrons.

electron micrograph *n.* a photograph of a specimen taken through an electron microscope.

electron microscope *n.* a powerful type of microscope that uses electrons, rather than light, and electron lenses to produce a magnified image.

electron multiplier *n. Physics.* a device for amplifying and measuring a flux of electrons. Each electron hits an anode surface and releases secondary electrons that are accelerated to a second surface; after several such stages a measurable pulse of current is obtained.

electron optics *n.* (*functioning as sing.*) the study and use of beams of electrons and of their deflection and focusing by electric and magnetic fields.

electron paramagnetic resonance *n. Physics.* another name for **electron spin resonance.** Abbrev.: **EPR.**

electron probe microanalysis *n.* a technique for the analysis of a very small amount of material by bombarding it with a narrow beam of electrons and examining the resulting x-ray emission spectrum.

electron spin resonance *n.* a technique for investigating paramagnetic substances by subjecting them to high-frequency radiation in a strong magnetic field. Changes in the spin of unpaired electrons cause radiation to be absorbed at certain frequencies. Abbrev.: **ESR.** See also **nuclear magnetic resonance.**

electron telescope *n.* an astronomical telescope with an attachment for converting the infrared radiation emitted from the surface of planets into a visible image.

electron transport *n. Biochem.* the metabolic process in mitochondria or chloroplasts, in which electrons are transferred in stages from energy-rich compounds to molecular oxygen with liberation of energy.

electron tube *n.* an electrical device, such as a valve, in which a flow of electrons between electrodes takes place. Sometimes shortened to **tube.**

electronvolt (ɪˌlɛktrɒnˈvəʊlt) *n.* a unit of energy equal to the work done on an electron accelerated through a potential difference of 1 volt. 1 electronvolt is equivalent to 1.602×10^{-19} joule. Symbol: eV

electro-osmosis *n.* movement of liquid through a capillary tube or membrane under the influence of an electric field: used in controlling rising damp. Also called: **electroendosmosis.**

electropalatography (ɪˌlɛktrəʊˌpæləˈtɒgrəfɪ) *n.* the study of the movements of the tongue during speech using touch-sensitive electrodes in the mouth linked to a computer.

electrophilic (ɪˌlɛktrəʊˈfɪlɪk) *adj. Chem.* having or involving an affinity for negative charge. Electrophilic reagents (**electrophiles**) are atoms, molecules, and ions that behave as electron acceptors. Compare **nucleophilic.** —**electrophile** (ɪˈlɛktrəʊˌfaɪl) *n.*

electrophone (ɪˈlɛktrəˌfəʊn) *n. Music.* any instrument whose sound is produced by the oscillation of an electric current, such as an electronic organ, synthesizer, etc. —**electrophonic** (ɪˌlɛktrəˈfɒnɪk) *adj.*

electrophoresis (ɪˌlɛktrəʊfəˈriːsɪs) *n.* the motion of charged particles in a colloid under the influence of an applied electric field. Also called: **cataphoresis.** —**electrophoretic** (ɪˌlɛktrəʊfəˈrɛtɪk) *adj.*

electrophorus (ɪlɛkˈtrɒfərəs, ˌiːlɛk-) *n.* an apparatus for generating static electricity. It consists of an insulating plate charged by friction and used to charge a metal plate by induction. [C18: from ELECTRO- + *-phorus,* from Greek *-phoros* bearing, from *pherein* to bear]

electrophysiology (ɪˌlɛktrəʊˌfɪzɪˈɒlədʒɪ) *n.* the branch of medical science concerned with the electrical activity associated with bodily processes. —**eˌlectroˌphysioˈlogical** *adj.* —**eˌlectroˌphysiˈologist** *n.*

electroplate (ɪˈlɛktrəʊˌpleɪt) *vb.* **1.** (*tr.*) to plate (an object) by electrolysis. ~*n.* **2.** electroplated articles collectively, esp. when plated with silver. ~*adj.* **3.** coated with metal by electrolysis; electroplated. —**eˈlectroˌplater** *n.*

electropositive (ɪˌlɛktrəʊˈpɒzɪtɪv) *adj.* **1.** having a positive electric charge. **2.** (of an atom, group, molecule, etc.) tending to release electrons and form positive ions or polarized bonds. Compare **electronegative.**

electroreceptor (ɪˈlɛktrəʊrɪˌsɛptə) *n. Zoology.* an organ, present in some fishes, that detects electrical discharges.

electrorheology (ɪˌlɛktrəʊrɪˈɒlədʒɪ) *n.* **1.** the study of the flow of fluids under the influence of electric fields. **2.** the way in which fluid flow is influenced by an electric field. —**eˌlectrorheoˈlogical** *adj.*

electroscope (ɪˈlɛktrəʊˌskəʊp) *n.* an apparatus for detecting an electric charge, typically consisting of a rod holding two gold foils that separate when a charge is applied. —**electroscopic** (ɪˌlɛktrəʊˈskɒpɪk) *adj.*

electroshock therapy (ɪˈlɛktrəʊˌʃɒk) *n.* another name for **electroconvulsive therapy.**

electrostatic (ɪˌlɛktrəʊˈstætɪk) *adj.* **1.** of, concerned with, producing, or caused by static electricity. **2.** concerned with electrostatics. —**eˌlectroˈstatically** *adv.*

electrostatic field *n.* an electric field associated with a static electric field.

electrostatic generator *n.* any device for producing a high voltage by building up a charge of static electricity.

electrostatic lens *n.* an electron lens consisting of a system of metal electrodes, the electrostatic field of which focuses the charged particles.

electrostatic precipitation *n. Chem.* the removal of suspended solid particles from a gas by giving them an electric charge and attracting them to charged plates.

electrostatics (ɪˌlɛktrəʊˈstætɪks) *n.* (*functioning as sing.*) the branch of physics concerned with static electricity.

electrostatic unit *n.* any unit that belongs to a system of electrical cgs units in which the electric constant is given the value of unity and is taken as a pure number. Abbrevs.: **ESU, e.s.u.** Compare **electromagnetic unit.**

electrostriction (ɪˌlɛktrəʊˈstrɪkʃən) *n.* the change in dimensions of a dielectric occurring as an elastic strain when an electric field is applied.

electrosurgery (ɪˌlɛktrəʊˈsɜːdʒərɪ) *n.* the surgical use of electricity, as in cauterization. —**eˌlectroˈsurgical** *adj.*

electrotechnics (ɪˌlɛktrəʊˈtɛknɪks) *n.* (*functioning as sing.*) another name for **electrotechnology.** —**eˌlectroˈtechnical** *adj.* —**eˌlectrotechˈnician** *n.*

electrotechnology (ɪˌlɛktrəʊtɛkˈnɒlədʒɪ) *n.* the technological use of electric power.

electrotherapeutics (ɪˌlɛktrəʊˌθɛrəˈpjuːtɪks) *n.* (*functioning as sing.*) the branch of medical science concerned with the use of electrotherapy. —**eˌlectroˌtheraˈpeutic** *or* **eˌlectroˌtheraˈpeutical** *adj.*

electrotherapy (ɪˌlɛktrəʊˈθɛrəpɪ) *n.* treatment in which electric currents are passed through the tissues to stimulate muscle function in paralysed patients. —**eˌlectroˈtherapist** *n.*

electrothermal (ɪˌlɛktrəʊˈθɜːməl) *or* **electrothermic** (ɪˌlɛktrəʊˈθɜːmɪk) *adj.* concerned with both electricity and heat, esp. the production of electricity by heat.

electrothermal printer (ɪˌlɛktrəʊˈθɜːməl) *n. Computer technol.* a printer that produces characters by burning the image on specially coated paper. Also called: **thermal printer.**

electrotint (ɪˈlɛktrəʊˌtɪnt) *n.* a printing block made by drawing on a metal plate with varnish and electrolytically depositing a layer of metal on the nonvarnished areas of the plate.

electrotonus (ɪlɛkˈtrɒtənəs, ˌiːlɛk-) *n. Physiol.* the change in the state of irritability and conductivity of a nerve or muscle caused by the passage of an electric current. [C19: from New Latin, from ELECTRO- + Latin *tonus* TONE] —**electrotonic** (ɪˌlɛktrəʊˈtɒnɪk) *adj.*

electrotype (ɪˈlɛktrəʊˌtaɪp) *n.* **1.** a duplicate printing plate made by electrolytically depositing a layer of copper or nickel onto a mould of the original. Sometimes shortened to **electro.** ~*vb.* **2.** (*tr.*) to make an electrotype of (printed matter, illustrations, etc.). —**eˈlectroˌtyper** *n.*

electrovalency (ɪˌlɛktrəʊˈveɪlənsɪ) *or* **electrovalence** *n. Chem.* the valency of a substance in forming ions, equal to the number of electrons gained or lost. —**eˌlectroˈvalent** *adj.* —**eˌlectroˈvalently** *adv.*

electrovalent bond *n.* a type of chemical bond in which one atom loses an electron to form a positive ion and the other atom gains the electron to form a negative ion. The resulting ions are held together by electrostatic attraction. Also called: **ionic bond.** Compare **covalent bond.**

electroweak interaction (ɪˌlɛktrəʊˈwiːk) *n. Physics.* a type of fundamental interaction combining both the electromagnetic interaction and the weak interaction. See also **electromagnetic interaction, weak interaction.**

electrum (ɪˈlɛktrəm) *n.* an alloy of gold (55–88 per cent) and silver used for jewellery and ornaments. [C14: from Latin, from Greek *ēlektron* amber]

electuary (ɪˈlɛktjʊərɪ) *n., pl.* **-aries.** *Med.* a paste taken orally, containing a drug mixed with syrup or honey. [C14: from Late Latin *ēlēctuārium,* probably from Greek *ekleikton* electuary, from *ekleikhein* to lick out, from *leikhein* to lick]

eleemosynary (ˌɛlɪiːˈmɒsɪnərɪ) *adj.* **1.** of, concerned with, or dependent on charity. **2.** given as an act of charity. [C17: from Church Latin *eleēmosyna* ALMS]

elegance (ˈɛlɪgəns) *or* **elegancy** *n., pl.* **-gances** *or* **-gancies. 1.** dignified grace in appearance, movement, or behaviour. **2.** good taste in design, style, arrangement, etc. **3.** something elegant; a refinement.

elegant (ˈɛlɪgənt) *adj.* **1.** tasteful in dress, style, or design. **2.** dignified and graceful in appearance, behaviour, etc. **3.** cleverly simple; ingenious: *an elegant solution to a problem.* [C16: from Latin *ēlegāns* tasteful, related to *ēligere* to select; see ELECT] —**ˈelegantly** *adv.*

elegiac (ˌɛlɪˈdʒaɪək) *adj.* **1.** resembling, characteristic of, relating to, or appropriate to an elegy. **2.** lamenting; mournful; plaintive. **3.** denoting or written in elegiac couplets or elegiac stanzas. ~*n.* 4. (*often pl.*) an elegiac couplet or stanza. —ˌel-e'**giacally** *adv.*

elegiac couplet *n. Classical prosody.* a couplet composed of a dactylic hexameter followed by a dactylic pentameter.

elegiac stanza *n. Prosody.* a quatrain in iambic pentameters with alternate lines rhyming.

elegize *or* **elegise** ('ɛlɪˌdʒaɪz) *vb.* 1. to compose an elegy or elegies (in memory of). 2. (*intr.*) to write elegiacally. —'**el-egist** *n.*

elegy ('ɛlɪdʒɪ) *n., pl.* **-gies.** 1. a mournful or plaintive poem or song, esp. a lament for the dead. 2. poetry or a poem written in elegiac couplets or stanzas. [C16: via French and Latin from Greek *elegeia,* from *elegos* lament sung to flute accompaniment]

elem. *abbrev. for:* 1. element(s). 2. elementary.

element ('ɛlɪmənt) *n.* 1. any of the 105 known substances (of which 93 occur naturally) that consist of atoms with the same number of protons in their nuclei. Compare **compound**[1] (sense 1). 2. one of the fundamental or irreducible components making up a whole. 3. a cause that contributes to a result; factor. 4. any group that is part of a larger unit, such as a military formation. 5. a small amount; hint: *an element of sarcasm in her voice.* 6. a distinguishable section of a social group: *he belonged to the stable element in the expedition.* 7. the most favourable environment for an animal or plant. 8. the situation in which a person is happiest or most effective (esp. in the phrases **in** or **out of one's element**). 9. the resistance wire and its former that constitute the electrical heater in a cooker, heater, etc. 10. *Electronics.* another name for **component** (sense 2). 11. one of the four substances thought in ancient and medieval cosmology to constitute the universe (earth, air, water, or fire). 12. (*pl.*) atmospheric conditions or forces, esp. wind, rain, and cold: *exposed to the elements.* 13. (*pl.*) the first principles of a subject. 14. *Geometry.* a point, line, plane, or part of a geometric figure. 15. *Maths.* **a.** any of the terms in the array of a determinant or matrix. **b.** one of the infinitesimally small quantities summed by an integral, often represented by the expression following the integral sign: *in* $\int_a^b f(x)dx$, $f(x)dx$ *is an element of area.* 16. *Maths, logic.* one of the objects or numbers that together constitute a set. 17. *Christianity.* the bread or wine consecrated in the Eucharist. 18. *Astronomy.* any of the numerical quantities, such as the major axis or eccentricity, used in describing the orbit of a planet, satellite, etc. 19. one of the vertical or horizontal rods forming a television or VHF radio receiving aerial. 20. *Physics.* a component of a compound lens. [C13: from Latin *elementum* a first principle, alphabet, element, of uncertain origin]

elemental (ˌɛlɪ'mɛntᵊl) *adj.* 1. fundamental; basic; primal: *the elemental needs of man.* 2. motivated by or symbolic of primitive and powerful natural forces or passions: *elemental rites of worship.* 3. of or relating to earth, air, water, and fire considered as elements. 4. of or relating to atmospheric forces, esp. wind, rain, and cold. 5. of, relating to, or denoting a chemical element. ~*n.* 6. *Rare.* a spirit or force that is said to appear in physical form. —ˌele'**mentally** *adv.* —ˌele'**mentalˌism** *n.*

elementary (ˌɛlɪ'mɛntərɪ, -trɪ) *adj.* 1. not difficult; simple; rudimentary. 2. of or concerned with the first principles of a subject; introductory or fundamental. 3. *Maths.* (of a function) having the form of an algebraic, exponential, trigonometric, or a logarithmic function, or any combination of these. 4. *Chem.* another word for **elemental** (sense 5). —ˌele'**mentarily** *adv.* —ˌele'**mentariness** *n.*

elementary particle *n.* any of several entities, such as electrons, neutrons, or protons, that are less complex than atoms and are regarded as the constituents of all matter. Also called: **fundamental particle.**

elementary school *n.* 1. *Brit.* a former name for **primary school.** 2. Also called (in the U.S.): **grade school, grammar school.** *U.S. and Canadian.* a state school in which instruction is given for the first six to eight years of a child's education.

elemi ('ɛlɪmɪ) *n., pl.* **-mis.** any of various fragrant resins obtained from tropical trees, esp. trees of the family *Burseraceae:* used in making varnishes, ointments, inks, etc. [C16: via Spanish from Arabic *al-lāmi* the elemi]

elenchus (ɪ'lɛŋkəs) *n., pl.* **-chi** (-kaɪ). *Logic.* 1. refutation of an argument by proving the contrary of its conclusion, esp. syllogistically. 2. **Socratic elenchus.** the drawing out of the consequences of a position in order to show them to be contrary to some accepted position. [C17: from Latin, from Greek *elenkhos* refutation, from *elenkhein* to put to shame, refute]

elenctic (ɪ'lɛŋktɪk) *adj. Logic.* refuting an argument by proving the falsehood of its conclusion. Compare **deictic** (sense 1).

eleoptene *or* **elaeoptene** (ˌɛlɪ'ɒptiːn) *n.* the liquid part of a volatile oil. [C20: from Greek *elaion* oil + *ptēnos* having wings, volatile; related to Greek *petesthai* to fly]

elephant ('ɛlɪfənt) *n., pl.* **-phants** *or* **-phant.** 1. either of the two proboscidean mammals of the family *Elephantidae.* The **African elephant** (*Loxodonta africana*) is the larger species, with large flapping ears and a less humped back than the **Indian elephant** (*Elephas maximus*), of S and SE Asia. 2. *Chiefly Brit.* a size of writing paper, 23 by 28 inches. [C13: from Latin *elephantus,* from Greek *elephas* elephant, ivory, of uncertain origin] —'**elephanˌtoid** *adj.*

elephant bird *n.* another name for **aepyornis.**

elephant grass *n.* any of various stout tropical grasses or grasslike plants, esp. *Pennisetum purpureum,* and *Typha elephantina,* a type of reed mace.

elephantiasis (ˌɛlɪfən'taɪəsɪs) *n. Pathol.* a complication of chronic filariasis, in which nematode worms block the lymphatic vessels, usually in the legs or scrotum, causing extreme enlargement of the affected area. See also **filariasis.** [C16: via Latin from Greek, from *elephas* ELEPHANT + -IASIS] —**elephantiasic** (ˌɛlɪˌfæntɪ'æsɪk, -fən'taɪəsɪk) *adj.*

elephantine (ˌɛlɪ'fæntaɪn) *adj.* 1. denoting, relating to, or characteristic of an elephant or elephants. 2. huge, clumsy, or ponderous.

elephant seal *n.* either of two large earless seals, *Mirounga leonina* of southern oceans or *M. angustirostris* of the N Atlantic, the males of which have a long trunklike snout.

elephant's-ear *n.* 1. any aroid plant of the genus *Colocasia,* of tropical Asia and Polynesia, having very large heart-shaped leaves: grown for ornament and for their edible tubers. See also **taro.** 2. any of various cultivated begonias with large showy leaves.

elephant's-foot *or* **elephant foot** *n.* a monocotyledonous plant, *Testudinaria elephantipes,* of southern Africa, with a very large starchy tuberous stem, covered in corky scales: family *Dioscoreaceae.*

elephant shrew *n.* any small active African mammal of the family *Macroscelididae,* having an elongated nose, large ears, and long hind legs: order *Insectivora* (insectivores).

Eleusinian mysteries (ˌɛlju'sɪnɪən) *pl. n.* a mystical religious festival of classical times, held in September at Eleusis, west of Athens, in which initiates celebrated Persephone, Demeter, and Dionysus.

elev. *or* **el.** *abbrev. for* elevation.

elevate ('ɛlɪˌveɪt) *vb.* (*tr.*) 1. to move to a higher place. 2. to raise in rank or status; promote. 3. to put in a cheerful mood; elate. 4. to put on a higher cultural plane; uplift: *to elevate the tone of a conversation.* 5. to raise the axis of a gun. 6. to raise the intensity or pitch of (the voice). 7. *R.C. Church.* to lift up (the Host) at Mass for adoration. [C15: from Latin *ēlevāre* from *levāre* to raise, from *levis* (adj.) light] —ˌele'**vatory** *adj.*

elevated ('ɛlɪˌveɪtɪd) *adj.* 1. raised to or being at a higher level. 2. inflated or lofty; exalted: *an elevated opinion of oneself.* 3. in a cheerful mood; elated. 4. *Informal.* slightly drunk. ~*n.* 5. *U.S.* short for **elevated railway** *or* **railroad.**

elevated railway *or* **railroad** *n. U.S.* an urban railway track built on supports above a road.

elevation (ˌɛlɪ'veɪʃən) *n.* 1. the act of elevating or the state of being elevated. 2. the height of something above a given or implied place, esp. above sea level. 3. a raised area; height. 4. nobleness or grandeur; loftiness: *elevation of thought.* 5. a drawing to scale of the external face of a building or structure. Compare **plan** (sense 3), **ground plan** (sense 1). 6. the external face of a building or structure. 7. a ballet dancer's ability to leap high. 8. *R.C. Church.* the lifting up of the Host at Mass for adoration. 9. *Astronomy.* another name for **altitude** (sense 3). 10. the angle formed between the muzzle of a gun and the horizontal. 11. *Surveying.* the angular distance between the plane through a point of observation and an object above it. Compare **depression** (sense 7). 12. *Linguistics.* another term for **amelioration.** —ˌele'**vational** *adj.*

elevator ('ɛlɪˌveɪtə) *n.* 1. a person or thing that elevates. 2. a mechanical hoist for raising something, esp. grain or coal, often consisting of a chain of scoops linked together on a conveyor belt. 3. the U.S. and Canadian name for **lift**[1] (sense 17a). 4. *Chiefly U.S. and Canadian.* a large granary equipped with an elevator and, usually, facilities for cleaning and grading the grain. 5. any muscle that raises a part of the body. 6. a surgical instrument for lifting a part of the body. 7. a control surface on the tailplane of an aircraft, for making it climb or descend.

eleven (ɪ'lɛvᵊn) *n.* 1. the cardinal number that is the sum of ten and one. 2. a numeral 11, XI, etc., representing this number. 3. something representing, represented by, or consisting of 11 units. 4. (*functioning as sing. or pl.*) a team of 11 players in football, cricket, hockey, etc. 5. Also called: **eleven o'clock.** eleven hours after noon or midnight. ~*determiner.* 6. **a.** amounting to eleven: *eleven chances.* **b.** (*as pronoun*): *have another eleven today.* [Old English *endleofan;* related to Old Norse *ellefo,* Gothic *ainlif,* Old Frisian *andlova,* Old High German *einlif*]

eleven-plus *n.* (esp. formerly) an examination, taken by children aged 11 or 12, that determines the type of secondary education a child will be given.

elevenses (ɪ'lɛvᵊnzɪz) *pl. n.* (*sometimes functioning as sing.*) *Brit. informal.* a light snack, usually with tea or coffee, taken in mid-morning.

eleventh (ɪ'lɛvᵊnθ) *adj.* 1. (*usually prenominal*) **a.** coming after the tenth in numbering or counting order, position, time, etc.; being the ordinal number of *eleven:* often written 11th. **b.** (*as pronoun*): *the eleventh in succession.* ~*n.* 2. **a.** one of 11 equal or nearly equal parts of an object, quantity, measurement, etc. **b.** (*as modifier*): *an eleventh part.* 3. the fraction equal to one divided by 11 (1/11). 4. *Music.* **a.** an interval of one octave plus one fourth. **b.** See **eleventh chord.**

eleventh chord *n.* a chord much used in jazz, consisting of a major or minor triad upon which are superimposed the seventh, ninth, and eleventh above the root.

eleventh hour *n.* **a.** the latest possible time; last minute. **b.** (*as modifier*): *an eleventh-hour decision.*

elevon ('ɛlɪˌvɒn) *n.* an aircraft control surface that combines the functions of an elevator and aileron, usually fitted to tailless or delta-wing aircraft. [C20: from ELEV(ATOR + AILER)ON]

elf (ɛlf) *n., pl.* **elves** (ɛlvz). **1.** (in folklore) one of a kind of legendary beings, usually characterized as small, manlike, and mischievous. **2.** a mischievous or whimsical child. [Old English *ælf;* related to Old Norse *elfr* elf, Middle Low German *alf* incubus, Latin *albus* white] —'**elf,like** *adj.*

ELF *abbrev. for* extremely low frequency.

elf-cup *n.* any of various cup-shaped ascomycetous fungi of the order *Pezizales,* often strikingly coloured, such as the **orange-peel elf-cup** (*Aleuria aurantia*), that is bright orange inside and dirty white outside, and the **scarlet elf-cup** (*sarcoscypha coccinea*).

elfin ('ɛlfɪn) *adj.* **1.** of, relating to, or like an elf or elves. **2.** small, delicate, and charming.

elfish ('ɛlfɪʃ) *or* **elvish** *adj.* **1.** of, relating to, or like an elf or elves; charmingly mischievous or sprightly; impish. ~*n.* **2.** the supposed language of elves. —'**elfishly** *or* '**elvishly** *adv.* —'**elfishness** *or* '**elvishness** *n.*

elfland ('ɛlfˌlænd) *n.* another name for **fairyland.**

elflock ('ɛlfˌlɒk) *n.* a lock of hair, fancifully regarded as having been tangled by the elves.

Elgin marbles ('ɛlgɪn) *pl. n.* a group of 5th-century B.C. Greek sculptures originally decorating the Parthenon in Athens, brought to England by Thomas Bruce, seventh Earl of Elgin (1766–1841), and now at the British Museum.

elicit (ɪ'lɪsɪt) *vb.* (*tr.*) **1.** to give rise to; evoke: *to elicit a sharp retort.* **2.** to bring to light: *to elicit the truth.* [C17: from Latin *ēlicere* to lure forth, from *licere* to entice] —**e'licitable** *adj.* —**eˌlici'tation** *n.* —**e'licitor** *n.*

elide (ɪ'laɪd) *vb. Phonetics.* to undergo or cause to undergo elision. [C16: from Latin *ēlīdere* to knock, from *laedere* to hit, wound] —**e'lidible** *adj.*

eligible ('ɛlɪdʒəbᵊl) *adj.* **1.** fit, worthy, or qualified, as for an office or function. **2.** desirable and worthy of being chosen, esp. as a spouse: *an eligible young man.* [C15: from Late Latin *ēligibilis* able to be chosen, from *ēligere* to ELECT] —ˌ**eligi'bility** *n.* —'**eligibly** *adv.*

eliminate (ɪ'lɪmɪˌneɪt) *vb.* (*tr.*) **1.** to remove or take out; get rid of. **2.** to reject as trivial or irrelevant; omit from consideration. **3.** to remove (a competitor, team, etc.) from a contest, usually by defeat. **4.** *Slang.* to murder in a cold-blooded manner. **5.** *Physiol.* to expel (waste matter) from the body. **6.** *Maths.* to remove (an unknown variable) from two or more simultaneous equations. [C16: from Latin *ēlīmināre* to turn out of the house, from *e-* out + *līmen* threshold] —**e'liminable** *adj.* —**eˌlimina'bility** *n.* —**e'liminant** *n.* —**e'liminative** *or* **e'liminatory** *adj.* —**e'limiˌnator** *n.*

elimination (ɪˌlɪmɪ'neɪʃən) *n.* **1.** the act of eliminating or the state of being eliminated. **2.** *Logic.* (qualified by the name of an operation) a syntactic rule specifying the conditions under which a formula or statement containing the specified operation may permit the derivation of others that do not contain it: *conjunction-elimination; universal elimination.* **3.** *Chem.* a type of chemical reaction involving the loss of a simple molecule, such as water or carbon dioxide.

ELISA (ɪ'laɪzə) *n. acronym for* enzyme-linked immunosorbent assay: an immunological technique for accurately measuring the amount of a substance, for example in a blood sample.

elision (ɪ'lɪʒən) *n.* **1.** the omission of a syllable or vowel at the beginning or end of a word, esp. when a word ending with a vowel is next to one beginning with a vowel. **2.** any omission of a part or parts. [C16: from Latin *ēlīsiō,* from *ēlīdere* to ELIDE]

elite *or* **élite** (ɪ'liːt, eɪ-) *n.* **1.** (*sometimes functioning as pl.*) the most powerful, rich, gifted, or educated members of a group, community, etc. **2.** Also called: **twelve pitch.** a typewriter typesize having 12 characters to the inch. ~*adj.* **3.** of, relating to, or suitable for an elite; exclusive. [C18: from French, from Old French *eslit* chosen, from *eslire* to choose, from Latin *ēligere* to ELECT]

elitism (ɪ'liːtɪzəm, eɪ-) *n.* **1. a.** the belief that society should be governed by a select group of gifted and highly educated individuals. **b.** such government. **2.** pride in or awareness of being one of an elite group. —**e'litist** *adj., n.*

elixir (ɪ'lɪksə) *n.* **1.** an alchemical preparation supposed to be capable of prolonging life indefinitely (**elixir of life**) or of transmuting base metals into gold. **2.** anything that purports to be a sovereign remedy; panacea. **3.** an underlying principle; quintessence. **4.** a liquid containing a medicinal drug with syrup, glycerin, or alcohol added to mask its unpleasant taste. [C14: from Medieval Latin, from Arabic *al iksīr* the elixir, probably from Greek *xērion* powder used for drying wounds, from *xēros* dry]

Eliz. *abbrev. for* Elizabethan.

Elizabethan (ɪˌlɪzə'biːθən) *adj.* **1.** of, characteristic of, or relating to England or its culture in the age of Elizabeth I (reigned 1558–1603) or to the United Kingdom or its culture in the age of Elizabeth II (reigned since 1952). **2.** of, relating to, or designating a style of architecture used in England during the reign of Elizabeth I, characterized by moulded and sculptured ornament based on German and Flemish models. ~*n.* **3.** a person who lived in England during the reign of Elizabeth I.

Elizabethan sonnet *n.* another term for **Shakespearean sonnet.**

elk (ɛlk) *n., pl.* **elks** *or* **elk.** **1.** a large deer, *Alces alces,* of N Europe and Asia, having large flattened palmate antlers: also occurs in North America, where it is called a moose. **2. American elk.** another name for **wapiti. 3.** a stout pliable waterproof leather made from calfskin or horsehide. [Old English *eolh;* related to Old Norse *elgr,* Old High German *elaho,* Latin *alcēs,* Greek *alkē, elaphos* deer]

elkhound ('ɛlkˌhaʊnd) *n.* a powerful breed of dog of the spitz type with a thick grey coat and tightly curled tail. Also called: **Norwegian elkhound.**

ell[1] (ɛl) *n.* an obsolete unit of length equal to approximately 45 inches. [Old English *eln* the forearm (the measure originally being from the elbow to the fingertips); related to Old High German *elina,* Latin *ulna,* Greek *ōlenē*]

ell[2] (ɛl) *n.* **1.** an extension to a building, usually at right angles and located at one end. **2.** a pipe fitting, pipe, or tube with a sharp right-angle bend. [C20: a spelling of *L,* indicating a right angle]

ellipse (ɪ'lɪps) *n.* a closed conic section shaped like a flattened circle and formed by an inclined plane that does not cut the base of the cone. Standard equation: $x^2/a^2 + y^2/b^2 = 1$, where $2a$ and $2b$ are the lengths of the major and minor axes. Area: πab. [C18: back formation from ELLIPSIS]

ellipsis (ɪ'lɪpsɪs) *n., pl.* **-ses** (-siːz). **1.** Also called: **eclipsis.** omission of parts of a word or sentence. **2.** *Printing.* a sequence of three dots (...) indicating an omission in text. [C16: from Latin, from Greek *elleipsis* omission, from *elleipein* to leave out, from *leipein* to leave]

ellipsoid (ɪ'lɪpsɔɪd) *n.* **a.** a geometric surface, symmetrical about the three coordinate axes, whose plane sections are ellipses or circles. Standard equation: $x^2/a^2 + y^2/b^2 + z^2/c^2 = 1$, where $\pm a$, $\pm b$, $\pm c$ are the intercepts on the x-, y-, and z-axes. **b.** a solid having this shape: *the earth is an ellipsoid.* —**ellipsoidal** (ɪlɪp'sɔɪdᵊl, ˌɛl-) *adj.*

ellipsoid of revolution *n.* a geometric surface produced by rotating an ellipse about one of its two axes and having circular plane surfaces perpendicular to the axis of revolution. Also called: **spheroid.**

elliptical (ɪ'lɪptɪkᵊl) *adj.* **1.** relating to or having the shape of an ellipse. **2.** relating to or resulting from ellipsis. **3.** (of speech, literary style, etc.) **a.** very condensed or concise, often so as to be obscure or ambiguous. **b.** circumlocutory or long-winded. ~Also (for senses 1 and 2): **elliptic.** —**el'liptically** *adv.* —**el'lipticalness** *n.*

▷**Usage.** The use of *elliptical* to mean *circumlocutory* is avoided by many careful speakers and writers.

elliptic geometry *n.* another name for **Riemannian geometry.**

ellipticity (ɪlɪp'tɪsɪtɪ, ˌɛl-) *n.* the degree of deviation from a circle or sphere of an elliptical or ellipsoidal shape or path, measured as the ratio of the major to the minor axes.

elm (ɛlm) *n.* **1.** any ulmaceous tree of the genus *Ulmus,* occurring in the N hemisphere, having serrated leaves and winged fruits (samaras): cultivated for shade, ornament, and timber. **2.** the hard heavy wood of this tree. ~See also **slippery elm, wahoo**[1], **wych-elm.** [Old English *elm;* related to Old Norse *almr,* Old High German *elm,* Latin *ulmus*]

El Niño (ɛl 'niːnjəʊ) *n. Meteorol.* a warming of the eastern tropical Pacific occurring every few years, which disrupts the weather pattern of the region. [from Spanish: The Child, i.e. Christ, referring to its original occurrence at Christmas time]

elocute ('ɛləˌkjuːt) *vb.* (*intr.*) *Facetious.* to speak as if practising elocution; declaim. [C19: back formation from ELOCUTION]

elocution (ˌɛlə'kjuːʃən) *n.* the art of public speaking, esp. of voice production, delivery, and gesture. [C15: from Latin *ēlocūtiō* a speaking out, from *ēloquī,* from *loquī* to speak] —ˌ**elo'cutionary** *adj.* —ˌ**elo'cutionist** *n.*

eloign *or* **eloin** (ɪ'lɔɪn) *vb.* (*tr.*) *Archaic.* to remove (oneself, one's property, etc.) to a distant place. [C16: from Anglo-French *esloigner* to go far away; related to Latin *longē* (adv.) far; compare ELONGATE] —**e'loigner** *or* **e'loiner** *n.* —**e'loignment** *or* **e'loinment** *n.*

elongate ('iːlɒŋgeɪt) *vb.* **1.** to make or become longer; stretch. ~*adj.* **2.** long and narrow; slender: *elongate leaves.* **3.** lengthened or tapered. [C16: from Late Latin *ēlongāre* to keep at a distance, from *ē-* away + Latin *longē* (adv.) far, but also later: to lengthen, as if from *ē-* + Latin *longus* (adj.) long]

elongation (ˌiːlɒŋ'geɪʃən) *n.* **1.** the act of elongating or state of being elongated; lengthening. **2.** something that is elongated. **3.** *Astronomy.* the difference between the celestial longitude of the sun and that of a planet or the moon.

elope (ɪ'ləʊp) *vb.* (*intr.*) to run away secretly with a lover, esp. in order to marry. [C16: from Anglo-French *aloper,* perhaps from Middle Dutch *lōpen* to run; see LOPE] —**e'lopement** *n.* —**e'loper** *n.*

eloquence ('ɛləkwəns) *n.* **1.** ease in using language to best effect. **2.** powerful and effective language. **3.** the quality of being persuasive or moving.

eloquent ('ɛləkwənt) *adj.* **1.** (of speech, writing, etc.) characterized by fluency and persuasiveness. **2.** visibly or vividly expressive, as of an emotion: *an eloquent yawn.* [C14: from Latin *ēloquēns,* from *ēloquī* to speak out, from *loquī* to speak] —'**eloquently** *adv.*

Elsan ('ɛlsæn) *n. Trademark.* a type of portable lavatory in which chemicals are used to kill bacteria and deodorize the sludge. [C20: from the initials of *E. L.* Jackson, the manufacturer + SAN(ITATION)]

else (ɛls) *determiner.* (*postpositive; used after an indefinite pronoun or an interrogative*) **1.** in addition; more: *there is nobody else here.* **2.** other; different: *where else could he be?* ~*adv.* **3. or else. a.** if not, then: *go away or else I won't finish my work today.* **b.** or something terrible will result: used as a threat: *sit down, or else!* [Old English *elles,* genitive of *el-* strange, foreign; related to Old High German *eli-* other, Gothic *alja,* Latin *alius,* Greek *allos*]

▷**Usage.** The possessive of the expressions *anybody else, everybody else, nobody else,* etc., is formed by adding *'s* to *else: this must be somebody else's letter. Who else* is an exception in that *whose else* is an acceptable alternative to *who else's: whose else can it be?* or *who else's can it be?* Careful writers and speakers avoid *whose else's* since it contains two possessives, one of which is redundant.

elsewhere (ˌɛls'wɛə) *adv.* in or to another place; somewhere else. [Old English *elles hwǣr;* see ELSE, WHERE]

ELT *abbrev. for* English Language Teaching: the teaching of English specifically to students whose native language is not English.

eluate ('ɛljuːˌeɪt) *n.* a solution of adsorbed material in the eluent obtained during the process of elution.

elucidate (ɪ'luːsɪˌdeɪt) *vb.* to make clear (something obscure or difficult); clarify. [C16: from Late Latin *ēlūcidāre* to enlighten; see LUCID] —**eˌluci'dation** *n.* —**e'luciˌdative** *or* **e'luciˌdatory** *adj.* —**e'luciˌdator** *n.*

elude (ɪ'luːd) *vb. (tr.)* **1.** to escape or avoid (capture, one's pursuers, etc.), esp. by cunning. **2.** to avoid fulfilment of (a responsibility, obligation, etc.); evade. **3.** to escape discovery, or understanding by; baffle: *the solution eluded her.* [C16: from Latin *ēlūdere* to deceive, from *lūdere* to play] —**e'luder** *n.* —**elusion** (ɪ'luːʒən) *n.*

eluent *or* **eluant** ('ɛljuːənt) *n.* a solvent used for eluting.

Elul (ɛ'luːl) *n.* (in the Jewish calendar) the sixth month of the year according to biblical reckoning and the twelfth month of the civil year, usually falling within August and September. [from Hebrew]

elusive (ɪ'luːsɪv) *adj.* **1.** difficult to catch: *an elusive thief.* **2.** preferring or living in solitude and anonymity. **3.** difficult to remember: *an elusive thought.* —**e'lusively** *adv.* —**e'lusiveness** *n.*

elusory (ɪ'luːsərɪ) *adj.* **1.** avoiding the issue; evasive: *elusory arguments.* **2.** difficult to grasp mentally; elusive: *elusory ideas.*

elute (iː'luːt, ɪ'luːt) *vb. (tr.)* to wash out (a substance) by the action of a solvent, as in chromatography. [C18: from Latin *ēlūtus* rinsed out, from *ēluere* to wash clean, from *luere* to wash, LAVE] —**e'lution** *n.*

elutriate (ɪ'luːtrɪˌeɪt) *vb. (tr.)* to purify or separate (a substance or mixture) by washing and straining or decanting. [C18: from Latin *ēlūtriāre* to wash out, from *ēluere,* from *ē-* out + *lavere* to wash] —**eˌlutri'ation** *n.* —**e'lutriˌator** *n.*

eluviation (ɪˌluːvɪ'eɪʃən) *n.* the process by which material suspended in water is removed from one layer of soil to another by the action of rainfall or chemical decomposition. [C20: from ELUVIUM]

eluvium (ɪ'luːvɪəm) *n., pl.* **-via** (-vɪə). a mass of sand, silt, etc.: a product of the erosion of rocks that has remained in its place of origin. [C19: New Latin, from Latin *ēluere* to wash out] —**e'luvial** *adj.*

elver ('ɛlvə) *n.* a young eel, esp. one migrating up a river from the sea. See also **leptocephalus.** [C17: variant of *eelfare* migration of young eels, literally: eel-journey; see EEL, FARE]

elves (ɛlvz) *n.* the plural of **elf.**

elvish ('ɛlvɪʃ) *adj.* a variant of **elfish.**

Elysian (ɪ'lɪzɪən) *adj.* **1.** of or relating to Elysium. **2.** *Literary.* delightful; glorious; blissful.

Elysium (ɪ'lɪzɪəm) *n.* a state or place of perfect bliss. [C16: from Latin, from Greek *Ēlusion pedion* Elysian (that is, blessed) fields]

elytron ('ɛlɪˌtrɒn) *or* **elytrum** ('ɛlɪtrəm) *n., pl.* **-tra** (-trə). either of the horny front wings of beetles and some other insects, which cover and protect the hind wings. [C18: from Greek *elutron* sheath, covering] —'**elyˌtroid** *or* '**elytrous** *adj.*

em (ɛm) *n. Printing.* **1.** Also called: **mutton, mut.** the square of a body of any size of type, used as a unit of measurement. **2.** Also called: **pica em, pica.** a unit of measurement used in printing, equal to one sixth of an inch. [C19: from the name of the letter *M*]

em- *prefix.* a variant of **en-**[1] and **en-**[2] before *b, m,* and *p.*

'em (əm) *pron.* an informal variant of **them.**

emaciate (ɪ'meɪsɪˌeɪt) *vb.* (*usually tr.*) to become or cause to become abnormally thin. [C17: from Latin *ēmaciāre* to make lean, from *macer* thin] —**e'maciˌated** *adj.* —**eˌmaci'ation** *n.*

E-mail ('iːmeɪl) *abbrev. for* electronic mail.

emanate ('ɛməˌneɪt) *vb.* **1.** (*intr.;* often foll. by *from*) to issue or proceed from or as from a source. **2.** (*tr.*) to send forth; emit. [C18: from Latin *ēmānāre* to flow out, from *mānāre* to flow] —**emanative** ('ɛmənətɪv) *adj.* —'**emaˌnator** *n.* —**emanatory** ('ɛməˌneɪtərɪ, -trɪ) *adj.*

emanation (ˌɛmə'neɪʃən) *n.* **1.** an act or instance of emanating. **2.** something that emanates or is produced; effusion. **3.** a gaseous product of radioactive decay, such as radon. —ˌ**ema'national** *adj.*

emancipate (ɪ'mænsɪˌpeɪt) *vb. (tr.)* **1.** to free from restriction or restraint, esp. social or legal restraint. **2.** (*often passive*) to free from the inhibitions imposed by conventional morality. **3.** to liberate (a slave) from bondage. [C17: from Latin *ēmancipāre* to give independence (to a son), from *mancipāre* to transfer property, from *manceps* a purchaser; see MANCIPLE] —**e'manciˌpated** *adj.* —**e'manciˌpative** *adj.* —**e'mancipist** *or* **e'manciˌpator** *n.* —**emancipatory** (ɪ'mænsɪpətərɪ, -trɪ) *adj.*

emancipation (ɪˌmænsɪ'peɪʃən) *n.* **1.** the act of freeing or state of being freed; liberation. **2.** *Informal.* freedom from inhibition and convention. —**eˌmanci'pationist** *n.*

emarginate (ɪ'mɑːdʒɪˌneɪt) *or* **emarginated** *adj.* having a notched tip or edge: *emarginate leaves.* [C17: from Latin *ēmargināre* to deprive of its edge, from *margō* MARGIN] —**e'margiˌnately** *adv.* —**eˌmargi'nation** *n.*

emasculate *vb.* (ɪ'mæskjʊˌleɪt). (*tr.*) **1.** to remove the testicles of; castrate; geld. **2.** to deprive of vigour, effectiveness, etc. **3.** *Botany.* to remove the stamens from (a flower) to prevent self-pollination for the purposes of plant breeding. ~*adj.* (ɪ'mæskjʊlɪt, -ˌleɪt). **4.** castrated; gelded. **5.** deprived of strength, effectiveness, etc. [C17: from Latin *ēmasculāre,* from *masculus* male; see MASCULINE] —**eˌmascu'lation** *n.* —**e'masculative** *or* **e'masculatory** *adj.* —**e'mascuˌlator** *n.*

embalm (ɪm'bɑːm) *vb. (tr.)* **1.** to treat (a dead body) with preservatives, as by injecting formaldehyde into the blood vessels, to retard putrefaction. **2.** to preserve or cherish the memory of. **3.** *Poetic.* to give a sweet fragrance to. [C13: from Old French *embaumer;* see BALM] —**em'balmer** *n.* —**em'balmment** *n.*

embank (ɪm'bæŋk) *vb. (tr.)* to protect, enclose, or confine (a waterway, road, etc.) with an embankment.

embankment (ɪm'bæŋkmənt) *n.* a man-made ridge of earth or stone that carries a road or railway or confines a waterway. See also **levee**[1].

embargo (ɛm'bɑːgəʊ) *n., pl.* **-goes. 1.** a government order prohibiting the departure or arrival of merchant ships in its ports. **2.** any legal stoppage of commerce: *an embargo on arms shipments.* **3.** a restraint, hindrance, or prohibition. ~*vb.* **-goes, -going, -goed.** (*tr.*) **4.** to lay an embargo upon. **5.** to seize for use by the state. [C16: from Spanish, from *embargar,* from Latin IM- + *barra* BAR[1]]

embark (ɛm'bɑːk) *vb.* **1.** to board (a ship or aircraft). **2.** (*intr.;* usually foll. by *on* or *upon*) to commence or engage (in) a new project, venture, etc. [C16: via French from Old Provençal *embarcar,* from EM- + *barca* boat, BARQUE] —ˌ**embar'kation** *n.* —**em'barkment** *n.*

embarras de richesses *French.* (ɑ̃bara də riʃɛs) *n.* a superfluous abundance of options, from which one finds it difficult to select. Also called: ***embarras de choix*** (də ʃwa). [C18: literally: embarrassment of riches]

embarrass (ɪm'bærəs) *vb.* (*mainly tr.*) **1.** (*also intr.*) to feel or cause to feel confusion or self-consciousness; disconcert; fluster. **2.** (*usually passive*) to involve in financial difficulties. **3.** *Archaic.* to make difficult; complicate. **4.** *Archaic.* to impede; obstruct; hamper. [C17 (in the sense: to impede): via French and Spanish from Italian *imbarrazzare,* from *imbarrare* to confine within bars; see EN-[1], BAR[1]] —**em'barrassed** *adj.* —**em'barrassedly** *adv.* —**em'barrassing** *adj.* —**em'barrassingly** *adv.*

embarrassment (ɪm'bærəsmənt) *n.* **1.** the state of being embarrassed. **2.** something that embarrasses. **3.** a financial predicament. **4.** an excessive amount; superfluity.

embassy ('ɛmbəsɪ) *n., pl.* **-sies. 1.** the residence or place of official business of an ambassador. **2.** an ambassador and his entourage collectively. **3.** the position, business, or mission of an ambassador. **4.** any important or official mission, duty, etc., esp. one undertaken by an agent. [C16: from Old French *ambassee,* from Old Italian *ambasciata,* from Old Provençal *ambaisada,* ultimately of Germanic origin; see AMBASSADOR]

embattle (ɪm'bætᵊl) *vb. (tr.)* **1.** to deploy (troops) for battle. **2.** to strengthen or fortify (a position, town, etc.). **3.** to provide (a building) with battlements. [C14: from Old French *embataillier;* see EN-[1], BATTLE]

embattled (ɪm'bætᵊld) *adj.* **1.** prepared for or engaged in conflict, controversy, or battle. **2.** *Heraldry.* having an indented edge resembling battlements.

embay (ɪm'beɪ) *vb. (tr.)* (*usually passive*) **1.** to form into a bay. **2.** to enclose in or as if in a bay. **3.** (esp. of the wind) to force (a ship, esp. a sailing ship) into a bay.

embayment (ɪm'beɪmənt) *n.* a shape resembling a bay.

Embden-Meyerhof pathway ('ɛmbdən'meɪəhɔːf) *n.* the metabolic reaction sequence in glycolysis by which glucose is converted to pyruvic acid with production of ATP. [C20: named after Gustav *Embden* (1874–1933) and Otto *Meyerhof* (1884–1951), German biochemists]

embed (ɪm'bɛd) *vb.* **-beds, -bedding, -bedded.** **1.** (usually foll. by *in*) to fix or become fixed firmly and deeply in a surrounding solid mass: *to embed a nail in wood.* **2.** (*tr.*) to surround closely: *hard rock embeds the roots.* **3.** (*tr.*) to fix or retain (a thought, idea, etc.) in the mind. **4.** (*tr.*) *Grammar.* to insert (a subordinate clause) into a sentence. ~Also: **imbed.** —**em'bedment** *n.*

embellish (ɪm'bɛlɪʃ) *vb.* (*tr.*) **1.** to improve or beautify by adding detail or ornament; adorn. **2.** to make (a story) more interesting by adding detail. **3.** to provide (a melody, part, etc.) with ornaments. See **ornament** (sense 5). [C14: from Old French *embelir,* from *bel* beautiful, from Latin *bellus*] —**em'bellisher** *n.* —**em'bellishment** *n.*

ember ('ɛmbə) *n.* **1.** a glowing or smouldering piece of coal or wood, as in a dying fire. **2.** the fading remains of a past emotion: *the embers of his love.* [Old English *ǣmyrge;* related to Old Norse *eimyrja* ember, *eimr* smoke, Old High German *eimuria* ember]

Ember days *pl. n. R.C. and Anglican Church.* any of four groups of three days (always Wednesday, Friday, and Saturday) of prayer and fasting, the groups occurring after Pentecost, after the first Sunday of Lent, after the feast of St Lucy (Dec. 13), and after the feast of the Holy Cross (Sept. 14). [Old English *ymbrendǣg,* from *ymbren,* perhaps from *ymbryne* a (recurring) period, from *ymb* around + *ryne* a course + *dǣg* day]

ember goose *n.* (*not in ornithological use*) another name for the **great northern diver.** [C18: from Norwegian *emmer-gaas*]

Ember week *n.* a week in which Ember days fall.

embezzle (ɪm'bɛz^{ə}l) *vb.* to convert (money or property entrusted to one) fraudulently to one's own use. [C15: from Anglo-French *embeseiller* to destroy, from Old French *beseiller* to make away with, of uncertain origin] —**em'bezzlement** *n.* —**em'bezzler** *n.*

embitter (ɪm'bɪtə) *vb.* (*tr.*) **1.** to make (a person) resentful or bitter. **2.** to aggravate (an already hostile feeling, difficult situation, etc.). —**em'bittered** *adj.* —**em'bitterer** *n.* —**em'bitterment** *n.*

emblaze (ɪm'bleɪz) *vb.* (*tr.*) *Archaic.* **1.** to cause to light up; illuminate. **2.** to set fire to.

emblazon (ɪm'bleɪz^{ə}n) *vb.* (*tr.*) **1.** to describe, portray, or colour (arms) according to the conventions of heraldry. **2.** to portray heraldic arms on (a shield, one's notepaper, etc.). **3.** to make bright or splendid, as with colours, flowers, etc. **4.** to glorify, praise, or extol, often so as to attract great publicity: *his feat was emblazoned on the front page.* —**em'blazonment** *n.*

emblazonry (ɪm'bleɪz^{ə}nrɪ) *n.* another name for **blazonry.**

emblem ('ɛmbləm) *n.* **1.** a visible object or representation that symbolizes a quality, type, group, etc., esp. the concrete symbol of an abstract idea: *the dove is an emblem of peace.* **2.** an allegorical picture containing a moral lesson, often with an explanatory motto or verses, esp. one printed in an **emblem book.** [C15: from Latin *emblēma* raised decoration, mosaic, from Greek, literally: something inserted, from *emballein* to insert, from *ballein* to throw] —ˌ**emblem'atic** *or* ˌ**emblem'atical** *adj.* —ˌ**emblem'atically** *adv.*

emblematize (ɛm'blɛməˌtaɪz), **emblemize** ('ɛmbləˌmaɪz), *or* **emblematise, emblemise** *vb.* (*tr.*) **1.** to function as an emblem of; symbolize. **2.** to represent by or as by an emblem.

emblements ('ɛmbləmənts) *pl. n. Law.* **1.** annual crops and vegetable products cultivated by man's labour. **2.** the profits from such crops. [C15: from Old French *emblaement,* from *emblaer* to sow with grain, from Medieval Latin *imblādāre,* from *blāda* grain, of Germanic origin; compare Old English *blǣd* grain]

embody (ɪm'bɒdɪ) *vb.* **-bodies, -bodying, -bodied.** (*tr.*) **1.** to give a tangible, bodily, or concrete form to (an abstract concept). **2.** to be an example of or express (an idea, principle, etc.), esp. in action: *his gentleness embodies a Christian ideal.* **3.** (often foll. by *in*) to collect or unite in a comprehensive whole, system, etc.; comprise; include: *all the different essays were embodied in one long article.* **4.** to invest (a spiritual entity) with a body or with bodily form; render incarnate. —**em'bodiment** *n.*

embolden (ɪm'bəʊld^{ə}n) *vb.* (*tr.*) to encourage; make bold.

embolectomy (ˌɛmbə'lɛktəmɪ) *n., pl.* **-mies.** the surgical removal of an embolus that is blocking a blood vessel.

embolic (ɛm'bɒlɪk) *adj.* **1.** of or relating to an embolus or embolism. **2.** *Embryol.* of, relating to, or resulting from invagination.

embolism ('ɛmbəˌlɪzəm) *n.* **1.** the occlusion of a blood vessel by an embolus. **2.** *Botany.* the blocking of a xylem vessel by an air bubble. **3.** the insertion of one or more days into a calendar, esp. the Jewish calendar; intercalation. **4.** *R.C. Church.* a prayer inserted in the canon of the Mass between the Lord's Prayer and the breaking of the bread. **5.** another name (not in technical use) for **embolus.** [C14: from Medieval Latin *embolismus,* from Late Greek *embolismos* intercalary; see EMBOLUS] —ˌ**embo'lismic** *adj.*

embolize *or* **embolise** ('ɛmbəˌlaɪz) *vb.* (*tr.*) to cause embolism in (a blood vessel). —ˌ**emboli'zation** *or* ˌ**emboli'sation** *n.*

embolus ('ɛmbələs) *n., pl.* **-li** (-ˌlaɪ). material, such as part of a blood clot or an air bubble, that is transported by the blood stream until it becomes lodged within a small vessel and impedes the circulation. Compare **thrombus.** [C17: via Latin from Greek *embolos* stopper, from *emballein* to insert, from *ballein* to throw; see EMBLEM]

emboly ('ɛmbəlɪ) *n., pl.* **-lies.** another name for **invagination** (sense 3). [C19: from Greek *embolē* an insertion, from *emballein* to throw in; see EMBLEM]

embonpoint *French.* (ɑ̃bɔ̃pwɛ̃) *n.* **1.** plumpness or stoutness. ~*adj.* **2.** plump; stout. [C18: from phrase *en bon point* in good condition]

embosom (ɪm'bʊzəm) *vb.* (*tr.*) *Archaic.* **1.** to enclose or envelop, esp. protectively. **2.** to clasp to the bosom; hug. **3.** to cherish.

emboss (ɪm'bɒs) *vb.* **1.** to mould or carve (a decoration or design) on (a surface) so that it is raised above the surface in low relief. **2.** to cause to bulge; make protrude. [C14: from Old French *embocer,* from EM- + *boce* BOSS[2]] —**em'bossed** *adj.* —**em'bosser** *n.* —**em'bossment** *n.*

embouchure (ˌɒmbʊ'ʃʊə) *n.* **1.** the mouth of a river or valley. **2.** *Music.* **a.** the correct application of the lips and tongue in playing a wind instrument. **b.** the mouthpiece of a wind instrument, esp. of the brass family. [C18: from French, from Old French *emboucher* to put to one's mouth, from *bouche* mouth, from Latin *bucca* cheek]

embourgeoisement (*French* ɑ̃burʒwaz'mɑ̃) *n.* the process of becoming middle class; the assimilation into the middle class of traditionally working-class people. [from French, from EN-[1] + BOURGEOIS[1]]

embow (ɪm'bəʊ) *vb.* (*tr.*) to design or create (a structure) in the form of an arch or vault. —**em'bowed** *adj.* —**em'bowment** *n.*

embowel (ɪm'baʊəl) *vb. Obsolete.* **1.** to bury or embed deeply. **2.** another word for **disembowel.**

embower (ɪm'baʊə) *vb.* (*tr.*) *Archaic.* to enclose in or as in a bower.

embrace[1] (ɪm'breɪs) *vb.* (*mainly tr.*) **1.** (*also intr.*) (of a person) to take or clasp (another person) in the arms, or (of two people) to clasp each other, as in affection, greeting, etc.; hug. **2.** to accept (an opportunity, challenge, etc.) willingly or eagerly. **3.** to take up (a new idea, faith, etc.); adopt: *to embrace Judaism.* **4.** to comprise or include as an integral part: *geology embraces the science of mineralogy.* **5.** to encircle or enclose: *an island embraced by the ocean.* **6.** *Rare.* to perceive or understand. ~*n.* **7.** the act of embracing. **8.** (*often pl.*) *Euphemistic.* sexual intercourse. [C14: from Old French *embracier,* from EM- + *brace* a pair of arms, from Latin *bracchia* arms] —**em'braceable** *adj.* —**em'bracement** *n.* —**em'bracer** *n.*

embrace[2] (ɪm'breɪs) *vb.* (*tr.*) *Criminal law.* to commit or attempt to commit embracery against (a jury, etc.). [C15: back formation from EMBRACEOR]

embraceor *or* **embracer** (ɪm'breɪsə) *n. Criminal law.* a person guilty of embracery. [C15: from Old French *embraseor,* from *embraser* to instigate, literally: to set on fire, from *braser* to burn, from *brese* live coals]

embracery (ɪm'breɪsərɪ) *n. Criminal law.* the offence of attempting by corrupt means to influence a jury or juror, as by bribery or threats.

embranchment (ɪm'brɑːntʃmənt) *n.* **1.** the process of branching out, esp. by a river. **2.** a branching out or ramification, as of a river or mountain range.

embrangle (ɪm'bræŋg^{ə}l) *vb.* (*tr.*) *Rare.* to confuse or entangle. [C17: from EM- + obsolete *brangle* to wrangle, perhaps a blend of BRAWL[1] + WRANGLE] —**em'branglement** *n.*

embrasure (ɪm'breɪʒə) *n.* **1.** *Fortifications.* an opening or indentation, as in a battlement, for shooting through. **2.** an opening forming a door or window, having splayed sides that increase the width of the opening in the interior. [C18: from French, from obsolete *embraser* to widen, of uncertain origin] —**em'brasured** *adj.*

embrocate ('ɛmbrəʊˌkeɪt) *vb.* (*tr.*) to apply a liniment or lotion to (a part of the body). [C17: from Medieval Latin *embrocāre,* from *embrocha* poultice, from Greek *embrokhē* lotion, infusion, from *brokhē* a moistening]

embrocation (ˌɛmbrəʊ'keɪʃən) *n.* a drug or agent for rubbing into the skin; liniment.

embroider (ɪm'brɔɪdə) *vb.* **1.** to do decorative needlework (upon). **2.** to add fictitious or fanciful detail to (a story). **3.** to add exaggerated or improbable details to (an account of an event, etc.). [C15: from Old French *embroder;* see *em-* EN-[1], BROIDER] —**em'broiderer** *n.*

embroidery (ɪm'brɔɪdərɪ) *n., pl.* **-deries.** **1.** decorative needlework done usually on loosely woven cloth or canvas, often being a picture or pattern. **2.** elaboration or exaggeration, esp. in writing or reporting; embellishment.

embroil (ɪm'brɔɪl) *vb.* (*tr.*) **1.** to involve (a person, oneself, etc.) in trouble, conflict, or argument. **2.** to throw (affairs) into a state of confusion or disorder; complicate; entangle. [C17: from French *embrouiller,* from *brouiller* to mingle, confuse] —**em'broiler** *n.* —**em'broilment** *n.*

embrue (ɪm'bruː) *vb.* **-brues, -bruing, -brued.** a variant spelling of **imbrue.** —**em'bruement** *n.*

embryectomy (ˌɛmbrɪ'ɛktəmɪ) *n., pl.* **-mies.** the surgical removal of an embryo.

embryo ('ɛmbrɪˌəʊ) *n., pl.* **-bryos.** **1.** an animal in the early stages of development following cleavage of the zygote and ending at birth or hatching. **2.** the human product of conception up to approximately the end of the second month of pregnancy. Compare **fetus.** **3.** a plant in the early stages of development: in higher plants, the plumule, cotyledons, and radicle within the seed. **4.** an undeveloped or rudimentary state (esp. in the phrase **in embryo**). **5.** something in an early stage of development: *an embryo of an idea.* [C16: from Late Latin, from Greek *embruon,* from *bruein* to swell] —'**embry,oid** *adj.*

embryogeny (ˌɛmbrɪˈɒdʒɪnɪ) *n.* **1.** Also called: **embryogenesis** (ˌɛmbrɪəʊˈdʒɛnəsɪs). the formation and development of an embryo. **2.** the study of these processes. —**embryogenic** (ˌɛmbrɪəʊˈdʒɛnɪk) *adj.*

embryol. *abbrev. for* embryology.

embryology (ˌɛmbrɪˈɒlədʒɪ) *n.* **1.** the branch of science concerned with the study of embryos. **2.** the structure and development of the embryo of a particular organism. —**embryological** (ˌɛmbrɪəˈlɒdʒɪkᵊl) *or* ˌ**embryo'logic** *adj.* —ˌ**embryo'logically** *adv.* —ˌ**embry'ologist** *n.*

embryonic (ˌɛmbrɪˈɒnɪk) *or* **embryonal** (ˈɛmbrɪənᵊl) *adj.* **1.** of or relating to an embryo. **2.** in an early stage; rudimentary; undeveloped. —ˌ**embry'onically** *adv.*

embryo sac *n.* the structure within a plant ovule that contains the egg cell; the megaspore of seed plants: contains the embryo plant and endosperm after fertilization.

embus (ɪmˈbʌs) *vb.* **-buses, -busing, -bused** *or* **-busses, -bussing, -bussed.** *Military.* to cause (troops) to board or (of troops) to board a transport vehicle.

embusqué *French.* (ɑ̃byske) *n., pl.* ***-qués*** (-ke). a man who avoids military conscription by obtaining a government job. [C20: from *embusquer* to lie in ambush, shirk]

emcee (ˌɛmˈsiː) *Informal.* ~*n.* **1.** a master of ceremonies. ~*vb.* **-cees, -ceeing, -ceed.** **2.** to act as master of ceremonies (for or at). [C20: from the abbreviation MC]

em dash *or* **rule** *n. Printing.* a dash (—) one em long.

-eme *suffix forming nouns. Linguistics.* indicating a minimal distinctive unit of a specified type in a language: *morpheme; phoneme.* [C20: via French, abstracted from PHONEME]

emend (ɪˈmɛnd) *vb. (tr.)* to make corrections or improvements in (a text) by critical editing. [C15: from Latin *ēmendāre* to correct, from *ē-* out + *mendum* a mistake] —**e'mendable** *adj.*

emendation (ˌiːmɛnˈdeɪʃən) *n.* **1.** a correction or improvement in a text. **2.** the act or process of emending. —'**emen,dator** *n.* —**emendatory** (ɪˈmɛndətərɪ, -trɪ) *adj.*

emerald (ˈɛmərəld, ˈɛmrəld) *n.* **1.** a green transparent variety of beryl: highly valued as a gem. **2. a.** the clear green colour of an emerald. **b.** (*as adj.*): *an emerald carpet.* **3.** (formerly) a size of printer's type approximately equal to 6½ point. **4.** short for **emerald moth.** [C13: from Old French *esmeraude,* from Latin *smaragdus,* from Greek *smaragdos;* related to Sanskrit *marakata* emerald]

emerald moth *n.* any of various green geometrid moths, esp. the **large emerald** (*Geometra papilionaria*) a handsome pale green moth with white wavy markings.

emerge (ɪˈmɜːdʒ) *vb. (intr.;* often foll. by *from)* **1.** to come up to the surface of or rise from water or other liquid. **2.** to come into view, as from concealment or obscurity: *he emerged from the cave.* **3.** (foll. by *from*) to come out (of) or live (through a difficult experience): *he emerged from his ordeal with dignity.* **4.** to become apparent: *several interesting things emerged from the report.* [C17: from Latin *ēmergere* to rise up from, from *mergere* to dip] —**e'merging** *adj.*

emergence (ɪˈmɜːdʒəns) *n.* **1.** the act or process of emerging. **2.** an outgrowth, such as a prickle, that contains no vascular tissue and does not develop into stem, leaf, etc.

emergency (ɪˈmɜːdʒənsɪ) *n., pl.* **-cies.** **1. a.** an unforeseen or sudden occurrence, esp. of a danger demanding immediate remedy or action. **b.** (*as modifier*): *an emergency exit.* **2. a.** a patient requiring urgent treatment. **b.** (*as modifier*): *an emergency ward.* **3. state of emergency.** a condition, declared by a government, in which martial law applies, usually because of civil unrest or natural disaster. **4.** *N.Z.* a player selected to stand by to replace an injured member of a team; reserve.

emergent (ɪˈmɜːdʒənt) *adj.* **1.** coming into being or notice: *an emergent political structure.* **2.** (of a nation) recently independent. ~*n.* **3.** an aquatic plant with stem and leaves above the water. —**e'mergently** *adv.*

emergent evolution *n. Philosophy.* the doctrine that, in the course of evolution, some entirely new properties, such as life and consciousness, appear at certain critical points, usually because of an unpredictable rearrangement of the already existing entities.

emeritus (ɪˈmɛrɪtəs) *adj.* (*usually postpositive*) retired or honourably discharged from full-time work, but retaining one's title on an honorary basis: *a professor emeritus.* [C19: from Latin, from *merēre* to deserve; see MERIT]

emersed (ɪˈmɜːst) *adj.* (of the leaves or stems of aquatic plants) protruding above the surface of the water.

emersion (ɪˈmɜːʃən) *n.* **1.** the act or an instance of emerging. **2.** Also called: **egress.** *Astronomy.* the reappearance of a celestial body after an eclipse or occultation. [C17: from Latin *ēmersus,* from *ēmergere;* see EMERGE]

emery (ˈɛmərɪ) *n.* **a.** a hard greyish-black mineral consisting of corundum with either magnetite or haematite: used as an abrasive and polishing agent, esp. as a coating on paper, cloth, etc. Formula: Al_2O_3. **b.** (*as modifier*): *emery paper.* [C15: from Old French *esmeril,* ultimately from Greek *smuris* powder for rubbing]

emery board *n.* a strip of cardboard or wood with a rough surface of crushed emery, for filing one's nails.

emery wheel *n.* a grinding or polishing wheel the surface of which is coated with abrasive emery particles.

emesis (ˈɛmɪsɪs) *n.* the technical name for **vomiting.** [C19: via New Latin from Greek, from *emein* to vomit]

emetic (ɪˈmɛtɪk) *adj.* **1.** causing vomiting. ~*n.* **2.** an emetic agent or drug. [C17: from Late Latin *ēmeticus,* from Greek *emetikos,* from *emein* to vomit] —**e'metically** *adv.*

emetine (ˈɛməˌtiːn, -tɪn) *or* **emetin** (ˈɛmətɪn) *n.* a white bitter poisonous alkaloid obtained from ipecac: the hydrochloride is used to treat amoebic infections. Formula: $C_{29}H_{40}O_4N_2$. [C19: from French *émétine;* see EMETIC, -INE[2]]

emf *or* **EMF** *abbrev. for* electromotive force.

-emia *n. combining form.* a U.S. variant of **-aemia.**

emigrant (ˈɛmɪɡrənt) *n.* **a.** a person who leaves one place or country, esp. a native country, to settle in another. Compare **immigrant. b.** (*as modifier*): *an emigrant worker.*

emigrate (ˈɛmɪˌɡreɪt) *vb. (intr.)* to leave one place or country, esp. one's native country, in order to settle in another. Compare **immigrate.** [C18: from Latin *ēmīgrāre,* from *mīgrāre* to depart, MIGRATE] —**emi,gratory** *adj.*

emigration (ˌɛmɪˈɡreɪʃən) *n.* **1.** the act or an instance of emigrating. **2.** emigrants considered collectively.

émigré (ˈɛmɪˌɡreɪ; *French* emigre) *n.* an emigrant, esp. one forced to leave his native country for political reasons. [C18: from French, from *émigrer* to EMIGRATE]

eminence (ˈɛmɪnəns) *n., pl.* **-nences.** **1.** a position of superiority, distinction, high rank, or fame. **2.** a high or raised piece of ground. **3.** *Anatomy.* a projection of an organ or part. ~Also: **eminency.** [C17: from French, from Latin *ēminentia* a standing out; see EMINENT]

Eminence (ˈɛmɪnəns) *or* **Eminency** *n., pl.* **-nences** *or* **-nencies.** (preceded by *Your* or *His*) a title used to address or refer to a cardinal.

éminence grise *French.* (eminɑ̃s ɡriz) *n., pl.* ***éminences grises*** (eminɑ̃s ɡriz). a person who wields power and influence unofficially or behind the scenes. [C19: literally: grey eminence, originally applied to Père Joseph (François Le Clerc du Tremblay; died 1638), French monk, secretary of Cardinal Richelieu]

eminent (ˈɛmɪnənt) *adj.* **1.** above others in rank, merit, or reputation; distinguished: *an eminent scientist.* **2.** (*prenominal*) noteworthy, conspicuous, or outstanding: *eminent good sense.* **3.** projecting or protruding; prominent. [C15: from Latin *ēminēre* to project, stand out, from *minēre* to stand] —'**eminently** *adv.*

eminent domain *n. Law.* the right of a state to confiscate private property for public use, payment usually being made to the owners in compensation.

emir (ɛˈmɪə) *n.* (in the Islamic world) **1.** an independent ruler or chieftain. **2.** a military commander or governor. **3.** a descendant of Mohammed. ~Also spelled: **amir.** [C17: via French from Spanish *emir,* from Arabic *'amīr* commander]

emirate (ɛˈmɪərɪt, ˈɛmɪrɪt) *n.* **1.** the rank or office of an emir. **2.** the government, jurisdiction, or territory of an emir.

Emiscan (ˌɛmɪˈskæn) *n. Trademark.* a computerized radiological technique for examining the soft tissues of the body, esp. the brain, to detect the presence of tumours, abscesses, etc.

emissary (ˈɛmɪsərɪ, -ɪsrɪ) *n., pl.* **-saries.** **1. a.** an agent or messenger sent on a mission, esp. one who represents a government or head of state. **b.** (*as modifier*): *an emissary delegation.* **2.** an agent sent on a secret mission, as a spy. ~*adj.* **3.** (of veins) draining blood from sinuses in the dura mater to veins outside the skull. [C17: from Latin *ēmissārius* emissary, spy, from *ēmittere* to send out; see EMIT]

emission (ɪˈmɪʃən) *n.* **1.** the act of emitting or sending forth. **2.** energy, in the form of heat, light, radio waves, etc., emitted from a source. **3.** a substance, fluid, etc., that is emitted; discharge. **4.** a measure of the number of electrons emitted by a cathode or electron gun: *at 1000°C the emission is 3 mA.* See also **secondary emission, thermionic emission.** **5.** *Physiol.* any bodily discharge, esp. an involuntary release of semen during sleep. **6.** an issue, as of currency. [C17: from Latin *ēmissiō,* from *ēmittere* to send forth, EMIT] —**e'missive** *adj.*

emission nebula *n.* a type of nebula that emits radiation. See **nebula.**

emission spectrum *n.* the continuous spectrum or pattern of bright lines or bands seen when the electromagnetic radiation emitted by a substance is passed into a spectrometer. The spectrum is characteristic of the emitting substance and the type of excitation to which it is subjected. Compare **absorption spectrum.**

emissivity (ɪmɪˈsɪvɪtɪ, ˌɛm-) *n.* a measure of the ability of a surface to radiate energy; the ratio of the radiant flux emitted per unit area to that emitted by a black body at the same temperature. Symbol: ε

emit (ɪˈmɪt) *vb.* **emits, emitting, emitted.** *(tr.)* **1.** to give or send forth; discharge: *the pipe emitted a stream of water.* **2.** to give voice to; utter: *she emitted a shrill scream.* **3.** *Physics.* to give off (radiation or particles). **4.** to put (currency) into circulation. [C17: from Latin *ēmittere* to send out, from *mittere* to send]

emitter (ɪ'mɪtə) *n.* **1.** a person or thing that emits. **2.** a radioactive substance that emits radiation: *a beta emitter.* **3.** the region in a transistor in which the charge-carrying holes or electrons originate.

emmenagogue (ɪ'mɛnəˌgɒg, -'miː-) *n.* **1.** a drug or agent that increases menstrual flow. ~*adj.* also **emmenagogic** (ɪˌmɛnə'gɒdʒɪk). **2.** inducing or increasing menstrual flow. [C18: from Greek *emmēna* menses, (from *mēn* month) + -AGOGUE]

Emmenthal, Emmental ('ɛmənˌtɑːl), *or* **Emmenthaler, Emmentaler** *n.* a hard Swiss cheese with holes in it, similar to Gruyère. [C20: named after *Emmenthal,* a valley in Switzerland]

emmer ('ɛmə) *n.* a variety of wheat, *Triticum dicoccum,* grown in mountainous parts of Europe as a cereal crop and for livestock food: thought to be an ancestor of many other varieties of wheat. [C20: from German; related to Old High German *amari* spelt]

emmet ('ɛmɪt) *n. Brit.* an archaic or dialect word for **ant.** [Old English *ǣmette* ANT; related to Old Norse *meita,* Old High German *āmeiza,* Gothic *maitan*]

emmetropia (ˌɛmɪ'trəʊpɪə) *n.* the normal condition of perfect vision, in which parallel light rays are focused on the retina without the need for accommodation. [C19: from New Latin, from Greek *emmetros* in due measure + -OPIA] —**emmetropic** (ˌɛmɪ'trɒpɪk) *adj.*

Emmy ('ɛmɪ) *n., pl.* **-mys** *or* **-mies.** (in the U.S.) one of the gold-plated statuettes awarded annually for outstanding television performances and productions. [C20: alteration of *Immy,* short for *image orthicon tube*]

emollient (ɪ'mɒljənt) *adj.* **1.** softening or soothing, esp. to the skin. ~*n.* **2.** any preparation or substance that has a softening or soothing effect, esp. when applied to the skin. [C17: from Latin *ēmollīre* to soften, from *mollis* soft] —**e'mollience** *n.*

emolument (ɪ'mɒljʊmənt) *n.* the profit arising from an office or employment, usually in the form of fees or wages. [C15: from Latin *ēmolumentum* benefit; originally, fee paid to a miller, from *ēmolere,* from *molere* to grind]

emote (ɪ'məʊt) *vb.* (*intr.*) to display exaggerated emotion, as in acting; behave theatrically. [C20: back formation from EMOTION] —**e'moter** *n.*

emotion (ɪ'məʊʃən) *n.* any strong feeling, as of joy, sorrow, or fear. [C16: from French, from Old French *esmovoir* to excite, from Latin *ēmovēre* to disturb, from *movēre* to MOVE] —**e'motionless** *adj.*

emotional (ɪ'məʊʃənᵊl) *adj.* **1.** of, characteristic of, or expressive of emotion. **2.** readily or excessively affected by emotion. **3.** appealing to or arousing emotion: *an emotional piece of music.* **4.** caused, determined, or actuated by emotion rather than reason: *an emotional argument.* —**eˌmotion'ality** *n.* —**e'motionally** *adv.*

emotionalism (ɪ'məʊʃənəˌlɪzəm) *n.* **1.** emotional nature, character, or quality. **2.** a tendency to yield readily to the emotions. **3.** an appeal to the emotions, esp. an excessive appeal, as to an audience. **4.** a doctrine stressing the value of deeply felt responses in ethics and the arts. —**e'motionalist** *n.* —**eˌmotional'istic** *adj.*

emotionalize *or* **emotionalise** (ɪ'məʊʃənəˌlaɪz) *vb.* (*tr.*) to make emotional; subject to emotional treatment. —**eˌmotionali'zation** *or* **eˌmotionali'sation** *n.*

emotive (ɪ'məʊtɪv) *adj.* **1.** tending or designed to arouse emotion. **2.** of or characterized by emotion. —**e'motively** *adv.* —**e'motiveness** *or* **ˌemo'tivity** *n.*

emotivism (ɪ'məʊtɪˌvɪzəm) *n. Ethics.* the theory that moral utterances do not have a truth value but express the feelings of the speaker, so that *murder is wrong* is equivalent to *down with murder.* Also called: **boo-hurrah theory.** Compare **prescriptivism, descriptivism.**

Emp. *abbrev. for:* **1.** Emperor. **2.** Empire. **3.** Empress.

empale (ɪm'peɪl) *vb.* a less common spelling of **impale.** —**em'palement** *n.* —**em'paler** *n.*

empanel *or* **impanel** (ɪm'pænᵊl) *vb.* **-els, -elling, -elled** *or U.S.* **-els, -eling, -eled.** (*tr.*) *Law.* **1.** to enter on a list (names of persons to be summoned for jury service). **2.** to select (a jury) from the names on such a list. —**em'panelment** *or* **im'panelment** *n.*

empathic (ɛm'pæθɪk) *or* **empathetic** (ˌɛmpə'θɛtɪk) *adj.* of or relating to empathy. —**em'pathically** *or* **ˌempa'thetically** *adv.*

empathize *or* **empathise** ('ɛmpəˌθaɪz) *vb.* (*intr.*) to engage in or feel empathy.

empathy ('ɛmpəθɪ) *n.* **1.** the power of understanding and imaginatively entering into another person's feelings. See also **identification** (sense 3b.). **2.** the attribution to an object, such as a work of art, of one's own emotional or intellectual feelings about it. [C20: from Greek *empatheia* affection, passion, intended as a rendering of German *Einfühlung,* literally: a feeling in; see EN-[2], -PATHY] —'**empathist** *n.*

empennage (ɛm'pɛnɪdʒ; *French* ɑ̃pɛnaʒ) *n.* the rear part of an aircraft, comprising the fin, rudder, and tailplane. [C20: from French: feathering, from *empenner* to feather an arrow, from *penne* feather, from Latin *pinna*]

emperor ('ɛmpərə) *n.* **1.** a monarch who rules or reigns over an empire. **2.** Also called: **emperor moth.** any of several large saturniid moths with eyelike markings on each wing, esp. *Saturnia pavonia* of Europe. See also **giant peacock moth. 3.** See **purple emperor.** [C13: from Old French *empereor,* from Latin *imperātor* commander-in-chief, from *imperāre* to command, from IM- + *parāre* to make ready] —'**emperorˌship** *n.*

emperor penguin *n.* an Antarctic penguin, *Aptenodytes forsteri,* with orange-yellow patches on the neck: the largest penguin, reaching a height of 1.3 m (4 ft.).

empery ('ɛmpərɪ) *n., pl.* **-peries.** *Archaic.* dominion or power; empire. [C13 (in the sense: the status of an emperor): from Anglo-French *emperie,* from Latin *imperium* power; see EMPIRE]

emphasis ('ɛmfəsɪs) *n., pl.* **-ses** (-siːz). **1.** special importance or significance. **2.** an object, idea, etc., that is given special importance or significance. **3.** stress made to fall on a particular syllable, word, or phrase in speaking. **4.** force or intensity of expression: *he spoke with special emphasis on the subject of civil rights.* **5.** sharpness or clarity of form or outline: *the sunlight gave emphasis to the shape of the mountain.* [C16: via Latin from Greek: meaning, (in rhetoric) significant stress; see EMPHATIC]

emphasize *or* **emphasise** ('ɛmfəˌsaɪz) *vb.* (*tr.*) to give emphasis or prominence to; stress.

emphatic (ɪm'fætɪk) *adj.* **1.** expressed, spoken, or done with emphasis. **2.** forceful and positive; definite; direct: *an emphatic personality.* **3.** sharp or clear in form, contour, or outline. **4.** important or significant; stressed: *the emphatic points in an argument.* **5.** *Phonetics.* denoting certain dental consonants of Arabic that are pronounced with accompanying pharyngeal constriction. ~*n.* **6.** *Phonetics.* an emphatic consonant, as used in Arabic. [C18: from Greek *emphatikos* expressive, forceful, from *emphainein* to exhibit, display, from *phainein* to show] —**em'phatically** *adv.*

emphysema (ˌɛmfɪ'siːmə) *n. Pathol.* **1.** Also called: **pulmonary emphysema.** a condition in which the air sacs of the lungs are grossly enlarged, causing breathlessness and wheezing. **2.** the abnormal presence of air in a tissue or part. [C17: from New Latin, from Greek *emphusēma,* a swelling up, from *emphusan* to inflate, from *phusan* to blow] —**emphysematous** (ˌɛmfɪ'sɛmətəs, -'siː-) *adj.*

empire ('ɛmpaɪə) *n.* **1.** an aggregate of peoples and territories, often of great extent, under the rule of a single person, oligarchy, or sovereign state. **2.** any monarchy that for reasons of history, prestige, etc., has an emperor rather than a king as head of state. **3.** the period during which a particular empire exists. **4.** supreme power; sovereignty. **5.** a large industrial organization with many ramifications, esp. a multinational corporation. [C13: from Old French, from Latin *imperium* rule, from *imperāre* to command, from *parāre* to prepare]

Empire ('ɛmpaɪə) *adj.* **1.** denoting, characteristic of, or relating to the British Empire. **2.** denoting, characteristic of, or relating to either French Empire (1804–15; 1852–70), esp. the first: in particular, denoting the neoclassical style of architecture and furniture and the high-waisted style of women's dresses characteristic of the period.

empire-builder *n. Informal.* a person who seeks extra power for its own sake, esp. by increasing the number of his subordinates or staff. —'**empire-ˌbuilding** *n., adj.*

empiric (ɛm'pɪrɪk) *n.* **1.** a person who relies on empirical methods. **2.** a medical quack; charlatan. ~*adj.* **3.** a variant of **empirical.** [C16: from Latin *empīricus,* from Greek *empeirikos* practised, from *peiran* to attempt]

empirical (ɛm'pɪrɪkᵊl) *adj.* **1.** derived from or relating to experiment and observation rather than theory. **2.** (of medical treatment) based on practical experience rather than scientific proof. **3.** *Philosophy.* **a.** (of knowledge) derived from experience rather than by logic from first principles. Compare **a priori, a posteriori. b.** (of a proposition) subject, at least theoretically, to verification. Compare **analytic** (sense 4), **synthetic** (sense 4). **4.** of or relating to medical quackery. ~*n.* **5.** *Statistics.* the posterior probability of an event derived on the basis of its observed frequency in a sample. Compare **mathematical probability.** See also **posterior probability.** —**em'pirically** *adv.* —**em'piricalness** *n.*

empirical formula *n.* **1.** a chemical formula indicating the proportion of each element present in a molecule: $C_6H_{12}O_6$ *is the molecular formula of sucrose whereas* CH_2O *is its empirical formula.* Compare **molecular formula, structural formula. 2.** a formula or expression obtained from experimental data rather than theory.

empiricism (ɛm'pɪrɪˌsɪzəm) *n.* **1.** *Philosophy.* the doctrine that all knowledge of matters of fact derives from experience and that the mind is not furnished with a set of concepts in advance of experience. Compare **intuitionism, rationalism. 2.** the use of empirical methods. **3.** medical quackery; charlatanism. —**em'piricist** *n., adj.*

emplace (ɪm'pleɪs) *vb.* (*tr.*) to put in place or position.

emplacement (ɪm'pleɪsmənt) *n.* **1.** a prepared position for the siting of a gun or other weapon. **2.** the act of putting or state of being put in place. [C19: from French, from obsolete *emplacer* to put in position, from PLACE]

emplane (ɪm'pleɪn) *vb.* to board or put on board an aeroplane.

employ (ɪm'plɔɪ) *vb.* (*tr.*) **1.** to engage or make use of the services of (a person) in return for money; hire. **2.** to provide work or occupation for; keep busy; occupy: *collecting stamps employs a lot of his time.* **3.** to use as a means: *to employ secret measures to get one's ends.* ~*n.* **4.** the state of being employed (esp. in the phrase **in someone's employ**). [C15: from Old French *emploier,* from Latin *implicāre* to entangle, engage, from *plicāre* to fold] —**em'ployable** *adj.* —**em,ploya'bility** *n.*

employee (ɛm'plɔiː, ˌɛmplɔɪ'iː) *or U.S.* **employe** *n.* a person who is hired to work for another or for a business, firm, etc., in return for payment. Also called (esp. formerly): **employé.**

employee association *n.* an organization, other than a trade union, whose members comprise employees of a single employing organization. The aims of the association may be social, recreational, or professional.

employer (ɪm'plɔɪə) *n.* **1.** a person, business, firm, etc., that employs workers. **2.** a person who employs; user.

employers' association *n.* a body of employers, usually from the same sector of the economy, associated to further the interests of member companies by conducting negotiations with trade unions, providing advice, making representations to other bodies, etc.

employment (ɪm'plɔɪmənt) *n.* **1.** the act of employing or state of being employed. **2.** the work or occupation in which a person is employed. **3.** the purpose for which something is used.

employment agency *n.* a private firm whose business is placing people in jobs.

employment exchange *n. Brit.* a former name for **employment office.**

employment office *n. Brit.* any of a number of government offices established to collect and supply to the unemployed information about job vacancies and to employers information about availability of prospective workers. Former names: **employment exchange, labour exchange.** See also **Jobcentre.**

empoison (ɪm'pɔɪzᵊn) *vb.* (*tr.*) **1.** *Rare.* to embitter or corrupt. **2.** an archaic word for **poison** (senses 6–9). —**em'poisonment** *n.*

empolder (ɪm'pəʊldə) *vb.* a variant spelling of **impolder.**

emporium (ɛm'pɔːrɪəm) *n., pl.* **-riums** *or* **-ria** (-rɪə). a large and often ostentatious retail shop offering for sale a wide variety of merchandise. [C16: from Latin, from Greek *emporion,* from *emporos* merchant, from *poros* a journey]

empoverish (ɪm'pɒvərɪʃ) *vb.* an obsolete spelling of **impoverish.** —**em'poverisher** *n.* —**em'poverishment** *n.*

empower (ɪm'paʊə) *vb.* (*tr.*) **1.** to give or delegate power or authority to; authorize. **2.** to give ability to; enable or permit. —**em'powerment** *n.*

empress ('ɛmprɪs) *n.* **1.** the wife or widow of an emperor. **2.** a woman who holds the rank of emperor in her own right. **3.** a woman of great power and influence. [C12: from Old French *empereriz,* from Latin *imperātrix* feminine of *imperātor* EMPEROR]

emprise (ɛm'praɪz) *n. Archaic.* **1.** a chivalrous or daring enterprise; adventure. **2.** chivalrous daring or prowess. [C13: from Old French, from *emprendre* to undertake; see ENTERPRISE]

empt (ɛmpt, ɛmt) *vb.* (*tr.*) *Dialect.* to empty. [from Old English *ǣmtian* to be without duties; compare EMPTY]

empty ('ɛmptɪ) *adj.* **-tier, -tiest. 1.** containing nothing. **2.** without inhabitants; vacant or unoccupied. **3.** carrying no load, passengers, etc. **4.** without purpose, substance, or value: *an empty life.* **5.** insincere or trivial: *empty words.* **6.** not expressive or vital; vacant: *she has an empty look.* **7.** *Informal.* hungry. **8.** (*postpositive,* foll. by *of*) devoid; destitute: *a life empty of happiness.* **9.** *Informal.* drained of energy or emotion: *after the violent argument he felt very empty.* **10.** *Maths, logic.* (of a set or class) containing no members. **11.** *Philosophy, logic.* (of a name or description) having no reference. ~*vb.* **-ties, -tying, -tied. 12.** to make or become empty. **13.** (when *intr.,* foll. by *into*) to discharge (contents). **14.** (*tr.;* often foll. by *of*) to unburden or rid (oneself): *to empty oneself of emotion.* ~*n., pl.* **-ties. 15.** an empty container, esp. a bottle. [Old English *ǣmtig,* from *æmetta* free time, from *æ-* without + *-metta,* from *mōtan* to be obliged to; see MUST[1]] —**'emptiable** *adj.* —**'emptier** *n.* —**'emptily** *adv.* —**'emptiness** *n.*

empty cow *n.* a cow that does not produce calves during the breeding season.

empty-handed *adj.* **1.** carrying nothing in the hands. **2.** having gained nothing: *they returned from the negotiations empty-handed.*

empty-headed *adj.* lacking intelligence or sense; frivolous.

empty-nester *n. Informal.* a married person whose children have grown up and left home.

empyema (ˌɛmpaɪ'iːmə) *n., pl.* **-emata** (-'iːmətə) *or* **-emas.** a collection of pus in a body cavity, esp. in the chest. [C17: from Medieval Latin, from Greek *empuēma* abscess, from *empuein* to suppurate, from *puon* pus] —ˌ**empy'emic** *adj.*

empyrean (ˌɛmpaɪ'riːən) *n.* **1.** *Archaic.* the highest part of the (supposedly spherical) heavens, thought in ancient times to contain the pure element of fire and by early Christians to be the abode of God and the angels. **2.** *Poetic.* the heavens or sky. ~*adj. also* **empyreal. 3.** of or relating to the sky, the heavens, or the empyrean. **4.** heavenly or sublime. **5.** *Archaic.* composed of fire. [C17: from Medieval Latin *empyreus,* from Greek *empuros* fiery, from *pur* fire]

empyreuma (ˌɛmpɪ'ruːmə) *n., pl.* **-mata** (-mətə). the smell and taste associated with burning vegetable and animal matter. [C17: from Greek, from *empureuein* to set on fire]

EMS *abbrev. for* European Monetary System.

emu ('iːmjuː) *n.* **1.** a large Australian flightless bird, *Dromaius novaehollandiae,* similar to the ostrich but with three-toed feet and grey or brown plumage: order *Casuariiformes.* See also **ratite. 2.** *Austral. informal.* a person who picks up discarded betting tickets in the hope of a lucky find. [C17: changed from Portuguese *ema* ostrich, from Arabic *Na-'amah* ostrich]

EMU 1. *abbrev. for* economic and monetary union: a stage in the progress towards a federal Europe. **2.** see **e.m.u.**

e.m.u. *or* **EMU** *abbrev. for* electromagnetic unit.

emu-bobber *n. Austral. informal.* a person employed to pick up sticks after clearing or burning off in the bush. —**'emu-bobbing** *n.*

emu bush *n.* any of various Australian shrubs, esp. those of the genus *Eremophila* (family Myoporaceae), whose fruits are eaten by emus.

emulate ('ɛmjʊˌleɪt) *vb.* (*tr.*) **1.** to attempt to equal or surpass, esp. by imitation. **2.** to rival or compete with. **3.** to make one computer behave like (another different type of computer) so that the imitating system can operate on the same data and execute the same programs as the imitated system. [C16: from Latin *aemulārī,* from *aemulus* competing with; probably related to *imitārī* to IMITATE] —**'emulative** *adj.* —**'emulatively** *adv.* —**'emuˌlator** *n.*

emulation (ˌɛmjʊ'leɪʃən) *n.* **1.** the act of emulating or imitating. **2.** the effort or desire to equal or surpass another or others. **3.** *Archaic.* jealous rivalry.

emulous ('ɛmjʊləs) *adj.* **1.** desiring or aiming to equal or surpass another; competitive. **2.** characterized by or arising from emulation or imitation. **3.** *Archaic.* envious or jealous. [C14: from Latin *aemulus* rivalling; see EMULATE] —**'emulously** *adv.* —**'emulousness** *n.*

emulsifier (ɪ'mʌlsɪˌfaɪə) *n.* an agent that forms or preserves an emulsion, esp. any food additive, such as lecithin, that prevents separation of sauces or other processed foods.

emulsify (ɪ'mʌlsɪˌfaɪ) *vb.* **-fies, -fying, -fied.** to make or form into an emulsion. —**eˌmulsi'fiable** *or* **e'mulsible** *adj.* —**eˌmulsifi'cation** *n.*

emulsion (ɪ'mʌlʃən) *n.* **1.** *Photog.* a light-sensitive coating on a base, such as paper or film, consisting of fine grains of silver bromide suspended in gelatin. **2.** *Chem.* a colloid in which both phases are liquids: *an oil-in-water emulsion.* **3.** Also called: **emulsion paint.** a type of paint in which the pigment is suspended in a vehicle, usually a synthetic resin, that is dispersed in water as an emulsion. It usually gives a mat finish. **4.** *Pharmacol.* a mixture in which an oily medicine is dispersed in another liquid. **5.** any liquid resembling milk. [C17: from New Latin *ēmulsiō,* from Latin *ēmulsus* milked out, from *ēmulgēre* to milk out, drain out, from *mulgēre* to milk] —**e'mulsive** *adj.*

emulsoid (ɪ'mʌlsɔɪd) *n. Chem.* a sol with a liquid disperse phase.

emunctory (ɪ'mʌŋktərɪ) *adj.* **1.** of or relating to a bodily organ or duct having an excretory function. ~*n., pl.* **-ries. 2.** an excretory organ or duct, such as a skin pore. [C16: from New Latin *ēmunctōrium,* from Latin *ēmungere* to wipe clean, from *mungere* to wipe]

emu parade *n. Austral.* an army exercise devoted to emu-bobbing.

emu-wren *n.* any Australian wren of the genus *Stipiturus,* having long plumy tail feathers.

en (ɛn) *n. Printing.* a unit of measurement, half the width of an em. Also called: **nut.** See also **ennage.**

EN (in Britain) *abbrev. for* enrolled nurse.

en-[1] *or* **em-** *prefix forming verbs.* **1.** (*from nouns*) **a.** put in or on: *entomb; enthrone.* **b.** go on or into: *enplane.* **c.** surround or cover with: *enmesh.* **d.** furnish with: *empower.* **2.** (*from adjectives and nouns*) cause to be in a certain condition: *enable; encourage; enrich; enslave.* [via Old French from Latin *in-* IN-[2]]

en-[2] *or* **em-** *prefix forming nouns and adjectives.* in; into; inside: *endemic.* [from Greek (often via Latin); compare IN-[1], IN-[2]]

-en[1] *suffix forming verbs from adjectives and nouns.* cause to be; become; cause to have: *blacken; heighten.* [Old English *-n-,* as in *fæst-n-ian* to fasten, of common Germanic origin; compare Icelandic *fastna*]

-en[2] *suffix forming adjectives from nouns.* of; made of; resembling: *ashen; earthen; wooden.* [Old English *-en;* related to Gothic *-eins,* Latin *-īnus* -INE[1]]

enable (ɪn'eɪbᵊl) *vb.* (*tr.*) **1.** to provide (someone) with adequate power, means, opportunity, or authority (to do something). **2.** to make possible. **3.** to put (a digital electronic circuit element) into an operative condition by supplying a suitable input pulse. —**en'ablement** *n.* —**en'abler** *n.*

enabling act *n.* a legislative act conferring certain specified powers on a person or organization.

enact (ɪn'ækt) *vb.* (*tr.*) **1.** to make into an act or statute. **2.** to establish by law; ordain or decree. **3.** to represent or perform in or as if in a play; to act out. —**en'actable** *adj.* —**en'active** *or* **en'actory** *adj.* —**en'actment** *or* **en'action** *n.* —**en'actor** *n.*

enamel (ɪ'næməl) *n.* **1.** a coloured glassy substance, translucent or opaque, fused to the surface of articles made of metal, glass, etc., for ornament or protection. **2.** an article or articles ornamented with enamel. **3.** an enamel-like paint or varnish. **4.** any smooth glossy coating resembling enamel. **5.** another word for **nail polish. 6.** the hard white calcified substance that covers the crown of each tooth. **7.** (*modifier*) **a.** decorated or covered with enamel: *an enamel ring.* **b.** made with enamel:

enamel paste. ~*vb.* **-els, -elling, -elled** *or U.S.* **-els, -eling, -eled.** (*tr.*) **8.** to inlay, coat, or otherwise decorate with enamel. **9.** to ornament with glossy variegated colours, as if with enamel. **10.** to portray in enamel. [C15: from Old French *esmail,* of Germanic origin; compare Old High German *smalz* lard; see SMELT[1]] —**e'nameller, e'namellist** *or U.S.* **e'nameler, e'namelist** *n.* —**e'namel,work** *n.*

enamour *or U.S.* **enamor** (ɪn'æmə) *vb.* (*tr.; usually passive* and foll. by *of*) to inspire with love; captivate; charm. [C14: from Old French *enamourer,* from *amour* love, from Latin *amor*] —**en'amoured** *or U.S.* **en'amored** *adj.*

enantiomer (ɛn'æntɪəmə) *n. Chem.* a molecule that exhibits stereoisomerism because of the presence of one or more chiral centres.

enantiomorph (ɛn'æntɪə,mɔːf) *n.* either of the two crystal forms of a substance that are mirror images of each other. [C19: from Greek *enantios* opposite + -MORPH] —**en,antio'morphic** *adj.* —**en,antio'morphism** *n.*

enarthrosis (,ɛnɑː'θrəʊsɪs) *n., pl.* **-ses** (-siːz). *Anatomy.* a ball-and-socket joint, such as that of the hip. [C17: via New Latin from Greek, from *arthrōsis,* from *arthron* a joint + -OSIS] —,**enar'throdial** *adj.*

enate ('iːneɪt) *adj. also* **enatic** (iː'nætɪk). **1.** *Biology.* growing out or outwards. **2.** related on the side of the mother. ~*n.* **3.** a relative on the mother's side. [C17: from Latin *ēnātus,* from *ēnāscī* to be born from, from *nāscī* to be born]

en attendant *French.* (ɑ̃n atɑ̃dɑ̃) *adv.* in the mean time; while waiting.

en bloc *French.* (ɑ̃ blɔk) *adv.* in a lump or block; as a body or whole; all together.

en brochette *French.* (ɑ̃ brɔʃɛt) *adj., adv.* (esp. of meat) roasted or grilled on a skewer. [literally: on a skewer]

en brosse *French.* (ɑ̃ brɔs) *adj., adv.* (of the hair) cut very short so that the hair stands up stiffly. [literally: in the style of a brush]

enc. *abbrev. for:* **1.** enclosed. **2.** enclosure.

encaenia (ɛn'siːnɪə) *n. Rare.* a festival of dedication or commemoration. [C14: via Late Latin from Greek *enkainia,* from *kainos* new]

encage (ɪn'keɪdʒ) *vb.* (*tr.*) to confine in or as in a cage.

encamp (ɪn'kæmp) *vb.* to lodge or cause to lodge in a camp.

encampment (ɪn'kæmpmənt) *n.* **1.** the act of setting up a camp. **2.** the place where a camp, esp. a military camp, is set up.

encapsulate *or* **incapsulate** (ɪn'kæpsjʊ,leɪt) *vb.* **1.** to enclose or be enclosed in or as if in a capsule. **2.** (*tr.*) to put in a short or concise form; condense; abridge. —**en,capsu'lation** *or* **in,capsu'lation** *n.*

encarnalize *or* **encarnalise** (ɪn'kɑːnə,laɪz) *vb.* (*tr.*) *Rare.* **1.** to provide with a bodily form; incarnate. **2.** to make carnal, gross, or sensual.

encase *or* **incase** (ɪn'keɪs) *vb.* (*tr.*) to place or enclose in or as if in a case. —**en'casement** *or* **in'casement** *n.*

encash (ɪn'kæʃ) *vb.* (*tr.*) *Brit., formal.* to exchange (a cheque) for cash. —**en'cashable** *adj.* —**en'cashment** *n.*

encastré (ɛn'kɑːstreɪ) *adj. Civil engineering.* (of a beam) fixed at the ends; built into its supports. [from French, past participle of *encastrer,* from Latin *incastrare* to cut in; see CASTRATE]

encaustic (ɪn'kɒstɪk) *Ceramics, etc.* ~*adj.* **1.** decorated by any process involving burning in colours, esp. by inlaying coloured clays and baking or by fusing wax colours to the surface. ~*n.* **2.** the process of burning in colours. **3.** a product of such a process. [C17: from Latin *encausticus,* from Greek *enkaustikos,* from *enkaiein* to burn in, from *kaiein* to burn] —**en'caustically** *adv.*

-ence *or* **-ency** *suffix forming nouns.* indicating an action, state, condition, or quality: *benevolence; residence; patience.* [via Old French from Latin *-entia,* from *-ēns,* present participial ending]

enceinte[1] (ɒn'sænt; *French* ɑ̃sɛ̃t) *adj.* another word for **pregnant.** [C17: from French, from Latin *inciēns* pregnant; related to Greek *enkuos,* from *kuein* to be pregnant]

enceinte[2] (ɒn'sænt; *French* ɑ̃sɛ̃t) *n.* **1.** a boundary wall enclosing a defended area. **2.** the area enclosed. [C18: from French: enclosure, from *enceindre* to encompass, from Latin *incingere,* from *cingere* to gird]

encephalalgia (ɛn,sɛfə'lældʒɪə) *n. Med.* pain in the head; headache.

encephalic (,ɛnsɪ'fælɪk, ,ɛnkɪ-) *adj.* of or relating to the brain.

encephalin (ɛn'sɛfəlɪn) *n.* a variant of **enkephalin.**

encephalitis (,ɛnsɛfə'laɪtɪs, ,ɛnkɛf-) *n.* inflammation of the brain. —**encephalitic** (,ɛnsɛfə'lɪtɪk) *adj.*

encephalitis lethargica (lɪ'θɑːdʒɪkə) *n. Pathol.* a technical name for **sleeping sickness** (sense 2).

encephalo- *or before a vowel* **encephal-** *combining form.* indicating the brain: *encephalogram; encephalitis.* [from New Latin, from Greek *enkephalos,* from *en-* in + *kephalē* head]

encephalogram (ɛn'sɛfələ,græm) *n.* **1.** an x-ray photograph of the brain, esp. one (a **pneumoencephalogram**) taken after replacing some of the cerebrospinal fluid with air or oxygen so that the brain cavities show clearly. **2.** short for **electroencephalogram.**

encephalograph (ɛn'sɛfələ,grɑːf, -,græf) *n.* **1.** short for **electroencephalograph. 2.** any other apparatus used to produce an encephalogram.

encephalography (,ɛnsɛfə'lɒgrəfɪ) *n.* **1.** the branch of medical science concerned with taking and analysing x-ray photographs of the brain. **2.** another name for **electroencephalography.** —**encephalographic** (ɛn,sɛfələ'græfɪk) *adj.* —**en,cephalo'graphically** *adv.*

encephaloma (,ɛnsɛfə'ləʊmə) *n., pl.* **-mas** *or* **-mata** (-mətə). a brain tumour.

encephalomyelitis (ɛn,sɛfələʊ,maɪə'laɪtɪs) *n.* acute inflammation of the brain and spinal cord. —**encephalomyelitic** (ɛn,sɛfələʊ,maɪə'lɪtɪk) *adj.*

encephalon (ɛn'sɛfə,lɒn) *n., pl.* **-la** (-lə). a technical name for **brain.** [C18: from New Latin, from Greek *enkephalos* brain (literally: that which is in the head), from EN-[2] + *kephalē* head] —**en'cephalous** *adj.*

encephalopathy (ɛn,sɛfə'lɒpəθɪ) *n.* any degenerative disease of the brain, often associated with toxic conditions. See also **BSE.**

enchain (ɪn'tʃeɪn) *vb.* (*tr.*) **1.** to bind with chains. **2.** to hold fast or captivate (the attention, etc.). —**en'chainment** *n.*

enchant (ɪn'tʃɑːnt) *vb.* (*tr.*) **1.** to cast a spell on; bewitch. **2.** to delight or captivate utterly; fascinate; charm. [C14: from Old French *enchanter,* from Latin *incantāre* to chant a spell, from *cantāre* to chant, from *canere* to sing] —**en'chanted** *adj.* —**en'chanter** *n.* —**en'chantress** *fem. n.*

enchanter's nightshade *n.* any of several onagraceous plants of the genus *Circaea,* esp. *C. lutetiana,* having small white flowers and bristly fruits.

enchanting (ɪn'tʃɑːntɪŋ) *adj.* pleasant; delightful. —**en'chantingly** *adv.*

enchantment (ɪn'tʃɑːntmənt) *n.* **1.** the act of enchanting or state of being enchanted. **2.** a magic spell or act of witchcraft. **3.** great charm or fascination.

enchase (ɪn'tʃeɪs) *vb.* (*tr.*) a less common word for **chase**[3]. [C15: from Old French *enchasser* to enclose, set, from EN-[1] + *casse* CASE[2]] —**en'chaser** *n.*

enchilada (,ɛntʃɪ'lɑːdə) *n.* a Mexican dish consisting of a tortilla fried in hot fat, filled with meat, and served with a chilli sauce. [C19: American Spanish, feminine of *enchilado* seasoned with chilli, from *enchilar* to spice with chilli, from *chile* CHILLI]

enchiridion (,ɛnkaɪ'rɪdɪən) *n., pl.* **-ions** *or* **-ia** (-ɪə). *Rare.* a handbook or manual. [C16: from Late Latin, from Greek *enkheiridion,* from EN-[2] + *kheir* hand]

enchondroma (,ɛnkən'drəʊmə) *n., pl.* **-mas** *or* **-mata** (-mətə). *Pathol.* a benign cartilaginous tumour, most commonly in the bones of the hands or feet. [C19: New Latin from Greek, from EN-[2] + *khondros* cartilage] —,**enchon'dromatous** *adj.*

enchorial (ɛn'kɔːrɪəl) *or* **enchoric** *adj.* of or used in a particular country: used esp. of the popular (demotic) writing of the ancient Egyptians. [C19: via Late Latin from Greek *enkhōrios,* from EN-[2] + *khōra* country]

-enchyma *combining form.* denoting cellular tissue: *aerenchyma.* [C20: abstracted from PARENCHYMA]

encipher (ɪn'saɪfə) *vb.* (*tr.*) to convert (a message, document, etc.) from plain text into code or cipher; encode. —**en'cipherer** *n.* —**en'cipherment** *n.*

encircle (ɪn'sɜːkᵊl) *vb.* (*tr.*) to form a circle around; enclose within a circle; surround. —**en'circlement** *n.* —**en'circling** *adj.*

encl. *abbrev. for:* **1.** enclosed. **2.** enclosure.

en clair *French.* (ɑ̃ klɛr) *adv., adj.* in ordinary language; not in cipher. [literally: in clear]

enclasp (ɪn'klɑːsp) *vb.* (*tr.*) to clasp; embrace.

enclave ('ɛnkleɪv) *n.* a part of a country entirely surrounded by foreign territory: viewed from the position of the surrounding territories. Compare **exclave.** [C19: from French, from Old French *enclaver* to enclose, from Vulgar Latin *inclāvāre* (unattested) to lock up, from Latin IN-[2] + *clavis* key]

enclitic (ɪn'klɪtɪk) *adj.* **1. a.** denoting or relating to a monosyllabic word or form that is treated as a suffix of the preceding word, as Latin *-que* in *populusque.* **b.** (in classical Greek) denoting or relating to a word that throws an accent back onto the preceding word. ~*n.* **2.** an enclitic word or linguistic form. ~Compare **proclitic.** [C17: from Late Latin *encliticus,* from Greek *enklitikos,* from *enklinein* to cause to lean, from EN-[2] + *klinein* to lean] —**en'clitically** *adv.*

enclose *or* **inclose** (ɪn'kləʊz) *vb.* (*tr.*) **1.** to close; hem in; surround. **2.** to surround (land) with or as if with a fence. **3.** to put in an envelope or wrapper, esp. together with a letter. **4.** to contain or hold. —**en'closable** *or* **in'closable** *adj.* —**en'closer** *or* **in'closer** *n.*

enclosed order *n.* a Christian religious order that does not permit its members to go into the outside world.

enclosure *or* **inclosure** (ɪn'kləʊʒə) *n.* **1.** the act of enclosing or state of being enclosed. **2.** a region or area enclosed by or as if by a fence. **3. a.** the act of appropriating land, esp. common land, by putting a hedge or other barrier around it. **b.** *History.* such acts as were carried out at various periods in England, esp. between the 12th and 14th centuries and finally in the 18th and 19th centuries. **4.** a fence, wall, etc., that serves to enclose. **5.** something, esp. a supporting document, enclosed within an envelope or wrapper, esp. together with a letter. **6.** *Brit.* a section of a sports ground, racecourse, etc., allotted to certain spectators.

encode (ɪnˈkəʊd) *vb. (tr.)* **1.** to convert (a message) from plain text into code. **2.** *Computer technol.* to convert (characters and symbols) into a digital form as a series of impulses. Compare **decode** (sense 2). **3.** to convert (an electrical signal) into a form suitable for transmission. **4.** to convert (a nerve signal) into a form that can be received by the brain. **5.** to use (a word, phrase, etc., esp. of a foreign language) in the construction appropriate to it in that language. —**enˈcodement** *n.* —**enˈcoder** *n.*

encomiast (ɛnˈkəʊmɪˌæst) *n.* a person who speaks or writes an encomium. [C17: from Greek *enkōmiastēs*, from *enkōmiazein* to utter an ENCOMIUM] —**enˌcomiˈastic** *or* **enˌcomiˈastical** *adj.* —**enˌcomiˈastically** *adv.*

encomium (ɛnˈkəʊmɪəm) *n., pl.* **-miums** *or* **-mia** (-mɪə). a formal expression of praise; eulogy; panegyric. [C16: from Latin, from Greek *enkōmion*, from EN-[2] + *kōmos* festivity]

encompass (ɪnˈkʌmpəs) *vb. (tr.)* **1.** to enclose within a circle; surround. **2.** to bring about; cause to happen; contrive: *he encompassed the enemy's ruin.* **3.** to include entirely or comprehensively: *this book encompasses the whole range of knowledge.* —**enˈcompassment** *n.*

encopresis (ˌɛnkəʊˈpriːsɪs) *n.* involuntary discharge of faeces, esp. when associated with psychiatric disturbance. [C20: from New Latin, from Greek EN-[2] + COPR-, + *-esis* as in ENURESIS] —**encopretic** (ˌɛnkəʊˈprɛtɪk) *adj.*

encore (ˈɒŋkɔː) *interj.* **1.** again; once more: used by an audience to demand an extra or repeated performance. ~*n.* **2.** an extra or repeated performance given in response to enthusiastic demand. ~*vb.* **3.** *(tr.)* to demand an extra or repeated performance of (a work, piece of music, etc.) by (a performer). [C18: from French: still, again, perhaps from Latin *in hanc hōram* until this hour]

encounter (ɪnˈkaʊntə) *vb.* **1.** to come upon or meet casually or unexpectedly. **2.** to come into conflict with (an enemy, army, etc.) in battle or contest. **3.** *(tr.)* to be faced with; contend with: *he encounters many obstacles in his work.* ~*n.* **4.** a meeting with a person or thing, esp. when casual or unexpected. **5.** a hostile meeting; contest or conflict. [C13: from Old French *encontrer*, from Vulgar Latin *incontrāre* (unattested), from Latin IN-[2] + *contrā* against, opposite] —**enˈcounterer** *n.*

encounter group *n.* a group of people who meet in order to develop self-awareness and mutual understanding by openly expressing their feelings, by confrontation, physical contact, etc.

encourage (ɪnˈkʌrɪdʒ) *vb. (tr.)* **1.** to inspire (someone) with the courage or confidence (to do something). **2.** to stimulate (something or someone to do something) by approval or help; support. —**enˈcouragement** *n.* —**enˈcourager** *n.* —**enˈcouraging** *adj.* —**enˈcouragingly** *adv.*

encrinite (ˈɛnkrɪˌnaɪt) *n.* a fossil crinoid, esp. one of the genus *Encrinus*. Sometimes shortened to **crinite.** [C19: from New Latin *encrinus* (from Greek EN-[2] + *krinon* lily) + -ITE[1]]

encroach (ɪnˈkrəʊtʃ) *vb. (intr.)* **1.** (often foll. by *on* or *upon*) to intrude gradually, stealthily, or insidiously upon the rights, property, etc., of another. **2.** to advance beyond the usual or proper limits. [C14: from Old French *encrochier* to seize, literally: fasten upon with hooks, from EN-[1] + *croc* hook, of Germanic origin; see CROOK] —**enˈcroacher** *n.* —**enˈcroachingly** *adv.* —**enˈcroachment** *n.*

encrust *or* **incrust** (ɪnˈkrʌst) *vb.* **1.** *(tr.)* to cover or overlay with or as with a crust or hard coating. **2.** to form or cause to form a crust or hard coating. **3.** *(tr.)* to decorate lavishly, as with jewels. —ˌ**encrusˈtation** *or* ˌ**incrusˈtation** *n.*

encrypt (ɪnˈkrɪpt) *vb. (tr.)* **1.** to put (a message) into code. **2.** to put (computer data) into a coded form. **3.** to distort (a television or other signal) so that it cannot be understood without the appropriate decryption equipment. [C20: from EN-[1] + *crypt*, as in CRYPTO-] —**enˈcrypted** *adj.* —**enˈcryption** *n.*

enculturation (ɛnˌkʌltʃʊˈreɪʃən) *n.* another word for **socialization.** —**enculturative** (ɛnˈkʌltʃʊrətɪv) *adj.*

encumber *or* **incumber** (ɪnˈkʌmbə) *vb. (tr.)* **1.** to hinder or impede; make difficult; hamper: *encumbered with parcels after going shopping at Christmas; his stupidity encumbers his efforts to learn.* **2.** to fill with superfluous or useless matter. **3.** to burden with debts, obligations, etc. [C14: from Old French *encombrer*, from EN-[1] + *combre* a barrier, from Late Latin *combrus*, of uncertain origin] —**enˈcumberingly** *or* **inˈcumberingly** *adv.*

encumbrance *or* **incumbrance** (ɪnˈkʌmbrəns) *n.* **1.** a thing that impedes or is burdensome; hindrance. **2.** *Law.* a burden or charge upon property, such as a mortgage or lien. **3.** *Rare.* a dependent person, esp. a child.

encumbrancer (ɪnˈkʌmbrənsə) *n. Law.* a person who holds an encumbrance on property belonging to another.

ency., encyc., *or* **encycl.** *abbrev. for* encyclopedia.

-ency *suffix forming nouns.* a variant of **-ence:** *fluency; permanency.*

encyclical (ɛnˈsɪklɪkəl) *n.* **1.** a letter sent by the pope to all Roman Catholic bishops throughout the world. ~*adj. also* **encyclic. 2.** (of letters) intended for general or wide circulation. [C17: from Late Latin *encyclicus*, from Greek *enkuklios* general, from *kuklos* circle]

encyclopedia *or* **encyclopaedia** (ɛnˌsaɪkləʊˈpiːdɪə) *n.* a book, often in many volumes, containing articles on various topics, often arranged in alphabetical order, dealing either with the whole range of human knowledge or with one particular subject: *a medical encyclopedia.* [C16: from New Latin *encyclopaedia*, erroneously for Greek *enkuklios paideia* general education, from *enkuklios* general (see ENCYCLICAL), + *paideia* education, from *pais* child]

encyclopedic *or* **encyclopaedic** (ɛnˌsaɪkləʊˈpiːdɪk) *adj.* **1.** of, characteristic of, or relating to an encyclopedia. **2.** covering a wide range of knowledge; comprehensive. —**enˌcycloˈpedically** *or* **enˌcycloˈpaedically** *adv.*

encyclopedist *or* **encyclopaedist** (ɛnˌsaɪkləʊˈpiːdɪst) *n.* a person who compiles or contributes to an encyclopedia. —**enˌcycloˈpedism** *or* **enˌcycloˈpaedism** *n.*

encyst (ɛnˈsɪst) *vb. Biology.* to enclose or become enclosed by a cyst, thick membrane, or shell. —**enˈcysted** *adj.* —**enˈcystment** *or* ˌ**encysˈtation** *n.*

end[1] (ɛnd) *n.* **1.** the extremity of the length of something, such as a road, line, etc. **2.** the surface at either extremity of a three-dimensional object. **3.** the extreme extent, limit, or degree of something. **4.** the most distant place or time that can be imagined: *the ends of the earth.* **5.** the time at which something is concluded. **6. a.** the last section or part. **b.** (*as modifier*): *the end office.* **7.** a share or part: *his end of the bargain; to keep one's end up.* **8.** (*often pl.*) a remnant or fragment (esp. in the phrase **odds and ends**). **9.** a final state, esp. death; destruction. **10.** the purpose of an action or existence. **11.** *Sport.* either of the two defended areas of a playing field, rink, etc. **12.** *Bowls.* a section of play from one side of the green to the other. **13.** *American and Canadian football.* a player at the extremity of the playing line; wing. **14. all ends up.** totally or completely. **15. a sticky end.** *Informal.* an unpleasant death. **16. at a loose end** *or* (*U.S. and Canadian*) **at loose ends.** without purpose or occupation. **17. at an end.** exhausted or completed. **18. come to an end.** to become completed or exhausted. **19. end on. a.** with the end pointing towards one. **b.** with the end adjacent to the end of another object. **20. go off the deep end.** *Informal.* to lose one's temper; react angrily. **21. in the end.** finally. **22. make (both) ends meet.** to spend no more than the money one has. **23. no end (of).** *Informal.* (intensifier): *I had no end of work.* **24. on end. a.** upright. **b.** without pause or interruption. **25. the end.** *Informal.* **a.** the worst, esp. something that goes beyond the limits of endurance. **b.** *Chiefly U.S.* the best in quality. **26. the end of the road.** the point beyond which survival or continuation is impossible. **27. throw (someone) in at the deep end.** to put (someone) into a new situation, job, etc., without preparation or introduction. Related adjs.: **final, terminal, ultimate.** ~*vb.* **28.** to bring or come to a finish; conclude. **29.** to die or cause to die. **30.** *(tr.)* surpass; outdo: *a novel to end all novels.* **31. end it all.** *Informal.* to commit suicide. ~See also **end up.** [Old English *ende;* related to Old Norse *endir*, Gothic *andeis*, Old High German *endi*, Latin *antiae* forelocks, Sanskrit *antya* last] —ˈ**ender** *n.*

end[2] (ɛnd) *vb. (tr.) Brit.* to put (hay or grain) into a barn or stack. [Old English *innian;* related to Old High German *innōn;* see INN]

end- *combining form.* a variant of **endo-** before a vowel.

-end *suffix forming nouns.* See **-and.**

end-all *n.* short for **be-all and end-all.**

endamage (ɛnˈdæmɪdʒ) *vb. (tr.)* to cause injury to; damage. —**enˈdamagement** *n.*

endamoeba *or U.S.* **endameba** (ˌɛndəˈmiːbə) *n., pl.* **-bae** (-biː) *or* **-bas.** variants of **entamoeba.**

endanger (ɪnˈdeɪndʒə) *vb. (tr.)* to put in danger or peril; imperil. —**enˈdangerment** *n.*

endangered (ɪnˈdeɪndʒəd) *adj.* in danger: used esp. of animals in danger of extinction: *the giant panda is an endangered species.*

endarch (ˈɛndˌɑːk) *adj. Botany.* (of a xylem strand) having the first-formed xylem internal to that formed later. Compare **exarch**[2], **mesarch.** [C20: from ENDO- + Greek *arkhē* beginning]

en dash *or* **rule** *n. Printing.* a dash (–) one en long.

end-blown *adj. Music.* (of a recorder) held downwards and blown through one end.

endbrain (ˈɛndˌbreɪn) *n. Anatomy.* another name for **telencephalon.**

endear (ɪnˈdɪə) *vb. (tr.)* to cause to be beloved or esteemed. —**enˈdearing** *adj.* —**enˈdearingly** *adv.*

endearment (ɪnˈdɪəmənt) *n.* **1.** something that endears, such as an affectionate utterance. **2.** the act or process of endearing or the condition of being endeared.

endeavour *or U.S.* **endeavor** (ɪnˈdɛvə) *vb.* **1.** to try (to do something). ~*n.* **2.** an effort to do or attain something. [C14 *endeveren*, from EN-[1] + *-deveren* from *dever* duty, from Old French *deveir;* see DEVOIRS] —**enˈdeavourer** *or U.S.* **enˈdeavorer** *n.*

endemic (ɛnˈdɛmɪk) *adj. also* **endemial** (ɛnˈdɛmɪəl) *or* **endemical. 1.** present within a localized area or peculiar to persons in such an area. ~*n.* **2.** an endemic disease or plant. [C18: from New Latin *endēmicus*, from Greek *endēmos* native, from EN-[2] + *dēmos* the people] —**enˈdemically** *adv.* —ˈ**endemism** *or* ˌ**endeˈmicity** *n.*

endergonic (ˌɛndəˈgɒnɪk) *adj.* (of a biochemical reaction) requiring energy to proceed. Compare **exergonic.** [C20: from END(O)- + Greek *ergon* work + -IC]

endermic (ɛnˈdɜːmɪk) *adj.* (of a medicine) acting by absorption through the skin. [C19: from EN-[2] + Greek *derma* skin]

endgame ('ɛnd,geɪm) *n.* **1.** Also called: **ending.** the closing stage of a game of chess, in which only a few pieces are left on the board. **2.** the closing stage of any of certain other games.

ending ('ɛndɪŋ) *n.* **1.** the act of bringing to or reaching an end. **2.** the last part of something, as a book, film, etc. **3.** the final part of a word, esp. a suffix. **4.** *Chess.* another word for **endgame.**

endive ('ɛndaɪv) *n.* a plant, *Cichorium endivia,* cultivated for its crisp curly leaves, which are used in salads: family *Compositae* (composites). Compare **chicory.** [C15: from Old French, from Medieval Latin *endīvia,* variant of Latin *intubus, entubus,* of uncertain origin]

endless ('ɛndlɪs) *adj.* **1.** having or seeming to have no end; eternal or infinite. **2.** continuing too long or continually recurring. **3.** formed with the ends joined: *an endless belt.* —'**endlessly** *adv.* —'**endlessness** *n.*

endlong ('ɛnd,lɒŋ) *adv. Archaic.* lengthways or on end.

end matter *n.* another name for **back matter.**

endmost ('ɛnd,məʊst) *adj.* nearest the end; most distant.

endo- *or before a vowel* **end-** *combining form.* inside; within: *endocrine.* [from Greek, from *endon* within]

endobiotic (,ɛndəʊbaɪ'ɒtɪk) *adj.* **1.** (of a plant) growing within another plant. **2.** formed within a host cell.

endoblast ('ɛndəʊ,blæst) *n.* **1.** *Embryol.* a less common name for **endoderm. 2.** another name for **hypoblast** (sense 1). —,**endo'blastic** *adj.*

endocardial (,ɛndəʊ'kɑːdɪəl) *or* **endocardiac** *adj.* **1.** of or relating to the endocardium. **2.** within the heart.

endocarditis (,ɛndəʊkɑː'daɪtɪs) *n.* inflammation of the endocardium. —**endocarditic** (,ɛndəʊkɑː'dɪtɪk) *adj.*

endocardium (,ɛndəʊ'kɑːdɪəm) *n., pl.* **-dia** (-dɪə). the membrane that lines the cavities of the heart and forms part of the valves. [C19: from New Latin, from ENDO- + Greek *kardia* heart]

endocarp ('ɛndə,kɑːp) *n.* the inner, usually woody, layer of the pericarp of a fruit, such as the stone of a peach or cherry. —,**endo'carpal** *or* ,**endo'carpic** *adj.*

endocentric (,ɛndəʊ'sɛntrɪk) *adj. Grammar.* (of a construction) fulfilling the grammatical role of one of its constituents; as in *three blind mice,* where the whole noun phrase fulfills the same role as its head noun *mice.* Compare **exocentric.**

endocranial cast (,ɛndəʊ'kreɪnɪəl) *n.* a cast made of the inside of a cranial cavity to show the size and shape of the brain: used esp. in anthropology. Sometimes shortened to **endocast.**

endocranium (,ɛndəʊ'kreɪnɪəm) *n., pl.* **-nia** (-nɪə). *Anatomy.* the thick fibrous membrane that lines the cranial cavity and forms the outermost layer of the dura mater.

endocrine ('ɛndəʊ,kraɪn, -krɪn) *adj. also* **endocrinal** (,ɛndəʊ'kraɪnᵊl), **endocrinic** (,ɛndəʊ'krɪnɪk), *or* **endocrinous** (ɛn'dɒkrɪnəs). **1.** of or denoting endocrine glands or their secretions: *endocrine disorders.* ~*n.* **2.** an endocrine gland. ~Compare **exocrine.** [C20: from ENDO- + *-crine,* from Greek *krinein* to separate]

endocrine gland *n.* any of the glands that secrete hormones directly into the bloodstream, including the pituitary, pineal, thyroid, parathyroid, adrenal, testes, ovaries, and the pancreatic islets of Langerhans. Also called: **ductless gland.**

endocrinology (,ɛndəʊkraɪ'nɒlədʒɪ, -krɪ-) *n.* the branch of medical science concerned with the endocrine glands and their secretions. —**endocrinologic** (,ɛndəʊ,krɪnə'lɒdʒɪk) *or* ,**endo,crino'logical** *adj.* —,**endocri'nologist** *n.*

endocrinopathy (,ɛndəʊkrɪ'nɒpəθɪ) *n.* any disease due to disorder of the endocrine system. —**endocrinopathic** (,ɛndəʊ,krɪnəʊ'pæθɪk) *adj.*

endocuticle ('ɛndəʊ,kjuːtɪkᵊl) *n.* the inner layer of the cuticle of an insect.

endocytosis (,ɛndəʊsaɪ'təʊsɪs) *n.* the process by which a living cell takes up molecules bound to its surface.

endoderm ('ɛndəʊ,dɜːm) *or* **entoderm** *n.* the inner germ layer of an animal embryo, which gives rise to the lining of the digestive and respiratory tracts. See also **ectoderm** and **mesoderm.** —,**endo'dermal,** ,**endo'dermic** *or* ,**ento'dermal,** ,**ento'dermic** *adj.*

endodermis (,ɛndəʊ'dɜːmɪs) *n. Botany.* the specialized innermost layer of cortex in roots and some stems, which controls the passage of water and dissolved substances between the cortex and stele. [C19: from New Latin, from ENDO- + Greek *derma* skin]

endodontics (,ɛndəʊ'dɒntɪks) *n.* (*functioning as sing.*) the branch of dentistry concerned with diseases of the dental pulp. [C19: from New Latin *endodontia,* from ENDO- + Greek *odōn* tooth] —,**endo'dontal** *or* ,**endo'dontic** *adj.* —,**endo'dontist** *n.*

endoenzyme (,ɛndəʊ'ɛnzaɪm) *n.* any of a group of enzymes, esp. endopeptidases, that act upon inner chemical bonds in a chain of molecules. Compare **exoenzyme** (sense 1).

endoergic (,ɛndəʊ'ɜːdʒɪk) *adj.* (of a nuclear reaction) occurring with absorption of energy, as opposed to *exoergic.* Compare **endothermic.** [from ENDO- + *-ergic* from Greek *ergon* work]

end of steel *n. Canadian.* **1.** a point up to which railway tracks have been laid. **2.** a town located at such a point.

endogamy (ɛn'dɒgəmɪ) *n.* **1.** *Anthropol.* marriage within one's own tribe or similar unit. Compare **exogamy** (sense 1). **2.** pollination between two flowers on the same plant. —**en'dogamous** *or* **endogamic** (,ɛndəʊ'gæmɪk) *adj.*

endogen ('ɛndəʊ,dʒɛn) *n.* a former name for **monocotyledon.**

endogenous (ɛn'dɒdʒɪnəs) *adj.* **1.** *Biology.* developing or originating within an organism or part of an organism: *endogenous rhythms.* **2.** having no apparent external cause: *endogenous depression.* —**en'dogenously** *adv.* —**en'dogeny** *n.*

endolithic (,ɛndəʊ'lɪθɪk) *adj.* (of plants, such as algae) growing inside rock.

endolymph ('ɛndəʊ,lɪmf) *n.* the fluid that fills the membranous labyrinth of the internal ear. —**endolymphatic** (,ɛndəʊlɪm'fætɪk) *adj.*

endometriosis (,ɛndəʊ,miːtrɪ'əʊsɪs) *n. Pathol.* the presence of endometrium in areas other than the lining of the uterus, as on the ovaries, resulting in premenstrual pain.

endometritis (,ɛndəʊmɪ'traɪtɪs) *n.* inflammation of the endometrium, which is caused by infection, as by bacteria, foreign bodies, etc.

endometrium (,ɛndəʊ'miːtrɪəm) *n., pl.* **-tria** (-trɪə). the mucous membrane that lines the uterus. [C19: New Latin, from ENDO- + Greek *mētra* uterus] —,**endo'metrial** *adj.*

endomitosis (,ɛndəʊmaɪ'təʊsɪs) *n. Biology.* the division of chromosomes but not of the cell nucleus, resulting in a polyploid cell.

endomorph ('ɛndəʊ,mɔːf) *n.* **1.** a person with a fat and heavy body build: said to be correlated with viscerotonia. Compare **ectomorph, mesomorph. 2.** a mineral that naturally occurs enclosed within another mineral, as within quartz. —,**endo'morphic** *adj.* —'**endo,morphy** *n.*

endomorphism (,ɛndəʊ'mɔː,fɪzəm) *n. Geology.* a type of metamorphism in which changes are induced in the cooling molten rock material by contact with the older rocks surrounding it.

endoneurium (,ɛndəʊ'njʊərɪəm) *n.* the delicate connective tissue surrounding nerve fibres within a bundle. [New Latin, from ENDO- + NEURO- + -IUM]

endonuclease (,ɛndəʊ'njuːklɪ,eɪz) *n.* an enzyme that is responsible for scission of a nucleic acid chain, the action of which is not confined to the terminal nucleotide. Compare **exonuclease.**

endoparasite (,ɛndəʊ'pærə,saɪt) *n.* a parasite, such as the tapeworm, that lives within the body of its host. —**endoparasitic** (,ɛndəʊ,pærə'sɪtɪk) *adj.*

endopeptidase (,ɛndəʊ'pɛptɪ,deɪz) *n.* any proteolytic enzyme, such as pepsin, that splits a protein into smaller peptide fragments. Also called: **proteinase.** Compare **exopeptidase.**

endophyte ('ɛndəʊ,faɪt) *n.* any plant, such as a parasitic fungus, that lives within another plant. —**endophytic** (,ɛndəʊ'fɪtɪk) *adj.* —,**endo'phytically** *adv.*

endoplasm ('ɛndəʊ,plæzəm) *n. Cytology.* the inner cytoplasm that in many cells is more granular and fluid than the outer cytoplasm (see **ectoplasm** (sense 1)). —,**endo'plasmic** *adj.*

endoplasmic reticulum *n.* an extensive intracellular membrane system in which certain proteins are synthesized by particles (ribosomes) attached to the membrane, for transport through or secretion from the cell.

end organ *n. Anatomy.* the expanded end of a peripheral motor or sensory nerve.

endorphin (ɛn'dɔːfɪn) *n.* any of a class of polypeptides, including enkephalin, occurring naturally in the brain, that bind to pain receptors and so block pain sensation. [C20: from ENDO- + MORPHINE]

endorse *or* **indorse** (ɪn'dɔːs) *vb.* (*tr.*) **1.** to give approval or sanction to. **2.** to sign (one's name) on the back of (a cheque, etc.) to specify oneself as payee. **3.** *Commerce.* **a.** to sign the back of (a negotiable document) to transfer ownership of the rights to a specified payee. **b.** to specify (a designated sum) as transferable to another as payee. **4.** to write (a qualifying comment, recommendation, etc.) on the back of a document. **5.** to sign (a document), as when confirming receipt of payment. **6.** *Chiefly Brit.* to record (a conviction) on (a driving licence). [C16: from Old French *endosser* to put on the back, from EN-[1] + *dos* back, from Latin *dorsum*] —**en'dorsable** *or* **in'dorsable** *adj.* —**en'dorser, en'dorsor** *or* **in'dorser, in'dorsor** *n.*

endorsee (ɪn,dɔː'siː, ,ɛndɔː-) *or* **indorsee** *n.* the person in whose favour a negotiable instrument is endorsed.

endorsement *or* **indorsement** (ɪn'dɔːsmənt) *n.* **1.** the act or an instance of endorsing. **2.** something that endorses, such as a signature or qualifying comment. **3.** approval or support. **4.** a record of a motoring offence on a driving licence. **5.** *Insurance.* a clause in or amendment to an insurance policy allowing for alteration of coverage.

endoscope ('ɛndəʊ,skəʊp) *n.* a long slender medical instrument for examining the interior of hollow organs including the lung, stomach, bladder and bowel. —**endoscopic** (,ɛndəʊ'skɒpɪk) *adj.* —**endoscopist** (ɛn'dɒskəpɪst) *n.* —**en'doscopy** *n.*

endoskeleton (,ɛndəʊ'skɛlɪtᵊn) *n.* the internal skeleton of an animal, esp. the bony or cartilaginous skeleton of vertebrates. Compare **exoskeleton.** —,**endo'skeletal** *adj.*

endosmosis (,ɛndɒs'məʊsɪs, -dɒz-) *n. Biology.* osmosis in which water enters a cell or organism from the surrounding solution. Compare **exosmosis.** —**endosmotic** (,ɛndɒs'mɒtɪk, -dɒz-) *adj.* —,**endos'motically** *adv.*

endosperm ('ɛndəʊ,spɜːm) *n.* the tissue within the seed of a flowering plant that surrounds and nourishes the developing embryo. —,**endo'spermic** *adj.*

endospore ('ɛndəʊ,spɔː) *n.* **1.** a small asexual spore produced by some bacteria and algae. **2.** the innermost wall of a spore or pollen grain. —**endosporous** (ɛn'dɒspərəs, ,ɛndəʊ'spɔːrəs) *adj.*

endosteum (ɛnˈdɒstɪəm) *n., pl.* **-tea** (-tɪə). a highly vascular membrane lining the internal surface of long bones, such as the femur and humerus. [C19: New Latin, from ENDO- + Greek *osteon* bone] —**enˈdosteal** *adj.*

endostosis (ˌɛndɒsˈtəʊsɪs) *n., pl.* **-ses** (-siːz). the conversion of cartilage into bone.

endosymbiosis (ˌɛndəʊˌsɪmbɪˈəʊsɪs) *n.* a type of symbiosis in which one organism lives inside the other, the two typically behaving as a single organism.

endothecium (ˌɛndəʊˈθiːʃɪəm, -sɪəm) *n., pl.* **-cia** (-ʃɪə, -sɪə). *Botany.* **1.** the inner mass of cells of the developing capsule in mosses. **2.** the fibrous tissue of the inner wall of an anther. [C19: New Latin, from ENDO- + Greek *thēkion* case; see THECA] —ˌ**endoˈthecial** *adj.*

endothelioma (ˌɛndəʊˌθiːlɪˈəʊmə) *n., pl.* **-mata** (-mətə). *Pathol.* a tumour originating in endothelial tissue, such as the lining of blood vessels.

endothelium (ˌɛndəʊˈθiːlɪəm) *n., pl.* **-lia** (-lɪə). a tissue consisting of a single layer of cells that lines the blood and lymph vessels, heart, and some other cavities. [C19: New Latin, from ENDO- + *-thelium,* from Greek *thēlē* nipple] —ˌ**endoˈthelial** *adj.* —ˌ**endoˈtheliˌoid** *adj.*

endothermic (ˌɛndəʊˈθɜːmɪk) *or* **endothermal** *adj.* (of a chemical reaction or compound) occurring or formed with the absorption of heat from the surroundings. Compare **exothermic, endoergic.** —ˌ**endoˈthermically** *adv.* —ˌ**endoˈthermism** *n.*

endotoxin (ˌɛndəʊˈtɒksɪn) *n.* a toxin contained within the protoplasm of an organism, esp. a bacterium, and liberated only at death. —ˌ**endoˈtoxic** *adj.*

endotrophic (ˌɛndəʊˈtrɒfɪk) *adj. Botany.* denoting a type of mycorrhiza in which the fungus lives within the cells of the roots of the plant. Compare **ectotrophic.**

endow (ɪnˈdaʊ) *vb. (tr.)* **1.** to provide with or bequeath a source of permanent income. **2.** (usually foll. by *with*) to provide (with qualities, characteristics, etc.). **3.** *Obsolete.* to provide with a dower. [C14: from Old French *endouer,* from EN-[1] + *douer* from Latin *dōtāre,* from *dōs* dowry] —**enˈdower** *n.*

endowment (ɪnˈdaʊmənt) *n.* **1. a.** the source of income with which an institution, etc., is endowed. **b.** the income itself. **2.** the act or process of endowing. **3.** (*usually pl.*) natural talents or qualities. **4.** *Austral.* Also called: **child endowment.** a social security payment for dependent children.

endowment assurance *or* **insurance** *n.* a form of life insurance that provides for the payment of a specified sum directly to the policyholder at a designated date or to his beneficiary should he die before this date.

endowment mortgage *n.* an arrangement whereby a person takes out a mortgage and pays the capital repayment instalments into a life assurance policy and only the interest to the mortgagee during the term of the policy. The loan is repaid by the policy either when it matures or on the prior death of the policyholder.

endozoic (ˌɛndəʊˈzəʊɪk) *adj. Botany.* **1.** (of a plant) living within an animal. **2.** denoting seed dispersal in which the seeds are swallowed by an animal and subsequently pass out in the faeces.

endpaper (ˈɛndˌpeɪpə) *n.* either of two leaves at the front and back of a book pasted to the inside of the board covers and the first leaf of the book to secure the binding.

end pin *n. Music.* the adjustable metal spike attached to the bottom of a cello, double bass, etc., that supports it while it is being played.

endplate (ˈɛndˌpleɪt) *n.* **1.** any usually flat platelike structure at the end of something. **2.** *Physiol.* the flattened end of a motor nerve fibre, which transmits impulses to muscle.

endplay (ˈɛndˌpleɪ) *Bridge.* ~*n.* **1.** a way of playing the last few tricks in a hand so that an opponent is forced to make a particular lead. ~*vb. (tr.)* **2.** to force (an opponent) to make a particular lead near the end of a hand: *declarer endplayed West for the jack of spades.*

end point *n.* **1.** *Chem.* the point at which a titration is complete, usually marked by a change in colour of an indicator. **2.** the point at which anything is complete.

end product *n.* the final result or outcome of a process, series, endeavour, etc., esp. in manufacturing.

end-stopped *adj.* (of verse) having a pause at the end of each line.

endue *or* **indue** (ɪnˈdjuː) *vb.* **-dues, -duing, -dued.** *(tr.)* **1.** (usually foll. by *with*) to invest or provide, as with some quality or trait. **2.** *Rare.* to don or assume. **3.** *Rare.* (foll. by *with*) to clothe or dress (in). [C15: from Old French *enduire,* from Latin *indūcere,* from *dūcere* to lead]

end up *vb. (adv.)* **1.** (*copula*) to become eventually; turn out to be: *he ended up a thief.* **2.** *(intr.)* to arrive, esp. by a circuitous or lengthy route or process: *to end up in prison.*

endurance (ɪnˈdjʊərəns) *n.* **1.** the capacity, state, or an instance of enduring. **2.** something endured; a hardship, strain, or privation.

endure (ɪnˈdjʊə) *vb.* **1.** to undergo (hardship, strain, privation, etc.) without yielding; bear. **2.** *(tr.)* to permit or tolerate. **3.** *(intr.)* to last or continue to exist. [C14: from Old French *endurer,* from Latin *indūrāre* to harden, from *dūrus* hard] —**enˈdurable** *adj.* —**enˌduraˈbility** *or* **enˈdurableness** *n.* —**enˈdurably** *adv.*

enduring (ɪnˈdjʊərɪŋ) *adj.* **1.** permanent; lasting. **2.** having forbearance; long-suffering. —**enˈduringly** *adv.* —**enˈduringness** *n.*

end user *n.* **1. a.** (in international trading) the person, organization, or nation that will be the ultimate recipient of goods, esp. such as arms or advanced technology. **b.** (*as modifier*): *an end-user certificate.* **2.** *Computer technol.* the ultimate destination, such as a program or operator, of information that is being transferred within a system.

endways (ˈɛndˌweɪz) *or esp. U.S. and Canadian* **endwise** (ˈɛndˌwaɪz) *adv.* **1.** having the end forwards or upwards. ~*adj.* **2.** vertical or upright. **3.** lengthways. **4.** standing or lying end to end.

endysis (ɛnˈdaɪsɪs) *n. Zoology.* the formation of new layers of integument after ecdysis.

end zone *n. American football.* the area behind the goals at each end of the field that the ball must cross for a touchdown to be awarded.

ENE *symbol for* east-northeast.

-ene *n. combining form.* (in chemistry) indicating an unsaturated compound containing double bonds: *benzene; ethylene.* [from Greek *-ēnē,* feminine patronymic suffix]

ENEA *abbrev. for* European Nuclear Energy Agency: the European body responsible for the development of nuclear-generated electric power.

enema (ˈɛnɪmə) *n., pl.* **-mas** *or* **-mata** (-mətə). *Med.* **1.** the introduction of liquid into the rectum to evacuate the bowels, medicate, or nourish. **2.** the liquid so introduced. [C15: from New Latin, from Greek: injection, from *enienai* to send in, from *hienai* to send]

enemy (ˈɛnəmɪ) *n., pl.* **-mies. 1.** a person hostile or opposed to a policy, cause, person, or group, esp. one who actively tries to do damage; opponent. **2. a.** an armed adversary; opposing military force. **b.** (*as modifier*): *enemy aircraft.* **3. a.** a hostile nation or people. **b.** (*as modifier*): *an enemy alien.* **4.** something that harms or opposes; adversary: *courage is the enemy of failure.* ~Related adj.: **inimical.** [C13: from Old French *enemi,* from Latin *inimīcus* hostile, from IN-[1] + *amīcus* friend]

energetic (ˌɛnəˈdʒɛtɪk) *adj.* having or showing much energy or force; vigorous. —ˌ**enerˈgetically** *adv.*

energetics (ˌɛnəˈdʒɛtɪks) *n.* (*functioning as sing.*) the branch of science concerned with energy and its transformations.

energid (ˈɛnədʒɪd) *n.* a biological unit that consists of nucleus and cytoplasm but does not constitute a cell. [C19: adapted from German, from ENERGY + -ID[1]]

energize *or* **energise** (ˈɛnəˌdʒaɪz) *vb.* **1.** to have or cause to have energy; invigorate. **2.** *(tr.)* to apply a source of electric current or electromotive force to (a circuit, field winding, etc.). —ˈ**enerˌgizer** *or* ˈ**enerˌgiser** *n.*

energumen (ˌɛnəˈgjuːmɛn) *n.* **1.** a person thought to be possessed by an evil spirit. **2.** a fanatic or zealot. [C18: via Late Latin from Greek *energoumenos* having been worked on, from *energein* to be in action, from *energos* effective; see ENERGY]

energy (ˈɛnədʒɪ) *n., pl.* **-gies. 1.** intensity or vitality of action or expression; forcefulness. **2.** capacity or tendency for intense activity; vigour. **3.** vigorous or intense action; exertion. **4.** *Physics.* **a.** the capacity of a body or system to do work. **b.** a measure of this capacity, expressed as the work that it does in changing to some specified reference state. It is measured in joules (SI units). Symbol: *E* See also **kinetic energy, potential energy.** [C16: from Late Latin *energīa,* from Greek *energeia* activity, from *energos* effective, from EN-[2] + *ergon* work]

energy band *n. Physics.* a range of energies associated with the quantum states of electrons in a crystalline solid. In a semiconductor or an insulator there is a **valence band** containing many states, most of which are occupied. Above this is a **forbidden band** with only a few isolated states caused by impurities. Above this is a **conduction band** containing many states most of which are empty. In a metal there is a continuous **valence-conduction band.** See also **energy gap.**

energy conversion *n.* the process of changing one form of energy into another, such as nuclear energy into heat or solar energy into electrical energy.

energy gap *n. Physics.* the difference of energy between the bottom of the conduction band and the top of the valence band of the electrons in a crystalline solid. For values below about 2eV the substance is considered to be a semiconductor whilst for higher values it is considered to be an insulator.

energy level *n. Physics.* **1.** a constant value of energy in the distribution of energies among a number of atomic particles. **2.** the energy of a quantum state of a system. The terms **energy level** and **energy state** are often used loosely to mean **quantum state.** This is avoided in precise communication.

enervate *vb.* (ˈɛnəˌveɪt). **1.** *(tr.)* to deprive of strength or vitality; weaken physically or mentally; debilitate. ~*adj.* (ɪˈnɜːvɪt). **2.** deprived of strength or vitality; weakened. [C17: from Latin *ēnervāre* to remove the nerves from, from *nervus* nerve, sinew] —ˈ**enerˌvating** *adj.* —ˌ**enerˈvation** *n.* —ˈ**enerˌvative** *adj.* —ˈ**enerˌvator** *n.*

enface (ɪnˈfeɪs) *vb. (tr.)* to write, print, or stamp (something) on the face of (a document). —**enˈfacement** *n.*

en face *French.* (ɑ̃ fas) *adj.* **1.** facing forwards. **2.** opposite; facing.

en famille *French.* (ɑ̃ famij) *adv.* **1.** with one's family; at home. **2.** in a casual way; informally.

enfant terrible *French.* (ɑ̃fɑ̃ tɛriblə) *n., pl.* ***enfants terribles*** (ɑ̃fɑ̃ tɛriblə). a person given to unconventional conduct or indiscreet remarks. [C19: literally: terrible child]

enfeeble (ɪn'fiːbᵊl) *vb.* (*tr.*) to make weak; deprive of strength. —**en'feeblement** *n.* —**en'feebler** *n.*

enfeoff (ɪn'fiːf) *vb.* (*tr.*) **1.** *Property law.* to invest (a person) with possession of a freehold estate in land. **2.** (in feudal society) to take (someone) into vassalage by giving a fee or fief in return for certain services. [C14: from Anglo-French *enfeoffer;* see FIEF] —**en'feoffment** *n.*

en fête *French.* (ɑ̃ fɛt) *adv.* **1.** dressed for a festivity. **2.** engaged in a festivity. [C19: literally: in festival]

Enfield rifle *n.* ('ɛnfiːld) **1.** a breech-loading bolt-action magazine rifle, usually .303 calibre, used by the British army until World War II and by other countries. **2.** a nineteenth-century muzzle-loading musket used by the British army. [C19: from *Enfield,* N London, where it was first made]

enfilade (ˌɛnfɪ'leɪd) *Military.* ~*n.* **1.** a position or formation subject to fire from a flank along the length of its front. ~*vb.* (*tr.*) **2.** to subject (a position or formation) to fire from a flank. **3.** to position (troops or guns) so as to be able to fire at a flank. [C18: from French: suite, from *enfiler* to thread on string, from *fil* thread]

enfleurage *French.* (ɑ̃flœraʒ) *n.* the process of exposing odourless oils to the scent of fresh flowers, used in perfume-making. [C19: literally: inflowering]

enfold *or* **infold** (ɪn'fəʊld) *vb.* (*tr.*) **1.** to cover by enclosing. **2.** to embrace. **3.** to form with or as with folds. —**en'folder** *or* **in'folder** *n.* —**en'foldment** *or* **in'foldment** *n.*

enforce (ɪn'fɔːs) *vb.* (*tr.*) **1.** to ensure observance of or obedience to (a law, decision, etc.). **2.** to impose (obedience, loyalty, etc.) by or as by force. **3.** to emphasize or reinforce (an argument, demand, etc.). —**en'forceable** *adj.* —**enˌforcea'bility** *n.* —**enforcedly** (ɪn'fɔːsɪdlɪ) *adv.* —**en'forcement** *n.* —**en'forcer** *n.*

enfranchise (ɪn'fræntʃaɪz) *vb.* (*tr.*) **1.** to grant the power of voting to, esp. as a right of citizenship. **2.** to liberate, as from servitude. **3.** (in England) to invest (a town, city, etc.) with the right to be represented in Parliament. **4.** *English law.* (formerly) to convert (copyhold land) to freehold. —**en'franchisement** *n.* —**en'franchiser** *n.*

eng (ɛŋ) *n. Phonetics.* another name for **agma.**

ENG *abbrev. for* electronic news gathering: TV news obtained at the point of action by means of modern video equipment.

eng. *abbrev. for:* **1.** engine. **2.** engineer. **3.** engineering. **4.** engraved. **5.** engraver. **6.** engraving.

Eng. *abbrev. for:* **1.** England. **2.** English.

engage (ɪn'geɪdʒ) *vb.* (*mainly tr.*) **1.** to secure the services of; employ. **2.** to secure for use; reserve: *engage a room.* **3.** to involve (a person or his attention) intensely; engross; occupy. **4.** to attract (the affection) of (a person): *her innocence engaged him.* **5.** to draw (somebody) into conversation. **6.** (*intr.*) to take part; participate: *he engages in many sports.* **7.** to promise (to do something). **8.** (*also intr.*) *Military.* to begin an action with (an enemy). **9.** to bring (a mechanism) into operation: *he engaged the clutch.* **10.** (*also intr.*) to undergo or cause to undergo interlocking, as of the components of a driving mechanism, such as a gear train. **11.** *Machinery.* to locate (a locking device) in its operative position or to advance (a tool) into a workpiece to commence cutting. [C15: from Old French *engagier,* from EN-[1] + *gage* a pledge, see GAGE[1]] —**en'gager** *n.*

engagé *or* (*fem.*) ***engagée*** *French.* (ɑ̃gaʒe) *adj.* (of a writer or artist) morally or politically committed to some ideology.

engaged (ɪn'geɪdʒd) *adj.* **1.** pledged to be married; betrothed. **2.** employed, occupied, or busy. **3.** *Architect.* built against or attached to a wall or similar structure: *an engaged column.* **4.** (of a telephone line) already in use. —**engagedly** (ɪn'geɪdʒɪdlɪ) *adv.*

engaged tone *n. Brit.* a repeated single note heard on a telephone when the number called is already in use. U.S. and Canadian equivalent: **busy signal.** Compare **ringing tone, dialling tone.**

engagement (ɪn'geɪdʒmənt) *n.* **1.** a pledge of marriage; betrothal. **2.** an appointment or arrangement, esp. for business or social purposes. **3.** the act of engaging or condition of being engaged. **4.** a promise, obligation, or other condition that binds. **5.** a period of employment, esp. a limited period. **6.** an action; battle. **7.** (*pl.*) financial obligations.

engagement ring *n.* a ring given by a man to a woman as a token of their betrothal.

engaging (ɪn'geɪdʒɪŋ) *adj.* pleasing, charming, or winning. —**en'gagingly** *adv.* —**en'gagingness** *n.*

en garde *French.* (ɑ̃ gard) *interj.* **1.** on guard; a call to a fencer to adopt a defensive stance in readiness for an attack or bout. ~*adj.* **2.** (of a fencer) in such a stance.

engender (ɪn'dʒɛndə) *vb.* **1.** (*tr.*) to bring about or give rise to; produce or cause. **2.** to be born or cause to be born; bring or come into being. [C14: from Old French *engendrer,* from Latin *ingenerāre,* from *generāre* to beget] —**en'genderer** *n.* —**en'genderment** *n.*

engin. *abbrev. for* engineering.

engine ('ɛndʒɪn) *n.* **1.** any machine designed to convert energy, esp. thermal energy, into mechanical work: *a steam engine; a petrol engine.* **2. a.** a railway locomotive. **b.** (*as modifier*): *the engine cab.* **3.** *Military.* any of various pieces of equipment formerly used in warfare, such as a battering ram or gun. **4.** *Obsolete.* any instrument or device: *engines of torture.* [C13: from Old French *engin,* from Latin *ingenium* nature, talent, ingenious contrivance, from IN-[2] + *-genium,* related to *gignere* to beget, produce]

engine driver *n. Chiefly Brit.* a man who drives a railway locomotive; train driver.

engineer (ˌɛndʒɪ'nɪə) *n.* **1.** a person trained in any branch of the profession of engineering. **2.** the originator or manager of a situation, system, etc. **3.** a mechanic; one who repairs or services machines. **4.** *U.S. and Canadian.* the driver of a railway locomotive. **5.** an officer responsible for a ship's engines. **6.** Informal name: **sapper.** a member of the armed forces, esp. the army, trained in engineering and construction work. ~*vb.* (*tr.*) **7.** to originate, cause, or plan in a clever or devious manner: *he engineered the minister's downfall.* **8.** to design, plan, or construct as a professional engineer. [C14 *enginer,* from Old French *engigneor,* from *engignier* to contrive, ultimately from Latin *ingenium* skill, talent; see ENGINE]

engineering (ˌɛndʒɪ'nɪərɪŋ) *n.* the profession of applying scientific principles to the design, construction, and maintenance of engines, cars, machines, etc. (**mechanical engineering**), buildings, bridges, roads, etc. (**civil engineering**), electrical machines and communication systems (**electrical engineering**), chemical plant and machinery (**chemical engineering**), or aircraft (**aeronautical engineering**). See also **military engineering.**

engineer officer *n.* a ship's officer who is qualified to be in charge of the vessel's propulsion and other machinery.

engine pod *n. Aeronautics.* an aircraft turbojet unit comprising the engine and its cowling suspended by a pylon, often below the wing.

engine room *n.* a place where engines are housed, esp. on a ship.

enginery ('ɛndʒɪnrɪ) *n., pl.* **-ries. 1.** a collection or assembly of engines; machinery. **2.** engines employed in warfare. **3.** *Rare.* skilful manoeuvring or contrivance.

englacial (ɪn'gleɪsɪəl) *adj.* embedded in, carried by, or running through a glacier: *englacial drift; an englacial river.* —**en'glacially** *adv.*

Engler degrees ('ɛŋlə) *n.* (*functioning as sing.*) a scale of measurement of viscosity based on the ratio of the time taken by a particular liquid to flow through a standard orifice to the time taken by water to flow through the same orifice. [named after C. *Engler* (1842–1925), German chemist, who proposed it]

English ('ɪŋglɪʃ) *n.* **1.** the official language of Britain, the U.S., most parts of the Commonwealth, and certain other countries. It is the native language of over 280 million people and is acquired as a second language by many more. It is an Indo-European language belonging to the West Germanic branch. **2. the English.** (*functioning as pl.*) the natives or inhabitants of England or (loosely) of Great Britain collectively. **3.** (formerly) a size of printer's type approximately equal to 14 point. **4.** an old style of black-letter typeface. **5.** (*often not cap.*) the usual U.S. and Canadian term for **side** (in billiards). ~*adj.* **6.** denoting, using, or relating to the English language. **7.** relating to or characteristic of England or the English. ~*vb.* (*tr.*) **8.** *Archaic.* to translate or adapt into English. —**'Englishness** *n.*

English bond *n.* a bond used in brickwork that has a course of headers alternating with a course of stretchers.

English Canadian *n.* a Canadian citizen whose first language is English, esp. one of English descent.

English disease *n.* (usually preceded by *the*) the pattern of strikes and industrial unrest supposed, esp. by foreigners and journalists, to be endemic in Great Britain and to weaken the British economy.

English flute *n. Music.* another name for **recorder** (sense 4).

English horn *n. Music.* another name for **cor anglais.**

Englishism ('ɪŋglɪˌʃɪzəm) *n. Chiefly U.S.* **1.** an English custom, practice, etc. **2.** a word or expression not found in forms of English other than British English; Anglicism. **3.** high regard for English customs, institutions, etc.

Englishman ('ɪŋglɪʃmən) *or* (*fem.*) **Englishwoman** *n., pl.* **-men** *or* **-women. 1.** a native or inhabitant of England. **2.** (loosely) a citizen of the United Kingdom.

Englishman's tie *or* **knot** *n.* a type of knot for tying together heavy ropes.

Englishry ('ɪŋglɪʃrɪ) *n. Now rare.* **1.** people of English descent, esp. in Ireland. **2.** the fact or condition of being an Englishman or Englishwoman, esp. by birth.

English setter *n.* a breed of setter having a white coat speckled with liver, brown, or yellowish markings.

English springer spaniel *n.* See **springer spaniel.**

englut (ɪn'glʌt) *vb.* **-gluts, -glutting, -glutted.** (*tr.*) *Literary.* **1.** to devour ravenously; swallow eagerly. **2.** to glut or sate (oneself); surfeit; satiate.

engorge (ɪn'gɔːdʒ) *vb.* (*tr.*) **1.** *Pathol.* to congest with blood. **2.** to eat (food) ravenously or greedily. **3.** to gorge (oneself); glut; satiate. —**en'gorgement** *n.*

engr *abbrev. for:* **1.** engineer. **2.** engraver.

engr. *abbrev. for* engraved.
engraft *or* **ingraft** (ɪnˈgrɑːft) *vb. (tr.)* **1.** to graft (a shoot, bud, etc.) onto a stock. **2.** to incorporate in a firm or permanent way; implant: *they engrafted their principles into the document.* —ˌ**engrafˈtation**, ˌ**ingrafˈtation** *or* **enˈgraftment, inˈgraftment** *n.*
engrail (ɪnˈgreɪl) *vb. (tr.)* to decorate or mark (the edge of) (a coin) with small carved notches. [C14: from Old French *engresler*, from EN-[1] + *gresle* slim, from Latin *gracilis* slender, graceful] —**enˈgrailment** *n.*
engrain (ɪnˈgreɪn) *vb.* a variant spelling of **ingrain.**
engram (ˈengræm) *n. Psychol.* the physical basis of an individual memory in the brain. See also **memory trace.** [C20: from German *Engramm*, from Greek *en-* IN + *gramma* letter] —**enˈgrammic** *or* ˌ**engramˈmatic** *adj.*
engrave (ɪnˈgreɪv) *vb. (tr.)* **1.** to inscribe (a design, writing, etc.) onto (a block, plate, or other surface used for printing) by carving, etching with acid, or other process. **2.** to print (designs or characters) from a printing plate so made. **3.** to fix deeply or permanently in the mind. [C16: from EN-[1] + GRAVE[3], on the model of French *engraver*] —**enˈgraver** *n.*
engraving (ɪnˈgreɪvɪŋ) *n.* **1.** the art of a person who engraves. **2.** a block, plate, or other surface that has been engraved. **3.** a print made from such a surface.
engross (ɪnˈgrəʊs) *vb. (tr.)* **1.** to occupy one's attention completely; absorb. **2.** to write or copy (manuscript) in large legible handwriting. **3.** *Law.* to write or type out formally (a deed, agreement, or other document) preparatory to execution. **4.** another word for **corner** (sense 21b). [C14 (in the sense: to buy up wholesale): from Old French *en gros* in quantity; C15 (in the sense: to write in large letters): probably from Medieval Latin *ingrossāre;* both from Latin *grossus* thick, GROSS] —**enˈgrossed** *adj.* —**engrossedly** (ɪnˈgrəʊsɪdlɪ) *adv.* —**enˈgrosser** *n.* —**enˈgrossing** *adj.*
engrossment (ɪnˈgrəʊsmənt) *n.* **1.** a deed or other document that has been engrossed. **2.** the state of being engrossed.
engulf *or* **ingulf** (ɪnˈgʌlf) *vb. (tr.)* **1.** to immerse, plunge, bury, or swallow up. **2.** (*often passive*) to overwhelm: *engulfed by debts.* —**enˈgulfment** *n.*
enhance (ɪnˈhɑːns) *vb. (tr.)* to intensify or increase in quality, value, power, etc.; improve; augment. [C14: from Old French *enhaucier*, from EN-[1] + *haucier* to raise, from Vulgar Latin *altiāre* (unattested), from Latin *altus* high] —**enˈhancement** *n.* —**enˈhancer** *n.* —**enˈhancive** *adj.*
enhanced oil recovery *n.* any of several techniques that make it possible to recover more oil than can be obtained by natural pressure, such as the injection of fluid or gases into an oilfield to force more oil to the surface.
enhanced radiation weapon *n.* a technical name for **neutron bomb.**
enharmonic (ˌenhɑːˈmɒnɪk) *adj. Music.* **1.** denoting or relating to a small difference in pitch between two notes such as A flat and G sharp: not present in instruments of equal temperament such as the piano, but significant in the intonation of stringed and wind instruments. **2.** denoting or relating to enharmonic modulation. [C17: from Latin *enharmonicus*, from Greek *enarmonios*, from EN-[2] + *harmonia;* see HARMONY] —ˌ**enharˈmonically** *adv.*
enharmonic modulation *n. Music.* a change of key achieved by regarding a note in one key as an equivalent note in another. Thus E flat in the key of A flat could be regarded as D sharp in the key of B major.
enigma (ɪˈnɪgmə) *n.* a person, thing, or situation that is mysterious, puzzling, or ambiguous. [C16: from Latin *aenigma*, from Greek *ainigma*, from *ainissesthai* to speak in riddles, from *ainos* fable, story] —**enigmatic** (ˌenɪgˈmætɪk) *or* ˌ**enigˈmatical** *adj.* —ˌ**enigˈmatically** *adv.*
enigmatize *or* **enigmatise** (ɪˈnɪgməˌtaɪz) *vb. (tr.)* to make enigmatic.
enisle (ɪnˈaɪl) *vb. (tr.) Poetic.* to put on or make into an island.
enjambment *or* **enjambement** (ɪnˈdʒæmmənt; *French* ɑ̃ʒɑ̃bmɑ̃) *n. Prosody.* the running over of a sentence from one line of verse into the next. [C19: from French, literally: a straddling, from *enjamber* to straddle, from EN-[1] + *jambe* leg; see JAMB] —**enˈjambed** *adj.*
enjoin (ɪnˈdʒɔɪn) *vb. (tr.)* **1.** to order (someone) to do (something); urge strongly; command. **2.** to impose or prescribe (a condition, mode of behaviour, etc.). **3.** *Law.* to require (a person) to do or refrain from doing (some act), esp. by issuing an injunction. [C13: from Old French *enjoindre*, from Latin *injungere* to fasten to, from IN-[2] + *jungere* to JOIN] —**enˈjoiner** *n.* —**enˈjoinment** *n.*
enjoy (ɪnˈdʒɔɪ) *vb. (tr.)* **1.** to receive pleasure from; take joy in. **2.** to have the benefit of; use with satisfaction. **3.** to have as a condition; experience: *the land enjoyed a summer of rain.* **4.** *Archaic.* to have sexual intercourse with. **5. enjoy oneself.** to have a good time. [C14: from Old French *enjoir*, from EN-[1] + *joir* to find pleasure in, from Latin *gaudēre* to rejoice] —**enˈjoyable** *adj.* —**enˈjoyableness** *n.* —**enˈjoyably** *adv.* —**enˈjoyer** *n.*
enjoyment (ɪnˈdʒɔɪmənt) *n.* **1.** the act or condition of receiving pleasure from something. **2.** the use or possession of something that is satisfying or beneficial. **3.** something that provides joy or satisfaction. **4.** the possession or exercise of a legal right.
enkephalin (enˈkefəlɪn) *or* **encephalin** (enˈsefəlɪn) *n.* a chemical occurring in the brain, having effects similar to those of morphine. See also **endorphin.**
enkindle (ɪnˈkɪndᵊl) *vb. (tr.)* **1.** to set on fire; kindle. **2.** to excite to activity or ardour; arouse. —**enˈkindler** *n.*
enl. *abbrev. for:* **1.** enlarge(d). **2.** enlisted.
enlace (ɪnˈleɪs) *vb. (tr.)* **1.** to bind or encircle with or as with laces. **2.** to entangle; intertwine. —**enˈlacement** *n.*
enlarge (ɪnˈlɑːdʒ) *vb.* **1.** to make or grow larger in size, scope, etc.; increase or expand. **2.** (*tr.*) to make (a photographic print) of a larger size than the negative. **3.** (*intr.;* foll. by *on* or *upon*) to speak or write (about) in greater detail; expatiate (on). —**enˈlargeable** *adj.*
enlargement (ɪnˈlɑːdʒmənt) *n.* **1.** the act of enlarging or the condition of being enlarged. **2.** something that enlarges or is intended to enlarge. **3.** a photographic print that is larger than the negative from which it is made.
enlarger (ɪnˈlɑːdʒə) *n.* an optical instrument for making enlarged photographic prints in which a negative is brightly illuminated and its enlarged image is focused onto a sheet of sensitized paper.
enlighten (ɪnˈlaɪtᵊn) *vb. (tr.)* **1.** to give information or understanding to; instruct; edify. **2.** to free from ignorance, prejudice, or superstition. **3.** to give spiritual or religious revelation to. **4.** *Poetic.* to shed light on. —**enˈlightener** *n.* —**enˈlightening** *adj.*
enlightened (ɪnˈlaɪtᵊnd) *adj.* **1.** factually well-informed, tolerant of alternative opinions, and guided by rational thought: *an enlightened administration; enlightened self-interest.* **2.** privy to or claiming a sense of spiritual or religious revelation of truth: *an enlightened spiritual master.*
enlightenment (ɪnˈlaɪtᵊnmənt) *n.* **1.** the act or means of enlightening or the state of being enlightened. **2.** *Buddhism.* the awakening to ultimate truth by which man is freed from the endless cycle of personal reincarnations to which all men are otherwise subject. **3.** *Hinduism.* a state of transcendent divine experience represented by Vishnu: regarded as a goal of all religion.
Enlightenment (ɪnˈlaɪtᵊnmənt) *n.* **the.** an 18th-century philosophical movement stressing the importance of reason and the critical reappraisal of existing ideas and social institutions.
enlist (ɪnˈlɪst) *vb.* **1.** to enter or persuade to enter into an engagement to serve in the armed forces. **2.** (*tr.*) to engage or secure (a person, his services, or his support) for a venture, cause, etc. **3.** (*intr.;* foll. by *in*) to enter into or join an enterprise, cause, etc. —**enˈlister** *n.* —**enˈlistment** *n.*
enlisted man *n. U.S.* a serviceman who holds neither a commission nor a warrant and is not under training for officer rank as a cadet or midshipman.
enliven (ɪnˈlaɪvᵊn) *vb. (tr.)* **1.** to make active, vivacious, or spirited; invigorate. **2.** to make cheerful or bright; gladden or brighten. —**enˈlivener** *n.* —**enˈlivening** *adj.* —**enˈlivenment** *n.*
en masse (*French* ɑ̃ mas) *adv.* in a group, body, or mass; as a whole; all together. [C19: from French]
enmesh, inmesh (ɪnˈmeʃ), *or* **immesh** *vb. (tr.)* to catch or involve in or as if in a net or snare; entangle. —**enˈmeshment** *n.*
enmity (ˈenmɪtɪ) *n., pl.* **-ties.** a feeling of hostility or ill will, as between enemies; antagonism. [C13: from Old French *enemistié*, from *enemi* ENEMY]
ennage (ˈenɪdʒ) *n. Printing.* the total number of ens in a piece of matter to be set in type.
ennead (ˈenɪˌæd) *n.* **1.** a group or series of nine. **2.** the sum of or number nine. [C17: from Greek *enneas*, from *ennea* nine] —ˌ**enneˈadic** *adj.*
enneagon (ˈenɪəgən) *n.* another name for **nonagon.**
enneahedron (ˌenɪəˈhiːdrən) *n., pl.* **-drons** *or* **-dra** (-drə). a solid figure having nine plane faces. See also **polyhedron.** —ˌ**enneaˈhedral** *adj.*
ennoble (ɪˈnəʊbᵊl) *vb. (tr.)* **1.** to make noble, honourable, or excellent; dignify; exalt. **2.** to raise to a noble rank; confer a title of nobility upon. —**enˈnoblement** *n.* —**enˈnobler** *n.* —**enˈnobling** *adj.*
ennui (ˈɒnwiː; *French* ɑ̃nɥi) *n.* a feeling of listlessness and general dissatisfaction resulting from lack of activity or excitement. [C18: from French: apathy, from Old French *enui* annoyance, vexation; see ANNOY]
ennuied, ennuyed (ˈɒnwiːd) *or* **ennuyé** (*French* ɑ̃nɥije) *adj.* affected with ennui; bored.
ENO *abbrev. for* English National Opera.
enol (ˈiːnɒl) *n.* any organic compound containing the group -CH:CO-, often existing in chemical equilibrium with the corresponding keto form. See **keto-enol tautomerism.** [C19: from -ENE + -OL[1]] —**eˈnolic** *adj.*
enology (iːˈnɒlədʒɪ) *n.* the usual U.S. spelling of **oenology.**
enormity (ɪˈnɔːmɪtɪ) *n., pl.* **-ties.** **1.** the quality or character of being outrageous; extreme wickedness. **2.** an act of great wickedness; atrocity. **3.** *Informal.* vastness of size or extent. [C15: from Old French *enormite*, from Late Latin *ēnormitās* hugeness; see ENORMOUS]
▷**Usage.** In careful usage, the noun *enormity* is not employed to convey the idea of great size, but that of something outrageous or horrifying: *the enormity of this crime leaves one astonished. The immensity* (rather than *enormity*) *of the area covered by the lake is astonishing.*

enormous (ɪˈnɔːməs) *adj.* **1.** unusually large in size, extent, or degree; immense; vast. **2.** *Archaic.* extremely wicked; heinous. [C16: from Latin *ēnormis*, from *ē-* out of, away from + *norma* rule, pattern] —**eˈnormously** *adv.* —**eˈnormousness** *n.*
enosis (ˈɛnəʊsɪs) *n.* the union of Greece and Cyprus: the aim of a group of Greek Cypriots. [C20: Modern Greek: from Greek *henoun* to unite, from *heis* one]
enough (ɪˈnʌf) *determiner.* **1. a.** sufficient to answer a need, demand, supposition, or requirement; adequate: *enough cake.* **b.** (*as pronoun*): *enough is now known.* **2. that's enough!** that will do: used to put an end to an action, speech, performance, etc. ~*adv.* **3.** so as to be adequate or sufficient; as much as necessary: *you have worked hard enough.* **4.** (*not used with a negative*) very or quite; rather: *she was pleased enough to see me.* **5.** (intensifier): *oddly enough; surprisingly enough.* **6.** just adequately; tolerably: *he did it well enough.* [Old English *genōh;* related to Old Norse *gnōgr*, Gothic *ganōhs*, Old High German *ginuog*]
enounce (ɪˈnaʊns) *vb.* (*tr.*) *Formal.* **1.** to enunciate. **2.** to pronounce. [C19: from French *énoncer*, from Latin *ēnuntiāre* ENUNCIATE] —**eˈnouncement** *n.*
enow (ɪˈnaʊ) *adj., adv.* an archaic word for **enough.**
en passant (ɒn pæˈsɑːnt; *French* ɑ̃ pasɑ̃) *adv.* in passing: in chess, said of capturing a pawn that has made an initial move of two squares to its fourth rank, bypassing the square where an enemy pawn on its own fifth rank could capture it. The capture is made as if the captured pawn had moved one square instead of two. [C17: from French]
en pension *French.* (ɑ̃ pɑ̃sjɔ̃) *adv.* in lodgings with all meals provided.
enphytotic (ˌɛnfaɪˈtɒtɪk) *adj.* (of plant diseases) causing a constant amount of damage each year. [C20: from EN-[2] + -PHYTE + -OTIC]
enplane (ɛnˈpleɪn) *vb.* (*intr.*) to board an aircraft.
en plein (*French* ɑ̃ plɛ̃) *adj.* (*postpositive*), *adv.* (of a gambling bet) placed entirely on a single number, etc. [from French: in full]
enprint (ˈɛnprɪnt) *n.* a standard photographic print (5 × 3.5 in.) produced from a negative.
en prise (*French* ɑ̃ priz) *adj.* (*postpositive*), *adv.* (of a chess piece) exposed to capture. [C19: from French; see PRIZE[1]]
enquire (ɪnˈkwaɪə) *vb.* a variant of **inquire.** —**enˈquirer** *n.* —**enˈquiry** *n.*
enrage (ɪnˈreɪdʒ) *vb.* (*tr.*) to provoke to fury; put into a rage; anger. —**enˈraged** *adj.* —**enragedly** (ɪnˈreɪdʒɪdlɪ) *adv.* —**enˈragement** *n.*
en rapport *French.* (ɑ̃ rapɔr) *adj.* (*postpositive*), *adv.* in sympathy, harmony, or accord.
enrapture (ɪnˈræptʃə) *vb.* (*tr.*) to fill with delight; enchant.
enrich (ɪnˈrɪtʃ) *vb.* (*tr.*) **1.** to increase the wealth of. **2.** to endow with fine or desirable qualities: *to enrich one's experience by travelling.* **3.** to make more beautiful; adorn; decorate: *a robe enriched with jewels.* **4.** to improve in quality, colour, flavour, etc. **5.** to increase the food value of by adding nutrients: *to enrich dog biscuits with calcium.* **6.** to make (soil) more productive, esp. by adding fertilizer. **7.** *Physics.* to increase the concentration or abundance of one component or isotope in (a solution or mixture); concentrate: *to enrich a solution by evaporation; enrich a nuclear fuel.* —**enˈriched** *adj.* —**enˈricher** *n.* —**enˈrichment** *n.*
enrobe (ɪnˈrəʊb) *vb.* (*tr.*) to dress in or as if in a robe; attire. —**enˈrober** *n.*
enrol *or U.S.* **enroll** (ɪnˈrəʊl) *vb.* **-rols** *or U.S.* **-rolls, -rolling -rolled.** (*mainly tr.*) **1.** to record or note in a roll or list. **2.** (*also intr.*) to become or cause to become a member; enlist; register. **3.** to put on record; record. **4.** *Rare.* to roll or wrap up. —**ˌenrolˈlee** *n.* —**enˈroller** *n.*
enrolment *or U.S.* **enrollment** (ɪnˈrəʊlmənt) *n.* **1.** the act of enrolling or state of being enrolled. **2.** a list of people enrolled. **3.** the total number of people enrolled.
enroot (ɪnˈruːt) *vb.* (*tr.; usually passive*) **1.** to establish (plants) by fixing their roots in the earth. **2.** to fix firmly, implant, or embed: *to enroot an idea in the mind.*
en route (ɒn ˈruːt; *French* ɑ̃ rut) *adv.* on or along the way; on the road. [C18: from French]
ens (ɛnz) *n., pl.* **entia** (ˈɛnʃɪə). *Metaphysics.* **1.** being or existence in the most general abstract sense. **2.** a real thing, esp. as opposed to an attribute; entity. [C16: from Late Latin, literally: being, from Latin *esse* to be]
Ens. *abbrev. for* Ensign.
ENSA (ˈɛnsə) *n. acronym for* Entertainments National Service Association: a British organization providing entertainment for the armed forces during World War II.
ensample (ɛnˈsɑːmpᵊl) *n.* an archaic word for **example.**
ensanguine (ɪnˈsæŋgwɪn) *vb.* (*tr.*) *Literary.* to cover or stain with or as with blood.
ensconce (ɪnˈskɒns) *vb.* (*tr.; often passive*) **1.** to establish or settle firmly or comfortably: *ensconced in a chair.* **2.** to place in safety; hide. [C16: see EN-[1], SCONCE[2]]
ensemble (ɒnˈsɒmbᵊl; *French* ɑ̃sɑ̃blə) *n.* **1.** all the parts of something considered together and in relation to the whole. **2.** a person's complete costume; outfit. **3. a.** the cast of a play other than the principals; supporting players. **b.** (*as modifier*): *an ensemble role.* **4.** *Music.* **a.** a group of soloists singing or playing together. **b.** (*as modifier*): *an ensemble passage.* **5.** *Music.* the degree of precision and unity exhibited by a group of instrumentalists or singers performing together: *the ensemble of the strings is good.* **6.** the general or total effect of something made up of individual parts. **7.** *Physics.* **a.** a set of systems (such as a set of collections of atoms) that are identical in all respects apart from the motions of their constituents. **b.** a single system (such as a collection of atoms) in which the properties are determined by the statistical behaviour of its constituents. ~*adv.* **8.** all together or at once. [C15: from French: together, from Latin *insimul*, from IN-[2] + *simul* at the same time]
enshrine *or* **inshrine** (ɪnˈʃraɪn) *vb.* (*tr.*) **1.** to place or enclose in or as if in a shrine. **2.** to hold as sacred; cherish; treasure. —**enˈshrinement** *n.*
enshroud (ɪnˈʃraʊd) *vb.* (*tr.*) to cover or hide with or as if with a shroud: *the sky was enshrouded in mist.*
ensiform (ˈɛnsɪˌfɔːm) *adj. Biology.* shaped like a sword blade: *ensiform leaves.* [C16: from Latin *ensis* sword]
ensign (ˈɛnsaɪn) *n.* **1.** (*also* ˈɛnsən). a flag flown by a ship, branch of the armed forces, etc., to indicate nationality, allegiance, etc. See also **Red Ensign, White Ensign. 2.** any flag, standard, or banner. **3.** a standard-bearer. **4.** a symbol, token, or emblem; sign. **5.** (in the U.S. Navy) a commissioned officer of the lowest rank. **6.** (in the British infantry) a colours bearer. **7.** (formerly in the British infantry) a commissioned officer of the lowest rank. [C14: from Old French *enseigne*, from Latin INSIGNIA] —**ˈensignˌship** *or* **ˈensigncy** *n.*
ensilage (ˈɛnsɪlɪdʒ) *n.* **1.** the process of ensiling green fodder. **2.** a less common name for **silage.**
ensile (ɛnˈsaɪl, ˈɛnsaɪl) *vb.* (*tr.*) **1.** to store and preserve (green fodder) in an enclosed pit or silo. **2.** to turn (green fodder) into silage by causing it to ferment in a closed pit or silo. [C19: from French *ensiler*, from Spanish *ensilar*, from EN-[1] + *silo* SILO] —**enˌsilaˈbility** *n.*
enslave (ɪnˈsleɪv) *vb.* (*tr.*) to make a slave of; reduce to slavery; subjugate. —**enˈslavement** *n.* —**enˈslaver** *n.*
ensnare *or* **insnare** (ɪnˈsnɛə) *vb.* (*tr.*) to catch or trap in or as if in a snare. —**enˈsnarement** *n.* —**enˈsnarer** *n.*
ensoul *or* **insoul** (ɪnˈsəʊl) *vb.* (*tr.*) **1.** to endow with a soul. **2.** to cherish within the soul. —**enˈsoulment** *or* **inˈsoulment** *n.*
ensphere *or* **insphere** (ɪnˈsfɪə) *vb.* (*tr.*) **1.** to enclose in or as if in a sphere. **2.** to make spherical in form.
enstatite (ˈɛnstəˌtaɪt) *n.* a grey, green, yellow, or brown pyroxene mineral consisting of magnesium silicate in orthorhombic crystalline form. Formula: $Mg_2Si_2O_6$. [C19: from Greek *enstatēs* adversary (referring to its refractory quality) + -ITE[1]]
ensue (ɪnˈsjuː) *vb.* **-sues, -suing, -sued. 1.** (*intr.*) to follow subsequently or in order; come next or afterwards. **2.** (*intr.*) to follow or occur as a consequence; result. **3.** (*tr.*) *Obsolete.* to pursue. [C14: from Anglo-French *ensuer*, from Old French *ensuivre*, from EN-[1] + *suivre* to follow, from Latin *sequī*] —**enˈsuing** *adj.*
en suite *French.* (ɑ̃ sɥit) *adv.* as part of a set; forming a unit: *a hotel room with bathroom en suite.* [C19: literally: in sequence]
ensure (ɛnˈʃʊə, -ˈʃɔː) *or* (*esp. U.S.*) **insure** *vb.* (*tr.*) **1.** (*may take a clause as object*) to make certain or sure; guarantee: *this victory will ensure his happiness.* **2.** to make safe or secure; protect. —**enˈsurer** *n.*
enswathe (ɪnˈsweɪð) *vb.* (*tr.*) to bind or wrap; swathe. —**enˈswathement** *n.*
ENT *Med. abbrev. for* ear, nose, and throat.
-ent *suffix forming adjectives and nouns.* causing or performing an action or existing in a certain condition; the agent that performs an action: *astringent; dependent.* [from Latin *-ent-, -ens*, present participial ending]
entablature (ɛnˈtæblətʃə) *n. Architect.* **1.** the part of a classical temple above the columns, having an architrave, a frieze, and a cornice. **2.** any construction of similar form. [C17: from French, from Italian *intavolatura* something put on a table, hence, something laid flat, from *tavola* table, from Latin *tabula* TABLE]
entablement (ɪnˈteɪbᵊlmənt) *n.* the platform of a pedestal, above the dado, that supports a statue. [C17: from Old French]
entail (ɪnˈteɪl) *vb.* (*tr.*) **1.** to bring about or impose by necessity; have as a necessary consequence: *this task entails careful thought.* **2.** *Property law.* to restrict (the descent of an estate) to a designated line of heirs. **3.** *Logic.* to have as a necessary consequence. ~*n.* **4.** *Property law.* **a.** the restriction imposed by entailing an estate. **b.** an estate that has been entailed. [C14 *entaillen*, from EN-[1] + *taille* limitation, TAIL[2]] —**enˈtailer** *n.*
entailment (ɪnˈteɪlmənt) *n.* **1.** the act of entailing or the condition of being entailed. **2.** *Philosophy, logic.* **a.** a relationship between propositions such that one must be true if the others are. **b.** a proposition whose truth depends on such a relationship. Usual symbol: ⥽ See **fish-hook** (sense 2).
entamoeba (ˌɛntəˈmiːbə), **endamoeba** *or U.S.* **entameba, endameba** *n., pl.* **-bae** (-biː) *or* **-bas.** any parasitic amoeba of the genus *Entamoeba* (or *Endamoeba*), esp. *E. histolytica*, which lives in the intestines of man and causes amoebic dysentery.
entangle (ɪnˈtæŋgᵊl) *vb.* (*tr.*) **1.** to catch or involve in or as if in a tangle; ensnare or enmesh. **2.** to make tangled or twisted; snarl. **3.** to make complicated; confuse. **4.** to involve in difficulties; entrap. —**enˈtangler** *n.*

entanglement (ɪnˈtæŋgəlmənt) *n.* **1.** something that entangles or is itself entangled. **2.** a sexual relationship regarded as unfortunate, damaging, or compromising.

entasis (ˈɛntəsɪs) *n., pl.* **-ses** (-siːz). **1.** a slightly convex curve given to the shaft of a column, pier, or similar structure, to correct the illusion of concavity produced by a straight shaft. **2.** Also called: **entasia** (ɛnˈteɪzɪə). *Physiol.* an involuntary or spasmodic muscular contraction. [C18: from Greek, from *enteinein* to stretch tight, from *teinein* to stretch]

entelechy (ɛnˈtɛlɪkɪ) *n., pl.* **-chies.** *Metaphysics.* **1.** (in the philosophy of Aristotle) actuality as opposed to potentiality. **2.** (in the system of Leibnitz) the soul or principle of perfection of an object or person; a monad or basic constituent. **3.** something that contains or realizes a final cause, esp. the vital force thought to direct the life of an organism. [C17: from Late Latin *entelechia,* from Greek *entelekheia,* from EN-[2] + *telos* goal, completion + *ekhein* to have]

entellus (ɛnˈtɛləs) *n.* an Old World monkey, *Presbytes entellus,* of S Asia. This langur is regarded as sacred in India. Also called: **hanuman.** [C19: New Latin, apparently from the name of the aged Sicilian character in Book V of Virgil's *Aeneid*]

entente (*French* ɑ̃tɑ̃t) *n.* **1.** short for **entente cordiale. 2.** the parties to an entente cordiale collectively. [C19: French: understanding]

entente cordiale (*French* ɑ̃tɑ̃t kɔrdjal) *n.* **1.** a friendly understanding between political powers: less formal than an alliance. **2.** (*often caps.*) the understanding reached by France and Britain in April 1904, which settled outstanding colonial disputes. [C19: French: cordial understanding]

enter (ˈɛntə) *vb.* **1.** to come or go into (a place, house, etc.). **2.** to penetrate or pierce. **3.** (*tr.*) to introduce or insert. **4.** to join (a party, organization, etc.). **5.** (when *intr.*, foll. by *into*) to become involved or take part (in): *to enter a game; to enter into an agreement.* **6.** (*tr.*) to record (an item such as a commercial transaction) in a journal, account, register, etc. **7.** (*tr.*) to record (a name, etc.) on a list. **8.** (*tr.*) to present or submit: *to enter a proposal.* **9.** (*intr.*) *Theatre.* to come on stage: used as a stage direction: *enter Juliet.* **10.** (when *intr.*, often foll. by *into, on,* or *upon*) to begin; start: *to enter upon a new career.* **11.** (*intr.*; often foll. by *upon*) to come into possession (of). **12.** (*tr.*) to place (evidence, a plea, etc.) before a court of law or upon the court records. **13.** (*tr.*) *Law.* **a.** to go onto and occupy (land). **b.** *Chiefly U.S.* to file a claim to (public lands). [C13: from Old French *entrer,* from Latin *intrāre* to go in, from *intrā* within] —ˈ**enterable** *adj.* —ˈ**enterer** *n.*

enterectomy (ˌɛntəˈrɛktəmɪ) *n.* surgical excision of part of the intestine.

enteric (ɛnˈtɛrɪk) *or* **enteral** (ˈɛntərəl) *adj.* intestinal. [C19: from Greek *enterikos,* from *enteron* intestine] —ˈ**enterally** *adv.*

enteric fever *n.* another name for **typhoid fever.**

enter into *vb.* (*intr., prep.*) **1.** to be considered as a necessary part of (one's plans, calculations, etc.). **2.** to be in sympathy with: *he enters into his patient's problems.*

enteritis (ˌɛntəˈraɪtɪs) *n.* inflammation of the intestine.

entero- *or before a vowel* **enter-** *combining form.* indicating an intestine: *enterovirus; enteritis.* [from New Latin, from Greek *enteron* intestine]

enterobacterium (ˌɛntərəʊbækˈtɪərɪəm) *n.* any of a class of Gram-negative rodlike bacteria that occur in the gut.

enterobiasis (ˌɛntərəʊˈbaɪəsɪs) *n.* a disease, common in children, caused by infestation of the large intestine with nematodes of the genus *Enterobius,* esp. the pinworm (*E. vermicularis*).

enterocolitis (ˌɛntərəʊkɒˈlaɪtɪs) *n.* inflammation of the small intestine and colon.

enterogastrone (ˌɛntərəʊˈgæstrəʊn) *n.* a hormone liberated by the upper intestinal mucosa when stimulated by fat: reduces peristalsis and secretion in the stomach. [C20: from ENTERO- + GASTRO- + (HORM)ONE]

enterokinase (ˌɛntərəʊˈkaɪneɪz) *n.* an enzyme in intestinal juice that converts trypsinogen to trypsin.

enteron (ˈɛntəˌrɒn) *n., pl.* **-tera** (-tərə). the alimentary canal, esp. of an embryo or a coelenterate. [C19: via New Latin from Greek: intestine; related to Latin *inter* between]

enterostomy (ˌɛntəˈrɒstəmɪ) *n., pl.* **-mies.** surgical formation of a permanent opening into the intestine through the abdominal wall, used as an artificial anus, for feeding, etc.

enterotomy (ˌɛntəˈrɒtəmɪ) *n., pl.* **-mies.** surgical incision into the intestine.

enterovirus (ˌɛntərəʊˈvaɪrəs) *n., pl.* **-viruses.** any of a group of viruses that occur in and cause diseases of the gastrointestinal tract.

enterprise (ˈɛntəˌpraɪz) *n.* **1.** a project or undertaking, esp. one that requires boldness or effort. **2.** participation in such projects. **3.** readiness to embark on new ventures; boldness and energy. **4. a.** initiative in business. **b.** (*as modifier*): *the enterprise culture.* **5.** a business unit; a company or firm. [C15: from Old French *entreprise* (n.), from *entreprendre* from *entre-* between (from Latin: INTER-) + *prendre* to take, from Latin *prehendere* to grasp] —ˈ**enterˌpriser** *n.*

Enterprise Allowance Scheme *n.* (in Britain) a scheme to provide a weekly allowance to an unemployed person who wishes to set up a business and is willing to invest a specified amount in it during its first year.

enterprise zone *n.* a designated zone in a depressed area, esp. an inner urban area, where firms are given tax concessions and various planning restrictions are lifted, in order to attract new industry and business to the area: first introduced in Britain in 1981.

enterprising (ˈɛntəˌpraɪzɪŋ) *adj.* ready to embark on new ventures; full of boldness and initiative. —ˈ**enterˌprisingly** *adv.*

entertain (ˌɛntəˈteɪn) *vb.* **1.** to provide amusement for (a person or audience). **2.** to show hospitality to (guests). **3.** (*tr.*) to hold in the mind: *to entertain an idea.* [C15: from Old French *entretenir,* from *entre-* mutually + *tenir* to hold, from Latin *tenēre*]

entertainer (ˌɛntəˈteɪnə) *n.* **1.** a professional singer, comedian, or other performer who takes part in public entertainments. **2.** any person who entertains.

entertaining (ˌɛntəˈteɪnɪŋ) *adj.* serving to entertain or give pleasure; diverting; amusing. —ˌ**enterˈtainingly** *adv.*

entertainment (ˌɛntəˈteɪnmənt) *n.* **1.** the act or art of entertaining or state of being entertained. **2.** an act, production, etc., that entertains; diversion; amusement.

enthalpy (ˈɛnθəlpɪ, ɛnˈθæl-) *n.* a thermodynamic property of a system equal to the sum of its internal energy and the product of its pressure and volume. Symbol: *H* Also called: **heat content, total heat.** [C20: from Greek *enthalpein* to warm in, from EN-[2] + *thalpein* to warm]

enthetic (ɛnˈθɛtɪk) *adj.* (esp. of infectious diseases) introduced into the body from without. [C19: from Greek *enthetikos,* from *entithenai* to put in]

enthral *or U.S.* **enthrall** (ɪnˈθrɔːl) *vb.* **-thrals** *or U.S.* **-thralls, -thralling, -thralled.** (*tr.*) **1.** to hold spellbound; enchant; captivate. **2.** *Obsolete.* to hold as thrall; enslave. [C16: from EN-[1] + THRALL] —**enˈthraller** *n.* —**enˈthralling** *adj.* —**enˈthralment** *or U.S.* **enˈthrallment** *n.*

enthrone (ɛnˈθrəʊn) *vb.* (*tr.*) **1.** to place on a throne. **2.** to honour or exalt. **3.** to assign authority to. —**enˈthronement** *n.*

enthuse (ɪnˈθjuːz) *vb.* to feel or show or cause to feel or show enthusiasm.

enthusiasm (ɪnˈθjuːzɪˌæzəm) *n.* **1.** ardent and lively interest or eagerness. **2.** an object of keen interest; passion. **3.** *Archaic.* extravagant or unbalanced religious fervour. **4.** *Obsolete.* possession or inspiration by a god. [C17: from Late Latin *enthūsiasmus,* from Greek *enthousiasmos,* from *enthousiazein* to be possessed by a god, from *entheos* inspired, from EN-[2] + *theos* god]

enthusiast (ɪnˈθjuːzɪˌæst) *n.* **1.** a person filled with or motivated by enthusiasm; fanatic. **2.** *Archaic.* a religious visionary, esp. one whose zeal for religion is extravagant or unbalanced. —**enˌthusiˈastic** *adj.* —**enˌthusiˈastically** *adv.*

enthymeme (ˈɛnθɪˌmiːm) *n. Logic.* **1.** an incomplete syllogism, in which one or more premises are unexpressed as their truth is considered to be self-evident. **2.** any argument some of whose premises are omitted as obvious. [C16: via Latin from Greek *enthumēma,* from *enthumeisthai* to infer (literally: to have in the mind), from EN-[2] + *thumos* mind] —ˌ**enthymeˈmatic** *or* ˌ**enthymeˈmatical** *adj.*

entice (ɪnˈtaɪs) *vb.* (*tr.*) to attract or draw towards oneself by exciting hope or desire; tempt; allure. [C13: from Old French *enticier,* from Vulgar Latin *intitiāre* (unattested) to incite, from Latin *titiō* firebrand] —**enˈticement** *n.* —**enˈticer** *n.* —**enˈticing** *adj.* —**enˈticingly** *adv.* —**enˈticingness** *n.*

entire (ɪnˈtaɪə) *adj.* **1.** (*prenominal*) whole; complete: *the entire project is going well.* **2.** (*prenominal*) without reservation or exception; total: *you have my entire support.* **3.** not broken or damaged; intact. **4.** consisting of a single piece or section; undivided; continuous. **5.** (of leaves, petals, etc.) having a smooth margin not broken up into teeth or lobes. **6.** not castrated: *an entire horse.* **7.** *Obsolete.* of one substance or kind; unmixed; pure. ~*n.* **8.** a less common word for **entirety. 9.** an uncastrated horse. **10.** *Philately.* **a.** a complete item consisting of an envelope, postcard, or wrapper with stamps affixed. **b. on entire.** (of a stamp) placed on an envelope, postcard, etc., and bearing postal directions. [C14: from Old French *entier,* from Latin *integer* whole, from IN-[1] + *tangere* to touch] —**enˈtireness** *n.*

entirely (ɪnˈtaɪəlɪ) *adv.* **1.** without reservation or exception; wholly; completely. **2.** solely or exclusively; only.

entirety (ɪnˈtaɪərɪtɪ) *n., pl.* **-ties. 1.** the state of being entire or whole; completeness. **2.** a thing, sum, amount, etc., that is entire; whole; total.

entitle (ɪnˈtaɪtəl) *vb.* (*tr.*) **1.** to give (a person) the right to do or have something; qualify; allow. **2.** to give a name or title to. **3.** to confer a title of rank or honour upon. [C14: from Old French *entituler,* from Late Latin *intitulāre,* from Latin *titulus* TITLE] —**enˈtitlement** *n.*

entity (ˈɛntɪtɪ) *n., pl.* **-ties. 1.** something having real or distinct existence; a thing, esp. when considered as independent of other things. **2.** existence or being. **3.** the essence or real nature. [C16: from Medieval Latin *entitās,* from *ēns* being; see ENS] —**entitative** (ˈɛntɪtətɪv) *adj.*

ento- *combining form.* inside; within: *entoderm.* [New Latin, from Greek *entos* within]

entoblast (ˈɛntəʊˌblæst) *n.* **1.** *Embryol.* a less common name for **endoderm. 2.** a less common name for **hypoblast.** —**entoblastic** (ˌɛntəʊˈblæstɪk) *adj.*

entoderm (ˈɛntəʊˌdɜːm) *n. Embryol.* another name for **endoderm.** —ˌ**entoˈdermal** *or* ˌ**entoˈdermic** *adj.*

entoil (ɪnˈtɔɪl) *vb.* (*tr.*) an archaic word for **ensnare.** —**enˈtoilment** *n.*

entomb (ɪnˈtuːm) *vb.* (*tr.*) **1.** to place in or as if in a tomb; bury; inter. **2.** to serve as a tomb for. —**enˈtombment** *n.*

entomic (ɛnˈtɒmɪk) *adj.* denoting or relating to insects. [C19: from Greek *entomon* (see ENTOMO-) + -IC]

entomo- *combining form.* indicating an insect: *entomology.* [from Greek *entomon* insect (literally: creature cut into sections), from *en-* in + *-tomon,* from *temnein* to cut]

entomol. *or* **entom.** *abbrev. for* entomology.

entomologize *or* **entomologise** (ˌɛntəˈmɒləˌdʒaɪz) *vb.* (*intr.*) to collect or study insects.

entomology (ˌɛntəˈmɒlədʒɪ) *n.* the branch of science concerned with the study of insects. —**entomological** (ˌɛntəməˈlɒdʒɪkᵊl) *or* ˌ**entomoˈlogic** *adj.* —ˌ**entomoˈlogically** *adv.* —ˌ**entoˈmologist** *n.*

entomophagous (ˌɛntəˈmɒfəgəs) *adj.* feeding mainly on insects; insectivorous.

entomophilous (ˌɛntəˈmɒfɪləs) *adj.* (of flowering plants such as orchids) pollinated by insects. Compare **anemophilous.** —ˌ**entoˈmophily** *n.*

entomostracan (ˌɛntəˈmɒstrəkən) *n.* **1.** any small crustacean of the group (formerly subclass) *Entomostraca,* including the branchiopods, ostracods, and copepods. ~*adj.* **2.** of, relating to, or belonging to the *Entomostraca.* [C19: from New Latin ENTOMO- + Greek *ostrakon* shell; see OSTRACIZE] —ˌ**entoˈmostracous** *adj.*

entophyte (ˈɛntəʊˌfaɪt) *n. Botany.* a variant of **endophyte.** —**entophytic** (ˌɛntəʊˈfɪtɪk) *adj.*

entopic (ɛnˈtɒpɪk) *adj. Anatomy.* situated in its normal place or position. See also **ectopia.** [from Greek *entopos* in a place, from *topos* place]

entoptic (ɛnˈtɒptɪk) *adj.* (of visual sensation) resulting from structures within the eye itself. [ENTO- + OPTIC]

entourage (ɒntʊˈrɑːʒ; *French* ɑ̃turaʒ) *n.* **1.** a group of attendants or retainers, esp. such as surround an important person; retinue. **2.** surroundings or environment. [C19: from French, from *entourer* to surround, from *entour* around, from *tour* circuit; see TOUR, TURN]

entozoic (ˌɛntəʊˈzəʊɪk) *adj.* **1.** of or relating to an entozoon. **2.** living inside an animal: *entozoic fungi.*

entozoon (ˌɛntəʊˈzəʊɒn) *or* **entozoan** *n., pl.* **-zoa** (-ˈzəʊə). any animal, such as a tapeworm, that lives within another animal, usually as a parasite.

entr'acte (ɒnˈtrækt; *French* ɑ̃trakt) *n.* **1.** an interval between two acts of a play or opera. **2.** (esp. formerly) an entertainment during an interval, such as dancing between acts of an opera. [C19: French, literally: between-act]

entrails (ˈɛntreɪlz) *pl. n.* **1.** the internal organs of a person or animal; intestines; guts. **2.** the innermost parts of anything. [C13: from Old French *entrailles,* from Medieval Latin *intrālia,* changed from Latin *interānea* intestines, ultimately from *inter* between]

entrain[1] (ɪnˈtreɪn) *vb.* to board or put aboard a train. —**enˈtrainment** *n.*

entrain[2] (ɪnˈtreɪn) *vb.* (*tr.*) **1.** (of a liquid or gas) to carry along (drops of liquid, bubbles, etc.), as in certain distillations. **2.** to disperse (air bubbles) through concrete in order to increase its resistance to frost. **3.** *Zoology.* to adjust (an internal rhythm of an organism) so that it synchronizes with an external cycle, such as that of light and dark. —**enˈtrainment** *n.*

entrammel (ɪnˈtræməl) *vb.* **-mels, -melling, -melled.** (*tr.*) to hamper or obstruct by entangling.

entrance[1] (ˈɛntrəns) *n.* **1.** the act or an instance of entering; entry. **2.** a place for entering, such as a door or gate. **3. a.** the power, liberty, or right of entering; admission. **b.** (*as modifier*): *an entrance fee.* **4.** the coming of an actor or other performer onto a stage. [C16: from French, from *entrer* to ENTER]

entrance[2] (ɪnˈtrɑːns) *vb.* (*tr.*) **1.** to fill with wonder and delight; enchant. **2.** to put into a trance; hypnotize. —**enˈtrancement** *n.* —**enˈtrancing** *adj.*

entrant (ˈɛntrənt) *n.* **1.** a person who enters. **2.** a new member of a group, society, or association. **3.** a person who enters a competition or contest; competitor. [C17: from French, literally: entering, from *entrer* to ENTER]

entrap (ɪnˈtræp) *vb.* **-traps, -trapping, -trapped.** (*tr.*) **1.** to catch or snare in or as if in a trap. **2.** to lure or trick into danger, difficulty, or embarrassment. —**enˈtrapper** *n.*

entrapment (ɪnˈtræpmənt) *n. Chiefly U.S.* the luring, by a police officer, of a person into committing a crime so that he may be prosecuted for it.

entreat *or* **intreat** (ɪnˈtriːt) *vb.* **1.** to ask (a person) earnestly; beg or plead with; implore. **2.** to make an earnest request or petition for (something). **3.** an archaic word for **treat** (sense 4). [C15: from Old French *entraiter,* from EN-[1] + *traiter* to TREAT] —**enˈtreatingly** *or* **inˈtreatingly** *adv.* —**enˈtreatment** *or* **inˈtreatment** *n.*

entreaty (ɪnˈtriːtɪ) *n., pl.* **-treaties.** an earnest request or petition; supplication; plea.

entrechat (*French* ɑ̃trəʃa) *n.* a leap in ballet during which the dancer repeatedly crosses his feet or beats them together. [C18: from French, from earlier *entrechase,* changed by folk etymology from Italian (*capriola*) *intrecciata,* literally: entwined (caper), from *intrecciare* to interlace, from IN-[2] + *treccia* TRESS]

entrecôte (*French* ɑ̃trəkot) *n.* a beefsteak cut from between the ribs. [C19: French *entrecôte,* from *entre-* INTER- + *côte* rib, from Latin *costa*]

Entre-Deux-Mers (*French* ɑ̃trədømɛr) *n.* any wine produced in the area of the Gironde between the rivers Dordogne and Garonne in S France.

entrée (ˈɒntreɪ) *n.* **1.** a dish served before a main course. **2.** *Chiefly U.S.* the main course of a meal. **3.** the power or right of entry. [C18: from French, from *entrer* to ENTER; in cookery, so called because formerly the course was served after an intermediate course called the *relevé* (remove)]

entremets (*French* ɑ̃trəmɛ) *n., pl.* **-mets** (*French* -mɛ). **1.** a dessert. **2.** a light dish, formerly served at formal dinners between the main course and the dessert. [C18: from French, from Old French *entremes,* from *entre-* between, INTER- + *mes* dish, MESS]

entrench *or* **intrench** (ɪnˈtrɛntʃ) *vb.* **1.** (*tr.*) to construct (a defensive position) by digging trenches around it. **2.** (*tr.*) to fix or establish firmly, esp. so as to prevent removal or change. **3.** (*intr.*; foll. by *on* or *upon*) to trespass or encroach; infringe. —**enˈtrenched** *or* **inˈtrenched** *adj.* —**enˈtrencher** *or* **inˈtrencher** *n.*

entrenchment *or* **intrenchment** (ɪnˈtrɛntʃmənt) *n.* **1.** the act of entrenching or state of being entrenched. **2.** a position protected by trenches. **3.** one of a series of deep trenches constructed as a shelter from gunfire.

entre nous (*French* ɑ̃trə nu) *adv.* between ourselves; in confidence. [C17: from French]

entrepôt (*French* ɑ̃trəpo) *n.* **1.** a warehouse for commercial goods. **2. a.** a trading centre or port at a geographically convenient location, at which goods are imported and re-exported without incurring liability for duty. **b.** (*as modifier*): *an entrepôt trade.* [C18: French, from *entreposer* to put in, from *entre-* between, INTER- + *poser* to place (see POSE); formed on the model of DEPOT]

entrepreneur (ˌɒntrəprəˈnɜː; *French* ɑ̃trəprənœr) *n.* **1.** the owner or manager of a business enterprise who, by risk and initiative, attempts to make profits. **2.** a middleman or commercial intermediary. [C19: from French, from *entreprendre* to undertake; see ENTERPRISE] —ˌ**entrepreˈneurial** *adj.* —ˌ**entrepreˈneurship** *n.*

entresol (ˌɒntrəˈsɒl; *French* ɑ̃trəsɔl) *n.* another name for **mezzanine** (sense 1). [C18: from French, literally: between floors, from *entre-* INTER- + *sol* floor, ground, from Latin *solum*]

entropy (ˈɛntrəpɪ) *n., pl.* **-pies.** **1.** a thermodynamic quantity that changes in a reversible process by an amount equal to the heat absorbed or emitted divided by the thermodynamic temperature. It is measured in joules per kelvin. Symbol: S See also **law of thermodynamics** (sense 1). **2.** a statistical measure of the disorder of a closed system expressed by $S = k\log P + c$ where P is the probability that a particular state of the system exists, k is the Boltzmann constant, and c is another constant. **3.** lack of pattern or organization; disorder. **4.** a measure of the efficiency of a system, such as a code or language, in transmitting information. [C19: from EN-[2] + -TROPE]

entrust *or* **intrust** (ɪnˈtrʌst) *vb.* (*tr.*) **1.** (usually foll. by *with*) to invest or charge (with a duty, responsibility, etc.). **2.** (often foll. by *to*) to put into the care or protection of someone. —**enˈtrustment** *or* **inˈtrustment** *n.*

entry (ˈɛntrɪ) *n., pl.* **-tries.** **1.** the act or an instance of entering; entrance. **2.** a point or place for entering, such as a door, gate, etc. **3. a.** the right or liberty of entering; admission; access. **b.** (*as modifier*): *an entry permit.* **4.** the act of recording an item, such as a commercial transaction, in a journal, account, register, etc. **5.** an item recorded, as in a diary, dictionary, or account. **6. a.** a person, horse, car, etc., entering a competition or contest; competitor. **b.** (*as modifier*): *an entry fee.* **7.** the competitors entering a contest considered collectively: *a good entry this year for the speed trials.* **8.** the people admitted at one time to a school, college, or course of study, etc., considered collectively; intake. **9.** the action of an actor in going on stage or his manner of doing this. **10.** *Criminal law.* the act of unlawfully going onto the premises of another with the intention of committing a crime. **11.** *Property law.* the act of going upon another person's land with the intention of asserting the right to possession. **12.** any point in a piece of music, esp. a fugue, at which a performer commences or resumes playing or singing. **13.** *Cards.* a card that enables one to transfer the lead from one's own hand to that of one's partner or to the dummy hand. **14.** *English dialect.* a passage between the backs of two rows of terraced houses. [C13: from Old French *entree,* past participle of *entrer* to ENTER]

entryism (ˈɛntrɪɪzəm) *n.* the policy or practice of members of a particular political group joining an existing political party with the intention of changing its principles and policies, instead of forming a new party. —ˈ**entryist** *n., adj.*

entwine *or* **intwine** (ɪnˈtwaɪn) *vb.* (of two or more things) to twine together or (of one or more things) to twine around (something else). —**enˈtwinement** *or* **inˈtwinement** *n.*

enucleate *vb.* (ɪˈnjuːklɪˌeɪt). (*tr.*) **1.** *Biology.* to remove the nucleus from (a cell). **2.** *Surgery.* to remove (a tumour or other structure) from its capsule without rupturing it. **3.** *Archaic.* to explain or disclose. ~*adj.* (ɪ'njuːklɪɪt, -ˌeɪt). **4.** (of cells) deprived of their nuclei. [C16: from Latin *ēnucleāre* to remove the kernel, from *nūcleus* kernel] —**eˌnucle'ation** *n.*

E number *n.* any of a series of numbers with the prefix E indicating a specific food additive recognized by the European Economic Community and used on labels of processed food.

enumerate (ɪ'njuːməˌreɪt) *vb.* **1.** (*tr.*) to mention separately or in order; name one by one; list. **2.** (*tr.*) to determine the number of; count. **3.** *Canadian.* to compile or enter (a name or names) in a voting list for an area. [C17: from Latin *ēnumerāre,* from *numerāre* to count, reckon; see NUMBER] —**e'numerable** *adj.* —**eˌnumer'ation** *n.* —**e'numerative** *adj.*

enumerator (ɪ'njuːməˌreɪtə) *n.* **1.** a person or thing that enumerates. **2.** *Canadian.* a person who compiles the voting list for an area. **3.** *Brit.* a person who issues and retrieves forms during a census of population.

enunciable (ɪ'nʌnsɪəbᵊl) *adj.* capable of being enunciated.

enunciate (ɪ'nʌnsɪˌeɪt) *vb.* **1.** to articulate or pronounce (words), esp. clearly and distinctly. **2.** (*tr.*) to state precisely or formally. [C17: from Latin *ēnuntiāre* to declare, from *nuntiāre* to announce, from *nuntius* messenger] —**eˌnunci'ation** *n.* —**e'nunciative** *or* **e'nunciatory** *adj.* —**e'nunciatively** *adv.* —**e'nunciˌator** *n.*

enure (ɪ'njʊə) *vb.* a variant spelling of **inure.** —**en'urement** *n.*

enuresis (ˌɛnjʊ'riːsɪs) *n.* involuntary discharge of urine, esp. during sleep. [C19: from New Latin, from Greek EN-[2] + *ourein* to urinate, from *ouron* urine] —**enuretic** (ˌɛnjʊ'rɛtɪk) *adj.*

envelop (ɪn'vɛləp) *vb.* (*tr.*) **-lops, -loping, -loped.** **1.** to wrap or enclose in or as if in a covering. **2.** to conceal or obscure, as from sight or understanding: *a plan enveloped in mystery.* **3.** to surround or partially surround (an enemy force). [C14: from Old French *envoluper,* from EN-[1] + *voluper, voloper,* of obscure origin] —**en'velopment** *n.*

envelope ('ɛnvəˌləʊp, 'ɒn-) *n.* **1.** a flat covering of paper, usually rectangular in shape and with a flap that can be folded over and sealed, used to enclose a letter, etc. **2.** any covering or wrapper. **3.** *Biology.* any enclosing structure, such as a membrane, shell, or skin. **4.** the bag enclosing the gas in a balloon. **5.** *Maths.* a curve or surface that is tangential to each one of a group of curves or surfaces. **6.** *Electronics.* the sealed glass or metal housing of a valve, electric light, etc. **7.** *Telecomm.* the outer shape of a modulated wave, formed by the peaks of successive cycles of the carrier wave. [C18: from French *enveloppe,* from *envelopper* to wrap around; see ENVELOP]

envenom (ɪn'vɛnəm) *vb.* (*tr.*) **1.** to fill or impregnate with venom; make poisonous. **2.** to fill with bitterness or malice.

enviable ('ɛnvɪəbᵊl) *adj.* exciting envy; fortunate or privileged. —**'enviableness** *n.* —**'enviably** *adv.*

envious ('ɛnvɪəs) *adj.* feeling, showing, or resulting from envy. [C13: from Anglo-Norman, ultimately from Latin *invidiōsus* full of envy, INVIDIOUS; see ENVY] —**'enviously** *adv.* —**'enviousness** *n.*

environ (ɪn'vaɪrən) *vb.* (*tr.*) to encircle or surround. [C14: from Old French *environner* to surround, from *environ* around, from EN-[1] + *viron* a circle, from *virer* to turn, VEER]

environment (ɪn'vaɪrənmənt) *n.* **1.** external conditions or surroundings, esp. those in which people live or work. **2.** *Ecology.* the external surroundings in which a plant or animal lives, which tend to influence its development and behaviour. **3.** the state of being environed; encirclement. **4.** *Computer technol.* an operating system, program, or integrated suite of programs that provides all the facilities necessary for a particular application: *a word-processing environment.* —**enˌviron'mental** *adj.* —**enˌviron'mentally** *adv.*

Environmental Health Officer *n.* (in Britain) an employee of the Environmental Health Service. Former names: **public health inspector, sanitary inspector.**

Environmental Health Service *n.* (in Britain) a service provided by a local authority, which deals with prevention of the spread of communicable diseases, food safety and hygiene, control of infestation by insects or rodents, etc.

environmentalism (ɪnˌvaɪrən'mɛntəˌlɪzəm) *n.* *Psychol.* the belief that a person's behaviour is affected chiefly by his environment. Compare **hereditarianism.**

environmentalist (ɪnˌvaɪrən'mɛntəlɪst) *n.* **1.** an adherent of environmentalism. **2.** a specialist in the maintenance of ecological balance and the conservation of the environment. **3.** a person concerned with issues that affect the environment, such as pollution.

environs (ɪn'vaɪrənz) *pl. n.* a surrounding area or region, esp. the suburbs or outskirts of a town or city; vicinity.

envisage (ɪn'vɪzɪdʒ) *vb.* (*tr.*) **1.** to form a mental image of; visualize; contemplate. **2.** to conceive of as a possibility in the future; foresee. **3.** *Archaic.* to look in the face of; confront. [C19: from French *envisager,* from EN-[1] + *visage* face, VISAGE] —**en'visagement** *n.*

▷ **Usage.** *Envisage,* followed by *that* and a clause, has come to be used in place of such verbs as *expect* and *think: the board envisages that there will be a high profit.* American writers in particular tend to prefer *envision* for this usage. In careful English, *envisage* is usually used with a direct object rather than a clause to refer to conceptions of future possibilities: *he envisaged great success for his project.*

envision (ɪn'vɪʒən) *vb.* (*tr.*) to conceive of as a possibility, esp. in the future; foresee.

envoy[1] ('ɛnvɔɪ) *n.* **1.** Formal name: **envoy extraordinary and minister plenipotentiary.** a diplomat of the second class, ranking between an ambassador and a minister resident. **2.** an accredited messenger, agent, or representative. [C17: from French *envoyé,* literally: sent, from *envoyer* to send, from Vulgar Latin *inviāre* (unattested) to send on a journey, from IN-[2] + *via* road] —**'envoyship** *n.*

envoy[2] *or* **envoi** ('ɛnvɔɪ) *n.* **1.** a brief dedicatory or explanatory stanza concluding certain forms of poetry, notably ballades. **2.** a postscript in other forms of verse or prose. [C14: from Old French *envoye,* from *envoyer* to send; see ENVOY[1]]

envy ('ɛnvɪ) *n., pl.* **-vies.** **1.** a feeling of grudging or somewhat admiring discontent aroused by the possessions, achievements, or qualities of another. **2.** the desire to have for oneself something possessed by another; covetousness. **3.** an object of envy. ~*vb.* **-vies, -vying, -vied.** **4.** to be envious of (a person or thing). [C13: via Old French from Latin *invidia,* from *invidēre* to eye maliciously, from IN-[2] + *vidēre* to see] —**'envier** *n.* —**'envyingly** *adv.*

enwind (ɪn'waɪnd) *vb.* **-winds, -winding, -wound.** (*tr.*) to wind or coil around; encircle.

enwomb (ɪn'wuːm) *vb.* (*tr.; often passive*) to enclose in or as if in a womb.

enwrap *or* **inwrap** (ɪn'ræp) *vb.* **-wraps, -wrapping, -wrapped.** (*tr.*) **1.** to wrap or cover up; envelop. **2.** (*usually passive*) to engross or absorb: *enwrapped in thought.*

enwreath (ɪn'riːð) *vb.* (*tr.*) to surround or encircle with or as with a wreath or wreaths.

Enzed ('ɛn'zɛd) *n.* *Austral. and N.Z. informal.* **1.** New Zealand. **2.** Also called: **'En'zedder.** a New Zealander.

enzootic (ˌɛnzəʊ'ɒtɪk) *adj.* **1.** (of diseases) affecting animals within a limited region. ~*n.* **2.** an enzootic disease. ~Compare **epizootic.** [C19: from EN-[2] + Greek *zōion* animal + -OTIC] —**ˌenzo'otically** *adv.*

enzyme ('ɛnzaɪm) *n.* any of a group of complex proteins or conjugated proteins that are produced by living cells and act as catalysts in specific biochemical reactions. [C19: from Medieval Greek *enzumos* leavened, from Greek EN-[2] + *zumē* leaven] —**enzymatic** (ˌɛnzaɪ'mætɪk, -zɪ-) *or* **enzymic** (ɛn'zaɪmɪk, -'zɪm-) *adj.*

enzyme-linked immunosorbent assay (ˌɪmjʊnəʊ'sɔːbənt) *n.* the full name for **ELISA.**

enzymology (ˌɛnzaɪ'mɒlədʒɪ) *n.* the branch of science concerned with the study of enzymes. —**enzymological** (ˌɛnzaɪmə'lɒdʒɪkᵊl) *adj.* —**ˌenzy'mologist** *n.*

enzymolysis (ˌɛnzaɪ'mɒlɪsɪs) *n.* a biochemical decomposition, such as a fermentation, that is catalysed by an enzyme. —**enzymolytic** (ˌɛnzaɪmə'lɪtɪk) *adj.*

e.o. *abbrev. for* ex officio.

eo- *combining form.* early or primeval: *Eocene; eohippus.* [from Greek, from *ēōs* dawn]

eobiont (ˌiːəʊ'baɪənt) *n.* a hypothetical chemical precursor of a living cell. [C20: from EO- + Greek *biōnt* stem of present participle of *biōn* to live, from *bios* life]

EOC *abbrev. for* Equal Opportunities Commission.

Eocene ('iːəʊˌsiːn) *adj.* **1.** of, denoting, or formed in the second epoch of the Tertiary period, which lasted for 20 000 000 years, during which hooved mammals appeared. ~*n.* **2.** **the.** the Eocene epoch or rock series. [C19: from EO- + -CENE]

Eogene ('iːəʊˌdʒiːn) *adj., n.* another word for **Palaeogene.**

eohippus (ˌiːəʊ'hɪpəs) *n., pl.* **-puses.** the earliest horse: an extinct Eocene dog-sized animal of the genus *Hyracotherium,* with four-toed forelegs, three-toed hindlegs, and teeth specialized for browsing. [C19: New Latin, from EO- + Greek *hippos* horse]

Eolic (iː'ɒlɪk, ɪ'əʊlɪk) *adj., n.* a variant spelling of **Aeolic.**

eolipile (iː'ɒlɪˌpaɪl) *n.* a variant spelling of **aeolipile.**

eolith ('iːəʊlɪθ) *n.* a stone, usually crudely broken, used as a primitive tool in Eolithic times.

Eolithic (ˌiːəʊ'lɪθɪk) *adj.* denoting, relating to, or characteristic of the early part of the Stone Age, characterized by the use of crude stone tools.

e.o.m. *Commerce. abbrev. for* end of the month.

eon ('iːən, 'iːɒn) *n.* **1.** the usual U.S. spelling of **aeon.** **2.** *Geology.* the longest division of geological time, comprising two or more eras.

eonian (iː'əʊnɪən) *adj.* **1.** the usual U.S. spelling of **aeonian.** **2.** *Geology.* the longest division of geological time, comprising two or more eras.

eonism ('iːəˌnɪzəm) *n.* *Psychiatry.* the adoption of female dress and behaviour by a male. See also **transvestite.** [C19: named after Charles Éon de Beaumont (died 1810), French transvestite]

eosin ('iːəʊsɪn) *or* **eosine** ('iːəʊsɪn, -ˌsiːn) *n.* **1.** Also called: **bromeosin.** a red crystalline water-insoluble derivative of fluorescein. Its soluble salts are used as dyes. Formula: $C_{20}H_8Br_4O_5$. **2.** any of several similar dyes. [C19: from Greek *ēōs* dawn + -IN; referring to the colour it gives to silk] —**ˌeo'sinic** *adj.* —**'eosin-ˌlike** *adj.*

eosinophil (ˌiːəʊ'sɪnəfɪl) *or* **eosinophile** (ˌiːəʊ'sɪnəˌfaɪl) *n.* a leucocyte with a bilobed nucleus and coarse granular cytoplasm that stains readily with acidic dyes such as eosin. —**ˌeoˌsino'philic** *or* **eosinophilous** (ˌiːəʊsɪ'nɒfɪləs) *adj.*

eosinophilia (ˌiːəʊˌsɪnəˈfɪlɪə) *n.* the presence of abnormally large numbers of eosinophils in the blood, occurring in various diseases and in response to certain drugs.

-eous *suffix of adjectives.* relating to or having the nature of: *gaseous.* Compare **-ious.** [from Latin *-eus*]

Eozoic (ˌiːəʊˈzəʊɪk) *adj.* of or formed in the part of the Precambrian era during which life first appeared.

EP *n.* **1.** Also called: **maxisingle.** an extended-play gramophone record: usually 7 inches (18 cm) in diameter with a longer recording on it than a single, designed to be played at 45 or $33\frac{1}{3}$ revolutions per minute. Compare **LP**[1]. ~*adj.* **2.** denoting such a record.

Ep. *abbrev. for* Epistle.

e.p. *Chess. abbrev. for* en passant.

ep- *prefix.* variant of **epi-** before a vowel: *epexegesis.*

EPA *abbrev. for* eicosapentaenoic acid: a fatty acid, found in certain fish oils, that can reduce blood cholesterol.

epact (ˈiːpækt) *n.* **1.** the difference in time, about 11 days, between the solar year and the lunar year. **2.** the number of days between the beginning of the calendar year and the new moon immediately preceding this. **3.** the difference in time between the calendar month and the synodic month. [C16: via Late Latin from Greek *epaktē,* from *epagein* to bring in, intercalate, from *agein* to lead]

epanalepsis (ɪˌpænəˈlɛpsɪs) *n. Rhetoric.* the repetition, after a more or less lengthy passage of subordinate or parenthetic text, of a word or clause that was used before. [C16: from Greek, from EPI- + ANA- + *lēpis* taking, from *lambanein* to take up] —ˌ**epanaˈleptic** *adj.*

epanaphora (ˌɛpəˈnæfərə) *n. Rhetoric.* another word for **anaphora.** —ˌ**epanaphˈoral** *adj.*

epanorthosis (ɪˌpænɔːˈθəʊsɪs) *n. Rhetoric.* the almost immediate replacement of a preceding word or phrase by a more correct or more emphatic one, as for example in *thousands, nay, millions.* [C16: from Greek: correction, from EPI- + ANA- + *orthos* straight] —ˌ**epanorˈthotic** *adj.*

eparch (ˈɛpɑːk) *n.* **1.** a bishop or metropolitan in charge of an eparchy (sense 1). **2.** a government official in charge of an eparchy (senses 2 or 3). [C17: from Greek *eparkhos,* from *epi-* over, on + -ARCH]

eparchy (ˈɛpɑːkɪ) *or* **eparchate** (ˈɛpɑːkɪt) *n., pl.* **-chies** *or* **-chates.** **1.** a diocese of the Eastern Christian Church. **2.** (in ancient Greece) a province. **3.** (in modern Greece) a subdivision of a province. —**epˈarchial** *adj.*

épatant *French.* (epatɑ̃) *adj.* startling or shocking, esp. through being unconventional. [C20: from present participle of *épater* to flabbergast]

epaulette *or U.S.* **epaulet** (ˈɛpəˌlɛt, -lɪt) *n.* a piece of ornamental material on the shoulder of a garment, esp. a military uniform. [C18: from French *épaulette,* from *épaule* shoulder, from Latin *spatula* shoulder blade; see SPATULA]

épée (ˈɛpeɪ; *French* epe) *n.* a sword similar to the foil but with a larger guard and a heavier blade of triangular cross section. [C19: from French: sword, from Latin *spatha,* from Greek *spathē* blade; see SPADE[1]]

épéeist (ˈɛpeɪɪst) *n. Fencing.* one who uses or specializes in using an épée.

epeiric (ɪˈpaɪrɪk) *adj. Geology.* in, of, or relating to a continent: *an epeiric sea.* [C20: from Greek *ēpeiros* continent + -IC]

epeirogeny (ˌɛpaɪˈrɒdʒɪnɪ) *or* **epeirogenesis** (ɪˌpaɪrəʊˈdʒɛnɪsɪs) *n.* the formation and submergence of continents by broad relatively slow displacements of the earth's crust. Also called: **epirogeny.** [C19: from Greek *ēpeiros* continent + -GENY] —**epeirogenic** (ɪˌpaɪrəʊˈdʒɛnɪk) *or* **epeirogenetic** (ɪˌpaɪrəʊdʒɪˈnɛtɪk) *adj.*

epencephalon (ˌɛpɛnˈsɛfəˌlɒn) *n., pl.* **-la** (-lə). *Anatomy.* **1.** the cerebellum and pons Varolii. **2.** the part of the embryonic brain that develops into this; metencephalon. [C19: New Latin; see EPI-, ENCEPHALON] —ˌ**epencephalic** (ˌɛpɛnsɪˈfælɪk) *adj.*

ependyma (ɪˈpɛndɪmə) *n.* the membrane lining the ventricles of the brain and the central canal of the spinal cord. —**eˈpendymal** *adj.*

epenthesis (ɛˈpɛnθɪsɪs) *n., pl.* **-ses** (-ˌsiːz). the insertion of a sound or letter into a word. [C17: via Late Latin from Greek, from *epentithenai* to insert, from EPI- + EN-[2] + *tithenai* to place] —**epenthetic** (ˌɛpɛnˈθɛtɪk) *adj.*

epergne (ɪˈpɜːn) *n.* an ornamental centrepiece for a table: a stand with holders for sweetmeats, fruit, flowers, etc. [C18: probably from French *épargne* a saving, from *épargner* to economize, of Germanic origin; compare SPARE]

epexegesis (ɛˌpɛksɪˈdʒiːsɪs) *n., pl.* **-ses** (-ˌsiːz). *Rhetoric.* **1.** the addition of a phrase, clause, or sentence to a text to provide further explanation. **2.** the phrase, clause, or sentence added for this purpose. [C17: from Greek; see EPI-, EXEGESIS] —**epexegetic** (ɛˌpɛksɪˈdʒɛtɪk) *or* **epˌexeˈgetical** *adj.* —**epˌexeˈgetically** *adv.*

Eph. *or* **Ephes.** *Bible. abbrev. for* Ephesians.

eph- *prefix.* a variant of **epi-** before an aspirate: *ephedra; ephedrine.*

ephah *or* **epha** (ˈiːfə) *n.* a Hebrew unit of dry measure equal to approximately one bushel or about 33 litres. [C16: from Hebrew *'ephāh,* of Egyptian origin]

ephebe (ɪˈfiːb, ˈɛfiːb) *n.* (in ancient Greece) a youth about to enter full citizenship, esp. one undergoing military training. [C19: from Latin *ephēbus,* from Greek *ephēbos,* from *hēbē* young manhood] —**eˈphebic** *adj.*

ephedra (ɪˈfɛdrə) *n.* any gymnosperm shrub of the genus *Ephedra,* of warm regions of America and Eurasia: the source of ephedrine: family *Ephedraceae,* order *Gnetales.* [C18: New Latin, from Latin, from Greek *ephedros* a sitting upon, from EPI- + *hedra* seat]

ephedrine *or* **ephedrin** (ɪˈfɛdrɪn, ˈɛfɪˌdriːn, -drɪn) *n.* a white crystalline alkaloid obtained from plants of the genus *Ephedra:* used for the treatment of asthma and hay fever; l-phenyl-2-methylaminopropanol. Formula: $C_6H_5CH(OH)CH(NHCH_3)CH_3$. [C19: from New Latin EPHEDRA + -INE[2]]

ephemera (ɪˈfɛmərə) *n., pl.* **-eras** *or* **-erae** (-əˌriː). **1.** a mayfly, esp. one of the genus *Ephemera.* **2.** something transitory or short-lived. **3.** (*functioning as pl.*) a class of collectable items not originally intended to last for more than a short time, such as tickets, posters, postcards, or labels. **4.** a plural of **ephemeron.** [C16; see EPHEMERAL]

ephemeral (ɪˈfɛmərəl) *adj.* **1.** lasting for only a short time; transitory; short-lived: *ephemeral pleasure.* ~*n.* **2.** a short-lived organism, such as the mayfly. [C16: from Greek *ephēmeros* lasting only a day, from *hēmera* day] —**eˈphemerally** *adv.* —**eˌphemerˈality** *or* **eˈphemeralness** *n.*

ephemerid (ɪˈfɛmərɪd) *n.* any insect of the order *Ephemeroptera* (or *Ephemerida*), which comprises the mayflies. Also called: **ephemeropteran.** [C19: from New Latin *Ephēmerida,* from Greek *ephēmeros* short-lived + -ID[2]]

ephemeris (ɪˈfɛmərɪs) *n., pl.* **ephemerides** (ˌɛfɪˈmɛrɪˌdiːz). **1.** a table giving the future positions of a planet, comet, or satellite. **2.** an annual publication giving the positions of the sun, moon, and planets during the course of a year, information concerning eclipses, astronomical constants, etc. **3.** *Obsolete.* a diary or almanac. [C16: from Latin, from Greek: diary, journal; see EPHEMERAL]

ephemeris time *n.* time based on the orbit of the earth around the sun rather than the axial rotation of the earth, one **ephemeris second** being 1/31 556 925.9747 of the tropical year 1900. It is used in astronomical calculations such as the construction of almanacs and ephemerides.

ephemeron (ɪˈfɛməˌrɒn) *n., pl.* **-era** (-ərə) *or* **-erons.** (*usually pl.*). something transitory or short-lived. [C16; see EPHEMERAL]

ephemeropteran (iːˌfɛməˈrɒptərən) *n.* **1.** another word for **ephemerid.** ~*adj.* **2.** of or relating to the *Ephemeroptera.*

Ephesian (ɪˈfiːʒən) *adj.* **1.** of or relating to Ephesus, a city of ancient Greece. ~*n.* **2.** an inhabitant or native of Ephesus.

ephod (ˈiːfɒd) *n. Old Testament.* an embroidered vestment believed to resemble an apron with shoulder straps, worn by priests in ancient Israel. [C14: from Hebrew *ēphōdh*]

ephor (ˈɛfɔː) *n., pl* **-ors** *or* **-ori** (-əˌraɪ). (in ancient Greece) one of a board of senior magistrates in any of several Dorian states, esp. the five Spartan ephors, who were elected by vote of all full citizens and who wielded effective power. [C16: from Greek *ephoros,* from *ephoran* to supervise, from EPI- + *horan* to look] —ˈ**ephoral** *adj.* —ˈ**ephorate** *n.*

epi-, eph-, *or before a vowel* **ep-** *prefix.* **1.** on; upon; above; over: *epidermis; epicentre.* **2.** in addition to: *epiphenomenon.* **3.** after: *epigenesis; epilogue.* **4.** near; close to: *epicalyx.* [from Greek, from *epi* (prep.)]

epibiosis (ˌɛpɪbaɪˈəʊsɪs) *n.* any relationship between two organisms in which one grows on the other but is not parasitic on it. See also **epiphyte, epizoite.** —**epibiotic** (ˌɛpɪbaɪˈɒtɪk) *adj.*

epiblast (ˈɛpɪˌblæst) *n. Embryol.* the outermost layer of an embryo, which becomes the ectoderm at gastrulation. Also called: **ectoblast.** —ˌ**epiˈblastic** *adj.*

epiblem (ˈɛpɪblɛm) *n. Botany.* the outermost cell layer of a root; epidermis.

epiboly (ɪˈpɪbəlɪ) *n., pl.* **-lies.** *Embryol.* a process that occurs during gastrulation in vertebrates, in which cells on one side of the blastula grow over and surround the remaining cells and yolk and eventually form the ectoderm. [C19: from Greek *epibolē* a laying on, from *epiballein* to throw on, from EPI- + *ballein* to throw] —**epibolic** (ˌɛpɪˈbɒlɪk) *adj.*

epic (ˈɛpɪk) *n.* **1.** a long narrative poem recounting in elevated style the deeds of a legendary hero, esp. one originating in oral folk tradition. **2.** the genre of epic poetry. **3.** any work of literature, film, etc., having heroic deeds for its subject matter or having other qualities associated with the epic: *a Hollywood epic.* **4.** an episode in the lives of men in which heroic deeds are performed or attempted: *the epic of Scott's expedition to the South Pole.* ~*adj.* **5.** denoting, relating to, or characteristic of an epic or epics. **6.** of heroic or impressive proportions: *an epic voyage.* [C16: from Latin *epicus,* from Greek *epikos,* from *epos* speech, word, song]

epicalyx (ˌɛpɪˈkeɪlɪks, -ˈkæl-) *n., pl.* **-lyxes** *or* **-lyces** (-lɪˌsiːz). *Botany.* a series of small sepal-like bracts forming an outer calyx beneath the true calyx in some flowers.

epicanthus (ˌɛpɪˈkænθəs) *n., pl.* **-thi** (-θaɪ). a fold of skin extending vertically over the inner angle of the eye: characteristic of Mongolian peoples and a congenital anomaly among other races. Also called: **epicanthic fold.** [C19: New Latin, from EPI- + Latin *canthus* corner of the eye, from Greek *kanthos*] —ˌepi'canthic *adj.*

epicardium (ˌɛpɪ'kɑːdɪəm) *n., pl.* **-dia** (-dɪə). *Anatomy.* the innermost layer of the pericardium, in direct contact with the heart. [C19: New Latin, from EPI- + Greek *kardia* heart] —ˌepi'cardiac *or* ˌepi'cardial *adj.*

epicarp ('ɛpɪˌkɑːp) *or* **exocarp** *n.* the outermost layer of the pericarp of fruits: forms the skin of a peach or grape. [C19: from French *épicarpe,* from EPI- + Greek *karpos* fruit]

epicedium (ˌɛpɪ'siːdɪəm) *n., pl.* **-dia** (-dɪə). *Rare.* a funeral ode. [C16: Latin, from Greek *epikēdeion,* from EPI- + *kēdos* care]

epicene ('ɛpɪˌsiːn) *adj.* **1.** having the characteristics of both sexes; hermaphroditic. **2.** of neither sex; sexless. **3.** effeminate. **4.** *Grammar.* **a.** denoting a noun that may refer to a male or a female, such as *teacher* as opposed to *businessman* or *shepherd.* **b.** (in Latin, Greek, etc.) denoting a noun that retains the same grammatical gender regardless of the sex of the referent. ~*n.* **5.** an epicene person or creature. **6.** an epicene noun. [C15: from Latin *epicoenus* of both genders, from Greek *epikoinos* common to many, from *koinos* common] —ˌepi'cenism *n.*

epicentre *or U.S.* **epicenter** ('ɛpɪˌsɛntə), *n., pl.* **-tres** *or U.S.* **-ters.** the point on the earth's surface directly above the focus of an earthquake or underground nuclear explosion. Compare **focus** (sense 6). [C19: from New Latin *epicentrum,* from Greek *epikentros* over the centre, from EPI- + *kentron* needle; see CENTRE] —ˌepi'central *adj.*

epiclesis (ˌɛpɪ'kliːsɪs) *n., pl.* **-ses** (-siːz). *Christianity.* the invocation of the Holy Spirit to consecrate the bread and wine of the Eucharist. [C19: from Greek, from EPI- + *klēsis* a prayer, from *kalein* to call]

epicontinental (ˌɛpɪˌkɒntɪ'nɛntᵊl) *adj.* (esp. of a sea) situated on a continental shelf or continent.

epicotyl (ˌɛpɪ'kɒtɪl) *n.* the part of an embryo plant stem above the cotyledons but beneath the terminal bud. [C19: from EPI- + Greek *kotulē;* see COTYLEDON]

epicrisis[1] (ɪ'pɪkrɪsɪs) *n. Rare.* a critical evaluation, esp. of a literary work. [C19: from Greek *epikrisis* a judgment, from *epikrinein* to decide, from EPI- + *krinein* to judge]

epicrisis[2] ('ɛpɪˌkraɪsɪs) *n. Pathol.* a secondary crisis occurring in the course of a disease. [C20: from EPI- + CRISIS]

epicritic (ˌɛpɪ'krɪtɪk) *adj.* (of certain nerve fibres of the skin) serving to perceive and distinguish fine variations of temperature or touch. [C20: from Greek *epikritikos* decisive; see EPICRISIS[1]]

epic simile *n.* an extended simile, as used in the epic poetry of Homer and other writers.

epicure ('ɛpɪˌkjʊə) *n.* **1.** a person who cultivates a discriminating palate for the enjoyment of good food and drink; gourmet. **2.** a person devoted to sensual pleasures. [C16: from Medieval Latin *epicūrus,* after *Epicurus;* see EPICUREAN] —'epicurˌism *n.*

epicurean (ˌɛpɪkjʊ'riːən) *adj.* **1.** devoted to sensual pleasures, esp. food and drink; hedonistic. **2.** suitable for an epicure: *an epicurean feast.* ~*n.* **3.** an epicure; gourmet. —ˌepicu'reanism *n.*

Epicurean (ˌɛpɪkjʊ'riːən) *adj.* **1.** of or relating to the philosophy of Epicurus (341–270 B.C.), Greek philosopher who held that the highest good is pleasure. ~*n.* **2.** a follower of the philosophy of Epicurus. —ˌEpicu'reanism *n.*

epicuticle ('ɛpɪˌkjuːtɪkᵊl) *n.* **1.** *Botany.* a waxy layer on the surface of the cuticle. **2.** *Zoology.* the outermost lipoprotein layer of the insect cuticle.

epicycle ('ɛpɪˌsaɪkᵊl) *n.* **1.** *Astronomy.* (in the Ptolemaic system) a small circle, around which a planet was thought to revolve, whose centre describes a larger circle (the **deferent**) centred on the earth. **2.** a circle that rolls around the inside or outside of another circle, so generating an epicycloid or hypocycloid. [C14: from Late Latin *epicyclus,* from Greek *epikuklos;* see EPI-, CYCLE] —**epicyclic** (ˌɛpɪ'saɪklɪk, -'sɪklɪk) *or* ˌepi'cyclical *adj.*

epicyclic train *n.* a cluster of gears consisting of a central gearwheel with external teeth (the sun), a coaxial gearwheel of greater diameter with internal teeth (the annulus), and one or more planetary gears engaging with both of them to provide a large gear ratio in a compact space.

epicycloid (ˌɛpɪ'saɪklɔɪd) *n.* the curve described by a point on the circumference of a circle as this circle rolls around the outside of another fixed circle, the two circles being coplanar. Compare **hypocycloid, cycloid** (sense 4). —ˌepicy'cloidal *adj.*

epicycloidal wheel *n.* one of the planetary gears of an epicyclic train.

epideictic (ˌɛpɪ'daɪktɪk) *adj.* designed to display something, esp. the skill of the speaker in rhetoric. Also: **epidictic** (ˌɛpɪ'dɪktɪk). [C18: from Greek *epideiktikos,* from *epideiknunai* to display, show off, from *deiknunai* to show]

epidemic (ˌɛpɪ'dɛmɪk) *adj.* **1.** (esp. of a disease) attacking or affecting many persons simultaneously in a community or area. ~*n.* **2.** a widespread occurrence of a disease: *an influenza epidemic.* **3.** a rapid development, spread, or growth of something, esp. something unpleasant: *an epidemic of strikes.* [C17: from French *épidémique,* via Late Latin from Greek *epidēmia* literally: among the people, from EPI- + *dēmos* people] —ˌepi'demically *adv.*

epidemic encephalitis *n. Pathol.* a technical name for **sleeping sickness** (sense 2).

epidemic meningitis *n.* another name for **cerebrospinal meningitis.**

epidemic parotitis *n.* another name for **mumps.**

epidemiology (ˌɛpɪˌdiːmɪ'ɒlədʒɪ) *n.* the branch of medical science concerned with the occurrence, transmission, and control of epidemic diseases. —**epidemiological** (ˌɛpɪˌdiːmɪə'lɒdʒɪkᵊl) *adj.* —ˌepiˌdemio'logically *adv.* —ˌepiˌdemi'ologist *n.*

epidermis (ˌɛpɪ'dɜːmɪs) *n.* **1.** Also called: **cuticle.** the thin protective outer layer of the skin, composed of stratified epithelial tissue. **2.** the outer layer of cells of an invertebrate. **3.** the outer protective layer of cells of a plant, which may be thickened by a cuticle. [C17: via Late Latin from Greek, from EPI- + *derma* skin] —ˌepi'dermal, ˌepi'dermic, *or* ˌepi'dermoid *adj.*

epidiascope (ˌɛpɪ'daɪəˌskəʊp) *n.* an optical device for projecting a magnified image onto a screen. See also **episcope.**

epididymis (ˌɛpɪ'dɪdɪmɪs) *n., pl.* **-didymides** (-dɪ'dɪmɪˌdiːz). *Anatomy.* a convoluted tube situated along the posterior margin of each testis, in which spermatozoa are stored and conveyed to the vas deferens. [C17: from Greek *epididumis,* from EPI- + *didumos* twin, testicle; see DIDYMOUS] —ˌepi'didymal *adj.*

epidote ('ɛpɪˌdəʊt) *n.* a green mineral consisting of hydrated calcium iron aluminium silicate in monoclinic crystalline form: common in metamorphic rocks. Formula: $Ca_2(Al,Fe)_3(SiO_4)_3(OH)$. [C19: from French *épidote,* ultimately from Greek *epididonai* to increase, from *didonai* to give; so called because two sides of its crystal are longer than the other two sides] —**epidotic** (ˌɛpɪ'dɒtɪk) *adj.*

epidural (ˌɛpɪ'djʊərəl) *adj.* **1.** Also: **extradural.** upon or outside the dura mater. ~*n.* **2.** Also called: **epidural anaesthesia. a.** injection of anaesthetic into the space outside the dura mater enveloping the spinal cord. **b.** anaesthesia induced by this method. [C19: from EPI- + DUR(A MATER) + -AL[1]]

epifocal (ˌɛpɪ'fəʊkᵊl) *adj. Geology.* situated or occurring at an epicentre.

epigamic (ˌɛpɪ'gæmɪk) *adj. Zoology.* attractive to the opposite sex: *epigamic coloration.*

epigastrium (ˌɛpɪ'gæstrɪəm) *n., pl.* **-tria** (-trɪə). the upper middle part of the abdomen, above the navel and below the breast. [C17: from New Latin, from Greek EPI- + *gastrion,* from *gastēr* stomach] —ˌepi'gastric *or* ˌepi'gastrial *adj.*

epigeal (ˌɛpɪ'dʒiːəl), **epigean,** *or* **epigeous** *adj.* **1.** of or relating to seed germination in which the cotyledons appear above the ground because of the growth of the hypocotyl. **2.** living or growing on or close to the surface of the ground. [C19: from Greek *epigeios* of the earth, from EPI- + *gē* earth]

epigene ('ɛpɪˌdʒiːn) *adj.* formed or taking place at the surface of the earth. Compare **hypogene.** [C19: from French *épigène,* ultimately from Greek *epigignesthai* to be born after, from *gignesthai* to be born]

epigenesis (ˌɛpɪ'dʒɛnɪsɪs) *n.* **1.** the widely accepted theory that an individual animal or plant develops by the gradual differentiation and elaboration of a fertilized egg cell. Compare **preformation** (sense 2). **2.** the formation of ore deposits after the surrounding rock has been formed. **3.** alteration of the mineral composition of a rock by external agents: a type of metamorphism. —ˌepi'genesist *or* **epigenist** (ɪ'pɪdʒɪnɪst) *n.* —**epigenetic** (ˌɛpɪdʒɪ'nɛtɪk) *adj.* —ˌepige'netically *adv.*

epigenous (ɪ'pɪdʒɪnəs) *adj. Biology.* growing on the surface, esp. the upper surface, of an organism or part: *an epigenous fungus.*

epigeous (ˌɛpɪ'dʒiːəs) *adj.* a variant of **epigeal.**

epiglottis (ˌɛpɪ'glɒtɪs) *n., pl.* **-tises** *or* **-tides** (-tɪˌdiːz). a thin cartilaginous flap that covers the entrance to the larynx during swallowing, preventing food from entering the trachea. —ˌepi'glottal *or* ˌepi'glottic *adj.*

epignathous (ˌɛpɪg'neɪθəs) *adj. Zoology.* having a protruding upper jaw.

epigone ('ɛpɪˌgəʊn) *or* **epigon** ('ɛpɪˌgɒn) *n. Rare.* an inferior follower or imitator. [C19: from Greek *epigonos* one born after, from *epigignesthai;* see EPIGENE]

epigram ('ɛpɪˌgræm) *n.* **1.** a witty, often paradoxical remark, concisely expressed. **2.** a short, pungent, and often satirical poem, esp. one having a witty and ingenious ending. [C15: from Latin *epigramma,* from Greek: inscription, from *epigraphein* to write upon, from *graphein* to write] —ˌepigram'matic *adj.* —ˌepigram'matically *adv.*

epigrammatize *or* **epigrammatise** (ˌɛpɪ'græməˌtaɪz) *vb.* to make an epigram or epigrams (about). —ˌepi'grammatism *n.* —ˌepi'grammatist *n.*

epigraph ('ɛpɪˌgrɑːf, -ˌgræf) *n.* **1.** a quotation at the beginning of a book, chapter, etc., suggesting its theme. **2.** an inscription on a monument or building. [C17: from Greek *epigraphē;* see EPIGRAM] —**epigraphic** (ˌɛpɪ'græfɪk) or ˌepi'graphical *adj.* —ˌepi'graphically *adv.*

epigraphy (ɪ'pɪgrəfɪ) *n.* **1.** the study of ancient inscriptions. **2.** epigraphs collectively. —e'pigraphist *or* e'pigrapher *n.*

epigynous (ɪ'pɪdʒɪnəs) *adj.* (of flowers) having the receptacle enclosing and fused with the gynoecium so that the other floral parts arise above it. [C19: from EPI- + Greek *gunē* (female organ, pistil) + -OUS] —e'pigyny *n.*

epilate ('ɛpɪˌleɪt) *vb. (tr.) Rare.* to remove hair from. [C19: from French *épiler* (modelled on *dépiler* DEPILATE) + -ATE[1]] —ˌepi'lation *n.*

epilator ('ɛpɪˌleɪtə) *n.* an electrical appliance consisting of a metal spiral head that rotates at high speed, plucking unwanted hair.

epilepsy ('ɛpɪˌlɛpsɪ) *n.* a disorder of the central nervous system characterized by periodic loss of consciousness with or without convulsions. In some cases it is due to brain damage but in others the cause is unknown. See also **grand mal, petit mal.** [C16: from Late Latin *epilēpsia,* from Greek, from *epilambanein* to attack, seize, from *lambanein* to take]

epileptic (ˌɛpɪ'lɛptɪk) *adj.* **1.** of, relating to, or having epilepsy. ~*n.* **2.** a person who has epilepsy. —ˌ**epi'leptically** *adv.*

epileptogenic (ˌɛpɪˌlɛptəʊ'dʒɛnɪk) *adj.* causing an epileptic attack.

epileptoid (ˌɛpɪ'lɛptɔɪd) *or* **epileptiform** (ˌɛpɪ'lɛptɪˌfɔːm) *adj.* resembling epilepsy.

epilimnion (ˌɛpɪ'lɪmnɪən) *n.* the upper layer of water in a lake. [C20: from EPI- + Greek *limnion,* diminutive of *limnē* lake]

epilithic (ˌɛpɪ'lɪθɪk) *adj.* (of plants) growing on the surface of rock.

epilogue ('ɛpɪˌlɒg) *n.* **1. a.** a speech, usually in verse, addressed to the audience by an actor at the end of a play. **b.** the actor speaking this. **2.** a short postscript to any literary work, such as a brief description of the fates of the characters in a novel. **3.** *Brit.* the concluding programme of the day on a radio or television station, often having a religious content. [C15: from Latin *epilogus,* from Greek *epilogos,* from *logos* word, speech] —**epilogist** (ɪ'pɪlədʒɪst) *n.*

epimere ('ɛpɪˌmɪə) *n. Embryol.* the dorsal part of the mesoderm of a vertebrate embryo, consisting of a series of segments (somites).

epimerism (ɪ'pɪməˌrɪzəm) *n.* optical isomerism in which isomers (**epimers**) can form about asymmetric atoms within the molecule, esp. in carbohydrates. [C20: from German *Epimer* (see EPI-, -MER) + -ISM] —**epimeric** (ˌɛpɪ'mɛrɪk) *adj.*

epimorphosis (ˌɛpɪmɔː'fəʊsɪs) *n.* a type of development in animals, such as certain insect larvae, in which segmentation of the body is complete before hatching. —ˌ**epi'morphic** *adj.*

epimysium (ˌɛpɪ'mɪzɪəm) *n., pl.* **-sia** (-zɪə). *Anatomy.* the sheath of connective tissue that encloses a skeletal muscle. [from New Latin, from EPI- + Greek *mus* mouse, MUSCLE]

epinasty ('ɛpɪˌnæstɪ) *n., pl.* **-ties.** increased growth of the upper surface of a plant part, such as a leaf, resulting in a downward bending of the part. Compare **hyponasty.** [C19: from EPI- + *-nasty,* from Greek *nastos* pressed down, from *nassein* to press] —ˌ**epi'nastic** *adj.*

epinephrine (ˌɛpɪ'nɛfrɪn, -riːn) *or* **epinephrin** *n.* a U.S. name for **adrenaline.** [C19: from EPI- + *nephro-* + -INE[2]]

epineurium (ˌɛpɪ'njʊərɪəm) *n.* a sheath of connective tissue around two or more bundles of nerve fibres. [C19: from New Latin, from EPI- + Greek *neuron* nerve + -IUM] —ˌ**epi'neurial** *adj.*

epipelagic (ˌɛpɪpə'lædʒɪk) *adj.* of, relating to, or inhabiting the upper zone of the ocean from just below the surface to approximately 100 metres deep.

epipetalous (ˌɛpɪ'pɛtələs) *adj. Botany.* (of stamens) attached to the petals.

Epiph. *abbrev. for* Epiphany.

epiphany (ɪ'pɪfənɪ) *n., pl.* **-nies. 1.** the manifestation of a supernatural or divine reality. **2.** any moment of great or sudden revelation. [C17: via Church Latin from Greek *epiphaneia* an appearing, from EPI- + *phainein* to show] —**epiphanic** (ˌɛpɪ'fænɪk) *adj.*

Epiphany (ɪ'pɪfənɪ) *n., pl.* **-nies.** a Christian festival held on Jan. 6, commemorating, in the Western Church, the manifestation of Christ to the Magi and, in the Eastern Church, the baptism of Christ.

epiphenomenalism (ˌɛpɪfɪ'nɒmɪnəˌlɪzəm) *n.* the dualistic doctrine that consciousness is merely a by-product of physiological processes and has no power to affect them. Compare **interactionism, parallelism.** —ˌ**epiphe'nomenalist** *n., adj.*

epiphenomenon (ˌɛpɪfɪ'nɒmɪnən) *n., pl.* **-na** (-nə). **1.** a secondary or additional phenomenon; by-product. **2.** *Pathol.* an unexpected or atypical symptom or occurrence during the course of a disease. —ˌ**epiphe'nomenal** *adj.* —ˌ**epiphe'nomenally** *adv.*

epiphragm ('ɛpɪˌfræm) *n.* a disc of calcium phosphate and mucilage secreted by snails over the aperture of their shells before hibernation. [C19: via New Latin from Greek *epiphragma* a lid, from *epiphrassein,* from EPI- + *phrassein* to place in an enclosure]

epiphyllous (ˌɛpɪ'fɪləs) *adj. Botany.* (of plants) growing on, or attached to, the leaf of another plant.

epiphysis (ɪ'pɪfɪsɪs) *n., pl.* **-ses** (-ˌsiːz). **1.** the end of a long bone, initially separated from the shaft (diaphysis) by a section of cartilage that eventually ossifies so that the two portions fuse together. **2.** Also called: **epiphysis cerebri** ('sɛrɪbraɪ). the technical name for **pineal gland.** [C17: via New Latin from Greek: a growth upon, from EPI- + *phusis* growth, from *phuein* to bring forth, produce] —**epiphyseal** *or* **epiphysial** (ˌɛpɪ'fɪzɪəl) *adj.*

epiphyte ('ɛpɪˌfaɪt) *n.* a plant, such as a moss, that grows on another plant but is not parasitic on it. —**epiphytic** (ˌɛpɪ'fɪtɪk), ˌ**epi'phytal,** *or* ˌ**epi'phytical** *adj.* —ˌ**epi'phytically** *adv.*

epiphytotic (ˌɛpɪfaɪ'tɒtɪk) *adj.* (of plant diseases and parasites) affecting plants over a wide geographical region. [from EPI- + -PHYTE + -OTIC]

epirogeny (ˌɛpaɪ'rɒdʒɪnɪ) *n.* a variant spelling of **epeirogeny.** —**epirogenic** (ɪˌpaɪrəʊ'dʒɛnɪk) *or* **epirogenetic** (ɪˌpaɪrəʊdʒɪ'nɛtɪk) *adj.*

Epis. *abbrev. for:* **1.** Also: **Episc.** Episcopal or Episcopalian. **2.** *Bible.* Also: **Epist.** Epistle.

episcopacy (ɪ'pɪskəpəsɪ) *n., pl.* **-cies. 1.** government of a Church by bishops. **2.** another word for **episcopate.**

episcopal (ɪ'pɪskəp^əl) *adj.* of, denoting, governed by, or relating to a bishop or bishops. [C15: from Church Latin *episcopālis,* from *episcopus* BISHOP] —**e'piscopally** *adv.*

Episcopal (ɪ'pɪskəp^əl) *adj.* belonging to or denoting the Episcopal Church. —**E'piscopally** *adv.*

Episcopal Church *n.* an autonomous branch of the Anglican Communion in Scotland and the U.S.

episcopalian (ɪˌpɪskə'peɪlɪən) *adj. also* **episcopal. 1.** practising or advocating the principle of Church government by bishops. ~*n.* **2.** an advocate of such Church government. —**eˌpisco'palianism** *n.*

Episcopalian (ɪˌpɪskə'peɪlɪən) *adj.* **1.** belonging to or denoting the Episcopal Church. ~*n.* **2.** a member or adherent of this Church.

episcopalism (ɪ'pɪskəpəˌlɪzəm) *n.* the belief that a Church should be governed by bishops.

episcopate (ɪ'pɪskəpɪt, -ˌpeɪt) *n.* **1.** the office, status, or term of office of a bishop. **2.** bishops collectively.

episcope ('ɛpɪˌskəʊp) *n. Brit.* an optical device that projects an enlarged image of an opaque object, such as a printed page or photographic print, onto a screen by means of reflected light. U.S. and Canadian name: **opaque projector.** See also **epidiascope.**

episematic (ˌɛpɪsɪ'mætɪk) *adj. Zoology.* (esp. of coloration) aiding recognition between animals of the same species.

episiotomy (əˌpiːzɪ'ɒtəmɪ) *n., pl.* **-mies.** surgical incision into the perineum during the late stages of labour to prevent its laceration during childbirth. [C20: from *episio-,* from Greek *epision* pubic region + -TOMY]

episode ('ɛpɪˌsəʊd) *n.* **1.** an incident, event, or series of events. **2.** any one of the sections into which a serialized novel or radio or television programme is divided. **3.** an incident, sequence, or scene that forms part of a narrative but may be a digression from the main story. **4.** (in ancient Greek tragedy) a section between two choric songs. **5.** *Music.* a contrasting section between statements of the subject, as in a fugue or rondo. [C17: from Greek *epeisodion* something added, from *epi-* (in addition) + *eisodios* coming in, from *eis-* in + *hodos* road]

episodic (ˌɛpɪ'sɒdɪk) *or* **episodical** *adj.* **1.** resembling or relating to an episode. **2.** divided into or composed of episodes. **3.** irregular, occasional, or sporadic. —ˌ**epi'sodically** *adv.*

episome ('ɛpɪˌsəʊm) *n.* any of various genetic particles, esp. viruses, that occur in bacteria and replicate either independently or in association with the chromosome.

epispastic (ˌɛpɪ'spæstɪk) *Med.* ~*adj.* **1.** producing a serous discharge or a blister. ~*n.* **2.** an epispastic agent. [C17: from Greek *epispastikos,* from *epispan* to attract, from *span* to draw; alluding to the ancient belief that blisters consisted of humours drawn to the surface of the skin]

Epist. *or* **Epis.** *Bible. abbrev. for* Epistle.

epistasis (ɪ'pɪstəsɪs) *n.* **1.** scum on the surface of a liquid, esp. on an old specimen of urine. **2.** *Med.* the arrest or checking of a bodily discharge, esp. bleeding. **3.** Also called: **hypostasis.** *Genetics.* the suppression by a gene of the effect of another gene that is not its allele. [C19: from Greek: a stopping, from *ephistanai* to stop, from EPI- + *histanai* to put] —**epistatic** (ˌɛpɪ'stætɪk) *adj.*

epistaxis (ˌɛpɪ'stæksɪs) *n.* the technical name for **nosebleed.** [C18: from Greek: a dropping, from *epistazein* to drop on, from *stazein* to drip]

epistemic (ˌɛpɪ'stiːmɪk) *adj.* **1.** of or relating to knowledge or epistemology. **2.** denoting the branch of modal logic that deals with the formalization of certain epistemological concepts, such as knowledge, certainty, and ignorance. ~See also **doxastic.** [C20: from Greek *epistēmē* knowledge] —ˌ**epis'temically** *adv.*

epistemics (ˌɛpɪ'stiːmɪks, -'stɛm-) *n.* (*functioning as sing.*) *Chiefly Brit.* the interdisciplinary study of knowledge and human information-processing, using the formal techniques of logic, linguistics, philosophy, and psychology. Compare **artificial intelligence.**

epistemological (ɪˌpɪstɪmə'lɒdʒɪk^əl) *adj.* **1.** concerned with or arising from epistemology. **2.** (of a philosophical problem) requiring an account of how knowledge of the given subject could be obtained. —**eˌpistemo'logically** *adv.*

epistemology (ɪˌpɪstɪ'mɒlədʒɪ) *n.* the theory of knowledge, esp. the critical study of its validity, methods, and scope. [C19: from Greek *epistēmē* knowledge] —**eˌpiste'mologist** *n.*

episternum (ˌɛpɪ'stɜːnəm) *n., pl.* **-na** (-nə). **1.** the manubrium of the sternum in mammals. **2.** another name for **interclavicle.** —ˌ**epi'sternal** *adj.*

epistle (ɪ'pɪs^əl) *n.* **1.** a letter, esp. one that is long, formal, or didactic. **2.** a literary work in letter form, esp. a dedicatory verse letter of a type originated by Horace. [Old English *epistol,* via Latin from Greek *epistolē,* from *epistellein* to send to, from *stellein* to prepare, send]

Epistle (ɪ'pɪs^əl) *n.* **1.** *New Testament.* any of the apostolic letters of Saints Paul, Peter, James, Jude, or John. **2.** a reading from one of the Epistles, forming part of the Eucharistic service in many Christian Churches.

epistler (ɪ'pɪslə, ɪ'pɪstlə) *or* **epistoler** (ɪ'pɪstᵊlə) *n.* (*often cap.*) **1.** a writer of an epistle or epistles. **2.** the person who reads the Epistle in a Christian religious service.

epistolary (ɪ'pɪstələrɪ) *or* (*archaic*) **epistolatory** *adj.* **1.** relating to, denoting, conducted by, or contained in letters. **2.** (of a novel or other work) constructed in the form of a series of letters.

epistrophe (ɪ'pɪstrəfɪ) *n. Rhetoric.* repetition of a word at the end of successive clauses or sentences. [C17: New Latin, from Greek, from EPI- + *strophē* a turning]

epistyle ('ɛpɪˌstaɪl) *n.* another name for **architrave** (sense 1). [C17: via Latin *epistȳlium* from Greek *epistulion*, from EPI- + *stulos* column, STYLE]

epitaph ('ɛpɪˌtɑːf, -ˌtæf) *n.* **1.** a commemorative inscription on a tombstone or monument. **2.** a speech or written passage composed in commemoration of a dead person. **3.** a final judgment on a person or thing. [C14: via Latin from Greek *epitaphion*, from *epitaphios* over a tomb, from EPI- + *taphos* tomb] —**epitaphic** (ˌɛpɪ'tæfɪk) *adj.* —'**epiˌtaphist** *n.*

epitasis (ɪ'pɪtəsɪs) *n.* (in classical drama) the part of a play in which the main action develops. Compare **protasis** (sense 2), **catastrophe** (sense 2). [C16: from Greek: a stretching, intensification, from *teinein* to stretch]

epitaxial transistor (ˌɛpɪ'tæksɪəl) *n.* a transistor made by depositing a thin pure layer of semiconductor material (**epitaxial layer**) onto a crystalline support by epitaxy. The layer acts as one of the electrode regions, usually the collector.

epitaxy ('ɛpɪˌtæksɪ) *or* **epitaxis** *n.* the growth of a thin layer on the surface of a crystal so that the layer has the same structure as the underlying crystal. —**epitaxial** (ˌɛpɪ'tæksɪəl) *adj.*

epithalamium (ˌɛpɪθə'leɪmɪəm) *or* **epithalamion** *n., pl.* **-mia** (-mɪə). a poem or song written to celebrate a marriage; nuptial ode. [C17: from Latin, from Greek *epithalamion* marriage song, from *thalamos* bridal chamber] —**epithalamic** (ˌɛpɪθə'læmɪk) *adj.*

epitheca (ˌɛpɪ'θiːkə) *n., pl.* **-cae** (-siː). the outer and older layer of the cell wall of a diatom. Compare **hypotheca.** [C19: from EPI- + THECA]

epithelioma (ˌɛpɪˌθiːlɪ'əʊmə) *n., pl.* **-mas** *or* **-mata** (-mətə). *Pathol.* a malignant tumour of epithelial tissue. —**epitheliomatous** (ˌɛpɪˌθiːlɪ'ɒmətəs) *adj.*

epithelium (ˌɛpɪ'θiːlɪəm) *n., pl.* **-liums** *or* **-lia** (-lɪə). an animal tissue consisting of one or more layers of closely packed cells covering the external and internal surfaces of the body. The cells vary in structure according to their function, which may be protective, secretory, or absorptive. [C18: New Latin, from EPI- + Greek *thēlē* nipple] —ˌ**epi'thelial** *adj.*

epithet ('ɛpɪˌθɛt) *n.* a descriptive word or phrase added to or substituted for a person's name: *"Lackland" is an epithet for King John.* [C16: from Latin *epitheton*, from Greek, from *epitithenai* to add, from *tithenai* to put] —ˌ**epi'thetic** *or* ˌ**epi'thetical** *adj.*

epitome (ɪ'pɪtəmɪ) *n.* **1.** a typical example of a characteristic or class; embodiment; personification: *he is the epitome of sloth.* **2.** a summary of a written work; abstract. [C16: via Latin from Greek *epitomē*, from *epitemnein* to abridge, from EPI- + *temnein* to cut] —**epitomical** (ˌɛpɪ'tɒmɪkᵊl) *or* ˌ**epi'tomic** *adj.*

epitomize *or* **epitomise** (ɪ'pɪtəˌmaɪz) *vb.* (*tr.*) **1.** to be a personification of; typify. **2.** to make an epitome of. —**e'pitomist** *n.* —**eˌpitomi'zation** *or* **eˌpitomi'sation** *n.* —**e'pitoˌmizer** *or* **e'pitoˌmiser** *n.*

epizoic (ˌɛpɪ'zəʊɪk) *adj.* **1.** (of an animal or plant) growing or living on the exterior of a living animal. **2.** (of plants) having seeds or fruit dispersed by animals. —ˌ**epi'zoism** *n.*

epizoite (ˌɛpɪ'zəʊɪt) *n.* an organism that lives on an animal but is not parasitic on it.

epizoon (ˌɛpɪ'zəʊɒn) *n., pl.* **-zoa** (-'zəʊə). an animal, such as a parasite, that lives on the body of another animal. [C19: New Latin, from EPI- + Greek *zōion* animal] —ˌ**epi'zoan** *adj.*

epizootic (ˌɛpɪzəʊ'ɒtɪk) *adj.* **1.** (of a disease) suddenly and temporarily affecting a large number of animals. *~n.* **2.** an epizootic disease. Compare **enzootic.** —ˌ**epizo'otically** *adv.*

e pluribus unum *Latin.* (eɪ 'plʊərɪbʊs 'uːnʊm) one out of many: the motto of the U.S.A.

EPNS *abbrev. for* electroplated nickel silver.

epoch ('iːpɒk) *n.* **1.** a point in time beginning a new or distinctive period: *the invention of nuclear weapons marked an epoch in the history of warfare.* **2.** a long period of time marked by some predominant or typical characteristic; era. **3.** *Astronomy.* a precise date to which information, such as coordinates, relating to a celestial body is referred. **4.** *Geology.* a unit of geological time within a period during which a series of rocks is formed: *the Pleistocene epoch.* **5.** *Physics.* the displacement of an oscillating or vibrating body at zero time. [C17: from New Latin *epocha*, from Greek *epokhē* cessation; related to *ekhein* to hold, have] —**epochal** ('ɛpˌɒkᵊl) *adj.* —'**epˌochally** *adv.*

epoch-making *adj.* of great importance; momentous.

epode ('ɛpəʊd) *n. Greek prosody.* **1.** the part of a lyric ode that follows the strophe and the antistrophe. **2.** a type of lyric poem composed of couplets in which a long line is followed by a shorter one, invented by Archilochus. [C16: via Latin from Greek *epōidos* a singing after, from *epaidein* to sing after, from *aidein* to sing]

eponym ('ɛpənɪm) *n.* **1.** a name, esp. a place name, derived from the name of a real or mythical person, as for example *Constantinople* from *Constantine I.* **2.** the name of the person from which such a name is derived: *in the Middle Ages, "Brutus" was thought to be the eponym of "Britain."* [C19: from Greek *epōnumos* giving a significant name] —**eponymous** (ɪ'pɒnɪməs) *or* ˌ**epo'nymic** *adj.* —**e'ponymously** *adv.*

eponymy (ɪ'pɒnɪmɪ) *n.* the derivation of names of places, etc., from those of persons.

epopee ('ɛpəʊˌpiː; *French* epɔpe) *or* **epopoeia** (ˌɛpə'piːə) *n.* **1.** an epic poem. **2.** epic poetry in general. [C17: from French *épopée*, from Greek *epopoiia*, from EPOS + *poiein* to make]

epos ('ɛpɒs) *n.* **1.** a body of poetry in which the tradition of a people is conveyed, esp. a group of poems concerned with a common epic theme. **2.** another word for **epic** (sense 1). [C19: via Latin from Greek: speech, word, epic poem, song; related to Latin *vōx* VOICE]

EPOS ('iːpɒs) *acronym for* electronic point of sale.

epoxide (ɪ'pɒksaɪd) *n.* **a.** a compound containing an oxygen atom joined to two different groups that are themselves joined to other groups. **b.** (*as modifier*): *epoxide resin.* [C20: from EPI- + OXIDE]

epoxy (ɪ'pɒksɪ) *adj. Chem.* **1.** of, consisting of, or containing an oxygen atom joined to two different groups that are themselves joined to other groups: *epoxy group.* **2.** of, relating to, or consisting of an epoxy resin. *~n., pl.* **epoxies. 3.** short for **epoxy resin.** [C20: from EPI- + OXY-[2]]

epoxy *or* **epoxide resin** *n.* any of various tough resistant thermosetting synthetic resins containing epoxy groups: used in surface coatings, laminates, and adhesives.

EPP *abbrev. for* executive pension plan.

EPR *abbrev. for* electron paramagnetic resonance.

EPROM ('iːprɒm) *n. Computer technol. acronym for* erasable programmable read only memory.

eps *abbrev. for* earnings per share.

epsilon ('ɛpsɪˌlɒn, ɛp'saɪlən) *n.* the fifth letter of the Greek alphabet (Ε, ε), a short vowel, transliterated as *e.* [Greek *e psilon*, literally: simple *e*]

Epsilon ('ɛpsɪˌlɒn, ɛp'saɪlən) *n.* (*foll. by the genitive case of a specified constellation*) the fifth brightest star in a constellation: *Epsilon Aurigae.*

Epsom salts ('ɛpsəm) *n.* (*functioning as sing. or pl.*) a medicinal preparation of hydrated magnesium sulphate, used as a purgative, to reduce inflammation, etc. [C18: named after *Epsom*, town in SE England, where they occur naturally in the water]

Epstein-Barr virus ('ɛpstaɪnˌbɑː) *n.* a virus belonging to the herpes family that causes infectious mononucleosis; it is also implicated in the development of Burkitt lymphoma. Abbrev.: **EBV.** [C20: named after Sir M. A. *Epstein* (born 1921), and Y. M. *Barr* (born 1932), British pathologists who discovered the virus]

epyllion (ɪ'pɪlɪən) *n., pl.* **-lia** (-lɪə). a miniature epic. [C19: from Greek, diminutive of EPOS]

eq. *abbrev. for:* **1.** equal. **2.** equation. **3.** equivalent.

equable ('ɛkwəbᵊl) *adj.* **1.** even-tempered; placid. **2.** unvarying; uniform: *an equable climate.* [C17: from Latin *aequābilis*, from *aequāre* to make equal] —ˌ**equa'bility** *or* '**equableness** *n.* —'**equably** *adv.*

equal ('iːkwəl) *adj.* **1.** (often foll. by *to* or *with*) identical in size, quantity, degree, intensity, etc.; the same (as). **2.** having identical privileges, rights, status, etc.: *all men are equal before the law.* **3.** having uniform effect or application: *equal opportunities.* **4.** evenly balanced or proportioned: *the game was equal between the teams.* **5.** (usually foll. by *to*) having the necessary or adequate strength, ability, means, etc. (for): *to be equal to one's work.* **6.** another word for **equivalent** (sense 3a). **7.** *Archaic.* tranquil; placid. *~n.* **8.** a person or thing equal to another, esp. in merit, ability, etc.: *he has no equal when it comes to boxing.* *~vb.* **equals, equalling, equalled** *or U.S.* **equals, equaling, equaled. 9.** (*tr.*) to be equal to; correspond to; match: *my offer equals his.* **10.** (*intr.*; usually foll. by *out*) to become equal or level. **11.** (*tr.*) to make, perform, or do something equal to: *to equal the world record.* **12.** (*tr.*) *Archaic.* to make equal. [C14: from Latin *aequālis*, from *aequus* level, of obscure origin] —'**equally** *adv.*

equal-area *n.* (*modifier*) (of a map projection) showing area accurately and therefore distorting shape and direction. Also: **homolographic.**

equali (ɪ'kwɑːlɪ) *pl. n. Music.* pieces for a group of instruments of the same kind: *Beethoven's Equali for four trombones.* [Italian: old pl. form of *uguale* equal]

equalitarian (ɪˌkwɒlɪ'tɛərɪən) *adj., n.* a less common word for **egalitarian.** —**eˌquali'tarianism** *n.*

equality (ɪ'kwɒlɪtɪ) *n., pl.* **-ties. 1.** the state of being equal. **2.** *Maths.* a statement, usually an equation, indicating that quantities or expressions on either side of an equal sign are equal in value.

equalize *or* **equalise** ('iːkwəˌlaɪz) *vb.* **1.** (*tr.*) to make equal or uniform; regularize. **2.** (*intr.*) (in sports) to reach the same score as one's opponent or opponents. —ˌ**equali'zation** *or* ˌ**equali'sation** *n.*

equalizer *or* **equaliser** ('iːkwəˌlaɪzə) *n.* **1.** a person or thing that equalizes, esp. a device to counterbalance opposing forces. **2.** an electronic network introduced into a transmission circuit to alter its response, esp. to reduce distortion by equalizing its response over a specified frequency range. 3. *Sport.* a goal, point, etc., that levels the score. 4. *U.S. slang.* a weapon, esp. a gun.

Equal Opportunities Commission *n.* (in Britain) a body appointed by the Government to enforce the provisions of the Equal Pay Act 1970 and the Sex Discrimination Act 1975. Abbrev.: **EOC.**

equal opportunity *n.* **a.** the offering of employment, pay, or promotion equally to all, without discrimination as to sex, race, colour, disability, etc. **b.** (*as modifier*): *our equal-opportunity policy; an equal-opportunities employer.*

equal pay *n.* the right of a man or woman to receive the same pay as a person of the opposite sex doing the same or similar work for the same or a similar employer.

equal sign *or* **equals sign** *n.* the symbol =, used to indicate a mathematical equality.

equanimity (ˌiːkwəˈnɪmɪtɪ, ˌɛkwə-) *n.* calmness of mind or temper; composure. [C17: from Latin *aequanimitās,* from *aequus* even, EQUAL + *animus* mind, spirit] —**equanimous** (ɪˈkwænɪməs) *adj.* —**eˈquanimously** *adv.*

equate (ɪˈkweɪt) *vb.* (*mainly tr.*) 1. to make or regard as equivalent or similar, esp. in order to compare or balance. 2. *Maths.* to indicate the equality of; form an equation from. 3. (*intr.*) to be equal; correspond. [C15: from Latin *aequāre* to make EQUAL] —**eˈquatable** *adj.* —**eˌquataˈbility** *n.*

equation (ɪˈkweɪʒən, -ʃən) *n.* 1. a mathematical statement that two expressions are equal: it is either an **identity,** in which the variables can assume any value, or a **conditional equation,** in which the variables have only certain values (roots). 2. the act of regarding as equal; equating. 3. the act of making equal or balanced; equalization. 4. the state of being equal, equivalent, or equally balanced. 5. See **chemical equation.** 6. *Astronomy.* See **personal equation.** —**eˈquational** *adj.* —**eˈquationally** *adv.*

equation of state *n.* any equation that expresses the relationship between the temperature, pressure, and volume of a substance.

equation of time *n.* the difference between apparent solar time and mean solar time, being at a maximum in February (over 14 minutes) and November (over 16 minutes).

equator (ɪˈkweɪtə) *n.* 1. the great circle of the earth with a latitude of 0°, lying equidistant from the poles; dividing the N and S hemispheres. 2. a circle dividing a sphere or other surface into two equal symmetrical parts. 3. See **magnetic equator.** 4. *Astronomy.* See **celestial equator.** [C14: from Medieval Latin (*circulus*) *aequātor* (*diei et noctis*) (circle) that equalizes (the day and night), from Latin *aequāre* to make EQUAL]

equatorial (ˌɛkwəˈtɔːrɪəl) *adj.* 1. of, like, or existing at or near the equator. 2. *Astronautics.* lying in the plane of the equator: *an equatorial orbit.* ~*n.* 3. an equatorial telescope or the mounting of such a telescope. —ˌ**equaˈtorially** *adv.*

equatorial telescope *n.* an astronomical telescope that is mounted on two mutually perpendicular axes, one of which is parallel to the earth's axis.

equerry (ˈɛkwərɪ; *at the British court* ɪˈkwɛrɪ) *n., pl.* **-ries.** 1. an officer attendant upon the British sovereign. 2. (formerly) an officer in a royal household responsible for the horses. [C16: alteration (through influence of Latin *equus* horse) of earlier *escuirie,* from Old French: stable, group of squires, from *escuyer* SQUIRE]

equestrian (ɪˈkwɛstrɪən) *adj.* 1. of or relating to horses and riding. 2. on horseback; mounted. 3. depicting or representing a person on horseback: *an equestrian statue.* 4. of, relating to, or composed of Roman equites. 5. of, relating to, or composed of knights, esp. the imperial free knights of the Holy Roman Empire. ~*n.* 6. a person skilled in riding and horsemanship. [C17: from Latin *equestris,* from *eques* horseman, knight, from *equus* horse] —**eˈquestrianˌism** *n.*

equestrienne (ɪˌkwɛstrɪˈɛn) *n.* a female rider on horseback, esp. one in a circus who performs acrobatics.

equi- *combining form.* equal or equally: *equidistant; equilateral.*

equiangular (ˌiːkwɪˈæŋgjʊlə) *adj.* having all angles equal.

equidistant (ˌiːkwɪˈdɪstənt) *adj.* distant by equal amounts from two or more places. —ˌ**equiˈdistance** *n.* —ˌ**equiˈdistantly** *adv.*

equilateral (ˌiːkwɪˈlætərəl) *adj.* 1. having all sides of equal length: *an equilateral triangle.* ~*n.* 2. a geometric figure having all its sides of equal length. 3. a side that is equal in length to other sides. —ˌ**equiˈlaterally** *adv.*

equilibrant (ɪˈkwɪlɪbrənt) *n.* a force capable of balancing another force and producing equilibrium.

equilibrate (ˌiːkwɪˈlaɪbreɪt, ɪˈkwɪlɪˌbreɪt) *vb.* to bring to or be in equilibrium; balance. [C17: from Late Latin *aequilībrāre,* from *aequilībris* in balance; see EQUILIBRIUM] —**equilibration** (ˌiːkwɪlaɪˈbreɪʃən, ɪˌkwɪlɪ-) *n.* —**equilibrator** (ɪˈkwɪlɪˌbreɪtə) *n.*

equilibrist (ɪˈkwɪlɪbrɪst) *n.* a person who performs balancing feats, esp. on a high wire. —**eˌquiliˈbristic** *adj.*

equilibrium (ˌiːkwɪˈlɪbrɪəm) *n., pl.* **-riums** *or* **-ria** (-rɪə). 1. a stable condition in which forces cancel one another. 2. a state or feeling of mental balance; composure. 3. any unchanging condition or state of a body, system, etc., resulting from the balance or cancelling out of the influences or processes to which it is subjected. See **thermodynamic equilibrium.** 4. *Physics.* a state of rest or uniform motion in which there is no resultant force on a body. 5. *Chem.* the condition existing when a chemical reaction and its reverse reaction take place at equal rates. 6. *Physics.* the condition of a system that has its total energy distributed among its component parts in the statistically most probable manner. 7. *Physiol.* a state of bodily balance, maintained primarily by special receptors in the inner ear. 8. the economic condition in which there is neither excess demand nor excess supply in a market. [C17: from Latin *aequilībrium,* from *aequi-* EQUI- + *lībra* pound, balance]

equimolecular (ˌiːkwɪməˈlɛkjʊlə) *adj.* (of substances, solutions, etc.) containing equal numbers of molecules.

equine (ˈɛkwaɪn) *adj.* 1. of, relating to, or resembling a horse. 2. of, relating to, or belonging to the family *Equidae,* which comprises horses, zebras, and asses. [C18: from Latin *equīnus,* from *equus* horse] —**ˈequinely** *adv.*

equine distemper *n.* another name for **strangles.**

equinoctial (ˌiːkwɪˈnɒkʃəl) *adj.* 1. relating to or occurring at either or both equinoxes. 2. (of a plant) having flowers that open and close at specific regular times. 3. *Astronomy.* of or relating to the celestial equator. ~*n.* 4. a storm or gale at or near an equinox. 5. another name for **celestial equator.** [C14: from Latin *aequinoctiālis* concerning the EQUINOX]

equinoctial circle *or* **line** *n.* another name for **celestial equator.**

equinoctial point *n.* either of the two points at which the celestial equator intersects the ecliptic.

equinoctial year *n.* another name for **solar year.** See **year** (sense 4).

equinox (ˈiːkwɪˌnɒks) *n.* 1. either of the two occasions, six months apart, when day and night are of equal length. See **vernal equinox, autumnal equinox.** 2. another name for **equinoctial point.** [C14: from Medieval Latin *equinoxium,* changed from Latin *aequinoctium,* from *aequi-* EQUI- + *nox* night]

equinumerous (ˌiːkwɪˈnjuːmərəs) *adj. Logic.* having the same number of members.

equip (ɪˈkwɪp) *vb.* **equips, equipping, equipped.** (*tr.*) 1. to furnish with (necessary supplies, etc.). 2. (*usually passive*) to provide with abilities, understanding, etc.: *her son was never equipped to be a scholar.* 3. to dress out; attire. [C16: from Old French *eschiper* to embark, fit out (a ship), of Germanic origin; compare Old Norse *skipa* to put in order, *skip* SHIP] —**eˈquipper** *n.*

equipage (ˈɛkwɪpɪdʒ) *n.* 1. a horse-drawn carriage, esp. one elegantly equipped and attended by liveried footmen. 2. (formerly) the stores and equipment of a military unit. 3. *Archaic.* **a.** a set of useful articles. **b.** a group of attendants; retinue.

equipartition (ˌɛkwɪpɑːˈtɪʃən) *n.* the equal division of the energy of a system in thermal equilibrium between different degrees of freedom. This principle was assumed to be exact in classical physics, but quantum theory shows that it is true only in certain special cases.

équipe (eɪˈkiːp) *n.* (esp. in motor racing) a team. [French]

equipment (ɪˈkwɪpmənt) *n.* 1. an act or instance of equipping. 2. the items so provided. 3. a set of tools, devices, kit, etc., assembled for a specific purpose, such as a soldier's kit and weapons.

equipoise (ˈɛkwɪˌpɔɪz) *n.* 1. even balance of weight or other forces; equilibrium. 2. a counterbalance; counterpoise. ~*vb.* 3. (*tr.*) to offset or balance in weight or force; balance.

equipollent (ˌiːkwɪˈpɒlənt) *adj.* 1. equal or equivalent in significance, power, or effect. 2. *Logic.* (of two propositions) logically deducible from each other; equivalent. 3. *Maths, logic.* (of two classes) having the same cardinality. ~*n.* 4. something that is equipollent. [C15: from Latin *aequipollēns* of equal importance, from EQUI- + *pollēre* to be able, be strong] —ˌ**equiˈpollence** *or* ˌ**equiˈpollency** *n.* —ˌ**equiˈpollently** *adv.*

equiponderate (ˌiːkwɪˈpɒndəˌreɪt) *vb.* (*tr.*) to equal or balance in weight, power, force, etc.; offset; counterbalance. [C17: from Medieval Latin *aequiponderāre,* from Latin EQUI- + *ponderāre* to weigh] —ˌ**equiˈponderance** *or* ˌ**equiˈponderancy** *n.* —ˌ**equiˈponderant** *adj.*

equipotential (ˌiːkwɪpəˈtɛnʃəl) *adj.* 1. having the same electric potential or uniform electric potential. 2. Also: **equipotent** (ˌiːkwɪˈpəʊtᵊnt). equivalent in power or effect. ~*n.* 3. an equipotential line or surface. —**equipoˌtentiˈality** *n.*

equiprobable (ˌiːkwɪˈprɒbəbᵊl) *adj.* equally probable. —ˌ**equiˌprobaˈbility** *n.*

equisetum (ˌɛkwɪˈsiːtəm) *n., pl.* **-tums** *or* **-ta** (-tə). any pteridophyte plant of the genus *Equisetum,* which comprises the horsetails. [C19: New Latin, changed from Latin *equisaetum,* from *equus* horse + *saeta* bristle]

equitable (ˈɛkwɪtəbᵊl) *adj.* 1. impartial or reasonable; fair; just: *an equitable decision.* 2. *Law.* relating to or valid in equity, as distinct from common law or statute law. 3. *Law.* (formerly) recognized in a court of equity only, as claims, rights, etc. [C17: from French *équitable,* from *équité* EQUITY] —**ˈequitableness** *n.* —**ˈequitably** *adv.*

equitant (ˈɛkwɪtᵊnt) *adj.* (of a leaf) having the base folded around the stem so that it overlaps the leaf above and opposite. [C19: from Latin *equitāns* riding, from *equitāre* to ride, from *equus* horse]

equitation (ˌɛkwɪˈteɪʃən) *n.* the study and practice of riding and horsemanship. [C16: from Latin *equitātiō*, from *equitāre* to ride, from *equus* horse]

equites (ˈɛkwɪˌtiːz) *pl. n.* (in ancient Rome) **1.** the cavalry. **2.** members of a social order distinguished by wealth and ranking just below the senators. ~Also called: **knights.** [from Latin, plural of *eques* horseman, from *equus* horse]

equities (ˈɛkwɪtɪz) *pl. n.* another name for **ordinary shares.**

equity (ˈɛkwɪtɪ) *n., pl.* **-ties. 1.** the quality of being impartial or reasonable; fairness. **2.** an impartial or fair act, decision, etc. **3.** *Law.* a system of jurisprudence founded on principles of natural justice and fair conduct. It supplements the common law and mitigates its inflexibility, as by providing a remedy where none exists at law. **4.** *Law.* an equitable right or claim: *equity of redemption.* **5.** the interest of ordinary shareholders in a company. **6.** the market value of a debtor's property in excess of all debts to which it is liable. [C14: from Old French *equité*, from Latin *aequitās*, from *aequus* level, EQUAL]

Equity (ˈɛkwɪtɪ) *n.* the actors' trade union. Full name: **Actors' Equity Association.**

equity capital *n.* the part of the share capital of a company owned by ordinary shareholders or in certain circumstances by other classes of shareholder.

equity-linked policy *n.* an insurance or assurance policy in which premiums are invested partially or wholly in ordinary shares for the eventual benefit of the beneficiaries of the policy.

equity of redemption *n. Property law.* the right that a mortgager has in equity to redeem his property on payment of the sum owing, even though the sum is overdue. See also **foreclose.**

equiv. *abbrev. for* equivalent.

equivalence (ɪˈkwɪvələns) *or* **equivalency** *n.* **1.** the state of being equivalent or interchangeable. **2.** *Maths, logic.* **a.** the relationship between two statements each of which implies the other. **b.** the binary truth-function that takes the value *true* when both component sentences are true or when both are false, corresponding to English *if and only if.* Symbol: ≡ or ↔ , as in $-(p \wedge q) \equiv -p \vee -q$ Also called: **biconditional.**

equivalence relation *n. Logic, maths.* a relation that is reflexive, symmetric, and transitive: it imposes a partition on its domain of definition so that two elements belong to the same subset if and only if the relation holds between them.

equivalency (ˌɛkwɪˈveɪlənsɪ) *or* **equivalence** *n. Chem.* the state of having equal valencies. —ˌ**equiˈvalent** *adj.*

equivalent (ɪˈkwɪvələnt) *adj.* **1.** equal or interchangeable in value, quantity, significance, etc. **2.** having the same or a similar effect or meaning. **3.** *Maths.* **a.** (of two geometric figures) having a particular property in common; equal. **b.** (of two equations or inequalities) having the same set of solutions. **c.** (of two sets) having the same cardinal number. **4.** *Maths, logic.* (of two propositions) having an equivalence between them. ~*n.* **5.** something that is equivalent. **6.** short for **equivalent weight.** [C15: from Late Latin *aequivalēns*, from *aequivalēre* to be equally significant, from Latin *aequi-* EQUI- + *valēre* to be worth] —**eˈquivalently** *adv.*

equivalent air speed *n.* the speed at sea level that would produce the same Pitot-static tube reading as that measured at altitude.

equivalent circuit *n.* an arrangement of simple electrical components that is electrically equivalent to a complex circuit and is used to simplify circuit analysis.

equivalent focal length *n. Optics.* the ratio of the size of an image of a small distant object near the optical axis to the angular distance of the object in radians.

equivalent weight *n.* the weight of an element or compound that will combine with or displace 8 grams of oxygen or 1.007 97 grams of hydrogen. Also called: **gram equivalent.**

equivocal (ɪˈkwɪvəkᵊl) *adj.* **1.** capable of varying interpretations; ambiguous. **2.** deliberately misleading or vague; evasive. **3.** of doubtful character or sincerity; dubious. [C17: from Late Latin *aequivocus*, from Latin EQUI- + *vōx* voice] —**eˈquivocally** *adv.* —**eˌquivoˈcality** *or* **eˈquivocalness** *n.*

equivocate (ɪˈkwɪvəˌkeɪt) *vb.* (*intr.*) to use vague or ambiguous language, esp. in order to avoid speaking directly or honestly; hedge. [C15: from Medieval Latin *aequivocāre*, from Late Latin *aequivocus* ambiguous, EQUIVOCAL] —**eˈquivoˌcatingly** *adv.* —**eˈquivoˌcator** *n.* —**eˈquivocatory** *adj.*

equivocation (ɪˌkwɪvəˈkeɪʃən) *n.* **1.** the act or an instance of equivocating. **2.** *Logic.* a fallacy based on the use of the same term in different senses, esp. as the middle term of a syllogism, as *the badger lives in the bank, and the bank is in the High Street, so the badger lives in the High Street.*

equivoque *or* **equivoke** (ˈɛkwɪˌvəʊk) *n.* **1.** a play on words; pun. **2.** an ambiguous phrase or expression. **3.** double meaning; ambiguity. [C14 *equivoc* EQUIVOCAL]

Equuleus (ɛˈkwʊlɪəs) *n., Latin genitive* **Equulei** (ɛˈkwʊlɪˌaɪ). a small faint constellation in the N hemisphere between Pegasus and Aquarius. [from Latin: a young horse, from *equus* horse]

er (ə, ɜː) *interj.* a sound made when hesitating in speech.

Er *the chemical symbol for* erbium.

ER *abbrev. for:* **1.** Elizabeth Regina. [Latin: Queen Elizabeth] **2.** Eduardus Rex. [Latin: King Edward]

-er[1] *suffix forming nouns.* **1.** a person or thing that performs a specified action: *reader; decanter; lighter.* **2.** a person engaged in a profession, occupation, etc.: *writer; baker; bootlegger.* **3.** a native or inhabitant of: *islander; Londoner; villager.* **4.** a person or thing having a certain characteristic: *newcomer; double-decker; fiver.* [Old English *-ere*; related to German *-er*, Latin *-ārius*]

-er[2] *suffix.* forming the comparative degree of adjectives (*deeper, freer, sunnier*, etc.) and adverbs (*faster, slower*, etc.). [Old English *-rd, -re* (adj.), *-or* (adv.)]

era (ˈɪərə) *n.* **1.** a period of time considered as being of a distinctive character; epoch. **2.** an extended period of time the years of which are numbered from a fixed point or event: *the Christian era.* **3.** a point in time, esp. one beginning a new or distinctive period: *the discovery of antibiotics marked an era in modern medicine.* **4.** *Geology.* a major division of geological time, divided into several periods: *the Mesozoic era.* [C17: from Latin *aera* counters, plural of *aes* brass, pieces of brass money]

ERA (ˈɪərə) *n.* (in Britain) *acronym for* Education Reform Act: the 1988 act which established the key elements of the National Curriculum and the Basic Curriculum.

eradiate (ɪˈreɪdɪˌeɪt) *vb.* a less common word for **radiate.** Compare **irradiate.** —**eˌradiˈation** *n.*

eradicate (ɪˈrædɪˌkeɪt) *vb.* (*tr.*) **1.** to obliterate; stamp out. **2.** to pull or tear up by the roots. [C16: from Latin *ērādīcāre* to uproot, from EX-[1] + *rādīx* root] —**eˈradicable** *adj.* —**eˈradicably** *adv.* —**eˌradiˈcation** *n.* —**eˈradicative** *adj.* —**eˈradiˌcator** *n.*

erase (ɪˈreɪz) *vb.* **1.** to obliterate or rub out (something written, typed, etc.). **2.** (*tr.*) to destroy all traces of; remove completely: *time erases grief.* **3.** to remove (a recording) from (magnetic tape). **4.** (*tr.*) *Computer technol.* to replace (data) on a storage device with characters representing an absence of data. [C17: from Latin *ērādere* to scrape off, from EX-[1] + *rādere* to scratch, scrape] —**eˈrasable** *adj.*

eraser (ɪˈreɪzə) *n.* an object, such as a piece of rubber or felt, used for erasing something written, typed, etc.: *a pencil eraser.*

erasion (ɪˈreɪʒən) *n.* **1.** the act of erasing; erasure. **2.** the surgical scraping away of tissue, esp. of bone.

Erastianism (ɪˈræstɪəˌnɪzəm) *n.* the theory that the state should have authority over the church in ecclesiastical matters. [C17: named after Thomas *Erastus* (1524–83), Swiss theologian to whom such views were attributed] —**Eˈrastian** *n., adj.*

erasure (ɪˈreɪʒə) *n.* **1.** the act or an instance of erasing. **2.** the place or mark, as on a piece of paper, where something has been erased.

erbium (ˈɜːbɪəm) *n.* a soft malleable silvery-white element of the lanthanide series of metals: used in special alloys, room-temperature lasers, and as a pigment. Symbol: Er; atomic no.: 68; atomic wt.: 167.26; valency: 3; relative density: 9.045; melting pt.: 1522°C; boiling pt.: 2510°C. [C19: from New Latin, from (*Ytt*)*erb*(*y*), Sweden, where it was first found + -IUM]

ERCP *abbrev. for* endoscopic retrograde cholangiopancreatography.

ere (ɛə) *conj., prep.* a poetic word for **before.** [Old English *ǣr*; related to Old Norse *ār* early, Gothic *airis* earlier, Old High German *ēr* earlier, Greek *eri* early]

erect (ɪˈrɛkt) *adj.* **1.** upright in posture or position; not bent or leaning: *an erect stance.* **2.** (of an optical image) having the same orientation as the object; not inverted. **3.** *Physiol.* (of the penis, clitoris, or nipples) firm or rigid after swelling with blood, esp. as a result of sexual excitement. **4.** (of plant parts) growing vertically or at right angles to the parts from which they arise. ~*vb.* (*mainly tr.*) **5.** to put up; construct; build. **6.** to raise to an upright position; lift up: *to erect a flagpole.* **7.** to found or form; set up. **8.** (*also intr.*) *Physiol.* to become or cause to become firm or rigid by filling with blood. **9.** to hold up as an ideal; exalt. **10.** *Optics.* to change (an inverted image) to an upright position. **11.** to draw or construct (a line, figure, etc.) on a given line or figure, esp. at right angles to it. [C14: from Latin *ērigere* to set up, from *regere* to control, govern] —**eˈrectable** *adj.* —**eˈrectly** *adv.* —**eˈrectness** *n.*

erectile (ɪˈrɛktaɪl) *adj.* **1.** *Physiol.* (of tissues or organs, such as the penis or clitoris) capable of becoming rigid or erect as the result of being filled with blood. **2.** capable of being erected. —**erectility** (ɪrɛkˈtɪlɪtɪ, ˌiːrɛk-) *n.*

erection (ɪˈrɛkʃən) *n.* **1.** the act of erecting or the state of being erected. **2.** something that has been erected; a building or construction. **3.** *Physiol.* the enlarged state or condition of erectile tissues or organs, esp. the penis, when filled with blood. **4.** an erect penis.

erector *or* **erecter** (ɪˈrɛktə) *n.* **1.** *Anatomy.* any muscle that raises a part or makes it erect. **2.** a person or thing that erects.

E region *or* **layer** *n.* a region of the ionosphere, extending from a height of 90 to about 150 kilometres. It reflects radio waves of medium wavelength. Also called: **Heaviside layer, Kennelly-Heaviside layer.** See also **ionosphere.**

erelong (ɛəˈlɒŋ) *adv. Archaic or poetic.* before long; soon.

eremite (ˈɛrɪˌmaɪt) *n.* a Christian hermit or recluse. Compare **coenobite.** [C13: see HERMIT] —**eremitic** (ˌɛrɪˈmɪtɪk) or ˌ**ereˈmitical** *adj.* —**eremitism** (ˈɛrɪmaɪˌtɪzəm) *n.*

erepsin (ɪˈrɛpsɪn) *n.* a mixture of proteolytic enzymes secreted by the small intestine. [C20: *er-*, from Latin *ēripere* to snatch (from *rapere* to seize) + (P)EPSIN]

erethism (ˈɛrɪˌθɪzəm) *n.* **1.** *Physiol.* an abnormally high degree of irritability or sensitivity in any part of the body. **2.** *Psychiatry.* an abnormal tendency to become aroused quickly, esp. sexually, as the result of a verbal or psychic stimulus. [C18: from French *éréthisme,* from Greek *erethismos* irritation, from *erethizein* to excite, irritate] —ˌ**ere'thismic,** ˌ**ere'thistic,** *or* ˌ**ere'thitic** *adj.*

Eretz Yisrael *or* **Eretz Israel** *Hebrew.* (*Hebrew* 'ɛrets jis'rɑeɪl; *Yiddish* 'ɛrets jisrɑ'eɪl) *n. Judaism.* **1.** the Holy Land; Israel. **2.** the concept, favoured by some extreme Zionists, of a Jewish state the territory of which matched the largest expanse of biblical Israel. [literally: Land of Israel]

erev ('ɛrɛv) *n.* (*in combination*) *Judaism.* the day before; the eve of: *erev Shabbat* (the Sabbath eve, i.e., Friday); *erev Pesach* (the day before Passover). [from Hebrew]

erewhile (ɛə'waɪl) *or* **erewhiles** *adv. Archaic.* a short time ago; a little while before.

erf (ɜːf) *n., pl.* **erven** ('ɜːvən). *S. African.* a plot of land, usually urban, marked off for building purposes. [Afrikaans]

Erf (ɜːf) *abbrev. for* electrorheological fluid: a man-made liquid that thickens or solidifies when an electric current passes through it and returns to a liquid when the current ceases.

erg[1] (ɜːg) *n.* the cgs unit of work or energy. 1 erg is equivalent to 10^{-7} joule. [C19: from Greek *ergon* work]

erg[2] (ɜːg) *n., pl.* **ergs** *or* **areg.** an area of shifting sand dunes in a desert, esp. the Sahara. [C19: from Arabic *'irj*]

ergastoplasm (ɜː'gæstəˌplæzəm) *n.* a former name for **endoplasmic reticulum.**

ergative ('ɜːgətɪv) *Linguistics.* ~*adj.* **1.** denoting a type of verb that takes the same noun as either direct object or as subject, with equivalent meaning. Thus, "fuse" is an ergative verb: "He fused the lights" and "The lights fused" have equivalent meaning. **2.** denoting a case of nouns in certain languages, for example, Eskimo or Basque, marking a noun used interchangeably as either the direct object of a transitive verb or the subject of an intransitive verb. **3.** denoting a language that has ergative verbs or ergative nouns. ~*n.* **4.** an ergative verb. **5.** an ergative noun or case of nouns. [C20: from Greek *ergatēs* a workman +-IVE]

ergatocracy (ˌɜːgə'tɒkrəsɪ) *n., pl.* **-cies.** *Rare.* government by the workers. [C20: from Greek *ergatēs* a workman, from *ergon* work, deed + -CRACY]

ergo ('ɜːgəʊ) *sentence connector.* therefore; hence. [C14: from Latin: therefore]

ergograph ('ɜːgəˌgrɑːf, -ˌgræf) *n.* an instrument that measures and records the amount of work a muscle does during contraction, its rate of fatigue, etc.

ergometer (ɜː'gɒmɪtə) *n.* a dynamometer. [C20: from Greek *ergon* work + -METER]

ergonomic (ˌɜːgə'nɒmɪk) *adj.* **1.** of or relating to ergonomics. **2.** designed to minimize physical effort and discomfort, and hence maximize efficiency.

ergonomics (ˌɜːgə'nɒmɪks) *n.* (*functioning as sing.*) the study of the relationship between workers and their environment, esp. the equipment they use. Also called: **biotechnology.** [C20: from Greek *ergon* work + (ECO)NOMICS] —**ergonomist** (ɜː'gɒnəmɪst) *n.*

ergosterol (ɜː'gɒstəˌrɒl) *n.* a plant sterol that is converted into vitamin D by the action of ultraviolet radiation. Formula: $C_{28}H_{43}OH$.

ergot ('ɜːgət, -gɒt) *n.* **1.** a disease of cereals and other grasses caused by ascomycete fungi of the genus *Claviceps,* esp. *C. purpurea,* in which the seeds or grain of the plants are replaced by the spore-containing bodies (sclerotia) of the fungus. **2.** any fungus causing this disease. **3.** the dried sclerotia of *C. purpurea,* used as the source of certain alkaloids used to treat haemorrhage, facilitate uterine contraction in childbirth, etc. [C17: from French: spur (of a cock), of unknown origin]

ergotism ('ɜːgəˌtɪzəm) *n.* ergot poisoning, producing either burning pains and eventually gangrene in the limbs or itching skin and convulsions. Also called: **Saint Anthony's fire.**

eric *or* **eriach** ('ɛrɪk) *n.* (in old Irish law) a fine paid by a murderer to the family of his victim. Compare **wergild.** [C16: from Irish *eiric*]

erica ('ɛrɪkə) *n.* any shrub of the ericaceous genus *Erica,* including the heaths and some heathers. [C19: via Latin from Greek *ereikē* heath]

ericaceous (ˌɛrɪ'keɪʃəs) *adj.* of, relating to, or belonging to the *Ericaceae,* a family of trees and shrubs with typically bell-shaped flowers: includes heather, rhododendron, azalea, and arbutus. [C19: from New Latin *Ericāceae,* from Latin *erīca* heath, from Greek *ereikē*]

ericoid ('ɛrɪˌkɔɪd) *adj. Botany.* (of leaves) small and tough, resembling those of heather.

Eridanus (ɛ'rɪdənəs) *n., Latin genitive* **Eridani** (ɛ'rɪdəˌnaɪ). a long twisting constellation in the S hemisphere extending from Orion to Hydrus and containing the first magnitude star Achernar. [from Greek *Eridanos* river in Italy (sometimes identified with the Po) into which, according to legend, Phaëthon fell]

Erie ('ɪərɪ) *n.* **1.** (*pl.* **Eries** *or* **Erie**) a member of a North American Indian people formerly living in the region south of Lake Erie. **2.** the language of this people, possibly belonging to the Iroquoian family.

erigeron (ɪ'rɪdʒərən, -'rɪg-) *n.* any plant of the genus *Erigeron,* whose flowers resemble asters but have narrower rays: family *Compositae* (composites). See also **fleabane** (sense 1). [C17: via Latin from Greek, from *ēri* early + *gerōn* old man; from the white down characteristic of some species]

erinaceous (ˌɛrɪ'neɪʃəs) *adj.* of, relating to, or resembling hedgehogs. [C18: from Latin *ērināceus* hedgehog]

eringo (ɪ'rɪŋgəʊ) *n., pl.* **-goes** *or* **-gos.** a variant spelling of **eryngo.**

erinus (ɪ'raɪnəs) *n.* any plant of the scrophulariaceous genus *Erinus,* native to S Africa and S Europe, esp. *E. alpinus,* grown as a rock plant for its white, purple, or carmine flowers. [New Latin, from Greek *erinos,* an unidentified plant]

eristic (ɛ'rɪstɪk) *adj. also* **eristical. 1.** of, relating, or given to controversy or logical disputation, esp. for its own sake. ~*n.* **2.** a person who engages in logical disputes; a controversialist. **3.** the art or practice of logical disputation, esp. if specious. [C17: from Greek *eristikos,* from *erizein* to wrangle, from *eris* discord]

Eritrean (ˌɛrɪ'treɪən) *adj.* **1.** of or relating to Eritrea, a province of N Ethiopia. ~*n.* **2.** a native or inhabitant of Eritrea.

erk (ɜːk) *n. Brit. slang.* an aircraftman or naval rating. [C20: perhaps a corruption of *AC* (aircraftman)]

erlang ('ɜːlæŋ) *n.* a unit of traffic intensity in a telephone system equal to the intensity for a specific period when the average number of simultaneous calls is unity. Abbrev.: **e.** [C20: named after A. K. *Erlang* (1878–1929), Danish mathematician]

Erlenmeyer flask ('ɜːlənˌmaɪə) *n.* a flask, for use in a laboratory, with a narrow neck, wide base, and conical shape; conical flask. [C19: named after Emil *Erlenmeyer* (1825–1909), German chemist]

erlking ('ɜːlˌkɪŋ) *n. German myth.* a malevolent spirit who carries children off to death. [C18: from German *Erlkönig,* literally: alder king, coined in 1778 by Herder, a mistranslation of Danish *ellerkonge* king of the elves]

ERM *abbrev. for* Exchange Rate Mechanism.

ermine ('ɜːmɪn) *n., pl.* **-mines** *or* **-mine. 1.** the stoat in northern regions, where it has a white winter coat with a black-tipped tail. **2.** the fur of this animal. **3.** one of the two principal furs used on heraldic shields, conventionally represented by a white field flecked with black ermine tails. Compare **vair. 4.** the dignity or office of a judge, noble, or king. **5.** short for **ermine moth.** [C12: from Old French *hermine,* from Medieval Latin *Armenius* (*mūs*) Armenian (mouse)]

ermine moth *n.* **1.** Also called: **ermine.** an arctiid moth of the genus *Spilosoma,* characterized by dark spots on the light coloured wings, and producing woolly bear caterpillars. **2. small ermine.** an unrelated micro, *Yponomeuta padella.*

Ermite ('ɜːmaɪt) *n.* a salty blue cheese made in Quebec, Canada. [via Canadian French from French *ermite* hermit, the cheese being made originally by monks]

erne *or* **ern** (ɜːn) *n.* another name for the (European) **sea eagle.** [Old English *earn;* related to Old Norse *örn* eagle, Old High German *aro* eagle, Greek *ornis* bird]

Ernie ('ɜːnɪ) *n.* (in Britain) a computer that randomly selects winning numbers of Premium Bonds. [C20: acronym of Electronic Random Number Indicator Equipment]

erode (ɪ'rəʊd) *vb.* **1.** to grind or wear down or away or become ground or worn down or away. **2.** to deteriorate or cause to deteriorate: *jealousy eroded the relationship.* **3.** (*tr.; usually passive*) *Pathol.* to remove (tissue) by ulceration. [C17: from Latin *ērōdere,* from EX-[1] + *rōdere* to gnaw] —**e'rodent** *adj., n.* —**e'rodible** *adj.*

erogenous (ɪ'rɒdʒɪnəs) *or* **erogenic** (ˌɛrə'dʒɛnɪk) *adj.* **1.** sensitive to sexual stimulation: *erogenous zones of the body.* **2.** arousing sexual desire or giving sexual pleasure. [C19: from Greek *erōs* love, desire + -GENOUS] —**erogeneity** (ˌɛrədʒɪ'niːɪtɪ) *n.*

Eros ('ɪərɒs, 'ɛrɒs) *n.* Also called: **life instinct.** (in Freudian theory) the group of instincts, esp. sexual, that govern acts of self-preservation and that tend towards uninhibited enjoyment of life. Compare **Thanatos.** [after *Eros,* the Greek god of love]

erose (ɪ'rəʊs, -'rəʊz) *adj.* jagged or uneven, as though gnawed or bitten: *erose leaves.* [C18: from Latin *ērōsus* eaten away, from *ērōdere* to ERODE] —**e'rosely** *adv.*

erosion (ɪ'rəʊʒən) *n.* **1.** the wearing away of rocks and other deposits on the earth's surface by the action of water, ice, wind, etc. **2.** the act or process of eroding or the state of being eroded. —**e'rosive** *or* **e'rosional** *adj.*

erotema (ˌɛrəʊ'tiːmə), **eroteme** ('ɛrəʊˌtiːm), *or* **erotesis** (ˌɛrəʊ'tiːsɪs) *n. Rhetoric.* a rhetorical question. [C16: New Latin, from Greek, from *erōtaein* to ask]

erotetic (ˌɛrəʊ'tɛtɪk) *adj.* **1.** *Rhetoric.* pertaining to a rhetorical question. **2.** *Grammar, philosophy.* pertaining to questions; interrogative.

erotic (ɪ'rɒtɪk) *adj. also* **erotical. 1.** of, concerning, or arousing sexual desire or giving sexual pleasure. **2.** marked by strong sexual desire or being especially sensitive to sexual stimulation. ~*n.* **3.** a person who has strong sexual desires or is especially responsive to sexual stimulation. [C17: from Greek *erōtikos* of love, from *erōs* love] —**e'rotically** *adv.*

erotica (ɪ'rɒtɪkə) *pl. n.* explicitly sexual literature or art. [C19: from Greek *erōtika,* neuter plural of *erōtikos* EROTIC]

eroticism (ɪ'rɒtɪˌsɪzəm) *or* **erotism** ('ɛrəˌtɪzəm) *n.* **1.** erotic quality or nature. **2.** the use of sexually arousing or pleasing symbolism in literature or art. **3.** sexual excitement or desire. **4.** a tendency to exalt sex. **5.** *Psychol.* an overt display of sexual behaviour.

eroto- *combining form.* denoting erotic desire, excitement, etc.: *erotogenic; erotology.* [from Greek *erōt-*, *erōs* love]

erotogenic (ɪˌrɒtəˈdʒɛnɪk) *adj.* originating from or causing sexual stimulation; erogenous.

erotology (ˌɛrəˈtɒlədʒɪ) *n.* **1.** the study of erotic stimuli and sexual behaviour. **2.** a description of such stimuli and behaviour. —**erotological** (ˌɛrətəˈlɒdʒɪkᵊl) *adj.* —ˌ**erotˈologist** *n.*

erotomania (ɪˌrɒtəʊˈmeɪnɪə) *n.* abnormally strong sexual desire. —**eˌrotoˈmaniac** *n.*

err (ɜː) *vb. (intr.)* **1.** to make a mistake; be incorrect. **2.** to stray from the right course or accepted standards; sin. **3.** to act with bias, esp. favourable bias: *to err on the side of justice.* [C14 *erren* to wander, stray, from Old French *errer*, from Latin *errāre*]

errancy (ˈɛrənsɪ) *n., pl.* **-cies.** **1.** the state or an instance of erring or a tendency to err. **2.** *Christianity.* the holding of views at variance with accepted doctrine.

errand (ˈɛrənd) *n.* **1.** a short trip undertaken to perform a necessary task or commission (esp. in the phrase **run errands**). **2.** the purpose or object of such a trip. [Old English *ǣrende;* related to *ār* messenger, Old Norse *erendi* message, Old High German *ārunti*, Swedish *ärende*]

errand boy *n.* (in Britain, esp. formerly) a boy employed by a shopkeeper to deliver goods and run other errands.

errant (ˈɛrənt) *adj. (often postpositive)* **1.** *Archaic or literary.* wandering in search of adventure. **2.** erring or straying from the right course or accepted standards. [C14: from Old French: journeying, from Vulgar Latin *iterāre* (unattested), from Latin *iter* journey; influenced by Latin *errāre* to ERR] —ˈ**errantly** *adv.*

errantry (ˈɛrəntrɪ) *n., pl.* **-ries.** the way of life of a knight errant.

errata (ɪˈrɑːtə) *n.* the plural of **erratum.**

▷**Usage.** *Errata* is sometimes used to mean a list of errata (in a book). Careful writers and speakers usually treat the word as plural: *the errata for this book are* (not *is*) *complete.*

erratic (ɪˈrætɪk) *adj.* **1.** irregular in performance, behaviour, or attitude; inconsistent and unpredictable. **2.** having no fixed or regular course; wandering. ~*n.* **3.** a piece of rock that differs in composition, shape, etc., from the rock surrounding it, having been transported from its place of origin, esp. by glacial action. **4.** an erratic person or thing. [C14: from Latin *errāticus*, from *errāre* to wander, ERR] —**erˈratically** *adv.*

erratum (ɪˈrɑːtəm) *n., pl.* **-ta** (-tə). **1.** an error in writing or printing. **2.** another name for **corrigendum.** [C16: from Latin: mistake, from *errāre* to ERR]

errhine (ˈɛraɪn, ˈɛrɪn) *Med.* ~*adj.* **1.** causing nasal secretion. ~*n.* **2.** an errhine drug or agent. [C17: from Greek *errhinos*, from EN-[2] + *rhis* nose]

erroneous (ɪˈrəʊnɪəs) *adj.* based on or containing error; mistaken; incorrect. [C14 (in the sense: deviating from what is right), from Latin *errōneus*, from *errāre* to wander] —**erˈroneously** *adv.* —**erˈroneousness** *n.*

error (ˈɛrə) *n.* **1.** a mistake or inaccuracy, as in action or speech: *a typing error.* **2.** an incorrect belief or wrong judgment. **3.** the condition of deviating from accuracy or correctness, as in belief, action, or speech: *he was in error about the train times.* **4.** deviation from a moral standard; wrongdoing: *he saw the error of his ways.* **5.** *Maths, statistics.* a measure of the difference between some quantity and an approximation to or estimate of it, often expressed as a percentage: *an error of ±5%.* **6.** *Statistics.* see **type I error, type II error.** [C13: from Latin, from *errāre* to ERR] —ˈ**error-ˌfree** *adj.*

error correction *n. Computer technol.* the automatic correction of errors in data that arise from missing or distorted digital pulses.

error message *n.* a message displayed on a visual display unit, printout, etc., indicating that an incorrect instruction has been given to the computer.

error of closure *n. Surveying.* the amount by which a computed, plotted, or observed quantity or position differs from the true or established one, esp. when plotting a closed traverse. Also called: **closing error.**

ERS *abbrev. for* earnings related supplement.

ersatz (ˈɛəzæts, ˈɜː-) *adj.* **1.** made in imitation of some natural or genuine product; artificial. ~*n.* **2.** an ersatz substance or article. [C20: German, from *ersetzen* to substitute]

Erse (ɜːs) *n.* **1.** another name for **Gaelic.** ~*adj.* **2.** of or relating to the Gaelic language. [C14: from Lowland Scots *Erisch* Irish; Irish being regarded as the literary form of Gaelic]

erst (ɜːst) *adv. Archaic.* **1.** long ago; formerly. **2.** at first. [Old English *ǣrest* earliest, superlative of *ǣr* early; see ERE; related to Old High German *ērist*, Dutch *eerst*]

erstwhile (ˈɜːstˌwaɪl) *adj.* **1.** former; one-time: *my erstwhile companions.* ~*adv.* **2.** *Archaic.* long ago; formerly.

erubescence (ˌɛrʊˈbɛsᵊns) *n.* the process of growing red or a condition of redness. [C18: from Latin *ērubescentia* blushing, from *rubēscere* to grow red, from *ruber* red] —ˌ**eruˈbescent** *adj.*

eruct (ɪˈrʌkt) *or* **eructate** *vb.* **1.** to raise (gas and often a small quantity of acid) from the stomach; belch. **2.** (of a volcano) to pour out (fumes or volcanic matter). [C17: from Latin *ēructāre*, from *ructāre* to belch] —**eructation** (ɪˌrʌkˈteɪʃən, ˌiːrʌk-) *n.* —**eructative** (ɪˈrʌktətɪv) *adj.*

erudite (ˈɛrʊˌdaɪt) *adj.* having or showing extensive scholarship; learned. [C15: from Latin *ērudītus*, from *ērudīre* to polish, from EX-[1] + *rudis* unpolished, rough] —ˈ**eruˌditely** *adv.* —**erudition** (ˌɛrʊˈdɪʃən) *or* ˈ**eruˌditeness** *n.*

erumpent (ɪˈrʌmpənt) *adj.* bursting out or (esp. of plant parts) developing as though bursting through an overlying structure. [C17: from Latin *ērumpere* to burst forth, from *rumpere* to shatter, burst]

erupt (ɪˈrʌpt) *vb.* **1.** to eject (steam, water, and volcanic material such as lava and ash) violently or (of volcanic material, etc.) to be so ejected. **2.** *(intr.)* (of a skin blemish) to appear on the skin; break out. **3.** *(intr.)* (of a tooth) to emerge through the gum and become visible during the normal process of tooth development. **4.** *(intr.)* to burst forth suddenly and violently, as from restraint: *to erupt in anger.* [C17: from Latin *ēruptus* having burst forth, from *ērumpere*, from *rumpere* to burst] —**eˈruptible** *adj.* —**eˈruption** *n.*

eruptive (ɪˈrʌptɪv) *adj.* **1.** erupting or tending to erupt. **2.** resembling or of the nature of an eruption. **3.** (of rocks) formed by solidification of magma; igneous. **4.** (of a disease) characterized by skin eruptions. —**eˈruptively** *adv.* —**eˌrupˈtivity** *or* **eˈruptiveness** *n.*

-ery *or* **-ry** *suffix forming nouns.* **1.** indicating a place of business or some other activity: *bakery; brewery; refinery.* **2.** indicating a class or collection of things: *cutlery; greenery.* **3.** indicating qualities or actions collectively: *snobbery; trickery.* **4.** indicating a practice or occupation: *husbandry.* **5.** indicating a state or condition: *slavery.* [from Old French *-erie*; see -ER[1], -Y[3]]

eryngium (ɪˈrɪndʒɪəm) *n.* any plant of the temperate and subtropical perennial genus *Eryngium*, with distinctive spiny foliage, metallic blue flower heads, and bluish stems, several species of which are grown as garden plants: family *Umbelliferae.* See also **sea holly.** [New Latin, from Greek *ēryngion* a species of thistle]

eryngo (ɪˈrɪŋgəʊ) *n., pl.* **-goes** *or* **-gos.** any umbelliferous plant of the genus *Eryngium*, such as the sea holly, having toothed or lobed leaves. Also called: **eringo.** [C16: from Latin *ēryngion* variety of thistle, from Greek *ērungion*, diminutive of *ērungos* thistle]

erysipelas (ˌɛrɪˈsɪpɪləs) *n.* an acute streptococcal infectious disease of the skin, characterized by fever, headache, vomiting, and purplish raised lesions, esp. on the face. Also called: **Saint Anthony's fire.** [C16: from Latin, from Greek *erusipelas*, from Greek *erusi-* red + *-pelas* skin] —**erysipelatous** (ˌɛrɪsɪˈpɛlətəs) *adj.*

erysipeloid (ˌɛrɪˈsɪpɪˌlɔɪd) *n.* an infective dermatitis mainly affecting the hands, characterized by inflammation and caused by the microorganism *Erysipelothrix rhusiopathiae* on contaminated meat, poultry, or fish: most prevalent among fishermen and butchers.

erythema (ˌɛrɪˈθiːmə) *n. Pathol.* redness of the skin, usually occurring in patches, caused by irritation or injury to the tissue. [C18: from New Latin, from Greek *eruthēma*, from *eruthros* red] —**erythematic** (ˌɛrɪθɪˈmætɪk), **erythematous** (ˌɛrɪˈθiːmətəs), *or* ˌ**eryˈthemal** *adj.*

erythraemia *or esp. U.S.* **erythremia** (ˌɛrɪˈθriːmɪə) *n. Med.* another name for **polycythaemia vera** (see **polycythaemia**).

erythrism (ɪˈrɪθrɪzəm) *n.* abnormal red coloration, as in plumage or hair. —**erythrismal** (ˌɛrɪˈθrɪzməl) *adj.*

erythrite (ɪˈrɪθraɪt) *n.* **1.** Also called: **cobalt bloom.** a pink to purple secondary mineral consisting of hydrated cobalt arsenate in monoclinic crystalline form. Formula: $Co_3(AsO_4)_2.8H_2O$. **2.** another name for **erythritol.**

erythritol (ɪˈrɪθrɪˌtɒl) *or* **erythrite** *n.* a sweet crystalline compound extracted from certain algae and lichens and used in medicine to dilate the blood vessels of the heart; 1,2,3,4-butanetetrol. Formula: $C_4H_{10}O_4$.

erythro- *or before a vowel* **erythr-** *combining form.* red: *erythrocyte.* [from Greek *eruthros* red]

erythroblast (ɪˈrɪθrəʊˌblæst) *n.* a nucleated cell in bone marrow that develops into an erythrocyte. —**eˌrythroˈblastic** *adj.*

erythroblastosis (ɪˌrɪθrəʊblæˈstəʊsɪs) *n.* **1.** the abnormal presence of erythroblasts in the circulating blood. **2.** an anaemic blood disease of a fetus or newborn child, characterized by erythroblasts in the circulating blood: caused by a blood incompatibility between mother and fetus.

erythrocyte (ɪˈrɪθrəʊˌsaɪt) *n.* a blood cell of vertebrates that transports oxygen and carbon dioxide, combined with the red pigment haemoglobin, to and from the tissues. Also called: **red blood cell.** —**erythrocytic** (ɪˌrɪθrəʊˈsɪtɪk) *adj.*

erythrocytometer (ɪˌrɪθrəʊsaɪˈtɒmɪtə) *n.* an instrument for counting the number or measuring the size of red blood cells in a sample of blood. —**eˌrythrocyˈtometry** *n.*

erythromycin (ɪˌrɪθrəʊˈmaɪsɪn) *n.* an antibiotic used in treating infections caused by Gram-positive bacteria. It is obtained from the bacterium *Streptomyces erythreus.* Formula: $C_{37}M_{67}NO_{13}$. [C20: from ERYTHRO- + Greek *mukēs* fungus + -IN]

erythronium (ˌɛrɪˈθrəʊnɪəm) *n.* any plant of the bulbous genus *Erythronium*, with decoratively mottled leaves and cyclamen-like yellow, rose, purple, or white flowers: family *Liliaceae.* See also **dogtooth violet.** [New Latin, from Greek *erythros* red]

erythropenia (ɪˌrɪθrəʊˈpiːnɪə) *n.* the presence of decreased numbers of erythrocytes in the blood, as occurs in some forms of anaemia. [from ERYTHRO- + Greek *penia* poverty]

erythropoiesis (ɪˌrɪθrəʊpɔɪˈiːsɪs) *n. Physiol.* the formation of red blood cells. [C19: from ERYTHRO- + Greek *poiēsis* a making, from *poiein* to make] —**eˌrythropoiˈetic** *adj.*

erythropoietin (ɪˌrɪθrəupɔɪˈiːtɪn) *n.* a hormone, secreted by the kidney in response to low levels of oxygen in the tissues, that increases the rate of erythropoiesis.

erythropsia (ˌɛrɪˈθrɒpsɪə) *n. Med.* a defect of vision in which objects appear red.

Es *the chemical symbol for* einsteinium.

-es *suffix.* **1.** a variant of **-s**[1] for nouns ending in *ch, s, sh, z,* postconsonantal *y,* for some nouns ending in a vowel, and nouns in *f* with *v* in the plural: *ashes; heroes; calves.* **2.** a variant of **-s**[2] for verbs ending in *ch, s, sh, z,* postconsonantal *y,* or a vowel: *preaches; steadies; echoes.*

ESA *abbrev. for* European Space Agency.

Esaki diode (ɪˈsɑːkɪ) *n.* another name for **tunnel diode.** [named after L. *Esaki* (born 1925), its Japanese designer]

ESB *abbrev. for* electrical stimulation of the brain.

escadrille (ˌɛskəˈdrɪl; *French* ɛskadrij) *n.* **1.** a French squadron of aircraft, esp. in World War I. **2.** a small squadron of ships. [from French: flotilla, from Spanish *escuadrilla,* from *escuadra* SQUADRON]

escalade (ˌɛskəˈleɪd) *n.* **1.** an assault by the use of ladders, esp. on a fortification. *~vb.* **2.** to gain access to (a place) by the use of ladders. [C16: from French, from Italian *scalata,* from *scalare* to mount, SCALE[3]] —ˌ**escaˈlader** *n.*

escalate (ˈɛskəˌleɪt) *vb.* to increase or be increased in extent, intensity, or magnitude: *to escalate a war; prices escalated because of inflation.* [C20: back formation from ESCALATOR] —ˌ**escaˈlation** *n.*

▷**Usage.** *Escalate,* as in *after the arrival of the troops the violence escalated,* is very commonly used in journalistic contexts in the sense of gradually increasing the intensity or scope of a war, etc. This word is, however, not yet completely accepted as appropriate in formal English.

escalator (ˈɛskəˌleɪtə) *n.* **1.** a moving staircase consisting of stair treads fixed to a conveyor belt, for transporting passengers between levels, esp. between the floors of a building. **2.** short for **escalator clause.** [C20: originally a trademark]

escalator clause *n.* a clause in a contract stipulating an adjustment in wages, prices, etc., in the event of specified changes in conditions, such as a large rise in the cost of living or price of raw materials.

escallonia (ˌɛskəˈləunɪə) *n.* any evergreen shrub of the South American saxifragaceous genus *Escallonia,* with white or red flowers: cultivated for ornament. [C19: from *Escallon,* 18th-century Spanish traveller who discovered it]

escallop (ɛˈskɒləp, ɛˈskæl-) *n., vb.* another word for **scallop.**

escalope (ˈɛskəˌlɒp) *n.* a thin slice of meat, usually veal, coated with egg and breadcrumbs, fried, and served with a rich sauce. [C19: from Old French: shell]

escapade (ˈɛskəˌpeɪd, ˌɛskəˈpeɪd) *n.* **1.** a wild or exciting adventure, esp. one that is mischievous or unlawful; scrape. **2.** any lighthearted or carefree episode; prank; romp. [C17: from French, from Old Italian *scappata,* from Vulgar Latin *excappāre* (unattested) to ESCAPE]

escape (ɪˈskeɪp) *vb.* **1.** to get away or break free from (confinements, captors, etc.): *the lion escaped from the zoo.* **2.** to manage to avoid (imminent danger, punishment, evil, etc.): *to escape death.* **3.** (*intr.;* usually foll. by *from*) (of gases, liquids, etc.) to issue gradually, as from a crack or fissure; seep; leak: *water was escaping from the dam.* **4.** (*tr.*) to elude; be forgotten by: *the actual figure escapes me.* **5.** (*tr.*) to be articulated inadvertently or involuntarily: *a roar escaped his lips.* **6.** (*intr.*) (of cultivated plants) to grow wild. *~n.* **7.** the act of escaping or state of having escaped. **8.** avoidance of injury, harm, etc.: *a narrow escape.* **9. a.** a means or way of escape. **b.** (*as modifier*): *an escape route.* **10.** a means of distraction or relief, esp. from reality or boredom: *angling provides an escape for many city dwellers.* **11.** a gradual outflow; leakage; seepage. **12.** Also called: **escape valve, escape cock.** a valve that releases air, steam, etc., above a certain pressure; relief valve. **13.** a plant that was originally cultivated but is now growing wild. [C14: from Old Northern French *escaper,* from Vulgar Latin *excappāre* (unattested) to escape (literally: to remove one's cloak, hence free oneself), from EX-[1] + Late Latin *cappa* cloak] —**esˈcapable** *adj.* —**esˈcaper** *n.*

escape clause *n.* a clause in a contract freeing one of the parties from his obligations in certain circumstances.

escapee (ɪˌskeɪˈpiː) *n.* a person who has escaped, esp. an escaped prisoner.

escape hatch *n.* a means of escape in an emergency, esp. from a submarine.

escape mechanism *n. Psychol.* any emotional or mental mechanism that enables a person to avoid acknowledging unpleasant or threatening realities. See also **escapism.**

escapement (ɪˈskeɪpmənt) *n.* **1.** *Horology.* a mechanism consisting of an escape wheel and anchor, used in timepieces to provide periodic impulses to the pendulum or balance. **2.** any similar mechanism that regulates movement, usually consisting of toothed wheels engaged by rocking levers. **3.** (in a piano) the mechanism that allows the hammer to clear the string after striking, so that the string can vibrate. **4.** an overflow channel. **5.** *Rare.* an act or means of escaping.

escape pipe *n.* a pipe for overflowing water, escaping steam, etc.

escape road *n.* a road, usually ending in a pile of sand, provided on a hill for a driver to drive into if his brakes fail or on a bend if he loses control of the turn.

escape routine *n. Computer technol.* a means of leaving a computer-program sequence before its end, in order to commence another sequence.

escape shaft *n.* a shaft in a mine through which miners can escape if the regular shaft is blocked.

escape velocity *n.* the minimum velocity that a body must have in order to escape from the gravitational field of the earth or other celestial body.

escape wheel *n. Horology.* a toothed wheel that engages intermittently with a balance wheel or pendulum, causing the mechanism to oscillate and thereby moving the hands of a clock or watch. Also called: **scapewheel.**

escapism (ɪˈskeɪpɪzəm) *n.* an inclination to or habit of retreating from unpleasant reality, as through diversion or fantasy. —**esˈcapist** *n., adj.*

escapologist (ˌɛskəˈpɒlədʒɪst) *n.* an entertainer who specializes in freeing himself from confinement. Also called: **escape artist.** —ˌ**escaˈpology** *n.*

escargot *French.* (ɛskargo) *n.* a variety of edible snail, usually eaten with a sauce made of melted butter and garlic.

escarp (ɪˈskɑːp) *n.* **1.** *Fortifications.* the inner side of the ditch separating besiegers and besieged. Compare **counterscarp.** *~vb.* **2.** a rare word for **scarp** (sense 3). [C17: from French *escarpe;* see SCARP]

escarpment (ɪˈskɑːpmənt) *n.* **1. a.** the long continuous steep face of a ridge or plateau formed by erosion; scarp. **b.** any steep slope, such as one resulting from faulting. **2.** a steep artificial slope immediately in front of the rampart of a fortified place.

-escent *suffix forming adjectives.* beginning to be, do, show, etc.: *convalescent; luminescent.* [via Old French from Latin *-ēscent-,* stem of present participial suffix of *-ēscere,* ending of inceptive verbs] —**-escence** *suffix forming nouns.*

eschalot (ˈɛʃəˌlɒt, ˌɛʃəˈlɒt) *n.* another name for a **shallot.** [C18: from Old French *eschalotte* a little SCALLION]

eschar (ˈɛskɑː) *n.* a dry scab or slough, esp. one following a burn or cauterization of the skin. [C16: from Late Latin *eschara* scab, from Greek *eskhara* hearth, pan of hot coals (which could inflict burns); see SCAR[1]]

escharotic (ˌɛskəˈrɒtɪk) *Med.* *~adj.* **1.** capable of producing an eschar. *~n.* **2.** a caustic or corrosive agent.

eschatology (ˌɛskəˈtɒlədʒɪ) *n.* the branch of theology or biblical exegesis concerned with the end of the world. [C19: from Greek *eskhatos* last] —**eschatological** (ˌɛskətəˈlɒdʒɪkᵊl) *adj.* —ˌ**eschatoˈlogically** *adv.* —ˌ**eschaˈtologist** *n.*

escheat (ɪsˈtʃiːt) *Law.* *~n.* **1.** (in England before 1926) the reversion of property to the Crown in the absence of legal heirs. **2.** (in feudal times) the reversion of property to the feudal lord in the absence of legal heirs or upon outlawry of the tenant. **3.** the property so reverting. *~vb.* **4.** to take (land) by escheat or (of land) to revert by escheat. [C14: from Old French *eschete,* from *escheoir* to fall to the lot of, from Late Latin *excadere* (unattested), from Latin *cadere* to fall] —**esˈcheatable** *adj.* —**esˈcheatage** *n.*

Escher figure (ˈɛʃə) *n.* another name for **impossible figure.** [named after M. C. *Escher* (1898–1970), Dutch graphic artist who produced many such drawings]

Escherichia (ˌɛʃəˈrɪkɪə) *n.* a genus of Gram-negative rodlike bacteria that form acid and gas in the presence of carbohydrates and are found in the intestines of man and many animals, esp. *E. coli,* which is sometimes pathogenic and is widely used in genetic research. [C19: named after Theodor *Escherich* (1857–1911), German paediatrician who first described *E. coli*]

eschew (ɪsˈtʃuː) *vb.* (*tr.*) to keep clear of or abstain from (something disliked, injurious, etc.); shun; avoid. [C14: from Old French *eschiver,* of Germanic origin; compare Old High German *skiuhan* to frighten away; see SHY[1], SKEW] —**esˈchewal** *n.* —**esˈchewer** *n.*

eschscholtzia *or* **eschscholzia** (ɛˈʃɒltsɪə) *n.* See **California poppy.** [named after J. F. von *Eschscholtz* (1743–1831), German naturalist]

escolar (ˌɛskəˈlɑː) *n., pl.* **-lars** *or* **-lar.** any slender spiny-finned fish of the family *Gempylidae,* of warm and tropical seas: similar and closely related to the scombroid fishes. Also called: **snake mackerel.** [from Spanish: SCHOLAR; so called from the rings round its eyes, suggestive of spectacles]

escort *n.* (ˈɛskɔːt). **1.** one or more persons, soldiers, vehicles, etc., accompanying another or others for protection, guidance, restraint, or as a mark of honour. **2.** a man or youth who accompanies a woman or girl: *he was her escort for the evening.* **3. a.** a person, esp. a young woman, who may be hired to accompany another for entertainment, etc. **b.** (*as modifier*): *an escort agency.* *~vb.* (ɪsˈkɔːt). **4.** (*tr.*) to accompany or attend as an escort. [C16: from French *escorte,* from Italian *scorta,* from *scorgere* to guide, from Latin *corrigere* to straighten; see CORRECT]

escribe (ɪˈskraɪb) *vb.* (*tr.*) to draw (a circle) so that it is tangential to one side of a triangle and to the other two sides produced. [C16 (meaning: to write out): from EX-[1] + Latin *scribere* to write]

escritoire (ˌɛskrɪˈtwɑː) *n.* a writing desk with compartments and drawers, concealed by a hinged flap, on a chest of drawers or plain stand. [C18: from French, from Medieval Latin *scriptōrium* writing room in a monastery, from Latin *scrībere* to write]

escrow (ˈɛskrəʊ, ɛˈskrəʊ) *Law.* ~*n.* **1.** money, goods, or a written document, such as a contract bond, delivered to a third party and held by him pending fulfilment of some condition. **2.** the state or condition of being an escrow (esp. in the phrase **in escrow**). ~*vb.* (*tr.*) **3.** to place (money, a document, etc.) in escrow. [C16: from Old French *escroe,* of Germanic origin; see SCREED, SHRED, SCROLL]

escuage (ˈɛskjuɪdʒ) *n.* (in medieval Europe) another word for **scutage.** [C16: from Old French, from *escu* shield, from Latin *scūtum*]

escudo (ɛˈskuːdəʊ; *Portuguese* ɪʃˈkuðu) *n., pl.* **-dos** (-dəʊz; *Portuguese* -ðuʃ). **1.** the standard monetary unit of Portugal, divided into 100 centavos. **2.** the standard monetary unit of Chile, divided into 100 centesimos. **3.** an old Spanish silver coin worth 10 reals. [C19: Spanish, literally: shield, from Latin *scūtum*]

esculent (ˈɛskjʊlənt) *n.* **1.** any edible substance. ~*adj.* **2.** edible. [C17: from Latin *ēsculentus* good to eat, from *ēsca* food, from *edere* to eat]

escutcheon (ɪˈskʌtʃən) *n.* **1.** a shield, esp. a heraldic one that displays a coat of arms. **2.** Also called: **escutcheon plate.** a plate or shield that surrounds a keyhole, door handle, light switch, etc., esp. an ornamental one protecting a door or wall surface. **3.** the place on the stern or transom of a vessel where the name is shown. **4. blot on one's escutcheon.** a stain on one's honour. [C15: from Old Northern French *escuchon,* ultimately from Latin *scūtum* shield] —**esˈcutcheoned** *adj.*

Esd. *Bible. abbrev. for* Esdras.

ESE *symbol. for* east-southeast.

-ese *suffix forming adjectives and nouns.* indicating place of origin, language, or style: *Cantonese; Japanese; journalese.*

esemplastic (ˌɛsɛmˈplæstɪk) *adj. Literature.* making into one; unifying. [C19 (first used by Samuel Taylor Coleridge): from Greek *es, eis* into + *em,* from *hen,* neuter of *heis* one + -PLASTIC]

eserine (ˈɛsəriːn, -rɪn) *n.* another name for **physostigmine.** [C19: *eser-,* of African origin + -INE[2]]

ESG (in Britain) *abbrev. for* Educational Support Grant: a government grant given to a Local Education Authority to fund educational schemes dealing with important social issues, such as drug abuse.

esker (ˈɛskə) *or* **eskar** (ˈɛskɑː, -kə) *n.* a long winding ridge of gravel, sand, etc., originally deposited by a meltwater stream running under a glacier. Also called: **os.** [C19: from Old Irish *escir* ridge]

Eskimo (ˈɛskɪˌməʊ) *n.* **1.** (*pl.* **-mos** *or* **-mo**) a member of a group of peoples inhabiting N Canada, Greenland, Alaska, and E Siberia, having a material culture adapted to an extremely cold climate. **2.** the language of these peoples. **3.** a family of languages that includes Eskimo and Aleut. ~*adj.* **4.** relating to, denoting, or characteristic of the Eskimos. ~Former spelling: **Esquimau.** See also **Inuit, Inuktitut.** [C18 *Esquimawes:* related to Abnaki *esquimantsic* eaters of raw flesh]

Eskimo dog *n.* a large powerful breed of sled dog with a long thick coat and curled tail.

Esky (ˈɛskɪ) *n., pl.* **-kies.** (*sometimes not cap.*) *Austral. trademark.* a portable insulated container for keeping food and drink cool. [C20: from ESKIMO, alluding to the Eskimos' cold habitat]

ESL *abbrev. for* English as a second language.

ESN *abbrev. for* educationally subnormal; used to designate a person of limited intelligence who needs special schooling.

esophagus (iːˈsɒfəgəs) *n., pl.* **-gi** (-ˌdʒaɪ) *or* **-guses.** the U.S. spelling of **oesophagus.** —**esophageal** (iːˌsɒfəˈdʒiːəl) *adj.*

esoteric (ˌɛsəʊˈtɛrɪk) *adj.* **1.** restricted to or intended for an enlightened or initiated minority, esp. because of abstruseness or obscurity: *an esoteric cult.* Compare **exoteric. 2.** difficult to understand; abstruse: *an esoteric statement.* **3.** not openly admitted; private: *esoteric aims.* [C17: from Greek *esōterikos,* from *esōterō* inner] —ˌ**esoˈterically** *adv.* —ˌ**esoˈteriˌcism** *n.*

ESP *abbrev. for:* **1.** English for specific (*or* Special) Purposes: the technique of teaching English to students who need it for a particular purpose, such as business dealings. **2.** extrasensory perception.

esp. *abbrev. for* especially.

espadrille (ˌɛspəˈdrɪl) *n.* a light shoe with a canvas upper, esp. with a braided cord sole. [C19: from French, from Provençal *espardilho,* diminutive of *espart* ESPARTO; so called from the use of esparto for the soles of such shoes]

espalier (ɪˈspæljə) *n.* **1.** an ornamental shrub or fruit tree that has been trained to grow flat, as against a wall. **2.** the trellis, framework, or arrangement of stakes on which such plants are trained. **3.** the method used to produce such plants. ~*vb.* **4.** (*tr.*) to train (a plant) on an espalier. [C17: from French: trellis, from Old Italian: shoulder supports, from *spalla* shoulder, from Late Latin SPATULA]

esparto *or* **esparto grass** (ɛˈspɑːtəʊ) *n., pl.* **-tos.** any of various grasses, esp. *Stipa tenacissima* of S Europe and N Africa, that yield a fibre used to make ropes, mats, etc. [C18: from Spanish, via Latin from Greek *sparton* rope made of rushes, from *spartos* a kind of rush]

especial (ɪˈspɛʃəl) *adj.* (*prenominal*) **1.** unusual; notable; exceptional: *he paid especial attention to her that evening.* **2.** applying to one person or thing in particular; not general; specific; peculiar: *he had an especial dislike of relatives.* [C14: from Old French, from Latin *speciālis* individual; see SPECIAL] —**esˈpecially** *adv.*

▷**Usage.** *Especial* and *especially* have a more limited use than *special* and *specially. Special* is always used in preference to *especial* when the sense is one of being out of the ordinary: *a special lesson; he has been specially trained. Special* is also used when something is referred to as being for a particular purpose: *the word was specially underlined for you.* Where an idea of pre-eminence or individuality is involved, either *especial* or *special* may be used: *he is my especial* (or *special*) *friend; he is especially* (or *specially*) *good at his job.* In informal English, however, *special* is usually preferred in all contexts.

esperance (ˈɛspərəns) *n. Archaic.* hope or expectation. [C15: from Old French, from Vulgar Latin *sperantia* (unattested), from Latin *spērāre* to hope, from *spēs* hope]

Esperanto (ˌɛspəˈræntəʊ) *n.* an international artificial language based on words common to the chief European languages, invented in 1887. [C19: literally: the one who hopes, pseudonym of Dr. L. L. Zamenhof (1859–1917), Polish philologist who invented it] —ˌ**Espeˈrantist** *n., adj.*

espial (ɪˈspaɪəl) *n. Archaic.* **1.** the act or fact of being seen or discovered. **2.** the act of noticing. **3.** the act of spying upon; secret observation.

espionage (ˈɛspɪəˌnɑːʒ, ˌɛspɪəˈnɑːʒ, ˈɛspɪənɪdʒ) *n.* **1.** the systematic use of spies to obtain secret information, esp. by governments to discover military or political secrets. **2.** the act or practice of spying. [C18: from French *espionnage,* from *espionner* to spy, from *espion* spy, from Old Italian *spione,* of Germanic origin; compare German *spähen* to SPY]

esplanade (ˌɛspləˈneɪd, -ˈnɑːd) *n.* **1.** a long open level stretch of ground for walking along, esp. beside the seashore. Compare **promenade** (sense 1). **2.** an open area in front of a fortified place, in which attackers are exposed to the defenders' fire. [C17: from French, from Old Italian *spianata,* from *spianare* to make level, from Latin *explānāre;* see EXPLAIN]

espousal (ɪˈspaʊzᵊl) *n.* **1.** adoption or support: *an espousal of new beliefs.* **2.** (*sometimes pl.*) *Archaic.* a marriage or betrothal ceremony.

espouse (ɪˈspaʊz) *vb.* (*tr.*) **1.** to adopt or give support to (a cause, ideal, etc.): *to espouse socialism.* **2.** *Archaic.* (esp. of a man) to take as spouse; marry. [C15: from Old French *espouser,* from Latin *spōnsāre* to affiance, espouse] —**esˈpouser** *n.*

espressivo (ˌɛspreˈsiːvəʊ) *adj., adv. Music.* (to be performed) in an expressive manner. [Italian]

espresso (ɛˈsprɛsəʊ) *n., pl.* **-sos. 1.** strong coffee made by forcing steam or boiling water through ground coffee beans. **2.** an apparatus for making coffee in this way. [C20: Italian, short for *caffè espresso,* literally: pressed coffee]

esprit (ɛˈspriː) *n.* spirit and liveliness, esp. in wit. [C16: from French, from Latin *spīritus* a breathing, SPIRIT]

esprit de corps (ɛˈspriː də ˈkɔː; *French* ɛspri də kɔr) *n.* consciousness of and pride in belonging to a particular group; the sense of shared purpose and fellowship.

espy (ɪˈspaɪ) *vb.* **-pies, -pying, -pied.** (*tr.*) to catch sight of or perceive (something distant or previously unnoticed); detect: *to espy a ship on the horizon.* [C14: from Old French *espier* to SPY, of Germanic origin] —**esˈpier** *n.*

Esq. *abbrev. for* esquire: used esp. in correspondence.

-esque *suffix forming adjectives.* indicating a specified character, manner, style, or resemblance: *picturesque; Romanesque; statuesque; Chaplinesque.* [via French from Italian *-esco,* of Germanic origin; compare -ISH]

Esquimau (ˈɛskɪˌməʊ) *n., pl.* **-maus** *or* **-mau,** *adj.* a former spelling of **Eskimo.**

esquire (ɪˈskwaɪə) *n.* **1.** *Chiefly Brit.* a title of respect, usually abbreviated *Esq.,* placed after a man's name. **2.** (in medieval times) the attendant and shield bearer of a knight, subsequently often knighted himself. **3.** *Rare.* a male escort. ~*vb.* **4.** (*tr.*) *Rare.* to escort (a woman). [C15: from Old French *escuier,* from Late Latin *scūtārius* shield bearer, from Latin *scūtum* shield]

ESR *abbrev. for* electron spin resonance.

ESRO (ˈɛzrəʊ) *n. acronym for* European Space Research Organization.

-ess *suffix forming nouns.* indicating a female: *waitress; lioness.* [via Old French from Late Latin *-issa,* from Greek]

▷**Usage.** The suffix *-ess* in such words as *poetess, authoress* is now often regarded as disparaging; a sexually neutral term *poet, author* is preferred.

essay *n.* (ˈɛseɪ; *senses 2,3 also* ɛˈseɪ). **1.** a short literary composition dealing with a subject analytically or speculatively. **2.** an attempt or endeavour; effort. **3.** a test or trial. ~*vb.* (ɛˈseɪ). (*tr.*) **4.** to attempt or endeavour; try. **5.** to test or try out. [C15: from Old French *essaier* to attempt, from *essai* an attempt, from Late Latin *exagium* a weighing, from Latin *agere* to do, compel, influenced by *exigere* to investigate]

essayist (ˈɛseɪɪst) *n.* a person who writes essays.

esse (ˈɛsɪ) *n. Philosophy.* **1.** existence. **2.** essential nature; essence. [C17: from Latin: to be]

essence (ˈɛsᵊns) *n.* **1.** the characteristic or intrinsic feature of a thing, which determines its identity; fundamental nature. **2.** the most distinctive element of a thing: *the essence of a problem.* **3.** a perfect or complete form of something, esp. a person who typifies an abstract quality: *he was the essence of gentility.* **4.** *Philosophy.* **a.** the unchanging and unchangeable nature of something which is necessary to its being the thing it is; its necessary properties. Compare **accident** (sense 4). **b.** the properties in virtue of which something is called by its name. **c.** the nature of something as distinct from, and logically prior to, its existence. **5.** *Theol.* an immaterial or spiritual entity. **6. a.** the constituent of a plant, usually an oil, alkaloid, or glycoside, that determines its chemical or pharmacological properties. **b.** an alcoholic solution of such a substance. **7.** the sense of a substance containing the properties of a plant or foodstuff in concentrated form: *vanilla essence.* **8.** a rare word for **perfume. 9. in essence.** essentially; fundamentally. **10. of the essence.** indispensable; vitally important. [C14: from Medieval Latin *essentia,* from Latin: the being (of something), from *esse* to be]

Essene ('ɛsiːn, ɛ'siːn) *n. Judaism.* a member of an ascetic sect that flourished in Palestine from the second century B.C. to the second century A.D., living in strictly organized communities. —**Essenian** (ɛ'siːnɪən) *or* **Essenic** (ɛ'sɛnɪk) *adj.*

essential (ɪ'sɛnʃəl) *adj.* **1.** vitally important; absolutely necessary. **2.** basic; fundamental: *the essential feature.* **3.** completely realized; absolute; perfect: *essential beauty.* **4.** *Biochem.* (of an amino acid or a fatty acid) necessary for the normal growth of an organism but not synthesized by the organism and therefore required in the diet. **5.** derived from or relating to an extract of a plant, drug, etc.: *an essential oil.* **6.** *Logic.* (of a property) guaranteed by the identity of the subject; necessary. Thus, if having the atomic number 79 is an essential property of gold, nothing can be gold unless it has that atomic number. **7.** *Music.* denoting or relating to a note that belongs to the fundamental harmony of a chord or piece. **8.** *Pathol.* (of a disease) having no obvious external cause: *essential hypertension.* **9.** *Geology.* (of a mineral constituent of a rock) necessary for defining the classification of a rock. Its absence alters the rock's name and classification. ~*n.* **10.** something fundamental or indispensable: *a sharp eye is an essential for a printer.* **11.** *Music.* an essential note. —**essentiality** (ɪˌsɛnʃɪ'ælɪtɪ) *or* **es'sentialness** *n.* —**es'sentially** *adv.*

essential element *n. Biochem.* any chemical element required by an organism for healthy growth. It may be required in large amounts (see **macronutrient**) or in very small amounts (see **trace element**).

essentialism (ɪ'sɛnʃəˌlɪzəm) *n.* **1.** *Philosophy.* one of a number of related doctrines which hold that there are necessary properties of things, that these are logically prior to the existence of the individuals which instantiate them, and that their classification depends upon their satisfaction of sets of necessary conditions. **2.** the doctrine that education should concentrate on teaching basic skills and encouraging intellectual self-discipline. —**es'sentialist** *n.*

essential oil *n.* any of various volatile organic oils present in plants, usually containing terpenes and esters and having the odour or flavour of the plant from which they are extracted: used in flavouring and perfumery. Compare **fixed oil.** See also **oleoresin.**

essonite ('ɛsəˌnaɪt) *n.* a variant spelling of **hessonite.**

est (ɛst) *n.* a treatment intended to help people towards psychological growth, in which they spend many hours in large groups, deprived of food and water and hectored by stewards. [*E*rhard *S*eminars *T*raining; after Werner Erhard, American businessman, who devised the system]

EST *abbrev. for:* **1.** (in the U.S. and Canada) Eastern Standard Time. **2.** electric-shock treatment.

est. *abbrev. for:* **1.** Also: **estab.** established. **2.** *Law.* estate. **3.** estimate(d). **4.** estuary.

-est[1] *suffix.* forming the superlative degree of adjectives and adverbs: *shortest; fastest.* [Old English *-est, -ost*]

-est[2] *or* **-st** *suffix.* forming the archaic second person singular present and past indicative tense of verbs: *thou goest; thou hadst.* [Old English *-est, -ast*]

establish (ɪ'stæblɪʃ) *vb.* (*usually tr.*) **1.** to make secure or permanent in a certain place, condition, job, etc.: *to establish one's usefulness; to establish a house.* **2.** to create or set up (an organization, etc.) on or as if on a permanent basis: *to establish a company.* **3.** to prove correct or free from doubt; validate: *to establish a fact.* **4.** to cause (a principle, theory, etc.) to be widely or permanently accepted: *to establish a precedent.* **5.** to give (a Church) the status of a national institution. **6.** (of a person) to become recognized and accepted: *he established himself as a reliable GP.* **7.** (in works of imagination) to cause (a character, place, etc.) to be credible and recognized: *the first scene established the period.* **8.** *Cards.* to make winners of (the remaining cards of a suit) by forcing out opponents' top cards. **9.** (*also intr.*) to cause (a plant) to grow or (of a plant) to grow in a new place: *the birch scrub has established over the past 25 years.* [C14: from Old French *establir,* from Latin *stabilīre* to make firm, from *stabilis* STABLE[2]] —**es'tablisher** *n.*

Established Church *n.* a Church that is officially recognized as a national institution, esp. the Church of England.

establishment (ɪ'stæblɪʃmənt) *n.* **1.** the act of establishing or state of being established. **2. a.** a business organization or other large institution. **b.** the place where a business is carried on. **3.** the staff and equipment of a commercial or other organization. **4.** the approved size, composition, and equipment of a military unit, government department, business division, etc., as formally promulgated. **5.** any large organization, institution, or system. **6.** a household or place of residence. **7.** a body of employees or servants. **8.** (*modifier*) belonging to or characteristic of the Establishment; orthodox or conservative: *the establishment view of history.*

Establishment (ɪ'stæblɪʃmənt) *n.* **the.** a group or class of people having institutional authority within a society, esp. those who control the civil service, the government, the armed forces, and the Church: usually identified with a conservative outlook.

establishmentarian (ɪˌstæblɪʃmən'tɛərɪən) *adj.* **1.** denoting or relating to an Established Church, esp. the Church of England. **2.** denoting or relating to the principle of a Church being officially recognized as a national institution. ~*n.* **3.** an upholder of this principle, esp. as applied to the Church of England. —**esˌtablishmen'tarianism** *n.*

estaminet *French.* (ɛstaminɛ) *n.* a small café, bar, or bistro, esp. a shabby one. [C19: from French, perhaps from Walloon dialect *staminet* manger]

estancia (ɪ'stænsɪə; *Spanish* es'tanθia) *n.* (in Spanish America) a large estate or cattle ranch. [C18: from American Spanish, from Spanish: dwelling, from Vulgar Latin *stantia* (unattested) a remaining, from Latin *stāre* to stand]

estate (ɪ'steɪt) *n.* **1.** a large piece of landed property, esp. in the country. **2.** *Chiefly Brit.* a large area of property development, esp. of new houses or (**trading estate**) of factories. **3.** *Property law.* **a.** property or possessions. **b.** the nature of interest that a person has in land or other property, esp. in relation to the right of others. **c.** the total extent of the real and personal property of a deceased person or bankrupt. **4.** Also called: **estate of the realm.** an order or class of persons in a political community, regarded collectively as a part of the body politic: usually regarded as being the lords temporal (peers), lords spiritual and commons. See also **fourth estate. 5.** state, period, or position in life, esp. with regard to wealth or social standing: *youth's estate; a poor man's estate.* **6.** *Archaic.* pomp; ceremony; grandeur. [C13: from Old French *estat,* from Latin *status* condition, STATE]

estate agent *n.* **1.** *Brit.* an agent concerned with the valuation, management, lease, and sale of property. Usual U.S. and Canadian name: **real-estate agent. 2.** the administrator of a large landed property, acting on behalf of its owner; estate manager.

estate car *n. Brit.* a car with a comparatively long body containing a large carrying space, reached through a rear door: usually the back seats can be folded forward to increase the carrying space. Also called (esp. U.S., Canadian, Austral., and N.Z.): **station wagon.**

estate duty *n.* another name for **death duty.**

esteem (ɪ'stiːm) *vb.* (*tr.*) **1.** to have great respect or high regard for: *to esteem a colleague.* **2.** *Formal.* to judge or consider; deem: *to esteem an idea improper.* ~*n.* **3.** high regard or respect; good opinion. **4.** *Archaic.* judgment; opinion. [C15: from Old French *estimer,* from Latin *aestimāre* ESTIMATE] —**es'teemed** *adj.*

ester ('ɛstə) *n. Chem.* any of a class of compounds produced by reaction between acids and alcohols with the elimination of water. Esters with low molecular weights, such as ethyl acetate, are usually volatile fragrant liquids; fats are solid esters. [C19: from German, probably a contraction of *Essigäther* acetic ether, from *Essig* vinegar (ultimately from Latin *acētum*) + *Äther* ETHER]

esterase ('ɛstəˌreɪs, -ˌreɪz) *n.* any of a group of enzymes that hydrolyse esters into alcohols and acids.

esterify (ɛ'stɛrəˌfaɪ) *vb.* **-fies, -fying, -fied.** *Chem.* to change or cause to change into an ester. —**esˌterifi'cation** *n.*

Esth. *Bible. abbrev. for* Esther.

esthesia (iːs'θiːzɪə) *n.* a U.S. spelling of **aesthesia.**

esthete ('iːsθiːt) *n.* a U.S. spelling of **aesthete.** —**esthetic** (ɛs'θɛtɪk) *or* **es'thetical** *adj.* —**es'thetically** *adv.* —**esthetician** (ˌiːsθɪ'tɪʃən) —**es'thetiˌcism** *n.* —**es'thetics** *n.*

estimable ('ɛstɪməbᵊl) *adj.* **1.** worthy of respect; deserving of admiration: *my estimable companion.* **2.** *Rare.* (of amounts, numbers, etc.) capable of being calculated. —'**estimableness** *n.* —'**estimably** *adv.*

estimate *vb.* ('ɛstɪˌmeɪt). **1.** to form an approximate idea of (distance, size, cost, etc.); calculate roughly; gauge. **2.** (*tr.; may take a clause as object*) to form an opinion about; judge: *to estimate one's chances.* **3.** to submit (an approximate price) for (a job) to a prospective client. **4.** (*tr.*) *Statistics.* to assign a value (a **point estimate**) or range of values (an **interval estimate**) to a parameter of a population on the basis of sampling statistics. See **estimator.** ~*n.* ('ɛstɪmɪt). **5.** an approximate calculation. **6.** a statement indicating the likely charge for or cost of certain work. **7.** a judgment; appraisal; opinion. [C16: from Latin *aestimāre* to assess the worth of, of obscure origin] —'**estimative** *adj.*

estimation (ˌɛstɪ'meɪʃən) *n.* **1.** a considered opinion; judgment: *what is your estimation of the situation?* **2.** esteem; respect. **3.** the act of estimating.

estimator ('ɛstɪˌmeɪtə) *n.* **1.** a person or thing that estimates. **2.** *Statistics.* a derived random variable that generates estimates of a parameter of a given distribution, such as $\bar{X}$, the mean of a number of identically distributed random variables X_i. If $\bar{X}$ is unbiased, $\bar{x}$, the observed value should be close to $E(X_i)$. See also **sampling statistic.**

estipulate (ɪˈstɪpjʊlɪt, -ˌleɪt) *adj.* a variant of **exstipulate.**

estival (iːˈstaɪvᵊl, ˈɛstɪ-) *adj.* the usual U.S. spelling of **aestival.**

estivate (ˈiːstɪˌveɪt, ˈɛs-) *vb. (intr.)* the usual U.S. spelling of **aestivate.** —**ˈestiˌvator** *n.*

estivation (ˌiːstɪˈveɪʃən, ˌɛs-) *n.* the usual U.S. spelling of **aestivation.**

Estonian *or* **Esthonian** (ɛˈstəʊnɪən, ɛˈsθəʊ-) *adj.* **1.** of, relating to, or characteristic of Estonia, a republic on the Gulf of Finland and the Baltic, its people, or their language. ~*n.* **2.** the official language of Estonia: belonging to the Finno-Ugric family. **3.** a native or inhabitant of Estonia.

estop (ɪˈstɒp) *vb.* **-tops, -topping, -topped.** *(tr.)* **1.** *Law.* to preclude by estoppel. **2.** *Archaic.* to stop. [C15: from Old French *estoper* to plug, ultimately from Latin *stuppa* tow; see STOP] —**esˈtoppage** *n.*

estoppel (ɪˈstɒpᵊl) *n. Law.* a rule of evidence whereby a person is precluded from denying the truth of a statement of facts he has previously asserted. See also **conclusion.** [C16: from Old French *estoupail* plug, from *estoper* to stop up; see ESTOP]

estovers (ɛˈstəʊvəz) *pl. n. Law.* necessaries allowed by law to tenants of land, esp. wood for fuel and repairs. [C15: from Anglo-French, plural of *estover*, n. use of Old French *estovoir* to be necessary, from Latin *est opus* there is need]

estrade (ɪsˈtrɑːd) *n.* a dais or raised platform. [C17: from French, from Spanish *estrado* carpeted floor, from Latin: STRATUM]

estradiol (ˌɛstrəˈdaɪɒl, ˌiːstrə-) *n.* the usual U.S. spelling of **oestradiol.**

estragon (ˈɛstrəˌgɒn) *n.* another name for **tarragon.**

estrange (ɪˈstreɪndʒ) *vb. (tr.)* to antagonize or lose the affection of (someone previously friendly); alienate. [C15: from Old French *estranger*, from Late Latin *extrāneāre* to treat as a stranger, from Latin *extrāneus* foreign; see STRANGE] —**esˈtranged** *adj.* —**esˈtrangement** *n.* —**esˈtranger** *n.*

estray (ɪˈstreɪ) *n. Law.* a stray domestic animal of unknown ownership. [C16: from Anglo-French, from Old French *estraier* to STRAY]

estreat (ɪˈstriːt) *Law.* ~*n.* **1.** a true copy of or extract from a court record. ~*vb. (tr.)* **2.** to enforce (a recognizance that has been forfeited) by sending an extract of the court record to the proper authority. [C14: from Old French *estraite*, feminine of *estrait* extracted, from *estraire* to EXTRACT]

estrin (ˈɛstrɪn, ˈiːstrɪn) *n.* the U.S. spelling of **oestrin.**

estriol (ˈɛstrɪˌɒl, ˈiːstrɪ-) *n.* the usual U.S. spelling of **oestriol.**

estrogen (ˈɛstrədʒən, ˈiːstrə-) *n.* the usual U.S. spelling of **oestrogen.** —**estrogenic** (ˌɛstrəˈdʒɛnɪk, ˌiːstrə-) *adj.* —ˌ**estroˈgenically** *adv.*

estrone (ˈɛstrəʊn, ˈiːstrəʊn) *n.* the usual U.S. spelling of **oestrone.**

estrus (ˈɛstrəs, ˈiːstrəs) *n.* the usual U.S. spelling of **oestrus.** —**ˈestrous** *adj.*

estuarine (ˈɛstjʊəˌraɪn, -rɪn) *adj.* **1.** formed or deposited in an estuary: *estuarine muds.* **2.** growing in, inhabiting, or found in an estuary: *an estuarine fauna.*

estuary (ˈɛstjʊərɪ) *n., pl.* **-aries.** **1.** the widening channel of a river where it nears the sea, with a mixing of fresh water and salt (tidal) water. **2.** an inlet of the sea. [C16: from Latin *aestuārium* marsh, channel, from *aestus* tide, billowing movement, related to *aestās* summer] —**estuarial** (ˌɛstjʊˈɛərɪəl) *adj.*

e.s.u. *or* **ESU** *abbrev. for* electrostatic unit.

esurient (ɪˈsjʊərɪənt) *adj.* greedy; voracious. [C17: from Latin *ēsurīre* to be hungry, from *edere* to eat] —**eˈsurience** *or* **eˈsuriency** *n.* —**eˈsuriently** *adv.*

E. Sussex *abbrev. for* East Sussex.

Et *the chemical symbol for* ethyl.

ET *abbrev. for* Employment Training: a government scheme offering training in technological and business skills to unemployed people.

-et *suffix of nouns.* small or lesser: *islet; baronet.* [from Old French *-et, -ete*]

eta¹ (ˈiːtə) *n.* the seventh letter in the Greek alphabet (Η, η), a long vowel sound, transliterated as *e* or *ē*. [Greek, of Phoenician origin; compare Hebrew HETH]

eta² (ˈeɪtə) *n., pl.* **eta** or **etas.** (in Japan, formerly) a member of a class of outcasts who did menial and dirty tasks. [C19: Japanese]

ETA¹ *abbrev. for* estimated time of arrival.

ETA² (ˈɛtə) *n. acronym for* Euzkadi ta Askatsuna: an organization of militant Basque nationalists attempting to gain independence for the Basques, esp. those ruled by Spain, by means of guerrilla warfare. [Basque, literally: Basque Nation and Liberty]

etaerio (ɛˈtɪərɪəʊ) *n.* an aggregate fruit, as one consisting of drupes (raspberry) or achenes (traveller's joy). [C19: from French *etairion*, from Greek *hetaireia* association]

étagère *French.* (etaʒɛr) *n.* a stand with open shelves for displaying ornaments, etc. [C19: from French, from *étage* shelf; see STAGE]

et al. *abbrev. for:* **1.** et alibi. [Latin: and elsewhere] **2.** et alii. [Latin: and others]

etalon (ˈɛtəˌlɒn) *n. Physics.* a device used in spectroscopy to measure wavelengths by interference effects produced by multiple reflections between parallel half-silvered glass or quartz plates. [C20: French *étalon* a fixed standard of weights and measures, from Old French *estalon*; see also STALLION]

etamine (ˈɛtəˌmiːn) *or* **etamin** (ˈɛtəmɪn) *n.* a cotton or worsted fabric of loose weave, used for clothing, curtains, etc. [C18: from French, from Latin *stāminea*, from *stāmineus* made of threads, from *stamen* thread, warp]

etaoin shrdlu (ˈɛtɪˌɔɪn ˈʃɜːdluː) *n. Printing.* a Linotype slug, used as a marker, produced by running the fingers down the first two rows of the keyboard.

etc. *abbrev. for* et cetera.

et cetera *or* **etcetera** (ɪt ˈsɛtrə) **1.** and the rest; and others; and so forth: used at the end of a list to indicate that other items of the same class or type should be considered or included. **2.** or the like; or something else similar. ~Abbrevs.: **etc., &c.** ~See also **etceteras.** [from Latin, from *et* and + *cetera* the other (things)]

▷**Usage.** Since *et cetera* (or *etc.*) means *and other things*, careful writers do not use the expression *and etc.* because *and* is redundant. The repetition of *etc.*, as in *he brought paper, ink, notebooks, etc., etc.*, is avoided except in informal contexts.

etceteras (ɪtˈsɛtrəz) *pl. n.* miscellaneous extra things or persons.

etch (ɛtʃ) *vb.* **1.** *(tr.)* to wear away the surface of (a metal, glass, etc.) by chemical action, esp. the action of an acid. **2.** to cut or corrode (a design, decoration, etc.) on (a metal or other plate to be used for printing) by using the action of acid on parts not covered by wax or other acid-resistant coating. **3.** *(tr.)* to cut with or as if with a sharp implement: *he etched his name on the table.* **4.** *(tr.; usually passive)* to imprint vividly: *the event was etched on her memory.* [C17: from Dutch *etsen*, from Old High German *azzen* to feed, bite] —**ˈetcher** *n.*

etchant (ˈɛtʃənt) *n.* any acid or corrosive used for etching.

etching (ˈɛtʃɪŋ) *n.* **1.** the art, act, or process of preparing etched surfaces or of printing designs from them. **2.** an etched plate. **3.** an impression made from an etched plate.

ETD *abbrev. for* estimated time of departure.

eternal (ɪˈtɜːnᵊl) *adj.* **1. a.** without beginning or end; lasting for ever: *eternal life.* **b.** *(as n.): the eternal.* **2.** *(often cap.)* denoting or relating to that which is without beginning and end, regarded as an attribute of God. **3.** unchanged by time, esp. being true or valid for all time; immutable: *eternal truths.* **4.** seemingly unceasing; occurring again and again: *eternal bickering.* [C14: from Late Latin *aeternālis*, from Latin *aeternus*; related to Latin *aevum* age] —ˌ**eterˈnality** *or* **eˈternalness** *n.* —**eˈternally** *adv.*

eternalize (ɪˈtɜːnəˌlaɪz), **eternize** (ɪˈtɜːnaɪz), *or* **eternalise, eternise** *vb. (tr.)* **1.** to make eternal. **2.** to make famous for ever; immortalize. —**eˌternaliˈzation, eˌterniˈzation** *or* **eˌternaliˈsation, eˌterniˈsation** *n.*

eternal triangle *n.* an emotional relationship in which there are conflicts involving a man and two women or a woman and two men.

eterne (ɪˈtɜːn) *adj.* an archaic or poetic word for **eternal.** [C14: from Old French, from Latin *aeternus*]

eternity (ɪˈtɜːnɪtɪ) *n., pl.* **-ties.** **1.** endless or infinite time. **2.** the quality, state, or condition of being eternal. **3.** *(usually pl.)* any of the aspects of life and thought that are considered to be timeless, esp. timeless and true. **4.** *Theol.* the condition of timeless existence, believed by some to characterize the afterlife. **5.** a seemingly endless period of time: *an eternity of waiting.*

eternity ring *n.* a ring given as a token of lasting affection, esp. one set all around with stones to symbolize continuity.

etesian (ɪˈtiːʒɪən) *adj.* (of NW winds) recurring annually in the summer in the E Mediterranean. [C17: from Latin *etēsius* yearly, from Greek *etēsios*, from *etos* year]

ETF *abbrev. for* electronic transfer of funds.

eth (ɛð, ɛθ) *n.* a variant of **edh.**

Eth. *abbrev. for:* **1.** Ethiopia(n). **2.** Ethiopic.

-eth¹ *suffix.* forming the archaic third person singular present indicative tense of verbs: *goeth; taketh.* [Old English *-eth, -th*]

-eth² *or* **-th** *suffix forming ordinal numbers.* a variant of **-th**²: *twentieth.*

ethambutol (ɛˈθæmbjʊˌtɒl) *n.* a compound used in the treatment of tuberculosis. [from ETH(YLENE) + AM(INE) + BUT(AN)OL]

ethanal (ˈɛθəˌnæl, ˈiːθə-) *n.* the modern name for **acetaldehyde.**

ethane (ˈiːθeɪn, ˈɛθ-) *n.* a colourless odourless flammable gaseous alkane obtained from natural gas and petroleum: used as a fuel and in the manufacture of organic chemicals. Formula: C_2H_6. [C19: from ETH(YL)+ -ANE]

ethanedioic acid (ˌiːθeɪndaɪˈəʊɪk, ˌɛθ-) *n.* the technical name for **oxalic acid.** [C20: from ETHANE + DI-¹ + -O- + -IC]

ethanediol (ˈiːθeɪnˌdaɪɒl, ˈɛθ-) *n.* a clear colourless syrupy soluble liquid substance, used as an antifreeze and solvent. Formula: CH_2OHCH_2OH. Also called: **glycol, ethylene glycol.** [C20: from ETHANE + DI-¹ + -OL¹]

ethanoic acid (ˌɛθəˈnəʊɪk, ˌiːθə-) *n.* the modern name for **acetic acid.**

ethanol (ˈɛθəˌnɒl, ˈiːθə-) *n.* the technical name for **alcohol** (sense 1).

ethanoyl (ˈɛθəˌnɔɪl) *n. (modifier)* of, consisting of, or containing the monovalent group CH_3CO-: *ethanoyl group or radical.* [C20: from ETH(YL) + -OYL]

ethanoyl chloride *n.* another name for **acetyl chloride.**

ethene (ˈɛθiːn) *n.* the technical name for **ethylene.**

ether ('iːθə) *n.* **1.** Also called: **diethyl ether, ethyl ether, ethoxyethane.** a colourless volatile highly flammable liquid with a characteristic sweetish odour, made by the reaction of sulphuric acid with ethanol: used as a solvent and anaesthetic. Formula: $C_2H_5OC_2H_5$. **2.** any of a class of organic compounds with the general formula ROR′ where R and R′ are alkyl groups, as in diethyl ether $C_2H_5OC_2H_5$. **3. the ether.** the hypothetical medium formerly believed to fill all space and to support the propagation of electromagnetic waves. **4.** *Greek myth.* the upper regions of the atmosphere; clear sky or heaven. **5.** a rare word for **air.** ~Also (for senses 3–5): **aether.** [C17: from Latin *aether,* from Greek *aithēr,* from *aithein* to burn] —**etheric** (iː'θɛrɪk) *adj.*

ethereal (ɪ'θɪərɪəl) *adj.* **1.** extremely delicate or refined; exquisite. **2.** almost as light as air; impalpable; airy. **3.** celestial or spiritual. **4.** of, containing, or dissolved in an ether, esp. diethyl ether: *an ethereal solution.* **5.** of or relating to the ether. [C16: from Latin *aethereus,* from Greek *aitherios,* from *aithēr* ETHER] —**eˌthere'ality** *or* **e'therealness** *n.* —**e'thereally** *adv.*

etherealize *or* **etherealise** (ɪ'θɪərɪəˌlaɪz) *vb. (tr.)* **1.** to make or regard as being ethereal. **2.** to add ether to or make into ether or something resembling ether. —**eˌtherealiˈzation** *or* **eˌtherealiˈsation** *n.*

etherify ('iːθərɪˌfaɪ, iː'θɛrɪ-) *vb.* **-fies, -fying, -fied.** *(tr.)* to change (a compound, such as an alcohol) into an ether. —**eˌtherifiˈcation** *n.*

etherize *or* **etherise** ('iːθəˌraɪz) *vb. (tr.) Obsolete.* to subject (a person) to the anaesthetic influence of ether fumes; anaesthetize. —ˌ**etheriˈzation** *or* ˌ**etheriˈsation** *n.* —**'etherˌizer** *or* **'etherˌiser** *n.*

Ethernet ('iːθəˌnɛt) *n. Trademark. Computer technol.* a widely used type of local area network.

ethic ('ɛθɪk) *n.* **1.** a moral principle or set of moral values held by an individual or group: *the Puritan ethic.* ~*adj.* **2.** another word for **ethical.** ~See also **ethics.** [C15: from Latin *ēthicus,* from Greek *éthikos,* from *ēthos* custom; see ETHOS]

ethical ('ɛθɪkᵊl) *adj.* **1.** in accordance with principles of conduct that are considered correct, esp. those of a given profession or group. **2.** of or relating to ethics. **3.** (of a medicinal agent) available legally only with a doctor's prescription or consent. —**'ethically** *adv.* —**'ethicalness** *or* ˌ**ethiˈcality** *n.*

ethicize *or* **ethicise** ('ɛθɪˌsaɪz) *vb. (tr.)* to make or consider as ethical.

ethics ('ɛθɪks) *n.* **1.** *(functioning as sing.)* the philosophical study of the moral value of human conduct and of the rules and principles that ought to govern it; moral philosophy. See also **meta-ethics. 2.** *(functioning as pl.)* a social, religious, or civil code of behaviour considered correct, esp. that of a particular group, profession, or individual. **3.** *(functioning as pl.)* the moral fitness of a decision, course of action, etc.: *he doubted the ethics of their verdict.* —**'ethicist** *n.*

Ethiop ('iːθɪˌɒp) *or* **Ethiope** ('iːθɪˌəʊp) *adj.* archaic words for **Negro.**

Ethiopian (ˌiːθɪ'əʊpɪən) *adj.* **1.** of, relating to, or characteristic of Ethiopia, a state in NE Africa, its people, or any of their languages. **2.** of or denoting a zoogeographical region consisting of Africa south of the Sahara. **3.** *Anthropol., obsolete.* of or belonging to a postulated racial group characterized by dark skin, an oval elongated face, and thin lips, living chiefly in Africa south of the Sahara. ~*n.* **4.** a native or inhabitant of Ethiopia. **5.** any of the languages of Ethiopia, esp. Amharic. ~*n., adj.* **6.** an archaic word for **Negro.**

Ethiopic (ˌiːθɪ'ɒpɪk, -'əʊpɪk) *n.* **1.** the ancient language of Ethiopia, belonging to the Semitic subfamily of the Afro-Asiatic family: a Christian liturgical language. See also **Ge'ez. 2.** the group of languages developed from this language, including Amharic, Tigre, and Tigrinya. ~*adj.* **3.** denoting or relating to this language or group of languages. **4.** a less common word for **Ethiopian.**

ethmoid ('ɛθmɔɪd) *Anatomy.* ~*adj. also* **ethmoidal. 1.** denoting or relating to a bone of the skull that forms part of the eye socket and the nasal cavity. ~*n.* **2.** the ethmoid bone. [C18: from Greek *ēthmoeidēs* like a sieve, from *ēthmos* sieve, from *ēthein* to sift]

ethnarch ('ɛθnɑːk) *n.* the ruler of a people or province, as in parts of the Roman and Byzantine Empires. [C17: from Greek *ethnarkhēs,* from *ethnos* nation + *arkhein* to rule] —**'ethnarchy** *n.*

ethnic ('ɛθnɪk) *or* **ethnical** *adj.* **1.** relating to or characteristic of a human group having racial, religious, linguistic, and certain other traits in common. **2.** relating to the classification of mankind into groups, esp. on the basis of racial characteristics. **3.** denoting or deriving from the cultural traditions of a group of people: *the ethnic dances of Bosnia.* **4.** characteristic of another culture, esp. a peasant culture: *the ethnic look; ethnic food.* ~*n.* **5.** *Chiefly U.S.* a member of an ethnic group, esp. a minority group. [C14 (in the senses: heathen, Gentile): from Late Latin *ethnicus,* from Greek *ethnikos,* from *ethnos* race] —**'ethnically** *adv.* —**ethnicity** (ɛθ'nɪsɪtɪ) *n.*

ethnic minority *n.* an immigrant or racial group regarded by those claiming to speak for the cultural majority as distinct and unassimilated.

ethno- *combining form.* indicating race, people, or culture: *ethnology.* [via French from Greek *ethnos* race]

ethnobotany (ˌɛθnəʊ'bɒtənɪ) *n.* the branch of botany concerned with the use of plants in folklore, religion, etc.

ethnocentrism (ˌɛθnəʊ'sɛnˌtrɪzəm) *n.* belief in the intrinsic superiority of the nation, culture, or group to which one belongs, often accompanied by feelings of dislike and contempt for other groups. —ˌ**ethno'centric** *adj.* —ˌ**ethno'centrically** *adv.* —ˌ**ethnocen'tricity** *n.*

ethnogeny (ɛθ'nɒdʒɪnɪ) *n.* the branch of ethnology that deals with the origin of races or peoples. —**ethnogenic** (ˌɛθnəʊ'dʒɛnɪk) *adj.* —**eth'nogenist** *n.*

ethnography (ɛθ'nɒgrəfɪ) *n.* the branch of anthropology that deals with the scientific description of individual human societies. —ˌ**eth'nographer** *n.* —**ethnographic** (ˌɛθnəʊ'græfɪk) *or* ˌ**ethno'graphical** *adj.* —ˌ**ethno'graphically** *adv.*

ethnol. *abbrev. for* ethnology.

ethnology (ɛθ'nɒlədʒɪ) *n.* the branch of anthropology that deals with races and peoples, their relations to one another, their origins, and their distinctive characteristics. —**ethnologic** (ˌɛθnə'lɒdʒɪk) *or* ˌ**ethno'logical** *adj.* —ˌ**ethno'logically** *adv.* —**eth'nologist** *n.*

ethnomethodology (ˌɛθnəʊmɛθə'dɒlədʒɪ) *n.* a method of studying linguistic communication that emphasizes common-sense views of conversation and the world. Compare **phenomenology.**

ethnomusicology (ˌɛθnəʊmjuːzɪ'kɒlədʒɪ) *n.* the study of the music of different cultures. —ˌ**ethnomusi'cologist** *n.*

ethology (ɪ'θɒlədʒɪ) *n.* the study of the behaviour of animals in their normal environment. [C17 (in the obsolete sense: mimicry): via Latin from Greek *ēthologia,* from *ēthos* character; current sense, C19] —**ethological** (ˌɛθə'lɒdʒɪkᵊl) *adj.* —ˌ**etho'logically** *adv.* —**e'thologist** *n.*

ethonone ('ɛθəˌnəʊn) *n.* another name for **ketene.**

ethos ('iːθɒs) *n.* the distinctive character, spirit, and attitudes of a people, culture, era, etc.: *the revolutionary ethos.* [C19: from Late Latin: habit, from Greek]

ethoxide (iː'θɒksaɪd) *n.* any of a class of saltlike compounds with the formula MOC_2H_5, where M is a metal atom. Also called: **ethylate.** [C20: from *ethox(yl)* (from ETH(YL) + OX(YGEN) + -YL) + -IDE]

ethoxyethane (ɛˌθɒksɪ'iːθeɪn) *n.* the technical name for **ether** (sense 1). [C20: from ETH(YL) + OXY-[2] +ETHANE]

ethyl ('iːθaɪl, 'ɛθɪl) *n. (modifier)* of, consisting of, or containing the monovalent group C_2H_5-: *ethyl group or radical.* [C19: from ETH(ER) + -YL] —**ethylic** (ɪ'θɪlɪk) *adj.*

ethyl acetate *n.* a colourless volatile flammable fragrant liquid ester, made from acetic acid and ethanol: used in perfumes and flavourings and as a solvent for plastics, lacquers, etc. Formula: $CH_3COOC_2H_5$.

ethyl alcohol *n.* another name for **alcohol** (sense 1).

ethylate ('ɛθɪˌleɪt) *vb.* **1.** to undergo or cause to undergo a chemical reaction in which an ethyl group is introduced into a molecule. ~*n.* **2.** another name for an **ethoxide.** —ˌ**ethyl'ation** *n.*

ethyl carbamate *n.* a colourless odourless crystalline ester used in the manufacture of pesticides, fungicides, and pharmaceuticals. Formula: $CO(NH_2)OC_2H_5$. Also called: **urethane.**

ethylene ('ɛθɪˌliːn) *n.* a colourless flammable gaseous alkene with a sweet odour, obtained from petroleum and natural gas and used in the manufacture of polythene and many other chemicals. Formula: $CH_2{:}CH_2$. Also called: **ethene.** —**ethylenic** (ˌɛθɪ'liːnɪk) *adj.*

ethylene glycol *n.* another name for **ethanediol.**

ethylene group *or* **radical** *n. Chem.* the divalent group, $-CH_2CH_2-$, derived from ethylene.

ethylene series *n. Chem.* the homologous series of unsaturated hydrocarbons that contain one double bond and have the general formula, C_nH_{2n}; alkene series.

ethyl ether *n.* a more formal name for **ether** (sense 1).

ethyne ('iːθaɪn, 'ɛθaɪn) *n.* another name for **acetylene.** [C20: from ETHYL + -INE]

etiolate ('iːtɪəʊˌleɪt) *vb.* **1.** *Botany.* to whiten (a green plant) through lack of sunlight. **2.** to become or cause to become pale and weak, as from malnutrition. [C18: from French *étioler* to make pale, probably from Old French *estuble* straw, from Latin *stipula*] —ˌ**etio'lation** *n.*

etiology (ˌiːtɪ'ɒlədʒɪ) *n., pl.* **-gies.** a variant spelling of **aetiology.** —**etiological** (ˌiːtɪə'lɒdʒɪkᵊl) *adj.* —ˌ**etio'logically** *adv.* —**eti'ologist** *n.*

etiquette ('ɛtɪˌkɛt, ˌɛtɪ'kɛt) *n.* **1.** the customs or rules governing behaviour regarded as correct or acceptable in social or official life. **2.** a conventional but unwritten code of practice followed by members of any of certain professions or groups: *medical etiquette.* [C18: from French, from Old French *estiquette* label, from *estiquier* to attach; see STICK[2]]

Eton collar ('iːtᵊn) *n.* a broad stiff white collar worn outside an Eton jacket.

Eton crop *n.* a very short mannish hairstyle worn by women in the 1920s.

Etonian (iː'təʊnɪən) *adj.* **1. a.** of or relating to Eton College, a public school for boys in Eton, S England. **b.** of or relating to a pupil of Eton College. **2.** of or relating to the town of Eton or its inhabitants, etc. ~*n.* **3.** a pupil, past or present, of Eton College: *Old Etonian.* **4.** a native or inhabitant of Eton.

Eton jacket *n.* a waist-length jacket with a V-shaped back, open in front, formerly worn by pupils of Eton College.

étrier (*French* etrije) *n. Mountaineering.* a short portable ladder or set of webbing loops that can be attached to a karabiner or fifi hook. U.S. name: **stirrup.** [C20: from French: stirrup]

Etruscan (ɪ'trʌskən) *or* **Etrurian** (ɪ'trʊərɪən) *n.* **1.** a member of an ancient people of Etruria in central Italy whose civilization greatly influenced the Romans, who had suppressed them by about 200 B.C. **2.** the non-Indo-European language of the ancient Etruscans, whose few surviving records have not been fully interpreted. ~*adj.* **3.** of, relating to, or characteristic of Etruria, the Etruscans, their culture, or their language.

et seq. *abbrev. for:* **1.** et sequens [Latin: and the following] **2.** Also: **et seqq.** et sequentia [Latin: and those that follow]

-ette *suffix of nouns.* **1.** small: *cigarette; kitchenette.* **2.** female: *majorette; suffragette.* **3.** (esp. in trade names) imitation: *Leatherette.* [from French, feminine of -ET]

étude ('eɪtju:d; *French* etyd) *n.* a short musical composition for a solo instrument, esp. one designed as an exercise or exploiting technical virtuosity. [C19: from French: STUDY]

étui (ɛ'twi:) *n., pl.* **étuis.** a small usually ornamented case for holding needles, cosmetics, or other small articles. [C17: from French, from Old French *estuier* to enclose; see TWEEZERS]

ety., etym., *or* **etymol.** *abbrev. for:* **1.** etymological. **2.** etymology.

etymologize *or* **etymologise** (ˌɛtɪ'mɒləˌdʒaɪz) *vb.* to trace, state, or suggest the etymology of (a word).

etymology (ˌɛtɪ'mɒlədʒɪ) *n., pl.* **-gies.** **1.** the study of the sources and development of words and morphemes. **2.** an account of the source and development of a word or morpheme. [C14: via Latin from Greek *etumologia;* see ETYMON, -LOGY] —**etymological** (ˌɛtɪmə'lɒdʒɪkəl) *adj.* —ˌ**etymo'logically** *adv.* —ˌ**ety'mologist** *n.*

etymon ('ɛtɪˌmɒn) *n., pl.* **-mons** *or* **-ma** (-mə). a form of a word or morpheme, usually the earliest recorded form or a reconstructed form, from which another word or morpheme is derived: *the etymon of English "ewe" is Indo-European "*owi".* [C16: via Latin, from Greek *etumon* basic meaning, from *etumos* true, actual]

Eu *the chemical symbol for* europium.

eu- *combining form.* well, pleasant, or good: *eupeptic; euphony.* [via Latin from Greek, from *eus* good]

eubacteria (ˌju:bæk'tɪərɪə) *pl. n., sing.* **-rium** (-rɪəm). a large group of bacteria characterized by a rigid cell wall and, in motile types, flagella; the true bacteria. [C20: via New Latin from Greek, from EU- (in the sense: true) + BACTERIUM]

eucaine (ju:'keɪn) *n.* a crystalline optically active substance formerly used as a local anaesthetic. Formula: $C_{15}H_{21}NO_2$.

eucalyptol (ˌju:kə'lɪptɒl) *or* **eucalyptole** (ˌju:kə'lɪptəʊl) *n.* a colourless oily liquid with a camphor-like odour and a spicy taste, obtained from eucalyptus oil and used in perfumery and as a flavouring. Formula: $C_{10}H_{18}O$. Also called: **cineol.**

eucalyptus (ˌju:kə'lɪptəs) *or* **eucalypt** ('ju:kəˌlɪpt) *n., pl.* **-lyptuses, -lypti** (-'lɪptaɪ), *or* **-lypts.** any myrtaceous tree of the mostly Australian genus *Eucalyptus,* such as the blue gum and ironbark, widely cultivated for the medicinal oil in their leaves (**eucalyptus oil**), timber, and ornament. [C19: New Latin, from EU- + Greek *kaluptos* covered, from *kaluptein* to cover, hide]

eucaryote (ju:'kærɪɒt) *n.* a variant spelling of **eukaryote.**

eucharis ('ju:kərɪs) *n.* any amaryllidaceous plant of the South American genus *Eucharis,* cultivated for their large white fragrant flowers. [C19: New Latin, from Late Latin: charming, from Greek *eukharis,* from EU- + *kharis* grace]

Eucharist ('ju:kərɪst) *n.* **1.** the Christian sacrament in which Christ's Last Supper is commemorated by the consecration of bread and wine. **2.** the consecrated elements of bread and wine offered in the sacrament. [C14: via Church Latin from Greek *eukharistia,* from *eukharistos* thankful, from EU- + *kharizesthai* to show favour, from *kharis* favour] —ˌ**Eucha'ristic** *or* ˌ**Eucha'ristical** *adj.* —ˌ**Eucha'ristically** *adv.*

euchlorine (ju:'klɔ:ri:n) *or* **euchlorin** (ju:'klɔ:rɪn) *n.* an explosive gaseous mixture of chlorine and chlorine dioxide.

euchre ('ju:kə) *n.* **1.** a U.S. and Canadian card game similar to écarté for two, three, or four players, using a poker pack with joker and jack high. **2.** an instance of euchring another player, preventing him from making his contracted tricks. ~*vb.* (*tr.*) **3.** to prevent (a player) from making his contracted tricks. **4.** (usually foll. by *out*) *U.S., Canadian, Austral., and N.Z. informal.* to outwit or cheat. **5.** *Austral. and N.Z. informal.* to ruin or exhaust. [C19: of unknown origin]

euchromatin (ju:'krəʊmətɪn) *n.* the part of a chromosome that constitutes the major genes and does not stain strongly with basic dyes when the cell is not dividing. Compare **heterochromatin.** —**euchromatic** (ˌju:krəʊ'mætɪk) *adj.*

Euclidean *or* **Euclidian** (ju:'klɪdɪən) *adj.* denoting a system of geometry based on the axioms of Euclid, 3rd-century B.C. Greek mathematician.

eucryphia (ju:'krɪfɪə) *n.* any tree or shrub of the mostly evergreen genus *Eucryphia,* native to Australia and S America, having leaves of a dark lustrous green and white flowers. [from Greek *eu* well + *kryphios* hidden, from *kryptein* to hide, referring to the sepals being joined at the top]

eudemon *or* **eudaemon** (ju:'di:mən) *n.* a benevolent spirit or demon. [C17: from Greek *eudaimōn,* from EU- + *daimōn* indwelling spirit; see DEMON]

eudemonia *or* **eudaemonia** (ˌju:dɪ'məʊnɪə) *n.* happiness, esp. (in the philosophy of Aristotle) that resulting from a rational active life.

eudemonics *or* **eudaemonics** (ˌju:dɪ'mɒnɪks) *n.* (*functioning as sing.*) **1.** the art or theory of happiness. **2.** another word for **eudemonism.** —ˌ**eude'monic** *or* ˌ**eudae'monic** *adj.*

eudemonism *or* **eudaemonism** (ju:'di:məˌnɪzəm) *n. Philosophy.* an ethical doctrine holding that the value of moral action lies in its capacity to produce happiness. —**eu'demonist** *or* **eu'daemonist** *n.* —**euˌdemon'istic, euˌdaemon'istic** *or* **euˌdemon'istical, euˌdaemon'istical** *adj.* —**euˌdemon'istically** *or* **euˌdaemon'istically** *adv.*

eudiometer (ˌju:dɪ'ɒmɪtə) *n.* a graduated glass tube used in the study and volumetric analysis of gas reactions. [C18: from Greek *eudios,* literally: clear skied (from EU- + *Dios,* genitive of *Zeus* god of the heavens) + -METER] —**eudiometric** (ˌju:dɪə'mɛtrɪk) *or* ˌ**eudio'metrical** *adj.* —ˌ**eudio'metrically** *adv.* —ˌ**eudi'ometry** *n.*

eugarie ('ju:gərɪ) *n. Queensland dialect.* another name for **pipi.**

eugenics (ju:'dʒɛnɪks) *n.* (*functioning as sing.*) the study of methods of improving the quality of the human race, esp. by selective breeding. [C19: from Greek *eugenēs* well-born, from EU- + *-genēs* born; see -GEN] —**eu'genic** *adj.* —**eu'genically** *adv.* —**eu'genicist** *n.* —**eugenist** ('ju:dʒənɪst) *n., adj.*

eugenol ('ju:dʒɪˌnɒl) *n.* a colourless or pale yellow oily liquid substance with a spicy taste and an odour of cloves, used in perfumery; 4-allyl-2-methoxyphenol. Formula: $C_{10}H_{12}O_2$. [C19: *eugen-,* from *Eugenia caryophyllata* kind of clove from which oil may be obtained + -OL[1]]

euglena (ju:'gli:nə) *n.* any freshwater flagellate protozoan of the genus *Euglena,* typically having holophytic nutrition. Because it has some plant characteristics *Euglena* is sometimes classified as an alga. [C19: from New Latin, from EU- + Greek *glēnē* eyeball, socket of a joint]

euhemerism (ju:'hi:məˌrɪzəm) *n.* **1.** the theory that gods arose out of the deification of historical heroes. **2.** any interpretation of myths that derives the gods from outstanding men and seeks the source of mythology in history. [C19: named after Euhemerus (?300 B.C.), Greek philosopher who propounded this theory] —**eu'hemerist** *n.* —**euˌhemer'istic** *adj.* —**euˌhemer'istically** *adv.*

euhemerize *or* **euhemerise** (ju:'hi:məˌraɪz) *vb.* to deal with or explain (myths) by euhemerism.

eukaryote *or* **eucaryote** (ju:'kærɪɒt) *n.* an organism having cells each with a distinct nucleus in which the genetic material is carried on chromosomes. All organisms except bacteria and blue-green algae are eukaryotes. Compare **prokaryote.** [from EU- + KARYO- + *-ote* as in *zygote*] —**eukaryotic** *or* **eucaryotic** (ˌju:kærɪ'ɒtɪk) *adj.*

eulachon ('ju:ləˌkɒn) *or* **eulachan** *n., pl.* **-chons, -chon** *or* **-chans, -chan.** another name for **candlefish.** [from Chinook Jargon *ulâkân*]

Euler's circles ('ɔɪləz) *pl. n. Logic.* a diagram in which the terms of categorial statements are represented by circles whose inclusion in one another represents the inclusion of the extensions of the terms in one another. Compare **Venn diagram.** [named after Leonhard *Euler* (1707–83), Swiss mathematician]

eulogia (ju:'ləʊdʒɪə) *n.* **1.** *Eastern Christian Church.* blessed bread distributed to members of the congregation after the liturgy, esp. to those who have not communed. **2.** *Archaic.* a blessing or something blessed. [C18: from Greek: blessing; see EULOGY]

eulogize *or* **eulogise** ('ju:ləˌdʒaɪz) *vb.* to praise (a person or thing) highly in speech or writing. —'**eulogist,** '**euloˌgizer,** *or* '**euloˌgiser** *n.* —ˌ**eulo'gistic** *or* ˌ**eulo'gistical** *adj.* —ˌ**eulo'gistically** *adv.*

eulogy ('ju:lədʒɪ) *n., pl.* **-gies.** **1.** a formal speech or piece of writing praising a person or thing, esp. a person who has recently died. **2.** high praise or commendation. ~Also called (archaic): **eulogium** (ju:'ləʊdʒɪəm). [C16: from Late Latin *eulogia,* from Greek: praise, from EU- + -LOGY; influenced by Latin *ēlogium* short saying, inscription]

Eumenides (ju:'mɛnɪˌdi:z) *pl. n.* another name for the **Furies,** used by the Greeks as a euphemism. [from Greek, literally: the benevolent ones, from *eumenēs* benevolent, from EU- + *menos* spirit]

eunuch ('ju:nək) *n.* **1.** a man who has been castrated, esp. (formerly) for some office such as a guard in a harem. **2.** *Informal.* an ineffective man: *a political eunuch.* [C15: via Latin from Greek *eunoukhos* attendant of the bedchamber, from *eunē* bed + *ekhein* to have, keep]

euonymus (ju:'ɒnɪməs) *or* **evonymus** *n.* any tree or shrub of the N temperate genus *Euonymus,* such as the spindle tree, whose seeds are each enclosed in a fleshy, typically red, aril: family *Celastraceae.* [C18: from Latin: spindle tree, from Greek *euōnumos* fortunately named, from EU- + *onoma* NAME]

eupatorium (ˌju:pə'tɔ:rɪəm) *n.* any plant of the genus *Eupatorium,* of tropical America and the West Indies: cultivated for their ornamental clusters of purple, pink, or white flowers: family *Compositae* (composites). [C16: from New Latin, from Greek *eupatorion* hemp agrimony, from *Eupator* surname of Mithridates VI, king of Pontus and traditionally the first to have used it medicinally]

eupatrid (juːˈpætrɪd) *n., pl.* **-patridae** (-ˈpætrɪˌdiː) *or* **-patrids.** (in ancient Greece) a hereditary noble or landowner. [C19: via Latin from Greek *eupatridēs,* literally: having a good father, from EU- + *patēr* father]

eupepsia (juːˈpɛpsɪə) *or* **eupepsy** (juːˈpɛpsɪ) *n. Physiol.* good digestion. [C18: from New Latin, from Greek, from EU- + *pepsis* digestion, from *peptein* to digest] —**eupeptic** (juːˈpɛptɪk) *adj.*

euphausiid (juːˈfɔːzɪɪd) *n.* any small pelagic shrimplike crustacean of the order *Euphausiacea:* an important constituent of krill. [C19: from New Latin *Euphausiacea,* perhaps from Greek EU- + *pha-* from *phainein* to reveal, show + *ousia* substance, stuff]

euphemism (ˈjuːfɪˌmɪzəm) *n.* **1.** an inoffensive word or phrase substituted for one considered offensive or hurtful, esp. one concerned with religion, sex, death, or excreta. Examples of euphemisms are: *sleep with* for *have sexual intercourse with; departed* for *dead; relieve oneself* for *urinate.* **2.** the use of such inoffensive words or phrases. [C17: from Greek *euphēmismos,* from EU- + *phēmē* speech] —ˌ**eupheˈmistic** *adj.* —ˌ**eupheˈmistically** *adv.*

euphemize *or* **euphemise** (ˈjuːfɪˌmaɪz) *vb.* to speak in euphemisms or refer to by means of a euphemism. —ˈ**eupheˌmizer** *or* ˈ**eupheˌmiser** *n.*

euphonic (juːˈfɒnɪk) *or* **euphonious** (juːˈfəʊnɪəs) *adj.* **1.** denoting or relating to euphony; pleasing to the ear. **2.** (of speech sounds) altered for ease of pronunciation. —**euˈphonically** *or* **euˈphoniously** *adv.* —**euˈphoniousness** *n.*

euphonium (juːˈfəʊnɪəm) *n.* a brass musical instrument with four valves; the tenor of the tuba family. It is used mainly in brass bands. [C19: New Latin, from EUPH(ONY + HARM)ONIUM]

euphonize *or* **euphonise** (ˈjuːfəˌnaɪz) *vb.* **1.** to make pleasant to hear; render euphonious. **2.** to change (speech sounds) so as to facilitate pronunciation.

euphony (ˈjuːfənɪ) *n., pl.* **-nies.** **1.** the alteration of speech sounds, esp. by assimilation, so as to make them easier to pronounce. **2.** a pleasing sound, esp. in speech. [C17: from Late Latin *euphōnia,* from Greek, from EU- + *phōnē* voice]

euphorbia (juːˈfɔːbɪə) *n.* any plant of the genus *Euphorbia,* such as the spurges and poinsettia: family *Euphorbiaceae.* [C14 *euforbia:* from Latin *euphorbea* African plant named after *Euphorbus,* first-century A.D. Greek physician]

euphorbiaceous (juːˌfɔːbɪˈeɪʃəs) *adj.* of, relating to, or belonging to the *Euphorbiaceae,* a family of plants typically having capsular fruits: includes the spurges, the castor oil and cassava plants, cascarilla, and poinsettia.

euphoria (juːˈfɔːrɪə) *n.* a feeling of great elation, esp. when exaggerated. [C19: from Greek: good ability to endure, from EU- + *pherein* to bear] —**euphoric** (juːˈfɒrɪk) *adj.*

euphoriant (juːˈfɔːrɪənt) *adj.* **1.** relating to or able to produce euphoria. ~*n.* **2.** a euphoriant drug or agent.

euphotic (juːˈfəʊtɪk, -ˈfɒt-) *adj. Ecology.* denoting or relating to the uppermost part of a sea or lake down to about 100 metres depth, which receives enough light to enable photosynthesis to take place. [C20: from EU- + PHOTIC]

euphrasy (ˈjuːfrəsɪ) *n., pl.* **-sies.** another name for **eyebright.** [C15 *eufrasie:* from Medieval Latin *eufrasia,* from Greek *euphrasia* gladness, from *euphrainein* to make glad, from EU- + *phrēn* mind]

euphroe *or* **uphroe** (ˈjuːfrəʊ, -vrəʊ) *n. Nautical.* a wooden block with holes through which the lines of a crowfoot are rove. [C19: from Dutch *juffrouw* maiden, earlier *joncfrouwe* (from *jonc* YOUNG + *frouwe* woman)]

euphuism (ˈjuːfjuːˌɪzəm) *n.* **1.** an artificial prose style of the Elizabethan period, marked by extreme use of antithesis, alliteration, and extended similes and allusions. **2.** any stylish affectation in speech or writing, esp. a rhetorical device or expression. [C16: after *Euphues,* prose romance by John Lyly] —ˈ**euphuist** *n.* —ˌ**euphuˈistic** *or* ˌ**euphuˈistical** *adj.* —ˌ**euphuˈistically** *adv.*

euplastic (juːˈplæstɪk) *adj.* healing quickly and well. [C19: from Greek *euplastos* readily moulded; see EU-, PLASTIC]

euploid (ˈjuːplɔɪd) *Biology.* ~*adj.* **1.** having chromosomes present in an exact multiple of the haploid number. ~*n.* **2.** a euploid cell or individual. ~Compare **aneuploid.** [C20: from EU- + *-ploid,* as in HAPLOID] —ˈ**euploidy** *n.*

eupnoea *or U.S.* **eupnea** (juːpˈnɪə) *n. Physiol.* normal relaxed breathing. Compare **dyspnoea.** [C18: from New Latin, from Greek *eupnoia,* from *eupnous* breathing easily, from EU- + *pnoē,* from *pnein* to breathe] —**eupˈnoeic** *or U.S.* **eupˈneic** *adj.*

Eur. *abbrev. for* Europe(an).

Eur- *combining form.* a variant of **Euro-** before a vowel.

Eurasian (jʊəˈreɪʃən, -ʒən) *adj.* **1.** of or relating to Europe and Asia considered as a whole. **2.** of mixed European and Asian descent. ~*n.* **3.** a person of mixed European and Asian descent.

Euratom (jʊəˈrætəm) *n.* short for **European Atomic Energy Community;** an authority established by the Common Market to develop peaceful uses of nuclear energy.

eureka (jʊˈriːkə) *interj.* an exclamation of triumph on discovering or solving something. [C17: from Greek *heurēka* I have found (it), from *heuriskein* to find; traditionally the exclamation of Archimedes when he realized, during bathing, that the volume of an irregular solid could be calculated by measuring the water displaced when it was immersed]

eurhythmic (juːˈrɪðmɪk), **eurhythmical** *or esp. U.S.* **eurythmic, eurythmical** *adj.* **1.** having a pleasing and harmonious rhythm, order, or structure. **2.** of or relating to eurhythmics.

eurhythmics *or esp. U.S.* **eurythmics** (juːˈrɪðmɪks) *n. (functioning as sing.)* **1.** a system of training through physical movement to music, originally taught by Émile Jaques-Dalcroze, to develop grace and musical understanding. **2.** dancing of this style, expressing the rhythm and spirit of the music through body movements.

eurhythmy *or esp. U.S. or* **eurythmy** (juːˈrɪðmɪ) *n.* **1.** rhythmical movement. **2.** harmonious structure. [C17: from Latin *eurythmia,* from Greek *eurhuthmia,* from EU- + *rhuthmos* proportion, RHYTHM]

euripus (jʊˈraɪpəs) *n., pl.* **-pi** (-paɪ). **1.** a strait or channel with a strong current or tide. **2.** *Rare.* a state of violent fluctuation. [C17: from Latin, from Greek *Euripos* the strait between Boeotia and Euboea, from *ripē* force, rush]

euro (ˈjuːrəʊ) *n., pl.* **euro** *or* **euros.** *Austral.* another name for the **wallaroo.** [from a native Australian language]

Euro- (ˈjʊərəʊ-) *or before a vowel* **Eur-** *combining form. (sometimes not cap.)* Europe or European: *Eurodollar.*

euro-ad (ˈjʊərəʊˌæd) *n.* an advertisement designed to be suitable for all countries in the European Community.

Eurobeach (ˈjʊərəʊˌbiːtʃ) *n.* a beach that has been designated as suitable for bathing from because it meets the limits set by European Community regulations for bacteria in bathing areas.

eurobond (ˈjʊərəʊˌbɒnd) *n. (sometimes cap.)* a bond issued in a eurocurrency.

eurocheque (ˈjʊərəʊˌtʃɛk) *n. (sometimes cap.)* a cheque drawn on a European bank that can be cashed at any bank or bureau de change displaying the EC sign or that can be used to pay for goods or services at any outlet displaying this sign.

Eurocommunism (ˌjʊərəʊˈkɒmjuˌnɪzəm) *n.* the policies, doctrines, and practices of Communist Parties in Western Europe, esp. insofar as these favour nonalignment with Russia or China. —ˌ**Euroˈcommunist** *n., adj.*

eurocrat (ˈjʊərəˌkræt) *n. (sometimes cap.)* a member, esp. a senior member, of the administration of the Common Market.

eurocurrency (ˈjʊərəʊˌkʌrənsɪ) *n. (sometimes cap.)* **a.** the currency of any country held on deposit in Europe outside its home market: used as a source of short- or medium-term finance, esp. in international trade, because of easy convertibility. **b.** (*as modifier*): *the eurocurrency market.*

eurodeposit (ˌjʊərəʊdɪˈpɒzɪt) *n. (sometimes cap.)* a deposit of the currency of any country in the eurocurrency market.

eurodollar (ˈjʊərəʊˌdɒlə) *n. (sometimes cap.)* a U.S. dollar as part of a European holding. See **eurocurrency.**

euromarket (ˈjʊərəʊˌmɑːkɪt) *n.* **1.** a market for financing international trade backed by the central banks and commercial banks of the European Community. **2.** the European Community treated as one large market for the sale of goods and services.

European (ˌjʊərəˈpɪən) *adj.* **1.** of or relating to the continent of Europe or its inhabitants. **2.** native to or derived from Europe. ~*n.* **3.** a native or inhabitant of Europe. **4.** a person of European descent. **5.** a supporter of the Common Market or of political union of the countries of Europe or a part of it, esp. Western Europe. —ˌ**EuroˈpeanˌIsm** *n.*

European Commission *n.* the executive body of the European Community formed in 1967, which initiates action in the community and mediates between member governments. Official name: **Commission of the European Communities.**

European Community *n.* the twelve nations (Belgium, Denmark, France, Germany, Greece, Ireland, Italy, Luxembourg, the Netherlands, Portugal, Spain, and the UK) that have formed an economic community, with some common monetary, social, and political objectives. Abbrev.: **EC.**

European Currency Unit *n.* See **ECU.**

European Economic Community *n.* the European common market set up by the six member states of the European Coal and Steel Community in 1957, which has since broadened into the European Community. Also called: **Common Market.** Abbrev.: **EEC.**

European Free Trade Association *n.* See **EFTA.**

Europeanize *or* **Europeanise** (ˌjʊərəˈpɪəˌnaɪz) *vb. (tr.)* **1.** to make European in culture, dress, etc. **2.** to integrate (a country, economy, etc.) into the European Community. —ˌ**Euroˌpeaniˈzation** *or* ˌ**EuroˌpeaniˈsationI** *n.*

European Monetary System *n.* the system used in the European Community for stabilizing exchange rates between the currencies of member states. It relies on the Exchange Rate Mechanism and the balance-of-payments support mechanism. Abbrev.: **EMS.**

European Parliament *n.* the assembly of the European Community in Strasbourg. It consists of 518 directly elected members and its role is largely advisory.

European plan *n. U.S.* a hotel rate of charging covering room and service but not meals. Compare **American plan.**

europium (jʊˈrəʊpɪəm) *n.* a soft ductile reactive silvery-white element of the lanthanide series of metals: used as the red phosphor in colour television and in lasers. Symbol: Eu; atomic no.: 63; atomic wt.: 151.96; valency: 2 or 3; relative density: 5.25;

melting pt.: 826°C; boiling pt.: 1439°C. [C20: named after *Europe* + -IUM]

Eurosterling ('jʊərəʊˌstɜːlɪŋ) *n.* sterling as part of a European holding. See **eurocurrency.**

Eurovision ('jʊərəʊˌvɪʒən) *n.* **a.** the network of the European Broadcasting Union for the exchange of news and television programmes amongst its member organizations and for the relay of news and programmes from outside the network. **b.** (*as modifier*): *the Eurovision song contest.*

eury- *combining form.* broad or wide: *eurythermal.* [New Latin, from Greek, from *eurus* wide]

euryhaline (ˌjʊərɪ'heɪliːn, -laɪn) *adj.* (of certain aquatic animals) able to tolerate a wide range of salinity. Compare **stenohaline.** [C20: from EURY- + *haline,* from Greek *hals* salt + -INE[1]]

eurypterid (jʊ'rɪptərɪd) *n.* any large extinct scorpion-like aquatic arthropod of the group *Eurypterida,* of Palaeozoic times, thought to be related to the horseshoe crabs. [C19: from New Latin *Eurypterida,* from EURY- + Greek *pteron* wing, feather]

eurythermal (ˌjʊərɪ'θɜːməl), **eurythermic,** *or* **eurythermous** *adj.* (of organisms) able to tolerate a wide range of temperatures in the environment. Compare **stenothermal.**

eurythmics (juː'rɪðmɪks) *n.* a variant spelling (esp. U.S.) of **eurhythmics.** —**eu'rythmic** *or* **eu'rythmical** *adj.* —**eu'rythmy** *n.*

eurytopic (ˌjʊərɪ'tɒpɪk) *adj. Ecology.* (of a species) able to tolerate a wide range of environmental changes. Compare **stenotopic.** [C20: from EURY- + *top* from Greek *topos* place + -IC]

eusporangiate (ˌjuːspɔː'rændʒɪɪt) *adj.* (of ferns) having each sporangium developing from a group of cells rather than a single cell. [from New Latin *eusporangiātus* (unattested), from EU- + SPORANGIUM]

Eustachian tube (juː'steɪʃən) *n.* a tube that connects the middle ear with the nasopharynx and equalizes the pressure between the two sides of the eardrum. [C18: named after Bartolomeo *Eustachio,* 16th-century Italian anatomist]

eustatic (juː'stætɪk) *adj.* denoting or relating to worldwide changes in sea level, caused by the melting of ice sheets, movements of the ocean floor, sedimentation, etc. [C20: from Greek, from EU- + STATIC] —**eustasy** ('juːstəsɪ) *n.* —**eu'statically** *adv.*

eutaxia (juː'tæksɪə) *n. Engineering.* the condition of being easily melted.

eutectic (juː'tɛktɪk) *adj.* **1.** (of a mixture of substances, esp. an alloy) having the lowest freezing point of all possible mixtures of the substances. **2.** concerned with or suitable for the formation of eutectic mixtures. ~*n.* **3.** a eutectic mixture. **4.** the temperature on a phase diagram at which a eutectic mixture forms. [C19: from Greek *eutēktos* melting readily, from EU- + *tēkein* to melt]

eutectoid (juː'tɛktɔɪd) *n.* **1.** a mixture of substances similar to a eutectic, but forming two or three constituents from a solid instead of from a melt. ~*adj.* **2.** concerned with or suitable for eutectoid mixtures. [C20: from EUTECT(IC) + -OID]

euthanasia (ˌjuːθə'neɪzɪə) *n.* the act of killing someone painlessly, esp. to relieve suffering from an incurable illness. Also called: **mercy killing.** [C17: via New Latin from Greek: easy death, from EU- + *thanatos* death]

euthenics (juː'θɛnɪks) *n.* (*functioning as sing.*) the study of the control of the environment, esp. with a view to improving the health and living standards of the human race. [C20: from Greek *euthēnein* to thrive] —**eu'thenist** *n.*

eutherian (juː'θɪərɪən) *adj.* **1.** of, relating to, or belonging to the *Eutheria,* a subclass of mammals all of which have a placenta and reach an advanced state of development before birth. The group includes all mammals except monotremes and marsupials. ~*n.* **2.** any eutherian mammal. ~Compare **metatherian, prototherian.** [C19: from New Latin *Euthēria,* from Greek EU- + *thēria,* plural of *thērion* beast]

euthymia (juː'θɪmɪə) *n. Psychol.* a pleasant state of mind. [EU- + -THYMIA]

eutrophic (juː'trɒfɪk, -'trəʊ-) *adj.* (of lakes and similar habitats) rich in organic and mineral nutrients and supporting an abundant plant life, which in the process of decaying depletes the oxygen supply for animal life. Compare **oligotrophic.** [C18: probably from *eutrophy,* from Greek *eutrophia* sound nutrition, from *eutrophos* well-fed, from EU- + *trephein* to nourish] —'**eutrophy** *n.*

eutrophication (juːˌtrɒfɪ'keɪʃən) *n.* a process by which pollution from such sources as sewage effluent or leachate from fertilized fields causes a lake, pond, or fen to become overrich in organic and mineral nutrients, so that algae grow rapidly and deplete the oxygen supply.

euxenite ('juːksɪˌnaɪt) *n.* a rare brownish-black mineral containing erbium, cerium, uranium, columbium, and yttrium. [C19: from Greek *euxenos* hospitable (literally: well-disposed to strangers), from EU- + *xenos* stranger; from its containing a number of rare elements]

eV *abbrev. for* electronvolt.

EV *abbrev. for* English Version (of the Bible).

EVA *Astronautics. abbrev. for* extravehicular activity.

evacuant (ɪ'vækjʊənt) *adj.* **1.** serving to promote excretion, esp. of the bowels. ~*n.* **2.** an evacuant agent.

evacuate (ɪ'vækjʊˌeɪt) *vb.* (*mainly tr.*) **1.** (*also intr.*) to withdraw or cause to withdraw from (a place of danger) to a place of greater safety. **2.** to make empty by removing the contents of. **3.** (*also intr.*) *Physiol.* **a.** to eliminate or excrete (faeces); defecate. **b.** to discharge (any waste product) from (a part of the body). **4.** (*tr.*) to create a vacuum in (a bulb, flask, reaction vessel, etc.). [C16: from Latin *ēvacuāre* to void, from *vacuus* empty] —**eˌvacu'ation** *n.* —**e'vacuative** *adj.* —**e'vacuˌator** *n.*

evacuee (ɪˌvækjʊ'iː) *n.* a person evacuated from a place of danger, esp. in wartime.

evade (ɪ'veɪd) *vb.* (*mainly tr.*) **1.** to get away from or avoid (imprisonment, captors, etc.); escape. **2.** to get around, shirk, or dodge (the law, a duty, etc.). **3.** (*also intr.*) to avoid answering (a question). [C16: from French *évader,* from Latin *ēvādere* to go forth, from *vādere* to go] —**e'vadable** *adj.* —**e'vader** *n.* —**e'vadingly** *adv.*

evaginate (ɪ'vædʒɪˌneɪt) *vb.* (*tr.*) *Med.* to turn (an organ or part) inside out; turn the outer surface (of an organ or part) back on itself. [C17: from Late Latin *ēvāgīnāre* to unsheathe, from *vāgīna* sheath] —**eˌvagi'nation** *n.*

evaluate (ɪ'væljʊˌeɪt) *vb.* (*tr.*) **1.** to ascertain or set the amount or value of. **2.** to judge or assess the worth of; appraise. **3.** *Maths, logic.* to determine the unique member of the range of a function corresponding to a given member of its domain. [C19: back formation from *evaluation,* from French, from *evaluer* to evaluate; see VALUE] —**eˌvalu'ation** *n.* —**e'valuˌator** *n.*

evaluative (ɪ'væljʊətɪv) *adj.* **1.** of, denoting, or based on an act of evaluating. **2.** *Philosophy.* expressing an attitude or value judgment; emotive.

evanesce (ˌɛvə'nɛs) *vb.* (*intr.*) (of smoke, mist, etc.) to fade gradually from sight; vanish. [C19: from Latin *ēvānēscere* to disappear; see VANISH]

evanescent (ˌɛvə'nɛsᵊnt) *adj.* **1.** passing out of sight; fading away; vanishing. **2.** ephemeral or transitory. —ˌ**eva'nescence** *n.* —ˌ**eva'nescently** *adv.*

evang. *or* **evan.** (*often cap.*) *abbrev. for* evangelical.

evangel (ɪ'vændʒəl) *n.* **1.** *Archaic.* the gospel of Christianity. **2.** (*often cap.*) any of the four Gospels of the New Testament. **3.** any body of teachings regarded as central or basic. **4.** *U.S.* an evangelist. [C14: from Church Latin *ēvangelium,* from Greek *evangelion* good news, from EU- + *angelos* messenger; see ANGEL]

evangelical (ˌiːvæn'dʒɛlɪkᵊl) *Christianity.* ~*adj.* **1.** of, based upon, or following from the Gospels. **2.** denoting or relating to any of certain Protestant sects or parties, which emphasize the importance of personal conversion and faith in atonement through the death of Christ as a means of salvation. **3.** another word for **evangelistic.** ~*n.* **4.** an upholder of evangelical doctrines or a member of an evangelical sect or party, esp. the Low-Church party of the Church of England. —ˌ**evan'gelicalism** *n.* —ˌ**evan'gelically** *adv.*

evangelism (ɪ'vændʒɪˌlɪzəm) *n.* **1.** the practice of spreading the Christian gospel. **2.** ardent or missionary zeal for a cause. **3.** the work, methods, or characteristic outlook of a revivalist or evangelist preacher. **4.** a less common word for **evangelicalism.**

evangelist (ɪ'vændʒɪlɪst) *n.* **1.** an occasional preacher, sometimes itinerant and often preaching at meetings in the open air. **2.** a preacher of the Christian gospel. **3.** any zealous advocate of a cause. **4.** another word for **revivalist** (sense 1).

Evangelist (ɪ'vændʒɪlɪst) *n.* **1.** any of the writers of the New Testament Gospels: Matthew, Mark, Luke, or John. **2.** a senior official or dignitary of the Mormon Church.

evangelistic (ɪˌvændʒɪ'lɪstɪk) *adj.* **1.** denoting, resembling, or relating to evangelists or their methods and attitudes: *evangelistic zeal.* **2.** zealously advocating a cause. **3.** (*often cap.*) of or relating to all or any of the four Evangelists. —**eˌvange'listically** *adv.*

evangelize *or* **evangelise** (ɪ'vændʒɪˌlaɪz) *vb.* **1.** to preach the Christian gospel or a particular interpretation of it (to). **2.** (*intr.*) to advocate a cause with the object of making converts. —**eˌvangeli'zation** *or* **eˌvangeli'sation** *n.* —**e'vangeˌlizer** *or* **e'vangeˌliser** *n.*

evanish (ɪ'vænɪʃ) *vb.* a poetic word for **vanish.** [C15: from Old French *esvanir,* from Latin *ēvānēscere* to VANISH] —**e'vanishment** *n.*

evaporate (ɪ'væpəˌreɪt) *vb.* **1.** to change or cause to change from a liquid or solid state to a vapour. Compare **boil**[1] (sense 1). **2.** to lose or cause to lose liquid by vaporization leaving a more concentrated residue. **3.** to disappear or cause to disappear; fade away or cause to fade away: *all her doubts evaporated.* **4.** (*tr.*) to deposit (a film, metal, etc.) by vaporization of a liquid or solid and the subsequent condensation of its vapour. [C16: from Late Latin *ēvapōrāre,* from Latin *vapor* steam; see VAPOUR] —**e'vaporable** *adj.* —**eˌvapora'bility** *n.* —**eˌvapo'ration** *n.* —**e'vaporative** *adj.* —**e'vapoˌrator** *n.*

evaporated milk *n.* thick unsweetened tinned milk from which some of the water has been evaporated.

evaporimeter (ɪˌvæpə'rɪmɪtə) *or* **evaporometer** (ɪˌvæpə'rɒmɪtə) *n.* another name for **atmometer.**

evaporite (ɪ'væpəˌraɪt) *n.* any sedimentary rock, such as rock salt, gypsum, or anhydrite, formed by evaporation of former seas or salt-water lakes. [C20: EVAPORATION + -ITE[1]]

evapotranspiration (ɪˌvæpəʊˌtrænspə'reɪʃən) *n.* the return of water vapour to the atmosphere by evaporation from land and water surfaces and by the transpiration of vegetation.

evasion (ɪ'veɪʒən) *n.* **1.** the act of evading or escaping, esp. from a distasteful duty, responsibility, etc., by trickery, cunning, or illegal means: *tax evasion.* **2.** trickery, cunning, or deception used to dodge a question, duty, etc.; means of evading. [C15: from Late Latin *ēvāsiō*, from Latin *ēvādere* to go forth; see EVADE]

evasive (ɪ'veɪsɪv) *adj.* **1.** tending or seeking to evade; avoiding the issue; not straightforward. **2.** avoiding or seeking to avoid trouble or difficulties: *to take evasive action.* **3.** hard to catch or obtain; elusive. —**e'vasively** *adv.* —**e'vasiveness** *n.*

eve (iːv) *n.* **1. a.** the evening or day before some special event or festival. **b.** (*cap. when part of a name*): *New Year's Eve.* **2.** the period immediately before an event: *on the eve of civil war.* **3.** an archaic word for **evening.** [C13: variant of EVEN[2]]

evection (ɪ'vɛkʃən) *n.* irregularity in the moon's motion caused by perturbations of the sun and planets. [C17: from Latin *ēvectiō* a going up, from *ēvehere* to lead forth, from *vehere* to carry] —**e'vectional** *adj.*

even[1] ('iːvᵊn) *adj.* **1.** level and regular; flat: *an even surface.* **2.** (*postpositive*; foll. by *with*) on the same level or in the same plane (as): *one surface even with another.* **3.** without variation or fluctuation; regular; constant: *an even rate of progress.* **4.** not readily moved or excited; placid; calm: *an even temper.* **5.** equally balanced between two sides: *an even game.* **6.** equal or identical in number, quantity, etc.: *two even spoonfuls of sugar.* **7. a.** (of a number) divisible by two. **b.** characterized or indicated by such a number: *maps are on the even pages.* Compare **odd** (sense 4). **8.** relating to or denoting two or either of two alternatives, events, etc., that have an equal probability: *an even chance of missing or catching a train.* **9.** having no balance of debt; neither owing nor being owed. **10.** just and impartial; fair: *an even division.* **11.** exact in number, amount, or extent: *an even pound.* **12.** equal, as in score; level: *now the teams are even.* **13.** *Maths.* (of a function) unchanged in value when the sign of the independent variable is changed, as in $y = z^2$. Compare **odd** (sense 8). **14. even money. a.** a bet in which the winnings are the same as the amount staked. **b.** (*as modifier*): *the even-money favourite.* **15. get even (with).** *Informal.* to exact revenge (on); settle accounts (with). **16. of even date.** *Legal, formal, or obsolete.* of the same or today's date. ~*adv.* **17.** (intensifier; used to suggest that the content of a statement is unexpected or paradoxical): *even an idiot can do that.* **18.** (intensifier; used with comparative forms): *this is even better.* **19.** notwithstanding; in spite of: *even having started late she soon caught him up.* **20.** used to introduce a more precise version of a word, phrase, or statement: *he is base, even depraved.* **21.** used preceding a clause of supposition or hypothesis to emphasize the implication that whether or not the condition in it is fulfilled, the statement in the main clause remains valid: *even if she died he wouldn't care.* **22.** *Archaic.* that is to say; namely (used for emphasis): *he, even he, hath spoken these things.* **23.** *Archaic.* all the way; fully: *I love thee even unto death.* **24. even as.** (*conj.*) at the very same moment or in the very same way that: *even as I spoke, it thundered.* **25. even so. a.** in spite of any assertion to the contrary: nevertheless. **b.** *Archaic.* yes; (that is) correct. ~*vb.* **26.** to make or become even. ~See also **break even, even out, evens, even up.** [Old English *efen*; related to Old Norse *jafn* even, equal, Gothic *ibns*, Old High German *eban*] —'**evener** *n.* —'**evenly** *adv.* —'**evenness** *n.*

even[2] ('iːvᵊn) *n.* an archaic word for **eve** or **evening.** [Old English *ǣfen*; related to Old Frisian *ēvend*, Old High German *āband*]

evenfall ('iːvᵊn,fɔːl) *n. Archaic.* early evening; dusk.

even-handed *adj.* dealing fairly with all; impartial. —,**even-'handedly** *adv.* —,**even-'handedness** *n.*

evening ('iːvnɪŋ) *n.* **1.** the latter part of the day, esp. from late afternoon until nightfall. **2.** the latter or concluding period: *the evening of one's life.* **3.** the early part of the night spent in a specified way: *an evening at the theatre.* **4.** an entertainment, meeting, or reception held in the early part of the night. **5.** *Southern U.S. and Brit. dialect.* the period between noon and sunset. **6.** (*modifier*) of, used, or occurring in the evening: *the evening papers.* ~See also **evenings.** [Old English *ǣfnung*; related to Old Frisian *ēvend*, Old High German *āband*]

evening class *n.* a class held in the evenings at certain colleges, normally for adults.

evening dress *n.* attire for wearing at a formal occasion during the evening, esp. (for men) a dinner jacket and black tie, or (less commonly, for women) a floor-length gown.

evening primrose *n.* any onagraceous plant of the American genus *Oenothera*, esp. *O. biennis*, typically having yellow flowers that open in the evening.

evening primrose oil *n.* an oil, obtained from the seeds of the evening primrose, that is claimed to stimulate the production of prostaglandins.

evenings ('iːvnɪŋz) *adv. Informal.* in the evening, esp. regularly.

evening star *n.* a planet, usually Venus, seen shining brightly in the west just after sunset. Compare **morning star.**

Evenki (ə'vɛŋkɪ) *n.* **1.** (*pl.* **Evenki**) a Tungus people of E Siberia. **2.** the language of this people.

even out *vb.* (*adv.*) to make or become even, as by the removal of bumps, inequalities, etc.: *the land evens out beyond that rise.*

evens ('iːvənz) *adj., adv.* **1.** (of a bet) winning the same as the amount staked if successful. **2.** (of a runner) offered at such odds.

evensong ('iːvᵊn,sɒŋ) *n.* **1.** Also called: **Evening Prayer, vespers.** *Church of England.* the daily evening service of Bible readings and prayers prescribed in the Book of Common Prayer. **2.** *Archaic.* another name for **vespers.** **3.** an archaic or poetic word for **evening.**

event (ɪ'vɛnt) *n.* **1.** anything that takes place or happens, esp. something important; happening; incident. **2.** the actual or final outcome; result (esp. in the phrases **in the event, after the event**). **3.** any one contest in a programme of sporting or other contests: *the high jump is his event.* **4.** *Philosophy.* **a.** an occurrence regarded as a bare instant of space-time as contrasted with an object which fills space and has endurance. **b.** an occurrence regarded in isolation from, or contrasted with, human agency. Compare **act** (sense 8). **5. at all events** *or* **in any event.** regardless of circumstances; in any case. **6. in the event of.** in case of; if (such a thing) happens: *in the event of rain the race will be cancelled.* **7. in the event that.** if it should happen that. ~*vb.* **8.** to take part or ride (a horse) in eventing. [C16: from Latin *ēventus* a happening, from *ēvenīre* to come forth, happen, from *venīre* to come]

even-tempered *adj.* not easily angered or excited; calm.

eventful (ɪ'vɛntfʊl) *adj.* full of events or incidents: *an eventful day.* —**e'ventfully** *adv.* —**e'ventfulness** *n.*

event horizon *n. Astronomy.* the spherical surface around a black hole enclosing the space from which electromagnetic radiation cannot escape due to excessive gravitational attraction. The radius is proportional to the mass of the black hole.

eventide ('iːvᵊn,taɪd) *n. Archaic or poetic.* another word for **evening.**

eventide home ('iːvᵊn,taɪd) *n. Euphemistic.* an old people's home.

eventing (ɪ'vɛntɪŋ) *n.* the sport of taking part in equestrian competitions (esp. **three-day events**), usually consisting of three sections: dressage, cross-country riding, and showjumping. —**e'venter** *n.*

eventration (,iːvɛn'treɪʃən) *n. Pathol.* protrusion of the bowel through the abdomen.

eventual (ɪ'vɛntʃʊəl) *adj.* **1.** (*prenominal*) happening in due course of time; ultimate: *the eventual outcome was his defeat.* **2.** *Archaic.* contingent or possible.

eventuality (ɪ,vɛntʃʊ'ælɪtɪ) *n., pl.* **-ties.** a possible event, occurrence, or result; contingency.

eventually (ɪ'vɛntʃʊəlɪ) *adv.* **1.** at the very end; finally. **2.** (*as sentence modifier*) after a long time or long delay: *eventually, he arrived.*

eventuate (ɪ'vɛntʃʊ,eɪt) *vb.* (*intr.*) **1.** (often foll. by *in*) to result ultimately (in). **2.** to come about as a result: *famine eventuated from the crop failure.* —**e,ventu'ation** *n.*

even up *vb.* (*adv.*) to make or become equal, esp. in respect of claims or debts; settle or balance.

ever ('ɛvə) *adv.* **1.** at any time: *have you ever seen it?* **2.** by any chance; in any case: *how did you ever find out?* **3.** at all times; always: *ever busy.* **4.** in any possible way or manner: *come as fast as ever you can.* **5.** *Informal, chiefly Brit.* (intensifier, in the phrases **ever so, ever such,** and **ever such a**): *ever so good; ever such bad luck; ever such a waste.* **6. ever and again** (*or* **anon**). *Archaic.* now and then; from time to time. **7. is he** *or* **she ever!** *U.S. and Canadian slang.* he or she displays the quality concerned in abundance. ~See also **for ever.** [Old English *ǣfre*, of uncertain origin]

Everest ('ɛvərɪst) *n.* any high point of ambition or achievement. [from Mount *Everest*, the world's highest peak]

evergreen ('ɛvə,griːn) *adj.* **1.** (of certain trees and shrubs) bearing foliage throughout the year; continually shedding and replacing leaves. Compare **deciduous.** **2.** remaining fresh and vital. ~*n.* **3.** an evergreen tree or shrub.

evergreen fund *n.* a fund that provides capital for new companies and makes regular injections of capital to support their development.

everlasting (,ɛvə'lɑːstɪŋ) *adj.* **1.** never coming to an end; eternal. **2.** lasting for an indefinitely long period. **3.** lasting so long or occurring so often as to become tedious; incessant: *I cannot bear her everlasting complaints.* ~*n.* **4.** endless duration; eternity. **5.** Also called: **everlasting flower.** another name for **immortelle.** See also **cat's-foot.** —,**ever'lastingly** *adv.* —,**ever'lastingness** *n.*

evermore (,ɛvə'mɔː) *adv.* (often preceded by *for*) all time to come.

evert (ɪ'vɜːt) *vb.* (*tr.*) to turn (an eyelid, the intestines, or some other bodily part) outwards or inside out. [C16: from Latin *ēvertere* to overthrow, from *vertere* to turn] —**e'versible** *adj.* —**e'version** *n.*

evertor (ɪ'vɜːtə) *n.* any muscle that turns a part outwards.

every ('ɛvrɪ) *determiner.* **1.** each one (of the class specified), without exception: *every child knows it.* **2.** (*not used with a negative*) the greatest or best possible: *every hope of success.* **3.** each: used before a noun phrase to indicate the recurrent, intermittent, or serial nature of a thing: *every third day; every now and then; every so often.* **4. every bit.** (used in comparisons with *as*) quite; just; equally: *every bit as funny as the other show.* **5. every other.** each alternate; every second: *every other day.* **6. every which way.** *U.S. and Canadian.* **a.** in all directions; everywhere: *I looked every which way for you.* **b.** from all sides: *stones coming at me every which way.* [C15 *everich*, from Old English *ǣfre ǣlc*, from *ǣfre* EVER + *ǣlc* EACH]

everybody ('ɛvrɪˌbɒdɪ) *pron.* every person; everyone.
▷**Usage.** See at **everyone.**

everyday ('ɛvrɪˌdeɪ) *adj.* **1.** happening each day; daily. **2.** commonplace or usual; ordinary. **3.** suitable for or used on ordinary days as distinct from Sundays or special days.

Everyman ('ɛvrɪˌmæn) *n.* **1.** a medieval English morality play in which the central figure represents mankind, whose earthly destiny is dramatized from the Christian viewpoint. **2.** (*often not cap.*) the ordinary person; common man.

everyone ('ɛvrɪˌwʌn, -wən) *pron.* every person; everybody.
▷**Usage.** *Everyone* and *everybody* are interchangeable, as are *no one* and *nobody*, and *someone* and *somebody*. *Everybody, everyone, none, no one, nobody, somebody, someone,* and *each* function as singular in careful English: *everyone nodded his head* (not *their heads*). The use of *their* in such constructions is, however, common in informal English. Careful writers distinguish between *everyone* and *someone* as single words and *every one* and *some one* as two words, using the latter form to refer to each individual person or thing in a particular group: *every one of them is wrong.*

every one *pron.* each person or thing in a group, without exception: *every one of the large cats is a fast runner.*

everyplace ('ɛvrɪˌpleɪs) *adv. U.S.* an informal word for **everywhere.**

everything ('ɛvrɪˌθɪŋ) *pron.* **1.** the entirety of a specified or implied class: *she lost everything in the War.* **2.** a great deal, esp. of something very important: *she means everything to me.*

everywhere ('ɛvrɪˌwɛə) *adv.* to or in all parts or places.

Eve's pudding (iːvz) *n. Brit.* a baked sponge pudding with a layer of apple at the bottom.

evict (ɪ'vɪkt) *vb.* (*tr.*) **1.** to expel (a tenant) from property by process of law; turn out. **2.** to recover (property or the title to property) by judicial process or by virtue of a superior title. [C15: from Late Latin *ēvincere*, from Latin: to vanquish utterly, from *vincere* to conquer] —**e'viction** *n.* —**e'victor** *n.*

evidence ('ɛvɪdəns) *n.* **1.** ground for belief or disbelief; data on which to base proof or to establish truth or falsehood. **2.** a mark or sign that makes evident; indication: *his pallor was evidence of ill health.* **3.** *Law.* matter produced before a court of law in an attempt to prove or disprove a point in issue, such as the statements of witnesses, documents, material objects, etc. See also **circumstantial evidence, direct evidence. 4. turn queen's (king's, state's) evidence.** (of an accomplice) to act as witness for the prosecution and testify against those associated with him in crime. **5. in evidence.** on display; apparent; conspicuous: *her engagement ring was in evidence.* ~*vb.* (*tr.*) **6.** to make evident; show clearly. **7.** to give proof of or evidence for.

evident ('ɛvɪdənt) *adj.* easy to see or understand; readily apparent. [C14: from Latin *ēvidēns*, from *vidēre* to see]

evidential (ˌɛvɪ'dɛnʃəl) *adj.* relating to, serving as, or based on evidence. —ˌ**evi'dentially** *adv.*

evidently ('ɛvɪdəntlɪ) *adv.* **1.** without question; clearly; undoubtedly. **2.** to all appearances; apparently: *they are evidently related.*

evil ('iːvəl) *adj.* **1.** morally wrong or bad; wicked: *an evil ruler.* **2.** causing harm or injury; harmful: *an evil plan.* **3.** marked or accompanied by misfortune; unlucky: *an evil fate.* **4.** (of temper, disposition, etc.) characterized by anger or spite. **5.** not in high esteem; infamous: *an evil reputation.* **6.** offensive or unpleasant: *an evil smell.* ~*n.* **7.** the quality or an instance of being morally wrong; wickedness: *the evils of war.* **8.** (*sometimes cap.*) a force or power that brings about wickedness or harm: *evil is strong in the world.* **9.** *Archaic.* an illness or disease, esp. scrofula (the **king's evil**). ~*adv.* **10.** (*now usually in combination*) in an evil manner; badly: *evil-smelling.* [Old English *yfel*, of Germanic origin; compare Old Frisian *evel*, Old High German *ubil* evil, Old Irish *adbal* excessive] —'**evilly** *adv.* —'**evilness** *n.*

evildoer ('iːvəlˌduːə) *n.* a person who does evil. —'**evilˌdoing** *n.*

evil eye *n.* **the. 1.** a look or glance superstitiously supposed to have the power of inflicting harm or injury. **2.** the power to inflict harm, etc., by such a look. —ˌ**evil-'eyed** *adj.*

evil-minded *adj.* inclined to evil thoughts; malicious or spiteful. —ˌ**evil-'mindedly** *adv.* —ˌ**evil-'mindedness** *n.*

Evil One *n.* **the.** the devil; Satan.

evince (ɪ'vɪns) *vb.* (*tr.*) to make evident; show (something, such as an emotion) clearly. [C17: from Latin *ēvincere* to overcome; see EVICT] —**e'vincible** *adj.* —**e'vincive** *adj.*

eviscerate (ɪ'vɪsəˌreɪt) *vb.* **1.** (*tr.*) to remove the internal organs of; disembowel. **2.** (*tr.*) to deprive of meaning or significance. **3.** (*tr.*) *Surgery.* to remove the contents of (the eyeball or other organ). **4.** (*intr.*) *Surgery.* (of the viscera) to protrude through a weakened abdominal incision after an operation. ~*adj.* **5.** having been disembowelled. [C17: from Latin *ēviscerāre* to disembowel, from *viscera* entrails] —**eˌviscer'ation** *n.* —**e'viscerˌator** *n.*

evitable ('ɛvɪtəbəl) *adj. Rare.* able to be avoided. [C16: from Latin *ēvītābilis*, from *ēvītāre*, from *vītāre* to avoid]

evite (ɪ'vaɪt) *vb.* an archaic word for **avoid.**

evocation (ˌɛvə'keɪʃən) *n.* **1.** the act or an instance of evoking. **2.** *French law.* the transference of a case from an inferior court for adjudication by a higher tribunal. **3.** another word for **induction** (sense 6). [C17: from Latin *ēvocātiō* a calling forth, from *ēvocāre* to EVOKE]

evocative (ɪ'vɒkətɪv) *adj.* tending or serving to evoke. —**e'vocatively** *adv.* —**e'vocativeness** *n.*

evocator ('ɛvəˌkeɪtə) *n.* **1.** a person or thing that evokes. **2.** *Embryol.* a substance or tissue that induces morphogenesis.

evoke (ɪ'vəʊk) *vb.* (*tr.*) **1.** to call or summon up (a memory, feeling, etc.), esp. from the past. **2.** to call forth or provoke; produce; elicit: *his words evoked an angry reply.* **3.** to cause (spirits) to appear; conjure up. [C17: from Latin *ēvocāre* to call forth, from *vocāre* to call] —**evocable** ('ɛvəkəbəl) *adj.* —**e'voker** *n.*

evolute ('ɛvəˌluːt) *n.* **1.** a geometric curve that describes the locus of the centres of curvature of another curve (the **involute**). The tangents to the evolute are at right angles to the involute. ~*adj.* **2.** *Biology.* having the margins rolled outwards. [C19: from Latin *ēvolūtus* unrolled, from *ēvolvere* to roll out, EVOLVE]

evolution (ˌiːvə'luːʃən) *n.* **1.** *Biology.* a gradual change in the characteristics of a population of animals or plants over successive generations: accounts for the origin of existing species from ancestors unlike them. See also **natural selection. 2.** a gradual development, esp. to a more complex form: *the evolution of modern art.* **3.** the act of throwing off, as heat, gas, vapour, etc. **4.** a pattern formed by a series of movements or something similar. **5.** an algebraic operation in which the root of a number, expression, etc., is extracted. Compare **involution** (sense 6). **6.** *Military.* an exercise carried out in accordance with a set procedure or plan. [C17: from Latin *ēvolūtiō* an unrolling, from *ēvolvere* to EVOLVE] —ˌ**evo'lutionary** *or* ˌ**evo'lutional** *adj.*

evolutionist (ˌiːvə'luːʃənɪst) *n.* **1.** a person who believes in a theory of evolution, esp. Darwin's theory of the evolution of plant and animal species. ~*adj.* **2.** of or relating to a theory of evolution. —ˌ**evo'lutionism** *n.* —ˌ**evolution'istic** *adj.*

evolutive (iː'vɒljʊtɪv) *adj.* relating to, tending to, or promoting evolution.

evolve (ɪ'vɒlv) *vb.* **1.** to develop or cause to develop gradually. **2.** (of animal or plant species) to undergo evolution of (organs or parts). **3.** (*tr.*) to yield, emit, or give off (heat, gas, vapour, etc.). [C17: from Latin *ēvolvere* to unfold, from *volvere* to roll] —**e'volvable** *adj.* —**e'volvement** *n.* —**e'volver** *n.*

evonymus (ɛ'vɒnɪməs) *n.* a variant of **euonymus.**

evulsion (ɪ'vʌlʃən) *n. Rare.* the act of extracting by force. [C17: from Latin *ēvulsiō*, from *ēvellere*, from *vellere* to pluck]

evzone ('ɛvzəʊn) *n.* a soldier in an elite Greek infantry regiment. [C19: from Modern Greek, from Greek *euzōnos* literally: well-girt, from EU- + *zōne* girdle]

ewe (juː) *n.* **a.** a female sheep. **b.** (*as modifier*): *a ewe lamb.* [Old English *ēowu*; related to Old Norse *ǣr* ewe, Old High German *ou*, Latin *ovis* sheep, Sanskrit *avi*]

Ewe ('ɛwɛ) *n.* **1.** (*pl.* **Ewe** *or* **Ewes**) a member of a Negroid people of W Africa living chiefly in the forests of E Ghana, Togo, and Benin. **2.** the language of this people, belonging to the Kwa branch of the Niger-Congo family.

ewe equivalent *n. N.Z.* the basic measure for calculating stock unit: *one Jersey cow is equal to 6.5 ewe equivalents.*

ewe-neck *n.* **1.** a condition in horses in which the neck is straight and sagging rather than arched. **2.** a horse or other animal with this condition. —'**ewe-ˌnecked** *adj.*

ewer ('juːə) *n.* a large jug or pitcher with a wide mouth. [C14: from Old French *evier*, from Latin *aquārius* water carrier, from *aqua* water]

EWO *abbrev. for* Educational Welfare Officer.

ex[1] (ɛks) *prep.* **1.** *Finance.* not participating in; excluding; without: *ex bonus; ex dividend; ex rights.* **2.** *Commerce.* without charge to the buyer until removed from: *ex quay; ex ship; ex works.* [C19: from Latin: out of, from]

ex[2] (ɛks) *n. Informal.* (a person's) former wife, husband, etc.

ex. *abbrev. for:* **1.** examination. **2.** examined. **3.** example. **4.** except(ed). **5.** exception. **6.** exchange. **7.** excursion. **8.** executed. **9.** executive. **10.** express. **11.** extra.

Ex. *Bible. abbrev. for* Exodus.

ex-[1] *prefix.* **1.** out of; outside of; from: *exclosure; exurbia.* **2.** former: *ex-wife.* [from Latin, from *ex* (prep.), identical in meaning and origin with Greek *ex, ek*; see EC-]

ex-[2] *combining form.* a variant of **exo-** before a vowel: *exergonic.*

exa- *prefix.* denoting 10^{18}: *exametres.* Symbol: E

exacerbate (ɪg'zæsəˌbeɪt, ɪk'sæs-) *vb.* (*tr.*) **1.** to make (pain, disease, emotion, etc.) more intense; aggravate. **2.** to exasperate or irritate (a person). [C17: from Latin *exacerbāre* to irritate, from *acerbus* bitter] —**exˌacer'bation** *n.*

exact (ɪg'zækt) *adj.* **1.** correct in every detail; strictly accurate: *an exact copy.* **2.** precise, as opposed to approximate; neither more nor less: *the exact sum.* **3.** (*prenominal*) specific; particular: *this exact spot.* **4.** operating with very great precision: *exact instruments.* **5.** allowing no deviation from a standard; rigorous; strict: *an exact mind.* **6.** based mainly on measurement and the formulation of laws, as opposed to description and classification: *physics is an exact science.* ~*vb.* (*tr.*) **7.** to force or compel (payment or performance); extort: *to exact tribute.* **8.** to demand as a right; insist upon: *to exact respect from one's employees.* **9.** to call for or require: *this work exacts careful effort.* [C16: from Latin *exactus* driven out, from *exigere* to drive forth, from *agere* to drive] —ex'actable *adj.* —ex'actness *n.* —ex'actor *or* ex'acter *n.*

exacting (ɪg'zæktɪŋ) *adj.* making rigorous or excessive demands: *an exacting job.* —**ex'actingly** *adv.* —**ex'actingness** *n.*

exaction (ɪg'zækʃən) *n.* **1.** the act or an instance of exacting, esp. money. **2.** an excessive or harsh demand, esp. for money; extortion. **3.** a sum or payment exacted.

exactitude (ɪg'zæktɪˌtjuːd) *n.* the quality of being exact; precision; accuracy.

exactly (ɪg'zæktlɪ) *adv.* **1.** in an exact manner; accurately or precisely. **2.** in every respect; just: *it is exactly what he wants.* ~*sentence substitute.* **3.** just so! precisely! **4. not exactly.** *Ironical.* not at all; by no means.

exacum ('ɛksəkəm) *n.* any plant of the annual or perennial tropical genus *Exacum;* some are grown as greenhouse biennials for their bluish-purple platter-shaped flowers: family *Gentianaceae.* [Latin, a name for centaury, from *ex* out + *agere* to drive]

exaggerate (ɪg'zædʒəˌreɪt) *vb.* **1.** to regard or represent as larger or greater, more important or more successful, etc., than is true. **2.** (*tr.*) to make greater, more noticeable, etc., than usual: *his new clothes exaggerated his awkwardness.* [C16: from Latin *exaggerāre* to magnify, from *aggerāre* to heap, from *agger* heap] —**ex'agger,atingly** *adv.* —**ex,agger'ation** *n.* —**ex'aggerative** *or* **ex'aggeratory** *adj.* —**ex'agger,ator** *n.*

exaggerated (ɪg'zædʒəˌreɪtɪd) *adj.* **1.** unduly or excessively magnified; enlarged beyond truth or reasonableness. **2.** *Pathol.* abnormally enlarged: *an exaggerated spleen.* —**ex'agger,atedly** *adv.*

ex all *adv. Finance.* without the right to any benefits: *shares quoted ex all.*

exalt (ɪg'zɔːlt) *vb.* (*tr.*) **1.** to raise or elevate in rank, position, dignity, etc. **2.** to praise highly; glorify; extol. **3.** to stimulate the mind or imagination of; excite. **4.** to increase the intensity of (a colour, etc.). **5.** to fill with joy or delight; elate. **6.** *Obsolete.* to lift up physically. [C15: from Latin *exaltāre* to raise, from *altus* high] —**ex'alter** *n.*

exaltation (ˌɛgzɔːl'teɪʃən) *n.* **1.** the act of exalting or state of being exalted. **2.** a feeling of intense well-being or exhilaration; elation; rapture. **3.** a flock of larks.

exalted (ɪg'zɔːltɪd) *adj.* **1.** high or elevated in rank, position, dignity, etc. **2.** elevated in character; noble; lofty: *an exalted ideal.* **3.** *Informal.* excessively high; inflated: *he has an exalted opinion of himself.* **4.** intensely excited; elated. —**ex'altedly** *adv.* —**ex'altedness** *n.*

exam (ɪg'zæm) *n.* short for **examination.**

examen (ɪg'zeɪmɛn) *n. R.C. Church.* an examination of conscience, usually made daily by Jesuits and others. [C17: from Latin: tongue of a balance, from *exigere* to thrust out, from *agere* to thrust]

examination (ɪgˌzæmɪ'neɪʃən) *n.* **1.** the act of examining or state of being examined. **2.** *Education.* **a.** written exercises, oral questions, or practical tasks, set to test a candidate's knowledge and skill. **b.** (*as modifier*): *an examination paper.* **3.** *Med.* **a.** physical inspection of a patient or parts of his body, in order to verify health or diagnose disease. **b.** laboratory study of secretory or excretory products, tissue samples, etc., esp. in order to diagnose disease. **4.** *Law.* the formal interrogation of a person on oath, esp. of an accused or a witness. —**ex,ami'national** *adj.*

examine (ɪg'zæmɪn) *vb.* (*tr.*) **1.** to look at, inspect, or scrutinize carefully or in detail; investigate. **2.** *Education.* to test the knowledge or skill of (a candidate) in (a subject or activity) by written or oral questions or by practical tests. **3.** *Law.* to interrogate (a witness or accused person) formally on oath. **4.** *Med.* to investigate the state of health of (a patient). [C14: from Old French *examiner,* from Latin *exāmināre* to weigh, from *exāmen* means of weighing; see EXAMEN] —**ex'aminable** *adj.* —**ex'aminer** *n.* —**ex'amining** *adj.*

examinee (ɪgˌzæmɪ'niː) *n.* a person who takes an examination.

examine-in-chief *vb.* (*tr.*) *Law.* to examine (one's own witness) in attempting to adduce a case. Compare **cross-examine.** —**ex,ami'nation-in-chief** *n.*

example (ɪg'zɑːmpᵊl) *n.* **1.** a specimen or instance that is typical of the group or set of which it forms part; sample. **2.** a person, action, thing, etc., that is worthy of imitation; pattern: *you must set an example to the younger children.* **3.** a precedent, illustration of a principle, or model: *an example in a maths book.* **4.** a punishment or the recipient of a punishment serving or intended to serve as a warning: *the headmaster made an example of him.* **5. for example.** as an illustration; for instance. ~*vb.* **6.** (*tr.; now usually passive*) to present an example of; exemplify. [C14: from Old French, from Latin *exemplum* pattern, from *eximere* to take out, from EX-[1] + *emere* to purchase]

exanimate (ɪg'zænɪmɪt, -ˌmeɪt) *adj. Rare.* lacking life; inanimate. [C16: from Latin *exanimāre* to deprive of air, kill, from *anima* breath, spirit] —**ex,ani'mation** *n.*

exanthema (ˌɛksæn'θiːmə) *or* **exanthem** (ɛk'sænθəm) *n., pl.* **-themata** (-'θiːmətə), **-themas,** *or* **-thems.** a skin eruption or rash occurring as a symptom in a disease such as measles or scarlet fever. [C17: via Late Latin from Greek, from *exanthein* to burst forth, from *anthein* to blossom, from *anthos* flower] —**exanthematous** (ˌɛksæn'θɛmətəs) *or* **exanthematic** (ɛkˌsænθɪ'mætɪk) *adj.*

exarate ('ɛksəˌreɪt) *adj.* (of the pupa of such insects as ants and bees) having the legs, wings, antennae, etc., free and movable. [C19: from Latin *exarātus,* literally: ploughed up (apparently referring to the way this type of pupa throws off the larval skin), from *exarāre,* from *arā* plough]

exarch[1] ('ɛksɑːk) *n.* **1.** the head of certain autonomous Orthodox Christian Churches, such as that of Bulgaria and Cyprus. **2.** any of certain Eastern Orthodox bishops, lower in rank than a patriarch but higher than a metropolitan. **3.** the governor of a province in the Byzantine Empire. [C16: from Late Latin *exarchus* overseer, from Greek *exarkhos,* from *exarkhein* to take the lead, from *arkhein* to rule] —**ex'archal** *adj.*

exarch[2] ('ɛksɑːk) *adj. Botany.* (of a xylem strand) having the first-formed xylem external to that formed later. Compare **endarch, mesarch.** [C19: from EX-[1] (outside) + Greek *arkhē* beginning, origin]

exarchate ('ɛksɑːˌkeɪt, ɛk'sɑːkeɪt) *or* **exarchy** ('ɛksɑːkɪ) *n., pl.* **-chates** *or* **-chies.** the office, rank, or jurisdiction of an exarch.

exasperate (ɪg'zɑːspəˌreɪt) *vb.* (*tr.*) **1.** to cause great irritation or anger to; infuriate. **2.** to cause (an unpleasant feeling, condition, etc.) to worsen; aggravate. ~*adj.* **3.** *Botany.* having a rough prickly surface because of the presence of hard projecting points. [C16: from Latin *exasperāre* to make rough, from *asper* rough] —**ex'asper,atedly** *adv.* —**ex'asper,ater** *n.* —**ex'asper,ating** *adj.* —**ex'asper,atingly** *adv.* —**ex,asper'ation** *n.*

exc. *abbrev. for:* **1.** excellent. **2.** except(ed). **3.** exception. **4.** excursion.

Exc. *abbrev. for* Excellency.

ex cathedra (ɛks kə'θiːdrə) *adj., adv.* **1.** with authority. **2.** *R.C. Church.* (of doctrines of faith or morals) defined by the pope as infallibly true, to be accepted by all Catholics. [Latin, literally: from the chair]

excaudate (ɛks'kɔːdeɪt) *adj. Zoology.* having no tail or tail-like process; tailless.

excavate ('ɛkskəˌveɪt) *vb.* **1.** to remove (soil, earth, etc.) by digging; dig out. **2.** to make (a hole, cavity, or tunnel) in (solid matter) by hollowing or removing the centre or inner part: *to excavate a tooth.* **3.** to unearth (buried objects) methodically in an attempt to discover information about the past. [C16: from Latin *excavāre,* from *cavāre* to make hollow, from *cavus* hollow] —ˌ**exca'vation** *n.*

excavator ('ɛkskəˌveɪtə) *n.* **1.** a powered machine for digging earth, gravel, sand, etc., esp. a caterpillar tractor so equipped. **2.** any person, animal, or thing that excavates.

exceed (ɪk'siːd) *vb.* **1.** to be superior to (a person or thing), esp. in size or quality; excel. **2.** (*tr.*) to go beyond the limit or bounds of: *to exceed one's income; exceed a speed limit.* **3.** to be greater in degree or quantity than (a person or thing). [C14: from Latin *excēdere* to go beyond, from *cēdere* to go] —**ex'ceedable** *adj.* —**ex'ceeder** *n.*

exceeding (ɪk'siːdɪŋ) *adj.* **1.** very great; exceptional or excessive. ~*adv.* **2.** an archaic word for **exceedingly.**

exceedingly (ɪk'siːdɪŋlɪ) *adv.* to a very great or unusual degree; extremely; exceptionally.

excel (ɪk'sɛl) *vb.* **-cels, -celling, -celled.** **1.** to be superior to (another or others); surpass. **2.** (*intr.;* foll. by *in* or *at*) to be outstandingly good or proficient: *he excels at tennis.* [C15: from Latin *excellere* to rise up]

excellence ('ɛksələns) *n.* **1.** the state or quality of excelling or being exceptionally good; extreme merit; superiority. **2.** an action, characteristic, feature, etc., in which a person excels. —'**excellent** *adj.* —'**excellently** *adv.*

Excellency ('ɛksələnsɪ) *or* **Excellence** *n., pl.* **-lencies** *or* **-lences.** **1.** (usually preceded by *Your, His,* or *Her*) a title used to address or refer to a high-ranking official, such as an ambassador or governor. **2.** *R.C. Church.* a title of bishops and archbishops in many non-English-speaking countries.

excelsior (ɪk'sɛlsɪˌɔː) *interj., adv., n.* **1.** excellent: used as a motto and as a trademark for various products, esp. in the U.S. for fine wood shavings used for packing breakable objects. **2.** upwards. [C19: from Latin: higher]

except (ɪk'sɛpt) *prep.* **1.** Also: **except for.** other than; apart from; with the exception of: *he likes everyone except you; except for this mistake, you did very well.* **2. except that.** (*conj.*) but for the fact that; were it not true that. ~*conj.* **3.** an archaic word for **unless.** **4.** *Informal; not standard in the U.S.* except that; but for the fact that: *I would have arrived earlier, except I lost my way.* ~*vb.* **5.** (*tr.*) to leave out; omit; exclude. **6.** (*intr.;* often foll. by *to*) *Rare.* to take exception; object. [C14: from Old French *excepter* to leave out, from Latin *exceptāre,* from *excipere* to take out, from *capere* to take]

excepting (ɪk'sɛptɪŋ) *prep.* **1.** excluding; except; except for (esp. in the phrase **not excepting**). ~*conj.* **2.** an archaic word for **unless.**

exception (ɪk'sɛpʃən) *n.* **1.** the act of excepting or fact of being excepted; omission. **2.** anything excluded from or not in conformance with a general rule, principle, class, etc. **3.** criticism, esp. when it is adverse; objection. **4.** *Law.* (formerly) a formal objection in the course of legal proceedings. **5.** *Law.* a clause or term in a document that restricts the usual legal effect of the document. **6. take exception. a.** (usually foll. by *to*) to make objections (to); demur (at). **b.** (often foll. by *at*) to be offended (by); be resentful (at).

exceptionable (ɪk'sɛpʃənəbᵊl) *adj.* open to or subject to objection; objectionable. —**ex'ceptionableness** *n.* —**ex'ceptionably** *adv.*
exceptional (ɪk'sɛpʃənᵊl) *adj.* **1.** forming an exception; not ordinary. **2.** having much more than average intelligence, ability, or skill. —**ex'ceptionally** *adv.*
exceptive (ɪk'sɛptɪv) *adj.* **1.** relating to or forming an exception. **2.** *Rare.* tending to take exception or find fault.
excerpt *n.* ('ɛksɜːpt). **1.** a part or passage taken from a book, speech, play, etc., and considered on its own; extract. ~*vb.* (ɛk'sɜːpt). **2.** (*tr.*) to take (a part or passage) from a book, speech, play, etc. [C17: from Latin *excerptum,* literally: (something) picked out, from *excerpere* to select, from *carpere* to pluck] —**ex'cerptor** *n.* —**ex'cerptible** *adj.* —**ex'cerption** *n.*
excess *n.* (ɪk'sɛs, 'ɛksɛs). **1.** the state or act of going beyond normal, sufficient, or permitted limits. **2.** an immoderate or abnormal amount, number, extent, or degree too much or too many: *an excess of tolerance.* **3.** the amount, number, extent, or degree by which one thing exceeds another. **4.** *Chem.* a quantity of a reagent that is greater than the quantity required to complete a reaction: *add an excess of acid.* **5.** overindulgence or intemperance. **6.** *Insurance, chiefly Brit.* a specified contribution towards the cost of a claim, stipulated on certain insurance policies as being payable by the policyholder. **7. in excess of.** of more than; over. **8. to excess.** to an inordinate extent; immoderately: *he drinks to excess.* ~*adj.* ('ɛksɛs, ɪk'sɛs). (*usually prenominal*) **9.** more than normal, necessary, or permitted; surplus: *excess weight.* **10.** payable as a result of previous underpayment: *excess postage; an excess fare for a railway journey.* [C14: from Latin *excessus,* from *excēdere* to go beyond; see EXCEED]
excess demand *n. Economics.* a situation in which the market demand for a commodity is greater than its market supply, thus causing its market price to rise.
excessive (ɪk'sɛsɪv) *adj.* exceeding the normal or permitted extents or limits; immoderate; inordinate. —**ex'cessively** *adv.* —**ex'cessiveness** *n.*
excess luggage *or* **baggage** *n.* luggage that is greater in weight or in number of pieces than an airline, etc., will carry free.
excess supply *n. Economics.* a situation in which the market supply of a commodity is greater than the market demand for it, thus causing its market price to fall.
exch. *abbrev. for:* **1.** exchange. **2.** exchequer.
exchange (ɪks'tʃeɪndʒ) *vb.* **1.** (*tr.*) to give up, part with, or transfer (one thing) for an equivalent: *to exchange gifts; to exchange francs for dollars.* **2.** (*tr.*) to give and receive (information, ideas, etc.); interchange. **3.** (*tr.*) to replace (one thing) with another, esp. to replace unsatisfactory goods. **4.** to transfer or hand over (goods) in return for the equivalent value in kind rather than in money; barter; trade. **5.** (*tr.*) *Chess.* to capture and surrender (pieces, usually of the same value) in a single sequence of moves. ~*n.* **6.** the act or process of exchanging. **7. a.** anything given or received as an equivalent, replacement, or substitute for something else. **b.** (*as modifier*): *an exchange student.* **8.** an argument or quarrel; altercation: *the two men had a bitter exchange.* **9.** Also called: **telephone exchange.** a switching centre in which telephone lines are interconnected. **10. a.** a place where securities or commodities are sold, bought, or traded, esp. by brokers or merchants: *a stock exchange; a corn exchange.* **b.** (*as modifier*): *an exchange broker.* **11. a.** the system by which commercial debts between parties in different places are settled by commercial documents, esp. bills of exchange, instead of by direct payment of money. **b.** the percentage or fee charged for accepting payment in this manner. **12.** a transfer or interchange of sums of money of equivalent value, as between different national currencies or different issues of the same currency. **13.** (*often pl.*) the cheques, drafts, bills, etc., exchanged or settled between banks in a clearing house. **14.** *Chess.* the capture by both players of pieces of equal value, usually on consecutive moves. **15. win** (*or* **lose**) **the exchange.** *Chess.* to win (or lose) a rook in return for a bishop or knight. **16.** *Med.* another word for **transfusion** (sense 2). **17.** *Physics.* a process in which a particle is transferred between two nucleons, such as the transfer of a meson between two nucleons. ~See also **bill of exchange, exchange rate, foreign exchange, labour exchange.** [C14: from Anglo-French *eschaungier,* from Vulgar Latin *excambiāre* (unattested), from Latin *cambīre* to barter] —**ex'changeable** *adj.* —**ex,changea'bility** *n.* —**ex'changeably** *adv.* —**ex'changer** *n.*
exchange force *n. Physics.* **1.** a force between two elementary particles resulting from the exchange of a virtual particle. **2.** the force causing the alignment of the magnetic dipole moments of atoms in ferromagnetic materials.
exchange rate *n.* the rate at which the currency unit of one country may be exchanged for that of another.
Exchange Rate Mechanism *n.* the mechanism used in the European Monetary System in which participating governments commit themselves to maintain the values of their currencies in relation to the ECU, taking action to correct any disparity in excess of 2.25% or, for some weaker currencies, 6%. Abbrev.: **ERM.**
exchequer (ɪks'tʃɛkə) *n.* **1.** (*often cap.*) *Government.* (in Britain and certain other countries) the accounting department of the Treasury, responsible for receiving and issuing funds. **2.** *Informal.* personal funds; finances. [C13 (in the sense: chessboard, counting table): from Old French *eschequier,* from *eschec* CHECK]
excide (ɪk'saɪd) *vb.* (*tr.*) *Rare.* to cut out; excise. [C18: from Latin *excīdere* to cut off, from *caedere* to cut]
excimer ('ɛk,saɪmə) *n. Physics.* an excited dimer formed by the association of excited and unexcited molecules, which would remain dissociated in the ground state.
excipient (ɪk'sɪpɪənt) *n.* an inert substance, such as sugar or gum, used to prepare drugs in a form suitable for oral administration. [C18: from Latin *excipiēns* excepting, from *excipere* to EXCEPT]
excisable (ɪk'saɪzəbᵊl) *adj.* liable to an excise tax.
excise[1] *n.* ('ɛksaɪz, ɛk'saɪz). **1.** Also called: **excise tax.** a tax on goods, such as spirits, produced for the home market. **2.** a tax paid for a licence to carry out various trades, sports, etc. **3.** *Brit.* that section of the government service responsible for the collection of excise, now the Board of Customs and Excise. ~*vb.* (ɪk'saɪz). **4.** (*tr.*) *Rare.* to compel (a person) to pay excise. [C15: probably from Middle Dutch *excijs,* probably from Old French *assise* a sitting, assessment, from Latin *assidēre* to sit beside, assist in judging, from *sedēre* to sit] —**ex'cisable** *adj.*
excise[2] (ɪk'saɪz) *vb.* (*tr.*) **1.** to delete (a passage, sentence, etc.); expunge. **2.** to remove (an organ, structure, or part) surgically. [C16: from Latin *excīdere* to cut down; see EXCIDE] —**excision** (ɪk'sɪʒən) *n.*
exciseman ('ɛksaɪz,mæn) *n., pl.* **-men.** *Brit.* (formerly) a government agent whose function was to collect excise and prevent smuggling.
excitable (ɪk'saɪtəbᵊl) *adj.* **1.** easily excited; volatile. **2.** (esp. of a nerve) ready to respond to a stimulus. —**ex,cita'bility** *or* **ex'citableness** *n.* —**ex'citably** *adv.*
excitant (ɪk'saɪtᵊnt, 'ɛksɪtənt) *adj. also* **excitative** (ɪk'saɪtətɪv) *or* **excitatory** (ɪk'saɪtətərɪ). **1.** able to excite or stimulate. ~*n.* **2.** something, such as a drug or other agent, able to excite; stimulant.
excitation (,ɛksɪ'teɪʃən) *n.* **1.** the act or process of exciting or state of being excited. **2.** a means of exciting or cause of excitement. **3. a.** the current in a field coil of a generator, motor, etc., or the magnetizing current in a transformer. **b.** (*as modifier*): *an excitation current.* **4.** the action of a stimulus on an animal or plant organ, inducing it to respond.
excite (ɪk'saɪt) *vb.* (*tr.*) **1.** to arouse (a person) to strong feeling, esp. to pleasurable anticipation or nervous agitation. **2.** to arouse or elicit (an emotion, response, etc.); evoke: *her answers excited curiosity.* **3.** to cause or bring about; stir up: *to excite a rebellion.* **4.** to arouse sexually. **5.** *Physiol.* to cause a response in or increase the activity of (an organ, tissue, or part); stimulate. **6.** to raise (an atom, molecule, electron, nucleus, etc.) from the ground state to a higher energy level. **7.** to supply electricity to (the coils of a generator or motor) in order to create a magnetic field. **8.** to supply a signal to a stage of a valve or transistor circuit. [C14: from Latin *excitāre,* from *exciēre* to stimulate, from *ciēre* to set in motion, rouse]
excited (ɪk'saɪtɪd) *adj.* **1.** emotionally aroused, esp. to pleasure or agitation. **2.** characterized by excitement: *an excited dance.* **3.** sexually aroused. **4.** (of an atom, molecule, etc.) having an energy level above the ground state. —**ex'citedly** *adv.* —**ex'citedness** *n.*
excitement (ɪk'saɪtmənt) *n.* **1.** the state of being excited. **2.** a person or thing that excites; stimulation or thrill.
exciter (ɪk'saɪtə) *n.* **1.** a person or thing that excites. **2.** a small generator that excites a larger machine. **3.** an oscillator producing a transmitter's carrier wave.
exciting (ɪk'saɪtɪŋ) *adj.* causing excitement; stirring; stimulating. —**ex'citingly** *adv.*
exciton ('ɛksaɪ,tɒn) *n.* a mobile neutral entity in a crystalline solid consisting of an excited electron bound to the hole produced by its excitation. [C20: from EXCIT(ATION) + -ON]
excitor (ɪk'saɪtə) *n.* **1.** a nerve that, when stimulated, causes increased activity in the organ or part it supplies. **2.** a variant spelling of **exciter.**
excl. *abbrev. for:* **1.** exclamation. **2.** excluding. **3.** exclusive.
exclaim (ɪk'skleɪm) *vb.* to cry out or speak suddenly or excitedly, as from surprise, delight, horror, etc. [C16: from Latin *exclāmāre,* from *clāmāre* to shout] —**ex'claimer** *n.*
exclamation (,ɛksklə'meɪʃən) *n.* **1.** an abrupt, emphatic, or excited cry or utterance; interjection; ejaculation. **2.** the act of exclaiming. —**,excla'mational** *adj.*
exclamation mark *or U.S.* **point** *n.* **1.** the punctuation mark ! used after exclamations and vehement commands. **2.** this mark used for any other purpose, as to draw attention to an obvious mistake, in road warning signs, (in chess commentaries) beside the notation of a move considered a good one, (in mathematics) as a symbol of the factorial function, or (in logic) occurring with an existential quantifier.
exclamatory (ɪk'sklæmətərɪ, -trɪ) *adj.* using, containing, or relating to exclamations. —**ex'clamatorily** *adv.*
exclaustration (,ɛksklɔː'streɪʃən) *n.* the return of a monk or nun to the outside world after being released from his or her religious vows. [from EX-[1] + Latin *claustrum* cloister]
exclave ('ɛkskleɪv) *n.* a part of a country entirely surrounded by foreign territory: viewed from the position of the home country.

Compare **enclave.** [C20: from EX-[1] + *-clave,* on the model of ENCLAVE]
exclosure (ɪk'skləʊʒə) *n.* an area of land, esp. in a forest, fenced round to keep out unwanted animals.
exclude (ɪk'sklu:d) *vb. (tr.)* **1.** to keep out; prevent from entering. **2.** to reject or not consider; leave out. **3.** to expel forcibly; eject. [C14: from Latin *exclūdere,* from *claudere* to shut] —**ex'cludable** *or* **ex'cludible** *adj.* —**ex'cluder** *n.*
excluded middle *n. Logic.* the principle that every proposition is either true or false, so that there is no third truth-value and no statements lack truth-value.
exclusion (ɪk'sklu:ʒən) *n.* the act or an instance of excluding or the state of being excluded. —**ex'clusionary** *adj.*
exclusionist (ɪk'sklu:ʒənɪst) *adj.* **1.** *Chiefly U.S.* denoting or relating to a policy of excluding various types of immigrants, imports, etc. ~*n.* **2.** a supporter of a policy of exclusion. —**ex'clusion,ism** *n.*
exclusion principle *n.* See **Pauli exclusion principle.**
exclusive (ɪk'sklu:sɪv) *adj.* **1.** excluding all else; rejecting other considerations, possibilities, events, etc.: *an exclusive preoccupation with money.* **2.** belonging to a particular individual or group and to no other; not shared: *exclusive rights; an exclusive story.* **3.** belonging to or catering for a privileged minority, esp. a fashionable clique: *an exclusive restaurant.* **4.** *(postpositive;* foll. by *to)* limited (to); found only (in): *this model is exclusive to Harrods.* **5.** single; unique; only: *the exclusive means of transport on the island was the bicycle.* **6.** separate and incompatible: *mutually exclusive principles.* **7.** *(immediately postpositive)* not including the numbers, dates, letters, etc., mentioned: *1980–84 exclusive.* **8.** *(postpositive;* foll. by *of)* except (for); not taking account (of): *exclusive of bonus payments, you will earn this amount.* **9.** *Commerce.* (of a contract, agreement, etc.) binding the parties to do business only with each other with respect to a class of goods or services. **10.** *Logic.* (of a disjunction) true if only one rather than both of its component propositions is true. Compare **inclusive** (sense 4). ~*n.* **11.** an exclusive story; a story reported in only one newspaper. —**ex'clusively** *adv.* —**ex'clusiveness** *or* **exclusivity** (,ɛksklu:'sɪvɪtɪ) *n.*
exclusive economic zone *n.* the coastal water and sea bed around a country's shores, to which it claims exclusive rights for fishing, oil exploration, etc. Sometimes shortened to **economic zone.**
exclusive or *n. Logic.* the connective that gives the value *true* to a disjunction if one or other, but not both, of the disjuncts are true. Also called: **exclusive disjunction.** Compare **inclusive or.**
exclusive OR circuit *or* **gate** *n. Electronics.* a computer logic circuit having two or more input wires and one output wire and giving a high-voltage output signal if a low-voltage signal is fed to one or more, but not all, of the input wires. Compare **OR circuit.**
excogitate (ɛks'kɒdʒɪ,teɪt) *vb. (tr.)* **1.** to devise, invent, or contrive. **2.** to think out in detail. [C16: from Latin *excōgitāre,* from *cōgitāre* to ponder, COGITATE] —**ex'cogitable** *adj.* —**ex,cogi'tation** *n.* —**ex'cogitative** *adj.* —**ex'cogi,tator** *n.*
excommunicate *R.C. Church.* ~*vb.* (,ɛkskə'mju:nɪ,keɪt). **1.** *(tr.)* to sentence (a member of the Church) to exclusion from the communion of believers and from the privileges and public prayers of the Church. ~*adj.* (,ɛkskə'mju:nɪkɪt, -,keɪt). **2.** having incurred such a sentence. ~*n.* (,ɛkskə'mju:nɪkɪt, -,keɪt). **3.** an excommunicated person. [C15: from Late Latin *excommūnicāre,* literally: to exclude from the community, from Latin *commūnis* COMMON] —,**excom'municable** *adj.* —,**ex-com,muni'cation** *n.* —,**excom'municative** *or* ,**excom'municatory** *adj.* —,**excom'municator** *n.*
excoriate (ɪk'skɔ:rɪ,eɪt) *vb. (tr.)* **1.** to strip (the skin) from (a person or animal); flay. **2.** *Med.* to lose (a superficial area of skin), as by scratching, the application of chemicals, etc. **3.** to denounce vehemently; censure severely. [C15: from Late Latin *excoriāre* to strip, flay, from Latin *corium* skin, hide] —**ex,cori'ation** *n.*
excrement ('ɛkskrɪmənt) *n.* waste matter discharged from the body, esp. faeces; excreta. [C16: from Latin *excrēmentum,* from *excernere* to sift, EXCRETE] —**excremental** (,ɛkskrɪ'mɛntᵊl) *or* **excrementitious** (,ɛkskrɪmɛn'tɪʃəs) *adj.*
excrescence (ɪk'skrɛsᵊns) *n.* a projection or protuberance, esp. an outgrowth from an organ or part of the body. —**excrescential** (,ɛkskrɪ'sɛnʃəl) *adj.*
excrescency (ɪk'skrɛsənsɪ) *n., pl.* **-cies.** **1.** the state or condition of being excrescent. **2.** another word for **excrescence.**
excrescent (ɪk'skrɛsᵊnt) *adj.* **1.** denoting, relating to, or resembling an abnormal outgrowth. **2.** uselessly added; not essential; superfluous. **3.** denoting or relating to a speech sound or letter inserted into a word without etymological justification, such as the *b* in *nimble.* [C17: from Latin *excrēscēns,* from *excrēscere,* from *crēscere* to grow] —**ex'crescently** *adv.*
excreta (ɪk'skri:tə) *pl. n.* waste matter, such as urine, faeces, or sweat, discharged from the body; excrement. [C19: New Latin, from Latin *excernere* to EXCRETE] —**ex'cretal** *adj.*
excrete (ɪk'skri:t) *vb.* **1.** to discharge (waste matter, such as urine, sweat, carbon dioxide, or faeces) from the body through the kidneys, skin, lungs, bowels, etc. **2.** (of plants) to eliminate (waste matter, such as carbon dioxide and salts) through the leaves, roots, etc. [C17: from Latin *excernere* to separate, discharge, from *cernere* to sift] —**ex'creter** *n.* —**ex'cretion** *n.* —**ex'cretive** *or* **ex'cretory** *adj.*
excruciate (ɪk'skru:ʃɪ,eɪt) *vb. (tr.)* **1.** to inflict mental suffering on; torment. **2.** *Obsolete.* to inflict physical pain on; torture. [C16: from Latin *excruciāre,* from *cruciāre* to crucify, from *crux* cross] —**ex,cruci'ation** *n.*
excruciating (ɪk'skru:ʃɪ,eɪtɪŋ) *adj.* **1.** unbearably painful; agonizing. **2.** intense; extreme: *he took excruciating pains to do it well.* **3.** *Informal.* irritating; trying. **4.** *Humorous.* very bad: *an excruciating pun.* —**ex'cruci,atingly** *adv.*
exculpate ('ɛkskʌl,peɪt, ɪk'skʌlpeɪt) *vb. (tr.)* to free from blame or guilt; vindicate or exonerate. [C17: from Medieval Latin *exculpāre,* from Latin EX-[1] + *culpāre* to blame, from *culpa* fault, blame] —**exculpable** (ɪk'skʌlpəbᵊl) *adj.* —,**excul'pation** *n.* —**ex'culpatory** *adj.*
excurrent (ɛk'skʌrənt) *adj.* **1.** *Zoology.* having an outward flow, as certain pores in sponges, ducts, etc. **2.** *Botany.* **a.** (of veins) extending beyond the margin of the leaf. **b.** having an undivided main stem or trunk, as the spruce and other conifers. **3.** flowing or running in an outward direction. [C19: from Latin *excurrere* to run forth; see EXCURSION]
excursion (ɪk'skɜ:ʃən, -ʒən) *n.* **1.** a short outward and return journey, esp. for relaxation, sightseeing, etc.; outing. **2.** a group of people going on such a journey. **3.** *(modifier)* of or relating to special reduced rates offered on certain journeys by rail: *an excursion ticket.* **4.** a digression or deviation; diversion: *an excursion into politics.* **5.** (formerly) a raid or attack. **6.** *Physics.* **a.** a movement from an equilibrium position, as in an oscillation. **b.** the magnitude of this displacement. **7.** the normal movement of a movable bodily organ or part from its resting position, such as the lateral movement of the lower jaw. **8.** *Machinery.* the locus of a point on a moving part, esp. the deflection of a whirling shaft. [C16: from Latin *excursiō* an attack, from *excurrere* to run out, from *currere* to run]
excursionist (ɪk'skɜ:ʃənɪst, -ʒənɪst) *n.* a person who goes on an excursion.
excursive (ɪk'skɜ:sɪv) *adj.* **1.** tending to digress. **2.** involving detours; rambling. [C17: from Latin *excursus,* from *excurrere* to run forth] —**ex'cursively** *adv.* —**ex'cursiveness** *n.*
excursus (ɛk'skɜ:səs) *n., pl.* **-suses** *or* **-sus.** an incidental digression from the main topic under discussion or from the main story in a narrative. [C19: from Latin: a running forth, from *excurrere* to run out]
excusatory (ɪk'skju:zətərɪ, -trɪ) *adj.* tending to or intended to excuse; apologetic.
excuse *vb.* (ɪk'skju:z). *(tr.)* **1.** to pardon or forgive: *he always excuses her unpunctuality.* **2.** to seek pardon or exemption for (a person, esp. oneself): *to excuse oneself for one's mistakes.* **3.** to make allowances for; judge leniently: *to excuse someone's ignorance.* **4.** to serve as an apology or explanation for; vindicate or justify: *her age excuses her behaviour.* **5.** to exempt from a task, obligation, etc.: *you are excused making breakfast.* **6.** to dismiss or allow to leave: *he asked them to excuse him.* **7.** to seek permission for (someone, esp. oneself) to leave: *he excused himself and left.* **8.** **be excused.** *Euphemistic.* to go to the lavatory. **9.** **excuse me!** an expression used to catch someone's attention or to apologize for an interruption, disagreement, or social indiscretion. ~*n.* (ɪk'skju:s). **10.** an explanation offered in defence of some fault or offensive behaviour or as a reason for not fulfilling an obligation, etc.: *he gave no excuse for his rudeness.* **11.** *Informal.* an inferior example of something specified; makeshift substitute: *she is a poor excuse for a hostess.* **12.** the act of excusing. [C13: from Latin *excusāre,* from EX-[1] + *-cūsare,* from *causa* cause, accusation] —**ex'cusable** *adj.* —**ex'cusableness** *n.* —**ex'cusably** *adv.*
excuse-me *n.* a dance in which a person may take another's partner.
ex-directory *adj. Chiefly Brit.* not listed in a telephone directory, by request, and not disclosed to inquirers. U.S. and Canadian term: **unlisted.**
ex div. *abbrev. for* ex dividend.
ex dividend *adv.* without the right to the current dividend: *to quote shares ex dividend.* Compare **cum dividend.**
exeat ('ɛksɪət) *n. Brit.* **1.** leave of absence from school or some other institution. **2.** a bishop's permission for a priest to leave his diocese in order to take up an appointment elsewhere. [C18: Latin, literally: he may go out, from *exīre*]
exec. *abbrev. for:* **1.** executive. **2.** executor.
execrable ('ɛksɪkrəbᵊl) *adj.* **1.** deserving to be execrated; abhorrent. **2.** of very poor quality: *an execrable meal.* [C14: from Latin *exsecrābilis,* from *exsecrārī* to EXECRATE] —**'execrableness** *n.* —**'execrably** *adv.*
execrate ('ɛksɪ,kreɪt) *vb.* **1.** *(tr.)* to loathe; detest; abhor. **2.** *(tr.)* to profess great abhorrence for; denounce; deplore. **3.** to curse (a person or thing); damn. [C16: from Latin *exsecrārī* to curse, from EX-[1] + *-secrārī* from *sacer* SACRED] —,**exe'cration** *n.* —**'exe,crative** *or* **'exe,cratory** *adj.* —**'exe,cratively** *adv.*
executant (ɪg'zɛkjutənt) *n.* a performer, esp. of musical works.
execute ('ɛksɪ,kju:t) *vb. (tr.)* **1.** to put (a condemned person) to death; inflict capital punishment upon. **2.** to carry out; complete; perform; do: *to execute an order.* **3.** to perform; accomplish; effect: *to execute a pirouette.* **4.** to make or produce: *to*

execute a drawing. **5.** to carry into effect (a judicial sentence, the law, etc.); enforce. **6.** *Law.* to comply with legal formalities in order to render (a deed, etc.) effective, as by signing, sealing, and delivering. **7.** to sign (a will) in the presence of witnesses and in accordance with other legal formalities. **8.** to carry out the terms of (a contract, will, etc.). [C14: from Old French *executer,* back formation from *executeur* EXECUTOR] —'**exe,cutable** *adj.* —'**exe,cuter** *n.*

execution (,ɛksɪ'kjuːʃən) *n.* **1.** the act or process of executing. **2.** the carrying out or undergoing of a sentence of death. **3.** the style or manner in which something is accomplished or performed; technique: *as a pianist his execution is poor.* **4. a.** the enforcement of the judgment of a court of law. **b.** the writ ordering such enforcement.

executioner (,ɛksɪ'kjuːʃənə) *n.* **1.** an official charged with carrying out the death sentence passed upon a condemned person. **2.** an assassin, esp. one appointed by a political or criminal organization.

executive (ɪg'zɛkjʊtɪv) *n.* **1. a.** a person or group responsible for the administration of a project, activity, or business. **b.** (*as modifier*): *executive duties; an executive position.* **2. a.** the branch of government responsible for carrying out laws, decrees, etc.; administration. **b.** any administration. Compare **judiciary, legislature.** ~*adj.* **3.** having the function or purpose of carrying plans, orders, laws, etc., into practical effect. **4.** of, relating to, or designed for an executive: *the executive suite.* **5.** *Informal.* of the most expensive or exclusive type: *executive housing; executive class.* —**ex'ecutively** *adv.*

Executive Council *n.* (in Australia and New Zealand) a body consisting of ministers of the Crown presided over by the Governor or Governor-General that formally approves Cabinet decisions, etc.

executive officer *n.* **1.** the second-in-command of any of certain military units. **2.** a specialist seaman officer, responsible under the captain for the routine efficient running of the ship in the U.S., British (formerly), and certain other navies.

executive session *n. U.S. government.* a session of the Senate for the discussion of executive business, such as the ratification of treaties: formerly held in secret.

executor (ɪg'zɛkjʊtə) *n.* **1.** *Law.* a person appointed by a testator to carry out the wishes expressed in his will. **2.** a person who executes. [C13: from Anglo-French *executour,* from Latin *execūtor,* from EX-[1] + *sequi* follow] —**ex,ecu'torial** *adj.* —**ex'ecutor,ship** *n.*

executory (ɪg'zɛkjʊtərɪ, -trɪ) *adj.* **1.** (of a law, agreement, etc.) coming into operation at a future date; not yet effective: *an executory contract.* **2.** executive; administrative.

executrix (ɪg'zɛkjʊtrɪks) *n., pl.* **executrices** (ɪg,zɛkjʊ'traɪsiːz) *or* **executrixes.** *Law.* a female executor.

exedra ('ɛksɪdrə, ɛk'siː-) *n.* **1.** a building, room, portico, or apse containing a continuous bench, used in ancient Greece and Rome for holding discussions. **2.** an outdoor bench in a recess. [C18: via Latin from Greek, from *hedra* seat]

exegesis (,ɛksɪ'dʒiːsɪs) *n., pl.* **-ses** (-siːz). explanation or critical interpretation of a text, esp. of the Bible. Compare **eisegesis.** [C17: from Greek, from *exēgeisthai* to interpret, from EX-[1] + *hēgeisthai* to guide]

exegete ('ɛksɪ,dʒiːt) *or* **exegetist** (,ɛksɪ'dʒiːtɪst, -'dʒɛt-) *n.* a person who practises exegesis. [C18: from Greek *exēgētēs,* from *exēgeisthai* to interpret; see EXEGESIS]

exegetic (,ɛksɪ'dʒɛtɪk) *or* **exegetical** *adj.* of or relating to exegesis; expository. —,**exe'getically** *adv.*

exegetics (,ɛksɪ'dʒɛtɪks) *n.* (*functioning as sing.*) the scientific study of exegesis and exegetical methods.

exemplar (ɪg'zɛmplə, -plɑː) *n.* **1.** a person or thing to be copied or imitated; model. **2.** a typical specimen or instance; example. **3.** a copy of a book or text on which further printings have been based. [C14: from Latin *exemplarium* model, from *exemplum* EXAMPLE]

exemplary (ɪg'zɛmplərɪ) *adj.* **1.** fit for imitation; model: *an exemplary performance.* **2.** serving as a warning; admonitory: *an exemplary jail sentence.* **3.** representative; typical: *an action exemplary of his conduct.* —**ex'emplarily** *adv.* —**ex'emplariness** *n.*

exemplary damages *pl. n. Law.* damages awarded to a plaintiff above the value of actual loss sustained so that they serve also as a punishment to the defendant and a deterrent to others.

exemplify (ɪg'zɛmplɪ,faɪ) *vb.* **-fies, -fying, -fied.** (*tr.*) **1.** to show by example. **2.** to serve as an example of. **3.** *Law.* **a.** to make an official copy of (a document from public records) under seal. **b.** to transcribe (a legal document). [C15: via Old French from Medieval Latin *exemplificāre,* from Latin *exemplum* EXAMPLE + *facere* to make] —**ex'empli,fiable** *adj.* —**ex,emplifi'cation** *n.* —**ex'emplifi,cative** *adj.* —**ex'empli,fier** *n.*

exempli gratia *Latin.* (ɪg'zɛmplaɪ 'grɑːtɪ,ɑː) for the sake of example. Abbrevs.: **e.g., eg, eg.**

exemplum (ɪg'zɛmpləm) *n., pl.* **-pla** (-plə). **1.** an anecdote that supports a moral point or sustains an argument, used esp. in medieval sermons. **2.** an example or illustration. [from Latin: EXAMPLE]

exempt (ɪg'zɛmpt) *vb.* **1.** (*tr.*) to release from an obligation, liability, tax, etc.; excuse: *to exempt a soldier from drill.* ~*adj.* (*sometimes postpositive*) **2.** freed from or not subject to an obligation, liability, tax, etc.; excused: *exempt gilts; tax-exempt bonus.* **3.** *Obsolete.* set apart; remote. ~*n.* **4.** a person who is exempt from an obligation, tax, etc. [C14: from Latin *exemptus* removed, from *eximere* to take out, from *emere* to buy, obtain] —**ex'emption** *n.*

exenterate *vb.* (ɪg'zɛntə,reɪt). (*tr.*) **1.** *Surgery.* to remove (internal organs, an eyeball, etc.); eviscerate. **2.** a rare word for **disembowel.** ~*adj.* (ɪg'zɛntə,reɪt, -rɪt). **3.** *Rare.* having been disembowelled. [C17: from Latin *exenterāre,* from EX-[1] + Greek *enteron* intestine] —**ex,enter'ation** *n.*

exequatur (,ɛksɪ'kweɪtə) *n.* **1.** an official authorization issued by a host country to a consular agent, permitting him to perform his official duties. **2.** an act by which the civil governments of certain nations permit the laws of the Roman Catholic Church to take effect in their territories. [C18: from Latin, literally: let him perform, from *exequī* to perform, from EX-[1] + *sequī* to follow]

exequies ('ɛksɪkwɪz) *pl. n., sing.* **-quy.** the rites and ceremonies used at funerals. [C14: from Latin *exequiae* (plural) funeral procession, rites, from *exequī* to follow to the end, from *sequī* to follow]

exercise ('ɛksə,saɪz) *vb.* (*mainly tr.*) **1.** to put into use; employ: *to exercise tact.* **2.** (*intr.*) to take exercise or perform exercises; exert one's muscles, etc., esp. in order to keep fit. **3.** to practise using in order to develop or train: *to exercise one's voice.* **4.** to perform or make proper use of: *to exercise one's rights.* **5.** to bring to bear; exert: *to exercise one's influence.* **6.** (*often passive*) to occupy the attentions of, esp. so as to worry or vex: *to be exercised about a decision.* **7.** *Military.* to carry out or cause to carry out, manoeuvres, simulated combat operations, etc. ~*n.* **8.** physical exertion, esp. for the purpose of development, training, or keeping fit. **9.** mental or other activity or practice, esp. in order to develop a skill. **10.** a set of movements, questions, tasks, etc., designed to train, improve, or test one's ability in a particular field: *piano exercises.* **11.** a performance or work of art done as practice or to demonstrate a technique. **12.** the performance of a function; discharge: *the exercise of one's rights; the object of the exercise is to win.* **13.** (*sometimes pl.*) *Military.* a manoeuvre or simulated combat operation carried out for training and evaluation. **14.** (*usually pl.*) *U.S. and Canadian.* a ceremony or formal routine, esp. at a school or college: *opening exercises; graduation exercises.* **15.** *Gymnastics.* a particular type of event, such as performing on the horizontal bar. [C14: from Old French *exercice,* from Latin *exercitium,* from *exercēre* to drill, from EX-[1] + *arcēre* to ward off] —'**exer,cisable** *adj.*

exercise bike *or* **cycle** *n.* a stationary exercise machine that is pedalled like a bicycle as a method of increasing cardiovascular fitness.

exercise book *n.* a notebook used by pupils and students.

exercise price *n. Stock exchange.* the price at which the holder of a traded option may exercise his right to buy (or sell) a security.

exerciser ('ɛksə,saɪzə) *n.* **1.** a device with springs or elasticated cords for muscular exercise. **2.** a person or thing that exercises.

exercitation (ɪg,zɜːsɪ'teɪʃən) *n.* a rare word for **exercise.** [C14: from Latin *exercitātiō,* from *exercitāre* frequentative of *exercēre* to EXERCISE]

exergonic (,ɛksə'gɒnɪk) *adj.* (of a biochemical reaction) producing energy and therefore occurring spontaneously. Compare **endergonic.** [C20: from EX(O)- + Greek *ergon* work + -IC]

exergue (ɛk'sɜːg) *n.* a space on the reverse of a coin or medal below the central design, often containing the date, place of minting, etc. [C17: from French, from Medieval Latin *exergum,* from Greek *ex* outside + *ergon* work] —**ex'ergual** *adj.*

exert (ɪg'zɜːt) *vb.* (*tr.*) **1.** to use (influence, authority, etc.) forcefully or effectively. **2.** to apply (oneself) diligently; make a strenuous effort. [C17 (in the sense: push forth, emit): from Latin *exserere* to thrust out, from EX-[1] + *serere* to bind together, entwine] —**ex'ertion** *n.* —**ex'ertive** *adj.*

exeunt ('ɛksɪ,ʌnt) *Latin.* they go out: used as a stage direction.

exeunt omnes ('ɛksɪ,ʌnt 'ɒmneɪz) *Latin.* they all go out: used as a stage direction.

exfoliate (ɛks'fəʊlɪ,eɪt) *vb.* **1.** (of bark, skin, etc.) to peel off in (layers, flakes, or scales). **2.** (*intr.*) (of rocks or minerals) to shed the thin outermost layer because of weathering or heating. **3.** (of some minerals, esp. mica) to split or cause to split into thin flakes: *a factory to exfoliate vermiculite.* [C17: from Late Latin *exfoliāre* to strip off leaves, from Latin *folium* leaf] —**ex,foli'ation** *n.* —**ex'foliative** *adj.*

ex gratia ('greɪʃə) *adj.* given as a favour or gratuitously where no legal obligation exists: *an ex gratia payment.* [New Latin, literally: out of kindness]

exhalant (ɛks'heɪlənt, ɪg'zeɪ-) *adj.* **1.** emitting a vapour or liquid; exhaling: *an exhalant siphon; exhalant duct.* ~*n.* **2.** an organ or vessel that emits a vapour or liquid.

exhale (ɛks'heɪl, ɪg'zeɪl) *vb.* **1.** to expel (breath, tobacco smoke, etc.) from the lungs; breathe out. **2.** to give off (air, vapour, fumes, etc.) or (of air, vapour, etc.) to be given off; emanate. [C14: from Latin *exhālāre* to breathe out, from *hālāre* to breathe] —**ex'halable** *adj.* —,**exha'lation** *n.*

exhaust (ɪg'zɔːst) *vb.* (*mainly tr.*) **1.** to drain the energy of; tire out: *to exhaust someone by constant questioning.* **2.** to deprive of resources, etc.: *a nation exhausted by war.* **3.** to deplete totally; expend, consume: *to exhaust food supplies.* **4.** to empty (a container) by drawing off or pumping out (the contents). **5.** to develop or discuss thoroughly so that no further interest remains: *to exhaust a topic of conversation.* **6.** to remove gas from (a vessel, etc.) in order to reduce the pressure or create a vacuum; evacuate. **7.** to remove or use up the active ingredients from (a drug, solution, etc.). **8.** to destroy the fertility of (soil) by excessive cultivation. **9.** (*intr.*) (of steam or other gases) to be emitted or to escape from an engine after being expanded. ~*n.* **10.** gases ejected from an engine as waste products. **11. a.** the expulsion of expanded gas or steam from an engine. **b.** (*as modifier*): *exhaust stroke.* **12. a.** the parts of an engine through which the exhausted gases or steam pass. **b.** (*as modifier*): *exhaust valve; exhaust pipe.* [C16: from Latin *exhaustus* made empty, from *exhaurīre* to draw out, from *haurīre* to draw, drain] —**ex'hausted** *adj.* —**ex'hauster** *n.* —**ex'haustible** *adj.* —**ex,hausti'bility** *n.* —**ex'hausting** *adj.*

exhaustion (ɪg'zɔːstʃən) *n.* **1.** extreme tiredness; fatigue. **2.** the condition of being used up; consumption: *exhaustion of the earth's resources.* **3.** the act of exhausting or the state of being exhausted.

exhaustive (ɪg'zɔːstɪv) *adj.* **1.** comprehensive in scope; thorough: *an exhaustive survey.* **2.** tending to exhaust. —**ex'haustively** *adv.* —**ex'haustiveness** *n.*

exhaust stroke *n.* another name for **scavenge stroke.**

exhibit (ɪg'zɪbɪt) *vb.* (*mainly tr.*) **1.** (*also intr.*) to display (something) to the public for interest or instruction: *this artist exhibits all over the world.* **2.** to manifest; display; show: *the child exhibited signs of distress.* **3.** *Law.* to produce (a document or object) in court to serve as evidence. ~*n.* **4.** an object or collection exhibited to the public. **5.** *Law.* a document or object produced in court and referred to or identified by a witness in giving evidence. [C15: from Latin *exhibēre* to hold forth, from *habēre* to have] —**ex'hibitory** *adj.*

exhibition (,ɛksɪ'bɪʃən) *n.* **1.** a public display of art, products, skills, activities, etc.: *a judo exhibition.* **2.** the act of exhibiting or the state of being exhibited. **3. make an exhibition of oneself.** to behave so foolishly in public that one excites notice or ridicule. **4.** *Brit. and Austral.* an allowance or scholarship awarded to a student at a university or school.

exhibitioner (,ɛksɪ'bɪʃənə) *n. Brit.* a student who has been awarded an exhibition.

exhibitionism (,ɛksɪ'bɪʃə,nɪzəm) *n.* **1.** a compulsive desire to attract attention to oneself, esp. by absurd or exaggerated behaviour or boasting. **2.** *Psychiatry.* a compulsive desire to expose one's genital organs publicly. —**,exhi'bitionist** *n., adj.* —**,exhi,bition'istic** *adj.*

exhibitive (ɪg'zɪbɪtɪv) *adj.* (*usually postpositive* and foll. by *of*) illustrative or demonstrative: *a masterpiece exhibitive of his talent.* —**ex'hibitively** *adv.*

exhibitor (ɪg'zɪbɪtə) *n.* **1.** a person or thing that exhibits. **2.** an individual or company that shows films, esp. the manager or owner of a cinema.

exhilarant (ɪg'zɪlərənt) *adj.* **1.** exhilarating; invigorating. ~*n.* **2.** something that exhilarates.

exhilarate (ɪg'zɪlə,reɪt) *vb.* (*tr.*) to make lively and cheerful; gladden; elate. [C16: from Latin *exhilarāre*, from *hilarāre* to cheer; see HILARIOUS] —**ex'hila,rating** *adj.* —**ex'hila,ratingly** *adv.* —**ex,hila'ration** *n.* —**ex'hilarative** *or* **ex'hilaratory** *adj.* —**ex'hila,rator** *n.*

exhort (ɪg'zɔːt) *vb.* to urge or persuade (someone) earnestly; advise strongly. [C14: from Latin *exhortārī*, from *hortārī* to urge] —**exhortative** (ɪg'zɔːtətɪv) *or* **ex'hortatory** *adj.* —**ex'horter** *n.*

exhortation (,ɛgzɔː'teɪʃən) *n.* **1.** the act or process of exhorting. **2.** a speech or written passage intended to persuade, inspire, or encourage.

exhume (ɛks'hjuːm) *vb.* (*tr.*) **1.** to dig up (something buried, esp. a corpse); disinter. **2.** to reveal; disclose; unearth: *don't exhume that old argument.* [C18: from Medieval Latin *exhumāre*, from Latin EX-[1] + *humāre* to bury, from *humus* the ground] —**exhumation** (,ɛkshjʊ'meɪʃən) *n.* —**ex'humer** *n.*

ex hypothesi (ɛks haɪ'pɒθəsɪ) *adv.* in accordance with or following from the hypothesis stated. [C17: New Latin]

exigency ('ɛksɪdʒənsɪ, ɪg'zɪdʒənsɪ) *or* **exigence** ('ɛksɪdʒəns) *n., pl.* **-gencies** *or* **-gences.** **1.** the state of being exigent; urgency. **2.** (*often pl.*) an urgent demand; pressing requirement. **3.** an emergency.

exigent ('ɛksɪdʒənt) *adj.* **1.** urgent; pressing. **2.** exacting; demanding. [C15: from Latin *exigere* to drive out, weigh out, from *agere* to drive, compel] —**'exigently** *adv.*

exigible ('ɛksɪdʒəbᵊl) *adj.* liable to be exacted or required: *part of the debt is exigible this month.* [C17: from French, from *exiger* to demand, from Latin *exigere*; see EXIGENT]

exiguous (ɪg'zɪgjʊəs, ɪk'sɪg-) *adj.* scanty or slender; meagre: *an exiguous income.* [C17: from Latin *exiguus*, from *exigere* to weigh out; see EXIGENT] —**exiguity** (,ɛksɪ'gjuːɪtɪ) *or* **ex'iguousness** *n.* —**ex'iguously** *adv.*

exile ('ɛgzaɪl, 'ɛksaɪl) *n.* **1.** a prolonged, usually enforced absence from one's home or country; banishment. **2.** the expulsion of a person from his native land by official decree. **3.** a person banished or living away from his home or country; expatriate. ~*vb.* **4.** to expel from home or country, esp. by official decree as a punishment; banish. [C13: from Latin *exsilium* banishment, from *exsul* banished person; perhaps related to Greek *alasthai* to wander] —**exilic** (ɛg'zɪlɪk, ɛk'sɪlɪk) *or* **ex'ilian** *adj.*

Exile ('ɛgzaɪl, 'ɛksaɪl) *n.* **the.** another name for the **Babylonian captivity** (of the Jews).

eximious (ɛg'zɪmɪəs) *adj. Rare.* select and distinguished; eminent. [C16: from Latin *eximius*, from *eximere* to take out, from *emere* to purchase] —**ex'imiously** *adv.*

exine ('ɛksɪn, -aɪn) *n.* another name for **extine.**

ex int. *Banking. abbrev. for* without [Latin *ex*] interest.

exist (ɪg'zɪst) *vb.* (*intr.*) **1.** to have being or reality; to be. **2.** to eke out a living; stay alive; survive: *he could barely exist on such a low wage.* **3.** to be living; live. **4.** to be present under specified conditions or in a specified place: *sharks exist in the Pacific.* **5.** *Philosophy.* **a.** to be actual rather than merely possible. **b.** to be a member of the domain of some theory, an element of some possible world, etc. **c.** to have contingent being while free, responsible, and aware of one's situation. [C17: from Latin *exsistere* to step forth, from EX-[1] + *sistere* to stand] —**ex'isting** *adj.*

existence (ɪg'zɪstəns) *n.* **1.** the fact or state of existing; being. **2.** the continuance or maintenance of life; living, esp. in adverse circumstances: *a struggle for existence; she has a wretched existence.* **3.** something that exists; a being or entity. **4.** everything that exists, esp. that is living.

existent (ɪg'zɪstənt) *adj.* **1.** in existence; extant; current. **2.** having existence; living. ~*n.* **3.** a person or a thing that exists. ▷**Usage.** See at **extant.**

existential (,ɛgzɪ'stɛnʃəl) *adj.* **1.** of or relating to existence, esp. human existence. **2.** *Philosophy.* pertaining to what exists, and is thus known by experience rather than reason; empirical as opposed to theoretical. **3.** *Logic.* denoting or relating to a formula or proposition asserting the existence of at least one object fulfilling a given condition; containing an existential quantifier. **4.** of or relating to existentialism. ~*n. Logic.* **5. a.** an existential statement or formula. **b.** short for **existential quantifier.** —**,exis'tentially** *adv.*

existentialism (,ɛgzɪ'stɛnʃə,lɪzəm) *n.* a modern philosophical movement stressing the importance of personal experience and responsibility and the demands that they make on the individual, who is seen as a free agent in a deterministic and seemingly meaningless universe. —**,exis'tentialist** *adj., n.*

existential quantifier *n. Logic.* a formal device, for which the conventional symbol is ∃, which indicates that the open sentence that follows is true of at least one member of the relevant universe of interpretation, as $(\exists x)\,Fx$ meaning "something is (an) F," "something Fs," or "there are (some) Fs."

exit ('ɛgzɪt, 'ɛksɪt) *n.* **1.** a way out; door or gate by which people may leave. **2.** the act or an instance of going out; departure. **3. a.** the act of leaving or right to leave a particular place. **b.** (*as modifier*): *an exit visa.* **4.** departure from life; death. **5.** *Theatre.* the act of going offstage. **6.** *Bridge, whist, etc.* **a.** the act of losing the lead deliberately. **b.** a card enabling one to do this. ~*vb.* (*intr.*) **7.** to go away or out; depart; leave. **8.** *Theatre.* to go offstage: used as a stage direction: *exit Hamlet.* **9.** *Bridge, whist, etc.* to lose the lead deliberately. **10.** (*sometimes tr.*) *Computer technol.* to leave (a computer program or system). [C17: from Latin *exitus* a departure, from *exīre* to go out, from EX-[1] + *īre* to go]

Exit ('ɛgzɪt, 'ɛksɪt) *n.* (in Britain) a society that seeks to promote the legitimization of voluntary euthanasia.

exitance ('ɛksɪtəns) *n.* a measure of the ability of a surface to emit radiation. See **luminous exitance, radiant exitance.**

exit poll *n.* a poll taken by an organization by asking people how they voted in an election as they leave a polling station.

ex lib. *abbrev. for* ex libris.

ex libris (ɛks 'liːbrɪs) *adj.* **1.** from the collection or library of: frequently printed on bookplates. ~*n.* **ex-libris.** **2.** a bookplate bearing the owner's name, coat of arms, etc. [C19: from Latin, literally: from the books (of)]

Exmoor ('ɛks,mʊə, -,mɔː) *n.* a small stocky breed of pony with a fawn-coloured nose, originally from Exmoor, an upland region in SW England.

ex new *adv., adj.* (of shares, etc.) without the right to take up any scrip issue or rights issue. Compare **cum new.**

exo- *combining form.* external, outside, or beyond: *exobiology; exothermal.* [from Greek *exō* outside]

exobiology (,ɛksəʊbaɪ'ɒlədʒɪ) *n.* another name for **astrobiology.** —**,exobi'ologist** *n.*

exocarp ('ɛksəʊ,kɑːp) *n.* another name for **epicarp.**

exocentric (,ɛksəʊ'sɛntrɪk) *adj. Grammar.* (of a construction) not fulfilling the grammatical role of any of its constituents; as in *until last Easter*, where the constituents are prepositional, adjectival, and nominal, while the whole construction is adverbial. Compare **endocentric.**

Exocet ('ɛksəʊsɛt) *n. Trademark.* a tactical missile with a high-explosive warhead, which is guided by computer and radar, travels at a very low altitude at high subsonic speed, and has a range of up to 70 km. It may be launched from a ship, aircraft, or submarine. [C20: from French, from New Latin *Exocoetus volitans* flying fish]

exocrine ('ɛksəʊ,kraɪn, -krɪn) *adj.* **1.** of or relating to exocrine glands or their secretions. ~*n.* **2.** an exocrine gland. ~Compare **endocrine.** [C20: EXO- + *-crine* from Greek *krinein* to separate]

exocrine gland *n.* any gland, such as a salivary or sweat gland, that secretes its products through a duct onto an epithelial surface.
exocuticle ('ɛksəʊˌkjuːtɪkᵊl) *n.* the layer of an insect's cuticle between the epicuticle and the endocuticle, which is often hard and dark in colour.
exocytosis (ˌɛksəʊsaɪ'təʊsɪs) *n.* a process by which material is exported from a biological cell.
Exod. *Bible. abbrev. for* Exodus.
exoderm ('ɛksəʊˌdɜːm) *n. Embryol.* another name for **ectoderm.**
exodontics (ˌɛksəʊ'dɒntɪks) *n. (functioning as sing.)* the branch of dental surgery concerned with the extraction of teeth. Also called: **exodontia** (ˌɛksəʊ'dɒnʃə). [C20: New Latin, from EX-[1] + *-odontia,* from Greek *odōn* tooth] —ˌ**exo'dontist** *n.*
exodus ('ɛksədəs) *n.* the act or an instance of going out. [C17: via Latin from Greek *exodos* from EX-[1] + *hodos* way]
exoenzyme (ˌɛksəʊ'ɛnzaɪm) *n.* **1.** any enzyme, esp. an exopeptidase, that acts upon terminal chemical bonds in a chain of molecules. Compare **endoenzyme. 2.** another name for **ectoenzyme.**
exoergic (ˌɛksəʊ'ɜːdʒɪk) *adj.* (of a nuclear reaction) occurring with evolution of energy. Compare **endoergic, exothermic.** [EXO- + *-ergic,* from Greek *ergon* work]
ex off. *abbrev. for* ex officio.
ex officio ('ɛks ə'fɪʃɪəʊ, ə'fɪsɪəʊ) *adv., adj.* by right of position or office. Abbrev.: **ex off.** [Latin]
exogamy (ɛk'sɒgəmɪ) *n.* **1.** *Sociol., anthropol.* the custom or an act of marrying a person belonging to another tribe, clan, or similar social unit. Compare **endogamy. 2.** *Biology.* fusion of gametes from parents that are not closely related. —**exogamous** (ɛk'sɒgəməs) *or* **exogamic** (ˌɛksəʊ'gæmɪk) *adj.*
exogenous (ɛk'sɒdʒɪnəs) *adj.* **1.** having an external origin. **2.** *Biology.* **a.** developing or originating outside an organism or part of an organism. **b.** of or relating to external factors, such as light, that influence an organism. **3.** *Psychiatry.* (of a mental illness) caused by external factors. —**ex'ogenously** *adv.*
exon[1] ('ɛksɒn) *n. Brit.* one of the four officers who command the Yeomen of the Guard. [C17: a pronunciation spelling of French *exempt* EXEMPT]
exon[2] ('ɛksɒn) *n.* any segment of a discontinuous gene the segments of which are separated by introns. Compare **intron.** [C20: from EX-[1] + -ON] —**ex'onic** *adj.*
exonerate (ɪg'zɒnəˌreɪt) *vb. (tr.)* **1.** to clear or absolve from blame or a criminal charge. **2.** to relieve from an obligation or task; exempt. [C16: from Latin *exonerāre* to free from a burden, from *onus* a burden] —**exˌoner'ation** *n.* —**ex'onerative** *adj.* —**ex'onerˌator** *n.*
exonuclease (ˌɛksəʊ'njuːklɪˌeɪz) *n.* an enzyme that is capable of detaching the terminal nucleotide from a nucleic acid chain. Compare **endonuclease.**
exonym ('ɛksəˌnɪm) *n.* a name given to a place by foreigners: *Londres is an exonym of London.* [C20: from Greek EX-[1] + -ONYM]
exoparasite (ˌɛksəʊ'pærəˌsaɪt) *n.* another word for **ectoparasite.** —**exoparasitic** (ˌɛksəʊˌpærə'sɪtɪk) *adj.*
exopeptidase (ˌɛksəʊ'pɛptɪˌdeɪz) *n.* any proteolytic enzyme, such as erepsin, that acts on the terminal bonds in a peptide chain. Compare **endopeptidase.**
exophoric (ˌɛksəʊ'fɒrɪk) *adj. Grammar.* denoting or relating to a pronoun such as "I" or "you", the meaning of which is determined by reference outside the discourse rather than by a preceding or following expression. Compare **anaphora.** [from EXO- + Greek *pherein* to carry]
exophthalmic goitre *n.* a form of hyperthyroidism characterized by enlargement of the thyroid gland, protrusion of the eyeballs, increased basal metabolic rate, and weight loss. Also called: **Graves' disease.**
exophthalmos (ˌɛksɒf'θælmɒs), **exophthalmus** (ˌɛksɒf'θælməs), *or* **exophthalmia** (ˌɛksɒf'θælmɪə) *n.* abnormal protrusion of the eyeball, as caused by hyperthyroidism. Also called: **proptosis, ocular proptosis.** [C19: via New Latin from Greek, from EX-[1] + *ophthalmos* eye] —ˌ**exoph'thalmic** *adj.*
exoplasm ('ɛksəʊˌplæzəm) *n.* another name for **ectoplasm.**
exor. ('ɛksɔː) *Brit. abbrev. for* executor.
exorable ('ɛksərəbᵊl) *adj.* able to be persuaded or moved by pleading. [C16: from Latin *exōrābilis,* from *exōrāre* to persuade, from *ōrāre* to beseech] —ˌ**exora'bility** *n.*
exorbitant (ɪg'zɔːbɪtᵊnt) *adj.* (of prices, demands, etc.) in excess of what is reasonable; excessive; extravagant; immoderate. [C15: from Late Latin *exorbitāre* to deviate, from Latin *orbita* track] —**ex'orbitance** *n.* —**ex'orbitantly** *adv.*
exorcize *or* **exorcise** ('ɛksɔːˌsaɪz) *vb. (tr.)* to expel or attempt to expel (one or more evil spirits) from (a person or place believed to be possessed or haunted), by prayers, adjurations, and religious rites. [C15: from Late Latin *exorcizāre,* from Greek *exorkizein,* from EX-[1] + *horkizein* to adjure] —'**exorˌcizer** *or* '**exorˌciser** *n.* —'**exorcism** *n.* —'**exorcist** *n.*
exordium (ɛk'sɔːdɪəm) *n., pl.* **-diums** *or* **-dia** (-dɪə). an introductory part or beginning, esp. of an oration or discourse. [C16: from Latin, from *exōrdīrī* to begin, from *ōrdīrī* to begin] —**ex'ordial** *adj.*
exoskeleton (ˌɛksəʊ'skɛlɪtᵊn) *n.* the protective or supporting structure covering the outside of the body of many animals, such as the thick cuticle of arthropods. Compare **endoskeleton.** —ˌ**exo'skeletal** *adj.*
exosmosis (ˌɛksɒz'məʊsɪs, -sɒs-) *n. Biology.* osmosis in which water flows from a cell or organism into the surrounding solution. Compare **endosmosis.** —**exosmotic** (ˌɛksɒz'mɒtɪk, -sɒs-) *or* **exosmic** (ɛk'sɒzmɪk, -'sɒs-) *adj.*
exosphere ('ɛksəʊˌsfɪə) *n.* the outermost layer of the earth's atmosphere. It extends from about 400 kilometres above the earth's surface.
exospore ('ɛksəʊˌspɔː) *n.* the outer layer of the spores of some algae and fungi. —ˌ**exo'sporous** *adj.*
exostosis (ˌɛksɒ'stəʊsɪs) *n., pl.* **-ses** (-siːz). an abnormal bony outgrowth from the surface of a bone. [C18: via New Latin from Greek, from EX-[1] + *osteon* bone]
exoteric (ˌɛksəʊ'tɛrɪk) *adj.* **1.** intelligible to or intended for more than a select or initiated minority: *an exoteric account of a philosophical doctrine.* **2.** external; exterior. [C17: from Latin *exōtericus* external, from Greek *exōterikos,* from *exōterō* further outside; see EXO-] —ˌ**exo'terically** *adv.* —ˌ**exo'teriˌcism** *n.*
exothermic (ˌɛksəʊ'θɜːmɪk) *or* **exothermal** *adj.* (of a chemical reaction or compound) occurring or formed with the evolution of heat. Compare **endothermic, exoergic.** —ˌ**exo'thermically** *or* ˌ**exo'thermally** *adv.*
exotic (ɪg'zɒtɪk) *adj.* **1.** originating in a foreign country, esp. one in the tropics; not native: *an exotic plant.* **2.** having a strange or bizarre allure, beauty, or quality. **3.** *N.Z.* (of trees, esp. pine trees) native to the northern hemisphere but cultivated in New Zealand: *an exotic forest.* **4.** of or relating to striptease. ~*n.* **5.** an exotic person or thing. [C16: from Latin *exōticus,* from Greek *exōtikos* foreign, from *exō* outside] —**ex'otically** *adv.* —**ex'otiˌcism** *n.* —**ex'oticness** *n.*
exotica (ɪg'zɒtɪkə) *pl. n.* exotic objects, esp. when forming a collection. [C19: Latin, neuter plural of *exōticus;* see EXOTIC]
exotic dancer *n.* a striptease dancer or belly dancer.
exotoxin (ˌɛksəʊ'tɒksɪn) *n.* a toxin produced by a microorganism and secreted into the surrounding medium. —ˌ**exo'toxic** *adj.*
exp *Maths. Symbol for* exponential (sense 2).
exp. *abbrev. for:* **1.** expenses. **2.** experiment(al). **3.** expired. **4.** export(ed). **5.** exporter. **6.** express.
expand (ɪk'spænd) *vb.* **1.** to make or become greater in extent, volume, size, or scope; increase. **2.** to spread out or be spread out; unfold; stretch out. **3.** *(intr.;* often foll. by *on)* to enlarge or expatiate on (a story, topic, etc.) in detail. **4.** *(intr.)* to become increasingly relaxed, friendly, or talkative. **5.** *Maths.* to express (a function or expression) as the sum or product of terms. [C15: from Latin *expandere* to spread out, from *pandere* to spread, extend] —**ex'pandable** *adj.* —**ex'pander** *n.*
expanded (ɪk'spændɪd) *adj.* **1.** Also: **extended.** (of printer's type) wider than usual for a particular height. Compare **condensed. 2.** (of a plastic) having been foamed during manufacture by the introduction of a gas in order to make a light packaging material or heat insulator: *expanded polystyrene.* See also **expanded metal.**
expanded metal *n.* an open mesh of metal produced by stamping out alternating slots in a metal sheet and stretching it into an open pattern. It is used for reinforcing brittle or friable materials and in fencing.
expander (ɪk'spændə) *n.* **1.** a device for exercising and developing the muscles of the body: *a chest expander.* **2.** an electronic device for increasing the variations in signal amplitude in a transmission system according to a specified law. Compare **compressor** (sense 5), **compander.**
expanding universe theory *n.* the theory, developed from the observed red shifts of celestial bodies, that all the galaxies are receding from each other at velocities that increase as the distance from earth increases. See also **oscillating universe theory.**
expanse (ɪk'spæns) *n.* **1.** an uninterrupted surface of something that spreads or extends, esp. over a wide area; stretch: *an expanse of water.* **2.** expansion or extension. [C17: from New Latin *expansum* the heavens, from Latin *expansus* spread out, from *expandere* to EXPAND]
expansible (ɪk'spænsəbᵊl) *adj.* able to expand or be expanded. —**exˌpansi'bility** *n.*
expansile (ɪk'spænsaɪl) *adj.* **1.** able to expand or cause expansion. **2.** of or relating to expansion.
expansion (ɪk'spænʃən) *n.* **1.** the act of expanding or the state of being expanded. **2.** something expanded; an expanded surface or part. **3.** the degree, extent, or amount by which something expands. **4.** an increase, enlargement, or development, esp. in the activities of a company. **5.** *Maths.* **a.** the form of an expression or function when it is written as the sum or product of its terms. **b.** the act or process of determining this expanded form. **6.** the part of an engine cycle in which the working fluid does useful work by increasing in volume. **7.** the increase in the dimensions of a body or substance when subjected to an increase in temperature, internal pressure, etc. —**ex'pansionary** *adj.*
expansion bend *n. Engineering.* a loop in a pipe conveying hot fluid that provides flexibility which takes up thermal expansion and thus reduces temperature-induced stress in the pipe to an acceptable level.
expansion bolt *n.* a bolt that expands on tightening, enabling it to be secured into an unthreaded hole.

expansionism (ɪk'spænʃəˌnɪzəm) *n.* the doctrine or practice of expanding the economy or territory of a country. —**ex'pansionist** *n., adj.* —**exˌpansion'istic** *adj.*

expansion joint *n. Engineering.* a gap in steel or concrete to allow for thermal expansion.

expansion slot *n.* a physical electronic interface provided in a computer system to enable extra facilities to be added at a later date.

expansive (ɪk'spænsɪv) *adj.* **1.** able or tending to expand or characterized by expansion. **2.** wide; extensive. **3.** friendly, open, or talkative: *an expansive person.* **4.** grand or extravagant: *an expansive way of life.* **5.** *Psychiatry.* lacking restraint in the expression of feelings, esp. in having delusions of grandeur or being inclined to overvalue oneself or one's work. —**ex'pansively** *adv.* —**ex'pansiveness** *n.*

expansivity (ˌɛkspæn'sɪvɪtɪ) *n.* **1.** the quality of being expansive. **2.** another name for **coefficient of expansion.**

ex parte (ɛks 'pɑːtɪ) *adj. Law.* (of an application in a judicial proceeding) on behalf of one side or party only: *an ex parte injunction.* [Latin]

expat (ˌɛks'pæt) *n., adj. Informal.* short for **expatriate.**

expatiate (ɪk'speɪʃɪˌeɪt) *vb.* (*intr.*) **1.** (foll. by *on* or *upon*) to enlarge (on a theme, topic, etc.) at length or in detail; elaborate (on). **2.** *Rare.* to wander about. [C16: from Latin *exspatiārī* to digress, from *spatiārī* to walk about] —**exˌpati'ation** *n.* —**ex'patiˌator** *n.*

expatriate *adj.* (ɛks'pætrɪɪt, -ˌeɪt). **1.** resident in a foreign country. **2.** exiled or banished from one's native country: *an expatriate American.* ~*n.* (ɛks'pætrɪɪt, -ˌeɪt). **3.** a person who lives in a foreign country. **4.** an exile; expatriate person. ~*vb.* (ɛks'pætrɪˌeɪt). (*tr.*) **5.** to exile (oneself) from one's native country or cause (another) to go into exile. **6.** to deprive (oneself or another) of citizenship. [C18: from Medieval Latin *expatriāre,* from Latin EX-[1] + *patria* native land] —**exˌpatri'ation** *n.*

expect (ɪk'spɛkt) *vb.* (*tr.; may take a clause as object or an infinitive*) **1.** to regard as probable or likely; anticipate: *he expects to win.* **2.** to look forward to or be waiting for: *we expect good news today.* **3.** to decide that (something) is requisite or necessary; require: *the teacher expects us to work late today.* ~See also **expecting.** [C16: from Latin *exspectāre* to watch for, from *spectāre* to look at] —**ex'pectable** *adj.* —**ex'pectably** *adv.*

expectancy (ɪk'spɛktənsɪ) *or* **expectance** *n.* **1.** something expected, esp. on the basis of a norm or average: *his life expectancy was 30 years.* **2.** anticipation; expectation. **3.** the prospect of a future interest or possession, esp. in property: *an estate in expectancy.*

expectant (ɪk'spɛktənt) *adj.* **1.** expecting, anticipating, or hopeful: *an expectant glance.* **2.** having expectations, esp. of possession of something or prosperity. **3.** pregnant: *an expectant mother.* ~*n.* **4.** a person who expects something. **5.** *Obsolete.* a candidate for office, esp. for ecclesiastical preferment. —**ex'pectantly** *adv.*

expectation (ˌɛkspɛk'teɪʃən) *n.* **1.** the act or state of expecting or the state of being expected. **2.** (*usually pl.*) something looked forward to, whether feared or hoped for: *we have great expectations for his future; their worst expectations.* **3.** an attitude of expectancy or hope; anticipation: *to regard something with expectation.* **4.** *Statistics.* **a.** the numerical probability that an event will occur. **b.** another term for **expected value.** —**expectative** (ɪk'spɛktətɪv) *adj.*

expected frequency *n. Statistics.* the number of occasions on which an event may be presumed to occur on average in a given number of trials.

expected utility *n. Statistics.* the weighted average utility of the possible outcomes of a probabilistic situation; the sum or integral of the product of the probability distribution and the utility function.

expected value *n. Statistics.* the sum or integral of all possible values of a random variable, or any given function of it, multiplied by the respective probabilities of the values of the variable. Symbol: $E(X)$. $E(X)$ is the mean of the distribution; $E(X - c) = E(X) - c$ where c is a constant. Also called: **mathematical expectation.**

expecting (ɪk'spɛktɪŋ) *adj. Informal.* pregnant.

expectorant (ɪk'spɛktərənt) *Med.* ~*adj.* **1.** promoting the secretion, liquefaction, or expulsion of sputum from the respiratory passages. ~*n.* **2.** an expectorant drug or agent.

expectorate (ɪk'spɛktəˌreɪt) *vb.* to cough up and spit out (sputum from the respiratory passages). [C17: from Latin *expectorāre,* literally: to drive from the breast, expel, from *pectus* breast] —**exˌpecto'ration** *n.* —**ex'pectoˌrator** *n.*

expediency (ɪk'spiːdɪənsɪ) *or* **expedience** *n., pl.* **-encies** *or* **-ences.** **1.** appropriateness; suitability. **2.** the use of or inclination towards methods that are advantageous rather than fair or just. **3.** another word for **expedient** (sense 3).

expedient (ɪk'spiːdɪənt) *adj.* **1.** suitable to the circumstances; appropriate. **2.** inclined towards methods or means that are advantageous rather than fair or just. ~*n. also* **expediency. 3.** something suitable or appropriate, esp. something used during an urgent situation. [C14: from Latin *expediēns* setting free; see EXPEDITE] —**ex'pediently** *adv.*

expediential (ɪkˌspiːdɪ'ɛnʃəl) *adj.* denoting, based on, or involving expediency. —**exˌpedi'entially** *adv.*

expedite ('ɛkspɪˌdaɪt) *vb.* (*tr.*) **1.** to hasten the progress of; hasten or assist. **2.** to do or process (something, such as business matters) with speed and efficiency. **3.** *Rare.* to dispatch (documents, messages, etc.). ~*adj. Obsolete.* **4.** unimpeded or prompt; expeditious. **5.** alert or prepared. [C17: from Latin *expedīre,* literally: to free the feet (as from a snare), hence, liberate, from EX-[1] + *pēs* foot]

expediter *or* **expeditor** ('ɛkspɪˌdaɪtə) *n.* a person who expedites something, esp. a person employed in an industry to ensure that work on each job progresses efficiently.

expedition (ˌɛkspɪ'dɪʃən) *n.* **1.** an organized journey or voyage for a specific purpose, esp. for exploration or for a scientific or military purpose. **2.** the people and equipment comprising an expedition. **3.** a pleasure trip; excursion. **4.** promptness in acting; dispatch. [C15: from Latin *expedītiō,* from *expedīre* to prepare, EXPEDITE]

expeditionary (ˌɛkspɪ'dɪʃənərɪ) *adj.* relating to or constituting an expedition, esp. a military one: *an expeditionary force.*

expeditious (ˌɛkspɪ'dɪʃəs) *adj.* characterized by or done with speed and efficiency; prompt; quick. —ˌ**expe'ditiously** *adv.* —ˌ**expe'ditiousness** *n.*

expel (ɪk'spɛl) *vb.* **-pels, -pelling, -pelled.** (*tr.*) **1.** to eject or drive out with force. **2.** to deprive of participation in or membership of a school, club, etc. [C14: from Latin *expellere* to drive out, from *pellere* to thrust, drive] —**ex'pellable** *adj.* —**expellee** (ˌɛkspɛ'liː) *n.* —**ex'peller** *n.*

expellant *or* **expellent** (ɪk'spɛlənt) *adj.* **1.** forcing out or having the capacity to force out. ~*n.* **2.** a medicine used to expel undesirable substances or organisms from the body, esp. worms from the digestive tract.

expellers (ɪk'spɛləz) *pl. n.* the residue remaining after an oilseed has been crushed to expel the oil, used for animal fodder: *groundnut expellers.* Compare **extractions.**

expend (ɪk'spɛnd) *vb.* (*tr.*) **1.** to spend; disburse. **2.** to consume or use up. [C15: from Latin *expendere,* from *pendere* to weigh] —**ex'pender** *n.*

expendable (ɪk'spɛndəbᵊl) *adj.* **1.** that may be expended or used up. **2.** not essential; not worth preserving. **3.** able to be sacrificed to achieve an objective, esp. a military one. ~*n.* **4.** something that is expendable. —**exˌpenda'bility** *n.*

expenditure (ɪk'spɛndɪtʃə) *n.* **1.** something expended, such as time or money. **2.** the act of expending.

expense (ɪk'spɛns) *n.* **1.** a particular payment of money; expenditure. **2.** money needed for individual purchases; cost; charge. **3.** (*pl.*) incidental money spent in the performance of a job, commission, etc., usually reimbursed by an employer or allowable against tax. **4.** something requiring money for its purchase or upkeep: *the car was more of an expense than he had expected.* **5.** **at the expense of.** to the detriment of: *he succeeded at the expense of his health.* ~*vb.* **6.** (*tr.*) *U.S. and Canadian.* to treat as an expense for book-keeping or tax purposes. [C14: from Late Latin *expēnsa,* from Latin *expēnsus* weighed out; see EXPEND]

expense account *n.* **1.** an arrangement by which expenses incurred in the course of a person's work are refunded by his employer or deducted from his income for tax purposes. **2.** a record of such expenses. **3.** (*modifier*) *Informal.* paid for by an employer or by money allowable against tax: *an expense-account lunch.*

expensive (ɪk'spɛnsɪv) *adj.* high-priced; costly; dear. —**ex'pensively** *adv.* —**ex'pensiveness** *n.*

experience (ɪk'spɪərɪəns) *n.* **1.** direct personal participation or observation; actual knowledge or contact: *experience of prison life.* **2.** a particular incident, feeling, etc., that a person has undergone: *an experience to remember.* **3.** accumulated knowledge, esp. of practical matters: *a man of experience.* **4. a.** the totality of characteristics, both past and present, that make up the particular quality of a person, place, or people. **b.** the impact made on an individual by the culture of a people, nation, etc.: *the American experience.* **5.** *Philosophy.* **a.** the content of a perception regarded as independent of whether the apparent object actually exists. Compare **sense datum. b.** the faculty by which a person acquires knowledge of contingent facts about the world, as contrasted with reason. **c.** the totality of a person's perceptions, feelings, and memories. ~*vb.* (*tr.*) **6.** to participate in or undergo. **7.** to be emotionally or aesthetically moved by; feel: *to experience beauty.* [C14: from Latin *experientia,* from *experīrī* to prove; related to Latin *perīculum* PERIL] —**ex'perienceable** *adj.*

experienced (ɪk'spɪərɪənst) *adj.* having become skilful or knowledgeable from extensive contact or participation or observation.

experience table *n. Insurance.* an actuarial table, esp. a mortality table based on past statistics.

experiential (ɪkˌspɪərɪ'ɛnʃəl) *adj. Philosophy.* relating to or derived from experience; empirical. —**exˌperi'entially** *adv.*

experiment *n.* (ɪk'spɛrɪmənt). **1.** a test or investigation, esp. one planned to provide evidence for or against a hypothesis: *a scientific experiment.* **2.** the act of conducting such an investigation or test; experimentation; research. **3.** an attempt at something new or different; an effort to be original: *a poetic experiment.* **4.** an obsolete word for **experience.** ~*vb.* (ɪk'spɛrɪˌmɛnt). **5.** (*intr.*) to make an experiment or experiments. [C14: from Latin *experīmentum* proof, trial, from *experīrī* to test; see EXPERIENCE] —**ex'periˌmenter** *n.*

experimental (ɪkˌspɛrɪˈmɛntᵊl) *adj.* **1.** relating to, based on, or having the nature of experiment: *an experimental study.* **2.** based on or derived from experience; empirical: *experimental evidence.* **3.** tending to experiment: *an experimental artist.* **4.** tentative or provisional: *an experimental rule in football.* —**exˌperiˈmentally** *adv.*

experimental condition *n. Statistics.* one of the distinct states of affairs or values of the independent variable for which the dependent variable is measured in order to carry out statistical tests or calculations. Also called: **condition.**

experimentalism (ɪkˌspɛrɪˈmɛntəˌlɪzəm) *n.* employment of or reliance upon experiments; empiricism. —**exˌperiˈmentalist** *n.*

experimentalize *or* **experimentalise** (ɪkˌspɛrɪˈmɛntəˌlaɪz) *vb.* (*intr.*) to engage in experiments.

experimental psychology *n.* the scientific study of the individual behaviour of man and other animals, esp. of perception, learning, memory, motor skills, and thinking.

experimentation (ɪkˌspɛrɪmɛnˈteɪʃən) *n.* the act, process, or practice of experimenting.

experimenter effect *n. Psychol.* the influence of an experimenter's expectations on his results.

expert (ˈɛkspɜːt) *n.* **1.** a person who has extensive skill or knowledge in a particular field. **2. the expert.** *Austral. informal.* the worker in a sheep-shearing shed responsible for the care of machinery. ~*adj.* **3.** skilful or knowledgeable. **4.** of, involving, or done by an expert: *an expert job.* [C14: from Latin *expertus* known by experience, from *experīrī* to test; see EXPERIENCE] —ˈ**expertly** *adv.* —ˈ**expertness** *n.*

expertise (ˌɛkspɜːˈtiːz) *n.* special skill, knowledge, or judgment; expertness. [C19: from French: expert skill, from EXPERT]

expertize *or* **expertise** (ˈɛkspɜːˌtaɪz) *vb. U.S.* to act as an expert or give an expert opinion (on).

expert system *n.* a computer program that can offer intelligent advice or make intelligent decisions using rule-based programs.

expiable (ˈɛkspɪəbᵊl) *adj.* capable of being expiated or atoned for.

expiate (ˈɛkspɪˌeɪt) *vb.* (*tr.*) to atone for or redress (sin or wrongdoing); make amends for. [C16: from Latin *expiāre,* from *pius* dutiful; see PIOUS] —ˈ**expiˌator** *n.*

expiation (ˌɛkspɪˈeɪʃən) *n.* the act, process, or a means of expiating; atonement.

expiatory (ˈɛkspɪətərɪ, -trɪ) *adj.* **1.** capable of making expiation. **2.** given or offered in expiation.

expiration (ˌɛkspɪˈreɪʃən) *n.* **1.** the finish of something; ending; expiry. **2.** the act, process, or sound of breathing out. **3.** *Rare.* a last breath; death.

expiratory (ɪkˈspaɪərətərɪ, -trɪ) *adj.* relating to the expulsion of air from the lungs during respiration.

expire (ɪkˈspaɪə) *vb.* **1.** (*intr.*) to finish or run out; cease; come to an end. **2.** to breathe out (air); exhale. **3.** (*intr.*) to die. [C15: from Old French *expirer,* from Latin *exspīrāre* to breathe out, from *spīrāre* to breathe] —**exˈpirer** *n.*

expiry (ɪkˈspaɪərɪ) *n., pl.* **-ries.** **1. a.** a coming to an end, esp. of a contract period; termination: *expiry of a lease.* **b.** (*as modifier*): *the expiry date.* **2.** death.

explain (ɪkˈspleɪn) *vb.* **1.** (when *tr., may take a clause as object*) to make (something) comprehensible, esp. by giving a clear and detailed account of the relevant structure, operation, surrounding circumstances, etc. **2.** (*tr.*) to justify or attempt to justify (oneself) by giving reasons for one's actions or words. [C15: from Latin *explānāre* to flatten, from *plānus* level] —**exˈplainable** *adj.* —**exˈplainer** *n.*

explain away *vb.* (*tr., adv.*) to offer excuses or reasons for (bad conduct, mistakes, etc.).

explanation (ˌɛkspləˈneɪʃən) *n.* **1.** the act or process of explaining. **2.** a statement or occurrence that explains. **3.** a clarification of disputed terms or points; reconciliation.

explanatory (ɪkˈsplænətərɪ, -trɪ) *or* **explanative** *adj.* serving or intended to serve as an explanation. —**exˈplanatorily** *adv.*

explant (ɛksˈplɑːnt) *vb.* **1.** to transfer (living tissue) from its natural site to a culture medium. ~*n.* **2.** a piece of tissue treated in this way. —ˌ**explanˈtation** *n.*

expletive (ɪkˈspliːtɪv) *n.* **1.** an exclamation or swearword; an oath or a sound expressing an emotional reaction rather than any particular meaning. **2.** any syllable, word, or phrase conveying no independent meaning, esp. one inserted in a line of verse for the sake of the metre. ~*adj. also* **expletory** (ɪkˈspliːtərɪ). **3.** expressing no particular meaning, esp. when filling out a line of verse. [C17: from Late Latin *explētīvus* for filling out, from *explēre,* from *plēre* to fill] —**exˈpletively** *adv.*

explicable (ˈɛksplɪkəbᵊl, ɪkˈsplɪk-) *adj.* capable of being explained.

explicate (ˈɛksplɪˌkeɪt) *vb.* (*tr.*) *Formal.* **1.** to make clear or explicit; explain. **2.** to formulate or develop (a theory, hypothesis, etc.). [C16: from Latin *explicāre* to unfold, from *plicāre* to fold] —**explicative** (ɪkˈsplɪkətɪv) *or* **explicatory** (ɪkˈsplɪkətərɪ, -trɪ) *adj.* —ˈ**expliˌcator** *n.*

explication (ˌɛksplɪˈkeɪʃən) *n.* **1.** the act or process of explicating. **2.** analysis or interpretation, esp. of a literary passage or work or philosophical doctrine. **3.** a comprehensive exposition or description.

explication de texte *French.* (ɛksplikasjɔ̃ də tɛkst) *n., pl.* ***explications de texte*** (ɛksplikasjɔ̃ də tɛkst). a close textual analysis of a literary work. [literally: explanation of (the) text]

explicit[1] (ɪkˈsplɪsɪt) *adj.* **1.** precisely and clearly expressed, leaving nothing to implication; fully stated: *explicit instructions.* **2.** graphically detailed, leaving little to the imagination: *sexually explicit scenes.* **3.** openly expressed without reservations; unreserved. **4.** *Maths.* (of a function) having an equation of the form $y = f(x)$, in which y is expressed directly in terms of x, as in $y = x^4 + x + z$. Compare **implicit** (sense 4). [C17: from Latin *explicitus* unfolded, from *explicāre;* see EXPLICATE] —**exˈplicitly** *adv.* —**exˈplicitness** *n.*

explicit[2] (ɪkˈsplɪsɪt) the end; an indication, used esp. by medieval scribes, of the end of a book, part of a manuscript, etc. [Late Latin, probably short for *explicitus est liber* the book is unfolded (or complete); shortened by analogy with INCIPIT]

explode (ɪkˈspləʊd) *vb.* **1.** to burst or cause to burst with great violence as a result of internal pressure, esp. through the detonation of an explosive; blow up. **2.** to destroy or be destroyed in this manner: *to explode a bridge.* **3.** (of a gas) to undergo or cause (a gas) to undergo a sudden violent expansion, accompanied by heat, light, a shock wave, and a loud noise, as a result of a fast uncontrolled exothermic chemical or nuclear reaction. **4.** (*intr.*) to react suddenly or violently with emotion, etc.: *to explode with anger.* **5.** (*intr.*) (esp. of a population) to increase rapidly. **6.** (*tr.*) to show (a theory, etc.) to be baseless; refute and make obsolete. **7.** (*tr.*) *Phonetics.* to pronounce (a stop) with audible plosion. ~Compare **implode.** [C16: from Latin *explōdere* to drive off by clapping, hiss (an actor) off, from EX-[1] + *plaudere* to clap] —**exˈploder** *n.*

exploded view *n.* a drawing or photograph of a complicated mechanism that shows the individual parts separately, usually indicating their relative positions.

exploding star *n.* an irregular variable star, such as a nova, supernova, or flare star, in which rapid increases in luminosity occur, caused by some form of explosion.

exploit *n.* (ˈɛksplɔɪt). **1.** a notable deed or feat, esp. one that is noble or heroic. ~*vb.* (ɪkˈsplɔɪt). (*tr.*) **2.** to take advantage of (a person, situation, etc.), esp. unethically or unjustly for one's own ends. **3.** to make the best use of: *to exploit natural resources.* [C14: from Old French: accomplishment, from Latin *explicitum* (something) unfolded, from *explicāre* to EXPLICATE] —**exˈploitable** *adj.* —ˌ**exploiˈtation** *n.* —**exˈploitive** *or* **exˈploitative** *adj.*

exploration (ˌɛkspləˈreɪʃən) *n.* **1.** the act or process of exploring. **2.** *Med.* examination of an organ or part for diagnostic purposes. **3.** an organized trip into unfamiliar regions, esp. for scientific purposes; expedition. —**exploratory** (ɪkˈsplɒrətərɪ, -trɪ) *or* **exˈplorative** *adj.*

explore (ɪkˈsplɔː) *vb.* **1.** (*tr.*) to examine or investigate, esp. systematically. **2.** to travel to or into (unfamiliar or unknown regions), esp. for organized scientific purposes. **3.** (*tr.*) *Med.* to examine (an organ or part) for diagnostic purposes. **4.** (*tr.*) *Obsolete.* to search for or out. [C16: from Latin *explōrāre,* from EX-[1] + *plōrāre* to cry aloud; probably from the shouts of hunters sighting prey] —**exˈplorer** *n.*

Explorer[1] (ɪkˈsplɔːrə) *n. U.S.* a member of the senior branch of the Scouts. Brit. equivalent: **Venture Scout.**

Explorer[2] (ɪkˈsplɔːrə) *n.* any of the first series of U.S. satellites. **Explorer 1,** launched in 1958, confirmed the existence of intense radiation belts around the earth.

explosion (ɪkˈspləʊʒən) *n.* **1.** the act or an instance of exploding. **2.** a violent release of energy resulting from a rapid chemical or nuclear reaction, esp. one that produces a shock wave, loud noise, heat, and light. Compare **implosion** (sense 1). **3.** a sudden or violent outburst of activity, noise, emotion, etc. **4.** a rapid increase, esp. in a population. **5.** *Phonetics.* another word for **plosion.** [C17: from Latin *explōsiō,* from *explōdere* to EXPLODE]

explosion welding *n. Engineering.* the welding of two parts forced together by a controlled explosion.

explosive (ɪkˈspləʊsɪv) *adj.* **1.** of, involving, or characterized by an explosion or explosions. **2.** capable of exploding or tending to explode. **3.** potentially violent or hazardous; dangerous: *an explosive situation.* **4.** *Phonetics.* another word for **plosive.** ~*n.* **5.** a substance that decomposes rapidly under certain conditions with the production of gases, which expand by the heat of the reaction. The energy released is used in firearms, blasting, and rocket propulsion. **6.** a plosive consonant; stop. —**exˈplosively** *adv.* —**exˈplosiveness** *n.*

explosive forming *n. Engineering.* a rapid method of forming a metal object in which components are made by subjecting the metal to very high pressures generated by a controlled explosion.

expo (ˈɛkspəʊ) *n., pl.* **-pos.** short for **exposition** (sense 3).

exponent (ɪkˈspəʊnənt) *n.* **1.** (usually foll. by *of*) a person or thing that acts as an advocate (of an idea, cause, etc.). **2.** a person or thing that explains or interprets. **3.** a performer or interpretive artist, esp. a musician. **4.** Also called: **power, index.** *Maths.* a number or variable placed as a superscript to the right of another number or quantity indicating the number of times the number or quantity is to be multiplied by itself. ~*adj.* **5.** offering a declaration, explanation, or interpretation. [C16: from Latin *expōnere* to set out, expound, from *pōnere* to set, place]

exponential (ˌɛkspəʊˈnɛnʃəl) *adj.* **1.** *Maths.* (of a function, curve, series, or equation) of, containing, or involving one or more numbers or quantities raised to an exponent, esp. e^x. **2.** *Maths.* raised to the power of e, the base of natural logarithms. Symbol:

exp 3. of or involving an exponent or exponents. 4. *Informal.* very rapid. ~*n.* 5. *Maths.* an exponential function, etc. —ˌ**ex·po'nentially** *adv.*

exponential distribution *n. Statistics.* a continuous single-parameter distribution used esp. when making statements about the length of life of certain materials or waiting times between randomly occurring events. Its density function is $p(x) = \lambda e^{-\lambda x}$ for positive λ and nonnegative *x*, and it is a special case of the gamma distribution.

exponential horn *n.* a horn for the radiation of acoustic or high-frequency electromagnetic waves, of which the cross-sectional area increases exponentially with the length.

export *n.* ('ɛkspɔːt). 1. (*often pl.*) **a.** goods (**visible exports**) or services (**invisible exports**) sold to a foreign country or countries. **b.** (*as modifier*): *an export licence; export finance.* ~*vb.* (ɪk'spɔːt, 'ɛkspɔːt). 2. to sell (goods or services) or ship (goods) to a foreign country or countries. 3. (*tr.*) to transmit or spread (an idea, social institution, etc.) abroad. ~Compare **import.** [C15: from Latin *exportāre* to carry away, from *portāre* to carry] —**ex'portable** *adj.* —**ex**ˌ**porta'bility** *n.* —**ex'porter** *n.*

exportation (ˌɛkspɔː'teɪʃən) *n.* 1. the act, business, or process of exporting goods or services. 2. *Chiefly U.S.* an exported product or service.

export reject *n.* an article that fails to meet a standard of quality required for export and that is sold on the home market.

expose (ɪk'spəʊz) *vb.* (*tr.*) 1. to display for viewing; exhibit. 2. to bring to public notice; disclose; reveal: *to expose the facts.* 3. to divulge the identity of; unmask. 4. (foll. by *to*) to make subject or susceptible (to attack, criticism, etc.). 5. to abandon (a child, animal, etc.) in the open to die. 6. (foll. by *to*) to introduce (to) or acquaint (with): *he was exposed to the classics at an early age.* 7. *Photog.* to subject (a photographic film or plate) to light, x-rays, or some other type of actinic radiation. 8. *R.C. Church.* to exhibit (the consecrated Eucharistic Host or a relic) for public veneration. 9. **expose oneself.** to display one's sexual organs in public. [C15: from Old French *exposer*, from Latin *expōnere* to set out; see EXPONENT] —**ex'posable** *adj.* —**ex'posal** *n.* —**ex'poser** *n.*

exposé (ɛks'pəʊzeɪ) *n.* 1. the act or an instance of bringing a scandal, crime, etc., to public notice. 2. an article, book, or statement that discloses a scandal, crime, etc.

exposed (ɪk'spəʊzd) *adj.* 1. not concealed; displayed for viewing. 2. without shelter from the elements. 3. susceptible to attack or criticism; vulnerable. 4. *Mountaineering.* (of a climb, pitch, or move) performed on a high, sheer, and unsheltered rock face. —**exposedness** (ɪk'spəʊzɪdnɪs) *n.*

exposition (ˌɛkspə'zɪʃən) *n.* 1. a systematic, usually written statement about, commentary on, or explanation of a specific subject. 2. the act of expounding or setting forth information or a viewpoint. 3. a large public exhibition, esp. of industrial products or arts and crafts. 4. the act of exposing or the state of being exposed. 5. the part of a play, novel, etc., in which the theme and main characters are introduced. 6. *Music.* the first statement of the subjects or themes of a movement in sonata form or a fugue. 7. *R.C. Church.* the exhibiting of the consecrated Eucharistic Host or a relic for public veneration. [C14: from Latin *expositiō* a setting forth, from *expōnere* to display; see EXPONENT] —ˌ**expo'sitional** *adj.*

expositor (ɪk'spɒzɪtə) *n.* a person who expounds.

expository (ɪk'spɒzɪtərɪ, -trɪ) *or* **expositive** *adj.* of, involving, or assisting in exposition; explanatory. —**ex'positorily** *or* **ex'positively** *adv.*

ex post facto (ɛks pəʊst 'fæktəʊ) *adj.* having retrospective effect: *an ex post facto law.* [C17: from Latin *ex* from + *post* afterwards + *factus* done, from *facere* to do]

expostulate (ɪk'spɒstjʊˌleɪt) *vb.* (*intr.*; usually foll. by *with*) to argue or reason (with), esp. in order to dissuade from an action or intention. [C16: from Latin *expostulāre* to require, from *postulāre* to demand; see POSTULATE] —**ex'postu**ˌ**latingly** *adv.* —**ex**ˌ**postu'lation** *n.* —**ex'postu**ˌ**lator** *n.* —**ex'postulatory** *or* **ex'postulative** *adj.*

exposure (ɪk'spəʊʒə) *n.* 1. the act of exposing or the condition of being exposed. 2. the position or outlook of a house, building, etc.; aspect: *the bedroom has a southern exposure.* 3. lack of shelter from the weather, esp. the cold: *to die of exposure.* 4. a surface that is exposed: *an exposure of granite.* 5. *Mountaineering.* the degree to which a climb, etc. is exposed (see **exposed** (sense 4)). 6. *Photog.* **a.** the act of exposing a photographic film or plate to light, x-rays, etc. **b.** an area on a film or plate that has been exposed to light, etc. **c.** (*as modifier*): *exposure control.* 7. *Photog.* **a.** the intensity of light falling on a photographic film or plate multiplied by the time for which it is exposed. **b.** a combination of lens aperture and shutter speed used in taking a photograph: *he used the wrong exposure.* 8. appearance or presentation before the public, as in a theatre, on television, or in films. 9. See **indecent exposure.**

exposure meter *n. Photog.* an instrument for measuring the intensity of light, usually by means of a photocell, so that the suitable camera settings of shutter speed and f-number (or lens aperture) can be determined. Also called: **light meter.**

expound (ɪk'spaʊnd) *vb.* (when *intr.*, foll. by *on* or *about*) to explain or set forth (an argument, theory, etc.) in detail: *to expound on one's theories; he expounded his reasoning.* [C13: from Old French *espondre*, from Latin *expōnere* to set forth, from *pōnere* to put] —**ex'pounder** *n.*

express (ɪk'sprɛs) *vb.* (*tr.*) 1. to transform (ideas) into words; utter; verbalize. 2. to show or reveal; indicate: *tears express grief.* 3. to communicate (emotion, etc.) without words, as through music, painting, etc. 4. to indicate through a symbol, formula, etc. 5. to force or squeeze out: *to express the juice from an orange.* 6. to send by rapid transport or special messenger. 7. **express oneself.** to communicate one's thoughts or ideas. ~*adj.* (*prenominal*) 8. clearly indicated or shown; explicitly stated: *an express wish.* 9. done or planned for a definite reason or goal; particular: *an express purpose.* 10. of, concerned with, or designed for rapid transportation of people, merchandise, mail, money, etc.: *express delivery; an express depot.* ~*n.* 11. **a.** a system for sending merchandise, mail, money, etc., rapidly. **b.** merchandise, mail, etc., conveyed by such a system. **c.** *Chiefly U.S. and Canadian.* an enterprise operating such a system. 12. Also called: **express train.** a fast train stopping at none or only a few of the intermediate stations between its two termini. 13. See **express rifle.** ~*adv.* 14. by means of a special delivery or express delivery: *it went express.* [C14: from Latin *expressus*, literally: squeezed out, hence, prominent, from *exprimere* to force out, from EX-[1] + *premere* to press] —**ex'presser** *n.* —**ex'pressible** *adj.*

expressage (ɪk'sprɛsɪdʒ) *n.* 1. the conveyance of merchandise by express. 2. the fee charged for such conveyance.

expression (ɪk'sprɛʃən) *n.* 1. the act or an instance of transforming ideas into words. 2. a manifestation of an emotion, feeling, etc., without words: *tears are an expression of grief.* 3. communication of emotion through music, painting, etc. 4. a look on the face that indicates mood or emotion: *a joyful expression.* 5. the choice of words, phrases, syntax, intonation, etc., in communicating. 6. a particular phrase used conventionally to express something: *a dialect expression.* 7. the act or process of forcing or squeezing out a liquid. 8. *Maths.* a variable, function, or some combination of constants, variables, or functions. 9. *Genetics.* the effect of a particular gene on the phenotype. —**ex'pressional** *adj.* —**ex'pressionless** *adj.* —**ex'pressionlessly** *adv.*

expressionism (ɪk'sprɛʃəˌnɪzəm) *n.* (*sometimes cap.*) an artistic and literary movement originating in Germany at the beginning of the 20th century, which sought to express emotions rather than to represent external reality: characterized by the use of symbolism and of exaggeration and distortion. —**ex'pressionist** *n., adj.* —**ex**ˌ**pression'istic** *adj.*

expression mark *n.* one of a set of musical directions, usually in Italian, indicating how a piece or passage is to be performed.

expressive (ɪk'sprɛsɪv) *adj.* 1. of, involving, or full of expression. 2. (*postpositive*; foll. by *of*) indicative or suggestive (of): *a look expressive of love.* 3. having a particular meaning, feeling, or force; significant. —**ex'pressively** *adv.* —**ex'pressiveness** *n.*

expressivity (ˌɛksprɛ'sɪvɪtɪ) *n.* 1. (esp. of a work of art) the quality of being expressive. 2. *Genetics.* the strength of the effect of a gene on the phenotype.

expressly (ɪk'sprɛslɪ) *adv.* 1. for an express purpose; with specific intentions. 2. plainly, exactly, or unmistakably.

expresso (ɪk'sprɛsəʊ) *n.* a variant of **espresso.**

express rifle *n.* a high-velocity hunting rifle for big game shooting.

expressway (ɪk'sprɛsˌweɪ) *n.* a motorway.

expropriate (ɛks'prəʊprɪˌeɪt) *vb.* (*tr.*) to deprive (an owner) of (property), esp. by taking it for public use. See also **eminent domain.** [C17: from Medieval Latin *expropriāre* to deprive of possessions, from *proprius* own] —**ex'propriable** *adj.* —**ex**ˌ**propri'ation** *n.* —**ex'propri**ˌ**ator** *n.*

exptl *abbrev. for* experimental.

expulsion (ɪk'spʌlʃən) *n.* the act of expelling or the fact or condition of being expelled. [C14: from Latin *expulsiō* a driving out, from *expellere* to EXPEL]

expulsive (ɪk'spʌlsɪv) *adj.* tending or serving to expel.

expunge (ɪk'spʌndʒ) *vb.* (*tr.*) 1. to delete or erase; blot out; obliterate. 2. to wipe out or destroy. [C17: from Latin *expungere* to blot out, from *pungere* to prick] —**expunction** (ɪk'spʌŋkʃən) *n.* —**ex'punger** *n.*

expurgate ('ɛkspəˌgeɪt) *vb.* (*tr.*) to amend (a book, text, etc.) by removing (obscene or offensive sections). [C17: from Latin *expurgāre* to clean out, from *purgāre* to purify; see PURGE] —ˌ**expur'gation** *n.* —'**expur**ˌ**gator** *n.* —**expurgatory** (ɛks'pɜːgətərɪ, -trɪ) *or* **expurgatorial** (ɛkˌspɜːgə'tɔːrɪəl) *adj.*

exquisite (ɪk'skwɪzɪt, 'ɛkskwɪzɪt) *adj.* 1. possessing qualities of unusual delicacy and fine craftsmanship: *jewels in an exquisite setting.* 2. extremely beautiful and pleasing: *an exquisite face.* 3. outstanding or excellent: *an exquisite victory.* 4. sensitive; discriminating: *exquisite taste.* 5. fastidious and refined. 6. intense or sharp in feeling: *exquisite pleasure; exquisite pain.* ~*n.* 7. *Obsolete.* a dandy. [C15: from Latin *exquīsītus* excellent, from *exquīrere* to search out, from *quaerere* to seek] —**ex'quisitely** *adv.* —**ex'quisiteness** *n.*

exr *abbrev. for* executor.

exsanguinate (ɪk'sæŋgwɪneɪt) *vb.* (*tr.*) *Rare.* to drain the blood from. [C19: from Latin *exsanguināre*] —**ex**ˌ**sanguin'ation** *n.*

exsanguine (ɪkˈsæŋgwɪn) *or* **exsanguinous** *adj.* without blood; bloodless or anaemic. [C17: from Latin *exsanguis*, from *sanguis* blood] —ˌ**exsanˈguinity** *n.*
exscind (ɛkˈsɪnd) *vb.* (*tr.*) to cut off or out; excise. [C17 *exscind*, from Latin *exscindere* to extirpate, destroy, from *scindere* to cut, tear, split]
exsect (ɛkˈsɛkt) *vb.* (*tr.*) to cut out. [C17 *exsect*, from Latin *exsecāre* to cut away, from *secāre* to cut] —**exsection** (ɛkˈsɛkʃən) *n.*
exsert (ɛkˈsɜːt) *vb.* **1.** (*tr.*) to thrust out; protrude. ~*adj. also* **exserted. 2.** protruded, stretched out, or (esp. of stamens) projecting beyond the corolla of a flower. [C19: from Latin *exserere* to thrust out; see EXERT] —**exˈsertion** *n.* —**exsertile** (ɛkˈsɜːtaɪl) *adj.*
ex-service *adj.* having formerly served in the armed forces.
ex-serviceman *or* (*fem.*) **ex-servicewoman** *n., pl.* **-men** *or* **-women.** a person who has served in the army, navy, or air force.
exsiccate (ˈɛksɪˌkeɪt) *vb.* to dry up; desiccate. [C15: from Latin *exsiccāre*, from *siccus* dry] —ˌ**exsicˈcation** *n.* —ˈ**exsiccative** *adj.* —ˈ**exsicˌcator** *n.*
ex silentio *Latin.* (ɛks sɪˈlɛnʃɪˌəʊ) *adv., adj.* (of a theory, assumption, etc.) based on a lack of evidence to the contrary. [literally: from silence]
exstipulate (ɛkˈstɪpjʊlɪt, -ˌleɪt) *or* **estipulate** *adj.* (of a flowering plant) having no stipules.
exstrophy (ˈɛkstrəfɪ) *n. Med.* congenital eversion of a hollow organ, esp. the urinary bladder. [C19: from Greek EX-[1] + *strophein* to turn]
ext *abbrev. for:* **1.** extinct. **2.** extract.
ext. *abbrev. for:* **1.** extension. **2.** external(ly). **3.** extra.
extant (ɛkˈstænt, ˈɛkstənt) *adj.* **1.** still in existence; surviving. **2.** *Archaic.* standing out; protruding. [C16: from Latin *exstāns* standing out, from *exstāre*, from *stāre* to stand]
▷**Usage.** Careful writers distinguish between *extant* and *existent.* Both are used of that which exists at the present time, but *extant* has a further connotation of survival. *Extant* is therefore used of that which still exists, although there would be reason for believing that it might have disappeared: *the species was believed extinct, but a small population was found to be still extant in Africa; in the existent circumstances this is impossible.*
extemporaneous (ɪkˌstɛmpəˈreɪnɪəs) *or* **extemporary** (ɪkˈstɛmpərərɪ, -prərɪ) *adj.* **1.** spoken, performed, etc., without planning or preparation; impromptu; extempore. **2.** done in a temporary manner; improvised. —**exˌtempoˈraneously** *or* **exˈtemporarily** *adv.* —**exˌtempoˈraneousness** *or* **exˈtemporariness** *n.*
extempore (ɪkˈstɛmpərɪ) *adv., adj.* without planning or preparation; impromptu. [C16: from Latin *ex tempore* instantaneously, from EX-[1] out of + *tempus* time]
extemporize *or* **extemporise** (ɪkˈstɛmpəˌraɪz) *vb.* **1.** to perform, speak, or compose (an act, speech, piece of music, etc.) without planning or preparation. **2.** to use (a temporary solution) for an immediate need; improvise. —**exˌtemporiˈzation** *or* **exˌtemporiˈsation** *n.* —**exˈtempoˌrizer** *or* **exˈtempoˌriser** *n.*
extend (ɪkˈstɛnd) *vb.* **1.** to draw out or be drawn out; stretch. **2.** to last for a certain time: *his schooling extended for three years.* **3.** (*intr.*) to reach a certain point in time or distance: *the land extends five miles.* **4.** (*intr.*) to exist or occur: *the trees extended throughout the area.* **5.** (*tr.*) to increase (a building, etc.) in size or area; add to or enlarge. **6.** (*tr.*) to broaden the meaning or scope of: *the law was extended.* **7.** (*tr.*) to put forth, present, or offer: *to extend greetings.* **8.** to stretch forth (an arm, etc.). **9.** (*tr.*) to lay out (a body) at full length. **10.** (*tr.*) to strain or exert (a person or animal) to the maximum. **11.** (*tr.*) to prolong (the time originally set) for payment of (a debt or loan), completion of (a task), etc. **12.** (*tr.*) *Book-keeping.* **a.** to carry forward. **b.** to calculate the amount of (a total, balance, etc.). **13.** (*tr.*) *Law.* (formerly in England) to value or assess (land). [C14: from Latin *extendere* to stretch out, from *tendere* to stretch] —**exˈtendible** *or* **exˈtendable** *adj.* —**exˌtendiˈbility** *or* **exˌtendaˈbility** *n.*
extended (ɪkˈstɛndɪd) *adj.* **1.** stretched out in time, space, influence, application, etc. **2.** (of a horse's pace) free-moving and with long steps: *an extended trot.* **3.** *Printing.* another word for **expanded** (sense 1). —**exˈtendedly** *adv.* —**exˈtendedness** *n.*
extended family *n. Sociol., anthropol.* a social unit that contains the nuclear family together with blood relatives, often spanning three or more generations.
extended-play *adj.* denoting an EP record.
extender (ɪkˈstɛndə) *n.* **1.** a person or thing that extends. **2.** a substance, such as French chalk or china clay, added to paints to give them body and decrease their rate of settlement. **3.** a substance added to glues and resins to dilute them or to modify their viscosity. **4.** a substance added to elastomers to assist the plasticizer. **5.** *Printing.* the part of certain lower-case letters that extends either above (the ascender) or below (the descender) the body of the letter.
extensible (ɪkˈstɛnsəbᵊl) *or* **extensile** (ɪkˈstɛnsaɪl) *adj.* capable of being extended. —**exˌtensiˈbility** *or* **exˈtensibleness** *n.*
extension (ɪkˈstɛnʃən) *n.* **1.** the act of extending or the condition of being extended. **2.** something that can be extended or that extends another object. **3.** the length, range, etc., over which something is extended; extent. **4.** an additional telephone set connected to the same telephone line as another set or other sets. **5.** a room or rooms added to an existing building. **6.** a delay, esp. one agreed by all parties, in the date originally set for payment of a debt or completion of a contract. **7.** the property of matter by which it occupies space; size. **8. a.** the act of straightening or extending an arm or leg. **b.** its position after being straightened or extended. **9.** *Med.* a steady pull applied to a fractured or dislocated arm or leg to restore it to its normal position. See also **traction** (sense 3). **10. a.** a service by which some of the facilities of an educational establishment, library, etc., are offered to outsiders. **b.** (*as modifier*): *a university extension course.* **11.** *Logic.* **a.** the class of entities to which a given word correctly applies: thus, the extension of *satellite of Mars* is the set containing only Deimos and Phobos. Compare **intension** (sense 1). **b. conservative extension.** a formal theory that includes among its theorems all the theorems of a given theory. [C14: from Late Latin *extensiō* a stretching out; see EXTEND]
extensional (ɪkˈstɛnʃənᵊl) *adj.* **1.** relating to or characterized by extension. **2.** *Logic.* explicable solely in terms of extensions; ignoring differences of meaning that do not affect the extension. See also **extensionality, substitutivity, transparent context.** —**exˈtensionally** *adv.* —**exˈtensionalism** *n.*
extensionality (ɪkˌstɛnʃəˈnælɪtɪ) *n. Logic.* the principle that sets are definable in terms of their elements alone, whatever way they may have been selected. Thus {a, b}={b, a}={first two letters of the alphabet}.
extension ring *or* **tube** *n. Photog.* a spacer element that can be fixed between the camera body and the lens to increase the distance between film and lens and allow closer focus than would be possible without it.
extensity (ɪkˈstɛnsɪtɪ) *n.* **1.** *Psychol.* that part of sensory perception relating to the spatial aspect of objects. **2.** *Rare.* the condition of being extensive or extended.
extensive (ɪkˈstɛnsɪv) *adj.* **1.** having a large extent, area, scope, degree, etc.; vast: *extensive deserts; an extensive inheritance.* **2.** widespread: *extensive coverage in the press.* **3.** *Agriculture.* involving or farmed with minimum expenditure of capital or labour, esp. depending on a large area of land. Compare **intensive** (sense 3). **4.** *Physics.* of or relating to a property, measurement, etc., that is dependent on mass: *heat is an extensive property.* Compare **intensive** (sense 7). **5.** *Logic.* **a.** of or relating to logical extension. **b.** (of a definition) in terms of the objects to which the term applies rather than its meaning. —**exˈtensively** *adv.* —**exˈtensiveness** *n.*
extensometer (ˌɛkstɛnˈsɒmɪtə) *or* **extensimeter** (ˌɛkstɛnˈsɪmɪtə) *n.* an apparatus for studying small changes of length, as in the thermal expansion or mechanical compression of a solid.
extensor (ɪkˈstɛnsə, -sɔː) *n.* any muscle that stretches or extends an arm, leg, or other bodily part. Compare **flexor.** [C18: from New Latin, from Latin *extensus* stretched out]
extent (ɪkˈstɛnt) *n.* **1.** the range over which something extends; scope: *the extent of the damage.* **2.** an area or volume: *a vast extent of concrete.* **3.** *U.S. law.* a writ authorizing a person to whom a debt is due to assume temporary possession of his debtor's lands. **4.** *Logic.* another word for **extension** (sense 11). [C14: from Old French *extente*, from Latin *extentus* extensive, from *extendere* to EXTEND]
extenuate (ɪkˈstɛnjʊˌeɪt) *vb.* (*tr.*) **1.** to represent (an offence, a fault, etc.) as being less serious than it appears, as by showing mitigating circumstances. **2.** to cause to be or appear less serious; mitigate. **3.** to underestimate or make light of. **4.** *Archaic.* **a.** to emaciate or weaken. **b.** to dilute or thin out. [C16: from Latin *extenuāre* to make thin, from *tenuis* thin, frail] —**exˈtenuˌating** *adj.* —**exˌtenuˈation** *n.* —**exˈtenuˌator** *n.* —**exˈtenuatory** *adj.*
exterior (ɪkˈstɪərɪə) *n.* **1.** a part, surface, or region that is on the outside. **2.** the observable outward behaviour or appearance of a person. **3.** a film or scene shot outside a studio. ~*adj.* **4.** of, situated on, or suitable for the outside: *exterior cleaning.* **5.** coming or acting from without; external: *exterior complications.* **6.** of or involving foreign nations. [C16: from Latin, comparative of *exterus* on the outside, from *ex* out of] —**exˈteriorly** *adv.*
exterior angle *n.* **1.** an angle of a polygon contained between one side extended and the adjacent side. **2.** any of the four angles made by a transversal that are outside the region between the two intersected lines.
exteriorize *or* **exteriorise** (ɪkˈstɪərɪəˌraɪz) *vb.* (*tr.*) **1.** *Surgery.* to expose (an attached organ or part) outside a body cavity, esp. in order to remove it from an operating area. **2.** another word for **externalize.** —**exˌterioriˈzation** *or* **exˌterioriˈsation** *n.*
exterminate (ɪkˈstɜːmɪˌneɪt) *vb.* (*tr.*) to destroy (living things, esp. pests or vermin) completely; annihilate; eliminate. [C16: from Latin *extermināre* to drive away, from *terminus* boundary] —**exˈterminable** *adj.* —**exˌtermiˈnation** *n.* —**exˈterminative** *or* **exˈterminatory** *adj.* —**exˈtermiˌnator** *n.*
extern *or* **externe** (ˈɛkstɜːn, ɪkˈstɜːn) *n. U.S.* a person, such as a physician at a hospital, who has an official connection with an institution but does not reside in it. [C16: from Latin *externus* EXTERNAL]
external (ɪkˈstɜːnᵊl) *adj.* **1.** of, situated on, or suitable for the outside; outer. **2.** coming or acting from without: *external evidence from an independent source.* **3.** of or involving foreign nations; foreign. **4.** of, relating to, or designating a medicine that

is applied to the outside of the body. **5.** *Anatomy.* situated on or near the outside of the body: *the external ear.* **6.** (of a student) studying a university subject extramurally. **7.** *Philosophy.* (of objects, etc.) taken to exist independently of a perceiving mind. ~*n.* **8.** (*often pl.*) an external circumstance or aspect, esp. one that is superficial or inessential. **9.** *Austral. and N.Z.* a student taking an extramural subject. [C15: from Latin *externus* outward, from *exterus* on the outside, from *ex* out of] —**exˈternally** *adv.*

external-combustion engine *n.* a heat engine in which the working fluid is heated in an external boiler or heat exchanger and is thus isolated from the process of fuel combustion.

external ear *n.* the part of the ear consisting of the auricle and the auditory canal.

externalism (ɪkˈstɜːnəˌlɪzəm) *n.* **1.** exaggerated emphasis on outward form, esp. in religious worship. **2.** a philosophical doctrine holding that only objects that can be perceived by the senses are real; phenomenalism. —**exˈternalist** *n.*

externality (ˌɛkstɜːˈnælɪtɪ) *n., pl.* **-ties. 1.** the state or condition of being external. **2.** something external. **3.** *Philosophy.* the quality of existing independently of a perceiving mind. **4.** an economic effect that results from an economic choice but is not reflected in market prices.

externalize (ɪkˈstɜːnəˌlaɪz), **exteriorize** (ɪkˈstɪərɪəˌraɪz) *or* **externalise, exteriorise** *vb.* (*tr.*) **1.** to make external; give outward shape to. **2.** *Psychol.* to attribute (one's own feelings) to one's surroundings. —**exˌternaliˈzation, exˌterioriˈzation** *or* **exˌternaliˈsation, exˌterioriˈsation** *n.*

exteroceptor (ˈɛkstərəʊˌsɛptə) *n.* any sensory organ or part of the body, such as the eye, able to receive stimuli from outside the body. Compare **interoceptor, proprioceptor.** [C20: *extero-*, from Latin *exterus* EXTERIOR outward + (RE)CEPTOR] —ˌ**exteroˈceptive** *adj.*

exterritorial (ˌɛkstɛrɪˈtɔːrɪəl) *adj.* a variant of **extraterritorial.** —**exˌterriˌtoriˈality** *n.* —ˌ**exterriˈtorially** *adv.*

extinct (ɪkˈstɪŋkt) *adj.* **1.** (of an animal or plant species) having no living representative; having died out. **2.** quenched or extinguished. **3.** (of a volcano) no longer liable to erupt; inactive. **4.** void or obsolete: *an extinct political office.* [C15: from Latin *exstinctus* quenched, from *exstinguere* to EXTINGUISH]

extinction (ɪkˈstɪŋkʃən) *n.* **1.** the act of making extinct or the state of being extinct. **2.** the act of extinguishing or the state of being extinguished. **3.** complete destruction; annihilation. **4.** *Physics.* reduction of the intensity of radiation as a result of absorption or scattering by matter. **5.** *Astronomy.* the absorption of light from a planet or star by the earth's atmosphere. **6.** *Psychol.* a process in which the frequency or intensity of a learned response is decreased as a result of reinforcement being withdrawn. Compare **habituation.**

extinctive (ɪkˈstɪŋktɪv) *adj.* tending or serving to extinguish or make extinct.

extine (ˈɛkstɪn, -tiːn, -taɪn) *or* **exine** (ˈɛksɪn, -aɪn) *n. Botany.* the outermost coat of a pollen grain or a spore. Compare **intine.** [C19: from Latin *extimus* outermost + -INE[1]]

extinguish (ɪkˈstɪŋgwɪʃ) *vb.* (*tr.*) **1.** to put out or quench (a light, flames, etc.). **2.** to remove or destroy entirely; annihilate. **3.** *Archaic.* to eclipse or obscure by or as if by superior brilliance. **4.** *Law.* to discharge (a debt). [C16: from Latin *exstinguere,* from *stinguere* to quench] —**exˈtinguishable** *adj.* —**exˈtinguisher** *n.* —**exˈtinguishment** *n.*

extinguishant (ɪkˈstɪŋgwɪʃənt) *n.* a substance, such as a liquid, foam, powder, etc., used in extinguishing fires.

extirpate (ˈɛkstəˌpeɪt) *vb.* (*tr.*) **1.** to remove or destroy completely. **2.** to pull up or out; uproot. **3.** to remove (an organ or part) surgically. [C16: from Latin *exstirpāre* to root out, from *stirps* root, stock] —ˌ**extirˈpation** *n.* —ˈ**extirˌpative** *adj.* —ˈ**extirˌpator** *n.*

extol *or U.S.* **extoll** (ɪkˈstəʊl) *vb.* **-tols, -tolling, -tolled** *or U.S.* **-tolls, -tolling, -tolled.** (*tr.*) to praise lavishly; exalt. [C15: from Latin *extollere* to elevate, from *tollere* to raise] —**exˈtoller** *n.* —**exˈtollingly** *adv.* —**exˈtolment** *n.*

extort (ɪkˈstɔːt) *vb.* (*tr.*) **1.** to secure (money, favours, etc.) by intimidation, violence, or the misuse of influence or authority. **2.** to obtain by importunate demands: *the children extorted a promise of a trip to the zoo.* **3.** to overcharge for (something, esp. interest on a loan). [C16: from Latin *extortus* wrenched out, from *extorquēre* to wrest away, from *torquēre* to twist, wrench] —**exˈtortion** *n.* —**exˈtortioner, exˈtortionist,** *or* **exˈtorter** *n.* —**exˈtortive** *adj.*

extortionate (ɪkˈstɔːʃənɪt) *adj.* **1.** (of prices, etc.) excessive; exorbitant. **2.** (of persons) using extortion. —**exˈtortionately** *adv.*

extra (ˈɛkstrə) *adj.* **1.** being more than what is usual or expected; additional. ~*n.* **2.** a person or thing that is additional. **3.** something for which an additional charge is made: *the new car had many extras.* **4.** an additional edition of a newspaper, esp. to report a new development or crisis. **5.** *Films.* an actor or person temporarily engaged, usually for crowd scenes. **6.** *Cricket.* a run not scored from the bat, such as a wide, no-ball, bye, or leg bye. **7.** *U.S.* something that is better than usual in quality. ~*adv.* **8.** unusually; exceptionally: *an extra fast car.* [C18: perhaps shortened from EXTRAORDINARY]

extra- *prefix.* outside or beyond an area or scope: *extrasensory; extraterritorial.* [from Latin *extrā* outside, beyond, changed from *extera,* from *exterus* outward]

extracanonical (ˌɛkstrəkəˈnɒnɪkᵊl) *adj. Christianity.* not included in the canon of Scripture.

extracellular (ˌɛkstrəˈsɛljʊlə) *adj. Biology.* situated or occurring outside a cell or cells. —ˌ**extraˈcellularly** *adv.*

extracorporeal (ˌɛkstrəkɔːˈpɔːrɪəl) *adj.* outside the body.

extra cover *n. Cricket.* a fielding position between cover and mid-off.

extract *vb.* (ɪkˈstrækt). (*tr.*) **1.** to withdraw, pull out, or uproot by force. **2.** to remove or separate. **3.** to derive (pleasure, information, etc.) from some source or situation. **4.** to deduce or develop (a doctrine, policy, etc.). **5.** *Informal.* to extort (money, etc.). **6.** to obtain (a substance) from a mixture or material by a chemical or physical process, such as digestion, distillation, the action of a solvent, or mechanical separation. **7.** to cut out or copy out (an article, passage, quotation, etc.) from a publication. **8.** to determine the value of (the root of a number). ~*n.* (ˈɛkstrækt). **9.** something extracted, such as a part or passage from a book, speech, etc. **10.** a preparation containing the active principle or concentrated essence of a material: *beef extract; yeast extract.* **11.** *Pharmacol.* a solution of plant or animal tissue containing the active principle. [C15: from Latin *extractus* drawn forth, from *extrahere,* from *trahere* to drag] —**exˈtractable** *adj.* —**exˌtractaˈbility** *n.*

extraction (ɪkˈstrækʃən) *n.* **1.** the act of extracting or the condition of being extracted. **2.** something extracted; an extract. **3. a.** the act or an instance of extracting a tooth or teeth. **b.** a tooth or teeth extracted. **4.** origin, descent, lineage, or ancestry: *of German extraction.*

extractions (ɪkˈstrækʃənz) *pl. n.* the residue remaining after an oilseed has had the oil extracted by a solvent. Used as a feed for animals: *groundnut extractions.* Compare **expellers.**

extractive (ɪkˈstræktɪv) *adj.* **1.** tending or serving to extract. **2.** of, involving, or capable of extraction. ~*n.* **3.** something extracted or capable of being extracted. **4.** the part of an extract that is insoluble.

extractor (ɪkˈstræktə) *n.* **1.** a person or thing that extracts. **2.** an instrument for pulling something out or for removing tight-fitting components. **3.** a device for extracting liquid from a solid, esp. a centrifugal dryer. **4.** short for **extractor fan. 5.** a fitting in many firearms for removing spent cartridges from the chamber.

extractor fan *or* **extraction fan** *n.* a fan used in kitchens, bathrooms, workshops, etc., to remove stale air or fumes.

extracurricular (ˌɛkstrəkəˈrɪkjʊlə) *adj.* **1.** taking place outside the normal school timetable: *extracurricular activities.* **2.** beyond the regular duties, schedule, etc.

extraditable (ˈɛkstrəˌdaɪtəbᵊl) *adj.* **1.** (of a crime) rendering the offender liable to extradition: *an extraditable offence.* **2.** (of a person) subject to extradition.

extradite (ˈɛkstrəˌdaɪt) *vb.* (*tr.*) **1.** to surrender (an alleged offender) for trial to a foreign state. **2.** to procure the extradition of. [C19: back formation from EXTRADITION]

extradition (ˌɛkstrəˈdɪʃən) *n.* the surrender of an alleged offender or fugitive to the state in whose territory the alleged offence was committed. [C19: from French, from Latin *trāditiō* a handing over; see TRADITION]

extrados (ɛkˈstreɪdɒs) *n., pl.* **-dos** (-dəʊz) *or* **-doses.** *Architect.* the outer curve or surface of an arch or vault. Compare **intrados.** [C18: from French, from EXTRA- + *dos* back, from Latin *dorsum*]

extradural (ˌɛkstrəˈdjʊərəl) *adj.* another word for **epidural** (sense 1).

extragalactic (ˌɛkstrəgəˈlæktɪk) *adj.* occurring or existing beyond the Galaxy.

extragalactic nebula *n.* the former name for **galaxy.**

extrajudicial (ˌɛkstrədʒuːˈdɪʃəl) *adj.* **1.** outside the ordinary course of legal proceedings: *extrajudicial evidence.* **2.** beyond the jurisdiction or authority of the court: *an extrajudicial opinion.* —ˌ**extrajuˈdicially** *adv.*

extramarital (ˌɛkstrəˈmærɪtᵊl) *adj.* (esp. of sexual relations) occurring outside marriage.

extramundane (ˌɛkstrəˈmʌndeɪn) *adj.* not of the physical world or universe.

extramural (ˌɛkstrəˈmjʊərəl) *adj.* **1.** connected with but outside the normal courses or programme of a university, college, etc.: *extramural studies.* **2.** located beyond the boundaries or walls of a city, castle, etc. —ˌ**extraˈmurally** *adv.*

extraneous (ɪkˈstreɪnɪəs) *adj.* **1.** not essential. **2.** not pertinent or applicable; irrelevant. **3.** coming from without; of external origin. **4.** not belonging; unrelated to that to which it is added or in which it is contained. [C17: from Latin *extrāneus* external, from *extrā* outside] —**exˈtraneously** *adv.* —**exˈtraneousness** *n.*

extranuclear (ˌɛkstrəˈnjuːklɪə) *adj. Biology.* situated or occurring in part of a cell outside the nucleus.

extraordinary (ɪkˈstrɔːdᵊnrɪ, -dᵊnərɪ) *adj.* **1.** very unusual, remarkable, or surprising. **2.** not in an established manner, course, or order. **3.** employed for particular events or purposes. **4.** (*usually postpositive*) (of an official, etc.) additional or subordinate to the usual one: *a minister extraordinary.* [C15: from

Latin *extraordinārius* beyond what is usual; see ORDINARY] —**ex'traordinarily** *adv.* —**ex'traordinariness** *n.*

extraordinary general meeting *n.* a meeting specially called to discuss a particular item of a company's business, usually one of some importance. The meeting may be called by a group of shareholders or by the directors. Abbrev.: **EGM.**

extraordinary ray *n. Optics.* the plane-polarized ray of light that does not obey the laws of refraction in a doubly refracting crystal. See **double refraction.** Compare **ordinary ray.**

extrapolate (ɪk'stræpəˌleɪt) *vb.* **1.** *Maths.* to estimate (a value of a function or measurement) beyond the values already known, by the extension of a curve. Compare **interpolate** (sense 4). **2.** to infer (something not known) by using but not strictly deducing from the known facts. [C19: EXTRA- + *-polate,* as in INTERPOLATE] —**exˌtrapo'lation** *n.* —**ex'trapolative** *or* **ex'trapolatory** *adj.* —**ex'trapoˌlator** *n.*

extraposition (ˌɛkstrəpə'zɪʃən) *n.* **1.** placement of something outside something else. **2.** *Transformational grammar.* a rule that moves embedded clauses out to the end of the main clause, converting, for example, *A man who will help has just arrived* into *A man has just arrived who will help.*

extrasensory (ˌɛkstrə'sɛnsərɪ) *adj.* of or relating to extrasensory perception.

extrasensory perception *n.* the supposed ability of certain individuals to obtain information about the environment without the use of normal sensory channels. Also called: **cryptaesthesia.** See also **clairvoyance** (sense 1), **telepathy.** Abbrev.: **ESP.**

extraterrestrial (ˌɛkstrətɪ'rɛstrɪəl) *adj.* **1.** occurring or existing beyond the earth's atmosphere. ~*n.* **2.** (in science fiction) a being from beyond the earth's atmosphere.

extraterritorial (ˌɛkstrəˌtɛrɪ'tɔːrɪəl) *or* **exterritorial** *adj.* **1.** beyond the limits of a country's territory. **2.** of, relating to, or possessing extraterritoriality. —**ˌextraˌterri'torially** *or* **ˌexterri'torially** *adv.*

extraterritoriality (ˌɛkstrəˌtɛrɪˌtɔːrɪ'ælɪtɪ) *n. International law.* **1.** the privilege granted to some aliens, esp. diplomats, of being exempt from the jurisdiction of the state in which they reside. **2.** the right or privilege of a state to exercise authority in certain circumstances beyond the limits of its territory.

extra time *n. Sport.* an additional period played at the end of a match, to compensate for time lost through injury or (in certain circumstances) to allow the teams to achieve a conclusive result.

extrauterine (ˌɛkstrə'juːtəˌraɪn) *adj.* situated or developing outside the cavity of the uterus.

extravagance (ɪk'strævɪgəns) *n.* **1.** excessive outlay of money; wasteful spending. **2.** immoderate or absurd speech or behaviour.

extravagant (ɪk'strævɪgənt) *adj.* **1.** spending money excessively or immoderately. **2.** going beyond usual bounds; unrestrained: *extravagant praise.* **3.** ostentatious; showy. **4.** exorbitant in price; overpriced. [C14: from Medieval Latin *extravagāns,* from Latin EXTRA- + *vagārī* to wander] —**ex'travagantly** *adv.*

extravaganza (ɪkˌstrævə'gænzə) *n.* **1.** an elaborately staged and costumed light entertainment. **2.** any lavish or fanciful display, literary or other composition, etc. [C18: from Italian: EXTRAVAGANCE]

extravagate (ɪk'strævəˌgeɪt) *vb.* (*intr.*) *Archaic.* **1.** to exceed normal limits or propriety. **2.** to roam at will. [C17: from Latin *extravagārī;* see EXTRAVAGANT] —**exˌtrava'gation** *n.*

extravasate (ɪk'strævəˌseɪt) *vb.* **1.** *Pathol.* to cause (blood or lymph) to escape or (of blood or lymph) to escape into the surrounding tissues from their proper vessels. **2.** to exude (molten material, such as lava) or (of molten material) to be exuded. ~*n.* **3.** *Pathol.* the material extravasated. [C17: from Latin EXTRA- + *vās* vessel] —**exˌtrava'sation** *n.*

extravascular (ˌɛkstrə'væskjʊlə) *adj. Anatomy.* situated or occurring outside a lymph or blood vessel.

extravehicular (ˌɛkstrəvɪ'hɪkjʊlə) *adj.* occurring or used outside a spacecraft, either in space or on the surface of the moon or another planet: *extravehicular activity.*

extraversion (ˌɛkstrə'vɜːʃən) *n.* a variant spelling of **extroversion.** —**ˌextra'versive** *adj.*

extravert ('ɛkstrəˌvɜːt) *n., adj.* a variant spelling of **extrovert.**

extra virgin *adj.* (of olive oil) of the highest quality, extracted by cold pressing rather than chemical treatment.

extremal (ɪk'striːməl) *n. Maths, logic.* the clause in a recursive definition that specifies that no items other than those generated by the stated rules fall within the definition, as in *1 is an integer, if n is an integer so is n+1, and nothing else is.*

extreme (ɪk'striːm) *adj.* **1.** being of a high or of the highest degree or intensity: *extreme cold; extreme difficulty.* **2.** exceeding what is usual or reasonable; immoderate: *extreme behaviour.* **3.** very strict, rigid, or severe; drastic: *an extreme measure.* **4.** (*prenominal*) farthest or outermost in direction: *the extreme boundary.* **5.** *Meteorol.* of, relating to, or characteristic of a **continental climate.** ~*n.* **6.** the highest or furthest degree (often in the phrases **in the extreme, go to extremes**). **7.** (*often pl.*) either of the two limits or ends of a scale or range of possibilities: *extremes of temperature.* **8.** *Maths.* **a.** the first or last term of a series or a proportion. **b.** a maximum or minimum value of a function. **9.** *Logic.* the subject or predicate of the conclusion of a syllogism. [C15: from Latin *extrēmus* outermost, from *exterus* on the outside; see EXTERIOR] —**ex'tremeness** *n.*

extremely (ɪk'striːmlɪ) *adv.* **1.** to the extreme; exceedingly. **2.** (intensifier): *she behaved extremely badly.*

▷**Usage.** See at **very.**

extremely high frequency *n.* a radio frequency between 30 000 and 300 000 megahertz. Abbrev.: **EHF.**

extreme unction *n. R.C. Church.* a former name for **anointing of the sick.**

extremist (ɪk'striːmɪst) *n.* **1.** a person who favours or resorts to immoderate, uncompromising, or fanatical methods or behaviour, esp. in being politically radical. ~*adj.* **2.** of, relating to, or characterized by immoderate or excessive actions, opinions, etc. —**ex'tremism** *n.*

extremity (ɪk'strɛmɪtɪ) *n., pl.* **-ties. 1.** the farthest or outermost point or section; termination. **2.** the greatest or most intense degree. **3.** an extreme condition or state, as of adversity or disease. **4.** a limb, such as a leg, arm, or wing, or the part of such a limb farthest from the trunk. **5.** (*usually pl.*) *Archaic.* a drastic or severe measure.

extricate ('ɛkstrɪˌkeɪt) *vb.* (*tr.*) **1.** to remove or free from complication, hindrance, or difficulty; disentangle. **2.** *Rare.* to free (a substance, gas, liquid, etc.) from chemical combination; liberate. [C17: from Latin *extrīcāre* to disentangle, from EX-[1] + *trīcae* trifles, vexations] —**'extricable** *adj.* —**ˌextri'cation** *n.*

extrinsic (ɛk'strɪnsɪk) *adj.* **1.** not contained or included within; extraneous. **2.** originating or acting from outside; external. [C16: from Late Latin *extrinsecus* (adj.) outward, from Latin (adv.) from without, on the outward side, from *exter* outward + *secus* alongside, related to *sequī* to follow] —**ex'trinsically** *adv.*

extrorse (ɛk'strɔːs) *or* **extrorsal** *adj. Botany.* turned or opening outwards or away from the axis: *extrorse anthers.* [C19: from Late Latin *extrorsus* in an outward direction, from Latin EXTRA- + *versus* turned towards]

extroversion *or* **extraversion** (ˌɛkstrə'vɜːʃən) *n.* **1.** *Psychol.* the directing of one's interest outwards, esp. towards social contacts. **2.** *Pathol.* a turning inside out of an organ or part. ~Compare **introversion.** [C17: from *extro-* (variant of EXTRA-, contrasting with INTRO-) + *-version,* from Latin *vertere* to turn] —**ˌextro'versive** *or* **ˌextra'versive** *adj.* —**ˌextro'versively** *or* **ˌextra'versively** *adv.*

extrovert *or* **extravert** ('ɛkstrəˌvɜːt) *Psychol.* ~*n.* **1.** a person concerned more with external reality than inner feelings. ~*adj.* **2.** of or characterized by extroversion: *extrovert tendencies.* ~Compare **introvert.** [C20: from *extro-* (variant of EXTRA-, contrasting with INTRO-) + *-vert,* from Latin *vertere* to turn] —**'extroˌverted** *or* **'extraˌverted** *adj.*

extrude (ɪk'struːd) *vb.* **1.** (*tr.*) to squeeze or force out. **2.** (*tr.*) to produce (moulded sections of plastic, metal, etc.) by ejection under pressure from a suitably shaped nozzle or die. **3.** (*tr.*) to chop up or pulverize (an item of food) and re-form it to look like a whole: *a factory-made rod of extruded egg.* **4.** a less common word for **protrude.** [C16: from Latin *extrūdere* to thrust out, from *trūdere* to push, thrust] —**ex'truded** *adj.*

extrusion (ɪk'struːʒən) *n.* **1.** the act or process of extruding. **2. a.** the movement of magma through volcano craters and cracks in the earth's crust, forming igneous rock. **b.** any igneous rock formed in this way. **3.** a component or material formed by the process of extruding. [C16: from Medieval Latin *extrūsiō,* from *extrūdere* to EXTRUDE] —**ex'trusible** *adj.*

extrusive (ɪk'struːsɪv) *adj.* **1.** tending to extrude. **2.** (of igneous rocks) formed from magma issuing from volcanoes or cracks in the earth's crust; volcanic. Compare **intrusive** (sense 2).

exuberant (ɪg'zjuːbərənt) *adj.* **1.** abounding in vigour and high spirits; full of vitality. **2.** lavish or effusive; excessively elaborate: *exuberant compliments.* **3.** growing luxuriantly or in profusion. [C15: from Latin *exūberāns,* from *ūberāre* to be fruitful, from *ūber* fertile] —**ex'uberance** *n.* —**ex'uberantly** *adv.*

exuberate (ɪg'zjuːbəˌreɪt) *vb.* (*intr.*) *Rare.* **1.** to be exuberant. **2.** to abound or grow in profusion. [C15: from Latin *exūberāre* to be abundant; see EXUBERANT]

exudation (ˌɛksjʊ'deɪʃən) *n.* **1.** the act of exuding or oozing out. **2.** Also called: **exudate** ('ɛksjʊˌdeɪt). an exuded substance, such as sweat or cellular debris. —**exudative** (ɪg'zjuːdətɪv) *adj.*

exude (ɪg'zjuːd) *vb.* **1.** to release or be released through pores, incisions, etc., as sweat from the body or sap from trees. **2.** (*tr.*) to make apparent by mood or behaviour: *he exuded confidence.* [C16: from Latin *exsūdāre,* from *sūdāre* to sweat]

exult (ɪg'zʌlt) *vb.* (*intr.*) **1.** to be joyful or jubilant, esp. because of triumph or success; rejoice. **2.** (often foll. by *over*) to triumph (over); show or take delight in the defeat or discomfiture (of). [C16: from Latin *exsultāre* to jump or leap for joy, from *saltāre* to leap] —**exultation** (ˌɛgzʌl'teɪʃən) *n.* —**ex'ultingly** *adv.*

exultant (ɪg'zʌltənt) *adj.* elated or jubilant, esp. because of triumph or success. —**ex'ultance** *or* **ex'ultancy** *n.* —**ex'ultantly** *adv.*

exurbia (ɛks'ɜːbɪə) *n. Chiefly U.S.* the region outside the suburbs of a city, consisting of residential areas (**exurbs**) that are occupied predominantly by rich commuters (**exurbanites**). Compare **stockbroker belt.** [C20: from EX-[1] + Latin *urbs* city, on pattern of *suburbia*] —**ex'urban** *adj.*

exuviae (ɪɡˈzjuːvɪˌiː) *pl. n.* layers of skin or cuticle shed by animals during ecdysis. [C17: from Latin: something stripped off (the body), from *exuere* to strip off] —**exˈuvial** *adj.*

exuviate (ɪɡˈzjuːvɪˌeɪt) *vb.* to shed (a skin or similar outer covering). —**exˌuviˈation** *n.*

ex voto *Latin.* (ɛks ˈvəʊtəʊ) *adv., adj.* **1.** in accordance with a vow. ~*n.* **2.** an offering made in fulfilment of a vow.

ex works *adv., adj.* (**ex-works** *when prenominal*) *Brit.* (of a price, value, etc.) excluding the cost of delivery from the factory and sometimes excluding the commission or profit of the distributor or retailer: *the price is £500 ex works.*

-ey *suffix.* a variant of **-y**^{1} and **-y**^{2}.

eyas (ˈaɪəs) *n.* a nestling hawk or falcon, esp. one reared for training in falconry. [C15: mistaken division of earlier *a nyas,* from Old French *niais* nestling, from Latin *nīdus* nest]

eye^{1} (aɪ) *n.* **1.** the organ of sight of animals, containing light-sensitive cells associated with nerve fibres, so that light entering the eye is converted to nervous impulses that reach the brain. In man and other vertebrates the iris controls the amount of light entering the eye and the lens focuses the light onto the retina. Related adjs.: **ocular, ophthalmic.** **2.** (*often pl.*) the ability to see; sense of vision: *weak eyes.* **3.** the visible external part of an eye, often including the area around it: *heavy-lidded eyes; piercing eyes.* **4.** a look, glance, expression, or gaze: *a stern eye.* **5.** a sexually inviting or provocative look (esp. in the phrases **give (someone) the (glad) eye, make eyes at**). **6.** attention or observation (often in the phrases **catch someone's eye, keep an eye on, cast an eye over**). **7.** ability to recognize, judge, or appreciate: *an eye for antiques.* **8.** (*often pl.*) opinion, judgment, point of view, or authority: *in the eyes of the law.* **9.** a structure or marking having the appearance of an eye, such as the bud on a twig or potato tuber or a spot on a butterfly wing. **10.** a small loop or hole, as at one end of a needle. **11.** a small area of low pressure and calm in the centre of a tornado. **12.** See **photocell.** **13.** *Informal.* See **private eye.** **14. all eyes.** *Informal.* acutely vigilant or observant: *the children were all eyes.* **15. (all) my eye.** *Informal.* rubbish; nonsense. **16. an eye for an eye.** retributive or vengeful justice; retaliation. **17. cut one's eye after, at,** *or* **on (someone).** *Caribbean.* to look rudely at (a person) and then turn one's face away sharply while closing one's eyes: a gesture of contempt. **18. eyes out.** *N.Z.* with every possible effort: *he went at the job eyes out.* **19. get one's eye in.** *Chiefly sports.* to become accustomed to the conditions, light, etc., with a consequent improvement in one's performance. **20. half an eye. a.** a modicum of perceptiveness: *anyone with half an eye can see she's in love.* **b.** continuing unobtrusive observation or awareness: *the dog had half an eye on the sheep.* **21. have eyes for.** to be interested in: *she has eyes only for him.* **22. in one's mind's eye.** pictured within the mind; imagined or remembered vividly. **23. in the public eye.** exposed to public curiosity or publicity. **24. keep an eye open** *or* **out (for).** to watch with special attention (for). **25. keep one's eyes skinned** (or **peeled**). to watch vigilantly (for). **26. lay, clap,** *or* **set eyes on.** (*usually used with a negative*) to see: *she had never laid eyes on him before.* **27. look (someone) in the eye.** to look openly and without shame or embarrassment at. **28. make (sheep's) eyes (at).** *Old-fashioned.* to ogle amorously. **29. more than meets the eye.** hidden motives, meaning, or facts. **30. pick the eyes out (of).** *Austral. and N.Z.* to select the best parts or pieces (of). **31. see eye to eye (with).** to agree (with). **32. shut one's eyes to** *or* **turn a blind eye to.** to pretend not to notice or ignore deliberately. **33. the eye of the wind.** *Nautical.* the direction from which the wind is blowing. **34. up to one's eyes (in).** extremely busy (with). **35. with a ... eye.** in a ... manner: *he regards our success with a jealous eye.* **36. with** *or* **having an eye to.** (*prep.*) **a.** regarding; with reference to: *with an eye to one's own interests.* **b.** with the intention or purpose of: *with an eye to reaching agreement.* **37. with one's eyes open.** in the full knowledge of all relevant facts. **38. with one's eyes shut. a.** with great ease, esp. as a result of thorough familiarity: *I could drive home with my eyes shut.* **b.** without being aware of all the facts. ~*vb.* **eyes, eyeing** *or* **eying, eyed.** (*tr.*) **39.** to look at carefully or warily. **40.** Also: **eye up.** to look at in a manner indicating sexual interest; ogle. ~See also **eyes.** [Old English *ēage;* related to Old Norse *auga,* Old High German *ouga,* Sanskrit *akṣi*] —ˈ**eyeless** *adj.* —ˈ**eyeˌlike** *adj.*

eye^{2} (aɪ) *n.* another word for **nye.**

eyeball (ˈaɪˌbɔːl) *n.* **1.** the entire ball-shaped part of the eye. **2. eyeball to eyeball.** in close confrontation.

eyebank (ˈaɪˌbæŋk) *n.* a place in which corneas are stored for use in corneal grafts.

eyebath (ˈaɪˌbɑːθ) *n.* a small vessel with a rim shaped to fit round the eye, used for applying medicated or cleansing solutions to the eyeball. Also called (U.S. and Canadian): **eyecup.**

eyeblack (ˈaɪˌblæk) *n.* another name for **mascara.**

eyebolt (ˈaɪˌbəʊlt) *n.* a threaded bolt, the head of which is formed into a ring or eye for lifting, pulling, or securing.

eyebright (ˈaɪˌbraɪt) *n.* any scrophulariaceous annual plant of the genus *Euphrasia,* esp. *E. nemorosa,* having small white-and-purple two-lipped flowers: formerly used in the treatment of eye disorders. Also called: **euphrasy.**

eyebrow (ˈaɪˌbraʊ) *n.* **1.** the transverse bony ridge over each eye. **2.** the arch of hair that covers this ridge. **3. raise an eyebrow.** See **raise** (sense 31).

eyebrow pencil *n.* a cosmetic in pencil form for applying colour and shape to the eyebrows.

eye-catching *adj.* tending to attract attention; striking. —ˈ**eyeˌcatcher** *n.*

eye contact *n.* a direct look between two people; meeting of eyes: *he maintained eye contact with his interrogator.*

eyecup (ˈaɪˌkʌp) *n.* a U.S. and Canadian name for an **eyebath.**

eyed (aɪd) *adj.* **a.** having an eye or eyes (as specified). **b.** (*in combination*): *one-eyed; brown-eyed.*

eye dog *n. N.Z.* a dog trained to control sheep by staring fixedly at them. Also called: **strong-eye dog.**

eyeful (ˈaɪfʊl) *n. Informal.* **1.** a view, glance, or gaze: *he got an eyeful of the secret before they blindfolded him.* **2.** a very beautiful or attractive sight, esp. a woman.

eyeglass (ˈaɪˌɡlɑːs) *n.* **1.** a lens for aiding or correcting defective vision, esp. a monocle. **2.** another word for **eyepiece.**

eyeglasses (ˈaɪˌɡlɑːsɪz) *pl. n. Now chiefly U.S.* another word for **spectacles.**

eyehole (ˈaɪˌhəʊl) *n.* **1.** a hole through which something, such as a rope, hook, or bar, is passed. **2.** the cavity that contains the eyeball; eye socket. **3.** another word for **peephole.**

eyehook (ˈaɪˌhʊk) *n.* a hook attached to a ring at the extremity of a rope or chain.

eyelash (ˈaɪˌlæʃ) *n.* **1.** any one of the short curved hairs that grow from the edge of the eyelids. **2.** a row or fringe of these hairs.

eyelet (ˈaɪlɪt) *n.* **1.** a small hole for a lace or cord to be passed through or for a hook to be inserted into. **2.** a small metal ring or tube with flared ends bent back, reinforcing an eyehole in fabric. **3.** a chink or small opening, such as a peephole in a wall. **4.** *Embroidery.* **a.** a small hole with finely stitched edges, forming part of an ornamental pattern. **b.** Also called: **eyelet embroidery.** a piece of embroidery decorated with such work. **5.** fabric decorated with such work produced by machine. **6.** a small eye or eyelike marking. ~*vb.* **7.** (*tr.*) to supply with an eyelet or eyelets. [C14: from Old French *oillet,* literally: a little eye, from *oill* eye, from Latin *oculus* eye; see EYE]

eyeleteer (ˌaɪlɪˈtɪə) *n.* a small bodkin or other pointed tool for making eyelet holes.

eyelevel (ˈaɪˌlɛvᵊl) *adj.* level with a person's eyes when looking straight ahead: *an eyelevel grill.*

eyelid (ˈaɪˌlɪd) *n.* **1.** either of the two muscular folds of skin that can be moved to cover the exposed portion of the eyeball. **2.** Also called: **clamshell.** *Aeronautics.* a set of movable parts at the rear of a jet engine that redirect the exhaust flow to assist braking during landing.

eyeliner (ˈaɪˌlaɪnə) *n.* a cosmetic used to outline the eyes.

eye of day *n. Poetic.* the sun.

eye-opener *n. Informal.* **1.** something startling or revealing. **2.** *U.S. and Canadian.* an alcoholic drink taken early in the morning.

eyepiece (ˈaɪˌpiːs) *n.* the lens or combination of lenses in an optical instrument nearest the eye of the observer.

eye rhyme *n.* a rhyme involving words that are similar in spelling but not in sound, such as *stone* and *none.*

eyes (aɪz) *pl. n. Nautical.* the part of the bows of a ship that are furthest forward at the level of the main deck.

eyes front *interj.* **1.** *Military.* a command to troops to look ahead. **2.** a demand for attention.

eyeshade (ˈaɪˌʃeɪd) *n.* an opaque or tinted translucent visor, worn on the head like a cap to protect the eyes from glare.

eye shadow *n.* a coloured cosmetic put around the eyes so as to enhance their colour or shape.

eyeshot (ˈaɪˌʃɒt) *n.* range of vision; view.

eyesight (ˈaɪˌsaɪt) *n.* the ability to see; faculty of sight.

eyes left *interj. Military.* a command to troops to look left, esp. as a salute when marching.

eye socket *n.* the nontechnical name for **orbit** (sense 3).

eyesore (ˈaɪˌsɔː) *n.* something very ugly.

eye splice *n.* an eye formed in a rope by splicing the end into its standing part.

eyespot (ˈaɪˌspɒt) *n.* **1.** a small area of light-sensitive pigment in some protozoans and algae and in other simple organisms. **2.** an eyelike marking, as on the wings of certain butterflies.

eyes right *interj. Military.* a command to troops to look right, esp. as a salute when marching.

eyestalk (ˈaɪˌstɔːk) *n.* a movable stalk bearing a compound eye at its tip: occurs in crustaceans and some molluscs.

eyestrain (ˈaɪˌstreɪn) *n.* fatigue or irritation of the eyes, resulting from excessive use, as from prolonged reading of small print, or uncorrected defects of vision.

Eyetie (ˈaɪtaɪ) *n., adj. Brit. slang, offensive.* Italian. [C20: based on a jocular mispronunciation of *Italian*]

eyetooth (ˌaɪˈtuːθ) *n., pl.* **-teeth.** **1.** either of the two canine teeth in the upper jaw. **2. give one's eyeteeth for.** to go to any lengths to achieve or obtain (something): *I'd give my eyeteeth for a radio as good as that.*

eyewash (ˈaɪˌwɒʃ) *n.* **1.** a mild solution for applying to the eyes for relief of irritation, etc. **2.** *Informal.* nonsense; rubbish.

eyewitness (ˈaɪˌwɪtnɪs) *n.* **a.** a person present at an event who can describe what happened. **b.** (*as modifier*): *an eyewitness account.*

eyot (aɪt) *n. Brit., obsolete except in place names.* island. [variant of AIT]
eyra ('ɛərə, 'aɪərə) *n.* a reddish-brown variety of the jaguarondi. [C19: from American Spanish, from Tupi *eirara*]
eyre (ɛə) *n. English legal history.* **1.** any of the circuit courts held in each shire from 1176 until the late 13th century. **2. justices in eyre.** the justices travelling on circuit and presiding over such courts. [C13: from Old French *erre* journey, from *errer* to travel, from Latin *errāre* to wander]
eyrie ('ɪərɪ, 'ɛərɪ, 'aɪərɪ) *or* **aerie** *n.* **1.** the nest of an eagle or other bird of prey, built in a high inaccessible place. **2.** the brood of a bird of prey, esp. an eagle. **3.** any high isolated position or place. [C16: from Medieval Latin *airea,* from Latin *ārea* open field, hence nest]
eyrir ('eɪrɪə) *n., pl.* **aurar** ('ɔːrɑː). an Icelandic monetary unit worth one hundredth of a krona. [Old Norse: ounce (of silver), money; related to Latin *aureus* golden]
Ez. *or* **Ezr.** *Bible. abbrev. for* Ezra.
Ezek. *Bible. abbrev. for* Ezekiel.

f *or* **F** (ɛf) *n., pl.* **f's, F's,** *or* **Fs.** **1.** the sixth letter and fourth consonant of the modern English alphabet. **2.** a speech sound represented by this letter, usually a voiceless labio-dental fricative, as in *fat.*

f *symbol for:* **1.** *Music.* forte: an instruction to play loudly. **2.** *Physics.* frequency. **3.** (in the Netherlands) guilder. [from Dutch: florin] **4.** *Maths.* function (of). **5.** *Physics.* femto-. **6.** *Chess.* See **algebraic notation.**

f, f/, *or* **f:** *symbol for* f-number.

F *symbol for:* **1.** *Music.* **a.** a note having a frequency of 349.23 hertz (**F above middle C**) or this value multiplied or divided by any power of 2; the fourth note of the scale of C major. **b.** a key, string, or pipe producing this note. **c.** the major or minor key having this note as its tonic. **2.** Fahrenheit. **3.** Fellow. **4.** *Chem.* fluorine. **5.** Helmholtz function. **6.** *Physics.* force. **7.** franc(s). **8.** farad(s). **9.** *Genetics.* a generation of filial offspring, F_1 being the first generation of offspring, F_2 being the second generation, etc. ~ **10.** *international car registration for* France.

f. *or* **F.** *abbrev. for:* **1.** fathom(s). **2.** female. **3.** *Grammar.* feminine. **4.** *Metallurgy.* fine. **5.** filly. **6.** (*pl.* **ff.** *or* **FF.**) folio. **7.** (*pl.* **ff.**) following (page). **8.** *Sport.* foul.

F- (of U.S. military aircraft) *abbrev. for* fighter: *F-106.*

fa (fɑː) *n. Music.* a variant spelling of **fah.**

FA *abbrev. for:* **1.** *Military.* field artillery. **2.** (in Britain) Football Association. See also **FA Cup.**

f.a. *or* **FA** *abbrev. for:* **1.** freight agent. **2.** fanny adams.

faa *or* **fa'** (fɔː) *vb.* a Scot. word for **fall.**

FAA *abbrev. for:* **1.** Fleet Air Arm. **2.** Fellow of the Australian Academy (of Science).

fab (fæb) *adj., interj. Informal, chiefly Brit.* short for **fabulous:** an expression of approval or enthusiasm.

fabaceous (fəˈbeɪʃəs) *adj.* a less common term for **leguminous.** [C18: from Late Latin *fabāceus* of beans, from Latin *faba* bean]

Fabian (ˈfeɪbɪən) *adj.* **1.** of, relating to, or resembling the delaying tactics of Quintus Fabius Maximus (died 203 B.C.), Roman general; cautious; circumspect. ~*n.* **2.** a member of or sympathizer with the Fabian Society. [C19: from Latin *Fabiānus* of Fabius]

Fabianism (ˈfeɪbɪəˌnɪzəm) *n.* the beliefs, principles, or practices of the Fabian Society. —**ˈFabianist** *n., adj.*

Fabian Society *n.* an association of British socialists advocating the establishment of democratic socialism by gradual reforms within the law: founded in 1884.

fable (ˈfeɪbᵊl) *n.* **1.** a short moral story, esp. one with animals as characters. **2.** a false, fictitious, or improbable account; fiction or lie. **3.** a story or legend about supernatural or mythical characters or events. **4.** legends or myths collectively. **5.** *Archaic.* the plot of a play or of an epic or dramatic poem. ~*vb.* **6.** to relate or tell (fables). **7.** (*intr.*) to speak untruthfully; tell lies. **8.** (*tr.*) to talk about or describe in the manner of a fable: *ghosts are fabled to appear at midnight.* [C13: from Latin *fābula* story, narrative, from *fārī* to speak, say] —**ˈfabler** *n.*

fabled (ˈfeɪbᵊld) *adj.* **1.** made famous in fable. **2.** fictitious.

fabliau (ˈfæblɪˌəʊ; *French* fɑblijo) *n., pl.* **fabliaux** (ˈfæblɪˌəʊz; *French* fɑblijo). a comic usually ribald verse tale, of a kind popular in France in the 12th and 13th centuries. [C19: from French: a little tale, from *fable* tale]

Fablon (ˈfæblən, -lɒn) *n. Trademark.* a brand of adhesive-backed plastic material used to cover and decorate shelves, worktops, etc., and for handicraft purposes.

fabric (ˈfæbrɪk) *n.* **1.** any cloth made from yarn or fibres by weaving, knitting, felting, etc. **2.** the texture of a cloth. **3.** a structure or framework: *the fabric of society.* **4.** a style or method of construction. **5.** *Rare.* a building. **6.** the texture, arrangement, and orientation of the constituents of a rock. [C15: from Latin *fabrica* workshop, from *faber* craftsman]

fabricant (ˈfæbrɪkənt) *n. Archaic.* a manufacturer.

fabricate (ˈfæbrɪˌkeɪt) *vb.* (*tr.*) **1.** to make, build, or construct. **2.** to devise, invent, or concoct (a story, lie, etc.). **3.** to fake or forge. [C15: from Latin *fabricāre* to build, make, from *fabrica* workshop; see FABRIC] —ˌ**fabriˈcation** *n.* —**ˈfabricative** *adj.* —**ˈfabriˌcator** *n.*

Fabrikoid (ˈfæbrɪˌkɔɪd) *n. Trademark.* a waterproof fabric made of cloth coated with pyroxylin.

fabulist (ˈfæbjʊlɪst) *n.* **1.** a person who invents or recounts fables. **2.** a person who lies or falsifies.

fabulous (ˈfæbjʊləs) *adj.* **1.** almost unbelievable; astounding; legendary: *fabulous wealth.* **2.** *Informal.* extremely good: *a fabulous time at the party.* **3.** of, relating to, or based upon fable: *a fabulous beast.* [C15: from Latin *fābulōsus* celebrated in fable, from *fābula* FABLE] —**ˈfabulously** *adv.* —**ˈfabulousness** *n.*

fac. *abbrev. for:* **1.** facsimile. **2.** factor. **3.** factory.

Fac. *abbrev. for* Faculty.

façade *or* **facade** (fəˈsɑːd, fæ-) *n.* **1.** the face of a building, esp. the main front. **2.** a front or outer appearance, esp. a deceptive one. [C17: from French, from Italian *facciata,* from *faccia* FACE]

face (feɪs) *n.* **1. a.** the front of the head from the forehead to the lower jaw; visage. **b.** (*as modifier*): *face flannel; face cream.* **2. a.** the expression of the countenance; look: *a sad face.* **b.** a distorted expression, esp. to indicate disgust; grimace: *she made a face.* **3.** *Informal.* make-up (esp. in the phrase **put one's face on.**) **4.** outward appearance: *the face of the countryside is changing.* **5.** appearance or pretence (esp. in the phrases **put a bold, good, bad,** etc., **face on).** **6.** worth in the eyes of others; dignity (esp. in the phrases **lose** or **save face).** **7.** *Informal.* impudence or effrontery. **8.** the main side of an object, building, etc., or the front: *the face of a palace; a cliff face.* **9.** the marked surface of an instrument, esp. the dial of a timepiece. **10.** the functional or working side of an object, as of a tool or playing card. **11. a.** the exposed area of a mine from which coal, ore, etc., may be mined. **b.** (*as modifier*): *face worker.* **12.** the uppermost part or surface: *the face of the earth.* **13.** Also called: **side.** any one of the plane surfaces of a crystal or other solid figure. **14.** *Mountaineering.* a steep side of a mountain, bounded by ridges. **15.** either of the surfaces of a coin, esp. the one that bears the head of a ruler. **16.** Also called: **typeface.** *Printing.* **a.** the printing surface of any type character. **b.** the style, the design, or sometimes the size of the character on the type. **c.** the print made from the type. **17.** *Nautical, aeronautics.* the aft or near side of a propeller blade. **18. fly in the face of.** to act in defiance of. **19. in one's face.** directly opposite or against one. **20. in (the) face of.** despite. **21. look (someone) in the face.** look directly at a person without fear or shame. **22. on the face of it.** to all appearances. **23. set one's face against.** to oppose with determination. **24. show one's face.** to make an appearance. **25. shut one's face.** *Slang.* (*often imperative*) to be silent. **26. to someone's face.** in someone's presence; directly and openly: *I told him the truth to his face.* ~*vb.* **27.** (when *intr.,* often foll. by *to, towards,* or *on*) to look or be situated or placed (in a specified direction): *the house faces on the square.* **28.** to be opposite: *facing page 9.* **29.** (*tr.*) to meet or be confronted by: *in his work he faces many problems.* **30.** (*tr.*) to provide with a surface of a different material: *the cuffs were faced with velvet.* **31.** to dress the surface of (stone or other material). **32.** (*tr.*) to expose (a card) with the face uppermost. **33.** *Military, chiefly U.S.* to order (a formation) to turn in a certain direction or (of a formation) to turn as required: *right face!* **34.** *Ice hockey.* **a.** (of the referee) to drop (the puck) between two opposing players, as when starting or restarting play. See also **face-off.** **b.** to start or restart play in this manner. **35. face the music.** *Informal.* to confront the consequences of one's actions. ~See also **face out, face up to.** [C13: from Old French, from Vulgar Latin *facia* (unattested), from Latin *faciēs* form, related to *facere* to make] —**ˈfaceable** *adj.*

FACE *abbrev. for* Fellow of the Australian College of Education.

face-ache *n.* **1.** neuralgia. **2.** *Slang.* an ugly or miserable-looking person.

facebar (ˈfeɪsˌbɑː) *n.* a wrestling hold in which a wrestler stretches the skin on his opponent's face backwards.

face card *n.* the usual U.S. and Canadian term for **court card.**

face-centred *adj.* (of a crystal) having a lattice point at the centre of each face of each unit cell as well as at the corners. Compare **body-centred.**

face cloth *or* **face flannel** *n. Brit.* a small piece of cloth used to wash the face and hands. U.S. equivalent: **washcloth.**

face-harden *vb.* (*tr.*) to harden the surface of (steel or iron) by the addition of carbon at high temperature.

faceless (ˈfeɪslɪs) *adj.* **1.** without a face. **2.** without identity; anonymous. —**ˈfacelessness** *n.*

face-lift *n.* **1.** cosmetic surgery for tightening sagging skin and smoothing unwanted wrinkles on the face. **2.** any improvement or renovation, as of a building, etc.

face-off *n.* **1.** *Ice hockey.* the method of starting a game, in which the referee drops the puck, etc. between two opposing players. **2.** a confrontation. ~*vb.* **face off.** (*adv.*) **3.** to start play by (a face-off).

face out *vb.* (*tr., adv.*) **1.** to endure (trouble). **2.** to defy or act boldly in spite of (criticism, blame, etc.). **3.** Also (esp. U.S. and Canadian): **face down.** to cause to concede by a bold stare.

face pack *n.* a cream treatment that cleanses and tones the skin.

faceplate (ˈfeɪsˌpleɪt) *n.* **1.** a perforated circular metal plate, attached to the headstock of a lathe, on which a workpiece can be mounted. **2.** Also called: **surface plate.** a flat rigid plate used to check the the flatness and squareness of the faces of a component. **3.** the part of a cathode-ray tube carrying the phosphor screen.

face powder *n.* a flesh-tinted cosmetic powder worn to make the face look less shiny, softer, etc.
facer ('feɪsə) *n.* **1.** a person or thing that faces. **2.** a lathe tool used to turn a face perpendicular to the axis of rotation. **3.** *Brit. informal.* a difficulty or problem.
face-saving *adj.* maintaining dignity or prestige. —'**face-ˌsaver** *n.*
facet ('fæsɪt) *n.* **1.** any of the surfaces of a cut gemstone. **2.** an aspect or phase, as of a subject or personality. **3.** *Architect.* the raised surface between the flutes of a column. **4.** any of the lenses that make up the compound eye of an insect or other arthropod. **5.** *Anatomy.* any small smooth area on a hard surface, as on a bone. ~*vb.* **-ets, -eting, -eted** *or* **-ets, -etting, -etted. 6.** (*tr.*) to cut facets in (a gemstone). [C17: from French *facette* a little FACE]
facetiae (fə'siːʃɪˌiː) *pl. n.* **1.** humorous or witty sayings. **2.** obscene or coarsely witty books. [C17: from Latin: jests, plural of *facētia* witticism, from *facētus* elegant]
facetious (fə'siːʃəs) *adj.* **1.** characterized by levity of attitude and love of joking: *a facetious person.* **2.** jocular or amusing, esp. at inappropriate times: *facetious remarks.* [C16: from Old French *facetieux,* from *facetie* witty saying; see FACETIAE] —**fa'cetiously** *adv.* —**fa'cetiousness** *n.*
face to face *adv., adj.* (**face-to-face** *as adj.*) **1.** opposite one another. **2.** in confrontation.
face up to *vb.* (*intr., adv. + prep.*) to accept (an unpleasant fact, reality, etc.).
face validity *n. Psychol.* the extent to which a psychological test appears to measure what it is intended to measure.
face value *n.* **1.** the value written or stamped on the face of a commercial paper or coin. **2.** apparent worth or value, as opposed to real worth.
facia ('feɪʃɪə) *n.* a variant spelling of **fascia.** —'**facial** *adj.*
facial ('feɪʃəl) *adj.* **1.** of or relating to the face. ~*n.* **2.** a beauty treatment for the face, involving cleansing, massage, and cosmetic packs. —'**facially** *adv.*
facial angle *n.* the angle formed between a line from the base of the nose to the opening of the ear and a line from the base of the nose to the most prominent part of the forehead: often used in comparative anthropology.
facial eczema *n.* a disease of sheep and cattle, occurring in warm areas of North Island, New Zealand. It is caused by a fungus, *Pithomyces chartarum,* and causes impairment of liver function and reddening, itching, scab formation, and swelling of the skin, esp. on the face.
facial index *n.* the ratio of the length of the face to the width of the face multiplied by 100: often used in comparative anthropology. Compare **cranial index.**
facial nerve *n.* the seventh cranial nerve, supplying the muscles controlling facial expression, glands of the palate and nose, and the taste buds in the anterior two-thirds of the tongue.
-facient *suffix forming adjectives and nouns.* indicating a state or quality: *absorbefacient; rubefacient.* [from Latin *facient-, faciēns,* present participle of *facere* to do]
facies ('feɪʃɪˌiːz) *n., pl.* **-cies. 1.** the general form and appearance of an individual or a group of plants or animals. **2.** the characteristics of a rock or series of rocks reflecting their appearance, composition, and conditions of formation. **3.** *Med.* the general facial expression of a patient, esp. when typical of a specific disease or disorder. [C17: from Latin: appearance, FACE]
facile ('fæsaɪl) *adj.* **1.** easy to perform or achieve. **2.** working or moving easily or smoothly. **3.** without depth; superficial: *a facile solution.* **4.** *Archaic.* relaxed in manner; easygoing. [C15: from Latin *facilis* easy, from *facere* to do] —'**facilely** *adv.* —'**facileness** *n.*
facile princeps *Latin.* ('fæsɪlɪ 'prɪnsɛps) *n.* an obvious leader. [literally: easily first]
facilitate (fə'sɪlɪˌteɪt) *vb.* (*tr.*) to make easier; assist the progress of. —**fa'cilitative** *adj.* —**fa'ciliˌtator** *n.*
facilitation (fəˌsɪlɪ'teɪʃən) *n.* **1.** the act or process of facilitating. **2.** *Physiol.* the increased ease of transmission of impulses in a nerve fibre, caused by prior excitation.
facility (fə'sɪlɪtɪ) *n., pl.* **-ties. 1.** ease of action or performance; freedom from difficulty. **2.** ready skill or ease deriving from practice or familiarity. **3.** (*often pl.*) the means or equipment facilitating the performance of an action. **4.** *Rare.* easy-going disposition. **5.** *Military.* an organization or building offering supporting capability. **6.** (*usually pl.*) a euphemistic word for **lavatory.** [C15: from Latin *facilitās,* from *facilis* easy; see FACILE]
facing ('feɪsɪŋ) *n.* **1.** a piece of material used esp. to conceal the seam of a garment and prevent fraying. **2.** (*usually pl.*) a piece of additional cloth, esp. in a different colour, on the collar, cuffs, etc., of the jacket of a military uniform, formerly used to denote the regiment. **3.** an outer layer or coat of material applied to the surface of a wall.
façonné *or* **faconne** ('fæsəˌneɪ) *adj.* **1.** denoting a fabric with the design woven in. ~*n.* **2.** such a fabric. [C19: French, from *façonner* to fashion]
facsimile (fæk'sɪmɪlɪ) *n.* **1. a.** an exact copy or reproduction. **b.** (*as modifier*): *a facsimile publication.* **2.** an image produced by facsimile transmission. ~*vb.* **-les, -leing, -led. 3.** (*tr.*) to make an exact copy of. [C17: from Latin *fac simile!* make something like it!, from *facere* to make + *similis* similar, like]
facsimile transmission *n.* an international system of transmitting a written, printed, or pictorial document over the telephone system by scanning it photoelectrically and reproducing the image xerographically after transmission. Often shortened to **fax.**
fact (fækt) *n.* **1.** an event or thing known to have happened or existed. **2.** a truth verifiable from experience or observation. **3.** a piece of information: *get me all the facts of this case.* **4.** *Law.* (*often pl.*) an actual event, happening, etc., as distinguished from its legal consequences. Questions of fact are decided by the jury, questions of law by the court or judge. **5.** *Philosophy.* a proposition that may be either true or false, as contrasted with an evaluative statement. **6. after** (*or* **before**) **the fact.** *Criminal law.* after (or before) the commission of the offence: *an accessory after the fact.* **7. as a matter of fact, in fact, in point of fact.** in reality or actuality. **8. fact of life.** an inescapable truth, esp. an unpleasant one. **9. the fact of the matter.** the truth. [C16: from Latin *factum* something done, from *factus* made, from *facere* to make] —'**factful** *adj.*
fact-finding *adj.* having the purpose of ascertaining facts: *a fact-finding tour of the Northeast.*
factice ('fæktɪs) *n.* a soft rubbery material made by reacting sulphur or sulphur chloride with vegetable oil. [C19: from Greek *faktis,* from Latin *factīcius* FACTITIOUS]
faction[1] ('fækʃən) *n.* **1.** a group of people forming a minority within a larger body, esp. a dissentious group. **2.** strife or dissension within a group. [C16: from Latin *factiō* a making, from *facere* to make, do] —'**factional** *adj.* —'**factionalˌism** *n.* —'**factionalist** *n.*
faction[2] ('fækʃən) *n.* a television programme, film, or literary work comprising a dramatized presentation of actual events. [C20: a blend of FACT and FICTION]
factious ('fækʃəs) *adj.* given to, producing, or characterized by faction. —'**factiously** *adv.* —'**factiousness** *n.*
factitious (fæk'tɪʃəs) *adj.* **1.** artificial rather than natural: *factitious demands created by the mass media.* **2.** not genuine; sham: *factitious enthusiasm.* [C17: from Latin *factīcius,* from *facere* to make, do] —**fac'titiously** *adv.* —**fac'titiousness** *n.*
factitive ('fæktɪtɪv) *adj. Grammar.* denoting a verb taking a direct object as well as a noun in apposition, as for example *elect* in *They elected John president,* where *John* is the direct object and *president* is the complement. [C19: from New Latin *factitīvus,* from Latin *factitāre* to do frequently, from *facere* to do] —'**factitively** *adv.*
factive ('fæktɪv) *adj. Logic, linguistics, philosophy.* (of a linguistic context) giving rise to the presupposition that a sentence occurring in that context is true, as *John regrets that Mary did not attend.*
factoid ('fæktɔɪd) *n.* a piece of unreliable information believed to be true because of the way it is presented or repeated in print. [C20: coined by Norman Mailer (born 1923), U.S. author, from FACT + -OID]
factor ('fæktə) *n.* **1.** an element or cause that contributes to a result. **2.** *Maths.* **a.** one of two or more integers or polynomials whose product is a given integer or polynomial: *2 and 3 are factors of 6.* **b.** an integer or polynomial that can be exactly divided into another integer or polynomial: *1, 2, 3, and 6 are all factors of 6.* **3.** a person who acts on another's behalf, esp. one who transacts business for another. **4.** *Commerce.* a business that makes loans in return for or on security of trade debts. **5.** former name for a **gene. 6.** *Commercial law.* a person to whom goods are consigned for sale and who is paid a factorage. **7.** (in Scotland) the manager of an estate. ~*vb.* **8.** (*intr.*) to engage in the business of a factor. [C15: from Latin: one who acts, from *facere* to do] —'**factorable** *adj.* —ˌ**factora'bility** *n.* —'**factorˌship** *n.*
factor VIII *n.* a protein that participates in the clotting of blood. It is extracted from donated serum and used in the treatment of the commonest type of haemophilia, in which it is absent.
factorage ('fæktərɪdʒ) *n.* the commission payable to a factor.
factor analysis *n. Statistics.* any of several techniques for deriving from a number of given variables a smaller number of different, more useful, variables.
factor cost *n.* (in social accounting) valuation of goods and services at their overall commercial cost, including markups but excluding indirect taxes and subsidies.
factorial (fæk'tɔːrɪəl) *Maths.* ~*n.* **1.** the product of all the positive integers from one up to and including a given integer. Factorial zero is assigned the value of one: *factorial four is* $1 \times 2 \times 3 \times 4$. Symbol: $n!$, $\underline{n|}$, where n is the given integer. ~*adj.* **2.** of or involving factorials or factors. —**fac'torially** *adv.*
factoring ('fæktərɪŋ) *n.* **1.** the business of a factor. **2.** the business of purchasing debts from clients at a discount and making a profit from their collection.
factorize *or* **factorise** ('fæktəˌraɪz) *vb.* (*tr.*) *Maths.* to resolve (an integer or polynomial) into factors. —ˌ**factori'zation** *or* ˌ**factori'sation** *n.*
factor of production *n.* a resource or input entering the production of wealth, such as land, labour, capital, etc. Also called: **agent of production.**

factor of safety *n.* the ratio of the breaking stress of a material or structure to the calculated maximum stress when in use. Also called: **safety factor.**

factory ('fæktərɪ) *n., pl.* **-ries.** **1. a.** a building or group of buildings containing a plant assembly for the manufacture of goods. **b.** (*as modifier*): *a factory worker.* **2.** *Rare.* a trading station maintained by factors in a foreign country. **3.** *Canadian.* (formerly) a main trading station for the exchange and transshipment of furs. [C16: from Late Latin *factorium*; see FACTOR] —'**factory-**ˌ**like** *adj.*

factory farm *n.* a farm in which animals are bred and fattened using modern industrial methods. —**factory farming** *n.*

factory ship *n. Whaling.* a vessel that processes whale carcasses supplied by a whale catcher.

factotum (fæk'təʊtəm) *n.* a person employed to do all kinds of work. [C16: from Medieval Latin, from Latin *fac!* do! + *tōtum,* from *tōtus* (adj.) all]

facts and figures *pl. n.* details; precise information.

factsheet ('fæktˌʃiːt) *n.* a printed sheet containing information relating to items covered in a television or radio programme.

facts of life *pl. n.* **the.** the details of sexual behaviour and reproduction, esp. as told to children.

factual ('fæktʃʊəl) *adj.* **1.** of, relating to, or characterized by facts. **2.** of the nature of fact; real; actual. —'**factualism** *n.* —'**factualist** *n.* —ˌ**factual'istic** *adj.* —'**factually** *adv.* —'**factualness** *or* ˌ**factu'ality** *n.*

facture ('fæktʃə) *n. Rare.* **1.** construction. **2.** workmanship; quality. [C15: from Old French, from Latin *factūra*]

facula ('fækjʊlə) *n., pl.* **-lae** (-ˌliː). any of the bright areas on the sun's surface, usually appearing just before a sunspot and subject to the same 11-year cycle. [C18: from Latin: little torch, from *fax* torch] —'**facular** *adj.*

facultative ('fækəltətɪv) *adj.* **1.** empowering but not compelling the doing of an act. **2.** *Philosophy.* that may or may not occur. **3.** *Insurance.* denoting a form of reinsurance in which the reinsurer has no obligation to accept a particular risk nor the insurer to reinsure, terms and conditions being negotiated for each reinsurance. **4.** *Biology.* able to exist under more than one set of environmental conditions: *a facultative parasite can exist as a parasite or a saprophyte.* Compare **obligate** (sense 4). **5.** of or relating to a faculty. —'**facultatively** *adv.*

faculty ('fækəltɪ) *n., pl.* **-ties.** **1.** one of the inherent powers of the mind or body, such as reason, memory, sight, or hearing. **2.** any ability or power, whether acquired or inherent. **3.** a conferred power or right. **4. a.** a department within a university or college devoted to a particular branch of knowledge. **b.** the staff of such a department. **c.** *Chiefly U.S. and Canadian.* all administrative and teaching staff at a university, college, school, etc. **5.** all members of a learned profession. **6.** *Archaic.* occupation. [C14 (in the sense: department of learning): from Latin *facultās* capability; related to Latin *facilis* easy]

Faculty of Advocates *n. Law.* the college or society of advocates in Scotland.

FA Cup *n. Soccer.* (in England) **1.** an annual knockout competition for a silver trophy, open to all member teams of the Football Association. **2.** the trophy itself.

fad (fæd) *n. Informal.* **1.** an intense but short-lived fashion; craze. **2.** a personal idiosyncrasy or whim. [C19: of uncertain origin] —'**faddish** *or* '**faddy** *adj.* —'**faddishness** *n.* —'**faddism** *n.* —'**faddist** *n.*

FAD *n. Biochem.* flavin adenine dinucleotide: an ester of riboflavin with ADP that acts as the prosthetic group for many flavoproteins. See also **FMN.**

fade (feɪd) *vb.* **1.** to lose or cause to lose brightness, colour, or clarity. **2.** (*intr.*) to lose freshness, vigour, or youth; wither. **3.** (*intr.;* usually foll. by *away* or *out*) to vanish slowly; die out. **4. a.** to decrease the brightness or volume of (a television or radio programme or film sequence) or (of a television programme, etc.) to decrease in this way. **b.** to decrease the volume of (a sound) in a recording system or (of a sound) to be so reduced in volume. **5.** (*intr.*) (of the brakes of a vehicle) to lose power. **6.** to cause (a golf ball) to veer from a straight line or (of a golf ball) to veer from a straight flight. ~*n.* **7.** the act or an instance of fading. [C14: from *fade* (adj.) dull, from Old French, from Vulgar Latin *fatidus* (unattested), probably blend of Latin *vapidus* VAPID + Latin *fatuus* FATUOUS] —'**fadable** *adj.* —'**fadedness** *n.* —'**fader** *n.*

fade-in *n.* **1.** *Films.* an optical effect in which a shot appears gradually out of darkness. **2.** a gradual increase in the volume in a radio or television broadcast. ~*vb.* **fade in** (*adv.*). **3.** Also: **fade up.** to increase or cause to increase gradually, as vision or sound in a film or broadcast.

fadeless ('feɪdlɪs) *adj.* not subject to fading.

fade-out *n.* **1.** *Films.* an optical effect in which a shot slowly disappears into darkness. **2.** a gradual reduction in signal strength in a radio or television broadcast. **3.** a gradual and temporary loss of a received radio or television signal due to atmospheric disturbances, magnetic storms, etc. **4.** a slow or gradual disappearance. ~*vb.* **fade out.** (*adv.*) **5.** to decrease or cause to decrease gradually, as vision or sound in a film or broadcast.

fadge (fædʒ) *vb.* (*intr.*) *Archaic or dialect.* **1.** to agree. **2.** to succeed. ~*n.* **3.** *N.Z.* a package of wool in a wool-bale that weighs less than 100 kilograms. [C16: of uncertain origin]

fading ('feɪdɪŋ) *n.* a variation in the strength of received radio signals due to variations in the conditions of the transmission medium.

fado *Portuguese.* ('fɑːdu) *n.* a type of melancholy Portuguese folk song. [literally: FATE]

fadometer (fə'dɒmɪtə) *n. Chem.* an instrument used to determine the resistance to fading of a pigment or dye.

faecal *or esp. U.S.* **fecal** ('fiːkəl) *adj.* of, relating to, or consisting of faeces.

faeces *or esp. U.S.* **feces** ('fiːsiːz) *pl. n.* bodily waste matter derived from ingested food and the secretions of the intestines and discharged through the anus. [C15: from Latin *faecēs,* plural of *faex* sediment, dregs]

faena *Spanish.* (fa'ena) *n. Bullfighting.* the matador's final series of passes with sword and cape before the kill. [literally: task, from obsolete Catalan (modern *feina*), from Latin *facienda* things to be done, from *facere* to do]

faerie *or* **faery** ('feɪərɪ, 'fɛərɪ) *n., pl.* **-ries.** *Archaic or poetic.* **1.** the land of fairies. **2.** enchantment. ~*adj., n.* **3.** a variant of **fairy.**

Faeroese *or* **Faroese** (ˌfɛərəʊ'iːz) *adj.* **1.** of or relating to the Faeroes, a group of islands in the North Atlantic, or to their inhabitants or language. ~*n.* **2.** the chief language of the Faeroes, closely related to Icelandic, although they are not mutually intelligible. **3.** (*pl.* **-ese**) a native or inhabitant of the Faeroes.

faff (fæf) *vb.* (*intr.;* often foll. by *about*) *Brit. informal.* to dither or fuss. [C19: of obscure origin]

fag[1] (fæg) *n.* **1.** *Informal.* a boring or wearisome task: *it's a fag having to walk all that way.* **2.** *Brit.* (esp. formerly) a young public school boy who performs menial chores for an older boy or prefect. ~*vb.* **fags, fagging, fagged.** **3.** (when *tr.,* often foll. by *out*) *Informal.* to become or cause to become exhausted by hard toil or work. **4.** (*usually intr.*) *Brit.* to do or cause to do menial chores in a public school: *Brown fags for Lee.* [C18: of obscure origin]

fag[2] (fæg) *n.* **1.** *Brit.* a slang word for **cigarette.** **2.** a fag end, as of cloth. [C16 (in the sense: something hanging loose, flap): of obscure origin]

fag[3] (fæg) *n. Slang, chiefly U.S. and Canadian.* short for **faggot**[2].

fagaceous (fə'geɪʃəs) *adj.* of, relating to, or belonging to the *Fagaceae,* a family of trees, including beech, oak, and chestnut, whose fruit is partly or wholly enclosed in a husk (cupule). [C19: from New Latin *Fāgāceae,* from Latin *fāgus* beech]

fag end *n.* **1.** the last and worst part, esp. when it is of little use. **2.** *Brit. informal.* the stub of a cigarette. [C17: see FAG[2]]

faggot[1] *or esp. U.S.* **fagot** ('fægət) *n.* **1.** a bundle of sticks or twigs, esp. when bound together and used as fuel. **2.** a bundle of iron bars, esp. a box formed by four pieces of wrought iron and filled with scrap to be forged into wrought iron. **3.** a ball of chopped meat, usually pork liver, bound with herbs and bread and eaten fried. **4.** a bundle of anything. ~*vb.* (*tr.*) **5.** to collect into a bundle or bundles. **6.** *Needlework.* to do faggoting on (a garment, piece of cloth, etc.). [C14: from Old French, perhaps from Greek *phakelos* bundle]

faggot[2] ('fægət) *n. Slang, chiefly U.S. and Canadian.* a male homosexual. Often shortened to **fag.** [C20: special use of FAGGOT[1]] —'**faggoty** *adj.*

faggoting *or esp. U.S.* **fagoting** ('fægətɪŋ) *n.* **1.** decorative needlework done by tying vertical threads together in bundles. **2.** a decorative way of joining two hems by crisscross stitches.

faggot vote *n.* (formerly) a vote created by the allotting of property to a person to give him the status of an elector. [C19: perhaps from the former use of FAGGOT[1] meaning a person spuriously entered on a military roll]

fah *or* **fa** (fɑː) *n. Music.* **1.** (in the fixed system of solmization) the note F. **2.** (in tonic sol-fa) the fourth degree of any major scale; subdominant. [C14: see GAMUT]

Fah. *or* **Fahr.** *abbrev. for* Fahrenheit.

FAHA *abbrev. for* Fellow of the Australian Academy of the Humanities.

fahlband ('fɑːlˌbænd) *n.* a thin bed of schistose rock impregnated with metallic sulphides. [C19: from German: pale band]

Fahrenheit ('færənˌhaɪt) *adj.* of or measured according to the Fahrenheit scale of temperature. Symbol: F

Fahrenheit scale *n.* a scale of temperatures in which 32° represents the melting point of ice and 212° represents the boiling point of pure water under standard atmospheric pressure. Compare **Celsius scale.** [named after Gabriel *Fahrenheit* (1686–1736), German physicist]

FAI *abbrev. for:* **1.** Fédération aéronautique internationale. [French: International Aeronautical Federation] **2.** Football Association of Ireland.

faïence (faɪ'ɑːns, feɪ-) *n.* **a.** tin-glazed earthenware, usually that of French, German, Italian, or Scandinavian origin. **b.** (*as modifier*): *a faïence cup.* [C18: from French, strictly: pottery from FAENZA]

fail[1] (feɪl) *vb.* **1.** to be unsuccessful in an attempt (at something or to do something). **2.** (*intr.*) to stop operating or working properly: *the steering failed suddenly.* **3.** to judge or be judged as being below the officially accepted standard required for success in (a course, examination, etc.). **4.** (*tr.*) to prove disappointing, undependable, or useless to (someone). **5.** (*tr.*) to neglect or be unable (to do something). **6.** (*intr.*) to prove partly or completely insufficient in quantity, duration, or extent. **7.** (*intr.*) to weaken; fade away. **8.** (*intr.*) to go bankrupt or become insolvent. *~n.* **9.** a failure to attain the required standard, as in an examination. **10. without fail.** definitely; with certainty. [C13: from Old French *faillir,* ultimately from Latin *fallere* to disappoint; probably related to Greek *phēlos* deceitful]

fail[2] (fel) *n. Scot.* a turf; sod. [perhaps from Scottish Gaelic *fàl*]

failing (ˈfeɪlɪŋ) *n.* **1.** a weak point; flaw. *~prep.* **2.** (*used to express a condition*) in default of: *failing a solution this afternoon, the problem will have to wait until Monday.* —ˈ**failingly** *adv.*

faille (feɪl; *French* faj) *n.* a soft light ribbed fabric of silk, rayon, or taffeta. [C16: from French: head covering, hence, fabric used for this, of obscure origin]

fail-safe *adj.* **1.** designed to return to a safe condition in the event of a failure or malfunction. **2.** (of a nuclear weapon) capable of being deactivated in the event of a failure or accident. **3.** unlikely to fail; foolproof. *~vb.* **4.** (*intr.*) to return to a safe condition in the event of a failure or malfunction.

failure (ˈfeɪljə) *n.* **1.** the act or an instance of failing. **2.** a person or thing that is unsuccessful or disappointing: *the evening was a failure.* **3.** nonperformance of something required or expected: *failure to attend will be punished.* **4.** cessation of normal operation; breakdown: *a power failure.* **5.** an insufficiency or shortage: *a crop failure.* **6.** a decline or loss, as in health or strength. **7.** the fact of not reaching the required standard in an examination, test, course, etc. **8.** the act or process of becoming bankrupt or the state of being bankrupt.

fain (feɪn) *adv.* **1.** (usually with *would*) *Archaic.* willingly; gladly: *she would fain be dead.* *~adj.* **2.** *Obsolete.* **a.** willing or eager. **b.** compelled. [Old English *fægen;* related to Old Norse *fegiun* happy, Old High German *gifehan* to be glad, Gothic *fahehs* joy; see FAWN[2]]

fainéant (ˈfeɪnɪənt; *French* fɛneɑ̃) *n.* **1.** a lazy person; idler. *~adj.* **2.** indolent. [C17: from French, modification of earlier *fait-nient* (he) does nothing, by folk etymology from Old French *faignant* shirker, from *faindre* to be lazy] —ˈ**faineance** *or* ˈ**faineancy** *n.*

fainites (ˈfeɪnaɪts) *or* **fains** (feɪnz) *interj. Dialect.* a cry for truce or respite from the rules of a game. [C19: from *fains I* I decline, from *feine* feign, from Old French *se feindre* in the sense: back out, esp. of battle]

fáinne (ˈfaːɲə) *n. Irish.* a small ring-shaped metal badge worn by advocates of the Irish language.

faint (feɪnt) *adj.* **1.** lacking clarity, brightness, volume, etc.: *a faint noise.* **2.** lacking conviction or force; weak: *faint praise.* **3.** feeling dizzy or weak as if about to lose consciousness. **4.** without boldness or courage; timid (esp. in the combination **faint-hearted**). **5. not the faintest (idea** *or* **notion)**. no idea whatsoever: *I haven't the faintest.* *~vb.* (*intr.*) **6.** to lose consciousness, esp. momentarily, as through weakness. **7.** *Archaic or poetic.* to fail or become weak, esp. in hope or courage. *~n.* **8.** a sudden spontaneous loss of consciousness, usually momentary, caused by an insufficient supply of blood to the brain. Technical name: **syncope.** [C13: from Old French, from *faindre* to be idle] —ˈ**fainter** *n.* —ˈ**faintingly** *adv.* —ˈ**faintish** *adj.* —ˈ**faintishness** *n.* —ˈ**faintly** *adv.* —ˈ**faintness** *n.*

faints (feɪnts) *pl. n.* a variant spelling of **feints.**

fair[1] (fɛə) *adj.* **1.** free from discrimination, dishonesty, etc.; just; impartial. **2.** in conformity with rules or standards; legitimate: *a fair fight.* **3.** (of the hair or complexion) light in colour. **4.** beautiful or lovely to look at. **5.** moderately or quite good: *a fair piece of work.* **6.** unblemished; untainted. **7.** (of the tide or wind) favourable to the passage of a vessel. **8.** sunny, fine, or cloudless. **9.** (*prenominal*) *Informal.* thorough; real: *a fair battle to get to the counter.* **10.** pleasant or courteous. **11.** apparently good or valuable, but really false: *fair words.* **12.** open or unobstructed: *a fair passage.* **13.** (of handwriting) clear and legible. **14. a fair crack of the whip** *or* (*Austral.*) **a fair shake of the dice, fair go.** *Informal.* a fair opportunity; fair chance. **15. fair and square.** in a correct or just way. **16. fair do's. a.** equal shares or treatment. **b.** an expression of appeal for equal shares or treatment. **17. fair enough!** an expression of agreement. **18. fair go!** *Austral. and N.Z.* come off it!; I don't believe it! **19. fair to middling.** about average. *~adv.* **20.** in a fair way; correctly: *act fair, now!* **21.** absolutely or squarely; quite: *the question caught him fair off his guard.* **22.** *Dialect.* really or very: *fair tired.* *~vb.* **23.** (*intr.*) *Dialect.* (of the weather) to become fine and mild. *~n.* **24.** *Archaic.* a person or thing that is beautiful or valuable, esp. a woman. [Old English *fæger;* related to Old Norse *fagr,* Old Saxon, Old High German *fagar,* Gothic *fagrs* suitable] —ˈ**fairness** *n.*

fair[2] (fɛə) *n.* **1.** a travelling entertainment with sideshows, rides, etc., esp. one that visits places at the same time each year. **2.** a gathering of producers of and dealers in a given class of products to facilitate business: *a world fair.* **3.** an event including sale of goods and amusements, esp. for a charity; bazaar. **4.** a regular assembly at a specific place for the sale of goods, esp. livestock. [C13: from Old French *feire,* from Late Latin *fēria* holiday, from Latin *fēriae* days of rest: related to *festus* FESTAL]

fair copy *n.* a clean copy of a document on which all corrections have been made.

fairfaced (ˈfɛəˌfeɪst) *adj.* (of brickwork) having a neat smooth unplastered surface.

fair game *n.* **1.** a legitimate object for ridicule or attack. **2.** *Hunting, archaic.* quarry that may legitimately be pursued according to the rules of a particular sport.

fairground (ˈfɛəˌgraʊnd) *n.* an open space used for a fair or exhibition.

fair-haired boy *n.* the usual U.S. name for **blue-eyed boy.**

fairing[1] (ˈfɛərɪŋ) *n.* an external metal structure fitted around parts of an aircraft, car, vessel, etc., to reduce drag. Also called: **fillet.** Compare **cowling.** [C20: FAIR[1] + -ING[1]]

fairing[2] (ˈfɛərɪŋ) *n.* **1.** *Archaic.* a present, esp. from a fair. **2.** a sweet circular biscuit made with butter.

fairish (ˈfɛərɪʃ) *adj.* **1.** moderately good, well, etc. **2.** (of the hair, complexion, etc.) moderately light in colour.

Fair Isle *n.* an intricate multicoloured pattern knitted with Shetland wool into various garments, such as sweaters. [C19: named after one of the Shetland Islands where the pattern originated]

fairlead (ˈfɛəˌliːd) *or* **fairleader** *n. Nautical.* a block or ring through which a line is rove to keep it clear of obstructions, prevent chafing, or maintain it at an angle.

fairly (ˈfɛəlɪ) *adv.* **1.** (*not used with a negative*) moderately. **2.** as deserved; justly. **3.** (*not used with a negative*) positively; absolutely: *the hall fairly rang with applause.* **4.** *Archaic.* clearly. **5.** *Obsolete.* courteously.

fair-minded *adj.* just or impartial. —ˌ**fair-**ˈ**mindedness** *n.*

fair play *n.* **1.** an established standard of decency, honesty, etc. **2.** abidance by this standard.

fair rent *n.* (in Britain) the rent for a private tenancy, fixed and registered by a rent officer, and based on the size, condition, and usefulness of the property, but not its scarcity value.

fair sex *n.* **the.** women collectively.

fair-spoken *adj.* civil, courteous, or elegant in speech. —ˌ**fair-**ˈ**spokenness** *n.*

fairway (ˈfɛəˌweɪ) *n.* **1.** Also called: **fair green.** (on a golf course) the areas of shorter grass between the tees and greens, esp. the avenue approaching a green bordered by rough. **2.** *Nautical.* **a.** the navigable part of a river, harbour, etc. **b.** the customary course followed by vessels.

fair-weather *adj.* **1.** suitable for use in fair weather only. **2.** not reliable or present in situations of hardship or difficulty (esp. in the phrase **fair-weather friend**).

fairy (ˈfɛərɪ) *n., pl.* **fairies. 1.** an imaginary supernatural being, usually represented in diminutive human form and characterized as clever, playful, and having magical powers. **2.** *Slang.* a male homosexual. *~adj.* (*prenominal*) **3.** of or relating to a fairy or fairies. **4.** resembling a fairy or fairies, esp. in being enchanted or delicate. [C14: from Old French *faerie* fairyland, from *feie* fairy, from Latin *Fāta* the Fates; see FATE, FAY[1]] —ˈ**fairy-**ˌ**like** *adj.*

fairy cycle *n.* a child's bicycle.

fairyfloss (ˈfɛərɪˌflɒs) *n.* the Australian word for **candyfloss.**

fairy godmother *n.* **1.** a character in certain fairy stories who brings unexpected benefits to the hero or heroine. **2.** any benefactress, esp. an unknown one.

fairyland (ˈfɛərɪˌlænd) *n.* **1.** the imaginary domain of the fairies; an enchanted or wonderful place. **2.** a fantasy world, esp. one resulting from a person's wild imaginings.

fairy lights *pl. n.* small coloured electric bulbs strung together and used for decoration, esp. on a Christmas tree.

fairy penguin *n.* a small penguin, *Eudyptula minor,* with a bluish head and back, found on the Australian coast. Also called: **little** or **blue penguin.**

fairy ring *n.* **1.** a ring of dark luxuriant vegetation in grassy ground corresponding to the outer edge of an underground fungal mycelium: popularly associated with the dancing of fairies: seasonally marked by a ring of mushrooms. **2.** short for **fairy ring mushroom,** *Marasmius oreades,* a dainty buff-coloured edible basidiomycetous fungus, characteristically forming rings in grassland.

fairy shrimp *n.* any small freshwater branchiopod crustacean of the genera *Chirocephalus, Artemia,* etc., having a transparent body with many appendages and habitually swimming on its back: order *Anostraca.*

fairy swallow *n.* (*sometimes caps.*) a variety of domestic fancy pigeon having blue-and-white plumage and heavily muffed feet.

fairy tale *or* **story** *n.* **1.** a story about fairies or other mythical or magical beings, esp. one of traditional origin told to children. **2.** a highly improbable account.

fairy-tale (ˈfɛərɪˌteɪl) *adj.* **1.** of or relating to a fairy tale. **2.** resembling a fairy tale, esp. in being extremely happy or fortunate: *a true story with a fairy-tale ending.* **3.** highly improbable: *he came out with a fairy-tale account of his achievements.*

fait accompli *French.* (fɛt akɔ̃pli) *n., pl.* ***faits accomplis*** (fɛz akɔ̃pli). something already done and beyond alteration. [literally: accomplished fact]

faites vos jeux *French.* (fɛt vo ʒø) place your bets! (a phrase used by croupiers in roulette and other casino gambling games).

faith (feɪθ) *n.* **1.** strong or unshakeable belief in something, esp. without proof or evidence. **2.** a specific system of religious beliefs: *the Jewish faith.* **3.** *Christianity.* trust in God and in his actions and promises. **4.** a conviction of the truth of certain doctrines of religion, esp. when this is not based on reason. **5.** complete confidence or trust in a person, remedy, etc. **6.** any set of firmly held principles or beliefs. **7.** allegiance or loyalty, as to a person or cause (esp. in the phrases **keep faith, break faith**). **8. bad faith.** insincerity or dishonesty. **9. good faith.** honesty or sincerity, as of intention in business (esp. in the phrase **in good faith**). **10.** (*modifier*) using, concerned with, or relating to the supposed ability to cure bodily ailments by means of religious faith: *a faith cure; a faith healer.* ~*interj.* **11.** *Archaic.* indeed; really (also in the phrases **by my faith, in faith**). [C12: from Anglo-French *feid,* from Latin *fidēs* trust, confidence]

faither ('feðər) *n.* a Scot. word for **father.**

faithful ('feɪθfʊl) *adj.* **1.** having faith; remaining true, constant, or loyal. **2.** maintaining sexual loyalty to one's lover or spouse. **3.** consistently reliable: *a faithful worker.* **4.** reliable or truthful: *a faithful source.* **5.** accurate in detail: *a faithful translation.* ~*n.* **6. the faithful. a.** the believers in and loyal adherents of a religious faith, esp. Christianity. **b.** any group of loyal and steadfast followers. —**'faithfully** *adv.* —**'faithfulness** *n.*

faithless ('feɪθlɪs) *adj.* **1.** unreliable or treacherous. **2.** dishonest or disloyal. **3.** having no faith or trust. **4.** lacking faith, esp. religious faith. —**'faithlessly** *adv.* —**'faithlessness** *n.*

faitour ('feɪtə) *n. Obsolete.* an impostor. [C14: from Anglo-French: cheat, from Old French *faitor,* from Latin: FACTOR]

fake[1] (feɪk) *vb.* **1.** (*tr.*) to cause (something inferior or not genuine) to appear more valuable, desirable, or real by fraud or pretence. **2.** to pretend to have (an illness, emotion, etc.): *to fake a headache.* **3.** to improvise (music, stage dialogue, etc.). ~*n.* **4.** an object, person, or act that is not genuine; sham, counterfeit, or forgery. ~*adj.* **5.** not genuine; spurious. [originally (C18) thieves' slang to mug or do someone; probably via Polari from Italian *facciare* to make or do] —**'faker** *n.* —**'fakery** *n.*

fake[2] (feɪk) *Nautical.* ~*vb.* **1.** (*tr.;* usually foll. by *down*) to coil (a rope) on deck. ~*n.* **2.** one round of a coil of rope. [Middle English *faken,* perhaps via Lingua Franca from Italian *facciare* to make or do; see FAKE[1]]

fakir, faqir (fə'kɪə, 'feɪkə), *or* **fakeer** (fə'kɪə) *n.* **1.** a member of any religious order of Islam. **2.** a Hindu ascetic mendicant or holy man. [C17: from Arabic *faqīr* poor]

fa-la *or* **fal la** (fɑː'lɑː) *n.* (esp. in 16th-century songs) a refrain sung to the syllables *fa-la-la.*

Falangist (fæ'lændʒɪst) *n.* **1.** a member or supporter of Falange, the Fascist movement founded in Spain in 1933; the one legal party in Spain under the Franco regime. ~*adj.* **2.** of or relating to Falange. [Spanish: PHALANX] —**Fa'langist** *n., adj.*

Falasha (fə'læʃə) *n., pl.* **-sha** *or* **-shas.** a member of a tribe of Black Ethiopian Jews. [from Amharic, from *fälasi* stranger]

falbala ('fælbələ) *n.* a gathered flounce, frill, or ruffle. [C18: from French, from (dialect) *ferbelà;* see FURBELOW]

falcate ('fælkeɪt) *or* **falciform** ('fælsɪˌfɔːm) *adj. Biology.* shaped like a sickle. [C19: from Latin *falcātus,* from *falx* sickle]

falchion ('fɔːltʃən, 'fɔːlʃən) *n.* **1.** a short and slightly curved medieval sword broader towards the point. **2.** an archaic word for **sword.** [C14: from Italian *falcione,* from *falce,* from Latin *falx* sickle]

falcon ('fɔːlkən, 'fɔːkən) *n.* **1.** any diurnal bird of prey of the family *Falconidae,* esp. any of the genus *Falco* (gyrfalcon, peregrine falcon, etc.), typically having pointed wings and a long tail. **2. a.** any of these or related birds, trained to hunt small game. **b.** the female of such a bird (compare **tercel**). **3.** a light-medium cannon used from the 15th to 17th centuries. [C13: from Old French *faucon,* from Late Latin *falcō* hawk, probably of Germanic origin; perhaps related to Latin *falx* sickle]

falconer ('fɔːlkənə, 'fɔːkə-) *n.* a person who breeds or trains hawks or who follows the sport of falconry.

falconet ('fɔːlkəˌnɛt, 'fɔːkə-) *n.* **1.** any of various small falcons, esp. any of the Asiatic genus *Microhierax.* **2.** a small light cannon used from the 15th to 17th centuries.

falcon-gentle *or* **falcon-gentil** *n. Falconry.* a female falcon, esp. a female peregrine falcon. [C14: from Old French *faucon-gentil* literally: noble falcon]

falconiform (fæl'kəʊnɪˌfɔːm) *adj.* of, relating to, or belonging to the order *Falconiformes,* which includes the vultures, hawks, eagles, buzzards, and falcons.

falconine ('fɔːlkəˌnaɪn, 'fɔːkə-) *adj.* **1.** of, relating to, or resembling a falcon. **2.** of, relating to, or belonging to the family *Falconidae,* which includes the falcons.

falconry ('fɔːlkənrɪ, 'fɔːkən-) *n.* **1.** the art of keeping falcons and training them to return from flight to a lure or to hunt quarry. **2.** the sport of causing falcons to return from flight to their trainer and to hunt quarry under his direction.

falcula ('fælkjʊlə) *n., pl.* **-lae** (-liː). *Zoology.* a sharp curved claw, esp. of a bird. —**'falculate** *adj.*

falderal ('fældɪˌræl), **falderol** ('fældɪˌrɒl), *or* **folderol** ('fɒldɪˌrɒl) *n.* **1.** a showy but worthless trifle. **2.** foolish nonsense. **3.** a nonsensical refrain in old songs.

faldstool ('fɔːldˌstuːl) *n.* a backless seat, sometimes capable of being folded, used by bishops and certain other prelates. [C11 *fyldestol,* probably a translation of Medieval Latin *faldistolium* folding stool, of Germanic origin; compare Old High German *faldstuol*]

Faliscan (fə'lɪskən) *n.* an ancient language of Italy, spoken in the area north of the Tiber. It was closely related to Latin, which displaced it before 200 B.C.

fall (fɔːl) *vb.* **falls, falling, fell** (fɛl), **fallen** ('fɔːlən). (*mainly intr.*) **1.** to descend by the force of gravity from a higher to a lower place. **2.** to drop suddenly from an erect position. **3.** to collapse to the ground, esp. in pieces. **4.** to become less or lower in number, quality, etc.: *prices fell in the summer.* **5.** to become lower in pitch. **6.** to extend downwards: *her hair fell to her waist.* **7.** to be badly wounded or killed. **8.** to slope in a downward direction. **9.** *Christianity.* to yield to temptation or sin. **10.** to diminish in status, estimation, etc. **11.** to yield to attack: *the city fell under the assault.* **12.** to lose power: *the government fell after the riots.* **13.** to pass into or take on a specified condition: *to fall asleep; fall in love.* **14.** to adopt a despondent expression: *her face fell.* **15.** to be averted: *her gaze fell.* **16.** to come by chance or presumption: *suspicion fell on the butler.* **17.** to occur; take place: *night fell; Easter falls early this year.* **18.** (of payments) to be due. **19.** to be directed to a specific point. **20.** (foll. by *back, behind,* etc.) to move in a specified direction. **21.** to occur at a specified place: *the accent falls on the last syllable.* **22.** (foll. by *to*) to return (to); be inherited (by): *the estate falls to the eldest son.* **23.** (often foll. by *into, under,* etc.) to be classified or included: *the subject falls into two main areas.* **24.** to issue forth: *a curse fell from her lips.* **25.** (of animals, esp. lambs) to be born. **26.** *Brit. dialect.* to become pregnant. **27.** (*tr.*) *Dialect, Austral., and N.Z.* to fell (trees). **28.** *Cricket.* (of a batsman's wicket) to be taken by the bowling side: *the sixth wicket fell for 96.* **29.** *Archaic.* to begin to do: *fall a-doing; fall to doing.* **30. fall flat.** to fail to achieve a desired effect. **31. fall foul of. a.** to come into conflict with. **b.** *Nautical.* to come into collision with. **32. fall short. a.** to prove inadequate. **b.** (often foll. by *of*) to fail to reach or measure up to (a standard). ~*n.* **33.** an act or instance of falling. **34.** something that falls: *a fall of snow.* **35.** *Chiefly U.S. and Canadian.* autumn. **36.** the distance that something falls: *a hundred-foot fall.* **37.** a sudden drop from an upright position. **38.** (*often pl.*) **a.** a waterfall or cataract. **b.** (*cap. when part of a name*): *Niagara Falls.* **39.** a downward slope or decline. **40.** a decrease in value, number, etc. **41.** a decline in status or importance. **42.** a moral lapse or failing. **43.** a capture or overthrow: *the fall of the city.* **44.** a long false hairpiece; switch. **45.** a piece of loosely hanging material, such as a veil on a hat. **46.** *Machinery, nautical.* the end of a tackle to which power is applied to hoist it. **47.** *Nautical.* one of the lines of a davit for holding, lowering, or raising a boat. **48.** Also called: **pinfall.** *Wrestling.* a scoring move, pinning both shoulders of one's opponent to the floor for a specified period. **49.** *Hunting.* **a.** another word for **deadfall. b.** (*as modifier*): *a fall trap.* **50. a.** the birth of an animal. **b.** the animals produced at a single birth. ~See also **fall about, fall among, fall away, fall back, fall behind, fall down, fall for, fall in, fall off, fall on, fallout, fall over, fall through, fall to.** [Old English *feallan;* related to Old Norse *falla,* Old Saxon, Old High German *fallan* to fall; see FELL[2]]

Fall (fɔːl) *n.* **the.** *Theol.* Adam's sin of disobedience and the state of innate sinfulness ensuing from this for himself and all mankind. See also **original sin.**

fall about *vb.* (*intr., adv.*) to laugh in an uncontrolled manner: *we fell about when we saw him.*

fallacious (fə'leɪʃəs) *adj.* **1.** containing or involving a fallacy; illogical; erroneous. **2.** tending to mislead. **3.** delusive or disappointing: *a fallacious hope.* —**fal'laciously** *adv.* —**fal'laciousness** *n.*

fallacy ('fæləsɪ) *n., pl.* **-cies. 1.** an incorrect or misleading notion or opinion based on inaccurate facts or invalid reasoning. **2.** unsound or invalid reasoning. **3.** the tendency to mislead. **4.** *Logic.* an error in reasoning that renders an argument logically invalid. [C15: from Latin *fallācia,* from *fallax* deceitful, from *fallere* to deceive]

fallacy of many questions *n. Logic.* the rhetorical trick of asking a question that cannot be answered without admitting a presupposition that may be false, as *have you stopped beating your wife?*

fallal (fæl'læl) *n.* a showy ornament, trinket, or article of dress. [C18: perhaps based on FALBALA] —**fal'lalery** *n.*

fall among *vb.* (*intr., prep.*) to enter the company of (a group of people), esp. by chance: *he fell among thieves.*

fall away *vb.* (*intr., adv.*) **1.** (of friendship) to be withdrawn. **2.** to slope down.

fall back *vb.* (*intr., adv.*) **1.** to recede or retreat. **2.** (foll. by *on* or *upon*) to have recourse (to). ~*n.* **fall-back. 3.** a retreat. **4.** a reserve, esp. money, that can be called upon in need. **5. a.** anything to which one can have recourse as a second choice. **b.** (*as modifier*): *a fall-back position.*

fall behind *vb.* (*intr., adv.*) **1.** to drop back; fail to keep up. **2.** to be in arrears, as with a payment.

fall down *vb.* (*intr., adv.*) **1.** to drop suddenly or collapse. **2.** (often foll. by *on*) *Informal.* to prove unsuccessful; fail.

fallen ('fɔːlən) *vb.* **1.** the past participle of **fall.** ~*adj.* **2.** having sunk in reputation or honour: *a fallen woman.* **3.** killed in battle with glory: *our fallen heroes.* **4.** defeated.

fallen arch *n.* collapse of the arch formed by the instep of the foot, resulting in flat feet.

faller ('fɔːlə) *n.* **1.** any device that falls or operates machinery by falling, as in a spinning machine. **2.** one that falls, esp. a horse that falls at a fence in a steeplechase. **3.** *Austral.* a person who fells trees.

fallfish ('fɔːlˌfɪʃ) *n., pl.* **-fish** *or* **-fishes.** a large North American freshwater cyprinid fish, *Semotilus corporalis,* resembling the chub.

fall for *vb. (intr., prep.)* **1.** to become infatuated with (a person). **2.** to allow oneself to be deceived by (a lie, trick, etc.).

fall guy *n. Informal.* **1.** a person who is the victim of a confidence trick. **2.** a scapegoat.

fallible ('fælɪbᵊl) *adj.* **1.** capable of being mistaken; erring. **2.** liable to mislead. [C15: from Medieval Latin *fallibilis,* from Latin *fallere* to deceive] —ˌ**falli'bility** *or* '**fallibleness** *n.* —'**fallibly** *adv.*

fall in *vb. (intr., adv.)* **1.** to collapse; no longer act as a support. **2.** to adopt a military formation, esp. as a soldier taking his place in a line. **3.** (of a lease) to expire. **4.** (of land) to come into the owner's possession on the expiry of the lease. **5.** (often foll. by *with*) **a.** to meet and join. **b.** to agree with or support a person, suggestion, etc. **6.** *Austral. and N.Z.* to make a mistake or come to grief. **7.** *N.Z.* to become pregnant. ~*sentence substitute.* **8.** the order to adopt a military formation.

falling band *n.* a man's large flat collar, often lace-trimmed, worn during the 17th century.

falling sickness *or* **evil** *n.* a former name (nontechnical) for **epilepsy.**

falling star *n.* an informal name for **meteor.**

fall line *n.* **1.** *Skiing.* the natural downward course between two points on a slope. **2.** the edge of a plateau.

fall off *vb. (intr.)* **1.** to drop unintentionally to the ground from (a high object, bicycle, etc.), esp. after losing one's balance. **2.** (*adv.*) to diminish in size, intensity, etc.; decline or weaken: *business fell off after Christmas.* **3.** (*adv.*) *Nautical.* to allow or cause a vessel to sail downwind of her former heading. ~*n.* **fall-off. 4.** a decline or drop.

fall on *vb. (intr., prep.)* **1.** Also: **fall upon.** to attack or snatch (an army, booty, etc.). **2. fall flat on one's face.** to fail, esp. in a ridiculous or humiliating manner. **3. fall on one's feet.** to emerge unexpectedly well from a difficult situation.

Fallopian tube (fə'ləʊpɪən) *n.* either of a pair of slender tubes through which ova pass from the ovaries to the uterus in female mammals. See **oviduct.** [C18: named after Gabriello *Fallopio* (1523–62), Italian anatomist who first described the tubes]

fallout ('fɔːlˌaʊt) *n.* **1.** the descent of solid material in the atmosphere onto the earth, esp. of radioactive material following a nuclear explosion. **2.** any solid particles that so descend. **3.** *Informal.* side-effects; secondary consequences. ~*vb.* **fall out.** (*intr., adv.*) **4.** *Informal.* to quarrel or disagree. **5.** (*intr.*) to happen or occur. **6.** *Military.* to leave a parade or disciplinary formation. ~*sentence substitute.* **7.** *Military.* the order to leave a parade or disciplinary formation.

fall over *vb. (intr., adv.)* **1.** to lose one's balance and collapse to the ground. **2.** to fall from an upright position: *the vase fell over.* **3. fall over oneself.** to do everything within one's power: *he fell over himself to be as helpful as possible.*

fallow¹ ('fæləʊ) *adj.* **1.** (of land) left unseeded after being ploughed and harrowed to regain fertility for a crop. **2.** (of an idea, state of mind, etc.) undeveloped or inactive, but potentially useful. ~*n.* **3.** land treated in this way. ~*vb.* **4.** (*tr.*) to leave (land) unseeded after ploughing and harrowing it. [Old English *fealga;* related to Greek *polos* ploughed field] —'**fallowness** *n.*

fallow² ('fæləʊ) *adj.* of a light yellowish-brown colour. [Old English *fealu;* related to Old Norse *fölr,* Old Saxon, Old High German *falo,* Latin *pallidus* Greek *polios* grey]

fallow deer *n.* either of two deer, *Dama dama* or *D. mesopotamica,* native to the Mediterranean region and Persia respectively. The antlers are flattened and the summer coat is reddish with white spots.

fall through *vb. (intr., adv.)* to miscarry or fail.

fall to *vb. (intr.)* **1.** (*adv.*) to begin some activity, as eating, working, or fighting. **2.** (*prep.*) to devolve on (a person): *the task fell to me.* **3. fall to the ground.** (of a plan, theory, etc.) to be rendered invalid, esp. because of lack of necessary information.

false (fɔːls) *adj.* **1.** not in accordance with the truth or facts. **2.** irregular or invalid: *a false start.* **3.** untruthful or lying: *a false account.* **4.** not genuine, real, or natural; artificial; fake: *false eyelashes.* **5.** being or intended to be misleading or deceptive: *a false rumour.* **6.** disloyal or treacherous: *a false friend.* **7.** based on mistaken or irrelevant ideas or facts: *false pride; a false argument.* **8.** (*prenominal*) (esp. of plants) superficially resembling the species specified: *false hellebore.* **9.** serving to supplement or replace, often temporarily: *a false keel.* **10.** *Music.* **a.** (of a note, interval, etc.) out of tune. **b.** (of the interval of a perfect fourth or fifth) decreased by a semitone. **c.** (of a cadence) interrupted or imperfect. ~*adv.* **11.** in a false or dishonest manner (esp. in the phrase **play (someone) false).** [Old English *fals,* from Latin *falsus,* from *fallere* to deceive] —'**falsely** *adv.* —'**falseness** *n.*

false acacia *n.* another name for the **locust tree** (see **locust** (sense 2)).

false alarm *n.* **1.** a needless alarm given in error or with intent to deceive. **2.** an occasion on which danger is perceived but fails to materialize.

false ankylosis *n.* a nontechnical name for **pseudarthrosis.**

false bedding *n.* another name for **cross bedding.**

false-card ('fɔːlsˌkɑːd) *vb. (intr.) Bridge.* to play a misleading card, esp. a high loser, in order to deceive an opponent.

false cirrus *n.* a type of thick cirrus cloud spreading from the top of a cumulonimbus cloud.

false colour *n.* colour used in a computer or photographic display to help in interpreting the image, as in the use of red to show high temperatures and blue to show low temperatures in an infrared image converter.

false colours *pl. n.* **1.** a flag to which one is not entitled, flown esp. in order to deceive: *the ship was sailing under false colours.* **2.** an assumed or misleading name or guise: *to trade under false colours.*

false dawn *n.* zodiacal light appearing just before sunrise.

false diamond *n.* any of a number of semiprecious stones that resemble diamond, such as zircon and white topaz.

false fruit *n.* another name for **pseudocarp.**

falsehood ('fɔːlsˌhʊd) *n.* **1.** the quality of being untrue. **2.** an untrue statement; lie. **3.** the act of deceiving or lying.

false imprisonment *n. Law.* the restraint of a person's liberty without lawful authority.

false joint *n.* a nontechnical name for **pseudarthrosis.**

false keel *n.* an extension to the keel of a vessel either for protecting the keel from damage or for reducing leeway.

false position *n.* a situation in which a person is forced to act or seems to be acting against his principles or interests.

false pregnancy *n.* another name for **phantom pregnancy.**

false pretences *pl. n.* **1.** *Criminal law.* a former name for **deception** (see **obtaining by deception**). **2.** a similar misrepresentation used to obtain anything, such as trust or affection (esp. in the phrase **under false pretences).**

false relation *n. Music.* a harmonic clash that occurs when a note in one part sounds simultaneously with or immediately before or after its chromatically altered (sharpened or flattened) equivalent appearing in another part. Also called (esp. U.S.): **cross relation.**

false ribs *pl. n.* any of the lower five pairs of ribs in man, attached behind to the thoracic vertebrae but in front not attached directly to the breastbone. See **floating rib.**

false scorpion *n.* any small predatory arachnid of the order *Pseudoscorpionida,* which includes the **book scorpion** and is named from the claw-shaped palps, which are poison organs.

false step *n.* **1.** an unwise action. **2.** a stumble; slip.

false teeth *pl. n.* a denture, esp. a removable complete set of artificial teeth for one or both jaws.

falsetto (fɔːl'sɛtəʊ) *n., pl.* **-tos.** a form of vocal production used by male singers to extend their range upwards beyond its natural compass by limiting the vibration of the vocal cords. [C18: from Italian, from *falso* FALSE]

false vampire *n.* any large insectivorous bat of of the family *Megadermatidae,* of Africa, S and SE Asia, and Australia. They eat insects and small vertebrates but do not feed on blood.

falsework ('fɔːlsˌwɜːk) *n.* a framework supporting something under construction.

falsies ('fɔːlsɪz) *pl. n. Informal.* pads of soft material, such as foam rubber, worn to exaggerate the size of or simulate the appearance of a woman's breasts.

falsify ('fɔːlsɪˌfaɪ) *vb.* **-fies, -fying, -fied. 1.** (*tr.*) to make (a report, evidence, accounts, etc.) false or inaccurate by alteration, esp. in order to deceive. **2.** (*tr.*) to prove false; disprove. [C15: from Old French *falsifier,* from Late Latin *falsificāre,* from Latin *falsus* FALSE + *facere* to make] —'**falsiˌfiable** *adj.* —**falsification** (ˌfɔːlsɪfɪ'keɪʃən) *n.* —'**falsiˌfier** *n.*

falsity ('fɔːlsɪtɪ) *n., pl.* **-ties. 1.** the state of being false or untrue. **2.** something false; a lie or deception.

Falstaffian (fɔːl'stɑːfɪən) *adj.* jovial, plump, and dissolute. [C19: after *Sir John Falstaff,* a character in Shakespeare's *Henry IV, Parts I–II* (1597)]

faltboat ('fæltˌbəʊt) *n.* a collapsible boat made of waterproof material stretched over a light framework. [German *Faltboot,* from *falten* to FOLD + *Boot* BOAT]

falter ('fɔːltə) *vb.* **1.** (*intr.*) to be hesitant, weak, or unsure; waver. **2.** (*intr.*) to move unsteadily or hesitantly; stumble. **3.** to utter haltingly or hesitantly; stammer. ~*n.* **4.** uncertainty or hesitancy in speech or action. **5.** a quavering or irregular sound. [C14: probably of Scandinavian origin; compare Icelandic *faltrast*] —'**falterer** *n.* —'**falteringly** *adv.*

fam. *abbrev. for:* **1.** familiar. **2.** family.

F.A.M. *abbrev. for* Free and Accepted Masons. See **Freemason.**

fame (feɪm) *n.* **1.** the state of being widely known or recognized; renown; celebrity. **2.** *Archaic.* rumour or public report. ~*vb.* **3.** (*tr.; now usually passive*) to make known or famous; celebrate: *he was famed for his ruthlessness.* [C13: from Latin *fāma* report; related to *fārī* to say] —'**fameless** *adj.*

familial (fə'mɪlɪəl) *adj.* **1.** of or relating to the family. **2.** occurring in the members of a family: *a familial disease.*

familiar (fə'mɪlɪə) *adj.* **1.** well-known; easily recognized: *a familiar figure.* **2.** frequent or customary: *a familiar excuse.* **3.** (*postpositive;* foll. by *with*) acquainted. **4.** friendly; informal. **5.**

close; intimate. **6.** more intimate than is acceptable; presumptuous. **7.** an archaic word for **familial.** ~*n.* **8.** Also called: **familiar spirit.** a supernatural spirit often assuming animal form, supposed to attend and aid a witch, wizard, etc. **9.** a person, attached to the household of the pope or a bishop, who renders service in return for support. **10.** an officer of the Inquisition who arrested accused persons. **11.** a friend or frequent companion. [C14: from Latin *familiāris* domestic, from *familia* FAMILY] —**fa'miliarly** *adv.* —**fa'miliarness** *n.*

familiarity (fəˌmɪlɪ'ærɪtɪ) *n., pl.* **-ties.** **1.** reasonable knowledge or acquaintance, as with a subject or place. **2.** close acquaintanceship or intimacy. **3.** undue intimacy. **4.** (*sometimes pl.*) an instance of unwarranted intimacy.

familiarize *or* **familiarise** (fə'mɪljəˌraɪz) *vb.* (*tr.*) **1.** to make (oneself or someone else) familiar, as with a particular subject. **2.** to make (something) generally known or accepted. —**faˌmiliari'zation** *or* **faˌmiliari'sation** *n.* —**fa'miliarˌizer** *or* **fa'miliarˌiser** *n.*

Familist ('fæmɪlɪst) *n.* a member of the Family of Love, a mystical Christian religious sect of the 16th and 17th centuries based upon love. —**'Familism** *n.*

famille *French.* (famij) *n.* a type of Chinese porcelain characterized either by a design on a background of yellow (***famille jaune***) or black (***famille noire***) or by a design in which the predominant colour is pink (***famille rose***) or green (***famille verte***). [C19: literally: family]

family ('fæmɪlɪ, 'fæmlɪ) *n., pl.* **-lies.** **1. a.** a primary social group consisting of parents and their offspring, the principal function of which is provision for its members. **b.** (*as modifier*): *family quarrels; a family unit.* **2.** one's wife or husband and one's children. **3.** one's children, as distinguished from one's husband or wife. **4.** a group of persons related by blood; a group descended from a common ancestor. Compare **extended family. 5.** all the persons living together in one household. **6.** any group of related things or beings, esp. when scientifically categorized. **7.** *Biology.* any of the taxonomic groups into which an order is divided and which contains one or more genera. *Felidae* (cat family) and *Canidae* (dog family) are two families of the order *Carnivora.* **8.** *Ecology.* a group of organisms of the same species living together in a community. **9.** a group of historically related languages assumed to derive from one original language. **10.** *Chiefly U.S.* an independent local group of the Mafia. **11.** *Maths.* a group of curves or surfaces whose equations differ from a given equation only in the values assigned to one or more constants in each curve: *a family of concentric circles.* **12.** *Physics.* the isotopes, collectively, that comprise a radioactive series. **13. in the family way.** *Informal.* pregnant. [C15: from Latin *familia* a household, servants of the house, from *famulus* servant]

family allowance *n.* **1.** (in Britain) a former name for **child benefit. 2.** (*caps.*) the Canadian equivalent of **child benefit.**

family benefit *n. N.Z.* a child allowance paid to the mothers of children under 18 years of age.

family Bible *n.* a large Bible used for family worship in which births, marriages, and deaths are recorded.

family circle *n.* **1.** members of a family regarded as a closed group. **2.** *Chiefly U.S.* the cheap seating area in a theatre behind or above the dress circle.

Family Compact *n. Canadian.* **1. the.** the ruling oligarchy in Upper Canada in the early 19th century. **2.** (*often not cap.*) any influential clique.

family credit *n.* (in Britain) a means-tested allowance paid to families who have at least one dependent child, and whose earnings from full-time work are low. It replaced Family Income Supplement.

Family Division *n. Brit. law.* a division of the High Court of Justice dealing with divorce, the custody of and rights of access to children, etc.

family doctor *n.* See **general practitioner.**

family grouping *n.* a system, used usually in the infant school, of grouping children of various ages together, esp. for project work. Also called: **vertical grouping.**

family man *n.* a man who is married and has children, esp. one who is devoted to his family.

family name *n.* **1.** a surname, esp. when regarded as representing the family honour. **2.** a first or middle name frequently used in a family, often originally a surname.

family planning *n.* the control of the number of children in a family and of the intervals between them, esp. by the use of contraceptives. See also **birth control.**

family skeleton *n.* a closely guarded family secret.

family therapy *n.* a form of psychotherapy in which the members of a family participate, with the aim of improving communications between them and the ways in which they relate to each other.

family tree *n.* a chart showing the genealogical relationships and lines of descent of a family. Also called: **genealogical tree.**

famine ('fæmɪn) *n.* **1.** a severe shortage of food, as through crop failure or overpopulation. **2.** acute shortage of anything. **3.** violent hunger. [C14: from Old French, via Vulgar Latin, from Latin *famēs* hunger]

famish ('fæmɪʃ) *vb.* **1.** (*now usually passive*) to be or make very hungry or weak. **2.** *Archaic.* to die or cause to die from starvation. **3.** *Irish.* to make very cold: *I was famished with the cold.* [C14: from Old French *afamer,* via Vulgar Latin, from Latin *famēs* FAMINE] —**'famishment** *n.*

famous ('feɪməs) *adj.* **1.** known to or recognized by many people; renowned. **2.** *Informal.* excellent; splendid. **3.** *Archaic.* of ill repute. [C14: from Latin *fāmōsus;* see FAME] —**'famously** *adv.* —**'famousness** *n.*

famulus ('fæmjʊləs) *n., pl.* **-li** (-ˌlaɪ). (formerly) the attendant of a sorcerer or scholar. [C19: from Latin: servant]

fan[1] (fæn) *n.* **1. a.** any device for creating a current of air by movement of a surface or number of surfaces, esp. a rotating device consisting of a number of blades attached to a central hub. **b.** a machine that rotates such a device. **2.** any of various hand-agitated devices for cooling onself, esp. a collapsible semicircular series of flat segments of paper, ivory, etc. **3.** something shaped like such a fan, such as the tail of certain birds. **4.** *Agriculture.* **a.** a kind of basket formerly used for winnowing grain. **b.** a machine equipped with a fan for winnowing or cleaning grain. ~*vb.* **fans, fanning, fanned.** (*mainly tr.*) **5.** to cause a current of air, esp. cool air, to blow upon, as by means of a fan: *to fan one's face.* **6.** to agitate or move (air, smoke, etc.) with or as if with a fan. **7.** to make fiercer, more ardent, etc.: *fan one's passion.* **8.** (*also intr.;* often foll. by *out*) to spread out or cause to spread out in the shape of a fan. **9. a.** to fire (an automatic gun) continuously by keeping the trigger depressed. **b.** to fire (a nonautomatic gun) several times by repeatedly chopping back the hammer with the palm. **10.** to winnow (grain) by blowing the chaff away from it. [Old English *fann,* from Latin *vannus*] —**'fanlike** *adj.* —**'fanner** *n.*

fan[2] (fæn) *n.* **1.** an ardent admirer of a pop star, film actor, football team, etc. **2.** a devotee of a sport, hobby, etc. [C17, re-formed C19: from FAN(ATIC)]

Fanagalo ('fænəgələʊ) *or* **Fanakalo** *n.* (in South Africa) a Zulu-based pidgin with English and Afrikaans components, esp. associated with the mines. [C20: from Fanagalo *fana go lo,* literally: to be like this; compare Zulu *fand* to be like, *ka-lo* of this]

fanatic (fə'nætɪk) *n.* **1.** a person whose enthusiasm or zeal for something is extreme or beyond normal limits. **2.** *Informal.* a person devoted to a particular hobby or pastime; fan: *a jazz fanatic.* ~*adj.* **3.** a variant of **fanatical.** [C16: from Latin *fānāticus* belonging to a temple, hence, inspired by a god, frenzied, from *fānum* temple]

fanatical (fə'nætɪk[ə]l) *adj.* surpassing what is normal or accepted in enthusiasm for or belief in something; excessively or unusually dedicated or devoted. —**fa'natically** *adv.*

fanaticism (fə'nætɪˌsɪzəm) *n.* wildly excessive or irrational devotion, dedication, or enthusiasm.

fanaticize *or* **fanaticise** (fə'nætɪˌsaɪz) *vb.* to make or become fanatical.

fan belt *n.* any belt that drives a fan, esp. the belt that drives a cooling fan together with a dynamo or alternator in a car engine.

fancied ('fænsɪd) *adj.* **1.** imaginary; unreal. **2.** thought likely to win or succeed: *a fancied runner.*

fancier ('fænsɪə) *n.* **1.** a person with a special interest in something. **2.** a person who breeds plants or animals, often as a pastime: *a bird fancier.*

fanciful ('fænsɪfʊl) *adj.* **1.** not based on fact; dubious or imaginary: *fanciful notions.* **2.** made or designed in a curious, intricate, or imaginative way. **3.** indulging in or influenced by fancy; whimsical. —**'fancifully** *adv.* —**'fancifulness** *n.*

fancy ('fænsɪ) *adj.* **-cier, -ciest.** **1.** not plain; ornamented or decorative: *a fancy cake; fancy clothes.* **2.** requiring skill to perform; intricate: *a fancy dance routine.* **3.** arising in the imagination; capricious or illusory. **4.** (often used ironically) superior in quality or impressive: *a fancy course in business administration.* **5.** higher than expected: *fancy prices.* **6.** (of a domestic animal) bred for particular qualities. ~*n., pl.* **-cies. 7.** a sudden capricious idea; whim. **8.** a sudden or irrational liking for a person or thing. **9.** the power to conceive and represent decorative and novel imagery, esp. in poetry. Fancy was held by Coleridge to be more casual and superficial than imagination. See **imagination** (sense 4). **10.** an idea or thing produced by this. **11.** a mental image. **12.** taste or judgment, as in art of dress. **13.** Also called: **fantasy, fantasia.** *Music.* a composition for solo lute, keyboard, etc., current during the 16th and 17th centuries. **14. the fancy.** *Archaic.* those who follow a particular sport, esp. prize fighting. ~*vb.* **-cies, -cying, -cied.** (*tr.*) **15.** to picture in the imagination. **16.** to suppose; imagine: *I fancy it will rain.* **17.** (*often used with a negative*) to like: *I don't fancy your chances!* **18.** (*reflexive*) to have a high or ill-founded opinion of oneself: *he fancied himself as a doctor.* **19.** *Informal.* to have a wish for; desire: *she fancied some chocolate.* **20.** *Brit. informal.* to be physically attracted to (another person). **21.** to breed (animals) for particular characteristics. ~*interj.* **22.** Also: **fancy that!** an exclamation of surprise or disbelief. [C15 *fantsy,* shortened from *fantasie;* see FANTASY] —**'fancily** *adv.* —**'fanciness** *n.*

fancy dress *n.* **a.** costume worn at masquerades, etc., usually representing a particular role, historical figure, etc. **b.** (*as modifier*): *a fancy-dress ball.*

fancy-free *adj.* having no commitments; carefree.

fancy goods *pl. n.* small decorative gifts; knick-knacks.

fancy man *n. Slang.* **1.** a woman's lover. **2.** a pimp.

fancy woman *n. Slang.* a mistress or prostitute.
fancywork ('fænsɪˌwɜːk) *n.* any ornamental needlework, such as embroidery or crochet.
fan dance *n.* a dance in which large fans are manipulated in front of the body, partially revealing or suggesting nakedness.
fandangle (fæn'dæŋgᵊl) *n. Informal.* **1.** elaborate ornament. **2.** nonsense. [C19: perhaps from FANDANGO]
fandango (fæn'dæŋgəʊ) *n., pl.* **-gos. 1.** an old Spanish courtship dance in triple time between a couple who dance closely and provocatively. **2.** a piece of music composed for or in the rhythm of this dance. [C18: from Spanish, of uncertain origin]
fane (feɪn) *n. Archaic or poetic.* a temple or shrine. [C14: from Latin *fānum*]
fanfare ('fænfɛə) *n.* **1.** a flourish or short tune played on brass instruments, used as a military signal, at a ceremonial event, etc. **2.** an ostentatious flourish or display. [C17: from French, back formation from *fanfarer* to play a flourish on trumpets; see FANFARONADE]
fanfaronade (ˌfænfərə'nɑːd) *n. Rare.* boasting or flaunting behaviour; bluster. [C17: via French from Spanish *fanfaronada,* from *fanfarron* boaster, from Arabic *farfār* garrulous]
fang (fæŋ) *n.* **1.** the long pointed hollow or grooved tooth of a venomous snake through which venom is injected. **2.** any large pointed tooth, esp. the canine or carnassial tooth of a carnivorous mammal. **3.** the root of a tooth. **4.** (*usually pl.*) *Brit. informal.* tooth: *clean your fangs.* [Old English *fang* what is caught, prey; related to Old Norse *fang* a grip, German *Fang* booty] —**fanged** *adj.* —'**fangless** *adj.* —'**fangˌlike** *adj.*
Fang (fæŋ, fɑːŋ) *n.* **1.** (*pl.* **Fangs** *or* **Fang**) a member of a Negroid people of W Africa, living chiefly in the rain forests of Gabon and Rio Muni: noted for their use of iron and copper money and for their sculpture. **2.** the language of this people, belonging to the Bantu group of the Niger-Congo family.
fango ('fæŋgəʊ) *n.* mud from thermal springs in Italy, used in the treatment of rheumatic disease. [from Italian]
fan heater *n.* a space heater consisting of an electrically heated element with an electrically driven fan to disperse the heat by forced convection.
fanion ('fænjən) *n.* a small flag used by surveyors to mark stations. [C18: from French, from *fanon* maniple, of Germanic origin]
fanjet ('fænˌdʒɛt) *n.* another name for **turbofan** (senses 1, 2).
fankle ('fæŋkᵊl) *Scot. dialect.* ~*vb.* (*tr.*) **1.** to entangle. ~*n.* **2.** a tangle; confusion. [from *fank* a coil of rope, from *fang,* obsolete variant of VANG]
fanlight ('fænˌlaɪt) *n.* **1.** a semicircular window over a door or window, often having sash bars like the ribs of a fan. **2.** a small rectangular window over a door. U.S name: **transom. 3.** another name for **skylight.**
fan mail *n.* mail sent to a famous person, such as a pop musician or film star, by admirers.
fanny ('fænɪ) *n., pl.* **-nies.** *Slang.* **1.** *Taboo, Brit.* the female pudendum. **2.** *Chiefly U.S. and Canadian.* the buttocks. [C20: perhaps from *Fanny,* pet name from *Frances*]
fanny adams *n. Brit. slang.* **1.** (usually preceded by *sweet*) absolutely nothing at all. Often shortened to **f.a., FA** *or* **SFA. 2.** *Chiefly nautical.* (formerly) tinned meat, esp. mutton. [C19: from the name of a young murder victim whose body was cut up into small pieces. For sense 1: a euphemism for *fuck all*]
fanon ('fænən) *n. R.C. Church.* **1.** a collar-shaped vestment worn by the pope when celebrating mass. **2.** (formerly) various pieces of embroidered fabric used in the liturgy. [Middle English, of Germanic origin; related to Old High German *fano* cloth]
fan palm *n.* any of various palm trees, such as the talipot and palmetto, that have fan-shaped leaves. Compare **feather palm.**
fantail ('fænˌteɪl) *n.* **1.** a breed of domestic pigeon having a large tail that can be opened like a fan. **2.** any Old World flycatcher of the genus *Rhipidura,* of Australia, New Zealand, and SE Asia, having a broad fan-shaped tail. **3.** a tail shaped like an outspread fan. **4.** *Architect.* a part or structure having a number of components radiating from a common centre. **5.** a burner that ejects fuel to produce a wide flat flame in a lamp or furnace. **6.** a flat jet of air and coal dust projected into the air stream of a pulverized-coal furnace. **7.** an auxiliary sail on the upper portion of a windmill that turns the mill to face the wind. **8.** *U.S.* a curved part of the deck projecting aft of the sternpost of a ship. —'**fanˌtailed** *adj.*
fan-tan *n.* **1.** a Chinese gambling game in which a random number of counters are placed under a bowl and wagers laid on how many will remain after they have been divided by four. **2.** a card game played in sequence, the winner being the first to use up all his cards. [C19: from Chinese (Cantonese) *fan t'an* repeated divisions, from *fan* times + *t'an* division]
fantasia (fæn'teɪzɪə, ˌfæntə'zɪə) *n.* **1.** any musical composition of a free or improvisatory nature. **2.** a potpourri of popular tunes woven freely into a loosely bound composition. **3.** another word for **fancy** (sense 13). [C18: from Italian: fancy; see FANTASY]
fantasize *or* **fantasise** ('fæntəˌsaɪz) *vb.* **1.** (when *tr.,* takes a clause as object) to conceive extravagant or whimsical ideas, images, etc. **2.** (*intr.*) to conceive pleasant or satisfying mental images.
fantasm ('fæntæzəm) *n.* an archaic spelling of **phantasm.** —**fan'tasmal** *or* **fan'tasmic** *adj.* —**fan'tasmally** *or* **fan'tasmically** *adv.*
fantast ('fæntæst) *n.* a dreamer or visionary. [C16: from German *Phantast,* from Greek *phantastēs* boaster; English word influenced in meaning by FANTASTIC]
fantastic (fæn'tæstɪk) *adj. also* **fantastical. 1.** strange, weird, or fanciful in appearance, conception, etc. **2.** created in the mind; illusory. **3.** extravagantly fanciful; unrealistic: *fantastic plans.* **4.** incredible or preposterous; absurd: *a fantastic verdict.* **5.** *Informal.* very large or extreme; great: *a fantastic fortune; he suffered fantastic pain.* **6.** *Informal.* very good; excellent. **7.** of, given to, or characterized by fantasy. **8.** not constant; capricious; fitful: *given to fantastic moods.* ~*n.* **9.** *Archaic.* a person who dresses or behaves eccentrically. [C14 *fantastik* imaginary, via Late Latin from Greek *phantastikos* capable of imagining, from *phantazein* to make visible] —ˌ**fantasti'cality** *or* **fan'tasticalness** *n.*
fantastically (fæn'tæstɪkəlɪ) *adv.* **1.** in a fantastic manner. **2.** *Informal.* (intensifier): *it's fantastically cheap.*
fantasy *or* **phantasy** ('fæntəsɪ) *n., pl.* **-sies. 1. a.** imagination unrestricted by reality. **b.** (*as modifier*): *a fantasy world.* **2.** a creation of the imagination, esp. a weird or bizarre one. **3.** *Psychol.* **a.** a series of pleasing mental images, usually serving to fulfil a need not gratified in reality. **b.** the activity of forming such images. **4.** a whimsical or far-fetched notion. **5.** an illusion, hallucination, or phantom. **6.** a highly elaborate imaginative design or creation. **7.** *Music.* another word for **fantasia** (senses 1, 2), **fancy** (sense 13), or (rare) **development** (sense 5). **8. a.** literature having a large fantasy content. **b.** a prose or dramatic composition of this type. ~*vb.* **-sies, -sying, -sied. 9.** a less common word for **fantasize.** [C14 *fantasie,* from Latin *phantasia,* from Greek *phantazein* to make visible]
Fanti ('fæntɪ) *n.* **1.** a language of Ghana: one of the two chief dialects of Akan. Compare **Twi. 2.** (*pl.* **-tis** *or* **-ti**) a member of a Negroid people who speak this language, inhabiting the rain forests of Ghana and the Ivory Coast.
fantoccini (ˌfæntə'tʃiːnɪ) *pl. n.* **1.** marionettes. **2.** puppet shows in which they are used. [C18: from Italian: little puppets, plural of *fantoccino,* from *fantoccio* puppet, from *fante* boy, from Latin *infāns* INFANT]
fantod ('fæntəd) *n.* **1.** crotchety or faddish behaviour. **2.** (*pl.*) a state of restlessness or unease. [C19: of uncertain origin]
fantom ('fæntəm) *n.* an archaic spelling of **phantom.**
fantoosh (fæn'tuːʃ) *adj. Scot.* pretentious; ostentatious. [of uncertain origin]
fan tracery *n. Architect.* the carved ornamentation on fan vaulting.
fan vaulting *n. Architect.* vaulting having ribs that radiate like those of a fan and spring from the top of a capital or corbel. Also called: **palm vaulting.**
fan worm *n.* any tube-dwelling polychaete worm of the family *Sabellidae,* having long tentacles that spread into a fan when the worm emerges from its tube.
FANY ('fænɪ) *n.* **1.** *acronym for* First Aid Nursing Yeomanry. **2.** Also called: **Fany, Fanny,** *pl.* **FANYs, Fanys, Fannies.** a member of this organization.
fanzine ('fænˌziːn) *n.* a small-circulation magazine produced by amateurs for fans of a specific interest, pop group, etc. [C20: from FAN² + (MAGA)ZINE]
FAO *abbrev. for* Food and Agriculture Organization (of the United Nations).
f.a.q. *abbrev. for:* **1.** *Commerce.* fair average quality. **2.** free alongside quay.
faqir (fə'kɪə, 'feɪkə) *n.* a variant spelling of **fakir.**
far (fɑː) *adv.* **farther** *or* **further, farthest** *or* **furthest. 1.** at, to, or from a great distance. **2.** at or to a remote time: *far in the future.* **3.** to a considerable degree; very much: *a far better plan.* **4. as far as. a.** to the degree or extent that. **b.** to the distance or place of. **5. by far.** by a considerable margin. **6. far and away.** by a very great margin. **7. far and wide.** over great distances; everywhere. **8. far be it from me.** I would not presume; on no account: *far be it from me to tell you what to do.* **9. far gone. a.** in an advanced state of deterioration. **b.** *Informal.* extremely drunk. **10. go far. a.** to be successful; achieve much: *your son will go far.* **b.** to be sufficient or last long: *the wine didn't go far.* **11. go too far.** to exceed reasonable limits. **12. how far?** to what extent, distance, or degree? **13. in so far as.** to the degree or extent that. **14. so far. a.** up to the present moment. **b.** up to a certain point, extent, degree, etc. **15. so far, so good.** an expression of satisfaction with progress made. ~*adj.* (*prenominal*) **16.** remote in space or time: *a far country; in the far past.* **17.** extending a great distance; long. **18.** more distant: *the far end of the room.* **19. a far cry. a.** a long way. **b.** something very different. **20. far from.** in a degree, state, etc., remote from: *he is far from happy.* [Old English *feorr;* related to Old Frisian *fir,* Old High German *ferro,* Latin *porro* forwards, Greek *pera* further] —'**farness** *n.*
farad ('færəd, -æd) *n. Physics.* the derived SI unit of electric capacitance; the capacitance of a capacitor between the plates of which a potential of 1 volt is created by a charge of 1 coulomb. Symbol: F [C19: named after Michael *Faraday* (1791–1867), British physicist]

faraday ('færəˌdeɪ) *n.* a quantity of electricity, used in electrochemical calculations, equivalent to unit amount of substance of electrons. It is equal to the product of the Avogadro number and the charge on the electron and has the value 96 487 coulombs per mole. Symbol: *F* [C20: named after Michael *Faraday*]

Faraday cage ('færəˌdeɪ) *n.* an earthed conducting cage or container used to protect electrical equipment against electric fields. [C20: named after Michael *Faraday*]

faradic (fə'rædɪk) *or* **faradaic** (ˌfærə'deɪɪk) *adj.* of or concerned with an intermittent asymmetric alternating current such as that induced in the secondary winding of an induction coil. [C19: from French *faradique,* from Michael *Faraday*]

faradism ('færəˌdɪzəm) *n.* the therapeutic use of faradic currents.

faradize *or* **faradise** ('færəˌdaɪz) *vb.* *(tr.)* to treat (an organ or part) with faradic currents. —ˌ**faradi'zation** *or* ˌ**faradi'sation** *n.* —'**faraˌdizer** *or* '**faraˌdiser** *n.*

farandole ('færənˌdəʊl; *French* farɑ̃dɔl) *n.* **1.** a lively dance in six-eight or four-four time from Provence. **2.** a piece of music composed for or in the rhythm of this dance. [C19: from French, from Provençal *farandoulo,* of uncertain origin; compare Spanish *farándula* itinerant group of actors]

faraway ('fɑːrəˌweɪ) *adj.* (**far away** *when postpositive*). **1.** very distant; remote. **2.** dreamy or absent-minded.

farce (fɑːs) *n.* **1.** a broadly humorous play based on the exploitation of improbable situations. **2.** the genre of comedy represented by works of this kind. **3.** a ludicrous situation or action. **4.** Also: **farcemeat.** another name for **forcemeat.** ~*vb.* *(tr.)* *Obsolete.* **5.** to enliven (a speech, etc.) with jokes. **6.** to stuff (meat, fowl, etc.) with forcemeat. [C14 (in the sense: stuffing): from Old French, from Latin *farcīre* to stuff, interpolate passages (in the mass, in religious plays, etc.)]

farceur (*French* farsœr) *n.* **1.** a writer of or performer in farces. **2.** a joker. —**far'ceuse** *fem. n.*

farci (fɑː'siː) *adj.* (of food) stuffed. [French: stuffed; see FARCE]

farcical ('fɑːsɪkᵊl) *adj.* **1.** ludicrous; absurd. **2.** of or relating to farce. —ˌ**farci'cality** *or* '**farcicalness** *n.* —'**farcically** *adv.*

farcy ('fɑːsɪ) *n., pl.* **-cies.** *Vet. science.* a form of glanders in which lymph vessels near the skin become thickened, with skin lesions and abscess-forming nodules. [C15: from Old French *farcin,* from Late Latin *farcīminum* glanders, from Latin *farcīmen* a sausage, from *farcīre* to stuff]

fard (fɑːd) *n. Archaic.* paint for the face, esp. white paint. [C15: from Old French *farder* to use facial cosmetics, of Germanic origin]

fardel ('fɑːdᵊl) *n. Archaic.* a bundle or burden. [C13: from Old French *farde,* ultimately from Arabic *fardah*]

fare (fɛə) *n.* **1.** the sum charged or paid for conveyance in a bus, train, aeroplane, etc. **2.** a paying passenger, esp. when carried by taxi. **3.** a range of food and drink; diet. ~*vb.* *(intr.)* **4.** to get on (as specified); manage: *he fared well.* **5.** (with *it* as a subject) to turn out or happen as specified: *it fared badly with him.* **6.** *Archaic.* to eat: *we fared sumptuously.* **7.** (often foll. by *forth*) *Archaic.* to go or travel. [Old English *faran;* related to Old Norse *fara* to travel, Old High German *faran* to go, Greek *poros* ford] —'**farer** *n.*

Far Eastern *adj.* of or relating to the Far East, the countries of E Asia.

fare stage *n.* **1.** a section of a bus journey for which a set charge is made. **2.** a bus stop marking the end of such a section.

fare-thee-well *or* **fare-you-well** *n. Informal, chiefly U.S.* a state of perfection: *the steak was cooked to a fare-thee-well.*

farewell (ˌfɛə'wel) *sentence substitute.* **1.** goodbye; adieu. ~*n.* **2.** a parting salutation. **3.** an act of departure; leave-taking. **4.** *(modifier)* expressing leave-taking: *a farewell speech.* ~*vb.* *(tr.)* **5.** *Austral. and N.Z.* to honour (a person) at his departure, retirement, etc.

far-fetched *adj.* improbable in nature; unlikely.

far-flung *adj.* **1.** widely distributed. **2.** far distant; remote.

farina (fə'riːnə) *n.* **1.** flour or meal made from any kind of cereal grain. **2.** *Chiefly Brit.* starch, esp. prepared from potato flour. [C18: from Latin *fār* spelt, coarse meal]

farinaceous (ˌfærɪ'neɪʃəs) *adj.* **1.** consisting or made of starch, such as bread, macaroni, and potatoes. **2.** having a mealy texture or appearance. **3.** containing starch: *farinaceous seeds.*

farinose ('færɪˌnəʊs, -ˌnəʊz) *adj.* **1.** similar to or yielding farina. **2.** *Botany.* covered with very short hairs resembling a whitish mealy dust. —'**fariˌnosely** *adv.*

farl *or* **farle** (fɑːl) *n.* a thin cake of oatmeal, often triangular in shape. [C18: from earlier *fardel* fourth part, from Old English *fēortha* fourth + Middle English *del* part]

farm (fɑːm) *n.* **1. a.** a tract of land, usually with house and buildings, cultivated as a unit or used to rear livestock. **b.** *(as modifier): farm produce.* **c.** *(in combination): farmland.* **2.** a unit of land or water devoted to the growing or rearing of some particular type of vegetable, fruit, animal, or fish: *a fish farm.* **3.** an installation for storage. **4.** a district of which one or more taxes are leased. **5.** *History.* **a.** a fixed sum paid by an individual or group for the right of collecting and retaining taxes, rents, etc. **b.** a fixed sum paid regularly by a town, county, etc., in lieu of taxes. **c.** the leasing of a source of revenue to an individual or group. **d.** a fixed tax, rent, etc., paid regularly. ~*vb.* **6.** *(tr.)* **a.** to cultivate (land). **b.** to rear (stock, etc.) on a farm. **7.** *(intr.)* to engage in agricultural work, esp. as a way of life. **8.** *(tr.)* to look after a child for a fixed sum. **9. a.** to collect the moneys due and retain the profits from (a tax district, business, etc.) for a specified period on payment of a sum or sums. **b.** to operate (a franchise) under similar conditions. ~See also **farm out.** [C13: from Old French *ferme* rented land, ultimately from Latin *firmāre* to settle] —'**farmable** *adj.*

farm-bike *n. N.Z.* a motorcycle built for off-road travel.

farmer ('fɑːmə) *n.* **1.** a person who operates or manages a farm. **2.** a person who obtains the right to collect and retain a tax, rent, etc., or operate a franchise for a specified period on payment of a fee. **3.** a person who looks after a child for a fixed sum.

farmer-general *n., pl.* **farmers-general.** (in France before 1789) a member of a group allowed to farm certain taxes. —'**farmer-'generalˌship** *n.*

farmer's lung *n.* inflammation of the alveoli of the lungs caused by an allergic response to fungal spores in hay.

farm-gate sale *n. N.Z.* the sale of produce direct from the producer.

farm hand *n.* a person who is hired to work on a farm.

farmhouse ('fɑːmˌhaʊs) *n.* **1.** a house attached to a farm, esp. the dwelling from which the farm is managed. **2.** Also called: **farmhouse loaf.** *Brit.* a large white loaf, baked in a tin, with slightly curved sides and top.

farming ('fɑːmɪŋ) *n.* **a.** the business, art, or skill of agriculture. **b.** *(as modifier): farming methods.*

farmland ('fɑːmˌlænd) *n.* land used or suitable for farming.

farm out *vb.* *(tr., adv.)* **1.** to send (work) to be done by another person, firm, etc.; subcontract. **2.** to put (a child, etc.) into the care of a private individual; foster. **3.** to lease to another for a rent or fee the right to operate (a business for profit, land, etc.) or the right to collect (taxes).

farmstead ('fɑːmˌsted) *n.* a farm or the part of a farm comprising its main buildings together with adjacent grounds.

farm-toun ('færmˌtʊn, 'fɑːmˌtʊn) *n. Scot.* a farmhouse together with its outbuildings.

farmyard ('fɑːmˌjɑːd) *n.* **a.** an area surrounded by or adjacent to farm buildings. **b.** *(as modifier): farmyard animals.*

farnesol ('fɑːnɪˌsɒl) *n.* a colourless aromatic sesquiterpene alcohol found in many essential oils and used in the form of its derivatives in perfumery; 3,7,11-trimethyl-2,6,10-dodecatrienol. Formula: $C_{15}H_{26}O$. [C20: from New Latin *(Acacia) farnesiāna;* named after Odoardo *Farnese,* C17 Italian cardinal]

faro ('fɛərəʊ) *n.* a gambling game in which players bet against the dealer on what cards he will turn up. [C18: probably spelling variant of *Pharoah*]

Faroese (ˌfɛərəʊ'iːz) *adj., n.* a variant spelling of **Faeroese.**

far-off *adj.* (**far off** *when postpositive*). remote in space or time; distant.

farouche *French.* (faruʃ) *adj.* **1.** sullen or shy. **2.** socially inept. [C18: from French, from Old French *faroche,* from Late Latin *forasticus* from without, from Latin *foras* out of doors]

far-out *Slang.* ~*adj.* (**far out** *when postpositive*) **1.** bizarre or avant-garde. **2.** excellent; wonderful. ~*interj.* **far out. 3.** an expression of amazement or delight.

farrago (fə'rɑːgəʊ) *n., pl.* **-gos** *or* **-goes.** a hotchpotch. [C17: from Latin: mash for cattle (hence, a mixture), from *fār* spelt] —**farraginous** (fə'rædʒɪnəs) *adj.*

far-reaching *adj.* extensive in influence, effect, or range.

farrier ('færɪə) *n. Chiefly Brit.* **1.** a person who shoes horses. **2.** another name for **veterinary surgeon. 3.** *Military.* a noncommissioned officer who looks after horses. [C16: from Old French *ferrier,* from Latin *ferrārius* smith, from *ferrum* iron]

farriery ('færɪərɪ) *n., pl.* **-eries.** *Chiefly Brit.* the art, work, or establishment of a farrier.

farrow[1] ('færəʊ) *n.* **1.** a litter of piglets. ~*vb.* **2.** (of a sow) to give birth to (a litter). [Old English *fearh;* related to Old High German *farah* young pig, Latin *porcus* pig, Greek *porkos*]

farrow[2] ('færəʊ) *adj.* (of a cow) not calving in a given year. [C15: from Middle Dutch *verwe-* (unattested) cow that has ceased to bear; compare Old English *fearr* ox]

far-seeing *adj.* having shrewd judgment; far-sighted.

Farsi ('fɑːsiː) *n.* the Indo-European language of modern Iran. See also **Persian** (sense 4).

far-sighted *adj.* **1.** possessing prudence and foresight. **2.** *Med.* of, relating to, or suffering from hyperopia. **3.** another word for **long-sighted.** —ˌ**far-'sightedly** *adv.* —ˌ**far-'sightedness** *n.*

fart (fɑːt) *Taboo.* ~*n.* **1.** an emission of intestinal gas from the anus, esp. an audible one. **2.** *Slang.* a contemptible person. ~*vb.* *(intr.)* **3.** to expel intestinal gas from the anus; to break wind. **4. fart about** *or* **around.** *Slang.* **a.** to behave foolishly or aimlessly. **b.** to waste time. [Middle English *farten;* related to Old Norse *freta,* Old High German *ferzan* to break wind, Sanskrit *pardatē* he breaks wind]

farther ('fɑːðə) *adv.* **1.** to or at a greater distance in space or time. **2.** in addition. ~*adj.* **3.** more distant or remote in space or time. **4.** additional. [C13: see FAR, FURTHER]

▷**Usage.** In careful usage, *farther* and *farthest* are preferred when referring to literal distance: *the farthest planet. Further* and *furthest* are regarded as more correct for figurative senses denoting greater or additional amount, time, etc.: *further to my letter. Further* and *furthest* are also preferred for figurative distance.

farthermost ('fɑːðəˌməʊst) *adj.* most distant or remote.

farthest ('fɑːðɪst) *adv.* **1.** to or at the greatest distance in space or time. ~*adj.* **2.** most distant in space or time. **3.** most extended. [C14 *ferthest,* from *ferther* FURTHER]

farthing ('fɑːðɪŋ) *n.* **1.** a former British bronze coin worth a quarter of an old penny that ceased to be legal tender in 1961. **2.** something of negligible value; jot. [Old English *fēorthing* from *fēortha* FOURTH + -ING[1]]

farthingale ('fɑːðɪŋˌgeɪl) *n.* a hoop or framework worn under skirts, esp. in the Elizabethan period, to shape and spread them. [C16: from French *verdugale,* from Old Spanish *verdugado,* from *verdugo* rod]

fartlek ('fɑːtlɛk) *n. Sport.* another name for **interval training.** [Swedish, literally: speed play]

FAS *or* **f.a.s.** *abbrev. for* free alongside ship.

fasces ('fæsiːz) *pl. n., sing.* **-cis** (-sɪs). **1.** (in ancient Rome) one or more bundles of rods containing an axe with its blade protruding; a symbol of a magistrate's power. **2.** (in modern Italy) such an object used as the symbol of Fascism. [C16: from Latin, plural of *fascis* bundle]

fascia *or* **facia** ('feɪʃɪə) *n., pl.* **-ciae** (-ʃɪˌiː). **1.** the flat surface above a shop window. **2.** *Architect.* a flat band or surface, esp. a part of an architrave or cornice. **3.** ('fæʃɪə). fibrous connective tissue occurring in sheets beneath the surface of the skin and between muscles and groups of muscles. **4.** *Biology.* a distinctive band of colour, as on an insect or plant. **5.** *Brit.* a less common name for **dashboard** (sense 1). [C16: from Latin: band: related to *fascis* bundle; see FASCES] —'**fascial** *or* '**facial** *adj.*

fasciate ('fæʃɪˌeɪt) *or* **fasciated** *adj.* **1.** *Botany.* **a.** (of stems and branches) abnormally flattened due to coalescence. **b.** growing in a bundle. **2.** (of birds, insects, etc.) marked by distinct bands of colour. [C17: probably from New Latin *fasciātus* (unattested) having bands; see FASCIA] —'**fasciˌately** *adv.*

fasciation (ˌfæʃɪ'eɪʃən) *n. Botany.* an abnormal flattening of stems due to failure of the lateral branches to separate from the main stem.

fascicle ('fæsɪkəl) *n.* **1.** a bundle or cluster of branches, leaves, etc. **2.** Also called: **fasciculus.** *Anatomy.* a small bundle of fibres, esp. nerve fibres. **3.** *Printing.* another name for **fascicule. 4.** any small bundle or cluster. [C15: from Latin *fasciculus* a small bundle, from *fascis* a bundle] —'**fascicled** *adj.* —**fascicular** (fə'sɪkjʊlə) *or* **fasciculate** (fə'sɪkjʊˌleɪt, -lɪt) *adj.* —**fas'ciculately** *adv.* —**fasˌcicu'lation** *n.*

fascicule ('fæsɪˌkjuːl) *n.* one part of a printed work that is published in instalments. Also called: **fascicle, fasciculus.**

fasciculus (fə'sɪkjʊləs) *n., pl.* **-li** (-ˌlaɪ). another name for **fascicle** (sense 2) or **fascicule.**

fascinate ('fæsɪˌneɪt) *vb. (mainly tr.)* **1.** to attract and delight by arousing interest or curiosity: *his stories fascinated me for hours.* **2.** to render motionless, as with a fixed stare or by arousing terror or awe. **3.** *Archaic.* to put under a spell. [C16: from Latin *fascināre,* from *fascinum* a bewitching] —'**fasciˌnatedly** *adv.* —ˌ**fasci'nation** *n.* —'**fascinative** *adj.*

fascinating ('fæsɪˌneɪtɪŋ) *adj.* **1.** arousing great interest. **2.** enchanting or alluring: *a fascinating woman.* —'**fasciˌnatingly** *adv.*

fascinator ('fæsɪˌneɪtə) *n. Rare.* a lace or crocheted head covering for women.

fascine (fæ'siːn, fə-) *n.* a bundle of long sticks used for filling in ditches and in the construction of embankments, roads, fortifications, etc. [C17: from French, from Latin *fascīna;* see FASCES]

fascism ('fæʃɪzəm) *n. (sometimes cap.)* **1.** any ideology or movement inspired by Italian Fascism, such as German National Socialism; any right-wing nationalist ideology or movement with an authoritarian and hierarchical structure that is fundamentally opposed to democracy and liberalism. **2.** any ideology, movement, programme, tendency, etc., that may be characterized as right-wing, chauvinist, authoritarian, etc. [C20: from Italian *fascismo,* from *fascio* political group, from Latin *fascis* bundle; see FASCES]

Fascism ('fæʃɪzəm) *n.* the political movement, doctrine, system, or regime of the dictator Benito Mussolini (1883–1945) in Italy (1922–43). Fascism encouraged militarism and nationalism, organizing the country along hierarchical authoritarian lines. —'**Fascist** *n., adj.*

fascist ('fæʃɪst) *(sometimes cap.)* ~*n.* **1.** an adherent or practitioner of fascism. **2.** any person regarded as having right-wing authoritarian views. ~*adj. also* **fascistic** (fə'ʃɪstɪk). **3.** characteristic of or relating to fascism. —**fa'scistically** *adv.*

fash (fæʃ) *Scot.* ~*n.* **1.** worry; trouble; bother. ~*vb.* **2.** to trouble; bother; annoy. [C16: from obsolete French *fascher* to annoy, ultimately from Latin *fastīdium* disgust, aversion]

fashion ('fæʃən) *n.* **1. a.** style in clothes, cosmetics, behaviour, etc., esp. the latest or most admired style. **b.** (*as modifier*): *a fashion magazine.* **2.** (*modifier*) (esp. of accessories) designed to be in the current fashion, but not necessarily to last. **3. a.** manner of performance; mode; way: *in a striking fashion.* **b.** (*in combination*): *crab-fashion.* **4.** a way of life that revolves around the activities, dress, interests, etc., that are most fashionable. **5.** shape, appearance, or form. **6.** sort; kind; type. **7. after** *or* **in a fashion. a.** in some manner, but not very well: *I mended it, after a fashion.* **b.** of a low order; of a sort: *he is a poet, after a fashion.* **8. after the fashion of.** like; similar to. **9. of fashion.** of high social standing. ~*vb. (tr.)* **10.** to give a particular form to. **11.** to make suitable or fitting. **12.** *Obsolete.* to contrive; manage. [C13 *facioun* form, manner, from Old French *faceon,* from Latin *factiō* a making, from *facere* to make] —'**fashioner** *n.*

fashionable ('fæʃənəbəl) *adj.* **1.** conforming to fashion; in vogue. **2.** of, characteristic of, or patronized by people of fashion: *a fashionable café.* **3.** (usually foll. by *with*) patronized (by); popular (with). —'**fashionableness** *n.* —'**fashionably** *adv.*

fashion house *n.* an establishment in which fashionable clothes are designed, made, and sold.

fashion plate *n.* **1.** an illustration of the latest fashion in dress. **2.** a fashionably dressed person.

fashion victim *n. Informal.* a person who slavishly follows fashion.

FASSA *abbrev. for* Fellow of the Academy of Social Sciences in Australia.

fast[1] (fɑːst) *adj.* **1.** acting or moving or capable of acting or moving quickly; swift. **2.** accomplished in or lasting a short time: *fast work; a fast visit.* **3.** (*prenominal*) adapted to or facilitating rapid movement: *the fast lane of a motorway.* **4.** requiring rapidity of action or movement: *a fast sport.* **5.** (of a clock, etc.) indicating a time in advance of the correct time. **6.** given to an active dissipated life. **7.** of or characteristic of such activity: *a fast life.* **8.** not easily moved; firmly fixed; secure. **9.** firmly fastened, secured, or shut. **10.** steadfast; constant (esp. in the phrase **fast friends). 11.** *Sport.* (of a playing surface, running track, etc.) conducive to rapid speed, as of a ball used on it or of competitors playing or racing on it. **12.** that will not fade or change colour readily: *a fast dye.* **13. a.** proof against fading: *the colour is fast to sunlight.* **b.** (*in combination*): *washfast.* **14.** *Photog.* **a.** requiring a relatively short time of exposure to produce a given density: *a fast film.* **b.** permitting a short exposure time: *a fast shutter.* **15.** *Cricket.* (of a bowler) characteristically delivering the ball rapidly. **16.** *Informal.* glib or unreliable; deceptive: *a fast talker.* **17.** *Archaic.* sound; deep: *a fast sleep.* **18. a fast one.** *Informal.* a deceptive or unscrupulous trick (esp. in the phrase **pull a fast one**). **19. fast worker.** a person who achieves results quickly, esp. in seductions. ~*adv.* **20.** quickly; rapidly. **21.** soundly; deeply: *fast asleep.* **22.** firmly; tightly. **23.** in quick succession. **24.** in advance of the correct time: *my watch is running fast.* **25.** in a reckless or dissipated way. **26. fast by** *or* **beside.** *Archaic.* close or hard by; very near. **27. play fast and loose.** *Informal.* to behave in an insincere or unreliable manner. ~*interj.* **28.** *Archery.* (said by the Field Captain to archers) stop shooting! [Old English *fæst* strong, tight; related to Old High German *festi* firm, Old Norse *fastr*]

fast[2] (fɑːst) *vb.* **1.** (*intr.*) to abstain from eating all or certain foods or meals, esp. as a religious observance. ~*n.* **2.** an act or period of fasting. [Old English *fæstan;* related to Old High German *fastēn* to fast, Gothic *fastan*] —'**faster** *n.*

fastback ('fɑːstˌbæk) *n.* **1.** a car having a back that forms one continuous slope from roof to rear. **2.** *Brit.* a type of pig developed from the landrace or large white and bred for lean meat.

fast-breeder reactor *n.* a nuclear reactor that uses little or no moderator and produces more fissionable material than it consumes. See also **breeder reactor, fast reactor.**

fasten ('fɑːsən) *vb.* **1.** to make or become fast or secure. **2.** to make or become attached or joined. **3.** to close or become closed by fixing firmly in place, locking, etc. **4.** (*tr.;* foll. by *in* or *up*) to enclose or imprison. **5.** (*tr.;* usually foll. by *on*) to cause (blame, a nickname, etc.) to be attached (to); place (on) or impute (to). **6.** (usually foll. by *on* or *upon*) to direct or be directed in a concentrated way; fix: *he fastened his gaze on the girl.* **7.** (*intr.;* usually foll. by *on*) take firm hold (of). [Old English *fæstnian;* related to Old Norse *fastna* to pledge, Old High German *fastinōn* to make fast; see FAST[1]] —'**fastener** *n.*

fastening ('fɑːsənɪŋ) *n.* something that fastens, such as a clasp or lock.

fast food *n.* **1.** food that requires little preparation before being served. ~*adj.* **fast-food. 2.** (of a restaurant, café, etc.) serving such food.

fast-forward *vb.* (*intr.*) to move rapidly. [C20: from the fast-forward wind control in a tape deck]

fastidious (fæ'stɪdɪəs) *adj.* **1.** very critical; hard to please. **2.** excessively particular about details. **3.** exceedingly delicate; easily disgusted. [C15: from Latin *fastīdiōsus* scornful, from *fastīdium* loathing, from *fastus* pride, + *taedium* weariness] —**fas'tidiously** *adv.* —**fas'tidiousness** *n.*

fastigiate (fæ'stɪdʒɪɪt, -ˌeɪt) *or* **fastigiated** *adj. Biology.* **1.** (of plants) having erect branches, often appearing to form a single column with the stem. **2.** (of parts or organs) united in a tapering group. [C17: from Medieval Latin *fastīgiātus* lofty, from Latin *fastigium* height]

fast lane *n.* **1.** the outside lane on a motorway or dual carriageway for vehicles overtaking or travelling at high speed. **2.** *Informal.* the quickest but most competitive route to success.

fast motion *n. Films.* action that appears to have occurred at a faster speed than that at which it was filmed. Compare **slow motion** (sense 1).

fastness ('fɑːstnɪs) *n.* **1.** a stronghold; fortress. **2.** the state or quality of being firm or secure. **3.** the ability of a dye to remain permanent and not run or fade. **4.** *Archaic.* swiftness. [Old English *fæstnes;* see FAST[1]]

fast neutron *n. Physics.* **a.** a neutron produced by nuclear fission that has lost little energy by collision; a neutron with a kinetic energy in excess of 0.1 MeV. **b.** a neutron with a kinetic energy in excess of 1.5 MeV, the fission threshold of uranium-238.

fast reactor *n.* a nuclear reactor using little or no moderator, fission being caused by fast neutrons.

fast talk *Slang.* ~*n.* **1.** fervent, deceptive patter. ~*vb.* **fast-talk.** **2.** to influence (a person) by means of such patter.

fast-track *adj.* taking the quickest but most competitive route to success or personal advancement: *fast-track executives.*

fat (fæt) *n.* **1.** any of a class of naturally occurring soft greasy solids that are esters of glycerol and certain fatty acids. They are present in some plants and in the adipose tissue of animals, forming a reserve energy source, and are used in making soap and paint and in the food industry. See also **oil** (sense 1). **2.** vegetable or animal tissue containing fat. **3.** corpulence, obesity, or plumpness. **4.** the best or richest part of something. **5.** a part in a play that gives an actor a good opportunity to show his talents. **6. chew the fat.** *Slang.* **a.** to argue over a point. **b.** to talk idly; gossip. **7. the fat is in the fire.** an irrevocable action has been taken, esp. one from which dire consequences are expected. **8. the fat of the land.** the best that is obtainable. ~*adj.* **fatter, fattest.** **9.** having much or too much flesh or fat. **10.** consisting of or containing fat; greasy: *fat pork.* **11.** profitable; lucrative: *a fat year.* **12.** affording great opportunities: *a fat part in the play.* **13.** fertile or productive: *a fat land.* **14.** thick, broad, or extended: *a fat log of wood.* **15.** having a high content of a particular material or ingredient, such as resin in wood or oil in paint. **16.** plentifully supplied: *a fat larder.* **17.** *Slang.* empty; stupid: *get this into your fat head.* **18.** *Slang.* very little or none; minimal (in phrases such as **a fat chance, a fat lot of good,** etc.). ~*vb.* **fats, fatting, fatted.** **19.** to make or become fat; fatten. [Old English *fǣtt*, past participle of *fǣtan* to cram; related to Old Norse *feita*, Old High German *feizen* to fatten; compare Gothic *fētjan* to adorn] —**'fatless** *adj.* —**'fat,like** *adj.* —**'fatly** *adv.* —**'fatness** *n.* —**'fattish** *adj.*

fatal ('feɪtᵊl) *adj.* **1.** resulting in or capable of causing death: *a fatal accident.* **2.** bringing ruin; disastrous. **3.** decisively important; fateful. **4.** decreed by fate; destined; inevitable. [C14: from Old French *fatal* or Latin *fātālis*, from *fātum*, see FATE]

fatalism ('feɪtə,lɪzəm) *n.* **1.** the philosophical doctrine that all events are predetermined so that man is powerless to alter his destiny. **2.** the acceptance of and submission to this doctrine. **3.** a lack of effort or action in the face of difficulty. —**'fatalist** *n.* —**,fatal'istic** *adj.* —**,fatal'istically** *adv.*

fatality (fə'tælɪtɪ) *n., pl.* **-ties.** **1.** an accident or disaster resulting in death. **2.** a person killed in an accident or disaster. **3.** the power of causing death or disaster; deadliness. **4.** the quality or condition of being fated. **5.** something caused or dictated by fate.

fatally ('feɪtəlɪ) *adv.* **1.** resulting in death or disaster. **2.** as decreed by fate; inevitably.

Fata Morgana ('fɑːtə mɔː'gɑːnə; *Italian* 'faːta mɔr'gaːna) *n.* a mirage, esp. one in the Strait of Messina attributed to the sorcery of Morgan le Fay. [C19: from Italian: *Morgan le Fay*, a sorceress of Arthurian legend]

fatback ('fæt,bæk) *n.* the fat, usually salted, from the upper part of a side of pork.

fat body *n. Zoology.* **1.** a mass of fatty tissue in insects, used as an energy source during hibernation and metamorphosis. **2.** a similar tissue mass in amphibians and reptiles.

fat cat *n. Slang, chiefly U.S.* **a.** a very wealthy or influential person. **b.** (*as modifier*): *a fat-cat industrialist.*

fate (feɪt) *n.* **1.** the ultimate agency that predetermines the course of events. **2.** the inevitable fortune that befalls a person or thing; destiny. **3.** the end or final result. **4.** a calamitous or unfavourable outcome or result; death, destruction, or downfall. ~*vb.* **5.** (*tr.; usually passive*) to predetermine; doom: *he was fated to lose the game.* [C14: from Latin *fātum* oracular utterance, from *fārī* to speak]

fated ('feɪtɪd) *adj.* **1.** destined. **2.** doomed to death or destruction.

fateful ('feɪtfʊl) *adj.* **1.** having important consequences; decisively important. **2.** bringing death or disaster. **3.** controlled by or as if by fate. **4.** prophetic. —**'fatefully** *adv.* —**'fatefulness** *n.*

fath. *abbrev. for* fathom.

fathead ('fæt,hɛd) *n. Informal.* a stupid person; fool. —**'fat,headed** *adj.*

fat hen *n.* a common plant, *Chenopodium album,* with small green flowers and whitish scales on the stem and leaves: family *Chenopodiaceae* (chenopods). Also called (U.S.): **pigweed, lamb's-quarters.**

father ('fɑːðə) *n.* **1.** a male parent. **2.** a person who founds a line or family; forefather. **3.** any male acting in a paternal capacity. **4.** (*often cap.*) a respectful term of address for an old man. **5.** a male who originates something: *the father of modern psychology.* **6.** a leader of an association, council, etc.; elder: *a city father.* **7.** *Brit.* the eldest or most senior member in a society, profession, etc.: *father of the House.* **8.** (*often pl.*) a senator or patrician in ancient Rome. **9. the father of.** *Informal.* a very large, severe, etc., example of a specified kind: *the father of a whipping.* ~*vb.* (*tr.*) **10.** to procreate or generate (offspring); beget. **11.** to create, found, originate, etc. **12.** to act as a father to. **13.** to acknowledge oneself as father or originator of. **14.** (foll. by *on* or *upon*) to impose or place without a just reason. [Old English *fæder;* related to Old Norse *fathir,* Old Frisian *feder,* Old High German *fater,* Latin *pater,* Greek *patēr,* Sanskrit *pitr*] —**'father,like** *adj.*

Father ('fɑːðə) *n.* **1.** God, esp. when considered as the first person of the Christian Trinity. **2.** Also called: **Church Father.** any of the writers on Christian doctrine of the pre-Scholastic period. **3.** a title used for Christian priests.

father confessor *n.* **1.** *Christianity.* a priest who hears confessions and advises on religious or moral matters. **2.** any person to whom one tells private matters.

fatherhood ('fɑːðə,hʊd) *n.* the state or responsibility of being a father.

father-in-law *n., pl.* **fathers-in-law.** the father of one's wife or husband.

fatherland ('fɑːðə,lænd) *n.* **1.** a person's native country. **2.** the country of a person's ancestors.

father lasher *n.* a large sea scorpion, *Myoxocephalus scorpius,* occurring in British and European coastal waters. Also called: **short-spined sea scorpion.**

fatherless ('fɑːðəlɪs) *adj.* having no father.

fatherly ('fɑːðəlɪ) *adj.* of, resembling, or suitable to a father. —**'fatherliness** *n.*

father of the chapel *n.* (in British trade unions in the publishing and printing industries) a shop steward. Abbrev.: **FoC.**

Father's Day *n.* a day observed as a day in honour of fathers; in Britain the third Sunday in June.

Father Time *n.* time personified as an old bearded man, usually carrying a scythe and an hourglass.

fathom ('fæðəm) *n.* **1.** a unit of length equal to six feet (1.829 metres), used to measure depths of water. **2.** *Mining.* a unit of volume usually equal to six cubic feet, used in measuring ore bodies. **3.** *Forestry.* a unit of volume equal to six cubic feet, used for measuring timber. ~*vb.* (*tr.*) **4.** to measure the depth of, esp. with a sounding line; sound. **5.** to penetrate (a mystery, problem, etc.); discover the meaning of. [Old English *fæthm;* related to Old Frisian *fethem* outstretched arms, Old Norse *fathmr* embrace, Old High German *fadum* cubit, Latin *patēre* to gape] —**'fathomable** *adj.* —**'fathomer** *n.*

Fathometer (fə'ðɒmɪtə) *n. Trademark.* a type of echo sounder used for measuring the depth of water.

fathomless ('fæðəmlɪs) *adj.* another word for **unfathomable.** —**'fathomlessly** *adv.* —**'fathomlessness** *n.*

fatidic (feɪ'tɪdɪk) *or* **fatidical** *adj. Rare.* prophetic. [C17: from Latin *fātidicus,* from *fātum* FATE + *dīcere* to say] —**fa'tidically** *adv.*

fatigue (fə'tiːg) *n.* **1.** physical or mental exhaustion due to exertion. **2.** a tiring activity or effort. **3.** *Physiol.* the temporary inability of an organ or part to respond to a stimulus because of overactivity. **4.** the weakening of a material subjected to alternating stresses, esp. vibrations. **5.** the temporary inability to respond to a situation or perform a function, because of overexposure or overactivity: *compassion fatigue.* **6. a.** any of the mainly domestic duties performed by military personnel, esp. as a punishment. **b.** (*as modifier*): *fatigue duties.* **7.** (*pl.*) special clothing worn by military personnel to carry out such duties. ~*vb.* **-tigues, -tiguing, -tigued.** **8.** to make or become weary or exhausted. **9.** to weaken or break (a material or part) by inducing fluctuating stresses in it, or (of a metal or part) to become weakened or fail as a result of fluctuating stresses. [C17: from French, from *fatiguer* to tire, from Latin *fatīgāre*] —**fatigable** ('fætɪgəbᵊl) *adj.* —**fa'tigueless** *adj.*

Fatimid ('fætɪmɪd) *n.* **1.** a member of the Moslem dynasty, descended from Fatima, daughter of Mohammed, and her husband Ali, that ruled over North Africa and parts of Egypt and Syria (909–1171). **2.** Also called: **Fatimite** ('fætɪ,maɪt). a descendant of Fatima and Ali.

fat lamb *n. Austral. and N.Z.* a lamb bred for its tender meat, esp. for export trade.

fatling ('fætlɪŋ) *n.* a young farm animal fattened for killing.

fat mouse *n.* any nocturnal African mouse of the genus *Steatomys,* of dry regions: eaten as a delicacy by Africans because of their high fat content: family *Muridae.*

fatshedera (fæts'hɛdərə) *n.* an evergreen garden shrub with shiny green leaves and umbels of pale green flowers; a bigeneric hybrid between *Fatsia japonica moseri* and *Hedera hibernica:* family *Araliaceae.*

fatsia ('fætsɪə) *n.* any shrub of the araliaceous genus *Fatsia,* esp. *F. japonica,* with large deeply palmate leaves and umbels of white flowers. [New Latin, from the Japanese name]

fatso ('fætsəʊ) *n., pl.* **-sos** *or* **-soes.** *Slang.* a fat person: used as an insulting or disparaging term of address.

fat-soluble *adj.* soluble in nonpolar substances, such as ether, chloroform, and oils. Fat-soluble compounds are often insoluble in water.

fat stock *n.* livestock fattened and ready for market.

fatten ('fætᵊn) *vb.* **1.** to grow or cause to grow fat or fatter. **2.** (*tr.*) to cause (an animal or fowl) to become fat by feeding it. **3.** (*tr.*) to make fuller or richer. **4.** (*tr.*) to enrich (soil) by adding fertilizing agents. —**'fattenable** *adj.* —**'fattener** *n.* —**'fattening** *adj.*

fatty ('fætɪ) *adj.* **-tier, -tiest.** **1.** containing, consisting of, or derived from fat. **2.** having the properties of fat; greasy; oily. **3.** (esp. of tissues, organs, etc.) characterized by the excessive accumulation of fat. ~*n., pl.* **-ties.** **4.** *Informal.* a fat person. —**'fattily** *adv.* —**'fattiness** *n.*

fatty acid *n.* **1.** any of a class of aliphatic carboxylic acids, such as palmitic acid, stearic acid, and oleic acid, that form part of a lipid molecule. **2.** another name for **carboxylic acid,** esp. a naturally occurring one.

fatty degeneration *n. Pathol.* the abnormal formation of tiny globules of fat within the cytoplasm of a cell.

fatty oil *n.* another name for **fixed oil.**

fatuity (fə'tju:ɪtɪ) *n., pl.* **-ties.** **1.** complacent foolishness; inanity. **2.** a fatuous remark, act, sentiment, etc. **3.** *Archaic.* idiocy. —**fa'tuitous** *adj.*

fatuous ('fætjʊəs) *adj.* complacently or inanely foolish. [C17: from Latin *fatuus;* related to *fatiscere* to gape] —**'fatuously** *adv.* —**'fatuousness** *n.*

fatwa *or* **fatwah** ('fætwə) *n.* a religious decree issued by a Muslim leader. [Arabic]

faubourg ('fəʊbʊəg; *French* fobur) *n.* a suburb or quarter, esp. of a French city. [C15: from French *fauxbourg,* perhaps a modification through folk etymology of Old French *forsborc,* from Latin *foris* outside + Old French *borc* BURG]

faucal ('fɔ:kᵊl) *or* **faucial** ('fɔ:ʃəl) *adj.* **1.** *Anatomy.* of or relating to the fauces. **2.** *Phonetics.* articulated in that part of the vocal tract between the back of the mouth and the larynx; pharyngeal.

fauces ('fɔ:si:z) *n., pl.* **-ces.** *Anatomy.* the area between the cavity of the mouth and the pharynx, including the surrounding tissues. [C16: from Latin: throat]

faucet ('fɔ:sɪt) *n.* **1.** a tap fitted to a barrel. **2.** the U.S. and Canadian name for a **tap**². [C14: from Old French *fausset,* from Provençal *falset,* from *falsar* to bore]

faugh (fɔ:) *interj.* an exclamation of disgust, scorn, etc.

fault (fɔ:lt) *n.* **1.** an imperfection; failing or defect; flaw. **2.** a mistake or error. **3.** an offence; misdeed. **4.** responsibility for a mistake or misdeed; culpability. **5.** *Electronics.* a defect in a circuit, component, or line, such as a short circuit. **6.** *Geology.* a fracture in the earth's crust resulting in the relative displacement and loss of continuity of the rocks on either side of it. **7.** *Tennis, squash, etc.* an invalid serve, such as one that lands outside a prescribed area. **8.** (in showjumping) a penalty mark given for failing to clear or refusing a fence, exceeding a time limit, etc. **9.** *Hunting.* an instance of the hounds losing the scent. **10.** deficiency; lack; want. **11. at fault. a.** guilty of error; culpable. **b.** perplexed. **c.** (of hounds) having temporarily lost the scent. **12. find fault (with).** to seek out minor imperfections or errors (in); carp (at). **13. to a fault.** excessively. ~*vb.* **14.** *Geology.* to undergo or cause to undergo a fault. **15.** (*tr.*) to find a fault in, criticize, or blame. **16.** (*intr.*) to commit a fault. [C13: from Old French *faute,* from Vulgar Latin *fallita* (unattested), ultimately from Latin *fallere* to fail]

fault-finding *n.* **1.** continual and usually trivial criticism. **2.** the systematic investigation of malfunctions in electronic apparatus. ~*adj.* **3.** given to finding fault. —**'fault-ˌfinder** *n.*

faultless ('fɔ:ltlɪs) *adj.* without fault; perfect or blameless. —**'faultlessly** *adv.* —**'faultlessness** *n.*

fault plane *n. Geology.* the surface of a fault fracture along which the rocks have been displaced.

faulty ('fɔ:ltɪ) *adj.* **faultier, faultiest.** **1.** defective or imperfect. **2.** *Archaic.* culpable. —**'faultily** *adv.* —**'faultiness** *n.*

faun (fɔ:n) *n.* (in Roman legend) a rural deity represented as a man with a goat's ears, horns, tail, and hind legs. [C14: back formation from *Faunes* (plural), from Latin *Faunus,* deity of forests] —**'faunˌlike** *adj.*

fauna ('fɔ:nə) *n., pl.* **-nas** *or* **-nae** (-ni:). **1.** all the animal life of a given place or time, esp. when distinguished from the plant life (flora). **2.** a descriptive list of such animals. [C18: from New Latin, from Late Latin *Fauna* a goddess, sister of *Faunus;* see FAUN] —**'faunal** *adj.* —**'faunally** *adv.*

faunula ('fɔ:njʊlə) *or* **faunule** ('fɔ:nju:l) *n., pl.* **-ulae** (-jʊli:) *or* **-ules.** **1.** the fauna of a small single environment. **2.** fossil fauna found in a single stratum or in several thin adjacent strata. [C20: from FAUNA + -ULE]

faur (fɔ:r) *adj.* a Scot. word for **far.**

Faustian ('faʊstɪən) *adj.* of, relating to, or characteristic of Faust (or Faustus), the magician and alchemist of German legend who sells his soul to the devil in exchange for knowledge and power.

faut (fɔ:t) *n., vb.* a Scot. word for **fault.**

faute de mieux *French.* (fot də mjø; *English* fəʊt də mjɜ:) for lack of anything better.

fauteuil ('fəʊtɜ:ɪ; *French* fotœj) *n.* an armchair, the sides of which are not upholstered. [C18: from French, from Old French *faudestuel,* folding chair, of Germanic origin; see FALDSTOOL]

Fauve (*French* fov) *n.* **1.** one of a group of French painters prominent from 1905, characterized by the use of bright colours and simplified forms. ~*adj.* **2.** (*often not cap.*) of this group or its style. [C20: from French, literally: wild beast, alluding to the violence of colours, etc.] —**'Fauvism** *n.* —**'Fauvist** *n., adj.*

faux-naïf (*French* fonaif) *adj.* **1.** appearing or seeking to appear simple and unsophisticated: *a faux-naïf narration.* ~*n.* **2.** a person who pretends to be naïve. [French: false naïve]

faux pas (fəʊ pɑ:; *French* fo pɑ) *n., pl.* **faux pas** (fəʊ pɑ:z; *French* fo pɑ). a social blunder or indiscretion. [C17: from French: false step]

favela (fɑ:'veɪlə) *n.* (in Brazil) a shanty or shantytown. [C20: from Portuguese]

faveolate (fə'vi:əˌleɪt) *or* **favose** ('fævəʊs) *adj.* pitted with cell-like cavities. [C19: from New Latin *faveolus* a little honeycomb, blend of Latin *favus* honeycomb + *alveolus* a small hollow]

favonian (fə'vəʊnɪən) *adj.* **1.** of or relating to the west wind. **2.** *Poetic.* favourable. [C17: from Latin *Favōniānus*]

favorite son *n.* (in the U.S.) a politician popular in his home state but little admired beyond it.

favour *or U.S.* **favor** ('feɪvə) *n.* **1.** an approving attitude; good will. **2.** an act performed out of good will, generosity, or mercy. **3.** prejudice and partiality; favouritism. **4.** a condition of being regarded with approval or good will (esp. in the phrases **in favour, out of favour**). **5.** *Archaic.* leave; permission. **6.** a token of love, goodwill, etc. **7.** a small gift or toy given to a guest at a party. **8.** *History.* a badge or ribbon worn or given to indicate loyalty, often bestowed on a knight by a lady. **9.** *Obsolete, chiefly Brit.* a communication, esp. a business letter. **10.** *Archaic.* appearance. **11. find favour with.** to be approved of by someone. **12. in favour of. a.** approving. **b.** to the benefit of. **c.** (of a cheque, etc.) made out to. **d.** in order to show preference for: *I rejected him in favour of George.* ~*vb.* (*tr.*) **13.** to regard with especial kindness or approval. **14.** to treat with partiality or favouritism. **15.** to support; advocate. **16.** to perform a favour for; oblige. **17.** to help; facilitate. **18.** *Informal.* to resemble: *he favours his father.* **19.** to wear habitually: *she favours red.* **20.** to treat gingerly or with tenderness; spare: *a footballer favouring an injured leg.* ~See also **favours.** [C14: from Latin, from *favēre* to protect] —**'favourer** *or U.S.* **'favorer** *n.* —**'favouringly** *or U.S.* **'favoringly** *adv.*

favourable *or U.S.* **favorable** ('feɪvərəbᵊl, 'feɪvrə-) *adj.* **1.** advantageous, encouraging, or promising. **2.** giving consent. —**'favourableness** *or U.S.* **'favorableness** *n.* —**'favourably** *or U.S.* **'favorably** *adv.*

favourable pressure gradient *n. Engineering.* a decrease of pressure in the direction of flow.

-favoured *adj.* (*in combination*) having an appearance (as specified): *ill-favoured.*

favourite *or U.S.* **favorite** ('feɪvərɪt, 'feɪvrɪt) *adj.* **1.** (*prenominal*) most liked; preferred above all others. ~*n.* **2. a.** a person or thing regarded with especial preference or liking. **b.** (*as modifier*): *a favourite book.* **3.** *Sport.* a competitor thought likely to win. [C16: from Italian *favorito,* from *favorire* to favour, from Latin *favēre*]

favouritism *or U.S.* **favoritism** ('feɪvərɪˌtɪzəm, 'feɪvrɪ-) *n.* **1.** the practice of giving special treatment to a person or group. **2.** the state of being treated as a favourite.

favours *or U.S.* **favors** ('feɪvəz) *pl. n.* sexual intimacy, as when consented to by a woman.

Favrile glass (fə'vri:l) *n.* a type of iridescent glass developed by L.C. Tiffany.

favus ('feɪvəs) *n.* an infectious fungal skin disease of man and some domestic animals, characterized by formation of a honeycomb-like mass of roundish dry cup-shaped crusts. [C19: from New Latin, from Latin: honeycomb]

fawn¹ (fɔ:n) *n.* **1.** a young deer of either sex aged under one year. **2. a.** a light greyish-brown colour. **b.** (*as adj.*): *a fawn raincoat.* **3. in fawn.** (of deer) pregnant. ~*vb.* **4.** (of deer) to bear (young). [C14: from Old French *faon,* from Latin *fētus* offspring; see FETUS] —**'fawnˌlike** *adj.*

fawn² (fɔ:n) *vb.* (*intr.;* often foll. by *on* or *upon*) **1.** to seek attention and admiration (from) by cringing and flattering. **2.** (of animals, esp. dogs) to try to please by a show of extreme friendliness and fondness (towards). [Old English *fægnian* to be glad, from *fægen* glad; see FAIN] —**'fawner** *n.* —**'fawningly** *adv.* —**'fawningness** *n.*

fawn lily *n.* another name for **dogtooth violet.**

fax (fæx) *n.* **1.** short for **facsimile transmission.** **2.** a message or document sent by fax. ~*vb.* **3.** (*tr.*) to send (a message, document, etc.) by fax.

fay¹ (feɪ) *n.* **1.** a fairy or sprite. ~*adj.* **2.** of or resembling a fay. **3.** *Informal.* pretentious or precious. [C14: from Old French *feie,* ultimately from Latin *fātum* FATE]

fay² (feɪ) *vb.* to fit or be fitted closely or tightly. [Old English *fēgan* to join; related to Old High German *fuogen,* Latin *pangere* to fasten]

fay³ (feɪ) *n.* an obsolete word for **faith.** [C13: from Anglo-French *feid;* see FAITH]

fayalite ('feɪəˌlaɪt, faɪ'ɑ:laɪt) *n.* a rare brown or black mineral of the olivine group, consisting of iron silicate. Formula: Fe_2SiO_4. [C19: named after *Fayal* (Faial), an island in the Azores]

faze (feɪz) *vb.* (*tr.*) to disconcert; worry; disturb. [C19: variant of FEEZE]

FBA *abbrev. for* Fellow of the British Academy.

FBI (in the U.S.) *abbrev. for* Federal Bureau of Investigation; an agency of the Justice Department responsible for investigating violations of Federal laws.

FBW *Aeronautics. abbrev. for* fly-by-wire.

fc *Printing. abbrev. for* follow copy.

FC (in Britain) *abbrev. for* Football Club.

FCA (in Britain) *abbrev. for* Fellow of the Institute of Chartered Accountants.
fcap *abbrev. for* foolscap.
FCC (in the U.S.) *abbrev. for* Federal Communications Commission.
FCCA (in Britain) *abbrev. for* Fellow of the Chartered Association of Certified Accountants.
FCII (in Britain) *abbrev. for* Fellow of the Chartered Insurance Institute.
F clef *n.* another name for **bass clef.**
FCO *abbrev. for* Foreign and Commonwealth Office.
FD *abbrev. for* Fidei Defensor. [Latin: Defender of the Faith]
F distribution *n. Statistics.* a continuous distribution obtained from the ratio of two chi-square distributions and used esp. to test the equality of the variances of two normally distributed variances.
fdm *abbrev. for* frequency-division multiplex. See **multiplex.**
FDP *abbrev. for* Freie Demokratische Partei. [German: Free Democratic Party]
Fe *the chemical symbol for* iron. [from New Latin *ferrum*]
feal (fiːl) *adj.* an archaic word for **faithful.** [C16: from Old French *feeil,* from Latin *fidēlis*]
fealty ('fiːəltɪ) *n., pl.* **-ties.** (in feudal society) the loyalty sworn to one's lord on becoming his vassal. See **homage** (sense 2). [C14: from Old French *fealte,* from Latin *fidēlitās* FIDELITY]
fear (fɪə) *n.* **1.** a feeling of distress, apprehension, or alarm caused by impending danger, pain, etc. **2.** a cause of this feeling. **3.** awe; reverence: *fear of God.* **4.** concern; anxiety. **5.** possibility; chance: *there is no fear of that happening.* **6. for fear of, that** *or* **lest.** to forestall or avoid. **7. no fear.** certainly not. **8. put the fear of God into.** to frighten. ~*vb.* **9.** to be afraid (to do something) or of (a person or thing); dread. **10.** (*tr.*) to revere; respect. **11.** (*tr.; takes a clause as object*) to be sorry: used to lessen the effect of an unpleasant statement: *I fear that you have not won.* **12.** (*intr.;* foll. by *for*) to feel anxiety about something. **13.** an archaic word for **frighten.** [Old English *fǣr;* related to Old High German *fāra,* Old Norse *fār* hostility, Latin *perīculum* danger] —'**fearer** *n.* —'**fearless** *adj.* —'**fearlessly** *adv.* —'**fearlessness** *n.*
fearful ('fɪəfʊl) *adj.* **1.** having fear; afraid. **2.** causing fear; frightening. **3.** *Informal.* very unpleasant or annoying: *a fearful cold.* —'**fearfulness** *n.*
fearfully ('fɪəfʊlɪ) *adv.* **1.** in a fearful manner. **2.** (intensifier): *you're fearfully kind.*
fearnought *or* **fearnaught** ('fɪə,nɔːt) *n.* **1.** a heavy woollen fabric. **2.** a coat made of such fabric.
fearsome ('fɪəsəm) *adj.* **1.** frightening. **2.** timorous; afraid. —'**fearsomely** *adv.* —'**fearsomeness** *n.*
feasibility study *n.* a study designed to determine the practicability of a system or plan.
feasible ('fiːzəb(ə)l) *adj.* **1.** able to be done or put into effect; possible. **2.** likely; probable: *a feasible excuse.* [C15: from Anglo-French *faisable,* from *faire* to do, from Latin *facere*] —,**feasi'bility** *or* '**feasibleness** *n.* —'**feasibly** *adv.*
feast (fiːst) *n.* **1.** a large and sumptuous meal, usually given as an entertainment for several people. **2.** a periodic religious celebration. **3.** something extremely pleasing or sumptuous: *a feast for the eyes.* **4. moveable feast.** a festival of variable date. ~*vb.* **5.** (*intr.*) **a.** to eat a feast. **b.** (usually foll. by *on*) to enjoy the eating (of), as if feasting: *to feast on cakes.* **6.** (*tr.*) to give a feast to. **7.** (*intr.;* foll. by *on*) to take great delight (in): *to feast on beautiful paintings.* **8.** (*tr.*) to regale or delight: *to feast one's mind or one's eyes.* [C13: from Old French *feste,* from Latin *festa,* neuter plural (later assumed to be feminine singular) of *festus* joyful; related to Latin *fānum* temple, *fēriae* festivals] —'**feaster** *n.*
Feast of Dedication *n. Judaism.* a literal translation of **Chanukah.**
Feast of Lanterns *n.* **1.** *Hinduism.* a five-day festival usually taking place in October or November, dedicated to the goddess of wealth. **2.** Also called: **Festival of Lanterns.** *Japanese Buddhism.* another name for **Bon.**
Feast of Lights *n. Judaism.* an English name for **Chanukah.**
Feast of Tabernacles *n. Judaism.* a literal translation of **Sukkoth.**
Feast of Weeks *n. Judaism.* a literal translation of **Shavuot.**
feat[1] (fiːt) *n.* a remarkable, skilful, or daring action; exploit; achievement: *feats of strength.* [C14: from Anglo-French *fait,* from Latin *factum* deed; see FACT]
feat[2] (fiːt) *adj. Archaic.* **1.** another word for **skilful.** **2.** another word for **neat**[1] or **suitable.** [C14: from Old French *fet,* from Latin *factus* made, from *facere* to make] —'**featly** *adv.*
feather ('fɛðə) *n.* **1.** any of the flat light waterproof epidermal structures forming the plumage of birds, each consisting of a hollow shaft having a vane of barbs on either side. They are essential for flight and help maintain body temperature. **2.** something resembling a feather, such as a tuft of hair or grass. **3.** *Archery.* **a.** a bird's feather or artificial substitute fitted to an arrow to direct its flight. **b.** the feathered end of an arrow, opposite the head. **4.** a strip, spline, or tongue of wood fitted into a groove. **5.** the wake created on the surface of the water by the raised periscope of a submarine. **6.** *Rowing.* the position of an oar turned parallel to the water between strokes. Compare **square** (sense 7). **7.** a step in ballroom dancing in which a couple maintain the conventional hold but dance side by side. **8.** condition of spirits; fettle: *in fine feather.* **9.** something of negligible value; jot: *I don't care a feather.* **10. birds of a feather.** people of the same type, character, or interests. **11. feather in one's cap.** a cause for pleasure at one's achievements: *your promotion is a feather in your cap.* **12. in full feather.** in good spirits. **13. not take** *or* **knock a feather out of (someone).** *Irish.* to fail to upset or injure (someone): *it didn't take a feather out of him.* ~*vb.* **14.** (*tr.*) to fit, cover, or supply with feathers. **15.** *Rowing.* to turn (an oar) parallel to the water during recovery between strokes, principally in order to lessen wind resistance. Compare **square** (sense 40). **16.** (in canoeing) to turn (a paddle) parallel to the direction of the canoe between strokes, while keeping it in the water, principally in order to move silently. **17.** to change the pitch of (an aircraft propeller) so that the chord lines of the blades are in line with the airflow. **18.** (*tr.*) to join (two boards) by means of a tongue-and-groove joint. **19.** (*intr.*) (of a bird) to grow feathers. **20.** (*intr.*) to move or grow like feathers. **21. feather one's nest.** to provide oneself with comforts, esp. financial. ~See also **feathers.** [Old English *fether;* related to Old Frisian *fethere,* Old Norse *fjöthr* feather, Old High German *fedara* wing, Greek *petesthai* to fly, Sanskrit *patati* he flies] —'**featherless** *adj.* —'**feather-,like** *adj.* —'**feathery** *adj.*
feather bed *n.* **1.** a mattress filled with feathers or down. ~*vb.* **featherbed, -beds, -bedding, -bedded.** **2.** (*tr.*) to pamper; spoil. **3.** (*intr.*) *U.S.* to be subject to or engage in featherbedding.
featherbedding ('fɛðə,bɛdɪŋ) *n.* the practice of limiting production, duplicating work, or overmanning, esp. in accordance with a union contract, in order to prevent redundancies or create jobs.
featherbrain ('fɛðə,breɪn) *or* **featherhead** *n.* a frivolous or forgetful person. —'**feather,brained** *or* '**feather,headed** *adj.*
featheredge ('fɛðər,ɛdʒ) *n.* a board or plank that tapers to a thin edge at one side. —'**feather,edged** *adj.*
feather grass *n.* a perennial grass, *Stipa pennata,* native to the steppes of Europe and N Asia, cultivated as an ornament for its feathery inflorescence.
feathering ('fɛðərɪŋ) *n.* **1.** the plumage of a bird; feathers. **2.** another word for **feathers** (sense 2). **3.** *Printing.* **a.** an imperfection in print caused by the spreading of ink. **b.** the use of additional space between lines in typesetting in order to fill the page.
feather palm *n.* any of various palm trees, such as the wax palm and date palm, that have pinnate or feather-like leaves. Compare **fan palm.**
feathers ('fɛðəz) *pl. n.* **1.** the plumage of a bird. **2.** Also called: **feathering.** the long hair on the legs or tail of certain breeds of horses and dogs. **3.** *Informal.* dress; attire: *her best feathers.*
feather star *n.* any free-swimming crinoid echinoderm of the genus *Antedon* and related genera, living on muddy sea bottoms and having ten feathery arms radiating from a small central disc.
featherstitch ('fɛðə,stɪtʃ) *n.* **1.** a zigzag embroidery stitch. ~*vb.* **2.** to decorate (cloth) with featherstitch.
feather-veined *adj.* (of a leaf) having a network of veins branching from the midrib to the margin.
featherweight ('fɛðə,weɪt) *n.* **1. a.** something very light or of little importance. **b.** (*as modifier*): *featherweight considerations.* **2. a.** a professional boxer weighing 118–126 pounds (53.5–57 kg). **b.** an amateur boxer weighing 54–57 kg (119–126 pounds). **c.** (*as modifier*): *the featherweight challenger.* **3.** a wrestler in a similar weight category (usually 126–139 pounds (57–63 kg)).
featly ('fiːtlɪ) *adv. Archaic.* **1.** neatly. **2.** fitly. —'**featliness** *n.*
feature ('fiːtʃə) *n.* **1.** any one of the parts of the face, such as the nose, chin, or mouth. **2.** a prominent or distinctive part or aspect, as of a landscape, building, book, etc. **3.** the principal film in a programme at a cinema. **4.** an item or article appearing regularly in a newspaper, magazine, etc.: *a gardening feature.* **5.** Also called: **feature story.** a prominent story in a newspaper, etc.: *a feature on prison reform.* **6.** a programme given special prominence on radio or television as indicated by attendant publicity. **7.** an article offered for sale as a special attraction, as in a large retail establishment. **8.** *Archaic.* general form or make-up. **9.** *Linguistics.* a quality of a linguistic unit at some level of description: *grammatical feature; semantic feature.* ~*vb.* **10.** (*tr.*) to have as a feature or make a feature of. **11.** to give prominence to (an actor, famous event, etc.) in a film or (of an actor, etc.) to have prominence in a film. **12.** (*tr.*) *Archaic.* to draw the main features or parts of. **13.** (*tr.*) *U.S. informal.* to imagine; consider: *I can't feature that happening.* **14.** (*tr.*) *Informal, archaic.* to resemble in looks. **15.** (*intr.;* often foll. by *with*) *Slang, archaic.* to have sexual intercourse (with). [C14: from Anglo-French *feture,* from Latin *factūra* a making, from *facere* to make]
-featured *adj.* (*in combination*) having features as specified: *heavy-featured.*
feature-length *adj.* (of a film or programme) similar in extent to a feature although not classed as such.
featureless ('fiːtʃəlɪs) *adj.* without distinctive points or qualities; undistinguished. —'**featurelessness** *n.*
feaze[1] (fiːz) *vb. Nautical.* to make or become unravelled or frayed. [C16: perhaps from obsolete Dutch *vese* fringe, from Middle Dutch *vese, veze* fringe; related to Old English *fæs*]

feaze[2] (fiːz) *vb., n.* a variant of **feeze** or **faze.**
Feb. *abbrev. for* February.
febri- *combining form.* indicating fever: *febrifuge.* [from Latin *febris* fever]
febricity (fɪˈbrɪsɪtɪ) *n. Rare.* the condition of having a fever. [C19: from Medieval Latin *febricitās,* from Latin *febris* fever]
febrifacient (ˌfɛbrɪˈfeɪʃənt) *adj.* **1.** producing fever. ~*n.* **2.** something that produces fever.
febrific (fɪˈbrɪfɪk) *or* **febriferous** *adj.* causing or having a fever.
febrifuge (ˈfɛbrɪˌfjuːdʒ) *n.* **1.** any drug or agent for reducing fever. ~*adj.* **2.** serving to reduce fever. [C17: from Medieval Latin *febrifugia* feverfew; see FEBRI-, -FUGE] —**febrifugal** (fɪˈbrɪfjʊgᵊl, ˌfɛbrɪˈfjuːgᵊl) *adj.*
febrile (ˈfiːbraɪl) *adj.* of or relating to fever; feverish. [C17: from medical Latin *febrīlis,* from Latin *febris* fever] —**febrility** (fɪˈbrɪlɪtɪ) *n.*
February (ˈfɛbrʊərɪ) *n., pl.* **-aries.** the second month of the year, consisting of 28 or (in a leap year) 29 days. [C13: from Latin *Februārius mēnsis* month of expiation, from *februa* Roman festival of purification held on February 15, from plural of *februum* a purgation]
fec. *abbrev. for* fecit.
fecal (ˈfiːkᵊl) *adj.* the usual U.S. spelling of **faecal.**
feces (ˈfiːsiːz) *pl. n.* the usual U.S. spelling of **faeces.**
fecht (fɛxt) *vb., n.* a Scot. word for **fight.** —ˈ**fechter** *n.*
fecit *Latin.* (ˈfeɪkɪt) (he or she) made it: used formerly on works of art next to the artist's name. Abbrev.: **fec.**
feck (fɛk) *n. Scot. obsolete.* **a.** worth; value. **b.** amount; quantity. **c.** the greater part; the majority. [C15 (Scottish dialect) *fek,* short for EFFECT]
feckless (ˈfɛklɪs) *adj.* feeble; weak; ineffectual; irresponsible. [C16: from obsolete *feck* value, effect + -LESS] —ˈ**fecklessly** *adv.* —ˈ**fecklessness** *n.*
fecula (ˈfɛkjʊlə) *n., pl.* **-lae** (-ˌliː). **1.** starch obtained by washing the crushed parts of plants, such as the potato. **2.** faecal material, esp. of insects. [C17: from Latin: burnt tartar, appearing as a crust in wine, from *faex* sediment]
feculent (ˈfɛkjʊlənt) *adj.* **1.** filthy, scummy, muddy, or foul. **2.** of the nature of or containing waste matter. [C15: from Latin *faeculentus;* see FAECES] —ˈ**feculence** *n.*
fecund (ˈfiːkənd, ˈfɛk-) *adj.* **1.** greatly productive; fertile. **2.** intellectually productive; prolific. [C14: from Latin *fēcundus;* related to Latin *fētus* offspring]
fecundate (ˈfiːkənˌdeɪt, ˈfɛk-) *vb. (tr.)* **1.** to make fruitful. **2.** to fertilize; impregnate. [C17: from Latin *fēcundāre* to fertilize] —ˌ**fecunˈdation** *n.* —ˈ**fecunˌdator** *n.* —**fecundatory** (fɪˈkʌndətərɪ, -trɪ) *adj.*
fecundity (fɪˈkʌndɪtɪ) *n.* **1.** fertility; fruitfulness. **2.** intellectual fruitfulness; creativity.
fed[1] (fɛd) *vb.* **1.** the past tense and past participle of **feed.** **2. fed to death** *or* **fed (up) to the (back) teeth.** *Informal.* bored or annoyed.
fed[2] (fɛd) *n. U.S. slang.* an agent of the FBI.
Fed. *or* **fed.** *abbrev. for:* **1.** Federal. **2.** Federation. **3.** Federated.
fedayee (fəˈdɑːjiː) *n., pl.* **-yeen** (-jiːn). *(sometimes cap.)* (in Arab states) a commando, esp. one fighting against Israel. [from Arabic *fidā'i* one who risks his life in a cause, from *fidā'* redemption]
federal (ˈfɛdərəl) *adj.* **1.** of or relating to a form of government or a country in which power is divided between one central and several regional governments. **2.** of or relating to a treaty between provinces, states, etc., that establishes a political unit in which power is so divided. **3.** of or relating to the central government of a federation. **4.** of or relating to any union or association of parties or groups that retain some autonomy. **5.** (of a university) comprised of relatively independent colleges. ~*n.* **6.** a supporter of federal union or federation. [C17: from Latin *foedus* league] —ˈ**federally** *adv.*
Federal (ˈfɛdərəl) *U.S. history.* ~*adj.* **1. a.** of or relating to the Federalist Party or Federalism. **b.** characteristic of or supporting the Union government during the American Civil War. ~*n.* **2. a.** a supporter of the Union government during the American Civil War. **b.** a Federalist.
Federal Bureau of Investigation *n.* See **FBI.**
federal district *or* **territory** *n.* an area used as the seat of central government in a federal system.
Federal Government *n.* the national government of a federated state, such as that of Australia located in Canberra.
federalism (ˈfɛdərəˌlɪzəm) *n.* **1.** the principle or a system of federal union. **2.** advocacy of federal union. —ˈ**federalist** *n., adj.* —ˌ**federalˈistic** *adj.*
Federalist (ˈfɛdərəlɪst) *U.S. history.* ~*n.* **1.** a supporter or member of the Federalist Party, founded in 1787 and advocating strong centralized government. ~*adj. also* ˌ**Federalˈistic. 2.** characteristic of the Federalists. —ˈ**Federalˌism** *n.*
federalize *or* **federalise** (ˈfɛdərəˌlaɪz) *vb. (tr.)* **1.** to unite in a federation or federal union; federate. **2.** to subject to federal control. —ˌ**federaliˈzation** *or* ˌ**federaliˈsation** *n.*
Federal Reserve note *n.* a bank note issued by the Federal Reserve Banks and now serving as the prevailing paper currency in circulation in the U.S.
Federal Reserve System *n.* (in the U.S.) a banking system consisting of twelve **Federal Reserve Districts,** each containing member banks regulated and served by a **Federal Reserve Bank.** It operates under the supervision of the **Federal Reserve Board** and performs functions similar to those of the Bank of England.
federate *vb.* (ˈfɛdəˌreɪt). **1.** to unite or cause to unite in a federal union. ~*adj.* (ˈfɛdərɪt). **2.** federal; federated. —ˈ**federative** *adj.*
federation (ˌfɛdəˈreɪʃən) *n.* **1.** the act of federating. **2.** the union of several provinces, states, etc., to form a federal union. **3.** a political unit formed in such a way. **4.** any league, alliance, or confederacy. **5.** a union of several parties, groups, etc. **6.** any association or union for common action.
Federation (ˌfɛdəˈreɪʃən) *n. Austral.* **1. the.** the federation of the Australian colonies in 1901. **2.** a style of domestic architecture of that period, characterized by red brick, terracotta roof tiles, sinuous curves, and heavy window frames.
Federation wheat *n. Austral.* an early-maturing drought-resistant variety of wheat developed by William Farrar in 1902.
fedora (fɪˈdɔːrə) *n.* a soft felt or velvet medium-brimmed hat, usually with a band. [C19: allegedly named after *Fédora* (1882), play by Victorien Sardou (1831–1908)]
fed up *adj. (usually postpositive) Informal.* annoyed, discontented, or bored: *I'm fed up with your conduct.*
fee (fiː) *n.* **1.** a payment asked by professional people or public servants for their services: *a doctor's fee; school fees.* **2.** a charge made for a privilege: *an entrance fee.* **3.** *Property law.* **a.** an interest in land capable of being inherited. See **fee simple, fee tail. b.** the land held in fee. **4.** (in feudal Europe) the land granted by a lord to his vassal. **5.** an obsolete word for a **gratuity. 6. in fee. a.** *Law.* (of land) in absolute ownership. **b.** *Archaic.* in complete subjection. ~*vb.* **fees, feeing, feed. 7.** *Rare.* to give a fee to. **8.** *Chiefly Scot.* to hire for a fee. [C14: from Old French *fie,* of Germanic origin; see FIEF] —ˈ**feeless** *adj.*
feeble (ˈfiːbᵊl) *adj.* **1.** lacking in physical or mental strength; frail; weak. **2.** inadequate; unconvincing: *feeble excuses.* **3.** easily influenced or indecisive. [C12: from Old French *feble, fleible,* from Latin *flēbilis* to be lamented, from *flēre* to weep] —ˈ**feebleness** *n.* —ˈ**feebly** *adv.*
feeble-minded *adj.* **1.** lacking in intelligence; stupid. **2.** mentally defective. **3.** lacking decision; irresolute. —ˌ**feeble-ˈmindedly** *adv.* —ˌ**feeble-ˈmindedness** *n.*
feed (fiːd) *vb.* **feeds, feeding, fed** (fɛd). *(mainly tr.)* **1.** to give food to: *to feed the cat.* **2.** to give as food: *to feed meat to the cat.* **3.** *(intr.)* to eat food: *the horses feed at noon.* **4.** to provide food for: *these supplies can feed 10 million people.* **5.** to provide what is necessary for the existence or development of: *to feed one's imagination.* **6.** to gratify; satisfy: *to feed one's eyes on a beautiful sight.* **7.** *(also intr.)* to supply (a machine, furnace, etc.) with (the necessary materials or fuel) for its operation, or (of such materials) to flow or move forwards into a machine, etc. **8.** to use (land) as grazing. **9.** *Theatre, informal.* to cue (an actor, esp. a comedian) with lines or actions. **10.** *Sport.* to pass a ball to (a teammate). **11.** *Electronics.* to introduce (electrical energy) into a circuit, esp. by means of a feeder. **12.** *(also intr.;* foll. by *on* or *upon)* to eat or cause to eat. ~*n.* **13.** the act or an instance of feeding. **14.** food, esp. that of animals or babies. **15.** the process of supplying a machine or furnace with a material or fuel. **16.** the quantity of material or fuel so supplied. **17.** the rate of advance of a cutting tool in a lathe, drill, etc. **18.** a mechanism that supplies material or fuel or controls the rate of advance of a cutting tool. **19.** *Theatre, informal.* a performer, esp. a straight man, who provides cues. **20.** an informal word for **meal**[1]. [Old English *fēdan;* related to Old Norse *fœtha* to feed, Old High German *fuotan,* Gothic *fōthjan;* see FOOD, FODDER] —ˈ**feedable** *adj.*
feedback (ˈfiːdˌbæk) *n.* **1. a.** the return of part of the output of an electronic circuit, device, or mechanical system to its input, so modifying its characteristics. In **negative feedback** a rise in output energy reduces the input energy; in **positive feedback** an increase in output energy reinforces the input energy. **b.** that part of the output signal fed back into the input. **2.** the return of part of the sound output by a loudspeaker to the microphone or pick-up so that a high-pitched whistle is produced. **3.** the whistling noise so produced. **4. a.** the effect of a product or action in a cyclic biological reaction on another stage in the same reaction. **b.** the substance or reaction causing such an effect, such as the release of a hormone in a biochemical pathway. **5.** information in response to an inquiry, experiment, etc.: *there was little feedback from our questionnaire.* ~*vb.* **feed back.** *(adv.)* **6.** *(tr.)* to return (part of the output of a system) to its input. **7.** to offer or suggest (information, ideas, etc.) in reaction to an inquiry, experiment, etc.
feedbag (ˈfiːdˌbæg) *n.* **1.** any bag in which feed for livestock is sacked. **2.** the usual U.S. and Canadian name for **nosebag.**
feeder (ˈfiːdə) *n.* **1.** a person or thing that feeds or is fed. **2.** a child's feeding bottle or bib. **3.** *Agriculture, chiefly U.S. and Canadian.* a head of livestock being fattened for slaughter. **4.** a person or device that feeds the working material into a system or machine. **5.** a tributary channel. **6. a.** a road, service, etc., that links secondary areas to the main traffic network. **b.** *(as modifier): a feeder bus.* **7. a.** a transmission line connecting an aerial

to a transmitter or receiver. **b.** a power line for transmitting electrical power from a generating station to a distribution network.

feeding bottle *n.* a bottle fitted with a rubber teat from which infants or young animals suck liquids. Also called: **nursing bottle.**

feedlot ('fiːdˌlɒt) *n.* an area or building where livestock are fattened rapidly for market.

feedstock ('fiːdˌstɒk) *n.* the main raw material used in the manufacture of a product.

feedthrough ('fiːdˌθruː) *n. Electronics.* a conductor used to connect two sides of a part, such as a printed circuit board.

feedwater ('fiːdˌwɔːtə) *n.* water, previously purified to prevent scale deposit or corrosion, that is fed to boilers for steam generation.

feel (fiːl) *vb.* **feels, feeling, felt** (fɛlt). **1.** to perceive (something) by touching. **2.** to have a physical or emotional sensation of (something): *to feel heat; to feel anger.* **3.** (*tr.*) to examine (something) by touch. **4.** (*tr.*) to find (one's way) by testing or cautious exploration. **5.** (*copula*) to seem or appear in respect of the sensation given: *I feel tired; it feels warm.* **6.** to have an indistinct, esp. emotional conviction; sense (esp. in the phrase **feel in one's bones**). **7.** (*intr.*; foll. by *for*) to show sympathy or compassion (towards): *I feel for you in your sorrow.* **8.** to believe, think, or be of the opinion (that): *he feels he must resign.* **9.** (*tr.*; *often foll. by up*) *Slang.* to pass one's hands over the sexual organs of. **10. feel like.** to have an inclination (for something or doing something): *I don't feel like going to the pictures.* **11. feel (quite) oneself.** to be fit and sure of oneself. **12. feel up to.** (*usually used with a negative or in a question*) to be fit enough for (something or doing something): *I don't feel up to going out tonight.* ~*n.* **13.** the act or an instance of feeling, esp. by touching. **14.** the quality of or an impression from something perceived through feeling: *the house has a homely feel about it.* **15.** the sense of touch: *the fabric is rough to the feel.* **16.** an instinctive aptitude; knack: *she's got a feel for this sort of work.* [Old English *fēlan*; related to Old High German *fuolen*, Old Norse *fālma* to grope, Latin *palma* PALM[1]]

▷**Usage.** The verbs *feel, look,* and *smell* can be followed by an adverb or an adjective according to the sense in which they are used. Where a quality of the subject is involved, an adjective is used: *I feel sick; he looks strong; this medicine smells bad.* For other senses an adverb would be used: *she feels strongly about that; I must look closely at his record; this animal smells inefficiently although its sight is well developed.*

feeler ('fiːlə) *n.* **1.** a person or thing that feels. **2.** an organ in certain animals, such as an antenna or tentacle, that is sensitive to touch. **3.** a remark designed to probe the reactions or intentions of other people.

feeler gauge *n.* a thin metal strip of known thickness used to measure a narrow gap or to set a gap between two parts.

feel-good *adj.* causing or characterized by a feeling of self-satisfaction: *feel-good factor.*

feeling ('fiːlɪŋ) *n.* **1.** the sense of touch. **2. a.** the ability to experience physical sensations, such as heat, pain, etc. **b.** the sensation so experienced. **3.** a state of mind. **4.** a physical or mental impression: *a feeling of warmth.* **5.** fondness; sympathy: *to have a great deal of feeling for someone.* **6.** an ability to feel deeply: *a person of feeling.* **7.** a sentiment: *a feeling that the project is feasible.* **8.** an impression or mood; atmosphere: *the feeling of a foreign city.* **9.** an emotional disturbance, esp. anger or dislike: *a lot of bad feeling about the increase in taxes.* **10.** intuitive appreciation and understanding: *a feeling for words.* **11.** sensibility in the performance of something. **12.** (*pl.*) emotional or moral sensitivity, as in relation to principles or personal dignity (esp. in the phrase **hurt** or **injure the feelings of**). ~*adj.* **13.** sentient; sensitive. **14.** expressing or containing emotion. **15.** warm-hearted; sympathetic. —'**feelingly** *adv.*

fee simple *n. Property law.* an absolute interest in land over which the holder has complete freedom of disposition during his life. Compare **fee tail.** [C15: from Anglo-French: fee (or fief) simple]

feet (fiːt) *n.* **1.** the plural of **foot. 2. at (someone's) feet.** as someone's disciple. **3. be run** *or* **rushed off one's feet.** to be very busy. **4. carry** *or* **sweep off one's feet.** to fill with enthusiasm. **5. feet of clay.** a weakness that is not widely known. **6. get one's feet wet.** to begin to participate in something. **7. have** (*or* **keep**) **one's feet on the ground.** to be practical and reliable. **8. on one's** *or* **its feet. a.** standing up. **b.** in good health. **c.** (of a business, company, etc.) thriving. **9. put one's feet up.** to rest. **10. to stand on one's own feet.** to be independent. —'**feetless** *adj.*

fee tail *n. Property law.* **a.** a freehold interest in land restricted to a particular line of heirs. **b.** an estate in land subject to such restriction. Compare **fee simple.** [C15: from Anglo-French *fee taillé* fee (or fief) determined, from *taillier* to cut]

feeze *or* **feaze** (fiːz) *Dialect.* ~*vb.* **1.** (*tr.*) to beat. **2.** to drive off. **3.** *Chiefly U.S.* to disconcert; worry. ~*n.* **4.** a rush. **5.** *Chiefly U.S.* a state of agitation. [Old English *fēsian*]

feign (feɪn) *vb.* **1.** to put on a show of (a quality or emotion); pretend: *to feign innocence.* **2.** (*tr.*) to make up; invent: *to feign an excuse.* **3.** (*tr.*) to copy; imitate: *to feign someone's laugh.* **4.** (*tr.*) *Archaic.* to portray. [C13: from Old French *feindre* to pretend, from Latin *fingere* to form, shape, invent] —'**feigner** *n.* —'**feigningly** *adv.*

feint[1] (feɪnt) *n.* **1.** a mock attack or movement designed to distract an adversary, as in a military manoeuvre or in boxing, fencing, etc. **2.** a misleading action or appearance. ~*vb.* **3.** (*intr.*) to make a feint. [C17: from French *feinte*, from *feint* pretended, from Old French *feindre* to FEIGN]

feint[2] (feɪnt) *n. Printing.* the narrowest rule used in the production of ruled paper. [C19: variant of FAINT]

feints *or* **faints** (feɪnts) *pl. n.* the leavings of the second distillation of Scotch malt whisky.

feisty ('faɪstɪ) *adj.* **feistier, feistiest.** *Informal, chiefly U.S. and Canadian.* **1.** frisky. **2.** irritable. [C19: from dialect *feist, fist* small dog; related to Old English *fīsting* breaking wind]

felafel *or* **falafel** (fəl'ɑːfəl) *n.* a ball or cake of ground spiced chickpeas, deep-fried and often served with pitta bread. [C20: from Arabic *felāfil*]

feldsher, feldscher, *or* **feldschar** ('fɛldʃə) *n.* (in Russia) a medical doctor's assistant. [C19: Russian, from German *Feldscher* a field surgeon, from *Feld* field + *Scherer* surgeon, from *scheren* to shear]

feldspar ('fɛldˌspɑː, 'fɛlˌspɑː) *or* **felspar** *n.* any of a group of hard rock-forming minerals consisting of aluminium silicates of potassium, sodium, calcium, or barium: the principal constituents of igneous rocks. The group includes orthoclase, microcline, and the plagioclase minerals. [C18: from German *feldspat(h)*, from *feld* field + *spat(h)* SPAR[3]] —**feldspathic** (fɛld'spæθɪk, fɛl'spæθ-), '**feldspathˌose** *or* **fel'spathic,** '**felspathˌose** *adj.*

feldspathoid ('fɛldspəˌθɔɪd) *n.* any of a group of rock-forming minerals, such as leucite and sodalite, that are similar to feldspars but contain less silica.

felicific (ˌfiːlɪ'sɪfɪk) *adj.* making or tending to make happy. [C19: from Latin *fēlix* happy + *facere* to make]

felicitate (fɪ'lɪsɪˌteɪt) *vb.* **1.** to wish joy to; congratulate. **2.** *Archaic.* to please. —**fe'liciˌtator** *n.*

felicitation (fɪˌlɪsɪ'teɪʃən) *n.* a less common word for **congratulation.**

felicitous (fɪ'lɪsɪtəs) *adj.* **1.** well-chosen; apt. **2.** possessing an agreeable style. **3.** producing or marked by happiness. —**fe'licitously** *adv.* —**fe'licitousness** *n.*

felicity (fɪ'lɪsɪtɪ) *n., pl.* **-ties. 1.** happiness; joy. **2.** a cause of happiness. **3.** an appropriate expression or style. **4.** the quality or display of such expressions or style. **5.** *Philosophy.* appropriateness (of a speech act). The performative *I appoint you ambassador* can only possess felicity if uttered by one in whom the authority for such appointments is vested. [C14: from Latin *fēlīcitās* happiness, from *fēlix* happy]

feline ('fiːlaɪn) *adj.* **1.** of, relating to, or belonging to the *Felidae*, a family of predatory mammals, including cats, lions, leopards, and cheetahs, typically having a round head and retractile claws: order *Carnivora* (carnivores). **2.** resembling or suggestive of a cat, esp. in stealth or grace. ~*n. also* **felid** ('fiːlɪd). **3.** any animal belonging to the family *Felidae*; a cat. [C17: from Latin *fēlīnus*, from *fēlēs* cat] —'**felinely** *adv.* —'**felineness** *or* **felinity** (fɪ'lɪnɪtɪ) *n.*

fell[1] (fɛl) *vb.* the past tense of **fall.**

fell[2] (fɛl) *vb.* (*tr.*) **1.** to cut or knock down: *to fell a tree; to fell an opponent.* **2.** *Needlework.* to fold under and sew flat (the edges of a seam). ~*n.* **3.** *U.S. and Canadian.* the timber felled in one season. **4.** a seam finished by felling. [Old English *fellan*; related to Old Norse *fella*, Old High German *fellen*; see FALL] —'**fellable** *adj.*

fell[3] (fɛl) *adj.* **1.** *Archaic.* cruel or fierce; terrible. **2.** *Archaic.* destructive or deadly: *a fell disease.* **3. one fell swoop.** a single hasty action or occurrence. [C13 *fel*, from Old French: cruel, from Medieval Latin *fellō* villain; see FELON[1]] —'**fellness** *n.*

fell[4] (fɛl) *n.* an animal skin or hide. [Old English; related to Old High German *fel* skin, Old Norse *berfjall* bearskin, Latin *pellis* skin; see PEEL[1]]

fell[5] (fɛl) *n.* (*often pl.*) *Northern English and Scot.* **a.** a mountain, hill, or tract of upland moor. **b.** (*in combination*): *fell-walking.* [C13: from Old Norse *fjall*; related to Old High German *felis* rock]

fellah ('fɛlə) *n., pl.* **fellahs, fellahin,** *or* **fellaheen** (ˌfɛlə'hiːn). a peasant in Arab countries. [C18: from Arabic, dialect variant of *fallāh*, from *falaha* to cultivate]

fellate (fɛ'leɪt, fɪ-) *vb.* (*tr.*) to perform fellatio on (a person). [C20: back formation from FELLATIO]

fellatio (fɪ'leɪʃɪəʊ, fɛ-) *or* **fellation** *n.* a sexual activity in which the penis is stimulated by the partner's mouth. Compare **cunnilingus.** [C19: New Latin, from Latin *fellāre* to suck] —**fel'lator** *n.* —**fel'latrix** *fem. n.*

feller[1] ('fɛlə) *n.* **1.** a person or thing that fells. **2.** an attachment on a sewing machine for felling seams.

feller[2] ('fɛlə) *n.* a nonstandard variant of **fellow.**

fellmonger ('fɛlˌmʌŋgə) *n.* a person who deals in animal skins or hides. —'**fellˌmongering** *or* '**fellˌmongery** *n.*

felloe ('fɛləʊ) *or* **felly** ('fɛlɪ) *n., pl.* **-loes** *or* **-lies.** a segment or the whole rim of a wooden wheel to which the spokes are attached and onto which a metal tyre is usually shrunk. [Old English *felge*; related to Old High German *felga*, Middle Dutch *velge*, of unknown origin]

fellow ('fɛləʊ) *n.* **1.** a man or boy. **2.** an informal word for **boyfriend. 3.** *Informal.* one or oneself: *a fellow has to eat.* **4.** a person considered to be of little importance or worth. **5. a.**

(*often pl.*) a companion; comrade; associate. **b.** (*as modifier*): *fellow travellers.* **6.** (at Oxford and Cambridge universities) a member of the governing body of a college, who is usually a member of the teaching staff. **7.** a member of the governing body or established teaching staff at any of various universities or colleges. **8.** a postgraduate student employed, esp. for a fixed period, to undertake research and, often, to do some teaching. **9. a.** a person in the same group, class, or condition: *the surgeon asked his fellows.* **b.** (*as modifier*): *fellow students; a fellow sufferer.* **10.** one of a pair; counterpart; mate: *looking for the glove's fellow.* ~*vb.* (*tr.*) *Rare.* **11.** to produce a counterpart for; match. **12.** to place on a par with; make equal to. [Old English *fēolaga,* from Old Norse *fēlagi,* one who lays down money, from *fē* money + *lag* a laying down]

Fellow ('fɛləʊ) *n.* a member of any of various learned societies: *Fellow of the British Academy.*

fellow feeling *n.* **1.** mutual sympathy or friendship. **2.** an opinion held in common.

fellowship ('fɛləʊˌʃɪp) *n.* **1.** the state of sharing mutual interests, experiences, activities, etc. **2.** a society of people sharing mutual interests, experiences, activities, etc.; club. **3.** companionship; friendship. **4.** the state or relationship of being a fellow. **5. a.** mutual trust and charitableness between Christians. **b.** a Church or religious association. **6.** *Education.* **a.** a financed research post providing study facilities, privileges, etc., often in return for teaching services. **b.** a foundation endowed to support a postgraduate research student. **c.** an honorary title carrying certain privileges awarded to a postgraduate student. **7.** (*often cap.*) the body of fellows in a college, university, etc.

fellow traveller *n.* **1.** a companion on a journey. **2.** a non-Communist who sympathizes with Communism.

felo de se ('fiːləʊ dɪ 'siː, 'fɛləʊ) *n., pl.* **felones de se** ('fiːləʊˌniːz dɪ 'siː, 'fɛl-) *or* **felos de se.** *Law.* **a.** suicide. **b.** a person who commits suicide. [C17: from Anglo-Latin, from *felō* felon, + Latin *dē* of, + *sē* oneself]

felon[1] ('fɛlən) *n.* **1.** *Criminal law.* (formerly) a person who has committed a felony. **2.** *Obsolete.* a wicked person. ~*adj.* **3.** *Archaic or poetic.* evil; cruel. [C13: from Old French: villain, from Medieval Latin *fellō,* of uncertain origin]

felon[2] ('fɛlən) *n.* a purulent inflammation of the end joint of a finger, sometimes affecting the bone. [C12: from Medieval Latin *fellō* sore, perhaps from Latin *fel* poison]

felonious (fɪ'ləʊnɪəs) *adj.* **1.** *Criminal law.* of, involving, or constituting a felony. **2.** *Obsolete.* wicked; base. —**fe'loniously** *adv.* —**fe'loniousness** *n.*

felonry ('fɛlənrɪ) *n., pl.* **-ries. 1.** felons collectively. **2.** (formerly) the convict population of a penal colony, esp. in Australia.

felony ('fɛlənɪ) *n., pl.* **-nies.** *Criminal law.* (formerly) a serious crime, such as murder or arson. All distinctions between felony and misdemeanour were abolished in England and Wales in 1967.

felsite ('fɛlsaɪt) *or* **felstone** ('fɛlˌstəʊn) *n.* any fine-grained igneous rock consisting essentially of quartz and feldspar. [C18: FELS(PAR) + -ITE[1]] —**felsitic** (fɛl'sɪtɪk) *adj.*

felspar ('fɛlˌspɑː) *n.* a variant (esp. Brit.) of **feldspar.** —**felspathic** (fɛl'spæθɪk) *or* '**felspathˌose** *adj.*

felt[1] (fɛlt) *vb.* the past tense and past participle of **feel.**

felt[2] (fɛlt) *n.* **1. a.** a matted fabric of wool, hair, etc., made by working the fibres together under pressure or by heat or chemical action. **b.** (*as modifier*): *a felt hat.* **2.** any material, such as asbestos, made by a similar process of matting. ~*vb.* **3.** (*tr.*) to make into or cover with felt. **4.** (*intr.*) to become matted. [Old English; related to Old Saxon *filt,* Old High German *filz* felt, Latin *pellere* to beat, Greek *pelas* close; see ANVIL, FILTER]

felting ('fɛltɪŋ) *n.* **1.** felted material; felt. **2.** the process of making felt. **3.** materials for making felt.

felt-tip pen *n.* a pen having a writing point made from pressed fibres. Also called: **fibre-tip pen.**

felucca (fɛ'lʌkə) *n.* a narrow lateen-rigged vessel of the Mediterranean. [C17: from Italian *felucca,* probably from obsolete Spanish *faluca,* from Arabic *fulūk* ships, from Greek *epholkion* small boat, from *ephelkein* to tow]

felwort ('fɛlˌwɜːt) *n.* a biennial gentianaceous plant, *Gentianella amarella,* of Europe and SW China, having purple flowers and rosettes of leaves. [Old English *feldwyrt;* see FIELD, WORT]

fem. *abbrev. for:* **1.** female. **2.** feminine.

female ('fiːmeɪl) *adj.* **1.** of, relating to, or designating the sex producing gametes (ova) that can be fertilized by male gametes (spermatozoa). **2.** of, relating to, or characteristic of a woman: *female charm.* **3.** for or composed of women or girls: *female suffrage; a female choir.* **4.** (of reproductive organs such as the ovary and carpel) capable of producing female gametes. **5.** (of gametes such as the ovum) capable of being fertilized by a male gamete in sexual reproduction. **6.** (of flowers) lacking, or having nonfunctional, stamens. **7.** having an internal cavity into which a projecting male counterpart can be fitted: *a female thread.* ~*n.* **8. a.** a female animal or plant. **b.** *Mildly offensive.* a woman or girl. [C14: from earlier *femelle* (influenced by *male*), from Latin *fēmella* a young woman, from *fēmina* a woman] —'**femaleness** *n.*

female impersonator *n.* a male theatrical performer who acts as a woman.

female suffrage *n. Chiefly U.S.* another name for **women's suffrage.**

feme (fɛm) *n. Law.* a woman or wife. [C16: from Anglo-French, ultimately from Latin *fēmina* woman]

feme covert *n. Law.* a married woman. [C16: from Anglo-French: a covered woman, one protected by marriage]

feme sole *n. Law.* **1.** a single woman, whether spinster, widow, or divorcee. **2.** a woman separated from her husband, or otherwise independent of him, as by owning her own property. [C16: from Anglo-French: a woman alone]

femineity (ˌfɛmɪ'neɪɪtɪ) *n.* the quality of being feminine; womanliness.

feminine ('fɛmɪnɪn) *adj.* **1.** suitable to or characteristic of a woman: *a feminine fashion.* **2.** possessing qualities or characteristics considered typical of or appropriate to a woman. **3.** effeminate; womanish. **4.** *Grammar.* **a.** denoting or belonging to a gender of nouns, occurring in many inflected languages, that includes all kinds of referents as well as some female animate referents. **b.** (*as n.*): *German* Zeit *"time" and* Ehe *"marriage" are feminines.* [C14: from Latin *fēminīnus,* from *fēmina* woman] —'**femininely** *adv.* —'**feminineness** *n.*

feminine ending *n. Prosody.* an unstressed syllable at the end of a line of verse.

feminine rhyme *n. Prosody.* a rhyme between words in which one, two, or more unstressed syllables follow a stressed one, as in *elation, nation* or *merrily, verily.* Compare **masculine rhyme.**

femininity (ˌfɛmɪ'nɪnɪtɪ) *n.* **1.** the quality of being feminine. **2.** womanhood.

feminism ('fɛmɪˌnɪzəm) *n.* a doctrine or movement that advocates equal rights for women. —'**feminist** *n., adj.*

feminize *or* **feminise** ('fɛmɪˌnaɪz) *vb.* **1.** to make or become feminine. **2.** to cause (a male animal) to develop female characteristics. —ˌ**feminiˈzation** *or* ˌ**feminiˈsation** *n.*

femme *French.* (fam; *English* fɛm) *n.* a woman or wife.

femme de chambre *French.* (fam də ʃɑ̃brə) *n., pl.* ***femmes de chambre*** (fam də ʃɑ̃brə). **1.** a chambermaid. **2.** *Rare.* a personal maid. [C18: woman of the bedroom]

femme fatale *French.* (fam fatal; *English* 'fɛm fə'tæl, -'tɑːl) *n., pl.* ***femmes fatales*** (fam fatal; *English* 'fɛm fə'tælz, -'tɑːlz). an alluring or seductive woman, esp. one who causes men to love her to their own distress. [fatal woman]

femoral ('fɛmərəl) *adj.* of or relating to the thigh or femur.

femto- *prefix.* denoting 10^{-15}: *femtometer.* Symbol: f [from Danish or Norwegian *femten* fifteen]

femur ('fiːmə) *n., pl.* **femurs** *or* **femora** ('fɛmərə). **1.** the longest thickest bone of the human skeleton, articulating with the pelvis above and the knee below. Nontechnical name: **thighbone. 2.** the corresponding bone in other vertebrates. **3.** the segment of an insect's leg nearest to the body. [C18: from Latin: thigh]

fen[1] (fɛn) *n.* low-lying flat land that is marshy or artificially drained. [Old English *fenn;* related to Old High German *fenna,* Old Norse *fen,* Gothic *fani* clay, Sanskrit *panka* mud]

fen[2] (fɛn) *n., pl.* **fen.** a monetary unit of the People's Republic of China worth one hundredth of a yuan. [from Mandarin Chinese]

fence (fɛns) *n.* **1.** a structure that serves to enclose an area such as a garden or field, usually made of posts of timber, concrete, or metal connected by wire, netting, rails, or boards. **2.** *Slang.* a dealer in stolen property. **3.** an obstacle for a horse to jump in steeplechasing or showjumping. **4.** *Machinery.* a guard or guide, esp. in a circular saw or plane. **5.** a projection usually fitted to the top surface of a sweptback aircraft wing to prevent movement of the airflow towards the wing tips. **6. mend one's fences. a.** *Chiefly U.S. and Canadian.* to restore a damaged position or reputation, esp. in politics. **b.** to re-establish friendly relations (with someone). **7. (sit) on the fence.** (to be) unable or unwilling to commit oneself. **8. over the fence.** *Austral. and N.Z. informal.* unreasonable, unfair, or unjust. ~*vb.* **9.** (*tr.*) to construct a fence on or around (a piece of land, etc.). **10.** (*tr.;* foll. by *in* or *off*) to close (in) or separate (off) with or as if with a fence: *he fenced in the livestock.* **11.** (*intr.*) to fight using swords or foils. **12.** (*intr.*) to evade a question or argument, esp. by quibbling over minor points. **13.** (*intr.*) to engage in skilful or witty debate, repartee, etc. **14.** (*intr.*) *Slang.* to receive stolen property. **15.** (*tr.*) *Archaic.* to ward off or keep out. [C14 *fens,* shortened from *defens* DEFENCE] —'**fenceless** *adj.* —'**fenceˌlike** *adj.*

fencer ('fɛnsə) *n.* **1.** a person who fights with a sword, esp. one who practises the art of fencing. **2.** *Chiefly Austral. and N.Z.* a person who erects and repairs fences.

fencible ('fɛnsəbᵊl) *adj.* **1.** a Scot. word for **defensible.** ~*n.* **2.** (formerly) a person who undertook military service in immediate defence of his homeland only.

fencing ('fɛnsɪŋ) *n.* **1.** the practice, art, or sport of fighting with swords, esp. the sport of using foils, épées, or sabres under a set of rules to score points. **2. a.** wire, stakes, etc., used as fences. **b.** fences collectively. **3.** skilful or witty debate. **4.** the avoidance of direct answers; evasiveness. **5.** *Slang.* the business of buying and selling stolen property.

fencing wire *n.* a heavy-gauge galvanized wire used for farm fences.

fend (fɛnd) *vb.* **1.** (*intr.;* foll. by *for*) to give support (to someone, esp. oneself); provide (for). **2.** (*tr.;* usually foll. by *off*) to ward off or turn aside (blows, questions, attackers, etc.). **3.** (*tr.*) *Archaic.* to defend or resist. **4.** (*intr.*) *Scot. and northern English dialect.*

to struggle; strive. *~n.* **5.** *Scot. and northern English dialect.* a shift or effort. [C13 *fenden,* shortened from *defenden* to DEFEND]

fender ('fɛndə) *n.* **1.** a low metal frame which confines falling coals to the hearth. **2.** *Chiefly U.S.* a metal frame fitted to the front of locomotives to absorb shock, clear the track, etc. **3.** a cushion-like device, such as a car tyre hung over the side of a vessel to reduce damage resulting from accidental contact or collision. **4.** the U.S. and Canadian name for **wing** (sense 10) or **mudguard.** —**fendered** *adj.*

Fender ('fɛndə) *n. Trademark.* a type of solid-body electric guitar. [C20: named after Leo *Fender,* its U.S. inventor (1951)]

fender pile *n.* an upright pile driven into the sea bed or a riverbed beside a berth to protect the dock wall or wharf from the impact of vessels.

fenestella (ˌfɛnɪ'stɛlə) *n., pl.* **-lae** (-liː). **1.** *R.C. Church.* a small aperture in the front of an altar, containing relics. **2.** *Ecclesiast.* a niche in the side wall of a chancel, in which the credence or piscina are set. **3.** *Architect.* a small window or an opening in a wall. [C18: from Latin: a little window, from *fenestra* window]

fenestra (fɪ'nɛstrə) *n., pl.* **-trae** (-triː). **1.** *Biology.* a small opening, esp. either of two openings between the middle and inner ears. **2.** *Zoology.* a transparent marking or spot, as on the wings of moths. **3.** *Architect.* a window or window-like opening in the outside wall of a building. [C19: via New Latin from Latin: wall opening, window] —**fe'nestral** *adj.*

fenestrated (fɪ'nɛsˌtreɪtɪd, 'fɛnɪˌstreɪtɪd) *or* **fenestrate** *adj.* **1.** *Architect.* having windows or window-like openings. **2.** *Biology.* perforated or having fenestrae.

fenestration (ˌfɛnɪ'streɪʃən) *n.* **1.** the arrangement and design of windows in a building. **2.** a surgical operation to restore hearing by making an artificial opening into the labyrinth of the ear.

F Eng *abbrev. for* Fellow of the Fellowship of Engineering.

Fenian ('fiːnɪən) *n.* **1.** (formerly) a member of an Irish revolutionary organization founded in the U.S. in the 19th century to fight for an independent Ireland. **2.** *Derogatory, offensive.* an Irish Catholic or a person of Irish Catholic descent. *~adj.* **3.** of or relating to the Fenians. [C19: from Irish Gaelic *féinne,* plural of *fian* band of warriors] —'**Fenianism** *n.*

fennec ('fɛnɛk) *n.* a very small nocturnal fox, *Fennecus zerda,* inhabiting deserts of N Africa and Arabia, having pale fur and enormous ears. [C18: from Arabic *fenek* fox]

fennel ('fɛnᵊl) *n.* **1.** a strong-smelling yellow-flowered umbelliferous plant, *Foeniculum vulgare,* whose seeds and feathery leaves are used to season and flavour food. See also **finocchio. 2. dog fennel.** another name for **mayweed.** [Old English *fenol,* from Latin *faeniculum* fennel, diminutive of *faenum* hay]

fennelflower ('fɛnᵊlˌflaʊə) *n.* any of various Mediterranean ranunculaceous plants of the genus *Nigella,* having finely divided leaves and white, blue, or yellow flowers. See also **love-in-a-mist.**

fenny ('fɛnɪ) *adj.* **1.** boggy or marshy: *fenny country.* **2.** found in, characteristic of, or growing in fens.

fentanyl ('fɛntəˌnaɪl) *n.* a narcotic drug used in medicine to relieve pain.

fenugreek ('fɛnjʊˌgriːk) *n.* an annual heavily scented Mediterranean leguminous plant, *Trigonella foenum-graecum,* with hairy stems and white flowers: cultivated for forage and for its medicinal seeds. [Old English *fēnogrēcum,* from Latin *fenum Graecum* literally: Greek hay]

feoff (fiːf) *Medieval history.* *~n.* **1.** a variant spelling of **fief.** *~vb.* **2.** (*tr.*) to invest with a benefice or fief. [C13: from Anglo-French *feoffer,* from *feoff* a FIEF] —'**feoffor** *or* '**feoffer** *n.*

feoffee (fɛ'fiː, fiː'fiː) *n.* (in feudal society) a vassal granted a fief by his lord.

feoffment ('fiːfmənt) *n.* (in medieval Europe) a lord's act of granting a fief to his man.

-fer *n. combining form.* indicating a person or thing that bears something specified: *crucifer; conifer.* [from Latin, from *ferre* to bear]

feral[1] ('fɪərəl, 'fɛr-) *or* **ferine** *adj.* **1.** (of animals and plants) existing in a wild or uncultivated state, esp. after being domestic or cultivated. **2.** savage; brutal. [C17: from Medieval Latin *ferālis,* from Latin *fera* a wild beast, from *ferus* savage] —**ferity** ('fɛrɪtɪ) *n.*

feral[2] ('fɪərəl, 'fɛr-) *adj. Archaic.* **1.** *Astrology.* associated with death. **2.** gloomy; funereal. [C17: from Latin *fērālis* relating to corpses; perhaps related to *ferre* to carry]

ferbam ('fɜːbæm) *n.* a black slightly water-soluble fluffy powder used as a fungicide. Formula: $[(CH_3)_2NCSS]_3Fe$. [C20: from *fer(ric dimethyldithiocar)bam(ate)*]

fer-de-lance (ˌfɛədə'lɑːns) *n.* a large highly venomous tropical American snake, *Trimeresurus* (or *Bothops*) *atrox,* with greyish-brown mottled coloration: family *Crotalidae* (pit vipers). [C19: from French, literally: iron (head) of a lance]

fere (fɪə; *Scot.* fiːr) *n. Archaic or Scot.* **1.** a companion. **2.** Also: **fier.** a husband or wife. [Old English *gefēra,* from *fēran* to travel; see FARE]

feretory ('fɛrɪtərɪ, -trɪ) *n., pl.* **-ries.** *Chiefly R.C. Church.* **1.** a shrine, usually portable, for a saint's relics. **2.** the chapel in which a shrine is kept. [C14: from Middle French *fiertre,* from Latin *feretrum* a bier, from Greek *pheretron,* from *pherein* to bear]

feria ('fɪərɪə) *n., pl.* **-rias** *or* **-riae** (-rɪˌiː). *R.C. Church.* a weekday, other than Saturday, on which no feast occurs. [C19: from Late Latin: day of the week (as in *prīma fēria* Sunday), singular of Latin *fēriae* festivals]

ferial ('fɪərɪəl) *adj.* **1.** of or relating to a feria. **2.** *Rare.* of or relating to a holiday.

ferine ('fɪəraɪn) *adj.* another word for **feral**[1]. [C17: from Latin *ferīnus* of wild animals, from *fera* wild beast]

ferity ('fɛrɪtɪ) *n., pl.* **-ties.** *Rare.* **1.** the state of being wild or uncultivated. **2.** savagery; ferocity. [C16: from Latin *feritās,* from *ferus* savage, untamed]

ferly ('fɛrlɪ) *Scot.* *~adj.* **1.** wonderful; strange. *~n., pl.* **-lies. 2.** a wonder; something strange or marvellous. *~vb.* (*intr.*) **-lies, -lying, -lied. 3.** to wonder; be surprised. [Old English *fǣrlic* sudden]

fermata (fə'mɑːtə) *n., pl.* **-tas** *or* **-te** (-tɪ). *Music.* another word for **pause** (sense 5). [from Italian, from *fermare* to stop, from Latin *firmāre* to establish; see FIRM[1]]

Fermat's last theorem (fɜː'mæts) *n.* (in number theory) the hypothesis that the equation $x^n + y^n = z^n$ has no integral solutions for *n* greater than two. [named after Pierre de *Fermat* (1601–65), French mathematician]

Fermat's principle *n. Physics.* the principle that a ray of light passes from one point to another in such a way that the time taken is a minimum.

ferment *n.* ('fɜːmɛnt). **1.** any agent or substance, such as a bacterium, mould, yeast, or enzyme, that causes fermentation. **2.** another word for **fermentation. 3.** commotion; unrest. *~vb.* (fə'mɛnt). **4.** to undergo or cause to undergo fermentation. **5.** to stir up or seethe with excitement. [C15: from Latin *fermentum* yeast, from *fervēre* to seethe] —**fer'mentable** *adj.* —**ferˌmenta'bility** *n.* —**fer'menter** *n.*

fermentation (ˌfɜːmɛn'teɪʃən) *n.* a chemical reaction in which a ferment causes an organic molecule to split into simpler substances, esp. the anaerobic conversion of sugar to ethyl alcohol by yeast. Also called: **ferment.** —**fer'mentative** *adj.* —**fer'mentatively** *adv.* —**fer'mentativeness** *n.*

fermentation lock *n.* a valve placed on the top of bottles of fermenting wine to allow bubbles to escape.

fermi ('fɜːmɪ) *n.* a unit of length used in nuclear physics equal to 10^{-15} metre.

Fermi-Dirac statistics ('fɜːmɪdɪ'ræk) *n. Physics.* the branch of quantum statistics used to calculate the permitted energy arrangements of the particles in a system in terms of the exclusion principle. Compare **Bose-Einstein statistics.** [C20: named after Enrico *Fermi* (1901–54), Italian physicist, and Paul *Dirac* (1902–84), British physicist]

Fermi energy *or* **level** *n.* the level in the distribution of electron energies in a solid at which a quantum state is equally likely to be occupied or empty. [C20: named after Enrico *Fermi*]

fermion ('fɜːmɪˌɒn) *n.* any of a group of elementary particles, such as a nucleon, that has half-integral spin and obeys Fermi-Dirac statistics. Compare **boson.** [C20: named after Enrico *Fermi;* see -ON]

fermium ('fɜːmɪəm) *n.* a transuranic element artificially produced by neutron bombardment of plutonium. Symbol: Fm; atomic no.: 100; half-life of most stable isotope, ^{257}Fm: 80 days (approx.). [C20: named after Enrico *Fermi*]

fern (fɜːn) *n.* **1.** any pteridophyte plant of the order *Filicales,* having roots, stems, and fronds and reproducing by spores formed in structures (sori) on the fronds. See also **tree fern. 2.** any of certain similar but unrelated plants, such as the sweet fern. [Old English *fearn;* related to Old High German *farn,* Sanskrit *parṇá* leaf] —'**fernˌlike** *adj.* —'**ferny** *adj.*

fernbird ('fɜːnˌbɜːd) *n.* a small brown and white New Zealand swamp bird, *Bowdleria punctata,* with a fernlike tail.

fernery ('fɜːnərɪ) *n., pl.* **-eries. 1.** a place where ferns are grown. **2.** a collection of ferns grown in such a place.

fern seed *n.* the minute particles by which ferns reproduce themselves, formerly thought to be invisible. Possession of them was thought to make a person invisible.

ferocious (fə'rəʊʃəs) *adj.* savagely fierce or cruel: *a ferocious tiger; a ferocious argument.* [C17: from Latin *ferox* fierce, untamable, warlike] —**fe'rociously** *adv.* —**ferocity** (fə'rɒsɪtɪ) *or* **fe'rociousness** *n.*

-ferous *adj. combining form.* bearing or producing: *coniferous; crystalliferous.* Compare **-gerous.** [from -FER + -OUS]

ferrate ('fɛreɪt) *n.* a salt containing the divalent ion, FeO_4^{2-}. Ferrates are derivatives of the hypothetical acid H_2FeO_4. [C19: from Latin *ferrum* iron]

ferredoxin (ˌfɛrɪ'dɒksɪn) *n.* any of certain iron-containing proteins, found in plants and some bacteria, that are involved in photosynthesis and nitrogen fixation.

ferreous ('fɛrɪəs) *adj.* containing or resembling iron: *a ferreous alloy; a ferreous substance.* [C17: from Latin *ferreus* made of iron, from *ferrum* iron]

ferret[1] ('fɛrɪt) *n.* **1.** a domesticated albino variety of the polecat *Mustela putorius,* bred for hunting rats, rabbits, etc. **2. black-footed ferret.** a musteline mammal, *Mustela nigripes,* of W North America, closely related to the weasels. *~vb.* **-rets, -reting, -reted. 3.** to hunt (rabbits, rats, etc.) with ferrets. **4.** (*tr.;* usually foll. by *out*) to drive from hiding: *to ferret out snipers.* **5.** (*tr.;* usually foll. by *out*) to find by persistent investigation. **6.**

(*intr.*) to search around. [C14: from Old French *furet*, from Latin *fur* thief] —'**ferreter** *n.* —'**ferrety** *adj.*

ferret[2] ('fɛrɪt) *or* **ferreting** *n.* silk binding tape. [C16: from Italian *fioretti* floss silk, plural of *fioretto:* a little flower, from *fiore* flower, from Latin *flōs*]

ferret badger *n.* any small badger of the genus *Melogale*, of SE Asia, resembling a ferret in appearance and smell.

ferri- *combining form.* indicating the presence of iron, esp. in the trivalent state: *ferricyanide; ferriferous.* Compare **ferro-**. [from Latin *ferrum* iron]

ferriage ('fɛrɪɪdʒ) *n.* **1.** transportation by ferry. **2.** the fee charged for passage on a ferry.

ferric ('fɛrɪk) *adj.* of or containing iron in the trivalent state: *ferric oxide*; designating an iron(III) compound. [C18: from Latin *ferrum* iron]

ferric oxide *n.* a red crystalline insoluble oxide of iron that occurs as haematite and rust and is made by heating ferrous sulphate: used as a pigment and metal polish (**jeweller's rouge**), and as a sensitive coating on magnetic tape. Formula: Fe_2O_3. Systematic name: **iron(III) oxide**.

ferricyanic acid (ˌfɛrɪsaɪ'ænɪk) *n.* a brown soluble unstable solid tribasic acid, usually known in the form of ferricyanide salts. Formula: $H_3Fe(CN)_6$.

ferricyanide (ˌfɛrɪ'saɪəˌnaɪd) *n.* any salt of ferricyanic acid.

ferriferous (fɛ'rɪfərəs) *adj.* producing or yielding iron; iron-bearing: *a ferriferous rock.*

ferrimagnetism (ˌfɛrɪ'mæɡnɪˌtɪzəm) *n.* a phenomenon exhibited by certain substances, such as ferrites, in which the magnetic moments of neighbouring ions are antiparallel and unequal in magnitude. The substances behave like ferromagnetic materials. See also **antiferromagnetism.** —**ferrimagnetic** (ˌfɛrɪmæɡ'nɛtɪk) *adj.*

Ferris wheel ('fɛrɪs) *n.* a fairground wheel having seats freely suspended from its rim; the seats remain horizontal throughout its rotation. [C19: named after G.W.G. *Ferris* (1859–96), American engineer]

ferrite ('fɛraɪt) *n.* **1.** any of a group of ferromagnetic highly resistive ceramic compounds with the formula MFe_2O_4, where M is usually a metal such as cobalt or zinc. **2.** any of the body-centred cubic allotropes of iron, such as alpha iron, occurring in steel, cast iron, etc. **3.** any of various microscopic grains, probably composed of iron compounds, in certain igneous rocks. [C19: from FERRI- + -ITE[1]]

ferrite-rod aerial *n.* a type of aerial, normally used in radio reception, consisting of a small coil of wire mounted on a ferrite core, the coil serving as a tuning inductance.

ferritin ('fɛrɪtɪn) *n. Biochem.* a protein that contains iron and plays a part in the storage of iron in the body. It occurs in the liver and spleen. [C20: from FERRITE + -IN]

ferro- *combining form.* **1.** indicating a property of iron or the presence of iron: *ferromagnetism; ferromanganese.* **2.** indicating the presence of iron in the divalent state: *ferrocyanide.* Compare **ferri-**. [from Latin *ferrum* iron]

ferrocene ('fɛrəʊˌsiːn) *n.* a reddish-orange insoluble crystalline compound. Its molecules have an iron atom sandwiched between two cyclopentadiene rings. Formula: $Fe(C_5H_5)_2$. [C20: from FERRO– + C(YCLOPENTADI)ENE]

ferrochromium (ˌfɛrəʊ'krəʊmɪəm) *or* **ferrochrome** *n.* an alloy of iron and chromium (60–72 per cent), used in the production of very hard steel.

ferroconcrete (ˌfɛrəʊ'kɒŋkriːt) *n.* another name for **reinforced concrete.**

ferrocyanic acid (ˌfɛrəʊsaɪ'ænɪk) *n.* a white volatile unstable solid tetrabasic acid, usually known in the form of ferrocyanide salts. Formula: $H_4Fe(CN)_6$.

ferrocyanide (ˌfɛrəʊ'saɪəˌnaɪd) *n.* any salt of ferrocyanic acid, such as potassium ferrocyanide, $K_4Fe(CN)_6$.

ferroelectric (ˌfɛrəʊɪ'lɛktrɪk) *adj.* **1.** (of a substance) exhibiting spontaneous polarization that can be reversed by the application of a suitable electric field. **2.** of or relating to ferroelectric substances. ~*n.* **3.** a ferroelectric substance. —ˌ**ferroe'lectrically** *adv.* —**ferroelectricity** (ˌfɛrəʊɪlɛk'trɪsɪtɪ, -ˌiːlɛk-) *n.*

ferromagnesian (ˌfɛrəʊmæɡ'niːʒən) *adj.* (of minerals such as biotite) containing a high proportion of iron and magnesium.

ferromagnetism (ˌfɛrəʊ'mæɡnɪˌtɪzəm) *n.* the phenomenon exhibited by substances, such as iron, that have relative permeabilities much greater than unity and increasing magnetization with applied magnetizing field. Certain of these substances retain their magnetization in the absence of the applied field. The effect is caused by the alignment of electron spin in regions called domains. Compare **diamagnetism, paramagnetism.** See also **magnet, Curie-Weiss law.** —**ferromagnetic** (ˌfɛrəʊmæɡ'nɛtɪk) *adj.*

ferromanganese (ˌfɛrəʊ'mæŋɡəˌniːz) *n.* an alloy of iron and manganese, used in making additions of manganese to cast iron and steel.

ferromolybdenum (ˌfɛrəʊmɒ'lɪbdɪnəm) *n.* an alloy of iron and molybdenum used in making alloy steels.

ferronickel (ˌfɛrəʊ'nɪkəl) *n.* an alloy of iron and nickel used in making nickel steels.

ferrosilicon (ˌfɛrəʊ'sɪlɪkən) *n.* an alloy of iron and silicon, used in making cast iron and steel.

ferrotype ('fɛrəʊˌtaɪp) *n.* **1.** a photographic print produced directly in a camera by exposing a sheet of iron or tin coated with a sensitized enamel. **2.** the process by which such a print is produced. ~Also called: **tintype.**

ferrous ('fɛrəs) *adj.* of or containing iron in the divalent state; designating an iron(II) compound. [C19: from FERRI- + -OUS]

ferrous sulphate *n.* an iron salt with a saline taste, usually obtained as greenish crystals of the heptahydrate, which are converted to the white monohydrate above 100°C: used in inks, tanning, water purification, and in the treatment of anaemia. Formula: $FeSO_4$. Systematic name: **iron(II) sulphate**. Also called: **copperas, green vitriol.**

ferruginous (fɛ'ruːdʒɪnəs) *adj.* **1.** (of minerals, rocks, etc.) containing iron: *a ferruginous clay.* **2.** rust-coloured. [C17: from Latin *ferrūgineus* of a rusty colour, from *ferrūgō* iron rust, from *ferrum* iron]

ferruginous duck *n.* a common European duck, *Aythyra nyroca*, having reddish-brown plumage with white wing bars.

ferrule *or* **ferule** ('fɛruːl, -rəl) *n.* **1.** a metal ring, tube, or cap placed over the end of a stick, handle, or post for added strength or to increase wear. **2.** a side opening in a pipe that gives access for inspection or cleaning. **3.** a bush, gland, small length of tube, etc., esp. one used for making a joint. ~*vb.* **4.** (*tr.*) to equip (a stick, etc.,) with a ferrule. [C17: from Middle English *virole*, from Old French *virol*, from Latin *viriola* a little bracelet, from *viria* bracelet; influenced by Latin *ferrum* iron]

ferry ('fɛrɪ) *n., pl.* **-ries.** **1.** Also called: '**ferryˌboat.** a vessel for transporting passengers and usually vehicles across a body of water, esp. as a regular service. **2. a.** such a service. **b.** (*in combination*): *a ferryman.* **3.** a legal right to charge for transporting passengers by boat. **4.** the act or method of delivering aircraft by flying them to their destination. ~*vb.* **-ries, -rying, -ried.** **5.** to transport or go by ferry. **6.** to deliver (an aircraft) by flying it to its destination. **7.** (*tr.*) to convey (passengers, goods, etc.): *the guests were ferried to the church in taxis.* [Old English *ferian* to carry, bring; related to Old Norse *ferja* to transport, Gothic *farjan;* see FARE]

fertile ('fɜːtaɪl) *adj.* **1.** capable of producing offspring. **2. a.** (of land) having nutrients capable of sustaining an abundant growth of plants. **b.** (of farm animals) capable of breeding stock. **3.** *Biology.* **a.** capable of undergoing growth and development: *fertile seeds; fertile eggs.* **b.** (of plants) capable of producing gametes, spores, seeds, or fruits. **4.** producing many offspring; prolific. **5.** highly productive; rich; abundant: *a fertile brain.* **6.** *Physics.* (of a substance) able to be transformed into fissile or fissionable material, esp. in a nuclear reactor. **7.** conducive to productiveness: *fertile rain.* [C15: from Latin *fertilis*, from *ferre* to bear] —'**fertilely** *adv.* —'**fertileness** *n.*

fertility (fɜː'tɪlɪtɪ) *n.* **1.** the ability to produce offspring, esp. abundantly. **2.** the state or quality of being fertile.

fertility cult *n.* the practice in some settled agricultural communities of performing religious or magical rites to ensure good weather and crops and the perpetuity of the tribe.

fertility symbol *n.* an object, esp. a phallic symbol, used in fertility-cult ceremonies to symbolize regeneration.

fertilization *or* **fertilisation** (ˌfɜːtɪlaɪ'zeɪʃən) *n.* **1.** the union of male and female gametes, during sexual reproduction, to form a zygote. **2.** the act or process of fertilizing. **3.** the state of being fertilized.

fertilize *or* **fertilise** ('fɜːtɪˌlaɪz) *vb.* (*tr.*) **1.** to provide (an animal, plant, or egg cell) with sperm or pollen to bring about fertilization. **2.** to supply (soil or water) with mineral and organic nutrients to aid the growth of plants. **3.** to make fertile or productive. —'**fertiˌlizable** *or* '**fertiˌlisable** *adj.*

fertilizer *or* **fertiliser** ('fɜːtɪˌlaɪzə) *n.* **1.** any substance, such as manure or a mixture of nitrates, added to soil or water to increase its productivity. **2.** an object or organism such as an insect that fertilizes an animal or plant.

ferula ('fɛrʊlə, 'fɛrjʊ-) *n., pl.* **-las** *or* **-lae** (-ˌliː). **1.** any large umbelliferous plant of the Mediterranean genus *Ferula*, having thick stems and dissected leaves: cultivated as the source of several strongly scented gum resins, such as galbanum. **2.** a rare word for **ferule**[1]. [C14: from Latin: giant fennel] —**ferulaceous** (ˌfɛruː'leɪʃəs, ˌfɛrjuː-) *adj.*

ferule[1] ('fɛruːl, -rəl) *n.* **1.** a flat piece of wood, such as a ruler, used in some schools to cane children on the hand. ~*vb.* **2.** (*tr.*) *Rare.* to punish with a ferule. [C16: from Latin *ferula* giant fennel, whip, rod; the stalk of the plant was used for punishment]

ferule[2] ('fɛruːl, -rəl) *n.* a variant spelling of **ferrule.**

fervency ('fɜːvənsɪ) *n., pl.* **-cies.** another word for **fervour.**

fervent ('fɜːvənt) *or* **fervid** ('fɜːvɪd) *adj.* **1.** intensely passionate; ardent: *a fervent desire to change society.* **2.** *Archaic or poetic.* boiling, burning, or glowing: *fervent heat.* [C14: from Latin *fervēre* to boil, glow] —'**fervently** *or* '**fervidly** *adv.* —'**ferventness** *or* '**fervidness** *n.*

Fervidor *French.* (fɛrvidɔr) *n.* another name for **Thermidor.** [probably from *ferveur* heat + THERMIDOR]

fervour *or U.S.* **fervor** ('fɜːvə) *n.* **1.** great intensity of feeling or belief; ardour; zeal. **2.** *Rare.* intense heat. [C14: from Latin: heat, from *fervēre* to glow, boil]

Fescennine ('fɛsɪˌnaɪn) *adj. Rare.* scurrilous or obscene. [C17: from Latin *Fescennīnus* of *Fescennia*, a city in Etruria noted for the production of mocking or obscene verse]

fescue ('fɛskjuː) *or* **fescue grass** *n.* any grass of the genus *Festuca:* widely cultivated as pasture and lawn grasses, having stiff narrow leaves. See also **meadow fescue, sheep's fescue.** [C14: from Old French *festu,* ultimately from Latin *festūca* stem, straw]

fesse *or* **fess** (fɛs) *n. Heraldry.* an ordinary consisting of a horizontal band across a shield, conventionally occupying a third of its length and being wider than a bar. [C15: from Anglo-French *fesse,* from Latin *fascia* band, fillet]

fesse point *n. Heraldry.* the midpoint of a shield.

festal ('fɛstᵊl) *adj.* another word for **festive.** [C15: from Latin *festum* holiday, banquet; see FEAST] —'**festally** *adv.*

fester ('fɛstə) *vb.* **1.** to form or cause to form pus. **2.** (*intr.*) to become rotten; decay. **3.** to become or cause to become bitter, irritated, etc., esp. over a long period of time; rankle: *resentment festered his imagination.* **4.** (*intr.*) *Informal, chiefly Brit.* to be idle or inactive. ~*n.* **5.** a small ulcer or sore containing pus. [C13: from Old French *festre* suppurating sore, from Latin: FISTULA]

festina lente *Latin.* (fɛs'tiːnə 'lɛntɪ) hasten slowly. [Latin]

festination (ˌfɛstɪ'neɪʃən) *n.* an involuntary quickening of gait, as in some persons with Parkinson's disease. [C16: from Latin *festīnātiō,* from *festīnāre* to hasten]

festival ('fɛstɪvᵊl) *n.* **1.** a day or period set aside for celebration or feasting, esp. one of religious significance. **2.** any occasion for celebration, esp. one which commemorates an anniversary or other significant event. **3.** an organized series of special events and performances, usually in one place: *a festival of drama.* **4.** *Archaic.* a time of revelry; merrymaking. **5.** (*modifier*) relating to or characteristic of a festival. [C14: from Church Latin *fēstivālis* of a feast, from Latin *festīvus* FESTIVE]

festive ('fɛstɪv) *adj.* appropriate to or characteristic of a holiday, etc.; merry. [C17: from Latin *festīvus* joyful, from *festus* of a FEAST] —'**festively** *adv.* —'**festiveness** *n.*

festivity (fɛs'tɪvɪtɪ) *n., pl.* **-ties.** **1.** merriment characteristic of a festival, party, etc. **2.** any festival or other celebration. **3.** (*pl.*) festive proceedings; celebrations.

festoon (fɛ'stuːn) *n.* **1.** a decorative chain of flowers, ribbons, etc., suspended in loops; garland. **2.** a carved or painted representation of this, as in architecture, furniture, or pottery. **3. a.** the scalloped appearance of the gums where they meet the teeth. **b.** a design carved on the base material of a denture to simulate this. **4. a.** either of two *Zerynthia* species of white pierid butterfly of southern Europe, typically mottled red, yellow, and brown. **b.** an ochreous brown moth, *Apoda avellana,* the unusual sluglike larvae of which feed on oak leaves. ~*vb.* (*tr.*) **5.** to decorate or join together with festoons. **6.** to form into festoons. [C17: from French *feston,* from Italian *festone* ornament for a feast, from *festa* FEAST]

festoon blind *n.* a window blind consisting of vertical rows of horizontally gathered fabric that may be drawn up to form a series of ruches.

festoonery (fɛ'stuːnərɪ) *n.* an arrangement of festoons.

festschrift ('fɛstˌʃrɪft) *n., pl.* **-schriften** (-ˌʃrɪftən) *or* **-schrifts.** a collection of essays or learned papers contributed by a number of people to honour an eminent scholar, esp. a colleague. [German, from *Fest* celebration, FEAST + *Schrift* writing]

FET *abbrev. for* field-effect transistor.

feta ('fɛtə) *n.* a white sheep or goat cheese popular in Greece. [Modern Greek, from the phrase *turi pheta,* from *turi* cheese + *pheta,* from Italian *fetta* a slice]

fetal *or* **foetal** ('fiːtᵊl) *adj.* of, relating to, or resembling a fetus.

fetal diagnosis *n.* prenatal determination of genetic or chemical abnormalities in a fetus, esp. by amniocentesis.

fetation *or* **foetation** (fiː'teɪʃən) *n.* **1.** the state of pregnancy. **2.** the process of development of a fetus.

fetch[1] (fɛtʃ) *vb.* (*mainly tr.*) **1.** to go after and bring back; get: *to fetch help.* **2.** to cause to come; bring or draw forth: *the noise fetched him from the cellar.* **3.** (*also intr.*) to cost or sell for (a certain price): *the table fetched six hundred pounds.* **4.** to utter (a sigh, groan, etc.). **5.** *Informal.* to deal (a blow, slap, etc.). **6.** (*also intr.*) *Nautical.* to arrive at or proceed by sailing. **7.** *Informal.* to attract: *to be fetched by an idea.* **8.** (used esp. as a command to dogs) to retrieve (shot game, an object thrown, etc.). **9.** *Rare.* to draw in (a breath, gasp, etc.), esp. with difficulty. **10.** **fetch and carry.** to perform menial tasks or run errands. ~*n.* **11.** the reach, stretch, etc., of a mechanism. **12.** a trick or stratagem. **13.** the distance in the direction of the prevailing wind that waves can travel continuously without obstruction before reaching the nearest coast. [Old English *feccan;* related to Old Norse *feta* to step, Old High German *sih fazzōn* to climb] —'**fetcher** *n.*

fetch[2] (fɛtʃ) *n.* the ghost or apparition of a living person. [C18: of unknown origin]

fetching ('fɛtʃɪŋ) *adj. Informal.* **1.** attractively befitting: *a fetching hat.* **2.** charming: *a fetching personality.* —'**fetchingly** *adv.*

fetch up *vb.* (*adv.*) **1.** (*intr.;* usually foll. by *at* or *in*) *Informal.* to arrive (at) or end up (in): *to fetch up in New York.* **2.** (*intr.*) *Nautical.* to stop suddenly, as from running aground: *to fetch up on a rock.* **3.** *Slang.* to vomit (food, etc.). **4.** (*tr.*) *Brit. dialect.* to rear (children, animals, etc.).

fête *or* **fete** (feɪt) *n.* **1.** a gala, bazaar, or similar entertainment, esp. one held outdoors in aid of charity. **2.** a feast day or holiday, esp. one of religious significance. **3.** *Caribbean informal.* an organized group entertainment, esp. a party or a dance. ~*vb.* **4.** (*tr.*) to honour or entertain with or as if with a fête: *the author was fêted by his publishers.* **5.** (*intr.*) *Caribbean informal.* to join in a fête. [C18: from French: FEAST]

fête champêtre *French.* (fɛt ʃɑ̃pɛtrə) *n., pl.* ***fêtes champêtres*** (fɛt ʃɑ̃pɛtrə). **1.** a garden party, picnic, or similar outdoor entertainment. **2.** Also called: ***fête galante*** (fɛt galɑ̃t). *Arts.* **a.** a genre of painting popular in France from the early 18th century, characterized by the depiction of figures in pastoral settings. Watteau was its most famous exponent. **b.** a painting in this genre. [C18: from French, literally: country festival]

fetial ('fiːʃəl) *n., pl.* **fetiales** (ˌfiːʃɪ'eɪliːz). **1.** (in ancient Rome) any of the 20 priestly heralds involved in declarations of war and in peace negotiations. ~*adj.* **2.** of or relating to the fetiales. **3.** a less common word for **heraldic.** [C16: from Latin *fētiālis,* probably from Old Latin *fētis* treaty]

feticide *or* **foeticide** ('fiːtɪˌsaɪd) *n.* the destruction of a fetus in the uterus; aborticide. —ˌ**feti'cidal** *or* ˌ**foeti'cidal** *adj.*

fetid *or* **foetid** ('fɛtɪd, 'fiː-) *adj.* having a stale nauseating smell, as of decay. [C16: from Latin *fētidus,* from *fētēre* to stink; related to *fūmus* smoke] —'**fetidly** *or* '**foetidly** *adv.* —'**fetidness** *or* '**foetidness** *n.*

fetiparous *or* **foetiparous** (fɪ'tɪpərəs) *adj.* (of marsupials, such as the kangaroo) giving birth to incompletely developed offspring. [C19: from FETUS + -PAROUS]

fetish *or* **fetich** ('fɛtɪʃ, 'fiːtɪʃ) *n.* **1.** something, esp. an inanimate object, that is believed in certain cultures to be the embodiment or habitation of a spirit or magical powers. **2. a.** a form of behaviour involving fetishism. **b.** any object that is involved in fetishism. **3.** any object, activity, etc., to which one is excessively or irrationally devoted: *to make a fetish of cleanliness.* [C17: from French *fétiche,* from Portuguese *feitiço* (n.) sorcery, from adj.: artificial, from Latin *factīcius* made by art, FACTITIOUS] —'**fetish-**ˌ**like** *or* '**fetich-**ˌ**like** *adj.*

fetishism *or* **fetichism** ('fɛtɪˌʃɪzəm, 'fiː-) *n.* **1.** a condition in which the handling of an inanimate object or a specific part of the body other than the sexual organs is a source of sexual satisfaction. **2.** belief in or recourse to a fetish for magical purposes. **3.** excessive attention or attachment to something. —'**fetishist** *or* '**fetichist** *n.* —ˌ**fetish'istic** *or* ˌ**fetich'istic** *adj.*

fetlock ('fɛtˌlɒk) *or* **fetterlock** *n.* **1.** a projection behind and above a horse's hoof: the part of the leg between the cannon bone and the pastern. **2.** Also called: **fetlock joint.** the joint at this part of the leg. **3.** the tuft of hair growing from this part. [C14 *fetlak;* related to Middle High German *vizzeloch* fetlock, from *vizzel* pastern + *-och;* see FOOT]

fetor *or* **foetor** ('fiːtə, -tɔː) *n.* an offensive stale or putrid odour; stench. [C15: from Latin, from *fētēre* to stink]

fetoscope ('fiːtəʊˌskəʊp) *n.* a fibreoptic instrument that can be passed through the abdomen of a pregnant woman to enable examination of the fetus and withdrawal of blood for sampling in prenatal diagnosis. —**fetoscopy** (fiː'tɒskəpɪ) *n.*

fetter ('fɛtə) *n.* **1.** (*often pl.*) a chain or bond fastened round the ankle; shackle. **2.** (*usually pl.*) a check or restraint: *in fetters.* ~*vb.* (*tr.*) **3.** to restrict or confine. **4.** to bind in fetters. [Old English *fetor;* related to Old Norse *fjöturr* fetter, Old High German *fezzera,* Latin *pedica* fetter, *impedīre* to hinder] —'**fetterer** *n.* —'**fetterless** *adj.*

fetter bone *n.* another name for **pastern** (sense 2).

fetterlock ('fɛtəˌlɒk) *n.* another name for **fetlock.**

fettle ('fɛtᵊl) *vb.* (*tr.*) **1.** to remove (excess moulding material and casting irregularities) from a cast component. **2.** to line or repair (the walls of a furnace). **3.** *Brit. dialect.* **a.** to prepare or arrange (a thing, oneself, etc.), esp. to put a finishing touch to. **b.** to repair or mend (something). ~*n.* **4.** state of health, spirits, etc. (esp. in the phrase **in fine fettle**). **5.** another name for **fettling.** [C14 (in the sense: to put in order): back formation from *fetled* girded up, from Old English *fetel* belt]

fettler ('fɛtlə) *n. Austral.* a person employed to maintain railway tracks.

fettling ('fɛtlɪŋ) *n.* a refractory material used to line the hearth of puddling furnaces. Also called: **fettle.**

fettucine, fettuccine, *or* **fettucini** (ˌfɛtuː'tʃiːnɪ) *n.* a type of pasta in the form of narrow ribbons. [Italian *fettuccine,* plural of *fettuccina,* diminutive of *fetta* slice]

fetus *or* **foetus** ('fiːtəs) *n., pl.* **-tuses.** the embryo of a mammal in the later stages of development, when it shows all the main recognizable features of the mature animal, esp. a human embryo from the end of the second month of pregnancy until birth. Compare **embryo** (sense 2). [C14: from Latin: offspring, brood]

feu (fjuː) *n.* **1.** *Scot. legal history.* **a.** a feudal tenure of land for which rent was paid in money or grain instead of by the performance of military service. **b.** the land so held. **2.** *Scots Law.* a right to the use of land in return for a fixed annual payment (**feu duty**). [C15: from Old French; see FEE]

feuar ('fjʊə) *n. Scot.* the tenant of a feu.

feud[1] (fjuːd) *n.* **1.** long and bitter hostility between two families, clans, or individuals; vendetta. **2.** a quarrel or dispute. ~*vb.* **3.** (*intr.*) to take part in or carry on a feud. [C13 *fede,* from Old French *feide,* from Old High German *fēhida;* related to Old English *fæhth* hostility; see FOE]

feud[2] *or* **feod** (fjuːd) *n. Feudal law.* land held in return for service. [C17: from Medieval Latin *feodum,* of Germanic origin; see FEE]

feudal[1] (ˈfjuːdᵊl) *adj.* **1.** of, resembling, relating to, or characteristic of feudalism or its institutions. **2.** of, characteristic of, or relating to a fief. Compare **allodial. 3.** *Disparaging.* old-fashioned, reactionary, etc. [C17: from Medieval Latin *feudālis,* from *feudum* FEUD[2]]

feudal[2] (ˈfjuːdᵊl) *adj.* of or relating to a feud or quarrel.

feudalism (ˈfjuːdəˌlɪzəm) *n.* **1.** Also called: **feudal system.** the legal and social system that evolved in W Europe in the 8th and 9th centuries, in which vassals were protected and maintained by their lords, usually through the granting of fiefs, and were required to serve under them in war. See also **vassalage, fief. 2.** any social system or society, such as medieval Japan or Ptolemaic Egypt, that resembles medieval European feudalism. —ˈ**feudalist** *n.* —ˌ**feudalˈistic** *adj.*

feudality (fjuːˈdælɪtɪ) *n., pl.* **-ties. 1.** the state or quality of being feudal. **2.** a fief or fee.

feudalize *or* **feudalise** (ˈfjuːdəˌlaɪz) *vb.* (*tr.*) to make feudal; create feudal institutions in (a society). —ˌ**feudaliˈzation** *or* ˌ**feudaliˈsation** *n.*

feudatory (ˈfjuːdətərɪ, -trɪ) (in feudal Europe) ~*n.* **1.** a person holding a fief; vassal. ~*adj.* **2.** relating to or characteristic of the relationship between lord and vassal. **3.** (esp. of a kingdom) under the overlordship of another sovereign. [C16: from Medieval Latin *feudātor*]

feu de joie (fø də ʒwa) *n.* a salute of musketry fired successively by each man in turn along a line and back. [C18: from French, literally: fire of joy]

feudist (ˈfjuːdɪst) *n. U.S.* a person who takes part in a feud or quarrel.

feuilleton (ˈfɜɪˌtɒn; *French* fœjtɔ̃) *n.* **1.** the part of a European newspaper carrying reviews, serialized fiction, etc. **2.** such a review or article. [C19: from French, from *feuillet* sheet of paper, diminutive of *feuille* leaf, from Latin *folium*] —ˈ**feuilletonism** *n.* —ˈ**feuilletonist** *n.* —ˌ**feuilletonˈistic** *adj.*

fever (ˈfiːvə) *n.* **1.** an abnormally high body temperature, accompanied by a fast pulse rate, dry skin, etc. Related adj.: **febrile. 2.** any of various diseases, such as yellow fever or scarlet fever, characterized by a high temperature. **3.** intense nervous excitement or agitation: *she was in a fever about her party.* ~*vb.* **4.** (*tr.*) to affect with or as if with fever. [Old English *fēfor,* from Latin *febris*] —ˈ**fevered** *adj.* —ˈ**feverless** *adj.*

fever blister *or* **sore** *n.* another name for **cold sore.**

feverfew (ˈfiːvəˌfjuː) *n.* a bushy European strong-scented perennial plant, *Chrysanthemum parthenium,* with white flower heads, formerly used medicinally: family *Compositae* (composites). [Old English *feferfuge,* from Late Latin *febrifugia,* from Latin *febris* fever + *fugāre* to put to flight]

feverish (ˈfiːvərɪʃ) *or* **feverous** *adj.* **1.** suffering from fever, esp. a slight fever. **2.** in a state of restless excitement. **3.** of, relating to, caused by, or causing fever. —ˈ**feverishly** *or* ˈ**feverously** *adv.* —ˈ**feverishness** *n.*

fever pitch *n.* a state of intense excitement: *things were at fever pitch with the election coming up.*

fever therapy *n.* a former method of treating disease by raising the body temperature. Compare **cryotherapy.**

fever tree *n. U.S.* **1.** any of several trees that produce a febrifuge or tonic, esp. *Pinckneya pubens,* a rubiaceous tree of SE North America. **2.** a tall mimosaceous swamp tree, *Acacia xanthophloea,* of southern Africa, with fragrant yellow flowers.

feverwort (ˈfiːvəˌwɜːt) *n. U.S.* any of several plants considered to have medicinal properties, such as horse gentian and boneset.

few (fjuː) *determiner.* **1. a.** a small number of; hardly any: *few men are so cruel.* **b.** (*as pronoun; functioning as pl.*): *many are called but few are chosen.* **2.** (preceded by *a*) **a.** a small number of: *a few drinks.* **b.** (*as pronoun; functioning as pl.*): *a few of you.* **3. a good few.** *Informal.* several. **4. few and far between. a.** at great intervals; widely spaced. **b.** not abundant; scarce. **5. have a few (too many).** to consume several (*or* too many) alcoholic drinks. **6. not** *or* **quite a few.** *Informal.* several. ~*n.* **7. the few.** a small number of people considered as a class: *the few who fell at Thermopylae.* Compare **many** (sense 4). [Old English *fēawa;* related to Old High German *fao* little, Old Norse *fār* little, silent] —ˈ**fewness** *n.*

▷**Usage.** See at **less.**

fey (feɪ) *adj.* **1.** interested in or believing in the supernatural; whimsical. **2.** attuned to the supernatural; clairvoyant; visionary. **3.** *Chiefly Scot.* fated to die; doomed. **4.** *Chiefly Scot.* in a state of high spirits or unusual excitement, formerly believed to presage death. [Old English *fǣge* marked out for death; related to Old Norse *feigr* doomed, Old High German *feigi*] —ˈ**feyness** *n.*

Feynman diagram (ˈfaɪnmən) *n. Physics.* a graphical representation of the interactions between elementary particles. [named after Richard *Feynman* (1918–88), U.S. physicist]

fez (fɛz) *n., pl.* **fezzes.** an originally Turkish brimless felt or wool cap, shaped like a truncated cone, usually red and with a tassel. [C19: via French from Turkish, from *Fez,* city in Morocco] —**fezzed** *adj.*

ff *symbol for:* **1.** Also: **ff.** folios. **2.** Also: **ff.** following (pages, lines, etc.). **3.** *Music.* fortissimo: an instruction to play very loudly.

ffa *Commerce. abbrev. for* free from alongside (ship).

FIA (in Britain) *abbrev. for* Fellow of the Institute of Actuaries.

fiacre (fɪˈɑːkrə) *n.* a small four-wheeled horse-drawn carriage, usually with a folding roof. [C17: named after the Hotel de St *Fiacre,* Paris, where these vehicles were first hired out]

fiancé *or* (*fem.*) **fiancée** (fɪˈɒnseɪ) *n.* a person who is engaged to be married. [C19: from French, from Old French *fiancier* to promise, betroth, from *fiance* a vow, from *fier* to trust, from Latin *fīdere*]

fianchetto (ˌfɪənˈtʃɛtəʊ, -ˈkɛtəʊ) *Chess.* ~*n., pl.* **-tos, -ti** (-tiː). **1.** the development of a bishop on the second rank of the neighbouring knight's file or the third rank of the nearer rook's file. ~*vb.* **-toes, -toing, -toed. 2.** to develop (a bishop) thus. [C19: from Italian diminutive of *fianco* FLANK]

fiasco (fɪˈæskəʊ) *n., pl.* **-cos** *or* **-coes.** a complete failure, esp. one that is ignominious or humiliating. [C19: from Italian, literally: FLASK; sense development obscure]

fiat (ˈfaɪət, -æt) *n.* **1.** official sanction; authoritative permission. **2.** an arbitrary order or decree. **3.** *Chiefly literary.* any command, decision, or act of will that brings something about. [C17: from Latin, literally: let it be done, from *fierī* to become]

fiat money *n. Chiefly U.S.* money declared by a government to be legal tender though it is not convertible into standard specie.

fib (fɪb) *n.* **1.** a trivial and harmless lie. ~*vb.* **fibs, fibbing, fibbed. 2.** (*intr.*) to tell such a lie. [C17: perhaps from *fibble-fable* an unlikely story; see FABLE] —ˈ**fibber** *n.*

fiber (ˈfaɪbə) *n.* the usual U.S. spelling of **fibre.**

Fibonacci sequence *or* **series** (ˌfɪbəˈnɑːtʃɪ) *n.* the infinite sequence of numbers, 0, 1, 1, 2, 3, 5, 8, etc., in which each member (**Fibonacci number**) is the sum of the previous two. [named after Leonardo *Fibonacci* (?1170–?1250), Italian mathematician]

fibre *or U.S.* **fiber** (ˈfaɪbə) *n.* **1.** a natural or synthetic filament that may be spun into yarn, such as cotton or nylon. **2.** cloth or other material made from such yarn. **3.** a long fine continuous thread or filament. **4.** the structure of any material or substance made of or as if of fibres; texture. **5.** essential substance or nature: *all the fibres of his being were stirred.* **6.** strength of character (esp. in the phrase **moral fibre**). **7.** See **dietary fibre. 8.** *Botany.* **a.** a narrow elongated thick-walled cell: a constituent of sclerenchyma tissue. **b.** such tissue extracted from flax, hemp, etc., used to make linen, rope, etc. **c.** a very small root or twig. **9.** *Anatomy.* any thread-shaped structure, such as a nerve fibre. [C14: from Latin *fibra* filament, entrails] —ˈ**fibred** *or U.S.* ˈ**fibered** *adj.* —ˈ**fibreless** *or U.S.* ˈ**fiberless** *adj.*

fibreboard *or U.S.* **fiberboard** (ˈfaɪbəˌbɔːd) *n.* a building material made of compressed wood or other plant fibres, esp. one in the form of a thin semirigid sheet.

fibrefill *or U.S.* **fiberfill** (ˈfaɪbəˌfɪl) *n.* a synthetic fibre used as a filling for pillows, quilted materials, etc.

fibreglass *or U.S.* **fiberglass** (ˈfaɪbəˌglɑːs) *n.* **1.** material consisting of matted fine glass fibres, used as insulation in buildings, in fireproof fabrics, etc. **2.** a fabric woven from this material or a light strong material made by bonding fibreglass with a synthetic resin; used for car bodies, boat hulls, etc. Also called: **glass fibre.**

fibre optics *n.* (*functioning as sing.*) the transmission of information modulated on light carried down very thin flexible fibres of glass. See also **optical fibre.** —ˌ**fibreˈoptic** *adj.*

fibrescope *or U.S.* **fiberscope** (ˈfaɪbəˌskəʊp) *n.* an endoscope that transmits images of the interior of a hollow organ by fibre optics.

fibriform (ˈfaɪbrɪˌfɔːm, ˈfɪb-) *adj.* having the form of a fibre or fibres.

fibril (ˈfaɪbrɪl) *or* **fibrilla** (faɪˈbrɪlə, fɪ-) *n., pl.* **-brils** *or* **-brillae** (-ˈbrɪliː). **1.** a small fibre or part of a fibre. **2.** *Biology.* a threadlike structure, such as a root hair or a thread of muscle tissue. [C17: from New Latin *fibrilla* a little FIBRE] —ˈ**fibrilar, fiˈbrillar,** *or* **fiˈbrillose** *adj.* —**fiˈbrilliˌform** *adj.*

fibrillation (ˌfaɪbrɪˈleɪʃən, ˌfɪb-) *n.* **1.** a local and uncontrollable twitching of muscle fibres, not affecting the entire muscle. **2.** irregular twitchings of the muscular wall of the heart, often interfering with the normal rhythmical contractions.

fibrin (ˈfɪbrɪn) *n.* a white insoluble elastic protein formed from fibrinogen when blood clots: forms a network that traps red cells and platelets.

fibrinogen (fɪˈbrɪnədʒən) *n.* a soluble protein, a globulin, in blood plasma, converted to fibrin by the action of the enzyme thrombin when blood clots. —**fibrinogenic** (ˌfaɪbrɪnəʊˈdʒɛnɪk) *or* **fibrinogenous** (ˌfaɪbrɪˈnɒdʒənəs) *adj.*

fibrinolysis (ˌfɪbrɪˈnɒlɪsɪs) *n.* the breakdown of fibrin in blood clots, esp. by enzymes. —**fibrinolytic** (ˌfaɪbrɪnəʊˈlɪtɪk) *adj.*

fibrinous (ˈfɪbrɪnəs) *adj.* of, containing, or resembling fibrin.

fibro (ˈfaɪbrəʊ) *n. Austral. informal.* **1. a.** short for **fibrocement. b.** (*as modifier*): *a fibro shack.* **2.** a house built of fibrocement.

fibro- *combining form.* **1.** indicating fibrous tissue: *fibroin; fibrosis.* **2.** indicating fibre: *fibrocement.* [from Latin *fibra* FIBRE]

fibroblast (ˈfaɪbrəʊˌblæst) *n.* a cell in connective tissue that synthesizes collagen. —ˌ**fibroˈblastic** *adj.*

fibrocement (ˌfaɪbrəʊsɪˈmɛnt) *n.* cement combined with asbestos fibre, used esp. in sheets for building.

fibroid (ˈfaɪbrɔɪd) *adj.* **1.** *Anatomy.* (of structures or tissues) containing or resembling fibres. ~*n.* **2.** a benign tumour, composed of fibrous and muscular tissue, occurring in the wall of the uterus and often causing heavy menstruation.

fibroin ('faɪbrəʊɪn) *n.* a tough elastic protein that is the principal component of spiders' webs and raw silk.

Fibrolite ('faɪbrəlaɪt) *n. N.Z. trademark.* a type of building board containing asbestos and cement.

fibroma (faɪ'brəʊmə) *n., pl.* **-mata** (-mətə) *or* **-mas.** a benign tumour derived from fibrous connective tissue. —**fibromatous** (faɪ'brɒmətəs) *adj.*

fibrosis (faɪ'brəʊsɪs) *n.* the formation of an abnormal amount of fibrous tissue in an organ or part as the result of inflammation, irritation, or healing. —**fibrotic** (faɪ'brɒtɪk) *adj.*

fibrositis (ˌfaɪbrə'saɪtɪs) *n.* inflammation of white fibrous tissue, esp. that of muscle sheaths.

fibrous ('faɪbrəs) *adj.* consisting of, containing, or resembling fibres: *fibrous tissue.* —'**fibrously** *adv.* —'**fibrousness** *n.*

fibrovascular (ˌfaɪbrəʊ'væskjʊlə) *adj. Botany.* (of a vascular bundle) surrounded by sclerenchyma or within sclerenchymatous tissue.

fibula ('fɪbjʊlə) *n., pl.* **-lae** (-ˌliː) *or* **-las.** **1.** the outer and thinner of the two bones between the knee and ankle of the human leg. Compare **tibia.** **2.** the corresponding bone in other vertebrates. **3.** a metal brooch resembling a safety pin, often highly decorated, common in Europe after 1300 B.C. [C17: from Latin: clasp, probably from *fīgere* to fasten] —'**fibular** *adj.*

-fic *suffix forming adjectives.* causing, making, or producing: *honorific.* [from Latin *-ficus,* from *facere* to do, make]

fiche (fiːʃ) *n.* See **microfiche, ultrafiche.**

fichu ('fiːʃuː) *n.* a woman's shawl or scarf of some light material, worn esp. in the 18th century. [C19: from French: small shawl, from *ficher* to fix with a pin, from Latin *fīgere* to fasten, FIX]

fickle ('fɪkᵊl) *adj.* changeable in purpose, affections, etc.; capricious. [Old English *ficol* deceitful; related to *fician* to wheedle, *befician* to deceive] —'**fickleness** *n.*

fico ('fiːkəʊ) *n., pl.* **-coes.** *Archaic.* **1.** a worthless trifle. **2.** another word for **fig**[1] (sense 7). [C16: from Italian: FIG[1]]

fictile ('fɪktaɪl) *adj.* **1.** moulded or capable of being moulded from clay; plastic. **2.** made of clay by a potter. **3.** relating to the craft of pottery. [C17: from Latin *fictilis* that can be moulded, hence, made of clay, from *fingere* to shape]

fiction ('fɪkʃən) *n.* **1.** literary works invented by the imagination, such as novels or short stories. **2.** an invented story or explanation; lie. **3.** the act of inventing a story or explanation. **4.** *Law.* something assumed to be true for the sake of convenience, though probably false. [C14: from Latin *fictiō* a fashioning, hence something imaginary, from *fingere* to shape] —'**fictional** *adj.* —'**fictionally** *adv.* —ˌ**fictio'neer** *or* '**fictionist** *n.*

fictionalize *or* **fictionalise** ('fɪkʃənəˌlaɪz) *vb.* (*tr.*) to make into fiction or give a fictional aspect to. —ˌ**fictionali'zation** *or* ˌ**fictionali'sation** *n.*

fictitious (fɪk'tɪʃəs) *adj.* **1.** not genuine or authentic; assumed; false: *to give a fictitious address.* **2.** of, related to, or characteristic of fiction; created by the imagination. —**fic'titiously** *adv.* —**fic'titiousness** *n.*

fictive ('fɪktɪv) *adj.* **1.** *Rare.* of, relating to, or able to create fiction. **2.** a rare word for **fictitious.** —'**fictively** *adv.*

ficus ('fiːkəs) *n.* any plant of the genus *Ficus,* which includes the edible fig and several greenhouse and house plants. See **rubber plant, weeping ivy.**

fid (fɪd) *n. Nautical.* **1.** a spike for separating strands of rope in splicing. **2.** a wooden or metal bar for supporting the heel of a topmast. [C17: of unknown origin]

-fid *adj. combining form.* divided into parts or lobes: *bifid; pinnatifid.* [from Latin *-fidus,* from *findere* to split]

Fid. Def. *or* **FID DEF** *abbrev. for* Fidei Defensor.

fiddle ('fɪdᵊl) *n.* **1.** *Informal or sometimes when used of a classical violin disparaging.* any instrument of the viol or violin family, esp. the violin. **2.** a violin played as a folk instrument. **3.** time-wasting or trifling behaviour; nonsense; triviality. **4.** *Nautical.* a small railing around the top of a table to prevent objects from falling off it in bad weather. **5.** *Brit. informal.* an illegal or fraudulent transaction or arrangement. **6.** *Brit. informal.* a manually delicate or tricky operation. **7. at** *or* **on the fiddle.** *Informal.* engaged in an illegal or fraudulent undertaking. **8. face as long as a fiddle.** *Informal.* a dismal or gloomy facial expression. **9. fit as a fiddle.** *Informal.* in very good health. **10. play second fiddle.** *Informal.* to be subordinate; play a minor part. ~*vb.* **11** to play (a tune) on the fiddle. **12.** (*intr.;* often foll. by *with*) to make restless or aimless movements with the hands. **13.** (when *intr.,* often foll. by *about* or *around*) *Informal.* to spend (time) or act in a careless or inconsequential manner; waste (time). **14.** (often foll. by *with*) *Informal.* to tamper or interfere (with). **15.** *Informal.* to contrive to do (something) by illicit means or deception: *he fiddled his way into a position of trust.* **16.** (*tr.*) *Informal.* to falsify (accounts, etc.); swindle. [Old English *fithele,* probably from Medieval Latin *vītula,* from Latin *vītulārī* to celebrate; compare Old High German *fidula* fiddle; see VIOLA[1]]

fiddle-back *n.* **1.** a chair with a fiddle-shaped back. **2.** a chasuble with a fiddle-shaped front.

fiddle-de-dee, fiddlededee, *or* **fiddledeedee** (ˌfɪdᵊldɪ'diː) *interj. Rare.* an exclamation of impatience, disbelief, or disagreement.

fiddle-faddle ('fɪdᵊlˌfædᵊl) *n., interj.* **1.** trivial matter; nonsense. ~*vb.* **2.** (*intr.*) to fuss or waste time, esp. over trivial matters. [C16: reduplication of FIDDLE] —'**fiddle-ˌfaddler** *n.*

fiddlehead ('fɪdᵊlˌhɛd) *or* **fiddleneck** *n.* **1.** *Nautical.* an ornamental carving, in the shape of the scroll at the head end of a fiddle, fitted to the top of the stem or cutwater. **2.** *U.S. and Canadian.* the edible coiled tip of a young fern frond.

fiddle pattern *n.* the style of a spoon or fork with a violin-shaped handle.

fiddler ('fɪdlə) *n.* **1.** a person who plays the fiddle, esp. in folk music. **2.** See **fiddler crab.** **3.** a person who wastes time or acts aimlessly. **4.** *Informal.* a cheat or petty rogue.

fiddler crab *n.* any of various burrowing crabs of the genus *Uca* of American coastal regions, the males of which have one of their anterior pincer-like claws very much enlarged. [C19: referring to the rapid fiddling movement of the enlarged anterior claw of the males, used to attract females]

fiddlestick ('fɪdᵊlˌstɪk) *n.* **1.** *Informal.* a violin bow. **2.** any meaningless or inconsequential thing; trifle. **3. fiddlesticks!** an expression of annoyance or disagreement.

fiddlewood ('fɪdᵊlˌwʊd) *n.* **1.** any of various tropical American verbenaceous trees of the genus *Citharexylum* and related genera. **2.** the hard durable wood of any of these trees.

fiddling ('fɪdlɪŋ) *adj.* trifling or insignificant; petty.

fiddly ('fɪdlɪ) *adj.* **-dlier, -dliest.** small and awkward to do or handle.

FIDE *abbrev. for* Fédération Internationale des Echecs: International Chess Federation.

fideicommissary (ˌfɪdɪaɪ'kɒmɪsərɪ) *Civil law.* ~*n., pl.* **-saries.** **1.** a person who receives a fideicommissum. ~*adj.* **2.** of, relating to, or resembling a fideicommissum.

fideicommissum (ˌfɪdɪaɪkə'mɪsəm) *n., pl.* **-sa** (-sə). *Civil law.* a gift of property, usually by will, to be held on behalf of another who cannot receive the gift directly. [C18: from Late Latin: (something) bequeathed in trust, from Latin *fidēs* trust, faith + *committere* to entrust]

Fidei Defensor *Latin.* ('faɪdɪˌaɪ dɪ'fɛnsɔː) *n.* defender of the faith; a title given to Henry VIII of England by Pope Leo X, and appearing on Brit. coins as FID DEF (before decimalization) or FD (after decimalization).

fideism ('fiːdeɪˌɪzəm) *n.* the theological doctrine that religious truth is a matter of faith and cannot be established by reason. Compare **natural theology.** [C19: from Latin *fidēs* faith] —'**fideist** *n.* —ˌ**fide'istic** *adj.*

Fidelism (fiː'dɛlɪzəm) *n.* belief in, adherence to, or advocacy of the principles of Fidel Castro. Also called: **Castroism.** —**Fi'delist** *n.*

fidelity (fɪ'dɛlɪtɪ) *n., pl.* **-ties.** **1.** devotion to duties, obligations, etc.; faithfulness. **2.** loyalty or devotion, as to a person or cause. **3.** faithfulness to one's spouse, lover, etc. **4.** adherence to truth; accuracy in reporting detail. **5.** *Electronics.* the degree to which the output of a system, such as an amplifier or radio, accurately reproduces the characteristics of the input signal. See also **high fidelity.** [C15: from Latin *fidēlitās,* from *fidēlis* faithful, from *fidēs* faith, loyalty]

fidge (fɪdʒ) *vb.* (*intr.*) an obsolete word for **fidget.** [C18: probably variant of dialect *fitch* to FIDGET]

fidget ('fɪdʒɪt) *vb.* **1.** (*intr.*) to move about restlessly. **2.** (*intr.;* often foll. by *with*) to make restless or uneasy movements (with something); fiddle: *he fidgeted with his pen.* **3.** (*tr.*) to cause to fidget. **4.** (*tr.*) to cause to worry; make uneasy. ~*n.* **5.** (*often pl.*) a state of restlessness or unease, esp. as expressed in continual motion: *he's got the fidgets.* **6.** a person who fidgets. [C17: from earlier *fidge,* probably from Old Norse *fīkjast* to desire eagerly] —'**fidgetingly** *adv.* —'**fidgety** *adj.*

fiducial (fɪ'djuːʃɪəl) *adj.* **1.** *Physics.* used as a standard of reference or measurement: *a fiducial point.* **2.** of or based on trust or faith. **3.** *Law.* a less common word for **fiduciary.** [C17: from Late Latin *fīdūciālis,* from Latin *fīdūcia* confidence, reliance, from *fīdere* to trust] —**fi'ducially** *adv.*

fiduciary (fɪ'duːʃɪərɪ) *Law.* ~*n.* **1.** a person bound to act for another's benefit, as a trustee in relation to his beneficiary. ~*adj.* **2. a.** having the nature of a trust. **b.** of or relating to a trust or trustee. [C17: from Latin *fīdūciārius* relating to something held in trust, from *fīdūcia* trust; see FIDUCIAL] —**fi'duciarily** *adv.*

fiduciary issue *n.* an issue of banknotes not backed by gold.

fidus Achates ('faɪdəs ə'keɪtiːz) *n.* a faithful friend or companion. [Latin, literally: faithful Achates, the name of the faithful companion of Aeneas in Virgil's *Aeneid*]

fie (faɪ) *interj. Obsolete or facetious.* an exclamation of distaste or mock dismay. [C13: from Old French *fi,* from Latin *fī,* exclamation of disgust]

fief *or* **feoff** (fiːf) *n.* (in feudal Europe) the property or fee granted to a vassal for his maintenance by his lord in return for service. [C17: from Old French *fie,* of Germanic origin; compare Old English *fēo* cattle, money, Latin *pecus* cattle, *pecūnia* money, Greek *pokos* fleece]

fiefdom ('fiːfdəm) *n.* **1.** (in feudal Europe) the property owned by a lord. **2.** an area over which a person or organization exerts authority or influence.

field (fiːld) *n.* **1.** an open tract of uncultivated grassland; meadow. Related adj.: **campestral.** **2.** a piece of land cleared of trees and undergrowth, usually enclosed with a fence or hedge and used for pasture or growing crops: *a field of barley.* **3.** a limited or marked off area, usually of mown grass, on which any of various sports, athletic competitions, etc., are held: *a soccer field.* **4.** an area that is rich in minerals or other natural resources: *a coalfield.* **5.** short for **battlefield** and **airfield.** **6.** the mounted followers that hunt with a pack of hounds. **7. a.** all the runners in a particular race or competitors in a competition. **b.** the runners in a race or competitors in a competition excluding the favourite. **8.** *Cricket.* the fielders collectively, esp. with regard to their positions. **9.** a wide or open expanse: *a field of snow.* **10. a.** an area of human activity: *the field of human knowledge.* **b.** a sphere or division of knowledge, interest, etc.: *his field is physics.* **11. a.** a place away from the laboratory, office, library, etc., usually out of doors, where practical work is done or original material or data collected. **b.** (*as modifier*): *a field course.* **12.** the surface or background, as of a flag, coin, or heraldic shield, on which a design is displayed. **13.** Also called: **field of view.** the area within which an object may be observed with a telescope, microscope, etc. **14.** *Physics.* **a.** See **field of force.** **b.** a region of space that is a vector field. **c.** a region of space under the influence of some scalar quantity, such as temperature. **15.** *Maths.* a set of entities subject to two binary operations, addition and multiplication, such that the set is a commutative group under addition and the set, minus the zero, is a commutative group under multiplication. **16.** *Maths, logic.* the set of elements that are either arguments or values of a function; the union of its domain and range. **17.** *Computer technol.* **a.** a set of one or more characters comprising a unit of information. **b.** the characters in a vertical column of a punched card. **c.** a predetermined section of a record. **18.** *Television.* one of two or more sets of scanning lines which when interlaced form the complete picture. **19.** *Obsolete.* the open country: *beasts of the field.* **20. hold** *or* **keep the field.** to maintain one's position in the face of opposition. **21. in the field. a.** *Military.* in an area in which operations are in progress. **b.** actively or closely involved with or working on something (rather than being in a more remote or administrative position). **22. leave the field.** *Informal.* to back out of a competition, contest, etc. **23. take the field.** to begin or carry on activity, esp. in sport or military operations. **24. play the field.** *Informal.* to disperse one's interests or attentions among a number of activities, people, or objects. **25.** (*modifier*) *Military.* of or relating to equipment, personnel, etc., specifically designed or trained for operations in the field: *a field gun; a field army.* ~*vb.* **26.** (*tr.*) *Sport.* to stop, catch, or return (the ball) as a fielder. **27.** (*tr.*) *Sport.* to send (a player or team) onto the field to play. **28.** (*intr.*) *Sport.* (of a player or team) to act or take turn as a fielder or fielders. **29.** (*tr.*) *Military.* to put (an army, a unit, etc.) in the field. **30.** (*tr.*) to enter (a person) in a competition: *each party fielded a candidate.* **31.** (*tr.*) *Informal.* to deal with or handle, esp. adequately and by making a reciprocal gesture: *to field a question.* [Old English *feld;* related to Old Saxon, Old High German *feld,* Old English *fold* earth, Greek *platus* broad]

field ambulance *n. Military.* a mobile medical unit that accepts casualties from forward units, treating the lightly wounded and stabilizing the condition of the seriously wounded before evacuating them to a hospital.

field army *n. Military.* the largest formation of a land force, usually consisting of two or more corps with supporting arms and services.

field artillery *n.* artillery capable of deployment in support of front-line troops, due mainly to its mobility.

field battery *n.* a small unit of usually four field guns.

field boot *n.* a close-fitting knee-length boot.

field captain *n.* the senior official at an archery meeting, responsible for safety.

field centre *n.* a centre equipped for field studies, usually situated in or near an area where field studies are carried out.

field corn *n. U.S.* any variety of corn that is grown as a feed for livestock.

field cornet *n. S. African.* a commander of burgher troops called up in time of war or in an emergency, esp. during the 19th century. Often shortened to **cornet.**

fieldcraft ('fiːldˌkrɑːft) *n.* ability and experience in matters concerned with living out-of-doors, esp. in a wild area.

field day *n.* **1.** a day spent in some special outdoor activity, such as nature study or sport. **2.** a day-long competition between amateur radio operators using battery or generator power, the aim being to make the most contacts with other operators around the world. **3.** *Military.* a day devoted to manoeuvres or exercises, esp. before an audience. **4.** *Informal.* a day or time of exciting or successful activity: *the children had a field day with their new toys.* **5.** *Austral.* **a.** a day or series of days devoted to the demonstration of farm machinery in country centres. **b.** a combined open day and sale on a stud property.

field drain *or* **tile** *n.* an earthenware channel used for draining fields.

field-effect transistor *n.* a unipolar transistor consisting of three or more electrode regions, the source, one or more gates, and the drain. A current flowing in a channel between the highly doped source and drain is controlled by the electric field arising from a voltage applied between source and gate. Abbrev.: **FET.** See also **JUGFET, IGFET.**

field emission *n.* the emission of electrons from a solid or liquid subjected to a high electric field.

fielder ('fiːldə) *n. Cricket, baseball, etc.* **a.** a player in the field. **b.** a member of the fielding rather than the batting side.

field event *n.* a competition, such as the discus, high jump, etc., that takes place on a field or similar area as opposed to those on the running track.

fieldfare ('fiːldˌfɛə) *n.* a large Old World thrush, *Turdus pilaris,* having a pale grey head and rump, brown wings and back, and a blackish tail. [Old English *feldefare;* see FIELD, FARE]

field glass *n.* **1.** a small telescope often incorporating a prism and held in one hand. **2.** a former name for **field glasses.**

field glasses *pl. n. or (formerly)* **field glass** *n.* another name for **binoculars.**

field goal *n.* **1.** *Basketball.* a goal worth two points scored while the ball is in normal play rather than from a free throw. **2.** *American football.* a score of three points made by kicking the ball through the opponent's goalposts above the crossbar.

field guidance *n.* a method of guiding a missile to a point within a gravitational or radio field by means of the properties of the field.

field gun *n.* a gun specially designed for service in direct support of front-line troops.

field hockey *n. U.S. and Canadian.* hockey played on a field, as distinguished from ice hockey.

field-holler *n.* a cry employing falsetto, portamento, and sudden changes of pitch, used in Negro work songs, later integrated into the techniques of the blues.

field hospital *n.* a temporary hospital set up near a battlefield equipped to provide remedial surgery and post-operative care.

field layer *n.* See **layer** (sense 2).

field magnet *n.* a permanent magnet or an electromagnet that produces the magnetic field in a generator, electric motor, or similar device.

field marshal *n.* an officer holding the highest rank in the British and certain other armies.

fieldmouse ('fiːldˌmaʊs) *n., pl.* **-mice. 1.** any nocturnal mouse of the genus *Apodemus,* inhabiting woods, fields, and gardens of the Old World: family *Muridae.* They have yellowish-brown fur and feed on fruit, vegetables, seeds, etc. **2.** a former name for **vole.**

field officer *n.* an officer holding **field rank,** namely that of major, lieutenant colonel, or colonel.

field of fire *n.* the area that a weapon or group of weapons can cover with fire from a given position.

field of force *n.* the region of space surrounding a body, such as a charged particle or a magnet, within which it can exert a force on another similar body not in contact with it. See also **electric field, magnetic field, gravitational field.**

field of honour *n.* the place or scene of a battle or duel, esp. of jousting tournaments in medieval times.

fieldpiece ('fiːldˌpiːs) *n.* a former name for **field gun.**

field poppy *n.* another name for **corn poppy.**

field post office *n.* a place to which mail intended for military units in the field is sent to be sorted and forwarded. Abbrev.: **FPO.**

fieldsman ('fiːldzmən) *n., pl.* **-men.** *Cricket.* another name for **fielder.**

field spaniel *n.* a robust, low-slung breed of spaniel developed by crossing the cocker spaniel with the Sussex spaniel.

field sports *pl. n.* sports carried on in the open countryside, such as hunting, shooting, or fishing.

fieldstone ('fiːldˌstəʊn) *n.* building stone found in fields.

field strength *n.* **1.** *Radio, television.* the intensity of an electromagnetic wave at any point in the area covered by a radio or television transmitter. **2.** *Physics.* the intensity of an electric or magnetic field. See **intensity.**

field study *n.* (*often pl.*) a research project carried out in the field. See **field** (sense 11).

field tile *n. Brit. and N.Z.* an earthenware drain used in farm drainage.

field trial *n.* **1.** *Hunting.* a test of or contest between gun dogs to determine their proficiency and standard of training in retrieving or pointing. **2.** (*often pl.*) a test to display performance, efficiency, or durability, as of a vehicle or invention.

field trip *n.* an expedition, as by a group of students or research workers, to study something at first hand.

field winding ('waɪndɪŋ) *n.* the insulated current-carrying coils on a field magnet that produce the magnetic field intensity required to set up the electrical excitation in a generator or motor.

fieldwork ('fiːldˌwɜːk) *n. Military.* a temporary structure used in defending or fortifying a place or position.

field work *n.* an investigation or search for material, data, etc., made in the field as opposed to the classroom, laboratory, or official headquarters. —**field worker** *n.*

fiend (fiːnd) *n.* **1.** an evil spirit; demon; devil. **2.** a person who is extremely wicked, esp. in being very cruel or brutal. **3.** *Informal.* **a.** a person who is intensely interested in or fond of something: *a fresh-air fiend; he is a fiend for cards.* **b.** an addict: *a drug fiend.* **4.** *Informal.* a mischievous or spiteful person, esp. a child. [Old English *fēond;* related to Old Norse *fjāndi* enemy, Gothic *fijands,* Old High German *fīant*] —'**fiendˌlike** *adj.*

fiendish (ˈfiːndɪʃ) *adj.* **1.** of or like a fiend. **2.** diabolically wicked or cruel. **3.** *Informal.* extremely difficult or unpleasant: *a fiendish problem.* —ˈ**fiendishly** *adv.* —ˈ**fiendishness** *n.*

fier *or* **fiere** (fiːr) *n. Scot.* variant spellings of **fere.**

fierce (fɪəs) *adj.* **1.** having a violent and unrestrained nature; savage: *a fierce dog.* **2.** wild or turbulent in force, action, or intensity: *a fierce storm.* **3.** vehement, intense, or strong: *fierce competition.* **4.** *Informal.* very disagreeable or unpleasant. [C13: from Old French *fiers,* from Latin *ferus*] —ˈ**fiercely** *adv.* —ˈ**fierceness** *n.*

fieri facias (ˈfaɪəˌraɪ ˈfeɪʃɪəs) *n. Law.* a writ ordering a levy on the belongings of an adjudged debtor to satisfy the debt. [C15: from Latin, literally: cause (it) to be done]

fiery (ˈfaɪərɪ) *adj.* **fierier, fieriest. 1.** of, containing, or composed of fire. **2.** resembling fire in heat, colour, ardour, etc.: *a fiery desert wind; a fiery speaker.* **3.** easily angered or aroused: *a fiery temper.* **4.** (of food) producing a burning sensation: *a fiery curry.* **5.** (of the skin or a sore) inflamed. **6.** flammable or containing flammable gas. **7.** (of a cricket pitch) making the ball bounce dangerously high. —ˈ**fierily** *adv.* —ˈ**fieriness** *n.*

fiery cross *n.* **1.** a burning cross, used as a symbol by the Ku Klux Klan. **2.** a wooden cross with ends charred or dipped in blood formerly used by Scottish Highlanders to summon the clans to battle.

fiesta (fɪˈɛstə; *Spanish* ˈfjesta) *n.* (esp. in Spain and Latin America) **1.** a religious festival or celebration, esp. on a saint's day. **2.** a holiday or carnival. [Spanish, from Latin *festa,* plural of *festum* festival; see FEAST]

FIFA (ˈfiːfə) *n. acronym for* Fédération Internationale de Football Association. [from French]

fife (faɪf) *n.* **1.** a small high-pitched flute similar to the piccolo and usually having no keys, used esp. in military bands. ~*vb.* **2.** to play (music) on a fife. [C16: from Old High German *pfīfa;* see PIPE[1]] —ˈ**fifer** *n.*

fife rail *n. Nautical.* a rail at the base of a mast of a sailing vessel, fitted with pins for belaying running rigging. Compare **pin rail.** [C18: of unknown origin]

fifi hook (ˈfiːfiː) *n. Mountaineering.* a metal hook at the top of an étrier for attaching it to a peg and also connected by a cord to the climber's harness to pull the étrier up and prevent it being dropped. [C20: of unknown origin]

FIFO (ˈfaɪfəʊ) *acronym for* first in, first out (as an accounting principle in costing stock). Compare **LIFO.**

fifteen (ˈfɪfˈtiːn) *n.* **1.** the cardinal number that is the sum of ten and five. **2.** a numeral, 15, XV, etc., representing this number. **3.** something represented by, representing, or consisting of 15 units. **4.** a rugby football team. ~*determiner.* **5. a.** amounting to fifteen: *fifteen jokes.* **b.** (*as pronoun*): *fifteen of us danced.* [Old English *fīftēne*]

fifteenth (ˈfɪfˈtiːnθ) *adj.* **1. a.** coming after the fourteenth in order, position, time, etc. Often written 15th. **b.** (*as n.*): *the fifteenth of the month.* ~*n.* **2. a.** one of 15 equal or nearly equal parts of something. **b.** (*as modifier*): *a fifteenth part.* **3.** the fraction equal to one divided by 15 (1/15). **4. a.** an interval of two octaves. **b.** one of two notes constituting such an interval in relation to the other, esp. the one higher in pitch. **c.** an organ stop of diapason quality sounding a note two octaves higher than that normally produced by the key depressed; a two-foot stop.

fifth (fɪfθ) *adj.* (*usually prenominal*) **1. a.** coming after the fourth in order, position, time, etc. Often written 5th. **b.** (*as n.*): *he came on the fifth.* ~*n.* **2. a.** one of five equal or nearly equal parts of an object, quantity, measurement, etc. **b.** (*as modifier*): *a fifth part.* **3.** the fraction equal to one divided by five (1/5). **4.** *Music.* **a.** the interval between one note and another five notes away from it counting inclusively along the diatonic scale. **b.** one of two notes constituting such an interval in relation to the other. See also **perfect** (sense 9), **diminished** (sense 2), **interval** (sense 5). **5.** an additional high gear fitted to some vehicles, esp. certain sports cars. ~*adv.* **6.** Also: **fifthly.** after the fourth person, position, event, etc. ~*sentence connector.* **7.** Also: **fifthly.** as the fifth point: linking what follows with the previous statements, as in a speech or argument. [Old English *fifta*]

Fifth Amendment *n.* **1.** an amendment to the U.S. Constitution stating that no person may be compelled to testify against himself and that no person may be tried for a second time on a charge for which he has already been acquitted. **2. take the fifth (amendment).** *U.S.* to refuse to answer a question on the grounds that it might incriminate oneself.

fifth column *n.* **1.** (originally) a group of Falangist sympathizers in Madrid during the Spanish Civil War who were prepared to join the four columns of insurgents marching on the city. **2.** any group of hostile or subversive infiltrators; an enemy in one's midst. —**fifth columnist** *n.*

fifth force *n.* a hypothetical non-Newtonian repulsive component of the force of gravity, postulated as an addition to the four known fundamental forces (gravitational, electromagnetic, strong, and weak).

fifth-generation *adj.* denoting developments in computer design to produce machines with artifical intelligence.

fifth wheel *n.* **1.** a spare wheel for a four-wheeled vehicle. **2.** a steering bearing that enables the front axle of a horse-drawn vehicle to rotate relative to the body. **3.** a superfluous or unnecessary person or thing.

fiftieth (ˈfɪftɪɪθ) *adj.* **1. a.** being the ordinal number of *fifty* in order, position, time, etc. Often written 50th. **b.** (*as n.*): *the fiftieth in the series.* ~*n.* **2. a.** one of 50 equal or approximately equal parts of something. **b.** (*as modifier*): *a fiftieth part.* **3.** the fraction equal to one divided by 50 (1/50).

fifty (ˈfɪftɪ) *n., pl.* **-ties. 1.** the cardinal number that is the product of ten and five. **2.** a numeral, 50, L, etc., representing this number. **3.** something represented by, representing, or consisting of 50 units. ~*determiner.* **4. a.** amounting to fifty: *fifty people.* **b.** (*as pronoun*): *fifty should be sufficient.* [Old English *fiftig*]

fifty-fifty *adj., adv. Informal.* shared or sharing equally; in equal parts.

fig[1] (fɪg) *n.* **1.** any moraceous tree or shrub of the tropical and subtropical genus *Ficus,* in which the flowers are borne inside a pear-shaped receptacle. **2.** the fruit of any of these trees, esp. of *F. carica,* which develops from the receptacle and has sweet flesh containing numerous seedlike structures. **3.** any of various plants or trees having a fruit similar to this. **4. Hottentot** *or* **sour fig.** a succulent plant, *Mesembryanthemum edule,* of southern Africa, having a capsular fruit containing edible pulp: family *Aizoaceae.* **5.** (*used with a negative*) something of negligible value; jot: *I don't care a fig for your opinion.* **6.** Also: **feg.** *Dialect.* a piece or segment from an orange. **7.** Also called: **fico.** an insulting gesture made with the thumb between the first two fingers or under the upper teeth. [C13: from Old French *figue,* from Old Provençal *figa,* from Latin *ficus* fig tree]

fig[2] (fɪg) *Slang.* ~*vb.* **figs, figging, figged.** (*tr.*) **1.** (foll. by *out* or *up*) to dress (up) or rig (out). **2.** to administer stimulating drugs to (a horse). ~*n.* **3.** dress, appearance, or array (esp. in the phrase **in full fig**). **4.** physical condition or form: *in bad fig.* [C17 *feague,* of uncertain origin]

fig. *abbrev. for:* **1.** figurative(ly). **2.** figure.

fig-bird *n.* any Australian oriole of the genus *Sphecotheres,* feeding on figs and other fruit.

fight (faɪt) *vb.* **fights, fighting, fought. 1.** to oppose or struggle against (an enemy) in battle. **2.** to oppose or struggle against (a person, thing, cause, etc.) in any manner. **3.** (*tr.*) to engage in or carry on (a battle, contest, etc.). **4.** (when *intr.,* often foll. by *for*) to uphold or maintain (a cause, ideal, etc.) by fighting or struggling: *to fight for freedom.* **5.** (*tr.*) to make or achieve (a way) by fighting. **6.** (*intr.*) *Boxing.* **a.** to box, as for a living. **b.** to use aggressive rough tactics. **7.** to engage (another or others) in combat. **8. fight it out.** to contend or struggle until a decisive result is obtained. **9. fight shy of.** to keep aloof from. ~*n.* **10.** a battle, struggle, or physical combat. **11.** a quarrel, dispute, or contest. **12.** resistance (esp. in the phrase **to put up a fight**). **13.** the desire to take part in physical combat (esp. in the phrase **to show fight**). **14.** a boxing match. ~See also **fight back, fight off.** [Old English *feohtan;* related to Old Frisian *fiuchta,* Old Saxon, Old High German *fehtan* to fight]

fight back *vb.* (*adv.*) **1.** (*intr.*) to resist an attack. **2.** (*intr.*) to counterattack. **3.** (*tr.*) to struggle to repress: *she tried to fight back her tears.* ~*n.* **fightback. 4.** an act or campaign of resistance. **5.** a counterattack.

fighter (ˈfaɪtə) *n.* **1.** a person who fights, esp. a professional boxer. **2.** a person who has determination. **3.** *Military.* an armed aircraft designed for destroying other aircraft.

fighter-bomber *n.* a high-performance aircraft that combines the roles of fighter and bomber.

fighting chance *n.* a slight chance of success dependent on a struggle.

fighting cock *n.* **1.** another name for **gamecock. 2.** a pugnacious person.

fighting fish *n.* any of various labyrinth fishes of the genus *Betta,* esp. the Siamese fighting fish.

fighting top *n.* one of the gun platforms on the lower masts of sailing men-of-war, used in attacking the crew of an enemy ship with swivel guns and muskets.

fight off *vb.* (*tr., adv.*) **1.** to repulse; repel. **2.** to struggle to avoid or repress: *to fight off a cold.*

fight-or-flight *n.* (*modifier*) involving or relating to an involuntary response to stress in which the hormone adrenaline is secreted into the blood in readiness for physical action, such as fighting or running away.

fig leaf *n.* **1.** a leaf from a fig tree. **2.** a representation of a leaf, usually a vine leaf rather than an actual fig leaf, used in painting or sculpture to cover the genitals of nude figures. **3.** a device intended to conceal something regarded as shameful or indecent.

fig marigold *n.* an erect species of mesembryanthemum, *M. tricolor,* grown as a garden annual for its red-orange flowers with yellow centres.

figment (ˈfɪgmənt) *n.* a fantastic notion, invention, or fabrication: *a figment of the imagination.* [C15: from Late Latin *figmentum* a fiction, from Latin *fingere* to shape]

figuline (ˈfɪgjʊˌlaɪn) *Rare.* ~*adj.* **1.** of or resembling clay. ~*n.* **2.** an article made of clay. [C17: from Latin *figulīnus* of a potter, from *figulus* a potter, from *fingere* to mould]

figural (ˈfɪgərəl) *adj.* composed of or relating to human or animal figures.

figurant (ˈfɪgjʊrənt) *n.* **1.** a ballet dancer who does group work but no solo roles. **2.** *Theatre.* a minor character, esp. one who does not speak. [C18: from French, from *figurer* to represent, appear, FIGURE] —**figurante** (ˌfɪgjʊˈrɒnt) *fem. n.*

figurate (ˈfɪgjʊrɪt) *adj.* **1.** *Music.* exhibiting or produced by figuration; florid or decorative. **2.** having a definite or particular shape or figure. [C15: from Latin *figūrāre* to shape] —ˈ**figurately** *adv.*

figuration (ˌfɪgəˈreɪʃən) *n.* **1.** *Music.* **a.** the employment of characteristic patterns of notes, esp. in variations on a theme. **b.** decoration or florid ornamentation in general. **2.** the act or an instance of representing figuratively, as by means of allegory or emblem. **3.** a figurative or emblematic representation. **4.** the act of decorating with a design.

figurative (ˈfɪgərətɪv) *adj.* **1.** of the nature of, resembling, or involving a figure of speech; not literal; metaphorical. **2.** using or filled with figures of speech. **3.** representing by means of an emblem, likeness, figure, etc. **4.** (in painting, sculpture, etc.) of, relating to, or characterized by the naturalistic representation of the external world. —ˈ**figuratively** *adv.* —ˈ**figurativeness** *n.*

figure (ˈfɪgə; *U.S.* ˈfɪgjər) *n.* **1.** any written symbol other than a letter, esp. a whole number. **2.** another name for **digit** (sense 2). **3.** an amount expressed numerically: *a figure of 1800 was suggested.* **4.** (*pl.*) calculations with numbers: *he's good at figures.* **5.** visible shape or form; outline. **6.** the human form, esp. as regards size or shape: *a girl with a slender figure.* **7.** a slim bodily shape (esp. in the phrases **keep** *or* **lose one's figure**). **8.** a character or personage, esp. a prominent or notable one; personality: *a figure in politics.* **9.** the impression created by a person through behaviour (esp. in the phrase **to cut a fine, bold,** etc., **figure**). **10. a.** a person as impressed on the mind: *the figure of Napoleon.* **b.** (*in combination*): *father-figure.* **11.** a representation in painting or sculpture, esp. of the human form. **12.** an illustration or explanatory diagram in a text. **13.** a representative object or symbol; emblem. **14.** a pattern or design, as on fabric or in wood. **15.** a predetermined set of movements in dancing or skating. **16.** *Geometry.* any combination of points, lines, curves, or planes. A **plane figure,** such as a circle, encloses an area; a **solid figure,** such as a sphere, encloses a volume. **17.** *Rhetoric.* See **figure of speech. 18.** *Logic.* one of the four possible arrangements of the three terms in the premises of a syllogism. Compare **mood**[2] (sense 2). **19.** *Music.* **a.** a numeral written above or below a note in a part. See **figured bass, thorough bass. b.** a characteristic short pattern of notes. ~*vb.* **20.** (when *tr.,* often foll. by *up*) to calculate or compute (sums, amounts, etc.). **21.** (*tr.; usually takes a clause as object*) *Informal, chiefly U.S., Canadian, and N.Z.* to think or conclude; consider. **22.** (*tr.*) to represent by a diagram or illustration. **23.** (*tr.*) to pattern or mark with a design. **24.** (*tr.*) to depict or portray in a painting, etc. **25.** (*tr.*) *Rhetoric.* to express by means of a figure of speech. **26.** (*tr.*) to imagine. **27.** (*tr.*) *Music.* **a.** to decorate (a melody line or part) with ornamentation. **b.** to provide figures above or below (a bass part) as an indication of the accompanying harmonies required. See **figured bass, thorough bass. 28.** (*intr.;* usually foll. by *in*) to be included: *his name figures in the article.* **29.** (*intr.*) *Informal.* to accord with expectation; be logical: *it figures that he wouldn't come.* ~See also **figure on, figure out.** [C13: from Latin *figūra* a shape, from *fingere* to mould] —ˈ**figureless** *adj.* —ˈ**figurer** *n.*

figured (ˈfɪgəd) *adj.* **1.** depicted as a figure in graphic art, painting, or sculpture. **2.** decorated or patterned with a design. **3.** having a form. **4.** *Music.* **a.** ornamental. **b.** (of a bass part) provided with numerals indicating accompanying harmonies.

figured bass (beɪs) *n.* a shorthand method of indicating a thorough-bass part in which each bass note is accompanied by figures indicating the intervals to be played in the chord above it in the realization.

figure-ground phenomenon *n.* the division of the perceptual field into background and objects that appear to stand out against it. The concept was evolved by the Gestalt psychologists, who invented *ambiguous* figures in which the same part could be seen either as figure or ground.

figurehead (ˈfɪgəˌhɛd) *n.* **1.** a person nominally having a prominent position, but no real authority. **2.** a carved bust or full-length figure at the upper end of the stems of some sailing vessels.

figure of eight *or* **figure eight** *n.* **1.** an outline of the number 8 traced on ice by a skater. **2.** a flight manoeuvre by an aircraft outlining a figure 8. **3. a.** a knot in the shape of a figure 8 made to prevent the unreeving of a rope. **b.** a climber's knot in the shape of a figure 8 made with a doubled rope to provide a secure loop. **c.** an angler's knot sometimes used to attach a fly to a leader or dropper.

figure of merit *n.* **1.** *Aeronautics.* a measure of the efficiency of a helicopter in hover. **2.** *Electrical engineering.* a measure of the efficiency of a component, such as a circuit.

figure of speech *n.* an expression of language, such as simile, metaphor, or personification, by which the usual or literal meaning of a word is not employed.

figure on *or* **upon** *vb.* (*intr., prep.*) *Informal, chiefly U.S. and Canadian.* **1.** to depend on (support or help.) **2.** to take into consideration.

figure out *vb.* (*tr., adv.; may take a clause as object*) *Informal.* **1.** to calculate or reckon. **2.** to understand.

figure skating *n.* ice skating in which the skater traces outlines of selected patterns. —**figure skater** *n.*

figurine (ˌfɪgəˈriːn) *n.* a small carved or moulded figure; statuette. [C19: from French, from Italian *figurina* a little FIGURE]

figwort (ˈfɪgˌwɜːt) *n.* any scrophulariaceous plant of the N temperate genus *Scrophularia,* having square stems and small greenish flowers.

Fijian (fiːˈdʒiːən) *n.* **1.** a member of the indigenous people of mixed Melanesian and Polynesian descent inhabiting Fiji, a republic in the SW Pacific. **2.** the language of this people, belonging to the Malayo-Polynesian family. ~*adj.* **3.** of, relating to, or characteristic of Fiji or its inhabitants. ~Also: **Fiji.**

filagree (ˈfɪləˌgriː) *n., adj., vb.* a less common variant of **filigree.**

filament (ˈfɪləmənt) *n.* **1.** the thin wire, usually tungsten, inside a light bulb that emits light when heated to incandescence by an electric current. **2.** *Electronics.* a high-resistance wire or ribbon, forming the cathode in some valves. **3.** a single strand of a natural or synthetic fibre; fibril. **4.** *Botany.* **a.** the stalk of a stamen. **b.** any of the long slender chains of cells into which some algae and fungi are divided. **5.** *Ornithol.* the barb of a down feather. **6.** *Anatomy.* any slender structure or part, such as the tail of a spermatozoon; filum. [C16: from New Latin *fīlāmentum,* from Medieval Latin *fīlāre* to spin, from Latin *fīlum* thread] —**filamentary** (ˌfɪləˈmɛntərɪ, -trɪ) *or* ˌ**filaˈmentous** *adj.*

filar (ˈfaɪlə) *adj.* **1.** of thread. **2.** (of an optical instrument) having fine threads across the eyepiece forming a reticle or set of cross wires. [C19: from Latin *fīlum* thread]

filaria (fɪˈlɛərɪə) *n., pl.* **-iae** (-ɪˌiː). any parasitic nematode worm of the family *Filariidae,* living in the blood and tissues of vertebrates and transmitted by insects: the cause of filariasis. [C19: New Latin (former name of genus), from Latin *fīlum* thread] —**fiˈlarial** *or* **fiˈlarian** *adj.*

filariasis (ˌfɪləˈraɪəsɪs, fɪˌlɛərɪˈeɪsɪs) *n.* a disease common in tropical and subtropical countries resulting from infestation of the lymphatic system with the nematode worms *Wuchereria bancrofti* or *Brugia malayi,* transmitted by mosquitoes: characterized by inflammation and obstruction of the lymphatic vessels. See also **elephantiasis.** [C19: from New Latin; see FILARIA]

filature (ˈfɪlətʃə) *n.* **1.** the act or process of spinning silk, etc., into threads. **2.** the reel used for this. **3.** a place where such spinning or reeling is done. [C18: from Medieval Latin *fīlātūra* the art of spinning, from *fīlāre* to spin thread; see FILAMENT]

filbert (ˈfɪlbət) *n.* **1.** any of several N temperate shrubs of the genus *Corylus,* esp. *C. maxima,* that have edible rounded brown nuts: family *Corylaceae.* **2.** Also called: **hazelnut, cobnut.** the nut of any of these shrubs. ~See also **hazel** (senses 1, 2). [C14: named after St *Philbert,* 7th-century Frankish abbot, because the nuts are ripe around his feast day, Aug. 22]

filch (fɪltʃ) *vb.* (*tr.*) to steal or take surreptitiously in small amounts; pilfer. [C16 *filchen* to steal, attack, perhaps from Old English *gefylce* band of men] —ˈ**filcher** *n.*

file[1] (faɪl) *n.* **1.** a folder, box, etc., used to keep documents or other items in order. **2.** the documents, etc., kept in this way. **3.** documents or information about a specific subject, person, etc.: *we have a file on every known thief.* **4.** an orderly line or row. **5.** a line of people in marching formation, one behind another. Compare **rank**[1] (sense 6). **6.** any of the eight vertical rows of squares on a chessboard. **7.** *Computer technol.* an organized collection of related records, usually held on a peripheral storage device and accessible via an assigned address. **8.** *Obsolete.* a list or catalogue. **9. on file.** recorded or catalogued for reference, as in a file. ~*vb.* **10.** to place (a document, letter, etc.) in a file. **11.** (*tr.*) to put on record, esp. to place (a legal document) on public or official record; register. **12.** (*tr.*) to bring (a suit, esp. a divorce suit) in a court of law. **13.** (*tr.*) to submit (copy) to a newspaper or news agency. **14.** (*intr.*) to march or walk in a file or files: *the ants filed down the hill.* [C16 (in the sense: string on which documents are hung): from Old French *filer,* from Medieval Latin *fīlāre;* see FILAMENT] —ˈ**filer** *n.*

file[2] (faɪl) *n.* **1.** a hand tool consisting essentially of a steel blade with small cutting teeth on some or all of its faces. It is used for shaping or smoothing metal, wood, etc. **2.** *Rare, Brit. slang.* a cunning or deceitful person. ~*vb.* **3.** (*tr.*) to shape or smooth (a surface) with a file. [Old English *fīl;* related to Old Saxon *fīla,* Old High German *fīhala* file, Greek *pikros* bitter, sharp] —ˈ**filer** *n.*

file[3] (faɪl) *vb.* (*tr.*) *Obsolete.* to pollute or defile. [Old English *fȳlan;* related to Middle Low German *vülen;* see DEFILE[1], FILTH, FOUL]

filecard (ˈfaɪlˌkɑːd) *n.* a type of brush with sharp steel bristles, used for cleaning the teeth of a file.

filefish (ˈfaɪlˌfɪʃ) *n., pl.* **-fish** *or* **-fishes.** any tropical triggerfish, such as *Alutera scripta,* having a narrow compressed body and a very long dorsal spine. [C18: referring to its file-like scales]

filename (ˈfaɪlˌneɪm) *n.* an arrangement of characters that enables a computer system to permit the user to have access to particular files.

filet (ˈfɪlɪt, ˈfɪleɪ; *French* filɛ) *n.* a variant spelling of **fillet** (senses 1-3). [C20: from French: net, from Old Provençal *filat,* from *fil* thread, from Latin *fīlum*]

filet mignon (ˈfɪleɪ ˈmiːnjɒn) *n.* a small tender boneless cut of beef from the inside of the loin. [from French, literally: dainty fillet]

filial ('fɪljəl) *adj.* **1.** of, resembling, or suitable to a son or daughter: *filial affection.* **2.** *Genetics.* designating any of the generations following the parental generation. Abbrev.: **F**; F_1 indicates the first filial generation, F_2 the second, etc. [C15: from Late Latin *fīliālis,* from Latin *fīlius* son] —'**filially** *adv.* —'**filialness** *n.*

filiate ('fɪlɪˌeɪt) *vb. (tr.)* **1.** *Law.* to fix judicially the paternity of (a child, esp. one born out of wedlock). **2.** *Law.* a less common word for **affiliate.** **3.** *Archaic.* to affiliate or associate. [C18: from Medieval Latin *fīliātus* acknowledged as a son, from Latin *fīlius* son]

filiation (ˌfɪlɪ'eɪʃən) *n.* **1.** line of descent; lineage; derivation. **2.** the fact of being the child of certain parents. **3.** *Law.* the act or process of filiating. **4.** *Law.* a less common word for **affiliation order.** **5.** the set of rules governing the attachment of children to their parents and its social consequences.

filibeg, fillibeg, *or* **philibeg** ('fɪlɪˌbɛg) *n.* the kilt worn by Scottish Highlanders. [C18: from Scottish Gaelic *fēileadhbeag,* from *fēileadh* kilt + *beag* small]

filibuster ('fɪlɪˌbʌstə) *n.* **1.** the process or an instance of obstructing legislation by means of long speeches and other delaying tactics. **2.** Also called: **filibusterer.** a legislator who engages in such obstruction. **3.** a buccaneer, freebooter, or irregular military adventurer, esp. a revolutionary in a foreign country. ~*vb.* **4.** to obstruct (legislation) with delaying tactics. **5.** *(intr.)* to engage in unlawful and private military action. [C16: from Spanish *filibustero,* from French *flibustier,* probably from Dutch *vrijbuiter* pirate, literally: one plundering freely; see FREEBOOTER] —'**filiˌbusterer** *n.* —'**filiˌbusterism** *n.*

filicide ('fɪlɪˌsaɪd) *n.* **1.** the act of killing one's own son or daughter. **2.** a person who does this. [C17: from Latin *fīlius* son or *fīlia* daughter + -CIDE] —ˌ**fili'cidal** *adj.*

filiform ('fɪlɪˌfɔːm, 'faɪ-) *adj. Biology.* having the form of a thread. [C18: from Latin *fīlum* thread]

filigree ('fɪlɪˌgriː), **filagree,** *or* **fillagree** *n.* **1.** delicate ornamental work of twisted gold, silver, or other wire. **2.** any fanciful delicate ornamentation. ~*adj.* **3.** made of or as if with filigree. ~*vb.* **-grees, -greeing, -greed.** **4.** *(tr.)* to decorate with or as if with filigree. [C17: from earlier *filigreen,* from French *filigrane,* from Latin *fīlum* thread + *grānum* GRAIN]

filing clerk *n.* an employee who maintains office files.

filings ('faɪlɪŋz) *pl. n.* shavings or particles removed by a file: *iron filings.*

Filipino (ˌfɪlɪ'piːnəʊ) *n., pl.* **-nos.** **1.** a native or inhabitant of the Philippines, a republic in SE Asia. **2.** another name for **Tagalog.** ~*adj.* **3.** of or relating to the Philippines or their inhabitants.

fill (fɪl) *vb. (mainly tr.;* often foll. by *up)* **1.** *(also intr.)* to make or become full: *to fill up a bottle; the bath fills in two minutes.* **2.** to occupy the whole of: *the party filled two floors of the house.* **3.** to plug (a gap, crevice, cavity, etc.). **4.** to meet (a requirement or need) satisfactorily. **5.** to cover (a page or blank space) with writing, drawing, etc. **6.** to hold and perform the duties of (an office or position). **7.** to appoint or elect an occupant to (an office or position). **8.** *Building trades.* to build up (ground) with fill. **9.** *(also intr.)* to swell or cause to swell with wind, as in manoeuvring the sails of a sailing vessel. **10.** to increase the bulk of by adding an inferior substance. **11.** *Poker.* to complete (a full house, etc.) by drawing the cards needed. **12.** *Chiefly U.S. and Canadian.* to put together the necessary materials for (a prescription or order). **13. fill the bill.** *Informal.* to serve or perform adequately. ~*n.* **14.** material such as gravel, stones, etc., used to bring an area of ground up to a required level. **15. one's fill.** the quantity needed to satisfy one: *to eat your fill.* ~See also **fill away, fill in, fill out, fill up.** [Old English *fyllan;* related to Old Frisian *fella,* Old Norse *fylla,* Gothic *fulljan,* Old High German *fullen;* see FULL[1], FULFIL]

fillagree ('fɪləˌgriː) *n., adj., vb.* a less common variant of **filigree.**

fill away *vb. (intr., adv.) Nautical.* to cause a vessel's sails to fill, either by steering it off the wind or by bracing the yards.

fille de joie *French.* (fij də ʒwa) *n., pl.* ***filles de joie*** (fij də ʒwa). a prostitute. [girl of pleasure]

filled gold *n.* another name (esp. U.S.) for **rolled gold.**

filler ('fɪlə) *n.* **1.** a person or thing that fills. **2.** an object or substance used to add weight or size to something or to fill in a gap. **3.** a paste, used for filling in cracks, holes, etc., in a surface before painting. **4.** *Architect.* a small joist inserted between and supported by two beams. **5. a.** the inner portion of a cigar. **b.** the cut tobacco for making cigarettes. **6.** *Journalism.* articles, photographs, etc., to fill space between more important articles in the layout of a newspaper or magazine. **7.** *Informal.* something, such as a musical selection, to fill time in a broadcast or stage presentation. **8.** a small radio or television transmitter used to fill a gap in coverage.

filler cap *n.* a device sealing the filling pipe to the petrol tank in a motor vehicle.

filler metal *n.* metal supplied in the form of a welding rod, sometimes flux coated, melted by an arc or a flame into a joint between components to be joined.

fillet ('fɪlɪt) *n.* **1. a.** Also called: **fillet steak.** a strip of boneless meat, esp. the undercut of a sirloin of beef. **b.** the boned side of a fish. **c.** the white meat of breast and wing of a chicken. **2.** a narrow strip of any material. **3.** a thin strip of ribbon, lace, etc., worn in the hair or around the neck. **4.** a narrow flat moulding, esp. one between other mouldings. **5.** a narrow band between two adjacent flutings on the shaft of a column. **6.** Also called: **fillet weld.** a narrow strip of welded metal used to join steel members at right angles. **7.** *Heraldry.* a horizontal division of a shield, one quarter of the depth of the chief. **8.** Also called: **listel, list.** the top member of a cornice. **9.** *Anatomy.* a band of sensory nerve fibres in the brain connected to the thalamus. Technical name: **lemniscus.** **10. a.** a narrow decorative line, impressed on the cover of a book. **b.** a wheel tool used to impress such lines. **11.** another name for **fairing**[1]. ~*vb. (tr.)* **-lets, -leting, -leted.** **12.** to cut or prepare (meat or fish) as a fillet. **13.** to cut fillets from (meat or fish). **14.** to bind or decorate with or as if with a fillet. ~Also (for senses 1-3): **filet.** [C14: from Old French *filet,* from *fil* thread, from Latin *fīlum*]

fill in *vb. (adv.)* **1.** *(tr.)* to complete (a form, drawing, etc.). **2.** *(intr.)* to act as a substitute: *a girl is filling in while the typist is away.* **3.** *(tr.)* to put material into (a hole or cavity), esp. so as to make it level with a surface. **4.** *(tr.) Informal.* to inform with facts or news. **5.** *(tr.) Brit. slang.* to attack and injure severely. ~*n.* **fill-in.** **6.** a substitute. **7.** *U.S. informal.* a briefing to complete one's understanding.

filling ('fɪlɪŋ) *n.* **1.** the substance or thing used to fill a space or container: *pie filling.* **2.** *Dentistry.* any of various substances (metal, plastic, etc.) for inserting into the prepared cavity of a tooth. **3.** *Textiles.* another term for **weft.** ~*adj.* **4.** (of food or a meal) substantial and satisfying.

filling station *n.* a place where petrol and other supplies for motorists are sold.

fillip ('fɪlɪp) *n.* **1.** something that adds stimulation or enjoyment. **2.** the action of holding a finger towards the palm with the thumb and suddenly releasing it outwards to produce a snapping sound. **3.** a quick blow or tap made by a finger snapped in this way. ~*vb.* **4.** *(tr.)* to stimulate or excite. **5.** *(tr.)* to strike or project sharply with a fillip. **6.** *(intr.)* to make a fillip. [C15 *philippe,* of imitative origin]

fillister, filister, *or* **fillester** ('fɪlɪstə) *n.* **1.** Also called: **fillister plane.** an adjustable plane for cutting rabbets, grooves, etc. **2.** Also called: **sash fillister.** a rabbet or groove, esp. one in a window sash bar for a pane of glass. [C19: of unknown origin]

fill light *n. Photog.* a light that supplements the key light without changing its character, used esp. to lighten shadows.

fill out *vb. (adv.)* **1.** to make or become fuller, thicker, or rounder: *her figure has filled out since her marriage.* **2.** to make more substantial: *the writers were asked to fill their stories out.* **3.** *(tr.) U.S. and Canadian.* to complete (a form, application, etc.).

fill up *vb. (adv.)* **1.** *(tr.)* to complete (a form, application, etc.). **2.** to make or become completely full. ~*n.* **fill-up.** **3.** the act of filling something completely, esp. the petrol tank of a car.

filly ('fɪlɪ) *n., pl.* **-lies.** **1.** a female horse or pony under the age of four. **2.** *Informal, rare.* a spirited girl or young woman. [C15: from Old Norse *fylja;* related to Old High German *fulihha;* see FOAL]

film (fɪlm) *n.* **1. a.** a sequence of images of moving objects photographed by a camera and providing the optical illusion of continuous movement when projected onto a screen. **b.** a form of entertainment, information, etc., composed of such a sequence of images and shown in a cinema, etc. **c.** *(as modifier): film techniques.* **2.** a thin flexible strip of cellulose coated with a photographic emulsion, used to make negatives and transparencies. **3.** a thin coating or layer. **4.** a thin sheet of any material, as of plastic for packaging. **5.** a fine haze, mist, or blur. **6.** a gauzy web of filaments or fine threads. **7.** *Pathol.* an abnormally opaque tissue, such as the cornea in some eye diseases. ~*vb.* **8. a.** to photograph with a cine camera. **b.** to make a film of (a screenplay, event, etc.). **9.** (often foll. by *over*) to cover or become covered or coated with a film. [Old English *filmen* membrane; related to Old Frisian *filmene,* Greek *pelma* sole of the foot; see FELL[4]] —'**filmic** *adj.*

film colour *n. Physiol.* a misty appearance produced when no lines or edges are present in the visual field.

film library *n.* a collection of films as archives or for loan or hire.

film noir (nwɑː) *n.* a gangster thriller, made esp. in the 1940s in Hollywood characterized by contrasty lighting and often somewhat impenetrable plots. [C20: French, literally: black film]

filmography (fɪl'mɒgrəfɪ) *n.* **1.** a list of the films made by a particular director, actor, etc. **2.** any writing that deals with films or the cinema.

film pack *n.* a box containing several sheets of film for use in a plate camera.

film set *n.* the scenery and props as arranged for shooting a film.

filmset ('fɪlmˌsɛt) *vb.* **-sets, -setting, -set.** *(tr.) Brit.* to set (type matter) by filmsetting. —'**filmˌsetter** *n.*

filmsetting ('fɪlmˌsɛtɪŋ) *n. Brit., printing.* typesetting by exposing type characters onto photographic film from which printing plates are made. U.S. and Canadian name: **photocomposition, photosetting.**

film speed *n.* **1.** the sensitivity to light of a photographic film, usually specified in terms of an ASA or DIN rating. **2.** the rate at which the film passes through a motion picture camera or projector.

film star *n.* a popular film actor or actress.

film strip *n.* a strip of film composed of different images projected separately as slides.
filmy ('fɪlmɪ) *adj.* **filmier, filmiest.** **1.** composed of or resembling film; transparent or gauzy. **2.** covered with or as if with a film; hazy; blurred. —'**filmily** *adv.* —'**filminess** *n.*
filmy fern *n.* any fern of the family *Hymenophyllaceae,* growing in humid regions and having thin translucent leaves.
filo ('fi:ləʊ) *n.* a type of Greek flaky pastry in very thin sheets. [C20: Modern Greek *phullon* leaf]
Filofax ('faɪləʊˌfæks) *n. Trademark.* a type of loose-leaf ring binder with sets of different-coloured paper, used as a portable personal filing system, including appointments, addresses, etc.
filoplume ('fɪləˌplu:m, 'faɪ-) *n. Ornithol.* any of the hairlike feathers that lack vanes and occur between the contour feathers. [C19: from New Latin *filoplūma,* from Latin *fīlum* thread + *plūma* feather]
filose ('faɪləʊs, -ləʊz) *adj. Biology.* resembling or possessing a thread or threadlike process: *filose pseudopodia.* [C19: from Latin *fīlum* thread]
filoselle (ˌfɪləʊ'sɛl) *n.* soft silk thread, used esp. for embroidery. [C17: from French: silk, silkworm, from Italian *filosello,* perhaps from Latin *folliculus* little bag]
fils[1] *French.* (fis) an addition to a French surname to specify the son rather than the father of the same name: *a book by Dumas fils.* Compare **père.** [French: son]
fils[2] (fɪls) *or* **fil** (fɪl) *n., pl.* **fils.** a fractional monetary unit of Iraq, Jordan, Kuwait, and Southern Yemen worth one thousandth of a dinar. [from Arabic]
filter ('fɪltə) *n.* **1.** a porous substance, such as paper or sand, that allows fluid to pass but retains suspended solid particles: used to clean fluids or collect solid particles. **2.** any device containing such a porous substance for separating suspensions from fluids. **3.** any of various porous substances built into the mouth end of a cigarette or cigar for absorbing impurities such as tar. **4.** any electronic, optical, or acoustic device that blocks signals or radiations of certain frequencies while allowing others to pass. See also **band-pass filter.** **5.** any transparent disc of gelatin or glass used to eliminate or reduce the intensity of given frequencies from the light leaving a lamp, entering a camera, etc. **6.** *Brit.* a traffic signal at a road junction consisting of a green arrow which when illuminated permits vehicles to turn either left or right when the main signals are red. ~*vb.* **7.** (often foll. by *out*) to remove or separate (suspended particles, wavelengths of radiation, etc.) from (a liquid, gas, radiation, etc.) by the action of a filter. **8.** (*tr.*) to obtain by filtering. **9.** (*intr.*; foll. by *through*) to pass (through a filter or something like a filter): *dust filtered through the screen.* **10.** (*intr.*) to flow slowly; trickle. [C16 *filtre,* from Medieval Latin *filtrum* piece of felt used as a filter, of Germanic origin; see FELT[2]]
filterable ('fɪltərəbᵊl) *or* **filtrable** ('fɪltrəbᵊl) *adj.* **1.** capable of being filtered. **2.** (of most viruses and certain bacteria) capable of passing through the pores of a fine filter. —ˌ**filtera'bility** *or* '**filterableness** *n.*
filter bed *n.* **1.** a layer of sand or gravel in a tank or reservoir through which a liquid is passed so as to purify it. Compare **bacteria bed.** **2.** any layer of material through which a liquid is passed so as to filter it.
filter cake *n. Chem.* the solid material accumulated by a filter press.
filter feeding *n. Zoology.* a method of feeding occurring in some aquatic animals, such as planktonic invertebrates and whalebone whales, in which minute food particles are filtered from the surrounding water. —**filter feeder** *n.*
filter out *or* **through** *vb.* (*intr., adv.*) to become known gradually; leak: *rumours filtered out about the divorce.*
filter paper *n.* a porous paper used for filtering liquids.
filter press *n.* an apparatus used for filtration consisting of a set of frames covered with filter cloth on both sides, between which the liquid to be filtered is pumped.
filter pump *n.* a vacuum pump used to assist laboratory filtrations in which a jet of water inside a glass tube entrains air molecules from the system to be evacuated.
filter tip *n.* **1.** an attachment to the mouth end of a cigarette for trapping impurities such as tar during smoking. It consists of any of various dense porous substances, such as cotton. **2.** a cigarette having such an attachment. —'**filter-**ˌ**tipped** *adj.*
filth (fɪlθ) *n.* **1.** foul or disgusting dirt; refuse. **2.** extreme physical or moral uncleanliness; pollution. **3.** vulgarity or obscenity, as in language. **4.** *Slang.* **the.** the police. [Old English *fӯlth;* related to Old Saxon, Old High German *fūlitha;* see FOUL, DEFILE]
filthy ('fɪlθɪ) *adj.* **filthier, filthiest.** **1.** characterized by or full of filth; very dirty or obscene. **2.** offensive or vicious: *that was a filthy trick to play.* **3.** *Informal, chiefly Brit.* extremely unpleasant: *filthy weather.* ~*adv.* **4.** extremely; disgustingly: *filthy rich.* —'**filthily** *adv.* —'**filthiness** *n.*
filtrate ('fɪltreɪt) *n.* **1.** a liquid or gas that has been filtered. ~*vb.* **2.** another name for **filter** (sense 7). [C17: from Medieval Latin *filtrāre* to FILTER] —'**filtratable** *adj.*
filtration (fɪl'treɪʃən) *n.* the act or process of filtering.
filum ('faɪləm) *n., pl.* **-la** (-lə). *Anatomy.* any threadlike structure or part. [Latin: thread, cord, fibre]
fimble ('fɪmbᵊl) *n.* the male plant of the hemp, which matures before the female plant. [C15: from Middle Dutch *femeel,* from Old French *chanvre femeile* female hemp, from *chanvre* hemp + *femelle* FEMALE]
fimbria ('fɪmbrɪə) *n., pl.* **-briae** (-brɪˌi:). *Anatomy.* a fringe or fringelike margin or border, esp. at the opening of the Fallopian tubes. [C18: from Late Latin, from Latin *fimbriae* threads, shreds] —'**fimbrial** *adj.*
fimbriate ('fɪmbrɪɪt, -ˌeɪt), **fimbriated,** *or* **fimbrillate** ('fɪmbrɪlɪt, -ˌleɪt) *adj.* having a fringed margin, as some petals, antennae, etc. —ˌ**fimbri'ation** *n.*
fimicolous (fɪ'mɪkələs) *adj. Botany.* (esp. of fungi) growing in or on dung. [C19: from Latin *fimus* dung + *colere* to inhabit]
fin[1] (fɪn) *n.* **1.** any of the firm appendages that are the organs of locomotion and balance in fishes and some other aquatic animals. Most fishes have paired and unpaired fins, the former corresponding to the limbs of higher vertebrates. **2.** a part or appendage that resembles a fin. **3. a.** *Brit.* a vertical surface to which the rudder is attached, usually placed at the rear of an aeroplane to give stability about the vertical axis. U.S. name: **vertical stabilizer. b.** a tail surface fixed to a rocket or missile to give stability. **4.** *Nautical.* a fixed or adjustable blade projecting under water from the hull of a vessel to give it stability or control. **5.** a projecting rib to dissipate heat from the surface of an engine cylinder, motor casing, or radiator. **6.** (*often pl.*) another name for **flipper** (sense 2). ~*vb.* **fins, finning, finned.** **7.** (*tr.*) to provide with fins. **8.** (*tr.*) to remove the fins from (a dead fish). **9.** (*intr.*) (esp. of a whale) to agitate the fins violently in the water. [Old English *finn;* related to Middle Dutch *vinne,* Old Swedish *fina,* Latin *pinna* wing] —'**finless** *adj.*
fin[2] (fɪn) *n. U.S. slang.* a five-dollar bill. [from Yiddish *finf* five, ultimately from Old High German *funf, finf*]
fin. *abbrev. for:* **1.** finance. **2.** financial. **3.** finish.
Fin. *abbrev. for:* **1.** Finland. **2.** Finnish.
finable *or* **fineable** ('faɪnəbᵊl) *adj.* liable to a fine. —'**finableness** *or* '**fineableness** *n.*
finagle (fɪ'neɪgᵊl) *vb. Informal.* **1.** (*tr.*) to get or achieve by trickery, craftiness, or persuasion; wangle. **2.** to use trickery or craftiness on (a person). [C20: probably changed from dialect *fainaigue*] —**fi'nagler** *n.*
final ('faɪnᵊl) *adj.* **1.** of or occurring at the end; concluding; ultimate; last. **2.** having no possibility for further discussion, action, or change; conclusive; decisive: *a final decree of judgment.* **3.** relating to or constituting an end or purpose: *a final clause may be introduced by "in order to".* **4.** *Phonetics.* at the end of a word: *"cat" has a final "t".* Compare **medial** (sense 1), **initial** (sense 1). **5.** *Music.* another word for **perfect** (sense 9b.). ~*n.* **6.** a terminal or last thing; end. **7.** a deciding contest between the winners of previous rounds in a competition. **8.** *Music.* the tonic note of a church mode. ~See also **finals.** [C14: from Latin *fīnālis,* from *fīnis* limit, boundary]
final cause *n. Philosophy.* the end or purpose of a thing or process, as opposed to its efficient cause. See **cause** (sense 7).
finale (fɪ'nɑ:lɪ) *n.* **1.** the concluding part of any performance or presentation. **2.** the closing section or movement of a musical composition. [C18: from Italian, n. use of adj. *finale,* from Latin *fīnālis* FINAL]
finalism ('faɪnəˌlɪzəm) *n. Philosophy.* the doctrine that final causes determine the course of all events. —ˌ**fina'listic** *adj.*
finalist ('faɪnəlɪst) *n.* a contestant who has reached the last and decisive stage of a sports or other competition.
finality (faɪ'nælɪtɪ) *n., pl.* **-ties.** **1.** the condition or quality of being final or settled; conclusiveness: *the finality of death.* **2.** a final or conclusive act. **3.** *Metaphysics.* the doctrine of the efficacy of final causes. Compare **teleology.**
finalize *or* **finalise** ('faɪnəˌlaɪz) *vb.* **1.** (*tr.*) to put into final form; settle: *to finalize plans for the merger.* **2.** (*intr.*) to complete arrangements or negotiations; reach agreement on a transaction. —ˌ**finali'zation** *or* ˌ**finali'sation** *n.*
▷**Usage.** Although *finalize* has been in widespread use for some time, it carries strong associations of bureaucratic or commercial jargon for many careful speakers and writers, who usually prefer *complete, conclude,* or *make final,* esp. in formal contexts.
finally ('faɪnəlɪ) *adv.* **1.** after a long delay; at last; eventually. **2.** at the end or final point; lastly. **3.** completely; conclusively; irrevocably. ~*sentence connector.* **4.** in the end; lastly: *finally, he put his tie on.* **5.** as the last or final point: linking what follows with the previous statements, as in a speech or argument.
finals ('faɪnᵊlz) *pl. n.* **1.** the deciding part or parts of a sports or other competition. **2.** *Education.* the last examination series in an academic or professional course.
finance (fɪ'næns, 'faɪnæns) *n.* **1.** the system of money, credit, etc., esp. with respect to government revenues and expenditures. **2.** funds or the provision of funds. **3.** (*pl.*) funds; financial condition. ~*vb.* **4.** (*tr.*) to provide or obtain funds, capital, or credit for. **5.** (*intr.*) to manage or secure financial resources. [C14: from Old French, from *finer* to end, settle by payment]
finance bill *n.* a legislative bill providing money for the public treasury.
finance company *or* **house** *n.* an enterprise engaged in the loan of money against collateral or speculatively to manufacturers and retailers, esp. one specializing in the financing of hire-purchase contracts.
financial (fɪ'nænʃəl, faɪ-) *adj.* **1.** of or relating to finance or finances. **2.** of or relating to persons who manage money, capi-

tal, or credit. 3. *Austral. and N.Z. informal.* having money; in funds. 4. *Austral. and N.Z.* (of a club member) fully paid-up. —**fi'nancially** *adv.*

Financial Ombudsman *n.* any of three British ombudsmen: the **Banking Ombudsman**, set up in 1986 to investigate complaints from bank customers; the **Building Societies Ombudsman**, set up in 1987 to investigate complaints from building society customers; and the **Insurance Ombudsman**, set up in 1981 to investigate complaints by policyholders; since 1988 this ombudsman has also operated a **Unit Trust Ombudsman** scheme.

Financial Times Industrial Ordinary Share Index *n.* an index of share prices produced by the *Financial Times,* designed to reflect general price trends: based on the average price of thirty British shares.

Financial Times Stock Exchange 100 Index *n.* an index of share prices produced by the *Financial Times* based on an average of 100 securities and giving the best indication of daily movements. Abbrev.: **FTSE 100 Index.** Informal name: **Footsie.**

financial year *n. Brit.* 1. any annual period at the end of which a firm's accounts are made up. 2. the annual period ending April 5, over which Budget estimates are made by the British Government and which functions as the income-tax year. ~U.S. and Canadian equivalent: **fiscal year.**

financier (fɪ'nænsɪə, faɪ-) *n.* a person who is engaged or skilled in large-scale financial operations.

financing gap *n.* the difference between a country's requirements for foreign exchange to finance its debts and imports and its income from overseas.

finback ('fɪn,bæk) *n.* another name for **rorqual.**

finch (fɪntʃ) *n.* 1. any songbird of the family *Fringillidae,* having a short stout bill for feeding on seeds and, in most species, a bright plumage in the male. Common examples are the goldfinch, bullfinch, chaffinch, siskin, and canary. 2. any of various similar or related birds. [Old English *finc;* related to Old High German *finko,* Middle Dutch *vinker,* Greek *spingos*]

find (faɪnd) *vb.* **finds, finding, found** (faʊnd). (*mainly tr.*) 1. to meet with or discover by chance. 2. to discover or obtain, esp. by search or effort: *to find happiness.* 3. (*may take a clause as object*) to become aware of; realize: *he found that nobody knew.* 4. (*may take a clause as object*) to regard as being; consider: *I find this wine a little sour.* 5. to look for and point out (something to be criticized): *to find fault.* 6. (*also intr.*) *Law.* to determine an issue after judicial inquiry and pronounce a verdict (upon): *the court found the accused guilty.* 7. to regain (something lost or not functioning): *to find one's tongue.* 8. to reach (a target): *the bullet found its mark.* 9. to provide, esp. with difficulty: *we'll find room for you too.* 10. to be able to pay: *I can't find that amount of money.* 11. **find oneself.** to realize and accept one's real character; discover one's true vocation. 12. **find one's feet.** to become capable or confident, as in a new job. ~*n.* 13. a person, thing, etc., that is found, esp. a valuable or fortunate discovery. [Old English *findan;* related to Old Norse *finna,* Gothic *finthan,* Old High German *fintan* to find) —'**findable** *adj.*

finder ('faɪndə) *n.* 1. a person or thing that finds. 2. *Physics.* a small low-power wide-angle telescope fitted to a more powerful larger telescope, used to locate celestial objects to be studied by the larger instrument. 3. *Photog.* short for **viewfinder.** 4. **finders keepers.** *Informal.* whoever finds something has the right to keep it.

fin de siècle *French.* (fɛ̃ də sjɛklə) *n.* 1. the end of the 19th century, when traditional social, moral, and artistic values were in transition. ~*adj.* ***fin-de-siècle.*** 2. of or relating to the close of the 19th century. 3. decadent, esp. in artistic tastes.

finding ('faɪndɪŋ) *n.* 1. a thing that is found or discovered. 2. *Law.* the conclusion reached after a judicial inquiry; verdict. 3. (*pl.*) *U.S.* the tools and equipment of an artisan.

find out *vb.* (*adv.*) 1. to gain knowledge of (something); learn: *he found out what he wanted.* 2. to detect the crime, deception, etc., of (someone).

find the lady *n.* another name for **three-card trick.**

fine[1] (faɪn) *adj.* 1. excellent or choice in quality; very good of its kind: *a fine speech.* 2. superior in skill, ability, or accomplishment: *a fine violinist.* 3. (of weather) clear and dry. 4. enjoyable or satisfying: *a fine time.* 5. (*postpositive*) *Informal.* quite well; in satisfactory health: *I feel fine.* 6. satisfactory; acceptable: *that's fine by me.* 7. of delicate composition or careful workmanship: *fine crystal.* 8. (of precious metals) pure or having a high or specified degree of purity: *fine silver; gold 98 per cent fine.* 9. subtle in perception; discriminating: *a fine eye for antique brasses.* 10. abstruse or subtle: *a fine point in argument.* 11. very thin or slender: *fine hair.* 12. very small: *fine dust; fine print.* 13. (of edges, blades, etc.) sharp; keen. 14. ornate, showy, or smart. 15. good-looking; handsome: *a fine young woman.* 16. polished, elegant, or refined: *a fine gentleman.* 17. morally upright and commendable: *a fine man.* 18. *Cricket.* (of a fielding position) oblique to and behind the wicket: *fine leg.* 19. (*prenominal*) *Informal.* disappointing or terrible: *a fine mess.* ~*adv.* 20. *Informal.* quite well; all right: *that suits me fine.* 21. a nonstandard word for **finely.** 22. *Billiards, etc.* (of a stroke on the cue ball) so as to merely brush the object ball. 23. **cut it fine.** to allow little margin of time, space, etc. ~*vb.* 24. to make or become finer; refine. 25. (often foll. by *down* or *away*) to make or become smaller. 26. (*tr.*) to clarify (wine, etc.) by adding finings. 27. (*tr.*) *Billiards.* to hit (a cue ball) fine. 28. (*intr.;* foll by *up*) *Austral. and N.Z. informal.* (of the weather) to become fine. [C13: from Old French *fin,* from Latin *fīnis* end, boundary, as in *fīnis honōrum* the highest degree of honour]

fine[2] (faɪn) *n.* 1. a certain amount of money exacted as a penalty: *a parking fine.* 2. a payment made by a tenant at the start of his tenancy to reduce his subsequent rent; premium. 3. *Feudal law.* a sum of money paid by a man to his lord, esp. for a privilege. 4. a method of transferring land in England by bringing a fictitious law suit: abolished 1833. 5. *Archaic.* a penalty of any sort. 6. **in fine. a.** in short; briefly. **b.** in conclusion; finally. ~*vb.* 7. (*tr.*) to impose a fine on. [C12 (in the sense: conclusion, settlement): from Old French *fin;* see FINE[1]]

fine[3] ('fiːneɪ) *n. Music.* 1. the point at which a piece is to end, usually after a *da capo* or *dal segno.* 2. an ending or finale. [Italian, from Latin *fīnis* end]

fine[4] *French.* (fin) *n.* brandy of ordinary quality. [literally: fine]

fineable ('faɪnəbᵊl) *adj.* a variant spelling of **finable.** —'**fineableness** *n.*

fine art *n.* 1. art produced chiefly for its aesthetic value, as opposed to applied art. 2. (*often pl.*) Also called: **beaux arts.** any of the fields in which such art is produced, such as painting, sculpture, and engraving.

fine-cut *adj.* (of tobacco) finely cut or shredded.

fine-draw *vb.* **-draws, -drawing, -drew, -drawn.** (*tr.*) 1. to sew together so finely that the join is scarcely noticeable. 2. to carry out the last drawing-out operation on (wire, tube, etc.) to reduce its diameter.

fine-drawn *adj.* 1. (of arguments, distinctions, etc.) precise or subtle. 2. (of wire) drawn out until very fine; attenuated. 3. (of features) delicate or refined.

fine-grain *adj. Photog.* having or producing an image with grain of inconspicuous size: *a fine-grain image; a fine-grain developer.*

fine-grained *adj.* (of wood, leather, etc.) having a fine smooth even grain.

fine leg *n. Cricket.* **a.** a fielding position between long leg and square leg. **b.** a fielder in this position.

finely ('faɪnlɪ) *adv.* 1. into small pieces; minutely. 2. precisely or subtly. 3. splendidly or delicately.

fineness ('faɪnnɪs) *n.* 1. the state or quality of being fine. 2. a measurement of the purity of precious metal, expressed as the number of parts per thousand that is precious metal.

fine print *n.* matter set in small type, as in a contract, esp. considered as containing unfavourable conditions that the signer might overlook. Also called: **small print.**

finery[1] ('faɪnərɪ) *n.* elaborate or showy decoration, esp. clothing and jewellery.

finery[2] ('faɪnərɪ) *n., pl.* **-eries.** a hearth for converting cast iron into wrought iron. [C17: from Old French *finerie,* from *finer* to refine; see FINE[1]]

fines herbes (*French* finz ɛrb) *pl. n.* a mixture of finely chopped herbs, used to flavour omelettes, salads, etc.

finespun ('faɪn'spʌn) *adj.* 1. spun or drawn out to a fine thread. 2. excessively subtle or refined; not practical.

finesse (fɪ'nɛs) *n.* 1. elegant skill in style or performance. 2. subtlety and tact in handling difficult situations. 3. *Bridge, whist.* an attempt to win a trick when opponents hold a high card in the suit led by playing a lower card, hoping the opponent who has already played holds the missing card. 4. a trick, artifice, or strategy. ~*vb.* 5. to manage or bring about with finesse. 6. to play (a card) as a finesse. [C15: from Old French, from *fin* fine, delicate; see FINE[1]]

fine structure *n.* the splitting of a spectral line into two or more closely spaced components as a result of interaction between the spin and orbital angular momenta of the atomic electrons. Compare **hyperfine structure.**

fine-tooth comb *or* **fine-toothed comb** *n.* 1. a comb with fine teeth set closely together. 2. **go over** (*or* **through**) **with a fine-tooth(ed) comb.** to examine very thoroughly.

fine-tune *vb.* (*tr.*) to make fine adjustments to (something) in order to obtain optimum performance.

finfoot ('fɪn,fʊt) *n., pl.* **-foots.** any aquatic bird of the tropical and subtropical family *Heliornithidae,* having broadly lobed toes, a long slender head and neck, and pale brown plumage: order *Gruiformes* (cranes, rails etc.). Also called: **sungrebe.**

finger ('fɪŋgə) *n.* 1. **a.** any of the digits of the hand, often excluding the thumb. Technical name: **digitus manus. b.** (*as modifier*): *a finger bowl.* **c.** (*in combination*): *a fingernail.* Related adj.: **digital.** 2. the part of a glove made to cover a finger. 3. something that resembles a finger in shape or function: *a finger of land.* 4. Also called: **digit.** the length or width of a finger used as a unit of measurement. 5. a quantity of liquid in a glass, etc., as deep as a finger is wide; tot. 6. a projecting machine part, esp. one serving as an indicator. 7. **burn one's fingers.** to suffer as a result of incautious or meddlesome action. 8. **get** *or* **pull one's finger out.** *Brit. informal.* to begin or speed up activity, esp. after initial delay or slackness. 9. **have a** (*or* **one's**) **finger in the pie. a.** to have an interest in or take part in some activity. **b.** to meddle or interfere. 10. **lay a finger on.** (*usually negative*) to harm. 11. **lay** *or* **put one's finger on.** to indicate, identify, or locate accurately. 12. **not lift** (*or* **raise**) **a finger.** (*foll. by an infinitive*) not to make any effort (to do something). 13. **let slip through one's fingers.** to allow to escape;

miss narrowly. **14. twist** *or* **wrap around one's little finger.** to have easy and complete control or influence over. **15. put the finger on.** *Informal.* **a.** to inform on or identify, esp. for the police. **b.** to choose (the victim or location of an intended crime). ~*vb.* **16.** (*tr.*) to touch or manipulate with the fingers; handle. **17.** (*tr.*) *Informal.* to put the finger on (see sense 15). **18.** (*intr.*) to extend like a finger. **19.** to use one's fingers in playing (an instrument, such as a piano or clarinet). **20.** to indicate on (a composition or part) the fingering required by a pianist, harpsichordist, etc. **21.** (*tr.; usually passive*) to arrange the keys of (a clarinet, flute, etc.) for playing in a certain way. [Old English; related to Old Norse *fingr,* Gothic *figgrs,* Old High German *fingar;* see FIVE, FIST] —'**fingerer** *n.* —'**fingerless** *adj.*

fingerboard ('fɪŋɡəˌbɔːd) *n.* the long strip of hard wood on a violin, guitar, or related stringed instrument upon which the strings are stopped by the fingers.

finger bowl *n.* a small bowl filled with water for rinsing the fingers at the table after a meal.

fingerbreadth ('fɪŋɡəˌbrɛdθ, -ˌbrɛtθ) *or* **finger's breadth** *n.* the width of a finger, used as an indication of length.

finger buffet ('bʊfeɪ) *n.* a buffet meal at which food that may be picked up with the fingers (**finger food**), such as canapés or vol-au-vents, is served.

fingered ('fɪŋɡəd) *adj.* **1.** marked or dirtied by handling. **2. a.** having a finger or fingers. **b.** (*in combination*): *nine-fingered; red-fingered.* **3.** (of a musical part) having numerals indicating the necessary fingering.

fingering[1] ('fɪŋɡərɪŋ) *n.* **1.** the technique or art of using one's fingers in playing a musical instrument, esp. the piano. **2.** the numerals in a musical part indicating this.

fingering[2] ('fɪŋɡərɪŋ) *n.* fine wool for knitting. [C17: from earlier *fingram,* perhaps from Old French *fin grain* fine grain]

fingerling ('fɪŋɡəlɪŋ) *n.* **1.** a very young fish, esp. the parr of salmon or trout. **2.** a diminutive creature or object.

fingermark ('fɪŋɡəˌmɑːk) *n.* a mark left by dirty or greasy fingers on paintwork, walls, etc.

fingernail ('fɪŋɡəˌneɪl) *n.* a thin horny translucent plate covering part of the dorsal surface of the end joint of each finger.

finger painting *n.* **1.** the process or art of painting with **finger paints** of starch, glycerin, and pigments, using the fingers, hand, or arm. **2.** a painting made in this way.

finger post *n.* a signpost showing a pointing finger or hand.

fingerprint ('fɪŋɡəˌprɪnt) *n.* **1.** an impression of the pattern of ridges on the palmar surface of the end joint of each finger and thumb. **2.** any identifying characteristic. **3.** *Biochem.* the pattern of fragments obtained when a protein is digested by a proteolytic enzyme, usually observed following two-dimensional separation by chromatography and electrophoresis. ~*vb.* **4.** (*tr.*) to take an inked impression of the fingerprints of (a person). **5.** to take a sample of (a person's) DNA.

fingerstall ('fɪŋɡəˌstɔːl) *n.* a protective covering for a finger. Also called: **cot, fingertip.**

finger tight *adj.* made as tight as possible by hand.

fingertip ('fɪŋɡəˌtɪp) *n.* **1.** the end joint or tip of a finger. **2.** another term for **fingerstall. 3. at one's fingertips.** readily available and within one's mental grasp.

finger trouble *n. Computer technol.* trouble caused by operator error, such as striking the wrong key.

finger wave *n. Hairdressing.* a wave set in wet hair by using fingers and comb only.

Fingo ('fɪŋɡəʊ) *n., pl.* **-go** *or* **-gos.** a member of a Xhosa-speaking people settled in southern Africa in the Ciskei and Transkei: originally refugees from the Zulu wars of conquest.

finial ('faɪnɪəl) *n.* **1.** an ornament on top of a spire, gable, etc., esp. in the form of a foliated fleur-de-lis. **2.** an ornament at the top of a piece of furniture, etc. [C14: from *finial* (adj.), variant of FINAL] —'**finialed** *adj.*

finical ('fɪnɪkᵊl) *adj.* another word for **finicky.** [C16: probably from slang FINE[1] + -ICAL] —ˌ**fini'cality** *n.* —'**finically** *adv.* —'**finicalness** *n.*

finicky ('fɪnɪkɪ) *or* **finicking** *adj.* **1.** excessively particular, as in tastes or standards; fussy. **2.** full of trivial detail; overelaborate. [C19: from FINICAL]

fining ('faɪnɪŋ) *n.* **1.** the process of removing undissolved gas bubbles from molten glass. **2.** the process of clarifying liquors by the addition of a coagulant. **3.** (*pl.*) a substance, such as isinglass, added to wine, beer, etc., to clarify it. [C17: from FINE[1] (in the sense: to clarify, refine)]

finis ('fɪnɪs) *n.* the end; finish: used at the end of books, films, etc. [C15: from Latin]

finish ('fɪnɪʃ) *vb.* (*mainly tr.*) **1.** to bring to an end; complete, conclude, or stop. **2.** (*intr.;* sometimes foll. by *up*) to be at or come to the end; use up. **3.** to bring to a desired or complete condition. **4.** to put a particular surface texture on (wood, cloth, etc.). **5.** (often foll. by *off*) to destroy or defeat completely. **6.** to train (a person) in social graces and talents. **7.** (*intr.;* foll. by *with*). **a.** to end a relationship or association. **b.** to stop punishing a person: *I haven't finished with you yet!* ~*n.* **8.** the final or last stage or part; end. **9. a.** the death, destruction, or absolute defeat of a person or one side in a conflict: *a fight to the finish.* **b.** the person, event, or thing that brings this about. **10. a.** the surface texture or appearance of wood, cloth, etc.: *a rough finish.* **b.** a preparation, such as varnish, used to produce such a texture. **11.** a thing, event, etc., that completes. **12.** completeness and high quality of workmanship. **13.** refinement in social graces. **14.** *Sport.* ability to sprint at the end of a race: *he has a good finish.* [C14: from Old French *finir,* from Latin *fīnīre* see FINE[1]]

finished ('fɪnɪʃt) *adj.* **1.** perfected. **2.** (*predicative*) at the end of a task, activity, etc.: *they were finished by four.* **3.** (*predicative*) without further hope of success or continuation: *she was finished as a prima ballerina.*

finisher ('fɪnɪʃə) *n.* **1.** a craftsman who carries out the final tasks in a manufacturing process. **2.** *Boxing.* a knockout blow.

finishing ('fɪnɪʃɪŋ) *n. Football.* the act or skill of goal scoring: *his finishing is deadly.*

finishing school *n.* a private school for girls that prepares them for society by teaching social graces and accomplishments.

finite ('faɪnaɪt) *adj.* **1.** bounded in magnitude or spatial or temporal extent: *a finite difference.* **2.** *Maths, logic.* having a countable number of elements; capable of being put into one-to-one correspondence with an initial segment of the natural numbers. Compare **denumerable, infinite** (sense 4). **3. a.** limited or restricted in nature: *human existence is finite.* **b.** (*as n.*): *the finite.* **4.** denoting any form or occurrence of a verb inflected for grammatical features such as person, number, and tense. [C15: from Latin *fīnītus* limited, from *fīnīre* to limit, end] —'**finitely** *adv.* —'**finiteness** *n.*

finitism ('faɪnaɪtˌɪzəm) *n. Philosophy, logic.* the view that only those entities may be admitted to mathematics that can be constructed in a finite number of steps, and only those propositions entertained whose truth can be proved in a finite number of steps. Compare **intuitionism.**

fink (fɪŋk) *Slang, chiefly U.S. and Canadian.* ~*n.* **1.** a strikebreaker; blackleg. **2.** an informer, such as one working for the police; spy. **3.** an unpleasant, disappointing, or contemptible person. ~*vb.* **4.** (*intr.;* often foll. by *on*) to inform (on someone), as to the police. [C20: of uncertain origin]

fin keel *n.* a projection from the keel of a vessel to give it additional stability.

fink out *vb.* (*intr., adv.*) *Slang, chiefly U.S.* to fail to carry something out or through; give up.

Finlandization *or* **Finlandisation** (ˌfɪnləndaɪ'zeɪʃən) *n.* neutralization of a small country by a superpower, using conciliation rather than confrontation, as the Soviet Union has in relation to Finland.

Finn (fɪn) *n.* **1.** a native, inhabitant, or citizen of Finland. **2.** a speaker of a Finnic language, esp. one of the original inhabitants of Russia, who were pushed northwards during the Slav migrations. [Old English *Finnas* (plural); related to Old Norse *Finnr* Finn, Latin *Fennī* the Finns, Greek *Phinnoi*]

finnan haddock ('fɪnən) *or* **haddie** ('hædɪ) *n.* smoked haddock. [C18: *finnan* after *Findon,* a village in Scotland south of Aberdeen + HADDOCK]

finned (fɪnd) *adj.* having one or more fins or finlike parts.

finner ('fɪnə) *n.* another name for **rorqual.** [C18: from FIN[1] + -ER[1]]

Finnic ('fɪnɪk) *n.* **1.** one of the two branches of the Finno-Ugric family of languages, including Finnish and several languages of the former Soviet Union in N Europe. Compare **Ugric.** ~*adj.* **2.** of or relating to this group of languages or to the Finns.

Finnish ('fɪnɪʃ) *adj.* **1.** of, relating to, or characteristic of Finland, the Finns, or their language. ~*n.* **2.** the official language of Finland, also spoken in the NW of the former Soviet Union, belonging to the Finno-Ugric family.

finnock ('fɪnək) *n.* a young sea trout on its first return to fresh water. [originally Scot.: from Gaelic *fionnag,* from *fionn* white]

Finno-Ugric ('fɪnəʊ'uːɡrɪk, -'juː-) *or* **Finno-Ugrian** *n.* **1.** a family of languages spoken in Scandinavia, Hungary, and the former Soviet Union, including Finnish, Estonian, Hungarian, Ostyak, and Vogul: generally regarded as a subfamily of Uralic. See also **Ural-Altaic.** ~*adj.* **2.** of, relating to, speaking, or belonging to this family of languages.

finny ('fɪnɪ) *adj.* **-nier, -niest. 1.** *Poetic.* relating to or containing many fishes. **2.** having or resembling a fin or fins.

fino ('fiːnəʊ) *n.* a very dry sherry. [from Spanish: FINE[1]]

finocchio *or* **finochio** (fɪ'nɒkɪˌəʊ) *n.* a variety of fennel, *Foeniculum vulgare dulce,* with thickened stalks that resemble celery and are eaten as a vegetable, esp. in S Europe. Also called: **Florence fennel.** [C18: from Italian: FENNEL]

fiord (fjɔːd) *n.* a variant spelling of **fjord.**

fiorin ('faɪərɪn) *n.* a temperate perennial grass, *Agrostis stolonifera.* Also called: **creeping bent grass.** See **bent grass.** [C19: from Irish Gaelic *fiorthann* wheat grass]

fioritura (ˌfjɔːrɪ'tʊərə, ˌfiːərɪ-) *n., pl.* **-ture** (-'tʊəreɪ). *Music.* embellishment, esp. ornamentation added by the performer. [Italian: a blossoming]

fipple ('fɪpᵊl) *n.* **1.** a wooden plug forming a flue in the end of a pipe, as the mouthpiece of a recorder. **2.** a similar device in an organ pipe with a flutelike tone. [C17: of unknown origin]

fipple flute *n.* an end-blown flute provided with a fipple, such as the recorder or flageolet.

fir (fɜː) *n.* **1.** any pyramidal coniferous tree of the N temperate genus *Abies,* having single needle-like leaves and erect cones: family *Pinaceae.* See also **red fir, silver fir, balsam fir. 2.** any of various other trees of the family *Pinaceae,* such as the Douglas fir. **3.** the wood of any of these trees. [Old English *furh;* related to Old Norse *fura,* Old High German *foraha* fir, Latin *quercus* oak]

fire (faɪə) *n.* **1.** the state of combustion in which inflammable material burns, producing heat, flames, and often smoke. **2. a.** a mass of burning coal, wood, etc., used esp. in a hearth to heat a room. **b.** (*in combination*): *firewood; firelighter.* **3.** a destructive conflagration, as of a forest, building, etc. **4.** a device for heating a room, etc. **5.** something resembling a fire in light or brilliance: *a diamond's fire.* **6.** a flash or spark of or as if of fire. **7. a.** the act of discharging weapons, artillery, etc. **b.** the shells, etc., fired. **8.** a burst or rapid volley: *a fire of questions.* **9.** intense passion; ardour. **10.** liveliness, as of imagination, thought, etc. **11.** a burning sensation sometimes produced by drinking strong alcoholic liquor. **12.** fever and inflammation. **13.** a severe trial or torment (esp. in the phrase **go through fire and water**). **14. between two fires.** under attack from two sides. **15. catch fire.** to ignite. **16. hang fire. a.** to delay firing. **b.** to delay or be delayed. **17. no smoke without fire.** the evidence strongly suggests something has indeed happened. **18. on fire. a.** in a state of ignition. **b.** ardent or eager. **19. open fire.** to start firing a gun, artillery, etc. **20. play with fire.** to be involved in something risky. **21. set fire to** *or* **set on fire. a.** to ignite. **b.** to arouse or excite. **22. set the world** *or* (*Brit.*) **the Thames** *or* (*Scot.*) **the heather on fire.** *Informal.* to cause a great sensation. **23. under fire.** being attacked, as by weapons or by harsh criticism. **24.** (*modifier*) *Astrology.* of or relating to a group of three signs of the zodiac, Aries, Leo, and Sagittarius. Compare **earth** (sense 10), **air** (sense 18), **water** (sense 12). ~*vb.* **25.** to discharge (a firearm or projectile) or (of a firearm, etc.) to be discharged. **26.** to detonate (an explosive charge or device), or (of such a charge or device) to be detonated. **27.** (*tr.*) *Informal.* to dismiss from employment. **28.** (*tr.*) *Ceramics.* to bake in a kiln to harden the clay, fix the glaze, etc. **29.** to kindle or be kindled; ignite. **30.** (*tr.*) to provide with fuel: *oil fires the heating system.* **31.** (*intr.*) to tend a fire. **32.** (*tr.*) to subject to heat. **33.** (*tr.*) to heat slowly so as to dry. **34.** (*tr.*) to arouse to strong emotion. **35.** to glow or cause to glow. **36.** (*intr.*) (of an internal combustion engine) to ignite. **37.** (*intr.*) (of grain) to become blotchy or yellow before maturity. **38.** *Vet. science.* another word for **cauterize. 39.** (*intr.*) *Austral. informal.* (of a sportsman, etc.) to play well or with enthusiasm. ~*sentence substitute.* **40.** a cry to warn others of a fire. **41.** the order to begin firing a gun, artillery, etc. [Old English *fȳr;* related to Old Saxon *fiur,* Old Norse *fūrr,* Old High German *fūir,* Greek *pur*] —ˈ**fireable** *adj.* —ˈ**fireless** *adj.* —ˈ**firer** *n.*

fire alarm *n.* **1.** a device to give warning of fire, esp. a bell, siren, or hooter. **2.** a shout to warn that a fire has broken out.

fire-and-brimstone *adj.* (of a sermon, preacher, etc.) zealous, esp. in threatening eternal damnation.

fire ant *n.* any mound-building predatory ant of the genus *Solenopsis,* of tropical and subtropical America, that can inflict a painful sting.

firearm (ˈfaɪərˌɑːm) *n.* a weapon, esp. a portable gun or pistol, from which a projectile can be discharged by an explosion caused by igniting gunpowder, etc.

fire away *vb.* (*intr., adv.; often imperative*) *Informal.* to begin to speak or to ask questions.

fireback (ˈfaɪəˌbæk) *n.* **1.** Also called: **reredos.** an ornamental iron slab against the back wall of a hearth. **2.** any pheasant of the genus *Lophura,* of SE Asia.

fireball (ˈfaɪəˌbɔːl) *n.* **1.** a ball-shaped discharge of lightning. **2.** the bright spherical region of hot ionized gas at the centre of a nuclear explosion. **3.** *Astronomy.* another name for **bolide. 4.** *Slang.* an energetic person.

firebird (ˈfaɪəˌbɜːd) *n. Chiefly U.S.* any of various songbirds having a bright red plumage, esp. the Baltimore oriole.

fire blight *n.* a disease of apples, pears, and similar fruit trees, caused by the bacterium *Erwinia amylovora* and characterized by blackening of the blossoms and leaves, and cankers on the branches.

fireboat (ˈfaɪəˌbəʊt) *n.* a motor vessel equipped with fire-fighting apparatus.

firebomb (ˈfaɪəˌbɒm) *n.* another name for **incendiary** (sense 6).

firebox (ˈfaɪəˌbɒks) *n.* **1.** the furnace chamber of a boiler in a steam locomotive. **2.** an obsolete word for **tinderbox.**

firebrand (ˈfaɪəˌbrænd) *n.* **1.** a piece of burning or glowing wood or other material. **2.** a person who causes unrest or is very energetic.

firebrat (ˈfaɪəˌbræt) *n.* a small primitive wingless insect, *Thermobia domestica,* that occurs in warm buildings, feeding on starchy food scraps, fabric, etc.: order *Thysanura* (bristletails).

firebreak (ˈfaɪəˌbreɪk), **fireguard** (ˈfaɪəˌgɑːd), *or* **fire line** *n.* a strip of open land in forest or prairie, serving to arrest the advance of a fire.

firebrick (ˈfaɪəˌbrɪk) *n.* a refractory brick made of fire clay, used for lining furnaces, flues, etc.

fire brigade *n. Chiefly Brit.* an organized body of fire fighters.

firebug (ˈfaɪəˌbʌg) *n. Informal.* a person who deliberately sets fire to property.

fire clay *n.* a heat-resistant clay used in the making of firebricks, furnace linings, etc.

fire company *n.* **1.** an insurance company selling policies relating to fire risk. **2.** *U.S.* an organized body of firemen.

fire control *n. Military.* the procedures by which weapons are brought to engage a target.

firecracker (ˈfaɪəˌkrækə) *n.* a small cardboard container filled with explosive powder and lit by a fuse.

firecrest (ˈfaɪəˌkrest) *n.* a small European warbler, *Regulus ignicapillus,* having a crown striped with yellow, black, and white.

fire-cure *vb.* (*tr.*) to cure (tobacco) by exposure to the smoke and heat of an open fire.

firedamp (ˈfaɪəˌdæmp) *n.* a mixture of hydrocarbons, chiefly methane, formed in coal mines. It forms explosive mixtures with air. See also **afterdamp.**

fire department *n. U.S. and Canadian.* the department of a local authority responsible for the prevention and extinguishing of fires.

firedog (ˈfaɪəˌdɒg) *n.* either of a pair of decorative metal stands used to support logs in an open fire.

fire door *n.* **1.** a door made of noncombustible material, the purpose of which is to prevent a fire from spreading within a building. **2.** a similar door, leading to the outside of a building, that can be easily opened from inside; emergency exit.

firedrake (ˈfaɪəˌdreɪk) *or* **firedragon** (ˈfaɪəˌdrægən) *n. Myth.* a fire-breathing dragon.

fire drill *n.* a rehearsal of duties or escape procedures to be followed in case of fire.

fire-eater *n.* **1.** a performer who simulates the swallowing of fire. **2.** a belligerent person. —ˈ**fire-ˌeating** *n., adj.*

fire engine *n.* a heavy road vehicle that carries firemen and fire-fighting equipment to a fire.

fire escape *n.* a means of evacuating persons from a building in the event of fire, esp. a metal staircase outside the building.

fire-extinguisher *n.* a portable device for extinguishing fires, usually consisting of a canister with a directional nozzle used to direct a spray of water, chemically generated foam, inert gas, or fine powder onto the fire.

firefighter (ˈfaɪəˌfaɪtə) *n.* a person who fights fires, usually a public employee or trained volunteer.

firefly (ˈfaɪəˌflaɪ) *n., pl.* **-flies. 1.** any nocturnal beetle of the family *Lampyridae,* common in warm and tropical regions, having luminescent abdominal organs. See also **glow-worm. 2.** any tropical American click beetle of the genus *Pyrophorus,* esp. *P. noctiluca,* that have luminescent thoracic organs.

fireguard (ˈfaɪəˌgɑːd) *n.* **1.** Also called: **fire screen.** a metal panel or meshed frame put before an open fire to protect against falling logs, sparks, etc. **2.** a less common word for **firebreak.**

fire hydrant *n.* a hydrant for use as an emergency supply for fighting fires, esp. one in a street. Also called (esp. U.S. and N.Z.): **fireplug.**

fire insurance *n.* insurance covering damage or loss caused by fire or lightning.

fire irons *pl. n.* metal fireside implements, such as poker, shovel, and tongs.

fireless cooker *n.* an insulated container that retains enough heat to cook food or keep it warm.

firelock (ˈfaɪəˌlɒk) *n.* **1.** an obsolete type of gunlock with a priming mechanism ignited by sparks. **2.** a gun or musket having such a lock.

fireman (ˈfaɪəmən) *n., pl.* **men. 1.** a man who fights fires, usually a public employee or trained volunteer. **2. a.** (on steam locomotives) the man who stokes the fire and controls the injectors feeding water to the boiler. **b.** (on diesel and electric locomotives) the driver's assistant. **3.** a man who tends furnaces; stoker. **4.** Also called: **deputy.** a mine official responsible for safety precautions. U.S. equivalent: **fire boss. 5.** *U.S. Navy.* a junior rating who works on marine engineering equipment.

fire marshal *n. U.S.* **1.** a public official responsible for investigating the causes of fires, enforcing fire prevention laws, etc. **2.** the head of a fire prevention organization.

fire opal *n.* an orange-red translucent variety of opal, valued as a gemstone.

firepan (ˈfaɪəˌpæn) *n.* a metal container for a fire in a room.

fireplace (ˈfaɪəˌpleɪs) *n.* **1.** an open recess in a wall of a room, at the base of a chimney, etc., for a fire; hearth. **2.** *Austral.* an authorized place or installation for outside cooking, esp. by a roadside.

fireplug (ˈfaɪəˌplʌg) *n.* another name (esp. U.S. and N.Z.) for **fire hydrant.**

fire power *n. Military.* **1.** the amount of fire that may be delivered by a unit or weapon. **2.** the capability of delivering fire.

fireproof (ˈfaɪəˌpruːf) *adj.* **1.** capable of resisting damage by fire. ~*vb.* **2.** (*tr.*) to make resistant to fire.

fire raiser *n.* a person who deliberately sets fire to property. —**fire raising** *n.*

fire screen *n.* **1.** a decorative screen placed in the hearth when there is no fire. **2.** a screen placed before a fire to protect the face from intense heat.

fire ship *n.* a vessel loaded with explosives and used, esp. formerly, as a bomb by igniting it and directing it to drift among an enemy's warships.

fireside (ˈfaɪəˌsaɪd) *n.* **1.** the hearth. **2.** family life; the home.

fire station *n.* a building where fire-fighting vehicles and equipment are stationed and where firefighters on duty wait. Also called (U.S.): ˈ**fireˌhouse, station house.**

firestone ('faɪəˌstəʊn) *n.* a sandstone that withstands intense heat, esp. one used for lining kilns, furnaces, etc.

firestorm ('faɪəˌstɔːm) *n.* an uncontrollable blaze sustained by violent winds that are drawn into the column of rising hot air over the burning area: often the result of heavy bombing.

firethorn ('faɪəˌθɔːn) *n.* any rosaceous evergreen spiny shrub of the genus *Pyracantha*, of SE Europe and Asia, having bright red or orange fruits: cultivated for ornament.

fire trail *n. Austral.* a permanent track cleared through the bush to provide access for fire-fighting.

firetrap ('faɪəˌtræp) *n.* a building that would burn easily or one without fire escapes.

fire walking *n.* a religious rite in which people walk barefoot over white-hot ashes, stones, etc.

fire wall *n.* a fireproof wall or partition used to impede the progress of a fire, as from one room or compartment to another.

firewarden ('faɪəˌwɔːdᵊn) *n. U.S. and Canadian.* an officer responsible for fire prevention and control in an area, esp. in a forest.

fire watcher *n.* a person who watches for fires, esp. those caused by aerial bombardment.

firewater ('faɪəˌwɔːtə) *n.* any strong spirit, esp. whisky.

fireweed ('faɪəˌwiːd) *n.* **1.** any of various plants that appear as first vegetation in burnt-over areas. **2.** Also called: **pilewort.** a weedy North American plant, *Erechtites hieracifolia*, having small white or greenish flowers: family *Compositae* (composites). **3.** another name for **rosebay willowherb.** See **rosebay** (sense 2).

firework ('faɪəˌwɜːk) *n.* a device, such as a Catherine wheel, Roman candle, or rocket, in which combustible materials are ignited and produce coloured flames, sparks, and smoke, sometimes accompanied by bangs.

fireworks ('faɪəˌwɜːks) *pl. n.* **1.** a show in which large numbers of fireworks are let off simultaneously. **2.** *Informal.* an exciting or spectacular exhibition, as of musical virtuosity or wit. **3.** *Informal.* a burst of temper.

firing ('faɪərɪŋ) *n.* **1.** the process of baking ceramics, etc., in a kiln or furnace: *a second firing.* **2.** the act of stoking a fire or furnace. **3.** a discharge of a firearm. **4.** something used as fuel, such as coal or wood. **5.** *U.S.* a scorching of plants, as a result of disease, drought, or heat.

firing line *n.* **1.** *Military.* **a.** the positions from which fire is delivered. **b.** the soldiers occupying these positions. **2.** the leading or most advanced position in an activity.

firing order *n.* the sequence of ignition in the cylinders of an internal-combustion engine.

firing party *n.* **1.** a military detachment detailed to fire a salute at a funeral. **2.** another name for **firing squad.**

firing pin *n.* the part of the firing mechanism of a firearm that ignites the charge by striking the primer.

firing squad *n.* a small military detachment formed to implement a death sentence by shooting.

firkin ('fɜːkɪn) *n.* **1.** a small wooden barrel or similar container. **2.** *Brit.* a unit of capacity equal to nine gallons. [C14 *fir*, from Middle Dutch *vierde* FOURTH + -KIN]

firm[1] (fɜːm) *adj.* **1.** not soft or yielding to a touch or pressure; rigid; solid. **2.** securely in position; stable or stationary. **3.** definitely established; decided; settled. **4.** enduring or steady; constant. **5.** having determination or strength; resolute. **6.** (of prices, markets, etc.) tending to rise. ~*adv.* **7.** in a secure, stable, or unyielding manner: *he stood firm over his obligation to pay.* ~*vb.* **8.** (sometimes foll. by *up*) to make or become firm. **9.** (*intr.*) *Austral. horse racing.* (of a horse) to shorten in odds. [C14: from Latin *firmus*] —'**firmly** *adv.* —'**firmness** *n.*

firm[2] (fɜːm) *n.* **1.** a business partnership. **2.** any commercial enterprise. **3.** a team of doctors and their assistants. [C16 (in the sense: signature): from Spanish *firma* signature, title of a partnership or business concern, from *firmar* to sign, from Latin *firmāre* to confirm, from *firmus* firm]

firmament ('fɜːməmənt) *n.* the expanse of the sky; heavens. [C13: from Late Latin *firmāmentum* sky (considered as fixed above the earth), from Latin: prop, support, from *firmāre* to make FIRM[1]] —**firmamental** (ˌfɜːmə'mentᵊl) *adj.*

firman (fɜː'mɑːn, 'fɜː-) *n.* **1.** an edict of an Oriental sovereign. **2.** any authoritative grant of permission. [C17: from Persian *fermān*]

firmer chisel ('fɜːmə) *n.* a chisel or gouge with a thin blade, used on wood. Sometimes shortened to **firmer.**

firmware ('fɜːmˌwɛə) *n. Computer technol.* a series of fixed instructions built into the hardware of a computer that can be changed only if the hardware itself is modified in some way.

firn (fɪən) *n.* another name for **névé** (sense 1). [C19: from German (Swiss dialect) *firn* of the previous year, from Old High German *firni* old]

firry ('fɜːrɪ) *adj.* **1.** of, relating to, or made from fir trees. **2.** abounding in or dominated by firs.

first (fɜːst) *adj.* (*usually prenominal*) **1. a.** coming before all others; earliest, best, or foremost. **b.** (*as n.*): *I was the first to arrive.* **2.** preceding all others in numbering or counting order; the ordinal number of *one.* Often written: 1st. **3.** rated, graded, or ranked above all other levels. **4.** denoting the lowest forward ratio of a gearbox in a motor vehicle. **5.** *Music.* **a.** denoting the highest part assigned to one of the voice parts in a chorus or one of the sections of an orchestra: *first soprano; the first violins.* **b.** denoting the principal player in a specific orchestral section: *he plays first horn.* **6. first thing.** as the first action of the day: *I'll see you first thing tomorrow.* **7. first things first.** things must be done in order of priority. **8. the first thing, idea, etc.** (*in negative constructions*) even one thing, etc.: *he doesn't know the first thing about me.* ~*n.* **9.** the beginning; outset: *I knew you were a rogue from the first; I couldn't see at first because of the mist.* **10.** *Education, chiefly Brit.* an honours degree of the highest class. Full term: **first-class honours degree. 11.** the lowest forward ratio of a gearbox in a motor vehicle; low gear. **12.** *Music.* **a.** the highest part in a particular section of a chorus or orchestra. **b.** the instrument or voice taking such a part. **c.** the chief or leading player in a section of an orchestra; principal. **13.** *Music.* a rare word for **prime** (sense 11). ~*adv.* **14.** Also: **firstly.** before anything else in order, time, preference, importance, etc.: *do this first.* **15. first and last.** on the whole; overall. **16. from first to last.** throughout. **17.** for the first time: *I've loved you since I first saw you.* **18.** (*sentence modifier*) in the first place or beginning of a series of actions: *first I want to talk about criminality.* ~See also **firsts.** [Old English *fyrest*; related to Old Saxon *furist*, Old Norse *fyrstr*, German *Fürst* prince, one who is first in rank]

first aid *n.* **1. a.** immediate medical assistance given in an emergency. **b.** (*as modifier*): *first-aid box.* **2.** (in Barbados) a small shop that sells domestic items after hours.

first base *n.* **1.** *Baseball.* **a.** the base that a runner must reach safely to score a hit, and the first of the three bases he must reach safely on the way to home plate in order to score a run. **b.** the fielding position nearest this base. **2. get to first base.** *Informal, chiefly U.S. and Canadian.* to accomplish the first step of an undertaking.

first-born *adj.* **1.** eldest of the children in a family. ~*n.* **2.** the eldest child in a family.

first cause *n.* **1.** a source or cause of something. **2.** (*often caps.*) (esp. in philosophy) God considered as the uncaused creator of all beings apart from himself.

first class *n.* **1.** the class or grade of the best or highest value, quality, etc. ~*adj.* (**first-class** *when prenominal*). **2.** of the best or highest class or grade: *a first-class citizen.* **3.** excellent; first-rate. **4.** of or denoting the most comfortable and expensive class of accommodation in a hotel, aircraft, train, etc. **5. a.** (in Britain) of or relating to letters that are handled faster than second-class letters. **b.** (in the U.S. and Canada) of or relating to mail that consists mainly of written letters, cards, etc. **6.** *Education.* See **first** (sense 10). ~*adv.* **first-class. 7.** by first-class mail, means of transportation, etc.

first-day cover *n. Philately.* a cover, usually an envelope, postmarked on the first day of the issue of its stamps.

first-degree burn *n. Pathol.* See **burn**[1] (sense 21).

first estate *n.* the first of the three estates of the realm, such as the Lords Spiritual in England or the clergy in France until the revolution.

First Fleet *n. Austral.* the fleet of convict ships that arrived at Port Jackson in 1788. —**First Fleeter** *n.*

first floor *n.* **1.** *Brit.* the floor or storey of a building immediately above the ground floor. U.S. and Canadian term: **second floor. 2.** *U.S. and Canadian.* another term for **ground floor.**

first-foot *Chiefly Scot.* ~*n. also* **first-footer. 1.** the first person to enter a household in the New Year. By Hogmanay tradition a dark-haired man who crosses the threshold at midnight brings good luck. ~*vb.* **2.** to enter (a house) as first-foot. —'**first-'footing** *n.*

first four ships *pl. n. N.Z.* **1.** the earliest settlers' ships to arrive in the Canterbury Province. **2. come with the first four ships.** to be a founder member of Canterbury.

first fruits *pl. n.* **1.** the first results, products, or profits of an undertaking. **2.** fruit that ripens first.

first-hand *adj., adv.* **1.** from the original source; direct or directly: *first-hand news; he got the news first-hand.* **2. at first hand.** from the original source; directly.

first lady *n.* (*often caps.*) **1.** (in the U.S.) the wife or official hostess of a chief executive, esp. of a state governor or a president. **2.** a woman considered to be at the top of her profession or art: *the first lady of jazz.*

first language *n.* a person's native language.

first lieutenant *n.* **1.** the officer responsible for the upkeep and maintenance of a warship, esp. the executive officer of a smaller ship in the Royal Navy. **2.** an officer holding commissioned rank in the U.S. Army, Air Force, Marine Corps, or in certain other forces, senior to a second lieutenant and junior to a captain.

first light *n.* the time when light first appears in the morning; dawn.

firstling ('fɜːstlɪŋ) *n.* the first, esp. the first offspring.

first-loss policy *n.* an insurance policy for goods in which a total loss is extremely unlikely and the insurer agrees to provide cover for a sum less than the total value of the property.

firstly ('fɜːstlɪ) *adv.* another word for **first** (sense 14).

first mate *n.* an officer second in command to the captain of a merchant ship. Also called: **first officer.**

first mortgage *n.* a mortgage that has priority over other mortgages on the same property, except for taxation and other statutory liabilities.

First Mover *n.* the Aristotelian conception of God as the unmoved mover of everything else.
first name *n.* another term for **Christian name.**
first night *n.* **a.** the first public performance of a play or other production. **b.** (*as modifier*): *first-night nerves.*
first-nighter *n.* a member of an opening night audience, esp. one who habitually attends first nights.
first offender *n.* a person convicted of any criminal offence for the first time.
first officer *n.* **1.** another name for **first mate. 2.** the member of an aircraft crew who is second in command to the captain.
first-order *adj. Logic.* quantifying only over individuals and not over predicates or clauses: **first-order predicate calculus** studies the logical properties of such quantification.
first-past-the-post *n.* (*modifier*) of or relating to a voting system in which a candidate may be elected by a simple majority rather than an absolute majority. Compare **proportional representation.**
first person *n.* a grammatical category of pronouns and verbs used by the speaker to refer to or talk about himself, either alone (**first person singular**) or together with others (**first person plural**).
first post *n. Brit.* the first of two military bugle calls ordering or giving notice of the time to retire for the night. The second is called **last post.**
first principle *n.* (*usually pl.*) **1.** one of the fundamental assumptions on which a particular theory or procedure is thought to be based. **2.** an axiom of a mathematical or scientific theory.
first quarter *n.* one of the four principal phases of the moon, occurring between new moon and full moon, when half of the lighted surface is visible from earth. Compare **last quarter.**
first-rate *adj.* **1.** of the best or highest rated class or quality. **2.** *Informal.* very good; excellent. ~*adv.* **3.** *Not standard.* very well; excellently.
first reading *n.* the introduction of a bill in a legislative assembly.
first refusal *n.* the chance of buying a house, merchandise, etc., before the offer is made to other potential buyers.
firsts (fɜːsts) *pl. n.* saleable goods of the highest quality.
first school *n. Brit.* a school for children aged between 5 and 8 or 9. Compare **middle school.**
first-strike *adj.* (of a nuclear missile) intended for use in an opening attack calculated to destroy the enemy's nuclear weapons.
first string *n.* **1.** the top player of a team in an individual sport, such as squash. ~*adj.* **first-string. 2.** being a regular member of a team rather than a substitute or reserve. **3.** being the top player of a team in an individual sport. **4.** of high rating; first-class.
first water *n.* **1.** the finest quality of diamond or other precious stone. **2.** the highest grade or best quality. **3.** the most extreme kind: *a fool of the first water.*
firth (fɜːθ) *or* **frith** *n.* a relatively narrow inlet of the sea, esp. in Scotland. [C15: from Old Norse *fjörthr* FIORD]
fisc (fɪsk) *n. Rare.* a state or royal treasury. [C16: from Latin *fiscus* treasury, originally money-bag]
fiscal (ˈfɪskəl) *adj.* **1.** of or relating to government finances, esp. tax revenues. **2.** of or involving financial matters. ~*n.* **3. a.** (in some countries) a public prosecutor. **b.** *Scot.* short for **procurator fiscal. 4.** a postage or other stamp signifying payment of a tax. [C16: from Latin *fiscālis* concerning the state treasury, from *fiscus* public money; see FISC] —ˈ**fiscally** *adv.*
fiscal drag *n. Economics.* the process by which, during inflation, rising incomes draw people into higher tax brackets, so that their real incomes may fall; this acts as a restraint on the expansion of the economy.
fiscal year *n.* the U.S. and Canadian term for **financial year.**
fish (fɪʃ) *n., pl.* **fish** *or* **fishes. 1. a.** any of a large group of cold-blooded aquatic vertebrates having jaws, gills, and usually fins and a skin covered in scales: includes the sharks and rays (class *Chondrichthyes:* **cartilaginous fishes**) and the teleosts, lungfish, etc. (class *Osteichthyes:* **bony fishes**). **b.** (*in combination*): *fishpond.* Related adj.: **piscine. 2.** any of various similar but jawless vertebrates, such as the hagfish and lamprey. **3.** (*not in technical use*) any of various aquatic invertebrates, such as the cuttlefish, jellyfish, and crayfish. **4.** the flesh of fish used as food. **5.** *Informal.* a person of little emotion or intelligence: *a poor fish.* **6.** short for **fishplate. 7.** Also called: **tin fish.** an informal word for **torpedo** (sense 1). **8. a fine kettle of fish.** an awkward situation; mess. **9. drink like a fish.** to drink to excess. **10. have other fish to fry.** to have other activities to do, esp. more important ones. **11. like a fish out of water.** out of one's usual place. **12. neither fish, flesh, nor fowl.** neither this nor that. **13. make fish of one and flesh of another.** *Irish.* to discriminate unfairly between people. ~*vb.* **14.** (*intr.*) to attempt to catch fish, as with a line and hook or with nets, traps, etc. **15.** (*tr.*) to fish in (a particular area of water). **16.** to search (a body of water) for something or to search for something, esp. in a body of water. **17.** (*intr.; foll. by for*) to seek something indirectly: *to fish for compliments.* **18. fish in troubled water.** to try to take advantage of confusion or trouble. ~See also **fish out.** [Old English *fisc;* related to Old Norse *fiskr,* Gothic *fiscs,* Russian *piskar,* Latin *piscis*] —ˈ**fishable** *adj.* —ˈ**fish,like** *adj.*
fish and chips *n.* fish fillets coated with batter and deep-fried, eaten with potato chips.
fish-and-chip shop *n.* (esp. in Britain) a place where fish and chips are cooked and sold.
fishbolt (ˈfɪʃˌbəʊlt) *n.* a bolt used for fastening a fishplate to a rail.
fishbowl (ˈfɪʃˌbəʊl) *n.* another name for **goldfish bowl.**
fish cake *n.* a fried ball of flaked fish mixed with mashed potatoes.
fish eagle *n.* another name for the **osprey.**
fisher (ˈfɪʃə) *n.* **1.** a person who fishes; fisherman. **2.** Also called: **pekan. a.** a large North American marten, *Martes pennanti,* having thick dark brown fur. **b.** the fur of this animal. **3. fisher of men.** an evangelist.
fisherman (ˈfɪʃəmən) *n., pl.* **-men. 1.** a person who fishes as a profession or for sport. **2.** a vessel used for fishing.
fisherman's bend *n.* a knot used to fasten a rope to an anchor, ring, or spar.
fisherman's knot *n.* a knot for joining two ropes of equal thickness consisting of an overhand knot or double overhand knot by each rope round the other, so that the two knots jam when pulled tight.
fishery (ˈfɪʃərɪ) *n., pl.* **-eries. 1. a.** the industry of catching, processing, and selling fish. **b.** a place where this is carried on. **2.** a place where fish are reared. **3.** a fishing ground. **4.** another word for **piscary** (sense 2).
Fishes (ˈfɪʃɪz) *n.* **the.** the constellation Pisces, the twelfth sign of the zodiac.
fish-eye lens *n. Photog.* a lens of small focal length, having a highly curved protruding front element, that covers an angle of view of almost 180°. It yields a circular image having considerable linear distortion.
fishfinger (ˈfɪʃˈfɪŋgə) *or U.S. and Canadian* **fish stick** *n.* an oblong piece of filleted or minced fish coated in breadcrumbs.
fish flake *n. Canadian.* a platform on which fish are dried.
fishgig (ˈfɪʃˌgɪg) *n.* a pole with barbed prongs for impaling fish. Also: **fizgig.** [C17: of uncertain origin; perhaps altered from Spanish *fisga* harpoon]
fish hawk *n.* another name for the **osprey.**
fish-hook *n.* **1.** a sharp hook used in angling, esp. one with a barb. **2.** *Logic.* a symbol (⥽) for entailment.
fishing (ˈfɪʃɪŋ) *n.* **1. a.** the occupation of catching fish. **b.** (*as modifier*): *a fishing match.* **2.** another word for **piscary** (sense 2).
fishing ground *n.* an area of water that is good for fishing.
fishing rod *n.* a long tapered flexible pole, often in jointed sections, for use with a fishing line and, usually, a reel.
fishing tackle *n.* all the equipment, such as rods, lines, bait, etc., used in angling.
fish joint *n.* a connection formed by fishplates at the meeting point of two rails, beams, etc., as on a railway.
fish ladder *n.* a row of ascending pools or weirs connected by short falls to allow fish to pass barrages or dams.
fish louse *n.* any small flat rounded crustacean of the subclass *Branchiura,* having sucking mouth parts: parasites of fish.
fish meal *n.* ground dried fish used as feed for farm animals, as a fertilizer, etc.
fishmonger (ˈfɪʃˌmʌŋgə) *n. Chiefly Brit.* a retailer of fish.
fishnet (ˈfɪʃˌnɛt) *n.* **1.** *Chiefly U.S. and Canadian.* a net for catching fish. **2. a.** an open mesh fabric resembling netting. **b.** (*as modifier*): *fishnet tights.*
fish out *vb.* (*tr., adv.*) to find or extract (something): *to fish keys out of a pocket.*
fishplate (ˈfɪʃˌpleɪt) *n.* a flat piece of metal joining one rail or beam to the next, esp. on railway tracks.
fishskin disease (ˈfɪʃˌskɪn) *n. Pathol.* a nontechnical name for **ichthyosis.**
fishtail (ˈfɪʃˌteɪl) *n.* **1.** an aeroplane manoeuvre in which the tail is moved from side to side to reduce speed. **2.** a nozzle having a long narrow slot at the top, placed over a Bunsen burner to produce a thin fanlike flame. ~*vb.* **3.** (*intr.*) to slow an aeroplane by moving the tail from side to side.
fish tail *n.* a step in ballroom dancing in which the feet are quickly crossed.
fishway (ˈfɪʃˌweɪ) *n. U.S. and Canadian.* another name for **fish ladder.**
fishwife (ˈfɪʃˌwaɪf) *n., pl.* **-wives. 1.** a woman who sells fish. **2.** a coarse scolding woman.
fishy (ˈfɪʃɪ) *adj.* **fishier, fishiest. 1.** of, involving, or suggestive of fish. **2.** abounding in fish. **3.** *Informal.* suspicious, doubtful, or questionable: *their leaving at the same time looked fishy.* **4.** dull and lifeless: *a fishy look.* —ˈ**fishily** *adv.* —ˈ**fishiness** *n.*
fissi- *combining form.* indicating a splitting or cleft: *fissirostral.* [from Latin *fissus,* past participle of *findere* to split]
fissile (ˈfɪsaɪl) *adj.* **1.** *Brit.* capable of undergoing nuclear fission as a result of the impact of slow neutrons. **2.** another word (esp. U.S. and Canadian) for **fissionable. 3.** tending to split or capable of being split. [C17: from Latin *fissilis,* from *fissus* split; see FISSI-] —**fissility** (fɪˈsɪlɪtɪ) *n.*
fission (ˈfɪʃən) *n.* **1.** the act or process of splitting or breaking into parts. **2.** *Biology.* a form of asexual reproduction in single-celled animals and plants involving a division into two or more

equal parts that develop into new cells. 3. short for **nuclear fission.** [C19: from Latin *fissiō* a cleaving]

fissionable (ˈfɪʃənəbᵊl) *adj.* capable of undergoing nuclear fission as a result of any process. Compare **fissile** (sense 1). —ˌ**fissionaˈbility** *n.*

fission bomb *n.* a bomb in which the energy is supplied by nuclear fission. See **atom bomb.**

fission-fusion bomb *n.* another name for **fusion bomb.**

fission product *n.* a nuclide produced either directly by nuclear fission or by the radioactive decay of such a nuclide.

fission reactor *n.* a nuclear reactor in which a fission reaction takes place.

fission-track dating *n.* the dating of samples of minerals by comparing the tracks in them by fission fragments of the uranium nuclei they contain, before and after irradiation by neutrons.

fissipalmate (ˌfɪsɪˈpælmeɪt) *adj.* (of some birds' feet) partially webbed, having lobes and fringes on separate toes.

fissiparous (fɪˈsɪpərəs) *adj. Biology.* reproducing by fission. —**fisˈsiparously** *adv.* —**fisˈsiparousness** *n.*

fissiped (ˈfɪsɪˌpɛd) *adj. also* **fissipedal** (fɪˈsɪpɪdᵊl, ˌfɪsɪˈpiːdᵊl). 1. having toes that are separated from one another, as dogs, cats, bears, and similar carnivores. ~*n.* 2. a fissiped animal. ~Compare **pinniped.**

fissirostral (ˌfɪsɪˈrɒstrəl) *adj.* 1. (of the beaks of some birds) broad and deeply cleft. 2. having such a beak, as swifts and swallows.

fissure (ˈfɪʃə) *n.* 1. any long narrow cleft or crack, esp. in a rock. 2. a weakness or flaw indicating impending disruption or discord: *fissures in a decaying empire.* 3. *Anatomy.* a narrow split or groove that divides an organ such as the brain, lung, or liver into lobes. See also **sulcus.** 4. a small unnatural crack in the skin or mucous membrane, as between the toes or at the anus. 5. a minute crack in the surface of a tooth, caused by imperfect joining of enamel during development. ~*vb.* 6. to crack or split apart. [C14: from medical Latin *fissūra,* from Latin *fissus* split]

fissure eruption *n.* the emergence of lava from a fissure in the ground rather than from a volcanic cone or vent.

fissure of Rolando (rəʊˈlændəʊ) *n.* another name for **central sulcus.** [C19: named after L. *Rolando* (died 1831), Italian anatomist]

fissure of Sylvius (ˈsɪlvɪəs) *n.* a deep horizontal cleft in each cerebral hemisphere: marks the separation of the temporal lobe from the frontal and parietal lobes. [named after Franciscus *Sylvius* (died 1652), German anatomist]

fist (fɪst) *n.* 1. a hand with the fingers clenched into the palm, as for hitting. 2. Also called: **fistful.** the quantity that can be held in a fist or hand. 3. an informal word for **hand** or **index** (sense 9). ~*vb.* 4. (*tr.*) to hit with the fist. [Old English *fȳst;* related to Old Frisian *fest,* Old Saxon, Old High German *fūst;* see FIVE]

fistic (ˈfɪstɪk) *adj.* of or relating to fisticuffs or boxing.

fisticuffs (ˈfɪstɪˌkʌfs) *pl. n.* combat with the fists. [C17: probably from *fisty* with the fist + CUFF[2]]

fistmele (ˈfɪstˌmiːl) *n. Archery.* a measure of the width of a hand and the extended thumb, used to calculate the approximate height of the string of a braced bow. [C17: from FIST + *mele,* variant of obsolete *meal* measure]

fistula (ˈfɪstjʊlə) *n., pl.* **-las** *or* **-lae** (-ˌliː). 1. *Pathol.* an abnormal opening between one hollow organ and another or between a hollow organ and the surface of the skin, caused by ulceration, congenital malformation, etc. 2. *Obsolete.* any musical wind instrument; a pipe. [C14: from Latin: pipe, tube, hollow reed, ulcer]

fistulous (ˈfɪstjʊləs), **fistular** (ˈfɪstjʊlə), *or* **fistulate** (ˈfɪstjʊlɪt) *adj.* 1. *Pathol.* containing, relating to, or resembling a fistula. 2. hollow, esp. slender and hollow; reedlike or tubular. 3. containing tubes or tubelike parts.

fit[1] (fɪt) *vb.* **fits, fitting, fitted.** 1. to be appropriate or suitable for (a situation, etc.). 2. to be of the correct size or shape for (a connection, container, etc.). 3. (*tr.*) to adjust in order to render appropriate: *they had to fit the idea to their philosophy.* 4. (*tr.*) to supply with that which is needed. 5. (*tr.*) to try clothes on (someone) in order to make adjustments if necessary. 6. (*tr.*) to make competent or ready: *the experience helped to fit him for the task.* 7. (*tr.*) to locate with care. 8. (*intr.*) to correspond with the facts or circumstances. ~*adj.* **fitter, fittest.** 9. suitable to a purpose or design; appropriate. 10. having the right qualifications; qualifying. 11. in good health. 12. worthy or deserving: *a book fit to be read.* 13. (*foll. by an infinitive*) in such an extreme condition that a specified consequence is likely: *she was fit to scream; you look fit to drop.* ~*n.* 14. the manner in which something fits. 15. the act or process of fitting. 16. *Statistics.* the correspondence between observed and predicted characteristics of a distribution or model. See **goodness of fit.** ~See also **fit in, fit out, fit up.** [C14: probably from Middle Dutch *vitten;* related to Old Norse *fitja* to knit] —ˈ**fittable** *adj.*

fit[2] (fɪt) *n.* 1. *Pathol.* a sudden attack or convulsion, such as an epileptic seizure. 2. a sudden spell of emotion: *a fit of anger.* 3. an impulsive period of activity or lack of activity; mood: *a fit of laziness.* 4. **by fits (and starts).** in spasmodic spells; irregularly. 5. **give (a person) a fit.** to surprise (a person) in an outrageous manner. 6. **have** *or* **throw a fit.** *Informal.* to become very angry or excited. [Old English *fitt* conflict; see FIT[3]]

fit[3] (fɪt) *n. Archaic.* a story or song or a section of a story or song. [Old English *fitt;* related to Old Norse *fit* hem, Old High German *fizza* yarn]

fitch (fɪtʃ) *or* **fitchet** (ˈfɪtʃɪt) *n.* 1. another name for **polecat** (sense 1). 2. the fur of the polecat. [C16: probably from *ficheux* FITCHEW]

fitchew (ˈfɪtʃuː) *n.* an archaic name for **polecat.** [C14 *ficheux,* from Old French *ficheau,* from Middle Dutch *vitsau,* of obscure origin]

fitful (ˈfɪtfʊl) *adj.* characterized by or occurring in irregular spells: *fitful sleep.* —ˈ**fitfully** *adv.* —ˈ**fitfulness** *n.*

fit in *vb.* 1. (*tr.*) to give a place or time to: *if my schedule allows it, I'll fit you in.* 2. (*intr., adv.*) to belong or conform, esp. after adjustment: *he didn't fit in with their plans.*

fitly (ˈfɪtlɪ) *adv.* in a proper manner or place or at a proper time.

fitment (ˈfɪtmənt) *n.* 1. *Machinery.* an accessory attached to an assembly of parts. 2. *Chiefly Brit.* a detachable part of the furnishings of a room.

fitness (ˈfɪtnɪs) *n.* 1. the state of being fit. 2. *Biology.* **a.** the degree of adaptation of an organism to its environment, determined by its genetic constitution. **b.** the ability of an organism to produce viable offspring capable of surviving to the next generation.

fit out *vb.* (*tr., adv.*) to equip; supply with necessary or new equipment, clothes, etc.

fitted (ˈfɪtɪd) *adj.* 1. designed for excellent fit: *a fitted suit.* 2. (of a carpet) cut, sewn, or otherwise adapted to cover a floor completely. 3. **a.** (of furniture) built to fit a particular space: *a fitted cupboard.* **b.** (of a room) equipped with fitted furniture: *a fitted kitchen.* 4. (of sheets) having ends that are elasticated and shaped to fit tightly over a mattress. 5. having accessory parts.

fitter (ˈfɪtə) *n.* 1. a person who fits a garment, esp. when it is made for a particular person. 2. a person who is skilled in the assembly and adjustment of machinery, esp. of a specified sort: *an electrical fitter.* 3. a person who supplies something for an expedition, activity, etc.

fitting (ˈfɪtɪŋ) *adj.* 1. appropriate or proper; suitable. ~*n.* 2. an accessory or part: *an electrical fitting.* 3. (*pl.*) furnishings or accessories in a building. 4. work carried out by a fitter. 5. the act of trying on clothes so that they can be adjusted to fit. 6. *Brit.* size in clothes or shoes: *a narrow fitting.* —ˈ**fittingly** *adv.* —ˈ**fittingness** *n.*

fit up *vb.* (*tr., adv.*) 1. (often foll. by *with*) to equip or provide: *the optician will soon fit you up with a new pair of glasses.* 2. *Brit. slang.* to incriminate (someone) on a false charge; frame: *he was fitted up for the bank job.* ~*n.* **fit-up.** 3. *Theatre slang.* a stage and accessories that can be erected quickly for plays. 4. *Brit. slang.* a frame-up.

Fitzgerald-Lorentz contraction (fɪtsˈdʒɛrəldlɔːˈrɛnts) *n. Physics.* the contraction that a moving body exhibits when its velocity approaches that of light. [C19: named after G. F. *Fitzgerald* (1851–1901), Irish physicist and H. A. *Lorentz* (1853–1928), Dutch physicist]

five (faɪv) *n.* 1. the cardinal number that is the sum of four and one. 2. a numeral, 5, V, etc., representing this number. 3. the amount or quantity that is one greater than four. 4. something representing, represented by, or consisting of five units, such as a playing card with five symbols on it. ~*determiner.* 5. **a.** amounting to five: *five minutes; five nights.* **b.** (*as pronoun*): *choose any five you like.* ~Related prefixes: **penta-, quinque-.** ~See also **fives.** [Old English *fīf;* related to Old Norse *fimm,* Gothic *fimf,* Old High German *finf,* Latin *quinque,* Greek *pente,* Sanskrit *pañca*]

five-a-side *n.* **a.** a version of soccer with five players on each side. **b.** (*as modifier*): *a five-a-side tournament.*

five-eighth *n. Austral., N.Z.* a rugby player positioned between the halfbacks and three-quarters.

five-faced bishop *n. Brit.* another name for **moschatel.**

five-finger *n.* any of various plants having five-petalled flowers or five lobed leaves, such as cinquefoil and Virginia creeper.

fivefold (ˈfaɪvˌfəʊld) *adj.* 1. equal to or having five times as many or as much. 2. composed of five parts. ~*adv.* 3. by or up to five times as many or as much.

five hundred *n.* a card game for three players, with 500 points for game.

five Ks *pl. n.* **the.** items traditionally worn or carried by Sikhs, each possessing a symbolic importance. See **kangha, kara, kesh, kirpan, kuccha.** [translation of Punjabi *panch kakke*]

five-o'clock shadow *n.* beard growth visible late in the day on a man's shaven face.

fivepenny (ˈfaɪfpənɪ) *adj.* (*prenominal*) *U.S.* (of a nail) one and three-quarters of an inch in length.

fivepins (ˈfaɪvˌpɪnz) *n.* (*functioning as sing.*) a bowling game using five pins, played esp. in Canada. —ˈ**fiveˌpin** *adj.*

fiver (ˈfaɪvə) *n. Informal.* 1. (in Britain) a five-pound note. 2. (in the U.S.) a five-dollar bill.

fives (faɪvz) *n.* (*functioning as sing.*) a ball game similar to squash but played with bats or the hands.

five-spot *n.* (in the U.S.) a five-dollar bill.

five-star *adj.* (of a hotel) first-class, top-quality, or offering exceptional luxury.

five stones *n.* the game of jacks played with five stones.

Five-Year Plan *n.* (in socialist economies) a government plan for economic development over a period of five years.

fix (fɪks) *vb.* (*mainly tr.*) **1.** (*also intr.*) to make or become firm, stable, or secure. **2.** to attach or place permanently: *fix the mirror to the wall.* **3.** (often foll. by *up*) to settle definitely; decide: *let us fix a date.* **4.** to hold or direct (eyes, attention, etc.) steadily: *he fixed his gaze on the woman.* **5.** to call to attention or rivet. **6.** to make rigid: *to fix one's jaw.* **7.** to place or ascribe: *to fix the blame on someone.* **8.** to mend or repair. **9.** *Informal.* to provide with: *how are you fixed for supplies?* **10.** *Informal.* to influence (a person, outcome of a contest, etc.) unfairly, as by bribery. **11.** *Slang.* to take revenge on; get even with, esp. by killing. **12.** *Informal.* to give (someone) his just deserts: *that'll fix him.* **13.** *Informal, chiefly U.S. and Canadian.* to arrange or put in order: *to fix one's hair.* **14.** *Informal, chiefly U.S. and Canadian.* to prepare: *to fix a meal.* **15.** *Dialect or informal.* to spay or castrate (an animal). **16.** *U.S. dialect or informal.* to prepare oneself: *I'm fixing to go out.* **17.** *Photog.* to treat (a film, plate, or paper) with fixer to make permanent the image rendered visible by developer. **18.** *Cytology.* to kill, preserve, and harden (tissue, cells, etc.) for subsequent microscopic study. **19.** to convert (atmospheric nitrogen) into nitrogen compounds, as in the manufacture of fertilizers or the action of bacteria in the soil. **20.** to reduce (a substance) to a solid or condensed state or a less volatile state. **21.** (*intr.*) *Slang.* to inject a drug. ~*n.* **22.** *Informal.* a predicament; dilemma. **23.** the ascertaining of the navigational position, as of a ship, by radar, observation, etc. **24.** *Slang.* an intravenous injection of a drug, esp. heroin. **25.** *Informal.* an act or instance of bribery. ~See also **fix up.** [C15: from Medieval Latin *fixāre,* from Latin *fixus* fixed, from Latin *figere*] —'**fixable** *adj.*

fixate ('fɪkseɪt) *vb.* **1.** to become or cause to become fixed. **2.** to direct the eye or eyes at a point in space so that the image of the point falls on the centre (fovea) of the eye or eyes. **3.** *Psychol.* to engage in fixation. **4.** (*tr.; usually passive*) *Informal.* to obsess or preoccupy. [C19: from Latin *fixus* fixed + -ATE[1]]

fixation (fɪk'seɪʃən) *n.* **1.** the act of fixing or the state of being fixed. **2.** a preoccupation or obsession. **3.** *Psychol.* **a.** the act of fixating. **b.** (in psychoanalytical schools) a strong attachment of a person to another person or an object in early life. **4.** *Chem.* **a.** the conversion of nitrogen in the air into a compound, esp. a fertilizer. **b.** the conversion of a free element into one of its compounds. **5.** the reduction of a substance from a volatile or fluid form to a nonvolatile or solid form.

fixative ('fɪksətɪv) *adj.* **1.** serving or tending to fix. ~*n.* **2.** a fluid usually consisting of a transparent resin, such as shellac, dissolved in alcohol and sprayed over drawings to prevent smudging. **3.** *Cytology.* a fluid, such as formaldehyde or ethanol, that fixes tissues and cells for microscopic study. **4.** a substance added to a liquid, such as a perfume, to make it less volatile.

fixed (fɪkst) *adj.* **1.** attached or placed so as to be immovable. **2.** not subject to change; stable: *fixed prices.* **3.** steadily directed: *a fixed expression.* **4.** established as to relative position: *a fixed point.* **5.** not fluctuating; always at the same time: *a fixed holiday.* **6.** (of ideas, notions, etc.) firmly maintained. **7.** (of an element) held in chemical combination: *fixed nitrogen.* **8.** (of a substance) nonvolatile. **9.** arranged. **10.** *Astrology.* of, relating to, or belonging to the group consisting of the four signs of the zodiac Taurus, Leo, Scorpio, and Aquarius, which are associated with stability. Compare **cardinal** (sense 9), **mutable** (sense 2). **11.** *Informal.* equipped or provided for, as with money, possessions, etc. **12.** *Informal.* illegally arranged: *a fixed trial.* —**fixedly** ('fɪksɪdlɪ) *adv.* —'**fixedness** *n.*

fixed assets *pl. n.* nontrading business assets of a relatively permanent nature, such as plant, fixtures, or goodwill. Also called: **capital assets.** Compare **current assets.**

fixed charge *n.* **1.** an invariable expense usually at regular intervals, such as rent. **2.** a legal charge on specific assets or property, as of a company.

fixed costs *pl. n.* **1.** another name for **overheads. 2.** costs that do not vary with output.

fixed-head coupé *n.* another name (esp. Brit.) for **coupé** (sense 1).

fixed idea *n.* an idea, esp. one of an obsessional nature, that is persistently maintained and not subject to change. Also called: ***idée fixe.***

fixed oil *n.* a natural animal or vegetable oil that is not volatile: a mixture of esters of fatty acids, usually triglycerides. Also called: **fatty oil.** Compare **essential oil.**

fixed point *n.* **1.** *Physics.* a reproducible invariant temperature; the boiling point, freezing point, or triple point of a substance, such as water, that is used to calibrate a thermometer or define a temperature scale. **2.** *Maths.* a point that is not moved by a given transformation.

fixed-point representation *n. Computer technol.* the representation of numbers by a single set of digits such that the radix point has a predetermined location, the value of the number depending on the position of each digit relative to the radix point. Compare **floating-point representation.**

fixed satellite *n.* a satellite revolving in a stationary orbit so that it appears to remain over a fixed point on the earth's surface.

fixed star *n.* **1.** any of the stars in the Ptolemaic system, all of which were thought to be attached to an outer crystal sphere thus explaining their apparent lack of movement. **2.** an extremely distant star whose position appears to be almost stationary over a long period of time.

fixer ('fɪksə) *n.* **1.** a person or thing that fixes. **2.** *Photog.* a solution containing one or more chemical compounds that is used, in fixing, to dissolve unexposed silver halides. It sometimes has an additive to stop the action of developer. **3.** *Slang.* a person who makes arrangements, esp. by underhand or illegal means.

fixing ('fɪksɪŋ) *n.* a means of attaching one thing to another, as a pipe to a wall, slate to a roof, etc.

fixings ('fɪksɪŋz) *pl. n. Chiefly U.S. and Canadian.* **1.** apparatus or equipment. **2.** accompaniments for a dish; trimmings.

fixity ('fɪksɪtɪ) *n., pl.* **-ties. 1.** the state or quality of being fixed; stability. **2.** something that is fixed; a fixture.

fixture ('fɪkstʃə) *n.* **1.** an object firmly fixed in place, esp. a household appliance. **2.** a person or thing regarded as fixed in a particular place or position. **3.** *Property law.* an article attached to land and regarded as part of it. **4.** a device to secure a workpiece in a machine tool. **5.** *Chiefly Brit.* **a.** a sports match or social occasion. **b.** the date of such an event. **6.** *Rare.* the act of fixing. [C17: from Late Latin *fixūra* a fastening (with *-t-* by analogy with *mixture*)] —'**fixtureless** *adj.*

fix up *vb.* (*tr., adv.*) **1.** to arrange: *let's fix up a date.* **2.** (often foll. by *with*) to provide: *I'm sure we can fix you up with a room.* **3.** *Informal, chiefly U.S. and Canadian.* to repair or rearrange: *to fix up one's house.*

fizgig ('fɪzˌgɪg) *n.* **1.** a frivolous or flirtatious girl. **2.** a firework or whirling top that fizzes as it moves. **3.** a variant of **fishgig.** [C16: probably from obsolete *fise* a breaking of wind + *gig* girl]

fizz (fɪz) *vb.* (*intr.*) **1.** to make a hissing or bubbling sound. **2.** (of a drink) to produce bubbles of carbon dioxide, either through fermentation or aeration. ~*n.* **3.** a hissing or bubbling sound. **4.** the bubbly quality of a drink; effervescence. **5.** any effervescent drink. [C17: of imitative origin] —'**fizzy** *adj.* —'**fizziness** *n.*

fizzer ('fɪzə) *n.* **1.** anything that fizzes. **2.** *Austral. slang.* a person or thing that disappoints, fails to succeed, etc.: *the horse proved to be a fizzer.*

fizzle ('fɪzᵊl) *vb.* (*intr.*) **1.** to make a hissing or bubbling sound. **2.** (often foll. by *out*) *Informal.* to fail or die out, esp. after a promising start. ~*n.* **3.** a hissing or bubbling sound; fizz. **4.** *Informal.* an outright failure; fiasco. [C16: probably from obsolete *fist* to break wind]

fjeld *or* **field** (fjɛld) *n.* a high rocky plateau with little vegetation in Scandinavian countries. [C19: Norwegian; related to Old Norse *fjall* mountain; see FELL[5]]

fjord *or* **fiord** (fjɔːd) *n.* a long narrow inlet of the sea between high steep cliffs. It is common in Norway and was probably formed by glacial action. [C17: from Norwegian, from Old Norse *fjörthr;* see FIRTH, FORD]

FL *abbrev. for:* **1.** Flight Lieutenant. **2.** Florida. ~ **3.** *international car registration for* Liechtenstein. [from German *Fürstentum Liechtenstein* Principality of Liechtenstein]

fl. *abbrev. for:* **1.** floor. **2.** floruit. **3.** fluid. ~**4.** (in the Netherlands) *symbol for* guilder.

Fl. *abbrev. for:* **1.** Flanders. **2.** Flemish.

Fla. *abbrev. for* Florida.

flab (flæb) *n.* unsightly or unwanted fat on the body; flabbiness. [C20: back formation from FLABBY]

flabbergast ('flæbəˌgɑːst) *vb.* (*tr.; usually passive*) *Informal.* to overcome with astonishment; amaze utterly; astound. [C18: of uncertain origin]

flabby ('flæbɪ) *adj.* **-bier, -biest. 1.** lacking firmness; loose or yielding: *flabby muscles.* **2.** having flabby flesh, esp. through being overweight. **3.** lacking vitality; weak; ineffectual. [C17: alteration of *flappy,* from FLAP + -Y[1]; compare Dutch *flabbe* drooping lip] —'**flabbily** *adv.* —'**flabbiness** *n.*

flabellate (flə'bɛlɪt, -eɪt) *or* **flabelliform** (flə'bɛlɪˌfɔːm) *adj. Biology.* shaped like a fan.

flabellum (flə'bɛləm) *n., pl.* **-la** (-lə). **1.** a fan-shaped organ or part, such as the tip of the proboscis of a honeybee. **2.** *R.C. Church.* a large ceremonial fan. [C19: from Latin: small fan, from *flābra* breezes, from *flāre* to blow]

flaccid ('flæksɪd, 'flæs-) *adj.* lacking firmness; soft and limp; flabby. [C17: from Latin *flaccidus,* from *flaccus*] —**flac'cidity** *or* '**flaccidness** *n.* —'**flaccidly** *adv.*

flack[1] (flæk) *n. Chiefly U.S. and Canadian.* a press or publicity agent. [C20: of unknown origin]

flack[2] (flæk) *n.* a variant spelling of **flak.**

flacon (*French* flakɔ̃) *n.* a small stoppered bottle or flask, such as one used for perfume. [C19: from French; see FLAGON]

flag[1] (flæg) *n.* **1.** a piece of cloth, esp. bunting, often attached to a pole or staff, decorated with a design and used as an emblem, symbol, or standard or as a means of signalling. **2.** a small paper flag, emblem, or sticker sold on flag days. **3.** an indicator, that may be set or unset, used to indicate a condition or to stimulate a particular reaction in the execution of a computer program. **4.** *Informal.* short for **flag officer** and **flagship. 5.** *Journalism.* another name for **masthead** (sense 2). **6.** the fringe of long hair, tapering towards the tip, on the underside of the tail of certain breeds of dog, such as setters. **7.** the conspicuously marked tail of a deer. **8.** a less common name for **bookmark. 9.** *Brit.,*

Austral., and N.Z. the part of a taximeter that is raised when a taxi is for hire. **10. the.** (in Victoria, Australia) the Australian Rules premiership. **11. show the flag. a.** to assert a claim, as to a territory or stretch of water, by military presence. **b.** *Informal.* to be present; make an appearance. **12. strike** (*or* **lower**) **the flag. a.** to relinquish command, esp. of a ship. **b.** to submit or surrender. ~*vb.* **flags, flagging, flagged.** (*tr.*) **13.** to decorate or mark with a flag or flags. **14.** (often foll. by *down*) to warn or signal (a vehicle) to stop. **15.** to send or communicate (messages, information, etc.) by flag. **16.** to decoy (game or wild animals) by waving a flag or similar object so as to attract their attention. **17.** to mark (a page in a book, card, etc.) for attention by attaching a small tab or flag. **18.** (foll. by *away*) *N.Z.* to consider unimportant; brush aside. ~See also **flags.** [C16: of uncertain origin] —'**flagger** *n.* —'**flagless** *adj.*

flag[2] (flæg) *n.* **1.** any of various plants that have long swordlike leaves, esp. the iris *Iris pseudacorus* (**yellow flag**). **2.** the leaf of any such plant. ~See also **sweet flag.** [C14: probably of Scandinavian origin; compare Dutch *flag*, Danish *flæg* yellow iris]

flag[3] (flæg) *vb.* **flags, flagging, flagged.** (*intr.*) **1.** to hang down; become limp; droop. **2.** to decline in strength or vigour; become weak or tired. [C16: of unknown origin]

flag[4] (flæg) *n.* **1.** short for **flagstone.** ~*vb.* **flags, flagging, flagged. 2.** (*tr.*) to furnish (a floor) with flagstones.

flag captain *n.* the captain of a flagship.

flag day *n. Brit.* a day on which money is collected by a charity and small flags, emblems, or stickers are given to contributors.

Flag Day *n.* June 14, the annual holiday in the U.S. to celebrate the adoption in 1777 of the Stars and Stripes.

flagellant ('flædʒɪlənt, flə'dʒɛlənt) *or* **flagellator** ('flædʒɪˌleɪtə) *n.* **1.** a person who whips himself or others either as part of a religious penance or for sexual gratification. **2.** (*often cap.*) (in medieval Europe) a member of a religious sect who whipped themselves in public. [C16: from Latin *flagellāre* to whip, from FLAGELLUM] —'**flagellantˌism** *n.*

flagellate *vb.* ('flædʒɪˌleɪt). **1.** (*tr.*) to whip; scourge; flog. ~*adj.* ('flædʒɪlɪt, -ˌleɪt), *also* **flagellated. 2.** possessing one or more flagella. **3.** resembling a flagellum; whiplike. ~*n.* ('flædʒɪlɪt, -ˌleɪt). **4.** a flagellate organism, esp. any protozoan of the class *Mastigophora.* —ˌ**flagel'lation** *n.*

flagelliform (flə'dʒɛlɪˌfɔːm) *adj.* slender, tapering, and whiplike, as the antennae of certain insects.

flagellin (flə'dʒɛlɪn) *n.* the structural protein of bacterial flagella.

flagellum (flə'dʒɛləm) *n., pl.* **-la** (-lə) *or* **-lums. 1.** *Biology.* a long whiplike outgrowth from a cell that acts as an organ of locomotion: occurs in some protozoans, gametes, spores, etc. **2.** *Botany.* a long thin supple shoot or runner. **3.** *Zoology.* the terminal whiplike part of an arthropod's appendage, esp. of the antenna of many insects. [C19: from Latin: a little whip, from *flagrum* a whip, lash] —**fla'gellar** *adj.*

flageolet (ˌflædʒə'lɛt) *n.* a high-pitched musical instrument of the recorder family having six or eight finger holes. [C17: from French, modification of Old French *flajolet* a little flute, from *flajol* flute, from Vulgar Latin *flabeolum* (unattested), from Latin *flāre* to blow]

flag fall *n. Brit. and Austral.* the minimum charge for hiring a taxi.

flagging ('flægɪŋ) *n.* flagstones or a flagged area.

flaggy[1] ('flægɪ) *adj.* **-gier, -giest.** drooping; limp.

flaggy[2] ('flægɪ) *adj.* made of or similar to flagstone.

flagitious (flə'dʒɪʃəs) *adj.* atrociously wicked; vicious; outrageous. [C14: from Latin *flāgitiōsus* infamous, from *flāgitium* a shameful act; related to Latin *flagrum* whip] —**fla'gitiously** *adv.* —**fla'gitiousness** *n.*

flag lieutenant *n.* an admiral's ADC.

flagman ('flægmən) *n., pl.* **-men.** a person who has charge of, carries, or signals with a flag, esp. a railway employee.

flag of convenience *n.* a national flag flown by a ship registered in that country to gain financial or legal advantage.

flag officer *n.* an officer in certain navies of the rank of rear admiral or above and entitled to fly its flag.

flag of truce *n.* a white flag indicating the peaceful intent of its bearer or an invitation to an enemy to negotiate.

flagon ('flægən) *n.* **1.** a large bottle of wine, cider, etc. **2.** a vessel having a handle, spout, and narrow neck. [C15: from Old French *flascon*, from Late Latin *flascō*, probably of Germanic origin; see FLASK]

flagpole ('flægˌpəʊl) *or* **flagstaff** ('flægˌstɑːf) *n., pl.* **-poles, -staffs,** *or* **-staves** (-ˌsteɪvz). a pole or staff on which a flag is hoisted and displayed.

flag rank *n.* the rank of a flag officer.

flagrant ('fleɪgrənt) *adj.* **1.** blatant; glaring; outrageous. **2.** *Obsolete.* burning or blazing. [C15: from Latin *flagrāre* to blaze, burn] —'**flagrancy,** '**flagrance,** *or* '**flagrantness** *n.* —'**flagrantly** *adv.*

flagrante delicto (flə'græntɪ dɪ'lɪktəʊ) *adv.* See **in flagrante delicto.**

flags (flægz) *pl. n. Rare.* the long feathers on the leg of a hawk or falcon.

flagship ('flægˌʃɪp) *n.* **1.** a ship, esp. in a fleet, aboard which the commander of the fleet is quartered. **2.** the most important ship belonging to a shipping company. **3.** a single item from a related group considered as the most important, often in establishing a public image: *the nine o'clock news is the flagship of the BBC.*

flagstone ('flægˌstəʊn) *or* **flag** *n.* **1.** a hard fine-textured rock, such as a sandstone or shale, that can be split up into slabs for paving. **2.** a slab of such a rock. [C15 *flag* (in the sense: sod, turf), from Old Norse *flaga* slab; compare Old English *flæcg* plaster, poultice]

flag-waving *n. Informal.* **a.** an emotional appeal or display intended to arouse patriotic or nationalistic feeling. **b.** (*as modifier*): *a flag-waving speech.* —'**flag-ˌwaver** *n.*

flail (fleɪl) *n.* **1.** an implement used for threshing grain, consisting of a wooden handle with a free-swinging metal or wooden bar attached to it. **2.** a weapon so shaped used in the Middle Ages. ~*vb.* **3.** (*tr.*) to beat or thrash with or as if with a flail. **4.** to move or be moved like a flail; thresh about: *with arms flailing.* [C12 *fleil*, ultimately from Late Latin *flagellum* flail, from Latin: whip]

flair[1] (flɛə) *n.* **1.** natural ability; talent; aptitude. **2.** instinctive discernment; perceptiveness. **3.** stylishness or elegance; dash: *to dress with flair.* **4.** *Hunting, rare.* **a.** the scent left by quarry. **b.** the sense of smell of a hound. [C19: from French, literally: sense of smell, from Old French: scent, from *flairier* to give off a smell, ultimately from Latin *frāgrāre* to smell sweet; see FRAGRANT]

flair[2] (fler) *n.* a Scot. word for **floor.**

flak *or* **flack** (flæk) *n.* **1.** anti-aircraft fire or artillery. **2.** *Informal.* a great deal of adverse criticism. [C20: from German *Fl(ieger)a(bwehr)k(anone)*, literally: aircraft defence gun]

flake[1] (fleɪk) *n.* **1.** a small thin piece or layer chipped off or detached from an object or substance; scale. **2.** a small piece or particle: *a flake of snow.* **3.** a thin layer or stratum. **4.** *Archaeol.* **a.** a fragment removed by chipping or hammering from a larger stone used as a tool or weapon. See also **blade. b.** (*as modifier*): *flake tool.* ~*vb.* **5.** to peel or cause to peel off in flakes; chip. **6.** to cover or become covered with or as with flakes. **7.** (*tr.*) to form into flakes. [C14: of Scandinavian origin; compare Norwegian *flak* disc, Middle Dutch *vlacken* to flutter] —'**flaker** *n.*

flake[2] (fleɪk) *n.* a rack or platform for drying fish or other produce. [C14: from Old Norse *flaki;* related to Dutch *vlaak* hurdle]

flake[3] (fleɪk) *vb. Nautical.* another word for **fake**[2].

flake[4] (fleɪk) *n.* (in Victoria, Australia) the commercial name for the meat of the gummy shark.

flake out *vb.* (*intr., adv.*) *Informal.* to collapse or fall asleep as through extreme exhaustion.

flake white *n.* a pigment made from flakes of white lead.

flak jacket *n.* a reinforced sleeveless jacket for protection against gunfire or shrapnel worn by soldiers, policemen, etc.

flaky ('fleɪkɪ) *adj.* **flakier, flakiest. 1.** like or made of flakes. **2.** tending to peel off or break easily into flakes. **3.** Also: **flakey.** *U.S. slang.* eccentric; crazy. —'**flakily** *adv.* —'**flakiness** *n.*

flaky pastry *n.* a rich pastry in the form of very thin layers, used for making pies, small cakes, etc.

flam[1] (flæm) *Now chiefly dialect.* ~*n.* **1.** a falsehood, deception, or sham. **2.** nonsense; drivel. ~*vb.* **flams, flamming, flammed. 3.** (*tr.*) to cheat or deceive. [C16: probably short for FLIMFLAM]

flam[2] (flæm) *n.* a drumbeat in which both sticks strike the head almost simultaneously but are heard to do so separately. [C18: probably imitative of the sound]

flambé *or* **flambée** ('flɑːmbeɪ, 'flæm-; *French* flɑ̃be) *adj.* **1.** (of food, such as steak or pancakes) served in flaming brandy. ~*vb.* **-béeing, -béed. 2.** (*tr.*) to pour brandy over (food) and ignite it. [French, past participle of *flamber* to FLAME]

flambeau ('flæmbəʊ) *n., pl.* **-beaux** (-bəʊ, -bəʊz) *or* **-beaus. 1.** a burning torch, as used in night processions. **2.** a large ornamental candlestick. [C17: from Old French: torch, literally: a little flame, from *flambe* FLAME]

flamboyant (flæm'bɔɪənt) *adj.* **1.** elaborate or extravagant; florid; showy. **2.** rich or brilliant in colour; resplendent. **3.** of, denoting, or relating to the French Gothic style of architecture characterized by flamelike tracery and elaborate carving. ~*n.* **4.** another name for **royal poinciana.** [C19: from French: flaming, from *flamboyer* to FLAME] —**flam'boyance** *or* **flam'boyancy** *n.* —**flam'boyantly** *adv.*

flame (fleɪm) *n.* **1.** a hot usually luminous body of burning gas often containing small incandescent particles, typically emanating in flickering streams from burning material or produced by a jet of ignited gas. **2.** (*often pl.*) the state or condition of burning with flames: *to burst into flames.* **3.** a brilliant light; fiery glow. **4. a.** a strong reddish-orange colour. **b.** (*as adj.*): *a flame carpet.* **5.** intense passion or ardour; burning emotion. **6.** *Informal.* a lover or sweetheart (esp. in the phrase **an old flame**). ~*vb.* **7.** to burn or cause to burn brightly; give off or cause to give off flame. **8.** (*intr.*) to burn or glow as if with fire; become red or fiery: *his face flamed with anger.* **9.** (*intr.*) to show great emotion; become angry or excited. **10.** (*tr.*) to apply a flame to (something). **11.** (*tr.*) *Archaic.* to set on fire, either physically or with emotion. ~See also **flameout.** [C14: from Anglo-French *flaume*, from Old French *flambe*, modification of *flamble*, from Latin *flammula* a little flame, from *flamma* flame] —'**flamer** *n.* —'**flameless** *adj.* —'**flamelet** *n.* —'**flameˌlike** *adj.* —'**flamy** *adj.*

flame-arc light *n. Electrical engineering.* an arc light that uses flame carbons to colour the arc.

flame carbon *n. Electrical engineering.* a carbon electrode containing metallic salts that colour the arc in a flame-arc light.
flame cell *n.* an organ of excretion in flatworms: a hollow cup-shaped cell containing a bunch of cilia, whose movement draws in waste products and wafts them to the outside through a connecting tubule.
flame cutting *n. Engineering.* a method of cutting ferrous metals in which the metal is heated by a torch to about 800°C and is oxidized by a stream of oxygen from the torch.
flame gun *n.* a type of flame-thrower for destroying garden weeds.
flame hardening *n. Engineering.* the surface hardening of ferrous metals by heating the metal with an oxyacetylene flame followed by rapid cooling.
flame lamp *n. Electrical engineering.* a filament lamp in which the bulb resembles the shape of a flame.
flamen ('fleɪmɛn) *n., pl.* **flamens** *or* **flamines** ('flæmɪˌniːz). (in ancient Rome) any of 15 priests who each served a particular deity. [C14: from Latin; probably related to Old English *blōtan* to sacrifice, Gothic *blotan* to worship]
flamenco (flə'mɛŋkəʊ) *n., pl.* **-cos.** **1.** a type of dance music for vocal soloist and guitar, characterized by elaborate melody and sad mood. **2.** the dance performed to such music. [from Spanish: like a gipsy, literally: Fleming, from Middle Dutch *Vlaminc* Fleming]
flame-of-the-forest *n.* **1.** (esp. in Malaysia) another name for **royal poinciana.** **2.** a papilionaceous tree, *Butea frondosa,* native to E India and Burma, having hanging clusters of scarlet flowers.
flameout ('fleɪmˌaʊt) *n.* **1.** the failure of an aircraft jet engine in flight due to extinction of the flame. ~*vb.* **flame out.** (*adv.*) **2.** (of a jet engine) to fail in flight or to cause (a jet engine) to fail in flight.
flameproof ('fleɪmˌpruːf) *adj.* **1.** not liable to catch fire or be damaged by fire. **2.** (of electrical apparatus) designed so that an internal explosion will not ignite external flammable gas.
flame retarder *n.* a material that, while not incombustible, does not itself maintain combustion without an external heat source and therefore retards the spread of fire.
flame test *n.* a test for detecting the presence of certain metals in compounds by the coloration they give to a flame. Sodium, for example, turns a flame yellow.
flame-thrower *n.* a weapon that ejects a stream or spray of burning fluid.
flame tree *n.* any of various tropical trees with red or orange flowers, such as flame-of-the-forest.
flaming ('fleɪmɪŋ) *adj.* **1.** burning with or emitting flames. **2.** glowing brightly; brilliant. **3.** intense or ardent; vehement; passionate: *a flaming temper.* **4.** *Informal.* (intensifier): *you flaming idiot.* **5.** an obsolete word for **flagrant.** —'**flamingly** *adv.*
flamingo (flə'mɪŋgəʊ) *n., pl.* **-gos** *or* **-goes.** **1.** any large wading bird of the family *Phoenicopteridae,* having a pink-and-red plumage and downward-bent bill and inhabiting brackish lakes: order *Ciconiiformes.* **2. a.** a reddish-orange colour. **b.** (*as adj.*): *flamingo gloves.* [C16: from Portuguese *flamengo,* from Provençal *flamenc,* from Latin *flamma* flame + Germanic suffix *-ing* denoting descent from or membership of; compare -ING[3]]
flammable ('flæməb^{ə}l) *adj.* liable to catch fire; readily combustible; inflammable. —ˌ**flamma'bility** *n.*
▷**Usage.** *Flammable* and *inflammable* are interchangeable when used of the properties of materials. *Flammable* is, however, often preferred for warning labels as there is less likelihood of misunderstanding (*inflammable* being sometimes taken to mean *not flammable*). *Inflammable* is preferred in figurative contexts: *his temperament could be described as inflammable.*
flan (flæn) *n.* **1.** an open pastry or sponge tart filled with fruit or a savoury mixture. **2.** a piece of metal ready to receive the die or stamp in the production of coins; shaped blank; planchet. [C19: from French, from Old French *flaon,* from Late Latin *fladō* flat cake, of Germanic origin]
flanch (flæntʃ) *n.* a variant of **flaunch.**
Flanders poppy ('flɑːndəz) *n.* another name for **corn poppy.**
flânerie *French.* (flɑnri) *n.* aimless strolling or lounging; idleness. [C19: from *flâner* to stroll, dawdle, ultimately from Old Norse *flana* to wander about]
flâneur *French.* (flɑnœr) *n.* an idler or loafer. [C19: see FLÂNERIE]
flange (flændʒ) *n.* **1.** a radially projecting collar or rim on an object for locating or strengthening it or for attaching it to another object. **2.** a flat outer face of a rolled-steel joist, esp. of an I- or H-beam. **3.** a tool for forming a flange. ~*vb.* **4.** (*tr.*) to attach or provide (a component) with a flange. **5.** (*intr.*) to take the form of a flange. [C17: probably changed from earlier *flaunche* curved segment at side of a heraldic field, from French *flanc* FLANK] —**flanged** *adj.* —'**flangeless** *adj.* —'**flanger** *n.*
flange coupling *n. Engineering.* a driving coupling between rotating shafts that consists of flanges (or **half couplings**) one of which is fixed at the end of each shaft, the two flanges being bolted together with a ring of bolts to complete the drive.
flanged rail *n.* another name for **flat-bottomed rail.**
flank (flæŋk) *n.* **1.** the side of a man or animal between the ribs and the hip. **2.** (loosely) the outer part of the human thigh. **3.** a cut of beef from the flank. **4.** the side of anything, such as a mountain or building. **5.** the side of a naval or military formation. ~*vb.* **6.** (when *intr.*, often foll. by *on* or *upon*) to be located at the side of (an object, building, etc.). **7.** *Military.* to position or guard on or beside the flank of (a formation, etc.). **8.** *Military.* to move past or go round (a flank). [C12: from Old French *flanc,* of Germanic origin]
flanker ('flæŋkə) *n.* **1.** one of a detachment of soldiers detailed to guard the flanks, esp. of a formation. **2.** a projecting fortification, used esp. to protect or threaten a flank.
flannel ('flæn^{ə}l) *n.* **1.** a soft light woollen fabric with a slight nap, used for clothing. **2.** (*pl.*) trousers or other garments made of flannel. **3.** See **cotton flannel.** **4.** *Brit.* a small piece of cloth used to wash the face and hands; face cloth. U.S. and Canadian equivalent: **washcloth.** **5.** *Brit. informal.* indirect or evasive talk; deceiving flattery. ~*vb.* **-nels, -nelling, -nelled** *or U.S.* **-nels, -neling, -neled.** (*tr.*) **6.** to cover or wrap with flannel. **7.** to rub, clean, or polish with flannel. **8.** *Brit. informal.* to talk evasively to; flatter in order to mislead. [C14: probably variant of *flanen* sackcloth, from Welsh *gwlanen* woollen fabric, from *gwlân* wool] —'**flannelly** *adj.*
flannelboard ('flæn^{ə}lˌbɔːd) *or* **flannelgraph** ('flæn^{ə}lˌgrɑːf, -ˌgræf) *n.* a visual aid used in teaching consisting of a board covered with flannel to which pictures, diagrams, etc. will stick when pressed on.
flannelette (ˌflæn^{ə}'lɛt) *n.* a cotton imitation of flannel.
flannel flower *n.* any Australian plant of the umbelliferous genus *Actinotus* having white flannel-like bracts beneath the flowers.
flap (flæp) *vb.* **flaps, flapping, flapped.** **1.** to move (wings or arms) up and down, esp. in or as if in flying, or (of wings or arms) to move in this way. **2.** to move or cause to move noisily back and forth or up and down: *the curtains flapped in the breeze.* **3.** (*intr.*) *Informal.* to become agitated or flustered; panic. **4.** to deal (a person or thing) a blow with a broad flexible object. **5.** (*tr.*; sometimes foll. by *down*) to toss, fling, slam, etc., abruptly or noisily. **6.** (*tr.*) *Phonetics.* to pronounce (an (r) sound) by allowing the tongue to give a single light tap against the alveolar ridge or uvula. ~*n.* **7.** the action, motion, or noise made by flapping: *with one flap of its wings the bird was off.* **8.** a piece of material, etc., attached at one edge and usually used to cover an opening, as on a tent, envelope, or pocket. **9.** a blow dealt with a flat object; slap. **10.** a movable surface fixed to the trailing edge of an aircraft wing that increases lift during takeoff and drag during landing. **11.** *Surgery.* a piece of tissue partially connected to the body, either following an amputation or to be used as a graft. **12.** *Informal.* a state of panic, distress, or agitation. **13.** *Phonetics.* an (r) produced by allowing the tongue to give a single light tap against the alveolar ridge or uvula. [C14: probably of imitative origin]
flapdoodle ('flæpˌduːd^{ə}l) *n. Slang.* foolish talk; nonsense. [C19: of unknown origin]
flapjack ('flæpˌdʒæk) *n.* **1.** a chewy biscuit made with rolled oats. **2.** *Chiefly U.S. and Canadian.* another word for **pancake.** [C17: from FLAP (in the sense: toss) + JACK[1]]
flapper ('flæpə) *n.* **1.** a person or thing that flaps. **2.** (in the 1920s) a young woman, esp. one flaunting her unconventional dress and behaviour.
flare (flɛə) *vb.* **1.** to burn or cause to burn with an unsteady or sudden bright flame. **2.** to spread or cause to spread outwards from a narrow to a wider shape. **3.** (*tr.*) to make a conspicuous display of. **4.** to increase the temperature of (a molten metal or alloy) until a gaseous constituent of the melt burns with a characteristic flame or (of a molten metal or alloy) to show such a flame. **5.** (*tr.*; sometimes foll. by *off*) (in the oil industry) to burn off (unwanted gas) at an oil well. ~*n.* **6.** an unsteady flame. **7.** a sudden burst of flame. **8. a.** a blaze of light or fire used to illuminate, identify, alert, signal distress, etc. **b.** the device producing such a blaze. **9.** a spreading shape or anything with a spreading shape: *a skirt with a flare.* **10.** a sudden outburst, as of emotion. **11.** *Optics.* **a.** the unwanted light reaching the image region of an optical device by reflections inside the instrument, etc. **b.** the fogged area formed on a negative by such reflections. **12.** *Astronomy.* short for **solar flare.** **13.** *Aeronautics.* the final transition phase of an aircraft landing, from the steady descent path to touchdown. **14.** an open flame used to burn off unwanted gas at an oil well. [C16 (to spread out): of unknown origin]
flare path *n.* an airstrip illuminated for use at night or in bad weather.
flares (flɛəz) *pl. n. Informal.* trousers with legs that widen below the knee, popular in the late 1960s and early 1970s.
flare star *n.* a red dwarf star in which outbursts, thought to be analogous to solar flares, occur, increasing the luminosity by several magnitudes in a few minutes.
flare-up *n.* **1.** a sudden burst of fire or light. **2.** *Informal.* a sudden burst of emotion or violence. ~*vb.* **flare up.** (*intr., adv.*). **3.** to burst suddenly into fire or light. **4.** *Informal.* to burst into anger.
flash (flæʃ) *n.* **1.** a sudden short blaze of intense light or flame: *a flash of sunlight.* **2.** a sudden occurrence or display, esp. one suggestive of brilliance: *a flash of understanding.* **3.** a very brief space of time: *over in a flash.* **4.** an ostentatious display: *a flash of her diamonds.* **5.** Also called: **newsflash.** a short news

announcement concerning a new event. 6. Also called: **patch.** *Chiefly Brit.* an insignia or emblem worn on a uniform, vehicle, etc., to identify its military formation. 7. a patch of bright colour on a dark background, such as light marking on an animal. 8. a volatile mixture of inorganic salts used to produce a glaze on bricks or tiles. 9. a. a sudden rush of water down a river or watercourse. b. a device, such as a sluice, for producing such a rush. 10. *Photog., informal.* short for **flashlight** (sense 2) or **flash photography.** 11. a ridge of thin metal or plastic formed on a moulded object by the extrusion of excess material between dies. 12. *Yorkshire and Lancashire dialect.* a pond, esp. one produced as a consequence of subsidence. 13. (*modifier*) involving, using, or produced by a flash of heat, light, etc.: *flash blindness; flash distillation.* 14. **flash in the pan.** a project, person, etc., that enjoys only short-lived success, notoriety, etc. ~*adj.* 15. *Informal.* ostentatious or vulgar. 16. *Informal.* of or relating to gamblers and followers of boxing and racing. 17. sham or counterfeit. 18. *Informal.* relating to or characteristic of the criminal underworld. 19. brief and rapid: **flash freezing.** ~*vb.* 20. to burst or cause to burst suddenly or intermittently into flame. 21. to emit or reflect or cause to emit or reflect light suddenly or intermittently. 22. (*intr.*) to move very fast: *he flashed by on his bicycle.* 23. (*intr.*) to come rapidly (into the mind or vision). 24. (*intr.; foll. by out or up*) to appear like a sudden light: *his anger really flashes out at times.* 25. a. to signal or communicate very fast: *to flash a message.* b. to signal by use of a light, such as car headlights. 26. (*tr.*) *Informal.* to display ostentatiously: *to flash money around.* 27. (*tr.*) *Informal.* to show suddenly and briefly. 28. (*intr.*) *Brit. slang.* to expose oneself indecently. 29. (*tr.*) to cover (a roof) with flashing. 30. to send a sudden rush of water down (a river, etc.), or to carry (a vessel) down by this method. 31. (in the making of glass) to coat (glass) with a thin layer of glass of a different colour. 32. (*tr.*) to subject to a brief pulse of heat or radiation. 33. (*tr.*) to change (a liquid) to a gas by causing it to hit a hot surface. 34. *Obsolete.* to splash or dash (water). [C14 (in the sense: to rush, as of water): of unknown origin]

flashback ('flæʃˌbæk) *n.* 1. a transition in a novel, film, etc., to an earlier scene or event. ~*vb.* **flash back.** 2. (*intr., adv.*) to return in a novel, film, etc., to a past event.

flashboard ('flæʃˌbɔːd) *n.* a board or boarding that is placed along the top of a dam to increase its height and capacity.

flashbulb ('flæʃˌbʌlb) *n. Photog.* a small expendable glass light bulb that is triggered, usually electrically, to produce a bright flash of light. Also called: **photoflash.** Compare **electronic flash.**

flashbulb memory *n. Psychol.* the clear recollections that a person may have of the circumstances associated with a dramatic event.

flash burn *n. Pathol.* a burn caused by momentary exposure to intense radiant heat.

flash card *n.* a card on which are written or printed words for children to look at briefly, used as an aid to learning.

flashcube ('flæʃˌkjuːb) *n.* a boxlike camera attachment, holding four flashbulbs, that turns so that each flashbulb can be used in quick succession.

flash eliminator *or* **suppressor** *n.* a device fitted to the muzzle of a firearm to reduce the flash made by the ignited propellant gases.

flasher ('flæʃə) *n.* 1. something that flashes, such as a direction indicator on a vehicle. 2. *Brit. slang.* a person who indecently exposes himself.

flash flood *n.* a sudden short-lived torrent, usually caused by a heavy storm, esp. in desert regions.

flash gun *n.* a device, attachable to or sometimes incorporated in a camera, for holding and electrically firing a flashbulb as the shutter opens. Compare **electronic flash.**

flashing ('flæʃɪŋ) *n.* a weatherproof material, esp. thin sheet metal, used to cover the valleys between the slopes of a roof, the junction between a chimney and a roof, etc.

flashlight ('flæʃˌlaɪt) *n.* 1. another word (esp. U.S.) for **torch.** 2. *Photog.* the brief bright light emitted by a flashbulb or electronic flash. Sometimes shortened to **flash.** 3. *Chiefly U.S. and Canadian.* a bright flashing light or its source.

flashover ('flæʃˌəʊvə) *n.* an electric discharge over or around the surface of an insulator.

flash photography *n.* photography in which a flashbulb or electronic flash is used to provide momentary illumination of a dark or insufficiently lit subject.

flash photolysis *n. Physics.* a technique for producing and investigating free radicals. A low-pressure gas is subjected to a flash of radiation to produce the radicals, subsequent flashes being used to identify them and assess their lifetimes by absorption spectroscopy.

flash point *or* **flashing point** *n.* 1. the lowest temperature at which the vapour above a liquid can be ignited in air. 2. a critical moment beyond which a situation will inevitably erupt into violence: *the political mood has reached flash point.*

flash set *n. Civil engineering.* undesirably rapid setting of cement in concrete.

flash smelting *n.* a smelting process for sulphur-containing ores in which the dried and powdered ore, mixed with oxygen, is ignited on discharge from a nozzle, melts, and drops to the bottom of a settling chamber. Sulphur is released mainly in its solid form, thus reducing atmospheric pollution.

flashy ('flæʃɪ) *adj.* **flashier, flashiest.** 1. brilliant and dazzling, esp. for a short time or in a superficial way. 2. cheap and ostentatious. —'**flashily** *adv.* —'**flashiness** *n.*

flask (flɑːsk) *n.* 1. a bottle with a narrow neck, esp. used in a laboratory or for wine, oil, etc. 2. Also called: **hip flask.** a small flattened container of glass or metal designed to be carried in a pocket, esp. for liquor. 3. See **powder flask.** 4. a container packed with sand to form a mould in a foundry. 5. See **vacuum flask.** 6. Also called: **cask, coffin.** *Engineering.* a container used for transporting irradiated nuclear fuel. [C14: from Old French *flasque, flaske,* from Medieval Latin *flasca, flasco,* perhaps of Germanic origin; compare Old English *flasce, flaxe*]

flasket ('flɑːskɪt) *n.* 1. a long shallow basket. 2. a small flask. [C15: from Old French *flasquet* a little FLASK]

flat[1] (flæt) *adj.* **flatter, flattest.** 1. horizontal; level: *flat ground; a flat roof.* 2. even or smooth, without projections or depressions: *a flat surface.* 3. lying stretched out at full length; prostrate: *he lay flat on the ground.* 4. having little depth or thickness; shallow: *a flat dish.* 5. (*postpositive;* often foll. by *against*) having a surface or side in complete contact with another surface: *flat against the wall.* 6. spread out, unrolled, or levelled. 7. (of a tyre) deflated, either partially or completely. 8. (of shoes) having an unraised or only slightly raised heel. 9. *Chiefly Brit.* a. (of races, racetracks, or racecourses) not having obstacles to be jumped. b. of, relating to, or connected with flat racing as opposed to steeplechasing and hurdling: *flat jockeys earn more.* 10. without qualification; total: *a flat denial.* 11. without possibility of change; fixed: *a flat rate.* 12. (*prenominal or immediately postpositive*) neither more nor less; exact: *he did the journey in thirty minutes flat; a flat thirty minutes.* 13. unexciting or lacking point or interest: *a flat joke.* 14. without variation or resonance; monotonous: *a flat voice.* 15. (of food) stale or tasteless. 16. (of beer, sparkling wines, etc.) having lost effervescence, as by exposure to air. 17. (of trade, business, a market, etc.) commercially inactive; sluggish. 18. (of a battery) fully discharged; dead. 19. (of a print, photograph, or painting) lacking contrast or shading between tones. 20. (of paint) without gloss or lustre; matt. 21. (of a painting) lacking perspective. 22. *adj.* (of lighting) diffuse. 23. *Music.* a. (*immediately postpositive*) denoting a note of a given letter name (or the sound it represents) that has been lowered in pitch by one chromatic semitone: *B flat.* b. (of an instrument, voice, etc.) out of tune by being too low in pitch. Compare **sharp** (sense 12). 24. *Phonetics.* another word for **lenis.** 25. *Phonetics.* **flat a.** the vowel sound of *a* as in the usual U.S. or S Brit. pronunciation of *hand, cat,* usually represented by the symbol (æ). ~*adv.* 26. in or into a prostrate, level, or flat state or position: *he held his hand out flat.* 27. completely or utterly; absolutely: *he went flat against the rules.* 28. exactly; precisely: *in three minutes flat.* 29. *Music.* a. lower than a standard pitch. b. too low in pitch: *she sings flat.* Compare **sharp** (sense 18). 30. **fall flat.** to fail to achieve a desired effect, etc. 31. **flat out.** *Informal.* a. with the maximum speed or effort. b. totally exhausted. ~*n.* 32. a flat object, surface, or part. 33. (*often pl.*) a low-lying tract of land, esp. a marsh or swamp. 34. (*often pl.*) a mud bank exposed at low tide. 35. *Music.* a. an accidental that lowers the pitch of the following note by one chromatic semitone. Usual symbol: ♭ b. a note affected by this accidental. Compare **sharp** (sense 19). 36. *Theatre.* a rectangular wooden frame covered with painted canvas, etc., used to form part of a stage setting. 37. a punctured car tyre. 38. (*often cap.;* preceded by *the*) *Chiefly Brit.* a. flat racing, esp. as opposed to steeplechasing and hurdling. b. the season of flat racing. 39. *Nautical.* a flatboat or lighter. ~*vb.* **flats, flatting, flatted.** 40. to make or become flat. 41. *Music.* the usual U.S. word for **flatten** (sense 3). ~See also **flats.** [C14: from Old Norse *flatr;* related to Old High German *flaz* flat, Greek *platus* flat, broad] —'**flatly** *adv.* —'**flatness** *n.*

flat[2] (flæt) *n.* 1. a set of rooms comprising a residence entirely on one floor of a building. Usual U.S. and Canadian name: **apartment.** 2. *Brit. and N.Z.* a portion of a house used as separate living quarters. 3. *N.Z.* a house shared with people who are not members of one's own family. ~*vb.* (*intr.*) 4. *Austral. informal. and N.Z.* to live in a flat (with someone). [Old English *flett* floor, hall, house; related to FLAT[1]]

flat-bed lorry ('flætˌbɛd) *n.* a lorry with a flat platform for its body.

flat-bed press *n.* a printing machine on which the type forme is carried on a flat bed under a revolving paper-bearing cylinder. Also called: **cylinder press.**

flatboat ('flætˌbəʊt) *n.* any boat with a flat bottom, usually for transporting goods on a canal or river.

flat-bottomed rail *n. Railways.* a rail having a cross section like an inverted T, with the top extremity enlarged slightly to form the head. Also called: **flanged rail.**

flat cap *n.* 1. another name for **cloth cap** (sense 1). 2. an Elizabethan man's hat with a narrow down-turned brim.

flatette (ˌflæt'ɛt) *n. Austral.* a flat having only a few rooms.

flatfish ('flætˌfɪʃ) *n., pl.* **-fish** *or* **-fishes.** any marine spiny-finned fish of the order *Heterosomata,* including the halibut, plaice, turbot, and sole, all of which (when adult) swim along the sea floor on one side of the body, which is highly compressed and has both eyes on the uppermost side.

flatfoot ('flæt,fʊt) *n.* **1.** Also called: **splayfoot.** a condition in which the entire sole of the foot is able to touch the ground because of flattening of the instep arch. **2.** (*pl.* **-foots** *or* **-feet**) a slang word (usually derogatory) for a **policeman.**

flat-footed (,flæt'fʊtɪd) *adj.* **1.** having flatfoot. **2.** *Brit. informal.* **a.** clumsy or awkward. **b.** downright and uncompromising. **3.** *Informal.* off guard or unawares (often in the phrase **catch flat-footed**). —,**flat-'footedly** *adv.* —,**flat-'footedness** *n.*

flathead ('flæt,hed) *n., pl.* **-head** *or* **-heads.** any Pacific scorpaenoid food fish of the family *Platycephalidae,* which resemble gurnards.

flatiron ('flæt,aɪən) *n.* (formerly) an iron for pressing clothes that was heated by being placed on a stove, etc.

flat knot *n.* another name for **reef knot.**

flatlet ('flætlɪt) *n.* a flat having only a few rooms.

flatling ('flætlɪŋ) *Archaic or dialect.* ~*adv.* **1.** in a flat or prostrate position. ~*adj., adv.* **2.** with the flat side, as of a sword. ~Also (for adv.): '**flatlings.**

flatmate ('flæt,meɪt) *n. Brit.* a person with whom one shares a flat.

flat racing *n.* **a.** the racing of horses on racecourses without jumps. **b.** (*as modifier*): *the flat-racing season.*

flats (flæts) *or* **flatties** ('flætɪz) *pl. n.* shoes with flat heels or no heels.

flat spin *n.* **1.** an aircraft spin in which the longitudinal axis is more nearly horizontal than vertical. **2.** *Informal.* a state of confusion; dither.

flat spot *n.* **1.** *Engineering.* a region of poor acceleration over a narrow range of throttle openings, caused by a weak mixture in the carburettor. **2.** any narrow region of poor performance in a mechanical device.

flatten ('flætᵊn) *vb.* **1.** (sometimes foll. by *out*) to make or become flat or flatter. **2.** (*tr.*) *Informal.* **a.** to knock down or injure; prostrate. **b.** to crush or subdue: *failure will flatten his self-esteem.* **3.** (*tr.*) *Music.* to lower the pitch of (a note) by one chromatic semitone. Usual U.S. word: **flat. 4.** (*intr.*; foll. by *out*) to manoeuvre an aircraft into horizontal flight, esp. after a dive. —'**flattener** *n.*

flatter[1] ('flætə) *vb.* **1.** to praise insincerely, esp. in order to win favour or reward. **2.** to show to advantage: *that dress flatters her.* **3.** (*tr.*) to make to appear more attractive, etc., than in reality. **4.** to play upon or gratify the vanity of (a person): *it flatters her to be remembered.* **5.** (*tr.*) to beguile with hope; encourage, esp. falsely: *this success flattered him into believing himself a champion.* **6.** (*tr.*) to congratulate or deceive (oneself): *I flatter myself that I am the best.* [C13: probably from Old French *flater* to lick, fawn upon, of Frankish origin] —'**flatterable** *adj.* —'**flatterer** *n.* —'**flatteringly** *adv.*

flatter[2] ('flætə) *n.* **1.** a blacksmith's tool, resembling a flat-faced hammer, that is placed on forged work and struck to smooth the surface of the forging. **2.** a die with a narrow rectangular orifice for drawing flat sections.

flattery ('flætərɪ) *n., pl.* **-teries. 1.** the act of flattering. **2.** excessive or insincere praise.

flattie ('flætɪ) *n. N.Z. informal.* a flounder or other flatfish.

flatties ('flætɪz) *pl. n.* another word for **flats.**

flatting ('flætɪŋ) *n.* **1.** *Metallurgy.* the process of flattening metal into a sheet by rolling. **2.** *N.Z.* the practice of sharing a house with people who are not members of one's own family. **3. go flatting.** *N.Z.* to leave the parental home and live independently in a flat, usually with people of the same age group.

flattish ('flætɪʃ) *adj.* somewhat flat.

flattop ('flæt,tɒp) *n. U.S.* an informal name for **aircraft carrier.**

flat top *n.* a style of haircut in which the hair is cut shortest on the top of the head so that it stands up from the scalp and appears flat from the crown to the forehead.

flat tuning *n.* the condition of a radio receiver that does not discriminate sharply between signals on different frequencies.

flatulent ('flætjʊlənt) *adj.* **1.** suffering from or caused by an excessive amount of gas in the alimentary canal, producing uncomfortable distension. **2.** generating excessive gas in the alimentary canal. **3.** pretentious or windy in style. [C16: from New Latin *flātulentus,* from Latin: FLATUS] —'**flatulence** *or* '**flatulency** *n.* —'**flatulently** *adv.*

flatus ('fleɪtəs) *n., pl.* **-tuses.** gas generated in the alimentary canal. [C17: from Latin: a blowing, snorting, from *flāre* to breathe, blow]

flatware ('flæt,wɛə) *n. U.S. and Canadian* **1.** cutlery. **2.** any relatively flat tableware such as plates, saucers, etc. Compare **hollowware.**

flatways ('flæt,weɪz) *or U.S.* **flatwise** *adv.* with the flat or broad side down or in contact with another surface.

flatworm ('flæt,wɜːm) *n.* any parasitic or free-living invertebrate of the phylum *Platyhelminthes,* including planarians, flukes, and tapeworms, having a flattened body with no circulatory system and only one opening to the intestine.

flat-woven *adj.* (of a carpet) woven without pile.

flaunch (flɔːntʃ) *n.* a cement or mortar slope around a chimney top, manhole, etc., to throw off water. Also called: **flaunching.** [C18: variant of FLANGE]

flaunt (flɔːnt) *vb.* **1.** to display (possessions, oneself, etc.) ostentatiously; show off. **2.** to wave or cause to wave freely; flutter. ~*n.* **3.** the act of flaunting. [C16: perhaps of Scandinavian origin; compare Norwegian dialect *flanta* to wander about] —'**flaunter** *n.* —'**flauntingly** *adv.*

flaunty ('flɔːntɪ) *adj.* **flauntier, flauntiest.** *Chiefly U.S.* characterized by or inclined to ostentatious display or flaunting. —'**flauntily** *adv.* —'**flauntiness** *n.*

flautist ('flɔːtɪst) *or U.S.* **flutist** ('fluːtɪst) *n.* a player of the flute. [C19: from Italian *flautista,* from *flauto* FLUTE]

flavescent (flə'vɛsᵊnt) *adj.* turning yellow; yellowish. [C19: from Latin *flāvēscere* to become yellow, from *flāvēre* to be yellow, from *flāvus* yellow]

flavin *or* **flavine** ('fleɪvɪn) *n.* **1.** a heterocyclic ketone that forms the nucleus of certain natural yellow pigments, such as riboflavin. Formula: $C_{10}H_6N_4O_2$. See **flavoprotein. 2.** any yellow pigment based on flavin. **3.** another name for **quercetin.** [C19: from Latin *flāvus* yellow]

flavine ('fleɪvɪn) *n.* **1.** another name for **acriflavine hydrochloride. 2.** a variant spelling of **flavin.**

flavone ('fleɪvəʊn) *n.* **1.** a crystalline compound occurring in plants. Formula: $C_{15}H_{10}O_2$. **2.** any of a class of yellow plant pigments derived from flavone. [C19: from German *Flavon,* from Latin *flāvus* yellow + -ONE]

flavonoid ('fleɪvə,nɔɪd) *n.* any of a group of organic compounds that occur as pigments in fruit and flowers. [C20: from FLAVONE + -OID]

flavoprotein (,fleɪvəʊ'prəʊtiːn) *n.* any of a group of enzymes that contain a derivative of riboflavin linked to a protein and catalyse oxidation in cells. Also called: **cytochrome reductase.** See also **FMN, FAD.** [C20: from FLAVIN + PROTEIN]

flavopurpurin (,fleɪvəʊ'pɜːpjʊrɪn) *n.* a yellow crystalline dye derived from anthraquinone. Formula: $C_{14}H_5O_2(OH)_3$. [C20: from Latin *flāvus* yellow + PURPURIN]

flavorous ('fleɪvərəs) *adj.* having flavour; tasty.

flavour *or U.S.* **flavor** ('fleɪvə) *n.* **1.** taste perceived in food or liquid in the mouth. **2.** a substance added to food, etc., to impart a specific taste. **3.** a distinctive quality or atmosphere; suggestion: *a poem with a Shakespearean flavour.* **4.** *Physics.* a property of quarks that enables them to be differentiated into six types: up, down, strange, charm, bottom (or beauty), and top (or truth). ~*vb.* **5.** (*tr.*) to impart a flavour, taste, or quality to. [C14: from Old French *flaour,* from Late Latin *flātor* (unattested) bad smell, breath, from Latin *flāre* to blow] —'**flavourer** *or U.S.* '**flavorer** *n.* —'**flavourless** *or U.S.* '**flavorless** *adj.* —'**flavoursome** *or U.S.* '**flavorsome** *adj.*

flavour enhancer *n.* another term for **monosodium glutamate.**

flavourful *or U.S.* **flavorful** ('fleɪvəfʊl) *adj.* having a full pleasant taste or flavour. —'**flavourfully** *or U.S.* '**flavorfully** *adv.*

flavouring *or U.S.* **flavoring** ('fleɪvərɪŋ) *n.* a substance used to impart a particular flavour to food: *rum flavouring.*

flaw[1] (flɔː) *n.* **1.** an imperfection, defect, or blemish. **2.** a crack, breach, or rift. **3.** *Law.* an invalidating fault or defect in a document or proceeding. ~*vb.* **4.** to make or become blemished, defective, or imperfect. [C14: probably from Old Norse *flaga* stone slab; related to Swedish *flaga* chip, flake, flaw] —'**flawless** *adj.* —'**flawlessly** *adv.* —'**flawlessness** *n.*

flaw[2] (flɔː) *n.* **1. a.** a sudden short gust of wind; squall. **b.** a spell of bad, esp. windy, weather. **2.** *Obsolete.* an outburst of strong feeling. [C16: of Scandinavian origin; related to Norwegian *flaga* squall, gust, Middle Dutch *vlāghe*] —'**flawy** *adj.*

flax (flæks) *n.* **1.** any herbaceous plant or shrub of the genus *Linum,* esp. *L. usitatissimum,* which has blue flowers and is cultivated for its seeds (flaxseed) and for the fibres of its stems: family *Linaceae.* **2.** the fibre of this plant, made into thread and woven into linen fabrics. **3.** any of various similar plants. **4.** *N.Z.* a swamp plant producing a fibre that is used by Maoris for decorative work, baskets, etc. [Old English *fleax;* related to Old Frisian *flax,* Old High German *flahs* flax, Greek *plekein* to plait]

flaxen ('flæksən) *or* **flaxy** *adj.* **1.** of, relating to, or resembling flax. **2.** of a soft yellow colour: *flaxen hair.*

flax kit *n. N.Z.* a basket woven from flax fibres.

flaxseed ('flæks,siːd) *n.* the seed of the flax plant, which yields linseed oil. Also called: **linseed.**

flay (fleɪ) *vb.* (*tr.*) **1.** to strip off the skin or outer covering of, esp. by whipping; skin. **2.** to attack with savage criticism. **3.** to strip of money or goods, esp. by cheating or extortion. [Old English *flēan;* related to Old Norse *flā* to peel, Lithuanian *plėšti* to tear] —'**flayer** *n.*

fld *abbrev. for* field.

fl. dr. *abbrev. for* fluid dram.

flea (fliː) *n.* **1.** any small wingless parasitic blood-sucking insect of the order *Siphonaptera,* living on the skin of mammals and birds and noted for its power of leaping. **2.** any of various invertebrates that resemble fleas, such as the water flea and flea beetle. **3. flea in one's ear.** *Informal.* a sharp rebuke. [Old English *flēah;* related to Old Norse *flō,* Old High German *flōh*]

fleabag ('fliː,bæg) *n. Slang.* **1.** *Brit.* a dirty or unkempt person, esp. a woman. **2.** *U.S.* a cheap or dirty hotel.

fleabane ('fliː,beɪn) *n.* **1.** any of several plants of the genus *Erigeron,* such as *E. acer,* having purplish tubular flower heads with orange centres: family *Compositae* (composites). **2.** any of several plants of the related genus *Pulicaria,* esp. the Eurasian *P. dysenterica,* which has yellow daisy-like flower heads. **3. Canadian fleabane.** a related plant, *Conyza* (or *Erigeron*) *canadensis,* with small white tubular flower heads. U.S. name:

horseweed. 4. any of various other plants reputed to ward off fleas.

flea beetle *n.* any small common beetle of the genera *Phyllotreta, Chalcoides,* etc., having enlarged hind legs and capable of jumping: family *Chrysomelidae.* The larvae of many species are very destructive to turnips and other cruciferous vegetables.

fleabite ('fliːˌbaɪt) *n.* **1.** the bite of a flea. **2.** a slight or trifling annoyance or discomfort.

flea-bitten *adj.* **1.** bitten by or infested with fleas. **2.** *Informal.* shabby or decrepit; mean. **3.** (of the coat of a horse) having reddish-brown spots on a lighter background.

fleam (fliːm) *n.* a lancet used for letting blood. [C16: from Old French *flieme,* alteration of Late Latin *phlebotomus* lancet (literally: vein cutter); see PHLEBOTOMY]

flea market *n.* an open-air market selling cheap and often second-hand goods.

fleapit ('fliːˌpɪt) *n. Informal.* a shabby cinema or theatre.

fleawort ('fliːˌwɜːt) *n.* **1.** any of various plants of the genus *Senecio,* esp. *S. integrifolius,* a European species with yellow daisy-like flowers and rosettes of downy leaves: family *Compositae* (composites). **2.** a Eurasian plantain, *Plantago psyllium* (or *P. indica*), whose seeds resemble fleas and were formerly used as a flea repellent. **3.** another name for **ploughman's spikenard.**

flèche (fleɪʃ, flɛʃ) *n.* **1.** Also called: **spirelet.** a slender spire, esp. over the intersection of the nave and transept ridges of a church roof. **2.** a pointed part of a fortification directed towards the attackers. [C18: from French: spire (literally: arrow), probably of Germanic origin; related to Middle Low German *flieke* long arrow]

fléchette (fleɪˈʃɛt) *n.* a steel dart or missile dropped from an aircraft, as in World War I. [from French; see FLÈCHE]

fleck (flɛk) *n.* **1.** a small marking or streak; speckle. **2.** a small particle; speck: *a fleck of dust.* ~*vb.* **3.** (*tr.*) Also: **'flecker.** to mark or cover with flecks; speckle. [C16: probably from Old Norse *flekkr* stain, spot; related to Old High German *flec* spot, plot of land]

flection ('flɛkʃən) *n.* **1.** the act of bending or the state of being bent. **2.** something bent; bend. **3.** *Grammar.* a less common word for **inflection.** ~See also **flexion.** [C17: from Latin *flexiō* a bending, from *flectere* to curve, bow] —**'flectional** *adj.* —**'flectionless** *adj.*

fled (flɛd) *vb.* the past tense and past participle of **flee**[1].

fledge (flɛdʒ) *vb.* **1.** (*tr.*) to feed and care for (a young bird) until it is able to fly. **2.** (*tr.*) Also called: **fletch.** to fit (something, esp. an arrow) with a feather or feathers. **3.** (*intr.*) (of a young bird) to grow feathers. **4.** (*tr.*) to cover or adorn with or as if with feathers. [Old English *-flycge,* as in *unflycge* unfledged; related to Old High German *flucki* able to fly; see FLY[1]]

fledgling *or* **fledgeling** ('flɛdʒlɪŋ) *n.* **1.** a young bird that has just fledged. **2.** a young and inexperienced person.

fledgy ('flɛdʒɪ) *adj.* **fledgier, fledgiest.** *Rare.* feathery or feathered.

flee[1] (fliː) *vb.* **flees, fleeing, fled.** **1.** to run away from (a place, danger, etc.); fly: *to flee the country.* **2.** (*intr.*) to run or move quickly; rush; speed: *she fled to the door.* [Old English *flēon;* related to Old Frisian *fliā,* Old High German *fliohan,* Gothic *thliuhan*] —**'fleer** *n.*

flee[2] (fliː) *vb.* **1.** a Scot. word for **fly**[1]. ~*n.* **2.** a Scot. word for **fly**[2].

fleece (fliːs) *n.* **1.** the coat of wool that covers the body of a sheep or similar animal and consists of a mass of crinkly hairs. **2.** the wool removed from a single sheep. **3.** something resembling a fleece in texture or warmth. **4.** sheepskin or a fabric with soft pile, used as a lining for coats, etc. ~*vb.* (*tr.*) **5.** to defraud or charge exorbitantly; swindle. **6.** another term for **shear** (sense 1). [Old English *flēos;* related to Middle High German *vlius,* Dutch *vlies* fleece, Latin *plūma* feather, down]

fleecie ('fliːsɪ) *n. N.Z.* a person who collects fleeces after shearing and prepares them for baling. Also called: **fleece-oh.**

fleecy ('fliːsɪ) *adj.* **fleecier, fleeciest.** of or resembling fleece; woolly. —**'fleecily** *adv.* —**'fleeciness** *n.*

fleein' ('fliːɪn) *adj. Scot. dialect.* drunk. [literally: flying, from FLEE[2]]

fleer (flɪə) *Archaic.* ~*vb.* **1.** to grin or laugh at; scoff; sneer. ~*n.* **2.** a derisory glance or grin. [C14: of Scandinavian origin; compare Norwegian *flire* to snigger] —**'fleeringly** *adv.*

fleet[1] (fliːt) *n.* **1.** a number of warships organized as a tactical unit. **2.** all the warships of a nation. **3.** a number of aircraft, ships, buses, etc., operating together or under the same ownership. [Old English *flēot* ship, flowing water, from *flēotan* to FLOAT]

fleet[2] (fliːt) *adj.* **1.** rapid in movement; swift. **2.** *Poetic.* fleeting; transient. ~*vb.* **3.** (*intr.*) to move rapidly. **4.** (*intr.*) *Archaic.* to fade away smoothly; glide. **5.** (*tr.*) *Nautical.* **a.** to change the position of (a hawser). **b.** to pass (a messenger or lead) to a hawser from a winch for hauling in. **c.** to spread apart (the blocks of a tackle). **6.** (*intr.*) *Obsolete.* to float or swim. **7.** (*tr.*) *Obsolete.* to cause (time) to pass rapidly. [probably Old English *flēotan* to float, glide rapidly; related to Old High German *fliozzan* to flow, Latin *pluere* to rain] —**'fleetly** *adv.* —**'fleetness** *n.*

fleet[3] (fliːt) *n. Chiefly southeastern Brit.* a small coastal inlet; creek. [Old English *flēot* flowing water; see FLEET[1]]

fleet admiral *n.* an officer holding the most senior commissioned rank in the U.S. and certain other navies.

Fleet Air Arm *n.* the aviation branch of the Royal Navy. Abbrev.: **FAA.**

fleet chief petty officer *n.* a noncommissioned officer in the Royal Navy comparable in rank to a warrant officer in the British Army or Royal Air Force.

fleeting ('fliːtɪŋ) *adj.* rapid and transient: *a fleeting glimpse of the sea.* —**'fleetingly** *adv.* —**'fleetingness** *n.*

fleet rate *or* **fleet rating** *n.* a reduced rate quoted by an insurance company to underwrite the risks to a fleet of vehicles, aircraft, etc.

Fleet Street *n.* **1.** a street in central London in which many newspaper offices were formerly situated. **2.** British journalism or journalists collectively.

fleishik *or* **fleishig** ('fleɪʃɪk, 'flaɪ-) *adj. Judaism.* (of food) containing or derived from meat or meat products and therefore to be prepared and eaten separately from dairy foods. Also: **meaty.** Compare **milchik.** See also **kashruth.**

Flem. *abbrev. for* Flemish.

Fleming ('flɛmɪŋ) *n.* a native or inhabitant of Flanders or a Flemish-speaking Belgian. Compare **Walloon.** [C14: from Middle Dutch *Vlaminc*]

Fleming's rules ('flɛmɪŋz) *pl. n. Physics.* two rules used as mnemonics for the relationship between the directions of current flow, motion, and magnetic field in electromagnetic induction. The hand is held with the thumb, first, and second fingers at right angles, respectively indicating the directions of motion, field, and electric current. The left hand is used for electric motors and the right hand for dynamos. [C19: named after Sir John Ambrose *Fleming* (1849–1945), the British electrical engineer who devised them]

Flemish ('flɛmɪʃ) *n.* **1.** one of the two official languages of Belgium, almost identical in form with Dutch. **2. the.** (*functioning as pl.*) the Flemings collectively. ~*adj.* **3.** of, relating to, or characteristic of Flanders, the Flemings, or their language.

Flemish bond *n.* a bond used in brickwork that has alternating stretchers and headers in each course, each header being placed centrally over a stretcher.

flense (flɛns), **flench** (flɛntʃ), *or* **flinch** (flɪntʃ) *vb.* (*tr.*) to strip (a whale, seal, etc.) of (its blubber or skin). [C19: from Danish *flense;* related to Dutch *flensen*] —**'flenser, 'flencher,** *or* **'flincher** *n.*

flesh (flɛʃ) *n.* **1.** the soft part of the body of an animal or human, esp. muscular tissue, as distinct from bone and viscera. **2.** *Informal.* excess weight; fat. **3.** *Archaic.* the edible tissue of animals as opposed to that of fish or, sometimes, fowl; meat. **4.** the thick usually soft part of a fruit or vegetable, as distinct from the skin, core, stone, etc. **5.** the human body and its physical or sensual nature as opposed to the soul or spirit. Related adj.: **carnal.** **6.** mankind in general. **7.** animate creatures in general. **8.** one's own family; kin (esp. in the phrase **one's own flesh and blood**). **9.** a yellowish-pink to greyish-yellow colour. **10.** *Christian Science.* erroneous belief on the physical plane, esp. the belief that matter has sensation. **11.** (*modifier*) *Tanning.* of or relating to the inner or under layer of a skin or hide: *a flesh split.* **12. in the flesh.** in person; actually present. **13. make one's flesh creep.** (esp. of something ghostly) to frighten and horrify one. ~*vb.* **14.** (*tr.*) *Hunting.* to stimulate the hunting instinct of (hounds or falcons) by giving them small quantities of raw flesh. **15.** to wound the flesh of with a weapon. **16.** *Archaic or poetic.* to accustom or incite to bloodshed or battle by initial experience. **17.** *Tanning.* to remove the flesh layer of (a hide or skin). **18.** to fatten; fill out. [Old English *flǣsc;* related to Old Norse *flesk* ham, Old High German *fleisk* meat, flesh]

flesher ('flɛʃə) *n.* **1.** a person or machine that fleshes hides or skins. **2.** *Scot.* a person who sells meat; butcher.

flesh fly *n.* any dipterous fly of the genus *Sarcophaga,* esp. *S. carnaria,* whose larvae feed on carrion or the tissues of living animals: family *Calliphoridae.*

fleshings ('flɛʃɪŋz) *pl. n.* **1.** flesh-coloured tights. **2.** bits of flesh scraped from the hides or skins of animals.

fleshly ('flɛʃlɪ) *adj.* **-lier, -liest.** **1.** relating to the body, esp. its sensual nature; carnal: *fleshly desire.* **2.** worldly as opposed to spiritual. **3.** fleshy; fat. —**'fleshliness** *n.*

flesh out *vb.* (*adv.*) **1.** (*tr.*) to give substance to (an argument, description, etc.). **2.** (*intr.*) to expand or become more substantial.

fleshpots ('flɛʃˌpɒts) *pl. n. Often facetious.* **1.** luxurious or self-indulgent living. **2.** places, such as striptease clubs, where bodily desires are gratified or titillated. [C16: from the Biblical use as applied to Egypt (Exodus 16:3)]

flesh wound (wuːnd) *n.* a wound affecting superficial tissues.

fleshy ('flɛʃɪ) *adj.* **fleshier, fleshiest.** **1.** fat; plump. **2.** related to or resembling flesh. **3.** *Botany.* (of some fruits, leaves, etc.) thick and pulpy. —**'fleshiness** *n.*

fletch (flɛtʃ) *vb.* another word for **fledge** (sense 2). [C17: probably back formation from FLETCHER]

fletcher ('flɛtʃə) *n.* a person who makes arrows. [C14: from Old French *flechier,* from *fleche* arrow; see FLÈCHE]

Fletcherism ('flɛtʃəˌrɪzəm) *n.* the practice of chewing food thoroughly and drinking liquids in small sips to aid digestion. [C20: named after Horace *Fletcher* (1849–1919), American nutritionist]

fletchings ('flɛtʃɪŋz) *pl. n.* arrow feathers. [plural of *fletching,* from FLETCH]

fleur-de-lis *or* **fleur-de-lys** (ˌflɜːdəˈliː) *n., pl.* **fleurs-de-lis** *or* **fleurs-de-lys** (ˌflɜːdəˈliːz). **1.** *Heraldry.* a charge representing a lily with three distinct petals. **2.** another name for **iris** (sense 2). [C19: from Old French *flor de lis,* literally: lily flower]

fleurette *or* **fleuret** (fluəˈrɛt, flɜː-) *n.* an ornament or motif resembling a flower. [C19: French, literally: a small flower, from *fleur* flower]

fleuron (ˈfluərɒn, -rən, ˈflɜː-) *n.* **1.** another name for **flower** (sense 8). **2.** *Cookery.* a decorative piece of pastry. [C14: from French, from Old French *floron,* from *flor* FLOWER]

flew[1] (fluː) *vb.* the past tense of **fly**[1].

flew[2] (fluː) *n.* a variant spelling of **flue**[3].

flews (fluːz) *pl. n.* the fleshy hanging upper lip of a bloodhound or similar dog. [C16: of unknown origin]

flex (flɛks) *n.* **1.** *Brit.* a flexible insulated electric cable, used esp. to connect appliances to mains. U.S. and Canadian name: **cord.** **2.** *Informal.* flexibility or pliability. ~*vb.* **3.** to bend or be bent: *he flexed his arm; his arm flexed.* **4.** to contract (a muscle) or (of a muscle) to contract. **5.** (*intr.*) to work according to flexitime. [C16: from Latin *flexus* bent, winding, from *flectere* to bend, bow]

flexible (ˈflɛksɪbᵊl) *adj.* **1.** Also: **flexile** (ˈflɛksaɪl). able to be bent easily without breaking; pliable. **2.** adaptable or variable: *flexible working hours.* **3.** able to be persuaded easily; tractable. —ˌ**flexiˈbility** *or* ˈ**flexibleness** *n.* —ˈ**flexibly** *adv.*

flexible disk *n.* another name for **floppy disk.**

flexion (ˈflɛkʃən) *n.* **1.** the act of bending a joint or limb. **2.** the condition of the joint or limb so bent. **3.** a variant spelling of **flection.** —ˈ**flexional** *adj.* —ˈ**flexionless** *adj.*

flexitime (ˈflɛksɪˌtaɪm) *or* **flextime** (ˈflɛksˌtaɪm) *n.* a system permitting flexibility of working hours at the beginning or end of the day, provided an agreed period of each day (**core time**) is spent at work.

flexo (ˈflɛksəʊ) *n., adj., adv.* short for **flexography, flexographic,** or **flexographically.**

flexography (flɛkˈsɒgrəfɪ) *n.* **1.** a method of rotary letterpress printing using a resilient printing plate and solvent-based ink: used characteristically for printing on metal foil or plastic. **2.** matter printed by this method. ~Abbrev.: **flexo.** —**flexographic** (ˌflɛksəˈgræfɪk) *adj.* —ˌ**flexoˈgraphically** *adv.*

flexor (ˈflɛksə) *n.* any muscle whose contraction serves to bend a joint or limb. Compare **extensor.** [C17: New Latin; see FLEX]

flexuous (ˈflɛksjʊəs) *or* **flexuose** (ˈflɛksjʊˌəʊs) *adj.* **1.** full of bends or curves; winding. **2.** variable; unsteady. [C17: from Latin *flexuōsus* full of bends, tortuous, from *flexus* a bending; see FLEX] —ˈ**flexuously** *adv.*

flexure (ˈflɛkʃə) *n.* **1.** the act of flexing or the state of being flexed. **2.** a bend, turn, or fold. —ˈ**flexural** *adj.*

flex-wing *n. Aeronautics.* a collapsible fabric delta wing, as used with hang-gliders.

fley *or* **flay** (fleɪ) *vb. Scot. and northern English dialect.* **1.** to be afraid or cause to be afraid. **2.** (*tr.*) to frighten away; scare. [Old English *āflēgan* to put to flight; related to Old Norse *fleygja*]

fleysome (ˈfleɪsəm) *adj. Scot. and northern English dialect.* frightening.

flibbertigibbet (ˈflɪbətɪˌdʒɪbɪt) *n.* an irresponsible, silly, or gossipy person. [C15: of uncertain origin]

flick[1] (flɪk) *vb.* **1.** (*tr.*) to touch with or as if with the finger or hand in a quick jerky movement. **2.** (*tr.*) to propel or remove by a quick jerky movement, usually of the fingers or hand: *to flick a piece of paper at someone.* **3.** to move or cause to move quickly or jerkily. **4.** (intr.; foll. by *through*) to read or look at (a book, newspaper, etc.) quickly or idly. **5.** to snap or click (the fingers) to produce a sharp sound. ~*n.* **6.** a tap or quick stroke with the fingers, a whip, etc. **7.** the sound made by such a stroke. **8.** a fleck, streak, or particle. **9. give (someone) the flick.** to dismiss (someone) from consideration. [C15: of imitative origin; compare French *flicflac*]

flick[2] (flɪk) *n. Slang.* **1.** a cinema film. **2.** (*pl.*) **the.** the cinema: *what's on at the flicks tonight?*

flicker[1] (ˈflɪkə) *vb.* **1.** (*intr.*) to shine with an unsteady or intermittent light: *a candle flickers.* **2.** (*intr.*) to move quickly to and fro; quiver, flutter, or vibrate. **3.** (*tr.*) to cause to flicker. ~*n.* **4.** an unsteady or brief light or flame. **5.** a swift quivering or fluttering movement. **6.** a visual sensation, often seen in a television image, produced by periodic fluctuations in the brightness of light at a frequency below that covered by the persistence of vision. [Old English *flicorian;* related to Dutch *flikkeren,* Old Norse *flökra* to flutter] —ˈ**flickeringly** *adv.* —ˈ**flickery** *adj.*

flicker[2] (ˈflɪkə) *n.* any North American woodpecker of the genus *Colaptes,* esp. *C. auratus* (**yellow-shafted flicker**), which has a yellow undersurface to the wings and tail. [C19: perhaps imitative of the bird's call]

flick knife *n.* a knife with a retractable blade that springs out when a button is pressed. U.S. and Canadian word: **switchblade.**

flier *or* **flyer** (ˈflaɪə) *n.* **1.** a person or thing that flies or moves very fast. **2.** an aviator or pilot. **3.** *Informal.* a long flying leap; bound. **4.** a fast-moving machine part, esp. one having periodic motion. **5.** a rectangular step in a straight flight of stairs. Compare **winder** (sense 5). **6.** *Athletics.* an informal word for **flying start.** **7.** *Chiefly U.S.* a speculative business transaction.

flight[1] (flaɪt) *n.* **1.** the act, skill, or manner of flying. **2.** a journey made by a flying animal or object. **3. a.** a scheduled airline journey. **b.** an aircraft flying on such a journey. **4.** a group of flying birds or aircraft: *a flight of swallows.* **5.** the basic tactical unit of a military air force. **6.** a journey through space, esp. of a spacecraft. **7.** rapid movement or progress. **8.** a soaring mental journey above or beyond the normal everyday world: *a flight of fancy.* **9. a.** a single line of hurdles across a track in a race. **b.** a series of such hurdles. **10.** a bird's wing or tail feather; flight feather. **11.** a feather or plastic attachment fitted to an arrow or dart to give it stability in flight. **12.** See **flight arrow.** **13.** the distance covered by a flight arrow. **14.** *Sport, esp. cricket.* **a.** a flighted movement imparted to a ball, dart, etc. **b.** the ability to flight a ball. **15.** *Angling.* a device on a spinning lure that revolves rapidly. **16.** a set of steps or stairs between one landing or floor and the next. **17.** a large enclosed area attached to an aviary or pigeon loft where the birds may fly but not escape. ~*vb.* **18.** (*tr.*) *Sport.* to cause (a ball, dart, etc.) to float slowly or deceptively towards its target. **19.** (*intr.*) (of wild fowl) to fly in groups. **20.** (*tr.*) to shoot (a bird) in flight. **21.** (*tr.*) to fledge (an arrow or a dart). [Old English *flyht;* related to Middle Dutch *vlucht,* Old Saxon *fluht*]

flight[2] (flaɪt) *n.* **1.** the act of fleeing or running away, as from danger. **2. put to flight.** to cause to run away; rout. **3. take (to) flight.** to run away or withdraw hastily; flee. [Old English *flyht* (unattested); related to Old Frisian *flecht,* Old High German *fluht,* Old Norse *flōtti*]

flight arrow *n.* a long thin arrow used for shooting long distances. Often shortened to **flight.**

flight deck *n.* **1.** the crew compartment in an airliner. Compare **cockpit** (sense 1). **2.** the upper deck of an aircraft carrier from which aircraft take off and on which they land.

flight engineer *n.* the member of an aircraft crew who is responsible for the operation of the aircraft's systems, including the engines, during flight.

flight feather *n.* any of the large stiff feathers that cover the wings and tail of a bird and are adapted for flying.

flight formation *n.* two or more aircraft flying together in a set pattern.

flightless (ˈflaɪtlɪs) *adj.* (of certain birds and insects) unable to fly. See also **ratite.**

flight level *n. Aeronautics.* a specified height at which an aircraft is allowed to fly.

flight lieutenant *n.* an officer holding a commissioned rank senior to a flying officer and junior to a squadron leader in the RAF and certain other air forces.

flight line *n.* an area of an airfield or airport on which aircraft, esp. military aircraft, are parked and serviced.

flight management systems *pl. n.* a suite of computer programs in a computer on board an aircraft used to calculate the most economical flying speeds and altitudes during a flight and to identify possible choices in emergencies.

flight path *n.* the course through the air of an aircraft, rocket, or projectile. Compare **approach** (sense 10), **glide path.**

flight plan *n.* a written statement of the details of a proposed aircraft flight.

flight recorder *n.* an electronic device fitted to an aircraft for collecting and storing information concerning its performance in flight. It is often used to determine the cause of a crash. Also called: **black box.**

flight sergeant *n.* a noncommissioned officer in the Royal Air Force junior in rank to a master aircrew.

flight simulator *n.* a ground-training device that reproduces exactly the conditions experienced on the flight deck of an aircraft. Compare **Link trainer.**

flight strip *n.* **1.** a strip of cleared land used as an emergency runway for aircraft. **2.** another name for **runway** (sense 1). **3.** a strip of continuous aerial photographs.

flight surgeon *n.* a medical officer specializing in aviation medicine in the U.S. and certain other air forces.

flighty (ˈflaɪtɪ) *adj.* **flightier, flightiest.** **1.** frivolous and irresponsible; capricious; volatile. **2.** mentally erratic, unstable, or wandering. **3.** flirtatious; coquettish. —ˈ**flightily** *adv.* —ˈ**flightiness** *n.*

flimflam (ˈflɪmˌflæm) *Informal.* ~*n.* **1. a.** nonsense; rubbish; foolishness. **b.** (*as modifier*): *flimflam arguments.* **2.** a deception; trick; swindle. ~*vb.* **-flams, -flamming, -flammed.** **3.** (*tr.*) to deceive; trick; swindle; cheat. [C16: probably of Scandinavian origin; compare Old Norse *flīm* mockery, Norwegian *flire* to giggle] —ˈ**flimˌflammer** *n.*

flimsy (ˈflɪmzɪ) *adj.* **-sier, -siest.** **1.** not strong or substantial; fragile: *a flimsy building.* **2.** light and thin: *a flimsy dress.* **3.** unconvincing or inadequate; weak: *a flimsy excuse.* ~*n.* **4.** thin paper used for making carbon copies of a letter, etc. **5.** a copy made on such paper. **6.** a slang word for **banknote.** [C17: of uncertain origin] —ˈ**flimsily** *adv.* —ˈ**flimsiness** *n.*

flinch[1] (flɪntʃ) *vb.* (*intr.*) **1.** to draw back suddenly, as from pain, shock, etc.; wince: *he flinched as the cold water struck him.* **2.** (often foll. by *from*) to avoid contact (with); shy away: *he never flinched from his duty.* ~*n.* **3.** the act or an instance of drawing back. **4.** a card game in which players build sequences. [C16: from Old French *flenchir;* related to Middle High German *lenken* to bend, direct] —ˈ**flincher** *n.* —ˈ**flinchingly** *adv.*

flinch[2] (flɪntʃ) *vb.* a variant of **flense.**
flinders ('flɪndəz) *pl. n. Rare.* small fragments or splinters (esp. in the phrase **fly into flinders**). [C15: probably of Scandinavian origin; compare Norwegian *flindra* thin piece of stone]
Flinders bar ('flɪndəz) *n. Navigation.* a bar of soft iron mounted on a binnacle to compensate for local magnetism causing error to the compass. [C19: named after Matthew *Flinders* (died 1814), English navigator]
fling (flɪŋ) *vb.* **flings, flinging, flung** (flʌŋ). (*mainly tr.*) **1.** to throw, esp. with force or abandon; hurl or toss. **2.** to put or send without warning or preparation: *to fling someone into jail.* **3.** (*also intr.*) to move (oneself or a part of the body) with abandon or speed: *he flung himself into a chair.* **4.** (usually foll. by *into*) to apply (oneself) diligently and with vigour (to). **5.** to cast aside; disregard: *she flung away her scruples.* **6.** to utter violently or offensively. **7.** *Poetic.* to give out; emit. ~*n.* **8.** the act or an instance of flinging; toss; throw. **9.** a period or occasion of unrestrained, impulsive, or extravagant behaviour: *to have a fling.* **10.** any of various vigorous Scottish reels full of leaps and turns, such as the Highland fling. **11.** a trial; try: *to have a fling at something different.* [C13: of Scandinavian origin; related to Old Norse *flengja* to flog, Swedish *flänga,* Danish *flænge*] —'**flinger** *n.*
flint (flɪnt) *n.* **1.** an impure opaque microcrystalline greyish-black form of quartz that occurs in chalk. It produces sparks when struck with steel and is used in the manufacture of pottery, flint glass, and road-construction materials. Formula: SiO_2. **2.** any piece of flint, esp. one used as a primitive tool or for striking fire. **3.** a small cylindrical piece of an iron alloy, used in cigarette lighters. **4.** Also called: **flint glass, white flint.** colourless glass other than plate glass. **5.** See **optical flint.** ~*vb.* **6.** (*tr.*) to fit or provide with a flint. [Old English; related to Old High German *flins,* Old Swedish *flinta* splinter of stone, Latin *splendēre* to shine]
flint glass *n.* another name for **optical flint, flint** (sense 4).
flintlock ('flɪntˌlɒk) *n.* **1.** an obsolete gunlock in which the charge is ignited by a spark produced by a flint in the hammer. **2.** a firearm having such a lock.
flinty ('flɪntɪ) *adj.* **flintier, flintiest. 1.** of, relating to, or resembling flint. **2.** hard or cruel; obdurate; unyielding. —'**flintily** *adv.* —'**flintiness** *n.*
flip (flɪp) *vb.* **flips, flipping, flipped. 1.** to throw (something light or small) carelessly or briskly; toss: *he flipped me an envelope.* **2.** to throw or flick (an object such as a coin) so that it turns or spins in the air. **3.** to propel by a sudden movement of the finger; flick: *to flip a crumb across the room.* **4.** (foll. by *through*) to read or look at (a book, newspaper, etc.) quickly, idly, or incompletely. **5.** (*intr.*) (of small objects) to move or bounce jerkily. **6.** (*intr.*) to make a snapping movement or noise with the finger and thumb. **7.** (*intr.*) *Slang.* to fly into a rage or an emotional outburst (also in the phrases **flip one's lid, flip one's top**). **8.** (*intr.*) *Slang.* to become ecstatic or very excited: *he flipped over the jazz group.* ~*n.* **9.** a snap or tap, usually with the fingers. **10.** a rapid jerk. **11.** a somersault, esp. one performed in the air, as in a dive, rather than from a standing position. **12.** any alcoholic drink containing beaten egg. ~*adj.* **13.** *Informal.* impertinent, flippant, or pert. [C16: probably of imitative origin; see FILLIP]
flip-flop *n.* **1.** a backward handspring. **2.** Also called: **bistable.** an electronic device or circuit that has one stable and one unstable state and that can be switched from one to the other by an input trigger pulse. **3.** a complete change of opinion, policy, etc. **4.** a repeated flapping or banging noise. **5.** Also called (U.S., Canadian, Austral., and N.Z.): **thong.** a rubber-soled sandal attached to the foot by a thong between the big toe and the next toe. ~*vb.* **-flops, -flopping, -flopped. 6.** (*intr.*) to move with repeated flaps. ~*adv.* **7.** with repeated flappings: *to go flip-flop.* [C16: reduplication of FLIP]
flippant ('flɪpənt) *adj.* **1.** marked by inappropriate levity; frivolous or offhand. **2.** impertinent; saucy. **3.** *Obsolete.* talkative or nimble. [C17: perhaps from FLIP] —'**flippancy** *n.* —'**flippantly** *adv.*
flipper ('flɪpə) *n.* **1.** the flat broad limb of seals, whales, penguins, and other aquatic animals, specialized for swimming. **2.** (*often pl.*) Also called: **fin.** either of a pair of rubber paddle-like devices worn on the feet as an aid in swimming, esp. underwater.
flipping ('flɪpɪŋ) *adj., adv. Brit. slang.* (intensifier): *a flipping idiot; it's flipping cold.* [C19: perhaps a euphemism for FUCKING]
flip side *n.* **1.** another term for **B-side. 2.** another, less familiar aspect of a person or thing: *the flip side of John Lennon.*
flirt (flɜːt) *vb.* **1.** (*intr.*) to behave or act amorously without emotional commitment; toy or play with another's affections; dally. **2.** (*intr.*; usually foll. by *with*) to deal playfully or carelessly (with something dangerous or serious); trifle: *the motorcyclist flirted with death.* **3.** (*intr.*; usually foll. by *with*) to think casually (about); toy (with): *to flirt with the idea of leaving.* **4.** (*intr.*) to move jerkily; dart; flit. **5.** (*tr.*) to subject to a sudden swift motion; flick or toss. ~*n.* **6.** a person who acts flirtatiously. [C16: of uncertain origin] —'**flirter** *n.* —'**flirty** *adj.* —'**flirtingly** *adv.*
flirtation (flɜː'teɪʃən) *n.* **1.** behaviour intended to arouse sexual feelings or advances without emotional commitment; coquetry. **2.** any casual involvement without commitment: *a flirtation with journalism.*
flirtatious (flɜː'teɪʃəs) *adj.* **1.** given to flirtation. **2.** expressive of playful sexual invitation: *a flirtatious glance.* —**flir'tatiously** *adv.* —**flir'tatiousness** *n.*
flit (flɪt) *vb.* **flits, flitting, flitted.** (*intr.*) **1.** to move along rapidly and lightly; skim or dart. **2.** to fly rapidly and lightly; flutter. **3.** to pass quickly; fleet: *a memory flitted into his mind.* **4.** *Scot. and northern English dialect.* to move house. **5.** *Brit. informal.* to depart hurriedly and stealthily in order to avoid obligations. **6.** an informal word for **elope.** ~*n.* **7.** the act or an instance of flitting. **8.** *Slang, chiefly U.S.* a male homosexual. **9.** *Brit. informal.* a hurried and stealthy departure in order to avoid obligations (esp. in the phrase **do a flit**). **10.** See **moonlight flit.** [C12: from Old Norse *flytja* to carry] —'**flitter** *n.*
flitch (flɪtʃ) *n.* **1.** a side of pork salted and cured. **2.** a steak cut from the side of certain fishes, esp. halibut. **3.** a piece of timber cut lengthways from a tree trunk, esp. one that is larger than 4 by 12 inches. ~*vb.* **4.** (*tr.*) to cut (a tree trunk) into flitches. [Old English *flicce;* related to Old Norse *flikki,* Middle Low German *vlicke,* Norwegian *flika;* see FLESH]
flite *or* **flyte** (flaɪt; *Scot.* fləɪt) *Scot. and northern English dialect.* ~*vb.* **1.** (*tr.*) to scold or rail at. ~*n.* **2.** a dispute or scolding. [Old English *flītan* to wrangle, of Germanic origin; related to Old Frisian *flīt* strife, Old High German *flīz* strife]
flitter ('flɪtə) *vb.* a less common word for **flutter.**
flittermouse ('flɪtəˌmaʊs) *n., pl.* **-mice.** a dialect name for **bat**[2] (the animal). [C16: translation of German *Fledermaus;* see FLITTER, MOUSE]
flivver ('flɪvə) *n.* an old, cheap, or battered car. [C20: of unknown origin]
float (fləʊt) *vb.* **1.** to rest or cause to rest on the surface of a fluid or in a fluid or space without sinking; be buoyant or cause to exhibit buoyancy: *oil floats on water; to float a ship.* **2.** to move or cause to move buoyantly, lightly, or freely across a surface or through air, water, etc.; drift: *fog floated across the road.* **3.** to move about aimlessly, esp. in the mind: *thoughts floated before him.* **4.** to suspend or be suspended without falling; hang: *lights floated above them.* **5.** (*tr.*) **a.** to launch or establish (a commercial enterprise, etc.). **b.** to offer for sale (stock or bond issues, etc.) on the stock market. **6.** (*tr.*) *Finance.* to allow (a currency) to fluctuate against other currencies in accordance with market forces. **7.** (*tr.*) to flood, inundate, or irrigate (land), either artificially or naturally. **8.** (*tr.*) to spread, smooth, or level (a surface of plaster, rendering, etc.). ~*n.* **9.** something that floats. **10.** *Angling.* an indicator attached to a baited line that sits on the water and moves when a fish bites. **11.** a small hand tool with a rectangular blade used for floating plaster, etc. **12.** *Chiefly U.S.* any buoyant object, such as a platform or inflated tube, used offshore by swimmers or, when moored alongside a pier, as a dock by vessels. **13.** Also called: **paddle.** a blade of a paddle wheel. **14.** *Brit.* a buoyant garment or device to aid a person in staying afloat. **15.** a hollow watertight structure fitted to the underside of an aircraft to allow it to land on water. **16.** another name for **air bladder** (sense 2). **17.** an exhibit carried in a parade, esp. a religious parade. **18.** a motor vehicle used to carry a tableau or exhibit in a parade, esp. a civic parade. **19.** a small delivery vehicle, esp. one powered by batteries: *a milk float.* **20.** *Austral. and N.Z.* a vehicle for transporting horses. **21.** *Banking, chiefly U.S.* the total value of uncollected cheques and other commercial papers. **22.** *Chiefly U.S. and Canadian.* a sum to be applied to minor expenses; petty cash. **23.** a sum of money used by shopkeepers to provide change at the start of the day's business, this sum being subtracted from the total at the end of the day when calculating the day's takings. **24.** the hollow floating ball of a ballcock. **25.** *Engineering.* a hollow cylindrical structure in a carburettor that actuates the fuel valve. **26.** *Chiefly U.S. and Canadian.* a carbonated soft drink with a scoop of ice cream in it. **27.** (in textiles) a single thread brought to or above the surface of a woven fabric, esp. to form a pattern. **28.** *Forestry.* a measure of timber equal to eighteen loads. ~See also **floats.** [Old English *flotian;* related to Old Norse *flota,* Old Saxon *flotōn;* see FLEET[2]] —'**floatable** *adj.* —ˌ**floata'bility** *n.*
floatage ('fləʊtɪdʒ) *n.* a variant spelling of **flotage.**
floatation (fləʊ'teɪʃən) *n.* a variant spelling of **flotation.**
float chamber *n.* a chamber in a carburettor in which a floating valve controls the entry and level of petrol.
floatcut file ('fləʊtˌkʌt) *n. Engineering.* a file having rows of parallel teeth.
floatel (fləʊ'tɛl) *n.* a variant spelling of **flotel.**
floater ('fləʊtə) *n.* **1.** a person or thing that floats. **2.** any of a number of dark spots that appear in one's vision as a result of dead cells or fragments in the lens or vitreous humour of the eye. **3.** *U.S. and Canadian.* **a.** a person of no fixed political opinion. **b.** a person who votes illegally in more than one district at one election. **c.** a voter who can be bribed. **4.** Also called: **floating policy.** *Insurance, U.S. and Canadian.* a policy covering loss or theft of or damage to movable property, such as jewels or furs, regardless of its location. **5.** *U.S. informal.* a person who often changes employment, residence, etc.; drifter. **6.** *Austral.* a loose gold- or opal-bearing rock. **7.** *Austral.* (esp. in Adelaide) a meat pie in a plate of pea soup.

float-feed *adj.* (of a fuel system) controlled by a float operating a needle valve.

float glass *n.* a type of flat polished transparent glass made by allowing the molten glass to harden as it floats on liquid of higher density.

floating ('fləʊtɪŋ) *adj.* **1.** having little or no attachment. **2.** (of an organ or part) displaced from the normal position or abnormally movable: *a floating kidney.* **3.** not definitely attached to one place or policy; uncommitted or unfixed: *the floating vote.* **4.** *Finance.* **a.** (of capital) not allocated or invested; available for current use. **b.** (of debt) short-term and unfunded, usually raised by a government or company to meet current expenses. **c.** (of a currency) free to fluctuate against other currencies in accordance with market forces. **5.** *Machinery.* operating smoothly through being free from external constraints. **6.** (of an electronic circuit or device) not connected to a source of voltage. —'**floatingly** *adv.*

floating assets *pl. n.* another term for **current assets.**

floating charge *n. Chiefly Brit.* an unsecured charge on the assets of an enterprise that allows such assets to be used commercially until the enterprise ceases to operate or the creditor intervenes to demand collateral.

floating debt *n.* short-term government borrowing, esp. by the issue of three-month Treasury bills.

floating dock *n.* a large boxlike structure that can be submerged to allow a vessel to enter it and then floated to raise the vessel out of the water for maintenance or repair. Also called: **floating dry dock.**

floating heart *n.* any perennial aquatic freshwater plant of the genus *Nymphoides,* esp. *N. lacunosum,* having floating heart-shaped leaves: family *Menyanthaceae.*

floating island *n.* a floating mass of soil held together by vegetation.

floating-point representation *n. Computer technol.* the representation of numbers by two sets of digits (a, b), the set a indicating the significant digits, the set b giving the position of the radix point. The number is the product ar^b, where r is the base of the number system used. Compare **fixed-point representation.**

floating policy *n.* **1.** (in marine insurance) a policy covering loss of or damage to specified goods irrespective of the ship in which they are consigned. **2.** another term for **floater** (sense 4).

floating rib *n.* any rib of the lower two pairs of ribs in man, which are not attached to the breastbone.

floating voter *n.* a person who does not vote consistently for any single political party.

floats (fləʊts) *pl. n. Theatre.* another word for **footlights.**

floaty ('fləʊtɪ) *adj.* **floatier, floatiest. 1.** filmy and light: *floaty material.* **2.** capable of floating; buoyant. **3.** (of a vessel) riding high in the water; of shallow draught.

floc (flɒk) *n.* another word for **floccule.** [C20: from Latin *floccus* a tuft of wool, FLOCK[2]]

floccose ('flɒkəʊs) *adj.* consisting of or covered with woolly tufts or hairs: *floccose growths of bacteria.* [C18: from Latin *floccōsus* full of flocks of wool]

flocculant ('flɒkjʊlənt) *n.* a substance added to a suspension to enhance aggregation of the suspended particles.

flocculate ('flɒkjʊˌleɪt) *vb.* to form or be formed into an aggregated flocculent mass. —ˌ**floccu'lation** *n.*

floccule ('flɒkjuːl), **flocculus, flock,** *or* **floc** *n.* **1.** a small aggregate of flocculent material. **2.** something resembling a tuft of wool. [C19: from Late Latin *flocculus* a little tuft; see FLOCK[2]]

flocculent ('flɒkjʊlənt) *adj.* **1.** like wool; fleecy. **2.** *Chem.* aggregated in woolly cloudlike masses: *a flocculent precipitate.* **3.** *Biology.* covered with tufts or flakes of a waxy or wool-like substance. —'**flocculence** *or* '**flocculency** *n.* —'**flocculently** *adv.*

flocculus ('flɒkjʊləs) *n., pl.* **-li** (-ˌlaɪ). **1.** a marking on the sun's surface or in its atmosphere, as seen on a spectroheliogram. It consists of calcium when lighter than the surroundings and of hydrogen when darker. **2.** *Anatomy.* a tiny ovoid prominence on each side of the cerebellum. **3.** another word for **floccule.**

floccus ('flɒkəs) *n., pl.* **flocci** ('flɒksaɪ). **1.** a downy or woolly covering, as on the young of certain birds. **2.** a small woolly tuft of hair. ~*adj.* **3.** (of a cloud) having the appearance of woolly tufts at odd intervals in its structure. [C19: from Latin: tuft of hair or wool, FLOCK[2]]

flock[1] (flɒk) *n.* (*sometimes functioning as pl.*) **1.** a group of animals of one kind, esp. sheep or birds. **2.** a large number of people; crowd. **3.** a body of Christians regarded as the pastoral charge of a priest, a bishop, the pope, etc. **4.** *Rare.* a band of people; group. ~*vb.* (*intr.*) **5.** to gather together or move in a flock. **6.** to go in large numbers: *people flocked to the church.* [Old English *flocc;* related to Old Norse *flokkr* crowd, Middle Low German *vlocke*]

flock[2] (flɒk) *n.* **1.** a tuft, as of wool, hair, cotton, etc. **2. a.** waste from fabrics such as cotton, wool, or other cloth used for stuffing mattresses, upholstered chairs, etc. **b.** (*as modifier*): *flock mattress.* **3.** very small tufts of wool applied to fabrics, wallpaper, etc., to give a raised pattern. **4.** another word for **floccule.** ~*vb.* **5.** (*tr.*) to fill, cover, or ornament with flock. [C13: from Old French *floc,* from Latin *floccus;* probably related to Old High German *floccho* down, Norwegian *flugsa* snowflake] —'**flocky** *adj.*

flock paper *n.* a type of wallpaper with a raised pattern. See also **flock**[2] (sense 3).

floe (fləʊ) *n.* See **ice floe.** [C19: probably from Norwegian *flo* slab, layer, from Old Norse; see FLAW[1]]

flog (flɒg) *vb.* **flogs, flogging, flogged. 1.** (*tr.*) to beat harshly, esp. with a whip, strap, etc. **2.** *Brit. slang.* to sell. **3.** (*intr.*) (of a sail) to flap noisily in the wind. **4.** (*intr.*) to make progress by painful work. **5.** *N.Z.* to steal. **6. flog** *or* **beat a dead horse.** *Chiefly Brit.* **a.** to harp on some long discarded subject. **b.** to pursue the solution of a problem long realized to be insoluble. **7. flog to death.** to persuade a person so persistently of the value of (an idea or venture) that he loses interest in it. [C17: probably from Latin *flagellāre;* see FLAGELLANT] —'**flogger** *n.*

flokati (flə'kɑːtɪ) *n.* a Greek hand-woven shaggy woollen rug. [C20: from Modern Greek *phlokatē* a peasant's blanket]

flong (flɒŋ) *n.* **1.** *Printing.* a material, usually pulped paper or cardboard, used for making moulds in stereotyping. **2.** *Journalism, slang.* material that is not urgently topical. [C20: variant of FLAN]

flood (flʌd) *n.* **1. a.** the inundation of land that is normally dry through the overflowing of a body of water, esp. a river. **b.** the state of a river that is at an abnormally high level (esp. in the phrase **in flood**). Related adj.: **diluvial. 2.** a great outpouring or flow: *a flood of words.* **3. a.** the rising of the tide from low to high water. **b.** (*as modifier*): *the flood tide.* Compare **ebb** (sense 3). **4.** *Theatre.* short for **floodlight. 5.** *Archaic.* a large body of water, as the sea or a river. ~*vb.* **6.** (of water) to inundate or submerge (land) or (of land) to be inundated or submerged. **7.** to fill or be filled to overflowing, as with a flood: *the children's home was flooded with gifts.* **8.** (*intr.*) to flow; surge: *relief flooded through him.* **9.** to supply an excessive quantity of petrol to (a carburettor or petrol engine) or (of a carburettor, etc.) to be supplied with such an excess. **10.** (*intr.*) to rise to a flood; overflow. **11.** (*intr.*) **a.** to bleed profusely from the uterus, as following childbirth. **b.** to have an abnormally heavy flow of blood during a menstrual period. [Old English *flōd;* related to Old Norse *flōth,* Gothic *flōdus,* Old High German *fluot* flood, Greek *plōtos* navigable; see FLOW, FLOAT] —'**floodable** *adj.* —'**flooder** *n.* —'**floodless** *adj.*

flood basalt *n.* a very extensive lava flow that has issued from a fissure, often to be found as part of a series of such flows one on top of another, forming a plateau. See **fissure eruption.**

flood control *n.* the technique or practice of preventing or controlling floods with dams, artificial channels, etc.

flooded gum *n.* any of various eucalyptus trees of Australia, esp. *Eucalyptus saligna* (the Sydney blue gum), that grow in damp soil.

floodgate ('flʌdˌgeɪt) *n.* **1.** Also called: **head gate, water gate.** a gate in a sluice that is used to control the flow of water. See also **sluicegate. 2.** (*often pl.*) a control or barrier against an outpouring or flow: *to open the floodgates to immigration.*

flooding ('flʌdɪŋ) *n. Psychol.* a method of eliminating anxiety in a given situation, by exposing a person to the situation until the anxiety subsides.

floodlight ('flʌdˌlaɪt) *n.* **1.** a broad intense beam of artificial light, esp. as used in the theatre or to illuminate the exterior of buildings. **2.** the lamp or source producing such light. ~*vb.* **-lights, -lighting, -lit. 3.** (*tr.*) to illuminate by or as if by a floodlight.

flood plain *n.* the flat area bordering a river, composed of sediment deposited during flooding.

floor (flɔː) *n.* **1.** Also called: **flooring.** the inner lower surface of a room. **2.** a storey of a building: *the second floor.* **3.** a flat bottom surface in or on any structure: *the floor of a lift; a dance floor.* **4.** the bottom surface of a tunnel, cave, river, sea, etc. **5.** *Mining.* an underlying stratum. **6.** *Nautical.* the bottom, or the lowermost framing members at the bottom, of a vessel. **7.** that part of a legislative hall in which debate and other business is conducted. **8.** the right to speak in a legislative or deliberative body (esp. in the phrases **get, have,** or **be given the floor**). **9.** the room in a stock exchange where trading takes place. **10.** the earth; ground. **11.** a minimum price charged or paid: *a wage floor.* **12. take the floor.** to begin dancing on a dance floor. ~*vb.* **13.** to cover with or construct a floor. **14.** (*tr.*) to knock to the floor or ground. **15.** (*tr.*) *Informal.* to disconcert, confound, or defeat: *to be floored by a problem.* [Old English *flōr;* related to Old Norse *flōrr,* Middle Low German *vlōr* floor, Latin *plānus* level, Greek *planan* to cause to wander]

floorage ('flɔːrɪdʒ) *n.* an area of floor; floor space.

floorboard ('flɔːˌbɔːd) *n.* one of the boards forming a floor.

flooring ('flɔːrɪŋ) *n.* **1.** the material used in making a floor, esp. the surface material. **2.** another word for **floor** (sense 1).

flooring saw *n.* a type of saw curved at the end for cutting through floorboards.

floor leader *n. U.S. government.* a member of a legislative body who organizes his party's activities.

floor manager *n.* **1.** the stage manager employed in the production of a television programme. **2.** a person in overall charge of one floor of a large shop or department store.

floor plan *n.* a drawing to scale of the arrangement of rooms on one floor of a building. Compare **elevation** (sense 5).

floor show *n.* a series of entertainments, such as singing, dancing, and comedy acts, performed in a nightclub.

floorwalker ('flɔːˌwɔːkə) *n.* the U.S. name for **shopwalker.**

floozy, floozie, *or* **floosie** ('fluːzɪ) *n., pl.* **-zies** *or* **-sies.** *Slang.* a disreputable woman. [C20: of unknown origin]

flop (flɒp) *vb.* **flops, flopping, flopped. 1.** (*intr.*) to bend, fall, or collapse loosely or carelessly: *his head flopped backwards.* **2.** (when *intr.*, often foll. by *into, onto,* etc.) to fall, cause to fall, or move with a sudden noise: *the books flopped onto the floor.* **3.** (*intr.*) *Informal.* to fail; be unsuccessful: *the scheme flopped.* **4.** (*intr.*) to fall flat onto the surface of water, hitting it with the front of the body. **5.** (*intr.;* often foll. by *out*) *Slang.* to go to sleep. ~*n.* **6.** the act of flopping. **7.** *Informal.* a complete failure. **8.** *U.S. and Canadian slang.* a place to sleep. **9.** *Athletics.* See **Fosbury flop.** [C17: variant of FLAP]

flophouse ('flɒpˌhaʊs) *n. Slang.* the U.S. and Canadian word for **dosshouse.**

floppy ('flɒpɪ) *adj.* **-pier, -piest. 1.** limp or hanging loosely: *a dog with floppy ears.* ~*n.* **2.** short for **floppy disk.** —'**floppily** *adv.* —'**floppiness** *n.*

floppy disk *n.* a flexible magnetic disk that stores information and can be used to store data for use in a microprocessor. Also called: **diskette, flexible disk.**

flor. *abbrev. for* floruit.

flora ('flɔːrə) *n., pl.* **-ras** *or* **-rae** (-riː). **1.** all the plant life of a given place or time. **2.** a descriptive list of such plants, often including a key for identification. **3.** short for **intestinal flora.** [C18: from New Latin, from Latin *Flōra* goddess of flowers, from *flōs* FLOWER]

floral ('flɔːrəl) *adj.* **1.** decorated with or consisting of flowers or patterns of flowers. **2.** of, relating to, or associated with flowers: *floral leaves.* —'**florally** *adv.*

floral envelope *n.* the part of a flower that surrounds the stamens and pistil: the calyx and corolla (considered together) or the perianth.

Floréal *French.* (flɔreal) *n.* the month of flowers: the eighth month of the French revolutionary calendar, extending from April 21 to May 20. [C19: ultimately from Latin *flōreus* of flowers, from *flōs* a flower]

floreat *Latin.* ('flɒrɪæt) *vb.* (*intr.*), *pl.* ***floreant.*** may (a person, institution, etc.) flourish: *floreat Oxonia!*

floreated ('flɔːrɪˌeɪtɪd) *adj.* a variant spelling of **floriated.**

Florence fennel ('flɒrəns) *n.* another name for **finocchio.**

Florence flask *n.* a round flat-bottomed glass flask with a long neck, used in chemical experiments.

Florentine ('flɒrənˌtaɪn) *adj.* **1.** of or relating to Florence, a city in central Italy. **2.** (*usually postpositive*) (of food) served or prepared with spinach. ~*n.* **3.** a native or inhabitant of Florence. **4.** a biscuit containing nuts and dried fruit and coated with chocolate. **5.** a type of domestic fancy pigeon somewhat resembling the Modena.

florescence (flɔː'rɛsəns) *n.* the process, state, or period of flowering. [C18: from New Latin *flōrēscentia,* from Latin *flōrēscere* to come into flower]

floret ('flɔːrɪt) *n.* a small flower, esp. one of many making up the head of a composite flower. [C17: from Old French *florete* a little flower, from *flor* FLOWER]

floriated *or* **floreated** ('flɔːrɪˌeɪtɪd) *adj. Architect.* having ornamentation based on flowers and leaves. [C19: from Latin *flōs* FLOWER]

floribunda (ˌflɔːrɪ'bʌndə) *n.* any of several varieties of cultivated hybrid roses whose flowers grow in large sprays. [C19: from New Latin, feminine of *flōribundus* flowering freely]

floriculture ('flɔːrɪˌkʌltʃə) *n.* the cultivation of flowering plants. —ˌ**flori'cultural** *adj.* —ˌ**flori'culturist** *n.*

florid ('flɒrɪd) *adj.* **1.** having a red or flushed complexion. **2.** excessively ornate; flowery: *florid architecture.* **3.** an archaic word for **flowery.** [C17: from Latin *flōridus* blooming] —**flo'ridity** *or* '**floridness** *n.* —'**floridly** *adv.*

floriferous (flɔː'rɪfərəs) *adj.* bearing or capable of bearing many flowers.

florigen ('flɒrɪdʒən) *n.* the hypothetical plant hormone that induces flowering, thought to be synthesized in the leaves as a photoperiodic response and transmitted to the flower buds. [C20: from Latin *flor-, flos* FLOWER + -GEN]

florilegium (ˌflɔːrɪ'liːdʒɪəm) *n., pl.* **-gia** (-dʒɪə). **1.** (formerly) a lavishly illustrated book on flowers. **2.** *Rare.* an anthology. [C17: Modern Latin, from Latin *florilegus* flower-collecting, from *flos* flower + *legere* to collect]

florin ('flɒrɪn) *n.* **1.** a former British coin, originally silver and later cupronickel, equivalent to ten (new) pence. **2.** (formerly) another name for **guilder** (sense 1). **3.** any of various gold coins of Florence, Britain, or Austria. [C14: from French, from Old Italian *fiorino* Florentine coin, from *fiore* flower, from Latin *flōs*]

florist ('flɒrɪst) *n.* a person who grows or deals in flowers.

floristic (flɒ'rɪstɪk) *adj.* of or relating to flowers or a flora. —**flo'ristically** *adv.*

floristics (flɒ'rɪstɪks) *n.* (*functioning as sing.*) the branch of botany concerned with the types, numbers, and distribution of plant species in a particular area.

-florous *adj. combining form.* indicating number or type of flowers: *tubuliflorous.*

floruit *Latin.* ('flɒruːɪt) *vb.* (he or she) flourished: used to indicate the period when a historical figure, whose birth and death dates are unknown, was most active. Abbrevs.: **fl., flor.**

florula ('flɒrjʊlə) *or* **florule** ('flɒrjuːl) *n., pl.* **-ulae** (-jʊliː) *or* **ules. 1.** the flora of a small single environment. **2.** a fossil flower found in a single stratum or in several thin adjacent strata. [C19: FLORA + -ULE]

flory ('flɔːrɪ) *or* **fleury** ('flʊərɪ, 'flɜːrɪ) *adj.* (*usually postpositive*) *Heraldry.* containing a fleur-de-lis. [C15: from Old French *floré,* from *flor* FLOWER]

flos ferri ('flɒs 'fɛrɪ) *n.* a variety of aragonite that is deposited from hot springs in the form of a white branching mass. [C18: from New Latin, literally: flower of iron]

floss (flɒs) *n.* **1.** the mass of fine silky fibres obtained from cotton and similar plants. **2.** any similar fine silky material, such as the hairlike styles and stigmas of maize or the fibres prepared from silkworm cocoons. **3.** untwisted silk thread used in embroidery, etc. **4.** See **dental floss.** [C18: perhaps from Old French *flosche* down]

flossy ('flɒsɪ) *adj.* **flossier, flossiest. 1.** consisting of or resembling floss. **2.** *U.S. and Canadian slang.* (esp. of dress) showy.

flotage *or* **floatage** ('fləʊtɪdʒ) *n.* **1.** the act or state of floating; flotation. **2.** buoyancy; power or ability to float. **3.** objects or material that float on the surface of the water; flotsam.

flotation *or* **floatation** (fləʊ'teɪʃən) *n.* **1. a.** the launching or financing of a commercial enterprise by bond or share issues. **b.** the raising of a loan or new capital by bond or share issues. **2.** power or ability to float; buoyancy. **3.** Also called: **froth flotation.** a process to concentrate the valuable ore in low-grade ores. The ore is ground to a powder, mixed with water containing surface-active chemicals, and vigorously aerated. The bubbles formed trap the required ore fragments and carry them to the surface froth, which is then skimmed off.

flotation bags *pl. n.* bags inflated to keep a spacecraft or helicopter afloat and upright when it lands in the sea.

flote grass (fləʊt) *n.* an aquatic perennial grass, *Glyceria fluitans,* whose metre-long stems and pale green leaves are often seen floating in still or sluggish water. The related **sweet grass** (*G. plicata*) has broader, darker leaves and owes its name to the fact that cattle like to eat it. [C16: *flote* obsolete spelling of FLOAT]

flotel *or* **floatel** (fləʊ'tɛl) *n.* (in the oil industry) an oil rig or boat used as accommodation for workers in off-shore oil fields. [C20: from *float + hotel*]

flotilla (flə'tɪlə) *n.* a small fleet or a fleet of small vessels. [C18: from Spanish *flota* fleet, from French *flotte,* ultimately from Old Norse *floti*]

flotsam ('flɒtsəm) *n.* **1.** wreckage from a ship found floating. Compare **jetsam** (sense 1), **lagan. 2.** useless or discarded objects; odds and ends (esp. in the phrase **flotsam and jetsam**). **3.** vagrants. [C16: from Anglo-French *floteson,* from *floter* to FLOAT]

flounce[1] (flaʊns) *vb.* **1.** (*intr.;* often foll. by *about, away, out,* etc.) to move or go with emphatic or impatient movements. ~*n.* **2.** the act of flouncing. [C16: of Scandinavian origin; compare Norwegian *flunsa* to hurry, Swedish *flunsa* to splash]

flounce[2] (flaʊns) *n.* an ornamental gathered ruffle sewn to a garment by its top edge. [C18: from Old French *fronce* wrinkle, from *froncir* to wrinkle, of Germanic origin]

flouncing ('flaʊnsɪŋ) *n.* material, such as lace or embroidered fabric, used for making flounces.

flounder[1] ('flaʊndə) *vb.* (*intr.*) **1.** to struggle; to move with difficulty, as in mud. **2.** to behave awkwardly; make mistakes. ~*n.* **3.** the act of floundering. [C16: probably a blend of FOUNDER[2] + BLUNDER; perhaps influenced by FLOUNDER[2]]

flounder[2] ('flaʊndə) *n., pl.* **-der** *or* **-ders. 1.** Also called: **fluke.** a European flatfish, *Platichthys flesus,* having a greyish-brown body covered with prickly scales: family *Pleuronectidae:* an important food fish. **2.** *U.S. and Canadian.* any flatfish of the families *Bothidae* (turbot, etc.) and *Pleuronectidae* (plaice, halibut, sand dab, etc.). [C14: probably of Scandinavian origin; compare Old Norse *flythra,* Norwegian *flundra*]

flour ('flaʊə) *n.* **1.** a powder, which may be either fine or coarse, prepared by sifting and grinding the meal of a grass, esp. wheat. **2.** any finely powdered substance. ~*vb.* **3.** (*tr.*) to make (grain) into flour. **4.** (*tr.*) to dredge or sprinkle (food or cooking utensils) with flour. **5.** (of mercury) to break into fine particles on the surface of a metal rather than amalgamating, or to produce such an effect on (a metal). The effect is caused by impurities, esp. sulphur. [C13 *flur* finer portion of meal, FLOWER] —'**floury** *adj.*

flourish ('flʌrɪʃ) *vb.* **1.** (*intr.*) to thrive; prosper. **2.** (*intr.*) to be at the peak of condition. **3.** (*intr.*) to be healthy: *plants flourish in the light.* **4.** to wave or cause to wave in the air with sweeping strokes. **5.** to display or make a display. **6.** to play (a fanfare, etc.) on a musical instrument. **7.** (*intr.*) to embellish writing, characters, etc., with ornamental strokes. **8.** to add decorations or embellishments to (speech or writing). **9.** (*intr.*) an obsolete word for **blossom.** ~*n.* **10.** the act of waving or brandishing. **11.** a showy gesture: *he entered with a flourish.* **12.** an ornamental embellishment in writing. **13.** a display of ornamental language or speech. **14.** a grandiose passage of music. **15.** an ostentatious display or parade. **16.** *Obsolete.* **a.** the state of flourishing. **b.** the state of flowering. [C13: from Old French *florir,* ultimately from Latin *flōrēre* to flower, from *flōs* a flower] —'**flourisher** *n.*

flour mite *n.* any of several mites that infest flour and other stored organic materials and may be a serious pest; some may cause itching in persons handling infected material.

flour moth *n.* a pyralid moth, *Ephestia Kuehniella,* the larvae of which are an important pest of flour mills and granaries.

flout (flaʊt) *vb.* (when *intr.*, usually foll. by *at*) to show contempt (for); scoff or jeer (at). [C16: perhaps from Middle English *flouten* to play the flute, from Old French *flauter;* compare Dutch *fluiten;* see FLUTE] —'**flouter** *n.* —'**floutingly** *adv.*

flow (fləʊ) *vb.* (*mainly intr.*) **1.** (of liquids) to move or be conveyed as in a stream. **2.** (of blood) to circulate around the body. **3.** to move or progress freely as if in a stream: *the crowd flowed into the building.* **4.** to proceed or be produced continuously and effortlessly: *ideas flowed from her pen.* **5.** to show or be marked by smooth or easy movement. **6.** to hang freely or loosely: *her hair flowed down her back.* **7.** to be present in abundance: *wine flows at their parties.* **8.** an informal word for **menstruate. 9.** (of tide water) to advance or rise. Compare **ebb** (sense 1). **10.** (*tr.*) to cover or swamp with liquid; flood. **11.** (of rocks such as slate) to yield to pressure without breaking so that the structure and arrangement of the constituent minerals are altered. ~*n.* **12.** the act, rate, or manner of flowing: *a fast flow.* **13.** a continuous stream or discharge. **14.** continuous progression. **15.** the advancing of the tide. **16.** a stream of molten or solidified lava. **17.** the amount of liquid that flows in a given time. **18.** an informal word for **menstruation. 19.** *Scot.* **a.** a marsh or swamp. **b.** an inlet or basin of the sea. **c.** (cap. when part of a name): *Scapa Flow.* **20. flow of spirits.** natural happiness. [Old English *flōwan;* related to Old Norse *flōa,* Middle Low German *vlōien,* Greek *plein* to float, Sanskrit *plavate* he swims]

flowage ('fləʊɪdʒ) *n.* **1.** the act of flowing or overflowing or the state of having overflowed. **2.** the liquid that flows or overflows. **3.** a gradual deformation or motion of certain solids, such as asphalt, which flow without fracture.

flow chart *or* **sheet** *n.* a diagrammatic representation of the sequence of operations or equipment in an industrial process, computer program, etc.

flower ('flaʊə) *n.* **1. a.** a bloom or blossom on a plant. **b.** a plant that bears blooms or blossoms. **2.** the reproductive structure of angiosperm plants, consisting of stamens and carpels surrounded by petals and sepals all borne on the receptacle. In some plants it is conspicuous and brightly coloured and attracts insects for pollination. Related adj.: **floral. 3.** any similar reproductive structure in other plants. **4.** the prime; peak: *in the flower of his youth.* **5.** the choice or finest product, part, or representative: *the flower of the young men.* **6.** a decoration or embellishment. **7.** *Printing.* a type ornament, used with others in borders, chapter headings, etc. **8.** Also called: **fleuron.** an embellishment or ornamental symbol depicting a flower. **9.** (*pl.*) fine powder, usually produced by sublimation: *flowers of sulphur.* ~*vb.* **10.** (*intr.*) to produce flowers; bloom. **11.** (*intr.*) to reach full growth or maturity. **12.** (*tr.*) to deck or decorate with flowers or floral designs. [C13: from Old French *flor,* from Latin *flōs;* see BLOW[3]] —'**flower-ˌlike** *adj.*

flowerage ('flaʊərɪdʒ) *n.* **1.** a mass of flowers. **2.** *Now rare.* the process or act of flowering.

flowerbed ('flaʊəˌbɛd) *n.* a plot of ground in which flowers are grown in a garden, park, etc.

flower bug *n.* any of a number of bugs of the family *Cimicidae,* related to the debris bugs but frequenting flowers and feeding on the small insects found there.

flower-de-luce ('flaʊədə'luːs) *n., pl.* **flowers-de-luce.** an archaic name for the **iris** (sense 2) and **lily** (sense 1). [C16: anglicized variant of French *fleur de lis*]

flowered ('flaʊəd) *adj.* **1.** having or abounding in flowers. **2.** decorated with flowers or a floral design.

flowerer ('flaʊərə) *n.* a plant that flowers at a specified time or in a specified way: *a late flowerer.*

floweret ('flaʊərɪt) *n.* another name for **floret.**

flower girl *n.* **1.** a girl or woman who sells flowers in the street. **2.** *U.S. and Scot.* a young girl who carries flowers in a procession, esp. at weddings.

flower head *n.* an inflorescence in which stalkless florets are crowded together at the tip of the stem.

flowering ('flaʊərɪŋ) *adj.* (of certain species of plants) capable of producing conspicuous flowers: *a flowering ash.*

flowering currant *n.* an ornamental shrub, *Ribes sanguineum,* growing to 2 to 3 metres (6 to 9ft.) in height, with red, crimson, yellow, or white flowers: family *Saxifragaceae.*

flowering maple *n.* any tropical shrub of the malvaceous genus *Abutilon,* esp. *A. hybridum,* having lobed leaves like those of the maple and brightly coloured flowers.

flowerless ('flaʊəlɪs) *adj.* designating any plant that does not produce seeds. See **cryptogam.**

flower-of-an-hour *n.* a malvaceous Old World herbaceous plant, *Hibiscus trionum,* having pale yellow flowers with a bladder-like calyx. Also called: **bladder ketmia.**

flower-pecker *n.* any small songbird of the family *Dicaeidae,* of SE Asia and Australasia, typically feeding on nectar, berries, and insects.

flowerpot ('flaʊəˌpɒt) *n.* a pot in which plants are grown.

flower power *n. Informal.* a youth cult of the late 1960s advocating peace and love, using the flower as a symbol; associated with drug-taking. Its adherents were known as **flower children** or **flower people.**

flowers of sulphur *pl. n.* minute crystals of sulphur obtained by condensing sulphur vapour on a cold surface.

flowery ('flaʊərɪ) *adj.* **1.** abounding in flowers. **2.** decorated with flowers or floral patterns. **3.** like or suggestive of flowers: *a flowery scent.* **4.** (of language or style) elaborate; ornate. —'**floweriness** *n.*

flowmeter ('fləʊˌmiːtə) *n.* an instrument that measures the rate of flow of a liquid or gas within a pipe or tube.

flown[1] (fləʊn) *vb.* the past participle of **fly**[1].

flown[2] (fləʊn) *adj.* relating to coloured (usually blue) decoration on porcelain that, during firing, has melted into the surrounding glaze giving a halo-like effect. [probably from the obsolete past participle of FLOW]

flow-on *n. Austral. and N.Z.* a wage or salary increase granted to one group of workers as a consequence of a similar increase granted to another group.

flow sheet *n.* another name for **flow chart.**

fl. oz. *abbrev. for* fluid ounce.

flu (fluː) *n. Informal.* **1.** (often preceded by *the*) short for **influenza. 2.** any of various viral infections, esp. a respiratory or intestinal infection.

fluctuant ('flʌktjʊənt) *adj.* inclined to vary or fluctuate; unstable.

fluctuate ('flʌktjʊˌeɪt) *vb.* **1.** to change or cause to change position constantly; be or make unstable; waver or vary. **2.** (*intr.*) to rise and fall like a wave; undulate. [C17: from Latin *fluctuāre,* from *fluctus* a wave, from *fluere* to flow]

fluctuation (ˌflʌktjʊ'eɪʃən) *n.* **1.** constant change; vacillation; instability. **2.** undulation. **3.** a variation in an animal or plant that is determined by environment rather than heredity.

flue[1] (fluː) *n.* **1.** a shaft, tube, or pipe, esp. as used in a chimney, to carry off smoke, gas, etc. **2.** *Music.* the passage in an organ pipe or flute within which a vibrating air column is set up. See also **flue pipe.** [C16: of unknown origin]

flue[2] (fluː) *n.* loose fluffy matter; down. [C16: from Flemish *vluwe,* from Old French *velu* shaggy] —'**fluey** *adj.*

flue[3] *or* **flew** (fluː) *n.* a type of fishing net. [Middle English, from Middle Dutch *vlūwe*]

flue[4] (fluː) *n.* another word for **fluke**[1] (senses 1, 3). —**flued** *adj.*

flue-cure *vb.* (*tr.*) to cure (tobacco) by means of radiant heat from pipes or flues connected to a furnace.

flue gas *n.* the smoke in the uptake of a boiler fire: it consists mainly of carbon dioxide, carbon monoxide, and nitrogen.

fluellin *or* **fluellen** (flʊ'ɛlən) *n.* **1.** either of two weedy scrophulariaceous annuals related to the toadflaxes, **round-leaved fluellin** (*Kickxia spuria*) and **sharp-leaved fluellin** (*K. elatine*). **2.** *Obsolete.* any of several speedwells, especially *Veronica officinalis.* [C16: shortened from Welsh *Ilysiau Llewelyn* Llewelyn's flower]

fluency ('fluːənsɪ) *n.* the quality of being fluent, esp. facility in speech or writing.

fluent ('fluːənt) *adj.* **1.** able to speak or write a specified foreign language with facility. **2.** spoken or written with facility: *his French is fluent.* **3.** easy and graceful in motion or shape. **4.** flowing or able to flow freely. [C16: from Latin: flowing, from *fluere* to flow] —'**fluently** *adv.*

flue pipe *or* **flue** *n.* an organ pipe or tubular instrument of the flute family whose sound is produced by the passage of air across a sharp-edged fissure in the side. This sets in motion a vibrating air column within the pipe or instrument.

flue stop *n.* an organ stop controlling a set of flue pipes.

fluff (flʌf) *n.* **1.** soft light particles, such as the down or nap of cotton or wool. **2.** any light downy substance. **3.** an object, matter, etc., of little importance; trifle. **4.** *Informal.* a mistake, esp. in speaking or reading lines or performing music. **5.** *Informal.* a young woman (esp. in the phrase **a bit of fluff**). ~*vb.* **6.** to make or become soft and puffy by shaking or patting; puff up. **7.** *Informal.* to make a mistake in performing (an action, dramatic speech, music, etc.). [C18: perhaps from FLUE[2]]

fluffy ('flʌfɪ) *adj.* **fluffier, fluffiest. 1.** of, resembling, or covered with fluff. **2.** soft and light: *fluffy hair.* —'**fluffily** *adv.* —'**fluffiness** *n.*

flugelhorn ('fluːgəlˌhɔːn) *n.* a type of valved brass instrument consisting of a tube of conical bore with a cup-shaped mouthpiece, used esp. in brass bands. It is a transposing instrument in B flat or C, and has the same range as the cornet in B flat. [German *Flügelhorn,* from *Flügel* wing + *Horn* HORN]

fluid ('fluːɪd) *n.* **1.** a substance, such as a liquid or gas, that can flow, has no fixed shape, and offers little resistance to an external stress. ~*adj.* **2.** capable of flowing and easily changing shape. **3.** of, concerned with, or using a fluid or fluids. **4.** constantly changing or apt to change. **5.** smooth in shape or movement; flowing. [C15: from Latin *fluidus,* from *fluere* to flow] —'**fluidal** *adj.* —'**fluidness** *n.* —'**fluidly** *or* '**fluidally** *adv.*

fluid dram *n.* another name for **drachm.**

fluid drive *n.* a type of coupling for transmitting power from the engine of a motor vehicle to the transmission, using a torque converter. Also called: **fluid coupling, fluid clutch, fluid flywheel.**

fluidextract ('flu:ɪd'ɛkstrækt) *n.* an alcoholic solution of a vegetable drug, one millilitre of which has an equivalent activity to one gram of the powdered drug.
fluidics (flu:'ɪdɪks) *n.* (*functioning as sing.*) the study and use of systems in which the flow of fluids in tubes simulates the flow of electricity in conductors. Such systems are used in place of electronics in certain applications, such as the control of apparatus. —**flu'idic** *adj.*
fluidity (flu:'ɪdɪtɪ) *n.* **1.** the state of being fluid. **2.** *Physics.* the reciprocal of viscosity.
fluidize *or* **fluidise** ('flu:ɪˌdaɪz) *vb.* (*tr.*) to make fluid, esp. to make (solids) fluid by pulverizing them so that they can be transported in a stream of gas as if they were liquids: *fluidized coal.* —ˌ**fluidi'zation** *or* ˌ**fluidi'sation** *n.* —'**fluidˌizer** *or* '**fluidˌiser** *n.*
fluidized bed *n. Chemical engineering.* a bed of fluidized solids used as a heat exchanger medium.
fluid lubrication *n. Engineering.* lubrication in which bearing surfaces are separated by an oil film sustained by the motion of the parts.
fluid mechanics *n.* (*functioning as sing.*) the study of the mechanical and flow properties of fluids, esp. as applied to practical engineering. Also called: **hydraulics.** See also **hydrodynamics, hydrostatics, hydrokinetics.**
fluid ounce *n.* a unit of capacity equal to the volume of one avoirdupois ounce of distilled water at 62°F: there are twenty fluid ounces in an Imperial pint and sixteen in a U.S. pint.
fluid pressure *n.* the pressure exerted by a fluid at any point inside it. The difference of pressure between two levels is determined by the product of the difference of height, the density, and the acceleration of free fall.
fluke[1] (flu:k) *n.* **1.** Also called: **flue.** a flat bladelike projection at the end of the arm of an anchor. **2.** either of the two lobes of the tail of a whale or related animal. **3.** Also called: **flue.** the barb or barbed head of a harpoon, arrow, etc. [C16: perhaps a special use of FLUKE[3] (in the sense: a flounder)]
fluke[2] (flu:k) *n.* **1.** an accidental stroke of luck. **2.** any chance happening. ~*vb.* **3.** (*tr.*) to gain, make, or hit by a fluke. [C19: of unknown origin]
fluke[3] (flu:k) *n.* **1.** any parasitic flatworm, such as the blood fluke and liver fluke, of the classes *Monogenea* and *Digenea* (formerly united in a single class *Trematoda*). **2.** another name for **flounder**[2] (sense 1). [Old English *flōc;* related to Old Norse *flōki* flounder, Old Saxon *flaka* sole, Old High German *flah* smooth]
fluky *or* **flukey** ('flu:kɪ) *adj.* **flukier, flukiest.** *Informal.* **1.** done or gained by an accident, esp. a lucky one. **2.** variable; uncertain: *fluky weather.* —'**flukiness** *n.*
flume (flu:m) *n.* **1.** a ravine through which a stream flows. **2.** a narrow artificial channel made for providing water for power, floating logs, etc. **3.** a slide in the form of a long and winding tube with a stream of water running through it that descends into a purpose-built pool. ~*vb.* **4.** (*tr.*) to transport (logs) in a flume. [C12: from Old French *flum,* ultimately from Latin *flūmen* stream, from *fluere* to flow]
flummery ('flʌmərɪ) *n., pl.* **-meries.** **1.** *Informal.* meaningless flattery; nonsense. **2.** *Chiefly Brit.* a cold pudding of oatmeal, etc. [C17: from Welsh *llymru*]
flummox ('flʌməks) *vb.* (*tr.*) to perplex or bewilder. [C19: of unknown origin]
flung (flʌŋ) *vb.* the past tense and past participle of **fling.**
flunk (flʌŋk) *Informal, chiefly U.S., Canadian, and N.Z.* ~*vb.* **1.** to fail or cause to fail to reach the required standard in (an examination, course, etc.). **2.** (*intr.;* foll. by *out*) to be dismissed from a school or college through failure in examinations. ~*n.* **3.** a low grade below the pass standard. [C19: perhaps from FLINCH[1] + FUNK[1]]
flunky *or* **flunkey** ('flʌŋkɪ) *n., pl.* **flunkies** *or* **flunkeys.** **1.** a servile or fawning person. **2.** a person who performs menial tasks. **3.** *Usually derogatory.* a manservant in livery. [C18: of unknown origin]
Fluon ('flu:ɒn) *n.* a trademark for **polytetrafluoroethylene.**
fluor ('flu:ɔ:) *n.* another name for **fluorspar.** [C17: from Latin: a flowing; so called from its use as a metallurgical flux]
fluor- *combining form.* a variant of **fluoro-** before a vowel: *fluorene; fluorine.*
fluorapatite (ˌflʊə'ræpətaɪt) *n.* a mineral consisting of calcium fluorophosphate; the most common form of apatite.
fluorene ('flʊəri:n) *n.* a white insoluble crystalline solid used in making dyes. Formula: $(C_6H_4)_2CH_2$.
fluoresce (ˌflʊə'rɛs) *vb.* (*intr.*) to exhibit fluorescence. [C19: back formation from FLUORESCENCE]
fluorescein *or* **fluoresceine** (ˌflʊə'rɛsɪɪn) *n.* an orange-red crystalline compound that in aqueous solution exhibits a greenish-yellow fluorescence in reflected light and is reddish-orange in transmitted light: used as a marker in sea water and as an indicator. Formula: $C_{20}H_{12}O_5$.
fluorescence (ˌflʊə'rɛsəns) *n.* **1.** *Physics.* **a.** the emission of light or other radiation from atoms or molecules that are bombarded by particles, such as electrons, or by radiation from a separate source. The bombarding radiation produces excited atoms, molecules, or ions and these emit photons as they fall back to the ground state. **b.** such an emission of photons that ceases as soon as the bombarding radiation is discontinued. **c.** such an emission of photons for which the average lifetime of the excited atoms and molecules is less than about 10^{-8} seconds. **2.** the radiation emitted as a result of fluorescence. Compare **phosphorescence.** [C19: FLUOR + *-escence* (as in *opalescence*)]
fluorescent (ˌflʊə'rɛsᵊnt) *adj.* exhibiting or having the property of fluorescence.
fluorescent lamp *n.* **1.** a type of lamp in which an electrical gas discharge is maintained in a tube with a thin layer of phosphor on its inside surface. The gas, which is often mercury vapour, emits ultraviolet radiation causing the phosphor to fluoresce. **2.** a type of lamp in which an electrical discharge is maintained in a tube containing a gas such as neon, mercury vapour, or sodium vapour at low pressure. Gas atoms in the discharge are struck by electrons and fluoresce.
fluorescent screen *n.* a transparent screen coated on one side with a phosphor that fluoresces when exposed to x-rays or cathode rays.
fluoric (flu:'ɔ:rɪk) *adj.* of, concerned with, or produced from fluorine or fluorspar.
fluoridate ('flʊərɪˌdeɪt) *vb.* to subject (water) to fluoridation.
fluoridation (ˌflʊərɪ'deɪʃən) *n.* the addition of about one part per million of fluorides to the public water supply as a protection against tooth decay.
fluoride ('flʊəˌraɪd) *n.* **1.** any salt of hydrofluoric acid, containing the fluoride ion, F^-. **2.** any compound containing fluorine, such as methyl fluoride.
fluorinate ('flʊərɪˌneɪt) *vb.* to treat or combine with fluorine. —ˌ**fluori'nation** *n.*
fluorine ('flʊəri:n) *or* **fluorin** ('flʊərɪn) *n.* a toxic pungent pale yellow gas of the halogen group that is the most electronegative and reactive of all the elements, occurring principally in fluorspar and cryolite: used in the production of uranium, fluorocarbons, and other chemicals. Symbol: F; atomic no.: 9; atomic wt.: 18.998; valency: 1; density: 1.696 kg/m³; freezing pt.: –219.62°C; boiling pt.: –188.1°C.
fluorite ('flʊəraɪt) *n.* the U.S. and Canadian name for **fluorspar.**
fluoro- *or before a vowel* **fluor-** *combining form.* **1.** indicating the presence of fluorine: *fluorocarbon.* **2.** indicating fluorescence: *fluoroscope.*
fluorocarbon (ˌflʊərəʊ'kɑ:bᵊn) *n.* any compound derived by replacing all or some of the hydrogen atoms in hydrocarbons by fluorine atoms. Many of them are used as lubricants, solvents, and coatings. See also **Freon, polytetrafluoroethylene, CFC.**
fluorochrome ('flʊərəʊˌkrəʊm) *n.* a chemical entity, such as a molecule or group, that exhibits fluorescence.
fluorography (flʊə'rɒgrəfɪ) *n.* the photographic recording of fluoroscopic images.
fluorometer (ˌflʊə'rɒmɪtə) *or* **fluorimeter** (ˌflʊə'rɪmɪtə) *n.* **1.** an instrument for inducing fluorescence by irradiation and for examination of the emission spectrum of the resulting fluorescent light. **2.** a device for detecting and measuring ultraviolet radiation by determining the amount of fluorescence that it produces from a phosphor. —**fluorometric** (ˌflʊərəʊ'mɛtrɪk) *or* **fluorimetric** (ˌflʊərɪ'mɛtrɪk) *adj.* —ˌ**fluo'rometry** *or* ˌ**fluo'rimetry** *n.*
fluorophore ('flʊərəʊˌfɔ:) *n.* a chemical group responsible for fluorescence.
fluoroscope ('flʊərəˌskəʊp) *n.* a device consisting of a fluorescent screen and an x-ray source that enables an x-ray image of an object, person, or part to be observed directly. —**fluoroscopic** (ˌflʊərə'skɒpɪk) *adj.* —ˌ**fluoro'scopically** *adv.*
fluoroscopy (flʊə'rɒskəpɪ) *n.* examination of a person or object by means of a fluoroscope.
fluorosis (flʊə'rəʊsɪs) *n.* fluoride poisoning, due to ingestion of too much fluoride in drinking water over a long period or to ingestion of pesticides containing fluoride salts. Chronic fluorosis results in mottling of the teeth of children.
fluorspar ('flʊəˌspɑ:), **fluor,** *or U.S. and Canadian* **fluorite** *n.* a white or colourless mineral sometimes fluorescent and often tinted by impurities, found in veins and as deposits from hot gases. It is used in the manufacture of glass, enamel, and jewellery, and is the chief ore of fluorine. Composition: calcium fluoride. Formula: CaF_2. Crystal structure: cubic.
flurry ('flʌrɪ) *n., pl.* **-ries.** **1.** a sudden commotion or burst of activity. **2.** a light gust of wind or rain or fall of snow. **3.** *Stock Exchange.* a sudden brief increase in trading or fluctuation in stock prices. **4.** the death spasms of a harpooned whale. ~*vb.* **-ries, -rying, -ried.** **5.** to confuse or bewilder or be confused or bewildered. [C17: from obsolete *flurr* to scatter, perhaps formed on analogy with HURRY]
flush[1] (flʌʃ) *vb.* **1.** to blush or cause to blush. **2.** to flow or flood or cause to flow or flood with or as if with water. **3.** to glow or shine or cause to glow or shine with a rosy colour. **4.** to send a volume of water quickly through (a pipe, channel, etc.) or into (a toilet) for the purpose of cleansing, emptying, etc. **5.** to cause (soluble substances in the soil) to be washed towards the surface, as by the action of underground springs, or (of such substances) to be washed towards the soil surface. **6.** (*tr.; usually passive*) to excite or elate. ~*n.* **7.** a rosy colour, esp. in the cheeks; blush. **8.** a sudden flow or gush, as of water. **9.** a feeling of excitement or elation: *the flush of success.* **10.** early bloom; freshness: *the flush of youth.* **11.** redness of the skin, esp. of the face, as from the effects of a fever, alcohol, etc. **12.** *Ecology.* an area of boggy land fed by ground water. ~*adj.* **13.** having a ruddy or height-

ened colour. [C16 (in the sense: to gush forth): perhaps from FLUSH³] —'**flusher** *n.*

flush² (flʌʃ) *adj.* (*usually postpositive*) **1.** level or even with another surface. **2.** directly adjacent; continuous. **3.** *Informal.* having plenty of money. **4.** *Informal.* abundant or plentiful, as money. **5.** full of vigour. **6.** full to the brim or to the point of overflowing. **7.** *Printing.* having an even margin, right or left, with no indentations. **8.** (of a blow) accurately delivered. **9.** (of a vessel) having no superstructure built above the flat level of the deck. ~*adv.* **10.** so as to be level or even. **11.** directly or squarely. ~*vb.* (*tr.*) **12.** to cause (surfaces) to be on the same level or in the same plane. **13.** to enrich the diet of (a ewe) during the breeding season. ~*n.* **14.** a period of fresh growth of leaves, shoots, etc. [C18: probably from FLUSH¹ (in the sense: spring out)] —'**flushness** *n.*

flush³ (flʌʃ) *vb.* (*tr.*) to rouse (game, wild creatures, etc. from their surroundings) and put to flight. [C13 *flusshen,* perhaps of imitative origin]

flush⁴ (flʌʃ) *n.* (in poker and similar games) a hand in which all the cards are from the same suit. See also **royal flush, straight flush.** [C16: from Old French *flus,* from Latin *fluxus* FLUX]

flushing ('flʌʃɪŋ) *n.* an extra feeding given to ewes before mating to increase the lambing percentage.

flushwork ('flʌʃˌwɜːk) *n. Architect.* decorative treatment of the surface of an outside wall with flints split to show their smooth black surface, combined with dressed stone to form patterns such as tracery or initials.

fluster ('flʌstə) *vb.* **1.** to make or become confused, nervous, or upset. ~*n.* **2.** a state of confusion or agitation. [C15: probably of Scandinavian origin; compare Icelandic *flaustr* to hurry, *flaustra* to bustle]

flute (fluːt) *n.* **1.** a wind instrument consisting of an open cylindrical tube of wood or metal having holes in the side stopped either by the fingers or by pads controlled by keys. The breath is directed across a mouth hole cut in the side, causing the air in the tube to vibrate. Range: about three octaves upwards from middle C. **2.** any pipe blown directly on the principle of a flue pipe, either by means of a mouth hole or through a fipple. **3.** *Architect.* a rounded shallow concave groove on the shaft of a column, pilaster, etc. **4.** a groove or furrow in cloth, etc. **5.** anything shaped like a flute. ~*vb.* **6.** to produce or utter (sounds) in the manner or tone of a flute. **7.** (*tr.*) to make grooves or furrows in. [C14: from Old French *flahute,* via Old Provençal, from Vulgar Latin *flabeolum* (unattested); perhaps also influenced by Old Provençal *laut* lute; see FLAGEOLET] —'**flute,like** *adj.* —'**fluty** *adj.*

fluted ('fluːtɪd) *adj.* **1.** (esp. of the shaft of a column) having flutes. **2.** sounding like a flute.

fluter ('fluːtə) *n.* **1.** a craftsman who makes flutes or fluting. **2.** a tool used to make flutes or fluting. **3.** a less common word, used esp. in folk music, for **flautist.**

fluting ('fluːtɪŋ) *n.* **1.** a design or decoration of flutes on a column, pilaster, etc. **2.** grooves or furrows, as in cloth.

flutist ('fluːtɪst) *n. Now chiefly U.S.* a variant of **flautist.**

flutter ('flʌtə) *vb.* **1.** to wave or cause to wave rapidly; flap. **2.** (*intr.*) (of birds, butterflies, etc.) to flap the wings. **3.** (*intr.*) to move, esp. downwards, with an irregular motion. **4.** (*intr.*) *Pathol.* (of the auricles of the heart) to beat abnormally rapidly, esp. in a regular rhythm. **5.** to be or make nervous or restless. **6.** (*intr.*) to move about restlessly. **7.** *Swimming.* to cause (the legs) to move up and down in a flutter kick or (of the legs) to move in this way. **8.** (*tr.*) *Brit. informal.* to wager or gamble (a small amount of money). ~*n.* **9.** a quick flapping or vibrating motion. **10.** a state of nervous excitement or confusion. **11.** excited interest; sensation; stir. **12.** *Brit. informal.* a modest bet or wager. **13.** *Pathol.* an abnormally rapid beating of the auricles of the heart (200 to 400 beats per minute), esp. in a regular rhythm, sometimes resulting in heart block. **14.** *Electronics.* a slow variation in pitch in a sound-reproducing system, similar to wow but occurring at higher frequencies. **15.** a potentially dangerous oscillation of an aircraft, or part of an aircraft, caused by the interaction of aerodynamic forces, structural elastic reactions, and inertia. **16.** *Swimming.* See **flutter kick. 17.** Also called: **flutter tonguing.** *Music.* a method of sounding a wind instrument, esp. the flute, with a rolling movement of the tongue. [Old English *floterian* to float to and fro; related to German *flattern;* see FLOAT] —'**flutterer** *n.* —'**flutteringly** *adv.* —'**fluttery** *adj.*

flutterboard ('flʌtəˌbɔːd) *n. U.S. and Canadian.* an oblong board or piece of polystyrene plastic used by swimmers in training or practice. Brit. word: **float.**

flutter kick *n.* a type of kick used in certain swimming strokes, such as the crawl, in which the legs are held straight and alternately moved up and down rapidly in the water.

fluvial ('fluːvɪəl) *or* **fluviatile** ('fluːvɪəˌtaɪl, -tɪl) *adj.* of, relating to, or occurring in a river: *fluvial deposits.* [C14: from Latin *fluviālis,* from *fluvius* river, from *fluere* to flow]

fluviomarine (ˌfluːvɪˌəʊmə'riːn) *adj.* **1.** (of deposits) formed by joint action of the sea and a river or stream. **2.** (esp. of fish) able to live in both rivers and the sea. [C19: *fluvio-,* from Latin *fluvius* river + MARINE]

fluvioterrestrial (ˌfluːvɪəʊtə'rɛstrɪəl) *adj.* (of animals) able to live in rivers and on land.

flux (flʌks) *n.* **1.** a flow or discharge. **2.** continuous change; instability. **3.** a substance, such as borax or salt, that gives a low melting-point mixture with a metal oxide. It is used for cleaning metal surfaces during soldering, etc., and for protecting the surfaces of liquid metals. **4.** *Metallurgy.* a chemical used to increase the fluidity of refining slags in order to promote the rate of chemical reaction. **5.** a similar substance used in the making of glass. **6.** *Physics.* **a.** the rate of flow of particles, energy, or a fluid, such as that of neutrons (**neutron flux**) or of light energy (**luminous flux**). **b.** the strength of a field in a given area expressed as the product of the area and the component of the field strength at right angles to the area: *magnetic flux; electric flux.* **7.** *Pathol.* an excessive discharge of fluid from the body, such as watery faeces in diarrhoea. **8.** the act or process of melting; fusion. **9.** (in the philosophy of Heraclitus) the state of constant change in which all things exist. ~*vb.* **10.** to make or become fluid. **11.** (*tr.*) to apply flux to (a metal, soldered joint, etc.). **12.** (*tr.*) an obsolete word for **purge.** [C14: from Latin *fluxus* a flow, from *fluere* to flow]

flux density *n. Physics.* the amount of flux per unit of cross-sectional area.

fluxion ('flʌkʃən) *n.* **1.** *Maths, obsolete.* the rate of change of a function; derivative. **2.** a less common word for **flux** (senses 1, 2). [C16: from Late Latin *fluxiō* a flowing] —'**fluxional** *or* '**fluxionary** *adj.* —'**fluxionally** *adv.*

fluxmeter ('flʌksˌmiːtə) *n.* any instrument for measuring magnetic flux, usually by measuring the charge that flows through a coil when the flux changes.

fly¹ (flaɪ) *vb.* **flies, flying, flew, flown. 1.** (*intr.*) (of birds, aircraft, etc.) to move through the air in a controlled manner using aerodynamic forces. **2.** to travel over (an area of land or sea) in an aircraft. **3.** to operate (an aircraft or spacecraft). **4.** to float, flutter, or be displayed in the air or cause to float, etc., in this way: *to fly a kite; they flew the flag.* **5.** to transport or be transported by or through the air by aircraft, wind, etc. **6.** (*intr.*) to move or be moved very quickly, forcibly, or suddenly: *she came flying towards me; the door flew open.* **7.** (*intr.*) to pass swiftly: *time flies.* **8.** to escape from (an enemy, place, etc.); flee: *he flew the country.* **9.** (*intr.*; may be foll. by *at* or *upon*) to attack a person. **10.** (*intr.*) to have a sudden outburst: *he flew into a rage again.* **11.** (*intr.*) (of money, etc.) to vanish rapidly. **12.** (*tr.*) *Falconry.* (of hawks) to fly at (quarry) in attack: *peregrines fly rooks.* **13.** (*tr.*) *Theatre.* to suspend (scenery) above the stage so that it may be lowered into view. **14. fly a kite. a.** to procure money by an accommodation bill. **b.** to release information or take a step in order to test public opinion. **15. fly high.** *Informal.* **a.** to have a high aim. **b.** to prosper or flourish. **16. fly in the face of.** See **face** (sense 18). **17. fly off the handle. Informal.** to lose one's temper. **18. fly the coop.** *U.S. and Canadian informal.* to leave suddenly. **19. go fly a kite.** *U.S. and Canadian informal.* go away. **20. let fly.** *Informal.* **a.** to lose one's temper (with a person): *she really let fly at him.* **b.** to shoot or throw (an object). ~*n., pl.* **flies. 21.** (*often pl.*) Also called: **fly front.** a closure that conceals a zip, buttons, or other fastening, by having one side overlapping, as on trousers. **22. a.** a flap forming the entrance to a tent. **b.** a piece of canvas drawn over the ridgepole of a tent to form an outer roof. **23.** short for **flywheel. 24.** the horizontal weighted arm of a fly press. **25. a.** the outer edge of a flag. **b.** the distance from the outer edge of a flag to the staff. Compare **hoist** (sense 9). **26.** *Brit.* a light one-horse covered carriage formerly let out on hire. **27.** *Austral. and N.Z.* an attempt: *I'll give it a fly.* **28.** *Printing.* **a.** a device for transferring printed sheets from the press to a flat pile. **b.** Also called: **flyhand.** a person who collects and stacks printed matter from a printing press. **c.** a piece of paper folded once in order to make four pages, with printing only on the first page. **29.** (*pl.*) *Theatre.* the space above the stage out of view of the audience, used for storing scenery, etc. **30.** *Rare.* the act of flying. [Old English *flēogan;* related to Old Frisian *fliāga,* Old High German *fliogan,* Old Norse *fljūga*] —'**flyable** *adj.*

fly² (flaɪ) *n., pl.* **flies. 1.** any dipterous insect, esp. the housefly, characterized by active flight. See also **horsefly, blowfly, tsetse fly, crane fly. 2.** any of various similar but unrelated insects, such as the caddis fly, firefly, dragonfly, and chalcid fly. **3.** *Angling.* a lure made from a fish-hook dressed with feathers, tinsel, etc., to resemble any of various flies or nymphs: used in fly-fishing. See also **dry fly, wet fly. 4.** (in southern Africa) an area that is infested with the tsetse fly. **5. drink with the flies.** *Austral. slang.* to drink alone. **6. fly in amber.** See **amber** (sense 2). **7. fly in the ointment.** *Informal.* a slight flaw that detracts from value, completeness, or enjoyment. **8. fly on the wall.** a person who watches others, while not being noticed himself. **9. there are no flies on him, her,** etc. *Informal.* he, she, etc., is no fool. [Old English *flēoge;* related to Old Norse *fluga,* Old High German *flioga;* see FLY¹] —'**flyless** *adj.*

fly³ (flaɪ) *adj. Slang, chiefly Brit.* knowing and sharp; smart. [C19: of uncertain origin]

fly agaric *n.* a saprophytic agaricaceous woodland fungus, *Amanita muscaria,* having a scarlet cap with white warts and white gills: poisonous but rarely fatal. See also **amanita.** [so named from its use as a poison on flypaper]

fly ash *n.* fine solid particles of ash carried into the air during combustion, esp. the combustion of pulverized fuel in power stations.
flyaway ('flaɪəˌweɪ) *adj.* **1.** (of hair or clothing) loose and fluttering. **2.** frivolous or flighty; giddy. *~n.* **3.** a person who is frivolous or flighty.
flyback ('flaɪˌbæk) *n.* the fast return of the spot on a cathode-ray tube after completion of each trace.
flyblow ('flaɪˌbləʊ) *vb.* **blows, blowing, blew, blown. 1.** (*tr.*) to contaminate, esp. with the eggs or larvae of the blowfly; taint. *~n.* **2.** (*usually pl.*) the egg or young larva of a blowfly, deposited on meat, paper, etc.
flyblown ('flaɪˌbləʊn) *adj.* **1.** covered with flyblows. **2.** contaminated; tainted.
flyboat ('flaɪˌbəʊt) *n.* any small swift boat.
flybook ('flaɪˌbʊk) *n.* a small case or wallet used by anglers for storing artificial flies.
flyby ('flaɪˌbaɪ) *n., pl.* **-bys.** a flight past a particular position or target, esp. the close approach of a spacecraft to a planet or satellite for investigation of conditions.
fly-by-light *n.* aircraft control through systems operated by optical fibres rather than mechanical rods. Abbrev.: **FBL.**
fly-by-night *Informal.* *~adj.* **1.** unreliable or untrustworthy, esp. in finance. **2.** brief; impermanent. *~n.* Also called: **fly-by-nighter. 3.** an untrustworthy person, esp. one who departs secretly or by night to avoid paying debts. **4.** a person who goes out at night to places of entertainment.
fly-by-wire *n.* aircraft control through systems operated by electronic circuits rather than mechanical rods. Abbrev.: **FBW.**
flycatcher ('flaɪˌkætʃə) *n.* **1.** any small insectivorous songbird of the Old World subfamily *Muscicapinae,* having small slender bills fringed with bristles: family *Muscicapidae.* See also **spotted flycatcher. 2.** any American passerine bird of the family *Tyrannidae.*
flyer ('flaɪə) *n.* a variant spelling of **flier.**
fly-fish *vb.* (*intr.*) *Angling.* to fish using artificial flies as lures. See **dry fly, wet fly.** —'**fly-ˌfisher** *n.* —'**fly-ˌfishing** *n.*
fly half *n. Rugby.* another name for **stand-off half.**
flying ('flaɪɪŋ) *adj.* **1.** (*prenominal*) hurried; fleeting: *a flying visit.* **2.** (*prenominal*) designed for fast action. **3.** (*prenominal*) moving or passing quickly on or as if on wings: *a flying leap; the flying hours.* **4.** hanging, waving, or floating freely: *flying hair.* **5.** *Nautical.* (of a sail) not hauled in tight against the wind. *~n.* **6.** the act of piloting, navigating, or travelling in an aircraft. **7.** (*modifier*) relating to, capable of, accustomed to, or adapted for flight: *a flying machine.* *~adv.* **8.** *Nautical.* freely flapping in the wind.
flying boat *n.* a seaplane in which the fuselage consists of a hull that provides buoyancy in the water.
flying bomb *n.* another name for the **V-1.**
flying bridge *n.* an auxiliary bridge of a vessel, usually built above or far outboard of the main bridge.
flying buttress *n.* a buttress supporting a wall or other structure by an arch or part of an arch that transmits the thrust outwards and downwards. Also called: **arc-boutant.**
flying circus *n.* **1.** an exhibition of aircraft aerobatics. **2.** the aircraft and men who take part in such exhibitions.
flying colours *pl. n.* conspicuous success; triumph: *he passed his test with flying colours.*
flying doctor *n.* (in areas of sparse or scattered population) a doctor who visits patients by aircraft.
flying field *n.* a small airport; an airfield.
flying fish *n.* any marine teleost fish of the family *Exocoetidae,* common in warm and tropical seas, having enlarged winglike pectoral fins used for gliding above the surface of the water.
flying fox *n.* **1.** any large fruit bat, esp. any of the genus *Pteropus* of tropical Africa and Asia: family *Pteropodidae.* **2.** *Austral. and N.Z.* a cable mechanism used for transportation across a river, gorge, etc.
flying frog *n.* any of several tropical frogs of the family *Rhacophoridae,* esp. *Rhacophorus reinwardtii* of Malaya, that glide between trees by means of long webbed digits.
flying gurnard *n.* any marine spiny-finned gurnard-like fish of the mostly tropical family *Dactylopteridae,* having enlarged fan-shaped pectoral fins used to glide above the surface of the sea.
flying jib *n.* the jib set furthest forward or outboard on a vessel with two or more jibs.
flying lemur *n.* either of the two arboreal mammals of the genus *Cynocephalus,* family *Cynocephalidae,* and order *Dermoptera,* of S and SE Asia. They resemble lemurs but have a fold of skin between the limbs enabling movement by gliding leaps. Also called: **colugo.**
flying lizard *or* **dragon** *n.* any lizard of the genus *Draco,* of S and SE Asia, having an extensible fold of skin on each side of the body, used to make gliding leaps: family *Agamidae* (agamas).
flying mare *n.* a wrestling throw in which a wrestler seizes his opponent's arm or head (**flying head mare**) and turns to throw him over his shoulder.
flying officer *n.* an officer holding commissioned rank senior to a pilot officer but junior to a flight lieutenant in the British and certain other air forces.
flying phalanger *n.* any nocturnal arboreal phalanger of the genus *Petaurus,* of E Australia and New Guinea, having black-striped greyish fur and moving with gliding leaps using folds of skin between the hind limbs and forelimbs. Also called: **glider.**
flying picket *n.* (in industrial disputes) a member of a group of pickets organized to be able to move quickly from place to place.
flying saucer *n.* any unidentified disc-shaped flying object alleged to come from outer space.
flying-spot *adj.* denoting an electronic system in which a rapidly moving spot of light is used to encode or decode data, for example to obtain a television signal by scanning a photographic film or slide.
flying squad *n.* a small group of police, soldiers, etc., ready to move into action quickly.
flying squirrel *n.* any nocturnal sciurine rodent of the subfamily *Petauristinae,* of Asia and North America. Furry folds of skin between the forelegs and hind legs enable these animals to move by gliding leaps.
flying start *n.* **1.** Also called (informal): **flier.** (in sprinting) a start by a competitor anticipating the starting signal. **2.** a start to a race or time trial in which the competitor is already travelling at speed as he passes the starting line. **3.** any promising beginning. **4.** an initial advantage over others.
flying wing *n.* **1.** an aircraft consisting mainly of one large wing and no fuselage or tailplane. **2.** (in Canadian football) the twelfth player, who has a variable position behind the scrimmage line.
flyleaf ('flaɪˌliːf) *n., pl.* **-leaves.** the inner leaf of the endpaper of a book, pasted to the first leaf.
flyman ('flaɪmən) *n., pl.* **-men.** *Theatre.* a stagehand who operates the scenery, curtains, etc., in the flies.
fly orchid *n.* a European orchid, *Ophrys insectifera,* whose flowers resemble and attract certain wasps: found in wood margins and scrub on chalk soils.
flyover ('flaɪˌəʊvə) *n.* **1.** Also called: **overpass.** *Brit.* **a.** an intersection of two roads at which one is carried over the other by a bridge. **b.** such a bridge. **2.** the U.S. name for a **fly-past.**
flypaper ('flaɪˌpeɪpə) *n.* paper with a sticky and poisonous coating, usually hung from the ceiling to trap flies.
fly-past *n.* a ceremonial flight of aircraft over a given area. Also called (esp. U.S.): **flyover.**
flyposting ('flaɪˌpəʊstɪŋ) *n.* the posting of advertising or political bills, posters, etc. in unauthorized places.
fly press *n.* a hand-operated press in which a horizontal beam with heavy steel balls attached to the ends gives additional momentum to the descending member.
fly rod *n.* a light flexible rod, now usually made of fibreglass or split cane, used in fly-fishing.
Flysch (flɪʃ) *n.* (*sometimes not cap.*) *n.* a sequence of sediments or sedimentary rocks comprising sandstones, conglomerates, marls, shales and clays that were formed by erosion during a period of mountain building and subsequently deformed as the mountain building continued. The phenomenon was first observed in the Alps. [Swiss German]
flyscreen ('flaɪˌskriːn) *n.* a wire-mesh screen over a window to prevent flies from entering a room.
fly sheet *n.* **1. a.** a flap forming the entrance to a tent. **b.** a piece of canvas drawn over the ridgepole of a tent to form an outer roof. **2.** a short handbill or circular.
flyspeck ('flaɪˌspɛk) *n.* **1.** the small speck of the excrement of a fly. **2.** a small spot or speck. *~vb.* **3.** (*tr.*) to mark with flyspecks.
fly spray *n.* a liquid used to destroy flies and other insects, sprayed from an aerosol.
flystrike ('flaɪstraɪk) *n. Austral. and N.Z.* the infestation of wounded sheep by blowflies or maggots.
flyte (flaɪt; *Scot.* fləɪt) *vb.* a variant spelling of **flite.**
fly-tipping *n.* the deliberate dumping of rubbish in an unauthorized place.
flytrap ('flaɪˌtræp) *n.* **1.** any of various insectivorous plants, esp. Venus's flytrap. **2.** a device for catching flies.
fly way *n.* the usual route used by birds when migrating.
flyweight ('flaɪˌweɪt) *n.* **1. a.** a professional boxer weighing not more than 112 pounds (51 kg). **b.** an amateur boxer weighing 48–51 kg (106–112 pounds). **c.** (*as modifier*): *a flyweight contest.* **2.** (in Olympic wrestling) a wrestler weighing not more than 115 pounds (52 kg).
flywheel ('flaɪˌwiːl) *n.* a heavy wheel that stores kinetic energy and smooths the operation of a reciprocating engine by maintaining a constant speed of rotation over the whole cycle.
fm *abbrev. for:* **1.** Also: **fm.** fathom. **2.** from.
Fm *the chemical symbol for* fermium.
FM *abbrev. for:* **1.** frequency modulation. **2.** Field Marshal. **3.** *Aeronautics.* figure of merit.
FMCG *abbrev. for* fast-moving consumer goods.
FMN *n. Biochem.* flavin mononucleotide; a phosphoric ester of riboflavin that acts as the prosthetic group for many flavoproteins. See also **FAD.**
FMS *Aeronautics abbrev. for* flight management systems.
f-number *or* **f number** *n. Photog.* the numerical value of the relative aperture. If the relative aperture is f8, 8 is the f-number and indicates that the focal length of the lens is 8 times the size of the lens aperture. See also **T-number.**
FO *abbrev. for:* **1.** *Army.* Field Officer. **2.** *Air Force.* Flying Officer. **3.** Foreign Office.

fo. *abbrev. for* folio.

foal (fəʊl) *n.* **1.** the young of a horse or related animal. *~vb.* **2.** to give birth to (a foal). [Old English *fola;* related to Old Frisian *fola,* Old High German *folo* foal, Latin *pullus* young creature, Greek *pōlos* foal]

foam (fəʊm) *n.* **1.** a mass of small bubbles of gas formed on the surface of a liquid, such as the froth produced by agitating a solution of soap or detergent in water. **2.** frothy saliva sometimes formed in and expelled from the mouth, as in rabies. **3.** the frothy sweat of a horse or similar animal. **4. a.** any of a number of light cellular solids made by creating bubbles of gas in the liquid material and solidifying it: used as insulators and in packaging. **b.** (*as modifier*): *foam rubber; foam plastic.* **5.** a colloid consisting of a gas suspended in a liquid. **6.** a mixture of chemicals sprayed from a fire extinguisher onto a burning substance to create a stable layer of bubbles which smothers the flames. **7.** a poetic word for the **sea.** *~vb.* **8.** to produce or cause to produce foam; froth. **9.** (*intr.*) to be very angry (esp. in the phrase **foam at the mouth**). [Old English *fām;* related to Old High German *feim,* Latin *spūma,* Sanskrit *phena*] —**'foamless** *adj.* —**'foam,like** *adj.*

foamflower ('fəʊm,flaʊə) *n.* a perennial saxifragaceous plant, *Tiarella cordifolia,* of North America and Asia, having spring-blooming white flowers.

foamy ('fəʊmɪ) *adj.* **foamier, foamiest.** of, resembling, consisting of, or covered with foam. —**'foamily** *adv.* —**'foaminess** *n.*

fob[1] (fɒb) *n.* **1.** a chain or ribbon by which a pocket watch is attached to a waistcoat. **2.** any ornament hung on such a chain. **3.** a small pocket in a man's waistcoat, for holding a watch. [C17: probably of Germanic origin; compare German dialect *Fuppe* pocket]

fob[2] (fɒb) *vb.* **fobs, fobbing, fobbed.** an archaic word for **cheat.** [C15: probably from German *foppen* to trick]

f.o.b. *or* **FOB** *Commerce. abbrev. for* free on board.

fob off *vb.* (*tr., adv.*) **1.** to appease or trick (a person) with lies or excuses. **2.** to dispose of (goods) by trickery.

FoC *abbrev. for* father of the chapel.

focal ('fəʊkəl) *adj.* **1.** of or relating to a focus. **2.** situated at, passing through, or measured from the focus. —**'focally** *adv.*

focal infection *n.* a bacterial infection limited to a specific part of the body, such as the tonsils or a gland.

focalize *or* **focalise** ('fəʊkə,laɪz) *vb.* a less common word for **focus.** —**,focali'zation** *or* **,focali'sation** *n.*

focal length *or* **distance** *n.* the distance from the focal point of a lens or mirror to the reflecting surface of the mirror or the centre point of the lens.

focal plane *n.* **1.** the plane that is perpendicular to the axis of a lens or mirror and passes through the focal point. **2.** the plane in a telescope, camera, or other optical instrument in which a real image is in focus.

focal point *n.* **1.** Also called: **principal focus, focus.** the point on the axis of a lens or mirror to which parallel rays of light converge or from which they appear to diverge after refraction or reflection. **2.** a central point of attention or interest.

focal ratio *n. Photog.* another name for **f-number.**

focometer (fəʊ'kɒmɪtə) *n.* an instrument for measuring the focal length of a lens.

fo'c's'le *or* **fo'c'sle** ('fəʊksəl) *n.* a variant spelling of **forecastle.**

focus ('fəʊkəs) *n., pl.* **-cuses** *or* **-ci** (-saɪ). **1.** a point of convergence of light or other electromagnetic radiation, particles, sound waves, etc., or a point from which they appear to diverge. **2.** another name for **focal point** (sense 1) or **focal length. 3.** *Optics.* the state of an optical image when it is distinct and clearly defined or the state of an instrument producing this image: *the picture is in focus; the telescope is out of focus.* **4.** a point upon which attention, activity, etc., is directed or concentrated. **5.** *Geometry.* a fixed reference point on the concave side of a conic section, used when defining its eccentricity. **6.** the point beneath the earth's surface at which an earthquake or underground nuclear explosion originates. Compare **epicentre. 7.** *Pathol.* the main site of an infection or a localized region of diseased tissue. *~vb.* **-cuses, -cusing, -cused. 8.** to bring or come to a focus or into focus. **9.** (*tr.;* often foll. by *on*) to fix attention (on); concentrate. [C17: via New Latin from Latin: hearth, fireplace] —**'focusable** *adj.* —**'focuser** *n.*

focus puller *n. Films.* the member of a camera crew who adjusts the focus of the lens as the camera is tracked in or out.

fodder ('fɒdə) *n.* **1.** bulk feed for livestock, esp. hay, straw, etc. **2.** raw experience or material: *fodder for the imagination.* *~vb.* **3.** (*tr.*) to supply (livestock) with fodder. [Old English *fōdor;* related to Old Norse *fōthr,* Old High German *fuotar;* see FOOD, FORAGE]

foe (fəʊ) *n. Formal or literary.* another word for **enemy.** [Old English *fāh* hostile; related to Old High German *fēhan* to hate, Old Norse *feikn* dreadful; see FEUD[1]]

FoE *or* **FOE** *abbrev. for* Friends of the Earth.

foehn (fɜːn; *German* føːn) *n. Meteorol.* a variant spelling of **föhn.**

foeman ('fəʊmən) *n., pl.* **-men.** *Archaic or poetic.* an enemy in war; foe.

foetal ('fiːtəl) *adj.* a variant spelling of **fetal.**

foetation (fiː'teɪʃən) *n.* a variant spelling of **fetation.**

foeticide ('fiːtɪ,saɪd) *n.* a variant spelling of **feticide.** —**,foeti'cidal** *adj.*

foetid ('fɛtɪd, 'fiː-) *adj.* a variant spelling of **fetid.** —**'foetidly** *adv.* —**'foetidness** *n.*

foetor ('fiːtə) *n.* a variant spelling of **fetor.**

foetus ('fiːtəs) *n., pl.* **-tuses.** a variant spelling of **fetus.**

fog[1] (fɒg) *n.* **1.** a mass of droplets of condensed water vapour suspended in the air, often greatly reducing visibility, corresponding to a cloud but at a lower level. **2.** a cloud of any substance in the atmosphere reducing visibility. **3.** a state of mental uncertainty or obscurity. **4.** *Photog.* a blurred or discoloured area on a developed negative, print, or transparency caused by the action of extraneous light, incorrect development, etc. **5.** a colloid or suspension consisting of liquid particles dispersed in a gas. *~vb.* **fogs, fogging, fogged. 6.** to envelop or become enveloped with or as if with fog. **7.** to confuse or become confused: *to fog an issue.* **8.** *Photog.* to produce fog on (a negative, print, or transparency) or (of a negative, print, or transparency) to be affected by fog. [C16: perhaps back formation from *foggy* damp, boggy, from FOG[2]]

fog[2] (fɒg) *n.* **a.** a second growth of grass after the first mowing. **b.** grass left to grow long in winter. [C14: probably of Scandinavian origin; compare Norwegian *fogg* rank grass]

fog bank *n.* a distinct mass of fog, esp. at sea.

fogbound ('fɒg,baʊnd) *adj.* **1.** prevented from operation by fog: *the airport was fogbound.* **2.** obscured by or enveloped in fog: *the skyscraper was fogbound.*

fogbow ('fɒg,bəʊ) *n.* a faint arc of light sometimes seen in a fog bank. Also called: **seadog, white rainbow.**

fogdog ('fɒg,dɒg) *n.* a whitish spot sometimes seen in fog near the horizon. Also called: **seadog.**

fogged (fɒgd) *or* **foggy** *adj. Photog.* affected or obscured by fog.

foggy ('fɒgɪ) *adj.* **-gier, -giest. 1.** thick with fog. **2.** obscure or confused. **3.** another word for **fogged. 4. not the foggiest (idea** *or* **notion).** no idea whatsoever: *I haven't the foggiest.* —**'foggily** *adv.* —**'fogginess** *n.*

foghorn ('fɒg,hɔːn) *n.* **1.** a mechanical instrument sounded at intervals to serve as a warning to vessels in fog. **2.** *Informal.* a loud deep resounding voice.

fog level *n.* the density produced by the development of photographic materials that have not been exposed to light or other actinic radiation. It forms part of the characteristic curve of a particular material.

fog signal *n.* a signal used to warn railway engine drivers in fog, consisting of a detonator placed on the line.

fogy *or* **fogey** ('fəʊgɪ) *n., pl.* **-gies** *or* **-geys.** an extremely fussy, old-fashioned, or conservative person (esp. in the phrase **old fogy).** [C18: of unknown origin] —**'fogyish** *or* **'fogeyish** *adj.* —**'fogyism** *or* **'fogeyism** *n.*

föhn *or* **foehn** (fɜːn; *German* føːn) *n.* a warm dry wind blowing down the northern slopes of the Alps. It originates as moist air blowing from the Mediterranean, rising on reaching the Alps and cooling at the saturated adiabatic lapse rate, and descending on the leeward side, warming at the dry adiabatic lapse rate, thus gaining heat. See also **lapse rate.** [German, from Old High German *phōnno,* from Latin *favōnius;* related to *fovēre* to warm]

foible ('fɔɪbəl) *n.* **1.** a slight peculiarity or minor weakness; idiosyncrasy. **2.** the most vulnerable part of a sword's blade, from the middle to the tip. Compare **forte**[1] (sense 2). [C17: from obsolete French, from obsolete adj.: FEEBLE]

foie gras (*French* fwagrɑ) *n.* See **pâté de foie gras.**

foil[1] (fɔɪl) *vb.* (*tr.*) **1.** to baffle or frustrate (a person, attempt, etc.). **2.** *Hunting.* (of hounds, hunters, etc.) to obliterate the scent left by a hunted animal or (of a hunted animal) to run back over its own trail. **3.** *Archaic.* to repulse or defeat (an attack or assailant). *~n.* **4.** *Hunting.* any scent that obscures the trail left by a hunted animal. **5.** *Archaic.* a setback or defeat. [C13 *foilen* to trample, from Old French *fouler,* from Old French *fuler* tread down, FULL[2]] —**'foilable** *adj.*

foil[2] (fɔɪl) *n.* **1.** metal in the form of very thin sheets: *gold foil; tin foil.* **2.** the thin metallic sheet forming the backing of a mirror. **3.** a thin leaf of shiny metal set under a gemstone to add brightness or colour. **4.** a person or thing that gives contrast to another. **5.** *Architect.* a small arc between cusps, esp. as used in Gothic window tracery. **6.** short for **aerofoil** or **hydrofoil.** *~vb.* (*tr.*) **7.** to back or cover with foil. **8.** Also: **foliate.** *Architect.* to ornament (windows) with foils. **9.** *Rare.* to act as a foil to. [C14: from Old French *foille,* from Latin *folia* leaves, plural of *folium*]

foil[3] (fɔɪl) *n.* a light slender flexible sword tipped by a button and usually having a bell-shaped guard. [C16: of unknown origin]

foilsman ('fɔɪlzmən) *n., pl.* **-men.** *Fencing.* a person who uses or specializes in using a foil.

foin (fɔɪn) *Archaic.* *~n.* **1.** a thrust or lunge with a weapon. *~vb.* **2.** to thrust with a weapon. [C14: probably from Old French *foine,* from Latin *fuscina* trident]

Foism ('fəʊ,ɪzəm) *n.* Chinese Buddhism, the version introduced from India from the 4th century A.D. onwards and essentially belonging to the Mahayana school. [from Mandarin Chinese *fo* BUDDHA] —**'Foist** *n., adj.*

foison ('fɔɪzən) *n. Archaic or poetic.* a plentiful supply or yield. [C13: from Old French, from Latin *fūsiō* a pouring out, from *fundere* to pour; see FUSION]

foist (fɔɪst) *vb.* (*tr.*) **1.** (often foll. by *off* or *on*) to sell or pass off (something, esp. an inferior article) as genuine, valuable, etc. **2.**

(usually foll. by *in* or *into*) to insert surreptitiously or wrongfully. [C16: probably from obsolete Dutch *vuisten* to enclose in one's hand, from Middle Dutch *vuist* fist]

Fokker ('fɒkə) *n.* an aircraft designed or built by the Dutch aeronautical engineer A. H. G. Fokker (1890–1939), characterized by its speed and climbing power, esp. as used by Germany in World War I.

FOL (in New Zealand) *abbrev. for* Federation of Labour.

fol. *abbrev. for:* **1.** folio. **2.** followed. **3.** following.

folacin ('fɒləsɪn) *n.* another name for **folic acid.** [C20: from FOL(IC) AC(ID) + -IN]

fold[1] (fəʊld) *vb.* **1.** to bend or be bent double so that one part covers another: *to fold a sheet of paper.* **2.** (*tr.*) to bring together and intertwine (the arms, legs, etc.): *she folded her hands.* **3.** (*tr.*) (of birds, insects, etc.) to close (the wings) together from an extended position. **4.** (*tr.; often foll. by up or in*) to enclose in or as if in a surrounding material. **5.** (*tr.; foll. by in*) to clasp (a person) in the arms. **6.** (*tr.; usually foll. by round, about, etc.*) to wind (around); entwine. **7.** (*tr.*) *Poetic.* to cover completely: *night folded the earth.* **8.** Also: **fold in.** (*tr.*) to mix (a whisked mixture) with other ingredients by gently turning one part over the other with a spoon. **9.** to produce a bend (in stratified rock) or (of stratified rock) to display a bend. **10.** (*intr.; often foll. by up*) *Informal.* to collapse; fail: *the business folded.* ~*n.* **11.** a piece or section that has been folded: *a fold of cloth.* **12.** a mark, crease, or hollow made by folding. **13.** a hollow in undulating terrain. **14.** a bend in stratified rocks that results from movements within the earth's crust and produces such structures as anticlines and synclines. **15.** *Anatomy.* another word for **plica** (sense 1). **16.** a coil, as in a rope, etc. **17.** an act of folding. ~See also **fold up.** [Old English *fealdan;* related to Old Norse *falda,* Old High German *faldan,* Latin *duplus* double, Greek *haploos* simple] —'**foldable** *adj.*

fold[2] (fəʊld) *n.* **1. a.** a small enclosure or pen for sheep or other livestock, where they can be gathered. **b.** the sheep or other livestock gathered in such an enclosure. **c.** a flock of sheep. **2.** a church or the members of it. **3.** any group or community sharing a way of life or holding the same values. ~*vb.* **4.** (*tr.*) to gather or confine (sheep or other livestock) in a fold. [Old English *falod;* related to Old Saxon *faled,* Middle Dutch *vaelt*]

-fold *suffix forming adjectives and adverbs.* having so many parts, being so many times as much or as many, or multiplied by so much or so many: *threefold; three-hundredfold.* [Old English *-fald, -feald*]

fold-and-thrust belt *n. Geology.* a linear or arcuate region of the earth's surface that has been subjected to severe folding and thrust faulting.

foldaway ('fəʊldəˌweɪ) *adj.* (*prenominal*) (of a bed) able to be folded and put away when not in use.

foldback ('fəʊldˌbæk) *n.* (in multitrack recording) a process for returning a signal to a performer instantly. Also called: **cueing.**

foldboat ('fəʊldˌbəʊt) *n.* another name for **faltboat.**

folded dipole *n.* a type of aerial, widely used with television and VHF radio receivers, consisting of two parallel dipoles connected together at their outer ends and fed at the centre of one of them. The length is usually half the operating wavelength.

folder ('fəʊldə) *n.* **1.** a binder or file for holding loose papers, etc. **2.** a folded circular. **3.** a machine for folding printed sheets. **4.** a person or thing that folds.

folderol ('fɒldəˌrɒl) *n.* a variant of **falderal.**

folding door *n.* a door in the form of two or more vertical hinged leaves that can be folded one against another.

folding money *n. Informal.* paper money.

folding press *n.* a fall in wrestling won by folding one's opponent's legs up to his head and pressing his shoulders to the floor.

foldout ('fəʊldˌaʊt) *n. Printing.* another name for **gatefold.**

fold up *vb.* (*adv.*) **1.** (*tr.*) to make smaller or more compact. **2.** (*intr.*) to collapse, as with laughter or pain.

foley *or* **foley artist** ('fəʊlɪ) *n. Films.* the U.S. name for **footsteps editor.** [C20: named after the inventor of the technique]

folia ('fəʊlɪə) *n.* the plural of **folium.**

foliaceous (ˌfəʊlɪ'eɪʃəs) *adj.* **1.** having the appearance of the leaf of a plant. **2.** bearing leaves or leaflike structures. **3.** *Geology.* (of certain rocks, esp. schists) consisting of thin layers. [C17: from Latin *foliāceus*]

foliage ('fəʊlɪɪdʒ) *n.* **1.** the green leaves of a plant. **2.** sprays of leaves used for decoration. **3.** an ornamental leaf-like design. [C15: from Old French *fuellage,* from *fuelle* leaf; influenced in form by Latin *folium*] —'**foliaged** *adj.*

foliar ('fəʊlɪə) *adj.* of or relating to a leaf or leaves. [C19: from French *foliaire,* from Latin *folium* leaf]

foliate *adj.* ('fəʊlɪɪt, -ˌeɪt). **1. a.** relating to, possessing, or resembling leaves. **b.** (*in combination*): *trifoliate.* **2.** (of certain metamorphic rocks, esp. schists) having the constituent minerals arranged in thin leaflike layers. ~*vb.* ('fəʊlɪˌeɪt). **3.** (*tr.*) to ornament with foliage or with leaf forms such as foils. **4.** to hammer or cut (metal) into thin plates or foil. **5.** (*tr.*) to coat or back (glass, etc.) with metal foil. **6.** (*tr.*) to number the leaves of (a book, manuscript, etc.). Compare **paginate.** **7.** (*intr.*) (of plants) to grow leaves. [C17: from Latin *foliātus* leaved, leafy]

foliated ('fəʊlɪˌeɪtɪd) *adj.* **1.** *Architect.* ornamented with or made up of foliage or foils. **2.** (of rocks and minerals, esp. schists) composed of thin easily separable layers. **3.** (esp. of parts of animals or plants) resembling a leaf.

foliation (ˌfəʊlɪ'eɪʃən) *n.* **1.** *Botany.* **a.** the process of producing leaves. **b.** the state of being in leaf. **c.** the arrangement of leaves in a leaf bud; vernation. **2.** *Architect.* **a.** ornamentation consisting of foliage. **b.** ornamentation consisting of cusps and foils. **3.** any decoration with foliage. **4.** the consecutive numbering of the leaves of a book. **5.** *Geology.* the arrangement of the constituents of a rock in leaflike layers, as in schists.

folic acid ('fəʊlɪk, 'fɒl-) *n.* any of a group of vitamins of the B complex, including pteroylglutamic acid and its derivatives: used in the treatment of megaloblastic anaemia. Also called: **folacin.** [C20: from Latin *folium* leaf; so called because it may be obtained from green leaves]

folie à deux ('fɒlɪ æ 'dɜː) *n. Psychiatry.* mental illness occurring simultaneously in two intimately related persons who share some of the elements of the illness, such as delusions. [French: madness involving two (people)]

folie de grandeur *French.* (fɔli də grɑ̃dœr) *n.* delusions of grandeur. [literally: madness of grandeur]

folio ('fəʊlɪəʊ) *n., pl.* **-lios.** **1.** a sheet of paper folded in half to make two leaves for a book or manuscript. **2.** a book or manuscript of the largest common size made up of such sheets. **3.** a leaf of paper or parchment numbered on the front side only. **4.** a page number in a book. **5.** *Law.* a unit of measurement of the length of legal documents, determined by the number of words, generally 72 or 90 in Britain and 100 in the U.S. ~*adj.* **6.** relating to or having the format of a folio: *a folio edition.* ~*vb.* **-lios, -lioing, -lioed.** **7.** (*tr.*) to number the leaves of (a book) consecutively. [C16: from Latin phrase *in foliō* in a leaf, from *folium* leaf]

foliolate ('fəʊlɪəˌleɪt; fəʊ'lɪəlɪt, -ˌleɪt) *adj. Botany.* possessing or relating to leaflets. [C19: from Late Latin *foliolum* little leaf, from Latin *folium* leaf]

foliose ('fəʊlɪˌəʊs, -ˌəʊz) *adj.* another word for **foliaceous** (senses 1, 2). [C18: from Latin *foliōsus* full of leaves]

folium ('fəʊlɪəm) *n., pl.* **-lia** (-lɪə). **1.** a plane geometrical curve consisting of a loop whose two ends, intersecting at a node, are asymptotic to the same line. Standard equation: $x^3 + y^3 = 3axy$ where $x = y + a$ is the equation of the line. **2.** any thin leaflike layer, esp. of some metamorphic rocks. [C19: from Latin, literally: leaf]

folk (fəʊk) *n., pl.* **folk** *or* **folks.** **1.** (*functioning as pl.; often pl. in form*) people in general, esp. those of a particular group or class: *country folk.* **2.** (*functioning as pl.; usually pl. in form*) *Informal.* members of a family. **3.** (*functioning as sing.*) *Informal.* short for **folk music.** **4.** a people or tribe. **5.** (*modifier*) relating to, originating from, or traditional to the common people of a country: *a folk song.* [Old English *folc;* related to Old Saxon, Old Norse, Old High German *folk*] —'**folkish** *adj.* —'**folkishness** *n.*

folk dance *n.* **1.** any of various traditional rustic dances often originating from festivals or rituals. **2.** a piece of music composed for such a dance. ~*vb.* **folk-dance.** (*intr.*) **3.** to perform a folk dance. —**folk dancing** *n.*

folk etymology *n.* **1.** the gradual change in the form of a word through the influence of a more familiar word or phrase with which it becomes associated, as for example *sparrow-grass* for *asparagus.* **2.** a popular but erroneous conception of the origin of a word.

folkie *or* **folky** ('fəʊkɪ) *n., pl.* **-ies.** *Informal.* a devotee of folk music.

folklore ('fəʊkˌlɔː) *n.* **1.** the unwritten literature of a people as expressed in folk tales, proverbs, riddles, songs, etc. **2.** the body of stories and legends attached to a particular place, group, activity, etc.: *Hollywood folklore; rugby folklore.* **3.** the anthropological discipline concerned with the study of folkloric materials. —'**folkˌloric** *adj.* —'**folkˌlorist** *n., adj.* —ˌ**folklor'istic** *adj.*

folk medicine *n.* the traditional art of medicine as practised among rustic communities and primitive peoples, consisting typically of the use of herbal remedies, fruits and vegetables thought to have healing power, etc.

folk memory *n.* the memory of past events as preserved in a community.

folkmoot ('fəʊkˌmuːt), **folkmote,** *or* **folkmot** ('fəʊkˌməʊt) *n.* (in early medieval England) an assembly of the people of a district, town, or shire. [Old English *folcmōt,* from *folc* FOLK + *mōt* from *mǣtan* to MEET]

folk music *n.* **1.** music that is passed on from generation to generation by oral tradition. Compare **art music.** **2.** any music composed in the idiom of this oral tradition.

folk-rock *n.* a combination of folk-orientated lyrics with a pop accompaniment.

folk singer *n.* a person who sings folk songs or other songs in the folk idiom. —**folk singing** *n.*

folk song *n.* **1.** a song of which the music and text have been handed down by oral tradition among the common people. **2.** a modern song which employs or reflects the folk idiom.

folksy ('fəʊksɪ) *adj.* **-sier, -siest.** **1.** of or like ordinary people; sometimes used derogatorily to describe affected simplicity. **2.** *Informal, chiefly U.S. and Canadian.* friendly; affable. **3.** of or relating to folk art. —'**folksiness** *n.*

folk tale *or* **story** *n.* a tale or legend originating among a people and typically becoming part of an oral tradition.

folkways (ˈfəʊkˌweɪz) *pl. n. Sociol.* traditional and customary ways of living.

folk weave *n.* a type of fabric with a loose weave.

foll. *abbrev. for:* **1.** followed. **2.** following.

follicle (ˈfɒlɪkᵊl) *n.* **1.** any small sac or cavity in the body having an excretory, secretory, or protective function: *a hair follicle.* **2.** *Botany.* a dry fruit, formed from a single carpel, that splits along one side only to release its seeds: occurs in larkspur and columbine. [C17: from Latin *folliculus* small bag, from *follis* pair of bellows, leather money-bag] —**follicular** (fɒˈlɪkjʊlə), **folliculate** (fɒˈlɪkjʊˌleɪt), *or* **folˈlicuˌlated** *adj.*

follicle-stimulating hormone *n.* a gonadotrophic hormone secreted by the pituitary gland that stimulates maturation of ovarian follicles in female mammals and growth of seminiferous tubules in males. Abbrev.: **FSH.** See also **luteinizing hormone, prolactin.**

folliculin (fɒˈlɪkjʊlɪn) *n.* another name for **oestrone.**

follow (ˈfɒləʊ) *vb.* **1.** to go or come after in the same direction: *he followed his friend home.* **2.** (*tr.*) to accompany; attend: *she followed her sister everywhere.* **3.** to come after as a logical or natural consequence. **4.** (*tr.*) to keep to the course or track of: *she followed the towpath.* **5.** (*tr.*) to act in accordance with; obey: *to follow instructions.* **6.** (*tr.*) to accept the ideas or beliefs of (a previous authority, etc.): *he followed Donne in most of his teachings.* **7.** to understand (an explanation, argument, etc.): *the lesson was difficult to follow.* **8.** to watch closely or continuously: *she followed his progress carefully.* **9.** (*tr.*) to have a keen interest in: *to follow athletics.* **10.** (*tr.*) to help in the cause of or accept the leadership of: *the men who followed Napoleon.* **11.** (*tr.*) *Rare.* to earn a living at or in: *to follow the Navy.* **12. follow suit. a.** *Cards.* to play a card of the same suit as the card played immediately before it. **b.** to do the same as someone else. ~*n.* **13.** *Billiards, etc.* **a.** a forward spin imparted to a cue ball causing it to roll after the object ball. **b.** a shot made in this way. See also **follow-on, follow out, follow through, follow up.** [Old English *folgian;* related to Old Frisian *folgia,* Old Saxon *folgōn,* Old High German *folgēn*] —ˈ**followable** *adj.*

follower (ˈfɒləʊə) *n.* **1.** a person who accepts the teachings of another; disciple; adherent: *a follower of Marx.* **2.** an attendant or henchman. **3.** an enthusiast or supporter, as of a sport or team. **4.** (esp. formerly) a male admirer. **5.** *Rare.* a pursuer. **6.** a machine part that derives its motion by following the motion of another part.

following (ˈfɒləʊɪŋ) *adj.* **1. a.** (*prenominal*) about to be mentioned, specified, etc.: *the following items.* **b.** (*as n.*): *will the following please raise their hands?* **2.** (of winds, currents, etc.) moving in the same direction as the course of a vessel. ~*n.* **3.** a group of supporters or enthusiasts: *he attracted a large following wherever he played.*

follow-my-leader *n.* a game in which the players must repeat the actions of the leader. U.S., Canadian, and Irish name: **follow-the-leader.**

follow-on *Cricket.* ~*n.* **1.** an immediate second innings forced on a team scoring a prescribed number of runs fewer than its opponents in the first innings. ~*vb.* **follow on. 2.** (*intr., adv.*) (of a team) to play a follow-on.

follow out *vb.* (*tr., adv.*) to implement (an idea or action) to a conclusion.

follow through *vb.* (*adv.*) **1.** *Sport.* to complete (a stroke or shot) by continuing the movement to the end of its arc. **2.** (*tr.*) to pursue (an aim) to a conclusion. ~*n.* **follow-through. 3.** *Sport.* **a.** the act of following through. **b.** the part of the stroke after the ball has been hit. **4.** the completion of a procedure, esp. after a first action.

follow up *vb.* (*tr., adv.*) **1.** to pursue or investigate (a person, evidence, etc.) closely. **2.** to continue (action) after a beginning, esp. to increase its effect. ~*n.* **follow-up. 3. a.** something done to reinforce an initial action. **b.** (*as modifier*): *a follow-up letter.* **4.** *Med.* a routine examination of a patient at various intervals after medical or surgical treatment.

folly (ˈfɒlɪ) *n., pl.* **-lies. 1.** the state or quality of being foolish; stupidity; rashness. **2.** a foolish action, mistake, idea, etc. **3.** a building in the form of a castle, temple, etc., built to satisfy a fancy or conceit, often of an eccentric kind. **4.** (*pl.*) *Theatre.* an elaborately costumed review. **5.** *Archaic.* **a.** evil; wickedness. **b.** lewdness; wantonness. [C13: from Old French *folie* madness, from *fou* mad; see FOOL[1]]

Folsom man (ˈfɒlsəm) *n.* a type of early man from a North American culture of the Pleistocene period, thought to have used flint tools and to have subsisted mainly by hunting bison. [C20: named after *Folsom,* a settlement in New Mexico, where archaeological evidence was found]

Fomalhaut (ˈfəʊməˌləʊt) *n.* the brightest star in the constellation Piscis Austrinus. Distance: 24 light years. [C16: from Arabic *fum'l-hūt* mouth of the fish, referring to its position in the constellation]

foment (fəˈmɛnt) *vb.* (*tr.*) **1.** to encourage or instigate (trouble, discord, etc.); stir up. **2.** *Med.* to apply heat and moisture to (a part of the body) to relieve pain and inflammation. [C15: from Late Latin *fōmentāre,* from Latin *fōmentum* a poultice, ultimately from *fovēre* to foster] —**fomentation** (ˌfəʊmɛnˈteɪʃən) *n.* —**foˈmenter** *n.*

fomes (ˈfəʊmiːz) *n., pl.* **-mites** (-mɪtiːz). *Med.* any material, such as bedding or clothing, that may harbour pathogens and therefore convey disease. [C18: from Latin *fōmes* tinder]

fond[1] (fɒnd) *adj.* **1.** (*postpositive;* foll. by *of*) predisposed (to); having a liking (for). **2.** loving; tender: *a fond embrace.* **3.** indulgent; doting: *a fond mother.* **4.** (of hopes, wishes, etc.) cherished but unlikely to be realized: *he had fond hopes of starting his own business.* **5.** *Archaic or dialect.* **a.** foolish. **b.** credulous. [C14 *fonned,* from *fonnen* to be foolish, from *fonne* a fool] —ˈ**fondly** *adv.* —ˈ**fondness** *n.*

fond[2] (fɒnd; *French* fɔ̃) *n.* **1.** the background of a design, as in lace. **2.** *Obsolete.* fund; stock. [C17: from French, from Latin *fundus* bottom; see FUND]

fondant (ˈfɒndənt) *n.* **1.** a thick flavoured paste of sugar and water, used in sweets and icings. **2.** a sweet made of this mixture. ~*adj.* **3.** (of a colour) soft; pastel. [C19: from French, literally: melting, from *fondre* to melt, from Latin *fundere;* see FOUND[3]]

fondle (ˈfɒndᵊl) *vb.* **1.** (*tr.*) to touch or stroke tenderly; caress. **2.** (*intr.*) *Archaic.* to act in a loving manner. [C17: from (obsolete) vb. *fond* to fondle; see FOND[1]] —ˈ**fondler** *n.* —ˈ**fondlingly** *adv.*

fondue (ˈfɒndjuː; *French* fɔ̃dy) *n.* a Swiss dish, consisting of cheese melted in white wine or cider, into which small pieces of bread are dipped and then eaten. [C19: from French, feminine of *fondu* melted, from *fondre* to melt; see FONDANT]

fondue Bourguignonne (ˈbʊəgɪˌnjɒn; *French* burgiɲɔn) *n.* a dish consisting of pieces of steak impaled on forks, cooked in oil at the table and dipped in sauces. [French: Burgundy fondue]

fons et origo *Latin.* (fɒnz ɛt ˈɒrɪgəʊ) *n.* the source and origin.

font[1] (fɒnt) *n.* **1. a.** a large bowl for baptismal water, usually mounted on a pedestal. **b.** a receptacle for holy water. **2.** the reservoir for oil in an oil lamp. **3.** *Archaic or poetic.* a fountain or well. [Old English, from Church Latin *fons* from Latin: fountain] —ˈ**fontal** *adj.*

font[2] (fɒnt) *n. Printing.* another name (esp. U.S. and Canadian) for **fount**[2].

fontanelle *or chiefly U.S.* **fontanel** (ˌfɒntəˈnɛl) *n. Anatomy.* any of several soft membranous gaps between the bones of the skull in a fetus or infant. [C16 (in the sense: hollow between muscles): from Old French *fontanele,* literally: a little spring, from *fontaine* FOUNTAIN]

food (fuːd) *n.* **1.** any substance containing nutrients, such as carbohydrates, proteins, and fats, that can be ingested by a living organism and metabolized into energy and body tissue. Related adj.: **alimentary. 2.** nourishment in more or less solid form as opposed to liquid form: *food and drink.* **3.** anything that provides mental nourishment or stimulus. [Old English *fōda;* related to Old Frisian *fōdia* to nourish, feed, Old Norse *fœthi,* Gothic *fōdeins* food; see FEED, FODDER] —ˈ**foodless** *adj.*

food additive *n.* any of various natural or synthetic substances, such as salt, monosodium glutamate, or citric acid, used in the commercial processing of food as preservatives, antioxidants, emulsifiers, etc., in order to preserve or add flavour, colour, or texture to processed food.

food body *n. Botany.* a mass of nutrients attached to a seed coat, which attracts ants and thus aids dispersal of the seed.

food chain *n. Ecology.* a series of organisms in a community, each member of which feeds on another in the chain and is eaten in turn by another member.

foodie *or* **foody** (ˈfuːdɪ) *n. Informal.* a person having an enthusiastic interest in the preparation and consumption of good food.

food poisoning *n.* an acute illness typically characterized by gastrointestinal inflammation, vomiting, and diarrhoea, caused by food that is either naturally poisonous or contaminated by pathogenic bacteria (esp. *Salmonella*).

food pollen *n.* infertile pollen produced by some plants that attracts insects and thus aids pollination.

food processor *n. Cookery.* an electric domestic appliance designed to speed the preparation and mixing of ingredients by automatic chopping, grating, blending, etc.

foodstuff (ˈfuːdˌstʌf) *n.* any material, substance, etc., that can be used as food.

food vacuole *n. Zoology.* a cavity surrounding ingested food particles in some protozoans.

fool[1] (fuːl) *n.* **1.** a person who lacks sense or judgement. **2.** a person who is made to appear ridiculous. **3.** (formerly) a professional jester living in a royal or noble household. **4.** *Obsolete.* an idiot or imbecile: *the village fool.* **5. act** *or* **play the fool.** to deliberately act foolishly; indulge in buffoonery. **6. form the fool.** *Caribbean.* to play the fool or behave irritatingly. **7. no fool.** a wise or sensible person. ~*vb.* **8.** (*tr.*) to deceive (someone), esp. in order to make him look ridiculous. **9.** (*intr.;* foll. by *with, around with,* or *about with*) *Informal.* to act or play (with) irresponsibly or aimlessly: *to fool around with a woman.* **10.** (*intr.*) to speak or act in a playful, teasing, or jesting manner. **11.** (*tr.;* foll. by *away*) to squander; fritter: *he fooled away a fortune.* **12.** *U.S.* **fool along.** to move or proceed in a leisurely way. ~*adj.* **13.** *Informal.* short for **foolish.** [C13: from Old French *fol* mad person, from Late Latin *follis* empty-headed fellow, from Latin: bellows; related to Latin *flāre* to blow]

fool[2] (fuːl) *n. Chiefly Brit.* a dessert made from a purée of fruit with cream or custard: *gooseberry fool.* [C16: perhaps from FOOL[1]]
foolery (ˈfuːlərɪ) *n., pl.* **-eries.** **1.** foolish behaviour. **2.** an instance of this, esp. a prank or trick.
foolhardy (ˈfuːlˌhɑːdɪ) *adj.* **-hardier, -hardiest.** heedlessly rash or adventurous. [C13: from Old French *fol hardi,* from *fol* foolish + *hardi* bold] —ˈ**fool,hardily** *adv.* —ˈ**fool,hardiness** *n.*
foolish (ˈfuːlɪʃ) *adj.* **1.** unwise; silly. **2.** resulting from folly or stupidity. **3.** ridiculous or absurd; not worthy of consideration. **4.** weak-minded; simple. **5.** an archaic word for **insignificant.** —ˈ**foolishly** *adv.* —ˈ**foolishness** *n.*
foolproof (ˈfuːlˌpruːf) *adj.* **1.** proof against failure; infallible: *a foolproof idea.* **2.** (esp. of machines) proof against human misuse, error, etc.
foolscap (ˈfuːlzˌkæp) *n.* **1.** *Chiefly Brit.* a size of writing or printing paper, 13½ by 17 inches or 13¼ by 16½ inches. **2.** a book size, 4¼ by 6¾ inches (**foolscap octavo**) or (chiefly Brit.) 6¾ by 8½ inches (**foolscap quarto**). **3.** a variant spelling of **fool's cap.** [C17: see FOOL[1], CAP; so called from the watermark formerly used on this kind of paper]
fool's cap *n.* **1.** a hood or cap with bells or tassels, worn by court jesters. **2.** a dunce's cap.
fool's errand *n.* a fruitless undertaking.
fool's gold *n.* any of various yellow minerals, esp. pyrite or chalcopyrite, that can be mistaken for gold.
fool's mate *n. Chess.* a checkmate achieved by Black's second move: the quickest possible mate.
fool's paradise *n.* illusory happiness.
fool's-parsley *n.* an evil-smelling Eurasian umbelliferous plant, *Aethusa cynapium,* with small white flowers: contains the poison coniine.
foot (fʊt) *n., pl.* **feet** (fiːt). **1.** the part of the vertebrate leg below the ankle joint that is in contact with the ground during standing and walking. Related adj.: **pedal.** **2.** any of various organs of locomotion or attachment in invertebrates, including molluscs. **3.** *Botany.* the lower part of some plants or plant structures, as of developing moss or fern sporophytes. **4. a.** a unit of length equal to one third of a yard or 12 inches. 1 Imperial foot is equivalent to 0.3048 metre. Abbrev.: **ft. b.** any of various units of length used at different times and places, typically about 10 per cent greater than the Imperial foot. **5.** any part resembling a foot in form or function: *the foot of a chair.* **6.** the lower part of something; base; bottom: *the foot of the page; the foot of a hill.* **7.** the end of a series or group: *the foot of the list.* **8.** manner of walking or moving; tread; step: *a heavy foot.* **9. a.** infantry, esp. in the British army. **b.** (*as modifier*): *a foot soldier.* **10.** any of various attachments on a sewing machine that hold the fabric in position, such as a presser foot for ordinary sewing and a zipper foot. **11.** *Music.* **a.** a unit used in classifying organ pipes according to their pitch, in terms of the length of an equivalent column of air. **b.** this unit applied to stops and registers on other instruments. **12.** *Printing.* **a.** the margin at the bottom of a page. **b.** the undersurface of a piece of type. **13.** *Prosody.* a group of two or more syllables in which one syllable has the major stress, forming the basic unit of poetic rhythm. **14. a foot in the door.** an action, appointment, etc., that provides an initial step towards a desired goal, esp. one that is not easily attainable. **15. kick with the wrong foot.** *Scot. and Irish.* to be of the opposite religion to that which is regarded as acceptable or to that of the person who is speaking. **16. my foot!** an expression of disbelief, often of the speaker's own preceding statement: *he didn't know, my foot! Of course he did!* **17. of foot.** *Archaic.* in manner of movement: *fleet of foot.* **18. on foot. a.** walking or running. **b.** in progress; astir; afoot. **19. one foot in the grave.** *Informal.* near to death. **20. on the wrong** (*or* **right**) **foot.** *Informal.* in an inauspicious (or auspicious) manner. **21. put a foot wrong.** to make a mistake. **22. put one's best foot forward. a.** to try to do one's best. **b.** to hurry. **23. put one's foot down.** *Informal.* **a.** to act firmly. **b.** to increase speed (in a motor vehicle) by pressing down on the accelerator. **24. put one's foot in it.** *Informal.* to blunder. **25. set on foot.** to initiate or start (something). **26. tread under foot.** to oppress. **27. under foot.** on the ground; beneath one's feet. ~*vb.* **28.** to dance to music (esp. in the phrase **foot it**). **29.** (*tr.*) to walk over or set foot on; traverse (esp. in the phrase **foot it**). **30.** (*tr.*) to pay the entire cost of (esp. in the phrase **foot the bill**). **31.** (usually foll. by *up*) *Archaic or dialect.* to add up. ~See also **feet, foots.** [Old English *fōt;* related to Old Norse *fōtr,* Gothic *fōtus,* Old High German *fuoz,* Latin *pēs,* Greek *pous,* Sanskrit *pad*] —ˈ**footless** *adj.*
footage (ˈfʊtɪdʒ) *n.* **1.** a length or distance measured in feet. **2. a.** the extent of film material shot and exposed. **b.** the sequences of filmed material. **3. a.** payment, by the linear foot of work done. **b.** the amount paid.
foot-and-mouth disease *n.* an acute highly infectious viral disease of cattle, pigs, sheep, and goats, characterized by the formation of vesicular eruptions in the mouth and on the feet, esp. around the hoofs. Also called: **hoof-and-mouth disease.**
football (ˈfʊtˌbɔːl) *n.* **1. a.** any of various games played with a round or oval ball and usually based on two teams competing to kick, head, carry, or otherwise propel the ball into each other's goal, territory, etc. See **association football, rugby, Australian rules, American football, Gaelic football. b.** (*as modifier*): *a football ground; a football supporter.* **2.** the ball used in any of these games or their variants. **3.** a problem, issue, etc., that is continually passed from one group or person to another and treated as a pretext for argument instead of being resolved: *he accused the government of using the strike as a political football.* —ˈ**foot,baller** *n.*
footboard (ˈfʊtˌbɔːd) *n.* **1.** a treadle or foot-operated lever on a machine. **2.** a vertical board at the foot of a bed.
footboy (ˈfʊtˌbɔɪ) *n.* a boy servant; page.
foot brake *n.* a brake operated by applying pressure to a foot pedal. Also called: **pedal brake.**
footbridge (ˈfʊtˌbrɪdʒ) *n.* a narrow bridge for the use of pedestrians.
foot-candle *n.* a former unit of illumination, equal to one lumen per square foot or 10.764 lux.
footcloth (ˈfʊtˌklɒθ) *n.* **1.** *Archaic.* a carpet or rug. **2.** an obsolete word for **caparison** (sense 1).
-footed *adj.* **1.** having a foot or feet as specified: *four-footed.* **2.** having a tread as specified: *heavy-footed.*
footer[1] (ˈfʊtə) *n.* **1.** *Archaic.* a person who goes on foot; walker. **2.** (*in combination*) a person or thing of a specified length or height in feet: *a six-footer.*
footer[2] (ˈfʊtə) *n. Brit. informal.* short for **football** (the game).
footer[3] *or* **fouter** (ˈfuːtər, ˈfuːtə) *Scot.* ~*vb.* (*intr.*) **1.** to potter; occupy oneself trivially or to little effect. ~*n.* **2.** a person who footers. [perhaps from French *foutre;* see FOOTLE]
footfall (ˈfʊtˌfɔːl) *n.* the sound of a footstep.
foot fault *n. Tennis.* a fault that occurs when the server fails to keep both feet behind the baseline until he has served.
footgear (ˈfʊtˌgɪə) *n.* another name for **footwear.**
foothill (ˈfʊtˌhɪl) *n.* (*often pl.*) a lower slope of a mountain or a relatively low hill at the foot of a mountain.
foothold (ˈfʊtˌhəʊld) *n.* **1.** a ledge, hollow, or other place affording a secure grip for the foot, as during climbing. **2.** a secure position from which further progress may be made: *a foothold for a successful career.*
footie (ˈfʊtɪ) *n.* a variant spelling of **footy.**
footing (ˈfʊtɪŋ) *n.* **1.** the basis or foundation on which something is established: *the business was on a secure footing.* **2.** the relationship or status existing between two persons, groups, etc.: *the two countries were on a friendly footing.* **3.** a secure grip by or for the feet. **4.** the lower part of a foundation of a column, wall, building, etc. **5.** *Chiefly U.S.* **a.** the act of adding a column of figures. **b.** the total obtained. **6.** *Rare.* a fee paid upon entrance into a craft, society, etc., or such an entrance itself.
foot-lambert *n.* a former unit of luminance equal to the luminance of a surface emitting or reflecting 1 lumen per square foot. A completely reflecting surface illuminated by 1 foot-candle has a luminance of 1 foot-lambert. Symbol: **ft-L.**
footle (ˈfuːtᵊl) *Informal.* ~*vb.* **1.** (*intr.;* often foll. by *around* or *about*) to loiter aimlessly; potter. **2.** (*intr.*) to talk nonsense. ~*n.* **3.** *Rare.* foolishness. [C19: probably from French *foutre* to copulate with, from Latin *futuere*]
footlights (ˈfʊtˌlaɪts) *pl. n. Theatre.* **1.** lights set in a row along the front of the stage floor and shielded on the audience side. **2.** *Informal.* the acting profession; the stage.
footling (ˈfuːtlɪŋ) *adj. Informal.* silly, trivial, or petty.
footloose (ˈfʊtˌluːs) *adj.* **1.** free to go or do as one wishes. **2.** eager to travel; restless: *to feel footloose.*
footman (ˈfʊtmən) *n., pl.* **-men.** **1.** a male servant, esp. one in livery. **2.** a low four-legged metal stand used in a fireplace for utensils, etc. **3.** (formerly) a foot soldier. **4.** any of several arctiid moths related to the tiger moths, esp. the **common footman** (*Eilema lurideola*), with yellowish hind wings and brown forewings with a yellow front stripe; they produce woolly bear larvae.
footmark (ˈfʊtˌmɑːk) *n.* a mark or trace of mud, wetness, etc., left by a person's foot on a surface.
footnote (ˈfʊtˌnəʊt) *n.* **1.** a note printed at the bottom of a page, to which attention is drawn by means of a reference mark in the body of the text. **2.** an additional comment, as to a main statement. ~*vb.* **3.** (*tr.*) to supply (a page, book, etc.) with footnotes.
footpace (ˈfʊtˌpeɪs) *n.* **1.** a normal or walking pace. **2.** Also called (in the Roman Catholic Church): **predella.** the platform immediately before an altar at the top of the altar steps.
footpad (ˈfʊtˌpæd) *n. Archaic.* a robber or highwayman, on foot rather than horseback.
footpath (ˈfʊtˌpɑːθ) *n.* a narrow path for walkers only.
footplate (ˈfʊtˌpleɪt) *n. Chiefly Brit.* **a.** a platform in the cab of a locomotive on which the crew stand to operate the controls. **b.** (*as modifier*): *a footplate man.*
foot-pound *n.* an fps unit of work or energy equal to the work done when a force of 1 pound moves through a distance of 1 foot. Abbrev.: **ft-lb.**
foot-poundal *n.* a unit of work or energy equal to the work done when a force of one poundal moves through a distance of one foot: it is equal to 0.042 14 joule.
foot-pound-second *n.* See **fps units.**
footprint (ˈfʊtˌprɪnt) *n.* **1.** an indentation or outline of the foot of a person or animal on a surface. **2.** an identifying characteristic on land or water, such as the area in which an aircraft's sonic boom can be heard or the area covered by the down-blast of a hovercraft. **3.** the area in which the signal from a direct broadcasting satellite is receivable.

footrest ('fʊtˌrɛst) *n.* something that provides a support for the feet, such as a low stool, rail, etc.
footrope ('fʊtˌrəʊp) *n. Nautical.* **1.** the part of a boltrope to which the foot of a sail is stitched. **2.** a rope fixed so as to hang below a yard to serve as a foothold.
foot rot *n. Vet. science.* See **rot**[1] (sense 11).
foot rule *n.* a rigid measure, one foot in length.
foots (fʊts) *pl. n.* (*sometimes sing.*) the sediment that accumulates at the bottom of a vessel containing any of certain liquids, such as vegetable oil or varnish; dregs.
footsie ('fʊtsɪ) *n. Informal.* flirtation involving the touching together of feet, knees, etc. (esp. in the phrase **play footsie**).
Footsie ('fʊtsɪ) *n.* an informal name for **Financial Times Stock Exchange 100 Index.**
footslog ('fʊtˌslɒg) *vb.* **-slogs, -slogging, -slogged.** (*intr.*) to march; tramp. —'**footˌslogger** *n.*
foot soldier *n.* an infantryman.
footsore ('fʊtˌsɔː) *adj.* having sore or tired feet, esp. from much walking. —'**footˌsoreness** *n.*
footstalk ('fʊtˌstɔːk) *n.* a small supporting stalk in animals and plants; a pedicel, peduncle, or pedicle.
footstall ('fʊtˌstɔːl) *n.* **1.** the pedestal, plinth, or base of a column, pier, or statue. **2.** the stirrup on a sidesaddle.
footstep ('fʊtˌstɛp) *n.* **1.** the action of taking a step in walking. **2.** the sound made by stepping or walking. **3.** the distance covered with a step; pace. **4.** a footmark. **5.** a single stair; step. **6. follow in someone's footsteps.** to continue the tradition or example of another.
footsteps editor *n. Brit. films.* the technician who adds sound effects, such as doors closing, rain falling, etc., during the postproduction sound-dubbing process. U.S. name: **foley** *or* **foley artist.**
footstock ('fʊtˌstɒk) *n.* another name for **tailstock.**
footstool ('fʊtˌstuːl) *n.* a low stool used for supporting or resting the feet of a seated person.
foot-ton *n.* a unit of work or energy equal to 2240 foot-pounds.
foot valve *n.* **1.** another name for **suction valve. 2.** a non-return valve at the inlet end of a pipe.
footwall ('fʊtˌwɔːl) *n.* the rocks on the lower side of an inclined fault plane or mineral vein. Compare **hanging wall.**
footway ('fʊtˌweɪ) *n.* a way or path for pedestrians, such as a raised walk along the edge of a bridge.
footwear ('fʊtˌwɛə) *n.* anything worn to cover the feet.
footwork ('fʊtˌwɜːk) *n.* skilful use of the feet, as in sports, dancing, etc.
footworn ('fʊtˌwɔːn) *adj.* **1.** Also: '**footˌweary.** footsore. **2.** worn away by the feet: *a footworn staircase.*
footy *or* **footie** ('fʊtɪ) *n. Informal, chiefly Austral. and N.Z.* **a.** football. **b.** (*as modifier*): *footy boots.*
foo yong ('fuː 'jɒŋ), **foo yoong** ('fuː 'jʊŋ), **foo yung,** *or* **fu yung** ('fuː 'jʌŋ) *n.* a Chinese dish made of eggs mixed with chicken, crab meat, etc., and cooked like an omelette. [from Chinese *fu yung* hibiscus]
foozle ('fuːzᵊl) *Chiefly golf.* ~*vb.* **1.** to bungle (a shot). ~*n.* **2.** a bungled shot. [C19: perhaps from German dialect *fuseln* to do slipshod work] —'**foozler** *n.*
fop (fɒp) *n.* a man who is excessively concerned with fashion and elegance. [C15: related to German *foppen* to trick; see FOB[2]] —'**foppish** *adj.* —'**foppishly** *adv.* —'**foppishness** *n.*
foppery ('fɒpərɪ) *n., pl.* **-peries.** the clothes, affectations, obsessions, etc., of or befitting a fop.
for (fɔː; *unstressed* fə) *prep.* **1.** intended to reach; directed or belonging to: *there's a phone call for you.* **2.** to the advantage of: *I only did it for you.* **3.** in the direction of: *heading for the border.* **4.** over a span of (time or distance): *working for six days; the river ran for six miles.* **5.** in favour of; in support of: *those for the proposal; vote for me.* **6.** in order to get or achieve: *I do it for money; he does it for pleasure; what did you do that for?* **7.** appropriate to; designed to meet the needs of; meant to be used in: *these kennels are for puppies.* **8.** in exchange for; at a cost of; to the amount of: *I got it for hardly any money.* **9.** such as explains or results in: *his reason for changing his job was not given.* **10.** in place of: *a substitute for the injured player.* **11.** because of; through: *she wept for pure relief.* **12.** with regard or consideration to the usual characteristics of: *he's short for a man; it's cool for this time of year.* **13.** concerning; as regards: *desire for money.* **14.** as being: *we took him for the owner; I know that for a fact.* **15.** at a specified time: *a date for the next evening.* **16.** to do or partake of: *an appointment for supper.* **17.** in the duty or task of: *that's for him to say.* **18.** to allow of: *too big a job for us to handle.* **19.** despite; notwithstanding: *she's a good wife, for all her nagging.* **20.** in order to preserve, retain, etc.: *to fight for survival.* **21.** as a direct equivalent to: *word for word; weight for weight.* **22.** in order to become or enter: *to go for a soldier; to train for the priesthood.* **23.** in recompense for: *I paid for it last week; he took the punishment for his crime.* **24. for it.** *Brit. informal.* liable for punishment or blame: *you'll be for it if she catches you.* **25. nothing for it.** no choice; no other course. ~*conj.* **26.** (*coordinating*) for the following reason; because; seeing that: *I couldn't stay, for the area was violent.* [Old English; related to Old Norse *fyr* for, Old High German *fora* before, Latin *per* through, *prō* before, Greek *pro* before, in front]
for. *abbrev. for:* **1.** foreign. **2.** forestry.
f.o.r. *or* **FOR** *Commerce. abbrev. for* free on rail.
for- *prefix.* **1.** indicating rejection or prohibition: *forbear; forbid.* **2.** indicating falsity or wrongness: *forswear.* **3.** used to give intensive force: *forgive; forlorn.* [Old English *for-;* related to German *ver-,* Latin *per-,* Greek *peri-*]
forage ('fɒrɪdʒ) *n.* **1.** food for horses or cattle, esp. hay or straw. **2.** the act of searching for food or provisions. **3.** *Military.* a raid or incursion. ~*vb.* **4.** to search (the countryside or a town) for food, provisions, etc. **5.** (*intr.*) *Military.* to carry out a raid. **6.** (*tr.*) to obtain by searching about. **7.** (*tr.*) to give food or other provisions to. **8.** (*tr.*) to feed (cattle or horses) with such food. [C14: from Old French *fourrage,* probably of Germanic origin; see FOOD, FODDER] —'**forager** *n.*
forage cap *n.* a soldier's undress cap.
forage mite *n.* a mite normally occurring in forage but sometimes infesting the skin of mammals, esp. horses, and birds.
foramen (fɒ'reɪmɛn) *n., pl.* **-ramina** (-'ræmɪnə) *or* **-ramens.** a natural hole, esp. one in a bone through which nerves and blood vessels pass. [C17: from Latin, from *forāre* to bore, pierce] —**foraminal** (fɒ'ræmɪnᵊl) *adj.*
foramen magnum *n.* the large opening at the base of the skull through which the spinal cord passes. [New Latin: large hole]
foraminifer (ˌfɒrə'mɪnɪfə) *n.* any rhizopod protozoan of the order *Foraminifera,* having a shell with numerous openings through which the pseudopodia protrude. See also **globigerina, nummulite.** [C19: from New Latin, from FORAMEN + -FER] —**foraminiferal** (fɒˌræmɪ'nɪfərəl) *or* **foˌrami'niferous** *adj.*
forasmuch as (fərəz'mʌtʃ) *conj.* (*subordinating*) *Archaic or legal.* seeing that; since.
foray ('fɒreɪ) *n.* **1.** a short raid or incursion. **2.** a first attempt or new undertaking. ~*vb.* **3.** to raid or ravage (a town, district, etc.). [C14: from *forrayen* to pillage, from Old French *forreier,* from *forrier* forager, from *fuerre* fodder; see FORAGE] —'**forayer** *n.*
forb (fɔːb) *n.* any herbaceous plant that is not a grass. [C20: from Greek *phorbē* food, from *pherbein* to graze]
forbade (fə'bæd, -'beɪd) *or* **forbad** (fə'bæd) *vb.* the past tense of **forbid.**
forbear[1] (fɔː'bɛə) *vb.* **-bears, -bearing, -bore, -borne. 1.** (when *intr.,* often foll. by *from* or an infinitive) to cease or refrain (from doing something). **2.** *Archaic.* to tolerate or endure (misbehaviour, mistakes, etc.). [Old English *forberan;* related to Gothic *frabairan* to endure] —**for'bearer** *n.* —**for'bearingly** *adv.*
forbear[2] ('fɔːˌbɛə) *n.* a variant spelling of **forebear.**
forbearance (fɔː'bɛərəns) *n.* **1.** the act of forbearing. **2.** self-control; patience. **3.** *Law.* abstention from or postponement of the enforcement of a legal right, esp. by a creditor allowing his debtor time to pay.
forbid (fə'bɪd) *vb.* **-bids, -bidding, -bade** *or* **-bad, -bidden** *or* **-bid.** (*tr.*) **1.** to prohibit (a person) in a forceful or authoritative manner (from doing something or having something). **2.** to make impossible; hinder. **3.** to shut out or exclude. **4. God forbid!** may it not happen. [Old English *forbēodan;* related to Old High German *farbiotan,* Gothic *faurbiudan;* see FOR-, BID] —**for'biddance** *n.* —**for'bidder** *n.*
forbidden (fə'bɪdᵊn) *adj.* **1.** not permitted by order or law. **2.** *Physics.* involving a change in quantum numbers that is not permitted by certain rules derived from quantum mechanics, esp. rules for changes in the electrical dipole moment of the system.
forbidden band *n.* See **energy band.**
forbidden fruit *n.* any pleasure or enjoyment regarded as illicit, esp. sexual indulgence.
forbidden transition *n. Physics.* an electronic transition in a molecule, etc., that has a very low probability of occurring.
forbidding (fə'bɪdɪŋ) *adj.* **1.** hostile or unfriendly. **2.** dangerous or ominous. —**for'biddingly** *adv.* —**for'biddingness** *n.*
forbore (fɔː'bɔː) *vb.* the past tense of **forbear**[1].
forborne (fɔː'bɔːn) *vb.* the past participle of **forbear**[1].
forby *or* **forbye** (fɔː'baɪ; *Scot.* fər'baɪ) *prep., adv. Scot.* **1.** besides; in addition (to). **2.** *Obsolete.* near; nearby.
force[1] (fɔːs) *n.* **1.** strength or energy; might; power: *the force of the blow; a gale of great force.* **2.** exertion or the use of exertion against a person or thing that resists; coercion. **3.** *Physics.* **a.** a dynamic influence that changes a body from a state of rest to one of motion or changes its rate of motion. The magnitude of the force is equal to the product of the mass of the body and its acceleration. **b.** a static influence that produces an elastic strain in a body or system or bears weight. Symbol: F **4.** *Physics.* any operating influence that produces or tends to produce a change in a physical quantity: *electromotive force; coercive force.* **5. a.** intellectual, social, political, or moral influence or strength: *the force of his argument; the forces of evil.* **b.** a person or thing with such influence: *he was a force in the land.* **6.** vehemence or intensity: *he spoke with great force.* **7.** a group of persons organized for military or police functions: *armed forces.* **8.** (*sometimes cap.;* preceded by *the*) *Informal.* the police force. **9.** a group of persons organized for particular duties or tasks: *a workforce.* **10.** *Criminal law.* violence unlawfully committed or threatened. **11.** *Philosophy, logic.* that which an expression is normally used to achieve. See **speech act, illocution, perlocution. 12. in force. a.** (of a law) having legal validity or binding effect. **b.** in great strength or numbers. **13. join forces.** to combine

strengths, efforts, etc. ~*vb.* (*tr.*) **14.** to compel or cause (a person, group, etc.) to do something through effort, superior strength, etc.; coerce. **15.** to acquire, secure, or produce through effort, superior strength, etc.: *to force a confession.* **16.** to propel or drive despite resistance: *to force a nail into wood.* **17.** to break down or open (a lock, safe, door, etc.). **18.** to impose or inflict: *he forced his views on them.* **19.** to cause (plants or farm animals) to grow or fatten artificially at an increased rate. **20.** to strain or exert to the utmost: *to force the voice.* **21.** to rape; ravish. **22.** *Cards.* **a.** to compel (a player) to trump in order to take a trick. **b.** to compel a player by the lead of a particular suit to play (a certain card). **c.** (in bridge) to induce (a bid) from one's partner by bidding in a certain way. **23. force down.** to compel an aircraft to land. **24. force a smile.** to make oneself smile. **25. force the pace.** to adopt a high speed or rate of procedure. [C13: from Old French, from Vulgar Latin *fortia* (unattested), from Latin *fortis* strong] —ˈ**forceable** *adj.* —ˈ**forceless** *adj.* —ˈ**forcer** *n.* —ˈ**forcingly** *adv.*

force[2] (fɔːs) *n.* (in northern England) a waterfall. [C17: from Old Norse *fors*]

forced (fɔːst) *adj.* **1.** done because of force; compulsory: *forced labour.* **2.** false or unnatural: *a forced smile.* **3.** due to an emergency or necessity: *a forced landing.* **4.** *Physics.* caused by an external agency: *a forced vibration; a forced draught.* —**forcedly** (ˈfɔːsɪdlɪ) *adv.* —ˈ**forcedness** *n.*

forced development *n.* the processing of underexposed photographic film to increase the image density.

force de frappe (fɔs də fræp) *n.* a military strike force, esp. the independent nuclear strike force of France. [C20: French, literally: striking force]

forced march *n. Military.* a march in which normal needs are subordinated to the need for speed.

force-feed *vb.* **-feeds, -feeding, -fed.** (*tr.*) **1.** to force (a person or animal) to eat or swallow food. **2.** to force (someone) to receive opinions, propaganda, etc. ~*n.* **force feed. 3.** a method of lubrication in which a pump forces oil into the bearings of an engine, etc.

forceful (ˈfɔːsfʊl) *adj.* **1.** powerful. **2.** persuasive or effective. —ˈ**forcefully** *adv.* —ˈ**forcefulness** *n.*

force majeure (ˈfɔːs mæˈʒɜː, -ˈdʒʊə) *n. Law.* irresistible force or compulsion such as will excuse a party from performing his part of a contract. [from French: superior force]

forcemeat (ˈfɔːsˌmiːt) *n.* a mixture of chopped or minced ingredients used for stuffing. Also called: **farce, farcemeat.** [C17: from *force* (see FARCE) + MEAT]

forceps (ˈfɔːsɪps) *n., pl.* **-ceps** *or* **-cipes** (-sɪˌpiːz). **1. a.** a surgical instrument in the form of a pair of pincers, used esp. in the delivery of babies. **b.** (*as modifier*): *a forceps baby.* **2.** any pincer-like instrument. **3.** any part or structure of an organism shaped like a forceps. [C17: from Latin, from *formus* hot + *capere* to seize] —ˈ**forceps-ˌlike** *adj.*

force pump *n.* a pump that ejects fluid under pressure. Compare **lift pump.**

force-ripe *Caribbean.* ~*adj.* **1.** (of fruit) prematurely picked and ripened by squeezing or warm storage. **2.** precocious, esp. sexually. ~*vb.* **3.** (*tr.*) to ripen (prematurely picked fruit) by squeezing or warm storage.

Forces (ˈfɔːsɪz) *pl. n.* (usually preceded by *the*) the armed services of a nation.

forcible (ˈfɔːsəbᵊl) *adj.* **1.** done by, involving, or having force. **2.** convincing or effective: *a forcible argument.* —ˈ**forcibleness** *or* ˌ**forciˈbility** *n.* —ˈ**forcibly** *adv.*

forcing bid *n. Contract bridge.* a bid, often at a higher level than is required, that is understood to oblige the bidder's partner to reply.

forcing frequency *n. Physics.* the frequency of an oscillating force applied to a system. Compare **natural frequency.**

forcing house *n.* a place where growth or maturity (as of fruit, animals, etc.) is artificially hastened.

ford (fɔːd) *n.* **1.** a shallow area in a river that can be crossed by car, horseback, etc. ~*vb.* **2.** (*tr.*) to cross (a river, brook, etc.) over a shallow area. [Old English; related to Old Frisian *forda,* Old High German *furt* ford, Latin *porta* door, *portus* PORT[1]] —ˈ**fordable** *adj.*

fordo *or* **foredo** (fɔːˈduː) *vb.* **-does, -doing, -did, -done.** (*tr.*) *Archaic.* **1.** to destroy. **2.** to exhaust. [Old English *fordōn;* related to Old Saxon *fardōn,* Old High German *fartuon,* Dutch *verdoen;* see FOR-, DO[1]]

fore[1] (fɔː) *adj.* **1.** (*usually in combination*) located at, in, or towards the front: *the forelegs of a horse.* ~*n.* **2.** the front part. **3.** something located at, in, or towards the front. **4.** short for **foremast. 5. fore and aft.** located at or directed towards both ends of a vessel: *a fore-and-aft rig.* **6. to the fore. a.** to or into the front or conspicuous position. **b.** *Scot. and Irish.* alive or active: *is your grandfather still to the fore?* ~*adv.* **7.** at or towards a ship's bow. **8.** *Obsolete.* before. ~*prep., conj.* **9.** a less common word for **before.** [Old English; related to Old Saxon, Old High German *fora,* Gothic *faura,* Greek *para,* Sanskrit *pura*]

fore[2] (fɔː) *interj.* (in golf) a warning shout made by a player about to make a shot. [C19: probably short for BEFORE]

fore- *prefix.* **1.** before in time or rank: *foresight; forefather; foreman.* **2.** at or near the front; before in place: *forehead; forecourt.* [Old English, from *fore* (adv.)]

fore-and-after *n. Nautical.* **1.** any vessel with a fore-and-aft rig. **2.** a double-ended vessel.

forearm[1] (ˈfɔːrˌɑːm) *n.* the part of the arm from the elbow to the wrist. [C18: from FORE- + ARM[1]]

forearm[2] (fɔːrˈɑːm) *vb.* (*tr.*) to prepare or arm (someone, esp. oneself) in advance. [C16: from FORE- + ARM[2]]

forearm smash (ˈfɔːrˌɑːm) *n.* a blow like a punch delivered with the forearm in certain types of wrestling.

forebear *or* **forbear** (ˈfɔːˌbɛə) *n.* an ancestor; forefather.

forebode (fɔːˈbəʊd) *vb.* **1.** to warn of or indicate (an event, result, etc.) in advance. **2.** to have an intuition or premonition of (an event). —**foreˈboder** *n.*

foreboding (fɔːˈbəʊdɪŋ) *n.* **1.** a feeling of impending evil, disaster, etc. **2.** an omen or portent. ~*adj.* **3.** presaging something. —**foreˈbodingly** *adv.* —**foreˈbodingness** *n.*

forebrain (ˈfɔːˌbreɪn) *n.* the nontechnical name for **prosencephalon.**

forecast (ˈfɔːˌkɑːst) *vb.* **-casts, -casting, -cast** *or* **-casted. 1.** to predict or calculate (weather, events, etc.), in advance. **2.** (*tr.*) to serve as an early indication of. **3.** (*tr.*) to plan in advance. ~*n.* **4.** a statement of probable future weather conditions calculated from meteorological data. **5.** a prophecy or prediction. **6.** the practice or power of forecasting. —ˈ**foreˌcaster** *n.*

forecastle, fo'c's'le, *or* **fo'c'sle** (ˈfəʊksᵊl) *n.* the part of a vessel at the bow where the crew is quartered and stores, machines, etc., may be stowed.

foreclose (fɔːˈkləʊz) *vb.* **1.** *Law.* to deprive (a mortgagor, etc.) of the right to redeem (a mortgage or pledge). **2.** (*tr.*) to shut out; bar. **3.** (*tr.*) to prevent or hinder. **4.** (*tr.*) to answer or settle (an obligation, promise, etc.) in advance. **5.** (*tr.*) to make an exclusive claim to. [C15: from Old French *forclore,* from *for-* out + *clore* to close, from Latin *claudere*] —**foreˈclosable** *adj.* —**foreclosure** (fɔːˈkləʊʒə) *n.*

forecourse (ˈfɔːˌkɔːs) *n. Nautical.* the lowest foresail on a square-rigged vessel.

forecourt (ˈfɔːˌkɔːt) *n.* **1.** a courtyard in front of a building, as one in a filling station. **2.** Also called: **front court.** the front section of the court in tennis, badminton, etc., esp. the area between the service line and the net.

foredeck (ˈfɔːˌdɛk) *n. Nautical.* the deck between the bridge and the forecastle.

foredo (fɔːˈduː) *vb.* **-does, -doing, -did, -done.** (*tr.*) a variant spelling of **fordo.**

foredoom (fɔːˈduːm) *vb.* (*tr.*) to doom or condemn beforehand.

fore-edge *n.* the outer edge of the pages of a book.

forefather (ˈfɔːˌfɑːðə) *n.* an ancestor, esp. a male. —ˈ**foreˌfatherly** *adj.*

forefend (fɔːˈfɛnd) *vb.* (*tr.*) a variant spelling of **forfend.**

forefinger (ˈfɔːˌfɪŋgə) *n.* the finger next to the thumb. Also called: **index finger.**

forefoot (ˈfɔːˌfʊt) *n., pl.* **-feet. 1.** either of the front feet of a quadruped. **2.** *Nautical.* the forward end of the keel.

forefront (ˈfɔːˌfrʌnt) *n.* **1.** the extreme front. **2.** the position of most prominence, responsibility, or action.

foregather (fɔːˈgæðə) *vb.* a variant spelling of **forgather.**

forego[1] (fɔːˈgəʊ) *vb.* **-goes, -going, -went, -gone.** to precede in time, place, etc. [Old English *foregān*] —**foreˈgoer** *n.*

forego[2] (fɔːˈgəʊ) *vb.* **-goes, -going, -went, -gone.** (*tr.*) a variant spelling of **forgo.** —**foreˈgoer** *n.*

foregoing (fɔːˈgəʊɪŋ) *adj.* (*prenominal*) (esp. of writing or speech) going before; preceding.

foregone (fɔːˈgɒn, ˈfɔːˌgɒn) *adj.* gone or completed; past. —**foreˈgoneness** *n.*

foregone conclusion *n.* an inevitable result or conclusion.

foreground (ˈfɔːˌgraʊnd) *n.* **1.** the part of a scene situated towards the front or nearest to the viewer. **2.** the area of space in a perspective picture, depicted as nearest the viewer. **3.** a conspicuous or active position.

foreground processing *n. Computer technol.* the ability of a system to handle two or more processes virtually simultaneously so that it appears to be editing one text while printing another in the background.

foregut (ˈfɔːˌgʌt) *n.* **1.** the anterior part of the digestive tract of vertebrates, between the buccal cavity and the bile duct. **2.** the anterior part of the digestive tract of arthropods. ~See also **midgut, hindgut.**

forehand (ˈfɔːˌhænd) *adj.* (*prenominal*) **1.** *Tennis, squash, etc.* **a.** (of a stroke) made with the palm of the hand facing the direction of the stroke. **b.** of or relating to the right side of a right-handed player or the left side of a left-handed player. **2.** foremost or paramount. **3.** done or given beforehand. ~*n.* **4.** *Tennis, squash, etc.* **a.** a forehand stroke. **b.** the side on which such strokes are made. **5.** the part of a horse in front of the saddle. **6.** a frontal position. ~*adv.* **7.** *Tennis, squash, etc.* with a forehand stroke. ~*vb.* **8.** to play (a shot) forehand.

forehanded (ˌfɔːˈhændɪd) *adj.* **1.** *U.S.* **a.** thrifty. **b.** well-off. ~*adv., adj.* **2.** *Tennis, squash, etc.* a less common word for **forehand.** —ˌ**foreˈhandedly** *adv.* —ˌ**foreˈhandedness** *n.*

forehead (ˈfɒrɪd, ˈfɔːˌhɛd) *n.* the part of the face between the natural hairline and the eyes, formed skeletally by the frontal bone of the skull; brow. Related adj.: **frontal.** [Old English *forhēafod;* related to Old Frisian *forhāfd,* Middle Low German *vorhōved*]

forehock ('fɔːˌhɒk) *n.* a foreleg cut of bacon or pork.

foreign ('fɒrɪn) *adj.* **1.** of, involving, located in, or coming from another country, area, people, etc.: *a foreign resident.* **2.** dealing or concerned with another country, area, people, etc.: *a foreign office.* **3.** not pertinent or related: *a matter foreign to the discussion.* **4.** not familiar: strange. **5.** in an abnormal place or position: *foreign matter.* **6.** *Law.* outside the jurisdiction of a particular state; alien. [C13: from Old French *forain,* from Vulgar Latin *forānus* (unattested) situated on the outside, from Latin *foris* outside] —'**foreignly** *adv.* —'**foreignness** *n.*

foreign affairs *pl. n.* **1.** matters abroad that involve the homeland, such as relations with another country. **2.** matters that do not involve the homeland.

foreign aid *n.* economic and other assistance given by one country to another.

foreign bill *or* **draft** *n.* a bill of exchange that is drawn in one country and made payable in another: used extensively in foreign trade. Compare **inland bill.**

foreign correspondent *n. Journalism.* a reporter who visits or resides in a foreign country in order to report on its affairs.

foreigner ('fɒrɪnə) *n.* **1.** a person from a foreign country; alien. **2.** an outsider or interloper. **3.** something from a foreign country, such as a ship or product.

foreign exchange *n.* **1.** the system by which one currency is converted into another, enabling international transactions to take place without the physical transportation of gold. **2.** foreign bills and currencies.

foreignism ('fɒrɪˌnɪzəm) *n.* **1.** a custom, mannerism, idiom, etc., that is foreign. **2.** imitation of something foreign.

foreign legion *n.* a body of foreign volunteers serving in an army, esp. that of France.

foreign minister *or* **secretary** *n.* (*often caps.*) a cabinet minister who is responsible for a country's dealings with other countries. U.S. equivalent: **secretary of state.** —**foreign ministry** *n.*

foreign mission *n.* **1.** a body of persons sent to a non-Christian country in order to propagate Christianity. **2.** a diplomatic or other mission sent by one country to another.

foreign office *n.* the ministry of a country or state that is concerned with dealings with other states. U.S. equivalent: **State Department.** Canadian equivalent: **(department of) external affairs.**

foreign service *n. Chiefly U.S.* the diplomatic and usually consular personnel of a foreign affairs ministry or foreign office collectively who represent their country abroad, deal with foreign diplomats at home, etc.

forejudge[1] (fɔː'dʒʌdʒ) *vb.* to judge (someone or an event, circumstance, etc.) before the facts are known; prejudge.

forejudge[2] (fɔː'dʒʌdʒ) *vb. Law.* a variant spelling of **forjudge.** —**fore'judgment** *n.*

foreknow (fɔː'nəʊ) *vb.* **-knows, -knowing, -knew, -known.** (*tr.*) to know in advance. —**fore'knowable** *adj.* —**fore'knowledge** *n.* —**fore'knowingly** *adv.*

foreland ('fɔːlənd) *n.* **1.** a headland, cape, or promontory. **2.** land lying in front of something, such as water.

foreleg ('fɔːˌlɛg) *n.* either of the front legs of a horse, sheep, or other quadruped.

forelimb ('fɔːˌlɪm) *n.* either of the front or anterior limbs of a four-limbed vertebrate: a foreleg, flipper, or wing.

forelock[1] ('fɔːˌlɒk) *n.* **1.** a lock of hair growing or falling over the forehead. **2.** a lock of a horse's mane that grows forwards between the ears.

forelock[2] ('fɔːˌlɒk) *n.* **1.** a wedge or peg passed through the tip of a bolt to prevent withdrawal. ~*vb.* **2.** (*tr.*) to secure (a bolt) by means of a forelock.

foreman ('fɔːmən) *n., pl.* **-men. 1.** a person, often experienced, who supervises other workmen. Female equivalent: **forewoman. 2.** *Law.* the principal juror, who presides at the deliberations of a jury. —'**foreman,ship** *n.*

foremast ('fɔːˌmɑːst; *Nautical* 'fɔːməst) *n.* the mast nearest the bow on vessels with two or more masts.

foremilk ('fɔːˌmɪlk) *n.* **1.** another word for **colostrum. 2.** the first milk drawn from a cow's udder prior to milking.

foremost ('fɔːˌməʊst) *adj., adv.* first in time, place, rank, etc. [Old English *formest,* from *forma* first; related to Old Saxon *formo* first, Old High German *fruma* advantage]

forename ('fɔːˌneɪm) *n.* another term for **Christian name.**

forenamed ('fɔːˌneɪmd) *adj.* (*prenominal*) named or mentioned previously; aforesaid.

forenoon ('fɔːˌnuːn) *n.* **a.** the daylight hours before or just before noon. **b.** (*as modifier*): *a forenoon conference.*

forensic (fə'rɛnsɪk) *adj.* relating to, used in, or connected with a court of law: *forensic science.* [C17: from Latin *forēnsis* public, from FORUM] —**forensicality** (fəˌrɛnsɪ'kælɪtɪ) *n.* —**fo'rensically** *adv.*

forensic medicine *n.* the applied use of medical knowledge or practice, esp. pathology, to the purposes of the law, as in determining the cause of death. Also called: **medical jurisprudence, legal medicine.**

forensics (fə'rɛnsɪks) *n.* (*functioning as sing. or pl.*) the art or study of formal debating.

foreordain (ˌfɔːrɔː'deɪn) *vb.* (*tr.; may take a clause as object*) to determine (events, results, etc.) in the future. —ˌ**foreor'dainment** *or* **foreordination** (ˌfɔːrɔːdɪ'neɪʃən) *n.*

forepart ('fɔːˌpɑːt) *n.* the first or front part in place, order, or time.

forepaw ('fɔːˌpɔː) *n.* either of the front feet of most land mammals that do not have hoofs.

forepeak ('fɔːˌpiːk) *n. Nautical.* the interior part of a vessel that is furthest forward.

foreplay ('fɔːˌpleɪ) *n.* mutual sexual stimulation preceding sexual intercourse.

forequarter ('fɔːˌkwɔːtə) *n.* the front portion, including the leg, of half of a carcass, as of beef or lamb.

forequarters ('fɔːˌkwɔːtəz) *pl. n.* the part of the body of a horse or similar quadruped that consists of the forelegs, shoulders, and adjoining parts.

forereach (fɔː'riːtʃ) *vb.* **1.** (*intr.*) *Nautical.* to keep moving under momentum without engine or sails. **2.** (*tr.*) to surpass or outdo.

forerun (fɔː'rʌn) *vb.* **-runs, -running, -ran, -run.** (*tr.*) **1.** to serve as a herald for. **2.** to go before; precede. **3.** to prevent or forestall.

forerunner ('fɔːˌrʌnə) *n.* **1.** a person or thing that precedes another; precursor. **2.** a person or thing coming in advance to herald the arrival of someone or something; harbinger. **3.** an indication beforehand of something to follow; omen; portent.

foresaid ('fɔːˌsɛd) *adj.* a less common word for **aforesaid.**

foresail ('fɔːˌseɪl; *Nautical* 'fɔːsəl) *n. Nautical.* **1.** the aftermost headsail of a fore-and-aft rigged vessel. **2.** the lowest sail set on the foremast of a square-rigged vessel.

foresee (fɔː'siː) *vb.* **-sees, -seeing, -saw, -seen.** (*tr.; may take a clause as object*) to see or know beforehand: *he did not foresee that.* —**fore'seeable** *adj.* —**fore'seer** *n.*

foreshadow (fɔː'ʃædəʊ) *vb.* (*tr.*) to show, indicate, or suggest in advance; presage. —**fore'shadower** *n.*

foreshank ('fɔːˌʃæŋk) *n.* **1.** the top of the front leg of an animal. **2.** a cut of meat from this part.

foresheet ('fɔːˌʃiːt) *n.* **1.** the sheet of a foresail. **2.** (*pl.*) the part forward of the foremost thwart of a boat.

foreshock ('fɔːˌʃɒk) *n.* a relatively small earthquake heralding the arrival of a much larger one. Some large earthquakes are preceded by a series of foreshocks. Compare **aftershock.**

foreshore ('fɔːˌʃɔː) *n.* **1.** the part of the shore that lies between the limits for high and low tides. **2.** the part of the shore that lies just above the high-water mark.

foreshorten (fɔː'ʃɔːtən) *vb.* (*tr.*) **1.** to represent (a line, form, object, etc.) as shorter than actual length in order to give an illusion of recession or projection, in accordance with the laws of linear perspective. **2.** to make shorter or more condensed; reduce or abridge.

foreshow (fɔː'ʃəʊ) *vb.* **-shows, -showing, -showed, -shown.** (*tr.*) *Archaic.* to indicate in advance; foreshadow.

foreside ('fɔːˌsaɪd) *n.* **1.** the front or upper side or part. **2.** *U.S.* land extending along the sea.

foresight ('fɔːˌsaɪt) *n.* **1.** provision for or insight into future problems, needs, etc. **2.** the act or ability of foreseeing. **3.** the act of looking forward. **4.** *Surveying.* a reading taken looking forwards to a new station, esp. in levelling from a point of known elevation to a point the elevation of which is to be determined. Compare **backsight. 5.** the front sight on a firearm. —ˌ**fore'sighted** *adj.* —ˌ**fore'sightedly** *adv.* —ˌ**fore'sightedness** *n.*

foreskin ('fɔːˌskɪn) *n. Anatomy.* the nontechnical name for **prepuce** (sense 1).

forespeak (fɔː'spiːk) *vb.* **-speaks, -speaking, -spoke, -spoken.** (*tr.*) *Rare.* **1.** to predict; foresee. **2.** to arrange or speak of in advance.

forespent (fɔː'spɛnt) *adj.* a variant spelling of **forspent.**

forest ('fɒrɪst) *n.* **1.** a large wooded area having a thick growth of trees and plants. **2.** the trees of such an area. **3.** *N.Z.* an area planted with exotic pines or similar trees. Compare **bush**[1] (sense 4). **4.** something resembling a large wooded area, esp. in density: *a forest of telegraph poles.* **5.** *Law.* (formerly) an area of woodland, esp. one owned by the sovereign and set apart as a hunting ground with its own laws and officers. Compare **park** (sense 5). **6.** (*modifier*) of, involving, or living in a forest or forests: *a forest glade.* ~*vb.* **7.** (*tr.*) to create a forest (in); plant with trees. [C13: from Old French, from Medieval Latin *forestis* unfenced woodland, from Latin *foris* outside] —'**forestal** *or* **foresteal** (fə'rɛstɪəl) *adj.* —'**forested** *adj.* —'**forestless** *adj.* —'**forest,like** *adj.*

forestall (fɔː'stɔːl) *vb.* (*tr.*) **1.** to delay, stop, or guard against beforehand. **2.** to anticipate. **3. a.** to prevent or hinder sales at (a market, etc.) by buying up merchandise in advance, etc. **b.** to buy up (merchandise) for profitable resale. Compare **corner** (sense 21). [C14 *forestallen* to waylay, from Old English *foresteall* an ambush, from *fore-* in front of + *steall* place] —**fore'staller** *n.* —**fore'stalment** *or esp. U.S.* **fore'stallment** *n.*

forestation (ˌfɒrɪ'steɪʃən) *n.* the planting of trees over a wide area.

forestay ('fɔːˌsteɪ) *n. Nautical.* an adjustable stay leading from the truck of the foremast to the deck, stem, or bowsprit, for controlling the motion or bending of the mast.

forestaysail (fɔː'steɪˌseɪl; *Nautical* fɔː'steɪsəl) *n. Nautical.* the triangular headsail set aftermost on a vessel.

forester ('fɒrɪstə) *n.* **1.** a person skilled in forestry or in charge of a forest. **2.** any of various Old World moths of the genus *Ino,* characterized by brilliant metallic green wings: family *Zygaenidae.* **3.** a person or animal that lives in a forest. **4.** (*cap.*) a member of the Ancient Order of Foresters, a friendly society.

forest park *n. N.Z.* a recreational reserve which may include bush and exotic trees.
forest ranger *n. Chiefly U.S. and Canadian.* a government official who patrols and protects forests, wildlife, etc.
forestry ('fɒrɪstrɪ) *n.* **1.** the science of planting and caring for trees. **2.** the planting and management of forests. **3.** *Rare.* forest land.
foretaste *n.* ('fɔːˌteɪst). **1.** an early but limited experience or awareness of something to come. ~*vb.* (fɔː'teɪst). **2.** (*tr.*) to have a foretaste of.
foretell (fɔː'tɛl) *vb.* **-tells, -telling, -told.** (*tr.; may take a clause as object*) to tell or indicate (an event, a result, etc.) beforehand; predict. —**fore'teller** *n.*
forethought ('fɔːˌθɔːt) *n.* **1.** advance consideration or deliberation. **2.** thoughtful anticipation of future events; far-sightedness. —**fore'thoughtful** *adj.* —**fore'thoughtfully** *adv.* —**fore'thoughtfulness** *n.*
foretime ('fɔːˌtaɪm) *n.* time already gone; the past.
foretoken *n.* ('fɔːˌtəʊkən). **1.** a sign of a future event. ~*vb.* (fɔː'təʊkən). **2.** (*tr.*) to foreshadow.
foretooth ('fɔːˌtuːθ) *n., pl.* **-teeth** (-ˌtiːθ). *Dentistry.* another word for an **incisor.**
foretop ('fɔːˌtɒp; *Nautical* 'fɔːtəp) *n. Nautical.* a platform at the top of the foremast.
fore-topgallant (ˌfɔːtɒp'gælənt; *Nautical* ˌfɔːtə'gælənt) *adj. Nautical.* of, relating to, or being the topmost portion of a foremast, above the topmast: *the fore-topgallant mast.*
fore-topmast (fɔː'tɒpˌmɑːst; *Nautical* fɔː'tɒpməst) *n. Nautical.* a mast stepped above a foremast.
fore-topsail (fɔː'tɒpˌseɪl; *Nautical* fɔː'tɒpsᵊl) *n. Nautical.* a sail set on a fore-topmast.
foretriangle ('fɔːtraɪˌæŋgᵊl) *n.* the triangular area formed by the deck, foremast, and headstay of a sailing vessel.
for ever *or* **forever** (fɔː'rɛvə, fə-) *adv.* **1.** without end; everlastingly; eternally. **2.** at all times; incessantly. **3.** *Informal.* for a very long time: *he went on speaking for ever.* ~*n.* **forever. 4.** (*as object*) *Informal.* a very long time: *it took him forever to reply.* **5.** ... **for ever!** an exclamation expressing support or loyalty: *Scotland for ever!*
for evermore *or* **forevermore** (fɔːˌrɛvə'mɔː, fə-) *adv.* a more emphatic or emotive term for **for ever.**
forewarn (fɔː'wɔːn) *vb.* (*tr.*) to warn beforehand. —**fore'warner** *n.* —**fore'warningly** *adv.*
forewent (fɔː'wɛnt) *vb.* the past tense of **forego.**
forewind ('fɔːˌwɪnd) *n. Nautical.* a favourable wind.
forewing ('fɔːˌwɪŋ) *n.* either wing of the anterior pair of an insect's two pairs of wings.
foreword ('fɔːˌwɜːd) *n.* an introductory statement to a book. [C19: literal translation of German *Vorwort*]
foreworn (fɔː'wɔːn) *adj.* a variant spelling of **forworn.**
foreyard ('fɔːˌjɑːd) *n. Nautical.* a yard for supporting the foresail of a square-rigger.
forfaiting ('fɔːˌfeitɪŋ) *n.* the financial service of discounting, without recourse, a promissory note, bill of exchange, letter of credit, etc., received from an overseas buyer by an exporter; a form of debt discounting. [C20: from French *forfaire* to forfeit or surrender]
forfeit ('fɔːfɪt) *n.* **1.** something lost or given up as a penalty for a fault, mistake, etc. **2.** the act of losing or surrendering something in this manner. **3.** *Law.* something confiscated as a penalty for an offence, breach of contract, etc. **4.** (*sometimes pl.*) **a.** a game in which a player has to give up an object, perform a specified action, etc., if he commits a fault. **b.** an object so given up. ~*vb.* **5.** (*tr.*) to lose or be liable to lose in consequence of a mistake, fault, etc. **6.** (*tr.*) *Law.* **a.** to confiscate as punishment. **b.** to surrender (something exacted as a penalty). ~*adj.* **7.** surrendered or liable to be surrendered as a penalty. [C13: from Old French *forfet* offence, from *forfaire* to commit a crime, from Medieval Latin *foris facere* to act outside (what is lawful), from Latin *foris* outside + *facere* to do] —**'forfeitable** *adj.* —**'forfeiter** *n.*
forfeiture ('fɔːfɪtʃə) *n.* **1.** something forfeited. **2.** the act of forfeiting or paying a penalty.
forfend *or* **forefend** (fɔː'fɛnd) *vb.* (*tr.*) **1.** *U.S.* to protect or secure. **2.** *Obsolete.* to prohibit or prevent.
forfex ('fɔːfɛks) *n. Entomol.* a pair of pincers, esp. the paired terminal appendages of an earwig. [C18: Latin: a pair of scissors]
forficate ('fɔːfɪkɪt, -ˌkeɪt) *adj.* (esp. of the tails of certain birds) deeply forked. [C19: from Latin *forfex* scissors]
forfochen (fər'foxᵊn) *adj. Scot.* exhausted. [a variant of earlier *forfoughten* worn out by fighting]
forgat (fə'gæt) *vb. Archaic.* a past tense of **forget.**
forgather *or* **foregather** (fɔː'gæðə) *vb.* (*intr.*) **1.** to gather together; assemble. **2.** *Rare.* to meet, esp. unexpectedly. **3.** (foll. by *with*) to socialize.
forgave (fə'geɪv) *vb.* the past tense of **forgive.**
forge[1] (fɔːdʒ) *n.* **1.** a place in which metal is worked by heating and hammering; smithy. **2.** a hearth or furnace used for heating metal. **3.** a machine used to shape metals by hammering. ~*vb.* **4.** (*tr.*) to shape (metal) by heating and hammering. **5.** (*tr.*) to form, shape, make, or fashion (objects, articles, etc.). **6.** (*tr.*) to invent or devise (an agreement, understanding, etc.). **7.** to make or produce a fraudulent imitation of (a signature, banknote, etc.) or to commit forgery. [C14: from Old French *forgier* to construct, from Latin *fabricāre*, from *faber* craftsman] —**'forgeable** *adj.* —**'forger** *n.*
forge[2] (fɔːdʒ) *vb.* (*intr.*) **1.** to move at a steady and persevering pace. **2. forge ahead.** to increase speed; spurt. [C17: of unknown origin]
forgery ('fɔːdʒərɪ) *n., pl.* **-geries. 1.** the act of reproducing something for a deceitful or fraudulent purpose. **2.** something forged, such as a work of art or an antique. **3.** *Criminal law.* **a.** the false making or altering of any document, such as a cheque or character reference (and including a postage stamp), or any tape or disc on which information is stored, intending that anyone shall accept it as genuine and so act to his or another's prejudice. **b.** something forged. **4.** *Criminal law.* the counterfeiting of a seal or die with intention to defraud.
forget (fə'gɛt) *vb.* **-gets, -getting, -got, -gotten** *or* (*Archaic or dialect*) **-got. 1.** (when *tr., may take a clause as object or an infinitive*) to fail to recall (someone or something once known); be unable to remember. **2.** (*tr.; may take a clause as object or an infinitive*) to neglect, usually as the result of an unintentional error. **3.** (*tr.*) to leave behind by mistake. **4.** (*tr.*) to disregard intentionally. **5.** (when *tr., may take a clause as object*) to fail to mention. **6. forget oneself. a.** to act in an improper manner. **b.** to be unselfish. **c.** to be deep in thought. **7. forget it!** an exclamation of annoyed or forgiving dismissal of a matter or topic. [Old English *forgietan;* related to Old Frisian *forgeta*, Old Saxon *fargetan*, Old High German *firgezzan*] —**for'gettable** *adj.* —**for'getter** *n.*
forgetful (fə'gɛtfʊl) *adj.* **1.** tending to forget. **2.** (*often postpositive;* foll. by *of*) inattentive (to) or neglectful (of). **3.** *Poetic.* causing loss of memory. —**for'getfully** *adv.* —**for'getfulness** *n.*
forget-me-not *n.* any temperate low-growing plants of the mainly European boraginaceous genus *Myosotis*, esp. *M. scorpioides*, having clusters of small typically blue flowers. Also called: **scorpion grass.**
forging ('fɔːdʒɪŋ) *n.* **1.** the process of producing a metal component by hammering. **2.** the act of a forger. **3.** a metal component produced by this process. **4.** the collision of a horse's hind shoe and fore shoe.
forgive (fə'gɪv) *vb.* **-gives, -giving, -gave, -given. 1.** to cease to blame or hold resentment against (someone or something). **2.** to grant pardon for (a mistake, wrongdoing, etc.). **3.** (*tr.*) to free or pardon (someone) from penalty. **4.** (*tr.*) to free from the obligation of (a debt, payment, etc.). [Old English *forgiefan;* see FOR-, GIVE] —**for'givable** *adj.* —**for'givably** *adv.* —**for'giver** *n.*
forgiveness (fə'gɪvnɪs) *n.* **1.** the act of forgiving or the state of being forgiven. **2.** willingness to forgive.
forgiving (fə'gɪvɪŋ) *adj.* willing to forgive; merciful. —**for'givingly** *adv.* —**for'givingness** *n.*
forgo *or* **forego** (fɔː'gəʊ) *vb.* **-goes, -going, -went, -gone.** (*tr.*) **1.** to give up or do without. **2.** *Archaic.* to leave. [Old English *forgān;* see FOR-, GO[1]] —**for'goer** *or* **fore'goer** *n.*
forgot (fə'gɒt) *vb.* **1.** the past tense of **forget. 2.** *Archaic or dialect.* a past participle of **forget.**
forgotten (fə'gɒtᵊn) *vb.* a past participle of **forget.**
forint (*Hungarian* 'forint) *n.* the standard monetary unit of Hungary, divided into 100 fillér. [from Hungarian, from Italian *fiorino* FLORIN]
forjudge *or* **forejudge** (fɔː'dʒʌdʒ) *vb.* (*tr.*) *Law.* **1.** to deprive of a right by the judgment of a court. **2.** *Chiefly U.S.* to expel (an officer or attorney) from court for misconduct. —**for'judgment** *or* **fore'judgment** *n.*
fork (fɔːk) *n.* **1.** a small usually metal implement consisting of two, three, or four long thin prongs on the end of a handle, used for lifting food to the mouth or turning it in cooking, etc. **2.** an agricultural tool consisting of a handle and three or four metal prongs, used for lifting, digging, etc. **3.** a pronged part of any machine, device, etc. **4.** (of a road, river, etc.) **a.** a division into two or more branches. **b.** the point where the division begins. **c.** such a branch. **5.** *Chiefly U.S.* the main tributary of a river. **6.** *Chess.* a position in which two pieces are forked. ~*vb.* **7.** (*tr.*) to pick up, dig, etc., with a fork. **8.** (*tr.*) *Chess.* to place (two enemy pieces) under attack with one of one's own pieces, esp. a knight. **9.** (*tr.*) to make into the shape of a fork. **10.** (*intr.*) to be divided into two or more branches. **11.** to take one or other branch at a fork in a road, river, etc. [Old English *forca*, from Latin *furca*] —**'forkful** *n.*
forked (fɔːkt, 'fɔːkɪd) *adj.* **1. a.** having a fork or forklike parts. **b.** (*in combination*): *two-forked.* **2.** having sharp angles; zigzag. **3.** insincere or equivocal (esp. in the phrase **forked tongue**). —**forkedly** ('fɔːkɪdlɪ) *adv.* —**'forkedness** *n.*
forked lightning *n.* a zigzag form of lightning. Also called: **chain lightning.**
fork-lift truck *n.* a vehicle having two power-operated horizontal prongs that can be raised and lowered for loading, transporting, and unloading goods, esp. goods that are stacked on wooden pallets. Sometimes shortened to **forklift.**
fork out, over, *or* **up** *vb.* (*adv.*) *Slang.* to pay (money, goods, etc.), esp. with reluctance.
forlorn (fə'lɔːn) *adj.* **1.** miserable, wretched, or cheerless; desolate. **2.** deserted; forsaken. **3.** (*postpositive;* foll. by *of*) destitute;

bereft: *forlorn of hope.* **4.** desperate: *the last forlorn attempt.* [Old English *forloren* lost, from *forlēosan* to lose; related to Old Saxon *farliosan,* Gothic *fraliusan,* Greek *luein* to release] —**for'lornly** *adv.* —**for'lornness** *n.*

forlorn hope *n.* **1.** a hopeless or desperate enterprise. **2.** a faint hope. **3.** *Obsolete.* a group of soldiers assigned to an extremely dangerous duty. [C16 (in the obsolete sense): changed (by folk etymology) from Dutch *verloren hoop* lost troop, from *verloren,* past participle of *verliezen* to lose + *hoop* troop (literally: heap)]

form (fɔːm) *n.* **1.** the shape or configuration of something as distinct from its colour, texture, etc. **2.** the particular mode, appearance, etc., in which a thing or person manifests itself: *water in the form of ice; in the form of a bat.* **3.** a type or kind: *imprisonment is a form of punishment.* **4. a.** a printed document, esp. one with spaces in which to insert facts or answers: *an application form.* **b.** (*as modifier*): *a form letter.* **5.** physical or mental condition, esp. good condition, with reference to ability to perform: *off form.* **6.** the previous record of a horse, athlete, etc., esp. with regard to fitness. **7.** *Brit. slang.* a criminal record. **8.** style, arrangement, or design in the arts, as opposed to content. **9.** a fixed mode of artistic expression or representation in literary, musical, or other artistic works: *sonata form; sonnet form.* **10.** a mould, frame, etc., that gives shape to something. **11.** organized structure or order, as in an artistic work. **12.** *Education, chiefly Brit.* a group of children who are taught together; class. **13.** manner, method, or style of doing something, esp. with regard to recognized standards. **14.** behaviour or procedure, esp. as governed by custom or etiquette: *good form.* **15.** formality or ceremony. **16.** a prescribed set or order of words, terms, etc., as in a religious ceremony or legal document. **17.** *Philosophy.* **a.** the structure of anything as opposed to its constitution or content. **b.** essence as opposed to matter. **c.** (*often cap.*) (in the philosophy of Plato) the ideal universal that exists independently of the particulars which fall under it. See also **Form. d.** (in the philosophy of Aristotle) the constitution of matter to form a substance; by virtue of this its nature can be understood. **18.** See **logical form. 19.** *Brit.* a bench, esp. one that is long, low, and backless. **20.** the nest or hollow in which a hare lives. **21.** a group of organisms within a species that differ from similar groups by trivial differences, as of colour. **22.** *Linguistics.* **a.** the phonological or orthographic shape or appearance of a linguistic element, such as a word. **b.** a linguistic element considered from the point of view of its shape or sound rather than, for example, its meaning. **23.** *Crystallog.* See **crystal form. 24.** *Taxonomy.* a group distinguished from other groups by a single characteristic: ranked below a variety. *~vb.* **25.** to give shape or form to or to take shape or form, esp. a specified or particular shape. **26.** to come or bring into existence: *a scum formed on the surface.* **27.** to make, produce, or construct or be made, produced, or constructed. **28.** to construct or develop in the mind: *to form an opinion.* **29.** (*tr.*) to train, develop, or mould by instruction, discipline, or example. **30.** (*tr.*) to acquire, contract, or develop: *to form a habit.* **31.** (*tr.*) to be an element of, serve as, or constitute: *this plank will form a bridge.* **32.** (*tr.*) to draw up; organize: *to form a club.* [C13: from Old French *forme,* from Latin *forma* shape, model] —**'formable** *adj.*

Form (fɔːm) *n.* (in the philosophy of Plato) an ideal archetype existing independently of those individuals which fall under it, supposedly explaining their common properties and serving as the only objects of true knowledge as opposed to the mere opinion obtainable of matters of fact. Also called: **Idea.**

-form *adj. combining form.* having the shape or form of or resembling: *cruciform; vermiform.* [from New Latin *-formis,* from Latin, from *fŏrma* FORM]

formal[1] ('fɔːməl) *adj.* **1.** of, according to, or following established or prescribed forms, conventions, etc.: *a formal document.* **2.** characterized by observation of conventional forms of ceremony, behaviour, dress, etc.: *a formal dinner.* **3.** methodical, precise, or stiff. **4.** suitable for occasions organized according to conventional ceremony: *formal dress.* **5.** denoting or characterized by idiom, vocabulary, etc., used by educated speakers and writers of a language. **6.** acquired by study in academic institutions: *a formal education.* **7.** regular or symmetrical in form: *a formal garden.* **8.** of or relating to the appearance, form, etc., of something as distinguished from its substance. **9.** logically deductive: *formal proof.* **10.** *Philosophy.* **a.** of or relating to form as opposed to matter or content. **b.** pertaining to the essence or nature of something: *formal cause.* **c.** (in the writings of Descartes) pertaining to the correspondence between an image or idea and its object. **d.** being in the formal mode. **11.** denoting a second-person pronoun in some languages used when the addressee is a stranger, social superior, etc.: *in French the pronoun "vous" is formal, while "tu" is informal.* [C14: from Latin *formālis*] —**'formally** *adv.* —**'formalness** *n.*

formal[2] ('fɔːmæl) *n.* another name for **methylal.** [C19: from FORM(IC) + -AL[3]]

formaldehyde (fɔː'mældɪˌhaɪd) *n.* a colourless poisonous irritating gas with a pungent characteristic odour, made by the oxidation of methanol and used as formalin and in the manufacture of synthetic resins. Formula: HCHO. Systematic name: **methanal.** [C19: FORM(IC) + ALDEHYDE; on the model of German *Formaldehyd*]

formal equivalence *n. Logic.* the relation that holds between two open sentences when their universal closures are materially equivalent.

formalin ('fɔːməlɪn) *or* **formol** ('fɔːmɒl) *n.* a 40 per cent solution of formaldehyde in water, used as a disinfectant, preservative for biological specimens, etc.

formalism ('fɔːməˌlɪzəm) *n.* **1.** scrupulous or excessive adherence to outward form at the expense of inner reality or content. **2. a.** the mathematical or logical structure of a scientific argument as distinguished from its subject matter. **b.** the notation, and its structure, in which information is expressed. **3.** *Theatre.* a stylized mode of production. **4.** (in Marxist criticism) excessive concern with artistic technique at the expense of social values, etc. **5.** the philosophical theory that a mathematical statement has no meaning but that its symbols, regarded as physical objects, exhibit a structure that has useful applications. Compare **logicism, intuitionism.** —**'formalist** *n.* —**ˌformal'istic** *adj.* —**ˌformal'istically** *adv.*

formality (fɔː'mælɪtɪ) *n., pl.* **-ties. 1.** a requirement of rule, custom, etiquette, etc. **2.** the condition or quality of being formal or conventional. **3.** strict or excessive observance of form, ceremony, etc. **4.** an established, proper, or conventional method, act, or procedure.

formalize *or* **formalise** ('fɔːməˌlaɪz) *vb.* **1.** to be or make formal. **2.** (*tr.*) to make official or valid. **3.** (*tr.*) to give a definite shape or form to. **4.** *Logic.* to extract the logical form of (an expression), to express in the symbols of some formal system. —**ˌformali'zation** *or* **ˌformali'sation** *n.* —**'formalˌizer** *or* **'formalˌiser** *n.*

formal language *n.* **1.** a language designed for use in situations in which natural language is unsuitable, as for example in mathematics, logic, or computer programming. The symbols and formulas of such languages stand in precisely specified syntactic and semantic relations to one another. **2.** *Logic.* a logistic system for which an interpretation is provided: distinguished from formal calculus in that the semantics enable it to be regarded as *about* some subject matter.

formal logic *n.* **1.** the study of systems of deductive argument in which symbols are used to represent precisely defined categories of expressions. Also called: **symbolic logic.** Compare **philosophical logic. 2.** a specific formal system that can be interpreted as representing a fragment of natural argument.

formal mode *n. Philosophy.* the style in which words are explicitly mentioned rather than used of their subject matter. *"Fido" is a dog's name* is in the formal mode, while *"Fido is a dog"* is in the material mode. See also **mention** (sense 7).

formal system *n. Logic.* an uninterpreted symbolic system whose syntax is precisely defined, and on which a relation of deducibility is defined in purely syntactic terms; a logistic system. Also called: **formal theory, formal calculus.** Compare **formal language.**

formant ('fɔːmənt) *n. Acoustics, phonetics.* any of several frequency ranges within which the partials of a sound, esp. a vowel sound, are at their strongest, thus imparting to the sound its own special quality, tone colour, or timbre.

format ('fɔːmæt) *n.* **1.** the general appearance of a publication, including type style, paper, binding, etc. **2.** an approximate indication of the size of a publication as determined by the number of times the original sheet of paper is folded to make a leaf. See also **duodecimo, quarto. 3.** style, plan, or arrangement, as of a television programme. **4.** *Computer technol.* the arrangement of data on magnetic tape, paper tape, etc., to comply with a computer's specific input device. *~vb.* **-mats, -matting, -matted.** (*tr.*) **5.** to arrange (a book, page, etc.) into a specified format. [C19: via French from German, from Latin *liber formātus* volume formed]

formate ('fɔːmeɪt) *n.* any salt or ester of formic acid containing the ion $HCOO^-$ or the group HCOO-. [C19: from FORM(IC) + -ATE[1]]

formation (fɔː'meɪʃən) *n.* **1.** the act of giving or taking form, shape, or existence. **2.** something that is formed. **3.** the manner in which something is formed or arranged. **4.** a formal arrangement of a number of persons or things acting as a unit, such as a troop of soldiers, aircraft in flight, or a football team. **5.** a series of rocks with certain characteristics in common. **6.** *Ecology.* a community of plants, such as a tropical rain forest, extending over a very large area. —**for'mational** *adj.*

formation dance *n.* any dance in which a number of couples form a certain arrangement, such as two facing lines or a circle, and perform a series of figures within or based on that arrangement. —**formation dancing** *n.*

formation rules *pl. n. Logic.* the set of rules that specify the syntax of a formal system; the algorithm that generates the well-formed formulae.

formative ('fɔːmətɪv) *adj.* **1.** of or relating to formation, development, or growth: *formative years.* **2.** shaping; moulding: *a formative experience.* **3.** (of tissues and cells in certain parts of an organism) capable of growth and differentiation. **4.** functioning in the formation of derived, inflected, or compound words. *~n.* **5.** an inflectional or derivational affix. **6.** (in generative grammar) any of the minimum units of a sentence that have syntactic function. —**'formatively** *adv.* —**'formativeness** *n.*

formative assessment *n.* ongoing assessment of a pupil's educational development within a particular subject area. Compare **summative assessment.**

form class *n.* 1. another term for **part of speech.** 2. a group of words distinguished by common inflections, such as the weak verbs of English.

form criticism *n.* literary criticism concerned esp. with analysing the Bible in terms of the literary forms used, such as proverbs, songs, or stories, and relating them to their historical forms and background. —**form critic** *n.* —**form critical** *adj.*

form drag *n.* the drag on a body moving through a fluid as a result of the shape of the body. It can be reduced by streamlining.

forme *or U.S.* **form** (fɔːm) *n. Printing.* type matter, blocks, etc., assembled in a chase and ready for printing. [C15: from French: FORM]

former[1] (ˈfɔːmə) *adj.* (*prenominal*) 1. belonging to or occurring in an earlier time: *former glory.* 2. having been at a previous time: *a former colleague.* 3. denoting the first or first mentioned of two: *in the former case.* 4. near the beginning. ~*n.* 5. **the former.** the first or first mentioned of two: distinguished from *latter.*

former[2] (ˈfɔːmə) *n.* 1. a person or thing that forms or shapes. 2. *Electrical engineering.* a tool for giving a coil or winding the required shape, sometimes consisting of a frame on which the wire can be wound, the frame then being removed.

formerly (ˈfɔːməlɪ) *adv.* 1. at or in a former time; in the past. 2. *Obsolete.* in the immediate past; just now.

form genus *n.* a group of species (**form species**) that have similar structural characteristics but are not closely related.

formic (ˈfɔːmɪk) *adj.* 1. of, relating to, or derived from ants. 2. of, containing, or derived from formic acid. [C18: from Latin *formīca* ant; the acid occurs naturally in ants]

Formica (fɔːˈmaɪkə) *n. Trademark.* any of various laminated plastic sheets, containing melamine, used esp. for heat-resistant surfaces that can be easily cleaned.

formic acid *n.* a colourless corrosive liquid carboxylic acid found in some insects, esp. ants, and many plants: used in dyeing textiles and the manufacture of insecticides and refrigerants. Formula: HCOOH. Systematic name: **methanoic acid.**

formicary (ˈfɔːmɪkərɪ) *or* **formicarium** (ˌfɔːmɪˈkeərɪəm) *n., pl.* **-caries** *or* **-caria** (-ˈkeərɪə). less common names for **ant hill.** [C19: from Medieval Latin *formīcārium;* see FORMIC]

formicate (ˈfɔːmɪˌkeɪt) *vb.* (*intr.*) *Now rare.* 1. to crawl around like ants. 2. to swarm with ants or other crawling things. [C17: from Latin *formīcāre,* from *formīca* ant]

formication (ˌfɔːmɪˈkeɪʃən) *n.* a sensation of insects crawling on the skin; symptom of a nerve disorder.

formidable (ˈfɔːmɪdəbᵊl) *adj.* 1. arousing or likely to inspire fear or dread. 2. extremely difficult to defeat, overcome, manage, etc.: *a formidable problem.* 3. tending to inspire awe or admiration because of great size, strength, excellence, etc. [C15: from Latin *formīdābilis,* from *formīdāre* to dread, from *formīdō* fear] —ˌ**formidaˈbility** *or* ˈ**formidableness** *n.* —ˈ**formidably** *adv.*

formless (ˈfɔːmlɪs) *adj.* without a definite shape or form; amorphous. —ˈ**formlessly** *adv.* —ˈ**formlessness** *n.*

form letter *n.* a single copy of a letter that has been mechanically reproduced in large numbers for circulation.

formula (ˈfɔːmjʊlə) *n., pl.* **-las** *or* **-lae** (-ˌliː). 1. an established form or set of words, as used in religious ceremonies, legal proceedings, etc. 2. *Maths, physics.* a general relationship, principle, or rule stated, often as an equation, in the form of symbols. 3. *Chem.* a representation of molecules, radicals, ions, etc., expressed in the symbols of the atoms of their constituent elements. See **molecular formula, empirical formula, structural formula.** 4. **a.** a method, pattern, or rule for doing or producing something, often one proved to be successful. **b.** (*as modifier*): *formula fiction.* 5. *U.S. and Canadian.* **a.** a prescription for making up a medicine, baby's food, etc. **b.** a substance prepared according to such a prescription. 6. *Motor racing.* the specific category in which a particular type of car competes, judged according to engine size, weight, and fuel capacity. [C17: from Latin: diminutive of *forma* FORM] —**formulaic** (ˌfɔːmjʊˈleɪɪk) *adj.*

Formula One *n.* 1. the top class of professional motor racing. 2. the most important world championship in motor racing.

formularize *or* **formularise** (ˈfɔːmjʊləˌraɪz) *vb.* a less common word for **formulate** (sense 1). —ˌ**formulariˈzation** *or* ˌ**formulariˈsation** *n.* —ˈ**formularˌizer** *or* ˈ**formularˌiser** *n.*

formulary (ˈfɔːmjʊlərɪ) *n., pl.* **-laries.** 1. a book or system of prescribed formulas, esp. relating to religious procedure or doctrine. 2. a formula. 3. *Pharmacol.* a book containing a list of pharmaceutical products with their formulas and means of preparation. ~*adj.* 4. of, relating to, or of the nature of a formula.

formulate (ˈfɔːmjʊˌleɪt) *vb.* (*tr.*) 1. to put into or express in systematic terms; express in or as if in a formula. 2. to devise. —ˌ**formuˈlation** *n.* —ˈ**formuˌlator** *n.*

formulism (ˈfɔːmjʊˌlɪzəm) *n.* adherence to or belief in formulas. —ˈ**formulist** *n., adj.* —ˌ**formuˈlistic** *adj.*

formwork (ˈfɔːmˌwɜːk) *n.* an arrangement of wooden boards, bolts, etc., used to shape reinforced concrete while it is setting. Also called (esp. Brit.): **shuttering.**

formyl (ˈfɔːmaɪl) *n.* (*modifier*) of, consisting of, or containing the monovalent group HCO-: *a formyl group or radical.* [C19: from FORM(IC) + -YL]

Fornax (ˈfɔːnæks) *n., Latin genitive* **Fornacis** (fɔːˈneɪsɪs, -ˈnæs-). a faint constellation in the S hemisphere lying between Cetus and Phoenix. [Latin: oven, kiln]

fornenst (fɔːˈnɛnst) *prep. Scot. and northeast English dialect.* situated against or facing towards. [from Scottish, from FORE[1] + *anenst* a variant of archaic ANENT]

fornicate[1] (ˈfɔːnɪˌkeɪt) *vb.* (*intr.*) to indulge in or commit fornication. [C16: from Late Latin *fornicārī,* from Latin *fornix* vault, brothel situated therein] —ˈ**forniˌcator** *n.*

fornicate[2] (ˈfɔːnɪkɪt, -ˌkeɪt) *or* **fornicated** *adj. Biology.* arched or hoodlike in form. [C19: from Latin *fornicātus* arched, from *fornix* vault]

fornication (ˌfɔːnɪˈkeɪʃən) *n.* 1. voluntary sexual intercourse outside marriage. 2. *Law.* voluntary sexual intercourse between two persons of the opposite sex, where one is or both are unmarried. 3. *Bible.* sexual immorality in general, esp. adultery.

fornix (ˈfɔːnɪks) *n., pl.* **-nices** (-nɪˌsiːz). *Anatomy.* any archlike structure, esp. the arched band of white fibres at the base of the brain. [C17: from Latin; see FORNICATE[2]] —ˈ**fornical** *adj.*

forsake (fəˈseɪk) *vb.* **-sakes, -saking, -sook** (-ˈsʊk), **-saken** (-ˈseɪkən). (*tr.*) 1. to abandon. 2. to give up (something valued or enjoyed). [Old English *forsacan*] —**forˈsaker** *n.*

forsaken (fəˈseɪkən) *vb.* 1. the past participle of **forsake.** ~*adj.* 2. completely deserted or helpless; abandoned. —**forˈsakenly** *adv.* —**forˈsakenness** *n.*

forsook (fəˈsʊk) *vb.* the past tense of **forsake.**

forsooth (fəˈsuːθ) *adv. Archaic.* in truth; indeed. [Old English *forsōth*]

forspeak (fɔːˈspiːk) *vb.* **-speaks, -speaking, -spoke, -spoken.** (*tr.*) *Scot. archaic.* to bewitch.

forspent *or* **forespent** (fɔːˈspɛnt) *adj. Archaic.* tired out; exhausted.

forsterite (ˈfɔːstəˌraɪt) *n.* a white, yellow, or green mineral of the olivine group consisting of magnesium silicate. Formula: Mg_2SiO_4. [C19: named after J. R. *Forster* (1729–98), German naturalist]

forswear (fɔːˈswɛə) *vb.* **-swears, -swearing, -swore, -sworn.** 1. (*tr.*) to reject or renounce with determination or as upon oath. 2. (*tr.*) to deny or disavow absolutely or upon oath: *he forswore any knowledge of the crime.* 3. to perjure (oneself). [Old English *forswearian*] —**forˈswearer** *n.*

forsworn (fɔːˈswɔːn) *vb.* the past participle of **forswear.** —**forˈswornness** *n.*

forsythia (fɔːˈsaɪθɪə) *n.* any oleaceous shrub of the genus *Forsythia,* native to China, Japan, and SE Europe but widely cultivated for its showy yellow bell-shaped flowers, which appear in spring before the foliage. [C19: New Latin, named after William *Forsyth* (1737–1804), English botanist]

fort (fɔːt) *n.* 1. a fortified enclosure, building, or position able to be defended against an enemy. 2. **hold the fort.** *Informal.* to maintain or guard something temporarily. [C15: from Old French, from *fort* (adj.) strong, from Latin *fortis*]

fort. *abbrev. for:* 1. fortification. 2. fortified.

fortalice (ˈfɔːtəlɪs) *n.* a small fort or outwork of a fortification. [C15: from Medieval Latin *fortalitia,* from Latin *fortis* strong; see FORTRESS]

forte[1] (fɔːt, ˈfɔːteɪ) *n.* 1. something at which a person excels; strong point: *cooking is my forte.* 2. *Fencing.* the stronger section of a sword blade, between the hilt and the middle. Compare **foible.** [C17: from French *fort,* from *fort* (adj.) strong, from Latin *fortis*]

forte[2] (ˈfɔːtɪ) *Music.* ~*adj., adv.* 1. loud or loudly. Symbol: f ~*n.* 2. a loud passage in music. [C18: from Italian, from Latin *fortis* strong]

fortepiano (ˌfɔːtɪpɪˈænəʊ) *n.* an early type of piano popular in the late 18th century. [from Italian, loud-soft]

forte-piano (ˌfɔːtɪˈpjɑːnəʊ) *Music.* ~*adj., adv.* 1. loud and then immediately soft. Symbol: fp ~*n.* 2. a note played in this way.

forth (fɔːθ) *adv.* 1. forward in place, time, order, or degree. 2. out, as from concealment, seclusion, or inaction. 3. away, as from a place or country. 4. **and so forth.** and so on; et cetera. ~*prep.* 5. *Archaic.* out of; away from. [Old English; related to Middle High German *vort;* see FOR, FURTHER]

forthcoming (ˌfɔːθˈkʌmɪŋ) *adj.* 1. approaching in time: *the forthcoming debate.* 2. about to appear: *his forthcoming book.* 3. available or ready: *the money wasn't forthcoming.* 4. open or sociable. —ˌ**forthˈcomingness** *n.*

forthright *adj.* (ˈfɔːθˌraɪt). 1. direct and outspoken. ~*adv.* (ˌfɔːθˈraɪt, ˈfɔːθˌraɪt), *also* **forthrightly.** 2. in a direct manner; frankly. 3. at once. —ˈ**forthˌrightness** *n.*

forthwith (ˌfɔːθˈwɪθ, -ˈwɪð) *adv.* at once; immediately.

fortieth (ˈfɔːtɪɪθ) *adj.* 1. **a.** being the ordinal number of *forty* in numbering or counting order, position, time, etc.: often written 40th. **b.** (*as n.*): *he was the fortieth.* ~*n.* 2. **a.** one of 40 approximately equal parts of something. **b.** (*as modifier*): *a fortieth part.* 3. the fraction equal to one divided by 40 (1/40). [Old English *fēowertigotha*]

fortification (ˌfɔːtɪfɪˈkeɪʃən) *n.* 1. the act, art, or science of fortifying or strengthening. 2. **a.** a wall, mound, etc., used to fortify a place. **b.** such works collectively. **3.** any place that can be militarily defended.

fortified pa *n. N.Z. history.* a Maori hilltop dwelling with trenches and palisades for defensive occupation.

fortified wine *n.* wine treated by the addition of brandy or alcohol, such as port, marsala, and sherry.

fortify ('fɔːtɪˌfaɪ) *vb.* **-fies, -fying, -fied.** (*mainly tr.*) **1.** (*also intr.*) to make (a place) defensible, as by building walls, digging trenches, etc. **2.** to strengthen physically, mentally, or morally. **3.** to strengthen, support, or reinforce (a garment, structure, etc.). **4.** to add spirits or alcohol to (wine), in order to produce sherry, port, etc. **5.** to increase the nutritious value of (a food), as by adding vitamins and minerals. **6.** to support or confirm: *to fortify an argument with facts.* [C15: from Old French *fortifier,* from Late Latin *fortificāre,* from Latin *fortis* strong + *facere* to make] —'**fortiˌfiable** *adj.* —'**fortiˌfier** *n.* —'**fortiˌfyingly** *adv.*

fortis ('fɔːtɪs) *Phonetics.* ~*adj.* **1.** (of a consonant) articulated with considerable muscular tension of the speech organs or with a great deal of breath pressure or plosion. ~*n., pl.* **-tes** (-tiːz). **2.** a consonant, such as English *p* or *f,* pronounced with considerable muscular force or breath pressure. ~Compare **lenis.** [Latin: strong]

fortissimo (fɔːˈtɪsɪˌməʊ) *Music.* ~*adj., adv.* **1.** very loud. Symbol: ff ~*n.* **2.** a very loud passage in music. [C18: from Italian, from Latin *fortissimus,* from *fortis* strong]

fortitude ('fɔːtɪˌtjuːd) *n.* strength and firmness of mind; resolute endurance. [C15: from Latin *fortitūdō* courage] —ˌ**fortiˈtudinous** *adj.*

fortnight ('fɔːtˌnaɪt) *n.* a period of 14 consecutive days; two weeks. [Old English *fēowertīene niht* fourteen nights]

fortnightly ('fɔːtˌnaɪtlɪ) *Chiefly Brit.* ~*adj.* **1.** occurring or appearing once each fortnight. ~*adv.* **2.** once a fortnight. ~*n., pl.* **-lies.** **3.** a publication issued at intervals of two weeks.

FORTRAN *or* **Fortran** ('fɔːtræn) *n.* a high-level computer programming language for mathematical and scientific purposes, designed to facilitate and speed up the solving of complex problems. [C20: from *for(mula) tran(slation)*]

fortress ('fɔːtrɪs) *n.* **1.** a large fort or fortified town. **2.** a place or source of refuge or support. ~*vb.* **3.** (*tr.*) to protect with or as if with a fortress. [C13: from Old French *forteresse,* from Medieval Latin *fortalitia,* from Latin *fortis* strong]

fortuitism (fɔːˈtjuːɪˌtɪzəm) *n. Philosophy.* the doctrine that evolutionary adaptations are the result of chance. Compare **tychism.** —**forˈtuitist** *n., adj.*

fortuitous (fɔːˈtjuːɪtəs) *adj.* happening by chance, esp. by a lucky chance; unplanned; accidental. [C17: from Latin *fortuitus* happening by chance, from *forte* by chance, from *fors* chance, luck] —**forˈtuitously** *adv.* —**forˈtuitousness** *n.*

fortuity (fɔːˈtjuːɪtɪ) *n., pl.* **-ties.** **1.** a chance or accidental occurrence. **2.** fortuitousness. **3.** chance or accident.

fortunate ('fɔːtʃənɪt) *adj.* **1.** having good luck; lucky. **2.** occurring by or bringing good fortune or luck; auspicious. —'**fortunately** *adv.* —'**fortunateness** *n.*

fortune ('fɔːtʃən) *n.* **1.** an amount of wealth or material prosperity, esp., when unqualified, a great amount. **2. small fortune.** a large sum of money. **3.** a power or force, often personalized, regarded as being responsible for human affairs; chance. **4.** luck, esp. when favourable. **5.** (*often pl.*) a person's lot or destiny. ~*vb.* **6.** *Archaic.* **a.** (*tr.*) to endow with great wealth. **b.** (*intr.*) to happen by chance. [C13: from Old French, from Latin *fortūna,* from *fors* chance] —'**fortuneless** *adj.*

fortune-hunter *n.* a person who seeks to secure a fortune, esp. through marriage. —'**fortune-ˌhunting** *adj., n.*

fortune-teller *n.* a person who makes predictions about the future as by looking into a crystal ball, reading palms, etc. —'**fortune-ˌtelling** *adj., n.*

forty ('fɔːtɪ) *n., pl.* **-ties.** **1.** the cardinal number that is the product of ten and four. See also **number** (sense 1). **2.** a numeral, 40, XL, etc., representing this number. **3.** something representing, represented by, or consisting of 40 units. ~*determiner.* **4. a.** amounting to forty: *forty thieves.* **b.** (*as pronoun*): *there were forty in the herd.* [Old English *fēowertig*]

forty-five *n.* **1.** a gramophone record played at 45 revolutions per minute. **2.** *U.S. and Canadian.* a pistol having .45 calibre.

forty-niner *n.* (*sometimes cap.*) *U.S. history.* a prospector who took part in the California gold rush of 1849.

forty winks *n.* (*functioning as sing. or pl.*) *Informal.* a short light sleep; nap.

forum ('fɔːrəm) *n., pl.* **-rums** *or* **-ra** (-rə). **1.** a meeting or assembly for the open discussion of subjects of public interest. **2.** a medium for open discussion, such as a magazine. **3.** a public meeting place for open discussion. **4.** a court; tribunal. **5.** (in ancient Italy) an open space, usually rectangular in shape, serving as a city's marketplace and centre of public business. [C15: from Latin: public place; related to Latin *foris* outside]

forward ('fɔːwəd) *adj.* **1.** directed or moving ahead. **2.** lying or situated in or near the front part of something. **3.** presumptuous, pert, or impudent: *a forward remark.* **4.** well developed or advanced, esp. in physical, material, or intellectual growth or development: *forward ideas.* **5.** *Archaic.* (*often postpositive*) ready, eager, or willing. **6. a.** of or relating to the future or favouring change; progressive. **b.** (*in combination*): *forward-looking.* **7.** *N.Z.* (of an animal) in good condition. ~*n.* **8. a.** an attacking player in any of various sports, such as soccer, hockey, or basketball. **b.** (in American football) a lineman. ~*adv.* **9.** a variant of **forwards.** **10.** ('fɔːwəd; *Nautical* 'fɒrəd). towards the front or bow of an aircraft or ship. **11.** into prominence or a position of being subject to public scrutiny; out; forth: *the witness came forward.* ~*vb.* (*tr.*) **12.** to send forward or pass on to an ultimate destination: *the letter was forwarded from a previous address.* **13.** to advance, help, or promote: *to forward one's career.* **14.** *Bookbinding.* to prepare (a book) for the finisher. [Old English *foreweard*] —'**forwardly** *adv.*

forward bias *or* **voltage** *n.* a voltage applied to a circuit or device, esp. a semiconductor device, in the direction that produces the larger current.

forward delivery *n.* (in commerce) delivery at a future date.

forwarder ('fɔːwədə) *n.* **1.** a person or thing that forwards. **2.** a person engaged in the bookbinding process of forwarding. **3.** another name for **forwarding agent.**

forwarding ('fɔːwədɪŋ) *n.* all the processes involved in the binding of a book subsequent to cutting and up to the fitting of its cover.

forwarding agent *n.* a person, agency, or enterprise that is engaged in the collection, shipment, and delivery of goods. Also called: **forwarder.**

forward market *n.* a market in which contracts are made to buy or sell currencies, commodities, etc., at some future date and at a price fixed at the date of the contract. Compare **spot market.**

forwardness ('fɔːwədnɪs) *n.* **1.** lack of modesty; presumption; boldness. **2.** willing readiness; eagerness. **3.** a state or condition of advanced progress or development.

forward pass *n. Rugby.* an illegal pass towards the opponent's dead-ball line. Also called: **throw-forward.**

forward quotation *n.* (in commerce) the price quoted for goods sent on forward delivery.

forward roll *n.* a gymnastic movement in which the body is turned heels over head with the back of the neck resting on the ground.

forwards ('fɔːwədz) *or* **forward** *adv.* **1.** towards or at a place ahead or in advance, esp. in space but also in time. **2.** towards the front.

forwent (fɔːˈwɛnt) *vb.* the past tense of **forgo.**

forwhy (fɔːˈwaɪ) *Archaic.* ~*adv.* **1.** for what reason; why. ~*conj.* **2.** (*subordinating*) because. [Old English *for hwī*]

forworn *or* **foreworn** (fɔːˈwɔːn) *adj. Archaic.* weary. [C16: past participle of obsolete *forwear* to wear out, from Middle English *forweren* to hollow out]

forza ('fɔːtsə) *n. Music.* force. [C19: Italian, literally: force]

forzando (fɔːˈtsændəʊ) *adj., adv., n.* another word for **sforzando.**

Fosbury flop ('fɒzbərɪ, -brɪ) *n. Athletics.* a modern high-jumping technique whereby the jumper clears the bar headfirst and backwards. [C20: named after Dick *Fosbury,* U.S. winner of men's high jump at Mexico Olympics in 1968, who perfected the technique]

fossa[1] ('fɒsə) *n., pl.* **-sae** (-siː). an anatomical depression, trench, or hollow area. [C19: from Latin: ditch, from *fossus* dug up, from *fodere* to dig up]

fossa[2] ('fɒsə) *n.* a large primitive catlike viverrine mammal, *Cryptoprocta ferox,* inhabiting the forests of Madagascar: order *Carnivora* (carnivores). It has thick reddish-brown fur and preys on lemurs, poultry, etc. [from Malagasy]

fosse *or* **foss** (fɒs) *n.* a ditch or moat, esp. a long narrow trench dug as a fortification. [C14: from Old French, from Latin *fossa;* see FOSSA[1]]

fossette (fɒˈsɛt) *n.* **1.** *Anatomy.* a small depression or fossa, as in a bone. **2.** *Pathol.* a small deep ulcer of the cornea. [C19: from French: dimple, from *fosse* ditch]

fossick ('fɒsɪk) *vb. Austral. and N.Z.* **1.** (*intr.*) to search for gold or precious stones in abandoned workings, rivers, etc. **2.** to rummage or search for (something). [C19: Australian, probably from English dialect *fussock* to bustle about, from FUSS] —'**fossicker** *n.*

fossil ('fɒsᵊl) *n.* **1. a.** a relic, remnant, or representation of a plant or animal that existed in a past geological age, occurring in the form of mineralized bones, shells, etc., as casts, impressions, and moulds, and as frozen perfectly preserved organisms. **b.** (*as modifier*): *fossil insects.* **2.** *Informal, derogatory.* **a.** a person, idea, thing, etc., that is outdated or incapable of change. **b.** (*as modifier*): *fossil politicians.* **3.** *Linguistics.* a form once current but now appearing only in one or two special contexts, as for example *stead,* which is found now only in *instead* (*of*) and in phrases like *in his stead.* **4.** *Obsolete.* any rock or mineral dug out of the earth. [C17: from Latin *fossilis* dug up, from *fodere* to dig]

fossil energy *n.* heat energy released by burning fossil fuel.

fossil fuel *n.* any naturally occurring carbon or hydrocarbon fuel, such as coal, petroleum, peat, and natural gas, formed by the decomposition of prehistoric organisms.

fossiliferous (ˌfɒsɪˈlɪfərəs) *adj.* (of sedimentary rocks) containing fossils.

fossilize *or* **fossilise** ('fɒsɪˌlaɪz) *vb.* **1.** to convert or be converted into a fossil. **2.** to become or cause to become antiquated or inflexible. —'**fossilˌizable** *or* '**fossilˌisable** *adj.* —ˌ**fossiliˈzation** *or* ˌ**fossiliˈsation** *n.*

fossorial (fɒˈsɔːrɪəl) *adj.* **1.** (of the forelimbs and skeleton of burrowing animals) adapted for digging. **2.** (of burrowing animals, such as the mole and armadillo) having limbs of this type. [C19: from Medieval Latin *fossōrius* from Latin *fossor* digger, from *fodere* to dig]

foster (ˈfɒstə) *vb.* (*tr.*) **1.** to promote the growth or development of. **2.** to bring up (a child, etc.); rear. **3.** to cherish (a plan, hope, etc.) in one's mind. **4.** *Chiefly Brit.* **a.** to place (a child) in the care of foster parents. **b.** to bring up under fosterage. ~*adj.* **5.** (*in combination*) of or involved in the rearing of a child by persons other than his natural or adopted parents: *foster parents; foster home.* [Old English *fōstrian* to feed, from *fōstor* FOOD] —ˈ**fosterer** *n.* —ˈ**fosteringly** *adv.*

fosterage (ˈfɒstərɪdʒ) *n.* **1.** the act of caring for or bringing up a foster child. **2.** the condition or state of being a foster child. **3.** the act of encouraging or promoting.

foster child *n.* a child looked after temporarily or brought up by people other than its natural or adoptive parents.

foster father *n.* a man who looks after or brings up a child or children as a father, in place of the natural or adoptive father.

fosterling (ˈfɒstəlɪŋ) *n.* a less common word for **foster child.**

foster mother *n.* a woman who looks after or brings up a child or children as a mother, in place of the natural or adoptive mother.

fou (fuː) *adj. Scot.* **1.** full. **2.** drunk. [perhaps a Scot. variant of *full*]

Foucault current (ˈfuːkəʊ) *n.* another name for **eddy current.** [named after Jean *Foucault* (1819–68), French physicist]

foudroyant (fuːˈdrɔɪənt) *adj.* **1.** (of a disease) occurring suddenly and with great severity. **2.** *Rare.* stunning, dazzling, or overwhelming. [C19: from French, from *foudroyer* to strike with lightning, from Old French *foudre* lightning, from Latin *fulgur*]

fouetté *French.* (fwete) *n.* a step in ballet in which the dancer stands on one foot and makes a whiplike movement with the other. [C19: French, past participle of *fouetter* to whip, from *fouet* a whip]

fought (fɔːt) *vb.* the past tense and past participle of **fight.**

foul (faʊl) *adj.* **1.** offensive to the senses; revolting. **2.** offensive in odour; stinking. **3.** charged with or full of dirt or offensive matter; filthy. **4.** (of food) putrid; rotten. **5.** morally or spiritually offensive; wicked; vile. **6.** obscene; vulgar: *foul language.* **7.** not in accordance with accepted standards or established rules; unfair: *to resort to foul means.* **8.** (esp. of weather) unpleasant or adverse. **9.** blocked or obstructed with dirt or foreign matter: *a foul drain.* **10.** entangled or impeded: *a foul anchor.* **11.** (of the bottom of a vessel) covered with barnacles and other growth that slow forward motion. **12.** *Printing.* (of a typecase) having type distributed in the wrong compartments. **13.** *Informal.* unsatisfactory or uninteresting; bad: *a foul book.* **14.** *Archaic.* ugly. ~*n.* **15.** *Sport.* **a.** a violation of the rules. **b.** (*as modifier*): *a foul shot; a foul blow.* **16.** something foul. **17.** an entanglement or collision, esp. in sailing or fishing. ~*vb.* **18.** to make or become dirty or polluted. **19.** to become or cause to become entangled or snarled. **20.** (*tr.*) to disgrace or dishonour. **21.** to become or cause to become clogged or choked. **22.** (*tr.*) *Nautical.* (of underwater growth) to cling to (the bottom of a vessel) so as to slow its motion. **23.** (*tr.*) *Sport.* to commit a foul against (an opponent). **24.** (*tr.*) *Baseball.* to hit (a ball) in an illegal manner. **25.** (*intr.*) *Sport.* to infringe the rules. **26.** to collide with (a boat, etc.). ~*adv.* **27.** in a foul or unfair manner. **28. fall foul of. a.** to come into conflict with. **b.** *Nautical.* to come into collision with. ~See also **foul up.** [Old English *fūl;* related to Old Norse *fūll,* Gothic *fūls* smelling offensively, Latin *pūs* PUS, Greek *puol* pus] —ˈ**foully** *adv.*

foulard (fuːˈlɑːd, ˈfuːlɑː) *n.* **1.** a soft light fabric of plain-weave or twill-weave silk or rayon, usually with a printed design. **2.** something made of this fabric, esp. a scarf or handkerchief. [C19: from French, of unknown origin]

foul marten *n.* another name for the **polecat** (sense 1). See also **sweet marten.**

foul-mouthed *adj.* given to using obscene, abusive, or blasphemous language.

foulness (ˈfaʊlnɪs) *n.* **1.** the state or quality of being foul. **2.** obscenity; vulgarity. **3.** viciousness or inhumanity. **4.** foul matter; filth.

foul play *n.* **1.** unfair or treacherous conduct esp. with violence. **2.** a violation of the rules in a game or sport.

foul shot *n. Basketball.* another term (esp. U.S. and Canadian) for **free throw.**

foul up *vb.* (*adv.*) **1.** (*tr.*) to bungle; mismanage. **2.** (*tr.*) to make dirty; contaminate. **3.** to be or cause to be blocked, choked, or entangled. ~*n.* **foul-up. 4.** a state of confusion or muddle caused by bungling.

foumart (ˈfuːmɑːt, -mət) *n.* a former name for the **polecat** (sense 1). [C15 *folmarde:* from Old English *fūl* foul + *mearth* a marten]

found[1] (faʊnd) *vb.* **1.** the past tense and past participle of **find.** ~*adj.* **2.** furnished, or fitted out: *the boat is well found.* **3.** *Brit.* with meals, heating, bed linen, etc., provided without extra charge (esp. in the phrase **all found**).

found[2] (faʊnd) *vb.* **1.** (*tr.*) to bring into being, set up, or establish (something, such as an institution, society, etc.). **2.** (*tr.*) to build or establish the foundation or basis of. **3.** (*also intr.;* foll. by *on* or *upon*) to have a basis (in); depend (on). [C13: from Old French *fonder,* from Latin *fundāre,* from *fundus* bottom]

found[3] (faʊnd) *vb.* (*tr.*) **1.** to cast (a material, such as metal or glass) by melting and pouring into a mould. **2.** to shape or make (articles) in this way; cast. [C14: from Old French *fondre,* from Latin *fundere* to melt]

foundation (faʊnˈdeɪʃən) *n.* **1.** that on which something is founded; basis. **2.** (*often pl.*) a construction below the ground that distributes the load of a building, wall, etc. **3.** the base on which something stands. **4.** the act of founding or establishing or the state of being founded or established. **5. a.** an endowment or legacy for the perpetual support of an institution such as a school or hospital. **b. on the foundation.** entitled to benefit from the funds of a foundation. **6.** an institution supported by an endowment, often one that provides funds for charities, research, etc. **7.** the charter incorporating or establishing a society or institution and the statutes or rules governing its affairs. **8.** a cosmetic in cream or cake form used as a base for make-up. **9.** See **foundation garment. 10.** *Cards.* a card on which a sequence may be built. —**foun'dational** *adj.* —**foun'dationally** *adv.* —**foun'dationary** *adj.*

foundation garment *n.* a woman's undergarment worn to shape and support the figure; brassiere or corset.

foundation stone *n.* a stone laid at a ceremony to mark the foundation of a new building.

foundation subjects *pl. n. Brit. Education.* the subjects studied as part of the National Curriculum, including the compulsory core subjects.

founder[1] (ˈfaʊndə) *n.* a person who establishes an institution, company, society, etc. [C14: see FOUND[2]]

founder[2] (ˈfaʊndə) *vb.* (*intr.*) **1.** (of a ship) to sink. **2.** to break down or fail: *the project foundered.* **3.** to sink into or become stuck in soft ground. **4.** to fall in or give way; collapse. **5.** (of a horse) to stumble or go lame. **6.** (of animals, esp. livestock) to become ill from overeating. ~*n.* **7.** *Vet. science.* another name for **laminitis.** [C13: from Old French *fondrer* to submerge, from Latin *fundus* bottom; see FOUND[2]]

founder[3] (ˈfaʊndə) *n.* **a.** a person who makes metal castings. **b.** (*in combination*): *an iron founder.* [C15: see FOUND[3]]

founders' shares *pl. n.* shares awarded to the founders of a company and often granting special privileges.

founder's type *n. Printing.* type cast by a typefounder for hand composition.

founding father *n.* (*often caps.*) a person who founds or establishes an important institution, esp. a member of the U.S. Constitutional Convention (1787).

foundling (ˈfaʊndlɪŋ) *n.* an abandoned infant whose parents are not known. [C13: *foundeling;* see FIND]

found object *n.* another name for ***objet trouvé.***

foundry (ˈfaʊndrɪ) *n., pl.* **-ries. 1.** a place in which metal castings are produced. **2.** the science or practice of casting metal. **3.** cast-metal articles collectively. [C17: from Old French *fonderie,* from *fondre;* see FOUND[3]]

foundry proof *n. Printing.* a proof taken from a forme before duplicate plates are made from it.

foundry sand *n.* silica-based sand mixed with clay, oil, etc., to improve its cohesive strength, used in moulding.

fount[1] (faʊnt) *n.* **1.** *Poetic.* a spring or fountain. **2.** source or origin. [C16: back formation from FOUNTAIN]

fount[2] (faʊnt, fɒnt) *n. Printing.* a complete set of type of one style and size. Also called (esp. U.S. and Canadian): **font.** [C16: from Old French *fonte* a founding, casting, from Vulgar Latin *funditus* (unattested) a casting, from Latin *fundere* to melt; see FOUND[3]]

fountain (ˈfaʊntɪn) *n.* **1.** a jet or spray of water or some other liquid. **2.** a structure from which such a jet or a number of such jets spurt, often incorporating figures, basins, etc. **3.** a natural spring of water, esp. the source of a stream. **4.** a stream, jet, or cascade of sparks, lava, etc. **5.** a principal source or origin. **6.** a reservoir or supply chamber, as for oil in a lamp. **7.** short for **drinking fountain** or **soda fountain.** [C15: from Old French *fontaine,* from Late Latin *fontāna,* from Latin *fons* spring, source] —ˈ**fountained** *adj.* —ˈ**fountainless** *adj.* —ˈ**fountain-ˌlike** *adj.*

fountainhead (ˈfaʊntɪnˌhɛd) *n.* **1.** a spring that is the source of a stream. **2.** a principal or original source.

fountain pen *n.* a pen the nib of which is supplied with ink from a cartridge or a reservoir in its barrel.

four (fɔː) *n.* **1.** the cardinal number that is the sum of three and one. **2.** a numeral, 4, IV, etc., representing this number. **3.** something representing, represented by, or consisting of four units, such as a playing card with four symbols on it. **4.** Also called: **four o'clock.** four hours after noon or midnight. **5.** *Cricket.* **a.** a shot that crosses the boundary after hitting the ground. **b.** the four runs scored for such a shot. **6.** *Rowing.* **a.** a racing shell propelled by four oarsmen pulling one oar each, with or without a cox. **b.** the crew of such a shell. ~*determiner.* **7. a.** amounting to four: *four thousand eggs; four times.* **b.** (*as pronoun*): *four are ready.* ~Related prefixes: **quadri-, tetra-.** [Old English *fēower;* related to Old Frisian *fiūwer,* Old Norse *fjōrir,* Old High German *fior,* Latin *quattuor,* Greek *tessares,* Sanskrit *catur*]

four-ball *n. Golf.* a match for two pairs in which each player uses his own ball, the better score of each pair being counted at every hole. Compare **foursome** (sense 2), **greensome.**

four-by-two *n. Austral. and N.Z.* a piece of timber with a cross section that measures 4 inches by 2 inches.

fourchette (fʊəˈʃɛt) *n.* **1.** *Anatomy.* the bandlike fold of skin, about one inch from the anus, forming the posterior margin of the vulva. **2.** a less common name for **furcula** or **frog**[3]. [C18: from French: a little fork, from Old French *forche,* from Latin *furca* FORK]

four-colour *n.* (*modifier*) (of a print or photographic process) using the principle in which four colours (magenta, cyan, yellow, and black) are used in combination to produce almost any other colour.

four-cycle *adj.* the U.S. and Canadian word for **four-stroke.**

four-deal bridge *n.* a version of bridge in which four hands only are played, the players then cutting for new partners.

four-dimensional *adj.* having or specified by four dimensions, esp. the three spatial dimensions and the dimension of time: *a four-dimensional continuum.*

Fourdrinier (fʊəˈdrɪnɪə) *n.* a particular type of paper-making machine that forms the paper in a continuous web. [C19: named after Henry (died 1854) and Sealy (died 1847) *Fourdrinier,* English paper makers]

four-eyed fish *n.* either of two viviparous tropical American freshwater cyprinodont fishes, *Anableps anableps* or *A. microlepis,* that swim at the surface of the water and have half of each eye specialized for seeing in air, the other half for seeing in water.

four-eyes *n.* a disparaging term of address for a person wearing spectacles. —ˈ**four-ˌeyed** *adj.*

four flush *n.* **1.** a useless poker hand, containing four of a suit and one odd card. ~*vb.* **four-flush.** (*intr.*) **2.** to bid confidently on a poor hand such as a four flush. **3.** *U.S. and Canadian.* a slang word for **bluff.**

four-flusher (ˈfɔːˌflʌʃə) *n. U.S. and Canadian slang.* a person who bluffs or attempts to deceive.

fourfold (ˈfɔːˌfəʊld) *adj.* **1.** equal to or having four times as many or as much. **2.** composed of four parts. ~*adv.* **3.** by or up to four times as many or as much.

four-four time *n. Music.* a form of simple quadruple time in which there are four crotchets to the bar, indicated by the time signature $^4_4$. Often shortened to **four-four.** Also called: **common time.**

fourgon *French.* (furgɔ̃) *n.* a long covered wagon, used mainly for carrying baggage, supplies, etc. [C19: from French: from Old French *forgon* poker, from *furgier* to search, ultimately from Latin *fūr* thief]

four-handed *adj.* **1.** (of a card game) arranged for four players. **2.** (of a musical composition) written for two performers at the same piano. —ˌ**four-ˈhandedly** *adv.*

Four Hundred *n.* **the.** *U.S.* the most exclusive or affluent social clique in a particular place.

Fourier analysis (ˈfʊərɪˌeɪ) *n.* the analysis of a periodic function into its simple sinusoidal or harmonic components, whose sum forms a Fourier series. [named after Jean Baptiste Joseph *Fourier* (1768–1830), French mathematician]

Fourierism (ˈfʊərɪəˌrɪzəm) *n.* the system of French social reformer Charles Fourier (1772–1837), under which society was to be organized into self-sufficient cooperatives. —ˈ**Fourierist** *or* **Fourierite** (ˈfʊərɪəˌraɪt) *n., adj.* —ˌ**Fourierˈistic** *adj.*

Fourier series *n.* an infinite trigonometric series of the form $\frac{1}{2}a_0 + a_1\cos x + b_1\sin x + a_2\cos 2x + b_2\sin 2x + \ldots$, where a_0, a_1, b_1, a_2, b_2 … are the **Fourier coefficients.** It is used, esp. in mathematics and physics, to represent or approximate any single-valued periodic function by assigning suitable values to the coefficients. [C19: named after Jean Baptiste Joseph *Fourier*]

Fourier transform *n.* an integral transform, used in many branches of science, of the form $F(x) = [1/\sqrt{(2\pi)}]\int e^{ixy}f(y)dy$, where the limits of integration are from $-\infty$ to $+\infty$ and the function F is the transform of the function f.

four-in-hand *n.* **1.** Also called: **tally-ho.** a road vehicle drawn by four horses and driven by one driver. **2.** a four-horse team in a coach or carriage. **3.** a long narrow tie formerly worn tied in a flat slipknot with the ends dangling.

four-leaf clover *or* **four-leaved clover** *n.* **1.** a clover with four leaves rather than three, supposed to bring good luck. **2.** another name for **cloverleaf** (sense 1).

four-letter word *n.* any of several short English words referring to sex or excrement: often used as swearwords and regarded generally as offensive or obscene.

four-o'clock *n.* **1.** Also called: **marvel-of-Peru.** a tropical American nyctaginaceous plant, *Mirabilis jalapa,* cultivated for its tubular yellow, red, or white flowers that open in late afternoon. **2.** an Australian name for **friarbird,** esp. the noisy friarbird (*Philemon corniculatus*): so called because of its cry.

four-part *adj. Music.* arranged for four voices or instruments.

fourpence (ˈfɔːpəns) *n.* a former English silver coin then worth four pennies.

fourpenny (ˈfɔːpənɪ) *adj.* **fourpenny one.** *Brit. slang.* a blow, esp. with the fist.

four-plus cover *n.* an advertising campaign in which members of the public are exposed to an advertisement at least four times.

four-poster *n.* a bed with posts at each corner supporting a canopy and curtains. Also called: **four-poster bed.**

fourragère (ˈfʊərəˌʒɛə; *French* furaʒɛr) *n.* an ornamental cord worn on the shoulder of a uniform for identification or as an award, esp. in the U.S. and French Armies. [French, feminine adj. of *fourrager* relating to forage, from *fourrage* FORAGE]

fourscore (ˌfɔːˈskɔː) *determiner.* an archaic word for **eighty.**

foursome (ˈfɔːsəm) *n.* **1.** a set or company of four. **2.** *Sport.* a game between two pairs of players, esp. a form of golf in which each partner in a pair takes alternate strokes at the same ball. Compare **four-ball, greensome.** **3.** (*modifier*) of or performed by a company of four: *a foursome competition.*

foursquare (ˌfɔːˈskwɛə) *adv.* **1.** squarely; firmly. ~*adj.* **2.** solid and strong. **3.** forthright; honest. **4.** a rare word for **square.** —ˌ**fourˈsquarely** *adv.* —ˌ**fourˈsquareness** *n.*

four-stroke *adj.* of, relating to, or designating an internal-combustion engine in which the piston makes four strokes for every explosion. U.S. and Canadian name: **four-cycle.** Compare **two-stroke.**

fourteen (ˈfɔːˈtiːn) *n.* **1.** the cardinal number that is the sum of ten and four. **2.** a numeral, 14, XIV, etc., representing this number. **3.** something represented by, representing, or consisting of 14 units. ~*determiner.* **4. a.** amounting to fourteen: *fourteen cats.* **b.** (*as pronoun*): *the fourteen who remained.* [Old English *fēowertīene*]

fourteenth (ˈfɔːˈtiːnθ) *adj.* **1. a.** coming after the thirteenth in order, position, time etc. Often written: 14th. **b.** (*as n.*): *the fourteenth in succession.* ~*n.* **2. a.** one of 14 equal or nearly equal parts of something. **b.** (*as modifier*): *a fourteenth part.* **3.** the fraction equal to one divided by 14 (1/14).

fourth (fɔːθ) *adj.* (*usually prenominal*) **1. a.** coming after the third in order, position, time, etc. Often written: 4th. **b.** (*as n.*): *the fourth in succession.* **2.** denoting the highest forward ratio of a gearbox in most motor vehicles. ~*n.* **3.** *Music.* **a.** the interval between one note and another four notes away from it counting inclusively along the diatonic scale. **b.** one of two notes constituting such an interval in relation to the other. See also **perfect** (sense 9), **interval** (sense 5), **diminished** (sense 2). **4.** the fourth forward ratio of a gearbox in a motor vehicle, usually the highest gear in cars; top gear: *he changed into fourth as soon as he had passed me.* **5.** a less common word for **quarter** (sense 2). ~*adv. also:* **fourthly.** **6.** after the third person, position, event, etc. ~*sentence connector. also:* **fourthly.** **7.** as the fourth point: linking what follows with the previous statements, as in a speech or argument.

fourth-class *U.S.* ~*adj.* **1.** of or relating to mail that is carried at the lowest rate. ~*adv.* **2.** by fourth-class mail.

fourth dimension *n.* **1.** the dimension of time, which is necessary in addition to three spatial dimensions to specify fully the position and behaviour of a point or particle. **2.** the concept in science fiction of a dimension in addition to three spatial dimensions, used to explain supranatural phenomena, events, etc. —ˌ**fourth-diˈmensional** *adj.*

fourth estate *n.* (*sometimes caps.*) journalists or their profession; the press. See **estate** (sense 4).

Fourth of July *n.* (preceded by *the*) a holiday in the United States, traditionally celebrated with fireworks: the day of the adoption of the Declaration of Independence in 1776. Official name: **Independence Day.**

Fourth World *n.* **1.** the poorest countries in the most undeveloped parts of the world in Africa, Asia, and Latin America. **2.** the poorest people in developed countries.

four-way *adj.* (*usually prenominal*) **1.** giving passage in four directions. **2.** made up of four elements.

four-wheel drive *n.* a system used in motor vehicles in which all four wheels are connected to the source of power.

fovea (ˈfəʊvɪə) *n., pl.* **-veae** (-vɪˌiː). **1.** *Anatomy.* any small pit or depression in the surface of a bodily organ or part. **2.** See **fovea centralis.** [C19: from Latin: a small pit] —ˈ**foveal** *adj.* —ˈ**foveate** *or* ˈ**foveˌated** *adj.*

fovea centralis (sɛnˈtrɑːlɪs) *n.* a small depression in the back of the retina, in the centre, that contains only cone cells and is therefore the area of sharpest vision. [C19: from New Latin: central fovea]

foveola (fəʊˈviːələ) *n., pl.* **-lae** (-ˌliː). *Biology.* a small fovea. [C19: from New Latin, diminutive of FOVEA] —**foˈveolar** *adj.* —**foveolate** (ˈfəʊvɪəˌleɪt) *or* ˈ**foveoˌlated** *adj.*

fowl (faʊl) *n.* **1.** See **domestic fowl.** **2.** any other bird, esp. any gallinaceous bird, that is used as food or hunted as game. See also **waterfowl, wildfowl.** **3.** the flesh or meat of fowl, esp. of chicken. **4.** an archaic word for any **bird.** ~*vb.* **5.** (*intr.*) to hunt or snare wildfowl. [Old English *fugol;* related to Old Frisian *fugel,* Old Norse *fogl,* Gothic *fugls,* Old High German *fogal*]

fowling (ˈfaʊlɪŋ) *n.* the shooting or trapping of birds for sport or as a livelihood. —ˈ**fowler** *n.*

fowl mite *n.* any of various mites parasitic in birds, usually bloodsucking and including the **red fowl mite** (*Dermanyssus gallinae*) and the **northern fowl mite** (*Ornithonyssus sylviarum*), both pests of poultry.

fowl pest *n.* **1.** an acute and usually fatal viral disease of domestic fowl, characterized by refusal to eat, high temperature, and discoloration of the comb and wattles. **2.** another name for **Newcastle disease.**

fox (fɒks) *n., pl.* **foxes** *or* **fox.** **1.** any canine mammal of the genus *Vulpes* and related genera. They are mostly predators that do not hunt in packs and typically have large pointed ears, a pointed muzzle, and a bushy tail. **2.** the fur of any of these animals, usually reddish-brown or grey in colour. **3.** a person who is cunning and sly. **4.** *Slang, chiefly U.S.* a sexually attractive woman. **5.** *Bible.* **a.** a jackal. **b.** an image of a false prophet. **6.** *Nautical.* small stuff made from yarns twisted together and then tarred. *~vb.* **7.** (*tr.*) *Informal.* to perplex or confound: *to fox a person with a problem.* **8.** to cause (paper, wood, etc.) to become discoloured with spots, or (of paper, etc.) to become discoloured, as through mildew. **9.** (*tr.*) to trick; deceive. **10.** (*intr.*) to act deceitfully or craftily. **11.** (*tr.*) *Austral. informal.* to pursue stealthily; tail. **12.** (*tr.*) *Austral. informal.* to chase and retrieve (a ball). **13.** (*tr.*) *Obsolete.* to befuddle with alcoholic drink. [Old English; related to Old High German *fuhs,* Old Norse *fōa* fox, Sanskrit *puccha* tail; see VIXEN] —**'fox,like** *adj.*

Fox (fɒks) *n.* **1.** (*pl.* **Fox** *or* **Foxes**) a member of a North American Indian people formerly living west of Lake Michigan along the Fox River. **2.** the language of this people, belonging to the Algonquian family.

foxfire ('fɒks,faɪə) *n.* a luminescent glow emitted by certain fungi on rotting wood. See also **bioluminescence.**

foxglove ('fɒks,glʌv) *n.* any Eurasian scrophulariaceous plant of the genus *Digitalis,* esp. *D. purpurea,* having spikes of purple or white thimble-like flowers. The soft wrinkled leaves are a source of digitalis.

fox grape *n.* a common wild grape, *Vitis labrusca* of the northern U.S., having purplish-black fruit and woolly leaves: the source of many cultivated grapes, including the catawba.

foxhole ('fɒks,həʊl) *n. Military.* a small pit dug during an action to provide individual shelter against hostile fire.

foxhound ('fɒks,haʊnd) *n.* either of two breeds (the English and the American) of dog having a short smooth coat and pendent ears. Though not large (height about 60 cm or 23 in.) they have great stamina and are usually kept for hunting foxes.

fox hunt *n.* **1. a.** the hunting of foxes with hounds. **b.** an instance of this. **2.** an organization for fox-hunting within a particular area.

fox-hunting *n.* a sport in which hunters follow a pack of hounds in pursuit of a fox. —**'fox-,hunter** *n.*

foxie ('fɒksɪ) *n. Austral.* an informal name for **fox terrier.**

foxing ('fɒksɪŋ) *n.* a piece of leather used to reinforce or trim part of the upper of a shoe.

fox moth *n.* a coppery-brown European eggar moth, *Macrothylacia rubi,* whose black-and-yellow woolly larvae are commonly found on heather and bramble.

fox squirrel *n.* a large squirrel, *Sciurus niger,* occurring in E North America.

foxtail ('fɒks,teɪl) *n.* **1.** any grass of the genus *Alopecurus,* esp. *A. pratensis,* of Europe, Asia, and South America, having soft cylindrical spikes of flowers: cultivated as a pasture grass. **2.** any of various similar and related grasses, esp. any of the genus *Setaria.*

fox terrier *n.* either of two breeds of small terrier, the wire-haired and the smooth, having a white coat with markings of black or tan or both.

foxtrot ('fɒks,trɒt) *n.* **1.** a ballroom dance in quadruple time, combining short and long steps in various sequences. *~vb.* **-trots, -trotting, -trotted.** **2.** (*intr.*) to perform this dance.

Foxtrot ('fɒks,trɒt) *n. Communications.* a code word for the letter *f.*

foxy ('fɒksɪ) *adj.* **foxier, foxiest.** **1.** of or resembling a fox, esp. in craftiness. **2.** smelling strongly like a fox. **3.** of a reddish-brown colour. **4.** (of paper, wood, etc.) spotted, esp. by mildew. **5.** (of wine) having the flavour of fox grapes. **6.** *Slang.* sexy; sexually attractive. —**'foxily** *adv.* —**'foxiness** *n.*

foyboat ('fɔɪ,bəʊt) *n. Tyneside dialect.* **a.** a small rowing boat. **b.** (*in combination*): *a foyboatman.* [C19: from *foy* to provide aid for ships, esp. those in distress]

foyer ('fɔɪeɪ, 'fɔɪə) *n.* a hall, lobby, or anteroom, used for reception and as a meeting place, as in a hotel, theatre, cinema, etc. [C19: from French: fireplace, from Medieval Latin *focārius,* from Latin *focus* fire]

fp **1.** *abbrev. for* fine point. *~***2.** *Music. symbol for* fortepiano.

FP *or* **fp** *abbrev. for:* **1.** freezing point. **2.** fully paid.

FPA *abbrev. for* Family Planning Association.

FPO *abbrev. for* field post office.

fps *abbrev. for:* **1.** feet per second. **2.** foot-pound-second. **3.** *Photog.* frames per second.

fps units *pl. n.* an Imperial system of units based on the foot, pound, and second as the units of length, mass, and time. For scientific and most technical purposes these units have been replaced by SI units.

Fr **1.** *Christianity. abbrev. for* **a.** Frater. [Latin: brother] **b.** Father. **2.** *the chemical symbol for* francium.

fr. *abbrev. for:* **1.** fragment. **2.** franc. **3.** from.

Fr. *abbrev. for:* **1.** *Christianity.* Father. **2.** France. **3.** French. *~***4.** the German equivalent of **Mrs.** [from German *Frau*]

Fra (frɑː) *n.* brother: a title given to an Italian monk or friar. [Italian, short for *frate* brother (in either natural or religious sense), from Latin *frāter* BROTHER]

fracas ('frækɑː) *n.* a noisy quarrel; brawl. [C18: from French, from *fracasser* to shatter, from Latin *frangere* to break, influenced by *quassāre* to shatter]

FRACP *abbrev. for* Fellow of the Royal Australasian College of Physicians.

FRACS *abbrev. for* Fellow of the Royal Australasian College of Surgeons.

fractal ('fræktəl) *Maths.* *~n.* **1.** a figure or surface generated by successive subdivisions of a simpler polygon or polyhedron, according to some iterative process. *~adj.* **2.** of, relating to, or involving such a process: *fractal geometry; fractal curve.* [C20: from Latin *frāctus* past participle of *frangere* to break]

fraction ('frækʃən) *n.* **1.** *Maths.* **a.** a ratio of two expressions or numbers other than zero. **b.** any rational number that can be expressed as the ratio of two integers, a/b, where b does not equal a, 1, or 0, and a does not equal 0. **2.** any part or subdivision: *a substantial fraction of the nation.* **3.** a small piece; fragment. **4.** *Chem.* a component of a mixture separated by a fractional process, such as fractional distillation. **5.** *Christianity.* the formal breaking of the bread in Communion. **6.** the act of breaking. *~vb.* **7.** (*tr.*) to divide. [C14: from Late Latin *fractiō* a breaking into pieces, from Latin *fractus* broken, from *frangere* to break]

fractional ('frækʃənᵊl) *adj.* **1.** relating to, containing, or constituting one or more fractions. **2.** of or denoting a process in which components of a mixture are separated by exploiting differences in their physical properties, such as boiling points, solubility, etc.: *fractional distillation; fractional crystallization.* **3.** very small or insignificant. **4.** broken up; fragmented. *~*Also called: **fractionary** ('frækʃənərɪ). —**'fractionally** *adv.*

fractional crystallization *n. Chem.* the process of separating the components of a solution on the basis of their different solubilities, by means of evaporating the solution until the least soluble component crystallizes out.

fractional currency *n.* paper or metal money of smaller denomination than the standard monetary unit.

fractional distillation *n.* **1.** the process of separating the constituents of a liquid mixture by heating it and condensing separately the components according to their different boiling points. **2.** a distillation in which the vapour is brought into contact with a countercurrent of condensed liquid to increase the purity of the final products. *~*Sometimes shortened to **distillation.**

fractionate ('frækʃə,neɪt) *vb.* **1.** to separate or cause to separate into constituents or into fractions containing concentrated constituents. **2.** (*tr.*) *Chem.* to obtain (a constituent of a mixture) by a fractional process. —**,fraction'ation** *n.* —**'fraction,ator** *n.*

fractionating column *n. Chem.* a long vertical cylinder used in fractional distillation, in which internal reflux enables separation of high and low boiling fractions to take place.

fractionize *or* **fractionise** ('frækʃə,naɪz) *vb.* to divide (a number or quantity) into fractions. —**,fractioni'zation** *or* **,fractioni'sation** *n.*

fractious ('frækʃəs) *adj.* **1.** irritable. **2.** unruly. [C18: from (obsolete) *fraction* discord + -OUS] —**'fractiously** *adv.* —**'fractiousness** *n.*

fractocumulus (,fræktəʊ'kjuːmjʊləs) *n., pl.* **-li** (-,laɪ). low ragged slightly bulbous cloud, often appearing below nimbostratus clouds during rain. Also called: **fractocumulus cloud.** [C19: from Latin *fractus* broken + CUMULUS]

fractostratus (,fræktəʊ'strɑːtəs, -'stræt-) *n., pl.* **-ti** (-taɪ). low ragged layered cloud often appearing below nimbostratus clouds during rain. [C19: from Latin *fractus* broken + STRATUS]

fracture ('fræktʃə) *n.* **1.** the act of breaking or the state of being broken. **2. a.** the breaking or cracking of a bone or the tearing of a cartilage. **b.** the resulting condition. See also **Colles' fracture, comminuted fracture, compound fracture, greenstick fracture, impacted** (sense 2), **simple fracture.** **3.** a division, split, or breach. **4.** *Mineralogy.* **a.** the characteristic appearance of the surface of a freshly broken mineral or rock. **b.** the way in which a mineral or rock naturally breaks. *~vb.* **5.** to break or cause to break; split. **6.** to break or crack (a bone) or (of a bone) to become broken or cracked. **7.** to tear (a cartilage) or (of a cartilage) to become torn. [C15: from Old French, from Latin *fractūra,* from *frangere* to break] —**'fracturable** *adj.* —**'fractural** *adj.*

frae (freɪ) *prep.* a Scot. word for **from.**

fraenum *or* **frenum** ('friːnəm) *n., pl.* **-na** (-nə). a fold of membrane or skin, such as the fold beneath the tongue, that supports an organ. [C18: from Latin: bridle]

frag (fræg) *vb.* **frags, fragging, fragged.** (*tr.*) *U.S. military slang.* to kill or wound (a fellow soldier or superior officer) deliberately with an explosive device. [C20: short for *fragmentation grenade,* as used in Vietnam] —**'fragging** *n.*

fragile ('frædʒaɪl) *adj.* **1.** able to be broken easily. **2.** in a weakened physical state. **3.** delicate; light: *a fragile touch.* **4.** slight; tenuous: *a fragile link with the past.* [C17: from Latin *fragilis,* from *frangere* to break] —**'fragilely** *adv.* —**fragility** (frə'dʒɪlɪtɪ) *or* **'fragileness** *n.*

fragile-X syndrome *n.* an inherited condition characterized by mental subnormality: affected individuals have an X-chromosome that is easily damaged under certain conditions.

fragment *n.* ('frægmənt). **1.** a piece broken off or detached: *fragments of rock.* **2.** an incomplete piece; portion: *fragments of a novel.* **3.** a scrap; morsel; bit. *~vb.* (fræg'mɛnt), *also U.S.* **fragmentize** ('frægmən,taɪz). **4.** to break or cause to break into fragments. [C15: from Latin *fragmentum*, from *frangere* to break]

fragmental (fræɡˈmɛntᵊl) *adj.* **1.** (of rocks or deposits) composed of fragments of pre-existing rocks and minerals. **2.** another word for **fragmentary.** —**fragˈmentally** *adv.*

fragmentary (ˈfræɡməntərɪ, -trɪ) *adj.* made up of fragments; disconnected; incomplete. Also: **fragmental.** —**ˈfragmentarily** *adv.* —**ˈfragmentariness** *n.*

fragmentation (ˌfræɡmɛnˈteɪʃən) *n.* **1.** the act of fragmenting or the state of being fragmented. **2.** the disintegration of norms regulating behaviour, thought, and social relationships. **3.** the steel particles of an exploded projectile. **4.** (*modifier*) of or relating to a weapon designed to explode into many small pieces, esp. as an antipersonnel weapon: *a fragmentation bomb.*

fragrance (ˈfreɪɡrəns) *or* **fragrancy** (-ɡrənsɪ) *n., pl.* **-grances** *or* **-grancies. 1.** a pleasant or sweet odour; scent; perfume. **2.** the state of being fragrant.

fragrant (ˈfreɪɡrənt) *adj.* having a pleasant or sweet smell. [C15: from Latin *frāgrāns*, from *frāgrāre* to emit a smell] —**ˈfragrantly** *adv.*

fragrant orchid *n.* another name for **scented orchid.**

frail[1] (freɪl) *adj.* **1.** physically weak and delicate. **2.** fragile: *a frail craft.* **3.** easily corrupted or tempted. [C13: from Old French *frele*, from Latin *fragilis*, FRAGILE] —**ˈfrailly** *adv.* —**ˈfrailness** *n.*

frail[2] (freɪl) *n.* **1.** a rush basket for figs or raisins. **2.** a quantity of raisins or figs equal to between 50 and 75 pounds. [C13: from Old French *fraiel*, of uncertain origin]

frailty (ˈfreɪltɪ) *n., pl.* **-ties. 1.** physical or moral weakness. **2.** (*often pl.*) a fault symptomatic of moral weakness.

fraise (freɪz) *n.* **1.** a neck ruff worn during the 16th century. **2.** a sloping or horizontal rampart of pointed stakes. **3. a.** a tool for enlarging a drill hole. **b.** a tool for cutting teeth on watch wheels. [C18: from French: mesentery of a calf, from Old French *fraiser* to remove a shell, from Latin *frendere* to crush]

Fraktur (*German* frakˈtuːr) *n.* a style of typeface, formerly used in German typesetting for many printed works. [German, from Latin *fractūra* a breaking, FRACTURE; from the curlicues that seem to interrupt the continuous line of a word]

framboesia *or U.S.* **frambesia** (fræmˈbiːzɪə) *n. Pathol.* another name for **yaws.** [C19: from New Latin, from French *framboise* raspberry; see FRAMBOISE; so called because of its raspberry-like excrescences]

framboise *French.* (frɑ̃bwaz) *n.* a brandy distilled from raspberries in the Alsace-Lorraine region. [C16: from Old French: raspberry, probably of Germanic origin]

frame (freɪm) *n.* **1.** an open structure that gives shape and support to something, such as the transverse stiffening ribs of a ship's hull or an aircraft's fuselage or the skeletal beams and uprights of a building. **2.** an enclosing case or border into which something is fitted: *the frame of a picture.* **3.** the system around which something is built up: *the frame of government.* **4.** the structure of the human body. **5.** a condition; state (esp. in the phrase **frame of mind**). **6. a.** one of a series of individual exposures on a strip of film used in making motion pictures. **b.** an individual exposure on a film used in still photography. **c.** an individual picture in a comic strip. **7. a.** a television picture scanned by one or more electron beams at a particular frequency. **b.** the area of the picture so formed. **8.** *Snooker, etc.* **a.** the wooden triangle used to set up the balls. **b.** the balls when set up. **c.** a single game finished when all the balls have been potted. U.S. and Canadian equivalent (for **a.** and **b.**): **rack. 9.** short for **cold frame. 10.** one of the sections of which a beehive is composed, esp. one designed to hold a honeycomb. **11.** a machine or part of a machine over which yarn is stretched in the production of textiles. **12.** (in language teaching, etc.) a syntactic construction with a gap in it, used for assigning words to syntactic classes by seeing which words may fill the gap. **13.** *Statistics.* an enumeration of a population for the purposes of sampling, esp. as the basis of a stratified sample. **14.** (in telecommunications, computers, etc.) one cycle of a regularly recurring number of pulses in a pulse train. **15.** *Slang.* another word for **frame-up. 16.** *Obsolete.* shape; form. ~*vb.* (*mainly tr.*) **17.** to construct by fitting parts together. **18.** to draw up the plans or basic details for; outline: *to frame a policy.* **19.** to compose, contrive, or conceive: *to frame a reply.* **20.** to provide, support, or enclose with a frame: *to frame a picture.* **21.** to form (words) with the lips, esp. silently. **22.** *Slang.* to conspire to incriminate (someone) on a false charge. **23.** *Slang.* to contrive the dishonest outcome of (a contest, match, etc.); rig. **24.** (*intr.*) *Yorkshire and northeastern English dialect.* **a.** (*usually imperative or dependent imperative*) to make an effort. **b.** to have ability. [Old English *framiae* to avail; related to Old Frisian *framia* to carry out, Old Norse *frama*] —**ˈframable** *or* **ˈframeable** *adj.* —**ˈframeless** *adj.* —**ˈframer** *n.*

frame aerial *n.* another name for **loop aerial.**

frame house *n.* a house that has a timber framework and cladding.

frame line *n. Films.* a black horizontal bar appearing between successive picture images.

frame of reference *n.* **1.** *Sociol.* a set of basic assumptions or standards that determines and sanctions behaviour. **2.** any set of planes or curves, such as the three coordinate axes, used to locate or measure movement of a point in space.

frame saw *n.* a saw with a thin blade held in a specially shaped frame. Also called: **span saw.**

frame-up *n. Slang.* **1.** a conspiracy to incriminate someone on a false charge. **2.** a plot to bring about a dishonest result, as in a contest.

framework (ˈfreɪmˌwɜːk) *n.* **1.** a structural plan or basis of a project. **2.** a structure or frame supporting or containing something. **3.** frames collectively. **4.** work such as embroidery or weaving done in or on a frame.

framing (ˈfreɪmɪŋ) *n.* **1.** a frame, framework, or system of frames. **2.** the way in which something is framed. **3.** adjustment of the longitudinal position of the film in a projector gate to secure proper vertical positioning of the picture on the screen.

franc (fræŋk; *French* frɑ̃) *n.* **1.** the standard monetary unit of France, French dependencies, and Monaco, divided into 100 centimes. **2.** the standard monetary and currency unit of Belgium and Luxembourg, divided into 100 centimes. **3.** the standard monetary and currency unit of Switzerland and Liechtenstein, divided into 100 centimes. **4.** the standard monetary and currency unit, comprising 100 centimes, of the following countries: Benin, Burkina-Faso, Burundi, Cameroon, the Central African Republic, Chad, Gabon, Guinea, the Ivory Coast, Madagascar, Mauritania, Niger, the Republic of the Congo, Senegal, Togo, Mali, and Rwanda. **5.** a Moroccan monetary unit worth one hundredth of a dirham. [C14: from Old French; from the Latin phrase *Rex Francōrum* King of the Franks, inscribed on 14th-century francs]

franchise (ˈfræntʃaɪz) *n.* **1.** (usually preceded by *the*) the right to vote, esp. for representatives in a legislative body; suffrage. **2.** any exemption, privilege, or right granted to an individual or group by a public authority, such as the right to use public property for a business. **3.** *Commerce.* authorization granted by a manufacturing enterprise to a distributor to market the manufacturer's products. **4.** the full rights of citizenship. **5.** (in marine insurance) a sum or percentage stated in a policy, below which the insurer disclaims all liability. ~*vb.* **6.** (*tr.*) *Commerce, chiefly U.S. and Canadian.* to grant (a person, firm, etc.) a franchise. **7.** an obsolete word for **enfranchise.** [C13: from Old French, from *franchir* to set free, from *franc* free; see FRANK] —**franchisement** (ˈfræntʃɪzmənt) *n.*

Franciscan (frænˈsɪskən) *n.* **a.** a member of any of several Christian religious orders of mendicant friars or nuns tracing their origins back to Saint Francis of Assisi; a Grey Friar. **b.** (*as modifier*): *a Franciscan friar.*

Francis turbine (ˈfrɑːnsɪs) *n.* a water turbine designed to produce high flow from a low head of pressure: used esp. in hydroelectric power generation. [named after J. B. *Francis* (1815–92), British-born hydraulic engineer, who invented it]

francium (ˈfrænsɪəm) *n.* an unstable radioactive element of the alkali-metal group, occurring in minute amounts in uranium ores. Symbol: Fr; atomic no.: 87; half-life of most stable isotope, ^{223}Fr: 22 minutes; valency: 1. [C20: from New Latin, from *France* + -IUM; so-called because first found in France]

Franco- (ˈfræŋkəʊ-) *combining form.* indicating France or French: *Franco-Prussian.* [from Medieval Latin *Francus*, from Late Latin: FRANK]

francolin (ˈfræŋkəʊlɪn) *n.* any African or Asian partridge of the genus *Francolinus.* [C17: from French, from Old Italian *francolino*, of unknown origin]

Franconian (fræŋˈkəʊnɪən) *n.* **1.** a group of medieval Germanic dialects spoken by the Franks in an area from N Bavaria and Alsace to the mouth of the Rhine. **Low Franconian** developed into Dutch, while **Upper Franconian** contributed to High German, of which it remains a recognizable dialect. See also **Old Low German, Old High German, Frankish.** ~*adj.* **2.** of or relating to Franconia, a medieval German duchy, the Franks, or their languages.

Francophile (ˈfræŋkəʊˌfaɪl) *or* **Francophil** (ˈfræŋkəʊfɪl) (*sometimes not cap.*) ~*n.* **1.** a person who admires France and the French. ~*adj.* **2.** marked by or possessing admiration of France and the French.

Francophobe (ˈfræŋkəʊˌfəʊb) *n.* (*sometimes not cap.*) a person who hates or despises France or its people.

Francophone (ˈfræŋkəʊˌfəʊn) (*often not cap.*) ~*n.* **1.** a person who speaks French, esp. a native speaker. ~*adj.* **2.** speaking French as a native language. **3.** using French as a lingua franca. ~Compare **Anglophone.**

franc-tireur *French.* (frɑ̃tirœr) *n.* **1.** a sniper. **2.** a guerrilla or irregular soldier. [C19: from *franc* free + *tireur* shooter, from *tirer* to shoot, of unknown origin]

franger (ˈfræŋə) *n. Austral. taboo slang.* a condom. [C20: perhaps related to FRENCH LETTER]

frangible (ˈfrændʒɪbᵊl) *adj.* breakable or fragile. [C15: from Old French, ultimately from Latin *frangere* to break] —ˌ**frangiˈbility** *or* **ˈfrangibleness** *n.*

frangipane (ˈfrændʒɪˌpeɪn) *n.* **1. a.** a pastry filled with cream and flavoured with almonds. **b.** a rich cake mixture containing ground almonds. **2.** a variant of **frangipani** (the perfume).

frangipani (ˌfrændʒɪˈpɑːnɪ) *n., pl.* **-panis** *or* **-pani. 1.** any tropical American apocynaceous shrub of the genus *Plumeria*, esp. *P. rubra*, cultivated for its waxy typically white or pink flowers, which have a sweet overpowering scent. **2.** a perfume prepared from this plant or resembling the odour of its flowers. **3. native frangipani.** *Austral.* an Australian evergreen tree, *Hymenosporum flavum,* with large fragrant yellow flowers: family *Pittosporaceae.* [C17: via French from Italian: perfume for scenting gloves, named after the Marquis Muzio *Frangipani,* 16th-century Roman nobleman who invented it]

Franglais (*French* frɑ̃glɛ) *n.* informal French containing a high proportion of words of English origin. [C20: from French *français* French + *anglais* English]

frank (fræŋk) *adj.* **1.** honest and straightforward in speech or attitude: *a frank person.* **2.** outspoken or blunt. **3.** open and avowed; undisguised: *frank interest.* **4.** an obsolete word for **free** or **generous.** ~*vb.* (*tr.*) **5.** *Chiefly Brit.* to put a mark on (a letter, parcel, etc.), either cancelling the postage stamp or in place of a stamp, ensuring free carriage. See also **postmark. 6.** to mark (a letter, parcel, etc.) with an official mark or signature, indicating the right of free delivery. **7.** to facilitate or assist (a person) to come and go, pass, or enter easily. **8.** to obtain immunity for or exempt (a person). ~*n.* **9.** an official mark or signature affixed to a letter, parcel, etc., ensuring free delivery or delivery without stamps. **10.** the privilege, issued to certain people and establishments, entitling them to delivery without postage stamps. [C13: from Old French *franc,* from Medieval Latin *francus* free; identical with FRANK (in Frankish Gaul only members of this people enjoyed full freedom)] —**'frankable** *adj.* —**'franker** *n.* —**'frankness** *n.*

Frank (fræŋk) *n.* a member of a group of West Germanic peoples who spread from the east bank of the middle Rhine into the Roman Empire in the late 4th century A.D., gradually conquering most of Gaul and Germany. The Franks achieved their greatest power under Charlemagne. [Old English *Franca;* related to Old High German *Franko;* perhaps from the name of a typical Frankish weapon (compare Old English *franca* javelin)]

frankalmoign ('fræŋkᵊl,mɔɪn) *n. English legal history.* a form of tenure by which religious bodies held lands, esp. on condition of praying for the soul of the donor. [C16: from Anglo-French *fraunke almoigne,* from *fraunke* FRANK + *almoign* church treasury, alms chest]

franked investment income *n.* dividends from one UK company received by another on which the paying company has paid corporation tax so that the receiving company has no corporation tax to pay; the tax credit included in the dividend can be set against the receiving company's advance corporation tax on its own dividends.

Frankenstein ('fræŋkɪn,staɪn) *n.* **1.** a person who creates something that brings about his ruin. **2.** Also called: **Frankenstein's monster.** a thing that destroys its creator. [C19: after Baron *Frankenstein,* who created a destructive monster from parts of corpses in the novel by Mary Shelley (1818)] —**,Franken'steinian** *adj.*

frankfurter ('fræŋk,fɜːtə) *n.* a light brown smoked sausage, made of finely minced pork or beef, often served in a bread roll. [C20: short for German *Frankfurter Wurst* sausage from *Frankfurt* (am Main), a city in central Germany]

frankincense ('fræŋkɪn,sɛns) *n.* an aromatic gum resin obtained from trees of the burseraceous genus *Boswellia,* which occur in Asia and Africa. Also called: **olibanum.** [C14: from Old French *franc* free, pure + *encens* INCENSE[1]; see FRANK]

Frankish ('fræŋkɪʃ) *n.* **1.** the ancient West Germanic language of the Franks, esp. the dialect that contributed to the vocabulary of modern French. See also **Franconian, Old High German.** ~*adj.* **2.** of or relating to the Franks or their language.

franklin ('fræŋklɪn) *n.* (in 14th- and 15th-century England) a substantial landholder of free but not noble birth. [C13: from Anglo-French *fraunclein,* from Old French *franc* free, on the model of CHAMBERLAIN]

franklinite ('fræŋklɪ,naɪt) *n.* a black mineral consisting of an oxide of iron, manganese, and zinc: a source of iron and zinc. Formula: $(Fe,Mn,Zn)(Fe,Mn)_2O_4$. [C19: from *Franklin,* New Jersey, where it is found, + -ITE[1]]

frankly ('fræŋklɪ) *adv.* **1.** (*sentence modifier*) in truth; to be honest: *frankly, I can't bear him.* **2.** in a frank manner.

frankpledge ('fræŋk,plɛdʒ) *n.* (in medieval England) **1.** the corporate responsibility of members of a tithing for the good behaviour of each other. **2.** a member of a tithing. **3.** a tithing itself. [C15: via Anglo-French from Old French *franc* free (see FRANK) + *plege* PLEDGE]

frantic ('fræntɪk) *adj.* **1.** distracted with fear, pain, joy, etc. **2.** marked by or showing frenzy: *frantic efforts.* **3.** *Archaic.* insane. [C14: from Old French *frenetique,* from Latin *phrenēticus* mad, FRENETIC] —**'frantically** or **'franticly** *adv.* —**'franticness** *n.*

frap (fræp) *vb.* **fraps, frapping, frapped.** (*tr.*) *Nautical.* to lash down or together. [C14: from Old French *fraper* to hit, probably of imitative origin]

frappé ('fræpeɪ; *French* frape) *n.* **1.** a drink consisting of a liqueur, etc., poured over crushed ice. ~*adj.* **2.** (*postpositive*) (esp. of drinks) chilled; iced. [C19: from French, from *frapper* to strike, hence, chill; see FRAP]

frass (fræs) *n.* excrement or other refuse left by insects and insect larvae. [C19: from German, from *fressen* to devour]

fratchy ('frætʃɪ) *adj.* **fratchier, fratchiest.** *Informal.* quarrelsome; irritable. [C19: from obsolete *fratch* to make a harsh noise; perhaps of imitative origin]

frater[1] ('freɪtə) *n.* a mendicant friar or a lay brother in a monastery or priory. [C16: from Latin: BROTHER]

frater[2] ('freɪtə) *n. Archaic.* a refectory. [C13: from Old French *fraiteur,* aphetic variant of *refreitor,* from Late Latin *rēfectōrium* REFECTORY]

fraternal (frə'tɜːnᵊl) *adj.* **1.** of or suitable to a brother; brotherly. **2.** of or relating to a fraternity. **3.** designating either or both of a pair of twins of the same or opposite sex that developed from two separate fertilized ova. Compare **identical** (sense 3). [C15: from Latin *frāternus,* from *frāter* brother] —**fra'ternalism** *n.* —**fra'ternally** *adv.*

fraternity (frə'tɜːnɪtɪ) *n., pl.* **-ties. 1.** a body of people united in interests, aims, etc.: *the teaching fraternity.* **2.** brotherhood. **3.** *U.S. and Canadian.* a secret society joined by male students, usually functioning as a social club and bearing a name composed of Greek letters.

fraternize or **fraternise** ('frætə,naɪz) *vb.* **1.** (*intr.;* often foll. by *with*) to associate on friendly terms. **2.** (*tr.*) *Rare.* to cause fraternal relations between. —**,fraterni'zation** or **,fraterni'sation** *n.* —**'frater,nizer** or **'frater,niser** *n.*

fratricide ('frætrɪ,saɪd, 'freɪ-) *n.* **1.** the act of killing one's brother. **2.** a person who kills his brother. **3.** *Military.* the destruction of or interference with a nuclear missile before it can strike its target caused by the earlier explosion of a warhead at a nearby target. [C15: from Latin *frātricīda;* see FRATER[1], -CIDE] —**,fratri'cidal** *adj.*

Frau (fraʊ) *n., pl.* **Frauen** ('fraʊən) or **Fraus.** a married German woman: usually used as a title equivalent to *Mrs* and sometimes extended to older unmarried women. [from Old High German *frouwa;* related to Dutch *vrouw*]

fraud (frɔːd) *n.* **1.** deliberate deception, trickery, or cheating intended to gain an advantage. **2.** an act or instance of such deception. **3.** something false or spurious: *his explanation was a fraud.* **4.** *Informal.* a person who acts in a false or deceitful way. [C14: from Old French *fraude,* from Latin *fraus* deception]

Fraud Squad *n.* (in Britain) the department of a police force that is concerned with criminal fraud.

fraudulent ('frɔːdjʊlənt) *adj.* **1.** acting with or having the intent to deceive. **2.** relating to or proceeding from fraud or dishonest action. [C15: from Latin *fraudulentus* deceitful] —**'fraudulence** or **'fraudulency** *n.* —**'fraudulently** *adv.*

fraughan ('frɒhən) *n.* an Irish word for **whortleberry** (senses 1, 2). [from Irish Gaelic fraochán, diminutive of *fraoch* heather]

fraught (frɔːt) *adj.* **1.** (*usually postpositive* and foll. by *with*) filled or charged; attended: *a venture fraught with peril.* **2.** *Informal.* showing or producing tension or anxiety: *she looks rather fraught; a fraught situation.* **3.** *Archaic.* (*usually postpositive* and foll. by *with*) freighted. ~*n.* **4.** an obsolete word for **freight.** [C14: from Middle Dutch *vrachten,* from *vracht* FREIGHT]

Fräulein (*German* 'frɔylain; *English* 'frɔːlaɪn, 'fraʊ-) *n., pl.* **-lein** or *English* **-leins.** an unmarried German woman: often used as a title equivalent to *Miss.* Abbrev.: **Frl.** [from Middle High German *vrouwelīn,* diminutive of *vrouwe* lady]

Fraunhofer lines ('fraʊn,həʊfə) *pl. n.* a set of dark lines appearing in the continuous emission spectrum of the sun. It is caused by the absorption of light of certain wavelengths coming from the hotter region of the sun by elements in the cooler outer atmosphere. [named after Joseph von *Fraunhofer* (1787–1826), German physicist]

fraxinella (,fræksɪ'nɛlə) *n.* another name for **gas plant.** [C17: from New Latin: a little ash tree, from Latin *frāxinus* ash]

fray[1] (freɪ) *n.* **1.** a noisy quarrel. **2.** a fight or brawl. **3.** an archaic word for **fright.** ~*vb. Archaic.* **4.** (*intr.*) to fight or disturb the peace. **5.** (*tr.*) to frighten. [C14: short for AFFRAY]

fray[2] (freɪ) *vb.* **1.** to wear or cause to wear away into tatters or loose threads, esp. at an edge or end. **2.** to make or become strained or irritated. **3.** to rub or chafe (another object) or (of two objects) to rub against one another. ~*n.* **4.** a frayed place, as in cloth. [C14: from French *frayer* to rub, from Latin *fricāre;* see FRICTION, FRIABLE]

frazil ('freɪzɪl) *n.* small pieces of ice that form in water moving turbulently enough to prevent the formation of a sheet of ice. [C19: from Canadian French *frasil,* from French *fraisil* cinders, ultimately from Latin *fax* torch]

frazzle ('fræzᵊl) *vb.* **1.** *Informal.* to make or become exhausted or weary; tire out. **2.** a less common word for **fray**[2] (sense 1). ~*n.* **3.** *Informal.* the state of being frazzled or exhausted. **4.** a frayed end or remnant. **5. to a frazzle.** *Informal.* absolutely; completely (esp. in the phrase **burnt to a frazzle**). [C19: probably from Middle English *faselen* to fray, from *fasel* fringe; influenced by FRAY[2]]

FRCM (in Britain) *abbrev. for* Fellow of the Royal College of Music.

FRCO (in Britain) *abbrev. for* Fellow of the Royal College of Organists.

FRCP (in Britain) *abbrev. for* Fellow of the Royal College of Physicians.

FRCS (in Britain) *abbrev. for* Fellow of the Royal College of Surgeons.

FRCVS (in Britain) *abbrev. for* Fellow of the Royal College of Veterinary Surgeons.

freak[1] (fri:k) *n.* **1.** a person, animal, or plant that is abnormal or deformed; monstrosity. **2. a.** an object, event, etc., that is abnormal or extremely unusual. **b.** (*as modifier*): *a freak storm.* **3.** a personal whim or caprice. **4.** *Informal.* a person who acts or dresses in a markedly unconventional or strange way. **5.** *Informal.* a person who is obsessed with something specified: *a jazz freak.* ~*vb.* **6.** See **freak out.** [C16: of obscure origin]

freak[2] (fri:k) *Rare.* ~*n.* **1.** a fleck or streak of colour. ~*vb.* **2.** (*tr.*) to streak with colour; variegate. [C17: from earlier *freaked,* probably coined by Milton, based on STREAK + obsolete *freckt* freckled; see FRECKLE]

freakish ('fri:kɪʃ) *adj.* **1.** of, related to, or characteristic of a freak; abnormal or unusual. **2.** unpredictable or changeable: *freakish weather.* —'**freakishly** *adv.* —'**freakishness** *n.*

freak out *vb.* (*adv.*) to be or cause to be in a heightened emotional state, such as that of anger, excitement, etc.

freaky ('fri:kɪ) *adj.* **freakier, freakiest. 1.** *Slang.* strange; unconventional; bizarre. **2.** another word for **freakish.** —'**freakily** *adv.* —'**freakiness** *n.*

freckle ('frɛkᵊl) *n.* **1.** a small brownish spot on the skin: a localized deposit of the pigment melanin, developed by exposure to sunlight. Technical name: **lentigo. 2.** any small area of discoloration; a spot. **3.** *Austral. slang.* the anus. ~*vb.* **4.** to mark or become marked with freckles or spots. [C14: from Old Norse *freknur* freckles; related to Swedish *fräkne,* Danish *fregne*] —'**freckled** *or* '**freckly** *adj.*

free (fri:) *adj.* **freer, freest. 1.** able to act at will; not under compulsion or restraint. **2. a.** having personal rights or liberty; not enslaved or confined. **b.** (*as n.*): *land of the free.* **3.** (*often postpositive* and foll. by *from*) not subject (to) or restricted (by some regulation, constraint, etc.); exempt: *a free market; free from pain.* **4.** (of a country, etc.) autonomous or independent. **5.** exempt from external direction or restriction; not forced or induced: *free will.* **6.** not subject to conventional constraints: *free verse.* **7.** (of jazz) totally improvised, with no preset melodic, harmonic, or rhythmic basis. **8.** not exact or literal: *a free translation.* **9.** costing nothing; provided without charge: *free entertainment.* **10.** *Law.* (of property) **a.** not subject to payment of rent or performance of services; freehold. **b.** not subject to any burden or charge, such as a mortgage or lien; unencumbered. **11.** (*postpositive;* often foll. by *of* or *with*) ready or generous in using or giving; liberal; lavish: *free with advice.* **12.** unrestrained by propriety or good manners; licentious. **13.** not occupied or in use; available: *a free cubicle.* **14.** not occupied or busy; without previous engagements: *I'm not free until Wednesday.* **15.** open or available to all; public. **16.** without charge to the subscriber or user: *freepost; freephone.* **17.** not fixed or joined; loose: *the free end of a chain.* **18.** without obstruction or impediment: *free passage.* **19.** *Chem.* chemically uncombined: *free nitrogen.* **20.** *Phonetics.* denoting a vowel that can occur in an open syllable, such as the vowel in *see* as opposed to the vowel in *cat.* **21.** *Grammar.* denoting a morpheme that can occur as a separate word. Compare **bound**[1] (sense 9). **22.** *Logic.* denoting an occurrence of a variable not bound by a quantifier. Compare **bound**[1] (sense 10). **23.** (of some materials, such as certain kinds of stone) easily worked. **24.** *Nautical.* (of the wind) blowing from the quarter. **25. free and easy.** casual or tolerant; easy-going. **26. for free.** *Nonstandard.* without charge or cost. **27. make free with.** to take liberties with; behave too familiarly towards. ~*adv.* **28.** in a free manner; freely. **29.** without charge or cost. **30.** *Nautical.* with the wind blowing from the quarter: *a yacht sailing free.* ~*vb.* **frees, freeing, freed.** (*tr.*) **31.** to set at liberty; release. **32.** to remove obstructions, attachments, or impediments from; disengage. **33.** (often foll. by *of* or *from*) to relieve or rid (of obstacles, pain, etc.). [Old English *frēo;* related to Old Saxon, Old High German *frī,* Gothic *freis* free, Sanskrit *priya* dear] —'**freer** *n.* —'**freely** *adv.* —'**freeness** *n.*

-free *adj. combining form.* free from: *trouble-free; lead-free petrol.*

free agent *n.* a person whose actions are not constrained by others.

free alongside ship *adj.* (of a shipment of goods) delivered to the dock without charge to the buyer, but excluding the cost of loading onto the vessel. Compare **free on board.** Abbrevs.: **FAS, f.a.s.** Also: **free alongside vessel.**

free association *n.* **1.** *Psychoanal.* a method of exploring a person's unconscious by eliciting words and thoughts that are associated with key words provided by a psychoanalyst. **2.** a spontaneous mental process whereby ideas, words, or images suggest other ideas, etc., in a nonlogical chain reaction.

freebase ('fri:ˌbeɪs) *vb. Slang.* to refine (cocaine) for smoking.

freebie ('fri:bɪ) *Slang.* ~*n.* **1.** something provided without charge. ~*adj.* **2.** without charge; free.

freeboard ('fri:ˌbɔ:d) *n.* the space or distance between the deck of a vessel and the waterline.

freeboot ('fri:ˌbu:t) *vb.* (*intr.*) to act as a freebooter; pillage.

freebooter ('fri:ˌbu:tə) *n.* **1.** a person, such as a pirate, living from plunder. **2.** *Informal.* a person, esp. an itinerant, who seeks pleasure, wealth, etc., without responsibility. [C16: from Dutch *vrijbuiter,* from *vrijbuit* booty; see FILIBUSTER]

freeborn ('fri:ˌbɔ:n) *adj.* **1.** not born in slavery. **2.** of, relating to, or suitable for people not born in slavery.

Free Church *n. Chiefly Brit.* **a.** any Protestant Church, esp. the Presbyterian, other than the Established Church. **b.** (*as modifier*): *Free-Church attitudes.*

free city *n.* a sovereign or autonomous city; city-state.

free climbing *n. Mountaineering.* climbing without using pitons, étriers, etc., as direct aids to ascent, but using ropes, belays, etc., at discretion for security. Compare **aid climbing.**

free coinage *n. U.S.* coinage of bullion brought to the mint by any individual.

free companion *n.* (in medieval Europe) a member of a company of mercenary soldiers.

free company *n. European history.* a band of mercenary soldiers during the Middle Ages.

freedman ('fri:dˌmæn) *n., pl.* **-men.** a man who has been freed from slavery. —'**freedˌwoman** *fem. n.*

freedom ('fri:dəm) *n.* **1.** personal liberty, as from slavery, bondage, serfdom, etc. **2.** liberation or deliverance, as from confinement or bondage. **3.** the quality or state of being free, esp. to enjoy political and civil liberties. **4.** (usually foll. by *from*) the state of being without something unpleasant or bad; exemption or immunity: *freedom from taxation.* **5.** the right or privilege of unrestricted use or access: *the freedom of a city.* **6.** autonomy, self-government, or independence. **7.** the power or liberty to order one's own actions. **8.** *Philosophy.* the quality, esp. of the will or the individual, of not being totally constrained; able to choose between alternative actions in identical circumstances. **9.** ease or frankness of manner; candour: *she talked with complete freedom.* **10.** excessive familiarity of manner; boldness. **11.** ease and grace, as of movement; lack of effort. [Old English *frēodōm*]

freedom fighter *n.* a militant revolutionary.

freedom of the seas *n. International law.* **1.** the right of ships of all nations to sail the high seas in peacetime. **2.** (in wartime) the immunity accorded to neutral ships from attack. **3.** the exclusive jurisdiction possessed by a state over its own ships sailing the high seas in peacetime.

freedom rider *n. U.S.* a person who participated, esp. in the 1960s, in an organized tour, usually by public transport in the South, in order to protest against racialism and put federal laws on integration to the test.

free electron *n.* any electron that is not attached to an ion, atom, or molecule and is free to move under the influence of an applied electric or magnetic field.

free energy *n.* a thermodynamic property that expresses the capacity of a system to perform work under certain conditions. See **Gibbs function, Helmholtz function.**

free enterprise *n.* an economic system in which commercial organizations compete for profit with little state control.

free fall *n.* **1.** free descent of a body in which the gravitational force is the only force acting on it. **2.** the part of a parachute descent before the parachute opens.

free flight *n.* the flight of a rocket, missile, etc., when its engine has ceased to produce thrust.

free-floating *adj.* unattached or uncommitted, as to a cause, a party, etc. —ˌ**free-'floater** *n.*

free-floating anxiety *n. Psychiatry.* chronic anxiety occurring for no identifiable cause.

Freefone ('fri:ˌfəʊn) *n. Brit. trademark.* a system of telephone use in which the cost of calls in response to an advertisement is borne by the advertiser.

free-for-all *n. Informal.* a disorganized brawl or argument, usually involving all those present.

free form *Arts.* ~*n.* **1.** an irregular flowing shape, often used in industrial or fabric design. ~*adj.* **free-form. 2.** freely flowing, spontaneous.

free gift *n.* something given away, esp. as an incentive to a purchaser.

free gold *n.* **1.** gold, uncombined with other minerals, found in a pure state. **2.** *U.S.* the excess of gold held by the Federal Reserve Banks over the legal reserve.

free hand *n.* **1.** unrestricted freedom to act (esp. in the phrase **give (someone) a free hand**). ~*adj., adv.* **freehand. 2.** (done) by hand without the use of guiding instruments: *a freehand drawing.*

free-handed *adj.* generous or liberal; unstinting. —ˌ**free-'handedly** *adv.* —ˌ**free-'handedness** *n.*

free-hearted *adj.* frank and spontaneous; open; generous. —ˌ**free-'heartedly** *adv.* —ˌ**free-'heartedness** *n.*

freehold ('fri:ˌhəʊld) *Property law.* ~*n.* **1. a.** tenure by which land is held in fee simple, fee tail, or for life. **b.** an estate held by such tenure. ~*adj.* **2.** relating to or having the nature of freehold.

freeholder ('fri:ˌhəʊldə) *n. Property law.* a person in possession of a freehold building or estate in land.

free house *n. Brit.* a public house not bound to sell only one brewer's products.

free kick *n. Soccer.* a place kick awarded for a foul or infringement, either direct, from which a goal may be scored, or indirect, from which the ball must be touched by at least one other player for a goal to be allowed.

free labour *n.* **1.** the labour of workers who are not members of trade unions. **2.** such workers collectively.

freelance ('friːˌlɑːns) *n.* **1. a.** Also called: **'freeˌlancer.** a self-employed person, esp. a writer or artist, who is not employed continuously but hired to do specific assignments. **b.** (*as modifier*): *a freelance journalist.* **2.** a person, esp. a politician, who supports several causes or parties without total commitment to any one. **3.** (in medieval Europe) a mercenary soldier or adventurer. ~*vb.* **4.** to work as a freelance on (an assignment, etc.). ~*adv.* **5.** as a freelance. [C19 (in sense 3): later applied to politicians, writers, etc.]

free list *n.* **1.** *Commerce, chiefly U.S.* a list of commodities not subject to tariffs. **2.** a list of people admitted free.

free-living *adj.* **1.** given to ready indulgence of the appetites. **2.** (of animals and plants) not parasitic; existing independently. —ˌ**free-'liver** *n.*

freeload ('friːˌləʊd) *vb.* (*intr.*) *Slang.* to act as a freeloader; sponge.

freeloader ('friːˌləʊdə) *n. Slang.* a person who habitually depends on the charity of others for food, shelter, etc. —'**freeˌloading** *n.*

free love *n.* the practice of sexual relationships without fidelity to a single partner or without formal or legal ties.

freeman ('friːmən) *n., pl.* **-men. 1.** a person who is not a slave or in bondage. **2.** a person who enjoys political and civil liberties; citizen. **3.** a person who enjoys a privilege or franchise, such as the freedom of a city.

free market *n.* **a.** an economic system that allows supply and demand to regulate prices, wages, etc., rather than government policy. **b.** (*as modifier*): *a free-market economy.*

freemartin ('friːˌmɑːtɪn) *n.* the female of a pair of twin calves of unlike sex that is imperfectly developed and sterile, probably due to the influence of the male hormones of its twin during development in the uterus. [C17: of uncertain origin]

freemason ('friːˌmeɪsᵊn) *n. Medieval history.* a member of a guild of itinerant skilled stonemasons, who had a system of secret signs and passwords with which they recognized each other. —**freemasonic** (ˌfriːmə'sɒnɪk) *adj.*

Freemason ('friːˌmeɪsᵊn) *n.* a member of the widespread secret order, constituted in London in 1717, of **Free and Accepted Masons,** pledged to brotherly love, faith, and charity. Sometimes shortened to **Mason.** —**Freemasonic** (ˌfriːmə'sɒnɪk) *adj.*

freemasonry ('friːˌmeɪsᵊnrɪ) *n.* natural or tacit sympathy and understanding.

Freemasonry ('friːˌmeɪsᵊnrɪ) *n.* **1.** the institutions, rites, practices, etc., of Freemasons. **2.** Freemasons collectively.

free on board *adj.* (of a shipment of goods) delivered on board ship or other carrier without charge to the buyer. Compare **free alongside ship.** Abbrevs.: **FOB, f.o.b.**

free on rail *adj.* (of a consignment of goods) delivered to a railway station and loaded onto a train without charge to the buyer. Abbrevs.: **FOR, f.o.r.**

free port *n.* **1.** a port open to all commercial vessels on equal terms. **2.** Also called: **free zone.** a zone adjoining a port that permits the duty-free entry of foreign goods intended for re-export.

Freepost ('friːˌpəʊst) *n. Brit. trademark.* a method of postage by which the cost of replies to an advertisement is borne by the advertiser.

free radical *n.* an atom or group of atoms containing at least one unpaired electron and existing for a brief period of time before reacting to produce a stable molecule. Sometimes shortened to **radical.** Compare **group** (sense 10).

free-range *adj. Chiefly Brit.* kept or produced in natural non-intensive conditions: *free-range hens; free-range eggs.*

free recall *n. Psychol.* the recollection of the members of a list of items without regard to their serial order.

free-running *adj.* **1.** (of a mechanism, material, etc.) moving smoothly and uninterruptedly. **2.** *Electronics.* of or relating to a periodic signal that is not synchronized to a timing source: *free-running interference produces moving patterns on a television screen.*

free-select *vb.* (*tr.*) *Austral. history.* to select (areas of crown land) and acquire the freehold by a series of annual payments. —ˌ**free-se'lection** *n.* —ˌ**free-se'lector** *n.*

freesheet ('friːˌʃiːt) *n.* a newspaper that is distributed free, paid for by its advertisers. Also called: **giveaway.**

freesia ('friːzɪə, 'friːʒə) *n.* any iridaceous plant of the genus *Freesia,* of southern Africa, cultivated for their white, yellow, or pink tubular fragrant flowers. [C19: New Latin, named after F. H. T. *Freese* (died 1876), German physician]

free silver *n.* the unlimited minting of silver coins, esp. when at a fixed ratio to gold.

free skating *n.* either the short programme of specified movements or the long programme chosen by a skater in a figure-skating competition.

free space *n.* a region that has no gravitational and electromagnetic fields: used as an absolute standard. Also called (no longer in technical usage): **vacuum.**

free speech *n.* the right to express one's opinions publicly.

free-spoken *adj.* speaking frankly or without restraint. —ˌ**free-'spokenly** *adv.* —ˌ**free-'spokenness** *n.*

freestanding (ˌfriː'stændɪŋ) *adj.* **1.** standing apart; not attached to or supported by another object. **2.** (in systemic grammar) denoting a clause that can stand alone as a sentence; denoting or being a main clause. Compare **bound**[1] (sense 9b).

freestone ('friːˌstəʊn) *n.* **1. a.** any fine-grained stone, esp. sandstone or limestone, that can be cut and worked in any direction without breaking. **b.** (*as modifier*): *a freestone house.* **2.** *Botany.* **a.** a fruit, such as a peach, in which the flesh separates readily from the stone. **b.** (*as modifier*): *a freestone peach.* Compare **clingstone.**

freestyle ('friːˌstaɪl) *n.* **1.** a competition or race, as in swimming, in which each participant may use a style of his or her choice instead of a specified style. **2. a. International freestyle.** an amateur style of wrestling with an agreed set of rules. **b.** Also called: **all-in wrestling.** a style of professional wrestling with no internationally agreed set of rules. **3.** a series of acrobatics performed in skiing, etc. **4.** (*as modifier*): *a freestyle event.*

free-swimming *adj.* (of aquatic animals or larvae) not sessile or attached to any object and therefore able to swim freely in the water. —ˌ**free-'swimmer** *n.*

freethinker (ˌfriː'θɪŋkə) *n.* a person who forms his ideas and opinions independently of authority or accepted views, esp. in matters of religion. —ˌ**free'thinking** *n., adj.*

free thought *n.* thought unrestrained and uninfluenced by dogma or authority, esp. in religious matters.

free throw *n. Basketball.* an unimpeded shot at the basket from the **free-throw line,** given for a technical fault (one free shot) or a foul (two free shots).

free trade *n.* **1.** international trade that is free of such government interference as import quotas, export subsidies, protective tariffs, etc. Compare **protection** (sense 3). **2.** *Archaic.* illicit trade; smuggling.

free-trader *n.* **1.** a person who supports or advocates free trade. **2.** *Archaic.* a smuggler or smuggling vessel.

free verse *n.* unrhymed verse without a metrical pattern.

free vote *n. Chiefly Brit.* a parliamentary division in which members are not constrained by a party whip.

freeway ('friːˌweɪ) *n. U.S.* **1.** another name for **expressway. 2.** a major road that can be used without paying a toll.

freewheel (ˌfriː'wiːl) *n.* **1.** a ratchet device in the rear hub of a bicycle wheel that permits the wheel to rotate freely while the pedals are stationary. **2.** a device in the transmission of some vehicles that automatically disengages the drive shaft when it rotates more rapidly than the engine shaft, so that the drive shaft can turn freely. ~*vb.* **3.** (*intr.*) to coast in a vehicle or on a bicycle using the freewheel.

freewheeling (ˌfriː'wiːlɪŋ) *adj.* **1.** relating to, operating as, or having a freewheel; coasting. **2.** *Informal, chiefly U.S. and Canadian.* free of restraints; carefree or uninhibited.

free will *n.* **1. a.** the apparent human ability to make choices that are not externally determined. **b.** the doctrine that such human freedom of choice is not illusory. Compare **determinism. c.** (*as modifier*): *a free-will decision.* **2.** the ability to make a choice without coercion: *he left of his own free will: I did not influence him.*

Free World *n.* **the.** the non-Communist countries collectively, esp. those that are actively anti-Communist.

freeze (friːz) *vb.* **freezes, freezing, froze** (frəʊz), **frozen** ('frəʊzᵊn). **1.** to change (a liquid) into a solid as a result of a reduction in temperature, or (of a liquid) to solidify in this way, esp. to convert or be converted into ice. **2.** (when *intr.*, sometimes foll. by *over* or *up*) to cover, clog, or harden with ice, or become so covered, clogged, or hardened: *the lake froze over last week.* **3.** to fix fast or become fixed (to something) because of the action of frost. **4.** (*tr.*) to preserve (food) by subjection to extreme cold, as in a freezer. **5.** to feel or cause to feel the sensation or effects of extreme cold. **6.** to die or cause to die of frost or extreme cold. **7.** to become or cause to become paralysed, fixed, or motionless, esp. through fear, shock, etc.: *he froze in his tracks.* **8.** (*tr.*) to cause (moving film) to stop at a particular frame. **9.** to decrease or cause to decrease in animation or vigour. **10.** to make or become formal, haughty, etc., in manner. **11.** (*tr.*) to fix (prices, incomes, etc.) at a particular level, usually by government direction. **12.** (*tr.*) to forbid by law the exchange, liquidation, or collection of (loans, assets, etc.). **13.** (*tr.*) to prohibit the manufacture, sale, or use of (something specified). **14.** (*tr.*) to stop (a process) at a particular stage of development. **15.** (*tr.*) *Informal.* to render (tissue or a part of the body) insensitive, as by the application or injection of a local anaesthetic. **16.** (*intr.*; foll. by *onto*) *Informal, chiefly U.S.* to cling. ~*n.* **17.** the act of freezing or state of being frozen. **18.** *Meteorol.* a spell of temperatures below freezing point, usually over a wide area. **19.** the fixing of incomes, prices, etc., by legislation. **20.** another word for **frost.** ~*sentence substitute.* **21.** *Chiefly U.S.* a command to stop still instantly or risk being shot. [Old English *frēosan;* related to Old Norse *frjōsa,* Old High German *friosan,* Latin *prūrīre* to itch; see FROST] —'**freezable** *adj.*

freeze-dry *vb.* **-dries, -drying, -dried.** (*tr.*) to preserve (a substance) by rapid freezing and subsequently drying in a vacuum.

freeze-frame *n.* **1.** *Films, television.* a single frame of a film repeated to give an effect like a still photograph. **2.** *Video.* a single frame of a video recording viewed as a still by stopping the tape.

freeze out *vb.* (*tr., adv.*) *Informal.* to force out or exclude, as by unfriendly behaviour, boycotting, etc.

freezer ('friːzə) *n.* **1.** Also called: **deepfreeze.** a device that freezes or chills, esp. an insulated cold-storage cabinet for long-term storage of perishable foodstuffs. **2.** a former name for a **refrigerator.**

freeze-up *n. Informal.* **1.** a period of freezing or extremely cold weather. **2.** *U.S., Canadian.* **a.** the freezing of lakes, rivers, and topsoil in autumn or early winter. **b.** the time of year when this occurs.

freezing mixture *n.* a mixture of two substances, usually salt and ice, to give a temperature below 0°C.

freezing point *n.* the temperature below which a liquid turns into a solid. It is equal to the melting point.

freezing works *n. Austral. and N.Z.* a slaughterhouse at which animal carcasses are frozen for export. See also **chain** (sense 9), **chamber** (sense 9).

free zone *n.* an area at a port where certain customs restrictions are not implemented. See also **free port.**

F region *n.* the highest region of the ionosphere, extending from a height of about 150 kilometres to about 1000 kilometres. It contains the highest proportion of free electrons and is the most useful region for long-range radio transmission. Also called: **Appleton layer.** See also **ionosphere.**

freight (freɪt) *n.* **1. a.** commercial transport that is slower and cheaper than express. **b.** the price charged for such transport. **c.** goods transported by this means. **d.** (*as modifier*): *freight insurance; freight transport.* **2.** *Chiefly Brit.* a ship's cargo or part of it. ~*vb.* (*tr.*) **3.** to load with goods for transport. **4.** *Chiefly U.S. and Canadian.* to convey commercially as or by freight. **5.** to load or burden; charge. [C16: from Middle Dutch *vrecht;* related to French *fret,* Spanish *flete,* Portuguese *frete*] —**'freightless** *adj.*

freightage ('freɪtɪdʒ) *n.* **1.** the commercial conveyance of goods. **2.** the goods so transported. **3.** the price charged for such conveyance.

freighter ('freɪtə) *n.* **1.** a ship or aircraft designed for transporting cargo. **2.** a person concerned with the loading or chartering of a ship.

freightliner ('freɪtˌlaɪnə) *n.* **1.** *Trademark.* a goods train carrying containers that can be transferred onto lorries or ships. **2.** (*cap.*) *Trademark.* a containerized transportation service involving both rail and road, operated by British Rail.

freight ton *n.* the full name for **ton**[1] (sense 4).

fremd (frɛmd, freɪmd) *adj. Archaic.* alien or strange. [Old English *fremde;* related to Old High German *fremidi*]

fremitus ('frɛmɪtəs) *n., pl.* **-tus.** *Med.* a vibration felt by the hand when placed on a part of the body, esp. the chest, or detected by auscultation, when the patient is speaking or coughing. [C19: from Latin: a roaring sound, a humming, from *fremere* to make a low roaring, murmur]

French (frɛntʃ) *n.* **1.** the official language of France: also an official language of Switzerland, Belgium, Canada, and certain other countries. It is the native language of approximately 70 million people; also used for diplomacy. Historically, French is an Indo-European language belonging to the Romance group. See also **Old French, Anglo-French.** **2. the French.** (*functioning as pl.*) the natives, citizens, or inhabitants of France collectively. **3.** See **French vermouth.** ~*adj.* **4.** relating to, denoting, or characteristic of France, the French, or their language. **5.** (in Canada) of or relating to French Canadians. [Old English *Frencisc* French, Frankish; see FRANK] —**'Frenchness** *n.*

French bean *n.* **1.** a small twining bushy or annual bean plant, *Phaseolus vulgaris,* with white or lilac flowers and slender green edible pods. **2.** the pod of this plant. See also **haricot.** ~Also called: **dwarf bean, kidney bean.**

French bread *n.* white bread in a long slender loaf that is made from a water dough and has a crisp brown crust.

French bulldog *n.* a small stocky breed of dog with a sleek coat, usually brindled or pied, a large square head, and large erect rounded ears.

French Canadian *n.* **1.** a Canadian citizen whose native language is French. ~*adj.* **French-Canadian.** **2.** of or relating to French Canadians or their language.

French chalk *n.* a compact variety of talc used to mark cloth or remove grease stains from materials.

French cricket *n.* a child's game resembling cricket, in which the batsman's legs are used as the wicket.

French cuff *n.* a double cuff formed by a backward fold of the material.

French curve *n.* a thin plastic sheet with profiles of several curves, used by draughtsmen for drawing curves.

French doors *pl. n.* the U.S. and Canadian name for **French windows.**

French dressing *n.* a salad dressing made from oil and vinegar with seasonings; vinaigrette.

French fact *n.* (in Canada) the presence of French Canada as a distinct cultural force within Confederation.

French Foreign Legion *n.* a unit of the French Army serving outside France, esp. formerly in French North African colonies. It is largely recruited from foreigners.

French fried potatoes *pl. n.* a more formal name for **chips.** Also called (U.S. and Canadian): **French fries.**

French heel *n.* a fairly high and narrow-waisted heel on women's shoes. —**ˌFrench-'heeled** *adj.*

French horn *n. Music.* a valved brass instrument with a funnel-shaped mouthpiece and a tube of conical bore coiled into a spiral. It is a transposing instrument in F. Range: about three and a half octaves upwards from B on the second leger line below the bass staff. See **horn.**

Frenchify ('frɛntʃɪˌfaɪ) *vb.* **-fies, -fying, -fied.** *Informal.* to make or become French in appearance, behaviour, etc. —**ˌFrenchifi'cation** *n.*

French kiss *n.* a kiss involving insertion of the tongue into the partner's mouth.

French knickers *pl. n.* women's wide-legged underpants.

French knot *n.* an ornamental stitch made by looping the thread three or four times around the needle before putting it into the fabric.

French leave *n.* an unauthorized or unannounced absence or departure. [C18: alluding to a custom in France of leaving without saying goodbye to one's host or hostess]

French letter *n. Brit.* a slang term for **condom.**

French lilac *n.* another name for **goat's-rue** (sense 1).

Frenchman ('frɛntʃmən) *n., pl.* **-men.** a native, citizen, or inhabitant of France. —**'FrenchˌWoman** *fem. n.*

French mustard *n.* a mild mustard paste made with vinegar rather than water.

French navy *n.* **a.** a dark dull navy blue. **b.** (*as adj.*): *a French-navy dress.*

French pastry *n.* a rich pastry made esp. from puff pastry and filled with cream, fruit, etc.

French pleat *or* **roll** *n.* a woman's hair style with the hair gathered at the back into a cylindrical roll.

French polish *n.* **1.** a varnish for wood consisting of shellac dissolved in alcohol. **2.** the gloss finish produced by repeated applications of this polish.

French-polish *vb.* to treat with French polish or give a French polish (to).

French seam *n.* a seam in which the edges are not visible.

French sixth *n.* (in musical harmony) an augmented sixth chord having a major third and an augmented fourth between the root and the augmented sixth.

French stick *n. Brit.* a long straight notched stick loaf. Also called: **French stick loaf.**

French toast *n.* **1.** *Brit.* toast cooked on one side only. **2.** bread dipped in beaten egg and lightly fried.

French vermouth *n.* a dry aromatic white wine. Also called: **French.**

French windows *pl. n.* (*sometimes sing.*) *Brit.* a pair of casement windows extending to floor level and opening onto a balcony, garden, etc. U.S. and Canadian name: **French doors.**

Frenchy ('frɛntʃɪ) *adj.* **1.** *Informal.* characteristic of or resembling the French. ~*n., pl.* **-ies.** **2.** an informal name for a French person.

frenetic (frɪ'nɛtɪk) *adj.* distracted or frantic; frenzied. [C14: via Old French *frenetique* from Latin *phrenēticus,* from Greek *phrenetikos,* from *phrenitis* insanity, from *phrēn* mind] —**fre'netically** *adv.* —**fre'neticness** *n.*

Frenkel defect ('frɛŋkᵊl) *n. Physics.* a crystal defect in which a lattice ion has moved to an interstitial position leaving a vacant lattice site. [C20: named after I. I. *Frenkel* (1894–1952), Russian physicist]

frenulum ('frɛnjʊləm) *n., pl.* **-la** (-lə). **1.** a strong bristle or group of bristles on the hind wing of some moths and other insects, by which the forewing and hind wing are united during flight. **2.** a small fraenum. [C18: New Latin, diminutive of Latin *frēnum* bridle]

frenum ('friːnəm) *n., pl.* **-na** (-nə). a variant spelling (esp. U.S.) of **fraenum.**

frenzied ('frɛnzɪd) *adj.* filled with or as if with frenzy; wild; frantic. —**'frenziedly** *adv.*

frenzy ('frɛnzɪ) *n., pl.* **-zies.** **1.** violent mental derangement. **2.** wild excitement or agitation; distraction. **3.** a bout of wild or agitated activity: *a frenzy of preparations.* ~*vb.* **-zies, -zying, -zied.** **4.** (*tr.*) to make frantic; drive into a frenzy. [C14: from Old French *frenesie,* from Late Latin *phrēnēsis* madness, delirium, from Late Greek, ultimately from Greek *phrēn* mind; compare FRENETIC]

Freon ('friːɒn) *n. Trademark.* any of a group of chemically unreactive chlorofluorocarbons used as aerosol propellants, refrigerants, and solvents.

freq. *abbrev. for:* **1.** frequent(ly). **2.** frequentative.

frequency ('friːkwənsɪ) *n., pl.* **-cies.** **1.** the state of being frequent; frequent occurrence. **2.** the number of times that an event occurs within a given period; rate of recurrence. **3.** *Physics.* the number of times that a periodic function or vibration repeats itself in a specified time, often 1 second. It is usually measured in hertz. Symbol: ν or *f.* **4.** *Statistics.* **a.** the number of individuals in a class (**absolute frequency**). **b.** the ratio of this number to the total number of individuals under survey (**relative frequency**). **5.** *Ecology.* **a.** the number of individuals of a species within a given area. **b.** the percentage of quadrats that contains individuals of a species. ~Also called (for senses 1, 2): **frequence.** [C16: from Latin *frequentia* a large gathering, from *frequēns* numerous, crowded]

frequency band *n.* a continuous range of frequencies, esp. in the radio spectrum, between two limiting frequencies.

frequency distribution *n. Statistics.* the function of the distribution of a sample corresponding to the probability density function of the underlying population and tending to it as the sample size increases, the set of relative frequencies of sample points falling within given intervals of the range of the random variable.
frequency-division multiplex *n.* See **multiplex** (sense 1).
frequency modulation *n.* a method of transmitting information using a radio-frequency carrier wave. The frequency of the carrier wave is varied in accordance with the amplitude and polarity of the input signal, the amplitude of the carrier remaining unchanged. Abbrev.: **FM.** Compare **amplitude modulation.**
frequent *adj.* ('friːkwənt). **1.** recurring at short intervals. **2.** constant or habitual. ~*vb.* (frɪ'kwent). **3.** (*tr.*) to visit repeatedly or habitually. [C16: from Latin *frequēns* numerous; perhaps related to Latin *farcīre* to stuff] —**fre'quentable** *adj.* —**fre'quenter** *n.* —'**frequently** *adv.* —'**frequentness** *n.*
frequentation (ˌfriːkwɛn'teɪʃən) *n.* the act or practice of frequenting or visiting often.
frequentative (frɪ'kwɛntətɪv) *Grammar.* ~*adj.* **1.** denoting an aspect of verbs in some languages used to express repeated or habitual action. **2.** (in English) denoting a verb or an affix having meaning that involves repeated or habitual action, such as the verb *wrestle,* from *wrest.* ~*n.* **3. a.** a frequentative verb or affix. **b.** the frequentative aspect of verbs.
fresco ('frɛskəʊ) *n., pl.* **-coes** *or* **-cos. 1.** a very durable method of wall-painting using watercolours on wet plaster or, less properly, dry plaster (**fresco secco**), with a less durable result. **2.** a painting done in this way. [C16: from Italian: fresh plaster, coolness, from *fresco* (adj.) fresh, cool, of Germanic origin]
fresh (frɛʃ) *adj.* **1.** not stale or deteriorated; newly made, harvested, etc.: *fresh bread; fresh strawberries.* **2.** newly acquired, created, found, etc.: *fresh publications.* **3.** novel; original: *a fresh outlook.* **4.** latest; most recent: *fresh developments.* **5.** further; additional; more: *fresh supplies.* **6.** not canned, frozen, or otherwise preserved: *fresh fruit.* **7.** (of water) not salt. **8.** bright or clear: *a fresh morning.* **9.** chilly or invigorating: *a fresh breeze.* **10.** not tired; alert; refreshed. **11.** not worn or faded: *fresh colours.* **12.** having a healthy or ruddy appearance. **13.** newly or just arrived; straight: *fresh from the presses.* **14.** youthful or inexperienced. **15.** *Chiefly U.S.* designating a female farm animal, esp. a cow, that has recently given birth. **16.** *Informal.* presumptuous or disrespectful; forward. **17.** *Northern English dialect.* partially intoxicated; tipsy. ~*n.* **18.** the fresh part or time of something. **19.** another name for **freshet.** ~*vb.* **20.** *Obsolete.* to make or become fresh; freshen. ~*adv.* **21.** in a fresh manner; freshly. **22. fresh out of.** *Informal, chiefly U.S.* having just run out of supplies of. [Old English *fersc* fresh, unsalted; related to Old High German *frisc,* Old French *freis,* Old Norse *ferskr*] —'**freshly** *adv.* —'**freshness** *n.*
fresh breeze *n.* a fairly strong breeze of force five on the Beaufort scale.
freshen ('frɛʃən) *vb.* **1.** to make or become fresh or fresher. **2.** (often foll. by *up*) to refresh (oneself), esp. by washing. **3.** (*intr.*) (of the wind) to increase. **4.** to lose or cause to lose saltiness. **5.** (*intr.*) *Chiefly U.S.* **a.** (of farm animals) to give birth. **b.** (of cows) to commence giving milk after calving. —'**freshener** *n.*
fresher ('frɛʃə) *or* **freshman** ('frɛʃmən) *n., pl.* **-ers** *or* **-men.** a first-year student at college or university.
freshet ('frɛʃɪt) *n.* **1.** the sudden overflowing of a river caused by heavy rain or melting snow. **2.** a stream of fresh water emptying into the sea.
fresh gale *n.* a gale of force eight on the Beaufort scale.
fresh-run *adj.* (of fish) newly migrated upstream from the sea, esp. to spawn.
freshwater ('frɛʃˌwɔːtə) *n.* (*modifier*) **1.** of, relating to, or living in fresh water. **2.** (esp. of a sailor who has not sailed on the sea) unskilled or inexperienced. **3.** *U.S.* small and little known: *a freshwater school.*
fresnel ('freɪnɛl; *French* frenɛl) *n.* a unit of frequency equivalent to 10^{12} hertz. [C20: named after A. J. *Fresnel* (1788–1827), French physicist]
Fresnel lens ('freɪnɛl) *n.* a lens consisting of a number of smaller lenses arranged to give a flat surface of short focal length. [C20: named after A. J. *Fresnel*]
fret[1] (frɛt) *vb.* **frets, fretting, fretted. 1.** to distress or be distressed; worry. **2.** to rub or wear away. **3.** to irritate or be irritated; feel or give annoyance or vexation. **4.** to eat away or be eaten away by chemical action; corrode. **5.** (*intr.*) (of a road surface) to become loose so that potholes develop; scab. **6.** to agitate (water) or (of water) to be agitated. **7.** (*tr.*) to make by wearing away; erode. ~*n.* **8.** a state of irritation or anxiety. **9.** the result of fretting; corrosion. **10.** a hole or channel caused by fretting. [Old English *fretan* to EAT; related to Old High German *frezzan,* Gothic *fraitan,* Latin *peredere*]
fret[2] (frɛt) *n.* **1.** a repetitive geometrical figure, esp. one used as an ornamental border. **2.** such a pattern made in relief and with numerous small openings; fretwork. **3.** *Heraldry.* a charge on a shield consisting of a mascle crossed by a saltire. ~*vb.* **frets, fretting, fretted. 4.** (*tr.*) to ornament with fret or fretwork. [C14: from Old French *frete* interlaced design used on a shield, probably of Germanic origin] —'**fretless** *adj.*
fret[3] (frɛt) *n.* any of several small metal bars set across the fingerboard of a musical instrument of the lute, guitar, or viol family at various points along its length so as to produce the desired notes when the strings are stopped by the fingers. [C16: of unknown origin] —'**fretless** *adj.*
fret[4] (frɛt) *n.* short for **sea fret.**
fretful ('frɛtfʊl) *adj.* peevish, irritable, or upset. —'**fretfully** *adv.* —'**fretfulness** *n.*
fret saw *n.* a fine-toothed saw with a long thin narrow blade, used for cutting designs in thin wood or metal.
fretted ('frɛtɪd) *adj.* **1.** ornamented with angular designs or frets. **2.** decorated with fretwork.
fretwork ('frɛtˌwɜːk) *n.* **1.** decorative geometrical carving or openwork. **2.** any similar pattern of light and dark. **3.** ornamental work of three-dimensional frets.
Freudian ('frɔɪdɪən) *adj.* **1.** of or relating to the Austrian psychiatrist Sigmund Freud (1856–1939), the originator of psychoanalysis, or to his ideas. **2.** a person who follows or believes in the basic ideas of Sigmund Freud. —'**Freudianˌism** *n.*
Freudian slip *n.* any action, such as a slip of the tongue, that may reveal an unconscious thought.
FRG *abbrev. for* Federal Republic of Germany.
FRGS (in Britain) *abbrev. for* Fellow of the Royal Geographical Society.
Fri. *abbrev. for* Friday.
friable ('fraɪəbᵊl) *adj.* easily broken up; crumbly. [C16: from Latin *friābilis,* from *friāre* to crumble; related to Latin *fricāre* to rub down] —ˌ**fria'bility** *or* '**friableness** *n.*
friar ('fraɪə) *n.* a member of any of various chiefly mendicant religious orders of the Roman Catholic Church, the main orders being the **Black Friars** (Dominicans), **Grey Friars** (Franciscans), **White Friars** (Carmelites), and **Austin Friars** (Augustinians). [C13 *frere,* from Old French: brother, from Latin *frāter* BROTHER] —'**friarly** *adj.*
friarbird ('fraɪəˌbɜːd) *n.* any of various Australian honeyeaters of the genus *Philemon,* having a naked head.
Friar Minor *n., pl.* **Friars Minor.** *Christianity.* a member of either of two of the three orders into which the order founded by St Francis of Assisi came to be divided, namely the **Order of Friars Minor** and the **Order of Friars Minor Conventual.** Compare **Capuchin.**
friar's balsam *n.* a compound containing benzoin, mixed with hot water and used as an inhalant to relieve colds and sore throats.
friar's lantern *n.* another name for **will-o'-the-wisp.**
friary ('fraɪərɪ) *n., pl.* **-aries.** *Christianity.* a convent or house of friars.
frib (frɪb) *n. Austral. and N.Z.* a short heavy-conditioned piece of wool removed from a fleece during classing. [of unknown origin]
fribble ('frɪbᵊl) *vb.* **1.** (*tr.*) to fritter away; waste. **2.** (*intr.*) to act frivolously; trifle. ~*n.* **3.** a wasteful or frivolous person or action. ~*adj.* **4.** frivolous; trifling. [C17: of unknown origin] —'**fribbler** *n.*
fricandeau *or* **fricando** ('frɪkənˌdəʊ) *n., pl.* **-deaus, -deaux,** *or* **-does** (-ˌdəʊz). a larded and braised veal fillet. [C18: from Old French, probably based on FRICASSEE]
fricassee (ˌfrɪkə'siː, 'frɪkəsɪ, 'frɪkəˌseɪ) *n.* **1.** stewed meat, esp. chicken or veal, and vegetables, served in a thick white sauce. ~*vb.* **-sees, -seeing, -seed. 2.** (*tr.*) to prepare (meat) as a fricassee. [C16: from Old French, from *fricasser* to fricassee; probably related to *frire* to FRY[1]]
fricative ('frɪkətɪv) *n.* **1.** a continuant consonant produced by partial occlusion of the airstream, such as (f) or (z). ~*adj.* **2.** relating to or denoting a fricative. [C19: from New Latin *fricātivus,* from Latin *fricāre* to rub]
FRICS (in Britain) *abbrev. for* Fellow of the Royal Institute of Chartered Surveyors.
friction ('frɪkʃən) *n.* **1.** a resistance encountered when one body moves relative to another body with which it is in contact. **2.** the act, effect, or an instance of rubbing one object against another. **3.** disagreement or conflict; discord. **4.** *Phonetics.* the hissing element of a speech sound, such as a fricative. **5.** perfumed alcohol used on the hair to stimulate the scalp. [C16: from French, from Latin *frictiō* a rubbing, from *fricāre* to rub, rub down; related to Latin *friāre* to crumble] —'**frictional** *adj.* —'**frictionless** *adj.*
frictional soil *n.* another term for **cohesionless soil.**
frictional unemployment *n.* those people who are in the process of moving from one job to another and who therefore appear in the unemployment statistics collected at any given time.
friction clutch *n.* a mechanical clutch in which the drive is transmitted by the friction between surfaces, lined with cork, asbestos, or other fibrous materials, attached to the driving and driven shafts.
friction layer *n.* the atmospheric layer extending up to about 600 m, in which the aerodynamic effects of surface friction are appreciable.
friction match *n.* a match that ignites as a result of the heat produced by friction when it is struck on a rough surface. See also **safety match.**

friction rub *or* **murmur** *n. Med.* the sound, heard through a stethoscope, made by the rubbing together of the two inflamed layers of pericardium in patients with pericarditis.

friction tape *n.* the U.S. and Canadian name for **insulating tape.**

friction welding *n.* a form of welding in which the welding heat is generated by pressure and relative movement at the interface in the area of the weld.

Friday ('fraɪdɪ) *n.* **1.** the sixth day of the week; fifth day of the working week. **2.** See **girl Friday, man Friday.** [Old English *Frīgedæg,* literally: Freya's day; related to Old Frisian *frīadei,* Old High German *frīatag*]

fridge (frɪdʒ) *n. Informal.* short for **refrigerator.**

fried (fraɪd) *vb.* the past tense and past participle of **fry**[1].

friend (frɛnd) *n.* **1.** a person known well to another and regarded with liking, affection, and loyalty; an intimate. **2.** an acquaintance or associate. **3.** an ally in a fight or cause; supporter. **4.** a fellow member of a party, society, etc. **5.** a patron or supporter: *a friend of the opera.* **6. be friends (with).** to be friendly (with). **7. make friends (with).** to become friendly (with). ~*vb.* **8.** (*tr.*) an archaic word for **befriend.** [Old English *frēond;* related to Old Saxon *friund,* Old Norse *frǣndi,* Gothic *frijōnds,* Old High German *friunt*] —'**friendless** *adj.* —'**friendlessness** *n.* —'**friendship** *n.*

Friend[1] (frɛnd) *n.* a member of the Society of Friends; Quaker.

Friend[2] (frɛnd) *n. Mountaineering, trademark.* a device consisting of a shaft with double-headed spring-loaded cams that can be wedged in a crack to provide an anchor point.

friend at court *n.* an influential acquaintance who can promote one's interests.

friendly ('frɛndlɪ) *adj.* **-lier, -liest. 1.** showing or expressing liking, goodwill, or trust: *a friendly smile.* **2.** on the same side; not hostile. **3.** tending or disposed to help or support; favourable: *a friendly breeze helped them escape.* ~*n., pl.* **-lies. 4.** Also called: **friendly match.** *Sport.* a match played for its own sake, and not as part of a competition, etc. —'**friendlily** *adv.* —'**friendliness** *n.*

-friendly *adj. combining form.* helpful, easy, or good for the person or thing specified: *ozone-friendly.*

friendly firen *n. Military.* firing by one's own side, esp. when it harms one's own personnel.

friendly society *n. Brit.* an association of people who pay regular dues or other sums in return for old-age pensions, sickness benefits, etc. U.S. term: **benefit society.**

frier ('fraɪə) *n.* a variant spelling of **fryer.**

Friesian[1] ('friːʒən) *n. Brit.* any of several breeds of black-and-white dairy cattle having a high milk yield. Usual U.S. and Canadian name: **Holstein.**

Friesian[2] ('friːʒən) *n., adj.* a variant of **Frisian.**

frieze[1] (friːz) *n.* **1.** *Architect.* **a.** the horizontal band between the architrave and cornice of a classical entablature, esp. one that is decorated with sculpture. **b.** the upper part of the wall of a room, below the cornice, esp. one that is decorated. **2.** any ornamental band or strip on a wall. [C16: from French *frise,* perhaps from Medieval Latin *frisium,* changed from Latin *Phrygium* Phrygian (work), from *Phrygia* Phrygia, famous for embroidery in gold]

frieze[2] (friːz) *n.* a heavy woollen fabric with a long nap, used for coats, etc. [C15: from Old French *frise,* from Middle Dutch *friese, vriese,* perhaps from *Vriese* Frisian]

frig (frɪg) *vb.* **frigs, frigging, frigged.** *Taboo slang.* **1.** to have sexual intercourse with. **2.** to masturbate. **3.** (*intr.;* foll. by *around, about,* etc.) to behave foolishly or aimlessly. [C15 (in the sense: to wriggle): of uncertain origin; perhaps related to obsolete *frike* strong, or to Old English *frīgan* to love]

frigate ('frɪgɪt) *n.* **1.** a medium-sized square-rigged warship of the 18th and 19th centuries. **2. a.** *Brit.* a warship larger than a corvette and smaller than a destroyer. **b.** *U.S.* (formerly) a warship larger than a destroyer and smaller than a cruiser. **c.** *U.S.* a small escort vessel. [C16: from French *frégate,* from Italian *fregata,* of unknown origin]

frigate bird *n.* any bird of the genus *Fregata* and family *Fregatidae,* of tropical and subtropical seas, having a long bill with a downturned tip, a wide wingspan, and a forked tail: order *Pelecaniformes* (pelicans, cormorants, etc.). Also called: **man-of-war bird.**

frigging ('frɪgɪŋ) *adj. Taboo slang.* (intensifier, used as a milder word for *fucking*): *you frigging idiot.*

fright (fraɪt) *n.* **1.** sudden intense fear or alarm. **2.** a sudden alarming shock. **3.** *Informal.* a horrifying, grotesque, or ludicrous person or thing: *she looks a fright in that hat.* **4. take fright.** to become frightened. ~*vb.* **5.** a poetic word for **frighten.** [Old English *fryhto;* related to Gothic *faurhtei,* Old Frisian *fruchte,* Old High German *forhta*]

frighten ('fraɪtᵊn) *vb.* (*tr.*) **1.** to cause fear in; terrify; scare. **2.** to drive or force to go (away, off, out, in, etc.) by making afraid. —'**frightenable** *adj.* —'**frightener** *n.* —'**frighteningly** *adv.*

frightful ('fraɪtfʊl) *adj.* **1.** very alarming, distressing, or horrifying. **2.** unpleasant, annoying, or extreme: *a frightful hurry.* —'**frightfulness** *n.*

frightfully ('fraɪtfəlɪ) *adv.* (intensifier): *I'm frightfully glad.*

frigid ('frɪdʒɪd) *adj.* **1.** formal or stiff in behaviour or temperament; lacking in affection or warmth. **2.** (esp. of women) **a.** lacking sexual responsiveness. **b.** averse to sexual intercourse or unable to achieve orgasm during intercourse. **3.** characterized by physical coldness: *a frigid zone.* [C15: from Latin *frigidus* cold, from *frīgēre* to be cold, freeze; related to Latin *frīgus* frost] —**fri'gidity** *or* '**frigidness** *n.* —'**frigidly** *adv.*

frigorific (ˌfrɪgə'rɪfɪk) *adj. Obsolete.* causing cold or freezing. [C17: from French *frigorifique,* from Latin *frīgorificus,* from *frīgus* cold, coldness + *facere* to make]

frijol ('friːhəʊl; *Spanish* fri'xol) *n., pl.* **-joles** (-həʊlz; *Spanish* -'xoles). a variety of bean, esp. of the French bean, extensively cultivated for food in Mexico. [C16: from Spanish, ultimately from Latin *phaseolus,* diminutive of *phasēlus,* from Greek *phasēlos* bean with edible pod]

frill (frɪl) *n.* **1.** a gathered, ruched, or pleated strip of cloth sewn on at one edge only, as on garments, as ornament, or to give extra body. **2.** a ruff of hair or feathers around the neck of a dog or bird or a fold of skin around the neck of a reptile or amphibian. **3.** Full name: **oriental frill.** (*often cap.*) a variety of domestic fancy pigeon having a ruff of curled feathers on the chest and crop. **4.** *Photog.* a wrinkling or loosening of the emulsion at the edges of a negative or print. **5.** (*often pl.*) *Informal.* a superfluous or pretentious thing or manner; affectation: *he made a plain speech with no frills.* ~*vb.* **6.** (*tr.*) to adorn or fit with a frill or frills. **7.** to form into a frill or frills. **8.** (*intr.*) *Photog.* (of an emulsion) to develop a frill. [C14: perhaps of Flemish origin] —'**frilliness** *n.* —'**frilly** *adj.*

frilled lizard *n.* a large arboreal insectivorous Australian lizard, *Chlamydosaurus kingi,* having an erectile fold of skin around the neck: family *Agamidae* (agamas).

Frimaire *French.* (frimɛr) *n.* the frosty month: the third month of the French Revolutionary calendar, extending from Nov. 22 to Dec. 21. [C19: from French, from *frimas* hoarfrost, from Old French *frim,* of Germanic origin; related to Old Norse *hrīm* RIME[1]]

fringe (frɪndʒ) *n.* **1.** an edging consisting of hanging threads, tassels, etc. **2. a.** an outer edge; periphery. **b.** (*as modifier*): *fringe dwellers; a fringe area.* **3.** (*modifier*) unofficial; not conventional in form: *fringe theatre.* **4.** *Chiefly Brit.* a section of the front hair cut short over the forehead. **5.** an ornamental border or margin. **6.** *Physics.* any of the light and dark or coloured bands produced by diffraction or interference of light. ~*vb.* (*tr.*) **7.** to adorn or fit with a fringe or fringes. **8.** to be a fringe for: *fur fringes the satin.* [C14: from Old French *frenge,* ultimately from Latin *fimbria* fringe, border; see FIMBRIA] —'**fringeless** *adj.* —'**fringy** *adj.*

fringe benefit *n.* an incidental or additional advantage, esp. a benefit provided by an employer to supplement an employee's regular pay, such as a pension, company car, luncheon vouchers, etc.

fringed orchis *n.* any orchid of the genus *Habenaria,* having yellow, white, purple, or greenish flowers with fringed petals. See also **purple-fringed orchid.**

fringe tree *n.* either of two ornamental oleaceous shrubs or small trees of the genus *Chionanthus,* of North America and China, having clusters of white narrow-petalled flowers.

fringilline (frɪn'dʒɪlaɪn, -ɪn) *or* **fringillid** (frɪn'dʒɪlɪd) *adj.* of, relating to, or belonging to the *Fringillidae,* a family of songbirds that includes the finches. [C19: from New Latin *Fringilla* type genus, from Latin *fringilla* a small bird, perhaps a chaffinch]

fringing reef *n.* a coral reef close to the shore to which it is attached, having a steep seaward edge.

frippery ('frɪpərɪ) *n., pl.* **-peries. 1.** ornate or showy clothing or adornment. **2.** showiness; ostentation. **3.** unimportant considerations; trifles; trivia. [C16: from Old French *freperie,* from *frepe* frill, rag, old garment, from Medieval Latin *faluppa* a straw, splinter, of obscure origin]

frippet ('frɪpɪt) *n.* **1.** a frivolous or flamboyant young woman. **2.** *Informal.* young womanhood (esp. in the phrase **a (nice) bit of frippet**). [C20: of uncertain origin]

Fris. *abbrev. for* Frisian.

Frisbee ('frɪzbiː) *n. Trademark.* a light plastic disc, usually 20–25 centimetres in diameter, thrown with a spinning motion for recreation or in competition.

frisé ('friːzeɪ) *n.* a fabric with a long normally uncut nap used for upholstery and rugs. [from French, literally: curled]

frisette *or* **frizette** (frɪ'zɛt) *n.* a curly or frizzed fringe, often an artificial hairpiece, worn by women on the forehead. [C19: from French, literally: little curl, from *friser* to curl, shrivel up, probably from *frire* to FRY[1]]

friseur *French.* (frizœr) *n.* a hairdresser. [C18: literally: one who curls (hair); see FRISETTE]

Frisian ('frɪʒən) *or* **Friesian** *n.* **1.** a language spoken in the NW Netherlands and adjacent islands, belonging to the West Germanic branch of the Indo-European family: the nearest relative of the English language. **2.** a speaker of this language; a native or inhabitant of Friesland, a province of the N Netherlands. ~*adj.* **3.** of or relating to this language or its speakers. [C16: from Latin *Frīsiī* people of northern Germany]

frisk (frɪsk) *vb.* **1.** (*intr.*) to leap, move about, or act in a playful manner; frolic. **2.** (*tr.*) (esp. of animals) to whisk or wave briskly: *the dog frisked its tail.* **3.** (*tr.*) *Informal.* **a.** to search (someone) by feeling for concealed weapons, etc. **b.** to rob by searching in this way. ~*n.* **4.** a playful antic or movement;

frolic. 5. *Informal.* the act or an instance of frisking a person. [C16: from Old French *frisque,* of Germanic origin; related to Old High German *frisc* lively, FRESH] —'**frisker** *n.* —'**friskingly** *adv.*

frisket ('frɪskɪt) *n. Printing.* a light rectangular frame, attached to the tympan of a hand printing press, that carries a parchment sheet to protect the nonprinting areas. [C17: from French *frisquette,* of obscure origin]

frisky ('frɪskɪ) *adj.* **friskier, friskiest.** lively, high-spirited, or playful. —'**friskily** *adv.* —'**friskiness** *n.*

frisson *French.* (frisɔ̃) *n.* a shudder or shiver; thrill. [C18 (but in common use only from C20): literally: shiver]

frit *or* **fritt** (frɪt) *n.* 1. **a.** the basic materials, partially or wholly fused, for making glass, glazes for pottery, enamel, etc. **b.** a glassy substance used in some soft-paste porcelain. 2. the material used for making the glaze for artificial teeth. ~*vb.* **frits** *or* **fritts, fritting, fritted.** 3. (*tr.*) to fuse (materials) in making frit. [C17: from Italian *fritta,* literally: fried, from *friggere* to fry, from Latin *frīgere*]

frit fly *n.* a small black dipterous fly, *Oscinella frit,* whose larvae are destructive to barley, wheat, rye, oats, etc.: family *Chloropidae.*

frith (frɪθ) *n.* a variant of **firth.**

fritillary (frɪ'tɪlərɪ) *n., pl.* **-laries.** 1. any N temperate liliaceous plant of the genus *Fritillaria,* having purple or white drooping bell-shaped flowers, typically marked in a chequered pattern. See also **snake's head.** 2. any of various nymphalid butterflies of the genera *Argynnis, Boloria,* etc., having brownish wings chequered with black and silver. [C17: from New Latin *fritillāria,* from Latin *fritillus* dice box; probably with reference to the spotted markings]

fritter[1] ('frɪtə) *vb.* (*tr.*) 1. (usually foll. by *away*) to waste or squander: *to fritter away time.* 2. to break or tear into small pieces; shred. ~*n.* 3. a small piece; shred. [C18: probably from obsolete *fitter* to break into small pieces, ultimately from Old English *fitt* a piece] —'**fritterer** *n.*

fritter[2] ('frɪtə) *n.* a piece of food, such as apple or clam, that is dipped in batter and fried in deep fat. [C14: from Old French *friture,* from Latin *frictus* fried, roasted, from *frīgere* to fry, parch]

Friulian (frɪ'u:lɪən) *n.* 1. the Rhaetian dialect spoken in parts of Friuli, a historic region of SW Europe between the Carnic Alps and the Gulf of Venice. See also **Ladin, Romansch.** 2. an inhabitant of Friuli or a speaker of Friulian. ~*adj.* 3. of or relating to Friuli, its inhabitants, or their language.

frivol ('frɪvᵊl) *vb.* **-ols, -olling, -olled** *or U.S.* **-ols, -oling, -oled.** *Informal.* 1. (*intr.*) to behave frivolously; trifle. 2. (*tr.;* often foll. by *away*) to waste on frivolous pursuits. [C19: back formation from FRIVOLOUS] —'**frivoller** *or U.S.* '**frivoler** *n.*

frivolous ('frɪvələs) *adj.* 1. not serious or sensible in content, attitude, or behaviour; silly: *a frivolous remark.* 2. unworthy of serious or sensible treatment; unimportant: *frivolous details.* [C15: from Latin *frīvolus* silly, worthless] —'**frivolously** *adv.* —'**frivolousness** *or* **frivolity** (frɪ'vɒlɪtɪ) *n.*

frizette (frɪ'zɛt) *n.* a variant spelling of **frisette.**

frizz (frɪz) *vb.* 1. (of the hair, nap, etc.) to form or cause (the hair, etc.) to form tight wiry curls or crisp tufts. ~*n.* 2. hair that has been frizzed. 3. the state of being frizzed. [C19: from French *friser* to curl, shrivel up (see FRISETTE): influenced by FRIZZLE[1]] —'**frizzer** *n.*

frizzante (frɪ'zæntɪ; *Italian* frid'dzante) *adj.* (of wine) slightly effervescent. [Italian, from *frizzare* to sparkle]

frizzle[1] ('frɪzᵊl) *vb.* 1. to form (the hair) into tight crisp curls; frizz. ~*n.* 2. a tight crisp curl. [C16: probably related to Old English *frīs* curly, Old Frisian *frēsle* curl, ringlet] —'**frizzler** *n.* —'**frizzly** *adj.*

frizzle[2] ('frɪzᵊl) *vb.* 1. to scorch or be scorched, esp. with a sizzling noise. 2. (*tr.*) to fry (bacon, etc.) until crisp. [C16: probably blend of FRY[1] + SIZZLE]

frizzy ('frɪzɪ) *or* **frizzly** ('frɪzlɪ) *adj.* **-zier, -ziest** *or* **-zlier, -zliest.** (of the hair) in tight crisp wiry curls. —'**frizzily** *adv.* —'**frizziness** *or* '**frizzliness** *n.*

Frl. *abbrev. for* Fräulein. [German: Miss]

fro (frəʊ) *adv.* back or from. See **to and fro.** [C12: from Old Norse *frā;* related to Old English *fram* FROM]

frock (frɒk) *n.* 1. a girl's or woman's dress. 2. a loose garment of several types, such as a peasant's smock. 3. a coarse wide-sleeved outer garment worn by members of some religious orders. ~*vb.* 4. (*tr.*) to invest (a person) with the office or status of a cleric. [C14: from Old French *froc;* related to Old Saxon, Old High German *hroc* coat]

frock coat *n.* a man's single- or double-breasted skirted coat, as worn in the 19th century.

frocking ('frɒkɪŋ) *n.* coarse material suitable for making frocks or work clothes.

froe *or* **frow** (frəʊ) *n.* a cutting tool with handle and blade at right angles, used for stripping young trees, etc. [C16: from *frower,* from *froward* (in the sense: turned away)]

frog[1] (frɒg) *n.* 1. any insectivorous anuran amphibian of the family *Ranidae,* such as *Rana temporaria* of Europe, having a short squat tailless body with a moist smooth skin and very long hind legs specialized for hopping. 2. any of various similar amphibians of related families, such as the tree frog. 3. any spiked or perforated object used to support plant stems in a flower arrangement. 4. a recess in a brick to reduce its weight. 5. **a frog in one's throat.** phlegm on the vocal cords that affects one's speech. ~*vb.* **frogs, frogging, frogged.** 6. (*intr.*) to hunt or catch frogs. [Old English *frogga;* related to Old Norse *froskr,* Old High German *forsk*] —'**froggy** *adj.*

frog[2] (frɒg) *n.* 1. (*often pl.*) a decorative fastening of looped braid or cord, as on the front of a 19th-century military uniform. 2. a loop or other attachment on a belt to hold the scabbard of a sword, etc. 3. *Music.* another name (esp. U.S. and Canadian) for **nut** (sense 11). [C18: perhaps ultimately from Latin *floccus* tuft of hair, FLOCK[2]]

frog[3] (frɒg) *n.* a tough elastic horny material in the centre of the sole of a horse's foot. [C17: of uncertain origin]

frog[4] (frɒg) *n.* a grooved plate of iron or steel placed to guide train wheels over an intersection of railway lines. [C19: of uncertain origin; perhaps a special use of FROG[1]]

Frog (frɒg) *or* **Froggy** ('frɒgɪ) *n., pl.* **Frogs** *or* **Froggies.** *Brit. slang.* a derogatory word for a French person.

frog-bit *n.* a floating aquatic Eurasian plant, *Hydrocharis morsus-ranae,* with heart-shaped leaves and white flowers: family *Hydrocharitaceae.*

frogfish ('frɒg,fɪʃ) *n., pl.* **-fish** *or* **-fishes.** any angler (fish) of the family *Antennariidae,* in which the body is covered with fleshy processes, including a fleshy lure on top of the head.

frogged (frɒgd) *adj.* (of a coat) fitted with ornamental frogs.

frogging ('frɒgɪŋ) *n.* the ornamental frogs on a coat collectively.

froghopper ('frɒg,hɒpə) *n.* any small leaping herbivorous homopterous insect of the family *Cercopidae,* whose larvae secrete a protective spittle-like substance around themselves. Also called: **spittle insect, spittlebug.**

frog kick *n.* a type of kick used in swimming, as in the breast stroke, in which the legs are simultaneously drawn towards the body and bent at the knees with the feet together, straightened out with the legs apart, and then brought together again quickly.

frogman ('frɒgmən) *n., pl.* **-men.** a swimmer equipped with a rubber suit, flippers, and breathing equipment for working underwater.

frogmarch ('frɒg,mɑ:tʃ) *Chiefly Brit.* ~*n.* 1. a method of carrying a resisting person in which each limb is held by one person and the victim is carried horizontally and face downwards. 2. any method of making a resisting person move forward against his will. ~*vb.* 3. (*tr.*) to carry in a frogmarch or cause to move forward unwillingly.

frogmouth ('frɒg,maʊθ) *n.* any nocturnal insectivorous bird of the genera *Podargus* and *Batrachostomus,* of SE Asia and Australia, similar to the nightjars: family *Podargidae,* order *Caprimulgiformes.*

frog orchid *n.* any of several orchids having greenish flowers thought to resemble small frogs, esp. *Coeloglossum viride* of calcareous turf.

frogspawn ('frɒg,spɔ:n) *n.* a mass of fertilized frogs' eggs or developing tadpoles, each egg being surrounded by a protective nutrient jelly.

frog spit *or* **spittle** *n.* 1. another name for **cuckoo spit.** 2. a foamy mass of threadlike green algae floating on ponds.

frolic ('frɒlɪk) *n.* 1. a gay or light-hearted entertainment or occasion. 2. light-hearted activity; gaiety; merriment. ~*vb.* **-ics, -icking, -icked.** 3. (*intr.*) to caper about; act or behave playfully. ~*adj.* 4. *Archaic or literary.* full of merriment or fun; gay. [C16: from Dutch *vrolijk,* from Middle Dutch *vro* happy, glad; related to Old High German *frō* happy] —'**frolicker** *n.*

frolicsome ('frɒlɪksəm) *or* **frolicky** *adj.* given to frolicking; merry and playful. —'**frolicsomely** *adv.* —'**frolicsomeness** *n.*

from (frɒm; *unstressed* frəm) *prep.* 1. used to indicate the original location, situation, etc.: *from Paris to Rome; from behind the bushes; from childhood to adulthood.* 2. in a period of time starting at: *he lived from 1910 to 1970.* 3. used to indicate the distance between two things or places: *a hundred miles from here.* 4. used to indicate a lower amount: *from five to fifty pounds.* 5. showing the model of: *painted from life.* 6. used with the gerund to mark prohibition, restraint, etc.: *nothing prevents him from leaving.* 7. because of: *exhausted from his walk.* [Old English *fram;* related to Old Norse *frā,* Old Saxon, Old High German, Gothic *fram* from, Greek *promos* foremost]

▷ **Usage.** See at **off.**

fromage frais ('frɒmɑ:ʒ 'freɪ) *n.* a low-fat soft cheese with a smooth light texture. [French, literally: fresh cheese]

fromenty ('frəʊməntɪ) *n.* a variant of **frumenty.**

frond (frɒnd) *n.* 1. the compound leaf of a fern. 2. the leaf of a palm or a cycad. 3. the thallus of a seaweed or a lichen. [C18: from Latin *frōns*] —'**fronded** *adj.* —'**frondless** *adj.*

frondescence (frɒn'dɛsəns) *n.* 1. the process or state of producing leaves. 2. a less common name for **foliage.** [C19: from New Latin *frondēscentia,* from Latin *frondēscere* to put forth leaves, from *frōns* foliage; see FROND] —**fron'descent,** '**frondose,** *or* '**frondous** *adj.*

frons (frɒnz) *n., pl.* **frontes** ('frɒnti:z). an anterior cuticular plate on the head of some insects, in front of the clypeus. [C19: from Latin: forehead, brow, FRONT]

front (frʌnt) *n.* 1. that part or side that is forward, prominent, or most often seen or used. 2. a position or place directly before or ahead: *a fountain stood at the front of the building.* **3.** the beginning, opening, or first part: *the front of the book.* **4.** the position of leadership; forefront; vanguard: *in the front of scientific knowledge.* **5.** land bordering a lake, street, etc. **6.** land along a seashore or large lake, esp. a promenade. **7.** *Military.* **a.** the total area in which opposing armies face each other. **b.** the lateral space in which a military unit or formation is operating: *to advance on a broad front.* **c.** the direction in which troops are facing when in a formed line. **8.** *Meteorol.* the dividing line or plane between two air masses of different origins and having different characteristics. See also **warm front, cold front. 9.** outward aspect or bearing, as when dealing with a situation: *a bold front.* **10.** assurance, overconfidence, or effrontery. **11.** *Informal.* a business or other activity serving as a respectable cover for another, usually criminal, organization. **12.** *Chiefly U.S.* a nominal leader of an organization, etc., who lacks real power or authority; figurehead. **13.** *Informal.* outward appearance of rank or wealth. **14.** a particular field of activity involving some kind of struggle: *on the wages front.* **15.** a group of people with a common goal: *a national liberation front.* **16.** a false shirt front; a dicky. **17.** *Archaic.* the forehead or the face. ~*adj.* (*prenominal*) **18.** of, at, or in the front: *a front seat.* **19.** *Phonetics.* of, relating to, or denoting a vowel articulated with the blade of the tongue brought forward and raised towards the hard palate, as for the sound of *ee* in English *see* or *a* in English *hat.* ~*vb.* **20.** (when *intr.*, foll. by *on* or *onto*) to be opposite (to); face (onto): *this house fronts the river.* **21.** (*tr.*) to be a front of or for. **22.** (*tr.*) *Informal.* to appear as a presenter in (a television show). **23.** (*tr.*) to be the lead singer or player in (a band). **24.** (*tr.*) to confront, esp. in hostility or opposition. **25.** (*tr.*) to supply a front for. **26.** (*intr.;* often foll. by *up*) *Austral. and N.Z. informal.* to appear (at): *to front up at the police station.* [C13 (in the sense: forehead, face): from Latin *frōns* forehead, foremost part] —'**frontless** *adj.*

front. *abbrev. for* frontispiece.

frontage ('frʌntɪdʒ) *n.* **1.** the façade of a building or the front of a plot of ground. **2.** the extent of the front of a shop, plot of land, etc., esp. along a street, river, etc. **3.** the direction in which a building faces: *a frontage on the river.*

frontal ('frʌntᵊl) *adj.* **1.** of, at, or in the front. **2.** of or relating to the forehead: *frontal artery.* **3.** *Meteorol.* of, relating to, or resulting from a front or its passage: *frontal rainfall.* ~*n.* **4.** a decorative hanging for the front of an altar. **5.** See **frontal lobe, frontal bone. 6.** another name for **frontlet** (sense 1). [C14 (in the sense: adornment for forehead, altar cloth): via Old French *frontel,* from Latin *frontālia* (pl.) ornament worn on forehead, *frontellum* altar cloth, both from *frōns* forehead, FRONT] —'**frontally** *adv.*

frontal bone *n.* the bone that forms the front part of the skull.

frontality (frən'tælɪtɪ) *n. Fine arts.* a frontal view, as in a painting or other work of art.

frontal lobe *n. Anatomy.* the anterior portion of each cerebral hemisphere, situated in front of the central sulcus.

front bench *n. Brit.* **a.** the foremost bench of either the Government or Opposition in the House of Commons. **b.** the leadership (**frontbenchers**) of either group, who occupy this bench. **c.** (*as modifier*): *a front-bench decision.*

front door *n.* **1.** the main entrance to a house. **2.** an open legitimate means of obtaining a job, position, etc.: *to get in by the front door.*

front-end *adj.* (of money, costs, etc.) required or incurred in advance of a project in order to get it under way.

front-end load *n.* commission and other expenses paid for as a large proportion of the early payments made by an investor in an insurance policy or a long-term investment plan. —**front-end loading** *n.*

front-end processor *n.* a small computer that receives data from input devices and performs some initial processing tasks on it before passing it to a more powerful computer for final processing.

frontier ('frʌntɪə, frʌn'tɪə) *n.* **1. a.** the region of a country bordering on another or a line, barrier, etc., marking such a boundary. **b.** (*as modifier*): *a frontier post.* **2.** *U.S. and Canadian.* **a.** the edge of the settled area of a country. **b.** (*as modifier*): *the frontier spirit.* **3.** (*often pl.*) the limit of knowledge in a particular field: *the frontiers of physics have been pushed back.* **4.** *Maths.* the part of the closure of a topological set that lies outside its interior. [C14: from Old French *frontiere,* from *front* (in the sense: part which is opposite); see FRONT]

frontiersman ('frʌntɪəzmən, frʌn'tɪəz-) *or* (*fem.*) **frontierswoman** *n., pl.* **-men** *or* **-women.** (formerly) a person living on a frontier, esp. in a newly pioneered territory of the U.S.

frontispiece ('frʌntɪs,piːs) *n.* **1.** an illustration facing the title page of a book. **2.** the principal façade of a building; front. **3.** a pediment, esp. an ornamented one, over a door, window, etc. [C16 *frontispice,* from French, from Late Latin *frontispicium* façade, inspection of the forehead, from Latin *frōns* forehead + *specere* to look at; influenced by PIECE]

frontlet ('frʌntlɪt) *n.* **1.** Also called: **frontal.** a small decorative loop worn on a woman's forehead, projecting from under her headdress, in the 15th century. **2.** the forehead of an animal, esp. of a bird when it is a different colour from the rest of the head. **3.** the decorated border of an altar frontal. **4.** *Judaism.* a phylactery worn on the forehead. See also **Tefillin.** [C15: from Old French *frontelet* a little FRONTAL]

front line *n.* **1.** *Military.* the most advanced military units or elements in a battle. **2.** the most advanced, exposed, or conspicuous element in any activity or situation. **3.** (*modifier*) **a.** of, relating to, or suitable for the front line of a military formation: *frontline troops.* **b.** to the fore; advanced, conspicuous, etc.: *frontline news.* **c.** of or relating to a country bordering on or close to a hostile country or scene of armed conflict: *leaders of the frontline states attended the summit.*

front loader *n.* a washing machine with a door at the front which opens one side of the drum into which washing is placed.

front man *n. Informal.* **1.** a nominal leader of an organization, etc., who lacks real power or authority, esp. one who lends respectability to some nefarious activity. **2.** the leader or visual focus of a group of musicians, usually the singer. ~Also called: **front person.**

front matter *n.* another name for **prelims** (sense 1).

front of house *n.* the areas of a theatre, opera house, etc., used by the audience.

frontogenesis (,frʌntəʊ'dʒɛnɪsɪs) *n. Meteorol.* the formation or development of a front through the meeting of air masses from different origins. —**frontogenetic** (,frʌntəʊdʒə'nɛtɪk) *adj.* —,**frontoge'netically** *adv.*

frontolysis (frʌn'tɒlɪsɪs) *n. Meteorol.* the weakening or dissipation of a front.

fronton ('frɒntɒn, frɒn'tɒn) *n.* a wall against which pelota or jai alai is played. [C17: from Spanish *frontón,* from *frente* forehead, from Latin *frōns*]

front-page *n.* (*modifier*) important or newsworthy enough to be put on the front page of a newspaper.

frontrunner ('frʌnt,rʌnə) *n. Informal.* the leader or a favoured contestant in a race, election, etc.

frontrunning ('frʌnt,rʌnɪŋ) *n. Stock Exchange.* the practice by market makers of using advance information provided by their own investment analysts before it has been given to clients.

frontwards ('frʌntwədz) *or* **frontward** *adv.* towards the front.

frore (frɔː) *adj. Archaic.* very cold or frosty. [C13 *froren,* past participle of Old English *frēosan* to FREEZE]

frost (frɒst) *n.* **1.** a white deposit of ice particles, esp. one formed on objects out of doors at night. See also **hoarfrost. 2.** an atmospheric temperature of below freezing point, characterized by the production of this deposit. **3. degrees of frost.** degrees below freezing point: eight degrees of frost indicates a temperature of either −8°C or 24°F. **4.** *Informal.* something given a cold reception; failure. **5.** *Informal.* coolness of manner. **6.** the act of freezing. ~*vb.* **7.** to cover or be covered with frost. **8.** (*tr.*) to give a frostlike appearance to (glass, etc.), as by means of a fine-grained surface. **9.** (*tr.*) *Chiefly U.S. and Canadian.* to decorate (cakes, etc.) with icing or frosting. **10.** (*tr.*) to kill or damage (crops, etc.) with frost. [Old English *frost;* related to Old Norse, Old Saxon, Old High German *frost;* see FREEZE] —'**frost,like** *adj.*

frostbite ('frɒst,baɪt) *n.* **1.** destruction of tissues, esp. those of the fingers, ears, toes, and nose, by freezing, characterized by tingling, blister formation, and gangrene. **2.** *N.Z.* a type of small sailing dinghy.

frostbitten ('frɒst,bɪtᵊn) *adj.* of or affected with frostbite.

frosted ('frɒstɪd) *adj.* **1.** covered or injured by frost. **2.** covered with icing, as a cake. **3.** (of glass, etc.) having a surface roughened, as if covered with frost, to prevent clear vision through it.

frost heave *n.* the upthrust and cracking of a ground surface through the freezing and expansion of water underneath. Also called: **frost heaving.**

frost hollow *n.* a depression in a hilly area in which cold air collects, becoming very cold at night.

frosting ('frɒstɪŋ) *n.* **1.** a soft icing based on sugar and egg whites. **2.** another word (esp. U.S. and Canadian) for **icing. 3.** a rough or matt finish on glass, silver, etc.

frost line *n.* **1.** the deepest point in the ground to which frost will penetrate. **2.** the limit towards the equator beyond which frosts do not occur.

frostwork ('frɒst,wɜːk) *n.* **1.** the patterns made by frost on glass, metal, etc. **2.** similar artificial ornamentation.

frosty ('frɒstɪ) *adj.* **frostier, frostiest. 1.** characterized by frost: *a frosty night.* **2.** covered by or decorated with frost. **3.** lacking warmth or enthusiasm: *the new plan had a frosty reception.* **4.** like frost in appearance or colour; hoary. —'**frostily** *adv.* —'**frostiness** *n.*

froth (frɒθ) *n.* **1.** a mass of small bubbles of air or a gas in a liquid, produced by fermentation, detergent, etc. **2.** a mixture of saliva and air bubbles formed at the lips in certain diseases, such as rabies. **3.** trivial ideas, talk, or entertainment. ~*vb.* **4.** to produce or cause to produce froth. **5.** (*tr.*) to give out in the form of froth. **6.** (*tr.*) to cover with froth. [C14: from Old Norse *frotha* or *frauth;* related to Old English *āfrēothan* to foam, Sanskrit *prothati* he snorts] —'**frothy** *adj.* —'**frothily** *adv.* —'**frothiness** *n.*

froth flotation *n.* another name for **flotation** (in metallurgy).

frottage ('frɒtɑːʒ; *French* frɔtaʒ) *n.* **1.** the act or process of taking a rubbing from a rough surface, such as wood, for a work of art. **2.** sexual excitement obtained by rubbing against another person's clothed body. [French, from *frotter* to rub]

Froude number (fraʊd) *n.* a dimensionless number used in hydrodynamics for model simulation of actual conditions. [named after W. *Froude* (1810–79), British civil engineer]

froufrou ('fruːˌfruː) *n.* **1.** a swishing sound, as made by a long silk dress. **2.** elaborate dress or ornamentation, esp. worn by women. [C19: from French, of imitative origin]

frow (frəʊ) *n.* a variant spelling of **froe.**

froward ('frəʊəd) *adj. Archaic.* obstinate; contrary. [C14: see FRO, -WARD] —'**frowardly** *adv.* —'**frowardness** *n.*

frown (fraʊn) *vb.* **1.** (*intr.*) to draw the brows together and wrinkle the forehead, esp. in worry, anger, or concentration. **2.** (*intr.*; foll. by *on* or *upon*) to have a dislike (of); look disapprovingly (upon): *the club frowned upon political activity by its members.* **3.** (*tr.*) to express (worry, etc.) by frowning. **4.** (*tr.*; often foll. by *down*) to force, silence, etc., by a frowning look. ~*n.* **5.** the act of frowning. **6.** a show of dislike or displeasure. [C14: from Old French *froignier,* of Celtic origin; compare Welsh *ffroen* nostril, Middle Breton *froan*] —'**frowner** *n.* —'**frowningly** *adv.*

frowst (fraʊst) *n. Brit. informal.* a hot and stale atmosphere; fug. [C19: back formation from *frowsty* musty, stuffy, variant of FROWZY]

frowsty ('fraʊstɪ) *adj.* ill-smelling; stale; musty. —'**frowstiness** *n.*

frowzy, frouzy, *or* **frowsy** ('fraʊzɪ) *adj.* **frowzier, frowziest; frouzier, frouziest;** *or* **frowsier, frowsiest. 1.** untidy or unkempt in appearance; shabby. **2.** ill-smelling; frowsty. [C17: of unknown origin] —'**frowziness,** '**frouziness,** *or* '**frowsiness** *n.*

froze (frəʊz) *vb.* the past tense of **freeze.**

frozen ('frəʊzᵊn) *vb.* **1.** the past participle of **freeze.** ~*adj.* **2.** turned into or covered with ice. **3.** obstructed or blocked by ice. **4.** killed, injured, or stiffened by extreme cold. **5.** (of a region or climate) icy or snowy. **6.** (of food) preserved by a freezing process. **7. a.** (of prices, wages, etc.) arbitrarily pegged at a certain level. **b.** (of business assets) not convertible into cash, as by government direction or business conditions. **8.** frigid, unfeeling, or disdainful in manner. **9.** motionless or unyielding: *he was frozen with horror.* —'**frozenly** *adv.* —'**frozenness** *n.*

frozen shoulder *n. Pathol.* a painful stiffness in a shoulder joint.

FRPS (in Britain) *abbrev. for* Fellow of the Royal Photographic Society.

FRS (in Britain) *abbrev. for* Fellow of the Royal Society.

Frs. *abbrev. for* Frisian.

FRSC (in Britain) *abbrev. for* Fellow of the Royal Society of Chemistry.

FRSNZ *abbrev. for* Fellow of the Royal Society of New Zealand.

frt *abbrev. for* freight.

fructan ('frʌktən) *n.* a type of polymer of fructose, present in certain fruits.

Fructidor *French.* (fryktidɔr) *n.* the month of fruit: the twelfth month of the French Revolutionary calendar, extending from Aug. 19 to Sept. 22. [C18: from Latin *frūctus* fruit + Greek *dōron* gift]

fructiferous (frʌk'tɪfərəs, frʊk-) *adj.* (of plants or trees) bearing or yielding fruit. —**fruc'tiferously** *adv.*

fructification (ˌfrʌktɪfɪ'keɪʃən, ˌfrʊk-) *n.* **1.** the act or state of fructifying. **2.** the fruit of a seed-bearing plant. **3.** any spore-bearing structure in ferns, mosses, fungi, etc.

fructify ('frʌktɪˌfaɪ, 'frʊk-) *vb.* **-fies, -fying, -fied. 1.** to bear or cause to bear fruit. **2.** to make or become productive or fruitful. [C14: from Old French *fructifier,* from Late Latin *frūctificāre* to bear fruit, from Latin *frūctus* fruit + *facere* to make, produce] —'**fructiˌfier** *n.*

fructose ('frʌktəʊs, -təʊz, 'frʊk-) *n.* a white crystalline water-soluble sugar occurring in honey and many fruits. Formula: $C_6H_{12}O_6$. Also called: **laevulose, fruit sugar.** [C19: from Latin *frūctus* fruit + -OSE[2]]

fructuous ('frʌktjʊəs, 'frʊk-) *adj.* productive or fruitful; fertile. [C14: from Latin *frūctuōsus,* from *frūctus* fruit + -OUS] —'**fructuously** *adv.* —'**fructuousness** *n.*

frugal ('fruːgᵊl) *adj.* **1.** practising economy; living without waste; thrifty. **2.** not costly; meagre. [C16: from Latin *frūgālis,* from *frūgī* useful, temperate, from *frux* fruit] —**fru'gality** *or* '**frugalness** *n.* —'**frugally** *adv.*

frugivorous (fruː'dʒɪvərəs) *adj.* feeding on fruit; fruit-eating. [C18: from *frugi-* (as in FRUGAL) + -VOROUS]

fruit (fruːt) *n.* **1.** *Botany.* the ripened ovary of a flowering plant, containing one or more seeds. It may be dry, as in the poppy, or fleshy, as in the peach. **2.** any fleshy part of a plant, other than the above structure, that supports the seeds and is edible, such as the strawberry. **3.** the spore-producing structure of plants that do not bear seeds. **4.** any plant product useful to man, including grain, vegetables, etc. **5.** (*often pl.*) the result or consequence of an action or effort. **6.** *Brit. slang, old-fashioned.* chap; fellow: used as a term of address. **7.** *Slang, chiefly Brit.* a person considered to be eccentric or insane. **8.** *Slang, chiefly U.S. and Canadian.* a male homosexual. **9.** *Archaic.* offspring of man or animals; progeny. ~*vb.* **10.** to bear or cause to bear fruit. [C12: from Old French, from Latin *frūctus* enjoyment, profit, fruit, from *fruī* to enjoy] —'**fruitˌlike** *adj.*

fruitage ('fruːtɪdʒ) *n.* **1.** the process, state, or season of producing fruit. **2.** fruit collectively.

fruitarian (fruː'tɛərɪən) *n.* **1.** a person who eats only fruit. ~*adj.* **2.** of or relating to a fruitarian: *a fruitarian diet.* —**frui'tarianˌism** *n.*

fruit bat *n.* any large Old World bat of the suborder *Megachiroptera,* occurring in tropical and subtropical regions and feeding on fruit. Compare **insectivorous bat.**

fruit body *n.* the part of a fungus in which the spores are produced.

fruitcake ('fruːtˌkeɪk) *n.* **1.** a rich cake containing mixed dried fruit, lemon peel, nuts, etc. **2.** *Slang, chiefly Brit.* a person considered to be eccentric or insane.

fruit cocktail *n.* fruit salad consisting of small or diced fruits.

fruit cup *n.* a variety of fruits served in a cup or glass as an appetizer or dessert.

fruit drop *n.* **1.** the premature shedding of fruit from a tree before fully ripe. **2.** a boiled sweet with a fruity flavour.

fruiter ('fruːtə) *n.* **1.** a fruit grower. **2.** any tree that bears fruit, esp. edible fruit.

fruiterer ('fruːtərə) *n. Chiefly Brit.* a fruit dealer or seller.

fruit fly *n.* **1.** any small dipterous fly of the family *Trypetidae,* which feed on and lay their eggs in plant tissues. See also **gallfly. 2.** any dipterous fly of the genus *Drosophila.* See **drosophila.**

fruitful ('fruːtfʊl) *adj.* **1.** bearing fruit in abundance. **2.** productive or prolific, esp. in bearing offspring. **3.** causing or assisting prolific growth. **4.** producing results or profits: *a fruitful discussion.* —'**fruitfully** *adv.* —'**fruitfulness** *n.*

fruition (fruː'ɪʃən) *n.* **1.** the attainment or realization of something worked for or desired; fulfilment. **2.** enjoyment of this. **3.** the act or condition of bearing fruit. [C15: from Late Latin *fruitiō* enjoyment, from Latin *fruī* to enjoy]

fruit knife *n.* a small stainless knife for cutting fruit.

fruitless ('fruːtlɪs) *adj.* **1.** yielding nothing or nothing of value; unproductive; ineffectual. **2.** without fruit. —'**fruitlessly** *adv.* —'**fruitlessness** *n.*

fruit machine *n. Brit.* a gambling machine that pays out when certain combinations of diagrams, usually of fruit, appear on a dial.

fruit salad *n.* a dish consisting of sweet fruits cut up and served in a syrup: often sold canned.

fruit sugar *n.* another name for **fructose.**

fruit tree *n.* any tree that bears edible fruit.

fruity ('fruːtɪ) *adj.* **fruitier, fruitiest. 1.** of or resembling fruit. **2.** (of a voice) mellow or rich. **3.** ingratiating or unctuous. **4.** *Informal, chiefly Brit.* erotically stimulating; salacious. **5.** *Slang.* eccentric or insane. **6.** *Chiefly U.S. and Canadian.* a slang word for **homosexual.** —'**fruitiness** *n.* —'**fruitily** *adv.*

frumentaceous (ˌfruːmɛn'teɪʃəs) *adj.* resembling or made of wheat or similar grain. [C17: from Late Latin *frūmentāceus,* from Latin *frūmentum* corn, grain]

frumenty ('fruːməntɪ), **fromenty, furmenty,** *or* **furmety** *n. Brit.* a kind of porridge made from hulled wheat boiled with milk, sweetened, and spiced. [C14: from Old French *frumentee,* from *frument* grain, from Latin *frūmentum*]

frump (frʌmp) *n.* a woman who is dowdy, drab, or unattractive. [C16 (in the sense: to be sullen; C19: dowdy woman): from Middle Dutch *verrompelen* to wrinkle, RUMPLE] —'**frumpish** *or* '**frumpy** *adj.* —'**frumpishly** *or* '**frumpily** *adv.* —'**frumpishness** *or* '**frumpiness** *n.*

frusemide ('frʌsəˌmaɪd) *n.* a diuretic used to treat hypertension and to relieve oedema due to heart or kidney disease.

frustrate (frʌ'streɪt) *vb.* (*tr.*) **1.** to hinder or prevent (the efforts, plans, or desires) of; thwart. **2.** to upset, agitate, or tire: *her constant complaints began to frustrate him.* ~*adj.* **3.** *Archaic.* frustrated or thwarted; baffled. [C15: from Latin *frustrāre* to cheat, from *frustrā* in error] —**frus'trater** *n.*

frustrated (frʌ'streɪtɪd) *adj.* having feelings of dissatisfaction or lack of fulfilment.

frustration (frʌ'streɪʃən) *n.* **1.** the condition of being frustrated. **2.** something that frustrates. **3.** *Psychol.* **a.** the prevention or hindering of a potentially satisfying activity. **b.** the emotional reaction to such prevention that may involve aggression.

frustule ('frʌstjuːl) *n. Botany.* the hard siliceous cell wall of a diatom. [C19: from French, from Late Latin *frustulum* a small piece, from *frustum* a bit]

frustum ('frʌstəm) *n., pl.* **-tums** *or* **-ta** (-tə). **1.** *Geometry.* **a.** the part of a solid, such as a cone or pyramid, contained between the base and a plane parallel to the base that intersects the solid. **b.** the part of such a solid contained between two parallel planes intersecting the solid. **2.** *Architect.* a single drum of a column or a single stone used to construct a pier. [C17: from Latin: piece; probably related to Old English *brӯsan* to crush, BRUISE]

frutescent (fruː'tɛsᵊnt) *or* **fruticose** ('fruːtɪˌkəʊs, -ˌkəʊz) *adj.* having the appearance or habit of a shrub; shrubby. [C18: from Latin *frutex* shrub, bush] —**fru'tescence** *n.*

fry[1] (fraɪ) *vb.* **fries, frying, fried. 1.** (when *tr.,* sometimes foll. by *up*) to cook or be cooked in fat, oil, etc., usually over direct heat. **2.** (*intr.*) *Informal.* to be excessively hot. **3.** *Slang, chiefly U.S.* to kill or be killed by electrocution, esp. in the electric chair. ~*n., pl.* **fries. 4.** a dish of something fried, esp. the offal of a specified animal: *pig's fry.* **5.** *U.S. and Canadian.* a social occasion, often outdoors, at which the chief food is fried. **6. fry-up.** *Brit. informal*-

mal. the act of preparing a mixed fried dish or the dish itself. [C13: from Old French *frire,* from Latin *frīgere* to roast, fry]

fry[2] (fraɪ) *pl. n.* **1.** the young of various species of fish. **2.** the young of certain other animals, such as frogs. **3.** young children. ~See also **small fry.** [C14 (in the sense: young, offspring): perhaps via Norman French from Old French *freier* to spawn, rub, from Latin *fricāre* to rub]

fryer *or* **frier** (ˈfraɪə) *n.* **1.** a person or thing that fries. **2.** a young chicken suitable for frying.

frying pan *or U.S.* **fry-pan** *n.* **1.** a long-handled shallow pan used for frying. **2. out of the frying pan into the fire.** from a bad situation to a worse one.

f.s. *abbrev. for* foot-second.

FSA *abbrev. for* Fellow of the Society of Antiquaries.

FSH *abbrev. for* follicle-stimulating hormone.

FSK *Computer technol. abbrev. for* Frequency Shift Keying.

f-stop *n.* any of the settings for the f-number of a camera.

ft *abbrev. for* fort.

ft. *abbrev. for:* **1.** foot *or* feet. **2.** fortification.

fth. *or* **fthm.** *abbrev. for* fathom.

ft-lb *abbrev. for* foot-pound.

FT-SE 100 Index *abbrev. for* Financial Times Stock Exchange 100 Index.

FT Share Indexes *pl. n.* any of a number of share indexes published by the *Financial Times* to reflect various aspects of stock exchange prices. See **Financial Times Industrial Ordinary Share Index; Financial Times Stock Exchange 100 Index.**

fubsy (ˈfʌbzɪ) *adj.* **-sier, -siest.** *Archaic or dialect.* short and stout; squat. [C18: from obsolete *fubs* plump person]

fuchsia (ˈfjuːʃə) *n.* **1.** any onagraceous shrub of the mostly tropical genus *Fuchsia,* widely cultivated for their showy drooping purple, red, or white flowers. **2.** Also called: **California fuchsia.** a North American onagraceous plant, *Zauschneria californica,* with tubular scarlet flowers. **3. a.** a reddish-purple to purplish-pink colour. **b.** (*as adj.*): *a fuchsia dress.* [C18: from New Latin, named after Leonhard *Fuchs* (1501–66), German botanist]

fuchsin (ˈfuːksɪn) *or* **fuchsine** (ˈfuːksiːn, -sɪn) *n.* a greenish crystalline substance, the quaternary chloride of rosaniline, forming a red solution in water: used as a textile dye and a biological stain. Formula: $C_{20}H_{19}N_3HCl$. Also called: **magenta.** [C19: from FUCHS(IA) + -IN; from its similarity in colour to the flower]

fucivorous (fjuːˈkɪvərəs) *adj. Zoology.* feeding on seaweed. [C19: from Greek *phukos* seaweed + -VOROUS]

fuck (fʌk) *Taboo.* ~*vb.* **1.** to have sexual intercourse with (someone). ~*n.* **2.** an act of sexual intercourse. **3.** *Slang.* a partner in sexual intercourse, esp. one of specified competence or experience: *she was a good fuck.* **4. not care** *or* **give a fuck.** not to care at all. ~*interj.* **5.** *Offensive.* an expression of strong disgust or anger (often in exclamatory phrases such as **fuck you! fuck it!** etc.). [C16: of Germanic origin; related to Middle Dutch *fokken* to strike]

fuck about *or* **around** *vb. (adv.) Offensive taboo slang.* **1.** (*intr.*) to act in a stupid or aimless manner. **2.** (*tr.*) to treat (someone) in an inconsiderate or selfish way.

fucker (ˈfʌkə) *n. Taboo.* **1.** *Slang.* a despicable or obnoxious person. **2.** *Slang.* a person; fellow. **3.** a person who fucks.

fucking (ˈfʌkɪŋ) *adj. (prenominal), adv. Taboo slang.* (intensifier): *a fucking good time.*

fuck off *Offensive taboo slang.* ~*interj.* **1.** a forceful expression of dismissal or contempt. ~*vb.* **2.** (*intr., adv.*) to go away.

fuck up *Offensive taboo slang.* ~*vb. (tr., adv.)* **1.** to damage or bungle: *to fuck up a machine.* **2.** to make confused. ~*n.* **fuck-up. 3.** an act or an instance of bungling.

fuckwit (ˈfʌkwɪt) *n. Taboo slang.* a fool or idiot.

fucoid (ˈfjuːkɔɪd) *adj. also* **fucoidal** *or* **fucous** (ˈfjuːkəs). **1.** of, relating to, or resembling seaweeds of the genus *Fucus.* ~*n.* **2.** any seaweed of the genus *Fucus.*

fucoxanthin (ˌfjuːkəʊˈzænθɪn) *n.* a carotenoid pigment that gives brown algae and diatoms their colour: functions in photosynthesis. Formula: $C_{40}H_{56}O_6$ or $C_{40}H_{60}O_6$.

fucus (ˈfjuːkəs) *n., pl.* **-ci** (-saɪ) *or* **-cuses.** any seaweed of the genus *Fucus,* common in the intertidal regions of many shores and typically having greenish-brown slimy fronds. See also **wrack**[2] (sense 2). [C16: from Latin: rock lichen, from Greek *phukos* seaweed, dye, of Semitic origin]

fuddle (ˈfʌdᵊl) *vb.* **1.** (*tr.; often passive*) to cause to be confused or intoxicated. **2.** (*intr.*) to drink excessively; tipple. ~*n.* **3.** a muddled or confused state. [C16: of unknown origin]

fuddy-duddy (ˈfʌdɪˌdʌdɪ) *n., pl.* **-dies.** *Informal.* a person, esp. an elderly one, who is extremely conservative or dull. [C20: of uncertain origin]

fudge[1] (fʌdʒ) *n.* a soft variously flavoured sweet made from sugar, butter, cream, etc. [C19: of unknown origin]

fudge[2] (fʌdʒ) *n.* **1.** foolishness; nonsense. ~*interj.* **2.** a mild exclamation of annoyance. ~*vb.* **3.** (*intr.*) to talk foolishly or emptily. [C18: of uncertain origin]

fudge[3] (fʌdʒ) *n.* **1.** a small section of type matter in a box in a newspaper allowing late news to be included without the whole page having to be remade. **2.** the box in which such type matter is placed. **3.** the late news so inserted. **4.** a machine attached to a newspaper press for printing this. ~*vb.* **5.** (*tr.*) to make or adjust in a false or clumsy way. **6.** (*tr.*) to misrepresent; falsify. **7.** to evade (a problem, issue, etc.); dodge; avoid. [C19: see FADGE]

Fuegian (fjuːˈiːdʒɪən, ˈfweɪdʒ-) *adj.* **1.** of or relating to Tierra del Fuego, an archipelago S of South America, or its indigenous Indians. ~*n.* **2.** an Indian of Tierra del Fuego.

fuel (fjʊəl) *n.* **1.** any substance burned as a source of heat or power, such as coal or petrol. **2.** the material, containing a fissile substance such as uranium-235, that produces energy in a nuclear reactor. **3.** something that nourishes or builds up emotion, action, etc. ~*vb.* **fuels, fuelling, fuelled** *or U.S.* **fuels, fueling, fueled. 4.** to supply with or receive fuel. [C14: from Old French *feuaile,* from *feu* fire, ultimately from Latin *focus* fireplace, hearth] —ˈ**fueller** *or U.S.* ˈ**fueler** *n.*

fuel cell *n.* a cell in which the energy produced by oxidation of a fuel is converted directly into electrical energy.

fuel element *n.* a can containing nuclear fuel for use in a reactor.

fuel injection *n.* a system for introducing atomized liquid fuel under pressure directly into the combustion chambers of an internal-combustion engine without the use of a carburettor.

fuel oil *n.* a liquid petroleum product having a flash point above 37.8°C: used as a substitute for coal in industrial furnaces, domestic heaters, ships, and locomotives.

fuel rod *n.* a long tube, often made of a zirconium alloy and containing uranium-oxide pellets, that is stacked in bundles of about 200 to provide the fuel in certain types of nuclear reactor.

fug (fʌg) *n. Chiefly Brit.* a hot, stale, or suffocating atmosphere. [C19: perhaps variant of FOG[1]] —ˈ**fuggy** *adj.*

fugacious (fjuːˈgeɪʃəs) *adj.* **1.** passing quickly away; transitory; fleeting. **2.** *Botany.* lasting for only a short time: *fugacious petals.* [C17: from Latin *fugax* inclined to flee, swift, from *fugere* to flee; see FUGITIVE] —**fuˈgaciously** *adv.* —**fuˈgaciousness** *n.*

fugacity (fjuːˈgæsɪtɪ) *n.* **1.** Also called: **escaping tendency.** *Thermodynamics.* a property of a gas that expresses its tendency to escape or expand, given by $d(\log_e f) = d\mu/RT$, where μ is the chemical potential, R the gas constant, and T the thermodynamic temperature. Symbol: f **2.** the state or quality of being fugacious.

fugal (ˈfjuːgᵊl) *adj.* of, relating to, or in the style of a fugue. —ˈ**fugally** *adv.*

fugato (fjʊˈgɑːtəʊ) *Music.* ~*adv., adj.* **1.** in the manner or style of a fugue. ~*n.* **2.** a movement, section, or piece in this style. [C19: from Italian, from *fugare* to compose in the style of a FUGUE]

-fuge *n. combining form.* indicating an agent or substance that expels or drives away: *vermifuge.* [from Latin *fugāre* to expel, put to flight] —**-fugal** *adj. combining form.*

fugio (ˈfjuːdʒɪəʊ) *n., pl.* **-gios.** a former U.S. copper coin worth one dollar, the first authorized by Congress (1787). [C18: Latin: I flee; one of the words inscribed on the coin]

fugitive (ˈfjuːdʒɪtɪv) *n.* **1.** a person who flees. **2.** a thing that is elusive or fleeting. ~*adj.* **3.** fleeing, esp. from arrest or pursuit. **4.** not permanent; fleeting; transient. **5.** moving or roving about. [C14: from Latin *fugitīvus* fleeing away, from *fugere* to take flight, run away] —ˈ**fugitively** *adv.* —ˈ**fugitiveness** *n.*

fugitometer (ˌfjuːdʒɪˈtɒmɪtə) *n.* an instrument used for measuring the fastness to light of dyed materials.

fugleman (ˈfjuːgᵊlmən) *n., pl.* **-men. 1.** (formerly) a soldier used as an example for those learning drill. **2.** any person who acts as a leader or example. [C19: from German *Flügelmann,* from *Flügel* wing, flank + *Mann* MAN]

fugue (fjuːg) *n.* **1.** a musical form consisting essentially of a theme repeated a fifth above or a fourth below the continuing first statement. **2.** *Psychiatry.* a dreamlike altered state of consciousness, lasting from a few hours to several days, during which a person loses his memory for his previous life and often wanders away from home. [C16: from French, from Italian *fuga,* from Latin: a running away, flight] —ˈ**fugueˌlike** *adj.*

fuguist (ˈfjuːgɪst) *n.* a composer of fugues.

Führer *or* ***Fuehrer*** *German.* (ˈfyːrər; *English* ˈfjʊərə) *n.* a leader: applied esp. to Adolf Hitler (***der Führer***) while he was Chancellor. [German, from *führen* to lead]

-ful *suffix.* **1.** (*forming adjectives*) full of or characterized by: *painful; spiteful; restful.* **2.** (*forming adjectives*) able or tending to: *helpful; useful.* **3.** (*forming nouns*) indicating as much as will fill the thing specified: *mouthful; spoonful.* [Old English *-ful, -full,* from FULL]

▷**Usage.** Where the amount held by a spoon, etc., is used as a rough unit of measurement, the correct form is *spoonful,* etc.: *take a spoonful of this medicine every day. Spoon full* is used in a sentence such as *he left a spoon full of treacle,* where *full of* describes the spoon. The plural of a word like *spoonful* is *spoonfuls* and not *spoonsful.*

Fula (ˈfuːlə) *or* **Fulah** (ˈfuːlɑː) *n.* **1.** (*pl.* **-la, -las** *or* **-lah, -lahs**) a member of a pastoral nomadic people of W and central Africa, living chiefly in the sub-Sahara region from Senegal to N Cameroon: a racial mixture of light-skinned Berber peoples of the North and darker-skinned W Africans. **2.** the language of this people; Fulani.

Fulani (fuːˈlɑːnɪ, ˈfuːlənɪ) *n.* **1.** the language of the Fula, belonging to the West Atlantic branch of the Niger-Congo family, widely used as a trade pidgin in W Africa. **2.** (*pl.* **-nis, -ni**) another name for **Fula** (the people). **3.** (*pl.* **-nis, -ni**) a humped breed of cattle from W Africa. ~*adj.* **4.** of or relating to the Fula or their language.

fulcrum ('fʊlkrəm, 'fʌl-) *n., pl.* **-crums** *or* **-cra** (-krə). **1.** the pivot about which a lever turns. **2.** something that supports or sustains; prop. **3.** a spinelike scale occurring in rows along the anterior edge of the fins in primitive bony fishes such as the sturgeon. [C17: from Latin: foot of a couch, bedpost, from *fulcire* to prop up]

fulfil *or U.S.* **fulfill** (fʊl'fɪl) *vb.* **-fils** *or U.S.* **-fills, -filling, -filled.** (*tr.*) **1.** to bring about the completion or achievement of (a desire, promise, etc.). **2.** to carry out or execute (a request, etc.). **3.** to conform with or satisfy (regulations, demands, etc.). **4.** to finish or reach the end of: *he fulfilled his prison sentence.* **5. fulfil oneself.** to achieve one's potential or desires. [Old English *fulfyllan*] —**ful'filler** *n.* —**ful'filment** *or U.S.* **ful'fillment** *n.*

fulgent ('fʌldʒənt) *or* **fulgid** ('fʌldʒɪd) *adj. Poetic.* shining brilliantly; resplendent; gleaming. [C15: from Latin *fulgēre* to shine, flash] —**'fulgently** *adv.*

fulgurate ('fʌlgjʊˌreɪt) *vb.* (*intr.*) *Rare.* to flash like lightning. [C17: from Latin *fulgurāre,* from *fulgur* lightning] —**fulgurant** ('fʌlgjʊrənt) *adj.*

fulgurating ('fʌlgjʊˌreɪtɪŋ) *adj.* **1.** *Pathol.* (of pain) sudden and sharp; piercing. **2.** *Surgery.* of or relating to fulguration.

fulguration (ˌfʌlgjʊ'reɪʃən) *n. Surgery.* destruction of tissue by means of high-frequency (more than 10 000 per second) electric sparks.

fulgurite ('fʌlgjʊˌraɪt) *n.* a tube of glassy mineral matter found in sand and rock, formed by the action of lightning. [C19: from Latin *fulgur* lightning]

fulgurous ('fʌlgjʊrəs) *adj. Rare.* flashing like or resembling lightning; fulgurant. [C17: from Latin *fulgur* lightning]

fuliginous (fjuː'lɪdʒɪnəs) *adj.* **1.** sooty or smoky. **2.** of the colour of soot; dull greyish-black or brown. [C16: from Late Latin *fūlīginōsus* full of soot, from Latin *fūlīgō* soot] —**fu'liginously** *adv.* —**fu'liginousness** *n.*

full[1] (fʊl) *adj.* **1.** holding or containing as much as possible; filled to capacity or near capacity. **2.** abundant in supply, quantity, number, etc.: *full of energy.* **3.** having consumed enough food or drink. **4.** (esp. of the face or figure) rounded or plump; not thin. **5.** (*prenominal*) with no part lacking; complete: *a full dozen.* **6.** (*prenominal*) with all privileges, rights, etc.; not restricted: *a full member.* **7.** (*prenominal*) of, relating to, or designating a relationship established by descent from the same parents: *full brother.* **8.** filled with emotion or sentiment: *a full heart.* **9.** (*postpositive;* foll. by *of*) occupied or engrossed (with): *full of his own projects.* **10.** *Music.* **a.** powerful or rich in volume and sound. **b.** completing a piece or section; concluding: *a full close.* **11.** (of a garment, esp. a skirt) containing a large amount of fabric; of ample cut. **12.** (of sails, etc.) distended by wind. **13.** (of wine, such as a burgundy) having a heavy body. **14.** (of a colour) containing a large quantity of pure hue as opposed to white or grey; rich; saturated. **15.** *Informal.* drunk. **16. full and by.** *Nautical.* another term for **close-hauled.** **17. full of oneself.** full of pride or conceit; egoistic. **18. full up.** filled to capacity: *the cinema was full up.* **19. in full cry.** (esp. of a pack of hounds) in hot pursuit of quarry. **20. in full swing.** at the height of activity: *the party was in full swing.* ~*adv.* **21. a.** completely; entirely. **b.** (*in combination*): *full-grown; full-fledged.* **22.** exactly; directly; right: *he hit him full in the stomach.* **23.** very; extremely (esp. in the phrase **full well**). **24. full out.** with maximum effort or speed. ~*n.* **25.** the greatest degree, extent, etc. **26.** *Brit.* a ridge of sand or shingle along a seashore. **27. in full.** without omitting, decreasing, or shortening: *we paid in full for our mistake.* **28. to the full.** to the greatest extent; thoroughly; fully. ~*vb.* **29.** (*tr.*) *Needlework.* to gather or tuck. **30.** (*intr.*) (of the moon) to be fully illuminated. [Old English; related to Old Norse *fullr,* Old High German *foll,* Latin *plēnus,* Greek *plērēs;* see FILL] —**'fullness** *or esp. U.S.* **'fulness** *n.*

full[2] (fʊl) *vb.* (of cloth, yarn, etc.) to become or to make (cloth, yarn, etc.) heavier and more compact during manufacture through shrinking and beating or pressing. [C14: from Old French *fouler,* ultimately from Latin *fullō* a FULLER[1]]

fullback ('fʊlˌbæk) *n.* **1.** *Soccer, hockey.* one of two defensive players positioned in front of the goalkeeper. **2.** *Rugby.* a defensive player positioned close to his own line. **3.** the position held by any of these players.

full blood *n.* **1.** an individual, esp. a horse or similar domestic animal, of unmixed race or breed. **2.** the relationship between individuals having the same parents.

full-blooded *adj.* **1.** (esp. of horses) of unmixed ancestry; thoroughbred. **2.** having great vigour or health; hearty; virile. —ˌ**full-'bloodedness** *n.*

full-blown *adj.* **1.** characterized by the fullest, strongest, or best development. **2.** in full bloom.

full board *n.* **a.** the provision by a hotel of a bed and all meals. **b.** (*as modifier*): *full board accommodation.*

full-bodied *adj.* having a full rich flavour or quality.

full-bottomed *adj.* (of a wig) long at the back.

full-court press *n. Basketball.* the tactic of harrying the opposing team in all areas of the court, as opposed to the more usual practice of trying to defend one's own basket.

full-cream *adj.* denoting or made with whole unskimmed milk.

full dress *n.* **a.** a formal or ceremonial style of dress, such as white tie and tails for a man and a full-length evening dress for a woman. **b.** (*as modifier*): *full-dress uniform.*

full employment *n.* a state in which the labour force and other economic resources of a country are utilized to their maximum extent.

fuller[1] ('fʊlə) *n.* a person who fulls cloth for his living. [Old English *fullere,* from Latin *fullō*]

fuller[2] ('fʊlə) *n.* **1.** Also called: **fullering tool.** a tool for forging a groove. **2.** a tool for caulking a riveted joint. ~*vb.* **3.** (*tr.*) to forge (a groove) or caulk (a riveted joint) with a fuller. [C19: perhaps from the name *Fuller*]

fuller's earth *n.* a natural absorbent clay used, after heating, for decolorizing oils and fats, fulling cloth, etc.

fuller's teasel *n.* **1.** a Eurasian teasel plant, *Dipsacus fullonum,* whose prickly flower heads are used for raising the nap on woollen cloth. **2.** a similar and related plant, *Dipsacus sativum.*

full-faced *adj.* **1.** having a round full face. **2.** Also: **full face.** facing towards the viewer, with the entire face visible. **3.** another name for **bold face.** —**'full'face** *n., adv.*

full-fledged *adj.* See **fully fledged.**

full-frontal *adj.* **1.** *Informal.* (of a nude person or a photograph of a nude person) exposing the genitals to full view. **2.** all-out; unrestrained. ~*n.* **full frontal. 3.** a full-frontal photograph.

full house *n.* **1.** *Poker.* a hand with three cards of the same value and another pair. **2.** a theatre, etc., filled to capacity. **3.** (in bingo, etc.) the set of numbers needed to win.

full-length *n.* (*modifier*) **1.** extending to or showing the complete length: *a full-length mirror.* **2.** of the original or normal length; not abridged.

full moon *n.* **1.** one of the four phases of the moon, occurring when the earth lies between the sun and the moon so that the moon is visible as a fully illuminated disc. **2.** the moon in this phase. **3.** the time at which this occurs.

full-mouthed *adj.* **1.** (of livestock) having a full adult set of teeth. **2.** uttered loudly: *a full-mouthed oath.*

full nelson *n.* a wrestling hold, illegal in amateur wrestling, in which a wrestler places both arms under his opponent's arms from behind and exerts pressure with both palms on the back of the neck. Compare **half-nelson.**

full pitch *or* **full toss** *n. Cricket.* a bowled ball that reaches the batsman without bouncing.

full professor *n. U.S. and Canadian.* a university teacher of the highest academic rank. There can be several full professors in the same department.

full radiator *n. Physics.* another name for **black body.**

full-rigged *adj.* **1.** (of a sailing vessel) having three or more masts rigged square. **2.** *Rare.* fully equipped.

full sail *adv.* **1.** at top speed. ~*adj.* (*postpositive*), *adv.* **2.** with all sails set. —ˌ**full-'sailed** *adj.*

full-scale *n.* (*modifier*) **1.** (of a plan, etc.) of actual size; having the same dimensions as the original. **2.** done with thoroughness or urgency; using all resources; all-out.

full score *n.* the entire score of a musical composition, showing each part separately.

full stop *or* **full point** *n.* the punctuation mark (.) used at the end of a sentence that is not a question or exclamation, after abbreviations, etc. Also called (esp. U.S. and Canadian): **period.**

full time *n.* the end of a football or other match. Compare **half-time.**

full-time *adj.* **1.** for the entire time appropriate to an activity: *a full-time job; a full-time student.* ~*adv.* **full time. 2.** on a full-time basis: *he works full time.* ~Compare **part-time.** —ˌ**full-'timer** *n.*

full toss *n. Cricket.* another term for **full pitch.**

full-wave rectifier *n.* an electronic circuit in which both half-cycles of incoming alternating current are used to furnish the direct current output.

fully ('fʊlɪ) *adv.* **1.** to the greatest degree or extent; totally; entirely. **2.** amply; sufficiently; adequately: *they were fully fed.* **3.** at least: *it was fully an hour before she came.*

fully fashioned *adj.* (of stockings, knitwear, etc.) shaped and seamed so as to fit closely.

fully fledged *or* **full-fledged** *adj.* **1.** (of a young bird) having acquired its adult feathers and thus able to fly. **2.** developed or matured to the fullest degree. **3.** of full rank or status.

fulmar ('fʊlmə) *n.* any heavily built short-tailed oceanic bird of the genus *Fulmarus* and related genera, of polar regions: family *Procellariidae,* order *Procellariiformes* (petrels). [C17: of Scandinavian origin; related to Old Norse *fūlmār,* from *fūll* foul + *mār* gull]

fulminant ('fʌlmɪnənt, 'fʊl-) *adj.* **1.** sudden and violent; fulminating. **2.** *Pathol.* (of pain) sudden and sharp; piercing. [C17: from Latin *fulmināre* to cause lightning, from *fulmen* lightning that strikes]

fulminate ('fʌlmɪˌneɪt, 'fʊl-) *vb.* **1.** (*intr.;* often foll. by *against*) to make severe criticisms or denunciations; rail. **2.** to explode with noise and violence. **3.** (*intr.*) *Archaic.* to thunder and lighten. ~*n.* **4.** any salt or ester of fulminic acid, esp. the mercury salt, which is used as a detonator. [C15: from Medieval Latin *fulmināre;* see FULMINANT] —ˌ**fulmi'nation** *n.* —**'fulmiˌnator** *n.* —**'fulmiˌnatory** *adj.*

fulminating powder *n.* powder that detonates by percussion.

fulminic acid (fʌlˈmɪnɪk, fʊl-) *n.* an unstable volatile acid known only in solution and in the form of its salts and esters. Formula: HONC. Compare **cyanic acid.** [C19: from Latin *fulmen* lightning]
fulminous (ˈfʌlmɪnəs, ˈfʊl-) *adj. Rare.* **1.** harshly critical. **2.** of, involving, or resembling thunder and lightning.
fulsome (ˈfʊlsəm) *adj.* **1.** excessive or insincere, esp. in an offensive or distasteful way: *fulsome compliments.* **2.** *Archaic.* disgusting; loathsome. —ˈ**fulsomely** *adv.* —ˈ**fulsomeness** *n.*
fulvous (ˈfʌlvəs, ˈfʊl-) *adj.* of a dull brownish-yellow colour; tawny. [C17: from Latin *fulvus* reddish yellow, gold-coloured, tawny; probably related to *fulgēre* to shine]
fumaric acid (fjuːˈmærɪk) *n.* a colourless crystalline acid with a fruity taste, found in some plants and manufactured from benzene; *trans*-butenedioic acid: used esp. in synthetic resins. Formula: HCOOCH:CHCOOH. [C19: from New Latin *Fumāria* name of genus, from Late Latin: fumitory, from Latin *fūmus* smoke]
fumarole (ˈfjuːməˌrəʊl) *n.* a vent in or near a volcano from which hot gases, esp. steam, are emitted. [C19: from French *fumerolle,* from Late Latin *fūmāriolum* smoke hole, from Latin *fūmus* smoke] —**fumarolic** (ˌfjuːməˈrɒlɪk) *adj.*
fumatorium (ˌfjuːməˈtɔːrɪəm) *n., pl.* **-riums** *or* **-ria** (-rɪə). an airtight chamber in which insects and fungi on organic matter or plants are destroyed by fumigation. Also called: **fumatory.** [New Latin, from Latin *fūmāre* to smoke]
fumatory (ˈfjuːmətərɪ, -trɪ) *adj.* **1.** of or relating to smoking or fumigation. ~*n., pl.* **-ries. 2.** another name for a **fumatorium.**
fumble (ˈfʌmbᵊl) *vb.* **1.** (*intr.;* often foll. by *for* or *with*) to grope about clumsily or blindly, esp. in searching: *he was fumbling in the dark for the money he had dropped.* **2.** (*intr.;* foll. by *at* or *with*) to finger or play with, esp. in an absent-minded way. **3.** to say or do hesitantly or awkwardly: *he fumbled the introduction badly.* **4.** to fail to catch or grasp (a ball, etc.) cleanly. ~*n.* **5.** the act of fumbling. [C16: probably of Scandinavian origin; related to Swedish *fumla*] —ˈ**fumbler** *n.* —ˈ**fumblingly** *adv.* —ˈ**fumblingness** *n.*
fume (fjuːm) *vb.* **1.** (*intr.*) to be overcome with anger or fury; rage. **2.** to give off (fumes) or (of fumes) to be given off, esp. during a chemical reaction. **3.** (*tr.*) to subject to or treat with fumes; fumigate. ~*n.* **4.** (*often pl.*) a pungent or toxic vapour, gas, or smoke. **5.** a sharp or pungent odour. **6.** a condition of anger or fury. [C14: from Old French *fum,* from Latin *fūmus* smoke, vapour] —ˈ**fumeless** *adj.* —ˈ**fumeˌlike** *adj.* —ˈ**fumer** *n.* —ˈ**fumingly** *adv.* —ˈ**fumy** *adj.*
fume cupboard *n.* a ventilated enclosure for storing or experimenting with chemicals with harmful vapours.
fumed (fjuːmd) *adj.* (of wood, esp. oak) having a dark colour and distinctive grain from exposure to ammonia fumes.
fumet[1] (fjuːˈmɛt) *n.* a strong-flavoured liquor from cooking fish, meat, or game: used to flavour sauces. [French, literally: aroma]
fumet[2] (ˈfjuːmət) *n.* (*often pl.*) *Archaic.* the dropping of a deer. [C16 *fewmet:* probably via Old French from Latin *fimāre* to spread dung on, from *fimus* dung]
fumigant (ˈfjuːmɪgənt) *n.* a substance used for fumigating.
fumigate (ˈfjuːmɪˌgeɪt) *vb.* to treat (something contaminated or infected) with fumes or smoke. [C16: from Latin *fūmigāre* to smoke, steam, from *fūmus* smoke + *agere* to drive, produce] —ˌ**fumiˈgation** *n.* —ˈ**fumiˌgator** *n.*
fuming sulphuric acid *n.* a mixture of pyrosulphuric acid, $H_2S_2O_7$, and other condensed acids, made by dissolving sulphur trioxide in concentrated sulphuric acid. Also called: **oleum, Nordhausen acid** (ˈnɔːdhaʊzᵊn).
fumitory (ˈfjuːmɪtərɪ, -trɪ) *n., pl.* **-ries.** any plant of the chiefly European genus *Fumaria,* esp. *F. officinalis,* having spurred flowers and formerly used medicinally: family *Fumariaceae.* [C14: from Old French *fumetere,* from Medieval Latin *fūmus terrae,* literally: smoke of the earth; see FUME]
fun (fʌn) *n.* **1.** a source of enjoyment, amusement, diversion, etc. **2.** pleasure, gaiety, or merriment. **3.** jest or sport (esp. in the phrases **in** or **for fun**). **4. fun and games.** *Ironic or facetious.* gay amusement; frivolous activity. **5. like fun.** *Informal.* **a.** (*adv.*) quickly; vigorously. **b.** (*interj.*) not at all! certainly not! **6. make fun of** *or* **poke fun at.** to ridicule or deride. **7.** (*modifier*) full of amusement, diversion, gaiety, etc.: *a fun sport.* ~*vb.* **funs, funning, funned. 8.** (*intr.*) *Informal.* to act in a joking or sporting manner. [C17: perhaps from obsolete *fon* to make a fool of; see FOND[1]]
funambulist (fjuːˈnæmbjʊlɪst) *n.* a tightrope walker. [C18: from Latin *fūnambulus* rope dancer, from *fūnis* rope + ambulāre to walk] —**fuˈnambulism** *n.*
function (ˈfʌŋkʃən) *n.* **1.** the natural action or intended purpose of a person or thing in a specific role: *the function of a hammer is to hit nails into wood.* **2.** an official or formal social gathering or ceremony. **3.** a factor dependent upon another or other factors: *the length of the flight is a function of the weather.* **4. Also called: map, mapping.** *Maths, logic.* a relation between two sets that associates a unique element (the value) of the second (the range) with each element (the argument) of the first (the domain): a many-one relation. Symbol: f(x) The value of f(x) for $x = 2$ is f(2). ~*vb.* (*intr.*) **5.** to operate or perform as specified; work properly. **6.** (foll. by *as*) to perform the action or role (of something or someone else): *a coin may function as a screwdriver.* [C16: from Latin *functiō,* from *fungī* to perform, discharge] —ˈ**functionless** *adj.*
functional (ˈfʌŋkʃənᵊl) *adj.* **1.** of, involving, or containing a function or functions. **2.** practical rather than decorative; utilitarian: *functional architecture.* **3.** capable of functioning; working. **4.** *Psychol.* **a.** relating to the purpose or context of a behaviour. **b.** denoting a psychosis such as schizophrenia assumed not to have a direct organic cause, like deterioration or poisoning of the brain. ~*n.* **5.** *Maths.* a function whose domain is a set of functions and whose range is another set of functions that can be a set of numbers. —ˈ**functionally** *adv.*
functional calculus *n.* **1.** another name for **predicate calculus. 2.** the branch of mathematics that studies the properties of functions and operations upon functions.
functional disease *n.* a disease in which there is no observable change in the structure of an organ or part. Compare **organic disease.**
functional group *n. Chem.* the group of atoms in a compound, such as the hydroxyl group in an alcohol, that determines the chemical behaviour of the compound.
functional illiterate *n.* a person whose literacy is insufficient for most work and normal daily situations. —**functional illiteracy** *n.*
functionalism (ˈfʌŋkʃənəˌlɪzəm) *n.* **1.** the theory of design that the form of a thing should be determined by its use. **2.** any doctrine that stresses utility or purpose. **3.** *Psychol.* a system of thought based on the premise that all mental processes derive from their usefulness to the organism in adapting to the environment. —ˈ**functionalist** *n., adj.*
functionary (ˈfʌŋkʃənərɪ) *n., pl.* **-aries. 1.** a person acting in an official capacity, as for a government; an official. ~*adj.* **2.** a less common word for **functional** or **official.**
function key *n. Computer technol.* a key on the keyboard of a microcomputer, etc. that gives special commands to the computer.
function shift *or* **change** *n.* **1.** *Grammar.* a change in the syntactic function of a word, as when the noun *mushroom* is used as an intransitive verb. **2.** *Linguistics.* sound change involving a realignment of the phonemic system of a language.
function word *n. Grammar.* a word, such as *the,* with a particular grammatical role but little identifiable meaning. Compare **content word, grammatical meaning.**
fund (fʌnd) *n.* **1.** a reserve of money, etc., set aside for a certain purpose. **2.** a supply or store of something; stock: *it exhausted his fund of wisdom.* ~*vb.* (*tr.*) **3.** to furnish money to in the form of a fund. **4.** to place or store up in a fund. **5.** to convert (short-term floating debt) into long-term debt bearing fixed interest and represented by bonds. **6.** to provide a fund for the redemption of principal or payment of interest of. **7.** to accumulate a fund for the discharge of (a recurrent liability): *to fund a pension plan.* **8.** to invest (money) in government securities. ~See also **funds.** [C17: from Latin *fundus* the bottom, piece of land, estate; compare FOND[2]]
fundament (ˈfʌndəmənt) *n.* **1.** *Euphemistic or facetious.* the buttocks. **2.** the natural features of the earth's surface, unaltered by man. **3.** a base or foundation, esp. of a building. **4.** a theory, principle, or underlying basis. [C13: from Latin *fundāmentum* foundation, from *fundāre* to FOUND[2]]
fundamental (ˌfʌndəˈmɛntᵊl) *adj.* **1.** of, involving, or comprising a foundation; basic. **2.** of, involving, or comprising a source; primary. **3.** *Music.* denoting or relating to the principal or lowest note of a harmonic series. **4.** of or concerned with the component of lowest frequency in a complex vibration. ~*n.* **5.** a principle, law, etc., that serves as the basis of an idea or system. **6. a.** the principal or lowest note of a harmonic series. **b.** the bass note of a chord in root position. **7.** Also called: **fundamental frequency, first harmonic.** *Physics.* **a.** the component of lowest frequency in a complex vibration. **b.** the frequency of this component. —ˌ**fundamenˈtality** *or* ˌ**fundaˈmentalness** *n.* —ˌ**fundaˈmentally** *adv.*
fundamental interaction *n.* any of the four basic interactions that occur in nature: the gravitational, electromagnetic, strong, and weak interactions.
fundamentalism (ˌfʌndəˈmɛntəˌlɪzəm) *n.* **1.** *Christianity.* (esp. among certain Protestant sects) the belief that every word of the Bible is divinely inspired and therefore true. **2.** *Islam.* a movement favouring strict observance of the teachings of the Koran and Islamic law. **3.** strict adherence to the fundamental principles of any set of beliefs. —ˌ**fundaˈmentalist** *n., adj.* —ˌ**fundaˌmentalˈistic** *adj.*
fundamental law *n.* the law determining the constitution of the government of a state; organic law.
fundamental particle *n.* another name for **elementary particle.**
fundamental unit *n.* one of a set of unrelated units that form the basis of a system of units. For example, the metre, kilogram, and second are fundamental units of the SI system.
funded debt *n.* the part of the national debt, consisting mostly of consols, that the government has no obligation to repay by a specified date.
fundi (ˈfʊndiː) *n. E African.* a person skilled in repairing or maintaining machinery; mechanic. [C20: from Swahili]

funding operations *pl. n. Finance.* the conversion of government floating stock or short-term debt into holdings of long-term bonds.

fund manager *n.* an employee of an insurance company, pension fund, investment trust, etc., who manages its fund of investments.

funds (fʌndz) *pl. n.* **1.** money that is readily available. **2.** British government securities representing national debt.

fundus ('fʌndəs) *n., pl.* **-di** (-daɪ). *Anatomy.* the base of an organ or the part farthest away from its opening. [C18: from Latin, literally: the bottom, a farm, estate] —'**fundic** *adj.*

funeral ('fju:nərəl) *n.* **1. a.** a ceremony at which a dead person is buried or cremated. **b.** (*as modifier*): *a funeral service.* **2.** a procession of people escorting a corpse to burial. **3.** *Informal.* worry; concern; affair: *that's your funeral.* [C14: from Medieval Latin *fūnerālia*, from Late Latin *fūnerālis* (adj.), from Latin *fūnus* funeral]

funeral director *n.* an undertaker.

funeral parlour *n.* a place where the dead are prepared for burial or cremation. Usual U.S. name: **funeral home.**

funerary ('fju:nərərɪ) *adj.* of, relating to, or for a funeral.

funereal (fju:'nɪərɪəl) *adj.* suggestive of a funeral; gloomy or mournful. Also: **funebrial** (fju:'ni:brɪəl). [C18: from Latin *fūnereus*] —**fu'nereally** *adv.*

funfair ('fʌn,fɛə) *n. Brit.* an amusement park or fairground.

fun fur *n.* a relatively inexpensive synthetic fur garment.

fungal ('fʌŋgᵊl) *adj.* of, derived from, or caused by a fungus or fungi: *fungal spores; a fungal disease.*

fungi ('fʌŋgaɪ, 'fʌndʒaɪ, 'fʌndʒɪ) *n.* a plural of **fungus.**

fungi- *or before a vowel* **fung-** *combining form.* fungus: *fungicide; fungoid.*

fungible ('fʌndʒɪbᵊl) *Law.* ~*n.* **1.** (*often pl.*) moveable perishable goods of a sort that may be estimated by number or weight, such as grain, wine, etc. ~*adj.* **2.** having the nature or quality of fungibles. [C18: from Medieval Latin *fungibilis*, from Latin *fungī* to perform; see FUNCTION] —,**fungi'bility** *n.*

fungicide ('fʌndʒɪ,saɪd) *n.* a substance or agent that destroys or is capable of destroying fungi. —,**fungi'cidal** *adj.* —,**fungi'cidally** *adv.*

fungiform ('fʌndʒɪ,fɔ:m) *adj.* shaped like a mushroom or similar fungus: *the fungiform papillae of the tongue.*

fungistat ('fʌndʒɪ,stæt) *n.* a substance that inhibits the growth of fungi. —,**fungi'static** *adj.*

fungoid ('fʌŋgɔɪd) *adj.* resembling a fungus or fungi: *a fungoid growth.*

fungous ('fʌŋgəs) *adj.* **1.** appearing suddenly and spreading quickly like a fungus, but not lasting. **2.** a less common word for **fungal.**

fungus ('fʌŋgəs) *n., pl.* **fungi** ('fʌŋgaɪ, 'fʌndʒaɪ, 'fʌndʒɪ) *or* **funguses.** **1.** any one of a group of organisms, classified as plants by some authorities, that lacks chlorophyll, leaves, true stems, and roots, reproduces by spores, and lives as a saprophyte or parasite. The group includes moulds, mildews, rusts, yeasts, and mushrooms. **2.** something resembling a fungus, esp. in suddenly growing and spreading rapidly. **3.** *Pathol.* any soft tumorous growth. [C16: from Latin: mushroom, fungus; probably related to Greek *spongos* SPONGE] —**fungic** ('fʌndʒɪk) *adj.* —'**fungus-,like** *adj.*

funicle ('fju:nɪkᵊl) *n. Botany.* the stalk that attaches an ovule or seed to the wall of the ovary. Also called: **funiculus.** [C17: from Latin *fūniculus* a thin rope, from *fūnis* rope] —**funiculate** (fju'nɪkjʊlɪt, -,leɪt) *adj.*

funicular (fju:'nɪkjʊlə) *n.* **1.** Also called: **funicular railway.** a railway up the side of a mountain, consisting of two counterbalanced cars at either end of a cable passing round a driving wheel at the summit. ~*adj.* **2.** relating to or operated by a rope, cable, etc. **3.** of or relating to a funicle.

funiculus (fju:'nɪkjʊləs) *n., pl.* **-li** (-,laɪ). **1.** *Anatomy.* a cordlike part or structure, esp. a small bundle of nerve fibres in the spinal cord. **2.** a variant of **funicle.** [C17: from Latin; see FUNICLE]

funk[1] (fʌŋk) *Informal, chiefly Brit.* ~*n.* **1.** Also called: **blue funk.** a state of nervousness, fear, or depression (esp. in the phrase **in a funk**). **2.** a coward. ~*vb.* **3.** to flinch from (responsibility) through fear. **4.** (*tr.; usually passive*) to make afraid. [C18: university slang, perhaps related to FUNK[2]] —'**funker** *n.*

funk[2] (fʌŋk) *n. U.S. slang.* a strong foul odour. [C17 (in the sense: tobacco smoke): from *funk* (vb.) to smoke (tobacco), probably of French dialect origin; compare Old French *funkier* to smoke, from Latin *fūmigāre*]

funk[3] (fʌŋk) *n. Informal.* a type of polyrhythmic Black dance music with heavy syncopation. [C20: back formation from FUNKY[1]]

funk hole *n. Informal.* **1.** *Military.* a dugout. **2.** a job that affords exemption from military service.

funky[1] ('fʌŋkɪ) *adj.* **funkier, funkiest.** *Informal.* **1.** (of music) passionate, soulful; of or pertaining to funk. **2.** authentic; earthy. [C20: from FUNK[2], perhaps alluding to music that was smelly, that is, earthy (like the early blues)]

funky[2] ('fʌŋkɪ) *adj.* **funkier, funkiest.** *Slang, chiefly U.S.* evil-smelling; foul. [C18: from FUNK[2]]

funnel ('fʌnᵊl) *n.* **1.** a hollow utensil with a wide mouth tapering to a small hole, used for pouring liquids, powders, etc., into a narrow-necked vessel. **2.** something resembling this in shape or function. **3.** a smokestack for smoke and exhaust gases, as on a steamship or steam locomotive. **4.** a shaft or tube, as in a building, for ventilation. ~*vb.* **-nels, -nelling, -nelled** *or U.S.* **-nels, -neling, -neled.** **5.** to move or cause to move or pour through or as if through a funnel. **6.** to concentrate or focus or be concentrated or focused in a particular direction: *they funnelled their attention on the problem.* **7.** (*intr.*) to take on a funnel-like shape. [C15: from Old Provençal *fonilh*, ultimately from Latin *infundibulum* funnel, hopper (in a mill), from *infundere* to pour in] —'**funnel-,like** *adj.*

funnel cap *n.* any of various basidiomycetous fungi of the genus *Clitocybe*, characterized by the funnel-shaped caps and, usually, markedly decurrent gills.

funnel cloud *n.* a whirling column of cloud extending downwards from the base of a cumulonimbus cloud: part of a waterspout or tornado.

funnel-web *n. Austral.* any large poisonous black spider of the family *Dipluridae*, constructing funnel-shaped webs.

funnies ('fʌnɪz) *pl. n. U.S. and Canadian informal.* comic strips in a newspaper.

funny ('fʌnɪ) *adj.* **-nier, -niest.** **1.** causing amusement or laughter; humorous; comical. **2.** peculiar; odd. **3.** suspicious or dubious (esp. in the phrase **funny business**). **4.** *Informal.* faint or ill: *to feel funny.* ~*n., pl.* **-nies.** **5.** *Informal.* a joke or witticism. —'**funnily** *adv.* —'**funniness** *n.*

funny bone *n.* the area near the elbow where the ulnar nerve is close to the surface of the skin: when it is struck, a sharp tingling sensation is experienced along the forearm and hand. Also called (U.S.): **crazy bone.**

funny farm *n. Facetious.* a mental institution.

funny paper *n. U.S. and Canadian.* a section or separate supplement of a newspaper, etc., containing comic strips.

fun run *n.* a long run or part-marathon run for exercise and pleasure, often by large numbers of people.

fur (fɜ:) *n.* **1.** the dense coat of fine silky hairs on such mammals as the cat, seal, and mink. **2. a.** the dressed skin of certain fur-bearing animals, with the hair left on. **b.** (*as modifier*): *a fur coat.* **3.** a garment made of fur, such as a coat or stole. **4. a.** a pile fabric made in imitation of animal fur. **b.** a garment made from such a fabric. **5.** *Heraldry.* any of various stylized representations of animal pelts or their tinctures, esp. ermine or vair, used in coats of arms. **6. make the fur fly.** to cause a scene or disturbance. **7.** *Informal.* a whitish coating of cellular debris on the tongue, caused by excessive smoking, an upset stomach, etc. **8.** *Brit.* a whitish-grey deposit consisting chiefly of calcium carbonate precipitated from hard water onto the insides of pipes, boilers, and kettles. ~*vb.* **furs, furring, furred.** **9.** (*tr.*) to line or trim a garment, etc., with fur. **10.** (often foll. by *up*) to cover or become covered with a furlike lining or deposit. **11.** (*tr.*) to clothe (a person) in a fur garment or garments. [C14: from Old French *forrer* to line a garment, from *fuerre* sheath, of Germanic origin; related to Old English *fōdder* case, Old Frisian *fōder* coat lining] —'**furless** *adj.*

fur. *abbrev. for* furlong.

furaldehyde (fjʊə'rældə,haɪd) *n.* either of two aldehydes derived from furan, esp. **2-furaldehyde** (see **furfuraldehyde**). [C20: shortened from *furfuraldehyde*, from *furfurol* (see FURFUR, -OL[1]) + ALDEHYDE]

furan ('fjʊəræn, fjʊə'ræn) *n.* a colourless flammable toxic liquid heterocyclic compound, used in the synthesis of nylon. Formula: C_4H_4O. Also called: **furfuran.** [C19: shortened form of *furfuran*, from FURFUR]

furbelow ('fɜ:bɪ,ləʊ) *n.* **1.** a flounce, ruffle, or other ornamental trim. **2.** (*often pl.*) showy ornamentation. ~*vb.* **3.** (*tr.*) to put a furbelow on (a garment). [C18: by folk etymology from French dialect *farbella*; see FALBALA]

furbish ('fɜ:bɪʃ) *vb.* (*tr.*) **1.** to make bright by polishing; burnish. **2.** (often foll. by *up*) to improve the appearance or condition of; renovate; restore. [C14: from Old French *fourbir* to polish, of Germanic origin] —'**furbisher** *n.*

fur brigade *n. Canadian.* (formerly) a convoy of canoes, horses, or dog sleighs that transported furs and other goods between trading posts and towns or factories.

furca ('fɜ:kə) *n., pl.* **-cae** (-ki:). *Zoology.* any forklike structure, esp. in insects. [Latin: fork] —'**furcal** *adj.*

furcate *vb.* ('fɜ:keɪt). **1.** to divide into two parts; fork. ~*adj.* ('fɜ:keɪt, -kɪt) *or* **furcated.** **2.** forked; divided: *furcate branches.* [C19: from Late Latin *furcātus* forked, from Latin *furca* a fork] —**fur'cation** *n.*

furcula ('fɜ:kjʊlə) *or* **furculum** ('fɜ:kjʊləm) *n., pl.* **-lae** (-,li:) *or* **-la** (-lə). any forklike part or organ, esp. the fused clavicles (wishbone) of birds. [C19: from Latin: a forked support for a wall, diminutive of *furca* fork]

furfur ('fɜ:fə) *n., pl.* **furfures** ('fɜ:fjʊ,ri:z, -fə,ri:z). **1.** a scaling of the skin; dandruff. **2.** any scale of the epidermis. [C17: from Latin: bran, scurf]

furfuraceous (,fɜ:fjʊ'reɪʃəs, -fə'reɪ-) *adj.* **1.** relating to or resembling bran. **2.** *Med.* resembling dandruff; scaly. —,**furfu'raceously** *adv.*

furfuraldehyde (,fɜ:fjə'rældə,haɪd) *n.* a colourless flammable soluble mobile liquid with a penetrating odour, present in oat and rice hulls; 2-furaldehyde: used as a solvent and in the manufacture of resins. Formula: $C_5H_4O_2$. Also called: **furfural.**

furfuran (ˈfɜːfəˌræn, ˈfɜːfjʊ-) *n.* another name for **furan.**
furioso (ˌfjʊərɪˈəʊsəʊ) *Music.* ~*adj., adv.* **1.** in a frantically rushing manner. ~*n.* **2.** a passage or piece to be performed in this way. [C19: Italian, literally: furious; see FURY]
furious (ˈfjʊərɪəs) *adj.* **1.** extremely angry or annoyed; raging. **2.** violent, wild, or unrestrained, as in speed, vigour, energy, etc. —**ˈfuriously** *adv.* —**ˈfuriousness** *n.*
furl (fɜːl) *vb.* **1.** to roll up (an umbrella, a flag, etc.) neatly and securely or (of an umbrella, flag, etc.) to be rolled up in this way. **2.** (*tr.*) *Nautical.* to gather in (a square sail). **3.** (*intr.*) *Rare.* to disappear; vanish. ~*n.* **4.** the act or an instance of furling. **5.** a single rolled-up section. [C16: from Old French *ferlier* to bind tightly, from *ferm* tight (from Latin *firmus* FIRM[1]) + *lier* to tie, bind, from Latin *ligāre*] —**ˈfurlable** *adj.* —**ˈfurler** *n.*
furlong (ˈfɜːˌlɒŋ) *n.* a unit of length equal to 220 yards (201.168 metres). [Old English *furlang,* from *furh* FURROW + *lang* LONG[1]]
furlough (ˈfɜːləʊ) *n.* **1.** leave of absence from military duty. **2.** *U.S.* a temporary laying-off of employees, usually because there is insufficient work to occupy them. ~*vb.* (*tr.*) **3.** to grant a furlough to. **4.** *U.S.* to lay off (staff) temporarily. [C17: from Dutch *verlof,* from *ver-* FOR- + *lof* leave, permission; related to Swedish *förlof*]
furmenty (ˈfɜːməntɪ) *or* **furmety** (ˈfɜːmɪtɪ) *n.* variants of **frumenty.**
furnace (ˈfɜːnɪs) *n.* **1.** an enclosed chamber in which heat is produced to generate steam, destroy refuse, smelt or refine ores, etc. **2.** a very hot or stifling place. [C13: from Old French *fornais,* from Latin *fornax* oven, furnace; related to Latin *formus* warm] —**ˈfurnace-ˌlike** *adj.*
furnish (ˈfɜːnɪʃ) *vb.* (*tr.*) **1.** to provide (a house, room, etc.) with furniture, carpets, etc. **2.** to equip with what is necessary; fit out. **3.** to give; supply: *the records furnished the information required.* [C15: from Old French *fournir,* of Germanic origin; related to Old High German *frummen* to carry out] —**ˈfurnisher** *n.*
furnishings (ˈfɜːnɪʃɪŋz) *pl. n.* **1.** furniture and accessories, including carpets and curtains, with which a room, house, etc., is furnished. **2.** *U.S. and Canadian.* articles of dress and accessories.
furniture (ˈfɜːnɪtʃə) *n.* **1.** the movable, generally functional, articles that equip a room, house, etc. **2.** the equipment necessary for a ship, factory, etc. **3.** *Printing.* lengths of wood, plastic, or metal, used in assembling formes to create the blank areas and to surround the type. **4.** *Obsolete.* the full armour, trappings, etc., for a man and horse. **5.** See **door furniture** and **street furniture.** [C16: from French *fourniture,* from *fournir* to equip, FURNISH]
furniture beetle *n.* See **anobiid.**
furore (fjʊˈrɔːrɪ) *or esp. U.S.* **furor** (ˈfjʊərɔː) *n.* **1.** a public outburst, esp. of protest; uproar. **2.** a sudden widespread enthusiasm for something; craze. **3.** frenzy; rage; madness. [C15: from Latin: frenzy, rage, from *furere* to rave]
furphy (ˈfɜːfɪ) *n., pl.* **-phies.** *Austral. slang.* a rumour or fictitious story. [C20: from *Furphy* carts (used for water or sewage in World War I), made at a foundry established by the Furphy family]
furred (fɜːd) *adj.* **1.** made of, lined with, or covered in fur. **2.** wearing fur. **3.** (of animals) having fur. **4.** another word for **furry** (sense 4). **5.** Also: **furry.** provided with furring strips. **6.** (of a pipe, kettle, etc.) lined with hard lime or other salts deposited from water.
furrier (ˈfʌrɪə) *n.* a person whose occupation is selling, making, dressing, or repairing fur garments. [C14: *furour,* from Old French *fourrer* to trim or line with FUR]
furriery (ˈfʌrɪərɪ) *n., pl.* **-eries.** **1.** the occupation of a furrier. **2.** furs worn as a garment or trim collectively.
furring (ˈfɜːrɪŋ) *n.* **1. a.** short for **furring strip. b.** the fixing of furring strips. **c.** furring strips collectively. **2.** the formation of fur on the tongue. **3.** trimming of animal fur, as on a coat or other garment, or furs collectively.
furring strip *n.* a strip of wood or metal fixed to a wall, floor, or ceiling to provide a surface for the fixing of plasterboard, floorboards, etc. Sometimes shortened to **furring.**
furrow (ˈfʌrəʊ) *n.* **1.** a long narrow trench made in the ground by a plough or a trench resembling this. **2.** any long deep groove, esp. a deep wrinkle on the forehead. ~*vb.* **3.** to develop or cause to develop furrows or wrinkles. **4.** to make a furrow or furrows in (land). [Old English *furh;* related to Old Frisian *furch,* Old Norse *for,* Old High German *furuh, Latin porca* ridge between furrows] —**ˈfurrower** *n.* —**ˈfurrowless** *adj.* —**ˈfurrow-ˌlike** *or* **ˈfurrowy** *adj.*
furry (ˈfɜːrɪ) *adj.* **-rier, -riest. 1.** covered with fur or something furlike. **2.** of, relating to, or resembling fur. **3.** another word for **furred** (sense 5). **4.** Also: **furred.** (of the tongue) coated with whitish cellular debris. —**ˈfurrily** *adv.* —**ˈfurriness** *n.*
fur seal *n.* any of various eared seals, esp. of the genus *Arctocephalus,* that have a fine dense underfur and are hunted as a source of sealskin.
furth (fʌrθ) *adv. Scot.* out; outside; to the outside. [a Scot. variant of FORTH]
further (ˈfɜːðə) *adv.* **1.** in addition; furthermore. **2.** to a greater degree or extent. **3.** to or at a more advanced point. **4.** to or at a greater distance in time or space; farther. ~*adj.* **5.** additional; more. **6.** more distant or remote in time or space; farther. ~*vb.* **7.** (*tr.*) to assist the progress of; promote. ~See also **far, furthest.** [Old English *furthor;* related to Old Frisian *further,* Old Saxon *furthor,* Old High German *furdar;* see FORTH] —**ˈfurtherer** *n.*
▷**Usage.** See at **farther.**
furtherance (ˈfɜːðərəns) *n.* **1.** the act of furthering; advancement. **2.** something that furthers or advances.
further education *n.* (in Britain) formal education beyond school other than at a university or polytechnic.
furthermore (ˈfɜːðəˌmɔː) *adv.* in addition; moreover.
furthermost (ˈfɜːðəˌməʊst) *adj.* most distant; furthest.
furthest (ˈfɜːðɪst) *adv.* **1.** to the greatest degree or extent. **2.** to or at the greatest distance in time or space; farthest. ~*adj.* **3.** most distant or remote in time or space; farthest.
furtive (ˈfɜːtɪv) *adj.* characterized by stealth; sly and secretive. [C15: from Latin *furtīvus* stolen, clandestine, from *furtum* a theft, from *fūr* a thief; related to Greek *phōr* thief] —**ˈfurtively** *adv.* —**ˈfurtiveness** *n.*
furuncle (ˈfjʊərʌŋkəl) *n. Pathol.* the technical name for **boil**[2]. [C17: from Latin *fūrunculus* pilferer, petty thief, sore on the body, from *fūr* thief] —**furuncular** (fjʊˈrʌŋkjʊlə) *or* **fuˈrunculous** *adj.*
furunculosis (fjʊˌrʌŋkjʊˈləʊsɪs) *n.* **1.** a skin condition characterized by the presence of multiple boils. **2.** an infectious ulcerative disease of salmon and trout caused by the bacterium *Aeromonas salmonicida.*
fury (ˈfjʊərɪ) *n., pl.* **-ries. 1.** violent or uncontrolled anger; wild rage. **2.** an outburst of such anger. **3.** uncontrolled violence: *the fury of the storm.* **4.** a person, esp. a woman, with a violent temper. **5. like fury.** *Informal.* violently; furiously: *they rode like fury.* [C14: from Latin *furia* rage, from *furere* to be furious]
furze (fɜːz) *n.* another name for **gorse.** [Old English *fyrs*] —**ˈfurzy** *adj.*
fusain (fjuːˈzeɪn; *French* fyzɛ̃) *n.* **1.** a fine charcoal pencil or stick made from the spindle tree. **2.** a drawing done with such a pencil. **3.** a dull black brittle form of carbon resembling charcoal, found in certain coals. [C19: from French: spindle tree or charcoal made from it, from Vulgar Latin *fūsāgō* (unattested) a spindle (generally made from the spindle tree), from Latin *fūsus*]
fuscous (ˈfʌskəs) *adj.* of a brownish-grey colour. [C17: from Latin *fuscus* dark, swarthy, tawny]
fuse[1] *or U.S.* **fuze** (fjuːz) *n.* **1.** a lead of combustible black powder in a waterproof covering (**safety fuse**), or a lead containing an explosive (**detonating fuse**), used to fire an explosive charge. **2.** any device by which an explosive charge is ignited. ~*vb.* **3.** (*tr.*) to provide or equip with such a fuse. [C17: from Italian *fuso* spindle, from Latin *fūsus*] —**ˈfuseless** *adj.*
fuse[2] (fjuːz) *vb.* **1.** to unite or become united by melting, esp. by the action of heat: *to fuse borax and copper sulphate at a high temperature.* **2.** to become or cause to become liquid, esp. by the action of heat; melt. **3.** to join or become combined; integrate. **4.** (*tr.*) to equip (an electric circuit, plug, etc.) with a fuse. **5.** *Brit.* to fail or cause to fail as a result of the blowing of a fuse: *the lights fused.* ~*n.* **6.** a protective device for safeguarding electric circuits, etc., containing a wire that melts and breaks the circuit when the current exceeds a certain value. [C17: from Latin *fūsus* melted, cast, poured out, from *fundere* to pour out, shed; sense 5 influenced by FUSE[1]]
fuse box *n.* a housing for electric fuses.
fusee *or* **fuzee** (fjuːˈziː) *n.* **1.** (in early clocks and watches) a spirally grooved spindle, functioning as an equalizing force on the unwinding of the mainspring. **2.** a friction match with a large head, capable of remaining alight in a wind. **3.** an explosive fuse. [C16: from French *fusée* spindleful of thread, from Old French *fus* spindle, from Latin *fūsus*]
fuselage (ˈfjuːzɪˌlɑːʒ) *n.* the main body of an aircraft, excluding the wings, tailplane, and fin. [C20: from French, from *fuseler* to shape like a spindle, from Old French *fusel* spindle; see FUSEE]
fusel oil *or* **fusel** (ˈfjuːzəl) *n.* a mixture of amyl alcohols, propanol, and butanol: a by-product in the distillation of fermented liquors used as a source of amyl alcohols. [C19: from German *Fusel* bad spirits]
fusible (ˈfjuːzəbəl) *adj.* capable of being fused or melted. —**ˌfusiˈbility** *or* **ˈfusibleness** *n.* —**ˈfusibly** *adv.*
fusible metal *or* **alloy** *n.* any of various alloys with low melting points that contain bismuth, lead, and tin. They are used as solders and in safety devices.
fusiform (ˈfjuːzɪˌfɔːm) *adj.* elongated and tapering at both ends; spindle-shaped. [C18: from Latin *fūsus* spindle]
fusil[1] (ˈfjuːzɪl) *n.* a light flintlock musket. [C16 (in the sense: steel for a tinderbox): from Old French *fuisil,* from Vulgar Latin *focīlis* (unattested), from Latin *focus* fire]
fusil[2] (ˈfjuːzɪl) *n. Heraldry.* a charge shaped like a lengthened lozenge. [C15: from Old French *fusel,* ultimately from Latin *fūsus* spindle, FUSE[1] (the heraldic lozenge originally represented a spindle covered with tow for spinning)]
fusile (ˈfjuːzaɪl) *or* **fusil** *adj.* **1.** easily melted; fusible. **2.** formed by casting or melting; founded. [C14: from Latin *fūsilis* molten, from *fundere* to pour out, melt]
fusilier (ˌfjuːzɪˈlɪə) *n.* **1.** (formerly) an infantryman armed with a light musket. **2.** Also: ˌ**fusiˈleer. a.** a soldier, esp. a private, serving in any of certain British or other infantry regiments. **b.**

(*pl.; cap. when part of a name*): *the Royal Welsh Fusiliers.* [C17: from French; see FUSIL[1]]
fusillade (ˌfjuːzɪˈleɪd, -ˈlɑːd) *n.* **1.** a simultaneous or rapid continual discharge of firearms. **2.** a sudden outburst, as of criticism. *~vb.* **3.** (*tr.*) to attack with a fusillade. [C19: from French, from *fusiller* to shoot; see FUSIL[1]]
fusion (ˈfjuːʒən) *n.* **1.** the act or process of fusing or melting together; union. **2.** the state of being fused. **3.** something produced by fusing. **4.** See **nuclear fusion. 5.** the merging of juxtaposed speech sounds, morphemes, or words. **6.** a coalition of political parties or other groups, esp. to support common candidates at an election. **7.** a kind of popular music that is a blend of two or more styles, such as jazz and funk. **8.** *Psychol.* the processing by the mind of elements falling on the two eyes so that they yield a single percept. [C16: from Latin *fūsiō* a pouring out, melting, casting, from *fundere* to pour out, FOUND[3]]
fusion bomb *n.* a type of bomb in which most of the energy is provided by nuclear fusion, esp. the fusion of hydrogen isotopes. Also called: **thermonuclear bomb, fission-fusion bomb.** See also **hydrogen bomb.**
fusionism (ˈfjuːʒəˌnɪzəm) *n.* the favouring of coalitions among political groups. —ˈ**fusionist** *n., adj.*
fusion reactor *n.* a nuclear reactor in which a thermonuclear fusion reaction takes place.
fuss (fʌs) *n.* **1.** nervous activity or agitation, esp. when disproportionate or unnecessary. **2.** complaint or objection: *he made a fuss over the bill.* **3.** an exhibition of affection or admiration, esp. if excessive: *they made a great fuss over the new baby.* **4.** a quarrel; dispute. *~vb.* **5.** (*intr.*) to worry unnecessarily. **6.** (*intr.*) to be excessively concerned over trifles. **7.** (when *intr.*, usually foll. by *over*) to show great or excessive concern, affection, etc. (for). **8.** (*intr.*; foll. by *with*) *Jamaican.* to quarrel violently. **9.** (*tr.*) to bother (a person). [C18: of uncertain origin] —ˈ**fusser** *n.*
fusspot (ˈfʌsˌpɒt) *n. Brit. informal.* a person who fusses unnecessarily. Also called (U.S.): **fuss-budget.**
fussy (ˈfʌsɪ) *adj.* **fussier, fussiest. 1.** inclined to fuss over minor points. **2.** very particular about detail. **3.** characterized by overelaborate detail: *the furniture was too fussy to be elegant.* —ˈ**fussily** *adv.* —ˈ**fussiness** *n.*
fustanella (ˌfʌstəˈnɛlə) *or* **fustanelle** *n.* a white knee-length pleated skirt worn by men in Greece and Albania. [C19: from Italian, from Modern Greek *phoustani,* probably from Italian *fustagno* FUSTIAN]
fustian (ˈfʌstɪən) *n.* **1. a.** a hard-wearing fabric of cotton mixed with flax or wool with a slight nap. **b.** (*as modifier*): *a fustian jacket.* **2.** pompous or pretentious talk or writing. *~adj.* **3.** cheap; worthless. **4.** pompous; bombastic. [C12: from Old French *fustaigne,* from Medieval Latin *fustāneum,* from Latin *fustis* cudgel]
fustic (ˈfʌstɪk) *n.* **1.** Also called: **old fustic.** a large tropical American moraceous tree, *Chlorophora tinctoria.* **2.** the yellow dye obtained from the wood of this tree. **3.** any of various trees or shrubs that yield a similar dye, esp. *Rhus cotinus* (**young fustic**), a European sumach. [C15: from French *fustoc,* from Spanish, from Arabic *fustuq,* from Greek *pistakē* pistachio tree]
fustigate (ˈfʌstɪˌgeɪt) *vb.* (*tr.*) *Archaic.* to beat; cudgel. [C17: from Late Latin *fūstīgāre* to cudgel to death, from Latin *fūstis* cudgel] —ˌ**fustiˈgation** *n.* —ˈ**fustiˌgator** *n.* —ˌ**fustiˈgatory** *adj.*
fusty (ˈfʌstɪ) *adj.* **-tier, -tiest. 1.** smelling of damp or mould; musty. **2.** old-fashioned in attitude. [C14: from *fust* wine cask, from Old French: cask, tree trunk, from Latin *fūstis* cudgel, club] —ˈ**fustily** *adv.* —ˈ**fustiness** *n.*
fut. *abbrev. for* future.
futhark, futharc (ˈfuːθɑːk) *or* **futhorc, futhork** (ˈfuːθɔːk) *n.* a phonetic alphabet consisting of runes. [C19: from the first six letters: *f, u, th, a, r, k;* compare ALPHABET]
futile (ˈfjuːtaɪl) *adj.* **1.** having no effective result; unsuccessful. **2.** pointless; unimportant; trifling. **3.** inane or foolish: *don't be so futile!* [C16: from Latin *futtilis* pouring out easily, worthless, from *fundere* to pour out] —ˈ**futilely** *adv.* —ˈ**futileness** *n.*
futilitarian (fjuːˌtɪlɪˈtɛərɪən) *adj.* **1.** of or relating to the belief that human endeavour can serve no useful purpose. *~n.* **2.** one who holds this belief. [C19: facetious coinage from FUTILE + UTILITARIAN] —**fuˌtiliˈtarianˌism** *n.*
futility (fjuːˈtɪlɪtɪ) *n., pl.* **-ties. 1.** lack of effectiveness or success. **2.** lack of purpose or meaning. **3.** something futile.
futon (ˌfuːˈtɒn) *n.* a Japanese padded quilt, laid on the floor for use as a bed. [C19: from Japanese]
futtock (ˈfʌtək) *n. Nautical.* one of the ribs in the frame of a wooden vessel. [C13: perhaps variant of *foothook*]
futtock plate *n. Nautical.* a horizontal metal disc fixed at the top of a lower mast for holding the futtock shrouds.
futtock shroud *n. Nautical.* any of several metal rods serving as a brace between the futtock plate on a lower mast and the topmast.
future (ˈfjuːtʃə) *n.* **1.** the time yet to come. **2.** undetermined events that will occur in that time. **3.** the condition of a person or thing at a later date: *the future of the school is undecided.* **4.** likelihood of later improvement or advancement: *he has a future as a singer.* **5.** *Grammar.* **a.** a tense of verbs used when the action or event described is to occur after the time of utterance. **b.** a verb in this tense. **6. in future.** from now on; henceforth. *~adj.* **7.** that is yet to come or be. **8.** of or expressing time yet to come. **9.** (*prenominal*) destined to become: *a future president.* **10.** *Grammar.* in or denoting the future as a tense of verbs. *~*See also **futures.** [C14: from Latin *fūtūrus* about to be, from *esse* to be] —ˈ**futureless** *adj.*
future life *n.* a life after death; afterlife.
future perfect *Grammar.* *~adj.* **1.** denoting a tense of verbs describing an action that will have been performed by a certain time. In English this is formed with *will have* or *shall have* plus the past participle. *~n.* **2. a.** the future perfect tense. **b.** a verb in this tense.
futures (ˈfjuːtʃəz) *pl. n.* **a.** commodities bought or sold at an agreed price for delivery at a specified future date. **b.** (*as modifier*): *futures contract; futures market.*
future value *n.* the value that a sum of money invested at compound interest will have after a specified period.
futurism (ˈfjuːtʃəˌrɪzəm) *n.* an artistic movement that arose in Italy in 1909 to replace traditional aesthetic values with the characteristics of the machine age. —ˈ**futurist** *n., adj.*
futuristic (ˌfjuːtʃəˈrɪstɪk) *adj.* **1.** denoting or relating to design, technology, etc., that is thought likely to be current or fashionable at some future time; ultramodern. **2.** of or relating to futurism. —ˌ**futurˈistically** *adv.*
futurity (fjuːˈtjʊərɪtɪ) *n., pl.* **-ties. 1.** a less common word for **future. 2.** the quality of being in the future. **3.** a future event.
futurology (ˌfjuːtʃəˈrɒlədʒɪ) *n.* the study or prediction of the future of mankind. —ˌ**futurˈologist** *n.*
fuze (fjuːz) *n. Chiefly U.S.* a variant spelling of **fuse**[1].
fuzee (fjuːˈziː) *n.* a variant spelling of **fusee.**
fuzz[1] (fʌz) *n.* **1.** a mass or covering of fine or curly hairs, fibres, etc. **2.** a blur. *~vb.* **3.** to make or become fuzzy. **4.** to make or become indistinct; blur. [C17: perhaps from Low German *fussig* loose]
fuzz[2] (fʌz) *n.* a slang word for **police** or **policeman.** [C20: of uncertain origin]
fuzz box *n. Music.* an electronic device that breaks up the sound passing through it, used esp. by guitarists.
fuzzy (ˈfʌzɪ) *adj.* **fuzzier, fuzziest. 1.** of, resembling, or covered with fuzz. **2.** indistinct; unclear or distorted. **3.** not clearly thought out or expressed. **4.** (of the hair) tightly curled or very wavy. **5.** *Maths.* of or relating to a form of set theory in which set membership depends on a likelihood function: *fuzzy set; fuzzy logic.* —ˈ**fuzzily** *adv.* —ˈ**fuzziness** *n.*
fuzzy-wuzzy (ˈfʌzɪˌwʌzɪ) *n., pl.* **-ies** *or* **-y.** *Offensive slang.* a Black fuzzy-haired native of any of various countries.
fuzzy wuzzy angel *n. Austral. informal.* any native of Papua New Guinea who assisted as a stretcher-bearer in World War II.
fv *abbrev. for* folio verso. [Latin: on the reverse (that is left-hand) page]
fwd *abbrev. for* forward.
f.w.d. *abbrev. for:* **1.** four-wheel drive. **2.** front-wheel drive.
f-word *n.* **the** (*sometimes cap.*) a euphemistic way of referring to the word **fuck.** [from F(UCK) + WORD]
-fy *suffix forming verbs.* to make or become: *beautify; simplify; liquefy.* [from Old French *-fier,* from Latin *-ficāre,* verbal ending formed from *-ficus* -FIC]
fyke (faɪk) *n. U.S.* a fish trap consisting of a net suspended over a series of hoops, laid horizontally in the water. [C19: from Middle Dutch *fuycke*]
fylfot (ˈfaɪlfɒt) *n.* a rare word for **swastika.** [C16 (apparently meaning: a sign or device for the lower part or foot of a painted window): from *fillen* to FILL + *fot* FOOT]
fyrd (fɪəd, faɪəd) *n. History.* the local militia of an Anglo-Saxon shire, in which all freemen had to serve.
FZS *abbrev. for* Fellow of the Zoological Society.

g *or* **G** (dʒiː) *n., pl.* **g's, G's,** *or* **Gs. 1.** the seventh letter and fifth consonant of the modern English alphabet. **2.** a speech sound represented by this letter, in English usually either a voiced velar stop, as in *grass,* or a voiced palato-alveolar affricate, as in *page.*

g *symbol for:* **1.** gallon(s). **2.** gram(s). **3.** acceleration of free fall (due to gravity). **4.** grav. **5.** *Chess.* See **algebraic notation.**

G *symbol for:* **1.** *Music.* **a.** a note having a frequency of 392 hertz (**G above middle C**) or this value multiplied or divided by any power of 2; the fifth note of the scale of C major. **b.** a key, string, or pipe producing this note. **c.** the major or minor key having this note as its tonic. **2.** gauss. **3.** gravitational constant. **4.** *Physics.* conductance. **5.** German. **6.** Gibbs function. **7.** giga. **8.** good. **9.** *Slang, chiefly U.S.* grand (a thousand dollars or pounds). **10.** (in Australia) **a.** general exhibition (used to describe a category of film certified as suitable for viewing by anyone). **b.** (*as modifier*): *a G film.*

G. *or* **g.** *abbrev. for:* **1.** gauges. **2.** gelding. **3.** Gulf. **4.** guilder(s). **5.** guinea(s).

G3 *abbrev. for* Group of Three.

G5 *abbrev. for* Group of Five.

G7 *abbrev. for* Group of Seven.

G10 *abbrev. for* Group of Ten.

G77 *abbrev. for* Group of Seventy Seven.

Ga[1] *the chemical symbol for* gallium.

Ga[2] *or* **Gã** (gɑː) *n.* **1.** (*pl.* **Ga, Gas** *or* **Gã, Gãs**) a member of a Negroid people of W Africa living chiefly in S Ghana. **2.** the language of this people, belonging to the Kwa branch of the Niger-Congo family.

GA *abbrev. for:* **1.** General Assembly (of the United Nations). **2.** general average. **3.** Georgia (U.S. state).

Ga. *abbrev. for* Georgia (U.S. state).

GAA (in Ireland) *abbrev. for* Gaelic Athletic Association.

gab[1] (gæb) *Informal.* ~*vb.* **gabs, gabbing, gabbed. 1.** (*intr.*) to talk excessively or idly, esp. about trivial matters; gossip; chatter. ~*n.* **2.** idle or trivial talk. **3. gift of the gab.** ability to speak effortlessly, glibly, or persuasively. [C18: variant of Northern dialect *gob* mouth, probably from Irish Gaelic *gob* beak, mouth] —**'gabber** *n.*

gab[2] (gæb) *n.* **1.** a hook or open notch in a rod or lever that drops over the spindle of a valve to form a temporary connection for operating the valve. **2.** a pointed tool used in masonry. [C18: probably from Flemish *gabbe* notch, gash]

GABA ('gæbə) *n. acronym for* gamma-aminobutyric acid: a biologically active substance found in plants and in brain and other animal tissues; it is a neurotransmitter that inhibits activation of neurones.

Gabar ('gɑːbə), **Gheber,** *or* **Ghebre** *n.* **1.** a member of an Iranian religious sect practising a modern version of Zoroastrianism. ~*adj.* **2.** of, relating to, or characterizing the Gabar sect or its beliefs.

gabardine ('gæbəˌdiːn, ˌgæbə'diːn) *n.* a variant spelling of **gaberdine** (esp. sense 2).

gabble ('gæbᵊl) *vb.* **1.** to utter (words, etc.) rapidly and indistinctly; jabber. **2.** (*intr.*) (of geese and some other birds or animals) to utter rapid cackling noises. ~*n.* **3.** rapid and indistinct speech or noises. [C17: from Middle Dutch *gabbelen,* of imitative origin] —**'gabbler** *n.*

gabbro ('gæbrəʊ) *n., pl.* **-bros.** a dark coarse-grained basic plutonic igneous rock consisting of plagioclase feldspar, pyroxene, and often olivine. [C19: from Italian, probably from Latin *glaber* smooth, bald] —**gab'broic** *or* **ˌgabbro'itic** *adj.*

gabby ('gæbɪ) *adj.* **-bier, -biest.** *Informal.* inclined to chatter; talkative.

gabelle (gæ'bɛl) *n. French history.* a salt tax levied until 1790. [C15: from Old Italian *gabella,* from Arabic *qabālah* tribute, from *qabala* he received] —**ga'belled** *adj.*

gaberdine ('gæbəˌdiːn, ˌgæbə'diːn) *n.* **1.** a twill-weave worsted, cotton, or spun-rayon fabric. **2.** Also called: **gabardine.** an ankle-length loose coat or frock worn by men, esp. by Jews, in the Middle Ages. **3.** any of various other garments made of gaberdine, esp. a child's raincoat. [C16: from Old French *gauvardine* pilgrim's garment, from Middle High German *wallewart* pilgrimage; related to Spanish *gabardina*]

gaberlunzie (ˌgæbə'lʌnzɪ, -'luːnjɪ) *n. Scot. archaic or literary.* a wandering beggar. Also called: **gaberlunzie-man.** [C16: variant of earlier *gaberlungy*]

gabfest ('gæbfɛst) *n. Informal, chiefly U.S. and Canadian.* **1.** prolonged gossiping or conversation. **2.** an informal gathering for conversation.

gabion ('geɪbɪən) *n.* **1.** a cylindrical metal container filled with stones, used in the construction of underwater foundations. **2.** a wickerwork basket filled with stones or earth, used (esp. formerly) as part of a fortification. [C16: from French: basket, from Italian *gabbione,* from *gabbia* cage, from Latin *cavea;* see CAGE]

gabionade *or* **gabionnade** (ˌgeɪbɪə'neɪd) *n.* **1.** a row of gabions submerged in a waterway, stream, river, etc., to control the flow of water. **2.** a fortification constructed of gabions. [C18: from French; see GABION]

gable ('geɪbᵊl) *n.* **1.** the triangular upper part of a wall between the sloping ends of a pitched roof (**gable roof**). **2.** a triangular ornamental feature in the form of a gable, esp. as used over a door or window. **3.** the triangular wall on both ends of a gambrel roof. [C14: Old French *gable,* probably from Old Norse *gafl;* related to Old English *geafol* fork, Old High German *gibil* gable] —**'gabled** *adj.* —**'gable-ˌlike** *adj.*

gable end *n.* the end wall of a building on the side which is topped by a gable.

gablet ('geɪblɪt) *n.* a small gable.

gable window *n.* a window positioned in a gable or having a small gable over it.

Gabonese (ˌgæbə'niːz) *adj.* **1.** of or relating to Gabon, a republic in W central Africa, or its people. ~*n.* **2.** a native or inhabitant of Gabon.

gaboon (gə'buːn) *n.* the dark mahogany-like wood from a western and central African burseraceous tree, *Aucoumea klaineana,* used in plywood, for furniture, and as a veneer. [C20: altered from *Gabon*]

gaboon viper *n.* a large venomous viper, *Bitis gabonica,* that occurs in African rainforests. It has brown and purple markings and hornlike projections on its snout.

gaby ('geɪbɪ) *n., pl.* **-bies.** *Archaic or dialect.* a simpleton. [C18: of unknown origin]

gad[1] (gæd) *vb.* **gads, gadding, gadded. 1.** (*intr.;* often foll. by *about* or *around*) to go out in search of pleasure, esp. in an aimless manner; gallivant. ~*n.* **2.** carefree adventure (esp. in the phrase **on** *or* **upon the gad).** [C15: back formation from obsolete *gadling* companion, from Old English, from *gæd* fellowship; related to Old High German *gatuling*] —**'gadder** *n.*

gad[2] (gæd) *n.* **1.** *Mining.* a short chisel-like instrument for breaking rock or coal from the face. **2.** a goad for driving cattle. **3.** a western U.S. word for **spur** (sense 1). ~*vb.* **gads, gadding, gadded. 4.** (*tr.*) *Mining.* to break up or loosen with a gad. [C13: from Old Norse *gaddr* spike; related to Old High German *gart,* Gothic *gazds* spike]

Gad (gæd) *n., interj.* an archaic euphemism for **God:** used as or in an oath.

gadabout ('gædəˌbaʊt) *n. Informal.* a person who restlessly seeks amusement.

Gadarene ('gædəˌriːn) *adj.* relating to or engaged in a headlong rush. [C19: via Late Latin from Greek *Gadarēnos,* of Gadara (Palestine), alluding to the Biblical Gadarene swine (Matthew 8:28ff.)]

gadfly ('gædˌflaɪ) *n., pl.* **-flies. 1.** any of various large dipterous flies, esp. the horsefly, that annoy livestock by sucking their blood. **2.** a constantly irritating or harassing person. [C16: from GAD[2] (sting) + FLY[2]]

gadget ('gædʒɪt) *n.* **1.** a small mechanical device or appliance. **2.** any object that is interesting for its ingenuity or novelty rather than for its practical use. [C19: of uncertain origin] —**'gadgety** *adj.*

gadgeteer (ˌgædʒɪ'tɪə) *n.* a person who delights in gadgetry.

gadgetry ('gædʒɪtrɪ) *n.* **1.** gadgets collectively. **2.** use of or preoccupation with gadgets and their design.

Gadhelic (gæd'hɛlɪk) *n., adj.* another term for **Goidelic.** [C19: from Old Irish *Gaídel, Goídelc* the Gaelic language]

gadid ('geɪdɪd) *n.* **1.** any marine teleost fish of the family *Gadidae,* which includes the cod, haddock, whiting, and pollack. ~*adj.* **2.** of, relating to, or belonging to the *Gadidae.* [C19: see GADOID]

gadoid ('geɪdɔɪd) *adj.* **1.** of, relating to, or belonging to the *Anacanthini,* an order of marine soft-finned fishes typically having the pectoral and pelvic fins close together and small cycloid scales. The group includes gadid fishes and hake. ~*n.* **2.** any gadoid fish. [C19: from New Latin *Gadidae,* from *gadus* cod; see -OID]

gadolinite ('gædəlɪˌnaɪt) *n.* a rare brown or black mineral consisting of a silicate of iron, beryllium, and yttrium in monoclinic crystalline form. Formula: $2BeO.FeO.Y_2O_3.2SiO_2$. Also called: **ytterbite.** [C19: named after Johan *Gadolin* (1760–1852), Finnish mineralogist]

gadolinium (ˌgædə'lɪnɪəm) *n.* a ductile malleable silvery-white ferromagnetic element of the lanthanide series of metals: occurs principally in monazite and bastnaesite. Symbol: Gd; atomic no.: 64; atomic wt.: 157.25; valency: 3; relative density: 7.898;

melting pt.: 1312°C; boiling pt.: 3000°C (approx.). [C19: New Latin, from GADOLINITE] —ˌ**gado'linic** *adj.*

gadroon *or* **godroon** (gə'druːn) *n.* **1.** a moulding composed of a series of convex flutes and curves joined to form a decorative pattern, used esp. as an edge to silver articles. **2.** *Architect.* a carved ornamental moulding having a convex cross section. [C18: from French *godron,* perhaps from Old French *godet* cup, goblet, drinking vessel] —**ga'drooned** *or* **go'drooned** *adj.*

gadwall ('gædˌwɔːl) *n., pl.* **-walls** *or* **-wall.** a duck, *Anas strepera,* related to the mallard. The male has a grey body and black tail. [C17: of unknown origin]

gadzooks (gæd'zuːks) *interj. Archaic.* a mild oath. [C17: perhaps from *God's hooks* (the nails of the cross); see GAD]

gae (ge) *vb.* **gaes, gaun, gaed, gane.** a Scot. word for **go**[1].

Gaekwar *or* **Gaikwar** ('gaɪkwɑː) *n. History.* the title of the ruler of the former native state of Baroda in W India. [C19: from Marathi *Gaekvād,* literally: Guardian of the Cows, from Sanskrit *gauh* cow + *-vad* guardian]

Gael (geɪl) *n.* a person who speaks a Gaelic language, esp. a Highland Scot or an Irishman. [C19: from Gaelic *Gaidheal;* related to Old Irish *goidel,* Old Welsh *gwyddel* Irishman] —'**Gaeldom** *n.*

Gaelic ('geɪlɪk, 'gæl-) *n.* **1.** any of the closely related languages of the Celts in Ireland, Scotland, or (formerly) the Isle of Man. Compare **Goidelic.** ~*adj.* **2.** of, denoting, or relating to the Celtic people of Ireland, Scotland, or the Isle of Man or their language or customs.

Gaelic coffee *n.* another name for **Irish coffee.**

Gaelic football *n.* an Irish game played with 15 men on each side and goals resembling rugby posts with a net on the bottom part. Players are allowed to kick, punch, and bounce the ball and attempt to get it over the bar or in the net.

Gaeltacht ('geːltəxt) *or* **Gaedhealtacht** ('geɪlˌtæxt, 'gaɛl-) *n.* any of the regions in Ireland in which Irish Gaelic is the vernacular speech. The form *Gaeltacht* is sometimes also used to mean the region of Scotland in which Scottish Gaelic is spoken. See also **Gaidhealtachd.** [C20: from Irish Gaelic]

gaff[1] (gæf) *n.* **1.** *Angling.* a stiff pole with a stout prong or hook attached for landing large fish. **2.** *Nautical.* a boom hoisted aft of a mast to support a gaffsail. **3.** a metal spur fixed to the leg of a gamecock. ~*vb.* **4.** (*tr.*) *Angling.* to hook or land (a fish) with a gaff. **5.** (*tr.*) *Slang.* to cheat; hoax. [C13: from French *gaffe,* from Provençal *gaf* boathook]

gaff[2] (gæf) *n.* **1.** *Slang.* foolish talk; nonsense. **2. blow the gaff.** *Brit. slang.* to divulge a secret. **3. stand the gaff.** *Slang, chiefly U.S. and Canadian.* to endure ridicule, difficulties, etc. [C19: of unknown origin]

gaff[3] (gæf) *n. Brit. slang, archaic.* **1.** a person's home, esp. a flat. **2.** Also called: **penny-gaff.** a cheap or low-class place of entertainment, esp. a cheap theatre or music hall in Victorian England. [C18: of unknown origin]

gaffe (gæf) *n.* a social blunder, esp. a tactless remark. [C19: from French]

gaffer ('gæfə) *n.* **1.** an old man, esp. one living in the country: often used affectionately or patronizingly. Compare **gammer.** **2.** *Informal, chiefly Brit.* a boss, foreman, or owner of a factory, mine, etc. **3.** the senior electrician on a television or film set. [C16: alteration of GODFATHER]

gaffer tape *n. Brit.* strong adhesive tape used in electrical repairs.

gaff-rigged *adj.* (of a sailing vessel) rigged with one or more gaffsails.

gaffsail ('gæfˌseɪl, -səl) *n.* a quadrilateral fore-and-aft sail on a sailing vessel.

gaff-topsail *n.* a sail set above a gaffsail.

gag[1] (gæg) *vb.* **gags, gagging, gagged.** **1.** (*tr.*) to stop up (a person's mouth), esp. with a piece of cloth, etc., to prevent him from speaking or crying out. **2.** (*tr.*) to suppress or censor (free expression, information, etc.). **3.** to retch or cause to retch. **4.** (*intr.*) to struggle for breath; choke. **5.** (*tr.*) to hold (the jaws) of (a person or animal) apart with a surgical gag. **6.** (*tr.*) to apply a gag-bit to (a horse). ~*n.* **7.** a piece of cloth, rope, etc., stuffed into or tied across the mouth. **8.** any restraint on or suppression of information, free speech, etc. **9.** a surgical device for keeping the jaws apart, as during a tonsillectomy. **10.** *Parliamentary procedure.* another word for **closure** (sense 4). [C15 *gaggen;* perhaps imitative of a gasping sound]

gag[2] (gæg) *Informal.* ~*n.* **1.** a joke or humorous story, esp. one told by a professional comedian. **2.** a hoax, practical joke, etc.: *he did it for a gag.* ~*vb.* **gags, gagging, gagged.** **3.** (*intr.*) to tell jokes or funny stories, as comedians in nightclubs, etc. **4.** (often foll. by *up*) *Theatre.* **a.** to interpolate lines or business not in the actor's stage part, usually comic and improvised. **b.** to perform a stage jest, either spoken or based on movement. [C19: perhaps special use of GAG[1]]

gaga ('gɑːgɑː) *adj. Informal.* **1.** senile; doting. **2.** slightly crazy. [C20: from French, of imitative origin]

Gagauzi (gə'gɔːzɪ) *n.* a language spoken in the former Soviet Union, chiefly on the NW coast of the Black Sea, belonging to the Turkic branch of the Altaic family.

gag-bit *n.* a powerful type of bit used in breaking horses.

gage[1] (geɪdʒ) *n.* **1.** something deposited as security against the fulfilment of an obligation; pledge. **2.** (formerly) a glove or other object thrown down to indicate a challenge to combat. ~*vb.* **3.** (*tr.*) *Archaic.* to stake, pledge, or wager. [C14: from Old French *gage,* of Germanic origin; compare Gothic *wadi* pledge]

gage[2] (geɪdʒ) *n.* short for **greengage.**

gage[3] (geɪdʒ) *n. U.S. dated slang.* marijuana. [C20: of uncertain origin; compare GANJA]

gage[4] (geɪdʒ) *n., vb. U.S.* a variant spelling (esp. in technical senses) of **gauge.**

gager ('geɪdʒə) *n.* a variant spelling of **gauger.**

gagger ('gægə) *n.* **1.** a person or thing that gags. **2.** a wedge for a core in a casting mould.

gaggle ('gægᵊl) *vb.* **1.** (*intr.*) (of geese) to cackle. ~*n.* **2.** a flock of geese. **3.** *Informal.* a disorderly group of people. **4.** a gabbling or cackling sound. [C14: of Germanic origin; compare Old Norse *gagl* gosling, Dutch *gaggelen* to cackle, all of imitative origin]

gag rule *or* **resolution** *n. U.S.* any closure regulation adopted by a deliberative body.

gahnite ('gɑːnaɪt) *n.* a dark green mineral of the spinel group consisting of zinc aluminium oxide. Formula: $ZnAl_2O_4$. [C19: named after J. G. *Gahn* (1745–1818), Swedish chemist; see -ITE[1]]

Gaia hypothesis *or* **theory** ('gaɪə) *n.* the theory that the earth and everything on it constitutes a single self-regulating living entity. [C20: from *Gaia,* variant of *Gaea,* Greek goddess of the earth]

Gaidhealtachd ('geɪlˌtæxt, 'gaɛlˌtaxg) *n.* **1.** the area of Scotland in which Scottish Gaelic is the vernacular speech. See also **Gaeltacht.** **2.** the culture and traditions of the Scottish Gaels. [Scottish Gaelic]

gaiety ('geɪətɪ) *n., pl.* **-ties.** **1.** the state or condition of being merry, bright, or lively. **2.** festivity; merrymaking. ~Also: **gayety.**

Gaikwar ('gaɪkwɑː) *n.* a variant spelling of **Gaekwar.**

gaillardia (geɪ'lɑːdɪə) *n.* any plant of the North American genus *Gaillardia,* having ornamental flower heads with yellow or red rays and purple discs: family *Compositae* (composites). [C19: from New Latin, named after *Gaillard* de Marentonneau, 18th-century French amateur botanist]

gaily ('geɪlɪ) *adv.* **1.** in a gay manner; merrily. **2.** with bright colours; showily.

gain[1] (geɪn) *vb.* **1.** (*tr.*) to acquire (something desirable); obtain. **2.** (*tr.*) to win in competition: *to gain the victory.* **3.** to increase, improve, or advance: *the car gained speed; the shares gained in value.* **4.** (*tr.*) to earn (a wage, living, etc.). **5.** (*intr.;* usually foll. by *on* or *upon*) **a.** to get nearer (to) or catch up (on). **b.** to get farther away (from). **6.** (*tr.*) (esp. of ships) to get to; reach: *the steamer gained port.* **7.** (of a timepiece) to operate too fast, so as to indicate a time ahead of the true time or to run fast by a specified amount: *this watch gains; it gains ten minutes a day.* **8. gain ground.** to make progress or obtain an advantage. **9. gain time.** **a.** to obtain extra time by a delay or postponement. **b.** (of a timepiece) to operate too fast. ~*n.* **10.** something won, acquired, earned, etc.; profit; advantage. **11.** an increase in size, amount, etc. **12.** the act of gaining; attainment; acquisition. **13.** Also called: **amplification.** *Electronics.* the ratio of the output signal of an amplifier to the input signal, usually measured in decibels. ~See also **gains.** [C15: from Old French *gaaignier,* of Germanic origin; related to Old High German *weidenen* to forage, hunt] —'**gainable** *adj.*

gain[2] (geɪn) *n.* **1.** a notch, mortise, or groove, esp. one cut to take the flap of a butt hinge. ~*vb.* **2.** (*tr.*) to cut a gain or gains in. [C17: of obscure origin]

gainer ('geɪnə) *n.* **1.** a person or thing that gains. **2.** Also called: **full gainer.** a type of dive in which the diver leaves the board facing forward and completes a full backward somersault to enter the water feet first with his back to the diving board. Compare **half gainer.**

gainful ('geɪnful) *adj.* profitable; lucrative: *gainful employment.* —'**gainfully** *adv.* —'**gainfulness** *n.*

gainings ('geɪnɪŋz) *pl. n.* profits or earnings.

gainly ('geɪnlɪ) *Obsolete or dialect.* ~*adj.* **1.** graceful or well-formed; shapely. ~*adv.* **2.** conveniently or suitably. —'**gainliness** *n.*

gains (geɪnz) *pl. n.* profits or winnings: *ill-gotten gains.*

gainsay (geɪn'seɪ) *vb.* **-says, -saying, -said.** (*tr.*) *Archaic or literary.* to deny (an allegation, a statement, etc.); contradict. [C13 *gainsaien,* from *gain-* AGAINST + *saien* to SAY] —**gain'sayer** *n.*

'gainst *or* **gainst** (gɛnst, geɪnst) *prep. Poetic.* short for **against.**

gait (geɪt) *n.* **1.** manner of walking or running; bearing. **2.** (used esp. of horses and dogs) the pattern of footsteps at various speeds, as the walk, trot, canter, etc., each pattern being distinguished by a particular rhythm and footfall. ~*vb.* **3.** (*tr.*) to teach (a horse) a particular gait. [C16: variant of GATE[1]]

-gaited ('geɪtɪd) *adj.* (*in combination*) having a gait as specified: *slow-gaited.*

gaiter ('geɪtə) *n.* (*often pl.*) **1.** a cloth or leather covering for the leg or ankle buttoned on one side and usually strapped under the foot. **2.** Also called: **spat.** a similar covering extending from the ankle to the instep. **3.** a waterproof covering for the ankle worn by climbers and walkers to prevent snow, mud, or gravel entering over the top of the boot. [C18: from French *guêtre,* probably of Germanic origin and related to WRIST] —'**gaiterless** *adj.*

gal[1] (gæl) *n. Slang.* a girl.

gal[2] (gæl) *n.* a unit of acceleration equal to 1 centimetre per second per second. [C20: named after *Galileo* (1564–1642), Italian scientist]
gal. *or* **gall.** *abbrev. for* gallon.
Gal. *Bible. abbrev. for* Galatians.
gala ('gɑːlə, 'geɪlə) *n.* **1. a.** a celebration; festive occasion. **b.** (*as modifier*): *a gala occasion.* **2.** *Chiefly Brit.* a sporting occasion involving competitions in several events: *a swimming gala.* [C17: from French or Italian, from Old French *gale* pleasure, from Old French *galer* to make merry, probably of Germanic origin; compare GALLANT]
galactagogue (gə'læktə,gɒg) *adj.* **1.** inducing milk secretion. ~*n.* **2.** a galactagogue agent. [C19: from Greek *gala, galaktos,* milk + -AGOGUE]
galactic (gə'læktɪk) *adj.* **1.** *Astronomy.* of or relating to a galaxy, esp. the Galaxy: *the galactic plane.* **2.** *Med.* of or relating to milk. [C19: from Greek *galaktikos;* see GALAXY]
galactic equator *or* **circle** *n.* the great circle on the celestial sphere containing the galactic plane.
galactic halo *n. Astronomy.* a spheroidal aggregation of globular clusters, individual stars, dust, and gas that surrounds the Galaxy.
galactic plane *n.* the plane passing through the spiral arms of the Galaxy.
galactic poles *pl. n.* the two points on the celestial sphere, diametrically opposite each other, that can be joined by an imaginary line perpendicular to the galactic plane.
galacto- *or before a vowel* **galact-** *combining form.* milk or milky: *galactometer.* [from Greek *galakt-, gala*]
galactometer (,gælək'tɒmɪtə) *n.* an instrument, similar to a hydrometer, for measuring the relative density of milk. It is used to determine the fat content. —,**galac'tometry** *n.*
galactopoietic (gə,læktəʊpɔɪ'ɛtɪk) *adj.* **1.** inducing or increasing the secretion of milk. ~*n.* **2.** a galactopoietic agent. —**galactopoiesis** (gə,læktəʊpɔɪ'iːsɪs) *n.*
galactose (gə'læktəʊz, -əʊs) *n.* a white water-soluble monosaccharide found in lactose. Formula: $C_6H_{12}O_6$.
galago (gə'lɑːgəʊ) *n., pl.* **-gos.** another name for **bushbaby.** [C19: from New Latin, perhaps from Wolof *golokh* monkey]
galah (gə'lɑː) *n.* **1.** an Australian cockatoo, *Kakatoe roseicapilla,* having grey wings, back, and crest and a pink body. **2.** *Austral. slang.* a fool or simpleton. [C19: from a native Australian language]
Galahad ('gælə,hæd) *n.* a pure or noble man. [after the virtuous Sir *Galahad* of Arthurian legend]
galangal (gə'læŋgᵊl) *n.* **1.** another name for **galingale.** **2.** a zingiberaceous plant, *Alpinia officinarum,* of China and the East Indies. **3.** the pungent aromatic root of this plant, dried and used as a seasoning and in medicine.
galantine ('gælən,tiːn) *n.* a cold dish of meat or poultry, which is boned, cooked, stuffed, then pressed into a neat shape and glazed. [C14: from Old French, from Medieval Latin *galatina,* probably from Latin *gelātus* frozen, set; see GELATIN]
galanty show (gə'læntɪ) *n.* (formerly) a pantomime shadow play, esp. one in miniature using figures cut from paper. [C19: perhaps from Italian *galante* GALLANT]
galatea (,gælə'tɪə) *n.* a strong twill-weave cotton fabric, striped or plain, for clothing. [C19: named after the man-of-war H.M.S. *Galatea* (the fabric was at one time in demand for children's sailor suits)]
galaxy ('gæləksɪ) *n., pl.* **-axies.** **1.** any of a vast number of star systems held together by gravitational attraction in an asymmetric shape (an **irregular galaxy**) or, more usually, in a symmetrical shape (a **regular galaxy**), which is either a spiral or an ellipse. Former names: **island universe, extragalactic nebula.** **2.** a splendid gathering, esp. one of famous or distinguished people. [C14 (in the sense: the Milky Way), from Medieval Latin *galaxia,* from Latin *galaxias,* from Greek, from *gala* milk; related to Latin *lac* milk]
Galaxy ('gæləksɪ) *n.* **the.** the spiral galaxy, approximately 100 000 light years in diameter, that contains the solar system about three fifths of the distance from its centre. Also called: the **Milky Way System.** See also **Magellanic Cloud.**
galbanum ('gælbənəm) *n.* a bitter aromatic gum resin extracted from any of several Asian umbelliferous plants of the genus *Ferula,* esp. *F. galbaniflua,* and used in incense and medicinally as a counterirritant. [C14: from Latin, from Greek *khalbanē,* from Hebrew *helbenāh*]
gale[1] (geɪl) *n.* **1.** a strong wind, specifically one of force seven to ten on the Beaufort scale or from 45 to 90 kilometres per hour. **2.** (*often pl.*) a loud outburst, esp. of laughter. **3.** *Archaic and poetic.* a gentle breeze. [C16: of unknown origin]
gale[2] (geɪl) *n.* short for **sweet gale.** [Old English *gagel;* related to Middle Low German *gagel*]
galea ('geɪlɪə) *n., pl.* **-leae** (-lɪ,iː). a part or organ shaped like a helmet or hood, such as the petals of certain flowers. [C18: from Latin: helmet] —'**gale,ate** *or* '**gale,ated** *adj.* —'**galei,form** *adj.*
galena (gə'liːnə) *or* **galenite** (gə'liːnaɪt) *n.* a grey mineral, found in hydrothermal veins. It is the chief source of lead. Composition: lead sulphide. Formula: PbS. Crystal structure: cubic. [C17: from Latin: lead ore, dross left after melting lead]
Galenic (geɪ'lɛnɪk, gə-) *adj.* of or relating to Galen (?130–?200 A.D.), Greek physician, or his teachings or methods.
galenical (geɪ'lɛnɪkᵊl, gə-) *Pharmacol.* ~*n.* **1.** any drug obtained from plant or animal tissue, esp. vegetables, rather than being chemically synthesized. ~*adj.* **2.** denoting or belonging to this group of drugs. [C17: after *Galen*]
Galenism ('geɪlɪ,nɪzəm) *n.* a system of medicine based on the 84 surviving technical treatises of Galen, including the theory of the four bodily humours. —'**Galenist** *adj., n.*
galère *French.* (galɛr) *n.* **1.** a group of people having a common interest, esp. a coterie of undesirable people. **2.** an unpleasant situation. [C18: literally: a galley]
Galibi (gɑː'liːbɪ) *n.* **1.** (*pl.* **-bi** *or* **-bis**) a member of an American Indian people of French Guiana in NE South America. **2.** the language of this people, belonging to the Carib family.
Galician (gə'lɪʃɪən, -ʃən) *adj.* **1.** of or relating to Galicia in E central Europe. **2.** of or relating to Galicia in NW Spain. ~*n.* **3.** a native or inhabitant of either Galicia. **4.** the Romance language or dialect of Spanish Galicia, sometimes regarded as a dialect of Spanish, although historically it is more closely related to Portuguese.
Galilean[1] (,gælɪ'liːən) *n.* **1.** a native or inhabitant of Galilee in N Israel, scene of Christ's early ministry. **2. a. the.** an epithet of Jesus Christ. **b.** (*often pl.*) a Christian. ~*adj.* **3.** of Galilee.
Galilean[2] (,gælɪ'leɪən) *adj.* of or relating to Galileo (1564–1642), Italian scientist.
Galilean telescope (,gælɪ'leɪən) *n.* a type of telescope with a convex objective lens and a concave eyepiece; it produces an erect image and is suitable for terrestrial use.
galilee ('gælɪ,liː) *n.* a porch or chapel at the entrance to some medieval churches and cathedrals in England.
galimatias (,gælɪ'meɪʃɪəs, -'mætɪəs) *n. Rare.* confused talk; gibberish. [C17: from French, of unknown origin]
galingale ('gælɪŋ,geɪl) *or* **galangal** *n.* a European cyperaceous plant, *Cyperus longus,* with rough-edged leaves, reddish spikelets of flowers, and aromatic roots. [C13: from Old French *galingal,* from Arabic *khalanjān,* from Chinese *kaoliang-chiang,* from *Kaoliang* district in Kwangtung province + *chiang* ginger]
galiot *or* **galliot** ('gælɪət) *n.* **1.** a small swift galley formerly sailed on the Mediterranean. **2.** a shallow-draught ketch formerly used along the coasts of Germany and the Netherlands. [C14: from Old French *galiote,* from Italian *galeotta,* from Medieval Latin *galea* GALLEY]
galipot *or* **gallipot** ('gælɪ,pɒt) *n.* a resin obtained from several species of pine, esp. from the S European *Pinus pinaster.* [C18: from French, of unknown origin]
gall[1] (gɔːl) *n.* **1.** *Informal.* impudence. **2.** bitterness; rancour. **3.** something bitter or disagreeable. **4.** *Physiol.* an obsolete term for **bile.** **5.** an obsolete term for **gall bladder.** [from Old Norse, replacing Old English *gealla;* related to Old High German *galla,* Greek *kholē*]
gall[2] (gɔːl) *n.* **1.** a sore on the skin caused by chafing. **2.** something that causes vexation or annoyance: *a gall to the spirits.* **3.** irritation; exasperation. ~*vb.* **4.** *Pathol.* to abrade (the skin, etc.) as by rubbing. **5.** (*tr.*) to irritate or annoy; vex. [C14: of Germanic origin; related to Old English *gealla* sore on a horse, and perhaps to GALL[1]]
gall[3] (gɔːl) *n.* an abnormal outgrowth in plant tissue caused by certain parasitic insects, fungi, bacteria, or mechanical injury. [C14: from Old French *galle,* from Latin *galla*]
gall. *or* **gal.** *abbrev. for* gallon.
Galla ('gælə) *n.* **1.** (*pl.* **-las** *or* **-la**) a member of a tall dark-skinned people inhabiting Somalia and SE Ethiopia in NE Africa. **2.** the language of this people, belonging to the Cushitic subfamily of the Afro-Asiatic family of languages.
gallant *adj.* ('gælənt). **1.** brave and high-spirited; courageous and honourable; dashing: *a gallant warrior.* **2.** (gə'lænt, 'gælənt). (of a man) attentive to women; chivalrous. **3.** imposing; dignified; stately: *a gallant ship.* **4.** *Archaic.* showy in dress. ~*n.* ('gælənt, gə'lænt). *Archaic.* **5.** a woman's lover or suitor. **6.** a dashing or fashionable young man, esp. one who pursues women. **7.** a brave, high-spirited, or adventurous man. ~*vb.* (gə'lænt, 'gælənt). *Rare.* **8.** (when *intr.,* usually foll. by *with*) to court or flirt (with). **9.** (*tr.*) to attend or escort (a woman). [C15: from Old French *galant,* from *galer* to make merry, from *gale* enjoyment, pleasure, of Germanic origin; related to Old English *wela* WEAL[2]] —'**gallantly** *adv.* —'**gallantness** *n.*
gallantry ('gæləntrɪ) *n., pl.* **-ries.** **1.** conspicuous courage, esp. in war: *the gallantry of the troops.* **2.** polite attentiveness to women. **3.** a gallant action, speech, etc.
gallant soldier *n.* a South American plant, *Galinsoga parviflora,* widely distributed as a weed, having small daisy-like flowers surrounded by silvery scales: family *Compositae* (composites). Also called: **Joey Hooker.** [C20: by folk etymology from New Latin *Galinsoga*]
gall bladder *n.* a muscular sac, attached to the right lobe of the liver, that stores bile and ejects it into the duodenum.
galleass *or* **galliass** ('gælɪ,æs) *n. Nautical.* a three-masted lateen-rigged galley used as a warship in the Mediterranean from the 15th to the 18th centuries. [C16: from French *galleasse,* from Italian *galeazza,* from *galea* GALLEY]
galleon ('gælɪən) *n. Nautical.* a large sailing ship having three or more masts, lateen-rigged on the after masts and square-rigged

on the foremast and mainmast, used as a warship or trader from the 15th to the 18th centuries. [C16: from Spanish *galeón*, from French *galion*, from Old French *galie* GALLEY]

galleria (ˌgæləˈriːə) *n.* a central court through several storeys of a shopping centre or department store onto which shops or departments open at each level. [C20: from Italian; see GALLERY]

gallery (ˈgælərɪ) *n., pl.* **-leries.** **1.** a room or building for exhibiting works of art. **2.** a covered passageway open on one side or on both sides. See also **colonnade** (sense 1). **3. a.** a balcony running along or around the inside wall of a church, hall, etc. **b.** a covered balcony, sometimes with columns on the outside. **4.** *Theatre.* **a.** an upper floor that projects from the rear over the main floor and contains the cheapest seats. **b.** the seats there. **c.** the audience seated there. **5.** a long narrow room, esp. one used for a specific purpose: *a shooting gallery.* **6.** *Chiefly U.S.* a building or room where articles are sold at auction. **7.** an underground passage, as in a mine, the burrow of an animal, etc. **8.** *Theatre.* a narrow raised platform at the side or along the back of the stage for the use of technicians and stagehands. **9.** (in a TV studio) a glass-fronted soundproof room high up to one side of the studio looking into it. One gallery is used by the director and an assistant and one is for lighting, etc. **10.** *Nautical.* a balcony or platform at the quarter or stern of a ship, sometimes used as a gun emplacement. **11.** a small ornamental metal or wooden balustrade or railing on a piece of furniture, esp. one surrounding the top of a desk, table, etc. **12.** any group of spectators, as at a golf match. **13. play to the gallery.** to try to gain popular favour, esp. by crude appeals. [C15: from Old French *galerie*, from Medieval Latin *galeria*, probably from *galilea* GALILEE] —ˈ**galleried** *adj.*

gallery forest *n.* a stretch of forest along a river in an area of otherwise open country.

gallery tray *n.* a tray usually of silver with a raised rim, used for serving drinks.

galley (ˈgælɪ) *n.* **1.** any of various kinds of ship propelled by oars or sails used in ancient or medieval times as a warship or as a trader. **2.** the kitchen of a ship, boat, or aircraft. **3.** any of various long rowing boats. **4.** *Printing.* **a.** (in hot-metal composition) a tray open at one end for holding composed type. **b.** short for **galley proof.** [C13: from Old French *galie*, from Medieval Latin *galea*, from Greek *galaia*, of unknown origin; the sense development apparently is due to the association of a galley or slave ship with a ship's kitchen and hence with a hot furnace, trough, printer's tray, etc.]

galley proof *n.* a printer's proof, esp. one taken on a long strip of paper from type in a galley, used to make corrections before the matter has been split into pages. Often shortened to **galley.**

galley slave *n.* **1.** a criminal or slave condemned to row in a galley. **2.** *Informal.* a drudge.

galley-west *adv. Slang, chiefly U.S.* into confusion, inaction, or unconsciousness (esp. in the phrase **knock (someone** *or* **something) galley-west**). [C19: from English dialect *colly-west* awry, perhaps from *Collyweston*, a village in Northamptonshire]

gallfly (ˈgɔːlˌflaɪ) *n., pl.* **-flies.** any of several small insects that produce galls in plant tissues, such as the gall wasp and gall midge.

galliambic (ˌgælɪˈæmbɪk) *Prosody.* ~*adj.* **1.** of or relating to a metre consisting of four lesser Ionics, used in ancient Greek and Roman poetry and imitated by Tennyson (1809–92) in *Boadicea.* ~*n.* **2.** a verse in this metre. [C19: from Latin *galliambus* song of the *Galli* (priests of Cybele)]

galliard (ˈgæljəd) *n.* **1.** a spirited dance in triple time for two persons, popular in the 16th and 17th centuries. **2.** a piece of music composed for this dance. ~*adj.* **3.** *Archaic.* lively; spirited. [C14: from Old French *gaillard* valiant, perhaps of Celtic origin]

gallic[1] (ˈgælɪk) *adj.* of or containing gallium in the trivalent state. [C18: from GALL(IUM) + -IC]

gallic[2] (ˈgælɪk) *adj.* of, relating to, or derived from plant galls. [C18: from French *gallique*; see GALL[3]]

Gallic (ˈgælɪk) *adj.* **1.** of or relating to France. **2.** of or relating to ancient Gaul or the Gauls.

gallic acid *n.* a colourless crystalline compound obtained from tannin: used as a tanning agent and in making inks, paper, and pyrogallol; 3,4,5-trihydroxybenzoic acid. Formula: $C_6H_2(OH)_3COOH$.

Gallican (ˈgælɪkən) *adj.* **1.** of or relating to Gallicanism. ~*n.* **2.** an upholder of Gallicanism.

Gallicanism (ˈgælɪkəˌnɪzəm) *n.* a movement among French Roman Catholic clergy that favoured the restriction of papal control and greater autonomy for the French church. Compare **ultramontanism.**

Gallice (ˈgælɪsɪ) *adv.* in French. [C19: from Latin]

Gallicism (ˈgælɪˌsɪzəm) *n.* a word or idiom borrowed from French.

Gallicize *or* **Gallicise** (ˈgælɪˌsaɪz) *vb.* to make or become French in attitude, language, etc. —ˌ**Gallici'zation** *or* ˌ**Gallici'sation** *n.* —ˈ**Galliˌcizer** *or* ˈ**Galliˌciser** *n.*

galligaskins *or* **gallygaskins** (ˌgælɪˈgæskɪnz) *pl. n.* **1.** loose wide breeches or hose, esp. as worn by men in the 17th century. **2.** leather leggings, as worn in the 19th century. [C16: from obsolete French *garguesques*, from Italian *grechesco* Greek, from Latin *Graecus*]

gallimaufry (ˌgælɪˈmɔːfrɪ) *n., pl.* **-fries.** a jumble; hotchpotch. [C16: from French *galimafrée* ragout, hash, of unknown origin]

gallinacean (ˌgælɪˈneɪʃən) *n.* any gallinaceous bird.

gallinaceous (ˌgælɪˈneɪʃəs) *adj.* **1.** of, relating to, or belonging to the *Galliformes*, an order of birds, including domestic fowl, pheasants, grouse, etc., having a heavy rounded body, short bill, and strong legs. **2.** of, relating to, or resembling the domestic fowl. [C18: from Latin *gallīnāceus*, from *gallīna* hen]

galling (ˈgɔːlɪŋ) *adj.* **1.** irritating, exasperating, or bitterly humiliating. **2.** *Obsolete.* rubbing painfully; chafing. —ˈ**gallingly** *adv.*

gallinule (ˈgælɪˌnjuːl) *n.* **1.** any of various aquatic birds of the genera *Porphyrio* and *Porphyrula*, typically having a dark plumage, red bill, and a red shield above the bill: family *Rallidae* (rails). **2. common gallinule.** the U.S. name for **moorhen** (sense 1). [C18: from New Latin *Gallīnula* genus name, from Late Latin: pullet, chicken, from Latin *gallīna* hen]

galliot (ˈgælɪət) *n.* a variant spelling of **galiot.**

gallipot[1] (ˈgælɪˌpɒt) *n.* a small earthenware pot used by pharmacists as a container for ointments, etc. [C16: probably from GALLEY + POT[1]; so called because imported in galleys]

gallipot[2] (ˈgælɪˌpɒt) *n.* a variant spelling of **galipot.**

gallium (ˈgælɪəm) *n.* a silvery metallic element that is liquid for a wide temperature range. It occurs in trace amounts in some ores and is used in high-temperature thermometers and low-melting alloys. **Gallium arsenide** is used in semiconductors. Symbol: Ga; atomic no.: 31; atomic wt.: 69.72; valency: 2 or 3; relative density: 5.91; melting pt.: 29.78°C; boiling pt.: 2403°C. [C19: from New Latin, from Latin *gallus* cock, translation of French *coq* in the name of its discoverer, *Lecoq* de Boisbaudran, 19th-century French chemist]

gallivant, galivant, *or* **galavant** (ˈgælɪˌvænt) *vb.* (*intr.*) to go about in search of pleasure; gad about. [C19: perhaps whimsical modification of GALLANT]

galliwasp (ˈgælɪˌwɒsp) *n.* any lizard of the Central American genus *Diploglossus*, esp. *D. monotropis* of the West Indies: family *Anguidae.* [C18: of unknown origin]

gall midge *n.* any of various small fragile mosquito-like dipterous flies constituting the widely distributed family *Cecidomyidae*, many of which have larvae that produce galls on plants. Also called: **gallfly, gall gnat.** See also **Hessian fly.**

gall mite *n.* any of various plant-feeding mites of the family *Phytoptidae* that cause galls or blisters on buds, leaves, or fruit.

gallnut (ˈgɔːlˌnʌt) *or* **gall-apple** *n.* a type of plant gall that resembles a nut.

Gallo- (ˈgæləʊ) *combining form.* denoting Gaul or France: *Gallo-Roman.* [from Latin *Gallus* a Gaul]

galloglass *or* **gallowglass** (ˈgæləʊˌglɑːs) *n.* a heavily armed mercenary soldier, originally Hebridean (Gaelic-Norse), maintained by Irish and some other Celtic chiefs from about 1235 to the 16th century. [C16: from Irish Gaelic *gallóglach*, from *gall* foreigner + *óglach*, young warrior-servant, from *og* young + *-lach* a noun suffix]

gallon (ˈgælən) *n.* **1.** Also called: **imperial gallon.** *Brit.* a unit of capacity equal to 277.42 cubic inches. 1 Brit. gallon is equivalent to 1.20 U.S. gallons or 4.55 litres. **2.** *U.S.* a unit of capacity equal to 231 cubic inches. 1 U.S. gallon is equivalent to 0.83 imperial gallon or 3.79 litres. [C13: from Old Northern French *galon* (Old French *jalon*), perhaps of Celtic origin]

gallonage (ˈgælənɪdʒ) *n.* **1.** a capacity measured in gallons. **2.** the rate of pumping, transmission, or consumption of a fluid in gallons per unit of time.

galloon (gəˈluːn) *n.* a narrow band of cord, embroidery, silver or gold braid, etc., used on clothes and furniture. [C17: from French *galon*, from Old French *galonner* to trim with braid, of unknown origin] —**galˈlooned** *adj.*

galloot (gəˈluːt) *n.* a variant spelling of **galoot.**

gallop (ˈgæləp) *vb.* **-lops, -loping, -loped.** **1.** (*intr.*) (of a horse or other quadruped) to run fast with a two-beat stride in which all four legs are off the ground at once. **2.** to ride (a horse, etc.) at a gallop. **3.** (*intr.*) to move, read, talk, etc., rapidly; hurry. ~*n.* **4.** the fast two-beat gait of horses and other quadrupeds. **5.** an instance of galloping. [C16: from Old French *galoper*, of uncertain origin] —ˈ**galloper** *n.*

gallopade *or* **galopade** (ˌgæləˈpeɪd) *n.* another word for **galop.**

galloping (ˈgæləpɪŋ) *adj.* (*prenominal*) progressing at or as if at a gallop: *galloping consumption.*

Gallo-Romance *or* **Gallo-Roman** *n.* **1.** the vernacular language or group of dialects, of which few records survive, spoken in France between about 600 A.D. and 900 A.D.; the intermediate stage between Vulgar Latin and Old French. ~*adj.* **2.** denoting or relating to this language or the period during which it was spoken.

gallous (ˈgæləs) *adj.* of or containing gallium in the divalent state.

Galloway (ˈgæləˌweɪ) *n.* a breed of hardy black cattle originally bred in Galloway in SW Scotland.

gallows (ˈgæləʊz) *n., pl.* **-lowses** *or* **-lows.** **1.** a wooden structure usually consisting of two upright posts with a crossbeam from which a rope is suspended, used for hanging criminals. **2.** any timber structure resembling this, such as (in Australia and New Zealand) a frame for hoisting up the bodies of slaughtered cattle. **3. the gallows.** execution by hanging. [C13: from Old Norse

galgi, replacing Old English *gealga;* related to Old High German *galgo*]
gallows bird *n. Informal.* a person considered deserving of hanging.
gallows humour *n.* sinister and ironic humour.
gallows tree *or* **gallow tree** *n.* another name for **gallows** (sense 1).
gallsickness ('gɔːlˌsɪknɪs) *n.* a disease of cattle and sheep, caused by infection with rickettsiae of the genus *Anaplasma,* resulting in anaemia and jaundice. Also called: **anaplasmosis.**
gallstone ('gɔːlˌstəʊn) *n. Pathol.* a small hard concretion of cholesterol, bile pigments, and lime salts, formed in the gall bladder or its ducts. Also called: **bilestone.**
Gallup Poll ('gæləp) *n.* a sampling by the American Institute of Public Opinion or its British counterpart of the views of a representative cross section of the population, used esp. as a means of forecasting voting. [C20: named after G. H. *Gallup* (1901–84), U.S. statistician who devised it]
gallus ('gæləs) *adj. Scot.* bold; daring; reckless. [a variant of *gallows* used as an adjective, meaning fit for the gallows]
galluses ('gæləsɪz) *pl. n. Dialect.* braces for trousers. [C18: variant spelling of *gallowses,* from GALLOWS (in the obsolete sense: braces)]
gall wasp *n.* any small solitary wasp of the family *Cynipidae* and related families that produces galls in plant tissue, which provide shelter and food for the larvae.
Galois theory ('gælwɑː) *n. Maths.* the theory applying group theory to solving algebraic equations. [C19: named after Évariste *Galois* (1811–32), French mathematician]
galoot *or* **galloot** (gə'luːt) *n. Slang, chiefly U.S.* a clumsy or uncouth person. [C19: of unknown origin]
galop ('gæləp) *n.* **1.** a 19th-century couple dance in quick duple time. **2.** a piece of music composed for this dance. ~Also called: **gallopade.** [C19: from French; see GALLOP]
galore (gə'lɔː) *determiner.* (*immediately postpositive*) in great numbers or quantity: *there were daffodils galore in the park.* [C17: from Irish Gaelic *go leór* to sufficiency]
galoshes *or* **goloshes** (gə'lɒʃɪz) *pl. n.* (*sometimes sing.*) a pair of waterproof overshoes. [C14 (in the sense: wooden shoe): from Old French *galoche,* from Late Latin *gallicula* Gallic shoe]
galtonia (gɔːl'təʊnɪə) *n.* any plant of the bulbous genus *Galtonia,* esp. *G. candicans,* with lanceolate leaves, drooping racemes of waxy white flowers, and a fragrant scent: family *Liliaceae.* [named after Sir Francis *Galton* (1822–1911), British explorer and scientist]
galumph (gə'lʌmpf, -'lʌmf) *vb.* (*intr.*) *Informal.* to leap or move about clumsily or joyfully. [C19 (coined by Lewis Carroll (1832–98), British writer): probably a blend of GALLOP + TRIUMPH]
galv. *abbrev. for:* **1.** galvanic. **2.** galvanism.
galvanic (gæl'vænɪk) *or* **galvanical** *adj.* **1.** Also: **voltaic.** of, producing, or concerned with an electric current, esp. a direct current produced chemically: *a galvanic cell.* **2.** *Informal.* resembling the effect of an electric shock; convulsive, startling, or energetic: *galvanic reflexes.* [C18: after Luigi *Galvani* (1737–98), Italian physiologist] —**gal'vanically** *adv.*
galvanic pile *n.* another name for **voltaic pile.**
galvanic skin response *n.* a change in the electrical resistance of the skin occurring in moments of strong emotion; measurements of this change are used in lie detector tests. Abbrev.: **GSR.**
galvanism ('gælvəˌnɪzəm) *n.* **1.** *Obsolete.* electricity, esp. when produced by chemical means as in a cell or battery. **2.** *Med.* treatment involving the application of electric currents to tissues. [C18: via French from Italian *galvanismo,* after *Galvani:* see GALVANIC]
galvanize *or* **galvanise** ('gælvəˌnaɪz) *vb.* (*tr.*) **1.** to stimulate to action; excite; startle. **2.** to cover (iron, steel, etc.) with a protective zinc coating by dipping into molten zinc or by electrodeposition. **3.** to stimulate by application of an electric current. ~*n.* **4.** *Caribbean.* galvanized iron, usually in the form of corrugated sheets as used in roofing. —ˌ**galvani'zation** *or* ˌ**galvani'sation** *n.* —'**galvaˌnizer** *or* '**galvaˌniser** *n.*
galvanized iron *or* **galvanised iron** *n. Building trades.* iron, esp. a sheet of corrugated iron, covered with a protective coating of zinc.
galvano- *combining form.* indicating a galvanic current: *galvanometer.*
galvanometer (ˌgælvə'nɒmɪtə) *n.* any sensitive instrument for detecting or measuring small electric currents. —**galvanometric** (ˌgælvənəʊ'mɛtrɪk, gælˌvænə-) *or* ˌ**galvano'metrical** *adj.* —ˌ**galvano'metrically** *adv.* —ˌ**galva'nometry** *n.*
galvanoscope ('gælvənəˌskəʊp, gæl'vænə-) *n.* a galvanometer that depends for its action on the deflection of a magnetic needle in a magnetic field produced by the electric current that is to be detected. —**galvanoscopic** (ˌgælvənə'skɒpɪk, gælˌvænə-) *adj.* —ˌ**galva'noscopy** *n.*
galvanotropism (ˌgælvə'nɒtrəˌpɪzəm) *n.* the directional growth of an organism, esp. a plant, in response to an electrical stimulus. —**galvanotropic** (ˌgælvənəʊ'trɒpɪk, gælˌvænəʊ-) *adj.*
galvo ('gælvəʊ) *n., pl.* **-vos.** an informal name for a **galvanometer.**
Galwegian (gæl'wiːdʒən) *n.* **1.** a native or inhabitant of Galloway, an area of SW Scotland. **2.** a native or inhabitant of the town or county of Galway in W Ireland. ~*adj.* **3.** of or relating to Galloway. [C18: influenced by *Norway, Norwegian*]
galyak *or* **galyac** ('gæljæk, gæl'jæk) *n.* a smooth glossy fur obtained from the skins of newborn or premature lambs and kids. [from Russian (Uzbek dialect)]
gam[1] (gæm) *n.* **1.** a school of whales. **2.** *Nautical.* an informal visit between crew members of whalers. **3.** *N.Z.* a flock of large sea birds. ~*vb.* **gams, gamming, gammed.** **4.** (*intr.*) (of whales) to form a school. **5.** *Nautical.* (of members of the crews of whalers) to visit (each other) informally. **6.** (*tr.*) *U.S.* to visit or exchange visits with. [C19: perhaps dialect variant of GAME[1]]
gam[2] (gæm) *n. Slang.* a leg, esp. a woman's shapely leg. [C18: probably from Old Northern French *gambe* or Lingua Franca *gambe;* see JAMB]
gama grass ('gɑːmə) *n.* a tall perennial grass, *Tripsacum dactyloides,* of SE North America: cultivated for fodder. [C19: *gama,* probably changed from GRAMA]
gamahuche ('gæməˌhuːʃ) *or* **gamaruche** ('gæməˌruːʃ) *Taboo.* ~*vb.* (*tr.*) **1.** to practise cunnilingus or fellatio on. ~*n.* **2.** cunnilingus or fellatio. [C19: from French *gamahucher*]
gamba ('gæmbə) *n.* short for **viola da gamba.**
gambado[1] (gæm'beɪdəʊ) *n., pl.* **-dos** *or* **-does.** **1.** either of two leather holders for the feet attached to a horse's saddle like stirrups. **2.** either of a pair of leggings. [C17: from Italian *gamba* leg, from Late Latin: leg, hoof; see JAMB]
gambado[2] (gæm'beɪdəʊ) *or* **gambade** (gæm'beɪd, -'bɑːd) *n., pl.* **-bados, -badoes,** *or* **-bades.** **1.** *Dressage.* another word for **curvet.** **2.** a leap or gambol; caper. [C19: from French *gambade* spring (of a horse), ultimately from Spanish or Italian *gamba* leg]
gamba stop *n.* an organ stop with a tone resembling that of stringed instruments.
gambeson ('gæmbɪsᵊn) *n.* a quilted and padded or stuffed leather or cloth garment worn under chain mail in the Middle Ages and later as a doublet by men and women. [C13: from Old French, of Germanic origin; related to Old High German *wamba* belly; see WOMB]
Gambian ('gæmbɪən) *adj.* **1.** of or relating to The Gambia, a republic in W Africa, or its people. ~*n.* **2.** a native or inhabitant of The Gambia.
gambier *or* **gambir** ('gæmbɪə) *n.* an astringent resinous substance obtained from a rubiaceous tropical Asian woody climbing plant, *Uncaria gambir* (or *U. gambier*): used as an astringent and tonic and in tanning. [C19: from Malay]
gambit ('gæmbɪt) *n.* **1.** *Chess.* an opening move in which a chessman, usually a pawn, is sacrificed to secure an advantageous position. **2.** an opening comment, manoeuvre, etc., intended to secure an advantage or promote a point of view. [C17: from French, from Italian *gambetto* a tripping up, from *gamba* leg]
gamble ('gæmbᵊl) *vb.* **1.** (*intr.*) to play games of chance to win money. **2.** to risk or bet (money) on the outcome of an event, sport, etc. **3.** (*intr.;* often foll. by *on*) to act with the expectation of: *to gamble on its being a sunny day.* **4.** (often foll. by *away*) to lose by or as if by betting; squander. ~*n.* **5.** a risky act or venture. **6.** a bet, wager, or other risk or chance taken for possible monetary gain. [C18: probably variant of GAME[1]] —'**gambler** *n.* —'**gambling** *n.*
gamblers' fallacy *n. Psychol.* the fallacy that in a series of chance events the probability of one event occurring increases with the number of times another event has occurred in succession.
gamboge (gæm'bəʊdʒ, -'buːʒ) *n.* **1. a.** a gum resin used as the source of a yellow pigment and as a purgative. **b.** the pigment made from this resin. **2. gamboge tree.** any of several tropical Asian trees of the genus *Garcinia,* esp. *G. hanburyi,* that yield this resin: family *Guttiferae.* **3.** a strong yellow colour. ~Also called (for senses 1, 2): **cambogia.** [C18: from New Latin *gambaugium,* from *Cambodia,* country in SE Asia] —**gam'bogian** *adj.*
gambol ('gæmbᵊl) *vb.* **-bols, -bolling, -bolled** *or U.S.* **-bols, -boling, -boled.** **1.** (*intr.*) to skip or jump about in a playful manner; frolic. ~*n.* **2.** a playful antic; frolic. [C16: from French *gambade;* see GAMBADO[2], JAMB]
gambrel ('gæmbrəl) *n.* **1.** the hock of a horse or similar animal. **2.** a frame of wood or metal shaped like a horse's hind leg, used by butchers for suspending carcasses of meat. **3.** short for **gambrel roof.** [C16: from Old Northern French *gamberel,* from *gambe* leg]
gambrel roof *n.* **1.** *Chiefly Brit.* a hipped roof having a small gable at both ends. **2.** *Chiefly U.S. and Canadian.* a roof having two slopes on both sides, the lower slopes being steeper than the upper. Compare **mansard** (sense 1). ~Sometimes shortened to **gambrel.** —'**gambrel-ˌroofed** *adj.*
game[1] (geɪm) *n.* **1.** an amusement or pastime; diversion. **2.** a contest with rules, the result being determined by skill, strength, or chance. **3.** a single period of play in such a contest, sport, etc. **4.** the score needed to win a contest. **5.** a single contest in a series; match. **6.** (*pl.; often cap.*) an event consisting of various sporting contests, esp. in athletics: *Olympic Games; Highland Games.* **7.** equipment needed for playing certain games. **8.** style or ability in playing a game: *he is a keen player but his game is not good.* **9.** a scheme, proceeding, etc., practised like a game: *the game of politics.* **10.** an activity undertaken in a spirit of

levity; joke: *marriage is just a game to him.* **11. a.** wild animals, including birds and fish, hunted for sport, food, or profit. **b.** (*as modifier*): *game laws.* **12.** the flesh of such animals, used as food: generally taken not to include fish. **13.** an object of pursuit; quarry; prey (esp. in the phrase **fair game**). **14.** *Informal.* work or occupation. **15.** *Informal.* a trick, strategy, or device: *I can see through your little game.* **16.** *Obsolete.* pluck or courage; bravery. **17.** *Slang, chiefly Brit.* prostitution (esp. in the phrase **on the game**). **18. give the game away.** to reveal one's intentions or a secret. **19. make (a) game of.** to make fun of; ridicule; mock. **20. on** (*or* **off**) **one's game.** playing well (or badly). **21. play the game.** to behave fairly or in accordance with rules. **22. the game is up.** there is no longer a chance of success. ~*adj.* **23.** *Informal.* full of fighting spirit; plucky; brave. **24. (as) game as Ned Kelly.** *Austral. informal.* extremely brave; indomitable. **25.** (usually foll. by *for*) *Informal.* prepared or ready; willing: *I'm game for a try.* ~*vb.* **26.** (*intr.*) to play games of chance for money, stakes, etc.; gamble. [Old English *gamen;* related to Old Norse *gaman,* Old High German *gaman* amusement] —ˈ**game,like** *adj.*

game[2] (geɪm) *adj.* a less common word for **lame**[1] (esp. in the phrase **game leg**). [C18: probably from Irish *cam* crooked]

game-ball *adj. Irish.* **1.** (of a person) in perfect health. **2.** (of an arrangement, plan, etc.) excellent.

game bird *n.* a bird of any species hunted as game.

game chips *pl. n.* round thin potato chips served with game.

gamecock (ˈgeɪm,kɒk) *n.* a cock bred and trained for fighting. Also called: **fighting cock.**

game fish *n.* any fish providing sport for the angler.

game fowl *n.* any of several breeds of domestic fowl reared for cockfighting.

gamekeeper (ˈgeɪm,kiːpə) *n.* a person employed to take care of game and wildlife, as on an estate. —ˈ**game,keeping** *n.*

gamelan (ˈgæmɪ,læn) *n.* a type of percussion orchestra common in the East Indies. [from Javanese]

game laws *pl. n.* laws governing the hunting and preservation of game.

gamely (ˈgeɪmlɪ) *adv.* in a brave or sporting manner.

gameness (ˈgeɪmnɪs) *n.* courage or bravery; pluck.

game park *n.* (esp. in Africa) a large area of country set aside as a reserve for wild animals.

game plan *n.* **1.** a strategy. **2.** a plan of campaign, esp. in politics.

game point *n. Tennis, etc.* a stage at which winning one further point would enable one player or side to win a game.

gamesmanship (ˈgeɪmzmən,ʃɪp) *n. Informal.* the art of winning games or defeating opponents by clever or cunning practices without actually cheating. —ˈ**gamesman** *n.*

gamesome (ˈgeɪmsəm) *adj.* full of merriment; sportive. —ˈ**gamesomely** *adv.* —ˈ**gamesomeness** *n.*

gamester (ˈgeɪmstə) *n.* a person who habitually plays games for money; gambler.

gametangium (,gæmɪˈtændʒɪəm) *n., pl.* **-gia** (-dʒɪə). *Botany.* an organ or cell in which gametes are produced, esp. in algae and fungi. [C19: New Latin, from GAMETO- + Greek *angeion* vessel] —,**gameˈtangial** *adj.*

gamete (ˈgæmiːt, gəˈmiːt) *n.* a haploid germ cell, such as a spermatozoon or ovum, that fuses with another germ cell during fertilization. [C19: from New Latin, from Greek *gametē* wife, from *gamos* marriage] —**gaˈmetal** *or* **gametic** (gəˈmɛtɪk) *adj.*

gamete intrafallopian transfer (,ɪntrəfəˈləʊpɪən) *n.* the full name for **GIFT.**

game theory *n.* mathematical theory concerned with the optimum choice of strategy in situations involving a conflict of interest. Also called: **theory of games.** —,**game-,theoˈretic** *adj.*

gameto- *or sometimes before a vowel* **gamet-** *combining form.* gamete: *gametocyte.*

gametocyte (gəˈmiːtəʊ,saɪt) *n.* an animal or plant cell that develops into gametes by meiosis. See also **oocyte, spermatocyte.**

gametogenesis (,gæmɪtəʊˈdʒɛnɪsɪs) *or* **gametogeny** (,gæmɪˈtɒdʒɪnɪ) *n.* the formation and maturation of gametes. See also **spermatogenesis, oogenesis.** —,**gametoˈgenic** *or* ,**gameˈtogenous** *adj.*

gametophore (gəˈmiːtəʊ,fɔː) *n.* the part of a plant that bears the reproductive organs. —**ga,metoˈphoric** *adj.*

gametophyte (gəˈmiːtəʊ,faɪt) *n.* the plant body, in species showing alternation of generations, that produces the gametes. Compare **sporophyte.** —**gametophytic** (,gæmɪtəʊˈfɪtɪk) *adj.*

game warden *n.* a person who looks after game, as in a game reserve.

gamic (ˈgæmɪk) *adj.* (esp. of reproduction) requiring the fusion of gametes; sexual. [C19: from Greek *gamikos* of marriage; see GAMETE]

gamin (ˈgæmɪn; *French* gamɛ̃) *n.* a street urchin; waif. [from French]

gamine (ˈgæmiːn; *French* gamin) *n.* **a.** a slim and boyish girl or young woman; an elfish tomboy. **b.** (*as modifier*): *a gamine style of haircut.* [from French]

gaming (ˈgeɪmɪŋ) *n.* **a.** gambling on games of chance. **b.** (*as modifier*): *gaming house; gaming losses.*

gamma (ˈgæmə) *n.* **1.** the third letter in the Greek alphabet (Γ, γ), a consonant, transliterated as *g.* When double, it is transcribed and pronounced as *ng.* **2.** the third highest grade or mark, as in an examination. **3.** a unit of magnetic field strength equal to 10^{-5} oersted. 1 gamma is equivalent to $0.795\,775 \times 10^{-3}$ ampere per metre. **4.** *Photog., television.* the numerical value of the slope of the characteristic curve of a photographic emulsion or television camera; a measure of the contrast reproduced in a photographic or television image. **5.** (*modifier*) **a.** involving or relating to photons of very high energy: *a gamma detector.* **b.** relating to one of two or more allotropes or crystal structures of a solid: *gamma iron.* **c.** relating to one of two or more isomeric forms of a chemical compound, esp. one in which a group is attached to the carbon atom next but one to the atom to which the principal group is attached. [C14: from Greek; related to Hebrew *gīmel* third letter of the Hebrew alphabet (probably: camel)]

Gamma (ˈgæmə) *n.* (*foll. by the genitive case of a specified constellation*) the third brightest star in a constellation: *Gamma Leonis.*

gamma-aminobutyric acid (,gæməə,miːnəuːbjʊˈtɪrɪk) *n.* the full name for **GABA.**

gamma camera *n.* a medical apparatus that detects gamma rays emitted from a person's body after the administration of a radioactive drug and so produces images of the organ being investigated.

gammadion (gæˈmeɪdɪən) *n., pl.* **-dia** (-dɪə). a decorative figure composed of a number of Greek capital gammas, esp. radiating from a centre, as in a swastika. [C19: from Late Greek, literally: little GAMMA]

gamma distribution *n. Statistics.* a continuous two-parameter distribution from which the chi-square and exponential distributions are derived, written $Ga(2,v)$, and defined in terms of the gamma function.

gamma function *n. Maths.* a function that is defined by $\Gamma(x) = \int_0^\infty t^{x-1}e^{-t}dx$, where x is real and greater than zero.

gamma globulin *n.* any of a group of proteins in blood plasma that includes most known antibodies.

gamma iron *n.* an allotrope of iron that is nonmagnetic and exists between 910°C and 1400°C.

gamma radiation *n.* **1.** electromagnetic radiation emitted by atomic nuclei; the wavelength is generally in the range 1×10^{-10} to 2×10^{-13} metres. **2.** electromagnetic radiation of very short wavelength emitted by any source, esp. the portion of the electromagnetic spectrum with a wavelength less than about 1×10^{-11} metres.

gamma-ray astronomy *n.* the investigation of cosmic gamma rays, such as those from quasars.

gamma rays *pl. n.* streams of gamma radiation.

gamma stock *n.* any of the third rank of active securities on the London Stock Exchange. Prices displayed by market makers are given as an indication rather than an offer to buy or sell.

gammer (ˈgæmə) *n. Rare, chiefly Brit.* a dialect word for an old woman: now chiefly humorous or contemptuous. Compare **gaffer** (sense 1). [C16: probably alteration of GODMOTHER or GRANDMOTHER]

gammon[1] (ˈgæmən) *n.* **1.** a cured or smoked ham. **2.** the hindquarter of a side of bacon, cooked either whole or cut into large rashers. [C15: from Old Northern French *gambon,* from *gambe* leg; see GAMBREL]

gammon[2] (ˈgæmən) *n.* **1.** a double victory in backgammon in which one player throws off all his pieces before his opponent throws any. **2.** *Archaic.* the game of backgammon. ~*vb.* **3.** (*tr.*) to score a gammon over. [C18: probably special use of Middle English *gamen* GAME[1]]

gammon[3] (ˈgæmən) *Brit. informal.* ~*n.* **1.** deceitful nonsense; humbug. ~*vb.* **2.** to deceive (a person). [C18: perhaps special use of GAMMON[2]] —ˈ**gammoner** *n.*

gammon[4] (ˈgæmən) *vb.* (*tr.*) *Nautical.* to fix (a bowsprit) to the stemhead of a vessel. [C18: perhaps related to GAMMON[1], with reference to the tying up of a ham]

gammy (ˈgæmɪ) *adj.* **-mier, -miest.** *Brit. slang.* (esp. of the leg) malfunctioning, injured, or lame; game. U.S. equivalent: **gimpy.** [C19: from Shelta *gyamyath* bad, altered form of Irish *cam* crooked; see GAME[2]]

gamo- *or before a vowel* **gam-** *combining form.* **1.** indicating sexual union or reproduction: *gamogenesis.* **2.** united or fused: *gamopetalous.* [from Greek *gamos* marriage]

gamogenesis (,gæməʊˈdʒɛnɪsɪs) *n.* another name for **sexual reproduction.** —**gamogenetic** (,gæməʊdʒɪˈnɛtɪk) *or* ,**gamogeˈnetical** *adj.* —,**gamogeˈnetically** *adv.*

gamone (ˈgæməʊn) *n. Botany.* a chemical substance secreted by a gamete that attracts another gamete during sexual reproduction.

gamopetalous (,gæməʊˈpɛtələs) *adj.* (of flowers) having petals that are united or partly united, as the primrose. Also: **sympetalous.** Compare **polypetalous.**

gamophyllous (,gæməʊˈfɪləs) *adj.* (of flowers) having united leaves or perianth segments.

gamosepalous (,gæməʊˈsɛpələs) *adj.* (of flowers) having sepals that are united or partly united, as the primrose. Compare **polysepalous.**

-gamous *adj. combining form.* denoting marrying or uniting sexually: *monogamous.* [from Greek *gamos;* see -GAMY]

gamp (gæmp) *n. Brit. informal.* an umbrella. [C19: after Mrs Sarah *Gamp,* a nurse in Dickens' *Martin Chuzzlewit,* who carried a faded cotton umbrella]

gamut (ˈgæmət) *n.* **1.** entire range or scale, as of emotions. **2.** *Music.* **a.** a scale, esp. (in medieval theory) one starting on the G on the bottom line of the bass staff. **b.** the whole range of notes. **3.** *Physics.* the range of chromaticities that can be obtained by mixing three colours. [C15: from Medieval Latin, changed from *gamma ut,* from *gamma,* the lowest note of the hexachord as established by Italian musical theorist Guido d'Arezzo (?995–?1050 A.D.) + *ut* (now, *doh*), the first of the notes of the scale *ut, re, mi, fa, sol, la, si,* derived from a Latin hymn to St John: *Ut* queant laxis *re*sonare fibris, *Mi*ra gestorum *fa*muli tuorum, *Sol*ve polluti *la*bi reatum, Sancte *I*ohannes]

gamy *or* **gamey** (ˈgeɪmɪ) *adj.* **gamier, gamiest.** **1.** having the smell or flavour of game, esp. high game. **2.** *Informal.* spirited; plucky; brave. —ˈ**gamily** *adv.* —ˈ**gaminess** *n.*

-gamy *n. combining form.* denoting marriage or sexual union: *bigamy.* [from Greek *-gamia,* from *gamos* marriage]

gan[1] (gæn) *vb. Archaic or poetic.* the past tense of **gin**[3].

gan[2] (gæn) *vb.* **gans, ganning, ganned.** (*intr.*) *Northeast English dialect.* to go. [from Old English *gangan;* related to Old Norse *ganga.* See GANG[1]]

Ganda (ˈgændə) *n.* **1.** (*pl.* **-das** *or* **-da**) a member of the Buganda people of Uganda, whose kingdom was formerly the largest in E Africa. See also **Luganda.** **2.** the Luganda language of this people.

gander (ˈgændə) *n.* **1.** a male goose. **2.** *Informal.* a quick look (esp. in the phrase **take** (*or* **have**) **a gander**). **3.** *Informal.* a simpleton. [Old English *gandra, ganra;* related to Low German and Dutch *gander* and to GANNET]

Gandhian (ˈgændɪən) *adj.* **1.** of or relating to Mahatma Gandhi (1869–1948), Indian leader and social reformer, or his ideas. ~*n.* **2.** a follower of Gandhi or his ideas.

Gandhi cap (ˈgændɪ) *n.* a cap made of white hand-woven cloth worn by some men in India.

Gandhiism (ˈgændɪˌɪzəm) *or* **Gandhism** (ˈgænˌdɪzəm) *n.* the political principles of Mahatma Gandhi, esp. civil disobedience and passive resistance as means of achieving reform.

G & S *abbrev. for* Gilbert and Sullivan.

gandy dancer (ˈgændɪ) *n. Slang.* a railway track maintenance worker. [C20: of uncertain origin]

gane (gen) *vb.* the past participle of **gae.**

ganef, ganev, ganof (ˈgɑːnəf), **gonif,** *or* **gonof** *n. U.S. slang.* an unscrupulous opportunist who stoops to sharp practice. [from Yiddish, from Hebrew *gannābh* thief, from *gānnabh* he stole]

gang[1] (gæŋ) *n.* **1.** a group of people who associate together or act as an organized body, esp. for criminal or illegal purposes. **2.** an organized group of workmen. **3.** a herd of buffaloes or elks or a pack of wild dogs. **4.** *N.Z.* a group of shearers who travel to different shearing sheds, shearing, classing, and baling wool. **5.** **a.** a series of similar tools arranged to work simultaneously in parallel. **b.** (*as modifier*): *a gang saw.* ~*vb.* **6.** to form into, become part of, or act as a gang. **7.** (*tr.*) *Electronics.* to mount (two or more components, such as variable capacitors) on the same shaft, permitting adjustment by a single control. ~See also **gang up.** [Old English *gang* journey; related to Old Norse *gangr,* Old High German *gang,* Sanskrit *jangha* foot] —**ganged** *adj.*

gang[2] (gæŋ) *vb. Scot.* to go. [Old English *gangan* to GO[1]]

gang[3] (gæŋ) *n.* a variant spelling of **gangue.**

Ganga jal (ˈgʌŋgɑː dʒʌl) *n.* sacred water from the River Ganges in India. [Hindi, from *Ganga* Ganges + *jal* water]

gangbang (ˈgæŋˌbæŋ) *Taboo slang.* ~*n.* **1.** an instance of sexual intercourse between one woman and several men one after the other, esp. against her will. ~*vb.* **2.** (*tr.*) to force (a woman) to take part in a gangbang. **3.** (*intr.*) to take part in a gangbang. ~Also called: **gangshag** (ˈgæŋˌʃæg).

ganger (ˈgæŋə) *n. Chiefly Brit.* the foreman of a gang of labourers.

gang-gang (ˈgæŋˌgæŋ) *n.* a small black cockatoo, *Callocephalon fimbriatum,* of SE Australia, the male of which has a scarlet head. [C19: from a native Australian language]

gangland (ˈgæŋˌlænd, -lənd) *n.* the criminal underworld.

gangling (ˈgæŋglɪŋ) *or* **gangly** (ˈgæŋglɪ) *adj.* tall, lanky, and awkward in movement. [perhaps related to GANGREL; see GANG[2]]

ganglion (ˈgæŋglɪən) *n., pl.* **-glia** (-glɪə) *or* **-glions.** **1.** an encapsulated collection of nerve-cell bodies, usually located outside the brain and spinal cord. **2.** any concentration or centre of energy, activity, or strength. **3.** a cystic tumour on a tendon sheath or joint capsule. [C17: from Late Latin: swelling, from Greek: cystic tumour] —ˈ**ganglial** *or* ˈ**gangliar** *adj.* —ˌ**gangliˈonic** *or* ˈ**gangliˌated** *adj.*

gang nail *n.* an arrangement of nails on a metal plate, used as a connecting piece in strong timber joints.

gangplank (ˈgæŋˌplæŋk) *or* **gangway** *n. Nautical.* a portable bridge for boarding and leaving a vessel at dockside.

gang plough *n.* a plough having two or more shares, coulters, and mouldboards designed to work simultaneously.

gangrel (ˈgæŋgrəl, ˈgæŋrəl) *n. Scot. archaic or literary.* **1.** a wandering beggar. **2.** a child just able to walk; toddler. [C16: from Old English *gangan* to GO[1]]

gangrene (ˈgæŋgriːn) *n.* **1.** death and decay of tissue as the result of interrupted blood supply, disease, or injury. **2.** moral decay or corruption. ~*vb.* **3.** to become or cause to become affected with gangrene. [C16: from Latin *gangraena,* from Greek *gangraina* an eating sore; related to Greek *gran* to gnaw] —**gangrenous** (ˈgæŋgrɪnəs) *adj.*

gang saw *n.* a saw having several parallel blades making simultaneous cuts. —**gang sawyer** *n.*

gangster (ˈgæŋstə) *n.* a member of an organized gang of criminals, esp. one who resorts to violence.

gangue *or* **gang** (gæŋ) *n.* valueless and undesirable material, such as quartz in small quantities, in an ore. [C19: from French *gangue,* from German *Gang* vein of metal, course; see GANG[1]]

gang up *vb.* (often foll. by *on* or *against*) *Informal.* to combine in a group (against).

gangway (ˈgæŋˌweɪ) *n.* **1.** Also called: **logway.** *Chiefly U.S.* a ramp for logs leading into a sawmill. **2.** an opening in a ship's side to take a gangplank. **3.** another word for **gangplank.** **4.** *Brit.* an aisle between rows of seats. **5.** a main passage in a mine. **6.** temporary planks over mud or earth, as on a building site. ~*sentence substitute.* **7.** clear a path!

ganister *or* **gannister** (ˈgænɪstə) *n.* **1.** a highly refractory siliceous sedimentary rock occurring beneath coal seams: used for lining furnaces. **2.** a similar material synthesized from ground quartz and fireclay. [C19: of unknown origin]

ganja (ˈgɑːndʒə) *n.* a highly potent form of cannabis, usually used for smoking. [from Hindi *gājā,* from Sanskrit *grñja*]

gannet (ˈgænɪt) *n.* **1.** any of several heavily built marine birds of the genus *Morus* (or *Sula*), having a long stout bill and typically white plumage with dark markings: family *Sulidae,* order *Pelecaniformes* (pelicans, cormorants, etc.). See also **booby** (sense 3). **2.** *Slang.* a gluttonous or greedy person. [Old English *ganot;* related to Old High German *gannazzo* gander]

ganof (ˈgɑːnəf) *n.* a variant spelling of **ganef.**

ganoid (ˈgænɔɪd) *adj.* **1.** (of the scales of certain fishes) consisting of an inner bony layer and an outer layer of an enamel-like substance (ganoin). **2.** denoting fishes, including the sturgeon and bowfin, having such scales. ~*n.* **3.** a ganoid fish. [C19: from French *ganoïde,* from Greek *ganos* brightness + -OID]

gansey (ˈgænzɪ) *n. Dialect.* a jersey or pullover. [from the island of *Guernsey* in the English Channel]

gantlet[1] (ˈgæntlɪt, ˈgɔːnt-) *n.* **1.** a section of a railway where two tracks overlap. **2.** *U.S.* a variant spelling of **gauntlet**[2]. [C17 *gantlope* (modern spelling influenced by GAUNTLET[1]), from Swedish *gatlopp,* literally: passageway, from *gata* way (related to GATE[3]) + *lop* course]

gantlet[2] (ˈgæntlɪt, ˈgɔːnt-) *n.* a variant of **gauntlet**[1].

gantline (ˈgæntˌlaɪn, -lɪn) *n. Nautical.* a line rove through a sheave for hoisting men or gear. [C19: variant of *girtline;* see GIRT[1], LINE]

gantry (ˈgæntrɪ) *or* **gauntry** *n., pl.* **-tries.** **1.** a bridgelike framework used to support a travelling crane, signals over a railway track, etc. **2.** Also called: **gantry scaffold.** the framework tower used to attend to a large rocket on its launching pad. **3.** a supporting framework for a barrel or cask. **4.** **a.** the area behind a bar where bottles, esp. spirit bottles mounted in optics, are kept for use or display. **b.** the range or quality of the spirits on view: *this pub's got a good gantry.* [C16 (in the sense: wooden platform for barrels): from Old French *chantier,* from Medieval Latin *cantārius,* changed from Latin *canthērius* supporting frame, pack ass; related to Greek *kanthēlios* pack ass]

Ganymede (ˈgænɪˌmiːd) *n.* the third satellite of Jupiter and the largest in the solar system, discovered in 1610 by Galileo. Approximate diameter 5200 km (3200 miles).

gaol (dʒeɪl) *n., vb. Brit.* a variant spelling of **jail.** —ˈ**gaoler** *n.*

gap (gæp) *n.* **1.** a break or opening in a wall, fence, etc. **2.** a break in continuity; interruption; hiatus: *there is a serious gap in the accounts.* **3.** a break in a line of hills or mountains affording a route through. **4.** *Chiefly U.S.* a gorge or ravine. **5.** a divergence or difference; disparity: *there is a gap between his version of the event and hers; the generation gap.* **6.** *Electronics.* **a.** a break in a magnetic circuit that increases the inductance and saturation point of the circuit. **b.** See **spark gap.** **7.** **bridge, close, fill,** *or* **stop a gap.** to remedy a deficiency. ~*vb.* **gaps, gapping, gapped.** **8.** (*tr.*) to make a breach or opening in. [C14: from Old Norse *gap* chasm; related to *gapa* to GAPE, Swedish *gap,* Danish *gab* open mouth, opening] —ˈ**gapless** *adj.* —ˈ**gappy** *adj.*

gape (geɪp) *vb.* (*intr.*) **1.** to stare in wonder or amazement, esp. with the mouth open. **2.** to open the mouth wide, esp. involuntarily, as in yawning or hunger. **3.** to be or become wide open: *the crater gaped under his feet.* ~*n.* **4.** the act of gaping. **5.** a wide opening; breach. **6.** the width of the widely opened mouth of a vertebrate. **7.** a stare or expression of astonishment. ~See also **gapes.** [C13: from Old Norse *gapa;* related to Middle Dutch *gapen,* Danish *gabe*] —ˈ**gaping** *adj.* —ˈ**gapingly** *adv.*

gaper (ˈgeɪpə) *n.* **1.** a person or thing that gapes. **2.** any of various large marine bivalve molluscs of the genera *Mya* and *Lutraria* that burrow in muddy sand. *M. arenaria* is the American soft-shelled clam and the two species of *Lutraria* are the otter shells. The valves have a permanent gap at the hind end.

gapes (geɪps) *n.* (*functioning as sing.*) **1.** a disease of young domestic fowl, characterized by gaping or gasping for breath and caused by gapeworms. **2.** *Informal.* a fit of yawning. —ˈ**gapy** *adj.*

gapeworm ('geɪpˌwɜːm) *n.* a parasitic nematode worm, *Syngamus trachea,* that lives in the trachea of birds and causes gapes in domestic fowl: family *Syngamidae.*

gapped scale *n. Music.* a scale, such as a pentatonic scale, containing fewer than seven notes.

gapping ('gæpɪŋ) *n.* (in transformational grammar) a rule that deletes repetitions of a verb, as in the sentence *Bill voted for Smith, Sam for McKay, and Dave for Harris.*

gap-toothed *adj.* having wide spaces between the teeth.

gar[1] (gɑː) *n., pl.* **gar** *or* **gars.** short for **garpike** (sense 1).

gar[2] (gɑːr) *vb. (tr.) Scot.* to cause or compel. [from Old Norse]

garage ('gærɑːʒ, -rɪdʒ) *n.* **1.** a building or part of a building used to house a motor vehicle. **2.** a commercial establishment in which motor vehicles are repaired, serviced, bought, and sold, and which usually also sells motor fuels. *~vb.* **3.** (*tr.*) to put into, keep in, or take to a garage. [C20: from French, from *garer* to dock (a ship), from Old French: to protect, from Old High German *warōn;* see BEWARE]

garage band *n.* a rough-and-ready amateurish rock group. [perhaps from the practice of such bands rehearsing in a garage]

garage sale *n.* a sale of personal belongings or household effects held at a person's home, usually in the garage.

garaging ('gærədʒɪŋ) *n.* accommodation for housing a motor vehicle: *there is garaging for two cars.*

garam masala ('gɑːrəm mɑː'sɑːlə) *n.* an aromatic mixture of spices, extensively used in curries. [from Hindi]

Garamond ('gærəmɒnd) *n.* a typeface, designed by Claude Garamond (?1480–1561), French type founder.

Garand rifle ('gærənd, gə'rænd) *n.* another name for **M-1 rifle.** [C20: named after John C. *Garand* (1888–1974), U.S. gun designer]

garb (gɑːb) *n.* **1.** clothes, esp. the distinctive attire of an occupation or profession: *clerical garb.* **2.** style of dress; fashion. **3.** external appearance, covering, or attire. *~vb.* **4.** (*tr.*) to clothe or cover; attire. [C16: from Old French *garbe* graceful contour, from Old Italian *garbo* grace, probably of Germanic origin] —'**garbless** *adj.*

garbage ('gɑːbɪdʒ) *n.* **1.** worthless, useless, or unwanted matter. **2.** another word (esp. U.S. and Canadian) for **rubbish.** **3.** *Computer technol.* invalid data. [C15: probably from Anglo-French *garbelage* removal of discarded matter, of uncertain origin; compare Old Italian *garbuglio* confusion]

garbage can *n.* a U.S. and Canadian name for **dustbin.** Also called: **ash bin, ash can, trash can.**

garbage collection *n. Computer technol.* a systems routine for eliminating invalid or out-of-date data and releasing storage locations.

garbage truck *n.* a U.S. and Canadian name for **dustcart.**

garbanzo (gɑː'bænzəʊ) *n., pl.* **-zos.** another name for **chickpea.** [C18: from Spanish, from *arvanço,* probably of Germanic origin; compare Old High German *araweiz* pea]

garble ('gɑːbᵊl) *vb. (tr.)* **1.** to jumble (a story, quotation, etc.), esp. unintentionally. **2.** to distort the meaning of (an account, text, etc.), as by making misleading omissions; corrupt. **3.** *Rare.* to select the best part of. *~n.* **4. a.** the act of garbling. **b.** garbled matter. [C15: from Old Italian *garbellare* to strain, sift, from Arabic *gharbala,* from *ghirbāl* sieve, from Late Latin *crībellum* small sieve, from *crībrum* sieve] —'**garbled** *adj.* —'**garbler** *n.*

garbo ('gɑːbəʊ) *n., pl.* **garbos.** *Austral. informal.* a dustman. [C20: from GARBAGE]

garboard ('gɑːˌbɔːd) *n. Nautical.* the bottommost plank of a vessel's hull. Also called: **garboard plank, garboard strake.** [C17: from Dutch *gaarboord,* probably from Middle Dutch *gaderen* to GATHER + *boord* BOARD]

garboil ('gɑːbɔɪl) *n. Archaic.* confusion or disturbance; uproar. [C16: from Old French *garbouil,* from Old Italian *garbuglio,* ultimately from Latin *bullīre* to boil, hence, seethe with indignation]

garçon (*French* garsɔ̃) *n.* a waiter or male servant, esp. if French. [C19: from Old French *gars* lad, probably of Germanic origin]

garda ('gɑːrdə) *n., pl.* **gardaí** ('gɑːrdiː). a member of the **Garda Síochána.**

gardant ('gɑːdᵊnt) *adj.* a less common spelling of **guardant.**

Garda Síochána ('gɑːrdə ˌʃiə'xɑːnə) *n.* the police force of the Republic of Ireland. [C20: from Irish Gaelic *garda* guard + *síochána* of the peace, from *síocháin* peace]

garden ('gɑːdᵊn) *n.* **1.** *Brit.* **a.** an area of land, usually planted with grass, trees, flowerbeds, etc., adjoining a house. U.S. and Canadian word: **yard.** **b.** (*as modifier*): *a garden chair.* **2. a.** an area of land used for the cultivation of ornamental plants, herbs, fruit, vegetables, trees, etc. **b.** (*as modifier*): *garden tools.* Related adj.: **horticultural.** **3.** (*often pl.*) such an area of land that is open to the public, sometimes part of a park: *botanical gardens.* **4. a.** a fertile and beautiful region. **b.** (*as modifier*): *a garden paradise.* **5.** (*modifier*) provided with or surrounded by a garden or gardens: *a garden flat.* **6. lead (a person) up the garden path.** *Informal.* to mislead or deceive (a person). *~adj.* **7. common or garden.** *Informal.* ordinary; unexceptional. *~vb.* **8.** to work in, cultivate, or take care of (a garden, plot of land, etc.). [C14: from Old French *gardin,* of Germanic origin; compare Old High German *gart* enclosure; see YARD[2] (sense 1)] —'**gardenless** *adj.* —'**garden-ˌlike** *adj.*

garden centre *n.* a place where gardening tools and equipment, plants, seeds, etc., are sold.

garden city *n. Brit.* a planned town of limited size with broad streets and spacious layout, containing trees and open spaces and surrounded by a rural belt. See also **garden suburb.**

garden cress *n.* a pungent-tasting cruciferous plant, *Lepidium sativum,* with white or reddish flowers: cultivated for salads, as a garnish, etc.

gardener ('gɑːdnə) *n.* **1.** a person who works in or takes care of a garden as an occupation or pastime. **2.** any bowerbird of the genus *Amblyornis.*

garden flat *n.* a flat with direct access to a garden: typically, a garden flat consists of basement accommodation in prewar property, but some are in purpose-built blocks in urban areas.

garden frame *n.* another name for a **cold frame.**

gardenia (gɑː'diːnɪə) *n.* **1.** any evergreen shrub or tree of the Old World tropical rubiaceous genus *Gardenia,* cultivated for their large fragrant waxlike typically white flowers. **2.** the flower of any of these shrubs. [C18: New Latin, named after Dr Alexander *Garden* (1730–91), American botanist]

gardening ('gɑːdᵊnɪŋ) *n.* **a.** the planning and cultivation of a garden. **b.** (*as modifier*): *gardening gloves.*

garden party *n.* a social gathering held in the grounds of a house, school, etc., usually with light refreshments.

garden snail *n.* any of several land snails common in gardens, where they may become pests, esp. *Helix aspersa,* and sometimes including *Cepaea nemoralis,* common in woods and hedgerows.

garden suburb *n. Brit.* a suburb of a large established town or city, planned along the lines of a garden city.

garden warbler *n.* any of several small brownish-grey European songbirds of the genus *Sylvia* (warblers), esp. *S. borin,* common in woods and hedges: in some parts of Europe they are esteemed as a delicacy.

garderobe ('gɑːdˌrəʊb) *n. Archaic.* **1.** a wardrobe or the contents of a wardrobe. **2.** a bedroom or private room. **3.** a privy. [C14: from French, from *garder* to keep + *robe* dress, clothing; see WARDROBE]

garfish ('gɑːˌfɪʃ) *n., pl.* **-fish** *or* **-fishes.** **1.** another name for **garpike** (sense 1). **2.** an elongated European marine teleost fish, *Belone belone,* with long toothed jaws: related to the flying fishes. [Old English *gār* spear + FISH]

garganey ('gɑːgənɪ) *n.* a small Eurasian duck, *Anas querquedula,* closely related to the mallard. The male has a white stripe over each eye. [C17: from Italian dialect *garganei,* of imitative origin]

gargantuan (gɑː'gæntjʊən) *adj.* (*sometimes cap.*) huge; enormous. [after *Gargantua,* a gigantic king noted for his great capacity for food and drink, in Rabelais' satire *Gargantua and Pantagruel* (1534)]

garget ('gɑːgɪt) *n.* inflammation of the mammary gland of domestic animals, esp. cattle. [C16 (in the sense: throat): from Old French *gargate,* perhaps from Latin *gurges* gulf] —'**gargety** *adj.*

gargle ('gɑːgᵊl) *vb.* **1.** to rinse (the mouth and throat) with a liquid, esp. a medicinal fluid by slowly breathing out through the liquid. **2.** to utter (words, sounds, etc.) with the throaty bubbling noise of gargling. *~n.* **3.** the liquid used for gargling. **4.** the sound produced by gargling. [C16: from Old French *gargouiller* to gargle, make a gurgling sound, from *gargouille* throat, perhaps of imitative origin] —'**gargler** *n.*

gargoyle ('gɑːgɔɪl) *n.* **1.** a waterspout carved in the form of a grotesque face or creature and projecting from a roof gutter, esp. of a Gothic church. **2.** any grotesque ornament or projection, esp. on a building. **3.** a person with a grotesque appearance. [C15: from Old French *gargouille* gargoyle, throat; see GARGLE] —'**gargoyled** *adj.*

garibaldi (ˌgærɪ'bɔːldɪ) *n.* **1.** a woman's loose blouse with long sleeves popular in the 1860s, copied from the red flannel shirt worn by Garibaldi's soldiers. **2.** *Brit.* a type of biscuit having a layer of currants in the centre. [named after Giuseppe *Garibaldi* (1807–82), Italian patriot]

garish ('gɛərɪʃ) *adj.* gay or colourful in a crude or vulgar manner; gaudy. [C16: from earlier *gaure* to stare + -ISH] —'**garishly** *adv.* —'**garishness** *n.*

garland ('gɑːlənd) *n.* **1.** a wreath or festoon of flowers, leaves, etc., worn round the head or neck or hung up. **2.** a representation of such a wreath, as in painting, sculpture, etc. **3.** a collection of short literary pieces, such as ballads or poems; miscellany or anthology. **4.** *Nautical.* a ring or grommet of rope. *~vb.* **5.** (*tr.*) to deck or adorn with a garland or garlands. [C14: from Old French *garlande,* perhaps of Germanic origin]

garlic ('gɑːlɪk) *n.* **1.** a hardy widely cultivated Asian alliaceous plant, *Allium sativum,* having a stem bearing whitish flowers and bulbils. **2. a.** the bulb of this plant, made up of small segments (cloves) that have a strong odour and pungent taste and are used in cooking. **b.** (*as modifier*): *a garlic taste.* **3.** any of various other plants of the genus *Allium.* [Old English *gārlēac,* from *gār* spear + *lēac* LEEK]

garlicky ('gɑːlɪkɪ) *adj.* containing or resembling the taste or odour of garlic.

garlic mustard *n.* a cruciferous plant, *Alliaria petiolata,* of N temperate regions, with small white flowers and an odour of garlic. Also called: **jack-by-the-hedge, hedge garlic.** Compare **garlic.**

garment (ˈgɑːmənt) *n.* 1. (*often pl.*) an article of clothing. 2. outer covering. ~*vb.* 3. (*tr.; usually passive*) to cover or clothe. [C14: from Old French *garniment,* from *garnir* to equip; see GARNISH] —ˈ**garmentless** *adj.*

garner (ˈgɑːnə) *vb.* (*tr.*) 1. to gather or store in or as if in a granary. ~*n.* 2. an archaic word for **granary.** 3. a place for storage or safekeeping. [C12: from Old French *gernier* granary, from Latin *grānārium,* from *grānum* grain]

garnet[1] (ˈgɑːnɪt) *n.* any of a group of hard glassy red, yellow, or green minerals consisting of the silicates of calcium, iron, manganese, chromium, magnesium, and aluminium in cubic crystalline form: used as a gemstone and abrasive. Formula: $A_3B_2(SiO_4)_3$ where A is a divalent metal and B is a trivalent metal. [C13: from Old French *grenat,* from *grenat* (adj.) red, from *pome grenate* POMEGRANATE] —ˈ**garnet-**ˌ**like** *adj.*

garnet[2] (ˈgɑːnɪt) *n. Nautical.* a tackle used for lifting cargo. [C15: probably from Middle Dutch *garnaat*]

garnet paper *n.* sandpaper having powdered garnet as the abrasive.

garnierite (ˈgɑːnɪəˌraɪt) *n.* a green amorphous mineral consisting of hydrated nickel magnesium silicate: a source of nickel. [C19: named after Jules *Garnier* (died 1904), French geologist]

garnish (ˈgɑːnɪʃ) *vb.* (*tr.*) 1. to decorate; trim. 2. to add something to (food) in order to improve its appearance or flavour. 3. *Law.* **a.** to serve with notice of proceedings; warn. **b.** *Obsolete.* to summon to proceedings already in progress. **c.** to attach (a debt). 4. *Slang.* to extort money from. ~*n.* 5. a decoration; trimming. 6. something, such as parsley, added to a dish for its flavour or decorative effect. 7. *Obsolete slang.* a payment illegally extorted, as from a prisoner by his jailer. [C14: from Old French *garnir* to adorn, equip, of Germanic origin; compare Old High German *warnōn* to pay heed] —ˈ**garnisher** *n.*

garnishee (ˌgɑːnɪˈʃiː) *Law.* ~*n.* 1. a person upon whom a garnishment has been served. ~*vb.* **-nishees, -nisheeing, -nisheed.** (*tr.*) 2. to attach (a debt or other property) by garnishment. 3. to serve (a person) with a garnishment.

garnishment (ˈgɑːnɪʃmənt) *n.* 1. the act of garnishing. 2. decoration or embellishment; garnish. 3. *Law.* **a.** a notice or warning. **b.** *Obsolete.* a summons to court proceedings already in progress. **c.** a notice warning a person holding money or property belonging to a debtor whose debt has been attached to hold such property until directed by the court to apply it.

garniture (ˈgɑːnɪtʃə) *n.* decoration or embellishment. [C16: from French, from *garnir* to GARNISH]

garotte (gəˈrɒt) *n., vb.* a variant spelling of **garrotte.** —**gaˈrotter** *n.*

garpike (ˈgɑːˌpaɪk) *n.* 1. Also called: **garfish, gar.** any primitive freshwater elongated bony fish of the genus *Lepisosteus,* of North and Central America, having very long toothed jaws and a body covering of thick scales. 2. another name for **garfish** (sense 2).

garret (ˈgærɪt) *n.* another word for **attic** (sense 1). [C14: from Old French *garite,* watchtower, from *garir* to protect, of Germanic origin; see WARY]

garret window *n.* a skylight that lies along the slope of the roof.

garrison (ˈgærɪsᵊn) *n.* 1. the troops who maintain and guard a base or fortified place. 2. **a.** the place itself. **b.** (*as modifier*): *garrison town.* ~*vb.* 3. (*tr.*) to station (troops) in (a fort). [C13: from Old French *garison,* from *garir* to defend, of Germanic origin; compare Old Norse *verja* to defend, Old English, Old High German *werian*]

garron (ˈgærən) *n.* a small sturdy pony bred and used chiefly in Scotland and Ireland. [C16: from Gaelic *gearran*]

garrotte, garrote, *or* **garotte** (gəˈrɒt) *n.* 1. a Spanish method of execution by strangulation or by breaking the neck. 2. the device, usually an iron collar, used in such executions. 3. *Obsolete.* strangulation of one's victim while committing robbery. ~*vb.* (*tr.*) 4. to execute by means of the garrotte. 5. to strangle, esp. in order to commit robbery. [C17: from Spanish *garrote,* perhaps from Old French *garrot* cudgel; of obscure origin] —**garˈrotter, garˈroter,** *or* **gaˈrotter** *n.*

garrulous (ˈgærʊləs) *adj.* 1. given to constant and frivolous chatter; loquacious; talkative. 2. wordy or diffuse; prolix. [C17: from Latin *garrulus,* from *garrīre* to chatter] —ˈ**garrulously** *adv.* —ˈ**garrulousness** *or* **garrulity** (gæˈruːlɪtɪ) *n.*

garrya (ˈgærɪə) *n.* any ornamental catkin-bearing evergreen shrub of the North American genus *Garrya:* family *Garryaceae.* [C19: named after Nicholas *Garry* (1781–1856), an officer of the Hudson's Bay Company]

garryowen (ˌgærɪˈəʊɪn) *n.* (in rugby union) another term for **up-and-under.** [C20: named after *Garryowen* RFC, Ireland]

garter (ˈgɑːtə) *n.* 1. a band, usually of elastic, worn round the arm or leg to hold up a shirtsleeve, sock, or stocking. 2. the U.S. and Canadian word for **suspender.** ~*vb.* 3. (*tr.*) to fasten, support, or secure with or as if with a garter. [C14: from Old Northern French *gartier,* from *garet* bend of the knee, probably of Celtic origin]

Garter (ˈgɑːtə) *n.* **the.** 1. See **Order of the Garter.** 2. (*sometimes not cap.*) **a.** the badge of this Order. **b.** membership of this Order.

garter snake *n.* any nonvenomous North American colubrid snake of the genus *Thamnophis,* typically marked with longitudinal stripes.

garter stitch *n.* knitting in which all the rows are knitted in plain stitch instead of alternating with purl rows.

garth[1] (gɑːθ) *n.* 1. a courtyard surrounded by a cloister. 2. *Archaic.* a yard or garden. [C14: from Old Norse *garthr;* related to Old English *geard* YARD[2]]

garth[2] (gɑːθ) *n. Northern English dialect.* a child's hoop, often the rim of a bicycle wheel. [dialect variant of GIRTH]

gas (gæs) *n., pl.* **gases** *or* **gasses.** 1. a substance in a physical state in which it does not resist change of shape and will expand indefinitely to fill any container. If very high pressure is applied a gas may become liquid or solid, otherwise its density tends towards that of the condensed phase. Compare **liquid** (sense 1), **solid** (sense 1). 2. any substance that is gaseous at room temperature and atmospheric pressure. 3. any gaseous substance that is above its critical temperature and therefore not liquefiable by pressure alone. Compare **vapour** (sense 2). 4. **a.** a fossil fuel in the form of a gas, used as a source of domestic and industrial heat. See also **coal gas, natural gas. b.** (*as modifier*): *a gas cooker; gas fire.* 5. a gaseous anaesthetic, such as nitrous oxide. 6. *Mining.* firedamp or the explosive mixture of firedamp and air. 7. the usual U.S., Canadian, and New Zealand word for **petrol.** 8. **step on the gas.** *Informal.* **a.** to increase the speed of a motor vehicle; accelerate. **b.** to hurry. 9. a toxic or suffocating substance in suspension in air used against an enemy. 10. *Informal.* idle talk or boasting. 11. *Slang.* a delightful or successful person or thing: *his latest record is a gas.* ~*vb.* **gases** *or* **gasses, gassing, gassed.** 12. (*tr.*) to provide or fill with gas. 13. (*tr.*) to subject to gas fumes, esp. so as to asphyxiate or render unconscious. 14. (*intr.*) to give off gas, as in the charging of a battery. 15. (*tr.*) (in textiles) to singe (fabric) with a flame from a gas burner to remove unwanted fibres. 16. (*intr.*; foll. by *to*) *Informal.* to talk in an idle or boastful way (to a person). 17. (*tr.*) *Slang, chiefly U.S. and Canadian.* to thrill or delight. [C17 (coined by J. B. van Helmont (1577–1644), Flemish chemist): modification of Greek *khaos* atmosphere] —ˈ**gasless** *adj.*

gasbag (ˈgæsˌbæg) *Informal.* ~*n.* 1. a person who talks in a voluble way, esp. about unimportant matters. ~*vb.* **-bags, -bagging, -bagged.** 2. (*intr.*) *Irish.* to talk in a voluble way, esp. about unimportant matters.

gas black *n.* finely powdered carbon produced by burning natural gas. It is used as a pigment in paints, etc.

gas burner *n.* 1. Also called: **gas jet.** a jet or nozzle from which a combustible gas issues in order to form a stable flame. 2. an assembly of such jets or nozzles, used esp. in cooking.

gas chamber *or* **oven** *n.* an airtight room into which poison gas is introduced to kill people or animals.

gas chromatography *n.* a technique for analysing a mixture of volatile substances in which the mixture is carried by an inert gas through a column packed with a selective adsorbent and a detector records on a moving strip the conductivity of the gas leaving the tube. Peaks on the resulting graph indicate the presence of a particular component. Also called: **gas-liquid chromatography.**

gas coal *n.* coal that is rich in volatile hydrocarbons, making it a suitable source of domestic gas.

gascon (ˈgæskən) *n. Rare.* a boaster; braggart. [C14: from Old French *gascoun;* compare Latin *Vasconēs* Basque]

Gascon (ˈgæskən) *n.* 1. a native or inhabitant of Gascony in SW France. 2. the dialect of French spoken in Gascony. ~*adj.* 3. of or relating to Gascony, its inhabitants, or their dialect of French.

gasconade (ˌgæskəˈneɪd) *Rare.* ~*n.* 1. boastful talk, bragging, or bluster. ~*vb.* 2. (*intr.*) to boast, brag, or bluster. [C18: from French *gasconnade,* from *gasconner* to chatter, boast like a GASCON] —ˌ**gasconˈader** *n.*

gas constant *n.* the constant in the gas equation. It is equal to 8.3143 joules per kelvin per mole. Symbol: *R* Also called: **universal gas constant.**

gas-cooled reactor *n.* a nuclear reactor using a gas as the coolant. In the Mark I type the coolant is carbon dioxide, the moderator is graphite, and the fuel is uranium cased in magnox. See also **advanced gas-cooled reactor.**

gas-discharge tube *n. Electronics.* any tube in which an electric discharge takes place through a gas.

gaselier (ˌgæsəˈlɪə) *n.* a variant spelling of **gasolier.**

gas engine *n.* a type of internal-combustion engine using a flammable gas, such as coal gas or natural gas, as fuel.

gaseous (ˈgæsɪəs, -ʃəs, -ʃɪəs, ˈgeɪ-) *adj.* of, concerned with, or having the characteristics of a gas. —ˈ**gaseousness** *n.*

gas equation *n.* an equation that equates the product of the pressure and the volume of one mole of a gas to the product of its thermodynamic temperature and the **gas constant.** The equation is exact for an ideal gas and is a good approximation for real gases at low pressures. Also called: **ideal gas equation** *or* **law.**

gas fixture *n.* a wall or ceiling attachment for holding a gaslight.

gas gangrene *n.* gangrene resulting from infection of a wound by anaerobic bacteria (esp. *Clostridium welchii*) that cause gas bubbles and swelling in the surrounding tissues.

gash[1] (gæʃ) *vb.* 1. (*tr.*) to make a long deep cut or wound in; slash. ~*n.* 2. a long deep cut or wound. [C16: from Old French *garser* to scratch, wound, from Vulgar Latin *charissāre* (unattested), from Greek *kharassein* to scratch]

gash[2] (gæʃ) *adj. Slang.* surplus to requirements; unnecessary, extra, or spare. [C20: of unknown origin]
gasholder (ˈgæsˌhəʊldə) *n.* **1.** Also called: **gasometer.** a large tank for storing coal gas or natural gas prior to distribution to users. **2.** any vessel for storing or measuring a gas.
gasiform (ˈgæsɪˌfɔːm) *adj.* in a gaseous form.
gasify (ˈgæsɪˌfaɪ) *vb.* **-fies, -fying, -fied. 1.** to make into or become a gas. **2.** to subject (coal, etc.) to destructive distillation to produce gas, esp. for use as a fuel. —ˈ**gasiˌfiable** *adj.* —ˌ**gasifiˈcation** *n.* —ˈ**gasiˌfier** *n.*
gasket (ˈgæskɪt) *n.* **1.** a compressible packing piece of paper, rubber, asbestos, etc., sandwiched between the faces of a metal joint to provide a seal. **2.** *Nautical.* a piece of line used as a sail stop. **3. blow a gasket.** *Slang.* to burst out in anger. [C17 (in the sense: rope lashing a furled sail): probably from French *garcette* rope's end, literally: little girl, from Old French *garce* girl, feminine of *gars* boy, servant]
gaskin (ˈgæskɪn) *n.* the lower part of a horse's thigh, between the hock and the stifle. [C16: perhaps shortened from GALLIGASKINS]
gas laws *pl. n.* the physical laws obeyed by gases, esp. Boyle's law and Charles' law. See also **gas equation.**
gaslight (ˈgæsˌlaɪt) *n.* **1.** a type of lamp in which the illumination is produced by an incandescent mantle heated by a jet of gas. **2.** the light produced by such a lamp.
gas lighter *n.* **1.** a device for igniting a jet of gas. **2.** a cigarette lighter using a gas as fuel.
gas-liquid chromatography *n.* another name for **gas chromatography.**
gas main *n.* a large pipeline in which gas is carried for distribution through smaller pipes to consumers.
gasman (ˈgæsˌmæn) *n., pl.* **-men.** a man employed to read household gas meters, supervise gas fittings, etc.
gas mantle *n.* a mantle for use in a gaslight. See **mantle** (sense 4).
gas mask *n.* a mask fitted with a chemical filter to enable the wearer to breathe air free of poisonous or corrosive gases: used for military or industrial purposes. Also called (in Britain): **respirator.**
gas meter *n.* an apparatus for measuring and recording the amount of gas passed through it.
gasohol (ˈgæsəˌhɒl) *n.* a mixture of 80% or 90% petrol with 20% or 10% ethyl alcohol, for use as a fuel in internal-combustion engines.
gas oil *n.* a fuel oil obtained in the distillation of petroleum, intermediate in viscosity and boiling point between paraffin and lubricating oils. It boils above about 250°C.
gasolier *or* **gaselier** (ˌgæsəˈlɪə) *n.* a branched hanging fitting for gaslights. [C19: from GAS + (CHAND)ELIER]
gasoline *or* **gasolene** (ˈgæsəˌliːn) *n.* a U.S. and Canadian name for **petrol.** —**gasolinic** (ˌgæsəˈlɪnɪk) *adj.*
gasometer (gæsˈɒmɪtə) *n.* a nontechnical name for **gasholder.** —**gasometric** (ˌgæsəˈmɛtrɪk) *or* ˌ**gasoˈmetrical** *adj.*
gasometry (gæsˈɒmɪtrɪ) *n.* the measurement of quantities of gases.
gas oven *n.* **1.** a domestic oven heated by gas. **2.** a gas-fuelled cremation chamber. **3.** another name for **gas chamber.**
gasp (gɑːsp) *vb.* **1.** (*intr.*) to draw in the breath sharply, convulsively, or with effort, esp. in expressing awe, horror, etc. **2.** (*intr.*; foll. by *after* or *for*) to crave. **3.** (*tr.*; often foll. by *out*) to utter or emit breathlessly. ~*n.* **4.** a short convulsive intake of breath. **5.** a short convulsive burst of speech. **6. at the last gasp. a.** at the point of death. **b.** at the last moment. [C14: from Old Norse *geispa* to yawn; related to Swedish dialect *gispa,* Danish *gispe*] —**gaspingly** *adv.*
gasper (ˈgɑːspə) *n.* **1.** a person who gasps. **2.** *Brit. slang.* a cheap cigarette.
gas plant *n.* an aromatic white-flowered Eurasian rutaceous plant, *Dictamnus albus,* that emits a vapour capable of being ignited. Also called: **burning bush, dittany, fraxinella.**
gas poker *n.* a long tubular gas burner used to kindle a fire.
gas ring *n.* a circular assembly of gas jets, used esp. for cooking.
gassed (gæst) *adj. Slang.* drunk.
gasser (ˈgæsə) *n.* a drilling or well that yields natural gas.
gassing (ˈgæsɪŋ) *n.* **1.** the act or process of supplying or treating with gas. **2.** the affecting or poisoning of persons with gas or fumes. **3.** the evolution of a gas, esp. in electrolysis.
gas station *n. Chiefly U.S. and Canadian.* another term for **filling station.**
gassy (ˈgæsɪ) *adj.* **-sier, -siest. 1.** filled with, containing, or resembling gas. **2.** *Informal.* full of idle or vapid talk. —ˈ**gassiness** *n.*
gasteropod (ˈgæstərəˌpɒd) *n., adj.* a variant of **gastropod.**
gas thermometer *n.* a device for measuring temperature by observing the pressure of gas at a constant volume or the volume of a gas kept at a constant pressure.
gastight (ˈgæsˌtaɪt) *adj.* not allowing gas to enter or escape.
gastralgia (gæsˈtrældʒɪə) *n.* pain in the stomach. —**gasˈtralgic** *adj.*
gastrectomy (gæsˈtrɛktəmɪ) *n., pl.* **-mies.** surgical removal of all or part of the stomach.
gastric (ˈgæstrɪk) *adj.* of, relating to, near, or involving the stomach: *gastric pains.*
gastric juice *n.* a digestive fluid secreted by the stomach, containing hydrochloric acid, pepsin, rennin, etc.
gastric ulcer *n.* an ulcer of the mucous membrane lining the stomach. Compare **peptic ulcer.**
gastrin (ˈgæstrɪn) *n.* a polypeptide hormone secreted by the stomach: stimulates secretion of gastric juice.
gastritis (gæsˈtraɪtɪs) *n.* inflammation of the stomach. —**gastritic** (gæsˈtrɪtɪk) *adj.*
gastro- *or often before a vowel* **gastr-** *combining form.* stomach: *gastroenteritis; gastritis.* [from Greek *gastēr*]
gastrocolic (ˌgæstrəʊˈkɒlɪk) *adj.* of or relating to the stomach and colon: *gastrocolic reflex.*
gastroduodenostomy (ˌgæstrəʊˌdjuːəʊdiːˈnɒstəmɪ) *n.* a surgical operation in which the duodenum is joined to a new opening in the stomach, esp. to bypass an obstruction.
gastroenteric (ˌgæstrəʊɛnˈtɛrɪk) *adj.* another word for **gastrointestinal.**
gastroenteritis (ˌgæstrəʊˌɛntəˈraɪtɪs) *n.* inflammation of the stomach and intestines. —**gastroenteritic** (ˌgæstrəʊˌɛntəˈrɪtɪk) *adj.*
gastroenterology (ˌgæstrəʊˌɛntəˈrɒlədʒɪ) *n.* the branch of medical science concerned with diseases of the stomach and intestines. —ˌ**gastroˌenterˈologist** *n.*
gastroenterostomy (ˌgæstrəʊˌɛntəˈrɒstəmɪ) *n., pl.* **-mies.** surgical formation of an artificial opening between the stomach and the small intestine.
gastrointestinal (ˌgæstrəʊɪnˈtɛstɪnᵊl) *adj.* of or relating to the stomach and intestinal tract.
gastrolith (ˈgæstrəlɪθ) *n. Pathol.* a stone in the stomach; gastric calculus.
gastrology (gæsˈtrɒlədʒɪ) *n.* another name for **gastroenterology.** —**gastrological** (ˌgæstrəˈlɒdʒɪkᵊl) *adj.* —**gasˈtrologist** *n.*
gastronome (ˈgæstrəˌnəʊm), **gastronomer** (gæsˈtrɒnəmə), *or* **gastronomist** *n.* less common words for **gourmet.**
gastronomy (gæsˈtrɒnəmɪ) *n.* **1.** the art of good eating. **2.** the type of cookery of a particular region: *the gastronomy of Provence.* [C19: from French *gastronomie,* from Greek *gastronomia,* from *gastēr* stomach; see -NOMY] —**gastronomic** (ˌgæstrəˈnɒmɪk) *or* ˌ**gastroˈnomical** *adj.* —ˌ**gastroˈnomically** *adv.*
gastropod (ˈgæstrəˌpɒd) *or* **gasteropod** *n.* **1.** any mollusc of the class *Gastropoda,* typically having a flattened muscular foot for locomotion and a head that bears stalked eyes. The class includes the snails, whelks, limpets, and slugs. ~*adj.* **2.** of, relating to, or belonging to the *Gastropoda.* —**gastropodan** (gæsˈtrɒpədᵊn) *adj., n.* —**gasˈtropodous** *adj.*
gastroscope (ˈgæstrəˌskəʊp) *n.* a medical instrument used for examining the interior of the stomach. —**gastroscopic** (ˌgæstrəˈskɒpɪk) *adj.* —**gastroscopist** (gæsˈtrɒskəpɪst) *n.* —**gasˈtroscopy** *n.*
gastrostomy (gæsˈtrɒstəmɪ) *n., pl.* **-mies.** surgical formation of an artificial opening into the stomach from the skin surface: used for feeding.
gastrotomy (gæsˈtrɒtəmɪ) *n., pl.* **-mies.** surgical incision into the stomach.
gastrotrich (ˈgæstrətrɪk) *n.* any minute aquatic multicellular animal of the phylum *Gastrotricha,* having a wormlike body covered with cilia and bristles. [from New Latin *gastrotricha,* from GASTRO- + Greek *-trichos* -haired: see TRICHO-]
gastrovascular (ˌgæstrəʊˈvæskjʊlə) *adj.* (esp. of the body cavities of coelenterates) functioning in digestion and circulation.
gastrula (ˈgæstrʊlə) *n., pl.* **-las** *or* **-lae** (-ˌliː). a saclike animal embryo consisting of three layers of cells (see **ectoderm, mesoderm,** and **endoderm**) surrounding a central cavity (archenteron) with a small opening (blastopore) to the exterior. [C19: New Latin: little stomach, from Greek *gastēr* belly] —ˈ**gastrular** *adj.*
gastrulation (ˌgæstrʊˈleɪʃən) *n. Embryol.* the process in which a gastrula is formed from a blastula by the inward migration of cells.
gas turbine *n.* an internal-combustion engine in which the expanding gases emerging from one or more combustion chambers drive a turbine. A rotary compressor driven by the turbine compresses the air used for combustion, power being taken either as torque from the turbine or thrust from the expanding gases.
gas vacuole *n. Biology.* a gas-filled structure that provides buoyancy in some aquatic bacteria and blue-green algae.
gas welding *n.* a method of welding in which a combination of gases, usually oxyacetylene, is used to provide a hot flame.
gas well *n.* a well for obtaining natural gas.
gasworks (ˈgæsˌwɜːks) *n.* (*functioning as sing.*) a plant in which gas, esp. coal gas, is made.
gat[1] (gæt) *vb. Archaic.* a past tense of **get.**
gat[2] (gæt) *n. Slang, chiefly U.S.* a pistol or revolver. [C20: shortened from GATLING GUN]
gat[3] (gæt) *n.* a narrow channel of water. [C18: probably from Old Norse *gat* passage; related to GATE[1]]
gate[1] (geɪt) *n.* **1.** a movable barrier, usually hinged, for closing an opening in a wall, fence, etc. **2.** an opening to allow passage into or out of an enclosed place. **3.** any means of entrance or access. **4.** a mountain pass or gap, esp. one providing entry into another country or region. **5. a.** the number of people admitted

to a sporting event or entertainment. **b.** the total entrance money received from them. **6.** (in a large airport) any of the numbered exits leading to the airfield or aircraft: *passengers for Paris should proceed to gate 14.* **7.** *Horse racing.* short for **starting gate.** **8.** *Electronics.* **a.** a logic circuit having one or more input terminals and one output terminal, the output being switched between two voltage levels determined by the combination of input signals. **b.** a circuit used in radar that allows only a fraction of the input signal to pass. **9.** the electrode region or regions in a field-effect transistor that is biased to control the conductivity of the channel between the source and drain. **10.** a component in a motion-picture camera or projector that holds each frame flat and momentarily stationary behind the lens. **11.** a slotted metal frame that controls the positions of the gear lever in a motor vehicle. **12.** *Rowing.* a hinged clasp to prevent the oar from jumping out of a rowlock. **13.** a frame surrounding the blade or blades of a saw. *~vb.* (*tr.*) **14.** *Brit.* to restrict (a student) to the school or college grounds as a punishment. **15.** to select (part of a waveform) in terms of amplitude or time. [Old English *geat;* related to Old Frisian *jet* opening, Old Norse *gat* opening, passage] —'**gateless** *adj.* —'**gate,like** *adj.*

gate[2] (geɪt) *n. Dialect.* **1.** the channels by which molten metal is poured into a mould. **2.** the metal that solidifies in such channels. [C17: probably related to Old English *gyte* a pouring out, *geotan* to pour]

gate[3] (geɪt) *n. Scot. and northern English dialect.* **1.** a way, road, street, or path. **2.** a way or method of doing something. [C13: from Old Norse *gata* path; related to Old High German *gazza* road, street]

-gate *n. combining form.* indicating a person or thing that has been the cause of, or is associated with, a public scandal. [C20: on the analogy of WATERGATE]

gateau *or* **gâteau** ('gætəʊ) *n., pl.* **-teaux** (-təʊz). any of various elaborate cakes, usually layered with cream and richly decorated. [French: cake]

gate-crash *vb.* to gain entry to (a party, concert, etc.) without invitation or payment. —'**gate-,crasher** *n.*

gatefold ('geɪt,fəʊld) *n.* an oversize page in a book or magazine that is folded in. Also called: **foldout.**

gatefold sleeve *n.* a record sleeve that opens out like a book.

gatehouse ('geɪt,haʊs) *n.* **1.** a building above or beside an entrance gate to a city, university, etc., often housing a porter or guard, or (formerly) used as a fortification. **2.** a small house at the entrance to the grounds of a country mansion. **3.** a structure that houses the controls operating lock gates or dam sluices.

gatekeeper ('geɪt,kiːpə) *n.* **1.** a person who has charge of a gate and controls who may pass through it. **2.** any of several Eurasian butterflies of the genus *Pyronia,* esp. *P. tithonus,* having brown-bordered orange wings with a black-and-white eyespot on each forewing: family *Satyridae.*

gate-leg table *or* **gate-legged table** *n.* a table with one or two drop leaves that are supported when in use by a hinged leg swung out from the frame.

gate money *n.* the total receipts taken for admission to a sporting event or other entertainment.

gatepost ('geɪt,pəʊst) *n.* **1. a.** the post on which a gate is hung. **b.** the post to which a gate is fastened when closed. **2. between you, me, and the gatepost.** confidentially. **3.** *Logic.* another name for **turnstile** (sense 3).

gate valve *n.* a valve in a pipe or channel having a sliding plate that controls the flow.

gateway ('geɪt,weɪ) *n.* **1.** an entrance that may be closed by or as by a gate. **2.** a means of entry or access: *Bombay, gateway to India.*

Gatha ('gɑːtə) *n. Zoroastrianism.* any of a number of versified sermons in the Avesta that are in a more ancient dialect than the rest. [from Avestan *gāthā-;* related to Sanskrit *gāthā* song]

gather ('gæðə) *vb.* **1.** to assemble or cause to assemble. **2.** to collect or be collected gradually; muster. **3.** (*tr.*) to learn from information given; conclude or assume. **4.** (*tr.*) to pick or harvest (flowers, fruit, etc.). **5.** (*tr.;* foll. by *to* or *into*) to clasp or embrace: *the mother gathered the child into her arms.* **6.** (*tr.*) to bring close (to) or wrap (around): *she gathered her shawl about her shoulders.* **7.** to increase or cause to increase gradually, as in force, speed, intensity, etc. **8.** to contract (the brow) or (of the brow) to become contracted into wrinkles; knit. **9.** (*tr.*) to assemble (sections of a book) in the correct sequence for binding. **10.** (*tr.*) to collect by making a selection. **11.** (*tr.*) to prepare or make ready: *to gather one's wits.* **12.** to draw (material) into a series of small tucks or folds by passing a thread through it and then pulling it tight. **13.** (*intr.*) (of a boil or other sore) to come to a head; form pus. **14. be gathered to one's fathers.** *Euphemistic.* to die. *~n.* **15. a.** the act of gathering. **b.** the amount gathered. **16.** a small fold in material, as made by a tightly pulled stitch; tuck. **17.** *Printing.* an informal name for **section** (sense 17). [Old English *gadrian;* related to Old Frisian *gaderia,* Middle Low German *gaderen*] —'**gatherable** *adj.* —'**gatherer** *n.*

gathering ('gæðərɪŋ) *n.* **1.** a group of people, things, etc., that are gathered together; assembly. **2.** *Sewing.* a gather or series of gathers in material. **3. a.** the formation of pus in a boil. **b.** the pus so formed. **4.** *Printing.* an informal name for **section** (sense 17).

Gatling gun ('gætlɪŋ) *n.* a hand-cranked automatic machine gun equipped with a rotating cluster of barrels that are fired in succession using brass cartridges. [C19: named after R. J. *Gatling* (1818–1903), its U.S. inventor]

GATT (gæt) *n. acronym for* General Agreement on Tariffs and Trade: a multilateral international treaty signed in 1947 to promote trade, esp. by means of the reduction and elimination of tariffs and import quotas.

gauche (gəʊʃ) *adj.* lacking ease of manner; tactless. [C18: French: awkward, left, from Old French *gauchir* to swerve, ultimately of Germanic origin; related to Old High German *wankōn* to stagger] —'**gauchely** *adv.* —'**gaucheness** *n.*

gaucherie (,gəʊʃə'riː, 'gəʊʃərɪ; *French* goʃri) *n.* **1.** the quality of being gauche. **2.** a gauche act.

gaucho ('gaʊtʃəʊ) *n., pl.* **-chos.** a cowboy of the South American pampas, usually one of mixed Spanish and Indian descent. [C19: from American Spanish, probably from Quechuan *wáhcha* orphan, vagabond]

gaud (gɔːd) *n.* an article of cheap finery; trinket; bauble. [C14: probably from Old French *gaudir* to be joyful, from Latin *gaudēre*]

gaudeamus igitur (,gaʊdɪ'ɑːmʊs 'ɪgɪ,tʊə, ,gɔːdɪ'eɪməs 'ɪdʒɪtə) *interj.* let us therefore rejoice. [Latin, from a medieval student song]

gaudery ('gɔːdərɪ) *n., pl.* **-eries.** cheap finery or display.

gaudy[1] ('gɔːdɪ) *adj.* **gaudier, gaudiest.** gay, bright, or colourful in a crude or vulgar manner; garish. [C16: from GAUD] —'**gaudily** *adv.* —'**gaudiness** *n.*

gaudy[2] ('gɔːdɪ) *n., pl.* **gaudies.** *Brit.* a celebratory festival or feast held at some schools and colleges. [C16: from Latin *gaudium* joy, from *gaudēre* to rejoice]

gauffer ('gəʊfə) *n., vb.* a less common spelling of **goffer.**

gauge *or* **gage** (geɪdʒ) *vb.* (*tr.*) **1.** to measure or determine the amount, quantity, size, condition, etc., of. **2.** to estimate or appraise; judge. **3.** to check for conformity or bring into conformity with a standard measurement, dimension, etc. *~n.* **4.** a standard measurement, dimension, capacity, or quantity. **5.** any of various instruments for measuring a quantity: *a pressure gauge.* **6.** any of various devices used to check for conformity with a standard measurement. **7.** a standard or means for assessing; test; criterion. **8.** scope, capacity, or extent. **9.** the diameter of the barrel of a gun, esp. a shotgun. **10.** the thickness of sheet metal or the diameter of wire. **11.** the distance between the rails of a railway track: in Britain 4 ft. 8½ in. (1.435 m). **12.** the distance between two wheels on the same axle of a vehicle, truck, etc. **13.** *Nautical.* the position of a vessel in relation to the wind and another vessel. One vessel may be windward (**weather gauge**) or leeward (**lee gauge**) of the other. **14.** the proportion of plaster of Paris added to mortar to accelerate its setting. **15.** the distance between the nails securing the slates, tiles, etc., of a roof. **16.** a measure of the fineness of woven or knitted fabric, usually expressed as the number of needles used per inch. **17.** the width of motion-picture film or magnetic tape. *~adj.* **18.** (of a pressure measurement) measured on a pressure gauge that registers zero at atmospheric pressure; above or below atmospheric pressure: *5 bar gauge.* See also **absolute** (sense 10). [C15: from Old Northern French, probably of Germanic origin] —'**gaugeable** *or* '**gageable** *adj.* —'**gaugeably** *or* '**gageably** *adv.*

gauge boson *n. Physics.* a boson that mediates the interaction between elementary particles. There are four types: photons for electromagnetic interactions, gluons for strong interactions, intermediate vector bosons for weak interactions, and gravitons for gravitational interactions.

gauger *or* **gager** ('geɪdʒə) *n.* **1.** a person or thing that gauges. **2.** *Chiefly Brit.* a customs officer who inspects bulk merchandise, esp. liquor casks, for excise duty purposes. **3.** a collector of excise taxes.

gauge theory *n. Physics.* a type of theory of elementary particles designed to explain the strong, weak, and electromagnetic interactions in terms of exchange of virtual particles.

Gaul (gɔːl) *n.* **1.** a native of ancient Gaul, a region of W Europe corresponding to N Italy, France, Belgium, part of Germany, and the S Netherlands. **2.** a Frenchman.

Gauleiter ('gaʊ,laɪtə) *n.* **1.** a provincial governor in Germany under Hitler. **2.** (*sometimes not cap.*) *Informal.* a person in a position of petty or local authority who behaves in an overbearing authoritarian manner. [from German, from *Gau* district + *Leiter* LEADER]

Gaulish ('gɔːlɪʃ) *n.* **1.** the extinct language of the pre-Roman Gauls, belonging to the Celtic branch of the Indo-European family. *~adj.* **2.** of or relating to ancient Gaul, the Gauls, or their language.

Gaullism ('gəʊlɪzəm, 'gɔː-) *n.* **1.** the conservative French nationalist policies and principles associated with General Charles de Gaulle (1890–1970). **2.** a political movement founded on and supporting de Gaulle's principles and policies.

Gaullist ('gəʊlɪst, 'gɔː-) *n.* **1.** a supporter of Gaullism. *~adj.* **2.** of, characteristic of, supporting, or relating to Gaullism.

gault (gɔːlt) *n.* a stiff compact clay or thick heavy clayey soil. [C16: of obscure origin]

Gault (gɔːlt) *n.* **the.** the Lower Cretaceous clay formation in eastern England.

gaultheria (gɔːlˈθɪərɪə) *n.* any aromatic evergreen shrub of the ericaceous genus *Gaultheria,* of America, Asia, Australia, and New Zealand, esp. the wintergreen. [C19: New Latin, after Jean-François *Gaultier,* 18th-century Canadian physician and botanist]

gaumless ((ˈgɔːmlɪs) *adj.* a variant spelling of **gormless.**

gaun (gɔːn) *vb.* the present participle of **gae.**

gaunt (gɔːnt) *adj.* **1.** bony and emaciated in appearance. **2.** (of places) bleak or desolate. [C15: perhaps of Scandinavian origin; compare Norwegian dialect *gand* tall lean person] —ˈ**gauntly** *adv.* —ˈ**gauntness** *n.*

gauntlet[1] (ˈgɔːntlɪt) *or* **gantlet** *n.* **1.** a medieval armoured leather glove. **2.** a heavy glove with a long cuff. **3. take up** (*or* **throw down**) **the gauntlet.** to accept (or offer) a challenge. [C15: from Old French *gantelet,* diminutive of *gant* glove, of Germanic origin]

gauntlet[2] (ˈgɔːntlɪt) *n.* **1.** a punishment in which the victim is forced to run between two rows of men who strike at him as he passes: formerly a military punishment. **2. run the gauntlet. a.** to suffer this punishment. **b.** to endure an onslaught or ordeal, as of criticism. **3.** a testing ordeal; trial. **4.** a variant spelling of **gantlet**[1] (sense 1). [C15: changed (through influence of GAUNTLET[1]) from earlier *gantlope;* see GANTLET[1]]

gauntry (ˈgɔːntrɪ) *n., pl.* **-tries.** a variant of **gantry.**

gaup (gɔːp) *vb.* a variant spelling of **gawp.**

gaur (gaʊə) *n.* a large wild member of the cattle tribe, *Bos gaurus,* inhabiting mountainous regions of S Asia. [C19: from Hindi, from Sanskrit *gāūra*]

Gause's principle (ˈgaʊzəz) *n. Ecology.* the principle that similar species cannot coexist for long in the same ecological niche. [named after G. F. *Gause,* 20th-century Soviet biologist]

gauss (gaʊs) *n., pl.* **gauss.** the cgs unit of magnetic flux density; the flux density that will induce an emf of 1 abvolt (10^{-8} volt) per centimetre in a wire moving across the field at a velocity of 1 centimetre per second. 1 gauss is equivalent to 10^{-4} tesla. [after K. F. *Gauss* (1777–1855), German mathematician]

Gaussian distribution (ˈgaʊsɪən) *n.* another name for **normal distribution.**

gaussmeter (ˈgaʊsˌmiːtə) *n.* an instrument for measuring the intensity of a magnetic field.

gauze (gɔːz) *n.* **1. a.** a transparent cloth of loose plain or leno weave. **b.** (*as modifier*): *a gauze veil.* **2.** a surgical dressing of muslin or similar material. **3.** any thin openwork material, such as wire. **4.** a fine mist or haze. [C16: from French *gaze,* perhaps from *Gaza,* city in Israel, where it was believed to originate]

gauzy (ˈgɔːzɪ) *adj.* **gauzier, gauziest.** resembling gauze; thin and transparent. —ˈ**gauzily** *adv.* —ˈ**gauziness** *n.*

gavage (ˈgævɑːʒ) *n.* forced feeding by means of a tube inserted into the stomach through the mouth. [C19: from French, from *gaver,* from Old French (dialect) *gave* throat]

gave (geɪv) *vb.* the past tense of **give.**

gavel (ˈgævəl) *n.* **1.** a small hammer used by a chairman, auctioneer, etc., to call for order or attention. **2.** a hammer used by masons to trim rough edges off stones. [C19: of unknown origin]

gavelkind (ˈgævəlˌkaɪnd) *n.* **1.** a former system of land tenure peculiar to Kent based on the payment of rent to the lord instead of the performance of services by the tenant. **2.** the land subject to such tenure. **3.** *English law.* (formerly) land held under this system. [C13: from Old English *gafol* tribute + *gecynd* KIND[2]]

gavial (ˈgeɪvɪəl), **gharial,** *or* **garial** (ˈgærɪəl) *n.* **1.** a large fish-eating Indian crocodilian, *Gavialis gangeticus,* with a very long slender snout: family *Gavialidae.* **2. false gavial.** a SE Asian crocodile, *Tomistoma schlegeli,* similar to but smaller than the gavial. [C19: from French, from Hindi *ghariyāl*]

gavotte *or* **gavot** (gəˈvɒt) *n.* **1.** an old formal dance in quadruple time. **2.** a piece of music composed for or in the rhythm of this dance. [C17: from French, from Provençal *gavoto,* from *gavot* mountaineer, dweller in the Alps (where the dance originated), from *gava* goitre (widespread in the Alps), from Old Latin *gaba* (unattested) throat]

gawk (gɔːk) *n.* **1.** a clumsy stupid person; lout. ~*vb.* **2.** (*intr.*) to stare in a stupid way; gape. [C18: from Old Danish *gaukr;* probably related to GAPE]

gawky (ˈgɔːkɪ) *or* **gawkish** *adj.* **gawkier, gawkiest. 1.** clumsy or ungainly; awkward. **2.** *West Yorkshire dialect.* left-handed. —ˈ**gawkily** *or* ˈ**gawkishly** *adv.* —ˈ**gawkiness** *or* ˈ**gawkishness** *n.*

gawp *or* **gaup** (gɔːp) *vb.* (*intr.;* often foll. by *at*) *Brit. slang.* to stare stupidly; gape. [C14 *galpen;* probably related to Old English *gielpan* to boast, YELP. Compare Dutch *galpen* to yelp]

gay (geɪ) *adj.* **1. a.** homosexual. **b.** (*as n.*): *a group of gays.* **2. a.** carefree and merry: *a gay temperament.* **b.** brightly coloured; brilliant: *a gay hat.* **c.** given to pleasure, esp. in social entertainment: *a gay life.* [C13: from Old French *gai,* from Old Provençal, of Germanic origin] —ˈ**gayness** *n.*

gayal (gəˈjæl) *n., pl.* **gayal** *or* **gayals.** an ox of India and Burma, *Bibos frontalis,* possibly a semidomesticated variety of gaur, black or brown with white stockings. [C19: from Bengali *gayāl,* from Sanskrit *gāūra;* compare GAUR]

Gay Gordons (ˈgɔːdənz) *n.* (*functioning as sing.*) *Brit.* an energetic old-time dance.

Gay-Lussac's law (ˈgeɪˈluːsæks) *n.* **1.** the principle that gases react together in volumes (measured at the same temperature and pressure) that bear a simple ratio to each other and to the gaseous products. **2.** another name for **Charles' law.** [named after Joseph *Gay-Lussac* (1778–1850), French physicist and chemist]

gaz. *abbrev. for:* **1.** gazette. **2.** gazetteer.

gazania (gəˈzeɪnɪə) *n.* any plant of the S. African genus *Gazania,* grown for their showy rayed flowers in a range of variegated colours; the flowers close in the afternoon: family *Compositae.* Also called: **treasure flower.** [named after Theodore of *Gaza,* 1398–1478, translator of the botanical treatises of Theophrastus]

gaze (geɪz) *vb.* **1.** (*intr.*) to look long and fixedly, esp. in wonder or admiration. ~*n.* **2.** a fixed look; stare. [C14: from Swedish dialect *gasa* to gape at] —ˈ**gazer** *n.*

gazebo (gəˈziːbəʊ) *n., pl.* **-bos** *or* **-boes.** a summerhouse, garden pavilion, or belvedere, sited to command a view. [C18: perhaps a pseudo-Latin coinage based on GAZE]

gazehound (ˈgeɪzˌhaʊnd) *n.* a hound such as a greyhound that hunts by sight rather than by scent.

gazelle (gəˈzɛl) *n., pl.* **-zelles** *or* **-zelle.** any small graceful usually fawn-coloured antelope of the genera *Gazella* and *Procapra,* of Africa and Asia, such as *G. thomsoni* (**Thomson's gazelle**). [C17: from Old French, from Arabic *ghazāl*] —**gaˈzelle-ˌlike** *adj.*

gazette (gəˈzɛt) *n.* **1. a.** a newspaper or official journal. **b.** (*cap. when part of the name of a newspaper*): *the Thame Gazette.* **2.** *Brit.* an official document containing public notices, appointments, etc. Abbrev.: **gaz.** ~*vb.* **3.** (*tr.*) *Brit.* to announce or report (facts or an event) in a gazette. [C17: from French, from Italian *gazzetta,* from Venetian dialect *gazeta* news-sheet costing one *gazet,* small copper coin, perhaps from *gaza* magpie, from Latin *gaia, gaius* jay]

gazetted officer *n.* (in India) a senior official whose appointment is published in the government gazette.

gazetteer (ˌgæzɪˈtɪə) *n.* **1.** a book or section of a book that lists and describes places. Abbrev.: **gaz. 2.** *Archaic.* a writer for a gazette or newspaper; journalist.

gazpacho (gəzˈpɑːtʃəʊ, gæs-) *n.* a Spanish soup made from tomatoes, peppers, etc., and served cold. [from Spanish]

gazump (gəˈzʌmp) *Brit.* ~*vb.* **1.** to raise the price of something, esp. a house, after agreeing a price verbally with (an intending buyer). **2.** (*tr.*) to swindle or overcharge. ~*n.* **3.** the act or an instance of gazumping. [C20: of uncertain origin] —**gaˈzumper** *n.*

gazunder (gəˈzʌndə) *Brit.* ~*vb.* **1.** to reduce an offer on a property immediately before exchanging contracts, having previously agreed a higher price with (the seller). ~*n.* **2.** an act or instance of gazundering. [C20: modelled on GAZUMP] —**gaˈzunderer** *n.*

Gb *symbol for* gilbert.

GBA *international car registration for* Alderney.

GBE *abbrev. for* (Knight or Dame) Grand Cross of the British Empire (a Brit. title).

GBG *international car registration for* Guernsey.

GBH *abbrev. for* grievous bodily harm.

GBJ *international car registration for* Jersey.

GBM *international car registration for* Isle of Man.

GBS *abbrev. for* George Bernard Shaw.

GBZ *international car registration for* Gibraltar.

GC *abbrev. for* George Cross (a Brit. award for bravery).

GCA **1.** *Aeronautics. abbrev. for* ground control approach. ~ **2.** *international car registration for* Guatemala.

GCB *abbrev. for* (Knight) Grand Cross of the Bath (a Brit. title).

GCE (in Britain) *abbrev. for* General Certificate of Education: a public examination in specified subjects taken as qualifying examinations for entry into a university, college, etc. The GCSE has replaced it at O level. See also **A level, S level.**

GCF *or* **gcf** *abbrev. for* greatest common factor.

GCHQ (in Britain) *abbrev. for* Government Communications Headquarters.

G clef *n.* another name for **treble clef.**

GCM *or* **gcm** *abbrev. for* greatest common measure.

GCMG *abbrev. for* (Knight or Dame) Grand Cross of the Order of St Michael and St George (a Brit. title).

G-cramp *n.* another name for **cramp**[2] (sense 2).

GCSE (in Britain) *abbrev. for* General Certificate of Secondary Education: a public examination in specified subjects for 16-year-old schoolchildren. It replaces the GCE O-level and CSE.

GCVO *abbrev. for* (Knight or Dame) Grand Cross of the Royal Victorian Order (a Brit. title).

Gd *the chemical symbol for* gadolinium.

Gdns *abbrev. for* Gardens.

GDP *or* **gdp** *abbrev. for* gross domestic product.

GDR *abbrev. for* German Democratic Republic (now part of Germany).

gds *abbrev. for* goods.

Ge *the chemical symbol for* germanium.

gean (giːn) *n.* **1.** Also called: **wild cherry.** a white-flowered rosaceous tree, *Prunus avium,* of Europe, W Asia, and N Africa, the ancestor of the cultivated sweet cherries. **2.** see **sweet cherry** (sense 1).

geanticline (dʒiːˈæntɪˌklaɪn) *n.* a gently sloping anticline covering a large area. [C19: from Greek *gē* earth, land + ANTICLINE] —**geˌantiˈclinal** *adj.*

gear (gɪə) *n.* **1.** a toothed wheel that engages with another toothed wheel or with a rack in order to change the speed or direction of transmitted motion. **2.** a mechanism for transmitting motion by gears, esp. for a specific purpose: *the steering gear of a boat.* **3.** the engagement or specific ratio of a system of gears: *in gear; high gear.* **4.** personal equipment and accoutrements; belongings. **5.** equipment and supplies for a particular operation, sport, etc.: *fishing gear.* **6.** *Nautical.* all equipment or appurtenances belonging to a certain vessel, sailor, etc. **7.** short for **landing gear. 8.** *Informal.* up-to-date clothes and accessories, esp. those bought by young people. **9.** *Slang.* **a.** stolen goods. **b.** illegal drugs. **10.** a less common word for **harness** (sense 1). **11. out of gear.** out of order; not functioning properly. ~*vb.* **12.** (*tr.*) to adjust or adapt (one thing) so as to fit in or work with another: *to gear our output to current demand.* **13.** (*tr.*) to equip with or connect by gears. **14.** (*intr.*) to be in or come into gear. **15.** (*tr.*) to equip with harness. [C13: from Old Norse *gervi;* related to Old High German *garawī* equipment, Old English *gearwe*] —**ˈgearless** *adj.*

gearbox (ˈgɪəˌbɒks) *n.* **1.** the metal casing within which a train of gears is sealed. **2.** this metal casing and its contents, esp. in a motor vehicle.

gear cluster *n. Engineering.* an assembly of gears permanently attached to a shaft.

gear down *vb.* (*tr., adv.*) to adapt to a new situation by decreasing output, intensity of operations, etc.

gearing (ˈgɪərɪŋ) *n.* **1.** an assembly of gears designed to transmit motion. **2.** the act or technique of providing gears to transmit motion. **3.** Also called: **capital gearing.** *Accounting, Brit.* the ratio of a company's debt capital to its equity capital. U.S. word: **leverage.**

gear lever *or U.S. and Canadian* **gearshift** (ˈgɪəˌʃɪft) *n.* a lever used to move gearwheels relative to each other, esp. in a motor vehicle.

gear train *n. Engineering.* a system of gears that transmits power from one shaft to another.

gear up *vb.* (*adv.*) **1.** (*tr.*) to equip with gears. **2.** to prepare, esp. for greater efficiency: *is our industry geared up for the eighties?*

gearwheel (ˈgɪəˌwiːl) *n.* another name for **gear** (sense 1).

gecko (ˈgɛkəʊ) *n., pl.* **-os** *or* **-oes.** any small insectivorous terrestrial lizard of the family *Gekkonidae,* of warm regions. The digits have adhesive pads, which enable these animals to climb on smooth surfaces. [C18: from Malay *ge'kok,* of imitative origin]

gedact (gəˈdɑːkt, -ˈdækt) *or* **gedeckt** (gəˈdɛkt) *n. Music.* a flutelike stopped metal diapason organ pipe. [(*gedeckt*) from German: covered, from *decken* to cover]

gee[1] (dʒiː) *interj.* **1.** Also: **gee up!** an exclamation, as to a horse or draught animal, to encourage it to turn to the right, go on, or go faster. ~*vb.* **gees, geeing, geed. 2.** (usually foll. by *up*) to move (an animal, esp. a horse) ahead; urge on. ~*n.* **3.** *Slang.* See **gee-gee.** [C17: origin uncertain]

gee[2] (dʒiː) *interj. U.S. and Canadian informal.* a mild exclamation. Also: **gee whiz.** [C20: euphemism for JESUS]

geebung (ˈdʒiːbʌŋ) *n.* **1.** any of various trees and shrubs of the genus *Persoonia* of Australia having an edible but tasteless fruit. **2.** the fruit of these trees. **3.** (in the 19th century) an uncultivated Australian from the country districts. [from a native Australian language]

gee-gee (ˈdʒiːˌdʒiː) *n. Slang.* a horse. [C19: reduplication of GEE[1]]

geek (giːk) *n. Slang.* **1.** a stupid or ineffectual person. **2.** a degenerate. **3.** a sideshow performer who bites the heads off or eats live animals. [C19: probably variant of Scottish *geck* fool, from Middle Low German *geck*]

geelbek (ˈxɪəlˌbɛk) *n. S. African.* a yellow-jawed edible marine fish. [from Afrikaans *geel* yellow + *bek* mouth]

geepound (ˈdʒiːˌpaʊnd) *n.* another name for **slug**[2] (sense 1). [C20: from *gee,* representing G(RAVITY) + POUND[2]]

geese (giːs) *n.* the plural of **goose.**

geest (giːst) *n.* an area of sandy heathland in N Germany and adjacent areas. [C19: Low German *Geest* dry soil]

Ge'ez (ˈgiːɛz) *n.* the classical form of the ancient Ethiopic language, having an extensive Christian literature and still used in Ethiopia as a liturgical language.

geezer (ˈgiːzə) *n. Informal.* a man, esp. an old one regarded as eccentric. [C19: probably from dialect pronunciation of *guiser,* from GUISE + -ER[1]]

gefilte fish *or* **gefüllte fish** (gəˈfɪltə) *n. Jewish cookery.* a dish consisting of fish and matzo meal rolled into balls and poached, formerly served stuffed into the skin of a fish. [Yiddish, literally: filled fish]

gegenschein (ˈgeɪgənˌʃaɪn) *n.* a faint glow in the sky, just visible at a position opposite to that of the sun and having a similar origin to zodiacal light. Also called: **counterglow.** [German, from *gegen* against, opposite + *Schein* light; see SHINE]

Gehenna (gɪˈhɛnə) *n.* **1.** *New Testament, Judaism.* a place where the wicked are punished after death. **2.** a place or state of pain and torment. [C16: from Late Latin, from Greek *Geena,* from Hebrew *Gê' Hinnōm,* literally: valley of Hinnom, below Jerusalem, symbolic of hell]

gehlenite (ˈgeɪləˌnaɪt) *n.* a green mineral consisting of calcium aluminium silicate in tetragonal crystalline form. Formula: $Ca_2Al_2SiO_7$. [named after A.F. *Gehlen* (1775–1815), German chemist; see -ITE[1]]

Geiger counter (ˈgaɪgə) *or* **Geiger-Müller counter** (-ˈmʊlə) *n.* an instrument for detecting and measuring the intensity of ionizing radiation. It consists of a gas-filled tube containing a fine wire anode along the axis of a cylindrical cathode with a potential difference of several hundred volts. Any particle or photon which ionizes any number of gas molecules in the tube causes a discharge which is registered by electronic equipment. The magnitude of the discharge does not depend upon the nature or the energy of the ionizing particle. Compare **proportional counter.** [C20: named after Hans *Geiger* (1882–1945) and W. *Müller* (20th century), German physicists]

geisha (ˈgeɪʃə) *n., pl.* **-sha** *or* **-shas.** a professional female companion for men in Japan, trained in music, dancing, and the art of conversation. [C19: from Japanese, from *gei* art + *sha* person, from Ancient Chinese *ngi* and *che*]

Geissler tube (ˈgaɪslə) *n.* a glass or quartz vessel, usually having two bulbs containing electrodes separated by a capillary tube, for maintaining an electric discharge in a low-pressure gas as a source of visible or ultraviolet light for spectroscopy. [C19: named after Heinrich *Geissler* (1814–79), German mechanic]

geitonogamy (ˌgaɪtəˈnɒgəmɪ) *n. Botany.* the transfer of pollen to a stigma of a different flower on the same plant. [C19: from Greek *geitōn* neighbour + -GAMY]

gel (dʒɛl) *n.* **1.** a semirigid jelly-like colloid in which a liquid is dispersed in a solid: *nondrip paint is a gel.* **2.** See **hair gel. 3.** *Theatre, informal.* See **gelatin** (sense 4). ~*vb.* **gels, gelling, gelled. 4.** to become or cause to become a gel. **5.** a variant spelling of **jell.** [C19: by shortening from GELATIN]

gelada (ˈdʒɛlədə, ˈgɛl-; dʒɪˈlɑːdə, gɪ-) *n.* a NE African baboon, *Theropithecus gelada,* with dark brown hair forming a mane over the shoulders, a bare red chest, and a ridge muzzle: family *Cercopithecidae.* Also called: **gelada baboon.** [probably from Arabic *qilādah* mane]

Geländesprung *German.* (gəˈlɛndəˌʃprʊŋ) *or* **gelände jump** (gəˈlɛndə) *n. Skiing.* a jump made in downhill skiing, usually over an obstacle. [German, from *Gelände* terrain + *Sprung* jump]

gelatin (ˈdʒɛlətɪn) *or* **gelatine** (ˈdʒɛləˌtiːn) *n.* **1.** a colourless or yellowish water-soluble protein prepared by boiling animal hides and bones: used in foods, glue, photographic emulsions, etc. **2.** an edible jelly made of this substance, sweetened and flavoured. **3.** any of various substances that resemble gelatin. **4.** Also called (informal): **gel.** a translucent substance used for colour effects in theatrical lighting. [C19: from French *gélatine,* from Medieval Latin *gelātina,* from Latin *gelāre* to freeze]

gelatinize *or* **gelatinise** (dʒɪˈlætɪˌnaɪz) *vb.* **1.** to make or become gelatinous. **2.** (*tr.*) *Photog.* to coat (glass, paper, etc.) with gelatin. —**geˌlatiniˈzation** *or* **geˌlatiniˈsation** *n.* —**geˈlatiˌnizer** *or* **geˈlatiˌniser** *n.*

gelatinoid (dʒɪˈlætɪˌnɔɪd) *adj.* **1.** resembling gelatin. ~*n.* **2.** a gelatinoid substance, such as collagen.

gelatinous (dʒɪˈlætɪnəs) *adj.* **1.** consisting of or resembling jelly; viscous. **2.** of, containing, or resembling gelatin. —**geˈlatinously** *adv.* —**geˈlatinousness** *n.*

gelation[1] (dʒɪˈleɪʃən) *n.* the act or process of freezing a liquid. [C19: from Latin *gelātiō* a freezing; see GELATIN]

gelation[2] (dʒɪˈleɪʃən) *n.* the act or process of forming into a gel. [C20: from GEL]

geld[1] (gɛld) *vb.* **gelds, gelding, gelded** *or* **gelt.** (*tr.*) **1.** to castrate (a horse or other animal). **2.** to deprive of virility or vitality; emasculate; weaken. [C13: from Old Norse *gelda,* from *geldr* barren] —**ˈgelder** *n.*

geld[2] (gɛld) *n.* a tax on land levied in late Anglo-Saxon and Norman England. [Old English *gield* service, tax; related to Old Norse *gjald* tribute, Old Frisian *jeld,* Old High German *gelt* retribution, income]

gelding (ˈgɛldɪŋ) *n.* a castrated male horse. [C14: from Old Norse *geldingr;* see GELD[1], -ING[1]]

gelid (ˈdʒɛlɪd) *adj.* very cold, icy, or frosty. [C17: from Latin *gelidus* icy cold, from *gelu* frost] —**geˈlidity** *or* **ˈgelidness** *n.* —**ˈgelidly** *adv.*

gelignite (ˈdʒɛlɪgˌnaɪt) *n.* a type of dynamite in which the nitrogelatin is absorbed in a base of wood pulp and potassium or sodium nitrate. Also called (informal): **gelly** (ˈdʒɛlɪ). [C19: from GEL(ATIN) + Latin *ignis* fire + -ITE[1]]

gelsemium (dʒɛlˈsiːmɪəm) *n., pl.* **-miums** *or* **-mia** (-mɪə). **1.** any climbing shrub of the loganiaceous genus *Gelsemium,* of SE Asia and North America, esp. the yellow jasmine, having fragrant yellow flowers. **2.** the powdered root of the yellow jasmine, formerly used as a sedative. [C19: New Latin, from Italian *gelsomino* JASMINE]

gelt[1] (gɛlt) *vb. Archaic or dialect.* a past tense and past participle of **geld**[1].

gelt[2] (gɛlt) *n. Slang, chiefly U.S.* cash or funds; money. [C19: from Yiddish, from Old High German *gelt* reward]

gem (dʒɛm) *n.* **1.** a precious or semiprecious stone used in jewellery as a decoration; jewel. **2.** a person or thing held to be a perfect example; treasure. **3.** a size of printer's type, approximately equal to 4 point. **4.** *N.Z.* a type of small sweet cake. ~*vb.* **gems, gemming, gemmed.** **5.** (*tr.*) to set or ornament with gems. [C14: from Old French *gemme,* from Latin *gemma* bud, precious stone] —'**gem,like** *adj.* —'**gemmy** *adj.*

Gemara (gɛ'mɔrə; *Hebrew* gɛma'ra) *n. Judaism.* the main body of the Talmud, consisting of a record of ancient rabbinical debates about the interpretation of the Mishna and constituting the primary source of Jewish religious law. See also **Talmud.** [C17: from Aramaic *gemārā* completion, from *gemār* to complete] —**Ge'maric** *adj.* —**Ge'marist** *n.*

gemeinschaft (*German* gə'mainʃaft) *n., pl.* **-schaften** (*German* -ʃaftən). (*often cap.*) a social group united by common beliefs, family ties, etc. Compare **gesellschaft.** [German, literally: community]

gemfibrozil (dʒɛm'faɪbrəʊzɪl) *n.* a drug that lowers the level of low-density lipoproteins in the blood and is therefore used to treat patients with hypercholesterolaemia.

gemfish ('dʒɛm,fɪʃ) *n., pl.* **-fish** *or* **-fishes.** a food fish, *Rexea solandri* of Australia, having a delicate flavour.

geminate *adj.* ('dʒɛmɪnɪt, -,neɪt) *also* **geminated.** **1.** combined in pairs; doubled: *a geminate leaf; a geminate consonant.* ~*vb.* ('dʒɛmɪ,neɪt). **2.** to arrange or be arranged in pairs: *the "t"s in Italian "gatto" are geminated.* [C17: from Latin *gemināre* to double, from *geminus* born at the same time, twin] —'**geminately** *adv.*

gemination (,dʒɛmɪ'neɪʃən) *n.* **1.** the act or state of being doubled or paired. **2.** the doubling of a consonant. **3.** the immediate repetition of a word, phrase, or clause for rhetorical effect.

Gemini ('dʒɛmɪ,naɪ, -,niː) *n., Latin genitive* **Geminorum** (,dʒɛmɪ'nɔːrəm). **1.** *Astronomy.* a zodiacal constellation in the N hemisphere lying between Taurus and Cancer on the ecliptic and containing the stars Castor and Pollux. **2.** *Astronautics.* any of a series of manned U.S. spacecraft launched between the Mercury and Apollo projects to improve orbital rendezvous and docking techniques. **3.** *Astrology.* **a.** Also called: the **Twins.** the third sign of the zodiac, symbol ♊, having a mutable air classification and ruled by the planet Mercury. The sun is in this sign between about May 21 and June 20. **b.** a person born when the sun is in this sign. ~*adj.* **4.** *Astrology.* born under or characteristic of Gemini. ~Also (for senses 4b, 5): **Geminian** (,dʒɛmɪ'naɪən). [Latin: twins]

gem iron *n. N.Z.* a heavy, usually cast-iron oven dish used for baking small cakes (gems).

gemma ('dʒɛmə) *n., pl.* **-mae** (-miː). **1.** a small asexual reproductive structure in liverworts, mosses, etc., that becomes detached from the parent and develops into a new individual. **2.** *Zoology.* another name for **gemmule** (sense 1). [C18: from Latin: bud, GEM] —**gemmaceous** (dʒɛ'meɪʃəs) *adj.*

gemmate ('dʒɛmeɪt) *adj.* **1.** (of some plants and animals) having or reproducing by gemmae. ~*vb.* **2.** (*intr.*) to produce or reproduce by gemmae. —**gem'mation** *n.*

gemmiparous (dʒɛ'mɪpərəs) *adj.* (of plants and animals) reproducing by gemmae or buds. Also: **gemmiferous** (dʒɛ'mɪfərəs). —**gem'miparously** *adv.*

gemmulation (,dʒɛmjʊ'leɪʃən) *n.* the process of reproducing by or bearing gemmules.

gemmule ('dʒɛmjuːl) *n.* **1.** *Zoology.* a cell or mass of cells produced asexually by sponges and developing into a new individual; bud. **2.** *Botany.* a small gemma. **3.** a small hereditary particle postulated by Charles Darwin (1809–82) in his theory of pangenesis. [C19: from French, from Latin *gemmula* a little bud; see GEM]

gemology *or* **gemmology** (dʒɛ'mɒlədʒɪ) *n.* the branch of mineralogy that is concerned with gems and gemstones. —**gemological** *or* **gemmological** (,dʒɛmə'lɒdʒɪkᵊl) *adj.* —**gem'ologist** *or* **gem'mologist** *n.*

gemot *or* **gemote** (gɪ'məʊt) *n.* (in Anglo-Saxon England) a legal or administrative assembly of a community, such as a shire or hundred. [Old English *gemōt* MOOT]

gemsbok *or* **gemsbuck** ('gɛmz,bʌk) *n., pl.* **-bok, -boks** *or* **-buck, -bucks.** an oryx, *Oryx gazella,* of southern Africa, marked with a broad black band along its flanks. [C18: from Afrikaans, from German *Gemsbock,* from *Gemse* chamois + *Bock* BUCK[1]]

gemstone ('dʒɛm,stəʊn) *n.* a precious or semiprecious stone, esp. one cut and polished for setting in jewellery.

gemütlich *German.* (gə'myːtlɪç) *adj.* having a feeling or atmosphere of warmth and friendliness; cosy.

gen (dʒɛn) *n. Brit. informal.* information: *give me the gen on your latest project.* See also **gen up.** [C20: from *gen*(*eral information*)]

gen. *abbrev. for:* **1.** gender. **2.** general(ly). **3.** generic. **4.** genitive. **5.** genus.

Gen. *abbrev. for:* **1.** General. **2.** *Bible.* Genesis.

-gen *suffix forming nouns.* **1.** producing or that which produces: *hydrogen.* **2.** something produced: *carcinogen.* [via French *-gène,* from Greek *-genēs* born]

genappe (dʒə'næp) *n.* a smooth worsted yarn used for braid, etc. [C19: from *Genappe,* Belgium, where originally manufactured]

gendarme ('ʒɒndɑːm; *French* ʒɑ̃darm) *n.* **1.** a member of the police force in France or in countries formerly influenced or controlled by France. **2.** a slang word for a **policeman.** **3.** a sharp pinnacle of rock on a mountain ridge, esp. in the Alps. [C16: from French, from *gens d'armes* people of arms]

gendarmerie *or* **gendarmery** (ʒɒn'dɑːmərɪ; *French* ʒɑ̃darməri) *n.* **1.** the whole corps of gendarmes. **2.** the headquarters or barracks of a body of gendarmes.

gender ('dʒɛndə) *n.* **1.** a set of two or more grammatical categories into which the nouns of certain languages are divided, sometimes but not necessarily corresponding to the sex of the referent when animate. See also **natural gender.** **2.** any of the categories, such as masculine, feminine, neuter, or common, within such a set. **3.** *Informal.* the state of being male, female, or neuter. **4.** *Informal.* all the members of one sex: *the female gender.* [C14: from Old French *gendre,* from Latin *genus* kind] —'**genderless** *adj.*

gender-bender *n. Informal.* a person who adopts an androgynous style of dress, hair, make-up, etc.

gene (dʒiːn) *n.* a unit of heredity composed of DNA occupying a fixed position on a chromosome. A gene may determine a characteristic of an individual by specifying a polypeptide chain that forms a protein or part of a protein (**structural gene**); or regulate the operation of other genes (**operator genes**); or repress such operation (**repressor gene**). See also **operon.** [C20: from German *Gen,* shortened from *Pangen;* see PAN-, -GEN]

-gene *suffix forming nouns.* a variant of **-gen.**

geneal. *abbrev. for* genealogy.

genealogical tree *n.* another name for a **family tree.**

genealogy (,dʒiːnɪ'ælədʒɪ) *n., pl.* **-gies.** **1.** the direct descent of an individual or group from an ancestor. **2.** the study of the evolutionary development of animals and plants from earlier forms. **3.** a chart showing the relationships and descent of an individual, group, etc. [C13: from Old French *genealogie,* from Late Latin *geneālogia,* from Greek, from *genea* race] —**genealogical** (,dʒiːnɪə'lɒdʒɪkᵊl) *or* ,**genea'logic** *adj.* —,**genea'logically** *adv.* —,**gene'alogist** *n.*

gene bank *n. Botany.* a collection of seeds, plants, tissue cultures, etc., of potentially useful species, esp. species containing genes of significance to the breeding of crops.

genecology (,dʒɛnɪ'kɒlədʒɪ) *n.* the study of the gene frequency of a species in relation to its population distribution within a particular environment.

gene flow *n.* the movement and exchange of genes between interbreeding populations.

gene frequency *n.* the frequency of occurrence of a particular gene in a population in relation to the frequency of its alleles.

gene pool *n.* the sum of all the genes in an interbreeding population.

genera ('dʒɛnərə) *n.* a plural of **genus.**

generable ('dʒɛnərəbᵊl) *adj.* able to be generated. [C15: from Late Latin *generābilis,* from Latin *generāre* to beget]

general ('dʒɛnərəl, 'dʒɛnrəl) *adj.* **1.** common; widespread: *a general feeling of horror at the crime.* **2.** of, including, applying to, or participated in by all or most of the members of a group, category, or community. **3.** relating to various branches of an activity, profession, etc.; not specialized: *general office work.* **4.** including various or miscellaneous items: *general knowledge; a general store.* **5.** not specific as to detail; overall: *a general description of the merchandise.* **6.** not definite; vague: *give me a general idea of when you will finish.* **7.** applicable or true in most cases; usual. **8.** (*prenominal or immediately postpositive*) having superior or extended authority or rank: *general manager; consul general.* **9.** Also: **pass.** designating a degree awarded at some universities, studied at a lower academic standard than an honours degree. See **honours** (sense 2). **10.** *Med.* relating to or involving the entire body or many of its parts; systemic. **11.** *Logic.* (of a statement) not specifying an individual subject but quantifying over a domain. ~*n.* **12.** an officer of a rank senior to lieutenant general, esp. one who commands a large military formation. **13.** any person acting as a leader and applying strategy or tactics. **14.** a general condition or principle: opposed to *particular.* **15.** a title for the head of a religious order, congregation, etc. **16.** *Med.* short for **general anaesthetic.** **17.** *Archaic.* the people; public. **18. in general.** generally; mostly or usually. [C13: from Latin *generālis* of a particular kind, from *genus* kind] —'**generalness** *n.*

general anaesthetic *n.* a drug producing anaesthesia of the entire body, with loss of consciousness.

General Assembly *n.* **1.** the deliberative assembly of the United Nations. Abbrev.: **GA.** **2.** the supreme governing body of certain religious denominations, esp. of the Presbyterian Church.

general average *n. Insurance.* loss or damage to a ship or its cargo that is shared among the shipowners and all the cargo owners. Abbrev.: **GA.** Compare **particular average.**

General Certificate of Education *n.* See **GCE.**

General Certificate of Secondary Education *n.* See **GCSE.**

general delivery *n.* the U.S. and Canadian equivalent of **poste restante.**

general election *n.* **1.** an election in which representatives are chosen in all constituencies of a state. **2.** *U.S.* a final election from which successful candidates are sent to a legislative body. Compare **primary.** **3.** *U.S. and Canadian.* (in the U.S.) a national or state election or (in Canada) a federal or provincial election in contrast to a local election.

general hospital *n.* a hospital not specializing in the treatment of particular illnesses or of patients of a particular sex or age group.

generalissimo (ˌdʒɛnərəˈlɪsɪˌməʊ, ˌdʒɛnrə-) *n., pl.* **-mos.** a supreme commander of combined military, naval, and air forces, esp. one who wields political as well as military power. [C17: from Italian, superlative of *generale* GENERAL]

generalist (ˈdʒɛnərəlɪst, ˈdʒɛnrə-) *n.* **1. a.** a person who is knowledgeable in many fields of study. **b.** (*as modifier*): *a generalist profession.* **2.** *Ecology.* an organism able to utilize many food sources and therefore able to flourish in many habitats. Compare **specialist** (sense 3).

generality (ˌdʒɛnəˈrælɪtɪ) *n., pl.* **-ties. 1.** a principle or observation having general application, esp. when imprecise or unable to be proved. **2.** the state or quality of being general. **3.** *Archaic.* the majority.

generalization *or* **generalisation** (ˌdʒɛnrəlaɪˈzeɪʃən) *n.* **1.** a principle, theory, etc., with general application. **2.** the act or an instance of generalizing. **3.** *Psychol.* the evoking of a response learned to one stimulus by a different but similar stimulus. See also **conditioning. 4.** *Logic.* the derivation of a general statement from a particular one, formally by prefixing a quantifier and replacing a subject term by a bound variable. If the quantifier is universal (**universal generalization**) the argument is not in general valid; if it is existential (**existential generalization**) it is valid. **5.** *Logic.* any statement ascribing a property to every member of a class (**universal generalization**) or to one or more members (**existential generalization**).

generalize *or* **generalise** (ˈdʒɛnrəˌlaɪz) *vb.* **1.** to form (general principles or conclusions) from (detailed facts, experience, etc.); infer. **2.** (*intr.*) to think or speak in generalities, esp. in a prejudiced way. **3.** (*tr.; usually passive*) to cause to become widely used or known. **4.** (*intr.*) (of a disease) **a.** to spread throughout the body. **b.** to change from a localized infection or condition to a systemic one. —ˈ**generalˌizer** *or* ˈ**generalˌiser** *n.*

generalized other *n. Psychol.* an individual's concept of other people.

generally (ˈdʒɛnrəlɪ) *adv.* **1.** usually; as a rule. **2.** commonly or widely. **3.** without reference to specific details or facts; broadly.

general officer *n.* an officer holding a commission of brigadier's rank or above in the army, air force, or marine corps.

general paralysis of the insane *n.* a disease of the central nervous system: a late manifestation of syphilis, often occurring up to 15 years after the original infection, characterized by mental deterioration, speech defects, and progressive paralysis. Abbrev.: **GPI.** Also called: **general paresis, dementia paralytica.**

General Post Office *n.* **1.** (in Britain until 1969) the department of the central Government that provided postal and telephone services. **2.** the main post office in a locality.

general practitioner *n.* a physician who does not specialize but has a medical practice (**general practice**) in which he treats all illnesses. Informal name: **family doctor.** Abbrev.: **GP.**

general-purpose *adj.* having a range of uses or applications; not restricted to one function.

general semantics *n.* (*functioning as sing.*) a school of thought, founded by Alfred Korzybski, that stresses the arbitrary nature of language and other symbols and the problems that result from misunderstanding their nature.

generalship (ˈdʒɛnrəlˌʃɪp) *n.* **1.** the art or duties of exercising command of a major military formation or formations. **2.** tactical or administrative skill.

general staff *n.* officers assigned to advise commanders in the planning and execution of military operations.

general strike *n.* a strike by all or most of the workers of a country, province, city, etc., esp. (*caps.*) such a strike that took place in Britain in 1926.

General Synod *n.* the governing body, under Parliament, of the Church of England, made up of the bishops and elected clerical and lay representatives.

general theory of relativity *n.* the theory of gravitation, developed by Einstein in 1916, extending the special theory of relativity to include acceleration and leading to the conclusion that gravitational forces are equivalent to forces caused by acceleration.

general will *n.* (in the philosophy of Rousseau) the source of legitimate authority residing in the collective will as contrasted with individual interests.

generate (ˈdʒɛnəˌreɪt) *vb.* (*mainly tr.*) **1.** to produce or bring into being; create. **2.** (*also intr.*) to produce (electricity), esp. in a power station. **3.** to produce (a substance) by a chemical process. **4.** *Maths, linguistics.* to provide a precise criterion or specification for membership in (a set): *these rules will generate all the noun phrases in English.* **5.** *Geometry.* to trace or form by moving a point, line, or plane in a specific way: *circular motion of a line generates a cylinder.* [C16: from Latin *generāre* to beget, from *genus* kind]

generation (ˌdʒɛnəˈreɪʃən) *n.* **1.** the act or process of bringing into being; production or reproduction, esp. of offspring. **2.** a successive stage in natural descent of people or animals or the individuals produced at each stage. **3.** the normal or average time between two such generations of a species: about 35 years for humans. **4.** a phase or form in the life cycle of a plant or animal characterized by a particular type of reproduction: *the gametophyte generation.* **5.** all the people of approximately the same age, esp. when considered as sharing certain attitudes, etc. **6.** production of electricity, heat, etc. **7.** *Physics.* a set of nuclei formed directly from a preceding set in a chain reaction. **8.** (*modifier, in combination*) **a.** belonging to a generation specified as having been born in or as having parents, grandparents, etc., born in a given country: *a third-generation American.* **b.** belonging to a specified stage of development in manufacture, usually implying improvement: *a second-generation computer.* —ˌ**generˈational** *adj.*

generation gap *n.* the years separating one generation from the generation that precedes or follows it, esp. when regarded as representing the difference in outlook and the lack of understanding between them.

generative (ˈdʒɛnərətɪv) *adj.* **1.** of or relating to the production of offspring, parts, etc.: *a generative cell.* **2.** capable of producing or originating.

generative grammar *n.* a description of a language in terms of explicit rules that ideally generate all and only the grammatical sentences of the language. Compare **transformational grammar.**

generative semantics *n.* (*functioning as sing.*) a school of semantic theory based on the doctrine that syntactic and semantic structure are of the same formal nature and that there is a single system of rules that relates surface structure to meaning. Compare **interpretive semantics.**

generator (ˈdʒɛnəˌreɪtə) *n.* **1.** *Physics.* **a.** any device for converting mechanical energy into electrical energy by electromagnetic induction, esp. a large one as in a power station. **b.** a device for producing a voltage electrostatically. **c.** any device that converts one form of energy into another form: *an acoustic generator.* **2.** an apparatus for producing a gas. **3.** a person or thing that generates.

generatrix (ˈdʒɛnəˌreɪtrɪks) *n., pl.* **generatrices** (ˈdʒɛnəˌreɪtrɪˌsiːz). a point, line, or plane that is moved in a specific way to produce a geometric figure.

generic (dʒɪˈnɛrɪk) *or* **generical** *adj.* **1.** applicable or referring to a whole class or group; general. **2.** *Biology.* of, relating to, or belonging to a genus: *the generic name.* **3.** (of a drug, food product, etc.) not having a trademark. [C17: from French; see GENUS] —**geˈnerically** *adv.*

generosity (ˌdʒɛnəˈrɒsɪtɪ) *n., pl.* **-ties. 1.** willingness and liberality in giving away one's money, time, etc.; magnanimity. **2.** freedom from pettiness in character and mind. **3.** a generous act. **4.** abundance; plenty.

generous (ˈdʒɛnərəs, ˈdʒɛnrəs) *adj.* **1.** willing and liberal in giving away one's money, time, etc.; munificent. **2.** free from pettiness in character and mind. **3.** full or plentiful: *a generous portion.* **4.** (of wine) rich in alcohol. **5.** (of a soil type) fertile. [C16: via Old French from Latin *generōsus* nobly born, from *genus* race; see GENUS] —ˈ**generously** *adv.* —ˈ**generousness** *n.*

genesis (ˈdʒɛnɪsɪs) *n., pl.* **-ses** (-ˌsiːz). a beginning or origin of anything. [Old English: via Latin from Greek; related to Greek *gignesthai* to be born]

-genesis *n. combining form.* indicating genesis, development, or generation: *biogenesis; parthenogenesis.* [New Latin, from Latin: GENESIS] —**-genetic** *or* **-genic** *adj. combining form.*

genet[1] (ˈdʒɛnɪt) *or* **genette** (dʒɪˈnɛt) *n.* **1.** any agile catlike viverrine mammal of the genus *Genetta,* inhabiting wooded regions of Africa and S Europe, having an elongated head, thick spotted or blotched fur, and a very long tail. **2.** the fur of such an animal. [C15: from Old French *genette,* from Arabic *jarnayt*]

genet[2] (ˈdʒɛnɪt) *n.* an obsolete spelling of **jennet.**

gene therapy *n.* the replacement or alteration of defective genes in order to prevent the occurrence of such inherited diseases as haemophilia. Effected by genetic engineering techniques, it is still at the experimental stage.

genetic (dʒɪˈnɛtɪk) *or* **genetical** *adj.* of or relating to genetics, genes, or the origin of something. [C19: from GENESIS] —**geˈnetically** *adv.*

genetic code *n. Biochem.* the order in which the nitrogenous bases of DNA are arranged in the molecule, which determines the type and amount of protein synthesized in the cell. The four bases are arranged in groups of three in a specific order, each group acting as a unit (codon), which specifies a particular amino acid. See also **messenger RNA, transfer RNA.**

genetic counselling *n.* the provision of advice for couples with a history of inherited disorders who wish to have children, including the likelihood of having affected children, the course and management of the disorder, etc.

genetic engineering *n.* alteration of the DNA of a cell for purposes of research, as a means of manufacturing animal proteins, correcting genetic defects, or making improvements to plants and animals bred by man.

genetic fingerprinting *n.* the pattern of DNA unique to each individual that can be analysed in a sample of blood, saliva, or tissue: used as a means of identification.

geneticist (dʒɪˈnɛtɪsɪst) *n.* a person who studies or specializes in genetics.

genetic map *n.* a graphic representation of the order of genes within chromosomes by means of detailed analysis of the DNA. See also **chromosome map.** —**genetic mapping** *n.*

genetics (dʒɪˈnɛtɪks) *n.* **1.** (*functioning as sing.*) the study of heredity and variation in organisms. **2.** the genetic features and constitution of a single organism, species, or group.

Geneva bands (dʒɪˈniːvə) *pl. n.* a pair of white lawn or linen strips hanging from the front of the neck or collar of some ecclesiastical and academic robes. [C19: named after *Geneva*, city in Switzerland, where originally worn by Swiss Calvinist clergy]

Geneva gown *n.* a long loose black gown with very wide sleeves worn by academics or Protestant clerics. [C19: named after *Geneva*; see GENEVA BANDS]

Genevan (dʒɪˈniːvᵊn) *or* **Genevese** (ˌdʒɛnɪˈviːz) *adj.* **1.** of, relating to, or characteristic of the Swiss city of Geneva. **2.** of, adhering to, or relating to the teachings of Calvin or the Calvinists. ~*n., pl.* **-vans** *or* **-vese. 3.** a native or inhabitant of Geneva. **4.** a less common name for a **Calvinist.**

genial[1] (ˈdʒiːnjəl, -nɪəl) *adj.* **1.** cheerful, easy-going, and warm in manner or behaviour. **2.** pleasantly warm, so as to give life, growth, or health: *the genial sunshine.* [C16: from Latin *geniālis* relating to birth or marriage, from *genius* tutelary deity; see GENIUS] —**geniality** (ˌdʒiːnɪˈælɪtɪ) *or* ˈ**genialness** *n.* —ˈ**genially** *adv.*

genial[2] (dʒɪˈniːəl) *adj. Anatomy.* of or relating to the chin. [C19: from Greek *geneion*, from *genus* jaw]

genic (ˈdʒɛnɪk) *adj.* of or relating to a gene or genes.

-genic *adj. combining form.* **1.** relating to production or generation: *carcinogenic.* **2.** well suited to or suitable for: *photogenic.* [from -GEN + -IC]

genicular (dʒɪˈnɪkjʊlə) *adj. Anatomy.* of or relating to the knee: *genicular artery.* [C19: from Latin *genu* knee]

geniculate (dʒɪˈnɪkjʊlɪt, -ˌleɪt) *adj.* **1.** *Biology.* bent at a sharp angle: *geniculate antennae.* **2.** having a joint or joints capable of bending sharply. [C17: from Latin *geniculātus* jointed, from *geniculum* a little knee, small joint, from *genu* knee] —**geˈniculately** *adv.* —**geˌnicuˈlation** *n.*

genie (ˈdʒiːnɪ) *n.* **1.** (in fairy tales and stories) a servant who appears by magic and fulfils a person's wishes. **2.** another word for **jinni.** [C18: from French *génie*, from Arabic *jinni* demon, influenced by Latin *genius* attendant spirit; see GENIUS]

genii (ˈdʒiːnɪˌaɪ) *n.* the plural of **genius** (senses 5, 6).

genip (ˈdʒɛnɪp) *n.* another word for **genipap.** [C18: from Spanish *genipa*, from French, from Guarani]

genipap (ˈdʒɛnɪˌpæp) *or* **genip** *n.* **1.** an evergreen West Indian rubiaceous tree, *Genipa americana*, with reddish-brown edible orange-like fruits. **2.** the fruit of this tree. [C17: from Portuguese *genipapo*, from Tupi]

genit. *abbrev. for* genitive.

genital (ˈdʒɛnɪtᵊl) *adj.* **1.** of or relating to the sexual organs or to reproduction. **2.** *Psychoanal.* relating to the mature stage of psychosexual development in which an affectionate relationship with one's sex partner is established. Compare **anal** (sense 2), **oral** (sense 7), **phallic** (sense 2). [C14: from Latin *genitālis* concerning birth, from *gignere* to beget]

genital herpes *n.* a sexually transmitted disease caused by a variety of the herpes simplex virus in which painful blisters occur in the genital region.

genitals (ˈdʒɛnɪtᵊlz) *or* **genitalia** (ˌdʒɛnɪˈteɪlɪə, -ˈteɪljə) *pl. n.* the sexual organs; the testicles and penis of a male or the labia, clitoris, and vagina of a female. —**genitalic** (ˌdʒɛnɪˈtælɪk) *adj.*

genitive (ˈdʒɛnɪtɪv) *Grammar.* ~*adj.* **1.** denoting a case of nouns, pronouns, and adjectives in inflected languages used to indicate a relation of ownership or association, usually translated by English *of.* ~*n.* **2. a.** the genitive case. **b.** a word or speech element in this case. [C14: from Latin *genetīvus*, relating to birth, from *gignere* to produce] —**genitival** (ˌdʒɛnɪˈtaɪvᵊl) *adj.* —ˌ**geniˈtivally** *adv.*

genitor (ˈdʒɛnɪtə, -tɔː) *n.* the biological father as distinguished from the pater or legal father. [C15: from Latin, from *gignere* to beget]

genitourinary (ˌdʒɛnɪtəʊˈjʊərɪnərɪ) *adj.* of or relating to both the reproductive and excretory organs; urogenital.

genitourinary medicine *n.* the branch of medical science concerned with the study and treatment of diseases of the genital and urinary organs, esp. sexually transmitted diseases.

genius (ˈdʒiːnɪəs, -njəs) *n., pl.* **-uses** *or* (for senses 5, 6) **genii** (ˈdʒiːnɪˌaɪ). **1.** a person with exceptional ability, esp. of a highly original kind. **2.** such ability or capacity: *Mozart's musical genius.* **3.** the distinctive spirit or creative nature of a nation, era, language, etc. **4.** a person considered as exerting great influence of a certain sort: *an evil genius.* **5.** *Roman myth.* **a.** the guiding spirit who attends a person from birth to death. **b.** the guardian spirit of a place, group of people, or institution. **6.** *Arabic myth.* (*usually pl.*) a demon; jinn. [C16: from Latin, from *gignere* to beget]

genius loci *Latin.* (ˈdʒiːnɪəs ˈləʊsaɪ) *n.* **1.** the guardian spirit of a place. **2.** the special atmosphere of a particular place. [genius of the place]

genizah (gɛˈniːzə) *n. Judaism.* a repository (usually in a synagogue) for books and other sacred objects which can no longer be used but which may not be destroyed. [C19: from Hebrew, literally: a hiding place, from *gānaz* to hide, set aside]

Genl *or* **genl** *abbrev. for* General *or* general.

genoa (dʒɛnˈəʊə) *n. Yachting.* a large triangular jib sail, often with a foot that extends as far aft as the clew of the mainsail. Also called: **genoa jib.** Sometimes shortened to **genny, jenny.** [named after *Genoa*, port in NW Italy]

Genoa cake *n.* a fruit cake, usually decorated with almonds.

genocide (ˈdʒɛnəʊˌsaɪd) *n.* the policy of deliberately killing a nationality or ethnic group. [C20: from *geno-*, from Greek *genos* race + -CIDE] —ˌ**genoˈcidal** *adj.*

Genoese (ˌdʒɛnəʊˈiːz) *or* **Genovese** (ˌdʒɛnəˈviːz) *n., pl.* **-ese** *or* **-vese. 1.** a native or inhabitant of Genoa, a port in NW Italy. ~*adj.* **2.** of or relating to Genoa or its inhabitants.

genome *or* **genom** (ˈdʒiːnəʊm) *n.* the complement of haploid chromosomes contained in a single gamete or nucleus. [C20: from German *Genom*, from *Gen* GENE + (CHROMOS)OME]

genotype (ˈdʒɛnəʊˌtaɪp) *n.* **1.** the genetic constitution of an organism. **2.** a group of organisms with the same genetic constitution. ~Compare **phenotype.** —**genotypic** (ˌdʒɛnəʊˈtɪpɪk) *or* ˌ**genoˈtypical** *adj.* —ˌ**genoˈtypically** *adv.* —**genotypicity** (ˌdʒɛnəʊtɪˈpɪsɪtɪ) *n.*

-genous *adj. combining form.* **1.** yielding or generating: *androgenous; erogenous.* **2.** generated by or issuing from: *endogenous.* [from -GEN + -OUS]

genre (ˈʒɑːnrə) *n.* **1.** kind, category, or sort, esp. of literary or artistic work. **2. a.** a category of painting in which domestic scenes or incidents from everyday life are depicted. **b.** (*as modifier*): *genre painting.* [C19: from French, from Old French *gendre*; see GENDER]

genro (ˈgɛnˈrəʊ) *n.* **1.** (*functioning as sing. or pl.*) a group of highly respected elder statesmen in late 19th- and early 20th-century Japan. **2.** a member of this group. [C20: from Japanese, from Ancient Chinese *nguan lao*, from *nguan* first + *lao* elder]

gens (dʒɛnz) *n., pl.* **gentes** (ˈdʒɛntiːz). **1.** (in ancient Rome) any of a group of aristocratic families, having a common name and claiming descent from a common ancestor in the male line. **2.** *Anthropol.* a group based on descent in the male line. [C19: from Latin: race; compare GENUS, GENDER]

gent (dʒɛnt) *n. Informal.* short for **gentleman.**

genteel (dʒɛnˈtiːl) *adj.* **1.** affectedly proper or refined; excessively polite. **2.** respectable, polite, and well-bred: *a genteel old lady.* **3.** appropriate to polite or fashionable society: *genteel behaviour.* [C16: from French *gentil* well-born; see GENTLE] —**genˈteelly** *adv.* —**genˈteelness** *n.*

genteelism (dʒɛnˈtiːlɪzəm) *n.* a word or phrase used in place of a less genteel one.

gentian (ˈdʒɛnʃən) *n.* **1.** any gentianaceous plant of the genus *Gentiana*, having blue, yellow, white, or red showy flowers. **2.** the bitter-tasting dried rhizome and roots of *Gentiana lutea* (**European** or **yellow gentian**), used as a tonic. **3.** any of several similar plants, such as the horse gentian. [C14: from Latin *gentiāna*; perhaps named after *Gentius*, a second-century B.C. Illyrian king, reputedly the first to use it medicinally]

gentianaceous (ˌdʒɛnʃɪəˈneɪʃəs) *adj.* of, relating to, or belonging to the *Gentianaceae*, a family of flowering plants that includes centaury, felwort, and gentian.

gentian blue *n.* **a.** a purplish-blue colour. **b.** (*as adj.*): *gentian-blue shoes.*

gentianella (ˌdʒɛnʃəˈnɛlə, -ʃɪə-) *n.* any of various gentianaceous plants, esp. the alpine species *Gentiana acaulis*, which has showy blue flowers. [C17: from New Latin, literally: a little GENTIAN]

gentian violet *n.* a greenish crystalline substance, obtained from rosaniline, that forms a violet solution in water, used as an indicator, antiseptic, and in the treatment of burns. Also called: **crystal violet.**

gentile (ˈdʒɛntaɪl) *adj.* **1.** denoting an adjective or proper noun used to designate a place or the inhabitants of a place, as *Spanish* and *Spaniard.* **2.** of or relating to a tribe or people. [C14: from Late Latin *gentīlis*, from Latin: one belonging to the same tribe or family; see GENS]

Gentile (ˈdʒɛntaɪl) *n.* **1.** a person who is not a Jew. **2.** a Christian, as contrasted with a Jew. **3.** a person who is not a member of one's own church: used esp. by Mormons. **4.** a heathen or pagan. ~*adj.* **5.** of or relating to a race or religion that is not Jewish. **6.** Christian, as contrasted with Jewish. **7.** not being a member of one's own church: used esp. by Mormons. **8.** pagan or heathen.

gentilesse (ˈdʒɛntᵊˌlɛs) *n. Archaic.* politeness or good breeding. [C14: from Old French *gentillesse*; see GENTEEL]

gentility (dʒɛnˈtɪlɪtɪ) *n., pl.* **-ties. 1.** respectability and polite good breeding. **2.** affected politeness. **3.** noble birth or ancestry. **4.** people of noble birth. [C14: from Old French *gentilite*, from Latin *gentīlitās* relationship of those belonging to the same tribe or family; see GENS]

gentle (ˈdʒɛntᵊl) *adj.* **1.** having a mild or kindly nature or character. **2.** soft or temperate; mild; moderate: *a gentle scolding.* **3.** gradual: *a gentle slope.* **4.** easily controlled; tame: *a gentle horse.* **5.** *Archaic.* of good breeding; noble: *gentle blood.* **6.** *Archaic.* gallant; chivalrous. ~*vb.* (*tr.*) **7.** to tame or subdue (a horse). **8.** to appease or mollify. **9.** *Obsolete.* to ennoble or dignify. ~*n.* **10.** a maggot, esp. when used as bait in fishing. **11.** *Archaic.* a person who is of good breeding. [C13: from Old French *gentil* noble, from Latin *gentīlis* belonging to the same family; see GENS] —ˈ**gently** *adv.*

gentle breeze *n. Meteorol.* a light breeze of force three on the Beaufort scale, blowing at 8–12 mph.
gentlefolk ('dʒɛntᵊl,fəʊk) *or* **gentlefolks** *pl. n.* persons regarded as being of good breeding.
gentleman ('dʒɛntᵊlmən) *n., pl.* **-men.** **1.** a man regarded as having qualities of refinement associated with a good family. **2.** a man who is cultured, courteous, and well-educated. **3.** a polite name for a man. **4.** the personal servant of a gentleman (esp. in the phrase **gentleman's gentleman**). **5.** *British history.* a man of gentle birth, who was entitled to bear arms, ranking above a yeoman in social position. **6.** (formerly) a euphemistic word for a **smuggler.** —'**gentlemanly** *adj.* —'**gentlemanliness** *n.*
gentleman-at-arms *n., pl.* **gentlemen-at-arms.** a member of the guard who attend the British sovereign on ceremonial and state occasions.
gentleman-farmer *n., pl.* **gentlemen-farmers.** **1.** a person who engages in farming but does not depend on it for his living. **2.** a person who owns farmland but does not farm it personally.
gentlemen's agreement *or* **gentleman's agreement** *n.* a personal understanding or arrangement based on honour and not legally binding.
gentleness ('dʒɛntᵊlnɪs) *n.* **1.** the quality of being gentle. **2.** *Physics.* a property of elementary particles, conserved in certain strong interactions. See also **charm** (sense 7).
gentlewoman ('dʒɛntᵊl,wʊmən) *n., pl.* **-women.** **1.** *Archaic.* a woman regarded as being of good family or breeding; lady. **2.** *Rare.* a woman who is cultured, courteous, and well-educated. **3.** *History.* a woman in personal attendance on a high-ranking lady. —'**gentle,womanly** *adj.* —'**gentle,womanliness** *n.*
Gentoo ('dʒɛntuː) *n., pl.* **-toos.** (*sometimes not cap.*) *Archaic.* a Hindu, esp. as distinguished from a Muslim. [C17: from Portuguese *gentio* pagan (literally: GENTILE)]
gentrification (,dʒɛntrɪfɪ'keɪʃən) *n. Brit.* a process by which middle-class people take up residence in a traditionally working-class area of a city, changing the character of the area. [C20: from *gentrify* (to become GENTRY)] —'**gentri,fier** *n.*
gentry ('dʒɛntrɪ) *n.* **1.** persons of high birth or social standing; aristocracy. **2.** *Brit.* persons just below the nobility in social rank. **3.** *Informal, often derogatory.* people, esp. of a particular group or kind. [C14: from Old French *genterie,* from *gentil* GENTLE]
gents (dʒɛnts) *n.* (*functioning as sing.*) *Brit. informal.* a men's public lavatory.
genu ('dʒɛnjuː) *n., pl.* **genua** ('dʒɛnjʊə). *Anatomy.* **1.** the technical name for the **knee.** **2.** any kneelike bend in a structure or part. [Latin: knee]
genuflect ('dʒɛnjʊ,flɛkt) *vb.* (*intr.*) **1.** to act in a servile or deferential manner. **2.** *R.C. Church.* to bend one or both knees as a sign of reverence, esp. when passing before the Blessed Sacrament. [C17: from Medieval Latin *genūflectere,* from Latin *genu* knee + *flectere* to bend] —,**genu'flection** *or* (*esp. Brit.*) ,**genu'flexion** *n.* —'**genu,flector** *n.*
genuine ('dʒɛnjʊɪn) *adj.* **1.** not fake or counterfeit; original; real; authentic. **2.** not pretending; frank; sincere. **3.** being of authentic or original stock. [C16: from Latin *genuīnus* inborn, hence (in Late Latin) authentic, from *gignere* to produce] —'**genuinely** *adv.* —'**genuineness** *n.*
gen up *vb.* **gens up, genning up, genned up.** (*adv.; often passive;* when *intr.,* usually foll. by *on*) *Brit. informal.* to brief (someone) or study (something) in detail; make or become fully conversant with: *I can only take over this job if I am properly genned up.*
genus ('dʒiːnəs) *n., pl.* **genera** ('dʒɛnərə) *or* **genuses.** **1.** *Biology.* any of the taxonomic groups into which a family is divided and which contains one or more species. For example, *Vulpes* (foxes) is a genus of the dog family (*Canidae*). **2.** *Logic.* a class of objects or individuals that can be divided into two or more groups or species. **3.** a class, group, etc., with common characteristics. [C16: from Latin: race]
-geny *n. combining form.* indicating origin or manner of development: *phylogeny.* [from Greek *-geneia,* from *-genēs* born] — **-genic** *adj. combining form.*
geo *or* **gio** ('dʒiːəʊ) *n., pl.* **geos** *or* **gios.** (esp. in Shetland) a small fjord or gully. [C18: from Old Norse *gjā* ravine; related to Old English *gionian* to YAWN]
geo- *combining form.* indicating earth: *geomorphology.* [from Greek, from *gē* earth]
geocarpy ('dʒiːəʊ,kɑːpɪ) *n. Botany.* the ripening of fruits below ground, as occurs in the peanut.
geocentric (,dʒiːəʊ'sɛntrɪk) *adj.* **1.** having the earth at its centre: *the Ptolemaic system postulated a geocentric universe.* **2.** measured from or relating to the centre of the earth. —,**geo'centrically** *adv.*
geocentric parallax *n.* See **parallax** (sense 2).
geochemistry (,dʒiːəʊ'kɛmɪstrɪ) *n.* the chemistry of the earth's crust. —**geochemical** (,dʒiːəʊ'kɛmɪkᵊl) *adj.* —,**geo'chemist** *n.*
geochronology (,dʒiːəʊkrə'nɒlədʒɪ) *n.* the branch of geology concerned with ordering and dating of events in the earth's history, including the origin of the earth itself. —**geochronological** (,dʒiːəʊ,krɒnᵊ'lɒdʒɪkᵊl) *adj.*
geod. *abbrev. for:* **1.** geodesy. **2.** geodetic.
geode ('dʒiːəʊd) *n.* a cavity, usually lined with crystals, within a rock mass or nodule. [C17: from Latin *geōdēs* a precious stone, from Greek: earthlike; see GEO-, -ODE[1]] —**geodic** (dʒɪ'ɒdɪk) *adj.*
geodesic (,dʒiːəʊ'dɛsɪk, -'diː-) *adj.* **1.** Also: **geodetic, geodesical.** relating to or involving the geometry of curved surfaces. ~*n.* **2.** Also called: **geodesic line.** the shortest line between two points on a curved or plane surface.
geodesic dome *n.* a light structural framework arranged as a set of polygons in the form of a shell and covered with sheeting made of plastic, plywood, metal, etc.
geodesy (dʒɪ'ɒdɪsɪ) *or* **geodetics** (,dʒiːəʊ'dɛtɪks) *n.* the branch of science concerned with determining the exact position of geographical points and the shape and size of the earth. [C16: from French *géodésie,* from Greek *geōdaisia,* from GEO- + *daiein* to divide] —**ge'odesist** *n.*
geodetic (,dʒiːəʊ'dɛtɪk) *adj.* **1.** of or relating to geodesy. **2.** another word for **geodesic.** —,**geo'detically** *adv.*
geodetic surveying *n.* the surveying of the earth's surface, making allowance for its curvature and giving an accurate framework for smaller-scale surveys.
geodynamics (,dʒiːəʊdaɪ'næmɪks) *n.* (*functioning as sing.*) the branch of geology concerned with the forces and processes, esp. large-scale, of the earth's interior, particularly as regards their effects on the crust or lithosphere. —,**geody'namic** *adj.* —,**geody'namicist** *n.*
geog. *abbrev. for:* **1.** geographer. **2.** geographic(al). **3.** geography.
geognosy (dʒɪ'ɒgnəsɪ) *n.* the study of the origin and distribution of minerals and rocks in the earth's crust: superseded generally by the term **geology.** [C18: from French *géognosie,* from GEO- + Greek *gnōsis* a seeking to know, knowledge] —**geognostic** (,dʒiːɒg'nɒstɪk) *adj.*
geographical determinism *n. Sociol.* the theory that human activity is determined by geographical conditions.
geographical mile *n.* another name for **nautical mile.**
geographic north *n.* another name for **true north.**
geography (dʒɪ'ɒgrəfɪ) *n., pl.* **-phies.** **1.** the study of the natural features of the earth's surface, including topography, climate, soil, vegetation, etc., and man's response to them. **2.** the natural features of a region. **3.** an arrangement of constituent parts; plan; layout. —**ge'ographer** *n.* —**geographical** (,dʒɪə'græfɪkᵊl) *or* ,**geo'graphic** *adj.* —,**geo'graphically** *adv.*
geoid ('dʒiːɔɪd) *n.* **1.** a hypothetical surface that corresponds to mean sea level and extends at the same level under the continents. **2.** the shape of the earth.
geol. *abbrev. for:* **1.** geologic(al). **2.** geologist. **3.** geology.
geological cycle *n.* the series of events in which a rock of one type is converted to one or more other types and then back to the original type.
geological timescale *n.* any division of geological time into chronological units, whether relative (with units in the correct temporal sequence) or absolute (with numerical ages attached).
geologize *or* **geologise** (dʒɪ'ɒlə,dʒaɪz) *vb.* to study the geological features of (an area).
geology (dʒɪ'ɒlədʒɪ) *n.* **1.** the scientific study of the origin, history, structure, and composition of the earth. **2.** the geological features of a district or country. —**geological** (,dʒɪə'lɒdʒɪkᵊl) *or* ,**geo'logic** *adj.* —,**geo'logically** *adv.* —**ge'ologist** *or* **ge'ologer** *n.*
geom. *abbrev. for:* **1.** geometric(al). **2.** geometry.
geomagnetism (,dʒiːəʊ'mægnɪ,tɪzəm) *n.* **1.** the magnetic field of the earth. **2.** the branch of physics concerned with this. —**geomagnetic** (,dʒiːəʊmæg'nɛtɪk) *adj.*
geomancy ('dʒiːəʊ,mænsɪ) *n.* prophecy from the pattern made when a handful of earth is cast down or dots are drawn at random and connected with lines. —'**geo,mancer** *n.* —,**geo'mantic** *adj.*
geomechanics (,dʒiːəʊmɪ'kænɪks) *n.* (*functioning as sing.*) the study and application of rock and soil mechanics.
geometer (dʒɪ'ɒmɪtə) *or* **geometrician** (dʒɪ,ɒmɪ'trɪʃən, ,dʒiːəʊmɪ-) *n.* a person who is practised in or who studies geometry.
geometric (,dʒɪə'mɛtrɪk) *or* **geometrical** *adj.* **1.** of, relating to, or following the methods and principles of geometry. **2.** consisting of, formed by, or characterized by points, lines, curves, or surfaces: *a geometric figure.* **3.** (of design or ornamentation) composed predominantly of simple geometric forms, such as circles, rectangles, triangles, etc. —,**geo'metrically** *adv.*
geometric distribution *n. Statistics.* the distribution of the number, x, of independent trials required to obtain a first success: where the probability in each is p, the probability that $x = r$ is $p(1-p)^{r-1}$, with mean $1/p$. See also **Bernoulli trial.**
geometric mean *n.* the average value of a set of n integers, terms, or quantities, expressed as the nth root of their product. Compare **arithmetic mean.**
geometric pace *n.* a modern form of a Roman pace, a measure of length taken as 5 feet.
geometric progression *n.* a sequence of numbers, each of which differs from the succeeding one by a constant ratio, as 1, 2, 4, 8, ... Compare **arithmetic progression.**
geometric series *n.* a geometric progression written as a sum, as in 1 + 2 + 4 + 8.

geometrid (dʒɪˈɒmɪtrɪd) *n.* **1.** any moth of the family *Geometridae,* the larvae of which are called measuring worms, inchworms, or loopers. ~*adj.* **2.** of, relating to, or belonging to the *Geometridae.* [C19: from New Latin *Geōmetridae,* from Latin, from Greek *geometrēs:* land measurer, from the looping gait of the larvae]

geometrize *or* **geometrise** (dʒɪˈɒmɪˌtraɪz) *vb.* **1.** to use or apply geometric methods or principles (to). **2.** (*tr.*) to represent in geometric form.

geometry (dʒɪˈɒmɪtrɪ) *n.* **1.** the branch of mathematics concerned with the properties, relationships, and measurement of points, lines, curves, and surfaces. See also **analytical geometry, non-Euclidean geometry.** **2. a.** any branch of geometry using a particular notation or set of assumptions: *analytical geometry.* **b.** any branch of geometry referring to a particular set of objects: *solid geometry.* **3.** a shape, configuration, or arrangement. **4.** *Arts.* the shape of a solid or a surface. [C14: from Latin *geōmetria,* from Greek, from *geōmetrein* to measure the land]

geomorphic (ˌdʒiːəʊˈmɔːfɪk) *adj.* of, relating to, or resembling the earth's surface.

geomorphology (ˌdʒiːəʊmɔːˈfɒlədʒɪ) *or* **geomorphogeny** (ˌdʒiːəʊmɔːˈfɒdʒənɪ) *n.* the branch of geology concerned with the structure, origin, and development of the topographical features of the earth's crust. —**geomorphological** (ˌdʒiːəʊˌmɔːfəˈlɒdʒɪkᵊl) *or* ˌ**geo**ˌ**morpho**ˈ**logic** *adj.* —ˌ**geo**ˌ**morpho**ˈ**logically** *adv.*

geophagy (dʒɪˈɒfədʒɪ), **geophagia** (ˌdʒɪəˈfeɪdʒə, -dʒɪə), *or* **geophagism** (dʒɪˈɒfədʒɪzəm) *n.* **1.** the practice of eating earth, clay, chalk, etc., found in some primitive tribes. **2.** *Zoology.* the habit of some animals, esp. earthworms, of eating soil. —**ge**ˈ**ophagist** *n.* —**geophagous** (dʒɪˈɒfəgəs) *adj.*

geophysics (ˌdʒiːəʊˈfɪzɪks) *n.* (*functioning as sing.*) the study of the earth's physical properties and of the physical processes acting upon, above, and within the earth. It includes seismology, geomagnetism, meteorology, and oceanography. —ˌ**geo**ˈ**physical** *adj.* —ˌ**geo**ˈ**physicist** *n.*

geophyte (ˈdʒiːəʊˌfaɪt) *n.* a perennial plant that propagates by means of buds below the soil surface. —**geophytic** (ˌdʒiːəʊˈfɪtɪk) *adj.*

geopolitics (ˌdʒiːəʊˈpɒlɪtɪks) *n.* **1.** (*functioning as sing.*) the study of the effect of geographical factors on politics, esp. international politics; political geography. **2.** (*functioning as pl.*) the combination of geographical and political factors affecting a country or area. —**geopolitical** (ˌdʒiːəʊpəˈlɪtɪkᵊl) *adj.* —ˌ**geo**ˌ**poli**ˈ**tician** *n.*

geoponic (ˌdʒiːəʊˈpɒnɪk) *adj.* **1.** of or relating to agriculture, esp. as a science. **2.** rural; rustic. [C17: from Greek *geōponikos* concerning land cultivation, from *geōponein* to till the soil, from GEO- + *ponein* to labour]

geoponics (ˌdʒiːəʊˈpɒnɪks) *n.* (*functioning as sing.*) the science of agriculture.

Geordie (ˈdʒɔːdɪ) *Brit.* ~*n.* **1.** a person who comes from or lives in Tyneside, NE England. **2.** the dialect spoken by these people. ~*adj.* **3.** of or relating to these people or their dialect. [C19: a diminutive of *George*]

George (dʒɔːdʒ) *n. Brit. informal.* the automatic pilot in an aircraft. [C20: originally a slang name for an airman]

George Cross *n.* a British award for bravery, esp. of civilians: instituted 1940. Abbrev.: **GC.**

georgette *or* **georgette crepe** (dʒɔːˈdʒɛt) *n.* **a.** a thin silk or cotton crepe fabric with a mat finish. **b.** (*as modifier*): *a georgette blouse.* [C20: from the name Mme *Georgette,* a French modiste]

Georgian (ˈdʒɔːdʒjən) *adj.* **1.** of, characteristic of, or relating to any or all of the four kings who ruled Great Britain and Ireland from 1714 to 1830, or to their reigns. **2.** of or relating to George V of Great Britain and Northern Ireland or his reign (1910–36): *the Georgian poets.* **3.** of or relating to the former Soviet republic of Georgia, its people, or their language. **4.** of or relating to the American State of Georgia or its inhabitants. **5.** in or imitative of the style prevalent in England during the 18th century (reigns of George I, II, and III), esp. the Palladian style of architecture and the Sheraton style of furniture. ~*n.* **6.** the official language of the republic of Georgia, belonging to the South Caucasian family. **7.** a native or inhabitant of Georgia. **8.** an aboriginal inhabitant of the Caucasus. **9.** a native or inhabitant of the American State of Georgia. **10.** a person belonging to or imitating the styles of either of the Georgian periods in England.

georgic (ˈdʒɔːdʒɪk) *adj.* **1.** *Literary.* agricultural. ~*n.* **2.** a poem about rural or agricultural life. [C16: from Latin *geōrgicus,* from Greek *geōrgikos,* from *geōrgos* farmer, from *gē* land, earth + *-ourgos,* from *ergon* work]

geoscience (ˌdʒiːəʊˈsaɪəns) *n.* **1.** any science, such as geology, geophysics, geochemistry, or geodesy, concerned with the earth; an earth science. **2.** these sciences collectively.

geosphere (ˈdʒiːəʊˌsfɪə) *n.* another name for **lithosphere.**

geostatic (ˌdʒiːəʊˈstætɪk) *adj.* **1.** denoting or relating to the pressure exerted by a mass of rock or a similar substance. **2.** (of a construction) able to resist the pressure of a mass of earth or similar material.

geostatics (ˌdʒiːəʊˈstætɪks) *n.* (*functioning as sing.*) the branch of physics concerned with the statics of rigid bodies, esp. the balance of forces within the earth.

geostationary (ˌdʒiːəʊˈsteɪʃənərɪ) *or* **geosynchronous** (ˌdʒiːəʊˈsɪŋkrənəs) *adj.* (of a satellite) in an orbit in which it circles the earth once in 24 hours so that it appears stationary in relation to the earth's surface.

geostrategy (ˌdʒiːəʊˈstrætədʒɪ) *n.* the study of geopolitics and strategics, esp. as they affect the analysis of a region.

geostrophic (ˌdʒiːəʊˈstrɒfɪk) *adj.* of, relating to, or caused by the force produced by the rotation of the earth: *geostrophic wind.*

geosyncline (ˌdʒiːəʊˈsɪŋklaɪn) *n.* a broad elongated depression in the earth's crust containing great thicknesses of sediment. —ˌ**geosyn**ˈ**clinal** *adj.*

geotaxis (ˌdʒiːəʊˈtæksɪs) *n.* movement of an organism in response to the stimulus of gravity. —ˌ**geo**ˈ**tactic** *adj.* —ˌ**geo**ˈ**tactically** *adv.*

geotectonic (ˌdʒiːəʊtɛkˈtɒnɪk) *adj.* of or relating to the formation, arrangement, and structure of the rocks of the earth's crust.

geotextile (ˌdʒiːəʊˈtɛkstaɪl) *n.* any strong synthetic fabric used in civil engineering, as to retain an embankment.

geotherm (ˈdʒiːəʊˌθɜːm) *n.* **1.** a line or surface within or on the earth connecting points of equal temperature. **2.** the representation of such a line or surface on a map or diagram.

geothermal (ˌdʒiːəʊˈθɜːməl) *or* **geothermic** *adj.* of or relating to the heat in the interior of the earth.

geothermal power *n.* power generated using steam produced by heat emanating from the molten core of the earth.

geotropism (dʒɪˈɒtrəˌpɪzəm) *n.* the response of a plant part to the stimulus of gravity. Plant stems, which grow upwards irrespective of the position in which they are placed, show **negative geotropism.** —**geotropic** (ˌdʒiːəʊˈtrɒpɪk) *adj.* —ˌ**geo**ˈ**tropically** *adv.*

ger. *abbrev. for:* **1.** gerund. **2.** gerundive.

Ger. *abbrev. for:* **1.** German. **2.** Germany.

gerah (ˈgɪərə) *n.* **1.** an ancient Hebrew unit of weight. **2.** an ancient Hebrew coin equal to one twentieth of a shekel. [C16: from Hebrew *gērāh* bean]

geraniaceous (dʒɪˌreɪnɪˈeɪʃəs) *adj.* of, relating to, or belonging to the *Geraniaceae,* a family of plants with typically hairy stems and beaklike fruits: includes the geranium, pelargonium, storksbill, and cranesbill. [C19: from New Latin *Geraniāceae;* see GERANIUM]

geranial (dʒɪˈreɪnɪəl) *n.* the *cis-* isomer of citral. [C19: from GERANI(UM) + AL(DEHYDE)]

geraniol (dʒɪˈreɪnɪˌɒl, dʒɪˈrɑː-) *n.* a colourless or pale yellow terpine alcohol with an odour of roses, found in many essential oils: used in perfumery. Formula: $C_{10}H_{18}O$. [C19: from GERANI(UM + ALCOH)OL]

geranium (dʒɪˈreɪnɪəm) *n.* **1.** any cultivated geraniaceous plant of the genus *Pelargonium,* having scarlet, pink, or white showy flowers. See also **pelargonium, rose geranium, lemon geranium.** **2.** any geraniaceous plant of the genus *Geranium,* such as cranesbill and herb Robert, having divided leaves and pink or purplish flowers. **3.** a strong red to a moderate or strong pink colour. [C16: from Latin: cranesbill, from Greek *geranion,* from *geranos* CRANE]

geratology (ˌdʒɛrəˈtɒlədʒɪ) *n.* the branch of medicine concerned with the elderly and the phenomena associated with ageing; geriatrics and gerontology. [C19: from *gerato-,* from Greek *gēras* old age + -LOGY] —**geratologic** (ˌdʒɛrətəˈlɒdʒɪk) *adj.*

gerbera (ˈdʒɜːbərə) *n.* any plant of the perennial genus *Gerbera,* esp. the Baberton daisy from S. Africa, *G. jamesonii,* grown, usually as a greenhouse plant, for its large brightly coloured daisy-like flowers: family *Compositae.* [named after Traugott *Gerber* (died 1743), German naturalist]

gerbil *or* **gerbille** (ˈdʒɜːbɪl) *n.* any burrowing rodent of the subfamily *Gerbillinae,* inhabiting hot dry regions of Asia and Africa and having soft pale fur: family *Cricetidae.* [C19: from French *gerbille,* from New Latin *gerbillus* a little JERBOA]

gerent (ˈdʒɛrənt) *n. Rare.* a person who rules or manages. [C16: from Latin *gerēns* managing, from *gerere* to bear]

gerenuk (ˈgɛrɪˌnʊk) *n.* a slender E African antelope, *Litocranius walleri,* with a long thin neck and backward-curving horns. [from Somali *garanug*]

gerfalcon (ˈdʒɜːˌfɔːlkən, -ˌfɔːkən) *n.* a variant spelling of **gyrfalcon.**

geriatric (ˌdʒɛrɪˈætrɪk) *adj.* **1.** of or relating to geriatrics or to elderly people. **2.** *Facetious, derogatory, or offensive.* (of people or machines) old, obsolescent, worn out, or useless. ~*n.* **3.** an elderly person. **4.** *Derogatory.* an older person considered as one who may be disregarded as senile or irresponsible. ~See also **psychogeriatric.** [C20: from Greek *gēras* old age + IATRIC]

geriatrician (ˌdʒɛrɪəˈtrɪʃən) *or* **geriatrist** (ˌdʒɛrɪˈætrɪst) *n.* a physician who specializes in geriatrics.

geriatrics (ˌdʒɛrɪˈætrɪks) *n.* (*functioning as sing.*) the branch of medical science concerned with the diagnosis and treatment of diseases affecting elderly people. Compare **gerontology.**

germ (dʒɜːm) *n.* **1.** a microorganism, esp. one that produces disease in animals or plants. **2.** (*often pl.*) the rudimentary or initial form of something: *the germs of revolution.* **3.** a simple structure, such as a fertilized egg, that is capable of developing into a complete organism. [C17: from French *germe,* from Latin *germen* sprig, bud, sprout, seed]

german[1] ('dʒɜːmən) *n. U.S.* a dance consisting of complicated figures and changes of partners. [C19: shortened from *German cotillion*]

german[2] ('dʒɜːmən) *adj.* **1.** (used in combination) **a.** having the same parents as oneself: *a brother-german.* **b.** having a parent that is a brother or sister of either of one's own parents: *cousin-german.* **2.** a less common word for **germane.** [C14: via Old French *germain,* from Latin *germānus* of the same race, from *germen* sprout, offshoot]

German ('dʒɜːmən) *n.* **1.** the official language of Germany and Austria and one of the official languages of Switzerland; the native language of approximately 100 million people. It is an Indo-European language belonging to the West Germanic branch, closely related to English and Dutch. There is considerable diversity of dialects; modern standard German is a development of Old High German, influenced by Martin Luther's translation of the Bible. See also **Low German. 2.** a native, inhabitant, or citizen of Germany, a country in central Europe. **3.** a person whose native language is German: *Swiss Germans; Volga Germans.* ~*adj.* **4.** denoting, relating to, or using the German language. **5.** relating to, denoting, or characteristic of any German state or its people.

German cockroach *n.* a small cockroach, *Blattella germanica:* a common household pest. Also called (U.S.): **Croton bug.**

germander (dʒɜː'mændə) *n.* any of several plants of the genus *Teucrium,* esp. *T. chamaedrys* (**wall germander**) of Europe, having two-lipped flowers with a very small upper lip: family *Labiatae* (labiates). [C15: from Medieval Latin *germandrea,* from Late Greek *khamandrua,* from Greek *khamaidrus,* from *khamai* on the ground + *drus* oak tree]

germander speedwell *n.* a creeping scrophulariaceous Eurasian plant, *Veronica chamaedrys,* naturalized in North America, having small bright blue flowers with white centres. Usual U.S. name: **bird's-eye speedwell.**

germane (dʒɜː'meɪn) *adj.* (*postpositive;* usually foll. by *to*) related (to the topic being considered); akin; relevant: *an idea germane to the conversation.* [variant of GERMAN[2]] —**ger'manely** *adv.* —**ger'maneness** *n.*

germanic (dʒɜː'mænɪk) *adj.* of or containing germanium in the tetravalent state.

Germanic (dʒɜː'mænɪk) *n.* **1.** a branch of the Indo-European family of languages that includes English, Dutch, German, the Scandinavian languages, and Gothic. See **East Germanic, West Germanic, North Germanic.** Abbrev.: **Gmc. 2.** the unrecorded language from which all of these languages developed; Proto-Germanic. ~*adj.* **3.** of, denoting, or relating to this group of languages. **4.** of, relating to, or characteristic of Germany, the German language, or any people that speaks a Germanic language.

Germanism ('dʒɜːməˌnɪzəm) *n.* **1.** a word or idiom borrowed from or modelled on German. **2.** a German custom, trait, practice, etc. **3.** attachment to or high regard for German customs, institutions, etc.

germanite ('dʒɜːməˌnaɪt) *n.* a mineral consisting of a complex copper arsenic sulphide containing germanium, gallium, iron, zinc, and lead: an ore of germanium and gallium. [from GERMANIUM + -ITE[1]]

germanium (dʒɜː'meɪnɪəm) *n.* a brittle crystalline grey element that is a semiconducting metalloid, occurring principally in zinc ores and argyrodite: used in transistors, as a catalyst, and to strengthen and harden alloys. Symbol: Ge; atomic no.: 32; atomic wt.: 72.59; valency: 2 or 4; relative density: 5.32; melting pt.: 937.4°C; boiling pt.: 2830°C. [C19: New Latin, named after *Germany*]

Germanize *or* **Germanise** ('dʒɜːməˌnaɪz) *vb.* to adopt or cause to adopt German customs, speech, institutions, etc. —ˌ**Germani'zation** *or* ˌ**Germani'sation** *n.* —'**Germanˌizer** *or* '**Germanˌiser** *n.*

German measles *n.* (*functioning as sing.*) a nontechnical name for **rubella.**

Germanophile (dʒɜː'mænəˌfaɪl) *or* **Germanophil** *n.* a person having admiration for or devotion to Germany and the Germans. —**Germanophilia** (dʒɜːˌmænə'fɪlɪə) *n.*

Germanophobe (dʒɜː'mænəˌfəʊb) *n.* a person who hates Germany or its people. —**Gerˌmano'phobia** *n.*

germanous (dʒɜː'mænəs) *adj.* of or containing germanium in the divalent state.

German shepherd *or* **German shepherd dog** *n.* another name for **Alsatian** (sense 1).

German silver *n.* another name for **nickel silver.**

German sixth *n.* (in musical harmony) an augmented sixth chord having a major third and a perfect fifth between the root and the augmented sixth. Compare **Italian sixth, French sixth.**

germ cell *n.* a sexual reproductive cell; gamete. Compare **somatic cell.**

germen ('dʒɜːmən) *n., pl.* **-mens** *or* **-mina** (-mɪnə). *Biology.* the mass of undifferentiated cells that gives rise to the germ cells. [C17: from Latin; see GERM]

germicide ('dʒɜːmɪˌsaɪd) *n.* any substance that kills germs or other microorganisms. —ˌ**germi'cidal** *adj.*

germinal ('dʒɜːmɪnᵊl) *adj.* **1.** of, relating to, or like germs or a germ cell. **2.** of, or in the earliest stage of development; embryonic. [C19: from New Latin *germinālis,* from Latin *germen* bud; see GERM] —'**germinally** *adv.*

Germinal *French.* (ʒɛrminal) *n.* the month of buds: the seventh month of the French revolutionary calendar, from March 22 to April 20.

germinal vesicle *n. Biology.* the large nucleus of an oocyte before it develops into an ovum.

germinant ('dʒɜːmɪnənt) *adj.* in the process of germinating; sprouting.

germinate ('dʒɜːmɪˌneɪt) *vb.* **1.** to cause (seeds or spores) to sprout or (of seeds or spores) to sprout or form new tissue following increased metabolism. **2.** to grow or cause to grow; develop. **3.** to come or bring into existence; originate: *the idea germinated with me.* [C17: from Latin *germināre* to sprout; see GERM] —'**germinable** *or* '**germinative** *adj.* —ˌ**germi'nation** *n.* —'**germiˌnator** *n.*

germ layer *n. Embryol.* any of the three layers of cells formed during gastrulation. See **ectoderm, mesoderm, endoderm.**

germ line *n.* the lineage of cells culminating in the germ cells.

germ plasm *n.* **1. a.** the part of a germ cell that contains hereditary material; the chromosomes and genes. **b.** the germ cells collectively. Compare **somatoplasm. 2.** (in early theories) a type of protoplasm found only in the germ cells that is transmitted unchanged from generation to generation and gives rise to the body cells.

germ theory *n.* **1.** the theory that all infectious diseases are caused by microorganisms. **2.** the theory that living organisms develop from other living organisms by the growth and differentiation of germ cells.

germ tube *n. Botany.* a tube produced by a germinating spore, such as the pollen tube produced by a pollen grain.

germ warfare *n.* the military use of disease-spreading bacteria against an enemy. Also called: **bacteriological warfare.**

Geronimo (dʒə'rɒnɪˌməʊ) *n. U.S.* a shout given by paratroopers as they jump into battle. [from the name of the Apache Indian chief (1829–1909)]

gerontic (dʒɛ'rɒntɪk) *adj. Biology.* of or relating to the senescence of an organism.

geronto- *or before a vowel* **geront-** *combining form.* indicating old age: *gerontology; gerontophilia.* [from Greek *gerōn, geront-* old man]

gerontocracy (ˌdʒɛrɒn'tɒkrəsɪ) *n., pl.* **-cies. 1.** government by old people. **2.** a governing body of old people. —**gerontocratic** (dʒəˌrɒntə'krætɪk) *adj.*

gerontology (ˌdʒɛrɒn'tɒlədʒɪ) *n.* the scientific study of ageing and the problems associated with elderly people. Compare **geriatrics.** —**gerontological** (ˌdʒɛrɒntə'lɒdʒɪkᵊl) *adj.* —ˌ**geron'tologist** *n.*

-gerous *adj. combining form.* bearing or producing: *armigerous.* Compare **-ferous.** [from Latin *-ger* bearing + -OUS]

gerrymander ('dʒɛrɪˌmændə) *vb.* **1.** to divide the constituencies of (a voting area) so as to give one party an unfair advantage. **2.** to manipulate or adapt to one's advantage. ~*n.* **3.** an act or result of gerrymandering. [C19: from Elbridge *Gerry,* U.S. politician + (SALA)MANDER; from the salamander-like outline of an electoral district reshaped (1812) for political purposes while Gerry was governor of Massachusetts]

gerund ('dʒɛrənd) *n.* a noun formed from a verb, denoting an action or state. In English, the gerund, like the present participle, is formed in *-ing: the living is easy.* [C16: from Late Latin *gerundium,* from Latin *gerundum* something to be carried on, from *gerere* to wage] —**gerundial** (dʒɪ'rʌndɪəl) *adj.*

gerundive (dʒɪ'rʌndɪv) *n.* **1.** (in Latin grammar) an adjective formed from a verb, expressing the desirability of the activity denoted by the verb. ~*adj.* **2.** of or relating to the gerund or gerundive. [C17: from Late Latin *gerundīvus,* from *gerundium* GERUND] —**gerundival** (ˌdʒɛrən'daɪvᵊl) *adj.* —**ge'rundively** *adv.*

gesellschaft (*German* gə'zɛlʃaft) *n., pl.* **-schaften** (*German* -ʃaftən). (*often cap.*) a social group held together by practical concerns, formal and impersonal relationships, etc. Compare **gemeinschaft.** [German, literally: society]

gesneria (gɛs'nɪərɪə) *n.* any plant of the mostly tuberous-rooted S. American genus *Gesneria,* grown as a greenhouse plant for its large leaves and showy tubular flowers in a range of bright colours: family *Gesneriaceae.* [named after Conrad *Gesner,* 1516–65, Swiss naturalist]

gesso ('dʒɛsəʊ) *n.* **1.** a white ground of plaster and size, used esp. in the Middle Ages and Renaissance to prepare panels or canvas for painting or gilding. **2.** any white substance, esp. plaster of Paris, that forms a ground when mixed with water. [C16: from Italian: chalk, GYPSUM]

gest *or* **geste** (dʒɛst) *n. Archaic.* **1.** a notable deed or exploit. **2.** a tale of adventure or romance, esp. in verse. See also **chanson de geste.** [C14: from Old French, from Latin *gesta* deeds, from *gerere* to carry out]

Gestalt (gə'ʃtælt) *n., pl.* **-stalts** *or* **-stalten** (-'ʃtæltən). (*sometimes not cap.*) a perceptual pattern or structure possessing qualities as a whole that cannot be described merely as a sum of its parts. See also **Gestalt psychology.** [C20: German: form, from Old High German *stellen* to shape]

Gestalt psychology *n.* a system of thought, derived from experiments carried out by German psychologists, that regards all mental phenomena as being arranged in gestalts.

Gestalt psychotherapy *n.* a therapy devised in the U.S. in the 1960s in which patients are encouraged to concentrate on the immediate present and to express their true feelings.

Gestapo (gɛˈstɑːpəʊ; *German* geˈʃtaːpo) *n.* the secret state police in Nazi Germany, noted for its brutal methods of interrogation. [from German *Ge(heime) Sta(ats)po(lizei)*, literally: secret state police]

gestate (ˈdʒɛsteɪt) *vb.* **1.** (*tr.*) to carry (developing young) in the uterus during pregnancy. **2.** (*tr.*) to develop (a plan or idea) in the mind. **3.** (*intr.*) to be in the process of gestating. [C19: back formation from GESTATION]

gestation (dʒɛˈsteɪʃən) *n.* **1. a.** the development of the embryo of a viviparous mammal, between conception and birth: about 266 days in humans, 624 days in elephants, and 63 days in cats. **b.** (*as modifier*): *gestation period.* **2.** the development of an idea or plan in the mind. **3.** the period of such a development. [C16: from Latin *gestātiō* a bearing, from *gestāre* to bear, frequentative of *gerere* to carry] —**gesˈtational** *or* **gestative** (ˈdʒɛstətɪv, dʒɛˈsteɪ-) *adj.* —**ˈgestatory** *adj.*

gestatorial chair (ˌdʒɛstəˈtɔːrɪəl) *n.* a ceremonial chair on which the pope is carried.

gesticulate (dʒɛˈstɪkjʊˌleɪt) *vb.* to express by or make gestures. [C17: from Latin *gesticulārī,* from Latin *gesticulus* (unattested except in Late Latin) gesture, diminutive of *gestus* gesture, from *gerere* to bear, conduct] —**gesˈticulative** *adj.* —**gesˈticuˌlator** *n.*

gesticulation (dʒɛˌstɪkjʊˈleɪʃən) *n.* **1.** the act of gesticulating. **2.** an animated or expressive gesture. —**gesˈticulatory** *adj.*

gesture (ˈdʒɛstʃə) *n.* **1.** a motion of the hands, head, or body to emphasize an idea or emotion, esp. while speaking. **2.** something said or done as a formality or as an indication of intention: *a political gesture.* **3.** *Obsolete.* the manner in which a person bears himself; posture. ~*vb.* **4.** to express by or make gestures; gesticulate. [C15: from Medieval Latin *gestūra* bearing, from Latin *gestus,* past participle of *gerere* to bear] —**ˈgestural** *adj.* —**ˈgesturer** *n.*

gesundheit (*German* gəˈzʊnthait) *sentence substitute.* an expression used to wish good health to someone who has just sneezed. [from *gesund* healthy + *-heit* -HOOD; see SOUND[2]]

get (gɛt) *vb.* **gets, getting, got** (gɒt). (*mainly tr.*) **1.** to come into possession of; receive or earn. **2.** to bring or fetch. **3.** to contract or be affected by: *he got a chill at the picnic.* **4.** to capture or seize: *the police finally got him.* **5.** (*also intr.*) to become or cause to become or act as specified: *to get a window open; get one's hair cut; get wet.* **6.** (*intr.;* foll. by a preposition or adverbial particle) to succeed in going, coming, leaving, etc.: *get off the bus.* **7.** (*takes an infinitive*) to manage or contrive: *how did you get to be captain?* **8.** to make ready or prepare: *to get a meal.* **9.** to hear, notice, or understand: *I didn't get your meaning.* **10.** *U.S. and Canadian informal.* to learn or master by study. **11.** (*intr.;* often foll. by *to*) to come (to) or arrive (at): *we got home safely; to get to London.* **12.** to catch or enter: *to get a train.* **13.** to induce or persuade: *get him to leave at once.* **14.** to reach by calculation: *add 2 and 2 and you will get 4.* **15.** to receive (a broadcast signal). **16.** to communicate with (a person or place), as by telephone. **17.** (*also intr.;* foll. by *to*) *Informal.* to have an emotional effect (on): *that music really gets me.* **18.** *Informal.* to annoy or irritate: *her high voice gets me.* **19.** *Informal.* to bring a person into a difficult position from which he cannot escape. **20.** *Informal.* to puzzle; baffle. **21.** *Informal.* to hit: *the blow got him in the back.* **22.** *Informal.* to be revenged on, esp. by killing. **23.** *U.S. slang.* **a.** (foll. by *to*) to gain access (to a person) with the purpose of bribing him. **b.** (often foll. by *to*) to obtain access (to someone) and kill or silence him. **24.** *Informal.* to have the better of: *your extravagant habits will get you in the end.* **25.** (*intr.;* foll. by present participle) *Informal.* to begin: *get moving.* **26.** (used as a command) *Informal.* go! leave now! **27.** *Archaic.* to beget or conceive. **28. get even with.** See **even**[1] (sense 15). **29. get it (in the neck).** *Informal.* to be reprimanded or punished severely. **30. get with it.** *Slang.* to allow oneself to respond to new ideas, styles, etc. **31. get with child.** *Archaic.* to make pregnant. ~*n.* **32.** *Rare.* the act of begetting. **33.** *Rare.* something begotten; offspring. **34.** *Brit. slang.* a variant of **git. 35.** *Informal.* (in tennis) a successful return of a shot that was difficult to reach. ~See also **get about, get across, get ahead, get along, get at, get away, get back, get by, get down, get in, get into, get off, get on, get onto, get out, get over, get round, get through, get-together, get up, got, gotten.** [Old English *gietan;* related to Old Norse *geta* to get, learn, Old High German *bigezzan* to obtain] —**ˈgetable** *or* **ˈgettable** *adj.*

get about *or* **around** *vb.* (*intr., adv.*) **1.** to move around, as when recovering from an illness. **2.** to be socially active. **3.** (of news, rumour, etc.) to become known; spread.

get across *vb.* **1.** to cross or cause or help to cross. **2.** (*adv.*) to be or cause to be readily understood. **3.** (*intr., prep.*) *Informal.* to annoy: *her constant interference really got across him.*

get ahead *vb.* (*intr., adv.*) **1.** to be successful; prosper. **2.** (foll. by *of*) to surpass or excel.

get along *vb.* (*intr., adv.*) **1.** (often foll. by *with*) to be friendly or compatible: *my brother gets along well with everybody.* **2.** to manage, cope, or fare: *how are you getting along in your job?* **3.** (*also prep.; often imperative*) to go or move away; leave. ~*interj.* **4.** *Brit. informal.* an exclamation indicating mild disbelief.

get around *vb.* See **get about, get round.**

get at *vb.* (*intr., prep.*) **1.** to gain access to: *the dog could not get at the meat on the high shelf.* **2.** to mean or intend: *what are you getting at when you look at me like that?* **3.** to irritate or annoy persistently; criticize: *she is always getting at him.* **4.** to influence or seek to influence, esp. illegally by bribery, intimidation, etc.: *someone had got at the witness before the trial.*

get-at-able *adj. Informal.* accessible.

get away *vb.* (*adv., mainly intr.*) **1.** to make an escape; leave. **2.** to make a start. **3. get away with. a.** to steal and escape (with money, goods, etc.). **b.** to do (something wrong, illegal, etc.) without being discovered or punished or with only a minor punishment. ~*interj.* **4.** an exclamation indicating mild disbelief. ~*n.* **getaway. 5.** the act of escaping, esp. by criminals. **6.** a start or acceleration. **7.** (*modifier*) used for escaping: *a getaway car.*

get back *vb.* (*adv.*) **1.** (*tr.*) to recover or retrieve. **2.** (*intr.;* often foll. by *to*) to return, esp. to a former position or activity: *let's get back to the original question.* **3.** (*intr.;* foll. by *at*) to retaliate (against); wreak vengeance (on). **4. get one's own back.** *Informal.* to obtain one's revenge.

get by *vb.* **1.** to pass; go past or overtake. **2.** (*intr., adv.*) *Informal.* to manage, esp. in spite of difficulties: *I can get by with little money.* **3.** (*intr.*) to be accepted or permitted: *that book will never get by the authorities.*

get down *vb.* (*mainly adv.*) **1.** (*intr.; also prep.*) to dismount or descend. **2.** (*tr.; also prep.*) to bring down: *we could not get the wardrobe down the stairs.* **3.** (*tr.*) to write down. **4.** (*tr.*) to make depressed: *your nagging gets me down.* **5.** (*tr.*) to swallow: *he couldn't get the meal down.* **6.** (*intr.;* foll. by *to*) to attend seriously (to); concentrate (on) (esp. in the phrases **get down to business** *or* **brass tacks**). **7.** (*intr.*) *Informal, chiefly U.S.* to enjoy oneself uninhibitedly, esp. by dancing.

get in *vb.* (*mainly adv.*) **1.** (*intr.*) to enter a car, train, etc. **2.** (*intr.*) to arrive, esp. at one's home or place of work: *I got in at midnight.* **3.** (*tr.*) to bring in or inside: *get the milk in.* **4.** (*tr.*) to insert or slip in: *he got his suggestion in before anyone else.* **5.** (*tr.*) to gather or collect (crops, debts, etc.). **6.** (*tr.*) to ask (a person, esp. a specialist) to give a service: *shall I get the doctor in?* **7.** to be elected or cause to be elected: *he got in by 400 votes.* **8.** (*tr.*) to succeed in doing (something), esp. during a specified period: *I doubt if I can get this task in today.* **9.** (*intr.*) to obtain a place at university, college, etc. **10.** (foll. by *on*) to join or cause to join (an activity or organization). **11. get in with.** to be or cause to be on friendly terms with (a person). **12.** (*prep.*) See **get into.** ~*n.* **get-in. 13.** *Theatre.* the process of moving into a theatre the scenery, props, and costumes for a production.

get into *vb.* (*prep.*) **1.** (*intr.*) to enter. **2.** (*intr.*) to reach (a destination): *the train got into London at noon.* **3.** to get dressed in (clothes). **4.** (*intr.*) to preoccupy or obsess (a person's emotions or thoughts): *what's got into him tonight?* **5.** to assume or cause to assume (a specified condition, habit, etc.): *to get into debt; get a person into a mess.* **6.** to be elected to or cause to be elected to: *to get into Parliament.* **7.** (*usually intr.*) *Informal.* to become or cause to become familiar with (a skill): *once you get into driving you'll enjoy it.* **8.** (*usually intr.*) *Informal.* to develop or cause to develop an absorbing interest in (a hobby, subject, or book).

get off *vb.* **1.** (*intr., adv.*) to escape the consequences of an action: *he got off very lightly in the accident.* **2.** (*adv.*) to be or cause to be acquitted: *a good lawyer got him off.* **3.** (*adv.*) to depart or cause to depart: *to get the children off to school.* **4.** (*intr.*) to descend (from a bus, train, etc.); dismount: *she got off at the terminus.* **5.** to move or cause to move to a distance (from): *get off the field.* **6.** (*tr., adv.*) to remove; take off: *get your coat off.* **7.** (*adv.*) to go or send to sleep. **8.** (*adv.*) to send (letters) or (of letters) to be sent. **9.** (*intr., adv.*) *Slang.* to become high on or as on heroin or some other drug. **10. get off with.** *Brit. informal.* to establish an amorous or sexual relationship with. **11. tell (someone) where to get off.** *Informal.* to rebuke or criticize harshly.

get on *vb.* (*mainly adv.*) **1.** Also (when *prep.*): **get onto.** to board or cause or help to board (a bus, train, etc.). **2.** (*tr.*) to dress in (clothes as specified). **3.** (*intr.*) to grow late or (of time) to elapse: *it's getting on and I must go.* **4.** (*intr.*) (of a person) to grow old. **5.** (*intr.;* foll. by *for*) to approach (a time, age, amount, etc.): *she is getting on for seventy.* **6.** (*intr.*) to make progress, manage, or fare: *how did you get on in your exam?* **7.** (*intr.;* often foll. by *with*) to establish a friendly relationship: *he gets on well with other people.* **8.** (*intr.;* foll. by *with*) to continue to do: *get on with your homework!* ~*interj.* **9.** I don't believe you!

get onto *vb.* (*prep.*) **1.** Also: **get on.** to board or cause or help to board (a bus, train, etc.). **2.** (*intr.*) to make contact with; communicate with. **3.** (*intr.*) to become aware of (something illicit or secret): *the boss will get onto their pilfering unless they're careful.* **4.** (*intr.*) to deliver a demand, request, or rebuke to: *I'll get onto the manufacturers to replace these damaged goods.* See usage note at **onto.**

get out *vb.* (*adv.*) **1.** to leave or escape or cause to leave or escape: used in the imperative when dismissing a person. **2.** to make or become known; publish or be published. **3.** (*tr.*) to express with difficulty. **4.** (*tr.*; often foll. by *of*) to extract (information or money) (from a person): *to get a confession out of a criminal.* **5.** (*tr.*) to gain or receive something, esp. something of significance or value: *you get out of life what you put into it.* **6.** (foll. by *of*) to avoid or cause to avoid: *she always gets out of swimming.* **7.** (*tr.*) to solve (a puzzle or problem) successfully. **8.** *Cricket.* to dismiss or be dismissed. ~*n.* **get-out. 9.** an escape, as from a difficult situation. **10.** *Theatre.* the process of moving out of a theatre the scenery, props, and costumes after a production.

get over *vb.* **1.** to cross or surmount (something): *get the children over the fence.* **2.** (*intr., prep.*) to recover from (an illness, shock, etc.). **3.** (*intr., prep.*) to overcome or master (a problem): *you'll soon get over your shyness.* **4.** (*intr., prep.*) to appreciate fully: *I just can't get over seeing you again.* **5.** (*tr., adv.*) to communicate effectively: *he had difficulty getting the message over.* **6.** (*tr., adv.*; sometimes foll. by *with*) to bring (something necessary but unpleasant) to an end: *let's get this job over with quickly.*

get round *or* **around** *vb.* (*intr.*) **1.** (*prep.*) to circumvent or overcome: *he got round the problem by an ingenious trick.* **2.** (*prep.*) *Informal.* to have one's way with; cajole: *that girl can get round anyone.* **3.** (*prep.*) to evade (a law or rules). **4.** (*adv.*; foll. by *to*) to reach or come to at length: *I'll get round to that job in an hour.*

getter ('gɛtə) *n.* **1.** a person or thing that gets. **2.** a substance, usually a metal such as titanium, evaporated onto the walls of a vacuum tube, vessel, etc., to adsorb the residual gas and lower the pressure. ~*vb.* **3.** (*tr.*) to remove (a gas) by the action of a getter.

get through *vb.* **1.** to succeed or cause or help to succeed in an examination, test, etc. **2.** to bring or come to a destination, esp. after overcoming problems: *we got through the blizzards to the survivors.* **3.** (*intr., adv.*) to contact, as by telephone. **4.** (*intr., prep.*) to use, spend, or consume (money, supplies, etc.). **5.** to complete or cause to complete (a task, process, etc.): *to get a bill through Parliament.* **6.** (*adv.*; foll. by *to*) to reach the awareness and understanding (of a person): *I just can't get the message through to him.* **7.** (*intr., adv.*) *U.S. slang.* to obtain drugs.

get-together *n.* **1.** *Informal.* a small informal meeting or social gathering. ~*vb.* **get together.** (*adv.*) **2.** (*tr.*) to gather or collect. **3.** (*intr.*) (of people) to meet socially. **4.** (*intr.*) to discuss, esp. in order to reach an agreement. **5. get it together.** *Informal.* **a.** to achieve one's full potential, either generally as a person or in a particular field of activity. **b.** to achieve a harmonious frame of mind.

get up *vb.* (*mainly adv.*) **1.** to wake and rise from one's bed or cause to wake and rise from bed. **2.** (*intr.*) to rise to one's feet; stand up. **3.** (*also prep.*) to ascend or cause to ascend: *the old van couldn't get up the hill.* **4.** to mount or help to mount (a bicycle, horse, etc.). **5.** to increase or cause to increase in strength: *the wind got up at noon.* **6.** (*tr.*) *Informal.* to dress (oneself) in a particular way, esp. showily or elaborately. **7.** (*tr.*) *Informal.* to devise or create: *to get up an entertainment for Christmas.* **8.** (*tr.*) *Informal.* to study or improve one's knowledge of: *I must get up my history.* **9.** (*intr.*; foll. by *to*) *Informal.* to be involved in: *he's always getting up to mischief.* **10.** (*intr.*) *Austral. informal.* to win, esp. in a sporting event. ~*n.* **get-up. 11.** *Informal.* a costume or outfit, esp. one that is striking or bizarre. **12.** *Informal.* the arrangement or production of a book, etc.

get-up-and-go *n. Informal.* energy, drive, or ambition.

geum ('dʒiːəm) *n.* any herbaceous plant of the rosaceous genus *Geum,* having compound leaves and red, orange, yellow, or white flowers. See also **avens.** [C19: New Latin, from Latin: herb bennet, avens]

GeV *abbrev. for* giga-electronvolts (10^9 electronvolts). Sometimes written (esp. U.S. and Canadian) **BeV** (billion electronvolts).

gewgaw ('gjuːgɔː, 'guː-) *n.* **1.** a showy but valueless trinket. ~*adj.* **2.** showy and valueless; gaudy. [C15: of unknown origin]

Gewürztraminer (gə'vuətstrəˌmiːnə; *German* gə'vyrtstraˌmiːnər) *n.* **1.** a white grape grown in Alsace, Germany, and elsewhere, used for making wine. **2.** any of various fragrant white wines made from this grape. [German, from *Gewürz* spice, seasoning + *Traminer* a variety of grape first grown in the *Tramin* area of the South Tyrol]

gey (gaɪ; *Scot.* gəɪ) *adv. Scot. and Northumberland dialect.* (intensifier): *it's gey cold.* [variant of GAY]

geyser ('giːzə; *U.S.* 'gaɪzər) *n.* **1.** a spring that discharges steam and hot water. **2.** *Brit.* a domestic gas water heater. [C18: from Icelandic *Geysir,* from Old Norse *geysa* to gush]

geyserite ('giːzəˌraɪt) *n.* a mineral form of hydrated silica resembling opal, deposited from the waters of geysers and hot springs. Formula: $SiO_2.nH_2O$.

G-force *n.* the force of gravity.

GG *abbrev. for:* **1.** Girl Guides. **2.** Governor General.

GH *international car registration for* Ghana.

Ghan (gæn) *n. Austral.* short for **Afghan** (sense 3).

Ghanaian (gɑː'neɪən) *or* **Ghanian** ('gɑːnɪən) *adj.* **1.** of or relating to Ghana, a republic in W Africa, or its people. ~*n.* **2.** a native or inhabitant of Ghana.

gharial ('gærɪəl) *n.* another name for for **gavial.**

gharry *or* **gharri** ('gærɪ) *n., pl.* **-ries.** (in India) a horse-drawn vehicle available for hire. [C19: from Hindi *gārī*]

ghastly ('gɑːstlɪ) *adj.* **-lier, -liest. 1.** *Informal.* very bad or unpleasant. **2.** deathly pale; wan. **3.** *Informal.* extremely unwell; ill: *they felt ghastly the day after the party.* **4.** terrifying; horrible. ~*adv.* **5.** unhealthily; sickly: *ghastly pale.* **6.** *Archaic.* in a horrible or hideous manner. [Old English *gāstlīc* spiritual; see GHOSTLY] —'**ghastliness** *n.*

ghat (gɔːt) *n.* (in India) **1.** stairs or a passage leading down to a river. **2.** a mountain pass or mountain range. [C17: from Hindi *ghāt,* from Sanskrit *ghatta*]

ghaut (gʌt) *n. Caribbean.* a small cleft in a hill through which a rivulet runs down to the sea. [C17 *gaot,* a mountain pass, from Hindi: GHAT]

ghazi ('gɑːzɪ) *n., pl.* **-zis. 1.** a Muslim fighter against infidels. **2.** (*often cap.*) a Turkish warrior of high rank. [C18: from Arabic, from *ghazā* he made war]

Gheber *or* **Ghebre** ('geɪbə, 'giː-) *n.* other words for **Gabar.**

ghee (giː) *n.* butter, clarified by boiling, used in Indian cookery. [C17: from Hindi *ghī,* from Sanskrit *ghri* sprinkle]

gherao (gɛ'raʊ) *n.* a form of industrial action in India in which workers imprison their employers on the premises until their demands are met. [from Hindi *gherna* to besiege]

gherkin ('gɜːkɪn) *n.* **1.** the small immature fruit of any of various cucumbers, used for pickling. **2. a.** a tropical American cucurbitaceous climbing plant, *Cucumis anguria.* **b.** the small spiny edible fruit of this plant. [C17: from early modern Dutch *agurkkijn,* diminutive of *gurk,* from Slavonic, ultimately from Greek *angourion*]

ghetto ('gɛtəʊ) *n., pl.* **-tos** *or* **-toes. 1.** *Sociol.* a densely populated slum area of a city inhabited by a socially and economically deprived minority. **2.** an area in a European city in which Jews were formerly required to live. **3.** a group or class of people that is segregated in some way. [C17: from Italian, perhaps shortened from *borghetto,* diminutive of *borgo* settlement outside a walled city; or from the Venetian *ghetto* the medieval iron-founding district, largely inhabited by Jews]

ghetto blaster *n. Informal.* a large portable cassette recorder with built-in speakers.

Ghibelline ('gɪbɪˌlaɪn, -ˌliːn) *n.* **1.** a member of the political faction in medieval Italy originally based on support for the German emperor. **2.** (*modifier*) of or relating to the Ghibellines. Compare **Guelph.** [C16: from Italian *Ghibellino,* probably from Middle High German *Waiblingen,* a Hohenstaufen estate] —'**Ghibelˌlinism** *n.*

ghibli *or* **gibli** ('gɪblɪ) *n.* a fiercely hot wind of North Africa. [C20: from Arabic *gibliy* south wind]

ghillie ('gɪlɪ) *n.* **1.** a type of tongueless shoe with lacing up the instep, originally worn by the Scots. **2.** a variant spelling of **gillie.** [from Scottish Gaelic *gille* boy]

ghost (gəʊst) *n.* **1.** the disembodied spirit of a dead person, supposed to haunt the living as a pale or shadowy vision; phantom. Related adj.: **spectral. 2.** a haunting memory: *the ghost of his former life rose up before him.* **3.** a faint trace or possibility of something; glimmer: *a ghost of a smile.* **4.** the spirit; soul (archaic, except in the phrase **the Holy Ghost**). **5.** *Physics.* **a.** a faint secondary image produced by an optical system. **b.** a similar image on a television screen, formed by reflection of the transmitting waves or by a defect in the receiver. **6.** See **ghost word. 7.** Also called: **ghost edition.** an entry recorded in a bibliography of which no actual proof exists. **8.** See **ghostwriter. 9.** (*modifier*) falsely recorded as doing a particular job or fulfilling a particular function in order that some benefit, esp. money, may be obtained: *a ghost worker.* **10. give up the ghost.** to die. ~*vb.* **11.** See **ghostwrite. 12.** (*tr.*) to haunt. [Old English *gāst;* related to Old Frisian *jēst,* Old High German *geist* spirit, Sanskrit *hēda* fury, anger] —'**ghostˌlike** *adj.*

ghost dance *n.* a religious dance of certain North American Indians, connected with a political movement (from about 1888) that looked to reunion with the dead and a return to an idealized state of affairs before Europeans came.

ghost gum *n. Austral.* a eucalyptus tree with white trunk and branches.

ghostly ('gəʊstlɪ) *adj.* **-lier, -liest. 1.** of or resembling a ghost; spectral: *a ghostly face appeared at the window.* **2.** suggesting the presence of ghosts; eerie. **3.** *Archaic.* of or relating to the soul or spirit. —'**ghostliness** *n.*

ghost moth *n.* any of various large pale moths of the family *Hepialidae* that are active at dusk.

ghost town *n.* a deserted town, esp. one in the western U.S. that was formerly a boom town.

ghost word *n.* a word that has entered the language through the perpetuation, in dictionaries, etc., of an error.

ghostwrite ('gəʊstˌraɪt) *vb.* **-writes, -writing, -wrote, -written.** to write (an autobiographical or other article) on behalf of a person who is then credited as author. Often shortened to **ghost.** —'**ghostˌwriter** *n.*

ghoul (guːl) *n.* **1.** a malevolent spirit or ghost. **2.** a person interested in morbid or disgusting things. **3.** a person who robs graves. **4.** (in Muslim legend) an evil demon thought to eat human bodies, either stolen corpses or children. [C18: from Arabic *ghūl,* from *ghāla* he seized] —'**ghoulish** *adj.* —'**ghoulishly** *adv.* —'**ghoulishness** *n.*

GHQ *Military. abbrev. for* General Headquarters.
ghyll (gɪl) *n.* a variant spelling of **gill**[3].
Gi *Electronics. abbrev. for* gilbert.
GI[1] *n. U.S. informal.* 1. (*pl.* **GIs** *or* **GI's**). a soldier in the U.S. Army, esp. an enlisted man. ~*adj.* 2. conforming to U.S. Army regulations; of standard government issue. [C20: abbrev. of *government issue*]
GI[2] *or* **g.i.** *abbrev. for* gastrointestinal.
gi. *abbrev. for* gill (unit of measure).
giant (ˈdʒaɪənt) *n.* 1. Also (fem.): **giantess** (ˈdʒaɪəntɪs). a mythical figure of superhuman size and strength, esp. in folklore or fairy tales. 2. a person or thing of exceptional size, reputation, etc.: *a giant in the world of nuclear physics.* 3. *Pathol.* a person suffering from gigantism. 4. *Astronomy.* See **giant star.** 5. *Mining.* another word for **monitor** (sense 7). ~*adj.* 6. remarkably or supernaturally large. 7. *Architect.* another word for **colossal.** [C13: from Old French *geant,* from Vulgar Latin *gagās* (unattested), from Latin *gigant-, gigās,* from Greek] —ˈ**giant-ˌlike** *adj.*
giant cell *n. Histology.* an exceptionally large cell, often possessing several nuclei, such as an osteoclast.
giant hogweed *n.* an umbelliferous garden escape, *Heracleum mantegazzianum,* a tall species of cow parsley that grows up to 3½ metres (10 ft.) and whose irritant hairs and sap can cause a severe reaction if handled. Also called: **cartwheel flower.**
giantism (ˈdʒaɪənˌtɪzəm) *n.* another term for **gigantism.**
giant killer *n.* a person, sports team, etc., that defeats an apparently superior opponent.
giant panda *n.* See **panda** (sense 1).
giant peacock moth *n.* the largest European moth, an emperor, *Saturnia pyri,* reaching 15 cm (6 in.) in wingspan. It is mottled brown with a prominent ocellus on each wing and being night-flying can be mistaken for a bat.
giant planet *n.* any of the planets Jupiter, Saturn, Uranus, and Neptune, characterized by enormous mass, low density, and an extensive atmosphere.
giant powder *n.* dynamite composed of trinitroglycerin absorbed in kieselguhr.
giant slalom *n. Skiing.* a type of slalom in which the course is longer and the obstacles are further apart than in a standard slalom.
giant star *n.* any of a class of very bright stars, such as Capella and Arcturus, having an absolute magnitude between +2 and –2, a diameter up to 100 times that of the sun, and an extremely low mean density. Sometimes shortened to **giant.** Compare **supergiant.**
giant tortoise *n.* any of various very large tortoises of the genus *Testudo,* of the Galápagos, Seychelles, and certain other islands, weighing up to 225 kilograms (495 lbs.).
giaour (ˈdʒaʊə) *n.* a derogatory term for a non-Muslim, esp. a Christian, used esp. by the Turks. [C16: from Turkish *giaur* unbeliever, from Persian *gaur,* variant of *gäbr*]
giardiasis (ˌdʒaɪɑːˈdaɪəsɪs) *n.* infection with the parasitic protozoan *Giardia lamblia,* which may cause severe diarrhoea, nausea, etc.
gib[1] (gɪb) *n.* 1. a metal wedge, pad, or thrust bearing, esp. a brass plate let into a steam engine crosshead. ~*vb.* **gibs, gibbing, gibbed.** 2. (*tr.*) to fasten or supply with a gib. [C18: of unknown origin]
gib[2] (gɪb) *n.* a male cat, esp. a castrated one. [C14: probably a shortening and alteration of the proper name *Gilbert*]
gibber[1] (ˈdʒɪbə) *vb.* 1. to utter rapidly and unintelligibly; prattle. 2. (*intr.*) (of monkeys and related animals) to make characteristic chattering sounds. ~*n.* 3. a less common word for **gibberish.** [C17: of imitative origin]
gibber[2] (ˈdʒɪbə) *n. Austral.* 1. a stone or boulder. 2. (*modifier*) of or relating to a dry flat area of land covered with wind-polished stones: *gibber plains.* [C19: from a native Australian language]
gibberellic acid (ˌdʒɪbəˈrɛlɪk) *n.* a slightly soluble crystalline hormone extracted from fungi and other plants: a giberellin. Formula: $C_{19}H_{22}O_6$.
gibberellin (ˌdʒɪbəˈrɛlɪn) *n.* any of several plant hormones isolated from the fungus *Gibberella fujikuroi,* whose main action is to cause elongation of the stem: used in promoting the growth of plants, in the malting of barley, etc. [C20: from New Latin *Gibberella,* literally: a little hump, from Latin *gibber* hump + -IN]
gibberish (ˈdʒɪbərɪʃ) *n.* 1. rapid chatter like that of monkeys. 2. incomprehensible talk; nonsense.
gibbet (ˈdʒɪbɪt) *n.* 1. a. a wooden structure resembling a gallows, from which the bodies of executed criminals were formerly hung to public view. b. a gallows. ~*vb.* (*tr.*) 2. to put to death by hanging on a gibbet. 3. to hang (a corpse) on a gibbet. 4. to expose to public ridicule. [C13: from Old French *gibet* gallows, literally: little cudgel, from *gibe* cudgel; of uncertain origin]
Gib board *n. N.Z. informal.* short for **Gibraltar board.**
gibbon (ˈgɪbᵊn) *n.* any small agile arboreal anthropoid ape of the genus *Hylobates,* inhabiting forests in S Asia. [C18: from French, probably from an Indian dialect word]
gibbosity (gɪˈbɒsɪtɪ) *n., pl.* **-ties.** *Rare.* 1. the state of being gibbous. 2. *Biology.* a bulge or protuberance.
gibbous (ˈgɪbəs) *or* **gibbose** (ˈgɪbəʊs) *adj.* 1. (of the moon or a planet) more than half but less than fully illuminated. 2. having a hunchback; hunchbacked. 3. bulging. [C17: from Late Latin *gibbōsus* humpbacked, from Latin *gibba* hump] —ˈ**gibbously** *adv.* —ˈ**gibbousness** *n.*
Gibbs function (gɪbz) *n.* a thermodynamic property of a system equal to the difference between its enthalpy and the product of its temperature and its entropy. It is usually measured in joules. Symbol: *G* or (esp. U.S.) *F* Also called: **Gibbs free energy, free enthalpy.** Compare **Helmholtz function.** [C19: named after Josiah *Gibbs* (1839–1903), U.S. physicist]
gibbsite (ˈgɪbzaɪt) *n.* a mineral consisting of hydrated aluminium oxide: a constituent of bauxite and a source of alumina. Formula: $Al(OH)_3$. [C19: named after George *Gibbs* (died 1833), American mineralogist]
gibe[1] *or* **jibe** (dʒaɪb) *vb.* 1. to make jeering or scoffing remarks (at); taunt. ~*n.* 2. a derisive or provoking remark. [C16: perhaps from Old French *giber* to treat roughly, of uncertain origin] —ˈ**giber** *or* ˈ**jiber** *n.* —ˈ**gibingly** *or* ˈ**jibingly** *adv.*
gibe[2] (dʒaɪb) *vb., n. Nautical.* a variant spelling of **gybe.**
giblets (ˈdʒɪblɪts) *pl. n.* (*sometimes sing.*) the gizzard, liver, heart, and neck of a fowl. [C14: from Old French *gibelet* stew of game birds, probably from *gibier* game, of Germanic origin]
gibli (ˈgɪblɪ) *n.* a variant spelling of **ghibli.**
Gibraltar board (dʒɪˈbrɔːltə) *n. N.Z. trademark.* a type of lining board with a cardboard surface and a gypsum core.
Gibraltarian (ˌdʒɪbrɔːlˈtɛərɪən) *adj.* 1. of or relating to Gibraltar, a British crown colony at the tip of S Spain, or its inhabitants. ~*n.* 2. a native or inhabitant of Gibraltar.
Gibson (ˈgɪbsᵊn) *n. Chiefly U.S.* a cocktail consisting of four or more parts dry gin and one part dry vermouth, iced and served with a pickled pearl onion.
Gibson girl *n.* the ideal fashionable American girl of the late 1890s and early 1900s, as portrayed in the drawings of Charles Dana *Gibson,* 1867–1944, U.S. illustrator.
gibus (ˈdʒaɪbəs) *n.* another name for **opera hat.** [C19: named after *Gibus,* 19th-century Frenchman who invented it]
gid (gɪd) *n.* a disease of sheep characterized by an unsteady gait and staggering, caused by infestation of the brain with tapeworms (*Taenia caenuris*). [C17: back formation from GIDDY]
giddap (gɪˈdæp) *or* **giddy-up** (ˌgɪdɪˈʌp) *interj.* an exclamation used to make a horse go faster. [C20: colloquial form of *get up*]
gidday (gəˈdaɪ) *sentence substitute.* an Australian and N.Z. informal variant of **good day.**
giddy (ˈgɪdɪ) *adj.* **-dier, -diest.** 1. affected with a reeling sensation and feeling as if about to fall; dizzy. 2. causing or tending to cause vertigo. 3. impulsive; scatterbrained. 4. **my giddy aunt.** an exclamation of surprise. ~*vb.* **-dies, -dying, -died.** 5. to make or become giddy. [Old English *gydig* mad, frenzied, possessed by God; related to GOD] —ˈ**giddily** *adv.* —ˈ**giddiness** *n.*
Gideon Bible (ˈgɪdɪən) *n.* a Bible purchased by members of a Christian organization (**Gideons**) and placed in a hotel room, hospital ward, etc.
gidgee *or* **gidjee** (ˈgɪdʒiː) *n. Austral.* a small acacia tree, *Acacia cambagei,* yielding useful timber. [C19: from a native Australian language]
gie (giː) *vb.* a Scot. word for **give.**
gift (gɪft) *n.* 1. something given; a present. 2. a special aptitude, ability, or power; talent. 3. the power or right to give or bestow (esp. in the phrases **in the gift of, in (someone's) gift**). 4. the act or process of giving. 5. **look a gift-horse in the mouth.** (*usually negative*) to find fault with a free gift or chance benefit. ~*vb.* (*tr.*) 6. to present (something) as a gift to (a person). 7. *Rare.* to endow with; bestow. [Old English *gift* payment for a wife, dowry; related to Old Norse *gipt,* Old High German *gift,* Gothic *fragifts* endowment, engagement; see GIVE] —ˈ**giftless** *adj.*
GIFT (gɪft) *n. acronym for* gamete intrafallopian transfer: a technique, similar to in vitro fertilization, that enables some women who are unable to conceive to bear children. Egg cells are removed from the woman's ovary, mixed with sperm, and introduced into one of her Fallopian tubes.
gifted (ˈgɪftɪd) *adj.* having or showing natural talent or aptitude: *a gifted musician; a gifted performance.* —ˈ**giftedly** *adv.* —ˈ**giftedness** *n.*
gift of tongues *n.* an utterance, partly or wholly unintelligible, produced under the influence of ecstatic religious emotion and conceived to be a manifestation of the Holy Ghost: practised in certain Christian churches, usually called Pentecostal. Also called: **glossolalia.**
gift tax *n.* another name for **capital transfer tax.**
giftwrap (ˈgɪftˌræp) *vb.* **-wraps, -wrapping, -wrapped.** to wrap (an article intended as a gift) attractively.
gig[1] (gɪg) *n.* 1. a light two-wheeled one-horse carriage without a hood. 2. *Nautical.* a light tender for a vessel, often for the personal use of the captain. 3. a long light rowing boat, used esp. for racing. 4. a machine for raising the nap of a fabric. ~*vb.* **gigs, gigging, gigged.** 5. (*intr.*) to travel in a gig. 6. (*tr.*). to raise the nap of (fabric). [C13 (in the sense: flighty girl, spinning top): perhaps of Scandinavian origin; compare Danish *gig* top, Norwegian *giga* to shake about]
gig[2] (gɪg) *n.* 1. a cluster of barbless hooks drawn through a shoal of fish to try to impale them. 2. short for **fishgig.** ~*vb.* **gigs,**

gigging, gigged. **3.** to catch (fish) with a gig. [C18: shortened from FISHGIG]

gig[3] (gɪg) *Informal.* ~*n.* **1.** a job, esp. a single booking for jazz or pop musicians to play at a concert or club. **2.** the performance itself. ~*vb.* **gigs, gigging, gigged.** (*intr.*) **3.** to perform at a gig or gigs. [C20: of unknown origin]

giga- *combining form.* **1.** denoting 10^9: *gigavolt.* Symbol: G **2.** (in computer technology) denoting 2^{30}: *gigabyte.* [from Greek *gigas* GIANT]

gigabyte (ˈgaɪgəˌbaɪt) *n. Computer technol.* one thousand and twenty-four megabytes. See also **giga-** (sense 2).

gigaflop (ˈgaɪgəˌflɒp) *n. Computer technol.* a measure of processing speed, consisting of a thousand million floating-point operations a second. [C20: from GIGA- + *flo(ating) p(oint)*]

gigahertz (ˈgaɪgəˌhɜːts, ˈdʒɪg-) *n., pl.* **-hertz.** a unit of frequency equal to 10^9 hertz. Symbol: GHz

gigantic (dʒaɪˈgæntɪk) *adj.* **1.** very large; enormous: *a gigantic error.* **2.** Also: **gigantesque** (ˌdʒaɪgænˈtɛsk). of or suitable for giants. [C17: from Greek *gigantikos,* from *gigas* GIANT] —**giˈgantically** *adv.* —**giˈganticness** *n.*

gigantism (ˈdʒaɪgænˌtɪzəm, dʒaɪˈgæntɪzəm) *n.* **1.** Also called: **giantism.** excessive growth of the entire body, caused by overproduction of growth hormone by the pituitary gland during childhood or adolescence. Compare **acromegaly.** **2.** the state or quality of being gigantic.

gigantomachy (ˌdʒaɪgænˈtɒməkɪ) *or* **gigantomachia** (dʒaɪˌgæntəʊˈmeɪkɪə) *n., pl.* **-chies** or **-chias.** any battle fought between or as if between giants. [C17: from Greek *gigantomakhia,* from *gigas* giant + *makhē* battle]

giggle (ˈgɪgᵊl) *vb.* **1.** (*intr.*) to laugh nervously or foolishly. ~*n.* **2.** such a laugh. **3.** *Informal.* something or someone that provokes amusement. **4. the giggles.** a fit of prolonged and uncontrollable giggling. **5. for a giggle.** *Informal.* as a joke or prank; not seriously. [C16: of imitative origin] —**ˈgiggler** *n.* —**ˈgiggling** *n., adj.* —**ˈgigglingly** *adv.* —**ˈgiggly** *adj.*

giggle house *n. Austral. slang.* a mental hospital.

gig-lamps *pl. n.* an old-fashioned slang term for **spectacles.**

GIGO (ˈgaɪgəʊ) *n. Slang. Computer technol. acronym for* garbage in, garbage out.

gigolo (ˈʒɪgəˌləʊ) *n., pl.* **-los. 1.** a man who is kept by a woman, esp. an older woman. **2.** a man who is paid to dance with or escort women. [C20: from French, back formation from *gigolette* girl for hire as a dancing partner, prostitute, from *giguer* to dance, from *gigue* a fiddle; compare GIGOT, GIGUE, JIG]

gigot (ˈʒiːgəʊ, ˈdʒɪgət) *n.* **1.** a leg of lamb or mutton. **2.** a leg-of-mutton sleeve. [C16: from Old French: leg, a small fiddle, from *gigue* a fiddle, of Germanic origin]

gigue (ʒiːg) *n.* **1.** a piece of music, usually in six-eight time and often fugal, incorporated into the classical suite. **2.** a formal couple dance of the 16th and 17th centuries, derived from the jig. [C17: from French, from Italian *giga,* literally: a fiddle; see GIGOT]

GI Joe *n. U.S. informal.* a U.S. enlisted soldier; a GI.

Gila monster (ˈhiːlə) *n.* a large venomous brightly coloured lizard, *Heloderma suspectum,* inhabiting deserts of the southwestern U.S. and Mexico and feeding mostly on eggs and small mammals: family *Helodermatidae.*

gilbert (ˈgɪlbət) *n.* a unit of magnetomotive force; the magnetomotive force resulting from the passage of 4π abamperes through one turn of a coil. 1 gilbert is equivalent to $10/4\pi = 0.795\,775$ ampere-turn. Symbols: Gb or Gi [C19: named after William *Gilbert* (1540–1603), English physician and scientist]

Gilbertian (gɪlˈbɜːtɪən) *adj.* characteristic of or resembling the style or whimsical humour of the British librettist Sir W. S. Gilbert (1836–1911).

Gilbertine (ˈgɪlbətaɪn, -tɪn) *n.* **1.** a member of a Christian order founded in approximately 1135 by St Gilbert of Sempringham, composed of nuns who followed the Cistercian rule and Augustinian canons who ministered to them. It was the only religious order of English origin and never spread to Europe. ~*adj.* **2.** of, relating to, or belonging to this order.

gild[1] (gɪld) *vb.* **gilds, gilding, gilded** *or* **gilt** (gɪlt). (*tr.*) **1.** to cover with or as if with gold. **2. gild the lily. a.** to adorn unnecessarily something already beautiful. **b.** to praise someone inordinately. **3.** to give a falsely attractive or valuable appearance to. **4.** *Archaic.* to smear with blood. [Old English *gyldan,* from *gold* GOLD; related to Old Norse *gylla,* Middle High German *vergülden*] —**ˈgilder** *n.*

gild[2] (gɪld) *n.* a variant spelling of **guild** (sense 2). —**ˈgildsman** *n.*

gilder (ˈgɪldə) *n.* a variant spelling of **guilder.**

gilding (ˈgɪldɪŋ) *n.* **1.** the act or art of applying gilt to a surface. **2.** the surface so produced. **3.** another word for **gilt**[1] (sense 2).

gilet (dʒɪˈleɪ) *n.* **1.** a waist- or hip-length garment, usually sleeveless, fastening up the front; sometimes made from a quilted fabric, and designed to be worn over a blouse, shirt, etc. **2.** a bodice resembling a waistcoat in a woman's dress. **3.** such a bodice as part of a ballet dancer's costume. [C19: French, literally: waistcoat]

gilgai (ˈgɪlgaɪ) *n. Austral.* a natural water hole. [C19: from a native Australian language]

gill[1] (gɪl) *n.* **1.** the respiratory organ in many aquatic animals, consisting of a membrane or outgrowth well supplied with blood vessels. **External gills** occur in tadpoles, some molluscs, etc.; **internal gills,** within gill slits, occur in most fishes. **2.** any of the radiating leaflike spore-producing structures on the undersurface of the cap of a mushroom. ~*vb.* **3.** to catch (fish) or (of fish) to be caught in a gill net. **4.** (*tr.*) to gut (fish). ~See also **gills.** [C14: of Scandinavian origin; compare Swedish *gäl,* Danish *gjælle,* Greek *khelunē* lip] —**gilled** *adj.* —**ˈgill-less** *adj.* —**ˈgill-ˌlike** *adj.*

gill[2] (dʒɪl) *n.* **1.** a unit of liquid measure equal to one quarter of a pint. **2.** *Northern Brit. dialect.* half a pint, esp. of beer. [C14: from Old French *gille* vat, tub, from Late Latin *gillō* cooling vessel for liquids, of obscure origin]

gill[3] *or* **ghyll** (gɪl) *n. Dialect.* **1.** a narrow stream; rivulet. **2.** a wooded ravine. **3.** (*cap. when part of place name*) a deep natural hole in rock; pothole: *Gaping Gill.* [C11: from Old Norse *gil* steep-sided valley]

gill[4] (dʒɪl) *n.* **1.** *Archaic.* a girl or sweetheart. **2.** *Dialect.* Also spelt: **jill.** a female ferret. **3.** an archaic or dialect name for **ground ivy.** [C15: special use of *Gill,* short for *Gillian,* girl's name]

Gilles de la Tourette syndrome (dʒiːl də læ tʊəˈrɛt) *n.* another name for **Tourette syndrome.**

gill fungus (gɪl) *n.* any fungus of the basidiomycetous family *Agaricaceae,* in which the spores are produced on gills underneath a cap. See also **agaric.**

gillie, ghillie, *or* **gilly** (ˈgɪlɪ) *n., pl.* **-lies.** *Scot.* **1.** an attendant or guide for hunting or fishing. **2.** (formerly) a Highland chieftain's male attendant or personal servant. [C17: from Scottish Gaelic *gille* boy, servant]

gillion (ˈdʒɪljən) *n. Brit.* one thousand million. U.S. and Canadian equivalent: **billion.** [C20: from G(IGA-) + (M)ILLION]

gill net (gɪl) *n. Fishing.* a net suspended vertically in the water to trap fish by their gills in its meshes.

gill pouch (gɪl) *n.* any of a series of paired linear pouches in chordate embryos, arising as outgrowths of the wall of the pharynx. In fish and some amphibians they become the gill slits.

gills (gɪlz) *pl. n.* **1.** (*sometimes sing.*) the wattle of birds such as domestic fowl. **2. green around** *or* **about the gills.** *Informal.* looking or feeling nauseated.

gill slit (gɪl) *n.* any of a series of paired linear openings to the exterior from the sides of the pharynx in fishes and some amphibians. They contain the gills.

gillyflower *or* **gilliflower** (ˈdʒɪlɪˌflaʊə) *n.* **1.** any of several plants having fragrant flowers, such as the stock and wallflower. **2.** an archaic name for **carnation.** [C14: changed (through influence of *flower*) from *gilofre,* from Old French *girofle,* from Medieval Latin, from Greek *karuophullon* clove tree, from *karuon* nut + *phullon* leaf]

Gilsonite (ˈgɪlsəˌnaɪt) *n. Trademark.* a very pure form of asphalt found in Utah and Colorado; used for making paints, varnishes, and linoleum. [C19: named after S. H. *Gilson* of Salt Lake City, Utah, who discovered it]

gilt[1] (gɪlt) *vb.* **1.** a past tense and past participle of **gild**[1]. ~*n.* **2.** gold or a substance simulating it, applied in gilding. **3.** another word for **gilding** (senses 1, 2). **4.** superficial or false appearance of excellence; glamour. **5.** a gilt-edged security. **6. take the gilt off the gingerbread.** to destroy the part of something that gives it its appeal. ~*adj.* **7.** covered with or as if with gold or gilt; gilded.

gilt[2] (gɪlt) *n.* a young female pig, esp. one that has not had a litter. [C15: from Old Norse *gyltr;* related to Old English *gelte,* Old High German *gelza,* Middle Low German *gelte*]

gilt-edged *adj.* **1.** *Stock Exchange.* denoting government securities on which interest payments will certainly be met and that will certainly be repaid at par on the due date. **2.** of the highest quality: *the last track on the album is a gilt-edged classic.* **3.** (of books, papers, etc.) having gilded edges.

gilthead (ˈgɪltˌhɛd) *n.* **1.** a sparid fish, *Sparus aurata,* of Mediterranean and European Atlantic waters, having a gold-coloured band between the eyes. **2.** any similar or related fish.

gimbals (ˈdʒɪmbᵊlz, ˈgɪm-) *pl. n.* a device, consisting of two or three pivoted rings at right angles to each other, that provides free suspension in all planes for an object such as a gyroscope, compass, chronometer, etc. Also called: **gimbal ring.** [C16: variant of earlier *gimmal* finger ring, from Old French *gemel,* from Latin *gemellus,* diminutive of *geminus* twin]

gimcrack (ˈdʒɪmˌkræk) *adj.* **1.** cheap; shoddy. ~*n.* **2.** a cheap showy trifle or gadget. [C18: changed from C14 *gibecrake* little ornament, of unknown origin] —**ˈgimˌcrackery** *n.*

gimel (ˈgɪməl; *Hebrew* ˈgiːmɛl) *n.* the third letter of the Hebrew alphabet (ג) transliterated as *g* or, when final, *gh.* [literally: camel]

gimlet (ˈgɪmlɪt) *n.* **1.** a small hand tool consisting of a pointed spiral tip attached at right angles to a handle, used for boring small holes in wood. **2.** *U.S.* a cocktail consisting of half gin or vodka and half lime juice. **3.** a eucalyptus of W Australia having a twisted bole. ~*vb.* **4.** (*tr.*) to make holes in (wood) using a gimlet. ~*adj.* **5.** penetrating; piercing (esp. in the phrase **gimlet-eyed**). [C15: from Old French *guimbelet,* of Germanic origin, see WIMBLE]

gimme (ˈgɪmiː) *vb. Slang. contraction of* give me.

gimmick (ˈgɪmɪk) *n.* **1.** something designed to attract extra attention, interest, or publicity. **2.** any clever device, gadget, or stratagem, esp. one used to deceive. **3.** *Chiefly U.S.* a device or trick of legerdemain that enables a magician to deceive the audience. [C20: originally U.S. slang, of unknown origin] —'**gimmickry** *n.* —'**gimmicky** *adj.*

gimp *or* **guimpe** (gɪmp) *n.* a tapelike trimming of silk, wool, or cotton, often stiffened with wire. [C17: probably from Dutch *gimp,* of unknown origin]

gin[1] (dʒɪn) *n.* **1.** an alcoholic drink obtained by distillation and rectification of the grain of malted barley, rye, or maize, flavoured with juniper berries. **2.** any of various grain spirits flavoured with other fruit or aromatic essences: *sloe gin.* **3.** an alcoholic drink made from any rectified spirit. [C18: shortened from Dutch *genever* juniper, via Old French from Latin *jūniperus* JUNIPER]

gin[2] (dʒɪn) *n.* **1.** a primitive engine in which a vertical shaft is turned by horses driving a horizontal beam or yoke in a circle. **2.** Also called: **cotton gin.** a machine of this type used for separating seeds from raw cotton. **3.** a trap for catching small mammals, consisting of a noose of thin strong wire. **4.** a hand-operated hoist that consists of a drum winder turned by a crank. ~*vb.* **gins, ginning, ginned.** (*tr.*) **5.** to free (cotton) of seeds with a gin. **6.** to trap or snare (game) with a gin. [C13 *gyn,* shortened from ENGINE] —'**ginner** *n.*

gin[3] (gɪn) *vb.* **gins, ginning, gan, gun.** an archaic word for **begin.**

gin[4] (gɪn) *conj. Scot.* if. [perhaps related to *gif,* an earlier form of *if*]

gin[5] (dʒɪn) *n. Austral. derogatory slang.* an Aboriginal woman. [C19: from a native Australian language]

ging (gɪŋ) *n. Austral. informal.* a child's catapult. [of unknown origin]

ginger ('dʒɪndʒə) *n.* **1.** any of several zingiberaceous plants of the genus *Zingiber,* esp. *Z. officinale* of the East Indies, cultivated throughout the tropics for its spicy hot-tasting underground stem. See also **galangal.** Compare **wild ginger. 2.** the underground stem of this plant, which is used fresh or powdered as a flavouring or crystallized as a sweetmeat. **3.** any of certain related plants. **4. a.** a reddish-brown or yellowish-brown colour. **b.** (*as adj.*): *ginger hair.* **5.** *Informal.* liveliness; vigour. ~*vb.* **6.** (*tr.*) to add the spice ginger to (a dish). ~See also **ginger up.** [C13: from Old French *gingivre,* from Medieval Latin *gingiber,* from Latin *zinziberi,* from Greek *zingiberis,* probably from Sanskrit *śrṅgaveram,* from *śrṅga-* horn + *vera-* body, referring to its shape]

ginger ale *n.* a sweetened effervescent nonalcoholic drink flavoured with ginger extract.

ginger beer *n.* a slightly alcoholic drink made by fermenting a mixture of syrup and root ginger.

gingerbread ('dʒɪndʒəˌbrɛd) *n.* **1.** a moist brown cake, flavoured with ginger and treacle or syrup. **2. a.** a rolled biscuit, similarly flavoured, cut into various shapes and sometimes covered with icing. **b.** (*as modifier*): *gingerbread man.* **3. a.** an elaborate but unsubstantial ornamentation. **b.** (*as modifier*): *gingerbread style of architecture.*

gingerbread tree *n.* a W African rosaceous tree, *Parinarium macrophyllum,* with large mealy edible fruits (**gingerbread plums**): family *Chrysobalanaceae.*

ginger group *n. Chiefly Brit.* a group within a party, association, etc., that enlivens or radicalizes its parent body.

gingerly ('dʒɪndʒəlɪ) *adv.* **1.** in a cautious, reluctant, or timid manner. ~*adj.* **2.** cautious, reluctant, or timid. [C16: perhaps from Old French *gensor* dainty, from *gent* of noble birth; see GENTLE] —'**gingerliness** *n.*

ginger snap *or* **nut** *n.* a crisp biscuit flavoured with ginger.

ginger up *vb.* (*tr., adv.*) to enliven (an activity, group, etc.).

ginger wine *n.* an alcoholic drink made from fermented bruised ginger, sugar, and water.

gingery ('dʒɪndʒərɪ) *adj.* **1.** like or tasting of ginger. **2.** of or like the colour ginger. **3.** full of vigour; high-spirited. **4.** pointed; biting: *a gingery remark.*

gingham ('gɪŋəm) *n. Textiles.* **a.** a cotton fabric, usually woven of two coloured yarns in a checked or striped design. **b.** (*as modifier*): *a gingham dress.* [C17: from French *guingan,* from Malay *ginggang* striped cloth]

gingili, gingelli, *or* **gingelly** ('dʒɪndʒɪlɪ) *n.* **1.** the oil obtained from sesame seeds. **2.** another name for **sesame.** [C18: from Hindi *jingalī*]

gingiva ('dʒɪndʒɪvə, dʒɪn'dʒaɪvə) *n., pl.* **-givae** (-dʒɪˌviː, -'dʒaɪviː). *Anatomy.* the technical name for the **gum**[2]. [from Latin] —'**gingival** *adj.*

gingivitis (ˌdʒɪndʒɪ'vaɪtɪs) *n.* inflammation of the gums.

ginglymus ('dʒɪŋglɪməs, 'gɪŋ-) *n., pl.* **-mi** (-ˌmaɪ). *Anatomy.* a hinge joint. See **hinge** (sense 2). [C17: New Latin, from Greek *ginglumos* hinge]

gink (gɪŋk) *n. Slang.* a man or boy, esp. one considered to be odd. [C20: of unknown origin]

ginkgo ('gɪŋkgəʊ) *or* **gingko** ('gɪŋkəʊ) *n., pl.* **-goes** *or* **-koes.** a widely planted ornamental Chinese gymnosperm tree, *Ginkgo biloba,* with fan-shaped deciduous leaves and fleshy yellow fruit. Also called: **maidenhair tree.** [C18: from Japanese *ginkyō,* from Ancient Chinese *ngien* silver + *hang* apricot]

ginnel ('gɪnᵊl, 'dʒɪn-) *n. Northern English dialect.* a narrow passageway between buildings. [C17: perhaps a corruption of CHANNEL]

ginormous (dʒaɪ'nɔːməs) *adj. Informal.* very large. [C20: blend of *giant* or *gigantic* and *enormous*]

gin palace (dʒɪn) *n.* (formerly) a gaudy drinking house.

gin rummy (dʒɪn) *n.* a version of rummy in which a player may go out if the odd cards outside his sequences total less than ten points. Often shortened to **gin.** [C20: from GIN[1] + RUMMY[1], apparently from a humorous allusion to gin and rum]

ginseng ('dʒɪnsɛŋ) *n.* **1.** either of two araliaceous plants, *Panax schinseng* of China or *P. quinquefolius* of North America, whose forked aromatic roots are used medicinally in China. **2.** the root of either of these plants or a substance obtained from the roots, believed to possess stimulant, tonic, and energy-giving properties. [C17: from Mandarin Chinese *jen shen,* from *jen* man (from a resemblance of the roots to human legs) + *shen* ginseng]

gin sling (dʒɪn) *n.* an iced drink made from gin and water, sweetened, and flavoured with lemon or lime juice.

gio ('dʒiːəʊ) *n.* a variant spelling of **geo.**

Giorgi system ('dʒɔːdʒɪ) *n.* a system of units based on the metre, kilogram, second, and ampere, in which the magnetic constant has the value $4\pi \times 10^{-7}$ henries per metre. It was used as a basis for SI units. Also called: **MKSA system.** [C20: named after Giovanni *Giorgi* (1871–1950), Italian physicist]

gip (dʒɪp) *vb.* **gips, gipping, gipped. 1.** a variant spelling of **gyp**[1]. ~*n.* **2.** a variant spelling of **gyp**[2].

gipon (dʒɪ'pɒn, 'dʒɪpɒn) *n.* another word for **jupon.**

gippy ('dʒɪpɪ) *Slang.* ~*n., pl.* **-pies. 1.** an Egyptian person or thing. **2.** Also called: **gippo,** *pl.* **-poes.** a Gypsy. ~*adj.* **3.** Egyptian. **4. gippy tummy.** diarrhoea, esp. as experienced by visitors to hot climates. [C19: from GYPSY and EGYPTIAN]

Gipsy ('dʒɪpsɪ) *n., pl.* **-sies.** (*sometimes not cap.*) a variant spelling of **Gypsy.** —'**Gipsyish** *adj.* —'**Gipsydom** *n.* —'**Gipsyˌhood** *n.*—'**Gipsy-ˌlike** *adj.*

gipsy moth *n.* a European moth, *Lymantria dispar,* introduced into North America, where it is a serious pest of shade trees: family *Lymantriidae* (or *Liparidae*). See also **tussock moth.**

gipsywort ('dʒɪpsɪˌwɜːt) *n.* a hairy Eurasian plant, *Lycopus europaeus,* having two-lipped white flowers with purple dots on the lower lip: family *Labiatae* (labiates). See also **bugleweed** (sense 1).

giraffe (dʒɪ'rɑːf, -'ræf) *n., pl.* **-raffes** *or* **-raffe.** a large ruminant mammal, *Giraffa camelopardalis,* inhabiting savannas of tropical Africa: the tallest mammal, with very long legs and neck and a colouring of regular reddish-brown patches on a beige ground: family *Giraffidae.* [C17: from Italian *giraffa,* from Arabic *zarāfah,* probably of African origin]

girandole ('dʒɪrənˌdəʊl) *or* **girandola** (dʒɪ'rændələ) *n.* **1.** an ornamental branched wall candleholder, usually incorporating a mirror. **2.** an earring or pendant having a central gem surrounded by smaller ones. **3.** a kind of revolving firework. **4.** *Artillery.* a group of connected mines. [C17: from French, from Italian *girandola,* from *girare* to revolve, from Latin *gӯrāre* to GYRATE]

girasol, girosol, *or* **girasole** ('dʒɪrəˌsɒl, -ˌsəʊl) *n.* a type of opal that has a red or pink glow in bright light; fire opal. [C16: from Italian, from *girare* to revolve (see GYRATE) + *sole* the sun, from Latin *sōl*]

gird[1] (gɜːd) *vb.* **girds, girding, girded** *or* **girt.** (*tr.*) **1.** to put a belt, girdle, etc., around (the waist or hips). **2.** to bind or secure with or as if with a belt: *to gird on one's armour.* **3.** to surround; encircle. **4.** to prepare (oneself) for action (esp. in the phrase **gird (up) one's loins**). **5.** to endow with a rank, attribute, etc., esp. knighthood. [Old English *gyrdan,* of Germanic origin; related to Old Norse *gyrtha,* Old High German *gurten*]

gird[2] (gɜːd) *Northern English dialect.* ~*vb.* **1.** (when *intr.,* foll. by *at*) to jeer (at someone); mock. **2.** (*tr.*) to strike (a blow at someone). **3.** (*intr.*) to move at high speed. ~*n.* **4. a.** a blow or stroke. **b.** a taunt; gibe. **5.** a display of bad temper or anger (esp. in the phrases **in a gird; throw a gird**). [C13 *girden* to strike, cut, of unknown origin]

gird[3] (gɪrd) *n. Scot.* a hoop, esp. a child's hoop. Also: **girr.** [a Scot. variant of GIRTH]

girder ('gɜːdə) *n.* **1.** a large beam, esp. one made of steel, used in the construction of bridges, buildings, etc. **2.** *Botany.* the structure composed of tissue providing mechanical support for a stem or leaf.

girdle[1] ('gɜːdᵊl) *n.* **1.** a woman's elastic corset covering the waist to the thigh. **2.** anything that surrounds or encircles. **3.** a belt or sash. **4.** *Jewellery.* the outer edge of a gem. **5.** *Anatomy.* any encircling structure or part. See **pectoral girdle, pelvic girdle. 6.** the mark left on a tree trunk after the removal of a ring of bark. ~*vb.* (*tr.*) **7.** to put a girdle on or around. **8.** to surround or encircle. **9.** to remove a ring of bark from (a tree or branch), thus causing it to die. [Old English *gyrdel,* of Germanic origin; related to Old Norse *gyrthill,* Old Frisian *gerdel,* Old High German *gurtila;* see GIRD[1]] —'**girdle-ˌlike** *adj.*

girdle[2] ('gɜːdᵊl) *n. Scot. and northern English dialect.* another word for **griddle.**

girdler ('gɜːdlə) *n.* **1.** a person or thing that girdles. **2.** a maker of girdles. **3.** any insect, such as the twig girdler, that bores circular grooves around the stems or twigs in which it lays its eggs.

girdlescone ('gɜːdᵊlˌskəʊn, -ˌskɒn), **girdle scone,** *or* **girdlecake** ('gɜːdᵊlˌkeɪk) *n.* less common names for **drop scone.**

girdle traverse *n. Mountaineering.* a climb that consists of a complete traverse of a face or crag.
girl (gɜːl) *n.* **1.** a female child from birth to young womanhood. **2.** a young unmarried woman; lass; maid. **3.** *Informal.* a sweetheart or girlfriend. **4.** *Informal.* a woman of any age. **5.** an informal word for **daughter. 6.** a female employee, esp. a female servant. **7.** *S. African derogatory.* a Black female servant of any age. **8.** (*usually pl.* and preceded by *the*) *Informal.* a group of women, esp. acquaintances. [C13: of uncertain origin; perhaps related to Low German *Göre* boy, girl]
girl Friday *n.* a female employee who has a wide range of duties, usually including secretarial and clerical work. [C20: coined on the pattern of MAN FRIDAY]
girlfriend (ˈgɜːlˌfrɛnd) *n.* **1.** a female friend with whom a man or boy is romantically or sexually involved; sweetheart. **2.** any female friend.
Girl Guide *n.* See **Guide.**
girlhood (ˈgɜːlˌhʊd) *n.* the state or time of being a girl.
girlie (ˈgɜːlɪ) *n.* **1.** a little girl. **2.** (*modifier*) displaying or featuring nude or scantily dressed women: *a girlie magazine.*
girlish (ˈgɜːlɪʃ) *adj.* of or like a girl in looks, behaviour, innocence, etc. —ˈ**girlishly** *adv.* —ˈ**girlishness** *n.*
Girl Scout *n. U.S.* a member of the equivalent organization for girls to the Scouts. Brit. equivalent: **Guide.**
girn (gərn, gɜːn) *vb.* (*intr.*) *Scot. and northern English dialect.* **1.** to snarl. **2.** to grimace; pull grotesque faces. **3.** to complain fretfully or peevishly. [C14: a variant of GRIN]
giro (ˈdʒaɪrəʊ) *n., pl.* **-ros. 1.** a system of transferring money within the financial institutions of a country, such as banks and post offices, by which bills, etc. may be paid by filling in a giro form authorizing the debit of a specified sum from one's own account to the credit of the payee's account. **2.** *Brit. informal.* an unemployment or income support payment by giro cheque, posted fortnightly. [C20: ultimately from Greek *guros* circuit]
giron *or* **gyron** (ˈdʒaɪrɒn) *n. Heraldry.* a charge consisting of the lower half of a diagonally divided quarter, usually in the top left corner of the shield. [C16: from Old French *giron* a triangular piece of material, of Germanic origin; related to Old High German *gēro* triangular object; compare GORE[3]]
Girondist (dʒɪˈrɒndɪst) *n.* **1.** a member of a party of moderate republicans during the French Revolution, many of whom came from Gironde in SW France: overthrown (1793) by their rivals the Jacobins. See also **Jacobin** (sense 1). *~adj.* **2.** of or relating to the Girondists or their principles. —**Giˈrondism** *n.*
gironny *or* **gyronny** (dʒaɪˈrɒnɪ) *adj.* (*usually postpositive*) *Heraldry.* divided into segments from the fesse point.
girosol (ˈdʒɪrəˌsɒl, -ˌsəʊl) *n.* a variant spelling of **girasol.**
girr (gɪr) *n. Scot.* a variant of **gird**[3].
girt[1] (gɜːt) *vb.* **1.** a past tense and past participle of **gird**[1]. *~adj.* **2.** *Nautical.* moored securely to prevent swinging.
girt[2] (gɜːt) *vb.* **1.** (*tr.*) to bind or encircle; gird. **2.** to measure the girth of (something).
girth (gɜːθ) *n.* **1.** the distance around something; circumference. **2.** size or bulk: *a man of great girth.* **3.** a band around a horse's belly to keep the saddle in position. *~vb.* **4.** (usually foll. by *up*) to fasten a girth on (a horse). **5.** (*tr.*) to encircle or surround. [C14: from Old Norse *gjörth* belt; related to Gothic *gairda* GIRDLE[1]; see GIRD[1]]
gisarme (gɪˈzɑːm) *n.* a long-shafted battle-axe with a sharp point on the back of the axe head. [C13: from Old French *guisarme,* probably from Old High German *getīsarn* weeding tool, from *getan* to weed + *īsarn* IRON]
gismo *or* **gizmo** (ˈgɪzməʊ) *n., pl.* **-mos.** *Slang, chiefly U.S. and Canadian.* a device; gadget. [C20: of unknown origin]
gist (dʒɪst) *n.* **1.** the point or substance of an argument, speech, etc. **2.** *Law.* the essential point of an action. [C18: from Anglo-French, as in *cest action gist en* this action consists in, literally: lies in, from Old French *gésir* to lie, from Latin *jacēre,* from *jacere* to throw]
git (gɪt) *n. Brit. slang.* **1.** a contemptible person, often a fool. **2.** a bastard. [C20: from GET (in the sense: *to beget,* hence a bastard, fool)]
gîte (ʒiːt) *n.* a self-catering holiday cottage for let in France. [C20: French]
gittarone (ˌgɪtəˈrəʊnɪ) *n. Music.* an acoustic bass guitar.
gittern (ˈgɪtɜːn) *n. Music.* an obsolete medieval stringed instrument resembling the guitar. Compare **cittern.** [C14: from Old French *guiterne,* ultimately from Old Spanish *guitarra* GUITAR; see CITTERN]
giusto (ˈdʒuːstəʊ) *adv. Music.* (of a tempo marking) **a.** to be observed strictly. **b.** to be observed appropriately: *allegro giusto.* [Italian: just, proper]
give (gɪv) *vb.* **gives, giving, gave** (geɪv), **given** (ˈgɪvᵊn). (*mainly tr.*) **1.** (*also intr.*) to present or deliver voluntarily (something that is one's own) to the permanent possession of another or others. **2.** (often foll. by *for*) to transfer (something that is one's own, esp. money) to the possession of another as part of an exchange: *to give fifty pounds for a painting.* **3.** to place in the temporary possession of another: *I gave him my watch while I went swimming.* **4.** (when *intr.,* foll. by *of*) to grant, provide, or bestow: *give me some advice.* **5.** to administer: *to give a reprimand.* **6.** to award or attribute: *to give blame, praise,* etc. **7.** to be a source of: *he gives no trouble.* **8.** to impart or communicate: *to give news; give a person a cold.* **9.** to utter or emit: *to give a shout.* **10.** to perform, make, or do: *the car gave a jolt and stopped.* **11.** to sacrifice or devote: *he gave his life for his country.* **12.** to surrender: *to give place to others.* **13.** to concede or yield: *I will give you this game.* **14.** (*intr.*) *Informal.* to happen: *what gives?* **15.** (often foll. by *to*) to cause; lead: *she gave me to believe that she would come.* **16.** (foll. by *for*) to value (something) at: *I don't give anything for his promises.* **17.** to perform or present as an entertainment: *to give a play.* **18.** to propose as a toast: *I give you the Queen.* **19.** (*intr.*) to yield or break under force or pressure: *this surface will give if you sit on it; his courage will never give.* **20. give as good as one gets.** to respond to verbal or bodily blows to at least an equal extent as those received. **21. give battle.** to commence fighting. **22. give birth.** (often foll. by *to*) **a.** to bear (offspring). **b.** to produce, originate, or create (an idea, plan, etc.). **23. give (a person) five** *or* **some skin.** *Slang.* to greet or congratulate (someone) by slapping raised hands. **24. give ground.** to draw back or retreat. **25. give rise to.** to be the cause of. **26. give me.** *Informal.* I prefer: *give me hot weather any day!* **27. give or take.** plus or minus: *three thousand people came, give or take a few hundred.* **28. give way.** See **way** (sense 24). **29. give (a person) what for.** *Informal.* to punish or reprimand (a person) severely. *~n.* **30.** a tendency to yield under pressure; resilience: *there's bound to be some give in a long plank; there is no give in his moral views.* ~See also **give away, give in, give off, give onto, give out, give over, give up.** [Old English *giefan;* related to Old Norse *gefa,* Gothic *giban,* Old High German *geban,* Swedish *giva*] —ˈ**givable** *or* ˈ**giveable** *adj.* —ˈ**giver** *n.*
give-and-take *n.* **1.** mutual concessions, shared benefits, and cooperation. **2.** a smoothly flowing exchange of ideas and talk. *~vb.* **give and take.** (*intr.*) **3.** to make mutual concessions.
give away *vb.* (*tr., adv.*) **1.** to donate or bestow as a gift, prize, etc. **2.** to sell very cheaply. **3.** to reveal or betray (esp. in the phrases **give the game** *or* **show away**). **4.** to fail to use (an opportunity) through folly or neglect. **5.** to present (a bride) formally to her husband in a marriage ceremony. **6.** *Austral. and N.Z. informal.* to give up or abandon (something). *~n.* **giveaway. 7.** a betrayal or disclosure of information, esp. when unintentional. **8.** *Chiefly U.S. and Canadian.* something given, esp. with articles on sale, at little or no charge to increase sales, attract publicity, etc. **9.** *Journalism.* another name for **freesheet. 10.** *Chiefly U.S. and Canadian.* a radio or television programme characterized by the award of money and prizes. **11.** (*modifier*) **a.** very cheap (esp. in the phrase **giveaway prices**). **b.** free of charge: *a giveaway property magazine.*
give in *vb.* (*adv.*) **1.** (*intr.*) to yield; admit defeat. **2.** (*tr.*) to submit or deliver (a document).
given (ˈgɪvᵊn) *vb.* **1.** the past participle of **give.** *~adj.* **2.** (*postpositive;* foll. by *to*) tending (to); inclined or addicted (to). **3.** specific or previously stated. **4.** assumed as a premise. **5.** *Maths.* known or determined independently: *a given volume.* **6.** (on official documents) issued or executed, as on a stated date. *~n.* **7.** an assumed fact. **8.** *Philosophy.* the supposed raw data of experience. See also **sense datum.**
given name *n.* another term (Chiefly U.S.) for **Christian name.**
give off *vb.* (*tr., adv.*) to emit or discharge: *the mothballs gave off an acrid odour.*
give onto *vb.* (*intr.; prep.*) to afford a view or prospect of: *their new house gives onto the sea.*
give out *vb.* (*adv.*) **1.** (*tr.*) to emit or discharge. **2.** (*tr.*) to publish or make known: *the chairman gave out that he would resign.* **3.** (*tr.*) to hand out or distribute: *they gave out free chewing gum on the street.* **4.** (*intr.*) to become exhausted; fail: *the supply of candles gave out.* **5.** (*intr.;* foll. by *to*) *Irish informal.* to reprimand (someone) at length. **6.** (*tr.*) *Cricket.* (of an umpire) to declare (a batsman) dismissed.
give over *vb.* (*adv.*) **1.** (*tr.*) to transfer, esp. to the care or custody of another. **2.** (*tr.*) to assign or resign to a specific purpose or function: *the day was given over to pleasure.* **3.** *Informal.* to cease (an activity): *give over fighting, will you!*
give up *vb.* (*adv.*) **1.** to abandon hope (for). **2.** (*tr.*) to renounce (an activity, belief, etc.): *I have given up smoking.* **3.** (*tr.*) to relinquish or resign from: *he gave up the presidency.* **4.** (*tr.; usually reflexive*) to surrender: *the escaped convict gave himself up.* **5.** (*tr.*) to reveal or disclose (information). **6.** (*intr.*) to admit one's defeat or inability to do something. **7.** (*tr.; often passive or reflexive*) to devote completely (to): *she gave herself up to caring for the sick.*
gizzard (ˈgɪzəd) *n.* **1.** the thick-walled part of a bird's stomach, in which hard food is broken up by muscular action and contact with grit and small stones. **2.** a similar structure in many invertebrates. **3.** *Informal.* the stomach and entrails generally. [C14: from Old North French *guisier* fowl's liver, alteration of Latin *gigēria* entrails of poultry when cooked, of uncertain origin]
Gk *abbrev. for* Greek.
gl. *abbrev. for:* **1.** glass. **2.** gloss.
glabella (gləˈbɛlə) *n., pl.* **-lae** (-liː). *Anatomy.* a smooth elevation of the frontal bone just above the bridge of the nose: a reference point in physical anthropology or craniometry. [C19: New Latin, from Latin *glabellus* smooth, from *glaber* bald, smooth] —**glaˈbellar** *adj.*

glabrescent (gleɪˈbrɛsənt) *adj. Botany.* **1.** becoming hairless at maturity: *glabrescent stems.* **2.** nearly hairless. [C19: from Latin *glabrescere* to become smooth]

glabrous (ˈgleɪbrəs) *or* **glabrate** (ˈgleɪbreɪt, -brɪt) *adj. Biology.* without hair or a similar growth; smooth: *a glabrous stem.* [C17 *glabrous,* from Latin *glaber*] —ˈ**glabrousness** *n.*

glacé (ˈglæsɪ) *adj.* **1.** crystallized or candied: *glacé cherries.* **2.** covered in icing. **3.** (of leather, silk, etc.) having a glossy finish. **4.** *Chiefly U.S.* frozen or iced. ~*vb.* **-cés, -céing, -céed.** **5.** (*tr.*) to ice or candy (cakes, fruits, etc.). [C19: from French *glacé,* literally: iced, from *glacer* to freeze, from *glace* ice, from Latin *glaciēs*]

glacial (ˈgleɪsɪəl, -ʃəl) *adj.* **1.** characterized by the presence of masses of ice. **2.** relating to, caused by, or deposited by a glacier. **3.** extremely cold; icy. **4.** cold or hostile in manner: *a glacial look.* **5.** (of a chemical compound) of or tending to form crystals that resemble ice: *glacial acetic acid.* **6.** very slow in progress: *a glacial pace.* —ˈ**glacially** *adv.*

glacial acetic acid *n.* pure acetic acid (more than 99.8 per cent).

glacialist (ˈgleɪsɪəlɪst, -ʃəl-) *n.* a person who studies ice and its effects on the earth's surface.

glacial period *n.* **1.** any period of time during which a large part of the earth's surface was covered with ice, due to the advance of glaciers, as in the late Carboniferous period, and during most of the Pleistocene; glaciation. **2.** (*often caps.*) the Pleistocene epoch. ~Also called: **glacial epoch, ice age.**

glaciate (ˈgleɪsɪˌeɪt) *vb.* **1.** to cover or become covered with glaciers or masses of ice. **2.** (*tr.*) to subject to the effects of glaciers, such as denudation and erosion. —ˌ**glaciˈation** *n.*

glacier (ˈglæsɪə, ˈgleɪs-) *n.* a slowly moving mass of ice originating from an accumulation of snow. It can either spread out from a central mass (**continental glacier**) or descend from a high valley (**alpine glacier**). [C18: from French (Savoy dialect), from Old French *glace* ice, from Late Latin *glacia,* from Latin *glaciēs* ice]

glacier cream *n. Mountaineering.* a barrier cream, esp. against ultraviolet radiation, used when climbing above the snow line.

glacier milk *n.* water flowing in a stream from the snout of a glacier and containing particles of rock.

glacier table *n.* a rock sitting on a pillar of ice on top of a glacier, as a result of the ice immediately beneath the rock being protected from the heat of the sun and not melting.

glaciology (ˌglæsɪˈɒlədʒɪ, ˌgleɪ-) *n.* the study of the distribution, character, and effects of glaciers. —**glaciological** (ˌglæsɪəˈlɒdʒɪkᵊl, ˌgleɪ-) *or* ˌ**glacioˈlogic** *adj.* —ˌ**glaciˈologist** *or* ˈ**glacialist** *n.*

glacis (ˈglæsɪs, ˈglæsɪ, ˈgleɪ-) *n., pl.* **-ises** *or* **-is** (-iːz, -ɪz). **1.** a slight incline; slope. **2.** an open slope in front of a fortified place. **3.** short for **glacis plate.** [C17: from French, from Old French *glacier* to freeze, slip, from Latin *glaciāre,* from *glaciēs* ice]

glacis plate *n.* **1.** the frontal plate armour on a tank. **2.** a section of armour plate shielding an opening on a naval vessel.

glad[1] (glæd) *adj.* **gladder, gladdest.** **1.** happy and pleased; contented. **2.** causing happiness or contentment. **3.** (*postpositive;* foll. by *to*) very willing: *he was glad to help.* **4.** (*postpositive;* foll. by *of*) happy or pleased to have: *glad of her help.* ~*vb.* **glads, gladding, gladded.** **5.** an archaic word for **gladden.** [Old English *glǣd;* related to Old Norse *glathr,* Old High German *glat* smooth, shining, Latin *glaber* smooth, Lithuanian *glodùs* fitting closely] —ˈ**gladly** *adv.* —ˈ**gladness** *n.*

glad[2] (glæd) *n. Informal.* short for **gladiolus.** Also called (Austral.): **gladdie** (ˈglædɪ).

gladden (ˈglædᵊn) *vb.* to make or become glad and joyful. —ˈ**gladdener** *n.*

gladdon (ˈglædᵊn) *n.* another name for the **stinking iris.** [Old English, of uncertain origin]

glade (gleɪd) *n.* an open place in a forest; clearing. [C16: of uncertain origin; perhaps related to GLAD[1] (in obsolete sense: bright); see GLEAM] —ˈ**gladeˌlike** *adj.*

glad eye *n. Informal.* an inviting or seductive glance (esp. in the phrase **give (someone) the glad eye**).

glad hand *n.* **1. a.** a welcoming hand. **b.** a welcome. ~*vb.* **glad-hand.** **2.** (*tr.*) to welcome by or as if by offering a hand.

gladiate (ˈglædɪɪt, -ˌeɪt, ˈgleɪ-) *adj. Botany.* shaped like a sword: *gladiate leaves.* [C18: from Latin *gladius* sword]

gladiator (ˈglædɪˌeɪtə) *n.* **1.** (in ancient Rome and Etruria) a man trained to fight in arenas to provide entertainment. **2.** a person who supports and fights publicly for a cause. [C16: from Latin: swordsman, from *gladius* sword]

gladiatorial (ˌglædɪəˈtɔːrɪəl) *adj.* of, characteristic of, or relating to gladiators, combat, etc.

gladiolus (ˌglædɪˈəʊləs) *n., pl.* **-lus, -li** (-laɪ), *or* **-luses.** **1.** Also called: **sword lily, gladiola.** any iridaceous plant of the widely cultivated genus *Gladiolus,* having sword-shaped leaves and spikes of funnel-shaped brightly coloured flowers. **2.** *Anatomy.* the large central part of the breastbone. [C16: from Latin: a small sword, sword lily, from *gladius* a sword]

glad rags *pl. n. Informal.* best clothes or clothes used on special occasions.

gladsome (ˈglædsəm) *adj.* an archaic word for **glad**[1]. —ˈ**gladsomely** *adv.* —ˈ**gladsomeness** *n.*

Gladstone (ˈglædstən) *n.* a light four-wheeled horse-drawn vehicle. [C19: named after W. E. *Gladstone* (1809–98), British statesman]

Gladstone bag *n.* a piece of hand luggage consisting of two equal-sized hinged compartments. [C19: named after W. E. *Gladstone*]

Glagolitic (ˌglægəˈlɪtɪk) *adj.* of, relating to, or denoting a Slavic alphabet whose invention is attributed to Saint Cyril, preserved only in certain Roman Catholic liturgical books found in Dalmatia. [C19: from New Latin *glagoliticus,* from Serbo-Croatian *glagolica* the Glagolitic alphabet; related to Old Church Slavonic *glagolŭ* word]

glaikit *or* **glaiket** (ˈgleɪkɪt) *adj. Scot.* foolish; silly; thoughtless. [C15: of obscure origin] —ˈ**glaikitness** *or* ˈ**glaiketness** *n.*

glair (glɛə) *n.* **1.** white of egg, esp. when used as a size, glaze, or adhesive, usually in bookbinding. **2.** any substance resembling this. ~*vb.* **3.** (*tr.*) to apply glair to (something). [C14: from Old French *glaire,* from Vulgar Latin *clāria* (unattested) CLEAR, from Latin *clārus*] —ˈ**glairy** *or* ˈ**glaireous** *adj.* —ˈ**glairiness** *n.*

glaive (gleɪv) *n.* an archaic word for **sword.** [C13: from Old French: javelin, from Latin *gladius* sword] —**glaived** *adj.*

glam (glæm) *adj. Slang.* short for **glamorous.**

glamorize, glamorise, *or U.S.* (*sometimes*) **glamourize** (ˈglæməˌraɪz) *vb.* (*tr.*) to cause to be or seem glamorous; romanticize or beautify. —ˌ**glamoriˈzation** *or* ˌ**glamoriˈsation** *n.* —ˈ**glamorˌizer** *or* ˈ**glamorˌiser** *n.*

glamorous *or* **glamourous** (ˈglæmərəs) *adj.* **1.** possessing glamour; alluring and fascinating: *a glamorous career.* **2.** beautiful and smart, esp. in a showy way: *a glamorous woman.* —ˈ**glamorously** *or* ˈ**glamourously** *adv.* —ˈ**glamorousness** *or* ˈ**glamourousness** *n.*

glamour *or U.S.* (*sometimes*) **glamor** (ˈglæmə) *n.* **1.** charm and allure; fascination. **2. a.** fascinating or voluptuous beauty, often dependent on artifice. **b.** (*as modifier*): *a glamour girl.* **3.** *Archaic.* a magic spell; charm. [C18: Scottish variant of GRAMMAR (hence a magic spell, because occult practices were popularly associated with learning)]

glance[1] (glɑːns) *vb.* **1.** (*intr.*) to look hastily or briefly. **2.** (*intr.;* foll. by *over, through,* etc.) to look over briefly: *to glance through a report.* **3.** (*intr.*) to reflect, glint, or gleam: *the sun glanced on the water.* **4.** (*intr.;* usually foll. by *off*) to depart (from an object struck) at an oblique angle: *the arrow glanced off the tree.* **5.** (*tr.*) to strike at an oblique angle: *the arrow glanced the tree.* ~*n.* **6.** a hasty or brief look; peep. **7. at a glance.** from one's first look; immediately. **8.** a flash or glint of light; gleam. **9.** the act or an instance of an object glancing or glancing off another. **10.** a brief allusion or reference. **11.** *Cricket.* a stroke in which the ball is deflected off the bat to the leg side; glide. [C15: modification of *glacen* to strike obliquely, from Old French *glacier* to slide (see GLACIS); compare Middle English *glenten* to make a rapid sideways movement, GLINT] —ˈ**glancingly** *adv.*

glance[2] (glɑːns) *n.* any mineral having a metallic lustre, esp. a simple sulphide: *copper glance.* [C19: from German *Glanz* brightness, lustre]

gland[1] (glænd) *n.* **1.** a cell or organ in man and other animals that synthesizes chemical substances and secretes them for the body to use or eliminate, either through a duct (see **exocrine gland**) or directly into the bloodstream (see **endocrine gland**). **2.** a structure, such as a lymph node, that resembles a gland in form. **3.** a cell or organ in plants that synthesizes and secretes a particular substance. [C17: from Latin *glāns* acorn] —ˈ**glandˌlike** *adj.*

gland[2] (glænd) *n.* a device that prevents leakage of fluid along a rotating shaft or reciprocating rod passing through a boundary between areas of high and low pressure. It often consists of a flanged metal sleeve bedding into a stuffing box. [C19: of unknown origin]

glanders (ˈglændəz) *n.* (*functioning as sing.*) a highly infectious bacterial disease of horses, sometimes communicated to man, caused by *Actinobacillus mallei* and characterized by inflammation and ulceration of the mucous membranes of the air passages, skin and lymph glands. [C16: from Old French *glandres* enlarged glands, from Latin *glandulae,* literally: little acorns, from *glāns* acorn; see GLAND[1]] —ˈ**glandered** *adj.* —ˈ**glanderous** *adj.*

glandular (ˈglændjʊlə) *or* **glandulous** (ˈglændjʊləs) *adj.* of, relating to, containing, functioning as, or affecting a gland: *glandular tissue.* [C18: from Latin *glandula,* literally: a little acorn; see GLANDERS] —ˈ**glandularly** *or* ˈ**glandulously** *adv.*

glandular fever *n.* another name for **infectious mononucleosis.**

glandule (ˈglændjuːl) *n.* a small gland.

glans (glænz) *n., pl.* **glandes** (ˈglændiːz). *Anatomy.* any small rounded body or glandlike mass, such as the head of the penis (**glans penis**). [C17: from Latin: acorn; see GLAND[1]]

glare[1] (glɛə) *vb.* **1.** (*intr.*) to stare angrily; glower. **2.** (*tr.*) to express by glowering. **3.** (*intr.*) (of light, colour, etc.) to be very bright and intense. **4.** (*intr.*) to be dazzlingly ornamented or garish. ~*n.* **5.** an angry stare. **6.** a dazzling light or brilliance. **7.** garish ornamentation or appearance; gaudiness. [C13: probably from Middle Low German, Middle Dutch *glaren* to gleam; probably related to Old English *glæren* glassy; see GLASS] —ˈ**glareless** *adj.* —ˈ**glary** *adj.*

glare[2] (glɛə) *adj. Chiefly U.S. and Canadian.* smooth and glassy. [C16: special use of GLARE[1]]

glaring (ˈglɛərɪŋ) *adj.* **1.** conspicuous: *a glaring omission.* **2.** dazzling or garish. —ˈ**glaringly** *adv.* —ˈ**glaringness** *n.*

glasnost (ˈglæsˌnɒst) *n.* the policy of public frankness and accountability developed in the former USSR under the leadership of Mikhail Gorbachov (born 1931). [C20: Russian, literally: openness]

glass (glɑːs) *n.* **1. a.** a hard brittle transparent or translucent noncrystalline solid, consisting of metal silicates or similar compounds. It is made from a fused mixture of oxides, such as lime, silicon dioxide, phosphorus pentoxide, etc., and is used for making windows, mirrors, bottles, etc. **b.** (*as modifier*): *a glass bottle.* Related adj.: **vitreous. 2.** any compound that has solidified from a molten state into a noncrystalline form. **3.** something made of glass, esp. a drinking vessel, a barometer, or a mirror. **4.** Also called: **glassful.** the amount or volume contained in a drinking glass: *he drank a glass of wine.* **5.** glassware collectively. **6.** See **volcanic glass. 7.** See **fibreglass.** ~*vb.* **8.** (*tr.*) to cover with, enclose in, or fit with glass. [Old English *glæs;* related to Old Norse *gler,* Old High German *glas,* Middle High German *glast* brightness; see GLARE[1]] —ˈ**glassless** *adj.* —ˈ**glassˌlike** *adj.*

glass-blowing *n.* the process of shaping a mass of molten or softened glass into a vessel, shape, etc., by blowing air into it through a tube. —ˈ**glass-ˌblower** *n.*

glasses (ˈglɑːsɪz) *pl. n.* a pair of lenses for correcting faulty vision, in a frame that rests on the bridge of the nose and hooks behind the ears. Also called: **spectacles, eyeglasses.**

glass eye *n.* an artificial eye made of glass.

glass fibre *n.* another name for **fibreglass.**

glass harmonica *n.* a musical instrument of the 18th century consisting of a set of glass bowls of graduated pitches, played by rubbing the fingers over the moistened rims or by a keyboard mechanism. Sometimes shortened to **harmonica.** Also called: **musical glasses.**

glasshouse (ˈglɑːsˌhaʊs) *n.* **1.** *Brit.* a glass building, esp. a greenhouse, used for growing plants in protected or controlled conditions. **2.** *Informal, chiefly Brit.* a military detention centre. **3.** *U.S.* another word for **glassworks.**

glassine (glæˈsiːn) *n.* a glazed translucent paper used for book jackets.

glass jaw *n. Boxing, informal.* a jaw that is excessively fragile or susceptible to punches.

glass-maker *n.* a person who makes glass or glass objects. —ˈ**glass-ˌmaking** *n.*

glassman (ˈglɑːsmən) *n., pl.* **-men. 1.** a man whose work is making or selling glassware. **2.** a less common word for **glazier.**

glasspaper (ˈglɑːsˌpeɪpə) *n.* **1.** strong paper coated with powdered glass or other abrasive material for smoothing and polishing. ~*vb.* **2.** to smooth or polish with glasspaper.

glass snake *n.* any snakelike lizard of the genus *Ophisaurus,* of Europe, Asia, and North America, with vestigial hind limbs and a tail that breaks off easily: family *Anguidae.*

glass string *n.* (in Malaysia) the string of a kite used in kite fighting that has an abrasive coating of glue and crushed glass.

glassware (ˈglɑːsˌwɛə) *n.* articles made of glass, esp. drinking glasses.

glass wool *n.* fine spun glass massed into a wool-like bulk, used in insulation, filtering, etc.

glasswork (ˈglɑːsˌwɜːk) *n.* **1.** the production of glassware. **2.** the fitting of glass. **3.** articles of glass. —ˈ**glass-ˌworker** *n.*

glassworks (ˈglɑːsˌwɜːks) *n.* (*functioning as sing.*) a factory for the moulding of glass.

glasswort (ˈglɑːsˌwɜːt) *n.* **1.** Also called: **marsh samphire.** any plant of the chenopodiaceous genus *Salicornia,* of salt marshes, having fleshy stems and scalelike leaves: formerly used as a source of soda for glass-making. **2.** another name for **saltwort** (sense 1).

glassy (ˈglɑːsɪ) *adj.* **glassier, glassiest. 1.** resembling glass, esp. in smoothness, slipperiness, or transparency. **2.** void of expression, life, or warmth: *a glassy stare.* —ˈ**glassily** *adv.* —ˈ**glassiness** *n.*

Glaswegian (glæzˈwiːdʒən) *adj.* **1.** of or relating to the city of Glasgow or its inhabitants. ~*n.* **2.** a native or inhabitant of Glasgow. [C19: influenced by *Norway, Norwegian*]

Glauber's salt (ˈglaʊbəz) *or* **Glauber salt** (ˈglaʊbə) *n.* the crystalline decahydrate of sodium sulphate. [C18: named after J. R. *Glauber* (1604–68), German chemist]

glaucoma (glɔːˈkəʊmə) *n.* a disease of the eye in which increased pressure within the eyeball causes damage to the optic disc and impaired vision, sometimes progressing to blindness. [C17: from Latin, from Greek *glaukōma,* from *glaukos;* see GLAUCOUS] —**glauˈcomatous** *adj.*

glauconite (ˈglɔːkəˌnaɪt) *n.* a green mineral consisting of the hydrated silicate of iron, potassium, aluminium, and magnesium: found in greensand and other similar rocks. Formula: $K_2(Mg,Fe)_2Al_6(Si_4O_{10})_3(OH)_{12}$. [C19: from Greek *glaukon,* neuter of *glaukos* bluish-green + -ITE[1]; see GLAUCOUS] —**glauconitic** (ˌglɔːkəˈnɪtɪk) *adj.*

glaucous (ˈglɔːkəs) *adj.* **1.** *Botany.* covered with a waxy or powdery bloom. **2.** bluish-green. [C17: from Latin *glaucus* silvery, bluish-green, from Greek *glaukos*] —ˈ**glaucously** *adv.*

glaucous gull *n.* a gull, *Larus hyperboreus,* of northern and arctic regions, with a white head and tail and pale grey back and wings.

glaur (glɔːr) *n. Scot.* mud or mire. [C16: of unknown origin] —ˈ**glaury** *adj.*

glaze (gleɪz) *vb.* **1.** (*tr.*) to fit or cover with glass. **2.** (*tr.*) *Ceramics.* to cover with a vitreous solution, rendering impervious to liquid and smooth to the touch. **3.** (*tr.*) to cover (a painting) with a layer of semitransparent colour to modify the tones. **4.** (*tr.*) to cover (foods) with a shiny coating by applying beaten egg, sugar, etc. **5.** (*tr.*) to make glossy or shiny. **6.** (when *intr.,* often foll. by *over*) to become or cause to become glassy: *his eyes were glazing over.* ~*n.* **7.** *Ceramics.* **a.** a vitreous or glossy coating. **b.** the substance used to produce such a coating. **8.** a semitransparent coating applied to a painting to modify the tones. **9.** a smooth lustrous finish on a fabric produced by applying various chemicals. **10.** something used to give a glossy surface to foods: *a syrup glaze.* [C14 *glasen,* from *glas* GLASS] —**glazed** *adj.* —ˈ**glazer** *n.* —ˈ**glazy** *adj.*

glaze ice *or* **glazed frost** *n. Brit.* a thin clear layer of ice caused by the freezing of rain or water droplets in the air on impact with a cool surface or by refreezing after a thaw. Also called: **silver frost.** U.S. term: **glaze.**

glazier (ˈgleɪzɪə) *n.* a person who fits windows, doors, etc., with glass. —ˈ**glaziery** *n.*

glazing (ˈgleɪzɪŋ) *n.* **1.** the surface of a glazed object. **2.** glass fitted, or to be fitted, in a door, frame, etc.

glazing-bar *n.* a supporting or strengthening bar for a glass window, door, etc. Usual U.S. word: **muntin.**

GLC *abbrev. for* Greater London Council, abolished 1986.

gld *abbrev. for* guilder.

gleam (gliːm) *n.* **1.** a small beam or glow of light, esp. reflected light. **2.** a brief or dim indication: *a gleam of hope.* ~*vb.* (*intr.*) **3.** to send forth or reflect a beam of light. **4.** to appear, esp. briefly: *intelligence gleamed in his eyes.* [Old English *glǣm;* related to Old Norse *glja* to flicker, Old High German *gleimo* glow-worm, *glīmo* brightness, Old Irish *glē* bright] —ˈ**gleaming** *adj.* —ˈ**gleamingly** *adv.* —ˈ**gleamless** *adj.* —ˈ**gleamy** *adj.*

glean (gliːn) *vb.* **1.** to gather (something) slowly and carefully in small pieces: *to glean information from the newspapers.* **2.** to gather (the useful remnants of a crop) from the field after harvesting. [C14: from Old French *glener,* from Late Latin *glennāre,* probably of Celtic origin] —ˈ**gleanable** *adj.* —ˈ**gleaner** *n.*

gleanings (ˈgliːnɪŋz) *pl. n.* the useful remnants of a crop that can be gathered from the field after harvesting.

glebe (gliːb) *n.* **1.** *Brit.* land granted to a clergyman as part of his benefice. **2.** *Poetic.* land, esp. when regarded as the source of growing things. [C14: from Latin *glaeba*]

glede (gliːd) *or* **gled** (glɛd) *n.* a former Brit. name for the **red kite.** See **kite** (sense 4). [Old English *glida;* related to Old Norse *gletha,* Middle Low German *glede*]

glee (gliː) *n.* **1.** great merriment or delight, often caused by someone else's misfortune. **2.** a type of song originating in 18th-century England, sung by three or more unaccompanied voices. Compare **madrigal** (sense 1). [Old English *glēo;* related to Old Norse *glȳ*]

glee club *n. Now chiefly U.S. and Canadian.* a club or society organized for the singing of choral music.

gleeful (ˈgliːfʊl) *adj.* full of glee; merry. —ˈ**gleefully** *adv.* —ˈ**gleefulness** *n.*

gleeman (ˈgliːmən) *n., pl.* **-men.** *Obsolete.* a minstrel.

gleet (gliːt) *n.* **1.** inflammation of the urethra with a slight discharge of thin pus and mucus: a stage of chronic gonorrhoea. **2.** the pus and mucus discharged. [C14: from Old French *glette* slime, from Latin *glittus* sticky] —ˈ**gleety** *adj.*

Gleichschaltung (ˈglaɪkˌʃæltʊŋ) *n.* the enforcement of standardization and the elimination of all opposition within the political, economic, and cultural institutions of a state. [C20: German]

glen (glɛn) *n.* a narrow and deep mountain valley, esp. in Scotland or Ireland. [C15: from Scottish Gaelic *gleann,* from Old Irish *glend*] —ˈ**glenˌlike** *adj.*

glengarry (glɛnˈgærɪ) *n., pl.* **-ries.** a brimless Scottish woollen cap with a crease down the crown, often with ribbons dangling at the back. Also called: **glengarry bonnet.** [C19: after *Glengarry,* Scotland]

glenoid (ˈgliːnɔɪd) *adj. Anatomy.* **1.** resembling or having a shallow cavity. **2.** denoting the cavity in the shoulder blade into which the head of the upper arm bone fits. [C18: from Greek *glēnoeidēs,* from *glēnē* socket of a joint]

gley *or* **glei** (gleɪ) *n.* a bluish-grey compact sticky soil occurring in certain humid regions. [C20: from Russian *glei* clay]

glia (ˈgliːə) *n.* the delicate web of connective tissue that surrounds and supports nerve cells. Also called: **neuroglia.** —ˈ**glial** *adj.*

gliadin (ˈglaɪədɪn) *or* **gliadine** (ˈglaɪəˌdiːn, -dɪn) *n.* a protein of cereals, esp. wheat, with a high proline content: forms a sticky mass with water that binds flour into dough. Compare **glutelin.** [C19: from Italian *gliadina,* from Greek *glia* glue]

glib (glɪb) *adj.* **glibber, glibbest.** fluent and easy, often in an insincere or deceptive way. [C16: probably from Middle Low German *glibberich* slippery] —ˈ**glibly** *adv.* —ˈ**glibness** *n.*

glide (glaɪd) *vb.* **1.** to move or cause to move easily without jerks or hesitations: *to glide in a boat down the river.* **2.** (*intr.*) to pass slowly or without perceptible change: *to glide into sleep.* **3.** to cause (an aircraft) to come into land without engine power, or (of an aircraft) to land in this way. **4.** (*intr.*) to fly a glider. **5.** (*intr.*) *Music.* to execute a portamento from one note to another. **6.** (*intr.*) *Phonetics.* to produce a glide. ~*n.* **7.** a smooth easy movement. **8. a.** any of various dances featuring gliding steps. **b.** a step in such a dance. **9.** a manoeuvre in which an aircraft makes a gentle descent without engine power. See also **glide path. 10.** the act or process of gliding. **11.** *Music.* **a.** a long portion of tubing slipped in and out of a trombone to increase its length for the production of lower harmonic series. See also **valve** (sense 5). **b.** a portamento or slur. **12.** *Phonetics.* **a.** a transitional sound as the speech organs pass from the articulatory position of one speech sound to that of the next, as the (w) sound in some pronunciations of the word *doing.* **b.** another word for **semivowel. 13.** *Crystallog.* another name for **slip**[1] (sense 33). **14.** *Cricket.* another word for **glance**[1] (sense 11). [Old English *glīdan;* related to Old High German *glītan*] —'**glidingly** *adv.*

glide path *n.* the approach path of an aircraft when landing, usually defined by a radar beam.

glider ('glaɪdə) *n.* **1.** an aircraft capable of gliding and soaring in air currents without the use of an engine. See also **sailplane. 2.** a person or thing that glides. **3.** another name for **flying phalanger.**

glide time *n.* the New Zealand term for **flexitime.**

glim (glɪm) *n. Slang.* **1.** a light or lamp. **2.** an eye. [C17: probably short for GLIMMER; compare GLIMPSE]

glimmer ('glɪmə) *vb.* (*intr.*) **1.** (of a light, candle, etc.) to glow faintly or flickeringly. **2.** to be indicated faintly: *hope glimmered in his face.* ~*n.* **3.** a glow or twinkle of light. **4.** a faint indication. [C14: compare Middle High German *glimmern,* Swedish *glimra,* Danish *glimre*] —'**glimmeringly** *adv.*

glimpse (glɪmps) *n.* **1.** a brief or incomplete view: *to catch a glimpse of the sea.* **2.** a vague indication: *he had a glimpse of what the lecturer meant.* **3.** *Archaic.* a glimmer of light. ~*vb.* **4.** (*tr.*) to catch sight of briefly or momentarily. **5.** (*intr.;* usually foll. by *at*) *Chiefly U.S.* to look (at) briefly or cursorily; glance (at). **6.** (*intr.*) *Archaic.* to shine faintly; glimmer. [C14: of Germanic origin; compare Middle High German *glimsen* to glimmer] —'**glimpser** *n.*

glint (glɪnt) *vb.* **1.** to gleam or cause to gleam brightly. **2.** (*intr.*) *Archaic.* to move or pass quickly. ~*n.* **3.** a bright gleam or flash. **4.** brightness or gloss. **5.** a brief indication. [C15: probably of Scandinavian origin; compare Swedish dialect *glänta, glinta* to gleam]

glioma (glaɪ'əʊmə) *n., pl.* **-mata** (-mətə) *or* **-mas.** a tumour of the brain and spinal cord, composed of neuroglia cells and fibres. [C19: from New Latin, from Greek *glia* glue + -OMA] —**gli'omatous** *adj.*

glissade (glɪ'sɑːd, -'seɪd) *n.* **1.** a gliding step in ballet, in which one foot slides forwards, sideways, or backwards. **2.** a controlled slide down a snow slope. ~*vb.* **3.** (*intr.*) to perform a glissade. [C19: from French, from *glisser* to slip, from Old French *glicier,* of Frankish origin; compare Old High German *glītan* to GLIDE] —**glis'sader** *n.*

glissando (glɪ'sændəʊ) *n., pl.* **-di** (-diː) *or* **-dos. 1.** a rapidly executed series of notes on the harp or piano, each note of which is discretely audible. **2.** a portamento, esp. as executed on the violin, viola, etc. [C19: probably Italianized variant of GLISSADE]

glisten ('glɪsᵊn) *vb.* (*intr.*) **1.** (of a wet or glossy surface) to gleam by reflecting light: *wet leaves glisten in the sunlight.* **2.** (of light) to reflect with brightness: *the sunlight glistens on wet leaves.* ~*n.* **3.** *Rare.* a gleam or gloss. [Old English *glisnian;* related to *glisian* to glitter, Middle High German *glistern*] —'**glisteningly** *adv.*

glister ('glɪstə) *vb., n.* an archaic word for **glitter.** [C14: probably from Middle Dutch *glisteren*] —'**glisteringly** *adv.*

glitch (glɪtʃ) *n.* **1.** a sudden instance of malfunctioning or irregularity in an electronic system. **2.** a change in the rotation rate of a pulsar. [C20: of unknown origin]

glitter ('glɪtə) *vb.* (*intr.*) **1.** (of a hard, wet, or polished surface) to reflect light in bright flashes. **2.** (of light) to be reflected in bright flashes. **3.** (usually foll. by *with*) to be decorated or enhanced by the glamour (of): *the show glitters with famous actors.* ~*n.* **4.** sparkle or brilliance. **5.** show and glamour. **6.** tiny pieces of shiny decorative material used for ornamentation, as on the skin. **7.** *Canadian.* Also called: **silver thaw.** ice formed from freezing rain. [C14: from Old Norse *glitra;* related to Old High German *glīzan* to shine] —'**glitteringly** *adv.* —'**glittery** *adj.*

glitterati (,glɪtə'rɑːtiː) *pl. n. Informal.* the leaders of society, esp. the rich and beautiful; fashionable celebrities. [C20: from GLITTER + *-ati* as in LITERATI]

glitz (glɪts) *n. Slang.* ostentatious showiness; gaudiness or glitter. [C20: back formation from GLITZY]

glitzy ('glɪtsɪ) *adj.* **glitzier, glitziest.** *Slang.* showily attractive; flashy or glittery. [C20: originally U.S., probably via Yiddish from German *glitzern* to glitter]

gloaming ('gləʊmɪŋ) *n. Scot. or poetic.* twilight or dusk. [Old English *glōmung,* from *glōm;* related to Old Norse *glāmr* moon]

gloat (gləʊt) *vb.* **1.** (*intr.;* often foll. by *over*) to dwell (on) with malevolent smugness or exultation. ~*n.* **2.** the act of gloating. [C16: probably of Scandinavian origin; compare Old Norse *glotta* to grin, Middle High German *glotzen* to stare] —'**gloater** *n.* —'**gloatingly** *adv.*

glob (glɒb) *n. Informal.* a rounded mass of some thick fluid or pliable substance: *a glob of cream.* [C20: probably from GLOBE, influenced by BLOB]

global ('gləʊbᵊl) *adj.* **1.** covering, influencing, or relating to the whole world. **2.** comprehensive. —'**globally** *adv.*

globalization *or* **globalisation** (,gləʊbᵊlaɪ'zeɪʃən) *n.* **1.** the process enabling financial and investment markets to operate internationally, largely as a result of deregulation and improved communications. **2.** the process by which a company, etc., expands to operate internationally.

global product *n.* a commercial product, such as Coca Cola, that is marketed throughout the world under the same brand name.

global rule *n.* (in transformational grammar) a rule that makes reference to nonconsecutive stages of a derivation.

global search *n. Word processing.* an operation in which a complete computer file or set of files is searched for every occurrence of a particular word or other sequence of characters.

global village *n.* the whole world considered as being closely connected by modern telecommunications and as being interdependent economically, socially, and politically. [C20: coined by Marshal McLuhan (1911–80), Canadian writer]

global warming *n.* an increase in the average temperature worldwide believed to be caused by the greenhouse effect.

globate ('gləʊbeɪt) *or* **globated** *adj.* shaped like a globe.

globe (gləʊb) *n.* **1.** a sphere on which a map of the world or the heavens is drawn or represented. **2. the.** the world; the earth. **3.** a planet or some other astronomical body. **4.** an object shaped like a sphere, such as a glass lampshade or fish-bowl. **5.** *Chiefly Austral. and N.Z.* an electric light bulb. **6.** an orb, usually of gold, symbolic of authority or sovereignty. ~*vb.* **7.** to form or cause to form into a globe. [C16: from Old French, from Latin *globus*] —'**globe,like** *adj.*

globe artichoke *n.* See **artichoke** (senses 1, 2).

globefish ('gləʊb,fɪʃ) *n., pl.* **-fish** *or* **-fishes.** another name for **puffer** (sense 2) or **porcupine fish.**

globeflower ('gləʊb,flaʊə) *n.* any ranunculaceous plant of the genus *Trollius,* having pale yellow, white, or orange globe-shaped flowers.

globetrotter ('gləʊb,trɒtə) *n.* a habitual worldwide traveller, esp. a tourist or businessman. —'**globe,trotting** *n., adj.*

globigerina (gləʊ,bɪdʒə'raɪnə) *n., pl.* **-nas** *or* **-nae** (-niː). **1.** any marine protozoan of the genus *Globigerina,* having a rounded shell with spiny processes: order *Foraminifera* (foraminifers). **2. globigerina ooze.** a deposit on the ocean floor consisting of the shells of these protozoans. [C19: from New Latin, from Latin *globus* GLOBE + *gerere* to carry, bear]

globin ('gləʊbɪn) *n. Biochem.* the protein component of the pigments myoglobin and haemoglobin. [C19: from Latin *globus* ball, sphere + -IN]

globoid ('gləʊbɔɪd) *adj.* **1.** shaped approximately like a globe. ~*n.* **2.** a globoid body, such as any of those occurring in certain plant granules.

globose ('gləʊbəʊs, gləʊ'bəʊs) *or* **globous** ('gləʊbəs) *adj.* spherical or approximately spherical. [C15: from Latin *globōsus;* see GLOBE] —'**globosely** *adv.* —**globosity** (gləʊ'bɒsɪtɪ) *or* '**globoseness** *n.*

globular ('glɒbjʊlə) *or* **globulous** *adj.* **1.** shaped like a globe or globule. **2.** having or consisting of globules. —**globularity** (,glɒbjʊ'lærɪtɪ) *or* '**globularness** *n.* —'**globularly** *adv.*

globular cluster *n. Astronomy.* a densely populated spheroidal star cluster with the highest concentration of stars near its centre, found in the galactic halo.

globule ('glɒbjuːl) *n.* **1.** a small globe, esp. a drop of liquid. **2.** *Astronomy.* a small dark nebula thought to be a site of star formation. [C17: from Latin *globulus,* diminutive of *globus* GLOBE]

globuliferous (,glɒbjʊ'lɪfərəs) *adj.* producing, containing, or having globules.

globulin ('glɒbjʊlɪn) *n.* any of a group of simple proteins, including gamma globulin, that are generally insoluble in water but soluble in salt solutions and coagulated by heat. [C19: from GLOBULE + -IN]

globus ('gləʊbəs) *n. Anatomy.* any spherelike structure.

globus hystericus (hɪ'sterɪkəs) *n.* the technical name for a **lump in the throat.** See **lump** (sense 8).

glochidium (gləʊ'kɪdɪəm) *n., pl.* **-chidia** (-'kɪdɪə). **1.** any of the barbed hairs among the spore masses of some ferns and on certain other plants. **2.** a parasitic larva of certain freshwater mussels that attaches itself to the fins or gills of fish by hooks or suckers. [C19: from New Latin, from Greek *glōkhis* projecting point] —**glo'chidiate** *adj.*

glockenspiel ('glɒkən,spiːl, -,ʃpiːl) *n.* a percussion instrument consisting of a set of tuned metal plates played with a pair of small hammers. [C19: German, from *Glocken* bells + *Spiel* play]

glogg (glɒg) *n.* a hot alcoholic mixed drink, originally from Sweden, consisting of sweetened brandy, red wine, bitters or other flavourings, and blanched almonds. [from Swedish *glögg,* from *glödga* to burn]

glomerate ('glɒmərɪt) *adj.* **1.** gathered into a compact rounded mass. **2.** wound up like a ball of thread. **3.** *Anatomy.* (esp. of glands) conglomerate in structure. [C18: from Latin *glomerāre* to wind into a ball, from *glomus* ball]

glomeration (ˌglɒməˈreɪʃən) *n.* a conglomeration or cluster.

glomerule (ˈglɒməˌruːl) *n. Botany.* **1.** a cymose inflorescence in the form of a ball-like cluster of flowers. **2.** a ball-like cluster of spores. [C18: from New Latin GLOMERULUS] —**glomerulate** (glɒˈmɛrʊlɪt, -ˌleɪt) *adj.*

glomerulonephritis (glɒˌmɛrʊləʊnɪˈfraɪtɪs) *n.* any of various kidney diseases in which the glomeruli are affected.

glomerulus (glɒˈmɛrʊləs) *n., pl.* **-li** (-ˌlaɪ). **1.** a knot of blood vessels in the kidney projecting into the capsular end of a urine-secreting tubule. **2.** any cluster or coil of blood vessels, nerve fibres, etc., in the body. [C18: from New Latin, diminutive of *glomus* ball] —**gloˈmerular** *adj.*

gloom (gluːm) *n.* **1.** partial or total darkness. **2.** a state of depression or melancholy. **3.** an appearance or expression of despondency or melancholy. **4.** *Poetic.* a dim or dark place. ~*vb.* **5.** (*intr.*) to look sullen or depressed. **6.** to make or become dark or gloomy. [C14 *gloumben* to look sullen; related to Norwegian dialect *glome* to eye suspiciously] —ˈ**gloomful** *adj.* —ˈ**gloomfully** *adv.* —ˈ**gloomless** *adj.*

gloomy (ˈgluːmɪ) *adj.* **gloomier, gloomiest.** **1.** dark or dismal. **2.** causing depression, dejection, or gloom: *gloomy news.* **3.** despairing; sad. —ˈ**gloomily** *adv.* —ˈ**gloominess** *n.*

gloria (ˈglɔːrɪə) *n.* **1.** a silk, wool, cotton, or nylon fabric used esp. for umbrellas. **2.** a halo or nimbus, esp. as represented in art. [C16: from Latin: GLORY]

Gloria (ˈglɔːrɪə, -ˌɑː) *n.* **1.** any of several doxologies beginning with the word *Gloria,* esp. the Greater Doxology (**Gloria in Excelsis Deo**) or the Lesser Doxology (**Gloria Patri**). **2.** a musical setting of one of these.

glorification (ˌglɔːrɪfɪˈkeɪʃən) *n.* **1.** the act of glorifying or state of being glorified. **2.** *Informal.* an enhanced or favourably exaggerated version or account. **3.** *Brit. informal.* a celebration.

glorify (ˈglɔːrɪˌfaɪ) *vb.* **-fies, -fying, -fied.** (*tr.*) **1.** to make glorious. **2.** to make more splendid; adorn. **3.** to worship, exalt, or adore. **4.** to extol. **5.** to cause to seem more splendid or imposing than reality. —ˈ**gloriˌfiable** *adj.* —ˈ**gloriˌfier** *n.*

gloriole (ˈglɔːrɪˌəʊl) *n.* another name for a **halo** or **nimbus** (senses 2, 3). [C19: from Latin *glōriola,* literally: a small GLORY]

gloriosa (ˌglɔːrɪˈəʊsə) *n.* any plant of the bulbous tropical African genus *Gloriosa,* some species of which are grown as ornamental greenhouse climbers for their showy flowers of yellow, orange, and red: family *Liliaceae.* Also called: **glory lily.** [New Latin, from Latin *gloriosus* glorious]

glorious (ˈglɔːrɪəs) *adj.* **1.** having or full of glory; illustrious. **2.** conferring glory or renown: *a glorious victory.* **3.** brilliantly beautiful. **4.** delightful or enjoyable. **5.** *Informal.* drunk. —ˈ**gloriously** *adv.* —ˈ**gloriousness** *n.*

glory (ˈglɔːrɪ) *n., pl.* **-ries.** **1.** exaltation, praise, or honour, as that accorded by general consent: *the glory for the exploit went to the captain.* **2.** something that brings or is worthy of praise (esp. in the phrase **crowning glory**). **3.** thanksgiving, adoration, or worship: *glory be to God.* **4.** pomp; splendour: *the glory of the king's reign.* **5.** radiant beauty; resplendence: *the glory of the sunset.* **6.** the beauty and bliss of heaven. **7.** a state of extreme happiness or prosperity. **8.** another word for **halo** or **nimbus.** ~*vb.* **-ries, -rying, -ried.** **9.** (*intr.;* often foll. by *in*) to triumph or exult. **10.** (*intr.*) *Obsolete.* to brag. ~*interj.* **11.** *Informal.* a mild interjection to express pleasure or surprise (often in the exclamatory phrase **glory be!**). [C13: from Old French *glorie,* from Latin *glōria,* of obscure origin]

glory box *n. Austral. and N.Z.* a box in which a young woman stores clothes, etc., in preparation for marriage.

glory hole *n.* **1.** *Informal.* a room, cupboard, or other storage space that contains an untidy and miscellaneous collection of objects. **2.** *Nautical.* another term for **lazaretto** (sense 1).

glory-of-the-snow *n.* a small W Asian liliaceous plant, *Chionodoxa luciliae,* cultivated for its early-blooming blue flowers.

Glos *abbrev. for* Gloucestershire.

gloss[1] (glɒs) *n.* **1.** lustre or sheen, as of a smooth surface. **2.** a superficially attractive appearance. **3.** See **gloss paint.** **4.** a cosmetic preparation applied to the skin to give it a faint sheen: *lip gloss.* ~*vb.* **5.** to give a gloss to or obtain a gloss. ~See also **gloss over.** [C16: probably of Scandinavian origin; compare Icelandic *glossi* flame, Middle High German *glosen* to glow] —ˈ**glosser** *n.* —ˈ**glossless** *adj.*

gloss[2] (glɒs) *n.* **1.** a short or expanded explanation or interpretation of a word, expression, or foreign phrase in the margin or text of a manuscript, etc. **2.** an intentionally misleading explanation or interpretation. **3.** short for **glossary.** ~*vb.* (*tr.*) **4.** to add glosses to. [C16: from Latin *glōssa* unusual word requiring explanatory note, from Ionic Greek] —ˈ**glosser** *n.* —ˈ**glossingly** *adv.*

gloss. *abbrev. for* glossary.

glossa (ˈglɒsə) *n., pl.* **-sae** (-siː) *or* **-sas.** **1.** *Anatomy.* a technical word for the **tongue.** **2.** a paired tonguelike lobe in the labium of an insect. —ˈ**glossal** *adj.*

glossary (ˈglɒsərɪ) *n., pl.* **-ries.** an alphabetical list of terms peculiar to a field of knowledge with definitions or explanations. Sometimes called: **gloss.** [C14: from Late Latin *glossārium;* see GLOSS[2]] —**glossarial** (glɒˈsɛərɪəl) *adj.* —**glosˈsarially** *adv.* —ˈ**glossarist** *n.*

glossator (glɒˈseɪtə) *n.* **1.** Also called: **glossarist, glossist, glossographer.** a writer of glosses and commentaries, esp. (in the Middle Ages) an interpreter of Roman and Canon Law. **2.** a compiler of a glossary.

glossectomy (glɒˈsɛktəmɪ) *n., pl.* **-mies.** surgical removal of all or part of the tongue.

glosseme (ˈglɒsiːm) *n.* the smallest meaningful unit of a language, such as stress, form, etc. [C20: from Greek *glōssēma;* see GLOSS[2], -EME]

glossitis (glɒˈsaɪtɪs) *n.* inflammation of the tongue. —**glossitic** (glɒˈsɪtɪk) *adj.*

glosso- *or before a vowel* **gloss-** *combining form.* indicating a tongue or language: *glossolaryngeal.* [from Greek *glossa* tongue]

glossography (glɒˈsɒgrəfɪ) *n.* the art of writing textual glosses or commentaries. —**glosˈsographer** *n.*

glossolalia (ˌglɒsəˈleɪlɪə) *n.* **1.** another term for **gift of tongues.** **2.** *Psychol.* babbling in a nonexistent language. [C19: New Latin, from GLOSSO- + Greek *lalein* to babble]

glossology (glɒˈsɒlədʒɪ) *n.* an obsolete term for **linguistics.** —**glossological** (ˌglɒsəˈlɒdʒɪkᵊl) *adj.* —**glosˈsologist** *n.*

glossopharyngeal nerve (ˌglɒsəʊˌfærɪnˈdʒiːəl) *n.* the ninth cranial nerve, which supplies the muscles of the pharynx, the tongue, the middle ear, and the parotid gland.

gloss over *vb.* (*tr., adv.*) **1.** to hide under a deceptively attractive surface or appearance. **2.** to deal with (unpleasant facts) rapidly and cursorily, or to omit them altogether from an account of something.

gloss paint *n.* a type of paint composed of pigments ground up in a varnish medium, which produces a hard, shiny, and usually durable finish. Also called: **gloss.**

glossy (ˈglɒsɪ) *adj.* **glossier, glossiest.** **1.** smooth and shiny; lustrous. **2.** superficially attractive; plausible. **3.** (of a magazine) lavishly produced on shiny paper and usually with many colour photographs. ~*n., pl.* **glossies.** **4.** Also called (U.S.): **slick.** an expensively produced magazine, typically a sophisticated fashion or glamour magazine, printed on shiny paper and containing high quality colour photography. Compare **pulp** (sense 3). **5.** a photograph printed on paper that has a smooth shiny surface. —ˈ**glossily** *adv.* —ˈ**glossiness** *n.*

glottal (ˈglɒtᵊl) *adj.* **1.** of or relating to the glottis. **2.** *Phonetics.* articulated or pronounced at or with the glottis.

glottal stop *n.* a plosive speech sound produced as the sudden onset of a vowel in several languages, such as German, by first tightly closing the glottis and then allowing the air pressure to build up in the trachea before opening the glottis, causing the air to escape with force.

glottic (ˈglɒtɪk) *adj.* of or relating to the tongue or the glottis.

glottis (ˈglɒtɪs) *n., pl.* **-tises** *or* **-tides** (-tɪˌdiːz). the vocal apparatus of the larynx, consisting of the two true vocal cords and the opening between them. [C16: from New Latin, from Greek *glōttis,* from *glōtta,* Attic form of Ionic *glōssa* tongue; see GLOSS[2]] —**glottidean** (glɒˈtɪdɪən) *adj.*

glottochronology (ˌglɒtəʊkrəˈnɒlədʒɪ) *n.* the use of lexicostatistics to establish that languages are historically related. [C20 *glotto-,* from Greek *glōtta* tongue]

Gloucester Old Spot (ˈglɒstə) *n.* a hardy breed of pig, white with a few black markings, that originally lived off windfalls in orchards in the Severn valley in Gloucestershire.

glove (glʌv) *n.* **1.** (*often pl.*) a shaped covering for the hand with individual sheaths for the fingers and thumb, made of leather, fabric, etc. See also **gauntlet**[1] (sense 2). **2.** any of various large protective hand covers worn in sports, such as a boxing glove. **3. hand in glove.** *Informal.* in an intimate relationship or close association. **4. handle with kid gloves.** *Informal.* to treat with extreme care. **5. with the gloves off.** *Informal.* (of a dispute, argument, etc.) conducted mercilessly and in earnest, with no reservations. ~*vb.* **6.** (*tr.*) to cover or provide with or as if with gloves. [Old English *glōfe;* related to Old Norse *glōfi*] —ˈ**gloveless** *adj.* —ˈ**gloveˌlike** *adj.*

glove box *n.* a closed box in which toxic or radioactive substances can be handled by an operator who places his hands through protective gloves sealed to the box.

glove compartment *n.* a small compartment in a car dashboard for the storage of miscellaneous articles.

glove puppet *n.* a small figure of a person or animal that fits over and is manipulated by the hand.

glover (ˈglʌvə) *n.* a person who makes or sells gloves.

glow (gləʊ) *n.* **1.** light emitted by a substance or object at a high temperature. **2.** a steady even light without flames. **3.** brilliance or vividness of colour. **4.** brightness or ruddiness of complexion. **5.** a feeling of wellbeing or satisfaction. **6.** intensity of emotion; ardour. ~*vb.* (*intr.*) **7.** to emit a steady even light without flames. **8.** to shine intensely, as if from great heat. **9.** to be exuberant or high-spirited, as from excellent health or intense emotion. **10.** to experience a feeling of wellbeing or satisfaction: *to glow with pride.* **11.** (esp. of the complexion) to show a strong bright colour, esp. a shade of red. **12.** to be very hot. [Old English *glōwan;* related to Old Norse *glōa,* Old High German *gluoen,* Icelandic *glōra* to sparkle]

glow discharge *n.* a silent luminous discharge of electricity through a low-pressure gas.

glower ('glauə) *vb.* **1.** (*intr.*) to stare hard and angrily. ~*n.* **2.** a sullen or angry stare. [C16: probably of Scandinavian origin; related to Middle Low German *glūren* to watch] —'**gloweringly** *adv.*

glowing ('gləuɪŋ) *adj.* **1.** emitting a steady bright light without flames: *glowing embers.* **2.** warm and rich in colour: *the room was decorated in glowing shades of gold and orange.* **3.** flushed and rosy, as from exercise or excitement: *glowing cheeks.* **4.** displaying or indicative of extreme satisfaction, pride, or emotion: *he gave a glowing account of his son's achievements.* —'**glowingly** *adv.*

glow lamp *n.* a small light consisting of two or more electrodes in an inert gas, such as neon, at low pressure, across which an electrical discharge occurs when the voltage applied to the electrodes exceeds the ionization potential.

glow plug *n.* one of usually four plugs fitted to the cylinder block of a diesel engine that warms the engine chamber to facilitate starting in cold weather. Also called: **heater plug.**

glow-worm *n.* **1.** a European beetle, *Lampyris noctiluca,* the females and larvae of which bear luminescent organs producing a soft greenish light: family *Lampyridae.* **2.** any of various other beetles or larvae of the family *Lampyridae.* ~See also **firefly** (sense 1).

gloxinia (glɒk'sɪnɪə) *n.* any of several tropical plants of the genus *Sinningia,* esp. the South American *S. speciosa,* cultivated for its large white, red, or purple bell-shaped flowers: family *Gesneriaceae.* [C19: named after Benjamin P. *Gloxin,* 18th-century German physician and botanist who first described it]

gloze (gləuz) *Archaic.* ~*vb.* **1.** (*tr.;* often foll. by *over*) to explain away; minimize the effect or importance of. **2.** to make explanatory notes or glosses on (a text). **3.** to use flattery (on). ~*n.* **4.** flattery or deceit. **5.** an explanatory note or gloss. **6.** specious or deceptive talk or action. [C13: from Old French *glosser* to comment; see GLOSS[2]]

glt *Bookbinding. abbrev. for* gilt.

glucagon ('glu:kə,gɒn, -gən) *n.* a polypeptide hormone, produced in the pancreas by the islets of Langerhans, that stimulates the release of glucose into the blood. Compare **insulin.** [C20: from GLUC(OSE) + *-agon,* perhaps from Greek *agein* to lead]

glucan ('glu:,kæn) *n.* any polysaccharide consisting of a polymer of glucose, such as cellulose or starch.

glucinum (glu:'saɪnəm) *or* **glucinium** (glu:'sɪnɪəm) *n.* a former name for **beryllium.** [C19: New Latin *glucina* beryllium oxide, from Greek *glukus* sweet + -IN; alluding to the sweet taste of some of the salts]

glucocorticoid (,glu:kəu'kɔ:tɪ,kɔɪd) *n.* any of a class of corticosteroids that control carbohydrate, protein, and fat metabolism and have anti-inflammatory activity.

gluconeogenesis (,glu:kəu,ni:əu'dʒɛnɪsɪs) *n. Biochem.* the sequence of metabolic reactions by which glucose is synthesized, esp. in the liver, from noncarbohydrate sources, such as amino acids, pyruvic acid, or glycerol. Also called: **glyconeogenesis.**

glucophore ('glu:kəu,fɔ:) *n.* a chemical group responsible for sweetness of taste.

glucoprotein (,glu:kəu'prəuti:n) *n.* another name for **glycoprotein.**

glucose ('glu:kəuz, -kəus) *n.* **1.** a white crystalline monosaccharide sugar that has several optically active forms, the most abundant being dextrose: a major energy source in metabolism. Formula: $C_6H_{12}O_6$. **2.** a yellowish syrup (or, after desiccation, a solid) containing dextrose, maltose, and dextrin, obtained by incomplete hydrolysis of starch: used in confectionery, fermentation, etc. [C19: from French, from Greek *gleukos* sweet wine; related to Greek *glukus* sweet] —**glucosic** (glu:'kɒsɪk) *adj.*

glucoside ('glu:kəu,saɪd) *n. Biochem.* any of a large group of glycosides that yield glucose on hydrolysis. —,**gluco'sidal** *or* **glucosidic** (,glu:kəu'sɪdɪk) *adj.*

glucosuria (,glu:kəu'sjuərɪə) *n. Pathol.* a less common word for **glycosuria.** —,**gluco'suric** *adj.*

glue (glu:) *n.* **1.** any natural or synthetic adhesive, esp. a sticky gelatinous substance prepared by boiling animal products such as bones, skin, and horns. **2.** any other sticky or adhesive substance. ~*vb.* **glues, gluing, glued.** **3.** (*tr.*) to join or stick together with or as if with glue. [C14: from Old French *glu,* from Late Latin *glūs;* compare Greek *gloios*] —'**glue,like** *adj.* —'**gluer** *n.* —'**gluey** *adj.*

glue-sniffing *n.* the practice of inhaling the fumes of certain types of glue to produce intoxicating or hallucinatory effects. —'**glue-,sniffer** *n.*

gluhwein ('glu:,vaɪn) *n.* mulled wine. [German]

glum (glʌm) *adj.* **glummer, glummest.** silent or sullen, as from gloom. [C16: variant of GLOOM] —'**glumly** *adv.* —'**glumness** *n.*

glume (glu:m) *n. Botany.* one of a pair of dry membranous bracts at the base of the inflorescence, esp. the spikelet, of grasses. [C18: from Latin *glūma* husk of corn; related to Latin *glūbere* to remove the bark from] —**glu'maceous** *adj.* —'**glume,like** *adj.*

gluon ('glu:ɒn) *n.* a hypothetical particle believed to be exchanged between quarks in order to bind them together to form particles. [C20: from GLUE + -ON]

glut (glʌt) *n.* **1.** an excessive amount, as in the production of a crop, often leading to a fall in price. **2.** the act of glutting or state of being glutted. ~*vb.* **gluts, glutting, glutted.** (*tr.*) **3.** to feed or supply beyond capacity. **4.** to supply (a market) with a commodity in excess of the demand for it. **5.** to cram full or choke up: *to glut a passage.* [C14: probably from Old French *gloutir,* from Latin *gluttīre;* see GLUTTON[1]] —'**gluttingly** *adv.*

glutamate ('glu:tə,meɪt) *n.* any salt of glutamic acid, esp. its sodium salt (see **monosodium glutamate**). [C19: from GLUTAM(IC) + -ATE[1]]

glutamic acid (glu:'tæmɪk) *or* **glutaminic acid** (,glu:tə'mɪnɪk) *n.* a nonessential amino acid, occurring in proteins, that acts as a neurotransmitter and plays an important part in nitrogen metabolism.

glutamine ('glu:tə,mi:n, -mɪn) *n.* a nonessential amino acid occurring in proteins: plays an important role in protein metabolism. [C19: from GLUT(EN) + -AMINE]

glutaraldehyde (,glu:tə'ældɪ,haɪd) *n.* a water-soluble oil used as a disinfectant, tanning agent, and in resins. Formula: $C_5H_8O_2$.

glutathione (,glu:tə'θaɪəun, -θaɪ'əun) *n. Biochem.* a tripeptide consisting of glutamic acid, cysteine, and glycine: important in biological oxidations and the activation of some enzymes. Formula: $C_{10}H_{17}N_3O_6S$. [C20: from GLUTA(MIC ACID) + THI- + -ONE]

glutelin ('glu:tɪlɪn) *n.* any of a group of water-insoluble plant proteins found in cereals. They are precipitated by alcohol and are not coagulated by heat. Compare **gliadin.** [C20: See GLUTEN, -IN]

gluten ('glu:tᵊn) *n.* a protein consisting of a mixture of glutelin and gliadin, present in cereal grains, esp. wheat. A gluten-free diet is necessary in cases of coeliac disease. [C16: from Latin: GLUE] —'**glutenous** *adj.*

gluten bread *n.* bread made from flour containing a high proportion of gluten.

gluteus *or* **glutaeus** (glu'ti:əs) *n., pl.* **-tei** *or* **-taei** (-'ti:aɪ). any one of the three large muscles that form the human buttock and move the thigh, esp. the **gluteus maximus.** [C17: from New Latin, from Greek *gloutos* buttock, rump] —**glu'teal** *or* **glu'taeal** *adj.*

glutinous ('glu:tɪnəs) *adj.* resembling glue in texture; sticky. —'**glutinously** *adv.* —'**glutinousness** *or* **glutinosity** (,glu:tɪ'nɒsɪtɪ) *n.*

glutton[1] ('glʌtᵊn) *n.* **1.** a person devoted to eating and drinking to excess; greedy person. **2.** *Often ironical.* a person who has or appears to have a voracious appetite for something: *a glutton for punishment.* [C13: from Old French *glouton,* from Latin *glutto,* from *gluttīre* to swallow] —'**gluttonous** *adj.* —'**gluttonously** *adv.*

glutton[2] ('glʌtᵊn) *n.* another name for **wolverine.** [C17: from GLUTTON[1], apparently translating German *Vielfass* great eater]

gluttony ('glʌtənɪ) *n.* the act or practice of eating to excess.

glyceric (glɪ'sɛrɪk) *adj.* of, containing, or derived from glycerol.

glyceric acid *n.* a viscous liquid carboxylic acid produced by the oxidation of glycerol; 2,3-dihydroxypropanoic acid. Formula: $C_3H_6O_4$.

glyceride ('glɪsə,raɪd) *n.* any fatty-acid ester of glycerol.

glycerin ('glɪsərɪn) *or* **glycerine** ('glɪsərɪn, ,glɪsə'ri:n) *n.* another name (not in technical usage) for **glycerol.** [C19: from French *glycérine,* from Greek *glukeros* sweet + *-ine* -IN; related to Greek *glukus* sweet]

glycerol ('glɪsə,rɒl) *n.* a colourless or pale yellow odourless sweet-tasting syrupy liquid; 1,2,3-propanetriol: a by-product of soap manufacture, used as a solvent, antifreeze, plasticizer, and sweetener (**E422**). Formula: $C_3H_8O_3$. Also called (not in technical usage): **glycerin, glycerine.** [C19: from GLYCER(IN) + -OL[1]]

glyceryl ('glɪsərɪl) *n.* (*modifier*) derived from glycerol by replacing or removing one or more of its hydroxyl groups: *a glyceryl group or radical.*

glyceryl trinitrate *n.* another name for **nitroglycerin.**

glycine ('glaɪsi:n, glaɪ'si:n) *n.* a nonessential amino acid occurring in most proteins that acts as a neurotransmitter; aminoacetic acid. [C19: GLYCO- + -INE[2]]

glyco- *or before a vowel* **glyc-** *combining form.* indicating sugar: *glycogen.* [from Greek *glukus* sweet]

glycogen ('glaɪkəudʒən, -dʒɛn) *n.* a polysaccharide consisting of glucose units: the form in which carbohydrate is stored in the liver and muscles in man and animals. It can easily be hydrolysed to glucose. Also called: **animal starch.** —**glycogenic** (,glaɪkəu'dʒɛnɪk) *adj.*

glycogenesis (,glaɪkəu'dʒɛnɪsɪs) *n.* the formation of sugar, esp. (in animals) from glycogen. —**glycogenetic** (,glaɪkəudʒɪ'nɛtɪk) *adj.*

glycol ('glaɪkɒl) *n.* another name (not in technical usage) for **ethanediol** or a **diol.** —**glycolic** *or* **glycollic** (glaɪ'kɒlɪk) *adj.*

glycolic acid *n.* a colourless crystalline soluble hygroscopic compound found in sugar cane and sugar beet: used in tanning and in the manufacture of pharmaceuticals, pesticides, adhesives, and plasticizers; hydroxyacetic acid. Formula: $CH_2(OH)COOH$.

glycolipid (,glaɪkəu'lɪpɪd) *n.* any of a group of lipids containing a carbohydrate group, commonly glucose or galactose.

glycolysis (glaɪ'kɒlɪsɪs) *n. Biochem.* the breakdown of glucose by enzymes into pyruvic and lactic acids with the liberation of energy.

glyconeogenesis (ˌglaɪkəʊˌniːəʊˈdʒɛnɪsɪs) *n.* another name for **gluconeogenesis.**

glycophyte (ˈglaɪkəʊˌfaɪt) *n.* any plant that will only grow healthily in soils with a low content of sodium salts. —**glycophytic** (ˌglaɪkəʊˈfɪtɪk) *adj.*

glycoprotein (ˌglaɪkəʊˈprəʊtiːn), **glucoprotein,** *or* **glycopeptide** (ˌglaɪkəʊˈpɛptaɪd) *n.* any of a group of conjugated proteins containing small amounts of carbohydrates as prosthetic groups. See also **mucoprotein.**

glycose (ˈglaɪkəʊz, -kəʊs) *n.* **1.** an older word for **glucose. 2.** any of various monosaccharides.

glycoside (ˈglaɪkəʊˌsaɪd) *n.* any of a group of substances, such as digitoxin, derived from monosaccharides by replacing the hydroxyl group by another group. Many are important medicinal drugs. See also **glucoside.** —**glycosidic** (ˌglaɪkəʊˈsɪdɪk) *adj.*

glycosuria (ˌglaɪkəʊˈsjʊərɪə) *or* **glucosuria** *n.* the presence of excess sugar in the urine, as in diabetes. [C19: from New Latin, from French *glycose* GLUCOSE + -URIA] —ˌ**glycoˈsuric** *or* ˌ**glucoˈsuric** *adj.*

glycosylation (ˌglaɪkəʊsəˈleɪʃən) *n.* the process by which sugars are chemically attached to proteins to form glycoproteins. [from *glycosyl* radical derived from *glycose* + -ATION]

glyoxaline (glaɪˈɒksəlɪn) *n.* another name (not in technical usage) for **imidazole.**

glyph (glɪf) *n.* **1.** a carved channel or groove, esp. a vertical one as used on a Doric frieze. **2.** *Now rare.* another word for **hieroglyphic.** [C18: from French *glyphe,* from Greek *gluphē* carving, from *gluphein* to carve] —ˈ**glyphic** *adj.*

glyphography (glɪˈfɒgrəfɪ) *n.* a plate-making process in which an electrotype is made from an engraved copper plate. [C19: from Greek *gluphē* carving + -GRAPHY] —**glyphograph** (ˈglɪfəˌgrɑːf, -ˌgræf) *n.* —**glyˈphographer** *n.* —**glyphographic** (ˌglɪfəˈgræfɪk) *or* ˌ**glyphoˈgraphical** *adj.*

glyptal (ˈglɪptəl) *n.* an alkyd resin obtained from polyhydric alcohols and polybasic organic acids or their anhydrides; used for surface coatings. [C20: a trademark, perhaps from GLY(CEROL) + P(H)T(H)AL(IC)]

glyptic (ˈglɪptɪk) *adj.* of or relating to engraving or carving, esp. on precious stones. [C19: from French *glyptique,* from Greek *gluptikos,* from *gluptos,* from *gluphein* to carve]

glyptics (ˈglɪptɪks) *n.* (*functioning as sing.*) the art of engraving precious stones.

glyptodont (ˈglɪptəˌdɒnt) *n.* any extinct late Cenozoic edentate mammal of the genus *Glyptodon* and related genera, of South America, which resembled giant armadillos. [C19: from Greek *gluptos* carved + -ODONT]

glyptography (glɪpˈtɒgrəfɪ) *n.* the art of carving or engraving upon gemstones. —**glypˈtographer** *n.* —**glyptographic** (ˌglɪptəˈgræfɪk) *or* ˌ**glyptoˈgraphical** *adj.*

GM *abbrev. for:* **1.** general manager. **2.** (in Britain) George Medal. **3.** Grand Master.

G-man *n., pl.* **G-men. 1.** *U.S. slang.* an FBI agent. **2.** *Irish.* a political detective.

GMB *abbrev. for:* **1.** Grand Master Bowman; the highest standard of archer. **2.** General, Municipal, and Boilermakers (trades union).

GmbH (in Germany) *abbrev. for* Gesellschaft mit beschränkter Haftung; a limited company. [German: company with limited liabilities]

Gmc *abbrev. for* Germanic.

GMC *abbrev. for:* **1.** general management committee. **2.** General Medical Council.

GMT *abbrev. for* Greenwich Mean Time.

GMWU (in Britain) *abbrev. for* National Union of General and Municipal Workers.

gnamma hole (ˈnæmə) *n.* a variant spelling of **namma hole.**

gnarl[1] (nɑːl) *n.* **1.** any knotty protuberance or swelling on a tree. ~*vb.* **2.** (*tr.*) to knot or cause to knot. [C19: back formation from *gnarled,* probably variant of *knurled;* see KNURL]

gnarl[2] (nɑːl) *or* **gnar** (nɑː) *vb.* (*intr.*) *Obsolete.* to growl or snarl. [C16: of imitative origin]

gnarled (nɑːld) *or* **gnarly** (ˈnɑːlɪ) *adj.* **1.** having gnarls: *the gnarled trunk of the old tree.* **2.** (esp. of hands) rough, twisted, and weather-beaten in appearance. **3.** perverse or ill-tempered.

gnash (næʃ) *vb.* **1.** to grind (the teeth) together, as in pain or anger. **2.** (*tr.*) to bite or chew as by grinding the teeth. ~*n.* **3.** the act of gnashing the teeth. [C15: probably of Scandinavian origin; compare Old Norse *gnastan* gnashing of teeth, *gnesta* to clatter] —ˈ**gnashingly** *adv.*

gnat (næt) *n.* any of various small fragile biting dipterous insects of the suborder *Nematocera,* esp. *Culex pipiens* (**common gnat**), which abounds near stagnant water. [Old English *gnætt;* related to Middle High German *gnaz* scurf, German dialect *Gnitze* gnat] —ˈ**gnatˌlike** *adj.*

gnatcatcher (ˈnætˌkætʃə) *n.* any of various small American songbirds of the genus *Polioptila* and related genera, typically having a long tail and a pale bluish-grey plumage: family *Muscicapidae* (Old World flycatchers, etc.).

gnathic (ˈnæθɪk) *or* **gnathal** *adj. Anatomy.* of or relating to the jaw. [C19: from Greek *gnathos* jaw]

gnathion (ˈneɪθɪˌɒn, ˈnæθ-) *n.* the lowest point of the midline of the lower jaw: a reference point in craniometry. [C19: from New Latin, from Greek *gnathos* jaw]

gnathite (ˈneɪθaɪt, ˈnæθ-) *n. Zoology.* an appendage of an arthropod that is specialized for grasping or chewing; mouthpart. [C19: from Greek *gnathos* jaw]

gnathonic (næˈθɒnɪk) *adj. Literary.* deceitfully flattering; sycophantic. [C17: from Latin *gnathōnicus,* from *Gnathō,* such a character in the *Eunuchus,* Roman comedy by Terence (?190–159 B.C.)] —**gnaˈthonically** *adv.*

gnathostome (ˈneɪθəʊˌstəʊm) *n.* any vertebrate of the superclass *Gnathostomata,* having a mouth with jaws, including all vertebrates except the agnathans. [from New Latin *Gnathostomata,* from Greek *gnathos* jaw + *stoma* mouth] —ˌ**gnathoˈstomatous** *adj.*

-gnathous *adj. combining form.* indicating or having a jaw of a specified kind: *prognathous.* [from New Latin *-gnathus,* from Greek *gnathos* jaw]

gnaw (nɔː) *vb.* **gnaws, gnawing, gnawed; gnawed** *or* **gnawn** (nɔːn). **1.** (when *intr.,* often foll. by *at* or *upon*) to bite (at) or chew (upon) constantly so as to wear away little by little. **2.** (*tr.*) to form by gnawing: *to gnaw a hole.* **3.** to cause erosion of (something). **4.** (when *intr.,* often foll. by *at*) to cause constant distress or anxiety (to). ~*n.* **5.** the act or an instance of gnawing. [Old English *gnagan;* related to Old Norse *gnaga,* Old High German *gnagan*] —ˈ**gnawable** *adj.* —ˈ**gnawer** *n.* —ˈ**gnawing** *adj., n.*

gnawing (ˈnɔːɪŋ) *n.* a dull persistent pang or pain, esp. of hunger. —ˈ**gnawingly** *adv.*

GNC (in Britain) *abbrev. for* General Nursing Council.

gneiss (naɪs) *n.* any coarse-grained metamorphic rock that is banded or foliated: represents the last stage in the metamorphism of rocks before melting. [C18: from German *Gneis,* probably from Middle High German *ganeist* spark; related to Old Norse *gneista* to give off sparks] —ˈ**gneissic,** ˈ**gneissoid,** *or* ˈ**gneissose** *adj.*

gnocchi (ˈnɒkɪ, gəˈnɒkɪ, ˈgnɒkɪ) *pl. n.* dumplings made of pieces of semolina pasta, or sometimes potato, used to garnish soup or served alone with sauce. [Italian, plural of *gnocco* lump, probably of Germanic origin; compare Middle High German *knoche* bone]

gnome[1] (nəʊm) *n.* **1.** one of a species of legendary creatures, usually resembling small misshapen old men, said to live in the depths of the earth and guard buried treasure. **2.** the statue of a gnome, esp. in a garden. **3.** a very small or ugly person. **4.** *Facetious or derogatory.* an international banker or financier (esp. in the phrase **gnomes of Zürich**). [C18: from French, from New Latin *gnomus,* coined by Paracelsus, of obscure origin] —ˈ**gnomish** *adj.*

gnome[2] (nəʊm) *n.* a short pithy saying or maxim expressing a general truth or principle. [C16: from Greek *gnōmē,* from *gignōskein* to know]

gnomic (ˈnəʊmɪk, ˈnɒm-) *or* **gnomical** *adj.* **1.** consisting of, containing, or relating to gnomes or aphorisms. **2.** of or relating to a writer of such sayings. —ˈ**gnomically** *adv.*

gnomon (ˈnəʊmɒn) *n.* **1.** the stationary arm that projects the shadow on a sundial. **2.** a geometric figure remaining after a parallelogram has been removed from one corner of a larger parallelogram. [C16: from Latin, from Greek: interpreter, from *gignōskein* to know] —**gnoˈmonic** *adj.* —**gnoˈmonically** *adv.*

gnosis (ˈnəʊsɪs) *n., pl.* **-ses** (-siːz). supposedly revealed knowledge of various spiritual truths, esp. that said to have been possessed by ancient Gnostics. [C18: ultimately from Greek: knowledge, from *gignōskein* to know]

-gnosis *n. combining form.* (esp. in medicine) recognition or knowledge: *prognosis; diagnosis.* [via Latin from Greek: GNOSIS] —**-gnostic** *adj. combining form.*

gnostic (ˈnɒstɪk) *or* **gnostical** *adj.* of, relating to, or possessing knowledge, esp. esoteric spiritual knowledge. —ˈ**gnostically** *adv.*

Gnostic (ˈnɒstɪk) *n.* **1.** an adherent of Gnosticism. ~*adj.* **2.** of or relating to Gnostics or to Gnosticism. [C16: from Late Latin *Gnosticī* the Gnostics, from Greek *gnōstikos* relating to knowledge, from *gnōstos* known, from *gignōskein* to know]

Gnosticism (ˈnɒstɪˌsɪzəm) *n.* a religious movement characterized by a belief in gnosis, through which the spiritual element in man could be released from its bondage in matter: regarded as a heresy by the Christian Church.

Gnosticize *or* **Gnosticise** (ˈnɒstɪˌsaɪz) *vb.* **1.** (*intr.*) to maintain or profess Gnostic views. **2.** to put a Gnostic interpretation upon (something). —ˈ**Gnostiˌcizer** *or* ˈ**Gnostiˌciser** *n.*

gnotobiotics (ˌnəʊtəʊbaɪˈɒtɪks) *n.* (*functioning as sing.*) the study of organisms living in germ-free conditions or when inoculated with known microorganisms. [C20: from Greek, from *gnōtos,* from *gignōskein* to know + *bios* known life] —ˌ**gnotobiˈotic** *adj.* —ˌ**gnotobiˈotically** *adv.*

gnow (naʊ) *n. W Austral.* another name for **mallee fowl.**

GNP *abbrev. for* gross national product.

gnr. *abbrev. for* gunner.

GnRH *Biochem. abbrev. for* gonadotrophin-releasing hormone: a peptide that is released from the brain and stimulates the pituitary gland to secrete gonadotrophic hormones that act in turn on the sex glands.

gns. *abbrev. for* guineas.

gnu (nuː) *n., pl.* **gnus** *or* **gnu.** either of two sturdy antelopes, *Connochaetes taurinus* (**brindled gnu**) or the much rarer *C. gnou* (**white-tailed gnu**), inhabiting the savannas of Africa, having an oxlike head and a long tufted tail. Also called: **wildebeest.** [C18: from Xhosa *nqu*]

go[1] (gəʊ) *vb.* **goes, going, went, gone.** (*mainly intr.*) **1.** to move or proceed, esp. to or from a point or in a certain direction: *to go to London; to go home.* **2.** (*tr.; takes an infinitive,* often with *to* omitted or replaced by *and*) to proceed towards a particular person or place with some specified intention or purpose: *I must go and get that book.* **3.** to depart: *we'll have to go at eleven.* **4.** to start, as in a race: often used in commands. **5.** to make regular journeys: *this train service goes to the east coast.* **6.** to operate or function effectively: *the radio won't go.* **7.** (*copula*) to become: *his face went red with embarrassment.* **8.** to make a noise as specified: *the gun went bang.* **9.** to enter into a specified state or condition: *to go into hysterics; to go into action.* **10.** to be or continue to be in a specified state or condition: *to go in rags; to go in poverty.* **11.** to lead, extend, or afford access: *this route goes to the north.* **12.** to proceed towards an activity: *to go to supper; to go to sleep.* **13.** (*tr.; takes an infinitive*) to serve or contribute: *this letter goes to prove my point.* **14.** to follow a course as specified; fare: *the lecture went badly.* **15.** to be applied or allotted to a particular purpose or recipient: *her wealth went to her son; his money went on drink.* **16.** to be sold or otherwise transferred to a recipient: *the necklace went for three thousand pounds.* **17.** to be ranked; compare: *this meal is good as my meals go.* **18.** to blend or harmonize: *these chairs won't go with the rest of your furniture.* **19.** (foll. by *by* or *under*) to be known (by a name or disguise). **20.** to fit or extend: *that skirt won't go round your waist.* **21.** to have a usual or proper place: *those books go on this shelf.* **22.** (of music, poetry, etc.) to be sounded; expressed, etc.: *how does that song go?* **23.** to fail or give way: *my eyesight is going.* **24.** to break down or collapse abruptly: *the ladder went at the critical moment.* **25.** to die: *the old man went at 2 a.m.* **26.** (often foll. by *by*) **a.** (of time) to elapse: *the hours go by so slowly at the office.* **b.** to travel past: *the train goes by her house at four.* **c.** to be guided (by). **27.** to occur: *happiness does not always go with riches.* **28.** to be eliminated, abolished, or given up: *this entry must go to save space.* **29.** to be spent or finished: *all his money has gone.* **30.** to circulate or be transmitted: *the infection went around the whole community.* **31.** to attend: *go to school; go to church.* **32.** to join a stated profession: *go to the bar; go on the stage.* **33.** (foll. by *to*) to have recourse (to); turn: *to go to arbitration.* **34.** (foll. by *to*) to subject or put oneself (to): *she goes to great pains to please him.* **35.** to proceed, esp. up to or beyond certain limits: *you will go too far one day and then you will be punished.* **36.** to be acceptable or tolerated: *anything goes in this place.* **37.** to carry the weight of final authority: *what the boss says goes.* **38.** (foll. by *into*) to be contained in: *four goes into twelve three times.* **39.** (often foll. by *for*) to endure or last out: *we can't go for much longer without water in this heat.* **40.** (*tr.*) *Cards.* to bet or bid: *I go two hearts.* **41.** (*tr.*) *Informal, chiefly U.S.* to have as one's weight: *I went 112 pounds a year ago.* **42.** *U.S. and Canadian.* (*usually used in commands;* takes an infinitive without *to*) **a.** to start to act so as to: *go shut the door.* **b.** to leave so as to: *go blow your brains out.* **43.** *Informal.* to perform well; be successful: *that group can really go.* **44.** (*tr.*) *Nonstandard.* to say: widely used, esp. in the historic present, in reporting dialogue: *Then she goes, "Give it to me!" and she just snatched it.* **45. go and.** *Informal.* to be so foolish or unlucky as to: *then she had to go and lose her hat.* **46. be going.** to intend or be about to start (to do or be doing something): often used as an alternative future construction: *what's going to happen to us?* **47. go ape over.** *Slang.* to become crazy or extremely enthusiastic about. **48. go astray.** to be mislaid; go missing. **49. go bail.** to act as surety. **50. go bush.** See **bush** (sense 12). **51. go halves.** See **half** (sense 14). **52. go hard.** (often foll. by *with*) to cause trouble or unhappiness (to). **53. go it.** *Slang.* to do something or move energetically. **54. go it alone.** *Informal.* to act or proceed without allies or help. **55. go much on.** *Informal.* to approve of or be in agreement with (something): usually used in the negative: *I don't go much on the idea.* **56. go one better.** *Informal.* to surpass or outdo (someone). **57. go the whole hog.** *Informal.* See **hog** (sense 9). **58. let go. a.** to relax one's hold (on); release. **b.** *Euphemistic.* to dismiss (from employment). **c.** to discuss or consider no further. **59. let oneself go. a.** to act in an uninhibited manner. **b.** to lose interest in one's appearance, manners, etc. **60. to go. a.** remaining. **b.** *U.S. and Canadian informal.* (of food served by a restaurant) for taking away. ~*n., pl.* **goes. 61.** the act of going. **62.** *Informal.* **a.** an attempt or try: *he had a go at the stamp business.* **b.** an attempt at stopping a person suspected of a crime: *the police are not always in favour of the public having a go.* **c.** an attack, esp. verbal: *she had a real go at them.* **63.** a turn: *it's my go next.* **64.** *Informal.* the quality of being active and energetic: *she has much more go than I.* **65.** *Informal.* hard or energetic work: *it's all go.* **66.** *Informal.* a successful venture or achievement: *he made a go of it.* **67.** *Informal.* a bout or attack (of an illness): *he had a bad go of flu last winter.* **68.** *Informal.* an unforeseen, usually embarrassing or awkward, turn of events: *here's a rum go.* **69.** *Informal.* a bargain or agreement. **70. all the go.** *Informal.* very popular; in fashion. **71. from the word go.** *Informal.* from the very beginning. **72.** See **get-up-and-go. 73. no go.** *Informal.* impossible; abortive or futile: *it's no go, I'm afraid.* **74. on the go.** *Informal.* active and energetic. ~*adj.* **75.** (*postpositive*) *Informal.* functioning properly and ready for action: esp. used in astronautics: *all systems are go.* ~See also **go about, go against, go ahead, go along, go around, go at, go away, go back, go by, go down, go for, go forth, go in, going, go into, gone, go off, go on, go out, go over, go through, go to, go together, go under, go up, go with, go without.** [Old English *gān;* related to Old High German *gēn,* Greek *kikhanein* to reach, Sanskrit *jahāti* he forsakes]

go[2] (gəʊ) *or* **I-go** *n.* a game for two players in which stones are placed on a board marked with a grid, the object being to capture territory on the board. [from Japanese]

GO *Military. abbrev. for* general order.

goa ('gəʊə) *n.* a gazelle, *Procapra picticaudata,* inhabiting the plains of the Tibetan plateau, having a brownish-grey coat and backward-curving horns. [C19: from Tibetan *dgoba*]

go about *vb.* (*intr.*) **1.** (*adv.*) to move from place to place. **2.** (*prep.*) to busy oneself with: *to go about one's duties.* **3.** (*prep.*) to tackle (a problem or task). **4.** (*prep.*) to be actively and constantly engaged in (doing something): *he went about doing good.* **5.** to circulate (in): *there's a lot of flu going about.* **6.** (*adv.*) (of a sailing ship) to change from one tack to another.

goad (gəʊd) *n.* **1.** a sharp pointed stick for urging on cattle, etc. **2.** anything that acts as a spur or incitement. ~*vb.* **3.** (*tr.*) to drive with or as if with a goad; spur; incite. [Old English *gād,* of Germanic origin, related to Old English *gār,* Old Norse *geirr* spear] —'**goad,like** *adj.*

go against *vb.* (*intr., prep.*) **1.** to be contrary to (principles or beliefs). **2.** to be unfavourable to (a person): *the case went against him.*

go ahead *vb.* **1.** (*intr., adv.*) to start or continue, often after obtaining permission. ~*n.* **go-ahead. 2.** (usually preceded by *the*) *Informal.* permission to proceed. ~*adj.* **go-ahead. 3.** enterprising or ambitious.

goal (gəʊl) *n.* **1.** the aim or object towards which an endeavour is directed. **2.** the terminal point of a journey or race. **3.** (in various sports) the net, basket, etc. into or over which players try to propel the ball, puck, etc., to score. **4.** *Sport.* **a.** a successful attempt at scoring. **b.** the score so made. **5.** (in soccer, hockey, etc.) the position of goalkeeper. [C16: perhaps related to Middle English *gol* boundary, Old English *gǣlan* to hinder, impede] —'**goalless** *adj.*

goal area *n. Soccer.* a rectangular area to the sides and front of the goal, measuring 20 × 6 yards on a full-sized pitch, from which goal kicks are taken. Also called: **six-yard area.**

goalball ('gəʊl,bɔːl) *n.* **1.** a game played by two teams who compete to score goals by throwing a ball that emits audible sound when in motion. Players, who may be blind or sighted, are blindfolded during play. **2.** the ball used in this game.

goalie ('gəʊlɪ) *n. Informal.* short for **goalkeeper.**

goalkeeper ('gəʊl,kiːpə) *n. Sport.* a player in the goal whose duty is to prevent the ball, puck, etc., from entering or crossing it. —'**goal,keeping** *n.*

goal kick *n. Soccer.* a kick taken from the six-yard line by the defending team after the ball has been put out of play by an opposing player.

goal line *n. Sport.* the line marking each end of the pitch, on which the goals stand.

goalmouth ('gəʊl,maʊθ) *n. Soccer, hockey, etc.* the area in front of the goal.

go along *vb.* (*intr., adv.;* often foll. by *with*) to refrain from disagreement; assent.

goal post *n.* either of two upright posts supporting the crossbar of a goal.

goanna (gəʊ'ænə) *n.* any of various Australian monitor lizards. [C19: changed from IGUANA]

Goa powder ('gəʊə) *n.* another name for **araroba** (sense 2). [named after *Goa,* a state of India]

go around *or* **round** *vb.* (*intr.*) **1.** (*adv.*) to move about. **2.** (*adv.;* foll. by *with*) to frequent the society (of a person or group of people): *she went around with older men.* **3.** (*adv.*) to be sufficient: *are there enough sweets to go round?* **4.** to circulate (in): *measles is going round the school.* **5.** (*prep.*) to be actively and constantly engaged in (doing something): *she went around caring for the sick.* **6.** to be long enough to encircle: *will that belt go round you?*

goat (gəʊt) *n.* **1.** any sure-footed agile bovid mammal of the genus *Capra,* naturally inhabiting rough stony ground in Europe, Asia, and N Africa, typically having a brown-grey colouring and a beard. Domesticated varieties (*C. hircus*) are reared for milk, meat, and wool. Related adjs.: **caprine, hircine. 2.** short for **Rocky Mountain goat. 3.** *Informal.* a lecherous man. **4.** a bad or inferior member of any group (esp. in the phrase **separate the sheep from the goats**). **5.** short for **scapegoat. 6. act** (*or* **play**) **the** (**giddy**) **goat.** to fool around. **7. get** (**someone's**) **goat.** *Slang.* to cause annoyance to (someone). [Old English *gāt;* related to Old Norse *geit,* Old High German *geiz,* Latin *haedus* kid] —'**goat,like** *adj.*

Goat (gəʊt) *n.* **the.** the constellation Capricorn, the tenth sign of the zodiac.

go at *vb.* (*intr., prep.*) **1.** to make an energetic attempt at (something). **2.** to attack vehemently.

goat antelope *n.* any bovid mammal of the tribe *Rupicaprini,* including the chamois, goral, serow, and Rocky Mountain goat, having characteristics of both goats and antelopes.

goatee (gəʊˈtiː) *n.* a pointed tuftlike beard on the chin. [C19: from GOAT + -ee (see -Y[2])] —**goatˈeed** *adj.*

goatfish (ˈgəʊtˌfɪʃ) *n., pl.* **-fish** *or* **-fishes.** the U.S. name for the **red mullet.**

goatherd (ˈgəʊtˌhɜːd) *n.* a person employed to tend or herd goats.

goatish (ˈgəʊtɪʃ) *adj.* **1.** of, like, or relating to a goat. **2.** *Archaic or literary.* lustful or lecherous. —**ˈgoatishly** *adv.* —**ˈgoatishness** *n.*

goat moth *n.* a large European moth, *Cossus cossus,* with pale brownish-grey variably marked wings: family *Cossidae.*

goatsbeard *or* **goat's-beard** (ˈgəʊtsˌbɪəd) *n.* **1.** Also called: **Jack-go-to-bed-at-noon.** a Eurasian plant, *Tragopogon pratensis,* with woolly stems and large heads of yellow rayed flowers surrounded by large green bracts: family *Compositae* (composites). **2.** an American rosaceous plant, *Aruncus sylvester,* with long spikes of small white flowers.

goatskin (ˈgəʊtˌskɪn) *n.* **1.** the hide of a goat. **2. a.** something made from the hide of a goat, such as leather or a container for wine. **b.** (*as modifier*): *a goatskin rug.*

goat's-rue *n.* **1.** Also called: **French lilac.** a Eurasian leguminous plant, *Galega officinalis,* cultivated for its white, mauve, or pinkish flowers: formerly used medicinally. **2.** a North American leguminous plant, *Tephrosia virginiana,* with pink-and-yellow flowers.

goatsucker (ˈgəʊtˌsʌkə) *n.* the U.S. and Canadian name for **nightjar.**

go away *vb.* (*intr., adv.*) to leave, as when starting from home on holiday.

go-away bird *n.* any of several touracos of the genus *Corythaixoides.* [C19: imitative of its call]

gob[1] (gɒb) *n.* **1.** a lump or chunk, esp. of a soft substance. **2.** (*often pl.*) *Informal.* a great quantity or amount. **3.** *Mining.* **a.** waste material such as clay, shale, etc. **b.** a worked-out area in a mine often packed with this. **4.** a lump of molten glass used to make a piece of glassware. **5.** *Informal.* a globule of spittle or saliva. ~*vb.* **gobs, gobbing, gobbed. 6.** (*intr.*) *Brit. informal.* to spit. [C14: from Old French *gobe* lump, from *gober* to gulp down; see GOBBET]

gob[2] (gɒb) *n. U.S. slang.* an enlisted ordinary seaman in the U.S. Navy. [C20: of unknown origin]

gob[3] (gɒb) *n.* a slang word (esp. Brit.) for the **mouth.** [C16: perhaps from Gaelic *gob*]

go back *vb.* (*intr., adv.*) **1.** to return. **2.** (often foll. by *to*) to originate (in): *the links with France go back to the Norman Conquest.* **3.** (foll. by *on*) to change one's mind about; repudiate (esp. in the phrase **go back on one's word**). **4.** (of clocks and watches) to be set to an earlier time, as during British Summer Time: *when do the clocks go back this year?*

gobbet (ˈgɒbɪt) *n.* a chunk, lump, or fragment, esp. of raw meat. [C14: from Old French *gobet,* from *gober* to gulp down]

gobble[1] (ˈgɒbᵊl) *vb.* **1.** (when *tr.,* often foll. by *up*) to eat or swallow (food) hastily and in large mouthfuls. **2.** (*tr.;* often foll. by *up*) *Informal.* to snatch. [C17: probably from GOB[1]]

gobble[2] (ˈgɒbᵊl) *n.* **1.** the loud rapid gurgling sound made by male turkeys. ~*interj.* **2.** an imitation of this sound. ~*vb.* **3.** (*intr.*) (of a turkey) to make this sound. [C17: probably of imitative origin]

gobbledegook *or* **gobbledygook** (ˈgɒbᵊldɪˌguːk) *n.* pretentious language, esp. as characterized by obscure phraseology. [C20: whimsical formation from GOBBLE[2]]

gobbler (ˈgɒblə) *n. Informal.* a male turkey.

Gobelin (ˈgəʊbəlɪn; *French* gɔblɛ̃) *adj.* **1.** of or resembling tapestry made at the Gobelins' factory in Paris, having vivid pictorial scenes. ~*n.* **2.** a tapestry of this kind. [C19: from the *Gobelin* family, who founded the factory]

go-between *n.* a person who acts as agent or intermediary for two people or groups in a transaction or dealing.

gobioid (ˈgəʊbɪˌɔɪd) *adj.* **1.** of or relating to the *Gobioidea,* a suborder of spiny-finned teleost fishes that includes gobies and mudskippers (family *Gobiidae*) and sleepers (family *Eleotridae*). ~*n.* **2.** any gobioid fish. [C19: from New Latin *Gobioidea,* from Latin *gōbius* gudgeon]

goblet (ˈgɒblɪt) *n.* **1.** a vessel for drinking, usually of glass or metal, with a base and stem but without handles. **2.** *Archaic.* a large drinking cup shaped like a bowl. [C14: from Old French *gobelet* a little cup, from *gobel* ultimately of Celtic origin]

goblin (ˈgɒblɪn) *n.* (in folklore) a small grotesque supernatural creature, regarded as malevolent towards human beings. [C14: from Old French, from Middle High German *kobolt;* compare COBALT]

gobo (ˈgəʊbəʊ) *n., pl.* **-bos** *or* **-boes. 1.** a shield placed around a microphone to exclude unwanted sounds. **2.** a black screen placed around a camera lens, television lens, etc., to reduce the incident light. [C20: of unknown origin]

gobshite (ˈgɒbˌʃaɪt) *n. Irish taboo slang.* a stupid person. [C20: from GOB[3] + *shite* excrement; see SHIT]

gobsmacked (ˈgɒbˌsmækt) *adj. Brit. slang.* astounded; astonished. [C20: from GOB[3] + SMACK[2]]

gobstopper (ˈgɒbˌstɒpə) *n. Brit.* a large hard sweet consisting of different coloured concentric layers that are revealed as it is sucked.

goby (ˈgəʊbɪ) *n., pl.* **-by** *or* **-bies. 1.** any small spiny-finned fish of the family *Gobiidae,* of coastal or brackish waters, having a large head, an elongated tapering body, and the ventral fins modified as a sucker. **2.** any other gobioid fish. [C18: from Latin *gōbius* gudgeon, fish of little value, from Greek *kōbios*]

go-by *n. Slang.* a deliberate snub or slight (esp. in the phrase **give (a person) the go-by**).

go by *vb.* (*intr.*) **1.** to pass: *the cars went by; as the years go by we all get older; don't let those opportunities go by!* **2.** (*prep.*) to be guided by: *in the darkness we could only go by the stars.* **3.** (*prep.*) to use as a basis for forming an opinion or judgment: *it's wise not to go only by appearances.*

go-cart *n.* **1.** *Chiefly U.S. and Canadian.* a small wagon for young children to ride in or pull. **2.** *Chiefly U.S. and Canadian.* a light frame on casters or wheels that supports a baby while learning to walk. Brit. word: **baby-walker. 3.** *Motor racing.* See **kart. 4.** another word for **handcart.**

GOC(-in-C) *abbrev. for* General Officer Commanding(-in-Chief).

god (gɒd) *n.* **1.** a supernatural being, who is worshipped as the controller of some part of the universe or some aspect of life in the world or is the personification of some force. **2.** an image, idol, or symbolic representation of such a deity. **3.** any person or thing to which excessive attention is given: *money was his god.* **4.** a man who has qualities regarded as making him superior to other men. **5.** (*pl.*) the gallery of a theatre. [Old English *god;* related to Old Norse *goth,* Old High German *got,* Old Irish *guth* voice]

God (gɒd) *n.* **1.** *Theol.* the sole Supreme Being, eternal, spiritual, and transcendent, who is the Creator and ruler of all and is infinite in all attributes; the object of worship in monotheistic religions. ~*interj.* **2.** an oath or exclamation used to indicate surprise, annoyance, etc. (and in such expressions as **My God!** or **God Almighty!**).

godchild (ˈgɒdˌtʃaɪld) *n., pl.* **-children** (-ˌtʃɪldrən). a person, usually an infant, who is sponsored by adults at baptism.

goddamn (ˈgɒdˈdæm) *Informal, chiefly U.S. and Canadian.* ~*interj. also* **God damn. 1.** an oath expressing anger, surprise, etc. ~*adv. also* **goddam,** *adj. also* **goddam** *or* **goddamned. 2.** (intensifier): *a goddamn fool.*

goddaughter (ˈgɒdˌdɔːtə) *n.* a female godchild.

goddess (ˈgɒdɪs) *n.* **1.** a female divinity. **2.** a woman who is adored or idealized, esp. by a man. —**ˈgoddessˌhood** *or* **ˈgoddess-ˌship** *n.*

Gödel's proof (ˈgɜːdᵊlz) *n.* the principle that in a formal axiomatic system, such as logic or mathematics, it is impossible to prove consistency without using methods from outside the system. [C20: named after Kurt *Gödel* (1906–78), U.S. logician and mathematician who first proved it]

godet (ˈgəʊdeɪ, gəʊˈdɛt) *n.* a triangular piece of material inserted into a garment, such as into a skirt to create a flare. [C19: from French]

godetia (gəˈdiːʃə) *n.* any plant of the American onagraceous genus *Godetia,* esp. one grown as a showy-flowered annual garden plant. [C19: named after C. H. *Godet* (died 1879), Swiss botanist]

godfather (ˈgɒdˌfɑːðə) *n.* **1.** a male godparent. **2.** the head of a Mafia family or other organized criminal ring.

godfather offer *n. Informal.* a takeover bid pitched so high that the management of the target company is unable to dissuade shareholders from accepting it.

God-fearing *adj.* pious; devout: *a God-fearing people.*

godforsaken (ˈgɒdfəˌseɪkən, ˌgɒdfəˈseɪkən) *adj.* (*sometimes cap.*) **1.** (*usually prenominal*) desolate; dreary; forlorn. **2.** wicked.

Godhead (ˈgɒdˌhɛd) *n.* (*sometimes not cap.*) **1.** the essential nature and condition of being God. **2. the Godhead.** God.

godhood (ˈgɒdˌhʊd) *n.* the state of being divine.

godless (ˈgɒdlɪs) *adj.* **1.** wicked or unprincipled. **2.** lacking a god. **3.** refusing to acknowledge God. —**ˈgodlessly** *adv.* —**ˈgodlessness** *n.*

godlike (ˈgɒdˌlaɪk) *adj.* resembling or befitting a god or God; divine.

godly (ˈgɒdlɪ) *adj.* **-lier, -liest.** having a religious character; pious; devout: *a godly man.* —**ˈgodliness** *n.*

godmother (ˈgɒdˌmʌðə) *n.* a female godparent.

godown (ˈgəʊˌdaʊn) *n.* (in the East, esp. in India and Malaya) a warehouse. [C16: from Malay *godong*]

go down *vb.* (*intr., mainly adv.*) **1.** (*also prep.*) to move or lead to or as if to a lower place or level; sink, decline, decrease, etc.: *the ship went down this morning; prices are going down; the path goes down to the sea.* **2.** to be defeated; lose. **3.** to be remembered or recorded (esp. in the phrase **go down in history**). **4.** to be received: *his speech went down well.* **5.** (of food) to be swallowed. **6.** *Bridge.* to fail to make the number of tricks previously contracted for. **7.** *Brit.* to leave a college or university at the end of a term or the academic year. **8.** (usually foll. by *with*) to fall ill; be infected. **9.** (of a celestial body) to sink or set: *the sun went down before we arrived.* **10.** *Brit. slang.* to go to prison, esp. for a specified period: *he went down for six months.* **11.** *U.S. slang.* to happen.

godparent (ˈgɒdˌpɛərənt) *n.* a person who stands sponsor to another at baptism.

godroon (gəˈdruːn) *n.* a variant spelling of **gadroon.** —**goˈdrooned** *adj.*

God's acre *n. Literary.* a churchyard or burial ground. [C17: translation of German *Gottesacker*]

godsend (ˈgɒdˌsɛnd) *n.* a person or thing that comes unexpectedly but is particularly welcome. [C19: changed from C17 *God's send,* alteration of *goddes sand* God's message, from Old English *sand;* see SEND[1]]

godslot (ˈgɒdˌslɒt) *n. Informal.* a time in a television or radio schedule traditionally reserved for religious broadcasts.

godson (ˈgɒdˌsʌn) *n.* a male godchild.

Godspeed (ˈgɒdˈspiːd) *interj., n.* an expression of one's good wishes for a person's success and safety. [C15: from *God spede* may God prosper (you)]

godsquad (ˈgɒdˌskwɒd) *n. Informal, derogatory.* any group of evangelical Christians, members of which are regarded as intrusive and exuberantly pious.

godwit (ˈgɒdwɪt) *n.* any large shore bird of the genus *Limosa,* of northern and arctic regions, having long legs and a long upturned bill: family *Scolopacidae* (sandpipers, etc.), order *Charadriiformes.* [C16: of unknown origin]

goer (ˈgəʊə) *n.* **1. a.** a person who attends something regularly. **b.** (*in combination*): *filmgoer.* **2.** an energetic person. **3.** *Austral. informal.* an acceptable or feasible idea, proposal, etc. **4.** *Austral. and N.Z. informal.* a person trying to succeed.

goethite *or* **göthite** (ˈgəʊθaɪt; *German* ˈgøːtiːt) *n.* a black, brown, or yellow mineral consisting of hydrated iron oxide in the form of orthorhombic crystals or fibrous masses. Formula: FeO(OH). [C19: named after J. W. von *Goethe* (1749–1832), German writer and dramatist]

gofer (ˈgəʊfə) *n. Slang, chiefly U.S. and Canadian.* an employee or assistant whose duties include menial tasks such as running errands. [C20: originally U.S.: alteration of *go for*]

goffer *or* **gauffer** (ˈgəʊfə) *vb.* **1.** (*tr.*) to press pleats into (a frill). **2.** (*tr.*) to decorate (the gilt edges of a book) with a repeating pattern. ~*n.* **3.** an ornamental frill made by pressing pleats. **4.** the decoration formed by goffering books. **5.** the iron or tool used in making goffers. [C18: from French *gaufrer* to impress a pattern, from *gaufre,* from Middle Low German *wāfel;* see WAFFLE[1], WAFER]

go for *vb.* (*intr., prep.*) **1.** to go somewhere in order to have or fetch: *he went for a drink; shall I go for a doctor?* **2.** to seek to obtain: *I'd go for that job if I were you.* **3.** to apply to: *what I told him goes for you too.* **4.** to prefer or choose; like: *I really go for that new idea of yours.* **5.** to be to the advantage of: *you'll have great things going for you in the New Year.* **6.** to make a physical or verbal attack on. **7.** to be considered to be of a stated importance or value: *his twenty years went for nothing when he was made redundant.* **8. go for it.** *Informal.* to make the maximum effort to achieve a particular goal.

go forth *vb.* (*intr., adv.*) *Archaic or formal.* **1.** to be issued: *the command went forth that taxes should be collected.* **2.** to go out: *the army went forth to battle.*

go-getter *n. Informal.* an ambitious enterprising person. —ˈ**go-ˌgetting** *adj.*

gogga (ˈxɒxə) *n. S. African informal.* any small animal that crawls or flies, esp. an insect. [C20: from Hottentot *xoxon* insects collectively]

goggle (ˈgɒgᵊl) *vb.* **1.** (*intr.*) to stare stupidly or fixedly, as in astonishment. **2.** to cause (the eyes) to roll or bulge or (of the eyes) to roll or bulge. ~*n.* **3.** a fixed or bulging stare. **4.** (*pl.*) spectacles, often of coloured glass or covered with gauze: used to protect the eyes. [C14: from *gogelen* to look aside, of uncertain origin; see AGOG] —ˈ**goggly** *adj.*

gogglebox (ˈgɒgᵊlˌbɒks) *n. Brit. slang.* a television set.

goggle-eyed *adj.* (*often postpositive*) with a surprised, staring, or fixed expression.

goglet (ˈgɒglɪt) *or* **gurglet** *n.* a long-necked water-cooling vessel of porous earthenware, used esp. in India. Also called: **guglet** (ˈgʌglɪt). [C17: from Portuguese *gorgoleta* a little throat, from *gorja* throat; related to French *gargoule;* see GARGLE]

go-go *adj. Informal, chiefly U.S. and Canadian.* **1.** of or relating to discos or the lively music and dancing performed in them. **2.** dynamic or forceful. [C20: altered from French *à-gogo* aplenty, ad lib: sense influenced by English verb *go*]

go-go dancer *n.* a dancer, usually scantily dressed, who performs rhythmic and often erotic modern dance routines, esp. in a nightclub or disco.

Goidel (ˈgɔɪdᵊl) *n.* a Celt who speaks a Goidelic language; Gael. Compare **Brython.**

Goidelic, Goidhelic (gɔɪˈdɛlɪk), *or* **Gadhelic** *n.* **1.** the N group of Celtic languages, consisting of Irish Gaelic, Scottish Gaelic, and Manx. Compare **Brythonic.** ~*adj.* **2.** of, relating to, or characteristic of this group of languages. [C19: from Old Irish *Goidel* a Celt, from Old Welsh *gwyddel,* from *gwydd* savage]

go in *vb.* (*intr., mainly adv.*) **1.** to enter. **2.** (*prep.*) See **go into. 3.** (of the sun) to become hidden behind a cloud. **4.** to be assimilated or grasped: *nothing much goes in if I try to read in the evenings.* **5.** *Cricket.* to begin an innings. **6. go in for. a.** to enter as a competitor or contestant. **b.** to adopt as an activity, interest, or guiding principle: *she went in for nursing; some men go in for football in a big way.*

going (ˈgəʊɪŋ) *n.* **1.** a departure or farewell. **2.** the condition of a surface such as a road or field with regard to walking, riding, etc.: *muddy going.* **3.** *Informal.* speed, progress, etc.: *we made good going on the trip.* ~*adj.* **4.** thriving (esp. in the phrase **a going concern**). **5.** current or accepted, as from past negotiations or commercial operation: *the going rate for electricians; the going value of the firm.* **6.** (*postpositive*) available: *the best going.* **7. going, going, gone!** a statement by an auctioneer that the bidding has almost finished.

going-over *n., pl.* **goings-over.** *Informal.* **1.** a check, examination, or investigation. **2.** a castigation or thrashing.

goings-on *pl. n. Informal.* **1.** actions or conduct, esp. when regarded with disapproval. **2.** happenings or events, esp. when mysterious or suspicious: *there were strange goings-on up at the Hall.*

go into *vb.* (*intr., prep.*) **1.** to enter. **2.** to start a career in: *to go into publishing.* **3.** to investigate or examine: *to go into the problem of price increases.* **4.** to discuss: *we won't go into that now.* **5.** to dress oneself differently in: *to go into mourning.* **6.** to hit: *the car had gone into a lamppost.* **7.** to go to live in or be admitted to, esp. temporarily: *she went into hospital on Tuesday.* **8.** to enter a specified state: *she went into fits of laughter.*

goitre *or U.S.* **goiter** (ˈgɔɪtə) *n. Pathol.* a swelling of the thyroid gland, in some cases nearly doubling the size of the neck, usually caused by under- or overproduction of hormone by the gland. [C17: from French *goitre,* from Old French *goitron* ultimately from Latin *guttur* throat] —ˈ**goitred** *or U.S.* ˈ**goitered** *adj.* —ˈ**goitrous** *adj.*

go-kart *or* **go-cart** *n.* See **kart.**

Golconda (gɒlˈkɒndə) *n.* (*sometimes not cap.*) a source of wealth or riches, esp. a mine. [C18: after *Golconda,* former city in S central India renowned for its diamond mines]

gold (gəʊld) *n.* **1. a.** a dense inert bright yellow element that is the most malleable and ductile metal, occurring in rocks and alluvial deposits: used as a monetary standard and in jewellery, dentistry, and plating. The radioisotope gold-198 (**radiogold**), with a half-life of 2.69 days, is used in radiotherapy. Symbol: Au; atomic no.: 79; atomic wt.: 196.97; valency: 1 or 3; relative density: 19.32; melting pt.: 1063°C; boiling pt.: 2966°C. Related adjs.: **aurous, auric. b.** (*as modifier*): *a gold mine.* **2.** a coin or coins made of this metal. **3.** money; wealth. **4.** something precious, beautiful, etc., such as a noble nature (esp. in the phrase **heart of gold**). **5. a.** a deep yellow colour, sometimes with a brownish tinge. **b.** (*as adj.*): *a gold carpet.* **6.** *Archery.* the bull's eye of a target, scoring nine points. **7.** short for **gold medal.** [Old English *gold;* related to Old Norse *gull,* Gothic *gulth,* Old High German *gold*]

goldarn (gɒlˈdɑːn) *interj., adv. U.S. and Canadian slang.* a euphemistic variant of **goddamn.**

Goldbach's conjecture (ˈgəʊldˌbɑːxs) *n.* the hypothesis that every even number greater than two is the sum of two prime numbers. [named after C. *Goldbach* (1690–1764), German mathematician]

gold basis *n.* the gold standard as a criterion for the determination of prices.

goldbeater's skin (ˈgəʊldˌbiːtəz) *n.* animal membrane used to separate sheets of gold that are being hammered into gold leaf.

gold-beating *n.* the act, process, or skill of hammering sheets of gold into gold leaf. —ˈ**gold-ˌbeater** *n.*

gold beetle *or* **goldbug** (ˈgəʊldˌbʌg) *n.* any American beetle of the family *Chrysomelidae* having a bright metallic lustre.

gold brick *n.* **1.** something with only a superficial appearance of value. **2.** *U.S. slang.* an idler or shirker.

gold card *n.* a credit card issued by credit-card companies to favoured clients, entitling them to high unsecured overdrafts, some insurance cover, etc.

gold certificate *n.* (in the U.S.) **1.** a currency note issued exclusively to the Federal Reserve Banks by the U.S. Treasury. It forms a claim on gold reserves deposited by the Federal Reserve Banks at the Treasury and is used to transfer interbank balances within the Federal Reserve System. **2.** Also called: **gold note.** (formerly) a banknote issued by the U.S. Treasury to the public and redeemable in gold.

goldcrest (ˈgəʊldˌkrɛst) *n.* a small Old World warbler, *Regulus regulus,* having a greenish plumage and a bright yellow-and-black crown.

gold-digger *n.* **1.** a person who prospects or digs for gold. **2.** *Informal.* a woman who uses her sexual attractions to accumulate gifts and wealth or advance her social position. —ˈ**gold-ˌdigging** *n.*

gold disc *n.* **a.** (in Britain) an LP record certified to have sold 100 000 copies or a single certified to have sold 400 000 copies. **b.** (in the U.S.) an LP record or single certified to have sold 500 000 copies.

gold dust *n.* gold in the form of small particles or powder, as found in placer-mining.

golden (ˈgəʊldən) *adj.* **1.** of the yellowish or brownish-yellow metallic colour of gold: *golden hair.* **2.** made from or largely consisting of gold: *a golden statue.* **3.** happy or prosperous: *golden days.* **4.** (*sometimes cap.*) (of anniversaries) the 50th in a series: *Golden Jubilee; golden wedding.* **5.** *Informal.* very successful or destined for success: *the golden girl of tennis.* **6.**

extremely valuable or advantageous: *a golden opportunity.* —'**goldenly** *adv.* —'**goldenness** *n.*

golden age *n.* **1.** the most flourishing and outstanding period, esp. in the history of an art or nation: *the golden age of poetry.* **2.** the great classical period of Latin literature, occupying approximately the 1st century B.C. and represented by such writers as Cicero and Virgil.

golden aster *n.* any North American plant of the genus *Chrysopsis,* esp. *C. mariana* of the eastern U.S., having yellow rayed flowers: family *Compositae* (composites).

golden chain *n.* another name for **laburnum.**

Golden Delicious *n.* a variety of eating apple having sweet flesh and greenish-yellow skin.

golden eagle *n.* a large eagle, *Aquila chrysaetos,* of mountainous regions of the N hemisphere, having a plumage that is golden brown on the back and brown elsewhere.

goldeneye ('gəʊldən,aɪ) *n., pl.* **-eyes** *or* **-eye. 1.** either of two black-and-white diving ducks, *Bucephala clangula* or *B. islandica,* of northern regions. **2.** any lacewing of the family *Chrysopidae* that has a greenish body and eyes of a metallic lustre.

golden goose *n.* a goose in folklore that laid a golden egg a day until its greedy owner killed it in an attempt to get all the gold at once.

golden handcuffs *pl. n. Informal.* payments deferred over a number of years that induce a person to stay with a particular company or in a particular job.

golden handshake *n. Informal.* a sum of money, usually large, given to an employee, either on retirement in recognition of long or excellent service or as compensation for loss of employment.

golden hello *n. Informal.* a payment made to a sought-after recruit on signing a contract of employment with a company.

Golden Kiwi *n. N.Z.* **1.** a public lottery with valuable cash prizes. **2.** a grant made from the profits of a Golden Kiwi to the arts.

golden mean *n.* **1.** the middle course between extremes. **2.** another term for **golden section.**

golden number *n.* a number between 1 and 19, used to indicate the position of any year in the Metonic cycle, calculated as the remainder when 1 is added to the given year and the sum is divided by 19. If the remainder is zero the number is 19: *the golden number of 1984 is 9.*

golden oldie *n.* something old or long-established, esp. a hit record or song that has remained popular or is enjoying a revival. Also called: **oldie.**

golden oriole *n.* a European oriole, *Oriolus oriolus,* the male of which has a bright yellow head and body with black wings and tail.

golden parachute *n. Informal.* a clause in the employment contract of a senior executive providing for special benefits if the executive's employment is terminated as a result of a takeover.

golden perch *n.* another name for **callop.**

golden pheasant *n.* a brightly coloured pheasant, *Chrysolophus pictus,* of the mountainous regions of W and central Asia, the males of which have a crest and ruff.

golden plover *n.* any of several plovers of the genus *Pluvialis,* such as *P. apricaria* of Europe and Asia, that have golden brown back, head, and wings.

golden retriever *n.* a compact medium-sized breed of dog having a silky coat of flat or wavy hair of a gold or dark-cream colour, well-feathered on the legs and tail.

goldenrod (,gəʊldən'rɒd) *n.* **1.** any plant of the genus *Solidago,* of North America, Europe, and Asia, having spikes of small yellow flowers: family *Compositae* (composites). See also **yellowweed. 2.** any of various similar related plants, such as *Brachychaeta sphacelata* (**false goldenrod**) of the southern U.S.

golden rule *n.* **1.** any of a number of rules of fair conduct, such as *Whatsoever ye would that men should do to you, do ye even so to them* (Matthew 7:12) or *thou shalt love thy neighbour as thyself* (Leviticus 19:28). **2.** any important principle: *a golden rule of sailing is to wear a life jacket.* **3.** another name for **rule of three.**

goldenseal (,gəʊldən'siːl) *n.* a ranunculaceous woodland plant, *Hydrastis canadensis,* of E North America, whose thick yellow rootstock contains such alkaloids as berberine and hydrastine and was formerly used medicinally.

golden section *or* **mean** *n. Fine arts.* the proportion of the two divisions of a straight line or the two dimensions of a plane figure such that the smaller is to the larger as the larger is to the sum of the two. If the sides of a rectangle are in this proportion and a square is constructed internally on the shorter side, the rectangle that remains will also have sides in the same proportion.

golden share *n.* a share in a company that controls at least 51% of the voting rights, esp. one retained by the UK government in some privatization issues.

golden syrup *n. Brit.* a light golden-coloured treacle produced by the evaporation of cane sugar juice, used to sweeten and flavour cakes, puddings, etc.

golden triangle *n.* **the.** an opium-producing area of SE Asia, comprising parts of Burma, Laos, and Thailand.

golden wattle *n.* **1.** an Australian yellow-flowered mimosaceous plant, *Acacia pycnantha,* that yields a useful gum and bark. **2.** any of several similar and related plants, esp. *Acacia longifolia* of Australia.

gold-exchange standard *n.* a monetary system by which one country's currency, which is not itself based on the gold standard, is kept at a par with another currency that is based on the gold standard.

goldeye ('gəʊld,aɪ) *n., pl.* **-eyes** *or* **-eye.** a North American clupeoid fish, *Hiodon alosoides,* with yellowish eyes, silvery sides, and a dark blue back: family *Hiodontidae* (mooneyes).

goldfinch ('gəʊld,fɪntʃ) *n.* **1.** a common European finch, *Carduelis carduelis,* the male of which has a red-and-white face and yellow-and-black wings. **2.** any of several North American finches of the genus *Spinus,* esp. the yellow-and-black species *S. tristis.*

goldfinny ('gəʊld,fɪnɪ) *n., pl.* **-nies.** another name for **goldsinny.**

goldfish ('gəʊld,fɪʃ) *n., pl.* **-fish** *or* **-fishes. 1.** a freshwater cyprinid fish, *Carassius auratus,* of E Europe and Asia, esp. China, widely introduced as a pond or aquarium fish. It resembles the carp and has a typically golden or orange-red coloration. **2.** any of certain similar ornamental fishes, esp. the golden orfe (see **orfe**).

goldfish bowl *n.* **1.** Also called: **fishbowl.** a glass bowl, typically spherical, in which fish are kept as pets. **2.** a place or situation open to observation by onlookers.

gold foil *n.* thin gold sheet that is thicker than gold leaf.

goldilocks ('gəʊldɪ,lɒks) *n.* (*functioning as sing.*) **1.** a Eurasian plant, *Aster linosyris* (or *Linosyris vulgaris*), with clusters of small yellow flowers: family *Compositae* (composites). **2.** a Eurasian ranunculaceous woodland plant, *Ranunculus auricomus,* with yellow flowers. See also **buttercup. 3.** (*sometimes cap.*) a person, esp. a girl, with light blond hair.

gold leaf *n.* very thin gold sheet with a thickness between about 0.076 and 0.127 micrometre, produced by rolling or hammering gold and used for gilding woodwork, etc.

gold medal *n.* a medal of gold, awarded to the winner of a competition or race. Compare **silver medal, bronze medal.**

gold mine *n.* **1.** a place in which gold ore is mined. **2.** a source of great wealth, profit, etc. —'**gold-,miner** *n.* —'**gold-,mining** *n.*

gold note *n.* (in the U.S.) another name for **gold certificate.**

gold-of-pleasure *n.* a yellow-flowered Eurasian cruciferous plant, *Camelina sativa,* widespread as a weed, esp. in flax fields: formerly cultivated for its oil-rich seeds.

gold plate *n.* **1.** a thin coating of gold, usually produced by electroplating. **2.** vessels or utensils made of gold.

gold-plate *vb.* (*tr.*) to coat (other metal) with gold, usually by electroplating.

gold point *n. Finance.* either of two exchange rates (the **gold export point** and the **gold import point**) at which it is as cheap to settle international accounts by exporting or importing gold bullion as by selling or buying bills of exchange. Also called: **specie point.**

gold record *n.* a former name for **gold disc.**

gold reserve *n.* the gold reserved by a central bank to support domestic credit expansion, to cover balance of payments deficits, and to protect currency.

gold rush *n.* a large-scale migration of people to a territory where gold has been found.

goldsinny ('gəʊld,sɪnɪ) *n., pl.* **-nies.** any of various small European wrasses, esp. the brightly coloured *Ctenolabrus rupestris.* Also called: **goldfinny.** [origin obscure, but probably has reference to the colour of the fins and tail]

goldsmith ('gəʊld,smɪθ) *n.* **1. a.** a dealer in articles made of gold. **b.** an artisan who makes such articles. **2.** (formerly) a dealer or manufacturer of gold articles who also engaged in banking or other financial business. **3.** (in Malaysia) a Chinese jeweller.

goldsmith beetle *n.* any of various scarabaeid beetles that have a metallic golden lustre, esp. the rose chafer.

gold standard *n.* a monetary system in which the unit of currency is defined with reference to gold.

Gold Stick *n.* (*sometimes not caps.*) **1.** a gilt rod carried by the colonel of the Life Guards or the captain of the gentlemen-at-arms. **2.** the bearer of this rod.

goldstone ('gəʊld,stəʊn) *n.* another name for **aventurine** (senses 2, 3).

goldtail moth ('gəʊld,teɪl) *n.* a European moth, *Euproctis chrysorrhoea* (or *similis*), having white wings and a soft white furry body with a yellow tail tuft: its hairy caterpillars are known as palmer worms: family *Lymantriidae.* Also called: **yellowtail, yellowtail moth.**

goldthread ('gəʊld,θrɛd) *n.* **1.** a North American woodland ranunculaceous plant, *Coptis trifolia* (or *C. groenlandica*), with slender yellow roots. **2.** the root of this plant, which yields a medicinal tonic and a dye.

gold tranche *n.* former name for **reserve tranche.**

golem ('gəʊlɛm) *n.* (in Jewish legend) an artificially created human being brought to life by supernatural means. [from Yiddish *goylem,* from Hebrew *gōlem* formless thing]

golf (gɒlf) *n.* **1. a.** a game played on a large open course, the object of which is to hit a ball using clubs, with as few strokes as possible, into each of usually 18 holes. **b.** (*as modifier*): *a golf bag.* ~*vb.* **2.** (*intr.*) to play golf. [C15: perhaps from Middle Dutch *colf* CLUB]

Golf (gɒlf) *n. Communications.* a code word for the letter *g.*

golf ball *n.* **1.** a small resilient white ball of strands of rubber wound at high tension around a core with a cover made of gutta-percha, etc., used in golf. **2.** (in some electric typewriters) a small detachable metal sphere, around the surface of which type characters are arranged.

golf club *n.* **1.** any of various long-shafted clubs with wood or metal heads used to strike a golf ball. **2. a.** an association of golf players, usually having its own course and facilities. **b.** the premises of such an association.

golf course *n.* a general term for an area of ground, either inland or beside the sea, laid out for the playing of golf. Inland courses are often, though not necessarily, shorter than links courses.

golfer ('gɒlfə) *n.* **1.** a person who plays golf. **2.** a type of cardigan.

golf links *pl. n.* a large open undulating stretch of land beside the sea laid out for the playing of golf. See also **links.**

Golgi body, apparatus, *or* **complex** ('gɔldʒɪ) *n.* a membranous complex of vesicles, vacuoles, and flattened sacs in the cytoplasm of most cells: involved in intracellular secretion and transport. [C20: named after C. *Golgi* (1844–1926), Italian neurologist and histologist]

goliard ('gəʊljəd) *n.* one of a number of wandering scholars in 12th- and 13th-century Europe famed for their riotous behaviour, intemperance, and composition of satirical and ribald Latin verse. [C15: from Old French *goliart* glutton, from Latin *gula* gluttony] —**goliardic** (gəʊl'jɑːdɪk) *adj.*

goliardery (gəʊl'jɑːdərɪ) *n.* the poems of the goliards.

goliath beetle (gə'laɪəθ) *n.* any very large tropical scarabaeid beetle of the genus *Goliathus*, esp. *G. giganteus* of Africa, which may grow to a length of 20 centimetres.

goliath frog *n.* the largest living frog, *Rana goliath,* which occurs in the Congo region of Africa and can grow to a length of 30 centimetres.

golliwog *or* **golliwogg** ('gɒlɪˌwɒg) *n.* a soft doll with a black face, usually made of cloth or rags. [C19: from the name of a doll character in children's books by Bertha Upton (died 1912), U.S. writer, and Florence Upton (died 1922), U.S. illustrator]

gollop ('gɒləp) *vb.* to eat or drink (something) quickly or greedily. [dialect variant of GULP] —'**golloper** *n.*

golly[1] ('gɒlɪ) *interj.* an exclamation of mild surprise or wonder. [C19: originally a euphemism for GOD]

golly[2] ('gɒlɪ) *n., pl.* **-lies.** *Brit. informal.* short for **golliwog:** used chiefly by children.

golly[3] ('gɒlɪ) *Austral. slang.* ~*vb.* **-lies, -lying, -lied.** **1.** to spit. ~*n., pl.* **-lies.** **2.** a gob of spit. [C20: altered from *gollion* a gob of phlegm, probably of imitative origin]

goloshes (gə'lɒʃɪz) *pl. n.* a less common spelling of **galoshes.**

GOM *abbrev. for* Grand Old Man: used to describe an old and respected person or institution.

gombeenism ('gɒmbiːnɪzəm) *n. Irish.* the practice of usury. [C19: from Irish Gaelic *gaimbín* interest on a loan, from Middle English *cambie* exchange, barter, from Latin *cambium*]

gombeen-man ('gɒmbiːnˌmæn) *n. Irish.* a shopkeeper who practises usury.

gombroon (gɒm'bruːn) *n.* Persian and Chinese pottery and porcelain wares. [C17: named after *Gombroon,* Iran, from which it was originally exported]

gomeril ('gɒmərɪl) *n. Scot.* a slow-witted or stupid person. [C19: of uncertain origin]

Gomorrah *or* **Gomorrha** (gə'mɒrə) *n.* a place notorious for vice and depravity. [named after *Gomorrah,* a city destroyed by God as a punishment for the wickedness of its inhabitants (Genesis 19:24)] —**Go'morrean** *or* **Go'morrhean** *adj.*

gomphosis (gɒm'fəʊsɪs) *n., pl.* **-ses** (-siːz). *Anatomy.* a form of immovable articulation in which a peglike part fits into a cavity, as in the setting of a tooth in its socket. [C16: from New Latin, from Greek *gomphoein* to bolt together, from *gomphos* tooth, peg]

gomuti *or* **gomuti palm** (gə'muːtɪ) *n., pl.* **gomutis** *or* **gomuti palms.** **1.** an East Indian feather palm, *Arenga pinnata,* whose sweet sap is a source of sugar. **2.** a black wiry fibre obtained from the leafstalks of this plant, used for making rope, etc. **3.** a Malaysian sago palm, *Metroxylon sagu.* [from Malay *gĕmuti*]

gon- *combining form.* a variant of **gono-** before a vowel: *gonidium.*

-gon *n. combining form.* indicating a figure having a specified number of angles: *pentagon.* [from Greek *-gōnon,* from *gōnia* angle]

gonad ('gɒnæd) *n.* an animal organ in which gametes are produced, such as a testis or an ovary. [C19: from New Latin *gonas,* from Greek *gonos* seed] —'**gonadal, gonadial** (gɒ'neɪdɪəl), *or* **go'nadic** *adj.*

gonadotrophin (ˌgɒnədəʊ'trəʊfɪn) *or* **gonadotropin** (ˌgɒnədəʊ'trəʊpɪn) *n.* any of several glycoprotein hormones secreted by the pituitary gland and placenta that stimulate the gonads and control reproductive activity. See **chorionic gonadotrophin, follicle-stimulating hormone, luteinizing hormone, prolactin.** —ˌ**gonado'trophic** *or* ˌ**gonado'tropic** *adj.*

Gond (gɒnd) *n.* a member of a formerly tribal people now living in scattered enclaves throughout S central India.

Gondi ('gɒndɪ) *n.* the language or group of languages spoken by the Gonds, belonging to the Dravidian family of languages.

gondola ('gɒndələ) *n.* **1.** a long narrow flat-bottomed boat with a high ornamented stem and a platform at the stern where an oarsman stands and propels the boat by sculling or punting: traditionally used on the canals of Venice. **2. a.** a car or cabin suspended from an airship or balloon. **b.** a moving cabin suspended from a cable across a valley, etc. **3.** a flat-bottomed barge used on canals and rivers of the U.S. as far west as the Mississippi. **4.** *U.S. and Canadian.* a low open flat-bottomed railway goods wagon. **5.** a set of island shelves in a self-service shop: used for displaying goods. **6.** *Canadian.* a broadcasting booth built close to the roof over an ice-hockey arena, used by commentators. [C16: from Italian (Venetian dialect), from Medieval Latin *gondula,* perhaps ultimately from Greek *kondu* drinking vessel]

gondolier (ˌgɒndə'lɪə) *n.* a man who propels a gondola.

gone (gɒn) *vb.* **1.** the past participle of **go**[1]. ~*adj.* (*usually postpositive*) **2.** ended; past. **3.** lost; ruined (esp. in the phrases **gone goose** *or* **gosling**). **4.** dead or near to death. **5.** spent; consumed; used up. **6.** *Informal.* faint or weak. **7.** *Informal.* having been pregnant (for a specified time): *six months gone.* **8.** (usually foll. by *on*) *Slang.* in love (with). **9.** *Slang.* in an exhilarated state, as through music or the use of drugs. **10. gone out.** *Informal.* blankly and without comprehension, as if stupefied in surprise. ~*adv.* **11.** past: *it's gone midnight.*

goner ('gɒnə) *n. Slang.* a person or thing beyond help or recovery, esp. a person who is dead or about to die.

gonfalon ('gɒnfələn) *or* **gonfanon** ('gɒnfənən) *n.* **1.** a banner hanging from a crossbar, used esp. by certain medieval Italian republics or in ecclesiastical processions. **2.** a battle flag suspended crosswise on a staff, usually having a serrated edge to give the appearance of streamers. [C16: from Old Italian *gonfalone,* from Old French *gonfalon,* of Germanic origin; compare Old English *gūthfana* war banner, Old Norse *gunnfani*]

gonfalonier (ˌgɒnfələ'nɪə) *n.* the chief magistrate or other official of a medieval Italian republic, esp. the bearer of the republic's gonfalon.

gong (gɒŋ) *n.* **1.** Also called: **tam-tam.** a percussion instrument of indefinite pitch, consisting of a metal platelike disc struck with a soft-headed drumstick. **2.** a rimmed metal disc, hollow metal hemisphere, or metal strip, tube, or wire that produces a note when struck. It may be used to give alarm signals when operated electromagnetically. **3.** a fixed saucer-shaped bell, as on an alarm clock, struck by a mechanically operated hammer. **4.** *Brit. slang.* a medal, esp. a military one. ~*vb.* **5.** (*intr.*) to sound a gong. **6.** (*tr.*) (of traffic police) to summon (a driver) to stop by sounding a gong. [C17: from Malay, of imitative origin] —'**gong**ˌ**like** *adj.*

Gongorism ('gɒŋgəˌrɪzəm) *n.* **1.** an affected literary style characterized by intricate language and obscurity. **2.** an example of this. [C19: from Spanish *gongorismo,* in the style of *Góngora y Argote* (1561–1627), Spanish lyric poet] —'**Gongorist** *n.* —ˌ**Gongo'ristic** *adj.*

goniatite ('gəʊnɪəˌtaɪt) *n.* any extinct cephalopod mollusc of the genus *Goniatites* and related genera, similar to ammonites: a common fossil of Devonian and Carboniferous rocks. [C19: from Greek *gōnia* angle, referring to the angular sutures in some species + -ITE[1]]

gonidium (gə'nɪdɪəm) *n., pl.* **-ia** (-ɪə). **1.** a green algal cell in the thallus of a lichen. **2.** an asexual reproductive cell in some colonial algae. [C19: from New Latin, diminutive from GONO-] —**go'nidial** *or* **go'nidic** *adj.*

goniometer (ˌgəʊnɪ'ɒmɪtə) *n.* **1.** an instrument for measuring the angles between the faces of a crystal. **2.** an instrument consisting of a transformer circuit connected to two directional aerials, used to determine the bearing of a distant radio station. [C18: via French from Greek *gōnia* angle] —**goniometric** (ˌgəʊnɪə'metrɪk) *or* ˌ**gonio'metrical** *adj.* —ˌ**gonio'metrically** *adv.* —ˌ**goni'ometry** *n.*

gonion ('gəʊnɪən) *n., pl.* **-nia** (-nɪə). *Anatomy.* the point or apex of the angle of the lower jaw. [C19: from New Latin, from Greek *gōnia* angle]

gonioscope ('gəʊnɪəʊˌskəʊp) *n.* an instrument used for examining the structures of the eye between the cornea and the lens that are not directly visible.

-gonium *n. combining form.* indicating a seed or reproductive cell: *archegonium.* [from New Latin *gonium,* from Greek *gonos* seed]

gonna ('gɒnə) *vb. Slang. contraction of* going to.

gono- *or before a vowel* **gon-** *combining form.* sexual or reproductive: *gonorrhoea.* [New Latin, from Greek *gonos* seed]

gonococcus (ˌgɒnəʊ'kɒkəs) *n., pl.* **-cocci** (-'kɒksaɪ). a spherical Gram-negative bacterium, *Neisseria gonorrhoeae,* that causes gonorrhoea: family *Neisseriaceae.* —ˌ**gono'coccal** *or* ˌ**gono'coccic** *adj.* —ˌ**gono'coccoid** *adj.*

gonocyte ('gɒnəʊˌsaɪt) *n.* an oocyte or spermatocyte.

gonoduct ('gɒnəʊˌdʌkt) *n. Zoology.* a duct leading from a gonad to the exterior, through which gametes pass.

gonof *or* **gonif** ('gɒnəf) *n.* a variant of **ganef.**

gonophore ('gɒnəʊˌfɔː) *n.* **1.** *Zoology.* a polyp in certain coelenterates that bears gonads. **2.** *Botany.* an elongated structure in certain flowers that bears the stamens and pistil above the level of the other flower parts. —**gonophoric** (ˌgɒnəʊ'fɒrɪk) *or* **gonophorous** (gəʊ'nɒfərəs) *adj.*

gonopod ('gɒnəʊˌpɒd) *n. Zoology.* either member of a pair of appendages that are the external reproductive organs of insects and some other arthropods.

gonopore ('gɒnəˌpɔː) *n.* an external pore in insects, earthworms, etc., through which the gametes are extruded.

gonorrhoea *or esp. U.S.* **gonorrhea** (ˌgɒnə'rɪə) *n.* an infectious venereal disease caused by a gonococcus, characterized by a burning sensation when urinating and a mucopurulent discharge from the urethra or vagina. [C16: from Late Latin, from Greek, from *gonos* seed + *rhoia* flux, flow] —ˌ**gonor'rhoeal,** ˌ**gonor'rhoeic** *or esp. U.S.* ˌ**gonor'rheal,** ˌ**gonor'rheic** *adj.*

gonosome ('gɒnəʊˌsəʊm) *n. Zoology.* the individuals, collectively, in a colonial animal that are involved with reproduction.

-gony *n. combining form.* genesis, origin, or production: *cosmogony.* [from Latin *-gonia,* from Greek, *-goneia,* from *gonos* seed, procreation]

goo (guː) *n. Informal.* **1.** a sticky or viscous substance. **2.** coy or sentimental language or ideas. [C20: of uncertain origin]

goober *or* **goober pea** ('guːbə) *n.* another name for **peanut** (sense 1). [C19: of African (Angolan) origin; related to Kongo *nguba*]

gooby ('guːbɪ) *n., pl.* **goobies.** *N.Z. informal.* spittle.

good (gʊd) *adj.* **better, best. 1.** having admirable, pleasing, superior, or positive qualities; not negative, bad or mediocre: *a good idea; a good teacher.* **2. a.** morally excellent or admirable; virtuous; righteous: *a good man.* **b.** (*as collective n.;* preceded by *the*): *the good.* **3.** suitable or efficient for a purpose: *a good secretary; a good winter coat.* **4.** beneficial or advantageous: *vegetables are good for you.* **5.** not ruined or decayed; sound or whole: *the meat is still good.* **6.** kindly, generous, or approving: *you are good to him.* **7.** right or acceptable: *your qualifications are good for the job.* **8.** rich and fertile: *good land.* **9.** valid or genuine: *I would not do this without good reason.* **10.** honourable or held in high esteem: *a good family.* **11.** commercially or financially secure, sound, or safe: *good securities; a good investment.* **12.** (of a draft) drawn for a stated sum. **13.** (of debts) expected to be fully paid. **14.** clever, competent, or talented: *he's good at science.* **15.** obedient or well-behaved: *a good dog.* **16.** reliable, safe, or recommended: *a good make of clothes.* **17.** affording material pleasure or indulgence: *the good things in life; the good life.* **18.** having a well-proportioned, beautiful, or generally fine appearance: *a good figure; a good complexion.* **19.** complete; full: *I took a good look round the house.* **20.** propitious; opportune: *a good time to ask the manager for a rise.* **21.** satisfying or gratifying: *a good rest.* **22.** comfortable: *did you have a good night?* **23.** newest or of the best quality: *to keep the good plates for important guests.* **24.** fairly large, extensive, or long: *a good distance away.* **25.** sufficient; ample: *we have a good supply of food.* **26.** *U.S.* (of meat) of the third government grade, above *standard* and below *choice.* **27.** serious or intellectual: *good music.* **28.** used in a traditional description: *the good ship "Venus".* **29.** used in polite or patronizing phrases or to express anger (often intended ironically): *how is your good lady?; look here, my good man!* **30. a good one. a.** an unbelievable assertion. **b.** a very funny joke. **31. as good as.** virtually; practically: *it's as good as finished.* **32. as good as gold.** excellent; very good indeed. **33. be as** *or* **so good as to.** would you please. **34. come good.** to recover and perform well after a bad start or setback. **35. good and.** *Informal.* (intensifier): *good and mad.* **36.** (intensifier; used in mild oaths): *good grief! good heavens!* ~*interj.* **37.** an exclamation of approval, agreement, pleasure, etc. ~*n.* **38.** moral or material advantage or use; benefit or profit: *for the good of our workers; what is the good of worrying?* **39.** positive moral qualities; goodness; virtue; righteousness; piety. **40.** (*sometimes cap.*) moral qualities seen as a single abstract entity: *we must pursue the Good.* **41.** a good thing. **42.** *Economics.* a commodity or service that satisfies a human need. **43. for good (and all).** forever; permanently: *I have left them for good.* **44. make good. a.** to recompense or repair damage or injury. **b.** to be successful. **c.** to demonstrate or prove the truth of (a statement or accusation). **d.** to secure and retain (a position). **e.** to effect or fulfil (something intended or promised). **45. good on** *or* **for you (him,** etc.) well done, well said, etc.: a term of congratulation. **46. get any** (*or some*) **good of.** *Irish.* **a.** to handle to good effect: *I never got any good of this machine.* **b.** to understand properly: *I could never get any good of him.* **c.** to receive cooperation from. ~See also **goods.** [Old English *gōd;* related to Old Norse *gōthr,* Old High German *guot* good] —'**goodish** *adj.*

▷**Usage.** Careful speakers and writers of English do not use *good* and *bad* as adverbs: *she dances well* (not *good*); *he sings really badly* (not *really bad*).

good afternoon *sentence substitute.* a conventional expression of greeting or farewell used in the afternoon.

good arvo ('ɑːvəʊ) *sentence substitute. Austral.* good afternoon.

Good Book *n.* a name for the **Bible.** Also called: **the Book.**

goodbye (ˌgʊd'baɪ) *sentence substitute.* **1.** farewell: a conventional expression used at leave-taking or parting with people and at the loss or rejection of things or ideas. ~*n.* **2.** a leave-taking; parting: *they prolonged their goodbyes for a few more minutes.* **3.** a farewell: *they said goodbyes to each other.* [C16: contraction of *God be with ye*]

good day *sentence substitute.* a conventional expression of greeting or farewell used during the day.

good evening *sentence substitute.* a conventional expression of greeting or farewell used in the evening.

good-for-nothing *n.* **1.** an irresponsible or worthless person. ~*adj.* **2.** irresponsible; worthless.

Good Friday *n.* the Friday before Easter, observed as a commemoration of the Crucifixion of Jesus.

good hair *n. Caribbean.* hair showing evidence of some European strain in a person's blood.

good-humoured *adj.* being in or expressing a pleasant, tolerant, and kindly state of mind. —ˌ**good-'humouredly** *adv.* —ˌ**good-'humouredness** *n.*

goodies ('gʊdɪz) *pl. n.* any objects, rewards, prizes, etc., considered particularly desirable, attractive, or pleasurable.

Good King Henry *n.* a weedy chenopodiaceous plant, *Chenopodium bonus-henricus,* of N Europe, W Asia, and North America, having arrow-shaped leaves and clusters of small green flowers.

good-looker *n.* a handsome or pretty person.

good-looking *adj.* handsome or pretty.

good looks *pl. n.* personal attractiveness or beauty.

goodly ('gʊdlɪ) *adj.* **-lier, -liest. 1.** considerable: *a goodly amount of money.* **2.** *Obsolete.* attractive, pleasing, or fine: *a goodly man.* —'**goodliness** *n.*

goodman ('gʊdmən) *n., pl.* **-men.** *Archaic.* **1.** a husband. **2.** a man not of gentle birth: used as a title. **3.** a master of a household.

good morning *sentence substitute.* a conventional expression of greeting or farewell used in the morning.

good-natured *adj.* of a tolerant and kindly disposition. —ˌ**good-'naturedly** *adv.* —ˌ**good-'naturedness** *n.*

goodness ('gʊdnɪs) *n.* **1.** the state or quality of being good. **2.** generosity; kindness. **3.** moral excellence; piety; virtue. ~*interj.* **4.** a euphemism for **God:** used as an exclamation of surprise (often in phrases such as **goodness knows! thank goodness!**).

goodness of fit *n. Statistics.* the extent to which observed sample values of a variable approximate to values derived from a theoretical density, often measured by a chi-square test.

good night *sentence substitute.* a conventional expression of farewell, or, rarely, of greeting, used in the late afternoon, the evening, or at night, esp. when departing to bed.

good-oh *or* **good-o** ('gʊd'əʊ) *Informal.* ~*interj.* **1.** *Brit. and Austral.* an exclamation of pleasure, agreement, approval, etc. ~*adj., adv.* **2.** *Austral.* all right: *it was good-oh; I was getting on good-oh.*

good oil *n.* (usually preceded by *the*) *Austral. slang.* true or reliable facts, information, etc.

good people *pl. n.* **the.** *Folklore.* fairies.

good question *n.* a question that is hard to answer immediately.

goods (gʊdz) *pl. n.* **1.** possessions and personal property. **2.** (*sometimes sing.*) *Economics.* commodities that are tangible, usually movable, and generally not consumed at the same time as they are produced. Compare **services. 3.** articles of commerce; merchandise. **4.** *Chiefly Brit.* **a.** merchandise when transported, esp. by rail; freight. **b.** (*as modifier*): *a goods train.* **5. the goods. a.** *Informal.* that which is expected or promised: *to deliver the goods.* **b.** *Slang.* the real thing. **c.** *U.S. and Canadian slang.* incriminating evidence (esp. in the phrase **have the goods on someone**). **6. a piece of goods.** *Slang.* a person, esp. a woman.

Good Samaritan *n.* a kindly person who helps another in difficulty or distress. [named after the compassionate figure in one of Christ's parables (Luke 10:30–37)]

goods and chattels *pl. n.* any property that is not freehold, usually limited to include only moveable property.

Good Shepherd *n. New Testament.* a title given to Jesus Christ in John 10:11–12.

good-sized *adj.* quite large.

good sort *n. Informal.* **1.** a person of a kindly and likable disposition. **2.** *Austral.* an agreeable or attractive woman.

good-tempered *adj.* of a kindly and generous disposition.

good-time *adj.* (of a person) wildly seeking pleasure.

good turn *n.* a helpful and friendly act; good deed; favour.

goodwife ('gʊdˌwaɪf) *n., pl.* **-wives.** *Archaic.* **1.** the mistress of a household. **2.** a woman not of gentle birth: used as a title.

goodwill (ˌgʊd'wɪl) *n.* **1.** a feeling of benevolence, approval, and kindly interest. **2.** (*modifier*) resulting from, showing, or designed to show goodwill: *the government sent a goodwill mission to Moscow.* **3.** willingness or acquiescence. **4.** *Accounting.* an intangible asset taken into account in assessing the value of an enterprise and reflecting its commercial reputation, customer connections, etc.

goody[1] ('gʊdɪ) *interj.* **1.** a child's exclamation of pleasure and approval. ~*n., pl.* **goodies. 2.** short for **goody-goody. 3.** *Informal.* the hero in a film, book, etc. **4.** something particularly pleasant to have or (often) to eat. See also **goodies.**

goody[2] ('gʊdɪ) *n., pl.* **goodies.** *Archaic or literary.* a married woman of low rank: used as a title: *Goody Two-Shoes.* [C16: shortened from GOODWIFE]

goody-goody *n., pl.* **-goodies. 1.** *Informal.* a smugly virtuous or sanctimonious person. ~*adj.* **2.** smug and sanctimonious.

gooey ('guːɪ) *adj.* **gooier, gooiest.** *Informal.* **1.** sticky, soft, and often sweet. **2.** oversweet and sentimental. —'**gooily** *adv.*

goof (guːf) *Informal.* ~*n.* **1.** a foolish error or mistake. **2.** a stupid person. ~*vb.* **3.** to bungle (something); botch. **4.** (*intr.*; often foll. by *about* or *around*) to fool (around); mess (about). **5.** (*tr.*) to dope with drugs. **6.** (*intr.*; often foll. by *off*) *U.S.* to waste time; idle. [C20: probably from (dialect) *goff* simpleton, from Old French *goffe* clumsy, from Italian *goffo,* of obscure origin]

goofball (ˈguːfˌbɔːl) *n. U.S. and Canadian slang.* **1.** a barbiturate sleeping pill. **2.** a fool.

go off *vb.* (*intr.*) **1.** (*adv.*) (of power, a water supply, etc.) to cease to be available, running, or functioning: *the lights suddenly went off.* **2.** (*adv.*) to be discharged or activated; explode. **3.** (*adv.*) to occur as specified: *the meeting went off well.* **4.** to leave (a place): *the actors went off stage.* **5.** (*adv.*) (of a sensation) to gradually cease to be felt or perceived. **6.** (*adv.*) to fall asleep. **7.** (*adv.*) to enter a specified state or condition: *she went off into hysterics.* **8.** (*adv.*; foll. by *with*) to abscond (with). **9.** (*adv.*) (of concrete, mortar, etc.) to harden. **10.** (*adv.*) *Brit. informal.* (of food, milk, etc.) to become stale or rotten. **11.** (*prep.*) *Brit. informal.* to cease to like: *she went off him after their marriage.* **12.** (*adv.*) *Taboo slang.* to have an orgasm. **13.** (*adv.*) *Austral. slang.* (of premises) to be raided by the police. **14.** (*adv.*) *Austral. slang.* (of a racehorse) to win a fixed race. **15.** (*adv.*) *Austral. slang.* to be stolen.

goofy (ˈguːfɪ) *adj.* **goofier, goofiest.** *Informal.* **1.** foolish; silly; stupid. **2.** *Brit.* (of teeth) sticking out; protruding. —ˈ**goofily** *adv.* —ˈ**goofiness** *n.*

goofy-footer *n. Austral. informal.* a surfboard rider who stands with his right foot forward instead of his left foot forward.

goog (gʊg) *n. Austral. informal.* **1.** an egg. **2. full as a goog.** drunk.

googly (ˈguːglɪ) *n., pl.* **-lies.** *Cricket.* an off break bowled with a leg break action. [C20: Australian, of unknown origin]

googol (ˈguːgɒl, -gəl) *n.* the number represented as one followed by 100 zeros (10^{100}). [C20: coined by E. Kasner (1878–1955), American mathematician]

googolplex (ˈguːgɒlˌplɛks, -gəl-) *n.* the number represented as one followed by a googol (10^{100}) of zeros. [C20: from GOOGOL + (DU)PLEX]

gook (gʊk, guːk) *n. U.S.* **1.** *Slang.* a derogatory word for a person from a Far Eastern country. **2.** *Informal.* a messy sticky substance; muck. [C20: of uncertain origin]

goolie *or* **gooly** (ˈguːlɪ) *n., pl.* **-lies.** **1.** (*usually pl.*) *Taboo slang.* a testicle. **2.** *Austral. slang.* a stone or pebble. [from Hindustani *goli* a ball, bullet]

goon (guːn) *n.* **1.** a stupid or deliberately foolish person. **2.** *U.S. informal.* a thug hired to commit acts of violence or intimidation, esp. in an industrial dispute. [C20: partly from dialect *gooney* fool, partly after the character Alice the *Goon,* created by E. C. Segar (1894–1938), American cartoonist]

go on *vb.* (*intr., mostly adv.*) **1.** to continue or proceed. **2.** to happen or take place: *there's something peculiar going on here.* **3.** (of power, water supply, etc.) to start running or functioning. **4.** (*prep.*) to mount or board and ride on, esp. as a treat: *children love to go on donkeys at the seaside.* **5.** *Theatre.* to make an entrance on stage. **6.** to act or behave: *he goes on as though he's rich.* **7.** to talk excessively; chatter. **8.** to continue talking, esp. after a short pause: *"When I am Prime Minister," he went on, "we shall abolish taxes."* **9.** (foll. by *at*) to criticize or nag: *stop going on at me all the time!* **10.** (*prep.*) to use as a basis for further thought or action: *the police had no evidence at all to go on in the murder case.* **11.** (foll. by *for*) *Brit.* to approach (a time, age, amount, etc.): *he's going on for his hundredth birthday.* **12.** *Cricket.* to start to bowl. **13.** to take one's turn. **14.** (of clothes) to be capable of being put on. **15. go much on.** (*used with a negative*) *Brit.* to care for; like. **16. something to go on** *or* **to be going on with.** something that is adequate for the present time. ~*interj.* **17.** I don't believe what you're saying.

gooney bird (ˈguːnɪ) *n.* an informal name for **albatross,** esp. the black-footed albatross (*Diomedea nigripes*). [C19 *gony* (originally sailors' slang), probably from dialect *gooney* fool, of obscure origin; compare GOON]

goop (guːp) *n. U.S. and Canadian slang.* a rude or ill-mannered person. [C20: coined by G. Burgess (1866–1951), American humorist] —ˈ**goopy** *adj.*

goorie *or* **goory** (ˈguːrɪ) *n., pl.* **-ries.** *N.Z. informal.* See **kuri.**

goosander (guːˈsændə) *n.* a common merganser (a duck), *Mergus merganser,* of Europe and North America, having a dark head and white body in the male. [C17: probably from GOOSE[1] + Old Norse *önd* (genitive *andar*) duck]

goose[1] (guːs) *n., pl.* **geese** (giːs). **1.** any of various web-footed long-necked birds of the family *Anatidae:* order *Anseriformes.* They are typically larger and less aquatic than ducks and are gregarious and migratory. Related adj.: **anserine.** See also **brent goose, barnacle goose, greylag, snow goose. 2.** the female of such a bird, as opposed to the male (gander). **3.** *Informal.* a silly person. **4.** (*pl.* **gooses**). a pressing iron with a long curving handle, used esp. by tailors. **5.** the flesh of the goose, used as food. **6. all his geese are swans.** he constantly exaggerates the importance of a person or thing. **7. cook someone's goose.** *Informal.* **a.** to spoil someone's plans. **b.** to bring about someone's ruin, downfall, etc. **8. kill the goose that lays the golden eggs.** to sacrifice future benefits for the sake of momentary present needs. See also **golden goose.** [Old English *gōs;* related to Old Norse *gās,* Old High German *gans,* Old Irish *gēiss* swan, Greek *khēn,* Sanskrit *hainsas*]

goose[2] (guːs) *Slang.* ~*vb.* **1.** (*tr.*) to prod (a person) playfully in the behind. ~*n., pl.* **gooses. 2.** a playful prod in the behind. [C19: from GOOSE[1], probably from a comparison with the jabbing of a goose's bill]

goose barnacle *n.* any barnacle of the genus *Lepas,* living attached by a stalk to pieces of wood, having long feathery appendages (cirri) and flattened shells.

gooseberry (ˈgʊzbərɪ, -brɪ) *n., pl.* **-ries. 1.** a Eurasian shrub, *Ribes uva-crispa* (or *R. grossularia*), having greenish, purple-tinged flowers and ovoid yellow-green or red-purple berries: family *Grossulariaceae.* See also **currant** (sense 2). **2. a.** the berry of this plant. **b.** (*as modifier*): *gooseberry jam.* **3.** *Brit. informal.* an unwanted single person in a group of couples, esp. a third person with a couple (often in the phrase **play gooseberry**). **4. Cape gooseberry.** a tropical American solanaceous plant, *Physalis peruviana,* naturalized in southern Africa, having yellow flowers and edible yellow berries. See also **ground cherry.**

gooseberry bush *n.* **1.** See **gooseberry** (sense 1). **2. under a gooseberry bush.** used humorously in answering children's questions regarding their birth.

gooseberry stone *n.* another name for **grossularite.**

goosefish (ˈguːsˌfɪʃ) *n., pl.* **-fish** *or* **-fishes.** *U.S.* another name for **monkfish** (sense 1).

goose flesh *n.* the bumpy condition of the skin induced by cold, fear, etc., caused by contraction of the muscles at the base of the hair follicles with consequent erection of papillae: so called because of the resemblance to the skin of a freshly-plucked fowl. Also called: **goose bumps, goose pimples, goose skin.**

goosefoot (ˈguːsˌfʊt) *n., pl.* **-foots.** any typically weedy chenopodiaceous plant of the genus *Chenopodium,* having small greenish flowers and leaves shaped like a goose's foot. See also **Good King Henry, fat hen.**

goosegog (ˈgʊzgɒg) *or* **goosegob** *n. Brit.* a dialect or informal word for **gooseberry.** [from *goose* in GOOSEBERRY + *gog,* variant of GOB[1]]

goosegrass (ˈguːsˌgrɑːs) *n.* another name for **cleavers.**

gooseneck (ˈguːsˌnɛk) *n.* **1.** *Nautical.* a pivot between the forward end of a boom and a mast, to allow the boom to swing freely. **2.** something in the form of a neck of a goose. —ˈ**gooseˌnecked** *adj.*

goose step *n.* **1.** a military march step in which the leg is swung rigidly to an exaggerated height, esp. as in the German army in the Third Reich. ~*vb.* **goose-step, -steps, -stepping, -stepped. 2.** (*intr.*) to march in goose step.

goosy *or* **goosey** (ˈguːsɪ) *adj.* **goosier, goosiest. 1.** of or like a goose. **2.** having goose flesh. **3.** silly and foolish. —ˈ**goosiness** *n.*

go out *vb.* (*intr., adv.*) **1.** to depart from a room, house, country, etc. **2.** to cease to illuminate, burn, or function: *the fire has gone out.* **3.** to cease to be fashionable or popular: *that style went out ages ago!* **4.** to become unconscious or fall asleep: *she went out like a light.* **5.** (of a broadcast) to be transmitted. **6.** to go to entertainments, social functions, etc. **7.** (usually foll. by *with* or *together*) to associate (with a person of the opposite sex) regularly; date. **8.** (of workers) to begin to strike. **9.** (foll. by *to*) to be extended (to): *our sympathy went out to her on the death of her sister.* **10.** *Card games, etc.* to get rid of the last card, token, etc., in one's hand. **11. go all out.** to make a great effort to achieve or obtain something: *he went all out to pass the exam.*

go over *vb.* (*intr.*) **1.** to be received in a specified manner: *the concert went over very well.* **2.** (*prep.*) Also: **go through.** to examine and revise as necessary: *he went over the accounts.* **3.** (*prep.*) Also: **go through.** to clean: *she went over the room before her mother came.* **4.** (*prep.*) to check and repair: *can you go over my car please?* **5.** (*prep.*) Also: **go through.** to rehearse: *I'll go over my lines before the play.* **6.** (*adv.*; foll. by *to*) **a.** to change (to a different practice or system): *will Britain ever go over to driving on the right?* **b.** to change one's allegiances. **7.** (*prep.*) *Slang.* to do physical violence to: *they went over him with an iron bar.*

GOP (in the U.S.) *abbrev. for* Grand Old Party.

gopak (ˈgəʊˌpæk) *n.* a spectacular high-leaping Russian peasant dance for men. [from Russian, from Ukrainian *hopak,* from *hop!* a cry in the dance, from German *hopp!*]

gopher (ˈgəʊfə) *n.* **1.** Also called: **pocket gopher.** any burrowing rodent of the family *Geomyidae,* of North and Central America, having a thickset body, short legs, and cheek pouches. **2.** another name for **ground squirrel. 3.** any burrowing tortoise of the genus *Gopherus,* of SE North America. **4. gopher snake.** another name for **bull snake.** [C19: shortened from earlier *megopher* or *magopher,* of obscure origin]

gopherwood (ˈgəʊfəˌwʊd) *n. U.S.* another name for **yellowwood** (sense 1).

gopher wood *n.* the wood used in the construction of Noah's ark, thought to be a type of cypress (Genesis 6:14). [from Hebrew *gōpher*]

goral (ˈgɔːrəl) *n.* a small goat antelope, *Naemorhedus goral,* inhabiting mountainous regions of S Asia. It has a yellowish-grey and black coat and small conical horns. [C19: from Hindi, probably of Sanskrit origin]

gorblimey (gɔːˈblaɪmɪ) *interj.* a variant of **cor blimey.**

gorcock (ˈgɔːˌkɒk) *n.* the male of the red grouse. [C17: *gor-* (of unknown origin) + COCK[1]]

Gordian knot (ˈgɔːdɪən) *n.* a complicated and intricate problem (esp. in the phrase **cut the Gordian knot**). [after the complicated knot of Greek legend, tied by King *Gordius* and cut with a sword by Alexander the Great]

Gordon setter (ˈgɔːdən) *n.* a breed of setter originating in Scotland, with a black-and-tan coat. [C19: named after Alexander *Gordon* (1743–1827), Scottish nobleman who promoted this breed]

gore[1] (gɔː) *n.* **1.** blood shed from a wound, esp. when coagulated. **2.** *Informal.* killing, fighting, etc. [Old English *gor* dirt; related to Old Norse *gor* half-digested food, Middle Low German *göre*, Dutch *goor*]

gore[2] (gɔː) *vb.* (*tr.*) (of an animal, such as a bull) to pierce or stab (a person or another animal) with a horn or tusk. [C16: probably from Old English *gār* spear]

gore[3] (gɔː) *n.* **1.** a tapering or triangular piece of material used in making a shaped skirt, umbrella, etc. **2.** a similarly shaped piece, esp. of land. ~*vb.* **3.** (*tr.*) to make into or with a gore or gores. [Old English *gāra;* related to Old Norse *geiri* gore, Old High German *gēro*] —**gored** *adj.*

Gore-Tex (ˈgɔːˌtɛks) *n. Trademark.* a type of synthetic fabric which is waterproof yet allows the wearer's skin to breathe, used for sportswear.

gorge (gɔːdʒ) *n.* **1.** a deep ravine, esp. one through which a river runs. **2.** the contents of the stomach. **3.** feelings of disgust or resentment (esp. in the phrase **one's gorge rises**). **4.** an obstructing mass: *an ice gorge.* **5.** *Fortifications.* **a.** a narrow rear entrance to a work. **b.** the narrow part of a bastion or outwork. **6.** *Archaic.* the throat or gullet. ~*vb. also* **engorge. 7.** (*intr.*) *Falconry.* (of hawks) to eat until the crop is completely full. **8.** to swallow (food) ravenously. **9.** (*tr.*) to stuff (oneself) with food. [C14: from Old French *gorger* to stuff, from *gorge* throat, from Late Latin *gurga,* modification of Latin *gurges* whirlpool] —ˈ**gorgeable** *adj.* —ˈ**gorger** *n.*

gorgeous (ˈgɔːdʒəs) *adj.* **1.** strikingly beautiful or magnificent: *gorgeous array; a gorgeous girl.* **2.** *Informal.* extremely pleasing, fine, or good: *gorgeous weather.* [C15: from Old French *gorgias* elegant, from *gorgias* wimple, from *gorge;* see GORGE] —ˈ**gorgeously** *adv.* —ˈ**gorgeousness** *n.*

gorgerin (ˈgɔːdʒərɪn) *n. Architect.* another name for **necking.** [C17: from French, from *gorge* throat; see GORGE]

gorget (ˈgɔːdʒɪt) *n.* **1.** a collar-like piece of armour worn to protect the throat. **2.** a part of a wimple worn by women to cover the throat and chest, esp. in the 14th century. **3.** a band of distinctive colour on the throat of an animal, esp. a bird. [C15: from Old French, from *gorge;* see GORGE] —ˈ**gorgeted** *adj.*

Gorgio (ˈgɔːdʒəʊ, -dʒɪəʊ) *n., pl.* **-gios.** (*sometimes not cap.*) a word used by Gypsies for a non-Gypsy. [from Romany]

Gorgon (ˈgɔːgən) *n.* (*often not cap.*) *Informal.* a fierce or unpleasant woman. [named after the *Gorgons* of Greek mythology, winged clawed monstrous sisters with live snakes for hair; via Latin *Gorgō* from Greek, from *gorgos* terrible] —**Gorgonian** (gɔːˈgəʊnɪən) *adj.*

gorgoneion (ˌgɔːgəˈniːɒn) *n., pl.* **-neia** (-ˈniːə). a representation of a mythical Gorgon's head. [C19: from Greek, from *gorgoneios* of a GORGON]

gorgonian (gɔːˈgəʊnɪən) *n.* **1.** any coral of the order *Gorgonacea,* having a horny or calcareous branching skeleton: includes the sea fans and red corals. ~*adj.* **2.** of, relating to, or belonging to the *Gorgonacea.*

Gorgonzola *or* **Gorgonzola cheese** (ˌgɔːgənˈzəʊlə) *n.* a semihard blue-veined cheese of sharp flavour, made from pressed milk. [C19: named after *Gorgonzola,* Italian town where it originated]

gorilla (gəˈrɪlə) *n.* **1.** the largest anthropoid ape, *Gorilla gorilla,* inhabiting the forests of central W Africa. It is stocky and massive, with a short muzzle and coarse dark hair. **2.** *Informal.* a large, strong, and brutal-looking man. [C19: New Latin, from Greek *Gorillai,* an African tribe renowned for their hirsute appearance] —**goˈrilla-ˌlike** *adj.* —**goˈrillian** *or* **gorilline** (gəˈrɪlaɪn) *adj.* —**goˈrilloid** *adj.*

gormand (ˈgɔːmənd) *n.* a less common variant of **gourmand.**

gormandize *or* **gormandise** *vb.* (ˈgɔːmənˌdaɪz). **1.** to eat (food) greedily and voraciously. ~*n.* (ˈgɔːmənˌdiːz). **2.** a less common variant of **gourmandise.** —ˈ**gormandˌizer** *or* ˈ**gormandˌiser** *n.*

gormless (ˈgɔːmlɪs) *adj. Brit. informal.* stupid; dull. [C19: variant of C18 *gaumless,* from dialect *gome,* from Old English *gom, gome,* from Old Norse *gaumr* heed]

gorse (gɔːs) *n.* any evergreen shrub of the papilionaceous genus *Ulex,* esp. the European species *U. europeaus,* which has yellow flowers and thick green spines instead of leaves. Also called: **furze, whin.** [Old English *gors;* related to Old Irish *garb* rough, Latin *horrēre* to bristle, Old High German *gersta* barley, Greek *khēr* hedgehog] —ˈ**gorsy** *adj.*

Gorsedd (ˈgɔːsɛð) *n.* (in Wales) the bardic institution associated with the eisteddfod, esp. a meeting of bards and druids held daily before the eisteddfod. [from Welsh, literally: throne]

gory (ˈgɔːrɪ) *adj.* **gorier, goriest. 1.** horrific or bloodthirsty: *a gory story.* **2.** involving bloodshed and killing: *a gory battle.* **3.** covered in gore. —ˈ**gorily** *adv.* —ˈ**goriness** *n.*

gosh (gɒʃ) *interj.* an exclamation of mild surprise or wonder. [C18: euphemistic for *God,* as in *by gosh!*]

goshawk (ˈgɒsˌhɔːk) *n.* a large hawk, *Accipiter gentilis,* of Europe, Asia, and North America, having a bluish-grey back and wings and paler underparts: used in falconry. [Old English *gōshafoc;* see GOOSE[1], HAWK[1]]

gosling (ˈgɒzlɪŋ) *n.* **1.** a young goose. **2.** an inexperienced or youthful person. [C15: from Old Norse *gæslingr;* related to Danish *gäsling;* see GOOSE[1], -LING[1]]

go-slow *n.* **1.** *Brit.* **a.** a deliberate slackening of the rate of production by organized labour as a tactic in industrial conflict. **b.** (*as modifier*): *go-slow tactics.* U.S. and Canadian equivalent: **slowdown.** ~*vb.* **go slow. 2.** (*intr.*) to work deliberately slowly as a tactic in industrial conflict.

gospel (ˈgɒspəl) *n.* **1.** Also called: **gospel truth.** an unquestionable truth: *to take someone's word as gospel.* **2.** a doctrine maintained to be of great importance. **3.** Black religious music originating in the churches of the Southern states of the United States. **4.** the message or doctrine of a religious teacher. **5. a.** the story of Christ's life and teachings as narrated in the Gospels. **b.** the good news of salvation in Jesus Christ. **c.** (*as modifier*): *the gospel story.* [Old English *gōdspell,* from *gōd* GOOD + *spell* message; see SPELL[2]; compare Old Norse *guthspjall,* Old High German *guotspell*]

Gospel (ˈgɒspəl) *n.* **1.** any of the first four books of the New Testament, namely Matthew, Mark, Luke, and John. **2.** a reading from one of these in a religious service.

gospeller (ˈgɒspələ) *n.* **1.** a person who reads or chants the Gospel in a religious service. **2.** a person who professes to preach a gospel held exclusively by him and others of a like mind.

gospel oath *n.* an oath sworn on the Gospels.

gospodin *Russian.* (gəspaˈdin) *n., pl.* **-poda** (-paˈda). a Russian title of address, often indicating respect, equivalent to *sir* when used alone or to *Mr* when before a name. [literally: lord]

gossamer (ˈgɒsəmə) *n.* **1.** a gauze or silk fabric of the very finest texture. **2.** a filmy cobweb often seen on foliage or floating in the air. **3.** anything resembling gossamer in fineness or filminess. **4.** (*modifier*) made of or resembling gossamer: *gossamer wings.* [C14 (in the sense: a filmy cobweb): probably from *gos* GOOSE[1] + *somer* SUMMER[1]; the phrase refers to *St Martin's summer,* a period in November when goose was traditionally eaten; from the prevalence of the cobweb in the autumn; compare German *Gänsemonat,* literally: goosemonth, used for November] —ˈ**gossamery** *adj.*

gossip (ˈgɒsɪp) *n.* **1.** casual and idle chat: *to have a gossip with a friend.* **2.** a conversation involving malicious chatter or rumours about other people: *a gossip about the neighbours.* **3.** Also called: **gossipmonger.** a person who habitually talks about others, esp. maliciously. **4.** light easy communication: *to write a letter full of gossip.* **5.** *Archaic.* a close woman friend. ~*vb.* **-sips, -siping, -siped. 6.** (*intr.;* often foll. by *about*) to talk casually or maliciously (about other people). [Old English *godsibb* godparent, from GOD + SIB; the term came to be applied to familiar friends, esp. a woman's female friends at the birth of a child, hence a person, esp. a woman, fond of light talk] —ˈ**gossiper** *n.* —ˈ**gossiping** *n., adj.* —ˈ**gossipingly** *adv.* —ˈ**gossipy** *adj.*

gossipmonger (ˈgɒsɪpˌmʌŋgə) *n.* another word for **gossip** (sense 3).

gossoon (gɒˈsuːn) *n. Irish.* a boy, esp. a servant boy. [C17: from Old French *garçon*]

gossypol (ˈgɒsɪˌpɒl) *n.* a toxic crystalline pigment that is a constituent of cottonseed oil discovered to have medical applications and currently the subject of research as a male contraceptive. [C19: from Modern Latin *gossypium* cotton plant + -OL[1]]

goster (ˈgɒstə) *vb.* (*intr.*) *Northern English dialect.* to laugh uncontrollably. [C18: from earlier *gauster,* from Middle English *galstre,* of obscure origin]

got (gɒt) *vb.* **1.** the past tense and past participle of **get. 2. have got. a.** to possess: *he has got three apples.* **b.** (*takes an infinitive*) used as an auxiliary to express compulsion felt to be imposed by or upon the speaker: *I've got to get a new coat.* **3. have got it bad** *or* **badly.** *Informal.* to be infatuated.

Goth (gɒθ) *n.* **1.** a member of an East Germanic people from Scandinavia who settled south of the Baltic early in the first millennium A.D. They moved on to the Ukrainian steppes and raided and later invaded many parts of the Roman Empire from the 3rd to the 5th century. See also **Ostrogoth, Visigoth. 2.** a rude or barbaric person. **3.** (*sometimes not cap.*) Also called: **Gothic.** an aficionado of Goth music and fashion. ~*adj.* **4.** (*sometimes not cap.*) Also: **Gothic. a.** (of music) in a style halfway between heavy metal and punk. **b.** (of fashion) characterized by black clothes and deathly white make-up.

Goth. *abbrev. for* Gothic.

Gothic (ˈgɒθɪk) *adj.* **1.** denoting, relating to, or resembling the style of architecture that was used in W Europe from the 12th to the 16th centuries, characterized by the lancet arch, the ribbed vault, and the flying buttress. See also **Gothic Revival. 2.** of or relating to the style of sculpture, painting, or other arts as practised in W Europe from the 12th to the 16th centuries. **3.** (*sometimes not cap.*) of or relating to a literary style characterized by gloom, the grotesque, and the supernatural, popular esp. in the late 18th century: when used of modern literature, films, etc., sometimes spelt: **Gothick. 4.** of, relating to, or characteristic of the Goths or their language. **5.** (*sometimes not cap.*) primitive and barbarous in style, behaviour, etc. **6.** of or relating to the Middle Ages. **7.** another word for **Goth** (sense 4). ~*n.* **8.** Gothic architecture or art. **9.** the extinct language of the ancient Goths, known mainly from fragments of a translation of the Bible made in the 4th century by Bishop Wulfila. See also **East Germanic.** **10.** Also called (esp. Brit): **black letter.** the family of heavy script typefaces in use from about the 15th to 18th centuries. **11.** another word for **Goth** (sense 3). —'**Gothically** *adv.*

Gothic arch *n.* another name for **lancet arch.**

Gothicism ('gɒθɪˌsɪzəm) *n.* **1.** conformity to, use of, or imitation of the Gothic style, esp. in architecture. **2.** crudeness of manner or style.

Gothicize *or* **Gothicise** ('gɒθɪˌsaɪz) *vb.* (*tr.*) to make Gothic in style. —'**Gothiˌcizer** *or* '**Gothiˌciser** *n.*

Gothic Revival *n.* a Gothic style of architecture popular between the late 18th and late 19th centuries, exemplified by the Houses of Parliament in London (1840). Also called: **neogothic.**

go through *vb.* (*intr.*) **1.** (*adv.*) to be approved or accepted: *the amendment went through.* **2.** (*prep.*) to consume; exhaust: *we went through our supplies in a day; some men go through a pair of socks in no time.* **3.** (*prep.*) Also: **go over.** to examine and revise as necessary: *he went through the figures.* **4.** (*prep.*) to suffer: *she went through tremendous pain.* **5.** (*prep.*) Also: **go over.** to rehearse: *let's just go through the details again.* **6.** (*prep.*) Also: **go over.** to clean: *she went through the cupboards in the spring-cleaning.* **7.** (*prep.*) to participate in: *she went through the degree ceremony without getting too nervous.* **8.** (*adv.*; foll. by *with*) to bring to a successful conclusion, often by persistence. **9.** (*prep.*) (of a book) to be published in: *that book has gone through three printings this year alone.* **10.** (*adv.*) *Austral. informal.* to leave; depart.

go to *vb.* (*intr., prep.*) **1.** to be awarded to: *the Nobel prize last year went to a Scot.* **2.** **go to it.** to tackle a task vigorously. ~*interj.* **3.** *Archaic.* an exclamation expressing surprise, encouragement, etc.

go together *vb.* (*intr., adv.*) **1.** to be mutually suited; harmonize: *the colours go well together.* **2.** *Informal.* (of two people of opposite sex) to associate frequently with each other: *they had been going together for two years.*

gotta ('gɒtə) *vb. Slang. contraction of* got to.

gotten ('gɒtᵊn) *vb. U.S.* **1.** a past participle of **get.** **2.** **have gotten.** (*not usually in the infinitive*) **a.** to have obtained: *he had gotten a car for his 21st birthday.* **b.** to have become: *I've gotten sick of your constant bickering.*

gouache (gʊ'ɑːʃ) *n.* **1.** Also called: **body colour.** a painting technique using opaque watercolour paint in which the pigments are bound with glue and the lighter tones contain white. **2.** the paint used in this technique. **3.** a painting done by this method. [C19: from French, from Italian *guazzo* puddle, from Latin *aquātiō* a watering place, from *aqua* water]

Gouda ('gaʊdə) *n.* a large round Dutch cheese, mild and similar in taste to Edam. [named after *Gouda*, a town in the W Netherlands where it was originally made]

gouge (gaʊdʒ) *vb.* (*mainly tr.*) **1.** (usually foll. by *out*) to scoop or force (something) out of its position, esp. with the fingers or a pointed instrument. **2.** (sometimes foll. by *out*) to cut (a hole or groove) in (something) with a sharp instrument or tool. **3.** *U.S. and Canadian informal.* to extort from. **4.** (*also intr.*) *Austral.* to dig for (opal). ~*n.* **5.** a type of chisel with a blade that has a concavo-convex section. **6.** a mark or groove made with, or as if with, a gouge. **7.** *Geology.* a fine deposit of rock fragments, esp. clay, occurring between the walls of a fault or mineral vein. **8.** *U.S. and Canadian informal.* extortion; swindling. [C15: from French, from Late Latin *gulbia* a chisel, of Celtic origin]

gouger ('gaʊdʒə) *n.* **1.** a person or tool that gouges. **2.** *Irish dialect.* a low-class city lout.

goujon ('guːʒɒn) *n.* a small strip of fish or chicken, coated in breadcrumbs and deep-fried. [French, literally: gudgeon]

goulash ('guːlæʃ) *n.* **1.** Also called: **Hungarian goulash.** a rich stew, originating in Hungary, made of beef, lamb, or veal highly seasoned with paprika. **2.** *Bridge.* a method of dealing in threes and fours without first shuffling the cards, to produce freak hands. [C19: from Hungarian *gulyás hus* herdsman's meat, from *gulya* herd]

go under *vb.* (*intr., mainly adv.*) **1.** (*also prep.*) to sink below (a surface). **2.** to founder or drown. **3.** to be conquered or overwhelmed: *the firm went under in the economic crisis.*

go up *vb.* (*intr., mainly adv.*) **1.** (*also prep.*) to move or lead to or as if to a higher place or level; rise; increase: *prices are always going up; the curtain goes up at eight o'clock; new buildings are going up all around us.* **2.** to be destroyed: *the house went up in flames.* **3.** *Brit.* to go or return (to college or university) at the beginning of a term or academic year.

gourami ('gʊərəmɪ) *n., pl.* **-mi** *or* **-mis.** **1.** a large SE Asian labyrinth fish, *Osphronemus goramy,* used for food and (when young) as an aquarium fish. **2.** any of various other labyrinth fishes, such as *Helostoma temmincki* (**kissing gourami**), many of which are brightly coloured and popular aquarium fishes. [from Malay *gurami*]

gourd (gʊəd) *n.* **1.** the fruit of any of various cucurbitaceous or similar plants, esp. the bottle gourd and some squashes, whose dried shells are used for ornament, drinking cups, etc. **2.** any plant that bears this fruit. See also **sour gourd, dishcloth gourd, calabash.** **3.** a bottle or flask made from the dried shell of the bottle gourd. **4.** a small bottle shaped like a gourd. [C14: from Old French *gourde,* ultimately from Latin *cucurbita*] —'**gourdˌlike** *adj.* —'**gourd-ˌshaped** *adj.*

gourde (gʊəd) *n.* the standard monetary unit of Haiti, divided into 100 centimes. [C19: from French, feminine of *gourd* heavy, from Latin *gurdus* a stupid person]

gourmand ('gʊəmənd; *French* gurmɑ̃) *or* **gormand** *n.* a person devoted to eating and drinking, esp. to excess. [C15: from Old French *gourmant,* of uncertain origin] —'**gourmandˌism** *n.*

gourmandise (ˌgʊəmən'diːz) *or* **gormandize** *n.* a love of and taste for good food.

gourmet ('gʊəmeɪ; *French* gurmɛ) *n.* a person who cultivates a discriminating palate for the enjoyment of good food and drink. [C19: from French, from Old French *gromet* serving boy]

gout (gaʊt) *n.* **1.** a metabolic disease characterized by painful inflammation of certain joints, esp. of the big toe and foot, caused by deposits of sodium urate in them. **2.** *Archaic.* a drop or splash, esp. of blood. [C13: from Old French *goute* gout (thought to result from drops of humours), from Latin *gutta* a drop] —'**gouty** *adj.* —'**goutily** *adv.* —'**goutiness** *n.*

goût *French.* (gu) *n.* taste or good taste.

goutweed ('gaʊtˌwiːd) *n.* a widely naturalized Eurasian umbelliferous plant, *Aegopodium podagraria,* with white flowers and creeping underground stems. Also called: **bishop's weed, ground elder, herb Gerard.**

Gov. *or* **gov.** *abbrev. for:* **1.** government. **2.** governor.

govern ('gʌvᵊn) *vb.* (*mainly tr.*) **1.** (*also intr.*) to direct and control the actions, affairs, policies, functions, etc., of (a political unit, organization, nation, etc.); rule. **2.** to exercise restraint over; regulate or direct: *to govern one's temper.* **3.** to be a predominant influence on (something); decide or determine (something): *his injury governed his decision to avoid sports.* **4.** to control the speed of (an engine, machine, etc.) using a governor. **5.** to control the rate of flow of (a fluid) by using an automatic valve. **6.** (of a word) to determine the inflection of (another word): *Latin nouns govern adjectives that modify them.* [C13: from Old French *gouverner,* from Latin *gubernāre* to steer, from Greek *kubernan*] —'**governable** *adj.* —ˌ**governa'bility** *or* '**governableness** *n.*

governance ('gʌvənəns) *n.* **1.** government, control, or authority. **2.** the action, manner, or system of governing.

governess ('gʌvənɪs) *n.* a woman teacher employed in a private household to teach and train the children.

government ('gʌvənmənt, 'gʌvəmənt) *n.* **1.** the exercise of political authority over the actions, affairs, etc., of a political unit, people, etc., as well as the performance of certain functions for this unit or body; the action of governing; political rule and administration. **2.** the system or form by which a community, etc., is ruled: *tyrannical government.* **3. a.** the executive policy-making body of a political unit, community, etc.; ministry or administration: *yesterday we got a new government.* **b.** (*cap. when of a specific country*): *the British Government.* **4. a.** the state and its administration: *blame it on the government.* **b.** (*as modifier*): *a government agency.* **5.** regulation; direction. **6.** *Grammar.* the determination of the form of one word by another word. —**governmental** (ˌgʌvən'mɛntᵊl, ˌgʌvə'mɛntᵊl) *adj.* —ˌ**govern'mentally** *adv.*

government issue *adj. Chiefly U.S.* supplied by a government or government agency.

government man *n. Austral.* (in the 19th century) a convict.

governor ('gʌvənə) *n.* **1.** a person who governs. **2.** the ruler or chief magistrate of a colony, province, etc. **3.** the representative of the Crown in a British colony. **4.** *Brit.* the senior administrator or head of a society, prison, etc. **5.** the chief executive of any state in the U.S. **6.** a device that controls the speed of an engine, esp. by regulating the supply of fuel, etc., either to limit the maximum speed or to maintain a constant speed. **7.** *Grammar.* Also called: **head. a.** a word in a phrase or clause that is the principal item and gives the function of the whole, as *hat* in *the big red hat.* **b.** (*as modifier*): *a governor noun.* **8.** *Brit. informal.* a name or title of respect for a father, employer, etc. ~Related adj.: **gubernatorial.**

governor general *n., pl.* **governors general** *or* **governor generals.** **1.** the representative of the Crown in a dominion of the Commonwealth or a British colony; vicegerent. **2.** *Brit.* a governor with jurisdiction or precedence over other governors. —ˌ**governor-'generalˌship** *n.*

governorship ('gʌvənəˌʃɪp) *n.* the office, jurisdiction, or term of a governor.

Govt *or* **govt** *abbrev. for* government.

gowan ('gaʊən) *n. Scot.* any of various yellow or white flowers growing in fields, esp. the common daisy. [C16: variant of *gollan,* probably of Scandinavian origin; compare Old Norse *gullin* golden] —'**gowaned** *adj.* —'**gowany** *adj.*

go with *vb.* (*intr., prep.*) **1.** to accompany. **2.** to blend or harmonize: *that new wallpaper goes well with the furniture.* **3.** to be a normal part of: *three acres of land go with the house.* **4.** to be of the same opinion as: *I'm sorry I can't go with you on your new plan.* **5.** (of two people of the opposite sex) to associate frequently with (each other).

go without *vb. (intr.)* 1. *Chiefly Brit.* to be denied or deprived of (something, esp. food): *if you don't like your tea you can go without.* 2. **that goes without saying.** that is obvious or self-evident.

gowk (gaʊk) *n. Scot. and northern English dialect.* 1. a stupid person; fool. 2. a cuckoo. [from Old Norse *gaukr* cuckoo; related to Old High German *gouh*]

gown (gaʊn) *n.* 1. any of various outer garments, such as a woman's elegant or formal dress, a dressing robe, or a protective garment, esp. one worn by surgeons during operations. 2. a loose wide garment indicating status, such as worn by academics. 3. the members of a university as opposed to the other residents of the university town. Compare **town** (sense 7). ~*vb.* 4. *(tr.)* to supply with or dress in a gown. [C14: from Old French *goune,* from Late Latin *gunna* garment made of leather or fur, of Celtic origin]

goy (gɔɪ) *n., pl.* **goyim** ('gɔɪɪm) *or* **goys.** a Jewish word for a gentile. [from Yiddish, from Hebrew *goi* people] —'**goyish** *adj.*

GP *abbrev. for:* 1. general practitioner. 2. Gallup Poll. 3. (in Britain) graduated pension. 4. Grand Prix. 5. *Music.* general pause.

GPI *abbrev. for* general paralysis of the insane (general paresis).

GPO *abbrev. for* general post office.

GPS (in Australia) *abbrev. for* Great Public Schools; used of a group of mainly nonstate schools, and of sporting competitions between them.

GPU *abbrev. for* State Political Administration; the Soviet police and secret police from 1922 to 1923. [from Russian *Gosudarstvennoye politicheskoye upravlenie*]

GQ *Military. abbrev. for* general quarters.

GR *international car registration for* Greece.

gr. *abbrev. for:* 1. grade. 2. grain. 3. gross. 4. gram.

Gr. *abbrev. for:* 1. Grecian. 2. Greece. 3. Greek.

Graafian follicle ('grɑːfɪən) *n.* a fluid-filled vesicle in the mammalian ovary containing a developing egg cell. [C17: named after R. de *Graaf* (1641–73), Dutch anatomist]

grab (græb) *vb.* **grabs, grabbing, grabbed.** 1. to seize hold of (something). 2. *(tr.)* to seize illegally or unscrupulously. 3. *(tr.)* to arrest; catch. 4. *(intr.)* (of a brake or clutch in a vehicle) to grip and release intermittently causing juddering. 5. *(tr.) Informal.* to catch the attention or interest of; impress. ~*n.* 6. the act or an instance of grabbing. 7. a mechanical device for gripping objects, esp. the hinged jaws of a mechanical excavator. 8. something that is grabbed. [C16: probably from Middle Low German or Middle Dutch *grabben;* related to Swedish *grabba,* Sanskrit *grbhnāti* he seizes] —'**grabber** *n.*

grabble ('græbᵊl) *vb.* 1. *(intr.)* to scratch or feel about with the hands. 2. *(intr.)* to fall to the ground; sprawl. 3. *(tr.) Caribbean.* to seize rashly. [C16: probably from Dutch *grabbelen,* from *grabben* to GRAB] —'**grabbler** *n.*

graben ('grɑːbᵊn) *n.* an elongated trough of land produced by subsidence of the earth's crust between two faults. [C19: from German, from Old High German *graban* to dig]

grace (greɪs) *n.* 1. elegance and beauty of movement, form, expression, or proportion. 2. a pleasing or charming quality. 3. goodwill or favour. 4. the granting of a favour or the manifestation of goodwill, esp. by a superior. 5. a sense of propriety and consideration for others. 6. *(pl.)* **a.** affectation of manner (esp. in the phrase **airs and graces**). **b. in (someone's) good graces.** regarded favourably and with kindness by (someone). 7. mercy; clemency. 8. *Christianity.* **a.** the free and unmerited favour of God shown towards man. **b.** the divine assistance and power given to man in spiritual rebirth and sanctification. **c.** the condition of being favoured or sanctified by God. **d.** an unmerited gift, favour, etc., granted by God. 9. a short prayer recited before or after a meal to invoke a blessing upon the food or give thanks for it. 10. *Music.* a melodic ornament or decoration. 11. See **days of grace.** 12. **with (a) bad grace.** unwillingly or grudgingly. 13. **with (a) good grace.** willingly or cheerfully. ~*vb.* 14. *(tr.)* to add elegance and beauty to: *flowers graced the room.* 15. *(tr.)* to honour or favour: *to grace a party with one's presence.* 16. to ornament or decorate (a melody, part, etc.) with nonessential notes. [C12: from Old French, from Latin *grātia,* from *grātus* pleasing]

Grace (greɪs) *n.* (preceded by *your, his,* or *her*) a title used to address or refer to a duke, duchess, or archbishop.

grace-and-favour *n. (modifier) Brit.* (of a house, flat, etc.) owned by the sovereign and granted free of rent to a person to whom the sovereign wishes to express gratitude.

grace cup *n.* a cup, as of wine, passed around at the end of the meal for the final toast.

graceful ('greɪsfʊl) *adj.* characterized by beauty of movement, style, form, etc. —'**gracefully** *adv.* —'**gracefulness** *n.*

graceless ('greɪslɪs) *adj.* 1. lacking any sense of right and wrong; depraved. 2. lacking grace or excellence. —'**gracelessly** *adv.* —'**gracelessness** *n.*

grace note *n. Music.* a note printed in small type to indicate that it is melodically and harmonically nonessential.

gracile ('græsaɪl) *adj.* 1. gracefully thin or slender. 2. a less common word for **graceful.** [C17: from Latin *gracilis* slender] —**gracility** (græ'sɪlɪtɪ) *or* '**gracileness** *n.*

gracioso (ˌgræsɪ'əʊsəʊ; *Spanish* gra'θjoso) *n., pl.* **-sos.** a clown in Spanish comedy. [C17: from Spanish: GRACIOUS]

gracious ('greɪʃəs) *adj.* 1. characterized by or showing kindness and courtesy. 2. condescendingly courteous, benevolent, or indulgent. 3. characterized by or suitable for a life of elegance, ease, and indulgence: *gracious living; gracious furnishings.* 4. merciful or compassionate. 5. *Obsolete.* fortunate, prosperous, or happy. ~*interj.* 6. an expression of mild surprise or wonder (often in exclamatory phrases such as **good gracious! gracious me!**). —'**graciously** *adv.* —'**graciousness** *n.*

grackle ('grækᵊl) *n.* 1. Also called: **crow blackbird.** any American songbird of the genera *Quiscalus* and *Cassidix,* having a dark iridescent plumage: family *Icteridae* (American orioles). 2. any of various starlings of the genus *Gracula,* such as *G. religiosa* (**Indian grackle** or **hill myna**). [C18: from New Latin *Grăcula,* from Latin *grāculus* jackdaw]

grad (græd) *n. Informal.* a graduate.

grad. *abbrev. for:* 1. *Maths.* gradient. 2. *Education.* graduate(d).

gradable ('greɪdəbᵊl) *adj.* 1. capable of being graded. 2. *Linguistics.* denoting or relating to a word in whose meaning there is some implicit relationship to a standard: *"big" and "small" are gradable adjectives.* ~*n.* 3. *Linguistics.* a word of this kind. —ˌ**grada'bility** *or* '**gradableness** *n.*

gradate (grə'deɪt) *vb.* 1. to change or cause to change imperceptibly, as from one colour, tone, or degree to another. 2. *(tr.)* to arrange in grades or ranks.

gradation (grə'deɪʃən) *n.* 1. a series of systematic stages; gradual progression. 2. *(often pl.)* a stage or degree in such a series or progression. 3. the act or process of arranging or forming in stages, grades, etc., or of progressing evenly. 4. (in painting, drawing, or sculpture) transition from one colour, tone, or surface to another through a series of very slight changes. 5. *Linguistics.* any change in the quality or length of a vowel within a word indicating certain distinctions, such as inflectional or tense differentiations. See **ablaut.** 6. *Geology.* the natural levelling of land as a result of the building up or wearing down of pre-existing formations. —**gra'dational** *adj.* —**gra'dationally** *adv.*

grade (greɪd) *n.* 1. a position or degree in a scale, as of quality, rank, size, or progression: *small-grade eggs; high-grade timber.* 2. a group of people or things of the same category. 3. *Chiefly U.S.* a military or other rank. 4. a stage in a course of progression. 5. a mark or rating indicating achievement or the worth of work done, as at school. 6. *U.S. and Canadian.* a unit of pupils of similar age or ability taught together at school. 7. another word (esp. U.S. and Canadian) for **gradient** (senses 1, 2). 8. a unit of angle equal to one hundredth of a right angle or 0.9 degree. 9. *Stockbreeding.* **a.** an animal with one purebred parent and one of unknown or unimproved breeding. **b.** *(as modifier): a grade sheep.* ~Compare **crossbred, purebred** (sense 2). 10. *Linguistics.* one of the forms of the vowel in a morpheme when this vowel varies because of gradation. 11. **at grade. a.** on the same level. **b.** (of a river profile or land surface) at an equilibrium level and slope, because there is a balance between erosion and deposition. 12. **make the grade.** *Informal.* **a.** to reach the required standard. **b.** to succeed. ~*vb.* 13. *(tr.)* to arrange according to quality, rank, etc. 14. *(tr.)* to determine the grade of or assign a grade to. 15. *(intr.)* to achieve or deserve a grade or rank. 16. to change or blend (something) gradually; merge. 17. *(tr.)* to level (ground, a road, etc.) to a suitable gradient. 18. *(tr.) Stockbreeding.* to cross (one animal) with another to produce a grade animal. [C16: from French, from Latin *gradus* step, from *gradī* to step]

-grade *adj. combining form.* indicating a kind or manner of movement or progression: *plantigrade; retrograde.* [via French from Latin *-gradus,* from *gradus* a step, from *gradī* to walk]

grade cricket *n. Austral.* competitive cricket, in which cricket club teams are arranged in grades.

grade crossing *n.* the U.S. and Canadian name for **level crossing.**

graded post *n. Brit.* a position in a school having special responsibility for which additional payment is given.

gradely ('greɪdlɪ) *adj.* **-lier, -liest.** *Midland English dialect.* fine; excellent. [C13 *greithlic, greithli,* from Old Norse *greidhligr,* from *greidhr* ready]

grader ('greɪdə) *n.* 1. a person or thing that grades. 2. a machine, either self-powered or towed by a tractor, that levels earth, rubble, etc., as in road construction.

grade school *n. U.S.* another name for **elementary school.**

gradient ('greɪdɪənt) *n.* 1. Also called (esp. U.S.): **grade.** a part of a railway, road, etc., that slopes upwards or downwards; inclination. 2. Also called (esp. U.S. and Canadian): **grade.** a measure of such a slope, esp. the ratio of the vertical distance between two points on the slope to the horizontal distance between them. 3. *Physics.* a measure of the change of some physical quantity, such as temperature or electric potential, over a specified distance. 4. *Maths.* **a.** (of a curve) the slope of the tangent at any point on a curve with respect to the horizontal axis. **b.** (of a function, $f(x, y, z)$) the vector whose components along the axes are the partial derivatives of the function with respect to each variable, and whose direction is that in which the derivative of the function has its maximum value. Usually written: grad **f,** ∇f or $\nabla.f$. Compare **curl** (sense 11), **divergence** (sense 4). ~*adj.* 5. sloping uniformly. [C19: from Latin *gradiēns* stepping, from *gradī* to go]

gradient post *n.* a small white post beside a railway line at a point where the gradient changes having arms set at angles representing the gradients.

gradin (ˈgreɪdɪn) *or* **gradine** (grəˈdiːn) *n.* **1.** a ledge above or behind an altar on which candles, a cross, or other ornaments stand. **2.** one of a set of steps or seats arranged on a slope, as in an amphitheatre. [C19: from French, from Italian *gradino*, a little step, from *grado* step; see GRADE]

gradiometer (ˌgrædɪˈɒmɪtə) *n.* **1.** *Physics.* an instrument for measuring the gradient of a magnetic field. **2.** *Surveying.* an instrument used to ensure that a long gradient remains constant.

gradual (ˈgrædjʊəl) *adj.* **1.** occurring, developing, moving, etc., in small stages: *a gradual improvement in health.* **2.** not steep or abrupt: *a gradual slope.* ~*n.* **3.** (*often cap.*) *Christianity.* **a.** an antiphon or group of several antiphons, usually from the Psalms, sung or recited immediately after the epistle at Mass. **b.** a book of plainsong containing the words and music of the parts of the Mass that are sung by the cantors and choir. [C16: from Medieval Latin *graduālis* relating to steps, from Latin *gradus* a step] —ˈ**gradually** *adv.* —ˈ**gradualness** *n.*

gradualism (ˈgrædjʊəˌlɪzəm) *n.* **1.** the policy of seeking to change something or achieve a goal gradually rather than quickly or violently, esp. in politics. **2.** the theory that explains major changes in rock strata, fossils, etc. in terms of gradual evolutionary processes rather than sudden violent catastrophes. Compare **catastrophism.** —ˈ**gradualist** *n., adj.* —ˌ**gradualˈistic** *adj.*

graduand (ˈgrædjʊˌænd) *n. Chiefly Brit.* a person who is about to graduate. [C19: from Medieval Latin *graduandus*, gerundive of *graduārī* to GRADUATE]

graduate *n.* (ˈgrædjʊɪt). **1. a.** a person who has been awarded a first degree from a university or college. **b.** (*as modifier*): *a graduate profession.* **2.** *U.S. and Canadian.* a student who has completed a course of studies at a high school and received a diploma. **3.** *U.S.* a container, such as a flask, marked to indicate its capacity. ~*vb.* (ˈgrædjʊˌeɪt). **4.** to receive or cause to receive a degree or diploma. **5.** (*tr.*) *Chiefly U.S. and Canadian.* to confer a degree, diploma, etc. upon. **6.** (*tr.*) to mark (a thermometer, flask, etc.) with units of measurement; calibrate. **7.** (*tr.*) to arrange or sort into groups according to type, quality, etc. **8.** (*intr.*; often foll. by *to*) to change by degrees (from something to something else). [C15: from Medieval Latin *graduārī* to take a degree, from Latin *gradus* a step] —ˈ**graduˌator** *n.*

graduation (ˌgrædjʊˈeɪʃən) *n.* **1.** the act of graduating or the state of being graduated. **2.** the ceremony at which school or college degrees and diplomas are conferred. **3.** a mark or division or all the marks or divisions that indicate measure on an instrument or vessel.

gradus (ˈgreɪdəs) *n., pl.* **-duses.** **1.** a book of études or other musical exercises arranged in order of increasing difficulty. **2.** *Prosody.* a dictionary or textbook of prosody for use in writing Latin or Greek verse. [C18: shortened from Latin *Gradus ad Parnassum* a step towards Parnassus, a dictionary of prosody used in the 18th and 19th centuries]

Graecism *or esp. U.S.* **Grecism** (ˈgriːsɪzəm) *n.* **1.** Greek characteristics or style. **2.** admiration for or imitation of these, as in sculpture or architecture. **3.** a form of words characteristic or imitative of the idiom of the Greek language.

Graecize, Graecise, *or esp. U.S.* **Grecize** (ˈgriːsaɪz) *vb.* another word for **Hellenize.** [C17: from Latin *graecizāre* to imitate the Greeks, from Greek *graikizein*]

Graeco- *or esp. U.S.* **Greco-** (ˈgriːkəʊ, ˈgrɛkəʊ) *combining form.* Greek: *Graeco-Roman.*

Graeco-Roman *or esp. U.S.* **Greco-Roman** *adj.* **1.** of, characteristic of, or relating to Greek and Roman influences, as found in Roman sculpture. **2.** denoting a style of wrestling in which the legs may not be used to obtain a fall and no hold may be applied below the waist.

Graf *German.* (graːf) *n., pl.* ***Grafen*** (ˈgraːfən). a German or Swedish count: often used as a title. [German, from Old High German *grāvo*]

graffito (græˈfiːtəʊ) *n., pl.* **-ti** (-tiː). **1.** *Archaeol.* any inscription or drawing scratched or carved onto a surface, esp. rock or pottery. **2.** (*pl.; sometimes with sing. vb.*) drawings, messages, etc., often obscene, scribbled on the walls of public lavatories, advertising posters, etc. [C19: from Italian: a little scratch, from *graffio*, from Latin *graphium* stylus, from Greek *grapheion;* see GRAFT[1]] —**grafˈfitist** *n.*

graft[1] (grɑːft) *n.* **1.** *Horticulture.* **a.** a small piece of plant tissue (the scion) that is made to unite with an established plant (the stock), which supports and nourishes it. **b.** the plant resulting from the union of scion and stock. **c.** the point of union between the scion and the stock. **2.** *Surgery.* a piece of tissue or an organ transplanted from a donor or from the patient's own body to an area of the body in need of the tissue. **3.** the act of joining one thing to another by or as if by grafting. ~*vb.* **4.** *Horticulture.* **a.** to induce (a plant or part of a plant) to unite with another part or (of a plant or part of a plant) to unite in this way. **b.** to produce (fruit, flowers, etc.) by this means or (of fruit, flowers, etc.) to grow by this means. **5.** to transplant (tissue) or (of tissue) to be transplanted. **6.** to attach or incorporate or become attached or incorporated: *to graft a happy ending onto a sad tale.* [C15: from Old French *graffe*, from Medieval Latin *graphium*, from Latin: stylus, from Greek *grapheion*, from *graphein* to write] —ˈ**grafter** *n.* —ˈ**grafting** *n.*

graft[2] (grɑːft) *Informal.* ~*n.* **1.** work. (esp. in the phrase **hard graft**). **2. a.** the acquisition of money, power, etc., by dishonest or unfair means, esp. by taking advantage of a position of trust. **b.** something gained in this way, such as profit from government business. **c.** a payment made to a person profiting by such a practice. ~*vb.* **3.** (*intr.*) to work. **4.** to acquire by or practise graft. [C19: of uncertain origin] —ˈ**grafter** *n.*

graft hybrid *n.* a plant produced by grafting a scion and stock from dissimilar plants; chimera.

graham (ˈgreɪəm) *n.* (*modifier*) *Chiefly U.S. and Canadian.* made of graham flour: *graham crackers.* [C19: named after S. *Graham* (1794–1851), American dietetic reformer]

graham flour *n. Chiefly U.S. and Canadian.* unbolted wheat flour ground from whole-wheat grain, similar to whole-wheat flour.

grain (greɪn) *n.* **1.** the small hard seedlike fruit of a grass, esp. a cereal plant. **2.** a mass of such fruits, esp. when gathered for food. **3.** the plants, collectively, from which such fruits are harvested. **4.** a small hard particle: *a grain of sand.* **5. a.** the general direction or arrangement of the fibrous elements in wood: *to saw across the grain.* **b.** the pattern or texture of wood resulting from such an arrangement: *the attractive grain of the table.* **6.** the relative size of the particles of a substance: *sugar of fine grain.* **7. a.** the granular texture of a rock, mineral, etc. **b.** the appearance of a rock, mineral, etc., determined by the size and arrangement of its constituents. **8. a.** the outer (hair-side) layer of a hide or skin from which the hair or wool has been removed. **b.** the pattern on the outer surface of such a hide or skin. **9.** a surface artificially imitating the grain of wood, leather, stone, etc.; graining. **10.** the smallest unit of weight in the avoirdupois, Troy, and apothecaries' systems, based on the average weight of a grain of wheat: in the avoirdupois system it equals 1/7000 of a pound, and in the Troy and apothecaries' systems it equals 1/5760 of a pound. 1 grain is equal to 0.0648 gram. Abbrev.: **gr.** **11.** Also called: **metric grain.** a metric unit of weight used for pearls or diamonds, equal to 50 milligrams or one quarter of a carat. **12.** the threads or direction of threads in a woven fabric. **13.** *Photog.* any of a large number of particles in a photographic emulsion, the size of which limit the extent to which an image can be enlarged without serious loss of definition. **14.** *Television.* a granular effect in a television picture caused by electrical noise. **15.** cleavage lines in crystalline material, parallel to growth planes. **16.** *Chem.* any of a large number of small crystals forming a polycrystalline solid, each having a regular array of atoms that differs in orientation from that of the surrounding crystallites. **17.** a state of crystallization: *to boil syrup to the grain.* **18.** a very small amount: *a grain of truth.* **19.** natural disposition, inclination, or character (esp. in the phrase **go against the grain**). **20.** *Astronautics.* a homogenous mass of solid propellant in a form designed to give the required combustion characteristics for a particular rocket. **21.** (*not in technical usage*) kermes or a red dye made from this insect. **22.** *Dyeing.* an obsolete word for **colour.** **23. with a grain** *or* **pinch of salt.** without wholly believing: sceptically. ~*vb.* (*mainly tr.*) **24.** (*also intr.*) to form grains or cause to form into grains; granulate; crystallize. **25.** to give a granular or roughened appearance or texture to. **26.** to paint, stain, etc., in imitation of the grain of wood or leather. **27. a.** to remove the hair or wool from (a hide or skin) before tanning. **b.** to raise the grain pattern on (leather). [C13: from Old French, from Latin *grānum*] —ˈ**grainer** *n.* —ˈ**grainless** *adj.*

grain alcohol *n.* ethanol containing about 10 per cent of water, made by the fermentation of grain.

grain elevator *n.* a machine for raising grain to a higher level, esp. one having an endless belt fitted with scoops.

graining (ˈgreɪnɪŋ) *n.* **1.** the pattern or texture of the grain of wood, leather, etc. **2.** the process of painting, printing, staining, etc., a surface in imitation of a grain. **3.** a surface produced by such a process.

grains of paradise *pl. n.* the peppery seeds of either of two African zingiberaceous plants, *Aframomum melegueta* or *A. granum-paradisi* used as stimulants, diuretics, etc. Also called: **guinea grains.**

grainy (ˈgreɪnɪ) *adj.* **grainier, grainiest.** **1.** resembling, full of, or composed of grain; granular. **2.** resembling the grain of wood, leather, etc. **3.** *Photog.* having poor definition because of large grain size. —ˈ**graininess** *n.*

grallatorial (ˌgræləˈtɔːrɪəl) *adj.* of or relating to long-legged wading birds, such as cranes and storks. [C19: from New Latin *grallātōrius*, from Latin *grallātor* one who walks on stilts, from *grallae* stilts]

gralloch (ˈgræləx; *Scot.* ˈgrælɒx) *Brit.* ~*n.* **1.** the entrails of a deer. **2.** the act or an instance of disembowelling a deer killed in a hunt. ~*vb.* (*tr.*) **3.** to disembowel (a deer killed in a hunt). [C19: from Scottish Gaelic *grealach* intestines]

gram[1] *or* **gramme** (græm) *n.* a metric unit of mass equal to one thousandth of a kilogram. It is equivalent to 15.432 grains or 0.002 205 pounds. Symbol: g [C18: from French *gramme*, from Late Latin *gramma*, from Greek: small weight, from *graphein* to write]

gram[2] (græm) *n.* **1.** any of several leguminous plants, such as the beans *Phaseolus mungo* (**black gram** or **urd**) and *P. aureus* (**green gram**), whose seeds are used as food in India. **2.** the seed of any of these plants. [C18: from Portuguese *gram* (modern spelling: *grão*), from Latin *grānum* GRAIN]

gram[3] (grɑːm) *n.* (in India) a village. [Hindi]

gram. *abbrev. for:* **1.** grammar. **2.** grammatical.

-gram *n. combining form.* indicating a drawing or something written or recorded: *hexagram; telegram.* [from Latin *-gramma*, from Greek, from *gramma* letter and *grammē* line]

grama *or* **grama grass** (ˈgrɑːmə) *n.* any of various grasses of the genus *Bouteloua*, of W North America and South America: often used as pasture grasses. [C19: from Spanish, ultimately from Latin *grāmen* grass]

gramarye *or* **gramary** (ˈgræmərɪ) *n. Archaic.* magic, necromancy, or occult learning. [C14: from Old French *gramaire* GRAMMAR]

gram atom *or* **gram-atomic weight** *n.* an amount of an element equal to its atomic weight expressed in grams: now replaced by the mole. See **mole**[3].

gram calorie *n.* another name for **calorie.**

gram equivalent *or* **gram-equivalent weight** *n.* an amount of a substance equal to its equivalent weight expressed in grams.

gramercy (grəˈmɜːsɪ) *interj. Archaic.* **1.** many thanks. **2.** an expression of surprise, wonder, etc. [C13: from Old French *grand merci* great thanks]

gramicidin *or* **gramicidin D** (ˌgræmɪˈsaɪdɪn) *n.* an antibiotic used in treating local Gram-positive bacterial infections: obtained from the soil bacterium *Bacillus brevis.* [C20: from GRAM(-POSITIVE) + -CID(E) + -IN]

gramineous (grəˈmɪnɪəs) *adj.* **1.** of, relating to, or belonging to the grass family, *Gramineae.* **2.** resembling a grass; grasslike. ~Also: **graminaceous** (ˌgræmɪˈneɪʃəs). [C17: from Latin *grāmineus* of grass, grassy, from *grāmen* grass]

graminicolous (ˌgræmɪˈnɪkələs) *adj.* (esp. of parasitic fungi) living on grass.

graminivorous (ˌgræmɪˈnɪvərəs) *adj.* (of animals) feeding on grass. [C18: from Latin *grāmen* grass + -VOROUS]

grammar (ˈgræmə) *n.* **1.** the branch of linguistics that deals with syntax and morphology, sometimes also phonology and semantics. **2.** the abstract system of rules in terms of which a person's mastery of his native language can be explained. **3.** a systematic description of the grammatical facts of a language. **4.** a book containing an account of the grammatical facts of a language or recommendations as to rules for the proper use of a language. **5. a.** the use of language with regard to its correctness or social propriety, esp. in syntax: *the teacher told him to watch his grammar.* **b.** (*as modifier*): *a grammar book.* **6.** the elementary principles of a science or art: *the grammar of drawing.* [C14: from Old French *gramaire*, from Latin *grammatica*, from Greek *grammatikē* (*tekhnē*) the grammatical (art), from *grammatikos* concerning letters, from *gramma* letter] —ˈ**grammarless** *adj.*

grammarian (grəˈmɛərɪən) *n.* **1.** a person whose occupation is the study of grammar. **2.** the author of a grammar.

grammar school *n.* **1.** *Brit.* (esp. formerly) a state-maintained secondary school providing an education with an academic bias for children who are selected by the eleven-plus examination, teachers' reports, or other means. Compare **secondary modern school, comprehensive school. 2.** *U.S.* another term for **elementary school. 3.** *N.Z.* a secondary school forming part of the public education system.

grammatical (grəˈmætɪkᵊl) *adj.* **1.** of or relating to grammar. **2.** (of a sentence) well formed; regarded as correct and acceptable by native speakers of the language. —**gram**ˈ**matically** *adv.* —**gram**ˈ**maticalness** *n.*

grammatical meaning *n.* the meaning of a word by reference to its function within a sentence rather than to a world outside the sentence. Compare **lexical meaning, function word.**

grammatology (ˌgræməˈtɒlədʒɪ) *n.* the scientific study of writing systems. —ˌ**gramma**ˈ**tologist** *n.*

gramme (græm) *n.* a variant spelling of **gram**[1].

gram molecule *or* **gram-molecular weight** *n.* an amount of a compound equal to its molecular weight expressed in grams: now replaced by the mole. See **mole**[3]. —ˌ**gram-mo**ˈ**lecular** *or* **gram-molar** (ˌgræmˈməʊlə) *adj.*

Grammy (ˈgræmɪ) *n., pl.* **-mys** *or* **-mies.** (in the U.S.) one of the gold-plated discs awarded annually for outstanding achievement in the record industry. [C20: from GRAM(OPHONE) + *my* as in EMMY]

Gram-negative *adj.* designating bacteria that fail to retain the violet stain in Gram's method.

gramophone (ˈgræməˌfəʊn) *n.* **1. a.** Also called: **acoustic gramophone.** a device for reproducing the sounds stored on a record: now usually applied to the nearly obsolete type that uses a clockwork motor and acoustic horn. U.S. and Canadian name: **phonograph. b.** (*as modifier*): *a gramophone record.* **2.** the technique and practice of recording sound on disc: *the gramophone has made music widely available.* [C19: originally a trademark, perhaps based on an inversion of *phonogram;* see PHONO-, -GRAM] —**gramophonic** (ˌgræməˈfɒnɪk) *adj.*

Gram-positive *adj.* designating bacteria that retain the violet stain in Gram's method.

grampus (ˈgræmpəs) *n., pl.* **-puses. 1.** a widely distributed slaty-grey dolphin, *Grampus griseus*, with a blunt snout. **2.** another name for **killer whale.** [C16: from Old French *graspois*, from *gras* fat (from Latin *crassus*) + *pois* fish (from Latin *piscis*)]

Gram's method (græmz) *n. Bacteriol.* a staining technique used to classify bacteria, based on their ability to retain or lose a violet colour, produced by crystal violet and iodine, after treatment with a decolorizing agent. See also **Gram-negative, Gram-positive.** [C19: named after Hans Christian Joachim *Gram* (1853–1938), Danish physician]

granadilla (ˌgrænəˈdɪlə) *n.* **1.** any of various passionflowers, such as *Passiflora quadrangularis* (**giant granadilla**), that have edible egg-shaped fleshy fruit. **2.** Also called: **passion fruit.** the fruit of such a plant. [C18: from Spanish, diminutive of *granada* pomegranate, from Late Latin *grānātum*]

granary (ˈgrænərɪ; *U.S.* ˈgreɪnərɪ) *n., pl.* **-ries. 1.** a building or store room for storing threshed grain, farm feed, etc. **2.** a region that produces a large amount of grain. ~*adj.* **3.** (*cap.*) *Trademark.* (of bread, flour, etc.) containing malted wheat grain. [C16: from Latin *grānārium*, from *grānum* GRAIN]

gran cassa (*Italian* gran ˈkassa) *n. Music.* another name for **bass drum.** [Italian: great drum]

grand (grænd) *adj.* **1.** large or impressive in size, extent, or consequence: *grand mountain scenery.* **2.** characterized by or attended with magnificence or display; sumptuous: *a grand feast.* **3.** of great distinction or pretension; dignified or haughty. **4.** designed to impress: *he punctuated his story with grand gestures.* **5.** very good; wonderful. **6.** comprehensive; complete: *a grand total.* **7.** worthy of respect; fine: *a grand old man.* **8.** large or impressive in conception or execution: *grand ideas.* **9.** most important; chief: *the grand arena.* ~*n.* **10.** short for **grand piano. 11.** (*pl.* **grand**) *Slang.* a thousand pounds or dollars. [C16: from Old French, from Latin *grandis*] —ˈ**grandly** *adv.* —ˈ**grandness** *n.*

grand- *prefix.* (in designations of kinship) one generation removed in ascent or descent: *grandson; grandfather.* [from French *grand-*, on the model of Latin *magnus* in such phrases as *avunculus magnus* great-uncle]

grandam (ˈgrændəm, -dæm) *or* **grandame** (ˈgrændeɪm, -dəm) *n.* an archaic word for **grandmother.** [C13: from Anglo-French *grandame*, from Old French GRAND- + *dame* lady, mother]

grandaunt (ˈgrændˌɑːnt) *n.* another name for **great-aunt.**

grand chain *n.* a figure in formation dances, such as the lancers and Scottish reels, in which couples split up and move around in a circle in opposite directions, passing all other dancers until reaching their original partners.

grandchild (ˈgrænˌtʃaɪld) *n., pl.* **-children** (-ˌtʃɪldrən). the son or daughter of one's child.

granddad (ˈgrænˌdæd) *or* **granddaddy** (ˈgrænˌdædɪ) *n., pl.* **-dads** *or* **-daddies.** informal words for **grandfather.**

granddaughter (ˈgrænˌdɔːtə) *n.* a daughter of one's son or daughter.

grand duchess *n.* **1.** the wife or a widow of a grand duke. **2.** a woman who holds the rank of grand duke in her own right.

grand duchy *n.* the territory, state, or principality of a grand duke or grand duchess.

grand duke *n.* **1.** a prince or nobleman who rules a territory, state, or principality. **2.** a son or a male descendant in the male line of a Russian tsar. **3.** a medieval Russian prince who ruled over other princes.

grande dame *French.* (grɑ̃d dam) *n.* a woman regarded as the most experienced, prominent, or venerable member of her profession, etc.: *the* grande dame *of fashion.*

grandee (grænˈdiː) *n.* **1.** a Spanish or Portuguese prince or nobleman of the highest rank. **2.** a man of great rank or eminence. [C16: from Spanish *grande*] —**gran**ˈ**deeship** *n.*

grandeur (ˈgrændʒə) *n.* **1.** personal greatness, esp. when based on dignity, character, or accomplishments. **2.** magnificence; splendour. **3.** pretentious or bombastic behaviour.

grandfather (ˈgrænˌfɑːðə, ˈgrænd-) *n.* **1.** the father of one's father or mother. **2.** (*often pl.*) a male ancestor. **3.** (*often cap.*) a familiar term of address for an old man. **4.** *Dialect.* a caterpillar or woodlouse.

grandfather clause *n.* **1.** *U.S. history.* a clause in the constitutions of several Southern states that waived electoral literacy requirements for lineal descendants of people voting before 1867, thus ensuring the franchise for illiterate Whites: declared unconstitutional in 1915. **2.** a clause in legislation that forbids or regulates an activity so that those engaged in it are exempted from the ban.

grandfather clock *n.* any of various types of long-pendulum clocks in tall standing wooden cases. Also called: **longcase clock.**

grandfatherly (ˈgrænˌfɑːðəlɪ, ˈgrænd-) *adj.* of, resembling, or suitable to a grandfather, esp. in being kindly.

grand final *n. Austral.* the final game of the season in any of various sports, esp. football.

Grand Guignol *French.* (grɑ̃ giɲɔl) *n.* **a.** a brief sensational play intended to horrify. **b.** (*modifier*) of, relating to, or like plays of this kind. [C20: after *Le Grand Guignol*, a small theatre in Montmartre, Paris]

grandiloquent (grænˈdɪləkwənt) *adj.* inflated, pompous, or bombastic in style or expression. [C16: from Latin *grandiloquus*, from *grandis* great + *loquī* to speak] —**gran**ˈ**diloquence** *n.* —**gran**ˈ**diloquently** *adv.*

grandiose ('grændɪˌəʊs) *adj.* **1.** pretentiously grand or stately. **2.** imposing in conception or execution. [C19: from French, from Italian *grandioso,* from *grande* great; see GRAND] —'**grandiˌosely** *adv.* —**grandiosity** (ˌgrændɪ'ɒsɪtɪ) *n.*

grandioso (ˌgrændɪ'əʊsəʊ) *adj., adv. Music.* (to be played) in a grand manner.

grand jury *n. Law.* (esp. in the U.S. and, now rarely, in Canada) a jury of between 12 and 23 persons summoned to inquire into accusations of crime and ascertain whether the evidence is adequate to found an indictment. Abolished in Britain in 1948. Compare **petit jury.**

Grand Lama *n.* either of two high priests of Lamaism, the Dalai Lama or the Panchen Lama.

grand larceny *n.* **1.** (formerly in England) the theft of property valued at over 12 pence. Abolished in 1827. **2.** (in some states of the U.S.) the theft of property of which the value is above a specified figure, varying from state to state but usually being between $25 and $60. Compare **petit larceny.**

grandma ('grænˌmɑː, 'grænd-, 'græm-), **grandmama,** *or* **grandmamma** ('grænməˌmɑː, 'grænd-) *n.* informal words for **grandmother.**

grand mal (grɒn mæl; *French* grɑ̃ mal) *n.* a form of epilepsy characterized by loss of consciousness for up to five minutes and violent convulsions. Compare **petit mal.** [French: great illness]

Grand Marnier ('grɒn 'mɑːnɪˌeɪ; *French* grɑ̃ marnje) *n. Trademark.* a French cognac-based liqueur with an orange flavour.

grandmaster ('grændˌmɑːstə) *n. Chess.* **1. a.** one of the top chess players of a particular country. **b.** (*cap. as part of title*): *Grandmaster of the USSR.* **2.** Also called: **International Grandmaster.** a player who has been awarded the highest title by the Fédération Internationale des Échecs. **3.** a leading exponent of any of various arts.

Grand Master *n.* the title borne by the head of any of various societies, orders, and other organizations, such as the Templars or Freemasons, or the various martial arts.

grandmother ('grænˌmʌðə, 'grænd-) *n.* **1.** the mother of one's father or mother. **2.** (*often pl.*) a female ancestor. **3.** (*often cap.*) a familiar term of address for an old woman. **4. teach one's grandmother to suck eggs.** See **egg**[1] (sense 8).

grandmother clock *n.* a longcase clock with a pendulum, about two thirds the size of a grandfather clock.

grandmotherly ('grænˌmʌðəlɪ, 'grænd-) *adj.* of, resembling, or suitable to a grandmother, esp. in being protective, indulgent, or solicitous.

Grand Mufti *n.* **1.** the titular head of the Muslim community in Jerusalem and formerly the chief constitutional administrator there. **2.** (in Turkey) the former official head of the state religion.

Grand National *n.* **the.** an annual steeplechase run at Aintree, Liverpool, since 1839.

grandnephew ('grænˌnɛvjuː, -ˌnɛfjuː, 'grænd-) *n.* another name for **great-nephew.**

grandniece ('grænˌniːs, 'grænd-) *n.* another name for **great-niece.**

grand opera *n.* an opera that has a serious plot and is entirely in musical form, with no spoken dialogue.

grandpa ('grænˌpɑː, 'grænd-, 'græm-) *or* **grandpapa** ('grænpəˌpɑː, 'grænd-) *n.* informal words for **grandfather.**

grandparent ('grænˌpɛərənt, 'grænd-) *n.* the father or mother of either of one's parents.

grand piano *n.* a form of piano in which the strings are arranged horizontally. Grand pianos exist in three sizes (see **baby grand, boudoir grand, concert grand**). Compare **upright piano.**

Grand Prix (*French* grɑ̃ pri) *n.* **1. a.** any of a series of formula motor races held to determine the annual Drivers' World Championship. **b.** (*as modifier*): *a Grand Prix car.* **2.** *Horse racing.* a race for three-year-old horses run at Maisons Lafitte near Paris. **3.** a very important competitive event in various other sports, such as athletics, snooker, or powerboating. [French: great prize]

grand seigneur *French.* (grɑ̃ sɛɲœr) *n., pl.* ***grands seigneurs*** (grɑ̃ sɛɲœr). *Often ironic.* a dignified or aristocratic man. [literally: great lord]

grand siècle *French.* (grɑ̃ sjɛklə) *n., pl.* ***grands siècles*** (grɑ̃ sjɛklə). the 17th century in French art and literature, esp. the classical period of Louis XIV. [literally: great century]

grandsire[1] ('grænˌsaɪə, 'grænd-) *n.* an archaic word for **grandfather.**

grandsire[2] ('grændsə, -ˌsaɪə) *n. Bell-ringing.* a well-established method used in change-ringing. See **method** (sense 4).

grand slam *n.* **1.** *Bridge, etc.* the winning of 13 tricks by one player or side or the contract to do so. **2.** the winning of all major competitions in a season, esp. in tennis and golf.

grandson ('grænsʌn, 'grænd-) *n.* a son of one's son or daughter.

grandstand ('grænˌstænd, 'grænd-) *n.* **1. a.** a terraced block of seats, usually under a roof, commanding the best view at racecourses, football pitches, etc. **b.** (*as modifier*): *grandstand tickets.* **2.** the spectators in a grandstand. **3.** (*modifier*) as if from a grandstand; unimpeded (esp. in the phrase **grandstand view**). ~*vb.* **4.** (*intr.*) *U.S. and Canadian informal.* to behave ostentatiously in an attempt to impress onlookers. —'**grandˌstander** *n.*

grand tour *n.* **1.** (formerly) an extended tour through the major cities of Europe, esp. one undertaken by a rich or aristocratic Englishman to complete his education. **2.** *Informal.* an extended sightseeing trip, tour of inspection, etc.

granduncle ('grændˌʌŋkᵊl) *n.* another name for **great-uncle.**

Grand Unified Theory *n. Physics.* any of a number of theories of elementary particles and fundamental interactions designed to explain the electromagnetic, strong, and weak interactions in terms of a single mathematical formalism. Abbrev.: **GUT.**

grand vizier *n.* (formerly) the chief officer or minister of state in the Ottoman Empire and other Muslim countries.

grange (greɪndʒ) *n.* **1.** *Chiefly Brit.* a farm, esp. a farmhouse or country house with its various outbuildings. **2.** *History.* an outlying farmhouse in which a religious establishment or feudal lord stored crops and tithes in kind. **3.** *Archaic.* a granary or barn. [C13: from Anglo-French *graunge,* from Medieval Latin *grānica,* from Latin *grānum* GRAIN]

Grange (greɪndʒ) *n.* (in the U.S.) **1. the.** an association of farmers that strongly influenced state legislatures in the late 19th century. **2.** a lodge of this association.

grangerize *or* **grangerise** ('greɪndʒəˌraɪz) *vb.* (*tr.*) **1.** to illustrate (a book) by inserting prints, drawings, etc., taken from other works. **2.** to raid (books) to acquire material for illustrating another book. [C19: named after Joseph *Granger,* 18th-century English writer, whose *Biographical History of England* (1769) included blank pages for illustrations to be supplied by the reader] —'**grangerism** *n.* —ˌ**grangeri'zation** *or* ˌ**grangeri'sation** *n.* —'**grangerˌizer** *or* '**grangerˌiser** *n.*

grani- *combining form.* indicating grain: *graniform.* [from Latin, from *grānum* GRAIN]

granite ('grænɪt) *n.* **1.** a light-coloured coarse-grained acid plutonic igneous rock consisting of quartz, feldspars, and such ferromagnesian minerals as biotite or hornblende: widely used for building. **2.** great hardness, endurance, or resolution. **3.** another name for a **stone** (sense 9). [C17: from Italian *granito* grained, from *granire* to grain, from *grano* grain, from Latin *grānum*] —'**granite-ˌlike** *adj.* —**granitic** (grə'nɪtɪk) *or* '**granˌitˌoid** *adj.*

graniteware ('grænɪtˌwɛə) *n.* **1.** iron vessels coated with enamel of a granite-like appearance. **2.** a type of very durable white semivitreous pottery. **3.** a type of pottery with a speckled glaze.

granitite ('grænɪˌtaɪt) *n.* any granite with a high content of biotite.

granitization *or* **granitisation** (ˌgrænɪtaɪ'zeɪʃən) *n.* the metamorphic conversion of a rock into granite.

granivorous (græ'nɪvərəs) *adj.* (of animals) feeding on seeds and grain. —**granivore** ('grænɪˌvɔː) *n.*

grannies ('grænɪz) *pl. n. N.Z. informal.* Granny Smith apples.

grannom ('grænəm) *n.* a widespread caddis fly, *Brachycentrus subnubilus,* the larvae of which attach their cases to vegetation under running water and are esteemed as a bait by anglers. [C18: altered from *green tail*]

granny *or* **grannie** ('grænɪ) *n., pl.* **-nies. 1.** informal words for **grandmother.** Often shortened to **gran. 2.** *Informal.* an irritatingly fussy person. **3.** a revolving cap on a chimneypot that keeps out rain, etc. **4.** *Southern U.S.* a midwife or nurse. **5.** See **granny knot.**

granny bond *n.* (in Britain) an informal name for **retirement issue certificate,** an index-linked savings certificate, originally available only to people over retirement age.

granny flat *n.* self-contained accommodation within or built onto a house, suitable for an elderly parent. Also called: **granny annexe.**

granny knot *or* **granny's knot** *n.* a reef knot with the ends crossed the wrong way, making it liable to slip or jam.

Granny Smith *n.* a variety of hard green-skinned apple eaten raw or cooked. [C19: named after Maria Ann Smith, known as *Granny Smith* (died 1870), who first produced them at Eastwood, Sydney]

grano- *combining form.* of or resembling granite: *granolith.* [from German, from *Granit* GRANITE]

granodiorite (ˌgrænəʊ'daɪəˌraɪt) *n.* a coarse-grained acid igneous rock containing almost twice as much plagioclase as orthoclase: intermediate in structure between granite and diorite. [C19: from *grano* + DIORITE]

granolith ('grænəʊˌlɪθ) *n.* a paving material consisting of a mixture of cement and crushed granite or granite chippings. —ˌ**grano'lithic** *adj., n.*

granophyre ('grænəʊˌfaɪə) *n.* a fine-grained granitic rock in which irregular crystals of intergrown quartz and feldspar are embedded in a groundmass of these minerals. [C19: from GRAN(ITE) + *-phyre* after *porphyry*] —**granophyric** (ˌgrænəʊ'fɪrɪk) *adj.*

grant (grɑːnt) *vb.* (*tr.*) **1.** to consent to perform or fulfil: *to grant a wish.* **2.** (*may take a clause as object*) to permit as a favour, indulgence, etc.: *to grant an interview.* **3.** (*may take a clause as object*) to acknowledge the validity of; concede: *I grant what you say is true.* **4.** to bestow, esp. in a formal manner. **5.** to transfer (property) to another, esp. by deed; convey. **6. take for granted. a.** to accept or assume without question: *one takes certain amenities for granted.* **b.** to fail to appreciate the value, merit, etc., of (a person). ~*n.* **7.** a sum of money provided by a government or public fund to finance educational study, overseas aid, etc. **8.** a privilege, right, etc., that has been granted. **9.** the act of granting. **10.** a transfer of property by deed or other written instrument; conveyance. **11.** *U.S.* a territorial unit in Maine, New Hampshire, and Vermont, originally granted to an individual or organization. [C13: from Old French *graunter,* from Vulgar Latin *credentāre* (unattested), from Latin *crēdere* to believe] —'**grantable** *adj.* —'**granter** *n.*

grantee (grɑːn'tiː) *n. Law.* a person to whom a grant is made.

Granth *or* **Grant Sahib** (grʌnt) *n.* the sacred scripture of the Sikhs, believed by them to be the embodiment of the gurus. [from Hindi, from Sanskrit *grantha* a book]

grant-in-aid *n., pl.* **grants-in-aid.** **1.** a sum of money granted by one government to a lower level of government or to a dependency for a programme, etc. **2.** *Education.* a grant provided by the central government or local education authority to ensure consistent standards in buildings and other facilities.

grant-maintained *adj.* (**grant maintained** *when postpostive*). (of schools or educational institutions) funded directly by central government.

grant of probate *n. Law.* an instrument authorizing an executor to control and dispose of a deceased person's estate if a will has been made.

grantor (grɑːn'tɔː, 'grɑːntə) *n. Law.* a person who makes a grant.

gran turismo ('græn tʊə'rɪzməʊ) *n., pl.* **gran turismos.** the full form of **GT.** [C20: Italian, literally: great touring (i.e., touring on a grand scale)]

granular ('grænjʊlə) *adj.* **1.** of, like, containing, or resembling a granule or granules. **2.** having a grainy or granulated surface. —**granularity** (ˌgrænjʊ'lærɪtɪ) *n.* —'**granularly** *adv.*

granulate ('grænjʊˌleɪt) *vb.* **1.** (*tr.*) to make into grains. **2.** to make or become roughened in surface texture. **3.** (*intr.*) (of a wound, ulcer, etc.) to form granulation tissue. —'**granulative** *adj.* —'**granuˌlator** *or* '**granuˌlater** *n.*

granulated sugar *n.* a coarsely ground white sugar.

granulation (ˌgrænjʊ'leɪʃən) *n.* **1.** the act or process of granulating. **2.** a granulated texture or surface. **3.** a single bump or grain in such a surface. **4.** See **granulation tissue.** **5.** Also called: **granule.** *Astronomy.* any of numerous bright regions (approximate diameter 900 km) having a fine granular structure that can appear briefly on any part of the sun's surface.

granulation tissue *n.* a mass of new connective tissue and capillaries formed on the surface of a healing ulcer or wound, usually leaving a scar. Nontechnical name: **proud flesh.**

granule ('grænjuːl) *n.* **1.** a small grain. **2.** *Geology.* a single rock fragment in gravel, smaller than a pebble but larger than a sand grain. **3.** *Astronomy.* another name for **granulation** (sense 5). [C17: from Late Latin *grānulum* a small GRAIN]

granulite ('grænjʊˌlaɪt) *n.* a granular foliated metamorphic rock in which the minerals form a mosaic of equal-sized granules. —**granulitic** (ˌgrænjʊ'lɪtɪk) *adj.*

granulocyte ('grænjʊləˌsaɪt) *n.* any of a group of phagocytic leucocytes having cytoplasmic granules that take up various dyes. See also **eosinophil, neutrophil** (sense 1), **basophil** (sense 2). —**granulocytic** (ˌgrænjʊlə'sɪtɪk) *adj.*

granulocytopenia (ˌgrænjʊləʊˌsaɪtəʊ'piːnɪə) *n.* a diminished number of granulocytes in the blood, which occurs in certain forms of anaemia.

granuloma (ˌgrænjʊ'ləʊmə) *n., pl.* **-mas** *or* **-mata** (-mətə). a tumour composed of granulation tissue. —**granulomatous** (ˌgrænjʊ'lɒmətəs) *adj.*

granulose ('grænjʊˌləʊs, -ˌləʊz) *adj.* a less common word for **granular.**

grape (greɪp) *n.* **1.** the fruit of the grapevine, which has a purple or green skin and sweet flesh: eaten raw, dried to make raisins, currants, or sultanas, or used for making wine. **2.** any of various plants that bear grapelike fruit, such as the Oregon grape. **3.** See **grapevine** (sense 1). **4. the.** an informal term for **wine.** **5.** See **grapeshot.** **6. a grape on the business.** *Austral. slang.* a person whose presence spoils things for others. ~See also **grapes.** [C13: from Old French *grape* bunch of grapes, of Germanic origin; compare Old High German *krāpfo;* related to CRAMP[2], GRAPPLE] —'**grapeless** *adj.* —'**grapeˌlike** *adj.* —'**grapey** *or* '**grapy** *adj.*

grapefruit ('greɪpˌfruːt) *n., pl.* **-fruit** *or* **-fruits.** **1.** a tropical or subtropical evergreen rutaceous tree, *Citrus paradisi.* **2.** the large round edible fruit of this tree, which has yellow rind and juicy slightly bitter pulp.

grape hyacinth *n.* any of various Eurasian liliaceous plants of the genus *Muscari,* esp. *M. botryoides,* with clusters of rounded blue flowers resembling tiny grapes.

grape ivy *n.* See **rhoicissus.**

grapes (greɪps) *n.* (*functioning as sing.*) *Vet. science.* an abnormal growth, resembling a bunch of grapes, on the fetlock of a horse.

grapeshot ('greɪpˌʃɒt) *n.* ammunition for cannons consisting of a canvas tube containing a cluster of small iron balls that scatter after firing.

grape sugar *n.* another name for **dextrose.**

grapevine ('greɪpˌvaɪn) *n.* **1.** any of several vitaceous vines of the genus *Vitis,* esp. *V. vinifera* of E Asia, widely cultivated for its fruit (grapes): family *Vitaceae.* **2.** *Informal.* an unofficial means of relaying information, esp. from person to person. **3.** a wrestling hold in which a wrestler entwines his own leg around his opponent's and exerts pressure against various joints.

graph (grɑːf, græf) *n.* **1.** Also called: **chart.** a drawing depicting the relation between certain sets of numbers or quantities by means of a series of dots, lines, etc., plotted with reference to a set of axes. See also **bar graph.** **2.** *Maths.* a drawing depicting a functional relation between two or three variables by means of a curve or surface containing only those points whose coordinates satisfy the relation. **3.** *Linguistics.* a symbol in a writing system not further subdivisible into other such symbols. ~*vb.* **4.** (*tr.*) to draw or represent in a graph. [C19: short for *graphic formula*]

-graph *n. combining form.* **1.** an instrument that writes or records: *telegraph.* **2.** a writing, record, or drawing: *autograph; lithograph.* [via Latin from Greek *-graphos,* from *graphein* to write] —**-graphic** *or* **-graphical** *adj. combining form.* —**-graphically** *adv. combining form.*

grapheme ('græfiːm) *n. Linguistics.* one of a set of orthographic symbols (letters or combinations of letters) in a given language that serve to distinguish one word from another and usually correspond to or represent phonemes, e.g. the *f* in *fun,* the *ph* in *phantom,* and the *gh* in *laugh.* [C20: from Greek *graphēma* a letter] —**gra'phemically** *adv.*

-grapher *n. combining form.* **1.** indicating a person who writes about or is skilled in a subject: *geographer; photographer.* **2.** indicating a person who writes, records, or draws in a specified way: *stenographer; lithographer.*

graphic ('græfɪk) *or* **graphical** *adj.* **1.** vividly or clearly described: *a graphic account of the disaster.* **2.** of or relating to writing or other inscribed representations: *graphic symbols.* **3.** *Maths.* using, relating to, or determined by a graph: *a graphic representation of the figures.* **4.** of or relating to the graphic arts. **5.** *Geology.* having or denoting a texture formed by intergrowth of the crystals to resemble writing: *graphic granite.* [C17: from Latin *graphicus,* from Greek *graphikos,* from *graphein* to write; see CARVE] —'**graphically** *or* '**graphicly** *adv.* —'**graphicalness** *or* '**graphicness** *n.*

graphicacy ('græfɪkəsɪ) *n.* the ability to understand and use maps, plans, symbols, etc. [C20: formed on the model of *literacy*]

graphic arts *pl. n.* any of the fine or applied visual arts based on drawing or the use of line, as opposed to colour or relief, on a plane surface, esp. illustration and printmaking of all kinds.

graphic equalizer *n.* an electronic device for cutting or boosting selected frequencies, using small linear faders. Compare **parametric equalizer.**

graphic novel *n.* a novel in the form of a comic strip.

graphics ('græfɪks) *n.* **1.** (*functioning as sing.*) the process or art of drawing in accordance with mathematical principles. **2.** (*functioning as sing.*) the study of writing systems. **3.** (*functioning as pl.*) the drawings, photographs, etc., in the layout of a magazine or book, or in a television or film production. **4.** (*functioning as pl.*) the information displayed on a visual display unit or on a computer printout in the form of diagrams, graphs, pictures, and symbols.

graphite ('græfaɪt) *n.* a blackish soft allotropic form of carbon in hexagonal crystalline form: used in pencils, crucibles, and electrodes, as a lubricant, as a moderator in nuclear reactors, and, in a carbon fibre form, as a tough lightweight material for sporting equipment. Also called: **plumbago.** [C18: from German *Graphit;* from Greek *graphein* to write + -ITE[1]] —**graphitic** (grə'fɪtɪk) *adj.*

graphitize *or* **graphitise** ('græfɪˌtaɪz) *vb.* (*tr.*) **1.** to convert (a substance) into graphite, usually by heating. **2.** to coat or impregnate with graphite. —ˌ**graphiti'zation** *or* ˌ**graphiti'sation** *n.*

graphology (græ'fɒlədʒɪ) *n.* **1.** the study of handwriting, esp. to analyse the writer's character. **2.** *Linguistics.* the study of writing systems. —**graphologic** (ˌgræfə'lɒdʒɪk) *or* ˌ**grapho'logical** *adj.* —**gra'phologist** *n.*

graphomotor ('græfəˌməʊtə) *adj.* of or relating to the muscular movements used or required in writing.

graph paper *n.* paper printed with intersecting lines, usually horizontal and vertical and equally spaced, for drawing graphs, diagrams, etc.

-graphy *n. combining form.* **1.** indicating a form or process of writing, representing, etc.: *calligraphy; photography.* **2.** indicating an art or descriptive science: *choreography; oceanography.* [via Latin from Greek *-graphia,* from *graphein* to write]

grapnel ('græpnᵊl) *n.* **1.** a device with a multiple hook at one end and attached to a rope, which is thrown or hooked over a firm mooring to secure an object attached to the other end of the rope. **2.** a light anchor for small boats. [C14: from Old French *grapin* a little hook, from *grape* a hook; see GRAPE]

grappa ('græpə) *n.* a spirit distilled from the fermented remains of grapes after pressing. [Italian: grape stalk, of Germanic origin; see GRAPE]

grapple ('græpᵊl) *vb.* **1.** to come to grips with (one or more persons), esp. to struggle in hand-to-hand combat. **2.** (*intr.;* foll. by *with*) to cope or contend: *to grapple with a financial problem.* **3.** (*tr.*) to secure with a grapple. ~*n.* **4.** any form of hook or metal instrument by which something is secured, such as a grapnel. **5. a.** the act of gripping or seizing, as in wrestling. **b.**

a grip or hold. **6.** a contest of grappling, esp. a wrestling match. [C16: from Old French *grappelle* a little hook, from *grape* hook; see GRAPNEL] —ˈ**grappler** *n.*

grapple plant *n.* a herbaceous plant, *Harpagophytum procumbens,* of southern Africa, whose fruits are covered with large woody barbed hooks: family *Pedaliaceae.* Also called: **wait-a-bit.**

grappling (ˈɡræplɪŋ) *n.* **1.** the act of gripping or seizing, as in wrestling. **2.** a hook used for securing something.

grappling iron *or* **hook** *n.* a grapnel, esp. one used for securing ships.

graptolite (ˈɡræptəˌlaɪt) *n.* any extinct Palaeozoic colonial animal of the class *Graptolithina,* usually regarded as related to the coelenterates: a common fossil. [C19: from Greek *graptos* written, from *graphein* to write + -LITE]

grasp (ɡrɑːsp) *vb.* **1.** to grip (something) firmly with or as if with the hands. **2.** (when *intr.,* often foll. by *at*) to struggle, snatch, or grope (for). **3.** (*tr.*) to understand, esp. with effort. ~*n.* **4.** the act of grasping. **5.** a grip or clasp, as of a hand. **6.** the capacity to accomplish (esp. in the phrase **within one's grasp**). **7.** total rule or possession. **8.** understanding; comprehension. [C14: from Low German *grapsen;* related to Old English *græppian* to seize, Old Norse *grāpa* to steal] —ˈ**graspable** *adj.* —ˈ**grasper** *n.*

grasping (ˈɡrɑːspɪŋ) *adj.* greedy; avaricious; rapacious. —ˈ**graspingly** *adv.* —ˈ**graspingness** *n.*

grass (ɡrɑːs) *n.* **1.** any monocotyledonous plant of the family *Gramineae,* having jointed stems sheathed by long narrow leaves, flowers in spikes, and seedlike fruits. The family includes cereals, bamboo, etc. **2.** such plants collectively, in a lawn, meadow, etc. Related adj.: **verdant. 3.** any similar plant, such as knotgrass, deergrass, or scurvy grass. **4.** ground on which such plants grow; a lawn, field, etc. **5.** ground on which animals are grazed; pasture. **6.** a slang word for **marijuana. 7.** *Brit. slang.* a person who informs, esp. on criminals. **8.** short for **sparrowgrass. 9. let the grass grow under one's feet.** to squander time or opportunity. **10. put out to grass. a.** to retire (a racehorse). **b.** *Informal.* to retire (a person). ~*vb.* **11.** to cover or become covered with grass. **12.** to feed or be fed with grass. **13.** (*tr.*) to spread (cloth) out on grass for drying or bleaching in the sun. **14.** (*tr.*) *Sport.* to knock or bring down (an opponent). **15.** (*tr.*) to shoot down (a bird). **16.** (*tr.*) to land (a fish) on a river bank. **17.** (*intr.;* usually foll. by *on*) *Brit. slang.* to inform, esp. to the police. [Old English *græs;* related to Old Norse, Gothic, Old High German *gras,* Middle High German *gruose* sap] —ˈ**grassless** *adj.* —ˈ**grassˌlike** *adj.*

grass box *n.* a container attached to a lawn mower that receives grass after it has been cut.

grass cloth *n.* a cloth made from plant fibres, such as jute or hemp.

grass court *n.* a tennis court covered with grass. See also **hard court.**

grassfinch (ˈɡrɑːsˌfɪntʃ) *n.* any Australian weaverbird of the genus *Poephila* and related genera, many of which are brightly coloured and kept as cagebirds.

grass hockey *n. Canadian.* field hockey, as contrasted with ice hockey.

grasshook (ˈɡrɑːsˌhʊk) *n.* another name for **sickle.**

grasshopper (ˈɡrɑːsˌhɒpə) *n.* **1.** any orthopterous insect of the families *Acrididae* (**short-horned grasshoppers**) and *Tettigoniidae* (**long-horned grasshoppers**), typically terrestrial, feeding on plants, and producing a ticking sound by rubbing the hind legs against the leathery forewings. See also **locust** (sense 1), **katydid. 2. knee-high to a grasshopper.** *Informal.* very young or very small. **3.** an iced cocktail of equal parts of crème de menthe, crème de cacao, and cream. **4.** (*modifier*) unable to concentrate on any one subject for long: *a grasshopper mind.*

grassland (ˈɡrɑːsˌlænd) *n.* **1.** land, such as a prairie, on which grass predominates. **2.** land reserved for natural grass pasture.

grass moth *n.* any of a large subfamily of small night-flying pyralid moths, esp. *Crambus pratellus,* that during the day cling to grass stems.

grass-of-Parnassus *n.* a herbaceous perennial N temperate marsh plant, *Parnassia palustris,* with solitary whitish flowers: family *Parnassiaceae.*

grassquit (ˈɡrɑːsˌkwɪt) *n.* any tropical American finch of the genus *Tiaris* and related genera, such as *T. olivacea* (**yellow-faced grassquit**). [from GRASS + *quit,* a bird name in Jamaica]

grass roots *pl. n.* **1. a.** the ordinary people as distinct from the active leadership of a party or organization: used esp. of the rank-and-file members of a political party, or of the voters themselves. **b.** (*as modifier*): *the newly elected MP expressed a wish for greater contact with people at grass-roots level.* **2.** the origin or essentials. [C20: sense 1 originally U.S., with reference to rural areas in contrast to the towns]

grass snake *n.* **1.** a harmless nonvenomous European colubrid snake, *Natrix natrix,* having a brownish-green body with variable markings. **2.** any of several similar related European snakes, such as *Natrix maura* (**viperine grass snake**).

grass tree *n.* **1.** Also called: **blackboy.** any liliaceous plant of the Australian genus *Xanthorrhoea,* having a woody stem, stiff grasslike leaves, and a spike of small white flowers. Some species produce fragrant resins. See also **acaroid gum. 2.** any of several similar Australasian plants.

grass widow *or* (*masc.*) **grass widower** *n.* **1.** a person divorced, separated, or living away from his or her spouse. **2.** a person whose spouse is regularly away for a short period. [C16, meaning a discarded mistress: perhaps an allusion to a grass bed as representing an illicit relationship; compare BASTARD; C19 in the modern sense]

grassy (ˈɡrɑːsɪ) *adj.* **grassier, grassiest.** covered with, containing, or resembling grass. —ˈ**grassiness** *n.*

grate[1] (ɡreɪt) *vb.* **1.** (*tr.*) to reduce to small shreds by rubbing against a rough or sharp perforated surface: *to grate carrots.* **2.** to scrape (an object) against something or (objects) together, producing a harsh rasping sound, or (of objects) to scrape with such a sound. **3.** (*intr.;* foll. by *on* or *upon*) to annoy. **4.** (*tr.*) *Archaic.* to abrade; erode. ~*n.* **5.** a harsh rasping sound. [C15: from Old French *grater* to scrape, of Germanic origin; compare Old High German *krazzōn*]

grate[2] (ɡreɪt) *n.* **1.** a framework of metal bars for holding fuel in a fireplace, stove, or furnace. **2.** a less common word for **fireplace. 3.** another name for **grating**[1] (sense 1). **4.** *Mining.* a perforated metal screen for grading crushed ore. ~*vb.* **5.** (*tr.*) to provide with a grate or grates. [C14: from Old French *grate,* from Latin *crātis* hurdle]

grateful (ˈɡreɪtfʊl) *adj.* **1.** thankful for gifts, favours, etc.; appreciative. **2.** showing gratitude: *a grateful letter.* **3.** favourable or pleasant: *a grateful rest.* [C16: from obsolete *grate,* from Latin *grātus* + -FUL] —ˈ**gratefully** *adv.* —ˈ**gratefulness** *n.*

grater (ˈɡreɪtə) *n.* **1.** a kitchen utensil with sharp-edged perforations for grating carrots, cheese, etc. **2.** a person or thing that grates.

graticule (ˈɡrætɪˌkjuːl) *n.* **1.** the grid of intersecting lines of latitude and longitude on which a map is drawn. **2.** another name for **reticle. 3.** a transparent scale in front of a cathode-ray oscilloscope or other measuring instrument. [C19: from French, from Latin *crāticula,* from *crātis* wickerwork]

gratification (ˌɡrætɪfɪˈkeɪʃən) *n.* **1.** the act of gratifying or the state of being gratified. **2.** something that gratifies. **3.** an obsolete word for **gratuity.**

gratify (ˈɡrætɪˌfaɪ) *vb.* **-fies, -fying, -fied.** (*tr.*) **1.** to satisfy or please. **2.** to yield to or indulge (a desire, whim, etc.). **3.** *Obsolete.* to reward. [C16: from Latin *grātificārī* to do a favour to, from *grātus* grateful + *facere* to make] —ˈ**gratiˌfier** *n.* —ˈ**gratiˌfying** *adj.* —ˈ**gratiˌfyingly** *adv.*

gratin (*French* ɡratɛ̃) See **au gratin.**

grating[1] (ˈɡreɪtɪŋ) *n.* **1.** Also called: **grate.** a framework of metal bars in the form of a grille set into a wall, pavement, etc., serving as a cover or guard but admitting air and sometimes light. **2.** short for **diffraction grating.**

grating[2] (ˈɡreɪtɪŋ) *adj.* **1.** (of sounds) harsh and rasping. **2.** annoying; irritating. ~*n.* **3.** (*often pl.*) something produced by grating. —ˈ**gratingly** *adv.*

gratis (ˈɡreɪtɪs, ˈɡrætɪs, ˈɡrɑːtɪs) *adv., adj.* (*postpositive*) without payment; free of charge. [C15: from Latin: out of kindness, from *grātiīs,* ablative pl. of *grātia* favour]

gratitude (ˈɡrætɪˌtjuːd) *n.* a feeling of thankfulness or appreciation, as for gifts or favours. [C16: from Medieval Latin *grātitūdō,* from Latin *grātus* GRATEFUL]

gratuitous (ɡrəˈtjuːɪtəs) *adj.* **1.** given or received without payment or obligation. **2.** without cause; unjustified. **3.** *Law.* given or made without receiving any value in return: *a gratuitous contract.* [C17: from Latin *grātuītus,* from *grātia* favour] —**graˈtuitously** *adv.* —**graˈtuitousness** *n.*

gratuity (ɡrəˈtjuːɪtɪ) *n., pl.* **-ties. 1.** a gift or reward, usually of money, for services rendered; tip. **2.** something given without claim or obligation. **3.** *Military.* a financial award granted for long or meritorious service.

gratulate (ˈɡrætjʊˌleɪt) *vb.* (*tr.*) *Archaic.* **1.** to greet joyously. **2.** to congratulate. [C16: from Latin *grātulārī,* from *grātus* pleasing] —ˈ**gratulant** *adj.* —ˌ**gratuˈlation** *n.* —ˈ**gratulatory** *adj.*

graunch (ɡrɔːntʃ) *vb.* (*tr.*) *English dialect and N.Z.* to crush or destroy. [C19: of imitative origin]

graupel (ˈɡraʊpəl) *n.* soft hail or snow pellets. [German, from *Graupe,* probably from Serbo-Croatian *krupa;* related to Russian *krupá* peeled grain]

grav (ɡræv) *n.* a unit of acceleration equal to the standard acceleration of free fall. 1 grav is equivalent to 9.806 65 metres per second per second. Symbol: g

gravadlax (ˈɡrævədˌlæks) *n.* another name for **gravlax.**

gravamen (ɡrəˈveɪmɛn) *n., pl.* **-vamina** (-ˈvæmɪnə). **1.** *Law.* that part of an accusation weighing most heavily against an accused. **2.** *Law.* the substance or material grounds of a complaint. **3.** a rare word for **grievance.** [C17: from Late Latin: trouble, from Latin *gravāre* to load, from *gravis* heavy; see GRAVE[2]]

grave[1] (ɡreɪv) *n.* **1.** a place for the burial of a corpse, esp. beneath the ground and usually marked by a tombstone. Related adj.: **sepulchral. 2.** something resembling a grave or resting place: *the ship went to its grave.* **3.** (often preceded by *the*) a poetic term for **death. 4. have one foot in the grave.** *Informal.* to be near death. **5. to make (someone) turn (over) in his grave.** to do something that would have shocked or distressed (someone now dead): *many modern dictionaries would make Dr Johnson turn in* *his grave.* [Old English *græf;* related to Old Frisian *gref,* Old High German *grab,* Old Slavonic *grobŭ;* see GRAVE[3]]

grave[2] (greɪv) *adj.* **1.** serious and solemn: *a grave look.* **2.** full of or suggesting danger: *a grave situation.* **3.** important; crucial: *grave matters of state.* **4.** (of colours) sober or dull. **5.** (*also* grɑːv). *Phonetics.* **a.** (of a vowel or syllable in some languages with a pitch accent, such as ancient Greek) spoken on a lower or falling musical pitch relative to neighbouring syllables or vowels. **b.** of or relating to an accent (`) over vowels, denoting a pronunciation with lower or falling musical pitch (as in ancient Greek), with certain special quality (as in French), or in a manner that gives the vowel status as a syllable nucleus not usually possessed by it in that position (as in English *agèd*). Compare **acute** (sense 8), **circumflex.** ~*n.* **6.** (*also* grɑːv) a grave accent. [C16: from Old French, from Latin *gravis;* related to Greek *barus* heavy; see GRAVAMEN] —ˈ**gravely** *adv.* —ˈ**graveness** *n.*

grave[3] (greɪv) *vb.* **graves, graving, graved; graved** *or* **graven.** (*tr.*) *Archaic.* **1.** to cut, carve, sculpt, or engrave. **2.** to fix firmly in the mind. [Old English *grafan;* related to Old Norse *grafa,* Old High German *graban* to dig]

grave[4] (greɪv) *vb.* (*tr.*) *Nautical.* to clean and apply a coating of pitch to (the bottom of a vessel). [C15: perhaps from Old French *grave* GRAVEL]

grave[5] (ˈgrɑːvɪ) *adj., adv. Music.* to be performed in a solemn manner. [C17: from Italian: heavy, from Latin *gravis*]

grave clothes *pl. n.* the wrappings in which a dead body is interred.

gravel (ˈgrævəl) *n.* **1.** a mixture of rock fragments and pebbles that is coarser than sand. **2.** *Geology.* a mixture of rock fragments with diameters in the range 2-4 mm. **3.** *Pathol.* small rough calculi in the kidneys or bladder. ~*vb.* **-els, -elling, -elled** *or U.S.* **-els, -eling, -eled.** (*tr.*) **4.** to cover with gravel. **5.** to confound or confuse. **6.** *U.S. informal.* to annoy or disturb. [C13: from Old French *gravele,* diminutive of *grave* gravel, perhaps of Celtic origin] —ˈ**gravelish** *adj.*

gravel-blind *adj. Literary.* almost entirely blind. [C16: from GRAVEL + BLIND, formed on the model of SAND-BLIND]

gravelly (ˈgrævəlɪ) *adj.* **1.** consisting of or abounding in gravel. **2.** of or like gravel. **3.** (esp. of a voice) harsh and grating.

gravel-voiced *adj.* speaking in a rough and rasping tone.

graven (ˈgreɪvən) *vb.* **1.** a past participle of **grave**[3]. ~*adj.* **2.** strongly fixed.

graven image *n. Chiefly Bible.* a carved image used as an idol.

graveolent (ˈgrævɪələnt) *adj.* (of plants) having a strong fetid smell. [C17: from Latin *gravis* heavy + *olēre* to smell]

graver (ˈgreɪvə) *n.* any of various engraving, chasing, or sculpting tools, such as a burin.

Graves (grɑːv) *n.* **1.** (*sometimes not cap.*) a white or red wine from the district around Bordeaux, France. **2.** a dry or medium sweet white wine from any country: *Spanish Graves.*

Graves' disease (greɪvz) *n.* another name for **exophthalmic goitre.** [C19: named after R. J. *Graves* (1796–1853), Irish physician]

gravestone (ˈgreɪvˌstəʊn) *n.* a stone marking a grave and usually inscribed with the name and dates of the person buried.

Gravettian (grəˈvɛtɪən) *adj.* of, referring to, or characteristic of an Upper Palaeolithic culture, characterized esp. by small pointed blades with blunt backs. [C20: from *La Gravette* on the Dordogne, France]

grave-wax *n.* the nontechnical name for **adipocere.**

graveyard (ˈgreɪvˌjɑːd) *n.* a place for graves; a burial ground, esp. a small one or one in a churchyard.

graveyard orbit *n.* another name for **dump orbit.**

graveyard shift *n. U.S.* the working shift between midnight and morning.

gravid (ˈgrævɪd) *adj.* the technical word for **pregnant.** [C16: from Latin *gravidus,* from *gravis* heavy] —**graˈvidity** *or* ˈ**gravidness** *n.* —ˈ**gravidly** *adv.*

gravimeter (grəˈvɪmɪtə) *n.* **1.** an instrument for measuring the earth's gravitational field at points on its surface. **2.** an instrument for measuring relative density. [C18: from French *gravimètre,* from Latin *gravis* heavy] —**graˈvimetry** *n.*

gravimetric (ˌgrævɪˈmɛtrɪk) *or* **gravimetrical** *adj.* of, concerned with, or using measurement by weight. Compare **volumetric.** —ˌ**graviˈmetrically** *adv.*

gravimetric analysis *n. Chem.* quantitative analysis by weight, usually involving the precipitation, filtration, drying, and weighing of the precipitate. Compare **volumetric analysis.**

graving dock *n.* another term for **dry dock.**

graviperception (ˌgrævɪpəˈsɛpʃən) *n.* the perception of gravity by plants.

gravitate (ˈgrævɪˌteɪt) *vb.* (*intr.*) **1.** *Physics.* to move under the influence of gravity. **2.** (usually foll. by *to* or *towards*) to be influenced or drawn, as by strong impulses. **3.** to sink or settle. —ˈ**graviˌtater** *n.*

gravitation (ˌgrævɪˈteɪʃən) *n.* **1.** the force of attraction that bodies exert on one another as a result of their mass. **2.** any process or result caused by this interaction, such as the fall of a body to the surface of the earth. ~Also called: **gravity.** See also **Newton's law of gravitation.** —ˌ**graviˈtational** *adj.* —ˌ**graviˈtationally** *adv.*

gravitational constant *n.* the factor relating force to mass and distance in Newton's law of gravitation. It is a universal constant with the value 6.670×10^{-11} N m^2 kg^{-2}. Symbol: *G*

gravitational field *n.* the field of force surrounding a body of finite mass in which another body would experience an attractive force that is proportional to the product of the masses and inversely proportional to the square of the distance between them: *the gravitational field of the earth.*

gravitational interaction *or* **force** *n.* an interaction between particles or bodies resulting from their mass. It is very weak and occurs at all distances. See **interaction** (sense 2).

gravitational mass *n.* the mass of a body determined by the extent to which it responds to the force of gravity. Compare **inertial mass.**

gravitational wave *n. Physics.* another name for **gravity wave.**

gravitative (ˈgrævɪˌteɪtɪv) *adj.* **1.** of, involving, or produced by gravitation. **2.** tending or causing to gravitate.

graviton (ˈgrævɪˌtɒn) *n.* a postulated quantum of gravitational energy, usually considered to be a particle with zero charge and rest mass and a spin of 2. Compare **photon.**

gravity (ˈgrævɪtɪ) *n., pl.* **-ties.** **1.** the force of attraction that moves or tends to move bodies towards the centre of a celestial body, such as the earth or moon. **2.** the property of being heavy or having weight. See also **specific gravity, centre of gravity.** **3.** another name for **gravitation.** **4.** seriousness or importance, esp. as a consequence of an action or opinion. **5.** manner or conduct that is solemn or dignified. **6.** lowness in pitch. **7.** (*modifier*) of or relating to gravity or gravitation or their effects: *gravity wave; gravity feed.* [C16: from Latin *gravitās* weight, from *gravis* heavy]

gravity cell *n.* an electrolytic cell in which the electrodes lie in two different electrolytes, which are separated into two layers by the difference in their relative densities.

gravity dam *n.* a dam whose weight alone is great enough to prevent it from tipping over.

gravity fault *n.* a fault in which the rocks on the upper side of an inclined fault plane have been displaced downwards; normal fault.

gravity platform *n.* (in the oil industry) a drilling platform that rests directly on the sea bed and is kept in position by its own weight; it is usually made of reinforced concrete.

gravity scale *n.* See **API gravity scale.**

gravity wave *n. Physics.* **1.** a wave propagated in a gravitational field, predicted to occur as a result of an accelerating mass. **2.** a surface wave on water or other liquid propagated because of the weight of liquid in the crests. ~Also called: **gravitational wave.**

gravlax (ˈgrævˌlæks) *or* **gravadlax** *n.* dry-cured salmon, marinated in salt, sugar, and spices, as served in Scandinavia. [C20: from Norwegian, from *grav* grave (because the salmon is left to ferment) + *laks* or Swedish *lax* salmon]

gravure (grəˈvjʊə) *n.* **1.** a method of intaglio printing using a plate with many small etched recesses. See also **rotogravure.** **2.** See **photogravure.** **3.** matter printed by this process. [C19: from French, from *graver* to engrave, of Germanic origin; see GRAVE[3]]

gravy (ˈgreɪvɪ) *n., pl.* **-vies.** **1. a.** the juices that exude from meat during cooking. **b.** the sauce made by thickening and flavouring such juices. **2.** *Slang.* money or gain acquired with little effort, esp. above that needed for ordinary living. [C14: from Old French *gravé,* of uncertain origin]

gravy boat *n.* a small often boat-shaped vessel for serving gravy or other sauces.

gravy train *n. Slang.* a job requiring comparatively little work for good pay, benefits, etc.

gray[1] (greɪ) *adj., n., vb.* a variant spelling (now esp. U.S.) of **grey.** —ˈ**grayish** *adj.* —ˈ**grayly** *adv.* —ˈ**grayness** *n.*

gray[2] (greɪ) *n.* the derived SI unit of absorbed ionizing radiation dose or kerma equivalent to an absorption per unit mass of one joule per kilogram of irradiated material. Symbol: Gy 1 gray is equivalent to 100 rads. [C20: named after Louis Harold *Gray* (1905–65), British physicist]

Gray code (greɪ) *n.* a modification of a number system, esp. a binary code, in which any adjacent pair of numbers, in counting order, differ in their digits at one position only, the absolute difference being the value 1. [named after Frank *Gray,* 20th-century American physicist]

grayling (ˈgreɪlɪŋ) *n., pl.* **-ling** *or* **-lings.** **1.** any freshwater salmonoid food fish of the genus *Thymallus* and family *Thymallidae,* of the N hemisphere, having a long spiny dorsal fin, a silvery back, and greyish-green sides. **2.** any butterfly of the satyrid genus *Hipparchia* and related genera, esp. *H. semele* of Europe, having grey or greyish-brown wings.

graze[1] (greɪz) *vb.* **1.** to allow (animals) to consume the vegetation on (an area of land), or (of animals, esp. cows and sheep) to feed thus. **2.** (*tr.*) to tend (livestock) while at pasture. **3.** *Informal.* to eat snacks throughout the day rather than formal meals. **4.** *U.S.* to pilfer and eat sweets, vegetables, etc., from supermarket shelves while shopping. [Old English *grasian,* from *græs* GRASS; related to Old High German *grasōn,* Dutch *grazen,* Norwegian *grasa*]

graze[2] (greɪz) *vb.* **1.** (when *intr.,* often foll. by *against* or *along*) to brush or scrape (against) gently, esp. in passing. **2.** (*tr.*) to break the skin of (a part of the body) by scraping. ~*n.* **3.** the act of grazing. **4.** a scrape or abrasion made by grazing. [C17: probably special use of GRAZE[1]; related to Swedish *gräsa*] —'**grazer** *n.* —'**grazingly** *adv.*

grazier ('greɪzɪə) *n.* a rancher or farmer who rears or fattens cattle or sheep on grazing land.

grazing ('greɪzɪŋ) *n.* **1.** the vegetation on pastures that is available for livestock to feed upon. **2.** the land on which this is growing.

grease *n.* (gri:s, gri:z). **1.** animal fat in a soft or melted condition. **2.** any thick fatty oil, esp. one used as a lubricant for machinery, etc. **3.** Also called: **grease wool.** shorn fleece before it has been cleaned. **4.** *Vet. science.* inflammation of the skin of horses around the fetlocks, usually covered with an oily secretion. ~*vb.* (gri:z, gri:s). (*tr.*) **5.** to soil, coat, or lubricate with grease. **6.** to ease the course of: *his education greased his path to success.* **7. grease the palm** (*or* **hand**) **of.** *Slang.* to bribe; influence by giving money to. [C13: from Old French *craisse,* from Latin *crassus* thick] —'**greaseless** *adj.*

grease cup *n.* a container that stores grease and feeds it through a small hole into a bearing.

grease gun *n.* a device for forcing grease through nipples into bearings, usually consisting of a cylinder with a plunger and nozzle fitted to it.

grease monkey *n. Informal.* a mechanic, esp. one who works on cars or aircraft.

grease nipple *n.* a metal nipple designed to engage with a grease gun for injecting grease into a bearing, etc.

greasepaint ('gri:sˌpeɪnt) *n.* **1.** a waxy or greasy substance used as make-up by actors. **2.** theatrical make-up.

greaseproof paper ('gri:sˌpru:f) *n.* any paper that is resistant to penetration by greases and oils.

greaser ('gri:zə, 'gri:sə) *n. Brit. slang.* **1.** a mechanic, esp. of motor vehicles. **2.** a semiskilled engine attendant aboard a merchant ship. **3.** a young long-haired motorcyclist, usually one of a gang. **4.** an unpleasant person, esp. one who ingratiates himself with superiors.

greasewood ('gri:sˌwʊd) *or* **greasebush** ('gri:sˌbʊʃ) *n.* **1.** Also called: **chico.** a spiny chenopodiaceous shrub, *Sarcobatus vermiculatus* of W North America, that yields an oil used as a fuel. **2.** any of various similar or related plants, such as the creosote bush.

greasy ('gri:zɪ, -sɪ) *adj.* **greasier, greasiest.** **1.** coated or soiled with or as if with grease. **2.** composed of or full of grease. **3.** resembling grease. **4.** unctuous or oily in manner. ~*n., pl.* **greasies.** *Austral. slang.* **5.** a shearer. **6.** an outback cook, esp. cooking for a number of men. —'**greasily** *adv.* —'**greasiness** *n.*

greasy spoon *n. Slang.* a small, cheap, and often unsanitary restaurant, usually specializing in fried foods.

greasy wool *n.* untreated wool, still retaining the lanolin, which is used for waterproof clothing.

great (greɪt) *adj.* **1.** relatively large in size or extent; big. **2.** relatively large in number; having many parts or members: *a great assembly.* **3.** of relatively long duration: *a great wait.* **4.** of larger size or more importance than others of its kind: *the great auk.* **5.** extreme or more than usual: *great worry.* **6.** of significant importance or consequence: *a great decision.* **7. a.** of exceptional talents or achievements; remarkable: *a great writer.* **b.** (*as n.*): *the great; one of the greats.* **8.** arising from or possessing idealism in thought, action, etc.; heroic: *great deeds.* **9.** illustrious or eminent: *a great history.* **10.** impressive or striking: *a great show of wealth.* **11.** much in use; favoured: *poetry was a great convention of the Romantic era.* **12.** active or enthusiastic: *a great walker.* **13.** doing or exemplifying (a characteristic or pursuit) on a large scale: *what a great buffoon; he's not a great one for reading.* **14.** (often foll. by *at*) skilful or adroit: *a great carpenter; you are great at singing.* **15.** *Informal.* excellent; fantastic. **16.** *Brit. informal.* (intensifier): *a dirty great smack in the face.* **17.** (*postpositive;* foll. by *with*) *Archaic.* **a.** pregnant: *great with child.* **b.** full (of): *great with hope.* **18.** (intensifier, used in mild oaths): *Great Scott!* **19. be great on.** *Informal.* **a.** to be informed about. **b.** to be enthusiastic about or for. ~*adv.* **20.** *Informal.* very well; excellently: *it was working great.* ~*n.* **21.** Also called: **great organ.** the principal manual on an organ. Compare **choir** (sense 4), **swell** (sense 16). [Old English *grēat;* related to Old Frisian *grāt,* Old High German *grōz;* see GRIT, GROAT] —'**greatly** *adv.* —'**greatness** *n.*

great- *prefix.* **1.** being the parent of a person's grandparent (in the combinations **great-grandfather, great-grandmother, great-grandparent**). **2.** being the child of a person's grandchild (in the combinations **great-grandson, great-granddaughter, great-grandchild**).

great ape *n.* any of the larger anthropoid apes, such as the chimpanzee, orang-utan, or gorilla.

great auk *n.* a large flightless auk, *Pinguinus impennis,* extinct since the middle of the 19th century.

great-aunt *or* **grandaunt** *n.* an aunt of one's father or mother; sister of one's grandfather or grandmother.

Great Bear *n.* **the.** the English name for **Ursa Major.**

great circle *n.* a circular section of a sphere that has a radius equal to that of the sphere. Compare **small circle.**

greatcoat ('greɪtˌkəʊt) *n.* a heavy overcoat, now worn esp. by men in the armed forces. —'**greatˌcoated** *adj.*

great council *n.* (in medieval England) an assembly of the great nobles and prelates to advise the king.

great crested grebe *n.* a European grebe, *Podiceps cristatus,* having blackish ear tufts and, in the breeding season, a dark brown frill around the head.

Great Dane *n.* one of a very large powerful yet graceful breed of dog with a short smooth coat.

Great Dog *n.* **the.** the English name for **Canis Major.**

greaten ('greɪtᵊn) *vb. Archaic.* to make or become great.

Greater ('greɪtə) *adj.* (of a city) considered with the inclusion of the outer suburbs: *Greater London.*

greater celandine *n.* a Eurasian papaveraceous plant, *Chelidonium majus,* with yellow flowers and deeply divided leaves. Also called: **swallowwort.** Compare **lesser celandine.**

greatest ('greɪtɪst) *adj.* **1.** the superlative of **great.** ~*n.* **2. the greatest.** *Slang.* an exceptional person.

greatest common divisor *n.* another name for **highest common factor.**

greatest happiness principle *n.* the ethical principle that an action is right in so far as it promotes the greatest happiness of the greatest number of those affected. See **utilitarianism.**

great gross *n.* a unit of quantity equal to one dozen gross (or 1728).

great-hearted *adj.* benevolent or noble; magnanimous. —ˌ**great-'heartedness** *n.*

great mountain buttercup *n. N.Z.* See **Mount Cook lily.**

great-nephew *or* **grandnephew** *n.* a son of one's nephew or niece; grandson of one's brother or sister.

great-niece *or* **grandniece** *n.* a daughter of one's nephew or niece; granddaughter of one's brother or sister.

great northern diver *n.* a large northern bird, *Gavia immer,* with a black-and-white chequered back and a black head and neck in summer: family *Gaviidae* (divers).

great organ *n.* the full name for **great** (sense 21).

Great Power *n.* a nation that has exceptional political influence, resources, and military strength.

great primer *n.* (formerly) a size of printer's type approximately equal to 18 point.

Great Russian *n.* **1.** *Linguistics.* the technical name for **Russian.** Compare **Byelorussian, Ukrainian.** **2.** a member of the chief East Slavonic people of Russia. ~*adj.* **3.** of or relating to this people or their language.

Greats (greɪts) *pl. n.* (at Oxford University) **1.** the Honour School of Literae Humaniores, involving the study of Greek and Roman history and literature and philosophy. **2.** the final examinations at the end of this course.

great seal *n.* (*often caps.*) the principal seal of a nation, sovereign, etc., used to authenticate signatures and documents of the highest importance.

great tit *n.* a large common Eurasian tit, *Parus major,* with yellow-and-black underparts and a black-and-white head.

great-uncle *or* **granduncle** *n.* an uncle of one's father or mother; brother of one's grandfather or grandmother.

Great Vowel Shift *n. Linguistics.* a phonetic change that took place during the transition from Middle to Modern English, whereby the long vowels were raised (e: became i:, o: became u:, etc.). The vowels (i:) and (u:) underwent breaking and became the diphthongs (aɪ) and (aʊ).

Great Week *n. Eastern Church.* the week preceding Easter, the equivalent of Holy Week in the Western Church.

great white heron *n.* **1.** a large white heron, *Ardea occidentalis,* of S North America. **2.** a widely distributed white egret, *Egretta* (or *Casmerodius*) *albus.*

great year *n.* one complete cycle of the precession of the equinoxes; about 25 800 years.

greave (gri:v) *n.* (*often pl.*) a piece of armour worn to protect the shin from the ankle to the knee. [C14: from Old French *greve,* perhaps from *graver* to part the hair, of Germanic origin] —**greaved** *adj.*

greaves (gri:vz) *pl. n.* the residue left after the rendering of tallow. [C17: from Low German *greven;* related to Old High German *griubo*]

grebe (gri:b) *n.* any aquatic bird, such as *Podiceps cristatus* (**great crested grebe**), of the order *Podicipediformes,* similar to the divers but with lobate rather than webbed toes and a vestigial tail. [C18: from French *grèbe,* of unknown origin]

Grecian ('gri:ʃən) *adj.* **1.** (esp. of beauty or architecture) conforming to Greek ideals, esp. in being classically simple. ~*n.* **2.** a scholar of or expert in the Greek language or literature. ~*adj., n.* **3.** another word for **Greek.**

Grecism ('gri:ˌsɪzəm) *n.* a variant spelling (esp. U.S.) of **Graecism.**

Grecize ('gri:saɪz) *vb.* a variant spelling (esp. U.S.) of **Graecize.**

Greco- ('gri:kəʊ, 'grɛkəʊ) *combining form.* a variant (esp. U.S.) of **Graeco-.**

gree[1] (gri:) *n. Scot. archaic.* **1.** superiority or victory. **2.** the prize for a victory. [C14: from Old French *gré,* from Latin *gradus* step]

gree[2] (gri:) *n. Obsolete.* **1.** goodwill; favour. **2.** satisfaction for an insult or injury. [C14: from Old French *gré,* from Latin *grātum* what is pleasing; see GRATEFUL]

gree[3] (griː) *vb.* **grees, greeing, greed.** *Archaic or dialect.* to come or cause to come to agreement or harmony. [C14: variant of AGREE]

greed (griːd) *n.* **1.** excessive consumption of or desire for food; gluttony. **2.** excessive desire, as for wealth or power. [C17: back formation from GREEDY] —ˈ**greedless** *adj.*

greedy (ˈgriːdɪ) *adj.* **greedier, greediest. 1.** excessively desirous of food or wealth, esp. in large amounts; voracious. **2.** (*postpositive;* foll. by *for*) eager (for): *a man greedy for success.* [Old English *grǣdig;* related to Old Norse *grāthugr,* Gothic *grēdags* hungry, Old High German *grātac*] —ˈ**greedily** *adv.* —ˈ**greediness** *n.*

greedy guts *n.* (*functioning as sing.*) *Slang.* a glutton.

greegree (ˈgriːgriː) *n.* a variant spelling of **grigri.**

Greek (griːk) *n.* **1.** the official language of Greece, constituting the Hellenic branch of the Indo-European family of languages. See **Ancient Greek, Late Greek, Medieval Greek, Modern Greek. 2.** a native or inhabitant of Greece or a descendant of such a native. **3.** a member of the Greek Orthodox Church. **4.** *Informal.* anything incomprehensible (esp. in the phrase **it's (all) Greek to me**). **5. Greek meets Greek.** equals meet. ~*adj.* **6.** denoting, relating to, or characteristic of Greece, the Greeks, or the Greek language; Hellenic. **7.** of, relating to, or designating the Greek Orthodox Church. [from Old English *Grēcas* (plural), or Latin *Graecus,* from Greek *Graikos*] —ˈ**Greekness** *n.*

Greek Catholic *n.* **1.** a member of an Eastern Church in communion with the Greek patriarchal see of Constantinople. **2.** a member of one of the Uniat Greek Churches, which acknowledge the Pope's authority while retaining their own institutions, discipline, and liturgy.

Greek Church *n.* another name for the **Greek Orthodox Church.**

Greek cross *n.* a cross with each of the four arms of the same length.

Greek fire *n.* **1.** a Byzantine weapon employed in naval warfare from 670 A.D. It consisted of an unknown mixture that, when wetted, exploded and was projected, burning, from tubes. **2.** any of several other inflammable mixtures used in warfare up to the 19th century.

Greek gift *n.* a gift given with the intention of tricking and causing harm to the recipient. [C19: in allusion to Virgil's *Aeneid* ii 49; see also TROJAN HORSE]

Greek mallow *n.* See **sidalcea.**

Greek Orthodox Church *n.* **1.** Also called: **Greek Church.** the established Church of Greece, governed by the holy synod of Greece, in which the Metropolitan of Athens has primacy of honour. **2.** another name for **Orthodox Church.**

Greek Revival *n.* (*modifier*) denoting, relating to, or having the style of architecture used in Western Europe in the late 18th and early 19th centuries, based upon ancient Greek classical examples. —**Greek Revivalism** *n.* —**Greek Revivalist** *adj., n.*

green (griːn) *n.* **1.** any of a group of colours, such as that of fresh grass, that lie between yellow and blue in the visible spectrum in the wavelength range 575–500 nanometres. Green is the complementary colour of magenta and with red and blue forms a set of primary colours. Related adj.: **verdant. 2.** a dye or pigment of or producing these colours. **3.** something of the colour green. **4.** a small area of grassland, esp. in the centre of a village. **5.** an area of ground used for a purpose: *a putting green.* **6.** (*pl.*) **a.** the edible leaves and stems of certain plants, eaten as a vegetable. **b.** freshly cut branches of ornamental trees, shrubs, etc., used as a decoration. **7.** (*sometimes cap.*) a person, esp. a politician, who supports environmentalist issues (see sense 14). **8.** *Slang.* money. **9.** *Slang.* marijuana of low quality. **10.** (*pl.*) *Slang.* sexual intercourse. **11. green in one's eye.** an indication of immaturity or gullibility. ~*adj.* **12.** of the colour green. **13.** greenish in colour or having parts or marks that are greenish: *a green monkey.* **14.** (*sometimes cap.*) concerned with or relating to conservation of the world's natural resources and improvement of the environment: *green policies; the green consumer.* **15.** vigorous; not faded: *a green old age.* **16.** envious or jealous. **17.** immature, unsophisticated, or gullible. **18.** characterized by foliage or green plants: *a green wood; a green salad.* **19.** fresh, raw, or unripe: *green bananas.* **20.** unhealthily pale in appearance: *he was green after his boat trip.* **21.** denoting a unit of account that is adjusted in accordance with fluctuations between the currencies of the EC nations and is used to make payments to agricultural producers within the EC: *green pound; green franc.* **22.** (of pottery) not fired. **23.** (of meat) not smoked or cured; unprocessed: *green bacon.* **24.** *Metallurgy.* (of a product, such as a sand mould or cermet) compacted but not yet fired; ready for firing. **25.** (of timber) freshly felled; not dried or seasoned. **26.** (of concrete) not having matured to design strength. ~*vb.* **27.** to make or become green. [Old English *grēne;* related to Old High German *gruoni;* see GROW] —ˈ**greenish** *adj.* —ˈ**greenly** *adv.* —ˈ**greenness** *n.* —ˈ**greeny** *adj.*

green algae *pl. n.* the algae of the family *Chlorophyceae,* which possess the green pigment chlorophyll. The group includes sea lettuce and spirogyra.

greenback (ˈgriːnˌbæk) *n.* **1.** *U.S. informal.* an inconvertible legal-tender U.S. currency note originally issued during the Civil War in 1862. **2.** *U.S. slang.* a dollar bill.

green ban *n. Austral.* a trade union ban on any development that might be considered harmful to the environment.

green bean *n.* any bean plant, such as the French bean, having narrow green edible pods when unripe.

green belt *n.* a zone of farmland, parks, and open country surrounding a town or city: usually officially designated as such and preserved from urban development.

Green Beret *n.* an informal name for a British or U.S. commando.

greenbone (ˈgriːnˌbəʊn) *n. N.Z.* another name for **butterfish** (sense 2).

greenbottle (ˈgriːnˌbɒtᵊl) *n.* a common dipterous fly, *Lucilia caesar,* that has a dark greenish body with a metallic lustre and lays its eggs in carrion: family *Calliphoridae.*

greenbrier (ˈgriːnˌbraɪə) *n.* any of several prickly climbing plants of the liliaceous genus *Smilax,* esp. *S. rotundifolia* of the eastern U.S., which has small green flowers and blackish berries. Also called: **cat brier.**

green card *n.* **1.** an insurance document covering motorists against accidents abroad. **2.** *Social welfare.* (in Britain) an identification card issued by the Manpower Services Commission to a disabled person, to show registration for employment purposes and eligibility for special services. See also **handicap register, registered disabled.**

green corn *n.* another name for **sweet corn** (sense 1).

Green Cross Code *n.* (in Britain) a code for children giving rules for road safety: first issued in 1971.

green dragon *n.* a North American aroid plant, *Arisaema dracontium,* with a long slender spadix projecting from a green or white long narrow spathe. Also called: **dragonroot.**

greenery (ˈgriːnərɪ) *n., pl.* **-eries. 1.** green foliage or vegetation, esp. when used for decoration. **2.** *Rare.* a place where such foliage grows.

green-eyed *adj.* **1.** jealous or envious. **2. the green-eyed monster.** jealousy or envy.

greenfield (ˈgriːnˌfiːld) *n.* (*modifier*). denoting or located in a rural area which has not previously been built on: *new factories were erected on greenfield sites.*

greenfinch (ˈgriːnˌfɪntʃ) *n.* a common European finch, *Carduelis chloris,* the male of which has a dull green plumage with yellow patches on the wings and tail.

green fingers *pl. n.* considerable talent or ability to grow plants. U.S. and Canadian equivalent: **green thumb.**

green flash *n. Astronomy.* a flash of bright green light sometimes seen as the sun passes below the horizon, caused by the dispersion of blue light.

greenfly (ˈgriːnˌflaɪ) *n., pl.* **-flies.** a greenish aphid commonly occurring as a pest on garden and crop plants.

greengage (ˈgriːnˌgeɪdʒ) *n.* **1.** a cultivated variety of plum tree, *Prunus domestica italica,* with edible green plumlike fruits. **2.** the fruit of this tree. [C18: GREEN + *-gage,* after Sir W. *Gage* (1777–1864), English botanist who brought it from France]

green gland *n.* one of a pair of excretory organs in some crustaceans that open at the base of each antenna.

green glass *n.* glass in its natural colour, usually greenish as a result of metallic substances in the raw materials.

greengrocer (ˈgriːnˌgrəʊsə) *n. Chiefly Brit.* a retail trader in fruit and vegetables. —ˈ**greenˌgrocery** *n.*

greenhead (ˈgriːnˌhɛd) *n.* a male mallard.

greenheart (ˈgriːnˌhɑːt) *n.* **1.** Also called: **bebeeru.** a tropical American lauraceous tree, *Ocotea* (or *Nectandra*) *rodiaei,* that has dark green durable wood and bark that yields the alkaloid bebeerine. **2.** any of various similar trees. **3.** the wood of any of these trees.

green heron *n.* a small heron, *Butorides virescens,* of subtropical North America, with dark greenish wings and back.

greenhorn (ˈgriːnˌhɔːn) *n.* **1.** an inexperienced person, esp. one who is extremely gullible. **2.** *Chiefly U.S.* a newcomer or immigrant. [C17: originally an animal with *green* (that is, young) horns]

greenhouse (ˈgriːnˌhaʊs) *n.* **1.** a building with transparent walls and roof, usually of glass, for the cultivation and exhibition of plants under controlled conditions. ~*adj.* **2.** relating to or contributing to the greenhouse effect: *greenhouse gases such as carbon dioxide.*

greenhouse effect *n.* **1.** an effect occurring in greenhouses, etc., in which radiant heat from the sun passes through the glass warming the contents, the radiant heat from inside being trapped by the glass. **2.** the application of this effect to a planet's atmosphere; carbon dioxide and some other gases in the planet's atmosphere can absorb the infrared radiation emitted by the planet's surface as a result of exposure to solar ultraviolet radiation, thus increasing the mean temperature of the planet.

greenie (ˈgriːnɪ) *n. Austral. informal.* a conservationist.

greening (ˈgriːnɪŋ) *n.* the process of making or becoming more aware of environmental considerations. [C20: from GREEN (sense 14)]

green keeper *n.* a person in charge of a golf course or bowling green.

Greenlander (ˈgriːnləndə) *n.* a native or inhabitant of the Arctic island of Greenland.

Greenlandic (griːnˈlændɪk) *adj.* **1.** of, relating to, or characteristic of Greenland, the Greenlanders, or the Inuit dialect spoken in

Greenland. ~*n.* **2.** the dialect of Inuit Eskimo spoken in Greenland.

Greenland whale ('griːnlənd) *n.* an arctic right whale, *Balaena mysticetus,* that is black with a cream-coloured throat.

green leek *n.* any of several Australian parrots with a green or mostly green plumage.

greenlet ('griːnlɪt) *n.* a vireo, esp. one of the genus *Hylophilus.*

green light *n.* **1.** a signal to go, esp. a green traffic light. **2.** permission to proceed with a project.

greenling ('griːnlɪŋ) *n.* any scorpaenoid food fish of the family *Hexagrammidae* of the North Pacific Ocean.

greenmail ('griːnˌmeɪl) *n.* (esp. in the U.S.) the practice of a company buying sufficient shares in another company to threaten takeover and making a quick profit as a result of the threatened company buying back its shares at a higher price.

green manure *n.* **1.** a growing crop that is ploughed under to enrich the soil. **2.** manure that has not yet decomposed.

green monkey *n.* a W African variety of a common guenon monkey, *Cercopithecus aethiops,* having greenish-brown fur and a dark face. Compare **grivet, vervet.**

green monkey disease *n.* another name for **Marburg disease.**

green mould *n.* another name for **blue mould** (sense 1).

greenockite ('griːnəˌkaɪt) *n.* a rare yellowish mineral consisting of cadmium sulphide in hexagonal crystalline form: the only ore of cadmium. Formula: CdS. [C19: named after Lord C. C. *Greenock,* 19th-century English soldier]

green paper *n.* (*often caps.*) (in Britain) a command paper containing policy proposals to be discussed, esp. by Parliament.

green pepper *n.* **1.** the green unripe fruit of the sweet pepper, eaten raw or cooked. **2.** the unripe fruit of various other pepper plants, eaten as a green vegetable.

green plover *n.* another name for **lapwing.**

green pound *n.* a unit of account used in calculating Britain's contributions to and payments from the Community Agricultural Fund of the EC.

green revolution *n.* the introduction of high-yielding seeds and modern agricultural techniques in developing countries.

greenroom ('griːnˌruːm, -ˌrʊm) *n.* (esp. formerly) a backstage room in a theatre where performers may rest or receive visitors. [C18: probably from its original colour]

greensand ('griːnˌsænd) *n.* an olive-green sandstone consisting mainly of quartz and glauconite.

greenshank ('griːnˌʃæŋk) *n.* a large European sandpiper, *Tringa nebularia,* with greenish legs and a slightly upturned bill.

greensickness ('griːnˌsɪknɪs) *n.* another name for **chlorosis.** —'**greenˌsick** *adj.*

green soap *n. Med.* a soft or liquid alkaline soap made from vegetable oils, used in treating certain chronic skin diseases. Also called: **soft soap.**

greensome ('griːnsəm) *n. Golf.* a match for two pairs in which each of the four players tees off and after selecting the better drive the partners of each pair play that ball alternately. Compare **four-ball, foursome** (sense 2.).

greenstick fracture ('griːnˌstɪk) *n.* a fracture in children in which the bone is partly bent and splinters only on the convex side of the bend. [C20: alluding to the similar way in which a green stick splinters]

greenstone ('griːnˌstəʊn) *n.* **1.** any basic igneous rock that is dark green because of the presence of chlorite or epidote. **2.** a variety of jade used in New Zealand for ornaments and tools.

greenstuff ('griːnˌstʌf) *n.* green vegetables, such as cabbage or lettuce.

greensward ('griːnˌswɔːd) *n. Archaic or literary.* fresh green turf or an area of such turf.

green tea *n.* a sharp tea made from tea leaves that have been steamed and dried quickly without fermenting.

green thumb *n.* the U.S. and Canadian term for **green fingers.**

green turtle *n.* a mainly tropical edible turtle, *Chelonia mydas,* with greenish flesh used to prepare turtle soup: family *Chelonidae.*

green vitriol *n.* another name for **ferrous sulphate.**

green-wellie *n.* (*modifier*) characterizing or belonging to the upper-class set devoted to hunting, shooting, and fishing: *the green-wellie brigade.*

Greenwich Mean Time *or* **Greenwich Time** ('grɪnɪdʒ, -ɪtʃ, 'grɛn-) *n.* the local time of the 0° meridian passing through Greenwich, England: a standard time for Britain and a basis for calculating times throughout most of the world until 1972. See **universal time** (sense 2). Abbrev.: **GMT.**

greenwood ('griːnˌwʊd) *n.* a forest or wood when the leaves are green: the traditional setting of stories about English outlaws, esp. Robin Hood.

green woodpecker *n.* a European woodpecker, *Picus viridis,* with a dull green back and wings and a red crown.

greet[1] (griːt) *vb.* (*tr.*) **1.** to meet or receive with expressions of gladness or welcome. **2.** to send a message of friendship to. **3.** to receive in a specified manner: *her remarks were greeted by silence.* **4.** to become apparent to: *the smell of bread greeted him.* [Old English *grētan;* related to Old High German *gruozzen* to address] —'**greeter** *n.*

greet[2] (griːt) *Scot. or archaic.* ~*vb.* **1.** (*intr.*) to weep; lament. ~*n.* **2.** weeping; lamentation. [from Old English *grētan,* northern dialect variant of *grǣtan;* compare Old Norse *grāta,* Middle High German *grazen*]

greeting ('griːtɪŋ) *n.* **1.** the act or an instance of welcoming or saluting on meeting. **2.** (*often pl.*) **a.** an expression of friendly salutation. **b.** (*as modifier*): *a greetings card.*

gregarine ('grɛgəˌriːn, -rɪn) *n.* **1.** any parasitic protozoan of the order *Gregarinida,* typically occurring in the digestive tract and body cavity of other invertebrates: class *Sporozoa* (sporozoans). ~*adj. also* **gregarinian** (ˌgrɛgə'rɪnɪən). **2.** of, relating to, or belonging to the *Gregarinida.* [C19: from New Latin *Gregarīna* genus name, from Latin *gregārius;* see GREGARIOUS]

gregarious (grɪ'gɛərɪəs) *adj.* **1.** enjoying the company of others. **2.** (of animals) living together in herds or flocks. Compare **solitary** (sense 6). **3.** (of plants) growing close together but not in dense clusters. **4.** of, relating to, or characteristic of crowds or communities. [C17: from Latin *gregārius* belonging to a flock, from *grex* flock] —**gre'gariously** *adv.* —**gre'gariousness** *n.*

Gregorian (grɪ'gɔːrɪən) *adj.* relating to, associated with, or introduced by any of the popes named Gregory, esp. Gregory I or Gregory XIII.

Gregorian calendar *n.* the revision of the Julian calendar introduced in 1582 by Pope Gregory XIII and still in force, whereby the ordinary year is made to consist of 365 days and a leap year occurs in every year whose number is divisible by four, except those centenary years, such as 1900, whose numbers are not divisible by 400.

Gregorian chant *n.* another name for **plainsong.**

Gregorian telescope *n.* a form of reflecting astronomical telescope with a concave secondary mirror and the eyepiece set in the centre of the parabolic primary mirror. [C18: named after J. *Gregory* (died 1675), Scottish mathematician who invented it]

Gregorian tone *n.* a plainsong melody. See **tone** (sense 6).

Gregory's powder ('grɛgərɪz) *n.* a compound of rhubarb powder used as a laxative or purgative. [C19: named after Dr James *Gregory* (1753–1821), who first made it]

greige (greɪʒ) *Chiefly U.S.* ~*adj.* **1.** (of a fabric or material) not yet dyed. ~*n.* **2.** an unbleached or undyed cloth or yarn. [C20: from French *grège* raw]

greisen ('graɪzᵊn) *n.* a light-coloured metamorphic rock consisting mainly of quartz and white mica, formed by the pneumatolysis of granite. [C19: from German, from *greissen* to split]

gremial ('griːmɪəl) *n. R.C. Church.* a cloth spread upon the lap of a bishop when seated during Mass. [C17: from Latin *gremium* lap]

gremlin ('grɛmlɪn) *n.* **1.** an imaginary imp jokingly said to be responsible for mechanical troubles in aircraft, esp. in World War II. **2.** any mischievous troublemaker. [C20: of unknown origin]

grenade (grɪ'neɪd) *n.* **1.** a small container filled with explosive thrown by hand or fired from a rifle. **2.** a sealed glass vessel that is thrown and shatters to release chemicals, such as tear gas or a fire extinguishing agent. [C16: from French, from Spanish *granada* pomegranate, from Late Latin *grānāta,* from Latin *grānātus* seedy; see GRAIN]

grenadier (ˌgrɛnə'dɪə) *n.* **1.** *Military.* **a.** (in the British Army) a member of the senior regiment of infantry in the Household Brigade. **b.** (formerly) a member of a special formation, usually selected for strength and height. **c.** (formerly) a soldier trained to throw grenades. **2.** Also called: **rat-tail.** any deep-sea gadoid fish of the family *Macrouridae,* typically having a large head and trunk and a long tapering tail. **3.** any of various African weaverbirds of the genus *Estrilda.* See **waxbill.** [C17: from French; see GRENADE]

grenadine[1] (ˌgrɛnə'diːn) *n.* a light thin leno-weave fabric of silk, wool, rayon, or nylon, used esp. for dresses. [C19: from French, from earlier *grenade* silk with a grained texture, from *grenu* grained; see GRAIN]

grenadine[2] (ˌgrɛnə'diːn, 'grɛnəˌdiːn) *n.* **1.** a syrup made from pomegranate juice, used as a sweetening and colouring agent in various drinks. **2. a.** a moderate reddish-orange colour. **b.** (*as adj.*): *a grenadine coat.* [C19: from French: a little pomegranate, from *grenade* pomegranate; see GRENADE]

grenz rays (grɛnz) *n. Physics.* x-rays of long wavelength produced in a device when electrons are accelerated through 25 kilovolts or less. [C20: from *grenz* from German *Grenze* boundary]

Gresham's law *or* **theorem** ('grɛʃəmz) *n.* the economic hypothesis that bad money drives good money out of circulation; the superior currency will tend to be hoarded and the inferior will thus dominate the circulation. [C16: named after Sir Thomas *Gresham* (?1519–79), English financier]

gressorial (grɛ'sɔːrɪəl) *or* **gressorious** *adj.* **1.** (of the feet of certain birds) specialized for walking. **2.** (of birds, such as the ostrich) having such feet. [C19: from New Latin *gressōrius,* from *gressus* having walked, from *gradī* to step]

grevillea (grə'vɪljə) *n.* any of a large number of evergreen trees and shrubs comprising the genus *Grevillea,* native to Australia, Tasmania, and New Caledonia. [named after C. F. *Greville* (1749–1809), a founder of the Royal Horticultural Society]

grew (gruː) *vb.* the past tense of **grow.**

grewsome ('gruːsəm) *adj.* an archaic or U.S. spelling of **gruesome.**

grey *or now esp. U.S.* **gray** (greɪ) *adj.* **1.** of a neutral tone, intermediate between black and white, that has no hue and reflects and transmits only a little light. **2.** greyish in colour or having parts or marks that are greyish. **3.** dismal or dark, esp. from lack of light; gloomy. **4.** neutral or dull, esp. in character or opinion. **5.** having grey hair. **6.** of or relating to people of middle age or above: *grey power.* **7.** ancient; venerable. **8.** (of textiles) natural, unbleached, undyed, and untreated. *~n.* **9.** any of a group of grey tones. **10.** grey cloth or clothing: *dressed in grey.* **11.** an animal, esp. a horse, that is grey or whitish. *~vb.* **12.** to become or make grey. [Old English *grǣg;* related to Old High German *grāo,* Old Norse *grar*] —'**greyish** *or now esp. U.S.* '**grayish** *adj.* —'**greyly** *or now esp. U.S.* '**grayly** *adv.* —'**greyness** *or now esp. U.S.* '**grayness** *n.*

grey area *n.* **1.** (in Britain) a region in which unemployment is relatively high. **2.** an area or part of something existing between two extremes and having mixed characteristics of both. **3.** an area, situation, etc., lacking clearly defined characteristics.

greyback *or U.S.* **grayback** ('greɪˌbæk) *n.* any of various animals having a grey back, such as the grey whale and the hooded crow.

greybeard *or U.S.* **graybeard** ('greɪˌbɪəd) *n.* **1.** an old man, esp. a sage. **2.** a large stoneware or earthenware jar or jug for spirits. —'**greyˌbearded** *or U.S.* '**grayˌbearded** *adj.*

grey body *n. Physics.* a body that emits radiation in constant proportion to the corresponding black-body radiation.

grey eminence *n.* the English equivalent of ***éminence grise.***

grey fox *n.* **1.** a greyish American fox, *Urocyon cinereoargenteus,* inhabiting arid and woody regions from S North America to N South America. **2. island grey fox.** a similar and related animal, *U. littoralis,* inhabiting islands off North America.

Grey Friar *n.* a Franciscan friar.

grey ghost *n. Austral. informal.* a parking policeman. [from the colour of the uniform]

greyhen ('greɪˌhɛn) *n.* the female of the black grouse. Compare **blackcock.**

grey heron *n.* a large European heron, *Ardea cinerea,* with grey wings and back and a long black drooping crest.

greyhound ('greɪˌhaʊnd) *n.* a tall slender fast-moving dog of an ancient breed originally used for coursing.

greyhound racing *n.* a sport in which a mechanically propelled dummy hare is pursued by greyhounds around a race track.

grey knight *n. Informal.* an ambiguous intervener in a takeover battle, who makes a counterbid for the shares of the target company without having made his intentions clear. Compare **black knight, white knight.**

greylag *or* **greylag goose** ('greɪˌlæg) *n.* a large grey Eurasian goose, *Anser anser:* the ancestor of many domestic breeds of goose. U.S. spelling: **graylag.** [C18: from GREY + LAG[1], from its migrating later than other species]

grey market *n.* **1.** a system involving the secret but not illegal sale of goods at excessive prices. Compare **black market. 2.** *Stock Exchange.* a market in the shares of a new issue, in which market makers deal with investors who have applied for shares but not yet received an allotment.

grey matter *n.* **1.** the greyish tissue of the brain and spinal cord, containing nerve cell bodies, dendrites, and bare (unmyelinated) axons. Technical name: **substantia grisea.** Compare **white matter. 2.** *Informal.* brains or intellect.

grey mullet *n.* any teleost food fish of the family *Mugilidae,* mostly occurring in coastal regions, having a spindle-shaped body and a broad fleshy mouth. U.S. name: **mullet.** Compare **red mullet.**

grey sedge *n. Brit.* an angler's name for a greyish caddis fly, *Odontocerum albicorne,* that frequents running water, in which its larvae make cases from grains of sand.

grey squirrel *n.* a grey-furred squirrel, *Sciurus carolinensis,* native to E North America but now widely established.

grey-state *n.* (*modifier*) (of a fabric or material) not yet dyed.

greywacke *or U.S.* **graywacke** ('greɪˌwækə) *n.* any dark sandstone or grit having a matrix of clay minerals. [C19: partial translation of German *Grauwacke;* see WACKE]

grey warbler *n. N.Z.* a small bush bird that hatches the eggs of the shining cuckoo. Also called: **riroriro.**

grey-wave *adj. Informal.* denoting a company or an investment that is potentially profitable but is unlikely to fulfil expectations before the investor has grey hair.

greywether ('greɪˌwɛðə) *n. Geology.* another name for **sarsen.** [from its resemblance to a grey sheep; see WETHER]

grey whale *n.* a large N Pacific whalebone whale, *Eschrichtius glaucus,* that is grey or black with white spots and patches: family *Eschrichtidae.*

grey wolf *n.* another name for **timber wolf.**

GRF *Biochem. abbrev. for* growth hormone-releasing factor: a peptide that is released from the brain and stimulates the pituitary gland to secrete growth hormone.

gribble ('grɪbᵊl) *n.* any small marine isopod crustacean of the genus *Limnoria,* which bores into and damages wharves and other submerged wooden structures. [C19: perhaps related to GRUB]

gricer ('graɪsə) *n.* a railway enthusiast; an engine spotter. Also called: **grice.** [C20: origin obscure]

grid (grɪd) *n.* **1.** See **gridiron. 2.** a network of horizontal and vertical lines superimposed over a map, building plan, etc., for locating points. **3.** a grating consisting of parallel bars. **4. the grid.** the national network of transmission lines, pipes, etc., by which electricity, gas, or water is distributed. **5.** *N.Z.* short for **national grid. 6.** Also called: **control grid.** *Electronics.* **a.** an electrode situated between the cathode and anode of a valve usually consisting of a cylindrical mesh of wires, that controls the flow of electrons between cathode and anode. See also **screen grid, suppressor grid. b.** (*as modifier*): *the grid bias.* **7.** See **starting grid. 8.** a plate in an accumulator that carries the active substance. **9.** any interconnecting system of links: *the bus service formed a grid across the country.* [C19: back formation from GRIDIRON] —'**gridded** *adj.*

grid bias *n.* the fixed voltage applied between the control grid and cathode of a valve.

grid declination *n.* the angular difference between true north and grid north on a map.

griddle ('grɪdᵊl) *n.* **1.** Also called: **girdle.** *Brit.* a thick round iron plate with a half hoop handle over the top, for making scones, etc. **2.** any flat heated surface, esp. on the top of a stove, for cooking food. *~vb.* **3.** (*tr.*) to cook (food) on a griddle. [C13: from Old French *gridil,* from Late Latin *crātīculum* (unattested) fine wickerwork; see GRILL[1]]

griddlebread ('grɪdᵊlˌbrɛd) *or* **griddlecake** ('grɪdᵊlˌkeɪk) *n.* bread or cake made on a griddle.

gride (graɪd) *vb.* **1.** (*intr.*) *Literary.* to grate or scrape harshly. **2.** *Obsolete.* to pierce or wound. *~n.* **3.** *Literary.* a harsh or piercing sound. [C14: variant of *girde* GIRD[2]]

gridiron ('grɪdˌaɪən) *n.* **1.** a utensil of parallel metal bars, used to grill meat, fish, etc. **2.** any framework resembling this utensil. **3.** a framework above the stage in a theatre from which suspended scenery, lights, etc., are manipulated. **4. a.** the field of play in American football. **b.** an informal name for American football. **c.** (*as modifier*): *a gridiron hero.* ~Often shortened to **grid.** [C13 *gredire,* perhaps variant (through influence of *ire* IRON) of *gredile* GRIDDLE]

gridlock ('grɪdˌlɒk) *n. Chiefly U.S.* obstruction of urban traffic caused by queues of vehicles forming across junctions and causing further queues to form in the intersecting streets.

grid reference *n.* a method of locating a point on a map or plan by a number referring to the lines of a grid drawn upon the map or plan and to subdivisions of the space between the lines.

grid variation *n. Navigation.* the angle between grid north and magnetic north at a point on a map or chart. Also called: **grivation.**

grief (griːf) *n.* **1.** deep or intense sorrow or distress, esp. at the death of someone. **2.** something that causes keen distress or suffering. **3. come to grief.** *Informal.* to end unsuccessfully or disastrously. [C13: from Anglo-French *gref,* from *grever* to GRIEVE[1]] —'**griefless** *adj.*

grief-stricken *adj.* deeply affected by sorrow or distress.

grievance ('griːvᵊns) *n.* **1.** a real or imaginary wrong causing resentment and regarded as grounds for complaint. **2.** a feeling of resentment or injustice at having been unfairly treated. **3.** *Obsolete.* affliction or hardship. [C15 *grevance,* from Old French, from *grever* to GRIEVE]

grieve[1] (griːv) *vb.* **1.** to feel or cause to feel great sorrow or distress, esp. at the death of someone. **2.** (*tr.*) *Obsolete.* to inflict injury, hardship, or sorrow on. [C13: from Old French *grever,* from Latin *gravāre* to burden, from *gravis* heavy] —'**griever** *n.* —'**grieving** *n., adj.* —'**grievingly** *adv.*

grieve[2] (griːv) *n. Scot.* a farm manager or overseer. [C15: from Old English (Northumbrian) *grǣfa* reeve]

grievous ('griːvəs) *adj.* **1.** very severe or painful: *a grievous injury.* **2.** very serious; heinous: *a grievous sin.* **3.** showing or marked by grief: *a grievous cry.* **4.** causing great pain or suffering: *a grievous attack.* —'**grievously** *adv.* —'**grievousness** *n.*

grievous bodily harm *n. Criminal law.* really serious injury caused by one person to another. Abbrev.: **GBH.**

griff (grɪf) *n. Slang.* information; news. [C20: from GRIFFIN[2]]

griffe (grɪf) *n. Architect.* a carved ornament at the base of a column, often in the form of a claw. [C19: from French: claw, of Germanic origin]

griffin[1] ('grɪfɪn), **griffon,** *or* **gryphon** *n.* a winged monster with an eagle-like head and the body of a lion. [C14: from Old French *grifon,* from Latin *grȳphus,* from Greek *grups,* from *grupos* hooked]

griffin[2] ('grɪfɪn) *n.* a newcomer to the Orient, esp. one from W Europe. [C18: of unknown origin]

griffon[1] ('grɪfᵊn) *n.* **1.** any of various small wire-haired breeds of dog, originally from Belgium. **2.** any large vulture of the genus *Gyps,* of Africa, S Europe, and SW Asia, having a pale plumage with black wings: family *Accipitridae* (hawks). [C19: from French: GRIFFIN[1]]

griffon[2] ('grɪfᵊn) *n.* a variant of **griffin**[1].

grig (grɪg) *n. Dialect.* **1.** a lively person. **2.** a short-legged hen. **3.** a young eel. [C14: dwarf, perhaps of Scandinavian origin; compare Swedish *krik* a little creature]

Grignard reagent ('griːnjɑː; *French* griɲar) *n. Chem.* any of a class of organometallic reagents, having the general formula RMgX, where R is an organic group and X is a halogen atom: used in the synthesis of organic compounds. [C20: named after Victor *Grignard* (1871–1934), French chemist]

grigri, gris-gris, *or* **greegree** (ˈgriːgriː) *n., pl.* **-gris** (-griːz) *or* **-grees.** an African talisman, amulet, or charm. [of African origin]

grike *or* **gryke** (graɪk) *n.* a solution fissure, a vertical crack about 0.5 m wide formed by the dissolving of limestone by water, that divides an exposed limestone surface into sections or clints. [C20 in geological sense: from northern dialect]

Grikwa (ˈgriːkwə, ˈgrɪk-) *n., pl.* **-kwa** *or* **-kwas.** a variant spelling of **Griqua.**

grill[1] (grɪl) *vb.* **1.** to cook (meat, fish, etc.) by direct heat, as under a grill or over a hot fire, or (of meat, fish, etc.) to be cooked in this way. Usual U.S. and Canadian word: **broil. 2.** (*tr.; usually passive*) to torment with or as if with extreme heat: *the travellers were grilled by the scorching sun.* **3.** (*tr.*) *Informal.* to subject to insistent or prolonged questioning. ~*n.* **4.** a device with parallel bars of thin metal on which meat, fish, etc., may be cooked by a fire; gridiron. **5.** a device on a cooker that radiates heat downwards for grilling meat, fish, etc. **6.** food cooked by grilling. **7.** See **grillroom.** [C17: from French *gril* gridiron, from Latin *crātīcula* fine wickerwork; see GRILLE] —ˈ**griller** *n.*

grill[2] (grɪl) *n.* a variant spelling of **grille.** [C17: see GRILLE]

grillage (ˈgrɪlɪdʒ) *n.* an arrangement of beams and crossbeams used as a foundation on soft ground. [C18: from French, from *griller* to furnish with a grille]

grille *or* **grill** (grɪl) *n.* **1.** Also called: ˈ**grill,work.** a framework, esp. of metal bars arranged to form an ornamental pattern, used as a screen or partition. **2.** Also called: **radiator grille.** a grating, often chromium-plated, that admits cooling air to the radiator of a motor vehicle. **3.** a metal or wooden openwork grating used as a screen or divider. **4.** a protective screen, usually plastic or metal, in front of the loudspeaker in a radio, record player, etc. **5.** *Real Tennis.* the opening in one corner of the receiver's end of the court. **6.** a group of small pyramidal marks impressed in parallel rows into a stamp to prevent reuse. [C17: from Old French, from Latin *crātīcula* fine hurdlework, from *crātis* a hurdle]

grilled (grɪld) *adj.* **1.** cooked on a grill or gridiron. **2.** having a grille.

grillroom (ˈgrɪl,ruːm, -,rʊm) *n.* a restaurant or room in a restaurant, etc., where grilled steaks and other meat are served.

grilse (grɪls) *n., pl.* **grilses** *or* **grilse.** a salmon at the stage when it returns for the first time from the sea to fresh water. [C15 *grilles* (plural), of uncertain origin]

grim (grɪm) *adj.* **grimmer, grimmest. 1.** stern; resolute: *grim determination.* **2.** harsh or formidable in manner or appearance. **3.** harshly ironic or sinister: *grim laughter.* **4.** cruel, severe, or ghastly: *a grim accident.* **5.** *Archaic or poetic.* fierce: *a grim warrior.* **6.** *Informal.* unpleasant; disagreeable. **7. hold on like grim death.** to hold very firmly or resolutely. [Old English *grimm;* related to Old Norse *grimmr,* Old High German *grimm* savage, Greek *khremizein* to neigh] —ˈ**grimly** *adv.* —ˈ**grimness** *n.*

grimace (grɪˈmeɪs) *n.* **1.** an ugly or distorted facial expression, as of wry humour, disgust, etc. ~*vb.* **2.** (*intr.*) to contort the face. [C17: from French *grimace,* of Germanic origin; related to Spanish *grimazo* caricature; see GRIM] —**griˈmacer** *n.* —**griˈmacingly** *adv.*

Grimaldi man (grɪˈmɔːldɪ) *n. Anthropol.* a type of Aurignacian man having a negroid appearance, thought to be a race of Cro-Magnon man. [C20: named after the *Grimaldi* caves, Italy, where skeletons of this type were found]

grimalkin (grɪˈmælkɪn, -ˈmɔːl-) *n.* **1.** an old cat, esp. an old female cat. **2.** a crotchety or shrewish old woman. [C17: from GREY + MALKIN]

grim dig *n. N.Z. informal, obsolete.* an obdurate soldier.

grime (graɪm) *n.* **1.** dirt, soot, or filth, esp. when thickly accumulated or ingrained. ~*vb.* **2.** (*tr.*) to make dirty or coat with filth. [C15: from Middle Dutch *grime;* compare Flemish *grijm,* Old English *grīma* mask] —ˈ**grimy** *adj.* —ˈ**griminess** *n.*

Grimm's law (grɪmz) *n.* the rules accounting for systematic correspondences between consonants in the Germanic languages and consonants in other Indo-European languages; it states that Proto-Indo-European voiced aspirated stops, voiced unaspirated stops, and voiceless stops became voiced unaspirated stops, voiceless stops, and voiceless fricatives respectively. [C19: named after Jakob *Grimm* (1785–1863), German philologist and folklorist who formulated it]

grimoire (griːmˈwɑː) *n.* a textbook of sorcery and magic. [C19: from French, altered from *grammaire* GRAMMAR; compare GLAMOUR]

grin (grɪn) *vb.* **grins, grinning, grinned. 1.** to smile with the lips drawn back revealing the teeth or express (something) by such a smile: *to grin a welcome.* **2.** (*intr.*) to draw back the lips revealing the teeth, as in a snarl or grimace. **3. grin and bear it.** *Informal.* to suffer trouble or hardship without complaint. ~*n.* **4.** a broad smile. **5.** a snarl or grimace. [Old English *grennian;* related to Old High German *grennen* to snarl, Old Norse *grenja* to howl; see GRUNT] —ˈ**grinner** *n.* —ˈ**grinning** *adj., n.*

grind (graɪnd) *vb.* **grinds, grinding, ground. 1.** to reduce or be reduced to small particles by pounding or abrading: *to grind corn; to grind flour.* **2.** (*tr.*) to smooth, sharpen, or polish by friction or abrasion: *to grind a knife.* **3.** to scrape or grate together (two things, esp. the teeth) with a harsh rasping sound or (of such objects) to be scraped together. **4.** (*tr.;* foll. by *out*) to speak or say (something) in a rough voice. **5.** (*tr.;* often foll. by *down*) to hold down; oppress; tyrannize. **6.** (*tr.*) to operate (a machine) by turning a handle. **7.** (*tr.;* foll. by *out*) to produce in a routine or uninspired manner: *he ground out his weekly article for the paper.* **8.** (*tr.;* foll. by *out*) to continue to play in a dull or insipid manner: *the band only ground out old tunes all evening.* **9.** (*tr.;* often foll. by *into*) to instil (facts, information, etc.) by persistent effort: *they ground into the recruits the need for vigilance.* **10.** (*intr.*) *Informal.* to study or work laboriously. **11.** (*intr.*) *Chiefly U.S.* to dance erotically by rotating the pelvis (esp. in the phrase **bump and grind**). ~*n.* **12.** *Informal.* laborious or routine work or study. **13.** *Slang, chiefly U.S.* a person, esp. a student, who works excessively hard. **14.** a specific grade of pulverization, as of coffee beans: *coarse grind.* **15.** *Brit. slang.* the act of sexual intercourse. **16.** *Chiefly U.S.* a dance movement involving an erotic rotation of the pelvis. **17.** the act or sound of grinding. ~See also **grind on.** [Old English *grindan;* related to Latin *frendere,* Lithuanian *grendu* I rub, Low German *grand* sand] —ˈ**grindingly** *adv.*

grindelia (grɪnˈdiːlɪə) *n.* **1.** any coarse plant of the American genus *Grindelia,* having yellow daisy-like flower heads: family *Compositae* (composites). See also **gum plant. 2.** the dried leaves and tops of certain species of these plants, used in tonics and sedatives. [C19: named after David Hieronymus *Grindel* (1777–1836), Russian botanist]

grinder (ˈgraɪndə) *n.* **1.** a person who grinds, esp. one who grinds cutting tools. **2.** a machine for grinding. **3.** a molar tooth.

grindery (ˈgraɪndərɪ) *n., pl.* **-eries. 1.** a place in which tools and cutlery are sharpened. **2.** the equipment of a shoemaker.

grind in *vb.* (*tr., adv.*) *Engineering.* to make (a conical valve) fit its seating by grinding them together in the presence of an abrasive paste.

grinding wheel *n.* an abrasive wheel, usually a composite of hard particles in a resin filler, used for grinding.

grind on *vb.* (*intr., adv.*) to move further relentlessly: *the enemy's invasion ground slowly on.*

grindstone (ˈgraɪnd,stəʊn) *n.* **1. a.** a machine having a circular block of stone or composite abrasive rotated for sharpening tools or grinding metal. **b.** the stone used in this machine. **c.** any stone used for sharpening; whetstone. **2.** another name for **millstone. 3. keep** *or* **have one's nose to the grindstone.** to work hard and perseveringly.

gringo (ˈgrɪŋgəʊ) *n., pl.* **-gos.** a person from an English-speaking country: used as a derogatory term by Latin Americans. [C19: from Spanish: foreigner, probably from *griego* Greek, hence an alien]

griot (ˈgriːəʊ, griːˈɒt) *n.* (in Western Africa) a member of a caste responsible for maintaining an oral record of tribal history in the form of music, poetry, and storytelling. [C20: from French *guirot,* perhaps from Portuguese *criado* domestic servant]

grip[1] (grɪp) *n.* **1.** the act or an instance of grasping and holding firmly: *he lost his grip on the slope.* **2.** Also called: **handgrip.** the strength or pressure of such a grasp, as in a handshake: *a feeble grip.* **3.** the style or manner of grasping an object, such as a tennis racket. **4.** understanding, control, or mastery of a subject, problem, etc. (esp. in such phrases as **get** *or* **have a grip on**). **5. come** *or* **get to grips.** (often foll. by *with*) **a.** to deal with (a problem or subject). **b.** to tackle (an assailant). **6.** Also called: **handgrip.** a part by which an object is grasped; handle. **7.** Also called: **handgrip.** a travelling bag or holdall. **8.** See **hairgrip. 9.** any device that holds by friction, such as certain types of brake. **10.** a method of clasping or shaking hands used by members of secret societies to greet or identify one another. **11.** a spasm of pain: *a grip in one's stomach.* **12.** a worker in a camera crew or a stagehand who shifts sets and props, etc. **13.** a small drainage channel cut above an excavation to conduct surface water away from the excavation. ~*vb.* **grips, gripping, gripped. 14.** to take hold of firmly or tightly, as by a clutch. **15.** to hold the interest or attention of: *to grip an audience.* [Old English *gripe* grasp; related to Old Norse *gripr* property, Old High German *grif*] —ˈ**gripper** *n.* —ˈ**grippingly** *adv.*

grip[2] (grɪp) *n. Med.* a variant spelling of **grippe.**

gripe (graɪp) *vb.* **1.** (*intr.*) *Informal.* to complain, esp. in a persistent nagging manner. **2.** to cause sudden intense pain in the intestines of (a person) or (of a person) to experience this pain. **3.** (*intr.*) *Nautical.* (of a ship) to tend to come up into the wind in spite of the helm. **4.** *Archaic.* to clutch; grasp. **5.** (*tr.*) *Archaic.* to afflict. ~*n.* **6.** (*usually pl.*) a sudden intense pain in the intestines; colic. **7.** *Informal.* a complaint or grievance. **8.** *Now rare.* **a.** the act of gripping. **b.** a firm grip. **c.** a device that grips. **9.** (*in pl.*) *Nautical.* the lashings that secure a boat. [Old English *grīpan;* related to Gothic *greipan,* Old High German *grīfan* to seize, Lithuanian *greibiu*] —ˈ**griper** *n.* —ˈ**gripingly** *adv.*

gripe water *n. Brit.* a solution given to infants to relieve colic.

grippe *or* **grip** (grɪp) *n.* a former name for **influenza.** [C18: from French *grippe,* from *gripper* to seize, of Germanic origin; see GRIP[1]]

grip tape *n.* a rough tape for sticking to a surface to provide a greater grip.

Griqua *or* **Grikwa** (ˈgriːkwə, ˈgrɪk-) *n.* **1.** (*pl.* **-qua, -quas** *or* **-kwa, -kwas**) a member of a people of mixed ancestry, mainly

European and Hottentot, living chiefly in Griqualand in Cape Province, South Africa. 2. the language or dialect of Hottentot spoken by this people, belonging to the Khoisan family.

grisaille (grɪˈzeɪl; *French* grizɑj) *n.* 1. a technique of monochrome painting in shades of grey, as in an oil painting or a wall decoration, imitating the effect of relief. 2. a painting, stained glass window, etc., in this manner. [C19: from French, from *gris* grey]

griseofulvin (ˌgrɪzɪəʊˈfʊlvɪn) *n.* an antibiotic used to treat fungal infections of the hair and skin. [C20: from New Latin, from *Penicillium griseofulvum dierckx* (fungus from which it was isolated), from Medieval Latin *griseus* grey + Latin *fulvus* reddish yellow]

griseous (ˈgrɪsɪəs, ˈgrɪz-) *adj.* streaked or mixed with grey; somewhat grey. [C19: from Medieval Latin *griseus,* of Germanic origin]

grisette (grɪˈzɛt) *n.* 1. (esp. formerly) a French working girl, esp. a pretty or flirtatious one. 2. an edible toadstool of the genus *Amanita* of broad-leaved and birch woods. [C18: from French, from *grisette* grey fabric used for dresses, from *gris* grey]

gris-gris (ˈgriːgriː) *n., pl.* **-gris** (-griːz). a variant spelling of **grigri.**

griskin (ˈgrɪskɪn) *n. Brit.* the lean part of a loin of pork. [C17: probably from dialect *gris* pig, from Old Norse *griss*]

grisly[1] (ˈgrɪzlɪ) *adj.* **-lier, -liest.** causing horror or dread; gruesome. [Old English *grislic;* related to Old Frisian *grislik,* Old High German *grīsenlīh*] —ˈ**grisliness** *n.*

grisly[2] (ˈgrɪzlɪ) *n., pl* **-lies.** *Obsolete.* a variant spelling of **grizzly.**

grison (ˈgraɪsᵊn, ˈgrɪzᵊn) *n.* either of two musteline mammals, *Grison* (or *Galictis*) *cuja* or *G. vittata,* of Central and South America, having a greyish back and black face and underparts. [C18: from French, from *grison* grey animal, from Old French *gris* grey]

grist (grɪst) *n.* 1. a. grain intended to be or that has been ground. b. the quantity of such grain processed in one grinding. 2. *Brewing.* malt grains that have been cleaned and cracked. 3. **grist to** (*or* **for**) **the** (*or* **one's**) **mill.** anything that can be turned to profit or advantage. [Old English *grīst;* related to Old Saxon *grist-grimmo* gnashing of teeth, Old High German *grist-grimmōn*]

gristle (ˈgrɪsᵊl) *n.* cartilage, esp. when in meat. [Old English *gristle;* related to Old Frisian, Middle Low German *gristel*] —ˈ**gristly** *adj.* —ˈ**gristliness** *n.*

gristmill (ˈgrɪstˌmɪl) *n.* a mill, esp. one equipped with large grinding stones for grinding grain.

grit (grɪt) *n.* 1. small hard particles of sand, earth, stone, etc. 2. Also called: **gritstone.** any coarse sandstone that can be used as a grindstone or millstone. 3. the texture or grain of stone. 4. indomitable courage, toughness, or resolution. 5. *Engineering.* an arbitrary measure of the size of abrasive particles used in a grinding wheel or other abrasive process. ~*vb.* **grits, gritting, gritted.** 6. to clench or grind together (two objects, esp. the teeth). 7. to cover (a surface, such as icy roads) with grit. [Old English *grēot;* related to Old Norse *grjōt* pebble, Old High German *grioz;* see GREAT, GROATS, GRUEL] —ˈ**gritless** *adj.*

Grit (grɪt) *n., adj. Canadian.* an informal word for **Liberal.**

grith (grɪθ) *n.* 1. *English legal history.* security, peace, or protection, guaranteed either in a certain place, such as a church, or for a period of time. 2. a place of safety or protection. [Old English *grith;* related to Old Norse *grith* home]

grits (grɪts) *pl. n.* 1. hulled and coarsely ground grain. 2. *U.S.* See **hominy grits.** [Old English *grytt;* related to Old High German *gruzzi;* see GREAT, GRIT]

gritter (ˈgrɪtə) *n. Brit.* a vehicle which spreads grit on roads during icy weather, or when icy conditions are expected.

gritting (ˈgrɪtɪŋ) *n. Brit.* a. the spreading of grit on road surfaces to render them less slippery for vehicles during icy weather. b. (*as modifier*): *gritting lorries.*

gritty (ˈgrɪtɪ) *adj.* **-tier, -tiest.** 1. courageous; hardy; resolute. 2. of, like, or containing grit. —ˈ**grittily** *adv.* —ˈ**grittiness** *n.*

grivation (grɪˈveɪʃən) *n. Navigation.* short for **grid variation.**

grivet (ˈgrɪvɪt) *n.* an E African variety of a common guenon monkey, *Cercopithecus aethiops,* having long white tufts of hair on either side of the face. Compare **green monkey, vervet.** [C19: from French, of unknown origin]

grizzle[1] (ˈgrɪzᵊl) *vb.* 1. to make or become grey. ~*n.* 2. a grey colour. 3. grey or partly grey hair. 4. a grey wig. [C15: from Old French *grisel,* from *gris,* of Germanic origin; compare Middle High German *grīs* grey]

grizzle[2] (ˈgrɪzᵊl) *vb.* (*intr.*) *Informal, chiefly Brit.* 1. (esp. of a child) to fret; whine. 2. to sulk or grumble. [C18: of Germanic origin; compare Old High German *grist-grimmōn* gnashing of teeth, German *Griesgram* unpleasant person] —ˈ**grizzler** *n.*

grizzled (ˈgrɪzᵊld) *adj.* 1. streaked or mixed with grey; grizzly; griseous. 2. having grey or partly grey hair.

grizzly (ˈgrɪzlɪ) *adj.* **-zlier, -zliest.** 1. somewhat grey; grizzled. ~*n., pl.* **-zlies.** 2. See **grizzly bear.**

grizzly bear *n.* a variety of the brown bear, *Ursus arctos horribilis,* formerly widespread in W North America; its brown fur has cream or white hair tips on the back, giving a grizzled appearance. Often shortened to **grizzly.**

gro. *abbrev. for* gross (unit of quantity).

groan (grəʊn) *n.* 1. a prolonged stressed dull cry expressive of agony, pain, or disapproval. 2. a loud harsh creaking sound, as of a tree bending in the wind. 3. *Informal.* a grumble or complaint, esp. a persistent one. ~*vb.* 4. to utter (low inarticulate sounds) expressive of pain, grief, disapproval, etc.: *they all groaned at Larry's puns.* 5. (*intr.*) to make a sound like a groan. 6. (*intr.,* usually foll. by *beneath* or *under*) to be weighed down (by) or suffer greatly (under): *the country groaned under the dictator's rule.* 7. (*intr.*) *Informal.* to complain or grumble. [Old English *grānian;* related to Old Norse *grīna,* Old High German *grīnan;* see GRIN] —ˈ**groaner** *n.* —ˈ**groaning** *n., adj.* —ˈ**groaningly** *adv.*

groat (grəʊt) *n.* an English silver coin worth four pennies, taken out of circulation in the 17th century. [C14: from Middle Dutch *groot,* from Middle Low German *gros,* from Medieval Latin (*denarius*) *grossus* thick (coin); see GROSCHEN]

groats (grəʊts) *pl. n.* 1. the hulled and crushed grain of oats, wheat, or certain other cereals. 2. the parts of oat kernels used as food. [Old English *grot* particle; related to *grota* fragment, as in *meregrota* pearl; see GRIT, GROUT]

grocer (ˈgrəʊsə) *n.* a dealer in foodstuffs and other household supplies. [C15: from Old French *grossier,* from *gros* large; see GROSS]

groceries (ˈgrəʊsərɪz) *pl. n.* merchandise, esp. foodstuffs, sold by a grocer.

grocery (ˈgrəʊsərɪ) *n., pl.* **-ceries.** the business or premises of a grocer.

grockle (ˈgrɒkᵊl) *n. Devonshire dialect.* a tourist, esp. one from the Midlands or the North of England. [C20: of unknown origin]

grog (grɒg) *n.* 1. diluted spirit, usually rum, as an alcoholic drink. 2. *Informal, chiefly Austral. and N.Z.* alcoholic drink in general, esp. spirits. [C18: from Old *Grog,* nickname of Edward Vernon (1684–1757), British admiral, who in 1740 issued naval rum diluted with water; his nickname arose from his grogram cloak]

groggy (ˈgrɒgɪ) *adj.* **-gier, -giest.** *Informal.* 1. dazed or staggering, as from exhaustion, blows, or drunkenness. 2. faint or weak. —ˈ**groggily** *adv.* —ˈ**grogginess** *n.*

grogram (ˈgrɒgrəm) *n.* a coarse fabric of silk, wool, or silk mixed with wool or mohair, often stiffened with gum, formerly used for clothing. [C16: from French *gros grain* coarse grain; see GROSGRAIN]

grogshop (ˈgrɒgˌʃɒp) *n.* 1. *Rare.* a drinking place, esp. one of disreputable character. 2. *Austral. and N.Z. informal.* a shop where liquor can be bought for drinking off the premises.

groin (grɔɪn) *n.* 1. the depression or fold where the legs join the abdomen. 2. *Euphemistic.* the genitals, esp. the testicles. 3. a variant spelling (esp. U.S.) of **groyne.** 4. *Architect.* a curved arris formed where two intersecting vaults meet. ~*vb.* 5. (*tr.*) *Architect.* to provide or construct with groins. [C15: perhaps from English *grynde* abyss; related to GROUND[1]]

Grolier (ˈgrəʊlɪə; *French* grɔlje) *adj.* relating to or denoting a decorative style of bookbinding using interlaced leather straps, gilded ornamental scrolls, etc. [C19: named after Jean *Grolier de Servières* (1479–1565), French bibliophile]

grommet (ˈgrɒmɪt) *or* **grummet** *n.* 1. a ring of rubber or plastic or a metal eyelet designed to line a hole to prevent a cable or pipe passed through it from chafing. 2. a ring of rope hemp used to stuff the gland of a pipe joint. [C15: from obsolete French *gourmette* chain linking the ends of a bit, from *gourmer* bridle, of unknown origin]

gromwell (ˈgrɒmwəl) *n.* any of various hairy plants of the boraginaceous genus *Lithospermum,* esp. *L. officinale,* having small greenish-white, yellow, or blue flowers, and smooth nutlike fruits. See also **puccoon** (sense 1). [C13: from Old French *gromil,* from *gres* sandstone + *mil* millet, from Latin *milium*]

groom (gruːm, grʊm) *n.* 1. a person employed to clean and look after horses. 2. See **bridegroom.** 3. any of various officers of a royal or noble household. 4. *Archaic.* a male servant or attendant. 5. *Archaic and poetic.* a young man. ~*vb.* (*tr.*) 6. to make or keep (clothes, appearance, etc.) clean and tidy. 7. to rub down, clean, and smarten (a horse, dog, etc.). 8. to train or prepare for a particular task, occupation, etc.: *to groom someone for the Presidency.* [C13 *grom* manservant; perhaps related to Old English *grōwan* to GROW] —ˈ**groomer** *n.* —ˈ**grooming** *n.*

groomsman (ˈgruːmzmən, ˈgrʊmz-) *n., pl.* **-men.** a man who attends the bridegroom at a wedding, usually the best man.

groove (gruːv) *n.* 1. a long narrow channel or furrow, esp. one cut into wood by a tool. 2. the spiral channel, usually V-shaped, in a gramophone record. See also **microgroove.** 3. *Printing.* a channel across the bottom surface of a piece of type. 4. one of the spiral cuts in the bore of a gun. 5. *Anatomy.* any furrow or channel on a bodily structure or part; sulcus. 6. *Mountaineering.* a shallow fissure in a rock face or between two rock faces, forming an angle of more than 120°. 7. a settled existence, routine, etc., to which one is suited or accustomed, esp. one from which it is difficult to escape. 8. *Slang.* an experience, event, etc., that is groovy. 9. **in the groove.** a. *Jazz.* playing well and apparently effortlessly, with a good beat, etc. b. *U.S.* fashionable. ~*vb.* 10. (*tr.*) to form or cut a groove in. 11. (*intr.*) *Dated slang.* to enjoy oneself or feel in rapport with one's surroundings. 12. (*intr.*) *Jazz.* to play well, with a good beat, etc. [C15: from obsolete Dutch *groeve,* of Germanic origin; compare Old High

German *gruoba* pit, Old Norse *grof*] —'**grooveless** *adj.* —'**groove,like** *adj.*

grooving saw *n.* a circular saw used for making grooves.

groovy ('gruːvɪ) *adj.* **groovier, grooviest.** *Dated slang.* attractive, fashionable, or exciting.

grope (grəʊp) *vb.* **1.** (*intr.;* usually foll. by *for*) to feel or search about uncertainly (for something) with the hands. **2.** (*intr.;* usually foll. by *for* or *after*) to search uncertainly or with difficulty (for a solution, answer, etc.). **3.** (*tr.*) to find or make (one's way) by groping. **4.** (*tr.*) *Slang.* to feel or fondle the body of (someone) for sexual gratification. ~*n.* **5.** the act of groping. [Old English *grāpian;* related to Old High German *greifōn,* Norwegian *greipa;* compare GRIPE] —'**gropingly** *adv.*

groper ('grəʊpə) *or* **grouper** *n., pl.* **-er** *or* **-ers.** any large marine serranid fish of the genus *Epinephelus* and related genera, of warm and tropical seas. [C17: from Portuguese *garupa,* probably from a South American Indian word]

grosbeak ('grəʊs,biːk, 'grɒs-) *n.* **1.** any of various finches, such as *Pinicola enucleator* (**pine grosbeak**), that have a massive powerful bill. **2. cardinal grosbeak.** any of various mostly tropical American buntings, such as the cardinal and pyrrhuloxia, the males of which have brightly coloured plumage. [C17: from French *grosbec,* from Old French *gros* large, thick + *bec* BEAK[1]]

groschen ('grəʊʃən; *German* 'grɔʃən) *n., pl.* **-schen.** **1.** an Austrian monetary unit worth one hundredth of a schilling. **2.** a German coin worth ten pfennigs. **3.** a former German silver coin. [C17: from German: Bohemian dialect alteration of Middle High German *grosse,* from Medieval Latin (*denarius*) *grossus* thick (penny); see GROSS, GROAT]

gros de Londres *French.* (gro də lɔ̃drə) *n.* a lightweight shiny ribbed silk fabric, the ribs alternating between wide and narrow between different colours or between different textures of yarn. [literally: heavy (fabric) from London]

grosgrain ('grəʊ,greɪn) *n.* a heavy ribbed silk or rayon fabric or tape for trimming clothes, etc. [C19: from French *gros grain* coarse grain; see GROSS, GRAIN]

gros point ('grəʊ 'pɔɪnt; *French* gro pwɛ̃) *n.* **1.** a needlepoint stitch covering two horizontal and two vertical threads. **2.** work done in this stitch. ~Compare **petit point.**

gross (grəʊs) *adj.* **1.** repellently or excessively fat or bulky. **2.** with no deductions for expenses, tax, etc.; total: *gross sales; gross income.* Compare **net**[2] (sense 1). **3.** (of personal qualities, tastes, etc.) conspicuously coarse or vulgar. **4.** obviously or exceptionally culpable or wrong; flagrant: *gross inefficiency.* **5.** lacking in perception, sensitivity, or discrimination: *gross judgments.* **6.** (esp. of vegetation) dense; thick; luxuriant. **7.** *Obsolete.* coarse in texture or quality. **8.** *Rare.* rude; uneducated; ignorant. ~*interj. Slang.* **9.** an exclamation indicating disgust. ~*n.* **10.** *pl.* **gross.** a unit of quantity equal to 12 dozen. **11.** *pl.* **grosses. a.** the entire amount. **b.** the great majority. ~*vb.* (*tr.*) **12.** to earn as total revenue, before deductions for expenses, tax, etc. ~See also **gross out, gross up.** [C14: from Old French *gros* large, from Late Latin *grossus* thick] —'**grossly** *adv.* —'**grossness** *n.*

gross domestic product *n.* the total value of all goods and services produced domestically by a nation during a year. It is equivalent to gross national product minus net investment incomes from foreign nations. Abbrev.: **GDP.**

gross national product *n.* the total value of all final goods and services produced annually by a nation. Abbrev.: **GNP.**

gross out *U.S. slang.* ~*vb.* (*tr., adv.*) **1.** to cause (a person) to feel distaste or strong dislike for (something). ~*n.* **gross-out.** **2.** a person or thing regarded as disgusting or objectionable. ~*adj.* **gross-out.** **3.** disgusting, boring, or objectionable.

gross profit *n. Accounting.* the difference between total revenue from sales and the total cost of purchases or materials, with an adjustment for stock.

gross ton *n.* another name for **long ton:** see **ton**[1] (sense 1).

grossularite ('grɒsjʊlə,raɪt) *n.* a green or greenish-grey garnet, used as a gemstone. Formula: $Ca_3Al_2(SiO_4)_3$. Also called: **gooseberry stone.** [C19: from New Latin *grossulāria* gooseberry, from Old French *grosele* + -ITE[1]]

gross up *vb.* (*tr., adv.*) to increase (net income) to its pretax value.

gross weight *n.* total weight of an article inclusive of the weight of the container and packaging.

grosz (grɔːʃ) *n., pl.* **groszy** ('grɔːʃɪ). a Polish monetary unit worth one hundredth of a zloty. [from Polish, from Czech *grosh;* see GROSCHEN]

grot[1] (grɒt) *n. Slang.* rubbish; dirt. [C20: from GROTTY]

grot[2] (grɒt) *n.* a poetic word for **grotto.** [C16: from French *grotte,* from Old Italian *grotta;* see GROTTO]

grotesque (grəʊ'tɛsk) *adj.* **1.** strangely or fantastically distorted; bizarre: *a grotesque reflection in the mirror.* **2.** of or characteristic of the grotesque in art. **3.** absurdly incongruous; in a ludicrous context: *a grotesque turn of phrase.* ~*n.* **4.** a 16th-century decorative style in which parts of human, animal, and plant forms are distorted and mixed. **5.** a decorative device, as in painting or sculpture, in this style. **6.** *Printing.* the family of 19th-century sans serif display types. **7.** any grotesque person or thing. [C16: from French, from Old Italian (*pittura*) *grottesca* cave painting, from *grottesco* of a cave, from *grotta* cave; see GROTTO] —**gro'tesquely** *adv.* —**gro'tesqueness** *n.*

grotesquery *or* **grotesquerie** (grəʊ'tɛskərɪ) *n., pl.* **-queries.** **1.** the state of being grotesque. **2.** something that is grotesque, esp. an object such as a sculpture.

grotto ('grɒtəʊ) *n., pl.* **-toes** *or* **-tos.** **1.** a small cave, esp. one with attractive features. **2.** a construction in the form of a cave, esp. as in landscaped gardens during the 18th century. [C17: from Old Italian *grotta,* from Late Latin *crypta* vault; see CRYPT]

grotty ('grɒtɪ) *adj.* **-tier, -tiest.** *Brit. slang.* **1.** unpleasant, nasty, or unattractive. **2.** of poor quality or in bad condition; unsatisfactory or useless. [C20: from GROTESQUE]

grouch (graʊtʃ) *Informal.* ~*vb.* (*intr.*) **1.** to complain; grumble. ~*n.* **2.** a complaint, esp. a persistent one. **3.** a person who is always grumbling. [C20: from obsolete *grutch,* from Old French *grouchier* to complain; see GRUDGE] —'**grouchy** *adj.* —'**grouchily** *adv.* —'**grouchiness** *n.*

grough (grʌf) *n. Mountaineering.* a natural channel or fissure in a peat moor; a peat hag. [C20: possibly the same as *grough,* an obsolete variant of GRUFF in the obsolete sense: "rough" (of terrain)]

ground[1] (graʊnd) *n.* **1.** the land surface. **2.** earth or soil: *he dug into the ground outside his house.* **3.** (*pl.*) the land around a dwelling house or other building. **4.** (*sometimes pl.*) an area of land given over to a purpose: *football ground; burial grounds.* **5.** land having a particular characteristic: *level ground; high ground.* **6.** matter for consideration or debate; field of research or inquiry: *the lecture was familiar ground to him; the report covered a lot of ground.* **7.** a position or viewpoint, as in an argument or controversy (esp. in the phrases **give ground, hold, stand,** *or* **shift one's ground**). **8.** position or advantage, as in a subject or competition (esp. in the phrases **gain ground, lose ground,** etc.). **9.** (*often pl.*) reason; justification: *grounds for complaint.* **10.** *Arts.* **a.** the prepared surface applied to the support of a painting, such as a wall, canvas, etc., to prevent it reacting with or absorbing the paint. **b.** the support of a painting. **c.** the background of a painting or main surface against which the other parts of a work of art appear superimposed. **11. a.** the first coat of paint applied to a surface. **b.** (*as modifier*): *ground colour.* **12.** the bottom of a river or the sea. **13.** (*pl.*) sediment or dregs, esp. from coffee. **14.** *Chiefly Brit.* the floor of a room. **15.** *Cricket.* **a.** the area from the popping crease back past the stumps, in which a batsman may legally stand. **b.** ground staff. **16.** See **ground bass.** **17.** a mesh or network supporting the main pattern of a piece of lace. **18.** *Electrical.* the usual U.S. and Canadian word for **earth** (sense 8). **19. above ground.** alive. **20. below ground.** dead and buried. **21. break new ground.** to do something that has not been done before. **22. cut the ground from under someone's feet.** to anticipate someone's action or argument and thus make it irrelevant or meaningless. **23. (down) to the ground.** *Brit. informal.* completely; absolutely: *it suited him down to the ground.* **24. get off the ground.** *Informal.* to make a beginning, esp. one that is successful. **25. go to ground.** to go into hiding. **26. into the ground.** beyond what is requisite or can be endured; to exhaustion. **27. meet someone on his own ground.** to meet someone according to terms he has laid down himself. **28. touch ground. a.** (of a ship) to strike the sea bed. **b.** to arrive at something solid or stable after discussing or dealing with topics that are abstract or inconclusive. **29.** (*modifier*) situated on, living on, or used on the ground: *ground frost; ground forces.* **30.** (*modifier*) concerned with or operating on the ground, esp. as distinct from in the air: *ground crew; ground hostess.* **31.** (*modifier*) (used in names of plants) low-growing and often trailing or spreading. ~*vb.* **32.** (*tr.*) to put or place on the ground. **33.** (*tr.*) to instruct in fundamentals. **34.** (*tr.*) to provide a basis or foundation for; establish. **35.** (*tr.*) to confine (an aircraft, pilot, etc.) to the ground. **36.** the usual U.S. word for **earth** (sense 16). **37.** (*tr.*) *Nautical.* to run (a vessel) aground. **38.** (*tr.*) to cover (a surface) with a preparatory coat of paint. **39.** (*intr.*) to hit or reach the ground. [Old English *grund;* related to Old Norse *grunn* shallow, *grunnr, grund* plain, Old High German *grunt*]

ground[2] (graʊnd) *vb.* **1.** the past tense and past participle of **grind.** ~*adj.* **2.** having the surface finished, thickness reduced, or an edge sharpened by grinding. **3.** reduced to fine particles by grinding.

groundage ('graʊndɪdʒ) *n. Brit.* a fee levied on a vessel entering a port or anchored off a shore.

groundbait ('graʊnd,beɪt) *Angling.* ~*n.* **1.** bait, such as scraps of bread, maggots, etc., thrown into an area of water to attract fish. See **chum**[2]. ~*vb.* (*tr.*) **2.** to prepare (an area of water) with groundbait.

ground bass *or* **ground** (beɪs) *n. Music.* a short melodic bass line that is repeated over and over again.

ground beetle *n.* **1.** any beetle of the family *Carabidae,* often found under logs, stones, etc., having long legs and a dark coloration. **2.** any beetle of the family *Tenebrionidae,* feeding on plants and plant products. **3.** any of various other beetles that live close to or beneath the ground.

ground bug *n.* any member of a family (*Lygaeidae*) of hemipterous plant-eating insects, having generally dark bodies, sometimes marked with red, and lighter, yellowish wings.

ground cherry *n.* any of various American solanaceous plants of the genus *Physalis,* esp. *P. pubescens,* having round fleshy fruit enclosed in a bladder-like husk. See also **winter cherry, gooseberry** (sense 4).

ground control *n.* **1.** the personnel, radar, computers, etc., on the ground that monitor the progress of aircraft or spacecraft. **2.** a system for feeding continuous radio messages to an aircraft pilot to enable him to make a blind landing.

ground cover *n.* **a.** dense low herbaceous plants and shrubs that grow over the surface of the ground, esp., in a forest, preventing soil erosion or, in a garden, stifling weeds. **b.** (*as modifier*): *ground-cover plants.*

ground elder *n.* another name for **goutweed.**

ground engineer *n.* an engineer qualified and licensed to certify the airworthiness of an aircraft. Official name: **licensed aircraft engineer.**

ground floor *n.* **1.** the floor of a building level or almost level with the ground. **2. get in on** (*or* **start from**) **the ground floor.** *Informal.* **a.** to enter a business, organization, etc., at the lowest level. **b.** to be in a project, undertaking, etc., from its inception.

ground frost *n.* the condition resulting from a temperature reading of 0°C or below on a thermometer in contact with a grass surface.

ground game *n. Brit.* game animals, such as hares or deer, found on the earth's surface: distinguished from game birds.

ground glass *n.* **1.** glass that has a rough surface produced by grinding, used for diffusing light. **2.** glass in the form of fine particles produced by grinding, used as an abrasive.

groundhog ('graʊnd,hɒg) *n.* another name for **woodchuck.**

Groundhog Day *n.* (in the U.S. and Canada) February 2nd, when, according to tradition, the groundhog emerges from hibernation; if it sees its shadow, it returns to its burrow for six weeks as a sunny day indicates a late spring, while a cloudy day would mean an early spring.

ground ice *n.* ice formed below the surface of a body of water, either on the ground or on a submerged object.

grounding ('graʊndɪŋ) *n.* a basic knowledge of or training in a subject.

ground ivy *n.* a creeping or trailing Eurasian aromatic herbaceous plant, *Glechoma* (or *Nepeta*) *hederacea,* with scalloped leaves and purplish-blue flowers: family *Labiatae* (labiates).

ground layer *n.* See **layer** (sense 2).

groundless ('graʊndlɪs) *adj.* without reason or justification: *his suspicions were groundless.* —'**groundlessly** *adv.* —'**groundlessness** *n.*

groundling ('graʊndlɪŋ) *n.* **1.** any animal or plant that lives close to the ground or at the bottom of a lake, river, etc. **2. a.** (in Elizabethan theatre) a spectator standing in the yard in front of the stage and paying least. **b.** a spectator in the cheapest section of any theatre. **3.** a person on the ground as distinguished from one in an aircraft.

ground loop *n.* a sudden uncontrolled turn by an aircraft on the ground, while moving under its own power.

groundmass ('graʊnd,mæs) *n.* the matrix of igneous rocks, such as porphyry, in which larger crystals (phenocrysts) are embedded.

groundnut ('graʊnd,nʌt) *n.* **1.** a North American climbing leguminous plant, *Apios tuberosa,* with fragrant brown flowers and small edible underground tubers. **2.** the tuber of this plant. **3.** any of several other plants having underground nutlike parts. **4.** *Brit.* another name for **peanut** (sense 1).

ground pine *n.* **1.** a hairy plant, *Ajuga chamaepitys,* of Europe and N Africa, having two-lipped yellow flowers marked with red spots: family *Labiatae* (labiates). It smells of pine when crushed. See also **bugle**[2]. **2.** any of certain North American club mosses, esp. *Lycopodium obscurum.*

ground plan *n.* **1.** a drawing of the ground floor of a building, esp. one to scale. See also **plan** (sense 3). Compare **elevation** (sense 5). **2.** a preliminary or basic outline.

ground-plane aerial *n. Electronics.* a quarter-wave vertical dipole aerial in which the electrical image forming the other quarter-wave section is formed by reflection in a system of radially disposed metal rods or in a conductive sheet.

ground plate *n.* a joist forming the lowest member of a timber frame. Also called: **groundsill, soleplate.**

ground plum *n.* **1.** a North American leguminous plant, *Astragalus caryocarpus,* with purple or white flowers and green thick-walled plumlike edible pods. **2.** the pod of this plant.

ground provisions *pl. n. Caribbean.* starchy vegetables, esp. root crops and plantains.

ground rent *n. Law.* the rent reserved by a lessor on granting a lease, esp. one for a long period of years to enable the lessee to develop the land.

ground rule *n.* a procedural rule or principle.

ground run *n.* the distance taken by an aircraft to brake from its landing speed to its taxiing speed or a stop.

groundsel ('graʊnsəl) *n.* **1.** any of certain plants of the genus *Senecio,* esp. *S. vulgaris,* a Eurasian weed with heads of small yellow flowers: family *Compositae* (composites). See also **ragwort. 2. groundsel tree.** a shrub, *Baccharis halimifolia,* of E North America, with white plumelike fruits: family *Compositae.* [Old English *grundeswelge,* changed from *gundeswilge,* from *gund* pus + *swelgan* to swallow; after its use in poultices on abscesses]

groundsheet ('graʊnd,ʃiːt) *or* **ground cloth** *n.* **1.** a waterproof rubber, plastic, or polythene sheet placed on the ground in a tent, etc., to keep out damp. **2.** a similar sheet put over a sports field to protect it against rain.

groundsill ('graʊnd,sɪl) *n.* another name for **ground plate.**

groundsman ('graʊndzmən) *n., pl.* **-men.** a person employed to maintain a sports ground, park, etc.

groundspeed ('graʊnd,spiːd) *n.* the speed of an aircraft relative to the ground. Compare **airspeed.**

ground squirrel *n.* any burrowing sciurine rodent of the genus *Citellus* and related genera, resembling chipmunks and occurring in North America, E Europe, and Asia. Also called: **gopher.**

ground state *or* **level** *n.* the lowest energy state of an atom, molecule, particle, etc. Compare **excited** (sense 4).

ground stroke *n. Tennis.* any return made to a ball that has touched the ground, as opposed to a volley.

ground swell *n.* **1.** a considerable swell of the sea, often caused by a distant storm or earthquake or by the passage of waves into shallow water. **2.** a strong public feeling or opinion that is detectable even though not openly expressed: *a ground swell of discontent.*

ground water *n.* underground water that has come mainly from the seepage of surface water and is held in the soil and in pervious rocks.

ground wave *or* **ray** *n.* a radio wave that travels directly between a transmitting and a receiving aerial. Compare **sky wave.**

groundwork ('graʊnd,wɜːk) *n.* **1.** preliminary work as a foundation or basis. **2.** the ground or background of a painting, etc.

ground zero *n.* a point on the surface of land or water at or directly above or below the centre of a nuclear explosion.

group (gruːp) *n.* **1.** a number of persons or things considered as a collective unit. **2. a.** a number of persons bound together by common social standards, interests, etc. **b.** (*as modifier*): *group behaviour.* **3.** a small band of players or singers, esp. of pop music. **4.** a number of animals or plants considered as a unit because of common characteristics, habits, etc. **5.** *Grammar.* another word, esp. in systemic grammar, for **phrase** (sense 1). **6.** an association of companies under a single ownership and control, consisting of a holding company, subsidiary companies, and sometimes associated companies. **7.** two or more figures or objects forming a design or unit in a design, in a painting or sculpture. **8.** a military formation comprising complementary arms and services, usually for a purpose: *a brigade group.* **9.** an air force organization of higher level than a squadron. **10.** Also called: **radical.** *Chem.* two or more atoms that are bound together in a molecule and behave as a single unit: *a methyl group* $-CH_3$. Compare **free radical. 11.** a vertical column of elements in the periodic table that all have similar electronic structures, properties, and valencies. Compare **period** (sense 8). **12.** *Geology.* any stratigraphical unit, esp. the unit for two or more formations. **13.** *Maths.* a set under an operation involving any two members of the set such that the set is closed, associative, and contains both an identity and the inverse of each member. **14.** See **blood group.** ~*vb.* **15.** to arrange or place (things, people, etc.) in or into a group or (of things, etc.) to form into a group. [C17: from French *groupe,* of Germanic origin; compare Italian *gruppo;* see CROP]

group captain *n.* an officer holding commissioned rank senior to a wing commander but junior to an air commodore in the British RAF and certain other air forces.

group dynamics *n.* (*functioning as sing.*) *Psychol.* a field of social psychology concerned with the nature of human groups, their development, and their interactions with individuals, other groups, and larger organizations.

grouper ('gruːpə) *n.* a variant of **groper.**

groupie ('gruːpɪ) *n. Slang.* an ardent fan of a celebrity, esp. a pop star: originally, often a girl who followed the members of a pop group on tour in order to have sexual relations with them.

grouping ('gruːpɪŋ) *n.* a planned arrangement of things, people, etc., within a group.

group insurance *n. Chiefly U.S. and Canadian.* insurance relating to life, health, or accident and covering several persons, esp. the employees of a firm, under a single contract at reduced premiums.

group marriage *n.* an arrangement in which several males live together with several females, forming a conjugal unit.

Group of Five *n.* France, Japan, UK, U.S., and Germany acting as a group to stabilize their currency exchange rates. Abbrev.: **G5.**

Group of Seven *n.* the seven leading industrial nations excepting the USSR, i.e. Canada, France, Italy, Japan, UK, U.S., and Germany (formerly West Germany), whose heads of state and finance ministers meet regularly to coordinate economic policy. Abbrev.: **G7.**

Group of Seventy Seven *n.* the developing countries of the world. Abbrev.: **G77.**

Group of Ten *n.* the ten nations who met in Paris in 1961 to arrange the special drawing rights of the IMF; Belgium, Canada, France, Italy, Japan, Netherlands, Sweden, UK, U.S., and West Germany. Also called: **Paris Club.** Abbrev.: **G10.**

Group of Three *n.* Japan, U.S., and Germany (formerly West Germany), regarded as the largest western industrialized nations.

group practice *n.* a medical practice undertaken by a group of associated doctors who work together as partners or as specialists in different areas.

group speed *or* **velocity** *n. Physics.* the speed at which energy is propagated in a wave. This is the quantity which is determined when one measures the distance which the radiation travels in a given time. In a medium in which the speed increases with wavelength the group speed is less than the phase speed, and vice versa.

group therapy *n. Psychol.* the simultaneous treatment of a number of individuals who are members of a natural group or who are brought together to share their problems in group discussion.

grouse[1] (graʊs) *n., pl.* **grouse** *or* **grouses.** **1.** any gallinaceous bird of the family *Tetraonidae*, occurring mainly in the N hemisphere, having a stocky body and feathered legs and feet. They are popular game birds. See also **black grouse, red grouse.** *~adj.* **2.** *Austral. and N.Z. slang.* excellent. [C16: of unknown origin] —ˈ**grouse,like** *adj.*

grouse[2] (graʊs) *vb.* **1.** (*intr.*) to grumble; complain. *~n.* **2.** a persistent complaint. [C19: of unknown origin] —ˈ**grouser** *n.*

grout (graʊt) *n.* **1.** a thin mortar for filling joints between tiles, masonry, etc. **2.** a fine plaster used as a finishing coat. **3.** coarse meal or porridge. *~vb.* **4.** (*tr.*) to fill (joints) or finish (walls, etc.) with grout. [Old English *grūt;* related to Old Frisian *grēt* sand, Middle High German *grūz*, Middle Dutch *grūte* coarse meal; see GRIT, GROATS] —ˈ**grouter** *n.*

grouts (graʊts) *pl. n.* **1.** *Chiefly Brit.* sediment or grounds, as from making coffee. **2.** a variant of **groats.**

grouty (ˈgraʊtɪ) *adj.* **groutier, groutiest.** *Scot. and northern English dialect.* **1.** muddy; dirty. **2.** (of people's manners) rough; unpolished.

grove (grəʊv) *n.* **1.** a small wooded area or plantation. **2. a.** a road lined with houses and often trees, esp. in a suburban area. **b.** (*cap. as part of a street name*): *Ladbroke Grove.* [Old English *grāf;* related to *grǣfa* thicket, GREAVE, Norwegian *greivla* to intertwine]

grovel (ˈgrɒvᵊl) *vb.* **-els, -elling, -elled** *or U.S.* **-els, -eling, -eled.** (*intr.*) **1.** to humble or abase oneself, as in making apologies or showing respect. **2.** to lie or crawl face downwards, as in fear or humility. **3.** (often foll. by *in*) to indulge or take pleasure (in sensuality or vice). [C16: back formation from obsolete *groveling* (adv.), from Middle English *on grufe* on the face, of Scandinavian origin; compare Old Norse *ā grūfu,* from *grūfa* prone position; see -LING[2]] —ˈ**groveller** *n.* —ˈ**grovellingly** *adv.*

grovet (ˈgrɒvət) *n.* a wrestling hold in which a wrestler in a kneeling position grips the head of his kneeling opponent with one arm and forces his shoulders down with the other.

grow (grəʊ) *vb.* **grows, growing, grew** (gruː), **grown** (grəʊn). **1.** (of an organism or part of an organism) to increase in size or develop (hair, leaves, or other structures). **2.** (*intr.;* usually foll. by *out of* or *from*) to originate, as from an initial cause or source: *the federation grew out of the Empire.* **3.** (*intr.*) to increase in size, number, degree, etc.: *the population is growing rapidly.* **4.** (*intr.*) to change in length or amount in a specified direction: *some plants grow downwards; profits over the years grew downwards.* **5.** (*copula; may take an infinitive*) (esp. of emotions, physical states, etc.) to develop or come into existence or being gradually: *to grow cold; to grow morose; he grew to like her.* **6.** (*intr.;* usually foll. by *up*) to come into existence: *a close friendship grew up between them.* **7.** (*intr.;* foll. by *together*) to be joined gradually by or as by growth: *the branches on the tree grew together.* **8.** (*intr.;* foll. by *away, together,* etc.) to develop a specified state of friendship: *the lovers grew together gradually; many friends grow apart over the years.* **9.** (when *intr.*, foll. by *with*) to become covered with a growth: *the path grew with weeds.* **10.** to produce (plants) by controlling or encouraging their growth, esp. for home consumption or on a commercial basis. ~See also **grow into, grow on, grow out of, grow up.** [Old English *grōwan;* related to Old Norse *grōa,* Old Frisian *grōia,* Old High German *gruoen;* see GREEN, GRASS] —ˈ**growable** *adj.*

grow bag *n.* a plastic bag containing a sufficient amount of a sterile growing medium and nutrients to enable a plant, such as a tomato or pepper, to be grown to full size in it, usually for one season only. [C20: from *Gro-bag,* trademark for the first ones marketed]

grower (ˈgrəʊə) *n.* **1.** a person who grows plants: *a vegetable grower.* **2.** a plant that grows in a specified way: *a fast grower.*

growing pains *pl. n.* **1.** pains in muscles or joints sometimes experienced by children during a period of unusually rapid growth. **2.** difficulties besetting a new enterprise in the early stages of its development.

grow into *vb.* (*intr., prep.*) to become big or mature enough for: *his clothes were always big enough for him to grow into.*

growl (graʊl) *vb.* **1.** (of animals, esp. when hostile) to utter (sounds) in a low inarticulate manner: *the dog growled at us.* **2.** to utter (words) in a gruff or angry manner: *he growled an apology.* **3.** (*intr.*) to make sounds suggestive of an animal growling: *the thunder growled around the lake.* *~n.* **4.** the act or sound of growling. **5.** *Jazz.* an effect resembling a growl, produced at the back of the throat when playing a wind instrument. [C18: from earlier *grolle,* from Old French *grouller* to grumble] —ˈ**growlingly** *adv.*

growler (ˈgraʊlə) *n.* **1.** a person, animal, or thing that growls. **2.** *Brit. slang, obsolete.* a four-wheeled hansom cab. **3.** *Canadian.* a small iceberg that has broken off from a larger iceberg or from a glacier, often hazardous to shipping. **4.** *U.S. slang.* any container, such as a can, for draught beer.

grown (grəʊn) *adj.* **a.** developed or advanced: *fully grown.* **b.** (*in combination*): *half-grown.*

grown-up *adj.* **1.** having reached maturity; adult. **2.** suitable for or characteristic of an adult. *~n.* **3.** an adult.

grow on *vb.* (*intr., prep.*) to become progressively more acceptable or pleasant to: *I don't think much of your new record, but I suppose it will grow on me.*

grow out of *vb.* (*intr., adv. + prep.*) to become too big or mature for: *she soon grew out of her girlish ways.*

growth (grəʊθ) *n.* **1.** the process or act of growing, esp. this process in organisms following assimilation of food. **2.** an increase in size, number, significance, etc. **3.** something grown or growing: *a new growth of hair.* **4.** a stage of development: *a full growth.* **5.** any abnormal tissue, such as a tumour. **6.** (*modifier*) of, relating to, causing or characterized by growth: *a growth industry; growth hormone.*

growth curve *n.* a curve on a graph in which a variable is plotted against time to illustrate the growth of the variable.

growth factor *n.* any of several substances present in serum that induce growth of cells. Excessive amounts of growth factor may be associated with the production of cancer cells.

growth hormone *n.* a hormone synthesized in and secreted by the anterior lobe of the pituitary gland that promotes growth of the long bones in the limbs and increases the synthesis of protein essential for growth. Also called: **somatotrophin.**

growth ring *n.* another name for **annual ring.**

growth shares *pl. n. Finance.* ordinary shares with good prospects of appreciation in yield and value.

growth substance *n. Botany.* any substance, produced naturally by a plant or manufactured commercially, that, in very low concentrations, affects plant growth; a plant hormone.

grow up *vb.* (*intr., adv.*) **1.** to reach maturity; become adult. **2.** to come into existence; develop.

groyne *or esp. U.S.* **groin** (grɔɪn) *n.* a wall or jetty built out from a riverbank or seashore to control erosion. Also called: **spur, breakwater.** [C16: origin uncertain: perhaps altered from GROIN]

grozing iron (ˈgrəʊzɪŋ) *n.* an iron for smoothing joints between lead pipes. [C17: part translation of Dutch *gruisijzer,* from *gruizen* to crush, from *gruis* gravel + *yzer* iron]

GRU *abbrev.* the military intelligence service in the former Soviet Union, the military counterpart of the **KGB.** [from Russian *Glavnoye Razvedyvatelnoye Upravleniye* Main Intelligence Directorate]

grub (grʌb) *vb.* **grubs, grubbing, grubbed.** **1.** (when *tr.*, often foll. by *up* or *out*) to search for and pull up (roots, stumps, etc.) by digging in the ground. **2.** to dig up the surface of (ground, soil, etc.), esp. to clear away roots, stumps, etc. **3.** (*intr.;* often foll. by *in* or *among*) to search carefully. **4.** (*intr.*) to work unceasingly, esp. at a dull task or research. **5.** *Slang.* to provide (a person) with food or (of a person) to take food. **6.** (*tr.*) *Slang, chiefly U.S.* to scrounge: *to grub a cigarette.* *~n.* **7.** the short legless larva of certain insects, esp. beetles. **8.** *Slang.* food; victuals. **9.** a person who works hard, esp. in a dull plodding way. **10.** *Brit. informal.* a dirty child. [C13: of Germanic origin; compare Old High German *grubilōn* to dig, German *grübeln* to rack one's brain, Middle Dutch *grobben* to scrape together; see GRAVE[3], GROOVE]

grubber (ˈgrʌbə) *n.* **1.** a person who grubs. **2.** another name for **grub hoe.**

grubby (ˈgrʌbɪ) *adj.* **-bier, -biest.** **1.** dirty; slovenly. **2.** mean; beggarly. **3.** infested with grubs. —ˈ**grubbily** *adv.* —ˈ**grubbiness** *n.*

grub hoe *or* **grubbing hoe** *n.* a heavy hoe for grubbing up roots. Also called: **grubber.**

grub screw *n.* a small headless screw having a slot cut for a screwdriver or a socket for a hexagon key and used to secure a sliding component in a determined position.

grubstake (ˈgrʌb,steɪk) *n.* **1.** *U.S. and Canadian. informal.* supplies provided for a prospector on the condition that the donor has a stake in any finds. *~vb.* (*tr.*) **2.** *U.S. informal.* to furnish with such supplies. **3.** *Chiefly U.S. and Canadian.* to supply (a person) with a stake in a gambling game. —ˈ**grub,staker** *n.*

Grub Street *n.* **1.** the world or class of literary hacks, etc. *~adj. also* ˈ**Grub,street.** **2.** (*sometimes not cap.*) relating to or characteristic of hack literature. [named after *Grub Street,* a former street in London frequented by literary hacks and needy authors]

grudge (grʌdʒ) *n.* **1.** a persistent feeling of resentment, esp. one due to some cause, such as an insult or injury. *~vb.* **2.** (*tr.*) to give or allow unwillingly. **3.** to feel resentful or envious about (someone else's success, possessions, etc.). [C15: from Old French *grouchier* to grumble, probably of Germanic origin; compare Old High German *grunnizōn* to grunt] —ˈ**grudgeless** *adj.* —ˈ**grudger** *n.* —ˈ**grudging** *adj.* —ˈ**grudgingly** *adv.*

grue (gruː) *Scot.* ~*n.* **1.** a shiver or shudder; a creeping of the flesh. ~*vb.* (*intr.*) **2.** to shiver or shudder. **3.** to feel strong aversion. [C14: of Scandinavian origin; compare Old Swedish *grua,* Old Danish *grue;* related to German *grauen,* Dutch *gruwen* to abhor]

gruel (ˈgruːəl) *n.* a drink or thin porridge, made by boiling meal, esp. oatmeal, in water or milk. [C14: from Old French, of Germanic origin; see GROUT]

gruelling *or U.S.* **grueling** (ˈgruːəlɪŋ) *adj.* **1.** extremely severe or tiring: *a gruelling interview.* ~*n.* **2.** *Informal.* a severe or tiring experience, esp. punishment. [C19: from now obsolete vb. *gruel* to exhaust, punish]

gruesome (ˈgruːsəm) *adj.* inspiring repugnance and horror; ghastly. [C16: originally Northern English and Scottish; see GRUE, -SOME[1]] —ˈ**gruesomely** *adv.* —ˈ**gruesomeness** *n.*

gruff (grʌf) *adj.* **1.** rough or surly in manner, speech, etc.: *a gruff reply.* **2.** (of a voice, bark, etc.) low and throaty. [C16: originally Scottish, from Dutch *grof,* of Germanic origin; compare Old High German *girob;* related to Old English *hrēof,* Lithuanian *kraupùs*] —ˈ**gruffish** *adj.* —ˈ**gruffly** *adv.* —ˈ**gruffness** *n.*

grugru (ˈgruːgruː) *n.* **1.** any of several tropical American palms, esp. *Acrocomia sclerocarpa,* which has a spiny trunk and leaves and edible nuts. **2.** the large edible wormlike larva of a weevil, *Rhynchophorus palmarum,* that infests this palm. [C18: from American Spanish (Puerto Rican dialect) *grugrú,* of Cariban origin]

grumble (ˈgrʌmbᵊl) *vb.* **1.** to utter (complaints) in a nagging or discontented way. **2.** (*intr.*) to make low dull rumbling sounds. ~*n.* **3.** a complaint; grouse. **4.** a low rumbling sound. [C16: from Middle Low German *grommelen,* of Germanic origin; see GRIM] —ˈ**grumbler** *n.* —ˈ**grumblingly** *adv.* —ˈ**grumbly** *adj.*

grumbling appendix *n. Informal.* a condition in which the appendix causes intermittent pain or discomfort but appendicitis has not developed.

grummet (ˈgrʌmɪt) *n.* another word for **grommet.**

grumous (ˈgruːməs) *or* **grumose** (ˈgruːməʊs) *adj.* (esp. of plant parts) consisting of granular tissue. [C17: from *grume* a clot of blood, from Latin *grumus* a little heap; related to CRUMB]

grump (grʌmp) *Informal.* ~*n.* **1.** a surly or bad-tempered person. **2.** (*pl.*) a sulky or morose mood (esp. in the phrase **have the grumps**). ~*vb.* **3.** (*intr.*) to complain or grumble. [C18: dialect *grump* surly remark, probably of imitative origin]

grumpy (ˈgrʌmpɪ) *or* **grumpish** (ˈgrʌmpɪʃ) *adj.* **grumpier, grumpiest.** peevish; sulky. [C18: from GRUMP + -Y[1]] —ˈ**grumpily** *or* ˈ**grumpishly** *adv.* —ˈ**grumpiness** *or* ˈ**grumpishness** *n.*

Grundy (ˈgrʌndɪ) *n.* a narrow-minded person who keeps critical watch on the propriety of others. [C18: named after Mrs *Grundy,* the character in T. Morton's play *Speed the Plough* (1798)] —ˈ**Grundyˌism** *n.* —ˈ**Grundyist** *or* ˈ**Grundyite** *n.*

grunion (ˈgrʌnjən) *n.* a Californian marine teleost fish, *Leuresthes tenuis,* that spawns on beaches: family *Atherinidae* (silversides). [C20: probably from Spanish *gruñón* a grunter]

grunt (grʌnt) *vb.* **1.** (*intr.*) (esp. of pigs and some other animals) to emit a low short gruff noise. **2.** (when *tr., may take a clause as object*) to express something gruffly: *he grunted his answer.* ~*n.* **3.** the characteristic low short gruff noise of pigs, etc., or a similar sound, as of disgust. **4.** any of various mainly tropical marine sciaenid fishes, such as *Haemulon macrostomum* (**Spanish grunt**), that utter a grunting sound when caught. **5.** *U.S. slang.* an infantry soldier or U.S. marine, esp. in the Vietnam War. [Old English *grunnettan,* probably of imitative origin; compare Old High German *grunnizōn, grunni* moaning, Latin *grunnīre*] —ˈ**gruntingly** *adv.*

grunter (ˈgrʌntə) *n.* **1.** a person or animal that grunts, esp. a pig. **2.** another name for **grunt** (sense 4). **3.** *Austral. slang.* a promiscuous woman.

gruntled (ˈgrʌntᵊld) *adj. Informal.* happy or contented; satisfied. [C20: back formation from DISGRUNTLED]

gruppetto (grʊˈpɛtəʊ) *n., pl.* **-ti** (-tiː). *Music.* a turn. [C19: from Italian, diminutive of *gruppo* a group, a turn]

Grus (grʊs) *n., Latin genitive* **Gruis** (ˈgruːɪs). a constellation in the S hemisphere lying near Phoenix and Piscis Austrinus and containing two second magnitude stars. [via New Latin from Latin: crane]

Gruyère *or* **Gruyère cheese** (ˈgruːjɛə; *French* gryjɛr) *n.* a hard flat whole-milk cheese, pale yellow in colour and with holes. [C19: after *Gruyère,* Switzerland, where it originated]

gr. wt. *abbrev. for* gross weight.

gryke (graɪk) *n.* a variant spelling of **grike.**

gryphon (ˈgrɪfᵊn) *n.* a variant of **griffin**[1].

grysbok (ˈgraɪsˌbɒk) *n.* either of two small antelopes, *Raphicerus melanotis* or *R. sharpei,* of central and southern Africa, having small straight horns. [C18: Afrikaans, from Dutch *grijs* grey + *bok* BUCK[1]]

GS *abbrev. for:* **1.** General Secretary. **2.** General Staff.

gs. *abbrev. for* guineas.

GSR *abbrev. for* galvanic skin response.

G-string *n.* **1.** a piece of cloth worn by striptease artistes covering the pubic area only and attached to a very narrow waistband. **2.** a strip of cloth attached to the front and back of a waistband and covering the loins. **3.** *Music.* a string tuned to G, such as the lowest string of a violin.

G-suit *n.* a close-fitting garment covering the legs and abdomen that is worn by the crew of high-speed aircraft and can be pressurized to prevent blackout during certain manoeuvres. Also called: **anti-G suit.** [C20: from *g*(*ravity*) *suit*]

gt *abbrev. for:* **1.** *Bookbinding.* gilt. **2.** great.

GT *abbrev. for* **gran turismo,** a high-performance luxury sports car with a hard fixed roof, designed for covering long distances.

gt. *pl.* **gtt.** *Pharmacy. abbrev. for* gutta.

GTC *abbrev. for:* **1.** Also: **gtc.** (on a commercial order for goods) good till cancelled (*or* countermanded). **2.** (in Scotland) General Teaching Council.

gtd *abbrev. for* guaranteed.

g.u. *or* **GU** *abbrev. for* genitourinary.

guacamole *or* **guachamole** (ˌgwɑːkəˈməʊlɪ) *n.* **1.** a spread of mashed avocado, tomato pulp, mayonnaise, and seasoning. **2.** any of various Mexican or South American salads containing avocado. [from American Spanish, from Nahuatl *ahuacamolli,* from *ahuacatl* avocado + *molli* sauce]

guacharo (ˈgwɑːtʃəˌrəʊ) *n., pl.* **-ros.** another name for **oilbird.** [C19: from Spanish *guácharo*]

guaco (ˈgwɑːkəʊ) *n., pl.* **-cos. 1.** any of several tropical American plants whose leaves are used as an antidote to snakebite, esp. the climbers *Mikania guaco,* family *Compositae* (composites), or *Aristolochia maxima* (*A. serpentina*), family *Aristolochiaceae.* **2.** the leaves of any of these plants. [C19: from American Spanish]

guaiacol (ˈgwaɪəˌkɒl) *n.* a yellowish oily creosote-like liquid extracted from guaiacum resin and hardwood tar, used medicinally as an expectorant. Formula: $C_7H_8O_2$. [from GUAIAC(UM) + -OL[2]]

guaiacum *or* **guaiocum** (ˈgwaɪəkəm) *n.* **1.** any tropical American evergreen tree of the zygophyllaceous genus *Guaiacum,* such as the lignum vitae. **2.** the hard heavy wood of any of these trees. **3.** Also called: **guaiac** (ˈgwaɪæk). a brownish resin obtained from the lignum vitae, used medicinally and in making varnishes. [C16: New Latin, from Spanish *guayaco,* of Taino origin]

guan (gwɑːn) *n.* any gallinaceous bird of the genera *Penelope, Pipile,* etc., of Central and South America: family *Cracidae* (curassows). [C18: from American Spanish]

guanaco (gwɑːˈnɑːkəʊ) *n., pl.* **-cos.** a cud-chewing South American artiodactyl mammal, *Lama guanicoe,* closely related to the domesticated llama: family *Camelidae.* [C17: from Spanish, from Quechuan *huanacu*]

guanase (ˈgwɑːneɪz) *n.* an enzyme that converts guanine to xanthine by removal of an amino group. [C20: from GUAN(INE) + -ASE]

guanidine (ˈgwɑːnɪˌdiːn, -dɪn, ˈgwænɪ-) *or* **guanidin** (ˈgwɑːnɪdɪn, ˈgwænɪ-) *n.* a strongly alkaline crystalline substance, soluble in water and found in plant and animal tissues. It is used in organic synthesis. Formula: $HNC(NH_2)_2$. Also called: **carbamidine, iminourea.** [C19: from GUANO + -ID[3] + -INE[2]]

guanine (ˈgwɑːniːn, ˈguːəˌniːn) *n.* a white almost insoluble compound: one of the purine bases in nucleic acids. Formula: $C_5H_5N_5O$. [C19: from GUANO + -INE[2]]

guano (ˈgwɑːnəʊ) *n., pl.* **-nos. 1.** the dried excrement of fish-eating sea birds, deposited in rocky coastal regions of South America: contains the urates, oxalates, and phosphates of ammonium and calcium and is used as a fertilizer. **2.** any similar but artificially produced fertilizer. [C17: from Spanish, from Quechuan *huano* dung]

guanosine (ˈgwɑːnəˌsiːn, -ˌziːn) *n. Biochem.* a nucleoside consisting of guanine and ribose.

guanylic acid (gwəˈnɪlɪk) *n.* a nucleotide consisting of guanine, ribose or deoxyribose, and a phosphate group. It is a constituent of DNA or RNA. Also called: **guanosine monophosphate.**

guar (gwɑː) *n.* **1.** a leguminous Indian plant, *Cyamopsis tetragonolobus,* grown as a fodder crop and for the gum obtained from its seeds. **2.** Also called: **guar gum.** a gum obtained from the seeds of this plant, used as a stabilizer and thickening agent in food (E412) and as sizing for paper. [C19: from Hindi]

guarani (ˈgwɑːrənɪ) *n., pl.* **-ni** *or* **-nis.** the standard monetary unit of Paraguay, divided into 100 centimos.

Guarani (ˌgwɑːrəˈniː) *n.* **1.** (*pl.* **-ni** *or* **-nis**) a member of a South American Indian people of Paraguay, S Brazil, and Bolivia. **2.** the language of this people, belonging to the Tupi-Guarani family; one of the official languages of Paraguay, along with Spanish.

guarantee (ˌgærənˈtiː) *n.* **1.** a formal assurance, esp. in writing, that a product, service, etc., will meet certain standards or specifications. **2.** *Law.* a promise, esp. a collateral agreement, to answer for the debt, default, or miscarriage of another. **3. a.** a person, company, etc., to whom a guarantee is made. **b.** a person, company, etc., who gives a guarantee. **4.** a person who acts as a guarantor. **5.** something that makes a specified condition or outcome certain. **6.** a variant spelling of **guaranty.** ~*vb.* **-tees, -teeing, -teed.** (*mainly tr.*) **7.** (*also intr.*) to take responsibility for (someone else's debts, obligations, etc.). **8.** to serve as a guarantee for. **9.** to secure or furnish security for: *a small deposit will guarantee any dress.* **10.** (usually foll. by *from* or *against*) to undertake to protect or keep secure, as against injury, loss, etc. **11.** to ensure: *good planning will guarantee success.* **12.** (*may take a clause as object or an infinitive*) to promise or make certain. [C17: perhaps from Spanish *garante* or French *garant,* of Germanic origin; compare WARRANT]

guarantor (ˌgærənˈtɔː) *n.* a person who gives or is bound by a guarantee or guaranty; surety.

guaranty (ˈgærəntɪ) *n., pl.* **-ties.** **1.** a pledge of responsibility for fulfilling another person's obligations in case of that person's default. **2.** a thing given or taken as security for a guaranty. **3.** the act of providing security. **4.** a person who acts as a guarantor. *~vb.* **-ties, -tying, -tied.** **5.** a variant of **guarantee.** [C16: from Old French *garantie,* variant of *warantie,* of Germanic origin; see WARRANTY]

guard (gɑːd) *vb.* **1.** to watch over or shield (a person or thing) from danger or harm; protect. **2.** to keep watch over (a prisoner or other potentially dangerous person or thing), as to prevent escape. **3.** (*tr.*) to control: *to guard one's tongue.* **4.** (*intr.;* usually foll. by *against*) to take precautions. **5.** to control entrance and exit through (a gate, door, etc.). **6.** (*tr.*) to provide (machinery, etc.) with a device to protect the operator. **7.** (*tr.*) **a.** *Chess, cards.* to protect or cover (a chess man or card) with another. **b.** *Curling, bowling.* to protect or cover (a stone or bowl) by placing one's own stone or bowl between it and another player. **8.** (*tr.*) *Archaic.* to accompany as a guard. *~n.* **9.** a person or group who keeps a protecting, supervising, or restraining watch or control over people, such as prisoners, things, etc. Related adj.: **custodial.** **10.** a person or group of people, such as soldiers, who form a ceremonial escort: *guard of honour.* **11.** *Brit.* the official in charge of a train. **12.** **a.** the act or duty of protecting, restraining, or supervising. **b.** (*as modifier*): *guard duty.* **13.** *Irish.* another word for **garda.** **14.** a device, part, or attachment on an object, such as a weapon or machine tool, designed to protect the user against injury, as on the hilt of a sword or the trigger of a firearm. **15.** anything that provides or is intended to provide protection: *a guard against infection.* **16.** **a.** another name for **safety chain.** **b.** a long neck chain often holding a chatelaine. **17.** See **guard ring.** **18.** *Sport.* an article of light tough material worn to protect any of various parts of the body. **19.** *Basketball.* **a.** the position of either of the two defensive players in a team. **b.** a player in this position. **20.** the posture of defence or readiness in fencing, boxing, cricket, etc. **21.** **take guard.** *Cricket.* (of a batsman) to choose a position in front of the wicket to receive the bowling, esp. by requesting the umpire to indicate his position relative to the stumps. **22.** **give guard.** *Cricket.* (of an umpire) to indicate such a position to a batsman. **23.** **off (one's) guard.** having one's defences down; unprepared. **24.** **on (one's) guard.** prepared to face danger, difficulties, etc. **25.** **stand guard.** (of a military sentry, etc.) to keep watch. **26.** **mount guard.** **a.** (of a sentry) to begin to keep watch. **b.** (with *over*) to take up a protective or defensive stance (over something). [C15: from Old French *garde,* from *garder* to protect, of Germanic origin; compare Spanish *guardar;* see WARD] —ˈ**guardable** *adj.* —ˈ**guarder** *n.* —ˈ**guardless** *adj.* —ˈ**guard**ˌ**like** *adj.*

guardant *or* **gardant** (ˈgɑːdᵊnt) *adj.* (*usually postpositive*) *Heraldry.* (of a beast) shown full face. [C16: from French *gardant* guarding, from *garder* to GUARD]

guard band *n.* a space left vacant between two radio frequency bands, or between two tracks on a magnetic tape recording, to avoid mutual interference.

guard cell *n. Botany.* one of a pair of crescent-shaped cells that surround a pore (stoma) in the epidermis. Changes in the turgidity of the cells cause the opening and closing of the stoma.

guarded (ˈgɑːdɪd) *adj.* **1.** protected or kept under surveillance. **2.** prudent, restrained, or noncommittal: *a guarded reply.* —ˈ**guardedly** *adv.* —ˈ**guardedness** *n.*

guardee (ˌgɑːˈdiː) *n. Brit. informal.* a guardsman, esp. considered as representing smartness and dash.

guard hair *n.* any of the coarse hairs that form the outer fur in certain mammals, rising above the underfur.

guardhouse (ˈgɑːdˌhaʊs) *n. Military.* a building serving as the headquarters or a post for military police and in which military prisoners are detained.

guardian (ˈgɑːdɪən) *n.* **1.** one who looks after, protects, or defends: *the guardian of public morals.* **2.** **a.** *Law.* someone legally appointed to manage the affairs of a person incapable of acting for himself, as a minor or person of unsound mind. **b.** *Social welfare.* (in England) a local authority, or person accepted by it, named under the Mental Health Act 1983 as having the powers to require a mentally disordered person to live at a specified place, attend for treatment, and be accessible to a doctor or social worker. **3.** (*often cap.*) (in England) another word for **custos.** *~adj.* **4.** protecting or safeguarding. —ˈ**guardian**ˌ**ship** *n.*

guardrail (ˈgɑːdˌreɪl) *n.* **1.** a railing at the side of a staircase, road, etc., as a safety barrier. **2.** Also called (Brit.): **checkrail.** *Railways.* a short metal rail fitted to the inside of the main rail to provide additional support in keeping a train's wheels on the track.

guard ring *n.* **1.** Also called: **guard, keeper ring.** *Jewellery.* an extra ring worn to prevent another from slipping off the finger. **2.** an electrode used to counteract distortion of the electric fields at the edges of other electrodes in a capacitor or electron lens.

guardroom (ˈgɑːdˌruːm, -ˌrʊm) *n.* **1.** a room used by guards. **2.** a room in which prisoners are confined under guard.

Guards (gɑːdz) *pl. n.* **a.** (esp. in European armies) any of various regiments responsible for ceremonial duties and, formerly, the protection of the head of state: *the Life Guards; the Grenadier Guards.* **b.** (*as modifier*): *a Guards regiment.*

guardsman (ˈgɑːdzmən) *n., pl.* **-men.** **1.** (in Britain) a member of a Guards battalion or regiment. **2.** (in the U.S.) a member of the National Guard. **3.** a guard.

guard's van *n. Railways, Brit. and N.Z.* the van in which the guard travels, usually attached to the rear of a train. U.S. and Canadian equivalent: **caboose.**

Guarneri (gwɑːˈnɪərɪ; *Italian* gwarˈnɛːri), **Guarnieri** (*Italian* gwarˈnjɛːri), *or* **Guarnerius** (gwɑːˈnɛərɪəs) *n., pl.* **Guarneris, Guarnieris,** *or* **Guarneriuses.** a violin made in the 17th or 18th century by a member of the Italian Guarneri family.

Guat. *abbrev. for* Guatemala.

Guatemalan (ˌgwɑːtəˈmɑːlən) *adj.* **1.** of or relating to Guatemala, a republic in Central America, or its people. *~n.* **2.** a native or inhabitant of Guatemala.

guava (ˈgwɑːvə) *n.* **1.** any of various tropical American trees of the myrtaceous genus *Psidium,* esp. *P. guajava,* grown in tropical regions for their edible fruit. **2.** the fruit of such a tree, having yellow skin and pink pulp: used to make jellies, jams, etc. [C16: from Spanish *guayaba,* from a South American Indian word]

guayule (gwəˈjuːlɪ) *n.* **1.** a bushy shrub, *Parthenium argentatum,* of the southwestern U.S.: family *Compositae* (composites). **2.** rubber derived from the sap of this plant. [from American Spanish, from Nahuatl *cuauhuli,* from *cuahuitl* tree + *uli* gum]

gubbins (ˈgʌbɪnz) *n. Informal.* **1.** an object of little or no value. **2.** a small device or gadget. **3.** odds and ends; litter or rubbish. **4.** a silly person. [C16 (meaning: fragments): from obsolete *gobbon,* probably related to GOBBET]

gubernatorial (ˌgjuːbənəˈtɔːrɪəl, ˌguː-) *adj. Chiefly U.S.* of or relating to a governor. [C18: from Latin *gubernātor* governor]

guberniya *Russian.* (guˈbjɛrnɪjə) *n.* **1.** a territorial division of imperial Russia. **2.** a territorial and administrative subdivision in the former Soviet Union. [from Russian: government, ultimately from Latin *gubernāre* to GOVERN]

guck (gʌk, gʊk) *n.* slimy matter; gunk. [C20: perhaps a blend of GOO and MUCK]

guddle (ˈgʌdᵊl) *Scot.* *~vb.* **1.** to catch (fish) by groping with the hands under the banks or stones of a stream. *~n.* **2.** a muddle; confusion. [C19: of unknown origin]

gudgeon[1] (ˈgʌdʒən) *n.* **1.** a small slender European freshwater cyprinid fish, *Gobio gobio,* with a barbel on each side of the mouth: used as bait by anglers. **2.** any of various other fishes, such as the goby. **3.** bait or enticement. **4.** *Slang.* a person who is easy to trick or cheat. *~vb.* **5.** (*tr.*) *Slang.* to trick or cheat. [C15: from Old French *gougon,* probably from Latin *gōbius;* see GOBY]

gudgeon[2] (ˈgʌdʒən) *n.* **1.** the female or socket portion of a pinned hinge. **2.** *Nautical.* one of two or more looplike sockets, fixed to the transom of a boat, into which the pintles of a rudder are fitted. [C14: from Old French *goujon,* perhaps from Late Latin *gulbia* chisel]

gudgeon pin *n. Brit.* the pin through the skirt of a piston in an internal-combustion engine, to which the little end of the connecting rod is attached. U.S. and Canadian name: **wrist pin.**

guelder-rose (ˈgɛldəˌrəʊz) *n.* a Eurasian caprifoliaceous shrub, *Viburnum opulus,* with clusters of white flowers and small red fruits. [C16: from Dutch *geldersche roos,* from *Gelderland* or *Gelders,* province of the E Netherlands]

Guelph *or* **Guelf** (gwɛlf) *n.* **1.** a member of the political faction in medieval Italy that supported the power of the pope against the German emperors. Compare **Ghibelline.** **2.** a member of a secret society in 19th-century Italy opposed to foreign rule. —ˈ**Guelphic** *or* ˈ**Guelfic** *adj.* —ˈ**Guelphism** *or* ˈ**Guelfism** *n.*

guenon (gəˈnɒn) *n.* any slender agile Old World monkey of the genus *Cercopithecus,* inhabiting wooded regions of Africa and having long hind limbs and tail and long hair surrounding the face. [C19: from French, of unknown origin]

guerdon (ˈgɜːdᵊn) *Poetic.* *~n.* **1.** a reward or payment. *~vb.* **2.** (*tr.*) to give a guerdon to. [C14: from Old French *gueredon,* of Germanic origin; compare Old High German *widarlōn,* Old English *witherlēan;* final element influenced by Latin *dōnum* gift] —ˈ**guerdoner** *n.*

guereza (gəˈrɛzə) *n.* a handsome colobus monkey of the mountain forests of Ethiopia. [C19: its native name]

Guernsey (ˈgɜːnzɪ) *n.* **1.** a breed of dairy cattle producing rich creamy milk, originating from the island of Guernsey in the English Channel. **2.** (*sometimes not cap.*) a seaman's knitted woollen sweater. **3.** (*not cap.*) *Austral.* a sleeveless woollen shirt or jumper worn by a football player. **4.** **get a guernsey.** *Austral.* to be selected or gain recognition for something.

Guernsey lily *n.* See **nerine.**

guerrilla *or* **guerilla** (gəˈrɪlə) *n.* **a.** a member of an irregular usually politically motivated armed force that combats stronger regular forces, such as the army or police. **b.** (*as modifier*): *guerrilla warfare.* [C19: from Spanish, diminutive of *guerra* WAR] —**guer**ˈ**rillaism** *or* **gue**ˈ**rillaism** *n.*

guess (gɛs) *vb.* (when *tr., may take a clause as object*) **1.** (when *intr.,* often foll. by *at* or *about*) to form or express an uncertain estimate or conclusion (about something), based on insufficient information: *guess what we're having for dinner.* **2.** to arrive at a correct estimate of (something) by guessing: *he guessed my age.* **3.** *Informal, chiefly U.S. and Canadian.* to believe, think, or suppose (something): *I guess I'll go now.* **4. keep a person guessing.** to let a person remain in a state of uncertainty. *~n.* **5.** an estimate or conclusion arrived at by guessing: *a bad guess.* **6.** the act of guessing. **7. anyone's guess.** something difficult to predict. [C13: probably of Scandinavian origin; compare Old Swedish *gissa,* Old Danish *gitse,* Middle Dutch *gissen;* see GET] —**'guessable** *adj.* —**'guesser** *n.* —**'guessingly** *adv.*

guesstimate *or* **guestimate** *Informal.* *~n.* ('gɛstɪmɪt). **1.** an estimate calculated mainly or only by guesswork. *~vb.* ('gɛstɪˌmeɪt). **2.** to form a guesstimate of.

guesswork ('gɛsˌwɜːk) *n.* **1.** a set of conclusions, estimates, etc., arrived at by guessing. **2.** the process of making guesses.

guest (gɛst) *n.* **1.** a person who is entertained, taken out to eat, etc., and paid for by another. **2. a.** a person who receives hospitality at the home of another: *a weekend guest.* **b.** (*as modifier*): *the guest room.* **3. a.** a person who receives the hospitality of a government, establishment, or organization. **b.** (*as modifier*): *a guest speaker.* **4. a.** an actor, contestant, entertainer, etc., taking part as a visitor in a programme in which there are also regular participants. **b.** (*as modifier*): *a guest appearance.* **5.** a patron of a hotel, boarding house, restaurant, etc. **6.** *Zoology.* a nontechnical name for **inquiline.** **7. be my guest.** *Informal.* do as you like. *~vb.* **8.** (*intr.*) (in theatre and broadcasting) to be a guest: *to guest on a show.* [Old English *giest* guest, stranger, enemy; related to Old Norse *gestr,* Gothic *gasts,* Old High German *gast,* Old Slavonic *gostĭ,* Latin *hostis* enemy]

guest beer *n.* a draught beer stocked by a bar, often for a limited period, in addition to its usual range.

guesthouse ('gɛstˌhaʊs) *n.* a private home or boarding house offering accommodation, esp. to travellers.

guest rope *n. Nautical.* any line sent or trailed over the side of a vessel as a convenience for boats drawing alongside, as an aid in warping or towing, etc.

guff (gʌf) *n. Slang.* ridiculous or insolent talk. [C19: imitative of empty talk; compare dialect Norwegian *gufs* puff of wind]

guffaw (gʌ'fɔː) *n.* **1.** a crude and boisterous laugh. *~vb.* **2.** to laugh crudely and boisterously or express (something) in this way. [C18: of imitative origin]

Guianese (ˌgaɪə'niːz, ˌgɪə-) *or* **Guianan** (gaɪ'ænən, gɪ'ɑːnən) *adj.* **1.** of or relating to Guiana, a region of NE South America including Guyana, Surinam, and French Guiana. *~n.* **2.** a person inhabiting this region.

guichet ('giːʃeɪ) *n.* a grating, hatch, or small opening in a wall, esp. a ticket-office window. [C19: from French]

guid (gyd, gɪd) *adj.* a Scot. word for **good.**

guidance ('gaɪdᵊns) *n.* **1.** leadership, instruction, or direction. **2. a.** counselling or advice on educational, vocational, or psychological matters. **b.** (*as modifier*): *the marriage-guidance counsellor.* **3.** something that guides. **4.** any process by which the flight path of a missile is controlled in flight. See also **guided missile.**

guide (gaɪd) *vb.* **1.** to lead the way for (a person). **2.** to control the movement or course of (an animal, vehicle, etc.) by physical action; steer. **3.** to supervise or instruct (a person). **4.** (*tr.*) to direct the affairs of (a person, company, nation, etc.): *he guided the country through the war.* **5.** (*tr.*) to advise or influence (a person) in his standards or opinions: *let truth guide you always.* *~n.* **6. a.** a person, animal, or thing that guides. **b.** (*as modifier*): *a guide dog.* **7.** a person, usually paid, who conducts tour expeditions, etc. **8.** a model or criterion, as in moral standards or accuracy. **9.** See **guidebook.** **10.** a book that instructs or explains the fundamentals of a subject or skill: *a guide to better living.* **11.** a mark used to direct the reader's eye to a place on a page of printing. **12.** any device that directs the motion of a tool or machine part. **13. a.** a mark, sign, etc., that points the way. **b.** (*in combination*): *guidepost.* **14.** *Spiritualism.* a spirit believed to influence a medium so as to direct what he utters and convey messages through him. **15. a.** *Naval.* a ship in a formation used as a reference for manoeuvres, esp. with relation to maintaining the correct formation and disposition. **b.** *Military.* a soldier stationed to one side of a column or line to regulate alignment, show the way, etc. [C14: from (Old) French *guider,* of Germanic origin; compare Old English *wītan* to observe] —**'guidable** *adj.* —**'guideless** *adj.* —**'guider** *n.* —**'guiding** *adj., n.*

Guide (gaɪd) *n.* (*sometimes not cap.*) a member of an organization for girls equivalent to the Scouts. U.S. equivalent: **Girl Scout.**

guidebook ('gaɪdˌbʊk) *n.* a handbook with information for visitors to a place, as a historic building, museum, or foreign country. Also called: **guide.**

guided missile *n.* a missile, esp. one that is rocket-propelled, having a flight path controlled during flight either by radio signals or by internal preset or self-actuating homing devices. See also **command guidance, field guidance, homing guidance, inertial guidance, terrestrial guidance.**

guide dog *n.* a dog that has been specially trained to live with and accompany someone who is blind, enabling the blind person to move about safely.

guideline ('gaɪdˌlaɪn) *n.* **1.** a principle put forward to set standards or determine a course of action. **2.** *Printing.* a lightly marked line used to facilitate the alignment of letters, drawings, etc.

guidepost ('gaɪdˌpəʊst) *n.* **1.** a sign on a post by a road indicating directions. **2.** a principle or guideline.

Guider ('gaɪdə) *n.* (*sometimes not cap.*) **1.** in full: **Guide Guider.** a woman leader of a company of Guides. **2. Brownie Guider.** a woman leader of a pack of Brownie Guides.

guide rope *n.* **1.** a stay or rope attached to another rope that is lifting a load, either to steady the load or guide the rope. **2.** another name for **dragrope** (sense 2).

guide vanes *pl. n.* fixed aerofoils that direct air, gas, or water into the moving blades of a turbine or into or around bends in ducts with minimum loss of energy.

guidon ('gaɪdᵊn) *n.* **1.** a small pennant, used as a marker or standard, esp. by cavalry regiments. **2.** the man or vehicle that carries this. [C16: from French, from Old Provençal *guidoo,* from *guida* GUIDE]

guild *or* **gild** (gɪld) *n.* **1.** an organization, club, or fellowship. **2.** (esp. in medieval Europe) an association of men sharing the same interests, such as merchants or artisans: formed for mutual aid and protection and to maintain craft standards or pursue some other purpose such as communal worship. **3.** *Ecology.* a group of plants, such as a group of epiphytes, that share certain habits or characteristics. [C14: of Scandinavian origin; compare Old Norse *gjald* payment, *gildi* guild; related to Old English *gield* offering, Old High German *gelt* money]

guilder ('gɪldə) *or* **gulden** *n., pl.* **-ders, -der** *or* **-dens, -den.** **1.** Also: **gilder.** the standard monetary unit of the Netherlands, divided into 100 cents. **2.** the standard monetary unit of the Netherlands Antilles and Surinam, divided into 100 cents. **3.** any of various former gold or silver coins of Germany, Austria, or the Netherlands. [C15: changed from Middle Dutch *gulden,* literally: GOLDEN]

guildhall ('gɪldˌhɔːl) *n.* **1.** *Brit.* **a.** the hall of a guild or corporation. **b.** a town hall. **2.** Also: **gildhall.** the meeting place of a medieval guild.

guildsman, gildsman ('gɪldzmən) *or* (*fem.*) **guildswoman, gildswoman** *n., pl.* **-men** *or* **-women.** a member of a guild.

guild socialism *n.* a form of socialism advocated in Britain in the early 20th century. Industry was to be owned by the state but managed and controlled by worker-controlled guilds. —**guild socialist** *n.*

guile (gaɪl) *n.* clever or crafty character or behaviour. [C18: from Old French *guile,* of Germanic origin; see WILE] —**'guileful** *adj.* —**'guilefully** *adv.* —**'guilefulness** *n.*

guileless ('gaɪllɪs) *adj.* free from guile; ingenuous. —**'guilelessly** *adv.* —**'guilelessness** *n.*

guillemot ('gɪlɪˌmɒt) *n.* any northern oceanic diving bird of the genera *Uria* and *Cepphus,* having a black-and-white plumage and long narrow bill: family *Alcidae* (auks, etc.), order *Charadriiformes.* [C17: from French, diminutive of *Guillaume* William]

guilloche (gɪ'lɒʃ) *n.* an ornamental band or border with a repeating pattern of two or more interwoven wavy lines, as in architecture. [C19: from French: tool used in ornamental work, perhaps from *Guillaume* William]

guillotine *n.* ('gɪləˌtiːn). **1. a.** a device for beheading persons, consisting of a weighted blade set between two upright posts. **b. the guillotine.** execution by this instrument. **2.** a device for cutting or trimming sheet material, such as paper or sheet metal, consisting of a blade inclined at a small angle that descends onto the sheet. **3.** a surgical instrument for removing tonsils, growths in the throat, etc. **4.** Also called: **closure by compartment.** (in Parliament, etc.) a form of closure under which a bill is divided into compartments, groups of which must be completely dealt with each day. *~vb.* (ˌgɪlə'tiːn). (*tr.*) **5.** to behead (a person) by guillotine. **6.** (in Parliament, etc.) to limit debate on (a bill, motion, etc.) by the guillotine. [C18: from French, named after Joseph Ignace *Guillotin* (1738–1814), French physician, who advocated its use in 1789] —ˌ**guillo'tiner** *n.*

guilt (gɪlt) *n.* **1.** the fact or state of having done wrong or committed an offence. **2.** responsibility for a criminal or moral offence deserving punishment or a penalty. **3.** remorse or self-reproach caused by feeling that one is responsible for a wrong or offence. **4.** *Archaic.* sin or crime. [Old English *gylt,* of obscure origin]

guiltless ('gɪltlɪs) *adj.* free of all responsibility for wrongdoing or crime; innocent. —**'guiltlessly** *adv.* —**'guiltlessness** *n.*

guilty ('gɪltɪ) *adj.* **guiltier, guiltiest.** **1.** responsible for an offence or misdeed. **2.** *Law.* having committed an offence or adjudged to have done so: *the accused was found guilty.* **3. plead guilty.** *Law.* (of a person charged with an offence) to admit responsibility; confess. **4.** of, showing, or characterized by guilt. —**'guiltily** *adv.* —**'guiltiness** *n.*

guimpe (gɪmp, gæmp) *n.* **1.** a short blouse with sleeves worn under a pinafore dress. **2.** a fill-in for a low-cut dress. **3.** a piece of starched cloth covering the chest and shoulders of a nun's habit. **4.** a variant spelling of **gimp.** [C19: variant of GIMP]

Guin. *abbrev. for* Guinea.

guinea ('gɪnɪ) *n.* **1. a.** a British gold coin taken out of circulation in 1813, worth 21 shillings. **b.** the sum of 21 shillings (1.05), still used in some contexts, as in quoting professional fees. **2.** See **guinea fowl.** **3.** *U.S. slang, derogatory.* an Italian or a person of Italian descent. [C16: the coin was originally made of gold from Guinea in West Africa]

Guinean (ˈɡɪnɪən) *adj.* **1.** of or relating to Guinea, a republic in West Africa, or its people. ~*n.* **2.** a native or inhabitant of Guinea.
Guinea corn (ˈɡɪnɪ) *n.* another name for **durra.**
guinea fowl *or* **guinea** *n.* any gallinaceous bird, esp. *Numida meleagris,* of the family *Numididae* of Africa and SW Asia, having a dark plumage mottled with white, a naked head and neck, and a heavy rounded body.
guinea grains *pl. n.* another name for **grains of paradise.**
guinea hen *n.* a guinea fowl, esp. a female.
Guinea pepper *n.* a variety of the pepper plant *Capsicum frutescens,* from which cayenne pepper is obtained.
guinea pig *n.* **1.** a domesticated cavy, probably descended from *Cavia porcellus,* commonly kept as a pet and used in scientific experiments. **2.** a person or thing used for experimentation. [C17: origin uncertain: perhaps from old use of the name *Guinea* to mean any remote unknown land]
Guinea worm *n.* a parasitic nematode worm, *Dracunculus medinensis,* that lives beneath the skin in man and other vertebrates and is common in India and Africa.
guipure (ɡɪˈpjʊə) *n.* **1.** Also called: **guipure lace.** any of many types of heavy lace that have their pattern connected by brides, rather than supported on a net mesh. **2.** a heavy corded trimming; gimp. [C19: from Old French *guipure,* from *guiper* to cover with cloth, of Germanic origin; see WIPE, WHIP]
guise (ɡaɪz) *n.* **1.** semblance or pretence: *under the guise of friendship.* **2.** external appearance in general. **3.** *Archaic.* manner or style of dress. **4.** *Obsolete.* customary behaviour or manner. ~*vb.* **5.** *Dialect.* to disguise or be disguised in fancy dress. **6.** (*tr.*) *Archaic.* to dress or dress up. [C13: from Old French *guise,* of Germanic origin; see WISE²]
guiser (ˈɡaɪzə) *n.* a mummer, esp. at Christmas or Hallowe'en revels.
guitar (ɡɪˈtɑː) *n. Music.* a plucked stringed instrument originating in Spain, usually having six strings, a flat sounding board with a circular sound hole in the centre, a flat back, and a fretted fingerboard. Range: more than three octaves upwards from E on the first leger line below the bass staff. See also **electric guitar, bass guitar, Hawaiian guitar.** [C17: from Spanish *guitarra,* from Arabic *qītār,* from Greek *kithara* CITHARA] —**guiˈtarist** *n.* —**guiˈtar-ˌlike** *adj.*
guitarfish (ɡɪˈtɑːˌfɪʃ) *n., pl.* **-fish** *or* **-fishes.** any marine sharklike ray of the family *Rhinobatidae,* having a guitar-shaped body with a stout tail and occurring at the bottom of the sea.
Gujarati *or* **Gujerati** (ˌɡʊdʒəˈrɑːtɪ) *n.* **1.** (*pl.* **-ti**) a member of a people of India living chiefly in Gujarat. **2.** the state language of Gujarat, belonging to the Indic branch of the Indo-European family. ~*adj.* **3.** of or relating to Gujarat, its people, or their language.
Gulag (ˈɡuːlæɡ) *n.* the central administrative department of the Soviet security service, established in 1930, responsible for maintaining prisons and forced labour camps. [C20: from Russian *G(lavnoye) U(pravleniye Ispravitelno-Trudovykh) Lag(erei)* Main Administration for Corrective Labour Camps]
gular (ˈɡuːlə, ˈɡjuː-) *adj. Anatomy.* of, relating to, or situated in the throat or oesophagus. [C19: from Latin *gula* throat]
gulch (ɡʌltʃ) *n. U.S. and Canadian.* a narrow ravine cut by a fast stream. [C19: of obscure origin]
gulden (ˈɡʊldᵊn) *n., pl.* **-dens** *or* **-den.** a variant of **guilder.**
gules (ɡjuːlz) *adj.* (*usually postpositive*), *n. Heraldry.* red. [C14: from Old French *gueules* red fur worn around the neck, from *gole* throat, from Latin *gula* GULLET]
gulf (ɡʌlf) *n.* **1.** a large deep bay. **2.** a deep chasm. **3.** something that divides or separates, such as a lack of understanding. **4.** something that engulfs, such as a whirlpool. ~*vb.* **5.** (*tr.*) to swallow up; engulf. [C14: from Old French *golfe,* from Italian *golfo,* from Greek *kolpos*] —**ˈgulfˌlike** *adj.* —**ˈgulfy** *adj.*
Gulf (ɡʌlf) *n.* (*modifier*) of, relating to, or adjoining the Persian Gulf or the Gulf of Mexico: *Gulf country.*
Gulf Stream *n.* **1.** a relatively warm ocean current flowing northeastwards off the Atlantic coast of the U.S. from the Gulf of Mexico. **2.** another name for **North Atlantic Drift.**
gulfweed (ˈɡʌlfˌwiːd) *n.* any brown seaweed of the genus *Sargassum,* esp. *S. bacciferum,* having air bladders and forming dense floating masses in tropical Atlantic waters, esp. the Gulf Stream. Also called: **sargasso, sargasso weed.**
gull¹ (ɡʌl) *n.* any aquatic bird of the genus *Larus* and related genera, such as *L. canus* (**common gull** or **mew**) having long pointed wings, short legs, and a mostly white plumage: family *Laridae,* order *Charadriiformes.* [C15: of Celtic origin; compare Welsh *gwylan*] —**ˈgull-ˌlike** *adj.*
gull² (ɡʌl) *Archaic.* ~*n.* **1.** a person who is easily fooled or cheated. ~*vb.* **2.** (*tr.*) to fool, cheat, or hoax. [C16: perhaps from dialect *gull* unfledged bird, probably from *gul,* from Old Norse *gulr* yellow]
Gullah (ˈɡʌlə) *n.* **1.** (*pl.* **-lahs** *or* **-lah**) a member of a Negro people living on the Sea Islands off the coasts of South Carolina, Georgia, and NE Florida, or in the coastal regions of these states. **2.** the creolized English spoken by these people.
gullet (ˈɡʌlɪt) *n.* **1.** a less formal name for the **oesophagus.** **2.** the throat or pharynx. **3.** *Mining, quarrying.* a preliminary cut in excavating, wide enough to take the vehicle that removes the earth. [C14: from Old French *goulet,* diminutive of *goule* throat, from Latin *gula* throat]
gullible (ˈɡʌləbᵊl) *adj.* easily taken in or tricked. —ˌ**gulliˈbility** *n.* —ˈ**gullibly** *adv.*
gull-wing (ˈɡʌlˌwɪŋ) *adj.* **1.** (of a car door) opening upwards. **2.** (of an aircraft wing) having a short upward-sloping inner section and a longer horizontal outer section.
gully¹ *or* **gulley** (ˈɡʌlɪ) *n., pl.* **-lies** *or* **-leys.** **1.** a channel or small valley, esp. one cut by heavy rainwater. **2.** *N.Z.* a small bush-clad valley. **3.** a deep, wide fissure between two buttresses in a mountain face, sometimes containing a stream or scree. **4.** *Cricket.* **a.** a fielding position between the slips and point. **b.** a fielder in this position. **5.** either of the two channels at the side of a tenpin bowling lane. **6.** *Scot. and northern English dialect.* a path between fences or walls. ~*vb.* **-lies, -lying, -lied.** **7.** (*tr.*) to make (channels) in (the ground, sand, etc.). [C16: from French *goulet* neck of a bottle; see GULLET]
gully² (ˈɡʌlɪ) *n., pl.* **-lies.** *Scot.* a large knife, such as a butcher's knife. [C16: of obscure origin]
gulosity (ɡjʊˈlɒsɪtɪ) *n. Archaic.* greed or gluttony. [C16: from Late Latin *gulōsitās,* from Latin *gulōsus* gluttonous, from *gula* gullet]
gulp (ɡʌlp) *vb.* **1.** (*tr.*; often foll. by *down*) to swallow rapidly, esp. in large mouthfuls: *to gulp down food.* **2.** (*tr.*; often foll. by *back*) to stifle or choke: *to gulp back sobs.* **3.** (*intr.*) to swallow air convulsively, as while drinking, because of nervousness, surprise, etc. **4.** (*intr.*) to make a noise, as when swallowing too quickly. ~*n.* **5.** the act of gulping. **6.** the quantity taken in a gulp. [C15: from Middle Dutch *gulpen,* of imitative origin] —ˈ**gulper** *n.* —ˈ**gulpingly** *adv.* —ˈ**gulpy** *adj.*
gulper eel *or* **fish** *n.* any deep-sea eel-like fish of the genera *Eurypharynx* and *Saccopharynx* and order *Lyomeri,* having the ability to swallow large prey.
gum¹ (ɡʌm) *n.* **1.** any of various sticky substances that exude from certain plants, hardening on exposure to air and dissolving or forming viscous masses in water. **2.** any of various products, such as adhesives, that are made from such exudates. **3.** any sticky substance used as an adhesive; mucilage; glue. **4.** *N.Z.* short for **kauri gum.** **5.** See **chewing gum, bubble gum,** and **gumtree.** **6.** *Chiefly Brit.* a gumdrop. ~*vb.* **gums, gumming, gummed.** **7.** to cover or become covered, clogged, or stiffened with or as if with gum. **8.** (*tr.*) to stick together or in place with gum. **9.** (*intr.*) to emit or form gum. ~See also **gum up.** [C14: from Old French *gomme,* from Latin *gummi,* from Greek *kommi,* from Egyptian *kemai*] —ˈ**gumless** *adj.* —ˈ**gumˌlike** *adj.*
gum² (ɡʌm) *n.* the fleshy tissue that covers the jawbones around the bases of the teeth. Technical name: **gingiva.** Related adj.: **gingival.** [Old English *gōma* jaw; related to Old Norse *gōmr,* Middle High German *gūme,* Lithuanian *gomurīs*]
gum³ (ɡʌm) *n.* used in the mild oath *by gum!* [C19: euphemism for GOD]
gum accroides (əˈkrɔɪdiːz) *n.* another name for **acaroid gum.**
gum ammoniac *n.* another name for **ammoniac².**
gum arabic *n.* a gum exuded by certain acacia trees, esp. *Acacia senegal:* used in the manufacture of ink, food thickeners, pills, emulsifiers, etc. Also called: **acacia, gum acacia.**
gum benzoin *n.* another name for **benzoin.**
gumbo *or* **gombo** (ˈɡʌmbəʊ) *n., pl.* **-bos.** *U.S. and Canadian.* **1.** the mucilaginous pods of okra. **2.** another name for **okra.** **3.** a soup or stew thickened with okra pods. **4.** a fine soil in the W prairies that becomes muddy when wet. [C19: from Louisiana French *gombo,* of Bantu origin]
Gumbo (ˈɡʌmbəʊ) *n.* (*sometimes not cap.*) a French patois spoken by Creoles in Louisiana and the West Indies. [see GUMBO]
gumboil (ˈɡʌmˌbɔɪl) *n.* an abscess on the gums, often at the root of a decayed tooth. Also called: **parulis.**
gumboots (ˈɡʌmˌbuːts) *pl. n.* another name for **Wellington boots** (sense 1).
gumbotil (ˈɡʌmbətɪl) *n.* a sticky clay formed by the weathering of glacial drift. [C20: from GUMBO + TIL(L)⁴]
gum digger *n. N.Z.* a person who digs for fossilized kauri gum in a gum field.
gum digger's spear *n. N.Z.* a long steel probe used by gum diggers digging for kauri gum.
gumdrop (ˈɡʌmˌdrɒp) *n.* a small jelly-like sweet containing gum arabic and various colourings and flavourings. Also called (esp. Brit.): **gum.**
gum elastic *n.* another name for **rubber**¹ (sense 1).
gum elemi *n.* another name for **elemi.**
gum field *n. N.Z.* an area of land containing buried fossilized kauri gum.
gumlands (ˈɡʌmˌlændz) *pl. n. N.Z.* infertile land from which the original kauri bush has been removed or burnt producing only kauri gum.
gumma (ˈɡʌmə) *n., pl.* **-mas** *or* **-mata** (-mətə). *Pathol.* a rubbery tumour characteristic of advanced syphilis, occurring esp. on the skin, liver, brain or heart. [C18: from New Latin, from Latin *gummi* GUM¹] —ˈ**gummatous** *adj.*
gummite (ˈɡʌmaɪt) *n.* an orange or yellowish amorphous secondary mineral consisting of hydrated uranium oxides.
gummosis (ɡʌˈməʊsɪs) *n.* the abnormal production of excessive gum in certain trees, esp. fruit trees, as a result of wounding, infection, adverse weather conditions, severe pruning, etc. [C19: from New Latin; see GUMMA]

gummous ('gʌməs) *or* **gummose** ('gʌməʊs) *adj. Rare.* resembling or consisting of gum.

gummy[1] ('gʌmɪ) *adj.* **-mier, -miest.** **1.** sticky or tacky. **2.** consisting of, coated with, or clogged by gum or a similar substance. **3.** producing gum. [C14: from GUM[1] + -Y[1]] —'**gumminess** *n.*

gummy[2] ('gʌmɪ) *adj.* **-mier, -miest.** **1.** toothless; not showing one's teeth. ~*n., pl.* **-mies.** **2.** *Austral.* a small crustacean-eating shark, *Mustelus antarcticus,* with bony ridges resembling gums in its mouth. **3.** *N.Z.* an old ewe that has lost its incisor teeth. [C20: from GUM[2] + -Y[1]] —'**gummily** *adv.*

gum nut *n. Austral.* the hardened seed container of the gum tree *Eucalyptus gummifera.*

gum plant *or* **gumweed** ('gʌm,wi:d) *n.* any of several American yellow-flowered plants of the genus *Grindelia,* esp. *G. robusta,* that have sticky flower heads: family *Compositae* (composites).

gumption ('gʌmpʃən) *n. Informal.* **1.** *Brit.* common sense or resourcefulness. **2.** initiative or courage: *you haven't the gumption to try.* [C18: originally Scottish, of unknown origin]

gum resin *n.* a mixture of resin and gum obtained from various plants and trees. See also **bdellium, gamboge.**

gumshield ('gʌm,ʃi:ld) *n.* a plate or strip of soft waxy substance used by boxers to protect the teeth and gums. Also called: **mouthpiece.**

gumshoe ('gʌm,ʃu:) *n.* **1.** a waterproof overshoe. **2.** *U.S. and Canadian slang.* a detective or one who moves about stealthily. **3.** *U.S. and Canadian slang.* a stealthy action or movement. ~*vb.* **-shoes, -shoeing, -shoed.** **4.** (*intr.*) *U.S. and Canadian slang.* to act stealthily.

gumsucker ('gʌm,sʌkə) *n. Austral. informal.* (in the 19th century) **a.** a native-born Australian. **b.** a native of the state of Victoria.

gumtree ('gʌm,tri:) *n.* **1.** any of various trees that yield gum, such as the eucalyptus, sweet gum, and sour gum. Sometimes shortened to **gum.** **2.** Also called: **gumwood.** the wood of the eucalyptus tree. **3. up a gumtree.** *Informal.* in a very awkward position; in difficulties.

gum up *vb.* (*tr., adv.*) **1.** to cover, dab, or stiffen with gum. **2.** *Informal.* to make a mess of; bungle (often in the phrase **gum up the works**).

gun (gʌn) *n.* **1. a.** a weapon with a metallic tube or barrel from which a missile is discharged, usually by force of an explosion. It may be portable or mounted. In a military context the term applies specifically to a flat-trajectory artillery piece. **b.** (*as modifier*): *a gun barrel.* **2.** the firing of a gun as a salute or signal, as in military ceremonial. **3.** a member of or a place in a shooting party or syndicate. **4.** any device used to project something under pressure: *a grease gun; a spray gun.* **5.** *U.S. slang.* an armed criminal; gunman. **6.** *Austral. and N.Z. slang.* **a.** an expert. **b.** (*as modifier*): *a gun shearer; a gun batsman.* **7. give it the gun.** *Slang.* to increase speed, effort, etc., to a considerable or maximum degree. **8. go great guns.** *Slang.* to act or function with great speed, intensity, etc. **9. jump** *or* **beat the gun. a.** (of a runner, etc.) to set off before the starting signal is given. **b.** *Informal.* to act prematurely. **10. spike someone's guns.** See **spike**[1] (sense 15). **11. stick to one's guns.** *Informal.* to maintain one's opinions or intentions in spite of opposition. ~*vb.* **guns, gunning, gunned.** **12.** (when *tr.*, often foll. by *down*) to shoot (someone) with a gun. **13.** (*tr.*) to press hard on the accelerator of (an engine): *to gun the engine of a car.* **14.** (*intr.*) to hunt with a gun. ~See also **gun for.** [C14: probably from a female pet name shortened from the Scandinavian name *Gunnhildr* (from Old Norse *gunnr* war + *hildr* war)]

gunboat ('gʌn,bəʊt) *n.* a small shallow-draft vessel carrying mounted guns and used by coastal patrols, etc.

gunboat diplomacy *n.* diplomacy conducted by threats of military intervention, esp. by a major power against a militarily weak state.

gun carriage *n.* a mechanical frame on which a gun is mounted for adjustment and firing or for transportation.

guncotton ('gʌn,kɒtən) *n.* cellulose nitrate containing a relatively large amount of nitrogen: used as an explosive.

gun dog *n.* **1.** a dog trained to work with a hunter or gamekeeper, esp. in retrieving, pointing at, or flushing game. **2.** a dog belonging to any breed adapted to these activities.

gunfight ('gʌn,faɪt) *n. Chiefly U.S.* a fight between persons using firearms. —'**gun,fighter** *n.* —'**gun,fighting** *n.*

gunfire ('gʌn,faɪə) *n.* **1.** the firing of one or more guns, esp. when done repeatedly. **2.** the use of firearms, as contrasted with other military tactics.

gunflint ('gʌn,flɪnt) *n.* a piece of flint in a flintlock's hammer used to strike the spark that ignites the charge.

gun for *vb.* (*intr., prep.*) **1.** to search for in order to reprimand, punish, or kill. **2.** to try earnestly for: *he was gunning for promotion.*

gunge (gʌndʒ) *Informal.* ~*n.* **1.** sticky, rubbery, or congealed matter. ~*vb.* **2.** (*tr.; usually passive;* foll. by *up*) to block or encrust with gunge; clog. [C20: of imitative origin, perhaps influenced by GOO and SPONGE] —'**gungy** *adj.*

gung ho (gʌŋ həʊ) *adj.* **1.** extremely enthusiastic and enterprising, sometimes to excess. **2.** extremely keen to participate in military combat. [C20: pidgin English, from Mandarin Chinese *kung* work + *ho* together]

gunite ('gʌn,aɪt) *n. Civil engineering.* a cement-sand mortar that is sprayed onto formwork, walls, or rock by a compressed air ejector giving a very dense strong concrete layer: used to repair reinforced concrete, to line tunnel walls or mine airways, etc. [C20: from GUN + -ITE[1]]

gunk (gʌŋk) *n. Informal.* slimy, oily, or filthy matter. [C20: perhaps of imitative origin]

gunlock ('gʌn,lɒk) *n.* the mechanism in some firearms that causes the charge to be exploded.

gunman ('gʌnmən) *n., pl.* **-men.** **1.** a man who is armed with a gun, esp. unlawfully. **2.** a man who is skilled with a gun. **3.** *U.S.* a person who makes, repairs, or has expert knowledge of guns. —'**gunman,ship** *n.*

gunmetal ('gʌn,mɛtəl) *n.* **1.** a type of bronze containing copper (88 per cent), tin (8–10 per cent), and zinc (2–4 per cent): used for parts that are subject to wear or to corrosion, esp. by sea water. **2.** any of various dark grey metals used for toys, belt buckles, etc. **3.** a dark grey colour with a purplish or bluish tinge.

gun moll *n. Slang.* a female criminal or a woman who associates with criminals.

gunned (gʌnd) *adj.* **a.** having a gun or guns as specified: *heavily gunned.* **b.** (*in combination*): *three-gunned.*

Gunn effect (gʌn) *n.* a phenomenon observed in some semiconductors in which a steady electric field of magnitude greater than a threshold value generates electrical oscillations with microwave frequencies. [C20: named after John Battiscombe *Gunn* (born 1928), British physicist]

gunnel[1] ('gʌnəl) *n.* any eel-like blennioid fish of the family *Pholidae,* occurring in coastal regions of northern seas. See also **butterfish.** [C17: of unknown origin]

gunnel[2] ('gʌnəl) *n.* a variant spelling of **gunwale.**

gunner ('gʌnə) *n.* **1.** a serviceman who works with, uses, or specializes in guns. **2.** *Naval.* (formerly) a warrant officer responsible for the training of gun crews, their performance in action, and accounting for ammunition. **3.** (in the British Army) an artilleryman, esp. a private. Abbrev.: **gnr.** **4.** a person who hunts with a rifle or shotgun. —'**gunner,ship** *n.*

gunnera ('gʌnərə) *n.* any herbaceous perennial plant of the genus *Gunnera,* found throughout the S hemisphere and cultivated for its large leaves. [C18: named after J. E. *Gunnerus* (1718–73), Norwegian bishop and botanist]

gunnery ('gʌnərɪ) *n.* **1.** the art and science of the efficient design and use of ordnance, esp. artillery. **2.** guns collectively. **3.** the use and firing of guns. **4.** (*modifier*) of, relating to, or concerned with heavy guns, as in warfare: *a gunnery officer.*

gunning ('gʌnɪŋ) *n.* **1.** the act or an instance of shooting with guns. **2.** the art, practice, or act of hunting game with guns.

gunny ('gʌnɪ) *n., pl.* **-nies.** *Chiefly U.S.* **1.** a coarse hard-wearing fabric usually made from jute and used for sacks, etc. **2.** Also called: **gunny sack.** a sack made from this fabric. [C18: from Hindi *gōnī,* from Sanskrit *gonī* sack, probably of Dravidian origin]

gunpaper ('gʌn,peɪpə) *n.* a cellulose nitrate explosive made by treating paper with nitric acid.

gunplay ('gʌn,pleɪ) *n. Chiefly U.S.* the use of firearms, as by criminals.

gunpoint ('gʌn,pɔɪnt) *n.* **1.** the muzzle of a gun. **2. at gunpoint.** being under or using the threat of being shot.

gunpowder ('gʌn,paʊdə) *n.* an explosive mixture of potassium nitrate, charcoal, and sulphur (typical proportions are 75:15:10): used in time fuses, blasting, and fireworks. Also called: **black powder.** —'**gun,powdery** *adj.*

gunpowder tea *n.* a fine variety of green tea, each leaf of which is rolled into a pellet.

gun room *n.* **1.** (esp. in the Royal Navy) the mess allocated to subordinate or junior officers. **2.** a room where guns are stored.

gunrunning ('gʌn,rʌnɪŋ) *n.* the smuggling of guns and ammunition or other weapons of war into a country. —'**gun,runner** *n.*

gunsel ('gʌnsəl) *n. U.S. slang.* **1.** a catamite. **2.** a stupid or inexperienced person, esp. a youth. **3.** a criminal who carries a gun. [C20: probably from Yiddish *genzel;* compare German *ganslein* gosling, from *gans* GOOSE[1]]

gunshot ('gʌn,ʃɒt) *n.* **1. a.** shot fired from a gun. **b.** (*as modifier*): *gunshot wounds.* **2.** the range of a gun. **3.** the shooting of a gun.

gun-shy *adj.* afraid of a gun or the sound it makes: *a gun-shy dog is useless for shooting.*

gunslinger ('gʌn,slɪŋə) *n. Slang.* a gunfighter or gunman, esp. in the Old West. —'**gun,slinging** *n.*

gunsmith ('gʌn,smɪθ) *n.* a person who manufactures or repairs firearms, esp. portable guns. —'**gun,smithing** *n.*

gunstock ('gʌn,stɒk) *n.* the wooden or metallic handle or support to which is attached the barrel of a rifle.

gunter rig ('gʌntə) *n. Nautical.* a type of gaffing in which the gaff is hoisted parallel to the mast. [C18: named after Edmund *Gunter* (1581–1626), English mathematician and astronomer] —'**gunter-,rigged** *adj.*

Gunter's chain *n. Surveying.* a measuring chain 22 yards in length, or this length as a unit. See **chain** (sense 7). [C17: named after Edmund *Gunter*]

gunwale *or* **gunnel** ('gʌnəl) *n.* **1.** *Nautical.* the top of the side of a boat or the topmost plank of a wooden vessel. **2. full to the gunwales.** completely full; full to overflowing.

gunyah ('gʌnjɑː) *n. Austral.* a bush hut or shelter. [C19: from a native Australian language]

Günz (gʊnts) *n.* the first major Pleistocene glaciation of the Alps. See also **Mindel, Riss, Würm.** [named after the river *Günz* in Germany]

guppy ('gʌpɪ) *n., pl.* **-pies.** a small brightly coloured freshwater viviparous cyprinodont fish, *Lebistes reticulatus,* of N South America and the West Indies: a popular aquarium fish. [C20: named after R. J. L. *Guppy,* 19th-century clergyman of Trinidad who first presented specimens to the British Museum]

Gupta ('gʌptə) *n.* the dynasty ruling northern India from the early 4th century to the late 6th century A.D.: the period is famous for achievements in art, science, and mathematics.

Gur (gʊə) *n.* a small group of languages of W Africa, spoken chiefly in Burkina-Faso and Ghana, forming a branch of the Niger-Congo family. Also called: **Voltaic.**

gurdwara ('gɜːdwɑːrə) *n.* a Sikh place of worship. [C20: from Punjabi *gurduārā,* from Sanskrit *guru* teacher + *dvārā* DOOR]

gurgitation (ˌgɜːdʒɪ'teɪʃən) *n.* surging or swirling motion, esp. of water. [C16: from Late Latin *gurgitātus* engulfed, from *gurgitāre* to engulf, from Latin *gurges* whirlpool]

gurgle ('gɜːgᵊl) *vb.* (*intr.*) **1.** (of liquids, esp. of rivers, streams, etc.) to make low bubbling noises when flowing. **2.** to utter low throaty bubbling noises, esp. as a sign of contentment: *the baby gurgled with delight.* ~*n.* **3.** the act or sound of gurgling. [C16: perhaps from Vulgar Latin *gurgulāre,* from Latin *gurguliō* gullet] —'**gurgling** *adj.*

gurglet ('gɜːglɪt) *n.* another word for **goglet.**

Gurindji (gʊ'rɪndʒɪ) *n.* **1.** an Aboriginal people of N central Australia. **2.** the language of this people.

gurjun ('gɜːdʒən) *n.* **1.** any of several S or SE Asian dipterocarpaceous trees of the genus *Dipterocarpus* that yield a resin. **2.** Also called: **gurjun balsam.** the resin from any of these trees, used as a varnish. [C19: from Bengali *garjon*]

Gurkha ('gʊəkɑː, 'gɜːkə) *n., pl.* **-khas** *or* **-kha. 1.** a member of a Hindu people, descended from Brahmins and Rajputs, living chiefly in Nepal, where they achieved dominance after being driven from India by the Muslims. **2.** a member of this people serving as a soldier in the Indian or British army.

Gurkhali (ˌgʊə'kɑːlɪ, ˌgɜː-) *n.* the language of the Gurkhas, belonging to the Indic branch of the Indo-European family.

Gurmukhi ('gʊəmʊkɪ) *n.* the script used for writing the Punjabi language. [Sanskrit, from *guru* teacher + *mukh* mouth]

gurn (gərn, gɜːn) *vb.* (*intr.*) a variant spelling of **girn.**

gurnard ('gɜːnəd) *or* **gurnet** ('gɜːnɪt) *n., pl.* **-nard, -nards** *or* **-net, -nets.** any European marine scorpaenoid fish of the family *Triglidae,* such as *Trigla lucerna* (**tub** or **yellow gurnard**), having a heavily armoured head and finger-like pectoral fins. [C14: from Old French *gornard* grunter, from *grognier* to grunt, from Latin *grunnīre*]

gurrier ('gʌrɪər) *n. Dublin dialect.* a low-class tough ill-mannered person. [perhaps from CURRIER]

guru ('gʊruː, 'guːruː) *n.* **1.** a Hindu or Sikh religious teacher or leader, giving personal spiritual guidance to his disciples. **2.** *Often derogatory.* a leader or chief theoretician of a movement, esp. a spiritual or religious cult. [C17: from Hindi *gurū,* from Sanskrit *guruh* weighty] —'**guruˌship** *n.*

gush (gʌʃ) *vb.* **1.** to pour out or cause to pour out suddenly and profusely, usually with a rushing sound. **2.** to act or utter in an overeffusive, affected, or sentimental manner. ~*n.* **3.** a sudden copious flow or emission, esp. of liquid. **4.** something that flows out or is emitted. **5.** an extravagant and insincere expression of admiration, sentiment, etc. [C14: probably of imitative origin; compare Old Norse *gjósa,* Icelandic *gusa*] —'**gushing** *adj.* —'**gushingly** *adv.*

gusher ('gʌʃə) *n.* **1.** a person who gushes, as in being unusually effusive or sentimental. **2.** something, such as a spurting oil well, that gushes.

gushy ('gʌʃɪ) *adj.* **gushier, gushiest.** *Informal.* displaying excessive admiration or sentimentality. —'**gushily** *adv.* —'**gushiness** *n.*

gusset ('gʌsɪt) *n.* **1.** an inset piece of material used esp. to strengthen or enlarge a garment. **2.** a triangular metal plate for strengthening a corner joist between two structural members. **3.** a piece of mail fitted between armour plates or into the leather or cloth underclothes worn with armour, to give added protection. ~*vb.* **4.** (*tr.*) to put a gusset in (a garment). [C15: from Old French *gousset* a piece of mail, a diminutive of *gousse* pod, of unknown origin] —'**gusseted** *adj.*

gust (gʌst) *n.* **1.** a sudden blast of wind. **2.** a sudden rush of smoke, sound, etc. **3.** an outburst of emotion. ~*vb.* (*intr.*) **4.** to blow in gusts: *the wind was gusting to more than 50 mph.* [C16: from Old Norse *gustr;* related to *gjósa* to GUSH; see GEYSER]

gustation (gʌ'steɪʃən) *n.* the act of tasting or the faculty of taste. [C16: from Latin *gustātiō,* from *gustāre* to taste] —**gustatory** ('gʌstətərɪ, -trɪ) *or* '**gustative** *adj.*

gusto ('gʌstəʊ) *n.* vigorous enjoyment, zest, or relish, esp. in the performance of an action: *the aria was sung with great gusto.* [C17: from Spanish: taste, from Latin *gustus* a tasting; see GUSTATION]

gusty ('gʌstɪ) *adj.* **gustier, gustiest. 1.** blowing or occurring in gusts or characterized by blustery weather: *a gusty wind.* **2.** given to sudden outbursts, as of emotion or temperament. —'**gustily** *adv.* —'**gustiness** *n.*

gut (gʌt) *n.* **1. a.** the lower part of the alimentary canal; intestine. **b.** the entire alimentary canal. Related adj.: **visceral. 2.** (*often pl.*) the bowels or entrails, esp. of an animal. **3.** *Slang.* the belly; paunch. **4.** See **catgut. 5.** a silky fibrous substance extracted from silkworms, used in the manufacture of fishing tackle. **6.** a narrow channel or passage. **7.** (*pl.*) *Informal.* courage, willpower, or daring; forcefulness. **8.** (*pl.*) *Informal.* the essential part: *the guts of a problem.* **9. hate a person's guts.** *Informal.* to dislike a person very strongly. **10. sweat** *or* **work one's guts out.** *Informal.* to work very hard. ~*vb.* **guts, gutting, gutted.** (*tr.*) **11.** to remove the entrails from (fish, etc.). **12.** (esp. of fire) to destroy the inside of (a building). **13.** to plunder; despoil: *the raiders gutted the city.* **14.** to take out the central points of (an article), esp. in summary form. ~*adj.* **15.** *Informal.* arising from or characterized by what is basic, essential, or natural: *a gut problem; a gut reaction.* [Old English *gutt;* related to *gēotan* to flow; see FUSION] —'**gutˌlike** *adj.*

GUT (gʌt) *n. acronym for* Grand Unified Theory.

gutbucket ('gʌtˌbʌkɪt) *n.* a highly emotional style of jazz playing. [C20: from U.S. *gutbucket* a cheap gambling saloon where musicians could play for hand-outs]

gutless ('gʌtlɪs) *adj. Informal.* lacking courage or determination.

gut reaction *n.* a reaction to a situation derived from a person's instinct and experience.

gutser ('gʌtsə) *n.* **come a gutser.** *Austral. and N.Z. slang.* **1.** to fall heavily to the ground. **2.** to fail through error or misfortune. [C20: from *guts* + -ER[1]]

gutsy ('gʌtsɪ) *adj.* **gutsier, gutsiest.** *Slang.* **1.** gluttonous; greedy. **2.** full of courage, determination, or boldness.

gutta ('gʌtə) *n., pl.* **-tae** (-tiː). **1.** *Architect.* one of a set of small droplike ornaments, esp. as used on the architrave of a Doric entablature. **2.** *Med.* (formerly used in writing prescriptions) a technical name for **drop.** Abbrev.: **gt.** [C16: from Latin: a drop]

gutta-percha ('gʌtə'pɜːtʃə) *n.* **1.** any of several tropical trees of the sapotaceous genera *Palaquium* and *Payena,* esp. *Palaquium gutta.* **2.** a whitish rubber substance derived from the coagulated milky latex of any of these trees: used in electrical insulation and dentistry. [C19: from Malay *getah* gum + *percha* name of a tree that produces it]

guttate ('gʌteɪt) *or* **guttated** *adj. Biology.* **1.** (esp. of plants) covered with small drops or droplike markings, esp. oil glands. **2.** resembling a drop or drops. [C19: from Latin *guttātus* dappled, from *gutta* a drop] —**gut'tation** *n.*

gutted ('gʌtɪd) *adj. Informal.* disappointed and upset.

gutter ('gʌtə) *n.* **1.** a channel along the eaves or on the roof of a building, used to collect and carry away rainwater. **2.** a channel running along the kerb or the centre of a road to collect and carry away rainwater. **3.** either of the two channels running parallel to a tenpin bowling lane. **4.** *Printing.* **a.** the space between two pages in a forme. **b.** the white space between the facing pages of an open book. **5.** the space left between stamps on a sheet in order to separate them. **6.** *Austral.* (in gold-mining) the channel of a former watercourse that is now a vein of gold. **7. the gutter.** a poverty-stricken, degraded, or criminal environment. ~*vb.* **8.** (*tr.*) to make gutters in. **9.** (*intr.*) to flow in a stream or rivulet. **10.** (*intr.*) (of a candle) to melt away by the wax forming channels and running down in drops. **11.** (*intr.*) (of a flame) to flicker and be about to go out. [C13: from Anglo-French *goutiere,* from Old French *goute* a drop, from Latin *gutta*] —'**gutter-ˌlike** *adj.*

guttering ('gʌtərɪŋ) *n.* **1.** the gutters, downpipes, etc., that make up the rainwater disposal system on the outside of a building. **2.** the materials used in this system.

gutter press *n.* the section of the popular press that seeks sensationalism in its coverage.

guttersnipe ('gʌtəˌsnaɪp) *n.* **1.** a child who spends most of his time in the streets, esp. in a slum area. **2.** a person regarded as having the behaviour, morals, etc., of one brought up in squalor. [C19: originally a name applied to the common snipe (the bird), then to a person who gathered refuse from gutters in city streets] —'**gutterˌsnipish** *adj.*

guttural ('gʌtərəl) *adj.* **1.** *Anatomy.* of or relating to the throat. **2.** *Phonetics.* pronounced in the throat or the back of the mouth; velar or uvular. **3.** raucous. ~*n.* **4.** *Phonetics.* a guttural consonant. [C16: from New Latin *gutturālis* concerning the throat, from Latin *guttur* gullet] —'**gutturally** *adv.* —'**gutturalness,** ˌ**guttur'ality** *or* '**gutturalism** *n.*

gutturalize *or* **gutturalise** ('gʌtərəˌlaɪz) *vb.* **1.** (*tr.*) *Phonetics.* to change into a guttural speech sound or pronounce with guttural articulation or pharyngeal constriction. **2.** to speak or utter in harsh raucous tones. —ˌ**gutturali'zation** *or* ˌ**gutturali'sation** *n.*

gutty ('gʌtɪ) *n., pl.* **-ties.** *Irish dialect.* **1.** an urchin or delinquent. **2.** a low-class person. [probably from GUTTER, perhaps from the compound GUTTERSNIPE]

guv (gʌv) *or* **guv'nor** ('gʌvnə) *n. Brit.* an informal name for **governor.**

guy[1] (gaɪ) *n.* **1.** *Informal.* a man or youth. **2.** *Brit.* a crude effigy of Guy Fawkes, usually made of old clothes stuffed with straw or rags, that is burnt on top of a bonfire on Guy Fawkes Day. **3.** *Brit.* a person in shabby or ludicrously odd clothes. ~*vb.* **4.** (*tr.*)

to make fun of; ridicule. [C19: short for *Guy* Fawkes; see GUY FAWKES DAY]

guy[2] (gaɪ) *n.* **1.** a rope, chain, wire, etc., for anchoring an object, such as a radio mast, in position or for steadying or guiding it while being hoisted or lowered. ~*vb.* **2.** (*tr.*) to anchor, steady, or guide with a guy or guys. [C14: probably from Low German; compare Dutch *gei* brail, *geiblok* pulley, Old French *guie* guide, from *guier* to GUIDE]

Guyanese (ˌgaɪəˈniːz) *or* **Guyanan** (gaɪˈænən) *adj.* **1.** of or relating to Guyana, a republic in NE South America, or its people. ~*n.* **2.** a native or inhabitant of Guyana.

Guy Fawkes Day (gaɪ fɔːks) *n.* the anniversary of the discovery and capture in 1605 of Guy Fawkes (1570–1606), a conspirator involved in the Gunpowder Plot to blow up James I and Parliament at Westminster, celebrated on Nov. 5 in Britain with fireworks and bonfires.

guyot (ˈgiːˌəʊ) *n.* a flat-topped submarine mountain, common in the Pacific Ocean, thought to be an extinct volcano whose summit has been worn down by the erosive action of seawater. Compare **seamount.** [C20: named after A. H. *Guyot* (1807–84), Swiss geographer and geologist]

guzzle (ˈgʌzᵊl) *vb.* to consume (food or drink) excessively or greedily. [C16: of unknown origin] —**ˈguzzler** *n.*

gv *abbrev. for* gravimetric volume.

gwyniad (ˈgwɪnɪˌæd) *n.* a freshwater white fish, *Coregonus pennantii,* occurring in Lake Bala in Wales: related to the powan. [C17: Welsh, from *gwyn* white, related to Scottish Gaelic *fionn:* see FINNOCK]

Gyani (ˈgjɑːnɪ) *n.* (in India) a title placed before the name of a Punjabi scholar. [Hindi, from Sanskrit *gyan* knowledge]

gybe *or* **jibe** (dʒaɪb) *Nautical.* ~*vb.* **1.** (*intr.*) (of a fore-and-aft sail) to shift suddenly from one side of the vessel to the other when running before the wind, as the result of allowing the wind to catch the leech. **2.** to cause (a sailing vessel) to gybe or (of a sailing vessel) to undergo gybing. ~*n.* **3.** an instance of gybing. [C17: from obsolete Dutch *gijben* (now *gijpen*), of obscure origin]

gym (dʒɪm) *n., adj.* short for **gymnasium, gymnastics, gymnastic.**

gymkhana (dʒɪmˈkɑːnə) *n.* **1.** *Chiefly Brit.* an event in which horses and riders display skill and aptitude in various races and contests. **2.** (esp. in Anglo-India) a place providing sporting and athletic facilities. [C19: from Hindi *gend-khānā,* literally: ball house, from *khāna* house; influenced by GYMNASIUM]

gymnasiarch (dʒɪmˈneɪzɪˌɑːk) *n.* **1.** (in ancient Greece) an official who supervised athletic schools and contests. **2.** *Obsolete.* the governor or chief tutor of an academy or college. [C17: from Latin, from Greek *gymnasiarchos,* from *gymnasion* gymnasium + *-archos* ruling]

gymnasiast (dʒɪmˈneɪzɪˌæst) *n.* a student in a gymnasium.

gymnasium (dʒɪmˈneɪzɪəm) *n., pl.* **-siums** *or* **-sia** (-zɪə). **1.** a large room or hall equipped with bars, weights, ropes, etc., for games or physical training. **2.** (in various European countries) a secondary school that prepares pupils for university. [C16: from Latin: school for gymnastics, from Greek *gumnasion,* from *gumnazein* to exercise naked, from *gumnos* naked]

gymnast (ˈdʒɪmnæst) *n.* a person who is skilled or trained in gymnastics.

gymnastic (dʒɪmˈnæstɪk) *adj.* of, relating to, like, or involving gymnastics. —**gymˈnastically** *adv.*

gymnastics (dʒɪmˈnæstɪks) *n.* **1.** (*functioning as sing.*) practice or training in exercises that develop physical strength and agility or mental capacity. **2.** (*functioning as pl.*) gymnastic exercises.

gymno- *combining form.* naked, bare, or exposed: *gymnosperm.* [from Greek *gumnos* naked]

gymnosophist (dʒɪmˈnɒsəfɪst) *n.* one of a sect of naked Indian ascetics who regarded food or clothing as detrimental to purity of thought. [C16: from Latin *gymnosophistae,* from Greek *gumnosophistai* naked philosophers] —**gymˈnosophy** *n.*

gymnosperm (ˈdʒɪmnəʊˌspɜːm, ˈgɪm-) *n.* any seed-bearing plant of the division *Gymnospermae,* in which the ovules are borne naked on the surface of the megasporophylls, which are often arranged in cones; any conifer or related plant. Compare **angiosperm.** —ˌ**gymnoˈspermous** *adj.*

gympie (ˈgɪmpɪ) *n. Austral.* **1.** a tall tree with stinging hairs on its leaves. **2.** a hammer. [C19: from a native Australian language]

gym shoe *n.* another name for **plimsoll.**

gymslip (ˈdʒɪmˌslɪp) *n.* a tunic or pinafore dress worn by schoolgirls, often part of a school uniform.

gyn. *abbrev. for:* **1.** gynaecological. **2.** gynaecology.

gyn- *combining form.* variant of **gyno-** before a vowel.

gynaeceum (ˌdʒaɪnɪˈsiːəm) *n., pl.* **-cea** (-ˈsiːə). **1.** (in ancient Greece and Rome) the inner section of a house, used as women's quarters. **2.** (dʒaɪˈniːsɪəm, gaɪ-). a variant spelling of **gynoecium.** [C17: from Latin: women's apartments, from Greek *gunaikeion,* from *gunē* a woman]

gynaeco- *or U.S.* **gyneco-** *combining form.* relating to women; female: *gynaecology.* [from Greek, from *gunē, gunaik-* woman, female]

gynaecocracy *or U.S.* **gynecocracy** (ˌdʒaɪnɪˈkɒkrəsɪ, ˌgaɪ-) *n., pl.* **-cies.** government by women or by a single woman. Also called: **gynarchy.** —**gynaecocratic** *or U.S.* **gynecocratic** (dʒaɪˌniːkəˈkrætɪk, gaɪ-) *adj.*

gynaecoid *or U.S.* **gynecoid** (ˈdʒaɪnɪˌkɔɪd, ˈgaɪ-) *adj.* resembling, relating to, or like a woman.

gynaecol. *abbrev. for:* **1.** gynaecological. **2.** gynaecology.

gynaecology *or U.S.* **gynecology** (ˌgaɪnɪˈkɒlədʒɪ) *n.* the branch of medicine concerned with diseases in women, esp. those of the genitourinary tract. —**gynaecological** (ˌgaɪnɪkəˈlɒdʒɪkᵊl), ˌ**gynaecoˈlogic** *or U.S.* ˌ**gynecoˈlogical,** ˌ**gynecoˈlogic** *adj.* —ˌ**gynaeˈcologist** *or U.S.* ˌ**gyneˈcologist** *n.*

gynaecomastia *or U.S.* **gynecomastia** (ˌgaɪnɪkəʊˈmæstɪə) *n.* abnormal overdevelopment of the breasts in a man. [C19: from GYNAECO- + Greek *mastos* breast]

gynandromorph (dʒɪˈnændrəʊˌmɔːf, gaɪ-, dʒaɪ-) *n.* an abnormal organism, esp. an insect, that has both male and female physical characteristics. Compare **hermaphrodite** (sense 1). —**gyˌnandroˈmorphic** *or* **gyˌnandroˈmorphous** *adj.* —**gyˌnandroˈmorphism** *or* **gyˈnandroˌmorphy** *n.*

gynandrous (dʒaɪˈnændrəs, dʒɪ-, gaɪ-) *adj.* **1.** (of flowers such as the orchid) having the stamens and styles united in a column. **2.** hermaphroditic. [C19: from Greek *gunandros* of uncertain sex, from *gunē* woman + *anēr* man] —**gyˈnandry** *or* **gyˈnandrism** *n.*

gynarchy (ˈdʒaɪˌnɑːkɪ, ˈgaɪ-) *n., pl.* **-chies.** another word for **gynaecocracy.**

gynecium (dʒaɪˈniːsɪəm, gaɪ-) *n., pl.* **-cia** (-sɪə). a variant spelling (esp. U.S.) of **gynoecium.**

gyneco- *combining form.* a variant (esp. U.S.) of **gynaeco-.**

gyniatrics (ˌdʒaɪnɪˈætrɪks, ˌgaɪ-) *or* **gyniatry** (dʒaɪˈnaɪətrɪ, gaɪ-) *n. Med.* less common words for **gynaecology.**

gyno- *or before a vowel* **gyn-** *combining form.* **1.** relating to women; female: *gynarchy.* **2.** denoting a female reproductive organ: *gynophore.* [from Greek, from *gunē* woman]

gynodioecious (ˌgaɪnəʊdaɪˈiːʃəs) *adj.* (of a plant species) having some individuals bearing female flowers only and others bearing hermaphrodite flowers only.

gynoecium, gynaeceum, gynaecium, *or esp. U.S.* **gynecium** (dʒaɪˈniːsɪəm, gaɪ-) *n., pl.* **-cia** *or* **-cea** (-sɪə). the carpels of a flowering plant collectively. [C18: New Latin, from Greek *gunaikeion* women's quarters, from *gunaik-, gunē* woman + *-eion,* suffix indicating place]

gynomonoecious (ˌgaɪnəʊmɒˈniːʃəs) *adj.* (of a plant species) having each individual bearing both female and hermaphrodite flowers.

gynophore (ˈdʒaɪnəʊˌfɔː, ˈgaɪ-) *n.* a stalk in some plants that bears the gynoecium above the level of the other flower parts. —**gynophoric** (ˌdʒaɪnəʊˈfɒrɪk, ˌgaɪ-) *adj.*

-gynous *adj. combining form.* **1.** of or relating to women or females: *androgynous; misogynous.* **2.** relating to female organs: *epigynous.* [from New Latin *-gynus,* from Greek *-gunos,* from *gunē* woman] —**-gyny** *n. combining form.*

gyp[1] *or* **gip** (dʒɪp) *Slang.* ~*vb.* **gyps, gypping, gypped** *or* **gips, gipping, gipped. 1.** (*tr.*) to swindle, cheat, or defraud. ~*n.* **2.** an act of cheating. **3.** a person who gyps. [C18: back formation from GYPSY]

gyp[2] (dʒɪp) *n. Brit. and N.Z. slang.* severe pain; torture: *his arthritis gave him gyp.* [C19: probably a contraction of *gee up!;* see GEE[1]]

gyp[3] (dʒɪp) *n.* a college servant at the universities of Cambridge and Durham. Compare **scout**[1] (sense 5). [C18: perhaps from GYPSY, or from obsolete *gippo* a scullion]

gypsophila (dʒɪpˈsɒfɪlə) *n.* any caryophyllaceous plant of the Mediterranean genus *Gypsophila,* such as baby's-breath, having small white or pink flowers. [C18: New Latin, from Greek *gupsos* chalk + *philos* loving]

gypsum (ˈdʒɪpsəm) *n.* a colourless or white mineral sometimes tinted by impurities, found in beds as an evaporite. It is used in the manufacture of plaster of Paris, cement, paint, school chalk, glass, and fertilizer. Composition: hydrated calcium sulphate. Formula: $CaSO_4.2H_2O$. Crystal structure: monoclinic. [C17: from Latin, from Greek *gupsos* chalk, plaster, cement, of Semitic origin] —**gypseous** (ˈdʒɪpsɪəs) *adj.* —**gypsiferous** (dʒɪpˈsɪfərəs) *adj.*

Gypsy *or* **Gipsy** (ˈdʒɪpsɪ) *n., pl.* **-sies.** (*sometimes not cap.*) **1. a.** a member of a people scattered throughout Europe and North America, who maintain a nomadic way of life in industrialized societies. They migrated from NW India from about the 9th century onwards. **b.** (*as modifier*): *a Gypsy fortune-teller.* **2.** the language of the Gypsies; Romany. **3.** a person who looks or behaves like a Gypsy. [C16: from EGYPTIAN, since they were thought to have come originally from Egypt] —**ˈGypsydom** *or* **ˈGipsydom** *n.* —**ˈGypsyˌhood** *or* **ˈGipsyˌhood** *n.* —**ˈGypsyish** *or* **ˈGipsyish** *adj.* —**ˈGypsy-ˌlike** *or* **ˈGipsy-ˌlike** *adj.*

gypsy moth *n.* a variant spelling of **gipsy moth.**

gyral (ˈdʒaɪrəl) *adj.* **1.** having a circular, spiral, or rotating motion; gyratory. **2.** *Anatomy.* of or relating to a convolution (gyrus) of the brain. —**ˈgyrally** *adv.*

gyrate *vb.* (dʒɪˈreɪt, dʒaɪ-). **1.** (*intr.*) to rotate or spiral, esp. about a fixed point or axis. ~*adj.* (ˈdʒaɪrɪt, -reɪt). **2.** *Biology.* curved or coiled into a circle; circinate. [C19: from Late Latin *gȳrāre,* from Latin *gȳrus* circle, from Greek *guros*] —**gyratory** (ˈdʒaɪrətərɪ, -trɪ; dʒaɪˈreɪtərɪ) *adj.*

gyration (dʒaɪˈreɪʃən) *n.* **1.** the act or process of gyrating; rotation. **2.** any one of the whorls of a spiral-shaped shell.

gyrator (dʒaɪˈreɪtə) *n.* an electronic circuit that inverts the impedance.

gyre (dʒaɪə) *Chiefly literary.* ~*n.* **1.** a circular or spiral movement or path. **2.** a ring, circle, or spiral. ~*vb.* **3.** (*intr.*) to whirl. [C16: from Latin *gȳrus* circle, from Greek *guros*]

gyrfalcon *or* **gerfalcon** (ˈdʒɜːˌfɔːlkən, -ˌfɔːkən) *n.* a very large rare falcon, *Falco rusticolus,* of northern and arctic regions: often used for hunting. [C14: from Old French *gerfaucon,* perhaps from Old Norse *geirfalki,* from *geirr* spear + *falki* falcon]

gyro (ˈdʒaɪrəʊ) *n., pl.* **-ros. 1.** See **gyrocompass. 2.** See **gyroscope.**

gyro- *or before a vowel* **gyr-** *combining form.* **1.** indicating rotating or gyrating motion: *gyroscope.* **2.** indicating a spiral. **3.** indicating a gyroscope: *gyrocompass.* [via Latin from Greek *guro-,* from *guros* circle]

gyrocompass (ˈdʒaɪrəʊˌkʌmpəs) *n. Navigation.* a nonmagnetic compass that uses a motor-driven gyroscope to indicate true north. Sometimes shortened to **gyro.**

gyrodyne (ˈdʒaɪrəʊˌdaɪn) *n.* an aircraft that uses a powered rotor to take off and manoeuvre, but uses autorotation when cruising.

gyro horizon *n.* another name for **artificial horizon** (sense 1).

gyromagnetic (ˌdʒaɪrəʊmægˈnɛtɪk) *adj.* of or caused by magnetic properties resulting from the spin of a charged particle, such as an electron.

gyromagnetic ratio *n. Physics.* the ratio of the magnetic moment of a rotating charged particle, such as an electron, to its angular momentum.

gyron (ˈdʒaɪrɒn) *n.* a variant spelling of **giron.**

gyronny (dʒaɪˈrɒnɪ) *adj.* a variant spelling of **gironny.**

gyroplane (ˈdʒaɪrəˌpleɪn) *n.* another name for **autogiro.**

gyroscope (ˈdʒaɪrəˌskəʊp) *or* **gyrostat** *n.* a device containing a disc rotating on an axis that can turn freely in any direction so that the disc resists the action of an applied couple and tends to maintain the same orientation in space irrespective of the movement of the surrounding structure. Sometimes shortened to **gyro.** —**gyroscopic** (ˌdʒaɪrəˈskɒpɪk) *adj.* —ˌ**gyroˈscopically** *adv.* —ˌ**gyroˈscopics** *n.*

gyrose (ˈdʒaɪrəʊz) *adj. Botany.* marked with sinuous lines.

gyrostabilizer *or* **gyrostabiliser** (ˌdʒaɪrəʊˈsteɪbɪˌlaɪzə) *n.* a gyroscopic device used to stabilize the rolling motion of a ship.

gyrostatic (ˌdʒaɪrəʊˈstætɪk) *adj.* of or concerned with the gyroscope or with gyrostatics. —ˌ**gyroˈstatically** *adv.*

gyrostatics (ˌdʒaɪrəʊˈstætɪks) *n.* (*functioning as sing.*) the science of rotating bodies.

gyrus (ˈdʒaɪrəs) *n., pl.* **gyri** (ˈdʒaɪraɪ). another name for **convolution** (sense 3). [C19: from Latin; see GYRE]

gyve (dʒaɪv) *Archaic.* ~*vb.* **1.** (*tr.*) to shackle or fetter. ~*n.* **2.** (*usually pl.*) fetters. [C13: of unknown origin]

h *or* **H** (eɪtʃ) *n., pl.* **h's, H's,** *or* **Hs. 1.** the eighth letter and sixth consonant of the modern English alphabet. **2.** a speech sound represented by this letter, in English usually a voiceless glottal fricative, as in *hat.* **3. a.** something shaped like an H. **b.** (*in combination*): *an H-beam.*

h *symbol for:* **1.** *Physics.* Planck constant. **2.** hecto-. **3.** *Chess.* See **algebraic notation.**

H *symbol for:* **1.** *Chem.* hydrogen. **2.** *Physics.* **a.** magnetic field strength. **b.** Hamiltonian. **3.** *Electronics.* henry or henries. **4.** *Thermodynamics.* enthalpy. **5.** (on Brit. pencils, signifying degree of hardness of lead) hard: *H; 2H; 3H.* Compare **B** (sense 9). **6.** *Slang.* heroin. ~**7.** *international car registration for* Hungary.

h. *or* **H.** *abbrev. for:* **1.** harbour. **2.** hard(ness). **3.** height. **4.** high. **5.** *Music.* horn. **6.** hour. **7.** hundred. **8.** husband.

ha[1] *or* **hah** (hɑː) *interj.* **1.** an exclamation expressing derision, triumph, surprise, etc., according to the intonation of the speaker. **2.** (*reiterated*) a representation of the sound of laughter.

ha[2] *Symbol for* hectare.

h.a. *abbrev. for* hoc anno. [Latin: in this year]

HAA *abbrev. for* hepatitis-associated antigen; an antigen that occurs in the blood serum of some people, esp. those with serum hepatitis.

haaf (hɑːf) *n.* a deep-sea fishing ground off the Shetland and Orkney Islands. [Old English *hæf* sea; related to Old Norse *haf;* see HEAVE]

haar (hɑː) *n. Eastern Brit.* a cold sea mist or fog off the North Sea. [C17: related to Dutch dialect *harig* damp]

Hab. *Bible. abbrev. for* Habakkuk.

habanera (ˌhæbəˈnɛərə) *n.* **1.** a slow Cuban dance in duple time. **2.** a piece of music composed for or in the rhythm of this dance. [from Spanish *danza habanera* dance from Havana in Cuba]

Habanero (*Spanish* aβaˈnero) *n., pl.* **-ros** (-ros). a native or inhabitant of Havana, capital of Cuba.

habeas corpus (ˈheɪbɪəs ˈkɔːpəs) *n. Law.* a writ ordering a person to be brought before a court or judge, esp. so that the court may ascertain whether his detention is lawful. [C15: from the opening of the Latin writ, literally: you may have the body]

haberdasher (ˈhæbəˌdæʃə) *n.* **1.** *Brit.* a dealer in small articles for sewing, such as buttons, zips, and ribbons. **2.** *U.S.* a men's outfitter. [C14: from Anglo-French *hapertas* small items of merchandise, of obscure origin]

haberdashery (ˈhæbəˌdæʃərɪ) *n., pl.* **-eries.** the goods or business kept by a haberdasher.

habergeon (ˈhæbədʒən) *or* **haubergeon** *n.* a light sleeveless coat of mail worn in the 14th century under the plated hauberk. [C14: from Old French *haubergeon* a little HAUBERK]

Haber process (ˈhɑːbə) *n.* an industrial process for producing ammonia by reacting atmospheric nitrogen with hydrogen at about 200 atmospheres (2×10^7 pascals) and 500°C in the presence of a catalyst, usually iron. [named after Fritz *Haber* (1868–1934), German chemist]

habile (ˈhæbiːl) *adj.* **1.** *Rare.* skilful. **2.** *Obsolete.* fit. [C14: from Latin *habilis,* from *habēre* to have; see ABLE]

habiliment (həˈbɪlɪmənt) *n.* (*often pl.*) dress or attire. [C15: from Old French *habillement,* from *habiller* to dress, from *bille* log; see BILLET[2]]

habilitate (həˈbɪlɪˌteɪt) *vb.* **1.** (*tr.*) *U.S., chiefly Western.* to equip and finance (a mine). **2.** (*intr.*) to qualify for office. **3.** (*tr.*) *Archaic.* to clothe. [C17: from Medieval Latin *habilitāre* to make fit, from Latin *habilitās* aptness, readiness; see ABILITY] —**haˌbiliˈtation** *n.* —**haˈbiliˌtator** *n.*

habit (ˈhæbɪt) *n.* **1.** a tendency or disposition to act in a particular way. **2.** established custom, usual practice, etc. **3.** *Psychol.* a learned behavioural response that has become associated with a particular situation, esp. one frequently repeated. **4.** mental disposition or attitude: *a good working habit of mind.* **5. a.** a practice or substance to which a person is addicted: *drink has become a habit with him.* **b.** the state of being dependent on something, esp. a drug. **6.** *Botany, zoology.* the method of growth, type of existence, or general appearance of a plant or animal: *a climbing habit; a burrowing habit.* **7.** the customary apparel of a particular occupation, rank, etc., now esp. the costume of a nun or monk. **8.** Also called: **riding habit.** a woman's riding dress. **9.** *Crystallog.* short for **crystal habit.** ~*vb.* (*tr.*) **10.** to clothe. **11.** an archaic word for **inhabit** or **habituate.** [C13: from Latin *habitus* custom, from *habēre* to have]

habitable (ˈhæbɪtəbᵊl) *adj.* able to be lived in. —ˌ**habitaˈbility** *or* ˈ**habitableness** *n.* —ˈ**habitably** *adv.*

habitant (ˈhæbɪtᵊnt) *n.* **1.** a less common word for **inhabitant. 2.** (ˈhæbɪtᵊnt; *French* abitɑ̃). **a.** an early French settler in Canada or Louisiana in the U.S., esp. a small farmer. **b.** a descendant of these settlers, esp. a farmer.

habitat (ˈhæbɪˌtæt) *n.* **1.** the natural home of an animal or plant. **2.** the place in which a person, group, class, etc., is normally found. [C18: from Latin: it inhabits, from *habitāre* to dwell, from *habēre* to have]

habitation (ˌhæbɪˈteɪʃən) *n.* **1.** a dwelling place. **2.** occupation of a dwelling place. —ˌ**habiˈtational** *adj.*

habited (ˈhæbɪtɪd) *adj.* **1.** dressed in a habit. **2.** clothed.

habit-forming *adj.* (of an activity, indulgence, etc.) tending to become a habit or addiction.

habitual (həˈbɪtjʊəl) *adj.* **1.** (*usually prenominal*) done or experienced regularly and repeatedly: *the habitual Sunday walk.* **2.** (*usually prenominal*) by habit: *a habitual drinker.* **3.** customary; usual: *his habitual comment.* —**haˈbitually** *adv.* —**haˈbitualness** *n.*

habituate (həˈbɪtjʊˌeɪt) *vb.* **1.** to accustom; make used (to). **2.** *U.S. and Canadian archaic.* to frequent.

habituation (həˌbɪtjʊˈeɪʃən) *n.* **1.** the act or process of habituating. **2.** *Psychol.* the temporary waning of an innate response that occurs when it is elicited many times in succession. Compare **extinction** (sense 6).

habitude (ˈhæbɪˌtjuːd) *n. Rare.* habit or tendency. —ˌ**habiˈtudinal** *adj.*

habitué (həˈbɪtjʊˌeɪ) *n.* a frequent visitor to a place. [C19: from French, from *habituer* to frequent]

habitus (ˈhæbɪtəs) *n., pl.* **-tus. 1.** *Med.* general physical state, esp. with regard to susceptibility to disease. **2.** tendency or inclination, esp. of plant or animal growth; habit. [C19: from Latin: state, HABIT]

habu (ˈhɑːbuː) *n.* a large venomous snake, *Trimeresurus flavoviridis,* of Okinawa and other Ryukyu Islands: family *Crotalidae* (pit vipers). [the native name in the Ryukyu Islands of the W Pacific]

HAC *abbrev. for* Honourable Artillery Company.

háček (ˈhɑːtʃɛk) *n.* a diacritic mark (ˇ) placed over certain letters in order to modify their sounds, esp. used in Slavonic languages to indicate various forms of palatal articulation, as in the affricate č and the fricative trill ř used in Czech. [from Czech]

hachure (hæˈʃjʊə) *n.* **1.** another word for **hatching** (see **hatch**[3]). **2.** shading of short lines drawn on a relief map to indicate gradients. ~*vb.* **3.** (*tr.*) to mark or show by hachures. [C19: from French, from *hacher* to chop up, HATCH[3]]

hacienda (ˌhæsɪˈɛndə) *n.* (in Spain or Spanish-speaking countries) **1. a.** a ranch or large estate. **b.** any substantial stock-raising, mining, or manufacturing establishment in the country. **2.** the main house on such a ranch or plantation. [C18: from Spanish, from Latin *facienda* things to be done, from *facere* to do]

hack[1] (hæk) *vb.* **1.** (when *intr.,* usually foll. by *at* or *away*) to cut or chop (at) irregularly, roughly, or violently. **2.** to cut and clear (a way, path, etc.), as through undergrowth. **3.** (in sport, esp. rugby) to foul (an opposing player) by kicking or striking his shins. **4.** *Basketball.* to commit the foul of striking (an opposing player) on the arm. **5.** (*intr.*) to cough in short dry spasmodic bursts. **6.** (*tr.*) to reduce or cut (a story, article, etc.) in a damaging way. **7.** to manipulate a computer program skilfully, esp., to gain unauthorized access to another computer system. **8.** (*tr.*) *Slang, chiefly U.S., Canadian, and N.Z.* to tolerate; cope with: *I can't hack it.* **9. hack to bits.** to damage severely: *his reputation was hacked to bits.* ~*n.* **10.** a cut, chop, notch, or gash, esp. as made by a knife or axe. **11.** any tool used for shallow digging, such as a mattock or pick. **12.** a chopping blow. **13.** a dry spasmodic cough. **14.** a kick on the shins, as in rugby. **15.** a wound from a sharp kick. [Old English *haccian;* related to Old Frisian *hackia,* Middle High German *hacken*]

hack[2] (hæk) *n.* **1.** a horse kept for riding or (more rarely) for driving. **2.** an old, ill-bred, or overworked horse. **3.** a horse kept for hire. **4.** *Brit.* a country ride on horseback. **5.** a drudge. **6.** a person who produces mediocre literary or journalistic work. **7.** Also called: **hackney.** *U.S.* a coach or carriage that is for hire. **8.** Also called: **hackie.** *U.S. informal.* **a.** a cab driver. **b.** a taxi. ~*vb.* **9.** *Brit.* to ride (a horse) cross-country for pleasure. **10.** (*tr.*) to let (a horse) out for hire. **11.** (*tr.*) *Informal.* to write (an article) as or in the manner of a hack. **12.** (*intr.*) *U.S. informal.* to drive a taxi. ~*adj.* **13.** (*prenominal*) banal, mediocre, or unoriginal: *hack writing.* [C17: short for HACKNEY]

hack[3] (hæk) *n.* **1.** a rack used for fodder for livestock. **2.** a board on which meat is placed for a hawk. **3.** a pile or row of unfired bricks stacked to dry. ~*vb.* (*tr.*) **4.** to place (fodder) in a hack. **5.** to place (bricks) in a hack. [C16: variant of HATCH[2]]

hackamore (ˈhækəˌmɔː) *n. U.S. and N.Z.* a rope or rawhide halter used for unbroken foals. [C19: by folk etymology from Spanish *jáquima* headstall, from Old Spanish *xaquima,* from Arabic *shaqīmah*]

hackberry ('hæk,bɛrɪ) *n., pl.* **-ries.** **1.** any American tree or shrub of the ulmaceous genus *Celtis,* having edible cherry-like fruits. **2.** the fruit or soft yellowish wood of such a tree. [C18: variant of C16 *hagberry,* of Scandinavian origin; compare Old Norse *heggr* hackberry]
hackbut ('hækbʌt) *or* **hagbut** *n.* another word for **arquebus.** —,**hackbut'eer,** '**hackbutter,** *or* ,**hagbut'eer,** '**hagbutter** *n.*
hacker ('hækə) *n.* **1.** a person that hacks. **2.** *Slang.* a computer fanatic, esp. one who through a personal computer gains illegal access to the computer system of a company, government, etc.
hackery ('hækərɪ) *n.* **1.** *Ironic.* journalism; hackwork. **2.** *Informal.* the practice of gaining illegal access to a computer system.
hack hammer *n.* an adzelike tool, used for dressing stone.
hacking ('hækɪŋ) *adj.* (of a cough) harsh, dry, and spasmodic.
hacking jacket *or* **coat** *n. Chiefly Brit.* a riding jacket with side or back vents and slanting pockets.
hackle[1] ('hæk°l) *n.* **1.** any of the long slender feathers on the necks of poultry and other birds. **2.** *Angling.* **a.** parts of an artificial fly made from hackle feathers, representing the legs and sometimes the wings of a real fly. **b.** short for **hackle fly.** **3.** a feathered ornament worn in the headdress of some Highland regiments. **4.** a steel flax comb. ~*vb.* (*tr.*) **5.** to comb (flax) using a hackle. ~See also **hackles.** [C15 *hakell,* probably from Old English; variant of HECKLE; see HATCHEL] —'**hackler** *n.*
hackle[2] ('hæk°l) *vb. Rare.* to hack or be hacked; mangle. [C16: from HACK[1]; related to Middle Dutch *hakkelen*]
hackle fly *n. Angling.* an artificial fly in which the legs and wings are represented by hackle feathers.
hackles ('hæk°lz) *pl. n.* **1.** the hairs on the back of the neck and the back of a dog, cat, etc., which rise when the animal is angry or afraid. **2.** anger or resentment (esp. in the phrases **get one's hackles up, make one's hackles rise**).
hackney ('hæknɪ) *n.* **1.** a compact breed of harness horse with a high-stepping trot. **2. a.** a coach or carriage that is for hire. **b.** (*as modifier*): *a hackney carriage.* **3.** a popular term for **hack**[2] (sense 1). ~*vb.* **4.** (*tr.; usually passive*) to make commonplace and banal by too frequent use. [C14: probably after *Hackney* in NE London, where horses were formerly raised; sense 4 meaning derives from the allusion to a weakened hired horse] —'**hackneyism** *n.*
hackneyed ('hæknɪd) *adj.* (of phrases, fashions, etc.) used so often as to be trite, dull, and stereotyped.
hacksaw ('hæk,sɔː) *n.* **1.** a handsaw for cutting metal, with a hard-steel blade in a frame under tension. ~*vb.* **-saws, -sawing, -sawed, -sawed** *or* **-sawn** (-,sɔːn). **2.** (*tr.*) to cut with a hacksaw.
hackwork ('hæk,wɜːk) *n.* undistinguished literary work produced to order.
had (hæd) *vb.* the past tense and past participle of **have.**
hadal ('heɪd°l) *adj.* of, relating to, or constituting the zones of the oceans deeper than **abyssal:** below about 6000 metres (18 000 ft.). [C20: from French, from *Hadès* HADES]
hadaway (,hædə'weɪ) *sentence substitute. Northeastern English dialect.* an exclamation urging the hearer to refrain from delay in the execution of a task. [perhaps from HOLD[1] + AWAY]
haddock ('hædək) *n., pl.* **-docks** *or* **-dock.** a North Atlantic gadoid food fish, *Melanogrammus aeglefinus:* similar to but smaller than the cod. [C14: of uncertain origin]
hade (heɪd) *Geology* ~*n.* **1.** the angle made to the vertical by the plane of a fault or vein. ~*vb.* **2.** (*intr.*) (of faults or veins) to incline from the vertical. [C18: of unknown origin]
hadedah ('hɑːdɪ,dɑː) *n. S. African.* a large greyish-green ibis, *Hagedeshia hagedash,* having a greenish metallic sheen on the wing coverts and shoulders. [probably imitative of the bird's call]
Hades ('heɪdiːz) *n.* **1.** *Greek myth.* the underworld abode of the souls of the dead. **2.** (*often not cap.*) *Informal.* hell. —**Hadean** (heɪ'diːən, 'heɪdɪən) *adj.*
Hadith ('hædɪθ, hɑː'diːθ) *n.* the body of tradition and legend about Mohammed and his followers. [Arabic]
hadj (hædʒ) *n., pl.* **hadjes.** a variant spelling of **hajj.**
hadji ('hædʒɪ) *n., pl.* **hadjis.** a variant spelling of **hajji.**
hadn't ('hæd°nt) *vb. contraction of* had not.
hadron ('hædrɒn) *n.* any elementary particle capable of taking part in a strong nuclear interaction and therefore excluding leptons and photons. [C20: from Greek *hadros* heavy, from *hadēn* enough + -ON] —**had'ronic** *adj.*
hadrosaur ('hædrə,sɔː) *or* **hadrosaurus** (,hædrə'sɔːrəs) *n.* any bipedal Upper Cretaceous dinosaur of the genus *Anatosaurus* and related genera: partly aquatic, with a duck-billed skull and webbed feet. [C19: from Greek *hadros* thick, fat + -SAUR]
hadst (hædst) *vb. Archaic or dialect.* (used with the pronoun *thou*) a singular form of the past tense (indicative mood) of **have.**
hae (heɪ, hæ) *vb.* a Scottish variant of **have.**
haecceity (hɛk'siːɪtɪ, hiːk-) *n., pl.* **-ties.** *Philosophy.* the property that uniquely identifies an object. Compare **quiddity.** [C17: from Medieval Latin *haecceitas,* literally: thisness, from *haec,* feminine of *hic* this]
haem *or U.S.* **heme** (hiːm) *n. Biochem.* a complex red organic pigment containing ferrous iron, present in haemoglobin. [C20: shortened from HAEMATIN]
haem- *combining form.* a variant of **haemo-** before a vowel. Also (U.S.): **hem-.**
haema- *combining form.* a variant of **haemo-.** Also (U.S.): **hema-.**
haemachrome *or U.S.* **hemachrome** ('hiːmə,krəʊm, 'hɛm-) *n.* variants of **haemochrome.**
haemacytometer *or U.S.* **hemacytometer** (,hiːməsaɪ'tɒmɪtə) *n. Med.* variants of **haemocytometer.**
haemagglutinate *or U.S.* **hemagglutinate** (,hiːmə'gluːtɪ,neɪt, ,hɛm-) *vb.* (*tr.*) to cause the clumping of red blood cells in (a blood sample).
haemagglutinin *or U.S.* **hemagglutinin** (,hiːmə'gluːtɪnɪn, ,hɛm-) *n.* an antibody that causes the clumping of red blood cells.
haemagogue *or U.S.* **hemagogue, hemagog** ('hiːmə,gɒg) *adj.* **1.** promoting the flow of blood. ~*n.* **2.** a drug or agent that promotes the flow of blood, esp. the menstrual flow. [C18: from HAEMO- + Greek *agōgos* leading]
haemal *or U.S.* **hemal** ('hiːməl) *adj.* **1.** of or relating to the blood or the blood vessels. **2.** denoting or relating to the region of the body containing the heart.
haemangioma *or esp. U.S.* **hemangioma** (hɪ,mændʒɪ'əʊmə) *n., pl.* **-mas** *or* **-mata** (-mətə). a nonmalignant tumour of blood vessels, esp. affecting those of the skin. See **strawberry mark.** [from HAEM(O)- + ANGI(O)- + -OMA]
haematein *or U.S.* **hematein** (,hiːmə'tiːɪn, ,hɛm-) *n.* a dark purple water-insoluble crystalline substance obtained from logwood and used as an indicator and biological stain. Formula: $C_{16}H_{12}O_6$.
haematemesis *or U.S.* **hematemesis** (,hiːmə'tɛmɪsɪs, ,hɛm-) *n.* vomiting of blood, esp. as the result of a bleeding ulcer. Compare **haemoptysis.** [C19: from HAEMATO- + Greek *emesis* vomiting]
haematic *or U.S.* **hematic** (hiː'mætɪk) *adj.* **1.** Also: **haemic.** relating to, acting on, having the colour of, or containing blood. ~*n.* **2.** *Med.* another name for a **haematinic.**
haematin *or U.S.* **hematin** ('hɛmətɪn, 'hiː-) *n. Biochem.* a dark bluish or brownish pigment containing iron in the ferric state, obtained by the oxidation of haem.
haematinic *or U.S.* **hematinic** (,hɛmə'tɪnɪk, ,hiː-) *n.* **1.** Also called: **haematic.** an agent that stimulates the production of red blood cells or increases the amount of haemoglobin in the blood. ~*adj.* **2.** having the effect of enriching the blood.
haematite ('hiːmə,taɪt, 'hɛm-) *n.* a variant spelling of **hematite.** —**haematitic** (,hiːmə'tɪtɪk, ,hɛm-) *adj.*
haemato- *or before a vowel* **haemat-** *combining form.* indicating blood: *haematolysis.* Also: **haemo-** or (U.S.) **hemato-, hemat-.** [from Greek *haima, haimat-* blood]
haematoblast *or U.S.* **hematoblast** (hiː'mætəʊ,blæst) *n.* any of the undifferentiated cells in the bone marrow that develop into blood cells. —**hae,mato'blastic** *or U.S.* **he,mato'blastic** *adj.*
haematocele *or U.S.* **hematocele** ('hɛmətəʊ,siːl, 'hiː-) *n. Pathol.* a collection of blood in a body cavity, as in the space surrounding the testis; blood cyst.
haematocrit *or U.S.* **hematocrit** ('hɛmətəʊkrɪt, 'hiː-) *n.* **1.** a centrifuge for separating blood cells from plasma. **2.** Also called: **packed cell volume.** the ratio of the volume occupied by these cells, esp. the red cells, to the total volume of blood, expressed as a percentage. [C20: from HAEMATO- + Greek *kritēs* judge, from *krinein* to separate]
haematocryal *or U.S.* **hematocryal** (,hɛmətəʊ'kraɪəl, ,hiː-) *adj. Zoology.* another word for **poikilothermal.**
haematogenesis *or U.S.* **hematogenesis** (,hɛmətəʊ'dʒɛnɪsɪs, ,hiː-) *n.* another name for **haematopoiesis.** —,**haemato'genic, haematogenetic** (,hɛmətəʊdʒɪ'nɛtɪk, ,hiː-) *or U.S.* ,**hemato'genic,** ,**hematoge'netic** *adj.*
haematogenous *or U.S.* **hematogenous** (,hɛmə'tɒdʒɪnəs, ,hiː-) *adj.* **1.** producing blood. **2.** produced by, derived from, or originating in the blood. **3.** (of bacteria, cancer cells, etc.) borne by or distributed by the blood.
haematoid ('hiːmə,tɔɪd, 'hɛm-), **haemoid** *or U.S.* **hematoid, hemoid** *adj.* resembling blood.
haematology *or U.S.* **hematology** (,hiːmə'tɒlədʒɪ) *n.* the branch of medical science concerned with diseases of the blood and blood-forming tissues. —**haematologic** (,hiːmətə'lɒdʒɪk), ,**haemato'logical** *or U.S.* ,**hemato'logic,** ,**hemato'logical** *adj.* —,**haema'tologist** *or U.S.* ,**hema'tologist** *n.*
haematolysis *or U.S.* **hematolysis** (,hiːmə'tɒlɪsɪs) *n., pl.* **-ses** (-,siːz). another name for **haemolysis.**
haematoma *or U.S.* **hematoma** (,hiːmə'təʊmə, ,hɛm-) *n., pl.* **-mas** *or* **-mata** (-mətə). *Pathol.* a tumour of clotted or partially clotted blood.
haematophagous *or U.S.* **hematophagous** (,hiːmə'tɒfəgəs) *adj.* (of certain animals) feeding on blood.
haematopoiesis (,hɛmətəʊpɔɪ'iːsɪs, ,hiː-), **haemopoiesis** *or U.S.* **hematopoiesis, hemopoiesis** *n. Physiol.* the formation of blood. Also called: **haematosis, haematogenesis.** —**haematopoietic** (,hɛmətəʊpɔɪ'ɛtɪk, ,hiː-), **haemopoietic** (,hiːməpɔɪ'ɛtɪk, ,hɛm-) *or U.S.* ,**hematopoi'etic,** ,**hemopoi'etic** *adj.*
haematosis *or U.S.* **hematosis** (,hiːmə'təʊsɪs, ,hɛm-) *n. Physiol.* **1.** another word for **haematopoiesis.** **2.** the oxygenation of venous blood in the lungs.
haematothermal *or U.S.* **hematothermal** (,hɛmətəʊ'θɜːməl, ,hiː-) *adj. Zoology.* another word for **homoiothermic.**

haematoxylin *or U.S.* **hematoxylin** (ˌhiːməˈtɒksɪlɪn, ˌhɛm-) *n.* **1.** a colourless or yellowish crystalline compound that turns red on exposure to light: obtained from logwood and used in dyes and as a biological stain. Formula: $C_{16}H_{14}O_6.3H_2O$. **2.** a variant spelling of **haematoxylon.** [C19: from New Latin *Haematoxylon* genus name of logwood, from HAEMATO- + Greek *xulon* wood + -IN]

haematoxylon (ˌhiːməˈtɒksɪlɒn) *or* **haematoxylin** *n.* any thorny leguminous tree of the genus *Haematoxylon,* esp. the logwood, of tropical America and SW Africa. The heartwood yields the dye haematoxylin. [C19: see HAEMATOXYLIN] —**haematoxylic** (ˌhiːmətɒkˈsɪlɪk) *adj.*

haematozoon *or U.S.* **hematozoon** (ˌhiːmətəʊˈzəʊɒn, ˌhɛm-) *n., pl.* **-zoa** (-ˈzəʊə). any microorganism, esp. a protozoan, that is parasitic in the blood.

haematuria *or U.S.* **hematuria** (ˌhiːməˈtjʊərɪə, ˌhɛm-) *n. Pathol.* the presence of blood or red blood cells in the urine. —ˌ**haemaˈturic** *or U.S.* ˌ**hemaˈturic** *adj.*

-haemia *or esp. U.S.* **-hemia** *n. combining form.* variants of **-aemia.**

haemic *or U.S.* **hemic** (ˈhiːmɪk, ˈhɛm-) *adj.* another word for **haematic.**

haemin *or U.S.* **hemin** (ˈhiːmɪn) *n. Biochem.* haematin chloride; insoluble reddish-brown crystals formed by the action of hydrochloric acid on haematin in a test for the presence of blood. [C20: from HAEMO- + -IN]

haemo-, haema-, *or before a vowel* **haem-** *combining form.* denoting blood: *haemophobia.* Also: **haemato-** or (U.S.) **hemo-, hema-** or **hem-.** [from Greek *haima* blood]

haemochrome *or U.S.* **hemochrome** (ˈhiːməˌkrəʊm, ˈhɛm-) *n.* a blood pigment, such as haemoglobin, that carries oxygen.

haemocoel *or U.S.* **hemocoel** (ˈhiːməˌsiːl) *n.* the body cavity of many invertebrates, including arthropods and molluscs, developed from part of the blood system. [C19: from HAEMO- + New Latin *coel,* from Greek *koilos* hollow]

haemocyanin *or U.S.* **hemocyanin** (ˌhiːməʊˈsaɪənɪn) *n.* a blue copper-containing respiratory pigment in crustaceans and molluscs that functions as haemoglobin.

haemocyte *or U.S.* **hemocyte** (ˈhiːməʊˌsaɪt, ˈhɛm-) *n.* any blood cell, esp. a red blood cell.

haemocytometer (ˌhiːməʊsaɪˈtɒmɪtə), **haemacytometer** *or U.S.* **hemocytometer, hemacytometer** *n. Med.* an apparatus for counting the number of cells in a quantity of blood, typically consisting of a graduated pipette for drawing and diluting the blood and a ruled glass slide on which the cells are counted under a microscope.

haemodialysis *or U.S.* **hemodialysis** (ˌhiːməʊdaɪˈælɪsɪs) *n., pl.* **-ses** (-ˌsiːz). *Med.* the filtering of circulating blood through a semipermeable membrane in an apparatus (**haemodialyser** or **artificial kidney**) to remove waste products: performed in cases of kidney failure. Also called: **extracorporeal dialysis.** See also **dialysis.** [C20: from HAEMO- + DIALYSIS]

haemoflagellate *or U.S.* **hemoflagellate** (ˌhiːməˈflædʒəˌleɪt, ˌhɛm-) *n.* a flagellate protozoan, such as a trypanosome, that is parasitic in the blood.

haemoglobin *or U.S.* **hemoglobin** (ˌhiːməʊˈgləʊbɪn, ˌhɛm-) *n.* a conjugated protein, consisting of haem and the protein globin, that gives red blood cells their characteristic colour. It combines reversibly with oxygen and is thus very important in the transportation of oxygen to tissues. See also **oxyhaemoglobin.** [C19: shortened from *haematoglobulin,* from HAEMATIN + GLOBULIN the two components]

haemoglobinometer *or U.S.* **hemoglobinometer** (ˌhiːməʊgləʊbɪˈnɒmɪtə) *n.* an instrument used to determine the haemoglobin content of blood.

haemoglobinopathy *or U.S.* **hemoglobinopathy** (ˌhiːməʊgləʊbɪˈnɒpəθɪ) *n.* any of various inherited diseases, including sickle-cell anaemia and thalassaemia, characterized by abnormal haemoglobin.

haemoglobinuria *or U.S.* **hemoglobinuria** (ˌhiːməʊgləʊbɪˈnjʊərɪə, ˌhɛm-) *n. Pathol.* the presence of haemoglobin in the urine.

haemoid *or U.S.* **hemoid** (ˈhiːmɔɪd) *adj.* another word for **haematoid.**

haemolysin *or U.S.* **hemolysin** (ˌhiːməʊˈlaɪsɪn, ˌhɛməʊ-; hɪˈmɒlɪsɪn) *n. Biochem.* any substance, esp. an antibody, that causes the breakdown of red blood cells.

haemolysis (hɪˈmɒlɪsɪs), **haematolysis** *or U.S.* **hemolysis, hematolysis** *n., pl.* **-ses** (-ˌsiːz). the disintegration of red blood cells, with the release of haemoglobin, occurring in the living organism or in a blood sample. —**haemolytic** *or U.S.* **hemolytic** (ˌhiːməʊˈlɪtɪk, ˌhɛm-) *adj.*

haemophile *or U.S.* **hemophile** (ˈhiːməʊˌfaɪl, ˈhɛm-) *n.* **1.** another name for **haemophiliac. 2.** a haemophilic bacterium.

haemophilia *or U.S.* **hemophilia** (ˌhiːməʊˈfɪlɪə, ˌhɛm-) *n.* an inheritable disease, usually affecting only males but transmitted by women to their male children, characterized by loss or impairment of the normal clotting ability of blood so that a minor wound may result in fatal bleeding. —ˌ**haemoˈphiliˌoid** *or U.S.* ˌ**hemoˈphiliˌoid** *adj.*

haemophiliac *or U.S.* **hemophiliac** (ˌhiːməʊˈfɪlɪˌæk, ˌhɛm-) *n.* a person having haemophilia. Nontechnical name: **bleeder.** Also called: **haemophile.**

haemophilic *or U.S.* **hemophilic** (ˌhiːməʊˈfɪlɪk, ˌhɛm-) *adj.* **1.** of, relating to, or affected by haemophilia. **2.** (of bacteria) growing well in a culture medium containing blood.

haemopoiesis *or U.S.* **hemopoiesis** (ˌhiːməʊpɔɪˈiːsɪs, ˌhɛm-) *n. Physiol.* another name for **haematopoiesis.** —**haemopoietic** *or U.S.* **hemopoietic** (ˌhiːməʊpɔɪˈɛtɪk, ˌhɛm-) *adj.*

haemoptysis *or U.S.* **hemoptysis** (hɪˈmɒptɪsɪs) *n., pl.* **-ses** (-ˌsiːz). spitting or coughing up of blood or blood-streaked mucus, as in tuberculosis. Compare **haematemesis.** [C17: from HAEMO- + *-ptysis,* from Greek *ptyein* to spit]

haemorrhage *or U.S.* **hemorrhage** (ˈhɛmərɪdʒ) *n.* **1.** profuse bleeding from ruptured blood vessels. **2.** a steady or severe loss or depletion of resources, staff, etc. ~*vb.* **3.** (*intr.*) to bleed profusely. [C17: from Latin *haemorrhagia;* see HAEMO-, -RRHAGIA] —**haemorrhagic** *or U.S.* **hemorrhagic** (ˌhɛməˈrædʒɪk) *adj.*

haemorrhoidectomy *or U.S.* **hemorrhoidectomy** (ˌhɛmərɔɪˈdɛktəmɪ) *n., pl.* **-mies.** surgical removal of haemorrhoids.

haemorrhoids *or U.S.* **hemorrhoids** (ˈhɛməˌrɔɪdz) *pl. n. Pathol.* swollen and twisted veins in the region of the anus and lower rectum, often painful and bleeding. Nontechnical name: **piles.** [C14: from Latin *haemorrhoidae* (plural), from Greek, from *haimorrhoos* discharging blood, from *haimo-* HAEMO- + *rhein* to flow] —ˌ**haemorˈrhoidal** *or U.S.* ˌ**hemorˈrhoidal** *adj.*

haemostasis (ˌhiːməʊˈsteɪsɪs, ˌhɛm-), **haemostasia** (ˌhiːməʊˈsteɪʒɪə, -ʒə, ˌhɛm-) *or U.S.* **hemostasis, hemostasia** *n.* **1.** the stopping of bleeding or arrest of blood circulation in an organ or part, as during a surgical operation. **2.** stagnation of the blood. [C18: from New Latin, from HAEMO- + Greek *stasis* a standing still]

haemostat *or U.S.* **hemostat** (ˈhiːməʊˌstæt, ˈhɛm-) *n.* **1.** a surgical instrument that stops bleeding by compression of a blood vessel. **2.** a chemical agent that retards or stops bleeding.

haemostatic *or U.S.* **hemostatic** (ˌhiːməʊˈstætɪk, ˌhɛm-) *adj.* **1.** retarding or stopping the flow of blood within the blood vessels. **2.** retarding or stopping bleeding. ~*n.* **3.** a drug or agent that retards or stops bleeding.

haeremai (ˈhaɪrɪˌmaɪ) *interj. N.Z.* a Maori expression of welcome. [C18: Maori, literally: come hither]

haeres (ˈhɪəriːz) *n. pl.* **haeredes** (hɪˈriːdiːz). a variant spelling of **heres.**

haet (het) *n. Scot.* a whit; iota; the least amount. [C16: originally in the phrase *deil hae' it* devil have it]

hafiz (ˈhɑːfɪz) *n. Islam.* a title for a person who knows the Koran by heart. [from Persian, from Arabic *hāfiz,* from *hafiza* to guard]

hafnium (ˈhæfnɪəm) *n.* a bright metallic element found in zirconium ores: used in tungsten filaments and as a neutron absorber in nuclear reactors. Symbol: Hf; atomic no.: 72; atomic wt.: 178.49; valency: 4; relative density: 13.31; melting pt.: 2150°C; boiling pt.: 5400°C. [C20: New Latin, named after *Hafnia,* Latin name of Copenhagen + -IUM]

haft (hɑːft) *n.* **1.** the handle of an axe, knife, etc. ~*vb.* **2.** (*tr.*) to provide with a haft. [Old English *hæft;* related to Old Norse *hapt,* Old High German *haft* fetter, *hefti* handle] —ˈ**hafter** *n.*

Haftarah *or* **Haphtarah** (hɑːfˈtəʊrə; *Hebrew* haftaˈraː) *n., pl.* **-taroth** (-ˈtəʊrəʊt; *Hebrew* -taˈroːt) *Judaism.* a short reading from the Prophets which follows the reading from the Torah on Sabbaths and festivals, and relates either to the theme of the Torah reading or to the observances of the day. See also **maftir.**

hag[1] (hæg) *n.* **1.** an unpleasant or ugly old woman. **2.** a witch. **3.** short for **hagfish. 4.** *Obsolete.* a female demon. [Old English *hægtesse* witch; related to Old High German *hagazussa,* Middle Dutch *haghetisse*] —ˈ**haggish** *adj.* —ˈ**haggishly** *adv.* —ˈ**haggishness** *n.* —ˈ**hagˌlike** *adj.*

hag[2] (hæg, hɑːg) *n. Scot. and northern English dialect.* **1.** a firm spot in a bog. **2.** a soft place in a moor. [C13: of Scandinavian origin; compare Old Norse *högg* gap; see HEW]

Hag. *Bible. abbrev. for* Haggai.

hagbut (ˈhægbʌt) *n.* another word for **arquebus.** —ˌ**hagbutˈeer** *or* ˈ**hagbutter** *n.*

hagfish (ˈhægˌfɪʃ) *n., pl.* **-fish** *or* **-fishes.** any eel-like marine cyclostome vertebrate of the family *Myxinidae,* having a round sucking mouth and feeding on the tissues of other animals and on dead organic material. Often shortened to **hag.**

Haggadah *or* **Haggodoh** (həˈgɑːdə; *Hebrew* hagaˈdaː, -gɔˈdɔ) *n., pl.* **-dahs, -das** *or* **-doth** (*Hebrew* -ˈdoːt). *Judaism.* **1. a.** a book containing the order of service of the traditional Passover meal. **b.** the narrative of the Exodus from Egypt that constitutes the main part of that service. ~See also **Seder. 2.** another word for **Aggadah.** [C19: from Hebrew *haggādāh* a story, from *hagged* to tell] —**haggadic** (həˈgædɪk, -ˈgɑː-) *or* **hagˈgadical** *adj.*

haggadist (həˈgɑːdɪst) *n. Judaism.* **1.** a writer of Aggadoth. **2.** an expert in or a student of haggadic literature. —**haggadistic** (ˌhægəˈdɪstɪk) *adj.*

haggard[1] (ˈhægəd) *adj.* **1.** careworn or gaunt, as from lack of sleep, anxiety, or starvation. **2.** wild or unruly. **3.** (of a hawk) having reached maturity in the wild before being caught. ~*n.* **4.** *Falconry.* a hawk that has reached maturity before being caught. Compare **eyas, passage hawk.** [C16: from Old French *hagard* wild; perhaps related to HEDGE] —ˈ**haggardly** *adv.* —ˈ**haggardness** *n.*

haggard[2] ('hægərd) *n.* (in Ireland and the Isle of Man) an enclosure beside a farmhouse in which crops are stored. [C16: related to Old Norse *heygarthr,* from *hey* hay + *garthr* yard]

haggis ('hægɪs) *n.* a Scottish dish made from sheep's or calf's offal, oatmeal, suet, and seasonings boiled in a skin made from the animal's stomach. [C15: perhaps from *haggen* to HACK[1]]

haggle ('hæg^{ə}l) *vb.* **1.** (*intr.;* often foll. by *over*) to bargain or wrangle (over a price, terms of an agreement, etc.); barter. **2.** (*tr.*) *Rare.* to hack. [C16: of Scandinavian origin; compare Old Norse *haggva* to HEW] —'**haggler** *n.*

hagiarchy ('hægɪˌɑːkɪ) *n., pl.* **-archies. 1.** government by saints, holy men, or men in holy orders. **2.** an order of saints.

hagio- *or before a vowel* **hagi-** *combining form.* indicating a saint, saints, or holiness: *hagiography.* [via Late Latin from Greek, from *hagios* holy]

hagiocracy (ˌhægɪ'ɒkrəsɪ) *n., pl.* **-cies. 1.** government by holy men. **2.** a state, community, etc., governed by holy men.

Hagiographa (ˌhægɪ'ɒgrəfə) *n.* the third of the three main parts into which the books of the Old Testament are divided in Jewish tradition (the other two parts being the Law and the Prophets), comprising Psalms, Proverbs, Job, the Song of Solomon, Ruth, Lamentations, Ecclesiastes, Esther, Daniel, Ezra, Nehemiah, and Chronicles. Also called: **Writings.**

hagiographer (ˌhægɪ'ɒgrəfə) *or* **hagiographist** *n.* **1.** a person who writes about the lives of the saints. **2.** one of the writers of the Hagiographa.

hagiography (ˌhægɪ'ɒgrəfɪ) *n., pl.* **-phies. 1.** the writing of the lives of the saints. **2.** biography of the saints. **3.** any biography that idealizes or idolizes its subject. —**hagiographic** (ˌhægɪə'græfɪk) *or* ˌ**hagio'graphical** *adj.*

hagiolatry (ˌhægɪ'ɒlətrɪ) *n.* worship or veneration of saints. —ˌ**hagi'olater** *n.* —ˌ**hagi'olatrous** *adj.*

hagiology (ˌhægɪ'ɒlədʒɪ) *n., pl.* **-gies. 1.** literature concerned with the lives and legends of saints. **2. a.** a biography of a saint. **b.** a collection of such biographies. **3.** an authoritative canon of saints. **4.** a history of sacred writings. —**hagiologic** (ˌhægɪə'lɒdʒɪk) *or* ˌ**hagio'logical** *adj.* —ˌ**hagi'ologist** *n.*

hagioscope ('hægɪəˌskəʊp) *n. Architect.* another name for **squint** (sense 6). —**hagioscopic** (ˌhægɪə'skɒpɪk) *adj.*

hag-ridden *adj.* **1.** tormented or worried, as if by a witch. **2.** *Facetious.* (of a man) harassed by women.

hah (hɑː) *interj.* a variant spelling of **ha**[1].

ha-ha[1] ('hɑː 'hɑː) *or* **haw-haw** *interj.* **1.** a representation of the sound of laughter. **2.** an exclamation expressing derision, mockery, surprise, etc.

ha-ha[2] ('hɑː hɑː) *or* **haw-haw** *n.* a wall or other boundary marker that is set in a ditch so as not to interrupt the landscape. [C18: from French *haha,* probably based on *ha!* ejaculation denoting surprise]

hahnium ('hɑːnɪəm) *n.* a transuranic element artificially produced from californium. Symbol: Ha; atomic no.: 105; half-life of most stable isotope, ^{262}Ha: 40 seconds. [C20: named after Otto *Hahn* (1879–1968), German physicist]

Haida ('haɪdə) *n.* **1.** (*pl.* **-das** *or* **-da**) a member of a seafaring group of North American Indian peoples inhabiting the coast of British Columbia and SW Alaska. **2.** the language of these peoples, belonging to the Na-Dene phylum. —'**Haidan** *adj.*

Haiduk, Heyduck, *or* **Heiduc** ('haɪdʊk) *n.* a rural brigand in the European part of the Ottoman Empire. [C17: from Hungarian *hajdúk* brigands]

haik *or* **haick** (haɪk, heɪk) *n.* an Arab's outer garment of cotton, wool, or silk, for the head and body. [C18: from Arabic *hā'ik*]

haiku ('haɪkuː) *or* **hokku** *n., pl.* **-ku.** an epigrammatic Japanese verse form in 17 syllables. [from Japanese, from *hai* amusement + *ku* verse]

hail[1] (heɪl) *n.* **1.** small pellets of ice falling from cumulonimbus clouds when there are very strong rising air currents. **2.** a shower or storm of such pellets. **3.** words, ideas, etc., directed with force and in great quantity: *a hail of abuse.* **4.** a collection of objects, esp. bullets, spears, etc., directed at someone with violent force. ~*vb.* **5.** (*intr.;* with *it* as subject) to be the case that hail is falling. **6.** (often with *it* as subject) to fall or cause to fall as or like hail: *to hail criticism; bad language hailed about him.* [Old English *hægl;* related to Old Frisian *heil,* Old High German *hagal* hail, Greek *kakhlēx* pebble]

hail[2] (heɪl) *vb. (mainly tr.)* **1.** to greet, esp. enthusiastically: *the crowd hailed the actress with joy.* **2.** to acclaim or acknowledge: *they hailed him as their hero.* **3.** to attract the attention of by shouting or gesturing: *to hail a taxi; to hail a passing ship.* **4.** (*intr.;* foll. by *from*) to be a native (of); originate (in): *she hails from India.* ~*n.* **5.** the act or an instance of hailing. **6.** a shout or greeting. **7.** distance across which one can attract attention (esp. in the phrase **within hail**). ~*sentence substitute.* **8.** *Poetic.* an exclamation of greeting. [C12: from Old Norse *heill* WHOLE; see HALE[1], WASSAIL] —'**hailer** *n.*

hail-fellow-well-met *adj.* genial and familiar, esp. in an offensive or ingratiating way: *a hail-fellow-well-met slap on the back.*

Hail Mary *n.* **1.** *R.C. Church.* a prayer to the Virgin Mary, based on the salutations of the angel Gabriel (Luke 1:28) and Elizabeth (Luke 1:42) to her. Also called: **Ave Maria. 2.** *American football. Slang.* a very long high pass into the end zone, made in the final seconds of a half or of a game.

hailstone ('heɪlˌstəʊn) *n.* a pellet of hail.

hailstorm ('heɪlˌstɔːm) *n.* a storm during which hail falls.

hain't (heɪnt) *Archaic or dialect. contraction of* has not, have not, or is not.

hair (hɛə) *n.* **1.** any of the threadlike pigmented structures that grow from follicles beneath the skin of mammals and consist of layers of dead keratinized cells. **2.** a growth of such structures, as on the human head or animal body, which helps prevent heat loss from the body. **3.** *Botany.* any threadlike outgrowth from the epidermis, such as a root hair. **4. a.** a fabric or material made from the hair of some animals. **b.** (*as modifier*): *a hair carpet; a hair shirt.* **5.** another word for **hair's-breadth:** *to lose by a hair.* **6. get in someone's hair.** *Informal.* to annoy someone persistently. **7. hair of the dog (that bit one).** an alcoholic drink taken as an antidote to a hangover. **8. keep your hair on!** *Brit. informal.* keep calm. **9. let one's hair down.** to behave without reserve. **10. not turn a hair.** to show no surprise, anger, fear, etc. **11. split hairs.** to make petty and unnecessary distinctions. [Old English *hær;* related to Old Norse *hār,* Old High German *hār* hair, Norwegian *herren* stiff, hard, Lettish *sari* bristles, Latin *crescere* to grow] —'**hair**ˌ**like** *adj.*

hairball ('hɛəˌbɔːl) *n.* a compact mass of hair that forms in the stomach of cats, calves, etc., as a result of licking and swallowing the fur, and causes indigestion and convulsions.

hairbrush ('hɛəˌbrʌʃ) *n.* a brush for grooming the hair.

haircloth ('hɛəˌklɒθ) *n.* a cloth woven from horsehair, used in upholstery.

haircut ('hɛəˌkʌt) *n.* **1.** the act or an instance of cutting the hair. **2.** the style in which hair has been cut.

hairdo ('hɛəˌduː) *n., pl.* **-dos.** the arrangement of a person's hair, esp. after styling and setting.

hairdresser ('hɛəˌdrɛsə) *n.* **1.** a person whose business is cutting, curling, colouring and arranging hair, esp. that of women. **2.** a hairdresser's establishment. ~Related adj.: **tonsorial.** —'**hair**ˌ**dressing** *n.*

hair dryer *n.* **1.** a hand-held electric device that blows out hot air and is used to dry and, sometimes, assist in styling the hair, as in blow-drying. **2.** a device for drying the hair in which hot air is blown into a hood that surrounds the head of a seated person.

-haired *adj.* having hair as specified: *long-haired.*

hair follicle *n.* a narrow tubular cavity that contains the root of a hair, formed by an infolding of the epidermis and corium of the skin.

hair gel *n.* a jelly-like substance applied to the hair before styling in order to retain the shape of the style.

hair grass *n.* any grass of the genera *Aira, Deschampsia,* etc., having very narrow stems and leaves.

hairgrip ('hɛəˌgrɪp) *n. Chiefly Brit.* a small tightly bent metal hair clip. Also called (esp. U.S., Canadian, and N.Z.): **bobby pin.**

hairif ('hɛərɪf) *n.* another name for **cleavers.**

hair lacquer *n.* another name for **hair spray.**

hairless ('hɛəlɪs) *adj.* **1.** having little or no hair. **2.** *Brit. slang.* very angry; raging.

hairline ('hɛəˌlaɪn) *n.* **1.** the natural margin formed by hair on the head. **2. a.** a very narrow line. **b.** (*as modifier*): *a hairline crack.* **3.** *Printing.* **a.** a thin stroke in a typeface. **b.** any typeface consisting of such strokes. **c.** thin lines beside a character, produced by worn or poorly cast type. **4.** a rope or line of hair.

hairnet ('hɛəˌnɛt) *n.* any of several kinds of light netting worn over the hair to keep it in place.

hairpiece ('hɛəˌpiːs) *n.* **1.** a wig or toupee. **2.** Also called: **postiche.** a section of extra hair attached to a woman's real hair to give it greater bulk or length.

hairpin ('hɛəˌpɪn) *n.* **1.** a thin double-pronged pin used by women to fasten the hair. **2.** (*modifier*) (esp. of a bend in a road) curving very sharply.

hair-raising *adj.* inspiring horror; terrifying: *a hair-raising drop of 600 feet.* —'**hair-**ˌ**raiser** *n.*

hair restorer *n.* a lotion claimed to promote hair growth.

hair's-breadth *n.* **a.** a very short or imperceptible margin or distance. **b.** (*as modifier*): *a hair's-breadth escape.*

hair seal *n.* any earless seal, esp. the harbour seal, having a coat of stiff hair with no underfur.

hair sheep *n.* any variety of sheep growing hair instead of wool, yielding hides with a finer and tougher grain than those of wool sheep.

hair shirt *n.* **1.** a shirt made of haircloth worn next to the skin as a penance. **2.** a secret trouble or affliction.

hair slide *n.* a hinged clip with a tortoiseshell, bone, or similar back, used to fasten a girl's hair.

hair space *n. Printing.* the thinnest of the metal spaces used in setting type to separate letters or words.

hairsplitting ('hɛəˌsplɪtɪŋ) *n.* **1.** the making of petty distinctions. ~*adj.* **2.** occupied with or based on petty distinctions. —'**hair**ˌ**splitter** *n.*

hair spray *n.* a fixative solution sprayed onto the hair to keep a hairstyle in shape. Also called: **hair lacquer.**

hairspring ('hɛəˌsprɪŋ) *n. Horology.* a very fine spiral spring in some timepieces, which, in combination with the balance wheel, controls the timekeeping.

hairstreak ('hɛəˌstriːk) *n.* any small butterfly of the genus *Callophrys* and related genera, having fringed wings marked with narrow white streaks: family *Lycaenidae.*

hair stroke *n.* a very fine line in a written character.

hairstyle (ˈhɛəˌstaɪl) *n.* a particular mode of arranging, cutting, or setting the hair. —ˈ**hairˌstylist** *n.*

hairtail (ˈhɛəˌteɪl) *n.* any marine spiny-finned fish of the family *Trichiuridae,* most common in warm seas, having a long whiplike scaleless body and long sharp teeth. Usual U.S. name: **cutlass fish.**

hair trigger *n.* **1.** a trigger of a firearm that responds to very slight pressure. **2.** *Informal.* **a.** any mechanism, reaction, etc., set in operation by slight provocation. **b.** (*as modifier*): *a hair-trigger temper.*

hairweaving (ˈhɛəˌwiːvɪŋ) *n.* the interweaving of false hair with the hair on a balding person's head.

hairworm (ˈhɛəˌwɜːm) *n.* **1.** any hairlike nematode worm of the family *Trichostrongylidae,* such as the stomach worm, parasitic in the intestines of vertebrates. **2.** Also called: **horsehair worm.** any very thin long worm of the phylum (or class) *Nematomorpha,* the larvae of which are parasitic in arthropods.

hairy (ˈhɛərɪ) *adj.* **hairier, hairiest. 1.** having or covered with hair. **2.** *Slang.* **a.** difficult or problematic. **b.** scaring, dangerous, or exciting. —ˈ**hairiness** *n.*

hairy frog *n.* a W African frog, *Astylosternus robustus,* the males of which have glandular hairlike processes on the flanks.

hairy willowherb *n.* another name for **codlins-and-cream.**

Haitian *or* **Haytian** (ˈheɪʃɪən, hɑːˈiːʃən) *adj.* **1.** relating to or characteristic of the republic of Haiti in the Caribbean, its inhabitants, or their language. ~*n.* **2.** a native, citizen, or inhabitant of Haiti. **3.** the creolized French spoken in Haiti.

hajj *or* **hadj** (hædʒ) *n., pl.* **hajjes** *or* **hadjes.** the pilgrimage to Mecca that every Muslim is required to make at least once in his life. [from Arabic *hajj* pilgrimage]

hajji, hadji, *or* **haji** (ˈhædʒɪ) *n., pl.* **hajjis, hadjis,** *or* **hajis. 1.** a Muslim who has made a pilgrimage to Mecca: also used as a title. **2.** a Christian of the Greek Orthodox or Armenian Churches who has visited Jerusalem.

haka (ˈhɑkə) *n. N.Z.* **1.** a Maori war chant accompanied by gestures. **2.** a similar performance by a rugby team. [Maori]

hake[1] (heɪk) *n., pl.* **hake** *or* **hakes. 1.** any gadoid food fish of the genus *Merluccius,* such as *M. merluccius* (European hake), of the N hemisphere, having an elongated body with a large head and two dorsal fins. **2.** any North American fish of the genus *Urophycis,* similar and related to *Merluccius* species. **3.** *Austral.* another name for **barracouta.** [C15: perhaps from Old Norse *haki* hook; compare Old English *hacod* pike; see HOOK]

hake[2] (heɪk) *n.* a wooden frame for drying cheese or fish. [C18: variant of HECK[2]]

hakea (ˈhɑːkɪə, ˈheɪkɪə) *n.* any shrub or tree of the Australian genus *Hakea,* having a hard woody fruit and often yielding a useful wood: family *Proteaceae.* [C19: New Latin, named after C. L. von *Hake* (died 1818), German botanist]

Hakenkreuz *German* (ˈhɑːkənˌkrɔɪts) *n.* the swastika. [literally: hooked cross]

hakim *or* **hakeem** (hɑːˈkiːm, ˈhɑːkiːm) *n.* **1.** a Muslim judge, ruler, or administrator. **2.** a Muslim physician. [C17: from Arabic, from *hakama* to rule]

hal- *combining form.* a variant of **halo-** before a vowel.

Halacha, Halaka, *or* ***Halakha*** (*Hebrew* hɑlɑˈxɑː; *Yiddish* hɑˈlɔchə) *n.* **1. a.** Jewish religious law. **b.** a ruling on some specific matter. **2. a.** that part of the Talmud which is concerned with legal matters as distinct from homiletics. **b.** Jewish legal literature in general. ~Compare **Aggadah** (sense 1). [from Hebrew *hălākhāh* way]

Halafian (həˈlɑːfɪən) *adj.* of or relating to the Neolithic culture extending from Iran to the Mediterranean.

halal *or* **hallal** (hɑːˈlɑːl) *n.* **1.** meat from animals that have been killed according to Muslim law. ~*adj.* **2.** of or relating to such meat: *a halal butcher.* ~*vb.* **-als, -alling, -alled** (*tr.*) **3.** to kill (animals) in this way. [from Arabic: lawful]

halation (həˈleɪʃən) *n. Photog.* fogging usually seen as a bright ring surrounding a source of light: caused by reflection from the back of the film. [C19: from HALO + -ATION]

halberd (ˈhælbəd) *or* **halbert** (ˈhælbət) *n.* a weapon consisting of a long shaft with an axe blade and a pick, topped by a spearhead: used in 15th- and 16th-century warfare. [C15: from Old French *hallebarde,* from Middle High German *helm* handle, HELM[1] + *barde* axe, from Old High German *bart* BEARD] —ˌ**halberˈdier** *n.*

halcyon (ˈhælsɪən) *adj. also* **halcyonian** (ˌhælsɪˈəʊnɪən) *or* **halcyonic** (ˌhælsɪˈɒnɪk). **1.** peaceful, gentle, and calm. **2.** happy and carefree. ~*n.* **3.** *Greek myth.* a fabulous bird associated with the winter solstice. **4.** a poetic name for the **kingfisher. 5. halcyon days. a.** a fortnight of calm weather during the winter solstice. **b.** a period of peace and happiness. [C14: from Latin *alcyon,* from Greek *alkuōn* kingfisher, of uncertain origin]

hale[1] (heɪl) *adj.* **1.** healthy and robust (esp. in the phrase **hale and hearty**). **2.** *Scot. and northern English dialect.* whole. [Old English *hæl* WHOLE] —ˈ**haleness** *n.*

hale[2] (heɪl) *vb.* (*tr.*) **1.** to pull or drag; haul. **2.** *Rare.* to compel. [C13: from Old French *haler,* of Germanic origin; compare Old High German *halōn* to fetch, Old English *geholian* to acquire] —ˈ**haler** *n.*

haler (ˈhɑːlə) *n., pl.* **-lers** *or* **-leru** (-ləˌruː). a Czech monetary unit worth one hundredth of a koruna. Also called: **heller.** [Czech, from Middle High German *haller* a silver coin, after *Hall,* German town where the coins were minted]

half (hɑːf) *n., pl.* **halves** (hɑːvz). **1. a.** either of two equal or corresponding parts that together comprise a whole. **b.** a quantity equalling such a part: *half a dozen.* **2.** half a pint, esp. of beer. **3.** *Scot.* a small drink of spirits, esp. whisky. **4.** *Football, hockey, etc.* the half of the pitch regarded as belonging to one team. **5.** *Golf.* an equal score on a hole or round with an opponent. **6.** (in various games) either of two periods of play separated by an interval (the **first half** and **second half**). **7.** a half-price ticket on a bus, train, etc. **8.** short for **half-hour. 9.** short for **halfpenny** (sense 1). **10.** *Sport.* short for **halfback. 11.** *Obsolete.* a half-year period. **12. better half.** *Humorous.* a person's wife or husband. **13. by halves.** (*used with a negative*) without being thorough or exhaustive: *we don't do things by halves.* **14. go halves.** (often foll. by *on, in,* etc.) **a.** to share the expenses (of something with one other person). **b.** to share the whole amount (of something with another person): *to go halves on an orange.* ~*determiner.* **15. a.** being a half or approximately a half: *half the kingdom.* **b.** (*as pronoun; functioning as sing. or pl.*): *half of them came.* ~*adj.* **16.** not perfect or complete; partial: *he only did a half job on it.* ~*adv.* **17.** to the amount or extent of a half. **18.** to a great amount or extent. **19.** partially; to an extent. **20. by half.** by an excessive amount or to an excessive degree: *he's too arrogant by half.* **21. half two,** *etc. Informal.* 30 minutes after two o'clock. **22. have half a mind to.** to have the intention of. **23. not half.** *Informal.* **a.** not in any way: *he's not half clever enough.* **b.** *Brit.* really; very; indeed: *he isn't half stupid.* **c.** certainly; yes, indeed. [Old English *healf;* related to Old Norse *halfr,* Old High German *halb,* Dutch *half*]

half-a-crown *n.* another name for a **half-crown.**

half-a-dollar *n. Brit. slang.* another name for a **half-crown.**

half-and-half *n.* **1.** a mixture of half one thing and half another thing. **2.** a drink consisting of equal parts of beer and stout, or equal parts of bitter and mild. ~*adj.* **3.** of half one thing and half another thing. ~*adv.* **4.** in two equal parts.

half-assed *adj. U.S. and Canadian slang.* **1.** incompetent; inept. **2.** lacking efficiency or organization.

halfback (ˈhɑːfˌbæk) *n.* **1.** *Soccer.* any of three players positioned behind the line of forwards and in front of the fullbacks. **2.** *Rugby.* either the scrum half or the stand-off half. **3.** any of certain similar players in other team sports. **4.** the position of a player who is halfback.

half-baked *adj.* **1.** insufficiently baked. **2.** *Informal.* foolish; stupid. **3.** *Informal.* poorly planned or conceived.

half-ball *n.* **a.** a contact in billiards, etc., in which the player aims through the centre of the cue ball to the edge of the object ball, so that half the object ball is covered. **b.** (*as modifier*): *a half-ball stroke.*

halfbeak (ˈhɑːfˌbiːk) *n.* any marine and freshwater teleost fish of the tropical and subtropical family *Hemiramphidae,* having an elongated body with a short upper jaw and a long protruding lower jaw.

half-binding *n.* a type of bookbinding in which the backs are bound in one material and the sides in another.

half-blood *n.* **1. a.** the relationship between individuals having only one parent in common. **b.** an individual having such a relationship. **2.** a less common name for a **half-breed. 3.** a half-blooded domestic animal.

half-blooded *adj.* **1.** being related to another individual through only one parent. **2.** having parents of different races. **3.** (of a domestic animal) having only one parent of known pedigree.

half-blue *n.* (at Oxford and Cambridge universities) a sportsman who substitutes for a full blue or who represents the university in a minor sport. Compare **blue** (sense 4).

half board *n.* **a.** the daily provision by a hotel of bed, breakfast, and one main meal. **b.** (*as modifier*): *half-board accommodation.* ~Also called: **demi-pension.**

half-board *n.* a manoeuvre by a sailing ship enabling it to gain distance to windward by luffing up into the wind.

half-boot *n.* a boot reaching to the midcalf.

half-bound *adj.* (of a book) having a half-binding.

half-breed *n.* **1.** a person whose parents are of different races, esp. the offspring of a White person and an American Indian. ~*adj. also* **half-bred. 2.** of, relating to, or designating offspring of people or animals of different races or breeds.

half-brother *n.* the son of either of one's parents by another partner.

half-butt *n.* a snooker cue longer than an ordinary cue.

ˌ**half-aˈfraid** *adj.*
ˌ**half-aˈlive** *adj.*
ˌ**half-ˈangliˌcized** *or*
ˌ**half-ˈangliˌcised** *adj.*
ˌ**half-aˈshamed** *adj.*
ˌ**half-aˈsleep** *adj.*
ˌ**half-aˈwake** *adj.*
ˌ**half-ˈbarrel** *n.*
ˌ**half-ˈbegging** *adj.*
ˌ**half-beˈgun** *adj.*
ˌ**half-ˈbent** *adj.*
ˌ**half-ˈblind** *adj.*
ˌ**half-ˈbottle** *n.*
ˌ**half-ˈburied** *adj.*

half-caste *n.* **1.** a person having parents of different races, esp. the offspring of a European and an Indian. ~*adj.* **2.** of, relating to, or designating such a person.
half-cock *n.* **1.** on a single-action firearm, a halfway position in which the hammer can be set for safety; in this position the trigger is cocked by the hammer which cannot reach the primer to fire the weapon. **2. go off at half-cock** *or* **half-cocked. a.** to fail as a result of inadequate preparation or premature starting. **b.** to act or function prematurely.
half-cocked *adj.* (of a firearm) at half-cock.
half-crown *n.* a British silver or cupronickel coin worth two shillings and sixpence (now equivalent to 12½p), taken out of circulation in 1970. Also called: **half-a-crown.**
half-dead *adj. Brit. informal.* very tired.
half-dollar *n.* (in the U.S. and Canada) a 50-cent piece.
half eagle *n.* a former U.S. gold coin worth five dollars.
half-forward *n. Australian Rules football.* any of three forwards positioned between the centre line and the forward line.
half frame *n.* **a.** a photograph taking up half the normal area of a frame on a particular film, taken esp. on 35-millimetre film. **b.** (*as modifier*): *a half-frame camera.*
half gainer *n.* a type of dive in which the diver completes a half backward somersault to enter the water headfirst facing the diving board. Compare **gainer.**
half-hardy *adj.* (of a cultivated plant) able to survive out of doors except during severe frost.
half-hearted *adj.* without enthusiasm or determination. —ˌ**half-ˈheartedly** *adv.* —ˌ**half-ˈheartedness** *n.*
half-hitch *n.* a knot made by passing the end of a piece of rope around itself and through the loop thus made.
half holiday *n.* a day of which either the morning or the afternoon is a holiday.
half-hour *n.* **1. a.** a period of 30 minutes. **b.** (*as modifier*): *a half-hour stint.* **2. a.** the point of time 30 minutes after the beginning of an hour. **b.** (*as modifier*): *a half-hour chime.* —ˌ**half-ˈhourly** *adv., adj.*
half-hunter *n.* a watch with a hinged lid in which a small circular opening or crystal allows the approximate time to be read. See **hunter** (sense 5).
half-inch *n.* **1.** a measure of length approximately equivalent to 13 millimetres. ~*vb.* **2.** *Slang, old-fashioned.* to steal. [sense 2: from rhyming slang for *pinch*]
half-jack *n. S. African informal.* a flat pocket-sized bottle of alcohol. [C20 *jack,* probably from C16 *jack* a leather-covered vessel, from Old French *jaque,* of uncertain origin]
half landing *n.* a landing halfway up a flight of stairs.
half-leather *n.* a type of half-binding in which the backs and corners of a book are bound in leather.
half-length *adj.* **1.** (of a portrait) showing only the body from the waist up and including the hands. **2.** of half the entire or original length. ~*n.* **3.** a half-length portrait.
half-life *n.* **1.** the time taken for half of the atoms in a radioactive material to undergo decay. Symbol: τ. **2.** the time required for half of a quantity of radioactive material absorbed by a living tissue or organism to be naturally eliminated (**biological half-life**) or removed by both elimination and decay (**effective half-life**).
half-light *n.* a dim light, as at dawn or dusk.
half-marathon *n.* a race on foot of 13 miles 352 yards (21.243 kilometres).
half-mast *n.* **1.** the lower than normal position to which a flag is lowered on a mast as a sign of mourning or distress. ~*vb.* **2.** (*tr.*) to put (a flag) in this position.
half measure *n.* (*often pl.*) an inadequate measure.
half-miler *n.* a runner who specializes in running races over half a mile.
half-moon *n.* **1.** the moon at first or last quarter when half its face is illuminated. **2.** the time at which a half-moon occurs. **3. a.** something shaped like a half-moon. **b.** (*as modifier*): *half-moon spectacles.* **4.** *Anatomy.* a nontechnical name for **lunula.**
half-mourning *n.* dark grey clothes worn by some during a period after full formal mourning.
half-nelson *n.* a wrestling hold in which a wrestler places an arm under one of his opponent's arms from behind and exerts pressure with his palm on the back of his opponent's neck. Compare **full nelson.**
half-note *n.* the usual U.S. and Canadian name for **minim** (sense 2).
half-open *adj. Chess.* (of a file) having a pawn or pawns of only one colour on it.
half-p *n., pl.* **-ps.** an informal name for a **halfpenny** (sense 1).
half-pedalling *n.* a technique of piano playing in which the sustaining pedal is raised and immediately depressed thus allowing the lower strings to continue sounding.
halfpenny *or* **ha'penny** (ˈheɪpnɪ, for sense 1 ˈhɑːfˌpenɪ) *n.* **1.** (*pl.* **-pennies**) Also called: **half.** a small British coin worth half a new penny, withdrawn from circulation in 1985. **2.** (*pl.* **-pennies**) an old British coin worth half an old penny. **3.** (*pl.* **-pence**) the sum represented by half a penny. **4.** (*pl.* **-pence**) something of negligible value. **5.** (*modifier*) having the value or price of a halfpenny. **6.** (*modifier*) of negligible value.
halfpennyworth *or* **ha'p'orth** (ˈheɪpəθ) *n.* **1.** an amount that may be bought for a halfpenny. **2.** a trifling or very small amount.
half-pie *adj.* the N.Z. term for **half-baked** (sense 3). [from Maori *pai* good]
half-plate *n. Photography.* a size of plate measuring 16.5 cm by 10.8 cm.
half-price *adj., adv.* for half the normal price: *children go half-price.*
half-quartern *n. Brit.* a loaf having a weight, when baked, of 800 g.
half-rhyme *n.* a rhyme in which the vowel sounds are not identical, such as *years* and *yours.* See **consonance** (sense 2).
half-round chisel *n.* a cold chisel with a semicircular cutting edge used for making narrow channels.
half-round file *n. Engineering.* a file having a semicircular cross-section.
half seas over *adj. Brit. informal.* drunk.
half-section *n. Engineering.* a scale drawing of a section through a symmetrical object that shows only half the object.
half-silvered *adj.* (of a mirror) having an incomplete reflective coating, so that half the incident light is reflected and half transmitted: used in optical instruments and two-way mirrors.
half-sister *n.* the daughter of either of one's parents by another partner.
half-size *n.* any size, esp. in clothing, that is halfway between two sizes.
half-slip *n.* a woman's topless slip that hangs from the waist. Also called: **waist-slip.**
half-sole *n.* **1.** a sole from the shank of a shoe to the toe. ~*vb.* **2.** (*tr.*) to replace the half-sole of (a shoe).
half-step *n. Music, U.S. and Canadian.* another word for **semitone.**
half term *n. Brit. education.* **a.** a short holiday midway through an academic term. **b.** (*as modifier*): *a half-term holiday.*
half-tide *n.* the state of the tide between flood and ebb.
half-timbered *or* **half-timber** *adj.* (of a building, wall, etc.) having an exposed timber framework filled with brick, stone, or plastered laths, as in Tudor architecture. —ˌ**half-ˈtimbering** *n.*
half-time *n. Sport.* **a.** a rest period between the two halves of a game. **b.** (*as modifier*): *the half-time score.*

ˌ**half-ˈcentury** *n., pl.* **-ies.**
ˌ**half-ˈcircle** *n.*
ˌ**half-ˈciviˌlized** *or*
ˌ**half-ˈciviˌlised** *adj.*
ˌ**half-ˈcivilly** *adv.*
ˌ**half-ˈclad** *adj.*
ˌ**half-ˈclosed** *adj.*
ˌ**half-ˈclothed** *adj.*
ˌ**half-comˈpleted** *adj.*
ˌ**half-conˈcealed** *adj.*
ˌ**half-ˈconscious** *adj.*
ˌ**half-ˈconsciously** *adv.*
ˌ**half-conˈsumed** *adj.*
ˌ**half-conˈvinced** *adj.*
ˌ**half-conˈvincing** *adj.*
ˌ**half-conˈvincingly** *adv.*
ˌ**half-ˈcooked** *adj.*
ˌ**half-ˈcovered** *adj.*
ˌ**half-ˈcrazy** *adj.*
ˌ**half-ˈday** *n.*
ˌ**half-ˈdazed** *adj.*
ˌ**half-ˈdazedly** *adv.*
ˌ**half-ˈdeaf** *adj.*
ˌ**half-ˈdeafened** *adj.*
ˌ**half-deˈmented** *adj.*
ˌ**half-deˈserted** *adj.*
ˌ**half-deˈveloped** *adj.*
ˌ**half-diˈgested** *adj.*
ˌ**half-ˈdone** *adj.*
ˌ**half-ˈdozen** *n.*
ˌ**half-ˈdressed** *adj.*
ˌ**half-ˈdried** *adj.*
ˌ**half-ˈdrowned** *adj.*
ˌ**half-ˈdrunk** *adj.*
ˌ**half-ˈeaten** *adj.*
ˌ**half-ˈeduˌcated** *adj.*
ˌ**half-ˈempty** *adj.*
ˌ**half-ˈEnglish** *adj.*
ˌ**half-exˈpectant** *adj.*
ˌ**half-exˈpectantly** *adv.*
ˌ**half-ˈfamished** *adj.*
ˌ**half-ˈfilled** *adj.*
ˌ**half-ˈfinished** *adj.*
ˌ**half-forˈgotten** *adj.*
ˌ**half-ˈformed** *adj.*
ˌ**half-ˈfrozen** *adj.*
ˌ**half-fulˈfilled** *adj.*
ˌ**half-ˈfull** *adj.*
ˌ**half-ˈgrown** *adj.*
ˌ**half-ˈheard** *adj.*
ˌ**half-ˈhoping** *adj.*
ˌ**half-ˈhuman** *adj.*
ˌ**half-inˈclined** *adj.*
ˌ**half-inˈformed** *adj.*
ˌ**half-inˈstinctive** *adj.*
ˌ**half-inˈstinctively** *adv.*
ˌ**half-inˈtoxiˌcated** *adj.*
ˌ**half-ˈjoking** *adj.*
ˌ**half-ˈjokingly** *adv.*
ˌ**half-ˈknowledge** *n.*
ˌ**half-ˈlearned** *adj.*
ˌ**half-ˈlie** *n.*
ˌ**half-ˈmad** *adj.*
ˌ**half-ˈmeant** *adj.*
ˌ**half-ˈmile** *n.*
ˌ**half-ˈminute** *n.*
ˌ**half-ˈmonthly** *adj., adv.*
ˌ**half-ˈnaked** *adj.*
ˌ**half-ˈpagan** *adj., n.*
ˌ**half-ˈpay** *n.*
ˌ**half-ˈpetriˌfied** *adj.*
ˌ**half-ˈplayful** *adj.*
ˌ**half-ˈplayfully** *adv.*
ˌ**half-ˈpleased** *adj.*
ˌ**half-proˈtesting** *adj.*
ˌ**half-ˈproved** *adj.*
ˌ**half-ˈproven** *adj.*
ˌ**half-ˈquestioning** *adj.*
ˌ**half-ˈquestioningly** *adv.*
ˌ**half-ˈraw** *adj.*
ˌ**half-reˈluctant** *adj.*
ˌ**half-reˈluctantly** *adv.*
ˌ**half-reˈmembered** *adj.*
ˌ**half-reˈpentant** *adj.*
ˌ**half-ˈright** *adj.*
ˌ**half-ˈrotted** *adj.*
ˌ**half-ˈrotten** *adj.*
ˌ**half-ˈruined** *adj.*
ˌ**half-ˈsavage** *adj.*
ˌ**half-ˈsavagely** *adv.*
ˌ**half-ˈsecond** *n.*
ˌ**half-ˈseen** *adj.*
ˌ**half-ˈsensed** *adj.*
ˌ**half-ˈserious** *adj.*
ˌ**half-ˈseriously** *adv.*
ˌ**half-ˈshut** *adj.*
ˌ**half-ˈsmile** *n.*
ˌ**half-ˈstarved** *adj.*
ˌ**half-ˈstated** *adj.*
ˌ**half-subˈmerged** *adj.*

half-title *n.* **1.** the short title of a book as printed on the right-hand page preceding the title page. **2.** a title on a separate page preceding a section of a book.

halftone ('hɑːfˌtəʊn) *n.* **1. a.** a process used to reproduce an illustration by photographing it through a fine screen to break it up into dots. **b.** the etched plate thus obtained. **c.** the print obtained from such a plate. **2.** *Art.* a tonal value midway between highlight and dark shading. *~adj.* **3.** relating to, used in, or made by halftone.

half-track *n.* a vehicle with caterpillar tracks on the wheels that supply motive power only. —**'half-ˌtracked** *adj.*

half-truth *n.* a partially true statement intended to mislead. —**'half-'true** *adj.*

half volley *Sport.* *~n.* **1.** a stroke or shot in which the ball is hit immediately after it bounces. *~vb.* **half-volley. 2.** to hit or kick (a ball) immediately after it bounces.

halfway (ˌhɑːf'weɪ) *adv., adj.* **1.** at or to half the distance; at or to the middle. **2.** in or of an incomplete manner or nature. **3. meet halfway.** to compromise with.

halfway house *n.* **1.** a place to rest midway on a journey. **2.** the halfway point in any progression. **3.** a centre or hostel designed to facilitate the readjustment to private life of released prisoners, mental patients, etc.

halfwit ('hɑːfˌwɪt) *n.* **1.** a feeble-minded person. **2.** a foolish or inane person. —**ˌhalf'witted** *adj.* —**ˌhalf'wittedly** *adv.* —**ˌhalf'wittedness** *n.*

hali- *combining form.* a variant of **halo-.**

halibut ('hælɪbət) *or* **holibut** ('hɒlɪbət) *n., pl.* **-buts** *or* **-but. 1.** the largest flatfish: a dark green North Atlantic species, *Hippoglossus hippoglossus,* that is a very important food fish: family *Pleuronectidae.* **2.** any of several similar and related flatfishes, such as *Reinhardtius hippoglossoides* (**Greenland halibut**). [C15: from *hali* HOLY (because it was eaten on holy days) + *butte* flat fish, from Middle Dutch *butte*]

halide ('hælaɪd) *or* **halid** ('hælɪd) *n.* **1.** a binary compound containing a halogen atom or ion in combination with a more electropositive element. **2.** any organic compound containing halogen atoms in its molecules.

halidom ('hælɪdəm) *n. Archaic.* a holy place or thing. [Old English *hāligdōm;* see HOLY, -DOM]

haliplankton ('hælɪˌplæŋktən) *n.* plankton living in sea water.

halite ('hælaɪt) *n.* a colourless or white mineral sometimes tinted by impurities, found in beds as an evaporite. It is used to produce common salt and chlorine. Composition: sodium chloride. Formula: NaCl. Crystal structure: cubic. Also called: **rock salt.** [C19: from New Latin *halītes;* see HALO-, -ITE[2]]

halitosis (ˌhælɪ'təʊsɪs) *n.* the state or condition of having bad breath. [C19: New Latin, from Latin *hālitus* breath, from *hālāre* to breathe]

hall (hɔːl) *n.* **1.** a room serving as an entry area within a house or building. **2.** (*sometimes cap.*) a building for public meetings. **3.** (*often cap.*) the great house of an estate; manor. **4.** a large building or room used for assemblies, worship, concerts, dances, etc. **5.** a residential building, esp. in a university; hall of residence. **6. a.** a large room, esp. for dining, in a college or university. **b.** a meal eaten in this room. **7.** the large room of a house, castle, etc. **8.** *U.S. and Canadian.* a passage or corridor into which rooms open. **9.** (*often pl.*) *Informal.* short for **music hall.** [Old English *heall;* related to Old Norse *höll,* Old High German *halla* hall, Latin *cela* CELL, Old Irish *cuile* cellar, Sanskrit *śālā* hut; see HELL]

hallah ('hɑːlə; *Hebrew* xa'la) *n., pl.* **-lahs** *or* **-lot** (*Hebrew* -'lɔt). a variant spelling of **challah.**

Hall effect (hɔːl) *n.* the production of a potential difference across a conductor carrying an electric current when a magnetic field is applied in a direction perpendicular to that of the current flow. [named after Edwin Herbert *Hall* (1855–1938), American physicist who discovered it]

Hallel (*Hebrew* hɑ'lel; *Yiddish* hɑː'leɪl) *n. Judaism.* a section of the liturgy consisting of Psalms 113–18, read during the morning service on festivals, Chanukah, and Rosh Chodesh. [C18: from Hebrew *hallēl,* from *hellēl* to praise]

hallelujah, halleluiah (ˌhælɪ'luːjə), *or* **alleluia** (ˌælɪ'luːjə) *interj.* **1.** an exclamation of praise to God. **2.** an expression of relief or a similar emotion. *~n.* **3.** an exclamation of "Hallelujah". **4.** a musical composition that uses the word *Hallelujah* as its text. [C16: from Hebrew *hallelūyāh* praise the Lord, from *hellēl* to praise + *yāh* the Lord, YAHWEH]

Halley's Comet ('hælɪz) *n.* a comet revolving around the sun in a period of about 76 years and last seen in 1985–86.

halliard ('hæljəd) *n.* a variant spelling of **halyard.**

hallmark ('hɔːlˌmɑːk) *n.* **1.** *Brit.* an official series of marks stamped by the London Guild of Goldsmiths on gold, silver, or platinum articles to guarantee purity, date of manufacture, etc. **2.** a mark or sign of authenticity or excellence. **3.** an outstanding or distinguishing feature. *~vb.* **4.** (*tr.*) to stamp with or as if with a hallmark. ~Also (for senses 1 and 4): **platemark.** [C18: named after Goldsmiths' *Hall* in London, where items were graded and stamped]

hallo (hə'ləʊ) *sentence substitute, n.* **1.** a variant spelling of **hello.** *~sentence substitute, n., vb.* **2.** a variant spelling of **halloo.**

Hall of Fame *n. Chiefly U.S. and Canadian.* (*sometimes not caps.*) **1.** a building containing plaques or busts honouring famous people. **2.** a group of famous people.

hall of residence *n.* a residential block in or attached to a university, polytechnic, college, etc.

halloo (hə'luː), **hallo,** *or* **halloa** (hə'ləʊ) *sentence substitute.* **1.** a shout to attract attention, esp. to call hounds at a hunt. *~n., pl.* **-loos, -los,** *or* **-loas. 2.** a shout of "halloo". *~vb.* **-loos, -looing, -looed; -los, -loing, -loed,** *or* **-loas, -loaing, -loaed. 3.** to shout (something) to (someone). **4.** (*tr.*) to urge on or incite (dogs) with shouts. [C16: perhaps variant of *hallow* to encourage hounds by shouting]

hallow ('hæləʊ) *vb.* (*tr.*) **1.** to consecrate or set apart as being holy. **2.** to venerate as being holy. [Old English *hālgian,* from *hālig* HOLY] —**'hallower** *n.*

hallowed ('hæləʊd; *liturgical* 'hæləʊɪd) *adj.* **1.** set apart as sacred. **2.** consecrated or holy. —**'hallowedness** *n.*

Hallowe'en *or* **Halloween** (ˌhæləʊ'iːn) *n.* the eve of All Saints' Day celebrated on Oct. 31 by masquerading; Allhallows Eve. [C18: see ALLHALLOWS, EVEN[2]]

Hallowmas *or* **Hallowmass** ('hæləʊˌmæs) *n. Archaic.* the feast celebrating All Saints' Day. [C14: see ALLHALLOWS, MASS]

hall stand *or esp. U.S.* **hall tree** *n.* a piece of furniture for hanging coats, hats, etc., on.

Hallstatt ('hælstæt) *or* **Hallstattian** (hæl'stætɪən) *adj.* of or relating to a late Bronze Age culture extending from central Europe to Britain and lasting from the 9th to the 5th century B.C., characterized by distinctive burial customs, bronze and iron tools, etc. [C19: named after *Hallstatt,* Austrian village where remains were found]

hallucinate (hə'luːsɪˌneɪt) *vb.* (*intr.*) to experience hallucinations. [C17: from Latin *ālūcinārī* to wander in mind; compare Greek *aluein* to be distraught] —**hal'luciˌnator** *n.*

hallucination (həˌluːsɪ'neɪʃən) *n.* the alleged perception of an object when no object is present, occurring under hypnosis, in some mental disorders, etc. —**halˌluci'national, hal'lucinative** *or* **hal'lucinatory** *adj.*

hallucinogen (hə'luːsɪnəˌdʒɛn) *n.* any drug, such as LSD or mescaline, that induces hallucinations. —**hallucinogenic** (həˌluːsɪnəʊ'dʒɛnɪk) *adj.*

hallucinosis (həˌluːsɪ'nəʊsɪs) *n. Psychiatry.* a mental disorder the symptom of which is hallucinations, commonly associated with the ingestion of alcohol or other drugs.

hallux ('hæləks) *n.* the first digit on the hind foot of a mammal, bird, reptile, or amphibian; the big toe of man. [C19: New Latin, from Late Latin *allex* big toe]

hallux valgus *n.* an abnormal bending or deviation of the big toe towards the other toes of the same foot.

hallway ('hɔːlˌweɪ) *n.* a hall or corridor.

halm (hɔːm) *n.* a variant spelling of **haulm.**

halma ('hælmə) *n.* a board game in which players attempt to transfer their pieces from their own to their opponents' bases. [C19: from Greek *halma* leap, from *hallesthai* to leap]

halo ('heɪləʊ) *n., pl.* **-loes** *or* **-los. 1.** a disc or ring of light around the head of an angel, saint, etc., as in painting or sculpture. **2.** the aura surrounding an idealized, famous, or admired person, thing, or event. **3.** a circle of light around the sun or moon, caused by the refraction of light by particles of ice. **4.** *Astronomy.* a spherical cloud of stars surrounding the Galaxy and other spiral galaxies. *~vb.* **-loes** *or* **-los, -loing, -loed. 5.** to surround with or form a halo. [C16: from Medieval Latin, from Latin *halōs* circular threshing floor, from Greek] —**'halo-ˌlike** *adj.*

halo-, hali-, *or before a vowel* **hal-** *combining form.* **1.** indicating salt or the sea: *halophyte.* **2.** relating to or containing a halogen: *halothane.* [from Greek *hals, hal-* sea, salt]

halobiont (ˌhæləʊ'baɪɒnt) *n.* a plant or animal that lives in a salty environment such as the sea. [C20: from HALO- + *-biont* from Greek *bios* life] —**ˌhalobi'ontic** *adj.*

halo effect *n.* the tendency to evaluate too highly on many traits a person who is outstanding on one trait.

halogen ('hæləˌdʒɛn) *n.* any of the chemical elements fluorine, chlorine, bromine, iodine, and astatine. They are all monovalent and readily form negative ions. [C19: from Swedish; see HALO-, -GEN] —**'halogenˌoid** *adj.* —**halogenous** (hə'lɒdʒɪnəs) *adj.*

halogenate ('hælədʒəˌneɪt) *vb. Chem.* to treat or combine with a halogen. —**ˌhalogen'ation** *n.*

haloid ('hælɔɪd) *Chem.* *~adj.* **1.** resembling or derived from a halogen: *a haloid salt.* *~n.* **2.** a compound containing halogen atoms in its molecules; halide.

halon ('hælɒn) *n.* any of a class of chemical compounds derived from hydrocarbons by replacing one or more hydrogen atoms by bromine atoms and other hydrogen atoms by other halogen atoms (chlorine, fluorine, or iodine). Halons are stable com-

ˌ**half-'trained** *adj.*
ˌ**half-ˌunder'stood** *adj.*
ˌ**half-'used** *adj.*
ˌ**half-'veriˌfied** *adj.*
ˌ**half-'wild** *adj.*
ˌ**half-'wildly** *adv.*
ˌ**half-'wrong** *adj.*
ˌ**half-'year** *n.*
ˌ**half-'yearly** *adj., adv.*

pounds that are used in fire extinguishers, although they may contribute to depletion of the ozone layer.

halophile ('hæləʊˌfaɪl) *n.* an organism that thrives in media of very high salt concentration, such as in the Dead Sea. —ˌ**halo'philic** *adj.*

halophyte ('hæləʊˌfaɪt) *n.* a plant that grows in very salty soil, as in a salt marsh. —**halophytic** (ˌhælə'fɪtɪk) *adj.* —'**haloˌphytism** *n.*

halosere ('hæləʊˌsɪə) *n. Ecology.* a plant community that originates and develops in conditions of high salinity.

halothane ('hæləʊˌθeɪn) *n.* a colourless volatile slightly soluble liquid with an odour resembling that of chloroform; 2-bromo-2-chloro-1,1,1-trifluoroethane: a general anaesthetic. Formula: $CF_3CHBrCl$. [C20: from HALO- + *-thane*, as in METHANE]

halt[1] (hɔːlt) *n.* **1.** an interruption or end to activity, movement, or progress. **2.** *Chiefly Brit.* a minor railway station, without permanent buildings. **3. call a halt (to).** to put an end (to something); stop. ~*n., sentence substitute.* **4.** a command to halt, esp. as an order when marching. ~*vb.* **5.** to come or bring to a halt. [C17: from the phrase *to make halt*, translation of German *halt machen*, from *halten* to HOLD[1], stop]

halt[2] (hɔːlt) *vb.* (*intr.*) **1.** (esp. of logic or verse) to falter or be defective. **2.** to waver or be unsure. **3.** *Archaic.* to be lame. ~*adj.* **4.** *Archaic.* **a.** lame. **b.** (*as collective n.*; preceded by *the*): *the halt.* ~*n.* **5.** *Archaic.* lameness. [Old English *healt* lame; related to Old Norse *haltr*, Old High German *halz* lame, Greek *kólos* maimed, Old Slavonic *kladivo* hammer]

halter ('hɔːltə) *n.* **1.** a rope or canvas headgear for a horse, usually with a rope for leading. **2.** a style of woman's top fastened behind the neck and waist, leaving the back and arms bare. **3.** a rope having a noose for hanging a person. **4.** death by hanging. ~*vb.* (*tr.*) **5.** to secure with a halter or put a halter on. **6.** to hang (someone). [Old English *hælfter;* related to Old High German *halftra*, Middle Dutch *heliftra*]

haltere ('hæltɪə) *or* **halter** ('hæltə) *n., pl.* **halteres** (hæl'tɪəriːz). one of a pair of short projections in dipterous insects that are modified hind wings, used for maintaining equilibrium during flight. Also called: **balancer.** [C18: from Greek *haltēres* (plural) hand-held weights used as balancers or to give impetus in leaping, from *hallesthai* to leap]

halting ('hɔːltɪŋ) *adj.* **1.** hesitant: *halting speech.* **2.** lame. —'**haltingly** *adv.* —'**haltingness** *n.*

halutz *Hebrew.* (xɑ'lʊts; *English* hɑː'lʊts) *n.* a variant spelling of **chalutz.**

halvah, halva ('hælvɑː), *or* **halavah** ('hæləvɑː) *n.* an Eastern Mediterranean, Middle Eastern, or Indian sweetmeat made of honey and containing sesame seeds, nuts, rose water, saffron, etc. [from Yiddish *halva*, from Romanian, from Turkish *helve*, from Arabic *halwā* sweetmeat]

halve (hɑːv) *vb.* (*tr.*) **1.** to divide into two approximately equal parts. **2.** to share equally. **3.** to reduce by half, as by cutting. **4.** *Golf.* to take the same number of strokes on (a hole or round) as one's opponent. [Old English *hielfan;* related to Middle High German *helben;* see HALF]

halyard *or* **halliard** ('hæljəd) *n. Nautical.* a line for hoisting or lowering a sail, flag, or spar. [C14 *halier*, influenced by YARD[1]; see HALE[2]]

ham[1] (hæm) *n.* **1.** the part of the hindquarters of a pig or similar animal between the hock and the hip. **2.** the meat of this part, esp. when salted or smoked. **3.** *Informal.* **a.** the back of the leg above the knee. **b.** the space or area behind the knee. **4.** *Needlework.* a cushion used for moulding curves. [Old English *hamm;* related to Old High German *hamma* haunch, Old Irish *cnāim* bone, *camm* bent, Latin *camur* bent]

ham[2] (hæm) *n.* **1.** *Theatre, informal.* **a.** an actor who overacts or relies on stock gestures or mannerisms. **b.** overacting or clumsy acting. **c.** (*as modifier*): *a ham actor.* **2.** *Informal.* **a.** a licensed amateur radio operator. **b.** (*as modifier*): *a ham licence.* ~*vb.* **hams, hamming, hammed. 3.** *Informal.* to overact. [C19: special use of HAM[1]; in some senses probably influenced by AMATEUR]

hamadryad (ˌhæmə'draɪəd, -æd) *n.* **1.** *Classical myth.* one of a class of nymphs, each of which inhabits a tree and dies with it. **2.** another name for **king cobra.** [C14: from Latin *Hamādryas*, from Greek *Hamadruas*, from *hama* together with + *drus* tree; see DRYAD]

hamadryas (ˌhæmə'draɪəs) *n.* a baboon, *Papio* (or *Comopithecus*) *hamadryas*, of Arabia and NE Africa, having long silvery hair on the head, neck, and chest: regarded as sacred by the ancient Egyptians: family *Cercopithecidae.* Also called: **hamadryas baboon, sacred baboon.** [C19: via New Latin from Latin; see HAMADRYAD]

hamal, hammal, *or* **hamaul** (hə'mɑːl) *n.* (in the Orient) a porter, bearer, or servant. [from Arabic *hamala* to carry]

hamamelidaceous (ˌhæməˌmiːlɪ'deɪʃəs, -ˌmɛlɪ-) *adj.* of, relating to, or belonging to the *Hamamelidaceae*, a chiefly subtropical family of trees and shrubs that includes the witch hazel. [C19: from New Latin *Hamamelis* type genus, from Greek: medlar, from *hama* together with + *mēlon* fruit]

hamartiology (həˌmɑːtɪ'ɒlədʒɪ) *n.* the doctrine of sin in Christian theology. [C19: from Greek *hamartia* sin + -LOGY]

hamate ('heɪmeɪt) *adj. Rare.* hook-shaped. [C18: from Latin *hāmātus*, from *hāmus* hook]

hamba ('hæmbə) *interj. S. African, usually offensive.* go away; be off. [from Nguni *ukuttamba* to go]

Hambletonian (ˌhæmbᵊl'təʊnɪən) *n.* one of a breed of trotting horses descended from a stallion of that name.

hamburger ('hæmˌbɜːgə) *or* **hamburg** *n.* a flat fried cake of minced beef, often served in a bread roll. Also called: **Hamburger steak, beefburger.** [C20: shortened from *Hamburger steak* (that is, steak in the fashion of *Hamburg* in NW Germany)]

hame[1] (heɪm) *n.* either of the two curved bars holding the traces of the harness, attached to the collar of a draught animal. [C14: from Middle Dutch *hame;* related to Middle High German *hame* fishing rod]

hame[2] (hem) *n., adv.* a Scot. word for **home.**

hames (heɪmz) *n.* **make a hames of.** *Irish informal.* to spoil through clumsiness or ineptitude. [of unknown origin]

ham-handed *or* **ham-fisted** *adj.* **1.** *Informal.* lacking dexterity or elegance; clumsy. **2.** having large hands.

Hamiltonian (ˌhæməl'təʊnɪən) *Physics, maths.* ~*n.* **1.** a mathematical function of the coordinates and momenta of a system of particles used to express their equations of motion. **2.** a mathematical operator that generates such a function. Symbol: **H** ~*adj.* **3.** denoting or relating to the Irish mathematician Sir William Rowan Hamilton (1805–65), or the theory of mechanics or the mathematical operator devised by him.

Hamite ('hæmaɪt) *n.* a member of a group of peoples of N Africa supposedly descended from Noah's son Ham (Genesis 5:32, 10:6), including the ancient Egyptians, the Berbers, etc.

Hamitic (hæ'mɪtɪk, hə-) *n.* **1.** a group of N African languages related to Semitic. They are now classified in four separate subfamilies of the Afro-Asiatic family: Egyptian, Berber, Cushitic, and Chadic. ~*adj.* **2.** denoting, relating to, or belonging to this group of languages. **3.** denoting, belonging to, or characteristic of the Hamites.

Hamito-Semitic *n.* **1.** a former name for the **Afro-Asiatic** family of languages. ~*adj.* **2.** denoting or belonging to this family of languages.

hamlet ('hæmlɪt) *n.* **1.** a small village or group of houses. **2.** (in Britain) a village without its own church. [C14: from Old French *hamelet*, diminutive of *hamel*, from *ham*, of Germanic origin; compare Old English *hamm* plot of pasture, Low German *hamm* enclosed land; see HOME]

hammer ('hæmə) *n.* **1.** a hand tool consisting of a heavy usually steel head held transversely on the end of a handle, used for driving in nails, beating metal, etc. **2.** any tool or device with a similar function, such as the moving part of a door knocker, the striking head on a bell, etc. **3.** a power-driven striking tool, esp. one used in forging. A **pneumatic hammer** delivers a repeated blow from a pneumatic ram, a **drop hammer** uses the energy of a falling weight. **4.** a part of a gunlock that rotates about a fulcrum to strike the primer or percussion cap, either directly or via a firing pin. **5.** *Field sports.* **a.** a heavy metal ball attached to a flexible wire: thrown in competitions. **b.** the event or sport of throwing the hammer. **6.** an auctioneer's gavel. **7.** a device on a piano that is made to strike a string or group of strings causing them to vibrate. **8.** *Anatomy.* the nontechnical name for **malleus. 9. go** (or **come**) **under the hammer.** to be offered for sale by an auctioneer. **10. hammer and tongs.** with great effort or energy: *fighting hammer and tongs.* **11. on someone's hammer.** *Austral. and N.Z. slang.* in hot pursuit of someone. ~*vb.* **12.** to strike or beat (a nail, wood, etc.) with or as if with a hammer. **13.** (*tr.*) to shape or fashion with or as if with a hammer. **14.** (*tr.*; foll. by *in* or *into*) to impress or force (facts, ideas, etc.) into (someone) through constant repetition. **15.** (*intr.*) to feel or sound like hammering: *his pulse was hammering.* **16.** (*intr.*; often foll. by *away*) to work at constantly. **17.** (*tr.*) *Brit.* **a.** to question in a relentless manner. **b.** to criticize severely. **18.** *Informal.* to inflict a defeat on. **19.** (*tr.*) *Slang.* to beat, punish, or chastise. **20.** (*tr.*) *Stock Exchange.* **a.** to announce the default of (a member). **b.** to cause prices of (securities, the market, etc.) to fall by bearish selling. ~See also **hammer out.** [Old English *hamor;* related to Old Norse *hamarr* crag, Old High German *hamar* hammer, Old Slavonic *kamy* stone] —'**hammerer** *n.* —'**hammer-ˌlike** *adj.*

hammer and sickle *n.* **1.** the emblem on the flag of the former Soviet Union, representing the industrial workers and the peasants respectively. **2.** a symbolic representation of the former Soviet Union or of Communism in general.

hammer beam *n.* either of a pair of short horizontal beams that project from opposite walls to support arched braces and struts.

hammer drill *n.* **1.** a rock drill operated by compressed air in which the boring bit is not attached to the reciprocating piston. **2.** an electric hand drill providing hammering in addition to rotating action.

hammerhead ('hæməˌhɛd) *n.* **1.** any shark of the genus *Sphyrna* and family *Sphyrnidae*, having a flattened hammer-shaped head. **2.** a heavily built tropical African wading bird, *Scopus umbretta*, related to the herons, having a dark plumage and a long backward-pointing crest: family *Scopidae*, order *Ciconiiformes.* **3.** a large African fruit bat, *Hypsignathus monstrosus*, with a large square head and hammer-shaped muzzle. —'**hammerˌheaded** *adj.*

hammerless ('hæməlɪs) *adj.* (of a firearm) having the hammer enclosed so that it is not visible.

hammerlock ('hæmə,lɒk) *n.* a wrestling hold in which a wrestler twists his opponent's arm upwards behind his back.

hammer out *vb. (tr., adv.)* **1.** to shape or remove with or as if with a hammer. **2.** to settle or reconcile (differences, problems, etc.) after much dispute or conflict.

hammertoe ('hæmə,təʊ) *n.* **1.** a deformity of the bones of a toe causing the toe to be bent in a clawlike arch. **2.** such a toe.

hammock[1] ('hæmək) *n.* a length of canvas, net, etc., suspended at the ends and used as a bed. [C16: from Spanish *hamaca*, of Taino origin] —'**hammock-,like** *adj.*

hammock[2] ('hæmək) *n.* a variant of **hummock** (sense 3).

Hammond organ ('hæmənd) *n. Trademark.* an electric organ with two keyboards, electronic tone generation, and a wide variety of tone colours: invented in 1934. [C20: named after Laurens *Hammond* (1895–1973), U.S. mechanical engineer]

hammy ('hæmɪ) *adj.* **-mier, -miest.** *Informal.* **1.** (of an actor) overacting or tending to overact. **2.** (of a play, performance, etc.) overacted or exaggerated.

hamper[1] ('hæmpə) *vb.* **1.** *(tr.)* to prevent the progress or free movement of. ~*n.* **2.** *Nautical.* gear aboard a vessel that, though essential, is often in the way. [C14: of obscure origin; perhaps related to Old English *hamm* enclosure, *hemm* HEM[1]] —'**hamperedness** *n.* —'**hamperer** *n.*

hamper[2] ('hæmpə) *n.* **1.** a large basket, usually with a cover. **2.** *Brit.* such a basket and its contents, usually food. **3.** *U.S.* a laundry basket. [C14: variant of HANAPER]

hamshackle ('hæmʃækᵊl) *vb. (tr.)* to hobble (a cow, horse, etc.) by tying a rope around the head and one of the legs.

hamster ('hæmstə) *n.* any Eurasian burrowing rodent of the tribe *Cricetini*, such as *Mesocricetus auratus* (**golden hamster**), having a stocky body, short tail, and cheek pouches: family *Cricetidae*. They are popular pets. [C17: from German, from Old High German *hamustro*, of Slavic origin]

hamstring ('hæm,strɪŋ) *n.* **1.** *Anatomy.* one of the tendons at the back of the knee. **2.** the large tendon at the back of the hock in the hind leg of a horse, etc. ~*vb.* **-strings, -stringing, -strung** *(tr.)* **3.** to cripple by cutting the hamstring of. **4.** to ruin or thwart. [C16: HAM[1] + STRING]

hamulus ('hæmjʊləs) *n., pl.* **-li** (-,laɪ). *Biology.* a hook or hooklike process at the end of some bones or between the fore and hind wings of a bee or similar insect. [C18: from Latin: a little hook, from *hāmus* hook] —'**hamular,** '**hamu,late,** '**hamu,lose,** *or* '**hamulous** *adj.*

hamza *or* **hamzah** ('hɑːmzɑː, -zə) *n.* the sign used in Arabic to represent the glottal stop. [from Arabic *hamzah*, literally: a compression]

Han (hæn) *n.* **1.** the imperial dynasty that ruled China for most of the time from 206 B.C. to 221 A.D., expanding its territory and developing its bureaucracy. **2.** the Chinese people as contrasted to Mongols, Manchus, etc.

hanaper ('hænəpə) *n.* a small wickerwork basket, often used to hold official papers. [C15: from Old French *hanapier*, from *hanap* cup, of Germanic origin; compare Old High German *hnapf* bowl, Old English *hnæp*]

hance (hæns) *n.* a variant of **haunch** (sense 3).

hand (hænd) *n.* **1. a.** the prehensile part of the body at the end of the arm, consisting of a thumb, four fingers, and a palm. **b.** the bones of this part. Related adj.: **manual. 2.** the corresponding or similar part in animals. **3.** something resembling this in shape or function. **4. a.** the cards dealt to one or all players in one round of a card game. **b.** a player holding such cards. **c.** one round of a card game. **5.** agency or influence: *the hand of God.* **6.** a part in something done: *he had a hand in the victory.* **7.** assistance: *to give someone a hand with his work.* **8.** a pointer on a dial, indicator, or gauge, esp. on a clock: *the minute hand.* **9.** acceptance or pledge of partnership, as in marriage: *he asked for her hand; he gave me his hand on the merger.* **10.** a position or direction indicated by its location to the side of an object or the observer: *on the right hand; on every hand.* **11.** a contrastive aspect, condition, etc. (in the phrases **on the one hand, on the other hand**). **12.** (preceded by an ordinal number) source or origin: *a story heard at third hand.* **13.** a person, esp. one who creates something: *a good hand at painting.* **14.** a labourer or manual worker: *we've just taken on a new hand at the farm.* **15.** a member of a ship's crew: *all hands on deck.* **16.** *Printing.* another name for **index** (sense 9). **17.** a person's handwriting: *the letter was in his own hand.* **18.** a round of applause: *give him a hand.* **19.** ability or skill: *a hand for woodwork.* **20.** a manner or characteristic way of doing something: *the hand of a master.* **21.** a unit of length measurement equalling four inches, used for measuring the height of horses, usually from the front hoof to the withers. **22.** a cluster or bundle, esp. of bananas. **23.** a shoulder of pork. **24.** one of the two possible mirror-image forms of an asymmetric object, such as the direction of the helix in a screw thread. **25. a free hand.** freedom to do as desired. **26. a hand's turn.** *(usually used with a negative)* a small amount of work: *he hasn't done a hand's turn.* **27. a heavy hand.** tyranny, persecution, or oppression: *he ruled with a heavy hand.* **28. a high hand.** an oppressive or dictatorial manner. **29. (near) at hand.** very near or close, esp. in time. **30. at someone's hand(s).** from: *the acts of kindness received at their hands.* **31. by hand. a.** by manual rather than mechanical means. **b.** by messenger or personally: *the letter was delivered by hand.* **32. come to hand.** to become available; be received. **33. force someone's hand.** to force someone to act. **34. from hand to hand.** from one person to another. **35. from hand to mouth. a.** in poverty: *living from hand to mouth.* **b.** without preparation or planning. **36. hand and foot.** in all ways possible; completely: *they waited on him hand and foot.* **37. hand in glove.** in an intimate relationship or close association. **38. hand in hand. a.** together; jointly. **b.** clasping each other's hands. **39. hand over fist.** steadily and quickly; with rapid progress: *he makes money hand over fist.* **40. hold one's hand.** to stop or postpone a planned action or punishment. **41. hold someone's hand.** to support, help, or guide someone, esp. by giving sympathy or moral support. **42. in hand. a.** in possession. **b.** under control. **c.** receiving attention or being acted on. **d.** available for use; in reserve. **e.** with deferred payment: *he works a week in hand.* **43. keep one's hand in.** to continue or practise. **44. on hand.** close by; present: *I'll be on hand to help you.* **45. out of hand. a.** beyond control. **b.** without reservation or deeper examination: *he condemned him out of hand.* **46. set one's hand to. a.** to sign (a document). **b.** to start (a task or undertaking). **47. show one's hand.** to reveal one's stand, opinion, or plans. **48. take in hand.** to discipline; control. **49. throw one's hand in.** See **throw in** (sense 3). **50. to hand.** accessible. **51. try one's hand.** to attempt to do something. **52.** *(modifier)* **a.** of or involving the hand: *a hand grenade.* **b.** made to be carried in or worn on the hand: *hand luggage.* **c.** operated by hand: *a hand drill.* **53.** *(in combination)* made by hand rather than by a machine: *hand-sewn.* ~*vb. (tr.)* **54.** to transmit or offer by the hand or hands. **55.** to help or lead with the hand. **56.** *Nautical.* to furl (a sail). **57. hand it to someone.** to give credit to someone. ~See also **hand down, hand in, hand-off, hand on, hand-out, hand over, hands.** [Old English *hand*; related to Old Norse *hönd*, Gothic *handus*, Old High German *hant*] —'**handless** *adj.* —'**hand,like** *adj.*

handbag ('hænd,bæg) *n.* **1.** Also called: **bag, purse** (U.S. and Canadian), **pocketbook** (chiefly U.S.). a woman's small bag carried to contain personal articles. **2.** a small suitcase that can be carried by hand.

handball ('hænd,bɔːl) *n.* **1.** a game in which two or four people strike a ball against a wall or walls with the hand, usually gloved. **2.** the small hard rubber ball used in this game. **3.** *Soccer.* the offence committed when a player other than a goalkeeper in his own penalty area touches the ball with a hand. ~*vb.* **4.** *Australian Rules football.* to pass (the ball) with a blow of the fist. —'**hand,baller** *n.*

handbarrow ('hænd,bærəʊ) *n.* a flat tray for transporting loads, usually carried by two men.

handbell ('hænd,bɛl) *n.* a bell rung by hand, esp. one of a tuned set used in musical performance.

handbill ('hænd,bɪl) *n.* a small printed notice for distribution by hand.

handbook ('hænd,bʊk) *n.* a reference book listing brief facts on a subject or place or directions for maintenance or repair, as of a car: *a tourists' handbook.*

hand brace *n.* the full name for **brace** (sense 1).

handbrake ('hænd,breɪk) *n.* **1.** a brake operated by a hand lever. **2.** the lever that operates the handbrake.

handbreadth ('hænd,brɛtθ, -,brɛdθ) *or* **hand's-breadth** *n.* the width of a hand used as an indication of length.

h and c *abbrev. for* hot and cold (water).

handcart ('hænd,kɑːt) *n.* a simple cart, usually with one or two wheels, pushed or drawn by hand.

handclasp ('hænd,klɑːsp) *n. U.S.* another word for **handshake.**

handcraft ('hænd,krɑːft) *n.* **1.** another word for **handicraft.** ~*vb.* **2.** *(tr.)* to make by handicraft. —'**hand,crafted** *adj.*

handcuff ('hænd,kʌf) *vb.* **1.** *(tr.)* to put handcuffs on (a person); manacle. ~*n.* **2.** *(pl.)* a pair of locking metal rings joined by a short bar or chain for securing prisoners, etc.

hand down *vb. (tr., adv.)* **1.** to leave to a later period or generation; bequeath. **2.** to pass (an outgrown garment) on from one member of a family to a younger one. **3.** *U.S. and Canadian law.* to announce or deliver (a verdict).

-handed *adj.* **1.** having a hand or hands as specified: *broad-handed; a four-handed game of cards.* **2.** made as specified for either left- or right-hand operation or positioning.

handedness ('hændɪdnɪs) *n.* **1.** the tendency to use one hand more skilfully or in preference to the other. **2.** the property of some chemical substances of rotating the plane of polarized light in one direction rather than another. See also **dextrorotation, laevorotation. 3.** the relation between the vectors of spin and momentum of neutrinos and certain other elementary particles.

handfast ('hænd,fɑːst) *Archaic.* ~*n.* **1.** an agreement, esp. of marriage, confirmed by a handshake. **2.** a firm grip. ~*vb. (tr.)* **3.** to betroth or marry (two persons or another person) by joining the hands. **4.** to grip with the hand.

handfasting ('hænd,fɑːstɪŋ) *n.* **1.** an archaic word for **betrothal. 2.** (formerly) a kind of trial marriage marked by the formal joining of hands.

handfeed ('hænd,fiːd) *vb.* **-feeds, -feeding, -fed** (-,fɛd). *(tr.)* **1.** to feed (a person or an animal) by hand. **2.** *Agriculture.* to give food to (poultry or livestock) in fixed amounts and at fixed times, rather than use a self-feeding system.

handful ('hændful) *n., pl.* **-fuls.** **1.** the amount or number that can be held in the hand. **2.** a small number or quantity. **3.** *Informal.* a person or thing difficult to manage or control.

hand glass *n.* **1.** a magnifying glass with a handle. **2.** a small mirror with a handle. **3.** a small glazed frame for seedlings or plants.

hand grenade *n.* a small metal or plastic canister containing explosives, usually activated by a short fuse and used in close combat.

handgrip ('hænd,grɪp) *n.* **1.** another word for **grip**[1] (senses 2, 6, and 7). **2.** *Tennis, golf, etc.* a covering, usually of towelling or rubber, that makes the handle of a racket or club easier to hold.

handgun ('hænd,gʌn) *n. U.S. and Canadian.* a firearm that can be held, carried, and fired with one hand, such as a pistol.

hand-held *adj.* (of a film camera) held rather than mounted, as in close-up action shots.

handhold ('hænd,həuld) *n.* **1.** an object, crevice, etc., that can be used as a grip or support, as in climbing. **2.** a grip or secure hold with the hand or hands.

handicap ('hændɪ,kæp) *n.* **1.** something that hampers or hinders. **2. a.** a contest, esp. a race, in which contestants are given advantages or disadvantages of weight, distance, time, etc., in an attempt to equalize their chances of winning. **b.** the advantage or disadvantage prescribed. **3.** *Golf.* the number of strokes by which a player's averaged score exceeds the standard scratch score for the particular course: used as the basis for handicapping in competitive play. **4.** any physical disability or disadvantage resulting from physical, mental, or social impairment or abnormality. ~*vb.* **-caps, -capping, -capped.** (*tr.*) **5.** to be a hindrance or disadvantage to. **6.** to assign a handicap or handicaps to. **7.** to organize (a contest) by handicapping. **8.** *U.S. and Canadian.* **a.** to attempt to forecast the winner of (a contest, esp. a horse race). **b.** to assign odds for or against (a contestant). [C17: probably from *hand in cap,* a lottery game in which players drew forfeits from a cap or deposited money in it] —'**handi,capper** *n.*

handicapped ('hændɪ,kæpt) *adj.* **1.** physically disabled. **2.** *Psychol.* denoting a person whose social behaviour or emotional reactions are in some way impaired. **3.** (of a competitor) assigned a handicap.

handicapper ('hændɪ,kæpə) *n.* **1.** an official appointed to assign handicaps to competitors in such sports as golf and horse racing. **2.** a newspaper columnist employed to estimate the chances that horses have of winning races.

handicap register *n. Social welfare.* (in Britain) **1.** a list of the handicapped people in its area that a local authority has a duty to compile under the Chronically Sick and Disabled Persons Act 1970. Eligibility for certain welfare benefits may depend on registration. **2.** a different list of handicapped people, kept by the Manpower Services Commission for employment purposes. See also **green card, registered disabled.**

handicraft ('hændɪ,krɑːft) *n.* **1.** skill or dexterity in working with the hands. **2.** a particular skill or art performed with the hands, such as weaving, pottery, etc. **3.** the work produced by such a skill or art: *local handicraft is on sale.* ~Also called: **handcraft.** [C15: changed from HANDCRAFT through the influence of HANDIWORK, which was analysed as if HANDY + WORK] —'**handi,craftsman** *n.*

handily ('hændɪlɪ) *adv.* **1.** in a handy way or manner. **2.** conveniently or suitably: *handily nearby.* **3.** *U.S. and Canadian.* easily: *the horse won handily.*

hand in *vb.* (*tr., adv.*) to return or submit (something, such as an examination paper).

handiwork ('hændɪ,wɜːk) *n.* **1.** work performed or produced by hand, such as embroidery or pottery. **2.** the result of the action or endeavours of a person or thing. [Old English *handgeweorc,* from HAND + *geweorc,* from *ge-* (collective prefix) + *weorc* WORK]

handkerchief ('hæŋkətʃɪf, -tʃiːf) *n.* a small square of soft absorbent material, such as linen, silk, or soft paper, carried and used to wipe the nose, etc.

hand-knit *adj.* also **hand-knitted.** **1.** knitted by hand, not on a machine. ~*vb.* **-knits, -knitting, -knitted** *or* **-knit.** **2.** to knit (garments) by hand.

handle ('hænd[ə]l) *n.* **1.** the part of a utensil, drawer, etc., designed to be held in order to move, use, or pick up the object. **2.** *N.Z.* a glass beer mug with a handle. **3.** *Slang.* a person's name or title. **4.** *CB radio.* a slang name for **call sign.** **5.** an opportunity, reason, or excuse for doing something: *his background served as a handle for their mockery.* **6.** the quality, as of textiles, perceived by touching or feeling. **7.** the total amount of a bet on a horse race or similar event. **8. fly off the handle.** *Informal.* to become suddenly extremely angry. ~*vb.* (*mainly tr.*) **9.** to pick up and hold, move, or touch with the hands. **10.** to operate or employ using the hands: *the boy handled the reins well.* **11.** to have power or control over: *my wife handles my investments.* **12.** to manage successfully: *a secretary must be able to handle clients.* **13.** to discuss (a theme, subject, etc.). **14.** to deal with or treat in a specified way: *I was handled with great tact.* **15.** to trade or deal in (specified merchandise). **16.** (*intr.*) to react or respond in a specified way to operation or control: *the car handles well on bends.* [Old English; related to Old Saxon *handlon* (vb.), Old High German *hantilla* towel] —'**handleable** *adj.* —'**handled** *adj.* —'**handleless** *adj.*

handlebar moustache ('hænd[ə]l,bɑː) *n.* a bushy extended moustache with curled ends that resembles handlebars.

handlebars ('hænd[ə]l,bɑːz) *pl. n.* (*sometimes sing.*) a metal tube having its ends curved to form handles, used for steering a bicycle, motorcycle, etc.

handler ('hændlə) *n.* **1.** a person, esp. a police officer, in charge of a specially trained dog. **2.** a person who handles some specified thing: *a baggage handler.* **3.** a person who holds or incites a dog, gamecock, etc., esp. in a race or contest. **4.** the trainer or second of a boxer.

handling ('hændlɪŋ) *n.* **1.** the act or an instance of picking up, turning over, or touching something. **2.** treatment, as of a theme in literature. **3. a.** the process by which a commodity is packaged, transported, etc. **b.** (*as modifier*): *handling charges.* **4.** *Law.* the act of receiving property that one knows or believes to be stolen.

hand-loomed *adj.* (of a garment) made on a hand loom.

handmade (,hænd'meɪd) *adj.* made by hand, not by machine, esp. with care or craftsmanship.

handmaiden ('hænd,meɪd[ə]n) *or* **handmaid** *n.* **1.** a person or thing that serves a useful but subordinate purpose: *logic is the handmaid of philosophy.* **2.** *Archaic.* a female servant or attendant.

hand-me-down *n. Informal.* **1. a.** something, esp. an outgrown garment, passed down from one person to another. **b.** (*as modifier*): *a hand-me-down dress.* **2. a.** anything that has already been used by another. **b.** (*as modifier*): *hand-me-down ideas.*

hand-off *Rugby.* ~*n.* **1.** the act of warding off an opposing player with the open hand. ~*vb.* **hand off.** **2.** (*tr., adv.*) to ward off (an opponent) using a hand-off.

hand on *vb.* (*tr., adv.*) to pass to the next in a succession.

hand organ *n.* another name for **barrel organ.**

hand-out *n.* **1.** clothing, food, or money given to a needy person. **2.** a leaflet, free sample, etc., given out to publicize something. **3.** a statement or other document distributed to the press or an audience to confirm, supplement, or replace an oral presentation. ~*vb.* **hand out.** (*tr., adv.*) **4.** to distribute.

hand over *vb.* (*tr., adv.*) **1.** to surrender possession of; transfer. ~*n.* **handover.** **2.** a transfer, surrender.

hand-pick *vb.* (*tr.*) to choose or select with great care, as for a special job or purpose. —,**hand-'picked** *adj.*

hand-piece *n. Austral. and N.Z.* hand-held, power-operated shears used by a shearer. See also **comb** (sense 3).

handrail ('hænd,reɪl) *n.* a rail alongside a stairway, etc., at a convenient height to be grasped to provide support.

hands (hændz) *pl. n.* **1.** power or keeping: *your welfare is in his hands.* **2.** Also called: **handling.** *Soccer.* the infringement of touching the ball with any part of the hand or arm. **3. change hands.** to pass from the possession of one person or group to another. **4. clean hands.** freedom from guilt. **5. hands down.** without effort; easily. **6. hands off.** do not touch or interfere. **7. hands up!** raise the hands above the level of the shoulders, an order usually given by an armed robber to a victim, etc. **8. have one's hands full. a.** to be completely occupied. **b.** to be beset with problems. **9. have one's hands tied.** to be wholly unable to act. **10. in good hands.** in protective care. **11. join hands.** See **join** (sense 12). **12. lay hands on** *or* **upon. a.** to seize or get possession of. **b.** to beat up; assault. **c.** to find: *I just can't lay my hands on it anywhere.* **d.** *Christianity.* to confirm or ordain by the imposition of hands. **13. off one's hands.** for which one is no longer responsible. **14. on one's hands. a.** for which one is responsible: *I've got too much on my hands to help.* **b.** to spare: *time on my hands.* **15. throw up one's hands.** to give up in despair. **16. wash one's hands of.** to have nothing more to do with.

handsaw ('hænd,sɔː) *n.* any saw for use in one hand only.

hand's-breadth *n.* another name for **handbreadth.**

handsel *or* **hansel** ('hæns[ə]l) *Archaic or dialect.* ~*n.* **1.** a gift for good luck at the beginning of a new year, new venture, etc. ~*vb.* **-sels, -selling, -selled** *or U.S.* **-sels, -seling, -seled.** (*tr.*) **2.** to give a handsel to (a person). **3.** to begin (a venture) with ceremony; inaugurate. [Old English *handselen* delivery into the hand; related to Old Norse *handsal* promise sealed with a handshake, Swedish *handsöl* gratuity; see HAND, SELL]

handset ('hænd,sɛt) *n.* a telephone mouthpiece and earpiece mounted so that they can be held simultaneously to mouth and ear.

handshake ('hænd,ʃeɪk) *n.* the act of grasping and shaking a person's hand, as when being introduced or agreeing on a deal.

handshaking ('hænd,ʃeɪkɪŋ) *n. Computer technol.* communication between a computer system and an external device, by which each tells the other that data is ready to be transferred, and that the receiver is ready to accept it.

hands-off *adj.* (of a machine, device, etc.) without need of manual operation.

handsome ('hændsəm) *adj.* **1.** (of a man) good-looking, esp. in having regular, pleasing, and well-defined features. **2.** (of a woman) fine-looking in a dignified way. **3.** well-proportioned, stately, or comely: *a handsome room.* **4.** liberal or ample: *a handsome allowance.* **5.** gracious or generous: *a handsome action.* [C15 *handsom* easily handled; compare Dutch *handzaam;* see HAND, -SOME[1]] —'**handsomely** *adv.* —'**handsomeness** *n.*

hands-on *adj.* involving practical experience of equipment, etc.: *hands-on training in the use of computers.*
handspike ('hænd,spaɪk) *n.* a bar or length of pipe used as a lever.
handspring ('hænd,sprɪŋ) *n.* a gymnastic feat in which a person starts from a standing position and leaps forwards or backwards into a handstand and then onto his feet.
handstand ('hænd,stænd) *n.* the act or instance of supporting the body on the hands alone in an upside down position.
handstroke ('hænd,strəuk) *n. Bell-ringing.* the downward movement of the bell rope as the bell swings around allowing the ringer to grasp and pull it. Compare **backstroke** (sense 4).
hand-to-hand *adj., adv.* at close quarters: *they fought hand-to-hand.*
hand-to-mouth *adj., adv.* with barely enough money or food to satisfy immediate needs: *a hand-to-mouth existence.*
handwork ('hænd,wɜːk) *n.* work done by hand rather than by machine. —'**hand,worked** *adj.*
handwriting ('hænd,raɪtɪŋ) *n.* **1.** writing by hand rather than by typing or printing. **2.** a person's characteristic writing style: *that signature is in my handwriting.*
handwritten ('hænd,rɪtᵊn) *adj.* written by hand; not printed or typed.
handy ('hændɪ) *adj.* **handier, handiest. 1.** conveniently or easily within reach. **2.** easy to manoeuvre, handle, or use: *a handy tool.* **3.** skilful with one's hands. —'**handiness** *n.*
handyman ('hændɪ,mæn) *n., pl.* **-men. 1.** a man employed to do various tasks. **2.** a man skilled in odd jobs, etc.
hanepoot ('hɑːnə,puət) *n. S. African.* a variety of muscat grape used as a dessert fruit and in making wine. [from Afrikaans *hane* cock + *poot* claw]
hang (hæŋ) *vb.* **hangs, hanging, hung** (hʌŋ). **1.** to fasten or be fastened from above, esp. by a cord, chain, etc.; suspend: *the picture hung on the wall; to hang laundry.* **2.** to place or be placed in position as by a hinge so as to allow free movement around or at the place of suspension: *to hang a door.* **3.** (*intr.;* sometimes foll. by *over*) to be suspended or poised; hover: *a pall of smoke hung over the city.* **4.** (*intr.;* sometimes foll. by *over*) to be imminent; threaten. **5.** (*intr.*) to be or remain doubtful or unresolved (esp. in the phrase **hang in the balance**). **6.** (*past tense and past participle* **hanged**) to suspend or be suspended by the neck until dead. **7.** (*tr.*) to fasten, fix, or attach in position or at an appropriate angle: *to hang a scythe to its handle.* **8.** (*tr.*) to decorate, furnish, or cover with something suspended or fastened: *to hang a wall with tapestry.* **9.** (*tr.*) to fasten to or suspend from a wall: *to hang wallpaper.* **10.** to exhibit (a picture or pictures) by (a particular painter, printmaker, etc.) or (of a picture or a painter, etc.) to be exhibited in an art gallery, etc. **11.** to fall or droop or allow to fall or droop: *to hang one's head in shame.* **12.** (of cloth, clothing, etc.) to drape, fall, or flow, esp. in a specified manner: *her skirt hangs well.* **13.** (*tr.*) to suspend (game such as pheasant) so that it becomes slightly decomposed and therefore more tender and tasty. **14.** (of a jury) to prevent or be prevented from reaching a verdict. **15.** (*past tense and past participle* **hanged**) *Slang.* to damn or be damned: used in mild curses or interjections: *I'll be hanged before I'll go out in that storm.* **16.** (*intr.*) to pass slowly (esp. in the phrase **time hangs heavily**). **17. hang fire. a.** to be delayed. **b.** to procrastinate. See also **fire** (sense 16). ~*n.* **18.** the way in which something hangs. **19.** (*usually used with a negative*) *Slang.* a damn: *I don't care a hang for what you say.* **20. get the hang of.** *Informal.* **a.** to understand the technique of doing something. **b.** to perceive the meaning or significance of. ~See also **hang about, hang back, hang behind, hang in, hang on, hang out, hang together, hang up.** [Old English *hangian;* related to Old Norse *hanga,* Old High German *hangēn*]
hang about *or* **around** *vb.* (*intr.*) **1.** to waste time; loiter. **2.** (*adv.;* foll. by *with*) to frequent the company (of someone). ~*interj.* **3.** wait a moment! stop!
hangar ('hæŋə) *n.* a large workshop or building for storing and maintaining aircraft. [C19: from French: shed, perhaps from Medieval Latin *angārium* shed used as a smithy, of obscure origin]
hang back *vb.* (*intr., adv.;* often foll. by *from*) to be reluctant to go forward or carry on (with some activity).
hang behind *vb.* (*intr., adv.*) to remain in a place after others have left; linger.
hangbird ('hæŋ,bɜːd) *n. U.S. and Canadian.* any bird, esp. the Baltimore oriole, that builds a hanging nest.
hangdog ('hæŋ,dɒg) *adj.* **1.** downcast, furtive, or guilty in appearance or manner. ~*n.* **2.** a furtive or sneaky person.
hanger ('hæŋə) *n.* **1. a.** any support, such as a hook, strap, peg, or loop, on or by which something may be hung. **b.** See **coat hanger. 2. a.** a person who hangs something. **b.** (*in combination*): *paperhanger.* **3.** a bracket designed to attach one part of a mechanical structure to another, such as the one that attaches the spring shackle of a motor car to the chassis. **4.** a wood on a steep hillside, characteristically beech growing on chalk in southern England. **5. a.** a loop or strap on a sword belt from which a short sword or dagger was hung. **b.** the weapon itself.
hanger-on *n., pl.* **hangers-on.** a sycophantic follower or dependant, esp. one hoping for personal gain.
hang-glider *n.* an unpowered aircraft consisting of a large cloth wing stretched over a light framework from which the pilot hangs in a harness, using a horizontal bar to control the flight. —**hang-gliding** *n.*
hangi ('hʌŋiː) *n. N.Z.* **1.** an open-air cooking pit. **2.** the food cooked in it. **3.** the social gathering at the resultant meal. [Maori]
hang in *vb.* (*intr., prep.*) *Informal, chiefly U.S. and Canadian.* to persist: *just hang in there for a bit longer.*
hanging ('hæŋɪŋ) *n.* **1. a.** the putting of a person to death by suspending the body by the neck from a noose. **b.** (*as modifier*): *a hanging offence.* **2.** (*often pl.*) a decorative textile such as a tapestry or drapery hung on a wall or over a window. **3.** the act of a person or thing that hangs. ~*adj.* **4.** not supported from below; suspended. **5.** undecided; still under discussion. **6.** inclining or projecting downwards; overhanging. **7.** situated on a steep slope or in a high place. **8.** (*prenominal*) given to issuing harsh sentences, esp. death sentences: *a hanging judge.* **9.** *Chess.* See **hanging pawn.**
hanging glacier *n.* a glacier situated on a shelf above a valley or another glacier; it may be joined to the lower level by an icefall or separate from it.
hanging pawn *n. Chess.* one of two or more adjacent pawns on central half-open files with no pawns of the same colour on the files immediately to left and right of them.
hanging valley *n. Geography.* a tributary valley entering a main valley at a much higher level because of overdeepening of the main valley, esp. by glacial erosion.
hanging wall *n.* the rocks on the upper side of an inclined fault plane or mineral vein. Compare **footwall.**
hangman ('hæŋmən) *n., pl.* **-men.** an official who carries out a sentence of hanging on condemned criminals.
hangnail ('hæŋ,neɪl) *n.* a piece of skin torn away from, but still attached to, the base or side of a fingernail. [C17: from Old English *angnægl,* from *enge* tight + *nægl* NAIL; influenced by HANG]
hang on *vb.* (*intr.*) **1.** (*adv.*) to continue or persist in an activity, esp. with effort or difficulty: *hang on at your present job until you can get another.* **2.** (*adv.*) to cling, grasp, or hold: *she hangs on to her mother's arm.* **3.** (*prep.*) to be conditioned or contingent on; depend on: *everything hangs on this business deal.* **4.** (*prep.*) Also: **hang onto, hang upon.** to listen attentively to: *she hung on his every word.* **5.** (*adv.*) *Informal.* to wait or remain: *hang on for a few minutes.*
hang out *vb.* (*adv.*) **1.** to suspend, be suspended, or lean, esp. from an opening, as for display or airing: *to hang out the washing.* **2.** (*intr.*) *Informal.* to live at or frequent a place: *the police know where the thieves hang out.* **3.** (*intr.;* foll. by *with*) *Informal.* to frequent the company (of someone). **4.** *Slang.* to relax completely in an unassuming way (esp. in the phrase **let it all hang out**). **5.** (*intr.*) *U.S. informal.* to act or speak freely, in an open, cooperative, or indiscreet manner. ~*n.* **hang-out. 6.** *Informal.* a place where one lives or that one frequently visits.
hangover ('hæŋ,əuvə) *n.* **1.** the delayed aftereffects of drinking too much alcohol in a relatively short period of time, characterized by headache and sometimes nausea and dizziness. **2.** a person or thing left over from or influenced by a past age.
hang together *vb.* (*intr., adv.*) **1.** to be cohesive or united. **2.** to be consistent: *your statements don't quite hang together.*
hang up *vb.* (*adv.*) **1.** (*tr.*) to put on a hook, hanger, etc.: *please hang up your coat.* **2.** to replace (a telephone receiver) on its cradle at the end of a conversation, often breaking a conversation off abruptly. **3.** (*tr.; usually passive;* usually foll. by *on*) *Informal.* to cause to have an emotional or psychological preoccupation or problem: *he's really hung up on his mother.* ~*n.* **hang-up.** *Informal.* **4.** an emotional or psychological preoccupation or problem. **5.** a persistent cause of annoyance.
hank (hæŋk) *n.* **1.** a loop, coil, or skein, as of rope, wool, or yarn. **2.** *Nautical.* a ringlike fitting that can be opened to admit a stay for attaching the luff of a sail. **3.** a unit of measurement of cloth, yarn, etc., such as a length of 840 yards (767 m) of cotton or 560 yards (512 m) of worsted yarn. ~*vb.* **4.** (*tr.*) *Nautical.* to attach (a sail) to a stay by hanks. [C13: of Scandinavian origin; compare Old Norse *hanka* to coil, Swedish *hank* string]
hanker ('hæŋkə) *vb.* (foll. by *for, after,* or an infinitive) to have a yearning (for something or to do something). [C17: probably from Dutch dialect *hankeren*] —'**hankering** *n.*
hanky *or* **hankie** ('hæŋkɪ) *n., pl.* **hankies.** *Informal.* short for **handkerchief.**
hanky-panky ('hæŋkɪ'pæŋkɪ) *n. Informal.* **1.** dubious or suspicious behaviour. **2.** foolish behaviour or talk. **3.** illicit sexual relations. [C19: variant of HOCUS-POCUS]
Hanoverian (,hænə'vɪərɪən) *adj.* **1.** of, relating to, or situated in Hanover, city in N Germany. **2.** of or relating to the princely house of Hanover (1692–1815) or to the monarchs of Britain or their reigns from 1714 to 1901. ~*n.* **3.** a member or supporter of the house of Hanover.
Hansard ('hænsɑːd) *n.* **1.** the official verbatim report of the proceedings of the British Parliament. **2.** a similar report kept by other legislative bodies. [C19: named after L. *Hansard* (1752–1828) and his descendants, who compiled the reports until 1889]
Hanse (hæns) *or* **Hansa** ('hænsə, -zə) *n.* **1.** a medieval guild of merchants. **2.** a fee paid by the new members of a medieval trading guild. **3. a.** the Hanseatic League. b. (*as modifier*): *a*

Hanse town. [C12: of Germanic origin; compare Old High German *hansa,* Old English *hōs* troop]

Hanseatic (ˌhænsɪˈætɪk) *adj.* **1.** of or relating to the Hanseatic League of towns in N Germany formed in the mid-14th century to protect and control trade. ~*n.* **2.** a member of the Hanseatic League.

hansel (ˈhænsᵊl) *n., vb.* a variant spelling of **handsel.**

Hansen's disease (ˈhænsənz) *n. Pathol.* another name for **leprosy.** [C20: named after G. H. *Hansen* (1841–1912), Norwegian physician]

hansom (ˈhænsəm) *n.* (*sometimes cap.*) a two-wheeled one-horse carriage with a fixed hood. The driver sits on a high outside seat at the rear. Also called: **hansom cab.** [C19: short for *hansom cab,* named after its designer J. A. *Hansom* (1803–82)]

Hants (hænts) *abbrev. for* Hampshire.

Hanukkah (ˈhɑːnəkə, -nʊˌkɑː; *Hebrew* xanuˈka) *n.* a variant spelling of **Chanukah.**

hanuman (ˌhʌnʊˈmɑːn) *n.* another word for **entellus** (the monkey). [from Hindi *Hanumān,* monkey chief of Hindu mythology, from Sanskrit *hanumant* having (conspicuous) jaws, from *hanu* jaw]

hap[1] (hæp) *n. Archaic.* **1.** luck; chance. **2.** an occurrence. ~*vb.* **haps, happing, happed. 3.** (*intr.*) an archaic word for **happen.** [C13: from Old Norse *happ* good luck; related to Old English *gehæplic* convenient, Old Slavonic *kobŭ* fate]

hap[2] (hæp) *Scot. and eastern English dialect.* ~*vb.* (*tr.*) **1.** to cover up; wrap up warmly. ~*n.* **2.** a covering of any kind. [C14: perhaps of Norse origin]

hapaxanthic (ˌhæpəˈzænθɪk) *or* **hapaxanthous** (ˌhæpəˈzænθəs) *adj. Botany.* another word for **monocarpic.** [from Greek: fruiting only once]

hapax legomenon (ˈhæpæks ləˈgɒmɪˌnɒn) *n., pl.* **hapax legomena** (ləˈgɒmɪnə). another term for **nonce word.** [Greek: thing said only once]

ha'penny (ˈheɪpnɪ) *n., pl.* **-nies.** *Brit.* a variant spelling of **halfpenny.**

haphazard (hæpˈhæzəd) *adv., adj.* **1.** at random. ~*adj.* **2.** careless; slipshod. ~*n.* **3.** *Rare.* chance. —**hapˈhazardly** *adv.* —**hapˈhazardness** *n.*

Haphtarah (hɑːfˈtəʊrə; *Hebrew* haftaˈraː) *n., pl.* **-taroth** (-ˈtəʊrəʊt; *Hebrew* -taˈroːt) *or* **-tarahs.** a variant spelling of **Haftarah.**

hapless (ˈhæplɪs) *adj.* unfortunate; wretched. —ˈ**haplessly** *adv.* —ˈ**haplessness** *n.*

haplite (ˈhæplaɪt) *n.* a variant of **aplite.** —**haplitic** (hæpˈlɪtɪk) *adj.*

haplo- *or before a vowel* **hapl-** *combining form.* single or simple: *haplology; haplosis.* [from Greek *haplous* simple]

haplobiont (ˌhæpləʊˈbaɪɒnt) *n. Biology.* an organism, esp. a plant, that exists in either the diploid form or the haploid form (but never alternates between these forms) during its life cycle. —ˌ**haplobiˈontic** *adj.*

haplography (hæpˈlɒgrəfɪ) *n., pl.* **-phies.** the accidental writing of only one letter or syllable where there should be two similar letters or syllables, as in spelling *endodontics* as *endontics.* [C19: from Greek, from *haplous* single + -GRAPHY]

haploid (ˈhæplɔɪd) *Biology.* ~*adj.* also **haploidic. 1.** (esp. of gametes) having a single set of unpaired chromosomes. ~*n.* **2.** a haploid cell or organism. Compare **diploid.** [C20: from Greek *haploeidēs* single, from *haplous* single] —ˈ**haploidy** *n.*

haplology (hæpˈlɒlədʒɪ) *n.* omission of a repeated occurrence of a sound or syllable in fluent speech, as for example in the pronunciation of *library* as (ˈlaɪbrɪ). —**haplologic** (ˌhæpləˈlɒdʒɪk) *adj.*

haplont (ˈhæplɒnt) *n. Biology.* an organism, esp. a plant, that has the haploid number of chromosomes in its somatic cells. —**haˈplontic** *adj.*

haplosis (hæpˈləʊsɪs) *n. Biology.* the production of a haploid number of chromosomes during meiosis.

haplostemonous (ˈhæpləʊˈstiːmənəs, -ˈstem-) *adj.* (of plants) having the stamens arranged in a single whorl. [C19: from New Latin, from HAPLO- + *-stemonus* relating to a STAMEN]

haply (ˈhæplɪ) *adv.* (*sentence modifier*) an archaic word for **perhaps.**

ha'p'orth (ˈheɪpəθ) *n. Brit.* **1.** a variant spelling of **halfpennyworth. 2.** *Informal.* a person considered as specified: *daft ha'p'orth.*

happen (ˈhæpᵊn) *vb.* **1.** (*intr.*) (of an event in time) to come about or take place; occur. **2.** (*intr.;* foll. by *to*) (of some unforeseen circumstance or event, esp. death), to fall to the lot (of); be a source of good or bad fortune (to): *if anything happens to me it'll be your fault.* **3.** (*tr.*) to chance (to be or do something): *I happen to know him.* **4.** (*tr.; takes a clause as object*) to be the case, esp. if by chance, that: *it happens that I know him.* ~*adv., sentence substitute.* **5.** *Northern English dialect.* **a.** another word for **perhaps. b.** (*as sentence modifier*): *happen I'll see thee tomorrow.* [C14: see HAP, -EN[1]]

▷**Usage.** See at **occur.**

happen by, past, along, *or* **in** *vb.* (*intr., adv.*) *Informal, chiefly U.S.* to appear, arrive, or come casually or by chance.

happening (ˈhæpənɪŋ, ˈhæpnɪŋ) *n.* **1.** an occurrence; event. **2.** an improvised or spontaneous display or performance consisting of bizarre and haphazard events. ~*adj.* **3.** *Informal.* fashionable and up-to-the-minute.

happen on *or* **upon** *vb.* (*intr., prep.*) to find by chance: *I happened upon a pound note lying in the street.*

happenstance (ˈhæpənˌstæns) *n. U.S. and Canadian.* **1.** chance. **2.** a chance occurrence.

happy (ˈhæpɪ) *adj.* **-pier, -piest. 1.** feeling, showing, or expressing joy; pleased. **2.** causing joy or gladness. **3.** fortunate; lucky: *the happy position of not having to work.* **4.** aptly expressed; appropriate: *a happy turn of phrase.* **5.** (*postpositive*) *Informal.* slightly intoxicated. ~*interj.* **6.** (*in combination*): *happy birthday; happy Christmas.* ~See also **trigger-happy.** [C14: see HAP, -Y[1]] —ˈ**happily** *adv.* —ˈ**happiness** *n.*

happy event *n. Informal.* the birth of a child.

happy-go-lucky *adj.* carefree or easy-going.

happy hour *n.* a time, usually in the early evening, when some pubs or bars sell drinks at reduced prices.

happy hunting ground *n.* **1.** (in American Indian legend) the paradise to which a person passes after death. **2.** a productive or profitable area for a person with a particular interest or requirement: *jumble sales proved happy hunting grounds in her search for old stone jars.*

happy medium *n.* a course or state that avoids extremes.

happy release *n.* liberation, esp. by death, from an unpleasant condition.

Hapsburg (ˈhæpsˌbɜːg) *n.* **a.** a member of a royal dynasty that dominated Europe from the 15th to the 20th centuries, providing rulers for the Holy Roman Empire, Spain, Hungary, Austria, and Austria-Hungary. **b.** (*as modifier*): *the Hapsburg line.*

hapten (ˈhæptən) *or* **haptene** (ˈhæptiːn) *n. Immunol.* an incomplete antigen that can stimulate antibody production only in combination with a particular protein. [C20: from German, from Greek *haptein* to fasten]

hapteron (ˈhæptərɒn) *n.* a cell or group of cells that occurs in certain plants, esp. seaweeds, and attaches the plant to its substratum. [C20: from Greek *haptein* to make fast]

haptic (ˈhæptɪk) *adj.* relating to or based on the sense of touch. [C19: from Greek, from *haptein* to touch]

haptotropism (ˌhæptəʊˈtrəʊpɪzəm) *n.* another name for **thigmotropism.**

hapu (ˈhɑːpuː) *n. N.Z.* a subtribe. [Maori]

hapuka *or* **hapuku** (həˈpuːkə, ˈhɑːpʊkə) *n. N.Z.* another name for **groper.** [Maori]

hara-kiri (ˌhærəˈkɪrɪ) *or* **hari-kari** (ˌhærɪˈkɑːrɪ) *n.* (formerly, in Japan) ritual suicide by disembowelment with a sword when disgraced or under sentence of death. Also called: **seppuku.** [C19: from Japanese taboo slang, from *hara* belly + *kiri* cut]

harambee (ˌhɑːrɑːmˈbeɪ) *n.* **1.** a work chant used on the E African coast. **2.** a rallying cry used in Kenya. ~*interj.* **3.** a cry of harambee. [Swahili: pull together]

harangue (həˈræŋ) *vb.* **1.** to address (a person or crowd) in an angry, vehement, or forcefully persuasive way. ~*n.* **2.** a loud, forceful, or angry speech. [C15: from Old French, from Old Italian *aringa* public speech, probably of Germanic origin; related to Medieval Latin *harenga;* see HARRY, RING[1]] —**haˈranguer** *n.*

harass (ˈhærəs, həˈræs) *vb.* (*tr.*) to trouble, torment, or confuse by continual persistent attacks, questions, etc. [C17: from French *harasser,* variant of Old French *harer* to set a dog on, of Germanic origin; compare Old High German *harēn* to cry out] —ˈ**harassed** *adj.* —ˈ**harassing** *adj., n.* —ˈ**harassment** *n.*

harbinger (ˈhɑːbɪndʒə) *n.* **1.** a person or thing that announces or indicates the approach of something; forerunner. **2.** *Obsolete.* a person sent in advance of a royal party or army to obtain lodgings for them. ~*vb.* **3.** (*tr.*) to announce the approach or arrival of. [C12: from Old French *herbergere,* from *herberge* lodging, from Old Saxon *heriberga;* compare Old High German *heriberga* army shelter; see HARRY, BOROUGH]

harbour *or U.S.* **harbor** (ˈhɑːbə) *n.* **1.** a sheltered port. **2.** a place of refuge or safety. ~*vb.* **3.** (*tr.*) to give shelter to: *to harbour a criminal.* **4.** (*tr.*) to maintain secretly: *to harbour a grudge.* **5.** to shelter (a vessel) in a harbour or (of a vessel) to seek shelter. [Old English *herebeorg,* from *here* troop, army + *beorg* shelter; related to Old High German *heriberga* hostelry, Old Norse *herbergi*] —ˈ**harbourer** *or U.S.* ˈ**harborer** *n.* —ˈ**harbourless** *or U.S.* ˈ**harborless** *adj.*

harbourage *or U.S.* **harborage** (ˈhɑːbərɪdʒ) *n.* shelter or refuge, as for a ship, or a place providing shelter.

harbour master *n.* an official in charge of a harbour.

harbour seal *n.* a common earless seal, *Phoca vitulina,* that is greyish-black with paler markings: occurs off the coasts of North America, N Europe, and NE Asia.

hard (hɑːd) *adj.* **1.** firm or rigid; not easily dented, crushed, or pierced. **2.** toughened by or as if by physical labour; not soft or smooth: *hard hands.* **3.** difficult to do or accomplish; arduous: *a hard task.* **4.** difficult to understand or perceive: *a hard question.* **5.** showing or requiring considerable physical or mental energy, effort, or application: *hard work; a hard drinker.* **6.** stern, cold, or intractable: *a hard judge.* **7.** exacting; demanding: *a hard master.* **8.** harsh; cruel: *a hard fate.* **9.** inflicting pain, sorrow, distress, or hardship: *hard times.* **10.** tough or adamant: *a hard man.* **11.** forceful or violent: *a hard knock.* **12.** cool or uncompromising: *we took a long hard look at our profit factor.* **13.** indisputable; real: *hard facts.* **14.** *Chem.* (of water) impairing the formation of a lather by soap. See **hardness** (sense 3).

15. practical, shrewd, or calculating: *he is a hard man in business.* **16.** too harsh to be pleasant: *hard light.* **17. a.** (of cash, money, etc.) in coin and paper rather than cheques. **b.** (of currency) in strong demand, esp. as a result of a good balance of payments situation. **c.** (of credit) difficult to obtain; tight. **18.** (of alcoholic drink) being a spirit rather than a wine, beer, etc.: *the hard stuff.* **19.** (of a drug such as heroin, morphine, or cocaine) highly addictive. Compare **soft** (sense 20). **20.** *Physics.* (of radiation, such as gamma rays and x-rays) having high energy and the ability to penetrate solids. **21.** *Physics.* (of a vacuum) almost complete. **22.** *Chiefly U.S.* (of goods) durable. **23.** short for **hard-core. 24.** *Phonetics.* **a.** an older word for **fortis. b.** (not in modern technical usage) denoting the consonants *c* and *g* in English when they are pronounced as velar stops (k, g). **c.** (of consonants in the Slavonic languages) not palatalized. **25. a.** being heavily fortified and protected. **b.** (of nuclear missiles) located underground in massively reinforced silos. **26.** politically extreme: *the hard left.* **27.** *Brit. and N.Z. informal.* incorrigible or disreputable (esp. in the phrase **a hard case**). **28.** (of bread, etc.) stale and old. **29. a hard nut to crack. a.** a person not easily persuaded or won over. **b.** a thing not easily understood. **30. hard by.** near; close by. **31. hard doer.** *N.Z.* a tough worker at anything. **32. hard up.** *Informal.* **a.** in need of money; poor. **b.** (foll. by *for*) in great need (of): *hard up for suggestions.* **33. put the hard word on.** *Austral. and N.Z. informal.* to ask or demand something from. ~*adv.* **34.** with great energy, force, or vigour: *the team always played hard.* **35.** as far as possible; all the way: *hard left.* **36.** with application; earnestly or intently: *she thought hard about the formula.* **37.** with great intensity, force, or violence: *his son's death hit him hard.* **38.** (foll. by *on, upon, by,* or *after*) close; near: *hard on his heels.* **39.** (foll. by *at*) assiduously; devotedly. **40. a.** with effort or difficulty: *their victory was hard won.* **b.** (*in combination*): *hard-earned.* **41.** slowly and reluctantly: *prejudice dies hard.* **42. go hard with.** to cause pain or difficulty to (someone): *it will go hard with you if you don't tell the truth.* **43. hard at it.** working hard. **44. hard put (to it).** scarcely having the capacity (to do something): *he's hard put to get to work by 9:30.* ~*n.* **45.** any colorant that produces a harsh coarse appearance. **46.** *Brit.* a roadway across a foreshore. **47.** *Slang.* hard labour. **48.** *Taboo slang.* an erection of the penis (esp. in the phrase **get** or **have a hard on**). [Old English *heard;* related to Old Norse *harthr,* Old Frisian *herd,* Old High German *herti,* Gothic *hardus* hard, Greek *kratus* strong]

hard and fast *adj.* (**hard-and-fast** *when prenominal*) (esp. of rules) invariable or strict.

hardback ('hɑːdˌbæk) *n.* **1.** a book or edition with covers of cloth, cardboard, or leather. ~*adj.* **2.** Also: **casebound, hardbound** ('hɑːdˌbaʊnd), **hardcover** ('hɑːdˌkʌvə). of or denoting a hardback or the publication of hardbacks.

hardbake ('hɑːdˌbeɪk) *n.* almond toffee.

hard-bitten *adj.* tough and realistic.

hardboard ('hɑːdˌbɔːd) *n.* a thin stiff sheet made of compressed sawdust and woodchips bound together with plastic adhesive or resin under heat and pressure.

hard-boiled *adj.* **1.** (of an egg) boiled until the yolk and white are solid. **2.** *Informal.* **a.** tough, realistic. **b.** cynical.

hard bop *n.* a form of jazz originating in the late 1950s that is rhythmically less complex than bop.

hard card *n.* a hard disk, mounted on a card, that can be added to a personal computer.

hard cash *n.* money or payment in the form of coins or notes rather than cheques or credit.

hard cheese *sentence substitute, n. Brit. slang.* bad luck.

hard cider *n. U.S. and Canadian.* fermented apple juice. Compare **sweet cider.**

hard coal *n.* another name for **anthracite.** Compare **soft coal.**

hard copy *n.* computer output printed on paper, as contrasted with machine-readable output such as magnetic tape.

hardcore ('hɑːdˌkɔː) *n.* a style of rock music characterized by short fast numbers with minimal melody and aggressive delivery. [C20: short for *hard-core punk*]

hard core *n.* **1.** the members of a group or movement who form an intransigent nucleus resisting change. **2.** material, such as broken bricks, stones, etc., used to form a foundation for a road, paving, building, etc. ~*adj.* **hard-core. 3.** (of pornography) describing or depicting sexual acts in explicit detail. **4.** completely and enduringly established in a belief, etc.: *hard-core Communists.*

hard court *n.* a tennis court made of asphalt, concrete, etc. See also **grass court.**

hard disk *n.* a disk of rigid magnetizable material that is used to store data for computers: it usually has a storage capacity of many megabytes.

hard-edge *adj.* of, relating to, or denoting a style of painting in which vividly coloured subjects are clearly delineated.

harden[1] ('hɑːdᵊn) *vb.* **1.** to make or become hard or harder; freeze, stiffen, or set. **2.** to make or become more hardy, tough, or unfeeling. **3.** to make or become stronger or firmer: *they hardened defences.* **4.** to make or become more resolute or set: *hardened in his resolve.* **5.** (*intr.*) *Commerce.* **a.** (of prices, a market, etc.) to cease to fluctuate. **b.** (of price) to rise higher. ~See also **harden off, harden up.**

harden[2] ('hɑːdᵊn) *n.* a rough fabric made from hards.

hardened ('hɑːdᵊnd) *adj.* **1.** rigidly set, as in a mode of behaviour. **2.** toughened, as by custom; seasoned. **3.** (of a nuclear missile site) constructed to withstand a nuclear attack.

hardener ('hɑːdᵊnə) *n.* **1.** a person or thing that hardens. **2.** a substance added to paint or varnish to increase durability. **3.** an ingredient of certain adhesives and synthetic resins that accelerates or promotes setting.

hardening ('hɑːdᵊnɪŋ) *n.* **1.** the act or process of becoming or making hard. **2.** a substance added to another substance or material to make it harder.

hardening of the arteries *n.* a nontechnical name for **arteriosclerosis.**

harden off *vb.* (*adv.*) to accustom (a cultivated plant) or (of such a plant) to become accustomed to outdoor conditions by repeated exposure.

harden up *vb.* (*intr.*) *Nautical.* to tighten the sheets of a sailing vessel so as to prevent luffing.

hard feeling *n.* (*often pl.; often used with a negative*) resentment; ill will: *no hard feelings?*

hard fern *n.* a common tufted erect fern of the polypody family, *Blechnum spicant,* having dark-green lanceolate leaves: it prefers acid soils, and in the U.S. is sometimes grown as deer feed. U.S. name: **deer fern.**

hardhack ('hɑːdˌhæk) *n.* a woody North American rosaceous plant, *Spiraea tomentosa,* with downy leaves and tapering clusters of small pink or white flowers. Also called: **steeplebush.**

hard hat *n.* **1.** a hat made of a hard material for protection, worn esp. by construction workers, equestrians, etc. **2.** *Informal, chiefly U.S. and Canadian.* a construction worker. ~*adj.* **hard-hat. 3.** *Informal, chiefly U.S.* characteristic of the presumed conservative attitudes and prejudices typified by construction workers.

hard-headed *adj.* **1.** tough, realistic, or shrewd; not moved by sentiment. **2.** *Chiefly U.S. and Canadian.* stubborn; obstinate. —ˌ**hard-'headedly** *adv.* —ˌ**hard-'headedness** *n.*

hardheads ('hɑːdˌhɛdz) *n.* (*functioning as sing.*) a thistle-like plant, *Centaurea nigra,* native to Europe and introduced into North America and New Zealand, that has reddish-purple flower heads: family *Compositae* (composites). Also called: **knapweed.** See also **centaury** (sense 2).

hardhearted (ˌhɑːd'hɑːtɪd) *adj.* unkind or intolerant. —ˌ**hard-'heartedly** *adv.* —ˌ**hard'heartedness** *n.*

hard-hit *adj.* seriously affected or hurt: *hard-hit by taxation.*

hard hitter *n. N.Z. informal.* a bowler hat.

hard-hitting *adj.* uncompromising; tough: *a hard-hitting report on urban deprivation.*

hardihood ('hɑːdɪˌhʊd) *n.* courage, daring, or audacity.

hardily ('hɑːdɪlɪ) *adv.* in a hardy manner; toughly or boldly.

hardiness ('hɑːdɪnɪs) *n.* the condition or quality of being hardy, robust, or bold.

hard labour *n. Criminal law.* (formerly) the penalty of compulsory physical labour imposed in addition to a sentence of imprisonment: abolished in England in 1948.

hard landing *n.* **1.** a landing by a rocket or spacecraft in which the vehicle is destroyed on impact. **2.** a solution to a problem, esp. an economic problem, that involves hardship. Compare **soft landing.**

hard line *n.* **a.** an uncompromising course or policy. **b. hardline.** (*as modifier*): *a hardline policy.* —ˌ**hard'liner** *n.*

hard lines *sentence substitute, n. Brit. informal.* bad luck. Also: **hard cheese.**

hardly ('hɑːdlɪ) *adv.* **1.** scarcely; barely: *we hardly knew the family.* **2.** just; only just: *he could hardly hold the cup.* **3.** *Often used ironically.* almost or probably not or not at all: *he will hardly incriminate himself.* **4.** with difficulty or effort. **5.** *Rare.* harshly or cruelly.

▷**Usage.** Since *hardly, scarcely,* and *barely* already have negative force, it is redundant to use another negative in the same clause: *he had hardly had* (not *he hadn't hardly had*) *time to think; there was scarcely any* (not *scarcely no*) *bread left.*

hard-mouthed *adj.* **1.** (of a horse) not responding satisfactorily to a pull on the bit. **2.** stubborn; obstinate.

hard neck *n. Irish informal.* audacity; nerve.

hardness ('hɑːdnɪs) *n.* **1.** the quality or condition of being hard. **2.** one of several measures of resistance to indentation, deformation, or abrasion. See **Mohs scale, Brinell number. 3.** the quality of water that causes it to impair the lathering of soap: caused by the presence of certain calcium salts. **Temporary hardness** can be removed by boiling whereas **permanent hardness** cannot.

hard-nosed *adj. Informal.* tough, shrewd, and practical.

hard of hearing *adj.* **a.** deaf or partly deaf. **b.** (*as collective n.; preceded by the*): *the hard of hearing.*

hard pad *n.* (in dogs) an abnormal increase in the thickness of the foot pads: one of the clinical signs of canine distemper. See **distemper**[1] (sense 1).

hard palate *n.* the anterior bony portion of the roof of the mouth, extending backwards to the soft palate.

hardpan ('hɑːdˌpæn) *n.* a hard impervious layer of clay below the soil, resistant to drainage and root growth.

hard paste *n.* **a.** porcelain made with kaolin and petuntse, of Chinese origin and made in Europe from the early 18th century. **b.** (*as modifier*): *hard-paste porcelain.*
hard-pressed *adj.* **1.** in difficulties: *the swimmer was hard-pressed.* **2.** subject to severe competition. **3.** subject to severe attack. **4.** closely pursued.
hardrock ('hɑːdˌrɒk) *Canadian.* ~*adj.* **1.** (of mining) concerned with extracting minerals other than coal, usually from solid rock. ~*n.* **2.** *Slang.* a tough uncompromising man.
hard rock *n. Music.* a rhythmically simple and usually highly amplified style of rock and roll.
hard rubber *n.* a hard fairly inelastic material made by vulcanizing natural rubber. See **vulcanite.**
hards (hɑːdz) *or* **hurds** *pl. n.* coarse fibres and other refuse from flax and hemp. [Old English *heordan* (plural); related to Middle Dutch *hēde,* Greek *keskeon* tow]
hard sauce *n.* another name for **brandy butter.**
hard science *n.* **a.** one of the natural or physical sciences, such as physics, chemistry, biology, geology, or astronomy. **b.** (*as modifier*): *a hard-science lecture.* —**hard scientist** *n.*
hardscrabble ('hɑːdˌskræbᵊl) *n. U.S. informal.* **1.** (*modifier*) (of a place) difficult to make a living in; barren. **2.** great effort made in the face of difficulties.
hard sell *n.* an aggressive insistent technique of selling or advertising. Compare **soft sell.**
hard-shell *adj. also* **hard-shelled. 1.** *Zoology.* having a shell or carapace that is thick, heavy, or hard. **2.** *U.S.* strictly orthodox. ~*n.* **3.** another name for the **quahog.**
hard-shell clam *n.* another name for the **quahog.**
hard-shell crab *n.* a crab, esp. of the edible species *Cancer pagurus,* that has not recently moulted and therefore has a hard shell. Compare **soft-shell crab.**
hardship ('hɑːdʃɪp) *n.* **1.** conditions of life difficult to endure. **2.** something that causes suffering or privation.
hard shoulder *n. Brit.* a surfaced verge running along the edge of a motorway for emergency stops.
hard-spun *adj.* (of yarn) spun with a firm close twist.
hard standing *n.* a hard surface on which vehicles, such as cars or aircraft, may be parked.
hardtack ('hɑːdˌtæk) *n.* a kind of hard saltless biscuit, formerly eaten esp. by sailors as a staple aboard ship. Also called: **pilot biscuit, ship's biscuit, sea biscuit.**
hardtop ('hɑːdˌtɒp) *n.* **1.** a car equipped with a metal or plastic roof that is sometimes detachable. **2.** the detachable hard roof of some sports cars.
hard track *n. Irish informal.* whisky.
hardware ('hɑːdˌwɛə) *n.* **1.** metal tools, implements, etc., esp. cutlery or cooking utensils. **2.** *Computer technol.* the physical equipment used in a computer system, such as the central processing unit, peripheral devices, and memory. Compare **software. 3.** mechanical equipment, components, etc. **4.** heavy military equipment, such as tanks and missiles or their parts. **5.** *Informal.* a gun or guns collectively.
hard-wearing *adj.* resilient, durable, and tough.
hard wheat *n.* a type of wheat with hard kernels, yielding a strong flour and used for bread, macaroni, etc.
hard-wired *adj.* (of a circuit or instruction) permanently wired into a computer, replacing separate software.
hardwood ('hɑːdˌwʊd) *n.* **1.** the wood of any of numerous broad-leaved dicotyledonous trees, such as oak, beech, ash, etc., as distinguished from the wood of a conifer. **2.** any tree from which this wood is obtained. ~Compare **softwood.**
hard-working *adj.* (of a person) industrious; diligent.
hardy[1] ('hɑːdɪ) *adj.* **-dier, -diest. 1.** having or demanding a tough constitution; robust. **2.** bold; courageous. **3.** foolhardy; rash. **4.** (of plants) able to live out of doors throughout the winter. [C13: from Old French *hardi* bold, past participle of *hardir* to become bold, of Germanic origin; compare Old English *hierdan* to HARDEN, Old Norse *hertha,* Old High German *herten*]
hardy[2] ('hɑːdɪ) *n., pl.* **-dies.** any blacksmith's tool made with a square shank so that it can be lodged in a square hole in an anvil. [C19: probably from HARD]
hare (hɛə) *n., pl.* **hares** *or* **hare. 1.** any solitary leporid mammal of the genus *Lepus,* such as *L. europaeus* (**European hare**). Hares are larger than rabbits, having longer ears and legs, and live in shallow nests (forms). Related adj.: **leporine. 2. start a hare.** to raise a topic for conversation. **3. run with the hare and hunt with the hounds.** to be on good terms with both sides. **4. make a hare of (someone).** *Irish informal.* to defeat (someone) completely. ~*vb.* **5.** (*intr.;* often foll. by *off, after,* etc.) *Brit. informal.* to go or run fast or wildly. [Old English *hara;* related to Old Norse *heri,* Old High German *haso,* Swedish *hare,* Sanskrit *śaśá*] —'**hare,like** *adj.*
hare and hounds *n.* (*functioning as sing.*) a game in which certain players (**hares**) run across country scattering pieces of paper that the other players (**hounds**) follow in an attempt to catch the hares.
harebell ('hɛəˌbɛl) *n.* a N temperate campanulaceous plant, *Campanula rotundifolia,* having slender stems and leaves, and bell-shaped blue flowers. Also called (in Scotland): **bluebell.**
harebrained *or* **hairbrained** ('hɛəˌbreɪnd) *adj.* rash, foolish, or badly thought out: *harebrained schemes.*
Hare Krishna ('hɑːrɪ 'krɪʃnə) *n., pl.* **Hare Krishnas.** a member or follower of a Hindu sect devoted to a form of Hinduism (**Krishna Consciousness**) based on the worship of the god Krishna. [C20: from Hindi, literally: Lord Krishna (vocative): the opening words of a sacred verse often chanted in public by adherents of the movement]
harelip ('hɛəˌlɪp) *n.* a congenital cleft or fissure in the midline of the upper lip, resembling the cleft upper lip of a hare, often occurring with cleft palate. —'**hare,lipped** *adj.*
harem ('hɛərəm, hɑː'riːm) *or* **hareem** (hɑː'riːm) *n.* **1.** the part of an Oriental house reserved strictly for wives, concubines, etc. **2.** a Muslim's wives and concubines collectively. **3.** a group of female animals of the same species that are the mates of a single male. [C17: from Arabic *harīm* forbidden (place)]
hare's-foot *n.* a papilionaceous annual plant, *Trifolium arvense,* that grows on sandy soils in Europe and NW Asia and has downy heads of white or pink flowers. Also called: **hare's-foot clover.**
harestail ('hɛəsˌteɪl) *n.* a species of cotton grass, *Eriophorum vaginatum,* more tussocky than common cotton grass and having only a single flower head.
haricot ('hærɪkəʊ) *n.* **1.** a variety of French bean with light-coloured edible seeds, which can be dried and stored. **2.** another name for **French bean. 3.** the seed or pod of any of these plants, eaten as a vegetable. [C17: from French, perhaps from Nahuatl *ayecotli*]
Harijan ('hʌrɪdʒən) *n.* a member of certain classes in India, formerly considered inferior and untouchable. See **scheduled castes.** [Hindi, literally: man of God (so called by Mahatma Gandhi), from *Hari* god + *jan* man]
hari-kari (ˌhærɪ'kɑːrɪ) *n.* a non-Japanese variant of **hara-kiri.**
hark (hɑːk) *vb.* (*intr.; usually imperative*) to listen; pay attention. [Old English *heorcnian* to HEARKEN; related to Old Frisian *herkia,* Old High German *hōrechen;* see HEAR]
hark back *vb.* (*intr., adv.*) to return to an earlier subject, point, or position, as in speech or thought.
harken ('hɑːkən) *vb.* a variant spelling (esp. U.S.) of **hearken.** —'**harkener** *n.*
harl[1] (hærl, hɑːl) *Scot.* ~*vb.* **1.** (*tr.*) to drag (something) along the ground. **2.** (*intr.*) to drag oneself; trail along. **3.** (*tr.*) to cover (a building) with a mixture of lime and gravel; roughcast. **4.** (*intr.*) to troll for fish. ~*n.* **5.** the act of harling or dragging. **6.** a small quantity; a scraping. **7.** a mixture of lime and gravel; roughcast. [C18: of unknown origin] —'**harling** *n.*
harl[2] (hɑːl) *n. Angling.* a variant of **herl.**
harlequin ('hɑːlɪkwɪn) *n.* **1.** (*sometimes cap.*) *Theatre.* a stock comic character originating in the commedia dell'arte; the foppish lover of Columbine in the English harlequinade. He is usually represented in diamond-patterned multicoloured tights, wearing a black mask. **2.** a clown or buffoon. ~*adj.* **3.** varied in colour or decoration. **4.** (of certain animals) having a white coat with irregular patches of black or other dark colour: *harlequin Great Dane.* **5.** comic, ludicrous, etc. [C16: from Old French *Herlequin, Hellequin* leader of band of demon horsemen, perhaps from Middle English *Herle king* (unattested) King Herle, mythical being identified with the god Woden]
harlequinade (ˌhɑːlɪkwɪ'neɪd) *n.* **1.** (*sometimes cap.*) *Theatre.* a play or part of a pantomime in which harlequin has a leading role. **2.** buffoonery.
harlequin bug *n.* a brightly coloured heteropterous insect, *Murgantia histrionica,* of the U.S. and Central America: a pest of cabbages and related plants: family *Pentatomidae.*
harlequin duck *n.* a northern sea duck, *Histrionicus histrionicus,* the male of which has a blue and red plumage with black and white markings.
harlot ('hɑːlət) *n.* **1.** a prostitute or promiscuous woman. ~*adj.* **2.** *Archaic.* of or like a harlot. [C13: from Old French *herlot* rascal, of obscure origin] —'**harlotry** *n.*
harm (hɑːm) *n.* **1.** physical or mental injury or damage. **2.** moral evil or wrongdoing. ~*vb.* **3.** (*tr.*) to injure physically, morally, or mentally. [Old English *hearm;* related to Old Norse *harmr* grief, Old High German *harm* injury, Old Slavonic *sramŭ* disgrace] —'**harmer** *n.*
harmattan (hɑː'mætᵊn) *n.* a dry dusty wind from the Sahara blowing towards the W African coast, esp. from November to March. [C17: from Twi *haramata,* perhaps from Arabic *harām* forbidden thing; see HAREM]
harmful ('hɑːmfʊl) *adj.* causing or tending to cause harm; injurious. —'**harmfully** *adv.* —'**harmfulness** *n.*
harmless ('hɑːmlɪs) *adj.* not causing or tending to cause harm. —'**harmlessly** *adv.* —'**harmlessness** *n.*
harmolodics (ˌhɑːmə'lɒdɪks) *n.* (*functioning as sing.*) *Jazz.* the technique of each musician in a group simultaneously improvising around the melodic and rhythmic patterns in a tune, rather than one musician improvising on its underlying harmonic pattern while the others play an accompaniment. [C20: of unknown origin] —ˌ**harmo'lodic** *adj.*
harmonic (hɑː'mɒnɪk) *adj.* **1.** of, involving, producing, or characterized by harmony; harmonious. **2.** *Music.* of, relating to, or belonging to harmony. **3.** *Maths.* **a.** capable of expression in the form of sine and cosine functions. **b.** of or relating to numbers whose reciprocals form an arithmetic progression. **4.** *Physics.* of or concerned with an oscillation that has a frequency that is an integral multiple of a fundamental frequency. **5.** *Physics.* of

or concerned with harmonics. ~*n.* **6.** *Physics, music.* a component of a periodic quantity, such as a musical tone, with a frequency that is an integral multiple of the fundamental frequency. The **first harmonic** is the fundamental, the **second harmonic** (twice the fundamental frequency) is the **first overtone,** the **third harmonic** (three times the fundamental frequency) is the **second overtone,** etc. **7.** *Music.* (not in technical use) overtone: in this case, the first overtone is the first harmonic, etc. ~See also **harmonics.** [C16: from Latin *harmonicus* relating to HARMONY] —**harˈmonically** *adv.*

harmonica (hɑːˈmɒnɪkə) *n.* **1.** a small wind instrument of the reed organ family in which reeds of graduated lengths set into a metal plate enclosed in a narrow oblong box are made to vibrate by blowing and sucking. Also called: **mouth organ. 2.** See **glass harmonica.** [C18: from Latin *harmonicus* relating to HARMONY]

harmonic analysis *n.* **1.** the representation of a periodic function by means of the summation and integration of simple trigonometric functions. **2.** the study of this means of representation.

harmonic distortion *n. Electronics.* distortion caused by non-linear characteristics of electronic apparatus, esp. of audio amplifiers, that generate unwanted harmonics of the input frequencies.

harmonic mean *n.* the reciprocal of the arithmetic mean of the reciprocals of a set of specified numbers: the harmonic mean of 2, 3, and 4 is $3(\frac{1}{2} + \frac{1}{3} + \frac{1}{4})^{-1} = 36/13$.

harmonic minor scale *n. Music.* a minor scale modified from the state of being natural by the sharpening of the seventh degree. See **minor.** Compare **melodic minor scale.**

harmonic motion *n.* a periodic motion in which the displacement is symmetrical about a point or a periodic motion that is composed of such motions. See also **simple harmonic motion.**

harmonic progression *n.* a sequence of numbers whose reciprocals form an arithmetic progression, as 1, ½, ⅓, ...

harmonics (hɑːˈmɒnɪks) *n.* **1.** (*functioning as sing.*) the science of musical sounds and their acoustic properties. **2.** (*functioning as pl.*) the overtones of a fundamental note, as produced by lightly touching the string of a stringed instrument at one of its node points while playing. See **harmonic** (sense 6).

harmonic series *n.* **1.** *Maths.* a series whose terms are in harmonic progression, as in $1 + \frac{1}{2} + \frac{1}{3} + \ldots$ **2.** *Acoustics.* the series of tones with frequencies strictly related to one another and to the fundamental tone, as obtained by touching lightly the node points of a string while playing it. Its most important application is in the playing of brass instruments.

harmonious (hɑːˈməʊnɪəs) *adj.* **1.** (esp. of colours or sounds) fitting together well. **2.** having agreement or consensus. **3.** tuneful, consonant, or melodious. —**harˈmoniously** *adv.*

harmonist (ˈhɑːmənɪst) *n.* **1.** a person skilled in the art and techniques of harmony. **2.** a person who combines and collates parallel narratives. —ˌ**harmoˈnistic** *adj.* —ˌ**harmoˈnistically** *adv.*

harmonium (hɑːˈməʊnɪəm) *n.* a musical keyboard instrument of the reed organ family, in which air from pedal-operated bellows causes the reeds to vibrate. [C19: from French, from *harmonie* HARMONY]

harmonization *or* **harmonisation** (ˌhɑːmənaɪˈzeɪʃən) *n.* **1.** the act of harmonizing. **2.** a system, particularly used in the EC, whereby the blue-collar workers and the white-collar workers in an organization have similar status and any former differences in terms and conditions of employment are levelled up.

harmonize *or* **harmonise** (ˈhɑːməˌnaɪz) *vb.* **1.** to make or become harmonious. **2.** (*tr.*) *Music.* to provide a harmony for (a melody, tune, etc.). **3.** (*intr.*) to sing in harmony, as with other singers. **4.** to collate parallel narratives. —ˈ**harmoˌnizable** *or* ˈ**harmoˌnisable** *adj.*

harmonizer *or* **harmoniser** (ˈhɑːməˌnaɪzə) *n. Music.* **1.** a person skilled in the theory of composition of harmony. **2.** a device that electronically duplicates a signal at a different pitch or different pitches.

harmony (ˈhɑːmənɪ) *n., pl.* **-nies. 1.** agreement in action, opinion, feeling, etc.; accord. **2.** order or congruity of parts to their whole or to one another. **3.** agreeable sounds. **4.** *Music.* **a.** any combination of notes sounded simultaneously. **b.** the vertically represented structure of a piece of music. Compare **melody** (sense 1b), **rhythm** (sense 1). **c.** the art or science concerned with the structure and combinations of chords. **5.** a collation of the material of parallel narratives, esp. of the four Gospels. [C14: from Latin *harmonia* concord of sounds, from Greek: harmony, from *harmos* a joint]

harmotome (ˈhɑːməˌtəʊm) *n.* a mineral of the zeolite group consisting of hydrated aluminium barium silicate in the form of monoclinic twinned crystals. [C19: from French, from Greek *harmos* a joint + *tomē* a slice, from *temnein* to cut]

harness (ˈhɑːnɪs) *n.* **1.** an arrangement of leather straps buckled or looped together, fitted to a draught animal in order that the animal can be attached to and pull a cart. **2.** something resembling this, esp. for attaching something to the body: *a parachute harness.* **3.** *Mountaineering.* an arrangement of webbing straps that enables a climber to attach himself to the rope so that the impact of a fall is minimized. **4.** the total system of electrical leads for a vehicle or aircraft. **5.** *Weaving.* the part of a loom that raises and lowers the warp threads, creating the shed. **6.** *Archaic.* armour collectively. **7. in harness.** at one's routine work. ~*vb.* (*tr.*) **8.** to put harness on (a horse). **9.** (usually foll. by *to*) to attach (a draught animal) by means of harness to (a cart, etc.). **10.** to control so as to employ the energy or potential power of: *to harness the atom.* **11.** to equip or clothe with armour. [C13: from Old French *harneis* baggage, probably from Old Norse *hernest* (unattested) provisions, from *herr* army + *nest* provisions] —ˈ**harnesser** *n.* —ˈ**harnessless** *adj.* —ˈ**harness-ˌlike** *adj.*

harnessed antelope *n.* any of various antelopes with vertical white stripes on the back, esp. the bushbuck.

harness hitch *n.* a knot forming a loop with no free ends.

harness race *n. Horse racing.* a trotting or pacing race for standardbred horses driven in sulkies and harnessed in a special way to cause them to use the correct gait.

harp (hɑːp) *n.* **1.** a large triangular plucked stringed instrument consisting of a soundboard connected to an upright pillar by means of a curved crossbar from which the strings extend downwards. The strings are tuned diatonically and may be raised in pitch either one or two semitones by the use of pedals (**double-action harp**). Basic key: B major; range: nearly seven octaves. **2.** something resembling this, esp. in shape. **3.** an informal name (esp. in pop music) for **harmonica.** ~*vb.* **4.** (*intr.*) to play the harp. **5.** (*tr.*) *Archaic.* to speak; utter; express. **6.** (*intr.*; foll. by *on* or *upon*) to speak or write in a persistent and tedious manner. [Old English *hearpe;* related to Old Norse *harpa,* Old High German *harfa,* Latin *corbis* basket, Russian *korobit* to warp] —ˈ**harper** *or* ˈ**harpist** *n.*

harpings (ˈhɑːpɪŋz) *or* **harpins** (ˈhɑːpɪnz) *pl. n.* **1.** *Nautical.* wooden members used for strengthening the bow of a vessel. **2.** *Shipbuilding.* wooden supports used in construction. [C17: perhaps related to French *harpe* cramp iron]

harpoon (hɑːˈpuːn) *n.* **1. a.** a barbed missile attached to a long cord and hurled or fired from a gun when hunting whales, etc. **b.** (*as modifier*): *a harpoon gun.* ~*vb.* **2.** (*tr.*) to spear with or as if with a harpoon. [C17: probably from Dutch *harpoen,* from Old French *harpon* clasp, from *harper* to seize, perhaps of Scandinavian origin] —**harˈpooner** *or* ˌ**harpoonˈeer** *n.* —**harˈpoonˌlike** *adj.*

harp seal *n.* a brownish-grey earless seal, *Pagophilus groenlandicus,* of the North Atlantic and Arctic Oceans.

harpsichord (ˈhɑːpsɪˌkɔːd) *n.* a horizontally strung stringed keyboard instrument, triangular in shape, consisting usually of two manuals controlling various sets of strings plucked by pivoted plectra mounted on jacks. Some harpsichords have a pedal keyboard and stops by which the tone colour may be varied. [C17: from New Latin *harpichordium,* from Late Latin *harpa* HARP + Latin *chorda* CHORD[1]] —ˈ**harpsiˌchordist** *n.*

harpy (ˈhɑːpɪ) *n., pl.* **-pies.** a cruel grasping woman. [C16: from the *Harpies,* mythological woman-headed birds, from Latin *Harpyia,* from Greek *Harpuiai,* literally: snatchers, from *harpazein* to seize]

harpy eagle *n.* a very large tropical American eagle, *Harpia harpyja,* with a black-and-white plumage and a head crest.

harquebus (ˈhɑːkwɪbəs) *n., pl.* **-buses.** a variant of **arquebus.**

harquebusier (ˌhɑːkwɪbəˈsɪə) *n.* (formerly) a soldier armed with an arquebus. Also called: **arquebusier.**

harridan (ˈhærɪdᵊn) *n.* a scolding old woman; nag. [C17: of uncertain origin; perhaps related to French *haridelle,* literally: broken-down horse; of obscure origin]

harrier[1] (ˈhærɪə) *n.* **1.** a person or thing that harries. **2.** any diurnal bird of prey of the genus *Circus,* having broad wings and long legs and tail and typically preying on small terrestrial animals: family *Accipitridae* (hawks, etc.). See also **marsh harrier, Montagu's harrier.**

harrier[2] (ˈhærɪə) *n.* **1.** a smallish breed of hound used originally for hare-hunting. **2.** a cross-country runner. [C16: from HARE + -ER[1]; influenced by HARRIER[1]]

Harrier (ˈhærɪə) *n.* a British subsonic multipurpose military jet plane capable of vertical takeoff and landing by means of vectoring the engine thrust.

Harris Tweed (ˈhærɪs) *n. Trademark.* a loose-woven tweed made in the Outer Hebrides, esp. Lewis and Harris.

Harrovian (həˈrəʊvɪən) *n.* **1.** a person educated at Harrow School in NW Greater London. ~*adj.* **2.** of or concerning Harrow. [C19: from New Latin *Harrōvia* Harrow + -AN]

harrow[1] (ˈhærəʊ) *n.* **1.** any of various implements used to level the ground, stir the soil, break up clods, destroy weeds, etc., in soil. ~*vb.* **2.** (*tr.*) to draw a harrow over (land). **3.** (*intr.*) (of soil) to become broken up through harrowing. **4.** (*tr.*) to distress; vex. [C13: of Scandinavian origin; compare Danish *harv,* Swedish *harf;* related to Middle Dutch *harke* rake] —ˈ**harrower** *n.* —ˈ**harrowing** *adj., n.*

harrow[2] (ˈhærəʊ) *vb.* (*tr.*) *Archaic.* **1.** to plunder or ravish. **2.** (of Christ) to descend into (hell) to rescue righteous souls. [C13: variant of Old English *hergian* to HARRY] —ˈ**harrowment** *n.*

harrumph (həˈrʌmf) *vb.* (*intr.*) *Chiefly U.S. and Canadian.* to clear or make the noise of clearing the throat.

harry (ˈhærɪ) *vb.* **-ries, -rying, -ried. 1.** (*tr.*) to harass; worry. **2.** to ravage (a town, etc.), esp. in war. [Old English *hergian;* related to *here* army, Old Norse *herja* to lay waste, Old High German *heriōn*]

harsh (hɑːʃ) *adj.* **1.** rough or grating to the senses. **2.** stern, severe, or cruel. [C16: probably of Scandinavian origin; compare Middle Low German *harsch,* Norwegian *harsk* rancid] —ˈ**harshly** *adv.* —ˈ**harshness** *n.*

harslet (ˈhɑːzlɪt, ˈhɑːs-) *n.* a variant of **haslet.**

hart (hɑːt) *n., pl.* **harts** *or* **hart.** the male of the deer, esp. the red deer aged five years or more. [Old English *heorot;* related to Old Norse *hjörtr,* Old High German *hiruz* hart, Latin *cervus* stag, Lithuanian *kárve* cow; see HORN]

hartal (hɑːˈtɑːl) *n.* (in India) the act of closing shops or suspending work, esp. in political protest. [C20: from Hindi *hartāl,* from *hāt* shop (from Sanskrit *hatta*) + *tālā* bolt for a door (from Sanskrit: latch)]

hartebeest (ˈhɑːtɪˌbiːst) *or* **hartbeest** (ˈhɑːtˌbiːst) *n.* **1.** either of two large African antelopes, *Alcelaphus buselaphus* or *A. lichtensteini,* having an elongated muzzle, lyre-shaped horns, and a fawn-coloured coat. **2.** any similar and related animal, such as *Damaliscus hunteri* (**Hunter's hartebeest**). [C18: via Afrikaans from Dutch; see HART, BEAST]

hartshorn (ˈhɑːtsˌhɔːn) *n.* an obsolete name for **sal volatile** (sense 2). [Old English *heortes horn* hart's horn (formerly a chief source of ammonia)]

hart's-tongue *n.* an evergreen Eurasian fern, *Phyllitis scolopendrium,* with narrow undivided fronds bearing rows of sori: family *Polypodiaceae.*

harum-scarum (ˈhɛərəmˈskɛərəm) *adj., adv.* **1.** in a reckless way or of a reckless nature. ~*n.* **2.** a person who is impetuous or rash. [C17: perhaps from *hare* (in obsolete sense: harass) + *scare,* variant of STARE; compare HELTER-SKELTER]

haruspex (həˈrʌspɛks) *n., pl.* **haruspices** (həˈrʌspɪˌsiːz). (in ancient Rome) a priest who practised divination, esp. by examining the entrails of animals. [C16: from Latin, probably from *hīra* gut + *specere* to look] —**haruspical** (həˈrʌspɪkᵊl) *adj.* —**haruspicy** (həˈrʌspɪsɪ) *n.*

Harvard classification (ˈhɑːvəd) *n.* a classification of stars based on the characteristic spectral absorption lines and bands of the chemical elements present. See **spectral type.** [C20: named after the observatory at *Harvard,* Massachusetts, where it was prepared and published as part of *The Henry Draper Catalogue* (1924)]

harvest (ˈhɑːvɪst) *n.* **1.** the gathering of a ripened crop. **2.** the crop itself or the yield from it in a single growing season. **3.** the season for gathering crops. **4.** the product of an effort, action, etc.: *a harvest of love.* ~*vb.* **5.** to gather or reap (a ripened crop) from (the place where it has been growing). **6.** (*tr.*) to receive or reap (benefits, consequences, etc.). [Old English *hærfest;* related to Old Norse *harfr* harrow, Old High German *herbist* autumn, Latin *carpere* to pluck, Greek *karpos* fruit, Sanskrit *krpāna* shears] —ˈ**harvesting** *n.* —ˈ**harvestless** *adj.*

harvester (ˈhɑːvɪstə) *n.* **1.** a person who harvests. **2.** a harvesting machine, esp. a combine harvester.

harvest home *n.* **1.** the bringing in of the harvest. **2.** *Chiefly Brit.* a harvest supper.

harvestman (ˈhɑːvɪstmən) *n., pl.* **-men. 1.** a person engaged in harvesting. **2.** Also called (U.S. and Canadian): **daddy-longlegs.** any arachnid of the order *Opiliones* (or *Phalangida*), having a small rounded body and very long thin legs.

harvest mite *or* **tick** *n.* the bright red parasitic larva of any of various free-living mites of the genus *Trombicula* and related genera, which causes intense itching of human skin.

harvest moon *n.* the full moon occurring nearest to the autumnal equinox.

harvest mouse *n.* **1.** a very small reddish-brown Eurasian mouse, *Micromys minutus,* inhabiting cornfields, hedgerows, etc., and feeding on grain and seeds: family *Muridae.* **2. American harvest mouse.** any small greyish mouse of the American genus *Reithrodontomys:* family *Cricetidae.*

has (hæz) *vb.* (used with *he, she, it,* or a singular noun) a form of the present tense (indicative mood) of **have.**

has-been *n. Informal.* a person or thing that is no longer popular, successful, effective, etc.

hash[1] (hæʃ) *n.* **1.** a dish of diced cooked meat, vegetables, etc., reheated in a sauce. **2.** something mixed up. **3.** a reuse or rework of old material. **4. make a hash of.** *Informal.* **a.** to mix or mess up. **b.** to defeat or destroy. **5. settle** (*or* **fix**) **someone's hash.** *Informal.* to subdue or silence someone. ~*vb.* (*tr.*) **6.** to chop into small pieces. **7.** to mix or mess up. [C17: from Old French *hacher* to chop up, from *hache* HATCHET]

hash[2] (hæʃ) *n. Slang.* short for **hashish.**

hash browns *pl. n.* diced boiled potatoes mixed with chopped onion, shaped and fried until brown.

HaShem (hɑˈʃɛm) *Judaism.* a periphrastic way of referring to God in contexts other than prayer, scriptural reading, etc.: because the name itself is too holy for such use this expression is substituted for it. [from Hebrew, literally: The Name]

hash house *n. U.S. slang.* a cheap café or restaurant.

hashish (ˈhæʃiːʃ, -ɪʃ) *or* **hasheesh** (ˈhæʃiːʃ) *n.* **1.** a purified resinous extract of the dried flower tops of the female hemp plant, used as a hallucinogenic. See also **cannabis. 2.** any hallucinogenic substance prepared from this resin. [C16: from Arabic *hashīsh* hemp, dried herbage]

hask (hæsk, hʌsk) *Scot., Northern and north Midland English dialect.* ~*adj.* **1.** (esp. of a cough) dry or hoarse. ~*n.* **2.** a cough, usually of animals. [a dialect variant of *harsk,* an earlier form of HARSH]

haslet (ˈhæzlɪt) *or* **harslet** *n.* a loaf of cooked minced pig's offal, eaten cold. [C14: from Old French *hastelet* piece of spit roasted meat, from *haste* spit, of Germanic origin; compare Old High German *harsta* frying pan]

hasn't (ˈhæzᵊnt) *vb. contraction of* has not.

hasp (hɑːsp) *n.* **1.** a metal fastening consisting of a hinged strap with a slot that fits over a staple and is secured by a pin, bolt, or padlock. ~*vb.* **2.** (*tr.*) to secure (a door, window, etc.) with a hasp. [Old English *hæpse;* related to Old Norse *hespa,* Old High German *haspa* hasp, Dutch *haspel* reel, Sanskrit *capa* bow]

Hassidism *or* **Hasidism** (ˈhæsɪdˌɪzəm) *n.* variant spellings of **Chassidism.**

hassle (ˈhæsᵊl) *Informal.* ~*n.* **1.** a prolonged argument; wrangle. **2.** a great deal of trouble; difficulty; nuisance. ~*vb.* **3.** (*intr.*) to quarrel or wrangle. **4.** (*tr.*) to cause annoyance or trouble to (someone); harass. [C20: of unknown origin]

hassock (ˈhæsək) *n.* **1.** a firm upholstered cushion used for kneeling on, esp. in church. **2.** a thick clump of grass. [Old English *hassuc* matted grass]

hast (hæst) *vb. Archaic or dialect.* (used with the pronoun *thou* or its relative equivalent) a singular form of the present tense (indicative mood) of **have.**

hastate (ˈhæsteɪt) *adj.* (of a leaf) having a pointed tip and two outward-pointing lobes at the base. [C18: from Latin *hastātus* with a spear, from *hasta* spear]

haste (heɪst) *n.* **1.** speed, esp. in an action; swiftness; rapidity. **2.** the act of hurrying in a careless or rash manner. **3.** a necessity for hurrying; urgency. **4. make haste.** to hurry; rush. ~*vb.* **5.** a poetic word for **hasten.** [C14: from Old French *haste,* of Germanic origin; compare Old Norse *heifst* hate, Old English *hǣst* strife, Old High German *heisti* powerful] —ˈ**hasteful** *adj.* —ˈ**hastefully** *adv.*

hasten (ˈheɪsᵊn) *vb.* **1.** (*may take an infinitive*) to hurry or cause to hurry; rush. **2.** (*tr.*) to be anxious (to say something): *I hasten to add that we are just good friends.* —ˈ**hastener** *n.*

hasty (ˈheɪstɪ) *adj.* **-tier, -tiest. 1.** rapid; swift; quick. **2.** excessively or rashly quick. **3.** short-tempered. **4.** showing irritation or anger: *hasty words.* —ˈ**hastily** *adv.* —ˈ**hastiness** *n.*

hasty pudding *n.* **1.** *Brit.* a simple pudding made from milk thickened with tapioca, semolina, etc., and sweetened. **2.** *U.S.* a mush of cornmeal, served with treacle sugar.

hat (hæt) *n.* **1. a.** any of various head coverings, esp. one with a brim and a shaped crown. **b.** (*in combination*): *hatrack.* **2.** *Informal.* a role or capacity. **3. at the drop of a hat.** without hesitation or delay. **4. bad hat.** *Informal, chiefly Brit.* a bad or immoral person. **5. I'll eat my hat.** *Informal.* I will be greatly surprised if (something that proves me wrong) happens: *I'll eat my hat if this book comes out late.* **6. hat in hand.** humbly or servilely. **7. keep (something) under one's hat.** to keep (something) secret. **8. my hat.** (*interj.*) *Brit. informal.* **a.** my word! my goodness! **b.** nonsense! **9. old hat.** something stale or old-fashioned. **10. out of a hat. a.** as if by magic. **b.** at random. **11. pass** (*or* **send**) **the hat round.** to collect money, as for a cause. **12. take off one's hat to.** to admire or congratulate. **13. talk through one's hat. a.** to talk foolishly. **b.** to deceive or bluff. **14. throw one's hat at (it).** *Irish.* to give up all hope of getting or achieving (something): *you can throw your hat at it now.* **15. throw** (*or* **toss**) **one's hat in the ring.** to announce one's intentions to be a candidate or contestant. ~*vb.* **hats, hatting, hatted. 16.** (*tr.*) to supply (a person, etc.) with a hat or put a hat on (someone). [Old English *hætt;* related to Old Norse *höttr* cap, Latin *cassis* helmet; see HOOD[1]] —ˈ**hatless** *adj.* —ˈ**hatˌlike** *adj.*

hatband (ˈhætˌbænd) *n.* a band or ribbon around the base of the crown of a hat.

hatbox (ˈhætˌbɒks) *n.* a box or case for a hat or hats.

hatch[1] (hætʃ) *vb.* **1.** to cause (the young of various animals, esp. birds) to emerge from the egg or (of young birds, etc.) to emerge from the egg. **2.** to cause (eggs) to break and release the fully developed young or (of eggs) to break and release the young animal within. **3.** (*tr.*) to contrive or devise (a scheme, plot, etc.). ~*n.* **4.** the act or process of hatching. **5.** a group of newly hatched animals. [C13: of Germanic origin; compare Middle High German *hecken* to mate (used of birds), Swedish *häcka* to hatch, Danish *hække*] —ˈ**hatchable** *adj.* —ˈ**hatcher** *n.*

hatch[2] (hætʃ) *n.* **1.** a covering for a hatchway. **2.** short for **hatchway. 3.** Also called: **serving hatch.** an opening in a wall separating a kitchen from a dining area. **4.** the lower half of a divided door. **5.** a sluice or sliding gate in a dam, dyke, or weir. **6. down the hatch.** *Slang.* (used as a toast) drink up! **7. under hatches. a.** below decks. **b.** out of sight. **c.** brought low; dead. [Old English *hæcc;* related to Middle High German *heck,* Dutch *hek* gate]

hatch[3] (hætʃ) *vb. Drawing, engraving, etc.* to mark (a figure, shade, etc.) with fine parallel or crossed lines to indicate shading. Compare **hachure.** [C15: from Old French *hacher* to chop, from *hache* HATCHET] —ˈ**hatching** *n.*

hatchback (ˈhætʃˌbæk) *n.* **1. a.** a sloping rear end of a car having a single door that is lifted to open. **b.** (*as modifier*): *a hatchback model.* **2.** a car having such a rear end.

hatchel ('hætʃəl) *vb.* **-els, -elling, -elled** *or U.S.* **-els, -eling, -eled,** *n.* another word for **heckle** (senses 2, 3). [C13 *hechele,* of Germanic origin; related to Old High German *hāko* hook, Middle Dutch *hekele* HACKLE[1]] —'**hatcheller** *n.*

hatchery ('hætʃərɪ) *n., pl.* **-eries.** a place where eggs are hatched under artificial conditions.

hatchet ('hætʃɪt) *n.* **1.** a short axe used for chopping wood, etc. **2.** a tomahawk. **3.** (*modifier*) of narrow dimensions and sharp features: *a hatchet face.* **4. bury the hatchet.** to cease hostilities and become reconciled. [C14: from Old French *hachette,* from *hache* axe, of Germanic origin; compare Old High German *happa* knife] —'**hatchet-ˌlike** *adj.*

hatchet job *n. Informal.* a malicious or devastating verbal or written attack.

hatchet man *n. Informal.* **1.** a person carrying out unpleasant assignments for an employer or superior. **2.** *U.S. and Canadian.* a hired murderer. **3.** a severe or malicious critic.

hatchment ('hætʃmənt) *n. Heraldry.* a diamond-shaped tablet displaying the coat of arms of a dead person. Also called: **achievement.** [C16: changed from ACHIEVEMENT]

hatchway ('hætʃˌweɪ) *n.* **1.** an opening in the deck of a vessel to provide access below. **2.** a similar opening in a wall, floor, ceiling, or roof, usually fitted with a lid or door. ~Often shortened to **hatch.**

hate (heɪt) *vb.* **1.** to dislike (something) intensely; detest. **2.** (*intr.*) to be unwilling (to be or do something). ~*n.* **3.** intense dislike. **4.** *Informal.* a person or thing that is hated (esp. in the phrase **pet hate**). **5.** (*modifier*) expressing or arousing feelings of hatred: *hate mail.* [Old English *hatian;* related to Old Norse *hata,* Old Saxon *hatōn,* Old High German *hazzēn*] —'**hateable** *or* '**hatable** *adj.*

hateful ('heɪtfʊl) *adj.* **1.** causing or deserving hate; loathsome; detestable. **2.** full of or showing hate. —'**hatefully** *adv.* —'**hatefulness** *n.*

hath (hæθ) *vb. Archaic or dialect.* (used with the pronouns *he, she,* or *it* or a singular noun) a form of the present tense (indicative mood) of **have.**

hatha yoga ('hʌtə, 'hæθə) *n.* (*sometimes caps.*) a form of yoga concerned chiefly with the regulation of breathing by exercises consisting of various postures designed to maintain healthy functioning of the body and to induce mental calm. Compare **raja yoga.** [C20: from Sanskrit *hatha* force + YOGA]

hatpin ('hætˌpɪn) *n.* a sturdy pin used to secure a woman's hat to her hair, often having a decorative head.

hatred ('heɪtrɪd) *n.* a feeling of intense dislike; enmity.

hat stand *or esp. U.S.* **hat tree** *n.* a frame or pole equipped with hooks or arms for hanging up hats, coats, etc.

hatter ('hætə) *n.* **1.** a person who makes and sells hats. **2.** *Austral. informal.* a man, esp. a miner, who prefers to live and work alone, often considered eccentric. **3. mad as a hatter.** crazily eccentric.

hat trick *n.* **1.** *Cricket.* the achievement of a bowler in taking three wickets with three successive balls. **2.** any achievement of three successive points, victories, etc.

haubergeon ('hɔːbədʒən) *n.* a variant of **habergeon.**

hauberk ('hɔːbɜːk) *n.* a long coat of mail, often sleeveless. [C13: from Old French *hauberc,* of Germanic origin; compare Old High German *halsberc,* Old English *healsbeorg,* from *heals* neck + *beorg* protection, shelter]

haud (hɔːd, hʌd) *vb., n.* a Scot. word for **hold**[1].

hauf (hɔːf) *n., determiner, adj., adv.* a Scot. word for **half.**

haugh (hɑːk, hɑːf; *Scot.* hɒx) *n. Northern English dialect and Scot.* a low-lying often alluvial riverside meadow. [Old English *healh* corner of land; see HOLLOW]

haughty ('hɔːtɪ) *adj.* **-tier, -tiest.** **1.** having or showing arrogance. **2.** *Archaic.* noble or exalted. [C16: from Old French *haut,* literally: lofty, from Latin *altus* high] —'**haughtily** *adv.* —'**haughtiness** *n.*

haul (hɔːl) *vb.* **1.** to drag or draw (something) with effort. **2.** (*tr.*) to transport, as in a lorry. **3.** *Nautical.* to alter the course of (a vessel), esp. so as to sail closer to the wind. **4.** (*tr.*) *Nautical.* to draw or hoist (a vessel) out of the water onto land or a dock for repair, storage, etc. **5.** (*intr.*) *Nautical.* (of the wind) to blow from a direction nearer the bow. Compare **veer**[1] (sense 3b). **6.** (*intr.*) to change one's opinion or action. ~*n.* **7.** the act of dragging with effort. **8.** (esp. of fish) the amount caught at a single time. **9.** something that is hauled. **10.** the goods obtained from a robbery. **11.** a distance of hauling: *a three-mile haul.* **12.** the amount of a contraband seizure: *arms haul, drugs haul.* **13. in** (or **over**) **the long haul. a.** in a future time. **b.** over a lengthy period of time. [C16: from Old French *haler,* of Germanic origin; see HALE[2]]

haulage ('hɔːlɪdʒ) *n.* **1.** the act or labour of hauling. **2.** a rate or charge levied for the transportation of goods, esp. by rail.

haulier ('hɔːljə) *or U.S.* **hauler** ('hɔːlə) *n.* **1.** a person or firm that transports goods by lorry; one engaged in road haulage. **2.** a person that hauls, esp. a mine worker who conveys coal from the workings to the foot of the shaft.

haulm *or* **halm** (hɔːm) *n.* **1.** the stems or stalks of beans, peas, potatoes, grasses, etc., collectively, as used for thatching, bedding, etc. **2.** a single stem of such a plant. [Old English *healm;* related to Old Norse *halmr,* Old High German *halm* stem, straw, Latin *culmus* stalk, Greek *kalamos* reed, Old Slavonic *slama* straw]

haul off *vb.* (*intr., adv.*) **1.** (foll. by *and*) *U.S. and Canadian informal.* to draw back in preparation (esp. to strike or fight): *I hauled off and slugged him.* **2.** *Nautical.* to alter the course of a vessel so as to avoid an obstruction, shallow waters, etc.

haul up *vb.* (*adv.*) **1.** (*tr.*) *Informal.* to call to account or criticize. **2.** *Nautical.* to sail (a vessel) closer to the wind.

haunch (hɔːntʃ) *n.* **1.** the human hip or fleshy hindquarter of an animal, esp. a horse or similar quadruped. **2.** the leg and loin of an animal, used for food: *a haunch of venison.* **3.** Also called: **hance.** *Architect.* the part of an arch between the impost and the apex. [C13: from Old French *hanche;* related to Spanish, Italian *anca,* of Germanic origin; compare Low German *hanke*] —**haunched** *adj.*

haunch bone *n.* a nontechnical name for the **ilium** or **hipbone.**

haunt (hɔːnt) *vb.* **1.** to visit (a person or place) in the form of a ghost. **2.** (*tr.*) to intrude upon or recur to (the memory, thoughts, etc.): *he was haunted by the fear of insanity.* **3.** to visit (a place) frequently. **4.** to associate with (someone) frequently. ~*n.* **5.** (*often pl.*) a place visited frequently: *an old haunt of hers.* **6.** a place to which animals habitually resort for food, drink, shelter, etc. [C13: from Old French *hanter,* of Germanic origin; compare Old Norse *heimta* to bring home, Old English *hāmettan* to give a home to; see HOME] —'**haunter** *n.*

haunted ('hɔːntɪd) *adj.* **1.** frequented or visited by ghosts. **2.** (*postpositive*) obsessed or worried.

haunting ('hɔːntɪŋ) *adj.* **1.** (of memories) poignant or persistent. **2.** poignantly sentimental; enchantingly or eerily evocative. —'**hauntingly** *adv.*

Hausa ('haʊsə) *n.* **1.** (*pl.* **-sas** *or* **-sa**) a member of a Negroid people of W Africa, living chiefly in N Nigeria. **2.** the language of this people: the chief member of the Chadic subfamily of the Afro-Asiatic family of languages. It is widely used as a trading language throughout W Africa and the S Sahara.

hausfrau ('haʊsˌfraʊ) *n.* a German housewife. [German, from *Haus* HOUSE + *Frau* woman, wife]

haustellum (hɔː'stɛləm) *n., pl.* **-la** (-lə). the tip of the proboscis of a housefly or similar insect, specialized for sucking food. [C19: New Latin, diminutive of Latin *haustrum* device for drawing water, from *haurīre* to draw up; see EXHAUST] —**haus'tellate** *adj.*

haustorium (hɔː'stɔːrɪəm) *n., pl.* **-ria** (-rɪə). the organ of a parasitic plant that penetrates the host tissues and absorbs food and water from them. [C19: from New Latin, from Late Latin *haustor* a water-drawer; see HAUSTELLUM] —**haus'torial** *adj.*

hautboy ('əʊbɔɪ) *n.* **1.** Also called: **hautbois strawberry, hautbois** ('əʊbɔɪ). a strawberry, *Fragaria moschata,* of central Europe and Asia, with large fruit. **2.** an archaic word for **oboe.** [C16: from French *hautbois,* from *haut* high + *bois* wood, of Germanic origin; see BUSH[1]]

haute couture *French.* (ot kutyr) *n.* high fashion. [literally: high dressmaking]

haute cuisine *French.* (ot kwizin) *n.* high-class cooking. [literally: high cookery]

haute école *French.* (ot ekɔl) *n.* the classical art of riding. [literally: high school]

hauteur (əʊ'tɜː) *n.* pride; haughtiness. [C17: from French, from *haut* high; see HAUGHTY]

haut monde *French.* (o mɔ̃d) *n.* high society. [literally: high world]

Havana cigar (hə'vænə) *n.* any of various cigars manufactured in Cuba, known esp. for their high quality. Also called: **Havana.** [named after *Havana,* capital of Cuba]

havdalah *or* ***havdoloh*** *Hebrew.* (*Hebrew* hɑvdɑ'lɑ; *Yiddish* hav'dɔlə) *n. Judaism.* the ceremony marking the end of the sabbath or of a festival, including the blessings over wine, candles, and spices. [literally: separation]

have (hæv) *vb.* **has, having, had.** (*mainly tr.*) **1.** to be in material possession of; own: *he has two cars.* **2.** to possess as a characteristic quality or attribute: *he has dark hair.* **3.** to receive, take, or obtain: *she had a present from him; have a look.* **4.** to hold or entertain in the mind: *to have an idea.* **5.** to possess a knowledge or understanding of: *I have no German.* **6.** to experience or undergo: *to have a shock.* **7.** to be infected with or suffer from: *to have a cold.* **8.** to gain control of or advantage over: *you have me on that point.* **9.** (*usually passive*) *Slang.* to cheat or outwit: *he was had by that dishonest salesman.* **10.** (foll. by *on*) to exhibit (mercy, compassion, etc., towards): *have mercy on us, Lord.* **11.** to engage or take part in: *to have a conversation.* **12.** to arrange, carry out, or hold: *to have a party.* **13.** to cause, compel, or require to (be, do, or be done): *have my shoes mended.* **14.** (takes an infinitive with *to*) used as an auxiliary to express compulsion or necessity: *I had to run quickly to escape him.* **15.** to eat, drink, or partake of: *to have a good meal.* **16.** *Taboo slang.* to have sexual intercourse with: *he had her on the sofa.* **17.** (*used with a negative*) to tolerate or allow: *I won't have all this noise.* **18.** to declare, state, or assert: *rumour has it that they will marry.* **19.** to put or place: *I'll have the sofa in this room.* **20.** to receive as a guest: *to have three people to stay.* **21.** to beget or bear (offspring): *she had three children.* **22.** (*takes a past participle*) used as an auxiliary to form compound tenses expressing completed action: *I have gone; I shall have gone; I would have gone; I* *had gone.* **23. had better** *or* **best.** ought to: used to express compulsion, obligation, etc.: *you had better go.* **24. had rather** *or* **sooner.** to consider or find preferable that: *I had rather you left at once.* **25. have done.** See **done** (sense 3). **26. have had it.** *Informal.* **a.** to be exhausted, defeated, or killed. **b.** to have lost one's last chance. **c.** to become unfashionable. **27. have it.** to win a victory. **28. have it away** (*or* **off**). *Taboo, Brit. slang.* to have sexual intercourse. **29. have it coming.** *Informal.* to be about to receive or to merit punishment or retribution. **30. have it in for.** *Informal.* to wish or intend harm towards. **31. have it so good.** to have so many benefits, esp. material benefits. **32. have to do with. a.** to have dealings or associate with: *I have nothing to do with her.* **b.** to be of relevance to: *this has nothing to do with you.* **33. I have it.** *Informal.* I know the answer. **34. let (someone) have it.** *Slang.* to launch or deliver an attack on, esp. to discharge a firearm at (someone). **35. not having any.** (foll. by *of*) *Informal.* refusing to take part or be involved (in). ~*n.* **36.** (*usually pl.*) a person or group of people in possession of wealth, security, etc.: *the haves and the have-nots.* ~See also **have at, have in, have on, have out, have up.** [Old English *habban;* related to Old Norse *hafa,* Old Saxon *hebbian,* Old High German *habēn,* Latin *habēre*]

have at *vb.* (*intr., prep.*) *Archaic.* to make an opening attack on, esp. in fencing.

have in *vb.* (*tr., adv.*) **1.** to ask (a person) to give a service: *we must have the electrician in to mend the fire.* **2.** to invite to one's home.

havelock ('hævlɒk) *n.* a light-coloured cover for a service cap with a flap extending over the back of the neck to protect the head and neck from the sun. [C19: named after Sir H. *Havelock* (1795–1857), English general in India]

haven ('heɪvᵊn) *n.* **1.** a port, harbour, or other sheltered place for shipping. **2.** a place of safety or sanctuary; shelter. ~*vb.* **3.** (*tr.*) to secure or shelter in or as if in a haven. [Old English *hæfen,* from Old Norse *höfn;* related to Middle Dutch *havene,* Old Irish *cuan* to bend] —'**havenless** *adj.*

have-not *n.* (*usually pl.*) a person or group of people in possession of relatively little material wealth.

haven't ('hævᵊnt) *vb. contraction of* have not.

have on *vb.* (*tr.*) **1.** (*usually adv.*) to wear. **2.** (*usually adv.*) to have (a meeting or engagement) arranged as a commitment: *what does your boss have on this afternoon?* **3.** (*adv.*) *Informal.* to trick or tease (a person). **4.** (*prep.*) to have available (information or evidence, esp. when incriminating) about (a person): *the police had nothing on him, so they let him go.*

have out *vb.* (*tr., adv.*) **1.** to settle (a matter) or come to (a final decision), esp. by fighting or by frank discussion (often in the phrase **have it out**). **2.** to have extracted or removed: *I had two teeth out this morning.*

haver ('heɪvə) *vb.* (*intr.*) *Brit.* **1.** to dither. **2.** *Scot. and Northern English dialect.* to talk nonsense; babble. ~*n.* **3.** (*usually pl.*) *Scot.* nonsense. [C18: of unknown origin]

haversack ('hævəˌsæk) *n.* a canvas bag for provisions or equipment, carried on the back or shoulder. [C18: from French *havresac,* from German *Habersack* oat bag, from Old High German *habaro* oats + *Sack* SACK[1]]

Haversian canal (hæ'vɜːʃən) *n. Histology.* any of the channels that form a network in bone and contain blood vessels and nerves. [C19: named after C. *Havers* (died 1702), English anatomist who discovered them]

haversine ('hævəˌsaɪn) *n.* half the value of the versed sine. [C19: combination of *half* + *versed* + sine[1]]

have up *vb.* (*tr., adv.; usually passive*) to cause to appear for trial: *he was had up for breaking and entering.*

havildar ('hævɪlˌdɑː) *n.* a noncommissioned officer in the Indian army, equivalent in rank to sergeant. [C17: from Hindi, from Persian *hawāldār* one in charge]

havoc ('hævək) *n.* **1.** destruction; devastation; ruin. **2.** *Informal.* confusion; chaos. **3. cry havoc.** *Archaic.* to give the signal for pillage and destruction. **4. play havoc.** (often foll. by *with*) to cause a great deal of damage, distress, or confusion (to). ~*vb.* **-ocs, -ocking, -ocked. 5.** (*tr.*) *Archaic.* to lay waste. [C15: from Old French *havot* pillage, probably of Germanic origin] —'**havocker** *n.*

haw[1] (hɔː) *n.* **1.** the round or oval fruit (a pome) of the hawthorn, usually red or yellow, containing one to five seeds. **2.** another name for **hawthorn.** [Old English *haga,* identical with *haga* HEDGE; related to Old Norse *hagi* pasture]

haw[2] (hɔː) *n., interj.* **1.** an inarticulate utterance, as of hesitation, embarrassment, etc.; hem. ~*vb.* **2.** (*intr.*) to make this sound. **3. hem** (*or* **hum**) **and haw.** See **hem**[2] (sense 3). [C17: of imitative origin]

haw[3] (hɔː) *n. Archaic.* a yard or close. [of unknown origin]

haw[4] (hɔː) *n.* the nictitating membrane of a horse or other domestic animal. [C15: of unknown origin]

Hawaiian (hə'waɪən) *adj.* **1.** of or relating to Hawaii, US state and island group in the central Pacific, its people, or their language. ~*n.* **2.** a native or inhabitant of Hawaii, esp. one descended from Melanesian or Tahitian immigrants. **3.** a language of Hawaii belonging to the Malayo-Polynesian family.

Hawaiian guitar *n.* a lap-held steel-strung guitar with a wood or metal body, tuned to an open chord and played with a slide. Compare **Dobro, pedal steel guitar.**

hawfinch ('hɔːˌfɪntʃ) *n.* an uncommon European finch, *Coccothraustes coccothraustes,* having a very stout bill and brown plumage with black-and-white wings.

haw-haw[1] ('hɔː'hɔː) *interj.* a variant of **ha-ha**[1].

haw-haw[2] ('hɔːhɔː) *n.* a variant of **ha-ha**[2].

hawk[1] (hɔːk) *n.* **1.** any of various diurnal birds of prey of the family *Accipitridae,* such as the goshawk and Cooper's hawk, typically having short rounded wings and a long tail. **2.** *U.S. and Canadian.* any of various other falconiform birds, including the falcons but not the eagles or vultures. **3.** a person who advocates or supports war or warlike policies. Compare **dove**[1] (sense 2). **4.** a ruthless or rapacious person. **5. know a hawk from a handsaw.** to be able to judge things; be discerning. [from Shakespeare (*Hamlet* II:2:375); *handsaw* is probably a corruption of dialect *heronshaw* heron] ~*vb.* **6.** (*intr.*) to hunt with falcons, hawks, etc. **7.** (*intr.*) (of falcons or hawks) to fly in quest of prey. **8.** to pursue or attack on the wing, as a hawk. [Old English *hafoc;* related to Old Norse *haukr,* Old Frisian *havek,* Old High German *habuh,* Polish *kobuz*] —'**hawkish** *adj.* —'**hawkˌlike** *adj.*

hawk[2] (hɔːk) *vb.* **1.** to offer (goods) for sale, as in the street. **2.** (*tr.;* often foll. by *about*) to spread (news, gossip, etc.). [C16: back formation from HAWKER[1]]

hawk[3] (hɔːk) *vb.* **1.** (*intr.*) to clear the throat noisily. **2.** (*tr.*) to force (phlegm) up from the throat. **3.** *Brit.* a slang word for **spit**[1]. ~*n.* **4.** a noisy clearing of the throat. [C16: of imitative origin; see HAW[2]]

hawk[4] (hɔːk) *n.* a small square board with a handle underneath, used for carrying wet plaster or mortar. Also called: **mortar board.** [of unknown origin]

hawkbill ('hɔːkˌbɪl) *n.* another name for **hawksbill turtle.**

hawkbit ('hɔːkˌbɪt) *n.* any of three composite perennial plants of the genus *Leontodon,* with yellow dandelion-like flowers and lobed leaves in a rosette, erect or prostrate: found in grassland. [C18: from HAWK(WEED) + (DEVIL'S) BIT]

hawker[1] ('hɔːkə) *n.* a person who travels from place to place selling goods. [C16: probably from Middle Low German *hōker,* from *hōken* to peddle; see HUCKSTER]

hawker[2] ('hɔːkə) *n.* a person who hunts with hawks, falcons, etc. [Old English *hafecere;* see HAWK[1], -ER[1]]

hawk-eyed *adj.* **1.** having extremely keen sight. **2.** vigilant, watchful, or observant.

hawking ('hɔːkɪŋ) *n.* another name for **falconry.**

hawk moth *n.* any of various moths of the family *Sphingidae,* having long narrow wings and powerful flight, with the ability to hover over flowers when feeding from the nectar. Also called: **sphinx moth, hummingbird moth.** See also **death's-head moth.**

hawk owl *n.* a hawklike northern owl, *Surnia ulula,* with a long slender tail and brownish speckled plumage.

hawk's-beard *n.* any plant of the genus *Crepis,* having a ring of fine hairs surrounding the fruit and clusters of small dandelion-like flowers: family *Compositae* (composites).

hawksbill turtle *or* **hawksbill** ('hɔːksˌbɪl) *n.* a small tropical turtle, *Eretmochelys imbricata,* with a hooked beaklike mouth: a source of tortoiseshell: family *Chelonidae.* Also called: **hawkbill, tortoiseshell turtle.**

hawk's-eye *n.* a dark blue variety of the mineral crocidolite: a semiprecious gemstone.

hawkweed ('hɔːkˌwiːd) *n.* any typically hairy plant of the genus *Hieracium,* with clusters of dandelion-like flowers: family *Compositae* (composites).

hawse (hɔːz) *Nautical.* ~*n.* **1.** the part of the bows of a vessel where the hawseholes are. **2.** short for **hawsehole** or **hawsepipe. 3.** the distance from the bow of an anchored vessel to the anchor. **4.** the arrangement of port and starboard anchor ropes when a vessel is riding on both anchors. ~*vb.* **5.** (*intr.*) (of a vessel) to pitch violently when at anchor. [C14: from earlier *halse,* probably from Old Norse *háls;* related to Old English *heals* neck]

hawsehole ('hɔːzˌhəʊl) *n. Nautical.* one of the holes in the upper part of the bows of a vessel through which the anchor ropes pass. Often shortened to **hawse.**

hawsepipe ('hɔːzˌpaɪp) *n. Nautical.* a strong metal pipe through which an anchor rope passes. Often shortened to **hawse.**

hawser ('hɔːzə) *n. Nautical.* a large heavy rope. [C14: from Anglo-French *hauceour,* from Old French *haucier* to hoist, ultimately from Latin *altus* high]

hawser bend *n.* a knot for tying two ropes together.

hawser-laid *adj.* (of a rope) made up of three strands, the fibres (or yarns) of which have been twisted together in a left-handed direction. These three strands are then twisted together in a right-handed direction to make the rope.

hawthorn ('hɔːˌθɔːn) *n.* any of various thorny trees or shrubs of the N temperate rosaceous genus *Crataegus,* esp. *C. oxyacantha,* having white or pink flowers and reddish fruits (haws). Also called (in Britain): **may, may tree, mayflower.** [Old English *haguthorn* from *haga* hedge + *thorn* thorn; related to Old Norse *hagthorn,* Middle High German *hagendorn,* Dutch *haagdoorn*]

Hawthorne effect ('hɔːˌθɔːn) *n.* improvement in the performance of employees, students, etc., brought about by making changes in working methods, resulting from research into means of improving performance. Compare **iatrogenic, placebo effect.** [from the Western Electric Company's *Hawthorne* works in Chicago, U.S.A., where it was discovered during experiments in the 1920s]

hay[1] (heɪ) *n.* **1. a.** grass, clover, etc., cut and dried as fodder. **b.** (*in combination*): *a hayfield; a hayloft.* **2. hit the hay.** *Slang.* to go to bed. **3. make hay of.** to throw into confusion. **4. make hay while the sun shines.** to take full advantage of an opportunity. **5. roll in the hay.** *Informal.* sexual intercourse or heavy petting. ~*vb.* **6.** to cut, dry, and store (grass, clover, etc.) as fodder. **7.** (*tr.*) to feed with hay. [Old English *hieg;* related to Old Norse *hey,* Gothic *hawi,* Old Frisian *hē,* Old High German *houwi;* see HEW]

hay[2] *or* **hey** (heɪ) *n.* **1.** a circular figure in country dancing. **2.** a former country dance in which the dancers wove in and out of a circle. [C16: of uncertain origin]

haybox ('heɪˌbɒks) *n.* an airtight box full of hay or other insulating material used to keep partially cooked food warm and allow cooking by retained heat.

haycock ('heɪˌkɒk) *n.* a small cone-shaped pile of hay left in the field until dry enough to carry to the rick or barn.

hay fever *n.* an allergic reaction to pollen, dust, etc., characterized by sneezing, runny nose, and watery eyes due to inflammation of the mucous membranes of the eyes and nose. Technical name: **pollinosis.**

hayfork ('heɪˌfɔːk) *n.* a long-handled fork with two long curved prongs, used for moving or turning hay; pitchfork.

haymaker ('heɪˌmeɪkə) *n.* **1.** a person who helps to cut, turn, toss, spread, or carry hay. **2.** Also called: **hay conditioner.** either of two machines, one designed to crush stems of hay, the other to break and bend them, in order to cause more rapid and even drying. **3.** *Boxing slang.* a wild swinging punch. —'**hayˌmaking** *adj., n.*

haymow ('heɪˌmaʊ) *n.* **1.** a part of a barn where hay is stored. **2.** a quantity of hay stored in a barn or loft.

hayrack ('heɪˌræk) *n.* **1.** a rack for holding hay for feeding to animals. **2.** a rack fixed to a cart or wagon to increase the quantity of hay or straw that it can carry.

hayseed ('heɪˌsiːd) *n.* **1.** seeds or fragments of grass or straw. **2.** *U.S. and Canadian informal, derogatory.* a yokel.

haystack ('heɪˌstæk) *or* **hayrick** ('heɪˌrɪk) *n.* a large pile of hay, esp. one built in the open air and covered with thatch.

hayward ('heɪˌwɔːd) *n. Brit. obsolete.* a parish officer in charge of enclosures and fences.

haywire ('heɪˌwaɪə) *adj.* (*postpositive*) *Informal.* **1.** (of things) not functioning properly; disorganized (esp. in the phrase **go haywire**). **2.** (of people) erratic or crazy. [C20: alluding to the disorderly tangle of wire removed from bales of hay]

hazan *or* ***hazzan*** *Hebrew.* (xa'zan; *English* 'hɑːzᵊn) *n.* variant spellings of **chazan.**

hazard ('hæzəd) *n.* **1.** exposure or vulnerability to injury, loss, evil, etc. **2. at hazard.** at risk; in danger. **3.** a thing likely to cause injury, etc. **4.** *Golf.* an obstacle such as a bunker, a sand pit, etc. **5.** chance; accident (esp. in the phrase **by hazard**). **6.** a gambling game played with two dice. **7.** *Real Tennis.* **a.** the receiver's side of the court. **b.** one of the winning openings. **8.** *Billiards.* a scoring stroke made either when a ball other than the striker's is pocketed (**winning hazard**) or the striker's cue ball itself (**losing hazard**). ~*vb.* (*tr.*) **9.** to chance or risk. **10.** to venture (an opinion, guess, etc.). **11.** to expose to danger. [C13: from Old French *hasard,* from Arabic *az-zahr* the die] —'**hazardable** *adj.* —'**hazard-ˌfree** *adj.*

hazardous ('hæzədəs) *adj.* **1.** involving great risk. **2.** depending on chance. —'**hazardously** *adv.* —'**hazardousness** *n.*

hazard warning device *n.* an appliance fitted to a motor vehicle that operates a simultaneous flashing of all the direction indicators, used when the vehicle is stationary to indicate that the vehicle is temporarily obstructing traffic.

haze[1] (heɪz) *n.* **1.** *Meteorol.* **a.** reduced visibility in the air as a result of condensed water vapour, dust, etc., in the atmosphere. **b.** the moisture or dust causing this. **2.** obscurity of perception, feeling, etc. ~*vb.* **3.** (when *intr.,* often foll. by *over*) to make or become hazy. [C18: back formation from HAZY]

haze[2] (heɪz) *vb.* (*tr.*) **1.** *Chiefly U.S. and Canadian.* to subject (fellow students) to ridicule or abuse. **2.** *Nautical.* to harass with humiliating tasks. [C17: of uncertain origin] —'**hazer** *n.*

hazel ('heɪzᵊl) *n.* **1.** Also called: **cob.** any of several shrubs of the N temperate genus *Corylus,* esp. *C. avellana,* having oval serrated leaves and edible rounded brown nuts: family *Corylaceae.* **2.** the wood of any of these trees. **3.** short for **hazelnut. 4. a.** a light yellowish-brown colour. **b.** (*as adj.*): *hazel eyes.* [Old English *hæsel;* related to Old Norse *hasl,* Old High German *hasala,* Latin *corylus,* Old Irish *coll*]

hazelhen ('heɪzᵊlˌhɛn) *n.* a European woodland gallinaceous bird, *Tetrastes bonasia,* with a speckled brown plumage and slightly crested crown: family *Tetraonidae* (grouse).

hazelnut ('heɪzᵊlˌnʌt) *n.* the nut of a hazel shrub, having a smooth shiny hard shell. Also called: **filbert,** (Brit.) **cobnut, cob.**

hazy ('heɪzɪ) *adj.* **-zier, -ziest. 1.** characterized by reduced visibility; misty. **2.** indistinct; vague. [C17: of unknown origin] —'**hazily** *adv.* —'**haziness** *n.*

hazzan *Hebrew.* (xa'zan; *English* 'hɑːzᵊn) *n.* a variant spelling of **chazan.**

Hb *symbol for* haemoglobin.

HB (on Brit. pencils) *symbol for* hard-black: denoting a medium-hard lead. Compare **H** (sense 5), **B** (sense 9).

H-beam *n.* a rolled steel joist or girder with a cross section in the form of a capital letter *H.* Compare **I-beam.**

HBM (in Britain) *abbrev. for* His (*or* Her) Britannic Majesty.

H-bomb *n.* short for **hydrogen bomb.**

HC *abbrev. for:* **1.** Holy Communion. **2.** (in Britain) House of Commons.

HCF *or* **hcf** *abbrev. for* highest common factor.

HCG *abbrev. for* human chorionic gonadotrophin. See **gonadotrophin.**

hcp *abbrev. for* handicap.

hd *abbrev. for:* **1.** hand. **2.** head.

hdbk *abbrev. for* handbook.

HDL *abbrev. for* high-density lipoprotein.

hdqrs *abbrev. for* headquarters: replaced in military use by **HQ.**

HDR energy *n.* hot dry rock energy; energy extracted from hot rocks below the earth's surface by pumping water around a circuit in the hot region and back to the surface.

HDTV *abbrev. for* high definition television.

he[1] (hiː; *unstressed* iː) *pron.* (*subjective*) **1.** refers to a male person or animal: *he looks interesting; he's a fine stallion.* **2.** refers to an indefinite antecedent such as *one, whoever,* or *anybody: everybody can do as he likes in this country.* **3.** refers to a person or animal of unknown or unspecified sex: *a member of the party may vote as he sees fit.* ~*n.* **4. a.** a male person or animal. **b.** (*in combination*): *he-goat.* **5. a.** a children's game in which one player chases the others in an attempt to touch one of them, who then becomes the chaser. Compare **tag**[2]. **b.** the person chasing. Compare **it** (sense 7). [Old English *hē;* related to Old Saxon *hie,* Old High German *her* he, Old Slavonic *sĭ* this, Latin *cis* on this side]

he[2] (heɪ; *Hebrew* he) *n.* the fifth letter of the Hebrew alphabet (ה), transliterated as *h.* [from Hebrew]

he[3] (hiː, heɪ) *interj.* an expression of amusement or derision. Also: **he-he!** or **hee-hee!**

He *the chemical symbol for* helium.

HE *abbrev. for:* **1.** high explosive. **2.** His Eminence. **3.** His (*or* Her) Excellency.

head (hɛd) *n.* **1.** the upper or front part of the body in vertebrates, including man, that contains and protects the brain, eyes, mouth, and nose and ears when present. Related adj.: **cephalic. 2.** the corresponding part of an invertebrate animal. **3.** something resembling a head in form or function, such as the top of a tool. **4. a.** the person commanding most authority within a group, organization, etc. **b.** (*as modifier*): *head buyer.* **c.** (*in combination*): *headmaster.* **5.** the position of leadership or command: *at the head of his class.* **6. a.** the most forward part of a thing; a part that juts out; front: *the head of a queue.* **b.** (*as modifier*): *head point.* **7.** the highest part of a thing; upper end: *the head of the pass.* **8.** the froth on the top of a glass of beer. **9.** aptitude, intelligence, and emotions (esp. in the phrases **above** or **over one's head, have a head for, keep one's head, lose one's head,** etc.): *she has a good head for figures; a wise old head.* **10.** (*pl.* **head**) a person or animal considered as a unit: *the show was two pounds per head; six hundred head of cattle.* **11.** the head considered as a measure of length or height: *he's a head taller than his mother.* **12.** *Botany.* **a.** a dense inflorescence such as that of the daisy and other composite plants. **b.** any other compact terminal part of a plant, such as the leaves of a cabbage or lettuce. **13.** a culmination or crisis (esp. in the phrase **bring** or **come to a head**). **14.** the pus-filled tip or central part of a pimple, boil, etc. **15.** the head considered as the part of the body on which hair grows densely: *a fine head of hair.* **16.** the source or origin of a river or stream. **17.** (*cap. when part of name*) a headland or promontory, esp. a high one. **18.** the obverse of a coin, usually bearing a portrait of the head or a full figure of a monarch, deity, etc. Compare **tail. 19.** a main point or division of an argument, discourse, etc. **20.** (*often pl.*) the headline at the top of a newspaper article or the heading of a section within an article. **21.** *Nautical.* **a.** the front part of a ship or boat. **b.** (in sailing ships) the upper corner or edge of a sail. **c.** the top of any spar or derrick. **d.** any vertical timber cut to shape. **e.** (*often pl.*) a slang word for **lavatory. 22.** *Grammar.* another word for **governor** (sense 7). **23.** the taut membrane of a drum, tambourine, etc. **24. a.** the height of the surface of liquid above a specific point, esp. when considered or used as a measure of the pressure at that point: *a head of four feet.* **b.** pressure of water, caused by height or velocity, measured in terms of a vertical column of water. **c.** any pressure: *a head of steam in the boiler.* **25.** *Slang.* **a.** a person who regularly takes drugs, esp. LSD or cannabis. **b.** (*in combination*): *an acidhead.* **26.** *Mining.* a road driven into the coal face. **27. a.** the terminal point of a route. **b.** (*in combination*): *railhead.* **28.** a device on a turning or boring machine, such as a lathe, that is equipped with one or more cutting tools held to the work by this device. **29.** See **cylinder head. 30.** an electromagnet that can read, write, or erase information on a magnetic medium such as a magnetic tape, disk, or drum, used in computers, tape recorders, etc. **31.** *Informal.* short for **headmaster** *or* **headmistress. 32. a.** the head of a horse considered as a narrow margin in the outcome of a race (in the phrase **win by a head**). **b.** any narrow margin of victory (in the phrase **(win) by a head**). **33.** *Informal.* short for **head-**

ache. 34. *Curling.* the stones lying in the house after all 16 have been played. 35. **against the head.** *Rugby.* from the opposing side's put-in to the scrum. 36. **bite** *or* **snap someone's head off.** to speak sharply and angrily to someone. 37. **bring** *or* **come to a head. a.** to bring or be brought to a crisis: *matters came to a head.* **b.** (of a boil) to cause to be or be about to burst. 38. **get it into one's head.** to come to believe (an idea, esp. a whimsical one): *he got it into his head that the earth was flat.* 39. **give head.** *U.S. slang, taboo.* to perform fellatio. 40. **give someone** (*or* **something**) **his** (*or* **its**) **head. a.** to allow a person greater freedom or responsibility. **b.** to allow a horse to gallop by lengthening the reins. 41. **go to one's head. a.** to make one dizzy or confused, as might an alcoholic drink. **b.** to make one conceited: *his success has gone to his head.* 42. **head and shoulders above.** greatly superior to. 43. **head over heels. a.** turning a complete somersault. **b.** completely; utterly (esp. in the phrase **head over heels in love**). 44. **hold up one's head.** to be unashamed. 45. **keep one's head.** to remain calm. 46. **keep one's head above water.** to manage to survive a difficult experience. 47. **make head.** to make progress. 48. **make head or tail of.** (*used with a negative*). to attempt to understand (a problem, etc.): *he couldn't make head or tail of the case.* 49. **off** (*or* **out of**) **one's head.** *Slang.* insane or delirious. 50. **off the top of one's head.** without previous thought; impromptu. 51. **on one's (own) head.** at one's (own) risk or responsibility. 52. **one's head off.** *Slang.* loudly or excessively: *the baby cried its head off.* 53. **over someone's head. a.** without a person in the obvious position being considered, esp. for promotion: *the graduate was promoted over the heads of several of his seniors.* **b.** without consulting a person in the obvious position but referring to a higher authority: *in making his complaint he went straight to the director, over the head of his immediate boss.* **c.** beyond a person's comprehension. 54. **put (our, their,** *etc.*) **heads together.** *Informal.* to consult together. 55. **take it into one's head.** to conceive a notion, desire, or wish (to do something). 56. **turn someone's head.** to make someone vain, conceited, etc. ~*vb.* 57. (*tr.*) to be at the front or top of: *to head the field.* 58. (*tr.;* often foll. by *up*) to be in the commanding or most important position. 59. (often foll. by *for*) to go or cause to go (towards): *where are you heading?* 60. to turn or steer (a vessel) as specified: *to head into the wind.* 61. *Soccer.* to propel (the ball) by striking it with the head. 62. (*tr.*) to provide with or be a head or heading: *to head a letter; the quotation which heads chapter 6.* 63. (*tr.*) to cut the top branches or shoots off (a tree or plant). 64. (*intr.*) to form a head, as a boil or plant. 65. (*intr.;* often foll. by *in*) (of streams, rivers, etc.) to originate or rise in. 66. **head them.** *Austral.* to play two-up. ~See also **head for, head off, heads.** [Old English *hēafod;* related to Old Norse *haufuth,* Old Frisian *hāved,* Old Saxon *hōbid,* Old High German *houbit*] —'**head,like** *adj.*

-head *combining form.* indicating a person having a preoccupation as specified: *breadhead.*

headache ('hɛd,eɪk) *n.* 1. pain in the head, caused by dilation of cerebral arteries, muscle contraction, insufficient oxygen in the cerebral blood, reaction to drugs, etc. Technical name: **cephalalgia.** 2. *Informal.* any cause of worry, difficulty, or annoyance. —'**head,achy** *adj.*

head arrangement *n. Jazz.* a spontaneous orchestration.

headband ('hɛd,bænd) *n.* 1. a ribbon or band worn around the head. 2. a narrow cloth band attached to the top of the spine of a book for protection or decoration.

headbang ('hɛd,bæŋ) *vb.* (*intr.*) *Slang.* to nod one's head violently to the beat of loud rock music.

head-banger *n. Slang.* a heavy-metal rock fan.

headboard ('hɛd,bɔːd) *n.* a vertical board or terminal at the head of a bed.

head-butt *vb.* (*tr.*) 1. to deliberately strike (someone) with the head. ~*n.* **head butt.** 2. an act or an instance of deliberately striking someone with the head.

headcase ('hɛd,keɪs) *n. Informal.* an insane person.

headcheese ('hɛd,tʃiːz) *n.* the U.S. and Canadian name for **brawn** (sense 3).

head collar *n.* the part of a bridle that fits round a horse's head. Also called (esp. U.S.): **headstall.**

headdress ('hɛd,drɛs) *n.* any head covering, esp. an ornate one or one denoting a rank or occupation.

headed ('hɛdɪd) *adj.* 1. **a.** having a head or heads. **b.** (*in combination*): *two-headed; bullet-headed.* 2. having a heading: *headed notepaper.* 3. (*in combination*) having a mind or intellect as specified: *thickheaded.*

header ('hɛdə) *n.* 1. a machine that trims the heads from castings, forgings, etc., or one that forms heads, as in wire, to make nails. 2. a person who operates such a machine. 3. Also called: **header tank.** a reservoir, tank, or hopper that maintains a gravity feed or a static fluid pressure in an apparatus. 4. a brick or stone laid across a wall so that its end is flush with the outer surface. Compare **stretcher** (sense 5). 5. the action of striking a ball with the head. 6. *Informal.* a headlong fall or dive. 7. *Computer technol.* **a.** the first element of various information storage systems that contains information relevant to the main contents. **b.** (*as modifier*): *header card; header label.* 8. *Dialect.* a mentally unbalanced person.

headfast ('hɛdfɑːst) *n.* a mooring rope at the bows of a ship. [C16: from HEAD (in the sense: front) + *fast* a mooring rope, from Middle English *fest,* from Old Norse *festr;* related to FAST[1]]

headfirst ('hɛd'fɜːst) *adj., adv.* 1. with the head foremost; headlong: *he fell headfirst.* ~*adv.* 2. rashly or carelessly.

head for *vb.* (*prep.*) 1. to go or cause to go (towards). 2. to be destined for: *to head for trouble.*

head gate *n.* 1. a gate that is used to control the flow of water at the upper end of a lock. Compare **tail gate.** 2. another name for **floodgate** (sense 1).

headgear ('hɛd,gɪə) *n.* 1. any head covering, esp. a hat. 2. any part of a horse's harness that is worn on the head. 3. the hoisting mechanism at the pithead of a mine.

head-hunting *n.* 1. the practice among certain peoples of removing the heads of slain enemies and preserving them as trophies. 2. the recruitment, esp. through an agency, of executives from one company to another, often rival, company. 3. *U.S. slang.* the destruction or neutralization of political opponents. —'**head-,hunter** *n.*

heading ('hɛdɪŋ) *n.* 1. a title for a page, paragraph, chapter, etc. 2. a main division, as of a lecture, speech, essay, etc. 3. *Mining.* **a.** a horizontal tunnel. **b.** the end of such a tunnel. 4. the angle between the direction of an aircraft and a specified meridian, often due north. 5. the compass direction parallel to the keel of a vessel. 6. the act of heading. 7. anything that serves as a head.

heading dog *n. N.Z.* a dog that heads off a flock of sheep or a single sheep.

headland *n.* 1. ('hɛdlənd). a narrow area of land jutting out into a sea, lake, etc. 2. ('hɛd,lænd). a strip of land along the edge of an arable field left unploughed to allow space for machines.

headless ('hɛdlɪs) *adj.* 1. without a head. 2. without a leader. 3. foolish or stupid. 4. *Prosody.* another word for **catalectic.**

headlight ('hɛd,laɪt) *or* **headlamp** *n.* a powerful light, equipped with a reflector and attached to the front of a motor vehicle, locomotive, etc. See also **quartz-iodine lamp.**

headline ('hɛd,laɪn) *n.* 1. Also called: **head, heading. a.** a phrase at the top of a newspaper or magazine article indicating the subject of the article, usually in larger and heavier type. **b.** a line at the top of a page indicating the title, page number, etc. 2. (*usually pl.*) the main points of a television or radio news broadcast, read out before the full broadcast and summarized at the end. 3. **hit the headlines.** to become prominent in the news. ~*vb.* 4. (*tr.*) to furnish (a story or page) with a headline. 5. to have top billing (in).

headliner ('hɛd,laɪnə) *n. U.S.* a performer given prominent billing; star.

head-load *African.* ~*n.* 1. baggage or goods arranged so as to be carried on the heads of African porters. ~*vb.* 2. (*tr.*) to convey or carry (goods) on the head.

headlock ('hɛd,lɒk) *n.* a wrestling hold in which a wrestler locks his opponent's head between the crook of his elbow and the side of his body.

headlong ('hɛd,lɒŋ) *adv., adj.* 1. with the head foremost; headfirst. 2. with great haste. ~*adj.* 3. *Archaic.* (of slopes, etc.) very steep; precipitous.

headman ('hɛdmən) *n., pl.* **-men.** 1. *Anthropol.* a chief or leader. 2. a foreman or overseer.

headmaster (,hɛd'mɑːstə) *or* (*fem.*) **headmistress** *n.* the principal of a school. —,**head'master,ship** *or* (*fem.*) ,**head'mistress,ship** *n.*

headmasterly (,hɛd'mæstəlɪ) *or* (*fem.*) **headmistressy** (,hɛd'mɪstrɪsɪ) *adj.* relating to or typical of the duties and behaviour of a principal of a school.

head money *n.* 1. a reward paid for the capture or slaying of a fugitive, outlaw, etc. 2. an archaic term for **poll tax.**

headmost ('hɛd,məust) *adj.* a less common word for **foremost.**

head off *vb.* (*tr., adv.*) 1. to intercept and force to change direction: *to head off the stampede.* 2. to prevent or forestall (something that is likely to happen).

head of the river *n.* **a.** any of various annual rowing regattas held on particular rivers. **b.** the boat or team winning such a regatta: *Eton are head of the river again this year.*

head-on *adv., adj.* 1. with the front or fronts foremost: *a head-on collision.* 2. with directness or without compromise: *in his usual head-on fashion.*

headphones ('hɛd,fəunz) *pl. n.* an electrical device consisting of two earphones held in position by a flexible metallic strap passing over the head. Informal name: **cans.**

headpiece ('hɛd,piːs) *n.* 1. *Printing.* a decorative band at the top of a page, chapter, etc. 2. any covering for the head, esp. a helmet. 3. *Archaic.* the intellect. 4. a less common word for **crownpiece** (sense 2).

headpin ('hɛd,pɪn) *n. Tenpin bowling.* another word for **kingpin.**

headquarter (,hɛd'kwɔːtə) *vb. Informal, chiefly U.S.* to place in or establish as headquarters.

headquarters (,hɛd'kwɔːtəz) *pl. n.* (*sometimes functioning as sing.*) 1. any centre or building from which operations are directed, as in the military, the police, etc. 2. a military formation comprising the commander, his staff, and supporting echelons. ~Abbrevs.: **HQ, h.q.**

headrace ('hɛd,reɪs) *n.* a channel that carries water to a water wheel, turbine, etc. Compare **tailrace.**

headrail ('hɛd,reɪl) *n. Billiards, etc.* the end of the table from which play is started, nearest the baulkline.

headreach ('hɛd,riːtʃ) *Nautical.* ~*n.* **1.** the distance made to windward while tacking. ~*vb.* **2.** (*tr.*) to gain distance over (another boat) when tacking.

headrest ('hɛd,rɛst) *n.* a support for the head, as on a dentist's chair or car seat.

head restraint *n.* an adjustable support for the head, attached to a car seat, to prevent the neck from being jolted backwards sharply in the event of a crash or sudden stop.

headroom ('hɛd,rʊm, -,ruːm) *or* **headway** *n.* the height of a bridge, room, etc.; clearance.

heads (hɛdz) *interj., adv.* **1.** with the obverse side of a coin uppermost, esp. if it has a head on it: used as a call before tossing a coin. Compare **tails.** **2. the.** *Austral. informal.* people in authority.

headsail ('hɛd,seɪl; *Nautical* 'hɛdsəl) *n.* any sail set forward of the foremast.

headscarf ('hɛd,skɑːf) *n., pl.* **-scarves** (-,skɑːvz). a scarf for the head, often worn tied under the chin.

head sea *n.* a sea in which the waves run directly against the course of a ship.

headset ('hɛd,sɛt) *n.* a pair of headphones, esp. with a microphone attached.

headship ('hɛdʃɪp) *n.* **1.** the position or state of being a leader; command; leadership. **2.** *Education, Brit.* the position of headmaster or headmistress of a school.

headshrinker ('hɛd,ʃrɪŋkə) *n.* **1.** a slang name for **psychiatrist.** Often shortened to **shrink.** **2.** a head-hunter who shrinks the heads of his victims.

headsman ('hɛdzmən) *n., pl.* **-men.** (formerly) an executioner who beheaded condemned persons.

headspring ('hɛd,sprɪŋ) *n.* **1.** a spring that is the source of a stream. **2.** a spring using the head as a lever from a position lying on the ground. **3.** *Rare.* a source.

headsquare ('hɛd,skwɛə) *n.* a scarf worn on the head.

headstall ('hɛd,stɔːl) *n.* another word (esp. U.S.) for **head collar.**

headstand ('hɛd,stænd) *n.* the act or an instance of balancing on the head, usually with the hands as support.

head start *n.* an initial advantage in a competitive situation. [originally referring to a horse's having its head in front of others at the start of a race]

head station *n. Austral.* the main buildings on a large sheep or cattle farm.

headstock ('hɛd,stɒk) *n.* **1.** the part of a machine that supports and transmits the drive to the chuck. Compare **tailstock.** **2.** the wooden or metal block on which a church bell is hung.

headstone ('hɛd,stəʊn) *n.* **1.** a memorial stone at the head of a grave. **2.** *Architect.* another name for **keystone.**

headstream ('hɛd,striːm) *n.* a stream that is the source or a source of a river.

headstrong ('hɛd,strɒŋ) *adj.* **1.** self-willed; obstinate. **2.** (of an action) heedless; rash. —'**head,strongly** *adv.* —'**head,strongness** *n.*

head teacher *n.* a headmaster or headmistress.

head-up display *n.* the projection of readings from instruments onto a windscreen, enabling an aircraft pilot or car driver to see them without looking down.

head voice *or* **register** *n.* the high register of the human voice, in which the vibrations of sung notes are felt in the head.

head waiter *n.* a waiter who supervises the activities of other waiters and arranges the seating of guests.

headward ('hɛdwəd) *adj.* **1.** (of river erosion) cutting backwards or upstream above the original source, which recedes. ~*adv.* **2.** a variant of **headwards.**

headwards ('hɛdwədz) *or* **headward** *adv.* backwards beyond the original source: *a river erodes headwards.*

headwaters ('hɛd,wɔːtəz) *pl. n.* the tributary streams of a river in the area in which it rises; headstreams.

headway ('hɛd,weɪ) *n.* **1.** motion in a forward direction: *the vessel made no headway.* **2.** progress or rate of progress: *he made no headway with the problem.* **3.** another name for **headroom.** **4.** the distance or time between consecutive trains, buses, etc., on the same route.

headwind ('hɛd,wɪnd) *n.* a wind blowing directly against the course of an aircraft or ship. Compare **tailwind.**

headword ('hɛd,wɜːd) *n.* a key word placed at the beginning of a line, paragraph, etc., as in a dictionary entry.

headwork ('hɛd,wɜːk) *n.* **1.** mental work. **2.** the ornamentation of the keystone of an arch. —'**head,worker** *n.*

heady ('hɛdɪ) *adj.* **headier, headiest.** **1.** (of alcoholic drink) intoxicating. **2.** strongly affecting the mind or senses; extremely exciting. **3.** rash; impetuous. —'**headily** *adv.* —'**headiness** *n.*

heal (hiːl) *vb.* **1.** to restore or be restored to health. **2.** (*intr.*; often foll. by *over* or *up*) (of a wound, burn, etc.) to repair by natural processes, as by scar formation. **3.** (*tr.*) **a.** to treat (a wound, etc.) by assisting in its natural repair. **b.** to cure (a disease or disorder). **4.** to restore or be restored to friendly relations, harmony, etc. [Old English *hǣlan;* related to Old Norse *heila,* Gothic *hailjan,* Old High German *heilen;* see HALE[1], WHOLE] —'**healable** *adj.* —'**healer** *n.* —'**healing** *n., adj.*

heal-all *n.* another name for **selfheal.**

health (hɛlθ) *n.* **1.** the state of being bodily and mentally vigorous and free from disease. **2.** the general condition of body and mind: *in poor health.* **3.** the condition of any unit, society, etc.: *the economic health of a nation.* **4.** a toast to a person, wishing him or her good health, happiness, etc. **5.** (*modifier*) of or relating to food or other goods reputed to be beneficial to the health: *health food; a health store.* **6.** (*modifier*) of or relating to health, esp. to the administration of health: *a health committee; health resort; health service.* ~*interj.* **7.** an exclamation wishing someone good health as part of a toast (in the phrases **your health, good health,** etc.). [Old English *hǣlth;* related to *hāl* HALE[1]]

health camp *n. N.Z.* a camp, usually at the seaside, for children requiring health care.

health centre *n.* (in Britain) premises, owned by a local authority, providing health care for the local community and usually housing a group practice, nursing staff, a child-health clinic, x-ray facilities, etc.

health farm *n.* a residential establishment, often in the country, visited by those who wish to improve their health by losing weight, eating health foods, taking exercise, etc.

health food *n.* **a.** vegetarian food organically grown and with no additives, eaten for its dietary value and benefit to health. **b.** (*as modifier*): *a health-food shop.*

healthful ('hɛlθfʊl) *adj.* a less common word for **healthy** (senses 1–3). —'**healthfully** *adv.* —'**healthfulness** *n.*

health physics *n.* (*functioning as sing.*) the branch of physics concerned with the health and safety of people in medical, scientific, and industrial work, esp. with protection from the biological effects of ionizing radiation.

health salts *pl. n.* magnesium sulphate or similar salts taken as a mild laxative.

health stamp *n. N.Z.* a postage stamp with a surcharge that is used to support a health camp.

health visitor *n.* (in Britain) a nurse employed by a district health authority to visit people in their homes and give help and advice on health and social welfare, esp. to mothers of preschool children, to the handicapped, and to elderly people.

healthy ('hɛlθɪ) *adj.* **healthier, healthiest.** **1.** enjoying good health. **2.** functioning well or being sound: *the company's finances are not very healthy.* **3.** conducive to health; salutary. **4.** indicating soundness of body or mind: *a healthy appetite.* **5.** *Informal.* considerable in size or amount: *a healthy sum.* —'**healthily** *adv.* —'**healthiness** *n.*

heap (hiːp) *n.* **1.** a collection of articles or mass of material gathered together in one place. **2.** (*often pl.;* usually foll. by *of*) *Informal.* a large number or quantity. **3. give them heaps.** *Austral. slang.* to contend strenuously with an opposing sporting team. **4.** *Informal.* a place or thing that is very old, untidy, unreliable, etc.: *the car was a heap.* ~*adv.* **5. heaps.** (intensifier): *he said he was feeling heaps better.* ~*vb.* **6.** (often foll. by *up* or *together*) to collect or be collected into or as if into a heap or pile: *to heap up wealth.* **7.** (*tr.;* often foll. by *with, on,* or *upon*) to load or supply (with) abundantly: *to heap with riches.* [Old English *héap;* related to Old Frisian *hāp,* Old Saxon *hōp,* Old High German *houf*] —'**heaper** *n.*

heaping ('hiːpɪŋ) *adj. U.S. and Canadian.* (of a spoonful) heaped.

hear (hɪə) *vb.* **hears, hearing, heard** (hɜːd). **1.** (*tr.*) to perceive (a sound) with the sense of hearing. **2.** (*tr.; may take a clause as object*) to listen to: *did you hear what I said?* **3.** (when *intr.*, sometimes foll. by *of* or *about;* when *tr., may take a clause as object*) to be informed (of); receive information (about): *to hear of his success; have you heard?* **4.** *Law.* to give a hearing to (a case). **5.** (when *intr.*, usually foll. by *of* and used with a negative) to listen (to) with favour, assent, etc.: *she wouldn't hear of it.* **6.** (*intr.;* foll. by *from*) to receive a letter, news, etc. (from). **7. hear! hear!** an exclamation used to show approval of something said. **8. hear tell (of).** *Dialect.* to be told (about); learn (of). [Old English *hieran;* related to Old Norse *heyra,* Gothic *hausjan,* Old High German *hōren,* Greek *akouein*] —'**hearable** *adj.* —'**hearer** *n.*

hearing ('hɪərɪŋ) *n.* **1.** the faculty or sense by which sound is perceived. **2.** an opportunity to be listened to. **3.** the range within which sound can be heard; earshot. **4.** the investigation of a matter by a court of law, esp. the preliminary inquiry into an indictable crime by magistrates. **5.** a formal or official trial of an action or lawsuit.

hearing aid *n.* a device for assisting the hearing of partially deaf people, typically consisting of a small battery-powered electronic amplifier with microphone and earphone, worn by a deaf person in or behind the ear. Also called: **deaf aid.**

hearing loss *n.* an increase in the threshold of audibility caused by age, infirmity, or prolonged exposure to intense noise.

hearken *or U.S. (sometimes)* **harken** ('hɑːkən) *vb. Archaic.* to listen to (something). [Old English *heorcnian;* see HARK] —'**hearkener** *n.*

hear out *vb.* (*tr., adv.*) to listen in regard to every detail and give a proper or full hearing to.

hearsay ('hɪə,seɪ) *n.* gossip; rumour.

hearsay evidence *n. Law.* evidence based on what has been reported to a witness by others rather than what he has himself observed or experienced (not generally admissible as evidence).

hearse (hɜːs) *n.* a vehicle, such as a car or carriage, used to carry a coffin to the grave. [C14: from Old French *herce,* from Latin *hirpex* harrow]

heart (hɑːt) *n.* **1.** the hollow muscular organ in vertebrates whose contractions propel the blood through the circulatory system. In mammals it consists of a right and left atrium and a right and left ventricle. Related adj.: **cardiac. 2.** the corresponding organ or part in invertebrates. **3.** this organ considered as the seat of life and emotions, esp. love. **4.** emotional mood or disposition: *a happy heart; a change of heart.* **5.** tenderness or pity: *you have no heart.* **6.** courage or spirit; bravery. **7.** the inmost or most central part of a thing: *the heart of the city.* **8.** the most important or vital part: *the heart of the matter.* **9.** (of vegetables such as cabbage) the inner compact part. **10.** the core of a tree. **11.** the part nearest the heart of a person; breast: *she held him to her heart.* **12.** a dearly loved person: usually used as a term of address: *dearest heart.* **13.** a conventionalized representation of the heart, having two rounded lobes at the top meeting in a point at the bottom. **14. a.** a red heart-shaped symbol on a playing card. **b.** a card with one or more of these symbols or (*when pl.*) the suit of cards so marked. **15.** a fertile condition in land, conducive to vigorous growth in crops or herbage (esp. in the phrase **in good heart**). **16. after one's own heart.** appealing to one's own disposition, taste, or tendencies. **17. at heart.** in reality or fundamentally. **18. break one's** (*or* **someone's**) **heart.** to grieve (or cause to grieve) very deeply, esp. through love. **19. by heart.** by committing to memory. **20. cross my heart (and hope to die)!** I promise! **21. eat one's heart out.** to brood or pine with grief or longing. **22. from (the bottom of) one's heart.** very sincerely or deeply. **23. have a heart!** be kind or merciful. **24. have one's heart in it.** (*usually used with a negative*) to have enthusiasm for something. **25. have one's heart in one's boots.** to be depressed or down-hearted. **26. have one's heart in one's mouth** (*or* **throat**). to be full of apprehension, excitement, or fear. **27. have one's heart in the right place. a.** to be kind, thoughtful, or generous. **b.** to mean well. **28. have the heart.** (*usually used with a negative*) to have the necessary will, callousness, etc., (to do something): *I didn't have the heart to tell him.* **29. heart and soul.** absolutely; completely. **30. heart of hearts.** the depths of one's conscience or emotions. **31. heart of oak.** a brave person. **32. in one's heart.** secretly; fundamentally. **33. lose heart.** to become despondent or disillusioned (over something). **34. lose one's heart to.** to fall in love with. **35. near** *or* **close to one's heart.** cherished or important. **36. set one's heart on.** to have as one's ambition to obtain; covet. **37. take heart.** to become encouraged. **38. take to heart.** to take seriously or be upset about. **39. to one's heart's content.** as much as one wishes. **40. wear one's heart on one's sleeve.** to show one's feelings openly. **41. with all one's** (*or* **one's whole**) **heart.** very willingly. ~*vb.* **42.** (*intr.*) (of vegetables) to form a heart. **43.** an archaic word for **hearten.** ~See also **hearts.** [Old English *heorte;* related to Old Norse *hjarta,* Gothic *hairtō,* Old High German *herza,* Latin *cor,* Greek *kardia,* Old Irish *cride*]

heartache (ˈhɑːtˌeɪk) *n.* intense anguish or mental suffering.

heart attack *n.* any sudden severe instance of abnormal heart functioning, esp. coronary thrombosis.

heartbeat (ˈhɑːtˌbiːt) *n.* one complete pulsation of the heart. See **diastole, systole.**

heart block *n.* impaired conduction or blocking of the impulse that regulates the heartbeat, resulting in a lack of coordination between the beating of the atria and the ventricles. Also called: **Adams-Stokes syndrome, atrioventricular block.**

heartbreak (ˈhɑːtˌbreɪk) *n.* intense and overwhelming grief, esp. through disappointment in love. —**ˈheartˌbreaker** *n.*

heartbreaking (ˈhɑːtˌbreɪkɪŋ) *adj.* extremely sad, disappointing, or pitiful. —**ˈheartˌbreakingly** *adv.*

heartbroken (ˈhɑːtˌbrəʊkən) *adj.* suffering from intense grief. —**ˈheartˌbrokenly** *adv.* —**ˈheartˌbrokenness** *n.*

heartburn (ˈhɑːtˌbɜːn) *n.* a burning sensation beneath the breastbone caused by irritation of the oesophagus, as from regurgitation of the contents of the stomach. Technical names: **cardialgia, pyrosis.**

heart cherry *n.* a heart-shaped variety of sweet cherry.

-hearted *adj.* having a heart or disposition as specified: *good-hearted; cold-hearted; great-hearted; heavy-hearted.*

hearten (ˈhɑːtᵊn) *vb.* to make or become cheerful. —**ˈheartening** *adj.*

heart failure *n.* **1.** a condition in which the heart is unable to pump an adequate amount of blood to the tissues, usually resulting in breathlessness, swollen ankles, etc. **2.** sudden and permanent cessation of the heartbeat, resulting in death.

heartfelt (ˈhɑːtˌfɛlt) *adj.* sincerely and strongly felt.

hearth (hɑːθ) *n.* **1. a.** the floor of a fireplace, esp. one that extends outwards into the room. **b.** (*as modifier*): *hearth rug.* **2.** this part of a fireplace as a symbol of the home, etc. **3.** the bottom part of a metallurgical furnace in which the molten metal is produced or contained. [Old English *heorth;* related to Old High German *herd* hearth, Latin *carbō* charcoal]

hearthstone (ˈhɑːθˌstəʊn) *n.* **1.** a stone that forms a hearth. **2.** a less common word for **hearth** (sense 1). **3.** soft stone used to clean and whiten floors, steps, etc.

heartily (ˈhɑːtɪlɪ) *adv.* **1.** thoroughly or vigorously: *to eat heartily.* **2.** in a sincere manner: *he congratulated me heartily.*

heartland (ˈhɑːtˌlænd) *n.* **1.** the central region of a country or continent. **2.** the core or most vital area: *the industrial heartland of England.*

heartless (ˈhɑːtlɪs) *adj.* unkind or cruel; hard-hearted. —**ˈheartlessly** *adv.* —**ˈheartlessness** *n.*

heart-lung machine *n.* a machine used to maintain the circulation and oxygenation of the blood during heart surgery.

heart murmur *n.* an abnormal sound heard through a stethoscope over the region of the heart.

heart-rending *adj.* causing great mental pain and sorrow. —**ˈheart-ˌrendingly** *adv.*

hearts (hɑːts) *n.* (*functioning as sing.*) a card game in which players must avoid winning tricks containing hearts or the queen of spades. Also called: **Black Maria.**

heart-searching *n.* examination of one's feelings or conscience.

heartsease *or* **heart's-ease** (ˈhɑːtsˌiːz) *n.* **1.** another name for the **wild pansy. 2.** peace of mind.

heartsick (ˈhɑːtˌsɪk) *adj.* deeply dejected or despondent. —**ˈheartˌsickness** *n.*

heartsome (ˈhɑːtsəm) *adj. Chiefly Scot.* **1.** cheering or encouraging: *heartsome news.* **2.** gay; cheerful. —**ˈheartsomely** *adv.* —**ˈheartsomeness** *n.*

heart starter *n. Austral. slang.* the first drink of the day.

heartstrings (ˈhɑːtˌstrɪŋz) *pl. n. Often facetious.* deep emotions or feelings. [C15: originally referring to the tendons supposed to support the heart]

heart-throb *n.* **1.** an object of infatuation. **2.** a heart beat.

heart-to-heart *adj.* **1.** (esp. of a conversation or discussion) concerned with personal problems or intimate feelings. ~*n.* **2.** an intimate conversation or discussion.

heart urchin *n.* any echinoderm of the genus *Echinocardium,* having a heart-shaped body enclosed in a rigid spiny test: class *Echinoidea* (sea urchins).

heart-warming *adj.* **1.** pleasing; gratifying. **2.** emotionally moving.

heart-whole *adj. Rare.* **1.** not in love. **2.** sincere. **3.** stout-hearted. —**ˌheart-ˈwholeness** *n.*

heartwood (ˈhɑːtˌwʊd) *n.* the central core of dark hard wood in tree trunks, consisting of nonfunctioning xylem tissue that has become blocked with resins, tannins, and oils. Compare **sapwood.**

heartworm (ˈhɑːtˌwɜːm) *n.* a parasitic nematode worm, *Dirofilaria immitis,* that lives in the heart and bloodstream of vertebrates.

hearty (ˈhɑːtɪ) *adj.* **heartier, heartiest. 1.** warm and unreserved in manner or behaviour. **2.** vigorous and enthusiastic: *a hearty slap on the back.* **3.** sincere and heartfelt: *hearty dislike.* **4.** healthy and strong (esp. in the phrase **hale and hearty**). **5.** substantial and nourishing. ~*n. Informal.* **6.** a comrade, esp. a sailor. **7.** a vigorous sporting man: *a rugby hearty.* —**ˈheartiness** *n.*

heat (hiːt) *n.* **1.** the energy transferred as a result of a difference in temperature. Related adjs.: **thermal, calorific. 2.** the sensation caused in the body by heat energy; warmth. **3.** the state or quality of being hot. **4.** hot weather: *the heat of summer.* **5.** intensity of feeling; passion: *the heat of rage.* **6.** the most intense or active part: *the heat of the battle.* **7.** a period or condition of sexual excitement in female mammals that occurs at oestrus. **8.** *Sport.* **a.** a preliminary eliminating contest in a competition. **b.** a single section of a contest. **9.** *Slang.* police activity after a crime: *the heat is off.* **10.** *Chiefly U.S. slang.* criticism or abuse: *he took a lot of heat for that mistake.* **11. in** *or* **on heat. a.** Also: **in season.** (of some female mammals) sexually receptive. **b.** in a state of sexual excitement. **12. in the heat of the moment.** without pausing to think. **13. the heat.** *Slang.* the police. **14. turn on the heat.** *Informal.* to increase the intensity of activity, coercion, etc. ~*vb.* **15.** to make or become hot or warm. **16.** to make or become excited or intense. [Old English *hǣtu;* related to *hāt* HOT, Old Frisian *hēte* heat, Old High German *heizī*] —**ˈheatless** *adj.*

heat barrier *n.* another name for **thermal barrier.**

heat capacity *n.* the heat required to raise the temperature of a substance by unit temperature interval under specified conditions. Symbol: C_p (for constant pressure) or C_v (for constant volume).

heat content *n.* another name for **enthalpy.**

heat death *n. Thermodynamics.* the condition of any closed system when its total entropy is a maximum and it has no available energy. If the universe is a closed system it should eventually reach this state.

heated (ˈhiːtɪd) *adj.* **1.** made hot; warmed. **2.** impassioned or highly emotional. —**ˈheatedly** *adv.* —**ˈheatedness** *n.*

heat engine *n.* an engine that converts heat energy into mechanical energy.

heater (ˈhiːtə) *n.* **1.** any device for supplying heat, such as a hot-air blower, radiator, convector, etc. **2.** *U.S. slang.* a pistol. **3.** *Electronics.* a conductor carrying a current that indirectly heats the cathode in some types of valve.

heat exchanger *n.* a device for transferring heat from one fluid to another without allowing them to mix.

heat exhaustion *n.* a condition resulting from exposure to intense heat, characterized by dizziness, abdominal cramp, and prostration. Also called: **heat prostration.** Compare **heatstroke.**

heath (hiːθ) *n.* **1.** *Brit.* a large open area, usually with sandy soil and scrubby vegetation, esp. heather. **2.** Also called: **heather.** any low-growing evergreen ericaceous shrub of the Old World genus *Erica* and related genera, having small bell-shaped typically pink or purple flowers. **3.** any of several nonericaceous heathlike plants, such as sea heath. **4.** *Austral.* any of various heathlike plants of the genus *Epacris.* **5.** any of various small brown satyrid butterflies of the genus *Coenonympha,* with coppery-brown wings, esp. the **large heath** (*C. tullia*). [Old English *hǣth;* related to Old Norse *heithr* field, Old High German *heida* heather] —ˈ**heath,like** *adj.* —ˈ**heathy** *adj.*

heathberry (ˈhiːθˌbɛrɪ) *n., pl.* **-ries.** any of various plants that have berry-like fruits and grow on heaths, such as the bilberry and crowberry.

heath cock *n.* another name for **blackcock.**

heathen (ˈhiːðən) *n., pl.* **-thens** *or* **-then. 1.** a person who does not acknowledge the God of Christianity, Judaism, or Islam; pagan. **2.** an uncivilized or barbaric person. **3. the heathen.** (*functioning as pl.*) heathens collectively. ~*adj.* **4.** irreligious; pagan. **5.** unenlightened; uncivilized; barbaric. **6.** of or relating to heathen peoples or their religious, moral, and other customs, practices, and beliefs. [Old English *hǣthen;* related to Old Norse *heithinn,* Old Frisian *hēthin,* Old High German *heidan*] —ˈ**heathenism** *or* ˈ**heathenry** *n.* —ˈ**heathenness** *n.*

heathendom (ˈhiːðəndəm) *n.* heathen lands, peoples, or beliefs.

heathenish (ˈhiːðənɪʃ) *adj.* of, relating to, or resembling a heathen or heathen culture. —ˈ**heathenishly** *adv.* —ˈ**heathenishness** *n.*

heathenize *or* **heathenise** (ˈhiːðəˌnaɪz) *vb.* **1.** to render or become heathen, or bring or come under heathen influence. **2.** (*intr.*) to engage in heathen practices.

heather (ˈhɛðə) *n.* **1.** Also called: **ling, heath.** a low-growing evergreen Eurasian ericaceous shrub, *Calluna vulgaris,* that grows in dense masses on open ground and has clusters of small bell-shaped typically pinkish-purple flowers. **2.** any of certain similar plants. **3.** a purplish-red to pinkish-purple colour. ~*adj.* **4.** of a heather colour. **5.** of or relating to interwoven yarns of mixed colours: *heather mixture.* [C14: originally Scottish and Northern English, probably from HEATH] —ˈ**heathered** *adj.* —ˈ**heathery** *adj.*

heathfowl (ˈhiːθˌfaʊl) *n.* (in British game laws) an archaic name for the **black grouse.** Compare **moorfowl.**

heath grass *or* **heather grass** *n.* a perennial European grass, *Sieglingia decumbens,* with flat hairless leaves.

heath hen *n.* **1.** another name for **greyhen. 2.** a recently extinct variety of the prairie chicken.

Heath Robinson (hiːθ ˈrɒbɪnsᵊn) *adj.* (of a mechanical device) absurdly complicated in design and having a simple function. [C20: named after William *Heath Robinson* (1872–1944), British cartoonist and book illustrator]

heath wren *n.* either of two ground-nesting warblers of southern Australia, *Hylacola pyrrhopygia* or *H. cauta,* noted for their song and their powers of mimicry.

heating (ˈhiːtɪŋ) *n.* **1.** a device or system for supplying heat, esp. central heating, to a building. **2.** the heat supplied.

heating element *n.* a coil or other arrangement of wire in which heat is produced by an electric current.

heat-island *n. Meteorol.* the mass of air over a large city, characteristically having a slightly higher average temperature than that of the surrounding air.

heat lightning *n.* flashes of light seen near the horizon, esp. on hot evenings: reflections of more distant lightning.

heat of combustion *n. Chem.* the heat evolved when one mole of a substance is burnt in oxygen at constant volume.

heat of formation *n. Chem.* the heat evolved or absorbed when one mole of a compound is formed from its constituent atoms.

heat of reaction *n. Chem.* the heat evolved or absorbed when one mole of a product is formed at constant pressure.

heat of solution *n. Chem.* the heat evolved or absorbed when one mole of a substance dissolves completely in a large volume of solvent.

heat prostration *n.* another name for **heat exhaustion.**

heat pump *n.* a device, as used in a refrigerator, for extracting heat from a source and delivering it elsewhere at a much higher temperature.

heat rash *n.* a nontechnical name for **miliaria.**

heat-seeking *adj.* **1.** (of a detecting device) able to detect sources of infrared radiation: *a heat-seeking camera.* **2.** (of a missile) able to detect and follow a source of heat, as from an aircraft engine: *a heat-seeking missile.* —**heat seeker** *n.*

heat shield *n.* a coating or barrier for shielding from excessive heat, such as that experienced by a spacecraft on re-entry into the earth's atmosphere.

heat sink *n.* **1.** a metal plate specially designed to conduct and radiate heat from an electrical component, such as a rectifier. **2.** a layer of material placed within the outer skin of high-speed aircraft to absorb heat.

heatstroke (ˈhiːtˌstrəʊk) *n.* a condition resulting from prolonged exposure to intense heat, characterized by high fever and in severe cases convulsions and coma. See **sunstroke.**

heat-treat *vb.* (*tr.*) to apply heat to (a metal or alloy) in one or more temperature cycles to give it desirable properties. —**heat treatment** *n.*

heat wave *n.* **1.** a continuous spell of abnormally hot weather. **2.** an extensive slow-moving air mass at a relatively high temperature.

heaume (həʊm) *n.* (in the 12th and 13th centuries) a large helmet reaching and supported by the shoulders. [C16: from Old French *helme;* see HELMET]

heave (hiːv) *vb.* **heaves, heaving, heaved** *or* (*chiefly nautical*) **hove. 1.** (*tr.*) to lift or move with a great effort. **2.** (*tr.*) to throw (something heavy) with effort. **3.** to utter (sounds, sighs, etc.) or breathe noisily or unhappily: *to heave a sigh.* **4.** to rise and fall or cause to rise and fall heavily. **5.** (*past tense and past participle* **hove**) *Nautical.* **a.** to move or cause to move in a specified way, direction, or position: *to heave in sight.* **b.** (*intr.*) (of a vessel) to pitch or roll. **6.** (*tr.*) to displace (rock strata, mineral veins, etc.) in a horizontal direction. **7.** (*intr.*) to retch. ~*n.* **8.** the act or an instance of heaving. **9.** a fling. **10.** a horizontal displacement of rock strata at a fault. ~See also **heave down, heaves, heave to.** [Old English *hebban;* related to Old Norse *hefja,* Old Saxon *hebbian,* Old High German *heffen* to raise, Latin *capere* to take, Sanskrit *kapatī* two hands full] —ˈ**heaver** *n.*

heave down *vb.* (*intr., adv.*) *Naut.* to turn a vessel on its side for cleaning.

heave-ho *sentence substitute.* **1.** a sailors' cry, as when hoisting anchor. ~*n.* **2.** *Informal.* dismissal, as from employment.

heaven (ˈhɛvᵊn) *n.* **1.** (*sometimes cap.*) *Christianity.* **a.** the abode of God and the angels. **b.** a place or state of communion with God after death. Compare **hell. 2.** (*usually pl.*) the sky, firmament or space surrounding the earth. **3.** (in any of various mythologies) a place, such as Elysium or Valhalla, to which those who have died in the gods' favour are brought to dwell in happiness. **4.** a place or state of joy and happiness. **5.** (*sing.* or *pl.; sometimes cap.*) God or the gods, used in exclamatory phrases of surprise, exasperation, etc.: *for heaven's sake; heavens above.* **6. in seventh heaven.** ecstatically happy. **7. move heaven and earth.** to do everything possible (to achieve something). [Old English *heofon;* related to Old Saxon *heban*]

heavenly (ˈhɛvᵊnlɪ) *adj.* **1.** *Informal.* alluring, wonderful, or sublime. **2.** of or occurring in space: *a heavenly body.* **3.** divine; holy. —ˈ**heavenliness** *n.*

heaven-sent *adj.* providential; fortunate: *a heaven-sent opportunity.*

heavenward (ˈhɛvᵊnwəd) *adj.* **1.** directed towards heaven or the sky. ~*adv.* **2.** a variant of **heavenwards.**

heavenwards (ˈhɛvᵊnwədz) *or* **heavenward** *adv.* towards heaven or the sky.

heaves (hiːvz) *n.* (*functioning as sing. or pl.*) **1.** Also called: **broken wind.** a chronic respiratory disorder of animals of the horse family, of unknown cause. **2. the heaves.** *Slang.* an attack of vomiting or retching.

heave to *vb.* (*adv.*) to stop (a vessel) or (of a vessel) to stop, as by trimming the sails, etc. Also: **lay to.**

heavier-than-air *adj.* **1.** having a density greater than that of air. **2.** of or relating to an aircraft that does not depend on buoyancy for support but gains lift from aerodynamic forces.

Heaviside layer (ˈhɛvɪˌsaɪd) *n.* another name for **E region** (of the ionosphere). [C20: named after Oliver *Heaviside* (1850–1925), British physicist]

heavy (ˈhɛvɪ) *adj.* **heavier, heaviest. 1.** of comparatively great weight: *a heavy stone.* **2.** having a relatively high density: *lead is a heavy metal.* **3.** great in yield, quality, or quantity: *heavy rain; heavy traffic.* **4.** great or considerable: *heavy emphasis.* **5.** hard to bear, accomplish, or fulfil: *heavy demands.* **6.** sad or dejected in spirit or mood: *heavy at heart.* **7.** coarse or broad: *a heavy line; heavy features.* **8.** (of soil) having a high clay content; cloggy. **9.** solid or fat: *heavy legs.* **10.** (of an industry) engaged in the large-scale complex manufacture of capital goods or extraction of raw materials. Compare **light**[2] (sense 19). **11.** serious; grave. **12.** *Military.* **a.** armed or equipped with large weapons, armour, etc. **b.** (of guns, etc.) of a large and powerful type. **13.** (of a syllable) having stress or accentuation. Compare **light**[2] (sense 24). **14.** dull and uninteresting: *a heavy style.* **15.** prodigious: *a heavy drinker.* **16.** (of cakes, bread, etc.) insufficiently leavened. **17.** deep and loud: *a heavy thud.* **18.** (of music, literature, etc.). **a.** dramatic and powerful; grandiose. **b.** not immediately comprehensible or appealing. **19.** *Slang.* **a.** unpleasant or tedious. **b.** wonderful. **c.** (of rock music) having a powerful beat; hard. **20.** weighted; burdened: *heavy with child.* **21.** clumsy and slow: *heavy going.* **22.** permeating: *a heavy smell.* **23.** cloudy or overcast, esp. threatening rain: *heavy skies.* **24.** not easily digestible: *a heavy meal.* **25.** (of an element or compound) being or containing an isotope with greater atomic weight than that of the naturally occurring element: *heavy hydrogen; heavy water.* **26.** *Horse racing.* (of the going on a racecourse) soft and muddy. **27.** *Slang.* using, or prepared to use, violence or brutality: *the heavy mob.* **28. heavy on.** *Informal.* using large quantities of: *this car is heavy on petrol.* ~*n., pl.* **heavies. 29. a.** a villainous role. **b.** an actor who plays such a part. **30.** *Military.* **a.** a large fleet unit, esp. an aircraft carrier or battleship. **b.** a large calibre or weighty piece of artillery. **31.** *Informal.* (*usually pl.*, often preceded by *the*) a serious newspaper: *the Sunday heavies.* **32.** *Informal.* a heavyweight boxer, wrestler, etc. **33.** *Slang.* a man hired to threaten violence or deter others by his presence. **34.** *Scot.* strong bitter beer. ~*adv.* **35. a.** in a heavy manner; heavily: *time hangs heavy.* **b.** (*in combination*): *heavy-laden.* [Old English *hefig;* related to *hebban* to HEAVE, Old High German *hebīg*] —**'heavily** *adv.* —**'heaviness** *n.*

heavy breather *n.* **1.** a person who breathes stertorously or with difficulty. **2.** an anonymous telephone caller who imitates such sounds, as being suggestive of sexual excitement.

heavy chain *n. Immunol.* a type of polypeptide chain present in an immunoglobulin molecule.

heavy-duty *n.* (*modifier*) **1.** made to withstand hard wear, bad weather, etc.: *heavy-duty uniforms.* **2.** subject to high import or export taxes.

heavy earth *n.* another name for **barium oxide.**

heavy-footed *adj.* having a heavy or clumsy tread.

heavy-handed *adj.* **1.** clumsy. **2.** harsh and oppressive. —ˌ**heavy-'handedly** *adv.* —ˌ**heavy-'handedness** *n.*

heavy-hearted *adj.* sad; melancholy.

heavy hydrogen *n.* another name for **deuterium.**

heavy metal *n.* **1. a.** a type of rock music characterized by a strong beat and amplified instrumental effects. **b.** (*as modifier*): *a heavy-metal band.* **2.** a metal with a high specific gravity. **3.** *Military.* large guns or shot.

heavy oil *n.* a hydrocarbon mixture, heavier than water, distilled from coal tar.

heavy spar *n.* another name for **barytes.**

heavy water *n.* water that has been electrolytically decomposed to enrich it in the deuterium isotope in the form HDO or D_2O.

heavy-water reactor *n.* a nuclear reactor that uses heavy water as moderator.

heavyweight ('hɛvɪˌweɪt) *n.* **1.** a person or thing that is heavier than average. **2. a.** a professional boxer weighing more than 175 pounds (79 kg). **b.** an amateur boxer weighing more than 81 kg (179 pounds). **c.** (*as modifier*): *the world heavyweight championship.* **3.** a wrestler in a similar weight category (usually over 214 pounds (97 kg)). **4.** *Informal.* an important or highly influential person.

Heb. *or* **Hebr.** *abbrev. for:* **1.** Hebrew (language). **2.** *Bible.* Hebrews.

hebdomad ('hɛbdəˌmæd) *n.* **1.** *Obsolete.* the number seven or a group of seven. **2.** a rare word for **week.** [C16: from Greek, from *hebdomos* seventh, from *heptas* seven]

hebdomadal (hɛb'dɒmədᵊl) *or* **hebdomadary** (hɛb'dɒmədərɪ, -drɪ) *adj.* a rare word for **weekly.** —**heb'domadally** *adv.*

hebephrenia (ˌhiːbɪ'friːnɪə) *n.* a form of pubertal schizophrenia, characterized by hallucinations, delusions, foolish behaviour, and senseless laughter. [C20: New Latin, from Greek *hēbē* youth + *-phrenia* mental disorder, from *phrēn* mind] —**hebephrenic** (ˌhiːbɪ'frɛnɪk) *adj.*

hebetate ('hɛbɪˌteɪt) *adj.* **1.** (of plant parts) having a blunt or soft point. ~*vb.* **2.** *Rare.* to make or become blunted. [C16: from Latin *hebetāre* to make blunt, from *hebes* blunt] —ˌ**hebe'tation** *n.* —**'hebeˌtative** *adj.*

hebetic (hɪ'bɛtɪk) *adj.* of or relating to puberty. [C19: from Greek *hēbētikos* youth, from *hēbē* youth]

hebetude ('hɛbɪˌtjuːd) *n. Rare.* mental dullness or lethargy. [C17: from Late Latin *hebetūdō,* from Latin *hebes* blunt] —ˌ**hebe'tudinous** *adj.*

Hebraic (hɪ'breɪɪk), **Hebraical,** *or* **Hebrew** *adj.* of, relating to, or characteristic of the Hebrews or their language or culture. —**He'braically** *adv.*

Hebraism ('hiːbreɪˌɪzəm) *n.* a linguistic usage, custom, or other feature borrowed from or particular to the Hebrew language, or to the Jewish people or their culture.

Hebraist ('hiːbreɪɪst) *n.* a person who studies the Hebrew language and culture. —ˌ**Hebra'istic** *or* ˌ**Hebra'istical** *adj.* —ˌ**Hebra'istically** *adv.*

Hebraize *or* **Hebraise** ('hiːbreɪˌaɪz) *vb.* to become or cause to become Hebrew or Hebraic. —ˌ**Hebrai'zation** *or* ˌ**Hebrai'sation** *n.* —**'Hebraˌizer** *or* **'Hebraˌiser** *n.*

Hebrew ('hiːbruː) *n.* **1.** the ancient language of the Hebrews, revived as the official language of Israel. It belongs to the Canaanitic branch of the Semitic subfamily of the Afro-Asiatic family of languages. **2.** a member of an ancient Semitic people claiming descent from Abraham; an Israelite. **3.** *Archaic or offensive.* a Jew. ~*adj.* **4.** of or relating to the Hebrews or their language. **5.** *Archaic or offensive.* Jewish. [C13: from Old French *Ebreu,* from Latin *Hebraeus,* from Greek *Hebraios,* from Aramaic *'ibhray,* from Hebrew *'ibhrī* one from beyond (the river)]

Hebrew calendar *n.* another term for the **Jewish calendar.**

Hebridean *or* **Hebridian** (ˌhɛbrɪ'dɪən) **1.** of, relating to, or denoting the Hebrides, a group of islands off the W coast of Scotland, or their people. ~*n.* **2.** a native or inhabitant of the Hebrides.

hecatomb ('hɛkəˌtəʊm, -ˌtuːm) *n.* **1.** (in ancient Greece or Rome) any great public sacrifice and feast, originally one in which 100 oxen were sacrificed. **2.** a great sacrifice. [C16: from Latin *hecatombē,* from Greek *hekatombē,* from *hekaton* hundred + *bous* ox]

heck[1] (hɛk) *interj.* a mild exclamation of surprise, irritation, etc. [C19: euphemistic for *hell*]

heck[2] (hɛk) *n. Scot. and northern English dialect.* a frame for obstructing the passage of fish in a river. [C14: variant of HATCH[2]]

heckelphone ('hɛkəlˌfəʊn) *n. Music.* a type of bass oboe. [C20: named after W. *Heckel* (1856–1909), German inventor]

heckle ('hɛkᵊl) *vb.* **1.** to interrupt (a public speaker, performer, etc.) by comments, questions, or taunts. **2.** (*tr.*) Also: **hackle, hatchel.** to comb (hemp or flax). ~*n.* **3.** an instrument for combing flax or hemp. [C15: Northern and East Anglian form of HACKLE[1]] —**'heckler** *n.*

hectare ('hɛktɑː) *n.* one hundred ares. 1 hectare is equivalent to 10 000 square metres or 2.471 acres. Symbol: ha [C19: from French; see HECTO-, ARE[2]]

hectic ('hɛktɪk) *adj.* **1.** characterized by extreme activity or excitement. **2.** associated with, peculiar to, or symptomatic of tuberculosis (esp. in the phrases **hectic fever, hectic flush**). ~*n.* **3.** a hectic fever or flush. **4.** *Rare.* a person who is consumptive or who experiences a hectic fever or flush. [C14: from Late Latin *hecticus,* from Greek *hektikos* habitual, from *hexis* state, from *ekhein* to have] —**'hectically** *adv.*

hecto- *or before a vowel* **hect-** *prefix.* denoting 100: *hectogram.* Symbol: h [via French from Greek *hekaton* hundred]

hectocotylus (ˌhɛktəʊ'kɒtɪləs) *n., pl.* **-li** (-ˌlaɪ). a tentacle in certain male cephalopod molluscs, such as the octopus, that is specialized for transferring spermatozoa to the female. [C19: New Latin, from HECTO- + Greek *kotulē* cup]

hectogram *or* **hectogramme** ('hɛktəʊˌgræm) *n.* one hundred grams. 1 hectogram is equivalent to 3.527 ounces. Symbol: hg

hectograph ('hɛktəʊˌgrɑːf, -ˌgræf) *n.* **1.** Also called: **copygraph.** a process for copying type or manuscript from a glycerin-coated gelatin master to which the original has been transferred. **2.** a machine using this process. —**hectographic** (ˌhɛktəʊ'græfɪk) *adj.* —ˌ**hecto'graphically** *adv.* —**hectography** (hɛk'tɒgrəfɪ) *n.*

hectolitre *or U.S.* **hectoliter** ('hɛktəʊˌliːtə) *n.* one hundred litres. A measure of capacity equivalent to 3.531 cubic feet. Symbol: hl

hectometre *or U.S.* **hectometer** ('hɛktəʊˌmiːtə) *n.* one hundred metres: 1 hectometre is equivalent to 328.089 feet. Symbol: hm

hector ('hɛktə) *vb.* **1.** to bully or torment by teasing. ~*n.* **2.** a blustering bully. [C17: after *Hector* of Troy in classical mythology, in the sense: a bully]

he'd (hiːd; *unstressed* iːd, hɪd, ɪd) *contraction of* he had *or* he would.

heddle ('hɛdᵊl) *n.* one of a set of frames of vertical wires on a loom, each wire having an eye through which a warp thread can be passed. [Old English *hefeld* chain; related to Old Norse *hafald,* Middle Low German *hevelte*]

heder *Hebrew.* ('xɛdɛr; *English* 'heɪdə) *n., pl.* ***hadarim*** (xada'riːm). a variant spelling of **cheder.**

hedera ('hɛdərə) *n.* See **ivy** (sense 1). [Latin: ivy]

hedge (hɛdʒ) *n.* **1.** a row of shrubs or bushes forming a boundary to a field, garden, etc. **2.** a barrier or protection against something. **3.** the act or a method of reducing the risk of financial loss on an investment, bet, etc. **4.** a cautious or evasive statement. **5.** (*modifier; often in combination*) low, inferior, or illiterate: *a hedge lawyer.* ~*vb.* **6.** (*tr.*) to enclose or separate with or as if with a hedge. **7.** (*intr.*) to make or maintain a hedge, as by cutting and laying. **8.** (*tr.; often foll. by in, about,* or *around*) to hinder, obstruct, or restrict. **9.** (*intr.*) to evade decision or action, esp. by making noncommittal statements. **10.** (*tr.*) to guard against the risk of loss in (a bet, the paying out of a win, etc.), esp. by laying bets with other bookmakers. **11.** (*intr.*) to protect against financial loss through future price fluctuations, as by investing in futures. [Old English *hecg;* related to Old High German *heckia,* Middle Dutch *hegge;* see HAW[1]] —**'hedger** *n.* —**'hedging** *n.* —**'hedgy** *adj.*

hedge garlic *n.* another name for **garlic mustard.**

hedgehog ('hɛdʒˌhɒg) *n.* **1.** any small nocturnal Old World mammal of the genus *Erinaceus,* such as *E. europaeus,* and related genera, having a protective covering of spines on the back: family *Erinaceidae,* order *Insectivora* (insectivores). **2.** any other insectivores of the family *Erinaceidae,* such as the moon rat. **3.** *U.S.* any of various other spiny animals, esp. the porcupine.

hedgehop ('hɛdʒˌhɒp) *vb.* **-hops, -hopping, -hopped.** (*intr.*) (of an aircraft) to fly close to the ground, as in crop spraying. —**'hedgeˌhopper** *n.* —**'hedgeˌhopping** *n., adj.*

hedge hyssop *n.* any of several North American scrophulariaceous plants of the genus *Gratiola,* esp. *G. aurea,* having small yellow or white flowers.

hedge laying *n.* the art or practice of making or maintaining a hedge by cutting branches partway through, laying them horizontally, and pegging them in position in order to create a strong thick hedge.

hedgerow ('hɛdʒˌrəʊ) *n.* a hedge of shrubs or low trees growing along a bank, esp. one bordering a field or lane.

hedge-school *n. Irish history.* a school held out of doors in favourable weather, indoors in winter. —**'hedge-schoolˌmaster** *n.*

hedge sparrow *n.* a small brownish European songbird, *Prunella modularis:* family *Prunellidae* (accentors). Also called: **dunnock.**

hedonics (hiːˈdɒnɪks) *n.* (*functioning as sing.*) **1.** the branch of psychology concerned with the study of pleasant and unpleasant sensations. **2.** (in philosophy) the study of pleasure, esp. in its relation to duty.

hedonism (ˈhiːdəˌnɪzəm, ˈhɛd-) *n.* **1.** *Ethics.* **a.** the doctrine that moral value can be defined in terms of pleasure. See **utilitarianism. b.** the doctrine that the pursuit of pleasure is the highest good. **2.** the pursuit of pleasure as a matter of principle. **3.** indulgence in sensual pleasures. [C19: from Greek *hēdonē* pleasure] —**heˈdonic** *or* **ˌhedonˈistic** *adj.* —**ˈhedonist** *n.*

-hedron *n. combining form.* indicating a geometric solid having a specified number of faces or surfaces: *tetrahedron.* [from Greek *-edron* -sided, from *hedra* seat, base] —**-hedral** *adj. combining form.*

heebie-jeebies (ˈhiːbɪˈdʒiːbɪz) *pl. n.* **the.** *Slang.* apprehension and nervousness. [C20: coined by W. De Beck (1890–1942), American cartoonist]

heed (hiːd) *n.* **1.** close and careful attention; notice (often in the phrases **give, pay,** *or* **take heed**). ~*vb.* **2.** to pay close attention to (someone or something). [Old English *hēdan;* related to Old Saxon *hōdian,* Old High German *huoten*] —**ˈheeder** *n.* —**ˈheedful** *adj.* —**ˈheedfully** *adv.* —**ˈheedfulness** *n.*

heedless (ˈhiːdlɪs) *adj.* taking little or no notice; careless or thoughtless. —**ˈheedlessly** *adv.* —**ˈheedlessness** *n.*

heehaw (ˌhiːˈhɔː) *interj.* an imitation or representation of the braying sound of a donkey.

heel[1] (hiːl) *n.* **1.** the back part of the human foot from the instep to the lower part of the ankle. Compare **calcaneus. 2.** the corresponding part in other vertebrates. **3.** the part of a shoe, stocking, etc., designed to fit the heel. **4.** the outer part of a shoe underneath the heel. **5.** the part of the palm of a glove nearest the wrist. **6.** the lower, end, or back section of something: *the heel of a loaf.* **7.** *Horticulture.* the small part of the parent plant that remains attached to a young shoot cut for propagation and that ensures more successful rooting. **8.** *Nautical.* **a.** the bottom of a mast. **b.** the after end of a ship's keel. **9.** the back part of a golf club head where it bends to join the shaft. **10.** *Rugby.* possession of the ball as obtained from a scrum (esp. in the phrase **get the heel**). **11.** *Slang.* a contemptible person. **12. at** (*or* **on**) **one's heels.** just behind or following closely. **13. cool** (*or* **kick**) **one's heels.** to wait or be kept waiting. **14. dig one's heels in.** See **dig in** (sense 5). **15. down at heel. a.** shabby or worn. **b.** slovenly or careless. **16. rock back on one's heels.** to astonish or be astonished. **17. show a clean pair of heels.** to run off. **18. take to one's heels.** to run off. **19. to heel.** disciplined or under control, as a dog walking by a person's heel. ~*vb.* **20.** (*tr.*) to repair or replace the heel of (shoes, boots, etc.). **21.** to perform (a dance) with the heels. **22.** (*tr.*) *Golf.* to strike (the ball) with the heel of the club. **23.** *Rugby.* to kick (the ball) backwards using the sole and heel of the boot. **24.** to follow at the heels of (a person). **25.** (*tr.*) to arm (a gamecock) with spurs. **26.** (*tr.*) *N.Z.* (of a cattle dog) to drive (cattle) by biting their heels. [Old English *hēla;* related to Old Norse *hǣll,* Old Frisian *hêl*] —**ˈheelless** *adj.*

heel[2] (hiːl) *vb.* **1.** (of a vessel) to lean over; list. ~*n.* **2.** inclined position from the vertical: *the boat is at ten degrees of heel.* [Old English *hieldan;* related to Old Norse *hallr* inclined, Old High German *helden* to bow]

heel-and-toe *adj.* **1.** of or denoting a style of walking in which the heel of the front foot touches the ground before the toes of the rear one leave it. ~*vb.* **2.** (*intr.*) (esp. in motor racing) to use the heel and toe of the same foot to operate the brake and accelerator.

heelball (ˈhiːlˌbɔːl) *n.* **a.** a black waxy substance used by shoemakers to blacken the edges of heels and soles. **b.** a similar substance used to take rubbings, esp. brass rubbings.

heel bar *n.* a small shop or a counter in a department store where shoes are mended while the customer waits.

heel bone *n.* the nontechnical name for **calcaneus.**

heeled (hiːld) *adj.* **1. a.** having a heel or heels. **b.** (*in combination*): *high-heeled.* **2. well-heeled.** wealthy.

heeler (ˈhiːlə) *n.* **1.** *U.S.* See **ward heeler. 2.** a person or thing that heels. **3.** *Austral. and N.Z.* a dog that herds cattle by biting at their heels.

heel in *or* (*Dialect*) **hele in** *vb.* (*tr., adv.*) to insert (cuttings, shoots, etc.) into the soil before planting to keep them moist.

heelpiece (ˈhiːlˌpiːs) *n.* the piece of a shoe, stocking, etc., designed to fit the heel.

heelpost (ˈhiːlˌpəʊst) *n.* a post for carrying the hinges of a door or gate.

heeltap (ˈhiːlˌtæp) *n.* **1.** Also called: **lift.** a layer of leather, etc., in the heel of a shoe. **2.** a small amount of alcoholic drink left at the bottom of a glass after drinking.

heft (hɛft) *vb.* (*tr.*) *Brit. dialect and U.S. informal.* **1.** to assess the weight of (something) by lifting. **2.** to lift. ~*n.* **3.** weight. **4.** *U.S.* the main part. [C19: probably from HEAVE, by analogy with *thieve, theft, cleave, cleft*] —**ˈhefter** *n.*

hefty (ˈhɛftɪ) *adj.* **heftier, heftiest.** *Informal.* **1.** big and strong. **2.** characterized by vigour or force: *a hefty blow.* **3.** large, bulky, or heavy. **4.** sizable; involving a large amount of money: *a hefty bill; a hefty wage.* —**ˈheftily** *adv.* —**ˈheftiness** *n.*

Hegelian (hɪˈgeɪlɪən, heɪˈgiː-) *adj.* of or relating to G. W. F. Hegel (1770–1831), German philosopher, or his philosophical concepts. —**Heˈgelianˌism** *n.*

Hegelian dialectic *n. Philosophy.* an interpretive method in which the contradiction between a proposition (thesis) and its antithesis is resolved at a higher level of truth (synthesis).

hegemony (hɪˈgɛmənɪ) *n., pl.* **-nies.** ascendancy or domination of one power or state within a league, confederation, etc., or of one social class over others. [C16: from Greek *hēgemonia* authority, from *hēgemōn* leader, from *hēgeisthai* to lead] —**hegemonic** (ˌhɛgəˈmɒnɪk) *adj.*

Hegira *or* **Hejira** (ˈhɛdʒɪrə) *n.* **1.** the Muslim era, starting in 622 A.D., the date of Mohammed's departure from Mecca to Medina. See also **AH. 2.** (*often not cap.*) an emigration escape or flight. [C16: from Medieval Latin, from Arabic *hijrah* emigration or flight]

hegumen (hɪˈgjuːmɛn) *or* **hegumenos** (hɪˈgjuːmɪˌnəʊs) *n.* the head of a monastery of the Eastern Church. [C16: from Medieval Latin *hēgūmenus,* from Late Greek *hēgoumenos* leader, from Greek *hēgeisthai* to lead]

heh (heɪ) *interj.* an exclamation of surprise or inquiry.

heid (hiːd) *n.* a Scot. word for **head.**

Heidelberg man (ˈhaɪdəlˌbɜːg) *n.* a type of primitive man, *Homo heidelbergensis,* occurring in Europe in the middle Palaeolithic age, known only from a single fossil lower jaw. [C20: referring to the site where remains were found, at Mauer, near *Heidelberg,* Germany (1907)]

Heiduc (ˈhaɪdʊk) *n.* a variant spelling of **Haiduk.**

heifer (ˈhɛfə) *n.* a young cow. [Old English *heahfore;* related to Greek *poris* calf; see HIGH]

heigh-ho (ˈheɪˈhəʊ) *interj.* an exclamation of weariness, disappointment, surprise, or happiness.

height (haɪt) *n.* **1.** the vertical distance from the bottom or lowest part of something to the top or apex. **2.** the vertical distance of an object or place above the ground or above sea level; altitude. **3.** relatively great altitude or distance from the bottom to the top. **4.** the topmost point; summit. **5.** *Astronomy.* the angular distance of a celestial body above the horizon. **6.** the period of greatest activity or intensity: *the height of the battle.* **7.** an extreme example of its kind: *the height of rudeness.* **8.** (*often pl.*) an area of high ground. **9.** (*often pl.*) the state of being far above the ground: *I don't like heights.* **10.** (*often pl.*) a position of influence, fame, or power. [Old English *hīehthu;* related to Old Norse *hǣthe,* Gothic *hauhitha,* Old High German *hōhida;* see HIGH]

heighten (ˈhaɪtən) *vb.* **1.** to make or become high or higher. **2.** to make or become more extreme or intense. —**ˈheightened** *adj.* —**ˈheightener** *n.*

height of land *n. U.S. and Canadian.* a watershed.

height-to-paper *n.* the overall height of printing plates and type, standardized as 0.9175 inch (Brit.) and 0.9186 inch (U.S.).

Heimlich manoeuvre (ˈhaɪmlɪk) *n.* a technique in first aid to dislodge a foreign body in a person's windpipe by applying sudden upward pressure on the upper abdomen. Also called: **abdominal thrust.** [C20: named after Henry J. *Heimlich* (born 1920), American surgeon]

heinous (ˈheɪnəs, ˈhiː-) *adj.* evil; atrocious. [C14: from Old French *haineus,* from *haine* hatred, from *hair* to hate, of Germanic origin; see HATE] —**ˈheinously** *adv.* —**ˈheinousness** *n.*

heir (ɛə) *n.* **1.** *Civil law.* the person legally succeeding to all property of a deceased person, irrespective of whether such person died testate or intestate, and upon whom devolves as well as the rights the duties and liabilities attached to the estate. **2.** any person or thing that carries on some tradition, circumstance, etc., from a forerunner. **3.** an archaic word for **offspring.** [C13: from Old French, from Latin *hērēs;* related to Greek *khēros* bereaved] —**ˈheirless** *adj.*

heir apparent *n., pl.* **heirs apparent.** *Property law.* a person whose right to succeed to certain property cannot be defeated, provided such person survives his ancestor. Compare **heir presumptive.**

heir-at-law *n., pl.* **heirs-at-law.** *Property law.* the person entitled to succeed to the real property of a person who dies intestate.

heirdom (ˈɛədəm) *n. Property law.* succession by right of blood; inheritance.

heiress (ˈɛərɪs) *n.* **1.** a woman who inherits or expects to inherit great wealth. **2.** *Property law.* a female heir.

heirloom (ˈɛəˌluːm) *n.* **1.** an object that has been in a family for generations. **2.** *Property law.* an item of personal property inherited by special custom or in accordance with the terms of a will. [C15: from HEIR + *lome* tool; see LOOM[1]]

heir presumptive *n. Property law.* a person who expects to succeed to an estate but whose right may be defeated by the birth of one nearer in blood to the ancestor. Compare **heir apparent.**

heirship (ˈɛəʃɪp) *n. Law.* **1.** the state or condition of being an heir. **2.** the right to inherit; inheritance.

Heisenberg uncertainty principle (ˈhaɪzənˌbɜːg) *n.* a more formal name for **uncertainty principle.** [C20: named after Werner *Heisenberg* (1901–76), German physicist who formulated it]

heist (haɪst) *Slang, chiefly U.S. and Canadian.* ~*n.* **1.** a robbery. ~*vb.* **2.** (*tr.*) to steal or burgle. [variant of HOIST] —**ˈheister** *n.*

heitiki (heɪˈtiːkiː) *n. N.Z.* a Maori neck ornament of greenstone. [C19: from Maori, from *hei* to hang + TIKI]

Hejira ('hɛdʒɪrə) *n.* a variant spelling of **Hegira.**
held (hɛld) *vb.* the past tense and past participle of **hold**[1].
Heldentenor *German.* ('hɛldəntenoːr) *n., pl.* ***-tenöre*** (-te'nøːrə). a tenor with a powerful voice suited to singing heroic roles, esp. in Wagner. [literally: hero tenor]
hele in *vb.* (*tr., adv.*) a dialect variant of **heel in.** [Old English *helian* hide]
helenium (hə'liːnɪəm) *n.* any plant of the American genus *Helenium,* up to 1.6 m (5 ft.) tall, some species of which are grown as border plants for their daisy-like yellow or variegated flowers: family *Compositae.* [New Latin, from Greek *helenion,* a plant name]
heli- *combining form.* helicopter: *helistop.* [C20: shortened from HELICOPTER]
heliacal rising (hɪ'laɪəkᵊl) *n.* **1.** the rising of a celestial object at the same time as the rising of the sun. **2.** the date at which such a celestial object first becomes visible in the dawn sky. [C17: from Late Latin *hēliacus* relating to the sun, from Greek *hēliakos,* from *hēlios* the sun]
helianthemum (hiːlɪ'ænθəməm) *n.* any plant of the dwarf evergreen genus *Helianthemum,* some species of which are grown as rock-garden plants for their numerous papery yellow or orange flowers; related to the rockrose, which they resemble: family *Cistaceae.* Also called: **Cape primrose.** [New Latin, from Greek *hēlios* sun + *anthemon* flower]
helianthus (ˌhiːlɪ'ænθəs) *n., pl.* **-thuses.** any plant of the genus *Helianthus,* such as the sunflower and Jerusalem artichoke, typically having large yellow daisy-like flowers with yellow, brown, or purple centres: family *Compositae* (composites). [C18: New Latin, from Greek *hēlios* sun + *anthos* flower]
helical ('hɛlɪkᵊl) *adj.* of or shaped like a helix; spiral. —**'helically** *adv.*
helical gear *n.* a gearwheel having the tooth form generated on a helical path about the axis of the wheel.
helical scan *n.* (*modifier*) denoting a recording technique used with video tapes in which the recorded tracks on the tape are segments of a helix: *a helical-scan tape.*
helices ('hɛlɪˌsiːz) *n.* a plural of **helix.**
helichrysum (ˌhɛlɪ'kraɪzəm) *n.* any plant of the widely cultivated genus *Helichrysum,* whose flowers retain their shape and colour when dried: family *Compositae* (composites). [C16: from Latin, from Greek *helikhrusos,* from *helix* spiral + *khrusos* gold]
helicity (hɪ'lɪsɪtɪ) *n., pl.* **-ties.** *Physics.* the projection of the spin of an elementary particle on the direction of propagation. [C20: from HELIX + -ITY]
helicline ('hɛlɪˌklaɪn) *n. Architect.* a spiral-shaped ramp. [from HELICO- + -CLINE]
helico- *or before a vowel* **helic-** *combining form.* spiral or helical: *helicograph.* [from Latin, from Greek *helix* spiral]
helicograph ('hɛlɪkəʊˌgrɑːf, -ˌgræf) *n.* an instrument for drawing spiral curves.
helicoid ('hɛlɪˌkɔɪd) *adj. also* **helicoidal. 1.** *Biology.* shaped like a spiral: *a helicoid shell.* ~*n.* **2.** *Geometry.* any surface resembling that of a screw thread. —ˌ**heli'coidally** *adv.*
helicon ('hɛlɪkən) *n.* a bass tuba made to coil over the shoulder of a band musician. [C19: probably from *Helicon* (a mountain in Greece), associated with Greek *helix* spiral]
helicopter ('hɛlɪˌkɒptə) *n.* **1.** an aircraft capable of hover, vertical flight, and horizontal flight in any direction. Most get all of their lift and propulsion from the rotation of overhead blades. See also **autogiro.** ~*vb.* **2.** to transport (people or things) or (of people or things) to be transported by helicopter. [C19: from French *hélicoptère,* from HELICO- + Greek *pteron* wing]
helicopter gunship *n.* a large heavily armed helicopter used for ground attack.
helideck ('hɛlɪˌdɛk) *n.* a landing deck for helicopters on ships, oil platforms, etc. [C20: from HELI- + DECK]
helio- *or before a vowel* **heli-** *combining form.* indicating the sun: *heliocentric; heliolithic.* [from Greek, from *hēlios* sun]
heliocentric (ˌhiːlɪəʊ'sɛntrɪk) *adj.* **1.** having the sun at its centre. **2.** measured from or in relation to the centre of the sun. —ˌ**helio'centrically** *adv.* —**heliocentricity** (ˌhiːlɪəʊsɛn'trɪsɪtɪ) *or* **heliocentricism** (ˌhiːlɪəʊ'sɛntrɪˌsɪzəm) *n.*
heliocentric parallax *n.* See **parallax** (sense 2).
Heliochrome ('hiːlɪəʊˌkrəʊm) *n. Trademark.* a photograph that reproduces the natural colours of the subject. —ˌ**helio'chromic** *adj.*
heliodor ('hiːlɪəʊˌdɔː) *n.* a clear yellow form of beryl used as a gemstone.
heliograph ('hiːlɪəʊˌgrɑːf, -ˌgræf) *n.* **1.** an instrument with mirrors and a shutter used for sending messages in Morse code by reflecting the sun's rays. **2.** a device used to photograph the sun. —**heliographer** (ˌhiːlɪ'ɒgrəfə) *n.* —**heliographic** (ˌhiːlɪəʊ'græfɪk) *or* ˌ**helio'graphical** *adj.* —ˌ**heli'ography** *n.*
heliogravure (ˌhiːlɪəʊgrə'vjʊə) *n. Printing.* a former name for **photogravure.**
heliolatry (ˌhiːlɪ'ɒlətrɪ) *n.* worship of the sun. —ˌ**heli'olater** *n.* —ˌ**heli'olatrous** *adj.*
heliolithic (ˌhiːlɪəʊ'lɪθɪk) *adj.* of or relating to a civilization characterized by sun worship and megaliths.
heliometer (ˌhiːlɪ'ɒmɪtə) *n.* a refracting telescope having a split objective lens that is used to determine very small angular distances between celestial bodies. —**heliometric** (ˌhiːlɪəʊ'mɛtrɪk) *or* ˌ**helio'metrical** *adj.* —ˌ**helio'metrically** *adv.* —ˌ**heli'ometry** *n.*
heliophyte ('hiːlɪəʊˌfaɪt) *n.* any plant that grows best in direct sunlight.
heliosphere ('hiːlɪəʊˌsfɪə) *n.* the region around the sun taken to be the boundary outside which the sun's influence is negligible and interstellar space begins.
heliostat ('hiːlɪəʊˌstæt) *n.* an astronomical instrument used to reflect the light of the sun in a constant direction. —ˌ**helio'static** *adj.*
heliotaxis (ˌhiːlɪəʊ'tæksɪs) *n.* movement of an entire organism in response to the stimulus of sunlight. —**heliotactic** (ˌhiːlɪəʊ'tæktɪk) *adj.*
heliotherapy (ˌhiːlɪəʊ'θɛrəpɪ) *n.* the therapeutic use of sunlight.
heliotrope ('hiːlɪəˌtrəʊp, 'hɛljə-) *n.* **1.** any boraginaceous plant of the genus *Heliotropium,* esp. the South American *H. arborescens,* cultivated for its small fragrant purple flowers. **2. garden heliotrope.** a widely cultivated valerian, *Valeriana officinalis,* with clusters of small pink, purple, or white flowers. **3.** any of various plants that turn towards the sun. **4. a.** a bluish-violet to purple colour. **b.** (*as adj.*): *a heliotrope dress.* **5.** an instrument used in geodetic surveying employing the sun's rays reflected by a mirror as a signal for the sighting of stations over long distances. **6.** another name for **bloodstone.** [C17: from Latin *hēliotropium,* from Greek *hēliotropion,* from *hēlios* sun + *trepein* to turn]
heliotropin (ˌhiːlɪ'ɒtrəpɪn) *n.* another term for **piperonal.**
heliotropism (ˌhiːlɪ'ɒtrəˌpɪzəm) *n.* the growth of a plant in response to the stimulus of sunlight. —**heliotropic** (ˌhiːlɪəʊ'trɒpɪk) *adj.* —ˌ**helio'tropically** *adv.*
heliotype ('hiːlɪəʊˌtaɪp) *n.* **1.** a printing process in which an impression is taken in ink from a gelatin surface that has been exposed under a negative and prepared for printing. Also called: **heliotypy. 2.** the gelatin plate produced by such a process. **3.** a print produced from such a plate. —**heliotypic** (ˌhiːlɪəʊ'tɪpɪk) *adj.*
heliozoan (ˌhiːlɪəʊ'zəʊən) *n.* any protozoan of the mostly freshwater order *Heliozoa,* typically having a siliceous shell and stiff radiating pseudopodia: class *Sarcodina* (amoeba, etc.).
helipad ('hɛlɪˌpæd) *n.* a place for helicopters to land and take off. [C20: from HELI- + PAD[1]]
heliport ('hɛlɪˌpɔːt) *n.* an airport for helicopters. [C20: from HELI- + PORT[1]]
helium ('hiːlɪəm) *n.* a very light nonflammable colourless odourless element that is an inert gas, occurring in certain natural gases: used in balloons and in cryogenic research. Symbol: He; atomic no.: 2; atomic wt.: 4.0026; density: 0.178 kg/m^3; at normal pressures it is liquid down to absolute zero; boiling pt.: –268.9°C. See also **alpha particle.** [C19: New Latin, from HELIO- + -IUM; named from its having first been detected in the solar spectrum]
helix ('hiːlɪks) *n., pl.* **helices** ('hɛlɪˌsiːz) *or* **helixes. 1.** a curve that lies on a cylinder or cone, at a constant angle to the line segments making up the surface; spiral. **2.** a spiral shape or form. **3.** the incurving fold that forms the margin of the external ear. **4.** another name for **volute** (sense 2). **5.** any terrestrial gastropod mollusc of the genus *Helix,* which includes the garden snail (*H. aspersa*). [C16: from Latin, from Greek: spiral; probably related to Greek *helissein* to twist]
hell (hɛl) *n.* **1.** *Christianity.* (*sometimes cap.*) **a.** the place or state of eternal punishment of the wicked after death, with Satan as its ruler. **b.** forces of evil regarded as residing there. **2.** (*sometimes cap.*) (in various religions and cultures) the abode of the spirits of the dead. See also **Hades. 3.** pain, extreme difficulty, etc. **4.** *Informal.* a cause of such difficulty or suffering: *war is hell.* **5.** *U.S. and Canadian.* high spirits or mischievousness: *there's hell in that boy.* **6.** *Printing.* another name for **hellbox. 7.** a box used by a tailor for discarded material. **8.** *Now rare.* a gambling house, booth, etc. **9. as hell.** (intensifier): *tired as hell.* **10. for the hell of it.** *Informal.* for the fun of it. **11. give someone hell.** *Informal.* **a.** to give someone a severe reprimand or punishment. **b.** to be a source of annoyance or torment to someone. **12. hell of a** *or* **helluva.** *Informal.* (intensifier): *a hell of a good performance.* **13. hell for leather.** at great speed. **14. (come) hell or high water.** *Informal.* whatever difficulties may arise. **15. hell to pay.** *Informal.* serious consequences, as of a foolish action. **16. like hell.** *Informal.* **a.** (*adv.*) (intensifier): *he works like hell.* **b.** an expression of strong disagreement with a previous statement, request, order, etc. **17. play (merry) hell with.** *Informal.* to throw into confusion and disorder; disrupt. **18. raise hell. a.** to create a noisy disturbance, as in fun. **b.** to react strongly and unfavourably. **19. the hell.** *Informal.* **a.** (intensifier): used in such phrases as **what the hell, who the hell,** etc. **b.** an expression of strong disagreement or disfavour: *the hell I will.* See **like hell.** ~*interj.* **20.** *Informal.* an exclamation of anger, annoyance, surprise, etc. (Also in exclamations such as **hell's bells, hell's teeth,** etc.). [Old English *hell;* related to *helan* to cover, Old Norse *hel,* Gothic *halja* hell, Old High German *hella*]
he'll (hiːl; *unstressed* iːl, hɪl, ɪl) *contraction of* he will *or* he shall.
Helladic (hɛ'lædɪk) *adj.* of, characteristic of, or related to the Bronze Age civilization that flourished about 2900 to 1100 B.C. on the Greek mainland and islands. [from Greek *Hellas* Greece]

hellbender ('hɛlˌbɛndə) *n.* a very large dark grey aquatic salamander, *Cryptobranchus alleganiensis,* with internal gills: inhabits rivers in E and central U.S.: family *Cryptobranchidae.*
hellbent (ˌhɛl'bɛnt) *adj.* (*postpositive* and foll. by *on*) *Informal.* strongly or rashly intent.
hellbox ('hɛlˌbɒks) *n.* a receptacle used by printers for broken or unneeded type.
hellcat ('hɛlˌkæt) *n.* a spiteful fierce-tempered woman.
helldiver ('hɛlˌdaɪvə) *n. U.S. informal.* a small greyish-brown North American grebe, *Podilymbus podiceps,* with a small bill. Also called: **pied-billed grebe, dabchick.**
hellebore ('hɛlɪˌbɔː) *n.* **1.** any plant of the Eurasian ranunculaceous genus *Helleborus,* esp. *H. niger* (black hellebore), typically having showy flowers and poisonous parts. See also **Christmas rose. 2.** any of various liliaceous plants of the N temperate genus *Veratrum,* esp. *V. album,* which have greenish flowers and yield alkaloids used in the treatment of heart disease. [C14: from Greek *helleboros,* of uncertain origin]
helleborine (ˌhɛlɪ'bɔːriːn) *n.* any of various N temperate orchids of the genera *Cephalanthera* and *Epipactis.* [C16: ultimately from Greek *helleborinē* a plant resembling hellebore]
Hellene ('hɛliːn) *or* **Hellenian** (hɛ'liːnɪən) *n.* another name for a **Greek.** [from Greek *Hellēn,* legendary ancestor of the Greeks]
Hellenic (hɛ'lɛnɪk, -'liː-) *adj.* **1.** of or relating to the ancient or modern Greeks or their language. **2.** of or relating to ancient Greece or the Greeks of the classical period (776–323 B.C.). Compare **Hellenistic. 3.** another word for **Greek.** ~*n.* **4.** a branch of the Indo-European family of languages consisting of Greek in its various ancient and modern dialects. —**Hel'lenically** *adv.*
Hellenism ('hɛlɪˌnɪzəm) *n.* **1.** the principles, ideals, and pursuits associated with classical Greek civilization. **2.** the spirit or national character of the Greeks. **3.** conformity to, imitation of, or devotion to the culture of ancient Greece. **4.** the cosmopolitan civilization of the Hellenistic world.
Hellenist ('hɛlɪnɪst) *n.* **1.** Also called: **Hellenizer.** (in the Hellenistic world) a non-Greek, esp. a Jew, who adopted Greek culture. **2.** a student of the Greek civilization or language.
Hellenistic (ˌhɛlɪ'nɪstɪk) *or* **Hellenistical** *adj.* **1.** characteristic of or relating to Greek civilization in the Mediterranean world, esp. from the death of Alexander the Great (323 B.C.) to the defeat of Antony and Cleopatra (30 B.C.). **2.** of or relating to the Greeks or to Hellenism. —ˌ**Hellen'istically** *adv.*
Hellenize *or* **Hellenise** ('hɛlɪˌnaɪz) *vb.* to make or become like the ancient Greeks. —ˌ**Helleni'zation** *or* ˌ**Helleni'sation** *n.* —'**Hellenˌizer** *or* '**Hellenˌiser** *n.*
heller[1] ('hɛlə) *n., pl.* **-ler. 1.** any of various old German or Austrian coins of low denomination. **2.** another word for **haler.** [from German, after *Hall,* German town where the coins were minted]
heller[2] ('hɛlə) *n.* another word for **hellion.**
hellery ('hɛlərɪ) *n. Canadian slang.* wild or mischievous behaviour.
hellfire ('hɛlˌfaɪə) *n.* **1.** the torment and punishment of hell, envisaged as eternal fire. **2.** (*modifier*) characterizing sermons or preachers that emphasize this aspect of Christian belief.
hellgrammite ('hɛlgrəˌmaɪt) *n. U.S.* the larva of the dobsonfly, about 10 cm long with biting mouthparts: used as bait for bass. Also called: **dobson.** [C19: of unknown origin]
hellhole ('hɛlˌhəʊl) *n.* an unpleasant or evil place.
hellhound ('hɛlˌhaʊnd) *n.* **1.** a hound of hell. **2.** a fiend.
hellion ('hɛljən) *n. U.S. informal.* a rough or rowdy person, esp. a child; troublemaker. Also called: **heller.** [C19: probably from dialect *hallion* rogue, of unknown origin]
hellish ('hɛlɪʃ) *adj.* **1.** of or resembling hell. **2.** wicked; cruel. **3.** *Informal.* very difficult or unpleasant. ~*adv.* **4.** *Brit. informal.* (intensifier): *a hellish good idea.* —'**hellishly** *adv.* —'**hellishness** *n.*
hello, hallo, *or* **hullo** (hɛ'ləʊ, hə-; 'hɛləʊ) *sentence substitute.* **1.** an expression of greeting used on meeting a person or at the start of a telephone call. **2.** a call used to attract attention. **3.** an expression of surprise. ~*n., pl.* **-los. 4.** the act of saying or calling "hello". [C19: see HALLO]
helluva ('hɛləvə) *adv., adj. Informal.* (intensifier): *a helluva difficult job; he's a helluva guy.*
helm[1] (hɛlm) *n.* **1.** *Nautical.* **a.** the wheel, tiller, or entire apparatus by which a vessel is steered. **b.** the position of the helm: that is, on the side of the keel opposite from that of the rudder. **2.** a position of leadership or control (esp. in the phrase **at the helm**). ~*vb.* **3.** (*tr.*) to direct or steer. [Old English *helma;* related to Old Norse *hjalm* rudder, Old High German *halmo*] —'**helmless** *adj.*
helm[2] (hɛlm) *n.* **1.** an archaic or poetic word for **helmet.** ~*vb.* **2.** (*tr.*) *Archaic or poetic.* to supply with a helmet. [Old English *helm;* related to *helan* to cover, Old Norse *hjalmr,* Gothic *hilms,* Old High German *helm* helmet, Sanskrit *śárman* protection]
helmet ('hɛlmɪt) *n.* **1.** a piece of protective or defensive armour for the head worn by soldiers, policemen, firemen, divers, etc. **2.** *Biol.* a part or structure resembling a helmet, esp. the upper part of the calyx of certain flowers. [C15: from Old French, dim. of *helme,* of Germanic origin] —'**helmeted** *adj.*
Helmholtz function ('hɛlmhəʊlts) *n.* a thermodynamic property of a system equal to the difference between its internal energy and the product of its temperature and its entropy. Symbol: *A* or *F* Also called: **Helmholtz free energy.** [C20: named after Baron Hermann Ludwig Ferdinand von *Helmholtz* (1821–94), German physicist]
helminth ('hɛlmɪnθ) *n.* any parasitic worm, esp. a nematode or fluke. [C19: from Greek *helmins* parasitic worm] —**helminthoid** ('hɛlmɪnˌθɔɪd, hɛl'mɪnθɔɪd) *adj.*
helminthiasis (ˌhɛlmɪn'θaɪəsɪs) *n.* infestation of the body with parasitic worms. [C19: from New Latin, from Greek *helminthian* to be infested with worms]
helminthic (hɛl'mɪnθɪk) *adj.* **1.** of, relating to, or caused by parasitic worms. ~*n., adj.* **2.** another word for **vermifuge.**
helminthology (ˌhɛlmɪn'θɒlədʒɪ) *n.* the study of parasitic worms. —**helminthological** (ˌhɛlmɪnθə'lɒdʒɪkᵊl) *adj.* —ˌ**helmin'thologist** *n.*
helmsman ('hɛlmzmən) *n., pl.* **-men.** the person at the helm who steers the ship; steersman.
helophyte ('hɛləfaɪt) *n.* any perennial marsh plant that bears its overwintering buds in the mud below the surface. [C20: from Modern Greek *helos* marsh + -PHYTE]
Helot ('hɛlət, 'hiː-) *n.* **1.** (in ancient Greece, esp. Sparta) a member of the class of unfree men above slaves owned by the state. **2.** (*usually not cap.*) a serf or slave. [C16: from Latin *Hēlōtēs,* from Greek *Heilōtes,* alleged to have meant originally: inhabitants of Helos, who, after its conquest, were serfs of the Spartans]
helotism ('hɛləˌtɪzəm, 'hiː-) *n.* **1.** the condition or quality of being a Helot. **2.** a sociopolitical system in which a class, minority, nation, etc., is held in a state of subjection. **3.** *Zoology.* another name for **dulosis.** ~Also called (for senses 1, 2): **helotage.**
helotry ('hɛlətrɪ, 'hiː-) *n.* **1.** serfdom or slavery. **2.** serfs or slaves as a class.
help (hɛlp) *vb.* **1.** to assist or aid (someone to do something), esp. by sharing the work, cost, or burden of something: *he helped his friend to escape; she helped him climb out of the boat.* **2.** to alleviate the burden of (someone else) by giving assistance. **3.** (*tr.*) to assist (a person) to go in a specified direction: *help the old lady up from the chair.* **4.** to promote or contribute to: *to help the relief operations.* **5.** to cause improvement in (a situation, person, etc.): *crying won't help.* **6.** (*tr.;* preceded by *can, could,* etc.; *usually used with a negative*) **a.** to avoid or refrain from: *we can't help wondering who he is.* **b.** (usually foll. by *it*) to prevent or be responsible for: *I can't help it if it rains.* **7.** to alleviate (an illness, etc.). **8.** (*tr.*) to serve (a customer): *can I help you, madam?* **9.** (*tr.;* foll. by *to*) **a.** to serve (someone with food, etc.) (usually in the phrase **help oneself**): *may I help you to some more vegetables? help yourself to peas.* **b.** to provide (oneself with) without permission: *he's been helping himself to money out of the petty cash.* **10. cannot help but.** to be unable to do anything else except: *I cannot help but laugh.* **11. help a person on** *or* **off with.** to assist a person in the putting on or removal of (clothes). **12. so help me. a.** on my honour. **b.** no matter what: *so help me, I'll get revenge.* ~*n.* **13.** the act of helping, or being helped, or a person or thing that helps: *she's a great help.* **14.** a helping. **15. a.** a person hired for a job; employee, esp. a farm worker or domestic servant. **b.** (*functioning as sing.*) several employees collectively. **16.** a means of remedy: *there's no help for it.* ~*interj.* **17.** used to ask for assistance. ~See also **help out.** [Old English *helpan;* related to Old Norse *hjalpa,* Gothic *hilpan,* Old High German *helfan*] —'**helpable** *adj.* —'**helper** *n.*
helpful ('hɛlpfʊl) *adj.* serving a useful function; giving help. —'**helpfully** *adv.* —'**helpfulness** *n.*
helping ('hɛlpɪŋ) *n.* a single portion of food taken at a meal.
helping hand *n.* assistance: *many people lent a helping hand in making arrangements for the party.*
helpless ('hɛlplɪs) *adj.* **1.** unable to manage independently. **2.** made powerless or weak: *they were helpless from so much giggling.* **3.** without help. —'**helplessly** *adv.* —'**helplessness** *n.*
helpline ('hɛlpˌlaɪn) *n.* **1.** a telephone line operated by a charitable organization for people in distress. **2.** a telephone line operated by a commercial organization to provide information.
helpmate ('hɛlpˌmeɪt) *n.* a companion and helper, esp. a wife.
helpmeet ('hɛlpˌmiːt) *n.* a less common word for **helpmate.** [C17: from the phrase *an helpe meet* (suitable) *for him* Genesis 2:18]
help out *vb.* (*adv.*) **1.** to assist or aid (someone), esp. by sharing the burden. **2.** to share the burden or cost of something with (another person).
help screens *pl. n.* computer instructions displayed on a visual display unit.
helter-skelter ('hɛltə'skɛltə) *adj.* **1.** haphazard or carelessly hurried. ~*adv.* **2.** in a helter-skelter manner. ~*n.* **3.** *Brit.* a high spiral slide, as at a fairground. **4.** disorder or haste. [C16: probably of imitative origin]
helve (hɛlv) *n.* **1.** the handle of a hand tool such as an axe or pick. ~*vb.* **2.** (*tr.*) to fit a helve to (a tool). [Old English *hielfe;* related to Old Saxon *hèlvi,* Old High German *halb,* Lithuanian *kìlpa* stirrup; see HALTER]
Helvetian (hɛl'viːʃən) *adj.* **1.** another word for **Swiss.** ~*n.* **2.** a native or citizen of Switzerland. [from Latin *Helvetia* Switzerland]
Helvetic (hɛl'vɛtɪk) *adj.* **1.** Helvetian; Swiss. **2.** of or relating to the Helvetic Confessions or to Swiss Protestantism. ~*n.* **3.** a Swiss Protestant or reformed Calvinist who subscribes to one of

the two **Helvetic Confessions** (of faith) formulated in 1536 and 1566.
hem[1] (hɛm) *n.* **1.** an edge to a piece of cloth, made by folding the raw edge under and stitching it down. **2.** short for **hemline.** ~*vb.* **hems, hemming, hemmed.** (*tr.*) **3.** to provide with a hem. **4.** (usually foll. by *in, around,* or *about*) to enclose or confine. [Old English *hemm;* related to Old Frisian *hemme* enclosed land]
hem[2] (hɛm) *n., interj.* **1.** a representation of the sound of clearing the throat, used to gain attention, express hesitation, etc. ~*vb.* **hems, hemming, hemmed. 2.** (*intr.*) to utter this sound. **3. hem** (*or* **hum) and haw.** to hesitate in speaking or in making a decision.
hem- *combining form.* a U.S. variant of **haemo-** before a vowel.
hema- *combining form.* a U.S. variant of **haemo-.**
he-man *n., pl.* **-men.** *Informal.* a strongly built muscular man.
hematite ('hɛməˌtaɪt) *or* **haematite** ('hɛməˌtaɪt, 'hiːm-) *n.* a red, grey, or black mineral, found as massive beds and in veins and igneous rocks. It is the chief source of iron. Composition: iron (ferric) oxide. Formula: Fe_2O_3. Crystal structure: hexagonal (rhombohedral). [C16: via Latin from Greek *haimatitēs* resembling blood, from *haima* blood] —**hematitic** *or* **haematitic** (ˌhɛmə'tɪtɪk, ˌhiː-) *adj.*
hemato- *or before a vowel* **hemat-** *combining form.* U.S. variants of **haemato-.**
hemelytron (hɛ'mɛlɪˌtrɒn) *or* **hemielytron** *n., pl.* **-tra** (-trə). the forewing of plant bugs and related insects, having a thickened base and a membranous apex. [C19: from New Latin *hemielytron,* from HEMI- + Greek *elutron* a covering] —**hem'elytral** *or* **ˌhemi'elytral** *adj.*
hemeralopia (ˌhɛmərə'ləʊpɪə) *n.* inability to see clearly in bright light. Nontechnical name: **day blindness.** Compare **nyctalopia.** [C18: New Latin, from Greek *hēmeralōps,* from *hēmera* day + *alaos* blind + *ōps* eye] —**hemeralopic** (ˌhɛmərə'lɒpɪk) *adj.*
hemerocallis (ˌhɛmərəʊ'kælɪs) *n.* See **day lily.** [from Greek *hemera* day + *kallos* beautiful]
hemi- *prefix.* half: *hemicycle; hemisphere.* Compare **demi-** (sense 1), **semi-** (sense 1). [from Latin, from Greek *hēmi-*]
-hemia *n. combining form.* U.S. variant of **-aemia.**
hemialgia (ˌhɛmɪ'ældʒɪə) *n.* pain limited to one side of the body.
hemianopia (ˌhɛmɪæn'əʊpɪə) *n.* loss of vision in either the whole left or the whole right half of the field of vision. Also called: **hemianopsia** (ˌhɛmɪæn'ɒpsɪə). [C19: from HEMI- + AN- + Greek *opsis* sight]
hemicellulose (ˌhɛmɪ'sɛljʊˌləʊz) *n.* any of a group of plant polysaccharides that occur chiefly in the cell wall.
hemichordate (ˌhɛmɪ'kɔːˌdeɪt) *n.* **1.** any small wormlike marine animal of the subphylum *Hemichordata* (or *Hemichorda*), having numerous gill slits in the pharynx: phylum *Chordata* (chordates). ~*adj.* **2.** of, relating to, or belonging to the subphylum *Hemichordata.* ~See also **acorn worm.**
hemicryptophyte (ˌhɛmɪ'krɪptəˌfaɪt) *n.* any perennial plant that bears its overwintering buds at soil level, where they are often partly covered by surface debris. [C20: HEMI- + CRYPTOPHYTE]
hemicrystalline (ˌhɛmɪ'krɪstəˌlaɪn) *adj.* (of igneous rocks) having both glass and crystalline components. Also: **hypocrystalline.** Compare **holocrystalline.**
hemicycle ('hɛmɪˌsaɪkᵊl) *n.* **1.** a semicircular structure, room, arena, wall, etc. **2.** a rare word for **semicircle.** —**hemicyclic** (ˌhɛmɪ'saɪklɪk, -'sɪk-) *adj.*
hemidemisemiquaver (ˌhɛmɪˌdɛmɪ'sɛmɪˌkweɪvə) *n. Music.* a note having the time value of one sixty-fourth of a semibreve. Usual U.S. and Canadian name: **sixty-fourth note.**
hemielytron (ˌhɛmɪ'ɛlɪˌtrɒn) *n., pl.* **-tra** (-trə). a variant of **hemelytron.** —ˌ**hemi'elytral** *adj.*
hemihedral (ˌhɛmɪ'hiːdrəl) *adj.* (of a crystal) exhibiting only half the number of planes necessary for complete symmetry.
hemihydrate (ˌhɛmɪ'haɪdreɪt) *n. Chem.* a hydrate in which there are two molecules of substance to every molecule of water. —ˌ**hemi'hydrated** *adj.*
hemimorphic (ˌhɛmɪ'mɔːfɪk) *adj.* (of a crystal) having different forms at each end of an axis. —ˌ**hemi'morphism** *or* **'hemiˌmorphy** *n.*
hemimorphite (ˌhɛmɪ'mɔːfaɪt) *n.* a white mineral consisting of hydrated zinc silicate in orthorhombic crystalline form: a common ore of zinc. Formula: $Zn_4Si_2O_7(OH)_2.H_2O$.
hemiola (ˌhɛmɪ'əʊlə) *or* **hemiolia** *n. Music.* a rhythmical device involving the superimposition of, for example, two notes in the time of three. Also called: **sesquialtera.** [New Latin, from Greek *hēmiolia* ratio of one to one and a half, from HEMI- + (*h*)*olos* whole] —**hemiolic** (ˌhɛmɪ'ɒlɪk) *adj.*
hemiparasite (ˌhɛmɪ'pærɪˌsaɪt) *or* **semiparasite** *n.* **1.** a parasitic plant, such as mistletoe, that carries out photosynthesis but also obtains food from its host. **2.** an organism that can live independently or parasitically.
hemiplegia (ˌhɛmɪ'pliːdʒɪə) *n.* paralysis of one side of the body, usually as the result of injury to the brain. Compare **paraplegia, quadriplegia.** —ˌ**hemi'plegic** *adj.*
hemipode ('hɛmɪˌpəʊd) *or* **hemipod** ('hɛmɪˌpɒd) *n.* other names for **button quail.**
hemipteran (hɪ'mɪptərən) *n.* **1.** Also called: **hemipteron** (hɪ'mɪptəˌrɒn) any hemipterous insect. ~*adj.* **2.** another word for **hemipterous.** [C19: from HEMI- + Greek *pteron* wing]
hemipterous (hɪ'mɪptərəs) *or* **hemipteran** *adj.* of, relating to, or belonging to the *Hemiptera,* a large order of insects having sucking or piercing mouthparts specialized as a beak (rostrum). The group is divided into the suborders *Homoptera* (aphids, cicadas, etc.) and *Heteroptera* (water bugs, bedbugs, etc.).
hemisphere ('hɛmɪˌsfɪə) *n.* **1.** one half of a sphere. **2. a.** half of the terrestrial globe, divided into **northern** and **southern hemispheres** by the equator or into **eastern** and **western hemispheres** by some meridians, usually 0° and 180°. **b.** a map or projection of one of the hemispheres. **3.** either of the two halves of the celestial sphere that lie north or south of the celestial equator. **4.** *Anatomy.* short for **cerebral hemisphere.** —**hemispheric** (ˌhɛmɪ'sfɛrɪk) *or* ˌ**hemi'spherical** *adj.*
hemispheroid (ˌhɛmɪ'sfɪərɔɪd) *n.* half of a spheroid. —ˌ**hemispher'oidal** *adj.*
hemistich ('hɛmɪˌstɪk) *n. Prosody.* a half line of verse.
hemiterpene (ˌhɛmɪ'tɜːpiːn) *n.* any of a class of simple unsaturated hydrocarbons, such as isoprene, having the formula C_5H_8.
hemitrope ('hɛmɪˌtrəʊp) *n. Chem.* another name for **twin** (sense 3). —**hemitropic** (ˌhɛmɪ'trɒpɪk) *adj.* —ˌ**hemi'tropism** *or* **hemitropy** (hiː'mɪtrəpɪ) *n.*
hemizygous (ˌhɛmɪ'zaɪgəs) *adj. Genetics.* (of a chromosome or gene) not having a homologue; not paired in a diploid cell.
hemline ('hɛmˌlaɪn) *n.* the level to which the hem of a skirt or dress hangs; hem: *knee-length hemlines.*
hemlock ('hɛmˌlɒk) *n.* **1.** an umbelliferous poisonous Eurasian plant, *Conium maculatum,* having finely divided leaves, spotted stems, and small white flowers. U.S. name: **poison hemlock.** See also **water hemlock. 2.** a poisonous drug derived from this plant. **3.** Also called: **hemlock spruce.** any coniferous tree of the genus *Tsuga,* of North America and E Asia, having short flat needles: family *Pinaceae.* See also **western hemlock. 4.** the wood of any of these trees, used for lumber and as a source of wood pulp. [Old English *hymlic;* perhaps related to *hymele* hop plant, Middle Low German *homele,* Old Norwegian *humli,* Old Slavonic *chŭmeli*]
hemmer ('hɛmə) *n.* an attachment on a sewing machine for hemming.
hemo- *combining form.* a U.S. variant of **haemo-.**
hemp (hɛmp) *n.* **1.** Also called: **cannabis, marijuana.** an annual strong-smelling Asian moraceous plant, *Cannabis sativa,* having tough fibres, deeply lobed leaves, and small greenish flowers. See also **Indian hemp. 2.** the fibre of this plant, used to make canvas, rope, etc. **3.** any of several narcotic drugs obtained from some varieties of this plant, esp. from Indian hemp. See **bhang, cannabis, hashish, marijuana.** ~See also **bowstring hemp.** [Old English *hænep;* related to Old Norse *hampr,* Old High German *hanaf,* Greek *kannabis,* Dutch *hennep*] —**'hempen** *or* **'hempˌlike** *adj.*
hemp agrimony *n.* a Eurasian plant, *Eupatorium cannabinum,* with small clusters of reddish flowers: family *Compositae* (composites).
hemp nettle *n.* **1.** a hairy weedy plant, *Galeopsis tetrahit,* of northern regions, having helmet-shaped pink, purple, and white flowers and toothed leaves: family *Labiatae* (labiates). **2.** any of various other plants of the genus *Galeopsis.*
hemstitch ('hɛmˌstɪtʃ) *n.* **1.** a decorative edging stitch, usually for a hem, in which the cross threads are stitched in groups. ~*vb.* **2.** to decorate (a hem, etc.) with hemstitches. —**'hemˌstitcher** *n.*
hen (hɛn) *n.* **1.** the female of any bird, esp. the adult female of the domestic fowl. **2.** the female of certain other animals, such as the lobster. **3.** *Informal.* a woman regarded as gossipy or foolish. **4.** *Scot. dialect.* a term of address (often affectionate), used to women and girls. **5. scarce as a hen's teeth.** extremely rare. [Old English *henn;* related to Old High German *henna,* Old Frisian *henne*]
hen-and-chickens *n., pl.* **hens-and-chickens.** (*functioning as sing. or pl.*) any of several plants, such as the houseleek and ground ivy, that produce many offsets or runners.
henbane ('hɛnˌbeɪn) *n.* a poisonous solanaceous Mediterranean plant, *Hyoscyamus niger,* with sticky hairy leaves and funnel-shaped greenish flowers: yields the drug hyoscyamine.
henbit ('hɛnˌbɪt) *n.* a plant, *Lamium amplexicaule,* that is native to Europe and has toothed opposite leaves and small dark red flowers: family *Labiatae* (labiates).
hence (hɛns) *sentence connector.* **1.** for this reason; following from this; therefore. ~*adv.* **2.** from this time: *a year hence.* **3.** *Archaic.* **a.** from here or from this world; away. **b.** from this origin or source. ~*interj.* **4.** *Archaic.* begone! away! [Old English *hionane;* related to Old High German *hinana* away from here, Old Irish *cen* on this side]
henceforth ('hɛns'fɔːθ), **henceforwards,** *or* **henceforward** *adv.* from this time forward; from now on.
henchman ('hɛntʃmən) *n., pl.* **-men. 1.** a faithful attendant or supporter. **2.** *Archaic.* a squire; page. [C14 *hengestman,* from Old English *hengest* stallion + MAN; related to Old Norse *hestr* horse, Old High German *hengist* gelding]
hencoop ('hɛnˌkuːp) *n.* a cage for poultry.
hendeca- *combining form.* eleven: *hendecagon; hendecahedron; hendecasyllable.* [from Greek *hendeka,* from *hen,* neuter of *heis* one + *deka* ten]

hendecagon (hɛnˈdɛkəgən) *n.* a polygon having 11 sides. —**hendecagonal** (ˌhɛndɪˈkægənᵊl) *adj.*

hendecahedron (ˌhɛndɛkəˈhɛdrən, -ˈhiːdrən) *n., pl.* **-drons** *or* **-dra** (-drə). a solid figure having 11 plane faces. See also **polyhedron.**

hendecasyllable (ˈhɛndɛkəˌsɪləbᵊl) *n. Prosody.* a verse line of 11 syllables. [C18: via Latin from Greek *hendekasullabos*] —**hendecasyllabic** (hɛnˌdɛkəsɪˈlæbɪk) *adj.*

hendiadys (hɛnˈdaɪədɪs) *n.* a rhetorical device by which two nouns joined by a conjunction, usually *and,* are used instead of a noun and a modifier, as in *to run with fear and haste* instead of *to run with fearful haste.* [C16: from Medieval Latin, changed from Greek phrase *hen dia duoin,* literally: one through two]

henequen, henequin, *or* **heniquen** (ˈhɛnɪkɪn) *n.* **1.** an agave plant, *Agave fourcroydes,* that is native to Yucatán. **2.** the fibre of this plant, used in making rope, twine, and coarse fabrics. [C19: from American Spanish *henequén,* probably of Taino origin]

henge (hɛndʒ) *n.* a circular area, often containing a circle of stones or sometimes wooden posts, dating from the Neolithic and Bronze Ages. [back formation from *Stonehenge,* prehistoric monument in S England]

hen harrier *n.* a common harrier, *Circus cyaneus,* that flies over fields and marshes and nests in marshes and open land. U.S. and Canadian names: **marsh hawk, marsh harrier.**

henhouse (ˈhɛnˌhaʊs) *n.* a coop for hens.

Henle's loop (ˈhɛnlɪz) *n. Anatomy.* See **loop**[1] (sense 10b.). [C19: named after F. G. J. *Henle* (1809–85), German anatomist]

henna (ˈhɛnə) *n.* **1.** a lythraceous shrub or tree, *Lawsonia inermis,* of Asia and N Africa, with white or reddish fragrant flowers. **2.** a reddish dye obtained from the powdered leaves of this plant, used as a cosmetic and industrial dye. **3.** a reddish-brown or brown colour. ~*vb.* **4.** (*tr.*) to dye with henna. ~Archaic name (for senses 1, 2): **camphire.** [C16: from Arabic *hinnā'; see* ALKANET]

hennery (ˈhɛnərɪ) *n., pl.* **-neries.** a place or farm for keeping poultry.

hen night *n. Informal.* a party for women only, esp. held for a woman shortly before she is married. Compare **hen party, stag night.**

henotheism (ˈhɛnəʊθiːˌɪzəm) *n.* the worship of one deity (of several) as the special god of one's family, clan, or tribe. [C19: from Greek *heis* one + *theos* god] —**ˈhenotheist** *n.* —ˌ**henotheˈistic** *adj.*

hen party *n. Informal.* a party at which only women are present. Compare **hen night, stag night.**

henpeck (ˈhɛnˌpɛk) *vb.* (*tr.*) (of a woman) to harass or torment (a man, esp. her husband) by persistent nagging. —**ˈhenˌpecked** *adj.*

hen run *n.* an enclosure for hens, esp. one made of chicken wire.

henry (ˈhɛnrɪ) *n., pl.* **-ry, -ries,** *or* **-rys.** the derived SI unit of electric inductance; the inductance of a closed circuit in which an emf of 1 volt is produced when the current varies uniformly at the rate of 1 ampere per second. Symbol: H [C19: named after Joseph *Henry* (1797–1878), U.S. physicist]

Henry's law (ˈhɛnrɪz) *n. Chem.* the principle that the amount of a gas dissolved at equilibrium in a given quantity of a liquid is proportional to the pressure of the gas in contact with the liquid. [C19: named after William *Henry* (1774–1836), English chemist]

hent (hɛnt) *Archaic.* ~*vb.* **1.** (*tr.*) to seize; grasp. ~*n.* **2.** anything that has been grasped, esp. by the mind. [Old English *hentan* to pursue; related to *huntian* to HUNT]

hep (hɛp) *adj.* **hepper, heppest.** *Slang.* an earlier word for **hip**[4].

heparin (ˈhɛpərɪn) *n.* a polysaccharide, containing sulphate groups, present in most body tissues: an anticoagulant used in the treatment of thrombosis. [C20: from Greek *hēpar* the liver + -IN] —**ˈheparinˌoid** *adj.*

hepatic (hɪˈpætɪk) *adj.* **1.** of or relating to the liver. **2.** *Botany.* of or relating to the liverworts. **3.** having the colour of liver. ~*n.* **4.** any of various drugs for use in treating diseases of the liver. **5.** a less common name for a **liverwort.** [C15: from Latin *hēpaticus,* from Greek *hēpar* liver]

hepatica (hɪˈpætɪkə) *n.* any ranunculaceous woodland plant of the N temperate genus *Hepatica,* having three-lobed leaves and white, mauve, or pink flowers. [C16: from Medieval Latin: liverwort, from Latin *hēpaticus* of the liver]

hepatitis (ˌhɛpəˈtaɪtɪs) *n.* inflammation of the liver, characterized by fever, jaundice, and weakness. See **hepatitis A, hepatitis B, non-A, non-B hepatitis.**

hepatitis A *n.* a form of hepatitis caused by a virus transmitted in contaminated food or drink.

hepatitis B *n.* a form of hepatitis caused by a virus transmitted by infected blood transfusions or contaminated hypodermic needles. Also called: **serum hepatitis.**

hepato- *or before a vowel* **hepat-** *combining form.* denoting the liver: *hepatitis.* [from Greek *hēpat-, hēpar*]

hepatogenous (ˌhɛpəˈtɒdʒɪnəs) *adj.* originating in the liver.

hepatomegaly (ˌhɛpətəʊˈmɛgəlɪ) *n.* an abnormal enlargement of the liver, caused by congestion, inflammation, or a tumour. [C20: from HEPATO- + New Latin *megalia,* from Greek *megas* great]

hepcat (ˈhɛpˌkæt) *n. Obsolete slang.* a person who is hep, esp. a player or admirer of jazz and swing in the 1940s.

Hepplewhite (ˈhɛpᵊlˌwaɪt) *adj.* of, denoting, or made in a style of ornamental and carved 18th-century English furniture, of which oval or shield-shaped open chairbacks are characteristic. [C18: named after George *Hepplewhite* (died 1786), English cabinet-maker]

hepta- *or before a vowel* **hept-** *combining form.* seven: *heptameter.* [from Greek]

heptad (ˈhɛptæd) *n.* **1.** a group or series of seven. **2.** the number or sum of seven. **3.** an atom or element with a valency of seven. [C17: from Greek *heptas* seven]

heptadecanoic acid (ˌhɛptəˌdɛkəˈnəʊɪk) *n.* a colourless crystalline water-insoluble carboxylic acid used in organic synthesis. Formula: $CH_3(CH_2)_{15}COOH$. Also called: **margaric acid.**

heptagon (ˈhɛptəgən) *n.* a polygon having seven sides. —**heptagonal** (hɛpˈtægənᵊl) *adj.*

heptahedron (ˌhɛptəˈhiːdrən) *n.* a solid figure having seven plane faces. See also **polyhedron.** —ˌ**heptaˈhedral** *adj.*

heptamerous (hɛpˈtæmərəs) *adj.* (esp. of plant parts such as petals or sepals) arranged in groups of seven.

heptameter (hɛpˈtæmɪtə) *n. Prosody.* a verse line of seven metrical feet. —**heptametrical** (ˌhɛptəˈmɛtrɪkᵊl) *adj.*

heptane (ˈhɛpteɪn) *n.* an alkane existing in nine isomeric forms, esp. the isomer with a straight chain of carbon atoms (*n*-heptane), which is found in petroleum and used as an anaesthetic. Formula: C_7H_{16}. [C19: from HEPTA- + -ANE, so called because it has seven carbon atoms]

heptangular (hɛpˈtæŋgjʊlə) *adj.* having seven angles.

heptarchy (ˈhɛptɑːkɪ) *n., pl.* **-chies. 1.** government by seven rulers. **2.** a state divided into seven regions each under its own ruler. **3. a.** the seven kingdoms into which Anglo-Saxon England is thought to have been divided from about the 7th to the 9th centuries A.D.: Kent, East Anglia, Essex, Sussex, Wessex, Mercia, and Northumbria. **b.** the period when this grouping existed. —**ˈheptarch** *n.* —**hepˈtarchic** *or* **hepˈtarchal** *adj.*

heptastich (ˈhɛptəˌstɪk) *n. Prosody.* a poem, strophe, or stanza that consists of seven lines.

Heptateuch (ˈhɛptəˌtjuːk) *n.* the first seven books of the Old Testament. [C17: from Late Latin *Heptateuchos,* from Greek HEPTA- + *teukhos* book]

heptathlon (hɛpˈtæθlɒn) *n.* an athletic contest for women in which each athlete competes in seven different events. [C20: from HEPTA- + Greek *athlon* contest] —**hepˈtathlete.**

heptavalent (hɛpˈtævələnt, ˌhɛptəˈveɪlənt) *adj. Chem.* having a valency of seven. Also: **septivalent.**

heptose (ˈhɛptəʊs, -təʊz) *n.* any monosaccharide that has seven carbon atoms per molecule.

her (hɜː; *unstressed* hə, ə) *pron.* (*objective*) **1.** refers to a female person or animal: *he loves her; they sold her a bag; something odd about her; lucky her!* **2.** refers to things personified as feminine or traditionally to ships and nations. **3.** *Chiefly U.S.* a dialect word for **herself** when used as an indirect object: *she needs to get her a better job.* ~*determiner.* **4.** of, belonging to, or associated with her: *her silly ideas; her hair; her smoking annoys me.* [Old English *hire,* genitive and dative of *hēo* SHE, feminine of *hē* HE[1]; related to Old High German *ira,* Gothic *izōs,* Middle Dutch *hare*]

▷**Usage.** See at **me**[1].

her. *abbrev. for:* **1.** heraldic. **2.** heraldry.

Heraclid *or* **Heraklid** (ˈhɛrəklɪd) *n., pl.* **Heraclidae** *or* **Heraklidae** (ˌhɛrəˈklaɪdiː). any person claiming descent from Hercules (Heracles), esp. one of the Dorian aristocrats of Sparta. —**Heraclidan** *or* **Heraklidan** (ˌhɛrəˈklaɪdᵊn) *adj.*

herald (ˈhɛrəld) *n.* **1. a.** a person who announces important news. **b.** (*as modifier*): *herald angels.* **2.** *Often literary.* a forerunner; harbinger. **3.** the intermediate rank of heraldic officer, between king-of-arms and pursuivant. **4.** (in the Middle Ages) an official at a tournament. ~*vb.* (*tr.*) **5.** to announce publicly. **6.** to precede or usher in. [C14: from Old French *herault,* of Germanic origin; compare Old English *here* war; see WIELD]

heraldic (hɛˈrældɪk) *adj.* **1.** of or relating to heraldry. **2.** of or relating to heralds. —**heˈraldically** *adv.*

herald moth *n.* a noctuid moth, *Scoliopteryx libatrix,* having brownish cryptically mottled forewings and plain dull hind wings. The adult hibernates and has a prolonged life.

heraldry (ˈhɛrəldrɪ) *n., pl.* **-ries. 1.** the occupation or study concerned with the classification of armorial bearings, the allocation of rights to bear arms, the tracing of genealogies, etc. **2.** the duties and pursuit of a herald. **3.** armorial bearings, insignia, devices, etc. **4.** heraldic symbols or symbolism. **5.** the show and ceremony of heraldry. —**ˈheraldist** *n.*

heralds' college *n.* another name for **college of arms.**

herb (hɜːb; *U.S.* ɜːrb) *n.* **1.** a seed-bearing plant whose aerial parts do not persist above ground at the end of the growing season; herbaceous plant. **2. a.** any of various usually aromatic plants, such as parsley, rue, and rosemary, that are used in cookery and medicine. **b.** (*as modifier*): *a herb garden.* **3.** *Caribbean.* a slang term for **marijuana.** [C13: from Old French *herbe,* from Latin *herba* grass, green plants] —**ˈherbˌlike** *adj.*

herbaceous (hɜːˈbeɪʃəs) *adj.* **1.** designating or relating to plants or plant parts that are fleshy as opposed to woody: *a herbaceous plant.* **2.** (of petals and sepals) green and leaflike. **3.** of or relating to herbs. —**herˈbaceously** *adv.*

herbaceous border *n.* a flower bed that primarily contains perennials rather than annuals.

herbage (ˈhɜːbɪdʒ) *n.* **1.** herbaceous plants collectively, esp. the edible parts on which cattle, sheep, etc., graze. **2.** the vegetation of pasture land; pasturage.
herbal (ˈhɜːbᵊl) *adj.* **1.** of or relating to herbs. ~*n.* **2.** a book describing and listing the properties of plants.
herbalist (ˈhɜːbᵊlɪst) *n.* **1.** a person who grows, collects, sells, or specializes in the use of herbs, esp. medicinal herbs. **2.** (formerly) a descriptive botanist.
herbarium (hɜːˈbɛərɪəm) *n., pl.* **-iums** *or* **-ia** (-ɪə). **1.** a collection of dried plants that are mounted and classified systematically. **2.** a building, room, etc., in which such a collection is kept. —**herˈbarial** *adj.*
herb bennet *n.* a Eurasian and N African rosaceous plant, *Geum urbanum,* with yellow flowers. Also called: **wood avens, bennet.** [C13 *herbe beneit,* from Old French *herbe benoite,* literally: blessed herb, from Medieval Latin *herba benedicta*]
herb Christopher (ˈkrɪstəfə) *n., pl.* **herbs Christopher.** another name for **baneberry.** [C16: named after St *Christopher,* patron saint of travellers]
herb Gerard (ˈdʒɛˌrɑːd) *n., pl.* **herbs Gerard.** another name for **goutweed.** [C16: named after St *Gerard* (feast day April 23), who was invoked by those suffering from gout]
herbicide (ˈhɜːbɪˌsaɪd) *n.* a chemical that destroys plants, esp. one used to control weeds. —ˌ**herbiˈcidal** *adj.*
herbivore (ˈhɜːbɪˌvɔː) *n.* an animal that feeds on grass and other plants. [C19: from New Latin *herbivora* grass-eaters] —**herbivorous** (hɜːˈbɪvərəs) *adj.* —**herˈbivorously** *adv.* —**herˈbivorousness** *n.*
herb layer *n.* See **layer** (sense 2).
herb of grace *n.* an archaic name for **rue** (the plant).
herb Paris (ˈpærɪs) *n., pl.* **herbs Paris.** a Eurasian woodland plant, *Paris quadrifolia,* with a whorl of four leaves and a solitary yellow flower: formerly used medicinally: family *Trilliaceae.* [C16: from Medieval Latin *herba paris,* literally: herb of a pair: so called because the four leaves on the stalk look like a true lovers' knot; associated in folk etymology with *Paris,* France]
herb Robert (ˈrɒbət) *n., pl.* **herbs Robert.** a low-growing N temperate geraniaceous plant, *Geranium robertianum,* with strongly scented divided leaves and small purplish flowers. [C13: from Medieval Latin *herba Roberti* herb of Robert, probably named after St *Robert,* 11th-century French ecclesiastic]
herby (ˈhɜːbɪ) *adj.* **herbier, herbiest. 1.** abounding in herbs. **2.** of or relating to medicinal or culinary herbs.
herculean (ˌhɜːkjʊˈliːən) *adj.* **1.** requiring tremendous effort, strength, etc.: *a herculean task.* **2.** (*sometimes cap.*) resembling Hercules in strength, courage, etc.
Hercules[1] (ˈhɜːkjʊˌliːz) *n.* a man of outstanding strength or size. [after *Hercules,* hero of classical mythology] —ˌ**Hercuˈlean** *adj.*
Hercules[2] (ˈhɜːkjʊˌliːz) *n., Latin genitive* **Herculeis** (ˌhɜːkjʊˈliːɪs) a large constellation in the N hemisphere lying between Lyra and Corona Borealis.
hercules beetle *n.* a very large tropical American scarabaeid beetle, *Dynastes hercules:* the male has two large anterior curved horns.
Hercules'-club *n.* **1.** a prickly North American araliaceous shrub, *Aralia spinosa,* with medicinal bark and leaves. **2.** a prickly North American rutaceous tree, *Zanthoxylum clava-herculis,* with medicinal bark and berries.
Hercynian (hɜːˈsɪnɪən) *adj.* denoting a period of mountain building in Europe in the late Palaeozoic. [C16: from Latin *Hercynia silva* the Hercynian forest (i.e., the wooded mountains of central Germany, esp. the Erzgebirge)]
herd[1] (hɜːd) *n.* **1.** a large group of mammals living and feeding together, esp. a group of cattle, sheep, etc. **2.** *Often disparaging.* a large group of people. **3. the.** *Derogatory.* the large mass of ordinary people. ~*vb.* **4.** to collect or be collected into or as if into a herd. [Old English *heord;* related to Old Norse *hjörth,* Gothic *hairda,* Old High German *herta,* Greek *kórthus* troop]
herd[2] (hɜːd) *n.* **1. a.** *Archaic or dialect.* a man or boy who tends livestock; herdsman. **b.** (*in combination*): *goatherd, swineherd.* ~*vb.* (*tr.*) **2.** to drive forwards in a large group. **3.** to look after (livestock). [Old English *hirde;* related to Old Norse *hirthir,* Gothic *hairdeis,* Old High German *hirti,* Old Saxon *hirdi, herdi;* see HERD[1]]
herd-book *n.* a book containing the pedigrees of breeds of pigs, cattle, etc.
herder (ˈhɜːdə) *n. Chiefly U.S.* a person who cares for or drives herds of cattle or flocks of sheep, esp. on an open range. Brit. equivalent: **herdsman.**
herdic (ˈhɜːdɪk) *n. U.S.* a small horse-drawn carriage with a rear entrance and side seats. [C19: named after P. *Herdic,* 19th-century American inventor]
herd instinct *n. Psychol.* the inborn tendency to associate with others and follow the group's behaviour.
herdsman (ˈhɜːdzmən) *n., pl.* **-men.** *Chiefly Brit.* a person who breeds, rears, or cares for cattle or (rarely) other livestock in the herd. U.S. equivalent: **herder.**
herd tester *n. N.Z.* a technician trained to test the health and production of milk and butterfat of dairy cows. —**herd testing** *n.*
Herdwick (ˈhɜːdwɪk) *n.* a hardy breed of coarse-woolled sheep from NW England. [C19: from obsolete *herdwick* pasture, sheep farm (see HERD[1] (sense 4), WICK[2]); the breed is thought to have originated on the herdwicks of Furness Abbey in NW England]
here (hɪə) *adv.* **1.** in, at, or to this place, point, case, or respect: *we come here every summer; here, the policemen do not usually carry guns; here comes Roy.* **2. here and there.** at several places in or throughout an area. **3. here goes.** an exclamation indicating that the speaker is about to perform an action. **4. here's to.** a formula used in proposing a toast to someone or something. **5. here today, gone tomorrow.** short-lived; transitory. **6. here we go again.** an event or process is about to repeat itself. **7. neither here nor there.** of no relevance or importance. **8. this here.** See **this** (senses 1–3). ~*n.* **9.** this place: *they leave here tonight.* **10. (the) here and now.** the present time. [Old English *hēr;* related to Old Norse *hēr,* Old High German *hiar,* Old Saxon *hīr*]
hereabouts (ˈhɪərəˌbaʊts) *or* **hereabout** *adv.* in this region or neighbourhood; near this place.
hereafter (ˌhɪərˈɑːftə) *adv.* **1.** *Formal or law.* in a subsequent part of this document, matter, case, etc. **2.** a less common word for **henceforth. 3.** at some time in the future. **4.** in a future life after death. ~*n.* (usually preceded by *the*) **5.** life after death. **6.** the future.
hereat (ˌhɪərˈæt) *adv. Archaic.* because of this.
hereby (ˌhɪəˈbaɪ) *adv.* **1.** (used in official statements, proclamations, etc.) by means of or as a result of this. **2.** *Archaic.* nearby.
heredes (hɪˈriːdiːz) *n.* the plural of **heres.**
hereditable (hɪˈrɛdɪtəbᵊl) *adj.* a less common word for **heritable.** —**heˌreditaˈbility** *n.* —**heˈreditably** *adv.*
hereditament (ˌhɛrɪˈdɪtəmənt) *n. Property law.* **1.** any kind of property capable of being inherited. **2.** property that before 1926 passed to an heir if not otherwise disposed of by will.
hereditarianism (həˌrɛdɪˈtɛərɪəˌnɪzəm) *n. Psychol.* a school of thought that emphasizes the influence of heredity in the determination of human behaviour. Compare **environmentalism.**
hereditary (hɪˈrɛdɪtərɪ, -trɪ) *adj.* **1.** of, relating to, or denoting factors that can be transmitted genetically from one generation to another. **2.** *Law.* **a.** descending or capable of descending to succeeding generations by inheritance. **b.** transmitted or transmissible according to established rules of descent. **3.** derived from one's ancestors; traditional: *hereditary feuds.* **4.** *Maths, logic.* **a.** (of a set) containing all those elements which have a given relation to any element of the set. **b.** (of a property) transferred by the given relation, so that if x has the property R and xRy, then y also has the property. —**heˈreditarily** *adv.* —**heˈreditariness** *n.*
hereditist (həˈrɛdɪtɪst) *n.* any person who places the role of heredity above that of the environment as the determining factor in human or animal behaviour.
heredity (hɪˈrɛdɪtɪ) *n., pl.* **-ties. 1.** the transmission from one generation to another of genetic factors that determine individual characteristics: responsible for the resemblances between parents and offspring. **2.** the sum total of the inherited factors or their characteristics in an organism. [C16: from Old French *heredite,* from Latin *hērēditās* inheritance; see HEIR]
heredo-familial (həˌrɛdəʊfəˈmɪlɪəl) *adj.* denoting a condition or disease that may be passed from generation to generation and to several members of one family.
Hereford (ˈhɛrɪfəd) *n.* a hardy breed of beef cattle characterized by a red body, red and white head, and white markings, originating from the former county of Herefordshire in W England.
herein (ˌhɪərˈɪn) *adv.* **1.** *Formal or law.* in or into this place, thing, document, etc. **2.** *Rare.* in this respect, circumstance, etc.
hereinafter (ˌhɪərɪnˈɑːftə) *adv. Formal or law.* in a subsequent part or from this point on in this document, statement, etc.
hereinbefore (ˌhɪərɪnbɪˈfɔː) *adv. Formal or law.* in a previous part of or previously in this document, statement, etc.
hereinto (ˌhɪərˈɪntuː) *adv. Formal or law.* into this place, circumstance, etc.
hereof (ˌhɪərˈɒv) *adv. Formal or law.* of or concerning this.
hereon (ˌhɪərˈɒn) *adv.* an archaic word for **hereupon.**
Herero (həˈrɛərəʊ, ˈhɛərəˌrəʊ) *n.* **1.** (*pl.* **-ro** *or* **-ros**) a member of a formerly rich cattle-keeping Negroid people of southern Africa, living chiefly in central Namibia. **2.** the language of this people, belonging to the Bantu group of the Niger-Congo family.
heres *or* **haeres** (ˈhɪəriːz) *n., pl.* **heredes** *or* **haeredes** (hɪˈriːdiːz). *Civil law.* an heir. [from Latin]
heresiarch (hɪˈriːzɪˌɑːk) *n.* the leader or originator of a heretical movement or sect.
heresy (ˈhɛrəsɪ) *n., pl.* **-sies. 1. a.** an opinion or doctrine contrary to the orthodox tenets of a religious body or church. **b.** the act of maintaining such an opinion or doctrine. **2.** any opinion or belief that is or is thought to be contrary to official or established theory. **3.** belief in or adherence to unorthodox opinion. [C13: from Old French *eresie,* from Late Latin *haeresis,* from Latin: sect, from Greek *hairesis* a choosing, from *hairein* to choose]
heretic (ˈhɛrətɪk) *n.* **1.** *Now chiefly R.C. Church.* a person who maintains beliefs contrary to the established teachings of the Church. **2.** a person who holds unorthodox opinions in any field. —**heretical** (hɪˈrɛtɪkᵊl) *adj.* —**heˈretically** *adv.*
hereto (ˌhɪəˈtuː) *adv.* **1.** *Formal or law.* to this place, thing, matter, document, etc. **2.** an obsolete word for **hitherto.**

heretofore (ˌhɪətʊˈfɔː) *adv.* **1.** *Formal or law.* until now; before this time. ~*adj.* **2.** *Obsolete.* previous; former. ~*n.* **3.** (preceded by *the*) *Archaic.* the past.

hereunder (ˌhɪərˈʌndə) *adv. Formal or law.* **1.** (in documents, etc.) below this; subsequently; hereafter. **2.** under the terms or authority of this.

hereunto (ˌhɪərʌnˈtuː) *adv.* an archaic word for **hereto** (sense 1).

hereupon (ˌhɪərəˈpɒn) *adv.* **1.** following immediately after this; at this stage. **2.** *Formal or law.* upon this thing, point, subject, etc.

herewith (ˌhɪəˈwɪð, -ˈwɪθ) *adv.* **1.** *Formal.* together with this: *we send you herewith your statement of account.* **2.** a less common word for **hereby** (sense 1).

heriot (ˈhɛrɪət) *n.* (in medieval England) a death duty paid by villeins and free tenants to their lord, often consisting of the dead man's best beast or chattel. [Old English *heregeatwa,* from *here* army + *geatwa* equipment]

heritable (ˈhɛrɪtəbᵊl) *adj.* **1.** capable of being inherited; inheritable. **2.** *Chiefly law.* capable of inheriting. [C14: from Old French, from *heriter* to INHERIT] —ˌ**heritaˈbility** *n.* —ˈ**heritably** *adv.*

heritage (ˈhɛrɪtɪdʒ) *n.* **1.** something inherited at birth, such as personal characteristics, status, and possessions. **2.** anything that has been transmitted from the past or handed down by tradition. **3. a.** the evidence of the past, such as historical sites, buildings, and the unspoilt natural environment, considered collectively as the inheritance of present-day society. **b.** (*as modifier; cap. as part of name*): *Bannockburn Heritage Centre.* **4.** something that is reserved for a particular person or group or the outcome of an action, way of life, etc.: *the sea was their heritage; the heritage of violence.* **5.** *Law.* any property, esp. land, that by law has descended or may descend to an heir. **6.** *Bible.* **a.** the Israelites regarded as belonging inalienably to God. **b.** the land of Canaan regarded as God's gift to the Israelites. [C13: from Old French; see HEIR]

heritor (ˈhɛrɪtə) *n. Archaic or law.* a person who inherits; inheritor. —**heritress** (ˈhɛrɪtrɪs) *or* ˈ**heritrix** *fem. n.*

herl (hɜːl) *or* **harl** *n. Angling.* **1.** the barb or barbs of a feather, used to dress fishing flies. **2.** an artificial fly dressed with such barbs. [C15: from Middle Low German *herle,* of obscure origin]

herm (hɜːm) *or* **herma** (ˈhɜːmə) *n., pl.* **herms, hermae** (ˈhɜːmiː), *or* **hermai** (ˈhɜːmaɪ) (in ancient Greece) a stone head of Hermes, messenger and herald of the gods, surmounting a square stone pillar. [C16: from Latin *herma,* from Greek *hermēs* Hermes]

hermaphrodite (hɜːˈmæfrəˌdaɪt) *n.* **1.** *Biology.* an individual animal or flower that has both male and female reproductive organs. **2.** a person having both male and female sexual characteristics and genital tissues. **3.** a person or thing in which two opposite forces or qualities are combined. ~*adj.* **4.** having the characteristics of a hermaphrodite. [C15: from Latin *hermaphrodītus,* from Greek, after *Hermaphroditus,* a son of Hermes and the goddess Aphrodite who merged with the nymph Salmacis to form one body] —**herˌmaphroˈditic** *or* **herˌmaphroˈditical** *adj.* —**herˌmaphroˈditically** *adv.* —**herˈmaphroditˌism** *n.*

hermaphrodite brig *n.* a sailing vessel with two masts, rigged square on the foremast and fore-and-aft on the aftermast. Also called: **brigantine.**

hermeneutic (ˌhɜːmɪˈnjuːtɪk) *or* **hermeneutical** *adj.* **1.** of or relating to the interpretation of Scripture; using or relating to hermeneutics. **2.** interpretive. —ˌ**hermeˈneutically** *adv.* —ˌ**hermeˈneutist** *n.*

hermeneutics (ˌhɜːmɪˈnjuːtɪks) *n.* (*functioning as sing.*) **1.** the science of interpretation, esp. of Scripture. **2.** the branch of theology that deals with the principles and methodology of exegesis. **3.** *Philosophy.* **a.** the study and interpretation of human behaviour and social institutions. **b.** (in existentialist thought) discussion of the purpose of life. [C18: from Greek *hermēneutikos* expert in interpretation, from *hermēneuein* to interpret, from *hermēneus* interpreter, of uncertain origin]

hermetic (hɜːˈmɛtɪk) *or* **hermetical** *adj.* sealed so as to be airtight. [C17: from Medieval Latin *hermēticus* belonging to *Hermes Trismegistus,* (Greek, literally Hermes thrice-greatest), traditionally the inventor of a magic seal] —**herˈmetically** *adv.*

Hermetic (hɜːˈmɛtɪk) *adj.* **1.** of or relating to Hermes Trismegistus or the writings on mysticism and magic ascribed to him. **2.** of or relating to ancient science, esp. alchemy.

hermit (ˈhɜːmɪt) *n.* **1.** one of the early Christian recluses. **2.** any person living in solitude. [C13: from Old French *hermite,* from Late Latin *erēmīta,* from Greek *erēmitēs* living in the desert, from *erēmia* desert, from *erēmos* lonely] —**herˈmitic** *or* **herˈmitical** *adj.* —**herˈmitically** *adv.* —ˈ**hermit-ˌlike** *adj.*

hermitage (ˈhɜːmɪtɪdʒ) *n.* **1.** the abode of a hermit. **2.** any place where a person may live in seclusion; retreat.

Hermitage (ˈhɜːmɪtɪdʒ) *n.* a full-bodied red or white wine from the Rhône valley at Tain-l'Ermitage, in SE France.

hermit crab *n.* any small soft-bodied decapod crustacean of the genus *Pagurus* and related genera, living in and carrying about the empty shells of whelks or similar molluscs.

Hermitian conjugate (hɜːˈmɪtɪən) *n. Maths.* a matrix that is the transpose of the matrix of the complex conjugates of the entries of a given matrix. Also called: **adjoint.** [C19: named after Charles *Hermite* (1822–1901), French mathematician]

Hermitian matrix *n. Maths.* a matrix whose transpose is equal to the matrix of the complex conjugates of its entries. [C20: named after Charles *Hermite* (1822–1901), French mathematician]

hern (hɜːn) *n.* an archaic or dialect word for **heron.**

hernia (ˈhɜːnɪə) *n., pl.* **-nias** *or* **-niae** (-nɪˌiː). the projection of an organ or part through the lining of the cavity in which it is normally situated, esp. the protrusion of intestine through the front wall of the abdominal cavity. It is caused by muscular strain, injury, etc. Also called: **rupture.** [C14: from Latin] —ˈ**hernial** *adj.* —ˈ**herniˌated** *adj.*

herniorrhaphy (ˌhɜːnɪˈɒrəfɪ) *n., pl.* **-phies.** surgical repair of a hernia by means of a suturing operation.

hero (ˈhɪərəʊ) *n., pl.* **-roes. 1.** a man distinguished by exceptional courage, nobility, fortitude, etc. **2.** a man who is idealized for possessing superior qualities in any field. **3.** *Classical myth.* a being of extraordinary strength and courage, often the offspring of a mortal and a god, who is celebrated for his exploits. **4.** the principal male character in a novel, play, etc. [C14: from Latin *hērōs,* from Greek]

heroic (hɪˈrəʊɪk) *or* **heroical** *adj.* **1.** of, like, or befitting a hero. **2.** courageous but desperate. **3.** relating to or treating of heroes and their deeds. **4.** of, relating to, or resembling the heroes of classical mythology. **5.** (of language, manner, etc.) extravagant. **6.** *Prosody.* of, relating to, or resembling heroic verse. **7.** (of the arts, esp. sculpture) larger than life-size; smaller than colossal. ~See also **heroics.** —**heˈroically** *adv.* —**heˈroicalness** *or* **heˈroicness** *n.*

heroic age *n.* the period in an ancient culture, when legendary heroes are said to have lived.

heroic couplet *n. Prosody.* a verse form consisting of two rhyming lines in iambic pentameter.

heroics (hɪˈrəʊɪks) *pl. n.* **1.** *Prosody.* short for **heroic verse. 2.** extravagant or melodramatic language, behaviour, etc.

heroic stanza *n. Poetry.* a quatrain having the rhyme scheme a b a b.

heroic tenor *n.* a tenor with a dramatic voice.

heroic verse *n. Prosody.* a type of verse suitable for epic or heroic subjects, such as the classical hexameter, the French Alexandrine, or the English iambic pentameter.

heroin (ˈhɛrəʊɪn) *n.* a white odourless bitter-tasting crystalline powder derived from morphine: a highly addictive narcotic. Formula: $C_{17}H_{17}NO(C_2H_3O_2)_2$. Technical name: **diamorphine.** [C19: coined in German as a trademark, probably from HERO, referring to its aggrandizing effect on the personality]

heroine (ˈhɛrəʊɪn) *n.* **1.** a woman possessing heroic qualities. **2.** a woman idealized for possessing superior qualities. **3.** the main female character in a novel, play, film, etc.

heroism (ˈhɛrəʊˌɪzəm) *n.* the state or quality of being a hero.

heron (ˈhɛrən) *n.* any of various wading birds of the genera *Butorides, Ardea,* etc., having a long neck, slim body, and a plumage that is commonly grey or white: family *Ardeidae,* order *Ciconiiformes.* [C14: from Old French *hairon,* of Germanic origin; compare Old High German *heigaro,* Old Norse *hegri*]

heronry (ˈhɛrənrɪ) *n., pl.* **-ries.** a colony of breeding herons.

hero worship *n.* **1.** admiration for heroes or idealized persons. **2.** worship by the ancient Greeks and Romans of heroes. ~*vb.* **hero-worship, -ships, -shipping, -shipped** *or U.S.* **-ships, -shiping, -shiped. 3.** (*tr.*) to feel admiration or adulation for. —ˈ**hero-ˌworshipper** *n.*

herp., herpet., *or* **herpetol.** *abbrev. for* herpetology.

herpes (ˈhɜːpiːz) *n.* any of several inflammatory diseases of the skin, esp. herpes simplex, characterized by the formation of small watery blisters. See also **genital herpes.** [C17: via Latin from Greek: a creeping, from *herpein* to creep]

herpes labialis (ˌleɪbɪˈælɪs) *n.* a technical name for **cold sore.** [New Latin: herpes of the lip]

herpes simplex (ˈsɪmplɛks) *n.* an acute viral disease characterized by formation of clusters of watery blisters, esp. on the margins of the lips and nostrils or on the genitals. It can be sexually transmitted and may recur fitfully. [New Latin: simple herpes]

herpesvirus (ˈhɜːpiːzˌvaɪərəs) *n.* any one of a family of viruses that includes the agents causing herpes, the Epstein-Barr virus, and the cytomegalovirus.

herpes zoster (ˈzɒstə) *n.* a technical name for **shingles.** [New Latin: girdle herpes, from HERPES + Greek *zōstēr* girdle]

herpetic (hɜːˈpɛtɪk) *adj.* **1.** of or relating to any of the herpes diseases. ~*n.* **2.** a person suffering from any of the herpes diseases.

herpetology (ˌhɜːpɪˈtɒlədʒɪ) *n.* the study of reptiles and amphibians. [C19: from Greek *herpeton* creeping animal, from *herpein* to creep] —**herpetologic** (ˌhɜːpɪtəˈlɒdʒɪk) *or* ˌ**herpetoˈlogical** *adj.* —ˌ**herpetoˈlogically** *adv.* —ˌ**herpeˈtologist** *n.*

herptile (ˈhɜːpˌtaɪl) *adj. Chiefly U.S.* denoting, relating to, or characterizing both reptiles and amphibians. [from Greek *herp(eton)* (see HERPETOLOGY) + (REP)TILE]

Herr (*German* hɛr) *n., pl.* **Herren** (ˈhɛrən). a German man: used before a name as a title equivalent to *Mr.* [German, from Old High German *herro* lord]

Herrenvolk *German.* (ˈhɛrənfɔlk) *n.* See **master race.**

herring (ˈhɛrɪŋ) *n., pl.* **-rings** *or* **-ring.** any marine soft-finned teleost fish of the family *Clupeidae,* esp. *Clupea harengus,* an important food fish of northern seas, having an elongated body covered, except in the head region, with large fragile silvery scales. [Old English *hǣring;* related to Old High German *hāring,* Old Frisian *hēring,* Dutch *haring*]

herringbone (ˈhɛrɪŋˌbəʊn) *n.* **1. a.** a pattern used in textiles, brickwork, etc., consisting of two or more rows of short parallel strokes slanting in alternate directions to form a series of parallel Vs or zigzags. **b.** (*as modifier*): *a herringbone pattern.* **2.** *Skiing.* a method of ascending a slope by walking with the skis pointing outwards and one's weight on the inside edges. ~*vb.* **3.** to decorate (textiles, brickwork, etc.) with herringbone. **4.** (*intr.*) *Skiing.* to ascend a slope in herringbone fashion.

herringbone bond *n.* a type of bricklaying in which the bricks are laid on the slant to form a herringbone pattern.

herringbone gear *n.* a gearwheel having two sets of helical teeth, one set inclined at an acute angle to the other so that V-shaped teeth are formed. Also called: **double-helical gear.**

herring gull *n.* a common gull, *Larus argentatus,* that has a white plumage with black-tipped wings and pink legs.

hers (hɜːz) *pron.* **1.** something or someone belonging to or associated with her: *hers is the nicest dress; that cat is hers.* **2. of hers.** belonging to or associated with her. [C14 *hires;* see HER]

herself (həˈsɛlf) *pron.* **1. a.** the reflexive form of *she* or *her.* **b.** (intensifier): *the queen herself signed the letter.* **2.** (*preceded by a copula*) her normal or usual self: *she looks herself again after the operation.* **3.** *Irish and Scot.* the wife or woman of the house: *is herself at home?*

▷**Usage.** See at **myself.**

Herts (hɑːts) *abbrev. for* Hertfordshire.

hertz (hɜːts) *n., pl.* **hertz.** the derived SI unit of frequency; the frequency of a periodic phenomenon that has a periodic time of 1 second; 1 cycle per second. Symbol: Hz [C20: named after Heinrich Rudolph *Hertz* (1857–94), German physicist]

Hertzian wave (ˈhɜːtsɪən) *n.* an electromagnetic wave with a frequency in the range from about 3×10^{10} hertz to about 1.5×10^{5} hertz. [C19: named after H. R. *Hertz*]

Hertzsprung-Russell diagram (ˈhɜːtssprʌŋˈrʌsᵊl) *n.* a graph in which the spectral types of stars are plotted against their absolute magnitudes. Stars fall into different groupings in different parts of the graph. See also **main sequence.** [C20: named after Ejnar *Hertzsprung* (1873–1967), Danish astronomer and Henry N. *Russell* 1877–1957), U.S. astronomer]

he's (hiːz) *contraction of* he is *or* he has.

Heshvan (xɛʃˈvɑn) *n.* a variant spelling of **Cheshvan.**

hesitant (ˈhɛzɪtᵊnt) *adj.* wavering, hesitating, or irresolute. —**ˈhesitance** *or* **ˈhesitancy** *n.* —**ˈhesitantly** *adv.*

hesitate (ˈhɛzɪˌteɪt) *vb.* (*intr.*) **1.** to hold back or be slow in acting; be uncertain. **2.** to be unwilling or reluctant (to do something). **3.** to stammer or pause in speaking. [C17: from Latin *haesitāre,* from *haerēre* to cling to] —**ˈhesiˌtater** *or* **ˈhesiˌtator** *n.* —**ˈhesiˌtatingly** *adv.* —**ˌhesiˈtation** *n.* —**ˈhesiˌtative** *adj.*

Hesperian (hɛˈspɪərɪən) *adj.* **1.** *Poetic.* western. **2.** of or relating to the Hesperides, nymphs who guarded a garden of golden apples in the western Islands of the Blessed. ~*n.* **3.** a native or inhabitant of a western land. [from Latin *Hesperia* from Greek: land of the west, from *hesperos* western]

hesperidin (hɛˈspɛrɪdɪn) *n.* a glycoside extracted from orange peel or other citrus fruits and used to treat capillary fragility. [C19: from New Latin HESPERIDIUM + -IN]

hesperidium (ˌhɛspəˈrɪdɪəm) *n. Botany.* the fruit of citrus plants, in which the flesh consists of fluid-filled hairs and is protected by a tough rind. [C19: New Latin; alluding to the fruit in the garden of the *Hesperides*; see HESPERIAN]

Hesperus (ˈhɛspərəs) *n.* an evening star, esp. Venus. [from Latin, from Greek *Hesperos,* from *hesperos* western]

hessian (ˈhɛsɪən) *n.* a coarse jute fabric similar to sacking, used for bags, upholstery, etc. [C18: from *Hesse* (state in central Germany) + -IAN]

Hessian (ˈhɛsɪən) *n.* **1.** a native or inhabitant of Hesse in central Germany. **2. a.** a Hessian soldier in any of the mercenary units of the British Army in the War of American Independence or the Napoleonic Wars. **b.** *U.S.* any German mercenary in the British Army during the War of American Independence. **3.** *Chiefly U.S.* a mercenary or ruffian. ~*adj.* **4.** of or relating to Hesse or its inhabitants.

Hessian boots *pl. n.* men's high boots with tassels around the top, fashionable in England in the early 19th century.

Hessian fly *n.* a small dipterous fly, *Mayetiola destructor,* whose larvae damage wheat, barley, and rye: family *Cecidomyidae* (gall midges). [C18: so called because it was thought to have been introduced into America by Hessian soldiers]

hessite (ˈhɛsaɪt) *n.* a black or grey metallic mineral consisting of silver telluride in cubic crystalline form. Formula: Ag_2Te. [C19: from German *Hessit;* named after Henry *Hess,* 19th-century chemist of Swiss origin who worked in Russia; see -ITE[1]]

hessonite (ˈhɛsəˌnaɪt) *n.* an orange-brown variety of grossularite garnet. Also called: **essonite, cinnamon stone.** [C19: from French, from Greek *hēssōn* less, inferior + -ITE[1]; so called because it is less hard than genuine hyacinth]

hest (hɛst) *n.* an archaic word for **behest.** [Old English *hǣs;* related to *hātan* to promise, command]

Hesychast (ˈhɛsɪˌkæst) *n. Greek Orthodox Church.* a member of a school of mysticism developed by the monks of Mount Athos in the 14th century. [C18: from Medieval Latin *hesychasta* mystic, from Greek *hēsukhastēs,* from *hēsukhazein* to be tranquil, from *hēsukhos* quiet] —**ˌHesyˈchastic** *adj.*

het[1] (hɛt) *n. Slang.* short for **heterosexual.**

het[2] (hɛt) *vb.* **1.** *Archaic or dialect.* a past tense and past participle of **heat.** ~*adj.* **2.** a Scot. word for **hot.** ~See also **het up.**

hetaera (hɪˈtɪərə) *or* **hetaira** (hɪˈtaɪrə) *n., pl.* **-taerae** (-ˈtɪəriː) *or* **-tairai** (-ˈtaɪraɪ). (esp. in ancient Greece) a female prostitute, esp. an educated courtesan. [C19: from Greek *hetaira* concubine] —**heˈtaeric** *or* **heˈtairic** *adj.*

hetaerism (hɪˈtɪərɪzəm) *or* **hetairism** (hɪˈtaɪrɪzəm) *n.* **1.** the state of being a concubine. **2.** *Sociol., anthropol.* a social system attributed to some primitive societies, in which women are communally shared. —**heˈtaerist** *or* **heˈtairist** *n.* —**ˌhetaeˈristic** *or* **ˌhetaiˈristic** *adj.*

heterarchy (ˈhɛtərɑːkɪ) *n. Maths, linguistics.* a formal structure, usually represented by a diagram of connected nodes, without any single permanent uppermost node. Compare **hierarchy** (sense 5), **tree** (sense 6). [from Greek *heteros* other, different + *archē* sovereignty]

hetero (ˈhɛtərəʊ) *n., pl.* **-os.,** *adj. Informal.* short for **heterosexual.**

hetero- *combining form.* other, another, or different: *heterodyne; heterophony; heterosexual.* Compare **homo-.** [from Greek *heteros* other]

heteroblastic (ˌhɛtərəʊˈblæstɪk) *adj. Botany.* (of a plant or plant part) showing a marked difference in form between the juvenile and the adult structures. Compare **homoblastic.**

heterocercal (ˌhɛtərəʊˈsɜːkᵊl) *adj. Ichthyol.* of or possessing a tail in which the vertebral column turns upwards and extends into the upper, usually larger, lobe, as in sharks. Compare **homocercal.** [C19: from HETERO- + Greek *kerkos* tail]

heterochlamydeous (ˌhɛtərəʊkləˈmɪdɪəs) *adj.* (of a plant) having a perianth consisting of distinct sepals and petals. Compare **homochlamydeous.**

heterochromatic (ˌhɛtərəʊkrəʊˈmætɪk) *adj.* **1.** of or involving many different colours. **2.** *Physics.* consisting of or concerned with different frequencies or wavelengths. —**ˌheteroˈchromatism** *n.*

heterochromatin (ˌhɛtərəʊˈkrəʊmətɪn) *n.* the part of a chromosome that stains strongly with basic dyes in the interphase of cell division and has little genetic activity. Compare **euchromatin.**

heterochromosome (ˌhɛtərəʊˈkrəʊməˌsəʊm) *n.* an atypical chromosome, esp. a sex chromosome.

heterochromous (ˌhɛtərəʊˈkrəʊməs) *adj.* (esp. of plant parts) of different colours: *the heterochromous florets of a daisy flower.*

heteroclite (ˈhɛtərəˌklaɪt) *adj. also* **heteroclitic** (ˌhɛtərəˈklɪtɪk). **1.** (esp. of the form of a word) irregular or unusual. ~*n.* **2.** an irregularly formed word. [C16: from Late Latin *heteroclitus* declining irregularly, from Greek *heteroklitos,* from HETERO- + *klinein* to bend, inflect]

heterocyclic (ˌhɛtərəʊˈsaɪklɪk, -ˈsɪk-) *adj.* (of an organic compound) containing a closed ring of atoms, at least one of which is not a carbon atom. Compare **homocyclic.**

heterodactyl (ˌhɛtərəʊˈdæktɪl) *adj.* **1.** (of the feet of certain birds) having the first and second toes directed backwards and the third and fourth forwards. ~*n.* **2.** a bird with heterodactyl feet. ~Compare **zygodactyl.**

heterodont (ˈhɛtərəˌdɒnt) *adj.* (of most mammals) having teeth of different types. Compare **homodont.**

heterodox (ˈhɛtərəʊˌdɒks) *adj.* **1.** at variance with established, orthodox, or accepted doctrines or beliefs. **2.** holding unorthodox doctrines or opinions. [C17: from Greek *heterodoxos* holding another opinion, from HETERO- + *doxa* opinion] —**ˈheteroˌdoxy** *n.*

heterodyne (ˈhɛtərəʊˌdaɪn) *vb.* **1.** *Electronics.* to combine by intermodulation (two alternating signals, esp. radio signals) to produce two signals having frequencies corresponding to the sum and the difference of the original frequencies. See also **superheterodyne receiver.** ~*adj.* **2.** produced by, operating by, or involved in heterodyning two signals.

heteroecious (ˌhɛtəˈriːʃəs) *adj.* (of parasites, esp. rust fungi) undergoing different stages of the life cycle on different host species. Compare **autoecious.** [from HETERO- + *-oecious,* from Greek *oikia* house] —**ˌheterˈoecism** *n.*

heterogamete (ˌhɛtərəʊgæˈmiːt) *n.* a gamete that differs in size and form from the one with which it unites in fertilization. Compare **isogamete.**

heterogametic (ˌhɛtərəʊgəˈmɛtɪk) *adj. Genetics.* denoting the sex that possesses dissimilar sex chromosomes. In humans and many other mammals it is the male sex, possessing one X-chromosome and one Y-chromosome. Compare **homogametic.**

heterogamy (ˌhɛtəˈrɒgəmɪ) *n.* **1.** a type of sexual reproduction in which the gametes differ in both size and form. Compare **isogamy.** **2.** a condition in which different types of reproduction occur in successive generations of an organism. **3.** the presence of both male and female flowers in one inflorescence. Compare **homogamy** (sense 1). —**ˌheterˈogamous** *adj.*

heterogeneous (ˌhɛtərəʊˈdʒiːnɪəs) *adj.* **1.** composed of unrelated or differing parts or elements. **2.** not of the same kind or type. **3.** *Chem.* of, composed of, or concerned with two or more different phases. Compare **homogeneous.** [C17: from Medieval Latin *heterogeneus,* from Greek *heterogenēs,* from HETERO- +

genos sort] —**heterogeneity** (ˌhɛtərəʊdʒɪˈniːɪtɪ) *or* ˌ**hetero'geneousness** *n.* —ˌ**hetero'geneously** *adv.*

heterogenesis (ˌhɛtərəʊˈdʒɛnɪsɪs) *n.* another name for **alternation of generations** or **abiogenesis.** —**heterogenetic** (ˌhɛtərəʊdʒɪˈnɛtɪk) *or* ˌ**hetero'genic** *adj.* —ˌ**heteroge'netically** *adv.*

heterogenous (ˌhɛtəˈrɒdʒɪnəs) *adj. Biology, med.* not originating within the body; of foreign origin: *a heterogenous skin graft.* Compare **autogenous.**

heterogony (ˌhɛtəˈrɒgənɪ) *n.* **1.** *Biology.* the alternation of parthenogenetic and sexual generations in rotifers and similar animals. **2.** the condition in plants, such as the primrose, of having flowers that differ from each other in the length of their stamens and styles. Compare **homogony.** —ˌ**heter'ogonous** *adj.* —ˌ**heter'ogonously** *adv.*

heterograft (ˈhɛtərəʊˌgrɑːft) *n.* a tissue graft obtained from a donor of a different species from the recipient.

heterography (ˌhɛtəˈrɒgrəfɪ) *n.* **1.** the phenomenon of different letters or sequences of letters representing the same sound in different words, as for example *-ight* and *-ite* in *blight* and *bite.* **2.** any writing system in which this phenomenon occurs. —**heterographic** (ˌhɛtərəʊˈgræfɪk) *or* ˌ**hetero'graphical** *adj.*

heterogynous (ˌhɛtəˈrɒdʒɪnəs) *adj.* (of ants, bees, etc.) having two types of female, one fertile and the other infertile.

heterokaryon (ˌhɛtərəʊˈkærɪɒn) *n. Biology.* a fungal cell or mycelium containing two or more nuclei of different genetic constitution. [from HETERO- + *karyon,* from Greek *karuon* kernel]

heterolecithal (ˌhɛtərəʊˈlɛsɪθəl) *adj.* (of the eggs of birds) having an unequally distributed yolk. Compare **isolecithal.** [C19: HETERO- + Greek *lekithos* egg yolk]

heterologous (ˌhɛtəˈrɒləgəs) *adj.* **1.** *Pathol.* of, relating to, or designating cells or tissues not normally present in a particular part of the body. **2.** (esp. of parts of an organism or of different organisms) differing in structure or origin. —ˌ**heter'ology** *n.*

heterolysis (ˌhɛtəˈrɒlɪsɪs) *n.* **1.** the dissolution of the cells of one organism by the lysins of another. Compare **autolysis. 2.** Also called: **heterolytic fission.** *Chem.* the dissociation of a molecule into two ions with opposite charges. Compare **homolysis.** —**heterolytic** (ˌhɛtərəʊˈlɪtɪk) *adj.*

heteromerous (ˌhɛtəˈrɒmərəs) *adj. Biology.* having or consisting of parts that differ, esp. in number.

heteromorphic (ˌhɛtərəʊˈmɔːfɪk) *or* **heteromorphous** *adj. Biology.* **1.** differing from the normal form in size, shape, and function. **2.** (of pairs of homologous chromosomes) differing from each other in size or form. **3.** (esp. of insects) having different forms at different stages of the life cycle. —ˌ**hetero'morphism** *or* ˌ**hetero'morphy** *n.*

heteronomous (ˌhɛtəˈrɒnɪməs) *adj.* **1.** subject to an external law, rule, or authority. Compare **autonomous. 2.** (of the parts of an organism) differing in the manner of growth, development, or specialization. **3.** (in Kantian philosophy) directed to an end other than duty for its own sake. Compare **autonomous** (sense 4b). —ˌ**heter'onomously** *adv.* —ˌ**heter'onomy** *n.*

heteronym (ˈhɛtərəʊˌnɪm) *n.* one of two or more words pronounced differently but spelt alike: *the two English words spelt "bow" are heteronyms.* Compare **homograph.** [C17: from Late Greek *heteronumos,* from Greek HETERO- + *onoma* name] —**heteronymous** (ˌhɛtəˈrɒnɪməs) *adj.* —ˌ**heter'onymously** *adv.*

Heteroousian (ˌhɛtərəʊˈuːsɪən, -ˈaʊsɪən) *n.* **1.** a Christian who maintains that God the Father and God the Son are different in substance. ~*adj.* **2.** of or relating to this belief. [C17: from Late Greek *heteroousios,* from Greek HETERO- + *ousia* nature]

heterophony (ˌhɛtəˈrɒfənɪ) *n.* the simultaneous performance of different versions of the same melody by different voices or instruments.

heterophyllous (ˌhɛtərəʊˈfɪləs, ˌhɛtəˈrɒfɪləs) *adj.* (of plants such as arrowhead) having more than one type of leaf on the same plant. Also: **anisophyllous.** —ˈ**hetero**ˌ**phylly** *n.*

heterophyte (ˈhɛtərəʊˌfaɪt) *n.* any plant that lives as a parasite or saprophyte.

heteroplasty (ˈhɛtərəʊˌplæstɪ) *n., pl.* **-ties.** the surgical transplantation of tissue obtained from another person or animal. —ˌ**hetero'plastic** *adj.*

heteroploid (ˈhɛtərəʊˌplɔɪd) *adj.* **1.** of a chromosome number that is neither the haploid nor diploid number characteristic of the species. ~*n.* **2.** such a chromosome number.

heteropolar (ˌhɛtərəʊˈpəʊlə) *adj.* a less common word for **polar** (sense 5a). —**heteropolarity** (ˌhɛtərəʊpəʊˈlærɪtɪ) *n.*

heteropterous (ˌhɛtəˈrɒptərəs) *or* **heteropteran** *adj.* of, relating to, or belonging to the *Heteroptera,* a suborder of hemipterous insects, including bedbugs, water bugs, etc., in which the forewings are membranous but have leathery tips. Compare **homopterous.** [C19: from New Latin *Heteroptera,* from HETERO- + Greek *pteron* wing]

heteroscedastic (ˌhɛtərəʊskɪˈdæstɪk) *adj. Statistics.* **1.** (of several distributions) having different variances. **2.** (of a bivariate or multivariate distribution) not having any variable whose variance is the same for all values of the other or others. **3.** (of a random variable) having different variances for different values of the others in a multivariate distribution. ~Compare **homoscedastic.** [C20: from HETERO- + *scedastic,* from Greek *skedasis* a scattering, dispersion] —**heteroscedasticity** (ˌhɛtərəʊskɪdæsˈtɪsɪtɪ) *n.*

heterosexism (ˌhɛtərəʊˈsɛkˌsɪzəm) *n.* discrimination on the basis of sexual orientation, practised by heterosexuals against homosexuals. —ˌ**hetero'sexist** *adj., n.*

heterosexual (ˌhɛtərəʊˈsɛksjʊəl) *n.* **1.** a person who is sexually attracted to the opposite sex. ~*adj.* **2.** of or relating to heterosexuality. ~Compare **homosexual.**

heterosexuality (ˌhɛtərəʊˌsɛksjʊˈælɪtɪ) *n.* sexual attraction to or sexual relations with a person or persons of the opposite sex. Compare **homosexuality.**

heterosis (ˌhɛtəˈrəʊsɪs) *n. Biology.* another name for **hybrid vigour.** [C19: from Late Greek: alteration, from Greek *heteroioun* to alter, from *heteros* other, different]

heterosporous (ˌhɛtəˈrɒspərəs) *adj.* (of seed plants and some ferns) producing megaspores and microspores. Compare **homosporous.** —ˌ**heter'ospory** *n.*

heterostyly (ˈhɛtərəˌstaɪlɪ) *n.* the condition in certain plants, such as primroses, of having styles of different lengths, each type of style in flowers on different plants, which ensures cross-pollination. [C20: from Greek, from *heteros* different + *stylos* pillar] —ˌ**hetero'stylous** *adj.*

heterotaxis (ˌhɛtərəʊˈtæksɪs), **heterotaxy,** *or* **heterotaxia** *n.* an abnormal or asymmetrical arrangement of parts, as of the organs of the body or the constituents of a rock. —ˌ**hetero'tactic,** ˌ**hetero'tactous,** *or* ˌ**hetero'taxic** *adj.*

heterothallic (ˌhɛtərəʊˈθælɪk) *adj.* **1.** (of some algae and fungi) having male and female reproductive organs on different thalli. **2.** (of some fungi) having sexual reproduction that occurs only between two self-sterile mycelia. ~Compare **homothallic.** [C20: from HETERO- + Greek *thallos* green shoot, young twig] —ˌ**hetero'thallism** *n.*

heterotopia (ˌhɛtərəʊˈtəʊpɪə) *or* **heterotopy** (ˌhɛtəˈrɒtəpɪ) *n.* abnormal displacement of a bodily organ or part. [C19: from New Latin, from HETERO- + Greek *topos* place] —ˌ**hetero'topic** *or* ˌ**heter'otopous** *adj.*

heterotrophic (ˌhɛtərəʊˈtrɒfɪk) *adj.* (of animals and some plants) using complex organic compounds to manufacture their own organic constituents. Compare **autotrophic.** [C20: from HETERO- + Greek *trophikos* concerning food, from *trophē* nourishment] —ˈ**hetero**ˌ**troph** *n.*

heterotypic (ˌhɛtərəʊˈtɪpɪk) *or* **heterotypical** *adj.* denoting or relating to the first nuclear division of meiosis, in which the chromosome number is halved. Compare **homeotypic.**

heterozygote (ˌhɛtərəʊˈzaɪgəʊt, -ˈzɪgəʊt) *n.* an animal or plant that is heterozygous; a hybrid. Compare **homozygote.** —ˌ**heterozy'gosis** *n.*

heterozygous (ˌhɛtərəʊˈzaɪgəs) *adj. Genetics.* (of an organism) having dissimilar alleles for any one gene: *heterozygous for eye colour.* Compare **homozygous.**

heth *or* **cheth** (hɛt; *Hebrew* xɛt) *n.* the eighth letter of the Hebrew alphabet (ח), transliterated as *h* and pronounced as a pharyngeal fricative. [from Hebrew]

hetman (ˈhɛtmən) *n., pl.* **-mans.** another word for **ataman.** [C18: from Polish, from German *Hauptmann* headman]

het up *adj.* angry; excited: *don't get het up.*

heuchera (ˈhjuːkərə) *n.* any plant of the N. American genus *Heuchera,* with low-growing heart-shaped leaves and mostly red flowers carried in sprays on slender graceful stems: family *Saxifragaceae.* See also **alumroot.** [named after J. H. *Heucher* (1677–1747), German doctor and botanist]

heulandite (ˈhjuːlənˌdaɪt) *n.* a white, grey, red, or brown zeolite mineral that consists essentially of hydrated calcium aluminium silicate in the form of elongated tabular crystals. Formula: $Ca_2(Al_4Si_{14})O_{36}.12H_2O$. [C19: named after H. *Heuland,* 19th-century English mineral collector; see -ITE[1]]

heuristic (hjʊəˈrɪstɪk) *adj.* **1.** helping to learn; guiding in discovery or investigation. **2.** (of a method of teaching) allowing pupils to learn things for themselves. **3. a.** *Maths, science, philosophy.* using or obtained by exploration of possibilities rather than by following set rules. **b.** *Computer technol.* denoting a rule of thumb for solving a problem without the exhaustive application of an algorithm: *a heuristic solution.* ~*n.* **4.** (*pl.*) the science of heuristic procedure. [C19: from New Latin *heuristicus,* from Greek *heuriskein* to discover] —**heu'ristically** *adv.*

heuristics (hjʊəˈrɪstɪks) *n.* (*functioning as sing.*) *Maths, logic.* a method or set of rules for solving problems other than by algorithm. See also **algorithm** (sense 1), **artificial intelligence.**

hevea (ˈhiːvjə) *n.* any tree of the South American euphorbiaceous genus *Hevea,* having a milky sap which provides rubber: used esp. in electrical insulation. [C19: New Latin from native name *hevé*]

hew (hjuː) *vb.* **hews, hewing, hewed, hewed** *or* **hewn** (hjuːn). **1.** to strike (something, esp. wood) with cutting blows, as with an axe. **2.** (*tr.;* often foll. by *out*) to shape or carve from a substance. **3.** (*tr.;* often foll. by *away, down, from, off,* etc.) to sever from a larger or another portion. **4.** (*intr.;* often foll. by *to*) *U.S. and Canadian.* to conform (to a code, principle, etc.). [Old English *hēawan;* related to Old Norse *heggva,* Old Saxon *hāwa,* Old High German *houwan,* Latin *cūdere* to beat] —ˈ**hewer** *n.*

HEW (in the U.S.) *abbrev. for* Department of Health, Education, and Welfare.

hex[1] (hɛks) *n.* **a.** short for **hexadecimal notation** *or* **hexadecimal. b.** (*as modifier*): *hex code.*

hex[2] (hɛks) *U.S. and Canadian informal.* ~*vb.* **1.** (*tr.*) to bewitch. ~*n.* **2.** an evil spell or symbol of bad luck. **3.** a witch. [C19: via Pennsylvania Dutch from German *Hexe* witch, from Middle High German *hecse,* perhaps from Old High German *hagzissa;* see HAG[1]] —'**hexer** *n.*

hex. *abbrev. for:* **1.** hexachord. **2.** hexagon. **3.** hexagonal.

hexa- *or before a vowel* **hex-** *combining form.* six: *hexachord; hexameter.* [from Greek, from *hex* SIX]

hexachlorocyclohexane (ˌhɛksəˌklɔːrəˌsaɪkləʊ'hɛkseɪn) *n.* a white or yellowish powder existing in many isomeric forms. A mixture of isomers, including lindane, is used as an insecticide. Formula: $C_6H_6Cl_6$.

hexachloroethane (ˌhɛksəˌklɔːrəʊ'ɛθeɪn) *or* **hexachlorethane** *n.* a colourless crystalline insoluble compound with a camphor-like odour: used in pyrotechnics and explosives. Formula: C_2Cl_6.

hexachlorophene (ˌhɛksə'klɔːrəfiːn) *n.* an insoluble almost odourless white bactericidal substance used in antiseptic soaps, deodorants, etc. Formula: $(C_6HCl_3OH)_2CH_2$.

hexachord ('hɛksəˌkɔːd) *n.* (in medieval musical theory) any of three diatonic scales based upon C, F, and G, each consisting of six notes, from which solmization was developed.

hexacosanoic acid (ˌhɛksəkəʊsə'nəʊɪk) *n.* a white insoluble odourless wax present in beeswax, carnauba, and Chinese wax. Formula: $CH_3(CH_2)_{24}COOH$. Also called: **cerotic acid.**

hexad ('hɛksæd) *n.* **1.** a group or series of six. **2.** the number or sum of six. [C17: from Greek *hexas,* from *hex* six] —**hex'adic** *adj.*

hexadecane ('hɛksədɛˌkeɪn, ˌhɛksə'dɛkeɪn) *n.* the systematic name for **cetane.** [C19: from HEXA- + DECA- + -ANE]

hexadecanoic acid ('hɛksəˌdɛkənəʊɪk) *n.* the systematic name for **palmitic acid.**

hexadecimal notation *or* **hexadecimal** (ˌhɛksə'dɛsɪməl) *n.* a number system having a base 16; the symbols for the numbers 0–9 are the same as those used in the decimal system, and the numbers 10–15 are usually represented by the letters A–F. The system is used as a convenient way of representing the internal binary code of a computer.

hexaemeron (ˌhɛksə'ɛmərɒn) *or* **hexahemeron** *n.* **a.** the period of six days in which God created the world. **b.** the account of the Creation in Genesis 1. [C16: via Late Latin from Greek, from *hexaēmeros* (adj.) of six days, from HEXA- + *hēmera* day] —ˌ**hexa'emeric** *or* ˌ**hexa'hemeric** *adj.*

hexagon ('hɛksəgən) *n.* a polygon having six sides.

hexagonal (hɛk'sægənᵊl) *adj.* **1.** having six sides and six angles. **2.** of or relating to a hexagon. **3.** *Crystallog.* relating or belonging to the crystal system characterized by three equal coplanar axes inclined at 60° to each other and a fourth longer or shorter axis at right angles to their plane. See also **trigonal.** —**hex'agonally** *adv.*

hexagram ('hɛksəˌgræm) *n.* **1.** a star-shaped figure formed by extending the sides of a regular hexagon to meet at six points. **2.** a group of six broken or unbroken lines which may be combined into 64 different patterns, as used in the *I Ching,* an ancient Chinese book of divination. —ˌ**hexa'grammoid** *adj., n.*

hexahedron (ˌhɛksə'hiːdrən) *n.* a solid figure having six plane faces. A **regular hexahedron** (cube) has square faces. See also **polyhedron.** —ˌ**hexa'hedral** *adj.*

hexahydrate (ˌhɛksə'haɪdreɪt) *n.* a hydrate, such as magnesium chloride, $MgCl_2.6H_2O$, with six molecules of water per molecule of substance. —ˌ**hexa'hydrated** *adj.*

hexahydropiridine (ˌhɛksəhaɪdrəʊ'pɪrɪˌdiːn) *n.* the systematic name for **piperidine.**

hexahydropyrazine (ˌhɛksəhaɪdrəʊ'paɪrəˌziːn) *n.* the systematic name for **piperazine.**

hexamerous (hɛk'sæmərəs) *or* **hexameral** *adj.* (esp. of the parts of a plant) arranged in groups of six. —**hex'amerism** *n.*

hexameter (hɛk'sæmɪtə) *n. Prosody.* **1.** a verse line consisting of six metrical feet. **2.** (in Greek and Latin epic poetry) a verse line of six metrical feet, of which the first four are usually dactyls or spondees, the fifth almost always a dactyl, and the sixth a spondee or trochee. —**hexametric** (ˌhɛksə'mɛtrɪk), **hex'ametral,** *or* ˌ**hexa'metrical** *adj.*

hexamethylenetetramine (ˌhɛksəˌmɛθɪliːn'tɛtrəˌmiːn) *n.* a colourless crystalline organic compound used as a urinary antiseptic. Formula: $C_6H_{12}N_4$. Also called: **hexamine, methenamine.**

hexamine ('hɛksəmiːn) *n.* **1.** another name for **hexamethylenetetramine. 2.** a type of fuel produced in small solid blocks or tablets for use in miniature camping stoves.

hexane ('hɛkseɪn) *n.* a liquid alkane existing in five isomeric forms that are found in petroleum and used as solvents, esp. the isomer with a straight chain of carbon atoms (*n*-hexane). Formula: C_6H_{14}. [C19: from HEXA- + -ANE]

hexangular (hɛk'sæŋgjʊlə) *adj.* having six angles.

hexanoic acid (ˌhɛksə'nəʊɪk) *n.* an insoluble oily carboxylic acid found in coconut and palm oils and in milk. Formula: $C_5H_{11}COOH$. [C20: from HEXANE + *-oic*]

hexapla ('hɛksəplə) *n.* an edition of the Old Testament compiled by Origen, containing six versions of the text. [C17: from Greek *hexaploos* sixfold] —'**hexaplar, hexaplaric** (ˌhɛksə'plærɪk), *or* **hexaplarian** (ˌhɛksə'plɛərɪən) *adj.*

hexapod ('hɛksəˌpɒd) *n.* any arthropod of the class *Hexapoda* (or *Insecta);* an insect.

hexapody (hɛk'sæpədɪ) *n., pl.* **-dies.** *Prosody.* a verse measure consisting of six metrical feet. —**hexapodic** (ˌhɛksə'pɒdɪk) *adj.*

hexastich ('hɛksəˌstɪk) *or* **hexastichon** (hɛk'sæstɪˌkɒn) *n. Prosody.* a poem, stanza, or strophe that consists of six lines. —ˌ**hexa'stichic** *adj.*

hexastyle ('hɛksəˌstaɪl) *Architect.* ~*n.* **1.** a portico or façade with six columns. ~*adj.* **2.** having six columns.

Hexateuch ('hɛksəˌtjuːk) *n.* the first six books of the Old Testament. [C19: from HEXA- + Greek *teukhos* a book] —'**Hexaˌteuchal** *adj.*

hexavalent (ˌhɛksə'veɪlənt) *adj. Chem.* having a valency of six. Also: **sexivalent.**

hexone ('hɛksəʊn) *n.* another name for **methyl isobutyl ketone.**

hexosan ('hɛksəˌsæn) *n.* any of a group of polysaccharides that yield hexose on hydrolysis.

hexose ('hɛksəʊs, -əʊz) *n.* a monosaccharide, such as glucose, that contains six carbon atoms per molecule.

hexyl ('hɛksɪl) *n.* (*modifier*) of, consisting of, or containing the group of atoms C_6H_{13}, esp. the isomeric form of this group, $CH_3(CH_2)_4CH_2$-: *a hexyl group or radical.*

hexylresorcinol (ˌhɛksɪlrɪ'zɔːsɪˌnɒl) *n.* a yellowish-white crystalline phenol that has a fatty odour and sharp taste; 2,4- dihydroxy-1-hexylbenzene: used for treating bacterial infections of the urinary tract. Formula: $C_{12}H_{18}O_2$.

hey (heɪ) *interj.* **1.** an expression indicating surprise, dismay, discovery, etc., or calling for another's attention. **2. hey presto.** an exclamation used by conjurers to herald the climax of a trick. [C13: compare Old French *hay,* German *hei,* Swedish *hej*]

heyday ('heɪˌdeɪ) *n.* the time of most power, popularity, vigour, etc.; prime. [C16: probably based on HEY]

Heyduck ('haɪdʊk) *n.* a variant spelling of **Haiduk.**

hf *abbrev. for* half.

Hf *the chemical symbol for* hafnium.

HF *or* **h.f.** *abbrevs. for* high frequency.

hg *abbrev. for* hectogram.

Hg *the chemical symbol for* mercury. [from New Latin HYDRARGYRUM]

HG *abbrev. for:* **1.** High German. **2.** His (*or* Her) Grace. **3.** (in Britain) Home Guard.

HGH *abbrev. for* human growth hormone.

hgt *abbrev. for* height.

HGV (in Britain) *abbrev. for* heavy goods vehicle.

HH *abbrev. for* **1.** His (*or* Her) Highness. **2.** His Holiness (title of the Pope). ~**3.** (on Brit. pencils) *symbol for* double hard.

hhd *abbrev. for* hogshead.

H-hour *n. Military.* the specific hour at which any operation commences. Also called: **zero hour.**

hi[1] (haɪ) *sentence substitute.* an informal word for **hello.** [C20: originally U.S., from HIYA]

hi[2] (haɪ) *interj.* an expression used to attract attention. [C15: *hy;* compare HEY]

HI *abbrev. for:* **1.** Hawaii (state). **2.** Hawaiian Islands.

hiatus (haɪ'eɪtəs) *n., pl.* **-tuses** *or* **-tus. 1.** (esp. in manuscripts) a break or gap where something is missing. **2.** a break or interruption in continuity. **3.** a break between adjacent vowels in the pronunciation of a word. **4.** *Anatomy.* a natural opening or aperture; foramen. **5.** *Anatomy.* a less common word for **vulva.** [C16: from Latin: gap, cleft, aperture, from *hiāre* to gape, yawn] —**hi'atal** *adj.*

hiatus hernia *or* **hiatal hernia** *n.* protrusion of part of the stomach through the diaphragm at the oesophageal opening.

hibachi (hɪ'bɑːtʃɪ) *n.* a portable brazier for heating and cooking food. [from Japanese, from *hi* fire + *bachi* bowl]

hibakusha (hɪ'bɑːkʊʃə) *n., pl.* **-sha** or **-shas.** a survivor of either of the atomic-bomb attacks on Hiroshima and Nagasaki in 1945. [C20: from Japanese, from *hibaku* bombed + *-sha* -person]

hibernaculum (ˌhaɪbə'nækjʊləm) *or* **hibernacle** ('haɪbəˌnækᵊl) *n., pl.* **-ula** (-jʊlə) *or* **-les.** *Rare.* **1.** the winter quarters of a hibernating animal. **2.** the protective case or covering of a plant bud or animal. [C17: from Latin: winter residence; see HIBERNATE]

hibernal (haɪ'bɜːnᵊl) *adj.* of or occurring in winter. [C17: from Latin *hībernālis,* from *hiems* winter]

hibernate ('haɪbəˌneɪt) *vb.* (*intr.*) **1.** (of some mammals, reptiles, and amphibians) to pass the winter in a dormant condition with metabolism greatly slowed down. Compare **aestivate. 2.** to cease from activity. [C19: from Latin *hībernāre* to spend the winter, from *hībernus* of winter, from *hiems* winter] —ˌ**hiber'nation** *n.* —'**hiberˌnator** *n.*

Hibernian (haɪ'bɜːnɪən) *adj.* **1.** of, relating to, or characteristic of Ireland. ~*n.* **2.** a native or resident of Ireland. [from Latin *Hibernia* Ireland]

Hibernicism (haɪ'bɜːnɪˌsɪzəm) *or* **Hibernianism** (haɪ'bɜːnɪəˌnɪzəm) *n.* an Irish expression, idiom, trait, custom, etc.

hibiscus (haɪ'bɪskəs) *n., pl.* **-cuses.** any plant of the chiefly tropical and subtropical malvaceous genus *Hibiscus,* esp. *H. rosa-sinensis,* cultivated for its large brightly coloured flowers. [C18: from Latin, from Greek *hibiskos* marsh mallow]

hic (hɪk) *interj.* a representation of the sound of a hiccup.

hiccup ('hɪkʌp) *n.* **1.** a spasm of the diaphragm producing a sudden breathing in of air followed by a closing of the glottis, resulting in a characteristic sharp sound. Technical name: **singultus.** 2. the state or condition of having such spasms. 3. *Informal.* a minor difficulty or problem. ~*vb.* **-cups, -cuping, -cuped** *or* **-cups, -cupping, -cupped.** 4. (*intr.*) to make a hiccup or hiccups. 5. (*tr.*) to utter with a hiccup or hiccups. ~Also: **hiccough** ('hɪkʌp). [C16: of imitative origin]

hic jacet *Latin.* (hɪk 'jækɛt) (on gravestones) here lies.

hick (hɪk) *n. Informal, chiefly U.S. and Canadian.* **a.** a country person; bumpkin. **b.** (*as modifier*): *hick ideas.* [C16: after *Hick,* familiar form of *Richard*]

hickey ('hɪkɪ) *n. U.S. and Canadian informal.* 1. an object or gadget: used as a substitutive name when the correct name is unknown, forgotten, etc.; doodah. 2. a mark on the skin, esp. a lovebite. [C20: of unknown origin]

hickory ('hɪkərɪ) *n., pl.* **-ries.** 1. any juglandaceous tree of the chiefly North American genus *Carya,* having nuts with edible kernels and hard smooth shells. See also **pecan, pignut** (sense 1), **bitternut** (sense 1), **shagbark.** 2. the hard tough wood of any of these trees. 3. the nut of any of these trees. 4. a switch or cane made of hickory wood. [C17: from earlier *pohickery,* from Algonquian *pawcohiccora* food made from ground hickory nuts]

hid (hɪd) *vb.* the past tense and a past participle of **hide**[1].

hidalgo (hɪ'dælgəʊ; *Spanish* i'ðalyo) *n., pl.* **-gos** (-gəʊz; *Spanish* -yos). a member of the lower nobility in Spain. [C16: from Spanish, from Old Spanish *fijo dalgo* nobleman, from Latin *fīlius* son + *dē* of + *aliquid* something]

HIDB *abbrev. for* Highlands and Islands Development Board.

hidden ('hɪdᵊn) *vb.* 1. a past participle of **hide**[1]. ~*adj.* 2. concealed or obscured: *a hidden cave; a hidden meaning.* —'**hiddenly** *adv.* —'**hiddenness** *n.*

hiddenite ('hɪdəˌnaɪt) *n.* a green transparent variety of the mineral spodumene, used as a gemstone. [C19: named after W. E. *Hidden* (1853–1918), American mineralogist who discovered it]

hide[1] (haɪd) *vb.* **hides, hiding, hid** (hɪd), **hidden** ('hɪdᵊn) *or* **hid.** 1. to put or keep (oneself or an object) in a secret place; conceal (oneself or an object) from view or discovery: *to hide a pencil; to hide from the police.* 2. (*tr.*) to conceal or obscure: *the clouds hid the sun.* 3. (*tr.*) to keep secret. 4. (*tr.*) to turn (one's head, eyes, etc.) away. ~*n.* 5. *Brit.* a place of concealment, usually disguised to appear as part of the natural environment, used by hunters, birdwatchers, etc. U.S. and Canadian equivalent: **blind.** ~See also **hide-out.** [Old English *hȳdan;* related to Old Frisian *hēda,* Middle Low German *hüden,* Greek *keuthein*] —'**hidable** *adj.* —'**hider** *n.*

hide[2] (haɪd) *n.* 1. the skin of an animal, esp. the tough thick skin of a large mammal, either tanned or raw. 2. *Informal.* the human skin. 3. *Austral. and N.Z. informal.* impudence: *he had the hide to accuse me.* ~*vb.* **hides, hiding, hided.** 4. (*tr.*) *Informal.* to flog. [Old English *hȳd;* related to Old Norse *hūth,* Old Frisian *hēd,* Old High German *hūt,* Latin *cutis* skin, Greek *kutos;* see CUTICLE] —'**hideless** *adj.*

hide[3] (haɪd) *n.* an obsolete Brit. unit of land measure, varying in magnitude from about 60 to 120 acres. [Old English *hīgid;* related to *hīw* family, household, Latin *cīvis* citizen]

hide-and-seek *or U.S. and Canadian* **hide-and-go-seek** *n.* a game in which one player covers his eyes and waits while the others hide, and then he tries to find them.

hideaway ('haɪdəˌweɪ) *n.* a hiding place or secluded spot.

hidebound ('haɪdˌbaʊnd) *adj.* 1. restricted by petty rules, a conservative attitude, etc. 2. (of cattle, etc.) having the skin closely attached to the flesh as a result of poor feeding. 3. (of trees) having a very tight bark that impairs growth.

hideous ('hɪdɪəs) *adj.* 1. extremely ugly; repulsive: *a hideous person.* 2. terrifying and horrific. [C13: from Old French *hisdos,* from *hisde* fear; of uncertain origin] —'**hideously** *adv.* —'**hideousness** *or* **hideosity** (ˌhɪdɪ'ɒsɪtɪ) *n.*

hide-out *n.* 1. a hiding place, esp. a remote place used by outlaws, etc.; hideaway. ~*vb.* **hide out.** (*intr.*) 2. to remain deliberately concealed, esp. for a prolonged period of time.

hiding[1] ('haɪdɪŋ) *n.* 1. the state of concealment (esp. in the phrase **in hiding**). 2. **hiding place.** a place of concealment.

hiding[2] ('haɪdɪŋ) *n.* 1. *Informal.* a flogging; beating. 2. **be on a hiding to nothing.** to be bound to fail; to face impossible odds.

hidrosis (hɪ'drəʊsɪs) *n.* 1. a technical word for **perspiration** or **sweat.** 2. any skin disease affecting the sweat glands. 3. Also called: **hyperhidrosis** (ˌhaɪpəhɪ'drəʊsɪs, -haɪ'drəʊsɪs). *Pathol.* excessive perspiration. [C18: via New Latin from Greek: sweating, from *hidrōs* sweat] —**hidrotic** (hɪ'drɒtɪk) *adj.*

hidy-hole *or* **hidey-hole** ('haɪdɪˌhəʊl) *n. Informal.* a hiding place.

hie (haɪ) *vb.* **hies, hieing** *or* **hying, hied.** *Archaic or poetic.* to hurry; hasten; speed. [Old English *hīgian* to strive]

hieland ('hi:lənd) *adj. Scot. dialect.* 1. a variant of **Highland.** 2. characteristic of Highlanders, esp. alluding to their supposed gullibility or foolishness in towns or cities.

hiemal ('haɪəməl) *adj.* a less common word for **hibernal.** [C16: from Latin *hiems* winter; see HIBERNATE]

hieracosphinx (ˌhaɪə'reɪkəʊˌsfɪŋks) *n., pl.* **-sphinxes** *or* **-sphinges** (-ˌsfɪndʒi:z). (in ancient Egyptian art) a hawk-headed sphinx. [C18: from Greek *hierax* hawk + SPHINX]

hierarch ('haɪəˌrɑ:k) *n.* 1. **a.** a person in a position of high priestly authority. **b.** a person holding high rank in a religious hierarchy. 2. a person at a high level in a hierarchy. —ˌ**hier'archal** *adj.*

hierarchy ('haɪəˌrɑ:kɪ) *n., pl.* **-chies.** 1. a system of persons or things arranged in a graded order. 2. a body of persons in holy orders organized into graded ranks. 3. the collective body of those so organized. 4. a series of ordered groupings within a system, such as the arrangement of plants and animals into classes, orders, families, etc. 5. *Linguistics, etc.* a formal structure, usually represented by a diagram of connected nodes, with a single uppermost element. Compare **ordering, heterarchy, tree** (sense 6). 6. government by an organized priesthood. [C14: from Medieval Latin *hierarchia,* from Late Greek *hierarkhia,* from *hierarkhēs* high priest; see HIERO-, -ARCHY] —ˌ**hier'archical** *or* ˌ**hier'archic** *adj.* —ˌ**hier'archically** *adv.* —'**hierˌarchism** *n.*

hieratic (ˌhaɪə'rætɪk) *adj. also* **hieratical.** 1. of or relating to priests. 2. of or relating to a cursive form of hieroglyphics used by priests in ancient Egypt. 3. of or relating to styles in art that adhere to certain fixed types or methods, as in ancient Egypt. ~*n.* 4. the hieratic script of ancient Egypt. [C17: from Latin *hierāticus,* from Greek *hieratikos,* from *hiereus* a priest, from *hieros* holy] —ˌ**hier'atically** *adv.*

hiero- *or before a vowel* **hier-** *combining form.* holy or divine: *hierocracy; hierarchy.* [from Greek, from *hieros*]

hierocracy (ˌhaɪə'rɒkrəsɪ) *n., pl.* **-cies.** government by priests or ecclesiastics. —**hierocratic** (ˌhaɪərə'krætɪk) *or* ˌ**hiero'cratical** *adj.*

hierodule ('haɪərəˌdju:l) *n.* (in ancient Greece) a temple slave, esp. a sacral prostitute. [C19: from Greek *hierodoulos,* from HIERO- + *doulos* slave] —ˌ**hiero'dulic** *adj.*

hieroglyphic (ˌhaɪərə'glɪfɪk) *adj. also* **hieroglyphical.** 1. of or relating to a form of writing using picture symbols, esp. as used in ancient Egypt. 2. written with hieroglyphic symbols. 3. difficult to read or decipher. ~*n. also* **hieroglyph.** 4. a picture or symbol representing an object, concept, or sound. 5. a symbol or picture that is difficult to read or decipher. [C16: from Late Latin *hieroglyphicus,* from Greek *hierogluphikos,* from HIERO- + *gluphē* carving, from *gluphein* to carve] —ˌ**hiero'glyphically** *adv.* —**hieroglyphist** (ˌhaɪərə'glɪfɪst, ˌhaɪə'rɒg-) *n.*

hieroglyphics (ˌhaɪərə'glɪfɪks) *n.* (*functioning as sing. or pl.*) 1. a form of writing, esp. as used in ancient Egypt, in which pictures or symbols are used to represent objects, concepts, or sounds. 2. difficult or undecipherable writing.

hierogram ('haɪərəˌgræm) *n.* a sacred symbol.

hierology (ˌhaɪə'rɒlədʒɪ) *n., pl.* **-gies.** 1. sacred literature. 2. a biography of a saint. —**hierologic** (ˌhaɪərə'lɒdʒɪk) *or* ˌ**hiero'logical** *adj.* —ˌ**hier'ologist** *n.*

hierophant ('haɪərəˌfænt) *n.* 1. (in ancient Greece) an official high priest of religious mysteries, esp. those of Eleusis near Athens. 2. a person who interprets and explains esoteric mysteries. [C17: from Late Latin *hierophanta,* from Greek *hierophantēs,* from HIERO- + *phainein* to reveal] —ˌ**hiero'phantic** *adj.* —ˌ**hiero'phantically** *adv.*

hifalutin (ˌhaɪfə'lu:tɪn) *adj.* a variant spelling of **highfalutin.**

hi-fi ('haɪ'faɪ) *n. Informal.* 1. **a.** short for **high fidelity.** **b.** (*as modifier*): *hi-fi equipment.* 2. a set of high-quality sound-reproducing equipment.

higgle ('hɪgᵊl) *vb.* a less common word for **haggle.** —'**higgler** *n.*

higgledy-piggledy ('hɪgᵊldɪ'pɪgᵊldɪ) *Informal.* ~*adj., adv.* 1. in a jumble. ~*n.* 2. a muddle.

high (haɪ) *adj.* 1. being a relatively great distance from top to bottom; tall: *a high building.* 2. situated at or extending to a relatively great distance above the ground or above sea level: *a high plateau.* 3. **a.** (*postpositive*) being a specified distance from top to bottom: *three feet high.* **b.** (*in combination*): *a seven-foot-high wall.* 4. extending from an elevation: *a high dive.* 5. (*in combination*) coming up to a specified level: *knee-high.* 6. being at its peak or point of culmination: *high noon.* 7. of greater than average height: *a high collar.* 8. greater than normal in degree, intensity, or amount: *high prices; a high temperature; a high wind.* 9. of large or relatively large numerical value: *high frequency; high voltage; high mileage.* 10. (of sound) acute in pitch; having a high frequency. 11. (of latitudes) situated relatively far north or south from the equator. 12. (of meat) slightly decomposed or tainted, regarded as enhancing the flavour of game. 13. of great eminence; very important: *the high priestess.* 14. exalted in style or character; elevated: *high drama.* 15. expressing or feeling contempt or arrogance: *high words.* 16. elated; cheerful: *high spirits.* 17. (*predicative*) *Informal.* over-excited: *by the end of term the children are really high.* 18. *Informal.* being in a state of altered consciousness, characterized esp. by euphoria and often induced by the use of alcohol, narcotics, etc. 19. luxurious or extravagant: *high life.* 20. advanced in complexity or development: *high finance.* 21. (of a gear) providing a relatively great forward speed for a given engine speed. Compare **low**[1] (sense 21). 22. *Phonetics.* of, relating to, or denoting a vowel whose articulation is produced by raising the back of the tongue towards the soft palate or the blade towards the hard palate, such as for the *ee* in English *see* or *oo* in English *moon.* Compare **low**[1] (sense 20). 23. (*cap. when part of name*) formal and elaborate in style: *High Mass.* 24. (*usually cap.*) of or relating to the High Church. 25. remote, esp. in time. 26. *Cards.* **a.** having a relatively great value in a suit. **b.** able to win a trick. **27. high and dry.** stranded; helpless; destitute. **28. high and low.** in all places; everywhere. **29. high and mighty.** *Informal.* arrogant. **30. high as a kite.** *Informal.* **a.** very drunk. **b.** overexcited. **c.** euphoric from drugs. **31. high opinion.** a favourable opinion. ~*adv.* **32.** at or to a height: *he jumped high.* **33.** in a high manner. **34.** *Nautical.* close to the wind with sails full. ~*n.* **35.** a high place or level. **36.** *Informal.* a state of altered consciousness, often induced by alcohol, narcotics, etc. **37.** another word for **anticyclone. 38.** short for **high school. 39.** (*cap*) (esp. in Oxford) the High Street. **40.** *Electronics.* the voltage level in a logic circuit corresponding to logical one. Compare **low** (sense 30). **41. on high. a.** at a height. **b.** in heaven. [Old English *hēah;* related to Old Norse *hār,* Gothic *hauhs,* Old High German *hōh* high, Lithuanian *kaʼkas* bump, Russian *kúchča* heap, Sanskrit *kuča* bosom]

high altar *n.* the principal altar of a church.

highball (ˈhaɪˌbɔːl) *Chiefly U.S.* ~*n.* **1.** a long iced drink consisting of a spirit base with water, soda water, etc. **2.** (originally in railway use) a signal that the way ahead is clear and one may proceed. ~*vb.* **3.** (*intr.*) to move at great speed. **4.** (*tr.*) to drive (a vehicle) at great speed. [C19: (in sense 2) from the early railway signal consisting of a ball hoisted to the top of a pole]

highbinder (ˈhaɪˌbaɪndə) *n. U.S. informal.* **1.** a gangster. **2.** a corrupt politician. **3.** (formerly) a member of a Chinese-American secret society that engaged in blackmail, murder, etc. [C19: named after the *High-binders,* a New York city gang]

highborn (ˈhaɪˌbɔːn) *adj.* of noble or aristocratic birth.

highboy (ˈhaɪˌbɔɪ) *n. U.S. and Canadian.* a tall chest of drawers in two sections, the lower section being a lowboy. Brit. equivalent: **tallboy.**

high brass *n.* brass containing 65 per cent copper and 35 per cent zinc, used for most applications.

highbrow (ˈhaɪˌbraʊ) *Often disparaging.* ~*n.* **1.** a person of scholarly and erudite tastes. ~*adj. also* **highbrowed. 2.** appealing to highbrows: *highbrow literature.*

high camp *n.* a sophisticated form of **camp**[2] (the style).

high-carbon steel *n.* steel containing between 0.5 and 1.5 per cent carbon.

highchair (ˈhaɪˌtʃɛə) *n.* a long-legged chair for a child, esp. one with a table-like tray used at meal times.

High Church *n.* **1.** the party or movement within the Church of England stressing continuity with Catholic Christendom, the authority of bishops, and the importance of sacraments, rituals, and ceremonies. Compare **Broad Church, Low Church.** ~*adj.* **High-Church. 2.** of or relating to this party or movement. —ˈ**High-ˈChurchman** *n.*

high-class *adj.* **1.** of very good quality; superior: *a high-class grocer.* **2.** belonging to, associated with, or exhibiting the characteristics of an upper social class: *a high-class lady; a high-class prostitute.*

high-coloured *adj.* (of the complexion) deep red or purplish; florid.

high comedy *n.* comedy set largely among cultured and articulate people and featuring witty dialogue. Compare **low comedy.** —**high comedian** *n.*

high command *n.* the commander-in-chief and senior officers of a nation's armed forces.

high commissioner *n.* **1.** the senior diplomatic representative sent by one Commonwealth country to another instead of an ambassador. **2.** the head of an international commission. **3.** the chief officer in a colony or other dependency.

high country *n.* (often preceded by *the*) sheep pastures in the foothills of the Southern Alps, New Zealand.

High Court *n.* **1.** (in England and Wales) the High Court of Justice, one of the two divisions of the Supreme Court of Judicature. See also **Court of Appeal. 2.** (in Scotland) the High Court of Justiciary, the senior criminal court in Scotland, to which all cases of murder and rape and all cases involving heavy penalties are referred.

high day *n.* a day of celebration; festival (esp. in the phrase **high days and holidays**).

high definition television *n.* a television system offering a picture with superior definition, using 1000 or more scanning lines, and possibly a higher field repetition rate to reduce flicker effects. Abbrev.: **HDTV.**

high-energy physics *n.* another name for **particle physics.**

higher (ˈhaɪə) *adj.* **1.** the comparative of **high.** ~*n.* (*usually cap.*) (in Scotland) **2. a.** the advanced level of the Scottish Certificate of Education. **b.** (*as modifier*): *Higher Latin.* **3.** a pass in a particular subject at Higher level: *she has four Highers.*

higher criticism *n.* the use of scientific techniques of literary criticism to establish the sources of the books of the Bible. Compare **lower criticism.**

higher education *n.* education and training at colleges, universities, polytechnics, etc.

higher mathematics *n.* (*functioning as sing.*) mathematics, including number theory and topology, that is more abstract than normal arithmetic, algebra, geometry, and trigonometry.

higher-up *n. Informal.* a person of higher rank or in a superior position.

highest common factor *n.* the largest number or quantity that is a factor of each member of a group of numbers or quantities. Abbrev.: **HCF, h.c.f.** Also called: **greatest common divisor.**

high explosive *n.* an extremely powerful chemical explosive, such as TNT or gelignite.

highfalutin, hifalutin (ˌhaɪfəˈluːtɪn), *or* **highfaluting** *adj. Informal.* pompous or pretentious. [C19: from HIGH + *-falutin,* perhaps variant of *fluting,* from FLUTE]

high fashion *n.* another name for **haute couture.**

high fidelity *n.* **a.** the reproduction of sound using electronic equipment that gives faithful reproduction with little or no distortion. **b.** (*as modifier*): *a high-fidelity amplifier.* ~Often shortened to **hi-fi.**

high-five *n. Slang.* a gesture of greeting or congratulation in which two people slap raised right palms together.

high-flier *or* **high-flyer** *n.* **1.** a person who is extreme in aims, ambition, etc. **2.** a person of great ability, esp. in a career. —ˌ**high-ˈflying** *adj., n.*

high-flown *adj.* extravagant or pretentious in conception or intention: *high-flown ideas.*

high frequency *n.* a radio-frequency band or radio frequency lying between 30 and 3 megahertz. Abbrev.: **HF.**

High German *n.* **1.** the standard German language, historically developed from the form of West Germanic spoken in S Germany. Abbrev.: **HG.** See also **German, Low German. 2.** any of the German dialects of S Germany, Austria, or Switzerland.

high-handed *adj.* tactlessly overbearing and inconsiderate. —ˌ**high-ˈhandedly** *adv.* —ˌ**high-ˈhandedness** *n.*

high hat *n.* another name for **top hat.**

high-hat *adj.* **1.** *Informal.* snobbish and arrogant. ~*vb.* **-hats, -hatting, -hatted.** (*tr.*) **2.** *Informal, chiefly U.S. and Canadian.* to treat in a snobbish or offhand way. ~*n.* **3.** *Informal.* a snobbish person. **4.** two facing brass cymbals triggered by means of a foot pedal.

High Holidays *pl. n. Judaism.* the festivals of Rosh Hashanah and Yom Kippur, the period of repentance in the first ten days of the Jewish new year. Also called: **Days of Awe, Yamim Nora'im.**

high hurdles *n.* (*functioning as sing.*) a race in which competitors leap over hurdles 42 inches (107 cm) high.

highjack (ˈhaɪˌdʒæk) *vb., n.* a less common spelling of **hijack.** —ˈ**highˌjacker** *n.*

high jinks *or* **hijinks** (ˈhaɪˌdʒɪŋks) *n.* lively enjoyment.

high jump *n.* **1. a.** (usually preceded by *the*) an athletic event in which a competitor has to jump over a high bar set between two vertical supports. **b.** (*as modifier*): *high-jump techniques.* **2. be for the high jump.** *Brit. informal.* to be liable to receive a severe reprimand or punishment. —**high jumper** *n.* —**high jumping** *n.*

high-key *adj.* (of a photograph, painting, etc.) having a predominance of light grey tones or light colours. Compare **low-key** (sense 3).

high-keyed *adj.* **1.** having a high pitch; shrill. **2.** *U.S.* highly strung. **3.** bright in colour.

highland (ˈhaɪlənd) *n.* **1.** relatively high ground. **2.** (*modifier*) of or relating to a highland. —ˈ**highlander** *n.*

Highland (ˈhaɪlənd) *n.* (*modifier*) of, relating to, or denoting the Highlands of NW Scotland.

Highland cattle *n.* a breed of cattle with shaggy hair, usually reddish-brown in colour, and long horns.

Highland dress *n.* **1.** the historical costume, including the plaid, kilt or filibeg, and bonnet, as worn by Highland clansmen and soldiers. **2.** a modern version of this worn for formal occasions.

Highlander (ˈhaɪləndə) *n.* **1.** a native of the Highlands of Scotland. **2.** a member of a Scottish Highland regiment.

Highland fling *n.* a vigorous Scottish solo dance.

Highland Games *n.* (*functioning as sing. or pl.*) a meeting in which competitions in sport, piping, and dancing are held: originating in the Highlands of Scotland.

high-level *adj.* (of conferences, talks, etc.) involving very important people.

high-level language *n.* a computer programming language, such as Basic or Pascal, that is closer to human language or mathematical notation than to machine language. Compare **low-level language.**

high-level waste *n.* radioactive waste material, such as spent nuclear fuel, having a high activity and thus needing constant cooling for several decades by its producers before it can be disposed of. Compare **intermediate-level waste, low-level waste.**

highlife (ˈhaɪˌlaɪf) *n.* **a.** a style of music combining West African elements with U.S. jazz forms, found esp. in the cities of West Africa. **b.** (*as modifier*): *a highlife band.*

highlight (ˈhaɪˌlaɪt) *n.* **1.** an area of the lightest tone in a painting, drawing, photograph, etc. **2.** the most exciting or memorable part of an event or period of time. **3.** (*often pl.*) a bleached blond streak in the hair. ~*vb.* (*tr.*) **4.** *Painting, drawing, photog., etc.* to mark (any brightly illuminated or prominent part of a form or figure) with light tone. **5.** to bring notice or emphasis to. **6.** to be the highlight of. **7.** to produce blond streaks in (the hair) by bleaching.

highly (ˈhaɪlɪ) *adv.* **1.** (intensifier): *highly pleased; highly disappointed.* **2.** with great approbation or favour: *we spoke highly of it.* **3.** in a high position: *placed highly in class.* **4.** at or for a high price or cost.

highly strung *or U.S. and Canadian* **high-strung** *adj.* tense and easily upset; excitable; nervous.
High Mass *n.* a solemn and elaborate sung Mass. Compare **Low Mass.**
high-minded *adj.* **1.** having or characterized by high moral principles. **2.** *Archaic.* arrogant; haughty. —ˌ**high-ˈmindedly** *adv.* —ˌ**high-ˈmindedness** *n.*
high-muck-a-muck *n.* a conceited or haughty person. [C19: from Chinook Jargon *hiu muckamuck,* literally: plenty (of) food]
highness (ˈhaɪnɪs) *n.* the condition of being high or lofty.
Highness (ˈhaɪnɪs) *n.* (preceded by *Your, His,* or *Her*) a title used to address or refer to a royal person.
high-octane *adj.* (of petrol) having a high octane number.
high-pass filter *n. Electronics.* a filter that transmits all frequencies above a specified value, substantially attenuating frequencies below this value. Compare **low-pass filter, band-pass filter.**
high-pitched *adj.* **1.** pitched high in volume or tone. See **high** (sense 10). **2.** (of a roof) having steeply sloping sides. **3.** (of an argument, style, etc.) lofty or intense.
high place *n. Old Testament.* a place of idolatrous worship, esp. a hilltop.
high places *pl. n.* positions and offices of influence and importance: *a scandal in high places.*
high point *n.* a moment or occasion of great intensity, interest, happiness, etc.: *the award marked a high point in his life.*
high-powered *adj.* **1.** (of an optical instrument or lens) having a high magnification: *a high-powered telescope.* **2.** dynamic and energetic; highly capable. **3.** possessing great strength, power, etc.: *a high-powered engine.*
high-pressure *adj.* **1.** having, using, involving, or designed to withstand a pressure above normal pressure: *a high-pressure gas; a high-pressure cylinder.* **2.** *Informal.* (of selling) persuasive in an aggressive and persistent manner.
high priest *n.* **1.** *Judaism.* the priest of highest rank who alone was permitted to enter the holy of holies of the tabernacle and Temple. **2.** *Mormon Church.* a priest of the order of Melchizedek priesthood. **3.** Also (*fem.*) **high priestess.** the head of a group or cult. —**high priesthood** *n.*
high profile *n.* **a.** a position or approach characterized by a deliberate seeking of prominence or publicity. **b.** (*as modifier*): *a high-profile campaign.* ~Compare **low profile.**
high relief *n.* relief in which forms and figures stand out from the background to half or more than half of their natural depth. Also called: **alto-relievo.**
High Renaissance *n.* (*modifier*) denoting or relating to the period from about the 1490s to the 1520s in painting, sculpture, and architecture in Europe, esp. in Italy, when the Renaissance ideals were considered to have been attained: *High Renaissance art.*
high-rise *adj.* **a.** (*prenominal*) of or relating to a building that has many storeys, esp. one used for flats or offices: *a high-rise block.* Compare **low-rise. b.** (*as n.*): *a high-rise in Atlanta.*
high-risk *adj.* denoting a group, part, etc., that is particularly subject or exposed to a danger.
highroad (ˈhaɪˌrəʊd) *n.* **1.** a main road; highway. **2.** (usually preceded by *the*) the sure way: *the highroad to fame.*
high roller *n. Slang, chiefly U.S. and Canadian.* a person who spends money extravagantly or gambles recklessly. —**high rolling** *n., adj.*
high school *n.* **1.** *Brit.* another term for **grammar school. 2.** *U.S. and N.Z.* a secondary school from grade 7 to grade 12. **3.** *Canadian.* a secondary school, the grades covered depending on the province.
high seas *pl. n.* (*sometimes sing.*) the open seas of the world, outside the jurisdiction of any one nation.
high season *n.* the most popular time of year at a holiday resort, etc.
high society *n.* **a.** the upper classes, esp. when fashionable. **b.** (*as modifier*): *her high-society image.*
high-sounding *adj.* another term for **high-flown.**
high-speed *adj. Photog.* **1.** employing or requiring a very short exposure time: *high-speed film.* **2.** recording or making exposures at a rate usually exceeding 50 and up to several million frames per second. **3.** working, moving, or operating at a high speed.
high-speed steel *n.* any of various steels that retain their hardness at high temperatures and are thus suitable for making tools used on lathes and other high-speed machines.
high-spirited *adj.* vivacious, bold, or lively. —ˌ**high-ˈspiritedly** *adv.* —ˌ**high-ˈspiritedness** *n.*
high spot *n. Informal.* another word for **highlight** (sense 2).
high-stepper *n.* a horse trained to lift its feet high off the ground when walking or trotting.
High Street (*often not caps.*) *n.* (usually preceded by *the*) **1.** *Brit.* the main street of a town, usually where the principal shops are situated. **2.** the market constituted by the general public. **3.** (*modifier*) geared to meet the requirements of, and readily available for purchase by, the general public: *High-Street fashion.*
hight (haɪt) *vb.* (*tr.; used only as a past tense in the passive or as a past participle*) *Archaic and poetic.* to name; call: *a maid hight Mary.* [Old English *heht,* from *hatan* to call; related to Old Norse *heita,* Old Frisian *hēta,* Old High German *heizzan*]
high table *n.* (*sometimes caps.*) the table, sometimes elevated, in the dining hall of a school, college, etc., at which the principal teachers, fellows, etc., sit.
hightail (ˈhaɪˌteɪl) *vb.* (*intr.*) *Informal, chiefly U.S. and Canadian.* to go or move in a great hurry. Also: **hightail it.**
high tea *n. Brit.* See **tea** (sense 4c).
high tech (tɛk) *n.* a variant spelling of **hi tech.**
high technology *n.* highly sophisticated, often electronic, techniques used in manufacturing and other processes.
high-tension *n.* (*modifier*) subjected to, carrying, or capable of operating at a relatively high voltage: *a high-tension wire.* Abbrev.: **HT.**
high tide *n.* **1. a.** the tide at its highest level. **b.** the time at which it reaches this. **2.** a culminating point.
high time *Informal.* ~*adv.* **1.** the latest possible time; a time that is almost too late: *it's high time you mended this shelf.* ~*n.* **2.** Also called: **high old time.** an enjoyable and exciting time.
high-toned *adj.* **1.** having a superior social, moral, or intellectual quality. **2.** affectedly superior. **3.** high in tone.
high treason *n.* an act of treason directly affecting a sovereign or state.
high-up *n. Informal.* a person who holds an important or influential position.
highveld (ˈhaɪˌfɛlt, -ˌvɛlt) *n.* **the.** the high-altitude grassland region of the Transvaal, South Africa.
high water *n.* **1.** another name for **high tide** (sense 1). **2.** the state of any stretch of water at its highest level, as during a flood. ~Abbrev.: **HW.**
high-water mark *n.* **1. a.** the level reached by sea water at high tide or by other stretches of water in flood. **b.** the mark indicating this level. **2.** the highest point.
highway (ˈhaɪˌweɪ) *n.* **1.** a public road that all may use. **2.** *Now chiefly U.S. and Canadian except in legal contexts.* a main road, esp. one that connects towns or cities. **3.** a main route for any form of transport. **4.** a direct path or course.
highwayman (ˈhaɪˌweɪmən) *n., pl.* **-men.** (formerly) a robber, usually on horseback, who held up travellers.
highway robbery *n. Informal.* blatant overcharging.
high wire *n.* a tightrope stretched high in the air for balancing acts.
HIH *abbrev. for* His (*or* Her) Imperial Highness.
hi-hat *n.* a variant spelling of **high-hat** (sense 4).
hijack *or* **highjack** (ˈhaɪˌdʒæk) *vb.* **1.** (*tr.*) to seize, divert, or appropriate (a vehicle or the goods it carries) while in transit: *to hijack an aircraft.* **2.** to rob (a person or vehicle) by force: *to hijack a traveller.* **3.** (esp. in the U.S. during Prohibition) to rob (a bootlegger or smuggler) of his illicit goods or to steal (illicit goods) in transit. ~*n.* **4.** the act or an instance of hijacking. [C20: of unknown origin] —ˈ**hiˌjacker** *or* ˈ**highˌjacker** *n.*
hike (haɪk) *vb.* **1.** (*intr.*) to walk a long way, usually for pleasure or exercise, esp. in the country. **2.** (usually foll. by *up*) to pull or be pulled; hitch. **3.** (*tr.*) to increase (a price). ~*n.* **4.** a long walk. **5.** a rise in prices, wages, etc. [C18: of uncertain origin] —ˈ**hiker** *n.*
hike out *vb.* (*intr., adv.*) *Naut.* the U.S. and Canadian term for **sit out** (sense 3).
hilarious (hɪˈlɛərɪəs) *adj.* very funny or merry. [C19: from Latin *hilaris* glad, from Greek *hilaros*] —**hiˈlariously** *adv.* —**hiˈlariousness** *n.*
hilarity (hɪˈlærɪtɪ) *n.* mirth and merriment; cheerfulness.
Hilary term (ˈhɪlərɪ) *n.* the spring term at Oxford University, the Inns of Court, and some other educational establishments. [C16: named after Saint *Hilary* of Poitiers (?315–?367 A.D.), French bishop]
hill (hɪl) *n.* **1. a.** a conspicuous and often rounded natural elevation of the earth's surface, less high or craggy than a mountain. **b.** (*in combination*): *a hillside; a hilltop.* **2. a.** a heap or mound made by a person or animal. **b.** (*in combination*): *a dunghill.* **3.** an incline; slope. **4. hill and dale.** (of gramophone records) having or relating to vertical groove undulations. **5. over the hill. a.** *Informal.* beyond one's prime. **b.** *Military slang.* absent without leave or deserting. **6. up hill and down dale.** strenuously and persistently. ~*vb.* (*tr.*) **7.** to form into a hill or mound. **8.** to cover or surround with a mound or heap of earth. ~See also **hills.** [Old English *hyll;* related to Old Frisian *holla* head, Latin *collis* hill, Low German *hull* hill] —ˈ**hiller** *n.* —ˈ**hilly** *adj.*
hillbilly (ˈhɪlˌbɪlɪ) *n., pl.* **-lies. 1.** *Usually disparaging.* an unsophisticated person, esp. from the mountainous areas in the southeastern U.S. **2.** another name for **country and western.** [C20: from HILL + *Billy* (the nickname)]
hill climb *n.* a competition in which motor vehicles attempt singly to ascend a steep slope as fast as possible.
hill country *n. N.Z.* (in North Island) elevated pasture land for sheep or cattle.
hillfort (ˈhɪlˌfɔːt) *n. Archaeol.* a hilltop fortified with ramparts and ditches, dating from the second millennium B.C.
hill myna *n.* a starling, *Gracula religiosa,* of S and SE Asia: a popular cage bird because of its ability to talk. Also called: **Indian grackle.**
hillock (ˈhɪlək) *n.* a small hill or mound. [C14 *hilloc,* from HILL + -OCK] —ˈ**hillocked** *or* ˈ**hillocky** *adj.*

hills (hɪlz) *pl. n.* 1. **the.** a hilly and often remote region. 2. **as old as the hills.** very old.
hill station *n.* (in northern India) a settlement or resort at a high altitude.
hilt (hɪlt) *n.* 1. the handle or shaft of a sword, dagger, etc. 2. **to the hilt.** to the full. ~*vb.* 3. (*tr.*) to supply with a hilt. [Old English; related to Old Norse *hjalt,* Old Saxon *helta* oar handle, Old High German *helza*]
hilum ('haɪləm) *n., pl.* **-la** (-lə). 1. *Botany.* **a.** a scar on the surface of a seed marking its point of attachment to the seed stalk (funicle). **b.** the nucleus of a starch grain. 2. a rare word for **hilus.** [C17: from Latin: trifle; see NIHIL]
hilus ('haɪləs) *n.* a deep fissure or depression on the surface of a bodily organ around the point of entrance or exit of vessels, nerves, or ducts. [C19: via New Latin from Latin: a trifle] —'**hilar** *adj.*
him (hɪm; *unstressed* ɪm) *pron.* (*objective*) 1. refers to a male person or animal: *they needed him; she baked him a cake; not him again!* 2. *Chiefly U.S.* a dialect word for **himself** when used as an indirect object: *he ought to find him a wife.* [Old English *him,* dative of *hē* HE[1]]
▷**Usage.** See at **me.**
HIM *abbrev. for* His (*or* Her) Imperial Majesty.
Himalayan (ˌhɪmə'leɪən, hɪ'mɑːljən) *adj.* of, relating to, or denoting the Himalayas, a vast mountain system in S Asia and the highest range in the world.
Himalayan cat *n.* the U.S. name for **colourpoint cat.**
himation (hɪ'mætɪˌɒn) *n., pl.* **-ia** (-ɪə). (in ancient Greece) a cloak draped around the body. [C19: from Greek: a little garment, from *heima* dress, from *hennunai* to clothe]
himself (hɪm'sɛlf; *medially often* ɪm'sɛlf) *pron.* 1. **a.** the reflexive form of *he* or *him.* **b.** (intensifier): *the king himself waved to me.* 2. (*preceded by a copula*) his normal or usual self: *he seems himself once more.* 3. *Irish and Scot.* the man of the house: *how is himself?* [Old English *him selfum,* dative singular of *hē self;* see HE[1], SELF]
▷**Usage.** See at **myself.**
Himyarite ('hɪmjəˌraɪt) *n.* 1. a member of an ancient people of SW Arabia, sometimes regarded as including the Sabeans. ~*adj.* 2. of or relating to this people or their culture. [C19: named after *Himyar* legendary king in ancient Yemen]
Himyaritic (ˌhɪmjə'rɪtɪk) *n.* 1. the extinct language of the Himyarites, belonging to the SE Semitic subfamily of the Afro-Asiatic family. ~*adj.* 2. of, relating to, or using this language.
hin (hɪn) *n.* a Hebrew unit of capacity equal to about 12 pints or 3.5 litres. [from Late Latin, from Greek, from Hebrew *hīn,* from Egyptian *hnw*]
Hinayana (ˌhiːnə'jɑːnə) *n.* **a.** any of various early forms of Buddhism. **b.** (*as modifier*): *Hinayana Buddhism.* [from Sanskrit *hīnayāna,* from *hīna* lesser + *yāna* vehicle] —ˌ**Hina'yanist** *n.* —ˌ**Hinaya'nistic** *adj.*
hind[1] (haɪnd) *adj.* **hinder, hindmost** *or* **hindermost.** (*prenominal*) (esp. of parts of the body) situated at the back or rear: *a hind leg.* [Old English *hindan* at the back, related to German *hinten;* see BEHIND, HINDER[2]]
hind[2] (haɪnd) *n., pl.* **hinds** *or* **hind.** 1. the female of the deer, esp. the red deer when aged three years or more. 2. any of several marine serranid fishes of the genus *Epinephelus,* closely related and similar to the gropers. [Old English *hind;* related to Old High German *hinta,* Greek *kemas* young deer, Lithuanian *szmúlas* hornless]
hind[3] (haɪnd) *n.* (formerly) 1. a simple peasant. 2. (in N Britain) a skilled farm worker. 3. a steward. [Old English *hīne,* from *hīgna,* genitive plural of *hīgan* servants]
Hind. *abbrev. for:* 1. Hindi. 2. Hindu. 3. Hindustan. 4. Hindustani.
hindbrain ('haɪndˌbreɪn) *n.* the nontechnical name for **rhombencephalon.**
hinder[1] ('hɪndə) *vb.* 1. to be or get in the way of (someone or something); hamper. 2. (*tr.*) to prevent. [Old English *hindrian;* related to Old Norse *hindra,* Old High German *hintarōn*] —'**hinderer** *n.* —'**hindering** *adj., n.*
hinder[2] ('haɪndə) *adj.* (*prenominal*) situated at or further towards the back or rear; posterior. [Old English; related to Old Norse *hindri* latter, Gothic *hindar* beyond, Old High German *hintar* behind]
hindgut ('haɪndˌgʌt) *n.* 1. the part of the vertebrate digestive tract comprising the colon and rectum. 2. the posterior part of the digestive tract of arthropods. ~See also **foregut, midgut.**
Hindi ('hɪndɪ) *n.* 1. a language or group of dialects of N central India. It belongs to the Indic branch of the Indo-European family and is closely related to Urdu. See also **Hindustani.** 2. a formal literary dialect of this language, the official language of India, usually written in Nagari script. 3. a person whose native language is Hindi. [C18: from Hindi *hindī,* from *Hind* India, from Old Persian *Hindu* the river Indus]
hindmost ('haɪndˌməʊst) *or* **hindermost** ('haɪndəˌməʊst) *adj.* furthest back; last.
Hindoo ('hɪnduː, hɪn'duː) *n., pl.* **-doos,** *adj.* an older spelling of **Hindu.** —**Hindooism** ('hɪndʊˌɪzəm) *n.*
hindquarter ('haɪndˌkwɔːtə) *n.* 1. one of the two back quarters of a carcass of beef, lamb, etc. 2. (*pl.*) the rear, esp. of a four-legged animal.
hindrance ('hɪndrəns) *n.* 1. an obstruction or snag; impediment. 2. the act of hindering; prevention.
hindsight ('haɪndˌsaɪt) *n.* 1. the ability to understand, after something has happened, what should have been done or what caused the event. 2. a firearm's rear sight.
Hindu *or* **Hindoo** ('hɪnduː, hɪn'duː) *n., pl.* **-dus** *or* **-doos.** 1. a person who adheres to Hinduism. 2. an inhabitant or native of Hindustan or India, esp. one adhering to Hinduism. ~*adj.* 3. relating to Hinduism, Hindus, or India. [C17: from Persian *Hindū,* from *Hind* India; see HINDI]
Hinduism *or* **Hindooism** ('hɪndʊˌɪzəm) *n.* the complex of beliefs, values, and customs comprising the dominant religion of India, characterized by the worship of many gods, including Brahma as supreme being, a caste system, belief in reincarnation, etc.
Hindustani, Hindoostani (ˌhɪndʊ'stɑːnɪ), *or* **Hindostani** (ˌhɪndəʊ'stɑːnɪ) *n.* 1. the dialect of Hindi spoken in Delhi: used as a lingua franca throughout India. 2. a group of languages or dialects consisting of all spoken forms of Hindi and Urdu considered together. ~*adj.* 3. of or relating to these languages or to Hindustan, the areas in India where Hindi is the predominant language or where Hinduism predominates.
hinge (hɪndʒ) *n.* 1. a device for holding together two parts such that one can swing relative to the other, typically having two interlocking metal leaves held by a pin about which they pivot. 2. *Anatomy.* a type of joint, such as the knee joint, that moves only backwards and forwards; a joint that functions in only one plane. Technical name: **ginglymus.** 3. a similar structure in invertebrate animals, such as the joint between the two halves of a bivalve shell. 4. something on which events, opinions, etc., turn. 5. Also called: **mount.** *Philately.* a small thin transparent strip of gummed paper for affixing a stamp to a page. ~*vb.* 6. (*tr.*) to attach or fit a hinge to (something). 7. (*intr.*; usually foll. by *on* or *upon*) to depend (on). 8. (*intr.*) to hang or turn on or as if on a hinge. [C13: probably of Germanic origin; compare Middle Dutch *henge;* see HANG] —**hinged** *adj.* —'**hingeless** *adj.* —'**hingeˌlike** *adj.*
hinny[1] ('hɪnɪ) *n., pl.* **-nies.** the sterile hybrid offspring of a male horse and a female donkey or ass. Compare **mule**[1] (sense 1). [C17: from Latin *hinnus,* from Greek *hinnos*]
hinny[2] ('hɪnɪ) *vb.* **-nies, -nying, -nied.** a less common word for **whinny.**
hinny[3] ('hɪnɪ) *n. Scot. and northern English dialect.* a term of endearment, esp. for a woman or child. [variant of HONEY]
hint (hɪnt) *n.* 1. a suggestion or implication given in an indirect or subtle manner: *he dropped a hint.* 2. a helpful piece of advice or practical suggestion. 3. a small amount; trace. ~*vb.* 4. (when *intr.,* often foll. by *at;* when *tr., takes a clause as object*) to suggest or imply indirectly. [C17: of uncertain origin] —'**hinter** *n.* —'**hinting** *n.* —'**hintingly** *adv.*
hinterland ('hɪntəˌlænd) *n.* 1. land lying behind something, esp. a coast or the shore of a river. 2. remote or undeveloped areas of a country. 3. an area located near and dependent on a large city, esp. a port. [C19: from German, from *hinter* behind + *land* LAND; see HINDER[2]]
hip[1] (hɪp) *n.* 1. (*often pl.*) either side of the body below the waist and above the thigh, overlying the lateral part of the pelvis and its articulation with the thighbones. 2. another name for **pelvis** (sense 1). 3. short for **hip joint.** 4. the angle formed where two sloping sides of a roof meet or where a sloping side meets a sloping end. [Old English *hype;* related to Old High German *huf,* Gothic *hups,* Dutch *heup*] —'**hipless** *adj.* —'**hipˌlike** *adj.*
hip[2] (hɪp) *n.* the berry-like brightly coloured fruit of a rose plant: a swollen receptacle, rich in vitamin C, containing several small hairy achenes. Also called: **rosehip.** [Old English *héopa;* related to Old Saxon *hiopo,* Old High German *hiufo,* Dutch *joop,* Norwegian dialect *hjūpa*]
hip[3] (hɪp) *interj.* an exclamation used to introduce cheers (in the phrase **hip, hip, hurrah**). [C18: of unknown origin]
hip[4] (hɪp) *or* **hep** *adj.* **hipper, hippest** *or* **hepper, heppest.** *Slang.* 1. aware of or following the latest trends in music, ideas, fashion, etc. 2. (*often postpositive;* foll. by *to*) informed (about). [C20: variant of earlier *hep*]
hip bath *n.* a portable bath in which the bather sits.
hipbone ('hɪpˌbəʊn) *n.* the nontechnical name for **innominate bone.**
hip flask *n.* a small metal flask for spirits, etc., often carried in a hip pocket.
hip-hop ('hɪpˌhɒp) *n.* a U.S. pop culture movement of the 1980s comprising rap music, graffiti, and break dancing.
hip-huggers *pl. n. Chiefly U.S.* trousers that begin at the hips instead of the waist. Usual Brit. word: **hipsters.**
hip joint *n.* the ball-and-socket joint that connects each leg to the trunk of the body, in which the head of the femur articulates with the socket (acetabulum) of the pelvis.
hipparch ('hɪpɑːk) *n.* (in ancient Greece) a cavalry commander. [C17: from Greek *hippos* horse + -ARCH]
hippeastrum (hɪpɪ'æstrəm) *n.* any plant of the South American amaryllidaceous genus *Hippeastrum:* cultivated for their large funnel-shaped typically red flowers. [C19: New Latin, from Greek *hippeus* knight + *astron* star]
hipped[1] (hɪpt) *adj.* 1. **a.** having a hip or hips. **b.** (*in combination*): *broad-hipped; low-hipped.* 2. (esp. of cows, sheep, reindeer, elk, etc.) having an injury to the hip, such as a dislocation

of the bones. 3. *Architect.* having a hip or hips. See also **hipped roof.**

hipped[2] (hɪpt) *adj.* (*often postpositive;* foll. by *on*) *U.S. and Canadian dated slang.* very enthusiastic (about). [C20: from HIP[4]]

hipped roof *n.* a roof having sloping ends and sides.

hippie *or* **hippy** ('hɪpɪ) *n., pl.* **-pies. a.** (esp. during the 1960s) a person whose behaviour, dress, use of drugs, etc., implied a rejection of conventional values. **b.** (*as modifier*): *hippie language.* [C20: see HIP[4]]

hippo ('hɪpəʊ) *n., pl.* **-pos.** *Informal.* **1.** short for **hippopotamus. 2.** *S. Africa.* an armoured police car.

hippocampus (ˌhɪpəʊ'kæmpəs) *n., pl.* **-pi** (-paɪ). **1.** any marine teleost fish of the genus *Hippocampus,* having a horselike head. See **sea horse. 2.** a structure in the floor of the lateral ventricle of the brain, which in cross section has the shape of a sea horse. [C16: from Latin, from Greek *hippos* horse + *kampos* a sea monster] —ˌ**hippo'campal** *adj.*

hip pocket *n.* a pocket at the back of a pair of trousers.

hippocras ('hɪpəʊˌkræs) *n.* an old English drink of wine flavoured with spices. [C14 *ypocras,* from Old French: *Hippocrates,* probably referring to a filter called *Hippocrates' sleeve*]

Hippocratic ('hɪpəʊˌkrætɪk) *or* **Hippocratical** ('hɪpəʊˌkrætɪkᵊl) *adj.* of, denoting, or relating to Hippocrates (?460–?377 B.C.), Greek physician, commonly regarded as the father of medicine.

Hippocratic oath *n.* an oath taken by a doctor to observe a code of medical ethics derived from that of Hippocrates.

hippodrome ('hɪpəˌdrəʊm) *n.* **1.** a music hall, variety theatre, or circus. **2.** (in ancient Greece or Rome) an open-air course for horse and chariot races. [C16: from Latin *hippodromos,* from Greek *hippos* horse + *dromos* a race]

hippogriff *or* **hippogryph** ('hɪpəʊˌgrɪf) *n.* a monster of Greek mythology with a griffin's head, wings, and claws and a horse's body. [C17: from Italian *ippogrifo,* from *ippo-* horse (from Greek *hippos*) + *grifo* GRIFFIN[1]]

hippopotamus (ˌhɪpə'pɒtəməs) *n., pl.* **-muses** *or* **-mi** (-ˌmaɪ). **1.** a very large massive gregarious artiodactyl mammal, *Hippopotamus amphibius,* living in or around the rivers of tropical Africa: family *Hippopotamidae.* It has short legs and a thick skin sparsely covered with hair. **2. pigmy hippopotamus.** a related but smaller animal, *Choeropsis liberiensis.* [C16: from Latin, from Greek *hippopotamos* river horse, from *hippos* horse + *potamos* river]

hippuric acid (hɪ'pjʊərɪk) *n.* a crystalline solid excreted in the urine of mammals. Formula: $C_9H_9NO_3$.

hippy[1] ('hɪpɪ) *adj.* **-pier, -piest.** *Informal.* (esp. of a woman) having large hips.

hippy[2] ('hɪpɪ) *n., pl.* **-pies.** a variant spelling of **hippie.**

hip roof *n.* a roof having sloping ends and sides.

hipster ('hɪpstə) *n.* **1.** *Slang, now rare.* **a.** an enthusiast of modern jazz. **b.** an outmoded word for **hippie. 2.** (*modifier*) (of trousers) cut so that the top encircles the hips.

hipsters ('hɪpstəz) *pl. n. Brit.* trousers cut so that the top encircles the hips. Usual U.S. word: **hip-huggers.**

hiragana (ˌhɪərə'gɑːnə) *n.* one of the Japanese systems of syllabic writing based on Chinese cursive ideograms. The more widely used of the two current systems, it is employed in newspapers and general literature. Compare **katakana.** [from Japanese: flat kana]

hircine ('hɜːsaɪn, -sɪn) *adj.* **1.** *Archaic.* of or like a goat, esp. in smell. **2.** *Literary.* lustful; lascivious. [C17: from Latin *hircīnus,* from *hircus* goat]

hire ('haɪə) *vb.* (*tr.*) **1.** to acquire the temporary use of (a thing) or the services of (a person) in exchange for payment. **2.** to employ (a person) for wages. **3.** (often foll. by *out*) to provide (something) or the services of (oneself or others) for an agreed payment, usually for an agreed period. **4.** (*tr.;* foll. by *out*) *Chiefly Brit.* to pay independent contractors for (work to be done). ~*n.* **5. a.** the act of hiring or the state of being hired. **b.** (*as modifier*): *a hire car.* **6. a.** the price paid or payable for a person's services or the temporary use of something. **b.** (*as modifier*): *the hire charge.* **7. for** *or* **on hire.** available for service or temporary use in exchange for payment. [Old English *hȳrian;* related to Old Frisian *hēra* to lease, Middle Dutch *hūren*] —'**hirable** *or* '**hireable** *adj.* —'**hirer** *n.*

hireling ('haɪəlɪŋ) *n. Derogatory.* a person who works only for money, esp. one paid to do something unpleasant. [Old English *hȳrling;* related to Dutch *huurling;* see HIRE, -LING[1]]

hire-purchase *n. Brit.* **a.** a system for purchasing merchandise, such as cars or furniture, in which the buyer takes possession of the merchandise on payment of a deposit and completes the purchase by paying a series of regular instalments while the seller retains ownership until the final instalment is paid. **b.** (*as modifier*): *hire-purchase legislation.* Abbrev.: **HP, h.p.** U.S. and Canadian equivalents: **installment plan, instalment plan.**

Hiri Motu ('hɪərɪ 'məʊtuː) *n.* another name for **Motu** (the language).

hiring-fair *n.* (formerly, in rural areas) a fair or market at which agricultural labourers were hired.

hirple ('hɪrpᵊl) *Scot.* ~*vb.* (*intr.*) **1.** to limp. ~*n.* **2.** a limping gait. [C15: of unknown origin]

hirsute ('hɜːsjuːt) *adj.* **1.** covered with hair. **2.** (of plants or their parts) covered with long but not stiff hairs. **3.** (of a person) having long, thick, or untrimmed hair. [C17: from Latin *hirsūtus* shaggy; related to Latin *horrēre* to bristle, *hirtus* hairy; see HORRID] —'**hirsuteness** *n.*

hirudin (hɪ'ruːdɪn) *n. Med.* an anticoagulant extracted from the mouth glands of leeches. [C20: from Latin *hirudin-, hirudo* leech + -IN]

hirundine (hɪ'rʌndɪn, -daɪn) *adj.* **1.** of or resembling a swallow. **2.** belonging to the bird family *Hirundinidae,* which includes swallows and martins. [C19: from Late Latin *hirundineus,* from Latin *hirundō* a swallow]

his (hɪz; *unstressed* ɪz) *determiner.* **1. a.** of, belonging to, or associated with him: *his own fault; his knee; I don't like his being out so late.* **b.** (*as pronoun*): *his is on the left; that book is his.* **2. his and hers.** (of paired objects) for a man and woman respectively. ~*pron.* **3. of his.** belonging to or associated with him. [Old English *his,* genitive of *hē* HE[1] and of *hit* IT]

Hispanic (hɪ'spænɪk) *adj.* **1.** relating to, characteristic of, or derived from Spain or the Spanish. ~*n.* **2.** *U.S.* a U.S. citizen of Latin-American descent. [from Latin *Hispania* Spain]

Hispanicism (hɪ'spænɪˌsɪzəm) *n.* a word or expression borrowed from Spanish or modelled on the form of a Spanish word or expression.

Hispanicize *or* **Hispanicise** (hɪ'spænɪˌsaɪz) *vb.* (*tr.*) to make Spanish, as in custom or culture; bring under Spanish control or influence. —**His'panicist** *n.* —**His**ˌ**panici'zation** *or* **His**ˌ**panici'sation** *n.*

hispid ('hɪspɪd) *adj. Biology.* covered with stiff hairs or bristles. [C17: from Latin *hispidus* bristly] —**his'pidity** *n.*

hiss (hɪs) *n.* **1.** a voiceless fricative sound like that of a prolonged *s.* **2.** such a sound uttered as an exclamation of derision, contempt, etc., esp. by an audience or crowd. **3.** *Electronics.* receiver noise with a continuous spectrum, caused by thermal agitation, shot noise, etc. ~*interj.* **4.** an exclamation of derision or disapproval. ~*vb.* **5.** (*intr.*) to produce or utter a hiss. **6.** (*tr.*) to express with a hiss, usually to indicate derision or anger. **7.** (*tr.*) to show derision or anger towards (a speaker, performer, etc.) by hissing. [C14: of imitative origin] —'**hisser** *n.*

hist (hɪst) *interj.* an exclamation used to attract attention or as a warning to be silent.

hist. *abbrev. for:* **1.** histology. **2.** historical. **3.** history.

histaminase (hɪ'stæmɪˌneɪs) *n.* an enzyme, occurring in the digestive system, that inactivates histamine by removal of its amino group. Also called: **diamine oxidase.**

histamine ('hɪstəˌmiːn, -mɪn) *n.* an amine formed from histidine and released by the body tissues in allergic reactions, causing irritation. It also stimulates gastric secretions, dilates blood vessels, and contracts smooth muscle. Formula: $C_5H_9N_3$. See also **antihistamine.** [C20: from HIST(IDINE) + -AMINE] —**histaminic** (ˌhɪstə'mɪnɪk) *adj.*

histidine ('hɪstɪˌdiːn, -dɪn) *n.* a nonessential amino acid that occurs in most proteins: a precursor of histamine.

histiocyte ('hɪstɪəˌsaɪt) *n. Physiol.* a macrophage that occurs in connective tissue. [C20: alteration of German *histiozyt,* from Greek *histion* a little web, from *histos* web + -CYTE] —**histiocytic** (ˌhɪstɪə'sɪtɪk) *adj.*

histo- *or before a vowel* **hist-** *combining form.* indicating animal or plant tissue: *histology; histamine.* [from Greek, from *histos* web]

histochemistry (ˌhɪstəʊ'kɛmɪstrɪ) *n.* the chemistry of tissues, such as liver and bone, often studied with the aid of a microscope. —ˌ**histo'chemical** *adj.*

histocompatibility (ˌhɪstəʊkəmˌpætɪ'bɪlɪtɪ) *n.* the degree of similarity between the histocompatibility antigens of two individuals. Histocompatibility determines whether an organ transplant will be tolerated. —ˌ**histocom'patible** *adj.*

histocompatibility antigen *n.* a molecule occurring on the surface of tissue cells that can take several different forms. The differences between histocompatibility antigens are inherited and determine organ transplant rejection.

histogen ('hɪstəˌdʒɛn) *n.* any of several distinct regions in a plant that differentiate to produce new tissue.

histogenesis (ˌhɪstəʊ'dʒɛnɪsɪs) *or* **histogeny** (hɪ'stɒdʒənɪ) *n.* the formation of tissues and organs from undifferentiated cells. —**histogenetic** (ˌhɪstəʊdʒə'nɛtɪk) *or* ˌ**histo'genic** *adj.* —ˌ**histoge'netically** *or* ˌ**histo'genically** *adv.*

histogram ('hɪstəˌgræm) *n.* a statistical graph that represents the frequency of values of a quantity by vertical rectangles of varying heights and widths. The width of the rectangles is in proportion to the class interval under consideration, and their areas represent the relative frequency of the phenomenon in question. See also **stem and leaf diagram.** [C20: perhaps from HISTO(RY) + -GRAM]

histoid ('hɪstɔɪd) *adj.* (esp. of a tumour) **1.** resembling normal tissue. **2.** composed of one kind of tissue.

histology (hɪ'stɒlədʒɪ) *n.* **1.** the study, esp. the microscopic study, of the tissues of an animal or plant. **2.** the structure of a tissue or organ. —**histological** (ˌhɪstə'lɒdʒɪkᵊl) *or* ˌ**histo'logic** *adj.* —ˌ**histo'logically** *adv.* —**his'tologist** *n.*

histolysis (hɪ'stɒlɪsɪs) *n.* the disintegration of organic tissues. —**histolytic** (ˌhɪstə'lɪtɪk) *adj.* —ˌ**histo'lytically** *adv.*

histone ('hɪstəʊn) *n.* any of a group of basic proteins present in cell nuclei and implicated in the spatial organization of DNA.

histopathology (ˌhɪstəʊpəˈθɒlədʒɪ) *n.* the study of the microscopic structure of diseased tissues. —**histopathological** (ˌhɪstəʊˌpæθəˈlɒdʒɪkᵊl) *adj.*

histoplasmosis (ˌhɪstəʊplæzˈməʊsɪs) *n.* a severe fungal disease of the lungs caused by *Histoplasma capsulatum.*

historian (hɪˈstɔːrɪən) *n.* a person who writes or studies history, esp. one who is an authority on it.

historiated (hɪˈstɔːrɪˌeɪtɪd) *adj.* decorated with flowers or animals. Also: **storiated.** [C19: from Medieval Latin *historiāre* to tell a story in pictures, from Latin *historia* story]

historic (hɪˈstɒrɪk) *adj.* **1.** famous or likely to become famous in history; significant. **2.** a less common word for **historical** (senses 1–5). **3.** Also: **secondary.** *Linguistics.* (of Latin, Greek, or Sanskrit verb tenses) referring to past time.

▷**Usage.** In careful usage, a distinction is made between *historic* (important, significant) and *historical* (pertaining to history): *a historic decision; a historical perspective.*

historical (hɪˈstɒrɪkᵊl) *adj.* **1.** belonging to or typical of the study of history: *historical methods.* **2.** concerned with or treating of events of the past: *historical accounts.* **3.** based on or constituting factual material as distinct from legend or supposition. **4.** based on or inspired by history: *a historical novel.* **5.** occurring or prominent in history. **6.** a less common word for **historic** (sense 1). —**hisˈtorically** *adv.* —**hisˈtoricalness** *n.*

▷**Usage.** See at **historic.**

historical geology *n.* the branch of geology concerned with the evolution of the earth from its origins to the present.

historical linguistics *n. (functioning as sing.)* the study of language as it changes in the course of time, with a view either to discovering general principles of linguistic change or to establishing the correct genealogical classification of particular languages. Also called: **diachronic linguistics.** Compare **descriptive linguistics.**

historical materialism *n.* the part of Marxist theory maintaining that social structures derive from economic structures and that these are transformed as a result of class struggles, each ruling class producing another, which will overcome and destroy it, the final phase being the emergence of a communist society.

historical method *n.* a means of learning about something by considering its origins and development.

historical present *n.* the present tense used to narrate past events, usually employed in English for special effect or in informal use, as in *a week ago I'm walking down the street and I see this accident.*

historical school *n.* **1.** a group of 19th-century German economists who maintained that modern economies evolved from historical institutions. **2.** the school of jurists maintaining that laws are based on social and historical circumstances rather than made by a sovereign power.

historic episcopate *n. Christian Church.* the derivation of the episcopate of a Church in historic succession from the apostles.

historicism (hɪˈstɒrɪˌsɪzəm) *n.* **1.** the belief that natural laws govern historical events which in turn determine social and cultural phenomena. **2.** the doctrine that each period of history has its own beliefs and values inapplicable to any other, so that nothing can be understood independently of its historical context. **3.** the conduct of any enquiry in accordance with these views. **4.** excessive emphasis on history, historicism, past styles, etc. —**hisˈtoricist** *n., adj.*

historicity (ˌhɪstəˈrɪsɪtɪ) *n.* historical authenticity.

historiographer (hɪˌstɔːrɪˈɒgrəfə) *n.* **1.** a historian, esp. one concerned with historical method and the writings of other historians. **2.** a historian employed to write the history of a group or public institution.

historiography (ˌhɪstɔːrɪˈɒgrəfɪ) *n.* **1.** the writing of history. **2.** the study of the development of historical method, historical research, and writing. **3.** any body of historical literature. —**historiographic** (hɪˌstɔːrɪəˈgræfɪk) *or* **hisˌtorioˈgraphical** *adj.*

history (ˈhɪstərɪ, ˈhɪstrɪ) *n., pl.* **-ries. 1. a.** a record or account, often chronological in approach, of past events, developments, etc. **b.** *(as modifier): a history book; a history play.* **2.** all that is preserved or remembered of the past, esp. in written form. **3.** the discipline of recording and interpreting past events involving human beings. **4.** past events, esp. when considered as an aggregate. **5.** an event in the past, esp. one that has been forgotten or reduced in importance: *their quarrel was just history.* **6.** the past, background, previous experiences, etc., of a thing or person: *the house had a strange history.* **7.** a play that depicts or is based on historical events. **8.** a narrative relating the events of a character's life: *the history of Joseph Andrews.* ~Abbrev. (for senses 1,2,3): **hist.** [C15: from Latin *historia,* from Greek: enquiry, from *historein* to narrate, from *histōr* judge]

histrionic (ˌhɪstrɪˈɒnɪk) *or* **histrionical** *adj.* **1.** excessively dramatic, insincere, or artificial: *histrionic gestures.* **2.** *Now rare.* dramatic. ~*n.* **3.** *(pl.)* melodramatic displays of temperament. **4.** *Rare.* *(pl., functioning as sing.)* dramatics. [C17: from Late Latin *histriōnicus* of a player, from *histriō* actor] —ˌ**histriˈonically** *adv.*

hit (hɪt) *vb.* **hits, hitting, hit.** *(mainly tr.)* **1.** *(also intr.)* to deal (a blow or stroke) to (a person or thing); strike: *the man hit the child.* **2.** to come into violent contact with: *the car hit the tree.* **3.** to reach or strike with a missile, thrown object, etc.: *to hit a target.* **4.** to make or cause to make forceful contact; knock or bump: *I hit my arm on the table.* **5.** to propel or cause to move by striking: *to hit a ball.* **6.** *Cricket.* to score (runs). **7.** to affect (a person, place, or thing) suddenly or adversely: *his illness hit his wife very hard.* **8.** to become suddenly apparent to (a person): *the reason for his behaviour hit me and made the whole episode clear.* **9.** to achieve or reach: *to hit the jackpot; unemployment hit a new high.* **10.** to experience or encounter: *I've hit a slight snag here.* **11.** *Slang.* to murder (a rival criminal) in fulfilment of an underworld contract or vendetta. **12.** to accord or suit (esp. in the phrase **hit one's fancy). 13.** to guess correctly or find out by accident: *you have hit the answer.* **14.** *Informal.* to set out on (a road, path, etc.): *let's hit the road.* **15.** *Informal.* to arrive or appear in: *he will hit town tomorrow night.* **16.** *Informal, chiefly U.S. and Canadian.* to demand or request from: *he hit me for a pound.* **17.** *Slang.* to drink an excessive amount of (alcohol): *to hit the bottle.* **18. hit it.** *Music, slang.* start playing. **19. hit the sack** *(or* **hay).** *Slang.* to go to bed. **20. not know what has hit one.** to be completely taken by surprise. ~*n.* **21.** an impact or collision. **22.** a shot, blow, etc., that reaches its object. **23.** an apt, witty, or telling remark. **24.** *Informal.* **a.** a person or thing that gains wide appeal: *she's a hit with everyone.* **b.** *(as modifier): a hit record.* **25.** *Informal.* a stroke of luck. **26.** *Slang.* **a.** a murder carried out as the result of an underworld vendetta or rivalry. **b.** *(as modifier): a hit squad.* **27.** *Slang.* a drag on a cigarette, a swig from a bottle, a line of a drug, or an injection of heroin. **28. make** *(or* **score) a hit with.** *Informal.* to make a favourable impression on. ~See also **hit off, hit on, hit out.** [Old English *hittan,* from Old Norse *hitta*]

hit-and-run *adj. (prenominal)* **1. a.** involved in or denoting a motor-vehicle accident in which the driver leaves the scene without stopping to give assistance, inform the police, etc. **b.** *(as n.): a hit-and-run.* **2.** (of an attack, raid, etc.) relying on surprise allied to a rapid departure from the scene of operations for the desired effect: *hit-and-run tactics.* **3.** *Baseball.* denoting a play in which a base runner begins to run as the pitcher throws the ball to the batter.

hitch (hɪtʃ) *vb.* **1.** to fasten or become fastened with a knot or tie, esp. temporarily. **2.** (often foll. by *up*) to connect (a horse, team, etc.); harness. **3.** *(tr.;* often foll. by *up)* to pull up (the trousers, a skirt, etc.) with a quick jerk. **4.** *(intr.) Chiefly U.S.* to move in a halting manner: *to hitch along.* **5.** to entangle or become entangled: *the thread was hitched on the reel.* **6.** *(tr.; passive) Slang.* to marry (esp. in the phrase **get hitched). 7.** *Informal.* to obtain (a ride or rides) by hitchhiking. ~*n.* **8.** an impediment or obstacle, esp. one that is temporary or minor: *a hitch in the proceedings.* **9.** a knot for fastening a rope to posts, other ropes, etc., that can be undone by pulling against the direction of the strain that holds it. **10.** a sudden jerk; tug; pull: *he gave it a hitch and it came loose.* **11.** *Chiefly U.S.* a hobbling gait: *to walk with a hitch.* **12.** a device used for fastening. **13.** *Informal.* a ride obtained by hitchhiking. **14.** *U.S. and Canadian slang.* a period of time spent in prison, in the army, etc. [C15: of uncertain origin] —ˈ**hitcher** *n.*

hitchhike (ˈhɪtʃˌhaɪk) *vb. (intr.)* to travel by obtaining free lifts in motor vehicles. —ˈ**hitchˌhiker** *n.*

hitching post *n.* a post or rail to which the reins of a horse, etc., are tied.

hi tech *or* **high tech** (tɛk) *n.* **1.** short for **high technology. 2.** a style of interior design using features of industrial equipment. ~*adj.* **hi-tech** *or* **high-tech. 3.** designed for or using high technology. **4.** of or in the interior design style. ~Compare **low tech.**

hither (ˈhɪðə) *adv.* **1.** Also (archaic): **hitherward, hitherwards.** to or towards this place (esp. in the phrase **come hither). 2. hither and thither.** this way and that, as in a state of confusion. ~*adj.* **3.** *Archaic or dialect.* (of a side or part, esp. of a hill or valley) nearer; closer. [Old English *hider;* related to Old Norse *hethra* here, Gothic *hidrē,* Latin *citrā* on this side, *citrō*]

hithermost (ˈhɪðəˌməʊst) *adj. Now rare.* nearest to this place or in this direction.

Hitler (ˈhɪtlə) *n.* a person who displays dictatorial characteristics. [C20: named after Adolf *Hitler* (1889–1945), German Nazi dictator]

hitherto (ˈhɪðəˈtuː) *adv.* **1.** until this time: *hitherto, there have been no problems.* **2.** *Archaic.* to this place or point.

Hitlerism (ˈhɪtləˌrɪzəm) *n.* the policies, principles, and methods of the Nazi party as developed by Adolf Hitler.

hit list *n. Informal.* **1.** a list of people to be murdered: *a terrorist hit list.* **2.** a list of targets to be eliminated in some way: *a hit list of pits to be closed.*

hit man *n. Slang.* a hired assassin, esp. one employed by gangsters.

hit off *vb.* **1.** *(tr., adv.)* to represent or mimic accurately. **2. hit it off.** *Informal.* to have a good relationship with.

hit on *vb. (prep.)* **1.** *(tr.)* to strike. **2.** *(intr.)* Also: **hit upon.** to discover unexpectedly or guess correctly.

hit or miss *adj. (hit-or-miss when prenominal) Informal.* random; casual; haphazard: *his judgment is rather hit or miss; a hit-or-miss system.* Also: **hit and miss.**

hit out *vb. (intr., adv.;* often foll. by *at)* **1.** to direct blows forcefully and vigorously. **2.** to make a verbal attack (upon someone).

hit parade *n. Old-fashioned* a listing or playing of the current most popular songs.

hitter ('hɪtə) *n.* **1.** *Informal.* a boxer who has a hard punch rather than skill or finesse. **2.** a person who hits something.

Hittite ('hɪtaɪt) *n.* **1.** a member of an ancient people of Anatolia, who built a great empire in N Syria and Asia Minor in the second millennium B.C. **2.** the extinct language of this people, deciphered from cuneiform inscriptions found at Boğazköy, site of the ancient Hittite capital, and elsewhere. It is clearly related to the Indo-European family of languages, although the precise relationship is disputed. *~adj.* **3.** of or relating to this people, their civilization, or their language.

HIV *abbrev. for* human immunodeficiency virus; the cause of AIDS. Two strains have been identified: HIV-1 and HIV-2.

hive (haɪv) *n.* **1.** a structure in which social bees live and rear their young. **2.** a colony of social bees. **3.** a place showing signs of great industry (esp. in the phrase **a hive of activity**). **4.** a teeming crowd; multitude. **5.** an object in the form of a hive. *~vb.* **6.** to cause (bees) to collect or (of bees) to collect inside a hive. **7.** to live or cause to live in or as if in a hive. **8.** (*tr.*) (of bees) to store (honey, pollen, etc.) in the hive. **9.** (*tr.*; often foll. by *up* or *away*) to store, esp. for future use: *he used to hive away a small sum every week.* [Old English *hȳf*; related to Westphalian *hüwe*, Old Norse *hūfr* ship's hull, Latin *cūpa* barrel, Greek *kupē*, Sanskrit *kūpa* cave] —'**hive,like** *adj.*

hive bee *n.* another name for a **honeybee.**

hive dross *n.* another name for **propolis.**

hive off *vb.* (*adv.*) **1.** to transfer or be transferred from a larger group or unit. **2.** (*usually tr.*) to transfer (profitable activities of a nationalized industry) back to private ownership.

hives (haɪvz) *n.* (*functioning as sing. or pl.*) *Pathol.* a nontechnical name for **urticaria.** [C16: of uncertain origin]

hiya ('haɪjə, ,haɪ'jɑː) *sentence substitute.* an informal term of greeting. [C20: shortened from *how are you?*]

HJ (on gravestones) *abbrev. for* hic jacet. [Latin: here lies]

HJS (on gravestones) *abbrev. for* hic jacet sepultus. [Latin: here lies buried]

HK **1.** *abbrev. for* House of Keys (Manx Parliament). **2.** *international car registration for* Hong Kong.

HKJ *international car registration for* (Hashemite Kingdom of) Jordan.

hl *symbol for* hectolitre.

HL (in Britain) *abbrev. for* House of Lords.

HLA system *n.* human leucocyte antigen system; a group of the most important antigens responsible for tissue compatibility, together with the genes that encode them. For tissue and organ transplantation to be successful there needs to be a minimum number of HLA differences between the donor's and recipient's tissue.

hm *symbol for* hectometre.

HM *abbrev. for:* **1.** His (*or* Her) Majesty. **2.** heavy metal (sense 1). **3.** headmaster; headmistress.

h'm (*spelling pron.* hmmm) *interj.* used to indicate hesitation, doubt, assent, pleasure, etc.

HMAS *abbrev. for* His (*or* Her) Majesty's Australian Ship.

HMCS *abbrev. for* His (*or* Her) Majesty's Canadian Ship.

HMG *abbrev. for* His (*or* Her) Majesty's Government.

HMI (in Britain) *abbrev. for* Her Majesty's Inspector; a government official who examines and supervises schools.

H.M.S. *or* **HMS** *abbrev. for:* **1.** His (*or* Her) Majesty's Service. **2.** His (*or* Her) Majesty's Ship.

HMSO (in Britain) *abbrev. for* His (*or* Her) Majesty's Stationery Office.

HNC (in Britain) *abbrev. for* Higher National Certificate; a qualification recognized by many national technical and professional institutions.

HND (in Britain) *abbrev. for* Higher National Diploma; a qualification in technical subjects equivalent to an ordinary degree.

ho (həʊ) *interj.* **1.** Also: **ho-ho.** an imitation or representation of the sound of a deep laugh. **2.** an exclamation used to attract attention, announce a destination, etc.: *what ho! land ho! westward ho!* [C13: of imitative origin; compare Old Norse *hó*, Old French *ho!* halt!]

Ho *the chemical symbol for* holmium.

HO *or* **H.O.** *abbrev. for:* **1.** head office. **2.** *Brit. government.* Home Office.

ho. *abbrev. for* house.

hoactzin (həʊ'æktsɪn) *n.* a variant of **hoatzin.**

hoar (hɔː) *n.* **1.** short for **hoarfrost.** *~adj.* **2.** *Rare.* covered with hoarfrost. **3.** *Archaic.* a poetic variant of **hoary.** [Old English *hār*, related to Old Norse *hārr*, Old High German *hēr*, Old Slavonic *sĕrŭ* grey]

hoard (hɔːd) *n.* **1.** an accumulated store hidden away for future use. **2.** a cache of ancient coins, treasure, etc. *~vb.* **3.** to gather or accumulate (a hoard). [Old English *hord*; related to Old Norse *hodd*, Gothic *huzd*, German *Hort*, Swedish *hydda* hut] —'**hoarder** *n.*

hoarding ('hɔːdɪŋ) *n.* **1.** a large board used for displaying advertising posters, as by a road. Also called (esp. U.S. and Canadian): **billboard.** **2.** a temporary wooden fence erected round a building or demolition site. [C19: from C15 *hoard* fence, from Old French *hourd* palisade, of Germanic origin, related to Gothic *haurds*, Old Norse *hurth* door]

hoarfrost ('hɔː,frɒst) *n.* a deposit of needle-like ice crystals formed on the ground by direct condensation at temperatures below freezing point. Also called: **white frost.**

hoarhound ('hɔː,haʊnd) *n.* a variant spelling of **horehound.**

hoarse (hɔːs) *adj.* **1.** gratingly harsh or raucous in tone. **2.** low, harsh, and lacking in intensity: *a hoarse whisper.* **3.** having a husky voice, as through illness, shouting, etc. [C14: of Scandinavian origin; related to Old Norse *hās*, Old Saxon *hēs*] —'**hoarsely** *adv.* —'**hoarseness** *n.*

hoarsen ('hɔːsᵊn) *vb.* to make or become hoarse.

hoary ('hɔːrɪ) *adj.* **hoarier, hoariest.** **1.** having grey or white hair. **2.** white or whitish-grey in colour. **3.** ancient or venerable. —'**hoarily** *adv.* —'**hoariness** *n.*

hoary cress *n.* a perennial cruciferous Mediterranean plant, *Cardaria* (or *Lepidium*) *draba*, with small white flowers: a widespread troublesome weed.

hoast (host) *Scot.* *~n.* **1.** a cough. *~vb.* (*intr.*) **2.** to cough. [from Old Norse]

hoatching ('həʊtʃɪŋ) *adj. Scot.* infested; swarming: *this food's hoatching with flies.* [of unknown origin]

hoatzin (həʊ'ætsɪn) *or* **hoactzin** *n.* a unique South American gallinaceous bird, *Opisthocomus hoazin*, with a brownish plumage, a very small crested head, and clawed wing digits in the young: family *Opisthocomidae.* [C17: from American Spanish, from Nahuatl *uatzin* pheasant]

hoax (həʊks) *n.* **1.** a deception, esp. a practical joke. *~vb.* **2.** (*tr.*) to deceive or play a joke on (someone). [C18: probably from HOCUS] —'**hoaxer** *n.*

hob[1] (hɒb) *n.* **1.** the flat top part of a cooking stove, or a separate flat surface, containing hotplates or burners. **2.** a shelf beside an open fire, for keeping kettles, etc., hot. **3.** a steel pattern used in forming a mould or die in cold metal. **4.** a hard steel rotating cutting tool used in machines for cutting gears. *~vb.* **hobs, hobbing, hobbed.** **5.** (*tr.*) to cut or form with a hob. [C16: variant of obsolete *hubbe*, of unknown origin; perhaps related to HUB]

hob[2] (hɒb) *n.* **1.** a hobgoblin or elf. **2. raise** *or* **play hob.** *U.S. informal.* to cause mischief or disturbance. **3.** a male ferret. [C14: variant of *Rob*, short for *Robin* or *Robert*] —'**hob,like** *adj.*

Hobbesian ('hɒbzɪən) *adj.* **1.** of or relating to the English philosopher Thomas Hobbes (1588–1679) or his political philosophy, which stresses the necessity for a powerful sovereign to control human beings. *~n.* **2.** a proponent of Hobbesian philosophy. —'**Hobbism** *n.* —'**Hobbist** *n.*

hobble ('hɒbᵊl) *vb.* **1.** (*intr.*) to walk with a lame awkward movement. **2.** (*tr.*) to fetter the legs of (a horse) in order to restrict movement. **3.** to progress unevenly or with difficulty. *~n.* **4.** a strap, rope, etc., used to hobble a horse. **5.** a limping gait. **6.** *Brit. dialect.* a difficult or embarrassing situation. ~Also (for senses 2, 4): **hopple.** [C14: probably from Low German; compare Flemish *hoppelen*, Middle Dutch *hobbelen* to stammer] —'**hobbler** *n.*

hobbledehoy (,hɒbᵊldɪ'hɔɪ) *n. Archaic or dialect.* a clumsy or bad-mannered youth. [C16: from earlier *hobbard de hoy*, of uncertain origin]

hobble skirt *n.* a long skirt, popular between 1910 and 1914, cut so narrow at the ankles that it hindered walking.

hobby[1] ('hɒbɪ) *n., pl.* **-bies.** **1.** an activity pursued in spare time for pleasure or relaxation. **2.** *Archaic or dialect.* a small horse or pony. **3.** short for **hobbyhorse** (sense 1). **4.** an early form of bicycle, without pedals. [C14 *hobyn*, probably variant of proper name *Robin*; compare DOBBIN] —'**hobbyist** *n.*

hobby[2] ('hɒbɪ) *n., pl.* **-bies.** any of several small Old World falcons, esp. the European *Falco subbuteo*, formerly used in falconry. [C15: from Old French *hobet*, from *hobe* falcon; probably related to Middle Dutch *hobbelen* to roll, turn]

hobbyhorse ('hɒbɪ,hɔːs) *n.* **1.** a toy consisting of a stick with a figure of a horse's head at one end. **2.** another word for **rocking horse.** **3.** a figure of a horse attached to a performer's waist in a pantomime, morris dance, etc. **4.** a favourite topic or obsessive fixed idea (esp. in the phrase **on one's hobbyhorse**). *~vb.* **5.** (*intr.*) *Nautical.* (of a vessel) to pitch violently. [C16: from HOBBY[1], originally a small horse, hence sense 3; then generalized to apply to any pastime]

hobday ('hɒb,deɪ) *vb.* (*tr.*) to alleviate (a breathing problem in certain horses) by the surgical operation of pinning back the vocal fold. [C20: named after F. T. *Hobday* (1869–1939), English veterinary surgeon, who devised the operation] —'**hob,dayed** *adj.*

hobgoblin (,hɒb'gɒblɪn) *n.* **1.** an evil or mischievous goblin. **2.** a bogey; bugbear. [C16: from HOB[2] + GOBLIN]

hobnail ('hɒb,neɪl) *n.* **a.** a short nail with a large head for protecting the soles of heavy footwear. **b.** (*as modifier*): *hobnail boots.* [C16: from HOB[1] (in the archaic sense: peg) + NAIL] —'**hob,nailed** *adj.*

hobnob ('hɒb,nɒb) *vb.* **-nobs, -nobbing, -nobbed.** (*intr.*; often foll. by *with*) **1.** to socialize or talk informally. **2.** *Obsolete.* to drink (with). [C18: from *hob or nob* to drink to one another in turns, hence, to be familiar, ultimately from Old English *habban* to HAVE + *nabban* not to have]

hobo ('həʊbəʊ) *n., pl.* **-boes** *or* **-bos.** *Chiefly U.S. and Canadian.* **1.** a tramp; vagrant. **2.** a migratory worker, esp. an unskilled labourer. [C19 (U.S.): origin unknown] —'**hoboism** *n.*

hobson-jobson (ˌhɒbsənˈdʒɒbsən) *n.* another word for **folk etymology.** [C19: Anglo-Indian folk-etymological variant of Arabic *yā Hasan! yā Husayn!* O Hasan! O Husain! (ritual lament for the grandsons of Mohammed); influenced by the surnames *Hobson* and *Jobson*]

Hobson's choice (ˈhɒbsənz) *n.* the choice of taking what is offered or nothing at all. [C16: named after Thomas *Hobson* (1544–1631), English liveryman who gave his customers no choice but had them take the nearest horse]

Hochheimer (ˈhɒkˌhaɪmə; *German* ˈhoːxhaimər) *n.* a German white wine from the area around Hochheim near Mainz. Also called: **ˈHochˌheim.**

hock[1] (hɒk) *n.* **1.** the joint at the tarsus of a horse or similar animal, pointing backwards and corresponding to the human ankle. **2.** the corresponding joint in domestic fowl. ~*vb.* **3.** another word for **hamstring.** [C16: short for *hockshin,* from Old English *hōhsinu* heel sinew]

hock[2] (hɒk) *n.* **1.** any of several white wines from the German Rhine. **2.** (not in technical usage) any dry white wine. [C17: short for obsolete *hockamore* HOCHHEIMER]

hock[3] (hɒk) *Informal, chiefly U.S. and Canadian.* ~*vb.* **1.** (*tr.*) to pawn or pledge. ~*n.* **2.** the state of being in pawn (esp. in the phrase **in hock**). **3. in hock. a.** in prison. **b.** in debt. [C19: from Dutch *hok* prison, debt] —ˈ**hocker** *n.*

hockey[1] (ˈhɒkɪ) *n.* **1.** Also called (esp. U.S. and Canadian): **field hockey. a.** a game played on a field by two opposing teams of 11 players each, who try to hit a ball into their opponents' goal using long sticks curved at the end. **b.** (*as modifier*): *hockey stick; hockey ball.* **2.** See **ice hockey.** [C19: from earlier *hawkey,* of unknown origin]

hockey[2] (ˈhɒkɪ) *n. East Anglian dialect.* **a.** the feast at harvest home; harvest supper. **b.** (*as modifier*): *the hockey cart.* Also: **hawkey, horkey.** [C16: of unknown origin]

Hocktide (ˈhɒkˌtaɪd) *n. Brit. history.* a former festival celebrated on the second Monday and Tuesday after Easter. [C15: from *hock-, hoke-* (of unknown origin) +TIDE[1]]

hocus (ˈhəʊkəs) *vb.* **-cuses, -cusing, -cused** *or* **-cuses, -cussing, -cussed.** (*tr.*) *Now rare.* **1.** to take in; trick. **2.** to stupefy, esp. with a drug. **3.** to add a drug to (a drink).

hocus-pocus (ˈhəʊkəsˈpəʊkəs) *n.* **1.** trickery or chicanery. **2.** mystifying jargon. **3.** an incantation used by conjurers or magicians when performing tricks. **4.** conjuring skill or practice. ~*vb.* **-cuses, -cusing, -cused** *or* **-cuses, -cussing, -cussed. 5.** to deceive or trick (someone). [C17: perhaps a dog-Latin formation invented by jugglers]

hod (hɒd) *n.* **1.** an open wooden box attached to a pole, for carrying bricks, mortar, etc. **2.** a tall narrow coal scuttle. [C14: perhaps alteration of C13 dialect *hot,* from Old French *hotte* pannier, creel, probably from Germanic]

hod carrier *n.* a labourer who carries the materials in a hod for a mason, etc. Also called: **hodman.**

hodden (ˈhɒdən) *or* **hoddin** (ˈhɒdɪn) *n.* a coarse homespun cloth produced in Scotland: **hodden grey** is made by mixing black and white wools. [C18: Scottish, of obscure origin]

Hodge (hɒdʒ) *n.* a typical name for a farm labourer; rustic. [C14 *hogge,* from familiar form of *Roger*]

hodgepodge (ˈhɒdʒˌpɒdʒ) *n.* a variant (esp. U.S. and Canadian) of **hotchpotch.**

Hodgkin's disease (ˈhɒdʒkɪnz) *n.* a malignant disease characterized by enlargement of the lymph nodes, spleen, and liver. Also called: **lymphoadenoma, lymphogranulomatosis.** [C19: named after Thomas *Hodgkin* (1798–1866), London physician, who first described it]

hodman (ˈhɒdmən) *n., pl.* **-men.** *Brit.* another name for a **hod carrier.**

hodograph (ˈhɒdəˌgrɑːf, -ˌgræf) *n.* a curve of which the radius vector represents the velocity of a moving particle. [C19: from Greek *hodos* way + -GRAPH] —ˌ**hodoˈgraphic** *adj.*

hodometer (hɒˈdɒmɪtə) *n. U.S.* another name for **odometer.** —**hoˈdometry** *n.*

hodoscope (ˈhɒdəˌskəʊp) *n. Physics.* any device for tracing the path of a charged particle, esp. a particle found in cosmic rays. [C20: from Greek *hodos* way, path + -SCOPE]

hoe (həʊ) *n.* **1.** any of several kinds of long-handled hand implement equipped with a light blade and used to till the soil, eradicate weeds, etc. ~*vb.* **hoes, hoeing, hoed. 2.** to dig, scrape, weed, or till (surface soil) with or as if with a hoe. [C14: via Old French *houe* from Germanic: compare Old High German *houwā, houwan* to HEW, German *Haue* hoe] —ˈ**hoer** *n.* —ˈ**hoeˌlike** *adj.*

hoedown (ˈhəʊˌdaʊn) *n. U.S. and Canadian.* **1.** a boisterous square dance. **2.** a party at which hoedowns are danced.

hoe in *vb.* (*intr., adv.*) *Austral. and N.Z. informal.* to eat food heartily.

hoe into *vb.* (*intr., prep.*) *Austral. and N.Z. informal.* to eat (food) heartily.

hog (hɒg) *n.* **1.** a domesticated pig, esp. a castrated male weighing more than 102 kg. **2.** *U.S. and Canadian.* any artiodactyl mammal of the family *Suidae;* pig. **3.** Also: **hogget, hogg.** *Brit. dialect., Austral., and N.Z.* a sheep up to the age of one year that has yet to be sheared. **4.** *Brit. dialect, Austral., and N.Z.* the meat of this sheep. **5.** *Informal.* a selfish, greedy or slovenly person. **6.** *Nautical.* a stiff brush, for scraping a vessel's bottom. **7.** *Nautical.* the amount or extent to which a vessel is hogged. Compare **sag** (sense 6). **8.** another word for **camber** (sense 4). **9. go the whole hog.** *Informal.* to do something thoroughly or unreservedly. ~*vb.* **hogs, hogging, hogged.** (*tr.*) **10.** *Slang.* to take more than one's share of. **11.** to arch (the back) like a hog. **12.** to cut (the mane) of (a horse) very short. [Old English *hogg,* from Celtic; compare Cornish *hoch*] —ˈ**hogger** *n.* —ˈ**hogˌlike** *adj.*

hogan (ˈhəʊgən) *n.* a wooden dwelling covered with earth, typical of the Navaho Indians of N America. [from Navaho]

Hogarthian (həʊˈgɑːθɪən) *adj.* relating to or characteristic of William Hogarth (1697–1764), English engraver and painter, or his satirical artistic style.

hogback (ˈhɒgˌbæk) *n.* **1.** Also called: **hog's back.** a narrow ridge with sides that consist of steeply inclined rock strata. **2.** *Archaeol.* a Saxon or Scandinavian tomb with sloping sides.

hog badger *n.* a SE Asian badger, *Arctonyx collaris,* with a piglike mobile snout. Also called: **sand badger.**

hog cholera *n.* the U.S. term for **swine fever.**

hogfish (ˈhɒgˌfɪʃ) *n., pl.* **-fish** *or* **-fishes. 1.** a wrasse, *Lachnolaimus maximus,* that occurs in the Atlantic off the SE coast of North America. The head of the male resembles a pig's snout. **2.** another name for **pigfish** (sense 1).

hogged (hɒgd) *adj. Nautical.* (of a vessel) having a keel that droops at both ends. Compare **sag** (sense 6).

hogget (ˈhɒgɪt) *n. Brit. dialect, Austral., and N.Z.* another name for **hog** (senses 3, 4).

hoggin (ˈhɒgɪn) *or* **hogging** (ˈhɒgɪŋ) *n.* a finely sifted gravel used for making paths or roads. [C19: perhaps the same as *hogging* from HOG in the sense of arching the back, from the shape given to a road to facilitate drainage]

hoggish (ˈhɒgɪʃ) *adj.* selfish, gluttonous, or dirty. —ˈ**hoggishly** *adv.* —ˈ**hoggishness** *n.*

Hogmanay (ˌhɒgməˈneɪ) *n.* (*sometimes not cap.*) **a.** New Year's Eve in Scotland. **b.** (*as modifier*): *a Hogmanay party.* See also **first-foot.** [C17: Scottish and Northern English, perhaps from Norman French *hoguinane,* from Old French *aguillanneuf* the last day of the year; also, a New Year's eve gift]

hognosed skunk (ˈhɒgˌnəʊzd) *n.* any of several American skunks of the genus *Conepatus,* esp. *C. leuconotus,* having a broad snoutlike nose.

hognose snake (ˈhɒgˌnəʊz) *n.* any North American nonvenomous colubrid snake of the genus *Heterodon,* having a trowel-shaped snout and inflating the body when alarmed. Also called: **puff adder.**

hognut (ˈhɒgˌnʌt) *n.* another name for **pignut** (sense 1).

hog peanut *n.* a North American leguminous climbing plant, *Amphicarpa bracteata,* having fleshy curved one-seeded pods, which ripen in or on the ground.

hog's fennel *n.* any of several Eurasian umbelliferous marsh plants of the genus *Peucedanum,* esp. *P. officinale,* having clusters of small whitish flowers.

hogshead (ˈhɒgzˌhɛd) *n.* **1.** a unit of capacity, used esp. for alcoholic beverages. It has several values, being 54 imperial gallons in the case of beer and 52.5 imperial gallons in the case of wine. **2.** a large cask used for shipment of wines and spirits. [C14: of obscure origin]

hogtie (ˈhɒgˌtaɪ) *vb.* **-ties, -tying, -tied.** (*tr.*) *Chiefly U.S.* **1.** to tie together the legs or the arms and legs of. **2.** to impede, hamper, or thwart.

hogwash (ˈhɒgˌwɒʃ) *n.* **1.** nonsense. **2.** pigswill.

hogweed (ˈhɒgˌwiːd) *n.* any of several coarse weedy plants, esp. cow parsnip. See also **giant hogweed.**

hoick (hɔɪk) *vb. Informal.* to rise or raise abruptly and sharply: *to hoick an aircraft.* [C20: of unknown origin]

hoicks (hɔɪks) *interj.* a cry used to encourage hounds to hunt. Also: **yoicks.**

hoiden (ˈhɔɪdən) *n., adj., vb.* a variant spelling of **hoyden.** —ˈ**hoidenish** *adj.* —ˈ**hoidenishness** *n.*

hoi polloi (ˌhɔɪ pəˈlɔɪ) *n.* **the.** *Often derogatory.* the masses; common people. [Greek, literally: the many]

hoist (hɔɪst) *vb.* **1.** (*tr.*) to raise or lift up, esp. by mechanical means. **2. hoist with one's own petard.** See **petard** (sense 2). ~*n.* **3.** any apparatus or device for hoisting. **4.** the act of hoisting. **5.** See **rotary clothesline. 6.** *Nautical.* **a.** the amidships height of a sail bent to the yard with which it is hoisted. Compare **drop** (sense 15). **b.** the difference between the set and lowered positions of this yard. **7.** *Nautical.* the length of the luff of a fore-and-aft sail. **8.** *Nautical.* a group of signal flags. **9.** the inner edge of a flag next to the staff. Compare **fly**[1] (sense 25a). [C16: variant of *hoise,* probably from Low German; compare Dutch *hijschen,* German *hissen*] —ˈ**hoister** *n.*

hoity-toity (ˌhɔɪtɪˈtɔɪtɪ) *adj. Informal.* arrogant or haughty. [C17: rhyming compound based on C16 *hoit* to romp, of obscure origin]

hoke (həʊk) *vb.* (*tr.;* usually foll. by *up*) to overplay (a part, etc.). [C20: perhaps from HOKUM]

hokey (ˈhəʊkɪ) *adj. Slang, chiefly U.S. and Canadian.* **1.** corny; sentimental. **2.** contrived; phoney. [C20: from HOKUM]

hokey cokey (ˈhəʊkɪ ˈkəʊkɪ) *n.* a Cockney song with a traditional dance routine to match the words.

hokey-pokey (ˌhəʊkɪˈpəʊkɪ) *n.* another word for **hocus-pocus** (senses 1, 2).

hokku (ˈhɒkuː) *n., pl.* **-ku.** *Prosody.* another word for **haiku.** [from Japanese, from *hok* beginning + *ku* hemistich]

hokonui (həʊkəˈnuːiː) *n. N.Z.* illicit whisky. [from *Hokonui,* district of Southland Province, N.Z.]

hokum (ˈhəʊkəm) *n. Slang, chiefly U.S. and Canadian.* **1.** claptrap; bunk. **2.** obvious or hackneyed material of a sentimental nature in a play, film, etc. [C20: probably a blend of HOCUS-POCUS and BUNKUM]

hol- *combining form.* a variant of **holo-** before a vowel.

Holarctic (həʊˈlɑːktɪk) *adj.* of or denoting a zoogeographical region consisting of the Palaearctic and Nearctic regions. [C19: from HOLO- + ARCTIC]

hold[1] (həʊld) *vb.* **holds, holding, held** (hɛld). **1.** to have or keep (an object) with or within the hands, arms, etc.; clasp. **2.** (*tr.*) to support or bear: *to hold a drowning man's head above water.* **3.** to maintain or be maintained in a specified state or condition: *to hold one's emotions in check; hold firm.* **4.** (*tr.*) to set aside or reserve: *they will hold our tickets until tomorrow.* **5.** (when *intr., usually used in commands*) to restrain or be restrained from motion, action, departure, etc.: *hold that man until the police come.* **6.** (*intr.*) to remain fast or unbroken: *that cable won't hold much longer.* **7.** (*intr.*) (of the weather) to remain dry and bright: *how long will the weather hold?* **8.** (*tr.*) to keep the attention of: *her singing held the audience.* **9.** (*tr.*) to engage in or carry on: *to hold a meeting.* **10.** (*tr.*) to have the ownership, possession, etc., of: *he holds a law degree from London; who's holding the ace of spades?* **11.** (*tr.*) to have the use of or responsibility for: *to hold the office of director.* **12.** (*tr.*) to have the space or capacity for: *the carton will hold only eight books.* **13.** (*tr.*) to be able to control the outward effects of drinking beer, spirits, etc.: *he can hold his drink well.* **14.** (often foll. by *to* or *by*) to remain or cause to remain committed to: *hold him to his promise; he held by his views in spite of opposition.* **15.** (*tr.; takes a clause as object*) to claim: *he holds that the theory is incorrect.* **16.** (*intr.*) to remain relevant, valid, or true: *the old philosophies don't hold nowadays.* **17.** (*tr.*) to keep in the mind: *to hold affection for someone.* **18.** (*tr.*) to regard or consider in a specified manner: *I hold him very dear.* **19.** (*tr.*) to guard or defend successfully: *hold the fort against the attack.* **20.** (*intr.*) to continue to go: *hold on one's way.* **21.** (sometimes foll. by *on*) *Music.* to sustain the sound of (a note) throughout its specified duration: *to hold on a semibreve for its full value.* **22.** (*tr.*) *Computer technol.* to retain (data) in a storage device after copying onto another storage device or onto another location in the same device. Compare **clear** (sense 49). **23.** (*tr.*) to be in possession of illegal drugs. **24. hold (good) for.** to apply or be relevant to: *the same rules hold for everyone.* **25. hold it!** **a.** stop! wait! **b.** stay in the same position! as when being photographed. **26. hold one's head high.** to conduct oneself in a proud and confident manner. **27. hold one's own.** to maintain one's situation or position esp. in spite of opposition or difficulty. **28. hold one's peace** *or* **tongue.** to keep silent. **29. hold water.** to prove credible, logical, or consistent. **30. there is no holding him.** he is so spirited or resolute that he cannot be restrained. ~*n.* **31.** the act or method of holding fast or grasping, as with the hands. **32.** something to hold onto, as for support or control. **33.** an object or device that holds fast or grips something else so as to hold it fast. **34.** controlling force or influence: *she has a hold on him.* **35.** a short delay or pause. **36. on hold.** in a state of temporary postponement or delay. **37.** a prison or a cell in a prison. **38.** *Wrestling.* a way of seizing one's opponent: *a wrist hold.* **39.** *Music.* a pause or fermata. **40. a.** a tenure or holding, esp. of land. **b.** (*in combination*): *leasehold; freehold; copyhold.* **41.** a container. **42.** *Archaic.* a fortified place. **43. get hold of.** **a.** to obtain. **b.** to come into contact with. **44. no holds barred.** all limitations removed. ~See also **hold back, hold down, hold forth, hold in, hold off, hold on, hold out, hold over, hold together, hold-up, hold with.** [Old English *healdan;* related to Old Norse *halla,* Gothic *haldan,* German *halten*] —ˈ**holdable** *adj.*

hold[2] (həʊld) *n.* the space in a ship or aircraft for storing cargo. [C16: variant of HOLE]

holdall (ˈhəʊldˌɔːl) *n. Brit.* a large strong bag or basket. Usual U.S. and Canadian name: **carryall.**

hold back *vb.* (*adv.*) **1.** to restrain or be restrained. **2.** (*tr.*) to withhold: *he held back part of the payment.* ~*n.* **holdback. 3.** a strap of the harness joining the breeching to the shaft, so that the horse can hold back the vehicle. **4.** something that restrains or hinders.

hold down *vb.* (*tr., adv.*) **1.** to restrain or control. **2.** *Informal.* to manage to retain or keep possession of: *to hold down two jobs at once.*

holden (ˈhəʊldən) *vb. Archaic or dialect.* a past participle of **hold**[1].

holder (ˈhəʊldə) *n.* **1.** a person or thing that holds. **2. a.** a person, such as an owner, who has possession or control of something. **b.** (*in combination*): *householder.* **3.** *Law.* a person who has possession of a bill of exchange, cheque, or promissory note that he is legally entitled to enforce. —ˈ**holderˌship** *n.*

holdfast (ˈhəʊldˌfɑːst) *n.* **1. a.** the act of gripping strongly. **b.** such a grip. **2.** any device used to secure an object, such as a hook, clamp, etc. **3.** the organ of attachment of a seaweed or related plant.

hold forth *vb.* (*adv.*) **1.** (*intr.*) to speak for a long time or in public. **2.** (*tr.*) to offer (an attraction or enticement).

hold in *vb.* (*tr., adv.*) **1.** to curb, control, or keep in check. **2.** to conceal or restrain (feelings).

holding (ˈhəʊldɪŋ) *n.* **1.** land held under a lease and used for agriculture or similar purposes. **2.** (*often pl.*) property to which the holder has legal title, such as land, stocks, shares, and other investments. **3.** *Sport.* the obstruction of an opponent with the hands or arms, esp. in boxing. ~*adj.* **4.** *Austral. informal.* in funds; having money.

holding company *n.* a company with controlling shareholdings in one or more other companies.

holding operation *n.* a plan or procedure devised to prolong the existing situation.

holding paddock *n. Austral. and N.Z.* a paddock in which cattle or sheep are kept temporarily, as before shearing, etc.

holding pattern *n.* the oval or circular path of an aircraft flying around an airport awaiting permission to land.

hold off *vb.* (*adv.*) **1.** (*tr.*) to keep apart or at a distance. **2.** (*intr.;* often foll. by *from*) to refrain (from doing something): *he held off buying the house until prices fell slightly.*

hold on *vb.* (*intr., adv.*) **1.** to maintain a firm grasp: *she held on with all her strength.* **2.** to continue or persist. **3.** (foll. by *to*) to keep or retain: *hold on to those stamps as they'll soon be valuable.* **4.** to keep a telephone line open. ~*interj.* **5.** *Informal.* stop! wait!

hold out *vb.* (*adv.*) **1.** (*tr.*) to offer or present. **2.** (*intr.*) to last or endure. **3.** (*intr.*) to continue to resist or stand firm, as a city under siege or a person refusing to succumb to persuasion. **4.** *Chiefly U.S.* to withhold (something due or expected). **5. hold out for.** to wait patiently or uncompromisingly for (the fulfilment of one's demands). **6. hold out on.** *Informal.* to delay in or keep from telling (a person) some new or important information.

hold over *vb.* (*tr., mainly adv.*) **1.** to defer consideration of or action on. **2.** to postpone for a further period. **3.** to prolong (a note, chord, etc.) from one bar to the next. **4.** (*prep.*) to intimidate (a person) with (a threat). ~*n.* **holdover.** *U.S. and Canadian informal.* **5.** an elected official who continues in office after his term has expired. **6.** a performer or performance continuing beyond the original engagement.

hold together *vb.* (*adv.*) **1.** to cohere or remain or cause to cohere or remain in one piece: *your old coat holds together very well.* **2.** to stay or cause to stay united: *the children held the family together.*

hold-up *n.* **1.** a robbery, esp. an armed one. **2.** a delay; stoppage. **3.** *U.S.* an excessive charge; extortion. ~*vb.* **hold up.** (*adv.*) **4.** (*tr.*) to delay; hinder: *we were held up by traffic.* **5.** (*tr.*) to keep from falling; support. **6.** (*tr.*) to stop forcibly or waylay in order to rob, esp. using a weapon. **7.** (*tr.*) to exhibit or present: *he held up his achievements for our admiration.* **8.** (*intr.*) to survive or last: *how are your shoes holding up?* **9.** *Bridge.* to refrain from playing a high card, so delaying the establishment of (a suit).

hold with *vb.* (*intr., prep.*) to support; approve of.

hole (həʊl) *n.* **1.** an area hollowed out in a solid. **2.** an opening made in or through something. **3.** an animal's hiding place or burrow. **4.** *Informal.* an unattractive place, such as a town or a dwelling. **5.** *Informal.* a cell or dungeon. **6.** *U.S. informal.* a small anchorage. **7.** a fault (esp. in the phrase **pick holes in**). **8.** *Slang.* a difficult and embarrassing situation. **9.** the cavity in various games into which the ball must be thrust. **10.** (on a golf course) **a.** the cup on each of the greens. **b.** each of the divisions of a course (usually 18) represented by the distance between the tee and a green. **c.** the score made in striking the ball from the tee into the hole. **11.** *Physics.* **a.** a vacancy in a nearly full band of quantum states of electrons in a semiconductor or an insulator. Under the action of an electric field holes behave as carriers of positive charge. **b.** (*as modifier*): *hole current.* **c.** a vacancy in the nearly full continuum of quantum states of negative energy of fermions. A hole appears as the antiparticle of the fermion. **12. hole in the wall.** *Informal.* a small dingy place, esp. one difficult to find. **13. in holes.** so worn as to be full of holes: *his socks were in holes.* **14. in the hole.** *Chiefly U.S.* **a.** in debt. **b.** (of a card, the **hole card,** in stud poker) dealt face down in the first round. **15. make a hole in.** to consume or use a great amount of (food, drink, money, etc.): *to make a hole in a bottle of brandy.* ~*vb.* **16.** to make a hole or holes in (something). **17.** (when *intr.,* often foll. by *out*) *Golf.* to hit (the ball) into the hole. [Old English *hol;* related to Gothic *hulundi,* German *Höhle,* Old Norse *hylr* pool, Latin *caulis* hollow stem; see HOLLOW] —ˈ**holey** *adj.*

hole-and-corner *adj.* (*usually prenominal*) *Informal.* furtive or secretive.

hole in one *Golf.* ~*n.* **1.** a shot from the tee that finishes in the hole. ~*vb.* **2.** (*intr.*) to score a hole in one. ~Also (esp. U.S.): **ace.**

hole in the heart *n.* a defect of the heart in which there is an abnormal opening in any of the walls dividing the four heart chambers.

hole up *vb.* (*intr., adv.*). **1.** (of an animal) to hibernate, esp. in a cave. **2.** *Informal.* to hide or remain secluded.

Holi (ˈhɒˌliː) *n.* a Hindu spring festival, celebrated for two to five days, commemorating the god Krishna's dalliance with the cowgirls. Bonfires are lit and coloured powder and water thrown over celebrants. [named after *Holika,* legendary female demon]

-holic *suffix forming nouns.* indicating a person having an abnormal desire for or dependence on: *workaholic; chocaholic.* [C20: on the pattern of *alcoholic*]

holiday ('hɒlɪˌdeɪ, -dɪ) *n.* **1.** (*often pl.*) *Chiefly Brit.* **a.** a period in which a break is taken from work or studies for rest, travel, or recreation. U.S. and Canadian word: **vacation. b.** (*as modifier*): *a holiday mood.* **2.** a day on which work is suspended by law or custom, such as a religious festival, bank holiday, etc. Related adj.: **ferial.** ~*vb.* **3.** (*intr.*) *Chiefly Brit.* to spend a holiday. [Old English *hāligdæg,* literally: holy day]

holiday camp *n. Brit.* a place, esp. one at the seaside, providing accommodation, recreational facilities, etc., for holiday-makers.

holiday-maker *n. Brit.* a person who goes on holiday. U.S. and Canadian equivalents: **vacationer, vacationist.**

holily ('həʊlɪlɪ) *adv.* in a holy, devout, or sacred manner.

holiness ('həʊlɪnɪs) *n.* the state or quality of being holy.

Holiness ('həʊlɪnɪs) *n.* (preceded by *his* or *your*) a title once given to all bishops, but now reserved for the pope.

holism ('həʊlɪzəm) *n.* **1.** any doctrine that a system may have properties over and above those of its parts and their organization. **2.** the treatment of any subject as a whole integrated system, esp., in medicine, the consideration of the complete person, physically and psychologically, in the treatment of a disease. See also **alternative medicine. 3.** *Philosophy.* one of a number of methodological theses holding that the significance of the parts can only be understood in terms of their contribution to the significance of the whole and that the latter must therefore be epistemologically prior. Compare **reductionism, atomism** (sense 2). [C20: from HOLO- + -ISM] **—ho'listic** *adj.* **—ho'listically** *adv.*

holland ('hɒlənd) *n.* a coarse linen cloth, used esp. for furnishing. [C15: after *Holland* (the Netherlands), where it was made]

hollandaise sauce (ˌhɒlən'deɪz, 'hɒlənˌdeɪz) *n.* a rich sauce of egg yolks, butter, vinegar, etc., served esp. with fish. [C19: from French *sauce hollandaise* Dutch sauce]

Hollander ('hɒləndə) *n.* another name for a **Dutchman.**

Hollands ('hɒləndz) *n.* Dutch gin, often sold in stone bottles. [C18: from Dutch *hollandsch genever*]

holler ('hɒlə) *Informal.* ~*vb.* **1.** to shout or yell (something). ~*n.* **2.** a shout; call. [variant of C16 *hollow,* from *holla,* from French *holà* stop! (literally: ho there!)]

hollo ('hɒləʊ), **holla** ('hɒlə), *or* **holloa** (hə'ləʊ) *n., pl.* **-los, -las,** *or* **-loas** (-'ləʊz), *interj.* **1.** a cry for attention, or of encouragement. ~*vb.* **2.** (*intr.*) to shout. [C16: from French *holà* ho there!]

hollow ('hɒləʊ) *adj.* **1.** having a hole, cavity, or space within; not solid. **2.** having a sunken area; concave. **3.** recessed or deeply set: *hollow cheeks.* **4.** (of sounds) as if resounding in a hollow place. **5.** without substance or validity. **6.** hungry or empty. **7.** insincere; cynical. **8. a hollow leg** *or* **hollow legs.** the capacity to eat or drink a lot without ill effects. ~*adv.* **9. beat (someone) hollow.** *Brit. informal.* to defeat (someone) thoroughly and convincingly. ~*n.* **10.** a cavity, opening, or space in or within something. **11.** a depression or dip in the land. ~*vb.* (often foll. by *out,* usually when *tr.*) **12.** to make or become hollow. **13.** to form (a hole, cavity, etc.) or (of a hole, etc.) to be formed. [C12: from *holu,* inflected form of Old English *holh* cave; related to Old Norse *holr,* German *hohl;* see HOLE] **—'hollowly** *adv.* **—'hollowness** *n.*

hollow-back *n. Pathol.* the nontechnical name for **lordosis.** Compare **hunchback.**

hollow-eyed *adj.* with the eyes appearing to be sunk into the face, as from excessive fatigue.

hollowware ('hɒləʊˌwɛə) *n.* hollow articles made of metal, china, etc., such as pots, jugs, and kettles. Compare **flatware** (sense 2).

holly ('hɒlɪ) *n., pl.* **-lies. 1.** any tree or shrub of the genus *Ilex,* such as the Eurasian *I. aquifolium,* having bright red berries and shiny evergreen leaves with prickly edges. **2.** branches of any of these trees, used for Christmas decorations. **3. holly oak.** another name for **holm oak.** ~See also **sea holly.** [Old English *holegn;* related to Old Norse *hulfr,* Old High German *hulis,* German *Hulst,* Old Slavonic *kolja* prick]

hollyhock ('hɒlɪˌhɒk) *n.* a tall widely cultivated malvaceous plant, *Althaea rosea,* with stout hairy stems and spikes of white, yellow, red, or purple flowers. Also called (U.S.): **rose mallow.** [C16: from HOLY + *hock,* from Old English *hoc* mallow]

Hollywood ('hɒlɪˌwʊd) *n.* **a.** the American film industry, based at Hollywood, a suburb of Los Angeles, California. **b.** (*as modifier*): *a Hollywood star.*

holm[1] (həʊm) *n. Dialect, chiefly northwestern English.* **1.** an island in a river or lake. **2.** low flat land near a river. [Old English *holm* sea, island; related to Old Saxon *holm* hill, Old Norse *holmr* island, Latin *culmen* tip]

holm[2] (həʊm) *n.* **1.** short for **holm oak. 2.** *Chiefly Brit.* a dialect word for **holly.** [C14: variant of obsolete *holin,* from Old English *holegn* HOLLY]

holmic ('hɒlmɪk) *adj.* of or containing holmium.

holmium ('hɒlmɪəm) *n.* a malleable silver-white metallic element of the lanthanide series. Symbol: Ho; atomic no.: 67; atomic wt.: 164.93; valency: 3; relative density: 8.80; melting pt.: 1461°C; boiling pt.: 2600°C (approx.). [C19: from New Latin *Holmia* Stockholm, capital of Sweden]

holm oak *n.* an evergreen Mediterranean oak tree, *Quercus ilex,* with prickly leaves resembling holly. Also called: **holm, holly oak, ilex.**

holo- *or before a vowel* **hol-** *combining form.* whole or wholly: *holograph; holotype; Holarctic.* [from Greek *holos*]

holobenthic (ˌhɒlə'bɛnθɪk) *adj.* (of an animal) completing its life cycle in the ocean depths.

holoblastic (ˌhɒlə'blæstɪk) *adj. Embryol.* of or showing cleavage of the entire zygote into blastomeres, as in eggs with little yolk. Compare **meroblastic. —ˌholo'blastically** *adv.*

Holocaine ('hɒləˌkeɪn) *n.* a trademark for **phenacaine.**

holocaust ('hɒləˌkɔːst) *n.* **1.** great destruction or loss of life or the source of such destruction, esp. fire. **2.** (*usually cap.*) **the.** the mass murder by the Nazis of the Jews of continental Europe between 1940 and 1945. **3.** a rare word for **burnt offering.** [C13: from Late Latin *holocaustum* whole burnt offering, from Greek *holokauston,* from HOLO- + *kaustos,* from *kaiein* to burn] **—ˌholo'caustal** *or* **ˌholo'caustic** *adj.*

Holocene ('hɒləˌsiːn) *adj.* **1.** of, denoting, or formed in the second and most recent epoch of the Quaternary period, which began 10 000 years ago at the end of the Pleistocene. ~*n.* **2. the.** the Holocene epoch or rock series. ~Also: **Recent.**

holocrine ('hɒləkrɪn) *adj.* (of the secretion of glands) characterized by disintegration of the entire glandular cell in releasing its product, as in sebaceous glands. Compare **merocrine, apocrine.** [C20: from HOLO- + Greek *krinein* to separate, decide]

holocrystalline (ˌhɒlə'krɪstəˌlaɪn) *adj.* (of igneous rocks) having only crystalline components and no glass. Compare **hemicrystalline.**

holoenzyme (ˌhɒləʊ'ɛnzaɪm) *n.* an active enzyme consisting of a protein component (apoenzyme) and its coenzyme.

hologram ('hɒləˌgræm) *n.* a photographic record produced by illuminating the object with coherent light (as from a laser) and, without using lenses, exposing a film to light reflected from this object and to a direct beam of coherent light. When interference patterns on the film are illuminated by the coherent light a three-dimensional image is produced.

holograph ('hɒləˌgræf, -ˌgrɑːf) *n.* **a.** a book or document handwritten by its author; original manuscript; autograph. **b.** (*as modifier*): *a holograph document.*

holography (hɒ'lɒgrəfɪ) *n.* the science or practice of producing holograms. **—holographic** (ˌhɒlə'græfɪk) *adj.* **—ˌholo'graphically** *adv.*

holohedral (ˌhɒlə'hiːdrəl) *adj.* (of a crystal) exhibiting all the planes required for the symmetry of the crystal system. **—ˌholo'hedrism** *n.*

holomorphic (ˌhɒlə'mɔːfɪk) *adj. Maths.* another word for **analytic** (sense 5).

holophrastic (ˌhɒlə'fræstɪk) *adj.* **1.** denoting the stage in a child's acquisition of syntax when most utterances are single words. **2.** (of languages) tending to express in one word what would be expressed in several words in other languages; polysynthetic. [C19: from HOLO- + Greek *phrastikos* expressive, from *phrazein* to express]

holophytic (ˌhɒlə'fɪtɪk) *adj.* (of plants) capable of synthesizing their food from inorganic molecules, esp. by photosynthesis. **—holophyte** ('hɒləˌfaɪt) *n.*

holoplankton (ˌhɒlə'plæŋktən) *n.* organisms, such as diatoms and algae, that spend all stages of their life cycle as plankton. Compare **meroplankton.**

holothurian (ˌhɒlə'θjʊərɪən) *n.* **1.** any echinoderm of the class *Holothuroidea,* including the sea cucumbers, having a leathery elongated body with a ring of tentacles around the mouth. ~*adj.* **2.** of, relating to, or belonging to the *Holothuroidea.* [C19: from New Latin *Holothūria* name of type genus, from Latin: water polyp, from Greek *holothourion,* of obscure origin]

holotype ('hɒləˌtaɪp) *n. Biology.* another name for **type specimen. —holotypic** (ˌhɒlə'tɪpɪk) *adj.*

holozoic (ˌhɒlə'zəʊɪk) *adj.* (of animals) obtaining nourishment by feeding on plants or other animals.

holp (həʊlp) *vb. Archaic or dialect.* a past tense of **help.**

holpen ('həʊlpən) *vb. Archaic.* a past participle of **help.**

hols (hɒlz) *pl. n. Brit. school slang.* holidays.

Holstein ('həʊlstaɪn) *n.* the usual U.S. and Canadian name for **Friesian** (the cattle). [named after *Holstein* in N Germany]

holster ('həʊlstə) *n.* **1.** a sheathlike leather case for a pistol, attached to a belt or saddle. **2.** *Mountaineering.* a similar case for an ice axe or piton hammer. [C17: via Dutch *holster* from Germanic; compare Old Norse *hulstr* sheath, Old English *heolstor* darkness, Gothic *hulistr* cover] **—'holstered** *adj.*

holt[1] (həʊlt) *n. Archaic or poetic.* a wood or wooded hill. [Old English *holt;* related to Old Norse *holt,* Old High German *holz,* Old Slavonic *kladŭ* log, Greek *klados* twig]

holt[2] (həʊlt) *n.* the burrowed lair of an animal, esp. an otter. [C16: a phonetic variant of HOLD[2]]

holus-bolus ('həʊləs'bəʊləs) *adv. Informal.* all at once. [C19: pseudo-Latin based on *whole bolus;* see BOLUS]

holy ('həʊlɪ) *adj.* **holier, holiest. 1.** of, relating to, or associated with God or a deity; sacred. **2.** endowed or invested with extreme purity or sublimity. **3.** devout, godly, or virtuous. **4. holier-than-thou.** offensively sanctimonious or self-righteous: *a holier-than-thou attitude.* **5. holy terror. a.** a difficult or frightening person. **b.** *Irish informal.* a person who is an active gambler, womanizer, etc. ~*n., pl.* **-lies.** **6. a.** a sacred place. **b. the holy.** (*functioning as pl.*) persons or things invested with holiness. [Old English *hālig, hǣlig;* related to Old Saxon *hēlag,* Gothic *hailags,* German *heilig;* see HALLOW]

Holy Bible *n.* another name for the **Bible.**

Holy Communion *n.* **1.** the celebration of the Eucharist. **2.** the consecrated elements of the Eucharist. ~Often shortened to **Communion.**

holy day *n.* a day on which a religious festival is observed.

holy day of obligation *n.* a major feastday of the Roman Catholic Church on which Catholics are bound to attend Mass and refrain from servile work.

Holy Father *n. R.C. Church.* a title of the pope.

Holy Ghost *n.* another name for the **Holy Spirit.**

Holy Hour *n.* **1.** *R.C. Church.* an hour set aside for prayer and reflection. **2.** (*not caps.*) *Irish informal.* a period during the afternoon when public houses are obliged to close by law.

Holy Innocents' Day *n.* Dec. 28, a day commemorating the massacre of male children at Bethlehem by Herod's order (Matthew 2:16); Childermas.

Holy Joe *n. Informal.* **1.** a minister or chaplain. **2.** any sanctimonious or self-righteous person.

holy Mary *n. Irish.* a pietistic person: *he's a real holy Mary.*

holy of holies *n.* **1.** any place of special sanctity. **2.** (*caps.*) the innermost compartment of the Jewish tabernacle, and later of the Temple, where the Ark was enshrined.

holy orders *pl. n.* **1.** the sacrament or rite whereby a person is admitted to the Christian ministry. **2.** the grades of the Christian ministry. **3.** the rank or status of an ordained Christian minister. ~See also **orders.**

holy place *n.* **1.** the outer chamber of a Jewish sanctuary. **2.** a place of pilgrimage.

Holy Roller *n. Derogatory.* a member of a sect that expresses religious fervour in an ecstatic or frenzied way.

holy rood *n.* **1.** a cross or crucifix, esp. one placed upon the rood screen in a church. **2.** (*often cap.*) the cross on which Christ was crucified.

Holy Saturday *n.* the Saturday before Easter Sunday.

Holy Scripture *n.* another term for **Scripture.**

Holy See *n. R.C. Church.* **1.** the see of the pope as bishop of Rome and head of the Church. **2.** the Roman curia.

Holy Spirit *or* **Ghost** *n. Christianity.* the third person of the Trinity.

holystone ('həʊlɪˌstəʊn) *n.* **1.** a soft sandstone used for scrubbing the decks of a vessel. ~*vb.* **2.** (*tr.*) to scrub (a vessel's decks) with a holystone. [C19: perhaps so named from its being used in a kneeling position]

holy synod *n.* the governing body of any of the Orthodox Churches.

holytide ('həʊlɪˌtaɪd) *n. Archaic.* a season of special religious observances or one regarded as especially holy.

holy war *n.* a war waged in the cause of a religion.

holy water *n.* water that has been blessed by a priest for use in symbolic rituals of purification.

Holy Week *n.* the week preceding Easter Sunday.

Holy Willie ('wɪlɪ) *n.* a person who is hypocritically pious. [C18: from Burns' *Holy Willie's Prayer*]

Holy Writ *n.* another term for **Scripture.**

Holy Year *n. R.C. Church.* a period of remission from sin, esp. one granted every 25 years.

hom (hɒm) *or* **homa** ('hɒmə) *n.* **1.** a sacred plant of the Parsees and ancient Persians. **2.** a drink made from this plant. [from Persian, from Avestan *haoma*]

homage ('hɒmɪdʒ) *n.* **1.** a public show of respect or honour towards someone or something (esp. in the phrases **pay** *or* **do homage to**). **2.** (in feudal society) **a.** the act of respect and allegiance made by a vassal to his lord. See also **fealty. b.** something done in acknowledgment of vassalage. ~*vb.* (*tr.*) **3.** *Archaic or poetic.* to render homage to. [C13: from Old French, from *home* man, from Latin *homo*]

hombre[1] ('ɒmbreɪ, -brɪ) *n. Western U.S.* a slang word for **man.** [C19: from Spanish: man]

hombre[2] ('hɒmbə) *n.* a variant of **ombre.**

homburg ('hɒmbɜːg) *n.* a man's hat of soft felt with a dented crown and a stiff upturned brim. [C20: named after *Homburg,* in Germany, town where it was originally made]

home (həʊm) *n.* **1.** the place or a place where one lives: *have you no home to go to?* **2.** a house or other dwelling. **3.** a family or other group living in a house or other place. **4.** a person's country, city, etc., esp. viewed as a birthplace, a residence during one's early years, or a place dear to one. **5.** the environment or habitat of a person or animal. **6.** the place where something is invented, founded, or developed: *the U.S. is the home of baseball.* **7. a.** a building or organization set up to care for orphans, the aged, etc. **b.** an informal name for a **mental home. 8.** *Sport.* one's own ground: *the match is at home.* **9. a.** the objective towards which a player strives in certain sports. **b.** an area where a player is safe from attack. **10.** *Lacrosse.* **a.** one of two positions of play nearest the opponents' goal. **b.** a player assigned to such a position: *inside home.* **11.** *Baseball.* another name for **home plate. 12.** *N.Z. informal, obsolete.* Britain, esp. England. **13. a home from home.** a place other than one's own home where one can be at ease. **14. at home. a.** in one's own home or country. **b.** at ease, as if at one's own home. **c.** giving an informal party at one's own home. **d.** *Brit.* such a party. **15. at home in, on,** *or* **with.** familiar or conversant with. **16. home and dry.** *Brit. informal.* definitely safe or successful: *we will not be home and dry until the votes have been counted.* Austral. and N.Z. equivalent: **home and hosed. 17. near home.** concerning one deeply. ~*adj.* (*usually prenominal*) **18.** of, relating to, or involving one's home, country, etc.; domestic. **19.** (of an activity) done in one's house: *home taping.* **20.** effective or deadly: *a home thrust.* **21.** *Sport.* relating to one's own ground: *a home game.* **22.** *U.S.* central; principal: *the company's home office.* ~*adv.* **23.** to or at home: *I'll be home tomorrow.* **24.** to or on the point. **25.** to the fullest extent: *hammer the nail home.* **26.** (of nautical gear) into or in the best or proper position: *the boom is home.* **27. bring home to. a.** to make clear to. **b.** to place the blame on. **28. come home.** *Nautical.* (of an anchor) to fail to hold. **29. come home to.** to become absolutely clear to. **30. nothing to write home about.** *Informal.* to be of no particular interest: *the film was nothing to write home about.* ~*vb.* **31.** (*intr.*) (of birds and other animals) to return home accurately from a distance. **32.** (often foll. by *on* or *onto*) to direct or be directed onto a point or target, esp. by automatic navigational aids. **33.** to send or go home. **34.** to furnish with or have a home. **35.** (*intr.;* often foll. by *in* or *in on*) to be directed towards a goal, target, etc. [Old English *hām;* related to Old Norse *heimr,* Gothic *haims,* Old High German *heim,* Dutch *heem,* Greek *kōmi* village] —'**homeless** *adj., n.* —'**homelessness** *n.* —'**home,like** *adj.*

home aid *n. N.Z.* another name for **home help.**

home banking *n.* a system whereby a person at home or in an office can use a computer with a modem to call up information from a bank or to transfer funds electronically.

homebody ('həʊmˌbɒdɪ) *n., pl.* **-bodies.** *Informal.* a person whose life and interests are centred on the home.

homeboy ('həʊmˌbɔɪ) *n. Slang, chiefly U.S.* **1.** a close friend. **2.** a person from one's home town or neighbourhood. [C20: U.S. rap-music usage] —'**home,girl** *fem. n.*

homebred ('həʊmˌbrɛd) *adj.* **1.** raised or bred at home. **2.** lacking sophistication or cultivation; crude.

home-brew *n.* a beer or other alcoholic drink brewed at home rather than commercially. —'**home-'brewed** *adj.*

homecoming ('həʊmˌkʌmɪŋ) *n.* the act of coming home.

home economics *n.* (*functioning as sing. or pl.*) the study of diet, budgeting, child care, and other subjects concerned with running a home. —**home economist** *n.*

home farm *n. Brit.* (esp. formerly) a farm belonging to and providing food for a large country house.

home ground *n.* a familiar area or topic.

home-grown *adj.* (esp. of fruit and vegetables) produced in one's own country, district, estate, or garden.

Home Guard *n.* **1.** a volunteer part-time military force recruited for the defence of the United Kingdom in World War II. **2.** (in various countries) a civil defence and reserve militia organization.

home help *n. Social welfare.* (in Britain and New Zealand) **1.** a person, usually a woman, who is paid to do domestic chores for persons unable to look after themselves adequately. **2.** Also called: **home care.** such a service provided by a local authority social services department to those whom it judges most need it. ~Also called (N.Z.): **home aid.**

homeland ('həʊmˌlænd) *n.* **1.** the country in which one lives or was born. **2.** the official name for a **Bantustan.**

homelands movement *n. Austral.* the programme to resettle Australian Aborigines on their tribal lands.

home loan *n.* an informal name for **mortgage** (sense 1).

homely ('həʊmlɪ) *adj.* **-lier, -liest. 1.** characteristic of or suited to the ordinary home; unpretentious. **2.** (of a person) **a.** *Brit.* warm and domesticated in manner or appearance. **b.** *Chiefly U.S. and Canadian.* plain or ugly. —'**homeliness** *n.*

home-made *adj.* **1.** (esp. of cakes, jam, and other foods) made at home or on the premises, esp. of high-quality ingredients. **2.** crudely fashioned.

homemaker ('həʊmˌmeɪkə) *n. U.S. and Canadian.* **1.** a person, esp. a housewife, who manages a home. **2.** a social worker who manages a household during the incapacity of the housewife. —'**home,making** *n., adj.*

homeo-, homoeo-, *or* **homoio-** *combining form.* like or similar: *homeomorphism.* [from Latin *homoeo-,* from Greek *homoio-,* from *homos* same]

Home Office *n. Brit. government.* the national department responsible for the maintenance of law and order, immigration control, and all other domestic affairs not specifically assigned to another department.

homeomorphism *or* **homoeomorphism** (ˌhəʊmɪə'mɔːfɪzəm) *n.* **1.** the property, shown by certain chemical compounds, of having the same crystal form but different chemical composition. **2.** *Maths.* a one-to-one correspondence, continuous in both directions, between the points of two geometric figures or between two topological spaces. —ˌ**homeo'morphic,** ˌ**homeo'morphous,** *or* ˌ**homoeo'morphic,** ˌ**homoeo'morphous** *adj.*

homeopathy *or* **homoeopathy** (ˌhəʊmɪ'ɒpəθɪ) *n.* a method of treating disease by the use of small amounts of a drug that, in healthy persons, produces symptoms similar to those of the disease being treated. Compare **allopathy.** —**homeopathic**

or **homoeopathic** (ˌhəʊmɪəˈpæθɪk) *adj.* —ˌ**homeoˈpathically** *or* ˌ**homoeoˈpathically** *adv.* —**homeopathist, homoeopathist** (ˌhəʊmɪˈɒpəθɪst) *or* **homeopath, homoeopath** (ˈhəʊmɪəˌpæθ) *n.*

homeostasis *or* **homoeostasis** (ˌhəʊmɪəʊˈsteɪsɪs) *n.* **1.** the maintenance of metabolic equilibrium within an animal by a tendency to compensate for disrupting changes. **2.** the maintenance of equilibrium within a social group, person, etc. —**homeostatic** *or* **homoeostatic** (ˌhəʊmɪəʊˈstætɪk) *adj.*

homeotypic (ˌhəʊmɪəʊˈtɪpɪk), **homeotypical** *or* **homoeotypic, homoeotypical** *adj.* denoting or relating to the second nuclear division of meiosis, which resembles mitosis. Compare **heterotypic.**

home plate *n. Baseball.* a flat often five-sided piece of hard rubber or other material that serves to define the area over which the pitcher must throw the ball for a strike and that a base runner must safely reach on his way from third base to score a run. Also called: **plate, home, home base.**

home purpose benefit *n. N.Z.* an allowance made by the Department of Social Welfare to a single mother and her children.

homer (ˈhəʊmə) *n.* **1.** another word for **homing pigeon. 2.** *U.S. and Canadian.* an informal word for **home run.**

home range *n. Ecology.* the area in which an animal normally ranges.

Homeric (həʊˈmerɪk) *or* **Homerian** (həʊˈmɪərɪən) *adj.* **1.** of, relating to, or resembling the Greek poet Homer (born c. 800 B.C.) or his poems. **2.** imposing or heroic. **3.** of or relating to the archaic form of Greek used by Homer. See **epic.** —**Hoˈmerically** *adv.*

Homeric laughter *n.* loud unrestrained laughter, as that of the gods.

home rule *n.* **1.** self-government, esp. in domestic affairs. **2.** *U.S. government.* the partial autonomy of cities and (in some states) counties, under which they manage their own affairs, with their own charters, etc., within the limits set by the state constitution and laws. **3.** the partial autonomy sometimes granted to a national minority or a colony.

home run *n. Baseball.* a hit that enables the batter to run round all four bases, usually by hitting the ball out of the playing area.

Home Secretary *n. Brit. government.* short for **Secretary of State for the Home Department;** the head of the Home Office.

homesick (ˈhəʊmˌsɪk) *adj.* depressed or melancholy at being away from home and family. —ˈ**homeˌsickness** *n.*

homespun (ˈhəʊmˌspʌn) *adj.* **1.** having plain or unsophisticated character. **2.** woven or spun at home. ~*n.* **3.** cloth made at home or made of yarn spun at home. **4.** a cloth resembling this but made on a power loom.

homestead (ˈhəʊmˌstɛd, -stɪd) *n.* **1.** a house or estate and the adjoining land, buildings, etc., esp. a farm. **2.** (in the U.S.) a house and adjoining land designated by the owner as his fixed residence and exempt under the homestead laws from seizure and forced sale for debts. **3.** (in western Canada) a piece of land, usually 160 acres, granted to a settler by the federal government. **4.** *Austral. and N.Z.* the owner's or manager's residence on a sheep or cattle station; in New Zealand the term includes all outbuildings.

homesteader (ˈhəʊmˌstɛdə) *n.* **1.** a person owning a homestead. **2.** *U.S. and Canadian.* a person who acquires or possesses land under a homestead law. **3.** a person taking part in a homesteading scheme.

homesteading (ˈhəʊmˌstɛdɪŋ) *n.* (in Britain) **a.** a scheme whereby council tenants are enabled to buy derelict property from the council and renovate it with the aid of Government grants. **b.** (*as modifier*): *a homesteading scheme.*

homestead law *n.* (in the U.S. and Canada) any of various laws conferring certain privileges on owners of homesteads.

home straight *n.* **1.** *Horse racing.* the section of a racecourse forming the approach to the finish. **2.** the final stage of an undertaking or journey. ~Also (chiefly U.S.) **home stretch.**

home teacher *n. Brit.* a teacher who educates ill or disabled children in their homes.

home truth *n.* (*often pl.*) an unpleasant fact told to a person about himself.

home unit *n. Austral. and N.Z.* a self-contained residence which is part of a series of similar residences. Often shortened to **unit.**

homeward (ˈhəʊmwəd) *adj.* **1.** directed or going home. **2.** (of a ship, part of a voyage, etc.) returning to the home port. ~*adv. also* **homewards. 3.** towards home.

homework (ˈhəʊmˌwɜːk) *n.* **1.** school work done out of lessons, esp. at home. **2.** any preparatory study. **3.** work done at home for pay.

homeworker (ˈhəʊmˌwɜːkə) *n.* a person who does paid work, esp. piecework, at home.

homey (ˈhəʊmɪ) *adj.* **homier, homiest. 1.** a variant spelling (esp. U.S.) of **homy.** ~*n.* **2.** *N.Z. informal.* a British person. —ˈ**homeyness** *n.*

homicidal (ˌhɒmɪˈsaɪdᵊl) *adj.* **1.** of, involving, or characterized by homicide. **2.** likely to commit homicide: *a homicidal maniac.* —ˌ**homiˈcidally** *adv.*

homicide (ˈhɒmɪˌsaɪd) *n.* **1.** the killing of a human being by another person. **2.** a person who kills another. [C14: from Old French, from Latin *homo* man + *caedere* to slay]

homiletic (ˌhɒmɪˈlɛtɪk) *or* **homiletical** *adj.* **1.** of or relating to a homily or sermon. **2.** of, relating to, or characteristic of homiletics. —ˌ**homiˈletically** *adv.*

homiletics (ˌhɒmɪˈlɛtɪks) *n.* (*functioning as sing.*) the art of preaching or writing sermons. [C17: from Greek *homilētikos* cordial, from *homilein* to converse with; see HOMILY]

homily (ˈhɒmɪlɪ) *n., pl.* **-lies. 1.** a sermon or discourse on a moral or religious topic. **2.** moralizing talk or writing. [C14: from Church Latin *homīlia,* from Greek: discourse, from *homilein* to converse with, from *homilos* crowd, from *homou* together + *ilē* crowd] —ˈ**homilist** *n.*

homing (ˈhəʊmɪŋ) *n.* (*modifier*) **1.** *Zoology.* relating to the ability to return home after travelling great distances: *homing instinct.* **2.** (of an aircraft, a missile, etc.) capable of guiding itself onto a target or to a specified point.

homing guidance *n.* a method of missile guidance in which internal equipment enables it to steer itself onto the target, as by sensing the target's heat radiation.

homing pigeon *n.* any breed of pigeon developed for its homing instinct, used for carrying messages or for racing. Also called: **homer.**

hominid (ˈhɒmɪnɪd) *n.* **1.** any primate of the family *Hominidae,* which includes modern man (*Homo sapiens*) and the extinct precursors of man. ~*adj.* **2.** of, relating to, or belonging to the *Hominidae.* [C19: via New Latin from Latin *homo* man + -ID²]

hominoid (ˈhɒmɪˌnɔɪd) *adj.* **1.** of or like man; manlike. **2.** of, relating to, or belonging to the primate superfamily *Hominoidea,* which includes the anthropoid apes and man. ~*n.* **3.** a hominoid animal. [C20: from Latin *homin-, homo* man + -OID]

hominy (ˈhɒmɪnɪ) *n. Chiefly U.S.* coarsely ground maize prepared as a food by boiling in milk or water. [C17: probably of Algonquian origin]

hominy grits *pl. n. U.S.* finely ground hominy. Often shortened to **grits.**

homo (ˈhəʊməʊ) *n., pl.* **-mos.** *Informal.* short for **homosexual.**

Homo (ˈhəʊməʊ) *n.* a genus of hominids including modern man (see ***Homo sapiens***) and several extinct species of primitive man, including *H. habilis* and *H. erectus.* [Latin: man]

homo- *combining form.* being the same or like: *homologous; homosexual.* Compare **hetero-.** [via Latin from Greek, from *homos* same]

homoblastic (ˌhəʊməˈblæstɪk) *adj.* (of a plant or plant part) showing no difference in form between the juvenile and the adult structures. Compare **heteroblastic.**

homocentric (ˌhəʊməʊˈsɛntrɪk, ˌhɒm-) *adj.* having the same centre; concentric. —ˌ**homoˈcentrically** *adv.*

homocercal (ˌhəʊməʊˈsɜːkᵊl, ˌhɒm-) *adj. Ichthyol.* of or possessing a symmetrical tail that extends beyond the end of the vertebral column, as in most bony fishes. Compare **heterocercal.** [C19: from HOMO- + Greek *kerkos* tail]

homochlamydeous (ˌhəʊməkləˈmɪdɪəs) *adj.* (of a plant) having a perianth in which the sepals and petals are fused together and indistinguishable. Compare **heterochlamydeous.**

homochromatic (ˌhəʊməʊkrəʊˈmætɪk, ˌhɒm-) *adj.* a less common word for **monochromatic** (sense 1). —**homochromatism** (ˌhəʊməʊˈkrəʊməˌtɪzəm, ˌhɒm-) *n.*

homochromous (ˌhəʊməˈkrəʊməs, ˌhɒm-) *adj.* (esp. of plant parts) of only one colour.

homocyclic (ˌhəʊməʊˈsaɪklɪk, -ˈsɪk-, ˌhɒm-) *adj.* (of an organic compound) containing a closed ring of atoms of the same kind, esp. carbon atoms. Compare **heterocyclic.**

homodont (ˈhəʊməˌdɒnt) *adj.* (of most nonmammalian vertebrates) having teeth that are all of the same type. Compare **heterodont.** [C19: from HOMO- + -ODONT]

homoeo- *combining form.* a variant of **homeo-.**

homoeroticism (ˌhəʊməʊɪˈrɒtɪˌsɪzəm) *or* **homoerotism** (ˌhəʊməʊˈɛrəˌtɪzəm) *n.* eroticism centred on or aroused by persons of one's own sex. —ˌ**homoeˈrotic** *adj.*

homogametic (ˌhəʊməgəˈmɛtɪk) *adj. Genetics.* denoting the sex that possesses two similar sex chromosomes. In humans and many other mammals it is the female sex, possessing two X-chromosomes. Compare **heterogametic.**

homogamy (hɒˈmɒgəmɪ) *n.* **1.** a condition in which all the flowers of an inflorescence are either of the same sex or hermaphrodite. Compare **heterogamy** (sense 3). **2.** the maturation of the anthers and stigmas of a flower at the same time, ensuring self-pollination. Compare **dichogamy.** —**hoˈmogamous** *adj.*

homogenate (hɒˈmɒdʒɪnɪt, -ˌneɪt) *n.* a substance produced by homogenizing. [C20: from HOMOGENIZE + -ATE¹]

homogeneous (ˌhəʊməˈdʒiːnɪəs, ˌhɒm-) *adj.* **1.** composed of similar or identical parts or elements. **2.** of uniform nature. **3.** similar in kind or nature. **4.** having a constant property, such as density, throughout. **5.** *Maths.* **a.** (of a polynomial) containing terms of the same degree with respect to all the variables, as in $x^2 + 2xy + y^2$. **b.** (of a function) containing a set of variables such that when each is multiplied by a constant, this constant can be eliminated without altering the value of the function, as in $\cos x/y + x/y$. **c.** (of an equation) containing a homogeneous function made equal to 0. **6.** *Chem.* of, composed of, or concerned with a single phase. Compare **heterogeneous.** ~Also (for senses 1–4): **homogenous.** —**homogeneity** (ˌhəʊməʊdʒɪˈniːɪtɪ, ˌhɒm-) *n.* —ˌ**homoˈgeneously** *adv.* —ˌ**homoˈgeneousness** *n.*

homogenize *or* **homogenise** (hɒˈmɒdʒɪˌnaɪz) *vb.* **1.** (*tr.*) to break up the fat globules in (milk or cream) so that they are evenly distributed. **2.** to make or become homogeneous. —**hoˌmogeniˈzation** *or* **hoˌmogeniˈsation** *n.* —**hoˈmogeˌnizer** *or* **hoˈmogeˌniser** *n.*

homogenous (həˈmɒdʒɪnəs) *adj.* **1.** another word for **homogeneous** (senses 1–4). **2.** of, relating to, or exhibiting homogeny.

homogeny (hɒˈmɒdʒɪnɪ) *n. Biology.* similarity in structure of individuals or parts because of common ancestry. [C19: from Greek *homogeneia* community of origin, from *homogenēs* of the same kind]

homogony (hɒˈmɒgənɪ) *n.* the condition in a plant of having stamens and styles of the same length in all the flowers. Compare **heterogony** (sense 2). —**hoˈmogonous** *adj.* —**hoˈmogonously** *adv.*

homograft (ˈhɒməˌgrɑːft) *n.* a tissue graft obtained from an organism of the same species as the recipient.

homograph (ˈhɒməˌgræf, -ˌgrɑːf) *n.* one of a group of words spelt in the same way but having different meanings. Compare **heteronym.** —ˌ**homoˈgraphic** *adj.*

homoio- *combining form.* a variant of **homeo-**.

homoiothermic (həʊˌmɔɪəˈθɜːmɪk) *or* **homothermal** *adj.* (of birds and mammals) having a constant body temperature, usually higher than the temperature of the surroundings; warm-blooded. Compare **poikilothermic.** —**hoˈmoioˌthermy** *or* **ˈhomoˌthermy** *n.*

Homoiousian (ˌhəʊmɔɪˈuːsɪən, -ˈaʊ-, ˌhɒm-) *n.* **1.** a Christian who believes that the Son is of like (and not identical) substance with the Father. Compare **Homoousian.** ~*adj.* **2.** of or relating to the Homoiousians. [C18: from Late Greek *homoiousios* of like substance, from Greek *homoio-* like + *ousia* nature] —ˌ**Homoiˈousianism** *n.*

homologate (hɒˈmɒləˌgeɪt) *vb.* (*tr.*) **1.** *Law, chiefly Scots.* to approve or ratify (a deed or contract, esp. one that is defective). **2.** *Law.* to confirm (a proceeding, etc.). **3.** to recognize (a particular type of car or car component) as a production model or component rather than a prototype, as in making it eligible for a motor race. [C17: from Medieval Latin *homologāre* to agree, from Greek *homologein* to approve, from *homologos* agreeing, from HOMO- + *legein* to speak] —**hoˌmoloˈgation** *n.*

homologize *or* **homologise** (hɒˈmɒləˌdʒaɪz) *vb.* to be, show to be, or make homologous. —**hoˈmoloˌgizer** *or* **hoˈmoloˌgiser** *n.*

homologous (həʊˈmɒləgəs, hɒ-), **homological** (ˌhəʊməˈlɒdʒɪkəl, ˌhɒm-), *or* **homologic** *adj.* **1.** having a related or similar position, structure, etc. **2.** *Chem.* (of a series of organic compounds) having similar characteristics and structure but differing by a number of CH_2 groups. **3.** *Med.* **a.** (of two or more tissues) identical in structure. **b.** (of a vaccine) prepared from the infecting microorganism. **4.** *Biology.* (of organs and parts) having the same evolutionary origin but different functions: *the wing of a bat and the paddle of a whale are homologous.* Compare **analogous** (sense 2). **5.** *Maths.* (of elements) playing a similar role in distinct figures or functions. —ˌ**homoˈlogically** *adv.*

homologous chromosomes *pl. n.* two chromosomes, one of paternal origin, the other of maternal origin, that are identical in appearance and pair during meiosis.

homolographic (həʊˌmɒləˈgræfɪk) *or* **homalographic** *adj. Cartography.* another term for **equal-area.**

homologue *or U.S.* (*sometimes*) **homolog** (ˈhɒməˌlɒg) *n.* **1.** *Biology.* a homologous part or organ. **2.** *Chem.* any homologous compound.

homology (həʊˈmɒlədʒɪ) *n., pl.* **-gies. 1.** the condition of being homologous. **2.** *Chem.* the similarities in chemical behaviour shown by members of a homologous series. **3.** *Zoology.* the measurable likenesses between animals, as used in grouping them according to the theory of cladistics. [C17: from Greek *homologia* agreement, from *homologos* agreeing; see HOMOLOGATE]

homolosine projection (hɒˈmɒləˌsaɪn) *n.* a map projection of the world on which the oceans are distorted to allow for greater accuracy in representing the continents, combining the sinusoidal and equal-area projections. [C20: from HOMOLOGRAPHIC + SINE[1]]

homolysis (hɒˈmɒlɪsɪs) *n.* the dissociation of a molecule into two neutral fragments. Also called: **homolytic fission.** Compare **heterolysis** (sense 2). —**homolytic** (ˌhəʊməʊˈlɪtɪk, ˌhɒm-) *adj.*

homomorphism (ˌhəʊməʊˈmɔːfɪzəm, ˌhɒm-) *or* **homomorphy** *n. Biology.* similarity in form, as of the flowers of a plant. —ˌ**homoˈmorphic** *or* ˌ**homoˈmorphous** *adj.*

homonym (ˈhɒmənɪm) *n.* **1.** one of a group of words pronounced or spelt in the same way but having different meanings. Compare **homograph, homophone. 2.** a person with the same name as another. **3.** *Biology.* a specific or generic name that has been used for two or more different organisms. [C17: from Latin *homōnymum,* from Greek *homōnumon,* from *homōnumos* of the same name; see HOMO-, -ONYM] —ˌ**homoˈnymic** *or* **hoˈmonymous** *adj.* —ˌ**homoˈnymity** *or* **hoˈmonymy** *n.*

Homoousian (ˌhəʊməʊˈuːsɪən, -ˈaʊ-, ˌhɒm-) *n.* **1.** a Christian who believes that the Son is of the same substance as the Father. Compare **Homoiousian.** ~*adj.* **2.** of or relating to the Homoousians. [C16: from Late Greek *homoousios* of the same substance, from Greek HOMO- + *ousia* nature] —ˌ**Homoˈousianism** *n.*

homophile (ˈhəʊməˌfaɪl, ˈhɒm-) *n.* a rare word for **homosexual.**

homophobia (ˌhəʊməʊˈfəʊbɪə) *n.* intense hatred or fear of homosexuals or homosexuality. [C20: from HOMO(SEXUAL) + -PHOBIA] —ˈ**homoˌphobe** *n.* —ˌ**homoˈphobic** *adj.*

homophone (ˈhɒməˌfəʊn) *n.* **1.** one of a group of words pronounced in the same way but differing in meaning or spelling or both, as for example *bear* and *bare.* **2.** a written letter or combination of letters that represents the same speech sound as another: *"ph" is a homophone of "f" in English.*

homophonic (ˌhɒməˈfɒnɪk) *adj.* **1.** of or relating to homophony. **2.** of or relating to music in which the parts move together rather than independently. —ˌ**homoˈphonically** *adv.*

homophonous (hɒˈmɒfənəs) *adj.* of, relating to, or denoting a homophone.

homophony (hɒˈmɒfənɪ) *n.* **1.** the linguistic phenomenon whereby words of different origins become identical in pronunciation. **2.** part music composed in a homophonic style.

homophyly (hɒˈmɒfəlɪ) *n.* resemblance due to common ancestry. [C19: from Greek, from HOMO- + PHYLUM] —**homophyllic** (ˌhəʊməˈfɪlɪk, ˌhɒm-) *adj.*

homoplastic (ˌhəʊməʊˈplæstɪk, ˌhɒm-) *adj.* **1.** (of a tissue graft) derived from an individual of the same species as the recipient. **2.** another word for **analogous** (sense 2). —ˌ**homoˈplastically** *adv.* —ˈ**homoˌplasty** *n.* —**homoplasy** (ˈhəʊməʊˌpleɪsɪ, ˈhɒm-) *n.*

homopolar (ˌhəʊməʊˈpəʊlə) *adj. Chem.* of uniform charge; not ionic; covalent: *a homopolar bond.* —**homopolarity** (ˌhəʊməʊpəʊˈlærɪtɪ, ˌhɒm-) *n.*

homopterous (həʊˈmɒptərəs) *or* **homopteran** *adj.* of, relating to, or belonging to the *Homoptera,* a suborder of hemipterous insects, including cicadas, aphids, and scale insects, having wings of a uniform texture held over the back at rest. Compare **heteropterous.** [C19: from Greek *homopteros,* from HOMO- + *pteron* wing]

homorganic (ˌhɒmɔːˈgænɪk, ˌhɒm-) *adj. Phonetics.* (of a consonant) articulated at the same point in the vocal tract as a consonant in a different class. Thus ŋ is the homorganic nasal of *k.*

Homo sapiens (ˈsæpɪˌɛnz) *n.* the specific name of modern man; the only extant species of the genus *Homo.* This species also includes extinct types of primitive man such as Cro-Magnon man. See also **man** (sense 5). [New Latin, from Latin *homo* man + *sapiens* wise]

homoscedastic (ˌhəʊməʊskɪˈdæstɪk) *adj. Statistics.* **1.** (of several distributions) having equal variance. **2.** (of a bivariate or multivariate distribution) having one variable whose variance is the same for all values of the other or others. **3.** (of a random variable) having this property. ~Compare **heteroscedastic.** [C20: from HOMO- + *scedastic,* from Greek *skedasis* a scattering, dispersion] —**homoscedasticity** (ˌhəʊməʊskɪdæsˈtɪsɪtɪ) *n.*

homosexual (ˌhəʊməʊˈsɛksjʊəl, ˌhɒm-) *n.* **1.** a person who is sexually attracted to members of the same sex. ~*adj.* **2.** of or relating to homosexuals or homosexuality. **3.** of or relating to the same sex. ~Compare **heterosexual.**

homosexuality (ˌhəʊməʊˌsɛksjʊˈælɪtɪ, ˌhɒm-) *n.* sexual attraction to or sexual relations with members of the same sex. Compare **heterosexuality.**

homosporous (hɒˈmɒspərəs, ˌhəʊməʊˈspɔːrəs) *adj.* (of some ferns) producing spores of one kind only, which develop into hermaphrodite gametophytes. Compare **heterosporous.** —**homospory** (həʊˈmɒspərɪ) *n.*

homotaxis (ˌhəʊməʊˈtæksɪs, ˌhɒm-) *n.* similarity of composition and arrangement in rock strata of different ages or in different regions. —ˌ**homoˈtaxic** *or* ˌ**homoˈtaxial** *adj.* —ˌ**homoˈtaxially** *adv.*

homothallic (ˌhəʊməʊˈθælɪk) *adj.* (of some algae and fungi) having both male and female reproductive organs on the same thallus, which is self-fertilizing. Compare **heterothallic.** [C20: from HOMO- + Greek *thallos* green shoot] —ˌ**homoˈthallism** *n.*

homothermal (ˌhəʊməʊˈθɜːməl, ˌhɒm-) *adj.* another word for **homoiothermic.**

homozygote (ˌhəʊməʊˈzaɪgəʊt, -ˈzɪg-, ˌhɒm-) *n.* an animal or plant that is homozygous and breeds true to type. Compare **heterozygote.** —ˌ**homozyˈgosis** *n.* —**homozygotic** (ˌhəʊməʊzaɪˈgɒtɪk, -zɪ-, ˌhɒm-) *adj.*

homozygous (ˌhəʊməʊˈzaɪgəs, -ˈzɪg-, ˌhɒm-) *adj. Genetics.* (of an organism) having identical alleles for any one gene: *these two fruit flies are homozygous for red eye colour.* Compare **heterozygous.** —ˌ**homoˈzygously** *adv.*

homunculus (hɒˈmʌŋkjʊləs) *n., pl.* **-li** (-ˌlaɪ). **1.** a miniature man; midget. **2.** (in early biological theory) a fully-formed miniature human being existing in a spermatozoon or egg. ~Also called: **homuncule** (həʊˈmʌŋkjuːl). [C17: from Latin, diminutive of *homo* man] —**hoˈmuncular** *adj.*

homy *or esp. U.S.* **homey** (ˈhəʊmɪ) *adj.* **homier, homiest.** like a home, esp. in comfort or informality; cosy. —ˈ**hominess** *or esp. U.S.* ˈ**homeyness** *n.*

hon. *abbrev. for:* **1.** honorary. **2.** honourable.

Hon. *abbrev. for* Honourable (title).

honan (ˈhəʊˈnæn) *n.* (*sometimes cap.*) a silk fabric of rough weave. [C20: from *Honan,* former name of *Henan* in N central China, where it is made]

honcho ('hɒntʃəʊ) *Informal, chiefly U.S.* ~*n., pl.* **-chos.** **1.** the person in charge; the boss. ~*vb.* **2.** to supervise or be in charge of. [C20: from Japanese *han'chō* group leader]

Hond. *abbrev. for* Honduras.

Honduran (hɒn'djʊərən) *adj.* **1.** of or relating to Honduras, a republic in Central America, or its people. ~*n.* **2.** a native or inhabitant of Honduras.

hone[1] (həʊn) *n.* **1.** a fine whetstone, esp. for sharpening razors. **2.** a tool consisting of a number of fine abrasive slips held in a machine head, rotated and reciprocated to impart a smooth finish to cylinder bores, etc. ~*vb.* **3.** (*tr.*) to sharpen or polish with or as if with a hone. [Old English *hān* stone; related to Old Norse *hein*]

hone[2] (həʊn) *vb.* (*intr.*) *Dialect.* **1.** (often foll. by *for* or *after*) to yearn or pine. **2.** to moan or grieve. [C17: from Old French *hogner* to growl, probably of Germanic origin; compare Old High German *hōnen* to revile]

honest ('ɒnɪst) *adj.* **1.** not given to lying, cheating, stealing, etc.; trustworthy. **2.** not false or misleading; genuine. **3.** just or fair: *honest wages.* **4.** characterized by sincerity and candour: *an honest appraisal.* **5.** without pretensions or artificial traits: *honest farmers.* **6.** *Archaic.* (of a woman) respectable. **7. honest broker.** a mediator in disputes, esp. international ones. **8. make an honest woman of.** to marry (a woman, esp. one who is pregnant) to prevent scandal. **9. honest Injun.** (*interj.*) *School slang.* genuinely, really. **10. honest to God** (*or* **goodness**). **a.** (*adj.*) completely authentic. **b.** (*interj.*) an expression of affirmation or surprise. [C13: from Old French *honeste,* from Latin *honestus* distinguished, from *honōs* HONOUR] —'**honestness** *n.*

honestly ('ɒnɪstlɪ) *adv.* **1.** in an honest manner. **2.** (intensifier): *I honestly don't believe it.* ~*interj.* **3.** an expression of disgust, surprise, etc.

honesty ('ɒnɪstɪ) *n., pl.* **-ties.** **1.** the condition of being honest. **2.** sincerity or fairness. **3.** *Archaic.* virtue or respect. **4.** a purple-flowered SE European cruciferous plant, *Lunaria annua,* cultivated for its flattened silvery pods, which are used for indoor decoration. Also called: **moonwort, satinpod.**

honewort ('həʊn,wɜːt) *n.* **1.** a European umbelliferous plant, *Trinia glauca,* with clusters of small white flowers. **2.** any of several similar and related plants. [C17: apparently from obsolete dialect *hone* a swelling, of obscure origin; the plant was believed to relieve swellings]

honey ('hʌnɪ) *n.* **1.** a sweet viscid substance made by bees from nectar and stored in their nests or hives as food. It is spread on bread or used as a sweetening agent. **2.** any similar sweet substance, esp. the nectar of flowers. **3.** anything that is sweet or delightful. **4.** (*often cap.*) *Chiefly U.S. and Canadian.* a term of endearment. **5.** *Informal, chiefly U.S. and Canadian.* something considered to be very good of its kind: *a honey of a car.* **6.** (*modifier*) of, concerned with, or resembling honey. ~*vb.* **honeys, honeying, honeyed** *or* **honied.** **7.** (*tr.*) to sweeten with or as if with honey. **8.** (often foll. by *up*) to talk to (someone) in a fond or flattering way. [Old English *huneg;* related to Old Norse *hunang,* Old Saxon *hanig,* German *Honig,* Greek *knēkos* yellowish, Sanskrit *kánaka-* gold] —'**honey-,like** *adj.*

honey badger *n.* another name for **ratel.**

honey bear *n.* another name for **kinkajou** (sense 1) or **sun bear.**

honeybee ('hʌnɪ,biː) *n.* any of various social honey-producing bees of the genus *Apis,* esp. *A. mellifera,* which has been widely domesticated as a source of honey and beeswax. Also called: **hive bee.**

honeybunch ('hʌnɪ,bʌntʃ) *or* **honeybun** ('hʌnɪ,bʌn) *n. Informal, chiefly U.S.* honey; darling: a term of endearment.

honey buzzard *n.* a common European bird of prey, *Pernis apivorus,* having broad wings and a typically dull brown plumage with white-streaked underparts: family *Accipitridae* (hawks, buzzards, etc.). It feeds on grubs and honey from bees' nests.

honeycomb ('hʌnɪ,kəʊm) *n.* **1.** a waxy structure, constructed by bees in a hive, that consists of adjacent hexagonal cells in which honey is stored, eggs are laid, and larvae develop. **2.** something resembling this in structure or appearance. **3.** *Zoology.* another name for **reticulum** (sense 2). ~*vb.* (*tr.*) **4.** to pierce or fill with holes, cavities, etc. **5.** to permeate: *honeycombed with spies.*

honeycomb moth *n.* another name for the **wax moth.**

honey creeper *n.* **1.** any small tropical American songbird of the genus *Dacnis* and related genera, closely related to the tanagers and buntings, having a slender downward-curving bill and feeding on nectar. **2.** any bird of the family *Drepanididae* of Hawaii.

honeydew ('hʌnɪ,djuː) *n.* **1.** a sugary substance excreted by aphids and similar insects. **2.** a similar substance exuded by certain plants. **3.** short for **honeydew melon.** —'**honey-,dewed** *adj.*

honeydew melon *n.* a variety of muskmelon with a smooth greenish-white rind and sweet greenish flesh.

honey-eater ('hʌnɪ,iːtə) *n.* any small arboreal songbird of the Australasian family *Meliphagidae,* having a downward-curving bill and a brushlike tongue specialized for extracting nectar from flowers.

honeyed *or* **honied** ('hʌnɪd) *adj. Poetic.* **1.** flattering or soothing. **2.** made sweet or agreeable: *honeyed words.* **3.** of, full of, or resembling honey. —'**honeyedly** *or* '**honiedly** *adv.*

honey fungus *n.* an edible basidiomycetous fungus, *Armillaria mellea,* having a yellow-spotted cap and wrinkled stems, parasitic on the roots of woody plants, which it may kill by root rot. It spreads by thin black underground strands. Also called: **boot-lace fungus.**

honey guide *n.* any small bird of the family *Indicatoridae,* inhabiting tropical forests of Africa and Asia and feeding on beeswax, honey, and insects: order *Piciformes* (woodpeckers, etc.).

honey locust *n.* **1.** a thorny mimosaceous tree, *Gleditsia triacanthos* of E North America, that has long pods containing a sweet-tasting pulp. **2.** another name for **mesquite.**

honey mesquite *n.* another name for **mesquite.**

honeymoon ('hʌnɪ,muːn) *n.* **1. a.** a holiday taken by a newly married couple. **b.** (*as modifier*): *a honeymoon cottage.* **2.** a holiday considered to resemble a honeymoon: *a second honeymoon.* **3.** the early, usually calm period of a relationship, such as a political or business one. ~*vb.* **4.** (*intr.*) to take a honeymoon. [C16: traditionally explained as an allusion to the feelings of married couples as changing with the phases of the moon] —'**honey,mooner** *n.*

honey mouse *or* **phalanger** *n.* a small agile Australian marsupial, *Tarsipes spenserae,* having dark-striped pale brown fur, a long prehensile tail, and a very long snout and tongue with which it feeds on honey, pollen, and insects: family *Phalangeridae.* Also called: **honeysucker.**

honey plant *n.* any of various plants that are particularly useful in providing bees with nectar.

honeysucker ('hʌnɪ,sʌkə) *n.* **1.** any bird, esp. a honey-eater, that feeds on nectar. **2.** another name for **honey mouse.**

honeysuckle ('hʌnɪ,sʌkᵊl) *n.* **1.** any temperate caprifoliaceous shrub or vine of the genus *Lonicera:* cultivated for their fragrant white, yellow, or pink tubular flowers. **2.** any of several similar plants. **3.** any of various Australian trees or shrubs of the genus *Banksia,* having flowers in dense spikes: family *Proteaceae.* [Old English *hunigsūce,* from HONEY + SUCK; see SUCKLE] —'**honey-,suckled** *adj.*

honeysuckle ornament *n. Arts.* another term for **anthemion.**

honey-sweet *adj.* sweet or endearing.

hong (hɒŋ) *n.* **1.** (in China) a factory, warehouse, etc. **2.** (formerly, in Canton) a foreign commercial establishment. [C18: from Chinese (Cantonese dialect)]

hongi ('hɒŋiː) *n. N.Z.* a form of salutation expressed by touching noses. [Maori]

honied ('hʌnɪd) *adj.* a variant spelling of **honeyed.** —'**honiedly** *adv.*

honi soit qui mal y pense *French.* (ɔni swa ki mal i pɑ̃s) shamed be he who thinks evil of it: the motto of the Order of the Garter.

Honiton ('hɒnɪtᵊn, 'hʌn-) *or* **Honiton lace** *n.* a type of lace with a floral sprig pattern. [C19: named after *Honiton,* Devon, where it was first made]

honk (hɒŋk) *n.* **1.** a representation of the sound made by a goose. **2.** any sound resembling this, esp. a motor horn. ~*vb.* **3.** to make or cause (something) to make such a sound. **4.** (*intr.*) *Brit.* a slang word for **vomit.**

honker ('hɒŋkə) *n.* **1.** a person or thing that honks. **2.** *Canadian.* an informal name for the **Canada goose.** **3.** *Slang.* a nose, esp. a large nose.

honky ('hɒŋkɪ) *n., pl.* **honkies.** *Derogatory slang, chiefly U.S.* a White man or White men collectively. [C20: of unknown origin]

honky-tonk ('hɒŋkɪ,tɒŋk) *n.* **1.** *U.S. and Canadian slang.* **a.** a cheap disreputable nightclub, bar, etc. **b.** (*as modifier*): *a honky-tonk district.* **2.** a style of ragtime piano-playing, esp. on a tinny-sounding piano. **3.** a type of country music, usually performed by a small band with electric and steel guitars. **4.** (*as modifier*): *honky-tonk music.* [C19: rhyming compound based on HONK]

honor ('ɒnə) *n., vb.* the U.S. spelling of **honour.**

honorarium (,ɒnə'rɛərɪəm) *n., pl.* **-iums** *or* **-ia** (-ɪə). a fee paid for a nominally free service. [C17: from Latin: something presented on being admitted to a post of HONOUR]

honorary ('ɒnərərɪ, 'ɒnrərɪ) *adj.* (*usually prenominal*) **1. a.** (esp. of a position, title, etc.) held or given only as an honour, without the normal privileges or duties: *an honorary degree.* **b.** (of a secretary, treasurer, etc.) unpaid. **2.** having such a position or title. **3.** depending on honour rather than legal agreement.

honorific (,ɒnə'rɪfɪk) *adj.* **1.** showing or conferring honour or respect. **2. a.** (of a pronoun, verb inflection, etc.) indicating the speaker's respect for the addressee or his acknowledgment of inferior status. **b.** (*as n.*): *a Japanese honorific.* —,**honor'ifically** *adv.* ***honoris causa*** *Latin.* (hɒ'nɔːrɪs 'kaʊzɑː) for the sake of honour.

honour *or U.S.* **honor** ('ɒnə) *n.* **1.** personal integrity; allegiance to moral principles. **2. a.** fame or glory. **b.** a person or thing that wins this for another: *he is an honour to the school.* **3.** (*often pl.*) great respect, regard, esteem, etc., or an outward sign of this. **4.** (*often pl.*) high or noble rank. **5.** a privilege or pleasure: *it is an honour to serve you.* **6.** a woman's virtue or chastity. **7. a.** *Bridge, poker, etc.* any of the top five cards in a suit or any of the four aces at no trumps. **b.** *Whist.* any of the top four cards. **8.**

Golf. the right to tee off first. **9. do honour to. a.** to pay homage to. **b.** to be a credit to. **10. do the honours. a.** to serve as host or hostess. **b.** to perform a social act, such as carving meat, proposing a toast, etc. **11. honour bright.** *Brit. school slang.* an exclamation pledging honour. **12. in honour bound.** under a moral obligation. **13. in honour of.** out of respect for. **14. on** (*or* **upon**) **one's honour.** on the pledge of one's word or good name. ~*vb.* (*tr.*) **15.** to hold in respect or esteem. **16.** to show courteous behaviour towards. **17.** to worship. **18.** to confer a distinction upon. **19.** to accept and then pay when due (a cheque, draft, etc.). **20.** to keep (one's promise); fulfil (a previous agreement). **21.** to bow or curtsy to (one's dancing partner). ~See also **honours.** [C12: from Old French *onor,* from Latin *honor* esteem] —'**honourer** *or U.S.* '**honorer** *n.* —'**honourless** *or U.S.* '**honorless** *adj.*

Honour ('ɒnə) *n.* (preceded by *Your, His,* or *Her*) **a.** a title used to or of certain judges. **b.** (in Ireland) a form of address in general use.

honourable *or U.S.* **honorable** ('ɒnərəbᵊl, 'ɒnrəbᵊl) *adj.* **1.** possessing or characterized by high principles: *honourable intentions.* **2.** worthy of or entitled to honour or esteem. **3.** consistent with or bestowing honour. —'**honourableness** *or U.S.* '**honorableness** *n.* —'**honourably** *or U.S.* '**honorably** *adv.*

Honourable *or U.S.* **Honorable** ('ɒnərəbᵊl, 'ɒnrəbᵊl) *adj.* (*prenominal*) **the.** a title of respect placed before a name: employed before the names of various officials in the English-speaking world, as a courtesy title in Britain for the children of viscounts and barons and the younger sons of earls, and in Parliament by one member speaking of another. Abbrev.: **Hon.**

honourable discharge *n.* See **discharge** (sense 15).

Honour Moderations *pl. n.* (at Oxford University) the first public examination, in which candidates are placed into one of three classes of honours. Sometimes shortened to **Moderations** or **Mods.**

honours *or U.S.* **honors** ('ɒnəz) *pl. n.* **1.** observances of respect. **2.** (*often cap.*) **a.** (in a university degree or degree course) a rank of the highest academic standard. **b.** (*as modifier*): *an honours degree.* Abbrev.: **Hons.** Compare **general** (sense 9), **pass** (sense 35). **3.** a high mark awarded for an examination; distinction. **4. last** (*or* **funeral**) **honours.** observances of respect at a funeral. **5. military honours.** ceremonies performed by troops in honour of royalty, at the burial of an officer, etc.

honour school *n.* (at Oxford University) one of the courses of study leading to an honours degree.

honours list *n. Brit.* a list of those who have had or are having an honour, esp. a peerage or membership of an order of chivalry, conferred on them.

honours of war *pl. n. Military.* the honours granted by the victorious to the defeated, esp. as of marching out with all arms and flags flying.

Hon. Sec. *abbrev. for* Honorary Secretary.

hoo (huː) *pron. West Yorkshire and south Lancashire dialect.* she. [from Old English *heo*]

hooch *or* **hootch** (huːtʃ) *n. Informal, chiefly U.S. and Canadian.* alcoholic drink, esp. illicitly distilled spirits. [C20: shortened from Tlingit *Hootchinoo,* name of a tribe that distilled a type of liquor]

hood[1] (hʊd) *n.* **1.** a loose head covering either attached to a cloak or coat or made as a separate garment. **2.** something resembling this in shape or use. **3.** the U.S. and Canadian name for **bonnet** (of a car). **4.** the folding roof of a convertible car. **5.** a hoodlike garment worn over an academic gown, indicating its wearer's degree and university. **6.** *Falconry.* a close-fitting cover, placed over the head and eyes of a falcon to keep it quiet when not hunting. **7.** *Biology.* a structure or marking, such as the fold of skin on the head of a cobra, that covers or appears to cover the head or some similar part. ~*vb.* **8.** (*tr.*) to cover or provide with or as if with a hood. [Old English *hōd;* related to Old High German *huot* hat, Middle Dutch *hoet,* Latin *cassis* helmet; see HAT] —'**hoodless** *adj.* —'**hood,like** *adj.*

hood[2] (hʊd) *n. Slang.* short for **hoodlum** (gangster).

-hood *suffix forming nouns.* **1.** indicating state or condition of being: *manhood.* **2.** indicating a body of persons: *knighthood; priesthood.* [Old English *-hād*]

hooded ('hʊdɪd) *adj.* covered with, having, or shaped like a hood.

hooded crow *n.* a subspecies of the carrion crow, *Corvus corone cornix,* that has a grey body and black head, wings, and tail. Also called (Scot.): **hoodie** ('hʊdɪ), **hoodie crow.**

hooded seal *n.* a large greyish earless seal, *Cystophora cristata,* of the N Atlantic and Arctic Oceans, having an inflatable hoodlike sac over the nasal region. Also called: **bladdernose.**

hoodlum ('huːdləm) *n.* **1.** a petty gangster or ruffian. **2.** a lawless youth. [C19: perhaps from Southern German dialect *Haderlump* ragged good-for-nothing] —'**hoodlumism** *n.*

hoodman-blind *n. Brit., archaic.* blind man's buff.

hood mould *n.* another name for **dripstone** (sense 2).

hoodoo ('huːduː) *n., pl.* **-doos. 1.** a variant of **voodoo. 2.** *Informal.* a person or thing that brings bad luck. **3.** *Informal.* bad luck. **4.** (in the western U.S. and Canada) a strangely shaped column of rock. ~*vb.* **-doos, -dooing, -dooed. 5.** (*tr.*) *Informal.* to bring bad luck to. [C19: variant of VOODOO] —'**hoodooism** *n.*

hoodwink ('hʊd,wɪŋk) *vb.* (*tr.*) **1.** to dupe; trick. **2.** *Obsolete.* to cover or hide. [C16: originally, to cover the eyes with a hood, blindfold] —'**hood,winker** *n.*

hooey ('huːɪ) *n., interj. Slang.* nonsense; rubbish. [C20: of unknown origin]

hoof (huːf) *n., pl.* **hooves** (huːvz) *or* **hoofs. 1. a.** the horny covering of the end of the foot in the horse, deer, and all other ungulate mammals. **b.** (*in combination*): *a hoofbeat.* Related adj.: **ungular. 2.** the foot of an ungulate mammal. **3.** a hoofed animal. **4.** *Facetious.* a person's foot. **5. on the hoof.** (of livestock) alive. ~*vb.* **6.** (*tr.*) to kick or trample with the hoofs. **7. hoof it.** *Slang.* **a.** to walk. **b.** to dance. [Old English *hōf;* related to Old Norse *hōfr,* Old High German *huof* (German *Huf*), Sanskrit *saphás*] —'**hoofless** *adj.* —'**hoof,like** *adj.*

hoofbound ('huːf,baʊnd) *adj. Vet. science.* (of a horse) having dry contracted hooves, with resultant pain and lameness.

hoofed (huːft) *adj.* **a.** having a hoof or hoofs. **b.** (*in combination*): *four-hoofed; cloven-hoofed.*

hoo-ha ('huː,hɑː) *n.* a noisy commotion or fuss. [C20: of unknown origin]

hook (hʊk) *n.* **1.** a piece of material, usually metal, curved or bent and used to suspend, catch, hold, or pull something. **2.** short for **fish-hook. 3.** a trap or snare. **4.** *Chiefly U.S.* something that attracts or is intended to be an attraction. **5.** something resembling a hook in design or use. **6. a.** a sharp bend or angle in a geological formation, esp. a river. **b.** a sharply curved spit of land. **7.** *Boxing.* a short swinging blow delivered from the side with the elbow bent. **8.** *Cricket.* a shot in which the ball is hit square on the leg side with the bat held horizontally. **9.** *Golf.* a shot that causes the ball to go to the player's left. **10.** *Surfing.* the top of a breaking wave. **11.** Also called: **hookcheck.** *Ice hockey.* the act of hooking an opposing player. **12.** a hook-shaped stroke used in writing or printing, such as a serif or (in writing) any part of a letter extending above or below the line. **13.** *Music.* a stroke added to the stem of a written or printed note to indicate time values shorter than a crotchet. **14.** a catchy musical phrase in a pop song. **15.** another name for a **sickle. 16.** a nautical word for **anchor. 17. by hook or (by) crook.** by any means. **18. get the hook.** *U.S. and Canadian slang.* to be dismissed from employment. **19. hook, line, and sinker.** *Informal.* completely: *he fell for it hook, line, and sinker.* **20. off the hook. a.** *Slang.* out of danger; free from obligation or guilt. **b.** (of a telephone receiver) not on the support, so that incoming calls cannot be received. **21. on one's own hook.** *Slang, chiefly U.S.* on one's own initiative. **22. on the hook.** *Slang.* **a.** waiting. **b.** in a dangerous or difficult situation. **23. sling one's hook.** *Brit. slang.* to leave. ~*vb.* **24.** (often foll. by *up*) to fasten or be fastened with or as if with a hook or hooks. **25.** (*tr.*) to catch (something, such as a fish) on a hook. **26.** to curve like or into the shape of a hook. **27.** (*tr.*) (of bulls, elks, etc.) to catch or gore with the horns. **28.** (*tr.*) to make (a rug) by hooking yarn through a stiff fabric backing with a special instrument. **29.** (*tr.;* often foll. by *down*) to cut (grass or herbage) with a sickle: *to hook down weeds.* **30.** *Boxing.* to hit (an opponent) with a hook. **31.** *Ice hockey.* to impede (an opposing player) by catching hold of him with the stick. **32.** *Golf.* to play (a ball) with a hook. **33.** *Rugby.* to obtain and pass (the ball) backwards from a scrum to a member of one's team, using the feet. **34.** *Cricket.* to play (a ball) with a hook. **35.** (*tr.*) *Informal.* to trick. **36.** (*tr.*) a slang word for **steal. 37. hook it.** *Slang.* to run or go quickly away. ~See also **hook-up.** [Old English *hōc;* related to Middle Dutch *hōk,* Old Norse *haki*] —'**hookless** *adj.* —'**hook,like** *adj.*

hookah *or* **hooka** ('hʊkə) *n.* an oriental pipe for smoking marijuana, tobacco, etc., consisting of one or more long flexible stems connected to a container of water or other liquid through which smoke is drawn and cooled. Also called: **hubble-bubble, kalian, narghile, water pipe.** [C18: from Arabic *huqqah*]

hook and eye *n.* a fastening for clothes consisting of a small hook hooked onto a small metal or thread loop.

hooked (hʊkt) *adj.* **1.** bent like a hook. **2.** having a hook or hooks. **3.** caught or trapped. **4.** a slang word for **married. 5.** *Slang.* addicted to a drug. **6.** (often foll. by *on*) obsessed (with). —**hookedness** ('hʊkɪdnɪs) *n.*

hooker[1] ('hʊkə) *n.* **1.** a commercial fishing boat using hooks and lines instead of nets. **2.** a sailing boat of the west of Ireland formerly used for cargo and now for pleasure sailing and racing. [C17: from Dutch *hoeker*]

hooker[2] ('hʊkə) *n.* **1.** a person or thing that hooks. **2.** *U.S. and Canadian slang.* **a.** a draught of alcoholic drink, esp. of spirits. **b.** a prostitute. **3.** *Rugby.* the central forward in the front row of a scrum whose main job is to hook the ball.

Hooke's law (hʊks) *n.* the principle that the stress imposed on a solid is directly proportional to the strain produced, within the elastic limit. [C18: named after Robert *Hooke* (1635–1703), English scientist]

hooknose ('hʊk,nəʊz) *n.* a nose with a pronounced outward and downward curve; aquiline nose. —'**hook,nosed** *adj.*

hook-tip *n.* **1.** any of several moths of the genus *Daepana,* characterized by the hooked point on each forewing. **2. beautiful hook-tip.** a similar but unrelated species, *Laspeyria flexula.*

hook-up *n.* **1.** the contact of an aircraft in flight with the refuelling hose of a tanker aircraft. **2.** an alliance or relationship, esp. an unlikely one, between people, countries, etc. **3.** the linking of broadcasting equipment or stations to transmit a special programme. ~*vb.* **hook up** (*adv.*). 4. to connect (two or more people or things). 5. (often foll. by *with*) *Slang.* to get married (to).

hookworm ('hʊk,wɜːm) *n.* any parasitic blood-sucking nematode worm of the family *Ancylostomatidae,* esp. *Ancylostoma duodenale* or *Necator americanus,* both of which cause disease. They have hooked mouthparts and enter their hosts by boring through the skin.

hookworm disease *n.* the nontechnical name for **ancylostomiasis.**

hooky *or* **hookey** ('hʊkɪ) *n. Informal, chiefly U.S., Canadian, and N.Z.* truancy, usually from school (esp. in the phrase **play hooky**). [C20: perhaps from *hook it* to escape]

hooley *or* **hoolie** ('huːlɪ) *n., pl.* **-leys** *or* **-lies.** *Chiefly Irish and N.Z.* a lively party. [C19: of unknown origin]

hooligan ('huːlɪgən) *n. Slang.* a rough lawless young person. [C19: perhaps variant of *Houlihan,* Irish surname] —'**hooliganism** *n.*

hoon (huːn) *n.* 1. *N.Z. informal.* a hooligan. 2. *Austral. slang.* a pimp. [of unknown origin]

hoop[1] (huːp) *n.* 1. a rigid circular band of metal or wood. 2. something resembling this. 3. **a.** a band of iron that holds the staves of a barrel or cask together. **b.** (*as modifier*): *hoop iron.* 4. a child's toy shaped like a hoop and rolled on the ground or whirled around the body. 5. *Croquet.* any of the iron arches through which the ball is driven. 6. **a.** a light curved frame to spread out a skirt. **b.** (*as modifier*): *a hoop skirt; a hoop petticoat.* 7. *Basketball.* the round metal frame to which the net is attached to form the basket. 8. a large ring through which performers or animals jump. 9. *Jewellery.* **a.** an earring consisting of one or more circles of metal, plastic, etc. **b.** the part of a finger ring through which the finger fits. 10. *Austral. informal.* a jockey. 11. **go** *or* **be put through the hoop.** to be subjected to an ordeal. ~*vb.* 12. (*tr.*) to surround with or as if with a hoop. [Old English *hōp;* related to Dutch *hoep,* Old Norse *hōp* bay, Lithuanian *kabē* hook] —**hooped** *adj.* —'**hoop,like** *adj.*

hoop[2] (huːp) *n., vb.* a variant spelling of **whoop.**

hooper ('huːpə) *n.* a rare word for **cooper.**

hoopla ('huːplɑː) *n.* 1. *Brit.* a fairground game in which a player tries to throw a hoop over an object and so win it. 2. *U.S. and Canadian slang.* noise; bustle. 3. *U.S. slang.* nonsense; ballyhoo. [C20: see WHOOP, LA[2]]

hoopoe ('huːpuː) *n.* an Old World bird, *Upupa epops,* having a pinkish-brown plumage with black-and-white wings and an erectile crest: family *Upupidae,* order *Coraciiformes* (kingfishers, etc.). [C17: from earlier *hoopoop,* of imitative origin; compare Latin *upupa*]

hoop pine *n.* a fast-growing timber tree of Australia, *Araucaria cunninghamii,* having rough bark with hoop-like cracks around the trunk and branches: family *Araucariaceae.*

hoop snake *n.* any of various North American snakes, such as the mud snake (*Farancia abacura*), that were formerly thought to hold the tail in the mouth and roll along like a hoop.

hooray (huː'reɪ) *or* **hoorah** (huː'rɑː) *interj., n., vb.* 1. variants of **hurrah.** ~*interj.* 2. Also: **hooroo** (huː'ruː). *Austral. and N.Z.* goodbye; cheerio.

Hooray Henry *n., pl.* **Hooray Henries** *or* **-rys.** a young upper-class man, often with affectedly hearty voice and manners. Sometimes shortened to **Hooray.**

hoosegow *or* **hoosgow** ('huːsgaʊ) *n. U.S.* a slang word for **jail.** [C20: from Mexican Spanish *jusgado* prison, from Spanish: court of justice, from *juzgar* to judge, from Latin *judicāre,* from *judex* a JUDGE; compare JUG]

hoot[1] (huːt) *n.* 1. the mournful wavering cry of some owls. 2. a similar sound, such as that of a train whistle. 3. a jeer of derision. 4. *Informal.* an amusing person or thing. 5. **not give a hoot.** not to care at all. ~*vb.* 6. (often foll. by *at*) to jeer or yell (something) contemptuously (at someone). 7. (*tr.*) to drive (political speakers, actors on stage, etc.) off or away by hooting. 8. (*intr.*) to make a hoot. 9. (*intr.*) *Brit.* to blow a horn. [C13 *hoten,* of imitative origin]

hoot[2] (huːt) *or* **hoots** (huːts) *interj.* an exclamation of impatience or dissatisfaction: a supposed Scotticism. [C17: of unknown origin]

hoot[3] (huːt) *n. Austral. and N.Z.* a slang word for **money.** [from Maori *utu* price]

hootch (huːtʃ) *n.* a variant spelling of **hooch.**

hootenanny ('huːtᵊ,nænɪ) *or* **hootnanny** ('huːt,nænɪ) *n., pl.* **-nies.** 1. *U.S. and Canadian.* an informal performance by folk singers. 2. *Chiefly U.S.* something the name of which is unspecified or forgotten. [C20: of unknown origin]

hooter ('huːtə) *n. Chiefly Brit.* 1. a person or thing that hoots, esp. a car horn. 2. *Slang.* a nose.

hoot owl *n.* any owl that utters a hooting cry, as distinct from a screech owl.

Hoover ('huːvə) *n.* 1. *Trademark.* a type of vacuum cleaner. ~*vb.* (*usually not cap.*) 2. to vacuum-clean (a carpet, furniture, etc.).

hooves (huːvz) *n.* a plural of **hoof.**

hop[1] (hɒp) *vb.* **hops, hopping, hopped.** 1. (*intr.*) to make a jump forwards or upwards, esp. on one foot. 2. (*intr.*) (esp. of frogs, birds, rabbits, etc.) to move forwards in short jumps. 3. (*tr.*) to jump over: *he hopped the hedge.* 4. (*intr.*) *Informal.* to move or proceed quickly (in, on, out of, etc.): *hop on a bus.* 5. (*tr.*) *Informal.* to cross (an ocean) in an aircraft: *they hopped the Atlantic in seven hours.* 6. (*tr.*) *U.S. and Canadian informal.* to travel by means of (an aircraft, bus, etc.): *he hopped a train to Chicago.* 7. *U.S. and Canadian.* to bounce or cause to bounce: *he hopped the flat stone over the lake's surface.* 8. (*intr.*) *U.S. and Canadian informal.* to begin intense activity, esp. work. 9. (*intr.*) another word for **limp**[1]. 10. **hop it** (*or* **off**). *Brit. slang.* to go away. ~*n.* 11. the act or an instance of hopping. 12. *Informal.* a dance, esp. one at which popular music is played: *we're all going to the school hop tonight.* 13. *Informal.* a trip, esp. in an aircraft. 14. *U.S.* a bounce, as of a ball. 15. **on the hop.** *Informal.* **a.** active or busy. **b.** *Brit.* unawares or unprepared: *the new ruling caught me on the hop.* ~See also **hop into.** [Old English *hoppian;* related to Old Norse *hoppa* to hop, Middle Low German *hupfen*]

hop[2] (hɒp) *n.* 1. any climbing plant of the N temperate genus *Humulus,* esp. *H. lupulus,* which has green conelike female flowers and clusters of small male flowers: family *Cannabiaceae* (or *Cannabidaceae*). See also **hops.** 2. **hop garden.** a field of hops. 3. *Obsolete slang.* opium or any other narcotic drug. ~See also **hop up.** [C15: from Middle Dutch *hoppe;* related to Old High German *hopfo,* Norwegian *hupp* tassel]

hop clover *n.* the U.S. name for **hop trefoil.**

hope (həʊp) *n.* 1. (*sometimes pl.*) a feeling of desire for something and confidence in the possibility of its fulfilment: *his hope for peace was justified; their hopes were dashed.* 2. a reasonable ground for this feeling: *there is still hope.* 3. a person or thing that gives cause for hope. 4. a thing, situation, or event that is desired: *my hope is that prices will fall.* 5. **not a hope** *or* **some hope.** used ironically to express little confidence that expectations will be fulfilled. ~*vb.* 6. (*tr.; takes a clause as object or an infinitive*) to desire (something) with some possibility of fulfilment: *we hope you can come; I hope to tell you.* 7. (*intr.;* often foll. by *for*) to have a wish (for a future event, situation, etc.). 8. (*tr.; takes a clause as object*) to trust, expect, or believe: *we hope that this is satisfactory.* [Old English *hopa;* related to Old Frisian *hope,* Dutch *hoop,* Middle High German *hoffe*] —'**hoper** *n.*

hope chest *n.* the U.S., Canadian, and N.Z. name for **bottom drawer.**

hopeful ('həʊpfʊl) *adj.* 1. having or expressing hope. 2. giving or inspiring hope; promising. ~*n.* 3. a person considered to be on the brink of success (esp. in the phrase **a young hopeful**). —'**hopefulness** *n.*

hopefully ('həʊpfʊlɪ) *adv.* 1. in a hopeful manner. 2. *Informal.* it is hoped: *hopefully they will be married soon.*

hopeless ('həʊplɪs) *adj.* 1. having or offering no hope. 2. impossible to analyse or solve. 3. unable to learn, function, etc. 4. *Informal.* without skill or ability. —'**hopelessly** *adv.* —'**hopelessness** *n.*

hophead ('hɒp,hɛd) *n. Slang, chiefly U.S.* a heroin or opium addict. [C20: from obsolete slang *hop* opium; see HOP[2]]

Hopi ('həʊpɪ) *n.* 1. (*pl.* **-pis** *or* **-pi**) a member of a North American Indian people of NE Arizona. 2. the language of this people, belonging to the Shoshonean subfamily of the Uto-Aztecan family. [from Hopi *Hópi* peaceful]

hop into *vb.* (*intr., prep.*) *Austral. and N.Z. slang.* 1. to attack (a person). 2. to start or set about (a task).

hoplite ('hɒplaɪt) *n.* (in ancient Greece) a heavily armed infantryman. [C18: from Greek *hoplitēs,* from *hoplon* weapon, from *hepein* to prepare] —**hoplitic** (hɒp'lɪtɪk) *adj.*

hoplology (hɒp'lɒlədʒɪ) *n.* the study of weapons or armour. [C19: from Greek, from *hoplon* weapon + -LOGY] —**hop'lologist** *n.*

hopper ('hɒpə) *n.* 1. a person or thing that hops. 2. a funnel-shaped chamber or reservoir from which solid materials can be discharged under gravity into a receptacle below, esp. for feeding fuel to a furnace, loading a railway truck with grain, etc. 3. a machine used for picking hops. 4. any of various long-legged hopping insects, esp. the grasshopper, leaf hopper, and immature locust. 5. Also called: **hoppercar.** an open-topped railway truck for bulk transport of loose minerals, etc., unloaded through doors on the underside. 6. *Computer technol.* a device for holding punched cards and feeding them to a card punch or card reader.

hop-picker *n.* a person employed or a machine used to pick hops.

hopping ('hɒpɪŋ) *n.* 1. the action of a person or animal that hops. 2. *Tyneside dialect.* a fair, esp. (**the Hoppings**) an annual fair in Newcastle. ~*adj.* 3. **hopping mad.** in a terrible rage.

hopple ('hɒpᵊl) *vb., n.* a less common word for **hobble** (senses 2, 4). —'**hoppler** *n.*

Hoppus foot ('hɒpəs) *n.* a unit of volume equal to 1.27 cubic feet, applied to timber in the round, the cross-sectional area being taken as the square of one quarter of the circumference. [C20: named after Edward *Hoppus,* 18th-century British surveyor]

hops (hɒps) *pl. n.* the dried ripe flowers, esp. the female flowers, of the hop plant, used to give a bitter taste to beer.

hopsack ('hɒp,sæk) *n.* 1. a roughly woven fabric of wool, cotton, etc., used for clothing. 2. Also called: **hopsacking.** a coarse fabric used for bags, etc., made generally of hemp or jute.

hopscotch ('hɒp,skɒtʃ) *n.* a children's game in which a player throws a small stone or other object to land in one of a pattern of squares marked on the ground and then hops over to it to pick it up. [C19: HOP[1] + SCOTCH[1]]

hop, step, and jump *n.* **1.** an older term for **triple jump. 2.** Also called: **hop, skip, and jump.** a short distance: *the shops are only a hop, step, and jump from our house.*

hop trefoil *n.* a leguminous plant, *Trifolium campestre,* of N temperate grasslands, with globular yellow flower heads and trifoliate leaves. U.S. and Canadian name: **hop clover.**

hop up *vb.* (*tr., adv.*) **1.** *Dated.* to make intoxicated, esp. by narcotics. **2.** to invigorate, excite, etc. **3.** *U.S. and Canadian slang.* another term for **soup up.** ~*n.* **hop-up. 4.** *Dated.* a drug, chemical, etc., intended to hop up a person or thing.

hor. *abbrev. for:* **1.** horizon. **2.** horizontal.

hora ('hɔːrə) *n.* a traditional Israeli or Romanian circle dance. [from Modern Hebrew *hōrāh,* from Romanian *horă,* from Turkish]

horal ('hɔːrəl) *adj.* a less common word for **hourly.** [C18: from Late Latin *hōrālis* of an HOUR]

horary ('hɔːrərɪ) *adj. Archaic.* **1.** relating to the hours. **2.** hourly. [C17: from Medieval Latin *hōrārius;* see HOUR]

Horatian (hə'reɪʃən) *adj.* of, relating to, or characteristic of Horace (65–8 B.C.), Roman poet and satirist, or his poetry.

Horatian ode *n.* an ode of several stanzas, each of the same metrical pattern. Also called: **Sapphic ode.**

horde (hɔːd) *n.* **1.** a vast crowd; throng; mob. **2.** a local group of people in a nomadic society. **3.** a nomadic group of people, esp. an Asiatic group. **4.** a large moving mass of animals, esp. insects. ~*vb.* **5.** (*intr.*) to form, move in, or live in a horde. [C16: from Polish *horda,* from Turkish *ordū* camp; compare *Urdu*]

hordein ('hɔːdiːɪn) *n.* a simple protein, rich in proline, that occurs in barley. [C19: from French *hordéine,* from Latin *hordeum* barley + French *-ine* -IN]

horehound *or* **hoarhound** ('hɔːˌhaʊnd) *n.* **1.** Also called: **white horehound.** a downy perennial herbaceous Old World plant, *Marrubium vulgare,* with small white flowers that contain a bitter juice formerly used as a cough medicine and flavouring: family *Labiatae* (labiates). See also **black horehound. 2. water horehound.** another name for **bugleweed** (sense 1). [Old English *hārhūne,* from *hār* grey + *hūne* horehound, of obscure origin]

hori ('hɔːriː) *n., pl.* **horis.** *N.Z. informal, derogatory.* a Maori. [Maori]

horizon (hə'raɪzᵊn) *n.* **1.** Also called: **visible horizon, apparent horizon.** the apparent line that divides the earth and the sky. **2.** *Astronomy.* **a.** Also called: **sensible horizon.** the circular intersection with the celestial sphere of the plane tangential to the earth at the position of the observer. **b.** Also called: **celestial horizon.** the great circle on the celestial sphere, the plane of which passes through the centre of the earth and is parallel to the sensible horizon. **3.** the range or limit of scope, interest, knowledge, etc. **4.** a layer of rock within a stratum that has a particular composition, esp. of fossils, by which the stratum may be dated. **5.** a layer in a soil profile having particular characteristics. See **A horizon, B horizon, C horizon.** [C14: from Latin, from Greek *horizōn kuklos* limiting circle, from *horizein* to limit, from *horos* limit] —**ho'rizonless** *adj.*

horizontal (ˌhɒrɪ'zɒntᵊl) *adj.* **1.** parallel to the plane of the horizon; level; flat. Compare **vertical** (sense 1). **2.** of or relating to the horizon. **3.** measured or contained in a plane parallel to that of the horizon. **4.** applied uniformly or equally to all members of a group. **5.** *Economics.* relating to identical stages of commercial activity: *horizontal integration.* ~*n.* **6.** a horizontal plane, position, line, etc. —ˌ**hori'zontalness** *or* ˌ**horizon'tality** *n.* —ˌ**hori'zontally** *adv.*

horizontal bar *n. Gymnastics.* a raised bar on which swinging and vaulting exercises are performed. Also called: **high bar.**

horizontal mobility *n. Sociol.* the movement of groups or individuals to positions that differ from those previously held but do not involve any change in class, status, or power. Compare **vertical mobility.** See also **upward mobility, downward mobility.**

horizontal stabilizer *n.* the U.S. name for **tailplane.**

horizontal union *n.* another name (esp. U.S.) for **craft union.**

horme ('hɔːmɪ) *n.* (in Jungian psychology) fundamental vital energy. [C20: from Greek *hormē* impulse] —**'hormic** *adj.*

hormone ('hɔːməʊn) *n.* **1.** a chemical substance produced in an endocrine gland and transported in the blood to a certain tissue, on which it exerts a specific effect. **2.** an organic compound produced by a plant that is essential for growth. **3.** any synthetic substance having the same effects. [C20: from Greek *hormōn,* from *horman* to stir up, urge on, from *hormē* impulse, assault] —**hor'monal** *adj.*

hormone replacement therapy *n.* a form of oestrogen treatment used to control menopausal symptoms and in the prevention of osteoporosis. Abbrev.: **HRT.**

horn (hɔːn) *n.* **1.** either of a pair of permanent outgrowths on the heads of cattle, antelopes, sheep, etc., consisting of a central bony core covered with layers of keratin. Related adj.: **corneous. 2.** the outgrowth from the nasal bone of a rhinoceros, consisting of a mass of fused hairs. **3.** any hornlike projection or process, such as the eyestalk of a snail. **4.** the antler of a deer. **5. a.** the constituent substance, mainly keratin, of horns, hooves, etc. **b.** (*in combination*): *horn-rimmed spectacles.* **6.** a container or device made from this substance or an artificial substitute: *a shoe horn; a drinking horn.* **7.** an object or part resembling a horn in shape, such as the points at either end of a crescent, the point of an anvil, the pommel of a saddle, or a cornucopia. **8.** a primitive musical wind instrument made from the horn of an animal. **9.** any musical instrument consisting of a pipe or tube of brass fitted with a mouthpiece, with or without valves. See **hunting horn, French horn, cor anglais. 10.** *Jazz slang.* any wind instrument. **11. a.** a device for producing a warning or signalling noise. **b.** (*in combination*): *a foghorn.* **12.** (*usually pl.*) the hornlike projection attributed to certain devils, deities, etc. **13.** (*usually pl.*) the imaginary hornlike parts formerly supposed to appear on the forehead of a cuckold. **14.** Also called: **horn balance.** an extension of an aircraft control surface that projects in front of the hinge providing aerodynamic assistance in moving the control. **15. a.** Also called: **acoustic horn, exponential horn.** a hollow conical device coupled to the diaphragm of a gramophone to control the direction and quality of the sound. **b.** a similar device attached to an electrical loudspeaker, esp. in a public-address system. **c.** Also called: **horn antenna.** a microwave aerial, formed by flaring out the end of a waveguide. **16.** *Geology.* another name for **pyramidal peak. 17.** a stretch of land or water shaped like a horn. **18.** *Brit. taboo slang.* an erection of the penis. **19.** *Bible.* a symbol of power, victory, or success: *in my name shall his horn be exalted.* **20. blow one's own horn.** *U.S. and Canadian.* to boast about oneself; brag. Brit. equivalent: **blow one's own trumpet. 21. draw** (*or* **pull**) **in one's horns. a.** to suppress or control one's feelings, esp. of anger, enthusiasm, or passion. **b.** to withdraw a previous statement. **c.** to economize. **22. on the horns of a dilemma. a.** in a situation involving a choice between two equally unpalatable alternatives. **b.** in an awkward situation. ~*vb.* (*tr.*) **23.** to provide with a horn or horns. **24.** to gore or butt with a horn. ~See also **horn in.** [Old English; related to Old Norse *horn,* Gothic *haurn,* Latin *cornu* horn] —**'hornless** *adj.* —**'hornˌlike** *adj.*

hornbeam ('hɔːnˌbiːm) *n.* **1.** any tree of the betulaceous genus *Carpinus,* such as *C. betulus* of Europe and Asia, having smooth grey bark and hard white wood. **2.** the wood of any of these trees. ~Also called: **ironwood.** [C14: from HORN + BEAM, referring to its tough wood]

hornbill ('hɔːnˌbɪl) *n.* any bird of the family *Bucerotidae* of tropical Africa and Asia, having a very large bill with a basal bony protuberance: order *Coraciiformes* (kingfishers, etc.).

hornblende ('hɔːnˌblɛnd) *n.* a black or greenish-black mineral of the amphibole group, found in igneous and metamorphic rocks. Composition: calcium magnesium iron sodium aluminium aluminosilicate. General formula: $Ca_2Na(Mg,Fe)_4(Al,Fe)(Si,Al)_8O_{22}$. Crystal structure: monoclinic. [C18: from German *Horn* horn + BLENDE] —ˌ**horn'blendic** *adj.*

hornbook ('hɔːnˌbʊk) *n.* **1.** a page bearing a religious text or the alphabet, held in a frame with a thin window of flattened cattle horn over it. **2.** any elementary primer.

horned (hɔːnd) *adj.* having a horn, horns, or hornlike parts. —**hornedness** ('hɔːnɪdnɪs) *n.*

horned owl *n.* any large owl of the genus *Bubo,* having prominent ear tufts: family *Strigidae.*

horned poppy *n.* any of several Eurasian papaveraceous plants of the genera *Glaucium* and *Roemeria,* having large brightly coloured flowers and long curved seed capsules.

horned pout *n.* a North American catfish, *Ameiurus* (or *Ictalurus*) *nebulosus,* with a sharp spine on the dorsal and pectoral fins and eight long barbels around the mouth: family *Ameiuridae.* Also called: **brown bullhead.**

horned toad *or* **lizard** *n.* any small insectivorous burrowing lizard of the genus *Phrynosoma,* inhabiting desert regions of America, having a flattened toadlike body covered with spines: family *Iguanidae* (iguanas).

horned viper *n.* a venomous snake, *Cerastes cornutus,* that occurs in desert regions of N Africa and SW Asia and has a small horny spine above each eye: family *Viperidae* (vipers). Also called: **sand viper.**

hornet ('hɔːnɪt) *n.* **1.** any of various large social wasps of the family *Vespidae,* esp. *Vespa crabro* of Europe, that can inflict a severe sting. **2. hornet's nest.** a strongly unfavourable reaction (often in the phrase **stir up a hornet's nest**). [Old English *hyrnetu;* related to Old Saxon *hornut,* Old High German *hornuz*]

hornet clearwing *n.* See **clearwing.**

hornfels ('hɔːnfɛlz) *n.* a hard compact fine-grained metamorphic rock formed by the action of heat on clay rocks. Also called: **hornstone.** [German: literally, horn rock]

horn in *vb.* (*intr., adv.;* often foll. by *on*) *Slang.* to interrupt or intrude: *don't horn in on our conversation.*

horn of plenty *n.* **1.** another term for **cornucopia. 2.** an edible basidiomycetous fungus, *Craterellus cornucopioides,* related to the chanterelle and like it funnel shaped but dark brown inside and dark grey outside: found in broad-leaved woodland.

hornpipe ('hɔːnˌpaɪp) *n.* **1.** an obsolete reed instrument with a mouthpiece made of horn. **2.** an old British solo dance to a hornpipe accompaniment, traditionally performed by sailors. **3.** a piece of music for such a dance.

horn silver *n.* another name for **cerargyrite.**

hornstone ('hɔːnˌstəʊn) *n.* another name for **chert** or **hornfels.** [C17: translation of German *Hornstein;* so called from its appearance]

hornswoggle ('hɔːnˌswɒgᵊl) *vb. (tr.) Slang.* to cheat or trick; bamboozle. [C19: of unknown origin]

horntail ('hɔːnˌteɪl) *n.* any of various large wasplike insects of the hymenopterous family *Siricidae,* the females of which have a strong stout ovipositor and lay their eggs in the wood of felled trees. Also called: **wood wasp.**

hornwort ('hɔːnˌwɜːt) *n.* any aquatic plant of the genus *Ceratophyllum,* forming submerged branching masses in ponds and slow-flowing streams: family *Ceratophyllaceae.*

hornwrack ('hɔːnˌræk) *n.* a yellowish bryozoan or sea mat sometimes found on beaches after a storm.

horny ('hɔːnɪ) *adj.* **hornier, horniest. 1.** of, like, or hard as horn. **2.** having a horn or horns. **3.** *Slang.* aroused sexually. —'**hornily** *adv.* —'**horniness** *n.*

horol. *abbrev. for* horology.

horologe ('hɒrəˌlɒdʒ) *n.* a rare word for **timepiece.** [C14: from Latin *hōrologium,* from Greek *hōrologion,* from *hōra* HOUR + *-logos* from *legein* to tell]

horologist (hɒ'rɒlədʒɪst) *or* **horologer** (hɒ'rɒlədʒə) *n.* a person skilled in horology, esp. an expert maker of timepieces.

horologium (ˌhɒrə'ləʊdʒɪəm) *n., pl.* **-gia** (-dʒɪə). **1.** a clocktower. **2.** Also called: **horologion.** (in the Eastern Church) a liturgical book of the offices for the canonical hours, corresponding to the Western breviary. [C17: from Latin; see HOROLOGE]

Horologium (ˌhɒrə'ləʊdʒɪəm) *n., Latin genitive* **Horologii** (ˌhɒrə'ləʊdʒɪaɪ). a faint constellation in the S hemisphere lying near Eridanus and Hydrus.

horology (hɒ'rɒlədʒɪ) *n.* the art or science of making timepieces or of measuring time. —**horologic** (ˌhɒrə'lɒdʒɪk) *or* ˌ**horo'logical** *adj.*

horopter (hɒ'rɒptə) *n. Optics.* the locus of all points in space that stimulate points on each eye that yield the same visual direction as each other. [C18: from Greek *horos* boundary + *optēr,* from *ops* eye]

horoscope ('hɒrəˌskəʊp) *n.* **1.** the prediction of a person's future based on a comparison of the zodiacal data for the time of birth with the data from the period under consideration. **2.** the configuration of the planets, the sun, and the moon in the sky at a particular moment. **3.** Also called: **chart.** a diagram showing the positions of the planets, sun, moon, etc., at a particular time and place. [Old English *horoscopus,* from Latin, from Greek *hōroskopos* ascendant birth sign, from *hōra* HOUR + -SCOPE] —**horoscopic** (ˌhɒrə'skɒpɪk) *adj.*

horoscopy (hɒ'rɒskəpɪ) *n., pl.* **-pies.** the casting and interpretation of horoscopes.

horrendous (hɒ'rɛndəs) *adj.* another word for **horrific.** [C17: from Latin *horrendus* fearful, from *horrēre* to bristle, shudder, tremble; see HORROR] —**hor'rendously** *adv.*

horrible ('hɒrəbᵊl) *adj.* **1.** causing horror; dreadful. **2.** disagreeable; unpleasant. **3.** *Informal.* cruel or unkind. [C14: via Old French from Latin *horribilis,* from *horrēre* to tremble] —'**horribleness** *n.*

horribly ('hɒrɪblɪ) *adv.* **1.** in a horrible manner. **2.** (intensifier): *I'm horribly bored.*

horrid ('hɒrɪd) *adj.* **1.** disagreeable; unpleasant: *a horrid meal.* **2.** repulsive or frightening. **3.** *Informal.* unkind. [C16 (in the sense: bristling, shaggy): from Latin *horridus* prickly, rough, from *horrēre* to bristle] —'**horridly** *adv.* —'**horridness** *n.*

horrific (hɒ'rɪfɪk, hə-) *adj.* provoking horror; horrible. —**hor'rifically** *adv.*

horrify ('hɒrɪˌfaɪ) *vb.* **-fies, -fying, -fied.** *(tr.)* **1.** to cause feelings of horror in; terrify; frighten. **2.** to dismay or shock greatly. —ˌ**horrifi'cation** *n.* —'**horrified** *adj.* —'**horriˌfying** *adj.* —'**horriˌfyingly** *adv.*

horripilation (hɒˌrɪpɪ'leɪʃən) *n. Physiol.* **1.** a technical name for **goose flesh. 2.** the erection of any short bodily hairs. [C17: from Late Latin *horripilātiō* a bristling, from Latin *horrēre* to stand on end + *pilus* hair]

horror ('hɒrə) *n.* **1.** extreme fear; terror; dread. **2.** intense loathing; hatred. **3.** *(often pl.)* a thing or person causing fear, loathing, etc. **4.** *(modifier)* having a frightening subject, esp. a supernatural one: *a horror film.* [C14: from Latin: a trembling with fear; compare HIRSUTE]

horrors ('hɒrəz) *pl. n.* **1.** *Slang.* a fit of depression or anxiety. **2.** *Informal.* See **delirium tremens.** *~interj.* **3.** an expression of dismay, sometimes facetious.

horror-struck *or* **horror-stricken** *adj.* shocked; horrified.

hors concours *French.* (ɔr kɔ̃kur) *adj. (postpositive), adv.* **1.** (of an artist, exhibitor, etc.) excluded from competing. **2.** without equal; unrivalled. [literally: out of the competition]

hors de combat *French.* (ɔr də kɔ̃ba) *adj. (postpositive), adv.* disabled or injured. [literally: out of (the) fight]

hors d'oeuvre (ɔː 'dɜːvr; *French* ɔr dœvrə) *n., pl.* **hors d'oeuvre** *or* **hors d'oeuvres** ('dɜːvr; *French* dœvrə). an additional dish served as an appetizer, usually before the main meal. [C18: from French, literally: outside the work, not part of the main course]

horse (hɔːs) *n.* **1.** a domesticated perissodactyl mammal, *Equus caballus,* used for draught work and riding: family *Equidae.* Related adj.: **equine. 2.** the adult male of this species; stallion. **3. wild horse. a.** a horse (*Equus caballus*) that has become feral. **b.** another name for **Przewalski's horse. 4. a.** any other member of the family *Equidae,* such as the zebra or ass. **b.** *(as modifier): the horse family.* **5.** *(functioning as pl.)* horsemen, esp. cavalry: *a regiment of horse.* **6.** Also called: **buck.** *Gymnastics.* a padded apparatus on legs, used for vaulting, etc. **7.** a narrow board supported by a pair of legs at each end, used as a frame for sawing or as a trestle, barrier, etc. **8.** a contrivance on which a person may ride and exercise. **9.** a slang word for **heroin. 10.** *Mining.* a mass of rock within a vein of ore. **11.** *Nautical.* a rod, rope, or cable, fixed at the ends, along which something may slide by means of a thimble, shackle, or other fitting; traveller. **12.** *Chess.* an informal name for **knight. 13.** *Informal.* short for **horsepower. 14.** *(modifier)* drawn by a horse or horses: *a horse cart.* **15. be** *(or* **get) on one's high horse.** *Informal.* to be disdainfully aloof. **16. flog** *or* **beat a dead horse.** See **flog** (sense 6). **17. hold one's horses.** to hold back; restrain oneself. **18. a horse of another** *or* **a different colour.** a completely different topic, argument, etc. **19. horses for courses.** a policy, course of action, etc. modified slightly to take account of specific circumstances without departing in essentials from the original. **20. the horse's mouth.** the most reliable source. **21. to horse!** an order to mount horses. *~vb.* **22.** *(tr.)* to provide with a horse or horses. **23.** to put or be put on horseback. **24.** *(tr.)* to move (something heavy) into position by sheer physical strength. [Old English *hors;* related to Old Frisian *hors,* Old High German *hros,* Old Norse *hross*] —'**horseless** *adj.* —'**horseˌlike** *adj.*

horse around *or* **about** *vb. (intr., adv.) Informal.* to indulge in horseplay.

horseback ('hɔːsˌbæk) *n.* **a.** a horse's back (esp. in the phrase **on horseback**). **b.** *Chiefly U.S. and Canadian. (as modifier): horseback riding.*

horse bean *n.* another name for **broad bean.**

horsebox ('hɔːsˌbɒks) *n. Brit.* a van or trailer used for carrying horses.

horse brass *n.* a decorative brass ornament, usually circular, originally attached to a horse's harness.

horse chestnut *n.* **1.** any of several trees of the genus *Aesculus,* esp. the Eurasian *A. hippocastanum,* having palmate leaves, erect clusters of white, pink, or red flowers, and brown shiny inedible nuts enclosed in a spiky bur: family *Hippocastanaceae.* **2.** Also called: **conker.** the nut of this tree. [C16: so called from its having been used in the treatment of respiratory disease in horses]

horseflesh ('hɔːsˌflɛʃ) *n.* **1.** horses collectively. **2.** the flesh of a horse, esp. edible horse meat.

horsefly ('hɔːsˌflaɪ) *n., pl.* **-flies.** any large stout-bodied dipterous fly of the family *Tabanidae,* the females of which suck the blood of mammals, esp. horses, cattle, and man. Also called: **gadfly, cleg.**

horse gentian *n.* any caprifoliaceous plant of the genus *Triosteum,* of Asia and North America, having small purplish-brown flowers. Also called: **feverwort.**

horsehair ('hɔːsˌhɛə) *n.* **a.** hair taken chiefly from the tail or mane of a horse, used in upholstery and for fabric, etc. **b.** *(as modifier): a horsehair mattress.*

horsehair toadstool *or* **fungus** *n.* a small basidiomycetous fungus, *Marasmius androsaceus,* having a rusty coloured cap and very slender black stems. It is related to the fairy ring mushroom, but is commonly found among conifers and heather.

horsehair worm *n.* another name for **hairworm** (sense 2).

horsehide ('hɔːsˌhaɪd) *n.* **1.** the hide of a horse. **2.** leather made from this hide. **3.** *(modifier)* made of horsehide.

horse latitudes *pl. n. Nautical.* the latitudes near 30°N or 30°S at sea, characterized by baffling winds, calms, and high barometric pressure. [C18: referring either to the high mortality of horses on board ship in these latitudes or to *dead horse* (nautical slang: advance pay), which sailors expected to work off by this stage of a voyage]

horse laugh *n.* a coarse, mocking, or raucous laugh; guffaw.

horseleech ('hɔːsˌliːtʃ) *n.* **1.** any of several large carnivorous freshwater leeches of the genus *Haemopis,* esp. *H. sanguisuga.* **2.** an archaic name for a **veterinary surgeon.**

horse mackerel *n.* **1.** Also called: **scad.** a mackerel-like carangid fish, *Trachurus trachurus,* of European Atlantic waters, with a row of bony scales along the lateral line. Sometimes called (U.S.): **saurel. 2.** any of various large tunnies or related fishes.

horseman ('hɔːsmən) *n., pl.* **-men. 1.** a person who is skilled in riding or horsemanship. **2.** a person who rides a horse. —'**horseˌwoman** *fem. n.*

horsemanship ('hɔːsmənˌʃɪp) *n.* **1.** the art of riding on horseback. **2.** skill in riding horses.

horse marine *n. U.S.* **1.** (formerly) a mounted marine or cavalryman serving in a ship. **2.** someone out of his natural element, as if a member of an imaginary body of marine cavalry.

horsemint ('hɔːsˌmɪnt) *n.* **1.** a hairy European mint plant, *Mentha longifolia,* with small mauve flowers: family *Labiatae* (labiates). **2.** any of several similar and related plants, such as *Monarda punctata* of North America.

horse mushroom *n.* a large edible agaricaceous field mushroom, *Agaricus arvensis,* with a white cap and greyish gills.

horse nettle *n.* a weedy solanaceous North American plant, *Solanum carolinense,* with yellow prickles, white or blue flowers, and yellow berries.

horse opera *n. Informal.* another term for **Western** (sense 4).
horse pistol *n.* a large holstered pistol formerly carried by horsemen.
horseplay ('hɔːsˌpleɪ) *n.* rough, boisterous, or rowdy play.
horsepower ('hɔːsˌpaʊə) *n.* **1.** an fps unit of power, equal to 550 foot-pounds per second (equivalent to 745.7 watts). **2.** a U.S. standard unit of power, equal to 746 watts. ~Abbrevs.: **HP, h.p.**
horsepower-hour *n.* an fps unit of work or energy equal to the work done by 1 horsepower in 1 hour. 1 horsepower-hour is equivalent to 2.686×10^6 joules.
horseradish ('hɔːsˌrædɪʃ) *n.* **1.** a coarse Eurasian cruciferous plant, *Armoracia rusticana,* cultivated for its thick white pungent root. **2.** the root of this plant, which is ground and combined with vinegar, etc., to make a sauce.
horse sense *n.* another term for **common sense.**
horseshit ('hɔːsˌʃɪt) *n. Taboo slang.* rubbish; nonsense.
horseshoe ('hɔːsˌʃuː) *n.* **1.** a piece of iron shaped like a U with the ends curving inwards that is nailed to the underside of the hoof of a horse to protect the soft part of the foot from hard surfaces: commonly thought to be a token of good luck. **2.** an object of similar shape. ~*vb.* **-shoes, -shoeing, -shoed. 3.** (*tr.*) to fit with a horseshoe; shoe.
horseshoe arch *n.* an arch formed in the shape of a horseshoe, esp. as used in Moorish architecture.
horseshoe bat *n.* any of numerous large-eared Old World insectivorous bats, mostly of the genus *Rhinolophus,* with a fleshy growth around the nostrils, used in echolocation: family *Rhinolophidae.*
horseshoe crab *n.* any marine chelicerate arthropod of the genus *Limulus,* of North America and Asia, having a rounded heavily armoured body with a long pointed tail: class *Merostomata.* Also called: **king crab.**
horseshoes ('hɔːsˌʃuːz) *n.* (*functioning as sing.*) a game in which the players try to throw horseshoes so that they encircle a stake in the ground some distance away.
horsetail ('hɔːsˌteɪl) *n.* **1.** any pteridophyte plant of the genus *Equisetum* and order *Equisetales,* having jointed stems with whorls of small dark toothlike leaves. **2.** a stylized horse's tail formerly used as the emblem of a pasha, the number of tails increasing with rank.
horse trading *n.* hard bargaining to obtain equal concessions by both sides in a dispute.
horseweed ('hɔːsˌwiːd) *n.* the U.S. name for **Canadian fleabane** (see **fleabane** (sense 3)).
horsewhip ('hɔːsˌwɪp) *n.* **1.** a whip, usually with a long thong, used for managing horses. ~*vb.* **-whips, -whipping, -whipped. 2.** (*tr.*) to flog with such a whip. —**'horseˌwhipper** *n.*
horst (hɔːst) *n.* a ridge of land that has been forced upwards between two parallel faults. [C20: from German: thicket]
horsy *or* **horsey** ('hɔːsɪ) *adj.* **horsier, horsiest. 1.** of or relating to horses: *a horsy smell.* **2.** dealing with or devoted to horses. **3.** like a horse: *a horsy face.* —**'horsily** *adv.* —**'horsiness** *n.*
hort. *abbrev. for:* **1.** horticultural. **2.** horticulture.
hortatory ('hɔːtətərɪ, -trɪ) *or* **hortative** ('hɔːtətɪv) *adj.* tending to exhort; encouraging. [C16: from Late Latin *hortātōrius,* from Latin *hortārī* to EXHORT] —**hor'tation** *n.* —**'hortatorily** *or* **'hortatively** *adv.*
horticulture ('hɔːtɪˌkʌltʃə) *n.* the art or science of cultivating gardens. [C17: from Latin *hortus* garden + CULTURE, on the model of AGRICULTURE] —**ˌhorti'cultural** *adj.* —**ˌhorti'culturally** *adv.* —**ˌhorti'culturist** *n.*
hortus siccus ('hɔːtəs 'sɪkəs) *n.* a less common name for **herbarium.** [C17: Latin, literally: dry garden]
Hos. *Bible. abbrev. for* Hosea.
hosanna (həʊ'zænə) *interj.* **1.** an exclamation of praise, esp. one to God. ~*n.* **2.** the act of crying "hosanna". [Old English *osanna,* via Late Latin from Greek, from Hebrew *hōshi 'āh nnā* save now, we pray]
hose[1] (həʊz) *n.* **1.** a flexible pipe, for conveying a liquid or gas. ~*vb.* **2.** (sometimes foll. by *down*) to wash, water, or sprinkle (a person or thing) with or as if with a hose. [C15: later use of HOSE[2]]
hose[2] (həʊz) *n., pl.* **hose** *or* **hosen. 1.** stockings, socks, and tights collectively. **2.** *History.* a man's garment covering the legs and reaching up to the waist; worn with a doublet. **3. half-hose.** socks. [Old English *hosa;* related to Old High German *hosa,* Dutch *hoos,* Old Norse *hosa*]
hosier ('həʊzɪə) *n.* a person who sells stockings, etc.
hosiery ('həʊzɪərɪ) *n.* stockings, socks, and knitted underclothing collectively.
hosp. *abbrev. for* hospital.
hospice ('hɒspɪs) *n., pl.* **hospices. 1.** a nursing home that specializes in caring for the terminally ill. **2.** Also called: **hospitium** (hɒ'spɪtɪəm), *pl.* **hospitia** (hɒ'spɪtɪə). *Archaic.* a place of shelter for travellers, esp. one kept by a monastic order. [C19: from French, from Latin *hospitium* hospitality, from *hospes* guest, HOST[1]]
hospitable ('hɒspɪtəbᵊl, hɒ'spɪt-) *adj.* **1.** welcoming to guests or strangers. **2.** fond of entertaining. **3.** receptive: *hospitable to new ideas.* [C16: from Medieval Latin *hospitāre* to receive as a guest, from Latin *hospes* guest, HOST[1]] —**'hospitableness** *n.* —**'hospitably** *adv.*
hospital ('hɒspɪtᵊl) *n.* **1.** an institution for the medical, surgical, obstetric, or psychiatric care and treatment of patients. **2.** (*modifier*) having the function of a hospital: *a hospital ship.* **3.** a repair shop for something specified: *a dolls' hospital.* **4.** *Archaic.* a charitable home, hospice, or school. [C13: from Medieval Latin *hospitāle* hospice, from Latin *hospitālis* relating to a guest, from *hospes, hospit-* guest, HOST[1]]
hospital corner *n.* a corner of a made-up bed in which the bedclothes have been neatly and securely folded, esp. as in hospitals.
hospitality (ˌhɒspɪ'tælɪtɪ) *n., pl.* **-ties. 1.** kindness in welcoming strangers or guests. **2.** receptiveness.
hospitality suite *n.* a room or suite, as at a conference, where free drinks are offered.
hospitalization *or* **hospitalisation** (ˌhɒspɪtəlaɪ'zeɪʃən) *n.* **1.** the act or an instance of being hospitalized. **2.** the duration of a stay in a hospital.
hospitalize *or* **hospitalise** ('hɒspɪtəˌlaɪz) *vb.* (*tr.*) to admit or send (a person) into a hospital.
hospitaller *or U.S.* **hospitaler** ('hɒspɪtələ) *n.* a person, esp. a member of certain religious orders, dedicated to hospital work, ambulance services, etc. [C14: from Old French *hospitalier,* from Medieval Latin *hospitālārius,* from *hospitāle* hospice; see HOSPITAL]
Hospitaller *or U.S.* **Hospitaler** ('hɒspɪtələ) *n.* a member of the military religious order of the Knights Hospitallers, founded (*c.* 1096–99) in Jerusalem by European Crusaders.
hospodar ('hɒspəˌdɑː) *n.* (formerly) the governor or prince of Moldavia or Wallachia (present-day Romania) under Ottoman rule. [C17: via Romanian from Ukrainian, from *hospod'* lord; related to Russian *gospodin* courtesy title, Old Slavonic *gospodĭ* lord]
host[1] (həʊst) *n.* **1.** a person who receives or entertains guests, esp. in his own home. **2.** the compere of a show or television programme. **3.** *Biology.* **a.** an animal or plant that nourishes and supports a parasite. **b.** an animal, esp. an embryo, into which tissue is experimentally grafted. **4.** the owner or manager of an inn. ~*vb.* **5.** to be the host of (a party, programme, etc.): *to host one's own show.* **6.** (*tr.*) *U.S. informal.* to leave (a restaurant) without paying the bill. [C13: from French *hoste,* from Latin *hospes* guest, foreigner, from *hostis* enemy]
host[2] (həʊst) *n.* **1.** a great number; multitude. **2.** an archaic word for **army.** [C13: from Old French *hoste,* from Latin *hostis* stranger, enemy]
Host (həʊst) *n.* the bread consecrated in the Eucharist. [C14: from Old French *oiste,* from Latin *hostia* victim]
hosta ('hɒstə) *n.* any plant of the liliaceous genus *Hosta,* of China and Japan: cultivated esp. for their ornamental foliage. [C19: New Latin, named after N. T. *Host* (1761–1834), Austrian physician]
hostage ('hɒstɪdʒ) *n.* **1.** a person given to or held by a person, organization, etc., as a security or pledge or for ransom, release, exchange for prisoners, etc. **2.** the state of being held as a hostage. **3.** any security or pledge. **4. give hostages to fortune.** to place oneself in a position in which misfortune may strike through the loss of what one values most. [C13: from Old French, from *hoste* guest, HOST[1]]
hostel ('hɒstᵊl) *n.* **1.** a building providing overnight accommodation, as for the homeless, etc. **2.** See **youth hostel. 3.** *Brit.* a supervised lodging house for nurses, workers, etc. **4.** *Archaic.* another word for **hostelry.** [C13: from Old French, from Medieval Latin *hospitāle* hospice; see HOSPITAL]
hosteller *or U.S.* **hosteler** ('hɒstələ) *n.* **1.** a person who stays at youth hostels. **2.** an archaic word for **innkeeper.**
hostelling *or U.S.* **hosteling** ('hɒstəlɪŋ) *n.* the practice of staying at youth hostels when travelling.
hostelry ('hɒstəlrɪ) *n., pl.* **-ries.** *Archaic or facetious.* an inn.
hostel school *n.* (in N Canada) a government boarding school for Indian and Inuit students.
hostess ('həʊstɪs) *n.* **1.** a woman acting as host. **2.** a woman who receives and entertains patrons of a club, restaurant, etc. **3.** See **air hostess.**
hostie ('həʊstɪ) *n. Austral. informal.* short for **air hostess.**
hostile ('hɒstaɪl) *adj.* **1.** antagonistic; opposed. **2.** of or relating to an enemy. **3.** unfriendly. ~*n.* **4.** a hostile person; enemy. [C16: from Latin *hostīlis,* from *hostis* enemy] —**'hostilely** *adv.*
hostile witness *n.* a witness who gives evidence against the party calling him.
hostility (hɒ'stɪlɪtɪ) *n., pl.* **-ties. 1.** enmity or antagonism. **2.** an act expressing enmity or opposition. **3.** (*pl.*) fighting; warfare.
hostler ('ɒslə) *n.* another name (esp. Brit.) for **ostler.**
hot (hɒt) *adj.* **hotter, hottest. 1.** having a relatively high temperature. **2.** having a temperature higher than desirable. **3.** causing or having a sensation of bodily heat. **4.** causing a burning sensation on the tongue: *hot mustard; a hot curry.* **5.** expressing or feeling intense emotion, such as embarrassment, anger, or lust. **6.** intense or vehement: *a hot argument.* **7.** recent; fresh; new: *a hot trial; hot from the press.* **8.** *Ball games.* (of a ball) thrown or struck hard, and so difficult to respond to. **9.** much favoured or approved: *a hot tip; a hot favourite.* **10.** *Informal.* having a dangerously high level of radioactivity: *a hot laboratory.* **11.** *Slang.* (of goods or money) stolen, smuggled, or otherwise illegally obtained. **12.** *Slang.* (of people) being sought

by the police. **13.** (of a colour) intense; striking: *hot pink.* **14.** close or following closely: *hot on the scent.* **15.** *Informal.* at a dangerously high electric potential: *a hot terminal.* **16.** *Physics.* having an energy level higher than that of the ground state: *a hot atom.* **17.** *Slang.* impressive or good of its kind (esp. in the phrase **not so hot**). **18.** *Jazz slang.* arousing great excitement or enthusiasm by inspired improvisation, strong rhythms, etc. **19.** *Informal.* dangerous or unpleasant (esp. in the phrase **make it hot for someone**). **20.** (in various searching or guessing games) very near the answer or object to be found. **21.** *Metallurgy.* (of a process) at a sufficiently high temperature for metal to be in a soft workable state. **22.** *Austral. and N.Z. informal.* (of a price, charge, etc.) excessive. **23. give it (to someone) hot.** to punish or thrash (someone). **24. hot on.** *Informal.* **a.** very severe: *the police are hot on drunk drivers.* **b.** particularly skilled at or knowledgeable about: *he's hot on vintage cars.* **25. hot under the collar.** *Informal.* aroused with anger, annoyance, etc. **26. in hot water.** *Informal.* in trouble, esp. with those in authority. ~*adv.* **27.** in a hot manner; hotly. ~See also **hots, hot up.** [Old English *hāt;* related to Old High German *heiz,* Old Norse *heitr,* Gothic *heito* fever] —'**hotly** *adv.* —'**hotness** *n.*

hot air *n. Informal.* empty and usually boastful talk.

hot-air balloon *n.* a lighter-than-air craft in which air heated by a flame is trapped in a large fabric bag.

hotbed ('hɒt,bɛd) *n.* **1.** a glass-covered bed of soil, usually heated by fermenting material, used for propagating plants, forcing early vegetables, etc. **2.** a place offering ideal conditions for the growth of an idea, activity, etc., esp. one considered bad: *a hotbed of insurrection.*

hot-blooded *adj.* **1.** passionate or excitable. **2.** (of a horse) being of thoroughbred stock. —,**hot-'bloodedness** *n.*

hotchpot ('hɒtʃ,pɒt) *n. Property law.* the collecting of property so that it may be redistributed in equal shares, esp. on the intestacy of a parent who has given property to his children in his lifetime. [C14: from Old French *hochepot,* from *hocher* to shake, of Germanic origin + POT[1]]

hotchpotch ('hɒtʃ,pɒtʃ) *or esp. U.S. and Canadian* **hodgepodge** *n.* **1.** a jumbled mixture. **2.** a thick soup or stew made from meat and vegetables. [C15: variant of HOTCHPOT]

hot cockles *n.* (*functioning as sing.*) (formerly) a children's game in which one blindfolded player has to guess which other player has hit him.

hot cross bun *n.* a yeast bun with spices, currants, and sometimes candied peel, marked with a cross and traditionally eaten on Good Friday.

hot dog[1] *n.* a sausage, esp. a frankfurter, served hot in a long roll split lengthways. [C20: from the supposed resemblance of the sausage to a dachshund]

hot dog[2] *n.* **1.** *Chiefly U.S.* a person who performs showy acrobatic manoeuvres when skiing or surfing. ~*vb.* **hot-dog, -dogs, -dogging, -dogged. 2.** (*intr.*) to perform a series of manoeuvres in skiing, surfing, etc., esp. in a showy manner. [C20: from U.S. *hot dog!,* exclamation of pleasure, approval, etc.]

hotel (həʊ'tɛl) *n.* **1.** a commercially run establishment providing lodging and usually meals for guests. **2.** *Austral. and N.Z.* a public house. [C17: from French *hôtel,* from Old French *hostel;* see HOSTEL]

Hotel (həʊ'tɛl) *n. Communications.* a code word for the letter *h.*

hotelier (həʊ'tɛljeɪ) *n.* an owner or manager of one or more hotels.

hot fence *n. N.Z.* an electric fence surrounding a farm.

hot flush *or U.S.* **hot flash** *n.* a sudden unpleasant hot feeling in the skin, caused by endocrine imbalance, esp. experienced by women at the time of their menopause.

hotfoot ('hɒt,fʊt) *adv.* **1.** with all possible speed; quickly. ~*vb.* **2.** to move quickly.

hot-gospeller *n. Informal.* a revivalist preacher with a highly enthusiastic style of addressing his audience.

hothead ('hɒt,hɛd) *n.* an excitable or fiery person.

hot-headed *adj.* impetuous, rash, or hot-tempered. —,**hot-'headedly** *adv.* —,**hot-'headedness** *n.*

hothouse ('hɒt,haʊs) *n.* **1. a.** a greenhouse in which the temperature is maintained at a fixed level above that of the surroundings. **b.** (*as modifier*): *a hothouse plant.* **2.** (*modifier*) *Informal, often disparaging.* sensitive or delicate.

hot line *n.* **1.** a direct telephone, teletype, or other communications link between heads of government, for emergency use. **2.** any such direct line kept for urgent use.

hot metal *n.* **a.** metallic type cast into shape in the molten state. **b.** (*as modifier*): *hot-metal printing.*

hot money *n.* capital that is transferred from one financial centre to another seeking the highest interest rates or the best opportunity for short-term gain, esp. from anticipated changes in exchange rates.

hot pants *pl. n.* **1.** very brief skin-tight shorts, worn by young women. **2.** *Taboo slang.* a feeling of sexual arousal: *he has hot pants for her.*

hot pepper *n.* **1.** any of several varieties of the pepper *Capsicum frutescens,* esp. chilli pepper. **2.** the pungent usually small fruit of any of these plants.

hotplate ('hɒt,pleɪt) *n.* **1.** an electrically heated plate on a cooker. **2.** a portable device, heated electrically or by spirit lamps, etc., on which food can be kept warm.

hotpot ('hɒt,pɒt) *n.* **1.** *Brit.* a baked stew or casserole made with meat or fish and covered with a layer of potatoes. **2.** *Austral. slang.* a heavily backed horse.

hot potato *n. Slang.* an awkward or delicate matter.

hot-press *n.* **1.** a machine for applying a combination of heat and pressure to give a smooth surface to paper, to express oil from it, etc. ~*vb.* **2.** (*tr.*) to subject (paper, cloth, etc.) to heat and pressure to give it a smooth surface or extract oil.

hot rod *n.* a car with an engine that has been radically modified to produce increased power.

hots (hɒts) *pl. n.* **the.** *Slang.* intense sexual desire; lust (esp. in the phrase **have the hots for someone**).

hot seat *n.* **1.** *Informal.* a precarious, difficult, or dangerous position. **2.** *U.S.* a slang term for **electric chair.**

hot shoe *n. Photog.* an accessory shoe on a camera through which electrical contact is made for the operation of an electronic flash device.

hotshot ('hɒt,ʃɒt) *n. Informal.* an important person or expert, esp. when showy.

hot spot *n.* **1.** an area of potential violence or political unrest. **2.** a lively nightclub or other place of entertainment. **3. a.** any local area of high temperature in a part of an engine, etc. **b.** part of the inlet manifold of a paraffin engine that is heated by exhaust gases to vaporize the fuel. **4.** *Med.* **a.** a small area on the surface of or within a body with an exceptionally high concentration of radioactivity or of some chemical or mineral considered harmful. **b.** a similar area that generates an abnormal amount of heat, as revealed by thermography. **5.** *Genetics.* a part of a chromosome that has a tendency for mutation or recombination.

hot spring *n.* a natural spring of mineral water at a temperature of 21°C (70°F) or above, found in areas of volcanic activity. Also called: **thermal spring.**

hotspur ('hɒt,spɜː) *n.* an impetuous or fiery person. [C15: from *Hotspur,* nickname of Sir Henry *Percy* (1364–1403), English rebel]

hot stuff *n. Informal.* **1.** a person, object, etc., considered important, attractive, sexually exciting, etc. **2.** a pornographic or erotic book, play, film, etc.

Hottentot ('hɒtᵊn,tɒt) *n.* **1.** (*pl.* **-tot** *or* **-tots**) a member of a race of people of southern Africa, of low stature and a dark yellowish-brown complexion, who formerly occupied the region near the Cape of Good Hope and are now almost extinct. **2.** any of the languages of this people, belonging to the Khoisan family. [C17: from Afrikaans, of uncertain origin]

Hottentot fig *n.* a perennial plant, *Mesembryanthemum* (or *Carpobrotus*) *edule,* originally South African, having fleshy prostrate leaves, showy yellow or purple flowers, and edible fruits.

hottie ('hɒtɪ) *n. Austral. and N.Z. informal.* a hot-water bottle.

hottish ('hɒtɪʃ) *adj.* fairly hot.

hot up *vb.* (*adv.*) *Informal.* **1.** to make or become more exciting, active, or intense: *the chase was hotting up.* **2.** (*tr.*) another term for **soup up.**

hot-water bottle *n.* a receptacle, now usually made of rubber, designed to be filled with hot water, used for warming a bed or parts of the body.

hot-wire *vb.* (*tr.*) *Slang.* to start the engine of (a motor vehicle) by bypassing the ignition switch.

hot-work *vb.* (*tr.*) to shape (metal) when hot.

hot zone *n. Computer technol.* a variable area towards the end of a line of text that informs the operator that a decision must be taken as to whether to hyphenate or begin a new line.

houdah ('haʊdə) *n.* a variant spelling of **howdah.**

Houdan ('huːdæn) *n.* a breed of light domestic fowl originally from France, with a distinctive full crest. [C19: named after *Houdan,* village near Paris where the breed originated]

hough (hɒk) *Brit.* ~*n.* **1.** another word for **hock**[1]. **2.** (hɒx). in Scotland, a cut of meat corresponding to shin. ~*vb.* (*tr.*) **3.** to hamstring (cattle, horses, etc.). [C14: from Old English *hōh* heel]

hoummos, houmous, *or* **houmus** ('huːməs) *n.* variant spellings of **hummus.**

hound[1] (haʊnd) *n.* **1. a.** any of several breeds of dog used for hunting. **b.** (*in combination*): *an otterhound; a deerhound.* **2. the hounds.** a pack of foxhounds, etc. **3.** a dog, esp. one regarded as annoying. **4.** a despicable person. **5.** (in hare and hounds) a runner who pursues a hare. **6.** *Slang, chiefly U.S. and Canadian.* an enthusiast: *an autograph hound.* **7.** short for **houndfish.** See also **nursehound. 8. ride to hounds** *or* **follow the hounds.** to take part in a fox hunt with hounds. ~*vb.* (*tr.*) **9.** to pursue or chase relentlessly. **10.** to urge on. [Old English *hund;* related to Old High German *hunt,* Old Norse *hundr,* Gothic *hunds*] —'**hounder** *n.*

hound[2] (haʊnd) *n.* **1.** either of a pair of horizontal bars that reinforce the running gear of a horse-drawn vehicle. **2.** *Nautical.* either of a pair of fore-and-aft braces that serve as supports for a topmast. [C15: of Scandinavian origin; related to Old Norse *hūnn* knob, cube]

houndfish ('haʊnd,fɪʃ) *n., pl.* **-fish** *or* **-fishes.** a name given to various small sharks or dogfish. See also **nursehound.**

hound's-tongue *n.* any boraginaceous weedy plant of the genus *Cynoglossum,* esp. the Eurasian *C. officinale,* which has small reddish-purple flowers and spiny fruits. Also called: **dog's-tongue.** [Old English *hundestunge,* translation of Latin *cyn-*

oglōssos, from Greek *kunoglōssos,* from *kuōn* dog + *glōssa* tongue; referring to the shape of its leaves]

hound's-tooth check *n.* a pattern of broken or jagged checks, esp. one printed on or woven into cloth. Also called: **dog's-tooth check, dogtooth check.**

hour (aʊə) *n.* **1.** a period of time equal to 3600 seconds; 1/24th of a calendar day. Related adjs.: **horal, horary. 2.** any of the points on the face of a timepiece that indicate intervals of 60 minutes. **3. the hour.** an exact number of complete hours: *the bus leaves on the hour.* **4.** the time of day as indicated by a watch, clock, etc. **5.** the period of time allowed for or used for something: *the lunch hour; the hour of prayer.* **6.** a special moment or period: *our finest hour.* **7. the hour.** the present time: *the man of the hour.* **8.** the distance covered in an hour: *we live an hour from the city.* **9.** *Astronomy.* an angular measurement of right ascension equal to 15° or a 24th part of the celestial equator. **10. one's hour. a.** a time of success, fame, etc. **b.** Also: **one's last hour.** the time of one's death: *his hour had come.* **11. take one's hour.** *Irish informal.* to do something in a leisurely manner. ~See also **hours.** [C13: from Old French *hore,* from Latin *hōra,* from Greek: season]

hour angle *n.* the angular distance along the celestial equator from the meridian of the observer to the hour circle of a particular celestial body.

hour circle *n.* a great circle on the celestial sphere passing through the celestial poles and a specified point, such as a star.

hourglass (ˈaʊəˌglɑːs) *n.* **1.** a device consisting of two transparent chambers linked by a narrow channel, containing a quantity of sand that takes a specified time to trickle to one chamber from the other. **2.** (*modifier*) well-proportioned with a small waist: *an hourglass figure.*

hour hand *n.* the pointer on a timepiece that indicates the hour. Compare **minute hand, second hand.**

houri (ˈhʊərɪ) *n., pl.* **-ris. 1.** (in Muslim belief) any of the nymphs of Paradise. **2.** any alluring woman. [C18: from French, from Persian *hūri,* from Arabic *hūr,* plural of *haurā'* woman with dark eyes]

hourlong (ˈaʊəˌlɒŋ) *adj., adv.* lasting an hour.

hourly (ˈaʊəlɪ) *adj.* **1.** of, occurring, or done every hour. **2.** done in or measured by the hour: *we are paid an hourly rate.* **3.** continual or frequent. ~*adv.* **4.** every hour. **5.** at any moment or time.

hours (aʊəz) *pl. n.* **1.** a period regularly or customarily appointed for work, business, etc. **2.** one's times of rising and going to bed (esp. in the phrases **keep regular, irregular,** or **late hours**). **3. the small hours.** the hours just after midnight. **4. till all hours.** until very late. **5.** an indefinite period of time. **6.** Also called (in the Roman Catholic Church): **canonical hours. a.** the seven times of the day laid down for the recitation of the prayers of the divine office. **b.** the prayers recited at these times.

house *n.* (haʊs), *pl.* **houses** (ˈhaʊzɪz). **1. a.** a building used as a home; dwelling. **b.** (*as modifier*): *house dog.* **2.** the people present in a house, esp. its usual occupants. **3. a.** a building used for some specific purpose. **b.** (*in combination*): *a schoolhouse.* **4.** (*often cap.*) a family line including ancestors and relatives, esp. a noble one: *the House of York.* **5. a.** a commercial company; firm: *a publishing house.* **b.** (*as modifier*): *house style; a house journal.* **6.** an official deliberative or legislative body, such as one chamber of a bicameral legislature. **7.** a quorum in such a body (esp. in the phrase **make a house**). **8.** a dwelling for a religious community. **9.** *Astrology.* any of the 12 divisions of the zodiac. See also **planet** (sense 3). **10. a.** any of several divisions, esp. residential, of a large school. **b.** (*as modifier*): *house spirit.* **11. a.** a hotel, restaurant, bar, inn, club, etc., or the management of such an establishment. **b.** (*as modifier*): *house rules.* **c.** (*in combination*): *steakhouse.* **12.** the audience in a theatre or cinema. **13.** an informal word for **brothel. 14.** a hall in which an official deliberative or legislative body meets. **15.** See **full house. 16.** *Curling.* the 12-foot target circle around the tee. **17.** *Nautical.* any structure or shelter on the weather deck of a vessel. **18. bring the house down.** *Theatre.* to win great applause. **19. house and home.** an emphatic form of **home. 20. keep open house.** to be always ready to provide hospitality. **21. like a house on fire.** *Informal.* very well, quickly, or intensely. **22. on the house.** (usually of drinks) paid for by the management of the hotel, bar, etc. **23. put one's house in order.** to settle or organize one's affairs. **24. safe as houses.** *Brit.* very secure. ~*vb.* (haʊz). **25.** (*tr.*) to provide with or serve as accommodation. **26.** to give or receive shelter or lodging. **27.** (*tr.*) to contain or cover, esp. in order to protect. **28.** (*tr.*) to fit (a piece of wood) into a mortise, joint, etc. **29.** (*tr.*) *Nautical.* **a.** to secure or stow. **b.** to secure (a topmast). **c.** to secure and stow (an anchor). [Old English *hūs;* related to Old High German *hūs,* Gothic *gudhūs* temple, Old Norse *hūs* house] —ˈ**houseless** *adj.*

House (haʊs) **the.** *n.* **1.** See **House of Commons. 2.** *Brit. informal.* the Stock Exchange.

house agent *n. Brit.* another name for **estate agent.**

house arrest *n.* confinement to one's own home.

houseboat (ˈhaʊsˌbəʊt) *n.* a stationary boat or barge used as a home.

housebound (ˈhaʊsˌbaʊnd) *adj.* unable to leave one's house because of illness, injury, etc.

houseboy (ˈhaʊsˌbɔɪ) *n.* a male domestic servant.

housebreaking (ˈhaʊsˌbreɪkɪŋ) *n. Criminal law.* the act of entering a building as a trespasser for an unlawful purpose. Assimilated with burglary, 1968. —ˈ**houseˌbreaker** *n.*

house-broken *adj.* another word for **house-trained.**

housecarl (ˈhaʊsˌkɑːl) *n.* (in medieval Europe) a household warrior of Danish kings and noblemen. [Old English *hūscarl,* from Old Norse *hūskarl* manservant, from *hūs* HOUSE + *karl* man; see CHURL]

housecoat (ˈhaʊsˌkəʊt) *n.* a woman's loose robelike informal garment.

house-craft *n.* skill in domestic management.

house factor *n.* a Scottish term for **estate agent.**

housefather (ˈhaʊsˌfɑːðə) *n.* a man in charge of the welfare of a particular group of children in an institution such as a children's home or approved school. —ˈ**houseˌmother** *fem. n.*

housefly (ˈhaʊsˌflaɪ) *n., pl.* **-flies.** a common dipterous fly, *Musca domestica,* that frequents human habitations, spreads disease, and lays its eggs in carrion, decaying vegetables, etc.: family *Muscidae.*

house group *or* **church** *n.* a group of Christians who regularly meet to worship, study the Bible, etc. in someone's house.

house guest *n.* a guest at a house, esp. one who stays for a comparatively long time.

household (ˈhaʊsˌhəʊld) *n.* **1.** the people living together in one house collectively. **2.** (*modifier*) of, relating to, or used in the running of a household; domestic: *household management.*

householder (ˈhaʊsˌhəʊldə) *n.* a person who owns or rents a house. —ˈ**houseˌholderˌship** *n.*

household gods *pl. n.* **1.** (in ancient Rome) deities of the home; lares and penates. **2.** *Brit. informal.* the essentials of domestic life.

household name *or* **word** *n.* a person or thing that is very well known.

household troops *pl. n.* the infantry and cavalry regiments that carry out escort and guard duties for a head of state.

househusband (ˈhaʊsˌhʌzbənd) *n.* a married man who keeps house, usually without having paid employment.

housekeeper (ˈhaʊsˌkiːpə) *n.* **1.** a person, esp. a woman, employed to run a household. **2. good** (*or* **bad**) **housekeeper.** a person who is (or is not) an efficient and thrifty domestic manager.

housekeeping (ˈhaʊsˌkiːpɪŋ) *n.* **1.** the running of a household. **2.** money allocated for the running of a household. **3.** organization and tidiness in general, as of an office, shop, etc. **4.** the general maintenance of a computer storage system, including removal of obsolete files, documentation, etc.

housel (ˈhaʊzᵊl) *n.* **1.** a medieval name for **Eucharist.** ~*vb.* **-sels, -selling, -selled** *or U.S.* **-sels, -seling, -seled. 2.** (*tr.*) to give the Eucharist to (someone). [Old English *hūsl;* related to Gothic *hunsl* sacrifice, Old Norse *hūsl*]

houseleek (ˈhaʊsˌliːk) *n.* any Old World crassulaceous plant of the genus *Sempervivum,* esp. *S. tectorum,* which has a rosette of succulent leaves and pinkish flowers: grows on walls. Also called: **hen-and-chickens.**

house lights *pl. n.* the lights in the auditorium of a theatre, cinema, etc.

houseline (ˈhaʊsˌlaɪn) *n. Nautical.* tarred marline. Also called: **housing.**

housemaid (ˈhaʊsˌmeɪd) *n.* a girl or woman employed to do housework, esp. one who is resident in the household.

housemaid's knee *n.* inflammation and swelling of the bursa in front of the kneecap, caused esp. by constant kneeling on a hard surface. Technical name: **prepatellar bursitis.**

houseman (ˈhaʊsmən) *n., pl.* **-men.** *Med.* a junior doctor who is a member of the medical staff of a hospital. U.S. and Canadian equivalent: **intern.**

house martin *n.* a Eurasian swallow, *Delichon urbica,* with a slightly forked tail and a white and bluish-black plumage.

housemaster (ˈhaʊsˌmɑːstə) *n.* a teacher, esp. in a boarding school, responsible for the pupils in his house. —**housemistress** (ˈhaʊsˌmɪstrɪs) *fem. n.*

house moth *n.* either of two species of micro moth, esp. the **brown house moth** (*Hofmannophila pseudospretella*) which, although it usually inhabits birds' nests, sometimes enters houses where its larvae can be very destructive of stored fabrics and foodstuffs.

house mouse *n.* any of various greyish mice of the Old World genus *Mus,* esp. *M. musculus,* a common household pest in most parts of the world: family *Muridae.*

House music *or* **House** *n.* a type of disco music of the late 1980s, based on funk, with fragments of other recordings edited in electronically.

House of Assembly *n.* a legislative assembly or the lower chamber of such an assembly, esp. in various British colonies and countries of the Commonwealth.

house of cards *n.* an unstable situation, plan, etc.

House of Commons *n.* (in Britain, Canada, etc.) the lower chamber of Parliament.

house of correction *n.* (formerly) a place of confinement for persons convicted of minor offences.

house of God *n.* a church, temple, or chapel.

house of ill repute *or* **ill fame** *n.* a euphemistic name for **brothel.**
House of Lords *n.* (in Britain) the upper chamber of Parliament, composed of the peers of the realm.
House of Representatives *n.* **1.** (in the U.S.) the lower chamber of Congress. **2.** (in Australia) the lower chamber of Parliament. **3.** the sole chamber of New Zealand's Parliament: formerly the lower chamber. **4.** (in the U.S.) the lower chamber in many state legislatures.
house organ *n.* a periodical published by an organization for its employees or clients.
house party *n.* **1.** a party, usually in a country house, at which guests are invited to stay for several days. **2.** the guests who are invited.
house physician *or* **doctor** *n.* a physician who lives in a hospital or other institution where he is employed. Compare **resident** (sense 7).
house plant *n.* a plant that can be grown indoors.
house-proud *adj.* proud of the appearance, cleanliness, etc., of one's house, sometimes excessively so.
houseroom ('haʊsˌrʊm, -ˌruːm) *n.* **1.** room for storage or lodging. **2. give (something) houseroom.** (*used with a negative*) to have or keep (something) in one's house: *I wouldn't give that vase houseroom.*
Houses of Parliament *n.* (in Britain) **1.** the building in which the House of Commons and the House of Lords assemble. **2.** these two chambers considered together.
house sparrow *n.* a small Eurasian weaverbird, *Passer domesticus,* now established in North America and Australia. It has a brown streaked plumage with grey underparts. Also called (U.S.): **English sparrow.**
house spider *n.* any largish dark spider of the genus *Tegenaria* that is common in houses, such as the cardinal spider.
housetop ('haʊsˌtɒp) *n.* **1.** the roof of a house. **2. proclaim from the housetops.** to announce (something) publicly.
house-train *vb.* (*tr.*) *Brit.* to train (pets) to urinate and defecate outside the house or in a special place.
house-warming *n.* **a.** a party given after moving into a new home. **b.** (*as modifier*): *a house-warming party.*
housewife ('haʊsˌwaɪf) *n. pl.* **-wives. 1.** a woman, typically a married woman, who keeps house, usually without having paid employment. **2.** ('hʌzɪf) Also called: **hussy, huswife.** *Chiefly Brit.* a small sewing kit issued to soldiers. —**housewifery** ('haʊsˌwɪfərɪ, -ˌwɪfrɪ) *n.*
housewifely ('haʊsˌwaɪflɪ) *adj.* prudent and neat; domestic: *housewifely virtues.* —'**houseˌwifeliness** *n.*
housework ('haʊsˌwɜːk) *n.* the work of running a home, such as cleaning, cooking, etc. —'**houseˌworker** *n.*
housey-housey ('haʊzɪ'haʊzɪ) *n.* another name for **bingo** or **lotto.** [C20: so called from the cry of "house!" shouted by the winner of a game, probably from FULL HOUSE]
housing[1] ('haʊzɪŋ) *n.* **1. a.** houses or dwellings collectively. **b.** (*as modifier*): *a housing problem.* **2.** the act of providing with accommodation. **3.** a hole, recess, groove, or slot made in one wooden member to receive another. **4.** a part designed to shelter, cover, contain, or support a component, such as a bearing, or a mechanism, such as a pump or wheel: *a bearing housing; a motor housing; a wheel housing.* **5.** another word for **houseline.**
housing[2] ('haʊzɪŋ) *n.* (*often pl.*) *Archaic.* another word for **trappings** (sense 2). [C14: from Old French *houce* covering, of Germanic origin]
housing association *n. Social welfare.* (in Britain) a non-profit-making body whose purpose is to build, convert, or improve houses for letting at fair rents.
housing benefit *n. Social welfare.* (in Britain) a payment made by a local authority in the form of a rent rebate to a council tenant, a rent allowance to a private tenant, or a rate rebate to a tenant or home-owner.
housing estate *n.* a planned area of housing, often with its own shops and other amenities.
housing scheme *n.* **1.** a local-authority housing plan. **2.** the houses built according to such a plan; housing estate. ~Often shortened to **scheme.**
houstonia (huː'stəʊnɪə) *n.* any small North American rubiaceous plant of the genus *Houstonia,* having blue, white or purple flowers. [C19: named after Dr. William *Houston* (died 1733), Scottish botanist]
houting ('haʊtɪŋ) *n.* a European whitefish, *Coregonus oxyrhynchus,* that lives in salt water but spawns in freshwater lakes: a valued food fish. [C19: from Dutch, from Middle Dutch *houtic,* of uncertain origin]
hove (həʊv) *vb. Chiefly nautical.* a past tense and past participle of **heave.**
hovel ('hʌvᵊl, 'hɒv-) *n.* **1.** a ramshackle dwelling place. **2.** an open shed for livestock, carts, etc. **3.** the conical building enclosing a kiln. ~*vb.* **-els, -elling, -elled** *or U.S.* **-els, -eling, -eled. 4.** to shelter or be sheltered in a hovel. [C15: of unknown origin]
hover ('hɒvə) *vb.* (*intr.*) **1.** to remain suspended in one place. **2.** (of certain birds, esp. hawks) to remain in one place in the air by rapidly beating the wings. **3.** to linger uncertainly in a nervous or solicitous way. **4.** to be in a state of indecision: *she was hovering between the two suitors.* ~*n.* **5.** the act of hovering. [C14 *hoveren,* variant of *hoven,* of obscure origin] —'**hoverer** *n.* —'**hoveringly** *adv.*
hovercraft ('hɒvəˌkrɑːft) *n.* a vehicle that is able to travel across both land and water on a cushion of air. The cushion is produced by fans or a peripheral ring of nozzles.
hover fly *n.* any dipterous fly of the family *Syrphidae,* with a typically hovering flight, esp. *Syrphus ribesii,* which mimics a wasp.
hoverport ('hɒvəˌpɔːt) *n.* a port for hovercraft.
hovertrain ('hɒvəˌtreɪn) *n.* a train that moves over a concrete track and is supported while in motion by a cushion of air supplied by powerful fans.
how[1] (haʊ) *adv.* **1.** in what way? in what manner? by what means?: *how did it happen?* Also used in indirect questions: *tell me how he did it.* **2.** to what extent?: *how tall is he?* **3.** how good? how well? what...like?: *how did she sing? how was the holiday?* **4. how about?** used to suggest something: *how about asking her? how about a cup of tea?* **5. how are you?** what is your state of health? **6. how come?** *Informal.* what is the reason (that)?: *how come you told him?* **7. how's that for...? a.** is this satisfactory as regards...: *how's that for size?* **b.** an exclamation used to draw attention to a quality, deed, etc.: *how is that for endurance?* **8. how's that? a.** what is your opinion? **b.** *Cricket.* Also written: **howzat** (haʊ'zæt). (an appeal to the umpire) is the batsman out? **9. how now?** *or* **how so?** *Archaic.* what is the meaning of this? **10.** Also: **as how.** *Not standard.* that: *he told me as how the shop was closed.* **11.** in whatever way: *do it how you wish.* **12. and how!** (intensifier) very much so! **13. here's how!** (as a toast) good health! ~*n.* **14.** the way a thing is done: *the how of it.* [Old English *hu;* related to Old Frisian *hū,* Old High German *hweo*]
how[2] (haʊ) *sentence substitute.* a greeting supposed to be or have been used by American Indians and often used humorously. [C19: of Siouan origin; related to Dakota *háo*]
howbeit (haʊ'biːɪt) *Archaic.* ~*sentence connector.* **1.** however. ~*conj.* **2.** (*subordinating*) though; although.
howdah *or* **houdah** ('haʊdə) *n.* a seat for riding on an elephant's back, esp. one with a canopy. [C18: from Hindi *haudah,* from Arabic *haudaj* load carried by elephant or camel]
how do you do *sentence substitute.* **1.** Also: **how do?, how d'ye do?** a formal greeting said by people who are being introduced to each other or are meeting for the first time. ~*n.* **how-do-you-do. 2.** *Informal.* a difficult situation.
howdy ('haʊdɪ) *sentence substitute. Chiefly U.S.* an informal word for **hello.** [C16: from the phrase *how d'ye do*]
howe (haʊ) *n. Scot. and northern English dialect.* a depression in the earth's surface, such as a basin or valley. [C16: from HOLE]
howe'er (haʊ'ɛə) *sentence connector, adv.* a poetic contraction of **however.**
however (haʊ'ɛvə) *sentence connector.* **1.** still; nevertheless. **2.** on the other hand; yet. ~*adv.* **3.** by whatever means; in whatever manner. **4.** (*used with adjectives expressing or admitting of quantity or degree*) no matter how: *however long it takes, finish it.* **5.** an emphatic form of **how**[1] (sense 1).
howf *or* **howff** (hauf, həʊf) *n. Scot.* a haunt, esp. a public house. [C16: of uncertain origin]
howitzer ('haʊɪtsə) *n.* a cannon having a short or medium barrel with a low muzzle velocity and a steep angle of fire. [C16: from Dutch *houwitser,* from German *Haubitze,* from Czech *houfnice* stone-sling]
howk (haʊk) *vb. Scot.* to dig (out or up). [C17: from earlier *holk*]
howl (haʊl) *n.* **1.** a long plaintive cry or wail characteristic of a wolf or hound. **2.** a similar cry of pain or sorrow. **3.** *Slang.* **a.** a person or thing that is very funny. **b.** a prolonged outburst of laughter. **4.** *Electronics.* an unwanted prolonged high-pitched sound produced by a sound-producing system as a result of feedback. ~*vb.* **5.** to express in a howl or utter such cries. **6.** (*intr.*) (of the wind, etc.) to make a wailing noise. **7.** (*intr.*) *Informal.* to shout or laugh. [C14 *houlen;* related to Middle High German *hiuweln,* Middle Dutch *hūlen,* Danish *hyle*]
howl down *vb.* (*tr., adv.*) to prevent (a speaker) from being heard by shouting disapprovingly.
howler ('haʊlə) *n.* **1.** Also called: **howler monkey.** any large New World monkey of the genus *Alouatta,* inhabiting tropical forests in South America and having a loud howling cry. **2.** *Informal.* a glaring mistake. **3.** *Brit.* (formerly) a device that produces a loud tone in a telephone receiver to attract attention when the receiver is incorrectly replaced. **4.** a person or thing that howls.
howlet ('haʊlɪt) *n. Archaic, poetic.* another word for **owl.** [C15: diminutive of *howle* OWL]
howling ('haʊlɪŋ) *adj.* (*prenominal*) *Informal.* (intensifier): *a howling success; a howling error.* —'**howlingly** *adv.*
howlround ('haʊlˌraʊnd) *n.* the condition, resulting in a howling noise, when sound from a loudspeaker is fed back into the microphone of a public-address or recording system. Also called: '**howlˌback.**
howsoever (ˌhaʊsəʊ'ɛvə) *sentence connector, adv.* a less common word for **however.**
howtowdie (haʊ'taʊdɪ) *n.* a Scottish dish of boiled chicken with poached eggs and spinach. [C18: from Old French *hétoudeau, estaudeau* a fat young chicken for cooking]

hoy[1] (hɔɪ) *n. Nautical.* **1.** a freight barge. **2.** a coastal fishing and trading vessel, usually sloop-rigged, used during the 17th and 18th centuries. [C15: from Middle Dutch *hoei*]

hoy[2] (hɔɪ) *interj.* a cry used to attract attention or drive animals. [C14: variant of HEY]

hoya ('hɔɪə) *n.* any plant of the asclepiadaceous genus *Hoya,* of E Asia and Australia, esp. the waxplant. [C19: named after Thomas *Hoy* (died 1821), English gardener]

hoyden *or* **hoiden** ('hɔɪdᵊn) *n.* a wild boisterous girl; tomboy. [C16: perhaps from Middle Dutch *heidijn* heathen] —'**hoydenish** *or* '**hoidenish** *adj.* —'**hoydenishness** *or* '**hoidenishness** *n.*

HP *or* **h.p.** *abbrev. for:* **1.** *Brit.* hire purchase. **2.** horsepower. **3.** high pressure. **4.** (in Britain) Houses of Parliament.

HPV *abbrev. for* human papilloma virus.

HQ *or* **h.q.** *abbrev. for* headquarters.

hr *abbrev. for* hour.

HR *abbrev. for:* **1.** *Brit.* Home Rule. **2.** *U.S.* House of Representatives.

HRE *abbrev. for* Holy Roman Emperor *or* Empire.

HRH *abbrev. for* His (*or* Her) Royal Highness.

HRT *abbrev. for* hormone replacement therapy.

HS *abbrev. for:* **1.** High School. **2.** (in Britain) Home Secretary.

h.s. *abbrev. for* hoc sensu. [Latin: in this sense]

HSH *abbrev. for* His (*or* Her) Serene Highness.

HSM *abbrev. for* His (*or* Her) Serene Majesty.

HST (in Britain) *abbrev. for* high speed train.

ht *abbrev. for* height.

HT *Physics. abbrev. for* high tension.

HTLV *abbrev. for* human T-cell lymphotrophic virus: any one of a small family of viruses that cause certain rare diseases in the T-cells of human beings; for instance, HTLV I causes a form of leukaemia.

Hts (in place names) *abbrev. for* Heights.

hub (hʌb) *n.* **1.** the central portion of a wheel, propeller, fan, etc., through which the axle passes. **2.** the focal point. [C17: probably variant of HOB[1]]

hubble-bubble ('hʌbᵊl'bʌbᵊl) *n.* **1.** another name for **hookah.** **2.** hubbub; turmoil. **3.** a bubbling or gargling sound. [C17: rhyming jingle based on BUBBLE]

Hubble classification ('hʌbᵊl) *n.* a method of classifying galaxies depending on whether they are elliptical, spiral, barred spiral, or irregular. [C20: named after E. P. *Hubble* (1889–1953), U.S. astronomer who devised it]

Hubble constant *n.* the ratio of the recessional velocity of a galaxy to its distance, the recessional velocity being determined from its red shift. It is equal to approximately 0.12 m s^{-1}parsec^{-1}. [C20: named after E. P. *Hubble*]

Hubble's law *n. Astronomy.* a law stating that the velocity of recession of a galaxy is proportional to its distance from the observer. [C20: named after E. P. *Hubble*]

Hubble telescope *n.* a telescope launched into orbit around the earth in 1990 to provide information about the universe in the visible, infrared, and ultraviolet ranges. It is hoped to repair a malfunctioning mirror in 1993. [C20: named after E. P. *Hubble*]

hubbub ('hʌbʌb) *n.* **1.** a confused noise of many voices. **2.** uproar. [C16: probably from Irish *hooboobbes;* compare Scottish Gaelic *ubub!* an exclamation of contempt]

hubby ('hʌbɪ) *n., pl.* **-bies.** an informal word for **husband.** [C17: by shortening and altering]

hubcap ('hʌbˌkæp) *n.* a metal cap fitting onto the hub of a wheel, esp. a stainless steel or chromium-plated one.

hubris ('hjuːbrɪs) *or* **hybris** *n.* **1.** pride or arrogance. **2.** (in Greek tragedy) an excess of ambition, pride, etc., ultimately causing the transgressor's ruin. [C19: from Greek] —**hu'bristic** *or* **hy'bristic** *adj.*

huckaback ('hʌkəˌbæk) *n.* a coarse absorbent linen or cotton fabric used for towels and informal shirts, etc. Also called: **huck** (hʌk). [C17: of unknown origin]

huckery ('hʌkərɪ) *adj. N.Z. informal.* ugly.

huckle ('hʌkᵊl) *n. Rare.* **1.** the hip or haunch. **2.** a projecting or humped part. [C16: diminutive of Middle English *huck* hip, haunch; perhaps related to Old Norse *hūka* to squat]

huckleberry ('hʌkᵊlˌbɛrɪ) *n., pl.* **-ries.** **1.** any American ericaceous shrub of the genus *Gaylussacia,* having edible dark blue berries with large seeds. **2.** the fruit of any of these shrubs. **3.** another name for **blueberry.** **4.** a Brit. name for **whortleberry** (sense 1). [C17: probably a variant of *hurtleberry,* of unknown origin]

hucklebone ('hʌkᵊlˌbəʊn) *n. Archaic.* **1.** the anklebone; talus. **2.** the hipbone; innominate bone.

huckster ('hʌkstə) *n.* **1.** a person who uses aggressive or questionable methods of selling. **2.** *Now rare.* a person who sells small articles or fruit in the street. **3.** *U.S.* a person who writes for radio or television advertisements. *~vb.* **4.** (*tr.*) to peddle. **5.** (*tr.*) to sell or advertise aggressively or questionably. **6.** to haggle (over). [C12: perhaps from Middle Dutch *hoekster,* from *hoeken* to carry on the back] —'**hucksterism** *n.*

HUD *abbrev. for* head-up display.

huddle ('hʌdᵊl) *n.* **1.** a heaped or crowded mass of people or things. **2.** *Informal.* a private or impromptu conference (esp. in the phrase **go into a huddle**). *~vb.* **3.** to crowd or cause to crowd or nestle closely together. **4.** (often foll. by *up*) to draw or hunch (oneself), as through cold. **5.** (*intr.*) *Informal.* to meet and confer privately. **6.** (*tr.*) *Chiefly Brit.* to do (something) in a careless way. **7.** (*tr.*) *Rare.* to put on (clothes) hurriedly. [C16: of uncertain origin; compare Middle English *hoderen* to wrap up] —'**huddler** *n.*

hudibrastic (ˌhjuːdɪ'bræstɪk) *adj.* mock-heroic in style. [C18: after *Hudibras,* poem by Samuel Butler (1612–80), English poet]

Hudson seal ('hʌdsən) *n.* muskrat fur that has been dressed and dyed to resemble sealskin. [after *Hudson* Bay, NE Canada]

hue (hjuː) *n.* **1.** the attribute of colour that enables an observer to classify it as red, green, blue, purple, etc., and excludes white, black, and shades of grey. See also **colour.** **2.** a shade of a colour. **3.** aspect; complexion: *a different hue on matters.* [Old English *hīw* beauty; related to Old Norse *hȳ* fine hair, Gothic *hiwi* form]

hue and cry *n.* **1.** (formerly) the pursuit of a suspected criminal with loud cries in order to raise the alarm. **2.** any loud public outcry. [C16: from Anglo-French *hu et cri,* from Old French *hue* outcry, from *huer* to shout, from *hu!* shout of warning + *cri* CRY]

hued (hjuːd) *adj. Archaic or poetic.* **a.** having a hue or colour as specified. **b.** (*in combination*): *rosy-hued dawn.*

huff (hʌf) *n.* **1.** a passing mood of anger or pique (esp. in the phrase **in a huff**). *~vb.* **2.** to make or become angry or resentful. **3.** (*intr.*) to blow or puff heavily. **4.** Also: **blow.** *Draughts.* to remove (an opponent's draught) from the board for failure to make a capture. **5.** (*tr.*) *Obsolete.* to bully. **6. huffing and puffing.** empty threats or objections; bluster. [C16: of imitative origin; compare PUFF] —'**huffish** *or* '**huffy** *adj.* —'**huffily** *or* **huffishly** *adv.* —'**huffiness** *or* '**huffishness** *n.*

hug (hʌg) *vb.* **hugs, hugging, hugged.** (*mainly tr.*) **1.** (*also intr.*) to clasp (another person or thing) tightly or (of two people) to cling close together; embrace. **2.** to keep close to a shore, kerb, etc. **3.** to cling to (beliefs, etc.); cherish. **4.** to congratulate (oneself); be delighted with (oneself). *~n.* **5.** a tight or fond embrace. [C16: probably of Scandinavian origin; related to Old Norse *hugga* to comfort, Old English *hogian* to take care of] —'**huggable** *adj.* —'**hugger** *n.*

huge (hjuːdʒ) *adj.* extremely large in size, amount, or scope. Archaic form: **hugeous.** [C13: from Old French *ahuge,* of uncertain origin] —'**hugeness** *n.*

hugely ('hjuːdʒlɪ) *adv.* very much; enormously.

huggermugger ('hʌgəˌmʌgə) *n.* **1.** confusion. **2.** *Rare.* secrecy. *~adj., adv. Archaic.* **3.** with secrecy. **4.** in confusion. *~vb. Obsolete.* **5.** (*tr.*) to keep secret. **6.** (*intr.*) to act secretly. [C16: of uncertain origin]

Hughie ('hjuːɪ) *n. Austral. and N.Z. informal.* the god of rain and the god of surf (esp. in the phrases **send her down, Hughie!, send 'em up, Hughie**).

hug-me-tight *n.* a woman's knitted jacket.

Huguenot ('hjuːgəˌnəʊ, -ˌnɒt) *n.* **1.** a French Calvinist, esp. of the 16th or 17th centuries. *~adj.* **2.** designating the French Protestant Church. [C16: from French, from Genevan dialect *eyguenot* one who opposed annexation by Savoy, ultimately from Swiss German *Eidgenoss* confederate; influenced by *Hugues,* surname of 16th-century Genevan burgomaster] —ˌ**Hugue'notic** *adj.* —'**Hugueˌnotism** *n.*

huh (*spelling pron.* hʌ) *interj.* an exclamation of derision, bewilderment, inquiry, etc.

huhu ('huːhuː) *n.* a New Zealand beetle, *Prionoplus reticularis,* with a hairy body. [Maori]

hui ('huːɪ) *n., pl.* **huies.** *N.Z.* **1.** a Maori social gathering. **2.** *Informal.* any party. [Maori]

huia ('huɪjə) *n.* an extinct bird of New Zealand, *Heteralocha acutirostris,* prized by early Maoris for its distinctive tail feathers. [Maori]

hula ('huːlə) *or* **hula-hula** *n.* a Hawaiian dance performed by a woman. [from Hawaiian]

Hula-Hoop *n. Trademark.* a light hoop that is whirled around the body by movements of the waist and hips.

hula skirt *n.* a skirt made of long grass attached to a waistband and worn by hula dancers.

hulk (hʌlk) *n.* **1.** the body of an abandoned vessel. **2.** *Disparaging.* a large or unwieldy vessel. **3.** *Disparaging.* a large ungainly person or thing. **4.** (*often pl.*) the frame or hull of a ship, used as a storehouse, etc., or (esp. in 19th-century Britain) as a prison. *~vb.* **5.** (*intr.*) *Brit. informal.* to move clumsily. **6.** (*intr.;* often foll. by *up*) to rise massively. [Old English *hulc,* from Medieval Latin *hulca,* from Greek *holkas* barge, from *helkein* to tow]

hulking ('hʌlkɪŋ) *adj.* big and ungainly. Also: '**hulky.**

hull (hʌl) *n.* **1.** the main body of a vessel, tank, flying boat, etc. **2.** the shell or pod of peas or beans; the outer covering of any fruit or seed; husk. **3.** the persistent calyx at the base of a strawberry, raspberry, or similar fruit. **4.** the outer casing of a missile, rocket, etc. *~vb.* **5.** to remove the hulls from (fruit or seeds). **6.** (*tr.*) to pierce the hull of (a vessel, tank, etc.). [Old English *hulu;* related to Old High German *helawa,* Old English *helan* to hide] —'**huller** *n.* —'**hull-less** *adj.*

hullabaloo *or* **hullaballoo** (ˌhʌləbə'luː) *n., pl.* **-loos.** loud confused noise, esp. of protest; commotion. [C18: perhaps from interjection HALLO + Scottish *baloo* lullaby]

hull down *adj.* **1.** (of a ship) having its hull concealed by the horizon. **2.** (of a tank) having only its turret visible.

hullo (hʌ'ləʊ) *sentence substitute, n.* a variant of **hello.**

hum (hʌm) *vb.* **hums, humming, hummed.** 1. (*intr.*) to make a low continuous vibrating sound like that of a prolonged *m.* 2. (*intr.*) (of a person) to sing with the lips closed. 3. (*intr.*) to utter an indistinct sound, as in hesitation; hem. 4. (*intr.*) *Informal.* to be in a state of feverish activity. 5. (*intr.*) *Brit. and Irish slang.* to smell unpleasant. 6. (*intr.*) *Austral. slang.* to scrounge. 7. **hum and haw.** See **hem**[2] (sense 3). ~*n.* 8. a low continuous murmuring sound. 9. *Electronics.* an undesired low-frequency noise in the output of an amplifier or receiver, esp. one caused by the power supply. 10. *Austral. slang.* a scrounger; cadger. 11. *Brit. and Irish slang.* an unpleasant odour. ~*interj., n.* 12. an indistinct sound of hesitation, embarrassment, etc.; hem. [C14: of imitative origin; compare Dutch *hommelen,* Old High German *humbal* bumblebee] —'**hummer** *n.*

human ('hjuːmən) *adj.* 1. of, characterizing, or relating to man and mankind: *human nature.* 2. consisting of people: *the human race; a human chain.* 3. having the attributes of man as opposed to animals, divine beings, or machines: *human failings.* 4. a. kind or considerate. b. natural. ~*n.* 5. a human being; person. [C14: from Latin *hūmānus;* related to Latin *homō* man] —'**human-ˌlike** *adj.* —'**humanness** *n.*

human being *n.* a member of any of the races of *Homo sapiens;* person; man, woman, or child.

human capital *n. Economics.* the abilities and skills of any individual, esp. those acquired through investment in education and training, that enhance potential income earning.

humane (hjuː'meɪn) *adj.* 1. characterized by kindness, mercy, sympathy, etc. 2. inflicting as little pain as possible: *a humane killing.* 3. civilizing or liberal (esp. in the phrases **humane studies, humane education**). [C16: variant of HUMAN] —**hu'manely** *adv.* —**hu'maneness** *n.*

humane society *n.* an organization for promotion of humane ideals, esp. in dealing with animals.

human interest *n.* (in a newspaper story, news broadcasting, etc.) reference to individuals and their emotions.

humanism ('hjuːməˌnɪzəm) *n.* 1. the denial of any power or moral value superior to that of humanity; the rejection of religion in favour of a belief in the advancement of humanity by its own efforts. 2. a philosophical position that stresses the autonomy of human reason in contradistinction to the authority of the Church. 3. (*often cap.*) a cultural movement of the Renaissance, based on classical studies. 4. interest in the welfare of people. —'**humanist** *n.* —ˌ**human'istic** *adj.*

humanistic psychology *n.* approach to psychology advocated by some that emphasizes feelings and emotions and the better understanding of the self in terms of observation of oneself and one's relations with others.

humanitarian (hjuːˌmænɪ'tɛərɪən) *adj.* 1. having the interests of mankind at heart. 2. of or relating to ethical or theological humanitarianism. ~*n.* 3. a philanthropist. 4. an adherent of humanitarianism.

humanitarianism (hjuːˌmænɪ'tɛərɪəˌnɪzəm) *n.* 1. humanitarian principles. 2. *Ethics.* a. the doctrine that man's duty is to strive to promote the welfare of mankind. b. the doctrine that man can achieve perfection through his own resources. 3. *Theol.* the belief that Jesus Christ was only a mortal man. —**huˌmani'tarianist** *n.*

humanity (hjuː'mænɪtɪ) *n., pl.* **-ties.** 1. the human race. 2. the quality of being human. 3. kindness or mercy. 4. (*pl.*) (usually preceded by *the*) the study of literature, philosophy, and the arts. 5. the study of Ancient Greek and Roman language, literature, etc.

humanize *or* **humanise** ('hjuːməˌnaɪz) *vb.* 1. to make or become human. 2. to make or become humane. —ˌ**humani'zation** *or* ˌ**humani'sation** *n.* —'**humanˌizer** *or* '**humanˌiser** *n.*

humankind (ˌhjuːmən'kaɪnd) *n.* the human race; humanity.

humanly ('hjuːmənlɪ) *adv.* 1. by human powers or means. 2. in a human or humane manner.

human nature *n.* 1. the qualities common to humanity. 2. ordinary human behaviour, esp. considered as less than perfect. 3. *Sociol.* the unique elements that form a basic part of human life and distinguish it from other animal life.

humanoid ('hjuːməˌnɔɪd) *adj.* 1. like a human being in appearance. ~*n.* 2. a being with human rather than anthropoid characteristics. 3. (in science fiction) a robot or creature resembling a human being.

human papilloma virus *n.* any one of a class of viruses that cause tumours, including warts, in humans. Certain strains infect the cervix and have been implicated as a cause of cervical cancer. Abbrev.: **HPV**

human resources *pl. n.* 1. the actual workforce, including sometimes the potential workforce, of an organization. 2. the contribution to an employing organization which its workforce could provide in effort, skills, knowledge, etc.

human rights *pl. n.* the rights of individuals to liberty, justice, etc.

humble ('hʌmbᵊl) *adj.* 1. conscious of one's failings. 2. unpretentious; lowly: *a humble cottage; my humble opinion.* 3. deferential or servile. ~*vb.* (*tr.*) 4. to cause to become humble; humiliate. 5. to lower in status. [C13: from Old French, from Latin *humilis* low, from *humus* the ground] —'**humbled** *adj.* —'**humbleness** *n.* —'**humbler** *n.* —'**humbling** *adj.* —'**humblingly** *adv.* —'**humbly** *adv.*

humblebee ('hʌmbᵊlˌbiː) *n.* another name for the **bumblebee.** [C15: related to Middle Dutch *hommel* bumblebee, Old High German *humbal;* see HUM]

humble pie *n.* 1. (formerly) a pie made from the heart, entrails, etc., of a deer. 2. **eat humble pie.** to behave or be forced to behave humbly; be humiliated. [C17: earlier *an umble pie,* by mistaken word division from *a numble pie,* from *numbles* offal of a deer, from Old French *nombles,* ultimately from Latin *lumbulus* a little loin, from *lumbus* loin]

Humboldt Current ('hʌmbəʊlt) *n.* a cold ocean current of the S Pacific, flowing north along the coasts of Chile and Peru. Also called: **Peru Current.** [named after Baron Alexander von *Humboldt* (1769–1859), German scientist and explorer]

humbucker ('hʌmˌbʌkə) *n.* a twin-coil guitar pick-up.

humbug ('hʌmˌbʌg) *n.* 1. a person or thing that tricks or deceives. 2. nonsense; rubbish. 3. *Brit.* a hard boiled sweet, usually flavoured with peppermint and often having a striped pattern. ~*vb.* **-bugs, -bugging, -bugged.** 4. to cheat or deceive (someone). [C18: of unknown origin] —'**humˌbugger** *n.* —'**humˌbuggery** *n.*

humdinger ('hʌmˌdɪŋə) *n. Slang.* an excellent person or thing: *a humdinger of a party.* [C20: of unknown origin]

humdrum ('hʌmˌdrʌm) *adj.* 1. ordinary; dull. ~*n.* 2. a monotonous routine, task, or person. [C16: rhyming compound, probably based on HUM] —'**humˌdrumness** *n.*

humectant (hjuː'mɛktənt) *adj.* 1. producing moisture. ~*n.* 2. a substance added to another substance to keep it moist. [C17: from Latin *ūmectāre* to wet, from *ūmēre* to be moist, from *ūmor* moisture; see HUMOUR]

humeral ('hjuːmərəl) *adj.* 1. *Anatomy.* of or relating to the humerus. 2. of or near the shoulder.

humeral veil *n. R.C. Church.* a silk shawl worn by a priest at High Mass, etc. Often shortened to **veil.**

humerus ('hjuːmərəs) *n., pl.* **-meri** (-məˌraɪ). 1. the bone that extends from the shoulder to the elbow. 2. the corresponding bone in other vertebrates. [C17: from Latin *umerus;* related to Gothic *ams* shoulder, Greek *ōmos*]

Hume's law (hjuːmz) *n.* the philosophical doctrine that an evaluative statement cannot be derived from purely factual premises, often formulated as: *one can't derive an "ought" from an "is".* See also **naturalistic fallacy.** [named after David *Hume* (1711–76), British empiricist philosopher]

humic ('hjuːmɪk) *adj.* of, relating to, or derived from humus: *humic acids.* [C19: from Latin *humus* ground + -IC]

humicole ('hjuːmɪˌkəʊl) *n.* any plant that thrives on humus. —**humicolous** (hjuː'mɪkələs) *adj.*

humid ('hjuːmɪd) *adj.* moist; damp: *a humid day.* [C16: from Latin *ūmidus,* from *ūmēre* to be wet; see HUMECTANT, HUMOUR] —'**humidly** *adv.* —'**humidness** *n.*

humidifier (hjuː'mɪdɪˌfaɪə) *n.* a device for increasing or controlling the water vapour in a room, building, etc.

humidify (hjuː'mɪdɪˌfaɪ) *vb.* **-fies, -fying, -fied.** (*tr.*) to make (air) humid or damp. —**huˌmidifi'cation** *n.*

humidistat (hjuː'mɪdɪˌstæt) *n.* a device for maintaining constant humidity. Also called: **hygrostat.**

humidity (hjuː'mɪdɪtɪ) *n.* 1. the state of being humid; dampness. 2. a measure of the amount of moisture in the air. See **relative humidity, absolute humidity.**

humidor ('hjuːmɪˌdɔː) *n.* a humid place or container for storing cigars, tobacco, etc.

humify ('hjuːmɪˌfaɪ) *vb.* **-fies, -fying, -fied.** to convert or be converted into humus. —ˌ**humifi'cation** *n.*

humiliate (hjuː'mɪlɪˌeɪt) *vb.* (*tr.*) to lower or hurt the dignity or pride of. [C16: from Late Latin *humiliāre,* from Latin *humilis* HUMBLE] —**hu'miliˌated** *adj.* —**hu'miliˌating** *adj.* —**hu'miliˌatingly** *adv.* —**huˌmili'ation** *n.* —**humiliative** (hjuː'mɪljətɪv) *adj.* —**hu'miliˌator** *n.* —**hu'miliatory** *adj.*

humility (hjuː'mɪlɪtɪ) *n., pl.* **-ties.** the state or quality of being humble.

hummel ('hʌmᵊl) *adj. Scot.* 1. (of cattle) hornless. 2. (of grain) awnless. [C15: of Germanic origin; compare Low German *hummel* hornless animal]

hummingbird ('hʌmɪŋˌbɜːd) *n.* any very small American bird of the family *Trochilidae,* having a brilliant iridescent plumage, long slender bill, and wings specialized for very powerful vibrating flight: order *Apodiformes.*

hummingbird moth *n. U.S.* another name for the **hawk moth.**

humming top *n.* a top that hums as it spins.

hummock ('hʌmək) *n.* 1. a hillock; knoll. 2. a ridge or mound of ice in an ice field. 3. Also called: **hammock.** *Chiefly southern U.S.* a wooded area lying above the level of an adjacent marsh. [C16: of uncertain origin; compare HUMP, HAMMOCK] —'**hummocky** *adj.*

hummus, hoummos, *or* **houmous** ('hʊməs) *n.* a creamy dip originating in the Middle East, made from puréed chickpeas, tahina, etc. [from Turkish *humus*]

humongous *or* **humungous** (hjuː'mɒŋgəs, -'mʌŋgəs) *adj. U.S. slang.* exceptionally large; huge or enormous. [C20: of uncertain origin]

humoral ('hjuːmərəl) *adj.* 1. *Immunol.* denoting or relating to a type of immunity caused by free antibodies circulating in the blood. 2. *Obsolete.* of or relating to the four bodily fluids (humours).

humoresque (ˌhjuːməˈrɛsk) *n.* a short lively piece of music. [C19: from German *Humoreske,* ultimately from English HUMOUR]

humorist (ˈhjuːmərɪst) *n.* a person who acts, speaks, or writes in a humorous way. —ˌ**humorˈistic** *adj.*

humorous (ˈhjuːmərəs) *adj.* **1.** funny; comical; amusing. **2.** displaying or creating humour. **3.** *Archaic.* another word for **capricious.** —ˈ**humorously** *adv.* —ˈ**humorousness** *n.*

humour *or U.S.* **humor** (ˈhjuːmə) *n.* **1.** the quality of being funny. **2.** Also called: **sense of humour.** the ability to appreciate or express that which is humorous. **3.** situations, speech, or writings that are thought to be humorous. **4. a.** a state of mind; temper; mood. **b.** (*in combination*): *ill humour; good humour.* **5.** temperament or disposition. **6.** a caprice or whim. **7.** any of various fluids in the body, esp. the aqueous humour and vitreous humour. **8.** Also called: **cardinal humour.** *Archaic.* any of the four bodily fluids (blood, phlegm, choler or yellow bile, melancholy or black bile) formerly thought to determine emotional and physical disposition. **9. out of humour.** in a bad mood. ~*vb.* (*tr.*) **10.** to attempt to gratify; indulge: *he humoured the boy's whims.* **11.** to adapt oneself to: *to humour someone's fantasies.* [C14: from Latin: liquid; related to Latin *ūmēre* to be wet, Old Norse *vökr* moist, Greek *hugros* wet] —ˈ**humourful** *or U.S.* ˈ**humorful** *adj.* —ˈ**humourless** *or U.S.* ˈ**humorless** *adj.* —ˈ**humourlessness** *or U.S.* ˈ**humorlessness** *n.*

humoursome *or U.S.* **humorsome** (ˈhjuːməsəm) *adj.* **1.** capricious; fanciful. **2.** inclined to humour (someone).

hump (hʌmp) *n.* **1.** a rounded protuberance or projection, as of earth, sand, etc. **2.** *Pathol.* a rounded deformity of the back in persons with kyphosis, consisting of a convex spinal curvature. **3.** a rounded protuberance on the back of a camel or related animal. **4. the hump.** *Brit. informal.* a fit of depression or sulking (esp. in the phrase **it gives me the hump**). **5. over the hump.** past the largest or most difficult portion of work, time, etc. ~*vb.* **6.** to form or become a hump; hunch; arch. **7.** (*tr.*) *Brit. slang.* to carry or heave. **8.** *Taboo slang.* to have sexual intercourse with (someone). **9. hump one's swag.** *Austral. and N.Z. informal.* (of a tramp) to carry one's belongings from place to place on one's back. [C18: probably from earlier HUMPBACKED] —ˈ**hump**ˌ**like** *adj.*

humpback (ˈhʌmpˌbæk) *n.* **1.** another word for **hunchback. 2.** Also called: **humpback whale.** a large whalebone whale, *Megaptera novaeangliae,* closely related and similar to the rorquals but with a humped back and long flippers: family *Balaenopteridae.* **3.** a Pacific salmon, *Oncorhynchus gorbuscha,* the male of which has a humped back and hooked jaws. **4.** Also called: **humpback bridge.** *Brit.* a road bridge having a sharp incline and decline and usually a narrow roadway. [C17: alteration of earlier *crumpbacked,* perhaps influenced by HUNCHBACK; perhaps related to Dutch *homp* lump] —ˈ**hump**ˌ**backed** *adj.*

humph (*spelling pron.* hʌmf) *interj.* an exclamation of annoyance, indecision, dissatisfaction, etc.

humpty (ˈhʌmptɪ) *n. Brit.* a low padded seat; pouffe. [C20: from *humpty* hunchbacked, perhaps influenced by *Humpty Dumpty* (nursery rhyme)]

humpty dumpty (ˈhʌmptɪ ˈdʌmptɪ) *n. Chiefly Brit.* **1.** a short fat person. **2.** a person or thing that once overthrown or broken cannot be restored or mended. [C18: after the nursery rhyme *Humpty Dumpty*]

humpy[1] (ˈhʌmpɪ) *adj.* **humpier, humpiest. 1.** full of humps. **2.** *Brit. informal.* angry or gloomy. —ˈ**humpiness** *n.*

humpy[2] (ˈhʌmpɪ) *n., pl.* **humpies.** *Austral.* a primitive hut. [C19: from a native Australian language]

hum tone *n.* a note produced by a bell when struck, lying an octave or (in many English bells) a sixth or seventh below the strike tone. Also called (esp. Brit.): **hum note.**

humus (ˈhjuːməs) *n.* a dark brown or black colloidal mass of partially decomposed organic matter in the soil. It improves the fertility and water retention of the soil and is therefore important for plant growth. [C18: from Latin: soil, earth]

Hun (hʌn) *n.* **1.** a member of any of several Asiatic nomadic peoples speaking Mongoloid or Turkic languages who dominated much of Asia and E Europe from before 300 B.C., invading the Roman Empire in the 4th and 5th centuries A.D. **2.** *Informal.* (esp. in World War I) a derogatory name for a **German. 3.** *Informal.* a vandal. [Old English *Hūnas,* from Late Latin *Hūnī,* from Turkish *Hun-yū*] —ˈ**Hun**ˌ**like** *adj.*

hunch (hʌntʃ) *n.* **1.** an intuitive guess or feeling. **2.** another word for **hump. 3.** a lump or large piece. ~*vb.* **4.** to bend or draw (oneself or a part of the body) up or together. **5.** (*intr.;* usually foll. by *up*) to sit in a hunched position. [C16: of unknown origin]

hunchback (ˈhʌntʃˌbæk) *n.* **1.** a person having an abnormal convex curvature of the thoracic spine. **2.** such a curvature. ~Also called: **humpback.** See **kyphosis.** Compare **hollow-back.** [C18: from earlier *hunchbacked, huckbacked* hump-backed, influenced by *bunchbacked,* from *bunch* (in obsolete sense of *hump*) + BACKED] —ˈ**hunch**ˌ**backed** *adj.*

hundred (ˈhʌndrəd) *n., pl.* **-dreds** *or* **-dred. 1.** the cardinal number that is the product of ten and ten; five score. See also **number** (sense 1). **2.** a numeral, 100, C, etc., representing this number. **3.** (*often pl.*) a large but unspecified number, amount, or quantity: *there will be hundreds of people there.* **4. the hundreds. a.** the numbers 100 to 109: *the temperature was in the hundreds.* **b.** the numbers 100 to 199: *his score went into the hundreds.* **c.** the numbers 100 to 999: *the price was in the hundreds.* **5.** (*pl.*) the 100 years of a specified century: *in the sixteen hundreds.* **6.** something representing, represented by, or consisting of 100 units. **7.** *Maths.* the position containing a digit representing that number followed by two zeros: *in 4376, 3 is in the hundred's place.* **8.** an ancient division of a county in England, Ireland, and parts of the U.S. ~*determiner.* **9. a.** amounting to or approximately a hundred: *a hundred reasons for that.* **b.** (*as pronoun*): *the hundred I chose.* **10.** amounting to 100 times a particular scientific quantity: *a hundred volts.* Related prefix: **hecto-.** [Old English; related to Old Frisian *hunderd,* Old Norse *hundrath,* German *hundert,* Gothic *hund,* Latin *centum,* Greek *hekaton*]

hundred-percenter *n. U.S.* an extreme or unjustified nationalist. —ˈ**hundred-per**ˈ**centism** *n.*

hundreds and thousands *pl. n.* tiny beads of brightly coloured sugar, used in decorating cakes, sweets, etc.

hundredth (ˈhʌndrədθ) *adj.* **1.** (*usually prenominal*) **a.** being the ordinal number of 100 in numbering or counting order, position, time, etc. **b.** (*as n.*): *the hundredth in line.* ~*n.* **2. a.** one of 100 approximately equal parts of something. **b.** (*as modifier*): *a hundredth part.* **3.** one of 100 equal divisions of a particular scientific quantity. Related prefix: **centi-:** *centimetre.* **4.** the fraction equal to one divided by 100 (1/100).

hundredweight (ˈhʌndrədˌweɪt) *n., pl.* **-weights** *or* **-weight. 1.** Also called: **long hundredweight.** *Brit.* a unit of weight equal to 112 pounds or 50.802 35 kilograms. **2.** Also called: **short hundredweight.** *U.S. and Canadian.* a unit of weight equal to 100 pounds or 45.359 24 kilograms. **3.** Also called: **metric hundredweight.** a metric unit of weight equal to 50 kilograms. ~Abbrev. (for senses 1, 2): **cwt.**

hung (hʌŋ) *vb.* **1.** the past tense and past participle of **hang** (except in the sense of *to execute* or in the idiom *I'll be hanged*). ~*adj.* **2. a.** (of a legislative assembly) not having a party with a working majority: *a hung parliament.* **b.** unable to reach a decision: *a hung jury.* **c.** (of a situation) unable to be resolved. **3. hung over.** *Informal.* suffering from the effects of a hangover. **4. hung up.** *Slang.* **a.** impeded by some difficulty or delay. **b.** in a state of confusion; emotionally disturbed. **5. hung up on.** *Slang.* obsessively or exclusively interested in: *he's hung up on modern art these days.*

Hung. *abbrev. for:* **1.** Hungarian. **2.** Hungary.

Hungarian (hʌŋˈgɛərɪən) *n.* **1.** the official language of Hungary, a republic in central Europe, also spoken in Romania and elsewhere, belonging to the Finno-Ugric family and most closely related to the Ostyak and Vogul languages of NW Siberia. **2.** a native, inhabitant, or citizen of Hungary. **3.** a Hungarian-speaking person who is not a citizen of Hungary. ~*adj.* **4.** of or relating to Hungary, its people, or their language. ~Compare **Magyar.**

Hungarian goulash *n.* the full name of **goulash.**

hunger (ˈhʌŋgə) *n.* **1.** a feeling of pain, emptiness, or weakness induced by lack of food. **2.** an appetite, desire, need, or craving: *hunger for a woman.* ~*vb.* **3.** to have or cause to have a need or craving for food. **4.** (*intr.;* usually foll. by *for* or *after*) to have a great appetite or desire (for). [Old English *hungor;* related to Old High German *hungar,* Old Norse *hungr,* Gothic *hūhrus*]

hunger march *n.* a procession of protest or demonstration by the unemployed.

hunger strike *n.* a voluntary fast undertaken, usually by a prisoner, as a means of protest. —**hunger striker** *n.*

hungry (ˈhʌŋgrɪ) *adj.* **-grier, -griest. 1.** desiring food. **2.** experiencing pain, weakness, or nausea through lack of food. **3.** (*postpositive;* foll. by *for*) having a craving, desire, or need (for). **4.** expressing or appearing to express greed, craving, or desire. **5.** lacking fertility; poor. **6.** *N.Z.* (of timber) dry and bare. —ˈ**hungrily** *or* ˈ**hungeringly** *adv.* —ˈ**hungriness** *n.*

hunk (hʌŋk) *n.* **1.** a large piece. **2.** Also called: **hunk of a man.** *Slang.* a sexually attractive man. [C19: probably related to Flemish *hunke;* compare Dutch *homp* lump]

hunker (ˈhʌŋkə) *vb.* (*intr.*) (often foll. by *down*) to squat; crouch.

hunkers (ˈhʌŋkəz) *pl. n.* haunches. [C18: of uncertain origin]

hunks (hʌŋks) *n.* (*functioning as sing.*) *Rare.* **1.** a crotchety old person. **2.** a miserly person. [C17: of unknown origin]

hunky-dory (ˌhʌŋkɪˈdɔːrɪ) *adj. Informal.* very satisfactory; fine. [C20: of uncertain origin]

Hunnish (ˈhʌnɪʃ) *adj.* **1.** of, relating to, or characteristic of the Huns. **2.** barbarously destructive; vandalistic. —ˈ**Hunnishly** *adv.* —ˈ**Hunnishness** *n.*

hunt (hʌnt) *vb.* **1.** to seek out and kill or capture (game or wild animals) for food or sport. **2.** (*intr.;* often foll. by *for*) to look (for); search (for): *to hunt for a book; to hunt up a friend.* **3.** (*tr.*) to use (hounds, horses, etc.) in the pursuit of wild animals, game, etc.: *to hunt a pack of hounds.* **4.** (*tr.*) to search or draw (country) to hunt wild animals, game, etc.: *to hunt the parkland.* **5.** (*tr.;* often foll. by *down*) to track or chase diligently, esp. so as to capture: *to hunt down a criminal.* **6.** (*tr.; usually passive*) to persecute; hound. **7.** (*intr.*) (of a gauge indicator, engine speed, etc.) to oscillate about a mean value or position. **8.** (*intr.*) (of an aircraft, rocket, etc.) to oscillate about a flight path. ~*n.* **9.** the act or an instance of hunting. **10.** chase or search, esp. of animals or game. **11.** the area of a hunt. **12.** a party or institution organized for the pursuit of wild animals or game, esp. for sport. **13.** the participants in or members of such a party or institution. ~See also **hunt down, hunt up.** [Old English *huntian;* related to Old English *hentan,* Old Norse *henda* to grasp] —'**huntedly** *adv.*

huntaway ('hʌntəˌweɪ) *n. N.Z.* a dog trained to drive sheep at a long distance from the shepherd.

hunt down *vb. (adv.)* **1.** *(tr.)* to pursue successfully by diligent searching and chasing: *they finally hunted down the killer in Mexico.* **2.** *(intr.)* (of a bell) to be rung progressively later during a set of changes.

hunted ('hʌntɪd) *adj.* harassed and worn: *he has a hunted look.*

hunter ('hʌntə) *n.* **1.** a person or animal that seeks out and kills or captures game. Fem. equivalent: **huntress** ('hʌntrɪs). **2. a.** a person who looks diligently for something. **b.** *(in combination): a fortune-hunter.* **3.** a specially bred horse used in hunting, usually characterized by strength and stamina. **4.** a specially bred dog used to hunt game. **5.** a watch with a hinged metal lid or case (**hunting case**) to protect the crystal. Also called: **hunting watch.** See also **half-hunter.**

hunter-killer *adj.* denoting a type of naval vessel, esp. a submarine, designed and equipped to pursue and destroy enemy craft.

hunter's moon *n.* the full moon following the harvest moon.

hunting ('hʌntɪŋ) *n.* **a.** the pursuit and killing or capture of game and wild animals, regarded as a sport. **b.** *(as modifier): hunting boots; hunting lodge.*

hunting cat *or* **leopard** *n.* another name for **cheetah.**

hunting ground *n.* **1.** the area of a hunt. **2.** Also called: **happy hunting ground.** any place containing a supply of what is wanted or in which a search is conducted: *some resorts are a happy hunting ground for souvenirs.*

hunting horn *n.* **1.** a long straight metal tube with a flared end and a cylindrical bore, used in giving signals in hunting. See **horn** (sense 9). **2.** an obsolete brass instrument from which the modern French horn was developed.

hunting knife *n.* a knife used for flaying and cutting up game and sometimes for killing it.

hunting spider *n.* another name for **wolf spider.**

Huntington's chorea ('hʌntɪŋtənz) *n.* a rare hereditary type of chorea, marked by involuntary jerky movements, impaired speech, and increasing dementia. [C19: named after George *Huntington* (1850–1916), U.S. neurologist]

huntsman ('hʌntsmən) *n., pl.* **-men. 1.** a person who hunts. **2.** a person who looks after and trains hounds, beagles, etc., and manages them during a hunt.

huntsman's-cup *n. U.S.* any of various pitcher plants of the genus *Sarracenia,* whose leaves are modified to form tubular pitchers.

hunt the slipper *n.* a children's game in which the players look for a hidden slipper or other object, such as a thimble (**hunt the thimble**).

hunt up *vb. (adv.)* **1.** *(tr.)* to search for, esp. successfully: *I couldn't hunt up a copy of it anywhere.* **2.** *(intr.)* (of a bell) to be rung progressively earlier during a set of changes.

Huon pine ('hjuːɒn) *n.* a taxaceous tree, *Dacrydium franklinii,* of Australasia, SE Asia, and Chile, with scalelike leaves and cup-shaped berry-like fruits. [named after the *Huon* River, Tasmania]

huppah ('hʊpə) *n.* a variant spelling of **chuppah.**

hurdies ('hʌrdɪz) *pl. n. Scot.* the buttocks or haunches. [C16: of unknown origin]

hurdle ('hɜːdᵊl) *n.* **1. a.** *Athletics.* one of a number of light barriers over which runners leap in certain events. **b.** a low barrier used in certain horse races. **2.** an obstacle to be overcome: *the next hurdle in his career.* **3.** a light framework of interlaced osiers, wattle, etc., used as a temporary fence. **4.** *Brit.* a sledge on which criminals were dragged to their executions. ~*vb.* **5.** to jump (a hurdle, etc.), as in racing. **6.** *(tr.)* to surround with hurdles. **7.** *(tr.)* to overcome. [Old English *hyrdel;* related to Gothic *haurds* door, Old Norse *hurth* door, Old High German *hurd,* Latin *crātis,* Greek *kurtos* basket] —'**hurdler** *n.*

hurds (hɜːdz) *pl. n.* another word for **hards.**

hurdy-gurdy ('hɜːdɪ'gɜːdɪ) *n., pl.* **-dies. 1.** any mechanical musical instrument, such as a barrel organ. **2.** a medieval instrument shaped like a viol in which a rosined wheel rotated by a handle sounds the strings. [C18: rhyming compound, probably of imitative origin]

hurl (hɜːl) *vb.* **1.** *(tr.)* to throw or propel with great force. **2.** *(tr.)* to utter with force; yell: *to hurl insults.* **3.** (hʌrl). *Scot.* to transport or be transported in a driven vehicle. ~*n.* **4.** the act or an instance of hurling. **5.** (hʌrl). *Scot.* a ride in a driven vehicle. [C13: probably of imitative origin] —'**hurler** *n.*

hurley ('hɜːlɪ) *n.* **1.** *Chiefly Brit.* another word for **hurling** (the game). **2.** Also called: **hurley stick.** the stick used in playing hurling.

hurling ('hɜːlɪŋ) *n.* a traditional Irish game resembling hockey and lacrosse, played with sticks and a ball between two teams of 15 players each.

hurly-burly ('hɜːlɪ'bɜːlɪ) *n., pl.* **hurly-burlies. 1.** confusion or commotion. ~*adj.* **2.** turbulent. [C16: from earlier *hurling and burling,* rhyming phrase based on *hurling* in obsolete sense of uproar]

Huron ('hjʊərən) *n.* **1.** *(pl.* **-rons** *or* **-ron)** a member of a North American Indian people formerly living in the region east of Lake Huron, one of the Great Lakes. **2.** the Iroquoian language of this people.

hurrah (hʊ'rɑː), **hooray** (huː'reɪ), *or* **hoorah** (huː'rɑː) *interj., n.* **1.** a cheer of joy, victory, etc. ~*vb.* **2.** to shout "hurrah". [C17: probably from German *hurra;* compare HUZZAH]

hurricane ('hʌrɪkᵊn, -keɪn) *n.* **1.** a severe, often destructive storm, esp. a tropical cyclone. **2. a.** a wind of force 12 or above on the Beaufort scale. **b.** *(as modifier): a wind of hurricane force.* **3.** anything acting like such a wind. [C16: from Spanish *huracán,* from Taino *hurakán,* from *hura* wind]

hurricane deck *n.* a ship's deck that is covered by a light deck as a sunshade.

hurricane lamp *n.* a paraffin lamp, with a glass covering to prevent the flame from being blown out. Also called: **storm lantern.**

hurried ('hʌrɪd) *adj.* performed with great or excessive haste: *a hurried visit.* —'**hurriedly** *adv.* —'**hurriedness** *n.*

hurry ('hʌrɪ) *vb.* **-ries, -rying, -ried. 1.** *(intr.;* often foll. by *up)* to hasten (to do something); rush. **2.** *(tr.;* often foll. by *along)* to speed up the completion, progress, etc., of. ~*n.* **3.** haste. **4.** urgency or eagerness. **5. in a hurry.** *Informal.* **a.** easily: *you won't beat him in a hurry.* **b.** willingly: *we won't go there again in a hurry.* [C16 *horyen,* probably of imitative origin; compare Middle High German *hurren;* see SCURRY] —'**hurrying** *n., adj.* —'**hurryingly** *adv.*

hurry-scurry *adv.* **1.** in frantic haste. ~*adj.* **2.** hasty and disorderly. ~*n.* **3.** disordered haste. ~*vb. (intr.)* **4.** to rush about in confusion. [C18: reduplication of HURRY; compare HELTER-SKELTER]

hurst (hɜːst) *n. Archaic.* **1.** a wood. **2.** a sandbank. [Old English *hyrst;* related to Old High German *hurst*]

hurt[1] (hɜːt) *vb.* **hurts, hurting, hurt. 1.** to cause physical pain to (someone or something). **2.** to cause emotional pain or distress to (someone). **3.** to produce a painful sensation in (someone): *the bruise hurts.* **4.** *(intr.) Informal.* to feel pain. ~*n.* **5.** physical, moral, or mental pain or suffering. **6.** a wound, cut, or sore. **7.** damage or injury; harm. ~*adj.* **8.** injured or pained physically or emotionally: *a hurt knee; a hurt look.* [C12 *hurten* to hit, from Old French *hurter* to knock against, probably of Germanic origin; compare Old Norse *hrūtr* ram, Middle High German *hurt* a collision] —'**hurter** *n.*

hurt[2] (hɜːt) *or* **whort** (hwɜːt) *n. Southern English dialect.* another name for **whortleberry.**

hurter ('hɜːtə) *n.* an object or part that gives protection, such as a concrete block that protects a building from traffic or the shoulder of an axle against which the hub strikes. [C14 *hurtour,* from Old French *hurtoir* something that knocks or strikes, from *hurter* to HURT[1]]

hurtful ('hɜːtfʊl) *adj.* causing distress or injury: *to say hurtful things.* —'**hurtfully** *adv.* —'**hurtfulness** *n.*

hurtle ('hɜːtᵊl) *vb.* **1.** to project or be projected very quickly, noisily, or violently. **2.** *(intr.) Rare.* to collide or crash. [C13 *hurtlen,* from *hurten* to strike; see HURT[1]]

husband ('hʌzbənd) *n.* **1.** a woman's partner in marriage. **2.** *Archaic.* **a.** a manager of an estate. **b.** a frugal person. ~*vb.* **3.** to manage or use (resources, finances, etc.) thriftily. **4.** *Archaic.* **a.** *(tr.)* to find a husband for. **b.** (of a woman) to marry (a man). **5.** *(tr.) Obsolete.* to till (the soil). [Old English *hūsbonda,* from Old Norse *hūsbōndi,* from *hūs* house + *bōndi* one who has a household, from *bōa* to dwell] —'**husbander** *n.* —'**husbandless** *adj.*

husbandman ('hʌzbəndmən) *n., pl.* **-men.** *Archaic.* a farmer.

husbandry ('hʌzbəndrɪ) *n.* **1.** farming, esp. when regarded as a science, skill, or art. **2.** management of affairs and resources.

hush[1] (hʌʃ) *vb.* **1.** to make or become silent; quieten. **2.** to soothe or be soothed. ~*n.* **3.** stillness; silence. **4.** an act of hushing. ~*interj.* **5.** a plea or demand for silence. [C16: probably from earlier *husht* quiet!, the *-t* being thought to indicate a past participle] —**hushed** *adj.*

hush[2] (hʌʃ) *Mining, northern English.* ~*vb. (tr.)* **1.** to run water over the ground to erode (surface soil), revealing the underlying strata and any valuable minerals present. **2.** to wash (an ore) by removing particles of earth with rushing water. ~*n.* **3.** a gush of water, esp. when artificially produced. [C18: of imitative origin]

hushaby ('hʌʃəˌbaɪ) *interj.* **1.** used in quietening a baby or child to sleep. ~*n.* **2.** a lullaby. [C18: from HUSH[1] + *by,* as in BYE-BYE]

hush-hush *adj. Informal.* (esp. of official work, documents, etc.) secret; confidential.

hush money *n. Slang.* money given to a person, such as an accomplice, to ensure that something is kept secret.

hush up *vb. (tr., adv.)* to suppress information or rumours about.

husk (hʌsk) *n.* **1.** the external green or membranous covering of certain fruits and seeds. **2.** any worthless outer covering. ~*vb.* **3.** *(tr.)* to remove the husk from. [C14: probably based on Middle Dutch *huusken* little house, from *hūs* house; related to Old English *hosu* husk, *hūs* HOUSE] —'**husker** *n.* —'**huskˌlike** *adj.*

husky[1] ('hʌskɪ) *adj.* **huskier, huskiest.** **1.** (of a voice, an utterance, etc.) slightly hoarse or rasping. **2.** of, like, or containing husks. **3.** *Informal.* big, strong, and well-built. [C19: probably from HUSK, from the toughness of a corn husk] —**'huskily** *adv.* —**'huskiness** *n.*

husky[2] ('hʌskɪ) *n., pl.* **huskies.** a breed of Arctic sled dog with a thick dense coat, pricked ears, and a curled tail. [C19: probably based on ESKIMO]

huss (hʌs) *n.* the flesh of the European dogfish, when used as food. [C15 *husk, huske,* C16 *huss*: of obscure origin]

hussar (hʊ'zɑː) *n.* **1. a.** a member of any of various light cavalry regiments in European armies, renowned for their elegant dress. **b.** (*pl.; cap. when part of a name*): *the Queen's own Hussars.* **2.** a Hungarian horseman of the 15th century. [C15: from Hungarian *huszár* hussar, formerly freebooter, from Old Serbian *husar,* from Old Italian *corsaro* CORSAIR]

Hussite ('hʌsaɪt) *n.* **1.** an adherent of the religious ideas of the Bohemian reformer John Huss (?1372–1415) or a member of the movement initiated by him. *~adj.* **2.** of or relating to John Huss, his teachings, followers, etc. —**'Hussism** *or* **'Hussitism** *n.*

hussy ('hʌsɪ, -zɪ) *n., pl.* **-sies.** **1.** *Contemptuous.* a shameless or promiscuous woman. **2.** *Dialect.* a folder for needles, thread, etc. [C16 (in the sense: housewife): from *hussif* HOUSEWIFE]

hustings ('hʌstɪŋz) *n.* (*functioning as pl. or sing.*) **1.** *Brit.* (before 1872) the platform on which candidates were nominated for Parliament and from which they addressed the electors. **2.** the proceedings at a parliamentary election. **3.** political campaigning. [C11: from Old Norse *hūsthing,* from *hūs* HOUSE + *thing* assembly]

hustle ('hʌsᵊl) *vb.* **1.** to shove or crowd (someone) roughly. **2.** to move or cause to move hurriedly or furtively: *he hustled her out of sight.* **3.** (*tr.*) to deal with or cause to proceed hurriedly: *to hustle legislation through.* **4.** *Slang.* to earn or obtain (something) forcefully. **5.** *U.S. and Canadian slang.* (of procurers and prostitutes) to solicit. *~n.* **6.** an instance of hustling. **7.** undue activity. **8.** a disco dance of the 1970s. [C17: from Dutch *husselen* to shake, from Middle Dutch *hutsen*] —**'hustler** *n.*

hustle up *vb.* (*tr.*) *Informal, chiefly U.S. and Canadian.* to prepare quickly.

hut (hʌt) *n.* **1.** a small house or shelter, usually made of wood or metal. **2. the.** *Austral.* (on a sheep or cattle station) accommodation for the shearers, stockmen, etc. **3.** *N.Z.* a shelter for mountaineers, skiers, etc. *~vb.* **4.** to furnish with or live in a hut. [C17: from French *hutte,* of Germanic origin; related to Old High German *hutta* a crude dwelling] —**'hut,like** *adj.*

hutch (hʌtʃ) *n.* **1.** a cage, usually of wood and wire mesh, for small animals. **2.** *Informal, derogatory.* a small house. **3.** a cart for carrying ore. **4.** a trough, esp. one used for kneading dough or (in mining) for washing ore. *~vb.* **5.** (*tr.*) to store or keep in or as if in a hutch. [C14 *hucche,* from Old French *huche,* from Medieval Latin *hutica,* of obscure origin]

hutchie ('hʌtʃɪ) *n. Austral.* a groundsheet draped over an upright stick, used as a temporary shelter. [C20: from HUTCH]

hut circle *n. Archaeol.* a circle of earth or stones representing the site of a prehistoric hut.

hutment ('hʌtmənt) *n. Chiefly military.* a number or group of huts.

Hutu ('huː,tuː) *n.* **1.** (*pl.* **-tu** *or* **-tus**) a member of a Negroid people of Rwanda in central Africa. **2.** the language of this people, belonging to the Bantu group of the Niger-Congo family.

hutzpah ('xʊtspə) *n.* a variant spelling of **chutzpah.**

Huygens' eyepiece ('haɪgənz, 'hɔɪgənz) *n. Physics.* a telescope eyepiece consisting of two planoconvex lenses separated by a distance equal to half the sum of their focal lengths, which are in the ratio of three to one, and oriented so that their curved surfaces face the incident light. [C19: named after Christiaan *Huygens* (1629–95), Dutch physicist]

huzzah (hə'zɑː) *interj., n., vb.* an archaic word for **hurrah.** [C16: of unknown origin]

HV *or* **h.v.** *abbrev. for* high voltage.

HW *or* **h.w.** *abbrev. for:* **1.** high water. **2.** *Cricket.* hit wicket.

hwan (hwɑːn, wɑːn) *n.* another name for **won**[2] (senses 1, 2). [Korean]

HWM *abbrev. for* high-water mark.

hwyl ('huːɪl) *n.* emotional fervour, as in the recitation of poetry. [C19: Welsh]

hyacinth ('haɪəsɪnθ) *n.* **1.** any liliaceous plant of the Mediterranean genus *Hyacinthus,* esp. any cultivated variety of *H. orientalis,* having a thick flower stalk bearing white, blue, or pink fragrant flowers. **2.** the flower or bulb of such a plant. **3.** any similar or related plant, such as the grape hyacinth. **4.** Also called: **jacinth.** a red or reddish-brown transparent variety of the mineral zircon, used as a gemstone. **5.** *Greek myth.* a flower which sprang from the blood of the dead Hyacinthus. **6.** any of the varying colours of the hyacinth flower or stone. [C16: from Latin *hyacinthus,* from Greek *huakinthos*] —**hyacinthine** (,haɪə'sɪnθaɪn) *adj.*

Hyades ('haɪə,diːz) *or* **Hyads** ('haɪædz) *pl. n.* an open cluster of stars in the constellation Taurus. Compare **Pleiades.** [C16: via Latin from Greek *huades,* perhaps from *huein* to rain]

hyaena (haɪ'iːnə) *n.* a variant spelling of **hyena.** —**hy'aenic** *adj.*

hyalin ('haɪəlɪn) *n.* glassy translucent substance, such as occurs in certain degenerative skin conditions or in hyaline cartilage.

hyaline ('haɪəlɪn) *adj.* **1.** *Biology.* clear and translucent, with no fibres or granules. **2.** *Archaic.* transparent. *~n.* **3.** *Archaic.* a glassy transparent surface. [C17: from Late Latin *hyalinus,* from Greek *hualinos* of glass, from *hualos* glass]

hyaline cartilage *n.* a common type of cartilage with a translucent matrix containing little fibrous tissue.

hyalite ('haɪə,laɪt) *n.* a clear and colourless variety of opal in globular form.

hyalo- *or before a vowel* **hyal-** *combining form.* of, relating to, or resembling glass: *hyaloplasm.* [from Greek *hualos* glass]

hyaloid ('haɪə,lɔɪd) *adj. Anatomy, zoology.* clear and transparent; glassy; hyaline. [C19: from Greek *hualoeidēs*]

hyaloid membrane *n.* the delicate transparent membrane enclosing the vitreous humour of the eye.

hyaloplasm ('haɪələʊ,plæzəm) *n.* the clear nongranular constituent of cell cytoplasm. —,**hyalo'plasmic** *adj.*

hyaluronic acid (,haɪəlʊ'rɒnɪk) *n.* a viscous polysaccharide with important lubricating properties, present, for example, in the synovial fluid in joints. [C20: HYALO- + Greek *ouron* urine + -IC] —,**hyalu'ronic** *adj.*

hyaluronidase (,haɪəlʊ'rɒnɪ,deɪs, -,deɪz) *n.* an enzyme that breaks down hyaluronic acid, thus decreasing the viscosity of the medium containing the acid. [C20: HYALO- + Greek *ouron* urine + -ID[3] + -ASE]

hybrid ('haɪbrɪd) *n.* **1.** an animal or plant resulting from a cross between genetically unlike individuals. Hybrids between different species are usually sterile. **2.** anything of mixed ancestry. **3.** a word, part of which is derived from one language and part from another, such as *monolingual,* which has a prefix of Greek origin and a root of Latin origin. *~adj.* **4.** denoting or being a hybrid; of mixed origin. **5.** *Physics.* (of an electromagnetic wave) having components of both electric and magnetic field vectors in the direction of propagation. **6.** *Electronics.* **a.** (of a circuit) consisting of transistors and valves. **b.** (of an integrated circuit) consisting of one or more fully integrated circuits and other components, attached to a ceramic substrate. Compare **monolithic** (sense 3). [C17: from Latin *hibrida* offspring of a mixed union (human or animal)] —**'hybridism** *n.* —**hy'bridity** *n.*

hybrid antibody *n.* a synthetic antibody that is able to combine with two different antigens.

hybrid bill *n.* (in Parliament) a public bill to which the standing orders for private business apply; a bill having a general application as well as affecting certain private interests.

hybrid computer *n.* a computer that uses both analogue and digital techniques.

hybridize *or* **hybridise** ('haɪbrɪ,daɪz) *vb.* to produce or cause to produce hybrids; crossbreed. —**'hybrid,izable** *or* **'hybrid,isable** *adj.* —,**hybridi'zation** *or* ,**hybridi'sation** *n.* —**'hybrid,izer** *or* **'hybrid,iser** *n.*

hybridoma (,haɪbrə'dəʊmə) *n.* a hybrid cell formed by the fusion of two different types of cell, esp. one capable of producing antibodies, but of limited lifespan, fused with an immortal tumour cell. [C20: from HYBRID + -OMA]

hybrid rock *n.* an igneous rock formed by molten magma incorporating pre-existing rock through which it passes.

hybrid vigour *n. Biology.* the increased size, strength, etc., of a hybrid as compared to either of its parents. Also called: **heterosis.**

hybris ('haɪbrɪs) *n.* a variant of **hubris.** —**hy'bristic** *adj.*

hydantoin (haɪ'dæntəʊɪn) *n.* a colourless odourless crystalline compound present in beet molasses: used in the manufacture of pharmaceuticals and synthetic resins. Formula: $C_3H_4N_2O_2$. [C20: from HYD(ROGEN + *all*)*antoin* product occurring in allantoic fluid]

hydathode ('haɪdə,θəʊd) *n.* a pore in plants, esp. on the leaves, specialized for excreting water. [C19: from Greek, from *hudor* water + *hodos* way]

hydatid ('haɪdətɪd) *n.* **1.** a large bladder containing encysted larvae of the tapeworm *Echinococcus:* causes serious disease in man. **2.** a sterile fluid-filled cyst produced in man and animals during infestation by *Echinococcus* larval forms. Also called: **hydatid cyst.** [C17: from Greek *hudatis* watery vesicle, from *hudōr, hudat-* water]

hydnocarpate (,hɪdnəʊ'kɑːpeɪt) *n.* any salt or ester of hydnocarpic acid.

hydnocarpic acid (,hɪdnəʊ'kɑːpɪk) *n.* a cyclic fatty acid occurring in the form of its glycerides in chaulmoogra oil. Formula: $C_{16}H_{28}O_2$. [C20: from Greek *hudnon* truffle + *karpos* fruit + -IC]

hydr- *combining form.* a variant of **hydro-** before a vowel.

hydra ('haɪdrə) *n., pl.* **-dras** *or* **-drae** (-driː). **1.** any solitary freshwater hydroid coelenterate of the genus *Hydra,* in which the body is a slender polyp with tentacles around the mouth. **2.** a persistent trouble or evil: *the hydra of the Irish problem.* [C16: from Latin, from Greek *hudra* water serpent; compare OTTER]

Hydra ('haɪdrə) *n., Latin genitive* **Hydrae** ('haɪdriː). a very long faint constellation lying mainly in the S hemisphere and extending from near Virgo to Cancer.

hydracid (haɪ'dræsɪd) *n.* an acid, such as hydrochloric acid, that does not contain oxygen.

hydragogue ('haɪdrəˌgɒg) *n. Med.* any purgative that causes evacuation of water from the bowels.

hydrangea (haɪ'dreɪndʒə) *n.* any shrub or tree of the Asian and American genus *Hydrangea,* cultivated for their large clusters of white, pink, or blue flowers: family *Hydrangeaceae.* [C18: from New Latin, from Greek *hudōr* water + *angeion* vessel: probably from the cup-shaped fruit]

hydrant ('haɪdrənt) *n.* an outlet from a water main, usually consisting of an upright pipe with a valve attached, from which water can be tapped for fighting fires. See also **fire hydrant.** [C19: from HYDRO- + -ANT]

hydranth ('haɪdrænθ) *n.* a polyp in a colony of hydrozoan coelenterates that is specialized for feeding rather than reproduction. [C19: from HYDRA + Greek *anthos* flower]

hydrargyria (ˌhaɪdrɑː'dʒaɪrɪə) *or* **hydrargyrism** (haɪ'drɑːdʒɪrɪzəm) *n. Med.* mercury poisoning. [C17: see HYDRARGYRUM]

hydrargyrum (haɪ'drɑːdʒɪrəm) *n.* an obsolete name for **mercury** (sense 1). [C16: from New Latin, from Latin *hydrargyrus* from Greek *hydrarguros,* from HYDRO- + *arguros* silver] —**hydrargyric** (ˌhaɪdrɑː'dʒɪərɪk) *adj.*

hydrastine (haɪ'dræstiːn, -tɪn) *n.* a white poisonous alkaloid extracted from the roots of the goldenseal: has been used in medicine (in the form of one of its water-soluble salts) to contract the uterus and arrest haemorrhage. Formula: $C_{21}H_{21}NO_6$. [C19: from HYDRAST(IS) + -INE[2]]

hydrastinine (haɪ'dræstɪˌniːn) *n.* a colourless crystalline water-soluble compound whose pharmacological action resembles that of hydrastine. Formula: $C_{11}H_{13}NO_3$.

hydrastis (haɪ'dræstɪs) *n.* any ranunculaceous plant of the genus *Hydrastis,* of Japan and E North America, such as goldenseal, having showy foliage and ornamental red fruits. [C18: New Latin, from Greek HYDRO- + *-astis,* of unknown origin]

hydrate ('haɪdreɪt) *n.* **1.** a chemical compound containing water that is chemically combined with a substance and can usually be expelled without changing the constitution of the substance. **2.** a chemical compound that can dissociate reversibly into water and another compound. For example sulphuric acid (H_2SO_4) dissociates into sulphur trioxide (SO_3) and water (H_2O). **3.** *(not in technical usage)* a chemical compound, such as a carbohydrate, that contains hydrogen and oxygen atoms in the ratio two to one. ~*vb.* **4.** to undergo or cause to undergo treatment or impregnation with water. [C19: from HYDRO- + ATE[1]] —**hy'dration** *n.* —**'hydrator** *n.*

hydrated ('haɪdreɪtɪd) *adj.* (of a compound) chemically bonded to water molecules.

hydraulic (haɪ'drɒlɪk) *adj.* **1.** operated by pressure transmitted through a pipe by a liquid, such as water or oil. **2.** of, concerned with, or employing liquids in motion. **3.** of or concerned with hydraulics. **4.** hardening under water: *hydraulic cement.* [C17: from Latin *hydraulicus* of a water organ, from Greek *hudraulikos,* from *hudraulos* water organ, from HYDRO- + *aulos* pipe, reed instrument] —**hy'draulically** *adv.*

hydraulic brake *n.* a type of brake, used in motor vehicles, in which the braking force is transmitted from the brake pedal to the brakes by a liquid under pressure.

hydraulic coupling *n.* another name for **torque converter.**

hydraulic press *n.* a press that utilizes liquid pressure to enable a small force applied to a small piston to produce a large force on a larger piston. The small piston moves through a proportionately greater distance than the larger.

hydraulic ram *n.* **1.** the larger or working piston of a hydraulic press. **2.** a form of water pump utilizing the kinetic energy of running water to provide static pressure to raise water to a reservoir higher than the source.

hydraulics (haɪ'drɒlɪks) *n. (functioning as sing.)* another name for **fluid mechanics.**

hydraulic suspension *n.* a system of motor-vehicle suspension using hydraulic members, often with hydraulic compensation between front and rear systems (**hydroelastic suspension**).

hydrazide ('haɪdrəˌzaɪd) *n.* any of a class of chemical compounds that result when hydrogen in hydrazine or any of its derivatives is replaced by an acid radical.

hydrazine ('haɪdrəˌziːn, -zɪn) *n.* a colourless basic liquid made from sodium hypochlorite and ammonia: a strong reducing agent, used chiefly as a rocket fuel. Formula: N_2H_4. [C19: from HYDRO- + AZO- + -INE[2]]

hydrazoic acid (ˌhaɪdrə'zəʊɪk) *n.* a colourless highly explosive liquid. Formula: HN_3. See also **azide.**

hydria ('haɪdrɪə) *n.* (in ancient Greece and Rome) a large water jar. [C19: from Latin, from Greek *hudria,* from *hudōr* water]

hydric ('haɪdrɪk) *adj.* **1.** of or containing hydrogen. **2.** containing or using moisture.

hydride ('haɪdraɪd) *n.* any compound of hydrogen with another element, including ionic compounds such as sodium hydride (NaH), covalent compounds such as borane (B_2H_6), and the transition metal hydrides formed when certain metals, such as palladium, absorb hydrogen.

hydrilla (haɪ'drɪlə) *n.* any aquatic plant of the Eurasian genus *Hydrilla,* growing underwater and forming large masses: used as an oxygenator in aquaria and pools. It was introduced in the S U.S. where it has become a serious problem, choking fish and hindering navigation. [C20: New Latin, probably from HYDRA]

hydriodic acid (ˌhaɪdrɪ'ɒdɪk) *n.* the colourless or pale yellow aqueous solution of hydrogen iodide: a strong acid. [C19: from HYDRO- + IODIC]

hydro[1] ('haɪdrəʊ) *n., pl.* **-dros.** *Brit.* (esp. formerly) a hotel or resort, often near a spa, offering facilities for hydropathic treatment.

hydro[2] ('haɪdrəʊ) *adj.* **1.** short for **hydroelectric.** ~*n.* **2.** a Canadian name for **electricity** as supplied to a residence, business, institution, etc.

hydro- *or sometimes before a vowel* **hydr-** *combining form.* **1.** indicating or denoting water, liquid, or fluid: *hydrolysis; hydrodynamics.* **2.** indicating the presence of hydrogen in a chemical compound: *hydrochloric acid.* **3.** indicating a hydroid: *hydrozoan.* [from Greek *hudōr* water]

hydroacoustics (ˌhaɪdrəʊə'kuːstɪks) *n. (functioning as sing.) Physics.* the study of sound travelling through water.

hydrobromic acid (ˌhaɪdrəʊ'brəʊmɪk) *n.* the colourless or faintly yellow aqueous solution of hydrogen bromide: a strong acid.

hydrocarbon (ˌhaɪdrəʊ'kɑːbᵊn) *n.* any organic compound containing only carbon and hydrogen, such as the alkanes, alkenes, alkynes, terpenes, and arenes.

hydrocele ('haɪdrəʊˌsiːl) *n.* an abnormal collection of fluid in any saclike space, esp. around the testicles [C16: from HYDRO- + -CELE].

hydrocellulose (ˌhaɪdrəʊ'sɛljʊˌləʊs, -ˌləʊz) *n.* a gelatinous material consisting of hydrated cellulose, made by treating cellulose with water, acids, or alkalis: used in making paper, viscose rayon, and mercerized cotton.

hydrocephalus (ˌhaɪdrəʊ'sɛfələs) *or* **hydrocephaly** (ˌhaɪdrəʊ'sɛfəlɪ) *n.* accumulation of cerebrospinal fluid within the ventricles of the brain because its normal outlet has been blocked by congenital malformation or disease. In infancy it usually results in great enlargement of the head. Nontechnical name: **water on the brain.** —**hydrocephalic** (ˌhaɪdrəʊse'fælɪk), ˌ**hydro'cephaloid,** *or* ˌ**hydro'cephalous** *adj.*

hydrochloric acid (ˌhaɪdrə'klɒrɪk) *n.* the colourless or slightly yellow aqueous solution of hydrogen chloride: a strong acid used in many industrial and laboratory processes. Formerly called: **muriatic acid.**

hydrochloride (ˌhaɪdrə'klɔːraɪd) *n.* a quaternary salt formed by the addition of hydrochloric acid to an organic base, such as aniline hydrochloride, $[C_6H_5NH_3]^+ Cl^-$.

hydrocoral (ˌhaɪdrə'kɒrəl) *or* **hydrocoralline** *n.* any hydrozoan coelenterate of the order *Milleporina* (or *Hydrocorallinae*), which includes the millepores. [C20: from HYDRO- + CORAL]

hydrocortisone (ˌhaɪdrəʊ'kɔːtɪˌzəʊn) *n.* the principal glucocorticoid secreted by the adrenal cortex; 17-hydroxycorticosterone. The synthesized form is used mainly in treating rheumatic, allergic, and inflammatory disorders. Formula: $C_{21}H_{30}O_5$. Also called: **cortisol.**

hydrocyanic acid (ˌhaɪdrəʊsaɪ'ænɪk) *n.* another name for **hydrogen cyanide,** esp. when in aqueous solution.

hydrodynamic (ˌhaɪdrəʊdaɪ'næmɪk, -dɪ-) *or* **hydrodynamical** *adj.* **1.** of or concerned with the mechanical properties of fluids. **2.** of or concerned with hydrodynamics. —ˌ**hydrody'namically** *adv.*

hydrodynamics (ˌhaɪdrəʊdaɪ'næmɪks, -dɪ-) *n.* **1.** *(functioning as sing.)* the branch of science concerned with the mechanical properties of fluids, esp. liquids. Also called: **hydromechanics.** See also **hydrokinetics, hydrostatics. 2.** another name for **hydrokinetics.**

hydroelastic suspension (ˌhaɪdrəʊɪ'læstɪk) *n.* See **hydraulic suspension.**

hydroelectric (ˌhaɪdrəʊɪ'lɛktrɪk) *adj.* **1.** generated by the pressure of falling water: *hydroelectric power.* **2.** of or concerned with the generation of electricity by water pressure: *a hydroelectric scheme.* —**hydroelectricity** (ˌhaɪdrəʊɪlɛk'trɪsɪtɪ, -ˌiːlɛk-) *n.*

hydrofluoric acid (ˌhaɪdrəʊfluː'ɒrɪk) *n.* the colourless aqueous solution of hydrogen fluoride: a strong acid that attacks glass.

hydrofoil ('haɪdrəˌfɔɪl) *n.* **1.** a fast light vessel the hull of which is raised out of the water on one or more pairs of fixed vanes. **2.** any of these vanes.

hydroforming ('haɪdrəʊˌfɔːmɪŋ) *n. Chem.* **1.** the catalytic reforming of petroleum to increase the proportion of aromatic and branched-chain hydrocarbons. **2.** *Engineering.* a forming process in which a metal component is shaped by a metal punch forced against a die, consisting of a flexible bag containing a fluid.

hydrogel ('haɪdrəˌdʒɛl) *n.* a gel in which the liquid constituent is water.

hydrogen ('haɪdrɪdʒən) *n.* **a.** a flammable colourless gas that is the lightest and most abundant element in the universe. It occurs mainly in water and in most organic compounds and is used in the production of ammonia and other chemicals, in the hydrogenation of fats and oils, and in welding. Symbol: H; atomic no.: 1; atomic wt.: 1.007 97; valency: 1; density: 0.0899 kg/m^3; melting pt.: –259.14°C; boiling pt.: –252.5°C. See also **deuterium, tritium. b.** *(as modifier): hydrogen bomb.* [C18: from French *hydrogène,* from HYDRO- + -GEN; so called because its combustion produces water]

hydrogenate ('haɪdrədʒɪˌneɪt, haɪ'drɒdʒɪˌneɪt), **hydrogenize,** *or* **hydrogenise** ('haɪdrədʒɪˌnaɪz, haɪ'drɒdʒɪˌnaɪz) *vb.* to undergo or cause to undergo a reaction with hydrogen: *to hydrogenate*

ethylene. —ˌ**hydrogen'ation,** ˌ**hydrogeni'zation,** *or* ˌ**hydrogeni'sation** *n.* —'**hydrogenˌator** *n.*
hydrogen bomb *n.* a type of bomb in which energy is released by fusion of hydrogen nuclei to give helium nuclei. The energy required to initiate the fusion is provided by the detonation of an atom bomb, which is surrounded by a hydrogen-containing substance such as lithium deuteride. Also called: **H-bomb.** See also **fusion bomb.**
hydrogen bond *n.* a weak chemical bond between an electronegative atom, such as fluorine, oxygen, or nitrogen, and a hydrogen atom bound to another electronegative atom. Hydrogen bonds are responsible for the properties of water and many biological molecules.
hydrogen bromide *n.* **1.** a colourless pungent gas used in organic synthesis. Formula: HBr. **2.** an aqueous solution of hydrogen bromide; hydrobromic acid.
hydrogen carbonate *n.* another name for **bicarbonate.**
hydrogen chloride *n.* **1.** a colourless pungent corrosive gas obtained by the action of sulphuric acid on sodium chloride: used in making vinyl chloride and other organic chemicals. Formula: HCl. **2.** an aqueous solution of hydrogen chloride; hydrochloric acid.
hydrogen cyanide *n.* a colourless poisonous liquid with a faint odour of bitter almonds, usually made by a catalysed reaction between ammonia, oxygen, and methane. It forms prussic acid in aqueous solution and is used for making plastics and dyes and as a war gas. Formula: HCN. Also called: **hydrocyanic acid.**
hydrogen embrittlement (ɪm'brɪtᵊlmənt) *n. Engineering.* the weakening of metal by the sorption of hydrogen during a pickling process, such as that used in plating.
hydrogen fluoride *n.* **1.** a colourless poisonous corrosive gas or liquid made by reaction between calcium fluoride and sulphuric acid: used as a fluorinating agent and catalyst. Formula: HF. **2.** an aqueous solution of hydrogen fluoride; hydrofluoric acid.
hydrogen iodide *n.* **1.** a colourless poisonous corrosive gas obtained by a catalysed reaction between hydrogen and iodine vapour: used in making iodides. Formula: HI. **2.** an aqueous solution of this gas; hydriodic acid.
hydrogen ion *n.* **1.** an ionized hydrogen atom, occurring in plasmas and in aqueous solutions of acids, in which it is solvated by one or more water molecules; proton. Formula: H^+ **2.** an ionized hydrogen molecule; hydrogen molecular ion. Formula: H_2^+
hydrogenize *or* **hydrogenise** ('haɪdrədʒɪˌnaɪz, haɪ'drɒdʒɪˌnaɪz) *vb.* variants of **hydrogenate.** —ˌ**hydrogeni'zation** *or* ˌ**hydrogeni'sation** *n.*
hydrogenolysis (ˌhaɪdrəʊdʒɪ'nɒlɪsɪs) *n.* a chemical reaction in which a compound is decomposed by hydrogen.
hydrogenous (haɪ'drɒdʒɪnəs) *adj.* of or containing hydrogen.
hydrogen peroxide *n.* a colourless oily unstable liquid, usually used in aqueous solution. It is a strong oxidizing agent used as a bleach for textiles, wood pulp, hair, etc., and as an oxidizer in rocket fuels. Formula: H_2O_2.
hydrogen sulphate *n.* another name for **bisulphate.**
hydrogen sulphide *n.* a colourless poisonous soluble flammable gas with an odour of rotten eggs: used as a reagent in chemical analysis. Formula: H_2S. Also called: **sulphuretted hydrogen.**
hydrogen sulphite *n.* another name for **bisulphite.**
hydrogen tartrate *n.* another name for **bitartrate.**
hydrogeology (ˌhaɪdrədʒɪ'ɒlədʒɪ) *n.* the branch of geology dealing with the waters below the earth's surface and with the geological aspects of surface waters. —ˌ**hydrogeo'logical** *adj.* —ˌ**hydroge'ologist** *n.*
hydrograph ('haɪdrəˌgrɑːf, -ˌgræf) *n.* a graph showing the seasonal variation in the level, velocity, or discharge of a body of water.
hydrography (haɪ'drɒgrəfɪ) *n.* **1.** the study, surveying, and mapping of the oceans, seas, and rivers. Compare **hydrology. 2.** the oceans, seas, and rivers as represented on a chart. —**hy'drographer** *n.* —**hydrographic** (ˌhaɪdrə'græfɪk) *or* ˌ**hydro'graphical** *adj.* —ˌ**hydro'graphically** *adv.*
hydroid ('haɪdrɔɪd) *adj.* **1.** of or relating to the *Hydroida,* an order of colonial hydrozoan coelenterates that have the polyp phase dominant. **2.** (of coelenterate colonies or individuals) having or consisting of hydra-like polyps. ~*n.* **3.** a hydroid colony or individual. [C19: from HYDRA + -OID]
hydrokinetic (ˌhaɪdrəʊkɪ'nɛtɪk, -kaɪ-) *or* **hydrokinetical** *adj.* **1.** of or concerned with fluids that are in motion. **2.** of or concerned with hydrokinetics.
hydrokinetics (ˌhaɪdrəʊkɪ'nɛtɪks, -kaɪ-) *n.* (*functioning as sing.*) the branch of science concerned with the mechanical behaviour and properties of fluids in motion, esp. of liquids. Also called: **hydrodynamics.**
hydrolase ('haɪdrəˌleɪz) *n.* an enzyme, such as an esterase, that controls hydrolysis.
hydrologic cycle *n.* another name for **water cycle.**
hydrology (haɪ'drɒlədʒɪ) *n.* the study of the distribution, conservation, use, etc., of the water of the earth and its atmosphere. —**hydrologic** (ˌhaɪdrə'lɒdʒɪk) *or* ˌ**hydro'logical** *adj.* —ˌ**hydro'logically** *adv.* —**hy'drologist** *n.*
hydrolysate (haɪ'drɒlɪˌseɪt) *n.* a substance or mixture produced by hydrolysis. [C20: from HYDROLYSIS + -ATE[1]]
hydrolyse *or U.S.* **hydrolyze** ('haɪdrəˌlaɪz) *vb.* to subject to or undergo hydrolysis. —'**hydroˌlysable** *or U.S.* '**hydroˌlyzable** *adj.* —ˌ**hydroly'sation** *or U.S.* ˌ**hydroly'zation** *n.* —'**hydroˌlyser** *or U.S.* '**hydroˌlyzer** *n.*
hydrolysis (haɪ'drɒlɪsɪs) *n.* a chemical reaction in which a compound reacts with water to produce other compounds.
hydrolyte ('haɪdrəˌlaɪt) *n.* a substance subjected to hydrolysis.
hydrolytic (ˌhaɪdrə'lɪtɪk) *adj.* of, concerned with, producing, or produced by hydrolysis.
hydromagnetics (ˌhaɪdrəʊmæg'nɛtɪks) *n.* another name for **magnetohydrodynamics.** —ˌ**hydromag'netic** *adj.*
hydromancy ('haɪdrəʊˌmænsɪ) *n.* divination by water. —'**hydroˌmancer** *n.* —ˌ**hydro'mantic** *adj.*
hydromechanics (ˌhaɪdrəʊmɪ'kænɪks) *n.* another name for **hydrodynamics.** —ˌ**hydrome'chanical** *adj.*
hydromedusa (ˌhaɪdrəʊmɪ'djuːsə) *n., pl.* **-sas** *or* **-sae** (-siː). the medusa form of hydrozoan coelenterates. —ˌ**hydrome'dusan** *adj.*
hydromel ('haɪdrəʊˌmɛl) *n. Archaic.* another word for **mead** (the drink). [C15: from Latin, from Greek *hudromeli,* from HYDRO- + *meli* honey]
hydrometallurgy (ˌhaɪdrəʊ'mɛtᵊˌlɜːdʒɪ, -mɛ'tælədʒɪ) *n.* a technique for the recovery of a metal from an aqueous medium in which the metal or the gangue is preferentially dissolved. —ˌ**hydroˌmetal'lurgical** *adj.*
hydrometeor (ˌhaɪdrəʊ'miːtɪə) *n.* any weather condition produced by water in the atmosphere, such as rain or snow. —ˌ**hydroˌmeteoro'logical** *adj.* —ˌ**hydroˌmeteor'ology** *n.*
hydrometer (haɪ'drɒmɪtə) *n.* an instrument for measuring the relative density of a liquid, usually consisting of a sealed graduated tube with a weighted bulb on one end, the relative density being indicated by the length of the unsubmerged stem. —**hydrometric** (ˌhaɪdrəʊ'mɛtrɪk) *or* ˌ**hydro'metrical** *adj.* —ˌ**hydro'metrically** *adv.* —**hy'drometry** *n.*
hydronaut ('haɪdrəʊˌnɔːt) *n. U.S. Navy.* a person trained to operate deep submergence vessels. [C20: from Greek, from HYDRO- + *-naut,* as in *aeronaut, astronaut*]
hydronium ion (haɪ'drəʊnɪəm) *n. Chem.* another name for **hydroxonium ion.** [C20: from HYDRO- + (AMM)ONIUM]
hydropathy (haɪ'drɒpəθɪ) *n.* a pseudoscientific method of treating disease by the use of large quantities of water both internally and externally. Also called: **water cure.** Compare **hydrotherapy.** —**hydropathic** (ˌhaɪdrəʊ'pæθɪk) *or* ˌ**hydro'pathical** *adj.* —**hy'dropathist** *or* '**hydroˌpath** *n.*
hydrophane ('haɪdrəʊˌfeɪn) *n.* a white partially opaque variety of opal that becomes translucent in water. —**hydrophanous** (haɪ'drɒfənəs) *adj.*
hydrophilic (ˌhaɪdrəʊ'fɪlɪk) *adj. Chem.* tending to dissolve in, mix with, or be wetted by water: *a hydrophilic colloid.* Compare **hydrophobic.** —'**hydroˌphile** *n.*
hydrophilous (haɪ'drɒfɪləs) *adj. Botany.* growing in or pollinated by water. —**hy'drophily** *n.*
hydrophobia (ˌhaɪdrə'fəʊbɪə) *n.* **1.** another name for **rabies. 2.** a fear of drinking fluids, esp. that of a person with rabies, because of painful spasms when trying to swallow. Compare **aquaphobia.**
hydrophobic (ˌhaɪdrə'fəʊbɪk) *adj.* **1.** of or relating to hydrophobia. **2.** *Chem.* tending not to dissolve in, mix with, or be wetted by water: *a hydrophobic colloid.* Compare **hydrophilic.**
hydrophone ('haɪdrəˌfəʊn) *n.* an electroacoustic transducer that converts sound or ultrasonic waves travelling through water into electrical oscillations.
hydrophyte ('haɪdrəʊˌfaɪt) *n.* a plant that grows only in water or very moist soil. —**hydrophytic** (ˌhaɪdrəʊ'fɪtɪk) *adj.*
hydroplane ('haɪdrəʊˌpleɪn) *n.* **1.** a motorboat equipped with hydrofoils or with a shaped bottom that raises its hull out of the water at high speeds. **2.** an attachment to an aircraft to enable it to glide along the surface of water. **3.** another name (esp. U.S.) for a **seaplane. 4.** a horizontal vane on the hull of a submarine for controlling its vertical motion. ~*vb.* **5.** (*intr.*) (of a boat) to rise out of the water in the manner of a hydroplane.
hydroponics (ˌhaɪdrəʊ'pɒnɪks) *n.* (*functioning as sing.*) a method of cultivating plants by growing them in gravel, etc., through which water containing dissolved inorganic nutrient salts is pumped. Also called: **aquiculture.** [C20: from HYDRO- + (GEO)PONICS] —ˌ**hydro'ponic** *adj.* —ˌ**hydro'ponically** *adv.*
hydropower ('haɪdrəʊˌpaʊə) *n.* hydroelectric power.
hydroquinone (ˌhaɪdrəʊkwɪ'nəʊn) *or* **hydroquinol** (ˌhaɪdrəʊ'kwɪnɒl) *n.* a white crystalline soluble phenol used as a photographic developer; 1,4-dihydroxybenzene. Formula: $C_6H_4(OH)_2$. Also called: **quinol.**
hydroscope ('haɪdrəˌskəʊp) *n.* any instrument for making observations of underwater objects. —**hydroscopic** (ˌhaɪdrə'skɒpɪk) *or* ˌ**hydro'scopical** *adj.*
hydrosere ('haɪdrəʊsɪə) *n.* a sere that begins in an aquatic environment.
hydroski ('haɪdrəʊˌskiː) *n.* a hydrofoil used on some seaplanes to provide extra lift when taking off.
hydrosol ('haɪdrəˌsɒl) *n. Chem.* a sol that has water as its liquid phase.
hydrosome ('haɪdrəˌsəʊm) *or* **hydrosoma** (ˌhaɪdrə'səʊmə) *n. Zoology.* the body of a colonial hydrozoan. [C19: from *hydro-,* from HYDRA + -SOME[3]]

hydrosphere ('haɪdrəˌsfɪə) *n.* the watery part of the earth's surface, including oceans, lakes, water vapour in the atmosphere, etc. —ˌ**hydro'spheric** *adj.*
hydrostat ('haɪdrəʊˌstæt) *n.* a device that detects the presence of water as a prevention against drying out, overflow, etc., esp. one used as a warning in a steam boiler.
hydrostatic (ˌhaɪdrəʊ'stætɪk) *or* **hydrostatical** *adj.* **1.** of or concerned with fluids that are not in motion: *hydrostatic pressure.* **2.** of or concerned with hydrostatics. —ˌ**hydro'statically** *adv.*
hydrostatic balance *n.* a balance for finding the weight of an object submerged in water in order to determine the upthrust on it and thus determine its relative density.
hydrostatics (ˌhaɪdrəʊ'stætɪks) *n.* (*functioning as sing.*) the branch of science concerned with the mechanical properties and behaviour of fluids that are not in motion. See also **hydrodynamics.**
hydrosulphate (ˌhaɪdrəʊ'sʌlfeɪt) *n.* any quaternary acid salt formed by addition of an organic base to sulphuric acid, such as aniline hydrosulphate, $C_6H_5NH_3HSO_4$.
hydrosulphide (ˌhaɪdrəʊ'sʌlfaɪd) *n.* any salt derived from hydrogen sulphide by replacing one of its hydrogen atoms with a metal atom. Technical name: **hydrogen sulphide.**
hydrosulphite (ˌhaɪdrəʊ'sʌlfaɪt) *n.* another name (not in technical usage) for **dithionite.** [C20: from HYDROSULPH(UROUS) + -ITE[2]]
hydrosulphurous acid (ˌhaɪdrəʊ'sʌlfərəs) *n.* another name (not in technical usage) for **dithionous acid.**
hydrotaxis (ˌhaɪdrəʊ'tæksɪs) *n.* the directional movement of an organism or cell in response to the stimulus of water. —ˌ**hydro'tactic** *adj.*
hydrotherapeutics (ˌhaɪdrəʊˌθɛrə'pju:tɪks) *n.* (*functioning as sing.*) the branch of medical science concerned with hydrotherapy. —ˌ**hydroˌthera'peutic** *adj.*
hydrotherapy (ˌhaɪdrəʊ'θɛrəpɪ) *n. Med.* the treatment of certain diseases by the external use of water, esp. by exercising in water in order to mobilize stiff joints or strengthen weakened muscles. Also called: **water cure.** Compare **hydropathy.** —**hydrotherapic** (ˌhaɪdrəʊθɪ'ræpɪk) *adj.* —ˌ**hydro'therapist** *n.*
hydrothermal (ˌhaɪdrəʊ'θɜ:məl) *adj.* of or relating to the action of water under conditions of high temperature, esp. in forming rocks and minerals. —ˌ**hydro'thermally** *adv.*
hydrothorax (ˌhaɪdrəʊ'θɔ:ræks) *n. Pathol.* an accumulation of fluid in one or both pleural cavities, often resulting from disease of the heart or kidneys. —**hydrothoracic** (ˌhaɪdrəʊθɔ:'ræsɪk) *adj.*
hydrotropism (haɪ'drɒtrəˌpɪzəm) *n.* the directional growth of plants in response to the stimulus of water. —**hydrotropic** (ˌhaɪdrəʊ'trɒpɪk) *adj.* —ˌ**hydro'tropically** *adv.*
hydrous ('haɪdrəs) *adj.* **1.** containing water. **2.** (of a chemical compound) combined with water molecules: *hydrous copper sulphate,* $CuSO_4.5H_2O$.
hydrovane ('haɪdrəʊˌveɪn) *n.* a vane on a seaplane conferring stability on water (a sponson) or facilitating take off (a hydrofoil).
hydroxide (haɪ'drɒksaɪd) *n.* **1.** a base or alkali containing the ion OH^-. **2.** any compound containing an -OH group.
hydroxonium ion (ˌhaɪdrɒk'səʊnɪəm) *n.* a positive ion, H_3O^+, formed by the attachment of a proton to a water molecule: occurs in solutions of acids and behaves like a hydrogen ion. Also called: **hydronium ion.**
hydroxy (haɪ'drɒksɪ) *adj.* (of a chemical compound) containing one or more hydroxyl groups. [C19: HYDRO- + OXY(GEN)]
hydroxy- *combining form.* (in chemical compounds) indicating the presence of one or more hydroxyl groups or ions. [from HYDRO- + OXY(GEN)]
hydroxy acid *n.* **1.** any acid, such as sulphuric acid, containing hydroxyl groups in its molecules. **2.** any of a class of carboxylic acids that contain both a hydroxyl group and a carboxyl group in their molecules.
hydroxyl (haɪ'drɒksɪl) *n.* (*modifier*) of, consisting of, or containing the monovalent group -OH or the ion OH^-: *a hydroxyl group or radical.* —ˌ**hydrox'ylic** *adj.*
hydroxylamine (haɪˌdrɒksɪlə'mi:n, -'æmɪn, -'saɪləˌmi:n) *n.* a colourless crystalline compound that explodes when heated: a reducing agent. Formula: NH_2OH.
hydroxyproline (haɪˌdrɒksɪ'prəʊli:n, -lɪn) *n.* an amino acid occurring in some proteins, esp. collagen. Formula: $(OH)C_4H_7N(COOH)$.
hydroxytryptamine (haɪˌdrɒksɪ'trɪptəmi:n) *n.* 5-hydroxytryptamine: another name for **serotonin.** Abbrev.: **5HT.**
hydrozoan (ˌhaɪdrəʊ'zəʊən) *n.* **1.** any colonial or solitary coelenterate of the class *Hydrozoa,* which includes the hydra, Portuguese man-of-war, and the sertularians. ~*adj.* **2.** of, relating to, or belonging to the *Hydrozoa.*
Hydrus ('haɪdrəs) *n., Latin genitive* **Hydri** ('haɪdraɪ). a constellation near the S celestial pole lying close to Eridanus and Tucana and containing part of the Small Magellanic cloud. [C17: from Latin, from Greek *hudros* water serpent, from *hudōr* water]
hyena *or* **hyaena** (haɪ'i:nə) *n.* any of several long-legged carnivorous doglike mammals of the genera *Hyaena* and *Crocuta,* such as *C. crocuta* (**spotted** or **laughing hyena**), of Africa and S Asia: family *Hyaenidae,* order *Carnivora* (carnivores). See also **strandwolf.** [C16: from Medieval Latin, from Latin *hyaena,* from Greek *huaina,* from *hus* hog] —**hy'enic** *or* **hy'aenic** *adj.*
hyetal ('haɪɪtᵊl) *adj.* of or relating to rain, rainfall, or rainy regions. [C19: from Greek *huetos* rain + -AL[1]]
hyeto- *or before a vowel* **hyet-** *combining form.* indicating rain. [from Greek *huetos*]
hyetograph ('haɪɪtəˌgrɑ:f, -ˌgræf) *n.* **1.** a chart showing the distribution of rainfall of a particular area, usually throughout a year. **2.** a self-recording rain gauge.
hyetography (ˌhaɪɪ'tɒgrəfɪ) *n.* the study of the distribution and recording of rainfall. —**hyetographic** (ˌhaɪɪtə'græfɪk) *or* ˌ**hyeto'graphical** *adj.* —ˌ**hyeto'graphically** *adv.*
hygiene ('haɪdʒi:n) *n.* **1.** Also called: **hygienics.** the science concerned with the maintenance of health. **2.** clean or healthy practices or thinking: *personal hygiene.* [C18: from New Latin *hygiēna,* from Greek *hugieinē,* from *hugieinos* healthful, from *hugiēs* healthy]
hygienic (haɪ'dʒi:nɪk) *adj.* promoting health or cleanliness; sanitary. —**hy'gienically** *adv.*
hygienics (haɪ'dʒi:nɪks) *n.* (*functioning as sing.*) another word for **hygiene** (sense 1).
hygienist ('haɪdʒi:nɪst), **hygeist,** *or* **hygieist** ('haɪdʒi:ɪst) *n.* a person skilled in the practice of hygiene. See also **dental hygienist.**
hygristor (haɪ'grɪstə) *n.* an electronic component the resistance of which varies with humidity. [C20: from HYGRO- + (RES)ISTOR]
hygro- *or before a vowel* **hygr-** *combining form.* indicating moisture: *hygrometer.* [from Greek *hugros* wet]
hygrograph ('haɪgrəˌgrɑ:f, -ˌgræf) *n.* an automatic hygrometer that produces a graphic record of the humidity of the air.
hygrometer (haɪ'grɒmɪtə) *n.* any of various instruments for measuring humidity. —**hygrometric** (ˌhaɪgrə'mɛtrɪk) *adj.* —ˌ**hygro'metrically** *adv.* —**hy'grometry** *n.*
hygrophilous (haɪ'grɒfɪləs) *adj.* (of a plant) growing in moist places. —**hygrophile** ('haɪgrəʊˌfaɪl) *n.*
hygrophyte ('haɪgrəˌfaɪt) *n.* any plant that grows in wet or waterlogged soil. —**hygrophytic** (ˌhaɪgrə'fɪtɪk) *adj.*
hygroscope ('haɪgrəˌskəʊp) *n.* any device that indicates the humidity of the air without necessarily measuring it.
hygroscopic (ˌhaɪgrə'skɒpɪk) *adj.* (of a substance) tending to absorb water from the air. —ˌ**hygro'scopically** *adv.* —**hygroscopicity** (ˌhaɪgrəskəʊ'pɪsɪtɪ) *n.*
hygrostat ('haɪgrəˌstæt) *n.* another name for **humidistat.**
hying ('haɪɪŋ) *vb.* a present participle of **hie.**
hyla ('haɪlə) *n.* any tree frog of the genus *Hyla,* such as *H. leucophyllata* (**white-spotted hyla**) of tropical America. [C19: from New Latin, from Greek *hulē* forest, wood]
hylo- *or before a vowel* **hyl-** *combining form.* **1.** indicating matter (as distinguished from spirit): *hylozoism.* **2.** indicating wood: *hylophagous.* [from Greek *hulē* wood]
hylomorphism (ˌhaɪlə'mɔ:fɪzəm) *n.* the philosophical doctrine that identifies matter with the first cause of the universe.
hylophagous (haɪ'lɒfəgəs) *adj.* (esp. of insects) feeding on wood. [C19: from Greek *hulophagos,* from *hulē* wood + *phagein* to devour]
hylotheism (ˌhaɪlə'θi:ɪzəm) *n.* the doctrine that God is identical to matter.
hylozoism (ˌhaɪlə'zəʊɪzəm) *n.* the philosophical doctrine that life is one of the properties of matter. [C17: HYLO- + Greek *zōē* life] —ˌ**hylo'zoic** *adj.* —ˌ**hylo'zoist** *n.* —ˌ**hylozo'istic** *adj.* —ˌ**hylozo'istically** *adv.*
hymen ('haɪmɛn) *n. Anatomy.* a fold of mucous membrane that partly covers the entrance to the vagina and is usually ruptured when sexual intercourse takes place for the first time. [C17: from Greek: membrane] —'**hymenal** *adj.*
hymeneal (ˌhaɪmɛ'ni:əl) *adj.* **1.** *Chiefly poetic.* of or relating to marriage. ~*n.* **2.** a wedding song or poem.
hymenium (haɪ'mi:nɪəm) *n., pl.* **-nia** (-nɪə) *or* **-niums.** (in basidiomycetous and ascomycetous fungi) a layer of cells some of which produce the spores.
hymenophore (haɪ'mi:nəʊˌfɔ:) *n. Botany.* the fruit body of some basidiomycetous fungi. [from HYMENIUM + -PHORE]
hymenopteran (ˌhaɪmɪ'nɒptərən) *or* **hymenopteron** *n., pl.* **-terans, -tera** (-tərə), *or* **-terons.** any hymenopterous insect.
hymenopterous (ˌhaɪmɪ'nɒptərəs) *or* **hymenopteran** *adj.* of, relating to, or belonging to the *Hymenoptera,* an order of insects, including bees, wasps, ants, and sawflies, having two pairs of membranous wings and an ovipositor specialized for stinging, sawing, or piercing. [C19: from Greek *humenopteros* membrane wing; see HYMEN, -PTEROUS]
hymn (hɪm) *n.* **1.** a Christian song of praise sung to God or a saint. **2.** a similar song praising other gods, a nation, etc. ~*vb.* **3.** to express (praises, thanks, etc.) by singing hymns. [C13: from Latin *hymnus,* from Greek *humnos*] —**hymnic** ('hɪmnɪk) *adj.* —'**hymnˌlike** *adj.*
hymnal ('hɪmnᵊl) *n.* **1.** a book of hymns. ~*adj.* **2.** of, relating to, or characteristic of hymns.
hymn book *n.* a book containing the words and music of hymns.
hymnist ('hɪmnɪst), **hymnodist** ('hɪmnədɪst), *or* **hymnographer** (hɪm'nɒgrəfə) *n.* a person who composes hymns.
hymnody ('hɪmnədɪ) *n.* **1.** the composition or singing of hymns. **2.** hymns collectively. ~Also called: **hymnology.** [C18: from Medieval Latin *hymnōdia,* from Greek *humnōidia,* from

humnōidein to chant a hymn, from HYMN + *aeidein* to sing] —**hymnodical** (hɪmˈnɒdɪkᵊl) *adj.*

hymnology (hɪmˈnɒlədʒɪ) *n.* **1.** the study of hymn composition. **2.** another word for **hymnody.** —**hymnologic** (ˌhɪmnəˈlɒdʒɪk) *or* ˌ**hymnoˈlogical** *adj.* —**hymˈnologist** *n.*

hyoid (ˈhaɪɔɪd) *adj. also* **hyoidal** *or* **hyoidean. 1.** of or relating to the hyoid bone. ~*n. also* **hyoid bone. 2.** the horseshoe-shaped bone that lies at the base of the tongue and above the thyroid cartilage. **3.** a corresponding bone or group of bones in other vertebrates. [C19: from New Latin *hyoïdes,* from Greek *huoeidēs* having the shape of the letter UPSILON, from *hu* upsilon + -OID]

hyoscine (ˈhaɪəˌsiːn) *n.* another name for **scopolamine.** [C19: from HYOSC(YAMUS) + -INE[2]]

hyoscyamine (ˌhaɪəˈsaɪəˌmiːn, -mɪn) *n.* a poisonous alkaloid occurring in henbane and related plants: an optically active isomer of atropine, used in medicine in a similar way. Formula: $C_{17}H_{23}NO_3$.

hyoscyamus (ˌhaɪəˈsaɪəməs) *n.* any plant of the solanaceous genus *Hyoscyamus,* of Europe, Asia, and N Africa, including henbane. [C18: from New Latin, from Greek *huoskuamos,* from *hus* pig + *kuamos* bean; the plant was thought to be poisonous to pigs]

hyp. *abbrev. for:* **1.** hypotenuse. **2.** hypothesis. **3.** hypothetical.

hyp- *prefix.* a variant of **hypo-** before a vowel: *hypabyssal.*

hypabyssal (ˌhɪpəˈbɪsᵊl) *adj.* (of igneous rocks) derived from magma that has solidified close to the surface of the earth in the form of dykes, sills, etc.

hypaesthesia *or U.S.* **hypesthesia** (ˌhɪpiːsˈθiːzɪə, ˌhaɪ-) *n. Pathol.* a reduced sensibility to touch. —**hypaesthesic** *or U.S.* **hypesthesic** (ˌhɪpiːsˈθiːsɪk, ˌhaɪ-) *adj.*

hypaethral *or U.S.* **hypethral** (hɪˈpiːθrəl, haɪ-) *adj.* (esp. of a classical temple) having no roof. [C18: from Latin *hypaethrus* uncovered, from Greek *hupaithros,* from HYPO- + *aithros* clear sky]

hypalgesia (ˌhaɪpælˈdʒiːzɪə, -sɪə) *n. Pathol.* diminished sensitivity to pain. —ˌ**hypalˈgesic** *adj.*

hypallage (haɪˈpæləˌdʒiː) *n. Rhetoric.* a figure of speech in which the natural relations of two words in a statement are interchanged, as in *the fire spread the wind.* [C16: via Late Latin from Greek *hupallagē* interchange, from HYPO- + *allassein* to exchange]

hypanthium (haɪˈpænθɪəm) *n., pl.* **-thia** (-θɪə). *Botany.* the cup-shaped or flat receptacle of perigynous flowers. [C19: from New Latin, from HYPO- + Greek *anthion* a little flower, from *anthos* flower] —**hyˈpanthial** *adj.*

hype[1] (haɪp) *Slang.* ~*n.* **1.** a hypodermic needle or injection. ~*vb.* **2.** (*intr.;* usually foll. by *up*) to inject oneself with a drug. **3.** (*tr.*) to stimulate artificially or excite. [C20: shortened from HYPODERMIC]

hype[2] (haɪp) *n.* **1.** a deception or racket. **2.** intensive or exaggerated publicity or sales promotion: *media hype.* **3.** the person or thing so publicized. ~*vb.* (*tr.*) **4.** to market or promote (a product) using exaggerated or intensive publicity. **5.** to falsify or rig (something). **6.** (in the pop-music business) to buy (copies of a record) in such quantity as to increase its ratings in the charts. [C20: of unknown origin] —ˈ**hyper** *n.* —ˈ**hyping** *n.*

hyped up *adj. Slang.* stimulated or excited by or as if by the effect of a stimulating drug.

hyper (ˈhaɪpə) *adj. Informal.* overactive; overexcited. [C20: probably independent use of HYPER-]

hyper- *prefix.* **1.** above, over, or in excess: *hypercritical.* **2.** (in medicine) denoting an abnormal excess: *hyperacidity.* **3.** indicating that a chemical compound contains a greater than usual amount of an element: *hyperoxide.* [from Greek *huper* over]

hyperacidity (ˌhaɪpərəˈsɪdɪtɪ) *n.* excess acidity of the gastrointestinal tract, esp. the stomach, producing a burning sensation. —ˌ**hyperˈacid** *adj.*

hyperactive (ˌhaɪpərˈæktɪv) *adj.* abnormally active. —ˌ**hyperˈaction** *n.* —ˌ**hyperacˈtivity** *n.*

hyperaemia *or U.S.* **hyperemia** (ˌhaɪpərˈiːmɪə) *n. Pathol.* an excessive amount of blood in an organ or part. —ˌ**hyperˈaemic** *or U.S.* ˌ**hyperˈemic** *adj.*

hyperaesthesia *or U.S.* **hyperesthesia** (ˌhaɪpəriːsˈθiːzɪə) *n. Pathol.* increased sensitivity of any of the sense organs, esp. of the skin to cold, heat, pain, etc. —**hyperaesthetic** *or U.S.* **hyperesthetic** (ˌhaɪpəriːsˈθɛtɪk) *adj.*

hyperbaric (ˌhaɪpəˈbærɪk) *adj.* of, concerned with, or operating at pressures higher than normal.

hyperbaton (haɪˈpɜːbəˌtɒn) *n. Rhetoric.* a figure of speech in which the normal order of words is reversed, as in *cheese I love.* [C16: via Latin from Greek, literally: an overstepping, from HYPER- + *bainein* to step]

hyperbola (haɪˈpɜːbələ) *n., pl.* **-las** *or* **-le** (-ˌliː). a conic section formed by a plane that cuts both bases of a cone; it consists of two branches asymptotic to two intersecting fixed lines and has two foci. Standard equation: $x^2/a^2 - y^2/b^2 = 1$ where $2a$ is the distance between the two intersections with the x-axis and $b = a\surd(e^2 - 1)$, where e is the eccentricity. [C17: from Greek *huperbolē,* literally: excess, extravagance, from HYPER- + *ballein* to throw]

hyperbole (haɪˈpɜːbəlɪ) *n.* a deliberate exaggeration used for effect: *he embraced her a thousand times.* [C16: from Greek: from HYPER- + *bolē* a throw, from *ballein* to throw] —**hyˈperbolism** *n.*

hyperbolic (ˌhaɪpəˈbɒlɪk) *or* **hyperbolical** *adj.* **1.** of or relating to a hyperbola. **2.** *Rhetoric.* of or relating to a hyperbole. —ˌ**hyperˈbolically** *adv.*

hyperbolic function *n.* any of a group of functions of an angle expressed as a relationship between the distances of a point on a hyperbola to the origin and to the coordinate axes. The group includes sinh (**hyperbolic sine**), cosh (**hyperbolic cosine**), tanh (**hyperbolic tangent**), sech (**hyperbolic secant**), cosech (**hyperbolic cosecant**), and coth (**hyperbolic cotangent**).

hyperbolize *or* **hyperbolise** (haɪˈpɜːbəˌlaɪz) *vb.* to express (something) by means of hyperbole.

hyperboloid (haɪˈpɜːbəˌlɔɪd) *n.* a geometric surface consisting of one sheet, or of two sheets separated by a finite distance, whose sections parallel to the three coordinate planes are hyperbolas or ellipses. Equations: $x^2/a^2 + y^2/b^2 - z^2/c^2 = 1$ (one sheet) or $x^2/a^2 - y^2/b^2 - z^2/c^2 = 1$ (two sheets) where *a, b,* and *c* are constants.

Hyperborean (ˌhaɪpəˈbɔːrɪən) *n.* **1.** an inhabitant of the extreme north. ~*adj.* **2.** (*sometimes not cap.*) of or relating to the extreme north. [C16: from Latin *hyperboreus,* from Greek *huperboreos,* from HYPER- + *Boreas* the north wind]

hypercapnia (ˌhaɪpəˈkæpnɪə) *n.* an excess of carbon dioxide in the blood. Also: **hypercarbia.** [from HYPER- + Greek *kapnos* smoke] —ˌ**hyperˈcapnic** *adj.*

hypercatalectic (ˌhaɪpəˌkætəˈlɛktɪk) *adj. Prosody.* (of a line of verse) having extra syllables after the last foot.

hypercharge (ˈhaɪpəˌtʃɑːdʒ) *n.* a property of baryons that is used to account for the absence of certain strong interaction decays.

hypercholesterolaemia *or U.S.* **hypercholesterolemia** (ˌhaɪpəkəˌlɛstərɒlˈiːmɪə) *n.* the condition of having high levels of cholesterol in the blood. See **hyperlipidaemia.**

hypercorrect (ˌhaɪpəkəˈrɛkt) *adj.* **1.** excessively correct or fastidious. **2.** resulting from or characterized by hypercorrection. —ˌ**hypercorˈrectness** *n.*

hypercorrection (ˌhaɪpəkəˈrɛkʃən) *n.* a mistaken correction made through a desire to avoid nonstandard pronunciation or grammar: *"Between you and I" is a frequent hypercorrection for "Between you and me".*

hypercritical (ˌhaɪpəˈkrɪtɪkᵊl) *adj.* excessively or severely critical; carping; captious. —ˌ**hyperˈcritic** *n.* —ˌ**hyperˈcritically** *adv.* —ˌ**hyperˈcritiˌcism** *n.*

hypercube (ˈhaɪpəˌkjuːb) *n. Maths.* a figure in a space of four or more dimensions having all its sides equal and all its angles right angles.

hyperdulia (ˌhaɪpədjʊˈlɪə) *n. R.C. Church.* special veneration accorded to the Virgin Mary. Compare **dulia, latria.** [C16: from Latin HYPER- + Medieval Latin *dulia* service] —ˌ**hyperˈdulic** *or* ˌ**hyperˈdulical** *adj.*

hyperemia (ˌhaɪpərˈiːmɪə) *n. Pathol.* the usual U.S. spelling of **hyperaemia.** —ˌ**hyperˈemic** *adj.*

hyperesthesia (ˌhaɪpəriːsˈθiːzɪə) *n. Pathol.* the usual U.S. spelling of **hyperaesthesia.** —ˌ**hyperesˈthetic** *adj.*

hypereutectic (ˌhaɪpəjuːˈtɛktɪk) *or* **hypereutectoid** *adj.* (of a mixture or alloy with two components) containing more of the minor component than a eutectic mixture. Compare **hypoeutectic.**

hyperextension (ˌhaɪpərɪkˈstɛnʃən) *n.* extension of an arm or leg beyond its normal limits.

hyperfine structure (ˈhaɪpəˌfaɪn) *n.* the splitting of a spectral line of an atom or molecule into two or more closely spaced components as a result of interaction of the electrons with the magnetic moments of the nuclei or with external fields. Compare **fine structure.** See also **Zeeman effect.**

hyperfocal distance (ˌhaɪpəˈfəʊkᵊl) *n.* the distance from a camera lens to the point beyond which all objects appear sharp and clearly defined.

hypergamy (haɪˈpɜːgəmɪ) *n.* **1.** *Anthropol.* a custom that forbids a woman to marry a man of lower social status. **2.** any marriage with a partner of higher social status. [C19: from HYPER- + -GAMY] —ˌ**hyperˈgamous** *adj.*

hypergeometric (ˌhaɪpədʒɪəˈmɛtrɪk) *adj.* of or relating to operations or series that transcend ordinary geometrical operations or series.

ˌ**hyperaˈcute** *adj.*
ˌ**hyperˈciviˌlized** *or*
ˌ**hyperˈciviˌlised** *adj.*
ˌ**hyperˈclassical** *adj.*
ˌ**hyperˈconfidence** *n.*
ˌ**hyperconˈformity** *n.*
ˌ**hyperˈconscious** *adj.*
ˌ**hyperconˈservative** *adj.*
ˌ**hyperˈelegance** *n.*
ˌ**hypereˈmotional** *adj.*
ˌ**hyperˌenerˈgetic** *adj.*
ˌ**hyperenˈthusiasm** *n.*
ˌ**hyperexˈcitement** *n.*
ˌ**hyperˈfunctional** *adj.*
ˌ**hyperˌintelˈlectual** *adj.*
ˌ**hyperinˈtelligence** *n.*
ˌ**hyperˈlogical** *adj.*
ˌ**hyperˈmodest** *adj.*
ˌ**hyperˈnormal** *adj.*
ˌ**hyperˈorthoˌdox** *adj.*
ˌ**hyperˈpurist** *n.*
ˌ**hyperroˈmantic** *adj.*
ˌ**hyperˌsentiˈmental** *adj.*
ˌ**hypersoˈphistiˌcated** *adj.*
ˌ**hyperˈtechnical** *adj.*
ˌ**hyperˈtoxic** *adj.*
ˌ**hyperˈvigilant** *adj.*

hyperglycaemia *or U.S.* **hyperglycemia** (ˌhaɪpəglaɪˈsiːmɪə) *n. Pathol.* an abnormally large amount of sugar in the blood. [C20: from HYPER- + GLYCO- + -AEMIA] —ˌ**hypergly'caemic** *or U.S.* ˌ**hypergly'cemic** *adj.*

hypergolic (ˌhaɪpəˈgɒlɪk) *adj.* (of a rocket fuel) able to ignite spontaneously on contact with an oxidizer. [C20: from German *Hypergol* (perhaps from HYP(ER-) + ERG + -OL²) + -IC]

hypericum (haɪˈpɛrɪkəm) *n.* any herbaceous plant or shrub of the temperate genus *Hypericum*: family *Hypericaceae*. See **rose of Sharon** (sense 1), **Saint John's wort.** [C16: via Latin from Greek *hupereikon*, from HYPER- + *ereikē* heath]

hyperinflation (ˌhaɪpərɪnˈfleɪʃən) *n.* extremely high inflation, usually over 50 per cent per month, often involving social disorder. Also called: **galloping inflation.**

hyperinsulinism (ˌhaɪpərˈɪnsjʊlɪˌnɪzəm) *n. Pathol.* an excessive amount of insulin in the blood, producing hypoglycaemia, caused by oversecretion of insulin by the pancreas or overdosage of insulin in treating diabetes. See **insulin reaction.**

hyperkeratosis (ˌhaɪpəˌkɛrəˈtəʊsɪs) *n. Pathol.* overgrowth and thickening of the outer layer of the skin. —**hyperkeratotic** (ˌhaɪpəˌkɛrəˈtɒtɪk) *adj.*

hyperkinesia (ˌhaɪpəkɪˈniːzɪə, -kaɪ-) *or* **hyperkinesis** (ˌhaɪpəkɪˈniːsɪs, -kaɪ-) *n. Pathol.* **1.** excessive movement, as in a muscle spasm. **2.** extreme overactivity in children. [C20: from HYPER- + *-kinesia* from Greek *kinēsis* movement, from *kinein* to move] —**hyperkinetic** (ˌhaɪpəkɪˈnɛtɪk, -kaɪ-) *adj.*

hyperlipidaemia *or U.S.* **hyperlipidemia** (ˌhaɪpəˌlɪpɪˈdiːmɪə) *n.* an abnormally high level of lipids, esp. cholesterol, in the blood, predisposing to atherosclerosis and other arterial diseases.

hypermania (ˌhaɪpəˈmeɪnɪə) *n. Psychol.* a condition of extreme mania.

hypermarket (ˈhaɪpəˌmɑːkɪt) *n. Brit.* a huge self-service store, usually built on the outskirts of a town. [C20: translation of French *hypermarché*]

hypermeter (haɪˈpɜːmɪtə) *n. Prosody.* a verse line containing one or more additional syllables. —**hypermetric** (ˌhaɪpəˈmɛtrɪk) *or* ˌ**hyper'metrical** *adj.*

hypermetropia (ˌhaɪpəmɪˈtrəʊpɪə) *or* **hypermetropy** (ˌhaɪpəˈmɛtrəpɪ) *n. Pathol.* variants of **hyperopia.** [C19: from Greek *hupermetros* beyond measure (from HYPER- + *metron* measure) + -OPIA] —**hypermetropic** (ˌhaɪpəmɪˈtrɒpɪk) *or* ˌ**hyperme'tropical** *adj.*

hypermnesia (ˌhaɪpəmˈniːzɪə) *n. Psychol.* an unusually good ability to remember, found in some mental disorders and possibly in hypnosis. [C20: New Latin, from HYPER- + *-mnesia*, formed on the model of AMNESIA]

hypermodern school (ˌhaɪpəˈmɒdən) *n.* a style of chess characterized by control of the centre from the flanks.

hyperon (ˈhaɪpəˌrɒn) *n. Physics.* any baryon that is not a nucleon. [C20: from HYPER- + -ON]

hyperopia (ˌhaɪpəˈrəʊpɪə) *n.* inability to see near objects clearly because the images received by the eye are focused behind the retina; long-sightedness. Also called: **hypermetropia, hypermetropy.** Compare **myopia, presbyopia.** —**hyperopic** (ˌhaɪpəˈrɒpɪk).

hyperorexia (ˌhaɪpərɒˈrɛksɪə) *n.* compulsive overeating. [C20: from HYPER- + Greek *orexis* appetite]

hyperosmia (ˌhaɪpəˈɒzmɪə) *n.* an abnormally acute sense of smell. [C20: from HYPER- + Greek *osmē* odour]

hyperostosis (ˌhaɪpərɒˈstəʊsɪs) *n., pl.* **-ses** (-siːz). *Pathol.* **1.** an abnormal proliferation of bony tissue. **2.** a bony growth arising from the root of a tooth or from the surface of a bone. —**hyperostotic** (ˌhaɪpərɒˈstɒtɪk) *adj.*

hyperparasite (ˌhaɪpəˈpærəˌsaɪt) *n.* an organism that is parasitic on another parasite.

hyperphagia (ˌhaɪpəˈfeɪdʒɪə) *n. Psychol.* compulsive overeating over a prolonged period.

hyperphysical (ˌhaɪpəˈfɪzɪkᵊl) *adj.* beyond the physical; supernatural or immaterial. —ˌ**hyper'physically** *adv.*

hyperpituitarism (ˌhaɪpəpɪˈtjuːɪtəˌrɪzəm) *n. Pathol.* overactivity of the pituitary gland, sometimes resulting in acromegaly or gigantism. —ˌ**hyperpi'tuitary** *adj.*

hyperplane (ˈhaɪpəˌpleɪn) *n. Maths.* a higher dimensional analogue of a plane in three dimensions.

hyperplasia (ˌhaɪpəˈpleɪzɪə) *n.* enlargement of a bodily organ or part resulting from an increase in the total number of cells. Compare **hypertrophy.** —**hyperplastic** (ˌhaɪpəˈplæstɪk) *adj.*

hyperploid (ˈhaɪpəˌplɔɪd) *adj. Biology.* having or relating to a chromosome number that slightly exceeds an exact multiple of the haploid number. —ˈ**hyper**ˌ**ploidy** *n.*

hyperpnoea *or U.S.* **hyperpnea** (ˌhaɪpəpˈniːə, ˌhaɪpəˈniːə) *n.* an increase in the breathing rate or in the depth of breathing, as after strenuous exercise. [C20: from New Latin, from HYPER- + Greek *pnoia* breath, from *pnein* to breathe]

hyperprosexia (ˌhaɪpəprɒˈsɛksɪə) *n. Psychol.* a condition in which the whole attention is occupied by one object or idea to the exclusion of others. [C20: from HYPER- + Greek *prosexein* to heed]

hyperpyrexia (ˌhaɪpəpaɪˈrɛksɪə) *n. Pathol.* an extremely high fever, with a temperature of 41°C (106°F) or above. Also called: **hyperthermia, hyperthermy.** —**hyperpyretic** (ˌhaɪpəpaɪˈrɛtɪk) *or* ˌ**hyperpy'rexial** *adj.*

hypersensitive (ˌhaɪpəˈsɛnsɪtɪv) *adj.* **1.** having unduly vulnerable feelings. **2.** abnormally sensitive to an allergen, a drug, or other agent. —ˌ**hyper'sensitiveness** *or* ˌ**hyper**ˌ**sensi'tivity** *n.*

hypersensitize *or* **hypersensitise** (ˌhaɪpəˈsɛnsɪˌtaɪz) *vb.* (*tr.*) to treat (a photographic emulsion), usually after manufacture and shortly before exposure, to increase its speed. —ˌ**hyper**ˌ**sensiti'zation** *or* ˌ**hyper**ˌ**sensiti'sation** *n.*

hypersonic (ˌhaɪpəˈsɒnɪk) *adj.* concerned with or having a velocity of at least five times that of sound in the same medium under the same conditions. —ˌ**hyper'sonics** *n.*

hyperspace (ˌhaɪpəˈspeɪs) *n.* **1.** *Maths.* space having more than three dimensions: often used to describe a multi-dimensional environment. **2.** (in science fiction) a theoretical dimension within which conventional space-time relationship does not apply. —**hyperspatial** (ˌhaɪpəˈspeɪʃəl) *adj.*

hypersthene (ˈhaɪpəˌsθiːn) *n.* a green, brown, or black pyroxene mineral consisting of magnesium iron silicate in orthorhombic crystalline form. Formula: $(Mg,Fe)_2Si_2O_6$. [C19: from HYPER- + Greek *sthenos* strength] —**hypersthenic** (ˌhaɪpəˈsθɛnɪk) *adj.*

hypertension (ˌhaɪpəˈtɛnʃən) *n. Pathol.* abnormally high blood pressure. —**hypertensive** (ˌhaɪpəˈtɛnsɪv) *adj., n.*

hypertext (ˈhaɪpəˌtɛkst) *n.* computer software and hardware that allows users to store characters, images, and sound together and move between related items easily.

hyperthermia (ˌhaɪpəˈθɜːmɪə) *or* **hyperthermy** (ˌhaɪpəˈθɜːmɪ) *n. Pathol.* variants of **hyperpyrexia.** —ˌ**hyper'thermal** *adj.*

hyperthymia (ˌhaɪpəˈθaɪmɪə) *n.* excessive emotionalism. [C20: from HYPER- + Greek *thymos* spirit]

hyperthyroidism (ˌhaɪpəˈθaɪrɔɪˌdɪzəm) *n.* overproduction of thyroid hormone by the thyroid gland, causing nervousness, insomnia, sweating, palpitation, and sensitivity to heat. Also called: **thyrotoxicosis.** See **exophthalmic goitre.** —ˌ**hyper'thyroid** *adj., n.*

hypertonic (ˌhaɪpəˈtɒnɪk) *adj.* **1.** (esp. of muscles) being in a state of abnormally high tension. **2.** (of a solution) having a higher osmotic pressure than that of a specified, generally physiological, solution. Compare **hypotonic, isotonic.** —**hypertonicity** (ˌhaɪpətəʊˈnɪsɪtɪ) *n.*

hypertrophy (haɪˈpɜːtrəfɪ) *n., pl.* **-phies. 1.** enlargement of an organ or part resulting from an increase in the size of the cells. Compare **atrophy, hyperplasia.** ~*vb.* **-phies, -phying, -phied. 2.** to undergo or cause to undergo this condition. —**hypertrophic** (ˌhaɪpəˈtrɒfɪk) *adj.*

hyperventilation (ˌhaɪpəˌvɛntɪˈleɪʃən) *n.* an increase in the depth, duration, and rate of breathing, sometimes resulting in cramp and dizziness.

hypervitaminosis (ˌhaɪpəˌvɪtəmɪˈnəʊsɪs, -ˌvaɪ-) *n. Pathol.* the condition resulting from the chronic excessive intake of vitamins. [C20: from HYPER- + VITAMIN + -OSIS]

hypesthesia (ˌhɪpiːsˈθiːzɪə, ˌhaɪ-) *n.* the usual U.S. spelling of **hypaesthesia.** —**hypesthesic** (ˌhɪpiːsˈθiːsɪk, ˌhaɪ-) *adj.*

hypethral (hɪˈpiːθrəl, haɪ-) *adj.* the usual U.S. spelling of **hypaethral.**

hypha (ˈhaɪfə) *n., pl.* **-phae** (-fiː). any of the filaments that constitute the body (mycelium) of a fungus. [C19: from New Latin, from Greek *huphē* web] —ˈ**hyphal** *adj.*

hyphen (ˈhaɪfᵊn) *n.* **1.** the punctuation mark (-), used to separate the parts of some compound words, to link the words of a phrase, and between syllables of a word split between two consecutive lines of writing or printing. ~*vb.* **2.** (*tr.*) another word for **hyphenate.** [C17: from Late Latin (meaning: the combining of two words), from Greek *huphen* (adv.) together, from HYPO- + *heis* one]

hyphenate (ˈhaɪfᵊˌneɪt) *or* **hyphen** *vb.* (*tr.*) to separate (syllables, words, etc.) with a hyphen. —ˌ**hyphen'ation** *n.*

hyphenated (ˈhaɪfᵊˌneɪtɪd) *adj.* **1.** containing or linked with a hyphen. **2.** *Chiefly U.S.* having a nationality denoted by a hyphenated word: *American-Irish.*

hyphen help *n.* a word processing function that assists the operator to identify automatically those words that can be hyphenated at the end of a line of text.

hypnagogic *or* **hypnogogic** (ˌhɪpnəˈgɒdʒɪk) *adj. Psychol.* of or relating to the state just before one is fully asleep. See also **hypnagogic image, hypnopompic.** [C19: from French *hypnagogique*; see HYPNO-, -AGOGIC]

hypnagogic image *n. Psychol.* an image experienced by a person just before falling asleep, which often resembles a hallucination.

hypno- *or before a vowel* **hypn-** *combining form.* **1.** indicating sleep: *hypnophobia.* **2.** relating to hypnosis: *hypnotherapy.* [from Greek *hupnos* sleep]

hypnoanalysis (ˌhɪpnəʊəˈnælɪsɪs) *n. Psychol.* psychoanalysis conducted on a hypnotized person. —**hypnoanalytic** (ˌhɪpnəʊˌænəˈlɪtɪk) *adj.*

hypnogenesis (ˌhɪpnəʊˈdʒɛnɪsɪs) *n. Psychol.* the induction of sleep or hypnosis. —**hypnogenetic** (ˌhɪpnəʊdʒɪˈnɛtɪk) *adj.* —ˌ**hypnoge'netically** *adv.*

hypnoid (ˈhɪpˌnɔɪd) *or* **hypnoidal** (hɪpˈnɔɪdᵊl) *adj. Psychol.* of or relating to a state resembling sleep or hypnosis.

hypnology (hɪpˈnɒlədʒɪ) *n. Psychol.* the study of sleep and hypnosis. —**hypnologic** (ˌhɪpnəˈlɒdʒɪk) *or* ˌ**hypno'logical** *adj.* —**hyp'nologist** *n.*

hypnopaedia (ˌhɪpnəʊˈpiːdɪə) *n.* the learning of lessons heard during sleep. [C20: from HYPNO- + Greek *paideia* education]

hypnopompic (ˌhɪpnəʊˈpɒmpɪk) *adj. Psychol.* relating to the state existing between sleep and full waking, characterized by the persistence of dreamlike imagery. See also **hypnagogic.** [C20: from HYPNO- + Greek *pompē* a sending forth, escort + -IC; see POMP]

hypnosis (hɪpˈnəʊsɪs) *n., pl.* **-ses** (-siːz). an artificially induced state of relaxation and concentration in which deeper parts of the mind become more accessible: used clinically to reduce reaction to pain, to encourage free association, etc. See also **autohypnosis.**

hypnotherapy (ˌhɪpnəʊˈθɛrəpɪ) *n.* the use of hypnosis in the treatment of emotional and psychogenic problems.

hypnotic (hɪpˈnɒtɪk) *adj.* **1.** of, relating to, or producing hypnosis or sleep. **2.** (of a person) susceptible to hypnotism. ~*n.* **3.** a drug or agent that induces sleep. **4.** a person susceptible to hypnosis. [C17: from Late Latin *hypnōticus*, from Greek *hupnōtikos*, from *hupnoun* to put to sleep, from *hupnos* sleep] —**hypˈnotically** *adv.*

hypnotism (ˈhɪpnəˌtɪzəm) *n.* **1.** the scientific study and practice of hypnosis. **2.** the process of inducing hypnosis.

hypnotist (ˈhɪpnətɪst) *n.* a person skilled in the theory and practice of hypnosis.

hypnotize *or* **hypnotise** (ˈhɪpnəˌtaɪz) *vb. (tr.)* **1.** to induce hypnosis in (a person). **2.** to charm or beguile; fascinate. —ˈ**hypnoˌtizable** *or* ˈ**hypnoˌtisable** *adj.* —ˌ**hypnoˌtizaˈbility** *or* ˌ**hypnoˌtisaˈbility** *n.* —ˌ**hypnotiˈzation** *or* ˌ**hypnotiˈsation** *n.* —ˈ**hypnoˌtizer** *or* ˈ**hypnoˌtiser** *n.*

hypo[1] (ˈhaɪpəʊ) *n.* another name for **sodium thiosulphate,** esp. when used as a fixer in photographic developing. [C19: shortened from HYPOSULPHITE]

hypo[2] (ˈhaɪpəʊ) *n., pl.* **-pos.** *Informal.* short for **hypodermic syringe.**

hypo- *or before a vowel* **hyp-** *prefix.* **1.** under, beneath, or below: *hypodermic.* **2.** lower; at a lower point: *hypogastrium.* **3.** less than: *hypoploid.* **4.** (in medicine) denoting a deficiency or an abnormally low level: *hypothyroid.* **5.** incomplete or partial: *hypoplasia.* **6.** indicating that a chemical compound contains an element in a lower oxidation state than usual: *hypochlorous acid.* [from Greek, from *hupo* under]

Hypo- *prefix.* indicating a plagal mode in music: *Hypodorian.* [from Greek: beneath (it lies a fourth below the corresponding authentic mode)]

hypoacidity (ˌhaɪpəʊəˈsɪdɪtɪ) *n. Med.* abnormally low acidity, as of the contents of the stomach.

hypoallergenic (ˈhaɪpəʊˌæləˈdʒɛnɪk) *adj.* (of cosmetics, earrings, etc.) not likely to cause an allergic reaction.

hypoblast (ˈhaɪpəˌblæst) *n.* **1.** Also called: **endoblast.** *Embryol.* the inner layer of an embryo at an early stage of development that becomes the endoderm at gastrulation. **2.** a less common name for **endoderm.** —ˌ**hypoˈblastic** *adj.*

hypocaust (ˈhaɪpəˌkɔːst) *n.* an ancient Roman heating system in which hot air circulated under the floor and between double walls. [C17: from Latin *hypocaustum*, from Greek *hupokauston* room heated from below, from *hupokaiein* to light a fire beneath, from HYPO- + *kaiein* to burn]

hypocentre (ˈhaɪpəʊˌsɛntə) *n.* **1.** Also called: **ground zero.** the point on the ground immediately below the centre of explosion of a nuclear bomb in the atmosphere. **2.** another term for **focus** (sense 6).

hypochlorite (ˌhaɪpəˈklɔːraɪt) *n.* any salt or ester of hypochlorous acid.

hypochlorous acid (ˌhaɪpəˈklɔːrəs) *n.* an unstable acid known only in solution and in the form of its salts, formed when chlorine dissolves in water: a strong oxidizing and bleaching agent. Formula: HOCl.

hypochondria (ˌhaɪpəˈkɒndrɪə) *n.* chronic abnormal anxiety concerning the state of one's health, even in the absence of any evidence of disease on medical examination. Also called: **hypochondriasis** (ˌhaɪpəʊkɒnˈdraɪəsɪs). [C18: from Late Latin: the abdomen, supposedly the seat of melancholy, from Greek *hupokhondria*, from *hupokhondrios* of the upper abdomen, from HYPO- + *khondros* cartilage]

hypochondriac (ˌhaɪpəˈkɒndrɪˌæk) *n.* **1.** a person suffering from hypochondria. ~*adj. also* **hypochondriacal** (ˌhaɪpəkɒnˈdraɪəkəl). **2.** relating to or suffering from hypochondria. **3.** *Anatomy.* of or relating to the hypochondrium. —ˌ**hypochonˈdriacally** *adv.*

hypochondrium (ˌhaɪpəˈkɒndrɪəm) *n., pl.* **-dria** (-drɪə). *Anatomy.* the upper region of the abdomen on each side of the epigastrium, just below the lowest ribs. [C17: from New Latin, from Greek *hupokhondrion*; see HYPOCHONDRIA]

hypocorism (haɪˈpɒkəˌrɪzəm) *n.* **1.** a pet name, esp. one using a diminutive affix: *"Sally" is a hypocorism for "Sarah".* **2.** another word for **euphemism** (sense 1). [C19: from Greek *hupokorisma*, from *hupokorizesthai* to use pet names, from *hypo-* beneath + *korizesthai*, from *korē* girl, *koros* boy] —**hypocoristic** (ˌhaɪpəkɔːˈrɪstɪk) *adj.* —ˌ**hypocoˈristically** *adv.*

hypocotyl (ˌhaɪpəˈkɒtɪl) *n.* the part of an embryo plant between the cotyledons and the radicle. [C19: from HYPO- + COTYL(EDON)] —ˌ**hypoˈcotylous** *adj.*

hypocrisy (hɪˈpɒkrəsɪ) *n., pl.* **-sies.** **1.** the practice of professing standards, beliefs, etc., contrary to one's real character or actual behaviour, esp. the pretence of virtue and piety. **2.** an act or instance of this.

hypocrite (ˈhɪpəkrɪt) *n.* a person who pretends to be what he is not. [C13: from Old French *ipocrite*, via Late Latin, from Greek *hupokritēs* one who plays a part, from *hupokrinein* to feign, from *krinein* to judge] —ˌ**hypoˈcritical** *adj.* —ˌ**hypoˈcritically** *adv.*

hypocrystalline (ˌhaɪpəʊˈkrɪstəˌlaɪn) *adj.* another word for **hemicrystalline.**

hypocycloid (ˌhaɪpəˈsaɪklɔɪd) *n.* a curve described by a point on the circumference of a circle as the circle rolls around the inside of a fixed coplanar circle. Compare **epicycloid, cycloid** (sense 4). —ˌ**hypocyˈcloidal** *adj.*

hypoderm (ˈhaɪpəˌdɜːm) *n.* a variant of **hypodermis.** —ˌ**hypoˈdermal** *adj.*

hypodermic (ˌhaɪpəˈdɜːmɪk) *adj.* **1.** of or relating to the region of the skin beneath the epidermis. **2.** injected beneath the skin. ~*n.* **3.** a hypodermic syringe or needle. **4.** a hypodermic injection. —ˌ**hypoˈdermically** *adv.*

hypodermic syringe *n. Med.* a type of syringe consisting of a hollow cylinder, usually of glass or plastic, a tightly fitting piston, and a hollow needle (**hypodermic needle**), used for withdrawing blood samples, injecting medicine, etc.

hypodermis (ˌhaɪpəˈdɜːmɪs) *or* **hypoderm** *n.* **1.** *Botany.* a layer of thick-walled supportive or water-storing cells beneath the epidermis in some plants. **2.** *Zoology.* the epidermis of arthropods, annelids, etc., which secretes and is covered by a cuticle. [C19: from HYPO- + EPIDERMIS]

Hypodorian (ˌhaɪpəˈdɔːrɪən) *adj. Music.* denoting a plagal mode represented by the ascending diatonic scale from A to A. Compare **Dorian** (sense 3). See **Hypo-.**

hypoeutectic (ˌhaɪpəʊjuːˈtɛktɪk) *or* **hypoeutectoid** *adj.* (of a mixture or alloy with two components) containing less of the minor component than a eutectic mixture. Compare **hypereutectic.**

hypogastrium (ˌhaɪpəˈgæstrɪəm) *n., pl.* **-tria** (-trɪə). *Anatomy.* the lower front central region of the abdomen, below the navel. [C17: from New Latin, from Greek *hupogastrion*, from HYPO- + *gastrion*, diminutive of *gastēr* stomach] —ˌ**hypoˈgastric** *adj.*

hypogeal (ˌhaɪpəˈdʒiːəl) *or* **hypogeous** *adj.* **1.** occurring or living below the surface of the ground. **2.** *Botany.* of or relating to seed germination in which the cotyledons remain below the ground, because of the growth of the epicotyl. [C19: from Latin *hypogēus*, from Greek *hupogeios*, from HYPO- + *gē* earth]

hypogene (ˈhaɪpəˌdʒiːn) *adj.* formed, taking place, or originating beneath the surface of the earth. Compare **epigene.** —**hypogenic** (ˌhaɪpəˈdʒɛnɪk) *adj.*

hypogenous (haɪˈpɒdʒɪnəs) *adj. Botany.* produced or growing on the undersurface, esp. (of fern spores) growing on the undersurface of the leaves.

hypogeous (ˌhaɪpəˈdʒiːəs) *adj.* another word for **hypogeal.**

hypogeum (ˌhaɪpəˈdʒiːəm) *n., pl.* **-gea** (-ˈdʒiːə). an underground vault, esp. one used for burials. [C18: from Latin, from Greek *hupogeion*; see HYPOGEAL]

hypoglossal (ˌhaɪpəˈglɒsəl) *adj.* **1.** situated beneath the tongue. ~*n.* **2.** short for **hypoglossal nerve.**

hypoglossal nerve *n.* the twelfth cranial nerve, which supplies the muscles of the tongue.

hypoglycaemia *or U.S.* **hypoglycemia** (ˌhaɪpəʊglaɪˈsiːmɪə) *n. Pathol.* an abnormally small amount of sugar in the blood. [C20: from HYPO- + GLYCO- + -AEMIA] —ˌ**hypoglyˈcaemic** *or U.S.* ˌ**hypoglyˈcemic** *adj.*

hypognathous (haɪˈpɒgnəθəs) *adj.* **1.** having a lower jaw that protrudes beyond the upper jaw. **2.** (of insects) having downturned mouthparts. —**hyˈpognathism** *n.*

hypogynous (haɪˈpɒdʒɪnəs) *adj.* **1.** (of a flower) having the gynoecium situated above the other floral parts, as in the buttercup. **2.** of or relating to the parts of a flower arranged in this way. —**hyˈpogyny** *n.*

hypoid gear (ˈhaɪpɔɪd) *n.* a gear having a tooth form generated by a hypocycloidal curve; used extensively in motor vehicle transmissions to withstand a high surface loading. [C20: *hypoid*, shortened from HYPOCYCLOID]

hypolimnion (ˌhaɪpəʊˈlɪmnɪən) *n.* the lower and colder layer of water in a lake. [C20: from HYPO- + Greek *limnion*, diminutive of *limnē* lake]

Hypolydian (ˌhaɪpəˈlɪdɪən) *adj. Music.* denoting a plagal mode represented by the diatonic scale from D to D. Compare **Lydian** (sense 2). See **Hypo-.**

hypomania (ˌhaɪpəʊˈmeɪnɪə) *n. Psychiatry.* an abnormal condition of extreme excitement, milder than mania but characterized by great optimism and overactivity and often by reckless spending of money. —**hypomanic** (ˌhaɪpəʊˈmænɪk) *adj.*

hyponasty (ˈhaɪpəˌnæstɪ) *n.* increased growth of the lower surface of a plant part, resulting in an upward bending of the part. Compare **epinasty.** —ˌ**hypoˈnastic** *adj.* —ˌ**hypoˈnastically** *adv.*

hyponitrite (ˌhaɪpəˈnaɪtraɪt) *n.* any salt or ester of hyponitrous acid.

hyponitrous acid (ˌhaɪpəˈnaɪtrəs) *n.* a white soluble unstable crystalline acid: an oxidizing and reducing agent. Formula: $H_2N_2O_2$.

hyponym ('haɪpəʊnɪm) *n.* a word whose meaning is included in that of another word: *'scarlet', 'vermilion', and 'crimson' are hyponyms of 'red'.* Compare **superordinate** (sense 3), **synonym, antonym.** [C20: from HYPO- + Greek *onoma* name] —**hyponymy** (haɪ'pɒnəmɪ) *n.*

hypophosphate (ˌhaɪpə'fɒsfeɪt) *n.* any salt or ester of hypophosphoric acid.

hypophosphite (ˌhaɪpə'fɒsfaɪt) *n.* any salt of hypophosphorous acid.

hypophosphoric acid (ˌhaɪpəfɒs'fɒrɪk) *n.* a crystalline odourless deliquescent solid: a tetrabasic acid produced by the slow oxidation of phosphorus in moist air. Formula: $H_4P_2O_6$.

hypophosphorous acid (ˌhaɪpə'fɒsfərəs) *n.* a colourless or yellowish oily liquid or white deliquescent solid: a monobasic acid and a reducing agent. Formula: H_3PO_2.

hypophyge (haɪ'pɒfɪdʒɪ) *n. Architect.* another name for **apophyge.**

hypophysis (haɪ'pɒfɪsɪs) *n., pl.* **-ses** (-ˌsiːz). the technical name for **pituitary gland.** [C18: from Greek: outgrowth, from HYPO- + *phuein* to grow] —**hypophyseal** *or* **hypophysial** (ˌhaɪpə'fɪzɪəl, haɪˌpɒfɪ'sɪəl) *adj.*

hypopituitarism (ˌhaɪpəpɪ'tjuːɪtəˌrɪzəm) *n. Pathol.* underactivity of the pituitary gland. —ˌ**hypopi'tuitary** *adj.*

hypoplasia (ˌhaɪpəʊ'plæzɪə) *or* **hypoplasty** ('haɪpəʊˌplæstɪ) *n. Pathol.* incomplete development of an organ or part. —**hypoplastic** (ˌhaɪpəʊ'plæstɪk) *adj.*

hypoploid ('haɪpəˌplɔɪd) *adj.* having or designating a chromosome number that is slightly less than a multiple of the haploid number. —'**hypoˌploidy** *n.*

hypopnoea *or U.S.* **hypopnea** (haɪ'pɒpnɪə, ˌhaɪpə'niːə) *n. Pathol.* abnormally shallow breathing, usually accompanied by a decrease in the breathing rate. [C20: New Latin, from HYPO- + Greek *pnoia* breath, from *pnein* to breathe]

hyposensitize *or* **hyposensitise** (ˌhaɪpəʊ'sɛnsɪˌtaɪz) *vb. (tr.)* to desensitize; render less sensitive. —ˌ**hypoˌsensiti'zation** *or* ˌ**hypoˌsensiti'sation** *n.*

hypostasis (haɪ'pɒstəsɪs) *n., pl.* **-ses** (-ˌsiːz). **1.** *Metaphysics.* the essential nature of a substance as opposed to its attributes. **2.** *Christianity.* **a.** any of the three persons of the Godhead, together constituting the Trinity. **b.** the one person of Christ in which the divine and human natures are united. **3.** the accumulation of blood in an organ or part as the result of poor circulation. **4.** another name for **epistasis** (sense 3). [C16: from Late Latin: substance, from Greek *hupostasis* foundation, from *huphistasthai* to stand under, from HYPO- + *histanai* to cause to stand] —**hypostatic** (ˌhaɪpə'stætɪk) *or* ˌ**hypo'statical** *adj.* —ˌ**hypo'statically** *adv.*

hypostasize *or* **hypostasise** (haɪ'pɒstəˌsaɪz) *vb.* another word for **hypostatize.** —**hyˌpostasi'zation** *or* **hyˌpostasi'sation** *n.*

hypostatize *or* **hypostatise** (haɪ'pɒstəˌtaɪz) *vb. (tr.)* **1.** to regard or treat as real. **2.** to embody or personify. —**hyˌpostati'zation** *or* **hyˌpostati'sation** *n.*

hyposthenia (ˌhaɪpɒs'θiːnɪə) *n. Pathol.* a weakened condition; lack of strength. [C19: from HYPO- + Greek *sthenos* strength] —**hyposthenic** (ˌhaɪpɒs'θɛnɪk) *adj.*

hypostyle ('haɪpəʊˌstaɪl) *adj.* **1.** having a roof supported by columns. ~*n.* **2.** a building constructed in this way.

hyposulphite (ˌhaɪpə'sʌlfaɪt) *n.* **1.** another name for **sodium thiosulphate,** esp. when used as a photographic fixer. Often shortened to **hypo. 2.** another name for **dithionite.**

hyposulphurous acid (ˌhaɪpə'sʌlfərəs) *n.* another name for **dithionous acid.**

hypotaxis (ˌhaɪpəʊ'tæksɪs) *n. Grammar.* the subordination of one clause to another by a conjunction. Compare **parataxis.** —**hypotactic** (ˌhaɪpəʊ'tæktɪk) *adj.*

hypotension (ˌhaɪpəʊ'tɛnʃən) *n. Pathol.* abnormally low blood pressure. —**hypotensive** (ˌhaɪpəʊ'tɛnsɪv) *adj.*

hypotenuse (haɪ'pɒtɪˌnjuːz) *n.* the side in a right-angled triangle that is opposite the right angle. Abbrev.: **hyp.** [C16: from Latin *hypotēnūsa,* from Greek *hupoteinousa grammē* subtending line, from *hupoteinein* to subtend, from HYPO- + *teinein* to stretch]

hypoth. *abbrev. for:* **1.** hypothesis. **2.** hypothetical.

hypothalamus (ˌhaɪpə'θæləməs) *n., pl.* **-mi** (-ˌmaɪ). a neural control centre at the base of the brain, concerned with hunger, thirst, satiety, and other autonomic functions. —**hypothalamic** (ˌhaɪpəθə'læmɪk) *adj.*

hypothec (haɪ'pɒθɪk) *n. Roman and Scots law.* a charge on property in favour of a creditor. [C16: from Late Latin *hypotheca* a security, from Greek *hupothēkē* deposit, pledge, from *hupotithenai* to deposit as a security, place under, from HYPO- + *tithenai* to place]

hypotheca (ˌhaɪpəʊ'θiːkə) *n., pl.* **-cae** (-siː). the inner and younger layer of the cell wall of a diatom. Compare **epitheca.** [from HYPO- + THECA]

hypothecate (haɪ'pɒθɪˌkeɪt) *vb. (tr.) Law.* to pledge (personal property or a ship) as security for a debt without transferring possession or title. See also **bottomry.** —**hyˌpothe'cation** *n.* —**hy'potheˌcator** *n.*

hypothermal (ˌhaɪpəʊ'θɜːməl) *adj.* **1.** of, relating to, or characterized by hypothermia. **2.** (of rocks and minerals) formed at great depth under conditions of high temperature.

hypothermia (ˌhaɪpəʊ'θɜːmɪə) *n.* **1.** *Pathol.* an abnormally low body temperature, as induced in the elderly by exposure to cold weather. **2.** *Med.* the intentional reduction of normal body temperature, as by ice packs, to reduce the patient's metabolic rate: performed esp. in heart and brain surgery.

hypothesis (haɪ'pɒθɪsɪs) *n., pl.* **-ses** (-ˌsiːz). **1.** a suggested explanation for a group of facts or phenomena, either accepted as a basis for further verification (**working hypothesis**) or accepted as likely to be true. Compare **theory** (sense 5). **2.** an assumption used in an argument without it being endorsed; a supposition. **3.** an unproved theory; a conjecture. [C16: from Greek, from *hupotithenai* to propose, suppose, literally: put under; see HYPO-, THESIS] —**hy'pothesist** *n.*

hypothesis testing *n. Statistics.* the theory, methods, and practice of testing a hypothesis concerning the parameters of a population distribution (the **null hypothesis**) against another (the **alternative hypothesis**) which will be accepted only if its probability exceeds a predetermined significance level, generally on the basis of statistics derived from random sampling from the given population. Compare **statistical inference.**

hypothesize *or* **hypothesise** (haɪ'pɒθɪˌsaɪz) *vb.* to form or assume as a hypothesis. —**hy'potheˌsizer** *or* **hy'potheˌsiser** *n.*

hypothetical (ˌhaɪpə'θɛtɪkᵊl) *or* **hypothetic** *adj.* **1.** having the nature of a hypothesis. **2.** assumed or thought to exist. **3.** *Logic.* another word for **conditional** (sense 4). **4.** existing only as an idea or concept: *a time machine is a hypothetical device.* —ˌ**hypo'thetically** *adv.*

hypothetical imperative *n.* (esp. in Kantian philosophy) any conditional rule of action, concerned with means and ends rather than with duty for its own sake. Compare **categorical imperative.**

hypothetico-deductive (ˌhaɪpəˈθɛtɪkəʊdɪ'dʌktɪv) *adj.* pertaining to or governed by the supposed method of scientific progress whereby a general hypothesis is tested by deducing predictions that may be experimentally tested. When such a prediction is falsified the theory is rejected and a new hypothesis is required.

hypothymia (haɪpə'θaɪmɪə) **1.** a state of depression. **2.** a diminished emotional response. [C20: from HYPO- + Greek *thymos* spirit]

hypothyroidism (ˌhaɪpəʊ'θaɪrɔɪˌdɪzəm) *n. Pathol.* **1.** insufficient production of thyroid hormones by the thyroid gland. **2.** any disorder, such as cretinism or myxoedema, resulting from this. —ˌ**hypo'thyroid** *n., adj.*

hypotonic (ˌhaɪpə'tɒnɪk) *adj.* **1.** *Pathol.* (of muscles) lacking normal tone or tension. **2.** (of a solution) having a lower osmotic pressure than that of a specified, generally physiological, solution. Compare **hypertonic, isotonic.** —**hypotonicity** (ˌhaɪpətə'nɪsɪtɪ) *n.*

hypoxanthine (ˌhaɪpə'zænθiːn, -θɪn) *n.* a white or colourless crystalline compound that is a breakdown product of nucleoproteins. Formula: $C_5H_4N_4O$.

hypoxia (haɪ'pɒksɪə) *n.* deficiency in the amount of oxygen delivered to the body tissues. [C20: from HYPO- + OXY- + -IA] —**hypoxic** (haɪ'pɒksɪk) *adj.*

hypso- *or before a vowel* **hyps-** *combining form.* indicating height: *hypsometry.* [from Greek *hupsos*]

hypsochromic (ˌhɪpsə'krəʊmɪk) *adj. Chem.* denoting or relating to a shift to a shorter wavelength in the absorption spectrum of a compound. —'**hypsoˌchrome** *n.*

hypsography (hɪp'sɒgrəfɪ) *n.* **1.** the scientific study and mapping of the earth's topography above sea level. **2.** topography or relief, or a map showing this. **3.** another name for **hypsometry.** —**hypsographic** (ˌhɪpsə'græfɪk) *or* ˌ**hypso'graphical** *adj.*

hypsometer (hɪp'sɒmɪtə) *n.* **1.** an instrument for measuring altitudes by determining the boiling point of water at a given altitude. **2.** any instrument used to calculate the heights of trees by triangulation.

hypsometry (hɪp'sɒmɪtrɪ) *n.* (in mapping) the establishment of height above sea level. Also called: **hypsography.** —**hypsometric** (ˌhɪpsə'mɛtrɪk) *or* ˌ**hypso'metrical** *adj.* —ˌ**hypso'metrically** *adv.* —**hyp'sometrist** *n.*

hyracoid ('haɪrəˌkɔɪd) *adj.* **1.** of, relating to, or belonging to the mammalian order *Hyracoidea,* which contains the hyraxes. ~*n.* **2.** a hyrax. —ˌ**hyra'coidean** *adj., n.*

hyrax ('haɪræks) *n., pl.* **hyraxes** *or* **hyraces** ('haɪrəˌsiːz). any agile herbivorous mammal of the family *Procaviidae* and order *Hyracoidea,* of Africa and SW Asia, such as *Procavia capensis* (**rock hyrax**). They resemble rodents but have feet with hooflike toes. Also called: **dassie.** [C19: from New Latin, from Greek *hurax* shrewmouse; probably related to Latin *sōrex*]

hyson ('haɪsᵊn) *n.* a Chinese green tea, the early crop of which is known as **young hyson** and the inferior leaves as **hyson skin.** [C18: from Chinese (Cantonese) *hei-ch'un* bright spring]

hyssop ('hɪsəp) *n.* **1.** a widely cultivated Asian plant, *Hyssopus officinalis,* with spikes of small blue flowers and aromatic leaves, used as a condiment and in perfumery and folk medicine: family *Labiatae* (labiates). **2.** any of several similar or related plants such as the hedge hyssop. **3.** a Biblical plant, used for sprinkling in the ritual practices of the Hebrews. [Old English *ysope,* from Latin *hyssōpus,* from Greek *hussōpos,* of Semitic origin; compare Hebrew *ēzōv*]

hysterectomize *or* **hysterectomise** (ˌhɪstə'rɛktəˌmaɪz) *vb. (tr.)* to perform a hysterectomy on (someone).

hysterectomy (ˌhɪstə'rɛktəmɪ) *n., pl.* **-mies.** surgical removal of the uterus.

hysteresis (ˌhɪstəˈriːsɪs) *n. Physics.* the lag in a variable property of a system with respect to the effect producing it as this effect varies, esp. the phenomenon in which the magnetic induction of a ferromagnetic material lags behind the changing external field. [C19: from Greek *husterēsis* coming late, from *husteros* coming after] —**hysteretic** (ˌhɪstəˈrɛtɪk) *adj.* —ˌ**hysterˈetically** *adv.*

hysteresis loop *n.* a closed curve showing the variation of the magnetic induction of a ferromagnetic material with the external magnetic field producing it, when this field is changed through a complete cycle.

hysteria (hɪˈstɪərɪə) *n.* **1.** a mental disorder characterized by emotional outbursts, susceptibility to autosuggestion, and, often, symptoms such as paralysis that mimic the effects of physical disorders. ~See also **conversion hysteria.** **2.** any frenzied emotional state, esp. of laughter or crying. [C19: from New Latin, from Latin *hystericus* HYSTERIC]

hysteric (hɪˈstɛrɪk) *n.* **1.** a hysterical person. ~*adj.* **2.** hysterical. ~See also **hysterics.** [C17: from Latin *hystericus* literally: of the womb, from Greek *husterikos,* from *hustera* the womb; from the belief that hysteria in women originated in disorders of the womb]

hysterical (hɪˈstɛrɪkᵊl) *or* **hysteric** *adj.* **1.** of or suggesting hysteria: *hysterical cries.* **2.** suffering from hysteria. **3.** *Informal.* wildly funny. —**hysˈterically** *adv.*

hysterics (hɪˈstɛrɪks) *n.* (*functioning as pl. or sing.*) **1.** an attack of hysteria. **2.** *Informal.* wild uncontrollable bursts of laughter.

hystero- *or before a vowel* **hyster-** *combining form.* **1.** indicating the uterus: *hysterotomy.* **2.** hysteria: *hysterogenic.* [from Greek *hustera* womb]

hysterogenic (ˌhɪstərəˈdʒɛnɪk) *adj.* inducing hysteria. [C20: from HYSTERIA + -GENIC] —**hysterogeny** (ˌhɪstəˈrɒdʒənɪ) *n.*

hysteroid (ˈhɪstəˌrɔɪd) *or* **hysteroidal** *adj.* resembling hysteria.

hysteron proteron (ˈhɪstəˌrɒn ˈprɒtəˌrɒn) *n.* **1.** *Logic.* a fallacious argument in which the proposition to be proved is assumed as a premise. **2.** *Rhetoric.* a figure of speech in which the normal order of two sentences, clauses, etc., is reversed: *bred and born* (*for born and bred*). [C16: from Late Latin, from Greek *husteron proteron* the latter (placed as) former]

hysterotomy (ˌhɪstəˈrɒtəmɪ) *n., pl.* **-mies.** surgical incision into the uterus.

hystricomorph (hɪˈstraɪkəʊˌmɔːf) *n.* **1.** any rodent of the suborder *Hystricomorpha,* which includes porcupines, cavies, agoutis, and chinchillas. ~*adj. also* **hystricomorphic** (hɪˌstraɪkəʊˈmɔːfɪk). **2.** of, relating to, or belonging to the *Hystricomorpha.* [C19: from Latin *hystrix* porcupine, from Greek *hustrix*]

Hz *Symbol for* hertz.

I

i *or* **I** (aɪ) *n., pl.* **i's, I's,** *or* **Is.** **1.** the ninth letter and third vowel of the modern English alphabet. **2.** any of several speech sounds represented by this letter, in English as in *bite* or *hit*. **3. a.** something shaped like an I. **b.** (*in combination*): *an I-beam.* **4. dot one's i's and cross one's t's.** to pay meticulous attention to detail.

i *symbol for* the imaginary number √-1.

I[1] (aɪ) *pron.* (*subjective*) refers to the speaker or writer. [C12: reduced form of Old English *ic;* compare Old Saxon *ik,* Old High German *ih,* Sanskrit *ahám*]

I[2] symbol for: **1.** *Chem.* iodine. **2.** *Physics.* current. **3.** *Physics.* isospin. **4.** *Logic.* a particular affirmative categorial statement, such as *some men are married,* often symbolized as **SiP.** Compare **A, E, O.** [from Latin *(aff)i(rmo)* I affirm] ~ **5.** *the Roman numeral for* one. See **Roman numerals.** ~ **6.** *international car registration for* Italy.

i. *abbrev. for:* **1.** *Grammar.* intransitive. **2.** *Dentistry.* incisor. **3.** *Banking.* interest.

I. *abbrev. for:* **1.** Independence. **2.** Independent. **3.** Institute. **4.** International. **5.** Island *or* Isle.

-i *suffix forming adjectives.* of or relating to a region or people, esp. of the Middle East: *Iraqi; Bangladeshi.* [from an adjectival suffix in Semitic and in Indo-Iranian languages]

-i- *connective vowel.* used between elements in a compound word: *cuneiform, coniferous.* Compare **-o-.** [from Latin, stem vowel of nouns and adjectives in combination]

Ia. *or* **IA** *abbrev. for* Iowa.

-ia *suffix forming nouns.* **1.** occurring in place names: *Albania; Columbia.* **2.** occurring in names of diseases and pathological disorders: *pneumonia; aphasia.* **3.** occurring in words denoting condition or quality: *utopia.* **4.** occurring in names of botanical genera: *acacia; poinsettia.* **5.** occurring in names of zoological classes: *Reptilia.* **6.** occurring in collective nouns borrowed from Latin: *marginalia; memorabilia; regalia.* [(for senses 1–4) New Latin, from Latin and Greek, suffix of feminine nouns; (for senses 5–6) from Latin, neuter plural suffix]

IAA *abbrev. for* indoleacetic acid.

IAEA *abbrev. for* International Atomic Energy Agency.

IAF *abbrev. for* Indian Air Force.

-ial *suffix forming adjectives.* of; relating to; connected with: *managerial.* [from Latin *-iālis,* adj. suffix; compare -AL[1]]

iamb ('aɪæm, 'aɪæmb) *or* **iambus** (aɪ'æmbəs) *n., pl.* **iambs, iambi** (aɪ'æmbaɪ), *or* **iambuses.** *Prosody.* **1.** a metrical foot consisting of two syllables, a short one followed by a long one (˘–). **2.** a line of verse of such feet. [C19 *iamb,* from C16 *iambus,* from Latin, from Greek *iambos*]

iambic (aɪ'æmbɪk) *Prosody.* ~*adj.* **1.** of, relating to, consisting of, or using an iamb or iambs. **2.** (in Greek literature) denoting a type of satirical verse written in iambs. ~*n.* **3.** a metrical foot, line, or stanza of verse consisting of iambs. **4.** a type of ancient Greek satirical verse written in iambs. —**i'ambically** *adv.*

-ian *suffix.* a variant of **-an:** *Etonian; Johnsonian.* [from Latin *-iānus*]

-iana *suffix forming nouns.* a variant of **-ana.**

IARU *abbrev. for* International Amateur Radio Union.

IAS *Aeronautics. abbrev. for* indicated air speed.

-iasis *or* **-asis** *n. combining form.* (in medicine) indicating a diseased condition: *psoriasis.* Compare **-osis** (sense 2). [from New Latin, from Greek, suffix of action]

IATA (aɪ'ɑːtə, iː'ɑːtə) *n. acronym for* International Air Transport Association.

iatric (aɪ'ætrɪk) *or* **iatrical** *adj.* relating to medicine or physicians; medical. [C19: from Greek *iatrikos* of healing, from *iasthai* to heal]

-iatrics *n. combining form.* indicating medical care or treatment: *paediatrics.* Compare **-iatry.** [from IATRIC]

iatrogenic (aɪˌætrəʊ'dʒenɪk) *adj.* **1.** *Med.* (of an illness or symptoms) induced in a patient as the result of a physician's words or action. **2.** *Social welfare.* (of a problem) induced by the means of treating a problem but ascribed to the continuing natural development of the problem being treated. —**iatrogenicity** (aɪˌætrəʊdʒɪ'nɪsɪtɪ) *n.*

-iatry *n. combining form.* indicating healing or medical treatment: *psychiatry.* Compare **-iatrics.** [from New Latin *-iatria,* from Greek *iatreia* the healing art, from *iatros* healer, physician] —**-iatric** *adj. combining form.*

ib. See **ibid.**

IBA (in Britain) *abbrev. for* Independent Broadcasting Authority.

I-beam *n.* a rolled steel joist or a girder with a cross section in the form of a capital letter *I.* Compare **H-beam.**

Iberian (aɪ'bɪərɪən) *n.* **1.** a member of a group of ancient Caucasoid peoples who inhabited the Iberian Peninsula, now occupied by Spain and Portugal, in preclassical and classical times. See also **Celtiberian.** **2.** a native or inhabitant of the Iberian Peninsula; a Spaniard or Portuguese. **3.** a native or inhabitant of ancient Iberia in the Caucasus. ~*adj.* **4.** denoting, or relating to the pre-Roman peoples of the Iberian Peninsula or of Caucasian Iberia. **5.** of or relating to the Iberian Peninsula, its inhabitants, or any of their languages.

iberis (aɪ'bɪərɪs) *n.* any plant of the annual or perennial Eurasian genus *Iberis,* 12 to 25 cm (6-12 in.) in height, with white or purple flowers. *I. amara* and *I. umbellata* are the garden candytuft. Family *Cruciferae.* [New Latin, from *Iberia* Spain, where many species are common]

Ibero- ('aɪbərəʊ) *combining form.* indicating Iberia or Iberian: *Ibero-Caucasian.*

ibex ('aɪbɛks) *n., pl.* **ibexes, ibices** ('ɪbɪˌsiːz, 'aɪ-), *or* **ibex.** any of three wild goats, *Capra ibex, C. caucasica,* or *C. pyrenaica,* of mountainous regions of Europe, Asia, and North Africa, having large backward-curving horns. [C17: from Latin: chamois]

Ibibio (ɪ'bɪbɪəʊ) *n.* **1.** (*pl.* **-os** *or* **-o**) a member of a Negroid people of SE Nigeria, living esp. in and around Calabar. **2.** Also called: **Efik.** the language of this people.

ibid. *or* **ib.** (in annotations, bibliographies, etc., when referring to a book, article, chapter, or page previously cited) *abbrev. for* ibidem. [Latin: in the same place]

ibis ('aɪbɪs) *n., pl.* **ibises** *or* **ibis.** any of various wading birds of the family *Threskiornithidae,* such as *Threskiornis aethiopica* (**sacred ibis**), that occur in warm regions and have a long thin down-curved bill: order *Ciconiiformes* (herons, storks, etc.). Compare **wood ibis.** [C14: via Latin from Greek, from Egyptian *hby*]

-ible *suffix forming adjectives.* a variant of **-able.** —**-ibly** *suffix forming adverbs.* —**-ibility** *suffix forming nouns.*

Ibo *or* **Igbo** ('iːbəʊ) *n.* **1.** (*pl.* **-bos** *or* **-bo**) a member of a Negroid people of W Africa, living chiefly in S Nigeria. **2.** the language of this people, belonging to the Kwa branch of the Niger-Congo family: one of the chief literary and cultural languages of S Nigeria.

IBRD *abbrev. for* International Bank for Reconstruction and Development (the World Bank).

ibuprofen (ˌaɪbjuː'prəʊfən) *n.* a drug, isobutylphenylpropionic acid, that relieves pain and reduces inflammation: used to treat arthritis and muscular strains. Formula: $C_{13}H_{18}O_2$.

IC *abbrev. for:* **1.** internal-combustion. **2.** *Electronics.* integrated circuit. **3.** (in transformational grammar) immediate constituent. **4.** *Astrology.* Imum Coeli: the lowest point on the ecliptic below the horizon, lying directly opposite the Midheaven.

i/c *abbrev. for* in charge (of).

-ic *suffix forming adjectives.* **1.** of, relating to, or resembling: *allergic; Germanic; periodic.* See also **-ical.** **2.** (in chemistry) indicating that an element is chemically combined in the higher of two possible valence states: *ferric; stannic.* Compare **-ous** (sense 2). [from Latin *-icus* or Greek *-ikos; -ic* also occurs in nouns that represent a substantive use of adjectives (*magic*) and in nouns borrowed directly from Latin or Greek (*critic, music*)]

ICA *abbrev. for:* **1.** (in Britain) Institute of Contemporary Arts. **2.** International Cooperation Administration.

-ical *suffix forming adjectives.* a variant of **-ic,** but in some words having a less literal application than corresponding adjectives ending in *-ic: economical; fanatical.* [from Latin *-icālis*] —**-ically** *suffix forming adverbs.*

ICAO *abbrev. for* International Civil Aviation Organization.

Icarian (aɪ'kɛərɪən, ɪ-) *adj.* **1.** of or relating to Icaria, a Greek island in the Aegean Sea, or its inhabitants. ~*n.* **2.** an inhabitant of Icaria.

ICBM *abbrev. for* intercontinental ballistic missile: a missile with a range greater than 5500 km.

ice (aɪs) *n.* **1.** water in the solid state, formed by freezing liquid water. Related adj.: **glacial.** **2.** a portion of ice cream. **3.** *Slang.* a diamond or diamonds. **4.** the field of play in ice hockey. **5.** *Slang.* a concentrated and highly potent form of methamphetamine with dangerous side effects. **6. break the ice. a.** to relieve shyness, etc., esp. between strangers. **b.** to be the first of a group to do something. **7. cut no ice.** *Informal.* to fail to make an impression. **8. on ice.** in abeyance; pending. **9. on thin ice.** unsafe or unsafely; vulnerable or vulnerably. ~*vb.* **10.** (often foll. by *up, over,* etc.) to form or cause to form ice; freeze. **11.** (*tr.*) to mix with ice or chill (a drink, etc.). **12.** (*tr.*) to cover (a cake, etc.) with icing. **13.** (*tr.*) *U.S. slang.* to kill. [Old English *īs;* compare Old High German *īs,* Old Norse *īss*] —**'iceless** *adj.* —**'iceˌlike** *adj.*

ICE (in Britain) *abbrev. for* Institution of Civil Engineers.

Ice. *abbrev. for* Iceland(ic).

Ice age *n.* another name for **glacial period.**

ice axe *n.* a light axe used by mountaineers for cutting footholds in snow or ice, to provide an anchor point, or to control a slide on snow; it has a spiked tip and a head consisting of a pick and an adze.

ice bag *n.* **1.** a waterproof bag used as an ice pack. **2.** a strong bag, usually made of canvas and equipped with two handles, used for carrying blocks of ice.

iceberg ('aɪsbɜːg) *n.* **1.** a large mass of ice floating in the sea, esp. a mass that has broken off a polar glacier. **2. tip of the iceberg.** the small visible part of something, esp. a problem or difficulty, that is much larger. **3.** *Slang, chiefly U.S.* a person considered to have a cold or reserved manner. **4.** *Austral. informal.* a person who swims or surfs regularly in winter. [C18: probably part translation of Middle Dutch *ijsberg* ice mountain; compare Norwegian *isberg*]

iceberg lettuce *n.* a type of lettuce with very crisp pale leaves tightly enfolded.

iceblink ('aɪsˌblɪŋk) *n.* **1.** Also called: **blink.** a yellowish-white reflected glare in the sky over an ice field. **2.** a coastal ice cliff.

ice block *n. Scot., Austral., and N.Z.* a flavoured frozen water ice: in Australia and New Zealand, sometimes on a stick.

iceboat ('aɪsˌbəʊt) *n.* another name for **icebreaker** (sense 1) or **ice yacht.**

icebound ('aɪsˌbaʊnd) *adj.* covered or made immobile by ice; frozen in: *an icebound ship.*

icebox ('aɪsˌbɒks) *n.* **1.** a compartment in a refrigerator for storing or making ice. **2.** an insulated cabinet packed with ice for storing food.

icebreaker ('aɪsˌbreɪkə) *n.* **1.** Also called: **iceboat.** a vessel with a reinforced bow for breaking up the ice in bodies of water to keep channels open for navigation. **2.** any tool or device for breaking ice into smaller pieces. **3.** something intended to relieve mutual shyness at a gathering of strangers.

ice bucket *n.* a bucket-shaped container in which ice cubes are kept to be used for serving with drinks or into which a wine bottle is plunged to keep it cool at table.

icecap ('aɪsˌkæp) *n.* a thick mass of glacial ice and snow that permanently covers an area of land, such as either of the polar regions or the peak of a mountain.

ice cream *n.* a kind of sweetened frozen liquid, properly made from cream and egg yolks but often made from milk or a custard base, flavoured in various ways.

ice-cream cone *or* **cornet** *n.* **1.** a conical edible wafer for holding ice cream. **2.** such a cone containing ice cream.

ice-cream soda *n. Chiefly U.S.* ice cream served in a tall glass of carbonated water and a little milk, usually flavoured in various ways.

iced (aɪst) *adj.* **1.** covered, coated, or chilled with ice. **2.** covered with icing: *iced cakes.*

ice dance *n.* any of a number of dances, mostly based on ballroom dancing, performed by a couple skating on ice. —**ice dancer** *n.* —**ice dancing** *n.*

icefall ('aɪsˌfɔːl) *n.* a very steep part of a glacier that has deep crevasses and resembles a frozen waterfall.

ice field *n.* **1.** a very large flat expanse of ice floating in the sea; large ice floe. **2.** a large mass of ice permanently covering an extensive area of land.

ice fish *n.* any percoid fish of the family *Chaenichthyidae,* of Antarctic seas, having a semitransparent scaleless body.

ice floe *n.* a sheet of ice, of variable size, floating in the sea. See also **ice field** (sense 1).

ice foot *n.* a narrow belt of ice permanently attached to the coast in polar regions.

ice hockey *n.* a game played on ice by two opposing teams of six players each, who wear skates and try to propel a flat puck into their opponents' goal with long sticks having an offset flat blade at the end.

ice house *n.* a building for storing ice.

Icel. *abbrev. for* Iceland(ic).

Iceland agate ('aɪslənd) *n.* another name for **obsidian.**

Icelander ('aɪsˌlændə, 'aɪsləndə) *n.* a native, citizen, or inhabitant of Iceland.

Icelandic (aɪs'lændɪk) *adj.* **1.** of, relating to, or characteristic of Iceland, a republic in the N Atlantic, its people, or their language. ~*n.* **2.** the official language of Iceland, belonging to the North Germanic branch of the Indo-European family. See also **Old Icelandic.**

Iceland moss *n.* a lichen, *Cetraria islandica,* of arctic regions and N Europe, with brownish edible fronds.

Iceland poppy *n.* any of various widely cultivated arctic poppies, esp. *Papaver nudicaule,* with white or yellow nodding flowers.

Iceland spar *n.* a pure transparent variety of calcite with double-refracting crystals used in making polarizing microscopes.

ice lolly *n. Brit. informal.* an ice cream or water ice on a stick. Also called: **lolly.** U.S. and Canadian equivalent (trademark): **Popsicle.**

ice machine *n.* a machine that automatically produces ice for use in drinks, etc.

ice man *n. Chiefly U.S.* a man who sells or delivers ice.

ice needle *n. Meteorol.* one of many needle-like ice crystals that form cirrus clouds in clear cold weather.

ice pack *n.* **1.** a bag or folded cloth containing ice, applied to a part of the body, esp. the head, to cool, reduce swelling, etc. **2.** another name for **pack ice. 3.** a sachet containing a gel that can be frozen or heated and that retains its temperature for an extended period of time, used esp. in cool bags.

ice pick *n.* a pointed tool used for breaking ice.

ice plant *n.* a low-growing plant, *Mesembryanthemum* (or *Cryophytum*) *crystallinum,* of southern Africa, with fleshy leaves covered with icelike hairs and pink or white rayed flowers: family *Aizoaceae.*

ice point *n.* the temperature at which a mixture of ice and water are in equilibrium at a pressure of one atmosphere. It is 0° on the Celsius scale and 32° on the Fahrenheit scale. Compare **steam point.**

ice screw *n. Mountaineering.* a screwed tubular or solid steel rod with a ring at one end for inserting into ice as an anchor point.

ice sheet *n.* a thick layer of ice covering a large area of land for a long time, esp. the layer that covered much of the N hemisphere during the last glacial period.

ice shelf *n.* a thick mass of ice that is permanently attached to the land but projects into and floats on the sea.

ice show *n.* any entertainment performed by ice-skaters.

ice skate *n.* **1.** a boot having a steel blade fitted to the sole to enable the wearer to glide swiftly over ice. **2.** the steel blade on such a boot or shoe. ~*vb.* **ice-skate. 3.** (*intr.*) to glide swiftly over ice on ice skates. —'**ice-ˌskater** *n.*

ice station *n.* a scientific research station in polar regions, where ice movement, weather, and environmental conditions are monitored.

ice water *n.* **1.** water formed from ice. **2.** Also called: **iced water.** drinking water cooled by refrigeration or the addition of ice.

ice yacht *n.* a sailing craft having a cross-shaped frame with a cockpit and runners for travelling over ice. Also called: **iceboat.**

ICFTU *abbrev. for* International Confederation of Free Trade Unions.

I.Chem.E. *abbrev. for* Institution of Chemical Engineers.

ich-laut ('ɪçˌlaʊt, 'ɪk-) *n.* the voiceless palatal fricative sound that is written as *ch* in German *ich,* often allophonic with the ach-laut. See also **ach-laut.** [from German, from *ich* I + *laut* sound]

ichneumon (ɪk'njuːmən) *n.* a mongoose, *Herpestes ichneumon,* of Africa and S Europe, having greyish-brown speckled fur. [C16: via Latin from Greek, literally: tracker, hunter, from *ikhneuein* to track, from *ikhnos* a footprint; so named from the animal's alleged ability to locate the eggs of crocodiles]

ichneumon fly *or* **wasp** *n.* any hymenopterous insect of the family *Ichneumonidae,* whose larvae are parasitic in caterpillars and other insect larvae.

ichnite ('ɪknaɪt) *or* **ichnolite** ('ɪknəˌlaɪt) *n.* a fossilized footprint. [C19: from Greek *ikhnos* footprint, track + -ITE[1]]

ichnography (ɪk'nɒgrəfɪ) *n.* **1.** the art of drawing ground plans. **2.** the ground plan of a building, factory, etc. [C16: from Latin *ichnographia,* from Greek *ikhnographia,* from *ikhnos* trace, track] —**ichnographic** (ˌɪknə'græfɪk) *or* ˌ**ichno'graphical** *adj.* —ˌ**ichno'graphically** *adv.*

ichnology (ɪk'nɒlədʒɪ) *n.* the study of fossil footprints. [C19: from Greek *ikhnos* footprint, track] —**ichnological** (ˌɪknə'lɒdʒɪkᵊl) *adj.*

ichor ('aɪkɔː) *n.* **1.** *Greek myth.* the fluid said to flow in the veins of the gods. **2.** *Pathol.* a foul-smelling watery discharge from a wound or ulcer. [C17: from Greek *ikhōr,* of obscure origin] —'**ichorous** *adj.*

ichth. *abbrev. for* ichthyology.

ichthyic ('ɪkθɪɪk) *adj.* of, relating to, or characteristic of fishes. [C19: from Greek, from *ikhthus* fish]

ichthyo- *or before a vowel* **ichthy-** *combining form.* indicating or relating to fishes: *ichthyology.* [from Latin, from Greek *ikhthus* fish]

ichthyoid ('ɪkθɪˌɔɪd) *adj. also* **ichthyoidal. 1.** resembling a fish. ~*n.* **2.** a fishlike vertebrate.

ichthyol. *or* **ichth.** *abbrev. for* ichthyology.

ichthyolite ('ɪkθɪəˌlaɪt) *n. Rare.* any fossil fish. —**ichthyolitic** (ˌɪkθɪə'lɪtɪk) *adj.*

ichthyology (ˌɪkθɪ'ɒlədʒɪ) *n.* the study of the physiology, history, economic importance, etc., of fishes. —**ichthyologic** (ˌɪkθɪə'lɒdʒɪk) *or* ˌ**ichthyo'logical** *adj.* —ˌ**ichthyo'logically** *adv.* —ˌ**ichthy'ologist** *n.*

ichthyophagous (ˌɪkθɪ'ɒfəgəs) *adj.* feeding on fish. —**ichthyophagy** (ˌɪkθɪ'ɒfədʒɪ) *n.*

ichthyornis (ˌɪkθɪ'ɔːnɪs) *n.* an extinct Cretaceous sea bird of the genus *Ichthyornis,* thought to have resembled a tern. [C19: New Latin, from ICHTHY- + Greek *ornis* bird]

ichthyosaur ('ɪkθɪəˌsɔː) *or* **ichthyosaurus** (ˌɪkθɪə'sɔːrəs) *n., pl.* **-saurs, -sauruses,** *or* **-sauri** (-'sɔːraɪ). any extinct marine Mesozoic reptile of the order *Ichthyosauria,* which had a porpoise-like body with dorsal and tail fins and paddle-like limbs. See also **plesiosaur.**

ichthyosis (ˌɪkθɪ'əʊsɪs) *n.* a congenital disease in which the skin is coarse, dry, and scaly. Also called: **xeroderma.** Nontechnical name: **fishskin disease.** —**ichthyotic** (ˌɪkθɪ'ɒtɪk) *adj.*

ICI *abbrev. for* Imperial Chemical Industries.

-ician *suffix forming nouns.* indicating a person skilled or involved in a subject or activity: *physician; beautician.* [from French *-icien;* see -IC, -IAN]

icicle ('aɪsɪkᵊl) *n.* a hanging spike of ice formed by the freezing of dripping water. [C14: from ICE + *ickel*, from Old English *gicel* icicle, related to Old Norse *jökull* large piece of ice, glacier] —'**icicled** *adj.*
icily ('aɪsɪlɪ) *adv.* in an icy or reserved manner.
iciness ('aɪsɪnɪs) *n.* **1.** the condition of being icy or very cold. **2.** a manner that is cold or reserved; aloofness.
icing ('aɪsɪŋ) *n.* **1.** Also called (esp. U.S. and Canadian): **frosting.** a sugar preparation, variously flavoured and coloured, for coating and decorating cakes, biscuits, etc. **2.** the formation of ice, as on a ship or aircraft, due to the freezing of moisture in the atmosphere. **3.** any unexpected extra or bonus (esp. in **icing on the cake**).
icing sugar *n. Brit.* a very finely ground sugar used for icings, confections, etc. U.S. term: **confectioners' sugar.**
ICJ *abbrev. for* International Court of Justice.
icon *or* **ikon** ('aɪkɒn) *n.* **1.** a representation of Christ, the Virgin Mary, or a saint, esp. one painted in oil on a wooden panel, depicted in a traditional Byzantine style and venerated in the Eastern Church. **2.** an image, picture, representation, etc. **3.** a symbol resembling or analogous to the thing it represents. **4.** a person regarded as a sex symbol or as a symbol of a belief or cultural movement. **5.** a pictorial representation of a facility available on a computer system, that enables the facility to be activated by means of a screen cursor rather than by a textual instruction. [C16: from Latin, from Greek *eikōn* image, from *eikenai* to be like]
iconic (aɪ'kɒnɪk) *or* **iconical** *adj.* **1.** relating to, resembling, or having the character of an icon. **2.** (of memorial sculptures, esp. those depicting athletes of ancient Greece) having a fixed conventional style.
iconic memory *n. Psychol.* the temporary persistence of visual impressions after the stimulus has been removed. Compare **echoic memory.**
icono- *or before a vowel* **icon-** *combining form.* indicating an image or likeness: *iconology.* [from Greek: ICON]
iconoclasm (aɪ'kɒnəˌklæzəm) *n.* the acts or beliefs of an iconoclast.
iconoclast (aɪ'kɒnəˌklæst) *n.* **1.** a person who attacks established or traditional concepts, principles, laws, etc. **2. a.** a destroyer of religious images or sacred objects. **b.** an adherent of the heretical movement within the Greek Orthodox Church from 725 to 842 A.D., which aimed at the destruction of icons and religious images. [C16: from Late Latin *iconoclastes*, from Late Greek *eikonoklastes*, from *eikōn* icon + *klastēs* breaker] —**iˌcono'clastic** *adj.* —**iˌcono'clastically** *adv.*
iconography (ˌaɪkɒ'nɒgrəfɪ) *n., pl.* **-phies. 1. a.** the symbols used in a work of art or art movement. **b.** the conventional significance attached to such symbols. **2.** a collection of pictures of a particular subject, such as Christ. **3.** the representation of the subjects of icons or portraits, esp. on coins. —ˌ**ico'nographer** *n.* —**iconographic** (aɪˌkɒnə'græfɪk) *or* **iˌcono'graphical** *adj.*
iconolatry (ˌaɪkɒ'nɒlətrɪ) *n.* the worship or adoration of icons as idols. —ˌ**ico'nolater** *n.* —ˌ**ico'nolatrous** *adj.*
iconology (ˌaɪkɒ'nɒlədʒɪ) *n.* **1.** the study or field of art history concerning icons. **2.** icons collectively. **3.** the symbolic representation or symbolism of icons. —**iconological** (aɪˌkɒnə'lɒdʒɪkᵊl) *adj.* —ˌ**ico'nologist** *n.*
iconomatic (aɪˌkɒnə'mætɪk) *adj.* employing pictures to represent not objects themselves but the sound of their names. [C19: from Greek, from *eikon* image + *onoma* name] —**iconomaticism** (aɪˌkɒnə'mætɪˌsɪzəm) *n.*
iconoscope (aɪ'kɒnəˌskəʊp) *n.* a television camera tube in which an electron beam scans a photoemissive surface, converting an optical image into electrical pulses.
iconostasis (ˌaɪkəʊ'nɒstəsɪs) *or* **iconostas** (aɪ'kɒnəˌstæs) *n., pl.* **iconostases** (ˌaɪkəʊ'nɒstəˌsiːz *or* aɪ'kɒnəˌstæsɪz) *Eastern Church.* a screen with doors and icons set in tiers, which separates the bema (sanctuary) from the nave. [C19: Church Latin, from Late Greek *eikonostasion* shrine, literally: area where images are placed, from ICONO- + *histanai* to stand]
icosahedron (ˌaɪkəsə'hiːdrən) *n., pl.* **-drons** *or* **-dra** (-drə). a solid figure having 20 faces. The faces of a **regular icosahedron** are equilateral triangles. [C16: from Greek *eikosaedron*, from *eikosi* twenty + *-edron* -HEDRON] —ˌ**icosa'hedral** *adj.*
icositetrahedron (ˌaɪkəsɪˌtetrə'hiːdrən) *n.* a solid figure having 24 trapezoid faces, as occurring in some crystals.
ICS *abbrev. for* Indian Civil Service.
-ics *suffix forming nouns; functioning as sing.* **1.** indicating a science, art, or matters relating to a particular subject: *aeronautics; politics.* **2.** indicating certain activities or practices: *acrobatics.* [plural of *-ic*, representing Latin *-ica*, from Greek *-ika*, as in *mathēmatika* mathematics]
ICSH *abbrev. for* interstitial-cell-stimulating hormone.
icterus ('ɪktərəs) *n.* **1.** *Pathol.* another name for **jaundice. 2.** a yellowing of plant leaves, caused by excessive cold or moisture. [C18: from Latin: yellow bird, the sight of which reputedly cured jaundice, from Greek *ikteros*] —**icteric** (ɪk'terɪk) *adj.*
ictus ('ɪktəs) *n., pl.* **-tuses** *or* **-tus. 1.** *Prosody.* metrical or rhythmical stress in verse feet, as contrasted with the stress accent on words. **2.** *Med.* a sudden attack or stroke. [C18: from Latin *icere* to strike] —'**ictal** *adj.*
ICU *abbrev. for* intensive care unit.
icy ('aɪsɪ) *adj.* **icier, iciest. 1.** made of, covered with, or containing ice. **2.** resembling ice. **3.** freezing or very cold. **4.** cold or reserved in manner; aloof.
icy pole *n.* the Australian name for an **ice lolly.**
id (ɪd) *n. Psychoanal.* the mass of primitive instincts and energies in the unconscious mind that, modified by the ego and the superego, underlies all psychic activity. [C20: New Latin, from Latin: it; used to render German *Es*]
ID *abbrev. for:* **1.** Idaho. **2.** identification. **3.** Also: **i.d.** inside diameter. **4.** Intelligence Department. **5.** Also **i.d.** intradermal.
id. *abbrev. for* idem.
Id. *abbrev. for* Idaho.
I'd (aɪd) *contraction of* I had *or* I would.
-id[1] *suffix forming nouns.* **1.** indicating the names of meteor showers that appear to radiate from a specified constellation: *Orionids* (from Orion). **2.** indicating a particle, body, or structure of a specified kind: *energid.* [from Latin *-id-*, *-is*, from Greek, feminine suffix of origin]
-id[2] *suffix forming nouns and adjectives.* **1.** indicating members of a zoological family: *cyprinid.* **2.** indicating members of a dynasty: *Seleucid; Fatimid.* [from New Latin *-idae* or *-ida*, from Greek *-idēs* suffix indicating offspring]
-id[3] *suffix forming nouns.* a variant of **-ide.**
IDA *abbrev. for* International Development Association.
Ida. *abbrev.for* Idaho.
-idae *suffix forming nouns.* indicating names of zoological families: *Felidae; Hominidae.* [New Latin, from Latin, from Greek *-idai*, suffix indicating offspring]
IDB *Chiefly S. African. abbrev. for* illicit diamond buying.
IDC *abbrev. for* industrial development certificate.
ID card *n.* a card or document that serves to identify a person, or to prove his age, membership, etc.
ide (aɪd) *n.* another name for the **silver orfe.** See **orfe.** [C19: from New Latin *idus*, from Swedish *id*]
-ide *or* **-id** *suffix forming nouns.* **1.** (*added to the combining form of the nonmetallic or electronegative elements*) indicating a binary compound: *sodium chloride.* **2.** indicating an organic compound derived from another: *acetanilide.* **3.** indicating one of a class of compounds or elements: *peptide; lanthanide.* [from German *-id*, from French *oxide* OXIDE, based on the suffix of *acide* ACID]
idea (aɪ'dɪə) *n.* **1.** any content of the mind, esp. the conscious mind. **2.** the thought of something: *the very idea appals me.* **3.** a mental representation of something: *she's got a good idea of the layout of the factory.* **4.** the characterization of something in general terms; concept: *the idea of a square circle is self-contradictory.* **5.** an individual's conception of something: *his idea of honesty is not the same as yours and mine.* **6.** the belief that something is the case: *he has the idea that what he's doing is right.* **7.** a scheme, intention, plan, etc.: *here's my idea for the sales campaign.* **8.** a vague notion or indication; inkling: *he had no idea of what life would be like in Africa.* **9.** significance or purpose: *the idea of the game is to discover the murderer.* **10.** *Philosophy.* **a.** a private mental object, regarded as the immediate object of thought or perception. **b.** a Platonic Idea or Form. **11.** *Music.* a thematic phrase or figure; motif. **12.** *Obsolete.* a mental image. **13. get ideas.** to become ambitious, restless, etc. **14. not one's idea of.** not what one regards as (hard work, a holiday, etc.). **15. that's an idea.** that is worth considering. **16. the very idea!** that is preposterous, unreasonable, etc. [C16: via Late Latin from Greek: model, pattern, notion, from *idein* to see] —**i'dealess** *adj.*
Idea (aɪ'dɪə) *n.* another name for **Form.**
ideal (aɪ'dɪəl) *n.* **1.** a conception of something that is perfect, esp. that which one seeks to attain. **2.** a person or thing considered to represent perfection: *he's her ideal.* **3.** something existing only as an idea. **4.** a pattern or model, esp. of ethical behaviour. ~*adj.* **5.** conforming to an ideal. **6.** of, involving, or existing in the form of an idea. **7.** *Philosophy.* **a.** of or relating to a highly desirable and possible state of affairs. **b.** of or relating to idealism. —**ideality** (ˌaɪdɪ'ælɪtɪ) *n.* —**i'deally** *adv.* —**i'dealness** *n.*
ideal crystal *n. Chem.* a crystal in which there are no defects or impurities.
ideal element *n.* any element added to a mathematical theory in order to eliminate special cases. The ideal element $i = \sqrt{-1}$ allows all algebraic equations to be solved and the point at infinity (**ideal point**) ensures that any two lines in projective geometry intersect.
ideal gas *n.* a hypothetical gas which obeys Boyle's law exactly at all temperatures and pressures, and which has internal energy that depends only upon the temperature. Measurements upon real gases are extrapolated to zero pressure to obtain results in agreement with theories relating to an ideal gas, especially in thermometry. Also called: **perfect gas.**
idealism (aɪ'dɪəˌlɪzəm) *n.* **1.** belief in or pursuance of ideals. **2.** the tendency to represent things in their ideal forms, rather than as they are. **3.** any of a group of philosophical doctrines that share the monistic view that material objects and the external world do not exist in reality independently of the human mind but are variously creations of the mind or constructs of ideas. Compare **materialism** (sense 2), **dualism** (sense 2). —**i'dealist** *n.* —**iˌdeal'istic** *adj.* —**iˌdeal'istically** *adv.*

idealization *or* **idealisation** (aɪˌdɪəlaɪˈzeɪʃən) *n.* **1.** the representation of something as ideal. **2.** a conception of something that dwells on its advantages and ignores its deficiencies. **3.** a general theoretical account of natural phenomena that ignores features that are difficult to accommodate within a theory.

idealize *or* **idealise** (aɪˈdɪəˌlaɪz) *vb.* **1.** to consider or represent (something) as ideal. **2.** (*tr.*) to portray as ideal; glorify. **3.** (*intr.*) to form an ideal or ideals. —**iˈdealˌizer** *or* **iˈdealˌiser** *n.*

ideas of reference *pl. n.* a schizophrenic symptom in which the patient thinks that things completely disconnected from him are influencing him or conveying messages to him.

ideatum (ˌaɪdɪˈeɪtəm) *n., pl.* **-ata** (-ˈeɪtə). *Philosophy.* the objective reality with which human ideas are supposed to correspond. [C18: New Latin, from Latin: IDEA]

idée fixe *French.* (ide fiks) *n., pl.* ***idées fixes*** (ide fiks). a fixed idea; obsession.

idée reçue *French.* (ide rəsy) *n., pl.* ***idées reçues*** (ide rəsy). a generally held opinion or concept. [literally: received idea]

idem *Latin.* (ˈaɪdɛm, ˈɪdɛm) *pron., adj.* the same: used to refer to an article, chapter, etc., previously cited.

idempotent (ˈaɪdəmˌpəʊtənt, ˈɪd-) *adj. Maths.* (of a matrix, transformation, etc.) not changed in value following multiplication by itself. [C20: from Latin *idem* same + POTENT]

identic (aɪˈdɛntɪk) *adj.* **1.** *Diplomacy.* (esp. of opinions expressed by two or more governments) having the same wording or intention regarding another power: *identic notes.* **2.** an obsolete word for **identical.**

identical (aɪˈdɛntɪkᵊl) *adj.* **1.** Also called: **numerically identical.** being one and the same individual: *Cicero and Tully are identical.* **2.** Also called: **quantitatively identical.** exactly alike, equal, or agreeing. **3.** designating either or both of a pair of twins of the same sex who developed from a single fertilized ovum that split into two. Compare **fraternal** (sense 3). —**iˈdentically** *adv.* —**iˈdenticalness** *n.*

identical proposition *n. Logic.* a necessary truth, esp. a categorial identity, such as *whatever is triangular has three sides.*

identification (aɪˌdɛntɪfɪˈkeɪʃən) *n.* **1.** the act of identifying or the state of being identified. **2. a.** something that identifies a person or thing. **b.** (*as modifier*): *an identification card.* **3.** *Psychol.* **a.** the process of recognizing specific objects as the result of remembering. **b.** the process by which one incorporates aspects of another person's personality. **c.** the transferring of a response from one situation to another because the two bear similar features. See also **generalization** (sense 3).

identification parade *n.* a group of persons including one suspected of having committed a crime assembled for the purpose of discovering whether a witness can identify the suspect.

identify (aɪˈdɛntɪˌfaɪ) *vb.* **-fies, -fying, -fied.** (*mainly tr.*) **1.** to prove or recognize as being a certain person or thing; determine the identity of. **2.** to consider as the same or equivalent. **3.** (*also intr.;* often foll. by *with*) to consider (oneself) as similar to another. **4.** to determine the taxonomic classification of (a plant or animal). **5.** (*intr.;* usually foll. by *with*) *Psychol.* to engage in identification. —**iˈdentiˌfiable** *adj.* —**iˈdentiˌfiableness** *n.* —**iˈdentiˌfier** *n.*

Identikit (aɪˈdɛntɪˌkɪt) *n. Trademark.* **1. a.** a set of transparencies of various typical facial characteristics that can be superimposed on one another to build up, on the basis of a description, a picture of a person sought by the police. **b.** (*as modifier*): *an Identikit picture.* **2.** (*modifier*) artificially created by copying different elements in an attempt to form a whole: *an identikit pop group.*

identity (aɪˈdɛntɪtɪ) *n., pl.* **-ties.** **1.** the state of having unique identifying characteristics held by no other person or thing. **2.** the individual characteristics by which a person or thing is recognized. **3.** Also called: **numerical identity.** the property of being one and the same individual: *his loss of memory did not affect his identity.* **4.** Also called: **qualitative identity.** the state of being the same in nature, quality, etc.: *they were linked by the identity of their tastes.* **5.** the state of being the same as a person or thing described or claimed: *the identity of the stolen goods has not yet been established.* **6.** identification of oneself as: *moving to London destroyed his Welsh identity.* **7.** *Logic.* **a.** that relation that holds only between any entity and itself. **b.** an assertion that that relation holds, as *Cicero is Tully.* **8.** *Maths.* **a.** **an equation that is valid for all values of its variables, as in** $(x - y)(x + y) = x^2 - y^2$. Often denoted by the symbol ≡ **b.** Also called: **identity element.** a member of a set that when operating on another member, *x*, produces that member *x*: the identity for multiplication of numbers is 1 since $x.1 = 1.x = x$. See also **inverse** (sense 2b.). **9.** *Austral. and N.Z. informal.* a well-known person, esp. in a specified locality; figure (esp. in the phrase **an old identity**). [C16: from Late Latin *identitās,* from Latin *idem* the same]

identity card *n.* a card that establishes a person's identity, esp. one issued to all members of the population in wartime, to the staff of an organization, etc.

identity theory *n. Philosophy.* a form of materialism which holds mental states to be identical with certain states of the brain and so to have no separate existence, but regards this identity as contingent so that mentalistic and physicalistic language are not held to be synonymous. See also **anomalous monism, materialism** (sense 2).

ideo- *combining form.* of or indicating idea or ideas: *ideology.* [from French *idéo-,* from Greek *idea* IDEA]

ideogram (ˈɪdɪəʊˌgræm) *or* **ideograph** (ˈɪdɪəʊˌgrɑːf, -ˌgræf) *n.* **1.** a sign or symbol, used in such writing systems as those of China or Japan, that directly represents a concept, idea, or thing rather than a word or set of words for it. **2.** any graphic sign or symbol, such as %, @, &, etc.

ideography (ˌɪdɪˈɒgrəfɪ) *n.* the use of ideograms to communicate ideas.

ideologist (ˌaɪdɪˈɒlədʒɪst) *n.* **1.** a person who supports a particular ideology, esp. a political theorist. **2.** a person who studies an ideology or ideologies. **3.** a theorist or visionary. ~Also called: **ideologue** (ˈaɪdɪəˌlɒg).

ideology (ˌaɪdɪˈɒlədʒɪ) *n., pl.* **-gies.** **1.** a body of ideas that reflects the beliefs and interests of a nation, political system, etc. and underlies political action. **2.** *Philosophy, sociology.* the set of beliefs by which a group or society orders reality so as to render it intelligible. **3.** speculation that is imaginary or visionary. **4.** the study of the nature and origin of ideas. —**ideological** (ˌaɪdɪəˈlɒdʒɪkᵊl) *or* ˌ**ideoˈlogic** *adj.* —ˌ**ideoˈlogically** *adv.*

ideomotor (ˌaɪdɪəˈməʊtə) *adj. Physiol.* designating automatic muscular movements stimulated by ideas, as in absent-minded acts.

ides (aɪdz) *n.* (*functioning as sing.*) (in the Roman calendar) the 15th day in March, May, July, and October and the 13th day of each other month. See also **calends, nones.** [C15: from Old French, from Latin *īdūs* (plural), of uncertain origin]

id est *Latin.* (ˈɪd ˈɛst) the full form of **i.e.**

idio- *combining form.* indicating peculiarity, isolation, or that which pertains to an individual person or thing: *idiolect.* [from Greek *idios* private, separate]

idioblast (ˈɪdɪəʊˌblæst) *n.* a plant cell that differs from those around it in the same tissue. —ˌ**idioˈblastic** *adj.*

idiocy (ˈɪdɪəsɪ) *n., pl.* **-cies.** **1.** (*not in technical usage*) severe mental retardation. **2.** foolishness or senselessness; stupidity. **3.** a foolish act or remark.

idioglossia (ˌɪdɪəʊˈglɒsɪə) *n.* **1.** a private language, as invented by a child or between two children, esp. twins. **2.** a pathological condition in which a person's speech is so severely distorted that it is unintelligible. [C19: from Greek *idios* private, separate + *glossa* tongue]

idiogram (ˈɪdɪəʊˌgræm) *n.* another name for **karyogram.**

idiographic (ˌɪdɪəʊˈgræfɪk) *adj. Psychol.* of or relating to the study of individuals. Compare **nomothetic.**

idiolect (ˈɪdɪəˌlɛkt) *n.* the variety or form of a language used by an individual. —ˌ**idioˈlectal** *or* ˌ**idioˈlectic** *adj.*

idiom (ˈɪdɪəm) *n.* **1.** a group of words whose meaning cannot be predicted from the meanings of the constituent words, as for example (*It was raining*) *cats and dogs.* **2.** linguistic usage that is grammatical and natural to native speakers of a language. **3.** the characteristic vocabulary or usage of a specific human group or subject. **4.** the characteristic artistic style of an individual, school, period, etc. [C16: from Latin *idiōma* peculiarity of language, from Greek; see IDIO-] —**idiomatic** (ˌɪdɪəˈmætɪk) *or* ˌ**idioˈmatical** *adj.* —ˌ**idioˈmatically** *adv.* —ˌ**idioˈmaticalness** *n.*

idiomorphic (ˌɪdɪəʊˈmɔːfɪk) *adj.* (of minerals) occurring naturally in the form of well-developed crystals. —ˌ**idioˈmorphically** *adv.* —ˌ**idioˈmorphism** *n.*

idiopathy (ˌɪdɪˈɒpəθɪ) *n., pl.* **-thies.** any disease of unknown cause. —**idiopathic** (ˌɪdɪəʊˈpæθɪk) *adj.*

idiophone (ˈɪdɪəˌfəʊn) *n. Music.* a percussion instrument, such as a cymbal or xylophone, made of naturally sonorous material. —**idiophonic** (ˌɪdɪəˈfɒnɪk) *adj.*

idioplasm (ˈɪdɪəʊˌplæzəm) *n.* another name for **germ plasm.** —ˌ**idioˈplasmic** *or* **idioplasmatic** (ˌɪdɪəʊplæzˈmætɪk) *adj.*

idiosyncrasy (ˌɪdɪəʊˈsɪŋkrəsɪ) *n., pl.* **-sies.** **1.** a tendency, type of behaviour, mannerism, etc., of a specific person; quirk. **2.** the composite physical or psychological make-up of a specific person. **3.** an abnormal reaction of an individual to specific foods, drugs, or other agents. [C17: from Greek *idiosunkrasia,* from IDIO- + *sunkrasis* mixture, temperament, from *sun-* SYN- + *kerannunai* to mingle] —**idiosyncratic** (ˌɪdɪəʊsɪŋˈkrætɪk) *adj.* —ˌ**idiosynˈcratically** *adv.*

idiot (ˈɪdɪət) *n.* **1.** a person with severe mental retardation. **2.** a foolish or senseless person. [C13: from Latin *idiōta* ignorant person, from Greek *idiōtēs* private person, one who lacks professional knowledge, ignoramus; see IDIO-]

idiot board *n.* a slang name for **Autocue.**

idiot box *n. Slang.* a television set.

idiotic (ˌɪdɪˈɒtɪk) *adj.* of or resembling an idiot; foolish; senseless. —ˌ**idiˈotically** *adv.* —ˌ**idiˈoticalness** *n.*

idiotism (ˈɪdɪəˌtɪzəm) *n.* **1.** an archaic word for **idiocy.** **2.** an obsolete word for **idiom.**

idiot savant (ˈiːdjəʊ sæˈvɑ̃, ˈɪdɪət ˈsævənt) *n., pl.* **idiots savants** (ˈiːdjəʊ sæˈvɑ̃) *or* **idiot savants.** a person of subnormal intelligence who performs brilliantly at some specialized intellectual task, such as giving the day of the week for any calendar date past or present. [C19: from French: knowledgeable idiot]

idiot tape *n. Printing.* an input tape for a typesetting machine that contains text only, the typographical instructions being supplied by the typesetting machine itself.

idle (ˈaɪdᵊl) *adj.* **1.** unemployed or unoccupied; inactive. **2.** not operating or being used. **3.** (of money) not being used to earn interest or dividends. **4.** not wanting to work; lazy. **5.** (*usually prenominal*) frivolous or trivial: *idle pleasures.* **6.** ineffective or powerless; fruitless; vain. **7.** without basis; unfounded. *~vb.* **8.** (when *tr.*, often foll. by *away*) to waste or pass (time) fruitlessly or inactively: *he idled the hours away.* **9.** (*intr.*) to loiter or move aimlessly. **10.** (*intr.*) (of a shaft, etc.) to turn without doing useful work. **11.** (*intr.*) Also (Brit.): **tick over.** (of an engine) to run at low speed with the transmission disengaged. **12.** (*tr.*) *U.S. and Canadian.* to cause to be inactive or unemployed. [Old English *īdel;* compare Old High German *ītal* empty, vain] —**'idleness** *n.* —**'idly** *adv.*

idle pulley *or* **idler pulley** *n.* a freely rotating trolley used to control the tension or direction of a belt. Also called: **idler.**

idler ('aɪdlə) *n.* **1.** a person who idles. **2.** another name for **idle pulley** *or* **idle wheel. 3.** *Nautical.* a ship's crew member, such as a carpenter, sailmaker, etc., whose duties do not include standing regular watches.

idler shaft *n.* a shaft carrying one or more gearwheels that idles between a driver shaft and a driven shaft, usually to reverse the direction of rotation or provide different spacing of gearwheels, esp. in a gearbox.

idle time *n. Commerce.* time during which a machine or a worker could be working but is not, as when one job has been completed and tooling or materials for the next are not complete or available. Compare **down time.**

idle wheel *n.* a gearwheel interposed between two others to transmit torque without changing the direction of rotation to the velocity ratio. Also called: **idler.**

IDN *abbrev. for* in Dei nomine. Also: **IND.** [Latin: in the name of God]

Ido ('iːdəʊ) *n.* an artificial language; a modification of Esperanto. [C20: offspring, from Greek *-id* daughter of]

idocrase ('aɪdəˌkreɪs, 'ɪd-) *n.* another name for **vesuvianite.** [C19: from French, from Greek *eidos* form + *krasis* a mingling]

idol ('aɪdᵊl) *n.* **1.** a material object, esp. a carved image, that is worshipped as a god. **2.** *Christianity, Judaism.* any being (other than the one God) to which divine honour is paid. **3.** a person who is revered, admired, or highly loved. [C13: from Late Latin *īdōlum,* from Latin: image, from Greek *eidōlon,* from *eidos* shape, form]

idolatrize *or* **idolatrise** (aɪ'dɒləˌtraɪz) *vb.* **1.** (*tr.*) a less common word for **idolize. 2.** (*intr.*) to indulge in the worship of idols. —**i'dolaˌtrizer** *or* **i'dolaˌtriser** *n.*

idolatry (aɪ'dɒlətrɪ) *n.* **1.** the worship of idols. **2.** great devotion or reverence. —**i'dolater** *n. or* **i'dolatress** *fem. n.* —**i'dolatrous** *adj.* —**i'dolatrously** *adv.* —**i'dolatrousness** *n.*

idolize *or* **idolise** ('aɪdəˌlaɪz) *vb.* **1.** (*tr.*) to admire or revere greatly. **2.** (*tr.*) to worship as an idol. **3.** (*intr.*) to worship idols. —**i'dolism, ˌidoli'zation** *or* **ˌidoli'sation** *n.* —**'idolist, 'idolˌizer** *or* **'idolˌiser** *n.*

idolum (ɪ'dəʊləm) *n.* **1.** a mental picture; idea. **2.** a false idea, fallacy. [C17: from Latin: IDOL]

IDP *abbrev. for* integrated data processing.

id-ul-fitr (ˌɪdˌʊl'fɪtᵊr) *n.* a Muslim festival marking the end of the fast of Ramadan. [C18: from Arabic]

idyll *or U.S.* (*sometimes*) **idyl** ('ɪdɪl) *n.* **1.** a poem or prose work describing an idealized rural life, pastoral scenes, etc. **2.** any simple narrative or descriptive piece in poetry or prose. **3.** a charming or picturesque scene or event. **4.** a piece of music with a calm or pastoral character. [C17: from Latin *Idyllium,* from Greek *eidullion,* from *eidos* shape, (literary) form]

idyllic (ɪ'dɪlɪk, aɪ-) *adj.* **1.** of or relating to an idyll. **2.** charming; picturesque. —**i'dyllically** *adv.*

idyllist *or U.S.* **idylist** ('ɪdɪlɪst) *n.* a writer of idylls.

IE *abbrev. for* Indo-European (languages).

i.e. *abbrev. for* id est. [Latin: that is (to say); in other words]

-ie *suffix forming nouns.* a variant of **-y**[2].

iechyd da ('jækiːˌdɑː; *Welsh* 'jɛxəd dɑː) *interj. Welsh.* a drinking toast; good health; cheers. [Welsh: good health]

IEE *abbrev. for* Institution of Electrical Engineers.

-ier *suffix forming nouns.* a variant of **-eer:** *brigadier.* [from Old English *-ere* -ER[1] or (in some words) from Old French *-ier,* from Latin *-ārius* -ARY]

if (ɪf) *conj.* (*subordinating*) **1.** in case that, or on condition that: *if you try hard it might work; if he were poor, would you marry him?* **2.** used to introduce an indirect question. In this sense, *if* approaches the meaning of *whether.* **3.** even though: *an attractive if awkward girl.* **4. a.** used to introduce expressions of desire, with *only: if I had only known.* **b.** used to introduce exclamations of surprise, dismay, etc.: *if this doesn't top everything!* **5. as if.** as it would be if; as though: *he treats me as if I were junior to him.* *~n.* **6.** an uncertainty or doubt: *the big if is whether our plan will work at all.* **7.** a condition or stipulation: *I won't have any ifs or buts.* [Old English *gif;* related to Old Saxon *ef* if, Old High German *iba* whether, if]

IF *or* **i.f.** *Electronics. abbrev. for* intermediate frequency.

IFC *abbrev. for* International Finance Corporation.

-iferous *suffix forming adjectives.* containing or yielding: *carboniferous.*

iff (ɪf) *conj. Logic.* a shortened form of *if and only if:* it indicates that the two sentences so connected are necessary and sufficient conditions for one another. Usually *iff* is used for equivalence in the metalanguage, rather than as the biconditional in the object language.

IFF *Military abbrev. for* Identification, Friend or Foe: a system using radar transmissions to which equipment carried by friendly forces automatically responds with a precoded signal.

iffy ('ɪfɪ) *adj. Informal.* uncertain or subject to contingency: *this scheme sounds a bit iffy.* [C20: from IF + -Y[1]]

IFR *Aeronautics. abbrev. for* instrument flying regulations.

IFS *abbrev. for* Irish Free State (now called Republic of Ireland).

-ify *suffix forming verbs.* a variant of **-fy:** *intensify.* —**ification** *suffix forming nouns.*

IG *abbrev. for:* **1.** Indo-Germanic (languages). **2.** Inspector General.

Igbo ('iːbəʊ) *n., pl.* **-bo** *or* **-bos.** a variant spelling of **Ibo.**

IGFET ('ɪgfɛt) *n.* insulated-gate field-effect transistor; a type of field-effect transistor having one or more semiconductor gate electrodes. Compare **JUGFET.**

igloo *or* **iglu** ('ɪgluː) *n., pl.* **-loos** *or* **-lus. 1.** a dome-shaped Eskimo house, usually built of blocks of solid snow. **2.** a hollow made by a seal in the snow over its breathing hole in the ice. [C19: from Eskimo *igdlu* house]

IGM *Chess. abbrev. for* International Grandmaster.

ign. *abbrev. for:* **1.** ignites. **2.** ignition. **3.** ignotus. [Latin: unknown]

igneous ('ɪgnɪəs) *adj.* **1.** (of rocks) derived from magma or lava that has solidified on or below the earth's surface. Compare **sedimentary, metamorphic** (sense 2). **2.** of or relating to fire. [C17: from Latin *igneus* fiery, from *ignis* fire]

ignescent (ɪg'nɛsᵊnt) *adj.* **1.** giving off sparks when struck, as a flint. **2.** capable of bursting into flame. *~n.* **3.** an ignescent substance. [C19: from Latin *ignescere* to become inflamed]

ignimbrite ('ɪgnɪmˌbraɪt) *n.* a rock formed by the deposition at high temperature and the consolidation of a nuée ardente, being a complicated mixture of volcanic materials welded together by heat, hot gases, and pressure. Also called: **welded tuft.** See **tuft.** [C20: from Latin *ign(is)* fire + *imbr(is), imber* shower of rain + -ITE[1]]

ignis fatuus ('ɪgnɪs 'fætjʊəs) *n., pl.* **ignes fatui** ('ɪgniːz 'fætjʊˌaɪ). another name for **will-o'-the-wisp.** [C16: from Medieval Latin, literally: foolish fire]

ignite (ɪg'naɪt) *vb.* **1.** to catch fire or set fire to; burn or cause to burn. **2.** (*tr.*) *Chem.* to heat strongly. [C17: from Latin *ignīre* to set alight, from *ignis* fire] —**ig'nitable** *or* **ig'nitible** *adj.* —**igˌnita'bility** *or* **igˌniti'bility** *n.*

igniter (ɪg'naɪtə) *n.* **1.** a person or thing that ignites. **2.** a fuse to fire explosive charges. **3.** an electrical device for lighting a gas turbine. **4.** a subsidiary electrode in an ignitron.

ignition (ɪg'nɪʃən) *n.* **1.** the act or process of initiating combustion. **2.** the process of igniting the fuel in an internal-combustion engine. **3.** (usually preceded by *the*) the devices used to ignite the fuel in an internal-combustion engine.

ignition coil *n.* an induction coil that supplies the high voltage to the sparking plugs of an internal-combustion engine.

ignition key *n.* the key used in a motor vehicle to turn the switch that connects the battery to the ignition system and other electrical devices.

ignitron (ɪg'naɪtrɒn, 'ɪgnɪˌtrɒn) *n.* a mercury-arc rectifier controlled by a subsidiary electrode, the igniter, partially immersed in a mercury cathode. A current passed between igniter and cathode forms a hot spot sufficient to strike an arc between cathode and anode. [C20: from IGNITER + ELECTRON]

ignoble (ɪg'nəʊbᵊl) *adj.* **1.** dishonourable; base; despicable. **2.** of low birth or origins; humble; common. **3.** of low quality; inferior. **4.** *Falconry.* **a.** designating short-winged hawks that capture their quarry by swiftness and adroitness of flight. Compare **noble** (sense 7). **b.** designating quarry which is inferior or unworthy of pursuit by a particular species of hawk or falcon. [C16: from Latin *ignōbilis,* from IN-[1] + Old Latin *gnōbilis* NOBLE] —**ˌigno'bility** *or* **ig'nobleness** *n.* —**ig'nobly** *adv.*

ignominy ('ɪgnəˌmɪnɪ) *n., pl.* **-minies. 1.** disgrace or public shame; dishonour. **2.** a cause of disgrace; a shameful act. [C16: from Latin *ignōminia* disgrace, from *ig-* (see IN-[2]) + *nōmen* name, reputation] —**ˌigno'minious** *adj.* —**ˌigno'miniously** *adv.* —**ˌigno'miniousness** *n.*

ignoramus (ˌɪgnə'reɪməs) *n., pl.* **-muses.** an ignorant person; fool. [C16: from legal Latin, literally: we have no knowledge of, from Latin *ignōrāre* to be ignorant of; see IGNORE; modern usage originated from the use of *Ignoramus* as the name of an unlettered lawyer in a play by G. Ruggle, 17th-century English dramatist]

ignorance ('ɪgnərəns) *n.* lack of knowledge, information, or education; the state of being ignorant.

ignorant ('ɪgnərənt) *adj.* **1.** lacking in knowledge or education; unenlightened. **2.** (*postpositive;* often foll. by *of*) lacking in awareness or knowledge (of): *ignorant of the law.* **3.** resulting from or showing lack of knowledge or awareness: *an ignorant remark.* —**'ignorantly** *adv.*

ignoratio elenchi (ˌɪgnə'reɪʃɪəʊ ɪ'lɛŋkaɪ) *n. Logic.* **1.** a purported refutation of a proposition that does not in fact prove it false but merely establishes a related but strictly irrelevant proposition. **2.** the fallacy of arguing in this way. [Latin: an ignorance of proof, translating Greek *elenchou agnoia*]

ignore (ɪɡˈnɔː) *vb.* (*tr.*) **1.** to fail or refuse to notice; disregard. ~*n.* **2.** *Austral. informal.* disregard: *to treat someone with ignore.* [C17: from Latin *ignōrāre* not to know, from *ignārus* ignorant of, from *i-* IN-[1] + *gnārus* knowing; related to Latin *noscere* to know] —**igˈnorable** *adj.* —**igˈnorer** *n.*

ignotum per ignotius *Latin.* (ɪɡˈnəʊtʊm pər ɪɡˈnəʊtɪʊs) *n.* an explanation that is obscurer than the thing to be explained. [literally: the unknown by means of the more unknown]

Igorot (ˌɪɡəˈrəʊt, ˌiːɡə-) *or* **Igorrote** (ˌɪɡəˈrəʊtɪ, ˌiːɡə-) *n., pl.* **-rot, -rots** *or* **-rote, -rotes.** a member of a Negrito people of the mountains of N Luzon in the Philippines: noted as early exponents of mining.

iguana (ɪˈɡwɑːnə) *n.* **1.** either of two large tropical American arboreal herbivorous lizards of the genus *Iguana,* esp. *I. iguana* (**common iguana**), having a greyish-green body with a row of spines along the back: family *Iguanidae.* **2.** Also called: **iguanid** (ɪˈɡwɑːnɪd). any other lizard of the tropical American family *Iguanidae.* **3.** another name for **leguan.** [C16: from Spanish, from Arawak *iwana*] —**iˈguanian** *n., adj.*

iguanodon (ɪˈɡwɑːnəˌdɒn) *n.* a massive herbivorous long-tailed bipedal dinosaur of the genus *Iguanodon,* common in Europe and N Africa in Jurassic and Cretaceous times: suborder *Ornithopoda* (ornithopods). [C19: New Latin, from IGUANA + Greek *odōn* tooth]

IGY *abbrev. for* International Geophysical Year.

IHC (in New Zealand) *abbrev. for* intellectually handicapped child.

ihram (ɪˈrɑːm) *n.* the customary white robes worn by Muslim pilgrims to Mecca, symbolizing a sacred or consecrated state. [C18: from Arabic *ihrām,* from *harama* he forbade]

IHS the first three letters of the name Jesus in Greek (ΙΗΣΟΥΣ), often used as a Christian emblem.

iid *Statistics. abbrev. for* independent identically distributed (of random variables).

ikan (ˈiːkan) *n.* (in Malaysia) fish used esp. in names of cooked dishes: *assam ikan.* [from Malay]

ikat (ˈaɪkæt) *n.* a method of creating patterns in fabric by tie-dyeing the yarn before weaving. [C20: from Malay, literally: to tie, bind]

ikebana (ˌiːkəˈbɑːnə) *n.* the Japanese decorative art of flower arrangement.

ikon (ˈaɪkɒn) *n.* a variant spelling of **icon.**

IL *abbrev. for:* **1.** Illinois. ~**2.** *international car registration for* Israel.

il- *prefix.* variant of **in-**[1] and **in-**[2] before *l.*

ilang-ilang (ˈiːlæŋˈiːlæŋ) *n.* a variant spelling of **ylang-ylang.**

-ile *suffix forming adjectives and nouns.* indicating capability, liability, or a relationship with something: *agile; fragile; juvenile.* [via French from Latin or directly from Latin *-ilis*]

ILEA (ˈɪlɪə) *n.* (formerly) *abbrev. or acronym for* Inner London Education Authority.

ileac (ˈɪlɪˌæk) *or* **ileal** (ˈɪlɪəl) *adj.* **1.** *Anatomy.* of or relating to the ileum. **2.** *Pathol.* of or relating to ileus.

ileitis (ˌɪlɪˈaɪtɪs) *n.* inflammation of the ileum.

ileo- *or before a vowel* **ile-** *combining form.* indicating the ileum: *ileostomy.*

ileostomy (ˌɪlɪˈɒstəmɪ) *n., pl.* **-mies.** the surgical formation of a permanent opening through the abdominal wall into the ileum.

ileum (ˈɪlɪəm) *n.* **1.** the part of the small intestine between the jejunum and the caecum. **2.** the corresponding part in insects. [C17: New Latin, from Latin *īlium, īleum* flank, groin, of obscure origin]

ileus (ˈɪlɪəs) *n.* obstruction of the intestine, esp. the ileum, by mechanical occlusion or as the result of distension of the bowel following loss of muscular action. [C18: from Latin *īleos* severe colic, from Greek *eileos* a rolling, twisting, from *eilein* to roll]

ilex (ˈaɪlɛks) *n.* **1.** any of various trees or shrubs of the widely distributed genus *Ilex,* such as the holly and inkberry: family *Aquifoliaceae.* **2.** another name for the **holm oak.** [C16: from Latin]

ilia (ˈɪlɪə) *n.* the plural of **ilium.**

iliac (ˈɪlɪˌæk) *adj. Anatomy.* of or relating to the ilium.

Iliad (ˈɪlɪəd) *n.* a Greek epic poem describing the siege of Troy, attributed to Homer and probably composed before 700 B.C. —**Iliadic** (ˌɪlɪˈædɪk) *adj.*

ilium (ˈɪlɪəm) *n., pl.* **-ia** (-ɪə). the uppermost and widest of the three sections of the hipbone.

ilk[1] (ɪlk) *n.* **1.** a type; class; sort (esp. in the phrase **of that, his, her,** etc., **ilk**): *people of that ilk should not be allowed here.* **2. of that ilk.** *Scot.* of the place of the same name: used to indicate that the person named is proprietor or laird of the place named: *Moncrieff of that ilk.* [Old English *ilca* the same family, same kind; related to Gothic *is* he, Latin *is,* Old English *gelīc* like]

▷**Usage.** Although the use of *ilk* in the sense of sense 1 is often condemned as being the result of a misunderstanding of the original Scottish expression *of that ilk,* it is nevertheless well established and generally acceptable.

ilk[2] (ɪlk) *or* **ilka** (ˈɪlkə) *determiner. Scot.* each; every. [Old English *ǣlc* each (+A[1])]

ill (ɪl) *adj.* **worse, worst. 1.** (*usually postpositive*) not in good health; sick. **2.** characterized by or intending evil, harm, etc.; hostile: *ill deeds.* **3.** causing or resulting in pain, harm, adversity, etc.: *ill effects.* **4.** ascribing or imputing evil to something referred to: *ill repute.* **5.** promising an unfavourable outcome; unpropitious: *an ill omen.* **6.** harsh; lacking kindness: *ill will.* **7.** not up to an acceptable standard; faulty: *ill manners.* **8. ill at ease.** unable to relax; uncomfortable. ~*n.* **9.** evil or harm: *to wish a person ill.* **10.** a mild disease. **11.** misfortune; trouble. ~*adv.* **12.** badly: *the title ill befits him.* **13.** with difficulty; hardly: *he can ill afford the money.* **14.** not rightly: *she ill deserves such good fortune.* [C11 (in the sense: evil): from Old Norse *illr* bad]

ill. *abbrev. for:* **1.** illustrated. **2.** illustration.

Ill. *abbrev. for* Illinois.

I'll (aɪl) *contraction of* I will *or* I shall.

ill-advised *adj.* **1.** acting without reasonable care or thought: *you would be ill-advised to sell your house now.* **2.** badly thought out; not or insufficiently considered: *an ill-advised plan of action.* —ˌ**ill-adˈvisedly** *adv.*

ill-affected *adj.* (often foll. by *towards*) not well disposed; disaffected.

ill-assorted *adj.* badly matched; incompatible.

illation (ɪˈleɪʃən) *n.* a rare word for **inference.** [C16: from Late Latin *illātiō* a bringing in, from Latin *illātus* brought in, from *inferre* to bring in, from IN-[2] + *ferre* to bear, carry]

illative (ɪˈleɪtɪv) *adj.* **1.** of or relating to illation; inferential. **2.** *Grammar.* denoting a word or morpheme used to signal inference, for example *so* or *therefore.* **3.** (in the grammar of Finnish and other languages) denoting a case of nouns expressing a relation of motion or direction, usually translated by the English prepositions *into* or *towards.* Compare **elative** (sense 1). ~*n.* **4.** *Grammar.* **a.** the illative case. **b.** an illative word or speech element. [C16: from Late Latin *illātīvus* inferring, concluding] —**ilˈlatively** *adv.*

Illawarra (ˌɪləˈwɒrə) *n.* an Australian breed of shorthorn dairy cattle noted for its high milk yield and ability to survive on poor pastures. [named after *Illawarra,* a coastal district of E Australia]

ill-behaved *adj.* poorly behaved; lacking good manners.

ill-bred *adj.* badly brought up; lacking good manners. —ˌ**ill-ˈbreeding** *n.*

ill-considered *adj.* done without due consideration; not thought out: *an ill-considered decision.*

ill-defined *adj.* imperfectly defined; having no clear outline.

ill-disposed *adj.* (often foll. by *towards*) not kindly disposed.

illegal (ɪˈliːɡᵊl) *adj.* **1.** forbidden by law; unlawful; illicit. **2.** unauthorized or prohibited by a code of official or accepted rules. ~ *n.* **3.** a person who has entered or attempted to enter a country illegally. —**ilˈlegally** *adv.* —ˌ**illeˈgality** *n.*

illegalize *or* **illegalise** (ɪˈliːɡəˌlaɪz) *vb.* (*tr.*) to make illegal. —**il**ˌ**legaliˈzation** *or* **il**ˌ**legaliˈsation** *n.*

illegible (ɪˈlɛdʒɪbᵊl) *adj.* unable to be read or deciphered. —**il**ˌ**legiˈbility** *or* **ilˈlegibleness** *n.* —**ilˈlegibly** *adv.*

illegitimate (ˌɪlɪˈdʒɪtɪmɪt) *adj.* **1.** born of parents who were not married to each other at the time of birth; bastard. **2.** forbidden by law; illegal; unlawful. **3.** contrary to logic; incorrectly reasoned. ~*n.* **4.** an illegitimate person; bastard. —ˌ**illeˈgitimacy** *or* ˌ**illeˈgitimateness** *n.* —ˌ**illeˈgitimately** *adv.*

ill-fated *adj.* doomed or unlucky: *an ill-fated marriage.*

ill-favoured *or U.S.* **ill-favored** *adj.* **1.** unattractive or repulsive in appearance; ugly. **2.** offensive, disagreeable, or objectionable. —ˌ**ill-ˈfavouredly** *or U.S.* ˌ**ill-ˈfavoredly** *adv.* —ˌ**ill-ˈfavouredness** *or U.S.* ˌ**ill-ˈfavoredness** *n.*

ill feeling *n.* hostile feeling; animosity.

ill-founded *adj.* not founded on true or reliable premises; unsubstantiated: *an ill-founded rumour.*

ill-gotten *adj.* obtained dishonestly or illegally (esp. in the phrase **ill-gotten gains**).

ill humour *n.* a disagreeable or sullen mood; bad temper. —ˌ**ill-ˈhumoured** *adj.* —ˌ**ill-ˈhumouredly** *adv.*

illiberal (ɪˈlɪbərəl) *adj.* **1.** narrow-minded; prejudiced; bigoted; intolerant. **2.** not generous; mean. **3.** lacking in culture or refinement. —**il**ˌ**liberˈality, ilˈliberalness,** *or* **ilˈliberalism** *n.* —**ilˈliberally** *adv.*

illicit (ɪˈlɪsɪt) *adj.* **1.** another word for **illegal. 2.** not allowed or approved by common custom, rule, or standard: *illicit sexual relations.* —**ilˈlicitly** *adv.* —**ilˈlicitness** *n.*

illimitable (ɪˈlɪmɪtəbᵊl) *adj.* limitless; boundless. —**il**ˌ**limitaˈbility** *or* **ilˈlimitableness** *n.* —**ilˈlimitably** *adv.*

illinium (ɪˈlɪnɪəm) *n. Chem.* the former name for **promethium.** [C20: New Latin, from *Illinois* + -IUM]

illiquid (ɪˈlɪkwɪd) *adj.* **1.** (of an asset) not easily convertible into cash. **2.** (of an enterprise, organization, etc.) deficient in liquid assets.

illite (ˈɪlaɪt) *n.* a clay mineral of the mica group, found in shales and mudstones. Crystal structure: monoclinic. [C20: named after *Illinois,* a state in the U.S., where it was first found]

illiterate (ɪˈlɪtərɪt) *adj.* **1.** unable to read and write. **2.** violating accepted standards in reading and writing: *an illiterate scrawl.* **3.** uneducated, ignorant, or uncultured: *scientifically illiterate.* ~*n.* **4.** an illiterate person. —**ilˈliteracy** *or* **ilˈliterateness** *n.* —**ilˈliterately** *adv.*

ill-judged *adj.* rash; ill-advised.

ill-mannered *adj.* having bad manners; rude; impolite. —ˌ**ill-ˈmanneredly** *adv.*

ill-natured *adj.* naturally unpleasant and mean. —ˌ**ill-ˈnaturedly** *adv.* —ˌ**ill-ˈnaturedness** *n.*

illness ('ɪlnɪs) *n.* **1.** a disease or indisposition; sickness. **2.** a state of ill health. **3.** *Obsolete.* wickedness.

illocution (ˌɪlə'kjuːʃən) *n. Philosophy.* an act performed by a speaker by virtue of uttering certain words, as for example the acts of promising or of threatening. Also called: **illocutionary act.** See also **performative.** Compare **perlocution.** [C20: from IL- + LOCUTION] —ˌ**illo'cutionary** *adj.*

illogic (ɪ'lɒdʒɪk) *n.* reasoning characterized by lack of logic; illogicality.

illogical (ɪ'lɒdʒɪkəl) *adj.* **1.** characterized by lack of logic; senseless or unreasonable. **2.** disregarding logical principles. —**illogicality** (ɪˌlɒdʒɪ'kælɪtɪ) *or* **il'logicalness** *n.* —**il'logically** *adv.*

ill-omened *adj.* doomed to be unlucky; ill-fated.

ill-sorted *adj.* badly arranged or matched; ill-assorted.

ill-starred *adj.* unlucky; unfortunate; ill-fated.

ill temper *n.* bad temper; irritability. —ˌ**ill-'tempered** *adj.* —ˌ**ill-'temperedly** *adv.*

ill-timed *adj.* occurring at or planned for an unsuitable time.

ill-treat *vb.* (*tr.*) to behave cruelly or harshly towards; misuse; maltreat. —ˌ**ill-'treatment** *n.*

illude (ɪ'luːd) *vb. Literary.* to trick or deceive. [C15: from Latin *illūdere* to sport with, from *lūdus* game]

illume (ɪ'luːm) *vb.* (*tr.*) a poetic word for **illuminate.** [C17: shortened from ILLUMINE]

illuminance (ɪ'luːmɪnəns) *n.* the luminous flux incident on unit area of a surface. It is measured in lux. Symbol: E_v Sometimes called: **illumination.** Compare **irradiance.**

illuminant (ɪ'luːmɪnənt) *n.* **1.** something that provides or gives off light. ~*adj.* **2.** giving off light; illuminating.

illuminate *vb.* (ɪ'luːmɪˌneɪt). **1.** (*tr.*) to throw light in or into; light up: *to illuminate a room.* **2.** (*tr.*) to make easily understood; clarify. **3.** to adorn, decorate, or be decorated with lights. **4.** (*tr.*) to decorate (a letter, page, etc.) by the application of colours, gold, or silver. **5.** (*intr.*) to become lighted up. ~*adj.* (ɪ'luːmɪnɪt, -ˌneɪt). **6.** *Archaic.* made clear or bright with light; illuminated. ~*n.* (ɪ'luːmɪnɪt, -ˌneɪt). **7.** a person who has or claims to have special enlightenment. [C16: from Latin *illūmināre* to light up, from *lūmen* light] —**il'luminative** *adj.* —**il'lumiˌnator** *n.*

illuminati (ɪˌluːmɪ'nɑːtiː) *pl. n., sing.* **-to** (-təʊ). a group of persons claiming exceptional enlightenment on some subject, esp. religion. [C16: from Latin, literally: the enlightened ones, from *illūmināre* to ILLUMINATE]

illuminating (ɪ'luːmɪˌneɪtɪŋ) *adj.* serving to inform or clarify; instructive. —**il'lumiˌnatingly** *adv.*

illumination (ɪˌluːmɪ'neɪʃən) *n.* **1.** the act of illuminating or the state of being illuminated. **2.** a source of light. **3.** (*often pl.*) *Chiefly Brit.* a light or lights, esp. coloured lights, used as decoration in streets, parks, etc. **4.** spiritual or intellectual enlightenment; insight or understanding. **5.** the act of making understood; clarification. **6.** decoration in colours, gold, or silver used on some manuscripts or printed works. **7.** *Physics.* another name (not in technical usage) for **illuminance.** —**ilˌlumi'national** *adj.*

illumine (ɪ'luːmɪn) *vb.* a literary word for **illuminate.** [C14: from Latin *illūmināre* to make light; see ILLUMINATE] —**il'luminable** *adj.*

illuminism (ɪ'luːmɪˌnɪzəm) *n.* **1.** belief in and advocation of special enlightenment. **2.** the tenets and principles of the Illuminati or of any of several religious or political movements initiated by them. —**il'luminist** *n.*

ill-use *vb.* ('ɪl'juːz). **1.** to use badly or cruelly; abuse; maltreat. ~*n.* ('ɪl'juːs), *also* **ill-usage.** **2.** harsh or cruel treatment; abuse.

illusion (ɪ'luːʒən) *n.* **1.** a false appearance or deceptive impression of reality: *the mirror gives an illusion of depth.* **2.** a false or misleading perception or belief; delusion: *he has the illusion that he is really clever.* **3.** *Psychol.* a perception that is not true to reality, having been altered subjectively in some way in the mind of the perceiver. See also **hallucination.** **4.** a very fine gauze or tulle used for trimmings, veils, etc. [C14: from Latin *illūsiō* deceit, from *illūdere*; see ILLUDE] —**il'lusionary** *or* **il'lusional** *adj.* —**il'lusioned** *adj.*

illusionism (ɪ'luːʒəˌnɪzəm) *n.* **1.** *Philosophy.* the doctrine that the external world exists only in illusory sense perceptions. **2.** the use of highly illusory effects in art or decoration, esp. the use of perspective in painting to create an impression of three-dimensional reality.

illusionist (ɪ'luːʒənɪst) *n.* **1.** a person given to illusions; visionary; dreamer. **2.** *Philosophy.* a person who believes in illusionism. **3.** an artist who practises illusionism. **4.** a conjuror; magician. —**ilˌlusion'istic** *adj.*

illusory (ɪ'luːsərɪ) *or* **illusive** (ɪ'luːsɪv) *adj.* producing, produced by, or based on illusion; deceptive or unreal. —**il'lusorily** *or* **il'lusively** *adv.* —**il'lusoriness** *or* **il'lusiveness** *n.*

illust. *or* **illus.** *abbrev. for:* **1.** illustrated. **2.** illustration.

illustrate ('ɪləˌstreɪt) *vb.* **1.** to clarify or explain by use of examples, analogy, etc. **2.** (*tr.*) to be an example or demonstration of. **3.** (*tr.*) to explain or decorate (a book, text, etc.) with pictures. **4.** (*tr.*) an archaic word for **enlighten.** [C16: from Latin *illustrāre* to make light, explain, from *lustrāre* to purify, brighten; see LUSTRUM] —'**illusˌtratable** *adj.* —'**illusˌtrative** *adj.* —'**illusˌtratively** *adv.* —'**illusˌtrator** *n.*

illustration (ˌɪlə'streɪʃən) *n.* **1.** pictorial matter used to explain or decorate a text. **2.** an example or demonstration: *an illustration of his ability.* **3.** the act of illustrating or the state of being illustrated. —ˌ**illus'trational** *adj.*

illustrious (ɪ'lʌstrɪəs) *adj.* **1.** of great renown; famous and distinguished. **2.** glorious or great: *illustrious deeds.* **3.** *Obsolete.* shining. [C16: from Latin *illustris* bright, distinguished, famous, from *illustrāre* to make light; see ILLUSTRATE] —**il'lustriously** *adv.* —**il'lustriousness** *n.*

illuviation (ɪˌluːvɪ'eɪʃən) *n.* the process by which a material (**illuvium**), which includes colloids and mineral salts, is washed down from one layer of soil to a lower layer. [C20: from Latin *illuviēs* dirt, mud, from IL- + *-luviēs*, from *lavere* to wash] —**il'luvial** *adj.*

ill will *n.* hostile feeling; enmity; antagonism.

Illyrian (ɪ'lɪərɪən) *n.* **1.** a member of the group of related Indo-European peoples who occupied Illyria, an ancient region on the E Adriatic coast, from the late third millennium to the early first millennium B.C. **2.** the extinct and almost unrecorded language of these peoples: of uncertain relationship within the Indo-European family, but thought by some to be the ancestor of modern Albanian. ~*adj.* **3.** of, characteristic of, or relating to Illyria, its people, or their language.

ilmenite ('ɪlmɪˌnaɪt) *n.* a black mineral found in igneous rocks as sedimentary deposits and in veins. It is the chief source of titanium. Composition: iron titanium oxide. Formula: $FeTiO_3$. Crystal structure: hexagonal (rhombohedral). [C19: from *Ilmen*, mountain range in the southern Urals, Russia, + -ITE[1]]

ILO *abbrev. for* International Labour Organisation.

ILS *Aeronautics. abbrev. for* instrument landing system.

IM *abbrev. for:* **1.** Also: **i.m.** intramuscular. **2.** *Chess.* International Master.

I'm (aɪm) *contraction of* I am.

im- *prefix.* a variant of **in-**[1] and **in-**[2] before *b, m,* and *p.*

image ('ɪmɪdʒ) *n.* **1.** a representation or likeness of a person or thing, esp. in sculpture. **2.** an optically formed reproduction of an object, such as one formed by a lens or mirror. **3.** a person or thing that resembles another closely; double or copy. **4.** a mental representation or picture; idea produced by the imagination. **5.** the personality presented to the public by a person, organization, etc.: *a criminal charge is not good for a politician's image.* See also **corporate image.** **6.** the pattern of light that is focused onto the retina of the eye. **7.** *Psychol.* the mental experience of something that is not immediately present to the senses, often involving memory. See also **imagery, body image, hypnagogic image.** **8.** a personification of a specified quality; epitome: *the image of good breeding.* **9.** a mental picture or association of ideas evoked in a literary work, esp. in poetry. **10.** a figure of speech, such as a simile or metaphor. **11.** *Maths.* (of a point) the value of a function, f(x), corresponding to the point x. **12.** an obsolete word for **apparition.** ~*vb.* (*tr.*) **13.** to picture in the mind; imagine. **14.** to make or reflect an image of. **15.** *Computer technol.* to project or display on a screen or visual display unit. **16.** to portray or describe. **17.** to be an example or epitome of; typify. [C13: from Old French *imagene*, from Latin *imāgō* copy, representation; related to Latin *imitārī* to IMITATE] —'**imageable** *adj.* —'**imageless** *adj.*

image converter *or* **tube** *n.* a device for producing a visual image formed by other electromagnetic radiation such as infrared or ultraviolet radiation or x-rays.

image enhancement *n.* a method of improving the definition of a video picture by a computer program, which reduces the lowest grey values to black and the highest to white: used for pictures from microscopes, surveillance cameras, and scanners.

image intensifier *or* **tube** *n.* any of various devices for amplifying the intensity of an optical image, sometimes used in conjunction with an image converter.

image orthicon *n.* a television camera tube in which electrons, emitted from a photoemissive surface in proportion to the intensity of the incident light, are focused onto the target causing secondary emission of electrons.

imagery ('ɪmɪdʒrɪ, -dʒərɪ) *n., pl.* **-ries.** **1.** figurative or descriptive language in a literary work. **2.** images collectively. **3.** *Psychol.* **a.** the materials or general processes of the imagination. **b.** the characteristic kind of mental images formed by a particular individual. See also **image** (sense 7), **imagination** (sense 1). **4.** *Military.* the presentation of objects reproduced photographically (by infrared or electronic means) as prints or electronic displays.

image tube *n.* another name for **image converter** or **image intensifier.**

imaginal (ɪ'mædʒɪnəl) *adj.* **1.** of, relating to, or resembling an imago. **2.** of or relating to an image.

imaginary (ɪ'mædʒɪnərɪ, -dʒɪnrɪ) *adj.* **1.** existing in the imagination; unreal; illusory. **2.** *Maths.* involving or containing imaginary numbers. The imaginary part of a complex number, z, is usually written Imz. —**im'aginarily** *adv.* —**im'aginariness** *n.*

imaginary number *n.* any complex number of the form $a + ib$, where b is not zero and $i = \sqrt{-1}$.

imaginary part *n.* the coefficient b in a complex number $a + ib$, where $i = \sqrt{-1}$.

imagination (ɪˌmædʒɪ'neɪʃən) *n.* **1.** the faculty or action of producing ideas, esp. mental images of what is not present or has not been experienced. **2.** mental creative ability. **3.** the ability to deal resourcefully with unexpected or unusual problems, circumstances, etc. **4.** (in romantic literary criticism, esp. that of S. T. Coleridge) a creative act of perception that joins passive and active elements in thinking and imposes unity on the poetic material. Compare **fancy** (sense 9). **—im,agi'national** *adj.*

imaginative (ɪ'mædʒɪnətɪv) *adj.* **1.** produced by or indicative of a vivid or creative imagination: *an imaginative story.* **2.** having a vivid imagination. **—im'aginatively** *adv.* **—im'aginativeness** *n.*

imagine (ɪ'mædʒɪn) *vb.* **1.** (when *tr., may take a clause as object*) to form a mental image of. **2.** (when *tr., may take a clause as object*) to think, believe, or guess. **3.** (*tr.; takes a clause as object*) to suppose; assume: *I imagine he'll come.* **4.** (*tr.; takes a clause as object*) to believe or assume without foundation: *he imagines he knows the whole story.* **5.** an archaic word for **plot**[1]. *~sentence substitute.* **6.** Also: **imagine that!** an exclamation of surprise. [C14: from Latin *imāginārī* to fancy, picture mentally, from *imāgō* likeness; see IMAGE] **—im'aginable** *adj.* **—im'aginably** *adv.* **—im'aginer** *n.*

imagism ('ɪmɪ,dʒɪzəm) *n.* a poetic movement in England and America between 1912 and 1917, initiated chiefly by Ezra Pound, advocating the use of ordinary speech and the precise presentation of images. **—'imagist** *n., adj.* **—,imag'istic** *adj.* **—,imag'istically** *adv.*

imago (ɪ'meɪgəʊ) *n., pl.* **imagoes** *or* **imagines** (ɪ'mædʒə,ni:z). **1.** an adult sexually mature insect produced after metamorphosis. **2.** *Psychoanal.* an idealized image of another person, usually a parent, acquired in childhood and carried in the unconscious in later life. [C18: New Latin, from Latin: likeness; see IMAGE]

imam (ɪ'mɑ:m) *or* **imaum** (ɪ'mɑ:m, ɪ'mɔ:m) *n. Islam.* **1.** a leader of congregational prayer in a mosque. **2.** a caliph, as leader of a Muslim community. **3.** an honorific title applied to eminent doctors of Islam, such as the founders of the orthodox schools. **4.** any of a succession of either seven or twelve religious leaders of the Shiites, regarded by their followers as divinely inspired. [C17: from Arabic: leader, from *amma* he guided]

imamate (ɪ'mɑ:meɪt) *n. Islam.* **1.** the region or territory governed by an imam. **2.** the office, rank, or period of office of an imam.

IMarE *abbrev. for* Institute of Marine Engineers.

imaret (ɪ'mɑ:rɛt) *n.* (in Turkey) a hospice for pilgrims or travellers. [C17: from Turkish, from Arabic *'imārah* hospice, building, from *amara* he built]

imbalance (ɪm'bæləns) *n.* a lack of balance, as in emphasis, proportion, etc.: *the political imbalance of the programme.*

imbecile ('ɪmbɪ,si:l, -,saɪl) *n.* **1.** *Psychol.* a person of very low intelligence (IQ of 25 to 50), usually capable only of guarding himself against danger and of performing simple mechanical tasks under supervision. **2.** *Informal.* an extremely stupid person; dolt. *~adj.* also **imbecilic** (,ɪmbɪ'sɪlɪk). **3.** of or like an imbecile; mentally deficient; feeble-minded. **4.** stupid or senseless: *an imbecile thing to do.* [C16: from Latin *imbēcillus* feeble (physically or mentally)] **—'imbe,cilely** *or* **,imbe'cilically** *adv.* **—,imbe'cility** *n.*

imbed (ɪm'bɛd) *vb.* **-beds, -bedding, -bedded.** a less common spelling of **embed.**

imbibe (ɪm'baɪb) *vb.* **1.** to drink (esp. alcoholic drinks). **2.** *Literary.* to take in or assimilate (ideas, facts, etc.): *to imbibe the spirit of the Renaissance.* **3.** (*tr.*) to take in as if by drinking: *to imbibe fresh air.* **4.** to absorb or cause to absorb liquid or moisture; assimilate or saturate. [C14: from Latin *imbibere,* from *bibere* to drink] **—im'biber** *n.*

imbibition (,ɪmbɪ'bɪʃən) *n.* **1.** *Chem.* the absorption or adsorption of a liquid by a gel or solid. **2.** *Photog.* the absorption of dyes by gelatin, used in some colour printing processes. **3.** *Obsolete.* the act of imbibing.

imbricate *adj.* ('ɪmbrɪkɪt, -,keɪt), *also* **imbricated. 1.** *Architect.* relating to or having tiles, shingles, or slates that overlap. **2.** *Botany.* (of leaves, scales, etc.) overlapping each other. *~vb.* ('ɪmbrɪ,keɪt). **3.** (*tr.*) to decorate with a repeating pattern resembling scales or overlapping tiles. [C17: from Latin *imbricāre* to cover with overlapping tiles, from *imbrex* pantile] **—'imbricately** *adv.* **—,imbri'cation** *n.*

imbroglio (ɪm'brəʊlɪ,əʊ) *n., pl.* **-glios. 1.** a confused or perplexing political or interpersonal situation. **2.** *Obsolete.* a confused heap; jumble. [C18: from Italian, from *imbrogliare* to confuse, EMBROIL]

imbrue *or* **embrue** (ɪm'bru:) *vb.* **-brues, -bruing, -brued.** (*tr.*) *Rare.* **1.** to stain, esp. with blood. **2.** to permeate or impregnate. [C15: from Old French *embreuver,* from Latin *imbibere* IMBIBE] **—im'bruement** *or* **em'bruement** *n.*

imbue (ɪm'bju:) *vb.* **-bues, -buing, -bued.** (*tr.;* usually foll. by *with*) **1.** to instil or inspire (with ideals, principles, etc.): *his sermons were imbued with the spirit of the Reformation.* **2.** *Rare.* to soak, esp. with moisture, dye, etc. [C16: from Latin *imbuere* to stain, accustom] **—im'buement** *n.*

IMCO *abbrev. for* Intergovernmental Maritime Consultative Organization: the department of the United Nations concerned with international maritime safety, antipollution regulations, etc.

IMechE *abbrev. for* Institution of Mechanical Engineers.

IMF *abbrev. for* International Monetary Fund.

imidazole (,ɪmɪd'æzəʊl, -ɪdə'zəʊl) *n.* **1.** Also called: **glyoxaline, iminazole.** a white crystalline basic heterocyclic compound; 1,3-diazole. Formula: $C_3H_4N_2$. **2.** any substituted derivative of this compound. [C19: from IMIDE + AZOLE]

imide ('ɪmaɪd) *n.* any of a class of organic compounds whose molecules contain the divalent group -CONHCO-. [C19: alteration of AMIDE] **—imidic** (ɪ'mɪdɪk) *adj.*

imine (ɪ'mi:n, 'ɪmi:n) *n.* any of a class of organic compounds in which a nitrogen atom is bound to one hydrogen atom and to two alkyl or aryl groups. They contain the divalent group NH. [C19: alteration of AMINE]

IMinE *abbrev. for* Institution of Mining Engineers.

iminourea (ɪ,mi:nəʊjʊə'rɪə) *n.* another name for **guanidine.**

imipramine (ɪ'mɪprə,mi:n) *n.* a tricyclic antidepressant drug. Formula: $C_{19}H_{24}N_2$. [C20: from IMI(DE) + PR(OPYL) + AMINE]

imit. *abbrev. for:* **1.** imitation. **2.** imitative.

imitate ('ɪmɪ,teɪt) *vb.* (*tr.*) **1.** to try to follow the manner, style, character, etc., of or take as a model: *many writers imitated the language of Shakespeare.* **2.** to pretend to be or to impersonate, esp. for humour; mimic. **3.** to make a copy or reproduction of; duplicate; counterfeit. **4.** to make or be like; resemble or simulate: *her achievements in politics imitated her earlier successes in business.* [C16: from Latin *imitārī;* see IMAGE] **—imitable** ('ɪmɪtəb°l) *adj.* **—,imita'bility** *or* **'imitableness** *n.* **—'imi,tator** *n.*

imitation (,ɪmɪ'teɪʃən) *n.* **1.** the act, practice, or art of imitating; mimicry. **2.** an instance or product of imitating, such as a copy of the manner of a person; impression. **3. a.** a copy or reproduction of a genuine article; counterfeit. **b.** (*as modifier*): *imitation jewellery.* **4.** (in contrapuntal or polyphonic music) the repetition of a phrase or figure in one part after its appearance in another, as in a fugue. **5.** a literary composition that adapts the style of an older work to the writer's own purposes. **—,imi'tational** *adj.*

imitative ('ɪmɪtətɪv) *adj.* **1.** imitating or tending to imitate or copy. **2.** characterized by imitation. **3.** copying or reproducing the features of an original, esp. in an inferior manner: *imitative painting.* **4.** another word for **onomatopoeic. —'imitatively** *adv.* **—'imitativeness** *n.*

immaculate (ɪ'mækjʊlɪt) *adj.* **1.** completely clean; extremely tidy: *his clothes were immaculate.* **2.** completely flawless, etc.: *an immaculate rendering of the symphony.* **3.** morally pure; free from sin or corruption. **4.** *Biology.* of only one colour, with no spots or markings. [C15: from Latin *immaculātus,* from IM- (not) + *macula* blemish] **—im'maculacy** *or* **im'maculateness** *n.* **—im'maculately** *adv.*

Immaculate Conception *n. Christian theol., R.C. Church.* the doctrine that the Virgin Mary was conceived without any stain of original sin.

immanent ('ɪmənənt) *adj.* **1.** existing, operating, or remaining within; inherent. **2.** of or relating to the pantheistic conception of God, as being present throughout the universe. Compare **transcendent** (sense 3). [C16: from Latin *immanēre* to remain in, from IM- (in) + *manēre* to stay] **—'immanence** *or* **'immanency** *n.* **—'immanently** *adv.*

immanentism ('ɪmənən,tɪzəm) *n.* belief in the immanence of God. **—'immanentist** *n.*

immaterial (,ɪmə'tɪərɪəl) *adj.* **1.** of no real importance; inconsequential. **2.** not formed of matter; incorporeal; spiritual. **—,imma,teri'ality** *or* **,imma'terialness** *n.* **—,imma'terially** *adv.*

immaterialism (,ɪmə'tɪərɪə,lɪzəm) *n. Philosophy.* **1.** the doctrine that the material world exists only in the mind. **2.** the doctrine that only immaterial substances or spiritual beings exist. *~See also* **idealism** (sense 3). **—,imma'terialist** *n.*

immaterialize *or* **immaterialise** (,ɪmə'tɪərɪə,laɪz) *vb* (*tr.*) to make immaterial.

immature (,ɪmə'tjʊə, -'tʃʊə) *adj.* **1.** not fully grown or developed. **2.** deficient in maturity; lacking wisdom, insight, emotional stability, etc. **3.** *Geography.* a less common term for **youthful** (sense 4). **—,imma'turity** *or* **,imma'tureness** *n.* **—,imma'turely** *adv.*

immeasurable (ɪ'mɛʒərəb°l) *adj.* incapable of being measured, esp. by virtue of great size; limitless. **—im,measura'bility** *or* **im'measurableness** *n.* **—im'measurably** *adv.*

immediate (ɪ'mi:dɪət) *adj.* (*usually prenominal*) **1.** taking place or accomplished without delay: *an immediate reaction.* **2.** closest or most direct in effect or relationship: *the immediate cause of his downfall.* **3.** having no intervening medium; direct in effect: *an immediate influence.* **4.** contiguous in space, time, or relationship: *our immediate neighbour.* **5.** present; current: *the immediate problem is food.* **6.** *Philosophy.* of or relating to an object or concept that is directly known or intuited. **7.** *Logic.* (of an inference) deriving its conclusion from a single premise, esp. by conversion or obversion of a categorial statement. [C16: from Medieval Latin *immediātus,* from Latin IM- (not) + *mediāre* to be in the middle; see MEDIATE] **—im'mediacy** *or* **im'mediateness** *n.*

immediate annuity *n.* an annuity that starts less than a year after its purchase. Compare **deferred annuity.**

immediate constituent *n.* a constituent of a linguistic construction at the first step in an analysis; for example, the immediate constituents of a sentence are the subject and the predicate.

immediately (ɪˈmiːdɪətlɪ) *adv.* **1.** without delay or intervention; at once; instantly: *it happened immediately.* **2.** very closely or directly: *this immediately concerns you.* **3.** near or close by: *he's somewhere immediately in this area.* ~*conj.* **4.** (*subordinating*) *Chiefly Brit.* at the same time as; as soon as: *immediately he opened the door, there was a gust of wind.*

immedicable (ɪˈmɛdɪkəbᵊl) *adj.* (of wounds) unresponsive to treatment. —**imˈmedicableness** *n.* —**imˈmedicably** *adv.*

Immelmann turn *or* **Immelmann** (ˈɪməlˌmɑːn, -mən) *n.* an aircraft manoeuvre used to gain height while reversing the direction of flight. It consists of a half loop followed by a half roll. [C20: named after Max *Immelmann* (1890–1916), German aviator]

immemorial (ˌɪmɪˈmɔːrɪəl) *adj.* originating in the distant past; ancient (postpositive in the phrase **time immemorial**). [C17: from Medieval Latin *immemoriālis,* from Latin IM- (not) + *memoria* MEMORY] —ˌ**immeˈmorially** *adv.*

immense (ɪˈmɛns) *adj.* **1.** unusually large; huge; vast. **2.** without limits; immeasurable. **3.** *Informal.* very good; excellent. [C15: from Latin *immensus,* literally: unmeasured, from IM- (not) + *mensus* measured, from *mētīrī* to measure] —**imˈmensely** *adv.* —**imˈmenseness** *n.*

immensity (ɪˈmɛnsɪtɪ) *n., pl.* **-ties. 1.** the state or quality of being immense; vastness; enormity. **2.** enormous expanse, distance, or volume: *the immensity of space.* **3.** *Informal.* a huge amount: *an immensity of wealth.*

immensurable (ɪˈmɛnʃərəbᵊl) *adj.* a less common word for **immeasurable.**

immerge (ɪˈmɜːdʒ) *vb.* an archaic word for **immerse.** [C17: from Latin *immergere* to IMMERSE] —**imˈmergence** *n.*

immerse (ɪˈmɜːs) *vb.* (*tr.*) **1.** (often foll. by *in*) to plunge or dip into liquid. **2.** (*often passive;* often foll. by *in*) to involve deeply; engross: *to immerse oneself in a problem.* **3.** to baptize by immersion. [C17: from Latin *immergere,* from IM- (in) + *mergere* to dip] —**imˈmersible** *adj.*

immersed (ɪˈmɜːst) *adj.* **1.** sunk or submerged. **2.** (of plants) growing completely submerged in water. **3.** (of a plant or animal organ) embedded in another organ or part. **4.** involved deeply; engrossed.

immerser (ɪˈmɜːsə) *n.* an informal term for **immersion heater.**

immersion (ɪˈmɜːʃən) *n.* **1.** a form of baptism in which part or the whole of a person's body is submerged in the water. **2.** Also called: **ingress.** *Astronomy.* the disappearance of a celestial body prior to an eclipse or occultation. **3.** the act of immersing or state of being immersed.

immersion heater *n.* an electrical device, usually thermostatically controlled, for heating the liquid in which it is immersed, esp. as a fixture in a domestic hot-water tank.

immersionism (ɪˈmɜːʃəˌnɪzəm) *n.* the doctrine that immersion is the only true and valid form of Christian baptism. —**imˈmersionist** *n.*

immesh (ɪˈmɛʃ) *vb.* a variant of **enmesh.**

immethodical (ˌɪmɪˈθɒdɪkᵊl) *adj.* lacking in method or planning; disorganized. —ˌ**immeˈthodically** *adv.* —ˌ**immeˈthodicalness** *n.*

immigrant (ˈɪmɪgrənt) *n.* **1. a.** a person who immigrates. Compare **emigrant. b.** (*as modifier*): *an immigrant community.* **2.** *Brit.* a person who has been settled in a country of which he is not a native for less than ten years. **3.** an animal or plant that lives or grows in a region to which it has recently migrated.

immigrate (ˈɪmɪˌgreɪt) *vb.* **1.** (*intr.*) to come to a place or country of which one is not a native in order to settle there. Compare **emigrate. 2.** (*intr.*) (of an animal or plant) to migrate to a new geographical area. **3.** (*tr.*) to introduce or bring in as an immigrant. [C17: from Latin *immigrāre* to go into, from IM- + *migrāre* to move] —ˌ**immiˈgration** *n.* —ˌ**immiˈgrational** *or* ˈ**immiˌgratory** *adj.* —ˈ**immiˌgrator** *n.*

imminent (ˈɪmɪnənt) *adj.* **1.** liable to happen soon; impending. **2.** *Obsolete.* jutting out or overhanging. [C16: from Latin *imminēre* to project over, from IM- (in) + *-minēre* to project; related to *mons* mountain] —ˈ**imminence** *or* ˈ**imminentness** *n.* —ˈ**imminently** *adv.*

immingle (ɪˈmɪŋgᵊl) *vb. Archaic.* to blend or mix together; intermingle.

immiscible (ɪˈmɪsɪbᵊl) *adj.* (of two or more liquids) incapable of being mixed to form a homogeneous substance: *oil and water are immiscible.* —**imˌmisciˈbility** *n.* —**imˈmiscibly** *adv.*

immitigable (ɪˈmɪtɪgəbᵊl) *adj. Rare.* unable to be mitigated; relentless; unappeasable. —**imˈmitigably** *adv.* —**imˌmitigaˈbility** *n.*

immix (ɪˈmɪks) *vb.* (*tr.*) *Archaic.* to mix in; commix. —**imˈmixture** *n.*

immobile (ɪˈməʊbaɪl) *adj.* **1.** not moving; motionless. **2.** not able to move or be moved; fixed. —**immobility** (ˌɪməʊˈbɪlɪtɪ) *n.*

immobilism (ɪˈməʊbɪˌlɪzəm) *n.* a strongly reactionary political policy.

immobilize *or* **immobilise** (ɪˈməʊbɪˌlaɪz) *vb.* (*tr.*) **1.** to make or become immobile: *to immobilize a car.* **2.** *Finance.* **a.** to remove (specie) from circulation and hold it as a reserve. **b.** to convert (circulating capital) into fixed capital. —**imˌmobiliˈzation** *or* **imˌmobiliˈsation** *n.* —**imˈmobiˌlizer** *or* **imˈmobiˌliser** *n.*

immoderate (ɪˈmɒdərɪt, ɪˈmɒdrɪt) *adj.* **1.** lacking in moderation; excessive: *immoderate demands.* **2.** *Obsolete.* venial; intemperate: *immoderate habits.* —**imˈmoderately** *adv.* —**imˌmoderˈation** *or* **imˈmoderateness** *n.*

immodest (ɪˈmɒdɪst) *adj.* **1.** indecent, esp. with regard to sexual propriety; improper. **2.** bold, impudent, or shameless. —**imˈmodestly** *adv.* —**imˈmodesty** *n.*

immolate (ˈɪməʊˌleɪt) *vb.* (*tr.*) **1.** to kill or offer as a sacrifice. **2.** *Literary.* to sacrifice (something highly valued). [C16: from Latin *immolāre* to sprinkle an offering with sacrificial meal, sacrifice, from IM- (in) + *mola* spelt grain; see MILL[1]] —ˌ**immoˈlation** *n.* —ˈ**immoˌlator** *n.*

immoral (ɪˈmɒrəl) *adj.* **1.** transgressing accepted moral rules; corrupt. **2.** sexually dissolute; profligate or promiscuous. **3.** unscrupulous or unethical: *immoral trading.* **4.** tending to corrupt or resulting from corruption: *an immoral film; immoral earnings.* —**imˈmorally** *adv.*

immoralist (ɪˈmɒrəlɪst) *n.* a person who advocates or practises immorality.

immorality (ˌɪməˈrælɪtɪ) *n., pl.* **-ties. 1.** the quality, character, or state of being immoral. **2.** immoral behaviour, esp. in sexual matters; licentiousness; profligacy or promiscuity. **3.** an immoral act.

immortal (ɪˈmɔːtᵊl) *adj.* **1.** not subject to death or decay; having perpetual life. **2.** having everlasting fame; remembered throughout time. **3.** everlasting; perpetual; constant. **4.** of or relating to immortal beings or concepts. ~*n.* **5.** an immortal being. **6.** (*often pl.*) a person who is remembered enduringly, esp. an author: *Dante is one of the immortals.* —ˌ**immorˈtality** *n.* —**imˈmortally** *adv.*

immortalize *or* **immortalise** (ɪˈmɔːtəˌlaɪz) *vb.* (*tr.*) **1.** to give everlasting fame to, as by treating in a literary work: *Macbeth was immortalized by Shakespeare.* **2.** to give immortality to. —**imˌmortaliˈzation** *or* **imˌmortaliˈsation** *n.* —**imˈmortalˌizer** *or* **imˈmortalˌiser** *n.*

Immortals (ɪˈmɔːtᵊlz) *pl. n.* the members of the French Academy.

immortelle (ˌɪmɔːˈtɛl) *n.* any of various plants, mostly of the family *Compositae* (composites), that retain their colour when dried, esp. *Xeranthemum annuum.* Also called: **everlasting, everlasting flower.** [C19: from French *(fleur) immortelle* everlasting (flower)]

immotile (ɪˈməʊtaɪl) *adj.* (esp. of living organisms or their parts) not motile. —**immotility** (ˌɪməʊˈtɪlɪtɪ) *n.*

immovable *or* **immoveable** (ɪˈmuːvəbᵊl) *adj.* **1.** unable to move or be moved; fixed; immobile. **2.** unable to be diverted from one's intentions; steadfast. **3.** unaffected by feeling; impassive. **4.** unchanging; unalterable. **5.** (of feasts, holidays, etc.) occurring on the same date every year. **6.** *Law.* **a.** (of property) not liable to be removed; fixed. **b.** of or relating to immoveables. Compare **movable.** —**imˌmovaˈbility, imˌmoveaˈbility** *or* **imˈmovableness, imˈmoveableness** *n.* —**imˈmovably** *or* **imˈmoveably** *adv.*

immoveables (ɪˈmuːvəbᵊlz) *pl. n.* (in most foreign legal systems) real property.

immune (ɪˈmjuːn) *adj.* **1.** protected against a specific disease by inoculation or as the result of innate or acquired resistance. **2.** relating to or conferring immunity: *an immune body* (see **antibody**). **3.** (*usually postpositive;* foll. by *to*) unsusceptible (to) or secure (against): *immune to inflation.* **4.** exempt from obligation, penalty, etc. ~*n.* **5.** an immune person or animal. [C15: from Latin *immūnis* exempt from a public service, from IM- (not) + *mūnus* duty]

immune complex *or* **immunocomplex** (ˈɪmjʊnəʊˌkɒmplɛks) *n.* a complex formed between an antibody and an antigen.

immune response *n.* the reaction of an organism's body to foreign materials (antigens), including the production of antibodies.

immunity (ɪˈmjuːnɪtɪ) *n., pl.* **-ties. 1.** the ability of an organism to resist disease, through the activities of specialized blood cells or antibodies produced by them in response to natural exposure or inoculation. See also **acquired immunity, natural immunity. 2.** freedom from obligation or duty, esp. exemption from tax, duty, legal liability, etc. **3.** any special privilege granting immunity. **4.** the exemption of ecclesiastical persons or property from various civil obligations or liabilities.

immunize *or* **immunise** (ˈɪmjʊˌnaɪz) *vb.* to make immune, esp. by inoculation. —ˌ**immuniˈzation** *or* ˌ**immuniˈsation** *n.* —ˈ**immuˌnizer** *or* ˈ**immuˌniser** *n.*

immuno- *or before a vowel* **immun-** *combining form.* indicating immunity or immune: *immunology.*

immunoassay (ˌɪmjʊnəʊˈæseɪ) *n. Immunol.* a technique of identifying a substance, esp. a protein, through its action as an antigen. —ˈ**immunoˌassayist** *n.*

immunochemistry (ˌɪmjʊnəʊˈkɛmɪstrɪ) *n.* the study of the chemical reactions of immunity.

immunocompetence (ˌɪmjʊnəʊˈkɒmpɪtəns) *n.* the capacity of the immune system to carry out its function of distinguishing alien from endogenous material; ability of the body to resist disease.

immunodeficiency (ˌɪmjʊnəʊdɪˈfɪʃənsɪ) *n.* a deficiency in or breakdown of a person's immune system.

immunoelectrophoresis (ˌɪmjʊnəʊɪˌlɛktrəʊfəˈriːsɪs) *n.* a technique for identifying the antigens in a blood serum, which are separated into fractions by electrophoresis.

immunofluorescence (ˌɪmjʊnəʊfluəˈrɛsəns) *n.* a method used to determine the location of antibodies or antigens in which the antibodies or antigens are labelled with a fluorescent dye.

immunogen (ɪˈmjuːnəʊdʒən) *n.* **1.** any substance that evokes an immune response. **2.** any substance that stimulates immunity.

immunogenetics (ˌɪmjʊnəʊdʒɪˈnɛtɪks) *n.* (*functioning as sing.*) the study of the relationship between immunity and genetics. —ˌ**immunogeˈnetic** *or* ˌ**immunogeˈnetical** *adj.*

immunogenic (ˌɪmjʊnəʊˈdʒɛnɪk) *adj.* causing or producing immunity or an immune response. —ˌ**immunoˈgenically** *adv.*

immunoglobulin (ˌɪmjʊnəʊˈglɒbjʊlɪn) *n.* any of five classes of proteins, all of which show antibody activity. The most abundant ones are **immunoglobulin G** (**IgG**) and **immunoglobulin A** (**IgA**).

immunological tolerance *n.* the absence of antibody production in response to the presence of antigens, usually as a result of previous exposure to the antigens.

immunology (ˌɪmjʊˈnɒlədʒɪ) *n.* the branch of biological science concerned with the study of immunity. —**immunologic** (ˌɪmjʊnəˈlɒdʒɪk) *or* ˌ**immunoˈlogical** *adj.* —ˌ**immunoˈlogically** *adv.* —ˌ**immuˈnologist** *n.*

immunoreaction (ɪˌmjuːnəʊrɪˈækʃən) *n.* the reaction between an antigen and its antibody.

immunosuppression (ˌɪmjʊnəʊsəˈprɛʃən) *n.* medical suppression of the body's immune system, esp. in order to reduce the likelihood of rejection of a transplanted organ.

immunosuppressive (ˌɪmjʊnəʊsəˈprɛsɪv) *n.* **1.** any drug used for immunosuppression. ~*adj.* **2.** of or relating to such a drug. —ˌ**immunosupˈpressant** *n., adj.*

immunotherapy (ˌɪmjʊnəʊˈθɛrəpɪ) *n. Med.* the treatment of disease by stimulating the body's production of antibodies. —**immunotherapeutic** (ˌɪmjʊnəʊˈθɛrəpjuːtɪk) *adj.*

immure (ɪˈmjʊə) *vb.* (*tr.*) **1.** *Archaic or literary.* to enclose within or as if within walls; imprison. **2.** to shut (oneself) away from society. **3.** *Obsolete.* to build into or enclose within a wall. **4.** *Archaic.* to surround or fortify with walls. [C16: from Medieval Latin *immūrāre,* from Latin IM- (in) + *mūrus* a wall] —**imˈmurement** *n.*

immutable (ɪˈmjuːtəbəl) *adj.* unchanging through time; unalterable; ageless: *immutable laws.* —**imˌmutaˈbility** *or* **imˈmutableness** *n.* —**imˈmutably** *adv.*

imp (ɪmp) *n.* **1.** a small demon or devil; mischievous sprite. **2.** a mischievous child. ~*vb.* **3.** (*tr.*) *Falconry.* to insert (new feathers) into the stumps of broken feathers in order to repair the wing of a hawk or falcon. [Old English *impa* bud, graft, hence offspring, child, from *impian* to graft, ultimately from Greek *emphutos* implanted, from *emphuein* to implant, from *phuein* to plant]

imp. *abbrev. for:* **1.** imperative. **2.** imperfect. **3.** imperial. **4.** impersonal. **5.** import. **6.** important. **7.** importer. **8.** imprimatur.

Imp. *abbrev. for:* **1.** Imperator. [Latin: Emperor] **2.** Imperatrix. [Latin: Empress] **3.** Imperial.

impact *n.* (ˈɪmpækt). **1.** the act of one body, object, etc., striking another; collision. **2.** the force with which one thing hits another or with which two objects collide. **3.** the impression made by an idea, cultural movement, social group, etc.: *the impact of the Renaissance on Medieval Europe.* ~*vb.* (ɪmˈpækt). **4.** to drive or press (an object) firmly into (another object, thing, etc.) or (of two objects) to be driven or pressed firmly together. **5.** to have an impact or strong effect (on). [C18: from Latin *impactus* pushed against, fastened on, from *impingere* to thrust at, from *pangere* to drive in] —**imˈpaction** *n.*

impact adhesive *n.* a glue designed to give adhesion when two coated surfaces are pressed together.

impacted (ɪmˈpæktɪd) *adj.* **1.** (of a tooth) unable to erupt, esp. because of being wedged against another tooth below the gum. **2.** (of a fracture) having the jagged broken ends wedged into each other.

impactive (ɪmˈpæktɪv) *adj.* **1.** of or relating to a physical impact. **2.** making a strong impression.

impact printer *n.* any printing device in which the printing surface strikes the paper, such as a traditional typewriter or a line printer.

impair (ɪmˈpɛə) *vb.* (*tr.*) to reduce or weaken in strength, quality, etc.: *his hearing was impaired by an accident.* [C14: from Old French *empeirer* to make worse, from Late Latin *pējōrāre,* from Latin *pejor* worse; see PEJORATIVE] —**imˈpairable** *adj.* —**imˈpairer** *n.* —**imˈpairment** *n.*

impala (ɪmˈpɑːlə) *n., pl.* **-las** *or* **-la.** an antelope, *Aepyceros melampus,* of southern and eastern Africa, having lyre-shaped horns and able to move with enormous leaps when disturbed. [from Zulu]

impale *or* **empale** (ɪmˈpeɪl) *vb.* (*tr.*) **1.** (often foll. by *on, upon,* or *with*) to pierce with a sharp instrument: *they impaled his severed head on a spear.* **2.** *Archaic.* to enclose with pales or fencing; fence in. **3.** *Heraldry.* to charge (a shield) with two coats of arms placed side by side. [C16: from Medieval Latin *impālāre,* from Latin IM- (in) + *pālus* PALE[2]] —**imˈpalement** *or* **emˈpalement** *n.* —**imˈpaler** *or* **emˈpaler** *n.*

impalpable (ɪmˈpælpəbᵊl) *adj.* **1.** imperceptible, esp. to the touch: *impalpable shadows.* **2.** difficult to understand; abstruse. —**imˌpalpaˈbility** *n.* —**imˈpalpably** *adv.*

impanation (ˌɪmpæˈneɪʃən) *n. Christianity.* the embodiment of Christ in the consecrated bread and wine of the Eucharist. [C16: from Medieval Latin *impanātiō,* from *impanātus* embodied in bread, from Latin IM- (in) + *panis* bread]

impanel (ɪmˈpænᵊl) *vb.* **-els, -elling, -elled** *or U.S.* **-els, -eling, -eled.** a variant spelling (esp. U.S.) of **empanel.** —**imˈpanelment** *n.*

imparadise (ɪmˈpærədaɪs) *vb.* (*tr.*) **1.** to make blissfully happy; enrapture. **2.** to make into or like paradise.

imparipinnate (ˌɪmpærɪˈpɪneɪt, -ˈpɪnɪt) *adj.* (of pinnate leaves) having a terminal unpaired leaflet. Compare **paripinnate.**

imparisyllabic (ɪmˌpærsɪˈlæbɪk) *adj.* (of a noun or verb in inflected languages) having inflected forms with different numbers of syllables. Compare **parisyllabic.**

imparity (ɪmˈpærɪtɪ) *n., pl.* **-ties.** a less common word for **disparity** (sense 1). [C16: from Late Latin *imparitās,* from Latin *impar* unequal]

impart (ɪmˈpɑːt) *vb.* (*tr.*) **1.** to communicate (information); relate. **2.** to give or bestow (something, esp. an abstract quality): *to impart wisdom.* [C15: from Old French *impartir,* from Latin *impertīre,* from IM- (in) + *partīre* to share, from *pars* part] —**imˈpartable** *adj.* —ˌ**imparˈtation** *or* **imˈpartment** *n.* —**imˈparter** *n.*

impartial (ɪmˈpɑːʃəl) *adj.* not prejudiced towards or against any particular side or party; fair; unbiased. —**imˌpartiˈality** *or* **imˈpartialness** *n.* —**imˈpartially** *adv.*

impartible (ɪmˈpɑːtəbᵊl) *adj.* **1.** *Law.* (of land, an estate, etc.) incapable of partition; indivisible. **2.** capable of being imparted. —**imˌpartiˈbility** *n.* —**imˈpartibly** *adv.*

impassable (ɪmˈpɑːsəbᵊl) *adj.* (of terrain, roads, etc.) not able to be travelled through or over. —**imˌpassaˈbility** *or* **imˈpassableness** *n.* —**imˈpassably** *adv.*

impasse (æmˈpɑːs, ˈæmpɑːs, ɪmˈpɑːs, ˈɪmpɑːs) *n.* a situation in which progress is blocked; an insurmountable difficulty; stalemate; deadlock. [C19: from French; see IM-, PASS]

impassible (ɪmˈpæsəbᵊl) *adj. Rare.* **1.** not susceptible to pain or injury. **2.** impassive or unmoved. —**imˌpassiˈbility** *or* —**imˈpassibleness** *n.* —**imˈpassibly** *adv.*

impassion (ɪmˈpæʃən) *vb.* (*tr.*) to arouse the passions of; inflame.

impassioned (ɪmˈpæʃənd) *adj.* filled with passion; fiery; inflamed: *an impassioned appeal.* —**imˈpassionedly** *adv.* —**imˈpassionedness** *n.*

impassive (ɪmˈpæsɪv) *adj.* **1.** not revealing or affected by emotion; reserved. **2.** calm; serene; imperturbable. **3.** *Rare.* unconscious or insensible. —**imˈpassively** *adv.* —**imˈpassiveness** *or* **impassivity** (ˌɪmpæˈsɪvɪtɪ) *n.*

impaste (ɪmˈpeɪst) *vb.* (*tr.*) to apply paint thickly to. [C16: from Italian *impastare,* from *pasta* PASTE[1]] —**impastation** (ˌɪmpæsˈteɪʃən) *n.*

impasto (ɪmˈpæstəʊ) *n.* **1.** paint applied thickly, so that brush and palette knife marks are evident. **2.** the technique of applying paint in this way. [C18: from Italian, from *impastare;* see IMPASTE]

impatience (ɪmˈpeɪʃəns) *n.* **1.** lack of patience; intolerance of or irritability with anything that impedes or delays. **2.** restless desire for change and excitement.

impatiens (ɪmˈpeɪʃɪˌɛnz) *n., pl.* **-ens.** any balsaminaceous plant of the genus *Impatiens,* such as balsam, touch-me-not, busy Lizzie, and policeman's helmet. [C18: New Latin from Latin: impatient; from the fact that the ripe pods burst open when touched]

impatient (ɪmˈpeɪʃənt) *adj.* **1.** lacking patience; easily irritated at delay, opposition, etc. **2.** exhibiting lack of patience: *an impatient retort.* **3.** (*postpositive;* foll. by *of*) intolerant (of) or indignant (at): *impatient of indecision.* **4.** (*postpositive;* often foll. by *for*) restlessly eager (for something or to do something). —**imˈpatiently** *adv.*

impeach (ɪmˈpiːtʃ) *vb.* (*tr.*) **1.** *Criminal law.* to bring a charge or accusation against. **2.** *Brit. criminal law.* to accuse of a crime, esp. of treason or some other offence against the state. **3.** *Chiefly U.S.* to charge (a public official) with an offence committed in office. **4.** to challenge or question (a person's honesty, integrity, etc.). [C14: from Old French *empeechier,* from Late Latin *impedicāre* to entangle, catch, from Latin IM- (in) + *pedica* a fetter, from *pēs* foot] —**imˈpeacher** *n.*

impeachable (ɪmˈpiːtʃəbᵊl) *adj.* **1.** capable of being impeached or accused. **2.** (of an offence) making a person liable to impeachment. —**imˌpeachaˈbility** *n.*

impeachment (ɪmˈpiːtʃmənt) *n.* **1.** *Rare.* (in England) committal by the House of Commons, esp. of a minister of the Crown, for trial by the House of Lords. The last instance occurred in 1805. **2.** (in the U.S.) a proceeding brought against a federal government official. **3.** an accusation or charge. **4.** *Obsolete.* discredit; reproach.

impearl (ɪmˈpɜːl) *vb.* (*tr.*) *Archaic or poetic.* **1.** to adorn with pearls. **2.** to form into pearl-like shapes or drops.

impeccable (ɪmˈpɛkəbᵊl) *adj.* **1.** without flaw or error; faultless: *an impeccable record.* **2.** *Rare.* incapable of sinning. [C16: from Late Latin *impeccābilis* sinless, from Latin IM- (not) + *peccāre* to sin] —**imˌpeccaˈbility** *n.* —**imˈpeccably** *adv.*

impeccant (ɪmˈpɛkənt) *adj.* not sinning; free from sin. [C18: from IM- (not) + Latin *peccant-,* from *peccāre* to sin] —**imˈpeccancy** *n.*

impecunious (ˌɪmpɪˈkjuːnɪəs) *adj.* without money; penniless. [C16: from IM- (not) + *-pecunious,* from Latin *pecūniōsus* wealthy, from *pecūnia* money] —ˌ**impe'cuniously** *adv.* —ˌ**impe'cuniousness** *or* **impecuniosity** (ˌɪmpɪkjuːnɪ'ɒsɪtɪ) *n.*

impedance (ɪm'piːdᵊns) *n.* **1.** a measure of the opposition to the flow of an alternating current equal to the square root of the sum of the squares of the resistance and the reactance, expressed in ohms. Symbol: Z **2.** a component that offers impedance. **3.** Also called: **acoustic impedance.** the ratio of the sound pressure in a medium to the rate of alternating flow of the medium through a specified surface due to the sound wave. Symbol: Z_a **4.** Also called: **mechanical impedance.** the ratio of the mechanical force, acting in the direction of motion, to the velocity of the resulting vibration. Symbol: Z_m

impede (ɪm'piːd) *vb.* (*tr.*) to restrict or retard in action, progress, etc.; hinder; obstruct. [C17: from Latin *impedīre* to hinder, literally: shackle the feet, from *pēs* foot] —**im'peder** *n.* —**im'pedingly** *adv.*

impediment (ɪm'pɛdɪmənt) *n.* **1.** a hindrance or obstruction. **2.** a physical defect, esp. one of speech, such as a stammer. **3.** (*pl.* **-ments** *or* **-menta** (-'mɛntə)) *Law.* an obstruction to the making of a contract, esp. a contract of marriage by reason of closeness of blood or affinity. —**imˌpedi'mental** *or* **imˌpedi'mentary** *adj.*

impedimenta (ɪmˌpɛdɪ'mɛntə) *pl. n.* **1.** the baggage and equipment carried by an army. **2.** any objects or circumstances that impede progress. **3.** a plural of **impediment** (sense 3). [C16: from Latin, plural of *impedīmentum* hindrance; see IMPEDE]

impedor (ɪm'piːdə) *n. Physics.* a component, such as an inductor or resistor, that offers impedance.

impel (ɪm'pɛl) *vb.* **-pels, -pelling, -pelled.** (*tr.*) **1.** to urge or force (a person) to an action; constrain or motivate. **2.** to push, drive, or force into motion. [C15: from Latin *impellere* to push against, drive forward, from IM- (in) + *pellere* to drive, push, strike] —**im'pellent** *n., adj.*

impeller (ɪm'pɛlə) *n.* **1.** the vaned rotating disc of a centrifugal pump, compressor, etc. **2.** a compressor or centrifugal pump having such an impeller.

impend (ɪm'pɛnd) *vb.* (*intr.*) **1.** (esp. of something threatening) to be about to happen; be imminent. **2.** (foll. by *over*) *Rare.* to be suspended; hang. [C16: from Latin *impendēre* to overhang, from *pendēre* to hang] —**im'pendence** *or* **im'pendency** *n.* —**im'pending** *adj.*

impenetrable (ɪm'pɛnɪtrəbᵊl) *adj.* **1.** incapable of being pierced through or penetrated: *an impenetrable forest.* **2.** incapable of being understood; incomprehensible: *impenetrable jargon.* **3.** incapable of being seen through: *impenetrable gloom.* **4.** not susceptible to ideas, influence, etc.: *impenetrable ignorance.* **5.** *Physics.* (of a body) incapable of occupying the same space as another body. —**imˌpenetra'bility** *n.* —**im'penetrableness** *n.* —**im'penetrably** *adv.*

impenitent (ɪm'pɛnɪtənt) *adj.* not sorry or penitent; unrepentant. —**im'penitence, im'penitency,** *or* **im'penitentness** *n.* —**im'penitently** *adv.*

impennate (ɪm'pɛneɪt) *adj. Rare.* (of birds) lacking true functional wings or feathers.

imper. *abbrev. for* imperative.

imperative (ɪm'pɛrətɪv) *adj.* **1.** extremely urgent or important; essential. **2.** peremptory or authoritative: *an imperative tone of voice.* **3.** Also: **imperatival** (ɪmˌpɛrə'taɪvᵊl). *Grammar.* denoting a mood of verbs used in giving orders, making requests, etc. In English the verb root without any inflections is the usual form, as for example *leave* in *Leave me alone.* ~*n.* **4.** something that is urgent or essential. **5.** an order or command. **6.** *Grammar.* **a.** the imperative mood. **b.** a verb in this mood. [C16: from Late Latin *imperātīvus,* from Latin *imperāre* to command] —**im'peratively** *adv.* —**im'perativeness** *n.*

imperator (ˌɪmpə'rɑːtɔː) *n.* **1. a.** (in imperial Rome) a title of the emperor. **b.** (in republican Rome) a temporary title of honour bestowed upon a victorious general. **2.** a less common word for **emperor.** [C16: from Latin: commander, from *imperāre* to command] —**imperatorial** (ɪmˌpɛrə'tɔːrɪəl) *adj.* —**imˌpera'torially** *adv.* —ˌ**impe'ratorˌship** *n.*

imperceptible (ˌɪmpə'sɛptɪbᵊl) *adj.* too slight, subtle, gradual, etc., to be perceived. —ˌ**imperˌcepti'bility** *or* ˌ**imper'ceptibleness** *n.* —ˌ**imper'ceptibly** *adv.*

imperceptive (ˌɪmpə'sɛptɪv) *adj., also* **impercipient** (ˌɪmpə'sɪpɪənt). lacking in perception; obtuse. —ˌ**imper'ception** *n.* —ˌ**imper'ceptively** *adv.* —ˌ**impercep'tivity,** ˌ**imper'ceptiveness,** *or* ˌ**imper'cipience** *n.*

imperf. *abbrev. for:* **1.** Also: **impf.** imperfect. **2.** (of stamps) imperforate.

imperfect (ɪm'pɜːfɪkt) *adj.* **1.** exhibiting or characterized by faults, mistakes, etc.; defective. **2.** not complete or finished; deficient. **3.** *Botany.* **a.** (of flowers) lacking functional stamens or pistils. **b.** not involving or undergoing sexual reproduction: *imperfect fungi.* **4.** *Grammar.* denoting a tense of verbs used most commonly in describing continuous or repeated past actions or events, as for example *was walking* as opposed to *walked.* **5.** *Law.* (of a trust, an obligation, etc.) lacking some necessary formality to make effective or binding; incomplete; legally unenforceable. See also **executory** (sense 1). **6.** *Music.* **a.** (of a cadence) proceeding to the dominant from the tonic, subdominant, or any chord other than the dominant. **b.** of or relating to all intervals other than the fourth, fifth, and octave. Compare **perfect** (sense 9). ~*n.* **7.** *Grammar.* **a.** the imperfect tense. **b.** a verb in this tense. —**im'perfectly** *adv.* —**im'perfectness** *n.*

imperfect competition *n. Economics.* the market situation that exi sts when one or more of the necessary conditions for perfect competition do not hold.

imperfection (ˌɪmpə'fɛkʃən) *n.* **1.** the condition or quality of being imperfect. **2.** a fault or defect.

imperfective (ˌɪmpə'fɛktɪv) *Grammar.* ~*adj.* **1.** denoting an aspect of the verb in some languages, including English, used to indicate that the action is in progress without regard to its completion. Compare **perfective.** ~*n.* **2. a.** the imperfective aspect of a verb. **b.** a verb in this aspect. —ˌ**imper'fectively** *adv.*

imperforate (ɪm'pɜːfərɪt, -ˌreɪt) *adj.* **1.** not perforated. **2.** (of a postage stamp) not provided with perforation or any other means of separation. Abbrev.: **imperf.** Compare **perforate. 3.** *Anatomy.* (of a bodily part, such as the anus) without the normal opening. —**imˌperfo'ration** *n.*

imperia (ɪm'pɪərɪə) *n.* the plural of **imperium.**

imperial (ɪm'pɪərɪəl) *adj.* **1.** of or relating to an empire, emperor, or empress. **2.** characteristic of or befitting an emperor; majestic; commanding. **3.** characteristic of or exercising supreme authority; imperious. **4.** (esp. of products and commodities) of a superior size or quality. **5.** (*usually prenominal*) (of weights, measures, etc.) conforming to standards or definitions legally established in Great Britain: *an imperial gallon.* ~*n.* **6.** any of various book sizes, esp. 7½ by 11 inches (**imperial octavo**) or (chiefly Brit.) 11 by 15 inches (**imperial quarto**). **7.** a size of writing or printing paper, 23 by 31 inches (U.S. and Canadian) or 22 by 30 inches (Brit.). **8.** (formerly) a Russian gold coin originally worth ten roubles. **9.** *U.S.* **a.** the top of a carriage, such as a diligence. **b.** a luggage case carried there. **10.** *Architect.* a dome that has a point at the top. **11.** a small tufted beard popularized by the emperor Napoleon III. **12.** a member of an imperial family, esp. an emperor or empress. **13.** a red deer having antlers with fourteen points. [C14: from Late Latin *imperiālis,* from Latin *imperium* command, authority, empire] —**im'perially** *adv.* —**im'perialness** *n.*

Imperial (ɪm'pɪərɪəl) *adj.* **1.** (*sometimes not cap.*) of or relating to a specified empire, such as the British Empire. ~*n.* **2.** a supporter or soldier of the Holy Roman Empire.

imperial gallon *n.* a formal name for **gallon** (sense 1).

imperialism (ɪm'pɪərɪəˌlɪzəm) *n.* **1.** the policy or practice of extending a state's rule over other territories. **2.** an instance or policy of aggressive behaviour by one state against another. **3.** the extension or attempted extension of authority, influence, power, etc., by any person, country, institution, etc.: *cultural imperialism.* **4.** a system of imperial government or rule by an emperor. **5.** the spirit, character, authority, etc., of an empire. **6.** advocacy of or support for any form of imperialism. —**im'perialist** *adj., n.* —**imˌperial'istic** *adj.* —**imˌperial'istically** *adv.*

imperil (ɪm'pɛrɪl) *vb.* (*tr.*) to place in danger or jeopardy; endanger. —**im'perilment** *n.*

imperious (ɪm'pɪərɪəs) *adj.* **1.** domineering; arrogant; overbearing. **2.** *Rare.* urgent; imperative. [C16: from Latin *imperiōsus* from *imperium* command, power] —**im'periously** *adv.* —**im'periousness** *n.*

imperishable (ɪm'pɛrɪʃəbᵊl) *adj.* **1.** not subject to decay or deterioration: *imperishable goods.* **2.** not likely to be forgotten: *imperishable truths.* —**imˌperisha'bility** *or* **im'perishableness** *n.* —**im'perishably** *adv.*

imperium (ɪm'pɪərɪəm) *n., pl.* **-ria** (-rɪə). **1.** (in ancient Rome) the supreme power, held esp. by consuls and emperors, to command and administer in military, judicial, and civil affairs. **2.** the right to command; supreme power. **3.** a less common word for **empire.** [C17: from Latin: command, empire, from *imperāre* to command; see EMPEROR]

impermanent (ɪm'pɜːmənənt) *adj.* not permanent; fleeting; transitory. —**im'permanence** *or* **im'permanency** *n.* —**im'permanently** *adv.*

impermeable (ɪm'pɜːmɪəbᵊl) *adj.* (of a substance) not allowing the passage of a fluid through interstices; not permeable. —**imˌpermea'bility** *or* **im'permeableness** *n.* —**im'permeably** *adv.*

impermissible (ˌɪmpə'mɪsɪbᵊl) *adj.* not permissible; not allowed. —ˌ**imperˌmissi'bility** *n.* —ˌ**imper'missibly** *adv.*

impers. *abbrev. for* impersonal.

imperscriptible (ˌɪmpə'skrɪptɪbᵊl) *adj.* not supported by written authority. [C19: from IM- (not) + Latin *perscribere* to write down]

impersonal (ɪm'pɜːsənᵊl) *adj.* **1.** without reference to any individual person; objective: *an impersonal assessment.* **2.** devoid of human warmth or sympathy; cold: *an impersonal manner.* **3.** not having human characteristics: *an impersonal God.* **4.** *Grammar.* (of a verb) having no logical subject. Usually in English the pronoun *it* is used in such cases as a grammatical subject, as for example in *It is raining.* **5.** *Grammar.* (of a pronoun) not denoting a person. —**imˌperson'ality** *n.* —**im'personally** *adv.*

impersonalize *or* **impersonalise** (ɪm'pɜːsənəˌlaɪz) *vb.* (*tr.*) to make impersonal, esp. to rid of such human characteristics as sympathy, warmth, etc.; dehumanize. —**imˌpersonali'zation** *or* **imˌpersonali'sation** *n.*

impersonate (ɪm'pɜːsəˌneɪt) *vb.* (*tr.*) **1.** to pretend to be (another person). **2.** to imitate the character, mannerisms, etc., of (another person). 3. *Rare.* to play the part or character of. 4. an archaic word for **personify.** —**imˌpersonˈation** *n.* —**imˈpersonˌator** *n.*

impertinence (ɪmˈpɜːtɪnəns) *or* **impertinency** *n.* 1. disrespectful behaviour or language; rudeness; insolence. 2. an impertinent act, gesture, etc. 3. *Rare.* lack of pertinence; irrelevance; inappropriateness.

impertinent (ɪmˈpɜːtɪnənt) *adj.* 1. rude; insolent; impudent. 2. irrelevant or inappropriate. [C14: from Latin *impertinēns* not belonging, from Latin IM- (not) + *pertinēre* to be relevant; see PERTAIN] —**imˈpertinently** *adv.*

imperturbable (ˌɪmpɜːˈtɜːbəbᵊl) *adj.* not easily perturbed; calm; unruffled. —ˌ**imperˌturbaˈbility** *or* ˌ**imperˈturbableness** *n.* —ˌ**imperˈturbably** *adv.* —**imperturbation** (ˌɪmpɜːtɜːˈbeɪʃən) *n.*

impervious (ɪmˈpɜːvɪəs) *or* **imperviable** *adj.* 1. not able to be penetrated, as by water, light, etc.; impermeable. 2. (*often postpositive;* foll. by *to*) not able to be influenced (by) or not receptive (to): *impervious to argument.* —**imˈperviously** *adv.* —**imˈperviousness** *n.*

impetigo (ˌɪmpɪˈtaɪgəʊ) *n.* a contagious bacterial skin disease characterized by the formation of pustules that develop into yellowish crusty sores. [C16: from Latin: scabby eruption, from *impetere* to assail; see IMPETUS; for form, compare VERTIGO] —**impetiginous** (ˌɪmpɪˈtɪdʒɪnəs) *adj.*

impetrate (ˈɪmpɪˌtreɪt) *vb.* (*tr.*) 1. to supplicate or entreat for, esp. by prayer. 2. to obtain by prayer. [C16: from Latin *impetrāre* to procure by entreaty, from *-petrāre,* from *patrāre* to bring to pass, of uncertain origin; perhaps related to Latin *pater* a father] —ˌ**impeˈtration** *n.* —ˈ**impetrative** *adj.* —ˈ**impeˌtrator** *n.*

impetuous (ɪmˈpɛtjʊəs) *adj.* 1. liable to act without consideration; rash; impulsive. 2. resulting from or characterized by rashness or haste. 3. *Poetic.* moving with great force or violence; rushing: *the impetuous stream hurtled down the valley.* [C14: from Late Latin *impetuōsus* violent; see IMPETUS] —**imˈpetuously** *adv.* —**imˈpetuousness** *or* **impetuosity** (ɪmˌpɛtjʊˈɒsɪtɪ) *n.*

impetus (ˈɪmpɪtəs) *n., pl.* **-tuses.** 1. an impelling movement or force; incentive or impulse; stimulus. 2. *Physics.* the force that sets a body in motion or that tends to resist changes in a body's motion. [C17: from Latin: attack, from *impetere* to assail, from IM- (in) + *petere* to make for, seek out]

impf. *or* **imperf.** *abbrev. for* imperfect.

imp. gal. *or* **imp. gall.** *abbrev. for* imperial gallon.

impi (ˈɪmpɪ) *n., pl.* **-pi** *or* **-pies.** *Derogatory.* a group of Bantu warriors. [C19: from Zulu]

impiety (ɪmˈpaɪɪtɪ) *n., pl.* **-ties.** 1. lack of reverence or proper respect for a god. 2. any lack of proper respect. 3. an impious act.

impinge (ɪmˈpɪndʒ) *vb.* 1. (*intr.;* usually foll. by *on* or *upon*) to encroach or infringe; trespass: *to impinge on someone's time.* 2. (*intr.;* usually foll. by *on, against,* or *upon*) to collide (with); strike. [C16: from Latin *impingere* to drive at, dash against, from *pangere* to fasten, drive in] —**imˈpingement** *n.* —**imˈpinger** *n.*

impingement attack *n. Metallurgy.* a form of corrosion of metals caused by erosion of the oxide layer by a moving fluid in which there are suspended particles or air bubbles.

impious (ˈɪmpɪəs) *adj.* 1. lacking piety or reverence for a god; ungodly. 2. lacking respect; undutiful. —ˈ**impiously** *adv.* —ˈ**impiousness** *n.*

impish (ˈɪmpɪʃ) *adj.* of or resembling an imp; mischievous. —ˈ**impishly** *adv.* —ˈ**impishness** *n.*

implacable (ɪmˈplækəbᵊl) *adj.* 1. incapable of being placated or pacified; unappeasable. 2. inflexible; intractable. —**imˌplacaˈbility** *or* **imˈplacableness** *n.* —**imˈplacably** *adv.*

implacental (ˌɪmpləˈsɛntᵊl) *adj.* another word for **aplacental.**

implant *vb.* (ɪmˈplɑːnt). (*tr.*) 1. to establish firmly; inculcate; instil: *to implant sound moral principles.* 2. to plant or embed; infix; entrench. 3. *Surgery.* **a.** to graft (a tissue) into the body. **b.** to insert (a radioactive substance, hormone, etc.) into the tissues. ~*n.* (ˈɪmˌplɑːnt). 4. anything implanted, esp. surgically, such as a tissue graft. —**imˈplanter** *n.*

implantation (ˌɪmplɑːnˈteɪʃən) *n.* 1. the act of implanting or the state of being implanted. 2. Also called: **nidation.** the attachment of the blastocyst of a mammalian embryo to the wall of the uterus of the mother.

implausible (ɪmˈplɔːzəbᵊl) *adj.* not plausible; provoking disbelief; unlikely. —**imˌplausiˈbility** *or* **imˈplausibleness** *n.* —**imˈplausibly** *adv.*

implead (ɪmˈpliːd) *vb.* (*tr.*) *Law, rare.* 1. **a.** to sue or prosecute. **b.** to bring an action against. 2. to accuse. [C13: from Anglo-French *empleder;* see IM-, PLEAD] —**imˈpleadable** *adj.* —**imˈpleader** *n.*

implement *n.* (ˈɪmplɪmənt). 1. a piece of equipment; tool or utensil: *gardening implements.* 2. something used to achieve a purpose; agent. ~*vb.* (ˈɪmplɪˌmɛnt). (*tr.*) 3. to carry out; put into action; perform: *to implement a plan.* 4. *Rare.* to supply with tools. 5. *Archaic.* to complete, satisfy, or fulfil. [C17: from Late Latin *implēmentum,* literally: a filling up, from Latin *implēre* to fill up, satisfy, fulfil] —ˌ**impleˈmental** *adj.* —ˌ**implemenˈtation** *n.* —ˈ**impleˌmenter** *or* ˈ**impleˌmentor** *n.*

implicate (ˈɪmplɪˌkeɪt) *vb.* (*tr.*) 1. to show to be involved, esp. in a crime. 2. to involve as a necessary inference; imply: *his protest implicated censure by the authorities.* 3. to affect intimately: *this news implicates my decision.* 4. *Rare.* to intertwine or entangle. [C16: from Latin *implicāre* to involve, from IM- + *plicāre* to fold] —**implicative** (ɪmˈplɪkətɪv) *adj.* —**imˈplicatively** *adv.*

implication (ˌɪmplɪˈkeɪʃən) *n.* 1. the act of implicating or the state of being implicated. 2. something that is implied; suggestion: *the implication of your silence is that you're bored.* 3. *Logic.* **a.** the operator that forms a sentence from two given sentences and corresponds to the English *if ... then....* **b.** a sentence so formed. Usually written p→q or p⊃q, where p,q are the component sentences, it is true except when p (the antecedent) is true and q (the consequent) is false. **c.** the relation between such sentences. —ˌ**impliˈcational** *adj.*

implicature (ɪmˈplɪkətʃə) *n. Logic, philosophy.* 1. a proposition inferred from the circumstances of utterances of another proposition rather than from its literal meaning, as when an academic referee writes *the candidate's handwriting is excellent* to convey that he has nothing relevant to commend. 2. the relation between the uttered and the inferred statement.

implicit (ɪmˈplɪsɪt) *adj.* 1. not explicit; implied; indirect: *there was implicit criticism in his voice.* 2. absolute and unreserved; unquestioning: *you have implicit trust in him.* 3. (*when postpositive,* foll. by *in*) contained or inherent: *to bring out the anger implicit in the argument.* 4. *Maths.* (of a function) having an equation of the form $f(x,y) = 0$, in which y cannot be directly expressed in terms of x, as in $xy + x^2 + y^3x^2 = 0$. Compare **explicit**[1] (sense 4). 5. *Obsolete.* intertwined. [C16: from Latin *implicitus,* variant of *implicātus* interwoven; see IMPLICATE] —**imˈplicitly** *adv.* —**imˈplicitness** *or* **imˈplicity** *n.*

implied (ɪmˈplaɪd) *adj.* hinted at or suggested; not directly expressed: *an implied criticism.* —**impliedly** (ɪmˈplaɪɪdlɪ) *adv.*

implode (ɪmˈpləʊd) *vb.* 1. to collapse or cause to collapse inwards in a violent manner as a result of external pressure: *the vacuum flask imploded.* 2. (*tr.*) to pronounce (a consonant) with or by implosion. ~Compare **explode.** [C19: from IM- + (EX)PLODE]

implore (ɪmˈplɔː) *vb.* (*tr.*) 1. to beg or ask (someone) earnestly (to do something); plead with; beseech. 2. to ask earnestly or piteously for; supplicate; beg: *to implore someone's mercy.* [C16: from Latin *implōrāre,* from IM- + *plōrāre* to bewail] —ˌ**imploˈration** *n.* —**imˈploratory** *adj.* —**imˈplorer** *n.* —**imˈploringly** *adv.*

implosion (ɪmˈpləʊʒən) *n.* 1. the act or process of imploding: *the implosion of a light bulb.* 2. *Phonetics.* the suction or inhalation of breath employed in pronouncing an ingressive consonant.

implosive (ɪmˈpləʊsɪv) *adj.* 1. pronounced by or with implosion. ~*n.* 2. an implosive consonant. —**imˈplosively** *adv.*

imply (ɪmˈplaɪ) *vb.* **-plies, -plying, -plied.** (*tr.; may take a clause as object*) 1. to express or indicate by a hint; suggest: *what are you implying by that remark?* 2. to suggest or involve as a necessary consequence. 3. *Logic.* to enable (a conclusion) to be inferred. 4. *Obsolete.* to entangle or enfold. [C14: from Old French *emplier,* from Latin *implicāre* to involve; see IMPLICATE]

▷**Usage.** See at **infer.**

impolder (ɪmˈpəʊldə) *or* **empolder** *vb.* to make into a polder; reclaim (land) from the sea. [C19: from Dutch *inpolderen,* see IN-[2], POLDER]

impolicy (ɪmˈpɒlɪsɪ) *n., pl.* **-cies.** the act or an instance of being unjudicious or impolitic.

impolite (ˌɪmpəˈlaɪt) *adj.* discourteous; rude; uncivil. —ˌ**impoˈlitely** *adv.* —ˌ**impoˈliteness** *n.*

impolitic (ɪmˈpɒlɪtɪk) *adj.* not politic or expedient; unwise. —**imˈpoliticly** *adv.* —**imˈpoliticness** *n.*

imponderabilia (ɪmˌpɒndərəˈbɪlɪə) *pl. n.* imponderables. [C20: New Latin]

imponderable (ɪmˈpɒndərəbᵊl, -drəbᵊl) *adj.* 1. unable to be weighed or assessed. ~*n.* 2. something difficult or impossible to assess. —**imˌponderaˈbility** *or* **imˈponderableness** *n.* —**imˈponderably** *adv.*

imponent (ɪmˈpəʊnənt) *n.* a person who imposes a duty, etc.

import *vb.* (ɪmˈpɔːt, ˈɪmpɔːt). 1. to buy or bring in (goods or services) from a foreign country. Compare **export.** 2. (*tr.*) to bring in from an outside source: *to import foreign words into the language.* 3. *Rare.* to signify or be significant; mean; convey: *to import doom.* ~*n.* (ˈɪmpɔːt). 4. (*often pl.*) **a.** goods (**visible imports**) or services (**invisible imports**) that are bought from foreign countries. **b.** (*as modifier*): *an import licence.* 5. significance or importance: *a man of great import.* 6. meaning or signification. 7. *Canadian slang.* a sportsman who is not native to the area where he plays. [C15: from Latin *importāre* to carry in, from IM- + *portāre* to carry] —**imˈportable** *adj.* —**imˌportaˈbility** *n.* —**imˈporter** *n.*

importance (ɪmˈpɔːtᵊns) *n.* 1. the state of being important; significance. 2. social status; standing; esteem: *a man of importance.* 3. *Obsolete.* **a.** meaning or signification. **b.** an important matter. **c.** importunity.

important (ɪmˈpɔːtᵊnt) *adj.* 1. of great significance or value; outstanding: *Voltaire is an important writer.* 2. of social significance; notable; eminent; esteemed: *an important man in the town.* 3. (*when postpositive,* usually foll. by *to*) specially relevant or of great concern (to); valued highly (by): *your wishes are* *important to me.* 4. an obsolete word for **importunate.** [C16: from Old Italian *importante,* from Medieval Latin *importāre* to signify, be of consequence, from Latin: to carry in; see IMPORT] —**imˈportantly** *adv.*

importation (ˌɪmpɔːˈteɪʃən) *n.* 1. the act, business, or process of importing goods or services. 2. an imported product or service.

importunate (ɪmˈpɔːtjʊnɪt) *adj.* 1. persistent or demanding; insistent. 2. *Rare.* troublesome; annoying. —**imˈportunately** *adv.* —**imˈportunateness** *n.*

importune (ɪmˈpɔːtjuːn) *vb.* (*tr.*) 1. to harass with persistent requests; demand of (someone) insistently. 2. to beg for persistently; request with insistence. 3. *Obsolete.* **a.** to anger or annoy. **b.** to force; impel. [C16: from Latin *importūnus* tiresome, from *im-* IN-[1] + *-portūnus* as in *opportūnus* OPPORTUNE] —**imˈportunely** *adv.* —**imˈportuner** *n.* —ˌ**imporˈtunity** *or* **imˈportunacy** *n.*

impose (ɪmˈpəʊz) *vb.* (usually foll. by *on* or *upon*) 1. (*tr.*) to establish as something to be obeyed or complied with; enforce: *to impose a tax on the people.* 2. to force (oneself, one's presence, etc.) on another or others; obtrude. 3. (*intr.*) to take advantage, as of a person or quality: *to impose on someone's kindness.* 4. (*tr.*) *Printing.* to arrange (pages, type, etc.) for locking into a chase so that after printing and folding the pages will be in the correct order. 5. (*tr.*) to pass off deceptively; foist: *to impose a hoax on someone.* 6. (*tr.*) (of a bishop or priest) to lay (the hands) on the head of a candidate for certain sacraments. [C15: from Old French *imposer,* from Latin *impōnere* to place upon, from *pōnere* to place, set] —**imˈposable** *adj.* —**imˈposer** *n.*

imposing (ɪmˈpəʊzɪŋ) *adj.* grand or impressive: *an imposing building.* —**imˈposingly** *adv.* —**imˈposingness** *n.*

imposing stone *or* **table** *n. Printing.* a flat hard surface upon which pages are imposed.

imposition (ˌɪmpəˈzɪʃən) *n.* 1. the act of imposing. 2. something that is imposed unfairly on someone. 3. (in Britain) a task set as a school punishment. 4. the arrangement of pages for printing so that the finished work will have its pages in the correct order.

impossibility (ɪmˌpɒsəˈbɪlɪtɪ, ˌɪmpɒs-) *n., pl.* **-ties.** 1. the state or quality of being impossible. 2. something that is impossible.

impossible (ɪmˈpɒsəbᵊl) *adj.* 1. incapable of being done, undertaken, or experienced. 2. incapable of occurring or happening. 3. absurd or inconceivable; unreasonable: *it's impossible to think of him as a bishop.* 4. *Informal.* intolerable; outrageous: *those children are impossible.* —**imˈpossibleness** *n.* —**imˈpossibly** *adv.*

impossible figure *n.* a picture of an object that at first sight looks three-dimensional but cannot be a two-dimensional projection of a real three-dimensional object, for example a picture of a staircase that re-enters itself while appearing to ascend continuously. Also called: **Escher figure.**

impost[1] (ˈɪmpəʊst) *n.* 1. a tax, esp. a customs duty. 2. *Horse racing.* the specific weight that a particular horse must carry in a handicap race. ~*vb.* 3. (*tr.*) *U.S.* to classify (imported goods) according to the duty payable on them. [C16: from Medieval Latin *impostus* tax, from Latin *impositus* imposed; see IMPOSE] —ˈ**imposter** *n.*

impost[2] (ˈɪmpəʊst) *n. Architect.* a member at the top of a wall, pier, or column that supports an arch, esp. one that has a projecting moulding. [C17: from French *imposte,* from Latin *impositus* placed upon; see IMPOSE]

impostor *or* **imposter** (ɪmˈpɒstə) *n.* a person who deceives others, esp. by assuming a false identity; charlatan. [C16: from Late Latin: deceiver; see IMPOSE]

impostume (ɪmˈpɒstjuːm) *or* **imposthume** (ɪmˈpɒsθuːm) *n.* an archaic word for **abscess.** [C15: from Old French *empostume,* from Late Latin *apostēma,* from Greek, literally: separation (of pus), from *aphistanai* to remove, from *histanai* to stand]

imposture (ɪmˈpɒstʃə) *n.* the act or an instance of deceiving others, esp. by assuming a false identity. [C16: from French, from Late Latin *impostūra,* from Latin *impōnere;* see IMPOSE] —**impostrous** (ɪmˈpɒstrəs), **impostorous** (ɪmˈpɒstərəs), *or* **imˈposturous** *adj.*

impotent (ˈɪmpətənt) *adj.* 1. (*when postpositive, often takes an infinitive*) lacking sufficient strength; powerless. 2. (esp. of males) unable to perform sexual intercourse. 3. *Obsolete.* lacking self-control; unrestrained. —ˈ**impotence,** ˈ**impotency,** *or* ˈ**impotentness** *n.* —ˈ**impotently** *adv.*

impound (ɪmˈpaʊnd) *vb.* (*tr.*) 1. to confine (stray animals, illegally parked cars, etc.) in a pound. 2. **a.** to seize (chattels, etc.) by legal right. **b.** to take possession of (a document, evidence, etc.) and hold in legal custody. 3. to collect (water) in a reservoir or dam, as for irrigation. 4. to seize or appropriate. —**imˈpoundable** *adj.* —**imˈpoundage** *or* **imˈpoundment** *n.* —**imˈpounder** *n.*

impoverish (ɪmˈpɒvərɪʃ) *vb.* (*tr.*) 1. to make poor or diminish the quality of: *to impoverish society by cutting the grant to the arts.* 2. to deprive (soil, etc.) of fertility. [C15: from Old French *empovrir,* from *povre* POOR] —**imˈpoverisher** *n.* —**imˈpoverishment** *n.*

impower (ɪmˈpaʊə) *vb.* a less common spelling of **empower.**

impracticable (ɪmˈpræktɪkəbᵊl) *adj.* 1. incapable of being put into practice or accomplished; not feasible. 2. unsuitable for a desired use; unfit. 3. an archaic word for **intractable.** —**imˌpracticaˈbility** *or* **imˈpracticableness** *n.* —**imˈpracticably** *adv.*

impractical (ɪmˈpræktɪkᵊl) *adj.* 1. not practical or workable: *an impractical solution.* 2. not given to practical matters or gifted with practical skills: *he is intelligent but too impractical for commercial work.* —**imˌpractiˈcality** *or* **imˈpracticalness** *n.* —**imˈpractically** *adv.*

imprecate (ˈɪmprɪˌkeɪt) *vb.* 1. (*intr.*) to swear, curse, or blaspheme. 2. (*tr.*) to invoke or bring down (evil, a curse, etc.): *to imprecate disaster on the ship.* 3. (*tr.*) to put a curse on. [C17: from Latin *imprecārī* to invoke, from *im-* IN-[2] + *precārī* to PRAY] —ˈ**impreˌcatory** *adj.*

imprecation (ˌɪmprɪˈkeɪʃən) *n.* 1. the act of imprecating. 2. a malediction; curse.

imprecise (ˌɪmprɪˈsaɪs) *adj.* not precise; inexact or inaccurate. —ˌ**impreˈcisely** *adv.* —**imprecision** (ˌɪmprɪˈsɪʒən) *or* ˌ**impreˈciseness** *n.*

impredicative (ˌɪmprəˈdɪkətɪv) *adj. Logic.* (of a definition) given in terms that require quantification over a range that includes that which is to be defined, as *having all the properties of a great general* where one of the properties as ascribed must be that property itself. Compare **predicative** (sense 2).

impregnable[1] (ɪmˈprɛgnəbᵊl) *adj.* 1. unable to be broken into or taken by force: *an impregnable castle.* 2. unable to be shaken or overcome: *impregnable self-confidence.* 3. incapable of being refuted: *an impregnable argument.* [C15 *imprenable,* from Old French, from IM- (not) + *prenable* able to be taken, from *prendre* to take] —**imˌpregnaˈbility** *or* **imˈpregnableness** *n.* —**imˈpregnably** *adv.*

impregnable[2] (ɪmˈprɛgnəbᵊl) *or* **impregnatable** (ˌɪmprɛgˈneɪtəbᵊl) *adj.* able to be impregnated; fertile.

impregnate *vb.* (ˈɪmprɛgˌneɪt). (*tr.*) 1. to saturate, soak, or infuse: *to impregnate a cloth with detergent.* 2. to imbue or permeate; pervade. 3. to cause to conceive; make pregnant. 4. to fertilize (an ovum). 5. to make (land, soil, etc.) fruitful. ~*adj.* (ɪmˈprɛgnɪt, -ˌneɪt). 6. pregnant or fertilized. [C17: from Late Latin *impraegnāre* to make pregnant, from Latin *im-* IN-[2] + *praegnans* PREGNANT] —ˌ**impregˈnation** *n.* —**imˈpregnator** *n.*

impresa (ɪmˈpreɪzə) *or* **imprese** (ɪmˈpriːz) *n.* an emblem or device, usually a motto, as on a coat of arms. [C16: from Italian, literally: undertaking, hence deed of chivalry, motto, from *imprendere* to undertake; see EMPRISE]

impresario (ˌɪmprəˈsɑːrɪˌəʊ) *n., pl.* **-sarios.** 1. a producer or sponsor of public entertainments, esp. musical or theatrical ones. 2. the director or manager of an opera, ballet, or other performing company. [C18: from Italian, literally: one who undertakes; see IMPRESA]

imprescriptible (ˌɪmprɪˈskrɪptəbᵊl) *adj. Law.* immune or exempt from prescription. —ˌ**impreˌscriptiˈbility** *n.* —ˌ**impreˈscriptibly** *adv.*

impress[1] *vb.* (ɪmˈprɛs). (*tr.*) 1. to make an impression on; have a strong, lasting, or favourable effect on: *I am impressed by your work.* 2. to produce (an imprint, etc.) by pressure in or on (something): *to impress a seal in wax; to impress wax with a seal.* 3. (often foll. by *on*) to stress (something to a person); urge; emphasize: *to impress the danger of a situation on someone.* 4. to exert pressure on; press. 5. *Electronics.* to apply (a voltage) to a circuit or device. ~*n.* (ˈɪmprɛs). 6. the act or an instance of impressing. 7. a mark, imprint, or effect produced by impressing. [C14: from Latin *imprimere* to press into, imprint, from *premere* to PRESS[1]] —**imˈpresser** *n.* —**imˈpressible** *adj.*

impress[2] *vb.* (ɪmˈprɛs). 1. to commandeer or coerce (men or things) into government service; press-gang. ~*n.* (ˈɪmprɛs). 2. the act of commandeering or coercing into government service; impressment. [C16: see *im-* IN-[2], PRESS[2]]

impression (ɪmˈprɛʃən) *n.* 1. an effect produced in the mind by a stimulus; sensation: *he gave the impression of wanting to help.* 2. an imprint or mark produced by pressing: *he left the impression of his finger in the mud.* 3. a vague idea, consciousness, or belief: *I had the impression we had met before.* 4. a strong, favourable, or remarkable effect: *he made an impression on the managers.* 5. the act of impressing or the state of being impressed. 6. *Printing.* **a.** the act, process, or result of printing from type, plates, etc. **b.** one of a number of printings of a publication printed from the same setting of type with no or few alterations. Compare **edition** (sense 2). **c.** the total number of copies of a publication printed at one time. 7. *Dentistry.* an imprint of the teeth and gums, esp. in wax or plaster, for use in preparing crowns, inlays, or dentures. 8. an imitation or impersonation: *he did a funny impression of the politician.* —**imˈpressional** *adj.* —**imˈpressionally** *adv.*

impressionable (ɪmˈprɛʃənəbᵊl, -ˈprɛʃnə-) *adj.* easily influenced or characterized by susceptibility to influence: *an impressionable child; an impressionable age.* —**imˌpressionaˈbility** *or* **imˈpressionableness** *n.*

impressionism (ɪmˈprɛʃəˌnɪzəm) *n.* 1. (*often cap.*) a movement in French painting developed in the 1870s, having the aim of objectively recording experience by a system of fleeting impressions, esp. of natural light effects. 2. the technique in art, literature, or music of conveying experience by capturing fleeting impressions of reality or of mood.

impressionist (ɪmˈprɛʃənɪst) *n.* **1.** (*usually cap.*) any of the French painters of the late 19th century who were exponents of impressionism. **2.** (*sometimes cap.*) any artist, composer, or writer who uses impressionism. **3.** an entertainer who impersonates famous people. ~*adj.* **4.** (*often cap.*) denoting, of, or relating to impressionism or the exponents of this style. —**imˌpressionˈistic** *adj.*

impressive (ɪmˈprɛsɪv) *adj.* capable of impressing, esp. by size, magnificence, etc.; awe-inspiring; commanding. —**imˈpressively** *adv.* —**imˈpressiveness** *n.*

impressment (ɪmˈprɛsmənt) *n.* the commandeering or conscription of things or men into government service.

impressure (ɪmˈprɛʃə) *n.* an archaic word for **impression.** [C17: see IMPRESS[1], -URE; formed on the model of PRESSURE]

imprest (ɪmˈprɛst) *n.* **1.** a fund of cash from which a department or other unit pays incidental expenses, topped up periodically from central funds. **2.** *Chiefly Brit.* an advance from government funds for the performance of some public business or service. **3.** *Brit.* (formerly) an advance payment of wages to a sailor or soldier. [C16: probably from Italian *imprestare* to lend, from Latin *in-* towards + *praestāre* to pay, from *praestō* at hand; see PRESTO]

imprimatur (ˌɪmprɪˈmeɪtə, -ˈmɑː-) *n.* **1.** *R.C. Church.* a licence granted by a bishop certifying the Church's approval of a book to be published. **2.** sanction, authority, or approval, esp. for something to be printed. [C17: New Latin, literally: let it be printed]

imprimis (ɪmˈpraɪmɪs) *adv. Archaic.* in the first place. [C15: from Latin phrase *in prīmis,* literally: among the first things]

imprint *n.* (ˈɪmprɪnt). **1.** a mark or impression produced by pressure, printing, or stamping. **2.** a characteristic mark or indication; stamp: *the imprint of great sadness on his face.* **3.** the publisher's name and address, usually with the date of publication, in a book, pamphlet, etc. **4.** the printer's name and address on any printed matter. ~*vb.* (ɪmˈprɪnt). **5.** to produce (a mark, impression, etc.) on (a surface) by pressure, printing, or stamping: *to imprint a seal on wax; to imprint wax with a seal.* **6.** to establish firmly; impress; stamp: *to imprint the details on one's mind.* **7.** (of young animals) to undergo the process of imprinting. —**imˈprinter** *n.*

imprinting (ɪmˈprɪntɪŋ) *n.* the development through exceptionally fast learning in young animals of recognition of and attraction to members of their own species or to surrogates.

imprison (ɪmˈprɪzən) *vb.* (*tr.*) to confine in or as if in prison. —**imˈprisoner** *n.* —**imˈprisonment** *n.*

improbable (ɪmˈprɒbəbᵊl) *adj.* not likely or probable; doubtful; unlikely. —**imˌprobaˈbility** *or* **imˈprobableness** *n.* —**imˈprobably** *adv.*

improbity (ɪmˈprəʊbɪtɪ) *n., pl.* **-ties.** dishonesty, wickedness, or unscrupulousness.

impromptu (ɪmˈprɒmptjuː) *adj.* **1.** unrehearsed; spontaneous; extempore. **2.** produced or done without care or planning; improvised. ~*adv.* **3.** in a spontaneous or improvised way: *he spoke impromptu.* ~*n.* **4.** something that is impromptu. **5.** a short piece of instrumental music, sometimes improvisatory in character. [C17: from French, from Latin *in promptū* in readiness, from *promptus* (adj.) ready, PROMPT]

improper (ɪmˈprɒpə) *adj.* **1.** lacking propriety; not seemly or fitting. **2.** unsuitable for a certain use or occasion; inappropriate: *an improper use for a tool.* **3.** irregular or abnormal. —**imˈproperly** *adv.* —**imˈproperness** *n.*

improper fraction *n.* a fraction in which the numerator has a greater absolute value or degree than the denominator, as 7/6 or $(x^2 + 3)/(x + 1)$.

improper integral *n.* a definite integral having one or both limits infinite or having an integrand that becomes infinite within the limits of integration.

impropriate *vb.* (ɪmˈprəʊprɪˌeɪt). **1.** (*tr.*) to transfer (property, rights, etc.) from the Church into lay hands. ~*adj.* (ɪmˈprəʊprɪɪt, -ˌeɪt). **2.** transferred in this way. [C16: from Medieval Latin *impropriāre* to make one's own, from Latin *im-* IN-[2] + *propriāre* to APPROPRIATE] —**imˌpropriˈation** *n.* —**imˈpropriˌator** *n.*

impropriety (ˌɪmprəˈpraɪɪtɪ) *n., pl.* **-ties.** **1.** lack of propriety; indecency; indecorum. **2.** an improper act or use. **3.** the state of being improper.

improve (ɪmˈpruːv) *vb.* **1.** to make or become better in quality; ameliorate. **2.** (*tr.*) to make (buildings, land, etc.) more valuable by additions or betterment. **3.** (*intr.;* usually foll. by *on* or *upon*) to achieve a better standard or quality in comparison (with): *to improve on last year's crop.* ~*n.* **4. on the improve.** *Austral.* improving. [C16: from Anglo-French *emprouer* to turn to profit, from *en prou* into profit, from *prou* profit, from Late Latin *prōde* beneficial, from Latin *prōdesse* to be advantageous, from PRO-[1] + *esse* to be] —**imˈprovable** *adj.* —**imˌprovaˈbility** *or* **imˈprovableness** *n.* —**imˈprovably** *adv.* —**imˈprover** *n.* —**imˈprovingly** *adv.*

improvement (ɪmˈpruːvmənt) *n.* **1.** the act of improving or the state of being improved. **2.** something that improves, esp. an addition or alteration. **3.** alteration of the structure, fixtures, fittings, or decor of a building without changing its function. Compare **conversion** (sense 9). **4.** (*usually pl.*) *Austral. and N.Z.* a building or other works on a piece of land, adding to its value.

improvident (ɪmˈprɒvɪdənt) *adj.* **1.** not provident; thriftless, imprudent, or prodigal. **2.** heedless or incautious; rash. —**imˈprovidence** *n.* —**imˈprovidently** *adv.*

improvisation (ˌɪmprəvaɪˈzeɪʃən) *n.* **1.** the act or an instance of improvising. **2.** a product of improvising; something improvised. —**ˌimproviˈsational** *adj.*

improvise (ˈɪmprəˌvaɪz) *vb.* **1.** to perform or make quickly from materials and sources available, without previous planning. **2.** to perform (a poem, play, piece of music, etc.), composing as one goes along. [C19: from French, from Italian *improvvisare,* from Latin *imprōvīsus* unforeseen, from IM- (not) + *prōvīsus,* from *prōvidēre* to foresee; see PROVIDE] —**ˈimproˌviser** *n.*

imprudent (ɪmˈpruːdᵊnt) *adj.* not prudent; rash, heedless, or indiscreet. —**imˈprudence** *n.* —**imˈprudently** *adv.*

impudence (ˈɪmpjʊdəns) *or* **impudency** *n.* **1.** the quality of being impudent. **2.** an impudent act or statement. [C14: from Latin *impudēns* shameless, from IM- (not) + *pudēns* modest; see PUDENCY]

impudent (ˈɪmpjʊdənt) *adj.* **1.** mischievous, impertinent, or disrespectful. **2.** an obsolete word for **immodest.** —**ˈimpudently** *adv.* —**ˈimpudentness** *n.*

impudicity (ˌɪmpjʊˈdɪsɪtɪ) *n. Rare.* immodesty. [C16: from Old French *impudicite,* from Latin *impudīcus* shameless, from IN-[1] + *pudīcus* modest, virtuous]

impugn (ɪmˈpjuːn) *vb.* (*tr.*) to challenge or attack as false; assail; criticize. [C14: from Old French *impugner,* from Latin *impugnāre* to fight against, attack, from IM- + *pugnāre* to fight] —**imˈpugnable** *adj.* —**impugnation** (ˌɪmpʌgˈneɪʃən) *or* **imˈpugnment** *n.* —**imˈpugner** *n.*

impuissant (ɪmˈpjuːɪsᵊnt, ɪmˈpwiː-) *adj.* powerless, ineffectual, feeble, or impotent. [C17: from French: powerless] —**imˈpuissance** *n.*

impulse (ˈɪmpʌls) *n.* **1.** an impelling force or motion; thrust; impetus. **2.** a sudden desire, whim, or inclination: *I bought it on an impulse.* **3.** an instinctive drive; urge. **4.** tendency; current; trend. **5.** *Physics.* **a.** the product of the average magnitude of a force acting on a body and the time for which it acts. **b.** the change in the momentum of a body as a result of a force acting upon it. **6.** *Physiol.* See **nerve impulse.** **7.** *Electronics.* a less common word for **pulse**[1] (sense 2). **8. on impulse.** spontaneously or impulsively. [C17: from Latin *impulsus* a pushing against, incitement, from *impellere* to strike against; see IMPEL]

impulse buying *n.* the buying of retail merchandise prompted by a whim on seeing the product displayed. —**impulse buyer** *n.*

impulse turbine *n.* a turbine in which the expansion of the fluid is completed in a static nozzle, the torque being produced by the change in momentum of the fluid impinging on curved rotor blades. Compare **reaction turbine.**

impulsion (ɪmˈpʌlʃən) *n.* **1.** the act of impelling or the state of being impelled. **2.** motion produced by an impulse; propulsion. **3.** a driving force; compulsion.

impulsive (ɪmˈpʌlsɪv) *adj.* **1.** characterized by actions based on sudden desires, whims, or inclinations rather than careful thought: *an impulsive man.* **2.** based on emotional impulses or whims; spontaneous: *an impulsive kiss.* **3.** forceful, inciting, or impelling. **4.** (of physical forces) acting for a short time; not continuous. **5.** (of a sound) brief, loud, and having a wide frequency range. —**imˈpulsively** *adv.* —**imˈpulsiveness** *n.*

impunity (ɪmˈpjuːnɪtɪ) *n., pl.* **-ties.** **1.** exemption or immunity from punishment or recrimination. **2.** exemption or immunity from unpleasant consequences: *a successful career marked by impunity from early mistakes.* **3. with impunity. a.** with no unpleasant consequences. **b.** with no care or heed for such consequences. [C16: from Latin *impūnitās* freedom from punishment, from *impūnis* unpunished, from IM- (not) + *poena* punishment]

impure (ɪmˈpjʊə) *adj.* **1.** not pure; combined with something else; tainted or sullied. **2.** (in certain religions) **a.** (of persons) ritually unclean and as such debarred from certain religious ceremonies. **b.** (of foodstuffs, vessels, etc.) debarred from certain religious uses. **3.** (of a colour) mixed with another colour or with black or white. **4.** of more than one origin or style, as of architecture or other design. —**imˈpurely** *adv.* —**imˈpureness** *n.*

impurity (ɪmˈpjʊərɪtɪ) *n., pl.* **-ties.** **1.** the quality of being impure. **2.** an impure thing, constituent, or element: *impurities in the water.* **3.** *Electronics.* a small quantity of an element added to a pure semiconductor crystal to control its electrical conductivity. See also **acceptor** (sense 2), **donor** (sense 5).

imputable (ɪmˈpjuːtəbᵊl) *adj.* capable of being imputed; attributable; ascribable. —**imˌputaˈbility** *or* **imˈputableness** *n.* —**imˈputably** *adv.*

imputation system *n.* a taxation system in which some, or all, of the corporation tax on a company is treated as a tax credit on account of the income tax paid by its shareholders on their dividends. See also **advance corporation tax.**

impute (ɪmˈpjuːt) *vb.* (*tr.*) **1.** to attribute or ascribe (something dishonest or dishonourable, esp. a criminal offence) to a person. **2.** to attribute to a source or cause: *I impute your success to nepotism.* **3.** *Commerce.* to give (a notional value) to goods or services when the real value is unknown. [C14: from Latin *imputāre,* from IM- + *putāre* to think, calculate] —**ˌimpuˈtation** *n.* —**imˈputative** *adj.* —**imˈputer** *n.*

impv. *abbrev. for* imperative.

IMS *abbrev. for* Indian Medical Service.

IMunE *abbrev. for* Institution of Municipal Engineers.

in (ɪn) *prep.* **1.** inside; within: *no smoking in the auditorium.* **2.** at a place where there is: *lying in the shade; walking in the rain.* **3.** indicating a state, situation, or condition: *in a deep sleep; standing in silence.* **4.** before or when (a period of time) has elapsed: *come back in one year.* **5.** using (a language, etc.) as a means of communication: *written in code.* **6.** concerned or involved with, esp. as an occupation: *in journalism.* **7.** while or by performing the action of; as a consequence of or by means of: *in crossing the street he was run over.* **8.** used to indicate goal or purpose: *in honour of the president.* **9.** (used of certain animals) about to give birth to; pregnant with (specified offspring): *in foal; in calf.* **10.** a variant of **into:** *she fell in the water; he tore the paper in two.* **11. have it in one.** (often foll. by an infinitive) to have the ability (to do something). **12. in it.** *Austral. informal.* joining in; taking part. **13. in that** *or* **in so far as.** (*conj.*) because or to the extent that; inasmuch as: *I regret my remark in that it upset you.* **14. nothing, very little, quite a bit,** *etc.,* **in it.** no, a great, etc., difference or interval between two things. ~*adv.* (*particle*) **15.** in or into a particular place; inward or indoors: *come in; bring him in.* **16.** so as to achieve office, power, or authority: *the Conservatives got in at the last election.* **17.** so as to enclose: *block in; cover in a hole.* **18.** (in certain games) so as to take one's turn or one's team's turn at a certain aspect of the play; taking one's innings: *you have to get the other side out before you go in.* **19.** *Brit.* (of a fire) alight: *do you keep the fire in all night?* **20.** (*in combination*) indicating an activity or gathering, esp. one organized to protest against something: *teach-in; work-in.* **21. in at.** present at (the beginning, end, etc.). **22. in between.** between. **23. in for.** about to be affected by (something, esp. something unpleasant): *you're in for a shock.* **24. in on.** acquainted with or sharing in: *I was in on all his plans.* **25. in with.** associated with; friendly with; regarded highly by. **26. have (got) it in for.** *Informal.* to wish or intend harm towards. ~*adj.* **27.** (*stressed*) fashionable; modish: *the in thing to do.* **28.** *N.Z.* competing: *you've got to be in to win.* ~*n.* **29. ins and outs.** intricacies or complications; details: *the ins and outs of a computer system.* [Old English; compare Old High German *in,* Welsh *yn,* Old Norse *ī,* Latin *in,* Greek *en*]

In *the chemical symbol for* indium.

IN *abbrev. for* Indiana.

in. *abbrev. for* inch(es).

in-[1], **il-, im-,** *or* **ir-** *prefix.* not; non-: *incredible; insincere; illegal; imperfect; irregular.* Compare **un-.** [from Latin *in-;* related to *ne-, nōn* not]

in-[2], **il-, im-,** *or* **ir-** *prefix.* **1.** in; into; towards; within; on: *infiltrate; immigrate.* **2.** having an intensive or causative function: *inflame; imperil.* [from IN (prep., adv.)]

-in *suffix forming nouns.* **1.** indicating a neutral organic compound, including proteins, glucosides, and glycerides: *insulin; digitoxin; tripalmitin.* **2.** indicating an enzyme in certain nonsystematic names: *pepsin.* **3.** indicating a pharmaceutical substance: *penicillin; riboflavin; aspirin.* **4.** indicating a chemical substance in certain nonsystematic names: *coumarin.* [from New Latin *-ina;* compare -INE[2]]

inability (ˌɪnəˈbɪlɪtɪ) *n.* lack of ability or means; incapacity.

in absentia *Latin.* (ɪn æbˈsɛntɪə) *adv.* in the absence of (someone indicated): *he was condemned in absentia.*

inaccessible (ˌɪnækˈsɛsəb^{ə}l) *adj.* not accessible; unapproachable. —ˌ**inacˌcessiˈbility** *or* ˌ**inacˈcessibleness** *n.* —ˌ**inacˈcessibly** *adv.*

inaccuracy (ɪnˈækjʊrəsɪ) *n., pl.* **-cies.** **1.** lack of accuracy; imprecision. **2.** an error, a mistake, or a slip.

inaccurate (ɪnˈækjʊrɪt) *adj.* not accurate; imprecise, inexact, or erroneous. —**inˈaccurately** *adv.* —**inˈaccurateness** *n.*

inaction (ɪnˈækʃən) *n.* lack of action; idleness; inertia.

inactivate (ɪnˈæktɪˌveɪt) *vb.* (*tr.*) to render inactive. —**inˌactiˈvation** *n.*

inactive (ɪnˈæktɪv) *adj.* **1.** idle or inert; not active. **2.** sluggish, passive, or indolent. **3.** *Military.* of or relating to persons or equipment not in active service. **4.** *Chem.* (of a substance) having little or no reactivity. **5.** (of an element, isotope, etc.) having little or no radioactivity. —**inˈactively** *adv.* —ˌ**inacˈtivity** *or* **inˈactiveness** *n.*

inadequate (ɪnˈædɪkwɪt) *adj.* **1.** not adequate; insufficient. **2.** not capable or competent; lacking. —**inˈadequacy** *n.* —**inˈadequately** *adv.*

inadmissible (ˌɪnədˈmɪsəb^{ə}l) *adj.* not admissible or allowable. —ˌ**inadˌmissiˈbility** *n.* —ˌ**inadˈmissibly** *adv.*

inadvertence (ˌɪnədˈvɜːt^{ə}ns) *or* **inadvertency** *n.* **1.** lack of attention; heedlessness. **2.** an instance or an effect of being inadvertent; oversight; slip.

inadvertent (ˌɪnədˈvɜːt^{ə}nt) *adj.* **1.** failing to act carefully or considerately; inattentive. **2.** resulting from heedless action; unintentional. —ˌ**inadˈvertently** *adv.*

inadvisable (ˌɪnədˈvaɪzəb^{ə}l) *adj.* **1.** not advisable; not recommended. **2.** unwise; imprudent. —ˌ**inadˌvisaˈbility** *or* ˌ**inadˈvisableness** *n.* —ˌ**inadˈvisably** *adv.*

-inae *suffix forming plural proper nouns.* occurring in names of zoological subfamilies: *Felinae.* [New Latin, from Latin, feminine plural of *-īnus* -INE[1]]

in aeternum *Latin.* (ɪn iːˈtɜːnəm) *n.* forever; eternally.

inalienable (ɪnˈeɪljənəb^{ə}l) *adj.* not able to be transferred to another; not alienable: *the inalienable rights of the citizen.* —**inˌalienaˈbility** *or* **inˈalienableness** *n.* —**inˈalienably** *adv.*

inalterable (ɪnˈɔːltərəb^{ə}l) *adj.* not alterable; unalterable. —**inˌalteraˈbility** *or* **inˈalterableness** *n.* —**inˈalterably** *adv.*

inamorata (ɪnˌæməˈrɑːtə, ˌɪnæmə-) *or* (*masc.*) **inamorato** (ɪnˌæməˈrɑːtəʊ, ˌɪnæmə-) *n., pl.* **-tas** *or* (*masc.*) **-tos.** a person with whom one is in love; lover. [C17: from Italian *innamorata, innamorato,* from *innamorare* to cause to fall in love, from *amore* love, from Latin *amor*]

in-and-in *adj.* (of breeding) carried out repeatedly among closely related individuals of the same species to eliminate or intensify certain characteristics.

inane (ɪˈneɪn) *adj.* **1.** senseless, unimaginative, or empty; unintelligent: *inane remarks.* ~*n.* **2.** *Archaic.* something empty or vacant, esp. the void of space. [C17: from Latin *inānis* empty] —**inˈanely** *adv.*

inanga (ˈiːnʌŋə) *n.* another name for the New Zealand **whitebait** (sense 2). [Maori]

inanimate (ɪnˈænɪmɪt) *adj.* **1.** lacking the qualities or features of living beings; not animate: *inanimate objects.* **2.** lacking any sign of life or consciousness; appearing dead. **3.** lacking vitality; spiritless; dull. —**inˈanimately** *adv.* —**inˈanimateness** *or* **inanimation** (ɪnˌænɪˈmeɪʃən) *n.*

inanition (ˌɪnəˈnɪʃən) *n.* **1.** exhaustion resulting from lack of food. **2.** mental, social, or spiritual weakness or lassitude. [C14: from Late Latin *inānītio* emptiness, from Latin *inānis* empty; see INANE]

inanity (ɪˈnænɪtɪ) *n., pl.* **-ties.** **1.** lack of intelligence or imagination; senselessness; silliness. **2.** a senseless action, remark, etc. **3.** an archaic word for **emptiness.**

inappellable (ˌɪnəˈpɛləb^{ə}l) *adj.* incapable of being appealed against, as a court decision; unchallengeable. [C19: from IN-[1] + Latin *appellāre* to APPEAL]

inappetence (ɪnˈæpɪtəns) *or* **inappetency** *n. Rare.* lack of appetite or desire. —**inˈappetent** *adj.*

inapplicable (ɪnˈæplɪkəb^{ə}l, ˌɪnəˈplɪk-) *adj.* not applicable or suitable; irrelevant. —**inˌapplicaˈbility** *or* **inˈapplicableness** *n.* —**inˈapplicably** *adv.*

inapposite (ɪnˈæpəzɪt) *adj.* not appropriate or pertinent; unsuitable. —**inˈappositely** *adv.* —**inˈappositeness** *n.*

inappreciable (ˌɪnəˈpriːʃəb^{ə}l) *adj.* **1.** incapable of being appreciated. **2.** imperceptible; negligible. —ˌ**inapˈpreciably** *adv.*

inappreciative (ˌɪnəˈpriːʃətɪv) *adj.* lacking appreciation; unappreciative. —ˌ**inapˈpreciatively** *adv.* —ˌ**inapˌpreciˈation** *or* ˌ**inapˈpreciativeness** *n.*

inapprehensive (ˌɪnæprɪˈhɛnsɪv) *adj.* **1.** not perceiving or feeling fear or anxiety; untroubled. **2.** *Rare.* unable to understand; imperceptive. —ˌ**inappreˈhensively** *adv.* —ˌ**inappreˈhensiveness** *n.*

inapproachable (ˌɪnəˈprəʊtʃəb^{ə}l) *adj.* not accessible; unapproachable; unfriendly. —ˌ**inapˌproachaˈbility** *adv.* —ˌ**inapˈproachably** *adv.*

inappropriate (ˌɪnəˈprəʊprɪɪt) *adj.* not fitting or appropriate; unsuitable or untimely. —ˌ**inapˈpropriately** *adv.* —ˌ**inapˈpropriateness** *n.*

inapt (ɪnˈæpt) *adj.* **1.** not apt or fitting; inappropriate. **2.** lacking skill; inept. —**inˈaptiˌtude** *or* **inˈaptness** *n.* —**inˈaptly** *adv.*

inarch (ɪnˈɑːtʃ) *vb.* (*tr.*) to graft (a plant) by uniting stock and scion while both are still growing independently.

inarticulate (ˌɪnɑːˈtɪkjʊlɪt) *adj.* **1.** unable to express oneself fluently or clearly; incoherent. **2.** (of speech, language, etc.) unclear or incomprehensible; unintelligible: *inarticulate grunts.* **3.** unable to speak; dumb. **4.** unable to be expressed; unvoiced: *inarticulate suffering.* **5.** *Biology.* having no joints, segments, or articulation. —ˌ**inarˈticulately** *adv.* —ˌ**inarˈticulateness** *n.*

inartificial (ˌɪnɑːtɪˈfɪʃəl) *adj. Archaic.* **1.** not artificial; real; natural. **2.** inartistic. —ˌ**inartiˈficially** *adv.*

inartistic (ˌɪnɑːˈtɪstɪk) *adj.* lacking in artistic skill, appreciation, etc.; Philistine. —ˌ**inarˈtistically** *adv.*

inasmuch as (ˌɪnəzˈmʌtʃ) *conj.* (*subordinating*) **1.** in view of the fact that; seeing that; since. **2.** to the extent or degree that; in so far as.

inattentive (ˌɪnəˈtɛntɪv) *adj.* not paying attention; heedless; negligent. —ˌ**inatˈtention** *or* ˌ**inatˈtentiveness** *n.* —ˌ**inatˈtentively** *adv.*

inaudible (ɪnˈɔːdəb^{ə}l) *adj.* not loud enough to be heard; not audible. —**inˌaudiˈbility** *or* **inˈaudibleness** *n.* —**inˈaudibly** *adv.*

inaugural (ɪnˈɔːgjʊrəl) *adj.* **1.** characterizing or relating to an inauguration. ~*n.* **2.** a speech made at an inauguration, esp. by a president of the U.S.

inaugurate (ɪnˈɔːgjʊˌreɪt) *vb.* (*tr.*) **1.** to commence officially or formally; initiate. **2.** to place in office formally and ceremonially; induct. **3.** to open ceremonially; dedicate formally: *to inaugurate a factory.* [C17: from Latin *inaugurāre,* literally: to take omens, practise augury, hence to install in office after taking auguries; see IN-[2], AUGUR] —**inˌauguˈration** *n.* —**inˈauguˌrator** *n.* —**inauguratory** (ɪnˈɔːgjʊrətərɪ, -trɪ) *adj.*

Inauguration Day *n.* the day on which the inauguration of a president of the U.S. takes place, Jan. 20.

inauspicious (ˌɪnɔːˈspɪʃəs) *adj.* not auspicious; unlucky. —ˌ**inausˈpiciously** *adv.* —ˌ**inausˈpiciousness** *n.*

inbd *abbrev. for* inboard (on an aircraft, a boat, etc.).

inbeing ('ɪnˌbiːɪŋ) *n.* **1.** existence in something else; inherence. **2.** basic and inward nature; essence.

in-between *adj.* **1.** intermediate: *he's at the in-between stage, neither a child nor an adult.* ~*n.* **2.** an intermediate person or thing.

inboard ('ɪnˌbɔːd) *adj.* **1.** (esp. of a boat's motor or engine) situated within the hull. Compare **outboard** (sense 1). **2.** situated between the wing tip of an aircraft and its fuselage: *an inboard engine.* ~*adv.* **3.** towards the centre line of or within a vessel, aircraft, etc.

in-bond shop *n. Caribbean.* a duty-free shop.

inborn ('ɪn'bɔːn) *adj.* existing from birth; congenital; innate.

inbound ('ɪnˌbaʊnd) *adj.* coming in; inward bound: *an inbound ship.*

inbreathe (ɪn'briːð) *vb. (tr.) Rare.* to infuse or imbue.

inbred ('ɪn'brɛd) *adj.* **1.** produced as a result of inbreeding. **2.** deeply ingrained; innate: *inbred good manners.*

inbreed ('ɪn'briːd) *vb.* **-breeds, -breeding, -bred. 1.** to breed from unions between closely related individuals, esp. over several generations. **2.** *(tr.)* to develop within; engender. —**'in'breeding** *n., adj.*

in-built *adj.* built-in, integral.

inby (ɪn'baɪ) *adv.* **1.** *Scot.* into the house or an inner room; inside; within. **2.** *Scot. and northern English dialect.* towards or near the house. ~*adj.* **3.** *Scot. and northern English dialect.* located near or nearest to the house: *the inby field.* [C18: from IN (adv.) + BY (adv.)]

inc. *abbrev. for:* **1.** included. **2.** including. **3.** inclusive. **4.** income. **5.** incomplete. **6.** increase.

Inc. *or* **inc.** (esp. after the names of U.S. business organizations) *abbrev. for* incorporated. Brit. equivalent: **Ltd.**

Inca ('ɪŋkə) *n., pl.* **-ca** *or* **-cas. 1.** a member of a South American Indian people whose great empire centred on Peru lasted from about 1100 A.D. to the Spanish conquest in the early 1530s and is famed for its complex culture. **2.** the ruler or king of this empire or any member of his family. **3.** the language of the Incas. See also **Quechua.** [C16: from Spanish, from Quechua *inka* king]

incalculable (ɪn'kælkjʊləbᵊl) *adj.* beyond calculation; unable to be predicted or determined. —**inˌcalcula'bility** *or* **in'calculableness** *n.* —**in'calculably** *adv.*

incalescent (ˌɪnkə'lɛsᵊnt) *adj. Chem.* increasing in temperature. [C17: from Latin *incalescere,* from IN-[2] + *calescere* to grow warm, from *calēre* to be warm] —**ˌinca'lescence** *n.*

in camera (ɪn 'kæmərə) *adv., adj.* **1.** in a private or secret session; not in public. **2.** *Law.* **a.** in the privacy of a judge's chambers. **b.** in a court not open to the public. [Latin: in the chamber]

incandesce (ˌɪnkæn'dɛs) *vb. (intr.)* to exhibit incandescence.

incandescence (ˌɪnkæn'dɛsəns) *or* **incandescency** *n.* **1.** the emission of light by a body as a consequence of raising its temperature. Compare **luminescence. 2.** the light produced by raising the temperature of a body.

incandescent (ˌɪnkæn'dɛsᵊnt) *adj.* emitting light as a result of being heated to a high temperature; red-hot or white-hot. [C18: from Latin *incandescere* to become hot, glow, from IN-[2] + *candescere* to grow bright, from *candēre* to be white; see CANDID] —**ˌincan'descently** *adv.*

incandescent lamp *n.* a source of light that contains a heated solid, such as an electrically heated filament.

incantation (ˌɪnkæn'teɪʃən) *n.* **1.** ritual recitation of magic words or sounds. **2.** the formulaic words or sounds used; a magic spell. [C14: from Late Latin *incantātiō* an enchanting, from *incantāre* to repeat magic formulas, from Latin, from IN-[2] + *cantāre* to sing; see ENCHANT] —**ˌincan'tational** *or* **in'cantatory** *adj.*

incapable (ɪn'keɪpəbᵊl) *adj.* **1.** (when *postpositive,* often foll. by *of*) not capable (of); lacking the ability (to). **2.** powerless or helpless, as through injury or intoxication. **3.** *(postpositive;* foll. by *of)* not susceptible (to); not admitting (of): *a problem incapable of solution.* —**inˌcapa'bility** *or* **in'capableness** *n.* —**in'capably** *adv.*

incapacitant (ˌɪnkə'pæsɪtənt) *n.* a substance that can temporarily incapacitate a person, used esp. as a weapon in biological warfare.

incapacitate (ˌɪnkə'pæsɪˌteɪt) *vb. (tr.)* **1.** to deprive of power, strength, or capacity; disable. **2.** to deprive of legal capacity or eligibility. —**ˌincaˌpaci'tation** *n.*

incapacity (ˌɪnkə'pæsɪtɪ) *n., pl.* **-ties. 1.** lack of power, strength, or capacity; inability. **2.** *Law.* **a.** legal disqualification or ineligibility. **b.** a circumstance causing this.

Incaparina (ɪnˌkæpə'riːnə) *n.* a cheap high-protein food made of cottonseed, sorghum flours, maize, yeast, etc., used, esp. in Latin America, to prevent protein-deficiency diseases. [C20: from *Institute of Nutrition in Central America and Panama* + FARINA]

incapsulate (ɪn'kæpsjʊˌleɪt) *vb.* a less common spelling of **encapsulate.** —**inˌcapsu'lation** *n.*

in-car *adj.* installed or provided within a car: *an in-car hi-fi system.*

incarcerate *vb.* (ɪn'kɑːsəˌreɪt). **1.** *(tr.)* to confine or imprison. ~*adj.* (ɪn'kɑːsərɪt, -ˌreɪt). **2.** *Rare.* imprisoned. [C16: from Medieval Latin *incarcerāre,* from Latin IN-[2] + *carcer* prison] —**inˌcarcer'ation** *n.* —**in'carcerˌator** *n.*

incardinate (ɪn'kɑːdɪˌneɪt) *vb. (tr.) R.C. Church.* to transfer (a cleric) to the jurisdiction of a new bishop. [C17: from Late Latin *incardināre,* from IN-[2] + *cardinālis* CARDINAL]

incardination (ɪnˌkɑːdɪ'neɪʃən) *n.* **1.** the official acceptance by one diocese of a clergyman from another diocese. **2.** the promotion of a clergyman to the status of a cardinal.

incarnadine (ɪn'kɑːnəˌdaɪn) *Archaic or literary.* ~*vb.* **1.** *(tr.)* to tinge or stain with red. ~*adj.* **2.** of a pinkish or reddish colour similar to that of flesh or blood. [C16: from French *incarnadin* flesh-coloured, from Italian, from Late Latin *incarnātus* made flesh, INCARNATE]

incarnate *adj.* (ɪn'kɑːnɪt, -neɪt). *(usually immediately postpositive)* **1.** possessing bodily form, esp. the human form: *a devil incarnate.* **2.** personified or typified: *stupidity incarnate.* **3.** (esp. of plant parts) flesh-coloured or pink. ~*vb.* (ɪn'kɑːneɪt). *(tr.)* **4.** to give a bodily or concrete form to. **5.** to be representative or typical of. [C14: from Late Latin *incarnāre* to make flesh, from Latin IN-[2] + *carō* flesh]

incarnation (ˌɪnkɑː'neɪʃən) *n.* **1.** the act of manifesting or state of being manifested in bodily form, esp. human form. **2.** a bodily form assumed by a god, etc. **3.** a person or thing that typifies or represents some quality, idea, etc.: *the weasel is the incarnation of ferocity.*

Incarnation (ˌɪnkɑː'neɪʃən) *n. Christian theol.* the assuming of a human body by the Son of God.

incarvillea (ˌɪnkɑː'vɪlɪə) *n.* any plant of the genus *Incarvillea,* native to China, of which some species are grown as garden or greenhouse plants for their large usually carmine-coloured trumpet-shaped flowers, esp. *I. delavayi:* family *Bignoniaceae.* [named after Pierre *d'Incarville* (1706–57), French missionary]

incase (ɪn'keɪs) *vb.* a variant spelling of **encase.** —**in'casement** *n.*

incautious (ɪn'kɔːʃəs) *adj.* not careful or cautious. —**in'cautiously** *adv.* —**in'cautiousness** *or* **in'caution** *n.*

incendiarism (ɪn'sɛndɪəˌrɪzəm) *n.* **1.** the act or practice of illegal burning; arson. **2.** (esp. formerly) the creation of civil strife or violence for political reasons.

incendiary (ɪn'sɛndɪərɪ) *adj.* **1.** of or relating to the illegal burning of property, goods, etc. **2.** tending to create strife, violence, etc.; inflammatory. **3.** (of a substance) capable of catching fire, causing fires, or burning readily. ~*n., pl.* **-aries. 4.** a person who illegally sets fire to property, goods, etc.; arsonist. **5.** (esp. formerly) a person who stirs up civil strife, violence, etc., for political reasons; agitator. **6.** Also called: **incendiary bomb.** a bomb that is designed to start fires. **7.** an incendiary substance, such as phosphorus. [C17: from Latin *incendiārius* setting alight, from *incendium* fire, from *incendere* to kindle]

incense[1] ('ɪnsɛns) *n.* **1.** any of various aromatic substances burnt for their fragrant odour, esp. in religious ceremonies. **2.** the odour or smoke so produced. **3.** any pleasant fragrant odour; aroma. **4.** *Rare.* homage or adulation. ~*vb.* **5.** to burn incense in honour of (a deity). **6.** *(tr.)* to perfume or fumigate with incense. [C13: from Old French *encens,* from Church Latin *incensum,* from Latin *incendere* to kindle] —**ˌincen'sation** *n.*

incense[2] (ɪn'sɛns) *vb. (tr.)* to enrage greatly. [C15: from Latin *incensus* set on fire, from *incendere* to kindle] —**in'censement** *n.*

incensory ('ɪnsɛnsərɪ) *n., pl.* **-ries.** a less common name for a **censer.** [C17: from Medieval Latin *incensorium*]

incentive (ɪn'sɛntɪv) *n.* **1.** a motivating influence; stimulus. **2. a.** an additional payment made to employees as a means of increasing production. **b.** *(as modifier): an incentive scheme.* ~*adj.* **3.** serving to incite to action. [C15: from Late Latin *incentīvus* (adj.), from Latin: striking up, setting the tune, from *incinere* to sing, from IN-[2] + *canere* to sing] —**in'centively** *adv.*

incept (ɪn'sɛpt) *vb. (tr.)* **1.** (of organisms) to ingest (food). **2.** *Brit.* (formerly) to take a master's or doctor's degree at a university. ~*n.* **3.** *Botany.* a rudimentary organ. [C19: from Latin *inceptus* begun, attempted, from *incipere* to begin, take in hand, from IN-[2] + *capere* to take] —**in'ceptor** *n.*

inception (ɪn'sɛpʃən) *n.* the beginning, as of a project or undertaking.

inceptive (ɪn'sɛptɪv) *adj.* **1.** beginning; incipient; initial. **2.** Also called: **inchoative.** *Grammar.* denoting an aspect of verbs in some languages used to indicate the beginning of an action. ~*n.* **3.** *Grammar.* **a.** the inceptive aspect of verbs. **b.** a verb in this aspect. —**in'ceptively** *adv.*

incertitude (ɪn'sɜːtɪˌtjuːd) *n.* **1.** uncertainty; doubt. **2.** a state of mental or emotional insecurity.

incessant (ɪn'sɛsᵊnt) *adj.* not ceasing; continual. [C16: from Late Latin *incessāns,* from Latin IN-[1] + *cessāre* to CEASE] —**in'cessancy** *or* **in'cessantness** *n.* —**in'cessantly** *adv.*

incest ('ɪnsɛst) *n.* sexual intercourse between two persons commonly regarded as too closely related to marry. [C13: from Latin *incestus* incest (from adj.: impure, defiled), from IN-[1] + *castus* CHASTE]

incestuous (ɪn'sɛstjʊəs) *adj.* **1.** relating to or involving incest: *an incestuous union.* **2.** guilty of incest. **3.** *Obsolete.* resulting from incest: *an incestuous bastard.* **4.** resembling incest in excessive or claustrophobic intimacy. —**in'cestuously** *adv.* —**in'cestuousness** *n.*

inch[1] (ɪntʃ) *n.* **1.** a unit of length equal to one twelfth of a foot or 0.0254 metre. **2.** *Meteorol.* **a.** an amount of precipitation that would cover a surface with water one inch deep: *five inches of rain fell in January.* **b.** a unit of pressure equal to a mercury column one inch high in a barometer. **3.** a very small distance, degree, or amount. **4. every inch.** in every way; completely: *he was every inch an aristocrat.* **5. inch by inch.** gradually; little by little. **6. within an inch of.** very close to. ~*vb.* **7.** to move or be moved very slowly or in very small steps: *the car inched forward.* **8.** (*tr.*; foll. by *out*) to defeat (someone) by a very small margin. [Old English *ynce,* from Latin *uncia* twelfth part; see OUNCE]

inch[2] (ɪntʃ) *n. Scot. and Irish.* a small island. [C15: from Gaelic *innis* island; compare Welsh *ynys*]

inchmeal (ˈɪntʃˌmiːl) *adv.* gradually; inch by inch or little by little. [C16: from INCH[1] + *-mele,* from Old English *mælum* quantity taken at one time; compare PIECEMEAL]

inchoate *adj.* (ɪnˈkəʊeɪt, -ˈkəʊɪt). **1.** just beginning; incipient. **2.** undeveloped; immature; rudimentary. **3.** (of a legal document, promissory note, etc.) in an uncompleted state; not yet made specific or valid. ~*vb.* (ɪnˈkəʊeɪt). (*tr.*) **4.** to begin. [C16: from Latin *incohāre* to make a beginning, literally: to hitch up, from IN-[2] + *cohum* yokestrap] —**inˈchoately** *adv.* —**inˈchoateness** *n.* —**ˌinchoˈation** *n.* —**inchoative** (ɪnˈkəʊətɪv) *adj.*

inchworm (ˈɪntʃˌwɜːm) *n.* another name for a **measuring worm.**

incidence (ˈɪnsɪdəns) *n.* **1.** degree, extent, or frequency of occurrence; amount: *a high incidence of death from pneumonia.* **2.** the act or manner of impinging on or affecting by proximity or influence. **3.** *Physics.* the arrival of a beam of light or particles at a surface. See also **angle of incidence.** **4.** *Geometry.* the partial coincidence of two configurations, such as a point that lies on a circle.

incident (ˈɪnsɪdənt) *n.* **1.** a distinct or definite occurrence; event. **2.** a minor, subsidiary, or related event or action. **3.** a relatively insignificant event that might have serious consequences, esp. in international politics. **4.** a public disturbance: *the police had reports of an incident outside a pub.* ~*adj.* **5.** (*postpositive;* foll. by *to*) related (to) or dependent (on). **6.** (when *postpositive,* often foll. by *to*) having a subsidiary or minor relationship (with). **7.** (esp. of a beam of light or particles) arriving at or striking a surface: *incident electrons.* [C15: from Medieval Latin *incidens* an event, from Latin *incidere,* literally: to fall into, hence befall, happen, from IN-[2] + *cadere* to fall]

incidental (ˌɪnsɪˈdɛntᵊl) *adj.* **1.** happening in connection with or resulting from something more important; casual or fortuitous. **2.** (*postpositive;* foll. by *to*) found in connection (with); related (to). **3.** (*postpositive;* foll. by *upon*) caused (by). **4.** occasional or minor: *incidental expenses.* ~*n.* **5.** (*often pl.*) an incidental or minor expense, event, or action. —**ˌinciˈdentalness** *n.*

incidentally (ˌɪnsɪˈdɛntəlɪ) *adv.* **1.** as a subordinate or chance occurrence. **2.** (*sentence modifier*) by the way.

incidental music *n.* background music for a film, television programme, etc.

incinerate (ɪnˈsɪnəˌreɪt) *vb.* to burn up completely; reduce to ashes. [C16: from Medieval Latin *incinerāre,* from Latin IN-[2] + *cinis* ashes] —**inˌcinerˈation** *n.*

incinerator (ɪnˈsɪnəˌreɪtə) *n.* a furnace or apparatus for incinerating something, esp. refuse.

incipient (ɪnˈsɪpɪənt) *adj.* just starting to be or happen; beginning. [C17: from Latin *incipiēns,* from *incipere* to begin, take in hand, from IN-[2] + *capere* to take] —**inˈcipience** *or* **inˈcipiency** *n.* —**inˈcipiently** *adv.*

incipit (ˈɪnkɪpɪt) *Latin.* here begins: used as an introductory word at the beginning of some medieval manuscripts.

incise (ɪnˈsaɪz) *vb.* (*tr.*) to produce (lines, a design, etc.) by cutting into the surface of (something) with a sharp tool. [C16: from Latin *incīdere* to cut into, from IN-[2] + *caedere* to cut]

incised (ɪnˈsaɪzd) *adj.* **1.** cut into or engraved: *an incised surface.* **2.** made by cutting or engraving: *an incised design.* **3.** (of a wound) cleanly cut, as with a surgical knife. **4.** having margins that are sharply and deeply indented: *an incised leaf.*

incisiform (ɪnˈsaɪzɪˌfɔːm) *adj. Zoology.* having the shape of an incisor tooth.

incision (ɪnˈsɪʒən) *n.* **1.** the act of incising. **2.** a cut, gash, or notch. **3.** a cut made with a knife during a surgical operation. **4.** any indentation in an incised leaf. **5.** *Rare.* incisiveness.

incisive (ɪnˈsaɪsɪv) *adj.* **1.** keen, penetrating, or acute. **2.** biting or sarcastic; mordant: *an incisive remark.* **3.** having a sharp cutting edge: *incisive teeth.* —**inˈcisively** *adv.* —**inˈcisiveness** *n.*

incisor (ɪnˈsaɪzə) *n.* a chisel-edged tooth at the front of the mouth. In man there are four in each jaw.

incisure (ɪnˈsaɪʒə) *n. Anatomy.* an incision or notch in an organ or part. —**inˈcisural** *adj.*

incite (ɪnˈsaɪt) *vb.* (*tr.*) to stir up or provoke to action. [C15: from Latin *incitāre,* from IN-[2] + *citāre* to excite] —**ˌinciˈtation** *n.* —**inˈcitement** *n.* —**inˈciter** *n.* —**inˈcitingly** *adv.*

incivility (ɪnsɪˈvɪlɪtɪ) *n., pl.* **-ties.** **1.** lack of civility or courtesy; rudeness. **2.** an impolite or uncivil act or remark.

incl. *abbrev. for:* **1.** including. **2.** inclusive.

inclement (ɪnˈklɛmənt) *adj.* **1.** (of weather) stormy, severe, or tempestuous. **2.** harsh, severe, or merciless. —**inˈclemency** *or* **inˈclementness** *n.* —**inˈclemently** *adv.*

inclinable (ɪnˈklaɪnəbᵊl) *adj.* **1.** (*postpositive;* usually foll. by *to*) having an inclination or tendency (to); disposed (to). **2.** capable of being inclined.

inclination (ˌɪnklɪˈneɪʃən) *n.* **1.** (often foll. by *for, to, towards,* or an infinitive) a particular disposition, esp. a liking or preference; tendency: *I've no inclination for such dull work.* **2.** the degree of deviation from a particular plane, esp. a horizontal or vertical plane. **3.** a sloping or slanting surface; incline. **4.** the act of inclining or the state of being inclined. **5.** the act of bowing or nodding the head. **6.** *Maths.* **a.** the angle between a line on a graph and the positive limb of the *x*-axis. **b.** the smaller dihedral angle between one plane and another. **7.** *Astronomy.* the angle between the plane of the orbit of a planet or comet and another plane, usually that of the ecliptic. **8.** *Physics.* another name for **dip** (sense 27). —**ˌincliˈnational** *adj.*

incline *vb.* (ɪnˈklaɪn). **1.** to deviate or cause to deviate from a particular plane, esp. a vertical or horizontal plane; slope or slant. **2.** (when *tr.,* may take an infinitive) to be disposed or cause to be disposed (towards some attitude or to do something): *he inclines towards levity; that does not incline me to think that you are right.* **3.** to bend or lower (part of the body, esp. the head), as in a bow or in order to listen. **4. incline one's ear.** to listen favourably (to). ~*n.* (ˈɪnklaɪn, ɪnˈklaɪn). **5.** an inclined surface or slope; gradient. **6.** short for **inclined railway.** [C13: from Latin *inclīnāre* to cause to lean, from *clīnāre* to bend; see LEAN[1]] —**inˈcliner** *n.*

inclined (ɪnˈklaɪnd) *adj.* **1.** (*postpositive;* often foll. by *to*) having a disposition; tending. **2.** sloping or slanting.

inclined plane *n.* a plane whose angle to the horizontal is less than a right angle.

inclined railway *n. Chiefly U.S.* a cable railway used on particularly steep inclines unsuitable for normal adhesion locomotives.

inclinometer (ˌɪnklɪˈnɒmɪtə) *n.* **1.** an aircraft instrument for indicating the angle that an aircraft makes with the horizontal. **2.** another name for **dip circle.**

inclose (ɪnˈkləʊz) *vb.* a less common spelling of **enclose.** —**inˈclosable** *adj.* —**inˈcloser** *n.* —**inˈclosure** *n.*

include (ɪnˈkluːd) *vb.* (*tr.*) **1.** to have as contents or part of the contents; be made up of or contain. **2.** to add as part of something else; put in as part of a set, group, or category. **3.** to contain as a secondary or minor ingredient or element. [C15 (in the sense: to enclose): from Latin *inclūdere* to enclose, from IN-[2] + *claudere* to close] —**inˈcludable** *or* **inˈcludible** *adj.*

included (ɪnˈkluːdɪd) *adj.* (of the stamens or pistils of a flower) not protruding beyond the corolla. —**inˈcludedness** *n.*

include out *vb.* (*tr., adv.*) *Informal.* to exclude: *you can include me out of that deal.*

inclusion (ɪnˈkluːʒən) *n.* **1.** the act of including or the state of being included. **2.** something included. **3.** *Geology.* a solid fragment, liquid globule, or pocket of gas enclosed in a mineral or rock. **4.** *Maths.* **a.** the relation between two sets that obtains when all the members of the first are members of the second. Symbol: $x \subseteq y$. **b. strict** *or* **proper inclusion.** the relation that obtains between two sets when the first includes the second but not vice versa. Symbol: $x \subset y$. **5.** *Engineering.* a foreign particle in a metal, such as a particle of metal oxide.

inclusion body *n. Pathol.* any of the small particles found in cells infected with certain viruses.

inclusive (ɪnˈkluːsɪv) *adj.* **1.** (*postpositive;* foll. by *of*) considered together (with): *capital inclusive of profit.* **2.** (*postpositive*) including the limits specified: *Monday to Friday inclusive is five days.* **3.** comprehensive. **4.** *Logic.* (of a disjunction) true if at least one of its component propositions is true. Compare **exclusive** (sense 10). —**inˈclusively** *adv.* —**inˈclusiveness** *n.*

inclusive or *n. Logic.* the connective that gives the value *true* to a disjunction if either or both of the disjuncts are true. Also called: **inclusive disjunction.** Compare **exclusive or.**

incoercible (ˌɪnkəʊˈɜːsəbᵊl) *adj.* **1.** unable to be coerced or compelled. **2.** (of a gas) not capable of being liquefied by pressure alone.

incog. *abbrev. for* incognito.

incogitable (ɪnˈkɒdʒɪtəbᵊl) *adj. Rare.* not to be contemplated; unthinkable. —**inˌcogitaˈbility** *n.*

incogitant (ɪnˈkɒdʒɪtənt) *adj. Rare.* thoughtless. [C17: from Latin *incōgitāns,* from IN-[1] + *cōgitāre* to think]

incognito (ˌɪnkɒgˈniːtəʊ, ɪnˈkɒgnɪtəʊ) *or* (*fem.*) **incognita** *adv., adj.* (*postpositive*) **1.** under an assumed name or appearance; in disguise. ~*n., pl.* **-tos** *or* (*fem.*) **-tas.** **2.** a person who is incognito. **3.** the assumed name or disguise of such a person. [C17: from Italian, from Latin *incognitus* unknown, from IN-[1] + *cognitus* known]

incognizant (ɪnˈkɒgnɪzənt) *adj.* (*when postpositive,* often foll. by *of*) unaware (of). —**inˈcognizance** *n.*

incoherent (ˌɪnkəʊˈhɪərənt) *adj.* **1.** lacking in clarity or organization; disordered. **2.** unable to express oneself clearly; inarticulate. **3.** *Physics.* (of two or more waves) having the same frequency but not the same phase: *incoherent light.* —**ˌincoˈherence, ˌincoˈherency,** *or* **ˌincoˈherentness** *n.* —**ˌincoˈherently** *adv.*

incombustible (ˌɪnkəmˈbʌstəbᵊl) *adj.* **1.** not capable of being burnt; fireproof. ~*n.* **2.** an incombustible object or material. —**ˌincomˌbustiˈbility** *or* **ˌincomˈbustibleness** *n.* —**ˌincomˈbustibly** *adv.*

income (ˈɪnkʌm, ˈɪnkəm) *n.* **1.** the amount of monetary or other returns, either earned or unearned, accruing over a given period of time. **2.** receipts; revenue. **3.** *Rare.* an inflow or influx. [C13 (in the sense: arrival, entrance): from Old English *incumen* a coming in]

income bond *n.* a bond that pays interest at a rate in direct proportion to the issuer's earnings.

income group *n.* a group in a given population having incomes within a certain range.

incomer (ˈɪnkʌmə) *n.* a person who comes to live in a place in which he was not born.

incomes policy *n.* See **prices and incomes policy.**

income support *n.* (in Britain) a social-security payment for the unemployed and people on low incomes, replacing supplementary benefit from 1986.

income tax *n.* a personal tax, usually progressive, levied on annual income subject to certain deductions.

incoming (ˈɪnˌkʌmɪŋ) *adj.* **1.** coming in; entering. **2.** about to come into office; succeeding. **3.** (of interest, dividends, etc.) being received; accruing. ~*n.* **4.** the act of coming in; entrance. **5.** (*usually pl.*) income or revenue.

incommensurable (ˌɪnkəˈmɛnʃərəbᵊl) *adj.* **1.** incapable of being judged, measured, or considered comparatively. **2.** (*postpositive;* foll. by *with*) not in accordance; incommensurate. **3.** *Maths.* **a.** not having a common factor other than 1, such as 2 and √-5. **b.** not having units of the same dimension. **c.** unrelated to another measurement by integral multiples. ~*n.* **4.** something incommensurable. —**ˌincomˌmensuraˈbility** *or* **ˌincomˈmensurableness** *n.* —**ˌincomˈmensurably** *adv.*

incommensurate (ˌɪnkəˈmɛnʃərɪt) *adj.* **1.** (when *postpositive,* often foll. by *with*) not commensurate; disproportionate. **2.** incommensurable. —**ˌincomˈmensurately** *adv.* —**ˌincomˈmensurateness** *n.*

incommode (ˌɪnkəˈməʊd) *vb.* (*tr.*) to bother, disturb, or inconvenience. [C16: from Latin *incommodāre* to be troublesome, from *incommodus* inconvenient, from IN-[1] + *commodus* convenient; see COMMODE]

incommodious (ˌɪnkəˈməʊdɪəs) *adj.* **1.** insufficiently spacious; cramped. **2.** troublesome or inconvenient. —**ˌincomˈmodiously** *adv.* —**ˌincomˈmodiousness** *n.*

incommodity (ˌɪnkəˈmɒdɪtɪ) *n., pl.* **-ties.** a less common word for **inconvenience.**

incommunicable (ˌɪnkəˈmjuːnɪkəbᵊl) *adj.* **1.** incapable of being communicated. **2.** an obsolete word for **incommunicative.** —**ˌincomˌmunicaˈbility** *or* **ˌincomˈmunicableness** *n.* —**ˌincomˈmunicably** *adv.*

incommunicado (ˌɪnkəˌmjuːnɪˈkɑːdəʊ) *adv., adj.* (*postpositive*) deprived of communication with other people, as while in solitary confinement. [C19: from Spanish *incomunicado,* from *incomunicar* to deprive of communication; see IN-[1], COMMUNICATE]

incommunicative (ˌɪnkəˈmjuːnɪkətɪv) *adj.* tending not to communicate with others; taciturn. —**ˌincomˈmunicatively** *adv.* —**ˌincomˈmunicativeness** *n.*

incommutable (ˌɪnkəˈmjuːtəbᵊl) *adj.* incapable of being commuted; unalterable. —**ˌincomˌmutaˈbility** *or* **ˌincomˈmutableness** *n.* —**ˌincomˈmutably** *adv.*

incomparable (ɪnˈkɒmpərəbᵊl, -prəbᵊl) *adj.* **1.** beyond or above comparison; matchless; unequalled. **2.** lacking a basis for comparison; not having qualities or features that can be compared. —**inˌcomparaˈbility** *or* **inˈcomparableness** *n.* —**inˈcomparably** *adv.*

incompatible (ˌɪnkəmˈpætəbᵊl) *adj.* **1.** incapable of living or existing together in peace or harmony; conflicting or antagonistic. **2.** opposed in nature or quality; inconsistent. **3.** (of an office, position, etc.) only able to be held by one person at a time. **4.** *Med.* (esp. of two drugs or two types of blood) incapable of being combined or used together; antagonistic. **5.** *Logic.* (of two propositions) unable to be both true at the same time. **6.** (of plants) **a.** not capable of forming successful grafts. **b.** incapable of self-fertilization. **7.** *Maths.* another word for **inconsistent** (sense 4). ~*n.* **8.** (*often pl.*) a person or thing that is incompatible with another. —**ˌincomˌpatiˈbility** *or* **ˌincomˈpatibleness** *n.* —**ˌincomˈpatibly** *adv.*

incompetent (ɪnˈkɒmpɪtənt) *adj.* **1.** not possessing the necessary ability, skill, etc. to do or carry out a task; incapable. **2.** marked by lack of ability, skill, etc. **3.** *Law.* not legally qualified: *an incompetent witness.* **4.** (of rock strata, folds, etc.) yielding readily to pressure so as to undergo structural deformation. ~*n.* **5.** an incompetent person. —**inˈcompetence** *or* **inˈcompetency** *n.* —**inˈcompetently** *adv.*

incomplete (ˌɪnkəmˈpliːt) *adj.* **1.** not complete or finished. **2.** not completely developed; imperfect. **3.** *Logic.* **a.** (of a formal theory) not so constructed that the addition of a non-theorem to the axioms renders it inconsistent. **b.** (of an expression) not having a reference of its own but requiring completion by another expression. —**ˌincomˈpletely** *adv.* —**ˌincomˈpleteness** *or* **ˌincomˈpletion** *n.*

incompliant (ˌɪnkəmˈplaɪənt) *adj.* not compliant; unyielding or inflexible. —**ˌincomˈpliance** *or* **ˌincomˈpliancy** *n.* —**ˌincomˈpliantly** *adv.*

incomprehensible (ˌɪnkɒmprɪˈhɛnsəbᵊl, ɪnˌkɒm-) *adj.* **1.** incapable of being understood; unintelligible. **2.** *Archaic.* limitless; boundless. —**ˌincompreˌhensiˈbility** *or* **ˌincompreˈhensibleness** *n.* —**ˌincompreˈhensibly** *adv.*

incomprehension (ˌɪnkɒmprɪˈhɛnʃən, ɪnˌkɒm-) *n.* inability or failure to comprehend; lack of understanding.

incomprehensive (ˌɪnkɒmprɪˈhɛnsɪv, ɪnˌkɒm-) *adj.* not comprehensive; limited in range or scope. —**ˌincompreˈhensively** *adv.* —**ˌincompreˈhensiveness** *n.*

incompressible (ˌɪnkəmˈprɛsəbᵊl) *adj.* incapable of being compressed or condensed. —**ˌincomˌpressiˈbility** *or* **ˌincomˈpressibleness** *n.* —**ˌincomˈpressibly** *adv.*

incomputable (ˌɪnkəmˈpjuːtəbᵊl) *adj.* incapable of being computed; incalculable. —**ˌincomˌputaˈbility** *n.* —**ˌincomˈputably** *adv.*

inconceivable (ˌɪnkənˈsiːvəbᵊl) *adj.* incapable of being conceived, imagined, or considered. —**ˌinconˌceivaˈbility** *or* **ˌinconˈceivableness** *n.* —**ˌinconˈceivably** *adv.*

inconclusive (ˌɪnkənˈkluːsɪv) *adj.* not conclusive or decisive; not finally settled; indeterminate. —**ˌinconˈclusively** *adv.* —**ˌinconˈclusiveness** *n.*

incondensable *or* **incondensible** (ˌɪnkənˈdɛnsəbᵊl) *adj.* incapable of being condensed. —**ˌinconˌdensaˈbility** *or* **ˌinconˌdensiˈbility** *n.*

incondite (ɪnˈkɒndɪt, -daɪt) *adj. Rare.* **1.** poorly constructed or composed. **2.** rough or crude. [C17: from Latin *inconditus,* from IN-[1] + *conditus,* from *condere* to put together] —**inˈconditely** *adv.*

inconformity (ˌɪnkənˈfɔːmɪtɪ) *n.* lack of conformity; irregularity.

incongruity (ˌɪnkɒŋˈgruːɪtɪ) *n., pl.* **-ties.** **1.** something incongruous. **2.** the state or quality of being incongruous.

incongruous (ɪnˈkɒŋgrʊəs) *or* **incongruent** *adj.* **1.** (when *postpositive,* foll. by *with* or *to*) incompatible with (what is suitable); inappropriate. **2.** containing disparate or discordant elements or parts. —**inˈcongruously** *or* **inˈcongruently** *adv.* —**inˈcongruousness** *or* **inˈcongruence** *n.*

inconsecutive (ˌɪnkənˈsɛkjʊtɪv) *adj.* not consecutive; not in sequence. —**ˌinconˈsecutively** *adv.* —**ˌinconˈsecutiveness** *n.*

inconsequential (ˌɪnkɒnsɪˈkwɛnʃəl, ɪnˌkɒn-) *or* **inconsequent** (ɪnˈkɒnsɪkwənt) *adj.* **1.** not following logically as a consequence. **2.** trivial or insignificant. **3.** not in a logical sequence; haphazard. —**ˌinconseˌquentiˈality, ˌinconseˈquentialness, inˈconsequence,** *or* **inˈconsequentness** *n.* —**ˌinconseˈquentially** *or* **inˈconsequently** *adv.*

inconsiderable (ˌɪnkənˈsɪdərəbᵊl) *adj.* **1.** relatively small. **2.** not worthy of consideration; insignificant. —**ˌinconˈsiderableness** *n.* —**ˌinconˈsiderably** *adv.*

inconsiderate (ˌɪnkənˈsɪdərɪt) *adj.* **1.** lacking in care or thought for others; heedless; thoughtless. **2.** *Rare.* insufficiently considered. —**ˌinconˈsiderately** *adv.* —**ˌinconˈsiderateness** *or* **ˌinconˌsiderˈation** *n.*

inconsistency (ˌɪnkənˈsɪstənsɪ) *n., pl.* **-cies.** **1.** lack of consistency or agreement; incompatibility. **2.** an inconsistent feature or quality. **3.** *Logic.* **a.** the property of being inconsistent. **b.** a self-contradictory proposition.

inconsistent (ˌɪnkənˈsɪstənt) *adj.* **1.** lacking in consistency, agreement, or compatibility; at variance. **2.** containing contradictory elements. **3.** irregular or fickle in behaviour or mood. **4.** Also: **incompatible.** *Maths.* (of two or more equations) not having one common set of values of the variables: $x + 2y = 5$ and $x + 2y = 6$ are inconsistent. **5.** *Logic.* (of a set of propositions) enabling an explicit contradiction to be validly derived. —**ˌinconˈsistently** *adv.*

inconsolable (ˌɪnkənˈsəʊləbᵊl) *adj.* incapable of being consoled or comforted; disconsolate. —**ˌinconˌsolaˈbility** *or* **ˌinconˈsolableness** *n.* —**ˌinconˈsolably** *adv.*

inconsonant (ɪnˈkɒnsənənt) *adj.* lacking in harmony or compatibility; discordant. —**inˈconsonance** *n.* —**inˈconsonantly** *adv.*

inconspicuous (ˌɪnkənˈspɪkjʊəs) *adj.* not easily noticed or seen; not prominent or striking. —**ˌinconˈspicuously** *adv.* —**ˌinconˈspicuousness** *n.*

inconstant (ɪnˈkɒnstənt) *adj.* **1.** not constant; variable. **2.** fickle. —**inˈconstancy** *n.* —**inˈconstantly** *adv.*

inconsumable (ˌɪnkənˈsjuːməbᵊl) *adj.* **1.** incapable of being consumed or used up. **2.** *Economics.* providing an economic service without being consumed, as currency. —**ˌinconˈsumably** *adv.*

incontestable (ˌɪnkənˈtɛstəbᵊl) *adj.* incapable of being contested or disputed. —**ˌinconˌtestaˈbility** *or* **ˌinconˈtestableness** *n.* —**ˌinconˈtestably** *adv.*

incontinent[1] (ɪnˈkɒntɪnənt) *adj.* **1.** lacking in restraint or control, esp. sexually. **2.** relating to or exhibiting involuntary urination or defecation. **3.** (foll. by *of*) having little or no control (over). **4.** unrestrained; uncontrolled. [C14: from Old French, from Latin *incontinens,* from IN-[1] + *continere* to hold, restrain] —**inˈcontinence** *or* **inˈcontinency** *n.* —**inˈcontinently** *adv.*

incontinent[2] (ɪnˈkɒntɪnənt) *or* **incontinently** *adv.* obsolete words for **immediately.** [C15: from Late Latin *in continentī tempore,* literally: in continuous time, that is, with no interval]

incontrollable (ˌɪnkənˈtrəʊləbᵊl) *adj.* a less common word for **uncontrollable.** —**ˌinconˈtrollably** *adv.*

incontrovertible (ˌɪnkɒntrəˈvɜːtəbᵊl, ɪnˌkɒn-) *adj.* incapable of being contradicted or disputed; undeniable. —**ˌincontroˌvertiˈbility** *or* **ˌincontroˈvertibleness** *n.* —**ˌincontroˈvertibly** *adv.*

inconvenience (ˌɪnkənˈviːnjəns, -ˈviːnɪəns) *n.* **1.** the state or quality of being inconvenient. **2.** something inconvenient; a hindrance, trouble, or difficulty. ~*vb.* **3.** (*tr.*) to cause inconvenience to; trouble or harass.

inconvenient (ˌɪnkənˈviːnjənt, -ˈviːnɪənt) *adj.* not convenient; troublesome, awkward, or difficult. —ˌ**inconˈveniently** *adv.*

inconvertible (ˌɪnkənˈvɜːtəbᵊl) *adj.* **1.** incapable of being converted or changed. **2.** (of paper currency) **a.** not redeemable for gold or silver specie. **b.** not exchangeable for another currency. —ˌ**inconˌvertiˈbility** *or* ˌ**inconˈvertibleness** *n.* —ˌ**inconˈvertibly** *adv.*

inconvincible (ˌɪnkənˈvɪnsəbᵊl) *adj.* refusing or not able to be convinced. —ˌ**inconˌvinciˈbility** *or* ˌ**inconˈvincibleness** *n.* —ˌ**inconˈvincibly** *adv.*

incoordinate (ˌɪnkəʊˈɔːdɪnɪt) *adj.* **1.** not coordinate; unequal in rank, order, or importance. **2.** uncoordinated.

incoordination (ˌɪnkəʊˌɔːdɪˈneɪʃən) *n.* **1.** lack of coordination or organization. **2.** *Pathol.* a lack of muscular control when making a voluntary movement.

incorp. *or* **incor.** *abbrev. for* incorporated.

incorporable (ɪnˈkɔːpərəbᵊl) *adj.* capable of being incorporated or included.

incorporate[1] *vb.* (ɪnˈkɔːpəˌreɪt). **1.** to include or be included as a part or member of a united whole. **2.** to form or cause to form a united whole or mass; merge or blend. **3.** to form (individuals, an unincorporated enterprise, etc.) into a corporation or other organization with a separate legal identity from that of its owners or members. ~*adj.* (ɪnˈkɔːpərɪt, -prɪt). **4.** combined into a whole; incorporated. **5.** formed into or constituted as a corporation. [C14 (in the sense: put into the body of something else): from Late Latin *incorporāre* to embody, from Latin IN-[2] + *corpus* body] —**inˈcorporative** *adj.* —**inˌcorpoˈration** *n.*

incorporate[2] (ɪnˈkɔːpərɪt, -prɪt) *adj.* an archaic word for **incorporeal.** [C16: from Late Latin *incorporātus,* from Latin IN-[1] + *corporātus* furnished with a body]

incorporated (ɪnˈkɔːpəˌreɪtɪd) *adj.* **1.** united or combined into a whole. **2.** organized as a legal corporation, esp. in commerce. Abbrev.: **Inc.** *or* **inc.** —**inˈcorpoˌratedness** *n.*

incorporating (ɪnˈkɔːpəˌreɪtɪŋ) *adj. Linguistics.* another word for **polysynthetic.**

incorporator (ɪnˈkɔːpəˌreɪtə) *n.* **1.** a person who incorporates. **2.** *U.S. commerce.* **a.** any of the signatories of a certificate of incorporation. **b.** any of the original members of a corporation.

incorporeal (ˌɪnkɔːˈpɔːrɪəl) *adj.* **1.** without material form, body, or substance. **2.** spiritual or metaphysical. **3.** *Law.* having no material existence but existing by reason of its annexation of something material, such as an easement, touchline, copyright, etc.: *an incorporeal hereditament.* —ˌ**incorˈporeally** *adv.* —**incorporeity** (ɪnˌkɔːpəˈriːɪtɪ) *or* ˌ**incorporeˈality** *n.*

incorrect (ˌɪnkəˈrɛkt) *adj.* **1.** false; wrong: *an incorrect calculation.* **2.** not fitting or proper: *incorrect behaviour.* —ˌ**incorˈrectly** *adv.* —ˌ**incorˈrectness** *n.*

incorrigible (ɪnˈkɒrɪdʒəbᵊl) *adj.* **1.** beyond correction, reform, or alteration. **2.** firmly rooted; ineradicable. **3.** *Philosophy.* (of a belief) having the property that whoever honestly believes it cannot be mistaken. Compare **defeasible** (sense 2). ~*n.* **4.** a person or animal that is incorrigible. —**inˌcorrigiˈbility** *or* **inˈcorrigibleness** *n.* —**inˈcorrigibly** *adv.*

incorrupt (ˌɪnkəˈrʌpt) *adj.* **1.** free from corruption; pure. **2.** free from decay; fresh or untainted. **3.** (of a manuscript, text, etc.) relatively free from error or alteration. —ˌ**incorˈruptly** *adv.* —ˌ**incorˈruption** *or* ˌ**incorˈruptness** *n.*

incorruptible (ˌɪnkəˈrʌptəbᵊl) *adj.* **1.** incapable of being corrupted; honest; just. **2.** not subject to decay or decomposition. —ˌ**incorˌruptiˈbility** *or* ˌ**incorˈruptibleness** *n.* —ˌ**incorˈruptibly** *adv.*

incr. *abbrev. for:* **1.** increase. **2.** increased. **3.** increasing.

incrassate *adj.* (ɪnˈkræsɪt, -eɪt), *also* **incrassated.** **1.** *Biology.* thickened or swollen: *incrassate cell walls.* **2.** *Obsolete.* fattened or swollen. ~*vb.* (ɪnˈkræseɪt). **3.** *Obsolete.* to make or become thicker. [C17: from Late Latin *incrassāre,* from Latin *crassus* thick, dense] —ˌ**incrasˈsation** *n.*

increase *vb.* (ɪnˈkriːs). **1.** to make or become greater in size, degree, frequency, etc.; grow or expand. ~*n.* (ˈɪnkriːs). **2.** the act of increasing; augmentation. **3.** the amount by which something increases. **4. on the increase.** increasing, esp. becoming more frequent. [C14: from Old French *encreistre,* from Latin *incrēscere,* from IN-[2] + *crēscere* to grow] —**inˈcreasable** *adj.* —**increasedly** (ɪnˈkriːsɪdlɪ) *or* **inˈcreasingly** *adv.* —**inˈcreaser** *n.*

increate (ˌɪnkrɪˈeɪt, ˈɪnkrɪˌeɪt) *adj. Archaic, poetic.* (esp. of gods) never having been created. —ˌ**increˈately** *adv.*

incredible (ɪnˈkrɛdəbᵊl) *adj.* **1.** beyond belief or understanding; unbelievable. **2.** *Informal.* marvellous; amazing. —**inˌcrediˈbility** *or* **inˈcredibleness** *n.* —**inˈcredibly** *adv.*

incredulity (ˌɪnkrɪˈdjuːlɪtɪ) *n.* lack of belief; scepticism.

incredulous (ɪnˈkrɛdjʊləs) *adj.* (often foll. by *of*) not prepared or willing to believe (something); unbelieving. —**inˈcredulously** *adv.* —**inˈcredulousness** *n.*

increment (ˈɪnkrɪmənt) *n.* **1.** an increase or addition, esp. one of a series. **2.** the act of increasing; augmentation. **3.** *Maths.* a small positive or negative change in a variable or function. Symbol: Δ, as in Δ*x* or Δ*f*. [C15: from Latin *incrēmentum* growth, INCREASE] —**incremental** (ˌɪnkrɪˈmɛntᵊl) *adj.*

incremental plotter *n.* a device that plots graphs on paper from computer-generated instructions. See also **microfilm plotter.**

incremental recorder *n. Computer technol.* a device for recording data as it is generated, usually on paper tape or magnetic tape, and feeding it into a computer.

increscent (ɪnˈkrɛsᵊnt) *adj.* (esp. of the moon) increasing in size; waxing. [C16: from Latin *incrēscēns*]

incretion (ɪnˈkriːʃən) *n. Physiol.* **1.** direct secretion into the bloodstream, esp. of a hormone from an endocrine gland. **2.** the substance so secreted. [C20: from IN-[2] + (SE)CRETION] —**inˈcretionary** *or* **incretory** (ˈɪnkrɪtərɪ, -trɪ) *adj.*

incriminate (ɪnˈkrɪmɪˌneɪt) *vb.* (*tr.*) **1.** to imply or suggest the guilt or error of (someone). **2.** to charge with a crime or fault. [C18: from Late Latin *incrīmināre* to accuse, from Latin *crīmen* accusation; see CRIME] —**inˌcrimiˈnation** *n.* —**inˈcrimiˌnator** *n.* —**inˈcriminatory** *adj.*

incross (ˈɪnkrɒs) *n.* **1.** a plant or animal produced by continued inbreeding. ~*vb.* **2.** to inbreed or produce by inbreeding.

incrust (ɪnˈkrʌst) *vb.* a variant spelling of **encrust.** —**inˈcrustant** *n., adj.* —ˌ**incrusˈtation** *n.*

incubate (ˈɪnkjʊˌbeɪt) *vb.* **1.** (of birds) to supply (eggs) with heat for their development, esp. by sitting on them. **2.** to cause (eggs, embryos, bacteria, etc.) to develop, esp. in an incubator or culture medium. **3.** (*intr.*) (of eggs, embryos, bacteria, etc.) to develop in favourable conditions, esp. in an incubator. **4.** (*intr.*) (of disease germs) to remain inactive in an animal or human before causing disease. **5.** to develop or cause to develop gradually; foment or be fomented. [C18: from Latin *incubāre* to lie upon, hatch, from IN-[2] + *cubāre* to lie down] —ˌ**incuˈbation** *n.* —ˌ**incuˈbational** *adj.* —ˈ**incuˌbative** *or* ˈ**incuˌbatory** *adj.*

incubation period *n. Med.* the time between exposure to an infectious disease and the appearance of the first signs or symptoms. Sometimes shortened to **incubation.**

incubator (ˈɪnkjʊˌbeɪtə) *n.* **1.** *Med.* an enclosed transparent box-like apparatus for housing prematurely born babies under optimum conditions until they are strong enough to survive in the normal environment. **2.** a container kept at a constant temperature in which birds' eggs can be artificially hatched or bacterial cultures grown. **3.** a person, animal, or thing that incubates.

incubus (ˈɪnkjʊbəs) *n., pl.* **-bi** (-ˌbaɪ) *or* **-buses.** **1.** a demon believed in folklore to lie upon sleeping persons, esp. to have sexual intercourse with sleeping women. Compare **succubus.** **2.** something that oppresses, worries, or disturbs greatly, esp. a nightmare or obsession. [C14: from Late Latin, from *incubāre* to lie upon; see INCUBATE]

incudes (ɪnˈkjuːdiːz) *n.* the plural of **incus.**

inculcate (ˈɪnkʌlˌkeɪt, ɪnˈkʌlkeɪt) *vb.* (*tr.*) to instil by forceful or insistent repetition. [C16: from Latin *inculcāre* to tread upon, ram down, from IN-[2] + *calcāre* to trample, from *calx* heel] —ˌ**inculˈcation** *n.* —ˈ**inculˌcator** *n.*

inculpable (ɪnˈkʌlpəbᵊl) *adj.* incapable of being blamed or accused; guiltless. —**inˌculpaˈbility** *or* **inˈculpableness** *n.* —**inˈculpably** *adv.*

inculpate (ˈɪnkʌlˌpeɪt, ɪnˈkʌlpeɪt) *vb.* (*tr.*) to incriminate; cause blame to be imputed to. [C18: from Late Latin *inculpāre,* from Latin *culpāre* to blame, from *culpa* fault, blame] —ˌ**inculˈpation** *n.* —**inculpative** (ɪnˈkʌlpətɪv) *or* **inculpatory** (ɪnˈkʌlpətərɪ, -trɪ) *adj.*

incult (ɪnˈkʌlt) *adj. Rare.* **1.** (of land) uncultivated; untilled; naturally wild. **2.** lacking refinement and culture. [C16: from Latin *incultus,* from IN-[1] + *colere* to till]

incumbency (ɪnˈkʌmbənsɪ) *n., pl.* **-cies.** **1.** the state or quality of being incumbent. **2.** the office, duty, or tenure of an incumbent.

incumbent (ɪnˈkʌmbənt) *adj.* **1.** *Formal.* (often *postpositive* and foll. by *on* or *upon* and an infinitive) morally binding or necessary; obligatory: *it is incumbent on me to attend.* **2.** (usually *postpositive* and foll. by *on*) resting or lying (on). ~*n.* **3.** a person who holds an office, esp. a clergyman holding a benefice. [C16: from Latin *incumbere* to lie upon, devote one's attention to, from IN-[2] + *-cumbere,* related to Latin *cubāre* to lie down] —**inˈcumbently** *adv.*

incumber (ɪnˈkʌmbə) *vb.* a less common spelling of **encumber.** —**inˈcumberingly** *adv.* —**inˈcumbrance** *n.*

incunabula (ˌɪnkjʊˈnæbjʊlə) *pl. n., sing.* **-lum** (-ləm). **1.** any book printed before 1500. **2.** the infancy or earliest stages of something; beginnings. [C19: from Latin, originally: swaddling clothes, hence beginnings, from IN-[2] + *cūnābula* cradle] —ˌ**incuˈnabular** *adj.*

incur (ɪnˈkɜː) *vb.* **-curs, -curring, -curred.** (*tr.*) **1.** to make oneself subject to (something undesirable); bring upon oneself. **2.** to run into or encounter. [C16: from Latin *incurrere* to run into, from *currere* to run] —**inˈcurrable** *adj.*

incurable (ɪnˈkjʊərəbᵊl) *adj.* **1.** (esp. of a disease) not curable; unresponsive to treatment. ~*n.* **2.** a person having an incurable disease. —**inˌcuraˈbility** *or* **inˈcurableness** *n.* —**inˈcurably** *adv.*

incurious (ɪnˈkjʊərɪəs) *adj.* not curious; indifferent or uninterested. —**incuriosity** (ɪnˌkjʊərɪˈɒsɪtɪ) *or* **inˈcuriousness** *n.* —**inˈcuriously** *adv.*

incurrence (ɪnˈkʌrəns) *n.* the act or state of incurring.

incurrent (ɪnˈkʌrənt) *adj.* **1.** (of anatomical ducts, tubes, channels, etc.) having an inward flow. **2.** flowing or running in an inward direction. [C16: from Latin *incurrēns* running into; see INCUR]

incursion (ɪnˈkɜːʃən) *n.* **1.** a sudden invasion, attack, or raid. **2.** the act of running or leaking into; penetration. [C15: from Latin *incursiō* onset, attack, from *incurrere* to run into; see INCUR] —**incursive** (ɪnˈkɜːsɪv) *adj.*

incurvate *vb.* (ˈɪnkɜːˌveɪt), *also* **incurve** (ɪnˈkɜːv). **1.** to curve or cause to curve inwards. ~*adj.* (ɪnˈkɜːvɪt, -veɪt). **2.** curved inwards. [C16: from Latin *incurvāre* (*vb.*)] —ˌ**incurˈvation** *n.* —**incurvature** (ɪnˈkɜːvətʃə) *n.*

incus (ˈɪŋkəs) *n., pl.* **incudes** (ɪnˈkjuːdiːz). the central of the three small bones in the middle ear of mammals. Nontechnical name: **anvil.** Compare **malleus, stapes.** [C17: from Latin: anvil, from *incūdere* to forge] —**incudate** (ˈɪŋkjʊˌdeɪt) *or* **incudal** (ˈɪŋkjʊdᵊl) *adj.*

incuse (ɪnˈkjuːz) *n.* **1.** a design stamped or hammered onto a coin. ~*vb.* **2.** to impress (a design) in a coin or to impress (a coin) with a design by hammering or stamping. ~*adj.* **3.** stamped or hammered onto a coin. [C19: from Latin *incūsus* hammered; see INCUS]

IND **1.** Also: **IDN** *abbrev. for* in nomine Dei. [Latin: in the name of God] ~ **2.** *international car registration for* India.

ind. *abbrev. for:* **1.** independence. **2.** independent. **3.** index. **4.** indicative. **5.** indirect. **6.** industrial. **7.** industry.

Ind. *abbrev. for:* **1.** Independent. **2.** India. **3.** Indian. **4.** Indiana. **5.** Indies.

indaba (ɪnˈdɑːbə) *n.* **1.** *Anthropol., history.* (among Bantu peoples of southern Africa) a meeting to discuss a serious topic. **2.** *S. African informal.* a matter of concern or for discussion. [C19: from Zulu: topic]

indamine (ˈɪndəˌmiːn, -mɪn) *n.* **1.** an organic base used in the production of the dye safranine. Formula: $NH_2C_6H_4N{:}C_6H_4{:}NH$ **2.** any of a class of organic bases with a similar structure to this compound. Their salts are unstable blue and green dyes. [C20: from INDIGO + AMINE]

indebted (ɪnˈdɛtɪd) *adj.* (*postpositive*) **1.** owing gratitude for help, favours, etc; obligated. **2.** owing money.

indebtedness (ɪnˈdɛtɪdnɪs) *n.* **1.** the state of being indebted. **2.** the total of a person's debts.

indecency (ɪnˈdiːsənsɪ) *n., pl.* **-cies.** **1.** the state or quality of being indecent. **2.** an indecent act, etc.

indecent (ɪnˈdiːsᵊnt) *adj.* **1.** offensive to standards of decency, esp. in sexual matters. **2.** unseemly or improper (esp. in the phrase **indecent haste**). —**inˈdecently** *adv.*

indecent assault *n.* the act of taking indecent liberties with a person without his or her consent.

indecent exposure *n.* the offence of indecently exposing parts of one's body in public, esp. the genitals.

indeciduous (ˌɪndɪˈsɪdjʊəs) *adj.* **1.** (of leaves) not deciduous. **2.** another word for **evergreen** (sense 1).

indecipherable (ˌɪndɪˈsaɪfərəbᵊl, -frəbᵊl) *adj.* not decipherable; illegible. —ˌ**indeˌcipheraˈbility** *or* ˌ**indeˈcipherableness** *n.* —ˌ**indeˈcipherably** *adv.*

indecisive (ˌɪndɪˈsaɪsɪv) *adj.* **1.** (of a person) vacillating; irresolute. **2.** not decisive or conclusive. —ˌ**indeˈcision** *or* ˌ**indeˈcisiveness** *n.* —ˌ**indeˈcisively** *adv.*

indeclinable (ˌɪndɪˈklaɪnəbᵊl) *adj.* (of a noun or pronoun) having only one form; not declined for case or number. —ˌ**indeˈclinableness** *n.* —ˌ**indeˈclinably** *adv.*

indecorous (ɪnˈdɛkərəs) *adj.* improper or ungraceful; unseemly. —**inˈdecorously** *adv.* —**inˈdecorousness** *n.*

indecorum (ˌɪndɪˈkɔːrəm) *n.* indecorous behaviour or speech; unseemliness.

indeed (ɪnˈdiːd) *sentence connector.* **1.** certainly; actually: *indeed, it may never happen.* ~*adv.* **2.** (intensifier): *that is indeed amazing.* **3.** or rather; what is more: *a comfortable, indeed wealthy family.* ~*interj.* **4.** an expression of doubt, surprise, etc.

indef. *abbrev. for* indefinite.

indefatigable (ˌɪndɪˈfætɪgəbᵊl) *adj.* unable to be tired out; unflagging. [C16: from Latin *indēfatīgābilis*, from IN-[1] + *dēfatīgāre*, from *fatīgāre* to tire] —ˌ**indeˌfatigaˈbility** *or* ˌ**indeˈfatigableness** *n.* —ˌ**indeˈfatigably** *adv.*

indefeasible (ˌɪndɪˈfiːzəbᵊl) *adj. Law.* not liable to be annulled or forfeited. —ˌ**indeˌfeasiˈbility** *or* ˌ**indeˈfeasibleness** *n.* —ˌ**indeˈfeasibly** *adv.*

indefectible (ˌɪndɪˈfɛktɪbᵊl) *adj.* **1.** not subject to decay or failure. **2.** flawless. —ˌ**indeˌfectiˈbility** *n.* —ˌ**indeˈfectibly** *adv.*

indefensible (ˌɪndɪˈfɛnsəbᵊl) *adj.* **1.** not justifiable or excusable. **2.** capable of being disagreed with; untenable. **3.** incapable of defence against attack. —ˌ**indeˌfensiˈbility** *or* ˌ**indeˈfensibleness** *n.* —ˌ**indeˈfensibly** *adv.*

indefinable (ˌɪndɪˈfaɪnəbᵊl) *adj.* incapable of being defined or analysed: *there was an indefinable sense of terror.* —ˌ**indeˈfinableness** *n.* —ˌ**indeˈfinably** *adv.*

indefinite (ɪnˈdɛfɪnɪt) *adj.* **1.** not certain or determined; unsettled. **2.** without exact limits; indeterminate: *an indefinite number.* **3.** vague, evasive, or unclear. **4.** Also: **indeterminate.** *Botany.* **a.** too numerous to count: *indefinite stamens.* **b.** capable of continued growth at the tip of the stem, which does not terminate in a flower: *an indefinite inflorescence.* —**inˈdefinitely** *adv.* —**inˈdefiniteness** *n.*

indefinite article *n. Grammar.* a determiner that expresses nonspecificity of reference, such as *a, an,* or *some.* Compare **definite article.**

indefinite integral *n. Maths.* **a.** any function whose derivative is the given function, as x^2, $x^2 + 3$, $x^2 - 5$, etc. of $2x$. **b.** the schema representing all such functions, here $x^2 + k$. **c.** the symbolic representation of this as a function of the given function, written $\int f(x)\,dx$ where $f(x)$ is the given function. **d.** the symbol $\int$.

indefinite pronoun *n. Grammar.* a pronoun having no specific referent, such as *someone, anybody,* or *nothing.*

indehiscent (ˌɪndɪˈhɪsᵊnt) *adj.* (of fruits) not dehiscent; not opening to release seeds. —ˌ**indeˈhiscence** *n.*

indelible (ɪnˈdɛlɪbᵊl) *adj.* **1.** incapable of being erased or obliterated. **2.** making indelible marks: *indelible ink.* [C16: from Latin *indēlēbilis* indestructible, from IN-[1] + *delēre* to destroy] —**inˌdeliˈbility** *or* **inˈdelibleness** *n.* —**inˈdelibly** *adv.*

indelicate (ɪnˈdɛlɪkɪt) *adj.* **1.** coarse, crude, or rough. **2.** offensive, embarrassing, or tasteless. —**inˈdelicacy** *or* **inˈdelicateness** *n.* —**inˈdelicately** *adv.*

indemnify (ɪnˈdɛmnɪˌfaɪ) *vb.* **-fies, -fying, -fied.** (*tr.*) **1.** to secure against future loss, damage, or liability; give security for; insure. **2.** to compensate for loss, injury, expense, etc.; reimburse. —**inˌdemnifiˈcation** *n.* —**inˈdemniˌfier** *n.*

indemnity (ɪnˈdɛmnɪtɪ) *n., pl.* **-ties.** **1.** compensation for loss or damage; reimbursement; **2.** protection or insurance against future loss or damage. **3.** legal exemption from penalties or liabilities incurred through one's acts or defaults. **4.** **act of indemnity.** an act of Parliament granting exemption to public officers from technical penalties that they may have been compelled to incur. [C15: from Late Latin *indemnitās*, from *indemnis* uninjured, from Latin IN-[1] + *damnum* damage]

indemonstrable (ˌɪndɪˈmɒnstrəbᵊl) *adj.* incapable of being demonstrated or proved. —ˌ**indeˌmonstraˈbility** *n.* —ˌ**indeˈmonstrably** *adv.*

indene (ˈɪndiːn) *n.* a colourless liquid hydrocarbon extracted from petroleum and coal tar and used in making synthetic resins. Formula: C_9H_8. [C20: from INDOLE + -ENE]

indent[1] *vb.* (ɪnˈdɛnt). (*mainly tr.*) **1.** to place (written or printed matter, etc.) in from the margin, as at the beginning of a paragraph. **2.** to cut or tear (a document, esp. a contract or deed in duplicate) so that the irregular lines may be matched to confirm its authenticity. **3.** *Chiefly Brit.* (in foreign trade) to place an order for (foreign goods), usually through an agent. **4.** (when *intr.*, foll. by *for, on,* or *upon*) *Chiefly Brit.* to make an order on (a source or supply) or for (something). **5.** to notch (an edge, border, etc.); make jagged. **6.** to bind (an apprentice, etc.) by indenture. ~*n.* (ˈɪnˌdɛnt). **7.** *Chiefly Brit.* (in foreign trade) an order for foreign merchandise, esp. one placed with an agent. **8.** *Chiefly Brit.* an official order for goods. **9.** (in the late 18th-century U.S.) a certificate issued by federal and state governments for the principal or interest due on the public debt. **10.** another word for **indenture.** **11.** another word for **indentation** (sense 4). [C14: from Old French *endenter*, from EN-[1] + *dent* tooth, from Latin *dēns*] —**inˈdenter** *or* **inˈdentor** *n.*

indent[2] *vb.* (ɪnˈdɛnt). **1.** (*tr.*) to make a dent or depression in. ~*n.* (ˈɪnˌdɛnt). **2.** a dent or depression. [C15: from IN-[2] + DENT[1]]

indentation (ˌɪndɛnˈteɪʃən) *n.* **1.** a hollowed, notched, or cut place, as on an edge or on a coastline. **2.** a series of hollows, notches, or cuts. **3.** the act of indenting or the condition of being indented. **4.** Also called: **indention, indent.** the leaving of space or the amount of space left between a margin and the start of an indented line.

indention (ɪnˈdɛnʃən) *n.* another word for **indentation** (sense 4).

indenture (ɪnˈdɛntʃə) *n.* **1.** any deed, contract, or sealed agreement between two or more parties. **2.** (formerly) a deed drawn up in duplicate, each part having correspondingly indented edges for identification and security. **3.** (*often pl.*) a contract between an apprentice and his master. **4.** a formal or official list or certificate authenticated for use as a voucher, etc. **5.** a less common word for **indentation.** ~*vb.* **6.** (*intr.*) to enter into an agreement by indenture. **7.** (*tr.*) to bind (an apprentice, servant, etc.) by indenture. **8.** (*tr.*) *Obsolete.* to indent or wrinkle. —**inˈdentureˌship** *n.*

independence (ˌɪndɪˈpɛndəns) *n.* the state or quality of being independent. Also called: **independency.**

Independence Day *n.* the official name for the **Fourth of July.**

independency (ˌɪndɪˈpɛndənsɪ) *n., pl.* **-cies.** **1.** a territory or state free from the control of any other power. **2.** another word for **independence.**

Independency (ˌɪndɪˈpɛndənsɪ) *n.* (esp. in the Congregational Church) the principle upholding the independence of each local church or congregation.

independent (ˌɪndɪˈpɛndənt) *adj.* **1.** free from control in action, judgment, etc.; autonomous. **2.** not dependent on anything else for function, validity, etc.; separate: *two independent units make up this sofa.* **3.** not reliant on the support, esp. financial support, of others. **4.** capable of acting for oneself or on one's own: *a very independent little girl.* **5.** providing a large unearned sum towards one's support (esp. in the phrases **independent income, independent means**). **6.** living on an unearned income. **7.** *Maths.* (of a system of equations) not linearly dependent. See also **independent variable.** **8.** *Statistics.* **a.** (of two or more variables) distributed so that the value taken by one variable will have no effect on that taken by another or others. **b.** (of two or more events) such that the probability of all occurring equals the product of their individual probabilities. Compare **statistical dependence.** **9.** *Logic.* (of a set of propositions) **a.** not validly derivable from one another, so that if the propositions are the axioms of some theory none can be dispensed with. **b.** not logically related, so that in no case can the truth value of one be inferred from those of the others. ~*n.* **10.** an independent person or thing. **11.** a person who is not affiliated to or who acts independently of a political party. —ˌ**inde'pendently** *adv.*

Independent (ˌɪndɪ'pɛndənt) *n.* **1.** (in England) a member of the Congregational Church. ~*adj.* **2.** of or relating to Independency.

independent clause *n. Grammar.* a main or coordinate clause. Compare **dependent clause.**

independent school *n.* **1.** (in Britain) a school that is neither financed nor controlled by the government or local authorities. **2.** (in Australia) a school that is not part of the state system.

independent variable *n.* **1.** Also called: **argument.** a variable in a mathematical equation or statement whose value determines that of the dependent variable: in $y = f(x)$, x is the independent variable. **2.** *Statistics.* Also called: **predictor.** the variable which an experimenter deliberately manipulates in order to observe its relationship with some other quantity, or which defines the distinct conditions in an experiment. See also **experimental condition.**

in-depth *adj.* carefully worked out, detailed and thorough: *an in-depth study.*

indescribable (ˌɪndɪ'skraɪbəbᵊl) *adj.* beyond description; too intense, extreme, etc., for words. —ˌ**indeˌscriba'bility** *or* ˌ**inde'scribableness** *n.* —ˌ**inde'scribably** *adv.*

indestructible (ˌɪndɪ'strʌktəbᵊl) *adj.* incapable of being destroyed; very durable. —ˌ**indeˌstructi'bility** *or* ˌ**inde'structibleness** *n.* —ˌ**inde'structibly** *adv.*

indeterminable (ˌɪndɪ'tɜːmɪnəbᵊl) *adj.* **1.** incapable of being ascertained. **2.** incapable of being settled. —ˌ**inde'terminableness** *n.* —ˌ**inde'terminably** *adv.*

indeterminacy principle *n.* another name for **uncertainty principle.**

indeterminate (ˌɪndɪ'tɜːmɪnɪt) *adj.* **1.** uncertain in extent, amount, or nature. **2.** not definite; inconclusive: *an indeterminate reply.* **3.** unable to be predicted, calculated, or deduced. **4.** *Physics, etc.* (of an effect) not obeying the law of causality; noncausal. **5.** *Maths.* **a.** having no numerical meaning, as 0.00 and 0/0. **b.** (of an equation) having more than one variable and an unlimited number of solutions. **6.** *Botany.* another word for **indefinite** (sense 4). **7.** (of a structure, framework, etc.) comprising forces that cannot be fully analysed, esp. by vector analysis. —ˌ**inde'terminacy,** ˌ**indeˌtermi'nation,** *or* ˌ**inde'terminateness** *n.* —ˌ**inde'terminately** *adv.*

indeterminate sentence *n. Law.* a prison sentence the length of which depends on the prisoner's conduct.

indeterminism (ˌɪndɪ'tɜːmɪˌnɪzəm) *n.* the philosophical doctrine that behaviour is not entirely determined by motives. —ˌ**inde'terminist** *n., adj.* —ˌ**indeˌtermin'istic** *adj.*

index ('ɪndɛks) *n., pl.* **-dexes** *or* **-dices** (-dɪˌsiːz). **1.** an alphabetical list of persons, places, subjects, etc., mentioned in the text of a printed work, usually at the back, and indicating where in the work they are referred to. **2.** See **thumb index.** **3.** *Library science.* a systematic list of book titles or author's names, giving cross-references and the location of each book; catalogue. **4.** an indication, sign, or token. **5.** a pointer, needle, or other indicator, as on an instrument. **6.** *Maths.* **a.** another name for **exponent** (sense 4). **b.** a number or variable placed as a superscript to the left of a radical sign indicating by its value the root to be extracted, as in $\sqrt[3]{8} = 2$. **c.** a subscript or superscript to the right of a variable to show that the variable should be considered over a range of specified values: x_i *for the index* $i = 3$ *includes* x_1, x_2, and x_3. **7.** a numerical scale by means of which variables, such as levels of the cost of living, can be compared with each other or with some base number. **8.** a number or ratio indicating a specific characteristic, property, etc.: *refractive index.* **9.** Also called: **fist.** a printer's mark (☞) used to indicate notes, paragraphs, etc. **10.** *Obsolete.* a table of contents or preface. ~*vb.* (*tr.*) **11.** to put an index in (a book). **12.** to enter (a word, item, etc.) in an index. **13.** to point out; indicate. **14.** to index-link. **15.** to move (a machine or a workpiece held in a machine tool) so that one particular operation will be repeated at certain defined intervals. [C16: from Latin: pointer, hence forefinger, title, index, from *indicāre* to disclose, show; see INDICATE] —'**indexer** *n.* —'**indexless** *adj.*

indexation (ˌɪndɛk'seɪʃən) or **index-linking** *n.* the act of making wages, interest rates, etc., index-linked.

index case *n. Med.* the first case of a disease.

index finger *n.* the finger next to the thumb. Also called: **forefinger.**

index fossil *n.* a fossil species that characterizes and is used to delimit a geological zone. Also called: **zone fossil.**

indexical (ɪn'dɛksɪkᵊl) *adj.* **1.** arranged as or relating to an index or indexes. ~*n.* **2.** *Logic, linguistics.* a term whose reference depends on the context of utterance, such as *I, you, here, now,* or *tomorrow.* Also: **deictic.**

indexing head *n.* a circular plate mounted to rotate on its centre, inscribed with concentric circles, each accurately divided, the dimensions being marked by drilled holes. The plate can be moved round with a workpiece to facilitate the accurate location of holes or other machining operations on the workpiece.

Index Librorum Prohibitorum *Latin.* ('ɪndɛks laɪ'brɔːrʊm prəʊˌhɪbɪ'tɔːrʊm) *n. R.C. Church.* (formerly) an official list of proscribed books. Often called: **the Index.** [C17, literally: list of forbidden books]

index-linked *adj.* (of wages, interest rates, etc.) directly related to the cost-of-living index and rising or falling accordingly.

index number *n. Statistics.* a statistic indicating the relative change occurring in each successive period of time in the price, volume, or value of a commodity or in a general economic variable, such as the price level, national income, or gross output, with reference to a previous base period conventionally given the number 100.

Index of Industrial Production *n.* (in Britain) an index produced by the Central Statistical Office showing changes in the production of the primary British industries.

index of refraction *n.* another name for **refractive index.**

India ('ɪndɪə) *n. Communications.* a code word for the letter *i.*

Indiaman ('ɪndɪəmən) *n., pl.* **-men.** (formerly) a large merchant ship engaged in trade with India.

Indian ('ɪndɪən) *n.* **1.** a native, citizen, or inhabitant of the Republic of India, in S Asia. **2.** an American Indian. **3.** (*not in scholarly usage*) any of the languages of the American Indians. ~*adj.* **4.** of, relating to, or characteristic of India, its inhabitants, or any of their languages. **5.** of, relating to, or characteristic of the American Indians or any of their languages.

Indian agent *n.* an official who represents the U.S. or Canadian government to a group of North American Indians.

Indian bread *n.* another name for **corn bread.**

Indian cholera *n.* another name for **cholera.**

Indian club *n.* a bottle-shaped club, usually used in pairs by gymnasts, jugglers, etc.

Indian corn *n.* another name for **maize** (sense 1).

Indian file *n.* another term for **single file.**

Indian giver *n. U.S. and Canadian offensive.* a person who asks for the return of a present he has given. —**Indian giving** *n.*

Indian hemp *n.* **1.** another name for **hemp,** esp. the variety *Cannabis indica,* from which several narcotic drugs are obtained. **2.** Also called: **dogbane.** a perennial American apocynaceous plant, *Apocynum cannabinum,* whose fibre was formerly used by the Indians to make rope.

Indian ink *or esp. U.S. and Canadian* **India ink** *n.* **1.** a black pigment made from a mixture of lampblack and a binding agent such as gelatin or glue: usually formed into solid cakes and sticks. **2.** a black liquid ink made from this pigment. ~Also called: **China ink, Chinese ink.**

Indian liquorice *n.* a woody leguminous tropical Asian climbing plant, *Abrus precatorius,* with scarlet black-spotted poisonous seeds, used as beads, and roots used as a substitute for liquorice. Also called: **jequirity.**

Indian list *n. Informal.* (in Canada) a list of persons to whom spirits may not be sold. Also called: **interdict list.**

Indian mallow *n.* a tall malvaceous weedy North American plant, *Abutilon theophrasti,* with small yellow flowers and large velvety leaves.

Indian meal *n.* another name for **corn meal.**

Indian millet *n.* another name for **durra.**

Indian mulberry *n.* a small rubiaceous tree, *Morinda citrifolia,* of SE Asia and Australasia, with rounded yellow fruits: yields red and yellow dyes.

Indian pipe *n.* a white or pinkish saprophytic woodland plant, *Monotropa uniflora,* of the N hemisphere, with a solitary nodding flower resembling a pipe: family *Monotropaceae.*

Indian red *n.* **1.** a red pigment containing ferric oxide, used in paints and cosmetics and produced by oxidizing iron salts. **2.** a type of red soil containing ferric oxide, found in S Asia and used as a pigment and metal polish.

Indian reserve *or* **reservation** *n.* See **reservation** (sense 4).

Indian rice *n.* **1.** an annual erect aquatic North American grass, *Zizania aquatica,* with edible purplish-black grain. **2.** the grain of this plant. ~Also called: **wild rice.**

Indian rope-trick *n.* the supposed Indian feat of climbing an unsupported rope.

Indian sign *n. U.S.* a magic spell designed to place the victim in one's power or bring him bad luck.

indian summer *n.* **1.** a period of unusually settled warm weather after the end of summer proper. **2.** a period of ease and tranquillity or of renewed productivity towards the end of a person's life or of an epoch. ~See also **Saint Martin's summer.** [originally U.S.: probably so named because it was first noted in regions occupied by American Indians]

Indian sweater *n.* another name for **Cowichan sweater.**

Indian tobacco *n.* a poisonous North American campanulaceous plant, *Lobelia inflata,* with small pale blue flowers and rounded inflated seed capsules.

India paper *n.* **1.** a thin soft opaque printing paper made in the Orient. **2.** another name (not in technical usage) for **Bible paper.**

India print *n.* a colourful cotton fabric, with a block-printed pattern, made in India.
India rubber *n.* another name for **rubber**[1] (sense 1).
Indic (ˈɪndɪk) *adj.* **1.** denoting, belonging to, or relating to a branch of Indo-European consisting of the Indo-European languages of India, including Sanskrit, Hindi and Urdu, Punjabi, Gujerati, Bengali, and Sinhalese. ~*n.* **2.** this group of languages. ~Also: **Indo-Aryan.**
indic. *abbrev. for:* **1.** indicating. **2.** indicative. **3.** indicator.
indican (ˈɪndɪkən) *n.* a compound secreted in the urine, usually in the form of its potassium salt; indoxylsulphuric acid. Formula: $C_8H_6NOSO_2OH$. [C19: from Latin *indicum* INDIGO + -AN]
indicant (ˈɪndɪkənt) *n.* something that indicates.
indicate (ˈɪndɪˌkeɪt) *vb. (tr.)* **1.** (*may take a clause as object*) to be or give a sign or symptom of; imply: *cold hands indicate a warm heart.* **2.** to point out or show. **3.** (*may take a clause as object*) to state briefly; suggest: *he indicated what his feelings were.* **4.** (of instruments) to show a reading of: *the speedometer indicated 50 miles per hour.* **5.** (*usually passive*) to recommend or require: *surgery seems to be indicated for this patient.* [C17: from Latin *indicāre* to point out, from IN-[2] + *dicāre* to proclaim; compare INDEX] —ˈ**indiˌcatable** *adj.* —**indicatory** (ɪnˈdɪkətərɪ, -trɪ) *adj.*
indicated horsepower *n.* the power output of a piston engine calculated from the mean effective pressure in the cylinder as derived from an indicator diagram and the speed of the engine in revolutions per minute.
indication (ˌɪndɪˈkeɪʃən) *n.* **1.** something that serves to indicate or suggest; sign: *an indication of foul play.* **2.** the degree or quantity represented on a measuring instrument or device. **3.** the action of indicating. **4.** something that is indicated as advisable, necessary, or expedient.
indicative (ɪnˈdɪkətɪv) *adj.* **1.** (*usually postpositive;* foll. by *of*) serving as a sign; suggestive: *indicative of trouble ahead.* **2.** *Grammar.* denoting a mood of verbs used chiefly to make statements. Compare **subjunctive** (sense 1). ~*n.* **3.** *Grammar.* **a.** the indicative mood. **b.** a verb in the indicative mood. ~Abbrev.: **indic.** —**inˈdicatively** *adv.*
indicator (ˈɪndɪˌkeɪtə) *n.* **1.** something that provides an indication, esp. of trends. See **economic indicator. 2.** a device to attract attention, such as the pointer of a gauge or a warning lamp. **3.** an instrument that displays certain operating conditions in a machine, such as a gauge showing temperature, speed, pressure, etc. **4. a.** a device that records or registers something, such as the movements of a lift, or that shows information, such as arrival and departure times of trains. **b.** (*as modifier*): *indicator light.* **5.** Also called: **blinker.** a device for indicating that a motor vehicle is about to turn left or right, esp. two pairs of lights that flash when operated or a pair of trafficators. **6.** Also called: **dial gauge.** a delicate measuring instrument used to determine small differences in the height of mechanical components. It consists of a spring-loaded plunger that operates a pointer moving over a circular scale. **7.** *Chem.* **a.** a substance used in titrations to indicate the completion of a chemical reaction, usually by a change of colour. **b.** a substance, such as litmus, that indicates the presence of an acid or alkali. **8.** Also called: **indicator species.** *Ecology.* **a.** a plant or animal species that thrives only under particular environmental conditions and therefore indicates these conditions where it is found. **b.** a species of plant or animal whose well-being confirms the well-being of other species in the area.
indicator diagram *n.* a graphical or other representation of the cyclic variations of pressure and volume within the cylinder of a reciprocating engine obtained by using an indicator.
indices (ˈɪndɪˌsiːz) *n.* a plural of **index.**
indicia (ɪnˈdɪʃɪə) *pl. n., sing.* **-cium** (-ʃɪəm). distinguishing markings or signs; indications. [C17: from Latin, plural of *indicium* a notice, from INDEX] —**inˈdicial** *adj.*
indicolite (ˈɪndɪkəˌlaɪt) *or* **indigolite** *n.* a form of tourmaline ranging in colour from pale blue to blue-black. [C19: from Spanish *indico* INDIGO + -LITE]
indict (ɪnˈdaɪt) *vb. (tr.)* to charge (a person) with crime, esp. formally in writing; accuse. [C14: alteration of *enditen* to INDITE] —ˌ**indictˈee** *n.* —**inˈdicter** *or* **inˈdictor** *n.*
indictable (ɪnˈdaɪtəbᵊl) *adj. Criminal law.* **1.** (of a person) liable to be indicted. **2.** (of a crime) that makes a person liable to be indicted. —**inˈdictably** *adv.*
indiction (ɪnˈdɪkʃən) *n.* (in the Roman Empire and later in various medieval kingdoms) **1.** a recurring fiscal period of 15 years, often used as a unit for dating events. **2.** a particular year in this period or the number assigned it. **3.** (from the reign of Constantine the Great) **a.** a valuation of property made every 15 years as a basis for taxation. **b.** the tax based on this valuation. [C14: from Latin *indictiō* declaration, announcement of a tax; see INDITE] —**inˈdictional** *adj.*
indictment (ɪnˈdaɪtmənt) *n. Criminal law.* **1.** a formal written charge of crime formerly referred to and presented on oath by a grand jury. **2.** any formal accusation of crime. **3.** *Scot.* a charge of crime brought at the instance of the Lord Advocate. **4.** the act of indicting or the state of being indicted.
indie (ˈɪndɪ) *n. Informal.* **a.** an independent record company. **b.** (*as modifier*): *the indie charts.*
indifference (ɪnˈdɪfrəns, -fərəns) *n.* **1.** the fact or state of being indifferent; lack of care or concern. **2.** lack of quality; mediocrity. **3.** lack of importance; insignificance. **4.** See **principle of indifference.**
indifferent (ɪnˈdɪfrənt, -fərənt) *adj.* **1.** (often foll. by *to*) showing no care or concern; uninterested: *he was indifferent to my pleas.* **2.** unimportant; immaterial. **3. a.** of only average or moderate size, extent, quality, etc. **b.** not at all good; poor. **4.** showing or having no preferences; impartial. **5.** *Biology.* **a.** (of cells or tissues) not differentiated or specialized. **b.** (of a species) occurring in two or more different communities. [C14: from Latin *indifferēns* making no distinction] —**inˈdifferently** *adv.*
indifferentism (ɪnˈdɪfrənˌtɪzəm, -fərən-) *n.* systematic indifference, esp. in matters of religion. —**inˈdifferentist** *n.*
indigene (ˈɪndɪˌdʒiːn) *or* **indigen** (ˈɪndɪdʒən) *n.* an indigenous person, animal, or thing; native.
indigenous (ɪnˈdɪdʒɪnəs) *adj.* (when *postpositive,* foll. by *to*) **1.** originating or occurring naturally (in a country, region, etc.); native. **2.** innate (to); inherent (in). [C17: from Latin *indigenus,* from *indigena* indigene, from *indi-* in + *gignere* to beget] —**inˈdigenously** *adv.* —**inˈdigenousness** *or* **indigenity** (ˌɪndɪˈdʒɛnɪtɪ) *n.*
indigent (ˈɪndɪdʒənt) *adj.* **1.** so poor as to lack even necessities; very needy. **2.** (usually foll. by *of*) *Archaic.* lacking (in) or destitute (of). ~*n.* **3.** an impoverished person. [C14: from Latin *indigēre* to need, from *egēre* to lack] —ˈ**indigence** *n.* —ˈ**indigently** *adv.*
indigested (ˌɪndɪˈdʒɛstɪd) *adj. Archaic.* undigested.
indigestible (ˌɪndɪˈdʒɛstəbᵊl) *adj.* **1.** incapable of being digested or difficult to digest. **2.** difficult to understand or absorb mentally: *an indigestible book.* —ˌ**indiˌgestiˈbility** *or* ˌ**indiˈgestibleness** *n.* —ˌ**indiˈgestibly** *adv.*
indigestion (ˌɪndɪˈdʒɛstʃən) *n.* difficulty in digesting food, accompanied by abdominal pain, heartburn, and belching. Technical name: **dyspepsia.**
indigestive (ˌɪndɪˈdʒɛstɪv) *adj.* relating to or suffering from indigestion; dyspeptic.
indign (ɪnˈdaɪn) *adj. Obsolete or poetic.* **1.** undeserving; unworthy. **2.** unseemly; disgraceful. **3.** not deserved. [C15: from Old French *indigne,* from Latin *indignus* unworthy, from IN-[1] + *dignus* worthy; see DIGNITY]
indignant (ɪnˈdɪgnənt) *adj.* feeling or showing indignation. [C16: from Latin *indignārī* to be displeased with] —**inˈdignantly** *adv.*
indignation (ˌɪndɪgˈneɪʃən) *n.* anger or scorn aroused by something felt to be unfair, unworthy, or wrong.
indignity (ɪnˈdɪgnɪtɪ) *n., pl.* **-ties. 1.** injury to one's self-esteem or dignity; humiliation. **2.** *Obsolete.* disgrace or disgraceful character or conduct.
indigo (ˈɪndɪˌgəʊ) *n., pl.* **-gos** *or* **-goes. 1.** Also called: **indigotin.** a blue vat dye originally obtained from plants but now made synthetically. **2.** any of various tropical plants of the leguminous genus *Indigofera,* such as the anil, that yield this dye. Compare **wild indigo. 3. a.** any of a group of colours that have the same blue-violet hue; a spectral colour. **b.** (*as adj.*): *an indigo carpet.* [C16: from Spanish *indico,* via Latin from Greek *Indikos* of India] —**indigotic** (ˌɪndɪˈgɒtɪk) *adj.*
indigo blue *n., adj.* (**indigo-blue** *when prenominal*). the full name for **indigo** (the colour and the dye).
indigo bunting, bird, *or* **finch** *n.* a North American bunting, *Passerina cyanea,* the male of which is bright blue and the female brown.
indigoid (ˈɪndɪˌgɔɪd) *adj.* **1.** of, concerned with, or resembling indigo or its blue colour. ~*n.* **2.** any of a number of synthetic dyes or pigments related in chemical structure to indigo.
indigolite (ˈɪndɪgəˌlaɪt) *n.* a variant spelling of **indicolite.**
indigo snake *n.* a dark-blue nonvenomous North American colubrid snake, *Drymarchon corais couperi.*
indigotin (ɪnˈdɪgətɪn, ˌɪndɪˈgəʊ-) *n.* another name for **indigo** (the dye). [C19: from INDIGO + -IN]
indirect (ˌɪndɪˈrɛkt) *adj.* **1.** deviating from a direct course or line; roundabout; circuitous. **2.** not coming as a direct effect or consequence; secondary: *indirect benefits.* **3.** not straightforward, open, or fair; devious or evasive: *an indirect insult.* **4.** (of a title or an inheritance) not inherited in an unbroken line of succession from father to son. —ˌ**indiˈrectly** *adv.* —ˌ**indiˈrectness** *n.*
indirect costs *pl. n.* another name for **overheads.**
indirection (ˌɪndɪˈrɛkʃən) *n.* **1.** indirect procedure, courses, or methods. **2.** lack of direction or purpose; aimlessness. **3.** indirect dealing; deceit.
indirect labour *n. Commerce.* work done in administration and sales rather than in the manufacturing of a product. Compare **direct labour** (sense 1).
indirect lighting *n.* reflected or diffused light from a concealed source.
indirect object *n. Grammar.* a noun, pronoun, or noun phrase indicating the recipient or beneficiary of the action of a verb and its direct object, as *John* in the sentence *I bought John a newspaper.* Compare **direct object.**
indirect proof *n. Logic, maths.* proof of a conclusion by showing its negation to be self-contradictory; reductio ad absurdum. Compare **direct** (sense 17).

indirect question *n.* a question reported in indirect speech, as in *She asked why you came.* Compare **direct question.**
indirect speech *or esp. U.S.* **indirect discourse** *n.* the reporting of something said or written by conveying what was meant rather than repeating the exact words, as in the sentence *He asked me whether I would go* as opposed to *He asked me, "Will you go?"* Also called: **reported speech.**
indirect tax *n.* a tax levied on goods or services rather than on individuals or companies. Compare **direct tax.**
indiscernible (ˌɪndɪˈsɜːnəbᵊl) *adj.* **1.** incapable of being discerned. **2.** scarcely discernible or perceptible. —ˌ**indisˈcernibleness** *or* ˌ**indiscerniˈbility** *n.* —ˌ**indisˈcernibly** *adv.*
indiscipline (ɪnˈdɪsɪplɪn) *n.* lack of discipline.
indiscreet (ˌɪndɪˈskriːt) *adj.* not discreet; imprudent or tactless. —ˌ**indisˈcreetly** *adv.* —ˌ**indisˈcreetness** *n.*
indiscrete (ˌɪndɪˈskriːt) *adj.* not divisible or divided into parts. —ˌ**indisˈcretely** *adv.* —ˌ**indisˈcreteness** *n.*
indiscretion (ˌɪndɪˈskrɛʃən) *n.* **1.** the characteristic or state of being indiscreet. **2.** an indiscreet act, remark, etc. —ˌ**indisˈcretionary** *adj.*
indiscriminate (ˌɪndɪˈskrɪmɪnɪt) *adj.* **1.** lacking discrimination or careful choice; random or promiscuous. **2.** jumbled; confused. —ˌ**indisˈcriminately** *adv.* —ˌ**indisˈcriminateness** *n.* —ˌ**indisˌcrimiˈnation** *n.*
indispensable (ˌɪndɪˈspɛnsəbᵊl) *adj.* **1.** absolutely necessary; essential. **2.** not to be disregarded or escaped: *an indispensable role.* ~*n.* **3.** an indispensable person or thing. —ˌ**indisˌpensaˈbility** *or* ˌ**indisˈpensableness** *n.* —ˌ**indisˈpensably** *adv.*
indispose (ˌɪndɪˈspəʊz) *vb.* (*tr.*) **1.** to make unwilling or opposed; disincline. **2.** to cause to feel ill. **3.** to make unfit (for something or to do something).
indisposed (ˌɪndɪˈspəʊzd) *adj.* **1.** sick or ill. **2.** unwilling. [C15: from Latin *indispositus* disordered] —**indisposition** (ˌɪndɪspəˈzɪʃən) *n.*
indisputable (ˌɪndɪˈspjuːtəbᵊl) *adj.* beyond doubt; not open to question. —ˌ**indisˌputaˈbility** *or* ˌ**indisˈputableness** *n.* —ˌ**indisˈputably** *adv.*
indissoluble (ˌɪndɪˈsɒljʊbᵊl) *adj.* incapable of being dissolved or broken; permanent. —ˌ**indisˌsoluˈbility** *or* ˌ**indisˈsolubleness** *n.* —ˌ**indisˈsolubly** *adv.*
indistinct (ˌɪndɪˈstɪŋkt) *adj.* incapable of being clearly distinguished, as by the eyes, ears, or mind; not distinct. —ˌ**indisˈtinctly** *adv.* —ˌ**indisˈtinctness** *n.*
indistinctive (ˌɪndɪˈstɪŋktɪv) *adj.* **1.** without distinctive qualities. **2.** unable to make distinctions; undiscriminating. —ˌ**indisˈtinctively** *adv.* —ˌ**indisˈtinctiveness** *n.*
indistinguishable (ˌɪndɪˈstɪŋgwɪʃəbᵊl) *adj.* **1.** (*often postpositive; foll. by from*) identical or very similar (to): *twins indistinguishable from one another.* **2.** not easily perceptible; indiscernible. —ˌ**indisˌtinguishaˈbility** *or* ˌ**indisˈtinguishableness** *n.* —ˌ**indisˈtinguishably** *adv.*
indite (ɪnˈdaɪt) *vb.* (*tr.*) **1.** *Archaic.* to write. **2.** *Obsolete.* to dictate. [C14: from Old French *enditer,* from Latin *indīcere* to declare, from IN-[2] + *dīcere* to say] —**inˈditement** *n.* —**inˈditer** *n.*
indium (ˈɪndɪəm) *n.* a rare soft silvery metallic element associated with zinc ores: used in alloys, electronics, and electroplating. Symbol: In; atomic no.: 49; atomic wt.: 114.82; valency: 1, 2, or 3; relative density: 7.31; melting pt.: 156.61°C; boiling pt.: 2000°C (approx.). [C19: New Latin, from INDIGO + -IUM]
indiv. *or* **individ.** *abbrev. for* individual.
indivertible (ˌɪndɪˈvɜːtɪbᵊl) *adj.* incapable of being diverted or turned aside. —ˌ**indiˈvertibly** *adv.*
individual (ˌɪndɪˈvɪdjʊəl) *adj.* **1.** of, relating to, characteristic of, or meant for a single person or thing. **2.** separate or distinct, esp. from others of its kind; particular: *please mark the individual pages.* **3.** characterized by unusual and striking qualities; distinctive. **4.** *Obsolete.* indivisible; inseparable. ~*n.* **5.** a single person, esp. when regarded as distinct from others. **6.** *Biology.* **a.** a single animal or plant, esp. as distinct from a species. **b.** a single member of a compound organism or colony. **7.** *Logic.* **a.** Also called: **particular.** an object as opposed to a property or class. **b.** an element of the domain of discourse of a theory. [C15: from Medieval Latin *indīviduālis,* from Latin *indīviduus* indivisible, from IN-[1] + *dīviduus* divisible, from *dīvidere* to DIVIDE] —ˌ**indiˈvidually** *adv.*
▷**Usage.** In careful speech and writing, the noun *individual* is not loosely used as a synonym of *person,* although it is appropriate in that sense when a single person is being considered in contrast to a group, as in *in mass democracy the rights of the individual must be protected.*
individualism (ˌɪndɪˈvɪdjʊəˌlɪzəm) *n.* **1.** the action or principle of asserting one's independence and individuality; egoism. **2.** an individual quirk or peculiarity. **3.** another word for **laissez faire** (sense 1). **4.** *Philosophy.* the doctrine that only individual things exist and that therefore classes or properties have no reality. Compare **Platonism, realism** (sense 5).
individualist (ˌɪndɪˈvɪdjʊəlɪst) *n.* **1.** a person who shows independence and individuality in his behaviour, opinions, or actions. **2.** an advocate of individualism. —ˌ**indiˌvidualˈistic** *adj.* —ˌ**indiˌvidualˈistically** *adv.*
individuality (ˌɪndɪˌvɪdjʊˈælɪtɪ) *n., pl.* **-ties.** **1.** distinctive or unique character or personality: *a work of great individuality.* **2.** the qualities that distinguish one person or thing from another; identity. **3.** the state or quality of being a separate entity; discreteness. **4.** *Archaic.* indivisibility; inseparability.
individualize *or* **individualise** (ˌɪndɪˈvɪdjʊəˌlaɪz) *vb.* (*tr.*) **1.** to make or mark as individual or distinctive in character. **2.** to consider or treat individually; particularize. **3.** to make or modify so as to meet the special requirements of a person. —ˌ**indiˌvidualiˈzation** *or* ˌ**indiˌvidualiˈsation** *n.* —ˌ**indiˈvidualˌizer** *or* ˌ**indiˈvidualˌiser** *n.*
individuate (ˌɪndɪˈvɪdjʊˌeɪt) *vb.* (*tr.*) **1.** to give individuality or an individual form to. **2.** to distinguish from others of the same species or group; individualize. —ˌ**indiˈviduˌator** *n.*
individuation (ˌɪndɪˌvɪdjʊˈeɪʃən) *n.* **1.** the act or process of individuating. **2.** (in the psychology of Jung) the process by which the wholeness of the individual is established through the integration of consciousness and the collective unconscious. **3.** *Zoology.* the development of separate but mutually interdependent units, as in the development of zooids forming a colony.
indivisible (ˌɪndɪˈvɪzəbᵊl) *adj.* **1.** unable to be divided. **2.** *Maths.* leaving a remainder when divided by a given number: *8 is indivisible by 3.* —ˌ**indiˌvisiˈbility** *or* ˌ**indiˈvisibleness** *n.* —ˌ**indiˈvisibly** *adv.*
Indo- (ˈɪndəʊ-) *combining form.* denoting India or Indian: *Indo-European.*
Indo-Aryan *adj.* **1.** another word for **Indic** (sense 1). ~*n.* **2.** another name for **Indic** (sense 2). **3.** a native speaker of an Indo-Aryan language.
Indochinese *or* **Indo-chinese** (ˈɪndəʊtʃaɪˈniːz) *adj.* **1.** of or relating to Indochina, the peninsula in SE Asia consisting of Burma, Thailand, Laos, Cambodia, Vietnam, and Malaysia. ~*n.* **2.** (*pl.* **-ese**) a native or inhabitant of Indochina.
indocile (ɪnˈdəʊsaɪl) *adj.* difficult to discipline or instruct. —**indocility** (ˌɪndəʊˈsɪlɪtɪ) *n.*
indoctrinate (ɪnˈdɒktrɪˌneɪt) *vb.* (*tr.*) **1.** to teach (a person or group of people) systematically to accept doctrines, esp. uncritically. **2.** *Rare.* to impart learning to; instruct. —**inˌdoctriˈnation** *n.* —**inˈdoctriˌnator** *n.*
Indo-European *adj.* **1.** denoting, belonging to, or relating to a family of languages that includes English and many other culturally and politically important languages of the world: a characteristic feature, esp. of the older languages such as Latin, Greek, and Sanskrit, is inflection showing gender, number, and case. **2.** denoting or relating to the hypothetical parent language of this family, primitive Indo-European. **3.** denoting, belonging to, or relating to any of the peoples speaking these languages. ~*n.* **4.** the Indo-European family of languages. **5.** Also called: **primitive Indo-European, Proto-Indo-European.** the reconstructed hypothetical parent language of this family. **6.** a member of the prehistoric people who spoke this language. **7.** a descendant of this people or a native speaker of an Indo-European language.
Indo-Germanic *adj., n. Obsolete.* another term for **Indo-European.**
Indo-Hittite *n.* the Indo-European family of languages: used by scholars who regard Hittite not as a branch of Indo-European but as a related language.
Indo-Iranian *adj.* **1.** of or relating to the Indic and Iranian branches of the Indo-European family of languages. ~*n.* **2.** this group of languages, sometimes considered as forming a single branch of Indo-European.
indole (ˈɪndəʊl) *or* **indol** (ˈɪndəʊl, -dɒl) *n.* a white or yellowish crystalline heterocyclic compound extracted from coal tar and used in perfumery, medicine, and as a flavouring agent; 1-benzopyrrole. Formula: C_8H_7N. [C19: from IND(IGO) + -OLE[1]]
indoleacetic acid (ˌɪndəʊləˈsiːtɪk, -ˈsɛtɪk) *n.* an auxin that causes elongation of the cells of plant stems. Formula: $C_{10}H_9NO_2$. Abbrev.: **IAA.**
indolebutyric acid (ˌɪndəʊlbjuːˈtɪrɪk) *n.* a synthetic auxin used for stimulating plant growth and root formation. Formula: $C_8H_6N(CH_2)_3COOH$.
indolent (ˈɪndələnt) *adj.* **1.** disliking work or effort; lazy; idle. **2.** *Pathol.* causing little pain: *an indolent tumour.* **3.** (esp. of a painless ulcer) slow to heal. [C17: from Latin *indolēns* not feeling pain, from IN-[1] + *dolēns,* from *dolēre* to grieve, cause distress] —ˈ**indolence** *n.* —ˈ**indolently** *adv.*
Indologist (ɪnˈdɒlədʒɪst) *n.* a student of Indian literature, history, philosophy, etc. —**Inˈdology** *n.*
indomethacin (ˌɪndəʊˈmɛθəsɪn) *n.* a drug administered orally to relieve pain, fever, and inflammation, esp. in rheumatoid arthritis. Formula: $C_{19}H_{16}ClNO_4$. [C20: from INDOLE + METH- + ACETIC ACID + -IN]
indomitable (ɪnˈdɒmɪtəbᵊl) *adj.* (of courage, pride, etc.) difficult or impossible to defeat or subdue. [C17: from Late Latin *indomitābilis,* from Latin *indomitus* untamable, from IN-[1] + *domitus* subdued, from *domāre* to tame] —**inˌdomitaˈbility** *or* **inˈdomitableness** *n.* —**inˈdomitably** *adv.*
Indonesian (ˌɪndəʊˈniːzɪən) *adj.* **1.** of or relating to Indonesia, a republic in SE Asia, its people, or their language. ~*n.* **2.** a native or inhabitant of Indonesia. **3.** another name for **Bahasa Indonesia.**
indoor (ˈɪnˌdɔː) *adj.* (*prenominal*) of, situated in, or appropriate to the inside of a house or other building: *an indoor tennis court; indoor amusements.*

indoors (ˌɪnˈdɔːz) *adv., adj.* (*postpositive*) inside or into a house or other building.

Indo-Pacific *adj.* **1.** of or relating to the region of the Indian and W Pacific Oceans off the coast of SE Asia. ~*n.* **2.** a hypothetical family of languages relating the languages of New Guinea other than Malayo-Polynesian. Tentative affiliations with Malayo-Polynesian or Australian languages have been suggested.

indophenol (ˌɪndəʊˈfiːnɒl) *n.* **1.** a derivative of quinonimine. Formula: $HOC_6H_4NC_6H_4O$. **2.** any of a class of derivatives of this compound, esp. one of the blue or green dyes that are used for wool and cotton. [C19: from INDIGO + PHENOL]

indorse (ɪnˈdɔːs) *vb.* a variant spelling of **endorse.** —**inˈdorsable** *adj.* —**inˈdorsement** *n.* —**inˈdorser** *or* **inˈdorsor** *n.*

indorsee (ˌɪndɔːˈsiː, ɪnˈdɔːsiː) *n.* a variant of **endorsee.**

indoxyl (ɪnˈdɒksɪl) *n.* a yellow water-soluble crystalline compound occurring in woad as its glucoside and in urine as its ester. Formula: C_8H_7NO. See also **indican.** [C19: from INDIGO + HYDROXYL]

indraught *or U.S.* **indraft** (ˈɪnˌdrɑːft) *n.* **1.** the act of drawing or pulling in. **2.** an inward flow, esp. of air.

indrawn (ˌɪnˈdrɔːn) *adj.* **1.** drawn or pulled in. **2.** inward looking or introspective.

indris (ˈɪndrɪs) *or* **indri** (ˈɪndrɪ) *n., pl.* **-dris. 1.** a large Madagascan arboreal lemuroid primate, *Indri indri,* with thick silky fur patterned in black, white, and fawn: family *Indriidae.* **2. woolly indris.** a related nocturnal Madagascan animal, *Avahi laniger,* with thick grey-brown fur and a long tail. [C19: from French: lemur, from Malagasy *indry!* look! mistaken for the animal's name]

indubitable (ɪnˈdjuːbɪtəbᵊl) *adj.* incapable of being doubted; unquestionable. [C18: from Latin *indubitābilis,* from IN-[1] + *dubitāre* to doubt] —**inˌdubitaˈbility** *or* **inˈdubitableness** *n.* —**inˈdubitably** *adv.*

induc. *abbrev. for* induction.

induce (ɪnˈdjuːs) *vb.* (*tr.*) **1.** (often foll. by an infinitive) to persuade or use influence on. **2.** to cause or bring about. **3.** *Med.* to initiate or hasten (labour), as by administering a drug to stimulate uterine contractions. **4.** *Logic, obsolete.* to assert or establish (a general proposition, hypothesis, etc.) by induction. **5.** to produce (an electromotive force or electrical current) by induction. **6.** to transmit (magnetism) by induction. [C14: from Latin *indūcere* to lead in, from *dūcere* to lead] —**inˈducer** *n.* —**inˈducible** *adj.*

induced drag *n.* the former name for **trailing vortex drag.**

inducement (ɪnˈdjuːsmənt) *n.* **1.** the act of inducing. **2.** a means of inducing; persuasion; incentive. **3.** *Law.* (in pleading) the introductory part that leads up to and explains the matter in dispute.

induct (ɪnˈdʌkt) *vb.* (*tr.*) **1.** to bring in formally or install in an office, place, etc.; invest. **2.** (foll. by *to* or *into*) to initiate in knowledge (of). **3.** *U.S.* to enlist for military service; conscript. **4.** *Physics.* another word for **induce** (senses 5, 6). [C14: from Latin *inductus* led in, past participle of *indūcere* to introduce; see INDUCE]

inductance (ɪnˈdʌktəns) *n.* **1.** Also called: **induction.** the property of an electric circuit as a result of which an electromotive force is created by a change of current in the same circuit (see **self-inductance**) or in a neighbouring circuit (see **mutual inductance**). It is usually measured in henries. Symbol: L **2.** Also called: **inductor.** a component, such as a coil, in an electrical circuit, the main function of which is to produce inductance.

inductee (ˌɪndʌkˈtiː) *n. U.S.* a military conscript.

inductile (ɪnˈdʌktaɪl) *adj.* not ductile, pliant, or yielding. —ˌ**inducˈtility** *n.*

induction (ɪnˈdʌkʃən) *n.* **1.** the act of inducting or state of being inducted. **2.** the act of inducing. **3.** (in an internal-combustion engine) the part of the action of a piston by which mixed air and fuel are drawn from the carburettor to the cylinder. **4.** *Logic.* **a.** a process of reasoning, used esp. in science, by which a general conclusion is drawn from a set of premises, based mainly on experience or experimental evidence. The conclusion goes beyond the information contained in the premises, and does not follow necessarily from them. Thus an inductive argument may be highly probable, yet lead from true premises to a false conclusion. **b.** a conclusion reached by this process of reasoning. Compare **deduction** (sense 4). **5.** the process by which electrical or magnetic properties are transferred, without physical contact, from one circuit or body to another. See also **inductance. 6.** *Biology.* the effect of one tissue, esp. an embryonic tissue, on the development of an adjacent tissue. **7.** *Biochem.* the process by which synthesis of an enzyme is stimulated by the presence of its substrate. **8.** *Maths, logic.* **a.** a method of proving a proposition that all integers have a property, by first proving that 1 has the property and then that if the integer n has it so has $n + 1$. **b.** the application of recursive rules. **9. a.** a formal introduction or entry into an office or position. **b.** (*as modifier*): *induction course; induction period.* **10.** *U.S.* the formal enlistment of a civilian into military service. **11.** an archaic word for **preface.** —**inˈductional** *adj.*

induction coil *n.* a transformer for producing a high voltage from a low voltage. It consists of a cylindrical primary winding of few turns, a concentric secondary winding of many turns, and often a common soft-iron core. Sometimes shortened to **coil.**

induction hardening *n.* a process in which the outer surface of a metal component is rapidly heated by means of induced eddy currents. After rapid cooling the resulting phase transformations produce a hard wear-resistant skin.

induction heating *n.* the heating of a conducting material as a result of the electric currents induced in it by an externally applied alternating magnetic field.

induction loop system *n.* a system enabling partially deaf people to hear dialogue and sound in theatres, cinemas, etc., consisting of a loop of wire placed round the perimeter of a designated area. This emits an electromagnetic signal which is picked up by a hearing aid. Often shortened to **induction loop.**

induction motor *n.* a type of brushless electric motor in which an alternating supply fed to the windings of the stator creates a magnetic field that induces a current in the windings of the rotor. Rotation of the rotor results from the interaction of the magnetic field created by the rotor current with the field of the stator.

inductive (ɪnˈdʌktɪv) *adj.* **1.** relating to, involving, or operated by electrical or magnetic induction: *an inductive reactance.* **2.** *Logic, maths.* of, relating to, or using induction: *inductive reasoning.* **3.** serving to induce or cause. **4.** a rare word for **introductory. 5.** *Biology.* producing a reaction within an organism, esp. induction in embryonic tissue. —**inˈductively** *adv.* —**inˈductiveness** *n.*

inductor (ɪnˈdʌktə) *n.* **1.** a person or thing that inducts. **2.** another name for an **inductance** (sense 2).

indue (ɪnˈdjuː) *vb.* **-dues, -duing, -dued.** a variant spelling of **endue.**

indulge (ɪnˈdʌldʒ) *vb.* **1.** (when *intr.,* often foll. by *in*) to yield to or gratify (a whim or desire for): *to indulge a desire for new clothes; to indulge in new clothes.* **2.** (*tr.*) to yield to the wishes of; pamper: *to indulge a child.* **3.** (*tr.*) to allow oneself the pleasure of something: *at Christmas he liked to indulge himself.* **4.** (*tr.*) *Commerce.* to allow (a debtor) an extension of time for payment of (a bill, etc.). **5.** (*intr.*) *Informal.* to take alcoholic drink, esp. to excess. [C17: from Latin *indulgēre* to concede, from *-dulgēre,* probably related to Greek *dolikhos* long, Gothic *tulgus* firm] —**inˈdulger** *n.* —**inˈdulgingly** *adv.*

indulgence (ɪnˈdʌldʒəns) *n.* **1.** the act of indulging or state of being indulgent. **2.** a pleasure, habit, etc., indulged in; extravagance: *fur coats are an indulgence.* **3.** liberal or tolerant treatment. **4.** something granted as a favour or privilege. **5.** *R.C. Church.* a remission of the temporal punishment for sin after its guilt has been forgiven. **6.** *Commerce.* an extension of time granted as a favour for payment of a debt or as fulfilment of some other obligation. **7.** Also called: **Declaration of Indulgence.** a royal grant during the reigns of Charles II and James II of England giving Nonconformists and Roman Catholics a measure of religious freedom. ~*vb.* (*tr.*) **8.** *R.C. Church.* to designate as providing indulgence: *indulgenced prayers.*

indulgent (ɪnˈdʌldʒənt) *adj.* showing or characterized by indulgence. —**inˈdulgently** *adv.*

induline (ˈɪndjʊˌlaɪn) *or* **indulin** (ˈɪndjʊlɪn) *n.* any of a class of blue dyes obtained from aniline and aminoazobenzene. [C19: from INDIGO + -ULE + -INE[2]]

indult (ɪnˈdʌlt) *n. R.C. Church.* a faculty granted by the Holy See allowing a specific deviation from the Church's common law. [C16: from Church Latin *indultum* a privilege, from Latin *indulgēre* to INDULGE]

indumentum (ɪndjʊˈmɛntəm) *n., pl.* **-ta** *or* **-tums.** *Biology.* an outer covering, such as hairs or down on a plant or leaf, feathers, fur, etc. [C19: Latin, literally: garment]

induna (ɪnˈduːnə) *n.* (in South Africa) a Black African overseer in a factory, mine, etc. [C20: from Zulu *nduna* an official]

induplicate (ɪnˈdjuːplɪkɪt, -ˌkeɪt) *or* **induplicated** *adj.* (of the parts of a bud) bent or folded inwards with the edges touching but not overlapping. —**inˌdupliˈcation** *n.*

indurate *Rare.* ~*vb.* (ˈɪndjʊˌreɪt). **1.** to make or become hard or callous. **2.** to make or become hardy. ~*adj.* (ˈɪndjʊrɪt). **3.** hardened, callous, or unfeeling. [C16: from Latin *indūrāre* to make hard; see ENDURE] —ˌ**induˈration** *n.* —ˈ**induˌrative** *adj.*

Indus (ˈɪndəs) *n.* a faint constellation in the S hemisphere lying between Telescopium and Tucano.

indusium (ɪnˈdjuːzɪəm) *n., pl.* **-sia** (-zɪə). **1.** a membranous outgrowth on the undersurface of fern leaves that covers and protects the developing spores. **2.** an enveloping membrane, such as the amnion. [C18: New Latin, from Latin: tunic, from *induere* to put on] —**inˈdusial** *adj.*

industrial (ɪnˈdʌstrɪəl) *adj.* **1.** of, relating to, derived from, or characteristic of industry. **2.** employed in industry: *the industrial workforce.* **3.** relating to or concerned with workers in industry: *industrial conditions.* **4.** used in industry: *industrial chemicals.* —**inˈdustrially** *adv.*

industrial action *n. Brit.* any action, such as a strike or go-slow, taken by employees in industry to protest against working conditions, redundancies, etc.

industrial archaeology *n.* the study of past industrial machines, works, etc. —**industrial archaeologist** *n.*

industrial democracy *n.* control of an organization by the people who work for it, esp. by workers holding positions on its board of directors.

industrial design *n.* the art or practice of designing any object for manufacture. —**industrial designer** *n.*

industrial development certificate *n.* (in Britain) a certificate issued by the Department of the Environment to an industrial organization wishing to build or extend a factory, which has to accompany an application for planning permission. Abbrev.: **IDC.**

industrial diamond *n.* a small often synthetic diamond, valueless as a gemstone, used in cutting tools, abrasives, etc.

industrial disease *n.* any disease to which workers in a particular industry are prone.

industrial espionage *n.* attempting to obtain trade secrets by dishonest means, as by telephone- or computer-tapping, infiltration of a competitor's workforce, etc.

industrial estate *n. Brit.* another name for **trading estate.** U.S. equivalent: **industrial park.**

industrialism (ɪnˈdʌstrɪəˌlɪzəm) *n.* an organization of society characterized by large-scale mechanized manufacturing industry rather than trade, farming, etc.

industrialist (ɪnˈdʌstrɪəlɪst) *n.* a person who has a substantial interest in the ownership or control of industrial enterprise.

industrialize *or* **industrialise** (ɪnˈdʌstrɪəˌlaɪz) *vb.* **1.** (*tr.*) to develop industry on an extensive scale in (a country, region, etc.). **2.** (*intr.*) (of a country, region, etc.) to undergo the development of industry on an extensive scale. —**inˌdustrialiˈzation** *or* **inˌdustrialiˈsation** *n.*

industrial medicine *n.* the study and practice of the health care of employees of large organizations, including measures to prevent accidents, industrial diseases, and stress in the workforce and to monitor the health of executives.

industrial melanism *n.* See **melanism** (sense 1).

industrial misconduct *n.* behaviour by an employee which is considered to be negligent or irregular to such an extent that disciplinary action may be taken, usually by agreement between management and the employee's representatives.

industrial psychology *n.* the scientific study of human behaviour and cognitive processes in relation to the working environment.

industrial relations *n.* **1.** (*functioning as pl.*) those aspects of collective relations between management and workers' representatives which are normally covered by collective bargaining. **2.** (*functioning as sing.*) the management of relations between the employers or managers of an enterprise and their employees.

Industrial Revolution *n.* **the.** the transformation in the 18th and 19th centuries of first Britain and then other W European countries and the U.S. into industrial nations.

industrials (ɪnˈdʌstrɪəlz) *pl. n.* stocks, shares, and bonds of industrial enterprises.

industrial tribunal *n.* a tribunal that rules on disputes between employers and employees regarding unfair dismissal, redundancy, etc.

industrial union *n.* a labour organization in which all workers in a given industry are eligible for membership. Compare **craft union.**

industrious (ɪnˈdʌstrɪəs) *adj.* **1.** hard-working, diligent, or assiduous. **2.** an obsolete word for **skilful.** —**inˈdustriously** *adv.* —**inˈdustriousness** *n.*

industry (ˈɪndəstrɪ) *n., pl.* **-tries. 1.** organized economic activity concerned with manufacture, extraction and processing of raw materials, or construction. **2.** a branch of commercial enterprise concerned with the output of a specified product or service: *the steel industry.* **3. a.** industrial ownership and management interests collectively, as contrasted with labour interests. **b.** manufacturing enterprise collectively, as opposed to agriculture. **4.** diligence; assiduity. [C15: from Latin *industria* diligence, from *industrius* active, of uncertain origin]

indwell (ɪnˈdwɛl) *vb.* **-dwells, -dwelling, -dwelt. 1.** (*tr.*) (of a spirit, principle, etc.) to inhabit; suffuse. **2.** (*intr.*) to dwell; exist. —**inˈdweller** *n.*

-ine[1] *suffix forming adjectives.* **1.** of, relating to, or belonging to: *saturnine.* **2.** consisting of or resembling: *crystalline.* [from Latin *-īnus,* from Greek *-inos*]

-ine[2] *suffix forming nouns.* **1.** indicating a halogen: *chlorine.* **2.** indicating a nitrogenous organic compound, including amino acids, alkaloids, and certain other bases: *alanine; nicotine; purine.* **3.** Also: **-in.** indicating a chemical substance in certain nonsystematic names: *glycerine.* **4.** indicating a mixture of hydrocarbons: *benzine.* **5.** an obsolete equivalent of **-yne.** [via French from Latin *-ina* (from *-inus*) and Greek *-inē*]

inearth (ɪnˈɜːθ) *vb.* (*tr.*) a poetic word for **bury.**

inebriant (ɪnˈiːbrɪənt) *adj.* **1.** causing intoxication, esp. drunkenness. ~*n.* **2.** something that inebriates.

inebriate *vb.* (ɪnˈiːbrɪˌeɪt). (*tr.*) **1.** to make drunk; intoxicate. **2.** to arouse emotionally; make excited. ~*n.* (ɪnˈiːbrɪɪt). **3.** a person who is drunk, esp. habitually. ~*adj.* (ɪnˈiːbrɪɪt). *also* **inebriated. 4.** drunk, esp. habitually. [C15: from Latin *inēbriāre,* from IN-[2] + *ēbriāre* to intoxicate, from *ēbrius* drunk] —**inˌebriˈation** *n.* —**inebriety** (ˌɪnɪˈbraɪɪtɪ) *n.*

inedible (ɪnˈɛdɪbᵊl) *adj.* not fit to be eaten; uneatable. —**inˌediˈbility** *n.*

inedited (ɪnˈɛdɪtɪd) *adj.* **1.** not edited. **2.** not published.

ineducable (ɪnˈɛdjʊkəbᵊl) *adj.* incapable of being educated, esp. on account of mental retardation. —**inˌeducaˈbility** *n.*

ineffable (ɪnˈɛfəbᵊl) *adj.* **1.** too great or intense to be expressed in words; unutterable. **2.** too sacred to be uttered. **3.** indescribable; indefinable. [C15: from Latin *ineffābilis* unutterable, from IN-[1] + *effābilis,* from *effārī* to utter, from *fārī* to speak] —**inˌeffaˈbility** *or* **inˈeffableness** *n.* —**inˈeffably** *adv.*

ineffaceable (ˌɪnɪˈfeɪsəbᵊl) *adj.* incapable of being effaced; indelible. —**ˌinefˌfaceaˈbility** *n.* —**ˌinefˈfaceably** *adv.*

ineffective (ˌɪnɪˈfɛktɪv) *adj.* **1.** having no effect. **2.** incompetent or inefficient. —**ˌinefˈfectively** *adv.* —**ˌinefˈfectiveness** *n.*

ineffectual (ˌɪnɪˈfɛktʃʊəl) *adj.* **1.** having no effect or an inadequate effect. **2.** lacking in power or forcefulness; impotent: *an ineffectual ruler.* —**ˌinefˌfectuˈality** *or* **ˌinefˈfectualness** *n.* —**ˌinefˈfectually** *adv.*

inefficacious (ˌɪnɛfɪˈkeɪʃəs) *adj.* failing to produce the desired effect. —**ˌineffiˈcaciously** *adv.* —**inefficacy** (ɪnˈɛfɪkəsɪ), **ˌineffiˈcaciousness,** *or* **inefficacity** (ˌɪnɛfɪˈkæsɪtɪ) *n.*

inefficient (ˌɪnɪˈfɪʃənt) *adj.* **1.** unable to perform a task or function to the best advantage; wasteful or incompetent. **2.** unable to produce the desired result. —**ˌinefˈficiency** *n.* —**ˌinefˈficiently** *adv.*

inelastic (ˌɪnɪˈlæstɪk) *adj.* **1.** not elastic; not resilient. **2.** *Physics.* (of collisions) involving an overall decrease in translational kinetic energy. —**ineˈlastically** *adv.* —**inelasticity** (ˌɪnɪlæsˈtɪsɪtɪ) *n.*

inelegant (ɪnˈɛlɪgənt) *adj.* **1.** lacking in elegance or refinement; unpolished or graceless. **2.** coarse or crude. —**inˈelegance** *or* **inˈelegancy** *n.* —**inˈelegantly** *adv.*

ineligible (ɪnˈɛlɪdʒəbᵊl) *adj.* **1.** (often foll. by *for* or an infinitive) not fit or qualified: *ineligible for a grant; ineligible to vote.* ~*n.* **2.** an ineligible person. —**inˌeligiˈbility** *or* **inˈeligibleness** *n.* —**inˈeligibly** *adv.*

ineloquent (ɪnˈɛləkwənt) *adj.* lacking eloquence or fluency of expression. —**inˈeloquence** *n.* —**inˈeloquently** *adv.*

ineluctable (ˌɪnɪˈlʌktəbᵊl) *adj.* (esp. of fate) incapable of being avoided; inescapable. [C17: from Latin *inēluctābilis,* from IN-[1] + *ēluctārī* to escape, from *luctārī* to struggle] —**ˌineˌluctaˈbility** *n.* —**ˌineˈluctably** *adv.*

ineludible (ˌɪnɪˈluːdəbᵊl) *adj.* a rare word for **inescapable.** —**ˌineˌludiˈbility** *n.* —**ˌineˈludibly** *adv.*

inept (ɪnˈɛpt) *adj.* **1.** awkward, clumsy, or incompetent. **2.** not suitable, appropriate, or fitting; out of place. [C17: from Latin *ineptus,* from IN-[1] + *aptus* fitting, suitable] —**inˈeptiˌtude** *n.* —**inˈeptly** *adv.* —**inˈeptness** *n.*

inequable (ɪnˈɛkwəbᵊl) *adj.* uneven; not uniform.

inequality (ˌɪnɪˈkwɒlɪtɪ) *n., pl.* **-ties. 1.** the state or quality of being unequal; disparity. **2.** an instance of disparity. **3.** lack of smoothness or regularity. **4.** social or economic disparity. **5.** *Maths.* **a.** a statement indicating that the value of one quantity or expression is not equal to another, as in $x \neq y$: x may be greater than y, denoted by $x > y$, or less than y, denoted by $x < y$. **b.** the relation of being unequal. **6.** *Astronomy.* a departure from uniform orbital motion.

inequitable (ɪnˈɛkwɪtəbᵊl) *adj.* not equitable; unjust or unfair. —**inˈequitableness** *n.* —**inˈequitably** *adv.*

inequity (ɪnˈɛkwɪtɪ) *n., pl.* **-ties. 1.** lack of equity; injustice; unfairness. **2.** an unjust or unfair act, sentence, etc.

ineradicable (ˌɪnɪˈrædɪkəbᵊl) *adj.* not able to be removed or rooted out; inextirpable: *an ineradicable disease.* —**ˌineˈradicableness** *n.* —**ˌineˈradicably** *adv.*

inerrable (ɪnˈɛrəbᵊl) *or* **inerrant** (ɪnˈɛrənt) *adj.* less common words for **infallible.** —**inˌerraˈbility, inˈerrableness,** *or* **inˈerrancy** *n.* —**inˈerrably** *adv.*

inert (ɪnˈɜːt) *adj.* **1.** having no inherent ability to move or to resist motion. **2.** inactive, lazy, or sluggish. **3.** having only a limited ability to react chemically; unreactive. [C17: from Latin *iners* unskilled, from IN-[1] + *ars* skill; see ART[1]] —**inˈertly** *adv.* —**inˈertness** *n.*

inert gas *n.* **1.** Also called: **noble gas, rare gas, argonon.** any of the unreactive gaseous elements helium, neon, argon, krypton, xenon, and radon. **2.** (loosely) any gas, such as carbon dioxide, that is nonoxidizing.

inertia (ɪnˈɜːʃə, -ʃɪə) *n.* **1.** the state of being inert; disinclination to move or act. **2.** *Physics.* **a.** the tendency of a body to preserve its state of rest or uniform motion unless acted upon by an external force. **b.** an analogous property of other physical quantities that resist change: *thermal inertia.* —**inˈertial** *adj.*

inertia force *n.* an imaginary force supposed to act upon an accelerated body, equal in magnitude and opposite in direction to the resultant of the real forces. It is used in the theory of dynamics originated by d'Alembert.

inertial force *n.* an imaginary force which an accelerated observer postulates so that he can use the equations appropriate to an inertial observer. See also **Coriolis force.**

inertial fusion *n. Physics.* a type of nuclear fusion induced by impact, as by pulses of laser radiation or high-energy charged particles, rather than by high temperature.

inertial guidance *or* **navigation** *n.* a method of controlling the flight path of a missile by instruments contained within it. Velocities or distances covered, computed from the acceleration measured by these instruments, are compared with stored data and used to control the speed and direction of the missile. Compare **celestial guidance, terrestrial guidance.**

inertial mass *n.* the mass of a body as determined by its momentum, as opposed to gravitational mass. The acceleration of a falling body is inversely proportional to its inertial mass but directly proportional to its gravitational mass: as all falling bodies have the same constant acceleration the two types of mass must be equal.

inertial observer *n.* a hypothetical observer who is not accelerated with respect to an inertial system. Newton's laws of motion and the special theory of relativity apply to the measurements which would be made by such observers.

inertial system *n.* a frame of reference within which bodies are not accelerated unless acted upon by external forces. Also called: **inertial reference frame.**

inertia-reel seat belt *n.* a type of car seat belt in which the belt is free to unwind from a metal drum except when the drum locks as a result of rapid deceleration.

inertia selling *n.* (in Britain) the illegal practice of sending unrequested goods to householders followed by a bill for the price of the goods if they do not return them.

inescapable (ˌɪnɪ'skeɪpəbᵊl) *adj.* incapable of being escaped or avoided. —ˌ**ines'capably** *adv.*

inescutcheon (ˌɪnɪ'skʌtʃən) *n. Heraldry.* a small shield-shaped charge in the centre of a shield.

in esse (ɪn 'ɛsɪ) *adj.* actually existing. Compare **in posse.** [Latin, literally: in being]

inessential (ˌɪnɪ'sɛnʃəl) *adj.* **1.** not necessary. ~*n.* **2.** anything that is not essential. —ˌ**ines**ˌ**senti'ality** *n.*

inessive (ɪn'ɛsɪv) *adj.* **1.** (in the grammar of Finnish and related languages) denoting a case of nouns, etc., used when indicating the location of the referent. ~*n.* **2.** the inessive case. [C20: from Latin *inesse* to be in]

inestimable (ɪn'ɛstɪməbᵊl) *adj.* **1.** not able to be estimated; immeasurable. **2.** of immeasurable value. —**in**ˌ**estima'bility** *or* **in'estimableness** *n.* —**in'estimably** *adv.*

inevitable (ɪn'ɛvɪtəbᵊl) *adj.* **1.** unavoidable. **2.** sure to happen; certain. ~*n.* **3.** (often preceded by *the*) something that is unavoidable. [C15: from Latin *inēvītābilis,* from IN-[1] + *ēvītābilis,* from *ēvītāre* to shun, from *vītāre* to avoid] —**in**ˌ**evita'bility** *or* **in'evitableness** *n.* —**in'evitably** *adv.*

inexact (ˌɪnɪg'zækt) *adj.* not exact or accurate. —ˌ**inex'acti**ˌ**tude** *or* ˌ**inex'actness** *n.* —ˌ**inex'actly** *adv.*

inexcusable (ˌɪnɪk'skjuːzəbᵊl) *adj.* not able to be excused or justified. —ˌ**inex**ˌ**cusa'bility** *or* ˌ**inex'cusableness** *n.* —ˌ**inex'cusably** *adv.*

inexhaustible (ˌɪnɪg'zɔːstəbᵊl) *adj.* **1.** incapable of being used up; endless: *inexhaustible patience.* **2.** incapable or apparently incapable of becoming tired; tireless. —ˌ**inex**ˌ**hausti'bility** *or* ˌ**inex'haustibleness** *n.* —ˌ**inex'haustibly** *adv.*

inexistent (ˌɪnɪg'zɪstənt) *adj.* a rare word for **nonexistent.** —ˌ**inex'istence** *or* ˌ**inex'istency** *n.*

inexorable (ɪn'ɛksərəbᵊl) *adj.* **1.** not able to be moved by entreaty or persuasion. **2.** relentless. [C16: from Latin *inexōrābilis,* from IN-[1] + *exōrābilis,* from *exōrāre* to prevail upon, from *ōrāre* to pray] —**in**ˌ**exora'bility** *or* **in'exorableness** *n.* —**in'exorably** *adv.*

inexpedient (ˌɪnɪk'spiːdɪənt) *adj.* not suitable, advisable, or judicious. —ˌ**inex'pedience** *or* ˌ**inex'pediency** *n.* —ˌ**inex'pediently** *adv.*

inexpensive (ˌɪnɪk'spɛnsɪv) *adj.* not expensive; cheap. —ˌ**inex'pensively** *adv.* —ˌ**inex'pensiveness** *n.*

inexperience (ˌɪnɪk'spɪərɪəns) *n.* lack of experience or of the knowledge and understanding derived from experience. —ˌ**inex'perienced** *adj.*

inexpert (ɪn'ɛkspɜːt) *adj.* not expert; unskilled or unskilful; inept. —**in'expertly** *adv.* —**in'expertness** *n.*

inexpiable (ɪn'ɛkspɪəbᵊl) *adj.* **1.** incapable of being expiated; unpardonable. **2.** *Archaic.* implacable. —**in'expiableness** *n.* —**in'expiably** *adv.*

inexplicable (ˌɪnɪk'splɪkəbᵊl, ɪn'ɛksplɪkəbᵊl) *or* **inexplainable** *adj.* not capable of explanation; unexplainable. —ˌ**inexplica'bility,** ˌ**inex'plicableness** *or* ˌ**inex**ˌ**plaina'bility,** ˌ**inex'plainableness** *n.* —ˌ**inex'plicably** *or* ˌ**inex'plainably** *adv.*

inexplicit (ˌɪnɪk'splɪsɪt) *adj.* not explicit, clear, or precise; vague. —ˌ**inex'plicitly** *adv.* —ˌ**inex'plicitness** *n.*

inexpressible (ˌɪnɪk'sprɛsəbᵊl) *adj.* too great, etc., to be expressed or uttered; indescribable. —ˌ**inex**ˌ**pressi'bility** *or* ˌ**inex'pressibleness** *n.* —ˌ**inex'pressibly** *adv.*

inexpressive (ˌɪnɪk'sprɛsɪv) *adj.* **1.** lacking in expression: *an inexpressive face.* **2.** an archaic word for **inexpressible.** —ˌ**inex'pressively** *adv.* —ˌ**inex'pressiveness** *n.*

inexpugnable (ˌɪnɪk'spʌgnəbᵊl) *adj.* a rare word for **impregnable**[1]. —ˌ**inex**ˌ**pugna'bility** *or* ˌ**inex'pugnableness** *n.* —ˌ**inex'pugnably** *adv.*

inexpungible (ˌɪnɪks'pʌndʒɪbᵊl) *adj.* incapable of being expunged.

inextensible (ˌɪnɪk'stɛnsəbᵊl) *adj.* not capable of extension. —ˌ**inex**ˌ**tensi'bility** *n.*

in extenso *Latin.* (ɪn ɪk'stɛnsəʊ) *adv.* at full length.

inextinguishable (ˌɪnɪk'stɪŋgwɪʃəbᵊl) *adj.* not able to be extinguished, quenched, or put to an end. —ˌ**inex'tinguishableness** *n.* —ˌ**inex'tinguishably** *adv.*

inextirpable (ˌɪnɪk'stɜːpəbᵊl) *adj.* not able to be extirpated; ineradicable. —ˌ**inex'tirpableness** *n.*

in extremis *Latin.* (ɪn ɪk'striːmɪs) *adv.* **1.** in extremity; in dire straits. **2.** at the point of death. [literally: in the furthest reaches]

inextricable (ˌɪnɛks'trɪkəbᵊl) *adj.* **1.** not able to be escaped from: *an inextricable dilemma.* **2.** not able to be disentangled, etc.: *an inextricable knot.* **3.** extremely involved or intricate. —ˌ**inextrica'bility** *or* ˌ**inex'tricableness** *n.* —ˌ**inex'tricably** *adv.*

INF *abbrev. for* intermediate-range nuclear forces: land-based missiles and aircraft with a range between 500 and 5000 km.

inf. *abbrev. for:* **1.** inferior. **2.** infinitive. **3.** influence. **4.** information. **5.** infra. [Latin: below; after; later]

Inf. *or* **inf.** *abbrev. for* infantry.

infallibilism (ɪn'fælɪbᵊˌlɪzəm) *n. R.C. Church.* the principle of papal infallibility. —**in'fallibilist** *n.*

infallible (ɪn'fæləbᵊl) *adj.* **1.** not fallible; not liable to error. **2.** not liable to failure; certain; sure: *an infallible cure.* **3.** completely dependable or trustworthy. ~*n.* **4.** a person or thing that is incapable of error or failure. —**in**ˌ**falli'bility** *or* **in'fallibleness** *n.* —**in'fallibly** *adv.*

infamize *or* **infamise** ('ɪnfəˌmaɪz) *vb.* (*tr.*) to make infamous.

infamous ('ɪnfəməs) *adj.* **1.** having a bad reputation; notorious. **2.** causing or deserving a bad reputation; shocking: *infamous conduct.* **3.** *Criminal law.* (formerly) **a.** (of a person) deprived of certain rights of citizenship on conviction of certain offences. **b.** (of a crime or punishment) entailing such deprivation. —'**infamously** *adv.* —'**infamousness** *n.*

infamy ('ɪnfəmɪ) *n., pl.* **-mies. 1.** the state or condition of being infamous. **2.** an infamous act or event. [C15: from Latin *infāmis* of evil repute, from IN-[1] + *fāma* FAME]

infancy ('ɪnfənsɪ) *n., pl.* **-cies. 1.** the state or period of being an infant; childhood. **2.** an early stage of growth or development. **3.** infants collectively. **4.** the period of life prior to attaining legal majority (reached at 21 under common law, at 18 by statute); minority nonage.

infant ('ɪnfənt) *n.* **1.** a child at the earliest stage of its life; baby. **2.** *Law.* another word for **minor** (sense 10). **3.** *Brit.* a young schoolchild, usually under the age of seven. **4.** a person who is beginning or inexperienced in an activity. **5.** (*modifier*) **a.** of or relating to young children or infancy. **b.** designed or intended for young children. ~*adj.* **6.** in an early stage of development; nascent: *an infant science or industry.* **7.** *Law.* of or relating to the legal status of infancy. [C14: from Latin *infāns,* literally: speechless, from IN-[1] + *fārī* to speak] —'**infant**ˌ**hood** *n.*

infanta (ɪn'fæntə) *n.* **1.** (formerly) a daughter of a king of Spain or Portugal. **2.** the wife of an infante. [C17: from Spanish or Portuguese, feminine of INFANTE]

infante (ɪn'fæntɪ) *n.* (formerly) a son of a king of Spain or Portugal, esp. one not heir to the throne. [C16: from Spanish or Portuguese, literally: INFANT]

infanticide (ɪn'fæntɪˌsaɪd) *n.* **1.** the killing of an infant. **2.** the practice of killing newborn infants, still prevalent in some primitive tribes. **3.** a person who kills an infant. —**in**ˌ**fanti'cidal** *adj.*

infantile ('ɪnfənˌtaɪl) *adj.* **1.** like a child in action or behaviour; childishly immature; puerile. **2.** of, relating to, or characteristic of infants or infancy. **3.** in an early stage of development. —**infantility** (ˌɪnfən'tɪlɪtɪ) *n.*

infantile paralysis *n.* a former name for **poliomyelitis.**

infantilism (ɪn'fæntɪˌlɪzəm) *n.* **1.** *Psychol.* **a.** a condition in which an older child or adult is mentally or physically undeveloped. **b.** isolated instances of infantile behaviour in mature persons. **2.** childish speech; baby talk.

infant prodigy *n.* an exceptionally talented child.

infantry ('ɪnfəntrɪ) *n., pl.* **-tries. a.** soldiers or units of soldiers who fight on foot with small arms. **b.** (*as modifier*): *an infantry unit.* Abbrevs.: **Inf., inf.** [C16: from Italian *infanteria,* from *infante* boy, foot soldier; see INFANT]

infantryman ('ɪnfəntrɪmən) *n., pl.* **-men.** a soldier belonging to the infantry.

infant school *n. Brit.* a school for children aged between 5 and 7. Compare **junior school.**

infarct (ɪn'fɑːkt) *n.* a localized area of dead tissue (necrosis) resulting from obstruction of the blood supply to that part, esp. by an embolus. Also called: **infarction.** [C19: via New Latin from Latin *infarctus* stuffed into, from *farcīre* to stuff] —**in'farcted** *adj.*

infarction (ɪn'fɑːkʃən) *n.* **1.** the formation or development of an infarct. **2.** another word for **infarct.**

infare ('ɪnˌfɛə) *n. Dialect, chiefly Scot. and northern English.* a reception given on entering a new house or after a wedding. [Old English *innfær,* from *inn* in + *faran* to go; see FARE]

infatuate *vb.* (ɪn'fætjʊˌeɪt). (*tr.*) **1.** to inspire or fill with foolish, shallow, or extravagant passion. **2.** to cause to act foolishly. ~*adj.* (ɪn'fætjʊɪt, -ˌeɪt). **3.** an archaic word for **infatuated.** ~*n.* (ɪn'fætjʊɪt, -ˌeɪt). **4.** *Literary.* a person who is infatuated. [C16: from Latin *infatuāre,* from IN-[2] + *fatuus* FATUOUS]

infatuated (ɪn'fætjʊˌeɪtɪd) *adj.* (often foll. by *with*) possessed by a foolish or extravagant passion, esp. for another person. —**in'fatu**ˌ**atedly** *adv.*

infatuation (ɪnˌfætjʊˈeɪʃən) *n.* **1.** the act of infatuating or state of being infatuated. **2.** foolish or extravagant passion. **3.** an object of foolish or extravagant passion.

infeasible (ɪnˈfiːzəbᵊl) *adj.* a less common word for **impracticable.** —**inˌfeasiˈbility** *or* **inˈfeasibleness** *n.*

infect (ɪnˈfɛkt) *vb.* (*mainly tr.*) **1.** to cause infection in; contaminate (an organism, wound, etc.) with pathogenic microorganisms. **2.** (*also intr.*) to affect or become affected with a communicable disease. **3.** to taint, pollute, or contaminate. **4.** to affect, esp. adversely, as if by contagion. **5.** *Computer technol.* to affect or become affected with a computer virus. **6.** *Chiefly international law.* to taint with crime or illegality; expose to penalty or subject to forfeiture. ~*adj.* **7.** *Archaic.* contaminated or polluted with or as if with a disease; infected. [C14: from Latin *inficere* to dip into, stain, from *facere* to make] —**inˈfector** *or* **inˈfecter** *n.*

infection (ɪnˈfɛkʃən) *n.* **1.** invasion of the body by pathogenic microorganisms. **2.** the resulting condition in the tissues. **3.** an infectious disease. **4.** the act of infecting or state of being infected. **5.** an agent or influence that infects. **6.** persuasion or corruption, as by ideas, perverse influences, etc.

infectious (ɪnˈfɛkʃəs) *adj.* **1.** (of a disease) capable of being transmitted. Compare **contagious. 2.** (of a disease) caused by microorganisms, such as bacteria, viruses, or protozoa. **3.** causing or transmitting infection. **4.** tending or apt to spread, as from one person to another: *infectious mirth.* **5.** *International law.* **a.** tainting or capable of tainting with illegality. **b.** rendering liable to seizure or forfeiture. —**inˈfectiously** *adv.* —**inˈfectiousness** *n.*

infectious hepatitis *n.* any form of hepatitis caused by viruses. See **hepatitis A, hepatitis B.**

infectious mononucleosis *n.* an acute infectious disease, caused by Epstein-Barr virus, characterized by fever, sore throat, swollen and painful lymph nodes, and abnormal lymphocytes in the blood. Also called: **glandular fever.**

infective (ɪnˈfɛktɪv) *adj.* **1.** capable of causing infection. **2.** a less common word for **infectious.** —**inˈfectively** *adv.* —**inˈfectiveness** *or* **ˌinfecˈtivity** *n.*

infecund (ɪnˈfiːkənd) *adj.* a less common word for **infertile.** —**infecundity** (ˌɪnfɪˈkʌndɪtɪ) *n.*

infelicitous (ˌɪnfɪˈlɪsɪtəs) *adj.* **1.** not felicitous; unfortunate. **2.** inappropriate or unsuitable. —**ˌinfeˈlicitously** *adv.*

infelicity (ˌɪnfɪˈlɪsɪtɪ) *n., pl.* **-ties. 1.** the state or quality of being unhappy or unfortunate. **2.** an instance of bad luck or mischance; misfortune. **3.** something, esp. a remark or expression, that is inapt or inappropriate.

infer (ɪnˈfɜː) *vb.* **-fers, -ferring, -ferred.** (when *tr., may take a clause as object*) **1.** to conclude (a state of affairs, supposition, etc.) by reasoning from evidence; deduce. **2.** (*tr.*) to have or lead to as a necessary or logical consequence; indicate. **3.** (*tr.*) to hint or imply. [C16: from Latin *inferre* to bring into, from *ferre* to bear, carry] —**inˈferable, inˈferible, inˈferrable,** *or* **inˈferrible** *adj.* —**inˈferably** *adv.* —**inˈferrer** *n.*

▷**Usage.** The use of *infer* in the sense of *imply* often occurs in both speech and writing but is avoided by all careful speakers and writers of English.

inference (ˈɪnfərəns, -frəns) *n.* **1.** the act or process of inferring. **2.** an inferred conclusion, deduction, etc. **3.** any process of reasoning from premises to a conclusion. **4.** *Logic.* the specific mode of reasoning used. See also **deduction** (sense 4), **induction** (sense 4).

inferencing (ˈɪnfərənsɪŋ) *n. Psycholinguistics.* the practice of inferring the meaning of an unfamiliar word or expression from the meaning of familiar words occurring with it in a context together with one's knowledge of or beliefs about the world.

inferential (ˌɪnfəˈrɛnʃəl) *adj.* of, relating to, or derived from inference. —**ˌinferˈentially** *adv.*

inferential statistics *n.* (*functioning as sing.*) another name for **statistical inference.**

inferior (ɪnˈfɪərɪə) *adj.* **1.** lower in value or quality. **2.** lower in rank, position, or status; subordinate. **3.** not of the best; mediocre; commonplace. **4.** lower in position; situated beneath. **5.** (of a plant ovary) enclosed by and fused with the receptacle so that it is situated below the other floral parts. **6.** *Astronomy.* **a.** orbiting or occurring between the sun and the earth: *an inferior planet; inferior conjunction.* **b.** lying below the horizon. **7.** *Printing.* (of a character) printed at the foot of an ordinary character, as the 2 in H_2O. ~*n.* **8.** an inferior person. **9.** *Printing.* an inferior character. [C15: from Latin: lower, from *inferus* low] —**inferiority** (ɪnˌfɪərɪˈɒrɪtɪ) *n.* —**inˈferiorly** *adv.*

inferior court *n.* **1.** a court of limited jurisdiction. **2.** any court other than the Supreme Court of Judicature.

inferiority complex *n. Psychiatry.* a disorder arising from the conflict between the desire to be noticed and the fear of being humiliated, characterized by aggressiveness or withdrawal into oneself.

inferior planet *n.* either of the planets Mercury and Venus, whose orbits lie inside that of the earth.

infernal (ɪnˈfɜːnᵊl) *adj.* **1.** of or relating to an underworld of the dead. **2.** deserving hell or befitting its occupants; diabolic; fiendish. **3.** *Informal.* irritating; confounded. [C14: from Late Latin *infernālis,* from *infernus* hell, from Latin (adj.): lower, hellish; related to Latin *inferus* low] —**ˌinferˈnality** *n.* —**inˈfernally** *adv.*

infernal machine *n. Archaic.* a usually disguised explosive device or booby trap.

inferno (ɪnˈfɜːnəʊ) *n., pl.* **-nos. 1.** (*sometimes cap.; usually preceded by the*) hell; the infernal region. **2.** any place or state resembling hell, esp. a conflagration. [C19: from Italian, from Late Latin *infernus* hell]

infertile (ɪnˈfɜːtaɪl) *adj.* **1.** not capable of producing offspring; sterile. **2.** (of land) not productive; barren. —**inˈfertilely** *adv.* —**infertility** (ˌɪnfəˈtɪlɪtɪ) *n.*

infest (ɪnˈfɛst) *vb.* (*tr.*) **1.** to inhabit or overrun in dangerously or unpleasantly large numbers. **2.** (of parasites such as lice) to invade and live on or in (a host). [C15: from Latin *infestāre* to molest, from *infestus* hostile] —**ˌinfesˈtation** *n.* —**inˈfester** *n.*

infeudation (ˌɪnfjʊˈdeɪʃən) *n.* **1.** (in feudal society) **a.** the act of putting a vassal in possession of a fief. **b.** the deed conferring such possession. **c.** the consequent relationship of lord and vassal. **2.** the granting of tithes to laymen.

infibulate (ɪnˈfɪbjʊˌleɪt) *vb.* (*tr.*) *Rare.* to enclose (esp. the genitals, to prevent sexual intercourse) with a clasp. [C17: from Latin *infībulāre,* from IN-[2] + *fibula* clasp, FIBULA] —**inˌfibuˈlation** *n.*

infidel (ˈɪnfɪdᵊl) *n.* **1.** a person who has no religious belief; unbeliever. ~*adj.* **2.** rejecting a specific religion, esp. Christianity or Islam. **3.** of, characteristic of, or relating to unbelievers or unbelief. [C15: from Medieval Latin *infidēlis,* from Latin (adj.): unfaithful, from IN-[1] + *fidēlis* faithful; see FEAL]

infidelity (ˌɪnfɪˈdɛlɪtɪ) *n., pl.* **-ties. 1.** lack of faith or constancy, esp. sexual faithfulness. **2.** lack of religious faith; disbelief. **3.** an act or instance of disloyalty.

infield (ˈɪnˌfiːld) *n.* **1.** *Cricket.* the area of the field near the pitch. Compare **outfield. 2.** *Baseball.* **a.** the area of the playing field enclosed by the base lines and extending beyond them towards the outfield. **b.** the positions of the first baseman, second baseman, shortstop, third baseman, and sometimes the pitcher, collectively. Compare **outfield. 3.** *Agriculture.* **a.** the part of a farm nearest to the farm buildings. **b.** land from which crops are regularly taken.

infielder (ˈɪnˌfiːldə) *or* **infieldsman** (ˈɪnfiːldzmən) *n.* a player positioned in the infield.

infighting (ˈɪnˌfaɪtɪŋ) *n.* **1.** *Boxing.* combat at close quarters in which proper blows are inhibited and the fighters try to wear down each other's strength. **2.** intense competition, as between members of the same organization, esp. when kept secret from outsiders. —**ˈinˌfighter** *n.*

infill (ˈɪnfɪl) *or* **infilling** (ˈɪnfɪlɪŋ) *n.* **1.** the act of filling or closing gaps, etc., in something, such as a row of buildings. **2.** material used to fill a cavity, gap, hole, etc.

infiltrate (ˈɪnfɪlˌtreɪt) *vb.* **1.** to undergo or cause to undergo the process in which a fluid passes into the pores or interstices of a solid; permeate. **2.** *Military.* to pass undetected through (an enemy-held line or position). **3.** to gain or cause to gain entrance or access surreptitiously: *they infiltrated the party structure.* ~*n.* **4.** something that infiltrates. **5.** *Pathol.* any substance that passes into and accumulates within cells, tissues, or organs. [C18: from IN-[2] + FILTRATE] —**ˌinfilˈtration** *n.* —**ˈinfilˌtrative** *adj.* —**ˈinfilˌtrator** *n.*

infimum (ˈɪnfɪməm) *n., pl.* **-ma.** *Maths.* the greatest lower bound.

infin. *abbrev. for* infinitive.

infinite (ˈɪnfɪnɪt) *adj.* **1. a.** having no limits or boundaries in time, space, extent, or magnitude. **b.** (*as n.; preceded by the*): *the infinite.* **2.** extremely or immeasurably great or numerous: *infinite wealth.* **3.** all-embracing, absolute, or total: *God's infinite wisdom.* **4.** *Maths.* **a.** having an unlimited or uncountable number of digits, factors, terms, members, etc.: *an infinite series.* **b.** (of a set) able to be put in a one-to-one correspondence with part of itself. **c.** (of an integral) having infinity as one or both limits of integration. Compare **finite** (sense 2). —**ˈinfinitely** *adv.* —**ˈinfiniteness** *n.*

infinitesimal (ˌɪnfɪnɪˈtɛsɪməl) *adj.* **1.** infinitely or immeasurably small. **2.** *Maths.* of, relating to, or involving a small change in the value of a variable that approaches zero as a limit. ~*n.* **3.** *Maths.* an infinitesimal quantity. —**ˌinfiniˈtesimally** *adv.*

infinitesimal calculus *n.* another name for **calculus** (sense 1).

infinitive (ɪnˈfɪnɪtɪv) *n. Grammar.* a form of the verb not inflected for grammatical categories such as tense and person and used without an overt subject. In English, the infinitive usually consists of the word *to* followed by the verb. —**infinitival** (ˌɪnfɪnɪˈtaɪvᵊl) *adj.* —**inˈfinitively** *or* **ˌinfiniˈtivally** *adv.*

infinitive marker *n. Grammar.* a word or affix occurring with the verb stem in the infinitive, such as *to* in *to make.*

infinitude (ɪnˈfɪnɪˌtjuːd) *n.* **1.** the state or quality of being infinite. **2.** an infinite extent, quantity, degree, etc.

infinity (ɪnˈfɪnɪtɪ) *n., pl.* **-ties. 1.** the state or quality of being infinite. **2.** endless time, space, or quantity. **3.** an infinitely or indefinitely great number or amount. **4.** *Optics, photog.* a point that is far enough away from a lens, mirror, etc., for the light emitted by it to fall in parallel rays on the surface of the lens, etc. **5.** *Physics.* a dimension or quantity of sufficient size to be unaffected by finite variations. **6.** *Maths.* **a.** the concept of a value greater than any finite numerical value. **b.** the reciprocal of zero. **7.** a distant hypothetical point at which two parallel lines are assumed to meet. ~Symbol (for senses 4-7): ∞

infirm (ɪn'fɜːm) *adj.* **1. a.** weak in health or body, esp. from old age. **b.** (*as collective n.; preceded by the*): *the infirm.* **2.** lacking moral certainty; indecisive or irresolute. **3.** not stable, sound, or secure: *an infirm structure; an infirm claim.* **4.** *Law.* (of a law, custom, etc.) lacking legal force; invalid. —**in'firmly** *adv.* —**in'firmness** *n.*

infirmary (ɪn'fɜːmərɪ) *n., pl.* **-ries.** a place for the treatment of the sick or injured; dispensary; hospital.

infirmity (ɪn'fɜːmɪtɪ) *n., pl.* **-ties. 1.** the state or quality of being infirm. **2.** physical weakness or debility; frailty. **3.** a moral flaw or failing.

infix *vb.* (ɪn'fɪks, 'ɪnˌfɪks). **1.** (*tr.*) to fix firmly in. **2.** (*tr.*) to instil or inculcate. **3.** *Grammar.* to insert (an affix) or (of an affix) to be inserted into the middle of a word. ~*n.* ('ɪnˌfɪks). **4.** *Grammar.* an affix inserted into the middle of a word. —ˌ**infix'ation** *or* **infixion** (ɪn'fɪkʃən) *n.*

infl. *abbrev. for:* **1.** influence. **2.** influenced.

in flagrante delicto (ɪn flə'græntɪ dɪ'lɪktəʊ) *adv.* *Chiefly Law.* while committing the offence; red-handed. Also: **flagrante delicto.** [Latin, literally: with the crime still blazing]

inflame (ɪn'fleɪm) *vb.* **1.** to arouse or become aroused to violent emotion. **2.** (*tr.*) to increase or intensify; aggravate. **3.** to produce inflammation in (a tissue, organ, or part) or (of a tissue, etc.) to become inflamed. **4.** to set or be set on fire; kindle. **5.** (*tr.*) to cause to redden. —**in'flamer** *n.* —**in'flamingly** *adv.*

inflammable (ɪn'flæməbᵊl) *adj.* **1.** liable to catch fire; flammable. **2.** readily aroused to anger or passion. ~*n.* **3.** something that is liable to catch fire. —**inˌflamma'bility** *or* **in'flammableness** *n.* —**in'flammably** *adv.*

▷**Usage.** See at **flammable.**

inflammation (ˌɪnflə'meɪʃən) *n.* **1.** the reaction of living tissue to injury or infection, characterized by heat, redness, swelling, and pain. **2.** the act of inflaming or the state of being inflamed.

inflammatory (ɪn'flæmətərɪ, -trɪ) *adj.* **1.** characterized by or caused by inflammation. **2.** tending to arouse violence, strong emotion, etc. —**in'flammatorily** *adv.*

inflatable (ɪn'fleɪtəbᵊl) *n.* **1.** any of various large air-filled objects made of strong plastic or rubber, used for children to play on at fairs, carnivals, etc. ~*adj.* **2.** capable of being inflated.

inflate (ɪn'fleɪt) *vb.* **1.** to expand or cause to expand by filling with gas or air. **2.** (*tr.*) to cause to increase excessively; puff up; swell: *to inflate one's opinion of oneself.* **3.** (*tr.*) to cause inflation of (prices, money, etc.). **4.** (*tr.*) to raise in spirits; elate. **5.** (*intr.*) to undergo economic inflation. [C16: from Latin *inflāre* to blow into, from *flāre* to blow] —**in'flatedly** *adv.* —**in'flatedness** *n.* —**in'flater** *or* **in'flator** *n.*

inflation (ɪn'fleɪʃən) *n.* **1.** the act of inflating or state of being inflated. **2.** *Economics.* a progressive increase in the general level of prices brought about by an expansion in demand or the money supply (**demand-pull inflation**) or by autonomous increases in costs (**cost-push inflation**). Compare **deflation. 3.** *Informal.* the rate of increase of prices.

inflationary (ɪn'fleɪʃənərɪ) *adj.* of, relating to, causing, or characterized by inflation: *inflationary wage claims.*

inflationary gap *n.* the excess of total spending in an economy over the value, at current prices, of the output it can produce.

inflationary spiral *n.* the situation in which price and income increases may each induce further rises in the other.

inflationism (ɪn'fleɪʃəˌnɪzəm) *n.* the advocacy or policy of inflation through expansion of the supply of money and credit. —**in'flationist** *n., adj.*

inflect (ɪn'flɛkt) *vb.* **1.** *Grammar.* to change (the form of a word) or (of a word) to change in form by inflection. **2.** (*tr.*) to change (the voice) in tone or pitch; modulate. **3.** (*tr.*) to cause to deviate from a straight or normal line or course; bend. [C15: from Latin *inflectere* to curve round, alter, from *flectere* to bend] —**in'flectedness** *n.* —**in'flective** *adj.* —**in'flector** *n.*

inflection *or* **inflexion** (ɪn'flɛkʃən) *n.* **1.** modulation of the voice. **2.** *Grammar.* a change in the form of a word, usually modification or affixation, signalling change in such grammatical functions as tense, voice, mood, person, gender, number, or case. **3.** an angle or bend. **4.** the act of inflecting or the state of being inflected. **5.** *Maths.* a change in curvature from concave to convex or vice versa. See also **point of inflection.** —**in'flectional** *or* **in'flexional** *adj.* —**in'flectionally** *or* **in'flexionally** *adv.* —**in'flectionless** *or* **in'flexionless** *adj.*

inflexed (ɪn'flɛkst) *adj.* *Biology.* curved or bent inwards and downwards towards the axis: *inflexed leaves.*

inflexible (ɪn'flɛksəbᵊl) *adj.* **1.** not flexible; rigid; stiff. **2.** obstinate; unyielding. **3.** without variation; unalterable; fixed. [C14: from Latin *inflexībilis;* see INFLECT] —**inˌflexi'bility** *or* **in'flexibleness** *n.* —**in'flexibly** *adv.*

inflict (ɪn'flɪkt) *vb.* (*tr.*) **1.** (often foll. by *on* or *upon*) to impose (something unwelcome, such as pain, oneself, etc.). **2.** *Rare.* to cause to suffer; afflict (with). **3.** to deal out (blows, lashes, etc.). [C16: from Latin *inflīgere* to strike (something) against, dash against, from *flīgere* to strike] —**in'flictable** *adj.* —**in'flicter** *or* **in'flictor** *n.* —**in'fliction** *n.* —**in'flictive** *adj.*

in-flight *adj.* provided during flight in an aircraft: *in-flight meals.*

inflorescence (ˌɪnflɔː'rɛsəns) *n.* **1.** the part of a plant that consists of the flower-bearing stalks. **2.** the arrangement of the flowers on the stalks. **3.** the process of flowering; blossoming. [C16: from New Latin *inflōrēscentia,* from Late Latin *inflōrescere* to blossom, from *flōrescere* to bloom] —ˌ**inflo'rescent** *adj.*

inflow ('ɪnˌfləʊ) *n.* **1.** something, such as a liquid or gas, that flows in. **2.** the amount or rate of flowing in. **3.** Also called: **inflowing.** the act of flowing in; influx.

influence ('ɪnflʊəns) *n.* **1.** an effect of one person or thing on another. **2.** the power of a person or thing to have such an effect. **3.** power or sway resulting from ability, wealth, position, etc. **4.** a person or thing having influence. **5.** *Astrology.* an ethereal fluid or occult power regarded as emanating from the stars and affecting a person's actions, future, etc. **6. under the influence.** *Informal.* drunk. ~*vb.* (*tr.*) **7.** to persuade or induce. **8.** to have an effect upon (actions, events, etc.); affect. [C14: from Medieval Latin *influentia* emanation of power from the stars, from Latin *influere* to flow into, from *fluere* to flow] —'**influenceable** *adj.* —'**influencer** *n.*

influent ('ɪnflʊənt) *adj.* *also* **inflowing. 1.** flowing in. ~*n.* **2.** something flowing in, esp. a tributary. **3.** *Ecology.* an organism that has a major effect on the nature of its community.

influential (ˌɪnflʊ'ɛnʃəl) *adj.* having or exerting influence. —ˌ**influ'entially** *adv.*

influenza (ˌɪnflʊ'ɛnzə) *n.* a highly contagious and often epidemic viral disease characterized by fever, prostration, muscular aches and pains, and inflammation of the respiratory passages. Also called: **grippe.** Informal name: **flu.** [C18: from Italian, literally: INFLUENCE, hence, incursion, epidemic (first applied to influenza in 1743)] —ˌ**influ'enzal** *adj.*

influx ('ɪnˌflʌks) *n.* **1.** the arrival or entry of many people or things. **2.** the act of flowing in; inflow. **3.** the mouth of a stream or river. [C17: from Late Latin *influxus,* from *influere;* see INFLUENCE]

info ('ɪnfəʊ) *n.* *Informal.* short for **information.**

infold (ɪn'fəʊld) *vb.* a variant spelling of **enfold.** —**in'folder** *n.* —**in'foldment** *n.*

infopreneurial (ˌɪnfəʊprə'nɜːrɪəl) *adj.* of or relating to the manufacture or sales of electronic office or factory equipment designed to distribute information: *an infopreneurial industry.* [C20: INFO(RMATION) + (ENTRE)PRENEUR + -IAL]

inform[1] (ɪn'fɔːm) *vb.* **1.** (*tr.;* often foll. by *of* or *about*) to give information to; tell. **2.** (*tr.;* often foll. by *of* or *about*) to make conversant (with). **3.** (*intr.;* often foll. by *against* or *on*) to give information regarding criminals, as to the police, etc. **4.** to give form to. **5.** to impart some essential or formative characteristic to. **6.** (*tr.*) to animate or inspire. **7.** (*tr.*) *Obsolete.* **a.** to train or educate. **b.** to report. [C14: from Latin *informāre* to give form to, describe, from *formāre* to FORM] —**in'formable** *adj.* —**in'formedly** (ɪn'fɔːmɪdlɪ) *adv.* —**in'formingly** *adv.*

inform[2] (ɪn'fɔːm) *adj.* *Archaic.* without shape; unformed. [C16: from Latin *informis* from IN-[1] + *forma* shape]

informal (ɪn'fɔːməl) *adj.* **1.** not of a formal, official, or stiffly conventional nature: *an informal luncheon.* **2.** appropriate to everyday life or use: *informal clothes.* **3.** denoting or characterized by idiom, vocabulary, etc., appropriate to everyday conversational language rather than to formal written language. **4.** denoting a second-person pronoun in some languages used when the addressee is regarded as a friend or social inferior: *In French the pronoun "tu" is informal, while "vous" is formal.* —**in'formally** *adv.*

informality (ˌɪnfɔː'mælɪtɪ) *n., pl.* **-ties. 1.** the condition or quality of being informal. **2.** an informal act.

informal vote *n.* *Austral. and N.Z.* an invalid vote or ballot.

informant (ɪn'fɔːmənt) *n.* a person who gives information about a thing, a subject being studied, etc.

informatics (ˌɪnfə'mætɪks) *n.* (*functioning as sing.*) another term for **information science.**

information (ˌɪnfə'meɪʃən) *n.* **1.** knowledge acquired through experience or study. **2.** knowledge of specific and timely events or situations; news. **3.** the act of informing or the condition of being informed. **4. a.** an office, agency, etc., providing information. **b.** (*as modifier*): *information service.* **5. a.** a charge or complaint made before justices of the peace, usually on oath, to institute summary criminal proceedings. **b.** a complaint filed on behalf of the Crown, usually by the attorney general. **6.** *Computer technol.* **a.** the meaning given to data by the way in which it is interpreted. **b.** another word for **data** (sense 2). —ˌ**infor'mational** *adj.*

information processing *n.* *Computer technol.* the combined processing of numerical data, graphics, text, etc.

information question *n.* another term for **WH question.**

information retrieval *n.* *Computer technol.* the process of recovering specific information from stored data.

information science *n.* the science of the collection, evaluation, organization, and dissemination of information, often employing computers.

information technology *n.* the technology of the production, storage, and communication of information using computers and microelectronics. Abbrev.: **IT.**

information theory *n.* a collection of mathematical theories, based on statistics, concerned with methods of coding, transmitting, storing, retrieving, and decoding information.

informative (ɪn'fɔːmətɪv) *or* **informatory** *adj.* providing information; instructive. —**in'formatively** *adv.* —**in'formativeness** *n.*

informed (ɪnˈfɔːmd) *adj.* **1.** having much knowledge or education; learned or cultured. **2.** based on information: *an informed judgment.*
informer (ɪnˈfɔːmə) *n.* **1.** a person who informs against someone, esp. a criminal. **2.** a person who provides information: *he was the President's financial informer.*
infotainment (ˌɪnfəʊˈteɪnmənt) *n.* (in television) the practice of presenting serious or instructive subjects in a style designed primarily to be entertaining. [C20: from INFO + (ENTER)TAINMENT]
infra *Latin.* (ˈɪnfrə) *adv.* (esp. in textual annotation) below; further on.
infra- *prefix.* below; beneath; after: *infrasonic; infralapsarian.* [from Latin *infrā*]
infracostal (ˌɪnfrəˈkɒstᵊl) *adj. Anatomy.* situated beneath the ribs.
infract (ɪnˈfrækt) *vb. (tr.)* to violate or break (a law, an agreement, etc.). [C18: from Latin *infractus* broken off, from *infringere;* see INFRINGE] —**inˈfraction** *n.* —**inˈfractor** *n.*
infra dig (ˈɪnfrə ˈdɪg) *adj.* (*postpositive*) *Informal.* beneath one's dignity. [C19: from Latin phrase *infrā dignitātem*]
infralapsarian (ˌɪnfrəlæpˈsɛərɪən) *n. Christian theol., chiefly Calvinist.* a person who believes that foreknowledge of the Fall preceded God's decree of who was predestined to salvation and who was not. Compare **supralapsarian.** [C18: from INFRA- + *lapsarian* (see SUPRALAPSARIAN)] —ˌ**infralapˈsarianism** *n.*
infrangible (ɪnˈfrændʒɪbᵊl) *adj.* **1.** incapable of being broken. **2.** not capable of being violated or infringed. [C16: from Late Latin *infrangibilis,* from Latin IN-[1] + *frangere* to break] —**inˌfrangiˈbility** *or* **inˈfrangibleness** *n.* —**inˈfrangibly** *adv.*
infrared (ˌɪnfrəˈrɛd) *n.* **1.** the part of the electromagnetic spectrum with a longer wavelength than light but a shorter wavelength than radio waves; radiation with wavelength between 0.8 micrometres and 1 millimetre. ~*adj.* **2.** of, relating to, using, or consisting of radiation lying within the infrared: *infrared radiation.*
infrared astronomy *n.* the study of radiations from space in the infrared region of the electromagnetic spectrum.
infrared photography *n.* photography using film with an emulsion that is sensitive to infrared light, enabling it to be used in misty weather, in darkened interiors, or at night. It has applications in aerial surveys, the detection of forgeries, etc.
infrasound (ˈɪnfrəˌsaʊnd) *adj.* (of an oscillation, vibration, or pressure wave) soundlike waves having a frequency below the audible range, that is, below about 16Hz. —**infrasonic** (ˌɪnfrəˈsɒnɪk) *adj.*
infraspecific (ˌɪnfrəspəˈsɪfɪk) *adj. Biology.* occurring within or affecting all members of a species: *infraspecific variation.*
infrastructure (ˈɪnfrəˌstrʌktʃə) *n.* **1.** the basic structure of an organization, system, etc. **2.** the stock of fixed capital equipment in a country, including factories, roads, schools, etc., considered as a determinant of economic growth.
infrequent (ɪnˈfriːkwənt) *adj.* rarely happening or present; only occasional. —**inˈfrequency** *or* **inˈfrequence** *n.* —**inˈfrequently** *adv.*
infringe (ɪnˈfrɪndʒ) *vb.* **1.** (*tr.*) to violate or break (a law, an agreement, etc.). **2.** (*intr.;* foll. by *on* or *upon*) to encroach or trespass. [C16: from Latin *infringere* to break off, from *frangere* to break] —**inˈfringement** *n.* —**inˈfringer** *n.*
infulae (ˈɪnfjʊliː) *pl. n., sing.* **-la** (-lə). the two ribbons hanging from the back of a bishop's mitre. [C17: from Latin, plural of *infula,* woollen fillet worn on forehead by ancient Romans during religious rites]
infundibular (ˌɪnfʌnˈdɪbjʊlə) *adj.* funnel-shaped. [C18: from INFUNDIBULUM]
infundibuliform (ˌɪnfʌnˈdɪbjʊlɪˌfɔːm) *adj.* (of plant parts) shaped like a funnel.
infundibulum (ˌɪnfʌnˈdɪbjʊləm) *n., pl.* **-la** (-lə). *Anatomy.* any funnel-shaped part, esp. the stalk connecting the pituitary gland to the base of the brain. [C18: from Latin: funnel, from *infundere* to INFUSE] —ˌ**infunˈdibulate** *adj.*
infuriate *vb.* (ɪnˈfjʊərɪˌeɪt). **1.** (*tr.*) to anger; annoy. ~*adj.* (ɪnˈfjʊərɪɪt). **2.** *Archaic.* furious; infuriated. [C17: from Medieval Latin *infuriāre* (vb.); see IN-[2], FURY] —**inˈfuriately** *adv.* —**inˈfuriˌating** *adj.* —**inˈfuriatingly** *adv.* —**inˌfuriˈation** *n.*
infuscate (ɪnˈfʌskeɪt) *or* **infuscated** *adj.* (esp. of the wings of an insect) tinged with brown. [C17: from Latin *infuscāre* to darken, from *fuscus* dark]
infuse (ɪnˈfjuːz) *vb.* **1.** (*tr.;* often foll. by *into*) to instil or inculcate. **2.** (*tr.;* foll. by *with*) to inspire; emotionally charge. **3.** to soak or be soaked in order to extract flavour or other properties. **4.** *Rare.* (foll. by *into*) to pour. [C15: from Latin *infundere* to pour into] —**inˈfuser** *n.*
infuser (ɪnˈfjuːzə) *n.* any device used to make an infusion, esp. a tea maker.
infusible[1] (ɪnˈfjuːzəbᵊl) *adj.* not fusible; not easily melted; having a high melting point. [C16: from IN-[1] + FUSIBLE] —**inˌfusiˈbility** *or* **inˈfusibleness** *n.*
infusible[2] (ɪnˈfjuːzəbᵊl) *adj.* capable of being infused. [C17: from INFUSE + -IBLE] —**inˌfusiˈbility** *or* **inˈfusibleness** *n.*
infusion (ɪnˈfjuːʒən) *n.* **1.** the act of infusing. **2.** something infused. **3.** an extract obtained by soaking. **4.** *Med.* introduction of a liquid, such as a saline solution, into a vein. —**infusive** (ɪnˈfjuːsɪv) *adj.*
infusionism (ɪnˈfjuːʒəˌnɪzəm) *n. Christian theol.* the doctrine that at the birth of each individual a pre-existing soul is implanted in his body, to remain there for the duration of his earthly life. —**inˈfusionist** *n., adj.*
infusorial earth (ˌɪnfjʊˈzɔːrɪəl) *n.* another name for **diatomaceous earth.** See **diatomite.**
infusorian (ˌɪnfjʊˈzɔːrɪən) *n. Obsolete.* **1.** any of the microscopic organisms, such as protozoans and rotifers, found in infusions of organic material. **2.** any member of the subclass *Ciliata* (see **ciliate** (sense 3)). ~*adj.* **3.** of or relating to infusorians. [C18: from New Latin *Infusoria* former class name; see INFUSE] —ˌ**infuˈsorial** *adj.*
-ing[1] *suffix forming nouns.* **1.** (*from verbs*) the action of, process of, result of, or something connected with the verb: *coming; meeting; a wedding; winnings.* **2.** (*from other nouns*) something used in, consisting of, involving, etc.: *tubing; soldiering.* **3.** (*from other parts of speech*): *an outing.* [Old English *-ing, -ung*]
-ing[2] *suffix.* **1.** forming the present participle of verbs: *walking; believing.* **2.** forming participial adjectives: *a growing boy; a sinking ship.* **3.** forming adjectives not derived from verbs: *swashbuckling.* [Middle English *-ing, -inde,* from Old English *-ende*]
-ing[3] *suffix forming nouns.* a person or thing having a certain quality or being of a certain kind: *sweeting; whiting.* [Old English *-ing;* related to Old Norse *-ingr*]
ingather (ɪnˈgæðə) *vb.* (*tr.*) to gather together or in (a harvest). —**inˈgatherer** *n.*
ingeminate (ɪnˈdʒɛmɪˌneɪt) *vb.* (*tr.*) *Rare.* to repeat; reiterate. [C16: from Latin *ingemināre* to redouble, from IN-[2] + *gemināre* to GEMINATE] —**inˌgemiˈnation** *n.*
ingenerate[1] (ɪnˈdʒɛnərɪt) *adj. Rare.* inherent, intrinsic, or innate. [C17: from Late Latin *ingenerātus* not generated; see IN-[1], GENERATE]
ingenerate[2] (ɪnˈdʒɛnəˌreɪt) *vb.* (*tr.*) *Archaic.* to produce within; engender. [C16: from Latin *ingenerāre;* see IN-[2], GENERATE] —**inˌgenerˈation** *n.*
ingenious (ɪnˈdʒiːnjəs, -nɪəs) *adj.* **1.** possessing or done with ingenuity; skilful or clever. **2.** *Obsolete.* having great intelligence; displaying genius. [C15: from Latin *ingeniōsus,* from *ingenium* natural ability; see ENGINE] —**inˈgeniously** *adv.* —**inˈgeniousness** *n.*
ingénue (ˌænʒeɪˈnjuː; *French* ɛ̃ʒeny) *n.* an artless, innocent, or inexperienced girl or young woman. [C19: from French, feminine of *ingénu* INGENUOUS]
ingenuity (ˌɪndʒɪˈnjuːɪtɪ) *n., pl.* **-ties.** **1.** inventive talent; cleverness. **2.** an ingenious device, act, etc. **3.** *Archaic.* frankness; candour. [C16: from Latin *ingenuitās* a freeborn condition, outlook consistent with such a condition, from *ingenuus* native, freeborn (see INGENUOUS); meaning influenced by INGENIOUS]
ingenuous (ɪnˈdʒɛnjʊəs) *adj.* **1.** naive, artless, or innocent. **2.** candid; frank; straightforward. [C16: from Latin *ingenuus* freeborn, worthy of a freeman, virtuous, from IN-[2] + *-genuus,* from *gignere* to beget] —**inˈgenuously** *adv.* —**inˈgenuousness** *n.*
ingest (ɪnˈdʒɛst) *vb.* (*tr.*) **1.** to take (food or liquid) into the body. **2.** (of a jet engine) to suck in (an object, a bird, etc.). [C17: from Latin *ingerere* to put into, from IN-[2] + *gerere* to carry; see GEST] —**inˈgestible** *adj.* —**inˈgestion** *n.* —**inˈgestive** *adj.*
ingesta (ɪnˈdʒɛstə) *pl. n.* nourishment taken into the body through the mouth.
ingle (ˈɪŋgᵊl) *n. Archaic or dialect.* a fire in a room or a fireplace. [C16: probably from Scots Gaelic *aingeal* fire]
inglenook (ˈɪŋgᵊlˌnʊk) *n. Brit.* a corner by a fireplace; chimney corner.
inglorious (ɪnˈglɔːrɪəs) *adj.* **1.** without courage or glory; dishonourable, shameful, or disgraceful. **2.** unknown or obscure. —**inˈgloriously** *adv.* —**inˈgloriousness** *n.*
ingo (ˈɪngəʊ) *n. Scot.* a reveal. Also **ingoing.**
ingoing (ˈɪnˌgəʊɪŋ) *adj.* **1.** coming or going in; entering. ~*n.* **2.** (*often pl.*) *English law.* the sum paid by a new tenant for fixtures left behind by the outgoing tenant. **3.** *Scot.* another word for **ingo.**
ingot (ˈɪŋgət) *n.* **1.** a piece of cast metal obtained from a mould in a form suitable for storage, transporting, and further use. ~*vb.* **2.** (*tr.*) to shape (metal) into ingots. [C14: perhaps from IN-[2] + Old English *goten,* past participle of *geotan* to pour]
ingot iron *n.* a type of steel containing a small amount of carbon and very small quantities of other elements.
ingraft (ɪnˈgrɑːft) *vb.* a variant spelling of **engraft.** —**inˈgraftment** *or* ˌ**ingrafˈtation** *n.*
ingrain *or* **engrain** *vb.* (ɪnˈgreɪn). (*tr.*) **1.** to impress deeply on the mind or nature; instil. **2.** *Archaic.* to dye into the fibre of (a fabric). ~*adj.* (ˈɪnˌgreɪn). **3.** variants of **ingrained.** **4.** (of woven or knitted articles, esp. rugs and carpets) made of dyed yarn or of fibre that is dyed before being spun into yarn. ~*n.* (ˈɪnˌgreɪn). **5. a.** a carpet made from ingrained yarn. **b.** such yarn. [C18: from the phrase *dyed in grain* dyed with kermes through the fibre]
ingrained *or* **engrained** (ɪnˈgreɪnd) *adj.* **1.** deeply impressed or instilled: *his fears are deeply ingrained.* **2.** (*prenominal*) complete or inveterate; utter: *an ingrained fool.* **3.** (esp. of dirt) worked into or through the fibre, grain, pores, etc. —**ingrainedly** *or* **engrainedly** (ɪnˈgreɪnɪdlɪ) *adv.* —**inˈgrainedness** *or* **enˈgrainedness** *n.*

ingrate ('ɪngreɪt, ɪn'greɪt) *Archaic.* ~*n.* **1.** an ungrateful person. ~*adj.* **2.** ungrateful. [C14: from Latin *ingrātus* (*adj.*), from IN-[1] + *grātus* GRATEFUL] —'**ingrately** *adv.*

ingratiate (ɪn'greɪʃɪˌeɪt) *vb.* (*tr.*; often foll. by *with*) to place (oneself) purposely in the favour (of another). [C17: from Latin, from IN-[2] + *grātia* grace, favour] —**in'gratiˌating** *or* **in'gratiatory** *adj.* —**in'gratiˌatingly** *adv.* —**inˌgrati'ation** *n.*

ingratitude (ɪn'grætɪˌtjuːd) *n.* lack of gratitude; ungratefulness; thanklessness.

ingravescent (ˌɪngrə'vɛsᵊnt) *adj. Rare.* (esp. of a disease) becoming more severe. [C19: from Latin *ingravescere* to become heavier, from *gravescere* to grow heavy, from *gravis* heavy] —ˌ**ingra'vescence** *n.*

ingredient (ɪn'griːdɪənt) *n.* a component of a mixture, compound, etc., esp. in cooking. [C15: from Latin *ingrediēns* going into, from *ingredī* to enter; see INGRESS]

ingress ('ɪngrɛs) *n.* **1.** the act of going or coming in; an entering. **2.** a way in; entrance. **3.** the right or permission to enter. **4.** *Astronomy.* another name for **immersion** (sense 2). [C15: from Latin *ingressus,* from *ingredī* to go in, from *gradī* to step, go] —**ingression** (ɪn'grɛʃən) *n.*

ingressive (ɪn'grɛsɪv) *adj.* **1.** of or concerning ingress. **2.** (of a speech sound) pronounced with an inhalation rather than exhalation of breath. ~*n.* **3.** an ingressive speech sound, such as a Zulu click. —**in'gressiveness** *n.*

in-group *n. Sociol.* a highly cohesive and relatively closed social group characterized by the preferential treatment reserved for its members and the strength of loyalty between them. Compare **out-group.**

ingrowing ('ɪnˌgrəʊɪŋ) *adj.* **1.** (esp. of a toenail) growing abnormally into the flesh. **2.** growing within or into.

ingrown ('ɪnˌgrəʊn, ɪn'grəʊn) *adj.* **1.** (esp. of a toenail) grown abnormally into the flesh; covered by adjacent tissues. **2.** grown within; native; innate. **3.** excessively concerned with oneself, one's own particular group, etc. **4.** ingrained.

ingrowth ('ɪnˌgrəʊθ) *n.* **1.** the act of growing inwards: *the ingrowth of a toenail.* **2.** something that grows inwards.

inguinal ('ɪŋgwɪnᵊl) *adj. Anatomy.* of or relating to the groin. [C17: from Latin *inguinālis,* from *inguen* groin]

ingulf (ɪn'gʌlf) *vb.* a variant spelling of **engulf.** —**in'gulfment** *n.*

ingurgitate (ɪn'gɜːdʒɪˌteɪt) *vb.* to swallow (food) with greed or in excess; gorge. [C16: from Latin *ingurgitāre* to flood, from IN-[2] + *gurges* abyss] —**inˌgurgi'tation** *n.*

Ingush (ɪŋ'guːʃ) *n., pl.* **-gushes** *or* **-gush.** a member of a people speaking a Circassian language and chiefly inhabiting the former Checheno-Ingush ASSR.

inhabit (ɪn'hæbɪt) *vb.* **-its, -iting, -ited. 1.** (*tr.*) to live or dwell in; occupy. **2.** (*intr.*) *Archaic.* to abide or dwell. [C14: from Latin *inhabitāre,* from *habitāre* to dwell] —**in'habitable** *adj.* —**inˌhabita'bility** *n.* —**inˌhabi'tation** *n.*

inhabitant (ɪn'hæbɪtənt) *n.* a person or animal that is a permanent resident of a particular place or region. —**in'habitancy** *or* **in'habitance** *n.*

inhalant (ɪn'heɪlənt) *adj.* **1.** (esp. of a volatile medicinal preparation) inhaled for its soothing or therapeutic effect. **2.** inhaling. ~*n.* **3.** an inhalant medicinal preparation.

inhalation (ˌɪnhə'leɪʃən) *n.* **1.** the act of inhaling; breathing in of air or other vapours. **2.** an inhalant preparation.

inhalator ('ɪnhəˌleɪtə) *n.* a device for issuing a vapour which is breathed in to ease discomfort of or provide medication for the respiratory system.

inhale (ɪn'heɪl) *vb.* to draw (breath) into the lungs; breathe in. [C18: from IN-[2] + Latin *halāre* to breathe]

inhaler (ɪn'heɪlə) *n.* **1.** a device for breathing in therapeutic vapours, esp. one for relieving nasal congestion. **2.** a person who inhales.

inharmonious (ˌɪnhɑː'məʊnɪəs) *or* **inharmonic** (ˌɪnhɑː'mɒnɪk) *adj.* **1.** lacking harmony; discordant. **2.** lacking accord or agreement. —ˌ**inhar'moniously** *adv.* —ˌ**inhar'moniousness** *n.*

inhaul ('ɪnˌhɔːl) *or* **inhauler** *n. Nautical.* a line for hauling in a sail.

inhere (ɪn'hɪə) *vb.* (*intr.*; foll. by *in*) to be an inseparable part (of). [C16: from Latin *inhaerēre* to stick in, from *haerēre* to stick]

inherence (ɪn'hɪərəns, -'hɛr-) *or* **inherency** *n.* **1.** the state or condition of being inherent. **2.** *Metaphysics.* the relation of attributes, elements, etc., to the subject of which they are predicated, esp. if they are its essential constituents.

inherent (ɪn'hɪərənt, -'hɛr-) *adj.* existing as an inseparable part; intrinsic. —**in'herently** *adv.*

inherit (ɪn'hɛrɪt) *vb.* **-its, -iting, -ited. 1.** to receive (property, a right, title, etc.) by succession or under a will. **2.** (*intr.*) to succeed as heir. **3.** (*tr.*) to possess (a characteristic) through genetic transmission. **4.** (*tr.*) to receive (a position, attitude, property, etc.) from a predecessor. [C14: from Old French *enheriter,* from Late Latin *inhērēditāre* to appoint an heir, from Latin *hērēs* HEIR] —**in'herited** *adj.* —**in'heritor** *n.* —**in'heritress** *or* **in'heritrix** *fem. n.*

inheritable (ɪn'hɛrɪtəbᵊl) *adj.* **1.** capable of being transmitted by heredity from one generation to a later one. **2.** capable of being inherited. **3.** *Rare.* capable of inheriting; having the right to inherit. —**inˌherita'bility** *or* **in'heritableness** *n.* —**in'heritably** *adv.*

inheritance (ɪn'hɛrɪtəns) *n.* **1.** *Law.* **a.** hereditary succession to an estate, title, etc. **b.** the right of an heir to succeed to property on the death of an ancestor. **c.** something that may legally be transmitted to an heir. **2.** the act of inheriting. **3.** something inherited; heritage. **4.** the derivation of characteristics of one generation from an earlier one by heredity. **5.** *Obsolete.* hereditary rights.

inheritance tax *n.* **1.** (in Britain) a tax introduced in 1986 to replace capital transfer tax, consisting of a percentage levied on that part of an inheritance exceeding a specified allowance, and scaled charges on gifts made within seven years of death. **2.** (in the U.S.) a state tax imposed on an inheritance according to its size and the relationship of the beneficiary to the deceased.

inhesion (ɪn'hiːʒən) *n.* a less common word for **inherence** (sense 1). [C17: from Late Latin *inhaesiō,* from *inhaerēre* to INHERE]

inhibit (ɪn'hɪbɪt) *vb.* (*tr.*) **-its, -iting, -ited. 1.** to restrain or hinder (an impulse, a desire, etc.). **2.** to prohibit; forbid. **3.** to stop, prevent, or decrease the rate of (a chemical reaction). **4.** *Electronics.* **a.** to prevent the occurrence of (a particular signal) in a circuit. **b.** to prevent the performance of (a particular operation). [C15: from Latin *inhibēre* to restrain, from IN-[2] + *habēre* to have] —**in'hibitable** *adj.* —**in'hibitive** *or* **in'hibitory** *adj.*

inhibition (ˌɪnɪ'bɪʃən, ˌɪnhɪ-) *n.* **1.** the act of inhibiting or the condition of being inhibited. **2.** *Psychol.* **a.** a mental state or condition in which the varieties of expression and behaviour of an individual become restricted. **b.** the weakening of a learned response usually as a result of extinction or because of the presence of a distracting stimulus. **c.** (in psychoanalytical theory) the unconscious restraining of an impulse. See also **repression. 3.** the process of stopping or retarding a chemical reaction. **4.** *Physiol.* the suppression of the function or action of an organ or part, as by stimulation of its nerve supply. **5.** *Church of England.* an episcopal order suspending an incumbent.

inhibitor (ɪn'hɪbɪtə) *n.* **1.** Also called: **inhibiter.** a person or thing that inhibits. **2.** Also called: **anticatalyst.** a substance that retards or stops a chemical reaction. Compare **catalyst. 3.** *Biochem.* **a.** a substance that inhibits the action of an enzyme. **b.** a substance that inhibits a metabolic or physiological process: *a plant growth inhibitor.* **4.** any impurity in a solid that prevents luminescence. **5.** an inert substance added to some rocket fuels to inhibit ignition on certain surfaces.

inhomogeneous (ɪnˌhəʊmə'dʒiːnɪəs, -ˌhɒm-) *adj.* not homogeneous or uniform. —**inhomogeneity** (ɪnˌhəʊmədʒɪ'niːɪtɪ, -ˌhɒm-) *n.*

inhospitable (ɪn'hɒspɪtəbᵊl, ˌɪnhɒ'spɪt-) *adj.* **1.** not hospitable; unfriendly. **2.** (of a region, an environment, etc.) lacking a favourable climate, terrain, etc. —**in'hospitableness** *n.* —**in'hospitably** *adv.*

inhospitality (ˌɪnhɒspɪ'tælɪtɪ, ɪnˌhɒs-) *n.* the state or attitude of being inhospitable or unwelcoming.

in-house *adj., adv.* within an organization or group: *an in-house job; the job was done in-house.*

inhuman (ɪn'hjuːmən) *adj.* **1.** Also: **inhumane** (ˌɪnhjuː'meɪn). lacking humane feelings, such as sympathy, understanding, etc.; cruel; brutal. **2.** not human. —ˌ**inhu'manely** *adv.* —**in'humanly** *adv.* —**in'humanness** *n.*

inhumanity (ˌɪnhjuː'mænɪtɪ) *n., pl.* **-ties. 1.** lack of humane qualities. **2.** an inhumane act, decision, etc.

inhume (ɪn'hjuːm) *vb.* (*tr.*) to inter; bury. [C17: from Latin *inhumāre,* from IN-[2] + *humus* ground] —ˌ**inhu'mation** *n.* —**in'humer** *n.*

inimical (ɪ'nɪmɪkᵊl) *adj.* **1.** adverse or unfavourable. **2.** not friendly; hostile. [C17: from Late Latin *inimīcālis,* from *inimīcus,* from IN-[1] + *amīcus* friendly; see ENEMY] —**in'imically** *adv.* —**in'imicalness** *or* **inˌimi'cality** *n.*

inimitable (ɪ'nɪmɪtəbᵊl) *adj.* incapable of being duplicated or imitated; unique. —**inˌimita'bility** *or* **in'imitableness** *n.* —**in'imitably** *adv.*

inion ('ɪnɪən) *n. Anatomy.* the most prominent point at the back of the head, used as a point of measurement in craniometry. [C19: from Greek: back of the head]

iniquity (ɪ'nɪkwɪtɪ) *n., pl.* **-ties. 1.** lack of justice or righteousness; wickedness; injustice. **2.** a wicked act; sin. [C14: from Latin *inīquitās,* from *inīquus* unfair, from IN-[1] + *aequus* even, level; see EQUAL] —**in'iquitous** *adj.* —**in'iquitously** *adv.* —**in'iquitousness** *n.*

init. *abbrev. for:* **1.** initial. **2.** initio. [Latin: in the beginning]

initial (ɪ'nɪʃəl) *adj.* **1.** of, at, or concerning the beginning. ~*n.* **2.** the first letter of a word, esp. a person's name. **3.** *Printing.* a large sometimes highly decorated letter set at the beginning of a chapter or work. **4.** *Botany.* a cell from which tissues and organs develop by division and differentiation; a meristematic cell. ~*vb.* **-tials, -tialling, -tialled** *or U.S.* **-tials, -tialing, -tialed. 5.** (*tr.*) to sign with one's initials, esp. to indicate approval; endorse. [C16: from Latin *initiālis* of the beginning, from *initium* beginning, literally: an entering upon, from *inīre* to go in, from IN-[2] + *īre* to go] —**in'itialer** *or* **in'itialler** *n.* —**in'itially** *adv.*

initialize *or* **initialise** (ɪˈnɪʃəˌlaɪz) *vb.* (*tr.*) to assign an initial value to (a variable or storage location) in a computer program. —**inˌitialiˈzation** *or* **inˌitialiˈsation** *n.*

initiate *vb.* (ɪˈnɪʃɪˌeɪt). (*tr.*) **1.** to begin or originate. **2.** to accept (new members) into an organization such as a club, through often secret ceremonies. **3.** to teach fundamentals to: *she initiated him into the ballet.* ~*adj.* (ɪˈnɪʃɪɪt, -ˌeɪt). **4.** initiated; begun. ~*n.* (ɪˈnɪʃɪɪt, -ˌeɪt). **5.** a person who has been initiated, esp. recently. **6.** a beginner; novice. [C17: from Latin *initiāre* (vb.), from *initium;* see INITIAL] —**inˈitiatory** *adj.* —**inˈitiˌatress** *or* **inˈitiˌatrix** *fem. n.*

initiation (ɪˌnɪʃɪˈeɪʃən) *n.* **1.** the act of initiating or the condition of being initiated. **2.** the often secret ceremony initiating new members into an organization.

initiative (ɪˈnɪʃɪətɪv, -ˈnɪʃətɪv) *n.* **1.** the first step or action of a matter; commencing move: *he took the initiative; a peace initiative.* **2.** the right or power to begin or initiate something: *he has the initiative.* **3.** the ability or attitude required to begin or initiate something. **4.** *Government.* **a.** the right or power to introduce legislation, etc., in a legislative body. **b.** the procedure by which citizens originate legislation, as in many American states and Switzerland. **5. on one's own initiative.** without being prompted. ~*adj.* **6.** of or concerning initiation or serving to initiate; initiatory. —**inˈitiatively** *adv.*

initiator (ɪˈnɪʃɪeɪtə) *n.* **1.** a person or thing that initiates. **2.** *Chem.* a substance that starts a chain reaction. **3.** *Chem.* a very sensitive explosive used in detonators.

inject (ɪnˈdʒɛkt) *vb.* (*tr.*) **1.** *Med.* to introduce (a fluid) into (the body of a person or animal) by means of a syringe or similar instrument. **2.** (foll. by *into*) to introduce (a new aspect or element): *to inject humour into a scene.* **3.** to interject (a comment, idea, etc.). **4.** to place (a rocket, satellite, etc.) in orbit. [C17: from *injicere* to throw in, from *jacere* to throw] —**inˈjectable** *adj.*

injection (ɪnˈdʒɛkʃən) *n.* **1.** fluid injected into the body, esp. for medicinal purposes. **2.** something injected. **3.** the act of injecting. **4. a.** the act or process of introducing fluid under pressure, such as fuel into the combustion chamber of an engine. **b.** (*as modifier*): *injection moulding.* **5.** *Maths.* a function or mapping for which $f(x) = f(y)$ only if $x = y$ and for which the image of every element of the domain is contained in the image space. See also **surjection, bijection.** —**inˈjective** *adj.*

injector (ɪnˈdʒɛktə) *n.* **1.** a person or thing that injects. **2.** a device for spraying fuel into the combustion chamber of an internal-combustion engine. **3.** a device for forcing water into a steam boiler. Also called: **inspirator.**

injudicious (ˌɪndʒuˈdɪʃəs) *adj.* not discreet; imprudent. —ˌ**injuˈdiciously** *adv.* —ˌ**injuˈdiciousness** *n.*

Injun (ˈɪndʒən) *n.* **1.** *U.S.* an informal or dialect word for (American) **Indian. 2. honest Injun.** (*interj.*) *Slang.* genuinely; really.

injunction (ɪnˈdʒʌŋkʃən) *n.* **1.** *Law.* an instruction or order issued by a court to a party to an action, esp. to refrain from some act, such as causing a nuisance. **2.** a command, admonition, etc. **3.** the act of enjoining. [C16: from Late Latin *injunctiō*, from Latin *injungere* to ENJOIN] —**inˈjunctive** *adj.* —**inˈjunctively** *adv.*

injure (ˈɪndʒə) *vb.* (*tr.*) **1.** to cause physical or mental harm or suffering to; hurt or wound. **2.** to offend, esp. by an injustice. [C16: back formation from INJURY] —**ˈinjurable** *adj.* —**ˈinjured** *adj.* —**ˈinjurer** *n.*

injurious (ɪnˈdʒʊərɪəs) *adj.* **1.** causing damage or harm; deleterious; hurtful. **2.** abusive, slanderous, or libellous. —**inˈjuriously** *adv.* —**inˈjuriousness** *n.*

injury (ˈɪndʒərɪ) *n., pl.* **-ries. 1.** physical damage or hurt. **2.** a specific instance of this: *a leg injury.* **3.** harm done to a reputation. **4.** *Law.* a violation or infringement of another person's rights that causes him harm and is actionable at law. **5.** an obsolete word for **insult.** [C14: from Latin *injūria* injustice, wrong, from *injūriōsus* acting unfairly, wrongful, from IN-[1] + *jūs* right]

injury benefit *n.* (in the British National Insurance scheme) a weekly payment to a person injured while at work, varying according to the degree of injury.

injury time *n. Soccer, rugby, etc.* extra playing time added on to compensate for time spent attending to injured players during the match.

injustice (ɪnˈdʒʌstɪs) *n.* **1.** the condition or practice of being unjust or unfair. **2.** an unjust act.

ink (ɪŋk) *n.* **1.** a fluid or paste used for printing, writing, and drawing. **2.** a dark brown fluid ejected into the water for self-concealment by an octopus or related mollusc from a gland (**ink sac**) near the anus. ~*vb.* (*tr.*) **3.** to mark with ink. **4.** to coat (a printing surface) with ink. ~See also **ink in, ink up.** [C13: from Old French *enque*, from Late Latin *encaustum* a purplish-red ink, from Greek *enkauston* purple ink, from *enkaustos* burnt in, from *enkaiein* to burn in; see EN-[2], CAUSTIC] —**ˈinker** *n.*

inkberry (ˈɪŋkˌbɛrɪ) *n., pl.* **-ries. 1.** a North American holly tree, *Ilex glabra*, with black berry-like fruits. **2.** another name for the **pokeweed. 3.** the fruit of either of these plants.

inkblot (ˈɪŋkˌblɒt) *n. Psychol.* an abstract patch of ink, one of ten commonly used in the Rorschach test.

ink-cap *n.* any of several saprophytic agaricaceous fungi of the genus *Coprinus*, whose caps disintegrate into a black inky fluid after the spores mature. It includes the **shaggy ink-cap** (*Coprinus comatus*), also called **lawyer's wig,** a distinctive fungus having a white cylindrical cap covered with shaggy white or brownish scales.

inkhorn (ˈɪŋkˌhɔːn) *n.* (formerly) a small portable container for ink, usually made from horn.

inkhorn term *n.* an affectedly learned and obscure borrowing from another language, esp. Greek or Latin.

ink in *vb.* (*adv.*) **1.** (*tr.*) to use ink to go over pencil lines in (a drawing). **2.** to apply ink to (a printing surface) in preparing to print from it.

ink jet *n.* a method of printing using electrostatic fields to control the direction of streams of electrically charged ink.

inkle (ˈɪŋkᵊl) *n.* **1.** a kind of linen tape used for trimmings. **2.** the thread or yarn from which this tape is woven. [C16: of unknown origin]

inkling (ˈɪŋklɪŋ) *n.* a slight intimation or suggestion; suspicion. [C14: probably from *inclen* to hint at; related to Old English *inca*]

inkstand (ˈɪŋkˌstænd) *n.* a stand or tray on which are kept writing implements and containers for ink.

ink up *vb.* (*adv.*) to apply ink to (a printing machine) in preparing it for operation.

inkwell (ˈɪŋkˌwɛl) *n.* a small container for pen ink, often let into the surface of a desk.

inky (ˈɪŋkɪ) *adj.* **inkier, inkiest. 1.** resembling ink, esp. in colour; dark or black. **2.** of, containing, or stained with ink: *inky fingers.* —**ˈinkiness** *n.*

INLA *abbrev. for* Irish National Liberation Army; a Republican paramilitary organization in Ireland.

inlace (ɪnˈleɪs) *vb.* a variant spelling of **enlace.**

inlaid (ˈɪnˌleɪd, ɪnˈleɪd) *adj.* **1.** set in the surface, as a design in wood. **2.** having such a design or inlay: *an inlaid table.*

inland *adj.* (ˈɪnlənd). **1.** of, concerning, or located in the interior of a country or region away from a sea or border. **2.** *Chiefly Brit.* operating within a country or region; domestic; not foreign. ~*n.* (ˈɪnˌlænd, -lənd). **3.** the interior of a country or region. ~*adv.* (ˈɪnˌlænd, -lənd). **4.** towards or into the interior of a country or region. —**ˈinlander** *n.*

inland bill *n.* a bill of exchange that is both drawn and made payable in the same country. Compare **foreign bill.**

Inland Revenue *n.* (in Britain and New Zealand) a government board that administers and collects major direct taxes, such as income tax, corporation tax, and capital gains tax. Abbrev.: **IR.**

in-law *n.* **1.** a relative by marriage. ~*adj.* **2.** (*postpositive; in combination*) related by marriage: *a father-in-law.* [C19: back formation from *father-in-law*, etc.]

inlay *vb.* (ɪnˈleɪ), **-lays, -laying, -laid.** (*tr.*) **1.** to decorate (an article, esp. of furniture, or a surface) by inserting pieces of wood, ivory, etc., into prepared slots in the surface. ~*n.* (ˈɪnˌleɪ). **2.** *Dentistry.* a filling, made of gold, porcelain, etc., inserted into a cavity and held in position by cement. **3.** decoration made by inlaying. **4.** an inlaid article, surface, etc. —**ˈinˌlaid** *adj.* —**ˈinˌlayer** *n.*

inlet *n.* (ˈɪnˌlɛt). **1.** a narrow inland opening of the coastline. **2.** an entrance or opening. **3.** the act of letting someone or something in. **4.** something let in or inserted. **5. a.** a passage, valve, or part through which a substance, esp. a fluid, enters a device or machine. **b.** (*as modifier*): *an inlet valve.* ~*vb.* (ɪnˈlɛt), **-lets, -letting, -let. 6.** (*tr.*) to insert or inlay.

inlier (ˈɪnˌlaɪə) *n.* an outcrop of rocks that is entirely surrounded by younger rocks.

in-line *adj.* **1.** denoting a linked sequence of manufacturing processes. **2.** denoting an internal-combustion engine having its cylinders arranged in a line.

in loc. cit. (in textual annotation) *abbrev. for* in loco citato. [Latin: in the place cited]

in loco parentis *Latin.* (ɪn ˈləʊkəʊ pəˈrɛntɪs) in place of a parent: said of a person acting in a parental capacity.

inly (ˈɪnlɪ) *adv. Poetic.* inwardly; intimately.

inlying (ˈɪnˌlaɪɪŋ) *adj.* situated within or inside.

inmate (ˈɪnˌmeɪt) *n.* **1.** a person who is confined to an institution such as a prison or hospital. See also **resident** (sense 2). **2.** *Obsolete.* a person who lives with others in a house.

in medias res *Latin.* (ɪn ˈmiːdɪˌæs ˈreɪs) in or into the middle of events or a narrative. [literally: into the midst of things, taken from a passage in Horace's *Ars Poetica*]

in mem. *abbrev. for* in memoriam.

in memoriam (ɪn mɪˈmɔːrɪəm) in memory of; as a memorial to: used in obituaries, epitaphs, etc. [Latin]

inmesh (ɪnˈmɛʃ) *vb.* a variant spelling of **enmesh.**

inmigrant (ˈɪnˌmaɪgrənt) *adj.* **1.** coming in from another area of the same country: *an inmigrant worker.* ~*n.* **2.** an inmigrant person or animal.

inmost (ˈɪnˌməʊst) *adj.* another word for **innermost.**

inn (ɪn) *n.* **1.** a pub or small hotel providing food and accommodation. **2.** (formerly, in England) a college or hall of residence for students, esp. of law, now only in the names of such institutions as the **Inns of Court.** [Old English; compare Old Norse *inni* inn, house, place of refuge]

innards (ˈɪnədz) *pl. n. Informal.* **1.** the internal organs of the body, esp. the viscera. **2.** the interior parts or components of anything, esp. the working parts. [C19: colloquial variant of *inwards*]

innate (ɪˈneɪt, ˈɪneɪt) *adj.* **1.** existing in a person or animal from birth; congenital; inborn. **2.** being an essential part of the character of a person or thing. **3.** instinctive; not learned: *innate capacities.* **4.** *Botany.* (of anthers) joined to the filament by the base only. **5.** (in rationalist philosophy) (of ideas) present in the mind before any experience and knowable by pure reason. [C15: from Latin, from *innascī* to be born in, from *nascī* to be born] —**inˈnately** *adv.* —**inˈnateness** *n.*
innate releasing mechanism *n. Psychol.* the process by which a stimulus evokes a response when the connection between the two is inborn. Abbrev.: **IRM.**
inner (ˈɪnə) *adj.* (*prenominal*) **1.** being or located further inside: *an inner room.* **2.** happening or occurring inside: *inner movement.* **3.** relating to the soul, mind, spirit, etc.: *inner feelings.* **4.** more profound or obscure; less apparent: *the inner meaning.* **5.** exclusive or private: *inner regions of the party.* **6.** *Chem.* (of a compound) having a cyclic structure formed or apparently formed by reaction of one functional group in a molecule with another group in the same molecule: *an inner ester.* ~*n.* **7.** Also called: **red.** *Archery.* **a.** the red innermost ring on a target. **b.** a shot which hits this ring. —ˈ**innerly** *adv.* —ˈ**innerness** *n.*
inner bar *n. Brit.* all Queen's or King's Counsel collectively.
inner city *n.* **a.** the parts of a city in or near its centre, esp. when they are associated with poverty, unemployment, substandard housing, etc. **b.** (*as modifier*): *inner-city schools.*
inner-directed *adj.* guided by one's own conscience and values rather than external pressures to conform. Compare **other-directed.** —ˈ**inner-diˈrection** *n.*
inner ear *n.* another name for **internal ear.**
Inner Light *or* **Word** *n. Quakerism.* the presence and inner working of God in the soul acting as a guiding spirit that is superior even to Scripture and unites man to Christ.
inner man *or* (*fem.*) **inner woman** *n.* **1.** the mind or soul. **2.** *Jocular.* the stomach or appetite.
innermost (ˈɪnəˌməʊst) *adj.* **1.** being or located furthest within; central. **2.** intimate; private: *innermost beliefs.*
inner planet *n.* any of the planets Mercury, Venus, earth, and Mars, whose orbits lie inside the asteroid belt.
inner space *n.* **1.** the environment beneath the surface of the sea. **2.** the human mind regarded as being as unknown or as unfathomable as space.
inner tube *n.* an inflatable rubber tube that fits inside a pneumatic tyre casing.
innervate (ˈɪnɜːˌveɪt) *vb.* (*tr.*) **1.** to supply nerves to (a bodily organ or part). **2.** to stimulate (a bodily organ or part) with nerve impulses. —ˌ**innerˈvation** *n.*
innerve (ɪˈnɜːv) *vb.* (*tr.*) to supply with nervous energy; stimulate.
inning (ˈɪnɪŋ) *n.* **1.** *Baseball.* a division of the game consisting of a turn at bat and a turn in the field for each side. **2.** *Archaic.* the reclamation of land from the sea. [Old English *innung* a going in, from *innian* to go in]
innings (ˈɪnɪŋz) *n.* **1.** (*functioning as sing.*) *Cricket.* **a.** the batting turn of a player or team. **b.** the runs scored during such a turn. **2.** (*sometimes sing.*) a period of opportunity or action. **3.** (*functioning as pl.*) land reclaimed from the sea.
innkeeper (ˈɪnˌkiːpə) *n.* an owner or manager of an inn.
innocence (ˈɪnəsəns) *n.* the quality or state of being innocent. Archaic word: **innocency** (ˈɪnəsənsɪ). [C14: from Latin *innocentia* harmlessness, from *innocēns* doing no harm, blameless, from IN-[1] + *nocēns* harming, from *nocēre* to hurt, harm; see NOXIOUS]
innocent (ˈɪnəsənt) *adj.* **1.** not corrupted or tainted with evil or unpleasant emotion; sinless; pure. **2.** not guilty of a particular crime; blameless. **3.** (*postpositive;* foll. by *of*) free (of); lacking: *innocent of all knowledge of history.* **4. a.** harmless or innocuous: *an innocent game.* **b.** not cancerous: *an innocent tumour.* **5.** credulous, naive, or artless. **6.** simple-minded; slow-witted. ~*n.* **7.** an innocent person, esp. a young child or an ingenuous adult. **8.** a simple-minded person; simpleton. —ˈ**innocently** *adv.*
innocuous (ɪˈnɒkjʊəs) *adj.* having little or no adverse or harmful effect; harmless. [C16: from Latin *innocuus* harmless, from IN-[1] + *nocēre* to harm] —**inˈnocuously** *adv.* —**inˈnocuousness** *or* **innocuity** (ˌɪnəˈkjuːɪtɪ) *n.*
innominate (ɪˈnɒmɪnɪt) *adj.* **1.** having no name; nameless. **2.** a less common word for **anonymous.**
innominate bone *n.* either of the two bones that form the sides of the pelvis, consisting of three fused components, the ilium, ischium, and pubis. Nontechnical name: **hipbone.**
in nomine (ɪn ˈnɒmɪˌneɪ, -ˌniː) *n. Music.* any of several pieces of music of the 16th or 17th centuries for keyboard or for a consort of viols, based on a cantus firmus derived from the Vespers antiphon *Gloria tibi Trinitas.* [from Latin *in nomine Jesu* in the name of Jesus, the first words of an introit for which this type of music was originally composed]
innovate (ˈɪnəˌveɪt) *vb.* to invent or begin to apply (methods, ideas, etc.). [C16: from Latin *innovāre* to renew, from IN-[2] + *novāre* to make new, from *novus* new] —ˈ**innoˌvative** *or* ˈ**innoˌvatory** *adj.* —ˈ**innoˌvator** *n.*
innovation (ˌɪnəˈveɪʃən) *n.* **1.** something newly introduced, such as a new method or device. **2.** the act of innovating. —ˌ**innoˈvational** *adj.* —ˌ**innoˈvationist** *n.*
innoxious (ɪˈnɒkʃəs) *adj.* not noxious; harmless. —**inˈnoxiously** *adv.* —**inˈnoxiousness** *n.*
innuendo (ˌɪnjʊˈɛndəʊ) *n., pl.* **-dos** *or* **-does.** **1.** an indirect or subtle reference, esp. one made maliciously or indicating criticism or disapproval; insinuation. **2.** *Law.* (in pleading) a word introducing an explanatory phrase, usually in parenthesis. **3.** *Law.* (in an action for defamation) **a.** an explanation of the construction put upon words alleged to be defamatory where the defamatory meaning is not apparent. **b.** the words thus explained. [C17: from Latin, literally: by hinting, from *innuendum,* gerund of *innuere* to convey by a nod, from IN-[2] + *nuere* to nod]
Innuit (ˈɪnjuːɪt) *n.* a variant spelling of **Inuit.**
innumerable (ɪˈnjuːmərəbᵊl, ɪˈnjuːmrəbᵊl) *or* **innumerous** *adj.* so many as to be uncountable; extremely numerous. —**inˌnumeraˈbility** *or* **inˈnumerableness** *n.* —**inˈnumerably** *adv.*
innumerate (ɪˈnjuːmərɪt) *adj.* **1.** having neither knowledge nor understanding of mathematics or science. ~*n.* **2.** an innumerate person. —**inˈnumeracy** *n.*
innutrition (ˌɪnjuːˈtrɪʃən) *n.* lack or absence of nutrition. Compare **malnutrition.** —ˌ**innuˈtritious** *adj.*
inobservance (ˌɪnəbˈzɜːvəns) *n.* **1.** heedlessness. **2.** lack of compliance with or adherence to a law, religious duty, etc. —ˌ**inobˈservant** *adj.* —ˌ**inobˈservantly** *adv.*
inoculable (ɪˈnɒkjʊləbᵊl) *adj.* capable of being inoculated. —**inˌoculaˈbility** *n.*
inoculate (ɪˈnɒkjʊˌleɪt) *vb.* **1.** to introduce (the causative agent of a disease) into the body of (a person or animal), in order to induce immunity. **2.** (*tr.*) to introduce (microorganisms, esp. bacteria) into (a culture medium). **3.** (*tr.*) to cause to be influenced or imbued, as with ideas or opinions. [C15: from Latin *inoculāre* to implant, from IN-[2] + *oculus* eye, bud] —**inˌocuˈlation** *n.* —**inˈoculative** *adj.* —**inˈocuˌlator** *n.*
inoculum (ɪˈnɒkjʊləm) *or* **inoculant** *n., pl.* **-la** (-lə) *or* **-lants.** *Med.* the substance used in giving an inoculation. [C20: New Latin; see INOCULATE]
inodorous (ɪnˈəʊdərəs) *adj.* odourless; having no odour.
in-off *n. Billiards.* a shot that goes into a pocket after striking another ball.
inoffensive (ˌɪnəˈfɛnsɪv) *adj.* **1.** not giving offence; unobjectionable. **2.** not unpleasant, poisonous, or harmful. —ˌ**inofˈfensively** *adv.* —ˌ**inofˈfensiveness** *n.*
inofficious (ˌɪnəˈfɪʃəs) *adj.* contrary to moral obligation, as the disinheritance of a child by his parents: *an inofficious will.* —ˌ**inofˈficiously** *adv.* —ˌ**inofˈficiousness** *n.*
inoperable (ɪnˈɒpərəbᵊl, -ˈɒprə-) *adj.* **1.** incapable of being implemented or operated; unworkable. **2.** *Surgery.* not suitable for operation without risk, esp. (of a malignant tumour) because metastasis has rendered surgery useless. —**inˌoperaˈbility** *or* **inˈoperableness** *n.* —**inˈoperably** *adv.*
inoperative (ɪnˈɒpərətɪv, -ˈɒprə-) *adj.* **1.** not operating. **2.** useless or ineffective. —**inˈoperativeness** *n.*
inopportune (ɪnˈɒpəˌtjuːn) *adj.* not opportune; inappropriate or badly timed. —**inˈopporˌtunely** *adv.* —**inˈopporˌtuneness** *or* **inˌopporˈtunity** *n.*
inordinate (ɪnˈɔːdɪnɪt) *adj.* **1.** exceeding normal limits; immoderate. **2.** unrestrained, as in behaviour or emotion; intemperate. **3.** irregular or disordered. [C14: from Latin *inordinātus* disordered, from IN-[1] + *ordināre* to put in order] —**inˈordinacy** *or* **inˈordinateness** *n.* —**inˈordinately** *adv.*
inorg. *abbrev. for* inorganic.
inorganic (ˌɪnɔːˈgænɪk) *adj.* **1.** not having the structure or characteristics of living organisms; not organic. **2.** relating to or denoting chemical compounds that do not contain carbon. Compare **organic** (sense 4). **3.** not having a system, structure, or ordered relation of parts; amorphous. **4.** not resulting from or produced by growth; artificial. **5.** *Linguistics.* denoting or relating to a sound or letter introduced into the pronunciation or spelling of a word at some point in its history. —ˌ**inorˈganically** *adv.*
inorganic chemistry *n.* the branch of chemistry concerned with the elements and all their compounds except those containing carbon. Some simple carbon compounds, such as oxides, carbonates, etc., are treated as inorganic. Compare **organic chemistry.**
inosculate (ɪnˈɒskjʊˌleɪt) *vb.* **1.** *Physiol.* (of small blood vessels) to communicate by anastomosis. **2.** to unite or be united so as to be continuous; blend. **3.** to intertwine or cause to intertwine. [C17: from IN-[2] + Latin *ōsculāre* to equip with an opening, from *ōsculum,* diminutive of *ōs* mouth] —**inˌoscuˈlation** *n.*
inositol (ɪˈnəʊsɪˌtɒl) *n.* a cyclic alcohol, one isomer of which (*i*-inositol) is present in yeast and is a growth factor for some organisms; cyclohexanehexol. Formula: $C_6H_{12}O_6$. [C19: from Greek *in-, is* sinew + -OSE[2] + -ITE[1] + -OL[1]]
inotropic (ˌɪnəˈtrɒpɪk, ˌaɪnə-) *adj.* affecting or controlling the contraction of muscles, esp. those of the heart: *inotropic drugs.* [C20: from Greek, from *is* (stem *in-*) tendon + -TROPIC]
inpatient (ˈɪnˌpeɪʃənt) *n.* a patient living in the hospital where he is being treated. Compare **outpatient.**
in perpetuum *Latin.* (ɪn pɜːˈpɛtjʊəm) for ever.
in personam (ɪn pɜːˈsəʊnæm) *adj. Law.* (of a judicial act) directed against a specific person or persons. Compare **in rem.** [Latin]
in petto (ɪn ˈpɛtəʊ) *adj. R.C. Church.* not disclosed: used of the names of cardinals designate. [Italian, literally: in the breast]

in posse (ɪn ˈpɒsɪ) *adj.* possible; potential. Compare **in esse.** [Latin, literally: in possibility]

in propria persona *Latin.* (ɪn ˈprəʊprɪə pɜːˈsəʊnə) *adv. Chiefly law.* in person; personally.

input (ˈɪnˌpʊt) *n.* **1.** the act of putting in. **2.** that which is put in. **3.** (*often pl.*) a resource required for industrial production, such as capital goods, labour services, raw materials, etc. **4.** *Electronics.* **a.** the signal or current fed into a component or circuit. **b.** the terminals, or some other point, to which the signal is applied. **5.** *Computer technol.* the data fed into a computer from a peripheral device. **6.** (*modifier*) of or relating to electronic, computer, or other input: *input program.* ~*vb.* **7.** (*tr.*) to insert (data) into a computer.

input device *n. Computer technol.* a peripheral device that accepts data and feeds it into a computer.

input/output *n. Computer technol.* **1.** the data or information that is passed into or out of a computer. Abbrev.: **I/O.** **2.** (*modifier*) concerned with or relating to such passage of data or information.

input-output analysis *n. Economics.* an analysis of production relationships between the industries of an economy involving a study of each industry's inputs and outputs, esp. as used in social accounting.

inqilab (ˈɪnkɪˌlɑːb) *n.* (in India, Pakistan, etc.) revolution (esp. in the phrase **inqilab zindabad** long live the revolution). [Urdu]

inquest (ˈɪnˌkwɛst) *n.* **1.** an inquiry into the cause of an unexplained, sudden, or violent death, or as to whether or not property constitutes treasure trove, held by a coroner, in certain cases with a jury. **2.** *Informal.* any inquiry or investigation. [C13: from Medieval Latin *inquēsta,* from Latin IN-[2] + *quaesītus* investigation, from *quaerere* to examine]

inquietude (ɪnˈkwaɪɪˌtjuːd) *n.* restlessness, uneasiness, or anxiety. —**inquiet** (ɪnˈkwaɪət) *adj.* —**inˈquietly** *adv.*

inquiline (ˈɪnkwɪˌlaɪn) *n.* **1.** an animal that lives in close association with another animal without harming it. See also **commensal** (sense 1). ~*adj.* **2.** of or living as an inquiline. [C17: from Latin *inquilīnus* lodger, from IN-[2] + *colere* to dwell] —**inquilinism** (ˈɪnkwɪlɪˌnɪzəm) *or* **inquilinity** (ˌɪnkwɪˈlɪnɪtɪ) *n.* —**inquilinous** (ˌɪnkwɪˈlaɪnəs) *adj.*

inquire *or* **enquire** (ɪnˈkwaɪə) *vb.* **1. a.** to seek information; ask: *she inquired his age; she inquired about rates of pay.* **b.** (with *of*) to ask (a person) for information: *I'll inquire of my aunt when she is coming.* **2.** (*intr.;* often foll. by *into*) to make a search or investigation. [C13: from Latin *inquīrere* from IN-[2] + *quaerere* to seek] —**inˈquirer** *or* **enˈquirer** *n.*

inquiring (ɪnˈkwaɪərɪŋ) *adj.* seeking or tending to seek answers, information, etc.: *an inquiring mind.* —**inˈquiringly** *adv.*

inquiry *or* **enquiry** (ɪnˈkwaɪərɪ) *n.* **1.** a request for information; a question. **2.** an investigation, esp. a formal one conducted into a matter of public concern by a body constituted for that purpose by a government, local authority, or other organization.

inquisition (ˌɪnkwɪˈzɪʃən) *n.* **1.** the act of inquiring deeply or searchingly; investigation. **2.** a deep or searching inquiry, esp. a ruthless official investigation of individuals in order to suppress revolt or root out the unorthodox. **3.** an official inquiry, esp. one held by a jury before an officer of the Crown. **4.** another word for **inquest** (sense 2). [C14: from legal Latin *inquīsītiō,* from *inquīrere* to seek for; see INQUIRE] —ˌ**inquiˈsitional** *adj.* —ˌ**inquiˈsitionist** *n.*

Inquisition (ˌɪnkwɪˈzɪʃən) *n. History.* a judicial institution of the Roman Catholic Church (1232–1820) founded to discover and suppress heresy. See also **Spanish Inquisition.**

inquisitive (ɪnˈkwɪzɪtɪv) *adj.* **1.** excessively curious, esp. about the affairs of others; prying. **2.** eager to learn; inquiring. —**inˈquisitively** *adv.* —**inˈquisitiveness** *n.*

inquisitor (ɪnˈkwɪzɪtə) *n.* **1.** a person who inquires, esp. deeply, searchingly, or ruthlessly. **2.** (*often cap.*) an official of the ecclesiastical court of the Inquisition.

Inquisitor-General *n., pl.* **Inquisitors-General.** *History.* the head of the Spanish court of Inquisition.

inquisitorial (ɪnˌkwɪzɪˈtɔːrɪəl) *adj.* **1.** of, relating to, or resembling inquisition or an inquisitor. **2.** offensively curious; prying. **3.** *Law.* denoting criminal procedure in which one party is both prosecutor and judge, or in which the trial is held in secret. Compare **accusatorial** (sense 2). —**inˌquisiˈtorially** *adv.* —**inˌquisiˈtorialness** *n.*

inquorate (ɪnˈkwɔːreɪt) *adj. Brit.* not consisting of or being a quorum: *this meeting is inquorate.*

in re (ɪn ˈreɪ) *prep.* in the matter of: used esp. in bankruptcy proceedings. [C17: from Latin]

in rem (ɪn ˈrɛm) *adj. Law.* (of a judicial act) directed against property rather than against a specific person. Compare **in personam.** [Latin, literally: against the matter]

in rerum natura *Latin.* (ɪn ˈrɛərʊm næˈtʊərə) in the nature of things.

INRI *abbrev. for* Iesus Nazarenus Rex Iudaeorum (the inscription placed over Christ's head during the Crucifixion). [Latin: Jesus of Nazareth, King of the Jews]

inroad (ˈɪnˌrəʊd) *n.* **1.** an invasion or hostile attack; raid or incursion. **2.** an encroachment or intrusion.

inrush (ˈɪnˌrʌʃ) *n.* a sudden usually overwhelming inward flow or rush; influx. —ˈ**inˌrushing** *n., adj.*

INS *abbrev. for* International News Service.

ins. *abbrev. for:* **1.** inches. **2.** inspector. **3.** insulated. **4.** insulation. **5.** insurance.

insalivate (ɪnˈsælɪˌveɪt) *vb.* (*tr.*) to saturate (food) with saliva during mastication. —**inˌsaliˈvation** *n.*

insalubrious (ˌɪnsəˈluːbrɪəs) *adj.* not salubrious; unpleasant, unhealthy, or sordid. —ˌ**insaˈlubriously** *adv.* —**insalubrity** (ˌɪnsəˈluːbrɪtɪ) *n.*

insane (ɪnˈseɪn) *adj.* **1. a.** mentally deranged; crazy; of unsound mind. **b.** (*as collective n.;* preceded by *the*): *the insane.* **2.** characteristic of a person of unsound mind: *an insane stare.* **3.** irresponsible; very foolish; stupid. —**inˈsanely** *adv.* —**inˈsaneness** *n.*

insanitary (ɪnˈsænɪtərɪ, -trɪ) *adj.* not sanitary; dirty or infected. —**inˈsanitariness** *or* **inˌsaniˈtation** *n.*

insanity (ɪnˈsænɪtɪ) *n., pl.* **-ties.** **1.** relatively permanent disorder of the mind; state or condition of being insane. **2.** *Law.* (not in strict legal usage) a state of mind characterized by the inability to distinguish right from wrong. **3.** utter folly; stupidity.

insatiable (ɪnˈseɪʃəbᵊl, -ʃɪə-) *or* **insatiate** (ɪnˈseɪʃɪɪt) *adj.* not able to be satisfied or satiated; greedy or unappeasable. —**inˌsatiaˈbility, inˈsatiableness,** *or* **inˈsatiateness** *n.* —**inˈsatiably** *or* **inˈsatiately** *adv.*

inscape (ˈɪnskeɪp) *n.* the essential inner nature of a person, an object, etc. [C19: from IN-[2] + *-scape,* as in LANDSCAPE; coined by the British poet Gerard Manley Hopkins (1844–89)]

inscribe (ɪnˈskraɪb) *vb.* (*tr.*) **1.** to make, carve, or engrave (writing, letters, a design, etc.) on (a surface such as wood, stone, or paper). **2.** to enter (a name) on a list or in a register. **3.** to sign one's name on (a book, photograph, etc.) before presentation to another person. **4.** to draw (a geometric construction such as a circle, polygon, etc.) inside another construction so that the two are in contact but do not intersect. Compare **circumscribe** (sense 3). [C16: from Latin *inscrībere;* see INSCRIPTION] —**inˈscribable** *adj.* —**inˈscribableness** *n.* —**inˈscriber** *n.*

inscription (ɪnˈskrɪpʃən) *n.* **1.** something inscribed, esp. words carved or engraved on a coin, tomb, etc. **2.** a signature or brief dedication in a book or on a work of art. **3.** the act of inscribing. **4.** *Philosophy, linguistics.* an element of written language, esp. a sentence. Compare **utterance**[1] (sense 3). [C14: from Latin *inscriptiō* a writing upon, from *inscrībere* to write upon, from IN-[2] + *scrībere* to write] —**inˈscriptional** *or* **inˈscriptive** *adj.* —**inˈscriptively** *adv.*

inscrutable (ɪnˈskruːtəbᵊl) *adj.* incomprehensible; mysterious or enigmatic. [C15: from Late Latin *inscrūtābilis,* from Latin IN-[1] + *scrūtārī* to examine] —**inˌscrutaˈbility** *or* **inˈscrutableness** *n.* —**inˈscrutably** *adv.*

insect (ˈɪnsɛkt) *n.* **1.** any small air-breathing arthropod of the class *Insecta,* having a body divided into head, thorax, and abdomen, three pairs of legs, and (in most species) two pairs of wings. Insects comprise about five sixths of all known animal species, with a total of over one million named species. **2.** (loosely) any similar invertebrate, such as a spider, tick, or centipede. **3.** a contemptible, loathsome, or insignificant person. [C17: from Latin *insectum* (animal that has been) cut into, insect, from *insecāre,* from IN-[2] + *secāre* to cut; translation of Greek *entomon* insect] —**inˈsectean, inˈsectan,** *or* **inˈsectile** *adj.* —ˈ**insectˌlike** *adj.*

insectarium (ˌɪnsɛkˈtɛərɪəm) *or* **insectary** (ɪnˈsɛktərɪ) *n., pl.* **-tariums, -taria** (-ˈtɛərɪə), *or* **-taries.** a place where living insects are kept, bred, and studied.

insecticide (ɪnˈsɛktɪˌsaɪd) *n.* a substance used to destroy insect pests. —**inˌsectiˈcidal** *adj.*

insectivore (ɪnˈsɛktɪˌvɔː) *n.* **1.** any placental mammal of the order *Insectivora,* being typically small, with simple teeth, and feeding on invertebrates. The group includes shrews, moles, and hedgehogs. **2.** any animal or plant that derives nourishment from insects.

insectivorous (ˌɪnsɛkˈtɪvərəs) *adj.* **1.** feeding on or adapted for feeding on insects: *insectivorous plants.* **2.** of or relating to the order *Insectivora.*

insectivorous bat *n.* any bat of the suborder *Microchiroptera,* typically having large ears and feeding on insects. The group includes common bats (*Myotis* species), vampire bats, etc. Compare **fruit bat.**

insecure (ˌɪnsɪˈkjʊə) *adj.* **1.** anxious or afraid; not confident or certain. **2.** not adequately protected: *an insecure fortress.* **3.** unstable or shaky. —ˌ**inseˈcurely** *adv.* —ˌ**inseˈcureness** *n.* —ˌ**inseˈcurity** *n.*

inselberg (ˈɪnzᵊlˌbɜːg) *n.* an isolated rocky hill rising abruptly from a flat plain. [from German, from *Insel* island + *Berg* mountain]

inseminate (ɪnˈsɛmɪˌneɪt) *vb.* (*tr.*) **1.** to impregnate (a female) with semen. **2.** to introduce (ideas or attitudes) into the mind of (a person or group). [C17: from Latin *insēmināre,* from IN-[2] + *sēmināre* to sow, from *sēmen* seed] —**inˌsemiˈnation** *n.* —**inˈsemiˌnator** *n.*

insensate (ɪnˈsɛnseɪt, -sɪt) *adj.* **1.** lacking sensation or consciousness. **2.** insensitive; unfeeling. **3.** foolish; senseless. —**inˈsensately** *adv.* —**inˈsensateness** *n.*

insensible (ɪnˈsɛnsəbᵊl) *adj.* **1.** lacking sensation or consciousness. **2.** (foll. by *of* or *to*) unaware (of) or indifferent (to): *insensible to suffering.* **3.** thoughtless or callous. **4.** a less common word for **imperceptible.** —**inˌsensiˈbility** *or* **inˈsensibleness** *n.* —**inˈsensibly** *adv.*

insensitive (ɪnˈsɛnsɪtɪv) *adj.* **1.** lacking sensitivity; unfeeling. **2.** lacking physical sensation. **3.** (*postpositive;* foll. by *to*) not sensitive (to) or affected (by): *insensitive to radiation.* —**inˈsensitively** *adv.* —**inˈsensitiveness** *or* **inˌsensiˈtivity** *n.*

insentient (ɪnˈsɛnʃɪənt) *adj. Rare.* lacking consciousness or senses; inanimate. —**inˈsentience** *or* **inˈsentiency** *n.*

inseparable (ɪnˈsɛpərəbᵊl, -ˈsɛprə-) *adj.* incapable of being separated or divided. —**inˌseparaˈbility** *or* **inˈseparableness** *n.* —**inˈseparably** *adv.*

insert *vb.* (ɪnˈsɜːt). (*tr.*) **1.** to put in or between; introduce. **2.** to introduce, as into text, such as a newspaper; interpolate. ~*n.* (ˈɪnsɜːt). **3.** something inserted. **4. a.** a folded section placed in another for binding in with a book. **b.** a printed sheet, esp. one bearing advertising, placed loose between the leaves of a book, periodical, etc. **5.** another word for **cut-in** (sense 6). [C16: from Latin *inserere* to plant in, ingraft, from IN-[2] + *serere* to join] —**inˈsertable** *adj.* —**inˈserter** *n.*

inserted (ɪnˈsɜːtɪd) *adj.* **1.** *Anatomy.* (of a muscle) attached to the bone that it moves. **2.** *Botany.* (of parts of a plant) growing from another part, as stamens from the corolla.

insertion (ɪnˈsɜːʃən) *n.* **1.** the act of inserting or something that is inserted. **2.** a word, sentence, correction, etc., inserted into text, such as a newspaper. **3.** a strip of lace, embroidery, etc., between two pieces of material. **4.** *Anatomy.* the point or manner of attachment of a muscle to the bone that it moves. **5.** *Botany.* the manner or point of attachment of one part to another. —**inˈsertional** *adj.*

insertion element *or* **sequence** *n. Genetics.* a section of DNA that has been inserted into another chromosome. See **transposon.**

in-service *adj.* denoting training that is given to employees during the course of employment: *an in-service course.*

insessorial (ˌɪnsɛˈsɔːrɪəl) *adj.* **1.** (of feet or claws) adapted for perching. **2.** (of birds) having insessorial feet. [C19: from New Latin *Insessōrēs* birds that perch, from Latin: perchers, from *insidēre* to sit upon, from *sedēre* to sit]

inset *vb.* (ɪnˈsɛt), **-sets, -setting, -set.** **1.** (*tr.*) to set or place in or within; insert. ~*n.* (ˈɪnˌsɛt). **2.** something inserted. **3.** *Printing.* **a.** a small map or diagram set within the borders of a larger one. **b.** another name for **insert** (sense 4). **4.** a piece of fabric inserted into a garment, as to shape it or for decoration. **5.** a flowing in, as of the tide. —ˈ**inˌsetter** *n.*

inshallah (ɪnˈʃæla) *sentence substitute. Islam.* if Allah wills it. [C19: from Arabic]

inshore (ˈɪnˈʃɔː) *adj.* **1.** in or on the water, but close to the shore: *inshore weather.* ~*adv., adj.* **2.** towards the shore from the water: *an inshore wind; we swam inshore.*

inshrine (ɪnˈʃraɪn) *vb.* a variant spelling of **enshrine.**

inside *n.* (ˈɪnˈsaɪd). **1.** the interior; inner or enclosed part or surface. **2.** the side of a path away from the road or adjacent to a wall. **3.** (*also pl.*) *Informal.* the internal organs of the body, esp. the stomach and bowels. **4. inside of.** in a period of time less than; within. **5. inside out.** with the inside facing outwards. **6. know (something) inside out.** to know thoroughly or perfectly. ~*prep.* (ˌɪnˈsaɪd). **7.** in or to the interior of; within or to within; on the inside of. ~*adj.* (ˈɪnˌsaɪd). **8.** on or of an interior; on the inside: *an inside door.* **9.** (*prenominal*) arranged or provided by someone within an organization or building, esp. illicitly: *the raid was an inside job; inside information.* ~*adv.* (ˌɪnˈsaɪd). **10.** within or to within a thing or place; indoors. **11.** by nature; fundamentally: *inside, he's a good chap.* **12.** *Slang.* in or into prison.

▷**Usage.** See at **outside.**

inside forward *n. Soccer.* (esp. formerly) one of two players (the **inside right** and the **inside left**) having mainly midfield and attacking roles.

inside job *n. Informal.* a crime committed with the assistance of someone associated with the victim, such as a person employed on the premises burgled.

inside lane *n. Athletics.* the inside and advantageous position in a race that uses the curved parts of the track.

insider (ˌɪnˈsaɪdə) *n.* **1.** a member of a specified group. **2.** a person with access to exclusive information.

insider dealing *or* **trading** *n.* dealing in company securities on a recognized stock exchange, with a view to making a profit or avoiding a loss, by a person who has confidential information about the securities that, if generally known, would affect their price. Its practice by those connected with a company is illegal. —**insider dealer** *or* **trader** *n.*

inside track *n.* **1.** the inner and therefore shorter side of a racecourse. **2.** *Informal.* a position of advantage: *the local man has the inside track in this contest.*

insidious (ɪnˈsɪdɪəs) *adj.* **1.** stealthy, subtle, cunning, or treacherous. **2.** working in a subtle or apparently innocuous way, but nevertheless deadly: *an insidious illness.* [C16: from Latin *insidiōsus* cunning, from *insidiae* an ambush, from *insidēre* to sit in; see INSESSORIAL] —**inˈsidiously** *adv.* —**inˈsidiousness** *n.*

insight (ˈɪnˌsaɪt) *n.* **1.** the ability to perceive clearly or deeply; penetration. **2.** a penetrating and often sudden understanding, as of a complex situation or problem. **3.** *Psychol.* **a.** the capacity for understanding one's own or another's mental processes. **b.** the immediate understanding of the significance of an event or action. **4.** *Psychiatry.* the ability to understand one's own problems, sometimes used to distinguish between psychotic and neurotic disorders. —ˈ**inˌsightful** *adj.*

insignia (ɪnˈsɪgnɪə) *n., pl.* **-nias** *or* **-nia.** **1.** a badge or emblem of membership, office, or dignity. **2.** a distinguishing sign or mark. ~Also called (rare): **insigne** (ɪnˈsɪgniː). [C17: from Latin: marks, badges, from *insignis* distinguished by a mark, prominent, from IN-[2] + *signum* mark]

insignificant (ˌɪnsɪgˈnɪfɪkənt) *adj.* **1.** having little or no importance; trifling. **2.** almost or relatively meaningless. **3.** small or inadequate: *an insignificant wage.* **4.** not distinctive in character, etc. —ˌ**insigˈnificance** *or* ˌ**insigˈnificancy** *n.* —ˌ**insigˈnificantly** *adv.*

insincere (ˌɪnsɪnˈsɪə) *adj.* lacking sincerity; hypocritical. —ˌ**insinˈcerely** *adv.* —**insincerity** (ˌɪnsɪnˈsɛrɪtɪ) *n.*

insinuate (ɪnˈsɪnjʊˌeɪt) *vb.* **1.** (*may take a clause as object*) to suggest by indirect allusion, hints, innuendo, etc. **2.** (*tr.*) to introduce subtly or deviously. **3.** (*tr.*) to cause (someone, esp. oneself) to be accepted by gradual approaches or manoeuvres. [C16: from Latin *insinuāre* to wind one's way into, from IN-[2] + *sinus* curve] —**inˈsinuative** *or* **inˈsinuatory** *adj.* —**inˈsinuˌator** *n.*

insinuation (ɪnˌsɪnjʊˈeɪʃən) *n.* **1.** an indirect or devious hint or suggestion. **2.** the act or practice of insinuating.

insipid (ɪnˈsɪpɪd) *adj.* **1.** lacking spirit or interest; boring. **2.** lacking taste; unpalatable. [C17: from Latin *insipidus,* from IN-[1] + *sapidus* full of flavour, SAPID] —ˌ**insiˈpidity** *or* **inˈsipidness** *n.* —**inˈsipidly** *adv.*

insipience (ɪnˈsɪpɪəns) *n. Archaic.* lack of wisdom. [C15: from Latin *insipientia,* from IN-[1] + *sapientia* wisdom; see SAPIENT] —**inˈsipient** *adj.* —**inˈsipiently** *adv.*

insist (ɪnˈsɪst) *vb.* (when *tr., takes a clause as object;* when *intr.,* usually foll. by *on* or *upon*) **1.** to make a determined demand (for): *he insisted that his rights be respected; he insisted on his rights.* **2.** to express a convinced belief (in) or assertion (of): *he insisted that she was mad; he insisted on her madness.* [C16: from Latin *insistere* to stand upon, urge, from IN-[2] + *sistere* to stand] —**inˈsister** *n.* —**inˈsistingly** *adv.*

insistent (ɪnˈsɪstənt) *adj.* **1.** making continual and persistent demands. **2.** demanding notice or attention; compelling: *the insistent cry of a bird.* —**inˈsistence** *or* **inˈsistency** *n.* —**inˈsistently** *adv.*

in situ *Latin.* (ɪn ˈsɪtjuː) *adv., adj.* (*postpositive*) **1.** in the natural, original, or appropriate position. **2.** *Pathol.* (esp. of a cancerous growth or tumour) not seen to be spreading from a localized position.

insnare (ɪnˈsnɛə) *vb.* a less common spelling of **ensnare.** —**inˈsnarement** *n.* —**inˈsnarer** *n.*

insobriety (ˌɪnsəʊˈbraɪɪtɪ) *n.* lack of sobriety; intemperance.

in so far as *or U.S.* **insofar as** (ˌɪnsəʊˈfɑː) *adv.* to the degree or extent that.

insolate (ˈɪnsəʊˌleɪt) *vb.* (*tr.*) to expose to sunlight, as for drying or bleaching. [C17: from Latin *insōlāre* to place in the sun, from IN-[2] + *sōl* sun]

insolation (ˌɪnsəʊˈleɪʃən) *n.* **1.** the quantity of solar radiation falling upon a body or planet, esp. per unit area. **2.** exposure to the sun's rays. **3.** another name for **sunstroke.**

insole (ˈɪnˌsəʊl) *n.* **1.** the inner sole of a shoe or boot. **2.** a loose additional inner sole used to give extra warmth or to make a shoe fit.

insolent (ˈɪnsələnt) *adj.* offensive, impudent, or disrespectful. [C14: from Latin *insolens* from IN-[1] + *solēre* to be accustomed] —ˈ**insolence** *n.* —ˈ**insolently** *adv.*

insoluble (ɪnˈsɒljʊbᵊl) *adj.* **1.** incapable of being dissolved; incapable of forming a solution, esp. in water. **2.** incapable of being solved. —**inˌsoluˈbility** *or* **inˈsolubleness** *n.* —**inˈsolubly** *adv.*

insolvable (ɪnˈsɒlvəbᵊl) *adj.* another word for **insoluble** (sense 2). —**inˌsolvaˈbility** *n.* —**inˈsolvably** *adv.*

insolvency provision *n. Brit.* the right of employees of a firm that goes bankrupt or into receivership to receive money owed to them as wages, etc.

insolvent (ɪnˈsɒlvənt) *adj.* **1.** (of a person, company, etc.) having insufficient assets to meet debts and liabilities; bankrupt. **2.** of or relating to bankrupts or bankruptcy. ~*n.* **3.** a person who is insolvent; bankrupt. —**inˈsolvency** *n.*

insomnia (ɪnˈsɒmnɪə) *n.* chronic inability to fall asleep or to enjoy uninterrupted sleep. [C18: from Latin, from *insomnis* sleepless, from *somnus* sleep] —**inˈsomnious** *adj.*

insomniac (ɪnˈsɒmnɪˌæk) *adj.* **1.** exhibiting or causing insomnia. ~*n.* **2.** a person experiencing insomnia.

insomuch (ˌɪnsəʊˈmʌtʃ) *adv.* **1.** (foll. by *as* or *that*) to such an extent or degree. **2.** (foll. by *as*) because of the fact (that); inasmuch (as).

insouciant (ɪnˈsuːsɪənt) *adj.* carefree or unconcerned; lighthearted. [C19: from French, from IN-[1] + *souciant* worrying, from *soucier* to trouble, from Latin *sollicitāre;* compare SOLICITOUS] —**inˈsouciance** *n.* —**inˈsouciantly** *adv.*

insoul (ɪnˈsəʊl) *vb.* (*tr.*) a variant of **ensoul.**

insp. *abbrev. for:* **1.** inspected. **2.** inspector.

inspan (ɪnˈspæn) *vb.* **-spans, -spanning, -spanned.** (*tr.*) *Chiefly S. African.* to harness (animals) to (a vehicle); yoke. [C19: from

Afrikaans, from Middle Dutch *inspannen,* from *spannen* to stretch, yoke; see SPAN]

inspect (ɪnˈspɛkt) *vb. (tr.)* **1.** to examine closely, esp. for faults or errors. **2.** to scrutinize officially (a document, military personnel on ceremonial parade, etc.). [C17: from Latin *inspicere,* from *specere* to look] —**inˈspectable** *adj.* —**inˈspectingly** *adv.* —**inˈspection** *n.* —**inˈspectional** *adj.* —**inˈspective** *adj.*

inspection chamber *n.* a more formal name for **manhole** (sense 1).

inspector (ɪnˈspɛktə) *n.* **1.** a person who inspects, esp. an official who examines for compliance with regulations, standards, etc. **2.** a police officer ranking below a superintendent or chief inspector and above a sergeant. —**inˈspectoral** *or* **inspectorial** (ˌɪnspɛkˈtɔːrɪəl) *adj.* —**inˈspectorˌship** *n.*

inspectorate (ɪnˈspɛktərɪt) *n.* **1.** the office, rank, or duties of an inspector. **2.** a body of inspectors. **3.** a district under an inspector.

inspector general *n., pl.* **inspectors general. 1.** the head of an inspectorate or inspection system; an officer with wide investigative powers. **2.** a staff officer of the military, air, or naval service with the responsibility of conducting inspections and investigations.

inspector of taxes *n.* an official of the Inland Revenue whose work is to assess individuals' income tax liability.

insphere (ɪnˈsfɪə) *vb.* a variant spelling of **ensphere.**

inspiration (ˌɪnspɪˈreɪʃən) *n.* **1.** stimulation or arousal of the mind, feelings, etc., to special or unusual activity or creativity. **2.** the state or quality of being so stimulated or aroused. **3.** someone or something that causes this state. **4.** an idea or action resulting from such a state. **5.** the act or process of inhaling; breathing in.

inspirational (ˌɪnspɪˈreɪʃənᵊl) *adj.* **1.** of, relating to, or tending to arouse inspiration; inspiring. **2.** resulting from inspiration; inspired. —ˌ**inspiˈrationally** *adv.*

inspirator (ˈɪnspɪˌreɪtə) *n.* a device for drawing in or injecting a vapour, liquid, etc. Also called: **injector.**

inspiratory (ɪnˈspaɪərətərɪ, -trɪ) *adj.* of or relating to inhalation or the drawing in of air.

inspire (ɪnˈspaɪə) *vb.* **1.** to exert a stimulating or beneficial effect upon (a person); animate or invigorate. **2.** *(tr.;* foll. by *with* or *to; may take an infinitive)* to arouse (with a particular emotion or to a particular action); stir. **3.** *(tr.)* to prompt or instigate; give rise to: *her beauty inspired his love.* **4.** *(tr.; often passive)* to guide or arouse by divine influence or inspiration. **5.** to take or draw (air, gas, etc.) into the lungs; inhale. **6.** *(tr.) Archaic.* **a.** to breathe into or upon. **b.** to breathe life into. [C14 (in the sense: to breathe upon, blow into): from Latin *inspīrāre,* from *spīrāre* to breathe] —**inˈspirable** *adj.* —**inˈspirative** *adj.* —**inˈspirer** *n.* —**inˈspiringly** *adv.*

inspired (ɪnˈspaɪəd) *adj.* **1.** aroused or guided by or as if aroused or guided by divine inspiration: *an inspired performance; she was like one inspired.* **2.** extremely accurate or apt but based on intuition rather than knowledge or logical deduction: *an inspired guess.*

inspirit (ɪnˈspɪrɪt) *vb. (tr.)* to fill with vigour; inspire. —**inˈspiriter** *n.* —**inˈspiritingly** *adv.* —**inˈspiritment** *n.*

inspissate (ɪnˈspɪseɪt) *vb. Archaic.* to thicken, as by evaporation. [C17: from Late Latin *inspissātus* thickened, from Latin *spissāre* to thicken, from *spissus* thick] —ˌ**inspisˈsation** *n.* —ˈ**inspisˌsator** *n.*

inst. *abbrev. for:* **1.** instant (this month). **2.** instantaneous. **3.** instrumental.

Inst. *abbrev. for:* **1.** Institute. **2.** Institution.

instability (ˌɪnstəˈbɪlɪtɪ) *n., pl.* **-ties. 1.** lack of stability or steadiness. **2.** tendency to variable or unpredictable behaviour. **3.** *Physics.* a sudden deformation of a plasma due to a weakening of the confining field.

instable (ɪnˈsteɪbᵊl) *adj.* a less common word for **unstable.**

install *or* **instal** (ɪnˈstɔːl) *vb.* **-stalls, -stalling, -stalled** *or* **-stals, -stalling, -stalled.** *(tr.)* **1.** to place (machinery, equipment, etc.) in position and connect and adjust for use. **2.** to put in a position, rank, etc. **3.** to settle (a person, esp. oneself) in a position or state: *she installed herself in an armchair.* [C16: from Medieval Latin *installāre,* from IN-[2] + *stallum* STALL[1]] —**inˈstaller** *n.*

installant (ɪnˈstɔːlənt) *n.* **a.** a person who installs another in an office, etc. **b.** *(as modifier): an installant bishop.*

installation (ˌɪnstəˈleɪʃən) *n.* **1.** the act of installing or the state of being installed. **2.** a large device, system, or piece of equipment that has been installed. **3.** a military establishment usually serving in a support role.

installment plan *or esp. Canadian* **instalment plan** *n.* the U.S. and Canadian name for **hire-purchase.**

instalment[1] *or U.S.* **installment** (ɪnˈstɔːlmənt) *n.* **1.** one of the portions, usually equal, into which a debt is divided for payment at specified intervals over a fixed period. **2.** a portion of something that is issued, broadcast, or published in parts, such as a serial in a magazine. [C18: from obsolete *estallment,* probably from Old French *estaler* to fix, hence to agree rate of payment, from *estal* something fixed, place, from Old High German *stal* STALL[1]]

instalment[2] *or U.S.* **installment** (ɪnˈstɔːlmənt) *n.* another word for **installation** (sense 1).

instance (ˈɪnstəns) *n.* **1.** a case or particular example. **2. for instance.** for or as an example. **3.** a specified stage in proceedings; step (in the phrases **in the first, second,** etc., **instance). 4.** urgent request or demand (esp. in the phrase **at the instance of). 5.** *Logic.* **a.** an expression derived from another by instantiation. **b.** See **substitution** (sense 4b). **6.** *Archaic.* motive or reason. ~*vb. (tr.)* **7.** to cite as an example. [C14 (in the sense: case, example): from Medieval Latin *instantia* example, (in the sense: urgency) from Latin: a being close upon, presence, from *instāns* pressing upon, urgent; see INSTANT]

instancy (ˈɪnstənsɪ) *n. Rare.* **1.** the quality of being urgent or imminent. **2.** instantaneousness; immediateness.

instant (ˈɪnstənt) *n.* **1.** a very brief time; moment. **2.** a particular moment or point in time: *at the same instant.* **3. on the instant.** immediately; without delay. ~*adj.* **4.** immediate; instantaneous. **5.** (esp. of foods) prepared or designed for preparation with very little time and effort: *instant coffee.* **6.** urgent or imperative. **7.** *(postpositive) Rare except when abbreviated in formal correspondence.* **a.** of the present month: *a letter of the 7th instant.* Abbrev.: **inst.** Compare **proximo, ultimo. b.** currently under consideration. ~*adv.* **8.** a poetic word for **instantly.** [C15: from Latin *instāns,* from *instāre* to be present, press closely, from IN-[2] + *stāre* to stand]

instantaneous (ˌɪnstənˈteɪnɪəs) *adj.* **1.** occurring with almost no delay; immediate. **2.** happening or completed within a moment: *instantaneous death.* **3.** *Maths.* **a.** occurring at or associated with a particular instant. **b.** equal to the limit of the average value of a given variable as the time interval over which the variable is considered approaches zero: *instantaneous velocity.* —ˌ**instanˈtaneously** *adv.* —ˌ**instanˈtaneousness** *or* **instantaneity** (ɪnˌstæntəˈniːɪtɪ) *n.*

instanter (ɪnˈstæntə) *adv. Law.* without delay; (in connection with pleading) the same day or within 24 hours. [C17: from Latin: urgently, from *instans* INSTANT]

instantiate (ɪnˈstænʃɪˌeɪt) *vb. (tr.)* to represent by an instance. [C20: from Latin *instantia* (see INSTANCE) + -ATE[1]]

instantiation (ɪnˌstænʃɪˈeɪʃən) *n.* **1.** the act or an instance of instantiating. **2.** the representation of (an abstraction) by a concrete example. **3.** *Logic.* **a.** the process of deriving an individual statement from a general one by replacing the variable with a name or other referring expression. **b.** the valid inference of an instance from a universally quantified statement, as *David is rational* from *all men are rational.* **c.** a statement so derived.

instantly (ˈɪnstəntlɪ) *adv.* **1.** immediately; at once. **2.** *Archaic.* urgently or insistently.

instant replay *n.* another name for **action replay.**

instar (ˈɪnstɑː) *n.* the stage in the development of an insect between any two moults. [C19: New Latin from Latin: image]

instate (ɪnˈsteɪt) *vb. (tr.)* to place in a position or office; install. —**inˈstatement** *n.*

instauration (ˌɪnstɔːˈreɪʃən) *n. Rare.* restoration or renewal. [C17: from Latin *instaurātiō,* from *instaurāre* to renew] —ˈ**instauˌrator** *n.*

instead (ɪnˈstɛd) *adv.* **1.** as a replacement, substitute, or alternative. **2. instead of.** *(prep.)* in place of or as an alternative to. [C13: from phrase *in stead* in place]

instep (ˈɪnˌstɛp) *n.* **1.** the middle section of the human foot, forming the arch between the ankle and toes. **2.** the part of a shoe, stocking, etc., covering this. [C16: probably from IN-[2] + STEP]

instigate (ˈɪnstɪˌgeɪt) *vb. (tr.)* **1.** to bring about, as by incitement or urging: *to instigate rebellion.* **2.** to urge on to some drastic or inadvisable action. [C16: from Latin *instīgāre* to stimulate, incite; compare Greek *stizein* to prick] —ˈ**instiˌgatingly** *adv.* —ˌ**instiˈgation** *n.* —ˈ**instiˌgative** *adj.* —ˈ**instiˌgator** *n.*

instil *or U.S.* **instill** (ɪnˈstɪl) *vb.* **-stils** *or* **-stills, -stilling, -stilled.** *(tr.)* **1.** to introduce gradually; implant or infuse. **2.** *Rare.* to pour in or inject in drops. [C16: from Latin *instillāre* to pour in a drop at a time, from *stillāre* to drip] —**inˈstiller** *n.* —**inˈstilment,** *U.S.* **inˈstillment,** *or* ˌ**instilˈlation** *n.*

instinct (ˈɪnstɪŋkt) *n.* **1.** the innate capacity of an animal to respond to a given stimulus in a relatively fixed way. **2.** inborn intuitive power. **3.** a natural and apparently innate aptitude. ~*adj.* (ɪnˈstɪŋkt) **4.** *Rare.* *(postpositive;* often foll. by *with)* **a.** animated or impelled (by). **b.** imbued or infused (with). [C15: from Latin *instinctus* roused, from *instinguere* to incite; compare INSTIGATE]

instinctive (ɪnˈstɪŋktɪv) *or* **instinctual** *adj.* **1.** of, relating to, or resulting from instinct. **2.** conditioned so as to appear innate: *an instinctive movement in driving.* —**inˈstinctively** *or* **inˈstinctually** *adv.*

institute (ˈɪnstɪˌtjuːt) *vb. (tr.)* **1.** to organize; establish. **2.** to initiate: *to institute a practice.* **3.** to establish in a position or office; induct. **4.** (foll. by *in* or *into*) to install (a clergyman) in a church. ~*n.* **5.** an organization founded for particular work, such as education, promotion of the arts, or scientific research. **6.** the building where such an organization is situated. **7.** something instituted, esp. a rule, custom, or precedent. [C16: from Latin *instituere,* from *statuere* to place, stand] —ˈ**instiˌtutor** *or* ˈ**instiˌtuter** *n.*

institutes (ˈɪnstɪˌtjuːts) *pl. n.* a digest or summary, esp. of laws.

institution (ˌɪnstɪˈtjuːʃən) *n.* **1.** the act of instituting. **2.** an organization or establishment founded for a specific purpose, such as a hospital, church, company, or college. **3.** the building where such an organization is situated. **4.** an established custom, law, or relationship in a society or community. **5.** Also called: **institutional investor.** a large organization, such as an insurance company, bank, or pension fund, that has substantial sums to invest on a stock exchange. **6.** *Informal.* a constant feature or practice: *Jones' drink at the bar was an institution.* **7.** the appointment or admission of an incumbent to an ecclesiastical office or pastoral charge. **8.** *Christian theol.* the creation of a sacrament by Christ, esp. the Eucharist. —ˌ**instiˈtutionary** *adj.*

institutional (ˌɪnstɪˈtjuːʃənᵊl) *adj.* **1.** of, relating to, or characteristic of institutions. **2.** dull, routine, and uniform: *institutional meals.* **3.** relating to principles or institutes, esp. of law. —ˌ**instiˈtutionally** *adv.*

institutionalism (ˌɪnstɪˈtjuːʃənəˌlɪzəm) *n.* the system of or belief in institutions. —ˌ**instiˈtutionalist** *n.*

institutionalize *or* **institutionalise** (ˌɪnstɪˈtjuːʃənəˌlaɪz) *vb.* **1.** (*tr.; often passive*) to subject to the deleterious effects of confinement in an institution: *a mental patient who was institutionalized into boredom and apathy.* **2.** (*tr.*) to place in an institution. **3.** to make or become an institution. —ˌ**instiˌtutionaliˈzation** *or* ˌ**instiˌtutionaliˈsation** *n.*

institutive (ˈɪnstɪˌtjuːtɪv) *adj.* **1.** concerned with instituting and establishing. **2.** established by custom or law. —ˈ**instiˌtutively** *adv.*

in-store *adj.* available or taking place within a department store: *in-store banking facilities.*

instr. *abbrev. for:* **1.** instructor. **2.** instrument. **3.** instrumental.

instruct (ɪnˈstrʌkt) *vb.* (*tr.*) **1.** to direct to do something; order. **2.** to teach (someone) how to do (something). **3.** to furnish with information; apprise. **4.** *Law, chiefly Brit.* **a.** (esp. of a client to his solicitor or a solicitor to a barrister) to give relevant facts or information to. **b.** to authorize (a barrister or solicitor) to conduct a case on a person's behalf: *to instruct counsel.* [C15: from Latin *instruere* to construct, set in order, equip, teach, from *struere* to build] —**inˈstructible** *adj.*

instruction (ɪnˈstrʌkʃən) *n.* **1.** a direction; order. **2.** the process or act of imparting knowledge; teaching; education. **3.** Also called: **command.** *Computer technol.* a part of a program consisting of a coded command to the computer to perform a specified function. —**inˈstructional** *adj.*

instructions (ɪnˈstrʌkʃənz) *pl. n.* **1.** directions, orders, or recommended rules for guidance, use, etc. **2.** *Law.* the facts and details relating to a case given by a client to his solicitor or by a solicitor to a barrister with directions to conduct the case: *to take instructions.*

instructive (ɪnˈstrʌktɪv) *adj.* serving to instruct or enlighten; conveying information. —**inˈstructively** *adv.* —**inˈstructiveness** *n.*

instructor (ɪnˈstrʌktə) *n.* **1.** someone who instructs; teacher. **2.** *U.S. and Canadian.* a university teacher ranking below assistant professor. —**inˈstructorˌship** *n.* —**instructress** (ɪnˈstrʌktrɪs) *fem. n.*

instrument *n.* (ˈɪnstrəmənt). **1.** a mechanical implement or tool, esp. one used for precision work: *surgical instrument.* **2.** *Music.* any of various contrivances or mechanisms that can be played to produce musical tones or sounds. **3.** an important factor or agency in something: *her evidence was an instrument in his arrest.* **4.** *Informal.* a person used by another to gain an end; dupe; tool. **5.** a measuring device, such as a pressure gauge or ammeter. **6. a.** a device or system for use in navigation or control, esp. of aircraft. **b.** (*as modifier*): *instrument landing.* **7.** a formal legal document. ~*vb.* (ˈɪnstrəˌmɛnt). (*tr.*) **8.** another word for **orchestrate** (sense 1). **9.** to equip with instruments. [C13: from Latin *instrūmentum* tool, equipment, from *instruere* to erect, furnish; see INSTRUCT]

instrumental (ˌɪnstrəˈmɛntᵊl) *adj.* **1.** serving as a means or influence; helpful. **2.** of, relating to, or characterized by an instrument or instruments. **3.** played by or composed for musical instruments. **4.** *Grammar.* denoting a case of nouns, etc., in certain inflected languages, indicating the instrument used in performing an action, usually translated into English using the prepositions *with* or *by means of.* ~*n.* **5.** a piece of music composed for instruments rather than for voices. **6.** *Grammar.* **a.** the instrumental case. **b.** a word or speech element in the instrumental case. —ˌ**instrumenˈtality** *n.* —ˌ**instruˈmentally** *adv.*

instrumentalism (ˌɪnstrəˈmɛntəˌlɪzəm) *n.* **1.** a system of pragmatic philosophy holding that ideas are instruments, that they should guide our actions and can change the world, and that their value consists not in their truth but in their success. **2.** an antirealist philosophy of science that holds that theories are not true or false but are merely tools for deriving predictions from observational data.

instrumentalist (ˌɪnstrəˈmɛntəlɪst) *n.* **1.** a person who plays a musical instrument. **2.** *Philosophy.* a person who believes in the doctrines of instrumentalism. ~*adj.* **3.** of or relating to instrumentalism.

instrumental learning *n. Psychol.* a method of training in which the reinforcement is made contingent on the occurrence of the response. Compare **classical conditioning.**

instrumentation (ˌɪnstrəmɛnˈteɪʃən) *n.* **1.** the instruments specified in a musical score or arrangement. **2.** another word for **orchestration.** **3.** the study of the characteristics of musical instruments. **4.** the use of instruments or tools. **5.** means; agency.

instrument flying *n.* the navigation of an aircraft by the use of instruments only.

instrument landing *n.* an aircraft landing relying only upon instruments and ground radio devices, usually made when visibility is very poor.

instrument panel *or* **board** *n.* **1.** a panel on which instruments are mounted, as on a car. See also **dashboard.** **2.** an array of instruments, gauges, etc., mounted to display the condition or performance of a machine.

insubordinate (ˌɪnsəˈbɔːdɪnɪt) *adj.* **1.** not submissive to authority; disobedient or rebellious. **2.** not in a subordinate position or rank. ~*n.* **3.** an insubordinate person. —ˌ**insubˈordinately** *adv.* —ˌ**insubˌordiˈnation** *n.*

insubstantial (ˌɪnsəbˈstænʃəl) *adj.* **1.** not substantial; flimsy, tenuous, or slight. **2.** imaginary; unreal. —ˌ**insubˌstantiˈality** *n.* —ˌ**insubˈstantially** *adv.*

insufferable (ɪnˈsʌfərəbᵊl) *adj.* intolerable; unendurable. —**inˈsufferableness** *n.* —**inˈsufferably** *adv.*

insufficiency (ˌɪnsəˈfɪʃənsɪ) *n.* **1.** Also called: ˌ**insufˈficience.** the state of being insufficient. **2.** *Pathol.* failure in the functioning of an organ, tissue, etc.: *cardiac insufficiency.*

insufficient (ˌɪnsəˈfɪʃənt) *adj.* not sufficient; inadequate or deficient. —ˌ**insufˈficiently** *adv.*

insufflate (ˈɪnsʌˌfleɪt) *vb.* **1.** (*tr.*) to breathe or blow (something) into (a room, area, etc.). **2.** *Med.* to blow (air, medicated powder, etc.) into the lungs or into a body cavity. **3.** (*tr.*) to breathe or blow upon (someone or something) as a ritual or sacramental act, esp. so as to symbolize the influence of the Holy Spirit. —ˌ**insufˈflation** *n.* —ˈ**insufˌflator** *n.*

insula (ˈɪnsjʊlə) *n., pl.* **-lae** (-ˌliː). a pyramid-shaped area of the brain within each cerebral hemisphere beneath parts of the frontal and temporal lobes. Also called: **island of Reil.** [Latin, literally: island]

insular (ˈɪnsjʊlə) *adj.* **1.** of, relating to, or resembling an island. **2.** remote, detached, or aloof. **3.** illiberal or narrow-minded. **4.** isolated or separated. ~*n.* **5.** *Rare.* an inhabitant of an island. [C17: from Late Latin *insulāris,* from Latin *insula* island, ISLE] —ˈ**insularism** *or* **insularity** (ˌɪnsjʊˈlærɪtɪ) *n.* —ˈ**insularly** *adv.*

insulate (ˈɪnsjʊˌleɪt) *vb.* (*tr.*) **1.** to prevent or reduce the transmission of electricity, heat, or sound to or from (a body, device, or region) by surrounding with a nonconducting material. **2.** to isolate or detach. [C16: from Late Latin *insulātus:* made into an island]

insulating tape *n. Brit.* adhesive tape, impregnated with a moisture-repelling substance, used to insulate exposed electrical conductors. U.S. and Canadian name: **friction tape.**

insulation (ˌɪnsjʊˈleɪʃən) *n.* **1.** Also called: **insulant** (ˈɪnsjʊlənt). material used to insulate a body, device, or region. **2.** the act or process of insulating.

insulator (ˈɪnsjʊˌleɪtə) *n.* any material or device that insulates, esp. a material with a very low electrical conductivity or thermal conductivity or something made of such a material.

insulin (ˈɪnsjʊlɪn) *n.* a protein hormone, secreted in the pancreas by the islets of Langerhans, that controls the concentration of glucose in the blood. Insulin deficiency results in diabetes mellitus. [C20: from New Latin *insula* islet (of the pancreas) + -IN]

insulin reaction *or* **shock** *n.* the condition in a diabetic resulting from an overdose of insulin, causing a sharp drop in the blood sugar level with tremor, profuse sweating, and convulsions. See also **hyperinsulinism.**

insult *vb.* (ɪnˈsʌlt). **1.** (*tr.*) to treat, mention, or speak to rudely; offend; affront. **2.** (*tr.*) *Obsolete.* to assault; attack. ~*n.* (ˈɪnsʌlt). **3.** an offensive or contemptuous remark or action; affront; slight. **4.** a person or thing producing the effect of an affront: *some television is an insult to intelligence.* **5.** *Med.* an injury or trauma. [C16: from Latin *insultāre* to jump upon, from IN-[2] + *saltāre* to jump] —**inˈsulter** *n.*

insuperable (ɪnˈsuːpərəbᵊl, -prəbᵊl, -ˈsjuː-) *adj.* incapable of being overcome; insurmountable. —**inˌsuperaˈbility** *or* **inˈsuperableness** *n.* —**inˈsuperably** *adv.*

insupportable (ˌɪnsəˈpɔːtəbᵊl) *adj.* **1.** incapable of being endured; intolerable; insufferable. **2.** incapable of being supported or justified; indefensible. —ˌ**insupˈportableness** *n.* —ˌ**insupˈportably** *adv.*

insuppressible (ˌɪnsəˈprɛsəbᵊl) *adj.* incapable of being suppressed, overcome, or muffled: *an insuppressible giggle.* —ˌ**insupˈpressibly** *adv.*

insurable interest *n. Law.* a financial or other interest in the life or property covered by an insurance contract, without which the contract cannot be enforced.

insurance (ɪnˈʃʊərəns, -ˈʃɔː-) *n.* **1. a.** the act, system, or business of providing financial protection for property, life, health, etc., against specified contingencies, such as death, loss, or damage, and involving payment of regular premiums in return for a policy guaranteeing such protection. **b.** the state of having such protection. **c.** Also called: **insurance policy.** the policy providing such protection. **d.** the pecuniary amount of such protection. **e.** the premium payable in return for such protection. **f.** (*as modifier*): *insurance agent; insurance broker; insurance company.* **2.** a means of protecting or safeguarding against risk or injury.

insure (ɪnˈʃʊə, -ˈʃɔː) *vb.* **1.** (often foll. by *against*) to guarantee or protect (against risk, loss, etc.): *we insured against disappointment by making an early reservation.* **2.** (often foll. by *against*) to issue (a person) with an insurance policy or take out an insurance policy (on): *his house was heavily insured against fire; after all his car accidents the company refuses to insure him again.* **3.** another word (esp. U.S.) for **ensure** (senses 1, 2). ~Also (rare) (for senses 1, 2): **ensure.** —**inˈsurable** *adj.* —**inˌsuraˈbility** *n.*

insured (ɪnˈʃʊəd, -ˈʃɔːd) *adj.* **1.** covered by insurance: *an insured risk.* ~*n.* **2.** the person, persons, or organization covered by an insurance policy.

insurer (ɪnˈʃʊərə, -ˈʃɔː-) *n.* **1.** a person or company offering insurance policies in return for premiums. **2.** a person or thing that insures.

insurgence (ɪnˈsɜːdʒəns) *n.* rebellion, uprising, or riot.

insurgent (ɪnˈsɜːdʒənt) *adj.* **1.** rebellious or in revolt, as against a government in power or the civil authorities. ~*n.* **2.** a person who takes part in an uprising or rebellion; insurrectionist. **3.** *International law.* a person or group that rises in revolt against an established government or authority but whose conduct does not amount to belligerency. [C18: from Latin *insurgēns* rising upon or against, from *insurgere* to rise up, from *surgere* to rise] —**inˈsurgency** *n.*

insurmountable (ˌɪnsəˈmaʊntəbᵊl) *adj.* incapable of being overcome; insuperable. —ˌ**insurˌmountaˈbility** *or* ˌ**insurˈmountableness** *n.* —ˌ**insurˈmountably** *adv.*

insurrection (ˌɪnsəˈrɛkʃən) *n.* the act or an instance of rebelling against a government in power or the civil authorities; insurgency. [C15: from Late Latin *insurrectiō*, from *insurgere* to rise up] —ˌ**insurˈrectional** *adj.* —ˌ**insurˈrectionary** *n., adj.* —ˌ**insurˈrectionism** *n.* —ˌ**insurˈrectionist** *n., adj.*

insusceptible (ˌɪnsəˈsɛptəbᵊl) *adj.* (when *postpositive,* usually foll. by *to*) not capable of being affected (by); not susceptible (to). —ˌ**insusˌceptiˈbility** *n.* —ˌ**insusˈceptibly** *adv.*

inswing (ˈɪnˌswɪŋ) *n. Cricket.* the movement of a bowled ball from off to leg through the air. Compare **outswing.**

inswinger (ˈɪnˌswɪŋə) *n.* **1.** *Cricket.* a ball bowled so as to move from off to leg through the air. **2.** *Soccer.* a ball kicked, esp. from a corner, so as to move through the air in a curve towards the goal or the centre.

int. *abbrev. for:* **1.** interest. **2.** interim. **3.** interior. **4.** internal. **5.** Also: **Int.** international. **6.** interpreter. **7.** intelligence (military).

intact (ɪnˈtækt) *adj.* untouched or unimpaired; left complete or perfect. [C15: from Latin *intactus* not touched, from *tangere* to touch] —**inˈtactness** *n.*

intaglio (ɪnˈtɑːlɪˌəʊ) *n., pl.* **-lios** *or* **-li** (-ljiː). **1.** a seal, gem, etc., ornamented with a sunken or incised design, as opposed to a design in relief. Compare **cameo.** **2.** the art or process of incised carving. **3.** a design, figure, or ornamentation carved, engraved, or etched into the surface of the material used. **4.** any of various printing techniques using an etched or engraved plate. The whole plate is smeared with ink, the surface wiped clean, and the ink in the recesses then transferred to the paper or other material. **5.** an incised die used to make a design in relief. [C17: from Italian, from *intagliare* to engrave, from *tagliare* to cut, from Late Latin *tāliāre;* see TAILOR] —**intagliated** (ɪnˈtɑːlɪˌeɪtɪd) *adj.*

intake (ˈɪnˌteɪk) *n.* **1.** a thing or a quantity taken in: *an intake of students.* **2.** the act of taking in. **3.** the opening through which fluid enters a duct or channel, esp. the air inlet of a jet engine. **4.** a ventilation shaft in a mine. **5.** a contraction or narrowing: *an intake in a garment.*

intangible (ɪnˈtændʒɪbᵊl) *adj.* **1.** incapable of being perceived by touch; impalpable. **2.** imprecise or unclear to the mind: *intangible ideas.* **3.** (of property or a business asset) saleable though not possessing intrinsic productive value. ~*n.* **4.** something that is intangible. —**inˌtangiˈbility** *or* **inˈtangibleness** *n.* —**inˈtangibly** *adv.*

intarsia (ɪnˈtɑːsɪə) *or* **tarsia** *n.* **1.** a decorative or pictorial mosaic of inlaid wood or sometimes ivory of a style developed in the Italian Renaissance and used esp. on wooden wall panels. **2.** the art or practice of making such mosaics. **3.** (in knitting) an individually worked motif. [C19: changed from Italian *intarsio*]

integer (ˈɪntɪdʒə) *n.* **1.** any rational number that can be expressed as the sum or difference of a finite number of units, being a member of the set …–3, –2, –1, 0, 1, 2, 3… **2.** an individual entity or whole unit. [C16: from Latin: untouched, entire, from *tangere* to touch]

integral *adj.* (ˈɪntɪgrəl, ɪnˈtɛgrəl). **1.** (often foll. by *to*) being an essential part (of); intrinsic (to). **2.** intact; entire. **3.** formed of constituent parts; united. **4.** *Maths.* **a.** of or involving an integral. **b.** involving or being an integer. ~*n.* (ˈɪntɪgrəl). **5.** *Maths.* the sum of a large number of infinitesimally small quantities, summed either between stated limits (**definite integral**) or in the absence of limits (**indefinite integral**). Symbol: ∫ **6.** a complete thing; whole. —**integrality** (ˌɪntɪˈgrælɪtɪ) *n.* —ˈ**integrally** *adv.*

integral calculus *n.* the branch of calculus concerned with the determination of integrals and their application to the solution of differential equations, the determination of areas and volumes, etc. Compare **differential calculus.**

integrand (ˈɪntɪˌgrænd) *n.* a mathematical function to be integrated. [C19: from Latin: to be integrated]

integrant (ˈɪntəgrənt) *adj.* **1.** part of a whole; integral; constituent. ~*n.* **2.** an integrant thing or part.

integrate *vb.* (ˈɪntɪˌgreɪt). **1.** to make or be made into a whole; incorporate or be incorporated. **2.** (*tr.*) to designate (a school, park, etc.) for use by all races or groups; desegregate. **3.** to amalgamate or mix (a racial or religious group) with an existing community. **4.** *Maths.* to perform an integration on (a quantity, expression, etc.). ~*adj.* (ˈɪntɪgrɪt). **5.** made up of parts; integrated. [C17: from Latin *integrāre;* see INTEGER] —**integrable** (ˈɪntəgrəbᵊl) *adj.* —ˌ**integraˈbility** *n.* —ˈ**inteˌgrative** *adj.*

integrated (ˈɪntɪˌgreɪtɪd) *adj.* **1.** characterized by integration. **2.** denoting a works which combines various processes normally carried out at different locations: *an integrated steelworks.* **3.** *Biology.* denoting a virus the DNA of which is incorporated into the chromosomes of the host cell.

integrated circuit *n.* a very small electronic circuit consisting of an assembly of elements made from a chip of semiconducting material, such as crystalline silicon.

integrated school *n.* (in New Zealand) a private or church school that has joined the state school system.

integration (ˌɪntɪˈgreɪʃən) *n.* **1.** the act of combining or adding parts to make a unified whole. **2.** the act of amalgamating a racial or religious group with an existing community. **3.** the combination of previously racially segregated social facilities into a nonsegregated system. **4.** *Psychol.* organization into a unified pattern, esp. of different aspects of the personality into a hierarchical system of functions. **5.** the assimilation of nutritive material by the body during the process of anabolism. **6.** *Maths.* an operation used in calculus in which the integral of a function or variable is determined; the inverse of differentiation. —ˌ**inteˈgrationist** *n.*

integrative bargaining (ˈɪntɪˌgreɪtɪv) *n. Industrial relations.* a type of bargaining in which all parties involved recognize that there are common problems requiring mutual resolution.

integrator (ˈɪntɪˌgreɪtə) *n.* **1.** a person or thing that integrates, esp. a mechanical instrument that determines the value of a definite integral, as the area under a curve. See also **planimeter.** **2.** *Computer technol.* **a.** an arithmetic component with two input variables, *x* and *y,* whose output variable *z* is proportional to the integral of *y* with respect to *x.* **b.** an arithmetic component whose output variable is proportional to the integral of the input variable with respect to elapsed time.

integrity (ɪnˈtɛgrɪtɪ) *n.* **1.** adherence to moral principles; honesty. **2.** the quality of being unimpaired; soundness. **3.** unity; wholeness. [C15: from Latin *integritās;* see INTEGER]

integument (ɪnˈtɛgjʊmənt) *n.* any outer protective layer or covering, such as a cuticle, seed coat, rind, or shell. [C17: from Latin *integumentum,* from *tegere* to cover] —**inˌteguˈmental** *or* **inˌteguˈmentary** *adj.*

intellect (ˈɪntɪˌlɛkt) *n.* **1.** the capacity for understanding, thinking, and reasoning, as distinct from feeling or wishing. **2.** a mind or intelligence, esp. a brilliant one: *his intellect is wasted on that job.* **3.** *Informal.* a person possessing a brilliant mind; brain. **4.** those possessing the greatest mental power: *the intellect of a nation.* [C14: from Latin *intellectus* comprehension, intellect, from *intellegere* to understand; see INTELLIGENCE] —ˌ**intelˈlective** *adj.* —ˌ**intelˈlectively** *adv.*

intellection (ˌɪntɪˈlɛkʃən) *n.* **1.** mental activity; thought. **2.** an idea or thought.

intellectual (ˌɪntɪˈlɛktʃʊəl) *adj.* **1.** of or relating to the intellect, as opposed to the emotions. **2.** appealing to or characteristic of people with a developed intellect: *intellectual literature.* **3.** expressing or enjoying mental activity. ~*n.* **4.** a person who enjoys mental activity and has highly developed tastes in art, literature, etc. **5.** a person who uses or works with his intellect. **6.** a highly intelligent person. —ˌ**intelˌlectuˈality** *or* ˌ**intelˈlectualness** *n.* —ˌ**intelˈlectually** *adv.*

intellectualism (ˌɪntɪˈlɛktʃʊəˌlɪzəm) *n.* **1.** development and exercise of the intellect. **2.** the placing of excessive value on the intellect, esp. with disregard for the emotions. **3.** *Philosophy.* **a.** the doctrine that reason is the ultimate criterion of knowledge. **b.** the doctrine that deliberate action is consequent on a process of conscious or subconscious reasoning. —ˌ**intelˈlectualist** *n., adj.* —ˌ**intelˌlectualˈistic** *adj.* —ˌ**intelˌlectualˈistically** *adv.*

intellectualize *or* **intellectualise** (ˌɪntɪˈlɛktʃʊəˌlaɪz) *vb.* **1.** to make or become intellectual. **2.** (*tr.*) to treat or consider in an intellectual way; rationalize. —ˌ**intelˌlectualiˈzation** *or* ˌ**intelˌlectualiˈsation** *n.* —ˌ**intelˈlectualˌizer** *or* ˌ**intelˈlectualˌiser** *n.*

intellectual property *n.* an intangible asset, such as a copyright or patent.

intelligence (ɪnˈtɛlɪdʒəns) *n.* **1.** the capacity for understanding; ability to perceive and comprehend meaning. **2.** good mental capacity: *a person of intelligence.* **3.** *Old-fashioned.* news; information. **4.** military information about enemies, spies, etc. **5.** a group or department that gathers or deals with such information. **6.** (*often cap.*) an intelligent being, esp. one that is not embodied. **7.** (*modifier*) of or relating to intelligence: *an intelligence network.* [C14: from Latin *intellegentia,* from *intellegere* to discern, comprehend, literally: choose between, from INTER- + *legere* to choose] —**inˌtelliˈgential** *adj.*

intelligence quotient *n.* a measure of the intelligence of an individual derived from results obtained from specially designed tests. The quotient is traditionally derived by dividing an individual's mental age by his chronological age and multiplying the result by 100. Abbrev.: **IQ.**

intelligencer (ɪnˈtɛlɪdʒənsə) *n. Archaic.* an informant or spy.

intelligence test *n.* any of a number of tests designed to measure a person's mental skills. See also **Binet-Simon scale.**

intelligent (ɪnˈtɛlɪdʒənt) *adj.* **1.** having or indicating intelligence. **2.** having high intelligence; clever. **3.** indicating high intelligence; perceptive: *an intelligent guess.* **4.** guided by reason; rational. **5.** (of computerized functions) able to modify action in the light of ongoing events. **6.** (*postpositive;* foll. by *of*) *Archaic.* having knowledge or information: *they were intelligent of his whereabouts.* —**inˈtelligently** *adv.*

intelligent card *n.* another name for **smart card.**

intelligent knowledge-based system *n.* a computer system in which the properties of a data base and an expert system are combined to enable the system to store and process data and make deductions from stored data. Abbrev.: **IKBS.**

intelligentsia (ɪnˌtɛlɪˈdʒɛntsɪə) *n.* (usually preceded by *the*) the educated or intellectual people in a society or community. [C20: from Russian *intelligentsiya,* from Latin *intellegentia* INTELLIGENCE]

intelligent terminal *n.* a computer operating terminal that can carry out some data processing, as well as sending data to and receiving it from a central processor.

intelligible (ɪnˈtɛlɪdʒəbᵊl) *adj.* **1.** able to be understood; comprehensible. **2.** *Philosophy.* **a.** capable of being apprehended by the mind or intellect alone. **b.** (in metaphysical systems such as those of Plato or Kant) denoting that metaphysical realm which is accessible to the intellect as opposed to the world of mere phenomena accessible to the senses. [C14: from Latin *intellegibilis;* see INTELLECT] —**inˌtelligiˈbility** *or* **inˈtelligibleness** *n.* —**inˈtelligibly** *adv.*

Intelsat (ˈɪntɛlˌsæt) *n.* any of the series of communications satellites operated by the International Telecommunications Satellite Consortium.

intemerate (ɪnˈtɛmərɪt) *adj. Rare.* not defiled; pure; unsullied. [C15: from Latin *intemerātus* undefiled, pure, from IN-[1] + *temerāre* to darken, violate, from *temere* rashly] —**inˈtemerately** *adv.* —**inˈtemerateness** *n.*

intemperate (ɪnˈtɛmpərɪt, -prɪt) *adj.* **1.** consuming alcoholic drink habitually or to excess. **2.** indulging bodily appetites to excess; immoderate. **3.** unrestrained: *intemperate rage.* **4.** extreme or severe: *an intemperate climate.* —**inˈtemperance** *or* **inˈtemperateness** *n.* —**inˈtemperately** *adv.*

intend (ɪnˈtɛnd) *vb.* **1.** (*may take a clause as object*) to propose or plan (something or to do something); have in mind; mean. **2.** (*tr.;* often foll. by *for*) to design or destine (for a certain purpose, person, etc.): *that shot was intended for the President.* **3.** (*tr.*) to mean to express or indicate: *what do his words intend?* **4.** (*intr.*) to have a purpose as specified; mean: *he intends well.* **5.** (*tr.*) *Archaic.* to direct or turn (the attention, eyes, etc.). [C14: from Latin *intendere* to stretch forth, give one's attention to, from *tendere* to stretch] —**inˈtender** *n.*

intendance (ɪnˈtɛndəns) *n.* **1.** any of various public departments, esp. in France. **2.** a less common word for **superintendence.**

intendancy (ɪnˈtɛndənsɪ) *n.* **1.** the position or work of an intendant. **2.** intendants collectively. **3.** *History.* the district or area administered by an intendant.

intendant (ɪnˈtɛndənt) *n.* **1.** *History.* a provincial or colonial official of France, Spain, or Portugal. **2.** a senior administrator in some countries, esp. in Latin America. **3.** a superintendent or manager.

intended (ɪnˈtɛndɪd) *adj.* **1.** planned or future. ~*n.* **2.** *Informal.* a person whom one is to marry; fiancé or fiancée.

intendment (ɪnˈtɛndmənt) *n.* **1.** the meaning of something as fixed or understood by the law. **2.** *Obsolete.* intention, design, or purpose.

intenerate (ɪnˈtɛnəˌreɪt) *vb.* (*tr.*) *Rare.* to soften or make tender. [C16: from IN-[2] + Latin *tener* delicate, TENDER[1]] —**inˌtenerˈation** *n.*

intens. *abbrev. for:* **1.** intensifier. **2.** intensive.

intense (ɪnˈtɛns) *adj.* **1.** of extreme force, strength, degree, or amount: *intense heat.* **2.** characterized by deep or forceful feelings: *an intense person.* [C14: from Latin *intensus* stretched, from *intendere* to stretch out; see INTEND] —**inˈtensely** *adv.* —**inˈtenseness** *n.*

intensifier (ɪnˈtɛnsɪˌfaɪə) *n.* **1.** a person or thing that intensifies. **2.** a word, esp. an adjective or adverb, that has little semantic content of its own but that serves to intensify the meaning of the word or phrase that it modifies: *awfully* and *up* are intensifiers in the phrases *awfully sorry* and *cluttered up.* **3.** a substance, esp. one containing silver or uranium, used to increase the density of a photographic film or plate. Compare **reducer** (sense 1).

intensify (ɪnˈtɛnsɪˌfaɪ) *vb.* **-fies, -fying, -fied.** **1.** to make or become intense or more intense. **2.** (*tr.*) to increase the density of (a photographic film or plate). —**inˌtensifiˈcation** *n.*

intension (ɪnˈtɛnʃən) *n.* **1.** *Logic.* **a.** the set of characteristics or properties by which the referent or referents of a given word are determined: thus, the intension of *marsupial* is the set containing the characteristics *suckling its young* and *having a pouch.* Compare **extension** (sense 11). **b.** See **subjective intension.** **2.** a rare word for **intensity, determination,** or **intensification.**

intensional (ɪnˈtɛnʃənᵊl) *adj. Logic.* (of a predicate) incapable of explanation solely in terms of the set of objects to which it is applicable; requiring explanation in terms of meaning or understanding. Compare **extensional.** See also **opaque context, Electra paradox.** —**inˈtensionally** *adv.*

intensional object *n. Logic, philosophy.* the object of a propositional attitude that may or may not exist, as in *Robert is dreaming of the pot of gold at the end of the rainbow.* This must be an intensional (or opaque) context, for otherwise, since there is no pot of gold, Robert would be dreaming of nothing.

intensity (ɪnˈtɛnsɪtɪ) *n., pl.* **-ties.** **1.** the state or quality of being intense. **2.** extreme force, degree, or amount. **3.** *Physics.* **a.** a measure of field strength or of the energy transmitted by radiation. See **radiant intensity, luminous intensity.** **b.** (of sound in a specified direction) the average rate of flow of sound energy, usually in watts, for one period through unit area at right angles to the specified direction. Symbol: *I* **4.** Also called: **earthquake intensity.** *Geology.* a measure of the size of an earthquake based on observation of the effects of the shock at the earth's surface. Specified on the Mercalli scale. See **Mercalli scale, Richter scale.**

intensive (ɪnˈtɛnsɪv) *adj.* **1.** of, relating to, or characterized by intensity: *intensive training.* **2.** (*usually in combination*) using one factor of production proportionately more than others, as specified: *capital-intensive; labour-intensive.* **3.** *Agriculture.* involving or farmed using large amounts of capital or labour to increase production from a particular area. Compare **extensive** (sense 3). **4.** denoting or relating to a grammatical intensifier. **5.** denoting or belonging to a class of pronouns used to emphasize a noun or personal pronoun, such as *himself* in the sentence *John himself did it.* In English, intensive pronouns are identical in form with reflexive pronouns. **6.** of or relating to intension. **7.** *Physics.* of or relating to a property, measurement, etc., that is independent of mass. Compare **extensive** (sense 4). ~*n.* **8.** an intensifier or intensive pronoun or grammatical construction. —**inˈtensively** *adv.* —**inˈtensiveness** *n.*

intensive care *n.* extensive and continuous care and treatment provided for an acutely ill patient, usually in a specially designated section (**intensive care unit**) of a hospital.

intent (ɪnˈtɛnt) *n.* **1.** something that is intended; aim; purpose; design. **2.** the act of intending. **3.** *Law.* the will or purpose with which one does an act. **4.** implicit meaning; connotation. **5. to all intents and purposes.** for all practical purposes; virtually. ~*adj.* **6.** firmly fixed; determined; concentrated: *an intent look.* **7.** (*postpositive;* usually foll. by *on* or *upon*) having the fixed intention (of); directing one's mind or energy (to): *intent on committing a crime.* [C13 (in the sense: intention): from Late Latin *intentus* aim, intent, from Latin: a stretching out; see INTEND] —**inˈtently** *adv.* —**inˈtentness** *n.*

intention (ɪnˈtɛnʃən) *n.* **1.** a purpose or goal; aim: *it is his intention to reform.* **2.** *Law.* the resolve or design with which a person does or refrains from doing an act, a necessary ingredient of certain offences. **3.** *Med.* a natural healing process, as by **first intention,** in which the edges of a wound cling together with no tissue between, or by **second intention,** in which the wound edges adhere with granulation tissue. **4.** (*usually pl.*) design or purpose with respect to a proposal of marriage (esp. in the phrase **honourable intentions**). **5.** an archaic word for **meaning** or **intentness.**

intentional (ɪnˈtɛnʃənᵊl) *adj.* **1.** performed by or expressing intention; deliberate. **2.** of or relating to intention or purpose. **3.** *Philosophy.* **a.** of or relating to the capacity of the mind to refer to different kinds of objects. **b.** (of an object) existing only as the object of some mental attitude rather than in reality, as *a unicorn* in *she hopes to meet a unicorn.* See also **intensional.** —**inˌtentionˈality** *n.* —**inˈtentionally** *adv.*

inter (ɪnˈtɜː) *vb.* **-ters, -terring, -terred.** (*tr.*) to place (a body) in the earth; bury, esp. with funeral rites. [C14: from Old French *enterrer,* from Latin IN-[2] + *terra* earth]

inter. *abbrev. for* intermediate.

inter- *prefix.* **1.** between or among: *international.* **2.** together, mutually, or reciprocally: *interdependent; interchange.* [from Latin]

interact (ˌɪntərˈækt) *vb.* (*intr.*) to act on or in close relation with each other.

interaction (ˌɪntərˈækʃən) *n.* **1.** a mutual or reciprocal action or influence. **2.** *Physics.* the transfer of energy between elemen-

ˌ**interˌacaˈdemic** *adj.*

tary particles, between a particle and a field, or between fields. See **strong interaction, electromagnetic interaction, fundamental interaction, gravitational interaction, weak interaction,** and **electroweak interaction.** —ˌ**interˈactional** *adj.*

interactionism (ˌɪntərˈækʃəˌnɪzəm) *n. Philosophy.* the dualistic doctrine that holds that mind and body have a causal effect upon one another, as when pricking one's finger (physical) causes pain (mental), or an embarrassing memory (mental) causes one to blush (physical). Compare **parallelism** (sense 3).

interactive (ˌɪntərˈæktɪv) *adj.* **1.** allowing or relating to continuous two-way transfer of information between a user and the central point of a communication system, such as a computer or television. **2.** (of two or more persons, forces, etc.) acting upon or in close relation with each other; interacting. —ˌ**interacˈtivity** *n.*

interactive video *n.* a computer-optical disk system that displays still or moving video images as determined by computer program and user needs.

inter alia *Latin.* (ˈɪntər ˈeɪlɪə) *adv.* among other things.

inter alios *Latin.* (ˈɪntər ˈeɪlɪəʊs) *adv.* among other people.

interatomic (ˌɪntərəˈtɒmɪk) *adj.* existing or occurring between or among atoms. Compare **intra-atomic.**

interbedded (ˌɪntəˈbɛdɪd) *adj. Geology.* occurring between beds, esp. (of laval rock) occurring between strata of a different origin.

interbrain (ˈɪntəˌbreɪn) *n. Anatomy.* a nontechnical word for **diencephalon.**

interbreed (ˌɪntəˈbriːd) *vb.* **-breeds, -breeding, -bred. 1.** (*intr.*) to breed within a single family or strain so as to produce particular characteristics in the offspring. **2.** another term for **crossbreed** (sense 1).

interbroker dealer (ˌɪntəˈbrəʊkə) *n. Stock Exchange.* a specialist who matches the needs of different market makers and facilitates dealings between them.

intercalary (ɪnˈtɜːkələrɪ) *adj.* **1.** (of a day, month, etc.) inserted in the calendar. **2.** (of a particular year) having one or more days inserted. **3.** inserted, introduced, or interpolated. **4.** *Botany.* growing between the upper branches and the lower branches or bracts on a stem. [C17: from Latin *intercalārius;* see INTERCALATE] —**inˈtercalarily** *adv.*

intercalate (ɪnˈtɜːkəˌleɪt) *vb.* (*tr.*) **1.** to insert (one or more days) into the calendar. **2.** to interpolate or insert. [C17: from Latin *intercalāre* to insert, proclaim that a day has been inserted, from INTER- + *calāre* to proclaim] —**inˌtercaˈlation** *n.* —**inˈtercalative** *adj.*

intercede (ˌɪntəˈsiːd) *vb.* (*intr.*) **1.** (often foll. by *in*) to come between parties or act as mediator or advocate: *to intercede in the strike.* **2.** *Roman history.* (of a tribune or other magistrate) to interpose a veto. [C16: from Latin *intercēdere* to intervene, from INTER- + *cēdere* to move] —ˌ**interˈceder** *n.*

intercellular (ˌɪntəˈsɛljʊlə) *adj. Biology.* between or among cells: *intercellular fluid.*

intercensal (ˌɪntəˈsɛnsəl) *adj.* (of population figures, etc.) estimated at a time between official censuses. [C19: from INTER- + *censal,* irregularly formed from CENSUS]

intercept *vb.* (ˌɪntəˈsɛpt). (*tr.*) **1.** to stop, deflect, or seize on the way from one place to another; prevent from arriving or proceeding. **2.** *Sport.* to seize or cut off (a pass) on its way from one opponent to another. **3.** *Maths.* to cut off, mark off, or bound (some part of a line, curve, plane, or surface). ~*n.* (ˈɪntəˌsɛpt). **4.** *Maths.* **a.** a point at which two figures intersect. **b.** the distance from the origin to the point at which a line, curve, or surface cuts a coordinate axis. **c.** an intercepted segment. **5.** *Sport, U.S. and Canadian.* the act of intercepting an opponent's pass. [C16: from Latin *intercipere* to seize before arrival, from INTER- + *capere* to take] —ˌ**interˈception** *n.* —ˌ**interˈceptive** *adj.*

interceptor *or* **intercepter** (ˌɪntəˈsɛptə) *n.* **1.** a person or thing that intercepts. **2.** a fast highly manoeuvrable fighter aircraft used to intercept enemy aircraft.

intercession (ˌɪntəˈsɛʃən) *n.* **1.** the act or an instance of interceding. **2.** the act of interceding or offering petitionary prayer to God on behalf of others. **3.** such petitionary prayer. **4.** *Roman history.* the interposing of a veto by a tribune or other magistrate. [C16: from Latin *intercessio;* see INTERCEDE] —ˌ**interˈcessional** *or* ˌ**interˈcessory** *adj.* —ˌ**interˈcessor** *n.* —ˌ**intercesˈsorial** *adj.*

interchange *vb.* (ˌɪntəˈtʃeɪndʒ). **1.** to change places or cause to change places; alternate; exchange; switch. ~*n.* (ˈɪntəˌtʃeɪndʒ). **2.** the act of interchanging; exchange or alternation. **3.** a motorway junction of interconnecting roads and bridges designed to prevent streams of traffic crossing one another. —ˌ**interˈchangeable** *adj.* —ˌ**interˌchangeaˈbility** *or* ˌ**interˈchangeableness** *n.* —ˌ**interˈchangeably** *adv.*

intercity (ˌɪntəˈsɪtɪ) (in Britain) ~*adj.* **1.** denoting a fast train or rail service between main towns. ~*n.* **2.** such a train or rail service.

interclavicle (ˌɪntəˈklævɪkəl) *n.* a membrane bone between and beneath the clavicles, present in some fossil amphibians, all reptiles except snakes, and monotremes. —**interclavicular** (ˌɪntəkləˈvɪkjʊlə) *adj.*

intercolumniation (ˌɪntəkəˌlʌmnɪˈeɪʃən) *n. Architect.* **1.** the horizontal distance between two adjacent columns. **2.** the system of spacing for a set of columns. [C17: from Latin *intercolumnium* space between two columns] —ˌ**intercoˈlumnar** *adj.*

intercom (ˈɪntəˌkɒm) *n. Informal.* an internal telephone system for communicating within a building, an aircraft, etc. [C20: short for *intercommunication*]

intercommunicate (ˌɪntəkəˈmjuːnɪˌkeɪt) *vb.* (*intr.*) **1.** to communicate mutually. **2.** to interconnect, as two rooms. —ˌ**intercomˈmunicable** *adj.* —ˌ**intercomˌmunicaˈbility** *n.* —ˌ**intercomˌmuniˈcation** *n.* —ˌ**intercomˈmunicative** *adj.* —ˌ**intercomˈmuniˌcator** *n.*

intercommunion (ˌɪntəkəˈmjuːnjən) *n.* association between Churches, involving esp. mutual reception of Holy Communion.

intercontinental ballistic missile (ˌɪntəˌkɒntɪˈnɛntəl) *n.* a missile that follows a ballistic trajectory and has the range to carry a nuclear bomb over 5500 km. Abbrev.: **ICBM.**

intercooler (ˌɪntəˈkuːlə) *n.* a heat exchanger used in a supercharger or turbocharger.

intercostal (ˌɪntəˈkɒstəl) *adj. Anatomy.* between the ribs: *intercostal muscles.* [C16: via New Latin from Latin INTER- + *costa* rib]

intercourse (ˈɪntəˌkɔːs) *n.* **1.** communication or exchange between individuals; mutual dealings. **2.** See **sexual intercourse.** [C15: from Medieval Latin *intercursus* business, from Latin *intercurrere* to run between, from *currere* to run]

intercrop (ˌɪntəˈkrɒp) *n.* **1.** a crop grown between the rows of another crop. ~*vb.* **-crops, -cropping, -cropped. 2.** to grow (one crop) between the rows of (another).

intercross (ˌɪntəˈkrɒs) *vb., n.* another word for **crossbreed.**

intercurrent (ˌɪntəˈkʌrənt) *adj.* **1.** occurring during or in between; intervening. **2.** *Pathol.* (of a disease) occurring during the course of another disease. —ˌ**interˈcurrence** *n.* —ˌ**interˈcurrently** *adv.*

intercut (ˌɪntəˈkʌt) *vb.* **-cuts, -cutting, -cut.** *Films.* another word for **crosscut.**

interdental (ˌɪntəˈdɛntəl) *adj.* **1.** situated between teeth. **2.** *Phonetics.* (of a consonant) pronounced with the tip of the tongue lying between the upper and lower front teeth, as for the *th* sounds in English *thin* and *then.* —ˌ**interˈdentally** *adv.*

interdict *n.* (ˈɪntəˌdɪkt, -ˌdaɪt). **1.** *R.C. Church.* the exclusion of a person or all persons in a particular place from certain sacraments and other benefits, although not from communion. **2.** *Civil law.* any order made by a court or official prohibiting an act. **3.** *Scots Law.* an order having the effect of an injunction. **4.** *Roman history.* **a.** an order of a praetor commanding or forbidding an act. **b.** the procedure by which this order was sought. ~*vb.* (ˌɪntəˈdɪkt, -ˈdaɪt). (*tr.*) **5.** to place under legal or ecclesiastical sanction; prohibit; forbid. **6.** *Military.* to destroy (an enemy's lines of communication) by firepower. [C13: from Latin *interdictum* prohibition, from *interdīcere* to forbid, from INTER- + *dīcere* to say] —ˌ**interˈdictive** *or* ˌ**interˈdictory** *adj.* —ˌ**interˈdictively** *adv.* —ˌ**interˈdictor** *n.*

interdiction (ˌɪntəˈdɪkʃən) *n.* **1.** the act of interdicting or state of being interdicted. **2.** an interdict.

interdict list *n.* another name for **Indian list.**

interdigitate (ˌɪntəˈdɪdʒɪˌteɪt) *vb.* (*intr.*) to interlock like the fingers of clasped hands. [C19: from INTER- + Latin *digitus* (see DIGIT) + -ATE[1]]

interdisciplinary (ˌɪntəˈdɪsɪˌplɪnərɪ) *adj.* involving two or more academic disciplines.

interest (ˈɪntrɪst, -tərɪst) *n.* **1.** the sense of curiosity about or concern with something or someone. **2.** the power of stimulating such a sense: *to have great interest.* **3.** the quality of such stimulation. **4.** something in which one is interested; a hobby or pursuit. **5.** (*often pl.*) benefit; advantage: *in one's own interest.* **6.** (*often pl.*) **a.** a right, share, or claim, esp. in a business or property. **b.** the business, property, etc., in which a person has such concern. **7. a.** a charge for the use of credit or borrowed money. **b.** such a charge expressed as a percentage per time unit of the sum borrowed or used. **8.** (*often pl.*) a section of a community, etc., whose members have common aims: *we must not offend the landed interest.* **9. declare an interest.** to make known one's connection, esp. a prejudicial connection, with an affair. ~*vb.* (*tr.*) **10.** to arouse or excite the curiosity or concern of. **11.** to cause to become involved in something; concern. [C15: from Latin: it concerns, from *interesse;* from INTER- + *esse* to be]

ˌ**interalˈlied** *adj.*
ˌ**interˈbank** *adj.*
ˌ**interbelˈligerent** *adj.*
ˌ**interˈblend** *vb.*
ˌ**interˈbranch** *adj.*
ˌ**interˈcaste** *adj.*
ˌ**interˈclasp** *vb.*
ˌ**interˈclass** *adj.*
ˌ**interˈclub** *adj.*
ˌ**intercolˈlegiate** *adj.*
ˌ**intercoˈlonial** *adj.*
ˌ**intercomˈmunity** *adj.*
ˌ**interˈcompany** *adj.*
ˌ**interconˈnect** *vb.*
ˌ**interconˈnection** *n.*
ˌ**interˌconsoˈnantal** *adj.*
ˌ**interˌcontiˈnental** *adj.*
ˌ**interconˈvertible** *adj.*
ˌ**interˈcounty** *adj.*
ˌ**interˈcrural** *adj.*
ˌ**interdeˌnomiˈnational** *adj.*
ˌ**interˌdepartˈmental** *adj.*
ˌ**interˌdepartˈmentally** *adv.*
ˌ**interdeˈpend** *vb.*
ˌ**interdeˈpendence** *n.*
ˌ**interdeˈpendency** *n.*
ˌ**interdeˈpendent** *adj.*
ˌ**interdeˈpendently** *adv.*
ˌ**interˈdigital** *adj.*
ˌ**interˈdigitally** *adv.*

interested ('ɪntrɪstɪd, -tərɪs-) *adj.* **1.** showing or having interest. **2.** (*usually prenominal*) personally involved or implicated: *the interested parties met to discuss the business.* —**'interestedly** *adv.* —**'interestedness** *n.*

interesting ('ɪntrɪstɪŋ, -tərɪs-) *adj.* inspiring interest; absorbing. —**'interestingly** *adv.* —**'interestingness** *n.*

interface *n.* ('ɪntəˌfeɪs). **1.** *Physical chem.* a surface that forms the boundary between two bodies, liquids, or chemical phases. **2.** a common point or boundary between two things, subjects, etc. **3.** an electrical circuit linking one device, esp. a computer, with another. ~*vb.* (ˌɪntə'feɪs). **4.** (*tr.*) to design or adapt the input and output configurations of (two electronic devices) so that they may work together compatibly. **5.** to be or become an interface (with). **6.** to be or become interactive (with). —**interfacial** (ˌɪntə'feɪʃəl) *adj.* —ˌ**inter'facially** *adv.*

interfacing ('ɪntəˌfeɪsɪŋ) *n.* **1.** a piece of fabric sewn beneath the facing of a garment, usually at the neck, armholes, etc., to give shape and firmness. **2.** another name for **interlining.**

interfascicular (ˌɪntəfə'sɪkjʊlə) *adj. Botany.* between the vascular bundles of the stem: *interfascicular cambium.*

interfere (ˌɪntə'fɪə) *vb.* (*intr.*) **1.** (often foll. by *in*) to interpose, esp. meddlesomely or unwarrantedly; intervene. **2.** (often foll. by *with*) to come between or in opposition; hinder; obstruct. **3.** (foll. by *with*) *Euphemistic.* to assault sexually. **4.** to strike one against the other, as a horse's legs. **5.** *Physics.* to cause or produce interference. [C16: from Old French *s'entreferir* to collide, from *entre-* INTER- + *ferir* to strike, from Latin *ferīre*] —ˌ**inter'ferer** *n.* —ˌ**inter'fering** *adj.* —ˌ**inter'feringly** *adv.*

interference (ˌɪntə'fɪərəns) *n.* **1.** the act or an instance of interfering. **2.** *Physics.* the process in which two or more coherent waves combine to form a resultant wave in which the displacement at any point is the vector sum of the displacements of the individual waves. If the individual waves converge the resultant is a system of fringes. Two waves of equal or nearly equal intensity moving in opposite directions combine to form a standing wave. **3.** Also called: **radio interference.** any undesired signal that tends to interfere with the reception of radio waves. **4.** *Aeronautics.* the effect on the flow pattern around a body of objects in the vicinity. —**interferential** (ˌɪntəfə'rɛnʃəl) *adj.*

interference fit *n. Engineering.* a match between the size and shape of two parts, such that force is required for assembly as one part is slightly larger than the other.

interferometer (ˌɪntəfə'rɒmɪtə) *n.* **1.** *Physics.* any acoustic, optical, or microwave instrument that uses interference patterns or fringes to make accurate measurements of wavelength, wave velocity, distance, etc. **2.** *Astronomy.* a radio telescope consisting of two or more radio antennas separated by a known distance and connected to the same receiver so that radio waves from a source in space undergo interference, enabling the position of the source to be accurately determined. —**interferometric** (ˌɪntəˌfɛrə'mɛtrɪk) *adj.* —ˌ**interˌfero'metrically** *adv.* —ˌ**interfer'ometry** *n.*

interferon (ˌɪntə'fɪərɒn) *n. Biochem.* any of a family of proteins made by cells in response to virus infection that prevent the growth of the virus. Some interferons can prevent cell growth and have been tested for use in cancer therapy. [C20: from INTERFERE + -ON]

interfertile (ˌɪntə'fɜːtaɪl) *adj.* (of plants and animals) able to interbreed. —ˌ**interfer'tility** *n.*

interfile (ˌɪntə'faɪl) *vb.* (*tr.*) **1.** to place (one or more items) among other items in a file or arrangement. **2.** to combine (two or more sets of items) in one file or arrangement.

interflow (ˌɪntə'fləʊ) *vb.* (*intr.*) to flow together; merge.

interfluent (ɪn'tɜːflʊənt) *adj.* flowing together; merging. [C17: from Latin *interfluere,* from INTER- + *fluere* to flow]

interfluve ('ɪntəˌfluːv) *n.* a ridge or area of land dividing two river valleys. [C20: back formation from *interfluvial,* from INTER- + Latin *fluvius* river] —ˌ**inter'fluvial** *adj.*

interfuse (ˌɪntə'fjuːz) *vb.* **1.** to diffuse or mix throughout or become so diffused or mixed; intermingle. **2.** to blend or fuse or become blended or fused. —ˌ**inter'fusion** *n.*

interglacial (ˌɪntə'gleɪsɪəl, -ʃəl) *adj.* **1.** occurring or formed between periods of glacial action. ~*n.* **2.** a period of comparatively warm climate between two glaciations, esp. of the Pleistocene epoch.

intergrade *vb.* (ˌɪntə'greɪd). **1.** (*intr.*) (esp. of biological species, etc.) to merge one into another. ~*n.* ('ɪntəˌgreɪd). **2.** an intermediate stage or form. —ˌ**intergra'dation** *n.* —ˌ**intergra'dational** *adj.* —ˌ**inter'gradient** *adj.*

interim ('ɪntərɪm) *adj.* **1.** (*prenominal*) temporary, provisional, or intervening: *interim measures to deal with the emergency.* ~*n.* **2.** (usually preceded by *the*) the intervening time; the meantime (esp. in the phrase **in the interim**). ~*adv.* **3.** *Rare.* meantime. [C16: from Latin: meanwhile]

Interim Standard Atmosphere *n.* an agreed theoretical description of the atmosphere for altitudes between 50 and 80 km, pending refinement by further measurements. See **International Standard Atmosphere.**

interior (ɪn'tɪərɪə) *n.* **1.** a part, surface, or region that is inside or on the inside: *the interior of Africa.* **2.** inner character or nature. **3.** a film or scene shot inside a building, etc. **4.** a picture of the inside of a room or building, as in a painting or stage set. **5.** the inside of a building or room, with respect to design and decoration. ~*adj.* **6.** of, situated on, or suitable for the inside; inner. **7.** coming or acting from within; internal. **8.** of or involving a nation's domestic affairs; internal. **9.** (esp. of one's spiritual or mental life) secret or private; not observable. [C15: from Latin (adj.), comparative of *inter* within] —**in'teriorly** *adv.*

Interior (ɪn'tɪərɪə) *n.* (*in titles; usually preceded by the*) the domestic or internal affairs of any of certain countries: *Department of the Interior.*

interior angle *n.* **1.** an angle of a polygon contained between two adjacent sides. **2.** any of the four angles made by a transversal that lie inside the region between the two intersected lines.

interior decoration *n.* **1.** the colours, furniture, etc., of the interior of a house, etc. **2.** Also called: **interior design.** the art or business of an interior decorator.

interior decorator *n.* **1.** Also called: **interior designer.** a person whose profession is the planning of the decoration and furnishings of the interior of houses, shops, etc. **2.** a person whose profession is the painting and wallpapering of houses.

interiorize *or* **interiorise** (ɪn'tɪərɪəˌraɪz) *vb.* (*tr.*) another word for **internalize.**

interior monologue *n.* a literary attempt to present the mental processes of a character before they are formed into regular patterns of speech or logical sequence. See also **stream of consciousness.**

interior-sprung *adj.* (esp. of a mattress) containing springs.

interj. *abbrev. for* interjection.

interjacent (ˌɪntə'dʒeɪsᵊnt) *adj.* located in between; intervening. [C16: from Latin *interjacēnt-,* from *interjacēre,* from INTER- + *jacēre* to lie]

interject (ˌɪntə'dʒɛkt) *vb.* (*tr.*) **1.** to interpose abruptly or sharply; interrupt with; throw in: *she interjected clever remarks.* **2.** *Archaic.* to come between; interpose. [C16: from Latin *interjicere* to place between, from *jacere* to throw] —ˌ**inter'jector** *n.*

interjection (ˌɪntə'dʒɛkʃən) *n.* **1.** a word or remark expressing emotion; exclamation. **2.** the act of interjecting. **3.** a word or phrase that is characteristically used in syntactic isolation and that usually expresses sudden emotion; expletive. Abbrev.: **interj.** —ˌ**inter'jectional,** ˌ**inter'jectory,** *or* ˌ**inter'jectural** *adj.* —ˌ**inter'jectionally** *adv.*

interlace (ˌɪntə'leɪs) *vb.* **1.** to join together (patterns, fingers, etc.) by crossing, as if woven; intertwine. **2.** (*tr.*) to mingle or blend in an intricate way. **3.** (*tr.; usually foll. by with*) to change the pattern of; diversify; intersperse: *to interlace a speech with humour.* —**interlacedly** (ˌɪntə'leɪsɪdlɪ) *adv.* —ˌ**inter'lacement** *n.*

interlaced scanning *n.* a system of scanning a television picture, first along the even-numbered lines, then along the odd-numbered lines, in one complete scan.

interlaminate (ˌɪntə'læmɪˌneɪt) *vb.* (*tr.*) to place, stick, or insert (a sheet, layer, etc.) between (other layers). —ˌ**inter'laminar** *adj.* —ˌ**interˌlami'nation** *n.*

interlap (ˌɪntə'læp) *vb.* **-laps, -lapping, -lapped.** a less common word for **overlap.**

interlard (ˌɪntə'lɑːd) *vb.* (*tr.*) **1.** to scatter thickly in or between; intersperse: *to interlard one's writing with foreign phrases.* **2.** to occur frequently in; be scattered in or through: *foreign phrases interlard his writings.*

interlay *vb.* (ˌɪntə'leɪ). **-lays, -laying, -laid** (-'leɪd). **1.** (*tr.*) to insert (layers) between; interpose: *to interlay gold among the silver; to interlay the silver with gold.* ~*n.* ('ɪntəˌleɪ). **2.** material, such as paper, placed between a printing plate and its base, either all over to bring it up to type height, or in places to achieve the correct printing pressure all over the plate.

interleaf ('ɪntəˌliːf) *n., pl.* **-leaves.** a blank leaf inserted between the leaves of a book.

interleave (ˌɪntə'liːv) *vb.* (*tr.*) **1.** (often foll. by *with*) to intersperse (with), esp. alternately, as the illustrations in a book (with protective leaves). **2.** to provide (a book) with blank leaves for notes, etc., or to protect illustrations.

interleukin (ˌɪntə'luːkɪn) *n.* a substance extracted from white blood cells that stimulates their activity against infection and may be used to combat some forms of cancer.

interlibrary loan ('ɪntəˌlaɪbrərɪ) *n.* **1.** a system by which libraries borrow publications from other libraries. **2. a.** an instance of such borrowing. **b.** a publication so borrowed.

interline[1] (ˌɪntə'laɪn) *or* **interlineate** (ˌɪntə'lɪnɪˌeɪt) *vb.* (*tr.*) to write or print (matter) between the lines of (a text, book, etc.). —'**interˌlining** *or* ˌ**interˌline'ation** *n.*

interline[2] (ˌɪntə'laɪn) *vb.* (*tr.*) to provide (a part of a garment, such as a collar or cuff) with a second lining, esp. of stiffened material. —'**interˌliner** *n.*

interlinear (ˌɪntə'lɪnɪə) *or* **interlineal** *adj.* **1.** written or printed between lines of text. **2.** written or printed with the text in

ˌ**inter'factional** *adj.*
ˌ**interfi'brillar** *adj.*
ˌ**inter'fibrous** *adj.*
ˌ**inter'fold** *vb.*
ˌ**interga'lactic** *adj.*
ˌ**interˌgovern'mental** *adj.*
ˌ**inter'group** *adj.*
ˌ**interi'onic** *adj.*
ˌ**inter'knit** *vb.,* -'**knits,** -'**knitting,** -'**knitted** *or* -'**knit.**

different languages or versions on alternate lines. —ˌinter'linearly *or* ˌinter'lineally *adv.*

interlingua (ˌɪntə'lɪŋgwə) *n.* **1.** (*usually cap.*) an artificial language based on words common to English and the Romance languages. **2.** any artificial language used to represent the meaning of natural languages, as for purposes of machine translation. [C20: from Italian, from INTER- + *lingua* language]

interlining ('ɪntəˌlaɪnɪŋ) *n.* the material used to interline parts of garments, now often made of reinforced paper.

interlock *vb.* (ˌɪntə'lɒk). **1.** to join or be joined firmly, as by a mutual interconnection of parts. ~*n.* ('ɪntəˌlɒk). **2.** the act of interlocking or the state of being interlocked. **3.** a device, esp. one operated electromechanically, used in a logic circuit to prevent an activity being initiated unless preceded by certain events. **4.** a closely knitted fabric. ~*adj.* ('ɪntəˌlɒk). **5.** (of fabric) closely knitted. —**'interˌlocker** *n.*

interlocking directorates *pl. n.* boards of directors of different companies having sufficient members in common to ensure that the companies involved are under the same control.

interlocution (ˌɪntəlɒ'kju:ʃən) *n.* conversation, discussion, or dialogue.

interlocutor (ˌɪntə'lɒkjʊtə) *n.* **1.** a person who takes part in a conversation. **2.** Also called: **middleman.** the man in the centre of a troupe of minstrels who engages the others in talk or acts as announcer. **3.** *Scots Law.* a decree by a judge. —ˌ**inter'locutress,** ˌ**inter'locutrice,** *or* ˌ**inter'locutrix** *fem. n.*

interlocutory (ˌɪntə'lɒkjʊtərɪ, -trɪ) *adj.* **1.** *Law.* pronounced during the course of proceedings; provisional: *an interlocutory injunction.* **2.** interposed, as into a conversation, narrative, etc. **3.** of, relating to, or characteristic of dialogue. —ˌ**inter'locutorily** *adv.*

interloper ('ɪntəˌləʊpə) *n.* **1.** an intruder. **2.** a person who introduces himself into professional or social circles where he does not belong. **3.** a person who interferes in matters that are not his concern. **4.** a person who trades unlawfully. [C17: from INTER- + *loper,* from Middle Dutch *loopen* to leap]

interlude ('ɪntəˌlu:d) *n.* **1.** a period of time or different activity between longer periods, processes, or events; episode or interval. **2.** *Theatre.* a short dramatic piece played separately or as part of a longer entertainment, common in 16th-century England. **3.** a brief piece of music, dance, etc., given between the sections of another performance. [C14: from Medieval Latin *interlūdium,* from Latin INTER- + *lūdus* play]

interlunation (ˌɪntəlʊ'neɪʃən) *n.* the monthly period during which the moon is invisible. See **new moon.** —ˌ**inter'lunar** *adj.*

intermarry (ˌɪntə'mærɪ) *vb.* **-ries, -rying, -ried.** (*intr.*) **1.** (of different groups, races, religions, creeds, etc.) to become connected by marriage. **2.** to marry within one's own family, clan, group, etc. —ˌ**inter'marriage** *n.*

intermeddle (ˌɪntə'mɛdᵊl) *vb.* (*intr.*) *Rare.* another word for **meddle.** [C14 *entremedle,* from Anglo-Norman *entremedler,* from Old French; see INTER- + MEDDLE]

intermediary (ˌɪntə'mi:dɪərɪ) *n., pl.* **-aries.** **1.** a person who acts as a mediator or agent between parties. **2.** something that acts as a medium or means. **3.** an intermediate state or period. ~*adj.* **4.** acting as an intermediary. **5.** situated, acting, or coming between; intermediate.

intermediate *adj.* (ˌɪntə'mi:dɪɪt). **1.** occurring or situated between two points, extremes, places, etc.; in between. **2.** *Physics.* (of a neutron) having an energy between 100 and 100 000 electronvolts. **3.** *Geology.* (of such igneous rocks as syenite) containing between 55 and 66 per cent silica. ~*n.* (ˌɪntə'mi:dɪɪt). **4.** something intermediate. **5.** a substance formed during one of the stages of a chemical process before the desired product is obtained. ~*vb.* (ˌɪntə'mi:dɪˌeɪt). **6.** (*intr.*) to act as an intermediary or mediator. [C17: from Medieval Latin *intermediāre* to intervene, from Latin INTER- + *medius* middle] —ˌ**inter'mediacy** *or* ˌ**inter'mediateness** *n.* —ˌ**inter'mediately** *adv.* —ˌ**interˌmedi'ation** *n.* —ˌ**inter'mediˌator** *n.*

intermediate-acting *adj.* (of a drug) intermediate in its effects between long- and short-acting drugs. Compare **long-acting, short-acting.**

intermediate frequency *n. Electronics.* the frequency to which the signal carrier frequency is changed in a superheterodyne receiver and at which most of the amplification takes place.

intermediate host *n.* an animal that acts as host to a parasite that has not yet become sexually mature.

intermediate-level waste *n.* radioactive waste material, such as reactor and processing plant components, that is solidified before being mixed with concrete and stored in steel drums in deep mines or beneath the seabed in concrete chambers. Compare **high-level waste, low-level waste.**

intermediate range ballistic missile *n.* a missile that follows a ballistic trajectory with a medium range, normally of the order of 750–1500 miles. Abbrev.: **IRBM.**

intermediate school *n. N.Z.* a school for children aged between 11 and 13.

intermediate treatment *n. Social welfare.* a form of child care for young people in trouble that involves neither custody nor punishment and provides opportunities to learn constructive patterns of behaviour to replace potentially criminal ones.

intermediate vector boson *n. Physics.* a hypothetical particle believed to mediate the weak interaction between elementary particles.

interment (ɪn'tɜ:mənt) *n.* burial, esp. with ceremonial rites.

intermezzo (ˌɪntə'mɛtsəʊ) *n., pl.* **-zos** *or* **-zi** (-tsi:). **1.** a short piece of instrumental music composed for performance between the acts or scenes of an opera, drama, etc. **2.** an instrumental piece either inserted between two longer movements in an extended composition or intended for independent performance. **3.** another name for **interlude** (sense 3). [C19: from Italian, from Late Latin *intermedium* interval; see INTERMEDIATE]

intermigration (ˌɪntəmaɪ'greɪʃən) *n.* migration between two groups of people, animals, etc., resulting in an exchange of habitat.

interminable (ɪn'tɜ:mɪnəbᵊl) *adj.* endless or seemingly endless because of monotony or tiresome length. —**inˌtermina'bility** *or* **in'terminableness** *n.* —**in'terminably** *adv.*

intermission (ˌɪntə'mɪʃən) *n.* **1.** an interval, as between parts of a film. **2.** a period between events or activities; pause. **3.** the act of intermitting or the state of being intermitted. [C16: from Latin *intermissiō,* from *intermittere* to leave off, INTERMIT] —ˌ**inter'missive** *adj.*

intermit (ˌɪntə'mɪt) *vb.* **-mits, -mitting, -mitted.** to suspend (activity) or (of activity) to be suspended temporarily or at intervals. [C16: from Latin *intermittere* to leave off, from INTER- + *mittere* to send] —ˌ**inter'mittingly** *adv.* —ˌ**inter'mittor** *n.*

intermittent (ˌɪntə'mɪtᵊnt) *adj.* occurring occasionally or at regular or irregular intervals; periodic. —ˌ**inter'mittence** *or* ˌ**inter'mittency** *n.* —ˌ**inter'mittently** *adv.*

intermittent claudication *n. Pathol.* pain and cramp in the calf muscles, aggravated by walking and caused by an insufficient supply of blood.

intermittent fever *n.* any fever, such as malaria, characterized by intervals of periodic remission.

intermixture (ˌɪntə'mɪkstʃə) *n.* **1.** the act of intermixing or state of being intermixed. **2.** another word for **mixture.** **3.** an additional constituent or ingredient.

intermodal (ˌɪntə'məʊdᵊl) *adj.* **1.** (of a transport system) using different modes of conveyance in conjunction, such as ships, aircraft, road vehicles, etc. **2.** (of a container) able to be carried by different modes of conveyance without being unpacked. **3.** *Psychol.* denoting an interaction between different senses.

intermodulation ('ɪntəˌmɒdjʊ'leɪʃən) *n. Electronics.* **a.** interaction between two signals in electronic apparatus such that each affects the amplitude of the other. **b.** (*as modifier*): *intermodulation distortion.*

intermolecular (ˌɪntəmə'lɛkjʊlə) *adj.* occurring among or between molecules.

intermontane (ˌɪntəmɒn'teɪn) *adj.* occurring or situated between mountain ranges: *an intermontane basin.*

intern *vb.* **1.** (ɪn'tɜ:n). (*tr.*) to detain or confine (foreign or enemy citizens, ships, etc.), esp. during wartime. **2.** ('ɪntɜ:n). (*intr.*) *Chiefly U.S.* to serve or train as an intern. ~*n.* ('ɪntɜ:n). **3.** another word for **internee.** **4.** Also: **interne.** the approximate U.S. and Canadian equivalent of a British **houseman.** **5.** *Chiefly U.S.* a student teacher. **6.** *Chiefly U.S.* a student or recent graduate receiving practical training in a working environment. ~*adj.* (ɪn'tɜ:n). **7.** an archaic word for **internal.** [C19: from Latin *internus* internal]

internal (ɪn'tɜ:nᵊl) *adj.* **1.** of, situated on, or suitable for the inside; inner. **2.** coming or acting from within; interior. **3.** involving the spiritual or mental life; subjective. **4.** of or involving a nation's domestic as opposed to foreign affairs. **5.** (of examinations) set and marked within a school, college, or university rather than a public body. **6.** situated within, affecting, or relating to the inside of the body. ~*n.* **7.** *Euphemistic.* a medical examination of the vagina or uterus. [C16: from Medieval Latin *internālis,* from Late Latin *internus* inward] —ˌ**inter'nality** *or* **in'ternalness** *n.* —**in'ternally** *adv.*

internal-combustion engine *n.* a heat engine in which heat is supplied by burning the fuel in the working fluid (usually air).

internal ear *n.* the part of the ear that consists of the cochlea, vestibule, and semicircular canals. Also called: **inner ear, labyrinth.**

internal energy *n.* the thermodynamic property of a system that changes by an amount equal to the work done on the system when it suffers an adiabatic change. It is the sum of the kinetic and potential energies of its constituent atoms, molecules, etc. Symbol: *U* or *E*

internalize *or* **internalise** (ɪn'tɜ:nəˌlaɪz) *vb.* (*tr.*) *Psychol., sociol.* to make internal, esp. to incorporate within oneself (values, attitudes, etc.) through learning or socialization. Compare introject. Also: **interiorize.** —**inˌternali'zation** *or* **inˌternali'sation** *n.*

ˌ**inter'link** *vb.*
ˌ**inter'lobular** *adj.*
ˌ**inter'mesh** *vb.*
ˌ**interme'tallic** *adj.*
ˌ**inter'mingle** *vb.*
ˌ**inter'minglement** *n.*
ˌ**inter'mix** *vb.*
ˌ**inter'mixable** *adj.*
ˌ**inter'muscular** *adj.*

internal medicine *n.* the branch of medical science concerned with the diagnosis and nonsurgical treatment of disorders of the internal structures of the body.
internal resistance *n. Physics.* the resistance of a cell, accumulator, etc., usually given as $(E-V)/I$, where E is the emf of the cell, and V the potential difference between terminals when it is delivering a current I.
internal revenue *n. U.S.* government income derived from taxes, etc., within the country.
internal rhyme *n. Prosody.* rhyme that occurs between words within a verse line.
internal secretion *n. Physiol.* a secretion, esp. a hormone, that is absorbed directly into the blood.
internat. *abbrev. for* international.
international (ˌɪntəˈnæʃənᵊl) *adj.* **1.** of, concerning, or involving two or more nations or nationalities. **2.** established by, controlling, or legislating for several nations: *an international court; international fishing rights.* **3.** available for use by all nations: *international waters.* ~*n.* **4.** *Sport.* **a.** a contest between two national teams. **b.** a member of these teams. —**ˌinterˌnationˈality** *n.* —**ˌinterˈnationally** *adv.*
International (ˌɪntəˈnæʃənᵊl) *n.* **1.** any of several international socialist organizations, esp. **First International** (1864–76) or **Second International** (1889–1914). **2.** a member of any of these organizations.
International Atomic Time *n.* the scientific standard of time based on the SI unit, the second, used by means of atomic clocks and satellites to synchronize the time standards of the major nations. Abbrev.: **TAI.**
international candle *n.* a former international unit of luminous intensity, originally defined in terms of a standard candle and later in terms of a pentane-burning lamp. It has now been replaced by the candela.
International Criminal Police Organization *n.* See **Interpol.**
International Date Line *n.* the line approximately following the 180° meridian from Greenwich on the east side of which the date is one day earlier than on the west. Also called: **date line.**
Internationale (ˌɪntənæʃəˈnɑːl) *n.* **the.** a revolutionary socialist hymn, first sung in 1871 in France. [C19: shortened from French *chanson internationale* international song]
International Gothic *n.* a style in art during the late 14th and early 15th centuries characterized by elegant stylization of illuminated manuscripts, mosaics, stained glass, etc., and by increased interest in secular themes. Major contributors were Simone Martini, Giotto, and Pisanello.
International Grandmaster *n. Chess.* See **grandmaster** (sense 2).
internationalism (ˌɪntəˈnæʃənəˌlɪzəm) *n.* **1.** the ideal or practice of cooperation and understanding between nations. **2.** the state or quality of being international.
internationalist (ˌɪntəˈnæʃənəlɪst) *n.* **1.** an advocate of internationalism. **2.** a person versed in international law. **3.** (*cap.*) a member of an International.
internationalize *or* **internationalise** (ˌɪntəˈnæʃənəˌlaɪz) *vb.* (*tr.*) **1.** to make international. **2.** to put under international control. —**ˌinterˌnationaliˈzation** *or* **ˌinterˌnationaliˈsation** *n.*
international law *n.* the body of rules generally recognized by civilized nations as governing their conduct towards each other and towards each other's subjects.
International Master *n. Chess.* the second highest title awarded by the FIDE to a player: won by obtaining a certain number of points during specific international chess tournaments. Often shortened to **master.** Compare **grandmaster** (sense 2).
International Modernism *n.* See **International Style.**
international Morse code *n.* the full name for **Morse code.**
international nautical mile *n.* the full name for **nautical mile** (sense 1).
International Phonetic Alphabet *n.* a series of signs and letters propagated by the Association Phonétique Internationale for the representation of human speech sounds. It is based on the Roman alphabet but supplemented by modified signs or symbols from other writing systems, and is usually employed in its revised form of 1951. Abbrev.: **IPA.**
international pitch *n. Music.* the frequency of 435 hertz assigned to the A above middle C, widely used until 1939. See **pitch**¹ (sense 27b).
International Practical Temperature Scale *n.* a temperature scale adopted by international agreement in 1990 based on thermodynamic temperature and using experimental values to define 16 fixed points. The lowest is the triple point of an equilibrium mixture of orthohydrogen and parahydrogen (13.8033 K) and the highest the freezing point of copper (1357.77 K).
international screw thread *n. Engineering.* a metric system for screw threads relating the pitch to the diameter.
international sea and swell scale *n.* another name for the **Douglas scale.**
International Standard Atmosphere *n.* a theoretical vertical distribution of the physical properties of the atmosphere up to an altitude of 50 km established by international agreement. It permits the standardization of aircraft instruments and performance of all types of flying vehicles.
International Standards Organization *n.* an international organization for the standardization of units of measurement, technical terminology, etc. Founded in its present form in 1947, it has a secretariat in Geneva.
International Style *or* **Modernism** *n.* a twentieth-century architectural style characterized by undecorated rectilinear forms and the use of glass, steel, and reinforced concrete.
international telegram *n.* a telemessage sent from the U.K. to a foreign country.
interne (ˈɪntɜːn) *n.* a variant spelling of **intern** (sense 4).
internecine (ˌɪntəˈniːsaɪn) *adj.* **1.** mutually destructive or ruinous; maiming both or all sides: *internecine war.* **2.** of or relating to slaughter or carnage; bloody. **3.** of or involving conflict within a group or organization. [C17: from Latin *internecīnus,* from *internecāre* to destroy, from *necāre* to kill]
internee (ˌɪntɜːˈniː) *n.* a person who is interned, esp. an enemy citizen in wartime or a terrorism suspect.
interneuron (ˌɪntəˈnjʊərɒn) *n. Physiol.* any neuron that connects afferent and efferent neurons in a reflex arc. Also called: **internuncial neuron.**
internist (ˈɪntɜːnɪst, ɪnˈtɜːnɪst) *n.* a physician who specializes in internal medicine.
internment (ɪnˈtɜːnmənt) *n.* **a.** the act of interning or state of being interned, esp. of enemy citizens in wartime or of terrorism suspects. **b.** (*as modifier*): *an internment camp.*
internode (ˈɪntəˌnəʊd) *n.* **1.** the part of a plant stem between two nodes. **2.** the part of a nerve fibre between two nodes of Ranvier. —**ˌinterˈnodal** *adj.*
internship (ˈɪntɜːnʃɪp) *n. U.S. and Canadian.* the position of being an intern or the period during which a person is an intern.
internuncial (ˌɪntəˈnʌnʃəl) *adj.* **1.** *Physiol.* (esp. of neurons) interconnecting. See **internode.** **2.** of, relating to, or emanating from a papal internuncio.
internuncio (ˌɪntəˈnʌnʃɪˌəʊ) *n., pl.* **-cios.** **1.** an ambassador of the pope ranking immediately below a nuncio. **2.** a messenger, agent, or go-between. [C17: from Italian *internunzio,* from Latin *internuntius,* from INTER- + *nuntius* messenger]
interoceptor (ˌɪntərəʊˈsɛptə) *n. Physiol.* a sensory receptor of an internal organ (excluding the muscles). Compare **exteroceptor, proprioceptor.** [C20: from INTER(IOR) + (RE)CEPTOR] —**ˌinteroˈceptive** *adj.*
interosculate (ˌɪntərˈɒskjʊˌleɪt) *vb.* (*intr.*) *Biology.* (of two different species or groups of organisms) to share certain characteristics. —**ˌinterˌoscuˈlation** *n.*
interpage (ˌɪntəˈpeɪdʒ) *vb.* (*tr.*) **1.** to print (matter) on intervening pages. **2.** to insert (intervening pages) into a book.
interpellant (ˌɪntəˈpɛlənt) *adj.* **1.** causing an interpellation. ~*n.* **2.** a deputy who interpellates.
interpellate (ɪnˈtɜːpɛˌleɪt) *vb.* (*tr.*) *Parliamentary procedure.* (in European legislatures) to question (a member of the government) on a point of government policy, often interrupting the business of the day. [C16: from Latin *interpellāre* to disturb, from INTER- + *pellere* to push] —**inˌterpelˈlation** *n.* —**inˈterpelˌlator** *n.*
interpenetrate (ˌɪntəˈpɛnɪˌtreɪt) *vb.* **1.** to penetrate (something) thoroughly; pervade. **2.** to penetrate each other or one another mutually. —**ˌinterˈpenetrable** *adj.* —**ˌinterˈpenetrant** *adj.* —**ˌinterˌpeneˈtration** *n.* —**ˌinterˈpenetrative** *adj.* —**ˌinterˈpenetratively** *adv.*
interpersonal (ˌɪntəˈpɜːsənᵊl) *adj.* between persons; involving personal relationships.
interphase (ˈɪntəˌfeɪz) *n. Biology.* the period between two divisions of a cell.
interphone (ˈɪntəˌfəʊn) *n.* a telephone system for linking different rooms within a building, ship, etc.
interplay (ˈɪntəˌpleɪ) *n.* reciprocal and mutual action and reaction, as in circumstances, events, or personal relations.
interplead (ˌɪntəˈpliːd) *vb.* **-pleads, -pleading; -pleaded, -plead** (-ˈplɛd), *or* **-pled.** (*intr.*) *Law.* to institute interpleader proceedings.
interpleader (ˌɪntəˈpliːdə) *n. Law.* **1.** a process by which a person holding money or property claimed by two or more parties and having no interest in it himself can require the claimants to litigate with each other to determine the issue. **2.** a person who interpleads.
Interpol (ˈɪntəˌpɒl) *n. acronym for* International Criminal Police Organization, an association of over 100 national police forces, devoted chiefly to fighting international crime.
interpolate (ɪnˈtɜːpəˌleɪt) *vb.* **1.** to insert or introduce (a comment, passage, etc.) into (a conversation, text, etc.). **2.** to falsify or alter (a text, manuscript, etc.) by the later addition of (material, esp. spurious or valueless passages). **3.** (*intr.*) to make additions, interruptions, or insertions. **4.** *Maths.* to estimate (a value of a function) between the values already known or determined. Compare **extrapolate** (sense 1). [C17: from Latin *interpolāre* to give a new appearance to, from INTER- + *polīre* to

ˌ**interˈnuclear** *adj.*
ˌ**interˌoceˈanic** *adj.*
ˌ**interˈoffice** *adj.*
ˌ**interˈosseous** *adj.*
ˌ**interpaˈrietal** *adj.*
ˌ**interˈplait** *vb.*
ˌ**interˈplanetary** *adj.*
ˌ**interˈpolar** *adj.*

POLISH] —**inˈterpoˌlater** *or* **inˈterpoˌlator** *n.* —**inˈterpolative** *adj.*
interpolation (ɪnˌtɜːpəˈleɪʃən) *n.* **1.** the act of interpolating or the state of being interpolated. **2.** something interpolated.
interpose (ˌɪntəˈpəʊz) *vb.* **1.** to put or place between or among other things. **2.** to introduce (comments, questions, etc.) into a speech or conversation; interject. **3.** to exert or use power, influence, or action in order to alter or intervene in (a situation). [C16: from Old French *interposer,* from Latin *interpōnere,* from INTER- + *pōnere* to put] —ˌ**interˈposable** *adj.* —ˌ**interˈposal** *n.* —ˌ**interˈposer** *n.*
interposition (ˌɪntəpəˈzɪʃən) *n.* **1.** something interposed. **2.** the act of interposing or the state of being interposed.
interpret (ɪnˈtɜːprɪt) *vb.* **1.** (*tr.*) to clarify or explain the meaning of; elucidate. **2.** (*tr.*) to construe the significance or intention of: *to interpret a smile as an invitation.* **3.** (*tr.*) to convey or represent the spirit or meaning of (a poem, song, etc.) in performance. **4.** (*intr.*) to act as an interpreter; translate orally. [C14: from Latin *interpretārī,* from *interpres* negotiator, one who explains, from INTER- + *-pres,* probably related to *pretium* PRICE] —**inˈterpretable** *adj.* —**inˌterpretaˈbility** *or* **inˈterpretableness** *n.* —**inˈterpretably** *adv.*
interpretation (ɪnˌtɜːprɪˈteɪʃən) *n.* **1.** the act or process of interpreting or explaining; elucidation. **2.** the result of interpreting; an explanation. **3.** a particular view of an artistic work, esp. as expressed by stylistic individuality in its performance. **4.** explanation, as of the environment, a historical site, etc., provided by the use of original objects, personal experience, visual display material, etc. **5.** *Logic.* an allocation of significance to the terms of a purely formal system, by specifying ranges for the variables, denotations for the individual constants, etc.; a function from the formal language to such elements of a possible world. —**inˌterpreˈtational** *adj.*
interpreter (ɪnˈtɜːprɪtə) *n.* **1.** a person who translates orally from one language into another. **2.** a person who interprets the work of others. **3.** *Computer technol.* **a.** a program that translates a second program to machine code one statement at a time and causes the execution of the resulting code as soon as the translation is completed. **b.** a machine that interprets the holes in a punched card and prints the corresponding characters on that card. —**inˈterpreterˌship** *n.* —**inˈterpretress** *fem. n.*
interpretive (ɪnˈtɜːprɪtɪv) *or* **interpretative** (ɪnˈtɜːprɪtətɪv) *adj.* of, involving, or providing interpretation; expository. —**inˈterpretively** *or* **inˈterpretatively** *adv.*
interpretive centre *n.* (at a place of interest, such as a country park, historical site, etc.) a building or group of buildings that provides interpretation of the place of interest through a variety of media, such as video displays and exhibitions of material, and, often, includes facilities such as refreshment rooms and gift shops. Also called: **visitor centre.**
interpretive semantics *n.* (*functioning as sing.*) a school of semantic theory based on the doctrine that the rules that relate sentences to their meanings form an autonomous system, separate from the rules that determine what is grammatical in a language. Compare **generative semantics.**
interquartile range (ˌɪntəˈkwɔːtaɪl) *n. Statistics.* the difference between the value of a variable below which lie 25 per cent of the population, and that below which lie 75 per cent: a measure of the spread of the distribution.
interradial (ˌɪntəˈreɪdɪəl) *adj.* situated between two radii or rays, esp. between the radii of a sea urchin or similar animal. —ˌ**interˈradially** *adv.*
interregnum (ˌɪntəˈrɛgnəm) *n., pl.* **-nums** *or* **-na** (-nə). **1.** an interval between two reigns, governments, incumbencies, etc. **2.** any period in which a state lacks a ruler, government, etc. **3.** a period of absence of some control, authority, etc. **4.** a gap in a continuity. [C16: from Latin, from INTER- + *regnum* REIGN] —ˌ**interˈregnal** *adj.*
interrelate (ˌɪntərɪˈleɪt) *vb.* to place in or come into a mutual or reciprocal relationship. —ˌ**interreˈlation** *n.* —ˌ**interreˈlationˌship** *n.*
interrex (ˌɪntəˈrɛks) *n., pl.* **interreges** (ˌɪntəˈriːdʒiːz). a person who governs during an interregnum; provisional ruler. [C16: from Latin, from INTER- + *rēx* king]
interrog. *abbrev. for:* **1.** interrogate. **2.** interrogation. **3.** interrogative.
interrogate (ɪnˈtɛrəˌgeɪt) *vb.* to ask questions (of), esp. to question (a witness in court, spy, etc.) closely. [C15: from Latin *interrogāre* to question, examine, from *rogāre* to ask] —**inˈterroˌgatingly** *adv.*
interrogation (ɪnˌtɛrəˈgeɪʃən) *n.* **1.** the technique, practice, or an instance of interrogating. **2.** a question or query. **3.** *Telecomm.* the transmission of one or more triggering pulses to a transponder. —**inˌterroˈgational** *adj.*
interrogation mark *n.* a less common term for **question mark.**
interrogative (ˌɪntəˈrɒgətɪv) *adj.* **1.** asking or having the nature of a question. **2.** denoting a form or construction used in asking a question. **3.** denoting or belonging to a class of words, such as *which* and *whom,* that are determiners, adjectives, or pronouns and serve to question which individual referent or referents are intended. Compare **demonstrative, relative.** ~*n.* **4.** an interrogative word, phrase, sentence, or construction. **5.** a question mark. —ˌ**interˈrogatively** *adv.*
interrogator (ɪnˈtɛrəˌgeɪtə) *n.* **1.** a person who interrogates. **2.** a radio or radar transmitter used to send interrogating signals.
interrogatories (ˌɪntəˈrɒgətərɪz, -trɪz) *pl. n. Law.* written questions asked by one party to a suit, to which the other party has to give written answers under oath.
interrogatory (ˌɪntəˈrɒgətərɪ, -trɪ) *adj.* **1.** expressing or involving a question. ~*n., pl.* **-tories. 2.** a question or interrogation. —ˌ**interˈrogatorily** *adv.*
interrupt (ˌɪntəˈrʌpt) *vb.* **1.** to break the continuity of (an action, event, etc.) or hinder (a person) by intrusion. **2.** (*tr.*) to cease to perform (some action). **3.** (*tr.*) to obstruct (a view). **4.** to prevent or disturb (a conversation, discussion, etc.) by questions, interjections, or comment. ~*n.* **5.** the signal to initiate the stopping of the running of one computer program in order to run another, after which the running of the original program is usually continued. [C15: from Latin *interrumpere,* from INTER- + *rumpere* to break] —ˌ**interˈruptible** *adj.* —ˌ**interˈruptive** *adj.* —ˌ**interˈruptively** *adv.*
interrupted (ˌɪntəˈrʌptɪd) *adj.* **1.** broken, discontinued, or hindered. **2.** (of plant organs, esp. leaves) not evenly spaced along an axis. **3.** Also: **deceptive.** *Music.* (of a cadence) progressing from the dominant chord to any other, such as the subdominant or submediant. —ˌ**interˈruptedly** *adv.*
interrupted screw *n.* a screw with a slot or slots cut into the thread, esp. one used in the breech of some guns permitting both engagement and release of the block by a partial turn of the screw.
interrupter *or* **interruptor** (ˌɪntəˈrʌptə) *n.* **1.** a person or thing that interrupts. **2.** an electromechanical device for opening and closing an electric circuit.
interruption (ˌɪntəˈrʌpʃən) *n.* **1.** something that interrupts, such as a comment, question, or action. **2.** an interval or intermission. **3.** the act of interrupting or the state of being interrupted.
interscholastic (ˌɪntəskəˈlæstɪk) *adj.* **1.** (of sports events, competitions, etc.) occurring between two or more schools. **2.** representative of various schools.
inter se *Latin.* (ˈɪntə ˈseɪ) *adv.* among or between themselves.
intersect (ˌɪntəˈsɛkt) *vb.* **1.** to divide, cut, or mark off by passing through or across. **2.** (esp. of roads) to cross (each other). **3.** *Maths.* (often foll. by *with*) to have one or more points in common (with another configuration). [C17: from Latin *intersecāre* to divide, from INTER- + *secāre* to cut]
intersection (ˌɪntəˈsɛkʃən, ˈɪntəˌsɛk-) *n.* **1.** a point at which things intersect, esp. a road junction. **2.** the act of intersecting or the state of being intersected. **3.** *Maths.* **a.** a point or set of points common to two or more geometric configurations. **b.** Also called: **product.** the set of elements that are common to two sets. **c.** the operation that yields that set from a pair of given sets. Symbol: , as in *A B.* —ˌ**interˈsectional** *adj.*
intersex (ˈɪntəˌsɛks) *n. Zoology.* an individual with characteristics intermediate between those of a male and a female. Compare **gynandromorph, hermaphrodite** (sense 1).
intersexual (ˌɪntəˈsɛksjʊəl) *adj.* **1.** occurring or existing between the sexes. **2.** relating to or being an intersex. —ˌ**interˌsexuˈality** *or* ˌ**interˈsexualism** *n.* —ˌ**interˈsexually** *adv.*
interspace *vb.* (ˌɪntəˈspeɪs). **1.** (*tr.*) to make or occupy a space between. ~*n.* (ˈɪntəˌspeɪs). **2.** space between or among things. —**interspatial** (ˌɪntəˈspeɪʃəl) *adj.* —ˌ**interˈspatially** *adv.*
interspecific (ˌɪntəspəˈsɪfɪk) *adj.* hybridized from, relating to, or occurring between different species: *interspecific competition.*
intersperse (ˌɪntəˈspɜːs) *vb.* (*tr.*) **1.** to scatter or distribute among, between, or on. **2.** to diversify (something) with other things scattered here and there. [C16: from Latin *interspargere,* from INTER- + *spargere* to sprinkle] —**interspersedly** (ˌɪntəˈspɜːsɪdlɪ) *adv.* —**interspersion** (ˌɪntəˈspɜːʃən) *or* ˌ**interˈspersal** *n.*
interstadial (ˌɪntəˈsteɪdɪəl) *adj., n.* another word for **interglacial.** [C20: from New Latin, from INTER- + *stadium* stage]
interstate (ˈɪntəˌsteɪt) *adj.* **1.** between or involving two or more of the states of the U.S., Australia, etc. ~*adv.* **2.** *Austral.* to or into another state.
interstice (ɪnˈtɜːstɪs) *n.* (*usually pl.*) **1.** a minute opening or crevice between things. **2.** *Physics.* the space between adjacent atoms in a crystal lattice. [C17: from Latin *interstitium* interval, from *intersistere,* from INTER- + *sistere* to stand]
interstitial (ˌɪntəˈstɪʃəl) *adj.* **1.** of or relating to an interstice or interstices. **2.** *Physics.* forming or occurring in an interstice: *an interstitial atom.* **3.** *Chem.* containing interstitial atoms or ions: *an interstitial compound.* **4.** *Anatomy, zoology.* occurring in the spaces between organs, tissues, etc.: *interstitial cells.* ~*n.* **5.** *Chem.* an atom or ion situated in the interstices of a crystal lattice. —ˌ**interˈstitially** *adv.*

ˌ**interproˈfessional** *adj.*
ˌ**interproˈvincial** *adj.*
ˌ**interˈracial** *adj.*
ˌ**interˈregional** *adj.*
ˌ**interreˈligious** *adj.*
ˌ**interˈschool** *adj.*
ˌ**interˈseptal** *adj.*
ˌ**intersoˈcietal** *adj.*
ˌ**interˈspinal** *or* ˌ**interˈspinous** *adj.*
ˌ**interˈstellar** *adj.*

interstitial-cell-stimulating hormone *n.* another name for **luteinizing hormone.**

interstratify (ˌɪntəˈstrætɪˌfaɪ) *vb.* **-fies, -fying, -fied.** *(tr.; usually passive)* to arrange (a series of rock strata) in alternating beds. —ˌ**interˌstratifiˈcation** *n.*

intertexture (ˌɪntəˈtɛkstʃə) *n.* **1.** the act or process of interweaving or the condition of having been interwoven. **2.** something that has been interwoven.

intertidal (ˌɪntəˈtaɪdᵊl) *adj.* of or relating to the zone of the shore between the high-water mark and low-water mark.

intertrigo (ˌɪntəˈtraɪgəʊ) *n.* chafing between two moist closely opposed skin surfaces, as at the armpit. [C18: from INTER- + *-trigo,* from Latin *terere* to rub]

Intertropical Convergence Zone *n. Meteorol.* the zone of converging trade winds along the equator causing rising air currents and low atmospheric pressure. Abbrev.: **ITCZ.**

intertwine (ˌɪntəˈtwaɪn) *vb.* to unite or be united by twisting or twining together. Also: **intertwist.** —ˌ**interˈtwinement** *n.* —ˌ**interˈtwiningly** *adv.*

interval (ˈɪntəvəl) *n.* **1.** the period of time marked off by or between two events, instants, etc. **2.** the distance between two points, objects, etc. **3.** a pause or interlude, as between periods of intense activity. **4.** *Brit.* a short period between parts of a play, concert, film, etc.; intermission. **5.** *Music.* the difference of pitch between two notes, either sounded simultaneously (**harmonic interval**) or in succession as in a musical part (**melodic interval**). An interval is calculated by counting the (inclusive) number of notes of the diatonic scale between the two notes: *the interval between C and G is a fifth.* **6.** the ratio of the frequencies of two sounds. **7.** *Maths.* **a.** the set containing all real numbers or points between two given numbers or points, called the endpoints. A **closed interval** includes the endpoints, but an **open interval** does not. **b.** the set of points in *n*-dimensional space where coordinates satisfy the inequalities $a_i \le x_i \le b_i$ (**closed interval**) or $a_i < x_i < b_i$ (**open interval**) where $a_i < b_i$. **8. at intervals. a.** occasionally or intermittently. **b.** with spaces between. [C13: from Latin *intervallum,* literally: space between two palisades, from INTER- + *vallum* palisade, rampart] —**intervallic** (ˌɪntəˈvælɪk) *adj.*

interval estimate *n. Statistics.* an interval within which the true value of a parameter of a population is stated to lie with a predetermined probability on the basis of sampling statistics. Compare: **point estimate.**

intervalometer (ˌɪntəvəˈlɒmɪtə) *n.* an automatic device used to trigger an operation at regular intervals, esp. such a device operating the shutter of a camera.

interval scale *n. Statistics.* a scale of measurement of data according to which the differences between values can be quantified in absolute but not relative terms and for which any zero is merely arbitrary: for instance, dates are measured on an interval scale since differences can be measured in years, but no sense can be given to a ratio of times. Compare **ordinal scale, ratio scale, nominal scale.**

interval signal *n.* a characteristic snatch of music, chimes, etc., transmitted as an identifying signal by a radio station between programme items.

interval training *n.* a method of athletic training using alternate sprinting and jogging. Also called: **fartlek.**

intervene (ˌɪntəˈviːn) *vb. (intr.)* **1.** (often foll. by *in*) to take a decisive or intrusive role (in) in order to modify or determine events or their outcome. **2.** (foll. by *in* or *between*) to come or be (among or between). **3.** (of a period of time) to occur between events or points in time. **4.** (of an event) to disturb or hinder a course of action. **5.** *Economics.* to take action to affect the market forces of an economy, esp. to maintain the stability of a currency. **6.** *Law.* to interpose and become a party to a legal action between others, esp. in order to protect one's interests. [C16: from Latin *intervenīre* to come between, from INTER- + *venīre* to come] —ˌ**interˈvener** *or* ˌ**interˈvenor** *n.*

intervening variable *n. Maths, psychol., etc.* a hypothetical variable postulated to account for the way in which a set of independent variables control a set of dependent variables.

intervention (ˌɪntəˈvɛnʃən) *n.* **1.** the act of intervening. **2.** any interference in the affairs of others, esp. by one state in the affairs of another. **3.** *Economics.* the action of a central bank in supporting the international value of a currency by buying large quantities of the currency to keep the price up. **4.** *Commerce.* the action of the EEC in buying up surplus produce when the market price drops to a certain value. —ˌ**interˈventional** *adj.*

interventionist (ˌɪntəˈvɛnʃənɪst) *adj.* **1.** of, relating to, or advocating intervention, esp. in the affairs of a foreign country. ~*n.* **2.** an interventionist person or state. —ˌ**interˈventionism** *n.*

intervention price *n. Commerce.* the price at which the EEC intervenes to buy surplus produce.

intervertebral disc (ˌɪntəˈvɜːtəbrəl) *n.* any of the cartilaginous discs between individual vertebrae, acting as shock absorbers.

interview (ˈɪntəˌvjuː) *n.* **1.** a conversation with or questioning of a person, usually conducted for television, radio, or a newspaper. **2.** a formal discussion, esp. one in which an employer assesses an applicant for a job. ~*vb.* **3.** to conduct an interview with (someone). [C16: from Old French *entrevue;* see INTER-, VIEW] —ˌ**interviewˈee** *n.* —ˈ**interˌviewer** *n.*

inter vivos *Latin.* (ˈɪntə ˈviːvɒs) *adj. Law.* between living people: *an inter vivos gift.*

intervocalic (ˌɪntəvəʊˈkælɪk) *adj.* pronounced or situated between vowels. —ˌ**intervoˈcalically** *adv.*

interweave (ˌɪntəˈwiːv) *vb.* **-weaves, -weaving, -wove** *or* **-weaved; -woven, -wove,** *or* **-weaved.** to weave, blend, or twine together; intertwine. Also: **interwork.** —ˌ**interˈweavement** *n.* —ˈ**interˌweaver** *n.*

intestate (ɪnˈtɛsteɪt, -tɪt) *adj.* **1. a.** (of a person) not having made a will. **b.** (of property) not disposed of by will. ~*n.* **2.** a person who dies without having made a will. ~Compare **testate.** [C14: from Latin *intestātus,* from IN-[1] + *testātus,* from *testārī* to bear witness, make a will, from *testis* a witness] —**inˈtestacy** *n.*

intestinal flora *n.* harmless microorganisms that inhabit the lumen of the intestinal tract.

intestine (ɪnˈtɛstɪn) *n.* (*usually pl.*) the part of the alimentary canal between the stomach and the anus. See **large intestine, small intestine.** Related adj.: **alvine.** [C16: from Latin *intestīnum* gut, from *intestīnus* internal, from *intus* within] —**intestinal** (ɪnˈtɛstɪnᵊl, ˌɪntɛsˈtaɪnᵊl) *adj.* —**inˈtestinally** *adv.*

inti (ˈɪntɪ) *n.* the standard monetary unit of Peru. [C20: from Quechua]

intifada (ˌɪntɪˈfɑːdə) *n.* the Palestinian uprising against Israel in the West Bank and Gaza Strip that started at the end of 1987. [C20: Arabic, literally: uprising]

intima (ˈɪntɪmə) *n., pl.* **-mae** (-ˌmiː). *Anatomy, zoology.* the innermost layer of an organ or part, esp. of a blood vessel. [C19: from Latin, feminine of *intimus* innermost; see INTIMATE[1]] —ˈ**intimal** *adj.*

intimacy (ˈɪntɪməsɪ) *n., pl.* **-cies. 1.** close or warm friendship or understanding; personal relationship. **2.** (*often pl.*) *Euphemistic.* sexual relations.

intimate[1] (ˈɪntɪmɪt) *adj.* **1.** characterized by a close or warm personal relationship: *an intimate friend.* **2.** deeply personal, private, or secret. **3.** (*often postpositive;* foll. by *with*) *Euphemistic.* having sexual relations (with). **4. a.** (*postpositive;* foll. by *with*) having a deep or unusual knowledge (of) **b.** (of knowledge) deep; extensive. **5.** having a friendly, warm, or informal atmosphere: *an intimate nightclub.* **6.** of or relating to the essential part or nature of something; intrinsic. **7.** denoting the informal second person of verbs and pronouns in French and other languages. ~*n.* **8.** a close friend. [C17: from Latin *intimus* very close friend, from (adj.): innermost, deepest, from *intus* within] —ˈ**intimately** *adv.* —ˈ**intimateness** *n.*

intimate[2] (ˈɪntɪˌmeɪt) *vb. (tr.; may take a clause as object)* **1.** to hint; suggest. **2.** to proclaim; make known. [C16: from Late Latin *intimāre* to proclaim, from Latin *intimus* innermost] —ˈ**intiˌmater** *n.*

intimation (ˌɪntɪˈmeɪʃən) *n.* **1.** a hint or suggestion. **2.** *Rare.* an announcement or notice.

intimidate (ɪnˈtɪmɪˌdeɪt) *vb. (tr.)* **1.** to make timid or frightened; scare. **2.** to discourage, restrain, or silence illegally or unscrupulously, as by threats or blackmail. [C17: from Medieval Latin *intimidāre,* from Latin IN-[2] + *timidus* fearful, from *timor* fear] —**inˈtimiˌdating** *adj.* —**inˌtimiˈdation** *n.* —**inˈtimiˌdator** *n.*

intinction (ɪnˈtɪŋkʃən) *n. Christianity.* the practice of dipping the Eucharistic bread into the wine at Holy Communion. [C16: from Late Latin *intinctiō* a dipping in, from Latin *intingere* to dip in, from *tingere* to dip]

intine (ˈɪntɪn, -tiːn, -taɪn) *n.* the inner membrane of a pollen grain or a spore. Compare **extine.** [C19: from Latin *intimus* innermost + -INE[1]]

intitule (ɪnˈtɪtjuːl) *vb. (tr.) Parliamentary procedure.* (in Britain) to entitle (an Act). [C15: from Old French *intituler,* from Latin *titulus* TITLE]

intl *abbrev. for* international.

into (ˈɪntuː; *unstressed* ˈɪntə) *prep.* **1.** to the interior or inner parts of: *to look into a case.* **2.** to the middle or midst of so as to be surrounded by: *into the water; into the bushes.* **3.** against; up against: *he drove into a wall.* **4.** used to indicate the result of a transformation or change: *he changed into a monster.* **5.** *Maths.* used to indicate a dividend: *three into six is two.* **6.** *Informal.* interested or enthusiastically involved in: *I'm really into Freud these days.*

intolerable (ɪnˈtɒlərəbᵊl) *adj.* **1.** more than can be tolerated or endured; insufferable. **2.** *Informal.* extremely irritating or annoying. —**inˌtoleraˈbility** *or* **inˈtolerableness** *n.* —**inˈtolerably** *adv.*

intolerant (ɪnˈtɒlərənt) *adj.* **1.** lacking respect for practices and beliefs other than one's own. **2.** (*postpositive;* foll. by *of*) not able

ˌ**interˌterriˈtorial** *adj.*
ˌ**interˈtribal** *adj.*
ˌ**interˈtribally** *adv.*
ˌ**interˈtropical** *adj.*
ˌ**interˌuniˈversity** *adj.*
ˌ**interˈurban** *adj.*
ˌ**interˈvarsity** *adj.*
ˌ**interˈvertebral** *adj.*
ˌ**interˈvolve** *vb.*
ˌ**interˈwar** *adj.*
ˌ**interˈwind** *vb.*
ˌ**interˈwreathe** *vb.*
ˌ**interˈwrought** *adj.*

or willing to tolerate or endure: *intolerant of noise.* —**in'tolerance** *n.* —**in'tolerantly** *adv.*

intonate ('ɪntəʊˌneɪt) *vb.* (*tr.*) **1.** to pronounce or articulate (continuous connected speech) with a characteristic rise and fall of the voice. **2.** a less common word for **intone.**

intonation (ˌɪntəʊ'neɪʃən) *n.* **1.** the sound pattern of phrases and sentences produced by pitch variation in the voice. **2.** the act or manner of intoning. **3.** an intoned, chanted, or monotonous utterance; incantation. **4.** *Music.* the opening of a piece of plainsong, sung by a soloist. **5.** *Music.* **a.** the correct or accurate pitching of intervals. **b.** the capacity to play or sing in tune. See also **just intonation.** —ˌ**into'national** *adj.*

intonation pattern *or* **contour** *n. Linguistics.* a characteristic series of musical pitch levels that serves to distinguish between questions, statements, and other types of utterance in a language.

intone (ɪn'təʊn) *vb.* **1.** to utter, recite, or sing (a chant, prayer, etc.) in a monotonous or incantatory tone. **2.** (*intr.*) to speak with a particular or characteristic intonation or tone. **3.** to sing (the opening phrase of a psalm, etc.) in plainsong. [C15: from Medieval Latin *intonare,* from IN-[2] + TONE] —**in'toner** *n.*

intorsion (ɪn'tɔːʃən) *n. Botany.* a spiral twisting in plant stems or other parts.

in toto *Latin.* (ɪn 'təʊtəʊ) *adv.* totally; entirely; completely.

intoxicant (ɪn'tɒksɪkənt) *n.* **1.** anything that causes intoxication. ~*adj.* **2.** causing intoxication.

intoxicate (ɪn'tɒksɪˌkeɪt) *vb.* (*tr.*) **1.** (of an alcoholic drink) to produce in (a person) a state ranging from euphoria to stupor, usually accompanied by loss of inhibitions and control; make drunk; inebriate. **2.** to stimulate, excite, or elate so as to overwhelm. **3.** (of a drug) to poison. [C16: from Medieval Latin, from *intoxicāre* to poison, from Latin *toxicum* poison; see TOXIC] —**in'toxicable** *adj.* —**in'toxiˌcating** *adj.* —**in'toxiˌcatingly** *adv.* —**in'toxiˌcative** *adj.* —**in'toxiˌcator** *n.*

intoxication (ɪnˌtɒksɪ'keɪʃən) *n.* **1.** drunkenness; inebriation. **2.** great elation. **3.** the act of intoxicating. **4.** poisoning.

intr. *abbrev. for* intransitive.

intra- *prefix.* within; inside: *intravenous.* [from Latin *intrā* on the inside, within; see INTERIOR]

intra-atomic (ˌɪntrəə'tɒmɪk) *adj.* existing or occurring within an atom or atoms. Compare **interatomic.**

intracapsular (ˌɪntrə'kæpsjʊlə) *adj. Anatomy.* within a capsule, esp. within the capsule of a joint.

intracardiac (ˌɪntrə'kɑːdɪˌæk) *adj.* within the heart.

intracellular (ˌɪntrə'sɛljʊlə) *adj. Biology.* situated or occurring inside a cell or cells. —ˌ**intra'cellularly** *adv.*

intracranial (ˌɪntrə'kreɪnɪəl) *adj.* within the skull.

intractable (ɪn'træktəbᵊl) *adj.* **1.** difficult to influence or direct: *an intractable disposition.* **2.** (of a problem, illness, etc.) difficult to solve, alleviate, or cure. **3.** difficult to shape or mould, esp. with the hands. —**inˌtracta'bility** *or* **in'tractableness** *n.* —**in'tractably** *adv.*

intracutaneous (ˌɪntrəkjuː'teɪnɪəs) *adj. Anatomy.* within the skin. Also: **intradermal.** —ˌ**intracu'taneously** *adv.*

intradermal (ˌɪntrə'dɜːməl) *or* **intradermic** *adj. Anatomy.* other words for **intracutaneous.** Abbrev. (esp. of an injection) **ID, i.d.** —ˌ**intra'dermally** *or* ˌ**intra'dermically** *adv.*

intrados (ɪn'treɪdɒs) *n., pl.* **-dos** *or* **-doses.** *Architect.* the inner curve or surface of an arch or vault. Compare **extrados.** [C18: from French, from INTRA- + *dos* back, from Latin *dorsum*]

intrafascicular (ˌɪntrəfə'sɪkjʊlə) *adj. Botany.* between the xylem and phloem elements of a vascular bundle: *intrafascicular cambium.*

intramolecular (ˌɪntrəmə'lɛkjʊlə) *adj.* occurring within a molecule or molecules.

intramural (ˌɪntrə'mjʊərəl) *adj.* **1.** *Education, chiefly U.S. and Canadian.* operating within or involving those in a single establishment. **2.** *Anatomy.* within the walls of a cavity or hollow organ. —ˌ**intra'murally** *adv.*

intramuscular (ˌɪntrə'mʌskjʊlə) *adj. Anatomy.* within a muscle: *an intramuscular injection.* Abbrev. (esp. of an injection): **IM, i.m.** —ˌ**intra'muscularly** *adv.*

intranational (ˌɪntrə'næʃənᵊl) *adj.* within one nation.

intrans. *abbrev. for* intransitive.

intransigent (ɪn'trænsɪdʒənt) *adj.* **1.** not willing to compromise; obstinately maintaining an attitude. ~*n., also* **in'transigentist.** **2.** an intransigent person, esp. in politics. [C19: from Spanish *los intransigentes* the uncompromising (ones), a name adopted by certain political extremists, from IN-[1] + *transigir* to compromise, from Latin *transigere* to settle; see TRANSACT] —**in'transigence** *or* **in'transigency** *n.* —**in'transigently** *adv.*

intransitive (ɪn'trænsɪtɪv) *adj.* **1. a.** denoting a verb when it does not require a direct object. **b.** denoting a verb that customarily does not require a direct object. **c.** (*as n.*) a verb in either of these categories. **2.** denoting an adjective or noun that does not require any particular noun phrase as a referent. **3.** *Logic, maths.* (of a relation) having the property that if it holds between one argument and a second, and between the second and a third, it must fail to hold between the first and the third: *"being the mother of" is an intransitive relation.* ~Compare **transitive, pseudo-intransitive.** —**in'transitively** *adv.* —**inˌtransi'tivity** *or* **in'transitiveness** *n.*

intranuclear (ˌɪntrə'njuːklɪə) *adj.* situated or occurring within a nucleus.

intraocular (ˌɪntrə'ɒkjʊlə) *adj. Anatomy.* within an eyeball.

intrapartum (ˌɪntrə'pɑːtəm) *adj. Med.* of or relating to childbirth or delivery: *intrapartum care.* [C20: New Latin, from INTRA- + *partum,* from *partus* birth]

intrapreneur (ˌɪntrəprə'nɜː) *n.* a person who while remaining within a larger organization uses entrepreneurial skills to develop a new product or line of business as a subsidiary of the organization. [C20: from INTRA- + (ENTRE)PRENEUR]

intraspecific (ˌɪntrəspə'sɪfɪk) *adj.* relating to or occurring between members of the same species: *intraspecific competition.*

intrastate (ˌɪntrə'steɪt) *adj. Chiefly U.S.* of, relating to, or confined within a single state, esp. a state of the U.S.

intratelluric (ˌɪntrətə'ljʊərɪk) *adj.* (of rocks and their constituents, processes, etc.) formed or occurring below the surface of the earth.

intrauterine (ˌɪntrə'juːtəraɪn) *adj.* within the womb.

intrauterine device *n.* a metal or plastic device, in the shape of a loop, coil, or ring, inserted into the uterus to prevent conception. Abbrev.: **IUD.**

intravasation (ɪnˌtrævə'seɪʃən) *n.* the passage of extraneous material, such as pus, into a blood or lymph vessel. Compare **extravasate.**

intravenous (ˌɪntrə'viːnəs) *adj. Anatomy.* within a vein: *an intravenous injection.* Abbrevs. (esp. of an injection): **IV, i.v.** —ˌ**intra'venously** *adv.*

in-tray *n.* a tray for incoming papers requiring attention.

intrazonal soil (ˌɪntrə'zəʊnᵊl) *n.* a soil that has a well-developed profile determined by relief, parent material, age, etc.

intreat (ɪn'triːt) *vb.* an archaic spelling of **entreat.** —**in'treatingly** *adv.* —**in'treatment** *n.*

intrench (ɪn'trentʃ) *vb.* a less common spelling of **entrench.** —**in'trencher** *n.* —**in'trenchment** *n.*

intrepid (ɪn'trɛpɪd) *adj.* fearless; daring; bold. [C17: from Latin *intrepidus,* from IN-[1] + *trepidus* fearful, timid] —ˌ**intre'pidity** *or* **in'trepidness** *n.* —**in'trepidly** *adv.*

intricate ('ɪntrɪkɪt) *adj.* **1.** difficult to understand; obscure; complex; puzzling. **2.** entangled or involved: *intricate patterns.* [C15: from Latin *intrīcāre* to entangle, perplex, from IN-[2] + *trīcae* trifles, perplexities] —'**intricacy** *or* '**intricateness** *n.* —'**intricately** *adv.*

intrigant *or* **intriguant** ('ɪntrɪgənt; *French* ɛ̃trigɑ̃) *or* (*fem.*) **intrigante** *or* **intriguante** (ˌɪntrɪ'gɒnt; *French* ɛ̃trigɑ̃t) *n. Archaic.* a person who intrigues; intriguer.

intrigue *vb.* (ɪn'triːg), **-trigues, -triguing, -trigued.** **1.** (*tr.*) to make interested or curious: *I'm intrigued by this case, Watson.* **2.** (*intr.*) to make secret plots or employ underhand methods; conspire. **3.** (*intr.;* often foll. by *with*) to carry on a clandestine love affair. ~*n.* (ɪn'triːg, 'ɪntriːg). **4.** the act or an instance of secret plotting, etc. **5.** a clandestine love affair. **6.** the quality of arousing interest or curiosity; beguilement. [C17: from French *intriguer,* from Italian *intrigare,* from Latin *intrīcāre;* see INTRICATE] —**in'triguer** *n.*

intriguing (ɪn'triːgɪŋ) *adj.* arousing great interest or curiosity: *an intriguing mystery.* —**in'triguingly** *adv.*

intrinsic (ɪn'trɪnsɪk) *or* **intrinsical** *adj.* **1.** of or relating to the essential nature of a thing; inherent. **2.** *Anatomy.* situated within or peculiar to a part: *intrinsic muscles.* [C15: from Late Latin *intrinsecus* from Latin, inwardly, from *intrā* within + *secus* alongside; related to *sequī* to follow] —**in'trinsically** *adv.*

intrinsic factor *n. Biochem.* a glycoprotein, secreted by the stomach, the presence of which is necessary for the absorption of cyanocobalamin (vitamin B_{12}) in the intestine.

intrinsic semiconductor *n.* an almost pure semiconductor to which no impurities have been added and in which the electron and hole densities are equal at thermal equilibrium. Also called: **i-type semiconductor.**

intro ('ɪntrəʊ) *n., pl.* **-tros.** *Informal.* short for **introduction.**

intro. *or* **introd.** *abbrev. for:* **1.** introduction. **2.** introductory.

intro- *prefix.* in, into, or inward: *introvert.* [from Latin *intrō* towards the inside, inwardly, within]

introduce (ˌɪntrə'djuːs) *vb.* (*tr.*) **1.** (often foll. by *to*) to present (someone) by name (to another person) or (two or more people to each other). **2.** (foll. by *to*) to cause to experience for the first time: *to introduce a visitor to beer.* **3.** to present for consideration or approval, esp. before a legislative body: *to introduce a draft bill.* **4.** to bring in; establish: *to introduce decimal currency.* **5.** to present (a radio or television programme, etc.) verbally. **6.** (foll. by *with*) to start: *he introduced his talk with some music.* **7.** (often foll. by *into*) to insert or inject: *he introduced the needle into his arm.* **8.** to place (members of a species of plant or animal) in a new environment with the intention of producing a resident breeding population. [C16: from Latin *intrōdūcere* to bring inside, from INTRO- + *dūcere* to lead] —ˌ**intro'ducer** *n.* —ˌ**intro'ducible** *adj.*

introduction (ˌɪntrə'dʌkʃən) *n.* **1.** the act of introducing or fact of being introduced. **2.** a presentation of one person to another or others. **3.** a means of presenting a person to another person, group, etc., such as a **letter of introduction** or reference. **4.** a preliminary part, as of a book, speech, etc. **5.** *Music.* **a.** an instrumental passage preceding the entry of a soloist, choir, etc. **b.** an opening passage in a movement or composition that precedes the main material. **6.** something that has been or is introduced, esp. something that is not native to an area, country, etc. **7.** a basic or elementary work of instruction, reference, etc. **8.** *Logic.* (qualified by the name of an operation) a syntactic rule specifying the conditions under which a formula or statement containing the specified operator may be derived from others: *conjunction-introduction; negation-introduction.*

introductory (ˌɪntrəˈdʌktərɪ, -trɪ) *adj.* serving as an introduction; preliminary; prefatory. —ˌ**introˈductorily** *adv.* —ˌ**introˈductoriness** *n.*

introgression (ˌɪntrəˈɡrɛʃən) *n.* the introduction of genes from the gene pool of one species into that of another during hybridization.

introit (ˈɪntrɔɪt) *n. R.C. Church, Church of England.* a short prayer said or sung as the celebrant is entering the sanctuary to celebrate Mass or Holy Communion. [C15: from Church Latin *introitus* introit, from Latin: entrance, from *introīre* to go in, from INTRO- + *īre* to go] —**inˈtroital** *adj.*

introject (ˌɪntrəˈdʒɛkt) *vb. Psychol.* **1.** (*intr.*) (esp. of a child) to incorporate ideas of others, or (in fantasy) of objects. **2.** to turn (feelings for another) towards oneself. ~Compare **project.** See also **internalize.**

introjection (ˌɪntrəˈdʒɛkʃən) *n. Psychol.* the act or process of introjecting. [C20: from INTRO- + (PRO)JECTION] —ˌ**introˈjective** *adj.*

intromission (ˌɪntrəˈmɪʃən) *n.* a less common word for **insertion** or **introduction.** —ˌ**introˈmissive** *adj.*

intromit (ˌɪntrəˈmɪt) *vb.* **-mits, -mitting, -mitted.** (*tr.*) *Rare.* to enter or insert or allow to enter or be inserted. [C15: from Latin *intrōmittere* to send in, from INTRO- + *mittere* to send] —ˌ**introˈmissible** *adj.* —ˌ**introˌmissiˈbility** *n.* —ˌ**introˈmittent** *adj.* —ˌ**introˈmitter** *n.*

intron (ˈɪntrɒn) *n. Biochem.* a stretch of DNA that interrupts a gene and does not contribute to the specification of a protein. Compare **exon**[2]. [C20: from *intr(agenic) (regi)on*]

introrse (ɪnˈtrɔːs) *adj. Botany.* turned inwards or towards the axis, as anthers that shed their pollen towards the centre of the flower. [C19: from Latin *introrsus,* contraction of *intrōversus,* from INTRO- + *versus* turned, from *vertere* to turn] —**inˈtrorsely** *adv.*

introspect (ˌɪntrəˈspɛkt) *vb.* (*intr.*) to examine and analyse one's own thoughts and feelings.

introspection (ˌɪntrəˈspɛkʃən) *n.* the examination of one's own thoughts, impressions, and feelings, esp. for long periods. [C17: from Latin *intrōspicere* to look within, from INTRO- + *specere* to look] —ˌ**introˈspectional** *or* ˌ**introˈspective** *adj.* —ˌ**introˈspectionist** *n.* —ˌ**introˈspectively** *adv.* —ˌ**introˈspectiveness** *n.*

introversion (ˌɪntrəˈvɜːʃən) *n.* **1.** *Psychol.* the directing of interest inwards towards one's own thoughts and feelings rather than towards the external world or making social contacts. **2.** *Pathol.* the turning inside out of a hollow organ or part. ~Compare **extroversion.** —ˌ**introˈversive** *or* ˌ**introˈvertive** *adj.*

introvert *n.* (ˈɪntrəˌvɜːt). **1.** *Psychol.* a person prone to introversion. ~*adj.* (ˈɪntrəˌvɜːt). **2.** Also: **introverted.** characterized by introversion. ~*vb.* (ˌɪntrəˈvɜːt). **3.** (*tr.*) *Pathol.* to turn (a hollow organ or part) inside out. ~Compare **extrovert.** [C17: see INTRO-, INVERT]

intrude (ɪnˈtruːd) *vb.* **1.** (often foll. by *into, on,* or *upon*) to put forward or interpose (oneself, one's views, something) abruptly or without invitation. **2.** *Geology.* to force or thrust (rock material, esp. molten magma) or (of rock material) to be thrust between solid rocks. [C16: from Latin *intrūdere* to thrust in, from IN-[2] + *trūdere* to thrust] —**inˈtruder** *n.* —**inˈtrudingly** *adv.*

intrusion (ɪnˈtruːʒən) *n.* **1.** the act or an instance of intruding; an unwelcome visit, interjection, etc.: *an intrusion on one's privacy.* **2. a.** the movement of magma from within the earth's crust into spaces in the overlying strata to form igneous rock. **b.** any igneous rock formed in this way. **3.** *Property law.* an unlawful entry onto land by a stranger after determination of a particular estate of freehold and before the remainderman or reversioner has made entry. —**inˈtrusional** *adj.*

intrusive (ɪnˈtruːsɪv) *adj.* **1.** characterized by intrusion or tending to intrude. **2.** (of igneous rocks) formed by intrusion. Compare **extrusive** (sense 2). **3.** *Phonetics.* relating to or denoting a speech sound that is introduced into a word or piece of connected speech for a phonetic rather than a historical or grammatical reason, such as the (r) often pronounced between *idea* and *of* in *the idea of it.* —**inˈtrusively** *adv.* —**inˈtrusiveness** *n.*

intrust (ɪnˈtrʌst) *vb.* a less common spelling of **entrust.** —**inˈtrustment** *n.*

intubate (ˈɪntjʊˌbeɪt) *vb.* (*tr.*) *Med.* to insert a tube or cannula into (a hollow organ); cannulate. —ˌ**intuˈbation** *n.*

INTUC (ˈɪntʌk) *n. acronym for* Indian National Trade Union Congress.

intuit (ɪnˈtjuːɪt) *vb.* to know or discover by intuition. —**inˈtuitable** *adj.*

intuition (ˌɪntjʊˈɪʃən) *n.* **1.** knowledge or belief obtained neither by reason nor by perception. **2.** instinctive knowledge or belief. **3.** a hunch or unjustified belief. **4.** *Philosophy.* immediate knowledge of a proposition or object such as Kant's account of our knowledge of sensible objects. **5.** the supposed faculty or process by which we obtain any of these. [C15: from Late Latin *intuitiō* a contemplation, from Latin *intuērī* to gaze upon, from *tuērī* to look at] —ˌ**intuˈitional** *adj.* —ˌ**intuˈitionally** *adv.*

intuitionism (ˌɪntjʊˈɪʃəˌnɪzəm) *or* **intuitionalism** *n.* **1.** (in ethics) **a.** the doctrine that there are moral truths discoverable by intuition. **b.** the doctrine that there is no single principle by which to resolve conflicts between intuited moral rules. ~See also **deontological. 2.** *Philosophy.* the theory that general terms are used of a variety of objects in accordance with perceived similarities. Compare **nominalism, Platonism. 3.** *Logic.* the doctrine that logical axioms rest on prior intuitions concerning time, negation, and provability. **4. a.** the theory that mathematics cannot intelligibly comprehend the properties of infinite sets, and that only what can be shown to be provable can be justifiably asserted. **b.** the reconstruction of mathematics or logic in accordance with this view. ~Compare **formalism, logicism, finitism. 5.** the doctrine that knowledge, esp. of the external world, is acquired by intuition. —ˌ**intuˈitionist** *or* ˌ**intuˈitionalist** *n.*

intuitive (ɪnˈtjuːɪtɪv) *adj.* **1.** resulting from intuition: *an intuitive awareness.* **2.** of, characterized by, or involving intuition. —**inˈtuitively** *adv.* —**inˈtuitiveness** *n.*

intumesce (ˌɪntjʊˈmɛs) *vb.* (*intr.*) to swell or become swollen; undergo intumescence. [C18: from Latin *intumescere,* from *tumescere* to begin to swell, from *tumēre* to swell]

intumescence (ˌɪntjʊˈmɛsəns) *or* **intumescency** *n.* **1.** *Pathol.* a swelling up, as with blood or other fluid. **2.** *Pathol.* a swollen organ or part. **3.** *Chem.* the swelling of certain substances on heating, often accompanied by the escape of water vapour. —ˌ**intuˈmescent** *adj.*

intussuscept (ˌɪntəssəˈsɛpt) *vb.* (*tr.; usually passive*) *Pathol.* to turn or fold (an organ or a part) inwards; invaginate. —ˌ**intussusˈceptive** *adj.*

intussusception (ˌɪntəssəˈsɛpʃən) *n.* **1.** *Pathol.* invagination of a tubular organ or part, esp. the telescoping of one section of the intestinal tract into a lower section, causing obstruction. **2.** *Biology.* growth in the surface area of a cell by the deposition of new particles between the existing particles of the cell wall. Compare **apposition** (sense 3). [C18: from Latin *intus* within + *susceptiō* a taking up]

intwine (ɪnˈtwaɪn) *vb.* a less common spelling of **entwine.** —**inˈtwinement** *n.*

Inuit *or* **Innuit** (ˈɪnjuːɪt) *n., pl.* **-it** *or* **-its.** an Eskimo of N America or Greenland, as distinguished from one from Asia or the Aleutian Islands: the general name for an Eskimo in Canada. Compare **Yupik.** [from Eskimo *inuit* the people, pl. of *inuk* a man]

Inuktitut (ɪˈnʊktəˌtʊt) *n. Canadian.* the language of the Inuit; Eskimo. [from Eskimo *inuk* man + *titut* speech]

inulin (ˈɪnjʊlɪn) *n.* a fructose polysaccharide present in the tubers and rhizomes of some plants. Formula: $(C_6H_{10}O_5)_n$. [C19: from Latin *inula* elecampane + -IN]

inunction (ɪnˈʌŋkʃən) *n.* **1.** the application of an ointment to the skin, esp. by rubbing. **2.** the ointment so used. **3.** the act of anointing; anointment. [C15: from Latin *inunguere* to anoint, from *unguere;* see UNCTION]

inundate (ˈɪnʌnˌdeɪt) *vb.* (*tr.*) **1.** to cover completely with water; overflow; flood; swamp. **2.** to overwhelm, as if with a flood: *to be inundated with requests.* [C17: from Latin *inundāre* to flood, from *unda* wave] —ˈ**inundant** *or* **inˈundatory** *adj.* —ˌ**inunˈdation** *n.* —ˈ**inunˌdator** *n.*

inurbane (ˌɪnɜːˈbeɪn) *adj. Rare.* not urbane; lacking in courtesy or polish. —**inurbanity** (ˌɪnɜːˈbænɪtɪ) *n.* —ˌ**inurˈbanely** *adv.*

inure *or* **enure** (ɪˈnjʊə) *vb.* **1.** (*tr.; often passive;* often foll. by *to*) to cause to accept or become hardened to; habituate. **2.** (*intr.*) (esp. of a law, etc.) to come into operation; take effect. [C15 *enuren* to accustom, from *ure* use, from Old French *euvre* custom, work, from Latin *opera* works, plural of *opus*] —**inuredness** *or* **enuredness** (ɪˈnjʊərɪdnɪs) *n.* —**inˈurement** *or* **enˈurement** *n.*

inurn (ɪnˈɜːn) *vb.* (*tr.*) **1.** to place (esp. cremated ashes) in an urn. **2.** a less common word for **inter.** —**inˈurnment** *n.*

in utero *Latin.* (ɪn ˈjuːtəˌrəʊ) *adv.* within the womb.

inutile (ɪnˈjuːtaɪl) *adj. Rare.* useless; unprofitable. —**inˈutilely** *adv.* —ˌ**inuˈtility** *n.*

inv. *abbrev. for:* **1.** invented. **2.** invention. **3.** inventor. **4.** invoice.

in vacuo *Latin.* (ɪn ˈvækjʊˌəʊ) *adv.* **1.** in a vacuum. **2.** in isolation; without reference to facts or evidence.

invade (ɪnˈveɪd) *vb.* **1.** to enter (a country, territory, etc.) by military force. **2.** (*tr.*) to occupy in large numbers; overrun; infest. **3.** (*tr.*) to trespass or encroach upon (privacy, etc.). **4.** (*tr.*) to enter and spread throughout, esp. harmfully; pervade. **5.** (of plants, esp. weeds) to become established in (a place to which they are not native). [C15: from Latin *invādere,* from *vādere* to go] —**inˈvadable** *adj.* —**inˈvader** *n.*

invaginate *vb.* (ɪnˈvædʒɪˌneɪt). **1.** *Pathol.* to push one section of (a tubular organ or part) back into itself so that it becomes ensheathed; intussuscept. **2.** (*intr.*) (of the outer layer of an organism or part) to undergo invagination. ~*adj.* (ɪnˈvædʒɪnɪt, -ˌneɪt). **3.** (of an organ or part) folded back upon itself. [C19: from Medieval Latin *invāgīnāre,* from Latin IN-[2] + *vāgīna* sheath] —**inˈvaginable** *adj.*

invagination (ɪnˌvædʒɪˈneɪʃən) *n.* **1.** *Pathol.* the process of invaginating or the condition of being invaginated; intussusception. **2.** *Pathol.* an invaginated organ or part. **3.** an infolding of the outer layer of cells of an organism or part of an organism so as to form a pocket in the surface, as in the embryonic development of a gastrula from a blastula.

invalid[1] (ˈɪnvəˌliːd, -lɪd) *n.* **1. a.** a person suffering from disablement or chronic ill health. **b.** (*as modifier*): *an invalid chair.* ~*adj.* **2.** suffering from or disabled by injury, sickness, etc. ~*vb.* (*tr.*) **3.** to cause to become an invalid; disable. **4.** (usually foll. by *out; often passive*) *Chiefly Brit.* to require (a member of the armed forces) to retire from active service through wounds or illness. [C17: from Latin *invalidus* infirm, from IN-[1] + *validus* strong] —ˌ**invaˈlidity** *n.*

invalid[2] (ɪnˈvælɪd) *adj.* **1.** not valid; having no cogency or legal force. **2.** *Logic.* (of an argument) having a conclusion that does not follow from the premises: it may be false when the premises are all true; not valid. [C16: from Medieval Latin *invalidus* without legal force; see INVALID[1]] —**invalidity** (ˌɪnvəˈlɪdɪtɪ) *or* **inˈvalidness** *n.* —**inˈvalidly** *adv.*

invalidate (ɪnˈvælɪˌdeɪt) *vb.* (*tr.*) **1.** to render weak or ineffective, as an argument. **2.** to take away the legal force or effectiveness of; annul, as a contract. —**inˌvaliˈdation** *n.* —**inˈvaliˌdator** *n.*

invalidism (ˈɪnvəlɪˌdɪzəm) *n.* **1.** the state of being an invalid, esp. by reason of ill health. **2.** a state of being abnormally preoccupied with one's physical health.

invalidity benefit *n.* (in the British National Insurance scheme) a weekly payment to a person who has been off work through illness for more than six months. Abbrev.: **IVB.**

invaluable (ɪnˈvæljʊəbᵊl) *adj.* having great value that is impossible to calculate; priceless. —**inˈvaluableness** *n.* —**inˈvaluably** *adv.*

Invar (ɪnˈvɑː) *n. Trademark.* an alloy containing iron (63.8 per cent), nickel (36 per cent), and carbon (0.2 per cent). It has a very low coefficient of expansion and is used for the balance springs of watches, etc. [C20: shortened from INVARIABLE]

invariable (ɪnˈvɛərɪəbᵊl) *adj.* **1.** not subject to alteration; unchanging. ~*n.* **2.** a mathematical quantity having an unchanging value; a constant. —**inˌvariaˈbility** *or* **inˈvariableness** *n.* —**inˈvariably** *adv.*

invariant (ɪnˈvɛərɪənt) *n.* **1.** *Maths.* an entity, quantity, etc., that is unaltered by a particular transformation of coordinates: *a point in space, rather than its coordinates, is an invariant.* ~*adj.* **2.** *Maths.* (of a relationship or a property of a function, configuration, or equation) unaltered by a particular transformation of coordinates. **3.** a rare word for **invariable.** —**inˈvariance** *or* **inˈvariancy** *n.*

invasion (ɪnˈveɪʒən) *n.* **1.** the act of invading with armed forces. **2.** any encroachment or intrusion: *an invasion of rats.* **3.** the onset or advent of something harmful, esp. of a disease. **4.** *Pathol.* the spread of cancer from its point of origin into surrounding tissues. **5.** the movement of plants to an area to which they are not native.

invasive (ɪnˈveɪsɪv) *adj.* **1.** of or relating to an invasion, intrusion, etc. **2.** relating to or denoting cancer at the stage at which it has spread from its site of origin to other tissues. **3.** (of surgery) involving making a relatively large incision in the body to gain access to the target of the surgery, as opposed to making a small incision or gaining access endoscopically through a natural orifice.

invective (ɪnˈvɛktɪv) *n.* **1.** vehement accusation or denunciation, esp. of a bitterly abusive or sarcastic kind. ~*adj.* **2.** characterized by or using abusive language, bitter sarcasm, etc. [C15: from Late Latin *invectīvus* reproachful, scolding, from Latin *invectus* carried in; see INVEIGH] —**inˈvectively** *adv.* —**inˈvectiveness** *n.*

inveigh (ɪnˈveɪ) *vb.* (*intr.*; foll. by *against*) to speak with violent or invective language; rail. [C15: from Latin *invehī*, literally: to be carried in, hence, assail physically or verbally, from IN-[2] + *vehī* to be carried, ride] —**inˈveigher** *n.*

inveigle (ɪnˈviːgᵊl, -ˈveɪ-) *vb.* (*tr.*; often foll. by *into* or an infinitive) to lead (someone into a situation) or persuade (to do something) by cleverness or trickery; cajole: *to inveigle customers into spending more.* [C15: from Old French *avogler* to blind, deceive, from *avogle* blind, from Medieval Latin *ab oculis* without eyes] —**inˈveiglement** *n.* —**inˈveigler** *n.*

invent (ɪnˈvɛnt) *vb.* **1.** to create or devise (new ideas, machines, etc.). **2.** to make up (falsehoods); fabricate. [C15: from Latin *invenīre* to find, come upon, from IN-[2] + *venīre* to come] —**inˈventible** *or* **inˈventable** *adj.*

invention (ɪnˈvɛnʃən) *n.* **1.** the act or process of inventing. **2.** something that is invented. **3.** *Patent law.* the discovery or production of some new or improved process or machine that is both useful and is not obvious to persons skilled in the particular field. **4.** creative power or ability; inventive skill. **5.** *Euphemistic.* a fabrication; lie. **6.** (in traditional rhetoric) one of the five steps in preparing a speech or discourse: the process of finding suitable topics on which to talk or write. **7.** *Music.* a short piece consisting of two or three parts usually in imitative counterpoint. **8.** *Sociol.* the creation of a new cultural pattern or trait. —**inˈventional** *adj.* —**inˈventionless** *adj.*

inventive (ɪnˈvɛntɪv) *adj.* **1.** skilled or quick at contriving; ingenious; resourceful. **2.** characterized by inventive skill: *an inventive programme of work.* **3.** of or relating to invention. —**inˈventively** *adv.* —**inˈventiveness** *n.*

inventor (ɪnˈvɛntə) *n.* a person who invents, esp. as a profession. —**inˈventress** *fem. n.*

inventory (ˈɪnvəntərɪ, -trɪ) *n.* **1.** a detailed list of articles, goods, property, etc. **2.** (*often pl.*) *Accounting, chiefly U.S.* **a.** the amount or value of a firm's current assets that consist of raw materials, work in progress, and finished goods; stock. **b.** such assets individually. ~*vb.* **-tories, -torying, -toried. 3.** (*tr.*) to enter (items) in an inventory; make a list of. [C16: from Medieval Latin *inventōrium*; see INVENT] —ˈ**inventoriable** *adj.* —ˌ**invenˈtorial** *adj.* —ˌ**invenˈtorially** *adv.*

inveracity (ˌɪnvəˈræsɪtɪ) *n., pl.* **-ties.** *Formal or euphemistic.* **1.** lying; untruthfulness. **2.** an untruth; lie.

inverse (ɪnˈvɜːs, ˈɪnvɜːs) *adj.* **1.** opposite or contrary in effect, sequence, direction, etc. **2.** *Maths.* **a.** (of a relationship) containing two variables such that an increase in one results in a decrease in the other: *the volume of a gas is in inverse ratio to its pressure.* **b.** (of an element) operating on a specified member of a set to produce the identity of the set: *the additive inverse element of x is $-x$, the multiplicative inverse element of x is $1/x$.* **3.** (*usually prenominal*) upside-down; inverted: *in an inverse position.* ~*n.* **4.** *Maths.* **a.** another name for **reciprocal** (sense 7). **b.** an inverse element. **5.** *Logic.* a categorial proposition derived from another by changing both the proposition and its subject from affirmative to negative, or vice versa, as *all immortals are angels* from *no mortals are angels.* [C17: from Latin *inversus*, from *invertere* to INVERT] —**inˈversely** *adv.*

inverse function *n.* a function whose independent variable is the dependent variable of a given trigonometric or hyperbolic function: *the inverse function of* $\sin x$ is $\arcsin y$ (*also written* $\sin^{-1}y$).

inverse square law *n.* any natural law in which the magnitude of a physical quantity varies inversely with the square of the distance from its source.

inversion (ɪnˈvɜːʃən) *n.* **1.** the act of inverting or state of being inverted. **2.** something inverted, esp. a reversal of order, mutual functions, etc.: *an inversion of their previous relationship.* **3.** Also called: **anastrophe.** *Rhetoric.* the reversal of a normal order of words. **4.** *Chem.* **a.** the conversion of a dextrorotatory solution of sucrose into a laevorotatory solution of glucose and fructose by hydrolysis. **b.** any similar reaction in which the optical properties of the reactants are opposite to those of the products. **5.** *Music.* **a.** the process or result of transposing the notes of a chord (esp. a triad) such that the root, originally in the bass, is placed in an upper part. When the bass note is the third of the triad, the resulting chord is the **first inversion;** when it is the fifth, the resulting chord is the **second inversion.** See also **root position. b.** (in counterpoint) the modification of a melody or part in which all ascending intervals are replaced by corresponding descending intervals and vice versa. **c.** the modification of an interval in which the higher note becomes the lower or the lower one the higher. See **complement** (sense 8). **6.** *Pathol.* abnormal positioning of an organ or part, as in being upside down or turned inside out. **7.** *Psychiatry.* **a.** the adoption of the role or characteristics of the opposite sex. **b.** another word for **homosexuality. 8.** *Meteorol.* an abnormal condition in which the layer of air next to the earth's surface is cooler than an overlying layer. **9.** *Anatomy, phonetics.* another word for **retroflexion** (sense 2). **10.** *Computer technol.* an operation by which each digit of a binary number is changed to the alternative digit, as *10110* to *01001.* **11.** *Genetics.* a type of chromosomal mutation in which a section of a chromosome, and hence the order of its genes, is reversed. **12.** *Logic.* the process of deriving the inverse of a categorial proposition. **13.** *Maths.* a transformation of the set of points P to the new set of points P' about a fixed point O such that $OP \cdot OP' = a^2$, where a is a constant and P and P' lie on a straight line through O and on the same side of it. —**inˈversive** *adj.*

invert *vb.* (ɪnˈvɜːt). **1.** to turn or cause to turn upside down or inside out. **2.** (*tr.*) to reverse in effect, sequence, direction, etc. **3.** (*tr.*) *Phonetics.* **a.** to turn (the tip of the tongue) up and back. **b.** to pronounce (a speech sound) by retroflexion. **4.** *Logic.* to form the inverse of a categorial proposition. ~*n.* (ˈɪnvɜːt). **5.** *Psychiatry.* **a.** a person who adopts the role of the opposite sex. **b.** another word for **homosexual. 6.** *Architect.* **a.** the lower inner surface of a drain, sewer, etc. Compare **soffit** (sense 2). **b.** an arch that is concave upwards, esp. one used in foundations. [C16: from Latin *invertere*, from IN-[2] + *vertere* to turn] —**inˈvertible** *adj.* —**inˌvertiˈbility** *n.*

invertase (ɪnˈvɜːteɪz) *n.* an enzyme, occurring in the intestinal juice of animals and in yeasts, that hydrolyses sucrose to glucose and fructose. Also called: **saccharase.**

invertebrate (ɪnˈvɜːtɪbrɪt, -ˌbreɪt) *n.* **1.** any animal lacking a backbone, including all species not classified as vertebrates. ~*adj.* also **inˈvertebral. 2.** of, relating to, or designating invertebrates.

inverted comma *n.* another term for **quotation mark.**

inverted mordent *n. Music.* a melodic ornament consisting of the rapid single or double alternation of a principal note with a note one degree higher. Also called: **upper mordent.** See also **pralltriller.**

inverted pleat *n. Dressmaking.* a box pleat reversed so that the fullness of the material is turned inwards.

inverted snob *n.* a person who scorns the conventions or attitudes of his own class or social group by attempting to identify with people of a supposedly lower class.

inverter *or* **invertor** (ɪnˈvɜːtə) *n.* **1.** any device for converting a direct current into an alternating current. **2.** *Computer technol.* another name for **NOT circuit.**

invert sugar (ˈɪnvɜːt) *n.* a mixture of fructose and glucose obtained by the inversion of sucrose.

invest (ɪnˈvɛst) *vb.* **1.** (often foll. by *in*) to lay out (money or capital in an enterprise, esp. by purchasing shares) with the expectation of profit. **2.** (*tr.;* often foll. by *in*) to devote (effort, resources, etc., to a project). **3.** (*tr.;* often foll. by *in* or *with*) *Archaic or ceremonial.* to clothe or adorn (in some garment, esp. the robes of an office): *to invest a king in the insignia of an emperor.* **4.** (*tr.;* often foll. by *in*) to install formally or ceremoniously (in an official position, rank, etc.). **5.** (*tr.;* foll. by *in* or *with*) to place (power, authority, etc., in) or provide (with power or authority): *to invest new rights in the monarchy.* **6.** (*tr.; usually passive;* foll. by *in* or *with*) to provide or endow (a person with qualities, characteristics, etc.): *he was invested with great common sense.* **7.** (*tr.;* foll. by *with*) *Usually poetic.* to cover or adorn, as if with a coat or garment: *when spring invests the trees with leaves.* **8.** (*tr.*) *Rare.* to surround with military forces; besiege. **9.** (*intr.;* foll. by *in*) *Informal.* to purchase; buy. [C16: from Medieval Latin *investīre* to clothe, from Latin, from *vestīre,* from *vestis* a garment] —**inˈvestable** *or* **inˈvestible** *adj.* —**inˈvestor** *n.*

investigate (ɪnˈvɛstɪˌgeɪt) *vb.* to inquire into (a situation or problem, esp. a crime or death) thoroughly; examine systematically, esp. in order to discover the truth. [C16: from Latin *investīgāre* to search after, from IN-[2] + *vestīgium* track; see VESTIGE] —**inˈvestigable** *adj.* —**inˈvestigative** *or* **inˈvestigatory** *adj.*

investigation (ɪnˌvɛstɪˈgeɪʃən) *n.* the act or process of investigating; a careful search or examination in order to discover facts, etc. —**inˌvestiˈgational** *adj.*

investigator (ɪnˈvɛstɪˌgeɪtə) *n.* a person who investigates, such as a private detective.

investiture (ɪnˈvɛstɪtʃə) *n.* **1.** the act of presenting with a title or with the robes and insignia of an office or rank. **2.** (in feudal society) the formal bestowal of the possessory right to a fief or other benefice. **3.** a less common word for **investment** (sense 7). —**inˈvestitive** *adj.*

investment (ɪnˈvɛstmənt) *n.* **1. a.** the act of investing money. **b.** the amount invested. **c.** an enterprise, asset, etc., in which money is or can be invested. **2. a.** the act of investing effort, resources, etc. **b.** the amount invested. **3.** *Economics.* the amount by which the stock of capital (plant, machinery, materials, etc.) in an enterprise or economy changes. **4.** *Biology.* the outer layer or covering of an organ, part, or organism. **5.** a less common word for **investiture** (sense 1). **6.** the act of investing or state of being invested, as with an official robe, a specific quality, etc. **7.** *Rare.* the act of besieging with military forces, works, etc.

investment analyst *n.* a specialist in forecasting the prices of stocks and shares.

investment bond *n.* a single-premium life-assurance policy in which a fixed sum is invested in an asset-backed fund.

investment trust *n.* a financial enterprise that invests its subscribed capital in securities for its investors' benefit.

inveterate (ɪnˈvɛtərɪt) *adj.* **1.** long established, esp. so as to be deep-rooted or ingrained: *an inveterate feeling of hostility.* **2.** (*prenominal*) settled or confirmed in a habit or practice, esp. a bad one; hardened: *an inveterate smoker.* **3.** *Obsolete.* full of hatred; hostile. [C16: from Latin *inveterātus* of long standing, from *inveterāre* to make old, from IN-[2] + *vetus* old] —**inˈveteracy** *or* **inˈveterateness** *n.* —**inˈveterately** *adv.*

inviable (ɪnˈvaɪəbᵊl) *adj.* not viable, esp. financially; not able to survive: *an inviable company.* —**inˌviaˈbility** *or* **inˈviableness** *n.* —**inˈviably** *adv.*

invidious (ɪnˈvɪdɪəs) *adj.* **1.** incurring or tending to arouse resentment, unpopularity, etc.: *an invidious task.* **2.** (of comparisons or distinctions) unfairly or offensively discriminating. **3.** *Obsolete.* grudging; envious. [C17: from Latin *invidiōsus* full of envy, from *invidia* ENVY] —**inˈvidiously** *adv.* —**inˈvidiousness** *n.*

invigilate (ɪnˈvɪdʒɪˌleɪt) *vb.* (*intr.*) **1.** *Brit.* to watch examination candidates, esp. to prevent cheating. U.S. word: **proctor. 2.** *Archaic.* to keep watch. [C16: from Latin *invigilāre* to watch over, from IN-[2] + *vigilāre* to keep watch; see VIGIL] —**inˌvigiˈlation** *n.* —**inˈvigiˌlator** *n.*

invigorate (ɪnˈvɪgəˌreɪt) *vb.* (*tr.*) to give vitality and vigour to; animate; brace; refresh: *to be invigorated by fresh air.* [C17: from IN-[2] + Latin *vigor* VIGOUR] —**inˈvigorˌatingly** *adv.* —**inˌvigorˈation** *n.* —**inˈvigorative** *adj.* —**inˈvigoratively** *adv.* —**inˈvigorˌator** *n.*

invincible (ɪnˈvɪnsəbᵊl) *adj.* **1.** incapable of being defeated; unconquerable. **2.** unable to be overcome; insuperable: *invincible prejudices.* [C15: from Late Latin *invincibilis,* from Latin IN-[1] + *vincere* to conquer] —**inˌvinciˈbility** *or* **inˈvincibleness** *n.* —**inˈvincibly** *adv.*

in vino veritas *Latin.* (ɪn ˈviːnəʊ ˈvɛrɪˌtæs) in wine there is truth; people speak the truth when they are drunk.

inviolable (ɪnˈvaɪələbᵊl) *adj.* that must not or cannot be transgressed, dishonoured, or broken; to be kept sacred: *an inviolable oath.* —**inˌviolaˈbility** *or* **inˈviolableness** *n.* —**inˈviolably** *adv.*

inviolate (ɪnˈvaɪəlɪt, -ˌleɪt) *adj.* **1.** free from violation, injury, disturbance, etc. **2.** a less common word for **inviolable.** —**inˈviolacy** *or* **inˈviolateness** *n.* —**inˈviolately** *adv.*

invisible (ɪnˈvɪzəbᵊl) *adj.* **1.** not visible; not able to be perceived by the eye: *invisible rays.* **2.** concealed from sight; hidden. **3.** not easily seen or noticed: *invisible mending.* **4.** kept hidden from public view; secret; clandestine. **5.** *Economics.* of or relating to services rather than goods in relation to the invisible balance: *invisible earnings.* ~*n.* **6.** *Economics.* an invisible item of trade; service. —**inˌvisiˈbility** *or* **inˈvisibleness** *n.* —**inˈvisibly** *adv.*

invisible balance *n. Economics.* the difference in value between total exports of services plus payment of property incomes from abroad and total imports of services plus payment abroad of property incomes. Compare **balance of trade.**

invisible ink *n.* a liquid used for writing that does not become visible until it has been treated with chemicals, heat, ultraviolet light, etc.

invitation (ˌɪnvɪˈteɪʃən) *n.* **1. a.** the act of inviting, such as an offer of entertainment or hospitality. **b.** (*as modifier*): *an invitation dance; an invitation race.* **2.** the act of enticing or attracting; allurement.

invitatory (ɪnˈvaɪtətərɪ, -trɪ) *adj.* **1.** serving as or conveying an invitation. ~*n., pl.* **-tories. 2.** any of various invitations to prayer, such as Psalm 95 in a religious service.

invite *vb.* (ɪnˈvaɪt). (*tr.*) **1.** to ask (a person or persons) in a friendly or polite way (to do something, attend an event, etc.): *he invited them to dinner.* **2.** to make a request for, esp. publicly or formally: *to invite applications.* **3.** to bring on or provoke; give occasion for: *you invite disaster by your actions.* **4.** to welcome or tempt. ~*n.* (ˈɪnvaɪt). **5.** an informal word for **invitation.** [C16: from Latin *invītāre* to invite, entertain, from IN-[2] + *-vītāre,* probably related to Greek *hiesthai* to be desirous of] —**inˈviter** *n.*

inviting (ɪnˈvaɪtɪŋ) *adj.* tempting; alluring; attractive. —**inˈvitingly** *adv.* —**inˈvitingness** *n.*

in vitro (ɪn ˈviːtrəʊ) *adv., adj.* (of biological processes or reactions) made to occur outside the body of the organism in an artificial environment. [New Latin, literally: in glass]

in vitro fertilization *n.* a technique enabling some women who are unable to conceive to bear children. Egg cells removed from a woman's ovary are fertilized by sperm in vitro; some of the resulting fertilized egg cells are incubated until the blastocyst stage and then implanted into her uterus. Abbrev.: **IVF.**

in vivo (ɪn ˈviːvəʊ) *adv., adj.* (of biological processes or experiments) occurring or carried out in the living organism. [New Latin, literally: in a living (thing)]

invocate (ˈɪnvəˌkeɪt) *vb.* an archaic word for **invoke.** —**invocative** (ɪnˈvɒkətɪv) *adj.* —ˈ**invoˌcator** *n.*

invocation (ˌɪnvəˈkeɪʃən) *n.* **1.** the act of invoking or calling upon some agent for assistance. **2.** a prayer asking God for help, forgiveness, etc., esp. as part of a religious service. **3.** an appeal for inspiration and guidance from a Muse or deity at the beginning of a poem. **4. a.** the act of summoning a spirit or demon from another world by ritual incantation or magic. **b.** the incantation used in this act. —ˌ**invoˈcational** *adj.* —**invocatory** (ɪnˈvɒkətərɪ, -trɪ) *adj.*

invoice (ˈɪnvɔɪs) *n.* **1.** a document issued by a seller to a buyer listing the goods or services supplied and stating the sum of money due. **2.** *Rare.* a consignment of invoiced merchandise. ~*vb.* **3.** (*tr.*) **a.** to present (a customer) with an invoice. **b.** to list (merchandise sold) on an invoice. [C16: from earlier *invoyes,* from Old French *envois,* plural of *envoi* message; see ENVOY]

invoke (ɪnˈvəʊk) *vb.* (*tr.*) **1.** to call upon (an agent, esp. God or another deity) for help, inspiration, etc. **2.** to put (a law, penalty, etc.) into use: *the union invoked the dispute procedure.* **3.** to appeal to (an outside agent or authority) for confirmation, corroboration, etc. **4.** to implore or beg (help, etc.). **5.** to summon (a spirit, demon, etc.); conjure up. [C15: from Latin *invocāre* to call upon, appeal to, from *vocāre* to call] —**inˈvocable** *adj.* —**inˈvoker** *n.*

involucel (ɪnˈvɒljʊˌsɛl) *or* **involucellum** (ɪnˌvɒljʊˈsɛləm) *n., pl.* **-cels** *or* **-cella** (-ˈsɛlə). a ring of bracts at the base of the florets of a compound umbel. [C19: from New Latin *involūcellum* a little cover; see INVOLUCRE] —**inˌvoluˈcellate** *or* **inˌvoluˈcellated** *adj.*

involucre (ˈɪnvəˌluːkə) *or* **involucrum** (ˌɪnvəˈluːkrəm) *n., pl.* **-cres** *or* **-cra** (-krə). a ring of bracts at the base of an inflorescence in such plants as the *Compositae.* [C16 (in the sense: envelope): from New Latin *involucrum,* from Latin: wrapper, from *involvere* to wrap; see INVOLVE] —ˌ**invoˈlucral** *adj.* —ˌ**invoˈlucrate** *adj.*

involuntary (ɪnˈvɒləntərɪ, -trɪ) *adj.* **1.** carried out without one's conscious wishes; not voluntary; unintentional. **2.** *Physiol.* (esp. of a movement or muscle) performed or acting without conscious control. —**inˈvoluntarily** *adv.* —**inˈvoluntariness** *n.*

involute *adj.* (ˈɪnvəˌluːt), *also* **involuted. 1.** complex, intricate, or involved. **2.** *Botany.* (esp. of petals, leaves, etc., in bud) having margins that are rolled inwards. **3.** (of certain shells) closely coiled so that the axis is obscured. ~*n.* (ˈɪnvəˌluːt). **4.** *Geom.* the curve described by the free end of a thread as it is wound around another curve, the **evolute**, such that its normals are tangential to the evolute. *~vb.* (ˌɪnvəˈluːt). **5.** (*intr.*) to become involute. [C17: from Latin *involūtus*, from *involvere*; see INVOLVE] —**ˈin-voˌlutely** *adv.* —**ˌinvoˈlutedly** *adv.*

involute gear *n.* a gear tooth form that is generated by involute geometry.

involution (ˌɪnvəˈluːʃən) *n.* **1.** the act of involving or complicating or the state of being involved or complicated. **2.** something involved or complicated. **3.** *Zoology.* degeneration or structural deformation. **4.** *Biology.* an involute formation or structure. **5.** *Physiol.* reduction in size of an organ or part, as of the uterus following childbirth or as a result of ageing. **6.** an algebraic operation in which a number, variable, expression etc., is raised to a specified power. Compare **evolution** (sense 5). **7.** *Grammar.* an involved construction, such as one in which the subject is separated from the predicate by an additional clause. —**ˌinvoˈlutional** *adj.*

involve (ɪnˈvɒlv) *vb.* (*tr.*) **1.** to include or contain as a necessary part: *the task involves hard work.* **2.** to have an effect on; spread to: *the investigation involved many innocent people.* **3.** (*often passive*; usually foll. by *in* or *with*) to concern or associate significantly: *many people were involved in the crime.* **4.** (*often passive*) to make complicated; tangle: *the situation was further involved by her disappearance.* **5.** *Rare, often poetic.* to wrap or surround. **6.** *Archaic.* to coil up. **7.** *Maths, obsolete.* to raise to a specified power. [C14: from Latin *involvere* to roll in, surround, from IN-[2] + *volvere* to roll] —**inˈvolvement** *n.* —**inˈvolver** *n.*

involved (ɪnˈvɒlvd) *adj.* **1.** complicated; difficult to comprehend: *an involved literary style.* **2.** (*usually postpositive*) concerned or implicated: *one of the men involved.* **3.** (*postpositive*; foll. by *with*) *Euphemistic.* having sexual relations: *she was involved with a number of men.*

invt. or **invty** *abbrev. for* inventory.

invulnerable (ɪnˈvʌlnərəbᵊl, -ˈvʌlnrəbᵊl) *adj.* **1.** incapable of being wounded, hurt, damaged, etc., either physically or emotionally. **2.** incapable of being damaged or captured: *an invulnerable fortress.* —**inˌvulneraˈbility** or **inˈvulnerableness** *n.* —**inˈvulnerably** *adv.*

invultuation (ɪnˌvʌltʃʊˈeɪʃən) *n.* the use of or the act of making images of people, animals, etc., for witchcraft. [C19: from Medieval Latin *invultuāre* to make a likeness, from IN-[2] + *vultus* likeness]

inward (ˈɪnwəd) *adj.* **1.** going or directed towards the middle of or into something. **2.** situated within; inside. **3.** of, relating to, or existing in the mind or spirit: *inward meditation.* *~adv.* **4.** a variant of **inwards** (sense 1). *~n.* **5.** the inward part; inside. —**ˈinwardness** *n.*

inwardly (ˈɪnwədlɪ) *adv.* **1.** within the private thoughts or feelings; secretly: *inwardly troubled, he kept smiling.* **2.** not aloud: *to laugh inwardly.* **3.** with reference to the inside or inner part; internally. **4.** *Archaic.* intimately; essentially: *the most inwardly concerned of the plotters.*

inwards *adv.* (ˈɪnwədz) *also* **inward. 1.** towards the interior or middle of something. **2.** in, into, or towards the mind or spirit. *~pl. n.* (ˈɪnədz). **3.** a variant spelling of **innards.**

inweave (ɪnˈwiːv) *vb.* **-weaves, -weaving, -wove** or **-weaved; -woven** or **-weaved.** (*tr.*) to weave together into or as if into a design, fabric, etc.; interweave.

inwrap (ɪnˈræp) *vb.* **-wraps, -wrapping, -wrapped.** a less common spelling of **enwrap.**

inwrought (ˌɪnˈrɔːt) *adj.* **1.** worked or woven into material, esp. decoratively. **2.** *Rare.* blended with other things.

inyala (ɪnˈjɑːlə) *n.* another name for **nyala.**

I/O *abbrev. for* input/output.

IOC *abbrev. for* International Olympic Committee.

iodate (ˈaɪəˌdeɪt) *n.* **1.** a salt of iodic acid. *~vb.* **2.** (*tr.*) another word for **iodize.** —**ˌioˈdation** *n.*

iodic (aɪˈɒdɪk) *adj.* of or containing iodine, esp. in the pentavalent state.

iodic acid *n.* a colourless or pale yellow soluble crystalline substance that forms acidic aqueous solutions. Used as a reagent and disinfectant. Formula: HIO_3.

iodide (ˈaɪəˌdaɪd) *n.* **1.** a salt of hydriodic acid, containing the iodide ion, I^-. **2.** a compound containing an iodine atom, such as methyl iodide, CH_3I.

iodine (ˈaɪəˌdiːn) *n.* a bluish-black element of the halogen group that sublimates into a violet irritating gas. Its compounds are used in medicine and photography and in dyes. The radioisotope **iodine-131 (radioiodine)**, with a half-life of 8 days, is used in the diagnosis and treatment of thyroid disease. Symbol: I; atomic no.: 53; atomic wt.: 126.90; valency: 1, 3, 5, or 7; relative density: 4.93; melting pt.: 113.5°C; boiling pt.: 184.35°C. [C19: from French *iode*, from Greek *iōdēs* rust-coloured, but taken to mean violet-coloured, through a mistaken derivation from *ion* violet]

iodism (ˈaɪəˌdɪzəm) *n.* poisoning induced by ingestion of iodine or its compounds.

iodize or **iodise** (ˈaɪəˌdaɪz) *vb.* (*tr.*) to treat or react with iodine or an iodine compound. Also: **iodate.** —**ˌiodiˈzation** or **ˌiodiˈsation** *n.* —**ˈioˌdizer** or **ˈioˌdiser** *n.*

iodo- *or before a vowel* **iod-** *combining form.* indicating iodine: *iodoform; iodism.*

iodoform (aɪˈɒdəˌfɔːm) *n.* a yellow crystalline insoluble volatile solid with a penetrating sweet odour made by heating alcohol with iodine and an alkali: used as an antiseptic. Formula: CHI_3. Systematic name: **triiodomethane.**

iodometry (ˌaɪəˈdɒmɪtrɪ) *n. Chem.* a procedure used in volumetric analysis for determining the quantity of substance present that contains, liberates, or reacts with iodine. —**iodometric** (ˌaɪədəʊˈmɛtrɪk) or **ˌiodoˈmetrical** *adj.* —**ˌiodoˈmetrically** *adv.*

iodopsin (ˌaɪəˈdɒpsɪn) *n.* a violet light-sensitive pigment in the cones of the retina of the eye. Also called: **visual violet.** See also **rhodopsin.**

iodous (aɪˈɒdəs) *adj.* **1.** of or containing iodine, esp. in the trivalent state. **2.** concerned with or resembling iodine.

iolite (ˈaɪəˌlaɪt) *n.* another name for **cordierite.** [C19: from Greek *ion* a violet + -LITE]

IOM *abbrev. for* Isle of Man.

Io moth (ˈaɪəʊ) *n.* an American saturniid moth, *Automeris io*, bright yellow with a blue-and-pink eyelike spot on each of the hind wings. [C19: after *Io* (maiden in Greek mythology who was turned into a heifer and was tormented by a gadfly), referring to the sting of the larva]

ion (ˈaɪən, -ɒn) *n.* an electrically charged atom or group of atoms formed by the loss or gain of one or more electrons. See also **cation, anion.** [C19: from Greek, literally: going, from *ienai* to go]

-ion *suffix forming nouns.* indicating an action, process, or state: *creation; objection.* Compare **-ation, -tion.** [from Latin *-iōn-*, *-io*]

ion engine *n.* a type of rocket engine in which thrust is obtained by the electrostatic acceleration of charged positive ions. Compare **plasma engine.**

ion exchange *n.* the process in which ions are exchanged between a solution and an insoluble solid, usually a resin. It is used to soften water, to separate radioactive isotopes, and to purify certain industrial chemicals.

Ionian (aɪˈəʊnɪən) *n.* **1.** a member of a Hellenic people who settled in Attica in about 1100 B.C. and later colonized the islands and E coast of the Aegean Sea. *~adj.* **2.** of or relating to this people or their dialect of Ancient Greek; Ionic. **3.** of or relating to Ionia, an ancient region of W central Asia Minor. **4.** *Music.* relating to or denoting an authentic mode represented by the ascending natural diatonic scale from C to C and forming the basis of the modern major key. See also **Hypo-.**

ionic (aɪˈɒnɪk) *adj.* of, relating to, or occurring in the form of ions.

Ionic (aɪˈɒnɪk) *adj.* **1.** of, denoting, or relating to one of the five classical orders of architecture, characterized by fluted columns and capitals with scroll-like ornaments. See also **Doric, Composite, Tuscan, Corinthian.** **2.** of or relating to Ionia, its inhabitants, or their dialect of Ancient Greek. **3.** *Prosody.* of, relating to, designating, or employing Ionics in verse. *~n.* **4.** one of four chief dialects of Ancient Greek; the dialect spoken in Ionia. Compare **Aeolic, Arcadic, Doric.** See also **Attic** (sense 3). **5.** (in classical prosody) a type of metrical foot having either two long followed by two short syllables **(greater Ionic)**, or two short followed by two long syllables **(lesser Ionic)**.

ionic bond *n.* another name for **electrovalent bond.**

ion implantation *n.* a technique used in the manufacture of semiconductor devices in which impurities are implanted by means of beams of electrically accelerated ions.

ionium (aɪˈəʊnɪəm) *n. Obsolete.* a naturally occurring radioisotope of thorium with a mass number of 230. Symbol: Io [C20: from New Latin, from ION + -IUM]

ionization or **ionisation** (ˌaɪənaɪˈzeɪʃən) *n.* **a.** the formation of ions as a result of a chemical reaction, high temperature, electrical discharge, or radiation. **b.** (*as modifier*): *ionization temperature; ionization current.*

ionization chamber *n.* a device for detecting and measuring ionizing radiation, consisting of a tube containing a low pressure gas and two electrodes between which a high voltage is maintained. The current between the electrodes is a function of the intensity of the radiation.

ionization potential *n.* the energy required to remove an electron from an atom, molecule, or radical, measured in electronvolts. Symbol: *I* Compare **electron affinity.**

ionize or **ionise** (ˈaɪəˌnaɪz) *vb.* to change or become changed into ions. —**ˈionˌizable** or **ˈionˌisable** *adj.* —**ˈionˌizer** or **ˈionˌiser** *n.*

ionizing radiation *n.* electromagnetic or corpuscular radiation that is able to cause ionization.

ionone (ˈaɪəˌnəʊn) *n.* **1.** a yellowish liquid mixture of two isomers with an odour of violets, extracted from certain plants and used in perfumery. **2.** either of these two isomers. Formula: $C_{13}H_{20}O$.

ionopause (aɪˈɒnəˌpɔːz) *n.* the transitional zone in the atmosphere between the ionosphere and the exosphere, about 644 km (400 miles) from the earth's surface.

ionophore (aɪˈɒnəˌfɔː) *n.* a chemical compound capable of forming a complex with an ion and transporting it through a biological membrane. [C20: from ION + -O- + -PHORE]

ionosphere (aɪˈɒnəˌsfɪə) *n.* a region of the earth's atmosphere, extending from about 60 kilometres to 1000 km above the earth's surface, in which there is a high concentration of free electrons

formed as a result of ionizing radiation entering the atmosphere from space. See also **D region, E region, F region.** —**iono·spheric** (aɪˌɒnəˈsfɛrɪk) *adj.*
ionospheric wave *n.* another name for **sky wave.**
ionotropy (ˌaɪəˈnɒtrəpɪ) *n. Chem.* the reversible interconversion of a pair of organic isomers as a result of the migration of an ionic part of the molecule.
ion rocket *n.* a rocket propelled by an ion engine.
iontophoresis (aɪˌɒntəʊfəˈriːsɪs) *n. Biochem.* a technique for studying neurotransmitters in the brain by the application of experimental solutions to the tissues through fine glass electrodes. [C20: from Greek *iont-*, *ion*, from *ienai* to go + -PHORESIS]
IOOF *abbrev. for* Independent Order of Oddfellows.
iota (aɪˈəʊtə) *n.* **1.** the ninth letter in the Greek alphabet (Ι, ι), a vowel or semivowel, transliterated as *i* or *j*. **2.** (*usually used with a negative*) a very small amount; jot (esp. in the phrase **not one** *or* **an iota**). [C16: via Latin from Greek, of Semitic origin; see JOT]
iotacism (aɪˈəʊtəˌsɪzəm) *n.* a tendency of vowels and diphthongs, esp. in Modern Greek, to acquire the pronunciation of the vowel iota (iː).
IOU *n.* a written promise or reminder to pay a debt. [C17: representing *I owe you*]
-ious *suffix forming adjectives from nouns.* characterized by or full of: *ambitious; religious; suspicious.* Compare **-eous.** [from Latin *-ius* and *-iōsus* full of]
IOW *abbrev. for* Isle of Wight.
IPA *abbrev. for* International Phonetic Alphabet.
ipecac (ˈɪpɪˌkæk) *or* **ipecacuanha** (ˌɪpɪˌkækjʊˈænə) *n.* **1.** a low-growing South American rubiaceous shrub, *Cephaelis ipecacuanha.* **2.** a drug prepared from the dried roots of this plant, used as a purgative and emetic. [C18: from Portuguese *ipecacuanha*, from Tupi *ipekaaguéne*, from *ipeh* low + *kaa* leaves + *guéne* vomit]
ipomoea (ˌɪpəˈmɪə, ˌaɪ-) *n.* **1.** any tropical or subtropical convolvulaceous plant of the genus *Ipomoea*, such as the morning-glory, sweet potato, and jalap, having trumpet-shaped flowers. **2.** the dried root of a Mexican species, *I. orizabensis*, which yields a cathartic resin. [C18: New Latin, from Greek *ips* worm + *homoios* like]
ippon (ˈɪpɒn) *n. Judo, karate.* a winning point awarded in a sparring competition for a perfectly executed technique. [C20: Japanese, literally: one point]
ipse dixit *Latin.* (ˈɪpseɪ ˈdɪksɪt) *n.* an arbitrary and unsupported assertion. [C16, literally: he himself said it]
ipsilateral (ˌɪpsɪˈlætərəl) *adj.* on or affecting the same side of the body. [C20: irregularly formed from Latin *ipse* self + LATERAL]
ipsissima verba *Latin.* (ɪpˈsɪsɪmə ˈvɜːbə) *pl. n.* the very words; verbatim.
ipso facto (ˈɪpsəʊ ˈfæktəʊ) *adv.* by that very fact or act: *ipso facto his guilt was apparent.* [from Latin]
ipso jure (ˈɪpsəʊ ˈjʊərɪ) *adv.* by the law itself; by operation of law. [from Latin]
IQ *abbrev. for* intelligence quotient.
i.q. *abbrev. for* idem quod. [Latin: the same as]
Ir *the chemical symbol for* iridium.
IR *abbrev. for:* **1.** infrared. **2.** (in Britain) Inland Revenue. ~ **3**. *international car registration for* Iran.
Ir. *abbrev. for:* **1.** Ireland. **2.** Irish.
ir- *prefix.* a variant of **in-**[1] and **in-**[2] before *r*.
IRA *abbrev. for* Irish Republican Army.
iracund (ˈaɪərəˌkʌnd) *adj. Rare.* easily angered. [C19: from Latin *īrācundus*, from *īra* anger] —**ˌiraˈcundity** *n.*
irade (ɪˈrɑːdɛ) *n.* a written edict of a Muslim ruler. [C19: from Turkish: will, desire, from Arabic *irādah*]
Iran. *abbrev. for* Iranian.
Iranian (ɪˈreɪnɪən) *n.* **1.** a native, citizen, or inhabitant of Iran, a republic in SW Asia. **2.** a branch of the Indo-European family of languages, divided into **West Iranian** (including Old Persian, Pahlavi, modern Persian, Kurdish, Baluchi, and Tadzhiki) and **East Iranian** (including Avestan, Sogdian, Pashto, and Ossetic). **3.** the modern Persian language. ~*adj.* **4.** relating to, denoting, or characteristic of Iran, its inhabitants, or their language; Persian. **5.** belonging to or relating to the Iranian branch of Indo-European.
Iraqi (ɪˈrɑːkɪ) *adj.* **1.** of or relating to Iraq, a republic in SW Asia, or to its people, culture, etc. ~*n.* **2.** (*pl.* **-qis**) a native or inhabitant of Iraq.
irascible (ɪˈræsɪbᵊl) *adj.* **1.** easily angered; irritable. **2.** showing irritability: *an irascible action.* [C16: from Late Latin *īrascibilis*, from Latin *īra* anger] —**iˌrasciˈbility** *or* **iˈrascibleness** *n.* —**iˈrascibly** *adv.*
irate (aɪˈreɪt) *adj.* **1.** incensed with anger; furious. **2.** marked by extreme anger: *an irate letter.* [C19: from Latin *īrātus* enraged, from *īrascī* to be angry] —**iˈrately** *adv.*
IRBM *abbrev. for* intermediate range ballistic missile.
ire (aɪə) *n. Literary.* anger; wrath. [C13: from Old French, from Latin *īra*] —**ˈireful** *adj.* —**ˈirefully** *adv.* —**ˈirefulness** *n.* —**ˈireless** *adj.*
Ire. *abbrev. for* Ireland.
irenic, eirenic (aɪˈriːnɪk, -ˈrɛn-) *or* **irenical, eirenical** *adj.* tending to conciliate or promote peace. [C19: from Greek *eirēnikos*, from *eirēnē* peace] —**iˈrenically** *or* **eiˈrenically** *adv.*
irenicon (aɪˈriːnɪˌkɒn) *n.* a variant spelling of **eirenicon.**
irenics (aɪˈriːnɪks, -ˈrɛn-) *n.* (*functioning as sing.*) that branch of theology that is concerned with unity between Christian sects and denominations.
iridaceous (ˌɪrɪˈdeɪʃəs, ˌaɪ-) *adj.* of, relating to, or belonging to the *Iridaceae*, a family of monocotyledonous plants, including iris, crocus, and gladiolus, having swordlike leaves and showy flowers.
iridectomy (ˌɪrɪˈdɛktəmɪ, ˌaɪ-) *n., pl.* **-mies.** surgical removal of part of the iris.
iridescent (ˌɪrɪˈdɛsᵊnt) *adj.* displaying a spectrum of colours that shimmer and change due to interference and scattering as the observer's position changes. [C18: from IRIDO- + -ESCENT] —**ˌiriˈdescence** *n.* —**ˌiriˈdescently** *adv.*
iridic (aɪˈrɪdɪk, ɪˈrɪd-) *adj.* **1.** of or containing iridium, esp. in the tetravalent state. **2.** of or relating to the iris of the eye.
iridium (aɪˈrɪdɪəm, ɪˈrɪd-) *n.* a very hard inert yellowish-white transition element that is the most corrosion-resistant metal known. It occurs in platinum ores and is used as an alloy with platinum. Symbol: Ir; atomic no.: 77; atomic wt.: 192.2; valency: 3 or 4; relative density: 22.42; melting pt.: 2410°C; boiling pt.: 4130°C. [C19: New Latin, from IRIDO- + -IUM; from its colourful appearance when dissolving in certain acids]
irido- *or before a vowel* **irid-** *combining form.* **1.** denoting the iris of the eye or the genus of plants: *iridectomy; iridaceous.* **2.** denoting a rainbow: *iridescent.* [from Latin *irid-*, IRIS]
iridocyte (ˈɪrɪdəʊˌsaɪt) *n. Zoology.* a guanine-containing cell in the skin of fish and some cephalopods, giving these animals their iridescence.
iridology (ˌɪrɪˈdɒlədʒɪ) *n.* the practice of examining the iris of the eye as a method of medical diagnosis. —**ˌiriˈdologist** *n.*
iridosmine (ˌɪrɪˈdɒsmaɪn, ˌaɪrɪ-) *or* **iridosmium** *n.* other names for **osmiridium.** [C19: from IRIDO- + OSM(IUM) + -INE[2]]
iridotomy (ˌɪrɪˈdɒtəmɪ, ˌaɪrɪ-) *n., pl.* **-mies.** surgical incision into the iris, esp. to create an artificial pupil.
iris (ˈaɪrɪs) *n., pl.* **irises** *or* **irides** (ˈaɪrɪˌdiːz, ˈɪrɪ-). **1.** the coloured muscular diaphragm that surrounds and controls the size of the pupil. **2.** Also called: **fleur-de-lis.** any plant of the iridaceous genus *Iris*, having brightly coloured flowers composed of three petals and three drooping sepals. See also **flag**[2], **orris, stinking iris.** **3.** Also called: **rainbow quartz.** a form of quartz that reflects light polychromatically from internal fractures. **4.** a rare or poetic word for **rainbow.** **5.** something resembling a rainbow; iridescence. **6.** short for **iris diaphragm.** [C14: from Latin: rainbow, iris (flower), crystal, from Greek]
iris diaphragm *n.* an adjustable diaphragm that regulates the amount of light entering an optical instrument, esp. a camera. It usually consists of a number of thin metal leaves arranged so that they open out into an approximately circular aperture. Sometimes shortened to **iris.**
Irish (ˈaɪrɪʃ) *adj.* **1.** of, relating to, or characteristic of Ireland, its people, their Celtic language, or their dialect of English. **2.** *Informal, offensive.* ludicrous or illogical. ~*n.* **3. the Irish.** (*functioning as pl.*) the natives or inhabitants of Ireland. **4.** another name for **Irish Gaelic.**
Irish bull *n.* a ludicrously illogical statement. See also **bull**[2].
Irish coffee *n.* hot coffee mixed with Irish whiskey and topped with double cream.
Irish elk *n.* an extinct Eurasian giant deer of the Pleistocene genus *Megaloceros*, which had antlers up to 4 metres across.
Irish Gaelic *n.* the Goidelic language of the Celts of Ireland, now spoken mainly along the west coast; an official language of the Republic of Ireland since 1921.
Irishism (ˈaɪrɪˌʃɪzəm) *n.* an Irish custom or idiom.
Irishman (ˈaɪrɪʃmən) *or* (*fem.*) **Irishwoman** *n., pl.* **-men** *or* **-women.** a native, citizen, or inhabitant of Ireland or a descendant of one.
Irish moss *n.* another name for **carrageen.**
Irish potato *n. Chiefly U.S.* another name for the **potato.**
Irish setter *n.* a breed of setter developed in Ireland, having a flat soft brownish-red coat. Also called: **red setter.**
Irish stew *n.* a white stew made of mutton, lamb, or beef, with potatoes, onions, etc.
Irish terrier *n.* a breed of terrier with a wiry wheaten or reddish coat.
Irish water spaniel *n.* a breed of dog used to hunt duck and having a dense coat of a purplish-liver colour that falls in tight ringlets covering the whole body except for the face and tail.
Irish whiskey *n.* any of the whiskeys made in Ireland, usually from malt and subject to three distillations.
Irish wolfhound *n.* a large breed of hound with a rough thick coat.
iritis (aɪˈraɪtɪs) *n.* inflammation of the iris of the eye. —**iritic** (aɪˈrɪtɪk) *adj.*
irk (ɜːk) *vb.* (*tr.*) to irritate, vex, or annoy. [C13 *irken* to grow weary; probably related to Old Norse *yrkja* to work]
irksome (ˈɜːksəm) *adj.* causing vexation, annoyance, or boredom; troublesome or tedious. —**ˈirksomely** *adv.* —**ˈirksomeness** *n.*
IRL *international car registration for* Republic of Ireland.
IRM *abbrev. for* innate releasing mechanism.
IRO *abbrev. for:* **1.** (in Britain) Inland Revenue Office. **2.** International Refugee Organization.

iroko (ɪ'rəʊkəʊ) *n., pl.* **-kos.** 1. a tropical African hardwood tree of the genus *Chlorophora.* 2. the hard reddish-brown wood of this tree. [C19: from Yoruba]

iron ('aɪən) *n.* 1. **a.** a malleable ductile silvery-white ferromagnetic metallic element occurring principally in haematite and magnetite. It is widely used for structural and engineering purposes. See also **steel, cast iron, wrought iron, pig iron.** Symbol: Fe; atomic no.: 26; atomic wt.: 55.847; valency: 2,3,4, or 6; relative density: 7.874; melting pt.: 1535°C; boiling pt.: 2750°C. Related adjs.: **ferric, ferrous.** Related prefix: **ferro-. b.** (*as modifier*): *iron railings.* 2. any of certain tools or implements made of iron or steel, esp. for use when hot: *a grappling iron; a soldering iron.* 3. an appliance for pressing fabrics using dry heat or steam, esp. a small electrically heated device with a handle and a weighted flat bottom. 4. any of various golf clubs with metal heads, numbered from 2 to 10 according to the slant of the face, used esp. for approach shots: *a No. 6 iron.* 5. an informal word for **harpoon** (sense 1). 6. *U.S. slang.* a splintlike support for a malformed leg. 7. great hardness, strength, or resolve: *a will of iron.* 8. See **shooting iron.** 9. **strike while the iron is hot.** to act at an opportune moment. ~*adj.* 10. very hard, immovable, or implacable: *iron determination.* 11. very strong; extremely robust: *an iron constitution.* 12. cruel or unyielding: *he ruled with an iron hand.* ~*vb.* 13. to smooth (clothes or fabric) by removing (creases or wrinkles) using a heated iron; press. 14. (*tr.*) to furnish or clothe with iron. 15. (*tr.*) *Rare.* to place (a prisoner) in irons. ~See also **iron out, irons.** [Old English *īren;* related to Old High German *īsan,* Old Norse *jārn;* compare Old Irish *īarn*] —**'ironer** *n.* —**'ironless** *adj.* —**'iron,like** *adj.*

Iron Age *n.* **a.** the period following the Bronze Age characterized by the extremely rapid spread of iron tools and weapons, which began in the Middle East about 1100 B.C. **b.** (*as modifier*): *an Iron-Age weapon.*

ironbark ('aɪən,bɑːk) *n.* any of several Australian eucalyptus trees that have hard rough bark.

ironbound ('aɪən,baʊnd) *adj.* 1. bound with iron. 2. unyielding; inflexible. 3. (of a coast) rocky; rugged.

ironclad *adj.* (,aɪən'klæd). 1. covered or protected with iron: *an ironclad warship.* 2. inflexible; rigid: *an ironclad rule.* 3. not able to be assailed or contradicted: *an ironclad argument.* ~*n.* ('aɪən,klæd). 4. a large wooden 19th-century warship with armoured plating.

Iron Cross *n.* the highest decoration for bravery awarded to the German armed forces in wartime: instituted in 1813.

Iron Curtain *n.* **a.** (formerly) the guarded border between the countries of the Soviet bloc and the rest of Europe. **b.** (*as modifier*): *Iron Curtain countries.*

iron glance *n.* another name for **haematite.**

iron grey *n.* **a.** a neutral or dark grey colour. **b.** (*as adj.*): *iron-grey hair.*

iron hand *n.* harsh or rigorous control; overbearing or autocratic force: *he ruled with an iron hand.*

iron horse *n. Archaic.* 1. a steam-driven railway locomotive. 2. a bicycle or tricycle.

ironic (aɪ'rɒnɪk) *or* **ironical** *adj.* of, characterized by, or using irony. —**i'ronically** *adv.* —**i'ronicalness** *n.*

ironing ('aɪənɪŋ) *n.* 1. the act of ironing washed clothes. 2. clothes that are to be or that have been ironed.

ironing board *n.* a board, usually on legs, with a suitable covering on which to iron clothes.

ironize *or* **ironise** ('aɪrə,naɪz) *vb.* 1. (*intr.*) to use or indulge in irony. 2. (*tr.*) to make ironic or use ironically. —**'ironist** *n.*

iron lung *n.* 1. an airtight metal cylinder enclosing the entire body up to the neck and providing artificial respiration when the respiratory muscles are paralysed, as by poliomyelitis. 2. *Irish informal.* a gas container used in dispensing beer.

iron maiden *n.* a medieval instrument of torture, consisting of a hinged case (often shaped in the form of a woman) lined with iron spikes, which was forcibly closed on the victim.

iron man *n. Austral.* an event at a surf carnival in which contestants compete at swimming, surfing, running, etc.

ironmaster ('aɪən,mɑːstə) *n. Brit.* a manufacturer of iron, esp. (formerly) the owner of an ironworks.

iron meteorite *n.* a meteorite that is composed mainly of iron and nickel.

ironmonger ('aɪən,mʌŋgə) *n. Brit.* a dealer in metal utensils, hardware, locks, etc. U.S. and Canadian equivalent: **hardware dealer.** —**'iron,mongery** *n.*

iron out *vb.* (*tr., adv.*) 1. to smooth, using a heated iron. 2. to put right or settle (a problem or difficulty) as a result of negotiations or discussions. 3. *Austral. informal.* to knock unconscious.

iron pan *n. Geology.* a hard layer of precipitated iron salts often found below the surface of sands and gravels.

iron pyrites ('paɪraɪts) *n.* another name for **pyrite.**

iron rations *pl. n.* emergency food supplies, esp. for military personnel in action. See also **K ration.**

irons ('aɪənz) *pl. n.* 1. fetters or chains (often in the phrase **in** or **into irons**). 2. **in irons.** *Nautical.* (of a sailing vessel) headed directly into the wind without steerageway. 3. **have several irons in the fire.** to be involved in many projects, activities, etc.

ironsides ('aɪən,saɪdz) *n.* 1. a person with great stamina or resistance. 2. an ironclad ship. 3. (*often cap.*) (in the English Civil War) **a.** the cavalry regiment trained and commanded by Oliver Cromwell. **b.** Cromwell's entire army.

ironstone ('aɪən,stəʊn) *n.* 1. any rock consisting mainly of an iron-bearing ore. 2. Also called: **ironstone china.** a tough durable earthenware.

ironware ('aɪən,wɛə) *n.* domestic articles made of iron.

ironwood ('aɪən,wʊd) *n.* 1. any of various betulaceous trees, such as hornbeam, that have very hard wood. 2. a Californian rosaceous tree, *Lyonothamnus floribundus,* with very hard wood. 3. the wood of any of these trees.

ironwork ('aɪən,wɜːk) *n.* 1. work done in iron, esp. decorative work. 2. the craft or practice of working in iron. ~See also **ironworks.**

ironworker ('aɪən,wɜːkə) *n.* 1. a person who works in an ironworks. 2. a person who makes articles of iron.

ironworks ('aɪən,wɜːks) *n.* (*sometimes functioning as sing.*) a building in which iron is smelted, cast, or wrought.

irony[1] ('aɪrənɪ) *n., pl.* **-nies.** 1. the humorous or mildly sarcastic use of words to imply the opposite of what they normally mean. 2. an instance of this, used to draw attention to some incongruity or irrationality. 3. incongruity between what is expected to be and what actually is, or a situation or result showing such incongruity. 4. See **dramatic irony.** 5. *Philosophy.* See **Socratic irony.** [C16: from Latin *ironia,* from Greek *eirōneia,* from *eirōn* dissembler, from *eirein* to speak]

irony[2] ('aɪənɪ) *adj.* of, resembling, or containing iron.

Iroquoian (,ɪrə'kwɔɪən) *n.* 1. a family of North American Indian languages including Cherokee, Mohawk, Seneca, Oneida, and Onondaga: probably related to Siouan. ~*adj.* 2. of or relating to the Iroquois, their culture, or their languages.

Iroquois ('ɪrə,kwɔɪ, -,kwɔɪz) *n., pl.* **-quois.** 1. a member of any of a group of North American Indian peoples formerly living between the Hudson River and the St Lawrence and Lake Erie. 2. any of the Iroquoian languages. ~*adj.* 3. of or relating to the Iroquois, their language, or their culture.

IRQ *international car registration for* Iraq.

irradiance (ɪ'reɪdɪəns) *n.* the radiant flux incident on unit area of a surface. It is measured in watts per square metre. Symbol: E_e Also called: **irradiation.** Compare **illuminance.**

irradiant (ɪ'reɪdɪənt) *adj.* radiating light; shining brightly.

irradiate (ɪ'reɪdɪ,eɪt) *vb.* 1. (*tr.*) *Physics.* to subject to or treat with light or other electromagnetic radiation or with beams of particles. 2. (*tr.*) to expose (food) to electromagnetic radiation to kill bacteria and retard deterioration. 3. (*tr.*) to make clear or bright intellectually or spiritually; illumine. 4. a less common word for **radiate** (sense 1). 5. (*intr.*) *Obsolete.* to become radiant. —**ir'radiative** *adj.* —**ir'radi,ator** *n.*

irradiation (ɪ,reɪdɪ'eɪʃən) *n.* 1. the act or process of irradiating or the state of being irradiated. 2. the apparent enlargement of a brightly lit object when it is viewed against a dark background. 3. a shaft of light; beam or ray. 4. *Med.* **a.** the therapeutic or diagnostic use of radiation, esp. x-rays. **b.** exposure of a patient to such radiation. 5. another name for **radiation** or **irradiance.**

irrational (ɪ'ræʃənᵊl) *adj.* 1. inconsistent with reason or logic; illogical; absurd. 2. incapable of reasoning. 3. **a.** *Maths.* (of an equation, etc.) containing one or more variables in irreducible radical form or raised to a fractional power: $\sqrt{(x^2+1)} = x^{5/3}$. **b.** (*as n.*): *an irrational.* 4. *Prosody.* (in Greek or Latin verse) **a.** of or relating to a metrical irregularity, usually the occurrence of a long syllable instead of a short one. **b.** denoting a metrical foot where such an irregularity occurs. —**ir'rationally** *adv.* —**ir'rationalness** *n.*

irrationality (ɪ,ræʃə'nælɪtɪ) *or* **irrationalism** *n.* 1. the state or quality of being irrational. 2. irrational thought, action, or behaviour.

irrational number *n.* any real number that cannot be expressed as the ratio of two integers, such as π.

irreclaimable (,ɪrɪ'kleɪməbᵊl) *adj.* not able to be reclaimed. —**,irre,claima'bility** *or* **,irre'claimableness** *n.* —**,irre'claimably** *adv.*

irreconcilable (ɪ'rɛkᵊn,saɪləbᵊl, ɪ,rɛkᵊn'saɪ-) *adj.* 1. not able to be reconciled; uncompromisingly conflicting; incompatible. ~*n.* 2. a person or thing that is implacably hostile or uncompromisingly opposed. 3. (*usually pl.*) one of various principles, ideas, etc., that are incapable of being brought into agreement. —**ir,recon,cila'bility** *or* **ir'recon,cilableness** *n.* —**ir'recon,cilably** *adv.*

irrecoverable (,ɪrɪ'kʌvərəbᵊl, -'kʌvrə-) *adj.* 1. not able to be recovered or regained. 2. not able to be remedied or rectified. —**,irre'coverableness** *n.* —**,irre'coverably** *adv.*

irrecusable (,ɪrɪ'kjuːzəbᵊl) *adj.* not able to be rejected or challenged, as evidence, etc. —**,irre'cusably** *adv.*

irredeemable (,ɪrɪ'diːməbᵊl) *adj.* 1. (of bonds, debentures, shares, etc.) without a date of redemption of capital; incapable of being bought back directly or paid off. 2. (of paper money) not convertible into specie. 3. (of a sinner) not able to be saved or reformed. 4. (of a loss) not able to be recovered; irretrievable. 5. not able to be improved or rectified; irreparable. —**,irre,deema'bility** *or* **,irre'deemableness** *n.* —**,irre'deemably** *adv.*

irredentist (ˌɪrɪˈdɛntɪst) *n.* **1.** a person who favours the acquisition of territory that once was part of his country or is considered to have been. ~*adj.* **2.** of, relating to, or advocating this belief. [C19: from Italian *irredentista,* from the phrase *Italia irredenta,* literally: Italy unredeemed, from *ir-* IN-[1] + *redento* redeemed, from Latin *redemptus* bought back; see REDEEM] —ˌ**irreˈdentism** *n.*

Irredentist (ˌɪrɪˈdɛntɪst) *n.* (*sometimes not cap.*) a member of an Italian association prominent in 1878 that sought to recover for Italy certain neighbouring regions (***Italia irredenta***) with a predominantly Italian population that were under foreign control.

irreducible (ˌɪrɪˈdjuːsɪbəl) *adj.* **1.** not able to be reduced or lessened. **2.** not able to be brought to a simpler or reduced form. **3.** *Maths.* **a.** (of a polynomial) unable to be factorized into polynomials of lower degree, as $(x^2 + 1)$. **b.** (of a radical) incapable of being reduced to a rational expression, as $\sqrt{(x + 1)}$. —ˌ**irreˌduciˈbility** *or* ˌ**irreˈducibleness** *n.* —ˌ**irreˈducibly** *adv.*

irreflexive (ˌɪrɪˈflɛksɪv) *adj. Logic.* (of a relation) failing to hold between each member of its domain and itself: '... *is distinct from* ...' *is irreflexive.* Compare **reflexive** (sense 4), **nonreflexive.**

irrefragable (ɪˈrɛfrəgəbəl) *adj.* not able to be denied or refuted; indisputable. [C16: from Late Latin *irrefrāgābilis,* from Latin IR- + *refrāgārī* to resist, thwart] —**irˌrefragaˈbility** *or* **irˈrefragableness** *n.* —**irˈrefragably** *adv.*

irrefrangible (ˌɪrɪˈfrændʒəbəl) *adj.* **1.** not to be broken or transgressed; inviolable. **2.** *Physics.* incapable of being refracted. —ˌ**irreˌfrangiˈbility** *or* ˌ**irreˈfrangibleness** *n.* —ˌ**irreˈfrangibly** *adv.*

irrefutable (ɪˈrɛfjʊtəbəl, ˌɪrɪˈfjuːtəbəl) *adj.* impossible to deny or disprove; incontrovertible. —**irˌrefutaˈbility** *or* **irˈrefutableness** *n.* —**irˈrefutably** *adv.*

irreg. *abbrev. for* irregular(ly).

irregular (ɪˈrɛgjʊlə) *adj.* **1.** lacking uniformity or symmetry; uneven in shape, position, arrangement, etc. **2.** not occurring at expected or equal intervals: *an irregular pulse.* **3.** differing from the normal or accepted practice or routine. **4.** not according to established standards of behaviour; unconventional. **5.** (of the formation, inflections, or derivations of a word) not following the usual pattern of formation in a language, as English plurals ending other than in *-s* or *-es.* **6.** of or relating to guerrillas or volunteers not belonging to regular forces: *irregular troops.* **7.** (of flowers) having any of their parts, esp. petals, differing in size, shape, etc.; asymmetric. **8.** *U.S.* (of merchandise) not up to the manufacturer's standards or specifications; flawed; imperfect. ~*n.* **9.** a soldier not in a regular army. **10.** (*often pl.*) *U.S.* imperfect or flawed merchandise. Compare **second**[1] (sense 15). —**irˈregularly** *adv.*

irregularity (ɪˌrɛgjʊˈlærɪtɪ) *n., pl.* **-ties.** **1.** the state or quality of being irregular. **2.** something irregular, such as a bump in a smooth surface. **3.** a breach of a convention or normal procedure.

irrelative (ɪˈrɛlətɪv) *adj.* **1.** unrelated. **2.** a rare word for **irrelevant.** —**irˈrelatively** *adv.* —**irˈrelativeness** *n.*

irrelevant (ɪˈrɛləvənt) *adj.* not relating or pertinent to the matter at hand; not important. —**irˈrelevance** *or* **irˈrelevancy** *n.* —**irˈrelevantly** *adv.*

irrelievable (ˌɪrɪˈliːvəbəl) *adj.* not able to be relieved.

irreligion (ˌɪrɪˈlɪdʒən) *n.* **1.** lack of religious faith. **2.** indifference or opposition to religion. —ˌ**irreˈligionist** *n.* —ˌ**irreˈligious** *adj.* —ˌ**irreˈligiously** *adv.* —ˌ**irreˈligiousness** *n.*

irremeable (ɪˈrɛmɪəbəl, ɪˈriː-) *adj. Archaic or poetic.* affording no possibility of return. [C16: from Latin *irremeābilis,* from IR- + *remeāre* to return, from RE- + *meāre* to go] —**irˈremeably** *adv.*

irremediable (ˌɪrɪˈmiːdɪəbəl) *adj.* not able to be remedied; incurable or irreparable. —ˌ**irreˈmediableness** *n.* —ˌ**irreˈmediably** *adv.*

irremissible (ˌɪrɪˈmɪsəbəl) *adj.* **1.** unpardonable; inexcusable. **2.** that must be done, as through duty or obligation. —ˌ**irreˌmissiˈbility** *or* ˌ**irreˈmissibleness** *n.* —ˌ**irreˈmissibly** *adv.*

irremovable (ˌɪrɪˈmuːvəbəl) *adj.* not able to be removed. —ˌ**irreˌmovaˈbility** *or* ˌ**irreˈmovableness** *n.* —ˌ**irreˈmovably** *adv.*

irreparable (ɪˈrɛpərəbəl, ɪˈrɛprəbəl) *adj.* not able to be repaired or remedied; beyond repair. —**irˌreparaˈbility** *or* **irˈreparableness** *n.* —**irˈreparably** *adv.*

irrepealable (ˌɪrɪˈpiːləbəl) *adj.* not able to be repealed. —ˌ**irreˌpealaˈbility** *or* ˌ**irreˈpealableness** *n.* —ˌ**irreˈpealably** *adv.*

irreplaceable (ˌɪrɪˈpleɪsəbəl) *adj.* not able to be replaced: *an irreplaceable antique.* —ˌ**irreˈplaceably** *adv.*

irrepleviable (ˌɪrɪˈplɛvɪəbəl) *or* **irreplevisable** (ˌɪrɪˈplɛvɪsəbəl) *adj. Law.* not able to be replevied. [C16: see *ir-* IN-[1], REPLEVIN]

irrepressible (ˌɪrɪˈprɛsəbəl) *adj.* not capable of being repressed, controlled, or restrained. —ˌ**irreˌpressiˈbility** *or* ˌ**irreˈpressibleness** *n.* —ˌ**irreˈpressibly** *adv.*

irreproachable (ˌɪrɪˈprəʊtʃəbəl) *adj.* not deserving reproach; blameless. —ˌ**irreˌproachaˈbility** *or* ˌ**irreˈproachableness** *n.* —ˌ**irreˈproachably** *adv.*

irresistible (ˌɪrɪˈzɪstəbəl) *adj.* **1.** not able to be resisted or refused; overpowering: *an irresistible impulse.* **2.** very fascinating or alluring: *an irresistible woman.* —ˌ**irreˌsistiˈbility** *or* ˌ**irreˈsistibleness** *n.* —ˌ**irreˈsistibly** *adv.*

irresoluble (ɪˈrɛzəljʊbəl) *adj.* **1.** a less common word for **insoluble.** **2.** *Archaic.* not capable of being relieved. —**irˌresoluˈbility** *n.* —**irˈresolubly** *adv.*

irresolute (ɪˈrɛzəˌluːt) *adj.* lacking resolution; wavering; hesitating. —**irˈresoˌlutely** *adv.* —**irˈresoˌluteness** *or* **irˌresoˈlution** *n.*

irresolvable (ˌɪrɪˈzɒlvəbəl) *adj.* **1.** not able to be resolved into parts or elements. **2.** not able to be solved; insoluble. —ˌ**irreˌsolvaˈbility** *or* ˌ**irreˈsolvableness** *n.* —ˌ**irreˈsolvably** *adv.*

irrespective (ˌɪrɪˈspɛktɪv) *adj.* **1.** **irrespective of.** (*prep.*) without taking account of; regardless of. ~*adv.* **2.** *Informal.* regardless; without due consideration: *he carried on with his plan irrespective.* —ˌ**irreˈspectively** *adv.*

irrespirable (ɪˈrɛspɪrəbəl, ˌɪrɪˈspaɪərəbəl) *adj.* not fit for breathing or incapable of being breathed.

irresponsible (ˌɪrɪˈspɒnsəbəl) *adj.* **1.** not showing or done with due care for the consequences of one's actions or attitudes; reckless. **2.** not capable of bearing responsibility. **3.** *Archaic.* not answerable to a higher authority for one's actions. —ˌ**irreˌsponsiˈbility** *or* ˌ**irreˈsponsibleness** *n.* —ˌ**irreˈsponsibly** *adv.*

irresponsive (ˌɪrɪˈspɒnsɪv) *adj.* not responsive. —ˌ**irreˈsponsively** *adv.* —ˌ**irreˈsponsiveness** *n.*

irretentive (ˌɪrɪˈtɛntɪv) *adj.* not retentive. —ˌ**irreˈtentiveness** *n.*

irretrievable (ˌɪrɪˈtriːvəbəl) *adj.* not able to be retrieved, recovered, or repaired. —ˌ**irreˌtrievaˈbility** *or* ˌ**irreˈtrievableness** *n.* —ˌ**irreˈtrievably** *adv.*

irreverence (ɪˈrɛvərəns, ɪˈrɛvrəns) *n.* **1.** lack of due respect or veneration; disrespect. **2.** a disrespectful remark or act. **3.** *Rare.* disrepute; lack of reputation. —**irˈreverent** *or* **irˌreveˈrential** *adj.* —**irˈreverently** *adv.*

irreversible (ˌɪrɪˈvɜːsəbəl) *adj.* **1.** not able to be reversed: *the irreversible flow of time.* **2.** not able to be revoked or repealed; irrevocable. **3.** *Chem., physics.* capable of changing or producing a change in one direction only: *an irreversible reaction.* **4.** *Thermodynamics.* (of a change, process, etc.) occurring through a number of intermediate states that are not all in thermodynamic equilibrium. —ˌ**irreˌversiˈbility** *or* ˌ**irreˈversibleness** *n.* —ˌ**irreˈversibly** *adv.*

irrevocable (ɪˈrɛvəkəbəl) *adj.* not able to be revoked, changed, or undone; unalterable. —**irˌrevocaˈbility** *or* **irˈrevocableness** *n.* —**irˈrevocably** *adv.*

irrigate (ˈɪrɪˌgeɪt) *vb.* **1.** to supply (land) with water by means of artificial canals, ditches, etc., esp. to promote the growth of food crops. **2.** *Med.* to bathe or wash out a bodily part, cavity, or wound. **3.** (*tr.*) to make fertile, fresh, or vital by or as if by watering. [C17: from Latin *irrigāre,* from *rigāre* to moisten, conduct water] —ˈ**irrigable** *adj.* —ˌ**irriˈgation** *n.* —ˌ**irriˈgational** *or* ˈ**irriˌgative** *adj.* —ˈ**irriˌgator** *n.*

irriguous (ɪˈrɪgjʊəs) *adj. Archaic or poetic.* well-watered; watery. [C17: from Latin *irriguus* supplied with water, from *riguus* watered; *see* IRRIGATE]

irritable (ˈɪrɪtəbəl) *adj.* **1.** quickly irritated; easily annoyed; peevish. **2.** (of all living organisms) capable of responding to such stimuli as heat, light, and touch. **3.** *Pathol.* abnormally sensitive. —ˌ**irritaˈbility** *n.* —ˈ**irritableness** *n.* —ˈ**irritably** *adv.*

irritable bowel syndrome *n. Med.* a chronic condition of recurring abdominal pain with constipation or diarrhoea or both.

irritant (ˈɪrɪtənt) *adj.* **1.** causing irritation; irritating. ~*n.* **2.** something irritant. —ˈ**irritancy** *n.*

irritate (ˈɪrɪˌteɪt) *vb.* **1.** to annoy or anger (someone). **2.** (*tr.*) *Biology.* to stimulate (an organism or part) to respond in a characteristic manner. **3.** (*tr.*) *Pathol.* to cause (a bodily organ or part) to become excessively stimulated, resulting in inflammation, tenderness, etc. [C16: from Latin *irrītāre* to provoke, exasperate] —ˈ**irriˌtator** *n.*

irritation (ˌɪrɪˈteɪʃən) *n.* **1.** something that irritates. **2.** the act of irritating or the condition of being irritated. —ˈ**irriˌtative** *adj.*

irrupt (ɪˈrʌpt) *vb.* (*intr.*) **1.** to enter forcibly or suddenly. **2.** (of a plant or animal population) to enter a region suddenly and in very large numbers. **3.** (of a population) to increase suddenly and greatly. [C19: from Latin *irrumpere* to rush into, invade, from *rumpere* to break, burst] —**irˈruption** *n.*

irruptive (ɪˈrʌptɪv) *adj.* **1.** irrupting or tending to irrupt. **2.** of, involving, or causing irruption. **3.** (of igneous rocks) intrusive. —**irˈruptively** *adv.*

is (ɪz) *vb.* (used with *he, she, it,* and with singular nouns) a form of the present tense (indicative mood) of **be.** [Old English; compare Old Norse *es,* German *ist,* Latin *est,* Greek *esti*]

IS *international car registration for* Iceland. [Icelandic *Ísland*]

Is. *abbrev. for:* **1.** Also: **Isa.** *Bible.* Isaiah. **2.** Island(s) *or* Isle(s).

is- *combining form.* variant of **iso-** before a vowel: *isentropic.*

ISA *Aeronautics. abbrev. for:* **1.** International Standard Atmosphere. **2.** Interim Standard Atmosphere.

Isabella (ˌɪzəˈbɛlə) *or* **Isabel** (ˈɪzəˌbɛl) *n.* **a.** a greyish-yellow colour. **b.** Also: **Isabelline** (ˌɪzəˈbɛliːn). (*as adj.*): *an Isabella mohair coat.* [C17: from the name *Isabella*; original reference uncertain]

isagoge (ˈaɪsəˌgəʊdʒɪ, ˌaɪsəˈgəʊ-) *n.* an academic introduction to a specialized subject field or area of research. [C17: from Latin, from Greek *eisagōgē,* from *eisagein* to introduce, from *eis-* into + *agein* to lead]

isagogics (ˌaɪsəˈgɒdʒɪks) *n.* (*usually functioning as sing.*) introductory studies, esp. in the history of the Bible. —ˌ**isaˈgogic** *adj.*

isallobar (aɪˈsæləˌbɑː) *n. Meteorol.* a line on a map running through places experiencing equal pressure changes.

isatin (ˈaɪsətɪn) *or* **isatine** (ˈaɪsəˌtiːn) *n.* a yellowish-red crystalline compound soluble in hot water, used for the preparation of vat dyes. Formula: $C_8H_5NO_2$. [C19: from Latin *isatis* woad + -IN] —ˌ**isaˈtinic** *adj.*

ISBN *abbrev. for* International Standard Book Number.

ischaemia *or* **ischemia** (ɪˈskiːmɪə) *n. Pathol.* an inadequate supply of blood to an organ or part, as from an obstructed blood flow. [C19: from Greek *iskhein* to restrict, + -EMIA] —**ischaemic** *or* **ischemic** (ɪˈskɛmɪk) *adj.*

ischium (ˈɪskɪəm) *n., pl.* **-chia** (-kɪə). one of the three sections of the hipbone, situated below the ilium. [C17: from Latin: hip joint, from Greek *iskhion*] —ˈ**ischial** *adj.*

ISD *abbrev. for* international subscriber dialling.

-ise *suffix forming verbs.* a variant of **-ize.**

▷**Usage.** See at **-ize.**

isentropic (ˌaɪsɛnˈtrɒpɪk) *adj.* having or taking place at constant entropy.

-ish *suffix forming adjectives.* **1.** of or belonging to a nationality or group: *Scottish.* **2.** *Often derogatory.* having the manner or qualities of; resembling: *slavish; prudish; boyish.* **3.** somewhat; approximately: *yellowish; sevenish.* **4.** concerned or preoccupied with: *bookish.* [Old English *-isc;* related to German *-isch,* Greek *-iskos*]

Ishmaelite (ˈɪʃmeɪəˌlaɪt) *n.* **1.** a supposed descendant of Ishmael, the son of Abraham and Hagar; a member of a desert people of Old Testament times. **2.** *Rare.* an outcast. —ˈ**Ishmaelˌitism** *n.*

isinglass (ˈaɪzɪŋˌglɑːs) *n.* **1.** a gelatin made from the air bladders of freshwater fish, used as a clarifying agent and adhesive. **2.** another name for **mica.** [C16: from Middle Dutch *huysenblase,* literally: sturgeon bladder; influenced by English GLASS]

Isl. *abbrev. for:* **1.** Island. **2.** Isle.

Islam (ˈɪzlɑːm) *n.* **1.** Also called: **Islamism** (ɪzˈlɑːmɪzəm, ˈɪzləmɪzəm). the religion of Muslims, having the Koran as its sacred scripture and teaching that there is only one God and that Mohammed (570–632 A.D.) is his prophet; Mohammedanism. **2. a.** Muslims collectively and their civilization. **b.** the countries where the Muslim religion is predominant. [C19: from Arabic: surrender (to God), from *aslama* to surrender] —**Isˈlamic** *adj.*

Islamize *or* **Islamise** (ˈɪzləˌmaɪz) *vb.* (*tr.*) to convert or subject to the influence of Islam; Mohammedanize. —ˌ**Islamiˈzation** *or* ˌ**Islamiˈsation** *n.*

island (ˈaɪlənd) *n.* **1.** a mass of land that is surrounded by water and is smaller than a continent. **2.** something isolated, detached, or surrounded: *a traffic island.* **3.** *Anatomy.* a part, structure, or group of cells distinct in constitution from its immediate surroundings. ~Related adj.: **insular.** ~*vb.* (*tr.*) *Rare.* **4.** to cause to become an island. **5.** to intersperse with islands. **6.** to place on an island; insulate; isolate. [Old English *īgland,* from *īg* island + LAND; *s* inserted through influence of ISLE] —ˈ**island-ˌlike** *adj.*

island arc *n.* an arc-shaped chain of islands, such as the Aleutian Islands or the Japanese Islands, usually lying at the edge of a Benioff zone, indicating volcanic activity where the oceanic lithosphere is descending into the earth's interior.

islander (ˈaɪləndə) *n.* **1.** a native or inhabitant of an island. **2.** (*cap.*) *N.Z.* a native or inhabitant of the Pacific Islands.

island of Reil (raɪl) *n.* another name for **insula.** [after Johann *Reil* (died 1813), German physician]

islands council *n.* (in Scotland since 1975) any of the three divisions (Orkney, Shetland, and the Western Isles) into which the Scottish islands are divided for purposes of local government. See also **region** (sense 6).

island universe *n.* a former name for **galaxy.**

isle (aɪl) *n. Poetic except when cap. and part of place name.* an island, esp. a small one. [C13: from Old French *isle,* from Latin *insula* island]

islet (ˈaɪlɪt) *n.* a small island. [C16: from Old French *islette;* see ISLE]

islets of Langerhans *or* **islands of Langerhans** (ˈlæŋəˌhæns) *pl. n.* small groups of endocrine cells in the pancreas that secrete the hormones insulin and glucagon. [C19: named after Paul *Langerhans* (1847–88), German physician]

ism (ˈɪzəm) *n. Informal, often derogatory.* an unspecified doctrine, system, or practice.

-ism *suffix forming nouns.* **1.** indicating an action, process, or result: *criticism; terrorism.* **2.** indicating a state or condition: *paganism.* **3.** indicating a doctrine, system, or body of principles and practices: *Leninism; spiritualism.* **4.** indicating behaviour or a characteristic quality: *heroism.* **5.** indicating a characteristic usage, esp. of a language: *colloquialism; Scotticism.* **6.** indicating prejudice on the basis specified: *sexism; ageism.* [from Old French *-isme,* from Latin *-ismus,* from Greek *-ismos*]

Ismaili (ˌɪzmɑːˈiːlɪ) *or* **Ismailian** *n., pl.* **-lis.** *Islam.* a member of the Ismaili (or Isma'ili), a Shiah sect whose adherents believe that Ismail, son of the sixth imam, was the rightful seventh imam.

isna *or* **isnae** (ˈɪznɪ) *vb. Scot.* is not.

isn't (ˈɪzᵊnt) *vb. contraction of* is not.

ISO *abbrev. for* **1.** International Standards Organization. **2.** Imperial Service Order (a Brit. decoration).

iso- *or before a vowel* **is-** *combining form.* **1.** equal or identical: *isomagnetic.* **2.** indicating that a chemical compound is an isomer of a specified compound: *isobutane; isocyanic acid.* [from Greek *isos* equal]

isoagglutination (ˌaɪsəʊəˌgluːtɪˈneɪʃən) *n.* the agglutination of red blood cells of an organism by the blood serum of another organism of the same species. —ˌ**isoagˈglutinative** *adj.*

isoagglutinin (ˌaɪsəʊəˈgluːtɪnɪn) *n.* an antibody that causes agglutination of red blood cells in animals of the same species from which it was derived.

isoamyl acetate (ˌaɪsəʊˈæmɪl) *n.* a colourless volatile compound used as a solvent for cellulose lacquers and as a flavouring. Formula: $(CH_3)_2CHCH_2CH_2OOCCH_3$.

isoantigen (ˌaɪsəʊˈæntɪdʒən) *n. Immunol.* an antigen that stimulates antibody production in different members of the same species.

isobar (ˈaɪsəʊˌbɑː) *n.* **1.** a line on a map connecting places of equal atmospheric pressure, usually reduced to sea level for purposes of comparison, at a given time or period. **2.** *Physics.* any of two or more atoms that have the same mass number but different atomic numbers: *tin-115 and indium-115 are isobars.* Compare **isotope.** [C19: from Greek *isobarēs* of equal weight, from ISO- + *baros* weight] —ˈ**isobarˌism** *n.*

isobaric (ˌaɪsəʊˈbærɪk) *adj.* **1.** Also: **isopiestic.** having equal atmospheric pressure. **2.** of or relating to isobars.

isobaric spin *n.* See **isospin.**

isobath (ˈaɪsəʊˌbæθ) *n.* a line on a map connecting points of equal underwater depth. [C19: from Greek *isobathēs* of equal depth, from ISO- + *bathos* depth] —ˌ**isoˈbathic** *adj.*

isobilateral (ˌaɪsəʊbaɪˈlætərəl) *adj. Botany.* (esp. of a leaf) capable of being divided into symmetrical halves along two different planes.

isocheim *or* **isochime** (ˈaɪsəʊˌkaɪm) *n.* a line on a map connecting places with the same mean winter temperature. [C19: from ISO- + Greek *kheima* winter weather] —ˌ**isoˈcheimal,** ˌ**isoˈcheimenal,** *or* ˌ**isoˈchimal** *adj.*

isochor *or* **isochore** (ˈaɪsəʊˌkɔː) *n.* a line on a graph showing the variation of the temperature of a fluid with its pressure, when the volume is kept constant. [C19: from ISO- + Greek *khōros* place, space] —ˌ**isoˈchoric** *adj.*

isochromatic (ˌaɪsəʊkrəʊˈmætɪk) *adj.* **1. a.** having the same colour. **b.** of uniform colour. **2.** *Photog.* (of an early type of emulsion) sensitive to green light in addition to blue light but not to red light.

isochronal (aɪˈsɒkrənᵊl) *or* **isochronous** *adj.* **1.** having the same duration; equal in time. **2.** occurring at equal time intervals; having a uniform period of vibration or oscillation. [C17: from New Latin *isochronus,* from Greek *isokhronos,* from ISO- + *khronos* time] —**iˈsochronally** *or* **iˈsochronously** *adv.* —**iˈsochroˌnism** *n.*

isochronize *or* **isochronise** (aɪˈsɒkrəˌnaɪz) *vb.* (*tr.*) to make isochronal.

isochroous (aɪˈsɒkrəʊəs) *adj.* of uniform colour.

isoclinal (ˌaɪsəʊˈklaɪnᵊl) *or* **isoclinic** (ˌaɪsəʊˈklɪnɪk) *adj.* **1.** sloping in the same direction and at the same angle. **2.** *Geology.* (of folds) having limbs that are parallel to each other. ~*n.* **3.** Also called: **isocline, isoclinal line.** an imaginary line connecting points on the earth's surface having equal angles of dip.

isocline (ˈaɪsəʊˌklaɪn) *n.* **1.** a series of rock strata with isoclinal folds. **2.** another name for **isoclinal** (sense 3).

isocracy (aɪˈsɒkrəsɪ) *n., pl.* **-cies.** **1.** a form of government in which all people have equal powers. **2.** equality of political power. —**isocratic** (ˌaɪsəʊˈkrætɪk) *adj.*

isocyanic acid (ˌaɪsəʊsaɪˈænɪk) *n.* a hypothetical acid known only in the form of its compounds. Formula: HNCO.

isocyanide (ˌaɪsəʊˈsaɪəˌnaɪd) *n.* any salt or ester of isocyanic acid. Also called: **carbylamine, isonitrile.**

isodiametric (ˌaɪsəʊˌdaɪəˈmɛtrɪk) *adj.* **1.** having diameters of the same length. **2.** (of a crystal) having three equal axes. **3.** (of a cell or similar body) having a similar diameter in all planes.

isodiaphere (ˌaɪsəʊˈdaɪəˌfɪə) *n.* one of two or more nuclides in which the difference between the number of neutrons and the number of protons is the same: *a nuclide that has emitted an alpha particle, and its decay product, are isodiapheres.*

isodimorphism (ˌaɪsəʊdaɪˈmɔːfɪzəm) *n.* a property of a dimorphous substance such that it is isomorphous with another dimorphous substance in both its forms. —ˌ**isodiˈmorphous** *or* ˌ**isodiˈmorphic** *adj.*

isodose (ˈaɪsəʊˌdəʊs) *n. Med.* a dose of radiation applied to a part of the body in radiotherapy that is equal to the dose applied to a different part.

isodynamic (ˌaɪsəʊdaɪˈnæmɪk) *adj. Physics.* **1.** having equal force or strength. **2.** of or relating to an imaginary line on the earth's surface connecting points of equal horizontal magnetic intensity.

isoelectric (ˌaɪsəʊɪˈlɛktrɪk) *adj.* having the same electric potential.

isoelectric point *n. Biochem.* the pH value at which the net electric charge of a molecule, such as a protein or amino acid, is zero.

isoelectronic (ˌaɪsəʊɪlɛkˈtrɒnɪk) *adj.* (of atoms, radicals, or ions) having an equal number of electrons or a similar configuration of electrons.
isoenzyme (ˌaɪsəʊˈɛnzaɪm) *n.* another name for **isozyme.** —**isoenzymic** (ˌaɪsəʊɛnˈzaɪmɪk, -ˈzɪm-) *adj.*
isogamete (ˌaɪsəʊgæˈmiːt) *n.* a gamete that is similar in size and form to the one with which it unites in fertilization. Compare **heterogamete.** —**isogametic** (ˌaɪsəʊgæˈmɛtɪk) *adj.*
isogamy (aɪˈsɒgəmɪ) *n.* (in some algae and fungi) sexual fusion of gametes of similar size and form. Compare **heterogamy** (sense 1). —**iˈsogamous** *adj.*
isogenous (aɪˈsɒdʒɪnəs) *adj. Biology.* **1.** of similar origin, as parts derived from the same embryonic tissue. **2.** Also: **isogenic** (ˌaɪsəʊˈdʒɛnɪk). genetically uniform. —**iˈsogeny** *n.*
isogeotherm (ˌaɪsəʊˈdʒiːəʊˌθɜːm) *n.* an imaginary line below the surface of the earth connecting points of equal temperature. —ˌ**isoˌgeoˈthermal** *or* ˌ**isoˌgeoˈthermic** *adj.*
isogloss (ˈaɪsəʊˌglɒs) *n.* a line drawn on a map around the area in which a linguistic feature is to be found, such as a particular pronunciation of a given word. —ˌ**isoˈglossal** *or* ˌ**isoˈglottic** *adj.*
isogon (ˈaɪsəʊˌgɒn) *n.* an equiangular polygon.
isogonic (ˌaɪsəʊˈgɒnɪk) *or* **isogonal** (aɪˈsɒgənᵊl) *adj.* **1.** *Maths.* having, making, or involving equal angles. ~*n.* **2.** Also called: **isogonic line, isogonal line, isogone.** *Physics.* an imaginary line connecting points on the earth's surface having equal magnetic declination.
isogram (ˈaɪsəʊˌgræm) *n.* another name for **isopleth.**
isohel (ˈaɪsəʊˌhɛl) *n.* a line on a map connecting places with an equal period of sunshine. [C20: from ISO- + Greek *hēlios* sun]
isohydric (ˌaɪsəʊˈhaɪdrɪk) *adj. Chem.* having the same acidity or hydrogen-ion concentration.
isohyet (ˌaɪsəʊˈhaɪɪt) *n.* a line on a map connecting places having equal rainfall. [C19: from ISO- + *-hyet,* from Greek *huetos* rain]
isolate *vb.* (ˈaɪsəˌleɪt). (*tr.*) **1.** to place apart; cause to be alone. **2.** *Med.* to quarantine (a person or animal) having or suspected of having a contagious disease. **3.** to obtain (a compound) in an uncombined form. **4.** to obtain pure cultures of (bacteria, esp. those causing a particular disease). **5.** *Electronics.* to prevent interaction between (circuits, components, etc.); insulate. ~*n.* (ˈaɪsəlɪt). **6.** an isolated person or group. [C19: back formation from *isolated,* via Italian from Latin *insulātus,* literally: made into an island; see INSULATE] —ˈ**isolable** *adj.* —ˌ**isolaˈbility** *n.* —ˈ**isoˌlator** *n.*
isolated pawn *n. Chess.* a pawn without pawns of the same colour on neighbouring files.
isolating (ˈaɪsəˌleɪtɪŋ) *adj. Linguistics.* another word for **analytic.**
isolation (ˌaɪsəˈleɪʃən) *n.* **1.** the act of isolating or the condition of being isolated. **2.** (of a country, party, etc.) nonparticipation in or withdrawal from international politics. **3.** *Med.* **a.** social separation of a person who has or is suspected of having a contagious disease. Compare **quarantine. b.** (*as modifier*): *an isolation hospital.* **4.** *Sociol.* a lack of contact between persons, groups, or whole societies. **5.** *Social psychol.* the failure of an individual to maintain contact with others or genuine communication where interaction with others persists. **6. in isolation.** without regard to context, similar matters, etc.
isolationism (ˌaɪsəˈleɪʃəˌnɪzəm) *n.* **1.** a policy of nonparticipation in or withdrawal from international affairs. **2.** an attitude favouring such a policy. —ˌ**isoˈlationist** *n., adj.*
isolative (ˈaɪsəˌleɪtɪv, ˈaɪsələtɪv) *adj.* **1.** (of a sound change) occurring in all linguistic environments, as the change of Middle English /iː/ to Modern English /aɪ/, as in *time.* Compare **combinative** (sense 2). **2.** of, relating to, or concerned with isolation.
isolecithal (ˌaɪsəʊˈlɛsɪθəl) *adj.* (of the ova of mammals and certain other vertebrates) having an evenly distributed yolk. Compare **heterolecithal.**
isoleucine (ˌaɪsəʊˈluːsiːn, -sɪn) *n.* an essential amino acid that occurs in proteins and is formed by protein hydrolysis.
isolex (ˈaɪsəˌlɛks) *n. Linguistics.* an isogloss marking off the area in which a particular item of vocabulary is found [C20: from ISO(GLOSS) + Greek *lex(is)* word]
isoline (ˈaɪsəʊˌlaɪn) *n.* another term for **isopleth.**
isologous (aɪˈsɒləgəs) *adj.* (of two or more organic compounds) having a similar structure but containing different atoms of the same valency. [C19: from ISO- + (HOMO)LOGOUS] —**isologue** (ˈaɪsəʊˌlɒg) *n.*
isomagnetic (ˌaɪsəʊmægˈnɛtɪk) *adj.* **1.** having equal magnetic induction or force. ~*n.* **2.** Also called: **isomagnetic line.** an imaginary line connecting points on the earth's surface having equal magnetic intensity.
isomer (ˈaɪsəmə) *n.* **1.** *Chem.* a compound that exhibits isomerism with one or more other compounds. **2.** *Physics.* a nuclide that exhibits isomerism with one or more other nuclides. —**isomeric** (ˌaɪsəˈmɛrɪk) *adj.*
isomerase (aɪˈsɒməreɪs) *n.* any enzyme that catalyses the conversion of one isomeric form of a compound to another.
isomerism (aɪˈsɒməˌrɪzəm) *n.* **1.** the existence of two or more compounds having the same molecular formula but a different arrangement of atoms within the molecule. See also **stereoisomerism, optical isomerism. 2.** the existence of two or more nuclides having the same atomic numbers and mass numbers but different energy states.
isomerize *or* **isomerise** (aɪˈsɒməˌraɪz) *vb. Chem.* to change or cause to change from one isomer to another. —**iˌsomeriˈzation** *or* **iˌsomeriˈsation** *n.*
isomerous (aɪˈsɒmərəs) *adj.* **1.** having an equal number of parts or markings. **2.** (of flowers) having floral whorls with the same number of parts. Compare **anisomerous.**
isometric (ˌaɪsəʊˈmɛtrɪk) *adj. also* **isometrical. 1.** having equal dimensions or measurements. **2.** *Physiol.* of or relating to muscular contraction that does not produce shortening of the muscle. **3.** (of a crystal or system of crystallization) having three mutually perpendicular equal axes. **4.** *Crystallog.* another word for **cubic** (sense 4). **5.** *Prosody.* having or made up of regular feet. **6.** (of a method of projecting a drawing in three dimensions) having the three axes equally inclined and all lines drawn to scale. ~*n.* **7.** Also called: **isometric drawing.** a drawing made in this way. **8.** Also called: **isometric line.** a line on a graph showing variations of pressure with temperature at constant volume. [C19: from Greek *isometria* (see ISO- + -METRY) + -IC] —ˌ**isoˈmetrically** *adv.*
isometrics (ˌaɪsəʊˈmɛtrɪks) *n.* (*functioning as sing.*) physical exercise involving isometric contraction of muscles.
isometropia (ˌaɪsəʊmɪˈtrəʊpɪə) *n. Ophthalmol.* equal refraction of the two eyes. [from Greek *isometros* of equal measure + -OPIA]
isometry (aɪˈsɒmɪtrɪ) *n.* **1.** *Maths.* rigid motion of a plane or space such that the distance between any two points before and after this motion is unaltered. **2.** equality of height above sea level.
isomorph (ˈaɪsəʊˌmɔːf) *n.* a substance or organism that exhibits isomorphism.
isomorphism (ˌaɪsəʊˈmɔːfɪzəm) *n.* **1.** *Biology.* similarity of form, as in different generations of the same life cycle. **2.** *Chem.* the existence of two or more substances of different composition in a similar crystalline form. **3.** *Maths.* a one-to-one correspondence between the elements of two or more sets, such as those of Arabic and Roman numerals, and between the sums or products of the elements of one of these sets and those of the equivalent elements of the other set or sets. —ˌ**isoˈmorphic** *or* ˌ**isoˈmorphous** *adj.*
isoniazid (ˌaɪsəʊˈnaɪəzɪd) *n.* a soluble colourless crystalline compound used to treat tuberculosis. Formula: $C_6H_7N_3O$. [C20 *isoni(cotinic acid hydr)azid(e)*]
isonome (ˈaɪsəʊˌnəʊm) *n. Botany.* a line on a chart connecting points of equal abundance values of a plant species sampled in different sections of an area. Isonomes of different species from the same area are compared in studies of plant distribution. [C20: from ISO- + Greek *nomos* rule, law]
isonomy (aɪˈsɒnəmɪ) *n.* **1.** the equality before the law of the citizens of a state. **2.** the equality of civil or political rights. —**isonomic** (ˌaɪsəʊˈnɒmɪk) *or* **iˈsonomous** *adj.*
isooctane (ˌaɪsəʊˈɒkteɪn) *n.* a colourless liquid alkane hydrocarbon produced from petroleum and used in standardizing petrol. Formula: $(CH_3)_3CCH_2CH(CH_3)_2$. See also **octane number.**
isopach (ˈaɪsəʊˌpæk) *or* **isopachyte** (ˌaɪsəʊˈpækaɪt) *n. Geology.* a line on a map connecting points below which a particular rock stratum has the same thickness. [C20: from ISO- + Greek *pakhus* thick, *pakhutēs* thickness]
isophone (ˈaɪsəˌfəʊn) *n. Linguistics.* an isogloss marking off an area in which a particular feature of pronunciation is found. [C20: from *iso-* (as in ISOGLOSS) + *-phone* (as in PHONEME)]
isopiestic (ˌaɪsəʊpaɪˈɛstɪk) *adj.* another word for **isobaric** (sense 1). [C19: from ISO- + Greek *piestos* compressible, from *piezein* to press] —ˌ**isopiˈestically** *adv.*
isopleth (ˈaɪsəʊˌplɛθ) *n.* a line on a map connecting places registering the same amount or ratio of some geographical or meteorological phenomenon or phenomena. Also called: **isogram, isoline.** [C20: from Greek *isoplēthēs* equal in number, from ISO- + *plēthos* multitude, great number]
isopod (ˈaɪsəʊˌpɒd) *n.* **1.** any crustacean of the order *Isopoda,* including woodlice and pill bugs, in which the body is flattened dorsoventrally. ~*adj.* **2.** of, relating to, or belonging to the *Isopoda.* —**isopodan** (aɪˈsɒpədən) *or* **iˈsopodous** *adj.*
isoprene (ˈaɪsəʊˌpriːn) *n.* a colourless volatile liquid with a penetrating odour: used in making synthetic rubbers. Formula: $CH_2{:}CHC(CH_3){:}CH_2$. Systematic name: **methylbuta-1,3-diene.** [C20: from ISO- + PR(OPYL) + -ENE]
isopropyl (ˌaɪsəʊˈprəʊpɪl) *n.* (*modifier*) of, consisting of, or containing the group of atoms $(CH_3)_2CH$-, derived from propane: *an isopropyl group or radical.*
isopycnic (ˌaɪsəʊˈpɪknɪk) *n.* a line on a map connecting points of equal atmospheric density. [C19: from ISO- + Greek *puknos* thick]
ISO rating *n. Photog.* a measure of film speed in which the figures are the same as those on the ASA and DIN scales: ISO100/21° equals ASA100, DIN21°. [C20: from *I*nternational *S*tandards *O*rganization]
isorhythmic (ˌaɪsəˈrɪðmɪk) *adj. Music.* (of medieval motets) having a cantus firmus that is repeated according to a strict system of internal reiterated note values.
isosceles (aɪˈsɒsɪˌliːz) *adj.* **1.** (of a triangle) having two sides of equal length. **2.** (of a trapezium) having the two nonparallel sides of equal length. [C16: from Late Latin, from Greek *isoskelēs,* from ISO- + *skelos* leg]

isoseismal (ˌaɪsəʊˈsaɪzməl) *adj.* **1.** of or relating to equal intensity of earthquake shock. ~*n.* **2.** a line on a map connecting points at which earthquake shocks are of equal intensity. ~Also: **isoseismic.**

isosmotic (ˌaɪsɒzˈmɒtɪk) *adj.* another word for **isotonic** (sense 2).

isospin (ˈaɪsəʊˌspɪn) *n.* a quantity used in the classification of elementary particles. Particles which have very similar properties except for those associated with their charge are regarded as forms of the same fundamental particle with different components of the isospin in a certain direction in an imaginary space. Also called: **isobaric spin, isotopic spin.**

isospondylous (ˌaɪsəˈspɒndᵊləs) *adj.* of, relating to, or belonging to the *Isospondyli* (or *Clupeiformes*), an order of soft-finned teleost fishes that includes the herring, salmon, trout, and pike. [C20: from ISO- + Greek *spondulos* vertebra]

isostasy (aɪˈsɒstəsɪ) *n.* the state of balance, or equilibrium, which sections of the earth's lithosphere (whether continental or oceanic) are thought ultimately to achieve when the vertical forces upon them remain unchanged. The lithosphere floats upon the semifluid asthenosphere below. If a section of lithosphere is loaded, as by ice, it will slowly subside to a new equilibrium position; if a section of lithosphere is reduced in mass, as by erosion, it will slowly rise to a new equilibrium position. [C19: ISO- + *-stasy,* from Greek *stasis* a standing] —**isostatic** (ˌaɪsəʊˈstætɪk) *adj.*

isostemonous (ˌaɪsəʊˈstiːmənəs, -ˈstɛm-) *adj. Botany.* (of a flower) having the stamens arranged in a single whorl and equal to the number of petals. [C19: from ISO- + Greek *-stemonus* relating to a STAMEN]

isosteric (ˌaɪsəʊˈstɛrɪk) *adj.* (of two different molecules) having the same number of atoms and the same number and configuration of valency electrons, as carbon dioxide and nitrous oxide.

isotach (ˈaɪsəʊˌtæk) *n.* a line on a map connecting points of equal wind speed. [from ISO- + Greek *takhos* speed]

isotactic (ˌaɪsəʊˈtæktɪk) *adj. Chem.* (of a stereospecific polymer) having identical steric configurations of the groups on each asymmetric carbon atom on the chain. Compare **syndiotactic.**

isoteniscope (ˌaɪsəʊˈtɛnɪˌskəʊp) *n. Chem.* an instrument used to measure vapour pressure. [C20: from ISO- + TEN(SION) + -I- + -SCOPE]

isothere (ˈaɪsəʊˌθɪə) *n.* a line on a map linking places with the same mean summer temperature. Compare **isocheim.** [C19: from ISO- + Greek *theros* summer] —**isotheral** (aɪˈsɒθərəl) *adj.*

isotherm (ˈaɪsəʊˌθɜːm) *n.* **1.** a line on a map linking places of equal temperature. **2.** *Physics.* a curve on a graph that connects points of equal temperature. ~Also called: **isothermal, isothermal line.**

isothermal (ˌaɪsəʊˈθɜːməl) *adj.* **1.** (of a process or change) taking place at constant temperature. **2.** of or relating to an isotherm. ~*n.* **3.** another word for **isotherm.** —ˌ**isoˈthermally** *adv.*

isotone (ˈaɪsəˌtəʊn) *n.* one of two or more atoms of different atomic number that contain the same number of neutrons.

isotonic (ˌaɪsəʊˈtɒnɪk) *adj.* **1.** *Physiol.* (of two or more muscles) having equal tension. **2.** Also: **isosmotic.** (of two solutions) having the same osmotic pressure, commonly having physiological osmotic pressure. Compare **hypertonic, hypotonic. 3.** *Music.* of, relating to, or characterized by the equal intervals of the well-tempered scale: *isotonic tuning.* —**isotonicity** (ˌaɪsəʊtəʊˈnɪsɪtɪ) *n.*

isotope (ˈaɪsəˌtəʊp) *n.* one of two or more atoms with the same atomic number that contain different numbers of neutrons. [C20: from ISO- + Greek *topos* place] —**isotopic** (ˌaɪsəˈtɒpɪk) *adj.* —ˌ**isoˈtopically** *adv.* —**isotopy** (aɪˈsɒtəpɪ) *n.*

isotopic spin *n.* See **isospin.**

isotron (ˈaɪsəˌtrɒn) *n. Physics.* a device for separating small quantities of isotopes by ionizing them and separating the ions by an electric field, as in a mass spectrometer. [C20: from ISOTOPE + -TRON]

isotropic (ˌaɪsəʊˈtrɒpɪk) *or* **isotropous** (aɪˈsɒtrəpəs) *adj.* **1.** having uniform physical properties in all directions. **2.** *Biology.* not having predetermined axes: *isotropic eggs.* —ˌ**isoˈtropically** *adv.* —**iˈsotropy** *n.*

isozyme (ˈaɪsəʊˌzaɪm) *n.* any of a set of structural variants of an enzyme occurring in different tissues in a single species. Also called: **isoenzyme.** [from ISO- + (EN)ZYME] —**isozymic** (ˌaɪsəʊˈzaɪmɪk, -ˈzɪm-) *adj.*

I-spy *n.* a game in which one player specifies the initial letter of the name of an object that he can see, which the other players then try to guess.

Israeli (ɪzˈreɪlɪ) *n., pl.* **-lis** *or* **-li. 1.** a citizen or inhabitant of the state of Israel, in SW Asia. ~*adj.* **2.** of, relating to, or characteristic of the state of Israel or its inhabitants.

Israelite (ˈɪzrɪəˌlaɪt, -rə-) *n.* **1.** *Bible.* a member of the ethnic group claiming descent from Jacob; a Hebrew. **2.** *Bible.* a citizen of the kingdom of Israel (922 to 721 B.C.). **3.** a member of any of various Christian sects who regard themselves as God's chosen people. **4.** an archaic word for a **Jew.**

issuable (ˈɪʃjʊəbᵊl) *adj.* **1.** capable of issuing or being issued. **2.** *Chiefly law.* open to debate or litigation. **3.** authorized to be issued. —ˈ**issuably** *adv.*

issuance (ˈɪʃjʊəns) *n.* the act of issuing.

issuant (ˈɪʃjʊənt) *adj. Archaic or heraldry.* emerging or issuing.

issue (ˈɪʃjuː) *n.* **1.** the act of sending or giving out something; supply; delivery. **2.** something issued; an edition of stamps, a magazine, etc. **3.** the number of identical items, such as banknotes or shares in a company, that become available at a particular time. **4.** the act of emerging; outflow; discharge. **5.** something flowing out, such as a river. **6.** a place of outflow; outlet. **7.** the descendants of a person; offspring; progeny. **8.** a topic of interest or discussion. **9.** an important subject requiring a decision. **10.** an outcome or consequence; result. **11.** *Pathol.* **a.** a suppurating sore. **b.** discharge from a wound. **12.** *Law.* the matter remaining in dispute between the parties to an action after the pleadings. **13.** the yield from or profits arising out of land or other property. **14.** *Military.* the allocation of items of government stores, such as food, clothing, and ammunition. **15.** *Library science.* **a.** the system for recording current loans. **b.** the number of books loaned in a specified period. **16.** *Obsolete.* an act, deed, or proceeding. **17. at issue. a.** under discussion. **b.** in disagreement. **18. force the issue.** to compel decision on some matter. **19. join issue. a.** to join in controversy. **b.** to submit an issue for adjudication. **20. take issue.** to disagree. ~*vb.* **-sues, -suing, -sued. 21.** to come forth or emerge or cause to come forth or emerge. **22.** to publish or deliver (a newspaper, magazine, etc.). **23.** (*tr.*) to make known or announce. **24.** (*intr.*) to originate or proceed. **25.** (*intr.*) to be a consequence; result. **26.** (*intr.;* foll. by *in*) to end or terminate. **27.** (*tr.*) **a.** to give out or allocate (equipment, a certificate, etc.) officially to someone. **b.** (foll. by *with*) to supply officially (with). [C13: from Old French *eissue* way out, from *eissir* to go out, from Latin *exīre,* from EX-[1] + *īre* to go] —ˈ**issueless** *adj.* —ˈ**issuer** *n.*

issue price *n. Stock Exchange.* the price at which a new issue of shares is offered to the public.

issuing house *n. Brit.* a financial institution that engages in finding capital for established companies or for private firms wishing to convert to public companies, by issuing shares on their behalf.

-ist *suffix.* **1.** (*forming nouns*) a person who performs a certain action or is concerned with something specified: *motorist; soloist.* **2.** (*forming nouns*) a person who practises in a specific field: *physicist; typist.* **3.** (*forming nouns and adjectives*) a person who advocates a particular doctrine, system, etc., or relating to such a person or the doctrine advocated: *socialist.* **4.** (*forming nouns and adjectives*) a person characterized by a specified trait, tendency, etc., or relating to such a person or trait: *purist.* **5.** (*forming nouns and adjectives*) a person who is prejudiced on the basis specified: *sexist; ageist.* [via Old French from Latin *-ista, -istēs,* from Greek *-istēs*]

istana (iːˈstana) *n.* (in Malaysia) a royal palace. [from Malay]

Isth. *or* **isth.** *abbrev. for* isthmus.

isthmian (ˈɪsθmɪən) *adj.* relating to or situated in an isthmus.

Isthmian (ˈɪsθmɪən) *adj.* relating to or situated in the Isthmus of Corinth or the Isthmus of Panama.

isthmus (ˈɪsməs) *n., pl.* **-muses** *or* **-mi** (-maɪ). **1.** a narrow strip of land connecting two relatively large land areas. **2.** *Anatomy.* **a.** a narrow band of tissue connecting two larger parts of a structure. **b.** a narrow passage connecting two cavities. [C16: from Latin, from Greek *isthmos*] —ˈ**isthmoid** *adj.*

-istic *suffix forming adjectives.* equivalent to a combination of **-ist** and **-ic** but in some words having a less specific or literal application and sometimes a mildly pejorative force, as compared with corresponding adjectives ending in **-ist:** *communistic; impressionistic.* [from Latin *-isticus,* from Greek *istikos*]

istle (ˈɪstlɪ) *or* **ixtle** *n.* a fibre obtained from various tropical American agave and yucca trees used in making carpets, cord, etc. [C19: from Mexican Spanish *ixtle,* from Nahuatl *ichtli*]

it (ɪt) *pron.* (*subjective or objective*) **1.** refers to a nonhuman, animal, plant, or inanimate thing, or sometimes to a small baby: *it looks dangerous; give it a bone.* **2.** refers to an unspecified or implied antecedent or to a previous or understood clause, phrase, etc.: *it is impossible; I knew it.* **3.** used to represent human life or experience either in totality or in respect of the present situation: *how's it going?; I've had it; to brazen it out.* **4.** used as a formal subject (or object), referring to a following clause, phrase, or word: *it helps to know the truth; I consider it dangerous to go on.* **5.** used in the nominative as the formal grammatical subject of impersonal verbs. When *it* functions absolutely in such sentences, not referring to any previous or following clause or phrase, the context is nearly always a description of the environment or of some physical sensation: *it is raining; it hurts.* **6.** (used as complement with *be*) *Informal.* the crucial or ultimate point: *the steering failed and I thought that was it.* ~*n.* **7.** (in children's games) the player whose turn it is to try to touch another. Compare **he**[1] (sense 5b). **8.** *Informal.* **a.** sexual intercourse. **b.** sex appeal. **9.** *Informal.* a desirable quality or ability: *he's really got it.* [Old English *hit*]

IT *abbrev. for* information technology.

It. *abbrev. for:* **1.** Italian. **2.** Italy.

ITA (in Britain) *abbrev. for* Independent Television Authority: now superseded by the IBA.

i.t.a. *or* **ITA** *abbrev. for* initial teaching alphabet, a partly phonetic alphabet used to teach reading.

itacolumite (ˌɪtəˈkɒljʊˌmaɪt) *n.* a fine-grained micaceous sandstone that occurs in thin flexible slabs. [C19: named after *Itacolumi* mountain in Brazil where it is found]

itaconic acid (ˌɪtəˈkɒnɪk) *n.* a white colourless crystalline carboxylic acid obtained by the fermentation of carbohydrates and used in the manufacture of synthetic resins. Formula: CH_2:$C(COOH)CH_2COOH$.
ital. *abbrev. for* italic.
Ital. *abbrev. for:* 1. Italian. 2. Italy.
Italia irredenta *Italian.* (irreˈdɛnta) *n.* See **Irredentist.**
Italian (ɪˈtæljən) *n.* 1. the official language of Italy and one of the official languages of Switzerland: the native language of approximately 60 million people. It belongs to the Romance group of the Indo-European family, and there is a considerable diversity of dialects. 2. a native, citizen, or inhabitant of Italy, or a descendant of one. 3. See **Italian vermouth.** ~*adj.* 4. relating to, denoting, or characteristic of Italy, its inhabitants, or their language.
Italianate (ɪˈtæljənɪt, -ˌneɪt) *or* **Italianesque** (ɪˌtæljəˈnɛsk) *adj.* Italian in style or character.
Italian greyhound *n.* a breed of dog like a miniature greyhound.
Italianism (ɪˈtæljəˌnɪzəm) *or* **Italicism** (ɪˈtælɪˌsɪzəm) *n.* 1. an Italian custom or style. 2. Italian quality or life, or the cult of either.
Italianize *or* **Italianise** (ɪˈtæljəˌnaɪz) *vb.* to make or become Italian or like an Italian person or thing. —**Iˌtalianiˈzation** *or* **Iˌtalianiˈsation** *n.*
Italian sixth *n.* (in musical harmony) an augmented sixth chord characterized by having a major third and an augmented sixth above the root.
Italian sonnet *n.* another term for **Petrarchan sonnet.**
Italian vermouth *n.* sweet vermouth.
italic (ɪˈtælɪk) *adj.* 1. Also: **Italian.** of, relating to, or denoting a style of handwriting with the letters slanting to the right. ~*n.* 2. a style of printing type modelled on this, chiefly used to indicate emphasis, a foreign word, etc. Compare **roman.** 3. (*often pl.*) italic type or print. [C16 (after an edition of Virgil (1501) printed in Venice and dedicated to Italy): from Latin *Italicus* of Italy, from Greek *Italikos*]
Italic (ɪˈtælɪk) *n.* 1. a branch of the Indo-European family of languages that includes many of the ancient languages of Italy, such as Venetic and the Osco-Umbrian group, Latin, which displaced them, and the Romance languages. ~*adj.* 2. denoting, relating to, or belonging to this group of languages, esp. the extinct ones.
italicize *or* **italicise** (ɪˈtælɪˌsaɪz) *vb.* 1. to print (textual matter) in italic type. 2. (*tr.*) to underline (letters, words, etc.) with a single line to indicate italics. —**iˌtaliciˈzation** *or* **iˌtaliciˈsation** *n.*
Italo- (ɪˈtæləʊ-) *combining form.* indicating Italy or Italian: *Italophobia; Italo-German.*
ITC (in Britain) *abbrev. for* Independent Television Commission.
itch (ɪtʃ) *n.* 1. an irritation or tickling sensation of the skin causing a desire to scratch. 2. a restless desire. 3. any skin disorder, such as scabies, characterized by intense itching. ~*vb.* 4. (*intr.*) to feel or produce an irritating or tickling sensation. 5. (*intr.*) to have a restless desire (to do something). 6. *Not standard.* to scratch (the skin). 7. **itching palm.** a grasping nature; avarice. 8. **have itchy feet.** to be restless; have a desire to travel. [Old English *gīccean* to itch, of Germanic origin] —**ˈitchy** *adj.* —**ˈitchiness** *n.*
itch mite *n.* any mite of the family *Sarcoptidae,* all of which are skin parasites, esp. *Sarcoptes scabei,* which causes scabies.
-ite[1] *suffix forming nouns.* 1. a native or inhabitant of: *Israelite.* 2. a follower or advocate of; a member or supporter of a group: *Luddite; labourite.* 3. (in biology) indicating a division of a body or organ: *somite.* 4. indicating a mineral or rock: *nephrite; peridotite.* 5. indicating a commercial product: *vulcanite.* [via Latin *-ita* from Greek *-itēs* or directly from Greek]
-ite[2] *suffix forming nouns.* indicating a salt or ester of an acid having a name ending in *-ous: a nitrite is a salt of nitrous acid.* [from French, arbitrary alteration of -ATE[1]]
item *n.* (ˈaɪtəm). 1. a thing or unit, esp. included in a list or collection. 2. *Book-keeping.* an entry in an account. 3. a piece of information, detail, or note: *a news item.* 4. *Informal.* two people having a romantic or sexual relationship. ~*vb.* (ˈaɪtəm). 5. (*tr.*) an archaic word for **itemize.** ~*adv.* (ˈaɪtɛm). 6. likewise; also. [C14 (adv.) from Latin: in like manner]
itemize *or* **itemise** (ˈaɪtəˌmaɪz) *vb.* (*tr.*) to put on a list or make a list of. —ˌ**itemiˈzation** *or* ˌ**itemiˈsation** *n.* —ˈ**itemˌizer** *or* ˈ**itemˌiser** *n.*
item veto *n.* (in the U.S.) the power of a state governor to veto items in bills without vetoing the entire measure.
iterate (ˈɪtəˌreɪt) *vb.* (*tr.*) to say or do again; repeat. [C16: from Latin *iterāre,* from *iterum* again] —ˈ**iterant** *adj.* —ˌ**iterˈation** *or* ˈ**iterance** *n.*
iterative (ˈɪtərətɪv) *adj.* 1. repetitious or frequent. 2. *Maths, logic.* another word for **recursive.** 3. *Grammar.* another word for **frequentative.** —ˈ**iteratively** *adv.* —ˈ**iterativeness** *n.*
ither (ˈɪðər) *determiner.* a Scot. word for **other.**
ithyphallic (ˌɪθɪˈfælɪk) *adj.* 1. *Prosody.* (in classical verse) of or relating to the usual metre in hymns to Bacchus. 2. of or relating to the phallus carried in the ancient festivals of Bacchus. 3. (of sculpture and graphic art) having or showing an erect penis. ~*n.* 4. *Prosody.* a poem in ithyphallic metre. [C17: from Late Latin, from Greek *ithuphallikos,* from *ithuphallos* erect phallus, from *ithus* straight + *phallos* PHALLUS]
itinerancy (ɪˈtɪnərənsɪ, aɪ-) *or* **itineracy** *n.* 1. the act of itinerating. 2. *Chiefly Methodist Church.* the system of appointing a minister to a circuit of churches or chapels. 3. itinerants collectively.
itinerant (ɪˈtɪnərənt, aɪ-) *adj.* 1. itinerating. 2. working for a short time in various places, esp. as a casual labourer. ~*n.* 3. an itinerant worker or other person. [C16: from Late Latin *itinerārī* to travel, from *iter* a journey] —**iˈtinerantly** *adv.*
itinerary (aɪˈtɪnərərɪ, ɪ-) *n., pl.* **-aries.** 1. a plan or line of travel; route. 2. a record of a journey. 3. a guidebook for travellers. ~*adj.* 4. of or relating to travel or routes of travel. 5. a less common word for **itinerant.**
itinerate (aɪˈtɪnəˌreɪt, ɪ-) *vb.* (*intr.*) to travel from place to place. —**iˌtinerˈation** *n.*
-itious *suffix forming adjectives.* having the nature of; characterized by: *nutritious; suppositious.* [from Latin *-icius, -itious*]
-itis *suffix forming nouns.* 1. indicating inflammation of a specified part: *tonsillitis.* 2. *Informal.* indicating a preoccupation with or imaginary condition of illness caused by: *computeritis; telephonitis.* [New Latin, from Greek, feminine of *-itēs* belonging to; see -ITE[1]]
it'll (ˈɪtᵊl) *contraction of* it will *or* it shall.
ITO *abbrev. for* International Trade Organization.
-itol *suffix forming nouns.* indicating that certain chemical compounds are polyhydric alcohols: *inisitol; sorbitol.* [from -ITE[2] + -OL[1]]
its (ɪts) *determiner.* **a.** of, belonging to, or associated in some way with it: *its left rear wheel; I can see its logical consequence.* **b.** (*as pronoun*): *its is over there.*
it's (ɪts) *contraction of* it is *or* it has.
itself (ɪtˈsɛlf) *pron.* 1. **a.** the reflexive form of **it.** **b.** (intensifier): *even the money itself won't convince me.* 2. (*preceded by a copula*) its normal or usual self: *my cat doesn't seem itself these days.*
▷**Usage.** See at **myself.**
itsy-bitsy (ˈɪtsɪˈbɪtsɪ) *or* **itty-bitty** (ˈɪtɪˈbɪtɪ) *adj. Informal.* very small; tiny. [C20: baby talk alteration of *little bit*]
ITU *abbrev. for:* 1. Intensive Therapy Unit. 2. International Telecommunications Union.
ITV (in Britain) *abbrev. for* Independent Television.
-ity *suffix forming nouns.* indicating state or condition: *technicality.* [from Old French *-ite,* from Latin *-itās*]
i-type semiconductor *n.* another name for **intrinsic semiconductor.**
IU *abbrev. for:* 1. immunizing unit. 2. international unit.
IU(C)D *abbrev. for* intrauterine (contraceptive) device.
-ium *or sometimes* **-um** *suffix forming nouns.* 1. indicating a metallic element: *platinum; barium.* 2. (in chemistry) indicating groups forming positive ions: *ammonium chloride; hydroxonium ion.* 3. indicating a biological structure: *syncytium.* [New Latin, from Latin, from Greek *-ion,* diminutive suffix]
i.v. *abbrev. for:* 1. initial velocity. 2. Also: **IV.** intravenous(ly).
IVB *abbrev. for* invalidity benefit.
I've (aɪv) *contraction of* I have.
-ive *suffix.* 1. (*forming adjectives*) indicating a tendency, inclination, character, or quality: *divisive; prohibitive; festive; massive.* 2. (*forming nouns of adjectival origin*): *detective; expletive.* [from Latin *-īvus*]
ivermectin (ˌaɪvəˈmɛktɪn) *n.* a drug that kills parasitic nematode worms, mites, and insects. It is used to treat a variety of parasitic infections in domestic animals and has shown encouraging results in preliminary trials for treating onchocerciasis in humans.
IVF *abbrev. for* in vitro fertilization.
ivied (ˈaɪvɪd) *adj.* covered with ivy.
ivories (ˈaɪvərɪz, -vrɪz) *pl. n. Slang.* 1. the keys of a piano. 2. another word for **teeth.** 3. another word for **dice.**
ivory (ˈaɪvərɪ, -vrɪ) *n., pl.* **-ries.** 1. **a.** a hard smooth creamy white variety of dentine that makes up a major part of the tusks of elephants, walruses, and similar animals. **b.** (*as modifier*): *ivory ornaments.* 2. a tusk made of ivory. 3. **a.** a yellowish-white colour; cream. **b.** (*as adj.*): *ivory shoes.* 4. a substance resembling elephant tusk. 5. an ornament, etc., made of ivory. 6. **black ivory.** *Obsolete.* Negro slaves collectively. ~See also **ivories.** [C13: from Old French *ivurie,* from Latin *evoreus* made of ivory, from *ebur* ivory; related to Greek *elephas* ivory, ELEPHANT] —ˈ**ivory-ˌlike** *adj.*
ivory black *n.* a black pigment obtained by grinding charred scraps of ivory in oil.
ivory gull *n.* a white gull, *Pagophila* (or *Larus*) *eburneus,* mostly confined to arctic regions.
ivory nut *n.* 1. the seed of the ivory palm, which contains an ivory-like substance used to make buttons, etc. 2. any similar seed from other palms. ~Also called: **vegetable ivory.**
ivory palm *n.* a low-growing South American palm tree, *Phytelephas macrocarpa,* that yields the ivory nut.
ivory tower (ˈtaʊə) *n.* **a.** seclusion or remoteness of attitude regarding real problems, everyday life, etc. **b.** (*as modifier*): *ivory-tower aestheticism.* —ˌ**ivory-ˈtowered** *adj.*
ivorywood (ˈaɪvərɪˌwʊd) *n.* 1. the yellowish-white wood of an Australian tree, *Siphonodon australe,* used for engraving, inlaying, and turnery. 2. the tree itself: family *Siphonodontaceae.*
IVR *abbrev. for* International Vehicle Registration.

ivy (ˈaɪvɪ) *n., pl.* **ivies. 1.** any woody climbing or trailing araliaceous plant of the Old World genus *Hedera,* esp. *H. helix,* having lobed evergreen leaves and black berry-like fruits. **2.** any of various other climbing or creeping plants, such as Boston ivy, poison ivy, and ground ivy. [Old English *īfig;* related to Old High German *ebah,* perhaps to Greek *iphuon* a plant] —ˈ**ivy-ˌlike** *adj.*

Ivy League *n. U.S.* **a. the.** a group of eight universities (Brown, Columbia, Cornell, Dartmouth College, Harvard, Princeton, the University of Pennsylvania, and Yale) that have similar academic and social prestige in the U.S. to Oxford and Cambridge in Britain. **b.** (*as modifier*): *an Ivy-League education.*

iwi (ˈiːwɪ) *n. N.Z.* a tribe. [Maori]

iwis *or* **ywis** (ɪˈwɪs) *adv.* an archaic word for **certainly.** [C12: from Old English *gewiss* certain]

IWW *abbrev. for* Industrial Workers of the World.

ixia (ˈɪksɪə) *n.* any plant of the iridaceous genus *Ixia,* of southern Africa, having showy ornamental funnel-shaped flowers. [C18: New Latin from Greek *ixos* mistletoe, birdlime prepared from mistletoe berries]

ixtle (ˈɪkstlɪ, ˈɪst-) *n.* a variant of **istle.**

Iyar *or* **Iyyar** (iˈjar) *n.* (in the Jewish calendar) the second month of the year according to biblical reckoning and the eighth month of the civil year, usually falling within April and May. [from Hebrew]

izard (ˈɪzəd) *n.* (esp. in the Pyrenees) another name for **chamois.**

-ize *or* **-ise** *suffix forming verbs.* **1.** to cause to become, resemble, or agree with: *legalize.* **2.** to become; change into: *crystallize.* **3.** to affect in a specified way; subject to: *hypnotize.* **4.** to act according to some practice, principle, policy, etc.: *economize.* [from Old French *-iser,* from Late Latin *-izāre,* from Greek *-izein*]

▷**Usage.** In Britain and the U.S. *-ize* is the preferred ending for many verbs, but *-ise* is equally acceptable in British English. Certain words (chiefly those not formed by adding the suffix to an existing word) are, however, always spelt with *-ise* in both Britain and the U.S.: *advertise, revise.*

izzard (ˈɪzəd) *n. Archaic.* the letter *Z.* [C18: from earlier *ezed,* probably from Old French *et zède,* literally: and zed]

J

j *or* **J** (dʒeɪ) *n., pl.* **j's, J's,** *or* **Js. 1.** the tenth letter and seventh consonant of the modern English alphabet. **2.** a speech sound represented by this letter, in English usually a voiced palato-alveolar affricate, as in *jam.*

j *symbol for:* **1.** *Maths.* the unit vector along the *y*-axis. **2.** the imaginary number √−1.

J *symbol for:* **1.** *Cards.* jack. **2.** joule(s). **3.** current density. ~ **4.** *international car registration for* Japan.

J. *abbrev. for:* **1.** Journal. **2.** (*pl.* **JJ.**) Judge. **3.** (*pl.* **JJ.**) Justice.

JA *abbrev. for:* **1.** Also: **J/A.** *Banking.* joint account. **2.** Judge Advocate. ~ **3.** *international car registration for* Jamaica.

Ja. *abbrev. for* January.

jaap (jɑːp) *n. S. African.* a simpleton or country bumpkin. [from Afrikaans]

jab (dʒæb) *vb.* **jabs, jabbing, jabbed. 1.** to poke or thrust sharply. **2.** to strike with a quick short blow or blows. ~*n.* **3.** a sharp poke or stab. **4.** a quick short blow, esp. (in boxing) a straight punch with the leading hand. **5.** *Informal.* an injection: *polio jabs.* [C19: originally Scottish variant of JOB] —**'jabbingly** *adv.*

jabber ('dʒæbə) *vb.* **1.** to speak or say rapidly, incoherently, and without making sense; chatter. ~*n.* **2.** such talk. [C15: of imitative origin; compare GIBBER] —**'jabberer** *n.*

jabberwocky ('dʒæbəˌwɒkɪ) *n., pl.* **-wockies** nonsense verse. [C19: coined by Lewis Carroll (1832–98) as the title of a poem in *Through the Looking Glass* (1871)]

jabiru ('dʒæbɪˌruː) *n.* **1.** a large white tropical American stork, *Jabiru mycteria,* with a dark naked head and a dark bill. **2.** Also called: **black-necked stork, policeman bird.** a large Australian stork, *Xenorhyncus asiaticus,* having a white plumage, dark green back and tail, and red legs. **3.** another name for **saddlebill. 4.** (*not in ornithological usage*) another name for **wood ibis.** [C18: via Portuguese from Tupi-Guarani]

jaborandi (ˌdʒæbə'rændɪ) *n.* **1.** any of several tropical American rutaceous shrubs of the genus *Pilocarpus,* esp. *P. jaborandi.* **2.** the dried leaves of any of these plants, used to induce sweating. [C19: from Portuguese, from Tupi-Guarani *yaborandí*]

jabot ('ʒæbəʊ) *n.* a frill or ruffle on the breast or throat of a garment, originally to hide the closure of a shirt. [C19: from French: bird's crop, jabot; compare Old French *gave* throat]

jacamar ('dʒækəˌmɑː) *n.* any bird of the tropical American family *Galbulidae,* having an iridescent plumage and feeding on insects: order *Piciformes* (woodpeckers, etc.). [C19: from French, from Tupi *jacamá-ciri*]

jaçana (ˌʒɑːsə'nɑː, ˌdʒæ-) *n.* any bird of the family *Jacanidae,* of tropical and subtropical marshy regions, having long legs and very long toes that enable walking on floating plants: order *Charadriiformes.* Also called: **lily-trotter.** [C18: from Portuguese *jaçanã,* from Tupi-Guarani *jasaná*]

jacaranda (ˌdʒækə'rændə) *n.* **1.** any bignoniaceous tree of the tropical American genus *Jacaranda,* having fernlike leaves and pale purple flowers and widely cultivated in temperate areas of Australia. **2.** the fragrant ornamental wood of any of these trees. **3.** any of several related or similar trees or their wood. [C18: from Portuguese, from Tupi-Guarani *yacarandá*]

jacinth ('dʒæsɪnθ) *n.* another name for **hyacinth** (sense 4). [C13: from Medieval Latin *jacinthus,* from Latin *hyacinthus* plant, precious stone; see HYACINTH]

jack[1] (dʒæk) *n.* **1.** a man or fellow. **2.** a sailor. **3.** the male of certain animals, esp. of the ass or donkey. **4.** a mechanical or hydraulic device for exerting a large force, esp. to raise a heavy weight such as a motor vehicle. **5.** any of several mechanical devices that replace manpower, such as a contrivance for rotating meat on a spit. **6.** one of four playing cards in a pack, one for each suit, bearing the picture of a young prince; knave. **7.** *Bowls.* a small usually white bowl at which the players aim with their own bowls. **8.** *Electrical engineering.* a female socket with two or more terminals designed to receive a male plug (**jack plug**) that either makes or breaks the circuit or circuits. **9.** a flag, esp. a small flag flown at the bow of a ship indicating the ship's nationality. Compare **Union Jack. 10.** *Nautical.* either of a pair of crosstrees at the head of a topgallant mast used as standoffs for the royal shrouds. **11.** a part of the action of a harpsichord, consisting of a fork-shaped device on the end of a pivoted lever on which a plectrum is mounted. **12.** any of various tropical and subtropical carangid fishes, esp. those of the genus *Caranx,* such as *C. hippos* (**crevalle jack**). **13.** Also called: **jackstone.** one of the pieces used in the game of jacks. **14.** short for **applejack, bootjack, jackass, jackfish, jack rabbit,** and **lumberjack. 15.** *U.S.* a slang word for **money. 16. every man jack.** everyone without exception. ~*adj.* **17.** *Austral. slang.* tired or fed up (esp. in the phrase **be jack of** something). ~*vb.* (*tr.*) **18.** to lift or push (an object) with a jack. **19.** Also: **jacklight.** *U.S. and Canadian.* to hunt (fish or game) by seeking them out or dazzling them with a flashlight. ~See also **jack in, jacks, jack up.** [C16 *jakke,* variant of *Jankin,* diminutive of *John*]

jack[2] (dʒæk) *n.* short for **jackfruit.** [C17: from Portuguese *jaca;* see JACKFRUIT]

jack[3] (dʒæk) *n.* **1.** a short sleeveless coat of armour of the Middle Ages, consisting usually of a canvas base with metal plates. **2.** *Archaic.* a drinking vessel, often of leather. [C14: from Old French *jaque,* of uncertain origin]

Jack (dʒæk) *n.* **I'm all right, Jack.** *Brit. informal.* **a.** a remark indicating smug and complacent selfishness. **b.** (*as modifier*): *an "I'm all right, Jack" attitude.*

jackal ('dʒækɔːl) *n.* **1.** any of several African or S Asian canine mammals of the genus *Canis,* closely related to the dog, having long legs and pointed ears and muzzle: predators and carrion-eaters. **2.** a person who does menial tasks for another. **3.** a villain, esp. a swindler. [C17: from Turkish *chakāl,* from Persian *shagāl,* from Sanskrit *srgāla*]

jackanapes ('dʒækəˌneɪps) *n.* **1.** a conceited impertinent person. **2.** a mischievous child. **3.** *Archaic.* a monkey. [C16: variant of *Jakken-apes,* literally: Jack of the ape, nickname of William de la Pole (1396–1450), first Duke of Suffolk, whose badge showed an ape's ball and chain]

jackass ('dʒækˌæs) *n.* **1.** a male donkey. **2.** a stupid person; fool. **3. laughing jackass.** another name for **kookaburra.** [C18: from JACK[1] (male) + ASS[1]]

jack bean *n.* a tropical American leguminous plant, *Canavalia ensiformis,* that has clusters of purple flowers and long pods and is grown in the southern U.S. for forage.

jackboot ('dʒækˌbuːt) *n.* **1.** an all-leather military boot, extending up to or above the knee. **2. a.** arbitrary, cruel, and authoritarian rule or behaviour. **b.** (*as modifier*): *jackboot tactics.* —**'jackˌbooted** *adj.*

jack-by-the-hedge *n.* another name for **garlic mustard.**

jackdaw ('dʒækˌdɔː) *n.* a large common Eurasian passerine bird, *Corvus monedula,* in which the plumage is black and dark grey: noted for its thieving habits: family *Corvidae* (crows). [C16: from JACK[1] + DAW]

Jackeen (dʒæ'kiːn) *n. Irish.* a slick self-assertive lower-class Dubliner. [C19: from proper name *Jack* + *-een,* Irish diminutive suffix, from Irish Gaelic *-ín*]

jackeroo *or* **jackaroo** (ˌdʒækə'ruː) *n., pl.* **-roos.** *Austral. informal.* a young male management trainee on a sheep or cattle station. [C19: from JACK[1] + (KANG)AROO]

jacket ('dʒækɪt) *n.* **1.** a short coat, esp. one that is hip-length and has a front opening and sleeves. **2.** something that resembles this or is designed to be worn around the upper part of the body: *a life jacket.* **3.** any exterior covering or casing, such as the insulating cover of a boiler. **4.** the part of the cylinder block of an internal-combustion engine that encloses the coolant. **5.** See **dust jacket. 6. a.** the skin of a baked potato. **b.** (*as modifier*): *jacket potatoes.* **7.** a metal casing used in certain types of ammunition. **8.** *U.S.* a cover to protect a gramophone record. Brit. name: **sleeve. 9.** *Chiefly U.S.* a folder or envelope to hold documents. ~*vb.* **10.** (*tr.*) to put a jacket on (someone or something). [C15: from Old French *jaquet* short jacket, from *jacque* peasant, from proper name *Jacques* James] —**'jacketed** *adj.* —**'jacketˌlike** *adj.*

jackfish ('dʒækˌfɪʃ) *n., pl.* **-fish** *or* **-fishes.** a popular name for **pike** (the fish), esp. when small.

Jack Frost *n.* a personification of frost or winter.

jackfruit ('dʒækˌfruːt) *n.* **1.** a tropical Asian moraceous tree, *Artocarpus heterophyllus.* **2.** the edible fruit of this tree, which resembles breadfruit and can weigh up to 27 kilograms (60 pounds). ~Sometimes shortened to **jack.** [C19: from Portuguese *jaca,* from Malayalam *cakka*]

Jack-go-to-bed-at-noon *n.* another name for **goatsbeard** (sense 1).

jackhammer ('dʒækˌhæmə) *n.* a hand-held hammer drill, driven by compressed air, for drilling rocks, etc.

Jackie *or* **Jacky** ('dʒækɪ) *n., pl.* **Jackies.** *Austral. derogatory slang.* **1.** an Aborigine. **2.** Aborigines collectively. **3. sit up like Jackie.** to sit bolt upright, esp. cheekily.

jack in *vb.* (*tr., adv.*) *Slang.* to abandon or leave (an attempt or enterprise).

jack-in-office *n.* a self-important petty official.

jack-in-the-box *n., pl.* **jack-in-the-boxes** *or* **jacks-in-the-box.** a toy consisting of a figure on a compressed spring in a box, which springs out when the lid is opened.

jack-in-the-green *n.* (in England, formerly) a man who wore or supported a leaf-covered wooden framework while dancing in May-Day celebrations.

jack-in-the-pulpit *n.* **1.** an E North American aroid plant, *Arisaema triphyllum,* having a leaflike spathe partly arched over a clublike spadix. **2.** *Brit.* another name for **cuckoopint.**

Jack Ketch (kɛtʃ) *n. Brit. archaic.* a hangman. [C18: after *John Ketch* (died 1686), public executioner in England]

jackknife (ˈdʒækˌnaɪf) *n., pl.* **-knives. 1.** a knife with the blade pivoted to fold into a recess in the handle. **2.** a former name for a type of dive in which the diver bends at the waist in midair, with his legs straight and his hands touching his feet, finally straightening out and entering the water headfirst: forward pike dive. ~*vb.* (*intr.*) **3.** (of an articulated lorry) to go out of control in such a way that the trailer swings round at an angle to the cab. **4.** to make a jackknife dive.

jack ladder *n.* another name for **Jacob's ladder** (sense 2).

jack of all trades *n., pl.* **jacks of all trades.** a person who undertakes many different kinds of work.

jack-o'-lantern *n.* **1.** a lantern made from a hollowed pumpkin, which has holes cut in it to represent a human face. **2.** a will-o'-the-wisp or similar phenomenon.

jack pine *n.* a coniferous tree, *Pinus banksiana,* of North America, having paired needle-like leaves and small cones that remain on the branches for many years: family *Pinaceae.*

jack plane *n.* a carpenter's plane, usually with a wooden body, used for rough planing of timber.

jackpot (ˈdʒækˌpɒt) *n.* **1.** any large prize, kitty, or accumulated stake that may be won in gambling, such as a pool in poker that accumulates until the betting is opened with a pair of jacks or higher. **2. hit the jackpot. a.** to win a jackpot. **b.** *Informal.* to achieve great success, esp. through luck. [C20: probably from JACK[1] (playing card) + POT[1]]

jack rabbit *n.* any of various W North American hares, such as *Lepus townsendi* (**white-tailed jack rabbit**), having long hind legs and large ears. [C19: shortened from *jackass-rabbit,* referring to its long ears]

jack rafter *n.* a short rafter used in a hip roof.

Jack Robinson *n.* **before you could** (*or* **can**) **say Jack Robinson.** extremely quickly or suddenly.

Jack Russell *n.* a small short-legged terrier having a white coat with tan, black, or lemon markings: there are rough- and smooth-haired varieties. Also called: **Jack Russell terrier.** [named after John *Russell* (1795–1883), English clergyman who developed the breed]

jacks (dʒæks) *n.* (*functioning as sing.*) a game in which bone, metal, or plastic pieces (**jackstones**) are thrown and then picked up in various groups between bounces or throws of a small ball. Sometimes called: **knucklebones.** [C19: shortened from *jackstones,* variant of *checkstones* pebbles]

jackscrew (ˈdʒækˌskruː) *n.* another name for **screw jack.**

jackshaft (ˈdʒækˌʃɑːft) *n.* a short length of shafting that transmits power from an engine or motor to a machine.

jacksie *or* **jacksy** (ˈdʒæksɪ) *n. Brit. slang.* the buttocks or anus. Also called **jaxie, jaxy.** [C19: probably from JACK[1]]

jacksmelt (ˈdʒækˌsmɛlt) *n., pl.* **-smelts** *or* **-smelt.** a marine teleost food fish, *Atherinopsis californiensis,* of American coastal waters of the North Pacific: family *Atherinidae* (silversides).

jacksnipe (ˈdʒækˌsnaɪp) *n., pl.* **-snipe** *or* **-snipes. 1.** a small Eurasian short-billed snipe, *Lymnocryptes minima.* **2.** any of various similar birds, such as the pectoral sandpiper.

jackstay (ˈdʒækˌsteɪ) *n. Nautical.* **1.** a metal rod, wire rope, or wooden batten to which an edge of a sail is fastened along a yard. **2.** a support for the parrel of a yard.

jackstraws (ˈdʒækˌstrɔːz) *n.* (*functioning as sing.*) another name for **spillikins.**

Jack Tar *n. Now chiefly literary.* a sailor.

Jack-the-lad *n. Slang.* a young man who is regarded as a brash, loud show-off.

Jack-the-rags *n. South Wales dialect.* a rag-and-bone man.

jack towel *n.* another name for **roller towel.**

jack up *vb.* (*adv.*) **1.** (*tr.*) to increase (prices, salaries, etc.). **2.** (*tr.*) to raise an object, such as a car, with or as with a jack. **3.** (*intr.*) *Slang.* to inject oneself with a drug, usually heroin. **4.** (*intr.*) *Austral. informal.* to refuse to comply; rebel, esp. collectively. **5.** *N.Z. informal.* to initiate, organize, or procure.

Jacky (ˈdʒækɪ) *n.* See **Jackie.**

Jacky Howe *n. Austral. informal.* a sleeveless flannel shirt worn by shearers. [C19: named after *Jacky Howe* (1855–1922) who was the world champion shearer in 1892]

Jacob (ˈdʒeɪkəb) *n.* any of an ancient breed of sheep having a fleece with dark brown patches and two or four horns. Also called: **Jacob sheep.** [in allusion to *Jacob* separating the flock (Genesis 30:40)]

Jacobean (ˌdʒækəˈbɪən) *adj.* **1.** *History.* characteristic of or relating to James I of England or to the period of his rule (1603–25). **2.** of or relating to the style of furniture current at this time, characterized by the use of dark brown carved oak. **3.** denoting, relating to, or having the style of architecture used in England during this period, characterized by a combination of late Gothic and Palladian motifs. ~*n.* **4.** any writer or other person who lived in the reign of James I. [C18: from New Latin *jacōbaeus,* from *Jacōbus* James]

Jacobian (dʒəˈkəʊbɪən) *or* **Jacobian determinant** *n. Maths.* a function from n equations in n variables whose value at any point is the $n \times n$ determinant of the partial derivatives of those equations evaluated at that point. [named after K. G. J. *Jacobi* (1804–51), German mathematician]

Jacobin (ˈdʒækəbɪn) *n.* **1.** a member of the most radical club founded during the French Revolution, which overthrew the Girondists in 1793 and instituted the Reign of Terror. **2.** a leftist or extreme political radical. **3.** a French Dominican friar. **4.** (*sometimes not cap.*) a variety of fancy pigeon with a hood of feathers swept up over and around the head. ~*adj.* **5.** of, characteristic of, or relating to the Jacobins or their policies. [C14: from Old French, from Medieval Latin *Jacōbīnus,* from Late Latin *Jacōbus* James; applied to the Dominicans, from the proximity of the church of *St Jacques* (St James) to their first convent in Paris; the political club originally met in the convent in 1789] —ˌ**Jacoˈbinic** *or* ˌ**Jacoˈbinical** *adj.* —ˌ**Jacoˈbinically** *adv.* —ˈ**Jacobinism** *n.*

Jacobite (ˈdʒækəˌbaɪt) *n.* **1.** *British history.* an adherent of James II after his overthrow in 1688, or of his descendants in their attempts to regain the throne. **2. a.** a member of the Monophysite Church of Syria, which became a schismatic church in 451 A.D. **b.** *Rare.* a Monophysite Christian of the Coptic Church of Egypt. [C17: from Late Latin *Jacōbus* James + -ITE[1]] —**Jacobitic** (ˌdʒækəˈbɪtɪk) *adj.* —ˈ**JacoˌbitIsm** *n.*

Jacob sheep *n.* See **Jacob.**

Jacob's ladder *n.* **1.** **1.** Also called: **jack ladder.** a ladder made of wooden or metal steps supported by ropes or chains. **2.** a North American polemoniaceous plant, *Polemonium caeruleum,* with blue flowers and a ladder-like arrangement of leaves. **3.** any of several similar or related plants. [in allusion to the ladder reaching up to heaven that *Jacob* saw in a dream (Genesis 28:12–17)]

Jacob's staff *n.* a medieval instrument for measuring heights and distances.

jacobus (dʒəˈkəʊbəs) *n., pl.* **-buses.** an English gold coin minted in the reign of James I. [C17: from Late Latin: James]

jaconet (ˈdʒækənɪt) *n.* a light cotton fabric used for clothing, bandages, etc. [C18: from Urdu *jagannāthī,* from *Jagannāthpūrī,* India, where it was originally made]

Jacquard (ˈdʒækɑːd, dʒəˈkɑːd; *French* ʒakar) *n.* **1.** Also called: **Jacquard weave.** a fabric in which the design is incorporated into the weave instead of being printed or dyed on. **2.** Also called: **Jacquard loom.** the loom that produces this fabric. [C19: named after Joseph M. *Jacquard* (1752–1834), French inventor]

jactation (dʒækˈteɪʃən) *n.* **1.** *Rare.* the act of boasting. **2.** *Pathol.* another word for **jactitation** (sense 3). [C16: from Latin *jactātiō* bragging, from *jactāre* to flourish, from *jacere* to throw]

jactitation (ˌdʒæktɪˈteɪʃən) *n.* **1.** the act of boasting. **2.** a false boast or claim that tends to harm another person, esp. a false assertion that one is married to another, formerly actionable at law. **3.** Also called: **jactation.** *Pathol.* restless tossing in bed, characteristic of severe fevers and certain mental disorders. [C17: from Medieval Latin *jactitātiō,* from Latin *jacitāre* to utter publicly, from *jactitāre* to toss about; see JACTATION]

Jacuzzi (dʒəˈkuːzɪ) *n., pl.* **-zis. 1.** *Trademark.* a system of underwater jets that keep the water in a bath or pool constantly agitated. **2.** (*sometimes not cap.*) a bath or pool equipped with this.

jade[1] (dʒeɪd) *n.* **1. a.** a semiprecious stone consisting of either jadeite or nephrite. It varies in colour from white to green and is used for making ornaments and jewellery. **b.** (*as modifier*): *jade ornaments.* **2.** the green colour of jade. [C18: from French, from Italian *giada,* from obsolete Spanish *piedra de ijada* colic stone (literally: stone of the flank, because it was believed to cure renal colic); *ijada,* from Vulgar Latin *īliata* (unattested) flanks, from Latin *īlia,* plural of *īlium;* see ILEUM] —ˈ**jadeˌlike** *adj.*

jade[2] (dʒeɪd) *n.* **1.** an old overworked horse; nag; hack. **2.** *Derogatory or facetious.* a woman considered to be ill-tempered or disreputable. ~*vb.* **3.** to exhaust or make exhausted from work or use. [C14: of unknown origin] —ˈ**jadish** *adj.* —ˈ**jadishly** *adv.* —ˈ**jadishness** *n.*

jaded (ˈdʒeɪdɪd) *adj.* **1.** exhausted or dissipated. **2.** satiated. —ˈ**jadedly** *adv.* —ˈ**jadedness** *n.*

jade green *n., adj.* **a.** a colour varying from yellowish-green to bluish-green. **b.** (*as adj.*): *a jade-green carpet.*

jadeite (ˈdʒeɪdaɪt) *n.* a usually green or white mineral of the clinopyroxene group, found in igneous and metamorphic rocks. It is used as a gemstone (jade). Composition: sodium aluminium silicate. Formula: $NaAlSi_2O_6$. Crystal structure: monoclinic.

j'adoube *French.* (ʒadub) *interj. Chess.* an expression of an intention to touch a piece in order to adjust its placement rather than to make a move. [literally: I adjust]

jaeger (ˈjeɪgə) *n.* **1.** *Military.* a marksman in certain units of the German or Austrian armies. **2.** a member of a light or mountain infantry unit in some European armies. **3.** *U.S. and Canadian.* any of several skuas of the genus *Stercorarius.* **4.** *Rare.* a hunter or hunter's attendant. ~Also (for senses 1, 2, 4): **jager** or **jäger.** [C18: from German *Jäger* hunter, from *jagen* to hunt; see YACHT]

Jaffa (ˈdʒæfə, ˈdʒɑː-) *n.* a large variety of orange, having a thick skin. [named after *Jaffa,* a port in W Israel]

jag[1] *or* **jagg** (dʒæg) *vb.* **jags, jagging, jagged. 1.** (*tr.*) to cut unevenly; make jagged. **2.** *Austral.* to catch (fish) by impaling them on an unbaited hook. ~*n., vb.* **3.** an informal word for **jab.** ~*n.* **4.** a jagged notch or projection. [C14: of unknown origin]

jag[2] (dʒæg) *n. Slang.* **1. a.** intoxication from drugs or alcohol. **b.** a bout of drinking or drug taking. **2.** a period of uncontrolled activity: *a crying jag.* [of unknown origin]

Jag (dʒæg) *n. Informal.* a Jaguar car: often understood as a symbol of affluence.

JAG *abbrev. for* Judge Advocate General.

jaga ('dʒaga) (in Malaysia) ~*n.* **1.** a guard; sentry. ~*vb.* **2.** (*tr.*) to guard or watch: *jaga the door.* [from Malay]

jäger ('jeɪgə) *n.* See **jaeger.**

jagged ('dʒægɪd) *adj.* having sharp projecting notches; ragged; serrate. —'**jaggedly** *adv.* —'**jaggedness** *n.*

jaggery, jaggary, *or* **jagghery** ('dʒægərɪ) *n.* a coarse brown sugar made in the East Indies from the sap of the date palm. [C16: from Hindi *jāgrī*; compare Sanskrit *śárkarā* gritty substance, sugar]

jaggy ('dʒægɪ) *adj.* **-gier, -giest.** **1.** a less common word for **jagged.** **2.** *Scot.* prickly.

jaguar ('dʒægjʊə) *n.* a large feline mammal, *Panthera onca,* of S North America, Central America, and N South America, similar to the leopard but with a shorter tail and larger spots on its coat. [C17: from Portuguese, from Tupi *jaguara,* Guarani *yaguara*]

jaguarondi (ˌdʒægwə'rɒndɪ) *or* **jaguarundi** (ˌdʒægwə'rʌndɪ) *n., pl.* **-dis.** a feline mammal, *Felis yagouaroundi,* of Central and South America, with a reddish or grey coat, short legs, and a long tail. See also **eyra.** [C19: via Portuguese from Tupi]

Jahveh ('jɑːveɪ) *or* **Jahweh** ('jɑːweɪ) *n.* variant of **Yahweh.**

Jahvist ('jɑːvɪst) *or* **Jahwist** ('jɑːwɪst) *n.* variant of **Yahwist.**

Jahwism ('jɑːwɪzᵊm) *or* **Jahvism** ('jɑːvɪzəm) *n.* variants of **Yahwism** *or* **Yahvism.** —**Jah'wistic** *or* **Jah'vistic** *adj.*

jai (dʒæ) *n. Indian.* victory (to). [Hindi *jaya* victory]

jai alai ('haɪ 'laɪ, 'haɪ əˌlaɪ, ˌhaɪ ə'laɪ) *n.* a version of pelota played by two or four players. [via Spanish from Basque, from *jai* game, festival + *alai* merry]

Jai Hind (dʒæ 'hɪnd) victory to India: a political slogan and a form of greeting in India. [Hindi, from *jaya* victory + *Hind* India]

jail *or* **gaol** (dʒeɪl) *n.* **1.** a place for the confinement of persons convicted and sentenced to imprisonment or of persons awaiting trial to whom bail is not granted. ~*vb.* **2.** (*tr.*) to confine in prison. [C13: from Old French *jaiole* cage, from Vulgar Latin *caveola* (unattested), from Latin *cavea* enclosure; see CAGE: the two spellings derive from the forms of the word that developed in two different areas of France, and the spelling *gaol* represents a pronunciation in use until the 17th century] —'**jailless** *or* '**gaolless** *adj.* —'**jail-like** *or* '**gaol-like** *adj.*

jailbird *or* **gaolbird** ('dʒeɪlˌbɜːd) *n.* a person who is or has been confined to jail, esp. repeatedly; convict.

jailbreak *or* **gaolbreak** ('dʒeɪlˌbreɪk) *n.* an escape from jail.

jail delivery *n.* **1.** forcible and illegal liberation of prisoners from jail. **2.** *English law.* (formerly) a commission issued to assize judges when they come to a circuit town authorizing them to try all prisoners and release those acquitted.

jailer, jailor, *or* **gaoler** ('dʒeɪlə) *n.* a person in charge of prisoners in a jail.

jail fever *n.* a former name for **typhus,** once a common disease in jails.

jailhouse ('dʒeɪlˌhaʊs) *n. Southern U.S.* a jail; prison.

Jain (dʒaɪn) *or* **Jaina** ('dʒaɪnə) *n.* **1.** an adherent of Jainism. ~*adj.* **2.** of or relating to Jainism or the Jains. [C19: from Hindi *jaina* saint, literally: overcomer, from Sanskrit]

Jainism ('dʒaɪˌnɪzəm) *n.* an ancient Hindu religion, which has its own scriptures and believes that the material world is eternal, progressing endlessly in a series of vast cycles. —'**Jainist** *n., adj.*

jake (dʒeɪk) *adj. Austral. and N.Z. slang.* **1.** satisfactory, all right. **2. she's jake.** everything is under control. [probably from the name *Jake*]

jakes (dʒeɪks) *n.* **1.** an archaic slang word for **lavatory.** **2.** *Southwestern English dialect.* human excrement. [C16: probably from French *Jacques* James]

jalap *or* **jalop** ('dʒæləp) *n.* **1.** a Mexican convolvulaceous plant, *Exogonium* (or *Ipomoea*) *purga.* **2.** any of several similar or related plants. **3.** the dried and powdered root of any of these plants, used as a purgative. **4.** the resin obtained from any of these plants. [C17: from French, from Mexican Spanish *jalapa,* short for *purga de Jalapa* purgative of Jalapa] —**jalapic** (dʒə'læpɪk) *adj.*

jalopy *or* **jaloppy** (dʒə'lɒpɪ) *n., pl.* **-lopies** *or* **-loppies.** *Informal.* a dilapidated old car. [C20: of unknown origin]

jalouse (dʒə'luːz) *vb. Scot.* to suspect; infer. [C19: from French *jalouser* to be jealous of]

jalousie ('ʒæluˌziː) *n.* **1.** a window blind or shutter constructed from angled slats of wood, plastic, etc. **2.** a window made of similarly angled slats of glass. [C19: from Old French *gelosie* latticework screen, literally: JEALOUSY, perhaps because one can look through the screen without being seen]

jam[1] (dʒæm) *vb.* **jams, jamming, jammed.** **1.** (*tr.*) to cram or wedge into or against something: *to jam paper into an incinerator.* **2.** (*tr.*) to crowd or pack: *cars jammed the roads.* **3.** to make or become stuck or locked: *the switch has jammed.* **4.** (*tr.*; often foll. by *on*) to activate suddenly (esp. in the phrase **jam on the brakes**). **5.** (*tr.*) to block; congest: *to jam the drain with rubbish.* **6.** (*tr.*) to crush, bruise, or squeeze; smash. **7.** *Radio.* to prevent the clear reception of (radio communications or radar signals) by transmitting other signals on the same frequency. **8.** (*intr.*) *Musicians' slang.* to play in a jam session. ~*n.* **9.** a crowd or congestion in a confined space: *a traffic jam.* **10.** the act of jamming or the state of being jammed. **11.** *Informal.* a difficult situation; predicament: *to help a friend out of a jam.* **12.** See **jam session.** [C18: probably of imitative origin; compare CHAMP[1]] —'**jammer** *n.*

jam[2] (dʒæm) *n.* **1.** a preserve containing fruit, which has been boiled with sugar until the mixture sets. **2.** *Slang.* something desirable: *you want jam on it.* [C18: perhaps from JAM[1] (the act of squeezing)]

Jam. *abbrev. for:* **1.** Jamaica. **2.** *Bible.* James.

Jamaican (dʒə'meɪkən) *adj.* **1.** of or relating to Jamaica, an island state in the West Indies, or to its people, culture, etc. ~*n.* **2.** a native or inhabitant of Jamaica.

Jamaican ebony *n.* another name for **cocuswood.**

Jamaica pepper *n.* another name for **allspice.**

Jamaica rum *n.* a highly flavoured rum produced in Jamaica.

jamb *or* **jambe** (dʒæm) *n.* **1.** a vertical side member of a doorframe, window frame, or lining. **2.** a vertical inside face of an opening in a wall. [C14: from Old French *jambe* leg, jamb, from Late Latin *gamba* hoof, hock, from Greek *kampē* joint]

jambalaya (ˌdʒʌmbə'laɪə) *n.* a Creole dish made of shrimps, ham, rice, onions, etc. [C19: from Louisiana French, from Provençal *jambalaia* chicken and rice stew]

jambeau ('dʒæmbəʊ), **jambart** ('dʒæmbɑːt), *or* **jamber** ('dʒæmbə) *n., pl.* **-beaux** (-bəʊz), **-barts,** *or* **-bers.** (*often pl.*) other words for **greave.** [C14: from Anglo-French, from *jambe* leg; see JAMB]

jambo ('dʒambɔ) *sentence substitute.* an E African salutation. [C20: from Swahili]

jamboree (ˌdʒæmbə'riː) *n.* **1.** a large and often international gathering of Scouts. **2.** a party or spree. [C19: of uncertain origin]

Jamesian *or* **Jamesean** ('dʒeɪmzɪən) *adj.* relating to or characteristic of Henry James (1843–1916), U.S.-born British novelist and critic, or his brother William James (1842–1910), U.S. philosopher and psychologist.

James-Lange theory ('dʒeɪmz'lɑːŋə) *n. Psychol.* a theory that emotions are caused by bodily sensations; for example, we are sad because we weep. [named after William *James* + Carl *Lange* (1834–1900), Danish psychologist]

jamming ('dʒæmɪŋ) *n. Mountaineering.* a rock-climbing technique in which holds are got by wedging the hands and feet in suitable cracks.

jammy ('dʒæmɪ) *adj.* **-mier, -miest.** *Brit. slang.* **1.** pleasant; desirable. **2.** lucky.

jam-packed *adj.* crowded, packed, or filled to capacity.

jampan ('dʒæmˌpæn) *n.* a type of sedan chair used in India. [C19: from Bengali *jhāmpān*]

jam session *n. Slang.* an unrehearsed or improvised jazz or rock performance. [C20: probably from JAM[1]]

Jan. *abbrev. for* January.

Janata ('dʒʌnətɑː) *n.* (in India) the general public; the people. [Hindi]

Jandal ('dʒændᵊl) *n. N.Z. trademark.* a type of sandal with a strip of material between the big toe and the other toes and over the foot.

jane (dʒeɪn) *n. Slang, chiefly U.S.* a girl or woman.

Janeite ('dʒeɪˌnaɪt) *n.* a devotee of the works of Jane Austen (1775–1817), British novelist.

jangle ('dʒæŋgᵊl) *vb.* **1.** to sound or cause to sound discordantly, harshly, or unpleasantly: *the telephone jangled.* **2.** (*tr.*) to produce a jarring effect on: *the accident jangled his nerves.* **3.** an archaic word for **wrangle.** ~*n.* **4.** a harsh, unpleasant ringing noise. **5.** an argument or quarrel. [C13: from Old French *jangler,* of Germanic origin; compare Middle Dutch *jangelen* to whine, complain] —'**jangler** *n.*

janissary ('dʒænɪsərɪ) *or* **janizary** ('dʒænɪzərɪ) *n., pl.* **-saries** *or* **-zaries.** an infantryman in the Turkish army, originally a member of the sovereign's personal guard, from the 14th to the early 19th century. [C16: from French *janissaire,* from Italian *giannizzero,* from Turkish *yeniçeri,* from *yeni* new + *çeri* soldiery]

janitor ('dʒænɪtə) *n.* **1.** *Scot.* the caretaker of a building, esp. a school. **2.** *Chiefly U.S. and Canadian.* a person employed to clean and maintain a building, esp. the public areas in a block of flats or office building; porter. [C17: from Latin: doorkeeper, from *jānua* door, entrance, from *jānus* covered way (compare JANUS[1]); related to Latin *īre* to go] —**janitorial** (ˌdʒænɪ'tɔːrɪəl) *adj.* —'**janitress** *fem. n.*

Jansenism ('dʒænsəˌnɪzəm) *n.* **1.** *R.C. Church.* the doctrine of Cornelis Jansen (1585–1638), Dutch theologian, and his disciples, who maintained that salvation was limited to those subject to a supernatural determinism, the rest being destined to perdition. **2.** the religious movement arising from these doctrines. —'**Jansenist** *n., adj.* —ˌ**Jansen'istic** *or* ˌ**Jansen'istical** *adj.*

jansky ('dʒænskɪ) *n., pl.* **-skys.** a unit of flux density equal to 10^{-26} W m^{-2} Hz^{-1}, used in radio astronomy. Symbol: Jy [C20: named after K. G. *Jansky* (1905–50), U.S. electrical engineer]

January ('dʒænjʊərɪ) *n., pl.* **-aries.** the first month of the year, consisting of 31 days. [C14: from Latin *Jānuārius,* from adj.: (month) of *Janus,* Roman god of doorways depicted with two heads facing opposite ways]

Janus-faced (ˈdʒeɪnəs-) *adj.* two-faced; hypocritical; deceitful. [from *Janus*]
Jap (dʒæp) *n., adj. Informal, often derogatory.* short for **Japanese.**
japan (dʒəˈpæn) *n.* **1.** a glossy durable black lacquer originally from the Orient, used on wood, metal, etc. **2.** work decorated and varnished in the Japanese manner. **3.** a liquid used as a paint drier. ~*adj.* **4.** relating to or varnished with japan. ~*vb.* **-pans, -panning, -panned. 5.** (*tr.*) to lacquer with japan or any similar varnish.
Japan Current (dʒəˈpæn) *n.* a warm ocean current flowing northeastwards off the E coast of Japan towards the North Pacific. Also called: **Kuroshio.**
Japanese (ˌdʒæpəˈniːz) *adj.* **1.** of, relating to, or characteristic of Japan, its people, or their language. ~*n.* **2.** (*pl.* **-nese**) a native or inhabitant of Japan or a descendant of one. **3.** the official language of Japan: the native language of approximately 100 million people: considered by some scholars to be part of the Altaic family of languages.
Japanese andromeda *n.* an ericaceous Japanese shrub, *Pieris japonica,* with drooping clusters of small bell-shaped white flowers.
Japanese beetle *n.* a scarabaeid beetle, *Popillia japonica,* that eats the leaves and fruits of various plants: accidentally introduced into the U.S. from Japan.
Japanese cedar *n.* another name for **cryptomeria.**
Japanese ivy *n.* another name for **Virginia creeper** (sense 2).
Japanese lantern *n.* another name for **Chinese lantern** (sense 1).
Japanese persimmon *n.* an Asian persimmon tree, *Diospyros kaki,* with red or orange edible fruit. Also called: **kaki.**
Japanese river fever *n.* another name for **scrub typhus.**
Japanese slippers *pl. n.* (in Malaysia) casual sandals; flip-flops.
Japanese stranglehold *n.* a wrestling hold in which an opponent's wrists are pulled to cross his arms in front of his own neck and exert pressure on his windpipe.
Japanese umbrella pine *n.* a single aberrant species of pine, *Sciadopitys verticillata,* in which the leaves are fused in pairs and the crown is spire-shaped.
Japan wax *or* **tallow** *n.* a yellow wax obtained from the berries of plants of the genus *Rhus.* It is used in making matches, soaps, candles, and polishes.
jape (dʒeɪp) *n.* **1.** a jest or joke. ~*vb.* **2.** to joke or jest (about). [C14: perhaps from Old French *japper* to bark, yap, of imitative origin] —ˈ**japer** *n.* —ˈ**japery** *n.* —ˈ**japingly** *adv.*
Japhetic (dʒeɪˈfetɪk) *adj.* denoting a discredited grouping of languages that postulated a relationship between Basque, Etruscan, and Georgian among others. [C19: from New Latin *Japheti* descendants of *Japheth,* the second son of Noah, + -IC]
japonica (dʒəˈpɒnɪkə) *n.* **1.** Also called: **Japanese quince.** a Japanese rosaceous shrub, *Chaenomeles japonica,* cultivated for its red flowers and yellowish fruit. **2.** another name for the **camellia.** [C19: from New Latin, feminine of *japonicus* Japanese, from *Japonia* Japan]
jar[1] (dʒɑː) *n.* **1.** a wide-mouthed container that is usually cylindrical, made of glass or earthenware, and without handles. **2.** Also: ˈ**jarful.** the contents or quantity contained in a jar. **3.** *Brit. informal.* a glass of alcoholic drink, esp. beer: *to have a jar with someone.* **4.** *Obsolete.* a measure of electrical capacitance. [C16: from Old French *jarre,* from Old Provençal *jarra,* from Arabic *jarrah* large earthen vessel]
jar[2] (dʒɑː) *vb.* **jars, jarring, jarred. 1.** to vibrate or cause to vibrate. **2.** to make or cause to make a harsh discordant sound. **3.** (often foll. by *on*) to have a disturbing or painful effect (on the nerves, mind, etc.). **4.** (*intr.*) to disagree; clash. ~*n.* **5.** a jolt or shock. **6.** a harsh discordant sound. [C16: probably of imitative origin; compare Old English *cearran* to creak] —ˈ**jarring** *adj.* —ˈ**jarringly** *adv.*
jar[3] (dʒɑː) *n.* **on a** (*or* **the**) **jar.** (of a door) slightly open; ajar. [C17 (in the sense: turn): from earlier *char,* from Old English *cierran* to turn; see AJAR[1]]
jardinière (ˌʒɑːdɪˈnjɛə) *n.* **1.** an ornamental pot or trough for plants. **2.** a garnish of fresh vegetables, cooked, diced, and served around a dish of meat. [C19: from French, feminine of *jardinier* gardener, from *jardin* GARDEN]
jargon[1] (ˈdʒɑːgən) *n.* **1.** specialized language concerned with a particular subject, culture, or profession. **2.** language characterized by pretentious syntax, vocabulary, or meaning. **3.** gibberish. **4.** another word for **pidgin.** ~*vb.* **5.** (*intr.*) to use or speak in jargon. [C14: from Old French, perhaps of imitative origin; see GARGLE]
jargon[2] (ˈdʒɑːgɒn) *or* **jargoon** (dʒɑːˈguːn) *n. Mineralogy.* a golden yellow, smoky, or colourless variety of zircon. [C18: from French, from Italian *giargone,* ultimately from Persian *zargūn* of the golden colour; see ZIRCON]
jargonize *or* **jargonise** (ˈdʒɑːgəˌnaɪz) *vb.* **1.** (*tr.*) to translate into jargon. **2.** (*intr.*) to talk in jargon. —ˌ**jargoniˈzation** *or* ˌ**jargoniˈsation** *n.*
jarl (jɑːl) *n. Medieval history.* a Scandinavian chieftain or noble. [C19: from Old Norse; see EARL] —ˈ**jarldom** *n.*
Jarlsberg (ˈjɑːlzbɜːg) *n. Trademark.* a hard mild-tasting yellow-coloured cheese with holes in it. [C20: after *Jarlsberg,* Norway, where it originated]
jarosite (ˈdʒærəˌsaɪt) *n.* a yellow to brown secondary mineral consisting of basic hydrated sulphate of iron and potassium in masses or hexagonal crystals. Formula: $KFe_3(SO_4)_2(OH)_6$. [C19: from *Barranco Jaroso,* in Almeria, Spain + -ITE[1]]
jarp (dʒɑːp) *or* **jaup** (dʒɔːp) *vb.* (*tr.*) *Northeast English dialect.* to strike or smash, esp. to break the shell of (an egg) at Easter. [from Scottish *jaup, jawp* to dash or splash like water: perhaps of imitative origin]
jarrah (ˈdʒærə) *n.* a widely planted Australian eucalyptus tree, *Eucalyptus marginata,* that yields a valuable timber. [from a native Australian language]
jarvey *or* **jarvie** (ˈdʒɑːvɪ) *n. Brit. informal, obsolete.* a hackney coachman. [C19: from *Jarvey,* familiar form of personal name *Jarvis*]
Jas. *Bible. abbrev. for* James.
jasmine (ˈdʒæsmɪn, ˈdʒæz-) *n.* **1.** Also called: **jessamine.** any oleaceous shrub or climbing plant of the tropical and subtropical genus *Jasminum,* esp. *J. officinalis:* widely cultivated for their white, yellow, or red fragrant flowers, which are used in making perfume and in flavouring tea. See also **winter jasmine. 2.** any of several other shrubs with fragrant flowers, such as the Cape jasmine, yellow jasmine, and frangipani (**red jasmine**). **3.** a light to moderate yellow colour. [C16: from Old French *jasmin,* from Arabic *yāsamīn,* from Persian *yāsmīn*]
jaspé (ˈdʒæspeɪ) *adj.* resembling jasper; variegated. [C19: from French, from *jasper* to marble]
jasper (ˈdʒæspə) *n.* **1.** an opaque impure microcrystalline form of quartz, red, yellow, brown, or dark green in colour, used as a gemstone and for ornamental decoration. **2.** Also called: **jasper ware.** a dense hard stoneware, invented in 1775 by Wedgwood, capable of being stained throughout its substance with metallic oxides and used as background for applied classical decoration. [C14: from Old French *jaspe,* from Latin *jaspis,* from Greek *iaspis,* of Semitic origin; related to Assyrian *ashpū,* Arabic *yashb,* Hebrew *yāshpheh*]
Jat (dʒɑːt) *n., pl.* **Jat** *or* **Jats.** a member of an Indo-European people widely dispersed throughout the Punjab, Rajputana, and Uttar Pradesh.
jato (ˈdʒeɪtəʊ) *n., pl.* **-tos.** *Aeronautics.* jet-assisted takeoff. [C20 *j(et-)a(ssisted) t(ake)o(ff)*]
jaundice (ˈdʒɔːndɪs) *n.* **1.** Also called: **icterus.** yellowing of the skin and whites of the eyes due to the abnormal presence of bile pigments in the blood, as in hepatitis. **2.** a mental state of bitterness, jealousy, and ill humour resulting in distorted judgment. ~*vb.* **3.** to distort (the judgment, etc.) adversely: *jealousy had jaundiced his mind.* **4.** to affect with or as if with jaundice. [C14: from Old French *jaunisse,* from *jaune* yellow, from Latin *galbinus* yellowish, from *galbus*]
jaunt (dʒɔːnt) *n.* **1.** a short pleasurable excursion; outing. ~*vb.* **2.** (*intr.*) to go on such an excursion. [C16: of unknown origin] —ˈ**jauntingly** *adv.*
jaunting car *or* **jaunty car** *n.* a light two-wheeled one-horse car, formerly widely used in Ireland.
jaunty (ˈdʒɔːntɪ) *adj.* **-tier, -tiest. 1.** sprightly, self-confident, and cheerful; brisk: *a jaunty step.* **2.** smart; trim: *a jaunty hat.* [C17: from French *gentil* noble; see GENTEEL] —ˈ**jauntily** *adv.* —ˈ**jauntiness** *n.*
Jav. *abbrev. for* Javanese.
Java man (ˈdʒɑːvə) *n.* a type of primitive man, *Homo erectus* (formerly called *Pithecanthropus erectus*), that lived in the middle Palaeolithic Age in Java. Also called: **Trinil man.**
Javanese (ˌdʒɑːvəˈniːz) *adj.* **1.** of, relating to, or characteristic of Java, an island of Indonesia, its people, or the Javanese language. ~*n.* **2.** (*pl.* **-nese**) a native or inhabitant of Java. **3.** a Malayo-Polynesian language of Central and Eastern Java.
Java sparrow *n.* a small grey-and-pink finchlike Indonesian weaverbird, *Padda oryzivora:* a popular cage bird.
javelin (ˈdʒævlɪn) *n.* **1.** a long pointed spear thrown as a weapon or in competitive field events. **2. the javelin.** the event or sport of throwing the javelin. [C16: from Old French *javeline,* variant of *javelot,* of Celtic origin]
Javel water *or* **Javelle water** (ˈdʒævᵊl, dʒəˈvel) *n.* **1.** an aqueous solution containing sodium hypochlorite and some sodium chloride, used as a bleach and disinfectant. **2.** Also called: **eau de Javelle.** a similar solution made from potassium carbonate and chlorine. [C19: partial translation of French *eau de Javel,* from *Javel,* formerly a town, now part of Paris]
jaw (dʒɔː) *n.* **1.** the part of the skull of a vertebrate that frames the mouth and holds the teeth. In higher vertebrates it consists of the **upper jaw** (maxilla) fused to the cranium and the **lower jaw** (mandible). **2.** the corresponding part of an invertebrate, esp. an insect. **3.** a pair or either of a pair of hinged or sliding components of a machine or tool designed to grip an object. **4.** *Slang.* **a.** impudent talk; cheek. **b.** idle conversation; chat. **c.** moralizing talk; a lecture. ~*vb.* **5.** (*intr.*) *Slang.* **a.** to talk idly; chat; gossip. **b.** to lecture. ~See also **jaws.** [C14: probably from Old French *joue* cheek; related to Italian *gota* cheek] —ˈ**jawˌlike** *adj.*
Jawan (dʒəˈwɑːn) *n.* (in India) **1.** a soldier. **2.** a young man. [Urdu: young man]
jawbone (ˈdʒɔːˌbəʊn) *n.* **1.** a nontechnical name for **mandible** or (less commonly) **maxilla.** ~*vb.* **2.** *U.S.* to try to persuade or

bring pressure to bear (on) by virtue of one's high office or position, esp. in urging compliance with official policy.

jawbreaker (ˈdʒɔːˌbreɪkə) *n.* **1.** Also called: **jawcrusher.** a device having hinged jaws for crushing rocks and ores. **2.** *Informal.* a word that is hard to pronounce. —ˈ**jawˌbreaking** *adj.* —ˈ**jawˌbreakingly** *adv.*

jaws (dʒɔːz) *pl. n.* **1.** the narrow opening of some confined place such as a gorge. **2. the jaws.** a dangerously close position: *the jaws of death.*

jaws of life *pl. n.* (*functioning as sing.*) powerful shears used for cutting a vehicle open after a collision.

jay (dʒeɪ) *n.* **1.** any of various passerine birds of the family *Corvidae* (crows), esp. the Eurasian *Garrulus glandarius,* with a pinkish-brown body, blue-and-black wings, and a black-and-white crest. See also **blue jay. 2.** a foolish or gullible person. [C13: from Old French *jai,* from Late Latin *gāius,* perhaps from proper name *Gāius*]

Jaycee (ˈdʒeɪˈsiː) *n. Austral, N.Z., U.S., and Canadian.* a young person who belongs to a junior chamber of commerce. [C20: from the initials of *J*(unior) *C*(hamber), short for *United States Junior Chamber of Commerce*]

jaywalk (ˈdʒeɪˌwɔːk) *vb.* (*intr.*) to cross or walk in a street recklessly or illegally. [C20: from JAY (sense 2)] —ˈ**jayˌwalker** *n.* —ˈ**jayˌwalking** *n.*

jazz (dʒæz) *n.* **1. a.** a kind of music of American Negro origin, characterized by syncopated rhythms, solo and group improvisation, and a variety of harmonic idioms and instrumental techniques. It exists in a number of styles. Compare **blues.** See also: **bebop, bop, Dixieland, free** (sense 7), **hard bop, harmolodics, mainstream** (sense 2), **modern jazz, New Orleans jazz, swing** (sense 28), **trad. b.** (*as modifier*): *a jazz band.* **c.** (*in combination*): *a jazzman.* **2.** *Informal.* enthusiasm or liveliness. **3.** *Slang.* rigmarole; paraphernalia: *legal papers and all that jazz.* **4.** *U.S. Negro slang, obsolete.* sexual intercourse. ~*vb.* **5.** (*intr.*) to play or dance to jazz music. **6.** *U.S. Negro slang, obsolete.* to have sexual intercourse with (a person). [C20: of unknown origin] —ˈ**jazzer** *n.*

jazz age *n.* (*often caps.*) **the.** (esp. in the U.S.) the period between the end of World War I and the beginning of the Depression during which jazz became popular. [C20: popularized by U.S. writer F. Scott Fitzgerald (1896–1940), who called a collection of his short stories *Tales of the Jazz Age* (1922)]

jazz up *vb.* (*tr., adv.*) *Informal.* **1.** to imbue (a piece of music) with jazz qualities, esp. by improvisation or a quicker tempo. **2.** to make more lively, gaudy, or appealing.

jazzy (ˈdʒæzɪ) *adj.* **jazzier, jazziest.** *Informal.* **1.** of, characteristic of, or resembling jazz music. **2.** gaudy or flashy: *a jazzy car.* —ˈ**jazzily** *adv.* —ˈ**jazziness** *n.*

JC *abbrev. for* jurisconsult.

J.C. *abbrev for:* **1.** Jesus Christ. **2.** Julius Caesar.

JCB *n. Trademark.* a type of construction machine with a hydraulically operated shovel on the front and an excavator arm on the back. [named from the initials of *J*(oseph) *C*(yril) *B*(amford) (born 1916), its British manufacturer]

JCD *abbrev. for:* **1.** Doctor of Canon Law. [Latin: *Juris Canonici Doctor*] **2.** Doctor of Civil Law. [Latin: *Juris Civilis Doctor*]

JCL *Computer technol. abbrev. for* Job Control Language.

JCR *abbrev. for* junior common room.

JCS *abbrev. for* Joint Chiefs of Staff.

jct. *or* **jctn** *abbrev. for* junction.

JD *abbrev. for:* **1.** Doctor of Laws. [Latin: *Jurum Doctor*] **2.** juvenile delinquent.

jealous (ˈdʒɛləs) *adj.* **1.** suspicious or fearful of being displaced by a rival: *a jealous lover.* **2.** (often *postpositive* and foll. by *of*) resentful (of) or vindictive (towards), esp. through envy: *a child jealous of his brother.* **3.** (often *postpositive* and foll. by *of*) possessive and watchful in the maintenance or protection (of): *jealous of one's reputation.* **4.** characterized by or resulting from jealousy. **5.** *Obsolete except in biblical use.* demanding exclusive loyalty: *a jealous God.* **6.** an obsolete word for **zealous.** [C13: from Old French *gelos,* from Medieval Latin *zēlōsus,* from Late Latin *zēlus* emulation, jealousy, from Greek *zēlos* ZEAL] —ˈ**jealously** *adv.* —ˈ**jealousness** *n.*

jealousy (ˈdʒɛləsɪ) *n., pl.* **-ousies.** the state or quality of being jealous.

jean (dʒiːn) *n.* a tough twill-weave cotton fabric used for hard-wearing trousers, overalls, etc. See also **jeans.** [C16: short for *jean fustian,* from *Gene* Genoa, a port in NW Italy]

jeans (dʒiːnz) *pl. n.* informal trousers for casual wear, made esp. of denim or corduroy. [plural of JEAN]

jebel *or* **djebel** (ˈdʒɛbᵊl) *n.* a hill or mountain in an Arab country.

jeelie *or* **jeely** (ˈdʒiːlɪ) *n. Scot.* jelly or jam.

Jeep (dʒiːp) *n. Trademark.* a small military road vehicle with four-wheel drive. [C20: probably from the initials *GP,* for *general purpose* (*vehicle*)]

jeepers *or* **jeepers creepers** (ˈdʒiːpəz ˈkriːpəz) *interj. U.S. and Canadian slang.* a mild exclamation of surprise. [C20: euphemism for *Jesus*]

jeer (dʒɪə) *vb.* **1.** (often foll. by *at*) to laugh or scoff (at a person or thing); mock. ~*n.* **2.** a remark or cry of derision; gibe; taunt. [C16: of unknown origin] —ˈ**jeerer** *n.* —ˈ**jeering** *adj., n.* —ˈ**jeeringly** *adv.*

jefe (*Spanish* ˈxefe) *n.* (in Spanish-speaking countries) a military or political leader. [Spanish, from French *chef* CHIEF]

jehad (dʒɪˈhæd) *n.* a variant spelling of **jihad.**

Jehovah (dʒɪˈhəʊvə) *n. Old Testament.* the personal name of God, revealed to Moses on Mount Horeb (Exodus 3). [C16: from Medieval Latin, from Hebrew YHVH: the original vocalization was considered too sacred to be pronounced and the vowels of Eloah (God) were therefore substituted in the Masoretic text, whence Yetto Vah]

Jehovah's Witness *n.* a member of a Christian Church of American origin, the followers of which believe that the end of the present world system of government is near, that all other Churches and religions are false or evil, that all war is unlawful, and that the civil law must be resisted whenever it conflicts with their Church's own religious principles.

Jehovist (dʒɪˈhəʊvɪst) *n.* **1.** another name for the **Yahwist. 2.** a person who maintains that the name YHVH in the Hebrew text of the Old Testament was originally pronounced *Jehovah.* ~*adj.* **3.** of or relating to the Yahwist source of the Pentateuch. —**Je**ˈ**hovism** *n.* —**Jehovistic** (ˌdʒiːhəʊˈvɪstɪk) *adj.*

Jehu (ˈdʒiːhjuː) *n.* a fast driver, esp. one who is reckless (from the phrase **to drive like Jehu;** II Kings 9:20).

jejune (dʒɪˈdʒuːn) *adj.* **1.** simple; naive; unsophisticated. **2.** insipid; dull; dry. **3.** lacking nourishment; insubstantial or barren. [C17: from Latin *jējūnus* hungry, empty] —**je**ˈ**junely** *adv.* —**je**ˈ**juneness** *or* **je**ˈ**junity** *n.*

jejunostomy (dʒɪdʒuːˈnɒstəmɪ) *n.* the surgical formation of an opening from the jejunum to the surface of the body, through which food may be introduced.

jejunum (dʒɪˈdʒuːnəm) *n.* the part of the small intestine between the duodenum and the ileum. [C16: from Latin, from *jējūnus* empty; from the belief that the jejunum is empty after death] —**je**ˈ**junal** *adj.*

Jekyll and Hyde (ˈdʒɛkᵊl; haɪd) *n.* **a.** a person with two distinct personalities, one good, the other evil. **b.** (*as modifier*): *a Jekyll-and-Hyde personality.* [C19: after the principal character of Robert Louis Stevenson's novel *The Strange Case of Dr Jekyll and Mr Hyde* (1886)]

jell *or* **gel** (dʒɛl) *vb.* **jells, jelling, jelled** *or* **gels, gelling, gelled. 1.** to make or become gelatinous; congeal. **2.** (*intr.*) to assume definite form: *his ideas have jelled.* ~*n.* **3.** *U.S.* an informal word for **jelly.** [C19: back formation from JELLY[1]]

jellaba *or* **jellabah** (ˈdʒɛləbə) *n.* a kind of loose cloak with a hood, worn esp. in North Africa and the Middle East. [from Arabic *jallabah*]

jellied (ˈdʒɛlɪd) *adj.* **1.** congealed into jelly, esp. by cooling. **2.** containing, set in, or coated with jelly.

jellify (ˈdʒɛlɪˌfaɪ) *vb.* **-fies, -fying, -fied.** to make into or become jelly. —ˌ**jellifiˈcation** *n.*

jello (ˈdʒɛləʊ) *n.* the usual U.S. and Canadian name for **jelly**[1] (sense 1). [C20: from the trademark *Jell-O*]

jelly[1] (ˈdʒɛlɪ) *n., pl.* **-lies. 1.** a fruit-flavoured clear dessert set with gelatin. U.S. and Canadian name: **jello. 2.** a preserve made from the juice of fruit boiled with sugar and used as jam. **3.** a savoury food preparation set with gelatin or with a strong gelatinous stock and having a soft elastic consistency: *calf's-foot jelly.* **4.** anything having the consistency of jelly. **5.** *Informal.* a coloured gelatin filter that can be fitted in front of a stage or studio light. ~*vb.* **-lies, -lying, -lied. 6.** to jellify. [C14: from Old French *gelee* frost, jelly, from *geler* to set hard, from Latin *gelāre,* from *gelu* frost] —ˈ**jelly-**ˌ**like** *adj.*

jelly[2] (ˈdʒɛlɪ) *n. Brit.* a slang name for **gelignite.**

jelly baby *n. Brit.* a small sweet made from a gelatinous substance formed to resemble a baby in shape.

jelly bag *n.* a muslin bag used to strain off the juice from the fruit in making jelly (the preserve).

jellybean (ˈdʒɛlɪˌbiːn) *n.* a bean-shaped sweet with a brightly coloured coating around a gelatinous filling.

jellyfish (ˈdʒɛlɪˌfɪʃ) *n., pl.* **-fish** *or* **-fishes. 1.** any marine medusoid coelenterate of the class *Scyphozoa,* having a gelatinous umbrella-shaped body with trailing tentacles. **2.** any other medusoid coelenterate. **3.** *Informal.* a weak indecisive person.

jelly fungus *n.* a member of any of three orders (*Auriculariales, Tremellales,* and *Dacrymycetales*) of basidiomycetous fungi that grow on trees and have a jelly-like consistency when wet. They include the conspicuous **yellow brain fungus** (*Tremella mesenterica*), the black **witch's butter** (*Exidia plana*), and the pinky-red **jew's-ear** (*Auricularia auricula-judae*).

jelly mould *n.* the N.Z. term for **jelly fungus.**

jelutong (ˈdʒɛləˌtɒŋ) *n.* **1.** a Malaysian apocynaceous tree of the genus *Dyera,* esp. *D. costulata.* **2.** the latex obtained from this tree, used in the manufacture of chewing gum. **3.** the wood of this tree. [C19: from Malay]

jemadar (ˈdʒɛməˌdɑː) *n.* **1.** a native junior officer belonging to a locally raised regiment serving as mercenaries in India, esp. with the British Army (until 1947). **2.** an officer in the Indian police. [C18: from Urdu *jama 'dār,* from Persian *jama 'at* body of men + *dār* having]

jembe (ˈdʒɛmbɛ) *n. E African.* a hoe. [C19: from Swahili]

jemmy (ˈdʒɛmɪ) *or U.S.* **jimmy** *n., pl.* **-mies. 1.** a short steel crowbar used, esp. by burglars, for forcing doors and windows. ~*vb.* **-mies, -mying, -mied. 2.** (*tr.*) to prise (something) open with a jemmy. [C19: from the pet name for *James*]

je ne sais quoi *French.* (ʒənsekwa) *n.* an indefinable quality, esp. of personality. [literally: I don't know what]

jennet, genet, *or* **gennet** (ˈdʒɛnɪt) *n.* **1.** Also called: **jenny.** a female donkey or ass. **2.** a small Spanish riding horse. [C15: from Old French *genet*, from Catalan *ginet*, horse of the type used by the *Zenete*, from Arabic *Zanātah* the Zenete, a Moorish people renowned for their horsemanship]

jenny (ˈdʒɛnɪ) *n., pl.* **-nies. 1.** a hand-operated machine for turning up the edge of a piece of sheet metal in preparation for making a joint. **2.** the female of certain animals or birds, esp. a donkey, ass, or wren. **3.** short for **spinning jenny. 4.** *Billiards, etc.* an in-off. See **long jenny, short jenny.** [C17: from the name *Jenny*, diminutive of *Jane*]

jeopardize *or* **jeopardise** (ˈdʒɛpəˌdaɪz) *vb. (tr.)* **1.** to risk; hazard: *he jeopardized his job by being persistently unpunctual.* **2.** to put in danger; imperil.

jeopardy (ˈdʒɛpədɪ) *n.* (usually preceded by *in*) **1.** danger of injury, loss, death, etc.; risk; peril; hazard: *his health was in jeopardy.* **2.** *Law.* danger of being convicted and punished for a criminal offence. See also **double jeopardy.** [C14: from Old French *jeu parti*, literally: divided game, hence uncertain issue, from *jeu* game, from Latin *jocus* joke, game + *partir* to divide, from Latin *partīrī*]

jequirity *or* **jequerity** (dʒɪˈkwɪrɪtɪ) *n., pl.* **-ties. 1.** other names for **Indian liquorice. 2. jequirity bean.** the seed of the Indian liquorice. [C19: from Portuguese *jequiriti*, from Tupi-Guarani *jekiriti*]

Jer. *Bible. abbrev. for* Jeremiah.

jerbil (ˈdʒɜːbɪl) *n.* a variant spelling of **gerbil.**

jerboa (dʒɜːˈbəʊə) *n.* any small nocturnal burrowing rodent of the family *Dipodidae*, inhabiting dry regions of Asia and N Africa, having pale sandy fur, large ears, and long hind legs specialized for jumping. [C17: from New Latin, from Arabic *yarbūʻ*]

jeremiad (ˌdʒɛrɪˈmaɪəd) *n.* a long mournful lamentation or complaint.

Jeremiah (ˌdʒɛrɪˈmaɪə) *n.* a person who habitually prophesies doom or denounces contemporary society. [after *Jeremiah*, Old Testament prophet said to have written Lamentations]

jerepigo (ˌdʒɛrəˈpiːgəʊ) *n. S. African.* a usually red heavy dessert wine. [from Portuguese *geropiga*]

jerid (dʒəˈriːd) *n.* a wooden javelin used in Muslim countries in military displays on horseback. Also: **jereed, jerreed.**

jerk[1] (dʒɜːk) *vb.* **1.** to move or cause to move with an irregular or spasmodic motion. **2.** to throw, twist, pull, or push (something) abruptly or spasmodically. **3.** *(tr.;* often foll. by *out)* to utter (words, sounds, etc.) in a spasmodic, abrupt, or breathless manner. *~n.* **4.** an abrupt or spasmodic movement. **5.** an irregular jolting motion: *the car moved with a jerk.* **6.** *(pl.)* Also called: **physical jerks.** *Brit. informal.* physical exercises. **7.** *(pl.) U.S.* a slang word for **chorea. 8.** *Slang, chiefly U.S. and Canadian.* a person regarded with contempt, esp. a stupid or ignorant person. [C16: probably variant of *yerk* to pull stitches tight in making a shoe; compare Old English *gearcian* to make ready] —**ˈjerker** *n.* —**ˈjerking** *adj., n.*

jerk[2] (dʒɜːk) *vb. (tr.)* **1.** to preserve (venison, beef, etc.) by cutting into thin strips and curing by drying in the sun. *~n.* **2.** Also called: **jerky.** jerked meat, esp. beef. [C18: back formation from *jerky*, from CHARQUI]

jerkin (ˈdʒɜːkɪn) *n.* **1.** a sleeveless and collarless short jacket worn by men or women. **2.** a man's sleeveless and collarless fitted jacket, often made of leather, worn in the 16th and 17th centuries. [C16: of unknown origin]

jerk off *vb. (adv. often reflexive) Taboo slang.* (of a male) to masturbate.

jerkwater (ˈdʒɜːkˌwɔːtə) *adj. U.S. and Canadian slang.* inferior and insignificant: *a jerkwater town.* [C19: originally referring to railway locomotives for which water was taken on in buckets from streams along the route]

jerky[1] (ˈdʒɜːkɪ) *adj.* **jerkier, jerkiest.** characterized by jerks; spasmodic. —**ˈjerkily** *adv.* —**ˈjerkiness** *n.*

jerky[2] (ˈdʒɜːkɪ) *n.* another word for **jerk**[2] (sense 2).

jeroboam (ˌdʒɛrəˈbəʊəm) *n.* a wine bottle holding the equivalent of four normal bottles (approximately 104 ounces). Also called: **double-magnum.** [C19: humorous allusion to *Jeroboam*, described as a "mighty man of valour" (I Kings 11:28) who "made Israel to sin" (I Kings 14:16)]

jerreed (dʒəˈriːd) *n.* a variant spelling of **jerid.**

jerry (ˈdʒɛrɪ) *n., pl.* **-ries. 1.** *Brit.* an informal word for **chamber pot. 2.** short for **jeroboam.**

Jerry (ˈdʒɛrɪ) *n., pl.* **-ries.** *Brit. slang.* **1.** a German, esp. a German soldier. **2.** the Germans collectively: *Jerry didn't send his bombers out last night.*

jerry-build *vb.* **-builds, -building, -built.** *(tr.)* to build (houses, flats, etc.) badly using cheap materials. —**ˈjerry-ˌbuilder** *n.*

jerry can *n.* a flat-sided can with a capacity of between 4.5 and 5 gallons used for storing or transporting liquids, esp. motor fuel: originally a German design adopted by the British Army during World War II. [C20: from JERRY]

jersey (ˈdʒɜːzɪ) *n.* **1.** a knitted garment covering the upper part of the body. **2. a.** a machine-knitted slightly elastic cloth of wool, silk, nylon, etc., used for clothing. **b.** *(as modifier): a jersey suit.* **3.** *Austral. and N.Z.* a football shirt. [C16: from JERSEY, from the woollen sweaters traditionally worn by the fishermen]

Jersey (ˈdʒɜːzɪ) *n.* a breed of dairy cattle producing milk with a high butterfat content, originating from the island of Jersey in the English Channel.

Jerusalem (dʒəˈruːsələm) *n.* **the New Jerusalem. 1.** *Christianity.* Heaven. **2.** any ideal city. [named after *Jerusalem*, capital of modern Israel and of the historic Hebrew kingdom]

Jerusalem artichoke *n.* **1.** a North American sunflower, *Helianthus tuberosus*, widely cultivated for its underground edible tubers. **2.** the tuber of this plant, which is cooked and eaten as a vegetable. ~See also **artichoke** (senses 1, 2). [C17: by folk etymology from Italian *girasole articiocco;* see GIRASOL]

Jerusalem cherry *n.* a small South American solanaceous shrub, *Solanum pseudo-capsicum*, cultivated as a house plant for its white flowers and inedible reddish cherry-like fruit.

Jerusalem cross *n.* a cross the equal arms of which end in a bar. Also called: **cross potent.**

Jerusalem oak *n.* a weedy North American chenopodiaceous plant, *Chenopodium botrys*, that has lobed leaves and smells of turpentine.

jess (dʒɛs) *Falconry.* *~n.* **1.** a short leather strap, one end of which is permanently attached to the leg of a hawk or falcon while the other can be attached to a leash. *~vb.* **2.** *(tr.)* to put jesses on (a hawk or falcon). [C14: from Old French *ges*, from Latin *jactus* a throw, from *jacere* to throw] —**jessed** *adj.*

jessamine (ˈdʒɛsəmɪn) *n.* another name for **jasmine** (sense 1).

Jesse window (ˈdʒɛsɪ) *n.* a window in a church with a representation of Christ's descent from Jesse, usually in the form of a genealogical tree.

jessie (ˈdʒɛsɪ) *n. Scot. slang.* an effeminate, weak, or cowardly boy or man.

jest (dʒɛst) *n.* **1.** something done or said for amusement; joke. **2.** a frivolous mood or attitude; playfulness; fun: *to act in jest.* **3.** a jeer or taunt. **4.** an object of derision; laughing stock; butt. *~vb.* **5.** to act or speak in an amusing, teasing, or frivolous way; joke. **6.** to make fun of (a person or thing); scoff or mock. [C13: variant of GEST] —**ˈjestful** *adj.* —**ˈjesting** *adj., n.* —**ˈjestingly** *adv.*

jester (ˈdʒɛstə) *n.* a professional clown employed by a king or nobleman, esp. at courts during the Middle Ages.

Jesuit (ˈdʒɛzjʊɪt) *n.* **1.** a member of a Roman Catholic religious order (the **Society of Jesus**) founded by Ignatius Loyola in 1534 with the aims of defending the papacy and Catholicism against the Reformation and to undertake missionary work among the heathen. **2.** *(sometimes not cap.) Informal, offensive.* a person given to subtle and equivocating arguments; casuist. [C16: from New Latin *Jēsuita*, from Late Latin *Jēsus* + *-ita* -ITE[1]] —**ˌJesuˈitic** *or* **ˌJesuˈitical** *adj.* —**Jesuˈitically** *adv.*

Jesuitism (ˈdʒɛzjʊɪˌtɪzəm) *or* **Jesuitry** *n.* **1.** theology or practices of the Jesuits. **2.** *Informal, offensive.* subtle and equivocating arguments; casuistry.

Jesus (ˈdʒiːzəs) *interj. also* **Jesus wept.** used to express intense surprise, dismay, etc. [after *Jesus* CHRIST, via Latin from Greek *Iēsous*, from Hebrew *Yeshūaʻ*, shortened from *Yehōshūaʻ* God is help, Joshua]

Jesus freak *n. Informal.* a member of any of various Christian groups that combine a hippie communal way of life with zealous evangelicalism.

jet[1] (dʒɛt) *n.* **1.** a thin stream of liquid or gas forced out of a small aperture or nozzle. **2.** an outlet or nozzle for emitting such a stream. **3.** a jet-propelled aircraft. *~vb.* **jets, jetting, jetted. 4.** to issue or cause to issue in a jet: *water jetted from the hose; he jetted them with water.* **5.** to transport or be transported by jet aircraft. [C16: from Old French *jeter* to throw, from Latin *jactāre* to toss about, frequentative of *jacere* to throw]

jet[2] (dʒɛt) *n.* **a.** a hard black variety of lignite that takes a brilliant polish and is used for jewellery, ornaments, etc. **b.** *(as modifier): jet earrings.* [C14: from Old French *jaiet*, from Latin *gagātēs*, from Greek *lithos gagatēs* stone of *Gagai*, a town in Lycia, Asia Minor]

JET (dʒɛt) *n. acronym for* Joint European Torus; an apparatus at Culham, Oxfordshire, for research into energy production by nuclear fusion.

jet black *n.* **a.** a deep black colour. **b.** *(as adj.): jet-black hair.*

jet-boat *n. N.Z.* a power boat that is powered and steered by a jet of water under pressure.

jet condenser *n.* a steam condenser in which steam is condensed by jets of water.

jeté (ʒəˈteɪ) *n. Ballet.* a step in which the dancer springs from one leg and lands on the other. [French, literally: thrown, from *jeter;* see JET[1]]

jet engine *n.* a gas turbine, esp. one fitted to an aircraft.

jet lag *n.* a general feeling of fatigue and disorientation often experienced by travellers by jet aircraft who cross several time zones in relatively few hours.

jetliner (ˈdʒɛtˌlaɪnə) *n.* a commercial airliner powered by jet engines.

jet pipe *n.* the duct attached to the rear of a gas turbine through which the exhaust gases are discharged, esp. one fitted to an aircraft engine.

jet plane *n.* an aircraft powered by one or more jet engines.

jetport (ˈdʒɛtˌpɔːt) *n.* an airport for jet planes.

jet-propelled *adj.* **1.** driven by jet propulsion. **2.** *Informal.* very fast.

jet propulsion *n.* 1. propulsion by means of a jet of fluid. 2. propulsion by means of a gas turbine, esp. when the exhaust gases provide the propulsive thrust.

jetsam *or* **jetsom** ('dʒɛtsəm) *n.* 1. that portion of the equipment or cargo of a vessel thrown overboard to lighten her, as during a storm. Compare **flotsam** (sense 1), **lagan.** 2. another word for **flotsam** (sense 2). [C16: shortened from JETTISON]

jet set *n.* a. a rich and fashionable social set the members of which travel widely for pleasure. b. (*as modifier*): *jet-set travellers.* —'**jet-,setter** *n.* —'**jet-,setting** *adj.*

jet ski *n.* 1. a small self-propelled vehicle for one person resembling a scooter, which skims across water on a flat keel, and is steered by means of handlebars. ~*vb.* **jet-ski, -skis, -skiing, -skied** *or* **-ski'd.** (*intr.*) 2. to ride a jet ski. —**jet skier** *n.* —**jet skiing** *n.*

jet stream *n.* 1. *Meteorol.* a narrow belt of high-altitude winds (about 12 000 metres high) moving east at high speeds and having an important effect on frontogenesis. 2. the jet of exhaust gases produced by a gas turbine, rocket motor, etc.

jettison ('dʒɛtɪsᵊn, -zᵊn) *vb.* (*tr.*) **-sons, -soning, -soned.** 1. to throw away; abandon: *to jettison old clothes.* 2. to throw overboard. ~*n.* 3. another word for **jetsam** (sense 1). [C15: from Old French *getaison,* ultimately from Latin *jactātiō* a tossing about; see JACTATION]

jetton ('dʒɛtᵊn) *n.* a counter or token, esp. a chip used in such gambling games as roulette. [C18: from French *jeton,* from *jeter* to cast up (accounts); see JET[1]]

jetty[1] ('dʒɛtɪ) *n., pl.* **-ties.** 1. a structure built from a shore out into the water to direct currents or protect a harbour. 2. a landing pier; dock. [C15: from Old French *jetee* projecting part, literally: something thrown out, from *jeter* to throw; see JET[1]]

jetty[2] ('dʒɛtɪ) *adj.* of or resembling jet, esp. in colour or polish. —'**jettiness** *n.*

jeu d'esprit (*French* ʒø dɛspri) *n., pl.* ***jeux d'esprit*** (ʒø dɛspri). a light-hearted display of wit or cleverness, esp. in literature. [literally: play of spirit]

jeunesse dorée *French.* (ʒœnɛs dɔre) *n.* rich and fashionable young people. [literally: gilded youth]

Jew (dʒuː) *n.* 1. a member of the Semitic people who are notionally descended from the ancient Israelites, are spread throughout the world, and are linked by loose cultural or religious ties. 2. a person whose religion is Judaism. 3. (*modifier*) *Offensive.* Jewish: *a Jew boy.* 4. (*sometimes not cap.*) *Offensive.* a. a person who drives a hard bargain. b. a miserly person. c. *Obsolete.* a usurer. ~*vb.* 5. (*tr.; often not cap.*) *Offensive.* to drive a hard bargain (with), esp. in order to defraud. ~See also **Hebrew, Israeli, Israelite.** [C12: from Old French *juiu,* from Latin *jūdaeus,* from Greek *ioudaios,* from Hebrew *yehūdī,* from *yehūdāh* Judah]

Jew-baiting *n.* active persecution or harassment of Jews. —'**Jew-,baiter** *n.*

jewel ('dʒuːəl) *n.* 1. a precious or semiprecious stone; gem. 2. a person or thing resembling a jewel in preciousness, brilliance, etc. 3. a gemstone, often synthetically produced, used as a bearing in a watch. 4. a piece of jewellery. 5. an ornamental glass boss, sometimes faceted, used in stained glasswork. ~*vb.* **-els, -elling, -elled** *or U.S.* **-els, -eling, -eled.** 6. (*tr.*) to fit or decorate with a jewel or jewels. [C13: from Old French *jouel,* perhaps from *jeu* game, from Latin *jocus*] —'**jewelled** *or U.S.* '**jeweled** *adj.* —'**jewel-,like** *adj.*

jewelfish ('dʒuːəl,fɪʃ) *n., pl.* **-fish** *or* **-fishes.** an African cichlid, *Hemichromis bimaculatus*: a beautifully coloured and popular aquarium fish.

jeweller *or U.S.* **jeweler** ('dʒuːələ) *n.* a person whose business is the cutting, polishing, or setting of gemstones or the making, repairing, or selling of jewellery.

jeweller's rouge *n.* a finely powdered form of ferric oxide used as a metal polish. Also called: **crocus.** See also **colcothar.**

jewellery *or U.S.* **jewelry** ('dʒuːəlrɪ) *n.* 1. objects that are worn for personal adornment, such as bracelets, rings, necklaces, etc., considered collectively. 2. the art or business of a jeweller.

Jewess ('dʒuːɪs) *n.* a Jewish girl or woman.

jewfish ('dʒuː,fɪʃ) *n., pl.* **-fish** *or* **-fishes.** 1. any of various large dark serranid fishes, such as *Mycteroperca bonaci,* of warm or tropical seas. 2. *Austral.* a freshwater catfish. [C17: of uncertain origin]

Jewish ('dʒuːɪʃ) *adj.* 1. of, relating to, or characteristic of Jews. 2. *Offensive.* miserly. ~*n.* 3. a less common word for **Yiddish.** —'**Jewishly** *adv.* —'**Jewishness** *n.*

Jewish calendar *n.* the lunisolar calendar used by the Jews, in which time is reckoned from 3761 BC, regarded as the year of the Creation. See **Nisan, Iyar, Sivan, Tammuz, Av, Elul, Tishri, Cheshvan, Kislev, Tevet, Shevat, Adar.** Also called: **Hebrew calendar.**

jew lizard *n.* a large Australian lizard, *Amphibolus barbatus,* having a pouch beneath the jaw that is distended when the animal is threatened. Also called: **bearded lizard** *or* **dragon.**

Jewry ('dʒʊərɪ) *n., pl.* **-ries.** 1. a. Jews collectively. b. the Jewish religion or culture. 2. *Archaic.* (sometimes found in street names in England) a quarter of a town inhabited by Jews. 3. **the.** (in some anti-semitic literature) the Jews conceived of as an organized force seeking world domination.

jew's-ear *n.* See **jelly fungus.**

jew's-harp *n.* a musical instrument consisting of a small lyre-shaped metal frame held between the teeth, with a steel tongue plucked with the finger. Changes in pitch are produced by varying the size of the mouth cavities.

Jezebel ('dʒɛzə,bɛl, -bᵊl) (*sometimes not cap.*) a shameless or scheming woman. [after the Biblical *Jezebel,* who fostered worship of Baal and tried to destroy the prophets of Israel (1 Kings 18:4–13)]

JFK *abbrev. for* John Fitzgerald Kennedy.

jhatka ('dʒætkə) *n.* the slaughter of animals for food according to Sikh law. [Punjabi]

JHVH *or* **JHWH** *Old Testament.* variants of **YHVH.**

-ji (-dziː) *Indian.* a suffix placed after a person's name or title as a mark of respect. [Hindi]

jib[1] (dʒɪb) *n.* 1. *Nautical.* any triangular sail set forward of the foremast of a vessel. 2. **cut of someone's jib.** someone's manner, behaviour, style, etc. 3. *Obsolete.* a. the lower lip, usually when it protrudes forwards in a grimace. b. the face or nose. [C17: of unknown origin]

jib[2] (dʒɪb) *vb.* **jibs, jibbing, jibbed.** (*intr.*) *Chiefly Brit.* 1. (often foll. by *at*) to be reluctant (to); hold back (from); balk (at). 2. (of an animal) to stop short and refuse to go forwards: *the horse jibbed at the jump.* 3. *Nautical.* variant of **gybe.** [C19: of unknown origin] —'**jibber** *n.*

jib[3] (dʒɪb) *n.* the projecting arm of a crane or the boom of a derrick, esp. one that is pivoted to enable it to be raised or lowered. [C18: probably based on GIBBET]

jib[4] (dʒɪb) *n.* (*often pl.*) *South Wales dialect.* a contortion of the face; a face: *stop making jibs.* [special use of JIB[1] (in the sense: lower lip, face)]

jibbons ('dʒɪbᵊnz) *pl. n. Southwest Brit. dialect.* spring onions. [from Norman French *chiboule,* variant of French *ciboule* onion, ultimately from Latin *capulla* an onion patch, from *caepa* an onion]

jib boom *n. Nautical.* a spar forming an extension of the bowsprit.

jibe[1] (dʒaɪb), **jib,** *or* **jibb** (dʒɪb) *vb., n. Nautical.* variants of **gybe.**

jibe[2] (dʒaɪb) *vb.* a variant spelling of **gibe**[1]. —'**jiber** *n.* —'**jibingly** *adv.*

jibe[3] (dʒaɪb) *vb.* (*intr.*) *Informal.* to agree; accord; harmonize. [C19: of unknown origin]

jib-headed *adj. Nautical.* 1. (of a sail) pointed at the top or head. 2. (of a sailing vessel or rig) having sails that are triangular.

JICTAR ('dʒɪktɑː) *n. acronym for* Joint Industry Committee for Television Advertising Research.

jiffy ('dʒɪfɪ) *or* **jiff** (dʒɪf) *n., pl.* **jiffies** *or* **jiffs.** *Informal.* a very short time: *wait a jiffy.* [C18: of unknown origin]

Jiffy bag *n. Trademark.* a thickly padded but light envelope in which articles such as books are placed for protection in the post.

jig (dʒɪg) *n.* 1. any of several old rustic kicking and leaping dances. 2. a piece of music composed for or in the rhythm of this dance, usually in three-four time. 3. a mechanical device designed to hold and locate a component during machining and to guide the cutting tool. 4. *Angling.* any of various spinning lures that wobble when drawn through the water. 5. Also called: **jigger.** *Mining.* a device for separating ore or coal from waste material by agitation in water. 6. *Obsolete.* a joke or prank. ~*vb.* **jigs, jigging, jigged.** 7. to dance (a jig). 8. to jerk or cause to jerk up and down rapidly. 9. (often foll. by *up*) to fit or be fitted in a jig. 10. (*tr.*) to drill or cut (a workpiece) in a jig. 11. *Mining.* to separate ore or coal from waste material using a jig. 12. (*intr.*) to produce or manufacture a jig. 13. *Austral. slang.* to play truant from school. [C16 (originally: a dance or the music for it; applied to various modern devices because of the verbal sense: to jerk up and down rapidly): of unknown origin]

jigger[1] ('dʒɪgə) *n.* 1. a person or thing that jigs. 2. *Golf.* a club, an iron, usually No. 4. 3. any of a number of mechanical devices having a vibratory or jerking motion. 4. a light lifting tackle used on ships. 5. a small glass, esp. for whisky, with a capacity of about one and a half ounces. 6. *N.Z.* a light hand- or power-propelled vehicle used on railway lines. 7. *Engineering.* a type of hydraulic lift in which a hydraulic ram operates the lift through a block and tackle which increases the length of the stroke. 8. *Canadian.* a device used when setting a gill net beneath ice. 9. *Mining.* another word for **jig** (sense 5). 10. *Nautical.* short for **jiggermast.** 11. *Billiards.* another word for **bridge**[1] (sense 10). 12. *U.S. and Canadian informal.* a device or thing the name of which is unknown or temporarily forgotten. 13. *Liverpool dialect.* an alleyway.

jigger[2] *or* **jigger flea** ('dʒɪgə) *n.* other names for the **chigoe** (sense 1).

jiggered ('dʒɪgəd) *adj.* (*postpositive*) 1. *Informal.* damned; blowed: *I'm jiggered if he'll get away with it.* 2. (sometimes foll. by *up*) *Scot. and Northern English dialect.* tired out. [C19: probably euphemism for *buggered;* see BUGGER]

jiggermast ('dʒɪgə,mɑːst) *n. Nautical.* any small mast on a sailing vessel, esp. the mizzenmast of a yawl. Sometimes shortened to **jigger.**

jiggery-pokery ('dʒɪgərɪ'pəʊkərɪ) *n. Informal, chiefly Brit.* dishonest or deceitful behaviour or business; trickery. [C19: from Scottish dialect *joukery-pawkery*]

jiggle ('dʒɪgᵊl) *vb.* **1.** to move or cause to move up and down or to and fro with a short jerky motion: *to jiggle the door handle.* ~*n.* **2.** a short jerky motion. [C19: frequentative of JIG; compare JOGGLE] —'**jiggly** *adj.*

jigsaw ('dʒɪgˌsɔː) *n.* **1.** a mechanical saw with a fine steel blade for cutting intricate curves in sheets of material. **2.** See **jigsaw puzzle.** [C19: from JIG (to jerk up and down rapidly) + SAW[1]]

jigsaw puzzle *n.* a puzzle in which the player has to reassemble a picture that has been mounted on a wooden or cardboard base and cut into a large number of irregularly shaped interlocking pieces.

jihad *or* **jehad** (dʒɪ'hæd) *n.* **1.** *Islam.* a holy war against infidels undertaken by Muslims. **2.** *Rare.* a crusade in support of a cause. [C19: from Arabic *jihād* a conflict]

jill (dʒɪl) *n. Dialect.* a variant spelling of **gill**[4] (sense 2).

jillaroo (ˌdʒɪlə'ruː) *n., pl.* **-roos.** *Austral. informal.* a female jackeroo.

jillion ('dʒɪljən) *n. Informal.* an extremely large number or amount: *jillions of pounds.* [C20: fanciful coinage based on MILLION, BILLION, etc.] —'**jillionth** *adj.*

jilt (dʒɪlt) *vb.* **1.** (*tr.*) to leave or reject (a lover), esp. without previous warning: *she was jilted at the altar.* ~*n.* **2.** a woman who jilts a lover. [C17: from dialect *jillet* flighty girl, diminutive of proper name *Gill*] —'**jilter** *n.*

jim crow ('dʒɪm 'krəʊ) *n.* (*often caps.*) *U.S.* **1. a.** the policy or practice of segregating Negroes. **b.** (*as modifier*): *jim-crow laws.* **2. a.** a derogatory term for Negro. **b.** (*as modifier*): *a jim-crow saloon.* **3.** an implement for bending iron bars or rails. **4.** a crowbar fitted with a claw. [C19: from *Jim Crow,* name of song used as the basis of an act by Thomas Rice (1808–60), American entertainer] —'**jim-'crowism** *n.*

jimjams ('dʒɪmˌdʒæmz) *pl. n.* **1.** a slang word for **delirium tremens.** **2.** a state of nervous tension, excitement, or anxiety. [C19: whimsical formation based on JAM[1]]

jimmy ('dʒɪmɪ) *n., pl.* **-mies,** *vb.* **-mies, -mying, -mied.** the U.S. word for **jemmy.**

Jimmy ('dʒɪmɪ) *n. Central Scot. urban dialect.* an informal term of address to a male stranger.

Jimmy Woodser ('wʊdzə) *n. Austral. informal.* **1.** a man who drinks by himself. **2.** a drink taken alone.

jimson weed ('dʒɪmsᵊn) *n.* the U.S. and Canadian name for **thorn apple** (sense 1). [C17: from earlier *Jamestown weed,* from *Jamestown,* Virginia]

jingle ('dʒɪŋgᵊl) *vb.* **1.** to ring or cause to ring lightly and repeatedly. **2.** (*intr.*) to sound in a manner suggestive of jingling: *a jingling verse.* ~*n.* **3.** a sound of metal jingling: *the jingle of the keys.* **4.** a catchy and rhythmical verse, song, etc., esp. one used in advertising. [C16: probably of imitative origin; compare Dutch *jengelen*] —'**jingler** *n.* —'**jingly** *adj.*

jingo ('dʒɪŋgəʊ) *n., pl.* **-goes.** **1.** a loud and bellicose patriot; chauvinist. **2.** jingoism. **3. by jingo.** an exclamation of surprise. [C17: originally perhaps a euphemism for *Jesus;* applied to bellicose patriots after the use of *by Jingo!* in the refrain of a 19th-century music-hall song] —'**jingoish** *adj.*

jingoism ('dʒɪŋgəʊˌɪzəm) *n.* the belligerent spirit or foreign policy of jingoes; chauvinism. —'**jingoist** *n., adj.* —ˌ**jingo'istic** *adj.* —ˌ**jingo'istically** *adv.*

jink (dʒɪŋk) *vb.* **1.** to move swiftly or jerkily or make a quick turn in order to dodge or elude. ~*n.* **2.** a jinking movement. [C18: of Scottish origin, imitative of swift movement]

jinker ('dʒɪŋkə) *n. Austral.* **1.** a vehicle for transporting timber, consisting of a tractor and two sets of wheels for supporting the logs. **2.** a two-wheeled sulky. [of unknown origin]

jinks (dʒɪŋks) *pl. n.* boisterous or mischievous play (esp. in the phrase **high jinks**). [C18: of unknown origin]

jinn (dʒɪn) *n.* (*often functioning as sing.*) the plural of **jinni.**

jinni, jinnee, djinni, *or* **djinny** (dʒɪ'niː, 'dʒɪnɪ) *n., pl.* **jinn** *or* **djinn** (dʒɪn). a spirit in Muslim mythology who could assume human or animal form and influence man by supernatural powers. [C17: from Arabic]

jinrikisha, jinricksha, jinrickshaw, *or* **jinriksha** (dʒɪn'rɪkʃɔː, -ʃə) *n.* other names for **rickshaw.** [C19: from Japanese, from *jin* man + *riki* power + *sha* carriage]

jinx (dʒɪŋks) *n.* **1.** an unlucky or malevolent force, person, or thing. ~*vb.* **2.** (*tr.*) to be or put a jinx on. [C20: perhaps from New Latin *Jynx* genus name of the wryneck, from Greek *iunx* wryneck, the name of a bird used in magic]

jipijapa (ˌhiːpiː'hɑːpɑː) *n.* a palmlike plant, *Carludovica palmata,* of central and South America, whose fanlike leaves are bleached for making panama hats: family *Cyclanthaceae.* [American Spanish, after *Jipijapa,* Ecuador]

jissom ('dʒɪsəm) *n. Taboo.* an informal word for **semen.** [of unknown origin]

JIT *abbrev. for* **just-in-time.**

jitney ('dʒɪtnɪ) *n. U.S., now rare.* **1.** a small bus that carries passengers for a low price, originally five cents. **2.** *Slang.* a nickel; five cents. [C20: of unknown origin]

jitter ('dʒɪtə) *Informal.* ~*vb.* **1.** (*intr.*) to be anxious or nervous. ~*n.* **2. the jitters.** nervousness and anxiety. **3.** *Electronics.* small rapid variations in the amplitude or timing of a waveform arising from fluctuations in the voltage supply, mechanical vibrations, etc. [C20: of unknown origin] —'**jittery** *adj.* —'**jitteriness** *n.*

jitterbug ('dʒɪtəˌbʌg) *n.* **1.** a fast jerky American dance, usually to a jazz accompaniment, that was popular in the 1940s. **2.** a person who dances the jitterbug. **3.** a highly nervous or excitable person. ~*vb.* **-bugs, -bugging, -bugged.** **4.** (*intr.*) to perform such a dance.

jiujitsu *or* **jiujutsu** (dʒuː'dʒɪtsuː) *n.* variant spellings of **jujitsu.**

jive (dʒaɪv) *n.* **1.** a style of lively and jerky dance performed to jazz and, later, to rock and roll, popular esp. in the 1940s and 1950s. **2.** Also called: **jive talk.** a variety of American slang spoken chiefly by Blacks, esp. jazz musicians. **3. a.** *Slang, chiefly U.S.* deliberately misleading or deceptive talk. **b.** (*as modifier*): jive talk. ~*vb.* **4.** (*intr.*) to dance the jive. **5.** *Slang, chiefly U.S.* to mislead; tell lies (to). [C20: of unknown origin] —'**jiver** *n.*

jizz (dʒɪz) *n.* a term for the total combination of characteristics that serve to identify a particular species of bird or plant. [origin obscure]

JJ. *abbrev. for:* **1.** Judges. **2.** Justices.

jnd *abbrev. for* just noticeable difference.

Jnr *abbrev. for* junior.

jo *or* **joe** (dʒəʊ) *n., pl.* **joes.** a Scot. word for **sweetheart.** [C16: alteration of JOY]

joannes (dʒəʊ'æniːz) *n., pl.* **-nes.** a variant of **johannes.**

job (dʒɒb) *n.* **1.** an individual piece of work or task. **2.** an occupation; post of employment. **3.** an object worked on or a result produced from working. **4.** a duty or responsibility: *her job was to cook the dinner.* **5.** *Informal.* a difficult task or problem: *I had a job to contact him.* **6.** a state of affairs: *make the best of a bad job; it's a good job I saw you.* **7.** *Informal.* a damaging piece of work: *he really did a job on that.* **8.** *Informal.* a crime, esp. a robbery or burglary. **9.** *Informal.* an article or specimen: *the new car was a nice little job.* **10.** an instance of jobbery. **11.** *Computer technol.* a unit of work for a computer consisting of a single complete task submitted by a user. **12. jobs for the boys.** appointments given to or created for allies or favourites. **13. on the job. a.** actively engaged in one's employment. **b.** *Brit. taboo.* engaged in sexual intercourse. **14. just the job.** exactly what was required. ~*vb.* **jobs, jobbing, jobbed.** **15.** (*intr.*) to work by the piece or at casual jobs. **16.** to make a private profit out of (a public office, etc.). **17.** (*intr.;* usually foll. by *in*) **a.** to buy and sell (goods or services) as a middleman: *he jobs in government surplus.* **b.** *Brit.* to buy and sell stocks and shares as a stockjobber: *he jobs in blue chips.* **18.** (*tr.;* often foll. by *out*) to apportion (a contract, work, etc.) among several contractors, workers, etc. [C16: of uncertain origin]

Job (dʒəʊb) *n.* any person who withstands great suffering without despairing. [after *Job,* Old Testament patriarch whose faith withstood the test of afflictions sent by God]

job analysis *n.* the analysis of the contents of a job in order to provide a job description for such purposes as fitting the job into a grading structure or matching individual capabilities to job requirements.

jobber ('dʒɒbə) *n.* **1.** *Brit.* short for **stockjobber** (sense 1). **2.** a person who jobs.

jobbery ('dʒɒbərɪ) *n.* the practice of making private profit out of a public office; corruption or graft.

jobbing ('dʒɒbɪŋ) *adj.* working on occasional jobs or by the piece rather than in a regular job: *a jobbing gardener.*

jobbing printer *n.* one who prints mainly commercial and display work rather than books or newspapers.

Jobcentre ('dʒɒbˌsɛntə) *n. Brit.* any of a number of government offices having premises situated in the main shopping area of a town in which people seeking jobs can consult displayed advertisements in informal surroundings.

job club *n.* a group of unemployed people organized through a Jobcentre, which meets every day and is given advice on job seeking to increase its members' chances of finding employment.

job description *n.* a detailed written account, agreed between management and worker, of all the duties and responsibilities which together make up a particular job.

job enlargement *n.* a widening of the range of tasks performed by an employee in order to provide variety in the activities undertaken.

job evaluation *n.* the analysis of the relationship between jobs in an organization: often used as a basis for a wages structure.

jobless ('dʒɒblɪs) *adj.* **a.** unemployed. **b.** (*as collective n.;* preceded by *the*): *the jobless.* —'**joblessness** *n.*

job lot *n.* **1.** a miscellaneous collection of articles sold as a lot. **2.** a collection of cheap or trivial items.

job rotation *n.* the practice of transferring an employee from one work station or activity to another during the working day in order to add variety to a job: often used in assembly line work.

job satisfaction *n.* the extent to which a person's hopes, desires, and expectations about the employment he is engaged in are fulfilled.

Job's comforter *n.* a person who, while purporting to give sympathy, succeeds only in adding to distress.

job sharing *n.* the division of a job between two or more people such that each covers the same job for complementary parts of the day or week. —**job sharer** *n.*

Job's-tears *n.* **1.** (*functioning as sing.*) a tropical Asian grass, *Coix lacryma-jobi,* cultivated for its white beadlike modified leaves, which contain edible seeds. **2.** (*functioning as pl.*) the beadlike structures of this plant, used as rosary or ornamental beads.

jobsworth ('dʒɒbzˌwɜːθ) *n. Informal.* a person in a position of minor authority who invokes the letter of the law in order to avoid any action requiring initiative, cooperation, etc. [C20: from *it's more than my job's worth to ...*]

jock (dʒɒk) *n.* **1.** *Informal.* short for **disc jockey. 2.** *Informal.* short for **jockstrap. 3.** *U.S. informal.* an athlete. **4.** *N.Z. mining.* a pointed bar of steel inserted into the wheel of a mine vehicle used for emergency braking.

Jock (dʒɒk) *n.* a slang word or term of address for a Scot.

jockey ('dʒɒkɪ) *n.* **1.** a person who rides horses in races, esp. as a profession or for hire. ~*vb.* **2. a.** (*tr.*) to ride (a horse) in a race. **b.** (*intr.*) to ride as a jockey. **3.** (*intr.*) (often foll. by *for*) to try to obtain an advantage by manoeuvring, esp. literally in a race or metaphorically, as in a struggle for power (esp. in the phrase **jockey for position**). **4.** to trick or cheat (a person). [C16 (in the sense: lad): from name *Jock* + -EY]

jockey cap *n.* a cap with a long peak projecting from the forehead.

jocko ('dʒɒkəʊ) *n., pl.* **-os.** a W African name for **chimpanzee.** [C19: from French, based on Bantu *ngeko*]

jockstrap ('dʒɒkˌstræp) *n.* an elasticated belt with a pouch worn by men, esp. athletes, to support the genitals. Also called: **athletic support.** [C20: from slang *jock* penis + STRAP]

jocose (dʒə'kəʊs) *adj.* characterized by humour; merry. [C17: from Latin *jocōsus* given to jesting, from *jocus* JOKE] —**jo'cosely** *adv.* —**jo'coseness** *or* **jocosity** (dʒə'kɒsɪtɪ) *n.*

jocular ('dʒɒkjʊlə) *adj.* **1.** characterized by joking and good humour. **2.** meant lightly or humorously; facetious. [C17: from Latin *joculāris,* from *joculus* little JOKE] —**jocularity** (ˌdʒɒkjʊ'lærɪtɪ) *n.* —'**jocularly** *adv.*

jocund ('dʒɒkənd) *adj.* of a humorous temperament; merry. [C14: from Late Latin *jocundus,* from Latin *jūcundus* pleasant, from *juvāre* to please] —**jocundity** (dʒəʊ'kʌndɪtɪ) *or* '**jocundness** *n.* —'**jocundly** *adv.*

Jodhpuri coat ('dʒɒdpʊrɪ) *n.* a coat worn by men in India, similar to but shorter than a sherwani. [named after *Jodhpur,* a city in NW India]

jodhpurs ('dʒɒdpəz) *pl. n.* **1.** riding breeches, loose-fitting around the hips and tight-fitting from the thighs to the ankles. **2.** Also called: **jodhpur boots.** ankle-length leather riding boots. [C19: from the city of *Jodhpur*]

Joe (dʒəʊ) *n.* (*sometimes not cap.*) *Slang.* **1.** *U.S. and Canadian.* a man or fellow. **2.** *U.S.* a GI; soldier.

Joe Blake *n. Austral.* **1.** *Rhyming slang.* a snake. **2. the Joe Blakes.** the DT's.

Joe Bloggs (blɒgz) *n. Brit. slang.* an average or typical man. U.S., Canadian, and Austral. equivalent: **Joe Blow**. See also **Joe Six-Pack.**

Joe Public *n. Slang.* the general public.

joe-pye weed (dʒəʊ'paɪ) *n. U.S. and Canadian.* any of several North American plants of the genus *Eupatorium,* esp. *E. purpureum,* having pale purplish clusters of flower heads lacking rays: family *Compositae* (composites). [C19: of unknown origin]

joes (dʒəʊz) *pl. n. Austral. informal.* **the.** a fit of depression. [short for *the Joe Blakes*]

Joe Six-Pack ('sɪksˌpæk) *n. U.S. slang.* an average or typical man.

Joe Soap *n.* **1.** *Brit. slang.* a person who is regarded as unintelligent and imposed upon as a stooge or scapegoat. **2.** the N.Z. term for **Joe Bloggs.**

joey ('dʒəʊɪ) *n. Austral. informal.* **1.** a young kangaroo. **2.** a young animal or child. [C19: from a native Australian language]

Joey Hooker ('dʒəʊɪ 'hʊkə) *n.* another name for **gallant soldier** (a plant).

jog[1] (dʒɒg) *vb.* **jogs, jogging, jogged. 1.** (*intr.*) to run or move slowly or at a jog trot, esp. for physical exercise. **2.** (*intr.;* foll. by *on* or *along*) to continue in a plodding way. **3.** (*tr.*) to jar or nudge slightly; shake lightly. **4.** (*tr.*) to remind; stimulate: *please jog my memory.* **5.** (*tr.*) *Printing.* to even up the edges of (a stack of paper); square up. ~*n.* **6.** the act of jogging. **7.** a slight jar or nudge. **8.** a jogging motion; trot. [C14: probably variant of *shog* to shake, influenced by dialect *jot* to jolt]

jog[2] (dʒɒg) *n. U.S. and Canadian.* **1.** a sharp protruding point in a surface; jag. **2.** a sudden change in course or direction. [C18: probably variant of JAG[1]]

jogger ('dʒɒgə) *n.* **1.** a person who runs at a jog trot over some distance for exercise, usually regularly. **2.** *N.Z.* a cart with rubber-tyred wheels used on a farm.

jogger's nipple *n. Informal.* painful inflammation of the nipple, caused by friction with a garment when running for long distances.

jogging ('dʒɒgɪŋ) *n.* running at a slow regular pace usually over a long distance as part of an exercise routine.

joggle ('dʒɒgᵊl) *vb.* **1.** to shake or move (someone or something) with a slightly jolting motion. **2.** (*tr.*) to join or fasten (two pieces of building material) by means of a joggle. ~*n.* **3.** the act of joggling. **4.** a slight irregular shake; jolt. **5.** a joint between two pieces of building material by means of a projection on one piece that fits into a notch in the other; dowel. **6.** a shoulder designed to take the thrust of a strut or brace. [C16: frequentative of JOG[1]] —'**joggler** *n.*

joggle post *n.* a post or beam consisting of two timbers joined to each other by joggles.

jog trot *n.* **1.** an easy bouncy gait, esp. of a horse, midway between a walk and a trot. **2.** a monotonous or regular way of living or doing something. ~*vb.* **jog-trot, -trots, -trotting, -trotted. 3.** (*intr.*) to move at a jog trot.

johannes (dʒəʊ'hæniːz) *or* **joannes** *n., pl.* **-nes.** a Portuguese gold coin minted in the early 18th century. [C18: after *Joannes* (King John V) of Portugal, whose name was inscribed on the coin]

john (dʒɒn) *n.* **1.** *Chiefly U.S. and Canadian.* a slang word for **lavatory** (sense 1). **2.** *Austral. slang.* short for **John Hop.** [C20: special use of the proper name]

John Barleycorn *n. Usually humorous.* the personification of alcoholic drink, esp. of malt spirits.

John Bull *n.* **1.** a personification of England or the English people. **2.** a typical Englishman. [C18: name of a character intended to be representative of the English nation in *The History of John Bull* (1712) by John Arbuthnot] —**John Bullish** *adj.* —**John Bullishness** *n.* —**John Bullism** *n.*

John Doe *n.* See **Doe.**

John Dory ('dɔːrɪ) *n.* a European dory (the fish), *Zeus faber,* having a deep compressed body, spiny dorsal fins, and massive mobile jaws. [C18: from proper name *John* + DORY[1]; on the model of DOE]

John Hancock *n. U.S. and Canadian informal.* a person's signature: *put your John Hancock on this form.* Also called **John Henry.** [after *John Hancock* (1737–93), American statesman, from his clear and legible signature on the American Declaration of Independence]

John Hop *n. Austral. slang.* a policeman. [rhyming slang for COP[1]]

johnny ('dʒɒnɪ) *n., pl.* **-nies.** *Brit.* **1.** (*often cap.*) *Informal.* a man or boy; chap. **2.** a slang word for **condom.**

johnny cake *or* **johnny-cake** *n. Austral.* a thin cake of flour and water paste cooked in the ashes of a fire or in a pan.

Johnny Canuck ('dʒɒnɪ kə'nʌk) *n. Canadian.* **1.** an informal name for a **Canadian. 2.** a personification of Canada.

Johnny-come-lately *n., pl.* **Johnny-come-latelies** *or* **Johnnies-come-lately.** *Slang.* a brash newcomer, novice, or recruit.

Johnny-jump-up *n. U.S. and Canadian.* any of several violaceous plants, esp. the wild pansy. [C19: so called from its quick growth]

Johnny raw *n. Slang.* a novice; new recruit.

Johnny Reb *n. U.S. informal.* (in the American Civil War) a Confederate soldier. [C19: from REBEL (n.)]

Johnson grass ('dʒɒnsᵊn) *n.* a persistent perennial Mediterranean grass, *Sorghum halepense,* cultivated for hay and pasture in the U.S. where it also grows as a weed. See also **sorghum.** [C19: named after William *Johnson* (died 1859), American agriculturalist who introduced it]

Johnsonian (dʒɒn'səʊnɪən) *adj.* of, relating to, or characteristic of Samuel Johnson (1709–84), British lexicographer and critic, or of his works or his style of writing.

John Thomas *n. Slang.* a taboo name for **penis.**

joie de vivre *French.* (ʒwa də vivrə) *n.* joy of living; enjoyment of life; ebullience.

join (dʒɔɪn) *vb.* **1.** to come or bring together; connect. **2.** to become a member of (a club, organization, etc.). **3.** (*intr.;* often foll. by *with*) to become associated or allied. **4.** (*intr.;* usually foll. by *in*) to take part. **5.** (*tr.*) to meet (someone) as a companion. **6.** (*tr.*) to become part of; take a place in or with. **7.** (*tr.*) to unite (two people) in marriage. **8.** (*tr.*) *Geom.* to connect with a straight line or a curve. **9.** (*tr.*) an informal word for **adjoin. 10. join battle.** to start fighting. **11. join duty.** *Indian.* to report for work after a period of leave or a strike. **12. join hands. a.** to hold one's own hands together. **b.** (of two people) to hold each other's hands. **c.** (usually foll. by *with*) to work together in an enterprise or task. ~*n.* **13.** a joint; seam. **14.** the act of joining. **15.** *Maths.* another name for **union** (sense 9). ~See also **join up.** [C13: from Old French *joindre* from Latin *jungere* to yoke] —'**joinable** *adj.*

joinder ('dʒɔɪndə) *n.* **1.** the act of joining, esp. in legal contexts. **2.** *Law.* **a.** (in pleading) the stage at which the parties join issue (**joinder of issue**). **b.** the joining of two or more persons as coplaintiffs or codefendants (**joinder of parties**). **c.** the joining of two or more causes in one suit. [C17: from French *joindre* to JOIN]

joiner ('dʒɔɪnə) *n.* **1.** *Chiefly Brit.* a person trained and skilled in making finished woodwork, such as windows, doors, and stairs. **2.** a person or thing that joins. **3.** *Informal.* a person who joins many clubs, causes, etc.

joinery ('dʒɔɪnərɪ) *n.* **1.** the skill or craft of a joiner. **2.** work made by a joiner.

joint (dʒɔɪnt) *n.* **1.** a junction of two or more parts or objects. **2.** the part or space between two such junctions. **3.** *Anatomy.* the junction between two or more bones, usually formed of connective tissue and cartilage. **4.** the point of connection between movable parts in invertebrates, esp. insects and other arthropods. **5.** the part of a plant stem from which a branch or leaf grows. **6.** one of the parts into which a carcass of meat is cut by the butcher, esp. for roasting. **7.** *Geology.* a crack in a rock along which no displacement has occurred. **8.** *Slang.* **a.** a disreputable establishment, such as a bar or nightclub. **b.** *Often facetious.* a dwelling or meeting place. **9.** *Slang.* a cannabis cigarette. **10. out of joint. a.** dislocated. **b.** out of order or disorganized. **11. put someone's nose out of joint.** See **nose** (sense 18). ~*adj.* **12.** shared by or belonging to two or more: *joint property.* **13.** created by combined effort. **14.** sharing with others or with one another: *joint rulers.* **15.** *Law.* (of persons) combined in ownership or obligation; regarded as a single entity in law. ~*vb.* (*tr.*) **16.** to provide with or fasten by a joint or joints. **17.** to plane the edge of (a board, etc.) into the correct shape for a joint. **18.** to cut or divide (meat, fowl, etc.) into joints or at a joint. —'**jointly** *adv.*

joint account *n.* a bank account registered in the name of two or more persons, any of whom may make deposits and withdrawals.

joint consultation *n.* a formal system of communication between the management of an organization and the employees' representatives used prior to taking decisions affecting the workforce, usually effected through a joint consultative committee.

joint density function *n. Statistics.* a function of two or more random variables from which can be obtained a single probability that all the variables in the function will take specified values or fall within specified intervals.

jointed ('dʒɔɪntɪd) *adj.* **1. a.** having a joint or joints. **b.** (*in combination*): *large-jointed.* **2.** (of a plant stem or similar part) marked with constrictions, at which the stem breaks into separate portions. —'**jointedly** *adv.* —'**jointedness** *n.*

jointer ('dʒɔɪntə) *n.* **1.** a tool for pointing mortar joints, as in brickwork. **2.** Also called: **jointing plane.** a long plane for shaping the edges of planks so that they can be fitted together. **3.** a person or thing that makes joints.

joint resolution *n. U.S.* a resolution passed by both houses of a bicameral legislature, signed by the chief executive and legally binding.

jointress ('dʒɔɪntrɪs) *n. Law.* a woman entitled to a jointure.

joint stock *n.* capital funds held in common and usually divided into shares between the owners.

joint-stock company *n.* **1.** *Brit.* a business enterprise characterized by its separate legal existence and the sharing of ownership between shareholders, whose liability is limited. **2.** *U.S.* a business enterprise whose owners are issued shares of transferable stock but do not enjoy limited liability.

jointure ('dʒɔɪntʃə) *n.* **1.** *Law.* **a.** provision made by a husband for his wife by settling property upon her at marriage for her use after his death. **b.** the property so settled. **2.** *Obsolete.* the act of joining or the condition of being joined. [C14: from Old French, from Latin *junctūra* a joining]

jointworm ('dʒɔɪntˌwɜːm) *n. U.S.* the larva of chalcid flies of the genus *Harmolita,* esp. *H. tritici,* which form galls on the stems of cereal plants.

join up *vb.* (*adv.*) **1.** (*intr.*) to become a member of a military or other organization; enlist. **2.** (often foll. by *with*) to unite or connect.

joist (dʒɔɪst) *n.* **1.** a beam made of timber, steel, or reinforced concrete, used in the construction of floors, roofs, etc. See also **rolled-steel joist.** ~*vb.* **2.** (*tr.*) to construct (a floor, roof, etc.) with joists. [C14: from Old French *giste* beam supporting a bridge, from Vulgar Latin *jacitum* (unattested) support, from *jacēre* to lie]

jojoba (həʊ'həʊbə) *n.* a shrub or small tree of SW North America, *Simmondsia californica,* that has edible seeds containing a valuable oil used in cosmetics. [Mexican Spanish]

joke (dʒəʊk) *n.* **1.** a humorous anecdote. **2.** something that is said or done for fun; prank. **3.** a ridiculous or humorous circumstance. **4.** a person or thing inspiring ridicule or amusement; butt. **5.** a matter to be joked about or ignored. **6. joking apart.** seriously: said to recall a discussion to seriousness after there has been joking. **7. no joke.** something very serious. ~*vb.* **8.** (*intr.*) to tell jokes. **9.** (*intr.*) to speak or act facetiously or in fun. **10.** to make fun of (someone); tease. [C17: from Latin *jocus* a jest] —'**jokey** *or* '**joky** *adj.* —'**jokingly** *adv.*

joker ('dʒəʊkə) *n.* **1.** a person who jokes, esp. in an obnoxious manner. **2.** *Slang, often derogatory.* a person: *who does that joker think he is?* **3.** an extra playing card in a pack, which in many card games can substitute for or rank above any other card. **4.** *Chiefly U.S.* a clause or phrase inserted in a legislative bill in order to make the bill inoperative or to alter its apparent effect.

jolie laide *French.* (ʒɔli lɛd) *n., pl.* **jolies laides** (ʒɔli lɛd). a woman whose ugliness forms her chief fascination. [literally: pretty (attractive) ugly woman]

jollification (ˌdʒɒlɪfɪ'keɪʃən) *n.* a merry festivity.

jollify ('dʒɒlɪˌfaɪ) *vb.* **-fies, -fying, -fied.** to be or cause to be jolly.

jollities ('dʒɒlɪtɪz) *pl. n. Brit.* a party or celebration.

jollity ('dʒɒlɪtɪ) *n., pl.* **-ties.** the condition of being jolly.

jolly ('dʒɒlɪ) *adj.* **-lier, -liest.** **1.** full of good humour; jovial. **2.** having or provoking gaiety and merrymaking; festive. **3.** greatly enjoyable; pleasing. ~*adv.* **4.** *Brit.* (intensifier): *you're jolly nice.* ~*vb.* **-lies, -lying, -lied.** (*tr.*) *Informal.* **5.** (often foll. by *up* or *along*) to try to make or keep (someone) cheerful. **6.** to make good-natured fun of. ~*n.* **7.** *Informal, chiefly Brit.* a festivity or celebration. **8.** *Informal, chiefly Brit.* a trip, esp. one made for pleasure by a public official or committee at public expense. **9.** *Brit. slang.* a Royal Marine. [C14: from Old French *jolif,* probably from Old Norse *jōl* YULE] —'**jolliness** *n.*

jolly boat *n.* **1.** a small boat used as a utility tender for a vessel. **2.** a small sailing boat used for pleasure. [C18: *jolly* probably from Danish *jolle* YAWL[1]]

Jolly Roger *n.* the traditional pirate flag, consisting of a white skull and crossbones on a black field.

jolt (dʒəʊlt) *vb.* (*tr.*) **1.** to bump against with a jarring blow; jostle. **2.** to move in a jolting manner. **3.** to surprise or shock. ~*n.* **4.** a sudden jar or blow. **5.** an emotional shock. [C16: probably blend of dialect *jot* to jerk and dialect *joll* to bump] —'**jolter** *n.* —'**joltingly** *adv.* —'**jolty** *adj.*

Jon. *Bible. abbrev. for* Jonah.

Jonah ('dʒəʊnə) *or* **Jonas** ('dʒəʊnəs) *n.* a person believed to bring bad luck to those around him; a jinx. [after *Jonah,* Old Testament prophet who was swallowed by a great fish] —ˌ**Jonah**'**esque** *adj.*

Jonathan ('dʒɒnəθən) *n.* a variety of red apple that ripens in early autumn. [C19: named after *Jonathan* Hasbrouk (died 1846), American jurist]

jongleur (*French* ʒɔ̃glœr) *n.* (in medieval France) an itinerant minstrel. [C18: from Old French *jogleour,* from Latin *joculātor* joker, jester; see JUGGLE]

jonnock ('dʒɒnək) *or* **jannock** ('dʒænək) *Dialect.* ~*adj.* **1.** (*usually postpositive*) genuine; real. ~*adv.* **2.** honestly; truly; genuinely. [of uncertain origin]

jonquil ('dʒɒŋkwɪl) *n.* a Eurasian amaryllidaceous plant, *Narcissus jonquilla* with long fragrant yellow or white short-tubed flowers. [C17: from French *jonquille,* from Spanish *junquillo,* diminutive of *junco* reed; see JUNCO]

jook (dʒʊk) *or* **chook** *Caribbean informal.* ~*vb.* **1.** (*tr.*) to poke or puncture (the skin). ~*n.* **2.** a jab or the resulting wound. [C20: of uncertain origin]

Jordan almond ('dʒɔːdᵊn) *n.* **1.** a large variety of Spanish almond used in confectionery. **2.** a sugar-coated almond. [C15: by folk etymology from earlier *jardyne almaund,* literally: garden almond, from Old French *jardin* GARDEN]

Jordanian (dʒɔː'deɪnɪən) *adj.* **1.** of or relating to Jordan, a kingdom in SW Asia, or to its people, culture, etc. ~*n.* **2.** a native or inhabitant of Jordan.

jorum ('dʒɔːrəm) *n.* a large drinking bowl or vessel or its contents: *a jorum of punch.* [C18: probably named after *Jorum,* who brought vessels of silver, gold, and brass to King David (II Samuel 8:10)]

joseph ('dʒəʊzɪf) *n.* a woman's floor-length riding coat with a small cape, worn esp. in the 18th century. [perhaps from the story of Joseph and his long coat (Genesis 37:3)]

Josephson effect ('dʒəʊzɪfsən) *n. Physics.* any one of the phenomena which occur when an electric current passes through a very thin insulating layer between two superconducting substances. The applications include the very precise standardization of the volt. [C20: named after Brian David *Josephson* (born 1940), British physicist; shared the Nobel prize for physics in 1973]

josh (dʒɒʃ) *Slang, chiefly U.S. and Canadian.* ~*vb.* **1.** to tease (someone) in a bantering way. ~*n.* **2.** a teasing or bantering joke. [C19: perhaps from JOKE, influenced by BOSH[1]] —'**josher** *n.*

Josh. *Bible. abbrev. for* Joshua.

Joshua tree (dʒɒʃʊə) *n.* a treelike desert yucca plant, *Yucca brevifolia,* of the southwestern U.S., with sword-shaped leaves and greenish-white flowers. [named after the prophet *Joshua,* alluding to the extended branches of the tree]

joss (dʒɒs) *n.* a Chinese deity worshipped in the form of an idol. [C18: from pidgin English, from Portuguese *deos* god, from Latin *deus*]

josser ('dʒɒsə) *n. Slang.* **1.** *Brit.* a simpleton; fool. **2.** *Brit.* a fellow; chap. **3.** *Austral.* a clergyman. [C19: from JOSS + -ER[1]]

joss house *n.* a Chinese temple or shrine where an idol or idols are worshipped.

joss stick *n.* a stick of dried perfumed paste, giving off a fragrant odour when burnt as incense.

jostle ('dʒɒsᵊl) *vb.* **1.** to bump or push (someone) roughly. **2.** to come or bring into contact. **3.** to force (one's way) by pushing. ~*n.* **4.** the act of jostling. **5.** a rough bump or push. [C14: see JOUST] —'**jostlement** *n.* —'**jostler** *n.*

jot (dʒɒt) *vb.* **jots, jotting, jotted. 1.** (*tr.*; usually foll. by *down*) to write a brief note of. ~*n.* **2.** (*used with a negative*) a little bit (in phrases such as **not to care** (*or* **give**) **a jot**). [C16: from Latin *jota,* from Greek *iōta,* of Semitic origin; see IOTA]

jota (*Spanish* 'xota) *n.* a Spanish dance with castanets in fast triple time, usually to a guitar and voice accompaniment. [Spanish, probably modification of Old Spanish *sota,* from *sotar* to dance, from Latin *saltāre*]

jotter ('dʒɒtə) *n.* a small notebook.

jotting ('dʒɒtɪŋ) *n.* something jotted down.

joual (ʒwɑːl) *n.* nonstandard Canadian French dialect, esp. as associated with ill-educated speakers. [from the pronunciation in this dialect of French *cheval* horse]

jougs (dʒuːgz) *pl. n. Scot. history.* an iron ring, fastened by a chain to a wall, post, or tree, in which an offender was held by the neck: common in Scotland from the 16th to 18th century. [C16: probably from French *joug* yoke]

jouk (dʒʊk) *Scot.* ~*vb.* **1.** to duck or dodge. ~*n.* **2.** a sudden evasive movement. [C16: of uncertain origin]

joule (dʒuːl) *n.* the derived SI unit of work or energy; the work done when the point of application of a force of 1 newton is displaced through a distance of 1 metre in the direction of the force. 1 joule is equivalent to 1 watt-second, 10^7 ergs, 0.2390 calories, or 0.738 foot-pound. Symbol: J [C19: named after J. P. *Joule* (1818–89), British physicist]

Joule effect (dʒuːl) *n. Physics.* **1.** the production of heat as the result of a current flowing through a conductor. See **Joule's law** (sense 1). **2.** an increase in length of certain ferromagnetic materials when longitudinally magnetized. [C19: named after J. P. *Joule*]

Joule's law *n.* **1.** *Physics.* the principle that the heat produced by an electric current is equal to the product of the resistance of the conductor, the square of the current, and the time for which it flows. **2.** *Thermodynamics.* the principle that at constant temperature the internal energy of an ideal gas is independent of volume. Real gases change their internal energy with volume as a result of intermolecular forces. [C19: named after J. P. *Joule*]

Joule-Thomson effect (-ˈtɒmsən) *n.* a change in temperature of a thermally insulated gas when it is forced through a small hole or a porous material. For each gas there is a temperature of inversion above which the change is positive and below which it is negative. Also called: **Joule-Kelvin effect.** [C20: named after J. P. *Joule* and Sir William *Thomson*, 1st Baron *Kelvin* (1824–1907)]

jounce (dʒaʊns) *vb.* **1.** to shake or jolt or cause to shake or jolt; bounce. ~*n.* **2.** a jolting movement; shake; bump. [C15: probably a blend of dialect *joll* to bump + BOUNCE]

jour. *abbrev. for:* **1.** journal. **2.** journalist. **3.** journeyman.

journal (ˈdʒɜːnᵊl) *n.* **1.** a newspaper or periodical. **2.** a book in which a daily record of happenings, etc., is kept. **3.** an official record of the proceedings of a legislative body. **4.** *Book-keeping.* **a.** one of several books in which transactions are initially recorded to facilitate subsequent entry in the ledger. **b.** another name for **daybook. 5.** the part of a shaft or axle in contact with or enclosed by a bearing. **6.** a plain cylindrical bearing to support a shaft or axle. [C14: from Old French: daily, from Latin *diurnālis;* see DIURNAL]

journal box *n. Machinery.* a case enclosing or supporting a journal, often used as a means of retaining the lubricant.

journalese (ˌdʒɜːnᵊˈliːz) *n. Derogatory.* a superficial cliché-ridden style of writing regarded as typical of newspapers.

journalism (ˈdʒɜːnᵊˌlɪzəm) *n.* **1.** the profession or practice of reporting about, photographing, or editing news stories for one of the mass media. **2.** newspapers and magazines collectively; the press. **3.** the material published in a newspaper, magazine, etc.: *this is badly written journalism.* **4.** news reports presented factually without analysis.

journalist (ˈdʒɜːnᵊlɪst) *n.* **1.** a person whose occupation is journalism. **2.** a person who keeps a journal.

journalistic (ˌdʒɜːnᵊˈlɪstɪk) *adj.* of, relating to, or characteristic of journalism or journalists. —ˌ**journalˈistically** *adv.*

journalize *or* **journalise** (ˈdʒɜːnᵊˌlaɪz) *vb.* to record (daily events) in a journal. —ˌ**journaliˈzation** *or* ˌ**journaliˈsation** *n.* —ˈ**journalˌizer** *or* ˈ**journalˌiser** *n.*

journey (ˈdʒɜːnɪ) *n.* **1.** a travelling from one place to another; trip or voyage. **2. a.** the distance travelled in a journey. **b.** the time taken to make a journey. ~*vb.* **3.** (*intr.*) to make a journey. [C13: from Old French *journee* a day, a day's travelling, from Latin *diurnum* day's portion; see DIURNAL] —ˈ**journeyer** *n.*

journeyman (ˈdʒɜːnɪmən) *n., pl.* **-men. 1.** a craftsman, artisan, etc., who is qualified to work at his trade in the employment of another. **2.** a competent workman. **3.** (formerly) a worker hired on a daily wage. [C15: from JOURNEY (in obsolete sense: a day's work) + MAN]

journeywork (ˈdʒɜːnɪˌwɜːk) *n. Rare.* **1.** necessary, routine, and menial work. **2.** the work of a journeyman.

journo (ˈdʒɜːnəʊ) *n., pl.* **journos.** *Slang.* a journalist.

joust (dʒaʊst) *History.* ~*n.* **1.** a combat between two mounted knights tilting against each other with lances. A tournament consisted of a series of such engagements. ~*vb.* **2.** (*intr.;* often foll. by *against* or *with*) to encounter or engage in such a tournament: *he jousted with five opponents.* [C13: from Old French *jouste,* from *jouster* to fight on horseback, from Vulgar Latin *juxtāre* (unattested) to come together, from Latin *juxtā* close] —ˈ**jouster** *n.*

j'ouvert (ˈʒuːvɛət) *n. Chiefly Caribbean.* the eve of Mardi gras; the Monday morning on which the festivities begin. [from French *jour ouvert* the day having been opened]

Jove (dʒəʊv) *n.* **by Jove.** an exclamation of surprise or excitement. [C14: from Old Latin *Jovis* Jupiter, the Roman god]

jovial (ˈdʒəʊvɪəl) *adj.* having or expressing convivial humour; jolly. [C16: from Latin *joviālis* of (the planet) Jupiter, considered by astrologers to foster good humour] —ˌ**joviˈality** *or* ˈ**jovialness** *n.* —ˈ**jovially** *adv.*

Jovian (ˈdʒəʊvɪən) *adj.* **1.** of or relating to the god Jove (Jupiter). **2.** of, occurring on, or relating to the planet Jupiter. **3.** of or relating to the giant planets Jupiter, Saturn, Uranus, and Neptune: *the Jovian planets.* [C16: from Old Latin *Jovis* Jupiter]

jowl[1] (dʒaʊl) *n.* **1.** the jaw, esp. the lower one. **2.** (*often pl.*) a cheek, esp. a prominent one. **3. cheek by jowl.** See **cheek** (sense 7). [Old English *ceafl* jaw; related to Middle High German *kivel,* Old Norse *kjaptr*] —**jowled** *adj.*

jowl[2] (dʒaʊl) *n.* **1.** fatty flesh hanging from the lower jaw. **2.** a similar fleshy part in animals, such as the wattle of a fowl or the dewlap of a bull. [Old English *ceole* throat; compare Old High German *kela*]

joy (dʒɔɪ) *n.* **1.** a deep feeling or condition of happiness or contentment. **2.** something causing such a feeling; a source of happiness. **3.** an outward show of pleasure or delight; rejoicing. **4.** *Brit. informal.* success; satisfaction: *I went to the bank for a loan, but got no joy.* ~*vb.* **5.** (*intr.*) to feel joy. **6.** (*tr.*) *Obsolete.* to make joyful; gladden. [C13: from Old French *joie,* from Latin *gaudium* joy, from *gaudēre* to be glad]

joyance (ˈdʒɔɪəns) *n. Archaic.* a joyous feeling or festivity.

Joycean (ˈdʒɔɪsɪən) *adj.* **1.** of, relating to, or like, James Joyce (1882–1941), Irish novelist and short-story writer, or his works. ~*n.* **2.** a student or admirer of Joyce or his works.

joyful (ˈdʒɔɪfʊl) *adj.* **1.** full of joy; elated. **2.** expressing or producing joy: *a joyful look; a joyful occasion.* —ˈ**joyfully** *adv.* —ˈ**joyfulness** *n.*

joyless (ˈdʒɔɪlɪs) *adj.* having or producing no joy or pleasure. —ˈ**joylessly** *adv.* —ˈ**joylessness** *n.*

joyous (ˈdʒɔɪəs) *adj.* **1.** having a happy nature or mood. **2.** joyful. —ˈ**joyously** *adv.* —ˈ**joyousness** *n.*

joypop (ˈdʒɔɪˌpɒp) *vb.* **-pops, -popping, -popped.** (*intr.*) *Slang.* to take addictive drugs occasionally without becoming addicted.

joyride *n.* **1.** a ride taken for pleasure in a car, esp. in a stolen car driven recklessly. ~*vb.* **joy-ride, -rides, -riding, -rode, -ridden. 2.** (*intr.*) to take such a ride. —ˈ**joyˌrider** *n.* —ˈ**joyˌriding** *n.*

joystick (ˈdʒɔɪˌstɪk) *n.* **1.** *Informal.* the control stick of an aircraft or of any of various machines. **2.** *Computer technol.* a lever by means of which the movement of a cursor on a screen may be controlled.

JP *abbrev. for* Justice of the Peace.

J/psi particle *n.* a type of elementary particle thought to be formed from charmed quarks. See **charm**[1] (sense 7).

Jr *or* **jr** *abbrev. for* junior.

JSD *abbrev. for* Doctor of Juristic Science.

jt *abbrev. for* joint.

juba (ˈdʒuːbə) *n.* a lively Negro dance developed in the southern U.S. [C19: of Zulu origin]

jubbah (ˈdʒʊbə) *n.* a long loose outer garment with wide sleeves, worn by Muslim men and women, esp. in India. [C16: from Arabic]

jube[1] (ˈdʒuːbɪ) *n.* **1.** a gallery or loft over the rood screen in a church or cathedral. **2.** another name for **rood screen.** [C18: from French *jubé,* from opening words of Medieval Latin prayer *Jube, Domine, benedicere* Bid, Lord, a blessing; probably from the deacon's standing by the rood screen or in the rood loft to pronounce this prayer]

jube[2] (dʒuːb) *n. Austral. and N.Z. informal.* any jelly-like sweet. [C20: shortened from JUJUBE]

jubilant (ˈdʒuːbɪlənt) *adj.* feeling or expressing great joy. [C17: from Latin *jūbilāns* shouting for joy, from *jūbilāre* to give a joyful cry, from *jūbilum* a shout, wild cry] —ˈ**jubilance** *or* ˈ**jubilancy** *n.* —ˈ**jubilantly** *adv.*

jubilate (ˈdʒuːbɪˌleɪt) *vb.* (*intr.*) **1.** to have or express great joy; rejoice. **2.** to celebrate a jubilee. [C17: from Latin *jūbilāre* to raise a shout of joy; see JUBILANT]

Jubilate (ˌdʒuːbɪˈlɑːtɪ) *n.* **1.** *R.C. Church, Church of England.* the 100th psalm used as a canticle in the liturgy. **2.** a musical setting of this psalm. [from the opening word (*Jubilate* make a joyful noise) of the Vulgate version]

jubilation (ˌdʒuːbɪˈleɪʃən) *n.* a feeling of great joy and celebration.

jubilee (ˈdʒuːbɪˌliː, ˌdʒuːbɪˈliː) *n.* **1.** a time or season for rejoicing. **2.** a special anniversary, esp. a 25th or 50th one. **3.** *R.C. Church.* a specially appointed period, now ordinarily every 25th year, in which special indulgences are granted. **4.** *Old Testament.* a year that was to be observed every 50th year, during which Hebrew slaves were to be liberated, alienated property was to be restored, etc. **5.** a less common word for **jubilation.** [C14: from Old French *jubile,* from Late Latin *jubilaeus,* from Late Greek *iōbēlaios,* from Hebrew *yōbhēl* ram's horn, used for the proclamation of the year of jubilee; influenced by Latin *jūbilāre* to shout for joy]

JUD *abbrev. for* Doctor of Canon and Civil Law. [Latin *Juris Utriusque Doctor*]

Jud. *Bible. abbrev. for:* **1.** Also: **Judg.** Judges. **2.** Judith.

Judaean *or* **Judean** (dʒuːˈdɪən) *adj.* **1.** of or relating to Judaea, the S division of ancient Palestine, or to its people, customs, etc. ~*n.* **2.** a native or inhabitant of Judaea.

Judaeo- *or U.S.* **Judeo-** (dʒuːˈdeɪəʊ-, dʒuːˈdiːəʊ-) *combining form.* relating to Judaism: *Judaeo-Christian.*

Judaeo-German *n.* another name for **Yiddish.**

Judaeo-Spanish *n.* another name for **Ladino.**

Judaic (dʒuːˈdeɪɪk) *or* **Judaical** *adj.* **1.** of or relating to the Jews or Judaism. **2.** a less common word for **Jewish.** —**Juˈdaically** *adv.*

Judaica (dʒuːˈdeɪɪkə) *pl. n.* **1.** the literature, customs, culture, etc., of the Jews. **2.** books or artefacts of Jewish interest, esp. as a collection. [Latin, literally: Jewish matters]

Judaism (ˈdʒuːdeɪˌɪzəm) *n.* **1.** the religion of the Jews, based on the Old Testament and the Talmud and having as its central point a belief in the one God as transcendent creator of all things and the source of all righteousness. **2.** the religious and cultural traditions, customs, attitudes, and way of life of the Jews. —ˌ**Juda'istic** *adj.*

Judaize *or* **Judaise** (ˈdʒʊdeɪˌaɪz) *vb.* **1.** to conform or bring into conformity with Judaism. **2.** (*tr.*) to convert to Judaism. **3.** (*tr.*) to imbue with Jewish principles. —ˌ**Judai'zation** *or* ˌ**Judai'sation** *n.* —'**Judaˌizer** *or* '**Judaˌiser** *n.*

judas (ˈdʒuːdəs) *n.* (*sometimes cap.*) a peephole or a very small window in a door. Also called: **judas window, judas hole.** [C19: after JUDAS Iscariot]

Judas (ˈdʒuːdəs) *n.* **1.** a person who betrays a friend; traitor. *~adj.* **2.** denoting an animal or bird used to lure others of its kind or lead them to slaughter. [after *Judas* Iscariot, apostle in the New Testament who betrayed Jesus]

Judas tree *n.* small Eurasian leguminous tree, *Cercis siliquastrum,* with pinkish-purple flowers that bloom before the leaves appear: popularly thought to be the tree on which Judas hanged himself. See also **redbud.**

judder (ˈdʒʌdə) *Informal, chiefly Brit. ~vb.* **1.** (*intr.*) to shake or vibrate. *~n.* **2.** abnormal vibration in a mechanical system, esp. due to grabbing between friction surfaces, as in the clutch of a motor vehicle. **3.** a juddering motion. [probably blend of JAR[2] + SHUDDER]

judder bar *n.* a N.Z. name for **sleeping policeman.**

Judean (dʒuːˈdɪən) *adj., n.* a variant spelling of **Judaean.**

Judezmo (dʒʊˈdɛzməʊ) *n.* another name for **Ladino.** [from Ladino: Jewish]

judge (dʒʌdʒ) *n.* **1.** a public official with authority to hear cases in a court of law and pronounce judgment upon them. Compare **magistrate, justice** (senses 5, 6). **2.** a person who is appointed to determine the result of contests or competitions. **3.** a person qualified to comment critically: *a good judge of antiques.* **4.** a leader of the peoples of Israel from Joshua's death to the accession of Saul. *~vb.* **5.** to hear and decide upon (a case at law). **6.** (*tr.*) to pass judgment on; sentence. **7.** (when *tr., may take a clause as object or an infinitive*) to decide or deem (something) after inquiry or deliberation. **8.** to determine the result of (a contest or competition). **9.** to appraise (something) critically. **10.** (*tr.; takes a clause as object*) to believe (something) to be the case; suspect. [C14: from Old French *jugier,* from Latin *jūdicāre* to pass judgment, from *jūdex* a judge] —'**judgeable** *adj.* —'**judgeless** *adj.* —'**judgeˌlike** *adj.* —'**judger** *n.* —'**judgingly** *adv.*

judge advocate *n., pl.* **judge advocates.** an officer who superintends proceedings at a military court martial.

judge advocate general *n., pl.* **judge advocates general** *or* **judge advocate generals.** the civil adviser to the Crown on matters relating to courts martial and on military law generally.

judge-made *adj.* based on a judge's interpretation or decision (esp. in the phrase **judge-made law**).

judgeship (ˈdʒʌdʒˌʃɪp) *n.* the position, office, or function of a judge.

judges' rules *pl. n.* (in English law) a set of rules, not legally binding, governing the behaviour of police towards suspects, as in administering a caution to a person under arrest.

judgment *or* **judgement** (ˈdʒʌdʒmənt) *n.* **1.** the faculty of being able to make critical distinctions and achieve a balanced viewpoint; discernment. **2. a.** the verdict pronounced by a court of law. **b.** an obligation arising as a result of such a verdict, such as a debt. **c.** the document recording such a verdict. **d.** (*as modifier*): *a judgment debtor.* **3.** the formal decision of one or more judges at a contest or competition. **4.** a particular decision or opinion formed in a case in dispute or doubt. **5.** an estimation: *a good judgment of distance.* **6.** criticism or censure. **7.** *Logic.* **a.** the act of establishing a relation between two or more terms, esp. as an affirmation or denial. **b.** the expression of such a relation. **8. against one's better judgment.** contrary to a more appropriate or preferred course of action. **9. sit in judgment. a.** to preside as judge. **b.** to assume the position of critic. **10. in someone's judgment.** in someone's opinion.

Judgment (ˈdʒʌdʒmənt) *n.* **1.** the estimate by God of the ultimate worthiness or unworthiness of the individual (the **Particular Judgment**) or of all mankind (the **General Judgment** or **Last Judgment**). **2.** God's subsequent decision determining the final destinies of all individuals.

judgmental *or* **judgemental** (dʒʌdʒˈmɛntᵊl) *adj.* of or denoting an attitude in which judgments about other people's conduct are made.

Judgment Day *n.* the occasion of the Last (or General) Judgment by God at the end of the world. Also called: **Day of Judgment.** See **Last Judgment.**

judicable (ˈdʒuːdɪkəbᵊl) *adj.* capable of being judged, esp. in a court of law.

judicative (ˈdʒuːdɪkətɪv) *adj.* **1.** having the function of trying causes. **2.** competent to judge and pass sentence.

judicator (ˈdʒuːdɪˌkeɪtə) *n.* a person who acts as a judge.

judicatory (ˈdʒuːdɪkətərɪ) *adj.* **1.** of or relating to the administration of justice. *~n.* **2.** a court of law. **3.** the administration of justice. —ˌ**judica'torial** *adj.*

judicature (ˈdʒuːdɪkətʃə) *n.* **1.** the administration of justice. **2.** the office, function, or power of a judge. **3.** the extent of authority of a court or judge. **4.** a body of judges or persons exercising judicial authority; judiciary. **5.** a court of justice or such courts collectively.

judicial (dʒuːˈdɪʃəl) *adj.* **1.** of or relating to the administration of justice. **2.** of or relating to judgment in a court of law or to a judge exercising this function. **3.** inclined to pass judgment; discriminating. **4.** allowed or enforced by a court of law: *a decree of judicial separation.* **5.** having qualities appropriate to a judge. **6.** giving or seeking judgment, esp. determining or seeking determination of a contested issue. [C14: from Latin *jūdiciālis* belonging to the law courts, from *jūdicium* judgment, from *jūdex* a judge] —**ju'dicially** *adv.*

judicial separation *n. Family law.* a decree prohibiting a man and wife from cohabiting but not dissolving the marriage. See also **a mensa et thoro.** Compare **divorce.**

judiciary (dʒuːˈdɪʃɪərɪ, -ˈdɪʃərɪ) *adj.* **1.** of or relating to courts of law, judgment, or judges. *~n., pl.* **-aries. 2.** the branch of the central authority in a state concerned with the administration of justice. Compare **executive** (sense 2), **legislature. 3.** the system of courts in a country. **4.** the judges collectively; bench.

judicious (dʒuːˈdɪʃəs) *adj.* having or proceeding from good judgment. —**ju'diciously** *adv.* —**ju'diciousness** *n.*

judo (ˈdʒuːdəʊ) *n.* **a.** the modern sport derived from jujitsu, in which the object is to throw, hold to the ground, or otherwise force an opponent to submit, using the minimum of physical effort. **b.** (*as modifier*): *a judo throw.* [Japanese, from *jū* gentleness + *dō* art] —'**judoist** *n.*

judogi (dʒʊˈdəʊgɪ) *n.* a white two-piece cotton costume worn during judo contests. [from Japanese]

judoka (ˈdʒuːdəʊˌkæ) *n.* a competitor or expert in judo. [Japanese; see JUDO]

Judy (ˈdʒuːdɪ) *n., pl.* **-dies. 1.** the wife of Punch in the children's puppet show *Punch and Judy.* See **Punch. 2.** (*often not cap.*) *Brit. slang.* a girl or woman.

jug (dʒʌg) *n.* **1.** a vessel for holding or pouring liquids, usually having a handle and a spout or lip. U.S. equivalent: **pitcher. 2.** *Austral. and N.Z.* such a vessel used as a kettle: *an electric jug.* **3.** *U.S.* a large vessel with a narrow mouth. **4.** Also called: **jugful.** the amount of liquid held by a jug. **5.** *Brit. informal.* a glass of alcoholic drink, esp. beer. **6.** a slang word for **jail.** *~vb.* **jugs, jugging, jugged. 7.** to stew or boil (meat, esp. hare) in an earthenware container. **8.** (*tr.*) *Slang.* to put in jail. [C16: probably from *Jug,* nickname from girl's name *Joan*]

jugal (ˈdʒuːgᵊl) *adj.* **1.** of or relating to the zygomatic bone. *~n.* **2.** Also called: **jugal bone.** other names for **zygomatic bone.** [C16: from Latin *jugālis* of a yoke, from *jugum* a yoke]

jugate (ˈdʒuːgeɪt, -gɪt) *adj.* (esp. of compound leaves) having parts arranged in pairs. [C19: from New Latin *jugātus* (unattested), from Latin *jugum* a yoke]

jug band *n.* a small group playing folk or jazz music, using empty jugs that are played by blowing across their openings to produce bass notes.

Jugendstil *German.* (ˈjuːgəntʃtiːl) *n.* another name for **Art Nouveau.** [from *Jugend* literally: youth, name of illustrated periodical that first appeared in 1896, + *Stil* STYLE]

JUGFET (ˈdʒʌgfɛt) *n. acronym for* junction-gate field-effect transistor; a type of field-effect transistor in which the semiconductor gate region or regions form one or more p-n junctions with the conduction channel. Compare **IGFET.**

jugged hare *n.* a stew of hare cooked in an earthenware pot or casserole.

juggernaut (ˈdʒʌgəˌnɔːt) *n.* **1.** any terrible force, esp. one that destroys or that demands complete self-sacrifice. **2.** *Brit.* a very large lorry for transporting goods by road, esp. one that travels throughout Europe.

Juggernaut (ˈdʒʌgəˌnɔːt) *n. Hinduism.* **1.** a crude idol of Krishna worshipped at Puri and throughout Orissa and Bengal. At an annual festival the idol is wheeled through the town on a gigantic chariot and devotees are supposed to have formerly thrown themselves under the wheels in the hope of going straight to paradise. **2.** a form of Krishna miraculously raised by Brahma from the state of a crude idol to that of a living god. [C17: from Hindi *Jagannath,* from Sanskrit *Jagannātha* lord of the world (that is, Vishnu, chief of the Hindu gods), from *jagat* world + *nātha* lord]

juggins (ˈdʒʌgɪnz) *n. Brit. informal.* a silly person; simpleton. [C19: special use of the surname *Juggins*]

juggle (ˈdʒʌgᵊl) *vb.* **1.** to throw and catch (several objects) continuously so that most are in the air all the time, as an entertainment. **2.** to arrange or manipulate (facts, figures, etc.) so as to give a false or misleading picture. **3.** (*tr.*) to keep (several activities) in progress, esp. with difficulty. *~n.* **4.** an act of juggling. [C14: from Old French *jogler* to perform as a jester, from Latin *joculārī* to jest, from *jocus* a jest] —'**jugglery** *n.*

juggler (ˈdʒʌglə) *n.* **1.** a person who juggles, esp. a professional entertainer. **2.** a person who fraudulently manipulates facts or figures.

juglandaceous (ˌdʒuːglænˈdeɪʃəs) *adj.* of, relating to, or belonging to the *Juglandaceae,* a family of trees that includes walnut and hickory. [C19: via New Latin from Latin *juglans* walnut, from *ju-*, shortened from *Jovi-* of Jupiter + *glans* acorn]

Jugoslav ('juːgəʊˌslɑːv) *adj., n.* a variant spelling of **Yugoslav.**

jugular ('dʒʌgjʊlə) *adj.* **1.** of, relating to, or situated near the throat or neck. **2.** of, having, or denoting pelvic fins situated in front of the pectoral fins: *a jugular fish.* ~*n.* **3.** short for **jugular vein. 4. go for the jugular.** to make a savage and destructive attack on an enemy's weakest point. [C16: from Late Latin *jugulāris,* from Latin *jugulum* throat]

jugular vein *n.* any of three large veins of the neck that return blood to the heart from the head and face.

jugulate ('dʒʌgjʊˌleɪt) *vb. (tr.) Rare.* to check (a disease) by extreme measures or remedies. [C17 (in the obsolete sense: kill by cutting the throat of): from Latin *jugulāre,* from *jugulum* throat, from *jugum* yoke] —ˌ**jugu'lation** *n.*

jugum ('dʒuːgəm) *n.* **1.** a small process at the base of each forewing in certain insects by which the forewings are united to the hindwings during flight. **2.** *Botany.* a pair of opposite leaflets. [C19: from Latin, literally: YOKE]

juice (dʒuːs) *n.* **1.** any liquid that occurs naturally in or is secreted by plant or animal tissue: *the juice of an orange; digestive juices.* **2.** *Informal.* **a.** fuel for an engine, esp. petrol. **b.** electricity. **c.** alcoholic drink. **3. a.** vigour or vitality. **b.** essence or fundamental nature. **4. stew in one's own juice.** See **stew**[1] (sense 10). [C13: from Old French *jus,* from Latin] —'**juiceless** *adj.*

juice extractor *n.* a kitchen appliance, usually operated by electricity, for extracting juice from fruits and vegetables.

juice up *vb. (tr., adv.)* **1.** *U.S. slang.* to make lively: *to juice up a party.* **2.** *(often passive)* to cause to be drunk: *he got juiced up on Scotch last night.*

juicy ('dʒuːsɪ) *adj.* **juicier, juiciest. 1.** full of juice. **2.** provocatively interesting; spicy: *juicy gossip.* **3.** *Slang.* voluptuous or seductive: *she's a juicy bit.* **4.** *Chiefly U.S. and Canadian.* profitable: *a juicy contract.* —'**juicily** *adv.* —'**juiciness** *n.*

jujitsu, jujutsu, *or* **jiujutsu** (dʒuː'dʒɪtsuː) *n.* the traditional Japanese system of unarmed self-defence perfected by the samurai. See also **judo.** [C19: from Japanese, from *jū* gentleness + *jutsu* art]

juju ('dʒuːdʒuː) *n.* **1.** an object superstitiously revered by certain W African peoples and used as a charm or fetish. **2.** the power associated with a juju. **3.** a taboo effected by a juju. **4.** any process in which a mystery is exploited to confuse people. [C19: probably from Hausa *djudju* evil spirit, fetish] —'**jujuism** *n.* —'**jujuist** *n.*

jujube ('dʒuːdʒuːb) *n.* **1.** any of several Old World spiny rhamnaceous trees of the genus *Ziziphus,* esp. *Z. jujuba,* that have small yellowish flowers and dark red edible fruits. See also **Christ's-thorn. 2.** the fruit of any of these trees. **3.** a chewy sweet made of flavoured gelatin and sometimes medicated to soothe sore throats. ~Also called (for senses 1, 2): **Chinese date.** [C14: from Medieval Latin *jujuba,* modification of Latin *zīzyphum,* from Greek *zizuphon*]

jukebox ('dʒuːkˌbɒks) *n.* an automatic gramophone, usually in a large case, in which records may be selected by inserting coins and pressing appropriate buttons. [C20: from Gullah *juke* bawdy (as in *juke house* brothel) + BOX[1]]

jukskei ('jʊkˌskeɪ) *n. S. African.* a game in which a peg is thrown over a fixed distance at a stake driven into the ground. [from Afrikaans *juk* yoke + *skei* pin]

Jul. *abbrev. for* July.

julep ('dʒuːlɪp) *n.* **1.** a sweet drink, variously prepared and sometimes medicated. **2.** *Chiefly U.S.* short for **mint julep.** [C14: from Old French, from Arabic *julāb,* from Persian *gulāb* rose water, from *gul* rose + *āb* water]

Julian calendar ('dʒuːlɪən) *n.* the calendar introduced in 46 B.C. by the Roman emperor Julius Caesar (49–44 B.C.); it is identical to the present calendar in all but two aspects: the beginning of the year was not fixed on Jan. 1 and leap years occurred every fourth year and in every centenary year. Compare **Gregorian calendar.**

julienne (ˌdʒuːlɪ'ɛn) *adj.* **1.** (of vegetables) cut into thin shreds. ~*n.* **2.** a clear consommé to which a mixture of such vegetables has been added.

Juliet cap ('dʒuːlɪɪt) *n.* a close-fitting decorative cap, worn esp. by brides. [C20: after the heroine of Shakespeare's *Romeo and Juliet*]

Juliett (dʒʊlɪ'ɛt) *n. Communications.* a code word for the letter *j.*

July (dʒuː'laɪ, dʒə-, dʒʊ-) *n., pl.* **-lies.** the seventh month of the year, consisting of 31 days. [C13: from Anglo-French *julie,* from Latin *Jūlius,* after Gaius *Julius Caesar,* in whose honour it was named]

Jumada (dʒʊ'mɑːdə) *n.* either the fifth or the sixth month of the Muslim year, known respectively as **Jumada I** and **Jumada II.** [Arabic]

jumar ('dʒuːmə) *n. Mountaineering.* **1.** Also called: **jumar clamp.** a clamp with a handle that can move freely up a rope on which it is clipped but locks when downward pressure is applied. ~*vb. (intr.)* **2.** to climb (up a fixed rope) using jumars. [C20: Swiss name]

jumble ('dʒʌmbᵊl) *vb.* **1.** to mingle (objects, papers, etc.) in a state of disorder. **2.** *(tr.; usually passive)* to remember in a confused form; muddle. ~*n.* **3.** a disordered mass, state, etc. **4.** *Brit.* articles donated for a jumble sale. **5.** Also called: **jumbal.** a small thin cake, usually ring-shaped. [C16: of uncertain origin] —'**jumbler** *n.* —'**jumbly** *adj.*

jumble sale *n.* a sale of miscellaneous articles, usually cheap and predominantly secondhand, in aid of charity. U.S. and Canadian equivalent: **rummage sale.**

jumbo ('dʒʌmbəʊ) *n., pl.* **-bos. 1.** *Informal.* **a.** a very large person or thing. **b.** *(as modifier): a jumbo box of detergent.* **2.** See **jumbo jet.** [C19: after the name of a famous elephant exhibited by P. T. Barnum, from Swahili *jumbe* chief]

jumboize *or* **jumboise** ('dʒʌmbəʊˌaɪz) *vb. (tr.)* to extend (a ship, esp. a tanker) by cutting out the middle part and inserting a new larger part between the original bow and stern. [C20: from JUMBO + -IZE]

jumbo jet *n. Informal.* a type of large jet-propelled airliner that carries several hundred passengers.

jumbuck ('dʒʌmˌbʌk) *n. Austral.* an informal word for **sheep.** [C19: from a native Australian language]

jump (dʒʌmp) *vb.* **1.** *(intr.)* to leap or spring clear of the ground or other surface by using the muscles in the legs and feet. **2.** *(tr.)* to leap over or clear (an obstacle): *to jump a gap.* **3.** *(tr.)* to cause to leap over an obstacle: *to jump a horse over a hedge.* **4.** *(intr.)* to move or proceed hastily (into, onto, out of, etc.): *she jumped into a taxi and was off.* **5.** *(tr.) Informal.* to board so as to travel illegally on: *he jumped the train as it was leaving.* **6.** *(intr.)* to parachute from an aircraft. **7.** *(intr.)* to jerk or start, as with astonishment, surprise, etc.: *she jumped when she heard the explosion.* **8.** to rise or cause to rise suddenly or abruptly. **9.** to pass or skip over (intervening objects or matter): *she jumped a few lines and then continued reading.* **10.** *(intr.)* to change from one thing to another, esp. from one subject to another. **11.** *(tr.)* to drill by means of a jumper. **12.** *(intr.)* (of a film) **a.** to have sections of a continuous sequence omitted, as through faulty cutting. **b.** to flicker, as through faulty alignment of the film. **13.** *(tr.) U.S.* to promote in rank, esp. unexpectedly or to a higher rank than expected. **14.** *(tr.)* to start (a car) using jump leads. **15.** *Draughts.* to capture (an opponent's piece) by moving one of one's own pieces over it to an unoccupied square. **16.** *(intr.) Bridge.* to bid in response to one's partner at a higher level than is necessary, to indicate a strong hand. **17.** *(tr.)* to come off (a track, rail, etc.): *the locomotive jumped the rails.* **18.** *(intr.)* (of the stylus of a record player) to be jerked out of the groove. **19.** *(intr.) Slang.* to be lively: *the party was jumping when I arrived.* **20.** *(tr.) Informal.* to attack without warning: *thieves jumped the old man as he walked through the park.* **21.** *(tr.) Informal.* (of a driver or a motor vehicle) to pass through (a red traffic light) or move away from (traffic lights) before they change to green. **22.** *(tr.) Brit. slang.* (of a man) to have sexual intercourse with. **23. jump bail.** to forfeit one's bail by failing to appear in court, esp. by absconding. **24. jump down someone's throat.** *Informal.* to address or reply to someone with unexpected sharpness. **25. jump ship.** to desert, esp. to leave a ship in which one is legally bound to serve. **26. jump the queue.** See **queue-jump. 27. jump to it.** *Informal.* to begin something quickly and efficiently. ~*n.* **28.** an act or instance of jumping. **29.** a space, distance, or obstacle to be jumped or that has been jumped. **30.** a descent by parachute from an aircraft. **31.** *Sport.* any of several contests involving a jump: *the high jump.* **32.** a sudden rise: *the jump in prices last month.* **33.** a sudden or abrupt transition. **34.** a sudden jerk or involuntary muscular spasm, esp. as a reaction of surprise. **35.** a step or degree: *one jump ahead.* **36.** *Draughts.* a move that captures an opponent's piece by jumping over it. **37.** *Films.* **a.** a break in continuity in the normal sequence of shots. **b.** *(as modifier): a jump cut.* **38.** *Computer technol.* another name for **branch** (sense 7). **39.** *Brit. slang.* an act of sexual intercourse. **40. on the jump.** *Informal, chiefly U.S. and Canadian.* **a.** in a hurry. **b.** busy and energetic. **41. take a running jump.** *Brit. informal.* a contemptuous expression of dismissal. ~See also **jump at, jump-off, jump on, jump-up.** [C16: probably of imitative origin; compare Swedish *gumpa* to jump] —'**jumpable** *adj.* —'**jumpingly** *adv.*

jump at *vb. (intr., prep.)* to be glad to accept: *I would jump at the chance of going.*

jump ball *n. Basketball.* a ball thrown high by the referee between two opposing players to put it in play, as after a stoppage in which no foul or violation was committed.

jump bid *n. Bridge.* a bid by the responder at a higher level than is necessary.

jumped-up *adj. Informal.* suddenly risen in significance, esp. when appearing arrogant.

jumper[1] ('dʒʌmpə) *n.* **1.** *Chiefly Brit.* a knitted or crocheted garment covering the upper part of the body. **2.** the U.S. and Canadian term for **pinafore dress.** [C19: from obsolete *jump* man's loose jacket, variant of *jupe,* from Old French, from Arabic *jubbah* long cloth coat]

jumper[2] ('dʒʌmpə) *n.* **1.** a boring tool that works by repeated impact, such as a steel bit in a hammer drill used in boring rock. **2.** Also called: **jumper cable, jumper lead.** a short length of wire used to make a connection, usually temporarily, between terminals or to bypass a component. **3.** a type of sled with a high crosspiece. **4.** a person or animal that jumps. **5.** *Irish derogatory slang.* a person who changes religion; a convert.

jumping bean *n.* a seed of any of several Mexican euphorbiaceous plants, esp. species of *Sebastiania,* that contains a moth caterpillar whose movements cause it to jerk about.

jumping gene *n.* a fragment of nucleic acid, such as a plasmid or a transposon, that can become incorporated into the DNA of a cell.

jumping jack *n.* **1.** a firework having a long narrow tube filled with gunpowder, folded like an accordion so that when lit it burns with small explosions causing it to jump along the ground. **2.** a toy figure of a man with jointed limbs that can be moved by pulling attached strings.

jumping mouse *n.* any long-tailed small mouselike rodent of the family *Zapodidae,* of North America, E Asia, and N and E Europe, having long hind legs specialized for leaping.

jumping-off place *or* **point** *n.* **1.** a starting point, as in an enterprise. **2.** a final or extreme condition. **3.** *Canadian.* a place where one leaves civilization to go into the wilderness. **4.** *U.S.* a very remote spot.

jumping spider *n.* any spider of the family *Salticidae,* esp. *Attulus saltator,* that catch their prey by hunting and can jump considerable distances.

jump jet *n.* a fixed-wing jet aircraft that is capable of landing and taking off vertically.

jump jockey *n. Brit.* a jockey who rides in steeplechases, as opposed to one who rides in flat races.

jump leads (li:dz) *pl. n.* two heavy cables fitted with crocodile clips used to start a motor vehicle with a discharged battery by connecting the battery to an external battery. U.S. and Canadian name: **jumper cables.**

jump-off *n.* **1.** an extra round in a showjumping contest when two or more horses are equal first, the fastest round deciding the winner. ~*vb.* **jump off. 2.** (*intr., adv.*) to begin or engage in a jump-off.

jump on *vb.* (*intr., prep.*) *Informal.* to reprimand or attack suddenly and forcefully.

jump seat *n.* **1.** a folding seat for temporary use, as on the flight deck of some aircraft for an additional crew member. **2.** *Brit.* a folding seat in a motor vehicle such as in a London taxi.

jump shot *n. Basketball.* a shot at the basket made by a player releasing the ball at the highest point of a leap.

jump-start *vb.* **1.** to start the engine of (a car) by pushing or rolling it and then engaging the gears or (of a car) to start in this way. ~*n.* **2.** the act of starting a car in this way. ~Also (Brit.): **bump-start.**

jump suit *n.* a one-piece garment of combined trousers and jacket or shirt.

jump-up *n.* **1.** (in the Caribbean) an occasion of mass dancing and merrymaking, as in a carnival. ~*vb.* **jump up.** (*intr., adv.*) **2.** to stand up quickly and suddenly. **3.** (in the Caribbean) to take part in a jump-up.

jumpy ('dʒʌmpɪ) *adj.* **jumpier, jumpiest. 1.** nervous or apprehensive. **2.** moving jerkily or fitfully. —'**jumpily** *adv.* —'**jumpiness** *n.*

Jun. *abbrev. for:* **1.** June. **2.** Also: **jun.** junior.

junc. *abbrev. for* junction.

juncaceous (dʒʌŋ'keɪʃəs) *adj.* of, relating to, or belonging to the *Juncaceae,* a family of grasslike plants with small brown flowers: includes the rushes and woodrushes. Compare **cyperaceous.** [C19: via New Latin from Latin *juncus* a rush]

junco ('dʒʌŋkəʊ) *n., pl.* **-cos** *or* **-coes.** any North American bunting of the genus *Junco,* having a greyish plumage with white outer tail feathers. [C18: from Spanish: a rush, a marsh bird, from Latin *juncus* rush]

junction ('dʒʌŋkʃən) *n.* **1.** a place where several routes, lines, or roads meet, link, or cross each other: *a railway junction.* **2.** a point on a motorway where traffic may leave or join it. **3.** *Electronics.* **a.** a contact between two different metals or other materials: *a thermocouple junction.* **b.** a transition region between regions of differing electrical properties in a semiconductor: *a p-n junction.* **4.** a connection between two or more conductors or sections of transmission lines. **5.** the act of joining or the state of being joined. [C18: from Latin *junctiō* a joining, from *junctus* joined, from *jungere* to join] —'**junctional** *adj.*

junction box *n.* an earthed enclosure within which wires or cables can be safely connected.

junction transistor *n.* a bipolar transistor consisting of two p-n junctions combined to form either an n-p-n or a p-n-p transistor, having the three electrodes, the emitter, base, and collector.

juncture ('dʒʌŋktʃə) *n.* **1.** a point in time, esp. a critical one (often in the phrase **at this juncture**). **2.** *Linguistics.* **a.** a pause in speech or a feature of pronunciation that introduces, accompanies, or replaces a pause. **b.** the set of phonological features signalling a division between words, such as those that distinguish *a name* from *an aim.* **3.** a less common word for **junction.**

June (dʒu:n) *n.* the sixth month of the year, consisting of 30 days. [Old English *iunius,* from Latin *junius,* probably from *Junius* name of Roman gens]

Juneberry ('dʒu:n,bɛrɪ) *n., pl.* **-ries.** another name for **serviceberry** (senses 1, 2).

June bug *or* **beetle** *n.* any of various large brown North American scarabaeid beetles that are common in late spring and early summer, esp. any of the genus *Polyphylla.* Also called: **May beetle, May bug.**

Jungian ('jʊŋɪən) *adj.* of, following, or relating to the Swiss psychologist Carl Jung (1875–1961), his system of psychoanalysis, or to analytic psychology.

jungle ('dʒʌŋgᵊl) *n.* **1.** an equatorial forest area with luxuriant vegetation, often almost impenetrable. **2.** any dense or tangled thicket or growth. **3.** a place of intense competition or ruthless struggle for survival: *the concrete jungle.* **4.** *U.S. slang.* (esp. in the Depression) a gathering place for the unemployed, etc. [C18: from Hindi *jangal,* from Sanskrit *jāngala* wilderness] —'**jungly** *adj.*

jungle fever *n.* a serious malarial fever occurring in the East Indies.

jungle fowl *n.* **1.** any small gallinaceous bird of the genus *Gallus,* of S and SE Asia, the males of which have an arched tail and a combed and wattled head: family *Phasianidae* (pheasants). *G. gallus* (**red jungle fowl**) is thought to be the ancestor of the domestic fowl. **2.** *Austral.* any of several megapodes, esp. *Megapodius freycinet.*

jungle gym *n.* a climbing frame for young children. [from a trademark]

jungle juice *n.* a slang name for alcoholic liquor, esp. home-made liquor.

junior ('dʒu:njə) *adj.* **1.** lower in rank or length of service; subordinate. **2.** younger in years: *junior citizens.* **3.** of or relating to youth or childhood: *junior pastimes.* **4.** *Brit.* of or relating to schoolchildren between the ages of 7 and 11 approximately. **5.** *U.S.* of, relating to, or designating the third year of a four-year course at college or high school. ~*n.* **6.** *Law.* (in England) any barrister below the rank of Queen's Counsel. **7.** a junior person. **8.** *Brit.* a junior schoolchild. **9.** *U.S.* a junior student. [C17: from Latin: younger, from *juvenis* young]

Junior ('dʒu:njə) *adj. Chiefly U.S.* being the younger: usually used after a name to distinguish the son from the father with the same first name or names: *Charles Parker, Junior.* Abbrevs.: **Jnr, Jr, Jun., Junr.**

junior college *n. U.S. and Canadian.* **1.** an educational establishment providing a two-year course that either terminates with an associate degree or is the equivalent of the freshman and sophomore years of a four-year undergraduate course. **2.** the junior section of a college or university.

junior common room *n.* (in certain universities and colleges) a common room for the use of students. Compare **senior common room, middle common room.**

junior lightweight *n.* **a.** a professional boxer weighing 126–130 pounds (57–59 kg). **b.** (*as modifier*): *a junior-lightweight bout.*

junior middleweight *n.* **a.** a professional boxer weighing 147–154 pounds (66.5–70 kg). **b.** (*as modifier*): *the junior-middleweight championship.* Compare **light middleweight.**

junior school *n. Brit.* a school for children aged between 7 and 11. Compare **infant school.**

junior technician *n.* a rank in the RAF senior to aircraftman: comparable to that of private in the army.

junior welterweight *n.* **a.** a professional boxer weighing 135–140 pounds (61–63.5 kg). **b.** (*as modifier*): *a junior-welterweight fight.* Compare **light welterweight.**

juniper ('dʒu:nɪpə) *n.* **1.** any coniferous shrub or small tree of the genus *Juniperus,* of the N hemisphere, having purple berry-like cones. The cones of *J. communis* (**common** or **dwarf juniper**) are used as a flavouring in making gin. See also **red cedar** (sense 1). **2.** any of various similar trees, grown mainly as ornamentals. [C14: from Latin *jūniperus,* of obscure origin]

junk¹ (dʒʌŋk) *n.* **1.** discarded or secondhand objects, etc., collectively. **2.** *Informal.* **a.** rubbish generally. **b.** nonsense: *the play was absolute junk.* **3.** *Slang.* any narcotic drug, esp. heroin. ~*vb.* **4.** (*tr.*) *Informal.* to discard as junk; scrap. [C15 *jonke* old useless rope]

junk² (dʒʌŋk) *n.* a sailing vessel used in Chinese waters and characterized by a very high poop, flat bottom, and square sails supported by battens. [C17: from Portuguese *junco,* from Javanese *jon;* related to Dutch *jonk*]

junk bond *n. Finance.* a security that offers a high yield but often involves a high risk of default.

Junker ('jʊŋkə) *n.* **1.** *History.* any of the aristocratic landowners of Prussia who were devoted to maintaining their identity and extensive social and political privileges. **2.** an arrogant, narrow-minded, and tyrannical German army officer or official. **3.** (formerly) a young German nobleman. [C16: from German, from Old High German *junchērro* young lord, from *junc* young + *hērro* master, lord] —'**Junkerdom** *n.* —'**Junkerism** *n.*

junket ('dʒʌŋkɪt) *n.* **1.** a sweet dessert made of flavoured milk set to a curd with rennet. **2.** a feast or festive occasion. **3.** *U.S. and Canadian.* an excursion, esp. one made for pleasure at public expense by a public official or committee. ~*vb.* **4.** to have or entertain with a feast or festive gathering. **5.** (*intr.*) *U.S. and Canadian.* (of a public official, committee, etc.) to go on a junket. [C14 (in the sense: rush basket, hence custard served on rushes): from Old French (dialect) *jonquette,* from *jonc* rush, from Latin *juncus* reed] —'**junketer,** '**junketter,** *or* ,**junke'teer** *n.*

junk food *n.* food that is low in nutritional value, often highly processed or ready-prepared, and eaten instead of or in addition to well-balanced meals.

junkie *or* **junky** (ˈdʒʌŋkɪ) *n., pl.* **junkies.** an informal word for **drug addict,** esp. one who injects heroin into himself.
junk mail *n.* unlimited mail advertising goods or services.
junkman (ˈdʒʌŋkˌmæn) *n., pl.* **-men.** the U.S. and Canadian term for **rag-and-bone man.**
junk shop *n.* **1.** a shop selling miscellaneous secondhand goods. **2.** *Derogatory.* a shop selling antiques.
junkyard (ˈdʒʌŋkˌjɑːd) *n.* a place where junk is stored or collected for sale.
Junoesque (ˌdʒuːnəʊˈɛsk) *adj.* having stately bearing and regal beauty like the Roman goddess Juno.
Junr *or* **junr** *abbrev. for* junior.
junta (ˈdʒʊntə, ˈdʒʌn-; *chiefly U.S.* ˈhʊntə) *n.* **1.** a group of military officers holding the power in a country, esp. after a coup d'état. **2.** Also called: **junto.** a small group of men; cabal, faction, or clique. **3.** a legislative or executive council in some parts of Latin America. [C17: from Spanish: council, from Latin *junctus* joined, from *jungere* to JOIN]
junto (ˈdʒʊntəʊ, ˈdʒʌn-) *n., pl.* **-tos.** a variant of **junta** (sense 2). [C17: variant of JUNTA]
jupon (ˈʒuːpɒn) *n.* a short close-fitting sleeveless padded garment, used in the late 14th and early 15th centuries with armour. Also called: **gipon.** [C15: from Old French, from Old French *jupe;* see JUMPER[1]]
jura (ˈdʒʊərə) *n.* the plural of **jus.**
jural (ˈdʒʊərəl) *adj.* **1.** of or relating to law or to the administration of justice. **2.** of or relating to rights and obligations. [C17: from Latin *iūs* law + -AL[1]] —ˈ**jurally** *adv.*
Jurassic (dʒʊˈræsɪk) *adj.* **1.** of, denoting, or formed in the second period of the Mesozoic era, between the Triassic and Cretaceous periods, lasting for 45 million years during which dinosaurs and ammonites flourished. ~*n.* **2.** **the.** the Jurassic period or rock system. [C19: from French *jurassique,* after the *Jura* (Mountains), W central Europe]
jurat (ˈdʒʊəræt) *n.* **1.** *Law.* a statement at the foot of an affidavit, naming the parties, stating when, where, and before whom it was sworn, etc. **2.** (in England) a municipal officer of the Cinque Ports, having a similar position to that of an alderman. **3.** (in France and the Channel Islands) a magistrate. [C16: from Medieval Latin *jūrātus* one who has been sworn, from Latin *jūrāre* to swear]
juratory (ˈdʒʊərətərɪ, -trɪ) *adj. Law.* of, relating to, or expressed in an oath.
JurD *abbrev. for* Doctor of Law. [Latin: *Juris Doctor*]
jurel (huːˈrɛl) *n.* any of several carangid food fishes of the genus *Caranx,* of warm American Atlantic waters. [C18: from Spanish, from Catalan *sorell,* from Late Latin *saurus* horse mackerel, from Greek *sauros* lizard]
juridical (dʒʊˈrɪdɪkᵊl) *or* **juridic** *adj.* of or relating to law, to the administration of justice, or to the office or function of a judge; legal. [C16: from Latin *jūridicus,* from *iūs* law + *dicere* to say] —**juˈridically** *adv.*
juridical days *pl. n. Law.* days on which the courts are in session. Compare **dies non.**
jurisconsult (ˌdʒʊərɪsˈkɒnsʌlt) *n.* **1.** a person qualified to advise on legal matters. **2.** a master of jurisprudence. [C17: from Latin *jūris consultus;* see JUS, CONSULT]
jurisdiction (ˌdʒʊərɪsˈdɪkʃən) *n.* **1.** the right or power to administer justice and to apply laws. **2.** the exercise or extent of such right or power. **3.** power or authority in general. [C13: from Latin *jūrisdictiō* administration of justice; see JUS, DICTION] —ˌ**jurisˈdictional** *adj.* —ˌ**jurisˈdictionally** *adv.* —ˌ**jurisˈdictive** *adj.*
jurisp. *abbrev. for* jurisprudence.
jurisprudence (ˌdʒʊərɪsˈpruːdᵊns) *n.* **1.** the science or philosophy of law. **2.** a system or body of law. **3.** a branch of law: *medical jurisprudence.* [C17: from Latin *jūris prūdentia;* see JUS, PRUDENCE] —**jurisprudential** (ˌdʒʊərɪspruːˈdɛnʃəl) *adj.* —ˌ**jurispruˈdentially** *adv.*
jurisprudent (ˌdʒʊərɪsˈpruːdᵊnt) *adj.* **1.** skilled in jurisprudence or versed in the principles of law. ~*n.* **2.** a jurisprudent person.
jurist (ˈdʒʊərɪst) *n.* **1.** a person versed in the science of law, esp. Roman or civil law. **2.** a writer on legal subjects. **3.** a student or graduate of law. **4.** (in the U.S.) a lawyer. [C15: from French *juriste,* from Medieval Latin *jūrista;* see JUS]
juristic (dʒʊˈrɪstɪk) *or* **juristical** *adj.* **1.** of or relating to jurists. **2.** of, relating to, or characteristic of the study of law or the legal profession. —**juˈristically** *adv.*
juristic act *n.* **1.** a proceeding designed to have a legal effect. **2.** an act by an individual aimed at altering, terminating, or otherwise affecting a legal right.
juror (ˈdʒʊərə) *n.* **1.** a member of a jury. **2.** a person whose name is included on a panel from which a jury is selected. **3.** a person who takes an oath. [C14: from Anglo-French *jurour,* from Old French *jurer* to take an oath, from Latin *jūrāre*]
jury[1] (ˈdʒʊərɪ) *n., pl.* **-ries.** **1.** a group of twelve people sworn to deliver a true verdict according to the evidence upon a case presented in a court of law. See also **grand jury, petit jury.** **2.** a body of persons appointed to judge a competition and award prizes. [C14: from Old French *juree,* from *jurer* to swear; see JUROR]
jury[2] (ˈdʒʊərɪ) *adj. Chiefly nautical.* (in combination) makeshift: *jury-rigged.* [C17: of unknown origin]
jury box *n.* an enclosure where the jury sit in court.
juryman (ˈdʒʊərɪmən) *or* (*fem.*) **jurywoman** *n., pl.* **-men** *or* **-women.** a member of a jury.
jury process *n.* the writ used to summon jurors.
jury-rigged *adj. Chiefly nautical.* set up in a makeshift manner, usually as a result of the loss of regular gear.
jus (dʒʌs) *n., pl.* **jura** (ˈdʒʊərə). *Law.* **1.** a right, power, or authority. **2.** law in the abstract or as a system, as distinguished from specific enactments. [Latin: law]
jus. *or* **just.** *abbrev. for* justice.
jus canonicum (kəˈnɒnɪkəm) *n.* canon law. [from Latin]
jus civile (sɪˈviːlɪ) *n.* **1.** the civil law of the Roman state. **2.** the body of law derived from the principles of this law. Compare **jus gentium, jus naturale.** [from Latin]
jus divinum (dɪˈviːnəm) *n.* divine law. [from Latin]
jus gentium (ˈdʒɛntɪəm) *n. Roman law.* those rules of law common to all nations. [from Latin]
jus naturale (ˌnætjʊˈreɪlɪ) *n. Roman law.* **1.** (originally) a system of law based on fundamental ideas of right and wrong; natural law. **2.** (in later usage) another term for **jus gentium.** [from Latin]
jus sanguinis (ˈsæŋgwɪnɪs) *n. Law.* the principle that a person's nationality at birth is the same as that of his natural parents. Compare **jus soli.** [Latin, literally: law of blood]
jussive (ˈdʒʌsɪv) *adj. Grammar.* another word for **imperative** (sense 3). [C19: from Latin *jūssus* ordered, from *jubēre* to command]
jus soli (ˈsəʊlaɪ) *n. Law.* the principle that a person's nationality at birth is determined by the territory within which he was born. Compare **jus sanguinis.** [from Latin, literally: law of soil]
just *adj.* (dʒʌst). **1. a.** fair or impartial in action or judgment. **b.** (*as collective n.;* preceded by *the*): *the just.* **2.** conforming to high moral standards; honest. **3.** consistent with justice: *a just action.* **4.** rightly applied or given; deserved: *a just reward.* **5.** legally valid; lawful: *a just inheritance.* **6.** well-founded; reasonable: *just criticism.* **7.** correct, accurate, or true: *a just account.* ~*adv.* (dʒʌst; *unstressed* dʒəst). **8.** used with forms of *have* to indicate an action performed in the very recent past: *I have just closed the door.* **9.** at this very instant: *he's just coming in to land.* **10.** no more than; merely; only: *just an ordinary car.* **11.** exactly; precisely: *that's just what I mean.* **12.** by a small margin; barely: *he just got there in time.* **13.** (intensifier): *it's just wonderful to see you.* **14.** *Informal.* indeed; with a vengeance: *isn't it just.* **15.** **just about. a.** at the point of starting (to do something). **b.** very nearly; almost: *I've just about had enough.* **16. just a moment, second,** *or* **minute.** an expression requesting the hearer to wait or pause for a brief period of time. **17. just now. a.** a very short time ago. **b.** at this moment. **18. just on.** having reached exactly: *it's just on five o'clock.* **19. just so. a.** an expression of complete agreement or of unwillingness to dissent. **b.** arranged with precision. [C14: from Latin *jūstus* righteous, from *jūs* justice] —ˈ**justly** *adv.* —ˈ**justness** *n.*
justice (ˈdʒʌstɪs) *n.* **1.** the quality or fact of being just. **2.** *Ethics.* **a.** the principle of fairness that like cases should be treated alike. **b.** a particular distribution of benefits and burdens fairly in accordance with a particular conception of what are to count as like cases. **c.** the principle that punishment should be proportionate to the offence. **3.** the administration of law according to prescribed and accepted principles. **4.** conformity to the law; legal validity. **5.** a judge of the Supreme Court of Judicature. **6.** short for **justice of the peace.** **7.** good reason (esp. in the phrase **with justice**): *he was disgusted by their behaviour, and with justice.* **8. do justice to. a.** to show to full advantage: *the picture did justice to her beauty.* **b.** to show full appreciation of by action: *he did justice to the meal.* **c.** to treat or judge fairly. **9. do oneself justice.** to make full use of one's abilities. **10. bring to justice.** to capture, try, and usually punish (a criminal, an outlaw, etc.). [C12: from Old French, from Latin *jūstitia,* from *justus* JUST]
justice court *n.* an inferior court presided over by a justice of the peace.
justice of the peace *n.* a lay magistrate, appointed by the crown or acting *ex officio,* whose function is to preserve the peace in his area, try summarily such cases as are within his jurisdiction, and perform miscellaneous administrative duties.
justice of the peace court *n.* (in Scotland, formerly) a court with limited criminal jurisdiction held by justices of the peace in counties: replaced in 1975 by the **district court.**
justiceship (ˈdʒʌstɪsˌʃɪp) *n.* the rank or office of a justice.
justiciable (dʒʌˈstɪʃɪəbᵊl) *adj.* **1.** capable of being determined by a court of law. **2.** liable to be brought before a court for trial; subject to jurisdiction. —**jusˌticiaˈbility** *n.*
justiciar (dʒʌˈstɪʃɪˌɑː) *n. English legal history.* the chief political and legal officer from the time of William I to that of Henry III, who deputized for the king in his absence and presided over the kings' courts. Also called: **justiciary.** —**jusˈticiarˌship** *n.*
justiciary (dʒʌˈstɪʃɪərɪ) *adj.* **1.** of or relating to the administration of justice. ~*n., pl.* **-aries.** **2.** an officer or administrator of justice; judge. **3.** another word for **justiciar.**
justifiable (ˈdʒʌstɪˌfaɪəbᵊl) *adj.* capable of being justified; understandable. —ˌ**justiˌfiaˈbility** *or* ˈ**justiˌfiableness** *n.* —ˈ**justiˌfiably** *adv.*

justifiable homicide *n.* lawful killing, as in the execution of a death sentence.

justification (ˌdʒʌstɪfɪˈkeɪʃən) *n.* **1.** reasonable grounds for complaint, defence, etc. **2.** the act of justifying; proof, vindication, or exculpation. **3.** *Theol.* **a.** the act of justifying. **b.** the process of being justified or the condition of having been justified. **4.** *Printing, computer technol.* the process of adjusting interword spacing in text or data so that both right and left margins are straight. **5.** *Computer technol.* the process of moving data right or left so that the first or last character occurs in a predefined position.

justificatory (ˈdʒʌstɪfɪˌkeɪtərɪ, -trɪ) *or* **justificative** (ˈdʒʌstɪfɪˌkeɪtɪv) *adj.* serving as justification or capable of justifying; vindicatory.

justify (ˈdʒʌstɪˌfaɪ) *vb.* **-fies, -fying, -fied.** (*mainly tr.*) **1.** (*often passive*) to prove or see to be just or valid; vindicate: *he was certainly justified in taking the money.* **2.** to show to be reasonable; warrant or substantiate: *his behaviour justifies our suspicion.* **3.** to declare or show to be free from blame or guilt; absolve. **4.** *Law.* **a.** to show good reason in court for (some action taken). **b.** to show adequate grounds for doing (that with which a person is charged): *to justify a libel.* **5.** (*also intr.*) *Printing, computer technol.* to adjust the spaces between words in (a line of type or data) so that it is of the required length or (of a line of type or data) to fit exactly. **6. a.** *Protestant theol.* to account or declare righteous by the imputation of Christ's merits to the sinner. **b.** *R.C. theol.* to change from sinfulness to righteousness by the transforming effects of grace. **7.** (*also intr.*) *Law.* to prove (a person) to have sufficient means to act as surety, etc., or (of a person) to qualify to provide bail or surety. [C14: from Old French *justifier,* from Latin *justificāre,* from *jūstus* JUST + *facere* to make] —ˈ**justiˌfier** *n.*

Justinian Code (dʒʌˈstɪnɪən) *n.* a compilation of Roman imperial law made by order of Justinian I, Byzantine emperor (527–565), forming part of the **Corpus Juris Civilis.**

just-in-time *adj.* denoting or relating to an industrial method in which waste of resources is eliminated or reduced by producing production-line components, etc., as they are required, rather than holding large stocks. Abbrev.: **JIT.**

just intonation *n.* a form of tuning employing the pitch intervals of the untempered natural scale, sometimes employed in the playing of the violin, cello, etc.

justle (ˈdʒʌsəl) *vb.* a less common word for **jostle.**

just noticeable difference *n. Psychol.* another name for **difference threshold.** Abbrev.: **jnd.**

jut (dʒʌt) *vb.* **juts, jutting, jutted. 1.** (*intr.;* often foll. by *out*) to stick out or overhang beyond the surface or main part; protrude or project. ~*n.* **2.** something that juts out. [C16: variant of JET[1]] —ˈ**jutting** *adj.*

jute (dʒuːt) *n.* **1.** either of two Old World tropical yellow-flowered herbaceous plants, *Corchorus capsularis* or *C. olitorius,* cultivated for their strong fibre: family *Tiliaceae.* **2.** this fibre, used in making sacks, rope, etc. [C18: from Bengali *jhuto,* from Sanskrit *jūta* braid of hair, matted hair]

Jute (dʒuːt) *n.* a member of one of various Germanic tribes, some of whom invaded England in the 6th century A.D., settling in Kent.

Jutish (ˈdʒuːtɪʃ) *adj.* **1.** of or relating to the Jutes. ~*n.* **2.** another name for **Kentish.**

juvenal (ˈdʒuːvɪnəl) *adj. Ornithol.* a variant spelling (esp. U.S.) of **juvenile** (sense 4).

juvenescence (ˌdʒuːvɪˈnɛsəns) *n.* **1.** youth or immaturity. **2.** the act or process of growing from childhood to youth. **3.** restoration of youth; rejuvenation.

juvenescent (ˌdʒuːvɪˈnɛsənt) *adj.* becoming or being young or youthful. [C19: from Latin *juvenēscere* to grow up, regain strength, from *juvenis* youthful]

juvenile (ˈdʒuːvɪˌnaɪl) *adj.* **1.** young, youthful, or immature. **2.** suitable or designed for young people: *juvenile pastimes.* **3.** (of animals or plants) not yet fully mature. **4.** of or denoting young birds that have developed their first plumage of adult feathers. **5.** *Geology.* occurring at the earth's surface for the first time; new: *juvenile water; juvenile gases.* ~*n.* **6.** a juvenile person, animal, or plant. **7.** an actor who performs youthful roles. **8.** a book intended for young readers. [C17: from Latin *juvenīlis* youthful, from *juvenis* young] —ˈ**juveˌnilely** *adv.* —ˈ**juveˌnileness** *n.*

juvenile court *n.* a court that deals with juvenile offenders and children beyond parental control or in need of care.

juvenile delinquency *n.* antisocial or criminal conduct by juvenile delinquents.

juvenile delinquent *n.* a child or young person guilty of some offence, act of vandalism, or antisocial behaviour or whose conduct is beyond parental control and who may be brought before a juvenile court.

juvenile hormone *n.* a hormone, secreted by insects from a pair of glands behind the brain, that promotes the growth of larval characteristics and inhibits metamorphosis.

juvenilia (ˌdʒuːvɪˈnɪlɪə) *pl. n.* works of art, literature, or music produced in youth or adolescence, before the artist, author, or composer has formed a mature style. [C17: from Latin, literally: youthful things; see JUVENILE]

juvenility (ˌdʒuːvɪˈnɪlɪtɪ) *n., pl.* **-ties. 1.** the quality or condition of being juvenile, esp. of being immature. **2.** (*often pl.*) a juvenile act or manner. **3.** juveniles collectively.

juxtapose (ˌdʒʌkstəˈpəʊz) *vb.* (*tr.*) to place close together or side by side. [C19: back formation from *juxtaposition,* from Latin *juxta* next to + POSITION] —ˌ**juxtapoˈsition** *n.* —ˌ**juxtapoˈsitional** *adj.*

JWV *abbrev. for* Jewish War Veterans.

k *or* **K** (keɪ) *n., pl.* **k's, K's,** *or* **Ks.** **1.** the 11th letter and 8th consonant of the modern English alphabet. **2.** a speech sound represented by this letter, usually a voiceless velar stop, as in *kitten.* **3.** See **five Ks.**

k *symbol for:* **1.** kilo(s). **2.** *Maths.* the unit vector along the *z*-axis.

K *symbol for:* **1.** kelvin(s). **2.** *Chess.* king. **3.** *Chem.* potassium. [from New Latin *kalium*] **4.** *Physics.* kaon. **5.** *Currency.* **a.** kina. **b.** kip. **c.** kopeck. **d.** kwacha. **e.** kyat. **6.** one thousand. [from KILO-] **7.** *Computer technology.* originally or strictly, a unit of 1024 words, bits, or bytes: now often used to mean 1000.

K *or* **K.** *abbrev. for* Köchel: indicating the serial number in the catalogue (1862) of the works of Mozart made by Ludwig von Köchel, (1800–1877).

k. *abbrev. for:* **1.** karat. **2.** Also: **K.** king.

ka (kɑː) *n.* (in ancient Egypt) an attendant spirit supposedly dwelling as a vital force in a man or statue. [from Egyptian]

kab (kæb) *n.* a variant spelling of **cab**[2].

kabaka (kaˈbaka) *n.* any of the former rulers of the Baganda people of S Uganda. [C19: from Luganda]

kabaragoya (kəˌbɑːrəˈgəʊjə) *n.* a very large monitor lizard, *Varanus salvator,* of SE Asia: it grows to a length of three metres. Also called: **Malayan monitor.** [perhaps Tagalog]

Kabardian (kəˈbɑːdɪən) *n.* **1.** a member of a Circassian people of the North West Caucasus. **2.** the Eastern dialect of the Circassian language. Compare **Adygei.**

kabbala *or* **kabala** (kəˈbɑːlə) *n.* variant spellings of **cabbala.** —**kabbalism** *or* **kabalism** (ˈkæbəˌlɪzəm) *n.* —**ˈkabbalist** *or* **ˈkabalist** *n.* —**ˌkabbaˈlistic** *or* **ˌkabaˈlistic** *adj.*

kabob (kəˈbɒb) *n.* another name for **kebab.**

kabuki (kæˈbuːkɪ) *n.* a form of Japanese drama based on popular legends and characterized by elaborate costumes, stylized acting, and the use of male actors for all roles. See also **No**[1]. [Japanese, from *ka* singing + *bu* dancing + *ki* art]

Kabyle (kəˈbaɪl) *n.* **1.** (*pl.* **-byles** *or* **-byle**) a member of a Berber people inhabiting the E Atlas Mountains in Tunisia and Algeria. **2.** the dialect of Berber spoken by this people. [C19: from Arabic *qabā'il,* plural of *qabīlah* tribe]

kachang puteh (ˈkatʃaŋ puːˈteɪ) *n.* (in Malaysia) roasted or fried nuts or beans. [from Malay, literally: white beans]

kachina (kəˈtʃiːnə) *n.* any of the supernatural beings believed by the Hopi Indians to be the ancestors of living humans. [from Hopi *qačina* supernatural]

kadaitcha (kəˈdaɪtʃə) *n.* a variant spelling of **kurdaitcha.**

Kaddish (ˈkædɪʃ) *n., pl.* **Kaddishim** (kæˈdɪʃɪm). *Judaism.* **1.** an ancient Jewish liturgical prayer largely written in Aramaic and used in various forms to separate sections of the liturgy. Mourners have the right to recite some of these in public prayer during the year after, and on the anniversary of, a death. **2. say Kaddish.** to be a mourner. [C17: from Aramaic *qaddīsh* holy]

kadi (ˈkɑːdɪ, ˈkeɪdɪ) *n., pl.* **-dis.** a variant spelling of **cadi.**

Kaffir *or* **Kafir** (ˈkæfə) *n., pl.* **-firs** *or* **-fir.** **1.** *Offensive.* **a.** (in southern Africa) any Black African. **b.** (*as modifier*): *Kaffir farming.* **2.** a former name for the **Xhosa** language. **3.** *Offensive.* (among Muslims) a non-Muslim or infidel. [C19: from Arabic *kāfir* infidel, from *kafara* to deny, refuse to believe]

kaffir beer *n. S. African.* beer made from sorghum (kaffir corn) or millet.

kaffirboom (ˈkæfəˌbʊəm) *n. S. African.* a deciduous flowering tree, *Erythrina caffra,* having large clusters of brilliant orange or scarlet flowers. [from KAFFIR + Afrikaans *boom* tree]

kaffir corn *or U.S.* (*sometimes*) **kafir corn** *n.* a Southern African variety of sorghum, cultivated in dry regions for its grain and as fodder. Sometimes shortened to **kaffir** or (U.S.) **kafir.**

Kaffirs (ˈkæfəz) *pl. n. Stock Exchange.* South African mining shares.

kaffiyeh (kæˈfiːjə) *n.* a variant of **keffiyeh.**

Kafir (ˈkæfə) *n., pl.* **-irs** *or* **-ir.** **1.** another name for the **Nuri.** **2.** a variant spelling of **Kaffir.** [C19: from Arabic; see KAFFIR]

Kafkaesque (ˌkæfkəˈɛsk) *adj.* of or like the writings of Franz Kafka (1883–1924), Czech novelist, esp. in having a nightmarish dehumanized quality.

kaftan *or* **caftan** (ˈkæftæn, -ˌtɑːn) *n.* **1.** a long coatlike garment, usually worn with a belt and made of rich fabric, worn in the East. **2.** an imitation of this, worn, esp. by women, in the West, consisting of a loose dress with long wide sleeves. [C16: from Turkish *qaftān*]

kagoul *or* **kagoule** (kəˈguːl) *n.* variant spellings of **cagoule.**

kagu (ˈkɑːguː) *n.* a crested nocturnal bird, *Rhynochetos jubatus,* with a red bill and greyish plumage: occurs only in New Caledonia and is nearly extinct: family *Rhynochetidae,* order *Gruiformes* (cranes, rails, etc.). [native name in New Caledonia]

kahawai (ˈkɑːhəˌwaɪ) *n.* a large food and game fish of Australian and New Zealand coastal waters, *Arripis trutta,* that is greenish grey to silvery underneath and spotted with brown: resembles a salmon but is in fact a marine perch. Also called: **Australian salmon.** [Maori]

kahikatea (ˌkaɪkəˈtɪə) *n.* a tall New Zealand coniferous tree, *Podocarpus dacrydioides,* valued for its timber and resin. Also called: **white pine.** [Maori]

kai (kaɪ) *n. N.Z.* food. [Maori, from Melanesian pidgin *kaikai*]

kaiak (ˈkaɪæk) *n.* a variant of **kayak.**

kaif (kaɪf) *n.* a variant of **kif.**

kaik (kaɪk) *n. N.Z.* the South Island dialect word for **kainga.**

kail (keɪl) *n.* a variant spelling of **kale.**

kailyard (ˈkeɪlˌjɑːd) *n.* a variant spelling of **kaleyard.**

kain (keɪn) *n. History.* a variant spelling of **cain.**

kainga (ˈkaɪŋə) *n.* (in New Zealand) a Maori village or small settlement. Also called (on South Island): **kaik.** [Maori]

kainite (ˈkaɪnaɪt) *n.* a white mineral consisting of potassium chloride and magnesium sulphate: a fertilizer and source of potassium salts. Formula: $KCl.MgSO_4.3H_2O$. [C19: from German *Kainit,* from Greek *kainos* new + -ITE[1]]

kainogenesis (ˌkaɪnəʊˈdʒɛnɪsɪs) *n.* another name for **caenogenesis.** —**kainogenetic** (ˌkaɪnəʊdʒəˈnɛtɪk) *adj.* —**ˌkainogeˈnetically** *adv.*

Kaiser (ˈkaɪzə) *n.* (*sometimes not cap.*) *History.* **1.** any German emperor, esp. Wilhelm II (1888–1918). **2.** *Obsolete.* any Austro-Hungarian emperor. [C16: from German, ultimately from Latin *Caesar* emperor, from the cognomen of Gaius Julius CAESAR] —**ˈkaiserdom** *or* **ˈkaiserism** *n.*

kaka (ˈkɑːkə) *n.* a New Zealand parrot, *Nestor meridionalis,* with a long compressed bill. [C18: from Maori, perhaps imitative of its call]

kaka beak *n.* an evergreen climbing shrub, *Clianthus puniceus,* having pinnate leaves and clusters of bright red flowers in the shape of a parrot's beak. It is native to New Zealand but now rare except in cultivation. Also called: **red kowhai.**

kakapo (ˈkɑːkəˌpəʊ) *n., pl.* **-pos.** a ground-living nocturnal parrot, *Strigops habroptilus,* of New Zealand, resembling an owl. [C19: from Maori, literally: night kaka]

kakemono (ˌkækɪˈməʊnəʊ) *n., pl.* **-nos.** a Japanese paper or silk wall hanging, usually long and narrow, with a picture or inscription on it and a roller at the bottom. [C19: from Japanese, from *kake* hanging + *mono* thing]

kaki (ˈkɑːkɪ) *n., pl.* **kakis.** another name for **Japanese persimmon.** [Japanese]

kala-azar (ˌkɑːləəˈzɑː) *n.* a tropical infectious disease caused by the protozoan *Leishmania donovani* in the liver, spleen, etc., characterized by fever and weight loss; visceral leishmaniasis. [from Assamese *kālā* black + *āzār* disease]

kalanchoe (ˌkælənˈkəʊɪ) *n.* any plant of the tropical succulent genus *Kalanchoe,* grown as pot plants for their small bright red or white flowers, sometimes scented, and their dark shiny leaves: family *Crassulaceae.* [New Latin, from the Chinese name of one of the species]

kalashnikov (ˌkəˈlæʃnɪˌkɒf) *n.* a Russian-made sub-machine gun, used esp. by terrorists and guerrillas. [C20: from Russian]

kale *or* **kail** (keɪl) *n.* **1.** a cultivated variety of cabbage, *Brassica oleracea acephala,* with crinkled leaves: used as a potherb. See also **collard.** **2.** *Scot.* a cabbage. **3.** *U.S. slang.* money. ~Compare (for senses 1, 2) **sea kale.** [Old English *cāl;* see COLE]

kaleidoscope (kəˈlaɪdəˌskəʊp) *n.* **1.** an optical toy for producing symmetrical patterns by multiple reflections in inclined mirrors enclosed in a tube. Loose pieces of coloured glass, paper, etc., are placed between transparent plates at the far end of the tube, which is rotated to change the pattern. **2.** any complex pattern of frequently changing shapes and colours. **3.** a complicated set of circumstances. [C19: from Greek *kalos* beautiful + *eidos* form + -SCOPE] —**kaleidoscopic** (kəˌlaɪdəˈskɒpɪk) *adj.* —**kaˌleidoˈscopically** *adv.*

kalends (ˈkælɪndz) *pl. n.* a variant spelling of **calends.**

kaleyard *or* **kailyard** (ˈkeɪlˌjɑːd; *Scot.* -ˌjard) *n. Scot.* a vegetable garden. [C19: literally: cabbage garden]

kali (ˈkælɪ, ˈkeɪ-) *n.* another name for **saltwort** (sense 1).

kalian (kælˈjɑːn) *n.* another name for **hookah.** [C19: from Persian, from Arabic *qalyān*]

kalif (ˈkeɪlɪf, ˈkæl-) *n.* a variant spelling of **caliph.**

Kaliyuga (ˌkɑːlɪˈjuːgə) *n.* (in Hindu mythology) the fourth (present) age of the world, characterized by total decadence.

kalmia (ˈkælmɪə) *n.* any evergreen ericaceous shrub of the North American genus *Kalmia,* having showy clusters of white or pink flowers. See also: **mountain laurel.** [C18: named after Peter *Kalm* (1715–79), Swedish botanist and pupil of Linnaeus]

Kalmuck ('kælmʌk) *or* **Kalmyk** ('kælmɪk) *n.* **1.** (*pl.* **-mucks, -muck** *or* **-myks, -myk**) a member of a Mongoloid people of Buddhist tradition, who migrated from NE China in the 17th century. **2.** the language of this people, belonging to the Mongolic branch of the Altaic family.

kalong ('kɑːlɒŋ) *n.* any fruit bat of the genus *Pteropus;* a flying fox. [Javanese]

kalpa ('kælpə) *n.* (in Hindu cosmology) a period in which the universe experiences a cycle of creation and destruction. [C18: Sanskrit]

kalpak ('kælpæk) *n.* a variant spelling of **calpac.**

kalsomine ('kælsəˌmaɪn, -mɪn) *n.* a variant of **calcimine.**

kamacite ('kæməˌsaɪt) *n.* an alloy of iron and nickel, occurring in meteorites. [C19: from (obsolete) German *Kamacit,* from Greek *kamax* shaft, pole + -ITE[1]]

kamala (kə'mɑːlə, 'kæmələ) *n.* **1.** an East Indian euphorbiaceous tree, *Mallotus philippinensis.* **2.** a powder obtained from the seed capsules of this tree, used as a dye and formerly as a worm powder. [C19: from Sanskrit, probably of Dravidian origin; compare Kanarese *kōmale*]

Kamasutra (ˌkɑːmə'suːtrə) *n.* **the.** an ancient Hindu text on erotic pleasure and other topics. [Sanskrit: book on love, from *kāma* love + *sūtra* thread]

kame (keɪm) *n.* an irregular mound or ridge of gravel, sand, etc., deposited by water derived from melting glaciers. [C19: Scottish and northern English variant of COMB]

Kamerad *German.* (kamə'raːt; *English* 'kæməˌrɑːd) *n.* a shout of surrender, used by German soldiers. [German: COMRADE]

kamikaze (ˌkæmɪ'kɑːzɪ) *n.* (*often cap.*) **1.** (in World War II) one of a group of Japanese pilots who performed suicidal missions by crashing their aircraft, loaded with explosives, into an enemy target, esp. a ship. **2.** an aircraft used for such a mission. **3.** (*modifier*) (of an action) undertaken or (of a person) undertaking an action in the knowledge that it will result in the death of the person performing it in order that maximum damage may be inflicted on an enemy: *a kamikaze attack; a kamikaze bomber.* **4.** (*modifier*) extremely foolhardy and possibly self-defeating. [C20: from Japanese, from *kami* divine + *kaze* wind]

kamilaroi ('kæmələrɔɪ) *n.* an Australian Aboriginal language formerly used in NW New South Wales.

kampong ('kæmpɒŋ, kæm'pɒŋ) *n.* (in Malaysia) a village. [C19: from Malay]

kamseen (kæm'siːn) *or* **kamsin** ('kæmsɪn) *n.* variants of **khamsin.**

Kan. *abbrev. for* Kansas.

kana ('kɑːnə) *n.* the Japanese syllabary, which consists of two written varieties. See **hiragana, katakana.** [C18: from Japanese, literally: borrowed or provisional letters; compare KANJI, which are regarded as real letters]

Kanak (kə'næk) *n.* a native or inhabitant of New Caledonia who seeks independence from France. [C20: from Hawaiian: man]

Kanaka (kə'nækə, 'kænəkə) *n.* **1.** (esp. in Hawaii) a native Hawaiian. **2.** (*often not cap.*) *Austral.* any native of the South Pacific islands, esp. (formerly) one abducted to work in Australia. [C19: from Hawaiian: man, human being]

kanamycin (ˌkænə'maɪsɪn) *n.* an antibiotic obtained from the soil bacterium *Streptomyces kanamyceticus,* used in the treatment of various infections, esp. those caused by Gram-negative bacteria. Formula: $C_{18}H_{36}N_4O_{11}$. [C20: from New Latin *kanamyceticus*]

Kanarese *or* **Canarese** (ˌkænə'riːz) *n.* **1.** (*pl.* **-rese**) a member of a people of S India living chiefly in Kanara, a region in the southwest. **2.** the language of this people; Kannada.

kanga *or* **khanga** ('kɑːŋgɑː) *n.* a piece of gaily decorated thin cotton cloth used as a garment by women in E Africa. [from Swahili]

kangaroo (ˌkæŋgə'ruː) *n., pl.* **-roos. 1.** any large herbivorous marsupial of the genus *Macropus* and related genera, of Australia and New Guinea, having large powerful hind legs, used for leaping, and a long thick tail: family *Macropodidae.* See also **rat kangaroo, tree kangaroo. 2.** (*usually pl.*) *Stock Exchange.* an Australian share, esp. in mining, land, or a tobacco company. ~*vb.* **-roos, -rooing, -rooed. 3.** *Informal.* (of a car) to move forward or to cause (a car) to move forward with short sudden jerks, as a result of improper use of the clutch. [C18: probably from a native Australian language] —ˌ**kanga'roo-**ˌ**like** *adj.*

kangaroo closure *n. Parliamentary procedure.* a form of closure in which the chairman or speaker selects certain amendments for discussion and excludes others. Compare **guillotine** (sense 4).

kangaroo court *n.* an irregular court, esp. one set up by prisoners in a jail or by strikers to judge strikebreakers.

kangaroo dog *n.* an Australian breed of large rough-haired dog that resembles a greyhound and is bred to hunt kangaroos.

kangaroo grass *n.* a tall widespread Australian grass, *Themeda australis,* which is highly palatable to cattle and is used for fodder.

kangaroo paw *n.* any plant of the Australian genus *Anigozanthos,* having green-and-red hairy flowers: family *Haemodoraceae.*

kangaroo rat *n.* **1.** any small leaping rodent of the genus *Dipodomys,* related to the squirrels and inhabiting desert regions of North America, having a stocky body and very long hind legs and tails: family *Heteromyidae.* **2.** Also called: **kangaroo mouse.** any of several leaping murine rodents of the Australian genus *Notomys.*

kangaroo vine *n.* See **cissus.**

kangha ('kʌŋhə) *n.* the comb traditionally worn by Sikhs as a symbol of their religious and cultural loyalty: originally worn to keep the hair clean. See also **five Ks.** [Punjabi *kanghā*]

kanji ('kændʒɪ, 'kɑːn-) *n., pl.* **-ji** *or* **-jis. 1.** a Japanese writing system using characters mainly derived from Chinese ideograms. **2.** a character in this system. [Japanese, from Chinese *han* Chinese + *zi* character]

Kannada ('kɑːnədə, 'kæn-) *n.* a language of S India belonging to the Dravidian family of languages: the state language of Karnataka, also spoken in Madras and Maharashtra. Also called: **Kanarese.**

Kans. *abbrev. for* Kansas.

kantar (kæn'tɑː) *n.* a unit of weight used in E Mediterranean countries, equivalent to 100 pounds or 45 kilograms but varying from place to place. [C16: from Arabic *qinṭār,* from Late Greek *kentēnarion* weight of a hundred pounds, from Late Latin *centēnārium,* from *centum* hundred]

Kantian ('kæntɪən) *adj.* (of a philosophical theory) derived from or analogous to a position of Immanuel Kant (1724–1804), German philosopher, esp. his doctrines that there are synthetic a priori propositions which order our experience but are not derived from it, that metaphysical conclusions can be inferred from the nature of possible experience, that duty is to be done for its own sake and not as a means to any other end, and that there is a world of things-in-themselves to be distinguished from mere phenomena. See also **transcendental argument, transcendental idealism, categorical imperative, noumenon.** —'**Kantian**ˌ**ism** *or* '**Kantism** *n.*

KANU ('kɑːnuː) *n. acronym for* Kenya African National Union.

kanzu ('kænzuː) *n.* a long garment, usually white, with long sleeves, worn by E African men. [C20: from Swahili]

kaoliang (ˌkeɪəʊlɪ'æŋ) *n.* any of various E Asian varieties of the sorghum *Sorghum vulgare.* [from Chinese *kao* tall + *liang* grain]

kaolin *or* **kaoline** ('keɪəlɪn) *n.* a fine white clay used for the manufacture of hard-paste porcelain and bone china and in medicine as a poultice and gastrointestinal absorbent. Also called: **china clay, china stone.** [C18: from French, from Chinese *Kaoling* Chinese mountain where supplies for Europe were first obtained, from *kao* high + *ling* hill] —ˌ**kao'linic** *adj.* —ˌ**kaolin'ize** *vb.*

kaolinite ('keɪəlɪˌnaɪt) *n.* a white or grey clay mineral consisting of hydrated aluminium silicate in triclinic crystalline form, the main constituent of kaolin. Formula: $Al_2Si_2O_5(OH)_4$.

kaon ('keɪɒn) *n.* a meson that has a positive or negative charge and a rest mass of about 996 electron masses, or no charge and a rest mass of 964 electron masses. Also called: **K-meson.** [C20: *ka* representing the letter *k* + (MES)ON]

kapellmeister (kæ'pɛlˌmaɪstə) *n., pl.* **-ter.** a variant spelling of **capellmeister.**

kaph (kɔːf, kɑːf; *Hebrew* kaf) *n.* the 11th letter of the Hebrew alphabet (כ or, at the end of a word, ך) transliterated as *k* or, when final, *kh.* [Hebrew, literally: palm of the hand]

kapok ('keɪpɒk) *n.* a silky fibre obtained from the hairs covering the seeds of a tropical bombacaceous tree, *Ceiba pentandra* (**kapok tree** or **silk-cotton tree**): used for stuffing pillows, etc., and for sound insulation. Also called: **silk cotton.** [C18: from Malay]

Kaposi's sarcoma (kæ'pəʊsɪz) *n.* a form of skin cancer found in Africans and more recently in victims of AIDS. [C20: named after Moritz Kohn *Kaposi* (1837–1902), Austrian dermatologist who first described the sores that characterize the disease]

kappa ('kæpə) *n.* the tenth letter in the Greek alphabet (Κ, κ), a consonant, transliterated as *c* or *k.* [Greek, of Semitic origin]

kaput (kæ'pʊt) *adj.* (*postpositive*) *Informal.* ruined, broken, or not functioning. [C20: from German *kaputt* done for, from French *être capot* to have made no tricks (literally: to be hoodwinked), from *capot* hooded cloak]

kara ('kʌrə) *n.* the steel bangle traditionally worn by Sikhs as a symbol of their religious and cultural loyalty, symbolizing unity with God: originally worn as a wristguard by swordsmen. See also **five Ks.** [Punjabi *karā*]

karabiner (ˌkærə'biːnə) *n. Mountaineering.* a metal clip with a spring for attaching to a piton, belay, etc. Also called: **snaplink, krab.** [shortened from German *Karabinerhaken,* literally: carbine hook, that is, one used to attach carbines to a belt]

Karaite ('kɛərəˌaɪt) *n.* **1.** a member of a Jewish sect originating in the 8th century A.D., which rejected the Talmud, favoured strict adherence to and a literal interpretation of the Bible, and attempted to deduce a code of life from it. ~*adj.* **2.** of, relating to, or designating the Karaite sect. [C18: from Hebrew *qārāīm* members of the sect, scripturalists, from *qārā* to read]

Kara-Kalpak (kə'rɑːkəl'pɑːk) *n.* **1.** (*pl.* **-paks** *or* **-pak**) a member of a Mongoloid people of central Asia. **2.** the language of this people, belonging to the Turkic branch of the Altaic family.

karakul *or* **caracul** ('kærək[ə]l) *n.* **1.** a breed of sheep of central Asia having coarse black, grey, or brown hair: the lambs have soft curled usually black hair. **2.** the fur prepared from these lambs. ~See also **Persian lamb.** [C19: from Russian, from the name of a region in Bokhara where the sheep originated]

karaoke (ˌkɑːrəˈəʊkɪ) *n.* **a.** an entertainment of Japanese origin in which people take it in turns to sing well-known songs over a prerecorded backing tape. **b.** (*as modifier*): *a karaoke bar.* [from Japanese, from *kara* empty + *ōkesutora* orchestra]

karat (ˈkærət) *n.* the usual U.S. and Canadian spelling of **carat** (sense 2).

karate (kəˈrɑːtɪ) *n.* **a.** a traditional Japanese system of unarmed combat, employing smashes, chops, kicks, etc., made with the hands, feet, elbows, or legs. **b.** (*as modifier*): *karate chop.* [Japanese, literally: empty hand, from *kara* empty + *te* hand]

karateka (kəˈrɑːtɪˌkæ) *n.* a competitor or expert in karate. [Japanese; see KARATE]

Karelian (kəˈriːlɪən) *adj.* **1.** of or relating to Karelia, a region of NE Europe in Russia, or to its people or their language. ~*n.* **2.** a native or inhabitant of Karelia. **3.** the dialect of Finnish spoken in Karelia.

Karen (kəˈrɛn) *n.* **1.** (*pl.* **-rens** *or* **-ren**) a member of a Thai people of Burma. **2.** the language of this people, probably related to Thai and belonging to the Sino-Tibetan family.

Karitane (ˌkærɪˈtɑːnɪ) *n.* short for **Karitane nurse.**

Karitane hospital *n. N.Z.* a hospital for young babies and their mothers. [from *Karitane,* a town on South Island, New Zealand, headquarters of the Plunket Society]

Karitane nurse *n. N.Z.* a nurse trained in the care of young babies and their mothers according to the principles of the Plunket Society. Often shortened to **Karitane.**

karma (ˈkɑːmə) *n.* **1.** *Hinduism, Buddhism.* the principle of retributive justice determining a person's state of life and the state of his reincarnations as the effect of his past deeds. **2.** *Theosophy.* the doctrine of inevitable consequence. **3.** destiny or fate. [C19: from Sanskrit: action, effect, from *karoti* he does] —ˈ**karmic** *adj.*

Karmen vortex street (ˈkɑːmən) *n.* a regular stream of vortices shed from a body placed in a fluid stream: investigated by Karmen who advanced a formula for the frequency of the shed vortices in terms of the stream velocity and the dimensions of the body. See also **vortex street.** [named after Theodore Von *Karmen* (1881–1963), Hungarian-born engineer]

Karnatak music (kəˈnɑːtək) *n.* the classical music of South India. [named after *Karnataka,* Indian state]

Karoo *or* **Karroo** (kəˈruː) *n.* **1.** a period or rock system in Southern Africa equivalent to the period or system extending from the Upper Carboniferous to the Lower Jurassic: divided into **Lower** and **Upper Karoo.** ~*adj.* **2.** of, denoting, or formed in the Karoo period. [C18: from Afrikaans *karo,* probably from Hottentot *garo* desert]

kaross (kəˈrɒs) *n.* a garment of skins worn by indigenous peoples in southern Africa. [C18: from Afrikaans *karos,* perhaps from Dutch *kuras,* from French *cuirasse* CUIRASS]

karri (ˈkɑːrɪ) *n., pl.* **-ris.** **1.** an Australian eucalyptus tree, *Eucalyptus diversifolia.* **2.** the durable wood of this tree, used esp. for construction. [from a native Australian language]

karst (kɑːst) *n.* (*modifier*) denoting the characteristic scenery of a limestone region, including underground streams, gorges, etc. [C19: German, from *Karst,* limestone plateau near Trieste] —ˈ**karstic** *adj.*

kart (kɑːt) *n.* a light low-framed vehicle with small wheels and engine used for recreational racing (**karting**). Also called: **go-cart, go-kart.**

karyo- *or* **caryo-** *combining form.* indicating the nucleus of a cell: *karyogamy.* [from New Latin, from Greek *karuon* kernel, nut]

karyogamy (ˌkærɪˈɒgəmɪ) *n. Biology.* the fusion of two gametic nuclei during fertilization. —**karyogamic** (ˌkærɪəˈgæmɪk) *adj.*

karyogram (ˈkærɪəʊˌgræm) *n.* a diagram or photograph of the chromosomes of a cell, arranged in homologous pairs and in a numbered sequence. Also called: **idiogram.**

karyokinesis (ˌkærɪəʊkɪˈniːsɪs, -kaɪ-) *n.* another name for **mitosis.** [C19: from KARYO- + Greek *kinēsis* movement] —**karyokinetic** (ˌkærɪəʊkɪˈnɛtɪk, -kaɪ-) *adj.*

karyology (ˌkærɪˈɒlədʒɪ) *n.* the study of cell nuclei, esp. with reference to the structure of the chromosomes. —ˌ**kary**ˈ**ologist** *n.*

karyolymph (ˈkærɪəʊˌlɪmf) *n.* the liquid portion of the nucleus of a cell.

karyolysis (ˌkærɪˈɒlɪsɪs) *n. Cytology.* the disintegration of a cell nucleus, which occurs on death of the cell. [C20: from Greek, from *karyon* a nut + -LYSIS] —**karyolytic** (ˌkærɪəˈlɪtɪk) *adj.*

karyoplasm (ˈkærɪəʊˌplæzəm) *n.* another name for **nucleoplasm.** —ˌ**karyo**ˈ**plasmic** *adj.*

karyosome (ˈkærɪəʊˌsəʊm) *n.* **1.** any of the dense aggregates of chromatin in the nucleus of a cell: thought to be thickened segments of chromosomes. **2.** the nucleus of a cell.

karyotin (ˌkærɪˈəʊtɪn) *n.* a less common word for **chromatin.** [from KARYO- + (CHROMA)TIN]

karyotype (ˈkærɪəˌtaɪp) *n.* **1.** the appearance of the chromosomes in a somatic cell of an individual or species, with reference to their number, size, shape, etc. ~*vb.* (*tr.*) **2.** to determine the karyotype of (a cell). —**karyotypic** (ˌkærɪəˈtɪpɪk) *or* ˌ**karyo**ˈ**typical** *adj.*

kasbah *or* **casbah** (ˈkæzbɑː) *n.* (*sometimes cap.*) **1.** the citadel of any of various North African cities. **2.** the quarter in which a kasbah is located. Compare **medina.** [from Arabic *kāsbā* citadel]

kasha (ˈkɑːʃə) *n.* a dish originating in Eastern Europe, consisting of boiled or baked buckwheat. [from Russian]

kasher *Hebrew.* (ˈkɑːʃə) *vb.* (*tr.*) *Judaism.* to make fit for use; render kosher: for instance, to remove excess blood from (meat) by the prescribed process of washing and salting, or to remove all trace of previous nonkosher substances from (a utensil) by heating, immersion, etc. See also **kosher.** [see KOSHER]

kashmir (ˈkæʃmɪə) *n.* a variant spelling of **cashmere.**

Kashmir goat (kæʃˈmɪə) *n.* a Himalayan breed of goat having an undercoat of silky wool from which cashmere wool is obtained.

Kashmiri (kæʃˈmɪərɪ) *adj.* **1.** of or relating to Kashmir, a region of SW central Asia, or to its people or their language. ~*n.* **2.** (*pl.* **-miris** *or* **-miri**) a member of the people of Kashmir. **3.** the state language of Kashmir, belonging to the Dardic group of the Indo-European family of languages. —**Kash**ˈ**mirian** *adj., n.*

kashruth *or* ***kashrut*** *Hebrew.* (kaʃˈruːt) *n.* **1.** the condition of being fit for ritual use in general. **2.** the system of dietary laws which require ritual slaughter, the removal of excess blood from meat, and the complete separation of milk and meat, and prohibit such foods as pork and shellfish. ~See also **kosher** (sense 1). [literally: appropriateness, fitness]

kat *or* **khat** (kæt, kɑːt) *n.* a white-flowered evergreen shrub, *Catha edulis,* of Africa and Arabia, whose leaves have narcotic properties and are chewed or prepared as a drink. [C19: from Arabic *qāt*]

kata (ˈkætə) *n.* an exercise consisting of a sequence of the specific movements of a martial art, used in training and designed to show skill in technique. [C20: Japanese, literally: shape, pattern]

kata- *prefix.* a variant of **cata-.**

katabasis (kəˈtæbəsɪs) *n., pl.* **-ses** (-ˌsiːz). **1.** the retreat of the Greek mercenaries of Cyrus the Younger, after his death at Cunaxa, from the Euphrates to the Black Sea in 401–400 B.C. under the leadership of Xenophon: recounted in his *Anabasis.* Compare **anabasis. 2.** *Literary.* a retreat. [C19: from Greek: a going down, from *katabainein* to go down]

katabatic (ˌkætəˈbætɪk) *adj.* (of winds) blowing downhill through having become denser with cooling, esp. at night when heat is lost from the earth's surface. Compare **anabatic.**

katabolism (kəˈtæbəˌlɪzəm) *n.* a variant spelling of **catabolism.** —**katabolic** (ˌkætəˈbɒlɪk) *adj.* —ˌ**kata**ˈ**bolically** *adv.*

katakana (ˌkɑːtəˈkɑːnə) *n.* one of the two systems of syllabic writing employed for the representation of Japanese, based on Chinese ideograms. It is used mainly for foreign or foreign-derived words. [Japanese, from *kata* side + KANA]

Kathak (ˈkʌtək) *n.* a form of N Indian classical dancing that tells a story. [Bengali: narrator, from Sanskrit *kathayati* he tells]

Kathakali (ˌkɑːθəˈkɑːlɪ) *n. pl.* **-lis.** a form of dance drama of S India using mime and based on Hindu literature. [from Malayalam, from *katha* story + *kali* play]

Katharevusa *or* **Katharevousa** (ˌkɑːθəˈrɛvəˌsɑː) *n.* a literary style of Modern Greek, derived from the Attic dialect of Ancient Greek and including many archaic features. Compare **Demotic.**

katharometer (ˌkæθəˈrɒmɪtə) *n. Chem.* an instrument used for the analysis of gases by measurement of thermal conductivity.

katipo (ˈkætɪˌpəʊ, ˈkɑːd-) *n., pl.* **-pos.** a small venomous spider, *Latrodectus katipo,* of New Zealand, commonly black with a red or orange stripe on the abdomen. [Maori]

katydid (ˈkeɪtɪˌdɪd) *n.* any typically green long-horned grasshopper of the genus *Microcentrum* and related genera, living among the foliage of trees in North America. [C18: of imitative origin]

katzenjammer (ˈkætsənˌdʒæmə) *n. Chiefly U.S.* **1.** a confused uproar. **2.** a hangover. [German, literally: hangover, from *Katzen* cats + *jammer* misery, wailing]

kauri (ˈkaʊrɪ) *n., pl.* **-ris.** **1.** a New Zealand coniferous tree, *Agathis australis,* with oval leaves and round cones, cultivated for wood and resin: family *Araucariaceae.* **2.** the wood or resin of this tree. [C19: Maori]

kauri gum *n.* a hard resin from the kauri tree, found usually as a fossil in the soil where an extinct tree once grew: used chiefly in making varnishes.

kava (ˈkɑːvə) *n.* **1.** a Polynesian shrub, *Piper methysticum:* family *Piperaceae.* **2.** a drink prepared from the aromatic roots of this shrub. [C18: from Polynesian (Tongan): bitter]

kawakawa (ˈkɑːwəˌkɑːwə) *n.* an aromatic shrub or small tree of New Zealand, *Macropiper excelsum:* held to be sacred by the Maoris. Also called: **peppertree.** [Maori]

Kawasaki's disease (ˌkæwəˈsækɪ) *n.* a disease of children that causes a rash, fever, and swelling of the lymph nodes and often damages the heart muscle. [C20: named after T. *Kawasaki,* Japanese physician who first described it]

kayak *or* **kaiak** (ˈkaɪæk) *n.* **1.** a small light canoe-like boat used by Eskimos, consisting of a light frame covered with watertight animal skins. **2.** a fibreglass or canvas-covered canoe of similar design. [C18: from Eskimo (Greenland dialect)]

kayo *or* **KO** (ˈkeɪˈəʊ) *n., pl.* **kayos,** *vb.,* **kayoes** *or* **kayos, kayoing, kayoed.** *Boxing, slang.* another term for **knockout** or **knock out.** [C20: from the initial letters of *knock out*]

kazachok (ˌkɑːzəˈtʃɒk) *n.* a Russian folk dance in which the performer executes high kicks from a squatting position. [Russian]

Kazakh *or* **Kazak** (kəˈzɑːk, kɑː-) *n.* **1.** (*pl.* **-zakhs** *or* **-zaks**) a member of a traditionally Muslim Mongoloid people of the former Soviet republic of Kazakhstan. **2.** the language of this people, belonging to the Turkic branch of the Altaic family.
kazoo (kəˈzuː) *n., pl.* **-zoos.** a cigar-shaped musical instrument of metal or plastic with a membranous diaphragm of thin paper that vibrates with a nasal sound when the player hums into it. [C20: probably imitative of the sound produced]
kb *abbrev. for* kilobar.
KB (in Britain) *abbrev. for:* **1.** King's Bench. **2.** Knight Bachelor. **3.** *Computer technol.* kilobyte. **4.** *Chess. symbol for* king's bishop.
KBE *abbrev. for* Knight (Commander of the Order) of the British Empire.
KBP *Chess. symbol for* king's bishop's pawn.
kbyte *Computer technol. abbrev. for* kilobyte.
kc *abbrev. for* kilocycle.
KC (in Britain) *abbrev. for* **1.** King's Counsel. **2.** Kennel Club.
kcal *abbrev. for* kilocalorie.
KCB *abbrev. for* Knight Commander of the Bath (a Brit. title).
KCMG *abbrev. for* Knight Commander (of the Order) of St Michael and St George (a Brit. title).
Kčs. *abbrev. for* koruna. [Czech *koruna československá*]
KCVO *abbrev. for* Knight Commander of the Royal Victorian Order (a Brit. title).
KD *or* **k.d.** *Commerce. abbrev. for* knocked down: indicating furniture, machinery, etc., in separate parts.
KE *abbrev. for* kinetic energy.
kea (ˈkeɪə) *n.* a large New Zealand parrot, *Nestor notabilis,* with brownish-green plumage. [C19: from Maori, imitative of its call]
kebab (kəˈbæb) *n.* a dish consisting of small pieces of meat, tomatoes, onions, etc., threaded onto skewers and grilled, generally over charcoal. Also called: **shish kebab, kabob, cabob.** [C17: via Urdu from Arabic *kabāb* roast meat]
Kechua (ˈkɛtʃwə) *n.* a variant of **Quechua.**
keck[1] (kɛk) *vb.* (*intr.*) *Chiefly U.S.* **1.** to retch or feel nausea. **2.** to feel or express disgust. [C17: of imitative origin]
keck[2] (kɛk) *n.* another name for **cow parsnip** and **cow parsley.** [C17: from KEX, which was mistaken as a plural (as if *kecks*)]
ked (kɛd) *n.* See **sheep ked.** [C16: of unknown origin]
keddah (ˈkɛdə) *n.* a variant spelling of **kheda.**
kedge (kɛdʒ) *Nautical.* ~*vb.* **1.** to draw (a vessel) along by hauling in on the cable of a light anchor that has been dropped at some distance from it, or (of a vessel) to be drawn in this fashion. ~*n.* **2.** a light anchor, used esp. for kedging. [C15: from *caggen* to fasten]
kedgeree (ˌkɛdʒəˈriː) *n. Chiefly Brit.* a dish consisting of rice, cooked flaked fish, and hard-boiled eggs. [C17: from Hindi *khicarī,* from Sanskrit *khiccā,* of obscure origin]
keef (kiːf) *n.* a variant spelling of **kif.**
keek (kiːk) *n., vb.* a Scot. word for **peep**[1]. [C18: probably from Middle Dutch *kīken* to look]
keel[1] (kiːl) *n.* **1.** one of the main longitudinal structural members of a vessel to which the frames are fastened and that may extend into the water to provide lateral stability. **2. on an even keel.** well-balanced; steady. **3.** any structure corresponding to or resembling the keel of a ship, such as the central member along the bottom of an aircraft fuselage. **4.** *Biology.* a ridgelike part; carina. **5.** a poetic word for **ship.** ~*vb.* **6.** to capsize. ~See also **keel over.** [C14: from Old Norse *kjölr;* related to Middle Dutch *kiel,* KEEL[2]] —ˈ**keel-less** *adj.*
keel[2] (kiːl) *n. Eastern English dialect.* **1.** a flat-bottomed vessel, esp. one used for carrying coal. **2.** a measure of coal equal to about 21 tons. [C14 *kele,* from Middle Dutch *kiel;* compare Old English *cēol* ship]
keel[3] (kiːl) *n.* **1.** red ochre stain used for marking sheep, timber, etc. ~*vb.* (*tr.*) **2.** to mark with this stain. [Old English *cēlan,* from *cōl* COOL]
keel[4] (kiːl) *vb.* an archaic word for **cool** (esp. in the phrase **keel the pot**). [C15: probably from Scottish Gaelic *cīl*]
keel[5] (kiːl) *n.* a fatal disease of young ducks, characterized by intestinal bleeding. [C19: from KEEL[1]; see KEEL OVER]
keelage (ˈkiːlɪdʒ) *n.* a fee charged by certain ports to allow a ship to dock.
keel arch *n.* another name for **ogee arch.**
keelboat (ˈkiːlˌbəʊt) *n.* a river boat with a shallow draught and a keel, used for freight and moved by towing, punting, or rowing.
keelhaul (ˈkiːlˌhɔːl) *vb.* (*tr.*) **1.** to drag (a person) by a rope from one side of a vessel to the other through the water under the keel. **2.** to rebuke harshly. [C17: from Dutch *kielhalen;* see KEEL[1], HAUL]
keelie (ˈkiːlɪ) *n. Scot.* **1.** a kestrel. **2.** an urban ruffian; lower-class town or city dweller, esp. Glaswegian. [C19: of uncertain origin]
keel over *vb.* (*adv.*) **1.** to turn upside down; capsize. **2.** (*intr.*) *Informal.* to collapse suddenly.
keelson (ˈkɛlsən, ˈkiːl-) *or* **kelson** *n.* a longitudinal beam fastened to the keel of a vessel for strength and stiffness. [C17: probably from Low German *kielswin,* keel swine, ultimately of Scandinavian origin]
keen[1] (kiːn) *adj.* **1.** eager or enthusiastic. **2.** (*postpositive;* foll. by *on*) fond (of); devoted (to): *keen on a girl; keen on golf.* **3.** intellectually acute: *a keen wit.* **4.** (of sight, smell, hearing, etc.) capable of recognizing fine distinctions. **5.** having a sharp cutting edge or point. **6.** extremely cold and penetrating: *a keen wind.* **7.** intense or strong: *a keen desire.* **8.** *Chiefly Brit.* extremely low so as to be competitive: *keen prices.* **9.** *Slang, chiefly U.S. and Canadian.* very good. [Old English *cēne;* related to Old High German *kuoni* brave, Old Norse *koenn* wise; see CAN[1], KNOW] —ˈ**keenly** *adv.* —ˈ**keenness** *n.*
keen[2] (kiːn) *vb.* (*intr.*) **1.** to lament the dead. ~*n.* **2.** a dirge or lament for the dead. [C19: from Irish Gaelic *caoine,* from Old Irish *coīnim* I wail] —ˈ**keener** *n.*
keep (kiːp) *vb.* **keeps, keeping, kept** (kɛpt). **1.** (*tr.*) to have or retain possession of. **2.** (*tr.*) to have temporary possession or charge of: *keep my watch for me during the game.* **3.** (*tr.*) to store in a customary place: *I keep my books in the desk.* **4.** to remain or cause to remain in a specified state or condition: *keep the dog quiet; keep ready.* **5.** to continue or cause to continue: *keep the beat; keep in step.* **6.** (*tr.*) to have or take charge or care of: *keep the shop for me till I return.* **7.** (*tr.*) to look after or maintain for use, pleasure, etc.: *to keep chickens; keep two cars.* **8.** (*tr.*) to provide for the upkeep or livelihood of. **9.** (*tr.*) to support financially, esp. in return for sexual favours: *he keeps a mistress in the country.* **10.** to confine or detain or be confined or detained. **11.** to withhold or reserve or admit of withholding or reserving: *your news will keep till later.* **12.** (*tr.*) to refrain from divulging or violating: *to keep a secret; keep one's word.* **13.** to preserve or admit of preservation. **14.** (*tr.;* sometimes foll. by *up*) to observe with due rites or ceremonies: *to keep Christmas.* **15.** (*tr.*) to maintain by writing regular records in: *to keep a diary.* **16.** (when *intr.,* foll. by *in, on, to,* etc.) to stay in, on, or at (a place or position): *please keep your seats; keep to the path.* **17.** (*tr.*) to associate with (esp. in the phrase **keep bad company**). **18.** (*tr.*) to maintain in existence: *to keep court in the palace.* **19.** (*tr.*) *Chiefly Brit.* to have habitually in stock: *this shop keeps all kinds of wool.* **20. how are you keeping?** how are you? **21. keep tabs on.** *Informal.* to keep a watchful eye on. **22. keep track of.** See **track** (sense 14). **23. keep time.** See **time** (sense 42). **24. keep wicket.** to play as wicketkeeper in the game of cricket. **25. you can keep it.** *Informal.* I have no interest in what you are offering. ~*n.* **26.** living or support: *he must work for his keep.* **27.** *Archaic.* charge or care. **28.** Also called: **dungeon, donjon.** the main tower within the walls of a medieval castle or fortress. **29. for keeps.** *Informal.* **a.** completely; permanently. **b.** for the winner or possessor to keep permanently. ~See also **keep at, keep away, keep back, keep down, keep from, keep in, keep off, keep on, keep out, keep to, keep under, keep up.** [Old English *cēpan* to observe; compare Old Saxon *kapōn* to look, Old Norse *kōpa* to stare]
keep at *vb.* (*prep.*) **1.** (*intr.*) to persevere with or persist in. **2.** (*tr.*) to constrain (a person) to continue doing (a task).
keep away *vb.* (*adv.;* often foll. by *from*) **1.** to refrain or prevent from coming (near). **2.** to stop using, touching, etc.
keep back *vb.* (*adv.;* often foll. by *from*) **1.** (*tr.*) to refuse to reveal or disclose. **2.** to prevent, be prevented, or refrain from advancing, entering, etc.
keep down *vb.* (*adv., mainly tr.*) **1.** to repress; hold in submission. **2.** to restrain or control: *he had difficulty keeping his anger down.* **3.** to cause not to increase or rise: *prices were kept down for six months.* **4.** (*intr.*) not to show oneself to one's opponents; lie low. **5.** to cause (food) to stay in the stomach; not vomit.
keeper (ˈkiːpə) *n.* **1.** a person in charge of animals, esp. in a zoo. **2.** a person in charge of a museum, collection, or section of a museum. **3.** a person in charge of other people, such as a warder in a jail. **4.** See **goalkeeper, wicketkeeper, gamekeeper.** **5.** a person who keeps something. **6.** a device, such as a clip, for keeping something in place. **7.** a soft iron or steel bar placed across the poles of a permanent magnet to close the magnetic circuit when it is not in use. —ˈ**keeperless** *adj.* —ˈ**keeperˌship** *n.*
keeper ring *n.* another name for **guard ring.**
keep fit *n.* **a.** exercises designed to promote physical fitness if performed regularly. **b.** (*as modifier*): *keep-fit classes.*
keep from *vb.* (*prep.*) **1.** (foll. by a gerund) to prevent or restrain (oneself or another); refrain or cause to refrain. **2.** (*tr.*) to protect or preserve from.
keep in *vb.* (*mainly adv.*) **1.** (*intr.; also prep.*) to stay indoors. **2.** (*tr.*) to restrain (an emotion); repress. **3.** (*tr.*) to detain (a schoolchild) after hours as a punishment. **4.** (of a fire) to stay alight or to cause (a fire) to stay alight. **5.** (*tr., prep.*) to allow a constant supply of: *her prize money kept her in new clothes for a year.* **6. keep in with.** to maintain good relations with.
keeping (ˈkiːpɪŋ) *n.* **1.** conformity or harmony (esp. in the phrases **in** *or* **out of keeping**). **2.** charge or care: *valuables in the keeping of a bank.*
keepnet (ˈkiːpˌnɛt) *n.* a cylindrical net strung on wire hoops and sealed at one end, suspended in water by anglers to keep alive the fish they have caught.
keep off *vb.* **1.** to stay or cause to stay at a distance (from). **2.** (*prep.*) not to eat or drink or prevent from eating or drinking. **3.** (*prep.*) to avoid or cause to avoid (a topic). **4.** (*intr., adv.*) not to start: *the rain kept off all day.*
keep on *vb.* (*adv.*) **1.** to continue or persist in (doing something): *keep on running.* **2.** (*tr.*) to continue to wear. **3.** (*tr.*) to continue to employ: *the firm kept on only ten men.* **4.** (*intr.;* foll.

by *about*) to persist in talking (about). **5.** (*intr.*; foll. by *at*) to nag (a person).

keep out *vb.* (*adv.*) **1.** to remain or cause to remain outside. **2.** **keep out of. a.** to remain or cause to remain unexposed to: *keep out of the sun.* **b.** to avoid or cause to avoid: *the boss is in an angry mood, so keep out of his way.*

keepsake ('ki:pˌseɪk) *n.* a gift that evokes memories of a person or event with which it is associated.

keep to *vb.* (*prep.*) **1.** to adhere to or stand by or cause to adhere to or stand by: *to keep to a promise.* **2.** to confine or be confined to. **3.** **keep to oneself. a.** (*intr.*) to avoid the society of others. **b.** (*tr.*) to refrain from sharing or disclosing. **4.** **keep oneself to oneself.** to avoid the society of others.

keep under *vb.* **1.** to remain or cause to remain below (a surface). **2.** (*tr.*, *adv.*) to cause to remain unconscious. **3.** (*tr.*, *adv.*) to hold in submission.

keep up *vb.* (*adv.*) **1.** (*tr.*) to maintain (prices, one's morale) at the present level. **2.** (*intr.*) to maintain a pace or rate set by another. **3.** (*intr.*; often foll. by *with*) to remain informed: *to keep up with technological developments.* **4.** (*tr.*) to maintain in good condition. **5.** (*tr.*) to hinder (a person) from going to bed at night: *the excitement kept the children up well past their bedtime.* **6.** **keep it up.** to continue a good performance. **7.** **keep one's chin up.** to keep cheerful under difficult circumstances. **8.** **keep up with.** to remain in contact with, esp. by letter. **9.** **keep up with (the Joneses).** *Informal.* to compete with (one's neighbours) in material possessions, etc.

keeshond ('keɪsˌhɒnd, 'ki:s-) *n.*, *pl.* **-honds** *or* **-honden** (-ˌhɒndᵊn). a breed of dog of the spitz type with a shaggy greyish coat and tightly curled tail, originating in Holland. [C20: from Dutch, probably from *Kees* nickname for *Cornelis* Cornelius, from Latin + *hond* HOUND]

kef (kɛf) *n.* a variant of **kif.**

keffiyeh (kɛ'fi:jə), **kaffiyeh,** *or* **kufiyah** *n.* a cotton headdress worn by Arabs. [C19: from Arabic, perhaps from Late Latin *cofea* COIF]

keftedes (kɛf'tɛðɛs) *n.* a Greek dish of meatballs cooked with herbs and onions. [C20: from Modern Greek]

keg (kɛg) *n.* **1.** a small barrel with a capacity of between five and ten gallons. **2.** *Brit.* **a.** an aluminium container in which beer is transported and stored. **b.** Also called: **keg beer.** beer kept in a keg: it is infused with gas and served under pressure. [C17: variant of Middle English *kag*, of Scandinavian origin; related to Old Norse *kaggi* cask]

kegler ('kɛglə) *or* **kegeler** ('kɛgələ) *n. Informal, chiefly U.S.* a participant in a game of tenpin bowling. [from German, from *Kegel* pin, from Old High German *kegil* peg]

keister *or* **keester** ('ki:stə) *n. Slang, chiefly U.S.* **1.** the rump; buttocks. **2.** a suitcase, trunk, or box. [C20: of uncertain origin]

keitloa ('kaɪtləʊə, 'keɪt-) *n.* a southern African variety of the black two-horned rhinoceros, *Diceros bicornis.* [C19: from Tswana *khetlwa*]

Kekulé formula ('kɛkjəˌleɪ) *n.* a representation of the benzene molecule as six carbon atoms at the corners of a regular hexagon with alternate double and single bonds joining them and with one hydrogen atom bound to each carbon atom. See **benzene ring.** [C19: named after F. A. *Kekulé* von Stradonitz (1829–96), German chemist]

keloid *or* **cheloid** ('ki:lɔɪd) *n. Pathol.* a hard smooth pinkish raised growth of scar tissue at the site of an injury, tending to occur more frequently in dark-skinned races. [C19: from Greek *khēlē* claw] —**ke'loidal** *or* **che'loidal** *adj.*

kelp (kɛlp) *n.* **1.** any large brown seaweed, esp. any species of *Laminaria.* **2.** the ash of such seaweed, used as a source of iodine and potash. [C14: of unknown origin]

kelpie[1] *or* **kelpy** ('kɛlpɪ) *n.*, *pl.* **-pies.** an Australian breed of sheepdog, originally developed from Scottish collies, having a smooth coat of various colours and erect ears. [named after a particular specimen of the breed, c. 1870]

kelpie[2] ('kɛlpɪ) *n.* (in Scottish folklore) a water spirit in the form of a horse that drowned its riders. [C18: probably related to Scottish Gaelic *cailpeach* heifer, of obscure origin]

kelson ('kɛlsən) *n.* a variant of **keelson.**

kelt (kɛlt) *n.* a salmon that has recently spawned and is usually in poor condition. [C14: of unknown origin]

Kelt (kɛlt) *n.* a variant of **Celt.** —**'Keltic** *adj.* —**'Keltically** *adv.* —**'KeltiˌCism** *n.* —**'Kelticist** *or* **'Keltist** *n.*

kelter ('kɛltə) *n.* a variant of **kilter.**

kelvin ('kɛlvɪn) *n.* the basic SI unit of thermodynamic temperature; the fraction 1/273.16 of the thermodynamic temperature of the triple point of water. Symbol: K [named after William Thomson, 1st Baron *Kelvin* (1824–1907), British physicist]

Kelvin scale ('kɛlvɪn) *n.* a thermodynamic temperature scale based upon the efficiencies of ideal heat engines. The zero of the scale is absolute zero. Originally the degree was equal to that on the Celsius scale but it is now defined so that the triple point of water is exactly 273.16 kelvins. The International Practical Temperature Scale (1968) realizes the Kelvin scale over a wide range of temperatures. Compare **Rankine scale.**

kelyphitic rim *n. Geology.* a mineral shell enclosing another mineral in an igneous rock, formed by reaction of the interned mineral with the surrounding rock. [C19: from Greek *keluphos* pod + *-itic*; see -ITE[1]]

kemp (kɛmp) *n.* a coarse hair or strand of hair, esp. one in a fleece that resists dyeing. [C14: from Old Norse *kampr* beard, moustache] —**'kempy** *adj.*

kempt (kɛmpt) *adj.* (of hair) tidy; combed. See also **unkempt.** [C20: back formation from *unkempt;* originally past participle of dialect *kemb* to COMB]

ken (kɛn) *n.* **1.** range of knowledge or perception (esp. in the phrases **beyond** *or* **in one's ken**). ~*vb.* **kens, kenning, kenned** *or* **kent** (kɛnt). **2.** *Scot. and northern English dialect.* to know. **3.** *Scot. and northern English dialect.* to understand; perceive. **4.** (*tr.*) *Archaic.* to see. [Old English *cennan;* related to Old Norse *kenna* to perceive, Old High German *kennen* to make known; see CAN[1]]

Ken. *abbrev. for* Kentucky.

kenaf (kə'næf) *n.* another name for **ambary.** [from Persian]

Kendal green ('kɛndᵊl) *n.* **1.** a green woollen cloth, formerly worn by foresters. **2.** the colour of this cloth, produced by a dye obtained from the woad plant. See also **dyer's-greenweed.** [C14: from *Kendal*, NW England, where it originated]

kendo ('kɛndəʊ) *n.* the Japanese art of fencing with pliable bamboo staves or, sometimes, real swords: strict conventions are observed. [from Japanese]

kennel[1] ('kɛnᵊl) *n.* **1.** a hutlike shelter for a dog. U.S. name: **doghouse.** **2.** (*usually pl.*) an establishment where dogs are bred, trained, boarded, etc. **3.** the lair of a fox or other animal. **4.** a ramshackle house; hovel. **5.** a pack of hounds. ~*vb.* **-nels, -nelling, -nelled** *or U.S.* **-nels, -neling, -neled.** **6.** to put or go into a kennel; keep or stay in a kennel. [C14: from Old French *chenil*, from Vulgar Latin *canīle* (unattested), from Latin *canis* dog]

kennel[2] ('kɛnᵊl) *n. Archaic.* an open sewer or street gutter. [C16: variant of *cannel* CHANNEL[1]]

Kennelly-Heaviside layer ('kɛnəlɪ'hɛvɪˌsaɪd) *n.* See **E region.**

kenning ('kɛnɪŋ) *n.* a conventional metaphoric name for something, esp. in Old Norse and Old English poetry, such as Old English *bānhūs* (bone house) for "body." [C14: from Old Norse, from *kenna;* see KEN]

Kenny method *or* **treatment** ('kɛnɪ) *n.* a method of treating poliomyelitis by applying hot moist packs to the affected muscles alternated by passive and later active movement of the muscles. [C20: named after Sister Elizabeth *Kenny,* 1886–1952, Australian nurse who developed it]

keno, keeno, kino, *or* **quino** ('ki:no) *n. U.S. and Canadian.* a game of chance similar to bingo. [C19: of unknown origin]

kenogenesis (ˌki:nəʊ'dʒɛnɪsɪs) *n.* a secondary U.S. spelling of **caenogenesis.** —**kenogenetic** (ˌki:nəʊdʒə'nɛtɪk) *adj.* —ˌ**kenoge'netically** *adv.*

kenosis (kɪ'nəʊsɪs) *n. Christianity.* Christ's voluntary renunciation of certain divine attributes, in order to identify himself with mankind (Philippians 2:6–7). [C19: from Greek: an emptying, from *kenoun* to empty from *kenos* empty] —**kenotic** (kɪ'nɒtɪk) *adj.*, *n.*

kenspeckle ('kɛnˌspɛkᵊl) *adj. Scot.* easily seen or recognized. [C18: from dialect *kenspeck*, of Scandinavian origin; compare Old Norse *kennispecki* power of recognition; related to KEN]

kent (kɛnt) *vb.* a past tense and past participle of **ken.**

kente ('kɛntɪ) *n.* **1.** Also called: **kente cloth.** a brightly coloured handwoven cloth of Ghana, usually with some gold thread. **2.** the toga made of this cloth. [from a Ghanaian language, possibly Akan]

kentia ('kɛntɪə) *n.* a plant name formerly used to include palms now allotted to several different genera and still used commercially to denote the feather palm genus *Howea,* native to Lord Howe Island, popular as greenhouse or house plants for their decorative arching foliage: family *Palmaceae.* [named after W. *Kent* (fl. c. 1800), Dutch traveller and botanist]

Kentish ('kɛntɪʃ) *adj.* **1.** of or relating to Kent, a county of SE England. ~*n.* **2.** Also called: **Jutish.** the dialect of Old and Middle English that was spoken in Kent. See also **Anglian, West Saxon.**

Kentish glory *n.* a moth, *Endromis versicolora,* common in north and central Europe, having brown variegated front wings and, in the male, orange hindwings.

kentledge ('kɛntlɪdʒ) *n. Nautical.* scrap metal used as ballast in a vessel. [C17: perhaps from Old French *quintelage* ballast, from *quintal* hundredweight, ultimately from Arabic *qinṭār;* see KANTAR]

Kentucky bluegrass (kɛn'tʌkɪ) *n.* a Eurasian grass, *Poa pratensis,* grown for forage and naturalized throughout North America.

Kentucky coffee tree *n.* a North American leguminous tree, *Gymnocladus dioica,* whose seeds, in brown curved pulpy pods, were formerly used as a coffee substitute.

Kenyan ('kɛnjən) *adj.* **1.** of or relating to Kenya, a republic in E Africa, or to its people, customs, etc. ~*n.* **2.** a native or inhabitant of Kenya.

kep (kɛp) *vb.* **keps, kepping, keppit** ('kɛpɪt). (*tr.*) *Scot. and northern English dialect.* to catch. [from KEEP (in obsolete sense: to put oneself in the way of)]

kepi ('keɪpi:) *n.*, *pl.* **kepis.** a military cap with a circular top and a horizontal peak. [C19: from French *képi*, from German (Swiss dialect) *käppi* a little cap, from *kappe* CAP]

Kepler's laws ('kɛpləz) *pl. n.* three laws of planetary motion published by Johannes Kepler (1571–1630), German astronomer, between 1609 and 1619. The first states that the orbit of a planet describes an ellipse with the sun at one focus. The second states that, during one orbit, the straight line joining the sun and a planet sweeps out equal areas in equal times. The third states that the squares of the periods of any two planets are proportional to the cubes of their orbital major axes.
kept (kɛpt) *vb.* **1.** the past tense and past participle of **keep. 2. kept woman.** *Censorious.* a woman maintained by a man as his mistress.
keramic (kɪ'ræmɪk) *adj.* a rare variant of **ceramic.**
keramics (kɪ'ræmɪks) *n.* a rare variant of **ceramics.**
keratin ('kɛrətɪn) *or* **ceratin** *n.* a fibrous protein that occurs in the outer layer of the skin and in hair, nails, feathers, hooves, etc.
keratinize *or* **keratinise** (kɪ'rætɪˌnaɪz, 'kɛrətɪ-) *vb.* to become or cause to become impregnated with keratin. —**keˌratiniˈzation** *or* **keˌratiniˈsation** *n.*
keratitis (ˌkɛrə'taɪtɪs) *n.* inflammation of the cornea.
kerato- *or before a vowel* **kerat-** *combining form.* **1.** indicating horn or a horny substance: *keratin; keratogenous.* **2.** indicating the cornea: *keratoplasty.* [from Greek *kerat-, keras* horn]
keratogenous (ˌkɛrə'tɒdʒɪnəs) *adj.* developing or causing the growth of horny tissue.
keratoid ('kɛrəˌtɔɪd) *adj.* resembling horn; horny.
keratoplasty ('kɛrətəʊˌplæstɪ) *n., pl.* **-ties.** plastic surgery of the cornea, esp. involving corneal grafting. —ˌ**keratoˈplastic** *adj.*
keratose ('kɛrəˌtəʊs, -ˌtəʊz) *adj.* (esp. of certain sponges) having a horny skeleton.
keratosis (ˌkɛrə'təʊsɪs) *n. Pathol.* **1.** any skin condition marked by a horny growth, such as a wart. **2.** a horny growth.
keratotomy (ˌkɛrə'tɒtəmɪ) *n.* surgical incision of the cornea.
kerb *or U.S. and Canadian* **curb** (kɜːb) *n.* **1.** a line of stone or concrete forming an edge between a pavement and a roadway. ~*vb.* **2.** (*tr.*) to provide with or enclose with a kerb. [C17: from Old French *courbe* bent, from Latin *curvus;* see CURVE]
kerbaya ('kɛrbaja) *n.* a blouse worn by Malay women. [from Malay]
kerb crawling *n.* the act of driving slowly along the edge of the pavement seeking to entice someone into the car for sexual purposes. —**kerb crawler** *n.*
kerb drill *n.* a pedestrian's procedure for crossing a road safely, esp. as taught to children.
kerbing *or U.S. and Canadian* **curbing** ('kɜːbɪŋ) *n.* **1.** material used for a kerb. **2.** a less common word for **kerb** (sense 1).
kerb market *n. Stock Exchange.* **1.** an after-hours street market. **2.** a street market dealing in unquoted securities.
kerbstone *or U.S. and Canadian* **curbstone** ('kɜːbˌstəʊn) *n.* one of a series of stones that form a kerb.
kerb weight *n.* the weight of a motor car without occupants, luggage, etc.
kerchief ('kɜːtʃɪf) *n.* a piece of cloth worn tied over the head or around the neck. [C13: from Old French *cuevrechef,* from *covrir* to COVER + *chef* head; see CHIEF] —'**kerchiefed** *adj.*
kerf (kɜːf) *n.* the cut made by a saw, an axe, etc. [Old English *cyrf* a cutting; related to Old English *ceorfan* to CARVE]
kerfuffle, carfuffle, *or* **kurfuffle** (kə'fʌfᵊl) *n.* **1.** *Informal, chiefly Brit.* commotion; disorder; agitation. ~*vb.* **2.** (*tr.*) *Scot.* to put into disorder or disarray; ruffle or disarrange. [from Scottish *curfuffle, carfuffle,* from Scottish Gaelic *car* twist, turn + *fuffle* to disarrange]
kerma ('kɜːmə) *n. Physics.* the quotient of the sum of the initial kinetic energies of all the charged particles liberated by indirectly ionizing radiation in a volume element of a material divided by the mass of the volume element. The SI unit is the gray. [C20: *k*(inetic) *e*(nergy) *r*(eleased per unit) *ma*(ss)]
kermes ('kɜːmɪz) *n.* **1.** the dried bodies of female scale insects of the genus *Kermes,* esp. *K. ilices* of Europe and W Asia, used as a red dyestuff. **2.** a small evergreen Eurasian oak tree, *Quercus coccifera:* the host plant of kermes scale insects. [C16: from French *kermès,* from Arabic *qirmiz,* from Sanskrit *krmija-* red dye, literally: produced by a worm, from *krmi* worm + *ja-* produced]
kermis *or* **kirmess** ('kɜːmɪs) *n.* **1.** (formerly, esp. in Holland and Northern Germany) an annual country festival or carnival. **2.** *U.S. and Canadian.* a similar event, esp. one held to collect money for charity. [C16: from Middle Dutch *kercmisse,* from *kerc* church + *misse* MASS; originally a festival held to celebrate the dedication of a church]
kern[1] *or* **kerne** (kɜːn) *n.* **1.** the part of the character on a piece of printer's type that projects beyond the body. ~*vb.* **2.** (*tr.*) to furnish (a typeface) with a kern. [C17: from French *carne* corner of type, projecting angle, ultimately from Latin *cardō* hinge]
kern[2] (kɜːn) *n.* **1.** a lightly armed foot soldier in medieval Ireland or Scotland. **2.** a troop of such soldiers. **3.** *Archaic.* a loutish peasant. [C14: from Middle Irish *cethern* band of foot soldiers, from *cath* battle]
kern[3] (kɜːn) *n. Engineering.* the central area of a wall, column, etc., through which all compressive forces pass. [from German *Kern* core, heart]
kernel ('kɜːnᵊl) *n.* **1.** the edible seed of a nut or fruit within the shell or stone. **2.** the grain of a cereal, esp. wheat, consisting of the seed in a hard husk. **3.** the central or essential part of something. ~*vb.* **-nels, -nelling, -nelled** *or U.S.* **-nels, -neling, -neled. 4.** (*intr.*) *Rare.* to form kernels. [Old English *cyrnel* a little seed, from *corn* seed; see CORN[1]] —'**kernel-less** *adj.*
kernite ('kɜːnaɪt) *n.* a light soft colourless or white mineral consisting of a hydrated sodium borate in monoclinic crystalline form: an important source of borax and other boron compounds. Formula: $Na_2B_4O_7.4H_2O$. [C20: from *Kern* County, California, where it was found + -ITE[1]]
kernmantel rope ('kɜːnˌmæntᵊl) *n. Mountaineering.* a rope made of many straight nylon fibres within a plaited sheath; used for its tensile strength, freedom from twisting, and elasticity. [C20: from German *Kernmantel,* from *Kern* core + *Mantel* coat, casing]
Kero ('kɛrəʊ) *n. Austral. and N.Z.* short for **kerosene.**
kerogen ('kɛrədʒən) *n.* the solid organic material found in some rocks, such as oil shales, that produces hydrocarbons similar to petroleum when heated. [C20: from Greek *kērо(s)* wax + -GEN]
kerosene *or* **kerosine** ('kɛrəˌsiːn) *n.* **1.** another name (esp. U.S. and Canadian) for **paraffin** (sense 1). **2.** the general name for paraffin as a fuel for jet aircraft. [C19: from Greek *kēros* wax + -ENE]
▷**Usage.** the spelling *kerosine* is now the preferred form in technical and industrial usage.
Kerr effect (kɜː) *n.* **1.** Also called: **electro-optical effect.** the production of double refraction in certain transparent substances by the application of a strong electric field. **2.** Also called: **magneto-optical effect.** a slight elliptical polarization of plane polarized light when reflected from one of the poles of a strong magnet. [C19: named after John *Kerr* (1824–1907), Scottish physicist]
Kerry ('kɛrɪ) *n., pl.* **-ries.** a small black breed of dairy cattle, originally from Ireland. [C19: named after County *Kerry,* SW Ireland]
Kerry blue terrier *n.* an Irish breed of terrier with a soft silky wavy coat of a silvery-grey or smoky blue colour.
kersey ('kɜːzɪ) *n.* **1.** a smooth woollen cloth used for overcoats, etc. **2.** a twilled woollen cloth with a cotton warp. [C14: probably from *Kersey,* village in Suffolk]
kerseymere ('kɜːzɪˌmɪə) *n.* a fine soft woollen cloth of twill weave. [C18: from KERSEY + (CASSI)MERE]
kesh (keɪʃ) *n.* the beard and uncut hair, covered by the turban, traditionally worn by Sikhs as a symbol of their religious and cultural loyalty, symbolizing the natural life. See also **five Ks.** [Punjabi *keś*]
kestrel ('kɛstrəl) *n.* any of several small falcons, esp. the European *Falco tinnunculus,* that tend to hover against the wind and feed on small mammals on the ground. [C15: changed from Old French *cresserele,* from *cressele* rattle, from Vulgar Latin *crepicella* (unattested), from Latin *crepitāre* to crackle, from *crepāre* to rustle]
ketamine ('kɛtəmiːn) *n.* a drug, chemically related to PCP, that is used in medicine as a general anaesthetic, being administered by injection; cyclohexylamine.
ketch (kɛtʃ) *n.* a two-masted sailing vessel, fore-and-aft rigged, with a tall mainmast and a mizzen stepped forward of the rudderpost. Compare **yawl**[1] (sense 1). [C15 *cache,* probably from *cacchen* to hunt; see CATCH]
ketchup ('kɛtʃəp), **catchup,** *or* **catsup** *n.* any of various piquant sauces containing vinegar: *tomato ketchup.* [C18: from Chinese (Amoy) *kōetsiap* brine of pickled fish, from *kōe* seafood + *tsiap* sauce]
ketene ('kiːtiːn, 'kɛt-) *n.* a colourless irritating toxic gas used as an acetylating agent in organic synthesis. Formula: CH_2:CO. Also called: **ethonone.**
keto- *or before a vowel* **ket-** *combining form.* indicating that a chemical compound is a ketone or is derived from a ketone: *ketose; ketoxime.*
keto-enol tautomerism ('kiːtəʊ'iːnɒl) *n. Chem.* tautomerism in which the tautomers are an enol and a keto form. The change occurs by transfer of a hydrogen atom within the molecule.
keto form ('kiːtəʊ) *n.* the form of tautomeric compounds when they are ketones rather than enols. See **keto-enol tautomerism.**
ketogenic (ˌkiːtəʊ'dʒɛnɪk) *adj. Med.* forming or able to stimulate the production of ketone bodies: *a ketogenic diet.*
ketonaemia *or U.S.* **ketonemia** (ˌkiːtəʊ'niːmɪə) *n. Pathol.* an excess of ketone bodies in the blood.
ketone ('kiːtəʊn) *n.* any of a class of compounds with the general formula R'COR, where R and R' are alkyl or aryl groups. See also **acetone.** [C19: from German *Keton,* from *Aketon* ACETONE] —**ketonic** (kɪ'tɒnɪk) *adj.*
ketone body *n. Biochem.* any of three compounds (acetoacetic acid, 3-hydroxybutanoic acid, and acetone) produced when fatty acids are broken down in the liver to provide a source of energy. Excess ketone bodies are present in the blood and urine of people unable to use glucose as an energy source, as in diabetes and starvation. Also called: **acetone body.**
ketone group *n. Chem.* the functional group of ketones: a carbonyl group attached to the carbon atoms of two other organic groups.
ketonuria (ˌkiːtəʊ'njʊərɪə) *n. Pathol.* the presence of ketone bodies in the urine.
ketose ('kiːtəʊz) *n.* any monosaccharide that contains a ketone group.

ketosis (kɪˈtəʊsɪs) *n. Pathol.* the condition resulting from excess production of ketone bodies.

ketoxime (kiːˈtɒksiːm) *n.* an oxime formed by reaction between hydroxylamine and a ketone.

kettle (ˈkɛtᵊl) *n.* **1.** a metal container with a handle and spout for boiling water. **2.** any of various metal containers for heating liquids, cooking fish, etc. **3.** an open-topped refractory-lined steel vessel in which metals with low melting points are refined. **4.** short for **kettle hole.** [C13: from Old Norse *ketill;* related to Old English *cietel* kettle, Old High German *kezzil;* all ultimately from Latin *catillus* a little pot, from *catīnus* pot]

kettledrum (ˈkɛtᵊlˌdrʌm) *n.* a percussion instrument of definite pitch, consisting of a hollow bowl-like hemisphere covered with a skin or membrane, supported on a tripod or stand. The pitch may be adjusted by means of screws or pedals, which alter the tension of the skin. —**ˈkettleˌdrummer** *n.*

kettle hole *n.* a round hollow formed by the melting of a mass of buried ice. Often shortened to **kettle.**

kettle of fish *n.* **1.** a situation; state of affairs (often used ironically in the phrase **a pretty** or **fine kettle of fish**). **2.** case; matter for consideration: *that's quite a different kettle of fish.*

keV *abbrev. for* kilo-electronvolt.

kevel (ˈkɛvᵊl) *n.* **1.** *Nautical.* a strong bitt or bollard for securing heavy hawsers. **2.** *Building trades.* a hammer having an edged end and a pointed end, used for breaking and rough-shaping stone. [C14: from Old Northern French *keville,* from Latin *clāvicula* a little key, from *clāvis* key]

kewpie doll (ˈkjuːpɪ) *n. U.S. and Canadian.* **1.** any brightly coloured doll, commonly given as a prize at carnivals. **2.** (*caps.*) *Trademark.* a doll having rosy cheeks and a curl of hair on its head. [C20: *kewpie,* perhaps from *Cupid*]

kex (kɛks) *n.* **1.** any of several large hollow-stemmed umbelliferous plants, such as cow parsnip and chervil. **2.** the dried stalks of any of these plants. [C14: of obscure origin]

key[1] (kiː) *n.* **1.** a metal instrument, usually of a specifically contoured shape, that is made to fit a lock and, when rotated, operates the lock's mechanism. **2.** any instrument that is rotated to operate a valve, clock winding mechanism, etc. **3.** a small metal peg or wedge inserted into keyways. **4.** any of a set of levers operating a typewriter, computer, etc. **5.** any of the visible parts of the lever mechanism of a musical keyboard instrument that when depressed set in motion the action that causes the instrument to sound. **6. a.** Also called: **tonality.** any of the 24 major and minor diatonic scales considered as a corpus of notes upon which a piece of music draws for its tonal framework. **b.** the main tonal centre in an extended composition: *a symphony in the key of F major.* **c.** the tonic of a major or minor scale. **d.** See **tuning key. 7.** something that is crucial in providing an explanation or interpretation: *the key to adult behaviour lies in childhood.* **8.** a means of achieving a desired end: *the key to happiness.* **9.** a means of access or control: *Gibraltar is the key to the Mediterranean.* **10.** a list of explanations of symbols, codes, etc. **11.** a text that explains or gives information about a work of literature, art, or music. **12.** Also called: **key move.** the correct initial move in the solution of a set problem. **13.** *Biology.* a systematic list of taxonomic characteristics, used to identify animals or plants. **14.** *Photog., painting.* the dominant tonal value and colour intensity of a picture. See also **low-key** (sense 3), **high-key. 15.** *Electrical engineering.* **a.** a hand-operated device for opening or closing a circuit or for switching circuits. **b.** a hand-operated switch that is pressed to transmit coded signals, esp. Morse code. **16.** the grooving or scratching of a surface or the application of a rough coat of plaster, etc., to provide a bond for a subsequent finish. **17.** pitch: *he spoke in a low key.* **18.** a characteristic mood or style: *a poem in a melancholic key.* **19.** level of intensity: *she worked herself up to a high key.* **20.** *Railways.* a wooden wedge placed between a rail and a chair to keep the rail firmly in place. **21.** a wedge for tightening a joint or for splitting stone or timber. **22.** short for **keystone** (sense 1). **23.** *Botany.* any dry winged fruit, esp. that of the ash. **24.** (*modifier*) of great importance: *a key issue.* **25.** (*modifier*) *Photog.* determining the tonal value of a photograph: *flesh colour is an important key tone.* ~*vb.* (*mainly tr.*) **26.** (foll. by *to*) to harmonize (with): *to key one's actions to the prevailing mood.* **27.** to adjust or fasten with a key or some similar device. **28.** to provide with a key or keys. **29.** (often foll. by *up*) to locate the position of (a piece of copy, artwork, etc.) on a layout by the use of symbols. **30.** (*also intr.*) another word for **keyboard** (sense 3). **31.** to include a distinguishing device in (an advertisement, etc.), so that responses to it can be identified. **32.** to provide a keystone for (an arch). ~See also **key in, key up.** [Old English *cǣg;* related to Old Frisian *kēi,* Middle Low German *keie* spear] —**ˈkeyless** *adj.*

key[2] (kiː) *n.* a variant spelling of **cay.**

keyboard (ˈkiːˌbɔːd) *n.* **1. a.** a complete set of keys, usually hand-operated, as on a piano, organ, typewriter, or typesetting machine. **b.** (*as modifier*): *a keyboard instrument.* **2.** (*often pl.*) a musical instrument, esp. an electronic one, played by means of a keyboard. ~*vb.* **3.** to set (a text) in type, onto magnetic tape, or into some other medium, by using a keyboard machine. —**ˈkeyˌboarder** *n.*

keyboardist (ˈkiːˌbɔːdɪst) *n.* a person who plays a keyboard instrument, esp. an electronic musical instrument.

key fruit *n.* another name for **samara.**

key grip *n. Chiefly U.S.* the person in charge of moving and setting up camera tracks and scenery in a film or television studio. See also **grip**[1] (sense 12).

keyhole (ˈkiːˌhəʊl) *n.* **1.** an aperture in a door or a lock case through which a key may be passed to engage the lock mechanism. **2. a.** any small aperture resembling a keyhole in shape or function. **b.** (*as modifier*): *keyhole surgery.*

key in *vb.* (*tr., adv.*) to enter (information or instructions) in a computer or other device by means of a keyboard or keypad.

key light *n. Television, photog., etc.* the main stage or studio light that gives the required overall intensity of illumination.

key-man assurance *n.* an assurance policy taken out, esp. by a small company, on the life of a senior executive whose death would create a serious loss.

key money *n.* a fee payment required from a new tenant of a house or flat before he moves in.

Keynesian (ˈkeɪnzɪən) *adj.* **1.** of or relating to the works or theories of John Maynard Keynes (1st Baron Keynes; 1883–1946), British economist, esp. his view that government intervention in the economy is necessary to achieve high levels of employment. ~*n.* **2.** one who supports the ideas of Keynes. —**ˈKeynesianˌism** *n.*

keynote (ˈkiːˌnəʊt) *n.* **1. a.** a central or determining principle in a speech, literary work, etc. **b.** (*as modifier*): *a keynote speech.* **2.** the note upon which a scale or key is based; tonic. ~*vb.* (*tr.*) **3.** to deliver a keynote address to (a political convention, etc.). **4.** to outline (political issues, policy, etc.) in or as in a keynote address.

keypad (ˈkiːˌpæd) *n.* **1.** a small keyboard with push buttons, as on a pocket calculator, remote control unit for a television, etc. **2.** *Computer technol.* a data input device consisting of a limited number of keys, each with nominated functions.

key punch *n.* **1.** Also called: **card punch.** a device having a keyboard that is operated manually to transfer data onto punched cards, paper tape, etc. ~*vb.* **key-punch. 2.** to transfer (data) onto punched cards, paper tape, etc., by using a key punch.

keys (kiːz) *interj. Scot. dialect.* a children's cry for truce or respite from the rules of a game. [origin uncertain]

key signature *n. Music.* a group of sharps or flats appearing at the beginning of each stave line to indicate the key in which a piece, section, etc., is to be performed.

key stage *n. Brit. Education.* any one of four broad age-group divisions (5–7; 7–11; 11–14; 14–16) to which each level of the National Curriculum applies.

keystone (ˈkiːˌstəʊn) *n.* **1.** Also called: **headstone, quoin.** the central stone at the top of an arch or the top stone of a dome or vault. **2.** something that is necessary to connect or support a number of other related things.

keystroke (ˈkiːˌstrəʊk) *n.* a single operation of the mechanism of a typewriter or keyboard-operated typesetting machine by the action of a key.

key up *vb.* (*tr., adv.*) to raise the intensity, excitement, tension, etc., of.

keyway (ˈkiːˌweɪ) *n.* a longitudinal slot cut into a component to accept a key that engages with a similar slot on a mating component to prevent relative motion of the two components.

key word *n.* **1.** a word used as a key to a code. **2.** any significant word or thing, esp. a word used to describe the contents of a document.

kg **1.** *abbrev. for* keg. ~**2.** *symbol for* kilogram.

KG *abbrev. for* Knight of the Order of the Garter (a Brit. title).

KGB *abbrev.* the Soviet secret police since 1954. Compare **GRU.** [from Russian *Komitet Gosudarstvennoi Bezopasnosti* State Security Committee]

khaddar (ˈkɑːdə) *or* **khadi** (ˈkɑːdɪ) *n.* a cotton cloth of plain weave, produced in India. [from Hindi *khādar*]

khaki (ˈkɑːkɪ) *n., pl.* **-kis. 1. a.** a dull yellowish-brown colour. **b.** (*as adj.*): *a khaki background.* **2. a.** a hard-wearing fabric of this colour, used esp. for military uniforms. **b.** (*as modifier*): *a khaki jacket.* [C19: from Urdu, from Persian: dusty, from *khāk* dust]

khalif (ˈkeɪlɪf, ˈkæl-) *n.* a variant spelling of **caliph.**

Khalkha (ˈkælkə) *n.* the dialect of Mongolian that is the official language of the Mongolian Republic.

khamsin (ˈkæmsɪn, kæmˈsiːn), **kamseen,** *or* **kamsin** *n.* a hot southerly wind blowing from about March to May, esp. in Egypt. [C17: from Arabic, literally: fifty]

khan[1] (kɑːn) *n.* **1. a.** (formerly) a title borne by medieval Chinese emperors and Mongol and Turkic rulers: usually added to a name: *Kublai Khan.* **b.** such a ruler. **2.** a title of respect borne by important personages in Afghanistan and central Asia. [C14: from Old French *caan,* from Medieval Latin *caanus,* from Turkish *khān,* contraction of *khāqān* ruler]

khan[2] (kɑːn) *n.* an inn in Turkey, certain Arab countries, etc.; caravanserai. [C14: via Arabic from Persian]

khanate (ˈkɑːneɪt, ˈkæn-) *n.* **1.** the territory ruled by a khan. **2.** the position or rank of a khan.

khanga (ˈkæŋgə) *n.* a variant spelling of **kanga.**

kharif (kəˈriːf) *n.* (in Pakistan, India, etc.) a crop that is harvested at the beginning of winter. Compare **rabi.** [Urdu, ultimately from Arabic *kharafa* to gather]

khat (kæt, kɑːt) *n.* a variant spelling of **kat.**

khayal (kəˈjɑːl) *n.* a kind of Indian classical vocal music. [Urdu: literally: thought, imagination]

kheda, khedah, *or* **keddah** (ˈkɛdə) *n.* (in India, Burma, etc.) an enclosure into which wild elephants are driven to be captured. [from Hindi]

khedive (kɪˈdiːv) *n.* the viceroy of Egypt under Ottoman suzerainty (1867–1914). [C19: from French *khédive,* from Turkish *hidiv,* from Persian *khidīw* prince] —**kheˈdival** *or* **kheˈdivial** *adj.* —**kheˈdivate** *or* **kheˈdiviate** *n.*

Khmer (kmɛə, kmɜː) *n.* **1.** a member of a people of Cambodia, in SE Asia, noted for a civilization that flourished from about 800 A.D. to about 1370, remarkable for its architecture. **2.** the language of this people, belonging to the Mon-Khmer family: the official language of Cambodia. ~*adj.* **3.** of or relating to this people or their language. —**ˈKhmerian** *adj.*

Khoisan (ˈkɔɪsɑːn, kɔɪˈsɑːn) *n.* **1.** a family of languages spoken in southern Africa by the Hottentots and Bushmen and by two small groups in Tanzania. A characteristic phonological feature of these languages is the use of suction stops (clicks). ~*adj.* **2.** denoting, relating to, or belonging to this family of languages.

khurta (ˈkuətə) *n.* a variant spelling of **kurta.**

khuskhus (ˈkʊskʊs) *n.* an aromatic perennial Indian grass, *Vetiveria zizanioides* (or *Andropogon squarrosus*), whose roots are woven into mats, fans, and baskets. [Hindi]

kHz *symbol for* kilohertz.

kiaat (ˈkiːɑːt) *n.* **1.** a tropical African leguminous tree, *Pterocarpus angolensis.* **2.** the wood of this tree, used for furniture, floors, etc. [from Afrikaans, probably from a Bantu language]

kiang (kɪˈæŋ) *n.* a variety of the wild ass, *Equus hemionus,* that occurs in Tibet and surrounding regions. Compare **onager.** [C19: from Tibetan *rkyan*]

kia ora (ˌkɪə ˈɔːrə) *sentence substitute. N.Z.* greetings! good luck! [Maori, literally: be well!]

kibble[1] (ˈkɪbᵊl) *n. Brit.* a bucket used in wells or in mining for hoisting. [C17: from German *kübel;* related to Old English *cyfel,* ultimately from Medieval Latin *cuppa* CUP]

kibble[2] (ˈkɪbᵊl) *vb. (tr.)* to grind into small pieces. [C18: of unknown origin]

kibbutz (kɪˈbʊts) *n., pl.* **kibbutzim** (ˌkɪbʊtˈsiːm). a collective agricultural settlement in modern Israel, owned and administered communally by its members and on which children are reared collectively. [C20: from Modern Hebrew *qibbūs:* gathering, from Hebrew *qibbūtz*]

kibe (kaɪb) *n.* a chilblain, esp. an ulcerated one on the heel. [C14: probably from Welsh *cibi,* of obscure origin]

kibitka (kɪˈbɪtkə) *n.* **1.** (in Russia) a covered sledge or wagon. **2.** a felt tent used among the Tatars of central Asia. **3.** a Tatar family. [C18: Russian, from Tatar *kibits*]

kibitz (ˈkɪbɪts) *vb. (intr.) U.S. and Canadian informal.* to interfere or offer unwanted advice, esp. as a spectator at a card game. [C20: from Yiddish *kibitzen,* from German *kiebitzen* to be an onlooker, from *Kiebitz* busybody, literally: plover] —**ˈkibitzer** *n.*

kiblah *or* **kibla** (ˈkɪblɑː) *n. Islam.* the direction of Mecca, to which Muslims turn in prayer, indicated in mosques by a niche (mihrab) in the wall. [C18: from Arabic *qiblah* that which is placed opposite; related to *qabala* to be opposite]

kibosh (ˈkaɪˌbɒʃ) *Slang.* ~*n.* **1. put the kibosh on.** to put a stop to; prevent from continuing; halt. ~*vb.* **2.** *(tr.) Rare.* to put a stop to. [C19: of unknown origin]

kick (kɪk) *vb.* **1.** *(tr.)* to drive or impel with the foot. **2.** *(tr.)* to hit with the foot or feet. **3.** *(intr.)* to strike out or thrash about with the feet, as in fighting or swimming. **4.** *(intr.)* to raise a leg high, as in dancing. **5.** (of a gun, etc.) to recoil or strike in recoiling when fired. **6.** *(tr.) Rugby.* **a.** to make (a conversion or a drop goal) by means of a kick. **b.** to score (a goal) by means of a kicked conversion. **7.** *(tr.) Soccer.* to score (a goal) by a kick. **8.** *(intr.) Cricket.* (of a ball) to rear up sharply. **9.** *(intr.;* sometimes foll. by *against) Informal.* to object or resist. **10.** *(intr.) Informal.* to be active and in good health (esp. in the phrase **alive and kicking**). **11.** *Informal.* to change gear in (a car, esp. a racing car): *he kicked into third and passed the bigger car.* **12.** *(tr.) Informal.* to free oneself of (an addiction, etc.): *to kick heroin; to kick the habit.* **13. kick against the pricks.** See **prick** (sense 20). **14. kick into touch. a.** *Rugby, soccer.* to kick the ball out of the playing area and into touch. See **touch** (sense 15). **b.** *Informal.* to take some temporizing action so that a problem is shelved or a decision postponed. **15. kick one's heels.** to wait or be kept waiting. **16. kick over the traces.** See **trace**[2] (sense 3). **17. kick the bucket.** *Slang.* to die. **18. kick up one's heels.** *Informal.* to enjoy oneself without inhibition. ~*n.* **19.** a thrust or blow with the foot. **20.** any of certain rhythmic leg movements used in swimming. **21.** the recoil of a gun or other firearm. **22.** *Informal.* a stimulating or exciting quality or effect (esp. in the phrases **get a kick out of** or **for kicks**). **23.** *Informal.* the sudden stimulating or intoxicating effect of strong alcoholic drink or certain drugs. **24.** *Informal.* power or force. **25.** *Slang.* a temporary enthusiasm: *he's on a new kick every week.* **26. kick in the pants.** *Slang.* **a.** a reprimand or scolding designed to produce greater effort, enthusiasm, etc., in the person receiving it. **b.** a setback or disappointment. **27. kick in the teeth.** *Slang.* a humiliating rebuff. ~See also **kick about, kickback, kick in, kick off, kick out, kick up, kick upstairs.** [C14 *kiken,* perhaps of Scandinavian origin] —**ˈkickable** *adj.*

kick about *or* **around** *vb. (mainly adv.) Informal.* **1.** *(tr.)* to treat harshly. **2.** *(tr.)* to discuss (ideas, etc.) informally. **3.** *(intr.)* to wander aimlessly. **4.** *(intr.)* to lie neglected or forgotten. **5.** *(intr.; also prep.)* to be present in (some place).

kickback (ˈkɪkˌbæk) *n.* **1.** a strong reaction. **2.** part of an income paid to a person having influence over the size or payment of the income, esp. by some illegal arrangement. ~*vb.* **kick back.** *(adv.)* **3.** *(intr.)* to have a strong reaction. **4.** *(intr.)* (esp. of a gun) to recoil. **5.** to pay a kickback to (someone).

kick boxing *n.* a martial art that resembles boxing but permits blows with the feet as well as punches.

kickdown (ˈkɪkˌdaʊn) *n.* a method of changing gear in a car with automatic transmission, by fully depressing the accelerator.

kicker (ˈkɪkə) *n.* **1.** a person or thing that kicks. **2.** *Sport.* a player in a rugby or occasionally a soccer team whose task is to attempt to kick conversions, penalty goals, etc. **3.** *U.S. and Canadian slang.* a hidden and disadvantageous factor, such as a clause in a contract. **4.** *Informal.* any light outboard motor for propelling a boat.

kick in *vb. (adv.) Chiefly Austral. and N.Z. informal.* to contribute.

kick off *vb. (intr., adv.)* **1.** to start play in a game of football by kicking the ball from the centre of the field. **2.** *Informal.* to commence a discussion, job, etc. ~*n.* **kickoff. 3. a.** a place kick from the centre of the field in a game of football. **b.** the time at which the first such kick is due to take place: *kickoff is at 2.30 p.m.* **4.** *Informal.* **a.** the beginning of something. **b. for a kickoff.** to begin with.

kick on *vb. (adv.) Informal.* to continue.

kick out *vb. (tr., adv.) Informal.* to eject or dismiss.

kick pleat *n.* a back pleat at the hem of a straight skirt to allow the wearer greater ease in walking.

kickshaw (ˈkɪkˌʃɔː) *or* **kickshaws** *n.* **1.** a valueless trinket. **2.** *Archaic.* a small elaborate or exotic delicacy. [C16: back formation from *kickshaws,* by folk etymology from French *quelque chose* something]

kicksorter (ˈkɪkˌsɔːtə) *n. Physics.* a multichannel pulse-height analyser used esp. to distinguish between isotopes by sorting their characteristic pulses (kicks).

kickstand (ˈkɪkˌstænd) *n.* a short metal bar attached to and pivoting on the bottom of the frame of a motorcycle or bicycle, which when kicked into a vertical position holds the stationary vehicle upright.

kick-start (ˈkɪkˌstɑːt) *vb. (tr.)* to start (an engine, esp. of a motorcycle) by means of a pedal that is kicked downwards. —**ˈkick-ˌstarter** *n.*

kick turn *n. Skiing.* a standing turn performed by swivelling each ski separately through 180°.

kick up *vb. (adv.)* **1.** *Informal.* to cause (trouble, a fuss, etc.). **2. kick up bobsy-die.** See **bobsy-die.**

kick upstairs *vb. (tr., adv.) Informal.* to promote to a nominally higher but effectively powerless position.

kid[1] (kɪd) *n.* **1.** the young of a goat or of a related animal, such as an antelope. **2.** soft smooth leather made from the hide of a kid. **3.** *Informal.* **a.** a young person; child. **b.** *(modifier)* younger or being still a child: *kid brother; kid sister.* **4. our kid.** *Liverpool dialect.* my younger brother or sister. ~*vb.* **kids, kidding, kidded. 5.** (of a goat) to give birth to (young). [C12: of Scandinavian origin; compare Old Norse *kith,* Shetland Islands *kidi* lamb] —**ˈkiddishness** *n.* —**ˈkidˌlike** *adj.*

kid[2] (kɪd) *vb.* **kids, kidding, kidded.** (sometimes foll. by *on* or *along*) *Informal.* **1.** *(tr.)* to tease or deceive for fun. **2.** *(intr.)* to behave or speak deceptively for fun. **3.** *(tr.)* to delude or fool (oneself) into believing (something): *don't kid yourself that no-one else knows.* [C19: probably from KID[1]] —**ˈkidder** *n.* —**ˈkiddingly** *adv.*

kid[3] (kɪd) *n.* a small wooden tub. [C18: probably variant of KIT[1] (in the sense: barrel)]

kiddle (ˈkɪdᵊl) *n. Brit., archaic.* a device, esp. a barrier constructed of nets and stakes, for catching fish in a river or in the sea. [C13: from Anglo-French, from Old French *quidel,* of obscure origin]

Kiddush (ˈkɪdəʃ; *Hebrew* kɪˈdʊʃ) *n. Judaism.* **1.** a special blessing said before a meal on sabbaths and festivals, usually including the blessing for wine or bread. **2.** a reception usually for the congregants after a service at which drinks and snacks are served and this grace is said. [from Hebrew *qiddūsh* sanctification]

kiddy *or* **kiddie** (ˈkɪdɪ) *n., pl.* **-dies.** *Informal.* an affectionate word for **child.**

kid glove *n.* **1.** a glove made of kidskin. **2. handle with kid gloves.** to treat with great tact or caution. ~*adj.* **kidglove. 3.** overdelicate or overrefined. **4.** diplomatic; tactful: *a kidglove approach.*

kidnap (ˈkɪdnæp) *vb.* **-naps, -napping, -napped** *or U.S.* **-naps, -naping, -naped.** *(tr.)* to carry off and hold (a person), usually for ransom. [C17: KID[1] + obsolete *nap* to steal; see NAB] —**ˈkidnapper** *n.*

kidney (ˈkɪdnɪ) *n.* **1.** either of two bean-shaped organs at the back of the abdominal cavity in man, one on each side of the spinal column. They maintain water and electrolyte balance and filter waste products from the blood, which are excreted as urine. Related adj.: **renal. 2.** the corresponding organ in other animals. **3.** the kidneys of certain animals used as food. **4.** class, type, or disposition (esp. in the phrases **of the same** or **a different kidney**). [C14: of uncertain origin] —**'kidney,like** *adj.*

kidney bean *n.* **1.** any of certain bean plants having kidney-shaped seeds, esp. the French bean and scarlet runner. **2.** the seed of any of these beans.

kidney machine *n.* another name for **artificial kidney.** See **haemodialysis.**

kidney ore *n. Geology.* a form of hematite that occurs in kidney-shaped masses.

kidney-shaped *adj.* shaped like an oval with an inward curve at one side.

kidney stone *n.* **1.** *Pathol.* a hard mass formed in the kidney, usually composed of oxalates, phosphates, and carbonates. Also called: **renal calculus.** **2.** *Mineralogy.* another name for **nephrite.**

kidney vetch *n.* a silky papilionaceous perennial plant, *Anthyllis vulneraria,* of Europe and N Africa, with yellow or orange flowers. Also called: **ladies' fingers.**

kidology (kɪ'dɒlədʒɪ) *n. Brit. informal.* the art or practice of bluffing or deception. [C20: from KID[2] + OLOGY]

kidskin ('kɪd,skɪn) *n.* a soft smooth leather made from the hide of a young goat. Often shortened to **kid.**

kids' stuff *n. Slang.* **1.** something considered fit only for children. **2.** something considered simple or easy.

kidstakes ('kɪd,steɪks) *Austral. informal.* ~*pl. n.* **1.** pretence; nonsense: *cut the kidstakes!* ~*interj.* **2.** an exclamation of annoyance or disagreement.

kief (kiːf) *n.* a variant spelling of **kif.**

kiekie ('kɪə,kɪə, 'kiː,kiː) *n.* a climbing bush plant, *Freycinetia banksii,* of New Zealand, having elongated leaves and edible berries. [Maori]

kier (kɪə) *n.* a vat in which cloth is bleached. [C16: from Old Norse *ker* tub; related to Old High German *kar*]

kieselguhr ('kiːzᵊl,gʊə) *n.* an unconsolidated form of **diatomite.** [C19: from German *Kieselgur,* from *Kiesel* flint, pebble + *Gur* loose earthy deposit]

kieserite ('kiːzə,raɪt) *n.* a white mineral consisting of hydrated magnesium sulphate. Formula: $MgSO_4.H_2O$. [C19: named after Dietrich G. *Kieser* (died 1862), German physician; see -ITE[1]]

kif (kɪf, kiːf), **kaif, keef, kef,** *or* **kief** *n.* **1.** another name for **marijuana.** **2.** any drug or agent that when smoked is capable of producing a euphoric condition. **3.** the euphoric condition produced by smoking marijuana. [C20: from Arabic *kayf* pleasure]

kike (kaɪk) *n. U.S. and Canadian slang.* an offensive word for **Jew.** [C20: probably variant of *kiki,* reduplication of *-ki,* common name-ending among Jews from Slavic countries]

kikoi ('kiːkɔɪ) *n.* (in E Africa) **a.** a piece of cotton cloth with coloured bands, worn wrapped around the body. **b.** (*as modifier*): *kikoi material.* [C20: from Swahili]

kikumon ('kɪkuː,mɒn) *n.* the chrysanthemum emblem of the imperial family of Japan. [Japanese]

Kikuyu (kɪ'kuːjuː) *n.* **1.** (*pl.* **-yus** *or* **-yu**) a member of a Negroid people of E Africa, living chiefly in Kenya on the high foothills around Mount Kenya. **2.** the language of this people, belonging to the Bantu group of the Niger-Congo family.

kilderkin ('kɪldəkɪn) *n.* **1.** an obsolete unit of liquid capacity equal to 16 or 18 Imperial gallons or of dry capacity equal to 16 or 18 wine gallons. **2.** a cask capable of holding a kilderkin. [C14: from Middle Dutch *kindekijn,* from *kintal* hundredweight, from Medieval Latin *quintale;* see KENTLEDGE]

kiley ('kaɪlɪ) *n.* a variant spelling of **kylie.**

kilim (kɪ'lim, 'kiːlɪm) *n.* a pileless woven rug of intricate design made in the Middle East. [C19: from Turkish, from Persian *kilīm*]

kill[1] (kɪl) *vb.* (*mainly tr.*) **1.** (*also intr.;* when *tr.,* sometimes foll. by *off*) to cause the death of (a person or animal). **2.** to put an end to; destroy: *to kill someone's interest.* **3.** to make (time) pass quickly, esp. while waiting for something. **4.** to deaden (sound). **5.** *Informal.* to tire out; exhaust: *the effort killed him.* **6.** *Informal.* to cause to suffer pain or discomfort: *my shoes are killing me.* **7.** *Informal.* to cancel, cut, or delete: *to kill three lines of text.* **8.** *Informal.* to quash, defeat, or veto: *the bill was killed in the House of Lords.* **9.** *Informal.* to switch off; stop: *to kill a motor.* **10.** (*also intr.*) *Informal.* to overcome with attraction, laughter, surprise, etc.: *she was dressed to kill; his gags kill me.* **11.** *Slang.* to consume (alcoholic drink) entirely: *he killed three bottles of rum.* **12.** *Tennis, squash, etc.* to hit (a ball) so hard or so accurately that the opponent cannot return it. **13.** *Soccer.* to bring (a moving ball) under control; trap. **14. kill oneself.** *Informal.* to over-exert oneself: *don't kill yourself.* **15. kill two birds with one stone.** to achieve two results with one action. ~*n.* **16.** the act of causing death, esp. at the end of a hunt, bullfight, etc. **17.** the animal or animals killed during a hunt. **18.** *N.Z.* the seasonal tally of stock slaughtered at a freezing works. **19.** the destruction of a battleship, tank, etc. **20. in at the kill.** present at the end or climax of some undertaking. [C13 *cullen;* perhaps related to Old English *cwellan* to kill; compare German (Westphalian dialect) *küllen;* see QUELL]

kill[2] (kɪl) *n. U.S.* a channel, stream, or river (chiefly as part of place names). [C17: from Middle Dutch *kille;* compare Old Norse *kīll* small bay, creek]

killdeer ('kɪl,dɪə) *n., pl.* **-deer** *or* **-deers.** a large brown-and-white North American plover, *Charadrius vociferus,* with two black breast bands and a noisy cry. [C18: of imitative origin]

killer ('kɪlə) *n.* **1. a.** a person or animal that kills, esp. habitually. **b.** (*as modifier*): *a killer shark.* **2.** something, esp. a task or activity, that is particularly taxing or exhausting. **3.** *Austral. and N.Z.* an animal selected to be slaughtered for food.

killer bee *n.* an African honeybee, or one of its hybrids originating in Brazil, that is extremely aggressive when disturbed.

killer cell *n.* a type of white blood cell that is able to kill cells, such as cancer cells and cells infected with viruses.

killer whale *n.* a predatory black-and-white toothed whale, *Orcinus orca,* with a large erect dorsal fin, most common in cold seas: family *Delphinidae.* Also called: **killer, grampus, orc.**

killick ('kɪlɪk) *or* **killock** ('kɪlək) *n. Nautical.* a small anchor, esp. one made of a heavy stone. [C17: of unknown origin]

killifish ('kɪlɪ,fɪʃ) *n., pl.* **-fish** *or* **-fishes.** any of various chiefly American minnow-like cyprinodont fishes of the genus *Fundulus* and related genera, of fresh and brackish waters: used as aquarium fishes, to control mosquitoes, and as anglers' bait. [C19: see KILL[2], FISH]

killikinick (,kɪlɪkɪ'nɪk) *n.* a variant of **kinnikinnick.**

killing ('kɪlɪŋ) *Informal.* ~*adj.* **1.** very tiring; exhausting: *a killing pace.* **2.** extremely funny; hilarious. **3.** causing death; fatal. ~*n.* **4.** the act of causing death; slaying. **5.** a sudden stroke of success, usually financial, as in speculations on the stock market (esp. in the phrase **make a killing**). —**'killingly** *adv.*

killjoy ('kɪl,dʒɔɪ) *n.* a person who spoils other people's pleasure.

kill-time *n.* **a.** an occupation that passes the time. **b.** (*as modifier*): *kill-time pursuits.*

kiln (kɪln) *n.* **1.** a large oven for burning, drying, or processing something, such as porcelain or bricks. ~*vb.* **2.** (*tr.*) to fire or process in a kiln. [Old English *cylen,* from Late Latin *culīna* kitchen, from Latin *coquere* to COOK]

Kilner jar ('kɪlnə) *n. Trademark.* a glass preserving jar with an airtight lid, used for bottling fruit or vegetables.

kilo[1] ('kiːləʊ) *n., pl.* **kilos.** short for **kilogram** *or* **kilometre.**

kilo[2] ('kiːləʊ) *n. Communications.* a code word for the letter *k.*

kilo- *prefix.* **1.** denoting 10^3 (1000): *kilometre.* Symbol: k **2.** (in computer technology) denoting 2^{10} (1024): *kilobyte:* in computer usage, *kilo-* is restricted to sizes of storage (e.g. *kilobit*) when it means 1024; in other computer contexts it retains its usual meaning of 1000. [from French, from Greek *khilioi* thousand]

kilobyte ('kɪlə,baɪt) *n. Computer technol.* 1024 bytes. Abbrevs.: **KB, kbyte.** See also **kilo-** (sense 2).

kilocalorie ('kɪləʊ,kælərɪ) *n.* another name for **Calorie.**

kilocycle ('kɪləʊ,saɪkᵊl) *n.* short for kilocycle per second: a former unit of frequency equal to 1 kilohertz.

kilogram *or* **kilogramme** ('kɪləʊ,græm) *n.* **1.** one thousand grams. **2.** the basic SI unit of mass, equal to the mass of the international prototype held by the *Bureau International des Poids et Mesures.* One kilogram is equivalent to 2.204 62 pounds. Symbol: kg

kilogram calorie *n.* another name for **Calorie.**

kilohertz ('kɪləʊ,hɜːts) *n.* one thousand hertz; one thousand cycles per second. Symbol: kHz

kilometre *or U.S.* **kilometer** ('kɪlə,miːtə, kɪ'lɒmɪtə) *n.* one thousand metres, equal to 0.621 371 miles. Symbol: km —**kilometric** (,kɪləʊ'mɛtrɪk) *or* **,kilo'metrical** *adj.*

kiloton ('kɪləʊ,tʌn) *n.* **1.** one thousand tons. **2.** an explosive power, esp. of a nuclear weapon, equal to the power of 1000 tons of TNT. Abbrev.: **kt.**

kilovolt ('kɪləʊ,vəʊlt) *n.* one thousand volts. Symbol: kV

kilowatt ('kɪləʊ,wɒt) *n.* one thousand watts. Symbol: kW

kilowatt-hour *n.* a unit of energy equal to the work done by a power of 1000 watts in one hour. Symbol: kWh

kilt (kɪlt) *n.* **1.** a knee-length pleated skirt, esp. one in tartan, as worn by men in Highland dress. ~*vb.* (*tr.*) **2.** to tuck (the skirt) up around one's body. **3.** to put pleats in (cloth, a skirt, etc.). [C18: of Scandinavian origin; compare Danish *kilte* to tuck up, Old Swedish *kilta* lap] —**'kilted** *adj.* —**'kilt,like** *adj.*

kilter ('kɪltə) *or* **kelter** *n.* working order (esp. in the phrase **out of kilter**). [C17: origin unknown]

kimberlite ('kɪmbə,laɪt) *n.* an intrusive igneous rock consisting largely of peridotite and often containing diamonds. [C19: from *Kimberley,* a city in central South Africa, + -ITE[1]]

kimono (kɪ'məʊnəʊ) *n., pl.* **-nos.** **1.** a loose sashed ankle-length garment with wide sleeves, worn in Japan. **2.** any garment copied from this. [C19: from Japanese: clothing, from *ki* to wear + *mono* thing] —**ki'monoed** *adj.*

kin (kɪn) *n.* **1.** a person's relatives collectively; kindred. **2.** a class or group with similar characteristics. **3.** See **next of kin.** ~*adj.* **4.** (*postpositive*) related by blood. **5.** a less common word for **akin.** [Old English *cyn;* related to Old Norse *kyn* family, Old High German *kind* child, Latin *genus* kind]

-kin *suffix forming nouns.* small: *lambkin.* [from Middle Dutch, of West Germanic origin; compare German *-chen*]

kina ('kiːnə) *n.* the standard monetary unit of Papua New Guinea, divided into 100 toeas. [from a Papuan language]

kinaesthesia (,kɪnɪs'θiːzɪə, ,kaɪn-), **kinaesthesis** *or U.S.* **kinesthesia, kinesthesis** *n.* the sensation by which bodily position, weight, muscle tension, and movement are perceived. Also called: **muscle sense.** [C19: from New Latin, from Greek *kinein* to move + AESTHESIA] —**kinaesthetic** *or U.S.* **kinesthetic** (ˌkɪnɪsˈθɛtɪk, ˌkaɪn-) *adj.*

kinase (ˈkaɪneɪz, ˈkɪn-) *n.* **1.** any enzyme that can convert an inactive zymogen to the corresponding enzyme. **2.** any enzyme that brings about the phosphorylation of a molecule. [C20: from KIN(ETIC) + -ASE]

kincob (ˈkɪŋkɒb) *n.* a fine silk fabric embroidered with threads of gold or silver, of a kind made in India. [C18: from Urdu *kimkhāb*]

kind[1] (kaɪnd) *adj.* **1.** having a friendly or generous nature or attitude. **2.** helpful to others or to another: *a kind deed.* **3.** considerate or humane. **4.** cordial; courteous (esp. in the phrase **kind regards**). **5.** pleasant; agreeable; mild: *a kind climate.* **6.** *Informal.* beneficial or not harmful: *a detergent that is kind to the hands.* **7.** *Archaic.* loving. [Old English *gecynde* natural, native; see KIND[2]]

kind[2] (kaɪnd) *n.* **1.** a class or group having characteristics in common; sort; type: *two of a kind; what kind of creature?* **2.** an instance or example of a class or group, esp. a rudimentary one: *heating of a kind.* **3.** essential nature or character: *the difference is one of kind rather than degree.* **4.** *Archaic.* gender or sex. **5.** *Archaic.* nature; the natural order. **6. in kind. a.** (of payment) in goods or produce rather than in money. **b.** with something of the same sort: *to return an insult in kind.* **7. kind of.** (*adv.*) *Informal.* somewhat; rather: *kind of tired.* [Old English *gecynd* nature; compare Old English *cyn* KIN, Gothic *kuni* race, Old High German *kikunt,* Latin *gens*]

▷**Usage.** Careful users of English avoid the mixture of plural and singular constructions frequently used informally with *kind* and *sort,* as in *those kind* (instead of *kinds*) *of buildings seem badly designed* or *these sort* (instead of *sorts*) *of distinctions are becoming blurred.*

kindergarten (ˈkɪndəˌgɑːtᵊn) *n.* a class or small school for young children, usually between the ages of four and six to prepare them for primary education. Often shortened (in Australia) to **kinder** or (in Australia and New Zealand) to **kindy** or **kindie.** [C19: from German, literally: children's garden] —ˈ**kinderˌgartener** *n.*

kind-hearted *adj.* characterized by kindness; sympathetic. —ˌ**kind-ˈheartedly** *adv.* —ˌ**kind-ˈheartedness** *n.*

kindle (ˈkɪndᵊl) *vb.* **1.** to set alight or start to burn. **2.** to arouse or be aroused: *the project kindled his interest.* **3.** to make or become bright. [C12: from Old Norse *kynda,* influenced by Old Norse *kyndill* candle] —ˈ**kindler** *n.*

kindless (ˈkaɪndlɪs) *adj. Archaic.* **1.** heartless. **2.** against nature; unnatural. —ˈ**kindlessly** *adv.*

kindling (ˈkɪndlɪŋ) *n.* material for starting a fire, such as dry wood, straw, etc.

kindly (ˈkaɪndlɪ) *adj.* **-lier, -liest. 1.** having a sympathetic or warm-hearted nature. **2.** motivated by warm and sympathetic feelings: *a kindly act.* **3.** pleasant, mild, or agreeable: *a kindly climate.* **4.** *Archaic.* natural; normal. ~*adv.* **5.** in a considerate or humane way. **6.** with tolerance or forbearance: *he kindly forgave my rudeness.* **7.** cordially; pleasantly: *he greeted us kindly.* **8.** please (often used to express impatience or formality): *will you kindly behave yourself!* **9.** *Archaic.* in accordance with nature; appropriately. **10. take kindly.** to react favourably. —ˈ**kindliness** *n.*

kindness (ˈkaɪndnɪs) *n.* **1.** the practice or quality of being kind. **2.** a kind, considerate, or helpful act.

kindred (ˈkɪndrɪd) *adj.* **1.** having similar or common qualities, origin, etc. **2.** related by blood or marriage. **3. kindred spirit.** a person with whom one has something in common. ~*n.* **4.** relationship by blood. **5.** similarity in character. **6.** a person's relatives collectively. [C12 *kinred,* from KIN + *-red,* from Old English *rǣden* rule, from *rǣdan* to rule] —ˈ**kindredness** *or* ˈ**kindredˌship** *n.*

kindy *or* **kindie** (ˈkɪndɪ) *n. Austral. and N.Z. informal.* short for **kindergarten.**

kine (kaɪn) *n.* (*functioning as pl.*) an archaic word for **cows** or **cattle.** [Old English *cȳna* of cows, from *cū* COW[1]]

kinematics (ˌkɪnɪˈmætɪks, ˌkaɪ-) *n.* (*functioning as sing.*) the study of the motion of bodies without reference to mass or force. Compare **dynamics** (sense 1). [C19: from Greek *kinēma* movement; see CINEMA, -ICS] —ˌ**kineˈmatic** *adj.* —ˌ**kineˈmatically** *adv.*

kinematic viscosity *n.* a measure of the resistance to flow of a fluid, equal to its absolute viscosity divided by its density. Symbol: ν

kinematograph (ˌkɪnɪˈmætəˌgrɑːf, ˌkaɪnɪ-, -ˌgræf) *n.* a variant of **cinematograph.** —**kinematographer** (ˌkɪnəməˈtɒgrəfə) *n.* —**kinematographic** (ˌkɪnɪˌmætəˈgræfɪk, ˌkaɪnɪ-) *adj.* —ˌ**kinemaˈtography** *n.*

kinescope (ˈkɪnəskəʊp) *n.* the U.S. name for **television tube.**

kinesics (kɪˈniːsɪks) *n.* (*functioning as sing.*) the study of the role of body movements, such as winking, shrugging, etc., in communication.

kinesiology (kɪˌniːsɪˈɒlədʒɪ) *n.* the study of the mechanics and anatomy of human muscles.

kinesis (kɪˈniːsɪs, kaɪ-) *n. Biology.* the nondirectional movement of an organism or cell in response to a stimulus, the rate of movement being dependent on the strength of the stimulus.

kinesthesia (ˌkɪnɪsˈθiːzɪə, ˌkaɪn-) *or* **kinesthesis** *n.* the usual U.S. spelling of **kinaesthesia.**

kinetheodolite (ˌkɪnəθɪˈɒdəˌlaɪt) *n.* a type of theodolite containing a cine camera instead of a telescope and giving continuous film of a moving target together with a record of its altitude and azimuth: used in tracking a missile, satellite, etc.

kinetic (kɪˈnɛtɪk, kaɪ-) *adj.* relating to, characterized by, or caused by motion. [C19: from Greek *kinētikos,* from *kinein* to move] —**kiˈnetically** *adv.*

kinetic art *n.* art, esp. sculpture, that moves or has moving parts.

kinetic energy *n.* the energy of motion of a body, equal to the work it would do if it were brought to rest. The **translational kinetic energy** depends on motion through space, and for a rigid body of constant mass is equal to the product of half the mass times the square of the speed. The **rotational kinetic energy** depends on rotation about an axis, and for a body of constant moment of inertia is equal to the product of half the moment of inertia times the square of the angular velocity. In relativistic physics kinetic energy is equal to the product of the increase of mass caused by motion times the square of the speed of light. The SI unit is the joule but the electronvolt is often used in atomic physics. Symbol: E_k, *K*, or *T* Abbrev.: **KE.**

kinetics (kɪˈnɛtɪks, kaɪ-) *n.* (*functioning as sing.*) **1.** another name for **dynamics** (sense 2). **2.** the branch of mechanics, including both dynamics and kinematics, concerned with the study of bodies in motion. **3.** the branch of dynamics that excludes the study of bodies at rest. **4.** the branch of chemistry concerned with the rates of chemical reactions.

kinetic theory *n.* **the.** a theory of gases postulating that they consist of particles of negligible size moving at random and undergoing elastic collisions. In full: **Kinetic theory of gases.**

kinetoplast (kɪˈnɛtəˌplæst, -ˈniː-, -ˌplɑːst) *n.* a small granular cell body close to the nucleus in some flagellate protozoans. Also called: **kinetonucleus** (kɪˌnɛtəʊˈnjuːklɪəs). [C20: from Greek; see KINETIC, -PLAST]

kinfolk (ˈkɪnˌfəʊk) *pl. n. Chiefly U.S. and Canadian.* another word for **kinsfolk.**

king (kɪŋ) *n.* **1.** a male sovereign prince who is the official ruler of an independent state; monarch. Related adjs.: **royal, regal, monarchical. 2. a.** a ruler or chief: *king of the fairies.* **b.** (*in combination*): *the pirate king.* **3. a.** a person, animal, or thing considered as the best or most important of its kind. **b.** (*as modifier*): *a king bull.* **4.** any of four playing cards in a pack, one for each suit, bearing the picture of a king. **5.** the most important chess piece, although theoretically the weakest, being able to move only one square at a time in any direction. See also **check** (sense 30), **checkmate. 6.** *Draughts.* a piece that has moved entirely across the board and has been crowned, after which it may move backwards as well as forwards. **7. king of kings. a.** God. **b.** a title of any of various oriental monarchs. ~*vb.* (*tr.*) **8.** to make (someone) a king. **9. king it.** to act in a superior fashion. [Old English *cyning;* related to Old High German *kunig* king, Danish *konge*] —ˈ**kingˌhood** *n.* —ˈ**kingless** *adj.* —ˈ**kingˌlike** *adj.*

kingbird (ˈkɪŋˌbɜːd) *n.* any of several large American flycatchers of the genus *Tyrannus,* esp. *T. tyrannus* (**eastern kingbird** *or* **bee martin**).

kingbolt (ˈkɪŋˌbəʊlt) *or* **king rod** *n.* **a.** the pivot bolt that connects the body of a horse-drawn carriage to the front axle and provides the steering joint. **b.** a similar bolt placed between a railway carriage and the bogies.

King Charles spaniel *n.* **1.** a toy breed of spaniel with a short turned-up nose and a domed skull. **2. cavalier King Charles spaniel.** a similar breed that is slightly larger and has a longer nose. [C17: named after Charles II of England, who popularized the breed]

king cobra *n.* a very large venomous tropical Asian elapid snake, *Ophiophagus hannah,* that feeds on snakes and other reptiles and extends its neck into a hood when alarmed. Also called: **hamadryad.**

king crab *n.* another name for the **horseshoe crab.**

kingcraft (ˈkɪŋˌkrɑːft) *n. Archaic.* the art of ruling as a king, esp. by diplomacy and cunning.

kingcup (ˈkɪŋˌkʌp) *n. Brit.* any of several yellow-flowered ranunculaceous plants, esp. the marsh marigold.

kingdom (ˈkɪŋdəm) *n.* **1.** a territory, state, people, or community ruled or reigned over by a king or queen. **2.** any of the three groups into which natural objects may be divided: the animal, plant, and mineral kingdoms. **3.** *Theol.* the eternal sovereignty of God. **4.** an area of activity, esp. mental activity, considered as being the province of something specified: *the kingdom of the mind.* —ˈ**kingdomless** *adj.*

kingdom come *n.* **1.** the next world; life after death. **2.** *Informal.* the end of the world (esp. in the phrase **until kingdom come**). **3.** *Informal.* unconsciousness or death.

kingfish (ˈkɪŋˌfɪʃ) *n., pl.* **-fish** *or* **-fishes. 1.** any marine sciaenid food and game fish of the genus *Menticirrhus,* occurring in warm American Atlantic coastal waters. **2.** another name for **opah** (the fish). **3.** any of various other large food fishes, esp. the Spanish mackerel.

kingfisher (ˈkɪŋˌfɪʃə) *n.* any coraciiform bird of the family *Alcedinidae,* esp. the Eurasian *Alcedo atthis,* which has a greenish-blue and orange plumage. Kingfishers have a large head, short tail, and long sharp bill and tend to live near open water and feed on fish. [C15: originally *king's fisher*]

king-hit *Austral. informal.* ~*n.* **1.** a knockout blow, esp. an unfair one. ~*vb.* **-hits, -hitting, -hit.** (*tr.*) **2.** to deliver a knockout blow to.

King James Version *or* **Bible** *n.* **the.** another name for the **Authorized Version.**

kingklip ('kɪŋˌklɪp) *n. S. African.* an edible eel-like marine fish.

kinglet ('kɪŋlɪt) *n.* **1.** *Often derogatory.* the king of a small or insignificant territory. **2.** *U.S. and Canadian.* any of various small warblers of the genus *Regulus,* having a black-edged yellow crown: family *Muscicapidae.*

kingly ('kɪŋlɪ) *adj.* **-lier, -liest.** **1.** appropriate to a king; majestic. **2.** royal. ~*adv.* **3.** *Poetic or archaic.* in a manner appropriate to a king. —'**kingliness** *n.*

kingmaker ('kɪŋˌmeɪkə) *n.* a person who has control over appointments to positions of authority.

king-of-arms *n., pl.* **kings-of-arms.** **1.** the highest rank of heraldic officer. **2.** a person holding this rank.

king of the castle *n. Chiefly Brit.* **1.** a children's game in which each child attempts to stand alone on a mound, sandcastle, etc., by pushing other children off it. **2.** *Informal.* a person who is in a commanding or superior position.

king of the herrings *n.* another name for **oarfish** or **rabbitfish** (sense 1).

king penguin *n.* a large penguin, *Aptenodytes patagonica,* found on islands bordering the Antarctic Circle.

kingpin ('kɪŋˌpɪn) *n.* **1.** the most important person in an organization. **2.** the crucial or most important feature of a theory, argument, etc. **3.** Also called (Brit.): **swivel pin.** a pivot pin that provides a steering joint in a motor vehicle by securing the stub axle to the axle beam. **4.** *Tenpin bowling.* the front pin in the triangular arrangement of the ten pins. **5.** (in ninepins) the central pin in the diamond pattern of the nine pins.

king post *n.* a vertical post connecting the apex of a triangular roof truss to the tie beam. Also called: **joggle post.** Compare **queen post.**

king prawn *n.* any of several large prawns of the genus *Penaeus,* which are fished commercially in Australian waters.

king salmon *n.* another name for **Chinook salmon.**

King's Counsel *n.* (when the sovereign is male) another name for **Queen's Counsel.**

King's English *n.* (esp. when the British sovereign is male) standard Southern British English.

king's evidence *n.* (when the sovereign is male) another name for **queen's evidence** (esp. in the phrase **turn king's evidence**).

king's evil *n.* **the.** *Pathol.* a former name for **scrofula.** [C14: from the belief that the king's touch would heal scrofula]

king's highway *n.* (in Britain, esp. when the sovereign is male) any public road or right of way.

kingship ('kɪŋʃɪp) *n.* **1.** the position or authority of a king. **2.** the skill or practice of ruling as a king.

king-size *or* **king-sized** *adj.* larger or longer than a standard size.

king snake *n.* any nonvenomous North American colubrid snake of the genus *Lampropeltis,* feeding on other snakes, small mammals, etc.

king's peace *n.* **1.** (in early medieval England) the protection secured by the king for particular people or places. **2.** (in medieval England) the general peace secured to the entire realm by the law administered in the king's name.

King's proctor *n.* (in England when the sovereign is male) an official empowered to intervene in divorce and certain other cases when it is alleged that facts are being suppressed.

King's Regulations *pl. n.* (in Britain and the Commonwealth when the sovereign is male) the code of conduct for members of the armed forces that deals with discipline, aspects of military law, etc.

King's Scout *n.* (in Britain and the Commonwealth when the sovereign is male) another name for **Queen's Scout.** U.S. equivalent: **Eagle Scout.**

king's shilling *or, when the sovereign was female,* **queen's shilling** *n.* **1.** (until 1879) a shilling paid to new recruits to the British army. **2. take the king's** (*or* **queen's**) **shilling.** *Brit. archaic.* to enlist in the army.

King's speech *n.* (in Britain and the dominions of the Commonwealth when the sovereign is male) another name for the **speech from the throne.**

Kingwana (kɪŋ'wɑːnə) *n.* a language of Zaïre in W Africa, closely related to Swahili and used as a lingua franca.

kingwood ('kɪŋˌwʊd) *n.* **1.** the hard fine-grained violet-tinted wood of a Brazilian leguminous tree, *Dalbergia cearensis,* used in cabinetwork. **2.** the tree yielding this wood.

kinin ('kaɪnɪn) *n.* **1.** any of a group of polypeptides in the blood that cause dilation of the blood vessels and make smooth muscles contract. **2.** any of a group of plant hormones that promote cell division and retard ageing in plants. [C20: from Greek *kin(ēma)* motion + -IN]

kink (kɪŋk) *n.* **1.** a sharp twist or bend in a wire, rope, hair, etc., esp. one caused when it is pulled tight. **2.** a crick in the neck or similar muscular spasm. **3.** a flaw or minor difficulty in some undertaking or project. **4.** a flaw or idiosyncrasy of personality; quirk. **5.** *Brit. informal.* a sexual deviation. **6.** *U.S.* a clever or unusual idea. [C17: from Dutch: a curl in a rope; compare Middle Low German *kinke* kink, Old Norse *kinka* to nod]

kinkajou ('kɪŋkəˌdʒuː) *n.* **1.** Also called: **honey bear, potto.** an arboreal fruit-eating mammal, *Potos flavus,* of Central and South America, with a long prehensile tail: family *Procyonidae* (raccoons) order *Carnivora* (carnivores). **2.** another name for **potto** (sense 1). [C18: from French *quincajou,* from Algonquian; related to Ojibwa *gwingwâage* wolverine]

kinky ('kɪŋkɪ) *adj.* **kinkier, kinkiest.** **1.** *Slang.* given to unusual, abnormal, or deviant sexual practices. **2.** *Informal.* exhibiting unusual idiosyncrasies of personality; quirky; eccentric. **3.** *Informal.* attractive or provocative in a bizarre way: *kinky clothes.* **4.** tangled or tightly looped, as a wire or rope. **5.** tightly curled, as hair. —'**kinkily** *adv.* —'**kinkiness** *n.*

kinnikinnick, kinnikinic (ˌkɪnɪkɪ'nɪk), *or* **killikinick** *n.* **1.** the dried leaves and bark of certain plants, sometimes with tobacco added, formerly smoked by some North American Indians. **2.** any of the plants used for such a preparation, such as the sumach *Rhus glabra.* [C18: from Algonquian, literally: that which is mixed; related to Natick *kinukkinuk* mixture]

kino ('kiːnəʊ) *n.* a dark red resin obtained from various tropical plants, esp. an Indian leguminous tree, *Pterocarpus marsupium,* used as an astringent and in tanning. Also called: **kino gum.** [C18: of West African origin; related to Mandingo *keno*]

kin selection *n. Biology.* natural selection resulting from altruistic behaviour by animals towards members of the same species, esp. their offspring or other relatives.

kinsfolk ('kɪnzˌfəʊk) *pl. n.* one's family or relatives.

kinship ('kɪnʃɪp) *n.* **1.** blood relationship. **2.** the state of having common characteristics or a common origin.

kinsman ('kɪnzmən) *n., pl.* **-men.** **1.** a blood relation or a relation by marriage. **2.** a member of the same race, tribe, or ethnic stock. —'**kinsˌwoman** *fem. n.*

kiosk ('kiːɒsk) *n.* **1.** a small sometimes movable booth from which cigarettes, newspapers, light refreshments, etc., are sold. **2.** *Chiefly Brit.* a telephone box. **3.** *Chiefly U.S.* a thick post on which advertisements are posted. **4.** (in Turkey, Iran, etc., esp. formerly) a light open-sided pavilion. [C17: from French *kiosque* bandstand, from Turkish *kösk,* from Persian *kūshk* pavilion]

kip[1] (kɪp) *Slang.* ~*n.* **1.** *Brit.* sleep or slumber: *to get some kip.* **2.** *Brit.* a bed or lodging. **3.** *Obsolete* (*except Irish*). a brothel. ~*vb.* **kips, kipping, kipped.** (*intr.*) **4.** *Brit.* to sleep or take a nap. **5.** *Brit.* (foll. by *down*) to prepare for sleep. [C18: of uncertain origin; apparently related to Danish *kippe* common alehouse]

kip[2] (kɪp) *or* **kipskin** ('kɪpˌskɪn) *n.* the hide of a young animal, esp. a calf or lamb. [C16: from Middle Dutch *kipp;* related to Middle Low German *kip,* Old Norse *kippa* bundle]

kip[3] (kɪp) *n.* a unit of weight equal to one thousand pounds. [C20: from KI(LO) + P(OUND[2])]

kip[4] (kɪp) *n.* the standard monetary unit of Laos, divided into 100 at. [from Thai]

kip[5] (kɪp) *n. Austral.* a small board used to spin the coins in two-up. [C19: from KEP]

kippa (ki'pa) *n. Judaism.* a skullcap worn by orthodox male Jews at all times and by others for prayer, esp. a crocheted one worn by those with a specifically religious Zionist affiliation.

kipper[1] ('kɪpə) *n.* **1.** a fish, esp. a herring, that has been cleaned, salted, and smoked. **2.** a male salmon during the spawning season. **3.** *Austral. derogatory slang.* an Englishman. ~*vb.* **4.** (*tr.*) to cure (a fish, esp. a herring) by salting and smoking. [Old English *cypera,* perhaps from *coper* COPPER[1]; referring to its colour]

kipper[2] ('kɪpə) *n.* an Australian Aborigine youth who has completed an initiation rite. [from a native Australian language]

Kipp's apparatus (kɪps) *n.* a laboratory apparatus for producing a gas, usually hydrogen sulphide, by the action of a liquid on a solid without heating. [C19: named after Petrus Jacobus *Kipp* (1808–84), Dutch chemist]

kir (kɜː, kir) *n.* a drink made from dry white wine and cassis. [named after Canon F. *Kir* (1876–1968), mayor of Dijon, who is said to have invented it]

kirby grip ('kɜːbɪ) *n. Brit.* a hairgrip consisting of a piece of metal bent over to form a tight clip and having the upper part ridged to prevent it slipping on the hair. [from *Kerbigrip,* trademark for the original such hairgrip]

Kirchhoff's laws ('kɪəxhɒfs) *pl. n.* two laws describing the flow of currents in electric circuits. The first states that the algebraic sum of all the electric currents meeting at any point in a circuit is zero. The second states that in a closed loop of a circuit the algebraic sum of the products of the resistances and the currents flowing through them is equal to the algebraic sum of all the electromotive forces acting in the loop. [named after Gustav Robert *Kirchhoff* (1824–87), German physicist]

Kirghiz *or* **Kirgiz** ('kɜːgɪz) *n.* **1.** (*pl.* **-ghiz** or **-giz**) a member of a Mongoloid people inhabiting a vast area of central Siberia. **2.** the language of this people, belonging to the Turkic branch of the Altaic family.

kirigami (ˌkɪrɪ'gɑːmɪ) *n.* the art, originally Japanese, of folding and cutting paper into decorative shapes. Compare **origami.** [C20: from Japanese]

kirk (kɜːk; *Scot.* kɪrk) *n.* **1.** a Scot. word for **church.** **2.** a Scottish church. [C12: from Old Norse *kirkja,* from Old English *cirice* CHURCH]
Kirk (kɜːk; *Scot.* kɪrk) *n.* **the.** *Informal.* the Presbyterian Church of Scotland.
kirkman ('kɜːkmən; 'kɪrk-) *n., pl.* **-men.** *Scot.* **1.** a member or strong upholder of the Kirk. **2.** a churchman; clergyman.
kirk session *n.* the lowest court of the Presbyterian Church.
Kirlian photography ('kɜːlɪən) *n.* a process that is said to record directly on photographic film the field radiation of electricity emitted by an object to which an electric charge has been applied. [C20: named after Semyan D. and Valentina K. *Kirlian,* Russian researchers who described the process]
Kirman (kɪə'mɑːn) *n., pl.* **-mans.** a Persian carpet or rug. [named after *Kerman,* a city in SE Iran]
kirmess ('kɜːmɪs) *n.* a variant spelling of **kermis.**
kirpan (kɪr'pɑːn) the short sword traditionally carried by Sikhs as a symbol of their religious and cultural loyalty, symbolizing protection for the weak. See also **five Ks.** [Punjabi *kirpān*]
Kirsch (kɪəʃ) *or* **Kirschwasser** ('kɪəʃˌvɑːsə) *n.* a brandy distilled from cherries, made chiefly in the Black Forest in Germany and in the Jura and Vosges districts of France. [German *Kirschwasser* cherry water]
kirtle ('kɜːtᵊl) *n. Archaic.* **1.** a woman's skirt or dress. **2.** a man's coat. [Old English *cyrtel,* probably from *cyrtan* to shorten, ultimately from Latin *curtus* cut short]
Kirundi (kɪ'rʊndɪ) *n.* the official language of Burundi, belonging to the Bantu group of the Niger-Congo family and closely related to Rwanda.
kish (kɪʃ) *n. Metallurgy.* graphite formed on the surface of molten iron that contains a large amount of carbon. [C19: perhaps changed from German *Kies* gravel; related to Old High German *kisil* pebble]
kishke ('kɪʃkə) *n.* a beef or fowl intestine or skin stuffed with flour, onion, etc., and boiled and roasted. [Yiddish: gut, probably from Russian *kishka*]
Kislev (ki'slev) *n.* (in the Jewish calendar) the ninth month of the year according to biblical reckoning and the third month of the civil year, usually falling within November and December. [from Hebrew]
kismet ('kɪzmɛt, 'kɪs-) *n.* **1.** *Islam.* the will of Allah. **2.** fate or destiny. [C19: from Turkish, from Persian *qismat,* from Arabic, *qasama* he divided]
kiss (kɪs) *vb.* **1.** (*tr.*) to touch with the lips or press the lips against as an expression of love, greeting, respect, etc. **2.** (*intr.*) to join lips with another person in an act of love or desire. **3.** to touch (each other) lightly: *their hands kissed.* **4.** *Billiards.* (of balls) to touch (each other) lightly while moving. ~*n.* **5.** the act of kissing; a caress with the lips. **6.** a light touch. **7.** a small light sweet or cake, such as one made chiefly of egg white and sugar: *coffee kisses.* ~See also **kiss off.** [Old English *cyssan,* from *coss;* compare Old High German *kussen,* Old Norse *kyssa*] —'**kissable** *adj.*
kissagram ('kɪsəˌgræm) *n.* a greetings service in which a person is employed to present greetings by kissing the person celebrating. [C20: blend of *kiss* and *telegram*]
kiss-and-tell *modifier.* denoting the practice of publicizing one's former sexual relationship with a celebrity, esp. in the tabloid press: *a kiss-and-tell interview.*
kiss curl *n. Brit.* a circular curl of hair pressed flat against the cheek or forehead. U.S. and Canadian term: **spit curl.**
kissel ('kɪsᵊl) *n.* a Russian dessert of sweetened fruit purée thickened with arrowroot. [from Russian *kisel*]
kisser ('kɪsə) *n.* **1.** a person who kisses, esp. in a way specified. **2.** a slang word for **mouth** or **face.**
kissing bug *n.* a North American assassin bug, *Melanolestes picipes,* with a painful bite, usually attacking the lips or cheeks of man.
kissing gate *n.* a gate set in a U- or V-shaped enclosure, allowing only one person to pass through at a time.
kiss of death *n.* an act or relationship that has fatal or disastrous consequences. [from Judas' kiss that betrayed Jesus in the garden of Gethsemane (Mark 14:44–45)]
kiss off *Slang, chiefly U.S. and Canadian.* ~*vb.* **1.** (*tr., adv.*) to ignore or dismiss rudely and abruptly. ~*n.* **kiss-off. 2.** a rude and abrupt dismissal.
kiss of life *n.* **the. 1.** mouth-to-mouth resuscitation in which a person blows gently into the mouth of an unconscious person, allowing the lungs to deflate after each blow. **2.** something that revitalizes or reinvigorates.
kist[1] (kɪst) *n. Scot. and northern English dialect.* a large chest or coffer. [C14: from Old Norse *kista;* see CHEST]
kist[2] (kɪst) *n. Archaeol.* a variant spelling of **cist**[2].
kist[3] (kɪst) *n. S. African.* a large wooden chest in which linen is stored, esp. one used to store a bride's trousseau. [from Afrikaans, from Dutch: CHEST]
kit[1] (kɪt) *n.* **1.** a set of tools, supplies, construction materials, etc., for use together or for a purpose: *a first-aid kit; a model aircraft kit.* **2.** the case or container for such a set. **3. a.** a set of pieces of equipment ready to be assembled. **b.** (*as modifier*): *kit furniture.* **4.** clothing and other personal effects, esp. those of a traveller or soldier: *safari kit; battle kit.* **5. the whole kit** *or* **kit and caboodle.** *Informal.* everything or everybody. ~See also **kit out.** [C14: from Middle Dutch *kitte* tankard]
kit[2] (kɪt) *n.* a kind of small violin, now obsolete, used esp. by dancing masters in the 17th–18th centuries. [C16: of unknown origin]
kit[3] (kɪt) *n.* **1.** an informal or diminutive name for **kitten. 2.** a cub of various small mammals, such as the ferret or fox. [C16: by shortening]
kit[4] (kɪt) *n. N.Z.* a plaited flax basket. [from Maori *kete*]
kitbag ('kɪtˌbæg) *n.* a canvas or other bag for a serviceman's kit.
kitchen ('kɪtʃɪn) *n.* **a.** a room or part of a building equipped for preparing and cooking food. **b.** (*as modifier*): *a kitchen table.* [Old English *cycene,* ultimately from Late Latin *coquīna,* from Latin *coquere* to COOK; see KILN]
kitchen cabinet *n.* a group of unofficial advisers to a political leader, esp. when considered to be more influential than the official cabinet.
kitchen Dutch *n. S. African.* an impoverished form of Afrikaans, often with smatterings of English.
kitchenette *or* **kitchenet** (ˌkɪtʃɪ'nɛt) *n.* a small kitchen or part of another room equipped for use as a kitchen.
kitchen garden *n.* a garden where vegetables and sometimes also fruit are grown. —**kitchen gardener** *n.*
kitchen kaffir *n.* a derogatory term for **Fanagalo.**
kitchen midden *n. Archaeology.* the site of a large mound of domestic refuse marking a prehistoric settlement: usually including bones, potsherds, seashells, etc.
kitchen police *pl. n. U.S.* soldiers who have been detailed to work in the kitchen, esp. as a punishment. Abbrev.: **KP.**
kitchen sink *n.* **1.** a sink in a kitchen for washing dishes, vegetables, etc. **2. everything but the kitchen sink.** everything that can be conceived of. **3.** (*modifier*) denoting a type of drama or painting of the 1950s depicting the sordid aspects of domestic reality.
kitchen tea *n. Austral. and N.Z.* a party held before a wedding to which female guests bring items of kitchen equipment as wedding presents.
kitchenware ('kɪtʃɪnˌwɛə) *n.* pots and pans, knives, forks, spoons, and other utensils used in the kitchen.
kite[1] (kaɪt) *n.* **1.** a light frame covered with a thin material flown in the wind at the end of a length of string. **2.** *Brit. slang.* an aeroplane. **3.** (*pl.*) *Nautical.* any of various light sails set in addition to the working sails of a vessel. **4.** any diurnal bird of prey of the genera *Milvus, Elanus,* etc., typically having a long forked tail and long broad wings and usually preying on small mammals and insects: family *Accipitridae* (hawks, etc.). **5.** *Archaic.* a person who preys on others. **6.** *Commerce.* a negotiable paper drawn without any actual transaction or assets and designed to obtain money on credit, give an impression of affluence, etc. **7. fly a kite.** See **fly**[1] (sense 14). **8. high as a kite.** See **high** (sense 30). ~*vb.* **9.** to issue (fictitious papers) to obtain credit or money. **10.** (*tr.*) *U.S. and Canadian.* to write (a cheque) in anticipation of sufficient funds to cover it. **11.** (*intr.*) to soar and glide. [Old English *cȳta;* related to Middle High German *küze* owl, Old Norse *kȳta* to quarrel] —'**kiter** *n.*
kite[2] (kəɪt) *n.* a variant spelling of **kyte.**
kite fighting *n.* (in Malaysia) a game in which one player attempts to cut the string of his opponent's kite with the string of his own. See also **glass string.**
kite flying *n. Commerce.* the practice of drawing cheques on deposits which are already committed, assuming that the delay in clearing the cheque will allow time to replenish the account. Also called: **kiting.**
Kite mark *n. Brit.* the official mark of quality and reliability, in the form of a kite, on articles approved by the British Standards Institution.
kitenge (ki:'tɛŋgɛ) *n. E African.* **a.** a thick cotton cloth measuring 114 × 213 cm (45 × 84 inches), used in making garments. **b.** (*as modifier*): *a kitenge dress.* [C20: from Swahili]
kit fox *n.* another name for **swift fox.**
kith (kɪθ) *n.* one's friends and acquaintances (esp. in the phrase **kith and kin**). [Old English *cȳthth,* from *cūth;* see UNCOUTH]
kithara ('kɪθərə) *n.* a variant of **cithara.**
kit out *or* **up** *vb.* **kits, kitting, kitted.** (*tr., adv.*) *Chiefly Brit.* to provide with (a kit of personal effects and necessities).
kitsch (kɪtʃ) *n.* **a.** tawdry, vulgarized, or pretentious art, literature, etc., usually with popular or sentimental appeal. **b.** (*as modifier*): *a kitsch plaster bust of Beethoven.* [C20: from German] —'**kitschy** *adj.*
kitten ('kɪtᵊn) *n.* **1.** a young cat. **2. have kittens.** Also: **have a canary.** *Brit. informal.* to react with disapproval, anxiety, etc.: *she had kittens when she got the bill.* U.S. equivalent: **have a cow.** ~*vb.* **3.** (of cats) to give birth to (young). [C14: from Old Northern French *caton,* from CAT[1]; probably influenced by Middle English *kiteling*] —'**kitten-ˌlike** *adj.*
kittenish ('kɪtᵊnɪʃ) *adj.* **1.** like a kitten; lively. **2.** (of a woman) flirtatious, esp. coyly flirtatious. —'**kittenishly** *adv.* —'**kittenishness** *n.*
kitten moth *n.* any of three prominent moths, notably the **poplar kitten** (*furcula bifida*), that have larvae like those of the related puss moth.
kittiwake ('kɪtɪˌweɪk) *n.* either of two oceanic gulls of the genus *Rissa,* esp. *R. tridactyla,* having a white plumage with pale grey

black-tipped wings and a square-cut tail. [C17: of imitative origin]

kittle ('kɪtᵊl) *Scot.* ~*adj.* 1. capricious and unpredictable. ~*vb.* 2. to be troublesome or puzzling to (someone). 3. to tickle. [C16: probably from Old Norse *kitla* to TICKLE]

kitty[1] ('kɪtɪ) *n., pl.* **-ties.** a diminutive or affectionate name for a **kitten** or **cat**[1]. [C18: see KIT[3]]

kitty[2] ('kɪtɪ) *n., pl.* **-ties.** 1. the pool of bets in certain gambling games. 2. any shared fund of money, etc. 3. (in bowls) the jack. [C19: see KIT[1]]

kiva ('kiːvə) *n.* a large underground or partly underground room in a Pueblo Indian village, used chiefly for religious ceremonies. [from Hopi]

kiwi ('kiːwiː) *n., pl.* **kiwis.** 1. any nocturnal flightless New Zealand bird of the genus *Apteryx*, having a long beak, stout legs, and weakly barbed feathers: order *Apterygiformes* (see **ratite**). 2. short for **kiwi fruit.** 3. *Informal except in New Zealand.* a New Zealander. 4. short for **Golden Kiwi:** *he won the kiwi.* [C19: from Maori, of imitative origin]

kiwi fruit *n.* the edible oval fruit of the kiwi plant, *Actinidia chinensis*, a climbing plant native to Asia but grown extensively in New Zealand; it has a brown fuzzy skin and pale green flesh. Also called: **Chinese gooseberry.**

KKK *abbrev. for* Ku Klux Klan.

KKt *Chess. symbol for* king's knight.

KKtP *Chess. symbol for* king's knight's pawn.

kl *symbol for* kilolitre.

klangfarbe ('klɑːŋˌfɑːbə) *n.* (*often cap.*) instrumental timbre or tone colour. [German: tone colour]

Klansman ('klænzmən) *n., pl.* **-men.** a member of the Ku Klux Klan, a U.S. secret society active against the Blacks and other minority groups.

klaxon *or* **claxon** ('klæksᵊn) *n.* a type of loud horn formerly used on motor vehicles. [C20: former trademark, from the name of the manufacturing company]

Klebs-Löffler bacillus ('klɛbz'lʌflə; *German* 'kleːps'lœflər) *n.* a rodlike Gram-positive bacterium, *Corynebacterium diphtheriae*, that causes diphtheria: family *Corynebacteriaceae*. [C19: named after Edwin *Klebs* (1834–1913) and Friedrich A. J. *Löffler* (1852–1915), German bacteriologists]

Kleenex ('kliːnɛks) *n., pl.* **-ex** *or* **-exes.** *Trademark.* a kind of soft paper tissue, used esp. as a handkerchief.

Klein bottle (klaɪn) *n. Maths.* a three-dimensional surface having no interior, formed by inserting the smaller end of an open tapered tube through the surface of the tube and making this end contiguous with the other end. [named after Felix *Klein* (1849–1925) German mathematician]

klepht (klɛft) *n.* any of the Greeks who fled to the mountains after the 15th-century Turkish conquest of Greece and whose descendants survived as brigands into the 19th century. [C19: from Modern Greek *klephtēs*, from Greek *kleptēs* thief] —**'klephtic** *adj.*

kleptomania (ˌklɛptəʊ'meɪnɪə) *n. Psychol.* a strong impulse to steal, esp. when there is no obvious motivation. [C19: *klepto-* from Greek *kleptēs* thief, from *kleptein* to steal + -MANIA] —**ˌklepto'maniˌac** *n.*

kletterschuh ('klɛtəʃuː) *n., pl.* **kletterschuhe** ('klɛtəˌʃuːə) a lightweight climbing boot with a canvas or suede upper and Vibram (originally felt or cord) sole. Also called: **klett.** [C20: from German: climbing shoe]

klieg light (kliːg) *n.* an intense carbon-arc light used for illumination in producing films. [C20: named after John H. *Kliegl* (1869–1959) and his brother Anton (1872–1927), German-born American inventors in the field of lighting]

klipspringer ('klɪpˌsprɪŋə) *n.* a small agile antelope, *Oreotragus oreotragus*, inhabiting rocky regions of Africa south of the Sahara. [C18: from Afrikaans, from Dutch *klip* rock (see CLIFF) + *springer*, from *springen* to SPRING]

klong (klɒŋ) *n.* a type of canal in Thailand. [from Thai]

kloof (kluːf) *n.* a mountain pass or gorge in southern Africa. [C18: from Afrikaans, from Middle Dutch *clove* a cleft; see CLEAVE[1]]

klootchman ('kluːtʃmən) *n., pl.* **-mans** *or* **-men.** *Northwestern Canadian.* an Indian woman; squaw. Also called: **klootch, klooch.** [C19: from Chinook Jargon, from Nootka *hlotssma* woman, wife]

klutz (klʌts) *n. U.S. and Canadian slang.* a clumsy or stupid person. [from German *Klotz* dolt; compare CLOT] —**'klutzy** *adj.*

klystron ('klɪstrɒn, 'klaɪ-) *n.* an electron tube for the amplification or generation of microwaves by means of velocity modulation. [C20: *klys-*, from Greek *klus-*, *kluzein* to wash over, break over + -TRON]

km *symbol for* kilometre.

K-meson *n.* another name for **kaon.**

kn *abbrev. for:* 1. *Nautical.* knot. 2. krona. 3. krone.

KN *Chess. symbol for* king's knight.

knack (næk) *n.* 1. a skilful, ingenious, or resourceful way of doing something. 2. a particular talent or aptitude, esp. an intuitive one. [C14: probably variant of *knak* sharp knock, rap, of imitative origin]

knacker ('nækə) *Brit.* ~*n.* 1. a person who buys up old horses for slaughter. 2. a person who buys up old buildings and breaks them up for scrap. 3. (*usually pl.*) *Slang.* another word for testicle. 4. *Irish slang.* a despicable person. ~*vb.* 5. (*tr.; usually passive*) *Slang.* to exhaust; tire. [C16: probably from *nacker* saddler, probably of Scandinavian origin; compare Old Norse *hnakkur* saddle] —**'knackery** *n.*

knacker's yard *n. Brit.* 1. a slaughterhouse for horses. 2. *Informal.* destruction because of being beyond all usefulness (esp. in the phrase **ready for the knacker's yard**).

knackwurst *or* **knockwurst** ('nɒkˌwɜːst) *n.* a short fat highly seasoned sausage. [German, from *knacken* to make a cracking sound + *Wurst* sausage]

knag (næg) *n.* 1. a knot in wood. 2. a wooden peg. [C15: perhaps from Low German *knagge*]

knap[1] (næp) *n. Dialect.* the crest of a hill. [Old English *cnæpp* top; compare Old Norse *knappr* knob]

knap[2] (næp) *vb.* **knaps, knapping, knapped.** (*tr.*) *Dialect.* to hit, hammer, or chip. [C15 (in the sense: to strike with a sharp sound): of imitative origin; compare Dutch *knappen* to crack] —**'knapper** *n.*

knapping hammer *n.* a hammer used for breaking and shaping stones.

knapsack ('næpˌsæk) *n.* a canvas or leather bag carried strapped on the back or shoulder. [C17: from Low German *knappsack*, probably from *knappen* to bite, snap + *sack* bag; related to Dutch *knapzak;* see SACK[1]]

knapweed ('næpˌwiːd) *n.* any of several plants of the genus *Centaurea*, having purplish thistle-like flowers: family *Compositae* (composites). See also **centaury** (sense 2), **hardheads.** [C15 *knopwed;* see KNOP, WEED[1]]

knar (nɑː) *n.* a variant of **knur.** [C14 *knarre* rough stone, knot on a tree; related to Low German *knarre*] —**knarred** *or* **'knarry** *adj.*

knave (neɪv) *n.* 1. *Archaic.* a dishonest man; rogue. 2. another word for **jack** (the playing card). 3. *Obsolete.* a male servant. [Old English *cnafa;* related to Old High German *knabo* boy] —**'knavish** *adj.* —**'knavishly** *adv.* —**'knavishness** *n.*

knavery ('neɪvərɪ) *n., pl.* **-eries.** 1. a deceitful or dishonest act. 2. dishonest conduct; trickery.

knawel ('nɔːəl) *n.* any of several Old World caryophyllaceous plants of the genus *Scleranthus*, having heads of minute petalless flowers. [C16: from German *Knauel*, literally: ball of yarn, from Old High German *kliuwa* ball]

knead (niːd) *vb.* (*tr.*) 1. to work and press (a soft substance, such as bread dough) into a uniform mixture with the hands. 2. to squeeze, massage, or press with the hands. 3. to make by kneading. [Old English *cnedan;* related to Old Saxon *knedan*, Old Norse *knotha*] —**'kneader** *n.*

knee (niː) *n.* 1. the joint of the human leg connecting the tibia and fibula with the femur and protected in front by the patella. Technical name: **genu.** 2. **a.** the area surrounding and above this joint. **b.** (*modifier*) reaching or covering the knee: *knee breeches; knee socks.* 3. a corresponding or similar part in other vertebrates. 4. the part of a garment that covers the knee. 5. the upper surface of a seated person's thigh: *the child sat on her mother's knee.* 6. anything resembling a knee in action, such as a device pivoted to allow one member angular movement in relation to another. 7. anything resembling a knee in shape, such as an angular bend in a pipe. 8. any of the hollow rounded protuberances that project upwards from the roots of the swamp cypress: thought to aid respiration in waterlogged soil. 9. **bend** *or* **bow the knee.** to kneel or submit. 10. **bring someone to his knees.** to force someone into submission. ~*vb.* **knees, kneeing, kneed.** 11. (*tr.*) to strike, nudge, or push with the knee. [Old English *cnēow;* compare Old High German *kneo*, Old Norse *knē*, Latin *genu*]

kneecap ('niːˌkæp) *n.* 1. *Anatomy.* a nontechnical name for **patella.** 2. another word for **poleyn.** ~*vb.* **-caps, -capping, -capped.** (*tr.*) 3. (esp. of certain terrorist groups) to shoot (a person) in the kneecap, esp. as an act of retaliation.

knee-deep *adj.* 1. so deep as to reach or cover the knees: *knee-deep mud.* 2. (*postpositive;* often foll. by *in*) **a.** sunk or covered to the knees: *knee-deep in sand.* **b.** immersed; deeply involved: *knee-deep in work.*

knee drop *n.* a wrestling attack in which a wrestler lifts his opponent and drops him onto his bent knee.

knee-high *adj.* 1. another word for **knee-deep** (sense 1). 2. as high as the knee: *a knee-high child.*

kneehole ('niːˌhəʊl) *n.* **a.** a space for the knees, esp. under a desk. **b.** (*as modifier*): *a kneehole desk.*

knee jerk *n.* 1. *Physiol.* Also called: **patellar reflex.** an outward reflex kick of the lower leg caused by a sharp tap on the tendon just below the patella. ~*modifier.* **kneejerk.** 2. made or occurring as a predictable and automatic response, without thought: *kneejerk support.*

kneel (niːl) *vb.* **kneels, kneeling, knelt** *or* **kneeled.** 1. (*intr.*) to rest, fall, or support oneself on one's knees. ~*n.* 2. the act or position of kneeling. [Old English *cnēowlian;* see KNEE] —**'kneeler** *n.*

knee-length *adj.* reaching to the knee: *a knee-length skirt; knee-length boots.*

kneepad ('niːˌpæd) *n.* any of several types of protective covering for the knees. Also called: **kneecap.**

kneepan ('niːˌpæn) *n. Anatomy.* another word for **patella.**

knees-up *n., pl.* **knees-ups.** *Brit. informal.* **1.** a boisterous dance involving the raising of alternate knees. **2.** a lively noisy party or celebration, esp. one with dancing. [C20: from the song "Knees up Mother Brown" to which the dance is performed]

kneidel ('kneɪdᵊl, 'knaɪ-) *n.* (in Jewish cookery) a small dumpling, usually served in chicken soup. [from Yiddish]

knell (nɛl) *n.* **1.** the sound of a bell rung to announce a death or a funeral. **2.** something that precipitates or indicates death or destruction. ~*vb.* **3.** (*intr.*) to ring a knell. **4.** (*tr.*) to proclaim or announce by or as if by a tolling bell. [Old English *cnyll;* related to Middle High German *knüllen* to strike, Dutch *knallen* to bang]

knelt (nɛlt) *vb.* a past tense and past participle of **kneel.**

Knesset *or* **Knesseth** ('knɛsɪt) *n.* the unicameral parliament of Israel. [Hebrew, literally: gathering]

knew (njuː) *vb.* the past tense of **know.**

Knickerbocker ('nɪkəˌbɒkə) *n. U.S.* **1.** a descendant of the original Dutch settlers of New York. **2.** an inhabitant of New York. [C19: named after Diedrich *Knickerbocker,* fictitious Dutchman alleged to be the author of Washington Irving's *History of New York* (1809)]

knickerbocker glory *n.* a rich confection consisting of layers of ice cream, jelly, cream, and fruit served in a tall glass.

knickerbockers ('nɪkəˌbɒkəz) *pl. n.* baggy breeches fastened with a band at the knee or above the ankle. Also called (U.S.): **knickers.** [C19: regarded as the traditional dress of the Dutch settlers in America; see KNICKERBOCKER]

knickers ('nɪkəz) *pl. n.* **1.** an undergarment for women covering the lower trunk and sometimes the thighs and having separate legs or leg-holes. **2.** a U.S. variant of **knickerbockers. 3. get one's knickers in a twist.** *Slang.* to become agitated, flustered, or upset. [C19: contraction of KNICKERBOCKERS]

knick-knack *or* **nick-nack** ('nɪkˌnæk) *n.* **1.** a cheap ornament; trinket. **2.** an ornamental article of furniture, dress, etc. [C17: by reduplication from *knack,* in obsolete sense: toy] —'**knickˌknackery** *or* '**nick-ˌnackery** *n.*

knickpoint *or esp. U.S.* **nickpoint** ('nɪkˌpɔɪnt) *n.* a break in the slope of a river profile caused by renewed erosion by a rejuvenated river. [C20: partial translation of German *Knickpunkt,* from *knicken* to bend + *Punkt* POINT]

knife (naɪf) *n., pl.* **knives** (naɪvz). **1.** a cutting instrument consisting of a sharp-edged often pointed blade of metal fitted into a handle or onto a machine. **2.** a similar instrument used as a weapon. **3. have one's knife in someone.** to have a grudge against or victimize someone. **4. under the knife.** undergoing a surgical operation. ~*vb.* (*tr.*) **5.** to cut, stab, or kill with a knife. **6.** to betray, injure, or depose in an underhand way. [Old English *cnīf;* related to Old Norse *knīfr,* Middle Low German *knīf*] —'**knifeˌlike** *adj.* —'**knifer** *n.*

knife edge *n.* **1.** the sharp cutting edge of a knife. **2.** any sharp edge. **3.** a sharp-edged wedge of hard material on which the beam of a balance pivots or about which a pendulum is suspended. **4.** a critical point in the development of a situation, process of making a decision, etc.

knife grinder *n.* a person who makes and sharpens knives, esp. an itinerant one.

knife pleat *n.* a single pleat turned in one direction.

knife-point *n.* **1.** the tip of a knife blade. **2. at knife-point.** under threat of being stabbed.

kniferest ('naɪfˌrɛst) *n.* a support on which a carving knife or carving fork is placed at the table.

knife switch *n.* an electric switch in which a flat metal blade, hinged at one end, is pushed between fixed contacts.

knight (naɪt) *n.* **1.** (in medieval Europe) **a.** (originally) a person who served his lord as a mounted and heavily armed soldier. **b.** (later) a gentleman invested by a king or other lord with the military and social standing of this rank. **2.** (in modern times) a person invested by a sovereign with a nonhereditary rank and dignity usually in recognition of personal services, achievements, etc. A British knight bears the title *Sir* placed before his name: *Sir Winston Churchill.* **3.** a chess piece, usually shaped like a horse's head, that moves either two squares horizontally and one square vertically or one square horizontally and two squares vertically. **4.** a heroic champion of a lady or of a cause or principle. **5.** a member of the Roman class of the equites. ~*vb.* **6.** (*tr.*) to make (a person) a knight; dub. [Old English *cniht* servant; related to Old High German *kneht* boy]

knight bachelor *n., pl.* **knights bachelors** *or* **knights bachelor. 1.** a person who has been knighted but who does not belong to any of the orders of knights. **2.** another name for a **bachelor** (sense 3).

knight banneret *n., pl.* **knights bannerets.** another name for a **banneret.**

knight errant *n., pl.* **knights errant.** (esp. in medieval romance) a knight who wanders in search of deeds of courage, chivalry, etc.

knight errantry *n.* **1.** the practices of a knight errant. **2.** quixotic behaviour or practices.

knighthead ('naɪtˌhɛd) *n. Nautical.* either of a pair of vertical supports for each side of the bowsprit. [C18: originally decorated with carvings of knights' heads]

knighthood ('naɪthʊd) *n.* **1.** the order, dignity, or rank of a knight. **2.** the qualities of a knight; knightliness. **3.** knights collectively.

knightly ('naɪtlɪ) *adj.* of, relating to, resembling, or befitting a knight. —'**knightliness** *n.*

knight marshal *n.* another name for **marshal** (sense 5).

knight of the road *n. Informal or facetious.* **1.** a tramp. **2.** a commercial traveller. **3.** a lorry driver. **4.** *Obsolete.* a highwayman.

kniphofia (nɪ'fəʊfɪə) *n.* any plant of the perennial southern African genus *Kniphofia,* some species of which are cultivated for their conical spikes of bright red or yellow drooping tubular flowers: family *Liliaceae.* Also called: **red-hot poker.** [named after J. H. *Kniphof* (1704–1763), German doctor and botanist]

knish (knɪʃ) *n.* a piece of dough stuffed with potato, meat, or some other filling and baked or fried. [Yiddish, from Russian *knysh* cake; compare Polish *knysz*]

knit (nɪt) *vb.* **knits, knitting, knitted** *or* **knit. 1.** to make (a garment, etc.) by looping and entwining (yarn, esp. wool) by hand by means of long eyeless needles **(knitting needles)** or by machine **(knitting machine). 2.** to join or be joined together closely. **3.** to draw (the brows) together or (of the brows) to come together, as in frowning or concentrating. ~*n.* **4. a.** a fabric or garment made by knitting. **b.** (*in combination*): *a heavy knit.* [Old English *cnyttan* to tie in; related to Middle Low German *knütten* to knot together; see KNOT[1]] —'**knittable** *adj.* —'**knitter** *n.*

knitting ('nɪtɪŋ) *n.* **a.** knitted work or the process of producing it. **b.** (*as modifier*): *a knitting machine.*

knitwear ('nɪtˌwɛə) *n.* knitted clothes, esp. sweaters.

knives (naɪvz) *n.* the plural of **knife.**

knob (nɒb) *n.* **1.** a rounded projection from a surface, such as a lump on a tree trunk. **2.** a handle of a door, drawer, etc., esp. one that is rounded. **3.** a round hill or knoll or morainic ridge. **4.** *Brit. taboo.* a slang word for **penis. 5. and the same to you with (brass) knobs on.** *Brit. informal.* the same to you but even more so. ~*vb.* **knobs, knobbing, knobbed. 6.** (*tr.*) to supply or ornament with knobs. **7.** (*intr.*) to form into a knob; bulge. [C14: from Middle Low German *knobbe* knot in wood; see KNOP] —'**knobby** *adj.* —'**knobˌlike** *adj.*

knobbly ('nɒblɪ) *adj.* **-blier, -bliest.** having or covered with small knobs; bumpy.

knobkerrie ('nɒbˌkɛrɪ) *or* **knobstick** ('nɒbˌstɪk) *n.* a stick with a round knob at the end, used as a club or missile by South African tribesmen. [C19: from Afrikaans *knopkierie,* from *knop* knob, from Middle Dutch *cnoppe* + *kierie* stick, from Hottentot *kïrri*]

knock (nɒk) *vb.* **1.** (*tr.*) to give a blow or push to; strike. **2.** (*intr.*) to rap sharply with the knuckles, a hard object, etc., esp. to capture attention: *to knock at the door.* **3.** (*tr.*) to make or force by striking: *to knock a hole in the wall.* **4.** (*intr.;* usually foll. by *against*) to collide (with). **5.** (*tr.*) to bring into a certain condition by hitting or pushing: *to knock someone unconscious.* **6.** (*tr.*) *Informal.* to criticize adversely; belittle: *to knock someone's work.* **7.** (*intr.*) Also: **pink.** (of an internal-combustion engine) to emit a characteristic metallic noise as a result of faulty combustion. **8.** (*intr.*) (of a bearing, esp. one in an engine) to emit a regular characteristic sound as a result of wear. **9.** *Brit. slang.* to have sexual intercourse with (a person). **10. knock (a person) into the middle of next week.** *Informal.* to hit (a person) with a very heavy blow. **11. knock one's head against.** to have a violent or unpleasant encounter with (adverse facts or circumstances). **12. knock on the head. a.** to daze or kill (a person) by striking on the head. **b.** effectively to prevent the further development of (a plan). ~*n.* **13. a.** a blow, push, or rap: *he gave the table a knock.* **b.** the sound so caused. **14.** the sound of knocking in an engine or bearing. **15.** *Informal.* a misfortune, rebuff, or setback. **16.** *Informal.* unfavourable criticism. **17.** *Informal.* (in cricket) an innings or a spell of batting. **18. take the knock.** *Slang.* to suffer financially. ~See also **knock about, knock back, knock down, knock off, knock-on, knockout, knock up.** [Old English *cnocian,* of imitative origin; related to Old Norse *knoka* to hit]

knock about *or* **around** *vb.* **1.** (*intr., adv.*) to wander about aimlessly. **2.** (*intr., prep.*) to travel about, esp. as resulting in varied or exotic experience: *he's knocked about the world a bit.* **3.** (*intr., adv.;* foll. by *with*) to associate: *to knock about with a gang.* **4.** (*tr., adv.*) to treat brutally: *he knocks his wife about.* **5.** (*tr., adv.*) to consider or discuss informally: *to knock an idea about.* ~*n.* **knockabout. 6.** a sailing vessel, usually sloop-rigged, without a bowsprit and with a single jib. ~*adj.* **knockabout. 7.** rough; boisterous: *knockabout farce.*

knock back *vb.* (*tr., adv.*) **1.** *Informal.* to drink, esp. quickly. **2.** *Informal.* to cost. **3.** *Slang.* to reject or refuse: *you cannot possibly knock back such an offer.* **4.** *Slang.* to come as an unpleasant surprise to; disconcert. ~*n.* **knock-back. 5.** *Slang.* a refusal or rejection. **6.** *Prison slang.* failure to obtain parole.

knock down *vb.* (*tr., adv.*) **1.** to strike to the ground with a blow, as in boxing. **2.** (in auctions) to declare (an article) sold, as by striking a blow with a gavel. **3.** to demolish. **4.** to dismantle, for ease of transport. **5.** *Informal.* to reduce (a price, etc.). **6.** *Austral. slang.* to spend (a cheque). **7.** *Austral. slang.* to drink. ~*adj.* **knockdown.** (*prenominal*) **8.** overwhelming; powerful: *a knockdown blow.* **9.** *Chiefly Brit.* cheap: *I got the table at a* *knockdown price.* **10.** easily dismantled: *knockdown furniture.* ~*n.* **knockdown.** **11.** *U.S. and Austral. informal.* an introduction: *will you give me a knockdown to her?*

knocker ('nɒkə) *n.* **1.** an object, usually ornamental and made of metal, attached to a door by a hinge and used for knocking. **2.** *Informal.* a person who finds fault or disparages. **3.** (*usually pl.*) *Slang.* a female breast. **4.** a person or thing that knocks. **5. on the knocker.** *Austral. and N.Z. informal.* promptly; at once: *you pay on the knocker here.*

knock-for-knock *adj.* designating an agreement between vehicle insurers that in the event of an accident each will pay for the damage to the vehicle insured with him without attempting to establish blame for the accident.

knocking copy *n.* advertising or publicity material designed to denigrate a competing product.

knocking-shop *n. Brit.* a slang word for **brothel.**

knock-knee *n.* a condition in which the legs are bent inwards causing the knees to touch when standing. Technical name: **genu valgum.** —ˌ**knock-'kneed** *adj.*

knock off *vb.* (*mainly adv.*) **1.** (*intr., also prep.*) *Informal.* to finish work: *we knocked off an hour early.* **2.** (*tr.*) *Informal.* to make or do hastily or easily: *to knock off a novel in a week.* **3.** (*tr.; also prep.*) *Informal.* to reduce the price of (an article) by (a stated amount). **4.** (*tr.*) *Slang.* to kill. **5.** (*tr.*) *Slang.* to rob or steal: *to knock off a bank; to knock off a watch.* **6.** (*tr.*) *Slang.* to stop doing something, used as a command: *knock it off!* **7.** (*tr.*) *Slang.* to have sexual intercourse with; to seduce.

knock-on *adj.* **1.** resulting inevitably but indirectly from another event or circumstance: *the works closed with the direct loss of 3000 jobs and many more from the knock-on effect on the area.* ~*n.* **2.** *Rugby.* the infringement of playing the ball forward with the hand or arm. ~*vb.* **knock on** (*adv.*) **3.** *Rugby.* to play (the ball) forward with the hand or arm.

knockout ('nɒkˌaʊt) *n.* **1.** the act of rendering unconscious. **2.** a blow that renders an opponent unconscious. **3. a.** a competition in which competitors are eliminated progressively. **b.** (*as modifier*): *a knockout contest.* **4.** a series of absurd invented games, esp. obstacle races, involving physical effort or skill. **5.** *Informal.* a person or thing that is overwhelmingly impressive or attractive: *she's a knockout.* ~*vb.* **knock out.** (*tr., adv.*) **6.** to render unconscious, esp. by a blow. **7.** *Boxing.* to defeat (an opponent) by a knockout. **8.** to destroy, damage, or injure badly. **9.** to eliminate, esp. in a knockout competition. **10.** *Informal.* to overwhelm or amaze, esp. with admiration or favourable reaction: *I was knocked out by that new song.* **11.** to remove the ashes from (one's pipe) by tapping. **12. knock the bottom out of.** *Informal.* to invalidate (an argument).

knockout drops *pl. n. Slang.* a drug secretly put into someone's drink to cause stupefaction. See also **Mickey Finn.**

knock up *vb.* (*adv., mainly tr.*) **1.** Also: **knock together.** *Informal.* to assemble quickly; improvise: *to knock up a set of shelves.* **2.** *Brit. informal.* to waken; rouse: *to knock someone up early.* **3.** *Slang.* to make pregnant. **4.** *Brit. informal.* to exhaust: *the heavy work knocked him up.* **5.** *Cricket.* to score (runs). **6.** (*intr.*) *Tennis, squash, etc.* to practise or hit the ball about informally, esp. before a match. ~*n.* **knock-up.** **7.** a practice session at tennis, squash, or a similar game.

knockwurst ('nɒkˌwɜːst) *n.* a variant spelling of **knackwurst.**

knoll[1] (nəʊl) *n.* a small rounded hill. [Old English *cnoll;* compare Old Norse *knollr* hilltop] —'**knolly** *adj.*

knoll[2] (nəʊl) *n., vb.* an archaic or dialect word for **knell.** —'**knoller** *n.*

knop (nɒp) *n. Archaic.* a knob, esp. an ornamental one. [C14: from Germanic; compare Middle Dutch *cnoppe* bud, Old High German *knopf*]

knot[1] (nɒt) *n.* **1.** any of various fastenings formed by looping and tying a piece of rope, cord, etc., in upon itself, to another piece of rope, or to another object. **2.** a prescribed method of tying a particular knot. **3.** a tangle, as in hair or string. **4.** a decorative bow or fastening, as of ribbon or braid. **5.** a small cluster or huddled group. **6.** a tie or bond: *the marriage knot.* **7.** a difficult problem. **8.** a protuberance or lump of plant tissues, such as that occurring on the trunks of certain trees. **9. a.** a hard mass of wood at the point where a branch joins the trunk of a tree. **b.** a cross section of this, usually roundish and cross-grained, visible in a piece of timber. **10.** a sensation of constriction, caused by tension or nervousness: *his stomach was tying itself in knots.* **11. a.** *Pathol.* a lump of vessels or fibres formed in a part, as in a muscle. **b.** *Anatomy.* a protuberance on an organ or part. **12.** a unit of speed used by nautical vessels and aircraft, being one nautical mile (about 1.15 statute miles or 1.85 km) per hour. **13.** one of a number of equally spaced knots on a log line used to indicate the speed of a ship in nautical miles per hour. **14.** another term (not in technical use) for **nautical mile.** **15. at a rate of knots.** very fast. **16. tie (someone) in knots.** to completely perplex or confuse (someone). ~*vb.* **knots, knotting, knotted.** **17.** (*tr.*) to tie or fasten in a knot. **18.** to form or cause to form into a knot. **19.** (*tr.*) to ravel or entangle or become ravelled or entangled. **20.** (*tr.*) to make (an article or a design) by tying thread in an interlaced pattern of ornamental knots, as in macramé. [Old English *cnotta;* related to Old High German *knoto,* Old Norse *knūtr*] —'**knotter** *n.* —'**knotless** *adj.* —'**knotˌlike** *adj.*

knot[2] (nɒt) *n.* a small northern sandpiper, *Calidris canutus,* with a short bill and grey plumage. [C15: of unknown origin]

knot garden *n.* (esp. formerly) a formal garden of intricate design.

knotgrass ('nɒtˌgrɑːs) *n.* **1.** Also called: **allseed.** a widely distributed polygonaceous weedy plant, *Polygonum aviculare,* whose small green flowers produce numerous seeds. **2.** any of several related plants.

knothole ('nɒtˌhəʊl) *n.* a hole in a piece of wood where a knot has been.

knotted ('nɒtɪd) *adj.* **1.** (of wood, rope, etc.) having knots. **2. get knotted!** *Brit. slang.* used as a response to express disapproval or rejection.

knotting ('nɒtɪŋ) *n.* **1.** a sealer applied over knots in new wood before priming to prevent resin from exuding. **2.** (esp. formerly) a kind of decorative knotted fancywork.

knotty ('nɒtɪ) *adj.* **-tier, -tiest.** **1.** (of wood, rope, etc.) full of or characterized by knots. **2.** extremely difficult or intricate. —'**knottily** *adv.* —'**knottiness** *n.*

knotweed ('nɒtˌwiːd) *n.* any of several polygonaceous plants of the genus *Polygonum,* having small flowers and jointed stems.

knotwork ('nɒtˌwɜːk) *n.* ornamentation consisting of a mass of intertwined and knotted cords.

knout (naʊt) *n.* a stout whip used formerly in Russia as an instrument of punishment. [C17: from Russian *knut,* of Scandinavian origin; compare Old Norse *knūtr* knot]

know (nəʊ) *vb.* **knows, knowing, knew** (njuː), **known** (nəʊn). (*mainly tr.*) **1.** (*also intr.; may take a clause as object*) to be or feel certain of the truth or accuracy of (a fact, etc.). **2.** to be acquainted or familiar with: *she's known him five years.* **3.** to have a familiarity or grasp of, as through study or experience: *he knows French.* **4.** (*also intr.; may take a clause as object*) to understand, be aware of, or perceive (facts, etc.): *he knows the answer now.* **5.** (foll. by *how*) to be sure or aware of (how to be or do something). **6.** to experience, esp. deeply: *to know poverty.* **7.** to be intelligent, informed, or sensible enough (to do something): *she knew not to go home yet.* **8.** (*may take a clause as object*) to be able to distinguish or discriminate. **9.** *Archaic.* to have sexual intercourse with. **10. I know what.** I have an idea. **11. know what's what.** to know how one thing or things in general work. **12. you know.** *Informal.* a parenthetical filler phrase used to make a pause in speaking or add slight emphasis to a statement. **13. you never know.** things are uncertain. ~*n.* **14. in the know.** *Informal.* aware or informed. [Old English *gecnāwan;* related to Old Norse *knā* I can, Latin *noscere* to come to know] —'**knowable** *adj.* —'**knower** *n.*

know-all *n. Informal, disparaging.* a person who pretends or appears to know a great deal.

know-how *n. Informal.* **1.** ingenuity, aptitude, or skill; knack. **2.** commercial and saleable knowledge of how to do a particular thing; experience.

knowing ('nəʊɪŋ) *adj.* **1.** suggesting secret information or knowledge. **2.** wise, shrewd, or clever. **3.** deliberate; intentional. ~*n.* **4. there is no knowing.** one cannot tell. —'**knowingly** *adv.* —'**knowingness** *n.*

knowledge ('nɒlɪdʒ) *n.* **1.** the facts, feelings or experiences known by a person or group of people. **2.** the state of knowing. **3.** awareness, consciousness, or familiarity gained by experience or learning. **4.** erudition or informed learning. **5.** specific information about a subject. **6.** sexual intercourse (obsolete except in the legal phrase **carnal knowledge**). **7. come to one's knowledge.** to become known to one. **8. to my knowledge. a.** as I understand it. **b.** as I know. **9. grow out of one's knowledge.** *Irish.* to behave in a presumptuous or conceited manner.

knowledgeable *or* **knowledgable** ('nɒlɪdʒəbᵊl) *adj.* possessing or indicating much knowledge. —'**knowledgeableness** *or* '**knowledgableness** *n.* —'**knowledgeably** *or* '**knowledgably** *adv.*

known (nəʊn) *vb.* **1.** the past participle of **know.** ~*adj.* **2.** specified and identified: *a known criminal.* ~*n.* **3.** a fact or entity known.

KNP *Chess. symbol for* king's knight's pawn.

Knt *abbrev. for* Knight.

knuckle ('nʌkᵊl) *n.* **1.** a joint of a finger, esp. that connecting a finger to the hand. **2.** a joint of veal, pork, etc., consisting of the part of the leg below the knee joint, often used in making stews or stock. **3.** the cylindrical portion of a hinge through which the pin passes. **4.** an angle joint between two members of a structure. **5. near the knuckle.** *Informal.* approaching indecency. ~*vb.* **6.** (*tr.*) to rub or press with the knuckles. **7.** (*intr.*) to keep the knuckles on the ground while shooting a marble. ~See also **knuckle down, knuckle under.** [C14: related to Middle High German *knöchel,* Middle Low German *knoke* bone, Dutch *knok*] —'**knuckly** *adj.*

knucklebone ('nʌkᵊlˌbəʊn) *n.* any bone forming part of a knuckle or knuckle joint.

knucklebones ('nʌkᵊlˌbəʊnz) *n.* (*functioning as sing.*) a less common name for **jacks** (the game).

knuckle down *vb.* (*intr., adv.*) *Informal.* to apply oneself diligently: *to knuckle down to some work.*

knuckle-duster *n.* (*often pl.*) a metal bar fitted over the knuckles, often with holes for the fingers, for inflicting injury by a blow with the fist.

knucklehead ('nʌkᵊlˌhɛd) *n. Informal.* fool; idiot. —'**knuckle-ˌheaded** *adj.*

knuckle joint *n.* **1.** any of the joints of the fingers. **2.** *Mechanical engineering.* a hinged joint between two rods, often a ball and socket joint.

knuckle under *vb.* (*intr., adv.*) to give way under pressure or authority; yield.

knur, knurr (nɜː), *or* **knar** *n.* a knot or protuberance in a tree trunk or in wood. [C16 *knor;* related to Middle High German *knorre* knot; compare KNAR]

knurl *or* **nurl** (nɜːl) *vb.* (*tr.*) **1.** to impress with a series of fine ridges or serrations. ~*n.* **2.** a small ridge, esp. one of a series providing a rough surface that can be gripped. [C17: probably from KNUR]

knurly ('nɜːlɪ) *adj.* **knurlier, knurliest.** a rare word for **gnarled.**

KO *or* **k.o.** ('keɪ'əʊ) *vb.* **KO's, KO'ing, KO'd; k.o.'s, k.o.'ing, k.o.'d,** *n., pl.* **KO's** *or* **k.o.'s.** a slang term for **knock out** or **knockout.**

koa ('kəʊə) *n.* **1.** a Hawaiian mimosaceous tree, *Acacia koa,* yielding a hard wood. **2.** the reddish wood of this tree, used esp. for furniture. [C19: from Hawaiian]

koaea ('kəʊaɪə) *n. N.Z.* a Maori name for **butterfish** (sense 2).

koala *or* **koala bear** (kəʊ'ɑːlə) *n.* a slow-moving Australian arboreal marsupial, *Phascolarctus cinereus,* having dense greyish fur and feeding on eucalyptus leaves and bark. Also called (Austral.): **native bear.** [from a native Australian language]

koan ('kəʊæn) *n.* (in Zen Buddhism) a problem or riddle that admits no logical solution. [from Japanese]

kob (kɒb) *n.* any of several species of African antelope, esp. *Kobus kob:* similar to waterbucks. [C20: from a Niger-Congo language; compare Wolof *koba,* Fulani *kōba*]

kobold ('kɒbəʊld) *n. German myth.* **1.** a mischievous household sprite. **2.** a spirit that haunts subterranean places, such as mines. [C19: from German; see COBALT]

Köchel (*German* 'kœçəl) *n.* See **K**

kochia ('kəʊkɪə) *n.* any plant of the widely distributed annual genus *Kochia,* esp. *K. Scoparia trichophila,* grown for its foliage, which turns dark red in the late summer: family *Chenopodiaceae.* Also called: **burning bush, summer cypress.** [named after W. D. J. *Koch* (1771–1849), German botanist]

Kodiak bear *or* **Kodiak** ('kəʊdɪˌæk) *n.* a large variety of the brown bear, *Ursus arctos,* inhabiting the west coast of Alaska and neighbouring islands, esp. Kodiak.

koeksister ('kʊkˌsɪstə) *n. S. African.* a small cake of sweetened dough, usually dipped in syrup. [Afrikaans]

koel ('kəʊəl) *n.* any of several parasitic cuckoos of the genus *Eudynamys,* esp. *E. scolopacea,* of S and SE Asia and Australia. [C19: from Hindi, from Sanskrit *kokila*]

kofta ('kɒftə) *n.* an Indian dish of seasoned minced meat shaped into small balls and cooked. [Urdu]

koftgar ('kɒftgɑː) *n.* (in India) a person skilled in the art of inlaying steel with gold (**koftgari**). [C19: Urdu]

kohanga reo (kə'həŋgə 'rɛɔ) *n. N.Z.* an infant class in which the lessons are conducted in Maori. [Maori, literally: language nest]

Kohen *or* **Cohen** (kɒ'hɛn, kɔɪn) *n. Judaism.* a member of the priestly family of the Tribe of Levi, descended from Aaron, who has certain ritual privileges in the synagogue service. [from Hebrew, literally: priest]

kohl (kəʊl) *n.* a cosmetic powder used, originally esp. in Muslim and Asian countries, to darken the area around the eyes. It is usually powdered antimony sulphide. [C18: from Arabic *kohl;* see ALCOHOL]

kohlrabi (kəʊl'rɑːbɪ) *n., pl.* **-bies.** a cultivated variety of cabbage, *Brassica oleracea caulorapa* (or *gongylodes*), whose thickened stem is eaten as a vegetable. Also called: **turnip cabbage.** [C19: from German, from Italian *cavoli rape* (pl.), from *cavolo* cabbage (from Latin *caulis*) + *rapa* turnip (from Latin); influenced by German *Kohl* cabbage]

koine ('kɔɪniː) *n.* a common language among speakers of different languages; lingua franca. [from Greek *koinē dialektos* common language]

Koine ('kɔɪniː) *n.* (*sometimes not cap.*) **the.** the Ancient Greek dialect that was the lingua franca of the empire of Alexander the Great and was widely used throughout the E Mediterranean area in Roman times.

kokako ('kəʊˌkɑːkəʊ) *n., pl.* **-kos.** a dark grey long-tailed wattled crow of New Zealand, *Callaeas cinerea.* [Maori]

kokanee (kəʊ'kænɪ) *n.* a landlocked salmon, *Oncorhynchus nerka kennerlyi,* of lakes in W North America: a variety of sockeye. [probably from *Kokanee* Creek, in SE British Columbia]

kokobeh ('kʌkʌbe) *adj.* (of certain fruit) having a rough skin: *kokobeh breadfruit.* [from Twi: leprosy]

kola ('kəʊlə) *n.* a variant spelling of **cola**[1].

kola nut *n.* a variant spelling of **cola nut.**

kolinsky (kə'lɪnskɪ) *n., pl.* **-skies.** **1.** any of various Asian minks, esp. *Mustela sibirica* of Siberia. **2.** the rich tawny fur of this animal. [C19: from Russian *kolinski* of *Kola,* peninsula in NW Russia]

kolkhoz, kolkhos (kɒl'hɔːz; *Russian* kal'xɔs), *or* **kolkoz** (kɒl'kɔːz) *n.* a Russian collective farm. [C20: from Russian, short for *kollektivnoe khozyaistvo* collective farm]

Kol Nidre (kɔːl 'nɪdreɪ; *Hebrew* kɔl niː'dre) *n. Judaism.* **1.** the evening service with which Yom Kippur begins. **2.** the opening prayer of that service, declaring null in advance any purely religious vows one may come to make in the coming year. [Aramaic *kōl nidhrē* all the vows; the prayer's opening words]

kolo ('kəʊləʊ) *n., pl.* **-los.** **1.** a Serbian folk dance in which a circle of people dance slowly around one or more dancers in the centre. **2.** a piece of music composed for or in the rhythm of this dance. [Serbo-Croatian, from Old Slavonic: wheel; related to Old English *hwēol* WHEEL]

komatik ('kəʊmætɪk) *n.* a sledge having wooden runners and crossbars bound with rawhide, used by Eskimos. [C20: from Eskimo (Labrador)]

Komi ('kəʊmɪ) *n.* **1.** (*pl.* **Komi** *or* **Komis**) a member of a Finno-Ugric people living chiefly in the former ASSR of Komi, in NW Russia. **2.** the Finno-Ugric language of this people; Zyrian.

Komodo dragon *or* **lizard** (kə'məʊdəʊ) *n.* the largest monitor lizard, *Varanus komodoensis,* of Komodo and other East Indian islands: grows to a length of 3 m (about 10 ft.) and a weight of 135 kilograms (about 300 lbs.).

komondor ('kɒmənˌdɔː) *n.* a large powerful dog of an ancient Hungarian breed, originally used for sheep herding. It has a very long white coat that hangs in woolly or matted locks.

kondo ('kɒndəʊ) *n., pl.* **-dos.** (in Uganda) a thief or armed robber. [C20: from Luganda]

koneke ('kɒnˌɛkɪ) *n. N.Z.* a farm vehicle with runners in front and wheels at the rear. [Maori]

Kongo ('kɒŋgəʊ) *n.* **1.** (*pl.* **-gos** *or* **-go**) a member of a Negroid people of Africa living in the tropical forests of Zaïre, the Congo Republic, and Angola. **2.** the language of this people, belonging to the Bantu group of the Niger-Congo family.

kongoni (kəŋ'gəʊnɪ) *n., pl.* **-ni.** an E African hartebeest, *Alcelaphus buselaphus.* See **hartebeest** (sense 1). [Swahili]

konimeter (kəʊ'nɪmɪtə) *n.* a device for collecting samples of dust, etc., in the air by sucking the air through a hole and allowing it to pass over a glass plate coated with grease on which the particles collect. [C20: from Greek *konia* dust + -METER]

koniology *or* **coniology** (ˌkəʊnɪ'ɒlədʒɪ) *n.* the study of atmospheric dust and its effects. [C20: from Greek *konia* dust + -LOGY]

koodoo ('kuːduː) *n.* a variant spelling of **kudu.**

kook (kuːk) *n. U.S. and Canadian informal.* an eccentric, crazy, or foolish person. [C20: probably from CUCKOO]

kookaburra ('kʊkəˌbʌrə) *n.* a large arboreal Australian kingfisher, *Dacelo novaeguineae* (or *gigas*), with a cackling cry. Also called: **laughing jackass.** [C19: from a native Australian language]

kooky *or* **kookie** ('kuːkɪ) *adj.* **kookier, kookiest.** *U.S. and Canadian informal.* crazy, eccentric, or foolish.

koori ('kʊərɪ) *n., pl.* **-ries.** an Australian Aborigine. [C19: from a native Australian language]

kop (kɒp) *n.* a prominent isolated hill or mountain in southern Africa. See **inselberg.** [from Afrikaans: head, hence high part; compare German *Kopf* head; see COP[2]]

kopeck, kopek, *or* **copeck** ('kəʊpɛk) *n.* a Soviet monetary unit worth one hundredth of a rouble. [Russian *kopeika,* from *kopye* lance; so called because of the representation of Tsar Ivan IV on the coin with a lance in his hand]

koph *or* **qoph** (kɒf) *n.* the 19th letter in the Hebrew alphabet (ק) transliterated as *q,* and pronounced as a velar or uvular stop. [from Hebrew *qoph;* see QOPH]

kopje *or* **koppie** ('kɒpɪ) *n.* a small kop. [C19: from Afrikaans *koppie,* from Dutch *kopje,* literally: a little head, from *kop* head; see KOP]

koppa ('kɒpə) *n.* a consonantal letter in the Greek alphabet pronounced like kappa (K) with the point of articulation further back in the throat. It became obsolete in classical (Attic) Greek orthography, but was passed on to the Romans who incorporated it into their alphabet as Q [Greek, of Semitic origin]

kora ('kɔːrə) *n.* a West African instrument with twenty-one strings, combining features of the harp and the lute.

Koran (kɔː'rɑːn) *n.* the sacred book of Islam, believed by Muslims to be the infallible word of God dictated to Mohammed through the medium of the angel Gabriel. Also: **Qur'an.** [C17: from Arabic *qur'ān* reading, book; related to *qara'a* to read, recite] —**Ko'ranic** *adj.*

Korat cat ('kɔːræt) *n.* a rare type of cat originating in Thailand that has a blue-grey coat and, in the adult, brilliant green eyes. [named after the *Korat* Plateau in Thailand]

Kordofanian (ˌkɔːdəʊ'feɪnɪən) *n.* **1.** a group of languages spoken in the Kordofan and Nuba Hills of the S Sudan: classed as an independent family, probably distantly related to Niger-Congo. ~*adj.* **2.** denoting, relating to, or belonging to this group of languages. **3.** of or relating to Kordofan, a province of central Sudan.

Korean (kə'riːən) *adj.* **1.** of or relating to Korea, in E Asia, its people, or their language. ~*n.* **2.** a native or inhabitant of Korea. **3.** the official language of North and South Korea, considered by some scholars to be part of the Altaic family of languages.

Korero (kə'rɛrɔ) *n., pl.* **-ros.** *N.Z.* a talk or discussion; meeting. [Maori]

korfball ('kɔːfˌbɔːl) *n.* a game similar to basketball, in which each team consists of six men and six women. [C20: from Dutch *korfbal* basketball]

korma *or* **qorma** ('kɔːmə) *n.* any of a variety of Indian dishes consisting of meat or vegetables braised with water, stock, yoghurt, or cream. [from Urdu]

Korsakoffian (ˌkɔːsə'kɒfɪən) *adj.* **1.** relating to or suffering from Korsakoff's psychosis. ~*n.* **2.** a person suffering from Korsakoff's psychosis.

Korsakoff's psychosis *or* **syndrome** ('kɔːsəkɒfs) *n.* a mental illness involving severe confusion and inability to retain recent memories, usually caused by alcoholism. [C19: named after Sergei *Korsakoff* (1854–1900), Russian neuropsychiatrist, who described it]

koru ('kɒruː) *n. N.Z.* a stylized curved pattern used esp. in carving. [Maori]

koruna (kɒ'ruːnə) *n.* the standard monetary unit of Czechoslovakia, divided into 100 halers. [Czech, from Latin *corōna* crown, wreath; see CROWN]

kos (kəʊs) *n., pl.* **kos.** an Indian unit of distance having different values in different localities. It is usually between 1 and 3 miles or 1 and 5 kilometres. Also called: **coss.** [from Hindi *kōs*]

kosher ('kəʊʃə) *adj.* **1.** *Judaism.* conforming to religious law; fit for use: esp., (of food) prepared in accordance with the dietary laws. See also **kasher, kashruth.** **2.** *Informal.* **a.** genuine or authentic. **b.** legitimate or proper. [C19: from Yiddish, from Hebrew *kāshēr* right, proper]

koto ('kəʊtəʊ) *n., pl.* **kotos.** a Japanese stringed instrument, consisting of a rectangular wooden body over which are stretched silk strings, which are plucked with plectra or a nail-like device. [Japanese]

kotuku ('kəʊtʊkuː) *n., pl.* **-ku.** *N.Z.* the white heron, *Egretta alba,* having brilliant white plumage, black legs and yellow eyes and bill. [Maori]

koulibiaca *or* **coulibiaca** (ˌkəʊlɪ'bjɑːkə) *n.* a Russian baked dish consisting of flaked fish mixed with semolina encased in pastry. [from Russian]

koumis ('kuːmɪs) *n.* a variant spelling of **kumiss.**

kouprey ('kuːpreɪ) *n.* a large wild member of the cattle tribe, *Box sauveli,* of SE Asia, having a blackish-brown body and white legs: an endangered species. [C20: from French, from a Cambodian native name, from Pali *gō* cow + Khmer *brai* forest]

kowhai ('koːwaɪ) *n. N.Z.* a small leguminous tree, *Sophora tetraptera,* of New Zealand and Chile, with clusters of yellow flowers. [C19: from Maori]

kowtow (ˌkaʊ'taʊ) *vb. (intr.)* **1.** to touch the forehead to the ground as a sign of deference: a former Chinese custom. **2.** (often foll. by *to*) to be servile or obsequious (towards). ~*n.* **3.** the act of kowtowing. [C19: from Chinese *k'o t'ou,* from *k'o* to strike, knock + *t'ou* head] —ˌ**kow'tower** *n.*

KP *abbrev. for:* **1.** Knight (of the Order) of St Patrick. **2.** *U.S. military.* kitchen police. ~**3.** *Chess. symbol for* king's pawn.

kph *abbrev. for* kilometres per hour.

Kr **1.** *Currency. symbol for:* **a.** krona. **b.** krone. **2.** *the chemical symbol for* krypton.

KR *Chess. symbol for* king's rook.

kr. *abbrev. for:* **1.** krona. **2.** krone.

kraal (krɑːl) *S. African.* ~*n.* **1.** a hut village in southern Africa, esp. one surrounded by a stockade. **2.** an enclosure for livestock. ~*adj.* **3.** denoting or relating to the tribal aspects of the Black African way of life. ~*vb.* **4.** *(tr.)* to enclose (livestock) in a kraal. [C18: from Afrikaans, from Portuguese *curral* pen; see CORRAL]

kraft (krɑːft) *n.* strong wrapping paper, made from pulp processed with a sulphate solution. [from German: force]

krait (kraɪt) *n.* any nonaggressive brightly coloured venomous elapid snake of the genus *Bungarus,* of S and SE Asia. [C19: from Hindi *karait,* of obscure origin]

kraken ('krɑːkən) *n.* a legendary sea monster of gigantic size believed to dwell off the coast of Norway. [C18: from Norwegian, of obscure origin]

krameria (krə'mɪərɪə) *n.* another name for **rhatany** (plant or drug). [C18: New Latin, named (by Linnaeus) after J. G. H. *Kramer,* an Austrian botanist]

krans (krɑːns) *n. S. African.* a sheer rock face; precipice. [C18: from Afrikaans]

K ration *n.* a small package containing emergency rations used by U.S. and Allied forces in the field in World War II. [C20: *K,* from the initial of the surname of Ancel *Keys* (born 1904), U.S. physiologist who instigated it]

Kraut (kraʊt) *n., adj. Slang.* a derogatory word for **German.** [from German *(Sauer)kraut,* literally: (pickled) cabbage]

Krebs cycle (krɛbz) *n.* a stage of tissue respiration: a series of biochemical reactions occurring in mitochondria in the presence of oxygen by which acetate, derived from the break down of foodstuffs, is converted to carbon dioxide and water, with the release of energy. Also called: **citric acid cycle, tricarboxylic acid cycle.** [C20: named after Sir Hans *Krebs* (1900–81), British biochemist]

kremlin ('krɛmlɪn) *n.* the citadel of any Russian city. [C17: from obsolete German *Kremelin,* from Russian *kreml'*]

Kremlin ('krɛmlɪn) *n.* the central government of the former Soviet Union, housed in the citadel of the same name in Moscow.

Kremlinology (ˌkrɛmlɪn'ɒlədʒɪ) *n.* the study and analysis of the policies and practices of the Soviet government. —ˌ**Kremlin'ologist** *n.*

kreplach ('krɛplɑːk, -lɑːx) *pl. n.* small filled dough casings usually served in soup. [C20: from Yiddish]

kreutzer *or* **kreuzer** ('krɔɪtsə) *n.* any of various former copper and silver coins of Germany or Austria. [C16: from German *Kreuzer,* from *Kreuz* cross, from Latin *crux;* referring to the cross originally stamped upon such coins]

kriegspiel ('kriːgˌspiːl) *n.* **1.** *(sometimes cap.)* another word for **war game.** **2.** a variation of chess in which each player has his own board and men and does not see his opponent's board and men. The moves are regulated by an umpire on a third board out of sight of both players. [C19: from German *Kriegsspiel* war game]

krill (krɪl) *n., pl.* **krill.** any small shrimplike marine crustacean of the order *Euphausiacea:* the principal food of whalebone whales. [C20: from Norwegian *kril* young fish]

krimmer *or* **crimmer** ('krɪmə) *n.* a tightly curled light grey fur obtained from the skins of lambs from the Crimean region. [C20: from German, from *Krim,* Crimea]

Krio ('kriːəʊ) *n.* **1.** the English-based creole widely used as a lingua franca in Sierra Leone. Its principal language of admixture is Yoruba. **2.** *(pl.* **-os)** a native speaker of Krio. **3.** *(modifier)* of or relating to the Krio language or Krios: *Krio poetry.* [alteration of CREOLE]

Kriol ('krɪɒl) *n.* a creole language used by Aboriginal communities in the northern regions of Australia, developed from Northern Territory pidgin.

kris (krɪs) *n.* a Malayan and Indonesian stabbing or slashing knife with a scalloped edge. Also called: **crease, creese.** [C16: from Malay *kris*]

Krishna ('krɪʃnə) *n. Hinduism.* the most celebrated of the Hindu deities. [via Hindi from Sanskrit, literally: dark, black] —'**Krishnaism** *n.*

Kriss Kringle (ˌkrɪs 'krɪŋgᵊl) *n. Chiefly U.S.* another name for **Santa Claus.** [changed from German *Christkindl* little Christ child, from CHRIST + *Kindl,* from *Kind* child]

KRL *abbrev. for* knowledge representation language (in artificial intelligence).

kromesky (krə'mɛskɪ) *n., pl.* **-kies.** a croquette consisting of a piece of bacon wrapped round minced meat or fish. [C19: from Russian *kromochka,* diminutive of *kroma* slice of bread]

krona ('krəʊnə) *n., pl.* **krona** ('krəʊnə). the standard monetary unit of Sweden, divided into 100 öre.

króna ('krəʊnə) *n., pl.* **-nur** (-nə). the standard monetary unit of Iceland, divided into 100 aurar.

krone[1] ('krəʊnə) *n., pl.* **-ner** (-nə). **1.** the standard monetary unit of Denmark and its dependencies, divided into 100 øre. **2.** the standard monetary unit of Norway, divided into 100 øre. [C19: from Danish or Norwegian, from Middle Low German *krōne,* ultimately from Latin *corōna* CROWN]

krone[2] ('krəʊnə) *n., pl.* **-nen** (-nən). **1.** a former German gold coin worth ten marks. **2.** a former Austrian monetary unit. [C19: from German, literally: crown; see KRONE[1]]

Kronecker delta ('krɒnɪkə) *n. Maths.* a function of two variables, i and j, that has a value of zero unless $i = j$, when it has a value of unity. Symbol: δ_{ij} [named after Leopold *Kronecker* (1823–91), German mathematician]

kroon (kruːn) *n., pl.* **kroons** *or* **krooni** ('kruːnɪ). the monetary unit of Estonia before 1940. [Estonian *kron,* from German *krone* KRONE[2]]

KRP *Chess. symbol for* king's rook's pawn.

Krugerrand ('kruːgəˌrænd) *n.* a South African coin used for investment only and containing 1 troy ounce of gold. [C20: from S. J. P. *Kruger* (1825–1904), Boer statesman, + RAND[1]]

kruller ('krʌlə) *n.* a variant spelling of **cruller.**

krummholz ('krʊmˌhəʊlts) *n. Botany.* the zone of stunted windblown trees growing at high altitudes just above the timber line. [C20: from German *krumm* bent + *Holz* wood]

krummhorn ('krʌmˌhɔːn) *n.* a variant spelling of **crumhorn.**

krypton ('krɪptɒn) *n.* an inert gaseous element occurring in trace amounts in air and used in fluorescent lights and lasers. Symbol: Kr; atomic no.: 36; atomic wt.: 83.80; density: 3.733 kg/m^3; melting pt.: –169°C; boiling pt.: –151.7°C. [C19: from Greek, from *kruptos* hidden; see CRYPT]

krytron ('kraɪtrɒn) *n. Electronics.* a type of fast electronic gas-discharge switch, used as a trigger in nuclear weapons.

KS *abbrev. for* Kansas.

Kshatriya ('kʃætrɪə) *n.* a member of the second of the four main Hindu castes, the warrior caste. [C18: from Sanskrit, from *kshatra* rule]

KStJ *abbrev. for* Knight of the Order of St John.

kt *abbrev. for:* **1.** karat. **2.** *Nautical.* knot.

Kt **1.** Also: **Knt.** *abbrev. for* knight. ~**2.** Also: **N.** *Chess. symbol for* knight.

KT *abbrev. for:* **1.** Knight of the Order of the Thistle (a Brit. title). **2.** Knight Templar.

kt. *abbrev. for* kiloton.

K/T boundary *n. Geology.* **a.** Cretaceous/Tertiary boundary: the time zone comprising the end of the Cretaceous and the beginning of the Tertiary periods. **b.** (*as modifier*): *K/T boundary sediments.* [C20: *K* and *T*, symbols for Cretaceous and Tertiary, respectively]

kuccha ('kʌtʃtʃʌ) *n.* short trousers traditionally worn by Sikhs as a symbol of their religious and cultural loyalty: originally worn for ease of horse riding. See also **five Ks.** [Punjabi]

kuchen ('kuːxən) *n.* a breadlike cake containing apple, nuts, and sugar, originating from Germany. [German: CAKE]

kudos ('kjuːdɒs) *n.* (*functioning as sing.*) acclaim, glory, or prestige. [C18: from Greek]

kudu *or* **koodoo** ('kuːduː) *n.* either of two spiral-horned antelopes, *Tragelaphus strepsiceros* (**greater kudu**) or *T. imberbis* (**lesser kudu**), which inhabit the bush of Africa. [C18: from Afrikaans *koedoe*, probably from Xhosa *iqudu*]

kudzu ('kʊdzuː) *n.* a hairy leguminous climbing plant, *Pueraria thunbergiana*, of China and Japan, with trifoliate leaves and purple fragrant flowers. [from Japanese *kuzu*]

kueh ('kɔeɪ) *n.* (*functioning as sing. or pl.*) (in Malaysia) any cake of Malay, Chinese, or Indian origin. [from Malay]

Kufic *or* **Cufic** ('kuːfɪk, 'kjuː-) *adj.* **1.** of, relating to, or denoting an early form of the Arabic alphabet employed in making copies of the Koran. ~*n.* **2.** the script formed by the letters of this alphabet.

kufiyah (kʊ'fiːjə) *n.* a variant of **keffiyeh.**

Ku Klux Klan ('kuː 'klʌks 'klæn) *n.* **1.** a secret organization of White Southerners formed after the U.S. Civil War to fight Black emancipation and Northern domination. **2.** a secret organization of White Protestant Americans, mainly in the South, who use violence against Blacks, Jews, and other minority groups. [C19 *Ku Klux*, probably based on Greek *kuklos* CIRCLE + *Klan* CLAN] —**Ku Kluxer** *or* **Ku Klux Klanner** *n.* —**Ku Kluxism** *n.*

kukri ('kʊkrɪ) *n., pl.* **-ris.** a knife with a curved blade that broadens towards the point, esp. as used by Gurkhas. [from Hindi]

kukukuma ('kuːkʊˌkuːmə) *n.* the N.Z. name for **gurnard.** [Maori]

kula ('kuːlə) *n.* a ceremonial gift exchange practised among a group of islanders in the W Pacific, used to establish relations between islands. [of Melanesian origin]

kulak ('kuːlæk) *n.* (in Russia after 1906) a member of the class of peasants who became proprietors of their own farms. After the October Revolution the kulaks opposed collectivization of land, but in 1929 Stalin initiated their liquidation. [C19: from Russian fist, hence, tightfisted person; related to Turkish *kol* arm]

kulan ('kuːˌlɑːn) *n.* the Asiatic wild ass of the Russian steppes, probably a variety of kiang or onager. [C18: from Kirghiz]

Kultur (kʊl'tʊə) *n.* (often used ironically) German civilization, esp. as characterized by authoritarianism and earnestness. [German, from Latin *cultūra* CULTURE]

Kulturkampf (kʊl'tʊəˌkæmpf, 'kʊltə-) *n.* the struggle of the Prussian state against the Roman Catholic Church (1872–87), which took the form of laws designed to bring education, marriage, etc., under the control of the state. [German: culture struggle]

kumbaloi (ˌkʊmbə'lɔɪ) *pl. n.* another name for **worry beads.** [C20: Modern Greek]

kumera *or* **kumara** ('kuːmərə) *n.* the N.Z. name for **sweet potato.** [Maori]

kumiss, koumiss, koumis, *or* **koumyss** ('kuːmɪs) *n.* a drink made from fermented mare's or other milk, drunk by certain Asian tribes, esp. in Russia or used for dietetic and medicinal purposes. [C17: from Russian *kumys*, from Kazan Tatar *kumyz*]

kumite ('kuimɪˌteɪ) *n. Karate, etc.* freestyle sparring or fighting. [C20: Japanese, literally: sparring]

kümmel ('kʊməl; *German* 'kyməl) *n.* a German liqueur flavoured with aniseed and cumin. [C19: from German *Kümmel*, from Old High German *kumil*, probably variant of *kumin* CUMIN]

kummerbund ('kʌməˌbʌnd) *n.* a variant spelling of **cummerbund.**

kumquat *or* **cumquat** ('kʌmkwɒt) *n.* **1.** any of several small Chinese trees of the rutaceous genus *Fortunella.* **2.** the small round orange fruit of such a tree, with a sweet rind, used in preserves and confections. [C17: from Chinese (Cantonese) *kam kwat*, representing Mandarin Chinese *chin chü* golden orange]

kung fu ('kʌŋ 'fuː) *n.* a Chinese martial art combining principles of karate and judo. [from Chinese: martial art]

kunzite ('kʊntsaɪt) *n.* a lilac-coloured transparent variety of the mineral spodumene: a gemstone. [C20: named after George F. *Kunz* (1856–1932), U.S. gem expert]

kurchatovium (ˌkɜːtʃə'təʊvɪəm) *n.* another name for **rutherfordium,** esp. as used in the Soviet Union. [C20: from Russian, named after I. V. *Kurchatov* (1903–60), Soviet physicist]

Kurd (kɜːd) *n.* a member of a nomadic people living chiefly in E Turkey, N Iraq, and W Iran.

kurdaitcha (kə'daɪtʃə) *n.* (in certain Central Australian Aboriginal tribes) the man with the mission of avenging the death of a tribesman. Also: **kadaitcha.**

kurdaitcha shoes *pl. n.* (in certain Central Australian Aboriginal tribes) the emu-feather shoes worn by the kurdaitcha on his mission so that his footsteps may not be traced. Also: **kadaitcha shoes.**

Kurdish ('kɜːdɪʃ) *n.* **1.** the language of the Kurds, belonging to the West Iranian branch of the Indo-European family. ~*adj.* **2.** of or relating to the Kurds or their language.

kuri ('kuːrɪ) *n., pl.* **-ris.** *N.Z.* a mongrel dog. Also called **goorie.** [Maori]

kurrajong *or* **currajong** ('kʌrəˌdʒɒŋ) *n.* any of various Australian trees or shrubs, esp. *Brachychiton populneum*, a sterculiaceous tree that yields a tough durable fibre. [C19: from a native Australian language]

kursaal ('kɜːzᵊl) *n.* **1.** a public room at a health resort. **2.** an amusement park at a seaside or other resort. [from German, literally: cure room]

kurta *or* **khurta** ('kʊətə) *n.* a long loose garment like a shirt without a collar worn in India. [Hindi]

kurtosis (kə'təʊsɪs) *n. Statistics.* a measure of the concentration of a distribution around its mean, esp. the statistic $B_2 = m_4/m_2^2$ where m_2 and m_4 are respectively the second and fourth moment of the distribution around the mean. In a normal distribution $B_2 = 3$. See also **platykurtic, mesokurtic, leptokurtic.** Compare **skewness.** [from Greek: curvature, from *kurtos* arched]

kuru ('kʊruː) *n.* a degenerative disease of the nervous system, restricted to certain tribes in New Guinea, marked by loss of muscular control and thought to be caused by a slow virus. [C20: from a native name]

kurus (kʊ'ruːʃ) *n., pl.* **-rus.** another word for **piastre** (sense 2b). [from Turkish]

kutu ('kuːtuː) *n. N.Z.* a slang word for **body louse** (see **louse** (sense 1)). Also called: **cootie.** [Maori]

Kuwaiti (kʊ'weɪtɪ) *or* **Kowaiti** (kəʊ'weɪtɪ) *adj.* **1.** of or relating to Kuwait, a state on the NW Persian Gulf, or to its people, culture, etc. ~*n.* **2.** (*pl.* **-tis**) a native or inhabitant of Kuwait.

kV *abbrev. for* kilovolt.

KV *abbrev. for* Köchel Verzeichnis. See **K** [German, literally: Köchel catalogue]

kvass, kvas, *or* **quass** (kvɑːs) *n.* an alcoholic drink of low strength made in the Soviet Union and E Europe from cereals and stale bread. [C16: from Russian *kvas*; related to Old Slavic *kvasŭ* yeast, Latin *cāseus* cheese]

kW *abbrev. for* kilowatt.

Kwa (kwɑː) *n.* **1.** a group of languages, now generally regarded as a branch of the Niger-Congo family, spoken in an area of W Africa extending from the Ivory Coast to E Nigeria and including Akan, Ewe, Yoruba, and Ibo. ~*adj.* **2.** relating to or belonging to this group of languages.

kwacha ('kwɑːtʃɑː) *n.* **1.** the standard monetary unit of Zambia, divided into 100 ngwee. **2.** the standard monetary unit of Malawi. [from a native word in Zambia]

Kwakiutl (ˌkwɑːkɪ'uːtᵊl) *n.* **1.** (*pl.* **-utl** *or* **-utls**) a member of a North American Indian people of N Vancouver Island and the adjacent mainland. **2.** the language of this people, belonging to the Wakashan family.

kwanza ('kwænzə) *n.* the monetary unit of Angola. [from a Bantu language]

kwashiorkor (ˌkwæʃɪ'ɔːkə) *n.* severe malnutrition of infants and young children, esp. soon after weaning, resulting from dietary deficiency of protein. [C20: from a native word in Ghana]

Kwedien (kwɪ'diːn) *n.* an African boy, esp. one who has not yet undergone the rites of initiation. [from Xhosa *inKwenkwe* boy]

kwela ('kweɪlə, 'kwɛlə) *n.* a type of pop music popular among the Black communities of South Africa. [C20: said to be from Zulu or Xhosa: jump up]

kWh *abbrev. for* kilowatt-hour.

KWIC (kwɪk) *n. acronym for* key word in context (esp. in the phrase **KWIC index**).

KWOC (kwɒk) *n. acronym for* key word out of context.

KWT *international car registration for* Kuwait.

Ky. *or* **KY** *abbrev. for* Kentucky.

kyanite ('kaɪəˌnaɪt) *n.* a variant spelling of **cyanite.** —**kyanitic** (ˌkaɪə'nɪtɪk) *adj.*

kyanize *or* **kyanise** ('kaɪəˌnaɪz) *vb.* (*tr.*) to treat (timber) with corrosive sublimate to make it resistant to decay. [C19: after J. H. *Kyan* (died 1850), English inventor of the process] —ˌ**kyani'zation** *or* ˌ**kyani'sation** *n.*

kyat (kɪ'ɑːt) *n.* the standard monetary unit of Burma, divided into 100 pyas. [from Burmese]

kyle (kaɪl) *n. Scot.* (esp. in place names) a narrow strait or channel: *Kyle of Lochalsh.* [C16: from Gaelic *caol*, from *caol* narrow]

kylie *or* **kiley** ('kaɪlɪ) *n. Austral.* a boomerang that is flat on one side and convex on the other. [C19: from a native Australian language]

kylin ('kiː'lɪn) *n.* (in Chinese art) a mythical animal of composite form. [C19: from Chinese *ch'i-lin*, literally: male-female]

kylix *or* **cylix** ('kaɪlɪks, 'kɪl-) *n., pl.* **-likes** (-lɪˌkiːz). a shallow two-handled drinking vessel used in ancient Greece. [C19: from Greek *kulix* cup; compare CHALICE]

kyloe ('kaɪləʊ) *n.* a breed of small long-horned long-haired beef cattle from NW Scotland. [C19: of uncertain origin]

kymograph ('kaɪməˌgrɑːf, -ˌgræf) *or* **cymograph** *n.* **1.** *Med.* a rotatable drum for holding paper on which a tracking stylus continuously records variations in blood pressure, respiratory movements, etc. **2.** *Phonetics.* this device as applied to the measurement of variations in the muscular action of the articulatory organs. **3.** an instrument for recording the angular oscillations of an aircraft in flight. [C20: from Greek *kuma* wave + -GRAPH] —ˌ**kymo'graphic** *or* ˌ**cymo'graphic** *adj.*

Kymric ('kɪmrɪk) *n., adj.* a variant spelling of **Cymric.**

Kymry ('kɪmrɪ) *pl. n.* a variant spelling of **Cymry**.
kype (kaɪp) *n.* the hook on the lower jaw of a mature male salmon. [from Scot. *kip, kipp* anthing beaked or hooked; perhaps related to Low German *kippe* point, tip]
kyphosis (kaɪ'fəʊsɪs) *n. Pathol.* backward curvature of the thoracic spine, of congenital origin or resulting from injury or disease; hunchback. See also **Pott's disease.** Compare **lordosis, scoliosis.** [C19: from New Latin, from Greek *kuphōsis,* from *kuphos* humpbacked] —**kyphotic** (kaɪ'fɒtɪk) *adj.*
Kyrie eleison ('kɪrɪɪ ə'leɪsᵊn) *n.* **1.** a formal invocation used in the liturgies of the Roman Catholic, Greek Orthodox, and Anglican Churches. **2.** a musical setting of this. Often shortened to **Kyrie.** [C14: via Late Latin from Late Greek *kurie, eleēson* Lord, have mercy]
kyte *or* **kite** (kəɪt) *n. Scot.* the belly. [C16: of uncertain origin]
kyu (kjuː) *n. Judo.* **1.** one of the five student grades for inexperienced competitors. **2.** a student in the kyu grades. ~Compare **dan**[2]. [from Japanese]

l *or* **L** (ɛl) *n., pl.* **l's, L's,** *or* **Ls.** **1.** the 12th letter and ninth consonant of the modern English alphabet. **2.** a speech sound represented by this letter, usually a lateral, as in *label.* **3. a.** something shaped like an L. **b.** (*in combination*): *an L-shaped room.*

l *symbol for:* **1.** litre. **2.** *Physics.* lepton number.

L *symbol for:* **1.** ell (unit). **2.** lambert(s). **3.** large. **4.** Latin. **5.** (on British motor vehicles) learner driver. **6.** *Physics.* length. **7.** live. **8.** *Currency.* **a.** Usually written £ . pound. [Latin: *libra*] **b.** lempira. **c.** lek. **d.** leu. **e.** lire. **9.** *Aeronautics.* lift. **10.** *Electronics.* inductor (in circuit diagrams). **11.** *Physics.* latent heat. **12.** *Physics.* self-inductance. **13.** *Chem.* the Avogadro constant. **14.** *the Roman numeral for* 50. See **Roman numerals. 15.** *international car registration for* Luxembourg.

L. *or* **l.** *abbrev. for:* **1.** lake. **2.** law. **3.** leaf. **4.** league. **5.** left. **6.** length. **7.** liber. [Latin: book] **8.** (*pl.* **LL.** *or* **ll.**) line. **9.** link. **10.** low.

L. *abbrev. for:* **1.** *Politics.* Liberal. **2.** (in titles) Licentiate. **3.** Linnaeus. **4.** (fraternal) Lodge.

la[1] (lɑː) *n. Music.* a variant spelling of **lah.**

la[2] (lɔː) *interj.* an exclamation of surprise or emphasis. [Old English *lā* LO]

La *the chemical symbol for* lanthanum.

LA *abbrev. for:* **1.** Legislative Assembly. **2.** Library Association. **3.** local agent. **4.** Los Angeles. **5.** Louisiana.

La. *abbrev. for* Louisiana.

laager *or* **lager** (ˈlɑːgə) *n.* **1.** (in Africa) a camp, esp. one defended by a circular formation of wagons. **2.** *Military.* a place where armoured vehicles are parked. *~vb.* **3.** to form (wagons) into a laager. **4.** (*tr.*) to park (armoured vehicles) in a laager. [C19: from Afrikaans *lager,* via German from Old High German *legar* bed, lair]

lab (læb) *n. Informal.* short for: **1.** laboratory. **2.** Labrador retriever.

lab. *abbrev. for:* **1.** laboratory. **2.** labour.

Lab. *abbrev. for:* **1.** *Politics.* Labour. **2.** Labrador.

labarum (ˈlæbərəm) *n., pl.* **-ra** (-rə). **1.** a standard or banner carried in Christian religious processions. **2.** the military standard bearing a Christian monogram used by Constantine the Great. [C17: from Late Latin, of obscure origin]

labdanum (ˈlæbdənəm) *or* **ladanum** *n.* a dark resinous juice obtained from various rockroses of the genus *Cistus,* used in perfumery and in the manufacture of fumigants and medicinal plasters. [C16: Latin, from Greek *ladanon,* from *lēdon* rockrose, from Semitic]

labefaction (ˌlæbɪˈfækʃən) *or* **labefactation** (ˌlæbɪfækˈteɪʃən) *n. Rare.* deterioration; weakening. [C17: from Late Latin *labefactiō,* from Latin *labefacere* shake, from *lābī* to fall + *facere* to make]

label (ˈleɪbᵊl) *n.* **1.** a piece of paper, card, or other material attached to an object to identify it or give instructions or details concerning its ownership, use, nature, destination, etc.; tag. **2.** a brief descriptive phrase or term given to a person, group, school of thought, etc.: *the label "Romantic" is applied to many different kinds of poetry.* **3.** a word or phrase heading a piece of text to indicate or summarize its contents. **4.** a trademark or company or brand name on certain goods, esp. on gramophone records. **5.** another name for **dripstone** (sense 2). **6.** *Heraldry.* a charge consisting of a horizontal line across the chief of a shield with three or more pendants: the charge of an eldest son. **7.** *Computer technol.* a group of characters, such as a number or a word, appended to a particular statement in a program to allow its unique identification. **8.** *Chem.* a radioactive element used in a compound to trace the mechanism of a chemical reaction. *~vb.* **-bels, -belling, -belled** *or U.S.* **-bels, -beling, -beled.** (*tr.*) **9.** to fasten a label to. **10.** to mark with a label. **11.** to describe or classify in a word or phrase: *to label someone a liar.* **12.** to make (one or more atoms in a compound) radioactive, for use in determining the mechanism of a reaction. [C14: from Old French, from Germanic; compare Old High German *lappa* rag] —**ˈlabeller** *n.*

labellum (ləˈbɛləm) *n., pl.* **-la** (-lə). **1.** the part of the corolla of certain plants, esp. orchids, that forms a distinct, often lobed, lip. **2.** a lobe at the tip of the proboscis of a fly. [C19: New Latin, diminutive of Latin *labrum* lip] —**laˈbelloid** *adj.*

labia (ˈleɪbɪə) *n.* the plural of **labium.**

labial (ˈleɪbɪəl) *adj.* **1.** of, relating to, or near lips or labia. **2.** *Music.* producing sounds by the action of an air stream over a narrow liplike fissure, as in a flue pipe of an organ. **3.** *Phonetics.* relating to a speech sound whose articulation involves movement or use of the lips: *a labial click.* *~n.* **4.** Also called: **labial pipe.** *Music.* an organ pipe with a liplike fissure. **5.** *Phonetics.* a speech sound such as English *p* or *m,* whose articulation involves movement or use of the lips. [C16: from Medieval Latin *labiālis,* from Latin *labium* lip] —ˌ**labiˈality** *n.* —**ˈlabially** *adv.*

labialize *or* **labialise** (ˈleɪbɪəˌlaɪz) *vb.* (*tr.*) *Phonetics.* to pronounce with articulation involving rounded lips, such as for (k) before a close back vowel (uː) as in English *cool.* —**ˈlabialˌism,** ˌ**labialiˈzation,** *or* ˌ**labialiˈsation** *n.*

labia majora (məˈdʒɔːrə) *pl. n.* the two elongated outer folds of skin in human females surrounding the vaginal orifice. [C18: New Latin: greater lips]

labia minora (mɪˈnɔːrə) *pl. n.* the two small inner folds of skin in human females forming the margins of the vaginal orifice. [C18: New Latin: smaller lips]

labiate (ˈleɪbɪˌeɪt, -ɪt) *n.* **1.** any plant of the family *Labiatae,* having square stems, aromatic leaves, and a two-lipped corolla: includes mint, thyme, sage, rosemary, etc. *~adj.* **2.** of, relating to, or belonging to the family *Labiatae.* [C18: from New Latin *labiātus,* from Latin *labium* lip]

labile (ˈleɪbɪl) *adj.* **1.** *Chem.* (of a compound) prone to chemical change. **2.** liable to change or move. [C15: via Late Latin *lābilis,* from Latin *lābī* to slide, slip] —**lability** (ləˈbɪlɪtɪ) *n.*

labio- *or before a vowel* **labi-** *combining form.* relating to or formed by the lips and (another organ or part): *labiodental.* [from Latin *labium* lip]

labiodental (ˌleɪbɪəʊˈdɛntᵊl) *Phonetics.* *~adj.* **1.** pronounced by bringing the bottom lip into contact or near contact with the upper teeth, as for the fricative (f) in English *fat, puff.* *~n.* **2.** a labiodental consonant.

labionasal (ˌleɪbɪəʊˈneɪzᵊl) *Phonetics.* *~adj.* **1.** pronounced by making a complete closure of the air passage at the lips and lowering the soft palate allowing air to escape through the nasal cavity. *~n.* **2.** a labionasal consonant, such as *m.*

labiovelar (ˌleɪbɪəʊˈviːlə) *Phonetics.* *~adj.* **1.** relating to or denoting a speech sound pronounced with simultaneous articulation at the soft palate and the lips. *~n.* **2.** a labiovelar speech sound, such as some pronunciations of the consonant spelt *q* in English.

labium (ˈleɪbɪəm) *n., pl.* **-bia** (-bɪə). **1.** a lip or liplike structure. **2.** any one of the four lip-shaped folds of the female vulva. See **labia majora, labia minora. 3.** the fused pair of appendages forming the lower lip of insects. **4.** the lower lip of the corolla of labiate flowers. [C16: New Latin, from Latin: lip]

lablab (ˈlæbˌlæb) *n.* **1.** a twining leguminous plant, *Dolichos lablab* (or *Lablab niger*), of tropical Africa. **2.** the edible pod or bean of this plant. [from Arabic]

labor (ˈleɪbə) *vb., n.* the U.S. spelling of **labour.**

laboratory (ləˈbɒrətərɪ, -trɪ; *U.S.* ˈlæbrəˌtɔːrɪ) *n., pl.* **-ries. 1. a.** a building or room equipped for conducting scientific research or for teaching practical science. **b.** (*as modifier*): *laboratory equipment.* **2.** a place where chemicals or medicines are manufactured. ~Often shortened to **lab.** See also **language laboratory.** [C17: from Medieval Latin *labōrātōrium* workshop, from Latin *labōrāre* to LABOUR]

Labor Day *n.* **1.** (in the U.S. and Canada) a public holiday in honour of labour, held on the first Monday in September. **2.** (in Australia) a public holiday observed on different days in different states.

laborious (ləˈbɔːrɪəs) *adj.* **1.** involving great exertion or long effort. **2.** given to working hard. **3.** (of literary style, etc.) not fluent. —**laˈboriously** *adv.* —**laˈboriousness** *n.*

labor union *n.* the U.S. name for **trade union.**

labour *or U.S.* **labor** (ˈleɪbə) *n.* **1.** productive work, esp. physical toil done for wages. **2. a.** the people, class, or workers involved in this, esp. in contrast to management, capital, etc. **b.** (*as modifier*): *a labour dispute; labour relations.* **3. a.** difficult or arduous work or effort. **b.** (*in combination*): *labour-saving.* **4.** a particular job or task, esp. of a difficult nature. **5. a.** the process or effort of childbirth or the time during which this takes place. **b.** (*as modifier*): *labour pains.* *~vb.* **6.** (*intr.*) to perform labour; work. **7.** (*intr.;* foll. by *for,* etc.) to strive or work hard (for something). **8.** (*intr.;* usually foll. by *under*) to be burdened (by) or be at a disadvantage (because of): *to labour under a misapprehension.* **9.** (*intr.*) to make one's way with difficulty. **10.** (*tr.*) to deal with or treat too persistently: *to labour a point.* **11.** (*intr.*) (of a woman) to be in labour. **12.** (*intr.*) (of a ship) to pitch and toss. [C13: via Old French from Latin *labor;* perhaps related to *lābī* to fall] —**ˈlabouringly** *or U.S.* **ˈlaboringly** *adv.*

labour camp *n.* **1.** a penal colony involving forced labour. **2.** a camp for migratory labourers.

Labour Day *n.* a public holiday in many countries in honour of labour, usually held on May 1. See also **Labor Day.**

laboured *or U.S.* **labored** (ˈleɪbəd) *adj.* **1.** (of breathing) performed with difficulty. **2.** showing effort; contrived; lacking grace or fluency. —'**labouredly** *or U.S.* '**laboredly** *adv.* —'**labouredness** *or U.S.* '**laboredness** *n.*

labourer *or U.S.* **laborer** ('leɪbərə) *n.* a person engaged in physical work, esp. of an unskilled kind.

labour exchange *n. Brit.* a former name for **employment office.**

labour-intensive *adj.* of or denoting a task, organization, industry, etc., in which a high proportion of the costs are due to wages, salaries, etc.

labourism *or U.S.* **laborism** ('leɪbəˌrɪzəm) *n.* **1.** the dominance of the working classes. **2.** a political, social, or economic system that favours such dominance. **3.** support for workers' rights.

labourist *or U.S.* **laborist** ('leɪbərɪst) *n.* **1.** a person who supports workers' rights. **2.** a supporter of labourism.

Labourite ('leɪbəˌraɪt) *n.* **1.** an adherent of the Labour Party, a British political party generally supporting the interests of organized labour and advocating nationalization and social reform. **2.** an adherent of any similar party in any of various other countries.

labour law *n.* those areas of law which appertain to the relationship between employers and employees and between employers and trade unions.

labour relations *pl. n.* **a.** collective relations between the management of an organization and its employees or employees' representatives. **b.** a set of such relations in a wider context, such as in an industry, or in a national economy.

labra ('leɪbrə, 'læb-) *n.* the plural of **labrum.**

Labrador ('læbrəˌdɔː) *n.* (*often not cap.*) short for **Labrador retriever.**

labradorescent (ˌlæbrədɔː'rɛsənt) *adj.* (of minerals) displaying a brilliant play of colours, as that shown by some forms of labradorite.

labradorite (ˌlæbrə'dɔːraɪt) *n.* a blue, green, or reddish-brown feldspar mineral of the plagioclase series: used as a decorative stone. Formula: $CaAl_2Si_2O_8.NaAlSi_3O_8$. [C18: named after *Labrador,* NE Canada, where it was found; see -ITE[1]]

Labrador retriever *n.* a powerfully-built variety of retriever with a short dense black or golden-brown coat. Often shortened to **Labrador** or (informal) **lab.**

Labrador tea *n.* **1.** either of two arctic evergreen ericaceous shrubs, *Ledum groenlandicum* or *L. palustre* var. *decumbens.* **2.** (in Canada) an infusion brewed from the leaves of either of these plants.

labret ('leɪbrɛt) *n.* a piece of bone, shell, etc.; inserted into the lip as an ornament by certain peoples. [C19: from Latin *labrum* lip]

labroid ('læbrɔɪd, 'leɪ-) *or* **labrid** ('læbrɪd) *n.* **1.** any percoid fish of the family *Labridae* (wrasses). ~*adj.* **2.** of or relating to the *Labridae.* [C19: from New Latin *Labroidea,* from Latin *lābrus* a fish, from *labrum* lip]

labrum ('leɪbrəm, 'læb-) *n., pl.* **-bra** (-brə). a lip or liplike part, such as the cuticular plate forming the upper lip of insects. [C19: New Latin, from Latin]

laburnum (lə'bɜːnəm) *n.* any papilionaceous tree or shrub of the Eurasian genus *Laburnum,* having clusters of yellow drooping flowers: all parts of the plant are poisonous. [C16: New Latin, from Latin]

labyrinth ('læbərɪnθ) *n.* **1.** a mazelike network of tunnels, chambers, or paths, either natural or man-made. Compare **maze** (sense 1). **2.** any complex or confusing system of streets, passages, etc. **3.** a complex or intricate situation. **4. a.** any system of interconnecting cavities, esp. those comprising the internal ear. **b.** another name for **internal ear. 5.** *Electronics.* an enclosure behind a high-performance loudspeaker, consisting of a series of air chambers designed to absorb unwanted sound waves. [C16: via Latin from Greek *laburinthos,* of obscure origin]

labyrinth fish *n.* any tropical freshwater spiny-finned fish of the family *Anabantidae* of SE Asia and Africa, having a lunglike respiratory organ. See also **anabantid.**

labyrinthine (ˌlæbə'rɪnθaɪn), **labyrinthian** (ˌlæbə'rɪnθɪən), *or* **labyrinthic** (ˌlæbə'rɪnθɪk) *adj.* **1.** of or relating to a labyrinth. **2.** resembling a labyrinth in complexity. —ˌ**laby'rinthically** *adv.*

labyrinthitis (ˌlæbərɪn'θaɪtɪs) *n.* inflammation of the inner ear, causing loss of balance, vertigo, and vomiting. Also called: **otitis interna.**

labyrinthodont (ˌlæbə'rɪnθəˌdɒnt) *n.* any primitive amphibian of the order *Labyrinthodontia,* of late Devonian to Triassic times, having teeth with much-folded dentine. [C19: from Greek *laburinthos* LABYRINTH + -ODONT]

lac[1] (læk) *n.* a resinous substance secreted by certain lac insects, used in the manufacture of shellac. [C16: from Dutch *lak* or French *laque,* from Hindi *lākh* resin, ultimately from Sanskrit *lākshā*]

lac[2] (lɑːk) *n.* a variant spelling of **lakh.**

LAC *Brit. abbrev. for* leading aircraftman.

laccolith ('lækəlɪθ) *or* **laccolite** ('lækəˌlaɪt) *n.* a dome of igneous rock between two layers of older sedimentary rock: formed by the intrusion of magma, forcing the overlying strata into a dome. [C19: from Greek *lakkos* cistern + -LITH] —ˌ**lacco'lithic** *or* **laccolitic** (ˌlækə'lɪtɪk) *adj.*

lace (leɪs) *n.* **1.** a delicate decorative fabric made from cotton, silk, etc., woven in an open web of different symmetrical patterns and figures. **2.** a cord or string drawn through holes or eyelets or around hooks to fasten a shoe or garment. **3.** ornamental braid often used on military uniforms, etc. **4.** a dash of spirits added to a beverage. ~*vb.* **5.** to fasten (shoes, etc.) with a lace. **6.** (*tr.*) to draw (a cord or thread) through holes, eyes, etc., as when tying shoes. **7.** (*tr.*) to compress the waist of (someone), as with a corset. **8.** (*tr.*) to add a small amount of alcohol or drugs to (food or drink). **9.** (*tr.; usually passive* and foll. by *with*) to streak or mark with lines or colours: *the sky was laced with red.* **10.** (*tr.*) to intertwine; interlace. **11.** (*tr.*) *Informal.* to give a sound beating to. [C13 *las,* from Old French *laz,* from Latin *laqueus* noose] ~See also **lace into, lace up.** —'**laceˌlike** *adj.* —'**lacer** *n.*

lacebark ('leɪsbɑːk) *n.* another name for **ribbonwood.**

lace bug *n.* a small bug of the family *Tingidae,* having a delicate pattern in the wing venation. They are plant feeders and include the **thistle lace bugs** (*Tingis cardui* and *T. ampliata*) and the **rhododendron bug** (*Stephanitis rhododendri*).

Lacedaemonian (ˌlæsɪdɪ'məʊnɪən) *adj., n.* another word for **Spartan.**

lace into *vb.* (*intr., prep*) to attack violently, either verbally or physically.

lacerant ('læsərənt) *adj.* painfully distressing; harrowing.

lacerate *vb.* ('læsəˌreɪt). (*tr.*) **1.** to tear (the flesh, etc.) jaggedly. **2.** to hurt or harrow (the feelings, etc.). ~*adj.* ('læsəˌreɪt, -rɪt). **3.** having edges that are jagged or torn; lacerated: *lacerate leaves.* [C16: from Latin *lacerāre* to tear, from *lacer* mangled] —'**lacerable** *adj.* —ˌ**lacera'bility** *n.* —ˌ**lacer'ation** *n.* —'**lacerative** *adj.*

Lacerta (lə'sɜːtə) *n., Latin genitive* **Lacertae** (lə'sɜːtiː). a small faint constellation in the N hemisphere, part of which is crossed by the Milky Way, lying between Cygnus and Andromeda. [Latin: lizard]

lacertilian (ˌlæsə'tɪlɪən) *n. also* **lacertian** (lə'sɜːʃən). **1.** any reptile of the suborder *Lacertilia* (lizards). ~*adj.* **2.** of, relating to, or belonging to the *Lacertilia.* [C19: New Latin, from Latin *lacerta* lizard]

lace up *vb.* **1.** (*tr., adv.*) to tighten or fasten (clothes or footwear) with laces. ~*adj.* **lace-up. 2.** (of footwear) to be fastened with laces. ~*n.* **lace-up. 3.** a lace-up shoe or boot.

lacewing ('leɪsˌwɪŋ) *n.* any of various neuropterous insects, esp. any of the families *Chrysopidae* (**green lacewings**) and *Hemerobiidae* (**brown lacewings**), having lacy wings and preying on aphids and similar pests.

laches ('lætʃɪz) *n. Law.* negligence or unreasonable delay in pursuing a legal remedy. [C14 *lachesse,* via Old French *lasche* slack, from Latin *laxus* LAX]

lachryma Christi ('lækrəmə 'krɪstɪ) *n.* a red or white wine from the bay of Naples in S Italy. [C17: from Latin: Christ's tear]

lachrymal ('lækrɪməl) *adj.* a variant spelling of **lacrimal.**

lachrymator ('lækrɪˌmeɪtə) *n.* a variant spelling of **lacrimator.**

lachrymatory ('lækrɪmətərɪ, -trɪ) *n., pl.* **-ries. 1.** a small vessel found in ancient tombs, formerly thought to hold the tears of mourners. ~*adj.* **2.** a variant spelling of **lacrimatory.**

lachrymose ('lækrɪˌməʊs, -ˌməʊz) *adj.* **1.** given to weeping; tearful. **2.** mournful; sad. [C17: from Latin *lacrimōsus,* from *lacrima* a tear] —'**lachryˌmosely** *adv.* —**lachrymosity** (ˌlækrɪ'mɒsɪtɪ) *n.*

lacing ('leɪsɪŋ) *n.* **1.** *Chiefly Brit.* a course of bricks, stone, etc., for strengthening a rubble or flint wall. **2.** another word for **lace** (senses 2, 3). **3.** *Informal.* a severe beating (esp. in the phrase **give someone a lacing**).

laciniate (lə'sɪnɪˌeɪt, -ɪt) *or* **laciniated** *adj.* **1.** *Biology.* jagged: *a laciniate leaf.* **2.** having a fringe. [C17: from Latin *lacinia* flap] —**laˌcini'ation** *n.*

lac insect (læk) *n.* any of various homopterous insects of the family *Lacciferidae,* esp. *Laccifer lacca* of India, the females of which secrete lac.

lack (læk) *n.* **1.** an insufficiency, shortage, or absence of something required or desired. **2.** something that is required but is absent or in short supply. ~*vb.* **3.** (when *intr.;* often foll. by *in* or *for*) to be deficient (in) or have need (of): *to lack purpose.* [C12: related to Middle Dutch *laken* to be wanting]

lackadaisical (ˌlækə'deɪzɪkᵊl) *adj.* **1.** lacking vitality and purpose. **2.** lazy or idle, esp. in a dreamy way. [C18: from earlier *lackadaisy,* extended form of LACKADAY] —ˌ**lacka'daisically** *adv.* —ˌ**lacka'daisicalness** *n.*

lackaday ('lækəˌdeɪ) *interj. Archaic.* another word for **alas.** [C17: from *alack the day*]

lacker ('lækə) *n.* a variant spelling of **lacquer.**

lackey ('lækɪ) *n.* **1.** a servile follower; hanger-on. **2.** a liveried male servant or valet. **3.** a person who is treated like a servant. ~*vb.* **4.** (when *intr.,* often foll. by *for*) to act as a lackey (to). ~Also (rare): '**lacquey.** [C16: via French *laquais,* from Old French, perhaps from Catalan *lacayo, alacayo;* perhaps related to ALCALDE]

lackey moth *n.* a bombycid moth, *Malacosoma neustria,* whose brightly striped larvae live at first in a communal web often on fruit trees, of which they may become a pest.

lacklustre *or U.S.* **lackluster** ('lækˌlʌstə) *adj.* lacking force, brilliance, or vitality.

laconic (lə'kɒnɪk) *or* **laconical** *adj.* (of a person's speech) using few words; terse. [C16: via Latin from Greek *Lakōnikos,* from

Lakōn Laconian (of Laconia, ancient country of which Sparta was the capital); referring to the Spartans' terseness of speech] —**la'conically** *adv.*

laconism ('lækəˌnɪzəm) *or* **laconicism** (lə'kɒnɪˌsɪzəm) *n. Rare.* **1.** economy of expression. **2.** a terse saying.

lacquer ('lækə) *n.* **1.** a hard glossy coating made by dissolving cellulose derivatives or natural resins in a volatile solvent. **2.** a black resinous substance, obtained from certain trees, used to give a hard glossy finish to wooden furniture. **3. lacquer tree.** Also called: **varnish tree.** an E Asian anacardiaceous tree, *Rhus verniciflua,* whose stem yields a toxic exudation from which black lacquer is obtained. **4.** Also called: **hair lacquer.** a mixture of shellac and alcohol for spraying onto the hair to hold a style in place. **5.** *Art.* decorative objects coated with such lacquer, often inlaid. ~*vb.* (*tr.*) **6.** to apply lacquer to. [C16: from obsolete French *lacre* sealing wax, from Portuguese *laca* LAC[1]] —**'lacquerer** *n.*

lacrimal, lachrymal, *or* **lacrymal** ('lækrɪməl) *adj.* of or relating to tears or to the glands that secrete tears. [C16: from Medieval Latin *lachrymālis,* from Latin *lacrima* a tear]

lacrimal duct *n.* a short tube in the inner corner of the eyelid through which tears drain into the nose. Nontechnical name: **tear duct.**

lacrimal gland *n.* the compound gland that secretes tears and lubricates the surface of the eye and the conjunctiva of the eyelid.

lacrimation (ˌlækrɪ'meɪʃən) *n.* the secretion of tears.

lacrimator, lachrymator, *or* **lacrymator** ('lækrɪˌmeɪtə) *n.* a substance causing an increase in the flow of tears. See **tear gas.**

lacrimatory, lachrymatory, *or* **lacrymatory** ('lækrɪmətərɪ, -trɪ) *adj.* of, causing, or producing tears.

lacrosse (lə'krɒs) *n.* a ball game invented by American Indians, now played by two teams who try to propel a ball into each other's goal by means of long-handled hooked sticks that are loosely strung with a kind of netted pouch. [C19: Canadian French: the hooked stick, crosier]

lactalbumin (læk'tælbjʊmɪn) *n.* a protein occurring in milk that contains all the amino acids essential to man. See also **caseinogen.** [C19: from LACTO- + ALBUMIN]

lactam ('læktæm) *n. Chem.* any of a group of inner amides, derived from amino acids, having the characteristic group -CONH-. [C20: from LACT(ONE) + AM(IDE)]

lactary ('læktərɪ) *adj. Rare.* of or relating to milk. [C17: from Latin *lactārius,* from *lact-, lac* milk]

lactase ('lækteɪs, -teɪz) *n.* any of a group of enzymes that hydrolyse lactose to glucose and galactose. [C20: from LACTO- + -ASE]

lactate[1] ('lækteɪt) *n.* an ester or salt of lactic acid. [C18: from LACTO- + -ATE[1]]

lactate[2] ('lækteɪt) *vb.* (*intr.*) (of mammals) to produce or secrete milk.

lactation (læk'teɪʃən) *n.* **1.** the secretion of milk from the mammary glands after parturition. **2.** the period during which milk is secreted. —**lac'tational** *adj.* —**lac'tationally** *adv.*

lacteal ('læktɪəl) *adj.* **1.** of, relating to, or resembling milk. **2.** (of lymphatic vessels) conveying or containing chyle. ~*n.* **3.** any of the lymphatic vessels conveying chyle from the small intestine to the thoracic duct. [C17: from Latin *lacteus* of milk, from *lac* milk] —**'lacteally** *adv.*

lactescent (læk'tɛsənt) *adj.* **1.** (of plants and certain insects) secreting a milky fluid. **2.** milky or becoming milky. [C18: from Latin *lactescēns,* from *lactescēre* to become milky, from *lact-, lac* milk] —**lac'tescence** *n.*

lactic ('læktɪk) *adj.* relating to or derived from milk. [C18: from Latin *lact-, lac* milk]

lactic acid *n.* a colourless syrupy carboxylic acid found in sour milk and many fruits and used as a preservative (**E270**) for foodstuffs, such as soft margarine, and for making pharmaceuticals and adhesives. Formula: $CH_3CH(OH)COOH$. Systematic name: **2-hydroxypropanoic acid.**

lactiferous (læk'tɪfərəs) *adj.* **1.** producing, conveying, or secreting milk or a milky fluid: *lactiferous ducts.* **2.** *Botany.* containing latex; laticiferous. [C17: from Latin *lactifer,* from *lact-, lac* milk] —**lac'tiferousness** *n.*

lacto- *or before a vowel* **lact-** *combining form.* indicating milk: *lactobacillus.* [from Latin *lact-, lac* milk]

lactobacillus (ˌlæktəʊbə'sɪləs) *n., pl.* **-li** (-laɪ). any Gram-positive rod-shaped bacterium of the genus *Lactobacillus,* which ferments carbohydrates: family *Lactobacillaceae.*

lactoflavin (ˌlæktəʊ'fleɪvɪn) *n.* a less common name for **riboflavin.**

lactogenic (ˌlæktə'dʒɛnɪk) *adj.* inducing lactation: *lactogenic hormone.* See also **prolactin.**

lactoglobulin (ˌlæktəʊ'glɒbjʊlɪn) *n. Biochem.* any of a number of globular proteins found in milk.

lactometer (læk'tɒmɪtə) *n.* a hydrometer used to measure the relative density of milk and thus determine its quality. Also called: **galactometer.**

lactone ('læktəʊn) *n.* any of a class of organic compounds formed from hydroxy acids and containing the group -C(CO)OC-, where the carbon atoms are part of a ring. —**lactonic** (læk'tɒnɪk) *adj.*

lactoprotein (ˌlæktəʊ'prəʊtiːn) *n.* any protein, such as lactalbumin or caseinogen, that is present in milk.

lactoscope ('læktəˌskəʊp) *n.* an instrument for measuring the amount of cream in milk.

lactose ('læktəʊs, -təʊz) *n.* a white crystalline disaccharide occurring in milk and used in the manufacture of pharmaceuticals and baby foods. Formula: $C_{12}H_{22}O_{11}$. Also called: **milk sugar.**

lactosuria (ˌlæktə'sjʊrɪə) *n. Med.* the presence of lactose in the urine.

lacuna (lə'kjuːnə) *n., pl.* **-nae** (-niː) *or* **-nas. 1.** a gap or space, esp. in a book or manuscript. **2.** *Biology.* a cavity or depression, such as any of the spaces in the matrix of bone. **3.** another name for **coffer** (sense 3). [C17: from Latin *lacūna* pool, cavity, from *lacus* lake] —**la'cunose, la'cunal,** *or* **la'cunary** *adj.* —**lacunosity** (ˌlækjʊ'nɒsɪtɪ) *n.*

lacunar (lə'kjuːnə) *n., pl.* **lacunars** *or* **lacunaria** (ˌlækjʊ'nɛərɪə). **1.** Also called: **lequear.** a ceiling, soffit, or vault having coffers. **2.** another name for **coffer** (sense 3). ~*adj.* **3.** of, relating to, or containing a lacuna or lacunas. [C17: from Latin *lacūnar* panelled ceiling, from *lacūna* cavity; see LACUNA]

lacustrine (lə'kʌstraɪn) *adj.* **1.** of or relating to lakes. **2.** living or growing in or on the shores of a lake. [C19: from Italian *lacustre,* from Latin *lacus* lake]

LACW *Brit. abbrev. for* leading aircraftwoman.

lacy ('leɪsɪ) *adj.* **lacier, laciest.** made of or resembling lace. —**'lacily** *adv.* —**'laciness** *n.*

lad (læd) *n.* **1.** a boy or young man. **2.** *Informal.* a familiar form of address for any male. **3.** a lively or dashing man or youth (esp. in the phrase **a bit of a lad**). **4.** *Brit.* a boy or man who looks after horses. [C13 *ladde;* perhaps of Scandinavian origin]

ladanum ('lædənəm) *n.* another name for **labdanum.**

ladder ('lædə) *n.* **1.** a portable framework of wood, metal, rope, etc., in the form of two long parallel members connected by several parallel rungs or steps fixed to them at right angles, for climbing up or down. **2.** any hierarchy conceived of as having a series of ascending stages, levels, etc: *the social ladder.* **3. a.** anything resembling a ladder. **b.** (*as modifier*): *ladder stitch.* **4.** Also called: **run.** *Chiefly Brit.* a line of connected stitches that have come undone in knitted material, esp. stockings. **5.** See **ladder tournament.** ~*vb.* **6.** *Chiefly Brit.* to cause a line of interconnected stitches in (stockings, etc.) to undo, as by snagging, or (of a stocking) to come undone in this way. [Old English *hlǣdder;* related to Old High German *leitara*]

ladder back *n.* a type of chair in which the back is constructed of horizontal slats between two uprights.

ladder tournament *n.* a tournament in a sport or game in which each contestant in a list attempts to defeat and displace the contestant above him. Also called: **ladder.**

laddie ('lædɪ) *n. Chiefly Scot.* a familiar term for a male, esp. a young man; lad.

lade[1] (leɪd) *vb.* **lades, lading, laded, laden** ('leɪdᵊn) *or* **laded. 1.** to put cargo or freight on board (a ship, etc.) or (of a ship, etc.) to take on cargo or freight. **2.** (*tr.; usually passive* and foll. by *with*) to burden or oppress. **3.** (*tr.; usually passive* and foll. by *with*) to fill or load. **4.** to remove (liquid) with or as if with a ladle. [Old English *hladen* to load; related to Dutch *laden*] —**'lader** *n.*

lade[2] (led, leɪd) *n. Scot.* a watercourse, esp. a millstream. [of uncertain origin]

laden ('leɪdᵊn) *vb.* **1.** a past participle of **lade**[1]. ~*adj.* **2.** weighed down with a load; loaded. **3.** encumbered; burdened.

la-di-da, lah-di-dah, *or* **la-de-da** (ˌlɑːdiː'dɑː) *adj.* **1.** *Informal.* affecting exaggeratedly genteel manners or speech. ~*n.* **2.** a la-di-da person. [C19: mockingly imitative of affected speech]

ladies *or* **ladies' room** *n.* (*functioning as sing.*) *Informal.* a women's public lavatory.

ladies' fingers *n.* (*functioning as sing. or pl.*) another name for **kidney vetch** or **okra.**

ladies' gallery *n.* (in Britain, formerly) **1.** a gallery in the old House of Commons set aside for women spectators. **2.** a portion of the strangers' gallery of the new House of Commons similarly reserved.

ladies' man *or* **lady's man** *n.* a man who is fond of, attentive to, and successful with women.

ladies'-tresses *n.* (*functioning as sing. or pl.*) a variant spelling of **lady's-tresses.**

Ladin (læ'diːn) *n.* a Rhaetian dialect spoken in parts of South Tyrol. Compare **Friulian, Romansch.** [C19: from Italian *ladino,* from Latin *latīnus* Latin]

lading ('leɪdɪŋ) *n.* a load; cargo; freight.

ladino (lə'diːnəʊ) *n., pl.* **-nos.** an Italian variety of white clover grown as a forage crop in North America. [C20: perhaps from Italian *ladino* (see LADIN), referring to a person or thing from the Italian-speaking area of Switzerland, where the clover is grown]

Ladino (lə'diːnəʊ) *n.* a language of Sephardic Jews, based on Spanish with some Hebrew elements and usually written in Hebrew characters. Also called: **Judaeo-Spanish, Judezmo.** [from Spanish: Latin]

ladle ('leɪdᵊl) *n.* **1.** a long-handled spoon having a deep bowl for serving or transferring liquids: *a soup ladle.* **2.** a large bucket-shaped container for transferring molten metal. ~*vb.* **3.** (*tr.*) to lift or serve out with or as if with a ladle. [Old English *hlǣdel,* from *hladan* to draw out] —**'ladleˌful** *n.*

ladle out *vb.* (*tr., adv.*) *Informal.* to distribute (money, gifts, etc.) generously.

lad's love *n.* another name for **southernwood.**

lady ('leɪdɪ) *n., pl.* **-dies.** **1.** a woman regarded as having the characteristics of a good family and high social position; female counterpart of **gentleman** (sense 1). **2. a.** a polite name for a woman. **b.** (*as modifier*): *a lady doctor.* **3.** an informal name for **wife.** **4. lady of the house.** the female head of the household. **5.** *History.* a woman with proprietary rights and authority, as over a manor. Compare **lord** (sense 3). [Old English *hlǣfdīge,* from *hlāf* bread + *dīge* kneader, related to *dāh* dough]

Lady ('leɪdɪ) *n., pl.* **-dies.** **1.** (in Britain) a title of honour borne by various classes of women of the peerage. **2. my lady.** a term of address to holders of the title Lady, used esp. by servants. **3. Our Lady.** a title of the Virgin Mary. **4.** *Archaic.* an allegorical prefix for the personifications of certain qualities: *Lady Luck.* **5.** *Chiefly Brit.* the term of address by which certain positions of authority or respect are prefaced when held by women: *Lady Chairman.*

ladybird ('leɪdɪˌbɜːd) *n.* any of various small brightly coloured beetles of the family *Coccinellidae,* such as *Adalia bipunctata* **(two-spotted ladybird),** which has red elytra marked with black spots. Usual U.S. and Canadian name: **ladybug.** [C18: named after Our *Lady,* the Virgin Mary]

lady bountiful *n.* an ostentatiously charitable woman. [after a character in George Farquhar's play *The Beaux' Stratagem* (1707)]

Lady Chapel *n.* a chapel within a church or cathedral, dedicated to the Virgin Mary.

Lady Day *n.* March 25, the feast of the Annunciation of the Virgin Mary; one of the four quarter days in England, Wales and Ireland. Also called: **Annunciation Day.**

lady fern *n.* a large, graceful, but variable fern, *Athyrium filix-femina,* with bipinnate fronds, commonly found on damp acid soils in woods and on hillsides.

ladyfinger ('leɪdɪˌfɪŋgə) *or* **lady's finger** *n.* a small finger-shaped sponge cake.

ladyfy *or* **ladify** ('leɪdɪˌfaɪ) *vb.* **-fies, -fying, -fied.** (*tr.*) to make a lady of (someone).

lady-in-waiting *n., pl.* **ladies-in-waiting.** a lady of a royal household who attends a queen or princess.

lady-killer *n. Informal.* a man who is, or thinks he is, irresistibly fascinating to women. —**'lady-ˌkilling** *n., adj.*

ladylike ('leɪdɪˌlaɪk) *adj.* **1.** like or befitting a lady in manners and bearing; refined and fastidious. **2.** *Derogatory.* (of a man) effeminate. —**'ladyˌlikeness** *n.*

ladylove ('leɪdɪˌlʌv) *n. Now rare.* a beloved woman.

Lady Macbeth strategy *n. Informal.* a strategy in a takeover battle in which a third party makes a bid acceptable to the target company, appearing to act as a white knight but subsequently joining forces with the original (unwelcome) bidder. [C20: after *Lady Macbeth* in Shakespeare's *Macbeth*]

lady mayoress *n. Brit.* the wife of a lord mayor.

Lady Muck *n. Informal.* an ordinary woman behaving or being treated as if she were aristocratic. See also **Lord Muck.**

lady orchid *n.* a tall graceful orchid, *Orchis purpurea,* with faintly scented purple-brown and green flowers with a pinkish or white lip. [C19: named from a fancied resemblance to a lady in regency dress and bonnet]

lady's bedstraw *n.* a Eurasian rubiaceous plant, *Galium verum,* with clusters of small yellow flowers.

lady's finger *n.* another name for **bhindi.**

Ladyship ('leɪdɪʃɪp) *n.* (preceded by *your* or *her*) a title used to address or refer to any peeress except a duchess.

lady's maid *n.* a personal servant to a woman, esp. in matters of dress and toilet.

lady's man *n.* a variant spelling of **ladies' man.**

lady's mantle *n.* any of various rosaceous plants of the N temperate genus *Alchemilla,* having small green flowers.

lady's-slipper *n.* any of various orchids of the Eurasian genus *Cypripedium,* esp. *C. calceolus,* which has flowers with reddish twisted petals and a yellow inflated slipper-like lip. See also **moccasin flower, cypripedium.**

lady's-smock *n.* a N temperate cruciferous plant, *Cardamine pratensis,* with white or rose-pink flowers. Also called: **cuckooflower.**

lady's-thumb *n.* the usual U.S. name for **redshank** (the plant).

lady's-tresses *or* **ladies'-tresses** *n.* (*functioning as sing. or pl.*) any of various orchids of the genus *Spiranthes,* having spikes of small white fragrant flowers.

Laetrile ('leɪəˌtraɪl) *n. Trademark.* an extract of peach stones sold as a cure for cancer but judged useless and possibly dangerous by medical scientists.

laevo- *or U.S.* **levo-** *combining form.* **1.** on or towards the left: *laevorotatory.* **2.** (in chemistry) denoting a laevorotatory compound: *laevulose.* [from Latin *laevus* left]

laevogyrate (ˌliːvəʊ'dʒaɪreɪt) *adj.* another word for **laevorotatory.**

laevorotation (ˌliːvəʊrəʊ'teɪʃən) *n.* **1.** a rotation to the left. **2.** an anticlockwise rotation of the plane of polarization of plane-polarized light as a result of its passage through a crystal, liquid, or solution. ~Compare **dextrorotation.**

laevorotatory (ˌliːvəʊ'rəʊtətərɪ, -trɪ) *or* **laevorotary** *adj.* of, having, or causing laevorotation. Also: **laevogyrate.**

laevulin ('lɛvjʊlɪn) *n.* a polysaccharide occurring in the tubers of certain helianthus plants. [C19: from LAEVULOSE + -IN]

laevulose ('lɛvjʊˌləʊs, -ˌləʊz) *n.* another name for **fructose.** [C19: from LAEVO- + -ULE + -OSE[2]]

Laffer curve ('læfə) *n. Economics.* a curve on a graph showing government tax revenue plotted against percentage tax rates. It has been used to show that a cut in a high tax rate can increase government revenue. [C20: named after Arthur *Laffer* (born 1940), U.S. economist]

LAFTA ('læftə) *acronym for* Latin American Free Trade Area, the name before 1981 of the Latin American Integration Association. See **LAIA.**

lag[1] (læg) *vb.* **lags, lagging, lagged.** (*intr.*) **1.** (often foll. by *behind*) to hang (back) or fall (behind) in movement, progress, development, etc. **2.** to fall away in strength or intensity. **3.** to determine an order of play in certain games, as by rolling marbles towards a line or, in billiards, hitting cue balls up the table against the top cushion in an attempt to bring them back close to the headrail. ~*n.* **4.** the act or state of slowing down or falling behind. **5.** the interval of time between two events, esp. between an action and its effect. **6.** an act of lagging in a game, such as billiards. [C16: of obscure origin]

lag[2] (læg) *Slang.* ~*n.* **1.** a convict or ex-convict (esp. in the phrase **old lag**). **2.** a term of imprisonment. ~*vb.* **lags, lagging, lagged.** **3.** (*tr.*) to arrest or put in prison. [C19: of unknown origin]

lag[3] (læg) *vb.* **lags, lagging, lagged.** **1.** (*tr.*) to cover (a pipe, cylinder, etc.) with lagging to prevent loss of heat. ~*n.* **2.** the insulating casing of a steam cylinder, boiler, etc.; lagging. **3.** a stave or lath. [C17: of Scandinavian origin; related to Swedish *lagg* stave]

lagan ('lægən) *or* **ligan** ('laɪgən) *n.* goods or wreckage on the sea bed, sometimes attached to a buoy to permit recovery. Compare **flotsam, jetsam.** [C16: from Old French *lagan,* probably of Germanic origin; compare Old Norse *lögn* dragnet]

Lag b'Omer *Hebrew.* (lag bə'ɔmɛr; *English* læg 'bəʊmə) *n.* a Jewish holiday celebrated on the 18th day of Iyar. [Hebrew, literally: 33rd (day) of the Omer]

lagena (lə'dʒiːnə) *n.* **1.** a bottle with a narrow neck. **2.** an outgrowth of the sacculus in the ear of fishes and amphibians, thought to be homologous to the cochlea of mammals. [C19: Latin, a flask, from Greek *lagēnos*]

lager[1] ('lɑːgə) *n.* a light-bodied effervescent beer, stored for varying periods before use. [C19: from German *Lagerbier* beer for storing, from *Lager* storehouse]

lager[2] ('lɑːgə) *n.* a variant spelling of **laager.**

lager lout *n.* a rowdy or aggressive young drunk male, esp. one contributing to football hooliganism.

laggard ('lægəd) *n.* **1.** a person who lags behind. **2.** a dawdler or straggler. ~*adj.* **3.** *Rare.* sluggish, slow, or dawdling. —**'laggardly** *adv.* —**'laggardness** *n.*

lagging ('lægɪŋ) *n.* **1.** insulating material wrapped around pipes, boilers, etc., or laid in a roof loft, to prevent loss of heat. **2.** the act or process of applying lagging. **3.** a wooden frame used to support an arch during construction.

lagniappe *or* **lagnappe** (læn'jæp, 'lænjæp) *n. U.S.* **1.** a small gift, esp. one given to a customer who makes a purchase. **2.** something given or obtained as a gratuity or bonus. [C19: Louisiana French, from American Spanish *la ñapa,* from Quechua *yápa* addition]

lagomorph ('lægəʊˌmɔːf) *n.* any placental mammal of the order *Lagomorpha,* having two pairs of upper incisors specialized for gnawing: includes pikas, rabbits, and hares. [C19: via New Latin from Greek *lagōs* hare; see -MORPH] —**ˌlago'morphic** *or* **ˌlago'morphous** *adj.*

lagoon (lə'guːn) *n.* **1.** a body of water cut off from the open sea by coral reefs or sand bars. **2.** any small body of water, esp. one adjoining a larger one. ~Also (rare): **la'gune.** [C17: from Italian *laguna,* from Latin *lacūna* pool; see LACUNA]

Lagrangian point (lə'greɪndʒɪən) *n. Astronomy.* one of five points in the plane of revolution of two bodies in orbit around their common centre of gravity, at which a third body of negligible mass can remain in equilibrium with respect to the other two bodies. [named after J. L. *Lagrange* (1736–1813), French mathematician and astronomer]

lag screw *n.* a woodscrew with a square head. [from LAG[3]; the screw was originally used to fasten barrel staves]

lah (lɑː) *n. Music.* (in tonic sol-fa) the sixth note of any major scale; submediant. [C14: see GAMUT]

lahar ('lɑːhɑː) *n.* a landslide of volcanic debris mixed with water down the sides of a volcano, usually precipitated by heavy rainfall. [C20: from Javanese: lava]

lah-di-dah (ˌlɑːdiː'dɑː) *adj., n. Informal.* a variant spelling of **la-di-da.**

Lahnda ('lɑːndə) *n.* a language or group of dialects of Pakistan, belonging to the Indic branch of the Indo-European family and closely related to Punjabi.

Lahore (lə'hɔː) *n.* a variety of large domestic fancy pigeon having a black-and-white plumage.

LAIA *abbrev. for* Latin American Integration Association (before 1981, known as the Latin American Free Trade Area). An economic group, its members are Argentina, Bolivia, Brazil, Chile, Colombia, Ecuador, Mexico, Paraguay, Peru, Uruguay, and Venezuela.

laic ('leɪɪk) *adj.* *also* **laical.** **1.** of or involving the laity; secular. ~*n.* **2.** a rare word for **layman.** [C15: from Late Latin *lāicus* LAY[3]] —'**laically** *adv.* —'**laicism** *n.*

laicize *or* **laicise** ('leɪɪˌsaɪz) *vb.* (*tr.*) to withdraw clerical or ecclesiastical character or status from (an institution, building, etc.). —ˌ**laiciˈzation** *or* ˌ**laiciˈsation** *n.*

laid (leɪd) *vb.* the past tense and past participle of **lay**[1].

laid-back *adj.* *Informal.* relaxed in style, character, or behaviour; easy-going and unhurried.

laid paper *n.* paper with a regular mesh impressed upon it by the dandy roller on a paper-making machine. Compare **wove paper.**

laik (leɪk) *vb.* *Northern English dialect.* **1.** (when *intr.*, often foll. by *about*) to play (a game, etc.). **2.** (*intr.*) to be on holiday, esp. to take a day off work. **3.** (*intr.*) to be unemployed. [C14: *leiken,* from Old Norse *leika;* related to Old English *lacan* to manoeuvre; compare LARK[2]]

Lailat-ul-Qadr (ˌleɪlætʊlˈkɑːdə) *n.* a night of study and prayer observed annually by Muslims to mark the communication of the Koran: it usually follows the 27th day of Ramadan. [from Arabic: night of determination]

lain (leɪn) *vb.* the past participle of **lie**[2].

Laingian ('læŋɪən) *adj.* **1.** of or based on the theory of R. D. Laing (1927–89), British psychiatrist, that mental illnesses are understandable as natural responses to stress in family and social situations. ~*n.* **2.** a follower or adherent of Laing's teaching.

lair[1] (lɛə) *n.* **1.** the resting place of a wild animal. **2.** *Informal.* a place of seclusion or hiding. **3.** an enclosure or shed for farm animals. **4.** *Scot.* the ground for a grave in a cemetery. ~*vb.* **5.** (*intr.*) (esp. of a wild animal) to retreat to or rest in a lair. **6.** (*tr.*) to drive or place (an animal) in a lair. [Old English *leger;* related to LIE[2] and Old High German *leger* bed]

lair[2] (ler) *n., vb.* a Scot. word for **mire.** [from Old Norse *leir* mud]

lair[3] (lɛə) *Austral. slang.* ~*n.* **1.** a flashy man who shows off. ~*vb.* **2.** (*intr.*; foll. by *up* or *around*) to behave or dress like a lair. [perhaps from LEER]

lairage ('lɛərɪdʒ) *n.* accommodation for farm animals, esp. at docks or markets.

laird (lɛəd; *Scot.* lerd) *n.* *Scot.* a landowner, esp. of a large estate. [C15: Scottish variant of LORD]

lairy ('lɛərɪ) *adj.* **lairier, lairiest.** *Austral. slang.* gaudy or flashy. [C20: from LEERY]

laissez aller *or* ***laisser aller*** *French.* (lese ale) *n.* lack of constraint; freedom. [literally: let go]

laissez faire *or* **laisser faire** *French.* (lese fɛr; *English* ˌlɛseɪ ˈfɛə) *n.* **1. a.** Also called: **individualism.** the doctrine of unrestricted freedom in commerce, esp. for private interests. **b.** (*as modifier*): *a laissez-faire economy.* **2.** indifference or noninterference, esp. in the affairs of others. [French, literally: let (them) act] —ˌ**laissez-ˈfaireism** *or* ˌ**laisser-ˈfaireism** *n.*

laissez passer *or* ***laisser passer*** *French.* (lese pase) *n.* a document granting unrestricted access or movement to its holder. [literally: let pass]

laity ('leɪɪtɪ) *n.* **1.** laymen, as distinguished from clergymen. **2.** all people not of a specific occupation. [C16: from LAY[3]]

lake[1] (leɪk) *n.* **1.** an expanse of water entirely surrounded by land and unconnected to the sea except by rivers or streams. Related adj.: **lacustrine. 2.** anything resembling this. **3.** a surplus of a liquid commodity: *a wine lake.* [C13 *lac,* via Old French from Latin *lacus* basin]

lake[2] (leɪk) *n.* **1.** a bright pigment used in textile dyeing and printing inks, produced by the combination of an organic colouring matter with an inorganic compound, usually a metallic salt, oxide, or hydroxide. See also **mordant. 2.** a red dye obtained by combining a metallic compound with cochineal. [C17: variant of LAC[1]]

lake dwelling *n.* a dwelling, esp. in prehistoric villages, constructed on platforms supported by wooden piles driven into the bottom of a lake. —**lake dweller** *n.*

lake herring *n.* **1.** another name for **cisco. 2.** another name for **powan.**

Lakeland terrier ('leɪkˌlænd) *n.* a wire-haired breed of terrier, originally from the Lake District of NW England and used for hunting.

laker ('leɪkə) *n.* a cargo vessel used on lakes.

lakh *or* **lac** (lɑːk) *n.* (in India) the number 100 000, esp. when referring to this sum of rupees. [C17: from Hindi *lākh,* ultimately from Sanskrit *lakshā* a sign]

laksa ('læksa) *n.* (in Malaysia) a dish of Chinese origin consisting of rice noodles served in curry or hot soup. [from Malay: ten thousand]

laky ('leɪkɪ) *adj.* **lakier, lakiest.** of the reddish colour of the pigment lake.

Lala ('lɑːlɑː) *n.* a title or form of address, equivalent to *Mr,* used in India. [Hindi]

lalang ('lɑːlɑːŋ) *n.* a coarse weedy Malaysian grass, *Imperata arundinacea.* [Malay]

lalapalooza (ˌlɒləpəˈluːzə) *n.* a variant spelling of **lollapalooza.**

-lalia *combining form.* indicating a speech defect or abnormality: *coprolalia; echolalia.* [New Latin, from Greek *lalia* chatter, from *lalein* to babble]

Lallans ('lælənz) *or* **Lallan** ('lælən) *n.* **1.** a literary version of the variety of English spoken and written in the Lowlands of Scotland. **2.** (*modifier*) of or relating to the Lowlands of Scotland or their dialects. [Scottish variant of *Lowlands*]

lallation (læˈleɪʃən) *n.* *Phonetics.* a defect of speech consisting of the pronunciation of (r) as (l). [C17: from Latin *lallāre* to sing lullaby, of imitative origin]

lallygag ('lælɪˌgæg) *or* **lollygag** *vb.* **-gags, -gagging, -gagged.** (*intr.*) *U.S.* to loiter aimlessly. [C20: of unknown origin]

lam[1] (læm) *vb.* **lams, lamming, lammed.** *Slang.* **1.** (*tr.*) to thrash or beat. **2.** (*intr.*; usually foll. by *into* or *out*) to make a sweeping stroke or blow. [C16: from Scandinavian; related to Old Norse *lemja*]

lam[2] (læm) *U.S. and Canadian slang.* ~*n.* **1.** a sudden flight or escape, esp. to avoid arrest. **2. on the lam.** making an escape. **3. take it on the lam.** to escape or flee, esp. from the police. ~*vb.* **lams, lamming, lammed. 4.** (*intr.*) to escape or flee. [C19: perhaps from LAM[1] (hence, to be off)]

lam. *abbrev. for* laminated.

Lam. *Bible. abbrev. for* Lamentations.

lama ('lɑːmə) *n.* a priest or monk of Lamaism. [C17: from Tibetan *blama*]

Lamaism ('lɑːməˌɪzəm) *n.* the Mahayana form of Buddhism of Tibet and Mongolia. See also **Dalai Lama.** —'**Lamaist** *n., adj.* —ˌ**Lamaˈistic** *adj.*

Lamarckian (lɑːˈmɑːkɪən) *adj.* **1.** of or relating to Jean Baptiste de Monet Lamarck (1744–1829), French naturalist, or to Lamarckism. ~*n.* **2.** a supporter of Lamarckism.

Lamarckism (lɑːˈmɑːkɪzəm) *n.* the theory of organic evolution proposed by Lamarck, based on the principle that characteristics of an organism modified during its lifetime are inheritable. See also **acquired characteristic, Neo-Lamarckism.**

lamasery ('lɑːməsərɪ) *n., pl.* **-series.** a monastery of lamas. [C19: from French *lamaserie,* from LAMA + French *-serie,* from Persian *serāī* palace]

lamb (læm) *n.* **1.** the young of a sheep. **2.** the meat of a young sheep. **3.** a person, esp. a child, who is innocent, meek, good, etc. **4.** a person easily deceived. **5. like a lamb to the slaughter. a.** without resistance. **b.** innocently. ~*vb.* **6.** (*intr.*) Also **lamb down.** (of a ewe) to give birth. **7.** (*tr.; used in the passive*) (of a lamb) to be born. **8.** (*intr.*) (of a shepherd) to tend the ewes and newborn lambs at lambing time. ~See also **lamb down.** [Old English *lamb,* from Germanic; compare German *Lamm,* Old High German and Old Norse *lamb*] —'**lambˌlike** *adj.*

lambada (ˌlæmˈbɑːdə) *n.* **1.** an erotic dance, originating in Brazil, performed by two people who hold each other closely and gyrate their hips in synchronized movements. **2.** the music that accompanies the lambada, combining salsa, calypso, and reggae. [C20: from Portuguese, literally: the snapping of a whip]

lambaste (læmˈbeɪst) *or* **lambast** (læmˈbæst) *vb.* (*tr.*) **1.** to beat or whip severely. **2.** to reprimand or scold. [C17: perhaps from LAM[1] + BASTE[3]]

lambda ('læmdə) *n.* the 11th letter of the Greek alphabet (Λ, λ), a consonant transliterated as *l.* [C14: from Greek, from Semitic; related to LAMED]

lambda calculus *n.* *Logic, computer technol.* a formalized description of functions and the way in which they combine, developed by Alonzo Church and used in the theory of certain high-level programming languages. [C20: from the use of the symbol *lambda* (λ) to represent the mathematical functions]

lambdacism ('læmdəˌsɪzəm) *n.* *Phonetics.* **1.** excessive use or idiosyncratic pronunciation of *l.* **2.** another word for **lallation.** [C17: from Late Latin *labdacismus,* from Greek]

lambdoid ('læmdɔɪd) *or* **lambdoidal** *adj.* **1.** having the shape of the Greek letter lambda. **2.** of or denoting the suture near the back of the skull between the occipital and parietal bones. [C16: via French from Greek *lambdoeidēs*]

lamb down *vb.* (*tr., adv.*) **1.** another term for **lamb** (sense 6). **2.** *Austral. informal.* to persuade (someone) to spend all his money.

lambent ('læmbənt) *adj.* **1.** (esp. of a flame) flickering softly over a surface. **2.** glowing with soft radiance. **3.** (of wit or humour) light or brilliant. [C17: from the present participle of Latin *lambere* to lick] —'**lambency** *n.* —'**lambently** *adv.*

lambert ('læmbət) *n.* the cgs unit of illumination, equal to 1 lumen per square centimetre. Symbol: L [named after J. H. *Lambert* (1728–77), German mathematician and physicist]

Lambeth ('læmbəθ) *n.* the Archbishop of Canterbury in his official capacity. [from *Lambeth* Palace, the Archbishop's London residence]

Lambeth walk *n.* *Chiefly Brit.* a line dance popular in the 1930s.

lambing ('læmɪŋ) *n.* **1. a.** the birth of lambs. **b.** (*as modifier*): *lambing time.* **2.** the shepherd's work of tending the ewes and newborn lambs at this time.

lambkin ('læmkɪn) *or* **lambie** *n.* **1.** a small or young lamb. **2.** a term of affection for a small endearing child.

lambrequin ('læmbrɪkɪn, 'læmbə-) *n.* **1.** an ornamental hanging covering the edge of a shelf or the upper part of a window or door. **2. a.** a border pattern giving a draped effect, used on ceramics, etc. **b.** (*as modifier*): *a lambrequin pattern.* **3.** (*often pl.*) a scarf worn over a helmet. **4.** *Heraldry.* another name for **mantling.** [C18: from French, from Dutch *lamperkin* (unattested), diminutive of *lamper* veil]

lamb's ears *n.* (*functioning as sing.*) a perennial herb, *Stachys lanata,* planted for its foliage, which is covered with white woolly down; the purplish or striped flowers are small. Also called: **lamb's tongue,** (*Scot.*) **lamb's lugs.**

lamb's fry *n.* **1.** *Brit.* lamb's offal, esp. lamb's testicles, as food. **2.** *Austral. and N.Z.* lamb's liver as food.

lambskin (ˈlæmˌskɪn) *n.* **1.** the skin of a lamb, esp. with the wool still on. **2. a.** a material or garment prepared from this skin. **b.** (*as modifier*): *a lambskin coat.* **3.** a cotton or woollen fabric resembling this skin.

lamb's lettuce *n.* another name for **corn salad.**

lamb's-quarters *n., pl.* **lamb's-quarters.** a U.S. name for **fat hen.**

lamb's tails *pl. n.* the pendulous catkins of the hazel tree.

lamb's wool *n.* **a.** fine soft wool obtained from a lamb at its first shearing. **b.** (*as modifier*): *lamb's-wool jumpers.*

LAMDA *abbrev. for* London Academy of Music and Dramatic Art.

lame[1] (leɪm) *adj.* **1.** disabled or crippled in the legs or feet. **2.** painful or weak: *a lame back.* **3.** weak; unconvincing: *a lame excuse.* **4.** not effective or enthusiastic: *a lame try.* **5.** *U.S. slang.* conventional or uninspiring. ~*vb.* **6.** (*tr.*) to make lame. [Old English *lama;* related to Old Norse *lami,* German *lahm*] —ˈ**lamely** *adv.* —ˈ**lameness** *n.*

lame[2] (leɪm) *n.* one of the overlapping metal plates used in armour after about 1330; splint. [C16: via Old French from Latin *lāmina* a thin plate, LAMINA]

lamé (ˈlɑːmeɪ) *n.* **a.** a fabric of silk, cotton, or wool interwoven with threads of metal. **b.** (*as modifier*): *a gold lamé gown.* [from French, from Old French *lame* gold or silver thread, thin plate, from Latin *lāmina* thin plate]

lamebrain (ˈleɪmˌbreɪn) *n. Informal.* a stupid or slow-witted person.

lamed (ˈlɑːmɪd; *Hebrew* ˈlamɛd) *n.* the 12th letter in the Hebrew alphabet (ל), transliterated as *l.* Also: **lamedh** (ˈlamɛd). [from Hebrew, literally: ox goad (from its shape)]

lame duck *n.* **1.** a person or thing that is disabled or ineffectual. **2.** *Stock Exchange.* a speculator who cannot discharge his liabilities. **3.** a company with a large workforce and high prestige that is unable to meet foreign competition without government support. **4.** *U.S.* **a.** an elected official or body of officials remaining in office in the interval between the election and inauguration of a successor. **b.** (*as modifier*): *a lame-duck president.* **5.** (*modifier*) *U.S.* designating a term of office after which the officeholder will not run for re-election.

lamella (ləˈmɛlə) *n., pl.* **-lae** (-liː) *or* **-las.** **1.** a thin layer, plate, or membrane, esp. any of the calcified layers of which bone is formed. **2.** *Botany.* **a.** any of the spore-bearing gills of a mushroom. **b.** any of the membranes in a chloroplast. **c.** Also called: **middle lamella.** a layer of pectin cementing together adjacent cells. **3.** one of a number of timber, metal, or concrete members connected along a pattern of intersecting diagonal lines to form a framed vaulted roof structure. **4.** any thin sheet of material or thin layer in a fluid. [C17: New Latin, from Latin, diminutive of *lāmina* thin plate] —**laˈmellar, lamellate** (ˈlæmɪˌleɪt, -lɪt; ləˈmɛleɪt, -lɪt), *or* **lamellose** (ləˈmɛləʊs, ˈlæmɪˌləʊs) *adj.* —**laˈmellarly** *or* ˈ**lamellately** *adv.* —ˈ**lamelˌlated** *adj.* —ˌ**lamelˈlation** *n.* —**lamellosity** (ˌlæməˈlɒsɪtɪ) *n.*

lamelli- *combining form.* indicating lamella or lamellae: *lamellibranch.*

lamellibranch (ləˈmɛlɪˌbræŋk) *n., adj.* another word for **bivalve** (senses 1, 2). [C19: from New Latin *lamellibranchia* plate-gilled (animals); see LAMELLA, BRANCHIA] —**laˌmelliˈbranchiate** *adj., n.*

lamellicorn (ləˈmɛlɪˌkɔːn) *n.* **1.** any beetle of the superfamily *Lamellicornia,* having flattened terminal plates to the antennae: includes the scarabs and stag beetles. ~*adj.* **2.** of, relating to, or belonging to the *Lamellicornia.* **3.** designating antennae with platelike terminal segments. [C19: from New Latin *Lamellicornia* plate-horned (animals)]

lamelliform (ləˈmɛlɪˌfɔːm) *adj.* shaped like a lamella; platelike: *lamelliform antennae.*

lamellirostral (ləˌmɛlɪˈrɒstrəl) *or* **lamellirostrate** (ləˌmɛlɪˈrɒstreɪt) *adj.* (of ducks, geese, etc.) having a bill fringed with thin plates on the inner edge for straining water from food. [C19: from New Latin *lāmellirostris,* from LAMELLA + *rostrum* beak]

lament (ləˈmɛnt) *vb.* **1.** to feel or express sorrow, remorse, or regret (for or over). ~*n.* **2.** an expression of sorrow. **3.** a poem or song in which a death is lamented. [C16: from Latin *lāmentum*] —**laˈmenter** *n.* —**laˈmentingly** *adv.*

lamentable (ˈlæməntəb^{ə}l) *adj.* **1.** wretched, deplorable, or distressing. **2.** an archaic word for **mournful.** —ˈ**lamentableness** *n.* —ˈ**lamentably** *adv.*

lamentation (ˌlæmɛnˈteɪʃən) *n.* **1.** a lament; expression of sorrow. **2.** the act of lamenting.

lamented (ləˈmɛntɪd) *adj.* grieved for or regretted (often in the phrase **late lamented**): *our late lamented employer.* —**laˈmentedly** *adv.*

lamia (ˈleɪmɪə) *n., pl.* **-mias** *or* **-miae** (-mɪˌiː). **1.** *Classical myth.* one of a class of female monsters depicted with a snake's body and a woman's head and breasts. **2.** a vampire or sorceress. [C14: via Latin from Greek *Lamia*]

lamina (ˈlæmɪnə) *n., pl.* **-nae** (-ˌniː) *or* **-nas.** **1.** a thin plate, esp. of bone or mineral. **2.** *Botany.* the flat blade of a leaf, petal, or thallus. [C17: New Latin, from Latin: thin plate] —ˈ**laminar** *or* **laminose** (ˈlæmɪˌnəʊs, -ˌnəʊz) *adj.*

laminar flow *n.* nonturbulent motion of a fluid in which parallel layers have different velocities relative to each other. Compare **turbulent flow.** See also **streamline flow.**

laminaria (ˌlæmɪˈnɛərɪə) *n.* any brown seaweed of the genus *Laminaria,* having large fluted leathery fronds. [C19: genus name formed from Latin *lamina* plate]

laminarin (ˌlæmɪˈnɑːrɪn) *n.* a carbohydrate, consisting of repeated glucose units, that is the main storage product of brown algae. [C20: from LAMINAR(IA) + -IN]

laminate *vb.* (ˈlæmɪˌneɪt). **1.** (*tr.*) to make (material in sheet form) by bonding together two or more thin sheets. **2.** to split or be split into thin sheets. **3.** (*tr.*) to beat, form, or press (material, esp. metal) into thin sheets. **4.** (*tr.*) to cover or overlay with a thin sheet of material. ~*n.* (ˈlæmɪˌneɪt, -nɪt). **5.** a material made by bonding together two or more sheets. ~*adj.* (ˈlæmɪˌneɪt, -nɪt). **6.** having or composed of lamina; laminated. [C17: from New Latin *lāminātus* plated] —**laminable** (ˈlæmɪnəb^{ə}l) *adj.* —ˈ**lamiˌnator** *n.*

laminated (ˈlæmɪˌneɪtɪd) *adj.* **1.** composed of thin sheets (of plastic, wood, etc.) superimposed and bonded together by synthetic resins, usually under heat and pressure. **2.** covered with a thin protective layer of plastic or synthetic resin. **3.** another word for **laminate** (sense 6).

lamination (ˌlæmɪˈneɪʃən) *n.* **1.** the act of laminating or the state of being laminated. **2.** a layered structure. **3.** a layer; lamina. **4.** one of a set of iron plates forming the core of an electrical transformer. **5.** *Geology.* laminar stratification, typically shown by shales.

laminectomy (ˌlæmɪˈnɛktəmɪ) *n., pl.* **-mies.** surgical incision into the backbone to gain access to the spinal cord. Also called: **rachiotomy.**

lamington (ˈlæmɪŋtən) *n. Austral. and N.Z.* a cube of sponge cake coated in chocolate and dried coconut. [C20 (in the earlier sense: a homburg hat): named after Baron *Lamington,* governor of Queensland (1896–1901)]

laminitis (ˌlæmɪˈnaɪtɪs) *n.* inflammation of the laminated tissue structure to which the hoof of a horse is attached. Also called: **founder.** [C19: from New Latin, from LAMINA + -ITIS]

Lammas (ˈlæməs) *n.* **1.** *R.C. Church.* Aug. 1, held as a feast, commemorating St. Peter's miraculous deliverance from prison. **2.** Also called: **Lammas Day.** the same day formerly observed in England as a harvest festival. In Scotland Lammas is a quarter day. [Old English *hlāfmæsse,* loaf mass]

Lammastide (ˈlæməsˌtaɪd) *n. Archaic.* the season of Lammas.

lammergeier *or* **lammergeyer** (ˈlæməˌgaɪə) *n.* a rare vulture, *Gypaetus barbatus,* of S Europe, Africa, and Asia, with dark wings, a pale breast, and black feathers around the bill: family *Accipitridae* (hawks). Also called: **bearded vulture.** [C19: from German *Lämmergeier,* from *Lämmer* lambs + *Geier* vulture]

lamp (læmp) *n.* **1. a.** any of a number of devices that produce illumination: *an electric lamp; a gas lamp; an oil lamp.* **b.** (*in combination*): *lampshade.* **2.** a device for holding one or more electric light bulbs: *a table lamp.* **3.** a vessel in which a liquid fuel is burned to supply illumination. **4.** any of a variety of devices that produce radiation, esp. for therapeutic purposes: *an ultraviolet lamp.* [C13 *lampe,* via Old French from Latin *lampas,* from Greek, from *lampein* to shine]

lampas[1] (ˈlæmpəs) *or* **lampers** (ˈlæmpəz) *n.* a swelling of the mucous membrane of the hard palate of horses. [C16: from Old French; origin obscure]

lampas[2] (ˈlæmpəs) *n.* an ornate damask-like cloth of cotton or silk and cotton, used in upholstery. [C14 (a kind of crepe): probably from Middle Dutch *lampers*]

lampblack (ˈlæmpˌblæk) *n.* a finely divided form of almost pure carbon produced by the incomplete combustion of organic compounds, such as natural gas, used in making carbon electrodes and dynamo brushes and as a pigment.

lamp chimney *n.* a glass tube that surrounds the wick in an oil lamp.

lamper eel (ˈlæmpə) *n.* another name for **lamprey.** [C19 *lamper,* variant of LAMPREY]

lampern (ˈlæmpən) *n.* a migratory European lamprey, *Lampetra fluviatilis,* that spawns in rivers. Also called: **river lamprey.** [C14 *laumprun,* from Old French, from *lampreie* LAMPREY]

lampion (ˈlæmpɪən) *n.* an oil-burning lamp. [C19: from French via Italian *lampione,* from Old French *lampe* LAMP]

lamplighter (ˈlæmpˌlaɪtə) *n.* **1.** (formerly) a person who lit and extinguished street lamps, esp. gas ones. **2.** *Chiefly U.S. and Canadian.* any of various devices used to light lamps.

lampoon (læmˈpuːn) *n.* **1.** a satire in prose or verse ridiculing a person, literary work, etc. ~*vb.* **2.** (*tr.*) to attack or satirize in a lampoon. [C17: from French *lampon,* perhaps from *lampons* let us drink (frequently used as a refrain in poems)] —**lamˈpooner** *or* **lamˈpoonist** *n.* —**lamˈpoonery** *n.*

lamppost (ˈlæmpˌpəʊst) *n.* a post supporting a lamp, esp. in a street.

lamprey (ˈlæmprɪ) *n.* any eel-like cyclostome vertebrate of the family *Petromyzonidae,* having a round sucking mouth for clinging to and feeding on the blood of other animals. Also called: **lamper eel.** See also **sea lamprey.** [C13: from Old French *lamproie,* from Late Latin *lamprēda;* origin obscure]

lamprophyre (ˈlæmprəˌfaɪə) *n.* any of a group of basic igneous rocks consisting of feldspar and ferromagnesian minerals, esp. biotite: occurring as dykes and minor intrusions. [from Greek *lampros* bright + *-phyre*, from PORPHYRY]
lamp shell *n.* another name for a **brachiopod.** [C19: from its likeness in shape to an ancient Roman oil lamp]
lamp standard *n.* a tall metal or concrete post supporting a street lamp.
LAN *abbrev. for* local area network.
lanai (lɑːˈnɑːɪ, ləˈnaɪ) *n.* a Hawaiian word for **veranda.**
lanate (ˈleɪneɪt) *or* **lanose** (ˈleɪnəʊs, -nəʊz) *adj. Biology.* having or consisting of a woolly covering of hairs. [C18: from Latin *lānātus*, from *lāna* wool]
Lancashire (ˈlæŋkəˌʃɪə, -ʃə) *n.* a mild whitish-coloured cheese with a crumbly texture. [named after *Lancashire*, a county of NW England]
Lancastrian (læŋˈkæstrɪən) *n.* **1.** a native or resident of the county of Lancashire or the city of Lancaster, NW England. **2.** an adherent of the English royal house of Lancaster (reigned 1399–1461). Compare **Yorkist.** ~*adj.* **3.** of or relating to Lancashire or Lancaster. **4.** of or relating to the house of Lancaster.
lance (lɑːns) *n.* **1.** a long weapon with a pointed head used by horsemen to unhorse or injure an opponent. **2.** a similar weapon used for hunting, whaling, etc. **3.** *Surgery.* another name for **lancet.** **4.** short for **sand lance** (another name for **sand eel**). **5. break a lance (with).** to engage in argument (with someone). ~*vb.* (*tr.*) **6.** to pierce (an abscess or boil) with a lancet to drain off pus. **7.** to pierce with or as if with a lance. [C13 *launce*, from Old French *lance*, from Latin *lancea*]
lance corporal *n.* a noncommissioned officer of the lowest rank in the British Army.
lancejack (ˈlɑːnsˌdʒæk) *n. Brit. military slang.* a lance corporal.
lancelet (ˈlɑːnslɪt) *n.* any of several marine animals of the genus *Amphioxus*, esp. *A. lanceolatus*, that are closely related to the vertebrates: subphylum *Cephalochordata* (cephalochordates). Also called: **amphioxus.** [C19: referring to the slender shape]
lanceolate (ˈlɑːnsɪəˌleɪt, -lɪt) *adj.* narrow and tapering to a point at each end: *lanceolate leaves.* [C18: from Late Latin *lanceolātus*, from *lanceola* small LANCE]
lancer (ˈlɑːnsə) *n.* **1.** (formerly) a cavalryman armed with a lance. **2. a.** a member of a regiment retaining such a title. **b.** (*pl.; cap. when part of a name*): *the 21st Lancers.* ~See also **lancers.**
lance rest *n.* **1.** a hinged bracket on the breastplate of a medieval horseman on which the lance was rested in a charge. **2.** a similar structure on a knight's saddle.
lancers (ˈlɑːnsəz) *n.* (*functioning as sing.*) **1.** a quadrille for eight or sixteen couples. **2.** a piece of music composed for this dance.
lance sergeant *n.* a corporal acting as a sergeant, usually on a temporary basis and without additional pay.
lancet (ˈlɑːnsɪt) *n.* **1.** Also called: **lance.** a pointed surgical knife with two sharp edges. **2.** short for **lancet arch** or **lancet window.** [C15 *lancette*, from Old French: small LANCE]
lancet arch *n.* a narrow acutely pointed arch having two centres of equal radii. Sometimes shortened to **lancet.** Also called: **acute arch, Gothic arch, pointed arch, ogive.**
lanceted (ˈlɑːnsɪtɪd) *adj. Architect.* having one or more lancet arches or windows.
lancet fish *n.* either of two deep-sea teleost fishes, *Alepisaurus ferox* or *A. borealis*, having a long body with a long sail-like dorsal fin: family *Alepisauridae.*
lancet window *n.* a narrow window having a lancet arch. Sometimes shortened to **lancet.**
lancewood (ˈlɑːnsˌwʊd) *n.* **1.** any of various tropical trees, esp. *Oxandra lanceolata*, yielding a tough elastic wood: family *Annonaceae.* **2.** the wood of any of these trees.
lancinate (ˈlɑːnsɪˌneɪt) *adj.* (esp. of pain) sharp or cutting. [C17: from Latin *lancinātus* pierced, rent; related to *lacer* mangled] —ˌ**lanciˈnation** *n.*
Lancs (læŋks) *abbrev. for* Lancashire.
land (lænd) *n.* **1.** the solid part of the surface of the earth as distinct from seas, lakes, etc. Related adj.: **terrestrial.** **2. a.** ground, esp. with reference to its use, quality, etc. **b.** (*in combination*): *land-grabber.* **3.** rural or agricultural areas as contrasted with urban ones. **4.** farming as an occupation or way of life. **5.** *Law.* **a.** any tract of ground capable of being owned as property, together with any buildings on it, extending above and below the surface. **b.** any hereditament, tenement, or other interest; realty. **6. a.** a country, region, or area. **b.** the people of a country, etc. **7.** a realm, sphere, or domain. **8.** *Economics.* the factor of production consisting of all natural resources. **9.** the unindented part of a grooved surface, esp. one of the ridges inside a rifle bore. **10. how the land lies.** the prevailing conditions or state of affairs. ~*vb.* **11.** to transfer (something) or go from a ship or boat to the shore: *land the cargo.* **12.** (*intr.*) to come to or touch shore. **13.** to come down or bring (something) down to earth after a flight or jump. **14.** to come or bring to some point, condition, or state. **15.** (*tr.*) *Angling.* to retrieve (a hooked fish) from the water. **16.** (*tr.*) *Informal.* to win or obtain: *to land a job.* **17.** (*tr.*) *Informal.* to deliver (a blow). ~See also **lands, land up, land with.** [Old English; compare Old Norse, Gothic *land*, Old High German *lant*] —ˈ**landless** *adj.* —ˈ**landlessness** *n.*
Land (*German* lant) *n., pl.* ***Länder*** (ˈlɛndər) **a.** any of the federal states of Germany. **b.** any of the provinces of Austria. [German]
land agent *n.* **1.** a person who administers a landed estate and its tenancies. **2.** a person who acts as an agent for the sale of land. —**land agency** *n.*
landammann (ˈlændəmən) *n.* (*sometimes cap.*) the chairman of the governing council in any of several Swiss cantons. [C18: Swiss German, from *Land* country + *Ammann*, from *Amt* office + *Mann* MAN]
landau (ˈlændɔː) *n.* a four-wheeled horse-drawn carriage with two folding hoods that meet over the middle of the passenger compartment. [C18: named after *Landau* (a town in Bavaria), where it was first made]
landaulet *or* **landaulette** (ˌlændɔːˈlɛt) *n.* **1.** a small landau. **2.** *U.S.* an early type of car with a folding hood over the passenger seats and an open driver's seat.
land bank *n.* a bank that issues banknotes on the security of property.
land bridge *n.* (in zoogeography) a connecting tract of land between two continents, enabling animals to pass from one continent to the other.
land crab *n.* any of various crabs, esp. of the tropical family *Gecarcinidae*, that are adapted to a partly terrestrial life.
Landdrost (ˈlændrɒst) *n. S. African history.* the chief magistrate of a district. [Afrikaans]
landed (ˈlændɪd) *adj.* **1.** owning land: *landed gentry.* **2.** consisting of or including land: *a landed estate.*
Landeshauptmann (ˈlɑːndɪsˌhauptmən) *n.* the head of government in an Austrian state. [C20: from German, from *Land* country + *Hauptmann* leader]
landfall (ˈlændˌfɔːl) *n.* **1.** the act of sighting or nearing land, esp. from the sea. **2.** the land sighted or neared.
landfill (ˈlændˌfɪl) *n.* **a.** disposal of waste material by burying it under layers of earth. **b.** (*as modifier*): *landfill sites.*
land forces *pl. n.* armed forces serving on land.
landform (ˈlændˌfɔːm) *n. Geology.* any natural feature of the earth's surface, such as valleys and mountains.
land girl *n.* a girl or woman who does farm work, esp. in wartime.
land grant *n.* **1.** *U.S. and Canadian.* a grant of public land to a college, railway, etc. **2.** (*modifier*) *U.S.* designating a state university established with such a grant.
landgrave (ˈlændˌgreɪv) *n. German history.* **1.** (from the 13th century to 1806) a count who ruled over a specified territory. **2.** (after 1806) the title of any of various sovereign princes in central Germany. [C16: via German, from Middle High German *lantgrāve*, from *lant* land + *grāve* count]
landgraviate (lændˈgreɪvɪɪt, -ˌeɪt) *or* **landgravate** (ˈlændgrəˌveɪt) *n.* the domain or position of a landgrave or landgravine.
landgravine (ˈlændgrəˌviːn) *n.* **1.** the wife or widow of a landgrave. **2.** a woman who held the rank of landgrave.
land-holder *n.* a person who owns or occupies land. —ˈ**landˌholding** *adj., n.*
landing (ˈlændɪŋ) *n.* **1. a.** the act of coming to land, esp. after a flight or sea voyage. **b.** (*as modifier*): *landing place.* **2.** a place of disembarkation. **3.** the floor area at the top of a flight of stairs or between two flights of stairs.
landing beacon *n.* a radio transmitter that emits a landing beam.
landing beam *n.* a radio beam transmitted from a landing field to enable aircraft to make an instrument landing.
landing craft *n. Military.* any small vessel designed for the landing of troops and equipment on beaches.
landing field *n.* an area of land on which aircraft land and from which they take off.
landing gear *n.* another name for **undercarriage** (sense 1).
landing net *n. Angling.* a loose long-handled net on a triangular frame for lifting hooked fish from the water.
landing speed *n.* the minimum air speed at which an aircraft lands safely.
landing stage *n.* a platform used for landing goods and passengers from a vessel.
landing strip *n.* another name for **airstrip.**
landlady (ˈlændˌleɪdɪ) *n., pl.* **-dies.** **1.** a woman who owns and leases property. **2.** a landlord's wife. **3.** a woman who owns or runs a lodging house, pub, etc.
ländler (*German* ˈlɛntlər) *n.* **1.** an Austrian country dance in which couples spin and clap. **2.** a piece of music composed for or in the rhythm of this dance, in three-four time. [German, from dialect *Landl* Upper Austria]
land line *n.* a telecommunications wire or cable laid over land.
landlocked (ˈlændˌlɒkt) *adj.* **1.** (esp. of lakes) completely or almost completely surrounded by land. **2.** (esp. of certain salmon) living in fresh water that is permanently isolated from the sea.
landloper (ˈlændˌləʊpə) *n. Scot.* a vagabond or vagrant. [C16: from Dutch, from LAND + *loopen* to run, LEAP]
landlord (ˈlændˌlɔːd) *n.* **1.** a man who owns and leases property. **2.** a man who owns or runs a lodging house, pub, etc. **3.** *Brit. archaic.* the lord of an estate.
landlordism (ˈlændlɔːˌdɪzəm) *n.* the system by which land under private ownership is rented for a fixed sum to tenants.

landlubber ('lænd,lʌbə) *n. Nautical.* any person having no experience at sea. [C18: LAND + LUBBER]
landmark ('lænd,mɑːk) *n.* **1.** a prominent or well-known object in or feature of a particular landscape. **2.** an important or unique decision, event, fact, discovery, etc. **3.** a boundary marker or signpost.
landmass ('lænd,mæs) *n.* a large continuous area of land, as opposed to seas or islands.
land mine *n. Military.* an explosive charge placed in the ground, usually detonated by stepping or driving on it.
land office *n. U.S. and Canadian.* an office that administers the sale of public land.
land-office business *n. U.S. and Canadian informal.* a booming or thriving business.
land of milk and honey *n.* **1.** *Old Testament.* the land of natural fertility promised to the Israelites by God (Ezekiel 20:6). **2.** any fertile land, state, etc.
land of Nod *n.* an imaginary land of sleep. [C18: pun on the Biblical *Land of Nod* to which Cain went after he had killed Abel (Genesis 4:14)]
landowner ('lænd,əʊnə) *n.* a person who owns land. —'**land**,**owner**,**ship** *n.* —'**land**,**owning** *n., adj.*
land-poor *adj.* owning much unprofitable land and lacking the money to maintain its fertility or improve it.
landrace ('lænd,reɪs) *n.* **1.** *Chiefly Brit.* a white very long-bodied lop-eared breed of pork pig. **2.** *Botany.* an ancient or primitive cultivated variety of a crop plant. [from Danish, literally: land race]
land rail *n.* another name for **corncrake.**
land reform *n.* the redistributing of large agricultural holdings among the landless.
Landrost ('lændrɒst) *n.* a variant spelling of **Landdrost.**
lands (lændz) *pl. n.* **1.** holdings in land. **2.** *S. African.* the part of a farm on which crops are grown.
landscape ('lænd,skeɪp) *n.* **1.** an extensive area of land regarded as being visually distinct: *slagheaps dominated the landscape.* **2.** a painting, drawing, photograph, etc., depicting natural scenery. **3. a.** the genre including such pictures. **b.** (*as modifier*): *landscape painter.* **4.** the distinctive features of a given area of intellectual activity, regarded as an integrated whole: *the landscape of the European imagination.* ~*adj.* **5.** *Printing.* **a.** (of an illustration in a book, magazine, etc.) of greater width than depth. Compare **portrait** (sense 3). **b.** (of a page) carrying an illustration or table printed at right angles to the normal text. ~*vb.* **6.** (*tr.*) to improve the natural features of (a garden, park, etc.), as by creating contoured features and planting trees. **7.** (*intr.*) to work as a landscape gardener. [C16 *landskip* (originally a term in painting), from Middle Dutch *lantscap* region; related to Old English *landscipe* tract of land, Old High German *lantscaf* region]
landscape gardening *n.* the art of laying out grounds in imitation of natural scenery. Also called: **landscape architecture.** —**landscape gardener** *n.*
landscapist ('lænd,skeɪpɪst) *n.* a painter of landscapes.
landshark ('lænd,ʃɑːk) *n. Informal.* a person who makes inordinate profits by buying and selling land.
landside ('lænd,saɪd) *n.* **1.** the part of an airport farthest from the aircraft, the boundary of which is the security check, customs, passport control, etc. Compare **airside. 2.** the part of a plough that slides along the face of the furrow wall on the opposite side to the mouldboard.
landsknecht ('læntskə,nɛkt) *n.* a mercenary foot soldier in late 15th-, 16th-, and 17th-century Europe, esp. a German pikeman. [German, literally: landknight]
landslide ('lænd,slaɪd) *n.* **1.** Also called: **landslip. a.** the sliding of a large mass of rock material, soil, etc., down the side of a mountain or cliff. **b.** the material dislodged in this way. **2. a.** an overwhelming electoral victory. **b.** (*as modifier*): *a landslide win.*
Landsmål ('lɑntsmoːl) *n.* another name for **Nynorsk.**
landsman[1] ('lændzmən) *n., pl.* **-men. 1.** a person who works or lives on land, as distinguished from a seaman. **2.** a person with no experience at sea.
landsman[2] ('lændzmən) *n., pl.* **-men.** a Jewish compatriot from the same area of origin as another. [from Yiddish]
Landsturm *German.* ('lantʃtʊrm) *n.* (in German-speaking countries) **1.** a reserve force; militia. **2.** a general levy in wartime. [C19: literally: landstorm; originally a summons to arms by means of storm-warning bells]
Landtag ('lɑnt,tɑːk) *n.* **1.** the legislative assembly of each state in present-day Germany and Austria. **2.** the estates of principalities in medieval and modern Germany. **3.** the assembly of numerous states in 19th-century Germany. [C16: German: land assembly]
land tax *n.* (formerly) a tax payable annually by virtue of ownership of land, abolished in Britain in 1963.
land up *vb.* (*adv., usually intr.*) to arrive or cause to arrive at a final point: *after a summer in Europe, he suddenly landed up at home.*
landwaiter ('lænd,weɪtə) *n.* an officer of the Custom House.
landward ('lændwəd) *adj.* **1.** lying, facing, or moving towards land. **2.** in the direction of the land. ~*adv.* **3.** a variant of **landwards.**
landwards ('lændwədz) *or* **landward** *adv.* towards land.
Landwehr *German.* ('lantveːr) *n.* (in German-speaking countries) the army reserve. [C19: land defence]
land with *vb.* (*tr., prep.*) to give to, so as to put in difficulties; cause to be burdened with: *why did you land me with this extra work?*
lane[1] (leɪn) *n.* **1. a.** a narrow road or way between buildings, hedges, fences, etc. **b.** (*cap. as part of a street name*): *Drury Lane.* **2.** any narrow well-defined track or course, as for lines of traffic in a road, or for ships or aircraft. **3.** one of the parallel strips into which a running track or swimming bath is divided for races. **4.** the long strip of wooden flooring down which balls are bowled in a bowling alley. [Old English *lane, lanu,* of Germanic origin; related to Middle Dutch *lāne* lane]
lane[2] (leɪn) *Scot. dialect.* ~*adj.* **1.** lone or alone. **2. (on) one's lane.** on one's own.
lang (læŋ) *adj.* a Scot. word for **long.**
lang. *abbrev. for* language.
Langerhans islets ('læŋə,hæns) *or* **islands** *n. Anatomy.* see **islets of Langerhans.**
langlauf ('lɑːŋ,laʊf) *n.* cross-country skiing. [German, literally: long run] —**langläufer** ('lɑːŋ,lɔɪfə) *n.*
Langobard ('læŋgə,bɑːd) *n.* a less common name for a **Lombard.** [C18: from Late Latin *Langobardicus* Lombard]
Langobardic (,læŋgə'bɑːdɪk) *n.* **1.** the language of the ancient Lombards: a dialect of Old High German. ~*adj.* **2.** of or relating to the Lombards or their language.
langouste ('lɒnguːst, lɒŋ'guːst) *n.* another name for the **spiny lobster.** [French, from Old Provençal *langosta,* perhaps from Latin *lōcusta* lobster, locust]
langoustine (,lɒngʊ'stiːn) *n.* a large prawn or small lobster. [from French, diminutive of LANGOUSTE]
langrage ('læŋgrɪdʒ), **langrel** ('læŋgrəl), *or* **langridge** *n.* shot consisting of scrap iron packed into a case, formerly used in naval warfare. [C18: of unknown origin]
langsyne (,læŋ'saɪn, -'saɪn) *Scot.* ~*adv.* **1.** long ago; long since. ~*n.* **2.** times long past, esp. those fondly remembered. See also **auld lang syne.** [C16: Scottish: long since]
language ('læŋgwɪdʒ) *n.* **1.** a system for the expression of thoughts, feelings, etc., by the use of spoken sounds or conventional symbols. **2.** the faculty for the use of such systems, which is a distinguishing characteristic of man as compared with other animals. **3.** the language of a particular nation or people: *the French language.* **4.** any other systematic or nonsystematic means of communicating, such as gesture or animal sounds: *the language of love.* **5.** the specialized vocabulary used by a particular group: *medical language.* **6.** a particular manner or style of verbal expression: *your language is disgusting.* **7.** *Computer technol.* See **programming language. 8. speak the same language.** to communicate with understanding because of common background, values, etc. [C13: from Old French *langage,* ultimately from Latin *lingua* tongue]
language laboratory *n.* a room equipped with tape recorders, etc., for learning foreign languages.
langue (lɑːŋg) *n. Linguistics.* language considered as an abstract system or a social institution, being the common possession of a speech community. Compare **parole** (sense 5). [C19: from French: language]
langue de chat ('lɑːŋ də 'ʃɑː) *n.* **1.** a flat sweet finger-shaped biscuit. **2.** a piece of chocolate having the same shape. [French: cat's tongue]
Languedoc (*French* lɑ̃gdɔk) *n.* a wine from the region and former province of Languedoc in S France.
langue d'oc *French.* (lɑ̃g dɔk) *n.* the group of medieval French dialects spoken in S France: often regarded as including Provençal. Compare ***langue d'oïl.*** [literally: language of *oc* (form for the Provençal *yes*), ultimately from Latin *hoc* this]
langue d'oïl *French.* (lɑ̃g dɔj) *n.* the group of medieval French dialects spoken in France north of the Loire; the medieval basis of modern French. [literally: language of *oïl* (the northern form for *yes*), ultimately from Latin *hoc ille* (*fecit*) this he (did)]
languet ('læŋgwet) *n. Rare.* anything resembling a tongue in shape or function. [C15: from Old French *languette,* diminutive of *langue* tongue]
languid ('læŋgwɪd) *adj.* **1.** without energy or spirit. **2.** without interest or enthusiasm. **3.** sluggish; inactive. [C16: from Latin *languidus,* from *languēre* to languish] —'**languidly** *adv.* —'**languidness** *n.*
languish ('læŋgwɪʃ) *vb.* (*intr.*) **1.** to lose or diminish in strength or energy. **2.** (often foll. by *for*) to be listless with desire; pine. **3.** to suffer deprivation, hardship, or neglect: *to languish in prison.* **4.** to put on a tender, nostalgic, or melancholic expression. [C14 *languishen,* from Old French *languiss-,* stem of *languir,* ultimately from Latin *languēre*] —'**languishing** *adj.* —'**languishingly** *adv.* —'**languishment** *n.*
languor ('læŋgə) *n.* **1.** physical or mental laziness or weariness. **2.** a feeling of dreaminess and relaxation. **3.** oppressive silence or stillness. [C14 *langour,* via Old French from Latin *languor,* from *languēre* to languish; the modern spelling is directly from Latin]
languorous ('læŋgərəs) *adj.* **1.** characterized by or producing languor. **2.** another word for **languid.** —'**languorously** *adv.* —'**languorousness** *n.*

langur (lʌŋ'guə) *n.* any of various agile arboreal Old World monkeys of the genus *Presbytis* and related genera, of S and SE Asia having a slender body, long tail and hands, and long hair surrounding the face. [Hindi, perhaps related to Sanskrit *lāngūla* tailed]

laniard ('lænjəd) *n.* a variant spelling of **lanyard.**

laniary ('lænɪərɪ) *adj.* **1.** (esp. of canine teeth) adapted for tearing. ~*n., pl.* **-aries. 2.** a tooth adapted for tearing. [C19: from Latin *lanius* butcher, from *laniāre* to tear]

laniferous (lə'nɪfərəs) *or* **lanigerous** (lə'nɪdʒərəs) *adj. Biology.* bearing wool or fleecy hairs resembling wool. [C17: from Latin *lānifer,* from *lāna* wool]

lank (læŋk) *adj.* **1.** long and limp. **2.** thin or gaunt. [Old English *hlanc* loose] —'**lankly** *adv.* —'**lankness** *n.*

lanky ('læŋkɪ) *adj.* **lankier, lankiest.** tall, thin, and loose-jointed. —'**lankily** *adv.* —'**lankiness** *n.*

lanner ('lænə) *n.* **1.** a large falcon, *Falco biarmicus,* of Mediterranean regions, N Africa, and S Asia. **2.** *Falconry.* the female of this falcon. Compare **lanneret.** [C15: from Old French *(faucon) lanier* cowardly (falcon), from Latin *lanārius* wool worker, coward; referring to its sluggish flight and timid nature]

lanneret ('lænəˌrɛt) *n.* the male or tercel of the lanner falcon. [C15: diminutive of LANNER]

lanolin ('lænəlɪn) *or* **lanoline** ('lænəlɪn, -ˌliːn) *n.* a yellowish viscous substance extracted from wool, consisting of a mixture of esters of fatty acids: used in some ointments. Also called: **wool fat.** [C19: via German from Latin *lāna* wool + *oleum* oil; see -IN] —**lanolated** ('lænəˌleɪtɪd) *adj.*

lanose ('leɪnəʊs, -nəʊz) *adj.* another word for **lanate.** [C19: from Latin *lānosus*] —**lanosity** (leɪ'nɒsɪtɪ) *n.*

Lansker line ('lænskə) *n.* (in Pembrokeshire) the linguistic and ethnic division between the Welsh-speaking north and the English-speaking south. [C19: from Pembrokeshire dialect *lansker* boundary]

lansquenet ('lænskəˌnɛt) *n.* **1.** a gambling game of chance. **2.** an archaic spelling of **landsknecht.** [from French]

lantana (læn'teɪnə, -'tɑː-) *n.* any verbenaceous shrub or herbaceous plant of the tropical American genus *Lantana,* having spikes of yellow or orange flowers. It was introduced into Australia, where it is now regarded as a troublesome weed. [C18: New Latin, from Italian dialect *lantana* wayfaring tree]

lantern ('læntən) *n.* **1.** a light with a transparent or translucent protective case. **2.** a structure on top of a dome or roof having openings or windows to admit light or air. **3.** the upper part of a lighthouse that houses the light. **4.** *Photog.* short for **magic lantern.** [C13: from Latin *lanterna,* from Greek *lamptēr* lamp, from *lampein* to shine]

lantern fish *n.* any small deep-sea teleost fish of the family *Myctophidae,* having a series of luminescent spots along the body.

lantern fly *n.* any of various tropical insects of the homopterous family *Fulgoridae,* many species of which have a snoutlike process formerly thought to emit light.

lantern jaw *n.* (when *pl.,* refers to upper and lower jaw; when *sing.* usually to lower jaw) a long hollow jaw that gives the face a drawn appearance. —'**lantern-ˌjawed** *adj.*

lantern pinion *or* **wheel** *n.* a type of gearwheel, now used only in clocks, consisting of two parallel circular discs connected by a number of pins running parallel to the axis.

lantern slide *n.* (formerly) a photographic slide for projection, used in a magic lantern.

lanthanide ('lænθəˌnaɪd) *or* **lanthanon** ('lænθəˌnɒn) *n.* any element of the lanthanide series. Also called: **rare earth, rare-earth element.** [C19: from LANTHANUM + -IDE]

lanthanide series *n.* a class of 15 chemically related elements with atomic numbers from 57 (lanthanum) to 71 (lutecium).

lanthanum ('lænθənəm) *n.* a silvery-white ductile metallic element of the lanthanide series, occurring principally in bastnaesite and monazite: used in pyrophoric alloys, electronic devices, and in glass manufacture. Symbol: La; atomic no.: 57; atomic wt.: 138.91; valency: 3; relative density: 6.17; melting pt.: 920°C; boiling pt.: 3454°C. [C19: New Latin, from Greek *lanthanein* to lie unseen]

lanthorn ('læntˌhɔːn, 'læntən) *n.* an archaic word for **lantern.**

lanugo (lə'njuːgəʊ) *n., pl.* **-gos.** a layer of fine hairs, esp. the covering of the human fetus before birth. [C17: from Latin: down, from *lāna* wool] —**lanuginous** (lə'njuːdʒɪnəs) *or* **la'nugiˌnose** *adj.* —**la'nuginousness** *n.*

lanyard *or* **laniard** ('lænjəd) *n.* **1.** a cord, esp. one worn around the neck, to hold a whistle, knife, etc. **2.** a cord with an attached hook used in firing certain types of cannon. **3.** *Nautical.* a line rove through deadeyes for extending or tightening standing rigging. [C15 *lanyer,* from French *lanière,* from *lasne* strap, probably of Germanic origin]

Lao (laʊ) *or* **Laotian** ('laʊʃɪən) *n.* **1.** (*pl.* **Lao, Laos,** *or* **Laotians**) a member of a Buddhist people of Laos, a republic in SE Asia, and NE Thailand, related to the Thais. **2.** the language of this people, closely related to Thai. ~*adj.* **3.** of or relating to this people or their language or to Laos.

LAO *international car registration for* Laos.

laodicean (ˌleɪəʊdɪ'sɪən) *adj.* **1.** lukewarm and indifferent, esp. in religious matters. ~*n.* **2.** a person having a lukewarm attitude towards religious matters. [C17: referring to the early Christians of *Laodicea* in W Asia (Revelation 3:14–16)]

Laotian ('laʊʃɪən) *adj., n.* a variant of **Lao.**

lap[1] (læp) *n.* **1.** the area formed by the upper surface of the thighs of a seated person. **2.** Also called: **lapful.** the amount held in one's lap. **3.** a protected place or environment: *in the lap of luxury.* **4.** any of various hollow or depressed areas, such as a hollow in the land. **5.** the part of one's clothing that covers the lap. **6. drop in someone's lap.** give someone the responsibility of. **7. in the lap of the gods.** beyond human control and power. [Old English *læppa* flap; see LOBE, LAPPET, LOP[2]]

lap[2] (læp) *n.* **1.** one circuit of a racecourse or track. **2.** a stage or part of a journey, race, etc. **3. a.** an overlapping part or projection. **b.** the extent of overlap. **4.** the length of material needed to go around an object. **5.** a rotating disc coated with fine abrasive for polishing gemstones. **6.** any device for bedding mechanical components together using a fine abrasive to polish the mating surfaces. **7.** *Metallurgy.* a defect in rolled metals caused by the folding of a fin onto the surface. **8.** a sheet or band of fibres, such as cotton, prepared for further processing. ~*vb.* **laps, lapping, lapped. 9.** (*tr.*) to wrap or fold (around or over): *he lapped a bandage around his wrist.* **10.** (*tr.*) to enclose or envelop in: *he lapped his wrist in a bandage.* **11.** to place or lie partly or completely over or project beyond. **12.** (*tr.; usually passive*) to envelop or surround with comfort, love, etc.: *lapped in luxury.* **13.** (*intr.*) to be folded. **14.** (*tr.*) to overtake (an opponent) in a race so as to be one or more circuits ahead. **15.** (*tr.*) to polish or cut (a workpiece, gemstone, etc.) with a fine abrasive, esp. to hone (mating metal parts) against each other with an abrasive. **16.** to form (fibres) into a sheet or band. [C13 (in the sense: to wrap): probably from LAP[1]] —'**lapper** *n.*

lap[3] (læp) *vb.* **laps, lapping, lapped. 1.** (of small waves) to wash against (a shore, boat, etc.), usually with light splashing sounds. **2.** (often foll. by *up*) (esp. of animals) to scoop (a liquid) into the mouth with the tongue. ~*n.* **3.** the act or sound of lapping. **4.** a thin food for dogs or other animals. ~See also **lap up.** [Old English *lapian;* related to Old High German *laffan,* Latin *lambere,* Greek *laptein*] —'**lapper** *n.*

laparoscope ('læpərəˌskəʊp) *n.* a medical instrument consisting of a tube that is inserted through the abdominal wall and illuminated to enable a doctor to view the internal organs. [C19 (applied to various instruments used to examine the abdomen) and C20 (in the specific modern sense): from Greek *lapara* (see LAPAROTOMY) + -SCOPE] —ˌ**lapa'roscopy** *n.*

laparotomy (ˌlæpə'rɒtəmɪ) *n., pl.* **-mies. 1.** surgical incision through the abdominal wall, esp. to investigate the cause of an abdominal disorder. **2.** surgical incision into the loin. [C19: from Greek *lapara* flank, from *laparos* soft + -TOMY]

lapboard ('læpˌbɔːd) *n.* a flat board that can be used on the lap as a makeshift table or desk.

lap-chart *n. Motor racing.* a log of every lap covered by each car in a race, showing the exact position throughout.

lap dissolve *n. Films.* the technique of allowing the end of one scene to overlap the beginning of the next scene by fading out the former while fading in the latter.

lapdog ('læpˌdɒg) *n.* **1.** a pet dog small and docile enough to be cuddled in the lap. **2.** *Informal.* a person who attaches himself to someone in admiration or infatuation.

lapel (lə'pɛl) *n.* the continuation of the turned or folded back collar on a suit coat, jacket, etc. [C18: from LAP[1]] —**la'pelled** *adj.*

lapheld ('læpˌhɛld) *adj.* (esp. of a personal computer) small enough to be used on one's lap; portable.

lapidary ('læpɪdərɪ) *n., pl.* **-daries. 1.** a person whose business is to cut, polish, set, or deal in gemstones. ~*adj.* **2.** of or relating to gemstones or the work of a lapidary. **3.** Also: **lapidarian** (ˌlæpɪ'dɛərɪən). engraved, cut, or inscribed in a stone or gemstone. **4.** of sufficiently high quality to be engraved on a stone: *a lapidary inscription.* [C14: from Latin *lapidārius,* from *lapid-, lapis* stone] —ˌ**lapi'darian** *adj.*

lapidate ('læpɪˌdeɪt) *vb.* (*tr.*) *Literary.* **1.** to pelt with stones. **2.** to kill by stoning. [C17: from Latin *lapidāre,* from *lapis* stone] —ˌ**lapi'dation** *n.*

lapidicolous (ˌlæpɪ'dɪkələs) *adj. Zoology.* living under stones.

lapidify (lə'pɪdɪˌfaɪ) *vb.* **-fies, -fying, -fied.** to change into stone. [C17: from French *lapidifier,* from Medieval Latin *lapidificāre,* ultimately from Latin *lapis* stone] —**laˌpidifi'cation** *n.*

lapillus (lə'pɪləs) *n., pl.* **-li** (-laɪ). a small piece of lava thrown from a volcano. [C18: Latin: little stone]

lapis lazuli *or* **lazuli** ('læpɪs) *n.* **1.** a brilliant blue variety of the mineral lazurite, used as a gemstone. **2.** the deep blue colour of lapis lazuli. ~Also called: **lapis.** [C14: from Latin *lapis* stone + Medieval Latin *lazulī,* from *lazulum,* from Arabic *lāzaward,* from Persian *lāzhuward,* of obscure origin]

lap joint *n.* a joint made by placing one member over another and fastening them together. Also called: **lapped joint.** —'**lap-ˌjointed** *adj.*

Laplace operator (lə'plæs) *n. Maths.* the operator $\partial^2/\partial x^2 + \partial^2/\partial y^2 + \partial^2/\partial z^2$, used in differential analysis. Symbol: ∇^2 Also called: **Laplacian** (lə'pleɪʃɪən). [named after Pierre *Laplace* (1749–1827), French mathematician]

Laplander ('læpˌlændə) *n.* a native or inhabitant of Lapland, a mainly Arctic region of N Europe. See also **Lapp.**

lap of honour *n.* a ceremonial circuit of a racing track, etc., by the winner of a race.

Lapp (læp) *n.* **1.** a member of a nomadic people living chiefly in N Scandinavia and the Kola Peninsula of the former Soviet Union. **2.** the language of this people, belonging to the Finno-Ugric family. *~adj.* **3.** of or relating to this people or their language. —**'Lappish** *adj., n.*

lappet ('læpɪt) *n.* **1.** a small hanging flap or piece of lace, etc., such as one dangling from a headdress. **2.** *Zoology.* a lobelike hanging structure, such as the wattle on a bird's head. [C16: from LAP[1] + -ET] —**'lappeted** *adj.*

lappet moth *n.* a large purple-brown hairy eggar moth, *Gastropacha quercifolia,* whose grey furry caterpillars have lappets on each flank.

Lapsang Souchong ('læpsæŋ suː'ʃɒŋ) *n.* a large-leafed variety of China tea with a slightly smoky flavour.

lapse (læps) *n.* **1.** a drop in standard of an isolated or temporary nature: *a lapse of justice.* **2.** a break in occurrence, usage, etc.: *a lapse of five weeks between letters.* **3.** a gradual decline or a drop to a lower degree, condition, or state: *a lapse from high office.* **4.** a moral fall. **5.** *Law.* the termination of some right, interest, or privilege, as by neglecting to exercise it or through failure of some contingency. **6.** *Insurance.* the termination of coverage following a failure to pay the premiums. *~vb. (intr.)* **7.** to drop in standard or fail to maintain a norm. **8.** to decline gradually or fall in status, condition, etc. **9.** to be discontinued, esp. through negligence or other failure. **10.** (usually foll. by *into*) to drift or slide (into a condition): *to lapse into sleep.* **11.** (often foll. by *from*) to turn away (from beliefs or norms). **12.** *Law.* (of a devise or bequest) to become void, as on the beneficiary's predeceasing the testator. **13.** (of time) to slip away. [C15: from Latin *lāpsus* error, from *lābī* to glide] —**'lapsable** *or* **'lapsible** *adj.* —**lapsed** *adj.* —**'lapser** *n.*

lapse rate *n.* the rate of change of any meteorological factor with altitude, esp. atmospheric temperature, which usually decreases at a rate of 0.6°C per 100 metres (**environmental lapse rate**). Unsaturated air loses about 1°C per 100 m (**dry adiabatic lapse rate**), whereas saturated air loses an average 0.5°C per 100 m (**saturated adiabatic lapse rate**).

lapstrake ('læpˌstreɪk) *or* **lapstreak** ('læpˌstriːk) *Nautical.* *~adj.* **1.** another term for **clinker-built.** *~n.* **2.** a clinker-built boat. [C18: from LAP[2] + STRAKE]

lapsus ('læpsəs) *n., pl.* **-sus.** *Formal.* a lapse or error. [from Latin: LAPSE]

lapsus linguae ('lɪŋgwiː) *n.* a slip of the tongue. [Latin]

laptop ('læpˌtɒp) *adj.* (of a computer) small and light enough to be held on the user's lap.

lap up *vb. (tr., adv.)* **1.** to eat or drink. **2.** to relish or delight in: *he laps up old horror films.* **3.** to believe or accept eagerly and uncritically: *he laps up tall stories.*

lapwing ('læpˌwɪŋ) *n.* any of several plovers of the genus *Vanellus,* esp. *V. vanellus,* typically having a crested head, wattles, and spurs. Also called: **green plover, pewit, peewit.** [C17: altered form of Old English *hlēapewince,* plover, from *hlēapan* to LEAP + *wincian* to jerk, WINK[1]]

lar (lɑː) *n.* the singular of **lares.** See **lares and penates.** [Latin]

larboard ('lɑːbəd) *n., adj. Nautical.* a former word for **port**[2]. [C14 *laddeborde* (changed to *larboard* by association with *starboard*), from *laden* to load + *borde* BOARD]

larceny ('lɑːsɪnɪ) *n., pl.* **-nies.** *Law.* (formerly) a technical word for **theft.** [C15: from Old French *larcin,* from Latin *lātrōcinium* robbery, from *latrō* robber] —**'larcenist** *or* **'larcener** *n.* —**'larcenous** *adj.* —**'larcenously** *adv.*

larch (lɑːtʃ) *n.* **1.** any coniferous tree of the genus *Larix,* having deciduous needle-like leaves and egg-shaped cones: family *Pinaceae.* **2.** the wood of any of these trees. [C16: from German *Lärche,* ultimately from Latin *larix*]

lard (lɑːd) *n.* **1.** the rendered fat from a pig, esp. from the abdomen, used in cooking. **2.** *Informal.* excess fat on a person's body. *~vb. (tr.)* **3.** to prepare (lean meat, poultry, etc.) by inserting small strips of bacon or fat before cooking. **4.** to cover or smear (foods) with lard. **5.** to add extra material to (speech or writing); embellish. [C15: via Old French from Latin *lāridum* bacon fat] —**'lardˌlike** *adj.* —**'lardy** *adj.*

larder ('lɑːdə) *n.* a room or cupboard, used as a store for food. [C14: from Old French *lardier,* from LARD]

larder beetle *n.* See **dermestid.**

lardon ('lɑːdᵊn) *or* **lardoon** (lɑː'duːn) *n.* a strip of fat used in larding meat. [C15: from Old French, from LARD]

lard pig *n.* a large type of pig used principally for lard.

lardy cake ('lɑːdɪ) *n. Brit.* a rich sweet cake made of bread dough, lard, sugar, and dried fruit.

lares and penates ('lɛəriːz, 'lɑː-) *pl. n.* **1.** *Roman myth.* **a.** household gods. **b.** statues of these gods kept in the home. **2.** the valued possessions of a household.

large (lɑːdʒ) *adj.* **1.** having a relatively great size, quantity, extent, etc.; big. **2.** of wide or broad scope, capacity, or range; comprehensive: *a large effect.* **3.** having or showing great breadth of understanding: *a large heart.* **4.** *Nautical.* (of the wind) blowing from a favourable direction. **5.** *Rare.* overblown; pretentious. **6.** generous. **7.** *Obsolete.* (of manners and speech) gross; rude. *~n.* **8. at large. a.** (esp. of a dangerous criminal or wild animal) free; not confined. **b.** roaming freely, as in a foreign country. **c.** as a whole; in general. **d.** in full detail; exhaustively. **e. ambassador-at-large.** See **ambassador** (sense 4). **9. in (the) large.** as a totality or on a broad scale. *~adv.* **10.** *Nautical.* with the wind blowing from a favourable direction. **11. by and large. a.** (*sentence modifier*) generally; as a rule: *by and large, the man is the breadwinner.* **b.** *Nautical.* towards and away from the wind. **12. loom large.** to be very prominent or important. [C12 (originally: generous): via Old French from Latin *largus* ample, abundant] —**'largeness** *n.*

Large Black *n.* a heavy black breed of pig with long lop ears: used for crossbreeding.

large calorie *n.* another name for **Calorie.**

large-handed *adj.* generous; profuse.

large-hearted *adj.* kind; sympathetic. Also: **large-souled.**

large intestine *n.* the part of the alimentary canal consisting of the caecum, colon, and rectum. It extracts moisture from food residues, which are later excreted as faeces. Compare **small intestine.**

largely ('lɑːdʒlɪ) *adv.* **1.** principally; to a great extent. **2.** on a large scale or in a large manner.

large-minded *adj.* generous or liberal in attitudes. —ˌ**large-'mindedly** *adv.* —ˌ**large-'mindedness** *n.*

largemouth bass ('lɑːdʒˌmaʊθ 'bæs) *n.* a common North American freshwater black bass, *Micropterus salmoides:* a popular game fish.

largen ('lɑːdʒən) *vb. (tr.)* another word for **enlarge.**

large-scale *adj.* **1.** wide-ranging or extensive. **2.** (of maps and models) constructed or drawn to a big scale.

large-scale integration *n. Computer technol.* the process of integrating several thousand circuits on a single silicon chip. Abbrev.: **LSI.**

largess *or* **largesse** (lɑː'dʒɛs) *n.* **1.** the generous bestowal of gifts, favours, or money. **2.** the things so bestowed. **3.** generosity of spirit or attitude. [C13: from Old French, from LARGE]

large white *n.* **1.** Also called: **cabbage white.** a large white butterfly, *Pieris brassicae,* with scanty black markings, the larvae of which feed on brassica leaves. **2.** (*often caps.*) a white large-bodied breed of pig commonly kept for pork, bacon, and for fattening.

larghetto (lɑː'gɛtəʊ) *Music.* *~adj., adv.* **1.** to be performed moderately slowly. *~n., pl.* **-tos. 2.** a piece or passage to be performed in this way. [Italian: diminutive of LARGO]

largish ('lɑːdʒɪʃ) *adj.* fairly large.

largo ('lɑːgəʊ) *Music.* *~adj., adv.* **1.** to be performed slowly and broadly. *~n., pl.* **-gos. 2.** a piece or passage to be performed in this way. [C17: from Italian, from Latin *largus* LARGE]

lariat ('lærɪət) *n. U.S. and Canadian.* **1.** another word for **lasso. 2.** a rope for tethering animals. [C19: from Spanish *la reata* the LASSO]

larine ('læraɪn, -rɪn) *adj.* **1.** of, relating to, or resembling a gull. **2.** of, relating to, or belonging to the suborder *Lari,* which contains the gulls, terns, skuas, and skimmers. [C20: via New Latin from *Larus* genus name, from Greek *laros* a kind of gull]

lark[1] (lɑːk) *n.* **1.** any brown songbird of the predominantly Old World family *Alaudidae,* esp. the skylark: noted for their singing. **2.** short for **titlark** or **meadowlark. 3.** (*often cap.*) any of various slender but powerful fancy pigeons, such as the **Coburg Lark. 4. up with the lark.** up early in the morning. [Old English *lāwerce, lǣwerce,* of Germanic origin; related to German *Lerche,* Icelandic *lǣvirki*]

lark[2] (lɑːk) *Informal.* *~n.* **1.** a carefree adventure or frolic. **2.** a harmless piece of mischief. **3. what a lark!** how amusing! *~vb. (intr.)* **4.** (often foll. by *about*) to have a good time by frolicking. **5.** to play a prank. [C19: originally slang, perhaps related to LAIK] —**'larker** *n.* —**'larkish** *adj.* —**'larkishness** *n.* —**'larky** *adj.*

larkspur ('lɑːkˌspɜː) *n.* any of various ranunculaceous plants of the genus *Delphinium,* with spikes of blue, pink, or white irregular spurred flowers. [C16: LARK[1] + SPUR]

Larmor precession ('lɑːmɔː) *n.* precession of the orbit of an electron in an atom that is subjected to a magnetic field. [C20: named after Sir Joseph *Larmor* (1857–1942), British physicist]

larn (lɑːn) *vb. Not standard.* **1.** *Facetious.* to learn. **2.** (*tr.*) to teach (someone) a lesson: *that'll larn you!* [C18: from a dialect form of LEARN]

larnax ('lɑːnæks) *n. Archaeol.* a coffin made of terracotta. [from Greek; perhaps related to Late Greek *narnax* chest]

larrigan ('lærɪgən) *n.* a knee-high oiled leather moccasin boot worn by trappers, etc. [C19: of unknown origin]

larrikin ('lærɪkɪn) *n. Austral. and N.Z. slang.* **a.** a hooligan. **b.** (*as modifier*): *a larrikin bloke.* [C19: from English dialect: a mischievous youth]

larrup ('lærəp) *vb. (tr.) Dialect.* to beat or flog. [C19: of unknown origin] —**'larruper** *n.*

Larry ('lærɪ) *n. Brit., Austral., and N.Z. informal.* **(as) happy as Larry.** extremely happy. [of uncertain origin]

larum ('lærəm) *n.* an archaic word for **alarm.**

larva ('lɑːvə) *n., pl.* **-vae** (-viː). an immature free-living form of many animals that develops into a different adult form by metamorphosis. [C18: (C17 in the original Latin sense: ghost): New Latin] —**'larval** *adj.*

larvicide ('lɑːvɪˌsaɪd) *n.* a chemical used for killing larvae. —ˌ**lar'vi'cidal** *adj.*

laryngeal (ˌlærɪnˈdʒiːəl, ləˈrɪndʒɪəl) *or* **laryngal** (ləˈrɪŋgᵊl) *adj.* **1.** of or relating to the larynx. **2.** *Phonetics.* articulated at the larynx; glottal. [C18: from New Latin *laryngeus* of the LARYNX] —**larynˈgeally** *adv.*

laryngitis (ˌlærɪnˈdʒaɪtɪs) *n.* inflammation of the larynx. —**laryngitic** (ˌlærɪnˈdʒɪtɪk) *adj.*

laryngo- *or before a vowel* **laryng-** *combining form.* indicating the larynx: *laryngoscope.*

laryngology (ˌlærɪŋˈgɒlədʒɪ) *n.* the branch of medicine concerned with the larynx and its diseases. —**laryngological** (ləˌrɪŋgəˈlɒdʒɪkᵊl) *or* **laˌryngoˈlogic** *adj.* —**laˌryngoˈlogically** *adv.* —**ˌlarynˈgologist** *n.*

laryngoscope (ləˈrɪŋgəˌskəʊp) *n.* a medical instrument for examining the larynx. —**laryngoscopic** (ləˌrɪŋgəˈskɒpɪk) *adj.* —**laˌryngoˈscopically** *adv.* —**laryngoscopist** (ˌlærɪŋˈgɒskəpɪst) *n.* —**ˌlarynˈgoscopy** *n.*

laryngotomy (ˌlærɪŋˈgɒtəmɪ) *n., pl.* **-mies.** surgical incision into the larynx.

larynx (ˈlærɪŋks) *n., pl.* **larynges** (ləˈrɪndʒiːz) *or* **larynxes.** a cartilaginous and muscular hollow organ forming part of the air passage to the lungs: in higher vertebrates it contains the vocal cords. [C16: from New Latin *larynx,* from Greek *larunx*]

lasagne *or* **lasagna** (ləˈzænjə, -ˈsæn-) *n.* **1.** a form of pasta consisting of wide flat sheets. **2.** any of several dishes made from layers of lasagne and meat, cheese, etc. [from Italian *lasagna,* from Latin *lasanum* cooking pot]

lascar (ˈlæskə) *n.* a sailor from the East Indies. [C17: from Urdu *lashkar* soldier, from Persian: the army]

lascivious (ləˈsɪvɪəs) *adj.* **1.** lustful; lecherous. **2.** exciting sexual desire. [C15: from Late Latin *lascīviōsus,* from Latin *lascīvia* wantonness, from *lascīvus*] —**lasˈciviously** *adv.* —**lasˈciviousness** *n.*

lase (leɪz) *vb.* (*intr.*) (of a substance, such as carbon dioxide or ruby) to be capable of acting as a laser.

laser (ˈleɪzə) *n.* **1.** Also called: **optical maser.** a device for converting light of mixed frequencies into an intense narrow monochromatic beam of coherent light. It consists typically of a ruby rod or gas-filled tube illuminated by a light flash to excite its atoms. Light emitted by these atoms is reflected backwards and forwards along the tube and stimulates further emission. **2.** any similar device for producing a beam of any electromagnetic radiation, such as infrared or microwave radiation. See also **maser.** [C20: from *l*ight *a*mplification by *s*timulated *e*mission of *r*adiation]

laser card *n. Computer technol.* another name for **smart card.**

laser printer *n.* a quiet high-quality computer printer that uses a laser beam shining on a photoconductive drum to produce characters, which are then transferred to paper.

laser ring gyro *n. Aeronautics.* a system of aerial navigation in which rotation is sensed by the measuring of the frequency shift of laser light in a closed circuit in a horizontal plane.

lash[1] (læʃ) *n.* **1.** a sharp cutting blow from a whip or other flexible object: *twenty lashes was his punishment.* **2.** the flexible end or ends of a whip. **3.** a cutting or hurtful blow to the feelings, as one caused by ridicule or scolding. **4.** a forceful beating or impact, as of wind, rain, or waves against something. **5. have a lash (at).** *Austral. and N.Z. informal.* to make an attempt at or take part in (something). **6.** See **eyelash.** ~*vb.* (*tr.*) **7.** to hit (a person or thing) sharply with a whip, rope, etc., esp. as a punishment. **8.** (of rain, waves, etc.) to beat forcefully against. **9.** to attack with words, ridicule, etc. **10.** to flick or wave sharply to and fro: *the restless panther lashed his tail.* **11.** to urge or drive with or as if with a whip: *to lash the audience into a violent mood.* ~See also **lash out.** [C14: perhaps imitative] —**ˈlasher** *n.* —**ˈlashingly** *adv.*

lash[2] (læʃ) *vb.* (*tr.*) to bind or secure with rope, string, etc. [C15: from Old French *lachier,* ultimately from Latin *laqueāre* to ensnare, from *laqueus* noose] —**ˈlasher** *n.*

-lashed *adj.* having eyelashes as specified: *long-lashed.*

lashing[1] (ˈlæʃɪŋ) *n.* **1.** a whipping; flogging. **2.** a scolding. **3.** (*pl.;* usually foll. by *of*) *Brit. informal.* large amounts; lots.

lashing[2] (ˈlæʃɪŋ) *n.* rope, cord, etc., used for binding or securing.

lash out *vb.* (*intr., adv.*) **1.** to burst into or resort to verbal or physical attack. **2.** *Brit. informal.* to be extravagant, as in spending.

lash-up (ˈlæʃˌʌp) *n.* **a.** Also called: **hook-up.** a temporary connection of equipment for experimental or emergency use. **b.** (*as modifier*): *lash-up equipment.*

lasket (ˈlæskɪt) *n.* a loop at the foot of a sail onto which an extra sail may be fastened. [C18: perhaps an alteration of French *lacet* LATCHET, through the influence of GASKET]

lass (læs) *n.* a girl or young woman. [C13: origin uncertain]

Lassa fever (ˈlæsə) *n.* a serious viral disease of Central West Africa, characterized by high fever and muscular pains. [named after *Lassa,* the village in Nigeria where it was first identified]

lassie (ˈlæsɪ) *n. Informal.* a little lass; girl.

lassitude (ˈlæsɪˌtjuːd) *n.* physical or mental weariness. [C16: from Latin *lassitūdō,* from *lassus* tired]

lasso (læˈsuː, ˈlæsəʊ) *n., pl.* **-sos** *or* **-soes.** **1.** a long rope or thong with a running noose at one end, used (esp. in America) for roping horses, cattle, etc.; lariat. ~*vb.* **-sos** *or* **-soes; -soing, -soed.** **2.** (*tr.*) to catch with or as if with a lasso. [C19: from Spanish *lazo,* ultimately from Latin *laqueus* noose] —**lasˈsoer** *n.*

last[1] (lɑːst) *adj.* (*often prenominal*) **1.** being, happening, or coming at the end or after all others: *the last horse in the race.* **2.** being or occurring just before the present; most recent: *last Thursday.* **3. last but not least.** coming last in order but nevertheless important. **4. last but one.** next to last. **5.** only remaining: *one's last cigarette.* **6.** most extreme; utmost. **7.** least suitable, appropriate, or likely: *he was the last person I would have chosen.* **8.** (esp. relating to the end of a person's life or of the world) **a.** final or ultimate: *last rites.* **b.** (*cap.*): *the Last Judgment.* **9.** (*postpositive*) *Liverpool dialect.* inferior, unpleasant, or contemptible: *this ale is last.* ~*adv.* **10.** after all others; at or in the end: *he came last.* **11. a.** most recently: *he was last seen in the mountains.* **b.** (*in combination*): *last-mentioned.* **12.** (*sentence modifier*) as the last or latest item. ~*n.* **13. the last. a.** a person or thing that is last. **b.** the final moment; end. **14.** one's last moments before death. **15.** the last thing a person can do (esp. in the phrase **breathe one's last**). **16.** the final appearance, mention, or occurrence: *we've seen the last of him.* **17. at last.** in the end; finally. **18. at long last.** finally, after difficulty, delay, or irritation. ~See also **last out.** [variant of Old English *latest, lætest,* superlative of LATE]

last[2] (lɑːst) *vb.* **1.** (when *intr.,* often foll. by *for*) to remain in being (for a length of time); continue: *his hatred lasted for several years.* **2.** to be sufficient for the needs of (a person) for (a length of time): *it will last us until Friday.* **3.** (when *intr.,* often foll. by *for*) to remain fresh, uninjured, or unaltered (for a certain time or duration): *he lasted for three hours underground.* [Old English *lǣstan;* related to Gothic *laistjan* to follow] —**ˈlaster** *n.*

last[3] (lɑːst) *n.* **1.** the wooden or metal form on which a shoe or boot is fashioned or repaired. ~*vb.* **2.** (*tr.*) to fit (a shoe or boot) on a last. [Old English *lǣste,* from *lāst* footprint; related to Old Norse *leistr* foot, Gothic *laists*] —**ˈlaster** *n.*

last[4] (lɑːst) *n.* a unit of weight or capacity having various values in different places and for different commodities. Commonly used values are 2 tons, 2000 pounds, 80 bushels, or 640 gallons. [Old English *hlæst* load; related to *hladan* to LADE[1]]

last-cyclic *adj. Transformational grammar.* denoting rules that apply only to main clauses. Compare **cyclic** (sense 6), **postcyclic.**

last-ditch *n.* (*modifier*) made or done as a last desperate attempt or effort in the face of opposition.

last-gasp *n.* (*modifier*) done in desperation at the last minute: *a last-gasp attempt to save the talks.*

lasting (ˈlɑːstɪŋ) *adj.* **1.** permanent or enduring. ~*n.* **2.** a strong durable closely woven fabric used for shoe uppers, etc. —**ˈlastingly** *adv.* —**ˈlastingness** *n.*

Last Judgment *n.* **the.** the occasion, after the resurrection of the dead at the end of the world, when, according to biblical tradition, God will decree the final destinies of all men according to the good and evil in their earthly lives. Also called: **the Last Day, Doomsday, Judgment Day.**

lastly (ˈlɑːstlɪ) *adv.* **1.** at the end or at the last point. ~*sentence connector.* **2.** in the end; finally: *lastly, he put on his jacket.*

last-minute *n.* (*modifier*) given or done at the latest possible time: *last-minute preparations.*

last name *n.* another term for **surname** (sense 1).

last out *vb.* (*intr., adv.*) **1.** to be sufficient for one's needs: *how long will our supplies last out?* **2.** to endure or survive: *some old people don't last out the winter.*

last post *n.* (in the British military services) **1.** a bugle call that orders men to retire for sleep. **2.** a similar call sounded at military funerals.

last quarter *n.* one of the four principal phases of the moon, occurring between full moon and new moon, when half the lighted surface is visible. Compare **first quarter.**

last rites *pl. n. Christianity.* religious rites prescribed for those close to death.

last straw *n.* **the.** the final irritation or problem that stretches one's endurance or patience beyond the limit. [from the proverb, "It is the last straw that breaks the camel's back"]

last thing *adv.* as the final action, esp. before retiring to bed at night.

lat (læt) *n., pl.* **lats, latu** (ˈlætuː), *or* **lati** (ˈlætiː). the monetary unit of Latvia before 1940.

lat. *abbrev. for* latitude.

Lat. *abbrev. for* Latin.

latah (ˈlɑːtə) *n.* a psychological condition, observed esp. in Malaysian cultures, in which an individual, after experiencing a shock, becomes anxious and suggestible, often imitating the actions of another person. [C19: from Malay]

latch (lætʃ) *n.* **1.** a fastening for a gate or door that consists of a bar that may be slid or lowered into a groove, hole, etc. **2.** a spring-loaded door lock that can be opened by a key from outside. **3.** Also called: **latch circuit.** *Electronics.* a logic circuit that transfers the input states to the output states when signalled, the output thereafter remaining insensitive to changes in input status until signalled again. ~*vb.* **4.** to fasten, fit, or be fitted with or as if with a latch. [Old English *læccan* to seize, of Germanic origin; related to Greek *lazesthai*]

latchet (ˈlætʃɪt) *n. Archaic.* a shoe fastening, such as a thong or lace. [C14: from Old French *lachet,* from *las* LACE]

latchkey ('lætʃ,ki:) *n.* **1.** a key for an outside door or gate, esp. one that lifts a latch. **2. a.** a supposed freedom from restrictions. **b.** (*as modifier*): *a latchkey existence.*
latchkey child *n.* a child who has to let himself in at home on returning from school, as his parents are out at work.
latch on *vb.* (*intr., adv.*; often foll. by *to*) *Informal.* **1.** to attach oneself (to): *to latch on to a new acquaintance.* **2.** to understand: *he suddenly latched on to what they were up to.* **3.** *U.S. and Canadian.* to obtain; get.
latchstring ('lætʃ,strɪŋ) *n.* a length of string fastened to a latch and passed through a hole in the door so that it can be opened from the other side.
late (leɪt) *adj.* **1.** occurring or arriving after the correct or expected time: *the train was late.* **2.** (*prenominal*) occurring, scheduled for, or being at a relatively advanced time: *a late marriage.* **3.** (*prenominal*) towards or near the end: *the late evening.* **4.** at an advanced time in the evening or at night: *it was late.* **5.** (*prenominal*) occurring or being just previous to the present time: *his late remarks on industry.* **6.** (*prenominal*) having died, esp. recently: *my late grandfather.* **7.** (*prenominal*) just preceding the present or existing person or thing; former: *the late manager of this firm.* **8. of late.** recently; lately. ~*adv.* **9.** after the correct or expected time: *he arrived late.* **10.** at a relatively advanced age: *she married late.* **11.** recently; lately: *as late as yesterday he was selling books.* **12. late hours.** rising and going to bed later than is usual. **13. late in the day. a.** at a late or advanced stage. **b.** too late. [Old English *læt*; related to Old Norse *latr*, Gothic *lats*] —**'lateness** *n.*
latecomer ('leɪt,kʌmə) *n.* a person or thing that comes late.
lated ('leɪtɪd) *adj.* an archaic word for **belated.**
lateen (lə'ti:n) *adj. Nautical.* denoting a rig with a triangular sail (**lateen sail**) bent to a yard hoisted to the head of a low mast, used esp. in the Mediterranean. [C18: from French *voile latine* Latin sail]
lateenrigged (lə'ti:n,rɪgd) *adj. Nautical.* rigged with a lateen sail.
Late Greek *n.* the Greek language from about the 3rd to the 8th centuries A.D. Compare **Medieval Greek, Koine.**
Late Latin *n.* the form of written Latin used from the 3rd to the 7th centuries A.D. See also **Biblical Latin, Medieval Latin.**
lately ('leɪtlɪ) *adv.* in recent times; of late.
latency period *n. Psychoanal.* a period according to Freud, from the age of about five to puberty, when sexual interest is diminished.
La Tène (læ 'tɛn) *adj.* of or relating to a Celtic culture in Europe from about the 5th to the 1st centuries B.C., characterized by a distinctive type of curvilinear decoration. See also **Hallstatt.** [C20: from *La Tène*, a part of Lake Neuchâtel, Switzerland, where remains of this culture were first discovered]
latent ('leɪtᵊnt) *adj.* **1.** potential but not obvious or explicit. **2.** (of buds, spores, etc.) dormant. **3.** *Pathol.* (esp. of an infectious disease) not yet revealed or manifest. **4.** (of a virus) inactive in the host cell, its nucleic acid being integrated into, and replicated with, the host cell's DNA. **5.** *Psychoanal.* relating to that part of a dream expressive of repressed desires: *latent content.* Compare **manifest** (sense 2). [C17: from Latin *latent-*, from *latens* present participle of *latēre* to lie hidden] —**'latency** *n.* —**'latently** *adv.*
latent heat *n.* (*no longer in technical usage*) the heat evolved or liberated when a substance changes phase without any change in its temperature.
latent image *n. Photog.* the invisible image produced by the action of light, etc., on silver halide crystals suspended in the emulsion of a photographic material. It becomes visible after development.
latent learning *n. Psychol.* learning mediated neither by reward nor by the expectation of reward.
latent period *n.* **1.** the incubation period of an infectious disease, before symptoms appear. **2.** another name for **latent time.**
latent time *n. Psychol.* the time from the onset of a stimulus to that of the response. Also called: **latency, reaction time.**
later ('leɪtə) *adj., adv.* **1.** the comparative of **late.** ~*adv.* **2.** afterwards; subsequently. **3. see you later.** an expression of farewell. **4. sooner or later.** eventually; inevitably.
lateral ('lætərəl) *adj.* **1.** of or relating to the side or sides: *a lateral blow.* **2.** *Phonetics.* (of a speech sound like *l*) pronounced with the tip of the tongue touching the centre of the alveolar ridge, leaving space on one or both sides for the passage of the airstream. ~*n.* **3.** a lateral object, part, passage, or movement. **4.** *Phonetics.* a lateral speech sound. [C17: from Latin *laterālis*, from *latus* side] —**'laterally** *adv.*
laterality (,lætə'rælɪtɪ) *n. Psychol.* the difference in the mental functions controlled by the left and right cerebral hemispheres of the brain.
lateral line system *n.* a system of sensory organs in fishes and aquatic amphibians consisting of a series of cells on the head and along the sides of the body that detect pressure changes and vibrations.
lateral thinking *n.* a way of solving problems by rejecting traditional methods and employing unorthodox and apparently illogical means.
laterigrade ('lætərɪ,greɪd) *adj. Zoology.* (of some crabs) having a gait characterized by sideways movement.
laterite ('lætə,raɪt) *n.* any of a group of deposits consisting of residual insoluble deposits of ferric and aluminium oxides: formed by weathering of rocks in tropical regions. [C19: from Latin *later* brick, tile] —**lateritic** (,lætə'rɪtɪk) *adj.*
lateroversion (,lætərəʊ'vɜ:ʃən) *n.* abnormal lateral displacement of a bodily organ or part, esp. of the uterus. [C20: from LATERAL + *-version*, from Latin *versiō* a turning]
latest ('leɪtɪst) *adj., adv.* **1.** the superlative of **late.** ~*adj.* **2.** most recent, modern, or new: *the latest fashions.* ~*n.* **3. at the latest.** no later than the time specified. **4. the latest.** *Informal.* the most recent fashion or development.
latex ('leɪtɛks) *n., pl.* **latexes** *or* **latices** ('lætɪ,si:z). **1.** a whitish milky fluid containing protein, starch, alkaloids, etc., that is produced by many plants. Latex from the rubber tree is used in the manufacture of rubber. **2.** a suspension of synthetic rubber or plastic in water, used in the manufacture of synthetic rubber products, etc. [C19: New Latin, from Latin: liquid, fluid]
lath (lɑ:θ) *n., pl.* **laths** (lɑ:ðz, lɑ:θs). **1.** one of several thin narrow strips of wood used to provide a supporting framework for plaster, tiles, etc. **2.** expanded sheet metal, wire mesh, etc., used to provide backing for plaster or rendering. **3.** any thin strip of wood. ~*vb.* **4.** (*tr.*) to attach laths to (a ceiling, roof, floor, etc.). [Old English *lætt*; related to Dutch *lat*, Old High German *latta*] —**'lath,like** *adj.*
lathe[1] (leɪð) *n.* **1.** a machine for shaping, boring, facing, or cutting a screw thread in metal, wood, etc., in which the workpiece is turned about a horizontal axis against a fixed tool. ~*vb.* **2.** (*tr.*) to shape, bore, or cut a screw thread in or on (a workpiece) on a lathe. [perhaps C15 *lath* a support, of Scandinavian origin; compare Old Danish *lad* lathe, Old English *hlæd* heap]
lathe[2] (leɪð) *n. Brit. history.* any of the former administrative divisions of Kent. [Old English *læth* district]
lather ('lɑ:ðə, 'læ-) *n.* **1.** foam or froth formed by the action of soap or a detergent in water. **2.** foam formed by other liquid, such as the sweat of a horse. **3.** *Informal.* a state of agitation or excitement. ~*vb.* **4.** to coat or become coated with lather. **5.** (*intr.*) to form a lather. [Old English *lēathor* soap; related to Old Norse *lauthr* foam] —**'lathery** *adj.*
lathi ('lɑ:tɪ) *n.* a long heavy wooden stick used as a weapon in India, esp. by the police. [Hindi]
lathy ('lɑ:θɪ) *adj.* **lathier, lathiest.** resembling a lath, esp. in being tall and thin.
lathyrism ('læθərɪzəm) *n.* a neurological disease often resulting in weakness and paralysis of the legs: caused by eating the pealike seeds of the leguminous plant *Lathyrus sativus.*
latices ('lætɪ,si:z) *n.* a plural of **latex.**
laticifer (læ'tɪsɪfə) *n. Botany.* a cell or group of cells in a plant that contains latex. [C19: from New Latin *latic-* LATEX + -FER] —**laticiferous** (,lætɪ'sɪfərəs) *or* ,**lac'tiferous** *adj.*
latifundium (,lætɪ'fʌndɪəm) *n., pl.* **-dia** (-dɪə). a large agricultural estate, esp. one worked by slaves in ancient Rome. [C17: from Latin *lātus* broad + *fundus* farm, estate]
latimeria (,lætɪ'mɪərɪə) *n.* any coelacanth fish of the genus *Latimeria.* [C20: named after Marjorie Courtenay-*Latimer* (born 1902), South African museum curator]
Latin ('lætɪn) *n.* **1.** the language of ancient Rome and the Roman Empire and of the educated in medieval Europe, which achieved its classical form during the 1st century B.C. Having originally been the language of Latium, an ancient territory of W Asia, belonging to the Italic branch of the Indo-European family, it later formed the basis of the Romance group. See **Late Latin, Low Latin, Medieval Latin, New Latin, Old Latin.** See also **Romance. 2.** a member of any of those peoples whose languages are derived from Latin. **3.** an inhabitant of ancient Latium. ~*adj.* **4.** of or relating to the Latin language, the ancient Latins, or Latium. **5.** characteristic of or relating to those peoples in Europe and Latin America whose languages are derived from Latin. **6.** of or relating to the Roman Catholic Church. **7.** denoting or relating to the Roman alphabet. [Old English *latin* and *læden* Latin, language, from Latin *Latīnus* of Latium]
Latin alphabet *n.* another term for **Roman alphabet.**
Latin American *adj.* **1.** of or relating to those areas of America whose official languages are Spanish and Portuguese, derived from Latin: South America, Central America, Mexico, and certain islands in the Caribbean. ~*n.* **2.** a native or inhabitant of any of these regions.
Latinate ('lætɪ,neɪt) *adj.* (of writing, vocabulary, etc.) imitative of or derived from Latin.
Latin Church *n.* the Roman Catholic Church.
Latin cross *n.* a cross the lowest arm of which is longer than the other three.
Latinism ('lætɪ,nɪzəm) *n.* a word, idiom, or phrase borrowed from Latin.
Latinist ('lætɪnɪst) *n.* a person who studies or is proficient in Latin.
Latinity (lə'tɪnɪtɪ) *n.* **1.** facility in the use of Latin. **2.** Latin style, esp. in literature.
Latinize *or* **Latinise** ('lætɪ,naɪz) *vb.* (*tr.*) **1.** to translate into Latin or Latinisms. **2.** to transliterate into the Latin alphabet. **3.** to cause to acquire Latin style or customs. **4.** to bring Roman

Catholic influence to bear upon (the form of religious ceremonies, etc.). —ˌ**Latiniˈzation** *or* ˌ**Latiniˈsation** *n.* —ˈ**Latinˌizer** *or* ˈ**Latinˌiser** *n.*

Latino (læˈtiːnəʊ) *n., pl.,* **-nos.** *U.S.* an inhabitant of the U.S. who is of Latin American origin.

Latin square *n.* (in statistical analysis) one of a set of square arrays of *n* rows and columns, esp. as used in statistics and studied in combinatorial analysis, built up from *n* different symbols so that no symbol occurs more than once in any row or column.

latish (ˈleɪtɪʃ) *adj.* rather late.

latitude (ˈlætɪˌtjuːd) *n.* **1. a.** an angular distance in degrees north or south of the equator (latitude 0°), equal to the angle subtended at the centre of the globe by the meridian between the equator and the point in question. **b.** (*often pl.*) a region considered with regard to its distance from the equator. See **longitude** (sense 1). **2.** scope for freedom of action, thought, etc.; freedom from restriction: *his parents gave him a great deal of latitude.* **3.** *Photog.* the range of exposure over which a photographic emulsion gives an acceptable negative. **4.** *Astronomy.* See **celestial latitude.** [C14: from Latin *lātitūdō,* from *lātus* broad] —ˌ**latiˈtudinal** *adj.* —ˌ**latiˈtudinally** *adv.*

latitudinarian (ˌlætɪˌtjuːdɪˈnɛərɪən) *adj.* **1.** permitting or marked by freedom of attitude or behaviour, esp. in religious matters. **2.** (*sometimes cap.*) of or relating to a school of thought within the Church of England in the 17th century that minimized the importance of divine authority in matters of doctrine and stressed the importance of reason and personal judgment. ~*n.* **3.** a person with latitudinarian views. [C17: from Latin *lātitūdō* breadth, LATITUDE, influenced in form by TRINITARIAN] —ˌ**latiˌtudiˈnarianism** *n.*

latria (ləˈtraɪə) *n. R.C. Church, theol.* the adoration that may be offered to God alone. [C16: via Latin from Greek *latreia* worship]

latrine (ləˈtriːn) *n.* a lavatory, as in a barracks, camp, etc. [C17: from French, from Latin *lātrīna,* shortened form of *lavātrīna* bath, from *lavāre* to wash]

-latry *n. combining form.* indicating worship of or excessive veneration of: *idolatry; Mariolatry.* [from Greek *-latria,* from *latreia* worship] —**-latrous** *adj. combining form.*

latten (ˈlætᵊn) *n.* metal or alloy, esp. brass, made in thin sheets. [C14: from Old French *laton,* of unknown origin]

latter (ˈlætə) *adj.* (*prenominal*) **1. a.** denoting the second or second mentioned of two: distinguished from *former.* **b.** (*as n.; functioning as sing. or pl.*): *the latter is not important.* **2.** near or nearer the end: *the latter part of a film.* **3.** more advanced in time or sequence; later.

▷**Usage.** In careful usage, *latter* is used when only two items are in question: *he gave the money to Christopher and not to John, the latter being less in need of it. Last-named* is used to refer to the last-named of three or more items.

latter-day *adj.* present-day; modern.

Latter-day Saint *n.* a more formal name for a **Mormon.**

latterly (ˈlætəlɪ) *adv.* recently; lately.

lattermost (ˈlætəˌməʊst) *adj.* a less common word for **last**[1].

lattice (ˈlætɪs) *n.* **1.** Also called: ˈ**latticeˌwork.** an open framework of strips of wood, metal, etc., arranged to form an ornamental pattern. **2. a.** a gate, screen, etc., formed of such a framework. **b.** (*as modifier*): *a lattice window.* **3.** something, such as a decorative or heraldic device, resembling such a framework. **4.** an array of objects or points in a periodic pattern in two or three dimensions, esp. an array of atoms, ions, etc., in a crystal or an array of points indicating their positions in space. See also **Bravais lattice.** ~*vb.* **5.** to make, adorn, or supply with a lattice or lattices. [C14: from Old French *lattis,* from *latte* LATH] —ˈ**latticed** *adj.*

lattice energy *n. Chem.* the energy required to separate the ions of a crystal to an infinite distance, usually expressed in joules per mole.

latus rectum (ˈlɑːtəs ˈrɛktəm) *n., pl.* **latera recta** (ˈlætərə ˈrɛktə). *Geometry.* a chord that passes through the focus of a conic and is perpendicular to the major axis. [C18: New Latin: straight side]

Latvian (ˈlætvɪən) *adj.* **1.** of or relating to the republic of Latvia, in NE Europe, or to its people or their language. ~*n.* **2.** Also called: **Lettish.** the official language of Latvia, closely related to Lithuanian and belonging to the Baltic branch of the Indo-European family. **3.** a native or inhabitant of Latvia.

laud (lɔːd) *Literary.* ~*vb.* **1.** (*tr.*) to praise or glorify. ~*n.* **2.** praise or glorification. [C14: vb. from Latin *laudāre;* n. from *laudēs,* pl. of Latin *laus* praise] —ˈ**lauder** *n.*

laudable (ˈlɔːdəbᵊl) *adj.* deserving or worthy of praise; admirable; commendable. —ˈ**laudableness** *or* ˌ**laudaˈbility** *n.* —ˈ**laudably** *adv.*

laudanum (ˈlɔːdᵊnəm) *n.* **1.** a tincture of opium. **2.** (formerly) any medicine of which opium was the main ingredient. [C16: New Latin, name chosen by Paracelsus for a preparation probably containing opium, perhaps based on LABDANUM]

laudation (lɔːˈdeɪʃən) *n.* a formal word for **praise.**

laudatory (ˈlɔːdətərɪ, -trɪ) *or* **laudative** *adj.* expressing or containing praise; eulogistic.

Laudian (ˈlɔːdɪən) *adj. Church of England.* of or relating to the High-Church standards set up for the Church of England by William Laud, Archbishop of Canterbury (1633–45).

lauds (lɔːdz) *n.* (*functioning as sing. or pl.*) *Chiefly R.C. Church.* the traditional morning prayer of the Western Church, constituting with matins the first of the seven canonical hours. [C14: see LAUD]

laugh (lɑːf) *vb.* **1.** (*intr.*) to express or manifest emotion, esp. mirth or amusement, typically by expelling air from the lungs in short bursts to produce an inarticulate voiced noise, with the mouth open. **2.** (*intr.*) (esp. of certain mammals or birds) to make a noise resembling a laugh. **3.** (*tr.*) to utter or express with laughter: *he laughed his derision at the play.* **4.** (*tr.*) to bring or force (someone, esp. oneself) into a certain condition by laughter: *he laughed himself sick.* **5.** (*intr.;* foll. by *at*) to make fun (of); jeer (at). **6.** (intr.; foll. by *over*) to read or discuss something with laughter. **7. don't make me laugh.** *Informal.* I don't believe you for a moment. **8. laugh in a person's face.** to show open contempt or defiance towards a person. **9. laugh like a drain.** *Informal.* to laugh loudly and coarsely. **10. laugh up one's sleeve.** to laugh or have grounds for amusement, self-satisfaction, etc., secretly. **11. laugh on the other side of one's face.** to show sudden disappointment or shame after appearing cheerful or confident: *you'll laugh on the other side of your face when you see how bad your work is.* **12. be laughing.** *Informal.* to be in a favourable situation. ~*n.* **13.** the act or an instance of laughing. **14.** a manner of laughter. **15.** *Informal.* a person or thing that causes laughter: *that holiday was a laugh.* **16. the last laugh.** the final success in an argument, situation, etc., after previous defeat. ~See also **laugh away, laugh down, laugh off.** [Old English *lœhan, hliehhen;* related to Gothic *hlahjan,* Dutch *lachen*] —ˈ**laugher** *n.* —ˈ**laughing** *n., adj.* —ˈ**laughingly** *adv.*

laughable (ˈlɑːfəbᵊl) *adj.* **1.** producing scorn; ludicrous: *he offered me a laughable sum for the picture.* **2.** arousing laughter. —ˈ**laughableness** *n.* —ˈ**laughably** *adv.*

laugh away *vb.* (*tr., adv.*) **1.** to dismiss or dispel (something unpleasant) by laughter. **2.** to make (time) pass pleasantly by jesting.

laugh down *vb.* (*tr., adv.*) to silence by laughing contemptuously.

laughing gas *n.* another name for **nitrous oxide.**

laughing hyena *n.* another name for the **spotted hyena** (see **hyena**).

laughing jackass *n.* another name for the **kookaburra.**

laughing stock *n.* an object of humiliating ridicule: *his mistakes have made him a laughing stock.*

laugh off *vb.* (*tr., adv.*) to treat or dismiss lightly, esp. with stoicism: *he laughed off his injuries.*

laughter (ˈlɑːftə) *n.* **1.** the action of or noise produced by laughing. **2.** the experience or manifestation of mirth, amusement, scorn, or joy. [Old English *hleahtor;* related to Old Norse *hlātr*]

launce (lɑːns) *n.* another name for the **sand eel.**

launch[1] (lɔːntʃ) *vb.* **1.** to move (a vessel) into the water. **2.** to move (a newly built vessel) into the water for the first time. **3.** (*tr.*) **a.** to start off or set in motion: *to launch a scheme.* **b.** to put (a new product) on the market. **4.** (*tr.*) to propel with force. **5.** to involve (oneself) totally and enthusiastically: *to launch oneself into work.* **6.** (*tr.*) to set (a missile, spacecraft, etc.) into motion. **7.** (*tr.*) to catapult (an aircraft), as from the deck of an aircraft carrier. **8.** (*intr.;* foll. by *into*) to start talking or writing (about): *he launched into a story.* **9.** (*intr.;* usually foll. by *out*) to start (out) on a fresh course. **10.** (*intr.;* usually foll. by *out*) *Informal.* to spend a lot of money. ~*n.* **11.** an act or instance of launching. [C14: from Anglo-French *lancher,* from Late Latin *lanceāre* to use a lance, hence, to set in motion. See LANCE]

launch[2] (lɔːntʃ) *n.* **1.** a motor driven boat used chiefly as a transport boat. **2.** the largest of the boats of a man-of-war. [C17: via Spanish *lancha* and Portuguese from Malay *lancharan* boat, from *lanchar* speed]

launch complex *n.* an installation for the construction and launching of spacecraft, artificial satellites, or rockets.

launcher (ˈlɔːntʃə) *n.* any installation, vehicle, or other device for launching rockets, missiles, or other projectiles.

launching pad *or* **launch pad** *n.* a platform, esp. in a launch complex, from which a spacecraft, rocket, etc., is launched.

launching shoe *or* **launch shoe** *n.* an attachment to an aircraft from which a missile is launched.

launch vehicle *or* **launching vehicle** *n.* **1.** a rocket, without its payload, used to launch a spacecraft. **2.** another name for **booster** (sense 2).

launch window *n.* the limited period during which a spacecraft can be launched on a particular mission.

launder (ˈlɔːndə) *vb.* **1.** to wash, sometimes starch, and often also iron (clothes, linen, etc.). **2.** (*intr.*) to be capable of being laundered without shrinking, fading, etc. **3.** (*tr.*) to process (something acquired illegally) to make it appear respectable, esp. to process illegally acquired funds through a legitimate business or to send them to a foreign bank for subsequent transfer to a home bank. ~*n.* **4.** a water trough, esp. one used for washing ore in mining. [C14 (n., meaning: a person who washes linen): changed from *lavender* washerwoman, from Old French *lavandiere,* ultimately from Latin *lavāre* to wash] —ˈ**launderer** *n.*

Launderette (ˌlɔːndəˈrɛt, lɔːnˈdrɛt) *n. Brit. and N.Z. trademark.* a commercial establishment where clothes can be washed and dried, using coin-operated machines. Also called (U.S., Canadian, and N.Z.): **Laundromat.**

laundress ('lɔːndrɪs) *n.* a woman who launders clothes, sheets, etc., for a living.

laundrette (lɔːn'dret) *n.* a variant of **Launderette.**

Laundromat ('lɔːndrəˌmæt) *n. Trademark.* a U.S., Canadian, and N.Z. name for **Launderette.**

laundry ('lɔːndrɪ) *n., pl.* **-dries.** **1.** a place where clothes and linen are washed and ironed. **2.** the clothes or linen washed and ironed. **3.** the act of laundering. [C16: changed from C14 *lavendry;* see LAUNDER]

laundryman ('lɔːndrɪmən) *or (fem.)* **laundrywoman** *n., pl.* **-men** *or* **-women.** **1.** a person who collects or delivers laundry. **2.** a person who works in a laundry.

lauraceous (lɔː'reɪʃəs) *adj.* of, relating to, or belonging to the *Lauraceae,* a family of aromatic trees and shrubs having leathery leaves: includes the laurels and avocado.

laureate ('lɔːrɪɪt) *adj. (usually immediately postpositive)* **1.** *Literary.* crowned with laurel leaves as a sign of honour. **2.** *Archaic.* made of laurel. ~*n.* **3.** short for **poet laureate.** **4.** a person honoured with an award for art or science: *a Nobel laureate.* **5.** *Rare.* a person honoured with the laurel crown or wreath. [C14: from Latin *laureātus,* from *laurea* LAUREL] —**'laureateˌship** *n.* —**laureation** (ˌlɔːrɪ'eɪʃən) *n.*

laurel ('lɒrəl) *n.* **1.** Also called: **bay, bay laurel, sweet bay, true laurel.** a small Mediterranean lauraceous evergreen tree, *Laurus nobilis,* with glossy aromatic leaves, used for flavouring in cooking, and small blackish berries. **2.** a similar and related tree, *Laurus canariensis,* of the Canary Islands and Azores. **3.** short for **cherry laurel** or **mountain laurel.** **4. spurge laurel.** a European thymelaeaceous evergreen shrub, *Daphne laureola,* with glossy leaves and small green flowers. **5. spotted** or **Japan laurel.** an evergreen cornaceous shrub, *Aucuba japonica,* of S and SE Asia, the female of which has yellow-spotted leaves. **6.** *(pl.)* a wreath of true laurel, worn on the head as an emblem of victory or honour in classical times. **7.** *(pl.)* honour, distinction, or fame. **8. look to one's laurels.** to be on guard against one's rivals. **9. rest on one's laurels.** to be satisfied with distinction won by past achievements and cease to strive for further achievements. ~*vb.* **-rels, -relling, -relled** *or U.S.* **-rels, -reling, -reled.** **10.** *(tr.)* to crown with laurels. [C13 *lorer,* from old French *lorier* laurel tree, ultimately from Latin *laurus*]

Laurentian (lɔː'renʃən) *adj.* a variant spelling of **Lawrentian.**

lauric acid ('lɔːrɪk, 'lɒ-) *n.* another name for **dodecanoic acid.** [C19: from Latin *laurus* laurel; from its occurrence in the berries of the laurel (*Laurus nobilis*)]

laurustinus (ˌlɔːrə'staɪnəs) *n.* a Mediterranean caprifoliaceous shrub, *Viburnum tinus,* with glossy evergreen leaves and white or pink fragrant flowers. [C17: from New Latin, from Latin *laurus* laurel]

lauryl alcohol ('lɔːrɪl, 'lɒ-) *n.* a water-insoluble crystalline solid used in the manufacture of detergents; 1-dodecanol. Formula: $CH_3(CH_2)_{10}CH_2OH$. [C20: from LAUR(IC ACID) + -YL]

lav (læv) *n. Brit. informal.* short for **lavatory.**

lava ('lɑːvə) *n.* **1.** magma emanating from volcanoes and other vents. **2.** any extrusive igneous rock formed by the cooling and solidification of lava. [C18: from Italian (Neapolitan dialect), from Latin *lavāre* to wash]

lavabo (lə'veɪbəʊ) *n., pl.* **-boes** *or* **-bos.** *Chiefly R.C. Church.* **1. a.** the ritual washing of the celebrant's hands after the offertory at Mass. **b.** *(as modifier)*: *lavabo basin; lavabo towel.* **2.** another name for **washbasin.** **3.** a trough for washing in a convent or monastery. [C19: from Latin: I shall wash, the opening of Psalm 26:6]

lavage ('lævɪdʒ, læ'vɑːʒ) *n. Med.* the washing out of a hollow organ by flushing with water. [C19: via French, from Latin *lavāre* to wash]

lava-lava *n.* a draped skirtlike garment of printed cotton or calico worn by Polynesians. [Samoan]

lavatera (ˌlævə'tɪərə) *n.* any plant of the genus *Lavatera,* closely resembling mallow and grown for their purple, white, or rose-coloured flowers: family *Malvaceae.* [named after the two brothers *Lavater,* 18th-century Swiss doctors and naturalists]

lavation (læ'veɪʃən) *n. Formal or literary.* the act or process of washing. [C17: from Latin *lavātio,* from *lavāre* to wash] —**la'vational** *adj.*

lavatorial (ˌlævə'tɔːrɪəl) *adj.* **1.** of or in the style of decoration supposed to typify public lavatories: *white lavatorial tiling.* **2.** characterized by excessive mention of lavatories and the excretory functions; vulgar or scatological: *lavatorial humour.*

lavatory ('lævətərɪ, -trɪ) *n., pl.* **-ries.** **1.** Also called: **toilet, water closet, WC. a.** a sanitary installation for receiving and disposing of urine and faeces, consisting of a bowl fitted with a water-flushing device and connected to a drain. **b.** a room containing such an installation. **2.** the washing place in a convent or monastic establishment. [C14: from Late Latin *lavātōrium,* from Latin *lavāre* to wash]

lave (leɪv) *vb.* an archaic word for **wash.** [Old English *lafian,* perhaps from Latin *lavāre* to wash]

lavender ('lævəndə) *n.* **1.** any of various perennial shrubs or herbaceous plants of the genus *Lavandula,* esp. *L. vera,* cultivated for its mauve or blue flowers and as the source of a fragrant oil (**oil of lavender**): family *Labiatae* (labiates). See also **spike lavender.** Compare **sea lavender.** **2.** the dried parts of *L. vera,* used to perfume clothes. **3. a.** a pale or light bluish-purple to a very pale violet colour. **b.** *(as adj.)*: *lavender socks.* **4.** perfume scented with lavender. [C13: *lavendre,* via French from Medieval Latin *lavendula,* of obscure origin]

lavender bag *n.* a small fabric bag filled with dried lavender flowers and placed amongst clothes or linen to scent them.

lavender water *n.* a perfume made of essential oils of lavender and alcohol.

laver[1] ('leɪvə) *n.* **1.** *Old Testament.* a large basin of water used by the priests for ritual ablutions. **2.** the font or the water of baptism. [C14: from Old French *laveoir,* from Late Latin *lavātōrium* washing place]

laver[2] ('lɑːvə) *n.* any of several seaweeds of the genus *Porphyra* and related genera, with edible fronds: family *Rhodophyceae* (red algae). [C16: from Latin]

laver bread ('lɑːvə) *n.* laver seaweed fried as a breakfast food; popular in Wales.

laverock ('lævərək; *Scot. also* 'levərək, 'levrək) *n.* a Scot. and northern English dialect word for **skylark** (bird). [Old English *lǣwerce* LARK[1]]

lavish ('lævɪʃ) *adj.* **1.** prolific, abundant, or profuse. **2.** generous; unstinting; liberal. **3.** extravagant; prodigal; wasteful: *lavish expenditure.* ~*vb.* **4.** *(tr.)* to give, expend, or apply abundantly, generously, or in profusion. [C15: adj. use of *lavas* profusion, from Old French *lavasse* torrent, from Latin *lavāre* to wash] —**'lavisher** *n.* —**'lavishly** *adv.* —**'lavishment** *n.* —**'lavishness** *n.*

lavolta (lə'vɒltə) *n.* another word for **volta.** [C16: from Italian *la volta* the turn; see VOLTA]

law[1] (lɔː) *n.* **1.** a rule or set of rules, enforceable by the courts, regulating the government of a state, the relationship between the organs of government and the subjects of the state, and the relationship or conduct of subjects towards each other. **2. a.** a rule or body of rules made by the legislature. See **statute law.** **b.** a rule or body of rules made by a municipal or other authority. See **bylaw.** **3. a.** the condition and control enforced by such rules. **b.** *(in combination)*: *lawcourt.* **4.** a rule of conduct: *a law of etiquette.* **5.** one of a set of rules governing a particular field of activity: *the laws of tennis.* **6. the law. a.** the legal or judicial system. **b.** the profession or practice of law. **c.** *Informal.* the police or a policeman. **7.** a binding force or statement: *his word is law.* **8.** Also called: **law of nature.** a generalization based on a recurring fact or event. **9.** the science or knowledge of law; jurisprudence. **10.** the principles originating and formerly applied only in courts of common law. Compare **equity** (sense 3). **11.** a general principle, formula, or rule describing a phenomenon in mathematics, science, philosophy, etc.: *the laws of thermodynamics.* **12.** *Judaism.* *(cap.;* preceded by *the)* **a.** short for **Law of Moses.** **b.** the English term for **Torah.** ~See also **Oral Law, Written Law.** **13. a law unto itself (oneself, etc.)** a person or thing that is outside established laws. **14. go to law.** to resort to legal proceedings on some matter. **15. lay down the law.** to speak in an authoritative or dogmatic manner. **16. reading (of) the Law.** *Judaism.* that part of the morning service on Sabbaths, festivals, and Mondays and Thursdays during which a passage is read from the Torah scrolls. **17. take the law into one's own hands.** to ignore or bypass the law when redressing a grievance. ~Related adjs.: **judicial, juridical, legal.** [Old English *lagu,* from Scandinavian; compare Icelandic *lög* (pl.) things laid down, law]

law[2] (lɔː) *n. Scot.* a hill, esp. one rounded in shape. [Old English *hlǣw*]

law[3] (lɔː) *adj.* a Scot. word. for **low**[1].

law-abiding *adj.* adhering more or less strictly to the laws: *a law-abiding citizen.* —**'law-aˌbidingness** *n.*

law agent *n.* (in Scotland) a solicitor holding a certificate from the Law Society of Scotland and thereby entitled to appear for a client in any Sheriff Court.

law-and-order *n. (modifier)* favouring or advocating strong measures to suppress crime and violence: *a law-and-order candidate.*

lawbreaker ('lɔːˌbreɪkə) *n.* **1.** a person who breaks the law. **2.** *Informal.* something that does not conform with legal standards or requirements. —**'lawˌbreaking** *n., adj.*

law centre *n. Brit.* an independent service financed by a local authority, which provides free legal advice and information to the general public.

Law French *n.* a set of Anglo-Norman terms used in English laws and law books.

lawful ('lɔːfʊl) *adj.* allowed, recognized, or sanctioned by law; legal. —**'lawfully** *adv.* —**'lawfulness** *n.*

lawgiver ('lɔːˌgɪvə) *n.* **1.** the giver of a code of laws. **2.** Also called: **lawmaker.** a maker of laws. —**'lawˌgiving** *n., adj.*

lawin *or* **lawing** ('lɔːɪn) *n. Scot.* a bill or reckoning. [C16: from Old Norse *lag* market price]

lawks (lɔːks) *interj. Brit.* an expression of surprise or dismay. [C18: variant of *Lord!,* probably influenced in form by ALACK]

lawless ('lɔːlɪs) *adj.* **1.** without law. **2.** disobedient to the law. **3.** contrary to or heedless of the law. **4.** uncontrolled; unbridled: *lawless rage.* —**'lawlessly** *adv.* —**'lawlessness** *n.*

Law Lords *pl. n.* (in Britain) members of the House of Lords who sit as the highest court of appeal, although in theory the full House of Lords has this role.

lawman ('lɔːmən) *n., pl.* **-men.** *Chiefly U.S.* an officer of the law, such as a policeman or sheriff.
law merchant *n. Mercantile law.* the body of rules and principles determining the rights and obligations of the parties to commercial transactions; commercial law.
lawn[1] (lɔːn) *n.* **1.** a flat and usually level area of mown and cultivated grass. **2.** an archaic or dialect word for **glade.** [C16: changed form of C14 *launde,* from Old French *lande,* of Celtic origin; compare Breton *lann* heath; related to LAND] —'**lawny** *adj.*
lawn[2] (lɔːn) *n.* a fine linen or cotton fabric, used for clothing. [C15: probably from *Laon,* a town in France where linen was made] —'**lawny** *adj.*
lawn mower *n.* a hand-operated or power-operated machine with rotary blades for cutting grass on lawns.
lawn tennis *n.* **1.** tennis played on a grass court. **2.** the formal name for **tennis.**
law of averages *n.* (popularly) the expectation that a possible event is bound to occur regularly with a frequency approximating to its probability, as in the (actually false) example: *after five heads in a row the law of averages makes tails the better bet.* Compare **law of large numbers.**
law of large numbers *n.* the fundamental statistical result that the average of a sequence of *n* identically distributed independent random variables tends to their common mean as *n* tends to infinity, whence the frequency of the occurrence of an event in *n* independent repetitions of an experiment tends to its probability.
Law of Moses *n.* **1.** the first five books of the Old Testament; Pentateuch. **2.** *Judaism.* a law or body of laws derived from the Torah in accordance with interpretations (the Oral Law) traditionally believed to have been given to Moses on Mount Sinai together with the Written Law.
law of nations *n.* another term for **international law.**
law of nature *n.* **1.** an empirical truth of great generality, conceived of as a physical (but not a logical) necessity, and consequently licensing counterfactual conditionals. **2.** a system of morality conceived of as grounded in reason. See **natural law** (sense 2), **nomological** (sense 2). **3.** See **law** (sense 8).
law of supply and demand *n.* the theory that prices are determined by the interaction of supply and demand: an increase in supply will lower prices if not accompanied by increased demand, and an increase in demand will raise prices unless accompanied by increased supply.
law of the jungle *n.* a state of ruthless competition or self-interest.
law of thermodynamics *n.* **1.** any of three principles governing the relationships between different forms of energy. The **first law of thermodynamics** (law of conservation of energy) states that the change in the internal energy of a system is equal to the sum of the heat added to the system and the work done on it. The **second law of thermodynamics** states that heat cannot be transferred from a colder to a hotter body within a system without net changes occurring in other bodies within that system; in any irreversible process, entropy always increases. The **third law of thermodynamics** (Nernst heat theorem) states that it is impossible to reduce the temperature of a system to absolute zero in a finite number of steps. **2.** Sometimes called: the **zeroth law of thermodynamics.** the principle that if two bodies are each in thermal equilibrium with a third body then the first two bodies are in thermal equilibrium with each other.
lawrencium (lɒ'rɛnsɪəm, lɔː-) *n.* a transuranic element artificially produced from californium. Symbol: Lr; atomic no.: 103; half-life of most stable isotope, ^{256}Lr: 35 seconds; valency: 3. [C20: named after Ernest O. *Lawrence* (1901–58), U.S. physicist]
Lawrentian or **Laurentian** (lɔː'rɛnʃən) *adj.* relating to or characteristic of the style of either D. H. Lawrence (1885–1930), British novelist and poet, or of T. E. Lawrence (Lawrence of Arabia; 1888–1935), British soldier and writer.
law stationer *n.* **1.** a stationer selling articles used by lawyers. **2.** *Brit.* a person who makes handwritten copies of legal documents.
lawsuit ('lɔːˌsuːt, -ˌsjuːt) *n.* a proceeding in a court of law brought by one party against another, esp. a civil action.
law term *n.* **1.** an expression or word used in law. **2.** any of various periods of time appointed for the sitting of law courts.
lawyer ('lɔːjə, 'lɔɪə) *n.* **1.** a member of the legal profession, esp. a solicitor. See also **advocate, barrister, solicitor. 2.** a popular name for **burbot** (a fish). **3.** *Austral. and N.Z.* short for **bush lawyer** (sense 1). [C14: from LAW]
lawyer's wig *n.* another name for the **shaggy ink-cap:** see **ink-cap.**
lawyer vine *n. Austral.* any of various kinds of entangling and thorny vegetation, esp. in tropical areas. Also called: **lawyer cane, lawyer palm.**
lax (læks) *adj.* **1.** lacking firmness; not strict. **2.** lacking precision or definition. **3.** not taut. **4.** *Phonetics.* (of a speech sound) pronounced with little muscular effort and consequently having relatively imprecise accuracy of articulation and little temporal duration. In English the vowel *i* in *bit* is lax. **5.** (of flower clusters) having loosely arranged parts. [C14 (originally used with reference to the bowels): from Latin *laxus* loose] —'**laxly** *adv.* —'**laxity** *or* '**laxness** *n.*
laxation (læk'seɪʃən) *n.* **1.** the act of making lax or the state of being lax. **2.** *Physiol.* another word for **defecation.** [C14: from Latin *laxātio,* from *laxāre* to slacken]
laxative ('læksətɪv) *n.* **1.** an agent stimulating evacuation of faeces. ~*adj.* **2.** stimulating evacuation of faeces. [C14 (originally: relaxing): from Medieval Latin *laxātīvus,* from Latin *laxāre* to loosen]
lay[1] (leɪ) *vb.* **lays, laying, laid** (leɪd). (*mainly tr.*) **1.** to put in a low or horizontal position; cause to lie: *to lay a cover on a bed.* **2.** to place, put, or be in a particular state or position: *he laid his finger on his lips.* **3.** (*intr.*) *Dialect or not standard.* to be in a horizontal position; lie: *he often lays in bed all the morning.* **4.** (sometimes foll. by *down*) to establish as a basis: *to lay a foundation for discussion.* **5.** to place or dispose in the proper position: *to lay a carpet.* **6.** to arrange (a table) for eating a meal. **7.** to prepare (a fire) for lighting by arranging fuel in the grate. **8.** (*also intr.*) (of birds, esp. the domestic hen) to produce (eggs). **9.** to present or put forward: *he laid his case before the magistrate.* **10.** to impute or attribute: *all the blame was laid on him.* **11.** to arrange, devise, or prepare: *to lay a trap.* **12.** to place, set, or locate: *the scene is laid in London.* **13.** to apply on or as if on a surface: *to lay a coat of paint.* **14.** to impose as a penalty or burden: *to lay a fine.* **15.** to make (a bet) with (someone): *I lay you five to one on Prince.* **16.** to cause to settle: *to lay the dust.* **17.** to allay; suppress: *to lay a rumour.* **18.** to bring down forcefully: *to lay a whip on someone's back.* **19.** *Taboo slang.* to have sexual intercourse with. **20.** to press down or make smooth: *to lay the nap of cloth.* **21.** to cut (small trunks or branches of shrubs or trees) halfway through and bend them diagonally to form a hedge: *to lay a hedge.* **22.** to arrange and twist together (strands) in order to form (a rope, cable, etc.). **23.** *Military.* to apply settings of elevation and training to (a weapon) prior to firing. **24.** (foll. by *on*) *Hunting.* to put (hounds or other dogs) onto a scent. **25.** another word for **inlay. 26.** (*intr.;* often foll. by *to* or *out*) *Dialect or informal.* to plan, scheme, or devise. **27.** (*intr.*) *Nautical.* to move or go, esp. into a specified position or direction: *to lay close to the wind.* **28. lay aboard.** *Nautical.* (formerly) to move alongside a warship to board it. **29. lay a course. a.** *Nautical.* to sail on a planned course without tacking. **b.** to plan an action. **30. lay bare.** to reveal or explain: *he laid bare his plans.* **31. lay hands on.** See **hands** (sense 12). **32. lay hold of.** to seize or grasp. **33. lay oneself open.** to make oneself vulnerable (to criticism, attack, etc.). **34. lay open.** to reveal or disclose. **35. lay siege to.** to besiege (a city, etc.). ~*n.* **36.** the manner or position in which something lies or is placed. **37.** *Taboo slang.* **a.** an act of sexual intercourse. **b.** a sexual partner. **38.** a portion of the catch or the profits from a whaling or fishing expedition. **39.** the amount or direction of hoist in the strands of a rope. ~See also **layabout, lay aside, lay away, lay-by, lay down, lay in, lay into, lay off, lay on, lay out, lay over, lay to, lay up.** [Old English *lecgan;* related to Gothic *lagjan,* Old Norse *leggja*]
▷**Usage.** In careful English, the verb *lay* is used with an object and *lie* without one: *the soldier laid down his arms; the book was lying on the table.* In informal English, *lay* is frequently used for *lie: the book was laying on the table.* All careful writers and speakers observe the distinction even in informal contexts.
lay[2] (leɪ) *vb.* the past tense of **lie**[2].
lay[3] (leɪ) *adj.* **1.** of, involving, or belonging to people who are not clergymen. **2.** nonprofessional or nonspecialist; amateur. [C14: from Old French *lai,* from Late Latin *lāicus,* ultimately from Greek *laos* people]
lay[4] (leɪ) *n.* **1.** a ballad or short narrative poem, esp. one intended to be sung. **2.** a song or melody. [C13: from Old French *lai,* perhaps of Germanic origin]
layabout ('leɪəˌbaʊt) *n.* **1.** a lazy person; loafer. ~*vb.* **lay about. 2.** (*prep.,* usually *intr. or reflexive*) *Old-fashioned.* to hit out with violent and repeated blows in all directions.
lay analyst *n.* a person without medical qualifications who practises psychoanalysis.
lay aside *vb.* (*tr., adv.*) **1.** to abandon or reject. **2.** to store or reserve for future use.
lay away *vb.* (*tr., adv.*) **1.** to store or reserve for future use. **2.** to reserve (merchandise) for future delivery, while payments are being made.
layback ('leɪˌbæk) *n. Mountaineering.* a technique for climbing cracks by pulling on one side of the crack with the hands and pressing on the other with the feet.
lay brother *n.* a man who has taken the vows of a religious order but is not ordained and not bound to divine office.
lay-by *n.* **1.** *Brit.* a place for drivers to stop at the side of a main road. **2.** *Nautical.* an anchorage in a narrow waterway, away from the channel. **3.** a small railway siding where rolling stock may be stored or parked. **4.** *Austral. and N.Z.* a system of payment whereby a buyer pays a deposit on an article, which is reserved for him until he has paid the full price. ~*vb.* **lay by** (*adv.*) **5.** (*tr.*) to set aside or save for future needs. **6.** Also: **lay to.** to cause (a sailing vessel) to stop in open water or (of a sailing vessel) to stop.
lay days *pl. n.* **1.** *Commerce.* the number of days permitted for the loading or unloading of a ship without payment of demurrage. **2.** *Nautical.* the time during which a ship is kept from sailing because of loading, bad weather, etc.

lay down *vb.* (*tr., adv.*) **1.** to place on the ground, etc. **2.** to relinquish or discard: *to lay down one's life.* **3.** to formulate (a rule, principle, etc.). **4.** to build or begin to build: *the railway was laid down as far as Chester.* **5.** to record (plans) on paper. **6.** to convert (land) into pasture. **7.** to store or stock: *to lay down wine.* **8.** *Informal.* to wager or bet. **9.** (*tr., adv.*) *Informal.* to record (tracks) in a studio.

layer ('leɪə) *n.* **1.** a thickness of some homogeneous substance, such as a stratum or a coating on a surface. **2.** one of four levels of vegetation defined in ecological studies: the ground or moss layer, the field or herb layer, the shrub layer, and the tree layer. **3.** a laying hen. **4.** *Horticulture.* **a.** a shoot or branch rooted during layering. **b.** a plant produced as a result of layering. ~*vb.* **5.** to form or make a layer of (something). **6.** to take root or cause to take root by layering. [C14 *leyer, legger,* from LAY[1] + -ER[1]]

layer cake *n.* a cake made in layers with a filling.

layering ('leɪərɪŋ) *n.* **1.** *Horticulture.* a method of propagation that induces a shoot or branch to take root while it is still attached to the parent plant. **2.** *Geology.* the banded appearance of certain igneous rocks, each band being of a different mineral composition.

layette (leɪ'ɛt) *n.* a complete set of articles, including clothing, bedclothes, and other accessories, for a newborn baby. [C19: from French, from Old French, from *laie,* from Middle Dutch *laege* box]

lay figure *n.* **1.** an artist's jointed dummy, used in place of a live model, esp. for studying effects of drapery. **2.** a person considered to be subservient or unimportant. [C18: from obsolete *layman,* from Dutch *leeman,* literally: joint-man]

lay in *vb.* (*tr., adv.*) to accumulate and store: *we must lay in food for the party.*

laying on of hands *n.* (in Christian ordination, confirmation, faith healing, etc.) the act of laying hands on a person's head to confer spiritual blessing.

lay into *vb.* (*intr., prep.*) *Informal.* **1.** to attack forcefully. **2.** to berate severely.

layman ('leɪmən) *or* (*fem.*) **laywoman** *n., pl.* **-men** *or* **-women.** **1.** a person who is not a clergyman. **2.** a person who does not have specialized or professional knowledge of a subject: *science for the layman.*

lay off *vb.* **1.** (*tr., adv.*) to suspend (workers) from employment with the intention of re-employing them at a later date: *the firm had to lay off 100 men.* **2.** (*intr.*) *Informal.* to leave (a person, thing, or activity) alone: *lay off me, will you!* **3.** (*tr., adv.*) to mark off the boundaries of. **4.** (*tr., adv.*) *Soccer.* to pass or deflect (the ball) to a team-mate, esp. one in a more advantageous position. **5.** *Gambling.* another term for **hedge** (sense 10). ~*n.* **lay-off.** **6.** the act of suspending employees. **7.** a period of imposed unemployment.

lay on *vb.* (*tr., adv.*) **1.** to provide or supply: *to lay on entertainment.* **2.** *Brit.* to install: *to lay on electricity.* **3.** **lay it on.** *Informal.* **a.** to exaggerate, esp. when flattering. **b.** to charge an exorbitant price. **c.** to punish or strike harshly.

lay out *vb.* (*tr., adv.*) **1.** to arrange or spread out. **2.** to prepare (a corpse) for burial. **3.** to plan or contrive. **4.** *Informal.* to spend (money), esp. lavishly. **5.** *Informal.* to knock unconscious. **6.** *Informal.* to exert (oneself) or put (oneself) to an effort: *he laid himself out to please us.* ~*n.* **layout.** **7.** the arrangement or plan of something, such as a building. **8.** the arrangement of written material, photographs, or other artwork on an advertisement or page in a book, newspaper, etc. **9.** a preliminary plan indicating this. **10.** a drawing showing the relative disposition of parts in a machine, etc. **11.** the act of laying out. **12.** something laid out. **13.** the formation of cards on the table in various games, esp. in patience. **14.** *Informal, chiefly U.S.* a residence or establishment, esp. a large one.

lay over *U.S. and Canadian.* ~*vb.* (*adv.*) **1.** (*tr.*) to postpone for future action. **2.** (*intr.*) to make a temporary stop in a journey. ~*n.* **layover.** **3.** a break in a journey, esp. in waiting for a connection.

lay reader *n.* **1.** *Church of England.* a person licensed by a bishop to conduct religious services other than the Eucharist. **2.** *R.C. Church.* a layman chosen from among the congregation to read the epistle at Mass and sometimes other prayers.

layshaft ('leɪˌʃɑːft) *n.* an auxiliary shaft in a gearbox, running parallel to the main shaft, to and from which drive is transferred to enable varying ratios to be obtained.

lay to *vb.* (*intr. adv.*) *Nautical.* **1.** to bring a vessel into a haven. **2.** another term for **heave to.**

lay up *vb.* (*tr., adv.*) **1.** to store or reserve for future use. **2.** (*usually passive*) *Informal.* to incapacitate or confine through illness.

lazar ('læzə) *n.* an archaic word for **leper.** [C14: via Old French and Medieval Latin, after the diseased beggar *Lazarus* (Luke 16:19–31)] —'**lazar-ˌlike** *adj.*

lazaretto (ˌlæzə'rɛtəʊ), **lazaret,** *or* **lazarette** (ˌlæzə'rɛt) *n., pl.* **-rettos, -rets,** *or* **-rettes.** **1.** Also called: **glory hole.** *Nautical.* a small locker at the stern of a boat or a storeroom between decks of a ship. **2.** Also called: **lazar house, pesthouse.** (formerly) a hospital for persons with infectious diseases, esp. leprosy. [C16: Italian, from *lazzaro* LAZAR]

laze (leɪz) *vb.* **1.** (*intr.*) to be indolent or lazy. **2.** (*tr.*; often foll. by *away*) to spend (time) in indolence. ~*n.* **3.** the act or an instance of idling. [C16: back formation from LAZY]

lazuli ('læzjʊˌlaɪ) *n.* short for **lapis lazuli.**

lazulite ('læzjʊˌlaɪt) *n.* a blue mineral, consisting of hydrated magnesium iron phosphate, occurring in metamorphic rocks. Formula: $(Mg,Fe)Al_2(PO_4)_2(OH)_2$. [C19: from Medieval Latin *lāzulum* azure, LAPIS LAZULI]

lazurite ('læzjʊˌraɪt) *n.* a rare blue mineral consisting of a sodium aluminium silicate and sulphide: used as the gemstone lapis lazuli. Formula: $Na_{4-5}Al_3Si_3O_{12}S$. [C19: from Medieval Latin *lāzur* LAPIS LAZULI]

lazy ('leɪzɪ) *adj.* **lazier, laziest.** **1.** not inclined to work or exertion. **2.** conducive to or causing indolence. **3.** moving in a languid or sluggish manner: *a lazy river.* **4.** (of a brand letter or mark on livestock) shown as lying on its side. [C16: origin uncertain] —'**lazily** *adv.* —'**laziness** *n.*

lazy bed *n.* (in parts of Scotland and Ireland, formerly) a patch in which potatoes were cultivated by laying them on the surface and covering them with kelp and with soil from a trench on either side of the bed.

lazybones ('leɪzɪˌbəʊnz) *n. Informal.* a lazy person.

lazy daisy stitch *n.* an embroidery stitch consisting of a long chain stitch, usually used in making flower patterns.

lazy Susan ('suːzən) *n.* a revolving tray, often divided into sections, for holding condiments, etc.

lazy tongs *pl. n.* a set of tongs with extensible arms to allow objects to be grasped or handled at a distance.

lb *abbrev. for:* **1.** *Cricket.* leg bye. **2.** Also: **lb.** pound (weight). [Latin: *libra*]

LB *international car registration for* Liberia.

lbf *abbrev. for* pound force. See **pound**[2] (sense 4).

LBJ *abbrev. for* Lyndon Baines Johnson.

LBO *abbrev. for* leveraged buyout.

LBV *abbrev. for* Late Bottled Vintage: applied to port wine that has been matured in casks for six years and is then ready for drinking.

lbw *Cricket. abbrev. for* leg before wicket.

lc *abbrev. for:* **1.** left centre (of a stage, etc.). **2.** loco citato. [Latin: in the place cited] **3.** *Printing.* lower case.

LC (in the U.S.) *abbrev. for* Library of Congress.

L/C, l/c, *or* **lc** *abbrev. for* letter of credit.

LCC *abbrev. for* London County Council (a predecessor of the Greater London Council).

lcd *or* **LCD** *abbrevs. for* lowest common denominator.

LCD *abbrev. for* liquid-crystal display.

l'chaim (lə'xɑjim) *interj., n.* a variant spelling of **lechaim.**

LCJ *Brit. abbrev. for* Lord Chief Justice.

LCL *or* **lcl** *Commerce. abbrev. for* less than carload lot.

lcm *or* **LCM** *abbrev. for* lowest common multiple.

L/Cpl *abbrev. for* lance corporal.

ld *abbrev. for:* **1.** *Printing.* lead. **2.** load.

Ld *abbrev. for* Lord (title).

LD *abbrev. for:* **1.** lethal dosage: usually used with a subscript numeral showing what percentage of a test group of animals dies as a result of either being fed a substance being tested on them or being exposed to ionizing radiation, esp. in the median lethal dose: LD_{50}. **2.** Low Dutch.

L-D converter *n. Metallurgy.* a vessel in which steel is made from pig iron by blowing oxygen into the molten metal through a water-cooled tube. [C20: L(inz)-D(onawitz), from the Austrian towns of *Linz* and *Donawitz,* where the process was first used successfully]

Ldg *abbrev. for* leading: *Ldg seaman.*

LDL *abbrev. for* low-density lipoprotein.

L-dopa (ɛl'dəʊpə) *n.* a substance occurring naturally in the body and used to treat Parkinson's disease. Formula: $C_9H_{11}NO_4$. Also called: **levodopa.** [C20: from *L-d(ihydr)o(xy)p(henyl)a(lanine)*]

L-driver *n. Brit.* a learner-driver: a person who is learning to drive, has not yet passed the official driving test, and must be accompanied by a qualified driver and display L-plates on the car.

LDS *abbrev. for:* **1.** Latter-day Saints. **2.** laus Deo semper. [Latin: praise be to God for ever] **3.** (in Britain) Licentiate in Dental Surgery.

LE *abbrev. for* lupus erythematosus.

-le *suffix forming verbs.* denoting repeated or continuous action, often of a trivial nature: *twiddle; wriggle; wrestle.* [from Middle English *-len,* Old English *-lian,* with similar significance]

lea[1] (liː) *n.* **1.** *Poetic.* a meadow or field. **2.** land that has been sown with grass seed. [Old English *lēah;* related to German dialect *loh* thicket]

lea[2] (liː) *n.* **1.** a unit for measuring lengths of yarn, usually taken as 80 yards for wool, 120 yards for cotton and silk, and 300 yards for linen. **2.** a measure of yarn expressed as the length per unit weight, usually the number of leas per pound. [C14: of uncertain origin]

LEA (in Britain) *abbrev. for* Local Education Authority.

lea. *abbrev. for:* **1.** league. **2.** leather.

leach[1] (liːtʃ) *vb.* **1.** to remove or be removed from a substance by a percolating liquid. **2.** to lose or cause to lose soluble substances by the action of a percolating liquid. **3.** another word for **percolate** (senses 1, 2). ~*n.* **4.** the act or process of leaching.

5. a substance that is leached or the constituents removed by leaching. **6.** a porous vessel for leaching. [C17: variant of obsolete *letch* to wet, perhaps from Old English *leccan* to water; related to LEAK] —**'leacher** *n.*

leach[2] (liːtʃ) *n.* a variant spelling of **leech**[2].

leachate ('liːtʃeɪt) *n.* water that carries salts dissolved out of materials through which it has percolated, esp. polluted water from a refuse tip.

lead[1] (liːd) *vb.* **leads, leading, led** (lɛd). **1.** to show the way to (an individual or a group) by going with or ahead: *lead the party into the garden.* **2.** to guide or be guided by holding, pulling, etc.: *he led the horse by its reins.* **3.** (*tr.*) to cause to act, feel, think, or behave in a certain way; induce; influence: *he led me to believe that he would go.* **4.** (*tr.*) to phrase a question to (a witness) that tends to suggest the desired answer. **5.** (when *intr.*, foll. by *to*) (of a road, route, etc.) to serve as the means of reaching a place. **6.** (*tr.*) to go ahead so as to indicate (esp. in the phrase **lead the way**). **7.** to guide, control, or direct: *to lead an army.* **8.** (*tr.*) to direct the course of or conduct (water, a rope or wire, etc.) along or as if along a channel. **9.** to initiate the action of (something); have the principal part in (something): *to lead a discussion.* **10.** to go at the head of or have the top position in (something): *he leads his class in geography.* **11.** (*intr.*; foll. by *with*) to have as the first or principal item: *the newspaper led with the royal birth.* **12.** *Music.* **a.** *Brit.* to play first violin in (an orchestra). **b.** (*intr.*) (of an instrument or voice) to be assigned an important entry in a piece of music. **13.** to direct and guide (one's partner) in a dance. **14.** (*tr.*) **a.** to pass or spend: *I lead a miserable life.* **b.** to cause to pass a life of a particular kind: *to lead a person a dog's life.* **15.** (*intr.*; foll. by *to*) to tend (to) or result (in): *this will only lead to misery.* **16.** to initiate a round of cards by putting down (the first card) or to have the right to do this: *she led a diamond.* **17.** (*tr.*) to aim at a point in front of (a moving target) in shooting, etc., in order to allow for the time of flight. **18.** (*intr.*) *Boxing.* to make an offensive blow, esp. as one's habitual attacking punch: *southpaws lead with their right.* **19. lead astray.** to mislead so as to cause error or wrongdoing. **20. lead by the nose.** See **nose** (sense 12). ~*n.* **21. a.** the first, foremost, or most prominent place. **b.** (*as modifier*): *lead singer.* **22.** example, precedence, or leadership: *the class followed the teacher's lead.* **23.** an advance or advantage held over others: *the runner had a lead of twenty yards.* **24.** anything that guides or directs; indication; clue. **25.** another name for **leash. 26.** the act or prerogative of playing the first card in a round of cards or the card so played. **27.** the principal role in a play, film, etc., or the person playing such a role. **28. a.** the principal news story in a newspaper: *the scandal was the lead in the papers.* **b.** the opening paragraph of a news story. **c.** (*as modifier*): *lead story.* **29.** *Music.* an important entry assigned to one part usually at the beginning of a movement or section. **30.** a wire, cable, or other conductor for making an electrical connection. **31.** *Boxing.* **a.** one's habitual attacking punch. **b.** a blow made with this. **32.** *Nautical.* the direction in which a rope runs. **33.** a deposit of metal or ore; lode. **34.** the firing of a gun, missile, etc., ahead of a moving target to correct for the time of flight of the projectile. ~See also **lead off, lead on, lead up to.** [Old English *lǣdan*; related to *līthan* to travel, Old High German *līdan* to go]

lead[2] (lɛd) *n.* **1.** a heavy toxic bluish-white metallic element that is highly malleable: occurs principally as galena and used in alloys, accumulators, cable sheaths, paints, and as a radiation shield. Symbol: Pb; atomic no.: 82; atomic wt.: 207.2; valency: 2 or 4; relative density: 11.35; melting pt.: 327.5°C; boiling pt.: 1740°C. Related adjs.: **plumbic, plumbous. 2.** a lead weight suspended on a line used to take soundings of the depth of water. **3. swing the lead.** to malinger or make up excuses. **4.** lead weights or shot, as used in cartridges, fishing lines, etc. **5.** a thin grooved strip of lead for holding small panes of glass or pieces of stained glass. **6.** (*pl.*) **a.** thin sheets or strips of lead used as a roof covering. **b.** a flat or low-pitched roof covered with such sheets. **7.** Also called: **leading.** *Printing.* a thin strip of type metal used for spacing between lines. Compare **reglet** (sense 2). **8. a.** graphite or a mixture containing graphite, clay, etc., used for drawing. **b.** a thin stick of this material, esp. the core of a pencil. **9.** (*modifier*) of, consisting of, relating to, or containing lead. ~*vb.* (*tr.*) **10.** to fill or treat with lead. **11.** to surround, cover, or secure with lead or leads. **12.** *Printing.* to space (type) by use of leads. [Old English; related to Dutch *lood*, German *Lot*] —**'leadless** *adj.* —**'leady** *adj.*

lead acetate (lɛd) *n.* a white crystalline toxic solid used in dyeing cotton and in making varnishes and enamels. Formula: $Pb(CH_3CO)_2$. Systematic name: **lead(II) acetate.** Also called: **sugar of lead.**

lead arsenate (lɛd) *n.* a white insoluble toxic crystalline powder used as an insecticide and fungicide. Formula: $Pb_3(AsO_4)_2$.

lead chromate (lɛd) *n. Chem.* a yellow solid used as a pigment, as in chrome yellow. Formula: $PbCrO_4$.

lead colic (lɛd) *n.* a symptom of lead poisoning characterized by intense abdominal pain. Also called: **painter's colic.**

leaded ('lɛdɪd) *adj.* (of windows) composed of small panes of glass held in place by thin grooved strips of lead: *leaded lights.*

leaden ('lɛdᵊn) *adj.* **1.** heavy and inert. **2.** laboured or sluggish: *leaden steps.* **3.** gloomy, spiritless, or lifeless. **4.** made partly or wholly of lead. **5.** of a dull greyish colour: *a leaden sky.* —**'leadenly** *adv.* —**'leadenness** *n.*

leader ('liːdə) *n.* **1.** a person who rules, guides, or inspires others; head. **2.** *Music.* **a.** Also called (esp. U.S. and Canadian): **concertmaster.** the principal first violinist of an orchestra, who plays solo parts, and acts as the conductor's deputy and spokesman for the orchestra. **b.** *U.S.* a conductor or director of an orchestra or chorus. **3. a.** the first man on a climbing rope. **b.** the leading horse or dog in a team. **4.** *Chiefly U.S. and Canadian.* an article offered at a sufficiently low price to attract customers. See also **loss leader. 5.** a statistic or index that gives an advance indication of the state of the economy. **6.** *Chiefly Brit.* Also called: **leading article.** the leading editorial in a newspaper. **7.** *Angling.* another word for **trace**[2] (sense 2) or **cast** (sense 32a). **8.** *Nautical.* another term for **fairlead. 9.** a strip of blank film or tape used to facilitate threading a projector, developing machine, etc., and to aid identification. **10.** (*pl.*) *Printing.* rows of dots or hyphens used to guide the reader's eye across a page, as in a table of contents. **11.** *Botany.* any of the long slender shoots that grow from the stem or branch of a tree: usually removed during pruning. **12.** *Brit.* a member of the Government having primary authority in initiating legislative business (esp. in the phrases **Leader of the House of Commons** and **Leader of the House of Lords**). **13.** the senior barrister, usually a Queen's Counsel, in charge of the conduct of a case. Compare **junior** (sense 6). —**'leaderless** *adj.*

leadership ('liːdəʃɪp) *n.* **1.** the position or function of a leader. **2.** the period during which a person occupies the position of leader: *during her leadership very little was achieved.* **3. a.** the ability to lead. **b.** (*as modifier*): *leadership qualities.* **4.** the leaders as a group of a party, union, etc.: *the union leadership is now very reactionary.*

lead glass (lɛd) *n.* glass that contains lead oxide as a flux.

lead-in ('liːdˌɪn) *n.* **1. a.** an introduction to a subject. **b.** (*as modifier*): *a lead-in announcement.* **2.** the connection between a radio transmitter, receiver, etc., and the aerial or transmission line.

leading[1] ('liːdɪŋ) *adj.* **1.** guiding, directing, or influencing. **2.** (*prenominal*) principal or primary. **3.** in the first position: *the leading car in the procession.* **4.** *Maths.* (of a coefficient) associated with the term of highest degree in a polynomial containing one variable: *in* $5x^2 + 2x + 3$, *5 is the leading coefficient.* —**'leadingly** *adv.*

leading[2] ('lɛdɪŋ) *n. Printing.* another name for **lead**[2] (sense 7).

leading aircraftman ('liːdɪŋ) *n. Brit. airforce.* the rank above aircraftman. —**leading aircraftwoman** *fem. n.*

leading article ('liːdɪŋ) *n. Journalism.* **1.** another term for **leader** (sense 6). **2.** *Chiefly U.S.* the article given most prominence in a magazine or newspaper.

leading dog *n. N.Z.* a dog trained to lead a flock of sheep to prevent them breaking or stampeding.

leading edge ('liːdɪŋ) *n.* **1.** the forward edge of a propeller blade, aerofoil, or wing. Compare **trailing edge. 2.** *Electrical engineering.* the part of a pulse signal that has an increasing amplitude. ~*modifier.* **leading-edge. 3.** advanced; foremost: *leading-edge technology.*

leading light ('liːdɪŋ) *n.* **1.** an important or outstanding person, esp. in an organization or cause. **2.** *Nautical.* a less common term for **range light.**

leading man ('liːdɪŋ) *n.* a man who plays the main part in a film, play, etc. —**leading lady** *fem. n.*

leading note ('liːdɪŋ) *n. Music.* **1.** another word for **subtonic. 2.** (esp. in cadences) a note, usually the subtonic of a scale, that tends most naturally to resolve to the note lying one semitone above it.

leading question ('liːdɪŋ) *n.* a question phrased in a manner that tends to suggest the desired answer, such as *What do you think of the horrible effects of pollution?*

leading rating *n.* a rank in the Royal Navy comparable but junior to that of a corporal in the army.

leading reins *or U.S. and Canadian* **leading strings** ('liːdɪŋ) *pl. n.* **1.** straps or a harness and strap used to assist and control a child who is learning to walk. **2.** excessive guidance or restraint.

lead line (lɛd) *n. Nautical.* a length of line for swinging a lead, marked at various points to indicate multiples of fathoms.

lead monoxide (lɛd) *n.* a poisonous insoluble oxide of lead existing in red and yellow forms: used in making glass, glazes, and cements, and as a pigment. Formula: PbO. Systematic name: **lead(II) oxide.** Also called: **litharge, plumbous oxide.**

lead off (liːd) *vb.* (*adv.*) **1.** to initiate the action of (something); begin. ~*n.* **lead-off. 2.** an initial move or action. **3.** a person or thing that begins something.

lead on (liːd) *vb.* (*tr., adv.*) to lure or entice, esp. into trouble or wrongdoing.

lead pencil (lɛd) *n.* a pencil in which the writing material is a thin stick of a graphite compound.

lead poisoning (lɛd) *n.* **1.** Also called: **plumbism, saturnism.** acute or chronic poisoning by lead or its salts, characterized by abdominal pain, vomiting, convulsions, and coma. **2.** *U.S. slang.* death or injury resulting from being shot with bullets.

lead screw (liːd) *n.* a threaded rod that drives the tool carriage in a lathe when screw cutting, etc.

leadsman ('lɛdzmən) *n., pl.* **-men.** *Nautical.* a sailor who takes soundings with a lead line.
lead tetraethyl (lɛd) *n.* another name for **tetraethyl lead.**
lead time (liːd) *n.* **1.** *Manufacturing.* the time between the design of a product and its production. **2.** *Commerce.* the time from the placing of an order to the delivery of the goods.
lead up to (liːd) *vb.* (*intr., adv. + prep.*) **1.** to act as a preliminary or introduction to. **2.** to approach (a topic) gradually or cautiously.
leadwort ('lɛdˌwɜːt) *n.* any shrub of the plumbaginaceous genus *Plumbago,* of tropical and subtropical regions, with red, blue, or white flowers.
leaf (liːf) *n., pl.* **leaves** (liːvz). **1.** the main organ of photosynthesis and transpiration in higher plants, usually consisting of a flat green blade attached to the stem directly or by a stalk. **2.** foliage collectively. **3. in leaf.** (of shrubs, trees, etc.) having a full complement of foliage leaves. **4.** one of the sheets of paper in a book. **5.** a hinged, sliding, or detachable part, such as an extension to a table. **6.** metal in the form of a very thin flexible sheet: *gold leaf.* **7.** a foil or thin strip of metal in a composite material; lamina. **8.** short for **leaf spring. 9.** the inner or outer wall of a cavity wall. **10.** a crop that is harvested in the form of leaves. **11.** a metal strip forming one of the laminations in a leaf spring. **12.** a slang word for **marijuana. 13. take a leaf out of** (*or* **from) someone's book.** to imitate someone, esp. in one particular course of action. **14. turn over a new leaf.** to begin a new and improved course of behaviour. ~*vb.* **15.** (when *intr.,* usually foll. by *through*) to turn (through pages, sheets, etc.) cursorily. **16.** (*intr.*) (of plants) to produce leaves. [Old English; related to Gothic *laufs,* Icelandic *lauf*] —**'leafless** *adj.* —**'leaflessness** *n.* —**'leafˌlike** *adj.*
leafage ('liːfɪdʒ) *n.* a less common word for **foliage.**
leaf beet *n.* another name for **chard.**
leaf beetle *n.* any of a large family of beetles (*Chrysomelidae*) that includes more than 25,000 species, mostly leaf feeders and mostly brightly coloured, with a metallic sheen. It includes the notorious **Colorado beetle,** the **bloody-nosed beetle,** and the **flea beetles** (*Phyllotreta* species) which attack young cabbage plants.
leaf-climber *n.* a plant that climbs by using leaves specialized as tendrils.
leafcutter ant ('liːfˌkʌtə) *n.* any of various South American ants of the genus *Atta* that cut pieces of leaves and use them as fertilizer for the fungus on which they feed.
leafcutter bee *n.* any of various solitary bees of the genus *Megachile* that nest in soil or rotten wood, constructing the cells in which they lay their eggs from pieces of leaf.
leaf fat *n.* the dense fat that accumulates in layers around the kidneys of certain animals, esp. pigs.
leaf gap *n. Botany.* a region of parenchyma cells in the vascular tissue of flowering plants and some ferns, situated above a leaf trace.
leaf-hopper *n.* any homopterous insect of the family *Cicadellidae,* including various pests of crops.
leaf insect *n.* any of various mostly tropical Asian insects of the genus *Phyllium* and related genera, having a flattened leaflike body: order *Phasmida.* See also **stick insect.**
leaf-lard *n.* lard prepared from the leaf fat of a pig.
leaflet ('liːflɪt) *n.* **1.** a printed and usually folded sheet of paper for distribution, usually free and containing advertising material or information about a political party, charity, etc. **2.** any of the subdivisions of a compound leaf such as a fern leaf. **3.** any small leaf or leaflike part. ~*vb.* **4.** to distribute printed leaflets (to): *they leafleted every flat in the area.* —**'leafleter** *n.*
leaf miner *n.* **1.** any of various insect larvae that bore into and feed on leaf tissue, esp. the larva of dipterous flies of the genus *Philophylla* (family *Trypetidae*) and the caterpillar of moths of the family *Gracillariidae.* **2.** the adult insect of any of these larvae.
leaf monkey *n.* another name for **langur.**
leaf mould *n.* **1.** a nitrogen-rich material consisting of decayed leaves, etc., used as a fertilizer. **2.** any of various fungus diseases affecting the leaves of certain plants.
leaf sheath *n. Botany.* a sheath covering the base of a grass stem.
leaf sight *n.* a folding rear sight on certain rifles.
leaf spot *n.* any of various plant diseases, usually caused by fungi: characterized by dark lesions on the leaves.
leaf spring *n.* **1.** one of a number of metal strips bracketed together in length to form a compound spring. **2.** the compound spring so formed.
leafstalk ('liːfˌstɔːk) *n.* the stalk attaching a leaf to a stem or branch. Technical name: **petiole.**
leaf trace *n. Botany.* a vascular bundle connecting the vascular tissue of the stem with that of a leaf.
leafy ('liːfɪ) *adj.* **leafier, leafiest. 1.** covered with or having leaves. **2.** resembling a leaf or leaves. —**'leafiness** *n.*
league[1] (liːg) *n.* **1.** an association or union of persons, nations, etc., formed to promote the interests of its members. **2.** an association of sporting clubs that organizes matches between member teams of a similar standard. **3.** a class, category, or level: *he is not in the same league.* **4. in league (with).** working or planning together with. **5.** (*modifier*) of, involving, or belonging to a league: *a league game; a league table.* ~*vb.* **leagues, leaguing, leagued. 6.** to form or be formed into a league. [C15: from Old French *ligue,* from Italian *liga,* ultimately from Latin *ligāre* to bind]
league[2] (liːg) *n.* an obsolete unit of distance of varying length. It is commonly equal to 3 miles. [C14 *leuge,* from Late Latin *leuga, leuca,* of Celtic origin]
league football *n.* **1.** Also called: **league.** *Chiefly Austral.* rugby league football. **2.** *Austral.* an Australian Rules competition conducted within a league rather than a football association. Compare **association football** (sense 2).
leaguer[1] ('liːgə) *n. Archaic.* **1.** an encampment, esp. of besiegers. **2.** the siege itself. [C16: from Dutch *leger* siege; related to LAIR[1]]
leaguer[2] ('liːgə) *n. Chiefly U.S. and Canadian.* a member of a league.
league table *n. Brit.* **1.** a tabulated comparison of clubs or teams competing in a sporting league. **2.** a comparison of performance, merit, importance, etc. in any competitive situation: *a league table of wages.*
leak (liːk) *n.* **1. a.** a crack, hole, etc., that allows the accidental escape or entrance of fluid, light, etc. **b.** such escaping or entering fluid, light, etc. **2. spring a leak.** to develop a leak. **3.** something resembling this in effect: *a leak in the defence system.* **4.** the loss of current from an electrical conductor because of faulty insulation, etc. **5.** a disclosure, often intentional, of secret information. **6.** the act or an instance of leaking. **7.** a slang word for **urination.** ~*vb.* **8.** to enter or escape or allow to enter or escape through a crack, hole, etc. **9.** (when *intr.,* often foll. by *out*) to disclose (secret information), often intentionally, or (of secret information) to be disclosed. **10.** (*intr.*) a slang word for **urinate.** [C15: from Scandinavian; compare Old Norse *leka* to drip] —**'leaker** *n.*
leakage ('liːkɪdʒ) *n.* **1.** the act or an instance of leaking. **2.** something that escapes or enters by a leak. **3.** *Commerce.* an allowance made for partial loss (of stock, etc.) due to leaking. **4.** *Physics.* **a.** an undesired flow of electric current, neutrons, etc., **b.** (*as modifier*): *leakage current.*
leaky ('liːkɪ) *adj.* **leakier, leakiest.** leaking or tending to leak. —**'leakiness** *n.*
leal (liːl) *adj. Archaic or Scot.* loyal; faithful. [C13: from Old French *leial,* from Latin *lēgālis* LEGAL; related to LOYAL] —**'leally** *adv.* —**lealty** ('liːəltɪ) *n.*
lean[1] (liːn) *vb.* **leans, leaning; leant** *or* **leaned. 1.** (foll. by *against, on,* or *upon*) to rest or cause to rest against a support. **2.** to incline or cause to incline from a vertical position. **3.** (*intr.;* foll. by *to* or *towards*) to have or express a tendency or leaning. **4. lean over backwards.** *Informal.* to make a special effort, esp. in order to please. ~*n.* **5.** the condition of inclining from a vertical position. ~See also **lean on.** [Old English *hleonian, hlinian;* related to Old High German *hlinēn,* Latin *clīnāre* to INCLINE]
lean[2] (liːn) *adj.* **1.** (esp. of a person or an animal) having no surplus flesh or bulk; not fat or plump. **2.** not bulky or full. **3.** (of meat) having little or no fat. **4.** not rich, abundant, or satisfying. **5.** (of a mixture of fuel and air) containing insufficient fuel and too much air: *a lean mixture.* **6.** (of printer's type) having a thin appearance. **7.** (of a paint) containing relatively little oil. **8.** (of an ore) not having a high mineral content. **9.** (of concrete) made with a small amount of cement. ~*n.* **10.** the part of meat that contains little or no fat. [Old English *hlǣne,* of Germanic origin] —**'leanly** *adv.* —**'leanness** *n.*
lean-burn *adj.* (esp. of an internal-combustion engine) designed to use a lean mixture of fuel and air in order to reduce petrol consumption and exhaust emissions.
leaning ('liːnɪŋ) *n.* a tendency or inclination.
lean on *vb.* (*intr., prep.*) **1.** Also: **lean upon.** to depend on for advice, support, etc. **2.** *Informal.* to exert pressure on (someone), as by threats or intimidation.
leant (lɛnt) *vb.* a past tense and past participle of **lean**[1].
lean-to *n., pl.* **-tos. 1.** a roof that has a single slope with its upper edge adjoining a wall or building. **2.** a shed or outbuilding with such a roof.
leap (liːp) *vb.* **leaps, leaping; leapt** *or* **leaped. 1.** (*intr.*) to jump suddenly from one place to another. **2.** (*intr.;* often foll. by *at*) to move or react quickly. **3.** (*tr.*) to jump over. **4.** to come into prominence rapidly: *the thought leapt into his mind.* **5.** (*tr.*) to cause (an animal, esp. a horse) to jump a barrier. ~*n.* **6.** the act of jumping. **7.** a spot from which a leap was or may be made. **8.** the distance of a leap. **9.** an abrupt change or increase. **10.** Also called (U.S. and Canadian): **skip.** *Music.* a relatively large melodic interval, esp. in a solo part. **11. a leap in the dark.** an action performed without knowledge of the consequences. **12. by leaps and bounds.** with unexpectedly rapid progress. [Old English *hlēapan;* related to Gothic *hlaupan,* German *laufen*] —**'leaper** *n.*
leapfrog ('liːpˌfrɒg) *n.* **1.** a children's game in which each player in turn leaps over the others' bent backs, leaning on them with the hands and spreading the legs wide. ~*vb.* **-frogs, -frogging, -frogged. 2. a.** (*intr.*) to play leapfrog. **b.** (*tr.*) to leap in this way over (something). **3.** to advance or cause to advance by jumps or stages.
leap second *n.* a second added to or removed from a scale for reckoning time on one particular occasion, to synchronize it with another scale.
leapt (lɛpt, liːpt) *vb.* a past tense and past participle of **leap.**

leap year *n.* a calendar year of 366 days, February 29 (**leap day**) being the additional day, that occurs every four years (those whose number is divisible by four) except for century years whose number is not divisible by 400. It offsets the difference between the length of the solar year (365.2422 days) and the calendar year of 365 days.

lea-rig ('liː,rɪg) *n. Scot.* a ridge of unploughed land. [Old English *lǣghrycg*]

learn (lɜːn) *vb.* **learns, learning; learnt** *or* **learned** (lɜːnd). **1.** (when *tr., may take a clause as object*) to gain knowledge of (something) or acquire skill in (some art or practice). **2.** (*tr.*) to commit to memory. **3.** (*tr.*) to gain by experience, example, etc. **4.** (*intr.*; often foll. by *of* or *about*) to become informed; know. **5.** *Not standard.* to teach. [Old English *leornian;* related to Old High German *lirnen*] —**'learnable** *adj.* —**'learner** *n.*

learned ('lɜːnɪd) *adj.* **1.** having great knowledge or erudition. **2.** involving or characterized by scholarship. **3.** (*prenominal*) a title applied in referring to a member of the legal profession, esp. to a barrister: *my learned friend.* —**'learnedly** *adv.* —**'learnedness** *n.*

learned helplessness *n.* the act of giving up trying as a result of consistent failure to be rewarded in life, thought to be a cause of depression.

learner's chain *n. N.Z.* an inexperienced team of slaughtermen working in a freezing works.

learning ('lɜːnɪŋ) *n.* **1.** knowledge gained by study; instruction or scholarship. **2.** the act of gaining knowledge. **3.** *Psychol.* any relatively permanent change in behaviour that occurs as a direct result of experience.

learning curve *n.* a graphical representation of progress in learning: *I'm still only half way up the learning curve.*

learnt (lɜːnt) *vb.* a past tense and past participle of **learn.**

lease[1] (liːs) *n.* **1.** a contract by which property is conveyed to a person for a specified period, usually for rent. **2.** the instrument by which such property is conveyed. **3.** the period of time for which it is conveyed. **4.** a prospect of renewed health, happiness, etc.: *a new lease of life.* ~*vb.* (*tr.*) **5.** to grant possession of (land, buildings, etc.) by lease. **6.** to take a lease of (property); hold under a lease. [C15: via Anglo-French from Old French *lais* (n.), from *laissier* to let go, from Latin *laxāre* to loosen] —**'leasable** *adj.* —**'leaser** *n.*

lease[2] (liːz) *n. Dialect.* open pasture or common. [Old English *lǣs;* perhaps related to Old Norse *lāth* property]

leaseback ('liːs,bæk) *n.* a property transaction in which the buyer leases the property to the seller.

leasehold ('liːs,həʊld) *n.* **1.** land or property held under a lease. **2.** the tenure by which such property is held. **3.** (*modifier*) held under a lease.

leaseholder ('liːs,həʊldə) *n.* **1.** a person in possession of leasehold property. **2.** a tenant under a lease.

leash (liːʃ) *n.* **1.** a line or rope used to walk or control a dog or other animal; lead. **2.** something resembling this in function: *he kept a tight leash on his emotions.* **3.** *Hunting.* three of the same kind of animal, usually hounds, foxes, or hares. **4. straining at the leash.** eagerly impatient to begin something. ~*vb.* **5.** (*tr.*) to control or secure by or as if by a leash. [C13: from Old French *laisse,* from *laissier* to loose (hence, to let a dog run on a leash), ultimately from Latin *laxus* LAX]

least (liːst) *determiner.* **1. a. the.** the superlative of **little:** *you have the least talent of anyone.* **b.** (*as pronoun; functioning as sing.*): *least isn't necessarily worst.* **2. at least. a.** if nothing else: *you should at least try.* **b.** at the least. **3. at the least.** Also: **at least.** at the minimum: *at the least you should earn a hundred pounds.* **4. in the least.** (*usually used with a negative*) in the slightest degree; at all: *I don't mind in the least.* ~*adv.* **5. the least.** superlative of **little:** *they travel the least of all.* ~*adj.* **6.** of very little importance or rank. [Old English *lǣst,* superlative of *lǣssa* LESS]

least common denominator *n.* another name for **lowest common denominator.**

least common multiple *n.* another name for **lowest common multiple.**

least squares *n.* a method for determining the best value of an unknown quantity relating one or more sets of observations or measurements, esp. to find a curve that best fits a set of data. It states that the sum of the squares of the deviations of the experimentally determined value from its optimum value should be a minimum.

leastways ('liːst,weɪz) *or U.S. and Canadian* **leastwise** *adv. Informal.* at least; anyway; at any rate.

leat (liːt) *n. Brit.* a trench or ditch that conveys water to a mill wheel. [Old English *-gelǣt* (as in *wætergelǣt* water channel), from LET[1]]

leather ('lɛðə) *n.* **1. a.** a material consisting of the skin of an animal made smooth and flexible by tanning, removing the hair, etc. **b.** (*as modifier*): *leather goods.* **2.** something, such as a garment, made of leather. **3.** the flap of a dog's ear. ~*vb.* (*tr.*) **4.** to cover with leather. **5.** to whip with or as if with a leather strap. [Old English *lether-* (in compound words); related to Old High German *leder,* Old Norse *lethr-*]

leatherback ('lɛðə,bæk) *n.* a large turtle, *Dermochelys coriacea,* of warm and tropical seas, having a ridged leathery carapace: family *Dermochelidae.* Also called (in Britain): **leathery turtle.**

leather beetle *n.* see **dermestid.**

Leatherette (,lɛðə'rɛt) *n. Trademark.* an imitation leather made from paper, cloth, etc.

leatherhead ('lɛðə,hɛd) *n.* another name for **friarbird.**

leatherjacket ('lɛðə,dʒækɪt) *n.* **1.** any of various tropical carangid fishes of the genera *Oligoplites* and *Scomberoides,* having a leathery skin. **2.** any of various brightly coloured tropical triggerfishes of the genus *Monacanthus* and related genera. **3.** the greyish-brown tough-skinned larva of certain craneflies, esp. of the genus *Tipula,* which destroy the roots of grasses, etc.

leathern ('lɛðən) *adj. Archaic.* made of or resembling leather.

leatherneck ('lɛðə,nɛk) *n. Slang.* a member of the U.S. Marine Corps. [from the custom of facing the neckband of their uniform with leather]

leatherwood ('lɛðə,wʊd) *n.* **1.** Also called: **wicopy.** a North American thymelaeaceous shrub, *Dirca palustris,* with pale yellow flowers and tough flexible branches. **2.** any of various Australian shrubs of the family *Cunoniaceae.*

leathery ('lɛðərɪ) *adj.* having the appearance or texture of leather, esp. in toughness. —**'leatheriness** *n.*

leave[1] (liːv) *vb.* **leaves, leaving, left.** (*mainly tr.*) **1.** (*also intr.*) to go or depart (from a person or place). **2.** to cause to remain behind, often by mistake, in a place: *he often leaves his keys in his coat.* **3.** to cause to be or remain in a specified state: *paying the bill left him penniless.* **4.** to renounce or abandon: *to leave a political movement.* **5.** to refrain from consuming or doing something: *the things we have left undone.* **6.** to result in; cause: *childhood problems often leave emotional scars.* **7.** to allow to be or remain subject to another person or thing: *leave the past to look after itself.* **8.** to entrust or commit: *leave the shopping to her.* **9.** to submit in place of one's personal appearance: *will you leave your name and address?* **10.** to pass in a specified direction: *flying out of the country, we left the cliffs on our left.* **11.** to be survived by (members of one's family): *he leaves a wife and two children.* **12.** to bequeath or devise: *he left his investments to his children.* **13.** (*tr.*) to have as a remainder: *37 – 14 leaves 23.* **14.** *Not standard.* to permit; let. **15. leave be.** *Informal.* to leave undisturbed. **16. leave go** *or* **hold of.** *Not standard.* to stop holding. **17. leave it at that.** *Informal.* to take a matter no further. **18. leave much to be desired.** to be very unsatisfactory. **19. leave (someone) alone. a.** Also: **let alone.** See **let**[1] (sense 7). **b.** to permit to stay or be alone. **20. leave someone to himself.** not to control or direct someone. ~See also **leave behind, leave off, leave out.** [Old English *lǣfan;* related to *belīfan* to be left as a remainder] —**'leaver** *n.*

leave[2] (liːv) *n.* **1.** permission to do something: *he was granted leave to speak.* **2. by** *or* **with your leave.** with your permission. **3.** permission to be absent, as from a place of work or duty: *leave of absence.* **4.** the duration of such absence: *ten days' leave.* **5.** a farewell or departure (esp. in the phrase **take (one's) leave**). **6. on leave.** officially excused from work or duty. **7. take leave (of).** to say farewell (to). **8. take leave of one's senses.** to go mad or become irrational. [Old English *lēaf;* related to *alȳfan* to permit, Middle High German *loube* permission]

leave[3] (liːv) *vb.* **leaves, leaving, leaved.** (*intr.*) to produce or grow leaves.

leave behind *vb.* (*tr.*) **1.** (*adv.*) to forget or neglect to bring or take. **2.** to cause to remain as a result or sign of something: *the storm left a trail of damage behind.* **3.** to pass: *once the wind came up, we soon left the land behind us.*

leaved (liːvd) *adj.* **a.** having a leaf or leaves; leafed. **b.** (*in combination*): *a five-leaved stem.*

leaven ('lɛvᵊn) *n. also* **leavening. 1.** any substance that produces fermentation in dough or batter, such as yeast, and causes it to rise. **2.** a piece of such a substance kept to ferment a new batch of dough. **3.** an agency or influence that produces a gradual change. ~*vb.* (*tr.*) **4.** to cause fermentation in (dough or batter). **5.** to pervade, causing a gradual change, esp. with some moderating or enlivening influence. [C14: via Old French ultimately from Latin *levāmen* relief, (hence, raising agent, leaven), from *levāre* to raise]

leave of absence *n.* **1.** permission to be absent from work or duty. **2.** the period of absence.

leave off *vb.* **1.** (*intr.*) to stop; cease. **2.** (*tr., adv.*) to stop wearing or using.

leave out *vb.* (*tr., adv.*) **1.** to cause to remain in the open: *you can leave your car out tonight.* **2.** to omit or exclude.

leaves (liːvz) *n.* the plural of **leaf.**

leave-taking *n.* the act of departing; a farewell.

leavings ('liːvɪŋz) *pl. n.* something remaining, such as food on a plate, residue, refuse, etc.

Leavisite ('liːvɪs,aɪt) *adj.* **1.** of or relating to the works or ideas of F. R. Leavis (1895–1978), British literary critic. ~*n.* **2.** a supporter of the ideas of F. R. Leavis.

Lebanese (,lɛbə'niːz) *adj.* **1.** of or relating to Lebanon, a republic in W Asia, or its people, customs, etc. ~*n.* **2.** (*pl.* **-ese**) a native or inhabitant of Lebanon.

leben ('lɛbᵊn) *n.* a semiliquid food made from curdled milk in N Africa and the Levant. [C17: from Arabic *laban*]

Lebensraum ('leɪbənz,raʊm) *n.* territory claimed by a nation or state on the grounds that it is necessary for survival or growth. [German, literally: living space]

lebkuchen (ˈleɪbˌkuːkən) *n. pl.* **-chen.** a biscuit, originating from Germany, usually containing honey, spices, etc. [German: literally, loaf cake]

lech *or* **letch** (lɛtʃ) *Informal.* ~*vb.* **1.** (*intr.; usually foll. by after*) to behave lecherously (towards); lust (after). ~*n.* **2.** a lecherous act or indulgence. [C19: back formation from LECHER]

lechaim, lehaim, *or* **l'chaim** (ləˈxɑjim) *Judaism.* ~*interj.* **1.** a drinking toast. ~*n.* **2.** a small drink with which to toast something or someone. [from Hebrew, literally: to life]

Le Chatelier's principle (lə ʃæˈtɛljeɪz) *n. Chem.* the principle that if a system in chemical equilibrium is subjected to a disturbance it tends to change in a way that opposes this disturbance. [C19: named after H. L. *Le Chatelier* (1850–1936), French chemist]

lecher (ˈlɛtʃə) *n.* a promiscuous or lewd man. [C12: from Old French *lecheor* lecher, from *lechier* to lick, of Germanic origin; compare Old High German *leccōn* to lick]

lecherous (ˈlɛtʃərəs) *adj.* characterized by or inciting lechery. —ˈ**lecherously** *adv.*

lechery (ˈlɛtʃərɪ) *n., pl.* **-eries.** unrestrained and promiscuous sexuality.

lecithin (ˈlɛsɪθɪn) *n. Biochem.* any of a group of phospholipids that are found in many plant and animal tissues, esp. egg yolk: used in making candles, cosmetics, and inks, and as an emulsifier and stabilizer in foods (**E322**). Systematic name: **phosphatidylcholine.** [C19: from Greek *lekithos* egg yolk]

lecithinase (ləˈsɪθɪˌneɪs) *n.* any of a group of enzymes that remove the fatty-acid residue from lecithins: present in the venom of many snakes.

Leclanché cell (ləˈklɑːnʃeɪ) *n. Electrical engineering.* a primary cell with a carbon anode, surrounded by crushed carbon and manganese dioxide in a porous container, immersed in an electrolyte of aqueous ammonium chloride into which the zinc cathode dips. The common dry battery is a form of Leclanché cell. [C19: named after Georges *Leclanché* (1839–82), French engineer]

lect. *abbrev. for:* **1.** lecture. **2.** lecturer.

lectern (ˈlɛktən) *n.* **1.** a reading desk or support in a church. **2.** any similar desk or support. [C14: from Old French *lettrun,* from Late Latin *lectrum,* ultimately from *legere* to read]

lectin (ˈlɛktɪn) *n.* a type of protein possessing high affinity for a specific sugar; lectins are often highly toxic. [C20: from Latin *lectus,* past participle of *legere* to select + -IN]

lection (ˈlɛkʃən) *n.* a variant reading of a passage in a particular copy or edition of a text. [C16: from Latin *lectio* a reading, from *legere* to read, select]

lectionary (ˈlɛkʃənərɪ) *n., pl.* **-aries.** a book containing readings appointed to be read at divine services. [C15: from Church Latin *lectiōnārium,* from *lectio* LECTION]

lector (ˈlɛktɔː) *n.* **1.** a lecturer or reader in certain universities. **2.** *R.C. Church.* **a.** a person appointed to read lessons at certain services. **b.** (in convents or monastic establishments) a member of the community appointed to read aloud during meals. [C15: from Latin, from *legere* to read] —**lectorate** (ˈlɛktərɪt) *or* ˈ**lectorˌship** *n.*

lecture (ˈlɛktʃə) *n.* **1.** a discourse on a particular subject given or read to an audience. **2.** the text of such a discourse. **3.** a method of teaching by formal discourse. **4.** a lengthy reprimand or scolding. ~*vb.* **5.** to give or read a lecture (to an audience or class). **6.** (*tr.*) to reprimand at length. [C14: from Medieval Latin *lectūra* reading, from *legere* to read]

lecturer (ˈlɛktʃərə) *n.* **1.** a person who lectures. **2.** a teacher in higher education without professorial status.

lectureship (ˈlɛktʃəˌʃɪp) *n.* **1.** the office or position of lecturer. **2.** an endowment financing a series of lectures.

lecythus (ˈlɛsɪθəs) *n., pl.* **-thi** (-θaɪ). (in ancient Greece) a vase with a narrow neck. [from Greek *lēkuthos*]

led (lɛd) *vb.* the past tense and past participle of **lead**[1].

LED *Electronics. abbrev. for* light-emitting diode.

LED display *n.* a flat screen display using light-emitting diodes, used esp. in pocket calculators, digital timepieces, measuring instruments, and in some microcomputers.

lederhosen (ˈleɪdəˌhəʊzᵊn) *pl. n.* leather shorts with H-shaped braces, worn by men in Austria, Bavaria, etc. [German: leather trousers]

ledge (lɛdʒ) *n.* **1.** a narrow horizontal surface resembling a shelf and projecting from a wall, window, etc. **2.** a layer of rock that contains an ore; vein. **3.** a ridge of rock that lies beneath the surface of the sea. **4.** a narrow shelflike rock projection on a cliff or mountain. [C14 *legge,* perhaps from *leggen* to LAY[1]] —ˈ**ledgy** *or* **ledged** *adj.*

ledger (ˈlɛdʒə) *n.* **1.** *Book-keeping.* the principal book in which the commercial transactions of a company are recorded. **2.** a flat horizontal slab of stone. **3.** a horizontal scaffold pole fixed to two upright poles for supporting the outer ends of putlogs. **4.** *Angling.* **a.** a wire trace that allows the weight to rest on the bottom and the bait to float freely. **b.** (*as modifier*): *ledger tackle.* ~*vb.* **5.** (*intr.*) *Angling.* to fish using a ledger. [C15 *legger* book retained in a specific place, probably from *leggen* to LAY[1]]

ledger board *n.* **1.** a timber board forming the top rail of a fence or balustrade. **2.** Also called: **ribbon strip.** a timber board fixed horizontally to studding to support floor joists.

ledger line *n.* **1.** *Music.* a short line placed above or below the staff to accommodate notes representing pitches above or below the staff. **2.** *Angling.* a line using ledger tackle.

lee (liː) *n.* **1.** a sheltered part or side; the side away from the direction from which the wind is blowing. **2. by the lee.** *Nautical.* so that the wind is blowing on the wrong side of the sail. **3. under the lee.** *Nautical.* towards the lee. ~*adj.* **4.** (*prenominal*) *Nautical.* on, at, or towards the side or part away from the wind: *on a lee shore.* Compare **weather** (sense 5). [Old English *hlēow* shelter; related to Old Norse *hle*]

leeboard (ˈliːˌbɔːd) *n. Nautical.* one of a pair of large adjustable paddle-like boards that may be lowered along the lee side to reduce sideways drift or leeway.

leech[1] (liːtʃ) *n.* **1.** any annelid worm of the class *Hirudinea,* which have a sucker at each end of the body and feed on the blood or tissues of other animals. See also **horseleech, medicinal leech. 2.** a person who clings to or preys on another person. **3. a.** an archaic word for **physician. b.** (*in combination*): *leechcraft.* **4. cling like a leech.** to cling or adhere persistently to something. ~*vb.* (*tr.*) **5.** to use leeches to suck the blood of (a person), as a method of medical treatment. **6.** *Archaic.* to cure or heal. [Old English *lǣce, lœce;* related to Middle Dutch *lieke*] —ˈ**leechˌlike** *adj.*

leech[2] *or* **leach** (liːtʃ) *n. Nautical.* the after edge of a fore-and-aft sail or either of the vertical edges of a squaresail. [C15: of Germanic origin; compare Dutch *lijk*]

leek (liːk) *n.* **1.** Also called: **scallion.** an alliaceous plant, *Allium porrum,* with a slender white bulb, cylindrical stem, and broad flat overlapping leaves: used in cooking. **2.** any of several related species, such as *A. ampeloprasum* (wild leek). **3.** a leek, or a representation of one, as a national emblem of Wales. [Old English *lēac;* related to Old Norse *laukr,* Old High German *louh*]

leer (lɪə) *vb.* **1.** (*intr.*) to give an oblique, sneering, or suggestive look or grin. ~*n.* **2.** such a look. [C16: perhaps verbal use of obsolete *leer* cheek, from Old English *hlēor*] —ˈ**leering** *adj., n.* —ˈ**leeringly** *adv.*

leery *or* **leary** (ˈlɪərɪ) *adj.* **leerier, leeriest** *or* **learier, leariest. 1.** *Now chiefly dialect.* knowing or sly. **2.** *Slang.* (foll. by *of*) suspicious or wary. [C18: perhaps from obsolete sense (to look askance) of LEER] —ˈ**leeriness** *or* ˈ**leariness** *n.*

lees (liːz) *pl. n.* the sediment from an alcoholic drink. [C14: plural of obsolete *lee,* from Old French, probably from Celtic; compare Irish *lige* bed]

leet[1] (liːt) *n. English history.* **1.** Also called: **court-leet.** a special kind of manorial court that some lords were entitled to hold. **2.** the jurisdiction of this court. [C15: from Anglo-French, of unknown origin]

leet[2] (liːt) *n. Scot.* a list of candidates for an office. [C15: perhaps from Anglo-French *litte,* variant of LIST[1]]

leeward (ˈliːwəd; *nautical* ˈluːəd) *Chiefly nautical.* ~*adj.* **1.** of, in, or moving to the quarter towards which the wind blows. ~*n.* **2.** the point or quarter towards which the wind blows. **3.** the side towards the lee. ~*adv.* **4.** towards the lee. ~Compare **windward.**

lee wave *n. Meteorol.* a stationary wave sometimes formed in an air stream on the leeward side of a hill or mountain range.

leeway (ˈliːˌweɪ) *n.* **1.** room for free movement within limits, as in action or expenditure. **2.** sideways drift of a boat or aircraft.

left[1] (lɛft) *adj.* **1.** (*usually prenominal*) of or designating the side of something or someone that faces west when the front is turned towards the north. **2.** (*usually prenominal*) worn on a left hand, foot, etc. **3.** (*sometimes cap.*) of or relating to the political or intellectual left. **4.** (*sometimes cap.*) radical or progressive, esp. as compared to less radical or progressive groups, persons, etc. ~*adv.* **5.** on or in the direction of the left. ~*n.* **6.** a left side, direction, position, area, or part. Related adjs.: **sinister, sinistral. 7.** (*often cap.*) the supporters or advocates of varying degrees of social, political, or economic change, reform, or revolution designed to promote the greater freedom, power, welfare, or comfort of the common people. **8. to the left.** radical in the methods, principles, etc., employed in striving to achieve such change. **9.** *Boxing.* **a.** a blow with the left hand. **b.** the left hand. [Old English *left* idle, weak, variant of *lyft-* (in *lyftādl* palsy, literally: left-disease); related to Middle Dutch *lucht* left]

left[2] (lɛft) *vb.* the past tense and past participle of **leave**[1].

left-footer *n. Informal.* (esp. in Ireland) a Roman Catholic. [C20: from the Northern Irish saying that farm workers in Eire use the left foot to push a spade when digging]

left-hand *adj.* (*prenominal*) **1.** of, relating to, located on, or moving towards the left: *this car is left-hand drive; a left-hand bend.* **2.** for use by the left hand; left-handed.

left-handed *adj.* **1.** using the left hand with greater ease than the right. **2.** performed with the left hand. **3.** designed or adapted for use by the left hand. **4.** worn on the left hand. **5.** awkward or clumsy. **6.** ironically ambiguous: *a left-handed compliment.* **7.** turning from right to left; anticlockwise. **8.** *Law.* another term for **morganatic.** ~*adv.* **9.** with the left hand. —ˌ**left-**ˈ**handedly** *adv.* —ˌ**left-**ˈ**handedness** *n.*

left-hander *n.* **1.** a blow with the left hand. **2.** a left-handed person.

leftist (ˈlɛftɪst) *adj.* **1.** of, tending towards, or relating to the political left or its principles. ~*n.* **2.** a person who supports or belongs to the political left. —ˈ**leftism** *n.*

left-luggage office *n. Brit.* a place at a railway station, airport, etc., where luggage may be left for a small charge with an attendant for safekeeping. U.S. and Canadian name: **checkroom.**

leftover (ˈlɛftˌəʊvə) *n.* **1.** (*often pl.*) an unused portion or remnant, as of material or of cooked food. *~adj.* **2.** left as an unused portion or remnant.
leftward (ˈlɛftwəd) *adj.* **1.** on or towards the left. *~adv.* **2.** a variant of **leftwards.**
leftwards (ˈlɛftwədz) *or* **leftward** *adv.* towards or on the left.
left wing *n.* **1.** (*often cap.*) the leftist faction of an assembly, party, group, etc.; the radical or progressive wing. **2.** the units of an army situated on the left of a battle position. **3.** *Sports.* **a.** the left-hand side of the field of play from the point of view of either team facing its opponents' goal. **b.** a player positioned in this area in certain games. *~adj.* **left-wing. 4.** of, belonging to, or relating to the political left wing. —ˌ**left-ˈwinger** *n.*
lefty (ˈlɛftɪ) *n., pl.* **lefties.** *Informal.* **1.** a left-winger. **2.** *Chiefly U.S. and Canadian.* a left-handed person.
leg (lɛg) *n.* **1. a.** either of the two lower limbs, including the bones and fleshy covering of the femur, tibia, fibula, and patella. **b.** (*as modifier*): *leg guard; leg rest.* **2.** any similar or analogous structure in animals that is used for locomotion or support. **3.** this part of an animal, esp. the thigh, used for food: *leg of lamb.* **4.** something similar to a leg in appearance or function, such as one of the four supporting members of a chair. **5.** a branch, limb, or part of a forked or jointed object. **6.** the part of a garment that covers the leg. **7.** a section or part of a journey or course. **8.** a single stage, lap, length, etc., in a relay race. **9.** *Austral. and N.Z.* either one of two races on which a cumulative bet has been placed. **10.** either the opposite or adjacent side of a right-angled triangle. **11.** *Nautical.* **a.** the distance travelled without tacking. **b.** (in yacht racing) the course between any two marks. **12.** one of a series of games, matches, or parts of games. **13.** *Cricket.* **a.** the side of the field to the left of and behind a right-handed batsman as he faces the bowler. **b.** (*as modifier*): *a leg slip; leg stump.* **14. give (someone) a leg up. a.** to help (someone) to climb an obstacle by pushing upwards. **b.** to help (someone) to advance. **15. not have a leg to stand on.** to have no reasonable or logical basis for an opinion or argument. **16. on his, its, etc., last legs.** (of a person or thing) worn out; exhausted. **17. pull (someone's) leg.** *Informal.* to tease, fool, or make fun of (someone). **18. shake a leg.** *Informal.* **a.** to hurry up: usually used in the imperative. **b.** to dance. **19. show a leg.** *Informal.* to get up in the morning. **20. stretch one's legs.** See **stretch** (sense 17). *~vb.* **legs, legging, legged. 21.** (*tr.*) *Obsolete.* to propel (a canal boat) through a tunnel by lying on one's back and walking one's feet along the tunnel roof. **22. leg it.** *Informal.* to walk, run, or hurry. [C13: from Old Norse *leggr,* of obscure origin] —ˈ**legˌlike** *adj.*
leg. *abbrev. for:* **1.** legal. **2.** legate. **3.** legato. **4.** legislation. **5.** legislative. **6.** legislature.
legacy (ˈlɛgəsɪ) *n., pl.* **-cies. 1.** a gift by will, esp. of money or personal property. **2.** something handed down or received from an ancestor or predecessor. [C14 (meaning: office of a legate), C15 (meaning: bequest): from Medieval Latin *lēgātia* commission; see LEGATE]
legal (ˈliːgᵊl) *adj.* **1.** established by or founded upon law; lawful. **2.** of or relating to law. **3.** recognized, enforceable, or having a remedy at law rather than in equity. **4.** relating to or characteristic of the profession of law. [C16: from Latin *lēgālis,* from *lēx* law] —ˈ**legally** *adv.*
legal aid *n.* financial assistance available to persons unable to meet the full cost of legal proceedings.
legal cap *n. U.S.* ruled writing paper, about 8 by 13½ inches with the fold at the top, for use by lawyers.
legalese (ˌliːgəˈliːz) *n.* the conventional language in which legal documents, etc., are written.
legal holiday *n. U.S.* any of several weekdays which are observed as national holidays. Also called (Canadian): **statutory holiday.** Brit. equivalent: **bank holiday.**
legalism (ˈliːgəˌlɪzəm) *n.* strict adherence to the law, esp. the stressing of the letter of the law rather than its spirit. —ˈ**legalist** *n., adj.* —ˌ**legalˈistic** *adj.* —ˌ**legalˈistically** *adv.*
legality (lɪˈgælɪtɪ) *n., pl.* **-ties. 1.** the state or quality of being legal or lawful. **2.** adherence to legal principles.
legalize *or* **legalise** (ˈliːgəˌlaɪz) *vb.* (*tr.*) **1.** to make lawful or legal. **2.** to confirm or validate (something previously unlawful). —ˌ**legaliˈzation** *or* ˌ**legaliˈsation** *n.*
legal medicine *n.* another name for **forensic medicine.**
legal positivism *n.* another name for **positivism** (sense 2).
legal separation *n.* another term (esp. U.S.) for **judicial separation.**
legal tender *n.* currency in specified denominations that a creditor must by law accept in redemption of a debt.
legate (ˈlɛgɪt) *n.* **1.** a messenger, envoy, or delegate. **2.** *R.C. Church.* an emissary to a foreign state representing the Pope. [Old English, via Old French from Latin *lēgātus* deputy, from *lēgāre* to delegate; related to *lēx* law] —ˈ**legateˌship** *n.* —**legatine** (ˈlɛgəˌtaɪn) *adj.*
legatee (ˌlɛgəˈtiː) *n.* a person to whom a legacy is bequeathed. Compare **devisee.**
legation (lɪˈgeɪʃən) *n.* **1.** a diplomatic mission headed by a minister. **2.** the official residence and office of a diplomatic minister. **3.** the act of sending forth a diplomatic envoy. **4.** the mission or business of a diplomatic envoy. **5.** the rank or office of a legate. [C15: from Latin *lēgātiō,* from *lēgātus* LEGATE] —**leˈgationary** *adj.*
legato (lɪˈgɑːtəʊ) *Music.* *~adj., adv.* **1.** to be performed smoothly and connectedly. *~n., pl.* **tos. 2. a.** a style of playing in which no perceptible gaps are left between notes. **b.** (*as modifier*): *a legato passage.* [C19: from Italian, literally: bound]
legator (ˌlɛgəˈtɔː) *n.* a person who gives a legacy or makes a bequest. [C17: from Latin, from *lēgāre* to bequeath; see LEGATE] —ˌ**legaˈtorial** *adj.*
leg before wicket *n. Cricket.* a manner of dismissal on the grounds that a batsman has been struck on the leg by a bowled ball that otherwise would have hit the wicket. Abbrev.: **lbw.**
leg break *n. Cricket.* a bowled ball that spins from leg to off on pitching.
leg bye *n. Cricket.* a run scored after the ball has hit the batsman's leg or some other part of his body, except his hand, without touching the bat. Abbrev.: **lb.**
legend (ˈlɛdʒənd) *n.* **1.** a popular story handed down from earlier times whose truth has not been ascertained. **2.** a group of such stories: *the Arthurian legend.* **3.** a modern story that has taken on the characteristics of a traditional legendary tale. **4.** a person whose fame or notoriety makes him a source of exaggerated or romanticized tales or exploits. **5.** an inscription or title, as on a coin or beneath a coat of arms. **6.** explanatory matter accompanying a table, map, chart, etc. **7. a.** a story of the life of a saint. **b.** a collection of such stories. [C14 (in the sense: a saint's life or a collection of saints' lives): from Medieval Latin *legenda* passages to be read, from Latin *legere* to read] —ˈ**legendry** *n.*
legendary (ˈlɛdʒəndərɪ, -drɪ) *adj.* **1.** of or relating to legend. **2.** celebrated or described in a legend or legends. **3.** very famous or notorious.
legerdemain (ˌlɛdʒədəˈmeɪn) *n.* **1.** another name for **sleight of hand. 2.** cunning deception or trickery. [C15: from Old French: light of hand] —ˌ**legerdeˈmainist** *n.*
leger line (ˈlɛdʒə) *n.* a variant spelling of **ledger line.**
leges (ˈliːdʒiːz) *n.* the plural of **lex.**
legged (ˈlɛgɪd, lɛgd) *adj.* **a.** having a leg or legs. **b.** (*in combination*): *three-legged; long-legged.*
leggings (ˈlɛgɪŋz) *pl. n.* an extra outer covering for the lower legs. —ˈ**legginged** *adj.*
leggy (ˈlɛgɪ) *adj.* **-gier, -giest. 1.** having unusually long legs. **2.** (of a woman) having long and shapely legs. **3.** (of a plant) having an unusually long and weak stem. —ˈ**legginess** *n.*
leghorn (ˈlɛgˌhɔːn) *n.* **1.** a type of Italian wheat straw that is woven into hats. **2.** any hat made from this straw when plaited. [C19: named after *Leghorn* (Livorno), W Italy]
Leghorn (lɛˈgɔːn) *n.* a breed of domestic fowl laying white eggs.
legible (ˈlɛdʒəbᵊl) *adj.* **1.** (of handwriting, print, etc.) able to be read or deciphered. **2.** able to be discovered; discernible. [C14: from Late Latin *legibilis,* from Latin *legere* to read] —ˌ**legiˈbility** *or* ˈ**legibleness** *n.* —ˈ**legibly** *adv.*
legion (ˈliːdʒən) *n.* **1.** a military unit of the ancient Roman army made up of infantry with supporting cavalry, numbering some three to six thousand men. **2.** any large military force: *the French Foreign Legion.* **3.** (*usually cap.*) an association of ex-servicemen: *the British Legion.* **4.** (*often pl.*) any very large number, esp. of people. *~adj.* **5.** (*usually postpositive*) very large or numerous. [C13: from Old French, from Latin *legio,* from *legere* to choose]
legionary (ˈliːdʒənərɪ) *adj.* **1.** of or relating to a legion. *~n., pl.* **-aries. 2.** a soldier belonging to a legion.
legionary ant *n.* another name for the **army ant.**
legionnaire (ˌliːdʒəˈnɛə) *n.* (*often cap.*) a member of certain military forces or associations, such as the French Foreign Legion or the British Legion.
legionnaire's *or* **legionnaires' disease** *n.* a serious, sometimes fatal, infection, caused by the bacterium *Legionella pneumophila,* which has symptoms similar to those of pneumonia: believed to be spread by inhalation of contaminated water vapour from showers and air-conditioning plants. [C20: after the outbreak at a meeting of the American Legion at Philadelphia in 1976]
Legion of Honour *n.* an order for civil or military merit instituted by Napoleon in France in 1802. French name: **Légion d'Honneur** (leʒjɔ̃ dɔnœr).
legis. *abbrev. for:* **1.** legislation. **2.** legislative. **3.** legislature.
legislate (ˈlɛdʒɪsˌleɪt) *vb.* **1.** (*intr.*) to make or pass laws. **2.** (*tr.*) to bring into effect by legislation. [C18: back formation from LEGISLATOR]
legislation (ˌlɛdʒɪsˈleɪʃən) *n.* **1.** the act or process of making laws; enactment. **2.** the laws so made.
legislative (ˈlɛdʒɪslətɪv) *adj.* **1.** of or relating to legislation. **2.** having the power or function of legislating: *a legislative assembly.* **3.** of or relating to a legislature. *~n.* **4.** *Rare.* another word for **legislature.** —ˈ**legislatively** *adv.*
legislative assembly *n.* (*often caps.*) **1.** the bicameral legislature in 28 states of the U.S. **2.** the lower chamber of the bicameral state legislatures in several Commonwealth countries, such as Australia. **3.** the unicameral legislature in most Canadian provinces. **4.** any assembly with legislative powers.
legislative council *n.* (*often caps.*) **1.** the upper chamber of certain bicameral legislatures, such as those of the Indian and Australian states. **2.** the unicameral legislature of certain colo-

nies or dependent territories. **3.** (in the U.S.) a committee composed of members of both chambers of a state legislature, that meets to discuss problems, construct a legislative programme, etc.

legislator ('lɛdʒɪsˌleɪtə) *n.* **1.** a person concerned with the making or enactment of laws. **2.** a member of a legislature. [C17: from Latin *lēgis lātor,* from *lēx* law + *lātor* from *lātus,* past participle of *ferre* to bring] —'**legisˌlatorˌship** *n.* —'**legisˌlatress** *fem. n.*

legislatorial (ˌlɛdʒɪslə'tɔːrɪəl) *adj.* of or relating to a legislator or legislature.

legislature ('lɛdʒɪsˌleɪtʃə) *n.* a body of persons vested with power to make, amend, and repeal laws. Compare **executive, judiciary.**

legist ('liːdʒɪst) *n.* a person versed in the law. [C15: from Medieval Latin *lēgista,* from *lēx* law]

legit (lɪ'dʒɪt) *Slang.* ~*adj.* **1.** short for **legitimate.** ~*n.* **2.** legitimate or professionally respectable drama.

legitimate *adj.* (lɪ'dʒɪtɪmɪt). **1.** born in lawful wedlock; enjoying full filial rights. **2.** conforming to established standards of usage, behaviour, etc. **3.** based on correct or acceptable principles of reasoning. **4.** reasonable, sensible, or valid: *a legitimate question.* **5.** authorized, sanctioned by, or in accordance with law. **6.** of, relating to, or ruling by hereditary right: *a legitimate monarch.* **7.** of or relating to a body of famous long-established plays as distinct from films, television, vaudeville, etc.: *the legitimate theatre.* ~*vb.* (lɪ'dʒɪtɪˌmeɪt). **8.** (*tr.*) to make, pronounce, or show to be legitimate. [C15: from Medieval Latin *lēgitimātus* made legal, from *lēx* law] —**le'gitimacy** *or* **le'gitimateness** *n.* —**le'gitimately** *adv.* —**leˌgiti'mation** *n.*

legitimatize, legitimatise (lɪ'dʒɪtɪməˌtaɪz) *or* **legitimize, legitimise** (lɪ'dʒɪtɪˌmaɪz) *vb.* (*tr.*) to make legitimate; legalize. —**leˌgitimati'zation, leˌgitimati'sation** *or* **leˌgitimi'zation, leˌgitimi'sation** *n.*

legitimist (lɪ'dʒɪtɪmɪst) *n.* **1.** a monarchist who supports the rule of a legitimate dynasty or of its senior branch. **2.** (formerly) a supporter of the elder line of the Bourbon family in France. **3.** a supporter of legitimate authority. ~*adj. also* **legitimistic. 4.** of or relating to legitimists. —**le'gitimism** *n.*

legless ('lɛglɪs) *adj.* **1.** without legs. **2.** *Informal.* very drunk.

legman ('lɛgmən) *n., pl.* **-men.** *Chiefly U.S. and Canadian.* **1.** a newsman who reports on news stories from the scene of action or original source. **2.** a person employed to run errands, collect information, etc., outside an office.

Lego ('lɛgəʊ) *n. Trademark.* a construction toy consisting of plastic bricks and other standardized components that fit together with studs. [C20: from Danish *leg godt* play well]

leg-of-mutton *or* **leg-o'-mutton** *n.* (*modifier*) (of a sail, sleeve, etc.) tapering sharply or having a triangular profile.

leg-pull *n. Brit. informal.* a practical joke or mild deception.

legroom ('lɛgˌruːm) *n.* room to move one's legs comfortably, as in a car.

leg rope *n. Austral. and N.Z.* **1.** a rope used to secure an animal by its hind leg. ~*vb.* **leg-rope.** (*tr.*) **2** to restrain (an animal) by a leg rope.

leguan ('lɛgjʊən, 'lɛgʊˌɑːn) *n. S. African.* a large amphibious monitor lizard of the genus *Varanus,* esp. *V. niloticus* (the **water leguan**), which can grow up to 2 or 3 m. Also called: **iguana.** [from Afrikaans *likkewaan*]

legume ('lɛgjuːm, lɪ'gjuːm) *n.* **1.** the long dry dehiscent fruit produced by leguminous plants; a pod. **2.** any table vegetable of the superfamily *Leguminosae,* esp. beans or peas. **3.** any leguminous plant. [C17: from French *légume,* from Latin *legūmen* bean, from *legere* to pick (a crop)]

legumin (lɪ'gjuːmɪn) *n.* a protein obtained mainly from the seeds of leguminous plants. [C19: from LEGUME]

leguminous (lɪ'gjuːmɪnəs) *adj.* of, relating to, or belonging to the *Leguminosae* (or *Fabaceae*), a superfamily of flowering plants having pods (or legumes) as fruits and root nodules enabling storage of nitrogen-rich material: includes mimosaceous, caesalpiniaceous, and papilionaceous plants. [C17: from Latin *legūmen;* see LEGUME]

legwarmer ('lɛgˌwɔːmə) *n.* one of a pair of garments resembling stockings without feet, usually knitted and brightly coloured, often worn over jeans, tights, etc. or during exercise.

legwork ('lɛgˌwɜːk) *n. Informal.* work that involves travelling on foot or as if on foot.

lehaim (lə'xɑjim) *interj., n.* a variant spelling of **lechaim.**

lehr (lɪə) *n.* a long tunnel-shaped oven used for annealing glass. [from German: pattern, model]

lei[1] (leɪ) *n.* (in Hawaii) a garland of flowers, worn around the neck. [from Hawaiian]

lei[2] (leɪ) *n.* the plural of **leu.**

Leibnitz's law ('laɪbnɪtsɪz) *n. Logic, philosophy.* **1.** the principle that two expressions satisfy exactly the same predicates if and only if they both refer to the same subject. **2.** the weaker principle that if a=b whatever is true of a is true of b. [named after Gottfried Wilhelm von *Leibnitz* (1646–1716), German philosopher and mathematician]

Leicester ('lɛstə) *n.* **1.** a breed of sheep with long wool, originally from Leicestershire, a county in central England. **2.** a fairly mild dark orange whole-milk cheese, similar to Cheddar but looser and more moist.

Leics *abbrev. for* Leicestershire.

leishmania (liːʃ'meɪnɪə) *n.* any parasitic flagellate protozoan of the genus *Leishmania:* occurs in man and animals and causes certain skin diseases. [C20: New Latin, named after Sir W.B. *Leishman* (1865–1926), Scottish bacteriologist]

leishmaniasis (ˌliːʃmə'naɪəsɪs) *or* **leishmaniosis** (liːʃˌmeɪnɪ'əʊsɪs, -ˌmæn-) *n.* any disease, such as kala-azar, caused by protozoa of the genus *Leishmania.*

leister ('liːstə) *n.* **1.** a spear with three or more prongs for spearing fish, esp. salmon. ~*vb.* **2.** (*tr.*) to spear (a fish) with a leister. [C16: from Scandinavian; related to Old Norse *ljōstr,* from *ljōsta* to stab]

leisure ('lɛʒə; *U.S. also* 'liːʒər) *n.* **1. a.** time or opportunity for ease, relaxation, etc. **b.** (*as modifier*): *leisure activities.* **2.** ease or leisureliness. **3. at leisure. a.** having free time for ease, relaxation, etc. **b.** not occupied or engaged. **c.** without hurrying. **4. at one's leisure.** when one has free time. [C14: from Old French *leisir;* ultimately from Latin *licēre* to be allowed]

leisure centre *n.* a building designed to provide facilities for a range of leisure pursuits, such as a library, sports hall, café, and rooms for meetings.

leisured ('lɛʒəd) *adj.* **1.** (*usually prenominal*) having much leisure, as through unearned wealth: *the leisured classes.* **2.** unhurried or relaxed: *in a leisured manner.*

leisurely ('lɛʒəlɪ) *adj.* **1.** unhurried; relaxed. ~*adv.* **2.** without haste; in a relaxed way. —'**leisureliness** *n.*

leitmotiv *or* **leitmotif** ('laɪtməʊˌtiːf) *n.* **1.** *Music.* a recurring short melodic phrase or theme used, esp. in Wagnerian music dramas, to suggest a character, thing, etc. **2.** an often repeated word, phrase, image, or theme in a literary work. [C19: from German: leading motif]

lek[1] (lɛk) *n.* **1.** a small area in which birds of certain species, notably the black grouse, gather for sexual display and courtship. **2.** the act or practice of so gathering. [C19: perhaps from dialect *lake* (vb.) from Old English *lácan* to frolic, fight, or perhaps from Swedish *leka* to play]

lek[2] (lɛk) *n.* the standard monetary unit of Albania, divided into 100 qintars. [from Albanian]

lekker ('lɛkə) *adj. S. African slang.* pleasing, enjoyable, or likeable. [from Afrikaans, from Dutch]

LEM (lɛm) *n. acronym for* lunar excursion module.

leman ('lɛmən, 'liː-) *n. Archaic.* **1.** a beloved; sweetheart. **2.** a lover or mistress. [C13 *lemman, leofman,* from *leof* dear, LIEF + MAN]

lemma[1] ('lɛmə) *n., pl.* **-mas** *or* **-mata** (-mətə). **1.** a subsidiary proposition, assumed to be valid, that is used in the proof of another proposition. **2.** *Linguistics.* a word considered as its citation form together with all the inflected forms. For example, the lemma *go* consists of *go* together with *goes, going, went,* and *gone.* **3.** an argument or theme, esp. when used as the subject or title of a composition. [C16 (meaning: proposition), C17 (meaning: title, theme): via Latin from Greek: premise, from *lambanein* to take (for granted)]

lemma[2] ('lɛmə) *n., pl.* **-mas** *or* **-mata** (-mətə). the outer of two bracts surrounding each floret of a grass inflorescence. [C19: from Greek: rind, from *lepein* to peel]

lemmatize *or* **lemmatise** ('lɛməˌtaɪz) *vb.* (*tr.*) *Linguistics.* to group together the inflected forms of (a word) for analysis as a single item. —ˌ**lemmati'zation** *or* ˌ**lemmati'sation** *n.*

lemming ('lɛmɪŋ) *n.* **1.** any of various volelike rodents of the genus *Lemmus* and related genera, of northern and arctic regions of Europe, Asia, and North America: family *Cricetidae.* The Scandinavian variety, *Lemmus lemmus,* migrates periodically when its population reaches a peak. **2.** a member of any large group following an unthinking course towards mass destruction. [C17: from Norwegian; related to Latin *latrāre* to bark] —'**lemming-ˌlike** *adj.*

lemniscate ('lɛmnɪskɪt) *n.* a closed plane curve consisting of two symmetrical loops meeting at a node. Equation: $(x^2 + y^2)^2 = a^2(x^2 - y^2)$, where a is the greatest distance from the curve to the origin. The symbol for infinity (∞) is an example.

lemniscus (lɛm'nɪskəs) *n., pl.* **-nisci** (-'nɪsaɪ, -'nɪskiː). *Anatomy.* a technical name for **fillet** (sense 9). [C19: New Latin, from Latin, from Greek *lēmniskos* ribbon]

lemon ('lɛmən) *n.* **1.** a small Asian evergreen tree, *Citrus limon,* widely cultivated in warm and tropical regions, having pale green glossy leaves and edible fruits. Related adjs.: **citric, citrine, citrous. 2. a.** the yellow oval fruit of this tree, having juicy acidic flesh rich in vitamin C. **b.** (*as modifier*): *a lemon jelly.* **3.** Also called: **lemon yellow. a.** a greenish-yellow or strong yellow colour. **b.** (*as adj.*): *lemon wallpaper.* **4.** a distinctive tart flavour made from or in imitation of the lemon. **5.** *Slang.* a person or thing considered to be useless or defective. [C14: from Medieval Latin *lemōn-,* from Arabic *laymūn*] —'**lemonish** *adj.* —'**lemon-ˌlike** *adj.*

lemonade (ˌlɛmə'neɪd) *n.* a drink made from lemon juice, sugar, and water or from carbonated water, citric acid, etc.

lemon balm *n.* the full name of **balm** (sense 5).

lemon cheese *or* **curd** *n.* a soft paste made from lemons, sugar, eggs, and butter, used as a spread or filling.

lemon drop *n.* a lemon-flavoured boiled sweet.

lemon fish *n.* another name for **cobia.**

lemon geranium *n.* a cultivated geraniaceous plant, *Pelargonium limoneum,* with lemon-scented leaves.

lemon grass *n.* a perennial grass, *Cymbopogon citratus,* with a large flower spike: grown in tropical regions as the source of an aromatic oil (**lemon grass oil**).

lemon sole *n.* a European flatfish, *Microstomus kitt,* with a variegated brown body: highly valued as a food fish: family *Pleuronectidae.*

lemon squash *n. Brit.* a drink made from a sweetened lemon concentrate and water.

lemon squeezer *n.* **1.** any of various devices for extracting the juice from citrus fruit. **2.** *N.Z. informal.* a peaked hat with four indentations worn by the army on ceremonial occasions.

lemon verbena *n.* a tropical American verbenaceous shrub, *Lippia citriodora,* with slender lemon-scented leaves yielding an oil used in perfumery.

lemonwood ('lɛmən,wʊd) *n.* a small tree, *Pittosporum eugenioides,* of New Zealand having a white bark and lemon-scented flowers.

lemony ('lɛmənɪ) *adj.* **1.** having or resembling the taste or colour of a lemon. **2.** *Austral. slang.* angry or irritable.

lempira (lɛm'pɪərə) *n.* the standard monetary unit of Honduras, divided into 100 centavos. [American Spanish, after *Lempira,* Indian chief who opposed the Spanish]

lemur ('liːmə) *n.* **1.** any Madagascan prosimian primate of the family *Lemuridae,* such as *Lemur catta* (the **ring-tailed lemur**). They are typically arboreal, having foxy faces and long tails. **2.** any similar or closely related animal, such as a loris or indris. [C18: New Latin, adapted from Latin *lemurēs* ghosts; so named by Linnaeus for its ghost-like face and nocturnal habits] —'**lemur,like** *adj.*

lemuroid ('lɛmjʊ,rɔɪd) *or* **lemurine** ('lɛmjʊ,raɪn, -rɪn) *adj.* **1.** of, relating to, or belonging to the superfamily *Lemuroidea,* which includes the lemurs and indrises. **2.** resembling or closely related to a lemur. ~*n.* **3.** an animal that resembles or is closely related to a lemur.

lend (lɛnd) *vb.* **lends, lending, lent** (lɛnt). **1.** (*tr.*) to permit the use of (something) with the expectation of return of the same or an equivalent. **2.** to provide (money) temporarily, often at interest. **3.** (*intr.*) to provide loans, esp. as a profession. **4.** (*tr.*) to impart or contribute (something, esp. some abstract quality): *her presence lent beauty.* **5.** (*tr.*) to provide, esp. in order to assist or support: *he lent his skill to the company.* **6. lend an ear.** to listen. **7. lend itself.** to possess the right characteristics or qualities for: *the novel lends itself to serialization.* **8. lend oneself.** to give support, cooperation, etc. [C15 *lende* (originally the past tense), from Old English *lǣnan,* from *lǣn* LOAN[1]; related to Icelandic *lāna,* Old High German *lēhanōn*] —'**lender** *n.*

▷**Usage.** Although the use of *loan* as a verb equivalent to *lend* is widespread, it is avoided by careful speakers and writers except when referring to the formal lending of money: *the bank loaned him the money.*

lending library *n.* **1.** Also called (esp. U.S.): **circulating library.** the department of a public library providing books for use outside the building. **2.** a small commercial library.

lend-lease *n.* (during World War II) the system organized by the U.S. in 1941 by which equipment and services were provided for countries fighting Germany.

length (lɛŋkθ, lɛŋθ) *n.* **1.** the linear extent or measurement of something from end to end, usually being the longest dimension or, for something fixed, the longest horizontal dimension. **2.** the extent of something from beginning to end, measured in some more or less regular units or intervals: *the book was 600 pages in length.* **3.** a specified distance, esp. between two positions or locations: *the length of a race.* **4.** a period of time, as between specified limits or moments. **5.** something of a specified, average, or known size or extent measured in one dimension, often used as a unit of measurement: *a length of cloth.* **6.** a piece or section of something narrow and long: *a length of tubing.* **7.** the quality, state, or fact of being long rather than short. **8.** (*usually pl.*) the amount of trouble taken in pursuing or achieving something (esp. in the phrase **to great lengths**). **9.** (*often pl.*) the extreme or limit of action (in phrases such as **to any length(s), to what length(s) would someone go,** etc.). **10.** *Prosody, phonetics.* the metrical quantity or temporal duration of a vowel or syllable. **11.** the distance from one end of a rectangular swimming bath to the other. Compare **width** (sense 4). **12.** *Prosody.* the quality of a vowel, whether stressed or unstressed, that distinguishes it from another vowel of similar articulatory characteristics. Thus (iː) in English *beat* is of greater length than (ɪ) in English *bit.* **13.** *Cricket.* the distance from the batsman at which the ball pitches. **14.** *Bridge.* a holding of four or more cards in a suit. **15. at length. a.** in depth; fully. **b.** eventually. **c.** for a long time; interminably. [Old English *lengthu;* related to Middle Dutch *lengede,* Old Norse *lengd*]

lengthen ('lɛŋkθən, 'lɛŋθən) *vb.* to make or become longer. —'**lengthener** *n.*

lengthman ('lɛŋkθmən, 'lɛŋθ-) *n., pl.* **-men.** *Brit.* a person whose job it is to maintain a particular length of road or railway line.

lengthways ('lɛŋkθ,weɪz, 'lɛŋθ-) *or* **lengthwise** *adv., adj.* in, according to, or along the direction of length.

lengthy ('lɛŋkθɪ, 'lɛŋθɪ) *adj.* **lengthier, lengthiest.** of relatively great or tiresome extent or duration. —'**lengthily** *adv.* —'**lengthiness** *n.*

lenient ('liːnɪənt) *adj.* **1.** showing or characterized by mercy or tolerance. **2.** *Archaic.* caressing or soothing. [C17: from Latin *lēnīre* to soothe, from *lēnis* soft] —'**leniency** *or* '**lenience** *n.* —'**leniently** *adv.*

Leninism ('lɛnɪ,nɪzəm) *n.* **1.** the political and economic theories developed by Vladimir Ilyich Lenin (1870–1924), Russian statesman and Marxist theoretician. **2.** another name for **Marxism-Leninism.** —'**Leninist** *or* '**Leninite** *n., adj.*

lenis ('liːnɪs) *Phonetics.* ~*adj.* **1.** (of a consonant) articulated with weak muscular tension. ~*n., pl.* **lenes** ('liːniːz). **2.** a consonant, such as English *b* or *v,* pronounced with weak muscular force. ~Compare **fortis.** [C19: from Latin: gentle]

lenitive ('lɛnɪtɪv) *adj.* **1.** soothing or alleviating pain or distress. ~*n.* **2.** a lenitive drug. [C16: from Medieval Latin *lēnītīvus,* from Latin *lēnīre* to soothe]

lenity ('lɛnɪtɪ) *n., pl.* **-ties.** the state or quality of being lenient. [C16: from Latin *lēnitās* gentleness, from *lēnis* soft]

leno ('liːnəʊ) *n., pl.* **-nos.** **1.** (in textiles) a weave in which the warp yarns are twisted together in pairs between the weft or filling yarns. **2.** a fabric of this weave. [C19: probably from French *linon* lawn, from *lin* flax, from Latin *līnum.* See LINEN]

lens (lɛnz) *n.* **1.** a piece of glass or other transparent material, used to converge or diverge transmitted light and form optical images. **2.** Also called: **compound lens.** a combination of such lenses for forming images or concentrating a beam of light. **3.** a device that diverges or converges a beam of electromagnetic radiation, sound, or particles. See **electron lens.** **4.** *Anatomy.* See **crystalline lens.** [C17: from Latin *lēns* lentil, referring to the similarity of a lens to the shape of a lentil]

lens hood *n. Photog.* an extension piece fixed to a camera lens to shield it from a direct light source.

lent (lɛnt) *vb.* the past tense and past participle of **lend.**

Lent (lɛnt) *n.* **1.** *Christianity.* the period of forty weekdays lasting from Ash Wednesday to Holy Saturday, observed as a time of penance and fasting commemorating Jesus' fasting in the wilderness. **2.** (*modifier*) falling within or associated with the season before Easter: *Lent observance.* **3.** (*pl.*) (at Cambridge University) Lent term boat races. [Old English *lencten, lengten* spring, literally: lengthening (of hours of daylight)]

lentamente (,lɛntə'mɛntɪ) *adv. Music.* to be played slowly. [C18: Italian, from LENTO]

lenten ('lɛntən) *adj.* **1.** (*often cap.*) of or relating to Lent. **2.** *Archaic or literary.* spare, plain, or meagre: *lenten fare.* **3.** *Archaic.* cold, austere, or sombre: *a lenten lover.*

lentic ('lɛntɪk) *adj. Ecology.* of, relating to, or inhabiting still water: *a lentic fauna.* Compare **lotic.** [C20: from Latin *lentus* slow]

lenticel ('lɛntɪ,sɛl) *n.* any of numerous pores in the stem of a woody plant allowing exchange of gases between the plant and the exterior. [C19: from New Latin *lenticella,* from Latin *lenticula* diminutive of *lēns* LENTIL] —**lenticellate** (,lɛntɪ'sɛlɪt) *adj.*

lenticle ('lɛntɪkᵊl) *n. Geology.* a lens-shaped layer of mineral or rock embedded in a matrix of different constitution.

lenticular (lɛn'tɪkjʊlə) *or* **lentiform** ('lɛntɪ,fɔːm) *adj.* **1.** Also: **lentoid** ('lɛntɔɪd). shaped like a biconvex lens. **2.** of or concerned with a lens or lenses. **3.** shaped like a lentil seed. [C17: from Latin *lenticulāris* like a LENTIL]

lentigo (lɛn'taɪgəʊ) *n., pl.* **lentigines** (lɛn'tɪdʒɪ,niːz). a technical name for a **freckle.** [C14: from Latin, from *lēns* LENTIL] —**len'tiginous** *or* **len'tiginose** *adj.*

lentil ('lɛntɪl) *n.* **1.** a small annual leguminous plant, *Lens culinaris,* of the Mediterranean region and W Asia, having edible brownish convex seeds. **2.** any of the seeds of this plant, which are cooked and eaten as a vegetable, in soups, etc. [C13: from Old French *lentille,* from Latin *lenticula,* diminutive of *lēns* lentil]

lentissimo (lɛn'tɪsɪ,məʊ) *adj., adv. Music.* to be played very slowly. [Italian, superlative of *lento* slow]

lentivirus ('lɛntɪ,vaɪrəs) *n.* any of a group of slowly acting viruses, often affecting the nervous system. [C20: from Latin *lentus* slow + VIRUS]

lent lily *n.* another name for the **daffodil.**

lento ('lɛntəʊ) *Music.* ~*adj., adv.* **1.** to be performed slowly. ~*n., pl.* **-tos.** **2.** a movement or passage performed in this way. [C18: Italian, from Latin *lentus* slow]

Lent term *n.* the spring term at Cambridge University and some other educational establishments.

Lenz's law ('lɛntsɪz) *n. Physics.* the principle that the direction of the current induced in a circuit by a changing magnetic field is such that the magnetic field produced by this current will oppose the original field. [C19: named after H. F. E. *Lenz* (1804–65), German physicist]

Leo[1] ('liːəʊ) *n.* a name for a lion, used in children's tales, fables, etc. [from Latin: lion]

Leo[2] ('liːəʊ) *n., Latin genitive* **Leonis** (liː'əʊnɪs). **1.** *Astronomy.* a zodiacal constellation in the N hemisphere, lying between Cancer and Virgo on the ecliptic, that contains the star Regulus and the radiant of the Leonid meteor shower. **2.** *Astrology.* **a.** Also called: the **Lion.** the fifth sign of the zodiac, symbol ♌, having a fixed fire classification and ruled by the sun. The sun is in this sign between about July 23 and Aug. 22. **b.** a person born during a period when the sun is in this sign. ~*adj.* **3.** *Astrology.* born under or characteristic of Leo. ~Also (for senses 2b, 3): **Leonian** (liːˈəʊnɪən).

Leo Minor *n.* a small faint constellation in the N hemisphere lying near Leo and Ursa Major.

Leonardesque (ˌliːənɑːˈdɛsk) *adj.* of, relating to, or characteristic of the works or artistic style of Leonardo da Vinci (1452–1519), Italian painter, sculptor, architect, and engineer.

leone (liːˈəʊnɪ) *n.* the standard monetary unit of Sierra Leone, divided into 100 cents. [C20: from *Sierra Leone*]

leonine (ˈliːəˌnaɪn) *adj.* of, characteristic of, or resembling a lion. [C14: from Latin *leōnīnus,* from *leō* lion]

Leonine (ˈliːəˌnaɪn) *adj.* **1.** connected with one of the popes called Leo, esp. applied to certain prayers in the Mass prescribed by Leo XIII (1810–1903). ~*n.* **2.** Also called: **Leonine verse. a.** a type of medieval hexameter or elegiac verse having internal rhyme. **b.** a type of English verse with internal rhyme.

leontopodium (lɪˌɒntəˈpəʊdɪəm) *n.* any plant of the Eurasian alpine genus *Leontopodium,* esp. *L. alpinum.* See **edelweiss.** [New Latin, from Greek *leōn* lion + *podion,* diminutive of *pous* foot (from the shape of the flowers)]

leopard (ˈlɛpəd) *n.* **1.** Also called: **panther.** a large feline mammal, *Panthera pardus,* of forests of Africa and Asia, usually having a tawny yellow coat with black rosette-like spots. **2.** any of several similar felines, such as the snow leopard and cheetah. **3. clouded leopard.** a feline, *Neofelis nebulosa,* of SE Asia and Indonesia with a yellowish-brown coat marked with darker spots and blotches. **4.** *Heraldry.* a stylized leopard, painted as a lion with the face turned towards the front. **5.** the pelt of a leopard. [C13: from Old French *lepart,* from Late Latin *leōpardus,* from Late Greek *leópardos,* from *leōn* lion + *pardos* PARD[2] (the leopard was thought to be the result of cross-breeding)] —ˈ**leopardess** *fem. n.*

leopard lily *n.* a North American lily plant, *Lilium pardalinum,* cultivated for its large orange-red flowers, with brown-spotted petals and long stamens.

leopard moth *n.* a nocturnal European moth, *Zeuzera pyrina,* having white wings and body, both marked with black spots: family *Cossidae.*

leopard's-bane *n.* any of several Eurasian perennial plants of the genus *Doronicum,* esp. *D. plantagineum,* having clusters of yellow flowers: family *Compositae* (composites).

leotard (ˈlɪəˌtɑːd) *n.* a tight-fitting garment covering the body from the shoulders down to the thighs and worn by acrobats, ballet dancers, etc. [C19: named after Jules *Léotard,* French acrobat]

Lepcha (ˈlɛptʃə) *n.* **1.** (*pl.* **-cha** *or* **-chas**) a member of a Mongoloid people of Sikkim. **2.** the language of this people, belonging to the Tibeto-Burman branch of the Sino-Tibetan family. ~*adj.* **3.** of or relating to this people or their language.

leper (ˈlɛpə) *n.* **1.** a person who has leprosy. **2.** a person who is ignored or despised. [C14: via Late Latin from Greek *lepra,* noun use of *lepros* scaly, from *lepein* to peel]

lepido- *or before a vowel* **lepid-** *combining form.* scale or scaly: *lepidopterous.* [from Greek *lepis* scale; see LEPER]

lepidolite (lɪˈpɪdəˌlaɪt, ˈlɛpɪdəˌlaɪt) *n.* a lilac, pink, or greyish mica consisting of a hydrous silicate of lithium, potassium, aluminium, and fluorine, containing rubidium as an impurity: a source of lithium and rubidium. Formula: $K_2Li_3Al_4Si_7O_{21}(OH,F)_3$.

lepidopteran (ˌlɛpɪˈdɒptərən) *n., pl.* **-terans** *or* **-tera** (-tərə), *also* **lepidopteron. 1.** any of numerous insects of the order *Lepidoptera,* typically having two pairs of wings covered with fragile scales, mouthparts specialized as a suctorial proboscis, and caterpillars as larvae: comprises the butterflies and moths. ~*adj. also* **lepidopterous. 2.** of, relating to, or belonging to the order *Lepidoptera.* [C19: from New Latin *lepidoptera,* from LEPIDO- + Greek *pteron* wing]

lepidopterist (ˌlɛpɪˈdɒptərɪst) *n.* a person who studies or collects moths and butterflies.

lepidosiren (ˌlɛpɪdəʊˈsaɪərən) *n.* a South American lungfish, *Lepidosiren paradoxa,* having an eel-shaped body and whiplike paired fins.

lepidote (ˈlɛpɪˌdəʊt) *adj. Biology.* covered with scaly leaves or spots. [C19: via New Latin *lepidōtus,* from Greek, from *lepis* scale]

leporid (ˈlɛpərɪd) *adj.* **1.** of, relating to, or belonging to the *Leporidae,* a family of lagomorph mammals having long ears and limbs and a short tail: includes rabbits and hares. ~*n.* **2.** any animal belonging to the family *Leporidae.* [C19: from Latin *lepus* hare]

leporine (ˈlɛpəˌraɪn) *adj.* of, relating to, or resembling a hare. [C17: from Latin *leporīnus,* from *lepus* hare]

LEPRA (ˈlɛprə) *n. acronym for* Leprosy Relief Association.

leprechaun (ˈlɛprəˌkɔːn) *n.* (in Irish folklore) a mischievous elf, often believed to have a treasure hoard. [C17: from Irish Gaelic *leipreachān,* from Middle Irish *lūchorpān,* from *lū* small + *corp* body, from Latin *corpus* body]

leprosarium (ˌlɛprəˈsɛərɪəm) *n., pl.* **-ia** (-ɪə). a hospital or other centre for the treatment or care of lepers. [C20: from Medieval Latin: see LEPER]

leprose (ˈlɛprəʊs, -rəʊz) *adj. Biology.* having or denoting a whitish scurfy surface.

leprosy (ˈlɛprəsɪ) *n. Pathol.* a chronic infectious disease occurring mainly in tropical and subtropical regions, characterized by the formation of painful inflamed nodules beneath the skin and disfigurement and wasting of affected parts, caused by the bacillus *Mycobacterium leprae.* Also called: **Hansen's disease.** [C16: from LEPROUS + -Y[3]]

leprous (ˈlɛprəs) *adj.* **1.** having leprosy. **2.** relating to or resembling leprosy. **3.** *Biology.* a less common word for **leprose.** [C13: from Old French, from Late Latin *leprosus,* from *lepra* LEPER] —ˈ**leprously** *adv.* —ˈ**leprousness** *n.*

-lepsy *or sometimes* **-lepsia** *n. combining form.* indicating a seizure or attack: *catalepsy.* [from New Latin *-lepsia,* from Greek, from *lēpsis* a seizure, from *lambanein* to seize] —**-leptic** *adj. combining form.*

lepto- *or before a vowel* **lept-** *combining form.* fine, slender, or slight: *leptosome.* [from Greek *leptos* thin, literally: peeled, from *lepein* to peel]

leptocephalic (ˌlɛptəʊsɪˈfælɪk) *or* **leptocephalous** (ˌlɛptəʊˈsɛfələs) *adj.* having a narrow skull.

leptocephalus (ˌlɛptəʊˈsɛfələs) *n., pl.* **-li** (-ˌlaɪ). the slender transparent oceanic larva of eels of the genus *Anguilla* that migrates from its hatching ground near the West Indies to European freshwater habitats.

leptocercal (ˌlɛptəʊˈsɜːkəl) *adj. Zoology.* having a long thin tail. [from LEPTO- + Greek *kerkos* tail]

leptodactylous (ˌlɛptəʊˈdæktɪləs) *adj. Zoology.* having slender digits.

leptokurtic (ˌlɛptəʊˈkɜːtɪk) *adj. Statistics.* (of a distribution) having kurtosis B_2 greater than 3, more heavily concentrated about the mean than a normal distribution. Compare **platykurtic, mesokurtic.** [C20: from LEPTO- + Greek *kurtos* arched, bulging + -IC]

lepton[1] (ˈlɛptɒn) *n., pl.* **-ta** (-tə). **1.** a Greek monetary unit worth one hundredth of a drachma. **2.** a small coin of ancient Greece. [from Greek *lepton* (*nomisma*) small (coin)]

lepton[2] (ˈlɛptɒn) *n. Physics.* any of a group of elementary particles and their antiparticles, such as an electron, muon, or neutrino, that participate in electromagnetic and weak interactions and have a half-integral spin. [C20: from LEPTO- + -ON] —**lep**ˈ**tonic** *adj.*

lepton number *n. Physics.* a quantum number describing the behaviour of elementary particles, equal to the number of leptons present minus the number of antileptons. It is thought to be conserved in all processes. Symbol: **l**

leptophyllous (ˌlɛptəʊˈfɪləs) *adj.* (of plants) having long slender leaves.

leptorrhine (ˈlɛptərɪn) *adj.* another word for **catarrhine** (sense 2).

leptosome (ˈlɛptəˌsəʊm) *n.* a person with a small bodily frame and a slender physique. —ˌ**lepto**ˈ**somic** *or* **leptosomatic** (ˌlɛptəʊsəˈmætɪk) *adj.*

leptospirosis (ˌlɛptəʊspaɪˈrəʊsɪs) *n.* any of several infectious diseases caused by spirochaete bacteria of the genus *Leptospira,* transmitted to man by animals and characterized by jaundice, meningitis, and kidney failure. Also called: **Weil's disease.** [C20: from New Latin *Leptospira* (LEPTO- + Greek *speira* coil + -OSIS)]

leptotene (ˈlɛptəʊˌtiːn) *n.* the first stage of the prophase of meiosis during which the nuclear material becomes resolved into slender single-stranded chromosomes. [C20: from LEPTO- + *-tene,* from Greek *tainia* band, filament]

Lepus (ˈlɛpəs, ˈliː-) *n., Latin genitive* **Leporis** (ˈlɛpərɪs). a small constellation in the S hemisphere lying between Orion and Columba. [New Latin, from Latin: hare]

lequear (ləˈkwɪə) *n.* another name for **lacunar** (sense 1).

lesbian (ˈlɛzbɪən) *n.* **1.** a female homosexual. ~*adj.* **2.** of or characteristic of lesbians. [C19: from the homosexuality attributed to Sappho; see LESBIAN] —ˈ**lesbianism** *n.*

Lesbian (ˈlɛzbɪən) *n.* **1.** a native or inhabitant of Lesbos, an island in the E Aegean. **2.** the Aeolic dialect of Ancient Greek spoken in Lesbos. ~*adj.* **3.** of or relating to Lesbos. **4.** of or relating to the poetry of Lesbos, esp. that of the lyric poetess Sappho.

lese-majesty (ˈliːzˈmædʒɪstɪ) *n.* **1.** any of various offences committed against the sovereign power in a state; treason. **2.** an attack on authority or position. [C16: from French *lèse majesté,* from Latin *laesa mājestās* wounded majesty]

lesion (ˈliːʒən) *n.* **1.** any structural change in a bodily part resulting from injury or disease. **2.** an injury or wound. [C15: via Old French from Late Latin *laesiō* injury, from Latin *laedere* to hurt]

less (lɛs) *determiner.* **1. a.** the comparative of **little** (sense 1): *less sugar; less spirit than before.* **b.** (*as pronoun; functioning as sing. or pl.*): *she has less than she needs; the less you eat, the less you want.* **2.** (usually preceded by *no*) lower in rank or importance: *no less a man than the president; St. James the Less.* **3. no less.** *Informal.* used to indicate surprise or admiration, often sarcastic, at the preceding statement: *she says she's been to Italy, no less.* **4. less of.** to a smaller extent or degree: *we see less of John these days; less of a success than I'd hoped.* ~*adv.* **5.** the comparative of *a little: she walks less than she should; less quickly; less beautiful.* **6. much** *or* **still less.** used to reinforce a negative: *we don't like it, still less enjoy it.* **7. think less of.** to have a lower opinion of. ~*prep.* **8.** subtracting; minus: *three weeks less a day.* [Old English *lǣssa* (adj.), *lǣs* (adv., n.)]

▷**Usage.** *Less* should not be confused with *fewer*. *Less* refers strictly only to quantity and not to number: *there is less water than before.* *Fewer* means smaller in number: *there are fewer people than before.*

-less *suffix forming adjectives.* **1.** without; lacking: *speechless.* **2.** not able to (do something) or not able to be (done, performed, etc.): *countless.* [Old English *-lās*, from *lēas* lacking]

lessee (lɛˈsiː) *n.* a person to whom a lease is granted; a tenant under a lease. [C15: via Anglo-French from Old French *lessé*, from *lesser* to LEASE] —**lesˈseeship** *n.*

lessen (ˈlɛsᵊn) *vb.* **1.** to make or become less. **2.** (*tr.*) to make little of.

lesser (ˈlɛsə) *adj.* not as great in quantity, size, or worth.

lesser celandine *n.* a Eurasian ranunculaceous plant, *Ranunculus ficaria*, having yellow flowers and heart-shaped leaves. Also called: **pilewort.** Compare **greater celandine.**

lesser panda *n.* See **panda** (sense 2).

lesson (ˈlɛsᵊn) *n.* **1. a.** a unit, or single period of instruction in a subject; class: *an hour-long music lesson.* **b.** the content of such a unit. **2.** material assigned for individual study. **3.** something from which useful knowledge or principles can be learned; example. **4.** the principles, knowledge, etc., gained. **5.** a reprimand or punishment intended to correct. **6.** a portion of Scripture appointed to be read at divine service. ~*vb.* **7.** (*tr.*) *Rare.* to censure or punish. [C13: from Old French *leçon*, from Latin *lēctiō*, from *legere* to read]

lessor (ˈlɛsɔː, lɛˈsɔː) *n.* a person who grants a lease of property.

lest (lɛst) *conj.* (*subordinating; takes a subjunctive vb.*) **1.** so as to prevent any possibility that: *keep down lest anyone see us.* **2.** (*after verbs or phrases expressing fear, worry, anxiety, etc.*) for fear that; in case: *he was alarmed lest she should find out.* [Old English *thē lǣste*, earlier *thȳ lǣs the*, literally: whereby less that]

let[1] (lɛt) *vb.* **lets, letting, let.** (*tr.*; usually takes an infinitive without *to* or an implied infinitive) **1.** to permit; allow: *she lets him roam around.* **2.** (*imperative or dependent imperative*) **a.** used as an auxiliary to express a request, proposal, or command, or to convey a warning or threat: *let's get on; just let me catch you here again!* **b.** (in mathematical or philosophical discourse) used as an auxiliary to express an assumption or hypothesis: *let "a" equal "b".* **c.** used as an auxiliary to express resigned acceptance of the inevitable: *let the worst happen.* **3. a.** to allow the occupation of (accommodation) in return for rent. **b.** to assign (a contract for work). **4.** to allow or cause the movement of (something) in a specified direction: *to let air out of a tyre.* **5.** *Irish informal.* to utter: *to let a cry.* **6. let alone.** (*conj.*) much less; not to mention: *I can't afford wine, let alone champagne.* **7. let** *or* **leave alone** *or* **be.** to refrain from annoying or interfering with: *let the poor cat alone.* **8. let go.** See **go**[1] (sense 58). **9. let loose.** to set free. ~*n.* **10.** *Brit.* the act of letting property or accommodation: *the majority of new lets are covered by the rent regulations.* ~See also **let down, let in, let into, let off, let on, let out, let through, let up.** [Old English *lǣtan* to permit; related to Gothic *lētan*, German *lassen*]

let[2] (lɛt) *n.* **1.** an impediment or obstruction (esp. in the phrase **without let or hindrance**). **2.** *Tennis, squash, etc.* **a.** a minor infringement or obstruction of the ball, requiring a point to be replayed. **b.** the point so replayed. ~*vb.* **lets, letting, letted** *or* **let. 3.** (*tr.*) *Archaic.* to hinder; impede. [Old English *lettan* to hinder, from *læt* LATE; related to Old Norse *letja*]

-let *suffix forming nouns.* **1.** small or lesser: *booklet; starlet.* **2.** an article of attire or ornament worn on a specified part of the body: *anklet.* [from Old French *-elet*, from Latin *-āle*, neuter of adj. suffix *-ālis* or from Latin *-ellus*, diminutive suffix]

letch (lɛtʃ) *vb., n.* a variant spelling of **lech.** [C18: perhaps back formation from LECHER]

let down *vb.* (*tr., mainly adv.*) **1.** (*also prep.*) to lower. **2.** to fail to fulfil the expectations of (a person); disappoint. **3.** to undo, shorten, and resew (the hem) so as to lengthen (a dress, skirt, etc.). **4.** to untie (long hair that is bound up) and allow to fall loose. **5.** to deflate: *to let down a tyre.* ~*n.* **letdown. 6.** a disappointment. **7.** the gliding descent of an aircraft in preparation for landing.

lethal (ˈliːθəl) *adj.* **1.** able to cause or causing death. **2.** of or suggestive of death. [C16: from Latin *lēthālis*, from *lētum* death] —**lethality** (liːˈθælɪtɪ) *n.* —**ˈlethally** *adv.*

lethal dose *n.* the amount of a drug or other agent that if administered to an animal or human will prove fatal. Abbrev.: **LD.** See also **median lethal dose.**

lethargy (ˈlɛθədʒɪ) *n., pl.* **-gies. 1.** sluggishness, slowness, or dullness. **2.** an abnormal lack of energy, esp. as the result of a disease. [C14: from Late Latin *lēthargīa*, from Greek *lēthargos* drowsy, from *lēthē* forgetfulness] —**lethargic** (lɪˈθɑːdʒɪk) *or* **leˈthargical** *adj.* —**leˈthargically** *adv.*

Lethe (ˈliːθɪ) *n.* forgetfulness. [C16: after *Lethe* (the river in Hades that caused forgetfulness in those who drank its waters), via Latin from Greek, from *lēthē* oblivion] —**Lethean** (lɪˈθiːən) *adj.*

let in *vb.* (*tr., adv.*) **1.** to allow to enter. **2. let in for.** to involve (oneself or another) in (something more than is expected): *he let himself in for a lot of extra work.* **3. let in on.** to allow (someone) to know about or participate in.

let into *vb.* (*tr., prep.*) **1.** to allow to enter. **2.** to put into the surface of: *to let a pipe into the wall.* **3.** to allow (someone) to share (a secret).

let off *vb.* (*tr., mainly adv.*) **1.** (*also prep.*) to allow to disembark or leave. **2.** to explode or fire (a bomb, gun, etc.). **3.** (*also prep.*) to excuse from (work or other responsibilities): *I'll let you off for a week.* **4.** to allow to get away without the expected punishment, work, etc. **5.** to let (accommodation) in portions. **6.** to release (liquid, air, etc.). **7. let off steam.** See **steam** (sense 6). **8. let (someone) off with.** to give (a light punishment) to (someone).

let on *vb.* (*adv.*; when *tr., takes a clause as object*) *Informal.* **1.** to allow (something, such as a secret) to be known; reveal: *he never let on that he was married.* **2.** (*tr.*) to cause or encourage to be believed; pretend.

let out *vb.* (*adv., mainly tr.*) **1.** to give vent to; emit: *to let out a howl.* **2.** to allow to go or run free; release. **3.** (*may take a clause as object*) to reveal (a secret). **4.** to make available to tenants, hirers, or contractors. **5.** to permit to flow out: *to let air out of the tyres.* **6.** to make (a garment) larger, as by unpicking (the seams) and sewing nearer the outer edge. ~*n.* **let-out. 7.** a chance to escape.

let's (lɛts) *contraction of* let us: used to express a suggestion, command, etc., by the speaker to himself and his hearers.

Lett (lɛt) *n.* another name for a **Latvian.**

letter (ˈlɛtə) *n.* **1.** any of a set of conventional symbols used in writing or printing a language, each symbol being associated with a group of phonetic values in the language; character of the alphabet. **2.** a written or printed communication addressed to a person, company, etc., usually sent by post in an envelope. **3.** (*often preceded by the*) the strict legalistic or pedantic interpretation of the meaning of an agreement, document, etc.; exact wording as distinct from actual intention (esp. in the phrase **the letter of the law**). Compare **spirit**[1] (sense 10). **4.** *Printing, archaic.* a style of typeface: *a fancy letter.* **5. to the letter. a.** following the literal interpretation or wording exactly. **b.** attending to every detail. ~*vb.* **6.** to write or mark letters on (a sign, etc.), esp. by hand. **7.** (*tr.*) to set down or print using letters. ~See also **letters.** [C13: from Old French *lettre*, from Latin *littera* letter of the alphabet] —**ˈletterer** *n.*

letter bomb *n.* a thin explosive device inside an envelope, detonated when the envelope is opened.

letter box *n. Chiefly Brit.* **1. a.** a slot, usually covered with a hinged flap, through which letters, etc. are delivered to a building. **b.** a private box into which letters, etc., are delivered. **2.** Also called: **postbox.** a public box into which letters, etc., are put for collection and delivery.

letter card *n.* **1.** a card, usually one on which the postage is prepaid, that is sealed by being folded in half so that its gummed edges come into contact with each other. **2.** a long card consisting of a number of postcard views, with space for writing a letter on the backs, that is folded like a concertina for posting.

lettered (ˈlɛtəd) *adj.* **1.** well educated in literature, the arts, etc. **2.** literate. **3.** of or characterized by learning or culture. **4.** printed or marked with letters.

letterhead (ˈlɛtəˌhɛd) *n.* a sheet of paper printed with one's address, name, etc., for writing a letter on.

letter-high *adj.* another term for **type-high.**

lettering (ˈlɛtərɪŋ) *n.* **1.** the act, art, or technique of inscribing letters on to something. **2.** the letters so inscribed.

letter of advice *n.* a commercial letter giving a specific notification, such as the consignment of goods.

letter of attorney *n.* a less common term for **power of attorney.**

letter of credit *n.* **1.** a letter issued by a bank entitling the bearer to draw funds up to a specified maximum from that bank or its agencies. **2.** a letter addressed by a bank instructing the addressee to allow the person named to draw a specified sum on the credit of the addressor bank.

letter of intent *n.* a letter indicating that the writer has the serious intention of doing something, such as signing a contract in the circumstances specified. It does not constitute either a promise or a contract.

letter of introduction *n.* a letter given by one person to another, as an introduction to a third party.

letter of marque *or* **letters of marque** *n.* **1.** a licence granted by a state to a private citizen to arm a ship and seize merchant vessels of another nation. **2.** a similar licence issued by a nation allowing a private citizen to seize goods or citizens of another nation. ~Also called: **letter of marque and reprisal.**

letter-perfect *adj.* another term (esp. in the U.S.) for **word-perfect.**

letterpress (ˈlɛtəˌprɛs) *n.* **1. a.** a method of printing in which ink is transferred from raised surfaces to paper by pressure; relief printing. **b.** matter so printed. **2.** text matter as distinct from illustrations.

letter-quality printer *n. Computer technol.* a printer used to produce high quality output in printed form from a computer.

letters (ˈlɛtəz) *n.* (*functioning as pl. or sing.*) **1.** literary knowledge, ability, or learning: *a man of letters.* **2.** literary culture in general. **3.** an official title, degree, etc., indicated by an abbreviation: *letters after one's name.*

letterset (ˈlɛtəˌsɛt) *n.* a method of rotary printing in which ink is transferred from raised surfaces to paper via a rubber-covered cylinder. [C20: from LETTER(PRESS) + (OFF)SET]

letters of administration *pl. n. Law.* a formal document nominating a specified person to take over, administer, and dispose of an estate when there is no executor to carry out the testator's will.
letters of credence *or* **letters credential** *pl. n.* a formal document accrediting a diplomatic officer to a foreign court or government.
letters patent *pl. n.* See **patent** (sense 1).
let through *vb. (tr.)* to allow to pass (through): *the invalid was let through to the front of the queue.*
Lettish ('lɛtɪʃ) *n., adj.* another word for **Latvian.**
lettre de cachet *French.* (lɛtrə də kaʃɛ) *n., pl.* ***lettres de cachet*** (lɛtrə də kaʃɛ). *French history.* a letter under the sovereign's seal, often authorizing imprisonment without trial. [literally: letter with a seal]
lettuce ('lɛtɪs) *n.* **1.** any of various plants of the genus *Lactuca,* esp. *L. sativa,* which is cultivated in many varieties for its large edible leaves: family *Compositae* (composites). **2.** the leaves of any of these varieties, which are eaten in salads. **3.** any of various plants that resemble true lettuce, such as lamb's lettuce and sea lettuce. [C13: probably from Old French *laitues,* pl. of *laitue,* from Latin *lactūca,* from *lac-* milk, because of its milky juice]
let up *vb. (intr., adv.)* **1.** to diminish, slacken, or stop. **2.** (foll. by *on*) *Informal.* to be less harsh (towards someone). ~*n.* **let-up.** **3.** *Informal.* a lessening or abatement.
leu ('leɪuː) *n., pl.* **lei** (leɪ). the standard monetary unit of Romania, divided into 100 bani. [from Romanian: lion]
leucine ('luːsiːn) *or* **leucin** ('luːsɪn) *n.* an essential amino acid found in many proteins.
leucite ('luːsaɪt) *n.* a grey or white mineral consisting of potassium aluminium silicate: a source of potash for fertilizers and of aluminium. Formula: $KAlSi_2O_6$. —**leucitic** (luː'sɪtɪk) *adj.*
leuco-, leuko- *or before a vowel* **leuc-, leuk-** *combining form.* white or lacking colour: *leucocyte; leucorrhoea; leukaemia.* [from Greek *leukos* white]
leuco base ('luːkəʊ) *n.* a colourless compound formed by reducing a dye so that the original dye can be regenerated by oxidation.
leucoblast *or esp. U.S.* **leukoblast** ('luːkəʊˌblɑːst) *n.* an immature leucocyte.
leucocratic (ˌluːkə'krætɪk) *adj.* (of igneous rocks) light-coloured because of a low content of ferromagnesian minerals. [C20: from German *leukokrat,* from LEUCO- + Greek *kratein* to rule]
leucocyte *or esp. U.S.* **leukocyte** ('luːkəˌsaɪt) *n.* any of the various large unpigmented cells in the blood of vertebrates. Also called: **white blood cell, white (blood) corpuscle.** See also **lymphocyte, granulocyte, monocyte.** —**leucocytic** *or esp. U.S.* **leukocytic** (ˌluːkə'sɪtɪk) *adj.*
leucocytosis *or esp. U.S.* **leukocytosis** (ˌluːkəʊsaɪ'təʊsɪs) *n.* a gross increase in the number of white blood cells in the blood, usually as a response to an infection. —**leucocytotic** *or esp. U.S.* **leukocytotic** (ˌluːkəʊsaɪ'tɒtɪk) *adj.*
leucoderma *or esp. U.S.* **leukoderma** (ˌluːkəʊ'dɜːmə) *n.* any area of skin that is white from congenital (**albinism**; see **albino**) or acquired absence or loss of melanin pigmentation. Also called: **vitiligo.** —ˌ**leuco'dermal,** ˌ**leuco'dermic** *or esp. U.S.* ˌ**leuko'dermal,** ˌ**leuko'dermic** *adj.*
leucoma (luː'kəʊmə) *n. Pathol.* a white opaque scar of the cornea.
leucomaine ('luːkəˌmeɪn) *n. Biochem.* any of a group of toxic amines produced during animal metabolism. [C20: from LEUCO- + *-maine,* as in *ptomaine*]
leucopenia *or esp. U.S.* **leukopenia** (ˌluːkəʊ'piːnɪə) *n. Pathol.* an abnormal reduction in the number of white blood cells in the blood, characteristic of certain diseases. [C19: from LEUCO- + Greek *penia* poverty] —ˌ**leuco'penic** *or esp. U.S.* ˌ**leuko'penic** *adj.*
leucoplast ('luːkəˌplæst) *or* **leucoplastid** *n.* any of the small colourless bodies occurring in the cytoplasm of plant cells and used for storing food material, esp. starch.
leucopoiesis *or esp. U.S.* **leukopoiesis** (ˌluːkəʊpɔɪ'iːsɪs) *n. Physiol.* formation of leucocytes in the body. Also called: **leucocytopoiesis.** —**leucopoietic** *or esp. U.S.* **leukopoietic** (ˌluːkəʊpɔɪ'ɛtɪk) *adj.*
leucorrhoea *or esp. U.S.* **leukorrhea** (ˌluːkə'riːə) *n. Pathol.* a white or yellowish discharge of mucous material from the vagina, often an indication of infection. —ˌ**leucor'rhoeal** *or esp. U.S.* ˌ**leukor'rheal** *adj.*
leucotomy (luː'kɒtəmɪ) *n.* the surgical operation of cutting some of the nerve fibres in the frontal lobes of the brain for treating intractable mental disorders. See also **lobotomy.** [C20: from LEUCO- (with reference to the white brain tissue) + -TOMY]
leukaemia *or esp. U.S.* **leukemia** (luː'kiːmɪə) *n.* an acute or chronic disease characterized by a gross proliferation of leucocytes, which crowd into the bone marrow, spleen, lymph nodes, etc., and suppress the blood-forming apparatus. [C19: from LEUCO- + Greek *haima* blood]
leuko- *combining form.* a variant of **leuco-.**
leukotriene (ˌluːkəʊ'traɪiːn) *n.* one of a class of products of metabolic conversion of arachidonic acid; the active constituents of slow-reacting substance, responsible for bronchial constriction, contraction of smooth muscle, and inflammatory processes. [C20: from *leukocyte,* in which they were discovered + *triene* from the conjugated triene unit that they contain]
lev (lɛf) *n., pl.* **leva** ('lɛvə). the standard monetary unit of Bulgaria, divided into 100 stotinki. [from Bulgarian: lion]
Lev. *Bible. abbrev. for* Leviticus.
Levalloisian (ˌlɛvə'lɔɪzɪən) *or* **Levallois** (lə'vælwɑː) *adj.* of or relating to a Lower Palaeolithic culture in W Europe, characterized by a method of flaking flint tools so that one side of the core is flat and the other domed.
levant[1] (lɪ'vænt) *n.* a type of leather made from the skins of goats, sheep, or seals, having a pattern of irregular creases. [C19: shortened from *Levant morocco* (type of leather)]
levant[2] (lɪ'vænt) *vb. (intr.) Brit.* to bolt or abscond, esp. to avoid paying debts. [C18: perhaps from Spanish *levantar (el campo)* to break (camp).]
levanter[1] (lɪ'væntə) *n. (sometimes cap.)* **1.** an easterly wind in the W Mediterranean area, esp. in the late summer. **2.** an inhabitant of the Levant, an area of the E Mediterranean now occupied by Lebanon, Syria, and Israel.
levanter[2] (lɪ'væntə) *n. Brit.* a person who bolts or absconds.
levantine ('lɛvənˌtaɪn) *n.* a cloth of twilled silk.
Levantine ('lɛvənˌtaɪn) *adj.* **1.** of or relating to the Levant. ~*n.* **2.** (esp. formerly) an inhabitant of the Levant.
levator (lɪ'veɪtə, -tɔː) *n.* **1.** *Anatomy.* any of various muscles that raise a part of the body. **2.** *Surgery.* an instrument for elevating a part or structure. [C17: New Latin, from Latin *levāre* to raise]
levee[1] ('lɛvɪ) *n. U.S.* **1.** an embankment alongside a river, produced naturally by sedimentation or constructed by man to prevent flooding. **2.** an embankment that surrounds a field that is to be irrigated. **3.** a landing place on a river; quay. [C18: from French, from Medieval Latin *levāta,* from Latin *levāre* to raise]
levee[2] ('lɛvɪ, 'lɛveɪ) *n.* **1.** a formal reception held by a sovereign just after rising from bed. **2.** (in Britain) a public court reception for men, held in the early afternoon. [C17: from French, variant of *lever,* a rising, from Latin *levāre* to raise]
level ('lɛvᵊl) *adj.* **1.** on a horizontal plane. **2.** having a surface of completely equal height. **3.** being of the same height as something else. **4.** (of quantities to be measured, as in recipes) even with the top of the cup, spoon, etc. **5.** equal to or even with (something or someone else). **6.** not having or showing inconsistency or irregularities. **7.** Also: **level-headed.** even-tempered; steady. ~*vb.* **-els, -elling, -elled** *or U.S.* **-els, -eling, -eled. 8.** *(tr.;* sometimes foll. by *off)* to make (a surface) horizontal, level, or even. **9.** to make (two or more people or things) equal, as in position or status. **10.** *(tr.)* to raze to the ground. **11.** *(tr.)* to knock (a person) down by or as if by a blow. **12.** *(tr.)* to direct (a gaze, criticism, etc.) emphatically at someone. **13.** *(intr.;* often foll. by *with) Informal.* to be straightforward and frank. **14.** *(intr.;* foll. by *off* or *out)* to manoeuvre an aircraft into a horizontal flight path after a dive, climb, or glide. **15.** (often foll. by *at)* to aim (a weapon) horizontally. **16.** *Surveying.* to determine the elevation of a section of (land), sighting through a levelling instrument to a staff at successive pairs or points. ~*n.* **17.** a horizontal datum line or plane. **18.** a device, such as a spirit level, for determining whether a surface is horizontal. **19.** a surveying instrument consisting basically of a telescope with a spirit level attached, used for measuring relative heights of land. See **Abney level, dumpy level. 20.** a reading of the difference in elevation of two points taken with such an instrument. **21.** position or status in a scale of values. **22.** amount or degree of progress; stage. **23.** a specified vertical position; altitude. **24.** a horizontal line or plane with respect to which measurement of elevation is based: *sea level.* **25.** a flat even surface or area of land. **26.** a horizontal passage or drift in a mine. **27.** any of the successive layers of material that have been deposited with the passage of time to build up and raise the height of the land surface. **28.** *Physics.* the ratio of the magnitude of a physical quantity to an arbitrary magnitude: *sound-pressure level.* **29. do one's level best.** to make every possible effort; try one's utmost. **30. find one's level.** to find one's most suitable place socially, professionally, etc. **31. on a level.** on the same horizontal plane as another. **32. on the level.** *Informal.* sincere, honest, or genuine. [C14: from Old French *livel,* from Vulgar Latin *lībellum* (unattested), from Latin *lībella,* diminutive of *lībra* scales] —'**levelly** *adv.* —'**levelness** *n.*
level crossing *n. Brit.* a point at which a railway and a road cross, esp. one with barriers that close the road when a train is scheduled to pass. U.S. and Canadian name: **grade crossing.**
level-headed *adj.* even-tempered, balanced, and reliable; steady. —ˌ**level-'headedly** *adv.* —ˌ**level-'headedness** *n.*
leveller *or U.S.* **leveler** ('lɛvələ) *n.* **1.** a person or thing that levels. **2.** a person who works for the abolition of inequalities.
levelling screw *n.* a screw, often one of three, for adjusting the level of an apparatus.
level of attainment *n. Brit. Education.* one of ten groupings, each with its own attainment criteria based on pupil age and ability, within which a pupil is assessed.
level pegging *Brit. informal.* ~*n.* **1.** equality between two contestants. ~*adj.* **2.** (of two contestants) equal.
lever ('liːvə) *n.* **1.** a rigid bar pivoted about a fulcrum, used to transfer a force to a load and usually to provide a mechanical advantage. **2.** any of a number of mechanical devices employing this principle. **3.** a means of exerting pressure in order to accomplish something; strategic aid. ~*vb.* **4.** to prise or move (an object) with a lever. [C13: from Old French *leveour,* from

lever to raise, from Latin *levāre* from *levis* light] —**'lever-,like** *adj.*

leverage ('liːvərɪdʒ, -vrɪdʒ) *n.* **1.** the action of a lever. **2.** the mechanical advantage gained by employing a lever. **3.** power to accomplish something; strategic advantage. **4.** the enhanced power available to a large company: *the supermarket chains have greater leverage than single-outlet enterprises.* **5.** U.S. word for **gearing** (sense 3). **6.** the use made by a company of its limited assets to guarantee the substantial loans required to finance its business.

leveraged buyout ('liːvərɪdʒd) *n.* a takeover bid in which a small company makes use of its limited assets, and those of the usually larger target company, to raise the loans required to finance the takeover. Abbrev.: **LBO.**

leveret ('lɛvərɪt, -vrɪt) *n.* a young hare, esp. one less than one year old. [C15: from Norman French *levrete,* diminutive of *levre,* from Latin *lepus* hare]

Levi ('liːvaɪ; *Hebrew* 'levi) *or* **Levite** ('liːvaɪt) *n. Judaism.* a descendant of the tribe of Levi, third son of Jacob and Leah, who has certain privileges in the synagogue service.

leviable ('lɛvɪəbᵊl) *adj.* **1.** (of taxes, tariffs, etc.) liable to be levied. **2.** (of goods, etc.) liable to bear a levy; taxable.

leviathan (lɪ'vaɪəθən) *n.* **1.** *Bible.* a monstrous beast, esp. a sea monster. **2.** any huge or powerful thing. [C14: from Late Latin, ultimately from Hebrew *liwyāthān,* of obscure origin]

levigate ('lɛvɪ,geɪt) *vb. Chem.* **1.** (*tr.*) to grind into a fine powder or a smooth paste. **2.** to form or cause to form a homogeneous mixture, as in the production of gels. **3.** (*tr.*) to suspend (fine particles) by grinding in a liquid, esp. as a method of separating fine from coarse particles. ~*adj.* **4.** *Botany.* having a smooth polished surface; glabrous. [C17: from Latin *lēvigāre,* from *lēvis* smooth] —,**levi'gation** *n.* —**'levi,gator** *n.*

levin ('lɛvɪn) *n.* an archaic word for **lightning.** [C13: probably from Scandinavian; compare Danish *lygnild*]

levirate ('lɛvɪrɪt) *n.* the practice, required by Old Testament law, of marrying the widow of one's brother. [C18: from Latin *lēvir* a husband's brother] —**leviratic** (,lɛvɪ'rætɪk) *or* ,**levi'ratical** *adj.*

Levis ('liːvaɪz) *pl. n. Trademark.* jeans, usually blue and made of denim.

Levit. *Bible. abbrev. for* Leviticus.

levitate ('lɛvɪ,teɪt) *vb.* **1.** to rise or cause to rise and float in the air, usually attributed to supernatural intervention. **2.** (*tr.*) *Med.* to support (a patient) on a cushion of air in the treatment of severe burns. [C17: from Latin *levis* light + *-tate,* as in *gravitate*] —,**levi'tation** *n.* —**'levi,tator** *n.*

Levite ('liːvaɪt) *n. Judaism.* another word for **Levi.**

Levitical (lɪ'vɪtɪkᵊl) *or* **Levitic** *adj.* of or relating to the book of Leviticus in the Old Testament, containing moral precepts and many of the laws concerning the Temple ritual and construction. —**Le'vitically** *adv.*

levity ('lɛvɪtɪ) *n., pl.* **-ties.** **1.** inappropriate lack of seriousness. **2.** fickleness or instability. **3.** *Archaic.* lightness in weight. [C16: from Latin *levitās* lightness, from *levis* light]

levo- *combining form.* a U.S. variant of **laevo-.** [from Latin *laevus* left, on the left]

levodopa (,liːvəʊ'dəʊpə) *n.* another name for **L-dopa.**

levy ('lɛvɪ) *vb.* **levies, levying, levied.** (*tr.*) **1.** to impose and collect (a tax, tariff, fine, etc.). **2.** to conscript troops for service. **3.** to seize or attach (property) in accordance with the judgment of a court. ~*n., pl.* **levies.** **4. a.** the act of imposing and collecting a tax, tariff, etc. **b.** the money so raised. **5. a.** the conscription of troops for service. **b.** a person conscripted in this way. [C15: from Old French *levée* a raising, from *lever,* from Latin *levāre* to raise] —**'levier** *n.*

levy en masse ('lɛvɪ ɒn 'mæs) *n.* the conscription of the civilian population in large numbers in the face of impending invasion. Also called: **levée en masse** (*French* ləve ɑ̃ mas).

lewd (luːd) *adj.* **1.** characterized by or intended to excite crude sexual desire; obscene. **2.** *Obsolete.* **a.** wicked. **b.** ignorant. [C14: from Old English *lǣwde* lay, ignorant; see LAY[3]] —**'lewdly** *adv.* —**'lewdness** *n.*

lewis ('luːɪs) *or* **lewisson** *n.* a lifting device for heavy stone blocks consisting of a number of curved pieces of metal fitting into a dovetailed recess cut into the stone. [C18: perhaps from the name of the inventor]

Lewis acid ('luːɪs) *n.* a substance capable of accepting a pair of electrons from a base to form a covalent bond. Compare **Lewis base.** [C20: named after G. N. *Lewis* (1875–1946), U.S. chemist]

Lewis base *n.* a substance capable of donating a pair of electrons to an acid to form a covalent bond. Compare **Lewis acid.** [C20: named after G. N. *Lewis;* see LEWIS ACID]

Lewis gun *n.* a light air-cooled drum-fed gas-operated machine gun used chiefly in World War I. [C20: named after I. N. *Lewis* (1858–1931), U.S. soldier]

lewisite ('luːɪ,saɪt) *n.* a colourless oily poisonous liquid with an odour resembling that of geraniums, having a powerful vesicant action and used as a war gas; 1-chloro-2-dichloroarsinoethene. Formula: $ClCH{:}CHA_sCl_2$. [C20: named after W. L. *Lewis* (1878–1943), U.S. chemist]

lex (lɛks) *n., pl.* **leges** ('liːdʒiːz). **1.** a system or body of laws. **2.** a particular specified law. [Latin]

lex. *abbrev. for* lexicon.

lexeme ('lɛksiːm) *n. Linguistics.* a minimal meaningful unit of language, the meaning of which cannot be understood from that of its component morphemes. *Take off* (in the senses to mimic, to become airborne, etc.) is a lexeme, as well as the independent morphemes *take* and *off.* [C20: from LEX(ICON) + -EME]

lexical ('lɛksɪkᵊl) *adj.* **1.** of or relating to items of vocabulary in a language. **2.** of or relating to a lexicon. —**lexicality** (,lɛksɪ'kælɪtɪ) *n.* —**'lexically** *adv.*

lexical decision task *n. Psychol.* an experimental task in which subjects have to decide as fast as possible whether a given letter string is a word.

lexical insertion *n. Generative grammar.* the process in which actual morphemes of a language are substituted either for semantic material or for place-fillers in the course of a derivation of a sentence.

lexicalize *or* **lexicalise** ('lɛksɪkə,laɪz) *vb. Linguistics.* to form (a word or lexeme) or (of a word or lexeme) to be formed from constituent morphemes, words, or lexemes, as to form *cannot* from *can* and *not.* —,**lexicali'zation** *or* ,**lexicali'sation** *n.*

lexical meaning *n.* the meaning of a word in relation to the physical world or to abstract concepts, without reference to any sentence in which the word may occur. Compare **grammatical meaning, content word.**

lexical order *n.* the arrangement of a set of items in accordance with a recursive algorithm, such as the entries in a dictionary whose order depends on their first letter unless these are the same in which case it is the second which decides, and so on.

lexicog. *abbrev. for:* **1.** lexicographical. **2.** lexicography.

lexicography (,lɛksɪ'kɒgrəfɪ) *n.* the process or profession of writing or compiling dictionaries. —,**lexi'cographer** *n.* —**lexicographic** (,lɛksɪkə'græfɪk) *or* ,**lexico'graphical** *adj.* —,**lexico'graphically** *adv.*

lexicology (,lɛksɪ'kɒlədʒɪ) *n.* the study of the overall structure and history of the vocabulary of a language. —**lexicological** (,lɛksɪkə'lɒdʒɪkᵊl) *adj.* —,**lexico'logically** *adv.* —,**lexi'cologist** *n.*

lexicon ('lɛksɪkən) *n.* **1.** a dictionary, esp. one of an ancient language such as Greek or Hebrew. **2.** a list of terms relating to a particular subject. **3.** the vocabulary of a language or of an individual. **4.** *Linguistics.* the set of all the morphemes of a language. [C17: New Latin, from Greek *lexikon* n. use of *lexikos* relating to words, from Greek *lexis* word, from *legein* to speak]

lexicostatistics (,lɛksɪkəʊstə'tɪstɪks) *n.* (*functioning as sing.*) the statistical study of the vocabulary of a language, with special attention to the historical links with other languages. See also **glottochronology.**

lexigram ('lɛksɪ,græm) *n.* a figure or symbol that represents a word. [C20: from Greek *lexis* word + -GRAM]

lexigraphy (lɛk'sɪgrəfɪ) *n.* a system of writing in which each word is represented by a sign. [C19: from Greek *lexis* word + -GRAPHY]

lexis ('lɛksɪs) *n.* the totality of vocabulary items in a language, including all forms having lexical meaning or grammatical function. [C20: from Greek *lexis* word]

lex loci ('ləʊsaɪ, -kiː) *n.* the law of the place. [from Latin]

lex non scripta (nɒn 'skrɪptə) *n.* the unwritten law; common law. [from Latin]

lex scripta *n.* the written law; statute law. [from Latin]

lex talionis (,tælɪ'əʊnɪs) *n.* the law of revenge or retaliation. [C16: New Latin]

ley (leɪ, liː) *n.* **1.** arable land put down to grass; grassland or pastureland. **2.** Also called: **ley line.** a line joining two prominent points in the landscape, thought to be the line of a prehistoric track. [C14: variant of LEA[1]]

Leyden jar ('laɪdᵊn) *n. Physics.* an early type of capacitor consisting of a glass jar with the lower part of the inside and outside coated with tin foil. [C18: first made in the Dutch city of *Leyden* (Leiden)]

ley farming *n.* the alternation at intervals of several years of crop growing and grassland pasture.

lf *Printing. abbrev. for* light face.

LF *Radio. abbrev. for* low frequency.

LG *abbrev. for* Low German.

lg. *or* **lge** *abbrev. for* large.

lgth *abbrev. for* length.

LGU *abbrev. for* Ladies' Golf Union.

lh *or* **LH** *abbrev. for* left hand.

LH *abbrev. for* luteinizing hormone.

lhasa apso ('lɑːsə 'æpsəʊ) *n., pl.* **lhasa apsos.** a small dog of a Tibetan breed having a long straight dense coat, often gold or greyish, and a well-feathered tail carried curled over its back. [Tibetan]

lhd *abbrev. for* left-hand drive.

LH-RH *abbrev. for* luteinizing hormone-releasing hormone.

li (liː) *n.* a Chinese unit of length, approximately equal to 590 yards. [from Chinese]

Li *the chemical symbol for* lithium.

LI *abbrev. for:* **1.** Long Island. **2.** Light Infantry.

liabilities (,laɪə'bɪlɪtɪz) *pl. n. Accounting.* business obligations incurred but not discharged and entered as claims on the assets shown on the balance sheet. Compare **assets** (sense 1).

liability (,laɪə'bɪlɪtɪ) *n., pl.* **-ties.** **1.** the state of being liable. **2.** a financial obligation. **3.** a hindrance or disadvantage. **4.** likelihood or probability.

liable ('laɪəbᵊl) *adj.* (*postpositive*) **1.** legally obliged or responsible; answerable. **2.** susceptible or exposed; subject. **3.** probable, likely, or capable: *it's liable to happen soon.* [C15: perhaps via Anglo-French, from Old French *lier* to bind, from Latin *ligāre*] —'**liableness** *n.*

▷**Usage.** Careful users of English take *liable* to mean *responsible for* and *subject to* in sentences such as *he was liable for his employees' accidents* and *he was liable to accidents.* The use of *liable* in the sense of *likely* is avoided: *he was likely* (not *liable*) *to have accidents.*

liaise (lɪ'eɪz) *vb.* (*intr.*; usually foll. by *with*) to communicate and maintain contact (with). [C20: back formation from LIAISON]

liaison (lɪ'eɪzɒn) *n.* **1.** communication and contact between groups or units. **2.** (*modifier*) of or relating to liaison between groups or units: *a liaison officer.* **3.** a secretive or adulterous sexual relationship. **4.** the relationship between military units necessary to ensure unity of purpose. **5.** (in the phonology of several languages, esp. French) the pronunciation of a normally silent consonant at the end of a word immediately before another word commencing with a vowel, in such a way that the consonant is taken over as the initial sound of the following word. Liaison is seen between French *ils* (il) and *ont* (ɔ̃), to give *ils ont* (il zɔ̃). **6.** any thickening for soups, sauces, etc., such as egg yolks or cream. [C17: via French from Old French, from *lier* to bind, from Latin *ligāre*]

liaison officer *n.* **1.** a person who liaises between groups or units. **2.** *N.Z.* a university official who oversees the operation of the accrediting system in schools.

liana (lɪ'ɑːnə) *or* **liane** (lɪ'ɑːn) *n.* any of various woody climbing plants of tropical forests. [C19: changed from earlier *liane* (through influence of French *lier* to bind), from French, of obscure origin] —**li'anoid** *adj.*

liar ('laɪə) *n.* a person who has lied or lies repeatedly.

liard (lɪ'ɑːd) *n.* a former small coin of various European countries. [C16: after G. *Liard,* French minter]

liar paradox *n. Logic.* the paradox that *this statement is false* is true only if it is false and false only if it is true: attributed to Epimenides the Cretan in the form *all Cretans are liars.*

Lias ('laɪəs) *n.* the lowest series of rocks of the Jurassic system. [C15 (referring to a kind of limestone), C19 (geological sense) from Old French *liois,* perhaps from *lie* lees, dregs, so called from its appearance] —**Liassic** (laɪ'æsɪk) *adj.*

liatris (laɪ'ætrɪs) *n.* see **blazing star** (sense 2). [C18: New Latin, of uncertain origin]

lib (lɪb) *n. Informal, sometimes derogatory.* short for **liberation** (sense 2).

lib. *abbrev. for:* **1.** liber. [Latin: book] **2.** librarian. **3.** library.

Lib. *abbrev. for* Liberal.

libation (laɪ'beɪʃən) *n.* **1. a.** the pouring out of wine, etc., in honour of a deity. **b.** the liquid so poured out. **2.** *Usually facetious.* an alcoholic drink. [C14: from Latin *lībātiō,* from *lībāre* to pour an offering of drink] —**li'bational** *or* **li'bationary** *adj.*

libeccio (lɪ'betʃɪəʊ) *or* **libecchio** (lɪ'bɛkɪəʊ) *n.* a strong westerly or southwesterly wind blowing onto the W coast of Corsica. [Italian, via Latin, from Greek *libs*]

libel ('laɪbᵊl) *n.* **1.** *Law.* **a.** the publication of defamatory matter in permanent form, as by a written or printed statement, picture, etc. **b.** the act of publishing such matter. **2.** any defamatory or unflattering representation or statement. **3.** *Ecclesiastical law.* a plaintiff's written statement of claim. ~*vb.* **-bels, -belling, -belled** *or U.S.* **-bels, -beling, -beled.** (*tr.*) **4.** *Law.* to make or publish a defamatory statement or representation about (a person). **5.** to misrepresent injuriously. **6.** *Ecclesiastical law.* to bring an action against (a person) in the ecclesiastical courts. [C13 (in the sense: written statement), hence C14 legal sense: a plaintiff's statement, via Old French from Latin *libellus* a little book, from *liber* a book] —'**libeller** *or* '**libelist** *n.* —'**libellous** *or* '**libelous** *adj.*

libellant *or U.S.* **libelant** ('laɪbᵊlənt) *n.* **1.** a party who brings an action in the ecclesiastical courts by presenting a libel. **2.** a person who publishes a libel.

libellee *or U.S.* **libelee** (ˌlaɪbᵊ'liː) *n.* a person against whom a libel has been filed in an ecclesiastical court.

liber ('laɪbə) *n.* a rare name for **phloem.** [C18: from Latin, in original sense: tree bark]

liberal ('lɪbərəl, 'lɪbrəl) *adj.* **1.** relating to or having social and political views that favour progress and reform. **2.** relating to or having policies or views advocating individual freedom. **3.** giving and generous in temperament or behaviour. **4.** tolerant of other people. **5.** abundant; lavish: *a liberal helping of cream.* **6.** not strict; free: *a liberal translation.* **7.** of or relating to an education that aims to develop general cultural interests and intellectual ability. ~*n.* **8.** a person who has liberal ideas or opinions. [C14: from Latin *līberālis* of freedom, from *līber* free] —'**liberally** *adv.* —'**liberalness** *n.*

Liberal ('lɪbərəl, 'lɪbrəl) *n.* **1.** a member or supporter of the Liberal Party, a former political party favouring liberal policies. **2.** a member or supporter of any of various similar parties in other countries. ~*adj.* **3.** of or relating to a Liberal Party.

liberal arts *pl. n.* the fine arts, humanities, sociology, languages, and literature. Often shortened to **arts.**

Liberal Democrat *n.* a member or supporter of the Social and Liberal Democrats, a British political party of the centre.

liberalism ('lɪbərəˌlɪzəm, 'lɪbrə-) *n.* **1.** liberal opinions, practices, or politics. **2.** a movement in modern Protestantism that rejects biblical authority. —'**liberalist** *n., adj.* —ˌ**liberal'istic** *adj.*

liberality (ˌlɪbə'rælɪtɪ) *n., pl.* **-ties. 1.** generosity; bounty. **2.** the quality or condition of being liberal.

liberalize *or* **liberalise** ('lɪbərəˌlaɪz, 'lɪbrə-) *vb.* to make or become liberal. —ˌ**liberali'zation** *or* ˌ**liberali'sation** *n.* —'**liberalˌizer** *or* '**liberalˌiser** *n.*

liberal studies *n.* (*functioning as sing.*) *Brit.* a supplementary arts course for those specializing in scientific, technical, or professional studies.

Liberal Unionist *n.* a Liberal who opposed Gladstone's policy of Irish Home Rule in 1886 and after. —**Liberal Unionism** *n.*

liberate ('lɪbəˌreɪt) *vb.* (*tr.*) **1.** to give liberty to; make free. **2.** to release (something, esp. a gas) from chemical combination during a chemical reaction. **3.** to release from occupation or subjugation by a foreign power. **4.** to free from social prejudices or injustices. **5.** *Euphemistic or facetious.* to steal. —'**liberˌator** *n.*

liberated ('lɪbəˌreɪtɪd) *adj.* **1.** given liberty; freed; released. **2.** released from occupation or subjugation by a foreign power. **3.** (esp. in feminist theory) not bound by traditional sexual and social roles.

liberation (ˌlɪbə'reɪʃən) *n.* **1.** a liberating or being liberated. **2.** the seeking of equal status or just treatment for or on behalf of any group believed to be discriminated against: *women's liberation; animal liberation.* —ˌ**liber'ationist** *n., adj.*

liberation theology *n.* the belief that Christianity involves not only faith in the teachings of the Church but also a commitment to change social and political conditions from within in societies in which it is considered exploitation and oppression exist.

Liberian (laɪ'bɪərɪən) *adj.* **1.** of or relating to Liberia, a republic in W Africa on the Atlantic. ~*n.* **2.** a native or inhabitant of Liberia.

libero (*Italian* 'liːbero) *n.* another name for **sweeper** (sense 3).

libertarian (ˌlɪbə'tɛərɪən) *n.* **1.** a believer in freedom of thought, expression, etc. **2.** *Philosophy.* a believer in the doctrine of free will. Compare **determinism.** ~*adj.* **3.** of, relating to, or characteristic of a libertarian. [C18: from LIBERTY] —ˌ**liber'tarianism** *n.*

liberticide (lɪ'bɜːtɪˌsaɪd) *n.* **1.** a destroyer of freedom. **2.** the destruction of freedom. —**liˌberti'cidal** *adj.*

libertine ('lɪbəˌtiːn, -ˌtaɪn) *n.* **1.** a morally dissolute person. ~*adj.* **2.** morally dissolute. [C14 (in the sense: freedman, dissolute person): from Latin *lībertīnus* freedman, from *lībertus* freed, from *līber* free] —'**liberˌtinage** *or* '**libertinˌism** *n.*

liberty ('lɪbətɪ) *n., pl.* **-ties. 1.** the power of choosing, thinking, and acting for oneself; freedom from control or restriction. **2.** the right or privilege of access to a particular place; freedom. **3.** (*often pl.*) a social action regarded as being familiar, forward, or improper. **4.** (*often pl.*) an action that is unauthorized or unwarranted in the circumstances: *he took liberties with the translation.* **5. a.** authorized leave granted to a sailor. **b.** (*as modifier*): *liberty man; liberty boat.* **6. at liberty.** free, unoccupied, or unrestricted. **7. take liberties (with).** to be overfamiliar or overpresumptuous. **8. take the liberty (of** *or* **to).** to venture or presume (to do something). [C14: from Old French *liberté,* from Latin *lībertās,* from *līber* free]

liberty bodice *n.* a sleeveless vest-like undergarment made from thick cotton and covering the upper part of the body, formerly worn esp. by young children.

liberty cap *n.* **1.** a cap of soft felt worn as a symbol of liberty, esp. during the French Revolution, from the practice in ancient Rome of giving a freed slave such a cap. **2.** a poisonous hallucinogenic basidiomycetous fungus, *Psilocybe semilanceata,* yellowish-brown with a distinctive pointed cap, found in groups in grassland.

liberty hall *n.* (*sometimes caps.*) *Informal.* a place or condition of complete liberty.

liberty horse *n.* (in a circus) a riderless horse that performs movements to verbal commands.

liberty ship *n.* a supply ship of World War II.

libidinous (lɪ'bɪdɪnəs) *adj.* **1.** characterized by excessive sexual desire. **2.** of or relating to the libido. —**li'bidinously** *adv.* —**li'bidinousness** *n.*

libido (lɪ'biːdəʊ) *n., pl.* **-dos. 1.** *Psychoanal.* psychic energy emanating from the id. **2.** sexual urge or desire. [C20 (in psychoanalysis): from Latin: desire] —**libidinal** (lɪ'bɪdɪnᵊl) *adj.* —**li'bidinally** *adv.*

libra ('laɪbrə) *n., pl.* **-brae** (-briː). an ancient Roman unit of weight corresponding to 1 pound, but equal to about 12 ounces. [C14: from Latin, literally: scales]

Libra ('liːbrə) *n., Latin genitive* **Librae** ('liːbriː). **1.** *Astronomy.* a small faint zodiacal constellation in the S hemisphere, lying between Virgo and Scorpius on the ecliptic. **2.** *Astrology.* **a.** Also called: the **Scales,** the **Balance.** the seventh sign of the zodiac, symbol ♎, having a cardinal air classification and ruled by the planet Venus. The sun is in this sign between about Sept. 23 and Oct. 22. **b.** a person born under this sign. ~*adj.* **3.** *Astrology.* born under or characteristic of Libra. ~Also (for senses 2b, 3): **Libran** ('lɪbrən).

librarian (laɪˈbrɛərɪən) *n.* a person in charge of or assisting in a library.

librarianship (lɪˈbrɛərɪənʃɪp, laɪ-) *n.* the professional administration of library resources and services. Also called: **library science.**

library (ˈlaɪbrərɪ) *n., pl.* **-braries.** **1.** a room or set of rooms where books and other literary materials are kept. **2.** a collection of literary materials, films, tapes, gramophone records, children's toys, etc., kept for borrowing or reference. **3.** the building or institution that houses such a collection: *a public library.* **4.** a set of books published as a series, often in a similar format. **5.** *Computer technol.* a collection of standard programs and subroutines for immediate use, usually stored on disk or some other storage device. **6.** a collection of specific items for reference or checking against: *a library of genetic material.* [C14: from Old French *librairie,* from Medieval Latin *librāris,* n. use of Latin *librārius* relating to books, from *liber* book]

library edition *n.* an edition of a book having a superior quality of paper, binding, etc.

librate (ˈlaɪbreɪt) *vb. (intr.)* **1.** to oscillate or waver. **2.** to hover or be balanced. [C17: from Latin *librātus,* from *librāre* to balance] —**libratory** (ˈlaɪbrətərɪ, -trɪ) *adj.*

libration (laɪˈbreɪʃən) *n.* **1.** the act or an instance of oscillating. **2.** a real or apparent oscillation of the moon enabling approximately nine per cent of the surface facing away from earth to be seen. —**liˈbrational** *adj.*

librettist (lɪˈbrɛtɪst) *n.* the author of a libretto.

libretto (lɪˈbrɛtəʊ) *n., pl.* **-tos** *or* **-ti** (-tiː). a text written for and set to music in an opera, etc. [C18: from Italian, diminutive of *libro* book]

libriform (ˈlaɪbrɪˌfɔːm) *adj.* (of a fibre of woody tissue) elongated and having a pitted thickened cell wall.

Librium (ˈlɪbrɪəm) *n. Trademark.* a preparation of the drug chlordiazepoxide used as a tranquillizer. See also **benzodiazepine.**

Libyan (ˈlɪbɪən) *adj.* **1.** of or relating to Libya, a republic in N Africa, or to its people or language. ~*n.* **2.** a native or inhabitant of Libya. **3.** the extinct Hamitic language of ancient Libya.

lice (laɪs) *n.* the plural of **louse.**

licence *or U.S.* **license** (ˈlaɪsəns) *n.* **1.** a certificate, tag, document, etc., giving official permission to do something. **2.** formal permission or exemption. **3.** liberty of action or thought; freedom. **4.** intentional disregard of or deviation from conventional rules to achieve a certain effect: *poetic licence.* **5.** excessive freedom. **6.** licentiousness. [C14: via Old French and Medieval Latin *licentia* permission, from Latin: freedom, from *licet* it is allowed]

license (ˈlaɪsəns) *vb. (tr.)* **1.** to grant or give a licence for (something, such as the sale of alcohol). **2.** to give permission to or for. —**ˈlicensable** *adj.* —**ˈlicenser** *or* **ˈlicensor** *n.*

licensed aircraft engineer *n.* the official name for **ground engineer.**

licensee (ˌlaɪsənˈsiː) *n.* a person who holds a licence, esp. one to sell alcoholic drink.

license plate *or Canadian* **licence plate** *n.* the U.S. and Canadian term for **numberplate.**

licentiate (laɪˈsɛnʃɪɪt) *n.* **1.** a person who has received a formal attestation of professional competence to practise a certain profession or teach a certain skill or subject. **2.** a degree between that of bachelor and doctor awarded now only by certain chiefly European universities. **3.** a person who holds this degree. **4.** *Chiefly Presbyterian Church.* a person holding a licence to preach. [C15: from Medieval Latin *licentiātus,* from *licentiāre* to permit] —**liˈcentiateˌship** *n.* —**liˌcentiˈation** *n.*

licentious (laɪˈsɛnʃəs) *adj.* **1.** sexually unrestrained or promiscuous. **2.** *Now rare.* showing disregard for convention. [C16: from Latin *licentiōsus* capricious, from *licentia* LICENCE] —**liˈcentiously** *adv.* —**liˈcentiousness** *n.*

lichee (ˌlaɪˈtʃiː) *n.* a variant spelling of **litchi.**

lichen (ˈlaɪkən, ˈlɪtʃən) *n.* **1.** any plant of the division *Lichenes,* which are formed by the symbiotic association of a fungus and an alga and occur as crusty patches or bushy growths on tree trunks, bare ground, etc. **2.** *Pathol.* any of various eruptive disorders of the skin. [C17: via Latin from Greek *leikhēn,* from *leikhein* to lick] —**ˈlichened** *adj.* —**ˈlichen-ˌlike** *adj.* —**ˈlichenˌoid** *adj.* —**ˈlichenous** *or* **ˈlichenˌose** *adj.*

lichenin (ˈlaɪkənɪn) *n.* a complex polysaccharide occurring in certain species of mosses.

lichenology (ˌlaɪkəˈnɒlədʒɪ, ˌlɪ-) *n.* the study of the structure, physiology, and ecology of lichens.

lich gate *or* **lych gate** (lɪtʃ) *n.* a roofed gate to a churchyard, formerly used during funerals as a temporary shelter for the bier. [C15: *lich,* from Old English *līc* corpse]

lichi (ˌlaɪˈtʃiː) *n.* a variant spelling of **litchi.**

licht (lɪxt) *n., adj., vb.* a Scot. word for **light**[1] and **light**[2].

licit (ˈlɪsɪt) *adj.* a less common word for **lawful.** [C15: from Latin *licitus* permitted, from *licēre* to be permitted] —**ˈlicitly** *adv.* —**ˈlicitness** *n.*

lick (lɪk) *vb.* **1.** *(tr.)* to pass the tongue over, esp. in order to taste or consume. **2.** to flicker or move lightly over or round (something): *the flames licked around the door.* **3.** *(tr.) Informal.* **a.** to defeat or vanquish. **b.** to flog or thrash. **c.** to be or do much better than. **4. lick into shape.** to put into a satisfactory condition: from the former belief that bear cubs were born formless and had to be licked into shape by their mother. **5. lick one's lips.** to anticipate or recall something with glee or relish. **6. lick one's wounds.** to retire after a defeat or setback in order to husband one's resources. **7. lick the boots of.** See **boot**[1] (sense 14). ~*n.* **8.** an instance of passing the tongue over something. **9.** a small amount: *a lick of paint.* **10.** Also called: **salt lick.** a block of compressed salt or chemical matter provided for domestic animals to lick for medicinal purposes. **11.** a place to which animals go to lick exposed natural deposits of salt. **12.** *Informal.* a hit; blow. **13.** *Slang.* a short musical phrase, usually on one instrument. **14.** *Informal.* speed; rate of movement: *he was going at quite a lick when he hit it.* **15. a lick and a promise.** something hastily done, esp. a hurried wash. [Old English *liccian;* related to Old High German *leckon,* Latin *lingere,* Greek *leikhein*] —**ˈlicker** *n.*

lick-alike *adj. Irish informal.* very similar: *he and his father are lick-alike.*

lickerish *or* **liquorish** (ˈlɪkərɪʃ) *adj. Archaic.* **1.** lecherous or lustful. **2.** greedy; gluttonous. **3.** appetizing or tempting. [C16: changed from C13 *lickerous,* via Norman French from Old French *lechereus* lecherous; see LECHER] —**ˈlickerishly** *or* **ˈliquorishly** *adv.* —**ˈlickerishness** *or* **ˈliquorishness** *n.*

lickety-split (ˈlɪkɪtɪˈsplɪt) *adv. U.S. and Canadian informal.* very quickly; speedily. [C19: from LICK + SPLIT]

licking (ˈlɪkɪŋ) *n. Informal.* **1.** a beating. **2.** a defeat.

lickspittle (ˈlɪkˌspɪtᵊl) *n.* a flattering or servile person.

licorice (ˈlɪkərɪs) *n.* the usual U.S. and Canadian spelling of **liquorice.**

lictor (ˈlɪktə) *n.* one of a group of ancient Roman officials, usually bearing fasces, who attended magistrates, etc. [C16 *lictor,* C14 *littour,* from Latin *ligāre* to bind]

lid (lɪd) *n.* **1.** a cover, usually removable or hinged, for a receptacle: *a saucepan lid; a desk lid.* **2.** short for **eyelid.** **3.** *Botany.* another name for **operculum** (sense 2). **4.** *U.S. dated slang.* a quantity of marijuana, usually an ounce. **5. dip one's lid.** *Austral. informal.* to raise one's hat as a greeting, etc. **6. flip one's lid.** *Slang.* to become crazy or angry. **7. put the lid on.** *Informal.* **a.** *Brit.* to be the final blow to. **b.** to curb, prevent, or discourage. **8. take the lid off.** *Informal.* to make startling or spectacular revelations about. [Old English *hlid;* related to Old Friesian *hlid,* Old High German *hlit* cover] —**ˈlidded** *adj.*

lidless (ˈlɪdlɪs) *adj.* **1.** having no lid or top. **2.** (of animals) having no eyelids. **3.** *Archaic.* vigilant and watchful.

lido (ˈliːdəʊ) *n., pl.* **-dos.** *Brit.* a public place of recreation, including a pool for swimming or water sports. [C20: after the *Lido,* island bathing beach near Venice, from Latin *litus* shore]

lidocaine (ˈlaɪdəˌkeɪn) *n.* the U.S. name for **lignocaine.** [C20: from *acetanilid* + *-caine* as in *cocaine*]

lie[1] (laɪ) *vb.* **lies, lying, lied.** **1.** *(intr.)* to speak untruthfully with intent to mislead or deceive. **2.** *(intr.)* to convey a false impression or practise deception: *the camera does not lie.* ~*n.* **3.** an untrue or deceptive statement deliberately used to mislead. **4.** something that is deliberately intended to deceive. **5. give the lie to. a.** to disprove. **b.** to accuse of lying. ~Related adj.: **mendacious.** [Old English *lyge* (n.), *lēogan* (vb.); related to Old High German *liogan,* Gothic *liugan*]

lie[2] (laɪ) *vb.* **lies, lying, lay** (leɪ), **lain** (leɪn). *(intr.)* **1.** (often foll. by *down*) to place oneself or be in a prostrate position, horizontal to the ground. **2.** to be situated, esp. on a horizontal surface: *the pencil is lying on the desk; India lies to the south of Russia.* **3.** to be buried: *here lies Jane Brown.* **4.** *(copula)* to be and remain (in a particular state or condition): *to lie dormant.* **5.** to stretch or extend: *the city lies before us.* **6.** (usually foll. by *on* or *upon*) to rest or weigh: *my sins lie heavily on my mind.* **7.** (usually foll. by *in*) to exist or consist inherently: *strength lies in unity.* **8.** (foll. by *with*) **a.** to be or rest (with): *the ultimate decision lies with you.* **b.** *Archaic.* to have sexual intercourse (with). **9.** (of an action, claim, appeal, etc.) to subsist; be maintainable or admissible. **10.** *Archaic.* to stay temporarily. **11. lie in state.** See **state** (sense 13). **12. lie low. a.** to keep or be concealed or quiet. **b.** to wait for a favourable opportunity. ~*n.* **13.** the manner, place, or style in which something is situated. **14.** the hiding place or lair of an animal. **15.** *Golf.* **a.** the position of the ball after a shot: *a bad lie.* **b.** the angle made by the shaft of the club before the upswing. **16. lie of the land. a.** the topography of the land. **b.** the way in which a situation is developing or people are behaving. ~See also **lie down, lie in, lie to, lie up.** [Old English *licgan* akin to Old High German *ligen* to lie, Latin *lectus* bed]

▷**Usage.** See at **lay**[1].

Liebfraumilch (ˈliːbfraʊˌmɪlk; *German* ˈliːpfraumɪlç) *or* **Liebfrauenmilch** (*German* liːpˈfrauənmɪlç) *n.* a white table wine from the Rhine vineyards in W and central Europe. [German: from *Liebfrau* the Virgin Mary + *Milch* milk; after *Liebfrauenstift* convent where the wine was originally made]

Liebig condenser (ˈliːbɪg) *n. Chem.* a laboratory condenser consisting of a glass tube surrounded by a glass envelope through which cooling water flows. [named after Justus *Liebig* (1803–73), German chemist]

lied (liːd; *German* liːt) *n., pl.* **lieder** (ˈliːdə; *German* ˈliːdər). *Music.* any of various musical settings for solo voice and piano of a romantic or lyrical poem, for which composers such as Schubert, Schumann, and Wolf are famous. [from German: song]

lie detector *n.* a polygraph used esp. by a police interrogator to detect false or devious answers to questions, a sudden change in one or more involuntary physiological responses being considered a manifestation of guilt, fear, etc. See **polygraph** (sense 1), **galvanic skin response.**

lie down *vb. (intr., adv.)* **1.** to place oneself or be in a prostrate position in order to rest or sleep. **2.** to accept without protest or opposition (esp. in the phrases **lie down under, take something lying down**). ~*n.* **lie-down.** **3.** a rest.

lief (liːf) *adv.* **1.** *Now rare.* gladly; willingly: *I'd as lief go today as tomorrow.* ~*adj.* **2.** *Archaic.* **a.** ready; glad. **b.** dear; beloved. [Old English *leof;* related to *lufu* love]

liege (liːdʒ) *adj.* **1.** (of a lord) owed feudal allegiance (esp. in the phrase **liege lord**). **2.** (of a vassal or servant) owing feudal allegiance: *a liege subject.* **3.** of or relating to the relationship or bond between liege lord and liegeman: *liege homage.* **4.** faithful; loyal. ~*n.* **5.** a liege lord. **6.** a liegeman or true subject. [C13: from Old French *lige,* from Medieval Latin *līticus,* from *lītus, laetus* serf, of Germanic origin]

liegeman (ˈliːdʒˌmæn) *n., pl.* **-men.** **1.** (formerly) the subject of a sovereign or feudal lord; vassal. **2.** a loyal follower.

lie in *vb. (intr., adv.)* **1.** to remain in bed late in the morning. **2.** to be confined in childbirth. ~*n.* **lie-in.** **3.** a long stay in bed in the morning.

lien (ˈliːən, liːn) *n. Law.* a right to retain possession of another's property pending discharge of a debt. [C16: via Old French from Latin *ligāmen* bond, from *ligāre* to bind]

lienal (ˈlaɪənᵊl) *adj.* of or relating to the spleen. [C19: from Latin *lien* SPLEEN]

lientery (ˈlaɪəntərɪ, -trɪ) *n. Pathol.* the passage of undigested food in the faeces. [C16: from French, from Medieval Latin, from Greek *leienteria,* from *leios* smooth + *enteron* intestine] —ˌ**lienˈteric** *adj.*

lierne (lɪˈɜːn) *n. Architect.* a short secondary rib that connects the intersections of the primary ribs, esp. as used in Gothic vaulting. [C19: from French, perhaps related to *lier* to bind]

lie to *vb. (intr., adv.) Nautical.* (of a vessel) to be hove to with little or no swinging.

lieu (ljuː, luː) *n.* stead; place (esp. in the phrases **in lieu, in lieu of**). [C13: from Old French, ultimately from Latin *locus* place]

lie up *vb. (intr., adv.)* **1.** to go into or stay in one's room or bed, as through illness. **2.** to be out of commission or use: *my car has been lying up for months.*

Lieut *abbrev. for* lieutenant. Also: **Lt.**

lieutenant (lɛfˈtɛnənt; *U.S.* luːˈtɛnənt) *n.* **1.** a military officer holding commissioned rank immediately junior to a captain. **2.** a naval officer holding commissioned rank immediately junior to a lieutenant commander. **3.** *U.S.* an officer in a police or fire department ranking immediately junior to a captain. **4.** a person who holds an office in subordination to or in place of a superior. [C14: from Old French, literally: place-holding] —**lieuˈtenancy** *n.*

lieutenant colonel *n.* an officer holding commissioned rank immediately junior to a colonel in certain armies, air forces, and marine corps.

lieutenant commander *n.* an officer holding commissioned rank in certain navies immediately junior to a commander.

lieutenant general *n.* an officer holding commissioned rank in certain armies, air forces, and marine corps immediately junior to a general.

lieutenant governor *n.* **1.** a deputy governor. **2.** (in the U.S.) an elected official who acts as deputy to a state governor and succeeds him if he dies. **3. lieutenant-governor.** (in Canada) the representative of the Crown in a province: appointed by the federal government acting for the Crown.

life (laɪf) *n., pl.* **lives** (laɪvz). **1.** the state or quality that distinguishes living beings or organisms from dead ones and from inorganic matter, characterized chiefly by metabolism, growth, and the ability to reproduce and respond to stimuli. Related adj.: **animate.** **2.** the period between birth and death. **3.** a living person or being: *to save a life.* **4.** the time between birth and the present time. **5. a.** the remainder or extent of one's life. **b.** (*as modifier*): *a life sentence; life membership; life subscription; life work.* **6.** short for **life imprisonment.** **7.** the amount of time that something is active or functioning: *the life of a battery.* **8.** a present condition, state, or mode of existence: *my life is very dull here.* **9. a.** a biography. **b.** (*as modifier*): *a life story.* **10. a.** a characteristic state or mode of existence: *town life.* **b.** (*as modifier*): *life style.* **11.** the sum or course of human events and activities. **12.** liveliness or high spirits: *full of life.* **13.** a source of strength, animation, or vitality: *he was the life of the show.* **14.** all living things, taken as a whole: *there is no life on Mars; plant life.* **15.** sparkle, as of wines. **16.** strong or high flavour, as of fresh food. **17.** (*modifier*) *Arts.* drawn or taken from a living model: *life drawing; a life mask.* **18.** *Physics.* another name for **lifetime.** **19.** (in certain games) one of a number of opportunities of participation. **20. as large as life.** *Informal.* real and living. **21. larger than life.** in an exaggerated form. **22. come to life. a.** to become animate or conscious. **b.** to be realistically portrayed or represented. **23. for dear life.** urgently or with extreme vigour or desperation. **24. for the life of me (him, her,** etc.) though trying desperately. **25. go for your life.** *Austral. and N.Z. informal.* an expression of encouragement. **26. a matter of life and death.** a matter of extreme urgency. **27. not on your life.** *Informal.* certainly not. **28. the life and soul.** *Informal.* a person regarded as the main source of merriment and liveliness: *the life and soul of the party.* **29. the life of Riley.** *Informal.* an easy life. **30. to the life.** (of a copy or image) resembling the original exactly. **31. to save (one's) life.** *Informal.* in spite of all considerations or attempts: *he couldn't play football to save his life.* **32. the time of one's life.** a memorably enjoyable time. **33. true to life.** faithful to reality. [Old English *līf;* related to Old High German *lib,* Old Norse *līf* life, body]

life assurance *n.* a form of insurance providing for the payment of a specified sum to a named beneficiary on the death of the policyholder. Also called: **life insurance.**

life belt *n.* a ring filled with buoyant material or air, used to keep a person afloat when in danger of drowning.

lifeblood (ˈlaɪfˌblʌd) *n.* **1.** the blood, considered as vital to sustain life. **2.** the essential or animating force.

lifeboat (ˈlaɪfˌbəʊt) *n.* **1.** a boat, propelled by oars or a motor, used for rescuing people at sea, escaping from a sinking ship, etc. **2.** *Informal.* a fund set up by the dealers in a market to rescue any member who may become insolvent as a result of a collapse in market prices.

life buoy *n.* any of various kinds of buoyant device for keeping people afloat in an emergency.

life cycle *n.* the series of changes occurring in an animal or plant between one development stage and the identical stage in the next generation.

life estate *n.* property that may be held only for the extent of the holder's lifetime.

life expectancy *n.* the statistically determined average number of years of life remaining after a specified age for a given group of individuals. Also called: **expectation of life.**

life form *n.* **1.** *Biology.* the characteristic overall form and structure of a mature organism on the basis of which it can be classified. **2.** any living creature. **3.** (in science fiction) an alien.

lifeguard (ˈlaɪfˌgɑːd) *n.* a person present at a beach or pool to guard people against the risk of drowning. Also called: **life-saver.**

life history *n.* **1.** the series of changes undergone by an organism between fertilization of the egg and death. **2.** the series of events that make up a person's life.

life imprisonment *n.* an indeterminate sentence always given for murder and as a maximum sentence in several other crimes. There is no remission, although the Home Secretary may order the prisoner's release on licence.

life instinct *n. Psychoanal.* the instinct for reproduction and self-preservation.

life insurance *n.* another name for **life assurance.**

life interest *n.* interest (esp. from property) that is payable to a person during his life but ceases with his death.

life jacket *n.* an inflatable sleeveless jacket worn to keep a person afloat when in danger of drowning.

lifeless (ˈlaɪflɪs) *adj.* **1.** without life; inanimate; dead. **2.** not sustaining living organisms. **3.** having no vitality or animation. **4.** unconscious. —ˈ**lifelessly** *adv.* —ˈ**lifelessness** *n.*

lifelike (ˈlaɪfˌlaɪk) *adj.* closely resembling or representing life. —ˈ**lifeˌlikeness** *n.*

lifeline (ˈlaɪfˌlaɪn) *n.* **1.** a line thrown or fired aboard a vessel for hauling in a hawser for a breeches buoy. **2.** any rope or line attached to a vessel or trailed from it for the safety of passengers, crew, swimmers, etc. **3.** a line by which a deep-sea diver is raised or lowered. **4.** a vital line of access or communication.

lifelong (ˈlaɪfˌlɒŋ) *adj.* lasting for or as if for a lifetime.

life mask *n.* a cast taken from the face of a living person, usually using plaster of Paris.

life peer *n. Brit.* a peer whose title lapses at his death.

life preserver *n.* **1.** *Brit.* a club or bludgeon, esp. one kept for self-defence. **2.** *U.S. and Canadian.* a life belt or life jacket.

lifer (ˈlaɪfə) *n. Informal.* a prisoner sentenced to life imprisonment.

life raft *n.* a raft for emergency use at sea.

life-saver *n.* **1.** the saver of a person's life. **2.** another name for **lifeguard.** **3.** *Informal.* a person or thing that gives help in time of need. —ˈ**life-ˌsaving** *adj., n.*

life science *n.* any one of the branches of science concerned with the structure and behaviour of living organisms, such as biology, botany, zoology, physiology, or biochemistry. Compare **physical science.** See also **social science.**

life-size *or* **life-sized** *adj.* representing actual size.

life space *n. Psychol.* a spatial representation of all the forces that control a person's behaviour.

life span *n.* the period of time during which a human being, animal, machine, etc., may be expected to live or function under normal conditions.

lifestyle (ˈlaɪfˌstaɪl) *n.* **1.** a set of attitudes, habits, or possessions associated with a particular person or group. **2.** such attitudes, etc., regarded as fashionable or desirable.

life-support *adj.* of or providing the equipment required to sustain human life in an unnatural environment, such as in space, or in severe illness or disability.

life table *n.* another name for **mortality table.**

lifetime ('laɪfˌtaɪm) *n.* **1. a.** the length of time a person or animal is alive. **b.** (*as modifier*): *a lifetime supply.* **2.** the length of time that something functions, is useful, etc.. **3.** *Physics.* the average time of existence of an unstable or reactive entity, such as a nucleus or elementary particle, etc.; mean life.

LIFO ('laɪfəʊ) *acronym for* last in, first out (as an accounting principle in sorting stock). Compare **FIFO.**

lift[1] (lɪft) *vb.* **1.** to rise or cause to rise upwards from the ground or another support to a higher place: *to lift a sack.* **2.** to move or cause to move upwards: *to lift one's eyes.* **3.** (*tr.*) to take hold of in order to carry or remove: *to lift something down from a shelf.* **4.** (*tr.*) to raise in status, spirituality, estimation, etc.: *his position lifted him from the common crowd.* **5.** (*tr.*) to revoke or rescind: *to lift tax restrictions.* **6.** to make or become audible or louder: *to lift one's voice in song.* **7.** (*tr.*) to take (plants or underground crops) out of the ground for transplanting or harvesting. **8.** (*intr.*) to disappear by lifting or as if by lifting: *the fog lifted.* **9.** to transport in a vehicle. **10.** (*tr.*) *Informal.* to take unlawfully or dishonourably; steal. **11.** (*tr.*) *Informal.* to make dishonest use of (another person's idea, writing, etc.); plagiarize. **12.** (*tr.*) *Slang.* to arrest. **13.** (*tr.*) to perform a face-lift on. **14.** (*tr.*) *U.S. and Canadian.* to pay off (a mortgage, etc.). ~*n.* **15.** the act or an instance of lifting. **16.** the power or force available or used for lifting. **17. a.** *Brit.* a platform, compartment, or cage raised or lowered in a vertical shaft to transport persons or goods in a building. U.S. and Canadian word: **elevator. b.** See **chair lift, ski lift. 18.** the distance or degree to which something is lifted. **19.** a usually free ride as a passenger in a car or other vehicle. **20.** a rise in the height of the ground. **21.** a rise in morale or feeling of cheerfulness usually caused by some specific thing or event. **22.** the force required to lift an object. **23.** a layer of the heel of a shoe, etc., or a detachable pad inside the shoe to give the wearer added height. **24.** aid; help. **25.** *Mining.* **a.** the thickness of ore extracted in one operation. **b.** a set of pumps used in a mine. **26. a.** the component of the aerodynamic forces acting on a wing, etc., at right angles to the airflow. **b.** the upward force exerted by the gas in a balloon, airship, etc. **27.** See **airlift** (sense 1). [C13: from Scandinavian; related to Old Norse *lypta,* Old English *lyft* sky; compare LOFT] —'**liftable** *adj.* —'**lifter** *n.*

lift[2] (lɪft) *n. Scot.* the sky. [Old English *lyft*]

liftboy ('lɪftˌbɔɪ) *or* **liftman** *n., pl.* **-boys** *or* **-men.** a person who operates a lift, esp. in large public or commercial buildings and hotels.

lifting body *n.* a wingless aircraft or spacecraft that derives its aerodynamic lift from the shape of its body.

liftoff ('lɪftˌɒf) *n.* **1.** the initial movement or ascent of a rocket from its launching pad. **2.** the instant at which this occurs. ~*vb.* **lift off. 3.** (*intr., adv.*) (of a rocket) to leave its launching pad.

lift pump *n.* a pump that raises a fluid to a higher level. It usually consists of a piston and vertical cylinder with flap or ball valves in both piston and cylinder base. Compare: **force pump.**

ligament ('lɪgəmənt) *n.* **1.** *Anatomy.* any one of the bands or sheets of tough fibrous connective tissue that restrict movement in joints, connect various bones or cartilages, support muscles, etc. **2.** any physical or abstract connection or bond. [C14: from Medieval Latin *ligāmentum,* from Latin (in the sense: bandage), from *ligāre* to bind]

ligamentous (ˌlɪgə'mentəs), **ligamental,** *or* **ligamentary** *adj.* relating to or shaped like a ligament.

ligan ('laɪgən) *n.* a variant of **lagan.**

ligand ('lɪgənd, 'laɪ-) *n. Chem.* an atom, molecule, radical, or ion forming a complex with a central atom. [C20: from Latin *ligandum,* gerund of *ligāre* to bind]

ligase ('laɪˌgeɪz) *n.* any of a class of enzymes that catalyse the formation of covalent bonds and are important in the synthesis and repair of biological molecules, such as DNA.

ligate ('laɪgeɪt) *vb.* (*tr.*) to tie up or constrict (something) with a ligature. [C16: from Latin *ligātus,* from *ligāre* to bind] —**li'gation** *n.* —**ligative** ('lɪgətɪv) *adj.*

ligature ('lɪgətʃə, -ˌtʃʊə) *n.* **1.** the act of binding or tying up. **2.** something used to bind. **3.** a link, bond, or tie. **4.** *Surgery.* a thread or wire for tying around a vessel, duct, etc., as for constricting the flow of blood to a part. **5.** *Printing.* a character of two or more joined letters, such as, fi, fl, ffi, ffl, usually cast on the same piece of type. **6.** *Music.* **a.** a slur or the group of notes connected by it. **b.** (in plainsong notation) a symbol indicating two or more notes grouped together. ~*vb.* **7.** (*tr.*) to bind with a ligature; ligate. [C14: from Late Latin *ligātūra,* ultimately from Latin *ligāre* to bind]

liger ('laɪgə) *n.* the hybrid offspring of a female tiger and a male lion.

ligger ('lɪgə) *n. Slang.* (esp. in the entertainment industry and the media) a person who habitually takes advantage of what is freely available; hanger-on or freeloader. [C20: origin uncertain] —'**ligging** *n.*

light[1] (laɪt) *n.* **1.** the medium of illumination that makes sight possible. **2.** Also called: **visible radiation.** electromagnetic radiation that is capable of causing a visual sensation and has wavelengths from about 380 to about 780 nanometres. **3.** (*not in technical usage*) electromagnetic radiation that has a wavelength outside this range, esp. ultraviolet radiation: *ultraviolet light.* **4.** the sensation experienced when electromagnetic radiation within the visible spectrum falls on the retina of the eye. **5.** anything that illuminates, such as a lamp or candle. **6.** See **traffic light. 7.** a particular quality or type of light: *a good light for reading.* **8. a.** illumination from the sun during the day; daylight. **b.** the time this appears; daybreak; dawn. **9.** anything that allows the entrance of light, such as a window or compartment of a window. **10.** the condition of being visible or known (esp. in the phrases **bring** *or* **come to light**). **11.** an aspect or view: *he saw it in a different light.* **12.** mental understanding or spiritual insight. **13.** a person considered to be an authority or leader. **14.** brightness of countenance, esp. a sparkle in the eyes. **15. a.** the act of igniting or kindling something, such as a cigarette. **b.** something that ignites or kindles, esp. in a specified manner, such as a spark or flame. **c.** something used for igniting or kindling, such as a match. **16.** See **lighthouse. 17. a.** the effect of illumination on objects or scenes, as created in a picture. **b.** an area of brightness in a picture, as opposed to shade. **18.** a poetic or archaic word for **eyesight. 19.** the answer to a clue in a crossword. **20. in (the) light of.** in view of; taking into account; considering. **21. out like a light.** quickly asleep or unconscious. **22. see the light. a.** to gain sudden insight into or understanding of something. **b.** to experience a religious conversion. **23. see the light (of day). a.** to come into being. **b.** to come to public notice. **24. shed** (*or* **throw**) **light on.** to clarify or supply additional information on. **25. stand in a person's light. a.** to stand so as to obscure a person's vision. **b.** to impede a person's progress or prevent them gaining due recognition. **26. strike a light. a.** (*vb.*) to ignite something, esp. a match, by friction. **b.** (*interj.*) *Brit.* an exclamation of surprise. ~*adj.* **27.** full of light; well-lighted. **28.** (of a colour) reflecting or transmitting a large amount of light: *light yellow.* Compare **medium** (sense 2), **dark** (sense 2). **29.** *Phonetics.* relating to or denoting an (l) pronounced with front vowel resonance; clear: *the French "l" is much lighter than that of English.* Compare **dark** (sense 9). ~*vb.* **lights, lighting, lighted** *or* **lit** (lɪt). **30.** to ignite or cause to ignite. **31.** (often foll. by *up*) to illuminate or cause to illuminate. **32.** to make or become cheerful or animated. **33.** (*tr.*) to guide or lead by light. ~See also **lights**[1], **light up** [Old English *lēoht;* related to Old High German *lioht,* Gothic *liuhath,* Latin *lux*] —'**lightish** *adj.* —'**lightless** *adj.*

light[2] (laɪt) *adj.* **1.** not heavy; weighing relatively little. **2.** having relatively low density: *magnesium is a light metal.* **3.** lacking sufficient weight; not agreeing with standard or official weights. **4.** not great in degree, intensity, or number: *light rain; a light eater.* **5.** without burdens, difficulties, or problems; easily borne or done: *a light heart; light work.* **6.** graceful, agile, or deft: *light fingers.* **7.** not bulky or clumsy. **8.** not serious or profound; entertaining: *light verse.* **9.** without importance or consequence; insignificant: *no light matter.* **10.** frivolous or capricious. **11.** loose in morals. **12.** dizzy or unclear: *a light head.* **13.** (of bread, cake, etc.) spongy or well leavened. **14.** easily digested: *a light meal.* **15.** relatively low in alcoholic content: *a light wine.* **16.** (of a soil) having a crumbly texture. **17.** (of a vessel, lorry, etc.) **a.** designed to carry light loads. **b.** not loaded. **18.** carrying light arms or equipment: *light infantry.* **19.** (of an industry) engaged in the production of small consumer goods using light machinery. Compare **heavy** (sense 10). **20.** *Aeronautics.* (of an aircraft) having a maximum take-off weight less than 5670 kilograms (12 500 pounds). **21.** *Chem.* (of an oil fraction obtained from coal tar) having a boiling range between about 100° and 210°C. **22.** (of a railway) having a narrow gauge, or in some cases a standard gauge with speed or load restrictions not applied to a main line. **23.** *Bridge.* **a.** (of a bid) made on insufficient values. **b.** (of a player) having failed to take sufficient tricks to make his contract. **24.** *Phonetics, prosody.* (of a syllable, vowel, etc.) unaccented or weakly stressed; short. Compare **heavy** (sense 13). See also **light**[1] (sense 29). **25.** *Phonetics.* the least of three levels of stress in an utterance, in such languages as English. **26. light on.** *Informal.* lacking a sufficient quantity of (something). **27. make light of.** to treat as insignificant or trifling. ~*adv.* **28.** a less common word for **lightly. 29.** with little equipment, baggage, etc.: *to travel light.* ~*vb.* **lights, lighting, lighted** *or* **lit** (lɪt). (*intr.*) **30.** (esp. of birds) to settle or land after flight. **31.** to get down from a horse, vehicle, etc. **32.** (foll. by *on* or *upon*) to come upon unexpectedly. **33.** to strike or fall on: *the choice lighted on me.* ~See also **light into, light out, lights**[2]. [Old English *lēoht;* related to Dutch *licht,* Gothic *leihts*] —'**lightish** *adj.* —'**lightly** *adv.* —'**lightness** *n.*

Light (laɪt) *n.* **1.** God regarded as a source of illuminating grace and strength. **2.** *Quakerism.* short for **Inner Light.**

light air *n.* very light air movement of force one on the Beaufort scale.

light breeze *n.* a very light wind of force two on the Beaufort scale.

light bulb *n.* a glass bulb containing a gas, such as argon or nitrogen, at low pressure and enclosing a thin metal filament that emits light when an electric current is passed through it. Sometimes shortened to **bulb.**

light-emitting diode *n.* a diode of semiconductor material, such as gallium arsenide, that gives off light in proportion to the forward bias current applied. Abbrev.: **LED.**

lighten[1] ('laɪtᵊn) *vb.* **1.** to become or make light. **2.** (*intr.*) to shine; glow. **3.** (*intr.*) (of lightning) to flash. **4.** (*tr.*) *Archaic.* to cause to flash. **5.** (*tr.*) an archaic word for **enlighten.**
lighten[2] ('laɪtᵊn) *vb.* **1.** to make or become less heavy. **2.** to make or become less burdensome or oppressive; mitigate. **3.** to make or become more cheerful or lively.
light engine *n.* a railway locomotive in motion without drawing any carriages or wagons. U.S. equivalent: **wildcat.**
lightening ('laɪtᵊnɪŋ) *n. Obstetrics.* the sensation, experienced by many women late in pregnancy when the head of the fetus enters the pelvis, of a reduction in pressure on the diaphragm.
lighter[1] ('laɪtə) *n.* **1.** a small portable device for providing a naked flame or red-hot filament to light cigarettes, etc. **2.** a person or thing that ignites something.
lighter[2] ('laɪtə) *n.* a flat-bottomed barge used for transporting cargo, esp. in loading or unloading a ship. [C15: probably from Middle Dutch; compare C16 Dutch *lichter*]
lighterage ('laɪtərɪdʒ) *n.* **1.** the conveyance or loading and unloading of cargo by means of a lighter. **2.** the charge for this service.
lighter than air *adj.* (**lighter-than-air** *when prenominal*). **1.** having a lower density than that of air. **2.** of or relating to an aircraft, such as a balloon or airship, that depends on buoyancy for support in the air.
light face *n.* **1.** *Printing.* a weight of type characterized by light thin lines. Compare **bold face.** ~*adj. also* **light-faced. 2.** (of type) having this weight.
light-fast *adj.* (of a dye or dyed article) unaffected by light.
light-fingered *adj.* having nimble or agile fingers, esp. for thieving or picking pockets. —ˌ**light-'fingeredness** *n.*
light flyweight *n.* **a.** an amateur boxer weighing not more than 48 kg (106 pounds). **b.** (*as modifier*): *a light-flyweight fight.*
light-footed *adj.* having a light or nimble tread. —ˌ**light-'footedly** *adv.* —ˌ**light-'footedness** *n.*
light-headed *adj.* **1.** frivolous in disposition or behaviour. **2.** giddy; feeling faint or slightly delirious. —ˌ**light-'headedly** *adv.* —ˌ**light-'headedness** *n.*
light-hearted *adj.* cheerful or carefree in mood or disposition. —ˌ**light-'heartedly** *adv.* —ˌ**light-'heartedness** *n.*
light heavyweight *n.* **1.** Also called (in Brit.): **cruiserweight. a.** a professional boxer weighing 160–175 pounds (72.5–79.5 kg). **b.** an amateur boxer weighing 75–81 kg (165–179 pounds). **c.** (*as modifier*): *a light-heavyweight bout.* **2.** a wrestler in a similar weight category (usually 192–214 pounds (87–97 kg)).
light horse *n.* lightly armed and highly mobile cavalry. —ˌ**light-'horseman** *n.*
lighthouse ('laɪtˌhaʊs) *n.* a fixed structure in the form of a tower equipped with a light visible to mariners for warning them of obstructions, for marking harbour entrances, etc.
lighting ('laɪtɪŋ) *n.* **1.** the act or quality of illumination or ignition. **2.** the apparatus for supplying artificial light effects to a stage, film, or television set. **3.** the distribution of light on an object or figure, as in painting, photography, etc.
lighting cameraman *n. Films.* the person who designs and supervises the lighting of scenes to be filmed.
lighting-up time *n.* the time when vehicles are required by law to have their lights switched on.
light into *vb.* (*intr., prep.*) *Informal.* to assail physically or verbally.
light meter *n.* another name for **exposure meter.**
light middleweight *n.* **a.** an amateur boxer weighing 67–71 kg (148–157 pounds). **b.** (*as modifier*): *a light-middleweight bout.* Compare **junior middleweight.**
light music *n.* music for popular entertainment.
lightness ('laɪtnɪs) *n.* the attribute of an object or colour that enables an observer to judge the extent to which the object or colour reflects or transmits incident light. See also **colour.**
lightning ('laɪtnɪŋ) *n.* **1.** a flash of light in the sky, occurring during a thunderstorm and caused by a discharge of electricity, either between clouds or between a cloud and the earth. **2.** (*modifier*) fast and sudden: *a lightning raid.* [C14: variant of *lightening*]
lightning arrester *n.* a device that protects electrical equipment, such as an aerial, from an excessive voltage resulting from a lightning discharge or other accidental electric surge, by discharging it to earth.
lightning bug *n. U.S. and Canadian.* another name for the **firefly.**
lightning chess *n.* rapid chess in which either each move has a fixed time allowed (usually 10 seconds) or each player is allotted a fixed time (often 5 minutes) for all his moves. U.S. name: **rapid transit chess.**
lightning conductor *or* **rod** *n.* a metal strip terminating in a series of sharp points, attached to the highest part of a building, etc., to discharge the electric field before it can reach a dangerous level and cause a lightning strike.
light opera *n.* another term for **operetta.**
light out *vb.* (*intr., adv.*) *Informal.* to depart quickly, as if being chased.
light pen *n. Computer technol.* **a.** a rodlike device which, when applied to the screen of a cathode-ray tube, can detect the time of passage of the illuminated spot across that point thus enabling a computer to determine the position on the screen being pointed at. **b.** a penlike device, used to read bar codes, that emits light and determines the intensity of that light as reflected from a small area of an adjacent surface.
light reaction *n. Botany.* the stage of photosynthesis during which light energy is absorbed by chlorophyll and transformed into chemical energy stored in ATP. Compare **dark reaction.**
lights[1] (laɪts) *pl. n.* a person's ideas, knowledge, or understanding: *he did it according to his lights.*
lights[2] (laɪts) *pl. n.* the lungs, esp. of sheep, bullocks, and pigs, used for feeding pets and occasionally in human food. [C13: plural noun use of LIGHT[2], referring to the light weight of the lungs]
light-sensitive *adj. Physics.* (of a surface) having a photoelectric property, such as the ability to generate a current, change its electrical resistance, etc., when exposed to light.
lightship ('laɪtˌʃɪp) *n.* a ship equipped as a lighthouse and moored where a fixed structure would prove impracticable.
light show *n.* a kaleidoscopic display of moving lights, etc., projected onto a screen, esp. during pop concerts.
lightsome[1] ('laɪtsəm) *adj. Archaic or poetic.* **1.** lighthearted or gay. **2.** airy or buoyant. **3.** not serious; frivolous. —'**lightsomely** *adv.* —'**lightsomeness** *n.*
lightsome[2] ('laɪtsəm) *adj. Archaic or poetic.* **1.** producing or reflecting light. **2.** full of or flooded with light.
lights out *n.* **1.** the time when those resident at an institution, such as soldiers in barracks or children at a boarding school, are expected to retire to bed. **2.** a fanfare or other signal indicating or signifying this.
light table *n. Printing.* a translucent surface of ground glass or a similar substance, illuminated from below and used for the examination of positive or negative film.
light trap *n.* any mechanical arrangement that allows some form of movement to take place while excluding light, such as a light-proof door or the lips of a film cassette.
light up *vb.* (*adv.*) **1.** to light a cigarette, pipe, etc. **2.** to illuminate or cause to illuminate. **3.** to make or become cheerful or animated.
light water *n.* a name for water (H_2O), as distinct from heavy water.
lightweight ('laɪtˌweɪt) *adj.* **1.** of a relatively light weight. **2.** not serious; trivial. ~*n.* **3.** a person or animal of a relatively light weight. **4. a.** a professional boxer weighing 130–135 pounds (59–61 kg). **b.** an amateur boxer weighing 57–60 kg (126–132 pounds). **c.** (*as modifier*): *the lightweight contender.* **5.** a wrestler in a similar weight category (usually 115–126 pounds (52–57 kg)). **6.** *Informal.* a person of little importance or influence.
light welterweight *n.* **a.** an amateur boxer weighing 60–63.5 kg (132–140 pounds). **b.** (*as modifier*): *the light welterweight champion.* Compare **junior welterweight.**
light year *n.* a unit of distance used in astronomy, equal to the distance travelled by light in one mean solar year, i.e. 9.4607×10^{15} metres or 5.8784×10^{12} miles.
lignaloes (laɪ'næləʊz, lɪg-) *n.* (*functioning as sing.*) another name for **eaglewood** (sense 2). [C14 *ligne aloes,* from Medieval Latin *lignum aloēs* wood of the aloe]
ligneous ('lɪgnɪəs) *adj.* of or resembling wood. [C17: from Latin *ligneus,* from *lignum* wood]
ligni-, ligno-, *or before a vowel* **lign-** *combining form.* indicating wood: *lignocellulose.* [from Latin *lignum* wood]
lignicolous (lɪg'nɪkələs) *or* **lignicole** ('lɪgnɪˌkəʊl) *adj.* growing or living on or in wood. [C19: LIGNI- + -COLOUS]
ligniform ('lɪgnɪˌfɔːm) *adj.* having the appearance of wood.
lignify ('lɪgnɪˌfaɪ) *vb.* **-fies, -fying, -fied.** *Botany.* to make or become woody as a result of the deposition of lignin in the cell walls. —ˌ**lignifi'cation** *n.*
lignin ('lɪgnɪn) *n.* a complex polymer occurring in certain plant cell walls making the plant rigid.
lignite ('lɪgnaɪt) *n.* a brown carbonaceous sedimentary rock with woody texture that consists of accumulated layers of partially decomposed vegetation deposited in the late Cretaceous period: used as a fuel. Fixed carbon content: 46–60 per cent; calorific value: 1.28×10^7 to 1.93×10^7 J/kg (5500 to 8300 Btu/lb). Also called: **brown coal.** —**lignitic** (lɪg'nɪtɪk) *adj.*
lignivorous (lɪg'nɪvərəs) *adj.* (of animals) feeding on wood.
lignocaine ('lɪgnəˌkeɪn) *n.* a powerful local anaesthetic administered by injection, or topically to mucous membranes. Formula: $C_{14}H_{22}N_2O.HCl.H_2O$. U.S. name: **lidocaine.** [C20: from LIGNO- + *caine,* on the model of *cocaine*]
lignocellulose (ˌlɪgnəʊ'sɛljʊˌləʊs, -ˌləʊz) *n.* a compound of lignin and cellulose that occurs in the walls of xylem cells in woody tissue.
lignum ('lɪgnəm) *n. Austral.* another name for **polygonum.**
lignum vitae ('vaɪtɪ) *n.* **1.** either of two zygophyllaceous tropical American trees, *Guaiacum officinale* or *G. sanctum,* having blue or purple flowers. **2.** the heavy resinous wood of either of these trees, which is used in machine bearings, casters, etc.: formerly thought to have medicinal properties. ~See also **guaiacum.** [New Latin, from Late Latin, literally: wood of life]
ligroin ('lɪgrəʊɪn) *n.* a volatile fraction of petroleum containing aliphatic hydrocarbons of the paraffin series. It has an approximate boiling point range of 70°–130°C and is used as a solvent. [origin unknown]
ligula ('lɪgjʊlə) *n., pl.* **-lae** (-ˌliː) *or* **-las. 1.** *Entomol.* the terminal part of the labium of an insect consisting of paired lobes. **2.** a

variant spelling of **ligule.** [C18: New Latin; see LIGULE] —'**ligular** *adj.* —'**ligu,loid** *adj.*

ligulate ('lɪgjʊlɪt, -ˌleɪt) *adj.* **1.** having the shape of a strap. **2.** *Biology.* of, relating to, or having a ligule or ligula.

ligule ('lɪgjuːl) *or* **ligula** *n.* **1.** a strap-shaped membranous outgrowth at the junction between the leaf blade and sheath in many grasses. **2.** a strap-shaped corolla, such as that of the ray flower in the daisy. [C19: via French, from Latin *ligula* strap, variant of *lingula,* from *lingua* tongue]

ligure ('lɪgjʊə) *n. Old Testament.* any of the 12 precious stones used in the breastplates of high priests. [C14: from Late Latin *ligūrius,* from Late Greek *ligurion*]

likable *or* **likeable** ('laɪkəbᵊl) *adj.* easy to like; pleasing. —'**likableness** *or* '**likeableness** *n.*

like[1] (laɪk) *adj.* **1.** (*prenominal*) similar; resembling. ~*prep.* **2.** similar to; similarly to; in the manner of: *acting like a maniac; he's so like his father.* **3.** used correlatively to express similarity in certain proverbs: *like mother, like daughter.* **4.** such as: *there are lots of ways you might amuse yourself—like taking a long walk, for instance.* ~*adv.* **5.** a dialect word for **likely. 6.** *Not standard.* as it were: often used as a parenthetic filler: *there was this policeman just staring at us, like.* ~*conj.* **7.** *Not standard.* as though; as if: *you look like you've just seen a ghost.* **8.** in the same way as; in the same way that: *she doesn't dance like you do.* ~*n.* **9.** the equal or counterpart of a person or thing, esp. one respected or prized: *compare like with like; her like will never be seen again.* **10. the like.** similar things: *dogs, foxes, and the like.* **11. the likes** (*or* **like**) **of.** people or things similar to (someone or something specified): *we don't want the likes of you around here.* [shortened from Old English *gelīc;* compare Old Norse *glīkr* and *līkr* like]

like[2] (laɪk) *vb.* **1.** (*tr.*) to find (something) enjoyable or agreeable or find it enjoyable or agreeable (to do something): *he likes boxing; he likes to hear music.* **2.** (*tr.*) to be fond of. **3.** (*tr.*) to prefer or wish (to do something): *we would like you to go.* **4.** (*tr.*) to feel towards; consider; regard: *how did she like it?* **5.** (*intr.*) to feel disposed or inclined; choose; wish. **6.** (*tr.*) *Archaic.* to please; agree with: *it likes me not to go.* ~*n.* **7.** (*usually pl.*) a favourable feeling, desire, preference, etc. (esp. in the phrase **likes and dislikes**). [Old English *līcian;* related to Old Norse *līka,* Dutch *lijken*]

-like *suffix forming adjectives.* **1.** resembling or similar to: *lifelike; springlike.* **2.** having the characteristics of: *childlike; ladylike.* [from LIKE[1] (prep.)]

likelihood ('laɪklɪˌhʊd) *or* **likeliness** *n.* **1.** the condition of being likely or probable; probability. **2.** something that is probable. **3.** *Statistics.* the probability of a given sample being randomly drawn regarded as a function of the parameters of the population. The likelihood ratio is the ratio of this to the maximized likelihood. See also **maximum likelihood.**

likely ('laɪklɪ) *adj.* **1.** (usually foll. by an infinitive) tending or inclined; apt: *likely to rain.* **2.** probable: *a likely result.* **3.** believable or feasible; plausible. **4.** appropriate for a purpose or activity. **5.** having good possibilities of success: *a likely candidate.* **6.** *Dialect, chiefly U.S.* attractive, agreeable, or enjoyable: *her likely ways won her many friends.* ~*adv.* **7.** probably or presumably. **8. as likely as not.** very probably. [C14: from Old Norse *līkligr*]

▷ **Usage.** *Likely* as an adverb is preceded by another, intensifying adverb, as in *it will very likely rain* or *it will most likely rain.* Its use without an intensifier, as in *it will likely rain* is regarded as unacceptable by most users of British English, though it is common in colloquial U.S. English.

like-minded *adj.* agreeing in opinions, goals, etc. —ˌ**like-'mindedly** *adv.* —ˌ**like-'mindedness** *n.*

liken ('laɪkən) *vb.* (*tr.*) to see or represent as the same or similar; compare. [C14: from LIKE[1] (adj.)]

likeness ('laɪknɪs) *n.* **1.** the condition of being alike; similarity. **2.** a painted, carved, moulded, or graphic image of a person or thing. **3.** an imitative appearance; semblance.

likewise ('laɪkˌwaɪz) *adv.* **1.** in addition; moreover; also. **2.** in like manner; similarly.

liking ('laɪkɪŋ) *n.* **1.** the feeling of a person who likes; fondness. **2.** a preference, inclination, or pleasure.

likuta (liː'kuːtɑː) *n., pl.* **makuta** (mɑː'kuːtɑː). a coin of Zaïre worth one hundredth of a zaire. [C20: from Congolese]

lilac ('laɪlək) *n.* **1.** Also called: **syringa.** any of various Eurasian oleaceous shrubs or small trees of the genus *Syringa,* esp. *S. vulgaris* (**common lilac**) which has large sprays of purple or white fragrant flowers. **2. French lilac.** another name for **goat's-rue** (sense 1). **3. a.** a light or moderate purple colour, sometimes with a bluish or reddish tinge. **b.** (*as adj.*): *a lilac carpet.* [C17: via French from Spanish, from Arabic *līlak,* changed from Persian *nīlak* bluish, from *nīl* blue]

liliaceous (ˌlɪlɪ'eɪʃəs) *adj.* of, relating to, or belonging to the *Liliaceae,* a family of plants having showy flowers and a bulb or bulblike organ: includes the lily, tulip, bluebell, and onion. [C18: from Late Latin *līliāceus,* from *līlium* lily]

Lilliputian (ˌlɪlɪ'pjuːʃɪən) *n.* **1.** a tiny person or being. ~*adj.* **2.** tiny; very small. **3.** petty or trivial. [C18: from *Lilliput,* an imaginary country of tiny inhabitants in Jonathan Swift's *Gulliver's Travels* (1726)]

lilly-pilly ('lɪlɪˌpɪlɪ) *n. Austral.* a tall myrtaceous tree, *Eugenia smithii,* having dark green leaves, spikes of feathery flowers, and white to purplish edible berries.

Lilo ('laɪləʊ) *n., pl.* **-los.** *Trademark.* a type of inflatable plastic or rubber mattress.

lilt (lɪlt) *n.* **1.** (in music) a jaunty rhythm. **2.** a buoyant motion. ~*vb.* (*intr.*) **3.** (of a melody) to have a lilt. **4.** to move in a buoyant manner. [C14 *lulten,* origin obscure] —'**lilting** *adj.*

lily ('lɪlɪ) *n., pl.* **lilies. 1.** any liliaceous perennial plant of the N temperate genus *Lilium,* such as the Turk's-cap lily and tiger lily, having scaly bulbs and showy typically pendulous flowers. **2.** the bulb or flower of any of these plants. **3.** any of various similar or related plants, such as the water lily, plantain lily, and day lily. [Old English, from Latin *līlium;* related to Greek *leirion* lily] —'**lily-ˌlike** *adj.*

lily iron *n.* a harpoon, the head of which is detachable. [C19: from the shape of its shaft, which resembles lily leaves]

lily-livered *adj.* cowardly; timid.

lily of the valley *n., pl.* **lilies of the valley.** a small liliaceous plant, *Convallaria majalis,* of Eurasia and North America cultivated as a garden plant, having two long oval leaves and spikes of white bell-shaped flowers.

lily pad *n.* any of the floating leaves of a water lily.

lily-trotter *n.* another name for **jaçana.**

lily-white *adj.* **1.** of a pure white: *lily-white skin.* **2.** *Informal.* pure; irreproachable. **3.** *U.S. informal.* **a.** discriminating against Negroes: *a lily-white club.* **b.** racially segregated.

Lima ('liːmə) *n. Communications.* a code word for the letter *L.*

lima bean ('laɪmə, 'liː-) *n.* **1.** any of several varieties of the bean plant, *Phaseolus lunatus* (or *P. limensis*), native to tropical America but cultivated in the U.S. for its flat pods containing pale green edible seeds. **2.** the seed of such a plant. ~See also **butter bean.** [C19: named after *Lima,* capital of Peru]

limacine ('lɪməˌsaɪn, -sɪn, 'laɪ-) *adj.* **1.** of, or relating to slugs, esp. those of the genus *Limax.* **2.** Also: **limaciform** (lɪ'mæsɪˌfɔːm). resembling a slug. [C19: from New Latin, from Latin *līmax,* from *līmus* mud]

limaçon ('lɪməˌsɒn) *n.* a heart-shaped curve generated by a point lying on a line at a fixed distance from the intersection of the line with a fixed circle, the line rotating about a point on the circumference of the circle. [French, literally: snail (so named by Pascal)]

limb[1] (lɪm) *n.* **1.** an arm or leg, or the analogous part on an animal, such as a wing. **2.** any of the main branches of a tree. **3.** a branching or projecting section or member; extension. **4.** a person or thing considered to be a member, part, or agent of a larger group or thing. **5.** *Chiefly Brit.* a mischievous child (esp. in **limb of Satan** *or* **limb of the devil**). **6. out on a limb. a.** in a precarious or questionable position. **b.** *Brit.* isolated, esp. because of unpopular opinions. ~*vb.* **7.** (*tr.*) a rare word for **dismember.** [Old English *lim;* related to Old Norse *limr*] —**limbed** *adj.* —'**limbless** *adj.*

limb[2] (lɪm) *n.* **1.** the edge of the apparent disc of the sun, a moon, or a planet. **2.** a graduated arc attached to instruments, such as the sextant, used for measuring angles. **3.** *Botany.* **a.** the expanded upper part of a bell-shaped corolla. **b.** the expanded part of a leaf, petal, or sepal. **4.** either of the two halves of a bow. **5.** Also called: **fold limb.** either of the sides of a geological fold. [C15: from Latin *limbus* edge]

limbate ('lɪmbeɪt) *adj. Biology.* having an edge or border of a different colour from the rest: *limbate flowers.* [C19: from Late Latin *limbātus* bordered, from LIMBUS]

limbed (lɪmd) *adj.* **a.** having limbs. **b.** (*in combination*): *short-limbed; strong-limbed.*

limber[1] ('lɪmbə) *adj.* **1.** capable of being easily bent or flexed; pliant. **2.** able to move or bend freely; agile. [C16: origin uncertain] —'**limberly** *adv.* —'**limberness** *n.*

limber[2] ('lɪmbə) *n.* **1.** part of a gun carriage, consisting of an axle, pole, and two wheels, that is attached to the rear of an item of equipment, esp. field artillery. ~*vb.* **2.** (usually foll. by *up*) to attach the limber (to a gun, etc.). [C15 *lymour* shaft of a gun carriage, origin uncertain]

limber[3] ('lɪmbə) *n.* (*often pl.*) *Nautical.* (in the bilge of a vessel) a fore-and-aft channel through a series of holes in the frames (**limber holes**) where water collects and can be pumped out. [C17: probably changed from French *lumière* hole (literally: light)]

limber up *vb.* (*adv.*) **1.** (*intr.*) (esp. in sports) to exercise in order to be limber and agile. **2.** (*tr.*) to make flexible.

limbic system ('lɪmbɪk) *n.* the part of the brain bordering on the corpus callosum: concerned with basic emotion, hunger, and sex. [C19 *limbic,* from French *limbique,* from *limbe* limbus, from New Latin *limbus,* from Latin: border]

limbo[1] ('lɪmbəʊ) *n., pl.* **-bos. 1.** (*often cap.*) *Christianity.* the supposed abode of infants dying without baptism and the just who died before Christ. **2.** an imaginary place for lost, forgotten, or unwanted persons or things. **3.** an unknown intermediate place or condition between two extremes: *in limbo.* **4.** a prison or confinement. [C14: from Medieval Latin *in limbo* on the border (of hell)]

limbo[2] ('lɪmbəʊ) *n., pl.* **-bos.** a West Indian dance in which dancers pass, while leaning backwards, under a bar. [C20: origin uncertain]

Limburger (ˈlɪmbɜːgə) *n.* a semihard white cheese of very strong smell and flavour, originally made in the Belgian province of Limburg. Also called: **Limburg cheese.**

limbus (ˈlɪmbəs) *n., pl.* **-bi** (-baɪ). *Anatomy.* the edge or border of any of various structures or parts. [C15: from Latin: edge] —ˈ**limbic** *adj.*

lime[1] (laɪm) *n.* **1.** short for **quicklime, birdlime, slaked lime.** **2.** *Agriculture.* any of certain calcium compounds, esp. calcium hydroxide, spread as a dressing on lime-deficient land. ~*vb. (tr.)* **3.** to spread (twigs, etc.) with birdlime. **4.** to spread a calcium compound upon (land) to improve plant growth. **5.** to catch (animals, esp. birds) with or as if with birdlime. **6.** to whitewash or cover (a wall, ceiling, etc.) with a mixture of lime and water (**limewash**). [Old English *līm;* related to Icelandic *līm* glue, Latin *līmus* slime]

lime[2] (laɪm) *n.* **1.** a small Asian citrus tree, *Citrus aurantifolia,* with stiff sharp spines and small round or oval greenish fruits. **2. a.** the fruit of this tree, having acid fleshy pulp rich in vitamin C. **b.** *(as modifier): lime juice.* ~*adj.* **3.** having the flavour of lime fruit. [C17: from French, from Provençal, from Arabic *līmah*]

lime[3] (laɪm) *n.* a European linden tree, *Tilia europaea,* planted in many varieties for ornament. [C17: changed from obsolete *line,* from Old English *lind* LINDEN]

lime[4] (laɪm) *vb. (intr.) Caribbean slang.* (of young people) to sit or stand around on the pavement. [of unknown origin]

limeade (ˌlaɪmˈeɪd) *n.* a drink made from sweetened lime juice and plain or carbonated water.

lime burner *n.* a person whose job it is to burn limestone to make lime.

lime green *n.* **a.** a moderate greenish-yellow colour. **b.** *(as adj.): a lime-green dress.*

limekiln (ˈlaɪmˌkɪln) *n.* a kiln in which calcium carbonate is calcined to produce quicklime.

limelight (ˈlaɪmˌlaɪt) *n.* **1. the.** a position of public attention or notice (esp. in the phrase **in the limelight**). **2. a.** a type of lamp, formerly used in stage lighting, in which light is produced by heating lime to white heat. **b.** Also called: **calcium light.** brilliant white light produced in this way. —ˈ**limeˌlighter** *n.*

limen (ˈlaɪmɛn) *n., pl.* **limens** *or* **limina** (ˈlɪmɪnə). *Psychol.* another term for **threshold** (sense 4). See also **liminal.** [C19: from Latin]

lime pit *n.* (in tanning) a pit containing lime in which hides are placed to remove the hair.

limerick (ˈlɪmərɪk) *n.* a form of comic verse consisting of five anapaestic lines of which the first, second, and fifth have three metrical feet and rhyme together and the third and fourth have two metrical feet and rhyme together. [C19: allegedly from *will you come up to Limerick?,* a refrain sung between nonsense verses at a party]

limes (ˈlaɪmiːz) *n., pl.* **limites** (ˈlɪmɪˌtiːz). the fortified boundary of the Roman Empire. [from Latin]

limestone (ˈlaɪmˌstəʊn) *n.* a sedimentary rock consisting mainly of calcium carbonate, deposited as the calcareous remains of marine animals or chemically precipitated from the sea: used as a building stone and in the manufacture of cement, lime, etc.

limestone pavement *n. Geology.* a horizontal surface of exposed limestone in which the joints have been enlarged, cutting the surface into roughly rectangular blocks. See also **clint, grike.**

limewater (ˈlaɪmˌwɔːtə) *n.* **1.** a clear colourless solution of calcium hydroxide in water, sometimes used in medicine as an antacid. **2.** water that contains dissolved lime or calcium salts, esp. calcium carbonate or calcium sulphate.

limey (ˈlaɪmɪ) *U.S. and Canadian slang.* ~*n.* **1.** a British person. **2.** a British sailor or ship. ~*adj.* **3.** British. [abbreviated from C19 *lime-juicer,* because British sailors were required to drink lime juice as a protection against scurvy]

limicoline (laɪˈmɪkəˌlaɪn, -lɪn) *adj.* of, relating to, or belonging to the *Charadrii,* a suborder of birds containing the plovers, sandpipers, snipes, oystercatchers, avocets, etc. [C19: from New Latin *Limicolae* former name of order, from Latin *līmus* mud + *colere* to inhabit]

limicolous (laɪˈmɪkələs) *adj.* (of certain animals) living in mud or muddy regions.

liminal (ˈlɪmɪnᵊl) *adj. Psychol.* relating to the point (or threshold) beyond which a sensation becomes too faint to be experienced. [C19: from Latin *līmen* threshold]

limit (ˈlɪmɪt) *n.* **1.** *(sometimes pl.)* the ultimate extent, degree, or amount of something: *the limit of endurance.* **2.** *(often pl.)* the boundary or edge of a specific area: *the city limits.* **3.** *(often pl.)* the area of premises within specific boundaries. **4.** the largest quantity or amount allowed. **5.** *Maths.* **a.** a value to which a function f(x) approaches as closely as desired as the independent variable approaches a specified value (x = a) or approaches infinity. **b.** a value to which a sequence a_n approaches arbitrarily close as n approaches infinity. **c.** the limit of a sequence of partial sums of a convergent infinite series: *the limit of* 1 + ½ + ¼ + ⅛ + ... *is* 2. **6.** *Maths.* one of the two specified values between which a definite integral is evaluated. **7. the limit.** *Informal.* a person or thing that is intolerably exasperating. **8. off limits.** forbidden to military personnel without special permission to enter. **9. within limits.** to a certain or limited extent: *I approve of it within limits.* ~*vb. (tr.)* **-its, -iting, -ited. 10.** to restrict or confine, as to area, extent, time, etc. **11.** *Law.* to agree, fix, or assign specifically. [C14: from Latin *līmes* boundary] —ˈ**limitable** *adj.* —ˈ**limitableness** *n.* —ˈ**limitless** *adj.* —ˈ**limitlessly** *adv.* —ˈ**limitlessness** *n.*

limitarian (ˌlɪmɪˈtɛərɪən) *n. Christianity.* a person who regards salvation as limited to only a part of mankind.

limitary (ˈlɪmɪtərɪ, -trɪ) *adj.* **1.** of, involving, or serving as a limit. **2.** restricted or limited.

limitation (ˌlɪmɪˈteɪʃən) *n.* **1.** something that limits a quality or achievement. **2.** the act of limiting or the condition of being limited. **3.** *Law.* a certain period of time, legally defined, within which an action, claim, etc., must be commenced. **4.** *Property law.* a restriction upon the duration or extent of an estate.

limited (ˈlɪmɪtɪd) *adj.* **1.** having a limit; restricted; confined. **2.** without fullness or scope; narrow. **3.** (of governing powers, sovereignty, etc.) restricted or checked, by or as if by a constitution, laws, or an assembly: *limited government.* **4.** *U.S. and Canadian.* (of a train) stopping only at certain stations and having only a set number of cars for passengers. **5.** *Chiefly Brit.* (of a business enterprise) owned by shareholders whose liability for the enterprise's debts is restricted. ~*n.* **6.** *U.S. and Canadian.* a limited train, bus, etc. —ˈ**limitedly** *adv.* —ˈ**limitedness** *n.*

limited company *n. Brit.* a company whose owners enjoy limited liability for the company's debts and losses.

limited edition *n.* an edition of a book that is limited to a specified number of copies.

limited liability *n. Brit.* liability restricted to the unpaid portion (if any) of the par value of the shares of a limited company. It is a feature of share ownership.

limited monarchy *n.* another term for **constitutional monarchy.**

limited war *n.* a war in which the belligerents do not seek the total destruction of the enemy, esp. one in which nuclear weapons are deliberately not used.

limiter (ˈlɪmɪtə) *n.* an electronic circuit that produces an output signal whose positive or negative amplitude, or both, is limited to some predetermined value above which the peaks become flattened. Also called: **clipper.**

limit man *n.* (in a handicap sport or game) the competitor with the maximum handicap.

limit point *n. Maths.* a point in a topological space such that there is at least one other point of the space in every neighbourhood of the given point: 0 *is the limit point of the sequence* 1, ½, ¼, ⅛,.... Also called: **accumulation point.**

limitrophe (ˈlɪmɪˌtrəʊf) *adj.* (of a country or region) on or near a frontier. [C19: via French from Late Latin *limitrophus,* from *limit-* LIMIT + Greek *-trophus* supporting; originally referring to borderland that supported frontier troops]

limivorous (lɪˈmɪvərəs) *adj.* (of certain invertebrate animals) feeding on mud. [C19: from Latin *līmus* mud + -VOROUS]

limn (lɪm) *vb. (tr.)* **1.** to represent in drawing or painting. **2.** *Archaic.* to describe in words. **3.** an obsolete word for **illuminate.** [C15: from Old French *enluminer* to illumine (a manuscript) from Latin *inlūmināre* to brighten, from *lūmen* light] —**limner** (ˈlɪmnə) *n.*

limnetic (lɪmˈnɛtɪk) *adj.* of, relating to, or inhabiting the open water of lakes down to the depth of light penetration: *the limnetic zone.* [C20: from Greek *limnē* pool]

limnology (lɪmˈnɒlədʒɪ) *n.* the study of bodies of fresh water with reference to their plant and animal life, physical properties, geographical features, etc. [C20: from Greek *limnē* lake] —**limnological** (ˌlɪmnəˈlɒdʒɪkᵊl) *or* ˌ**limnoˈlogic** *adj.* —ˌ**limnoˈlogically** *adv.* —**limˈnologist** *n.*

limnophilous (lɪmˈnɒfɪləs) *adj.* (of animals) living in lakes or freshwater marshes.

limo (ˈlɪməʊ) *n., pl.* **-mos.** *Informal.* short for **limousine.**

limonene (ˈlɪməˌniːn) *n.* a liquid optically active terpene with a lemon-like odour, found in lemon, orange, peppermint, and other essential oils and used as a wetting agent and in the manufacture of resins. Formula: $C_{10}H_{16}$. [C19: from New Latin *limonum* lemon]

limonite (ˈlaɪməˌnaɪt) *n.* a common brown, black, or yellow amorphous secondary mineral that consists of hydrated ferric oxides and is a source of iron. Formula: $FeO(OH).nH_2O$. [C19: probably from Greek *leimōn,* translation of earlier German name, *Wiesenerz* meadow ore] —**limonitic** (ˌlaɪməˈnɪtɪk) *adj.*

limousine (ˈlɪməˌziːn, ˌlɪməˈziːn) *n.* **1.** any large and luxurious car, esp. one that has a glass division between the driver and passengers. **2.** a former type of car in which the roof covering the rear seats projects over the driver's compartment. [C20: from French, literally: cloak (originally one worn by shepherds in *Limousin*), hence later applied to the car]

limp[1] (lɪmp) *vb. (intr.)* **1.** to walk with an uneven step, esp. with a weak or injured leg. **2.** to advance in a labouring or faltering manner. ~*n.* **3.** an uneven walk or progress. [C16: probably a back formation from obsolete *limphalt* lame, from Old English *lempheалt;* related to Middle High German *limpfen* to limp] —ˈ**limper** *n.* —ˈ**limping** *adj., n.* —ˈ**limpingly** *adv.*

limp[2] (lɪmp) *adj.* **1.** not firm or stiff. **2.** not energetic or vital. **3.** (of the binding of a book) not stiffened with boards. [C18: probably of Scandinavian origin; related to Icelandic *limpa* looseness] —ˈ**limply** *adv.* —ˈ**limpness** *n.*

limpet ('lɪmpɪt) *n.* **1.** any of numerous marine gastropods, such as *Patella vulgata* (**common limpet**) and *Fissurella* (or *Diodora*) *apertura* (**keyhole limpet**), that have a conical shell and are found clinging to rocks. **2.** any of various similar freshwater gastropods, such as *Ancylus fluviatilis* (**river limpet**). **3.** (*modifier*) relating to or denoting certain weapons that are attached to their targets by magnetic or adhesive properties and resist removal: *limpet mines.* [Old English *lempedu,* from Latin *lepas,* from Greek]

limpid ('lɪmpɪd) *adj.* **1.** clear or transparent. **2.** (esp. of writings, style, etc.) free from obscurity. **3.** calm; peaceful. [C17: from French *limpide,* from Latin *limpidus* clear] —**lim'pidity** *or* **'limpidness** *n.* —**'limpidly** *adv.*

limpkin ('lɪmpkɪn) *n.* a rail-like wading bird, *Aramus guarauna,* of tropical American marshes, having dark brown plumage with white markings and a wailing cry: order *Gruiformes* (cranes, rails, etc.). Also called: **courlan.** [C19: named from its awkward gait]

limp-wristed *adj.* ineffectual; effete.

limulus ('lɪmjʊləs) *n., pl.* **-li** (-ˌlaɪ). any horseshoe crab of the genus *Limulus,* esp. *L. polyphemus.* [C19: from New Latin (name of genus), from Latin *līmus* sidelong]

limy[1] ('laɪmɪ) *adj.* **limier, limiest. 1.** of, like, or smeared with birdlime. **2.** containing or characterized by the presence of lime. —**'liminess** *n.*

limy[2] ('laɪmɪ) *adj.* **limier, limiest.** of or tasting of lime (the fruit).

lin. *abbrev. for:* **1.** lineal. **2.** linear.

linac ('lɪnæk) *n.* short for **linear accelerator.**

linage *or* **lineage** ('laɪnɪdʒ) *n.* **1.** the number of lines in a piece of written or printed matter. **2.** payment for written material calculated according to the number of lines. **3.** a less common word for **alignment.**

linalool (lɪ'nælәʊˌɒl, 'lɪnәˌluːl) *or* **linalol** ('lɪnәˌlɒl) *n.* an optically active colourless fragrant liquid found in essential oils and used in perfumery. Formula: $C_{10}H_{18}O$. [from LIGNALOES + -OL[1]]

linchpin ('lɪntʃˌpɪn) *n.* **1.** a pin placed transversely through an axle to keep a wheel in position. **2.** a person or thing regarded as an essential or coordinating element: *the linchpin of the company.* [C14 *lynspin,* from Old English *lynis*]

Lincoln ('lɪŋkәn) *n.* a breed of long-woolled sheep, originally from the county of Lincolnshire in E England.

Lincoln green *n., adj.* **1. a.** a yellowish-green or brownish-green colour. **b.** (*as adj.*): *a Lincoln-green suit.* **2.** a cloth of this colour. [C16: so named after a green fabric formerly made at *Lincoln,* a city in E England]

lincrusta (lɪn'krʌstә) *n.* a type of wallpaper having a hard embossed surface. [C19: from Latin *linum* flax + *crusta* rind]

Lincs (lɪŋks) *abbrev. for* Lincolnshire.

linctus ('lɪŋktәs) *n., pl.* **-tuses.** a syrupy medicinal preparation, taken to relieve coughs and sore throats. [C17 (in the sense: medicine to be licked with the tongue): from Latin, past participle of *lingere* to lick]

lindane ('lɪndeɪn) *n.* a white poisonous crystalline powder with a slight musty odour: used as an insecticide, weedkiller, and, in low concentrations, in treating scabies; 1,2,3,4,5,6-hexachlorocyclohexane. Formula: $C_6H_6Cl_6$. [C20: named after T. van der *Linden,* Dutch chemist]

linden ('lɪndәn) *n.* any of various tiliaceous deciduous trees of the N temperate genus *Tilia,* having heart-shaped leaves and small fragrant yellowish flowers: cultivated for timber and as shade trees. See also **lime**[3], **basswood.** [C16: n. use of obsolete adj. *linden,* from Old English *linde* lime tree]

line[1] (laɪn) *n.* **1.** a narrow continuous mark, as one made by a pencil, pen, or brush across a surface. **2.** such a mark cut into or raised from a surface. **3.** a thin indented mark or wrinkle. **4.** a straight or curved continuous trace having no breadth that is produced by a moving point. **5.** *Maths.* **a.** any straight one-dimensional geometrical element whose identity is determined by two points. A **line segment** lies between any two points on a line. **b.** a set of points (x, y) that satisfies the equation $y = mx + c$, where m is the gradient and c is the intercept with the y-axis. **6.** a border or boundary: *the county line.* **7.** *Sport.* **a.** a white or coloured band indicating a boundary or division on a field, track, etc. **b.** a mark or imaginary mark at which a race begins or ends. **8.** *American football.* **a.** See **line of scrimmage. b.** the players arranged in a row on either side of the line of scrimmage at the start of each play. **9.** a specified point of change or limit: *the dividing line between sanity and madness.* **10. a.** the edge or contour of a shape, as in sculpture or architecture, or a mark on a painting, drawing, etc., defining or suggesting this. **b.** the sum or type of such contours or marks, characteristic of a style or design: *the line of a draughtsman; the line of a building.* **11.** anything long, flexible, and thin, such as a wire or string: *a washing line; a fishing line.* **12.** a telephone connection: *a direct line to New York.* **13. a.** a conducting wire, cable, or circuit for making connections between pieces of electrical apparatus, such as a cable for electric-power transmission, telecommunications, etc. **b.** (*as modifier*): *the line voltage.* **14.** a system of travel or transportation, esp. over agreed routes: *a shipping line.* **15.** a company operating such a system. **16.** a route between two points on a railway. **17.** *Chiefly Brit.* **a.** a railway track, including the roadbed, sleepers, etc. **b.** one of the rails of such a track. **18.** *N.Z.* a roadway usually in a rural area. **19.** a course or direction of movement or advance: *the line of flight of a bullet.* **20.** a course or method of action, behaviour, etc.: *take a new line with him.* **21.** a policy or prescribed course of action or way of thinking (often in the phrases **bring** *or* **come into line**). **22.** a field of study, interest, occupation, trade, or profession: *this book is in your line.* **23.** alignment; true (esp. in the phrases **in line, out of line**). **24.** one kind of product or article: *a nice line in hats.* **25.** *N.Z.* a collection of bales of wool all of the one type. **26.** a row of persons or things: *a line of cakes on the conveyor belt.* **27.** a chronological or ancestral series, esp. of people: *a line of prime ministers.* **28.** a row of words printed or written across a page or column. **29.** a unit of verse consisting of the number of feet appropriate to the metre being used and written or printed with the words in a single row. **30.** a short letter; note: *just a line to say thank you.* **31.** a piece of useful information or hint about something: *give me a line on his work.* **32.** one of a number of narrow horizontal bands forming a television picture. **33.** a narrow band in an electromagnetic spectrum, resulting from a transition in an atom of a gas. **34.** *Music.* **a.** any of the five horizontal marks that make up the stave. Compare **space** (sense 9). **b.** the musical part or melody notated on one such set. **c.** a discernible shape formed by sequences of notes or musical sounds: *a meandering melodic line.* **d.** (in polyphonic music) a set of staves that are held together with a bracket or brace. **35.** a unit of magnetic flux equal to 1 maxwell. **36.** a defensive or fortified position, esp. one that marks the most forward position in war or a national boundary: *the front line.* **37. line ahead** *or* **line abreast.** a formation adopted by a naval unit for manoeuvring. **38.** a formation adopted by a body or a number of military units when drawn up abreast. **39.** the combatant forces of certain armies and navies, excluding supporting arms. **40.** *Fencing.* one of four divisions of the target on a fencer's body, considered as areas to which specific attacks are made. **41.** the scent left by a fox. **42. a.** the equator (esp. in the phrase **crossing the line**). **b.** any circle or arc on the terrestrial or celestial sphere. **43.** the amount of insurance written by an underwriter for a particular risk. **44.** a U.S. and Canadian word for **queue. 45.** *Slang.* a portion of a powdered drug for snorting. **46.** *Slang.* something said for effect, esp. to solicit for money, sex, etc.: *he gave me his usual line.* **47. above the line. a.** *Account.* denoting entries above a horizontal line on a profit and loss account, separating those that establish the profit or loss from those that show how the profit is distributed. **b.** denoting revenue transactions rather than capital transactions in a nation's accounts. **c.** *Marketing.* expenditure on media advertising through an agency, rather than internally arranged advertising, such as direct mail, free samples, etc. **d.** *Bridge.* denoting bonus points, marked above the horizontal line on the score card. **48. below the line. a.** *Account.* denoting entries below a horizontal line on a profit and loss account, separating those that establish the profit or loss from those that show how the profit is distributed. **b.** denoting capital transactions rather than revenue transactions in a nation's accounts. **c.** *Marketing.* denoting expenditure on advertising by other means than the traditional media, such as the provision of free gifts, special displays, direct-mail shots, etc. **d.** *Bridge.* denoting points scored towards game and rubber, marked below the horizontal line on the score card. **49. all along the line. a.** at every stage in a series. **b.** in every detail. **50. do a line (with).** *Irish and Austral. informal.* to associate (with a person of the opposite sex) regularly; go out (with): *he is doing a line with her.* **51. draw the line (at).** to reasonably object (to) or set a limit (on): *her father draws the line at her coming in after midnight.* **52. get a line on.** *Informal.* to obtain information about. **53. hold the line. a.** to keep a telephone line open. **b.** *Football.* to prevent the opponents from taking the ball forward. **c.** (of soldiers) to keep formation, as when under fire. **54. in line for.** in the running for; a candidate for: *he's in line for a directorship.* **55. in line with.** conforming to. **56. in the line of duty.** as a necessary and usually undesired part of the performance of one's responsibilities. **57. lay** *or* **put on the line. a.** to pay money. **b.** to speak frankly and directly. **c.** to risk (one's career, reputation, etc.) on something. **58. shoot a line.** *Informal.* to try to create a false image, as by boasting or exaggerating. **59. toe the line.** to conform to expected standards, attitudes, etc. ~*vb.* **60.** (*tr.*) to mark with a line or lines. **61.** (*tr.*) to draw or represent with a line or lines. **62.** (*tr.*) to be or put as a border to: *tulips lined the lawns.* **63.** to place in or form a row, series, or alignment. ~See also **lines, line-up.** [C13: partly from Old French *ligne,* ultimately from Latin *līnea,* n. use of *līneus* flaxen, from *līnum* flax; partly from Old English *līn,* ultimately also from Latin *līnum* flax] —**'linable** *or* **'lineable** *adj.* —**lined** *adj.* —**'lineˌlike** *adj.* —**'liny** *or* **'liney** *adj.*

line[2] (laɪn) *vb.* (*tr.*) **1.** to attach an inside covering to (a garment, curtain, etc.), as for protection, to hide the seaming, or so that it should hang well. **2.** to cover or fit the inside of: *to line the walls with books.* **3.** to fill plentifully: *a purse lined with money.* **4.** to reinforce the back of (a book) with fabric, paper, etc. [C14: ultimately from Latin *līnum* flax, since linings were often made of linen]

lineage[1] ('lɪnɪɪdʒ) *n.* **1.** direct descent from an ancestor, esp. a line of descendants from one ancestor. **2.** a less common word for **derivation.** [C14: from Old French *lignage*, from Latin *līnea* LINE[1]]

lineage[2] (ˈlaɪnɪdʒ) *n.* a variant spelling of **linage.**

lineal (ˈlɪnɪəl) *adj.* **1.** being in a direct line of descent from an ancestor. **2.** of, involving, or derived from direct descent. **3.** a less common word for **linear.** [C14: via Old French from Late Latin *līneālis*, from Latin *līnea* LINE[1]] —**ˈlineally** *adv.*

lineament (ˈlɪnɪəmənt) *n.* (*often pl.*) **1.** a facial outline or feature. **2.** a distinctive characteristic or feature. **3.** *Geology.* any long natural feature on the surface of the earth, such as a fault, esp. as revealed by aerial photography. [C15: from Latin: line, from *līneāre* to draw a line] —**lineamental** (ˌlɪnɪəˈmentᵊl) *adj.*

linear (ˈlɪnɪə) *adj.* **1.** of, in, along, or relating to a line. **2.** of or relating to length. **3.** resembling, represented by, or consisting of a line or lines. **4.** having one dimension. **5.** designating a style in the arts, esp. painting, that obtains its effects through line rather than colour or light and in which the edges of forms and planes are sharply defined. Compare **painterly. 6.** *Maths.* of or relating to the first degree: *a linear equation.* **7.** narrow and having parallel edges: *a linear leaf.* **8.** *Electronics.* **a.** (of a circuit, etc.) having an output that is directly proportional to input: *linear amplifier.* **b.** having components arranged in a line. [C17: from Latin *līneāris* of or by means of lines] —**linearity** (ˌlɪnɪˈærɪtɪ) *n.* —**ˈlinearly** *adv.*

Linear A *n.* a hitherto undeciphered script, partly syllabic and partly ideographic, found on tablets and pottery in Crete and dating mainly from the 15th century B.C.

linear accelerator *n.* an accelerator in which charged particles are accelerated along a linear path by potential differences applied to a number of electrodes along their path. Sometimes shortened to **linac.**

Linear B *n.* an ancient system of writing, apparently a modified form of Linear A, found on clay tablets and jars of the second millennium B.C. The earliest excavated examples, dating from about 1400, came from Knossos, in Crete, but all the later finds are at Pylos and Mycenae on the Greek mainland, dating from the 14th–12th centuries. The script is generally accepted as being an early representation of Mycenaean Greek.

linear equation *n.* a polynomial equation of the first degree, such as $x + y = 7$.

linear measure *n.* a unit or system of units for the measurement of length. Also called: **long measure.**

linear motor *n.* a form of electric motor in which the stator and the rotor are linear and parallel. It can be used to drive a train, one part of the motor being in the locomotive, the other in the track.

linear perspective *n.* the branch of perspective in which the apparent size and shape of objects and their position with respect to foreground and background are established by actual or suggested lines converging on the horizon.

linear programming *n. Maths.* a technique used in economics, etc., for determining the maximum or minimum of a linear function of non-negative variables subject to constraints expressed as linear equalities or inequalities.

lineate (ˈlɪnɪɪt, -ˌeɪt) *or* **lineated** *adj.* marked with lines; streaked. [C17: from Latin *līneātus* drawn with lines]

lineation (ˌlɪnɪˈeɪʃən) *n.* **1.** the act of marking with lines. **2.** an arrangement of or division into lines. **3.** an outline or contour. **4.** any linear arrangement involving rocks or minerals, such as a series of parallel rock strata.

line block *n.* a letterpress printing block made by a photoengraving process without the use of a screen.

line breeding *n.* selective inbreeding that produces individuals possessing one or more of the favourable characteristics of their common ancestor.

line call *n. Tennis.* the judgment of the umpire or linesman as to whether the ball has landed in or out of court.

linecaster (ˈlaɪnˌkɑːstə) *n.* a printing machine that casts metal type in lines.

line drawing *n.* a drawing made with lines only, gradations in tone being provided by the spacing and thickness of the lines.

line-engraving *n.* **1.** the art or process of hand-engraving in intaglio and copper plate. **2.** a plate so engraved. **3.** a print taken from such a plate. —**ˈline-enˌgraver** *n.*

lineman (ˈlaɪnmən) *n., pl.* **-men. 1.** another name for **platelayer. 2.** a person who does the chaining, taping, or marking of points for a surveyor. **3.** *Austral. and N.Z.* the member of a beach life-saving team who controls the line used to help drowning swimmers and surfers. **4.** *American football.* a member of the row of players who start each down, positioned on either side of the line of scrimmage. **5.** *U.S. and Canadian.* another word for **linesman** (sense 2).

line management *n. Commerce.* those managers in an organization who are responsible for the main activity or product of the organization, as distinct from those, such as transport, accounting, or personnel, who provide services to the line management. —**line manager** *n.*

linen (ˈlɪnɪn) *n.* **1. a.** a hard-wearing fabric woven from the spun fibres of flax. **b.** (*as modifier*): *a linen tablecloth.* **2.** yarn or thread spun from flax fibre. **3.** clothes, sheets, tablecloths, etc., made from linen cloth or from a substitute such as cotton. **4.** See **linen paper.** [Old English *linnen*, ultimately from Latin *līnum* flax, LINE[2]]

linen paper *n.* paper made from flax fibres or having a similar texture.

line of battle *n.* a formation adopted by a military or naval force when preparing for action.

line of credit *n. U.S. and Canadian.* another name for **credit line.**

line of fire *n.* the flight path of a missile discharged or to be discharged from a firearm.

line of force *n.* a line in a field of force, such as an electric or magnetic field, for which the tangent at any point is the direction of the force at that point.

line of scrimmage *n. American football.* an imaginary line, parallel to the goal lines, on which the ball is placed at the start of a down and on either side of which the offense and defense line up.

line of sight *n.* **1.** the straight line along which an observer looks or a beam of radiation travels. **2.** *Ophthalmol.* another term for **line of vision.**

line of vision *n. Ophthalmol.* a straight line extending from the fovea centralis of the eye to an object on which the eye is focused. Also called: **line of sight.**

lineolate (ˈlɪnɪəˌleɪt) *or* **lineolated** *adj. Biology.* marked with very fine parallel lines. [C19: from Latin *līneola*, diminutive of *līnea* LINE[1]]

line-out *n. Rugby Union.* the method of restarting play when the ball goes into touch, the forwards forming two parallel lines at right angles to the touchline and jumping for the ball when it is thrown in.

line printer *n.* an electromechanical device that prints a line of characters at a time rather than a character at a time, at speeds from about 200 to 3000 lines per minute: used in printing and in computer systems.

liner[1] (ˈlaɪnə) *n.* **1.** a passenger ship or aircraft, esp. one that is part of a commercial fleet. **2.** See **freightliner. 3.** Also called: **eye liner.** a cosmetic used to outline the eyes, consisting of a liquid or cake mixed with water and applied by brush or a grease pencil. **4.** a person or thing that uses lines, esp. in drawing or copying.

liner[2] (ˈlaɪnə) *n.* **1.** a material used as a lining. **2.** a person who supplies or fits linings. **3.** *Engineering.* a sleeve, usually of a metal that will withstand wear or corrosion, fixed inside or outside a structural component: *cylinder liner.*

liner notes *pl. n.* the U.S. name for **sleeve notes.**

lines (laɪnz) *pl. n.* **1.** general appearance or outline: *a car with fine lines.* **2.** a plan of procedure or construction: *built on traditional lines.* **3. a.** the spoken words of a theatrical presentation. **b.** the words of a particular role: *he forgot his lines.* **4.** *Informal, chiefly Brit.* a marriage certificate: *marriage lines.* **5.** luck, fate, or fortune (esp. in the phrase **hard lines). 6. a.** rows of buildings, temporary stabling, etc., in a military camp: *transport lines.* **b.** a defensive position, row of trenches, or other fortification: *we broke through the enemy lines.* **7. a.** a school punishment of writing the same sentence or phrase out a specified number of times. **b.** the phrases or sentences so written out: *a hundred lines.* **8. read between the lines.** to understand or find an implicit meaning in addition to the obvious one.

linesman (ˈlaɪnzmən) *n., pl.* **-men. 1.** an official who helps the referee or umpire in various sports, esp. by indicating when the ball has gone out of play. **2.** *Chiefly Brit.* a person who installs, maintains, or repairs telephone or electric-power lines. U.S. and Canadian name: **lineman.**

line squall *n.* a squall or series of squalls along a cold front.

line-up *n.* **1.** a row or arrangement of people or things assembled for a particular purpose: *the line-up for the football match.* **2.** the members of such a row or arrangement. **3.** *U.S.* an identity parade. ~*vb.* **line up.** (*adv.*) **4.** to form, put into, or organize a line-up. **5.** (*tr.*) to produce, organize, and assemble: *they lined up some questions.* **6.** (*tr.*) to align.

ling[1] (lɪŋ) *n., pl.* **ling** *or* **lings. 1.** any of several gadoid food fishes of the northern coastal genus *Molva*, esp. *M. molva*, having an elongated body with long fins. **2.** another name for **burbot** (a fish). [C13: probably from Low German; related to LONG[1]]

ling[2] (lɪŋ) *n.* another name for **heather** (sense 1). [C14: from Old Norse *lyng*] —**ˈlingy** *adj.*

ling. *abbrev. for* linguistics.

-ling[1] *suffix forming nouns.* **1.** *Often disparaging.* a person or thing belonging to or associated with the group, activity, or quality specified: *nestling; underling.* **2.** used as a diminutive: *duckling.* [Old English *-ling*, of Germanic origin; related to Icelandic *-lingr*, Gothic *-lings*]

-ling[2] *suffix forming adverbs.* in a specified condition, manner, or direction: *darkling; sideling.* [Old English *-ling*, adverbial suffix]

lingam (ˈlɪŋgəm) *or* **linga** (ˈlɪŋgə) *n.* **1.** (in Sanskrit grammar) the masculine gender. **2. a.** the Hindu phallic image of the god Siva. **b.** the penis. [C18: from Sanskrit]

lingcod (ˈlɪŋˌkɒd) *n., pl.* **-cod** *or* **-cods.** any scorpaenoid food fish of the family *Ophiodontidae*, esp. *Ophiodon elongatus*, of the North Pacific Ocean.

linger (ˈlɪŋgə) *vb.* (*mainly intr.*) **1.** to delay or prolong departure. **2.** to go in a slow or leisurely manner; saunter. **3.** to remain just alive for some time prior to death. **4.** to persist or continue, esp. in the mind. **5.** to be slow to act; dither; procrastinate. [C13 (northern dialect) *lengeren* to dwell, from *lengen* to prolong, from Old English *lengan;* related to Old Norse *lengja;* see LONG[1]] —'**lingerer** *n.* —'**lingering** *adj.* —'**lingeringly** *adv.*

lingerie ('lænʒərɪ) *n.* **1.** women's underwear and nightwear. **2.** *Archaic.* linen goods collectively. [C19: from French, from *linge,* from Latin *līneus* linen, from *līnum* flax]

lingo ('lɪŋgəʊ) *n., pl.* **-goes.** *Informal.* any foreign or unfamiliar language, jargon, etc. [C17: perhaps from LINGUA FRANCA; compare Portuguese *lingoa* tongue]

lingua ('lɪŋgwə) *n., pl.* **-guae** (-gwiː). *Anatomy.* **1.** the technical name for **tongue. 2.** any tongue-like structure. [C17: Latin]

lingua franca ('fræŋkə) *n., pl.* **lingua francas** *or* **linguae francae** ('frænsiː). **1.** a language used for communication among people of different mother tongues. **2.** a hybrid language containing elements from several different languages used in this way. **3.** any system of communication providing mutual understanding. [C17: Italian, literally: Frankish tongue]

Lingua Franca *n.* a particular lingua franca spoken from the time of the Crusades to the 18th century in the ports of the Mediterranean, based on Italian, Spanish, French, Arabic, Greek, and Turkish.

lingual ('lɪŋgwəl) *adj.* **1.** *Anatomy.* of or relating to the tongue or a part or structure resembling a tongue. **2. a.** *Rare.* of or relating to language or languages. **b.** (*in combination*): *polylingual.* **3.** articulated with the tongue. ~*n.* **4.** a lingual consonant, such as Scots (r). —'**lingually** *adv.*

linguiform ('lɪŋgwɪˌfɔːm) *adj.* shaped like a tongue.

linguini (lɪŋ'gwiːnɪ) *n.* a kind of pasta in the shape of thin flat strands. [from Italian: small tongues]

linguist ('lɪŋgwɪst) *n.* **1.** a person who has the capacity to learn and speak foreign languages. **2.** a person who studies linguistics. **3.** *West African, esp. Ghanaian.* the spokesman for a chief. [C16: from Latin *lingua* tongue]

linguistic (lɪŋ'gwɪstɪk) *adj.* **1.** of or relating to language. **2.** of or relating to linguistics. —**lin'guistically** *adv.*

linguistic atlas *n.* an atlas showing the distribution of distinctive linguistic features of languages or dialects.

linguistic borrowing *n.* another name for **loan word.**

linguistic geography *n.* the study of the distribution of dialectal speech elements. —**linguistic geographer** *n.*

linguistic philosophy *n.* the approach to philosophy common in the mid 20th century that tends to see philosophical problems as arising from inappropriate theoretical use of language and therefore as being resolved by detailed attention to the common use of expressions.

linguistics (lɪŋ'gwɪstɪks) *n.* (*functioning as sing.*) the scientific study of language. See also **historical linguistics, descriptive linguistics.**

lingulate ('lɪŋgjʊˌleɪt) *or* **lingulated** *adj.* shaped like a tongue: *a lingulate leaf.* [C19: from Latin *lingulātus*]

linhay ('lɪnɪ) *n. Dialect.* a farm building with an open front. [C17: of unknown origin]

liniment ('lɪnɪmənt) *n.* a medicated liquid, usually containing alcohol, camphor, and an oil, applied to the skin to relieve pain, stiffness, etc. [C15: from Late Latin *linīmentum,* from *linere* to smear, anoint]

linin ('laɪnɪn) *n.* the network of viscous material in the nucleus of a cell that connects the chromatin granules. [C19: from Latin *līnum* flax + -IN]

lining ('laɪnɪŋ) *n.* **1. a.** material used to line a garment, curtain, etc. **b.** (*as modifier*): *lining satin.* **2.** a material, such as mull or brown paper, used to strengthen the back of a book. **3.** *Civil engineering.* a layer of concrete, brick, or timber, etc., used in canals to prevent them leaking or in tunnels to prevent them falling in. **4.** any material used as an interior covering.

link[1] (lɪŋk) *n.* **1.** any of the separate rings, loops, or pieces that connect or make up a chain. **2.** something that resembles such a ring, loop, or piece. **3.** a road, rail, air, or sea connection, as between two main routes. **4.** a connecting part or episode. **5.** a connecting piece in a mechanism, often having pivoted ends. **6.** Also called: **radio link.** a system of transmitters and receivers that connect two locations by means of radio and television signals. **7.** a unit of length equal to one hundredth of a chain. 1 link of a Gunter's chain is equal to 7.92 inches, and of an engineer's chain to 1 foot. ~*vb.* **8.** (often foll. by *up*) to connect or be connected with or as if with links. **9.** (*tr.*) to connect by association, etc. [C14: from Scandinavian; compare Old Norse *hlekkr* link] —'**linkable** *adj.*

link[2] (lɪŋk) *n.* (formerly) a torch used to light dark streets. [C16: perhaps from Latin *lychnus,* from Greek *lukhnos* lamp]

linkage ('lɪŋkɪdʒ) *n.* **1.** the act of linking or the state of being linked. **2.** a system of interconnected levers or rods for transmitting or regulating the motion of a mechanism. **3.** *Electronics.* the product of the total number of lines of magnetic flux and the number of turns in a coil or circuit through which they pass. **4.** *Genetics.* the occurrence of two genes close together on the same chromosome so that they are unlikely to be separated during crossing over and tend to be inherited as a single unit.

linkboy ('lɪŋkˌbɔɪ) *or* **linkman** *n., pl.* **-boys** *or* **-men.** (formerly) a boy who carried a torch for pedestrians in dark streets.

linked list *n. Computer technol.* a list in which each item contains both data and a pointer to one or both neighbouring items, thus eliminating the need for the data items to be ordered in memory.

linker ('lɪŋkə) *n.* **1.** *Computer technol.* a program that adjusts two or more machine-language program segments so that they may be simultaneously loaded and executed as a unit. **2.** (in systemic grammar) a word that links one word, phrase, sentence, or clause to another; a co-ordinating conjunction or a sentence connector. Compare **binder** (sense 11).

linkman ('lɪŋkmən) *n., pl.* **-men. 1.** a presenter of a television or radio programme, esp. a sports transmission, consisting of a number of outside broadcasts from different locations. **2.** another word for **linkboy.**

link motion *n.* a mechanism controlling the valves of a steam engine, consisting of a slotted link terminating in a pair of eccentrics.

links (lɪŋks) *pl. n.* **1. a.** short for **golf links. b.** (*as modifier*): *a links course.* **2.** *Chiefly Scot.* undulating sandy ground near the shore. [Old English *hlincas* plural of *hlinc* ridge]

Link trainer (lɪŋk) *n. Trademark.* a ground-training device for training pilots and aircrew in the use of flight instruments. Compare **flight simulator.** [named after E. A. *Link* (1904–81), its U.S. inventor]

linkup ('lɪŋkˌʌp) *n.* **1.** the establishing of a connection or union between objects, groups, organizations, etc. **2.** the connection or union established.

linkwork ('lɪŋkˌwɜːk) *n.* **1.** something made up of links. **2.** a mechanism consisting of a series of links to impart or control motion; linkage.

linn (lɪn) *n. Chiefly Scot.* **1.** a waterfall or a pool at the foot of it. **2.** a ravine or precipice. [C16: probably from a confusion of two words, Scottish Gaelic *linne* pool and Old English *hlynn* torrent]

Linnean *or* **Linnaean** (lɪ'niːən, -'neɪ-) *adj.* **1.** of or relating to Carolus Linnaeus (1707–78), Swedish botanist who devised the binomial system of biological nomenclature. **2.** relating to the system of classification of plants and animals using binomial nomenclature.

linnet ('lɪnɪt) *n.* **1.** a brownish Old World finch, *Acanthis cannabina*: the male has a red breast and forehead. **2.** Also called: **house finch.** a similar and related North American bird, *Carpodacus mexicanus.* [C16: from Old French *linotte,* ultimately from Latin *līnum* flax (because the bird feeds on flaxseeds)]

lino ('laɪnəʊ) *n.* short for **linoleum.**

linocut ('laɪnəʊˌkʌt) *n.* **1.** a design cut in relief on linoleum mounted on a wooden block. **2.** a print made from such a design.

linoleate (lɪ'nəʊlɪˌeɪt) *n.* an ester or salt of linoleic acid.

linoleic acid (ˌlɪnəʊ'liːɪk) *n.* a colourless oily essential fatty acid found in many natural oils, such as linseed: used in the manufacture of soaps, emulsifiers, and driers. Formula: $C_{18}H_{32}O_2$. [C19: from Latin *linum* flax + OLEIC ACID; so named because it is found in linseed oil]

linolenic acid (ˌlɪnəʊ'lɛnɪk, -'liː-) *n.* a colourless unsaturated essential fatty acid found in drying oils, such as linseed oil, and used in making paints and synthetic resins; 9,12,15-octadecatrienoic acid. Formula: $C_{18}H_{30}O_2$.

linoleum (lɪ'nəʊlɪəm) *n.* a sheet material made of hessian, jute, etc., coated under pressure and heat with a mixture of powdered cork, linseed oil, rosin, and pigment, used as a floor covering. Often shortened to **lino.** [C19: from Latin *līnum* flax + *oleum* oil]

lino tile *n.* a tile made of linoleum or a similar substance, used as a floor covering.

Linotype ('laɪnəʊˌtaɪp) *n.* **1.** *Trademark.* a typesetting machine, operated by a keyboard, that casts an entire line on one solid slug of metal. **2.** type produced by such a machine.

linsang ('lɪnsæŋ) *n.* any of several forest-dwelling viverrine mammals, *Poiana richardsoni* of W Africa or either of the two species of *Prionodon* of S Asia: closely related to the genets, having a very long tail and a spotted or banded coat of thick fur. [C19: Malay]

linseed ('lɪnˌsiːd) *n.* another name for **flaxseed.** [Old English *līnsǣd,* from *līn* flax + *sǣd* seed]

linseed oil *n.* a yellow oil extracted from seeds of the flax plant. It has great drying qualities and is used in making oil paints, printer's ink, linoleum, etc.

linsey-woolsey ('lɪnzɪ'wʊlzɪ) *n.* **1.** a thin rough fabric of linen warp and coarse wool or cotton filling. **2.** a strange nonsensical mixture or confusion. [C15: probably from *Lindsey,* Suffolk village where the fabric was first made + WOOL (with rhyming suffix *-sey*)]

linstock ('lɪnˌstɒk) *n.* a long staff holding a lighted match, formerly used to fire a cannon. [C16: from Dutch *lontstok,* from *lont* match + *stok* stick]

lint (lɪnt) *n.* **1.** an absorbent cotton or linen fabric with the nap raised on one side, used to dress wounds, etc. **2.** shreds of fibre, yarn, etc. **3.** *Chiefly U.S.* staple fibre for making cotton yarn. [C14: probably from Latin *linteus* made of linen, from *līnum* flax] —'**linty** *adj.*

lintel ('lɪntᵊl) *n.* a horizontal beam, as over a door or window. [C14: via Old French probably from Late Latin *līmitāris* (unattested) of the boundary, influenced in meaning by *līminaris* of the threshold]

linter ('lɪntə) *n.* **1.** a machine for stripping the short fibres of ginned cotton seeds. **2.** (*pl.*) the fibres so removed.

lintie ('lɪntɪ) *n.* a Scot. word for **linnet** (sense 1).

lintwhite ('lɪnt,waɪt) *n. Archaic or poetic, chiefly Scot.* the linnet. [Old English *līnetwige,* probably from *līn* flax + *-twige,* perhaps related to Old High German *zwigon* to pluck]

linum ('laɪnəm) *n.* any plant of the annual or perennial genus *Linum,* of temperate regions, esp. *L. grandiflorum,* from N Africa, cultivated for its showy red or blue flowers: family *Linaceae.* See also **flax.** [Latin, from Greek *linon* flax]

lion ('laɪən) *n.* **1.** a large gregarious predatory feline mammal, *Panthera leo,* of open country in parts of Africa and India, having a tawny yellow coat and, in the male, a shaggy mane. Related adj.: **leonine. 2.** a conventionalized lion, the principal beast used as an emblem in heraldry. It has become the national emblem of Great Britain. **3.** a courageous, strong, or bellicose person. **4.** a celebrity or idol who attracts much publicity and a large following. **5. beard the lion in his den.** to approach a feared or influential person, esp. in order to ask a favour. **6. the lion's share.** the largest portion. [Old English *līo, lēo* (Middle English *lioun,* from Anglo-French *liun*), both from Latin *leo,* Greek *leōn*]

Lion ('laɪən) *n.* **the.** the constellation Leo, the fifth sign of the zodiac.

lioness ('laɪənɪs) *n.* a female lion.

lionfish ('laɪən,fɪʃ) *n., pl.* **-fish** *or* **-fishes.** any of various scorpion fishes of the tropical Pacific genus *Pterois,* having a striped body and elongated spiny fins.

lion-hearted *adj.* very brave; courageous. —**'lion-,heartedly** *adv.* —**'lion,heartedness** *n.*

lionize *or* **lionise** ('laɪə,naɪz) *vb.* (*tr.*) to treat as or make into a celebrity. —**,lioni'zation** *or* **,lioni'sation** *n.* —**'lion,izer** *or* **'lion,iser** *n.*

lip (lɪp) *n.* **1.** *Anatomy.* **a.** either of the two fleshy folds surrounding the mouth, playing an important role in the production of speech sounds, retaining food in the mouth, etc. Related adj.: **labial. b.** (*as modifier*): *lip salve.* **2.** the corresponding part in animals, esp. mammals. **3.** any structure resembling a lip, such as the rim of a crater, the margin of a gastropod shell, etc. **4.** a nontechnical word for **labium** and **labellum** (sense 1). **5.** *Slang.* impudent talk or backchat. **6.** the embouchure and control in the lips needed to blow wind and brass instruments. **7. bite one's lip. a.** to stifle one's feelings. **b.** to be annoyed or irritated. **8. button (up) one's lip.** *Slang.* to stop talking: often imperative. **9. keep a stiff upper lip.** to maintain one's courage or composure during a time of trouble without giving way to or revealing one's emotions. **10. lick** *or* **smack one's lips.** to anticipate or recall something with glee or relish. ~*vb.* **lips, lipping, lipped. 11.** (*tr.*) to touch with the lip or lips. **12.** (*tr.*) to form or be a lip or lips for. **13.** (*tr.*) *Rare.* to murmur or whisper. **14.** (*intr.*) to use the lips in playing a wind instrument. [Old English *lippa;* related to Old High German *leffur,* Norwegian *lepe,* Latin *labium*] —**'lipless** *adj.* —**'lip,like** *adj.*

lip- *combining form.* a variant of **lipo-** before a vowel.

lipaemia *or U.S.* **lipemia** (lɪ'piːmɪə) *n. Pathol.* an abnormally large amount of fat in the blood. [from Greek *lipos* fat + -AEMIA]

lipase ('laɪpeɪs, 'lɪpeɪs) *n.* any of a group of fat-digesting enzymes produced in the stomach, pancreas, and liver and also occurring widely in the seeds of plants. [C19: from Greek *lipos* fat + -ASE]

lip gloss *n.* a cosmetic preparation applied to the lips to give a sheen.

lipid *or* **lipide** ('laɪpɪd, 'lɪpɪd) *n. Biochem.* any of a large group of organic compounds that are esters of fatty acids (**simple lipids,** such as fats and waxes) or closely related substances (**compound lipids,** such as phospholipids): usually insoluble in water but soluble in alcohol and other organic solvents. They are important structural materials in living organisms. Former name: **lipoid.** [C20: from French *lipide,* from Greek *lipos* fat]

Lipizzaner (,lɪpɪt'sɑːnə) *n.* a breed of riding and carriage horse used by the Spanish Riding School in Vienna and nearly always grey in colour. [German, after *Lipizza,* Yugoslavia, where these horses were bred]

lip microphone *n.* a microphone designed and shaped to be held close to the mouth, for use in noisy environments.

lipo- *or before a vowel* **lip-** *combining form.* fat or fatty: *lipoprotein.* [from Greek *lipos* fat]

lipogenesis (,lɪpəʊ'dʒɛnɪsɪs) *adj. Biochem.* the synthesis of fatty acids in the body from glucose and other substrates.

lipography (lɪ'pɒgrəfɪ) *n.* the accidental omission of words or letters in writing. [C19: from Greek *lip-,* stem of *leipein* to omit + -GRAPHY]

lipoic acid *n. Biochem.* a sulphur-containing fatty acid, regarded as an element of the vitamin B complex, minute amounts of which are required for carbohydrate metabolism.

lipoid ('lɪpɔɪd, 'laɪ-) *adj. also* **lipoidal. 1.** resembling fat; fatty. ~*n.* **2.** a fatlike substance, such as wax. **3.** *Biochem.* a former name for **lipid.**

lipolysis (lɪ'pɒlɪsɪs) *n. Chem.* the hydrolysis of fats resulting in the production of carboxylic acids and glycerol. —**lipolytic** (,lɪpəʊ'lɪtɪk) *adj.*

lipoma (lɪ'pəʊmə) *n., pl.* **-mas** *or* **-mata** (-mətə). *Pathol.* a tumour composed of fatty tissue. [C19: New Latin] —**lipomatous** (lɪ'pɒmətəs) *adj.*

lipophilic (,lɪpəʊ'fɪlɪk) *or* **lipotropic** (,lɪpəʊ'trɒpɪk, ,laɪ-) *adj. Chem.* having an affinity for lipids.

lipoplast ('lɪpəʊ,plɑːst) *or* **lipidoplast** ('lɪpɪdəʊ,plɑːst) *n. Botany.* a small particle in plant cytoplasm, esp. that of seeds, in which fat is stored.

lipopolysaccaride (,lɪpəʊ,pɒlɪ'sækə,raɪd) *n.* a molecule, consisting of lipid and polysaccharide components, that is the main constituent of the cell walls of Gram-negative bacteria.

lipoprotein (,lɪpəʊ'prəʊtiːn, ,laɪ-) *n.* any of a group of proteins to which a lipid molecule is attached, important in the transport of lipids in the bloodstream. They exist in two main forms: high-density lipoproteins and low-density lipoproteins. See also **low-density lipoprotein.**

liposome ('lɪpəʊ,səʊm) *n.* a particle formed by lipids, consisting of a double layer similar to a natural biological membrane, enclosing an aqueous compartment.

liposuction ('lɪpəʊ,sʌkʃən) *n.* a cosmetic surgical operation in which subcutaneous fat is removed from the body by suction.

lipotropic (,lɪpəʊ'trɒpɪk) *adj. Biochem.* (of a substance) increasing the utilization of fat by the tissues.

-lipped *adj.* having a lip or lips as specified: *tight-lipped.*

lippie ('lɪpɪ) *n. Austral. informal.* lipstick.

Lippizaner (,lɪpɪt'zɑːnə) *n.* a variant spelling of **Lipizzaner.**

lippy ('lɪpɪ) *adj.* **-pier, -piest.** *U.S. and Canadian slang.* insolent or cheeky.

lip-read ('lɪp,riːd) *vb.* **-reads, -reading, -read** (-'rɛd). to interpret (words) by lip-reading.

lip-reading *n.* a method used by the deaf to comprehend spoken words by interpreting movements of the speaker's lips. Also called: **speech-reading.** —**'lip-,reader** *n.*

lip service *n.* insincere support or respect expressed but not put into practice.

lipstick ('lɪp,stɪk) *n.* a cosmetic for colouring the lips, usually in the form of a stick.

lip-synch *or* **lip-sync** ('lɪp,sɪŋk) *vb.* to mouth (prerecorded words) on television or film.

lipuria (lɪ'pjʊərɪə) *n. Pathol.* the presence of fat in the urine.

liq. *abbrev. for:* **1.** liquid. **2.** liquor.

liquate ('laɪkweɪt) *vb.* (*tr.;* often foll. by *out*) to separate one component of (an alloy, impure metal, or ore) by heating so that the more fusible part melts. [C17: from Latin *liquāre* to dissolve] —**li'quation** *n.*

liquefacient (,lɪkwɪ'feɪʃənt) *n.* **1.** a substance that liquefies or causes liquefaction. ~*adj.* **2.** becoming or causing to become liquid. [C19: from Latin *liquefacere* to make LIQUID]

liquefied natural gas *n.* a mixture of various gases, esp. methane, liquefied under pressure for transportation and used as an engine fuel. Abbrev.: **LNG.**

liquefied petroleum gas *n.* a mixture of various petroleum gases, esp. propane and butane, stored as a liquid under pressure and used as an engine fuel. See also **bottled gas.** Abbrev.: **LPG** *or* **LP gas.**

liquefy ('lɪkwɪ,faɪ) *vb.* **-fies, -fying, -fied.** (esp. of a gas) to become or cause to become liquid. [C15: via Old French from Latin *liquefacere* to make liquid] —**liquefaction** (,lɪkwɪ'fækʃən) *n.* —**,lique'factive** *adj.* —**'lique,fiable** *adj.* —**'lique,fier** *n.*

liquesce (lɪ'kwɛs) *vb.* (*intr.*) to become liquid.

liquescent (lɪ'kwɛsᵊnt) *adj.* (of a solid or gas) becoming or tending to become liquid. [C18: from Latin *liquescere*] —**li'quescence** *or* **li'quescency** *n.*

liqueur (lɪ'kjʊə; *French* likœr) *n.* **1. a.** any of several highly flavoured sweetened spirits such as kirsch or cointreau, intended to be drunk after a meal. **b.** (*as modifier*): *liqueur glass.* **2.** a small hollow chocolate sweet containing liqueur. [C18: from French; see LIQUOR]

liquid ('lɪkwɪd) *n.* **1.** a substance in a physical state in which it does not resist change of shape but does resist change of size. Compare **gas** (sense 1), **solid** (sense 1). **2.** a substance that is a liquid at room temperature and atmospheric pressure. **3.** *Phonetics.* a frictionless continuant, esp. (l) or (r). ~*adj.* **4.** of, concerned with, or being a liquid or having the characteristic state of liquids: *liquid wax.* **5.** shining, transparent, or brilliant. **6.** flowing, fluent, or smooth. **7.** (of assets) in the form of money or easily convertible into money. [C14: via Old French from Latin *liquidus,* from *liquēre* to be fluid] —**'liquidly** *adv.* —**'liquidness** *n.*

liquid air *n.* air that has been liquefied by cooling. It is a pale blue and consists mainly of liquid oxygen (boiling pt.: -182.9°C) and liquid nitrogen (boiling pt.: -195.7°C): used in the production of pure oxygen, nitrogen, and the inert gases, and as a refrigerant.

liquidambar (,lɪkwɪd'æmbə) *n.* **1.** any deciduous tree of the hamamelidaceous genus *Liquidambar,* of Asia and North and Central America, with star-shaped leaves, and exuding a yellow aromatic balsam. See also **sweet gum. 2.** the balsam of this tree, used in medicine. See also **storax** (sense 3). [C16: New Latin, from Latin *liquidus* liquid + Medieval Latin *ambar* AMBER]

liquidate ('lɪkwɪ,deɪt) *vb.* **1. a.** to settle or pay off (a debt, claim, etc.). **b.** to determine by litigation or agreement the amount of (damages, indebtedness, etc.). **2. a.** to terminate the operations of (a commercial firm, bankrupt estate, etc.) by assessment of liabilities and appropriation of assets for their settlement. **b.** (of a commercial firm, etc.) to terminate operations in this manner. 3. (*tr.*) to convert (assets) into cash. 4. (*tr.*) to eliminate or kill.

liquidation (ˌlɪkwɪˈdeɪʃən) *n.* 1. a. the process of terminating the affairs of a business firm, etc., by realizing its assets to discharge its liabilities. b. the state of a business firm, etc., having its affairs so terminated (esp. in the phrase **to go into liquidation**). 2. destruction; elimination.

liquidator (ˈlɪkwɪˌdeɪtə) *n.* a person assigned to supervise the liquidation of a business concern and whose legal authorization, rights, and duties differ according to whether the liquidation is compulsory or voluntary.

liquid crystal *n.* a liquid that has some crystalline characteristics, such as the presence of different optical properties in different directions; a substance in a mesomorphic state. See also **smectic, nematic.**

liquid-crystal display *n.* a display of numbers, esp. in an electronic calculator, using liquid-crystal cells that change their reflectivity or optical polarization when an electric field is applied to them. Abbrev.: **LCD.**

liquid fire *n.* inflammable petroleum or other liquid used as a weapon of war in flamethrowers, etc.

liquid glass *n.* another name for **water glass.**

liquidity (lɪˈkwɪdɪtɪ) *n.* 1. the possession of sufficient liquid assets to discharge current liabilities. 2. the state or quality of being liquid.

liquidity preference *n. Economics.* the desire to hold money rather than other assets, in Keynsian theory based on motives of transactions, precaution, and speculation.

liquidity ratio *n.* the ratio of those assets that can easily be exchanged for money to the total assets of a bank or other financial institution. Also called: **liquid assets ratio.**

liquidize *or* **liquidise** (ˈlɪkwɪˌdaɪz) *vb.* 1. to make or become liquid; liquefy. 2. (*tr.*) to pulverize (food) in a liquidizer so as to produce a fluid.

liquidizer *or* **liquidiser** (ˈlɪkwɪˌdaɪzə) *n.* a kitchen appliance with blades for cutting and puréeing vegetables, blending liquids, etc. Also called: **blender.**

liquid measure *n.* a unit or system of units for measuring volumes of liquids or their containers.

liquid oxygen *n.* the clear pale blue liquid state of oxygen produced by liquefying air and allowing the nitrogen to evaporate: used in rocket fuels. Also called: **lox.**

liquid paraffin *n.* a colourless almost tasteless oily liquid obtained by petroleum distillation and used as a laxative. Also called (esp. U.S. and Canadian): **mineral oil.**

liquor (ˈlɪkə) *n.* 1. any alcoholic drink, esp. spirits, or such drinks collectively. 2. any liquid substance, esp. that in which food has been cooked. 3. *Pharmacol.* a solution of a pure substance in water. 4. *Brewing.* warm water added to malt to form wort. 5. **in liquor.** drunk; intoxicated. ~*vb.* 6. *Brewing.* to steep (malt) in warm water to form wort; mash. [C13: via Old French from Latin, from *liquēre* to be liquid]

liquorice *or U.S. and Canadian* **licorice** (ˈlɪkərɪs, -ərɪʃ) *n.* 1. a perennial Mediterranean leguminous shrub, *Glycyrrhiza glabra,* having spikes of pale blue flowers and flat red-brown pods. 2. the dried root of this plant, used as a laxative and in confectionery. 3. a sweet having a liquorice flavour. [C13: via Anglo-Norman and Old French from Late Latin *liquirītia,* from Latin *glycyrrhīza,* from Greek *glukurrhiza,* from *glukus* sweet + *rhiza* root]

liquorish (ˈlɪkərɪʃ) *adj.* 1. a variant spelling of **lickerish.** 2. *Brit.* a variant of **liquorice.** —ˈ**liquorishly** *adv.* —ˈ**liquorishness** *n.*

liquor store *n. U.S.* See **package store.**

liquor up *vb.* (*adv.*) *U.S. and Canadian slang.* to become or cause to become drunk.

lira (ˈlɪərə; *Italian* ˈliːra) *n., pl.* **lire** (ˈlɪərɪ; *Italian* ˈliːre) *or* **liras.** 1. the standard monetary unit of Italy and San Marino. 2. Also called: **pound.** the standard monetary unit of Turkey, divided into 100 piastres. [Italian, from Latin *lībra* pound]

liriodendron (ˌlɪrɪəʊˈdɛndrən) *n., pl.* **-drons** *or* **-dra** (-drə). either of the two deciduous trees of the magnoliaceous genus *Liriodendron,* the tulip tree of North America or *L. chinense* of China. [C18: New Latin, from Greek *leiron* lily + *dendron* tree]

liripipe (ˈlɪrɪˌpaɪp) *or* **liripoop** (ˈlɪrɪˌpuːp) *n.* the tip of a graduate's hood. [C14: Medieval Latin *liripipium,* origin obscure]

lisle (laɪl) *n.* a. a strong fine cotton thread or fabric. b. (*as modifier*): *lisle stockings.* [C19: named after *Lisle* (now Lille), town in France where this type of thread was originally manufactured]

lisp (lɪsp) *n.* 1. the articulation of *s* and *z* like or nearly like the *th* sounds in English *thin* and *then* respectively. 2. the habit or speech defect of pronouncing *s* and *z* in this manner. 3. the sound of a lisp in pronunciation. ~*vb.* 4. to use a lisp in the pronunciation of (speech). 5. to speak or pronounce imperfectly or haltingly. [Old English *āwlispian,* from *wlisp* lisping (adj.), of imitative origin; related to Old High German *lispen*] —ˈ**lisper** *n.* —ˈ**lisping** *adj., n.* —ˈ**lispingly** *adv.*

LISP (lɪsp) *n.* a high-level computer-programming language suitable for work in artificial intelligence. [C20: from *lis(t) p(rocessing)*]

lis pendens (lɪs ˈpɛndɛnz) *n.* 1. a suit pending in a court that concerns the title to land. 2. a notice filed to warn interested persons of such a suit. [Latin: pending lawsuit]

Lissajous figure (ˈliːsəˌʒuː, ˌliːsəˈʒuː) *n.* a curve traced out by a point that undergoes two simple harmonic motions in mutually perpendicular directions. The shape of these curves is characteristic of the relative phases and frequencies of the motion; they are used to determine the frequencies and phases of alternating voltages. [C19: named after Jules A. *Lissajous* (1822–80), French physicist]

lissom *or* **lissome** (ˈlɪsəm) *adj.* 1. supple in the limbs or body; lithe; flexible. 2. agile; nimble. [C19: variant of LITHESOME] —ˈ**lissomly** *or* ˈ**lissomely** *adv.* —ˈ**lissomness** *or* ˈ**lissomeness** *n.*

list[1] (lɪst) *n.* 1. an item-by-item record of names or things, usually written or printed one under the other. 2. *Computer technol.* a linearly ordered data structure. 3. **be on the danger list.** to be in a critical medical or physical condition. ~*vb.* 4. (*tr.*) to make a list of. 5. (*tr.*) to include in a list. 6. (*tr.*) *Brit.* to declare to be a listed building. 7. (*tr.*) *Stock Exchange.* to obtain an official quotation for (a security) so that it may be traded on the recognized market. 8. an archaic word for **enlist.** [C17: from French, ultimately related to LIST[2]; compare Italian *lista* list of names (earlier: border, strip, as of paper), Old High German *līsta* border] —ˈ**listable** *adj.*

list[2] (lɪst) *n.* 1. a border or edging strip, esp. of cloth. 2. a less common word for **selvage.** 3. a strip of bark, sapwood, etc., trimmed from a board or plank. 4. another word for **fillet** (sense 8). 5. a strip, band, ridge or furrow. 6. *Agriculture.* a ridge in ploughed land formed by throwing two furrows together. ~*vb.* (*tr.*) 7. to border with or as if with a list or lists. 8. *Agriculture.* to plough (land) so as to form lists. 9. to cut a list from (a board, plank, etc.). ~See also **lists.** [Old English *līst;* related to Old High German *līsta*]

list[3] (lɪst) *vb.* 1. (esp. of ships) to lean over or cause to lean over to one side. ~*n.* 2. the act or an instance of leaning to one side. [C17: origin unknown]

list[4] (lɪst) *Archaic.* ~*vb.* 1. to be pleasing to (a person). 2. (*tr.*) to desire or choose. ~*n.* 3. a liking or desire. [Old English *lystan;* related to Old High German *lusten* and Gothic *lūston* to desire]

list[5] (lɪst) *vb.* an archaic or poetic word for **listen.** [Old English *hlystan;* related to Old Norse *hlusta*]

listed building *n.* (in Britain) a building officially recognized as having special historical or architectural interest and therefore protected from demolition or alteration.

listed company *n. Stock Exchange.* a company whose shares are quoted on the main market of the London Stock Exchange.

listed security *n. Stock Exchange.* a security that is quoted on the main market of the London Stock Exchange and appears in its *Official List of Securities.* Compare **Third Market, unlisted securities market.**

listel (ˈlɪstᵊl) *n.* another name for **fillet** (sense 8). [C16: via French from Italian *listello,* diminutive of *lista* band, LIST[2]]

listen (ˈlɪsᵊn) *vb.* (*intr.*) 1. to concentrate on hearing something. 2. to take heed; pay attention: *I told you many times but you wouldn't listen.* [Old English *hlysnan;* related to Old High German *lūstrēn*] —ˈ**listener** *n.*

listenable (ˈlɪsᵊnəbᵊl) *adj.* easy or pleasant to listen to. —ˌ**listenaˈbility** *n.*

listen in *vb.* (*intr., adv.;* often foll. by *to*) 1. to listen to the radio. 2. to intercept radio communications. 3. to listen but not contribute (to a discussion), esp. surreptitiously.

listening post *n.* 1. *Military.* a forward position set up to obtain early warning of enemy movement. 2. any strategic position or place for obtaining information about another country or area.

lister (ˈlɪstə) *n. U.S. and Canadian agriculture.* a plough with a double mouldboard designed to throw soil to either side of a central furrow. Also called: **lister plough, middlebreaker, middle buster.** [C19: from LIST[2]]

listeria (lɪsˈtɪərɪə) *n.* any rodlike Gram-positive bacterium of the genus *Listeria,* esp. *L. monocytogenes,* the cause of listeriosis. [C20: named after Joseph *Lister* (1827–1912), British surgeon] —**lisˈterial** *adj.*

listeriosis (lɪˌstɪərɪˈəʊsɪs) *n.* a serious form of food poisoning, caused by bacteria of the genus *Listeria.* Its symptoms can include meningitis and in pregnant women it may cause damage to the fetus.

Listerism (ˈlɪstəˌrɪzəm) *n. Surgery.* the use of or theory of using antiseptic techniques.

listing (ˈlɪstɪŋ) *n.* 1. a list or an entry in a list. 2. *Computer technol.* a printed copy of a program or file in a form that can be read by humans. 3. a place on the Official List of Securities of the London Stock Exchange obtained by a company that has fulfilled the listing requirements and whose shares are quoted on the main market. 4. (*pl.*) lists of concerts, films, and other events printed in newspapers or magazines, showing details, such as times and venues.

listless (ˈlɪstlɪs) *adj.* disinclined for any effort or exertion; lacking vigour, enthusiasm, or energy. [C15: from *list* desire + -LESS] —ˈ**listlessly** *adv.* —ˈ**listlessness** *n.*

list price *n.* the selling price of merchandise as quoted in a catalogue or advertisement.

list renting *n.* the practice of renting a list of potential customers to a direct-mail seller of goods or to the fund raisers of a charity.

lists (lɪsts) *pl. n.* **1.** *History.* **a.** the enclosed field of combat at a tournament. **b.** the barriers enclosing the field at a tournament. **2.** any arena or scene of conflict, controversy, etc. **3. enter the lists.** to engage in a conflict, controversy, etc. [C14: plural of LIST[2] (border, boundary)]

lit[1] (lɪt) *vb.* **1.** a past tense and past participle of **light**[1]. **2.** an alternative past tense and past participle of **light**[2].

lit[2] (lɪt) *or* **litas** ('liːtɑːs) *n., pl.* **lits, litai** ('liːteɪ), *or* **litu** ('liːtuː). the monetary unit of Lithuania before 1940.

lit. *abbrev. for:* **1.** literal(ly). **2.** literary. **3.** literature.

litany ('lɪtənɪ) *n., pl.* **-nies. 1.** *Christianity.* **a.** a form of prayer consisting of a series of invocations, each followed by an unvarying response. **b. the Litany.** the general supplication in this form included in the Book of Common Prayer. **2.** any long or tedious speech or recital. [C13: via Old French from Medieval Latin *litanīa* from Late Greek *litaneia* prayer, ultimately from Greek *litē* entreaty]

litchi, lichee, lichi, *or* **lychee** (ˌlaɪ'tʃiː) *n.* **1.** a Chinese sapindaceous tree, *Litchi chinensis*, cultivated for its round edible fruits. **2.** the fruit of this tree, which has whitish juicy pulp. [C16: from Cantonese *lai chi*]

-lite *n. combining form.* (in names of minerals) stone: *chrysolite.* Compare **-lith.** [from French *-lite* or *-lithe*, from Greek *lithos* stone]

liter ('liːtə) *n.* the U.S. spelling of **litre.**

literacy ('lɪtərəsɪ) *n.* **1.** the ability to read and write. **2.** the ability to use language proficiently.

literae humaniores ('lɪtəˌriː hjuːˌmænɪ'ɔːriːz) *n.* (at Oxford University) the faculty concerned with Greek and Latin literature, ancient history, and philosophy; classics. [Latin, literally: the more humane letters]

literal ('lɪtərəl) *adj.* **1.** in exact accordance with or limited to the primary or explicit meaning of a word or text. **2.** word for word. **3.** dull, factual, or prosaic. **4.** consisting of, concerning, or indicated by letters. **5.** true; actual. **6.** *Maths.* containing or using coefficients and constants represented by letters: $ax^2 + b$ is a literal expression. Compare **numerical** (sense 3a.). *~n.* **7.** Also called: **literal error.** a misprint or misspelling in a text. [C14: from Late Latin *litterālis* concerning letters, from Latin *littera* LETTER] **—'literalness** *or* **literality** (ˌlɪtə'rælɪtɪ) *n.*

literalism ('lɪtərəˌlɪzəm) *n.* **1.** the disposition to take words and statements in their literal sense. **2.** literal or realistic portrayal in art or literature. **—'literalist** *n.* **—ˌliteral'istic** *adj.* **—ˌliteral'istically** *adv.*

literally ('lɪtərəlɪ) *adv.* **1.** in a literal manner. **2.** (intensifier): *there were literally thousands of people.*

▷**Usage.** The use of *literally* as an intensifier is common, esp. in informal contexts. In some cases, it provides emphasis without adding to the meaning: *the house was literally only five minutes walk away.* Often, however, its use results in absurdity: *the news was literally an eye-opener to me.* It is therefore best avoided in formal contexts.

literary ('lɪtərərɪ, 'lɪtrərɪ) *adj.* **1.** of, relating to, concerned with, or characteristic of literature or scholarly writing: *a literary discussion; a literary style.* **2.** versed in or knowledgeable about literature: *a literary man.* **3.** (of a word) formal; not colloquial. [C17: from Latin *litterārius* concerning reading and writing. See LETTER] **—'literarily** *adv.* **—'literariness** *n.*

literary agent *n.* a person who manages the business affairs of an author. **—literary agency** *n.*

literate ('lɪtərɪt) *adj.* **1.** able to read and write. **2.** educated; learned. **3.** used to words rather than numbers as a means of expression. Compare **numerate.** *~n.* **4.** a literate person. [C15: from Latin *litterātus* learned. See LETTER] **—'literately** *adv.*

literati (ˌlɪtə'rɑːtiː) *pl. n.* literary or scholarly people. [C17: from Latin]

literatim (ˌlɪtə'rɑːtɪm) *adv.* letter for letter. [C17: from Medieval Latin, from Latin *littera* LETTER]

literation (ˌlɪtə'reɪʃən) *n.* the use of letters to represent sounds or words.

literator ('lɪtəˌreɪtə) *n.* another word for **littérateur.** [C18: from Latin, from *littera* letter]

literature ('lɪtərɪtʃə, 'lɪtrɪ-) *n.* **1.** written material such as poetry, novels, essays, etc., esp. works of imagination characterized by excellence of style and expression and by themes of general or enduring interest. **2.** the body of written work of a particular culture or people: *Scandinavian literature.* **3.** written or printed matter of a particular type or on a particular subject: *scientific literature; the literature of the violin.* **4.** printed material giving a particular type of information: *sales literature.* **5.** the art or profession of a writer. **6.** *Obsolete.* learning. [C14: from Latin *litterātūra* writing; see LETTER]

lith. *abbrev. for:* **1.** lithograph. **2.** lithography.

Lith. *abbrev. for* Lithuania(n).

-lith *n. combining form.* indicating stone or rock: *megalith.* Compare **-lite.** [from Greek *lithos* stone]

litharge ('lɪθɑːdʒ) *n.* another name for **lead monoxide.** [C14: via Old French from Latin *lithargyrus*, from Greek, from *lithos* stone + *arguros* silver]

lithe (laɪð) *adj.* flexible or supple. [Old English (in the sense: gentle; C15: supple); related to Old High German *lindi* soft, Latin *lentus* slow] **—'lithely** *adv.* **—'litheness** *n.*

lithesome ('laɪðsəm) *adj.* a less common word for **lissom.** [C18: from LITHE + -SOME[1]]

lithia ('lɪθɪə) *n.* **1.** another name for **lithium oxide. 2.** lithium present in mineral waters as lithium salts. [C19: New Latin, ultimately from Greek *lithos* stone]

lithiasis (lɪ'θaɪəsɪs) *n. Pathol.* the formation of a calculus. [C17: New Latin; see LITHO-, -IASIS]

lithia water *n.* a natural or artificial mineral water that contains lithium salts.

lithic ('lɪθɪk) *adj.* **1.** of, relating to, or composed of stone: *a lithic sandstone.* **2.** *Pathol.* of or relating to a calculus or calculi, esp. one in the urinary bladder. **3.** of or containing lithium. [C18: from Greek *lithikos* stony]

-lithic *adj. combining form.* (in anthropology) relating to the use of stone implements in a specified cultural period: *Neolithic.* [from Greek *lithikos*, from *lithos* stone]

lithification (ˌlɪθɪfɪ'keɪʃən) *n.* the consolidation of a loosely deposited sediment into a hard sedimentary rock.

lithium ('lɪθɪəm) *n.* a soft silvery element of the alkali metal series: the lightest known metal, used as an alloy hardener, as a reducing agent, and in batteries. Symbol: Li; atomic no.: 3; atomic wt.: 6.941; valency: 1; relative density: 0.534; melting pt.: 179°C; boiling pt.: 1317°C. [C19: New Latin, from LITHO- + -IUM]

lithium carbonate *n.* a white crystalline solid that is used in the treatment of manic-depressive illness and mania. Formula: Li_2CO_3.

lithium oxide *n.* a white crystalline compound. It absorbs carbon dioxide and water vapour.

litho ('laɪθəʊ) *n., pl.* **-thos,** *adj., adv.* short for **lithography, lithograph, lithographic,** or **lithographically.**

litho. *or* **lithog.** *abbrev. for:* **1.** lithograph. **2.** lithography.

litho- *or before a vowel* **lith-** *combining form.* stone: *lithograph.* [from Latin, from Greek, from *lithos* stone]

lithogenous (lɪ'θɒdʒɪnəs) *adj.* (of animals, esp. certain corals) rock-building.

lithograph ('lɪθəˌgrɑːf, -ˌgræf) *n.* **1.** a print made by lithography. *~vb.* **2.** *(tr.)* to reproduce (pictures, text, etc.) by lithography. **—lithographic** (ˌlɪθə'græfɪk) *or* **ˌlitho'graphical** *adj.* **—ˌlitho'graphically** *adv.*

lithography (lɪ'θɒgrəfɪ) *n.* a method of printing from a metal or stone surface on which the printing areas are not raised but made ink-receptive as opposed to ink-repellent. [C18: from New Latin *lithographia, from* LITHO- + -GRAPHY] **—li'thographer** *n.*

lithoid ('lɪθɔɪd) *or* **lithoidal** (lɪ'θɔɪdəl) *adj.* resembling stone or rock. [C19: from Greek *lithoeidēs*, from *lithos* stone]

lithol. *abbrev. for* lithology.

lithology (lɪ'θɒlədʒɪ) *n.* **1.** the physical characteristics of a rock, including colour, composition, and texture. **2.** the study of rocks. **—lithologic** (ˌlɪθə'lɒdʒɪk) *or* **ˌlitho'logical** *adj.* **—ˌlitho'logically** *adv.* **—li'thologist** *n.*

lithomarge ('lɪθəˌmɑːdʒ) *n.* a smooth compact type of kaolin: white or reddish and often mottled. [C18: from New Latin *lithomarga* from LITHO- + Latin *marga* marl]

lithometeor (ˌlɪθə'miːtɪə) *n.* a mass of solid particles, such as dust, sand, etc., suspended in the atmosphere.

lithophyte ('lɪθəˌfaɪt) *n.* **1.** a plant that grows on rocky or stony ground. **2.** an organism, such as a coral, that is partly composed of stony material. **—lithophytic** (ˌlɪθə'fɪtɪk) *adj.*

lithopone ('lɪθəˌpəʊn) *n.* a white pigment consisting of a mixture of zinc sulphide, zinc oxide, and barium sulphate. [C20: from LITHO- + Greek *ponos* work]

lithosol ('lɪθəˌsɒl) *n. Chiefly U.S.* a type of azonal soil consisting chiefly of unweathered or partly weathered rock fragments, usually found on steep slopes. [C20: from LITHO- + Latin *solum* soil]

lithosphere ('lɪθəˌsfɪə) *n.* the rigid outer layer of the earth, which has an average thickness of about 75 km and comprises the earth's crust and the solid part of the mantle above the asthenosphere.

lithotomy (lɪ'θɒtəmɪ) *n., pl.* **-mies.** the surgical removal of a calculus, esp. one in the urinary bladder. [C18: via Late Latin from Greek, from LITHO- + -TOMY] **—lithotomic** (ˌlɪθə'tɒmɪk) *or* **ˌlitho'tomical** *adj.* **—li'thotomist** *n.*

lithotripsy ('lɪθəʊˌtrɪpsɪ) *n.* **1.** the pulverization of gallstones or stones in the urinary tract *in situ*, by means of shock waves, often generated by a lithotripter. **2.** another name for lithotrity. [C20: from LITHO- + Greek *thruptein* to crush]

lithotripter ('lɪθəˌtrɪptə) *n.* a machine that localizes urinary stones or gallstones by ultrasound or x-rays and transmits shock waves to destroy them *in situ* as an alternative to their surgical removal.

lithotrity (lɪ'θɒtrɪtɪ) *n., pl.* **-ties.** *Surgery.* the crushing of a calculus in the bladder by means of an instrument (**lithotrite**) so that it can be expelled by urinating or can be removed by suction. Also called **lithotripsy.** [C19: from LITHO- + Latin *trītus*, from *terere* to crush]

Lithuanian (ˌlɪθjʊ'eɪnɪən) *adj.* **1.** of, relating to, or characteristic of the republic of Lithuania, in NE Europe, or of its people or their language. *~n.* **2.** the official language of Lithuania, belonging to the Baltic branch of the Indo-European family. **3.** a native or inhabitant of Lithuania.

litigable (ˈlɪtɪgəbᵊl) *adj. Law.* that may be the subject of litigation.
litigant (ˈlɪtɪgənt) *n.* **1.** a party to a lawsuit. ~*adj.* **2.** engaged in litigation.
litigate (ˈlɪtɪˌgeɪt) *vb.* **1.** to bring or contest (a claim, action, etc.) in a lawsuit. **2.** (*intr.*) to engage in legal proceedings. [C17: from Latin *lītigāre,* from *līt-,* stem of *līs* lawsuit + *agere* to carry on] —ˈ**litiˌgator** *n.*
litigation (ˌlɪtɪˈgeɪʃən) *n.* **1.** the act or process of bringing or contesting a lawsuit. **2.** a judicial proceeding or contest.
litigious (lɪˈtɪdʒəs) *adj.* **1.** excessively ready to go to law. **2.** of or relating to litigation. **3.** inclined to dispute or disagree. [C14: from Latin *lītigiōsus* quarrelsome, from *lītigium* strife] —**liˈtigiously** *adv.* —**liˈtigiousness** *n.*
litmus (ˈlɪtməs) *n.* a soluble powder obtained from certain lichens. It turns red under acid conditions and blue under basic conditions and is used, in the form of a solution or as **litmus paper**, as an indicator. [C16: perhaps from Scandinavian; compare Old Norse *litmosi,* from *litr* dye + *mosi* moss]
litotes (ˈlaɪtəʊˌtiːz) *n., pl.* **-tes.** understatement for rhetorical effect, esp. when achieved by using negation with a term in place of using an antonym of that term, as in "She was not a little upset" for "She was extremely upset." [C17: from Greek, from *litos* small]
litre *or U.S.* **liter** (ˈliːtə) *n.* **1.** one cubic decimetre. **2.** (formerly) the volume occupied by 1 kilogram of pure water at 4°C and 760 millimetres of mercury. This is equivalent to 1.000 028 cubic decimetres or about 1.76 pints. [C19: from French, from Medieval Latin *litra,* from Greek: a unit of weight]
LittB *or* **LitB** *abbrev. for* Bachelor of Letters *or* Bachelor of Literature. [Latin: *Litterarum Baccalaureus*]
LittD *or* **LitD** *abbrev. for* Doctor of Letters *or* Doctor of Literature. [Latin: *Litterarum Doctor*]
litter (ˈlɪtə) *n.* **1. a.** small refuse or waste materials carelessly dropped, esp. in public places. **b.** (*as modifier*): *litter bin.* **2.** a disordered or untidy condition or a collection of objects in this condition. **3.** a group of offspring produced at one birth by a mammal such as a sow. **4.** a layer of partly decomposed leaves, twigs, etc., on the ground in a wood or forest. **5.** straw, hay, or similar material used as bedding, protection, etc., by animals or plants. **6.** See **cat litter. 7.** a means of conveying people, esp. sick or wounded people, consisting of a light bed or seat held between parallel sticks. ~*vb.* **8.** to make (a place) untidy by strewing (refuse). **9.** to scatter (objects, etc.) about or (of objects) to lie around or upon (anything) in an untidy fashion. **10.** (of pigs, cats, etc.) to give birth to (offspring). **11.** (*tr.*) to provide (an animal or plant) with straw or hay for bedding, protection, etc. [C13 (in the sense: bed): via Anglo-French, ultimately from Latin *lectus* bed]
littérateur (ˌlɪtərəˈtɜː; *French* literatœr) *n.* an author, esp. a professional writer. [C19: from French from Latin *litterātor* a grammarian]
litter lout *or U.S. and Canadian* **litterbug** (ˈlɪtəˌbʌg) *n. Slang.* a person who tends to drop refuse in public places.
little (ˈlɪtᵊl) *determiner.* **1.** (often preceded by *a*) **a.** a small quantity, extent, or duration of: *the little hope there is left; very little milk.* **b.** (*as pronoun*): *save a little for me.* **2.** not much: *little damage was done.* **3. make little of.** See **make of** (sense 3). **4. not a little. a.** very. **b.** a lot. **5. quite a little.** a considerable amount. **6. think little of.** to have a low opinion of. ~*adj.* **7.** of small or less than average size. **8.** young: *a little boy; our little ones.* **9.** endearingly familiar; dear: *my husband's little ways.* **10.** contemptible, mean, or disagreeable: *your filthy little mind.* **11.** (of a region or district) resembling another country or town in miniature: *little Venice.* **12. little game.** a person's secret intention or business: *so that's his little game!* **13. no little.** considerable. ~*adv.* **14.** (usually preceded by *a*) in a small amount; to a small extent or degree; not a lot: *to laugh a little.* **15.** (*used preceding a verb*) not at all, or hardly: *he little realized his fate.* **16.** not much or often: *we go there very little now.* **17. little by little.** by small degrees. ~See also **less, lesser, least, littler, littlest.** [Old English *lȳtel;* related to *lȳr* few, Old High German *luzzil*]
Little Bear *n.* **the.** the English name for **Ursa Minor.**
Little Dipper *n.* **the.** a U.S. and Canadian name for **Ursa Minor.**
Little Dog *n.* **the.** the English name for **Canis Minor.**
little end *n. Brit.* **1.** Also called (in vertical engines): **top end.** the smaller end of a connecting rod in an internal-combustion engine or reciprocating pump. Compare: **big end. 2.** the bearing surface between the smaller end of a connecting rod and the gudgeon pin.
Little Englander (ˈɪŋgləndə) *n.* (esp. in the 19th century) a person opposed to the extension of the British Empire.
little grebe *n.* a small brownish European diving bird, *Podiceps ruficollis,* frequenting lakes, family *Podicipitidae* (grebes).
little hours *pl. n. R.C. Church.* the canonical hours of prime, terce, sext, and nones in the divine office.
little magazine *n.* a literary magazine that features experimental or other writing of interest only to a limited number of readers.
little man *n.* **1.** a man of no importance or significance. **2.** *Brit.* a tradesman or artisan operating on a small scale.
little office *n. R.C. Church.* a series of psalms and prayers similar to the divine office but shorter.
little owl *n.* a small Old World owl, *Athene noctua,* having a speckled brown plumage and flattish head.
little people *or* **folk** *pl. n. Folklore.* small supernatural beings, such as elves, pixies, or leprechauns.
littler (ˈlɪtlə) *determiner. Not standard.* the comparative of **little.**
Little Russian *n., adj.* a former word for **Ukrainian.**
little slam *n. Bridge, etc.* the winning of all tricks except one by one side, or the contract to do so. Also called: **small slam.**
littlest (ˈlɪtlɪst) *determiner. Not standard.* the superlative of **little.**
little theatre *n. Theatre, chiefly U.S. and Canadian.* experimental or avant-garde drama, usually amateur, originating from a theatrical movement of the 1920s.
little woman *n.* **the.** *Brit., old fashioned.* a facetious term for **wife.**
littoral (ˈlɪtərəl) *adj.* **1.** of or relating to the shore of a sea, lake, or ocean. **2.** *Biology.* inhabiting the shore of a sea or lake or the shallow waters near the shore: *littoral fauna.* ~*n.* **3.** a coastal or shore region. [C17: from Late Latin *littorālis,* from *lītorālis,* from *lītus* shore]
lit up *adj. Slang.* **1.** drunk. **2.** drugged, esp. on heroin.
liturgical (lɪˈtɜːdʒɪkᵊl) *or* **liturgic** *adj.* **1.** of or relating to public worship. **2.** of or relating to the liturgy. —**liˈturgically** *adv.*
liturgics (lɪˈtɜːdʒɪks) *n.* (*functioning as sing.*) the study of liturgies. Also called: **liturgiology** (lɪˌtɜːdʒɪˈɒlədʒɪ).
liturgist (ˈlɪtədʒɪst) *n.* a student or composer of liturgical forms. —ˈ**liturgism** *n.* —ˌ**liturˈgistic** *adj.*
liturgy (ˈlɪtədʒɪ) *n., pl.* **-gies. 1.** the forms of public services officially prescribed by a Church. **2.** (*often cap.*) Also called: **Divine Liturgy.** *Chiefly Eastern Churches.* the Eucharistic celebration. **3.** a particular order or form of public service laid down by a Church. [C16: via Medieval Latin, from Greek *leitourgia,* from *leitourgos* minister, from *leit-* people + *ergon* work]
livable *or* **liveable** (ˈlɪvəbᵊl) *adj.* **1.** (of a room, house, etc.) suitable for living in. **2.** worth living; tolerable. **3.** (foll. by *with*) pleasant to live (with). —ˈ**livableness,** ˈ**liveableness** *or* ˌ**livaˈbility,** ˌ**liveaˈbility** *n.*
live[1] (lɪv) *vb.* (*mainly intr.*). **1.** to show the characteristics of life; be alive. **2.** to remain alive or in existence. **3.** to exist in a specified way: *to live poorly.* **4.** (usually foll. by *in* or *at*) to reside or dwell: *to live in London.* **5.** (often foll. by *on*) to continue or last: *the pain still lives in her memory.* **6.** (usually foll. by *by*) to order one's life (according to a certain philosophy, religion, etc.). **7.** (foll. by *on, upon,* or *by*) to support one's style of life; subsist: *to live by writing.* **8.** (foll. by *with*) to endure the effects (of a crime, mistake, etc.). **9.** (foll. by *through*) to experience and survive: *he lived through the war.* **10.** (*tr.*) to pass or spend (one's life, etc.). **11.** to enjoy life to the full: *he knows how to live.* **12.** (*tr.*) to put into practice in one's daily life; express: *he lives religion every day.* **13. live and let live.** to refrain from interfering in others' lives; to be tolerant. **14. where one lives.** *U.S. informal.* in one's sensitive or defenceless position. ~See also **live down, live in, live out, live together, live up, live with.** [Old English *libban, lifian;* related to Old High German *libēn,* Old Norse *lifa*]
live[2] (laɪv) *adj.* **1.** (*prenominal*) showing the characteristics of life. **2.** (*usually prenominal*) of, relating to, or abounding in life: *the live weight of an animal.* **3.** (*usually prenominal*) of current interest; controversial: *a live issue.* **4.** actual: *a real live cowboy.* **5.** *Informal.* full of life and energy. **6.** (of a coal, ember, etc.) glowing or burning. **7.** (esp. of a volcano) not extinct. **8.** loaded or capable of exploding: *a live bomb.* **9.** *Radio, television, etc.* transmitted or present at the time of performance, rather than being a recording: *a live show.* **10.** (of a record) **a.** recorded in concert. **b.** recorded in one studio take, without overdubs or splicing. **11.** connected to a source of electric power: *a live circuit.* **12.** (esp. of a colour or tone) brilliant or splendid. **13.** acoustically reverberant: *a live studio.* **14.** *Sport.* (of a ball) in play. **15.** (of rocks, ores, etc.) not quarried or mined; native. **16.** being in a state of motion or transmitting power; positively connected to a driving member. **17.** *Printing.* **a.** (of copy) not yet having been set into type. **b.** (of type that has been set) still in use. ~*adv.* **18.** during, at, or in the form of a live performance: *the show went out live.* [C16: from *on live* ALIVE]
live axle *n.* an axle which rotates with the wheel.
live-bearer *n.* a fish, esp. a cyprinodont, that gives birth to living young.
live birth *n.* the birth of a living child. Compare **stillbirth.**
live centre (laɪv) *n.* a conically pointed rod mounted in the headstock of a lathe that locates and turns with the workpiece. Compare **dead centre** (sense 2).
-lived (-lɪvd) *adj.* having or having had a life as specified: *short-lived.*
lived-in *adj.* having a comfortable, natural, or homely appearance, as if subject to regular use or habitation.
livedo (lɪˈviːdəʊ) *n., pl.* **livedos.** *Med.* a reddish discoloured patch on the skin. [from Latin]
live down (lɪv) *vb.* (*tr., adv.*) to withstand the effects of (a crime, mistake, etc.) by waiting until others forget or forgive it.
live in (lɪv) *vb.* (*intr., adv.*) **1.** (of an employee, as in a hospital or hotel) to dwell at one's place of employment. ~*adj.* **live-in. 2.** living in the place at which one works: *a live-in maid.* **3.** living with someone else in that person's home: *a live-in lover.*

livelihood ('laɪvlɪˌhʊd) *n.* occupation or employment.
live load (laɪv) *n.* a variable weight on a structure, such as moving traffic on a bridge. Also called: **superload.** Compare **dead load.**
livelong ('lɪvˌlɒŋ) *adj. Chiefly poetic.* **1.** (of time) long or seemingly long, esp. in a tedious way (esp. in the phrase **all the livelong day**). **2.** whole; entire. ~*n.* **3.** *Brit.* another name for **orpine.**
lively ('laɪvlɪ) *adj.* **-lier, -liest. 1.** full of life or vigour. **2.** vivacious or animated, esp. when in company. **3.** busy; eventful. **4.** characterized by mental or emotional intensity; vivid. **5.** having a striking effect on the mind or senses. **6.** refreshing or invigorating: *a lively breeze.* **7.** springy or bouncy or encouraging springiness: *a lively ball.* **8.** (of a boat or ship) readily responsive to the helm. ~*adv. also* '**livelily. 9.** in a brisk or lively manner: *step lively.* **10. look lively.** (*interj.*) make haste. —'**liveliness** *n.*
liven ('laɪvᵊn) *vb.* (usually foll. by *up*) to make or become lively; enliven. —'**livener** *n.*
live oak (laɪv) *n.* a hard-wooded evergreen oak, *Quercus virginianus,* of S North America: used for shipbuilding.
live out (lɪv) *vb.* (*intr., adv.*) (of an employee, as in a hospital or hotel) to dwell away from one's place of employment.
liver[1] ('lɪvə) *n.* **1.** a multilobed highly vascular reddish-brown glandular organ occupying most of the upper right part of the human abdominal cavity immediately below the diaphragm. It secretes bile, stores glycogen, detoxifies certain poisons, and plays an important part in the metabolism of carbohydrates, proteins, and fat, helping to maintain a correct balance of nutrients. Related adj.: **hepatic. 2.** the corresponding organ in animals. **3.** the liver of certain animals used as food. **4.** a reddish-brown colour, sometimes with a greyish tinge. [Old English *lifer;* related to Old High German *lebrav,* Old Norse *lefr,* Greek *liparos* fat] —'**liverless** *adj.*
liver[2] ('lɪvə) *n.* a person who lives in a specified way: *a fast liver.*
liver extract *n.* an extract of raw mammalian liver containing a high concentration of vitamin B_{12}: sometimes used to treat pernicious anaemia.
liver fluke *n.* any of various parasitic flatworms, esp. *Fasciola hepatica,* that inhabit the bile ducts of sheep, cattle, etc., and have a complex life cycle: class *Digenea.* See also **trematode.**
liveried ('lɪvərɪd) *adj.* (esp. of servants or footmen) wearing livery.
liverish ('lɪvərɪʃ) *adj.* **1.** *Informal.* having a disorder of the liver. **2.** disagreeable; peevish. —'**liverishness** *n.*
liver of sulphur *n.* a mixture of potassium sulphides used as a fungicide and insecticide and in the treatment of skin diseases.
liver opal *n.* a form of opal having a reddish-brown coloration. Also called: **menilite.**
Liverpudlian (ˌlɪvə'pʌdlɪən) *n.* **1.** a native or inhabitant of Liverpool, a city in NW England. ~*adj.* **2.** of or relating to Liverpool. [C19: from *Liverpool,* with humorous alteration of *pool* to *puddle*]
liver salts *pl. n.* a preparation of mineral salts used to treat indigestion.
liver sausage *or esp. U.S.* **liverwurst** ('lɪvəˌwɜːst) *n.* a sausage made of or containing liver.
liverwort ('lɪvəˌwɜːt) *n.* any bryophyte plant of the class *Hepaticae,* growing in wet places and resembling green seaweeds or leafy mosses. See also **scale moss.** [late Old English *liferwyrt*]
livery[1] ('lɪvərɪ) *n., pl.* **-eries. 1.** the identifying uniform, badge, etc., of a member of a guild or one of the servants of a feudal lord. **2.** a uniform worn by some menservants and chauffeurs. **3.** an individual or group that wears such a uniform. **4.** distinctive dress or outward appearance. **5. a.** the stabling, keeping, or hiring out of horses for money. **b.** (*as modifier*): *a livery horse.* **6. at livery.** being kept in a livery stable. **7.** *Legal history.* an ancient method of conveying freehold land. [C14: via Anglo-French from Old French *livrée* allocation, from *livrer* to hand over, from Latin *līberāre* to set free]
livery[2] ('lɪvərɪ) *adj.* **1.** of or resembling liver. **2.** another word for **liverish.**
livery company *n. Brit.* one of the chartered companies of the City of London originating from the craft guilds.
liveryman ('lɪvərɪmən) *n., pl.* **-men. 1.** *Brit.* a member of a livery company. **2.** a worker in a livery stable.
livery stable *n.* a stable where horses are accommodated and from which they may be hired out.
lives (laɪvz) *n.* the plural of **life.**
live steam (laɪv) *n.* steam supplied directly from a boiler at full pressure, before it has performed any work.
livestock ('laɪvˌstɒk) *n.* (*functioning as sing. or pl.*) cattle, horses, poultry, and similar animals kept for domestic use but not as pets, esp. on a farm or ranch.
live together (lɪv) *vb.* (*intr., adv.*) (esp. of an unmarried couple) to dwell in the same house or flat; cohabit.
live trap (laɪv) *n.* **1.** a box constructed to trap an animal without injuring it. ~*vb.* **livetrap, -traps, -trapping, -trapped. 2.** (*tr.*) to catch (an animal) in such a box.
live up (lɪv) *vb.* **1.** (*intr., adv.;* foll. by *to*) to fulfil (an expectation, obligation, principle, etc.). **2. live it up.** *Informal.* to enjoy oneself, esp. flamboyantly.
liveware ('laɪvˌwɛə) *n.* the programmers, systems analysts, operating staff, and other personnel working in a computer system. Compare **hardware** (sense 2), **software.**
live wire (laɪv) *n.* **1.** *Informal.* an energetic or enterprising person. **2.** a wire carrying an electric current.
live with (lɪv) *vb.* (*tr., prep.*) to dwell with (a person to whom one is not married).
livid ('lɪvɪd) *adj.* **1.** (of the skin) discoloured, as from a bruise or contusion. **2.** of a greyish tinge or colour: *livid pink.* **3.** *Informal.* angry or furious. [C17: via French from Latin *līvidus,* from *līvēre* to be black and blue] —'**lividly** *adv.* —'**lividness** *or* **li'vidity** *n.*
living ('lɪvɪŋ) *adj.* **1. a.** possessing life; not dead. **b.** (*as collective n.* preceded by *the*): *the living.* **2.** having the characteristics of life (used esp. to distinguish organisms from nonliving matter). **3.** currently in use or valid: *living language.* **4.** seeming to be real: *a living image.* **5.** (of animals or plants) existing in the present age; extant. Compare **extinct** (sense 1). **6.** *Geology.* another word for **live**[2] (sense 15). **7.** presented by actors before a live audience: *living theatre.* **8.** (*prenominal*) (intensifier): *the living daylights.* ~*n.* **9.** the condition of being alive. **10.** the manner in which one conducts one's life: *fast living.* **11.** the means, esp. the financial means, whereby one lives. **12.** *Church of England.* another term for **benefice. 13.** (*modifier*) of, involving, or characteristic of everyday life: *living area.* **14.** (*modifier*) of or involving those now alive (esp. in the phrase **living memory**).
living death *n.* a life or lengthy experience of constant misery.
living fossil *n.* an animal or plant, such as the coelacanth and ginkgo, belonging to a group most of whose members are extinct.
living picture *n.* another term for **tableau vivant.**
living room *n.* a room in a private house or flat used for relaxation and entertainment of guests.
Livingstone daisy ('lɪvɪŋstən) *n.* a gardener's name for various species of *Mesembryanthemum,* especially *M. criniflorum,* grown as garden annuals (though several are perennial) for their brightly coloured showy flowers. [C20: of unknown origin]
living wage *n.* a wage adequate to permit a wage earner to live and support a family in reasonable comfort.
livraison (*French* livrɛzɔ̃) *n. Rare.* one of the numbers of a book published in parts. [literally: delivery (of goods)]
livre ('liːvrə; *French* livrə) *n.* a former French unit of money of account, equal to 1 pound of silver. [C16: via Old French from Latin *lībra* the Roman pound]
lixiviate (lɪk'sɪvɪˌeɪt) *vb.* (*tr.*) *Chem.* a less common word for **leach**[1] (senses 1, 2). [C17: from LIXIVIUM] —**lix'ivial** *adj.* —**lixˌivi'ation** *n.*
lixivium (lɪk'sɪvɪəm) *n., pl.* **-iums** *or* **-ia** (-ɪə). **1.** the alkaline solution obtained by leaching wood ash with water; lye. **2.** any solution obtained by leaching. [C17: from Late Latin, from *lix* lye]
lizard ('lɪzəd) *n.* **1.** any reptile of the suborder *Lacertilia* (or *Sauria*), esp. those of the family *Lacertidae* (Old World lizards), typically having an elongated body, four limbs, and a long tail: includes the geckos, iguanas, chameleons, monitors, and slow worms. **2. a.** leather made from the skin of such an animal. **b.** (*as modifier*): *a lizard handbag.* [C14: via Old French from Latin *lacerta*]
lizard fish *n.* any small teleost fish of the family *Synodontidae,* having a slender body and a lizard-like head and living at the bottom of warm seas.
lizard orchid *n.* a European orchid, *Orchis hircina,* rare in Britain, having a tangled spike of purplish and grey-green flowers.
LJ *Brit. abbrev. for* Lord Justice.
LL *abbrev. for:* **1.** Late Latin. **2.** Low Latin. **3.** Lord Lieutenant.
ll. *abbrev. for* lines (of written matter).
llama ('lɑːmə) *n.* **1.** a domesticated South American cud-chewing mammal, *Lama glama* (or *L. peruana*), that is used as a beast of burden and is valued for its hair, flesh, and hide: family *Camelidae* (camels). **2.** the cloth made from the wool of this animal. **3.** any other animal of the genus *Lama.* See **alpaca**[1], **guanaco.** [C17: via Spanish from Quechua]
llano ('lɑːnəʊ; *Spanish* 'ʎano) *n., pl.* **-nos** (-nəʊz; *Spanish* -nɔs). an extensive grassy treeless plain, esp. in South America. [C17: Spanish, from Latin *plānum* level ground]
LLB *abbrev. for* Bachelor of Laws. [Latin: *Legum Baccalaureus*]
LLD *abbrev. for* Doctor of Laws. [Latin: *Legum Doctor*]
LLM *abbrev. for* Master of Laws. [Latin: *Legum Magister*]
Lloyd's (lɔɪdz) *n.* an association of London underwriters, set up in the late 17th century. Originally concerned exclusively with marine insurance and a shipping information service, it now subscribes a variety of insurance policies and publishes a daily list (**Lloyd's List**) of shipping data and news. [C17: named after Edward *Lloyd* (died ?1726) at whose coffee house in London the underwriters originally carried on their business]
Lloyd's Register *n.* **1.** a society formed in 1760 by a group of merchants operating at Lloyd's coffee house to draw up rules concerning the construction of merchant ships. **2.** an annual publication giving details of all ships that have been built according to the various classifications established by this society. ~In full: **Lloyd's Register of Shipping.**
lm *symbol for* lumen.

LMS (in Britain) *abbrev. for* local management of schools: the system of making each school responsible for controlling its total budget, after the budget has been calculated by the Local Education Authority.

LMVD (in New Zealand) *abbrev. for* Licensed Motor Vehicle Dealer.

ln *abbrev. for* (natural) logarithm.

LNG *abbrev. for* liquefied natural gas.

lo (ləʊ) *interj.* look! see! (now often in the phrase **lo and behold**). [Old English *lā*]

loach (ləʊtʃ) *n.* any carplike freshwater cyprinoid fish of the family *Cobitidae*, of Eurasia and Africa, having a long narrow body with barbels around the mouth. [C14: from Old French *loche*, of obscure origin]

load (ləʊd) *n.* **1.** something to be borne or conveyed; weight. **2. a.** the usual amount borne or conveyed. **b.** (*in combination*): *a carload.* **3.** something that weighs down, oppresses, or burdens: *that's a load off my mind.* **4.** a single charge of a firearm. **5.** the weight that is carried by a structure. See also **dead load, live load. 6.** *Electrical engineering, electronics.* **a.** a device that receives or dissipates the power from an amplifier, oscillator, generator, or some other source of signals. **b.** the power delivered by a machine, generator, circuit, etc. **7.** the force acting on a component in a mechanism or structure. **8.** the resistance overcome by an engine or motor when it is driving a machine, etc. **9.** an external force applied to a component or mechanism. **10. a load of.** *Informal.* a quantity of: *a load of nonsense.* **11. get a load of.** *Informal.* pay attention to. **12. have a load on.** *U.S. and Canadian slang.* to be intoxicated. **13. shoot one's load.** *Taboo slang.* (of a man) to ejaculate at orgasm. ~*vb.* (*mainly tr.*) **14.** (*also intr.*) to place or receive (cargo, goods, etc.) upon (a ship, lorry, etc.). **15.** to burden or oppress. **16.** to supply or beset (someone) with in abundance or overwhelmingly: *they loaded her with gifts.* **17.** to cause to be biased: *to load a question.* **18.** (*also intr.*) to put an ammunition charge into (a firearm). **19.** *Photog.* to position (a film, cartridge, or plate) in (a camera). **20.** to weight or bias (a roulette wheel, dice, etc.). **21.** *Insurance.* to increase (a premium) to cover expenses, etc. **22.** to draw power from (an electrical device, such as a generator). **23.** to add material of high atomic number to (concrete) to increase its effectiveness as a radiation shield. **24.** to increase the power output of (an electric circuit). **25.** to increase the work required from (an engine or motor). **26.** to apply force to (a mechanism or component). **27.** *Computer technol.* to transfer (a program) to a memory. **28. load the dice. a.** to add weights to dice in order to bias them. **b.** to arrange to have a favourable or unfavourable position. ~See also **loads.** [Old English *lād* course; in meaning, influenced by LADE[1]; related to LEAD[1]]

load displacement *n. Nautical.* the total weight of a cargo vessel loaded so that its waterline reaches the summer load line.

loaded (ˈləʊdɪd) *adj.* **1.** carrying a load. **2.** (of dice, a roulette wheel, etc.) weighted or otherwise biased. **3.** (of a question or statement) containing a hidden trap or implication. **4.** charged with ammunition. **5.** (of concrete) containing heavy metals, esp. iron or lead, for use in making radiation shields. **6.** *Slang.* wealthy. **7.** (*postpositive*) *Slang, chiefly U.S. and Canadian.* **a.** drunk. **b.** drugged; influenced by drugs.

loader (ˈləʊdə) *n.* **1.** a person who loads a gun or other firearm. **2.** (*in combination*) designating a firearm or machine loaded in a particular way: *breech-loader; top-loader.* **3.** *Computer technol.* a system program that takes a program in a form close to machine code and places it into a memory for execution.

load factor *n.* **1.** the ratio of the average electric load to the peak load over a period of time. **2.** *Aeronautics.* **a.** the ratio of a given external load to the weight of an aircraft. **b.** the actual payload carried by an aircraft as a percentage of its maximum payload.

loading (ˈləʊdɪŋ) *n.* **1.** a load or burden; weight. **2.** the addition of an inductance to electrical equipment, such as a transmission line or aerial, to improve its performance. See **loading coil. 3.** an addition to an insurance premium to cover expenses, provide a safer profit margin, etc. **4.** the ratio of the gross weight of an aircraft to its engine power (**power loading**), wing area (**wing loading**), or some other parameter, or of the gross weight of a helicopter to its rotor disc area (**disc loading**). **5.** *Psychol.* the correlation of a factor, such as a personality trait, with a performance score derived from a psychological test. **6.** material, such as china clay or size, added to paper, textiles, or similar materials to produce a smooth surface, increase weight, etc. **7.** *Austral. and N.Z.* a payment made in addition to a basic wage or salary to reward special skills, compensate for unfavourable conditions, etc.

loading coil *n.* an inductance coil inserted at regular intervals and in series with the conductors of a transmission line in order to improve its characteristics.

load line *n. Nautical.* a pattern of lines painted on the hull of a ship, approximately midway between the bow and the stern, indicating the various levels that the waterline should reach if the ship is properly loaded under given circumstances.

loads (ləʊdz) *Informal.* ~*pl. n.* **1.** (often foll. by *of*) a lot: *loads to eat.* ~*adv.* **2.** (intensifier): *loads better; thanks loads.*

load shedding *n.* the act or practice of temporarily reducing the supply of electricity to an area to avoid overloading the generators.

loadstar (ˈləʊdˌstɑː) *n.* a variant spelling of **lodestar.**

loadstone (ˈləʊdˌstəʊn) *n.* a variant spelling of **lodestone.**

loaf[1] (ləʊf) *n., pl.* **loaves** (ləʊvz). **1.** a shaped mass of baked bread. **2.** any shaped or moulded mass of food, such as cooked meat. **3.** *Slang.* the head; sense: *use your loaf!* [Old English *hlāf*; related to Old High German *hleib* bread, Old Norse *hleifr*, Latin *libum* cake]

loaf[2] (ləʊf) *vb.* **1.** (*intr.*) to loiter or lounge around in an idle way. **2.** (*tr.*; foll. by *away*) to spend (time) idly: *he loafed away his life.* [C19: perhaps back formation from LOAFER]

loafer (ˈləʊfə) *n.* **1.** a person who avoids work; idler. **2.** *Chiefly U.S. and Canadian.* a moccasin-like shoe for casual wear. [C19: perhaps from German *Landläufer* vagabond]

loaf sugar *n.* (esp. formerly) **1.** a large conical mass of hard refined sugar; sugar loaf. **2.** small cube-shaped lumps of this, the form in which it was often sold.

loam (ləʊm) *n.* **1.** rich soil consisting of a mixture of sand, clay, and decaying organic material. **2.** a paste of clay and sand used for making moulds in a foundry, plastering walls, etc. ~*vb.* **3.** (*tr.*) to cover, treat, or fill with loam. [Old English *lām*; related to Old Swedish *lēmo* clay, Old High German *leimo*] —ˈ**loamy** *adj.* —ˈ**loaminess** *n.*

loan[1] (ləʊn) *n.* **1.** the act of lending: *the loan of a car.* **2. a.** property lent, esp. money lent at interest for a period of time. **b.** (*as modifier*): *loan holder.* **3.** the adoption by speakers of one language of a form current in another language. **4.** short for **loan word. 5. on loan. a.** lent out; borrowed. **b.** (esp. of personnel) transferred from a regular post to a temporary one elsewhere. ~*vb.* **6.** to lend (something, esp. money). [C13 *loon, lan*, from Old Norse *lān*; related to Old English *lǣn* loan; compare German *Lehen* fief, *Lohn* wages] —ˈ**loanable** *adj.* —ˈ**loaner** *n.*
▷**Usage.** See at **lend.**

loan[2] (ləʊn) *or* **loaning** (ˈləʊnɪŋ) *n. Scot. and northern English dialect.* **1.** a lane. **2.** a place where cows are milked. [Old English *lone*, variant of LANE[1]]

loanback (ˈləʊnˌbæk) *n.* **1.** a facility offered by some life-assurance companies in which an individual can borrow from his pension fund. ~*vb.* **loan back. 2.** to make use of this facility.

loan collection *n.* a number of works of art lent by their owners for a temporary public exhibition.

Loan Council *n.* (in Australia) a statutory body that controls borrowing by the states.

loan shark *n. Informal.* a person who lends funds at illegal or exorbitant rates of interest.

loan translation *n.* the adoption by one language of a phrase or compound word whose components are literal translations of the components of a corresponding phrase or compound in a foreign language: *English "superman" from German "Übermensch."* Also called: **calque.**

loan word *n.* a word adopted, often with some modification of its form, from one language into another.

loath *or* **loth** (ləʊθ) *adj.* **1.** (usually foll. by *to*) reluctant or unwilling. **2. nothing loath.** willing. [Old English *lāth* (in the sense: hostile); related to Old Norse *leithr*] —ˈ**loathness** *or* ˈ**lothness** *n.*

loathe (ləʊð) *vb.* (*tr.*) to feel strong hatred or disgust for. [Old English *lāthiān*, from LOATH] —ˈ**loather** *n.*

loathing (ˈləʊðɪŋ) *n.* abhorrence; disgust. —ˈ**loathingly** *adv.*

loathly[1] (ˈləʊθlɪ) *adv.* with reluctance; unwillingly.

loathly[2] (ˈləʊðlɪ) *adj.* an archaic word for **loathsome.**

loathsome (ˈləʊðsəm) *adj.* causing loathing; abhorrent. —ˈ**loathsomely** *adv.* —ˈ**loathsomeness** *n.*

loaves (ləʊvz) *n.* the plural of **loaf**[1].

lob[1] (lɒb) *Sport.* ~*n.* **1.** a ball struck in a high arc. **2.** *Cricket.* a ball bowled in a slow high arc. ~*vb.* **lobs, lobbing, lobbed. 3.** to hit or kick (a ball) in a high arc. **4.** *Informal.* to throw, esp. in a high arc. [C14: probably of Low German origin, originally in the sense: something dangling; compare Middle Low German *lobbe* hanging lower lip, Old English *loppe* spider]

lob[2] (lɒb) *n.* short for **lobworm.** [C17 (in the sense: pendulous object): related to LOB[1]]

lobar (ˈləʊbə) *adj.* of, relating to, or affecting a lobe.

lobate (ˈləʊbeɪt) *or* **lobated** *adj.* **1.** having or resembling lobes. **2.** (of birds) having separate toes that are each fringed with a weblike lobe. —ˈ**lobately** *adv.*

lobby (ˈlɒbɪ) *n., pl.* **-bies. 1.** a room or corridor used as an entrance hall, vestibule, etc. **2.** *Chiefly Brit.* a hall in a legislative building used for meetings between the legislators and members of the public. **3.** Also called: **division lobby.** *Chiefly Brit.* one of two corridors in a legislative building in which members vote. **4.** a group of persons who attempt to influence legislators on behalf of a particular interest. ~*vb.* **-bies, -bying, -bied. 5.** to attempt to influence (legislators, etc.) in the formulation of policy. **6.** (*intr.*) to act in the manner of a lobbyist. **7.** (*tr.*) to apply pressure or influence for the passage of (a bill, etc.). [C16: from Medieval Latin *lobia* portico, from Old High German *lauba* arbor, from *laub* leaf] —ˈ**lobbyer** *n.*

lobbyist (ˈlɒbɪɪst) *n.* a person employed by a particular interest to lobby. —ˈ**lobbyˌism** *n.*

lobe (ləʊb) *n.* **1.** any rounded projection forming part of a larger structure. **2.** any of the subdivisions of a bodily organ or part, delineated by shape or connective tissue. **3.** short for **ear lobe. 4.** any of the loops that form part of the graphic representation of the radiation pattern of a transmitting aerial. Compare **radiation pattern. 5.** any of the parts, not entirely separate from each other, into which a flattened plant part, such as a leaf, is divided. [C16: from Late Latin *lobus,* from Greek *lobos* lobe of the ear or of the liver]

lobectomy (ləʊ'bɛktəmɪ) *n., pl.* **-mies.** surgical removal of a lobe from any organ or gland in the body, esp. removal of tissue from the frontal lobe of the brain in an attempt to alleviate mental disorder.

lobelia (ləʊ'bi:lɪə) *n.* any plant of the genus *Lobelia,* having red, blue, white, or yellow five-lobed flowers with the three lower lobes forming a lip: family *Lobeliaceae.* [C18: from New Latin, named after Matthias de *Lobel* (1538–1616), Flemish botanist]

lobeline ('ləʊbəˌli:n) *n.* a crystalline alkaloid extracted from the seeds of the Indian tobacco plant, used as a smoking deterrent and respiratory stimulant. [C19: from LOBELIA]

loblolly ('lɒbˌlɒlɪ) *n., pl.* **-lies. 1.** a southern U.S. pine tree, *Pinus taeda,* with bright red-brown bark, green needle-like leaves, and reddish-brown cones. **2.** *Nautical or dialect.* a thick gruel. **3.** *U.S. dialect.* a mire; mudhole. [C16: perhaps from dialect *lob* to boil + obsolete dialect *lolly* thick soup]

loblolly boy *or* **man** *n. Brit., naval.* (formerly) a boy or man acting as a medical orderly on board ship. [C18: from LOBLOLLY sense 2, applied to a ship's doctor's medicines]

lobo ('ləʊbəʊ) *n., pl.* **-bos.** *Western U.S.* another name for **timber wolf.** [Spanish, from Latin *lupus* wolf]

lobola *or* **lobolo** (lɔ:'bɔ:lə, lə'bəʊ-) *n.* (in southern Africa) an African custom by which a bridegroom's family makes a payment in cattle or cash to the bride's family shortly before the marriage. [from Zulu]

lobotomized *or* **lobotomised** (ləʊ'bɒtəmaɪzd) *adj. Informal.* apathetic, sluggish, and zombie-like. [C20: from *lobotomize* (chiefly U.S.) to perform a lobotomy on]

lobotomy (ləʊ'bɒtəmɪ) *n., pl.* **-mies. 1.** surgical incision into a lobe of any organ. **2.** Also called: **prefrontal leucotomy.** surgical interruption of one or more nerve tracts in the frontal lobe of the brain: used in the treatment of intractable mental disorders. [C20: from LOBE + -TOMY]

lobscouse ('lɒbˌskaʊs) *n.* a sailor's stew of meat, vegetables, and hardtack. [C18: perhaps from dialect *lob* to boil + *scouse,* broth; compare LOBLOLLY]

lobster ('lɒbstə) *n., pl.* **-sters** *or* **-ster. 1.** any of several large marine decapod crustaceans of the genus *Homarus,* esp. *H. vulgaris,* occurring on rocky shores and having the first pair of limbs modified as large pincers. **2.** any of several similar crustaceans, esp. the spiny lobster. **3.** the flesh of any of these crustaceans, eaten as a delicacy. [Old English *loppestre,* from *loppe* spider]

lobster moth *n.* a large sombre-hued prominent moth, *Stauropus fagi,* that when at rest resembles dead leaves. The modified thoracic legs of the larva, carried curled over its body, look like a lobster's claw.

lobster Newburg ('nju:bɜ:g) *n.* lobster cooked in a rich cream sauce flavoured with sherry.

lobster pot *or* **trap** *n.* a round basket or trap made of open slats used to catch lobsters.

lobster thermidor ('θɜ:mɪˌdɔ:) *n.* a dish of cooked lobster, replaced in its shell with a creamy cheese sauce.

lobule ('lɒbju:l) *n.* a small lobe or a subdivision of a lobe. [C17: from New Latin *lobulus,* from Late Latin *lobus* LOBE] —**lobular** ('lɒbjʊlə), **lobulate** ('lɒbjʊlɪt), **'lobuˌlated,** *or* **'lobulose** *adj.* —ˌ**lobu'lation** *n.*

lobworm ('lɒbˌwɜ:m) *n.* **1.** another name for **lugworm.** Sometimes shortened to **lob. 2.** a large earthworm used as bait in fishing. [C17: from obsolete *lob* lump + WORM]

local ('ləʊkᵊl) *adj.* **1.** characteristic of or associated with a particular locality or area. **2.** of, concerned with, or relating to a particular place or point in space. **3.** *Med.* of, affecting, or confined to a limited area or part. Compare **general** (sense 10), **systemic** (sense 2). **4.** (of a train, bus, etc.) stopping at all stations or stops. ~*n.* **5.** a train, bus, etc., that stops at all stations or stops. **6.** an inhabitant of a specified locality. **7.** *Brit. informal.* a pub close to one's home or place of work. **8.** *Med.* short for **local anaesthetic. 9.** *U.S. and Canadian.* an item of local interest in a newspaper. **10.** *U.S. and Canadian.* a local or regional branch of an association. **11.** *Canadian.* a telephone extension. [C15: via Old French from Late Latin *locālis,* from Latin *locus* place, LOCUS] —**'localness** *n.*

local anaesthetic *n. Med.* a drug that produces local anaesthesia. Often shortened to **local.** See **anaesthesia** (sense 2).

local area network *n. Computer technol.* the linking of a number of different devices by cable within a system. Abbrev.: **LAN.**

local authority *n. Brit. and N.Z.* the governing body of a county, district, etc. U.S. equivalent: **local government.**

local colour *n.* the characteristic features or atmosphere of a place or time.

locale (ləʊ'kɑ:l) *n.* a place or area, esp. with reference to events connected with it. [C18: from French *local* (n. use of adj.); see LOCAL]

local examinations *pl. n.* any of various examinations, such as the GCE, set by university boards and conducted in local centres, schools, etc.

local government *n.* **1.** government of the affairs of counties, towns, etc., by locally elected political bodies. **2.** the U.S. equivalent of **local authority.**

Local Group *n. Astronomy.* the cluster of galaxies to which the Galaxy and the Andromeda Galaxy belong.

localism ('ləʊkəˌlɪzəm) *n.* **1.** a pronunciation, phrase, etc., peculiar to a particular locality. **2.** another word for **provincialism.** —**'localist** *n.* —ˌ**local'istic** *adj.*

locality (ləʊ'kælɪtɪ) *n., pl.* **-ties. 1.** a neighbourhood or area. **2.** the site or scene of an event. **3.** the fact or condition of having a location or position in space.

localize *or* **localise** ('ləʊkəˌlaɪz) *vb.* **1.** to make or become local in attitude, behaviour, etc. **2.** (*tr.*) to restrict or confine (something) to a particular area or part. **3.** (*tr.*) to assign or ascribe to a particular region. —**'localˌizable** *or* **'localˌisable** *adj.* —ˌ**locali'zation** *or* ˌ**locali'sation** *n.* —**'localˌizer** *or* **'localˌiser** *n.*

local loan *n.* (in Britain) a loan issued by a local government authority.

locally ('ləʊkəlɪ) *adv.* within a particular area or place.

local option *n.* (esp. in Scotland, New Zealand, and the U.S.) the privilege of a municipality, county, etc., to determine by referendum whether a particular activity, esp. the sale of liquor, shall be permitted there.

local oscillator *n. Electronics.* the oscillator in a superheterodyne receiver whose output frequency is mixed with the incoming modulated radio-frequency carrier signal to produce the required intermediate frequency.

local sign *n. Physiol.* the information from a receptor in the eye or the skin signifying respectively a direction in space or a given point on the body.

local time *n.* the time in a particular region or area expressed with reference to the meridian passing through it.

locate (ləʊ'keɪt) *vb.* **1.** (*tr.*) to discover the position, situation, or whereabouts of; find. **2.** (*tr.; often passive*) to situate or place: *located on the edge of the city.* **3.** (*intr.*) *U.S. and Canadian.* to become established or settled. —**lo'catable** *adj.* —**lo'cater** *n.*

location (ləʊ'keɪʃən) *n.* **1.** a site or position; situation. **2.** the act or process of locating or the state of being located. **3.** a place outside a studio where filming is done: *shot on location.* **4.** (in South Africa) **a.** a Black African or Coloured township, usually located near a small town. See also **township** (sense 4). **b.** a Black African tribal reserve in the E Cape Province. **5.** *Computer technol.* a position in a memory capable of holding a unit of information, such as a word, and identified by its address. **6.** *Roman and Scots Law.* the letting out on hire of a chattel or of personal services. [C16: from Latin *locatio,* from *locare* to place]

locative ('lɒkətɪv) *Grammar.* ~*adj.* **1.** (of a word or phrase) indicating place or direction. **2.** denoting a case of nouns, etc., that refers to the place at which the action described by the verb occurs. ~*n.* **3. a.** the locative case. **b.** a word or speech element in this case. [C19: LOCATE + -IVE, on the model of *vocative*]

loc. cit. (in textual annotation) *abbrev. for* loco citato. [Latin: in the place cited]

loch (lɒx, lɒk) *n.* **1.** a Scot. word for **lake. 2.** Also called: **sea loch.** a long narrow bay or arm of the sea in Scotland. [C14: from Gaelic]

lochan ('lɒxən, 'lɒkᵊn) *n. Scot.* a small inland loch. [C18: Gaelic, diminutive of LOCH]

lochia ('lɒkɪə) *n.* a vaginal discharge of cellular debris, mucus, and blood following childbirth. [C17: New Latin from Greek *lokhia,* from *lokhios,* from *lokhos* childbirth] —**'lochial** *adj.*

loci ('ləʊsaɪ) *n.* the plural of **locus.**

lock[1] (lɒk) *n.* **1.** a device fitted to a gate, door, drawer, lid, etc., to keep it firmly closed and often to prevent access by unauthorized persons. **2.** a similar device attached to a machine, vehicle, etc., to prevent use by unauthorized persons: *a steering lock.* **3. a.** a section of a canal or river that may be closed off by gates to control the water level and the raising and lowering of vessels that pass through it. **b.** (*as modifier*): *a lock gate.* **4.** the jamming, fastening, or locking together of parts. **5.** *Brit.* the extent to which a vehicle's front wheels will turn to the right or left: *this car has a good lock.* **6.** a mechanism that detonates the charge of a gun. **7. lock, stock, and barrel.** completely; entirely. **8.** any wrestling hold in which a wrestler seizes a part of his opponent's body and twists it or otherwise exerts pressure upon it. **9.** Also called: **lock forward.** *Rugby.* either of two players who make up the second line of the scrum and apply weight to the forwards in the front line. **10.** a gas bubble in a hydraulic system or a liquid bubble in a pneumatic system that stops or interferes with the fluid flow in a pipe, capillary, etc.: *an air lock.* ~*vb.* **11.** to fasten (a door, gate, etc.) or (of a door, etc.) to become fastened with a lock, bolt, etc., so as to prevent entry or exit. **12.** (*tr.*) to secure (a building) by locking all doors, windows, etc. **13.** to fix or become fixed together securely or inextricably. **14.** to become or cause to become rigid or immovable: *the front wheels of the car locked.* **15.** (when *tr., often passive*) to clasp or entangle (someone or each other) in a struggle or embrace. **16.** (*tr.*) to furnish (a canal) with locks. **17.** (*tr.*) to move (a vessel) through a system of locks. **18. lock horns.** (esp. of two equally matched opponents) to become engaged in argument or battle. **19. lock**

the stable door after the horse has bolted *or* **been stolen.** to take precautions after harm has been done. ~See also **lock on to, lock out, lock up.** [Old English *loc;* related to Old Norse *lok*] —'**lockable** *adj.*

lock[2] (lɒk) *n.* **1.** a strand, curl, or cluster of hair. **2.** a tuft or wisp of wool, cotton, etc. **3.** *(pl.) Chiefly literary.* hair, esp. when curly or fine. [Old English *loc;* related to Old Frisian *lok,* Old Norse *lokkr* lock of wool]

lockage ('lɒkɪdʒ) *n.* **1.** a system of locks in a canal. **2.** passage through a lock or the fee charged for such passage.

locker ('lɒkə) *n.* **1. a.** a small compartment or drawer that may be locked, as one of several in a gymnasium, etc., for clothes and valuables. **b.** *(as modifier): a locker room.* **2.** a person or thing that locks. **3.** *U.S. and Canadian.* a refrigerated compartment for keeping frozen foods, esp. one rented in an establishment.

locket ('lɒkɪt) *n.* a small ornamental case, usually on a necklace or chain, that holds a picture, keepsake, etc. [C17: from French *loquet* latch, diminutive of *loc* LOCK[1]]

lockjaw ('lɒk,dʒɔː) *n. Pathol.* a nontechnical name for **trismus** and (often) **tetanus.**

locknut ('lɒk,nʌt) *n.* **1.** a supplementary nut screwed down upon a primary nut to prevent it from shaking loose. **2.** a threaded nut having a feature, such as a nylon insert, to prevent it from shaking loose.

lock on to *vb. (intr., adv. + prep.)* (of a radar beam) to automatically follow (a target).

lock out *vb. (tr., adv.)* **1.** to prevent from entering by locking a door. **2.** to prevent (employees) from working during an industrial dispute, as by closing a factory. ~*n.* **lockout. 3.** the closing of a place of employment by an employer, in order to bring pressure on employees to agree to terms.

locksmith ('lɒk,smɪθ) *n.* a person who makes or repairs locks. —'**lock,smithery** *or* '**lock,smithing** *n.*

lock step *n.* a method of marching in step such that the men follow one another as closely as possible.

lock stitch *n.* a sewing-machine stitch in which the top thread interlocks with the bobbin thread.

lock up *vb. (adv.)* **1.** *(tr.)* Also: **lock in, lock away.** to imprison or confine. **2.** to lock or secure the doors, windows, etc., of (a building). **3.** *(tr.)* to keep or store securely: *secrets locked up in history.* **4.** *(tr.)* to invest (funds) so that conversion into cash is difficult. **5.** *Printing.* to secure (type, etc.) in a chase or in the bed of the printing machine by tightening the quoins. ~*n.* **lockup. 6.** the action or time of locking up. **7.** a jail or block of cells. **8.** *Brit.* a small shop with no attached quarters for the owner or shopkeeper. **9.** *Brit.* a garage or storage place separate from the main premises. **10.** *Stock Exchange.* an investment that is intended to be held for a relatively long period. **11.** *Printing.* the pages of type held in a chase by the positioning of quoins. ~*adj.* **12. lock-up.** *Brit. and N.Z.* (of premises) without living accommodation: *a lock-up shop.*

loco[1] ('ləʊkəʊ) *n. Informal.* short for **locomotive.**

loco[2] ('ləʊkəʊ) *adj.* **1.** *Slang, chiefly U.S.* insane. **2.** (of an animal) affected with loco disease. ~*n., pl.* **-cos. 3.** *U.S.* short for **locoweed.** ~*vb. (tr.)* **4.** to poison with locoweed. **5.** *U.S. slang.* to make insane. [C19: via Mexican Spanish from Spanish: crazy]

loco[3] ('ləʊkəʊ) *adj.* denoting a price for goods, esp. goods to be exported, that are in a place specified or known, the buyer being responsible for all transport charges from that place: *loco Bristol; a loco price.* [C20: from Latin *locō* from a place]

loco citato *Latin.* ('lɒkəʊ sɪ'tɑːtəʊ) in the place or passage quoted. Abbrevs.: **loc. cit., lc.**

loco disease *or* **poisoning** *n.* a disease of cattle, sheep, and horses characterized by paralysis and faulty vision, caused by ingestion of locoweed.

locoism ('ləʊkəʊ,ɪzəm) *n.* another word for **loco disease.**

locoman ('ləʊkəʊmən) *n., pl.* **-men.** *Brit. informal.* a railwayman, esp. an engine-driver.

locomotion (,ləʊkə'məʊʃən) *n.* the act, fact, ability, or power of moving. [C17: from Latin *locō* from a place, ablative of *locus* place + MOTION]

locomotive (,ləʊkə'məʊtɪv) *n.* **1. a.** Also called: **locomotive engine.** a self-propelled engine driven by steam, electricity, or diesel power and used for drawing trains along railway tracks. **b.** *(as modifier): a locomotive shed; a locomotive works.* ~*adj.* **2.** of or relating to locomotion. **3.** moving or able to move, as by self-propulsion. —,**loco'motively** *adv.* —,**loco'motiveness** *n.*

locomotor (,ləʊkə'məʊtə) *adj.* of or relating to locomotion. [C19: from Latin *locō* from a place, ablative of *locus* place + MOTOR (mover)]

locomotor ataxia *n. Pathol.* another name for **tabes dorsalis.**

locoweed ('ləʊkəʊ,wiːd) *n.* any of several perennial leguminous plants of the genera *Oxytropis* and *Astragalus* of W North America that cause loco disease in horses, cattle, and sheep.

locular ('lɒkjʊlə) *or* **loculate** ('lɒkjʊ,leɪt, -lɪt) *adj. Biology.* divided into compartments by septa: *the locular ovary of a plant.* [C19: from New Latin *loculāris* kept in boxes] —,**locu'lation** *n.*

locule ('lɒkjuːl) *or* **loculus** ('lɒkjʊləs) *n., pl.* **locules** *or* **loculi** ('lɒkjʊ,laɪ). **1.** *Botany.* any of the chambers of an ovary or anther. **2.** *Biology.* any small cavity or chamber. [C19: New Latin, from Latin: compartment, from *locus* place]

locum tenens ('ləʊkəm 'tiːnɛnz) *n., pl.* **locum tenentes** (tə'nɛntiːz). *Chiefly Brit.* a person who stands in temporarily for another member of the same profession, esp. for a physician, chemist, or clergyman. Often shortened to **locum.** [C17: Medieval Latin: (someone) holding the place (of another)]

locus ('ləʊkəs) *n., pl.* **loci** ('ləʊsaɪ). **1.** (in many legal phrases) a place or area, esp. the place where something occurred. **2.** *Maths.* a set of points or lines whose location satisfies or is determined by one or more specified conditions: *the locus of points equidistant from a given point is a circle.* **3.** *Genetics.* the position of a particular gene on a chromosome. [C18: Latin]

locus classicus ('klæsɪkəs) *n., pl.* **loci classici** ('klæsɪ,saɪ). an authoritative and often quoted passage from a standard work. [Latin: classical place]

locus sigilli (sɪ'dʒɪlaɪ) *n., pl.* **loci sigilli.** the place to which the seal is affixed on legal documents, etc. [Latin]

locus standi ('stændaɪ) *n. Law.* the right of a party to appear and be heard before a court. [from Latin: a place for standing]

locust ('ləʊkəst) *n.* **1.** any of numerous orthopterous insects of the genera *Locusta, Melanoplus,* etc., such as *L. migratoria,* of warm and tropical regions of the Old World, which travels in vast swarms, stripping large areas of vegetation. See also **grasshopper** (sense 1). Compare **seventeen-year locust. 2.** Also called: **locust tree, false acacia.** a North American leguminous tree, *Robinia pseudoacacia,* having prickly branches, hanging clusters of white fragrant flowers, and reddish-brown seed pods. **3.** the yellowish durable wood of this tree. **4.** any of several similar trees, such as the honey locust and carob. [C13 (the insect): from Latin *locusta* locust; applied to the tree (C17) because the pods resemble locusts] —'**locust-,like** *adj.*

locust bird *n.* any of various pratincoles, esp. *Glareola nordmanni* (**black-winged pratincole**), that feed on locusts.

locution (ləʊ'kjuːʃən) *n.* **1.** a word, phrase, or expression. **2.** manner or style of speech or expression. [C15: from Latin *locūtiō* an utterance, from *loquī* to speak] —**lo'cutionary** *adj.*

locutionary act *n. Philosophy.* the act of uttering a sentence considered only as such. Compare **illocution, perlocution.**

lode (ləʊd) *n.* **1.** a deposit of valuable ore occurring between definite limits in the surrounding rock; vein. **2.** a deposit of metallic ore filling a fissure in the surrounding rock. [Old English *lād* course. Compare LOAD]

loden ('ləʊdᵊn) *n.* **1.** a thick heavy waterproof woollen cloth with a short pile, used to make garments, esp. coats. **2.** a dark bluish-green colour, in which the cloth is often made. [German, from Old High German *lodo* thick cloth, perhaps related to Old English *lotha* cloak]

lodestar *or* **loadstar** ('ləʊd,stɑː) *n.* **1.** a star, esp. the North Star, used in navigation or astronomy as a point of reference. **2.** something that serves as a guide or model. [C14: literally, guiding star. See LODE]

lodestone *or* **loadstone** ('ləʊd,stəʊn) *n.* **1. a.** a rock that consists of pure or nearly pure magnetite and thus is naturally magnetic. **b.** a piece of such rock, which can be used as a magnet and which was formerly used as a primitive compass. **2.** a person or thing regarded as a focus of attraction. [C16: literally: guiding stone]

lodge (lɒdʒ) *n.* **1.** *Chiefly Brit.* a small house at the entrance to the grounds of a country mansion, usually occupied by a gatekeeper or gardener. **2.** a house or cabin used occasionally, as for some seasonal activity. **3.** *U.S. and Canadian.* a central building in a resort, camp, or park. **4.** *(cap. when part of a name)* a large house or hotel. **5.** a room for the use of porters in a university, college, etc. **6.** a local branch or chapter of certain societies. **7.** the building used as the meeting place of such a society. **8.** the dwelling place of certain animals, esp. the dome-shaped den constructed by beavers. **9.** a hut or tent of certain North American Indian peoples. **10.** (at Cambridge University) the residence of the head of a college. ~*vb.* **11.** to provide or be provided with accommodation or shelter, esp. rented accommodation. **12.** to live temporarily, esp. in rented accommodation. **13.** to implant, embed, or fix or be implanted, embedded, or fixed. **14.** *(tr.)* to deposit or leave for safety, storage, etc. **15.** *(tr.)* to bring (a charge or accusation) against someone. **16.** *(tr.;* often foll. by *in* or *with)* to place (authority, power, etc.) in the control (of someone). **17.** *(intr.;* often foll. by *in) Archaic.* to exist or be present (in). **18.** *(tr.)* (of wind, rain, etc.) to beat down (crops). [C15: from Old French *loge,* perhaps from Old High German *louba* porch] —'**lodgeable** *adj.*

lodger ('lɒdʒə) *n.* a person who pays rent in return for accommodation in someone else's house.

lodging ('lɒdʒɪŋ) *n.* **1.** a temporary residence. **2.** *(sometimes pl.)* sleeping accommodation. **3.** *(sometimes pl.)* (at Oxford University) the residence of the head of a college. ~See also **lodgings.**

lodging house *n.* a private home providing accommodation and meals for lodgers.

lodgings ('lɒdʒɪŋz) *pl. n.* a rented room or rooms in which to live, esp. in another person's house.

lodging turn *n.* a period of work or duty, esp. among railway workers, which involves sleeping away from home.

lodgment *or* **lodgement** ('lɒdʒmənt) *n.* **1.** the act of lodging or the state of being lodged. **2.** a blockage or accumulation. **3.** a small area gained and held in enemy territory.

lodicule (ˈlɒdɪˌkjuːl) *n.* any of two or three minute scales at the base of the ovary in grass flowers that represent the corolla. [C19: from Latin *lōdīcula,* diminutive of *lōdix* blanket]

loess (ˈləʊɪs; *German* lœs) *n.* a light-coloured fine-grained accumulation of clay and silt particles that have been deposited by the wind. [C19: from German *Löss,* from Swiss German dialect *lösch* loose] —**loessial** (ləʊˈɛsɪəl) *or* **loˈessal** *adj.*

loft (lɒft) *n.* **1.** the space inside a roof. **2.** a gallery, esp. one for the choir in a church. **3.** a room over a stable used to store hay. **4.** *U.S.* an upper storey of a warehouse or factory. **5.** a raised house or coop in which pigeons are kept. **6.** *Sport.* **a.** (in golf) the angle from the vertical made by the club face to give elevation to a ball. **b.** elevation imparted to a ball. **c.** a lofting stroke or shot. ~*vb.* (*tr.*) **7.** *Sport.* to strike or kick (a ball) high in the air. **8.** to store or place in a loft. **9.** *Golf.* to slant (the face of a golf club). **10.** to lay out a full-scale working drawing of (the lines of a vessel's hull). [Late Old English, from Old Norse *lopt* air, ceiling; compare Old Danish and Old High German *loft* (German *Luft* air)]

lofter (ˈlɒftə) *n. Golf.* a club; an iron with a wide-angled face for lofting. Also called: **lofting iron.**

loftsman (ˈlɒftsmən) *n., pl.* **-men.** a person who reproduces in actual size a draughtsman's design for a ship or an aircraft, working on the floor of a building (**mould loft**) with a large floor area.

lofty (ˈlɒftɪ) *adj.* **loftier, loftiest. 1.** of majestic or imposing height. **2.** exalted or noble in character or nature. **3.** haughty or supercilious. **4.** elevated, eminent, or superior. —ˈ**loftily** *adv.* —ˈ**loftiness** *n.*

log[1] (lɒg) *n.* **1. a.** a section of the trunk or a main branch of a tree, when stripped of branches. **b.** (*modifier*) constructed out of logs: *a log cabin.* **2. a.** a detailed record of a voyage of a ship or aircraft. **b.** a record of the hours flown by pilots and aircrews. **c.** a book in which these records are made; logbook. **3.** a written record of information about transmissions kept by radio stations, amateur radio operators, etc. **4. a.** a device consisting of a float with an attached line, formerly used to measure the speed of a ship. See also **chip log. b. heave the log.** to determine a ship's speed with such a device. **5.** *Austral.* a claim for better pay and conditions presented by a trade union to an employer. **6. like a log.** without stirring or being disturbed (in the phrase **sleep like a log**). ~*vb.* **logs, logging, logged. 7.** (*tr.*) to fell the trees of (a forest, area, etc.) for timber. **8.** (*tr.*) to saw logs from (trees). **9.** (*intr.*) to work at the felling of timber. **10.** (*tr.*) to enter (a distance, event, etc.) in a logbook or log. **11.** (*tr.*) to record the punishment received by (a sailor) in a logbook. **12.** (*tr.*) to travel (a specified distance or time) or move at (a specified speed). [C14: origin obscure]

log[2] (lɒg) *n.* short for **logarithm.**

-log *combining form.* a U.S. variant of **-logue.**

logagraphia (ˌlɒgəˈgræfɪə) *n. Med.* inability to express ideas in writing.

logan[1] (ˈləʊgən) *or* **logan-stone** *n.* other names for **rocking stone.** [C18: from *logging-stone,* from dialect *log* to rock]

logan[2] (ˈləʊgən) *n. Canadian.* another name for **bogan** (a backwater).

loganberry (ˈləʊgənbərɪ, -brɪ) *n., pl.* **-ries. 1.** a trailing prickly hybrid rosaceous plant, *Rubus loganobaccus,* cultivated for its edible fruit. **2. a.** the purplish-red acid fruit of this plant. **b.** (*as modifier*): *loganberry pie.* [C19: named after James H. *Logan* (1841–1928), American judge and horticulturist who first grew it (1881)]

loganiaceous (ləʊˌgeɪnɪˈeɪʃəs) *adj.* of, relating to, or belonging to the *Loganiaceae,* a tropical and subtropical family of plants that includes nux vomica, pinkroot, and gelsemium. [C19: from New Latin *Logania,* named after James *Logan* (1674–1751) Irish-American botanist]

logaoedic (ˌlɒgəˈiːdɪk) (in classical prosody) ~*adj.* **1.** of or relating to verse in which mixed metres are combined within a single line to give the effect of prose. ~*n.* **2.** a line or verse of this kind. [C19: via Late Latin from Greek *logaoidikos,* from *logos* speech + *aoidē* poetry]

logarithm (ˈlɒgəˌrɪðəm) *n.* the exponent indicating the power to which a fixed number, the base, must be raised to obtain a given number or variable. It is used esp. to simplify multiplication and division: if $a^x = M$, then the logarithm of M to the base a (written $\log_a M$) is x. Often shortened to **log.** See also **common logarithm, natural logarithm.** [C17: from New Latin *logarithmus,* coined 1614 by the inventor of logarithms, John Napier, from Greek, *logos* ratio, reckoning + *arithmos* number]

logarithmic (ˌlɒgəˈrɪðmɪk) *or* **logarithmical** *adj.* **1.** of, relating to, using, or containing logarithms of a number or variable. **2.** consisting of, relating to, or using points or lines whose distances from a fixed point or line are proportional to the logarithms of numbers. ~Abbrev.: **log.** —ˌ**logaˈrithmically** *adv.*

logarithmic function *n.* **a.** the mathematical function $y = \log x$. **b.** a function that can be expressed in terms of this function.

logbook (ˈlɒgˌbʊk) *n.* **1.** a book containing the official record of trips made by a ship or aircraft; log. **2.** *Brit.* (formerly) a document listing the registration, manufacture, ownership and previous owners, etc., of a motor vehicle. Compare **registration document.**

log chip *n. Nautical.* the chip of a chip log.

loge (ləʊʒ) *n.* **1.** a small enclosure or box in a theatre or opera house. **2.** the upper section in a theatre or cinema. [C18: French; see LODGE]

logger (ˈlɒgə) *n.* **1.** another word for **lumberjack. 2.** a tractor or crane for handling logs.

loggerhead (ˈlɒgəˌhɛd) *n.* **1.** Also called: **loggerhead turtle.** a large-headed turtle, *Caretta caretta,* occurring in most seas: family *Chelonidae.* **2. loggerhead shrike.** a North American shrike, *Lanius ludovicianus,* having a grey head and body, black-and-white wings and tail, and black facial stripe. **3.** a tool consisting of a large metal sphere attached to a long handle, used for warming liquids, melting tar, etc. **4.** a strong round upright post in a whaleboat for belaying the line of a harpoon. **5.** *Archaic or dialect.* a blockhead; dunce. **6. at loggerheads.** engaged in dispute or confrontation. [C16: probably from dialect *logger* wooden block + HEAD] —ˈ**loggerˌheaded** *adj.*

loggia (ˈlɒdʒə, ˈlɒdʒɪə) *n., pl.* **-gias** *or* **-gie** (-dʒɛ). **1.** a covered area on the side of a building, esp. one that serves as a porch. **2.** an open balcony in a theatre. [C17: Italian, from French *loge.* See LODGE]

logging (ˈlɒgɪŋ) *n.* the work of felling, trimming, and transporting timber.

logia (ˈlɒgɪə) *n.* **1.** a supposed collection of the sayings of Christ held to have been drawn upon by the writers of the gospels. **2.** the plural of **logion.**

logic (ˈlɒdʒɪk) *n.* **1.** the branch of philosophy concerned with analysing the patterns of reasoning by which a conclusion is properly drawn from a set of premises, without reference to meaning or context. See also **formal logic, deduction** (sense 4), **induction** (sense 4). **2.** any particular formal system in which are defined axioms and rules of inference. Compare **formal system, formal language. 3.** the system and principles of reasoning used in a specific field of study. **4.** a particular method of argument or reasoning. **5.** force or effectiveness in argument or dispute. **6.** reasoned thought or argument, as distinguished from irrationality. **7.** the relationship and interdependence of a series of events, facts, etc. **8. chop logic.** to use excessively subtle or involved logic or argument. See **chop-logic. 9.** *Electronics, computer technol.* **a.** the principles underlying the units in a computer system that perform arithmetical and logical operations. See also **logic circuit. b.** (*as modifier*): *a logic element.* [C14: from Old French *logique* from Medieval Latin *logica* (neuter plural, treated in Medieval Latin as feminine singular), from Greek *logikos* concerning speech or reasoning]

logical (ˈlɒdʒɪkᵊl) *adj.* **1.** relating to, used in, or characteristic of logic. **2.** using, according to, or deduced from the principles of logic: *a logical conclusion.* **3.** capable of or characterized by clear or valid reasoning. **4.** reasonable or necessary because of facts, events, etc.: *the logical candidate.* **5.** *Computer technol.* of, performed by, used in, or relating to the logic circuits in a computer. —ˌ**logiˈcality** *or* ˈ**logicalness** *n.* —ˈ**logically** *adv.*

logical atomism *n.* the philosophical theory of Russell and the early Wittgenstein which held that all meaningful expressions must be analysable into atomic elements which refer directly to atomic elements of the real world.

logical consequence *n.* the relation that obtains between the conclusion and the premises of a formally valid argument.

logical constant *n.* one of the connectives of a given system of formal logic, esp. those of the sentential calculus, *not, and, or,* and *if ... then ....*

logical form *n.* the syntactic structure that may be shared by different expressions as abstracted from their content and articulated by the logical constants of a particular logical system, esp. the structure of an argument by virtue of which it can be shown to be formally valid. Thus *John is tall and thin, so John is tall* has the same logical form as *London is large and dirty, so London is large,* namely *P & Q, so P.*

logically possible *adj.* capable of being described without self-contradiction.

logical operation *n. Computer technol.* an operation involving the use of logical functions, such as *and* or *or,* that are applied to the input signals of a particular logic circuit.

logical positivism *n.* a philosophical theory that holds to be meaningful only those propositions that can be analysed by the tools of logic into elementary propositions that are either tautological or are empirically verifiable. It therefore rejects metaphysics, theology, and sometimes ethics as meaningless.

logical sum *n.* another name for **disjunction** (sense 3).

logical truth *n.* **1.** another term for **tautology** (sense 2). **2.** the property of being logically tautologous.

logic array *n. Computer technol.* an integrated circuit consisting of interconnected logic gates.

logic bomb *n. Computer technol.* an unauthorized program that is inserted into a computer system; when activated it interferes with the operation of the computer.

logic circuit *n.* an electronic circuit used in computers to perform a logical operation on its two or more input signals. There are six basic circuits, the AND, NOT, NAND, OR, NOR, and exclusive OR circuits, which can be combined into more complex circuits.

logician (lɒˈdʒɪʃən) *n.* a person who specializes in or is skilled at logic.

logicism (ˈlɒdʒɪˌsɪzəm) *n.* the philosophical theory that all of mathematics can be deduced from logic. Compare **intuitionism, formalism.**

logic level *n.* the voltage level representing one or zero in an electronic logic circuit.

logic programming *n.* the study or implementation of computer programs capable of discovering or checking proofs of formal expressions or segments.

log in *vb. Computer technol.* to enter (an identification number, password, etc.) from a remote terminal to gain access to a multiaccess system.

logion (ˈlɒgɪˌɒn) *n., pl.* **logia** (ˈlɒgɪə). a saying of Christ regarded as authentic. See also **logia.** [C16: from Greek: a saying, oracle, from *logos* word]

logistic[1] (lɒˈdʒɪstɪk) *n.* **1.** an uninterpreted calculus or system of symbolic logic. Compare **formal language.** ~*adj.* **2.** *Maths.* (of a curve) having an equation of the form $y = k/(1 + e^{a+bx})$, where *b* is less than zero, and used to describe a continuously increasing function. **3.** *Rare.* of, relating to, or skilled in arithmetical calculations. [C17: via French, from Late Latin *logisticus* of calculation, from Greek *logistikos* rational, from *logos* word, reason]

logistic[2] (lɒˈdʒɪstɪk) *or* **logistical** *adj.* of or relating to logistics. —**loˈgistically** *adv.*

logistics (lɒˈdʒɪstɪks) *n.* (*functioning as sing. or pl.*) **1.** the science of the movement, supplying, and maintenance of military forces in the field. **2.** the management of materials flow through an organization, from raw materials through to finished goods. **3.** the detailed planning and organization of any large complex operation. [C19: from French *logistique,* from *loger* to LODGE] —**loˈgistically** *adv.* —**logistician** (ˌlɒdʒɪˈstɪʃən) *n.*

log jam *n. Chiefly U.S. and Canadian.* **1.** blockage caused by the crowding together of a number of logs floating in a river. **2.** a deadlock; standstill.

loglog (ˈlɒglɒg) *n.* the logarithm of a logarithm (in equations, etc.).

logo (ˈləugəu, ˈlɒg-) *n., pl.* **-os.** short for **logotype** (sense 2).

logo- *combining form.* indicating word or speech: *logogram.* [from Greek; see LOGOS]

log of wood *n. N.Z.* **the.** an informal name for **Ranfurly Shield.**

logogram (ˈlɒgəˌgræm) *or* **logograph** (ˈlɒgəˌgrɑːf, -ˌgræf) *n.* a single symbol representing an entire morpheme, word, or phrase, as for example the symbol (%) meaning *per cent.* —**logogrammatic** (ˌlɒgəgrəˈmætɪk), **logographic** (ˌlɒgəˈgræfɪk), *or* **ˌlogoˈgraphical** *adj.* —**ˌlogogramˈmatically** *or* **ˌlogoˈgraphically** *adv.*

logography (lɒˈgɒgrəfɪ) *n.* **1.** the use of logotypes in printing. **2.** (formerly) a method of longhand reporting. —**loˈgographer** *n.*

logogriph (ˈlɒgəuˌgrɪf) *n.* a word puzzle, esp. one based on recombination of the letters of a word. [C16: via French from LOGO- + Greek *grīphos* puzzle] —**ˌlogoˈgriphic** *adj.*

logomachy (lɒˈgɒməkɪ) *n., pl.* **-chies.** argument about words or the meaning of words. [C16: from Greek *logomakhia,* from *logos* word + *makhē* battle] —**loˈgomachist** *n.*

logopaedics *or U.S.* **logopedics** (ˌlɒgəˈpiːdɪks) *n.* (*functioning as sing.*) another name for **speech therapy.** —**ˌlogoˈpaedic** *or U.S.* **ˌlogoˈpedic** *adj.*

logorrhoea *or esp. U.S.* **logorrhea** (ˌlɒgəˈrɪə) *n.* excessive, uncontrollable, or incoherent talkativeness.

logos (ˈlɒgɒs) *n. Philosophy.* reason or the rational principle expressed in words and things, argument, or justification; esp. personified as the source of order in the universe. [C16: from Greek: word, reason, discourse, from *legein* to speak]

Logos (ˈlɒgɒs) *n.* the divine Word; the second person of the Trinity.

logotype (ˈlɒgəuˌtaɪp) *n.* **1.** *Printing.* a piece of type with several uncombined characters cast on it. **2.** Also called: **logo.** a trademark, company emblem, or similar device. —**ˈlogoˌtypy** *n.*

log out *vb. Computer technol.* to enter (an identification number, password, etc.) from a remote terminal to disconnect from a multiaccess system.

logroll (ˈlɒgˌrəul) *vb. Chiefly U.S.* to use logrolling in order to procure the passage of (legislation). —**ˈlogˌroller** *n.*

logrolling (ˈlɒgˌrəulɪŋ) *n.* **1.** *U.S.* the practice of undemocratic agreements between politicians involving mutual favours, the trading of votes, etc. **2.** another name for **birling.** See **birl**[1].

-logue *or U.S.* **-log** *n. combining form.* indicating speech or discourse of a particular kind: *travelogue; monologue.* [from French, from Greek *-logos*]

logway (ˈlɒgˌweɪ) *n.* another name for **gangway** (sense 1).

logwood (ˈlɒgˌwud) *n.* **1.** a leguminous tree, *Haematoxylon campechianum,* of the West Indies and Central America. **2.** the heavy reddish-brown wood of this tree, yielding the dye haematoxylin. See also **haematoxylon.**

logy (ˈləugɪ) *adj.* **logier, logiest.** *Chiefly U.S.* dull or listless. [C19: perhaps from Dutch *log* heavy] —**ˈloginess** *n.*

-logy *n. combining form.* **1.** indicating the science or study of: *musicology.* **2.** indicating writing, discourse, or body of writings: *trilogy; phraseology; martyrology.* [from Latin *-logia,* from Greek, from *logos* word; see LOGOS] —**-logical** *or* **-logic** *adj. combining form.* —**-logist** *n. combining form.*

lohan (ˈləuˈhɑːn) *n.* (*sometimes cap.*) another word for **Arhat.**

loin (lɔɪn) *n.* **1.** Also called: **lumbus.** *Anatomy.* the part of the lower back and sides between the pelvis and the ribs. Related adj.: **lumbar. 2.** a cut of meat from this part of an animal. ~See also **loins.** [C14: from Old French *loigne,* perhaps from Vulgar Latin *lumbra* (unattested), from Latin *lumbus* loin]

loincloth (ˈlɔɪnˌklɒθ) *n.* a piece of cloth worn round the loins. Also called: **breechcloth.**

loins (lɔɪnz) *pl. n.* **1.** the hips and the inner surface of the legs where they join the trunk of the body; crotch. **2. a.** *Euphemistic.* the reproductive organs. **b.** *Chiefly literary.* the womb.

loiter (ˈlɔɪtə) *vb.* (*intr.*) to stand or act aimlessly or idly. [C14: perhaps from Middle Dutch *löteren* to wobble: perhaps related to Old English *lūtian* to lurk] —**ˈloiterer** *n.* —**ˈloitering** *n., adj.*

loll (lɒl) *vb.* **1.** (*intr.*) to lie, lean, or lounge in a lazy or relaxed manner. **2.** to hang or allow to hang loosely. ~*n.* **3.** an act or instance of lolling. [C14: perhaps imitative; perhaps related to Middle Dutch *lollen* to doze] —**ˈloller** *n.* —**ˈlolling** *adj.*

lollapalooza (ˌlɒləpəˈluːzə) *or* **lalapalooza** *n. U.S. slang.* something excellent. [origin unknown]

Lollard (ˈlɒləd) *n. English history.* a follower of John Wycliffe during the 14th, 15th, and 16th centuries. [C14: from Middle Dutch; mutterer, from *lollen* to mumble (prayers)] —**ˈLollardy, ˈLollardry,** *or* **ˈLollardism** *n.*

lollipop (ˈlɒlɪˌpɒp) *n.* **1.** a boiled sweet or toffee stuck on a small wooden stick. **2.** *Brit.* another word for **ice lolly.** [C18: perhaps from Northern English dialect *lolly* the tongue (compare LOLL) + POP[1]]

lollipop man *or* **lady** *n.* (in Britain) a person wearing a white coat and carrying a pole bearing a circular warning sign who stops traffic to allow children travelling to or from school to cross a road safely. Official name: **school crossing patrol.**

lollop (ˈlɒləp) *vb.* (*intr.*) *Chiefly Brit.* **1.** to walk or run with a clumsy or relaxed bouncing movement. **2.** a less common word for **lounge.** [C18: probably from LOLL + *-op* as in GALLOP, to emphasize the contrast in meaning]

lollo rosso (ˈlɒləu ˈrɒsəu) *n.* a variety of lettuce originating in Italy, having curly red-tipped leaves and a slightly bitter taste.

lolly (ˈlɒlɪ) *n., pl.* **-lies. 1.** an informal word for **lollipop. 2.** *Brit.* short for **ice lolly. 3.** *Brit., Austral., and N.Z.* a slang word for **money. 4.** *Austral. and N.Z. informal.* a sweet, esp. a boiled one. **5. do the** (*or* **one's**) **lolly.** *Austral. informal.* to lose one's temper. [shortened from LOLLIPOP]

lollygag (ˈlɒlɪˌgæg) *vb.* **-gags, -gagging, -gagged.** (*intr.*) a variant of **lallygag.**

lolly water *n. Austral. and N.Z. informal.* any of various coloured soft drinks.

Lombard (ˈlɒmbəd, -bɑːd, ˈlʌm-) *n.* **1.** a native or inhabitant of Lombardy, a region of N central Italy. **2.** Also called: **Langobard.** a member of an ancient Germanic people who settled in N Italy after 568 A.D. ~*adj. also* **Lombardic. 3.** of or relating to Lombardy or the Lombards.

Lombard Street *n.* the British financial and banking world. [C16: from a street in London once occupied by Lombard bankers]

Lombardy poplar (ˈlɒmbədɪ) *n.* an Italian poplar tree, *Populus nigra italica,* with upwardly pointing branches giving it a columnar shape.

Lombrosian (lɒmˈbrəuzɪən) *adj.* of or relating to the doctrine propounded by Cesare Lombroso (1836–1909), Italian criminologist, that criminals are a product of hereditary and atavistic factors and can be classified as a definite abnormal type.

loment (ˈləumɛnt) *or* **lomentum** (ləuˈmɛntəm) *n., pl.* **-ments** *or* **-menta** (-ˈmɛntə). the pod of certain leguminous plants, constricted between each seed and breaking into one-seeded portions when ripe. [C19: from Latin *lomentum* bean meal] —**lomentaceous** (ˌləumənˈteɪʃəs) *adj.*

Londoner (ˈlʌndənə) *n.* a native or inhabitant of London.

London pride (ˈlʌndən) *n.* a saxifragaceous plant, a hybrid between *Saxifraga spathularis* and *S. umbrosa,* having a basal rosette of leaves and pinkish-white flowers.

lone (ləun) *adj.* (*prenominal*) **1.** unaccompanied; solitary. **2.** single or isolated: *a lone house.* **3.** a literary word for **lonely. 4.** unmarried or widowed. [C14: from the mistaken division of ALONE into *a lone*] —**ˈloneness** *n.*

lone hand *n.* **1.** (in card games such as euchre) an independent player or hand played without a partner. **2. play a lone hand.** to operate without assistance.

lonely (ˈləunlɪ) *adj.* **-lier, -liest. 1.** unhappy as a result of being without the companionship of others: *a lonely man.* **2.** causing or resulting from the state of being alone: *a lonely existence.* **3.** isolated, unfrequented, or desolate. **4.** without companions; solitary. —**ˈloneliness** *n.*

lonely hearts *adj.* (*often caps.*) of or for people who wish to meet a congenial companion or marriage partner: *a lonely hearts advertisement.*

lone pair *n. Chem.* a pair of valency electrons of opposite spin that are not shared between the atoms in a molecule and are responsible for the formation of coordinate bonds.

loner (ˈləunə) *n. Informal.* a person or animal who avoids the company of others or prefers to be alone.

lonesome (ˈləunsəm) *adj.* **1.** *Chiefly U.S. and Canadian.* another word for **lonely.** ~*n.* **2. on** *or* (*U.S.*) **by one's lonesome.**

Informal. on one's own. —ˈ**lonesomely** *adv.* —ˈ**lonesomeness** *n.*

lone wolf *n.* a person who prefers to be alone.

long[1] (lɒŋ) *adj.* **1.** having relatively great extent in space on a horizontal plane. **2.** having relatively great duration in time. **3. a.** (*postpositive*) of a specified number of units in extent or duration: *three hours long.* **b.** (*in combination*): *a two-foot-long line.* **4.** having or consisting of a relatively large number of items or parts: *a long list.* **5.** having greater than the average or expected range: *a long memory.* **6.** being the longer or longest of alternatives: *the long way to the bank.* **7.** having more than the average or usual quantity, extent, or duration: *a long match.* **8.** seeming to occupy a greater time than is really so: *she spent a long afternoon waiting in the departure lounge.* **9.** intense or thorough (esp. in the phrase **a long look**). **10.** (of drinks) containing a large quantity of nonalcoholic beverage. **11.** (of a garment) reaching to the wearer's ankles. **12.** *Informal.* (foll. by *on*) plentifully supplied or endowed (with): *long on good ideas.* **13.** *Phonetics.* (of a speech sound, esp. a vowel) **a.** of relatively considerable duration. **b.** classified as long, as distinguished from the quality of other vowels. **c.** (in popular usage) denoting the qualities of the five English vowels in such words as *mate, mete, mite, moat, moot,* and *mute.* **14.** from end to end; lengthwise. **15.** unlikely to win, happen, succeed, etc.: *a long chance.* **16.** *Prosody.* **a.** denoting a vowel of relatively great duration or (esp. in classical verse) followed by more than one consonant. **b.** denoting a syllable containing such a vowel. **c.** (in verse that is not quantitative) carrying the emphasis or ictus. **17.** *Finance.* having or characterized by large holdings of securities or commodities in anticipation of rising prices: *a long position.* **18.** *Cricket.* (of a fielding position) near the boundary: *long leg.* **19.** *Informal.* (of people) tall and slender. **20. in the long run.** See **run** (sense 82). **21. long in the tooth.** *Informal.* old or ageing. ~*adv.* **22.** for a certain time or period: *how long will it last?* **23.** for or during an extensive period of time: *long into the next year.* **24.** at a distant time; quite a bit of time: *long before I met you; long ago.* **25.** *Finance.* into a position with more security or commodity holdings than are required by sale contracts and therefore dependent on rising prices for profit: *to go long.* **26. as** (*or* **so**) **long as. a.** for or during just the length of time that. **b.** inasmuch as; since. **c.** provided that; if. **27. no longer.** not any more; formerly but not now. ~*n.* **28.** a long time (esp. in the phrase **for long**). **29.** a relatively long thing, such as a signal in Morse code. **30.** a clothing size for tall people, esp. in trousers. **31.** *Phonetics.* a long vowel or syllable. **32.** *Finance.* a person with large holdings of a security or commodity in expectation of a rise in its price; bull. **33.** *Music.* a note common in medieval music but now obsolete, having the time value of two breves. **34. before long.** soon. **35. the long and the short of it.** the essential points or facts. ~See also **longs.** [Old English *lang;* related to Old High German *lang,* Old Norse *langr,* Latin *longus*]

long[2] (lɒŋ) *vb.* (*intr.;* foll. by *for* or an infinitive) to have a strong desire. [Old English *langian;* related to LONG[1]]

long[3] (lɒŋ) *vb.* (*intr.*) *Archaic.* to belong, appertain, or be appropriate. [Old English *langian* to belong, from *gelang* at hand, belonging to; compare ALONG]

long. *abbrev. for* longitude.

long- *adv.* (*in combination*) for or lasting a long time: *long-awaited; long-established; long-lasting.*

long-acting *adj.* (of a drug) slowly effective after initial dosage, but maintaining its effects over a long period of time, being slowly absorbed and persisting in the tissues before being excreted. Compare **intermediate-acting, short-acting.**

longan (ˈlɒŋgən) *or* **lungan** *n.* **1.** a sapindaceous tree, *Euphoria longan,* of tropical and subtropical Asia, with small yellowish-white flowers and small edible fruits. **2.** the fruit of this tree, which is similar to but smaller than the litchi, having white juicy pulp and a single seed. [C18: from Chinese *lung yen* dragon's eye]

long-and-short work *n. Architect.* the alternation in masonry of vertical and horizontal blocks of stone.

longanimity (ˌlɒŋgəˈnɪmɪtɪ) *n. Now rare.* patience or forbearance. [C15: from Late Latin *longanimitās,* from *longanimis* forbearing, from *longus* long + *animus* mind, soul] —**longanimous** (lɒŋˈgænɪməs) *adj.*

long arm *n. Informal.* **1.** power, esp. far-reaching power: *the long arm of the law.* **2. make a long arm.** to reach out for something, as from a sitting position.

longboat (ˈlɒŋˌbəʊt) *n.* **1.** the largest boat carried aboard a commercial sailing vessel. **2.** another term for **longship.**

longbow (ˈlɒŋˌbəʊ) *n.* a large powerful hand-drawn bow, esp. as used in medieval England.

longcase clock (ˈlɒŋˌkeɪs) *n.* another name for **grandfather clock.**

long-chain *adj. Chemistry.* having a relatively long chain of atoms in the molecule.

longcloth (ˈlɒŋˌklɒθ) *n.* **1.** a fine plain-weave cotton cloth made in long strips. **2.** *U.S.* a light soft muslin.

long-coats *pl. n.* dress-like garments formerly worn by a baby. Archaic name: **long clothes.**

long-dated *adj.* (of a gilt-edged security) having more than 15 years to run before redemption. Compare **medium-dated, short-dated.**

long-day *adj.* (of certain plants) able to mature and flower only if exposed to long periods of daylight (more than 12 hours), each followed by a shorter period of darkness. Compare **short-day.**

long-distance *n.* **1.** (*modifier*) covering relatively long distances: *a long-distance driver.* **2.** (*modifier*) (of telephone calls, lines, etc.) connecting points a relatively long way apart. **3.** *Chiefly U.S.* a long-distance telephone call. **4.** a long-distance telephone system or its operator. ~*adv.* **5.** by a long-distance telephone line: *he phoned long-distance.*

long-drawn-out *adj.* over-prolonged or extended.

longe (lʌndʒ, lɒndʒ) *n.* an older variant of **lunge**[2]. [C17: via Old French from Latin *longus* LONG[1]]

long-eared owl *n.* a slender European owl, *Asio otus,* with long ear tufts: most common in coniferous forests.

longeron (ˈlɒndʒərən) *n.* a main longitudinal structural member of an aircraft. [C20: from French: side support, ultimately from Latin *longus* LONG[1]]

longevity (lɒnˈdʒɛvɪtɪ) *n.* **1.** long life. **2.** relatively long duration of employment, service, etc. [C17: from Late Latin *longaevitās,* from Latin *longaevus* long-lived, from *longus* LONG[1] + *aevum* age] —**longevous** (lɒnˈdʒiːvəs) *adj.*

long face *n.* a disappointed, solemn, or miserable facial expression. —ˌ**long-ˈfaced** *adj.*

long finger *n.* **put (something) on the long finger.** *Irish.* to postpone (something) for a long time.

longhand (ˈlɒŋˌhænd) *n.* ordinary handwriting, in which letters, words, etc., are set down in full, as opposed to shorthand or to typing.

long haul *n.* **1.** a journey over a long distance, esp. one involving the transport of goods. **2.** a lengthy job.

long-headed *adj.* astute; shrewd; sagacious. —ˌ**long-ˈheadedly** *adv.* —ˌ**long-ˈheadedness** *n.*

long hop *n. Cricket.* a short-pitched ball, which can easily be hit.

longhorn (ˈlɒŋˌhɔːn) *n.* **1.** Also called: **Texas longhorn.** a long-horned breed of beef cattle, usually red or variegated, formerly common in the southwestern U.S. **2.** a British breed of beef cattle with long curved horns.

long-horned beetle *n.* another name for **longicorn beetle** (see **longicorn** (sense 1)).

long house *n.* **1.** a long communal dwelling of the Iroquois and other North American Indian peoples. It often served as a council house as well. **2.** a long dwelling found in other parts of the world, such as Borneo.

long hundredweight *n.* the full name for **hundredweight** (sense 1).

longicorn (ˈlɒndʒɪˌkɔːn) *n.* **1.** Also called: **longicorn beetle, long-horned beetle.** any beetle of the family *Cerambycidae,* having a long narrow body, long legs, and long antennae. ~*adj.* **2.** *Zoology.* having or designating long antennae. [C19: from New Latin *longicornis* long-horned]

longing (ˈlɒŋɪŋ) *n.* **1.** a prolonged unfulfilled desire or need. ~*adj.* **2.** having or showing desire or need: *a longing look.* —ˈ**longingly** *adv.*

longipennate (ˌlɒndʒɪˈpɛneɪt) *adj.* (of birds) having long slender wings or feathers.

longirostral (ˌlɒndʒɪˈrɒstrəl) *adj.* (of birds) having a long beak.

longish (ˈlɒŋɪʃ) *adj.* rather long.

longitude (ˈlɒndʒɪˌtjuːd, ˈlɒŋg-) *n.* **1.** distance in degrees east or west of the prime meridian at 0° measured by the angle between the plane of the prime meridian and that of the meridian through the point in question, or by the corresponding time difference. See **latitude** (sense 1). **2.** *Astronomy.* short for **celestial longitude.** [C14: from Latin *longitūdō* length, from *longus* LONG[1]]

longitudinal (ˌlɒndʒɪˈtjuːdɪnᵊl, ˌlɒŋg-) *adj.* **1.** of or relating to longitude or length. **2.** placed or extended lengthways. Compare **transverse** (sense 1). **3.** *Psychol.* (of a study of behaviour) carried on over a protracted period of time. —ˌ**longiˈtudinally** *adv.*

longitudinal wave *n.* a wave that is propagated in the same direction as the displacement of the transmitting medium. Compare **transverse wave.**

long jenny *n. Billiards.* an in-off up the cushion into a far pocket. Compare **short jenny.** [from *Jenny,* pet form of *Janet*]

long johns *pl. n. Informal.* underpants with long legs.

long jump *n.* an athletic contest in which competitors try to cover the farthest distance possible with a running jump from a fixed board or mark. U.S. and Canadian equivalent: **broad jump.** —**long jumping** *n.*

longleaf pine (ˈlɒŋˌliːf) *n.* a North American pine tree, *Pinus palustris,* with long needle-like leaves and orange-brown bark: the most important timber tree of the southeastern U.S.

long lease *n.* (in England and Wales) a lease, originally for a period of over 21 years, on a whole house of low rent and ratable value, which is the occupants' only or main residence. Under the Leasehold Reform Act (1969) the leaseholder is entitled to buy the freehold, claim an extension of 50 years, or become a statutory tenant.

long leg *n. Cricket.* **a.** a fielding position on the leg side near the boundary almost directly behind the batsman's wicket. **b.** a fielder in this position.

long-legged (ˈlɒŋˌlɛgd, -ˌlɛgɪd) *adj.* **1.** having long legs. **2.** *Informal.* (of a person or animal) able to run fast.

long-lived *adj.* having long life, existence, or currency. —ˌ**long-ˈlivedness** *n.*
long mark *n.* another name for **macron.**
long measure *n.* another name for **linear measure.**
long metre *n.* a stanzaic form consisting of four octosyllabic lines, used esp. for hymns.
long moss *n.* another name for **Spanish moss.**
Longobard (ˈlɒŋgəˌbɑːd) *n., pl.* **-bards** *or* **-bardi** (-ˌbɑːdɪ). a rare name for an ancient **Lombard.** —ˌ**Longoˈbardian** *or* ˌ**Longoˈbardic** *adj.*
long-off *n. Cricket.* **a.** a fielding position on the off side near the boundary almost directly behind the bowler. **b.** a fielder in this position.
long-on *n. Cricket.* **a.** a fielding position on the leg side near the boundary almost directly behind the bowler. **b.** a fielder in this position.
long pig *n.* human flesh eaten by cannibals. [translation of a Maori and Polynesian term]
long-playing *adj.* of or relating to an LP (long-player).
long primer *n.* a size of printer's type, approximately equal to 10 point.
long purse *n. Informal.* wealth; riches.
long-range *adj.* **1.** of or extending into the future: *a long-range weather forecast.* **2.** (of vehicles, aircraft, etc.) capable of covering great distances without refuelling. **3.** (of weapons) made to be fired at a distant target.
longs (lɒŋz) *pl. n.* **1.** full-length trousers. **2.** long-dated gilt-edged securities. **3.** *Finance.* unsold securities or commodities held in anticipation of rising prices.
long s *n.* a lower-case *s*, printed ſ, formerly used in handwriting and printing. Also called: **long ess.**
longship (ˈlɒŋˌʃɪp) *n.* a narrow open vessel with oars and a square sail, used esp. by the Vikings during medieval times.
longshore (ˈlɒŋˌʃɔː) *adj.* situated on, relating to, or along the shore. [C19: shortened form of *alongshore*]
longshore drift *n.* the process whereby beach material is gradually shifted laterally as a result of waves meeting the shore at an oblique angle.
longshoreman (ˈlɒŋˌʃɔːmən) *n., pl.* **-men.** a U.S. and Canadian word for **docker**[1].
long shot *n.* **1.** a competitor, as in a race, considered to be unlikely to win. **2.** a bet against heavy odds. **3.** an undertaking, guess, or possibility with little chance of success. **4.** *Films, television.* a shot where the camera is or appears to be distant from the object to be photographed. **5. by a long shot.** by any means: *he still hasn't finished by a long shot.*
long-sighted *adj.* **1.** related to or suffering from hyperopia. **2.** able to see distant objects in focus. **3.** having foresight. —ˌ**long-ˈsightedly** *adv.* —ˌ**long-ˈsightedness** *n.*
longspur (ˈlɒŋˌspɜː) *n.* any of various Arctic and North American buntings of the genera *Calcarius* and *Rhyncophanes,* all of which have a long claw on the hind toe.
long-standing *adj.* existing or in effect for a long time.
long-suffering *adj.* **1.** enduring pain, unhappiness, etc., without complaint. ~*n. also* **long-sufferance.** **2.** long and patient endurance. —ˌ**long-ˈsufferingly** *adv.*
long suit *n.* **1. a.** the longest suit in a hand of cards. **b.** a holding of four or more cards of a suit. **2.** *Informal.* an outstanding advantage, personal quality, or talent.
long-tailed tit *n.* a small European songbird, *Aegithalos caudatus,* with a black, white, and pink plumage and a very long tail: family *Paridae* (tits).
long-term *adj.* **1.** lasting, staying, or extending over a long time: *long-term prospects.* **2.** *Finance.* maturing after a long period of time: *a long-term bond.*
long-term memory *n. Psychol.* that section of the memory storage system in which experiences are stored on a semipermanent basis. Compare **short-term memory.**
longtime (ˈlɒŋˌtaɪm) *adj.* of long standing.
long tin *n. Brit.* a tall long loaf of bread.
long tom *n.* **1.** a long swivel cannon formerly used in naval warfare. **2.** a long-range land gun. **3.** an army slang name for **cannon** (sense 1).
long ton *n.* the full name for **ton**[1] (sense 1).
longueur (*French* lɔ̃gœr) *n.* a period of boredom or dullness. [literally: length]
long vacation *n.* the long period of holiday in the summer during which universities, law courts, etc., are closed.
long view *n.* the consideration of events or circumstances likely to occur in the future.
long wave *n.* **a.** a radio wave with a wavelength greater than 1000 metres. **b.** (*as modifier*): *a long-wave broadcast.*
longways (ˈlɒŋˌweɪz) *or U.S. and Canadian* **longwise** (ˈlɒŋˌwaɪz) *adv.* another word for **lengthways.**
long weekend *n.* a weekend holiday extended by a day or days on either side.
long-winded *adj.* **1.** tiresomely long. **2.** capable of energetic activity without becoming short of breath. —ˌ**long-ˈwindedly** *adv.* —ˌ**long-ˈwindedness** *n.*
long-wire aerial *n.* a travelling-wave aerial consisting of one or more conductors, the length of which usually exceeds several wavelengths.
lonicera (lɒˈnɪsərə) *n.* See **honeysuckle.**
Lonsdale Belt (ˈlɒnzˌdeɪl) *n.* (in Britain) a belt conferred as a trophy on professional boxing champions, in various weight categories: if a champion wins it three times it becomes his personal property. [named after Hugh Cecil Lowther, 5th Earl of *Lonsdale* (1857–1944), who presented the first one]
loo[1] (luː) *n., pl.* **loos.** *Brit.* an informal word for **lavatory** (sense 1). [C20: perhaps from French *lieux d'aisance* water closet]
loo[2] (luː) *n., pl.* **loos.** **1.** a gambling card game. **2.** a stake used in this game. [C17: shortened form of *lanterloo,* via Dutch from French *lanterelu,* originally a meaningless word from the refrain of a popular song]
loo[3] (luː) *vb.* a variant spelling of **lou.**
looby (ˈluːbɪ) *n., pl.* **-bies.** a foolish or stupid person. [C14: of unknown origin]
loofah (ˈluːfə) *n.* **1.** the fibrous interior of the fruit of the dishcloth gourd, which is dried, bleached, and used as a bath sponge or for scrubbing. **2.** another name for **dishcloth gourd.** ~Also called (esp. U.S.): **loofa, luffa.** [C19: from New Latin *luffa,* from Arabic *lūf*]
look (lʊk) *vb.* (*mainly intr.*) **1.** (often foll. by *at*) to direct the eyes (towards): *to look at the sea.* **2.** (often foll. by *at*) to direct one's attention (towards): *let's look at the circumstances.* **3.** (often foll. by *to*) to turn one's interests or expectations (towards): *to look to the future.* **4.** (*copula*) to give the impression of being by appearance to the eye or mind; seem: *that looks interesting.* **5.** to face in a particular direction: *the house looks north.* **6.** to expect or hope (to do something): *I look to hear from you soon.* **7.** (foll. by *for*) **a.** to search or seek: *I looked for you everywhere.* **b.** to cherish the expectation (of); hope (for): *I look for success.* **8.** (foll. by *to*) **a.** to be mindful (of): *to look to the promise one has made.* **b.** to have recourse (to): *look to your swords, men!* **9.** to be a pointer or sign: *these early inventions looked towards the development of industry.* **10.** (foll. by *into*) to carry out an investigation: *to look into a mystery.* **11.** (*tr.*) to direct a look at (someone) in a specified way: *she looked her rival up and down.* **12.** (*tr.*) to accord in appearance with (something): *to look one's age.* **13. look alive** *or* **lively.** hurry up; get busy. **14. look daggers.** See **dagger** (sense 4). **15. look here.** an expression used to attract someone's attention, add emphasis to a statement, etc. **16. look sharp** *or* **smart.** (*imperative*) to hurry up; make haste. **17. not look at.** to refuse to consider: *they won't even look at my offer of £5000.* **18. not much to look at.** unattractive; plain. ~*n.* **19.** the act or an instance of looking: *a look of despair.* **20.** a view or sight (of something): *let's have a look.* **21.** (*often pl.*) appearance to the eye or mind; aspect: *the look of innocence; I don't like the looks of this place.* **22.** style; fashion: *the new look for summer.* ~*sentence connector.* **23.** an expression demanding attention or showing annoyance, determination, etc.: *look, I've had enough of this.* ~See also **look after, look back, look down, look forward to, look-in, look on, lookout, look over, look through, look up.** [Old English *lōcian;* related to Middle Dutch *læken,* Old High German *luogen* to look out]
▷**Usage.** See at **feel.**
look after *vb.* (*intr., prep.*) **1.** to take care of; be responsible for: *she looked after the child while I was out.* **2.** to follow with the eyes: *he looked after the girl thoughtfully.*
lookalike (ˈlʊkəˌlaɪk) *n.* **a.** a person, esp. a celebrity, or thing that is the double of another. **b.** (*as modifier*): *a lookalike Minister; a lookalike newspaper.*
look back *vb.* (*intr., adv.*) **1.** to cast one's mind to the past. **2. to never look back:** to become increasingly successful: *after his book was published, he never looked back.* **3.** *Chiefly Brit.* to pay another visit later.
look down *vb.* **1.** (*intr., adv.;* foll. by *on* or *upon*) to express or show contempt or disdain (for). **2. look down one's nose at.** *Informal.* to be contemptuous or disdainful of.
looker (ˈlʊkə) *n. Informal.* **1.** a person who looks. **2.** a very attractive person, esp. a woman or girl.
look forward to *vb.* (*intr., adv. + prep.*) to wait or hope for, esp. with pleasure.
look-in *Informal.* ~*n.* **1.** a chance to be chosen, participate, etc. **2.** a short visit. ~*vb.* **look in.** **3.** (*intr., adv.* often foll. by *on*) to pay a short visit.
looking glass *n.* **1.** a mirror, esp. a ladies' dressing mirror. ~*modifier.* **looking-glass.** **2.** with normal or familiar circumstances reversed; topsy-turvy: *a looking-glass world.* [sense 2 in allusion to Lewis Carroll's *Through the Looking-Glass*]
look on *vb.* (*intr.*) **1.** (*adv.*) to be a spectator at an event or incident. **2.** (*prep.*) Also: **look upon.** to consider or regard: *she looked on the whole affair as a joke; he looks on his mother-in-law with disapproval.* —ˌ**looker-ˈon** *n.*
lookout (ˈlʊkˌaʊt) *n.* **1.** the act of keeping watch against danger, etc. **2.** a person or persons instructed or employed to keep such a watch, esp. on a ship. **3.** a strategic point from which a watch is kept. **4.** *Informal.* worry or concern: *that's his lookout.* **5.** *Chiefly Brit.* outlook, chances, or view. ~*vb.* **look out.** (*adv., mainly intr.*) **6.** to heed one's behaviour; be careful: *look out for the children's health.* **7.** to be on the watch: *look out for my mother at the station.* **8.** (*tr.*) to search for and find: *I'll look out some curtains for your new house.* **9.** (foll. by *on* or *over*) to face in a particular direction: *the house looks out over the moor.*
look over *vb.* **1.** (*intr., prep.*) to inspect by making a tour of (a factory, house, etc.): *we looked over the country house.* **2.** (*tr.,*

adv.) to examine (a document, letter, etc.): *please look the papers over quickly.* ~*n.* **lookover.** 3. an inspection: often, specifically, a brief or cursory one.

look-see *n. Informal.* a brief inspection or look.

look through *vb.* 1. (*intr., prep.* or *tr., adv.*) to examine, esp. cursorily: *he looked through his notes before the lecture.* 2. (*intr., prep.*) to ignore (a person) deliberately: *whenever he meets his ex-girlfriend, she looks straight through him.*

look up *vb.* (*adv.*) 1. (*tr.*) to discover (something required to be known) by resorting to a work of reference, such as a dictionary. 2. (*intr.*) to increase, as in quality or value: *things are looking up.* 3. (*intr.;* foll. by *to*) to have respect (for): *I've always wanted a girlfriend I could look up to.* 4. (*tr.*) to visit or make contact with (a person): *I'll look you up when I'm in town.*

loom[1] (luːm) *n.* 1. an apparatus, worked by hand or mechanically (**power loom**), for weaving yarn into a textile. 2. the middle portion of an oar, which acts as a fulcrum swivelling in the rowlock. [C13 (meaning any kind of tool): variant of Old English *gelōma* tool; compare HEIRLOOM]

loom[2] (luːm) *vb.* (*intr.*) 1. to come into view indistinctly with an enlarged and often threatening aspect. 2. (of an event) to seem ominously close. 3. (often foll. by *over*) (of large objects) to dominate or overhang. ~*n.* 4. a rising appearance, as of something far away. [C16: perhaps from East Frisian *lomen* to move slowly]

loom[3] (luːm) *n. Archaic or dialect.* 1. another name for **diver** (the bird). 2. any of various other birds, esp. the guillemot. [C17: from Old Norse *lomr*]

loo mask *n.* a half-mask worn during the 18th century for masquerades, etc. Also called: **loup.** [C17 *loo,* from French *loup,* literally: wolf, from Latin *lupus*]

loom-state *adj.* (of a woven cotton fabric) not yet dyed.

loon[1] (luːn) *n.* the U.S. and Canadian name for **diver** (the bird). [C17: of Scandinavian origin; related to Old Norse *lōmr*]

loon[2] (luːn) *n.* 1. *Informal.* a simple-minded or stupid person. 2. *Northeast Scot. dialect.* a lad. 3. *Archaic.* a person of low rank or occupation (esp. in the phrase **lord and loon**). [C15: origin obscure]

loony, looney, *or* **luny** (ˈluːnɪ) *Slang.* ~*adj.* **loonier, looniest** *or* **lunier, luniest.** 1. lunatic; insane. 2. foolish or ridiculous. ~*n., pl.* **loonies, looneys,** *or* **lunies.** 3. a foolish or insane person. —ˈ**looniness** *or* ˈ**luniness** *n.*

loony bin *n. Slang.* a mental hospital or asylum.

loop[1] (luːp) *n.* 1. the round or oval shape formed by a line, string, etc., that curves around to cross itself. 2. any round or oval-shaped thing that is closed or nearly closed. 3. a piece of material, such as string, curved round and fastened to form a ring or handle for carrying by. 4. an intrauterine contraceptive device in the shape of a loop. 5. *Electronics.* a. a closed electric or magnetic circuit through which a signal can circulate, as in a feedback control system. b. short for **loop aerial.** 6. a flight manoeuvre in which an aircraft flies one complete circle in the vertical plane. 7. Also called: **loop line.** *Chiefly Brit.* a railway branch line which leaves the main line and rejoins it after a short distance. 8. *Maths, physics.* a closed curve on a graph: *hysteresis loop.* 9. another name for **antinode.** 10. *Anatomy.* a. the most common basic pattern of the human fingerprint, formed by several sharply rising U-shaped ridges. Compare **arch**[1] (sense 4b.). b. a bend in a tubular structure, such as the U-shaped curve in a kidney tubule (**Henle's loop** or **loop of Henle**). 11. *Computer technol.* a series of instructions in a program, performed repeatedly until some specified condition is satisfied. 12. *Skating.* a jump in which the skater takes off from a back outside edge, makes one, two, or three turns in the air, and lands on the same back outside edge. ~*vb.* 13. (*tr.*) to make a loop in or of (a line, string, etc.). 14. (*tr.*) to fasten or encircle with a loop or something like a loop. 15. Also: **loop the loop.** to cause (an aircraft) to perform a loop or (of an aircraft) to perform a loop. 16. (*intr.*) to move in loops or in a path like a loop. [C14: *loupe,* origin unknown]

loop[2] (luːp) *n.* an archaic word for **loophole.** [C14: perhaps related to Middle Dutch *lupen* to watch, peer]

loop aerial *n.* an aerial that consists of one or more coils of wire wound on a frame. Maximum radiation or reception is in the plane of the loop, the minimum occurring at right angles to it. Sometimes shortened to **loop.** Also called: **frame aerial.**

loop diuretic *n. Med.* any of a group of diuretics, including frusemide, that act by inhibiting resorption of salts from Henle's loop of the kidney tubule.

looper (ˈluːpə) *n.* 1. a person or thing that loops or makes loops. 2. another name for a **measuring worm.**

loophole (ˈluːpˌhəʊl) *n.* 1. an ambiguity, omission, etc., as in a law, by which one can avoid a penalty or responsibility. 2. a small gap or hole in a wall, esp. one in a fortified wall. ~*vb.* 3. (*tr.*) to provide with loopholes. [C16: from LOOP[2] + HOLE]

loop knot *n.* a knot that leaves a loop extending from it.

loopy (ˈluːpɪ) *adj.* **loopier, loopiest.** 1. full of loops; curly or twisted. 2. *Informal.* slightly mad, crazy, or stupid.

loose (luːs) *adj.* 1. free or released from confinement or restraint. 2. not close, compact, or tight in structure or arrangement. 3. not fitted or fitting closely: *loose clothing is cooler.* 4. not bundled, packaged, fastened, or put in a container: *loose nails.* 5. inexact; imprecise: *a loose translation.* 6. (of funds, cash, etc.) not allocated or locked away; readily available. 7. a. (esp. of women) promiscuous or easy. b. (of attitudes, ways of life, etc.) immoral or dissolute. 8. lacking a sense of responsibility or propriety: *loose talk.* 9. a. (of the bowels) emptying easily, esp. excessively; lax. b. (of a cough) accompanied by phlegm, mucus, etc. 10. (of a dye or dyed article) fading as a result of washing; not fast. 11. *Informal, chiefly U.S. and Canadian.* very relaxed; easy. ~*n.* 12. **the loose.** *Rugby.* the part of play when the forwards close round the ball in a ruck or loose scrum. See **scrum.** 13. **on the loose.** a. free from confinement or restraint. b. *Informal.* on a spree. ~*adv.* 14. a. in a loose manner; loosely. b. (*in combination*): *loose-fitting.* 15. **hang loose.** *Informal, chiefly U.S.* to behave in a relaxed, easy fashion. ~*vb.* 16. (*tr.*) to set free or release, as from confinement, restraint, or obligation. 17. (*tr.*) to unfasten or untie. 18. to make or become less strict, tight, firmly attached, compact, etc. 19. (when *intr.*, often foll. by *off*) to let fly (a bullet, arrow, or other missile). [C13 (in the sense: not bound): from Old Norse *lauss* free; related to Old English *lēas* free from, -LESS] —ˈ**loosely** *adv.* —ˈ**looseness** *n.*

loosebox (ˈluːsˌbɒks) *n.* an enclosed and covered stall with a door in which an animal can be confined.

loose change *n.* money in the form of coins suitable for small expenditures.

loose cover *n.* a fitted but easily removable cloth cover for a chair, sofa, etc. U.S. and Canadian name: **slipcover.**

loose end *n.* 1. a detail that is left unsettled, unexplained, or incomplete. 2. **at a loose end.** without purpose or occupation.

loose head *n. Rugby.* the prop on the hooker's left in the front row of a scrum. Compare **tight head.**

loose-jointed *adj.* 1. supple and easy in movement. 2. loosely built; with ill-fitting joints. —ˌ**loose-**ˈ**jointedness** *n.*

loose-leaf *adj.* 1. (of a binder, album, etc.) capable of being opened to allow removal and addition of pages. ~*n.* 2. a serial publication published in loose leaves and kept in such a binder.

loose-limbed *adj.* (of a person) having supple limbs.

loosen (ˈluːsᵊn) *vb.* 1. to make or become less tight, fixed, etc. 2. (often foll. by *up*) to make or become less firm, compact, or rigid. 3. (*tr.*) to untie. 4. (*tr.*) to let loose; set free. 5. (often foll. by *up*) to make or become less strict, severe, etc. 6. (*tr.*) to rid or relieve (the bowels) of constipation. [C14: from LOOSE] —ˈ**loosener** *n.*

loose order *n. Military.* a formation in which soldiers, units, etc., are widely separated from each other.

loose smut *n.* a disease of cereal grasses caused by smut fungi of the genus *Ustilago,* in which powdery spore masses replace the host tissue.

loosestrife (ˈluːsˌstraɪf) *n.* 1. any of various primulaceous plants of the genus *Lysimachia,* esp. the yellow-flowered *L. vulgaris* (**yellow loosestrife**). See also **moneywort.** 2. **purple loosestrife.** Also called: **willowherb.** a purple-flowered lythraceous marsh plant, *Lythrum salicaria.* 3. any of several similar or related plants, such as the primulaceous plant *Naumburgia thyrsiflora* (**tufted loosestrife**). [C16: LOOSE + STRIFE, an erroneous translation of Latin *lysimachia,* as if from Greek *lusimakhos* ending strife, instead of from the name of the supposed discoverer, *Lusimakhos*]

loose-tongued *adj.* careless or irresponsible in talking.

loosing *or* **lowsening** (ˈluːsɪŋ, -zɪŋ, ˈlɔɪ-) *n. Yorkshire dialect.* a celebration of one's 21st birthday.

loot (luːt) *n.* 1. goods stolen during pillaging, as in wartime, during riots, etc. 2. goods, money, etc., obtained illegally. 3. *Informal.* money or wealth. 4. the act of looting or plundering. ~*vb.* 5. to pillage (a city, settlement, etc.) during war or riots. 6. to steal (money or goods), esp. during pillaging. [C19: from Hindi *lūt*] —ˈ**looter** *n.*

lop[1] (lɒp) *vb.* **lops, lopping, lopped.** (*tr.;* usually foll. by *off*) 1. to sever (parts) from a tree, body, etc., esp. with swift strokes. 2. to cut out or eliminate from as excessive. ~*n.* 3. a part or parts lopped off, as from a tree. [C15 *loppe* branches cut off; compare LOB[1]] —ˈ**lopper** *n.*

lop[2] (lɒp) *vb.* **lops, lopping, lopped.** 1. to hang or allow to hang loosely. 2. (*intr.*) to slouch about or move awkwardly. 3. (*intr.*) a less common word for **lope.** [C16: perhaps related to LOP[1]; compare LOB[1]]

lop[3] (lɒp) *n. Northern English dialect.* a flea. [probably from Old Norse *hloppa* (unattested) flea, from *hlaupa* to LEAP]

lope (ləʊp) *vb.* 1. (*intr.*) (of a person) to move or run with a long swinging stride. 2. (*intr.*) (of four-legged animals) to run with a regular bounding movement. 3. to cause (a horse) to canter with a long easy stride or (of a horse) to canter in this manner. ~*n.* 4. a long steady gait or stride. [C15: from Old Norse *hlaupa* to LEAP; compare Middle Dutch *lopen* to run] —ˈ**loper** *n.*

lop-eared *adj.* (of animals) having ears that droop.

lopho- *combining form.* indicating a crested or tufted part: *lophophore.* [from Greek *lophos* crest]

lophobranch (ˈləʊfəˌbræŋk) *n.* 1. any teleost fish of the suborder *Lophobranchii,* having the gills arranged in rounded tufts: includes the pipefishes and sea horses. ~*adj.* 2. of, relating to, or belonging to the *Lophobranchii.* —**lophobranchiate** (ˌləʊfəˈbræŋkɪɪt, -ˌeɪt) *adj.*

lophophore (ˈləʊfəˌfɔː) *n.* a circle or horseshoe of ciliated tentacles surrounding the mouth and used for the capture of food in minute sessile animals of the phyla *Brachiopoda, Phoronida,* and *Ectoprocta.* —ˈ**lopho**ˈ**phorate** *adj.*

lopolith ('lɒpəlɪθ) *n.* a saucer-shaped body of intrusive igneous rock, formed by the penetration of magma between the beds or layers of existing rock. Compare **laccolith.** [C20: from Greek *lopas* dish + -LITH]

lopsided (ˌlɒp'saɪdɪd) *adj.* **1.** leaning or inclined to one side. **2.** greater in weight, height, or size on one side. —ˌ**lop'sidedly** *adv.* —ˌ**lop'sidedness** *n.*

loq. *abbrev. for* loquitur.

loquacious (lɒ'kweɪʃəs) *adj.* characterized by or showing a tendency to talk a great deal. [C17: from Latin *loquāx* from *loquī* to speak] —**lo'quaciously** *adv.* —**loquacity** (lɒ'kwæsɪtɪ) *or* **lo'quaciousness** *n.*

loquat ('ləʊkwɒt, -kwət) *n.* **1.** an ornamental evergreen rosaceous tree, *Eriobotrya japonica,* of China and Japan, having reddish woolly branches, white flowers, and small yellow edible plumlike fruits. **2.** the fruit of this tree. ~Also called: **Japan plum.** [C19: from Chinese (Cantonese) *lō kwat,* literally: rush orange]

loquitur *Latin.* ('lɒkwɪtə) he (or she) speaks: used, esp. formerly, as a stage direction. Usually abbreviated to **loq.**

lor (lɔː) *interj. Not standard.* an exclamation of surprise or dismay. [from LORD (interj.)]

loran ('lɔːrən) *n.* a radio navigation system operating over long distances. Synchronized pulses are transmitted from widely spaced radio stations to aircraft or shipping, the time of arrival of the pulses being used to determine position. [C20: *lo(ng-) ra(nge) n(avigation)*]

lord (lɔːd) *n.* **1.** a person who has power or authority over others, such as a monarch or master. **2.** a male member of the nobility, esp. in Britain. **3.** (in medieval Europe) a feudal superior, esp. the master of a manor. Compare **lady** (sense 5). **4.** a husband considered as head of the household (archaic except in the facetious phrase **lord and master**). **5.** *Astrology.* a planet having a dominating influence. **6. my lord.** a respectful form of address to a judge, bishop, or nobleman. ~*vb.* **7.** *(tr.) Now rare.* to make a lord of (a person). **8.** to act in a superior manner towards (esp. in the phrase **lord it over**). [Old English *hlāford* bread keeper; see LOAF[1], WARD] —**'lordless** *adj.* —**'lord,like** *adj.*

Lord (lɔːd) *n.* **1.** a title given to God or Jesus Christ. **2.** *Brit.* **a.** a title given to men of high birth, specifically to an earl, marquess, baron, or viscount. **b.** a courtesy title given to the younger sons of a duke or marquess. **c.** the ceremonial title of certain high officials or of a bishop or archbishop: *Lord Mayor; Lord of Appeal; Law Lord; Lord Bishop of Durham.* ~*interj.* **3.** *(sometimes not cap.)* an exclamation of dismay, surprise, etc.: *Good Lord!; Lord only knows!*

Lord Advocate *n.* (in Scotland) the chief law officer of the Crown: he acts as public prosecutor and is in charge of the administration of criminal justice.

Lord Chamberlain *n.* (in Britain) the chief official of the royal household.

Lord Chancellor *n. Brit. government.* the cabinet minister who is head of the judiciary in England and Wales and Speaker of the House of Lords.

Lord Chief Justice *n.* the judge who is second only to the Lord Chancellor in the English legal hierarchy; president of one division of the High Court of Justice.

Lord High Chancellor *n.* another name for the **Lord Chancellor.**

lording ('lɔːdɪŋ) *n.* **1.** *Archaic.* a gentleman; lord: used in the plural as a form of address. **2.** an obsolete word for **lordling.** [Old English *hlāfording,* from *hlāford* LORD + -ING[3], suffix indicating descent]

Lord Justice of Appeal *n.* an ordinary judge of the Court of Appeal.

Lord Lieutenant *n.* **1.** (in Britain) the representative of the Crown in a county. **2.** (formerly) the British viceroy in Ireland.

lordling ('lɔːdlɪŋ) *n. Now rare.* a young lord.

lordly ('lɔːdlɪ) *adj.* **-lier, -liest. 1.** haughty; arrogant; proud. **2.** of or befitting a lord. ~*adv.* **3.** *Archaic.* in the manner of a lord. —**'lordliness** *n.*

Lord Mayor *n.* the mayor in the City of London and in certain other important boroughs and large cities.

Lord Muck *n. Informal.* an ordinary man behaving or being treated as if he were aristocratic. See also **Lady Muck.**

Lord of Appeal *n. Brit.* one of several judges appointed to assist the House of Lords in hearing appeals.

Lord of Hosts *n.* Jehovah or God when regarded as having the angelic forces at his command.

Lord of Misrule *n.* (formerly, in England) a person appointed master of revels at a Christmas celebration.

lordosis (lɔː'dəʊsɪs) *n.* **1.** *Pathol.* forward curvature of the lumbar spine: congenital or caused by trauma or disease. Nontechnical name: **hollow-back.** Compare **kyphosis, scoliosis. 2.** *Zoology.* concave arching of the back occurring in many female animals during sexual stimulation. [C18: New Latin from Greek *lordōsis,* from *lordos* bent backwards] —**lordotic** (lɔː'dɒtɪk) *adj.*

Lord President of the Council *n.* (in Britain) the Cabinet minister who presides at meetings of the Privy Council.

Lord Privy Seal *n.* (in Britain) the senior cabinet minister without official duties.

Lord Provost *n.* the provost of one of the four major Scottish cities (Edinburgh, Glasgow, Aberdeen, and Dundee).

Lords (lɔːdz) *n.* **the.** short for **House of Lords.**

lords-and-ladies *n. (functioning as sing.)* another name for **cuckoopint.**

Lord's Day *n.* **the.** the Christian Sabbath; Sunday.

lordship ('lɔːdʃɪp) *n.* the position or authority of a lord.

Lordship ('lɔːdʃɪp) *n.* (preceded by *Your* or *His*) *Brit.* a title used to address or refer to a bishop, a judge of the high court, or any peer except a duke.

Lord's Prayer *n.* **the.** the prayer taught by Jesus Christ to his disciples, as in Matthew 6:9–13, Luke 11:2–4. Also called: **Our Father, Paternoster** (esp. Latin version).

Lords Spiritual *pl. n.* the two Anglican archbishops and 24 most senior bishops of England and Wales who sit as members of the House of Lords.

Lord's table *n.* **the.** *Chiefly Protestantism.* **1.** Holy Communion. **2.** another name for **altar.**

Lords Temporal *pl. n.* **the.** (in Britain) peers other than bishops in their capacity as members of the House of Lords.

lordy ('lɔːdɪ) *interj. Chiefly U.S. and Canadian.* an exclamation of surprise or dismay.

lore[1] (lɔː) *n.* **1.** collective knowledge or wisdom on a particular subject, esp. of a traditional nature. **2.** knowledge or learning. **3.** *Archaic.* teaching, or something that is taught. [Old English *lār;* related to *leornian* to LEARN]

lore[2] (lɔː) *n.* **1.** the surface of the head of a bird between the eyes and the base of the bill. **2.** the corresponding area in a snake or fish. [C19: from New Latin *lōrum,* from Latin: strap]

Lorentz-Fitzgerald contraction (lɒ'rɛntsˌfɪts'dʒɛrəld) *n.* the supposed contraction of a body in the direction of its motion through the ether, which is postulated to explain the result of the Michelson-Morley experiment. The special theory of relativity denies that any such real change can occur in a body as a result of uniform motion but shows that an observer moving with respect to the body will determine an apparent change given by a formula similar to that of Lorentz and Fitzgerald. [C20: named after H. A. *Lorentz* (1853–1928), Dutch physicist, and G. F. *Fitzgerald* (1851–1901), Irish physicist]

Lorentz transformation *n.* a set of equations relating the coordinates of space and time used by two hypothetical observers in uniform relative motion. According to the special theory of relativity the laws of physics are invariant under this transformation. [C20: named after H. A. *Lorentz*]

lorgnette (lɔː'njɛt) *n.* a pair of spectacles or opera glasses mounted on a handle. [C19: from French, from *lorgner* to squint, from Old French *lorgne* squinting]

lorgnon (*French* lɔrɲɔ̃) *n.* **1.** a monocle or pair of spectacles. **2.** another word for **lorgnette.** [C19: from French, from *lorgner;* see LORGNETTE]

lorica (lɒ'raɪkə) *n., pl.* **-cae** (-siː, -kiː). **1.** the hard outer covering of rotifers, ciliate protozoans, and similar animals. **2.** an ancient Roman cuirass of leather or metal. [C18: from New Latin, from Latin: leather cuirass; related to *lōrum* thong] —**loricate** ('lɒrɪˌkeɪt) *or* **'loriˌcated** *adj.*

lorikeet ('lɒrɪˌkiːt, ˌlɒrɪ'kiːt) *n.* any of various small lories, such as *Glossopsitta versicolor* (**varied lorikeet**) or *Trichoglossus moluccanus* (**rainbow lorikeet**). [C18: from LORY + *-keet,* as in PARAKEET]

lorimer ('lɒrɪmə) *or* **loriner** ('lɒrɪnə) *n. Brit.* (formerly) a person who made bits, spurs, and other small metal objects. [C15: from Old French, from *lorain* harness strap, ultimately from Latin *lōrum* strap]

loris ('lɔːrɪs) *n., pl.* **-ris.** any of several omnivorous nocturnal slow-moving prosimian primates of the family *Lorisidae,* of S and SE Asia, esp. *Loris tardigradus* (**slow loris**) and *Nycticebus coucang* (**slender loris**), having vestigial digits and no tails. [C18: from French; of uncertain origin]

lorn (lɔːn) *adj. Poetic.* forsaken or wretched. [Old English *loren,* past participle of *-lēosan* to lose] —**'lornness** *n.*

Lorraine cross (lɒ'reɪn) *n.* See **cross of Lorraine.**

lorry ('lɒrɪ) *n., pl.* **-ries. 1.** a large motor vehicle designed to carry heavy loads, esp. one with a flat platform. U.S. and Canadian name: **truck.** See also **articulated lorry. 2. off the back of a lorry.** *Brit. informal.* a phrase used humorously to imply that something has been dishonestly acquired: *it fell off the back of a lorry.* **3.** any of various vehicles with a flat load-carrying surface, esp. one designed to run on rails. [C19: perhaps related to northern English dialect *lurry* to pull, tug]

lory ('lɔːrɪ) *n., pl.* **-ries.** any of various small brightly coloured parrots of Australia and Indonesia, having a brush-tipped tongue with which to feed on nectar and pollen. [C17: via Dutch from Malay *lūrī,* variant of *nūrī*]

lose (luːz) *vb.* **loses, losing, lost.** *(mainly tr.)* **1.** to part with or come to be without, as through theft, accident, negligence, etc. **2.** to fail to keep or maintain: *to lose one's balance.* **3.** to suffer the loss or deprivation of: *to lose a parent.* **4.** to cease to have or possess. **5.** to fail to get or make use of: *to lose a chance.* **6.** *(also intr.)* to fail to gain or win (a contest, game, etc.): *to lose the match.* **7.** to fail to see, hear, perceive, or understand: *I lost the gist of his speech.* **8.** to waste: *to lose money gambling.* **9.** to wander from so as to be unable to find: *to lose one's way.* **10.** to cause the loss of: *his delay lost him the battle.* **11.** to allow to go astray or out of sight: *we lost him in the crowd.* **12.** *(usually passive)* to absorb or engross: *he was lost in contemplation.* **13.** *(usually passive)* to cause the death or destruction of: *two men were lost in the attack.* **14.** to outdistance or elude: *he soon lost his pursuers.* **15.** (*intr.*) to decrease or depreciate in value or effectiveness: *poetry always loses in translation.* **16.** (*also intr.*) (of a timepiece) to run slow (by a specified amount): *the clock loses ten minutes every day.* **17.** (of a physician) to fail to sustain the life of (a patient). **18.** (of a woman) to fail to give birth to (a viable baby), esp. as the result of a miscarriage. **19.** *Motor racing slang.* to lose control of (the car), as on a bend: *he lost it going into Woodcote.* [Old English *losian* to perish; related to Old English *-lēosan* as in *forlēosan* to forfeit. Compare LOOSE] —'**losable** *adj.* —'**losableness** *n.*

losel ('ləuzᵊl) *Archaic or dialect.* ~*n.* **1.** a worthless person. ~*adj.* **2.** (of a person) worthless, useless, or wasteful. [C14: from *losen,* from the past participle of LOSE]

lose out *vb. Informal.* **1.** (*intr., adv.*) to be defeated or unsuccessful. **2. lose out on.** to fail to secure or make use of: *we lost out on the sale.*

loser ('luːzə) *n.* **1.** a person or thing that loses. **2.** a person or thing that seems destined to be taken advantage of, fail, etc.: *a born loser.* **3.** *Bridge.* a card that will not take a trick.

losing ('luːzɪŋ) *adj.* unprofitable; failing: *the business was a losing concern.*

losings ('luːzɪŋz) *pl. n.* losses, esp. money lost in gambling.

loss (lɒs) *n.* **1.** the act or an instance of losing. **2.** the disadvantage or deprivation resulting from losing: *a loss of reputation.* **3.** the person, thing, or amount lost: *a large loss.* **4.** (*pl.*) military personnel lost by death or capture. **5.** (*sometimes pl.*) the amount by which the costs of a business transaction or operation exceed its revenue. **6.** a measure of the power lost in an electrical system expressed as the ratio of or difference between the input power and the output power. **7.** *Insurance.* **a.** an occurrence of something that has been insured against, thus giving rise to a claim by a policyholder. **b.** the amount of the resulting claim. **8. at a loss. a.** uncertain what to do; bewildered. **b.** rendered helpless (for lack of something): *at a loss for words.* **c.** at less than the cost of buying, producing, or maintaining (something): *the business ran at a loss for several years.* [C14: noun probably formed from *lost,* past participle of *losen* to perish, from Old English *lōsian* to be destroyed, from *los* destruction]

loss adjuster *n. Insurance.* a person qualified to adjust losses incurred through fire, explosion, accident, theft, natural disaster, etc., to agree the loss and the compensation to be paid.

loss leader *n.* an article offered below cost in the hope that customers attracted by it will buy other goods.

lossmaker ('lɒsˌmeɪkə) *n. Brit.* an organization, industry, or enterprise that consistently fails to make a profit. —'**lossˌmaking** *adj.*

loss ratio *n.* the ratio of the annual losses sustained to the premiums received by an insurance company.

lossy ('lɒsɪ) *adj.* (of a dielectric material, transmission line, etc.) designed to have a high attenuation; dissipating energy: *lossy line.* [C20: from LOSS]

lost (lɒst) *adj.* **1.** unable to be found or recovered. **2.** unable to find one's way or ascertain one's whereabouts. **3.** confused, bewildered, or helpless: *he is lost in discussions of theory.* **4.** (sometimes foll. by *on*) not utilized, noticed, or taken advantage of (by): *rational arguments are lost on her.* **5.** no longer possessed or existing because of defeat, misfortune, or the passage of time: *a lost art.* **6.** destroyed physically: *the lost platoon.* **7.** (foll. by *to*) no longer available or open (to). **8.** (foll. by *to*) insensible or impervious (to a sense of shame, justice, etc.). **9.** (foll. by *in*) engrossed (in): *he was lost in his book.* **10.** morally fallen: *a lost woman.* **11.** damned: *a lost soul.* **12. get lost.** (*usually imperative*) *Informal.* go away and stay away.

lost cause *n.* a cause with no chance of success.

lost tribes *pl. n.* **the.** *Old Testament.* the ten tribes deported from the N kingdom of Israel in 721 B.C. and believed never to have returned to Palestine.

lot (lɒt) *pron.* **1.** (*functioning as sing. or pl.; preceded by a*) a great number or quantity: *a lot to do; a lot of people; a lot of trouble.* ~*n.* **2.** a collection of objects, items, or people: *a nice lot of youngsters.* **3.** portion in life; destiny; fortune: *it falls to my lot to be poor.* **4.** any object, such as a straw or slip of paper, drawn from others at random to make a selection or choice (esp. in the phrase **draw** *or* **cast lots**). **5.** the use of lots in making a selection or choice (esp. in the phrase **by lot**). **6.** an assigned or apportioned share. **7.** an item or set of items for sale in an auction. **8.** *Chiefly U.S. and Canadian.* an area of land: *a parking lot.* **9.** *U.S. and Canadian.* a piece of land with fixed boundaries. **10.** *Chiefly U.S. and Canadian.* a film studio and the site on which it is located. **11. a bad lot.** an unpleasant or disreputable person. **12. cast** *or* **throw in one's lot with.** to join with voluntarily and share the fortunes of. **13. the lot.** the entire amount or number. ~*adv.* (preceded by *a*) *Informal.* **14.** to a considerable extent, degree, or amount; very much: *to delay a lot.* **15.** a great deal of the time or often: *to sing madrigals a lot.* ~*vb.* **lots, lotting, lotted. 16.** to draw lots for (something). **17.** (*tr.*) to divide (land, etc.) into lots. **18.** (*tr.*) another word for **allot.** ~See also **lots.** [Old English *hlot;* related to Old High German *lug* portion of land, Old Norse *hlutr* lot, share]

lota *or* **lotah** ('ləutə) *n.* a globular water container, usually of brass, used in India, Burma, etc. [C19: from Hindi *lotā*]

loth (ləuθ) *adj.* a variant spelling of **loath.** —'**lothness** *n.*

Lothario (ləu'θɑːrɪˌəu) *n., pl.* **-os.** (*sometimes not cap.*) a rake, libertine, or seducer. [C18: after a seducer in the tragedy *The Fair Penitent* (1703) by English dramatist Nicholas Rowe]

lotic ('ləutɪk) *adj. Ecology.* of, relating to, or designating natural communities living in rapidly flowing water. Compare **lentic.** [C20: from Latin *lotus,* a past participle of *lavāre* to wash]

lotion ('ləuʃən) *n.* a liquid preparation having a soothing, cleansing, or antiseptic action, applied to the skin, eyes, etc. [C14: via Old French from Latin *lōtiō* a washing, from *lōtus* past participle of *lavāre* to wash]

lots (lɒts) *Informal.* ~*pl. n.* **1.** (often foll. by *of*) great numbers or quantities: *lots of people; to eat lots.* ~*adv.* **2.** a great deal. **3.** (intensifier): *the journey is lots quicker by train.*

lottery ('lɒtərɪ) *n., pl.* **-teries. 1.** a game of chance in which tickets are sold, one or more of which may later qualify the holder for a prize. **2.** an activity or endeavour the success of which is regarded as a matter of fate or luck. [C16: from Old French *loterie,* from Middle Dutch *loterije.* See LOT]

lotto ('lɒtəu) *n.* **1.** Also called: **housey-housey.** a children's game in which numbered discs, counters, etc., are drawn at random and called out, while the players cover the corresponding numbers on cards, the winner being the first to cover all the numbers, a particular row, etc. Compare **bingo. 2.** *Austral.* a lottery with cash prizes based on this principle. [C18: from Italian, from Old French *lot,* from Germanic. See LOT]

lotus ('ləutəs) *n.* **1.** (in Greek mythology) a fruit that induces forgetfulness and a dreamy languor in those who eat it. **2.** the plant bearing this fruit, thought to be the date, the jujube, or any of various other plants. **3.** any of several water lilies of tropical Africa and Asia, esp. the **white lotus** (*Nymphaea lotus*), which was regarded as sacred in ancient Egypt. **4.** a related plant, *Nelumbo nucifera,* which is the sacred lotus of India, China, and Tibet: family *Nelumbonaceae.* **5.** a representation of such a plant, common in Hindu, Buddhist, and ancient Egyptian carving and decorative art. **6.** any leguminous plant of the genus *Lotus,* of the Old World and North America, having yellow, pink, or white pealike flowers. ~Also called (rare): **lotos.** [C16: via Latin from Greek *lōtos,* from Semitic; related to Hebrew *lōt* myrrh]

lotus-eater *n.* a person who lives a life of indolent ease and forgetfulness; daydreamer. [named after the people in Greek mythology who lived in indolence drugged by the fruit of the lotus]

lotus position *n.* a seated cross-legged position used in yoga, meditation, etc.

lou *or* **loo** (luː) *vb.* a Scot. word for **love.**

louche (luːʃ) *adj.* shifty or disreputable. [C19: from French, literally: squinting]

loud (laud) *adj.* **1.** (of sound) relatively great in volume: *a loud shout.* **2.** making or able to make sounds of relatively great volume: *a loud voice.* **3.** clamorous, insistent, and emphatic: *loud protests.* **4.** (of colours, designs, etc.) offensive or obtrusive to look at. **5.** characterized by noisy, vulgar, and offensive behaviour. ~*adv.* **6.** in a loud manner. **7. out loud.** audibly, as distinct from silently. [Old English *hlud;* related to Old Swedish *hlūd,* German *laut*] —'**loudly** *adv.* —'**loudness** *n.*

louden ('laudᵊn) *vb.* to make or become louder.

loud-hailer *n.* a portable loudspeaker having a built-in amplifier and microphone. Also called (U.S. and Canadian): **bullhorn.**

loudish ('laudɪʃ) *adj.* fairly loud; somewhat loud.

loudmouth ('laudˌmauθ) *n. Informal.* **1.** a person who brags or talks too loudly. **2.** a person who is gossipy or tactless. —**loud-mouthed** ('laudˌmauðd, -ˌmauθt) *adj.*

loudspeaker (ˌlaud'spiːkə) *n.* a device for converting audio-frequency signals into the equivalent sound waves by means of a vibrating conical diaphragm. Sometimes shortened to **speaker.** Also called: **reproducer.**

loudspeaker van *n.* a motor vehicle carrying a public address system. U.S. and Canadian name: **sound truck.**

lough (lɒx, lɒk) *n.* **1.** an Irish word for **lake. 2.** a long narrow bay or arm of the sea in Ireland. ~Compare **loch.** [C14: from Irish *loch* lake]

louis ('luːɪ; *French* lwi) *n., pl.* **louis** ('luːɪz; *French* lwi). short for **louis d'or.**

louis d'or (ˌluːɪ 'dɔː; *French* lwi dɔr) *n., pl.* **louis d'or** (ˌluːɪz 'dɔː; *French* lwi dɔr). **1.** a former French gold coin worth 20 francs. **2.** an old French coin minted in the reign (1610–43) of Louis XIII. ~Often shortened to **louis.** [C17: from French: golden louis, named after *Louis* XIII]

Louis Quatorze (kæ'tɔːz) *adj.* of or relating to the baroque style of furniture, decoration, and architecture of the time of Louis XIV of France (reigned 1643–1715) and characterized by massive forms and heavy ornamentation.

Louis Quinze (kænz) *adj.* of or relating to the rococo style of the furniture, decoration, and architecture of the time of Louis XV of France (reigned 1715–74).

Louis Seize (sɛz) *adj.* of or relating to the style of furniture, decoration, and architecture of the time of Louis XVI of France (reigned 1774–92), belonging to the late French rococo and early neoclassicism.

Louis Treize (trɛz) *adj.* of or relating to the style of furniture, decoration, and architecture of the time of Louis XIII of France (reigned 1610–43), with rich decorative features based on classical models.

lounge (laʊndʒ) *vb.* **1.** (*intr.*; often foll. by *about* or *around*) to sit, lie, walk, or stand in a relaxed manner. **2.** to pass (time) lazily or idly. ~*n.* **3. a.** a communal room in a hotel, ship, theatre, etc., used for waiting or relaxing in. **b.** (*as modifier*): *lounge chair.* **4.** *Chiefly Brit.* a living room in a private house. **5.** Also called: **lounge bar, saloon bar.** *Brit.* a more expensive bar in a pub or hotel. **6.** *Chiefly U.S. and Canadian.* **a.** an expensive bar, esp. in a hotel. **b.** short for **cocktail lounge. 7.** a sofa or couch, esp. one with a headrest and no back. **8.** the act or an instance of lounging. [C16: origin unknown]

lounge lizard *n. Informal.* an idle frequenter of places where rich or prominent people gather.

lounger (ˈlaʊndʒə) *n.* **1.** a comfortable sometimes adjustable couch or extending chair designed for someone to relax on. **2.** a loose comfortable leisure garment. **3.** a person who lounges.

lounge suit *n.* the customary suit of matching jacket and trousers worn by men for the normal business day.

loup[1] (luː) *n.* another name for **loo mask.** [C19: from French, from Latin *lupus* wolf]

loup[2] *or* **lowp** (laʊp) *vb., n.* a Scot. word for **leap.**

loupe (luːp) *n.* a magnifying glass used by jewellers, horologists, etc. [C20: from French (formerly an imperfect precious stone), from Old French, of obscure origin]

louping ill (ˈlaʊpɪŋ, ˈləʊ-) *n.* a viral disease of sheep causing muscular twitching and partial paralysis: caused by the bite of an infected tick (*Ixodes ricinus*). [C18 *louping,* from LOUP[2]]

lour *or* **lower** (laʊə) *vb.* (*intr.*) **1.** (esp. of the sky, weather, etc.) to be overcast, dark, and menacing. **2.** to scowl or frown. ~*n.* **3.** a menacing scowl or appearance. [C13 *louren* to scowl; compare German *lauern* to lurk] —ˈ**louring** *or* ˈ**lowering** *adj.* —ˈ**louringly** *or* ˈ**loweringly** *adv.*

lourie (ˈlaʊrɪ) *n. S. African.* any of several species of touraco: louries are divided into two groups, the arboreal species having a mainly green plumage and crimson wings and the species which inhabits the more open savanna areas having a plain grey plumage. [from Malay *luri*]

louse (laʊs) *n., pl.* **lice** (laɪs). **1.** any wingless bloodsucking insect of the order *Anoplura:* includes *Pediculus capitis* (**head louse**), *Pediculus corporis* (**body louse**), and the crab louse, all of which infest man. **2. biting** *or* **bird louse.** any wingless insect of the order *Mallophaga,* such as the chicken louse: external parasites of birds and mammals with biting mouthparts. **3.** any of various similar but unrelated insects, such as the plant louse and book louse. **4.** *pl.* **louses.** *Slang.* an unpleasant or mean person. ~*vb.* (*tr.*) **5.** to remove lice from. **6.** (foll. by *up*) *Slang.* to ruin or spoil. [Old English *lūs;* related to Old High German, Old Norse *lūs*]

louser (ˈlaʊzər) *n. Irish slang.* a mean nasty person. [C20: from *louse (up)* + -ER[1]]

lousewort (ˈlaʊsˌwɜːt) *n.* any of various N temperate scrophulariaceous plants of the genus *Pedicularis,* having spikes of white, yellow, or mauve flowers. See also **betony** (sense 3).

lousy (ˈlaʊzɪ) *adj.* **lousier, lousiest. 1.** *Slang.* very mean or unpleasant: *a lousy thing to do.* **2.** *Slang.* inferior or bad: *this is a lousy film.* **3.** infested with lice. **4.** (foll. by *with*) *Slang.* **a.** provided with an excessive amount (of): *he's lousy with money.* **b.** full of or teeming with. —ˈ**lousily** *adv.* —ˈ**lousiness** *n.*

lout[1] (laʊt) *n.* a crude or oafish person; boor. [C16: perhaps from LOUT[2]]

lout[2] (laʊt) *vb.* (*intr.*) *Archaic.* to bow or stoop. [Old English *lūtan;* related to Old Norse *lūta*]

loutish (ˈlaʊtɪʃ) *adj.* characteristic of a lout; unpleasant and uncouth. —ˈ**loutishly** *adv.* —ˈ**loutishness** *n.*

louvar (ˈluːvɑː) *n.* a large silvery whalelike scombroid fish, *Luvarus imperialis,* that occurs in most tropical and temperate seas and feeds on plankton: family *Luvaridae.* [from Italian (Calabrian and Sicilian dialect) *lùvaru,* perhaps from Latin *ruber* red]

louvre *or U.S.* **louver** (ˈluːvə) *n.* **1. a.** any of a set of horizontal parallel slats in a door or window, sloping outwards to throw off rain and admit air. **b.** Also called: **louvre boards.** the slats together with the frame supporting them. **2.** *Architect.* a lantern or turret that allows smoke to escape. [C14: from Old French *lovier,* of obscure origin]

louvred *or U.S.* **louvered** (ˈluːvəd) *adj.* (of a window, door, etc.) having louvres.

lovable *or* **loveable** (ˈlʌvəbᵊl) *adj.* attracting or deserving affection. —ˌ**lovaˈbility,** ˌ**loveaˈbility** *or* ˈ**lovableness,** ˈ**loveableness** *n.* —ˈ**lovably** *or* ˈ**loveably** *adv.*

lovage (ˈlʌvɪdʒ) *n.* **1.** a European umbelliferous plant, *Levisticum officinale,* with greenish-white flowers and aromatic fruits, which are used for flavouring food. **2.** a similar and related plant, *Ligusticum scoticum,* of N Europe. [C14 *loveache,* from Old French *luvesche,* from Late Latin *levisticum,* from Latin *ligusticum,* literally: Ligurian (plant)]

lovat (ˈlʌvət) *n.* a yellowish-green or bluish-green mixture, esp. in tweeds or woollens. [named after *Lovat,* Inverness-shire]

love (lʌv) *vb.* **1.** (*tr.*) to have a great attachment to and affection for. **2.** (*tr.*) to have passionate desire, longing, and feelings for. **3.** (*tr.*) to like or desire (to do something) very much. **4.** (*tr.*) to make love to. **5.** (*intr.*) to be in love. ~*n.* **6. a.** an intense emotion of affection, warmth, fondness, and regard towards a person or thing. **b.** (*as modifier*): *love song; love story.* **7.** a deep feeling of sexual attraction and desire. **8.** wholehearted liking for or pleasure in something. **9.** *Christianity.* **a.** God's benevolent attitude towards man. **b.** man's attitude of reverent devotion towards God. **10.** Also: **my love.** a beloved person: used esp. as an endearment. **11.** *Brit. informal.* a term of address, esp. but not necessarily for a person regarded as likable. **12.** (in tennis, squash, etc.) a score of zero. **13. fall in love.** to become in love. **14. for love.** without payment. **15. for love or money.** (*used with a negative*) in any circumstances: *I wouldn't eat a snail for love or money.* **16. for the love of.** for the sake of. **17. in love.** in a state of strong emotional attachment and usually sexual attraction. **18. make love (to). a.** to have sexual intercourse (with). **b.** *Now archaic.* to engage in courtship (with). [Old English *lufu;* related to Old High German *luba;* compare also Latin *libēre* (originally *lubēre*) to please]

love affair *n.* **1.** a romantic or sexual relationship, esp. a temporary one, between two people. **2.** a great enthusiasm or liking for something: *a love affair with ballet.*

love apple *n.* an archaic name for **tomato.**

lovebird (ˈlʌvˌbɜːd) *n.* **1.** any of several small African parrots of the genus *Agapornis,* often kept as cage birds. **2.** another name for **budgerigar. 3.** *Informal.* a lover: *the lovebirds are in the garden.*

lovebite (ˈlʌvˌbaɪt) *n.* a temporary red mark left on a person's skin by a partner's biting or sucking it during lovemaking.

love child *n. Euphemistic.* an illegitimate child; bastard.

love feast *n.* **1.** Also called: **agape.** (among the early Christians) a religious meal eaten with others as a sign of mutual love and fellowship. **2.** a ritual meal modelled upon this.

love game *n. Tennis.* a game in which the loser has a score of zero.

love-in-a-mist *n.* an erect S European ranunculaceous plant, *Nigella damascena,* cultivated as a garden plant, having finely cut leaves and white or pale blue flowers. See also **fennelflower.**

love-in-idleness *n.* another name for the **wild pansy.**

love knot *n.* a stylized bow, usually of ribbon, symbolizing the bond between two lovers. Also called: **lover's knot.**

loveless (ˈlʌvlɪs) *adj.* **1.** without love: *a loveless marriage.* **2.** receiving or giving no love. —ˈ**lovelessly** *adv.* —ˈ**lovelessness** *n.*

love letter *n.* **1.** a letter or note written by someone to his or her sweetheart or lover. **2.** (in Malaysia) a type of biscuit, made from eggs and rice flour and rolled into a cylinder.

love-lies-bleeding *n.* any of several amaranthaceous plants of the genus *Amaranthus,* esp. *A. caudatus,* having drooping spikes of small red flowers.

love life *n.* the part of a person's life consisting of his or her sexual relationships.

lovelock (ˈlʌvˌlɒk) *n.* a long lock of hair worn on the forehead.

lovelorn (ˈlʌvˌlɔːn) *adj.* miserable because of unrequited love or unhappiness in love. —ˈ**loveˌlornness** *n.*

lovely (ˈlʌvlɪ) *adj.* **-lier, -liest. 1.** very attractive or beautiful. **2.** highly pleasing or enjoyable: *a lovely time.* **3.** loving and attentive. **4.** inspiring love; lovable. ~*n.* **5.** *Slang.* a lovely woman. —ˈ**loveliness** *n.*

lovemaking (ˈlʌvˌmeɪkɪŋ) *n.* **1.** sexual play and activity between lovers, esp. including sexual intercourse. **2.** an archaic word for **courtship.**

love match *n.* a betrothal or marriage based on mutual love rather than any other considerations.

love nest *n.* a place suitable for or used for making love.

love potion *n.* any drink supposed to arouse sexual love in the one who drinks it.

lover (ˈlʌvə) *n.* **1.** a person, now esp. a man, who has an extramarital or premarital sexual relationship with another person. **2.** (*often pl.*) either of the two people involved in a love affair. **3. a.** someone who loves a specified person or thing: *a lover of music.* **b.** (*in combination*): *a music-lover; a cat-lover.*

love seat *n.* a small upholstered sofa for two people.

love set *n. Tennis.* a set in which the loser has a score of zero.

lovesick (ˈlʌvˌsɪk) *adj.* pining or languishing because of love. —ˈ**loveˌsickness** *n.*

lovey (ˈlʌvɪ) *n. Brit. informal.* another word for **love** (sense 11).

lovey-dovey *adj.* making an excessive or ostentatious display of affection.

loving (ˈlʌvɪŋ) *adj.* feeling, showing, or indicating love and affection. —ˈ**lovingly** *adv.* —ˈ**lovingness** *n.*

loving cup *n.* **1.** a large vessel, usually two-handled, out of which people drink in turn at a banquet. **2.** a similar cup awarded to the winner of a competition.

low[1] (ləʊ) *adj.* **1.** having a relatively small distance from base to top; not tall or high: *a low hill; a low building.* **2. a.** situated at a relatively short distance above the ground, sea level, the horizon, or other reference position: *low cloud.* **b.** (*in combination*): *low-lying.* **3. a.** involving or containing a relatively small amount of something: *a low supply.* **b.** (*in combination*): *low-pressure.* **4. a.** having little value or quality. **b.** (*in combination*): *low-grade.* **5.** of less than the usual or expected height, depth, or degree: *low temperature.* **6. a.** (of numbers) small. **b.** (of measurements) expressed in small numbers. **7.** unfavourable: *a low opinion.* **8.** not advanced in evolution: *a low form of plant life.* **9.** deep: *a low obeisance.* **10.** coarse or vulgar: *a low conversation.* **11. a.** inferior in culture or status. **b.** (*in combination*): *low-class.* **12.** in a physically or mentally depressed or weakened state. **13.** designed so as to reveal the wearer's neck and part of the bosom: *a low neckline.* **14.** with a hushed tone; quiet or soft: *a low whisper.* **15.** of relatively small price or monetary value: *low cost.* **16.** *Music.* relating to or characterized by a relatively low pitch. **17.** (of latitudes) situated not far north or south of the equator. **18.** having little or no money. **19.** abject or servile. **20.** *Phonetics.* of, relating to, or denoting a vowel whose articulation is produced by moving the back of the tongue away from the soft palate or the blade away from the hard palate, such as for the *a* in English *father.* Compare **high** (sense 22). **21.** (of a gear) providing a relatively low forward speed for a given engine speed. **22.** (*usually cap.*) of or relating to the Low Church. *~adv.* **23.** in a low position, level, degree, intensity, etc.: *to bring someone low.* **24.** at a low pitch; deep: *to sing low.* **25.** at a low price; cheaply: *to buy low.* **26. lay low. a.** to cause to fall by a blow. **b.** to overcome, defeat or destroy. **27. lie low. a.** to keep or be concealed or quiet. **b.** to wait for a favourable opportunity. *~n.* **28.** a low position, level, or degree: *an all-time low.* **29.** an area of relatively low atmospheric pressure, esp. a depression. **30.** *Electronics.* the voltage level in a logic circuit corresponding to logical zero. Compare **high** (sense 40). [C12 *lāh,* from Old Norse *lāgr;* related to Old Frisian *lēch* low, Dutch *laag*] —ˈ**lowness** *n.*

low[2] (ləʊ) *n. also* **lowing. 1.** the sound uttered by cattle; moo. *~vb.* **2.** to make or express by a low or moo. [Old English *hlōwan;* related to Dutch *loeien,* Old Saxon *hlōian*]

lowan (ˈləʊən) *n. Austral.* another name for **mallee fowl.**

lowborn (ˌləʊˈbɔːn) *or* **lowbred** (ˌləʊˈbrɛd) *adj. Now rare.* of ignoble or common parentage; not royal or noble.

lowboy (ˈləʊˌbɔɪ) *n. U.S. and Canadian.* a table fitted with drawers.

lowbrow (ˈləʊˌbraʊ) *Disparaging.* *~n.* **1.** a person who has uncultivated or nonintellectual tastes. *~adj. also* **lowbrowed. 2.** of or characteristic of such a person. —ˈ**low**ˌ**browism** *n.*

low camp *n.* an unsophisticated form of **camp** (the style).

low-carbon steel *n. Engineering.* steel containing between 0.04 and 0.25 per cent carbon.

Low Church *n.* **1.** the school of thought in the Church of England stressing evangelical beliefs and practices. Compare **Broad Church, High Church.** *~adj.* **Low-Church. 2.** of or relating to this school. —ˌ**Low-**ˈ**Churchman** *n.*

low comedy *n.* comedy characterized by slapstick and physical action. —**low comedian** *n.*

low-density lipoprotein *n.* a lipoprotein that is the form in which cholesterol is transported in the bloodstream to the cells and tissues of the body. High levels of low-density lipoprotein in the blood are associated with atheroma. Abbrev.: **LDL.**

low-down *Informal.* *~adj.* **1.** mean, underhand, or despicable. *~n.* **lowdown. 2.** information, esp. secret or true information.

lower[1] (ˈləʊə) *adj.* **1.** being below one or more other things: *the lower shelf; the lower animals.* **2.** reduced in amount or value: *a lower price.* **3.** *Maths.* (of a limit or bound) less than or equal to one or more numbers or variables. **4.** (*sometimes cap.*) *Geology.* denoting the early part or division of a period, system, formation, etc.: *Lower Silurian.* *~vb.* **5.** (*tr.*) to cause to become low or on a lower level; bring, put, or cause to move down. **6.** (*tr.*) to reduce or bring down in estimation, dignity, value, etc.: *to lower oneself.* **7.** to reduce or be reduced: *to lower one's confidence.* **8.** (*tr.*) to make quieter: *to lower the radio.* **9.** (*tr.*) to reduce the pitch of. **10.** (*tr.*) *Phonetics.* to modify the articulation of (a vowel) by bringing the tongue further away from the roof of the mouth. **11.** (*intr.*) to diminish or become less. [C12 (comparative of LOW[1]); C17 (vb.)] —ˈ**lowerable** *adj.*

lower[2] (ˈlaʊə) *vb.* a variant spelling of **lour.**

lower case *n.* **1.** the bottom half of a compositor's type case, in which the small letters are kept. *~adj.* **lower-case. 2.** of or relating to small letters. *~vb.* **lower-case. 3.** (*tr.*) to print with lower-case letters.

lower class *n.* **1.** the social stratum having the lowest position in the social hierarchy. Compare **middle class, upper class, working class.** *~adj.* **lower-class. 2.** of or relating to the lower class. **3.** inferior or vulgar.

lowerclassman (ˌləʊəˈklɑːsmən) *n., pl.* **-men.** *U.S.* a freshman or sophomore. Also called: **underclassman.**

lower criticism *n.* textual criticism, esp. the study of the extant manuscripts of the Scriptures in order to establish the original text. Compare **higher criticism.**

lower deck *n.* **1.** the deck of a ship situated immediately above the hold. **2.** *Informal.* the petty officers and seamen of a ship collectively.

lower house *n.* one of the two houses of a bicameral legislature: usually the larger and more representative house. Also called: **lower chamber.** Compare **upper house.**

lower mordent *n.* another term for **mordent.**

lowermost (ˈləʊəˌməʊst) *adj.* lowest.

Lower Palaeolithic *n.* **1.** the earliest of the three sections of the Palaeolithic, beginning about 3 million years ago and ending about 70 000 B.C. with the emergence of Neanderthal man. *~adj.* **2.** of or relating to this period.

lower regions *pl. n.* (usually preceded by *the*) hell.

lower school *n.* the younger pupils in a secondary school, usually those in the first three or four year groups.

lower world *n.* **1.** the earth as opposed to heaven or the spiritual world. **2.** another name for **hell.**

lowest common denominator *n.* the smallest integer or polynomial that is exactly divisible by each denominator of a set of fractions. Abbrevs.: **LCD, lcd.** Also called: **least common denominator.**

lowest common multiple *n.* the smallest number or quantity that is exactly divisible by each member of a set of numbers or quantities. Abbrevs.: **LCM, lcm.** Also called: **least common multiple.**

low explosive *n.* an explosive of relatively low power, as used in firearms.

low frequency *n.* a radio-frequency band or a frequency lying between 300 and 30 kilohertz. Abbrev.: **LF.**

Low German *n.* a language of N Germany, spoken esp. in rural areas: more closely related to Dutch than to standard High German. Also called: **Plattdeutsch.** Abbrev.: **LG.**

low-key *or* **low-keyed** *adj.* **1.** having a low intensity or tone. **2.** restrained, subdued, or understated. **3.** (of a photograph, painting, etc.) having a predominance of dark grey tones or dark colours with few highlights. Compare **high-key.**

lowland (ˈləʊlənd) *n.* **1.** relatively low ground. **2.** (*often pl.*) a low generally flat region. *~adj.* **3.** of or relating to a lowland or lowlands. —ˈ**lowlander** *n.*

Lowland (ˈləʊlənd) *n.* (*modifier*) of or relating to the Lowlands, a generally flat region of central Scotland, or the dialect of English spoken there.

Lowlander (ˈləʊləndə) *n.* a native or inhabitant of the Lowlands of Scotland.

Low Latin *n.* any form or dialect of Latin other than the classical, such as Vulgar or Medieval Latin.

low-level language *n.* a computer programming language that is closer to machine language than to human language. Compare **high-level language.**

low-level waste *n.* waste material contaminated by traces of radioactivity that can be disposed of in steel drums in concrete-lined trenches but not (since 1983) in the sea. Compare **high-level waste, intermediate-level waste.**

lowlife (ˈləʊˌlaɪf) *n., pl.* **-lifes.** *Slang.* **a.** a member or members of the underworld. **b.** (*as modifier*): *his lowlife friends.*

low-loader *n.* a road or rail vehicle for heavy loads with a low platform for ease of access.

lowly (ˈləʊlɪ) *Now rare.* *~adj.* **-lier, -liest. 1.** humble or low in position, rank, status, etc. **2.** full of humility; meek. **3.** simple, unpretentious, or plain. *~adv.* **4.** in a low or lowly manner. —ˈ**lowliness** *n.*

Low Mass *n.* a Mass that has a simplified ceremonial form and is spoken rather than sung. Compare **High Mass.**

low-minded *adj.* having a vulgar or crude mind and character. —ˌ**low-**ˈ**mindedly** *adv.* —ˌ**low-**ˈ**mindedness** *n.*

low-necked *adj.* (of a woman's garment) having a low neckline.

lowp (laʊp) *vb., n. Scot.* a variant spelling of **loup**[2].

low-pass filter *n. Electronics.* a filter that transmits all frequencies below a specified value, substantially attenuating frequencies above this value. Compare **high-pass filter, band-pass filter.**

low-pitched *adj.* **1.** pitched low in tone. **2.** (of a roof) having sides with a shallow slope.

low-pressure *adj.* **1.** having, using, or involving a pressure below normal: *a low-pressure gas.* **2.** relaxed or calm.

low profile *n.* **1. a.** a position or attitude characterized by a deliberate avoidance of prominence or publicity. **b.** (*as modifier*): *a low-profile approach.* *~adj.* **low-profile. 2.** (of a tyre) wide in relation to its height. ~Compare **high profile.**

low relief *n.* another term for **bas-relief.**

low-rise *adj.* **1.** of or relating to a building having only a few storeys. Compare **high-rise.** *~n.* **2.** such a building.

lowry *or* **lowrie** (ˈlaʊrɪ) *n.* another name for **lory.**

lowse (laʊz, laʊs) *Scot.* *~adj.* **1.** loose. *~vb.* **2.** (*tr.*) to release; loose. **3.** (*intr.*) to finish work. **4. lowsing time.** the time at which work or school finishes; knocking-off time. [a Scot. variant of LOOSE]

low-spirited *adj.* depressed, dejected, or miserable. —ˌ**low-**ˈ**spiritedly** *adv.* —ˌ**low-**ˈ**spiritedness** *n.*

Low Sunday *n.* the Sunday after Easter. [probably so named because of its relative unimportance in contrast with Easter Sunday]

low tech *n.* **1.** short for **low technology. 2.** a style of interior design using items associated with low technology. *~adj.* **low-tech. 3.** of or using low technology. **4.** of or in the interior design style. ~Compare **hi tech.**

low technology *n.* simple unsophisticated technology, often that used for centuries, that is limited to the production of basic necessities.

low-tension *adj.* subjected to, carrying, or capable of operating at a low voltage. Abbrev.: **LT.**

low tide *n.* **1.** the tide when it is at its lowest level or the time at which it reaches this. **2.** a lowest point.

low-velocity zone *n.* a layer or zone in the earth in which the velocity of seismic waves is slightly lower than in the layers above and below. The asthenosphere is thought to be such a zone. See **asthenosphere.**

low water *n.* **1.** another name for **low tide** (sense 1). **2.** the state of any stretch of water at its lowest level. **3.** a situation of difficulty or point of least success, excellence, etc.

low-water mark *n.* **1.** the level reached by seawater at low tide or by other stretches of water at their lowest level. **2.** the lowest point or level; nadir.

lox[1] (lɒks) *n.* a kind of smoked salmon. [C19: from Yiddish *laks,* from Middle High German *lahs* salmon]

lox[2] (lɒks) *n.* short for **liquid oxygen,** esp. when used as an oxidizer for rocket fuels.

loxodromic (ˌlɒksəˈdrɒmɪk) *or* **loxodromical** *adj.* of or relating to rhumb lines or to map projections on which rhumb lines appear straight, as on a Mercator projection. [C17: from Greek *loxos* oblique + *dromikos* relating to a course] —ˌ**loxoˈdromically** *adv.*

loxodromics (ˌlɒksəˈdrɒmɪks) *or* **loxodromy** (lɒkˈsɒdrəmɪ) *n.* *(functioning as sing.)* the technique of navigating using rhumb lines.

loy (lɔɪ) *n. Irish.* a narrow spade with a single footrest. [C18: from Irish Gaelic *láí*]

loyal (ˈlɔɪəl) *adj.* **1.** having or showing continuing allegiance. **2.** faithful to one's country, government, etc. **3.** of or expressing loyalty. [C16: from Old French *loial, leial,* from Latin *lēgālis* LEGAL] —ˈ**loyally** *adv.* —ˈ**loyalness** *n.*

loyalist (ˈlɔɪəlɪst) *n.* a patriotic supporter of his sovereign or government. —ˈ**loyalism** *n.*

Loyalist (ˈlɔɪəlɪst) *n.* **1.** (in Northern Ireland) any of the Protestants wishing to retain Ulster's link with Britain. **2.** (in North America) an American colonist who supported Britain during the War of American Independence. **3.** (during the Spanish Civil War) a supporter of the republican government.

loyalty (ˈlɔɪəltɪ) *n., pl.* **-ties. 1.** the state or quality of being loyal. **2.** *(often pl.)* a feeling of allegiance.

lozenge (ˈlɒzɪndʒ) *n.* **1.** Also called: **pastille, troche.** *Med.* a medicated tablet held in the mouth until it has dissolved. **2.** *Geometry.* another name for **rhombus. 3.** *Heraldry.* a diamond-shaped charge. [C14: from Old French *losange* of Gaulish origin; compare Vulgar Latin *lausa* flat stone]

lozenged (ˈlɒzɪndʒd) *adj.* decorated with lozenges.

lozengy (ˈlɒzɪndʒɪ) *adj.* *(usually postpositive) Heraldry.* divided by diagonal lines to form a lattice.

Lozi (ˈləʊzɪ) *n.* the language of the Barotse people of Zambia, belonging to the Bantu group of the Niger-Congo family.

LP[1] *n.* **a.** Also called: **long player.** a long-playing gramophone record: usually one 12 inches (30 cm) or 10 inches (25 cm) in diameter, designed to rotate at 33⅓ revolutions per minute. Compare **EP. b.** *(as modifier): an LP sleeve.*

LP[2] *abbrev. for* **1.** (in Britain) Lord Provost. **2.** Also: **lp.** low pressure.

L/P *Printing. abbrev. for* letterpress.

LPG *abbrev. for* liquefied petroleum gas.

L-plate *n. Brit.* a white rectangle with a red "L" sign fixed to the back and front of a motor vehicle to show that a driver using it may be a learner who has not passed the driving test.

LPO *abbrev. for* London Philharmonic Orchestra.

L'pool *abbrev. for* Liverpool.

LPS (in Britain) *abbrev. for* Lord Privy Seal.

Lr *the chemical symbol for* lawrencium.

LRSC *abbrev. for* Licentiate of the Royal Society of Chemistry.

ls (on a document) the place of the seal. [from Latin *locus sigilli*]

LS *international car registration for* Lesotho.

LSD *n.* lysergic acid diethylamide; a crystalline compound prepared from lysergic acid, used in experimental medicine and taken illegally as a hallucinogenic drug. Informal name (as an illegal hallucinogen): **acid.**

L.S.D., £.s.d., *or* **l.s.d.** (in Britain, esp. formerly) *abbrev. for* librae, solidi, denarii. [Latin: pounds, shillings, pence]

LSE *abbrev. for* London School of Economics.

LSI *Electronics. abbrev. for* large scale integration.

LSO *abbrev. for* London Symphony Orchestra.

LSZ (in New Zealand) *abbrev. for* limited speed zone.

lt *abbrev. for:* **1.** long ton. **2.** (esp. in the U.S.) local time.

Lt *abbrev. for* Lieutenant.

LT *abbrev. for* low-tension.

LTA *abbrev. for* Lawn Tennis Association.

Lt Cdr *abbrev. for* lieutenant commander.

Lt Col *abbrev. for* lieutenant colonel.

Ltd *or* **ltd** (esp. after the names of British business organizations) *abbrev. for* limited (liability). U.S. equivalent: **Inc.**

Lt Gen *abbrev. for* lieutenant general.

Lt Gov *abbrev. for* lieutenant governor.

Lu *the chemical symbol for* lutetium.

LU *Physics. abbrev. for* loudness unit.

luach (ˈlʊɑx) *n. Judaism.* a calendar that shows the dates of festivals and, usually, the times of start and finish of the Sabbath.

luau (luːˈaʊ, ˈluːaʊ) *n.* **1.** a feast of Hawaiian food. **2.** a dish of taro leaves usually prepared with coconut cream and octopus or chicken. [from Hawaiian *lu'au*]

Luba (ˈluːbə) *n.* **1.** *(pl.* **Luba)** a member of a Negroid people of Africa living chiefly in Shaba province of Zaïre. **2.** Also called: **Tshiluba.** the language of this people, belonging to the Bantu group of the Niger-Congo family.

lubber (ˈlʌbə) *n.* **1.** a big, awkward, or stupid person. **2.** short for **landlubber.** [C14 *lobre,* probably from Scandinavian. See LOB[1]] —ˈ**lubberly** *adj., adv.* —ˈ**lubberliness** *n.*

lubber line *n.* a mark on a ship's compass that designates the fore-and-aft axis of the vessel. Also called: **lubber's line.**

lubber's hole *n. Nautical.* a hole in a top or platform on a mast through which a sailor can climb.

lubra (ˈluːbrə) *n. Austral.* an Aboriginal woman. [C19: from a native Australian language]

lubricant (ˈluːbrɪkənt) *n.* **1.** a lubricating substance, such as oil. ~*adj.* **2.** serving to lubricate. [C19: from Latin *lūbricāns,* present participle of *lūbricāre.* See LUBRICATE]

lubricate (ˈluːbrɪˌkeɪt) *vb.* **1.** *(tr.)* to cover or treat with an oily or greasy substance so as to lessen friction. **2.** *(tr.)* to make greasy, slippery, or smooth. **3.** *(intr.)* to act as a lubricant. [C17: from Latin *lūbricāre,* from *lūbricus* slippery] —ˌ**lubriˈcation** *n.* —ˌ**lubriˈcational** *adj.* —ˈ**lubriˌcative** *adj.*

lubricator (ˈluːbrɪˌkeɪtə) *n.* **1.** a person or thing that lubricates. **2.** a device for applying lubricant.

lubricious (luːˈbrɪʃəs) *or* **lubricous** (ˈluːbrɪkəs) *adj.* **1.** *Formal or literary.* lewd, lascivious. **2.** *Rare.* oily or slippery. [C16: from Latin *lūbricus*] —**luˈbriciously** *or* ˈ**lubricously** *adv.*

lubricity (luːˈbrɪsɪtɪ) *n.* **1.** *Formal or literary.* lewdness or salaciousness. **2.** *Rare.* smoothness or slipperiness. **3.** capacity to lubricate. [C15 (lewdness), C17 (slipperiness): from Old French *lubricité,* from Medieval Latin *lubricitās,* from Latin, from *lūbricus* slippery]

lubritorium (ˌluːbrɪˈtɔːrɪəm) *n., pl.* **-ria** (-rɪə). *Chiefly U.S.* a place, as in a service station, for the lubrication of motor vehicles. [C20: from LUBRICATE + *-orium,* as in *sanatorium*]

Lucan (ˈluːkən) *adj.* of or relating to St. Luke or St. Luke's gospel.

lucarne (luːˈkɑːn) *n.* a type of dormer window. [C16: from French, from Provençal *lucana,* of obscure origin]

luce (luːs) *n.* another name for the **pike** (the fish). [C14: from Old French *lus,* from Late Latin *lūcius* pike]

lucent (ˈluːsᵊnt) *adj.* brilliant, shining, or translucent. [C16: from Latin *lūcēns,* present participle of *lūcēre* to shine] —ˈ**lucently** *adv.*

lucerne (luːˈsɜːn) *n. Brit.* another name for **alfalfa.**

lucid (ˈluːsɪd) *adj.* **1.** readily understood; clear. **2.** shining or glowing. **3.** *Psychiatry.* of or relating to a period of normality between periods of insane or irresponsible behaviour. [C16: from Latin *lūcidus* full of light, from *lūx* light] —**luˈcidity** *or* ˈ**lucidness** *n.* —ˈ**lucidly** *adv.*

lucifer (ˈluːsɪfə) *n.* a friction match: originally a trade name for a match manufactured in England in the 19th century.

Lucifer (ˈluːsɪfə) *n.* **1.** the leader of the rebellion of the angels: usually identified with Satan. **2.** the planet Venus when it rises as the morning star. [Old English, from Latin *Lūcifer,* light-bearer, from *lūx* light + *ferre* to bear]

luciferin (luːˈsɪfərɪn) *n. Biochem.* a substance occurring in bioluminescent organisms, such as glow-worms and fireflies. It undergoes an enzyme-catalysed oxidation and emits light on decaying to its ground state. [C20: from Latin *lucifer* (literally: light-bearer) + -IN]

luciferous (luːˈsɪfərəs) *adj. Rare.* bringing or giving light.

lucifugous (luːˈsɪfjʊgəs) *adj.* avoiding light. [C17: from Latin *lucifugus,* from *lux* (genitive *lūcis*) light + *fugere* to flee + -OUS]

luck (lʌk) *n.* **1.** events that are beyond control and seem subject to chance; fortune. **2.** success or good fortune. **3.** something considered to bring good luck. **4. down on one's luck.** having little or no good luck to the point of suffering hardships. **5. no such luck.** *Informal.* unfortunately not. **6. try one's luck.** to attempt something that is uncertain. ~*vb.* **7.** *(intr.;* foll. by *out) U.S. and Canadian informal.* to succeed with (something). [C15: from Middle Dutch *luc;* related to Middle High German *gelücke,* late Old Norse *lukka, lykka*]

luckless (ˈlʌklɪs) *adj.* having no luck; unlucky. —ˈ**lucklessly** *adv.* —ˈ**lucklessness** *n.*

luckpenny (ˈlʌkˌpɛnɪ) *n., pl.* **-nies.** *Brit.* **1.** a coin kept for luck. **2.** a small amount of money returned for luck by a seller to a customer.

lucky (ˈlʌkɪ) *adj.* **luckier, luckiest. 1.** having or bringing good fortune. **2.** happening by chance, esp. as desired. —ˈ**luckily** *adv.* —ˈ**luckiness** *n.*

lucky dip *n. Brit.* **1.** a barrel or box filled with sawdust and small prizes for which children search. **2.** *Informal.* an undertaking of uncertain outcome.

lucrative (ˈluːkrətɪv) *adj.* producing a profit; profitable; remunerative. [C15: from Old French *lucratif;* see LUCRE] —ˈ**lucratively** *adv.* —ˈ**lucrativeness** *n.*

lucre (ˈluːkə) *n. Usually facetious.* money or wealth (esp. in the phrase **filthy lucre**). [C14: from Latin *lūcrum* gain; related to Old English *lēan* reward, German *Lohn* wages]

Lucretian (luːˈkriːʃən) *adj.* denoting or relating to the style of Titus Lucretius Carus. (?96–55 B.C.), Roman poet and philosopher.

lucubrate (ˈluːkjʊˌbreɪt) *vb. (intr.)* to write or study, esp. at night. [C17: from Latin *lūcubrāre* to work by lamplight] —ˈ**lucuˌbrator** *n.*

lucubration (ˌluːkjʊˈbreɪʃən) *n.* **1.** laborious study, esp. at night. **2.** (*often pl.*) a solemn literary work.
luculent (ˈluːkjʊlənt) *adj. Rare.* **1.** easily understood; lucid. **2.** bright or shining; glowing. [C15: from Latin *lūculentus* full of light, from *lūx* light] —ˈ**luculently** *adv.*
lud (lʌd) *Brit.* ~*n.* **1.** lord (in the phrase **my lud, m'lud**): used when addressing a judge in court. ~*interj.* **2.** *Archaic.* an exclamation of dismay or surprise.
Luddite (ˈlʌdaɪt) *n. English history.* **1.** any of the textile workers opposed to mechanization who rioted and organized machine-breaking between 1811 and 1816. **2.** any opponent of industrial change or innovation. ~*adj.* **3.** of or relating to the Luddites. [C19: alleged to be named after Ned *Ludd,* an 18th-century Leicestershire workman, who destroyed industrial machinery] —ˈ**Luddism** *n.*
luderick (ˈluːdərɪk) *n.* an estuarine and rock fish, *Girella tricuspidata,* of Australia, usually black or dark brown in colour: a kind of blackfish. [C19: from a native Australian language]
ludicrous (ˈluːdɪkrəs) *adj.* absurd or incongruous to the point of provoking ridicule or laughter. [C17: from Latin *lūdicrus* done in sport, from *lūdus* game; related to *lūdere* to play] —ˈ**ludicrously** *adv.* —ˈ**ludicrousness** *n.*
Ludlow (ˈlʌdləʊ) *n. Trademark.* a machine for casting type from matrices set by hand, used esp. for headlines.
ludo (ˈluːdəʊ) *n. Brit.* a simple board game in which players advance counters by throwing dice. [C19: from Latin: I play]
lues (ˈluːiːz) *n., pl.* **lues.** *Rare.* **1.** any venereal disease. **2.** a pestilence. [C17: from New Latin, from Latin: calamity] —**luetic** (luːˈɛtɪk) *adj.* —**luˈetically** *adv.*
luff (lʌf) *n.* **1.** *Nautical.* the leading edge of a fore-and-aft sail. ~*vb.* **2.** *Nautical.* to head (a sailing vessel) into the wind so that her sails flap. **3.** (*intr.*) *Nautical.* (of a sail) to flap when the wind is blowing equally on both sides. **4.** to move the jib of (a crane) or raise or lower the boom of (a derrick) in order to shift a load. [C13 (in the sense: steering gear): from Old French *lof,* perhaps from Middle Dutch *loef* peg of a tiller; compare Old High German *laffa* palm of hand, oar blade, Russian *lapa* paw]
luffa (ˈlʌfə) *n.* **1.** any tropical climbing plant of the cucurbitaceous genus *Luffa,* esp. the dishcloth gourd. **2.** *U.S.* another name for **loofah.**
lug[1] (lʌg) *vb.* **lugs, lugging, lugged. 1.** to carry or drag (something heavy) with great effort. **2.** (*tr.*) to introduce (an irrelevant topic) into a conversation or discussion. **3.** (*tr.*) (of a sailing vessel) to carry too much (sail) for the amount of wind blowing. ~*n.* **4.** the act or an instance of lugging. [C14: probably from Scandinavian; apparently related to Norwegian *lugge* to pull by the hair]
lug[2] (lʌg) *n.* **1.** a projecting piece by which something is connected, supported, or lifted. **2.** Also called: **tug.** a leather loop used in harness for various purposes. **3.** a box or basket for vegetables or fruit with a capacity of 28 to 40 pounds. **4.** *Informal or Scot.* another word for **ear. 5.** *Slang.* a man, esp. a stupid or awkward one. [C15 (Scots dialect) *lugge* ear, perhaps related to LUG[1] (in the sense: to pull by the ear)]
lug[3] (lʌg) *n. Nautical.* short for **lugsail.**
lug[4] (lʌg) *n.* short for **lugworm.** [C16: origin uncertain]
Luganda (luːˈgændə, -ˈgɑːndə) *n.* the language of the Buganda, spoken chiefly in Uganda, belonging to the Bantu group of the Niger-Congo family.
luge (luːʒ) *n.* **1.** a racing toboggan on which riders lie on their backs, descending feet first. ~*vb.* (*intr.*) **2.** to ride on a luge. [C20: from French]
Luger (ˈluːgə) *n. Trademark.* a German 9 mm calibre automatic pistol.
luggage (ˈlʌgɪdʒ) *n.* suitcases, trunks, etc., containing personal belongings for a journey; baggage. [C16: perhaps from LUG[1], influenced in form by BAGGAGE]
luggage van *n. Brit.* a railway carriage used to transport passengers' luggage, bicycles, etc. U.S. and Canadian name: **baggage car.**
lugger (ˈlʌgə) *n. Nautical.* a small working boat rigged with a lugsail. [C18: from LUGSAIL]
lughole (ˈlʌgˌhəʊl) *n. Brit.* an informal word for **ear**[1]. See also **lug**[2] (sense 4).
lugsail (ˈlʌgsəl) *or* **lug** (lʌg) *n. Nautical.* a four-sided sail bent and hoisted on a yard. [C17: perhaps from Middle English (now dialect) *lugge* pole, or from *lugge* ear]
lug screw *n.* a small screw without a head.
lugubrious (lʊˈguːbrɪəs) *adj.* excessively mournful; doleful. [C17: from Latin *lūgubris* mournful, from *lūgēre* to grieve] —**luˈgubriously** *adv.* —**luˈgubriousness** *n.*
lugworm (ˈlʌgˌwɜːm) *n.* any polychaete worm of the genus *Arenicola,* living in burrows on sandy shores and having tufted gills: much used as bait by fishermen. Sometimes shortened to **lug.** Also called: **lobworm.** [C17: of uncertain origin]
lug wrench *n.* a spanner with a lug or lugs projecting from its jaws to engage the component to be rotated.
lukewarm (ˌluːkˈwɔːm) *adj.* **1.** (esp. of water) moderately warm; tepid. **2.** having or expressing little enthusiasm or conviction. [C14 *luke* probably from Old English *hlēow* warm; compare German *lauwarm*] —ˌ**lukeˈwarmly** *adv.* —ˌ**lukeˈwarmness** *n.*
lull (lʌl) *vb.* **1.** to soothe (a person or animal) by soft sounds or motions (esp. in the phrase **lull to sleep**). **2.** to calm (someone or someone's fears, suspicions, etc.), esp. by deception. ~*n.* **3.** a short period of calm or diminished activity. [C14: possibly imitative of crooning sounds; related to Middle Low German *lollen* to soothe, Middle Dutch *lollen* to talk drowsily, mumble] —ˈ**lulling** *adj.*
lullaby (ˈlʌləˌbaɪ) *n., pl.* **-bies. 1.** a quiet song to lull a child to sleep. **2.** the music for such a song. ~*vb.* **-bies, -bying, -bied. 3.** (*tr.*) to quiet or soothe with or as if with a lullaby. [C16: perhaps a blend of LULL + GOODBYE]
lulu (ˈluːluː) *n. Slang.* a person or thing considered to be outstanding in size, appearance, etc. [C19: probably from the nickname for *Louise*]
lum (lʌm) *n. Scot.* a chimney. [C17: of obscure origin]
lumbago (lʌmˈbeɪgəʊ) *n.* pain in the lower back; backache affecting the lumbar region. [C17: from Late Latin *lumbāgo,* from Latin *lumbus* loin]
lumbar (ˈlʌmbə) *adj.* of, near, or relating to the part of the body between the lowest ribs and the hipbones. [C17: from New Latin *lumbāris,* from Latin *lumbus* loin]
lumbar puncture *n. Med.* insertion of a hollow needle into the lower region of the spinal cord to withdraw cerebrospinal fluid, introduce drugs, etc.
lumber[1] (ˈlʌmbə) *n.* **1.** *Chiefly U.S. and Canadian.* **a.** logs; sawn timber. **b.** cut timber, esp. when sawn and dressed ready for use in joinery, carpentry, etc. **c.** (*as modifier*): *the lumber trade.* **2.** *Brit.* **a.** useless household articles that are stored away. **b.** (*as modifier*): *lumber room.* ~*vb.* **3.** (*tr.*) to pile together in a disorderly manner. **4.** (*tr.*) to fill up or encumber with useless household articles. **5.** *Chiefly U.S. and Canadian.* to convert (the trees) of (a forest) into marketable timber. **6.** (*tr.*) *Brit. informal.* to burden with something unpleasant, tedious, etc. **7.** (*tr.*) *Austral.* to arrest; imprison. [C17: perhaps from a noun use of LUMBER[2]] —ˈ**lumberer** *n.*
lumber[2] (ˈlʌmbə) *vb.* (*intr.*) **1.** to move or proceed in an awkward heavy manner. **2.** an obsolete word for **rumble.** [C14 *lomeren;* perhaps related to *lome* LAME, Swedish dialect *loma* to move ponderously]
lumbering[1] (ˈlʌmbərɪŋ) *n. Chiefly U.S. and Canadian.* the business or trade of cutting, transporting, preparing, or selling timber.
lumbering[2] (ˈlʌmbərɪŋ) *adj.* **1.** awkward or heavy in movement. **2.** moving with a rumbling sound. —ˈ**lumberingly** *adv.* —ˈ**lumberingness** *n.*
lumberjack (ˈlʌmbəˌdʒæk) *n.* (esp. in North America) a person whose work involves felling trees, transporting the timber, etc. [C19: from LUMBER[1] + JACK[1] (man)]
lumberjacket (ˈlʌmbəˌdʒækɪt) *n.* a boldly coloured, usually checked jacket in warm cloth, as worn by lumberjacks. U.S. name: **lumberjack.**
lumberyard (ˈlʌmbəˌjɑːd) *n.* the U.S. and Canadian word for **timberyard.**
lumbricalis (ˌlʌmbrɪˈkeɪlɪs) *n. Anatomy.* any of the four wormlike muscles in the hand or foot. [C18: New Latin, from Latin *lumbrīcus* worm] —**lumbrical** (ˈlʌmbrɪk[ə]l) *adj.*
lumbricoid (ˈlʌmbrɪˌkɔɪd) *adj.* **1.** *Anatomy.* designating any part or structure resembling a worm. **2.** of, relating to, or resembling an earthworm. [C19: from New Latin *lumbricoides,* from Latin *lumbrīcus* worm]
lumen (ˈluːmɪn) *n., pl.* **-mens** *or* **-mina** (-mɪnə). **1.** the derived SI unit of luminous flux; the flux emitted in a solid angle of 1 steradian by a point source having a uniform intensity of 1 candela. Symbol: lm **2.** *Anatomy.* a passage, duct, or cavity in a tubular organ. **3.** a cavity within a plant cell enclosed by the cell walls. [C19: New Latin, from Latin: light, aperture] —ˈ**lumenal** *or* ˈ**luminal** *adj.*
lum-hat (ˌlʌmˈhæt) *n. Scot.* a top hat. [C19: from LUM]
luminance (ˈluːmɪnəns) *n.* **1.** a state or quality of radiating or reflecting light. **2.** a measure (in candelas per square metre) of the brightness of a point on a surface that is radiating or reflecting light. It is the luminous intensity in a given direction of a small element of surface area divided by the orthogonal projection of this area onto a plane at right angles to the direction. Symbol: *L* [C19: from Latin *lūmen* light]
luminary (ˈluːmɪnərɪ) *n., pl.* **-naries. 1.** a person who enlightens or influences others. **2.** a famous person. **3.** *Literary.* something, such as the sun or moon, that gives off light. ~*adj.* **4.** of, involving, or characterized by light or enlightenment. [C15: via Old French, from Latin *lūmināre* lamp, from *lūmen* light]
luminesce (ˌluːmɪˈnɛs) *vb.* (*intr.*) to exhibit luminescence. [back formation from LUMINESCENT]
luminescence (ˌluːmɪˈnɛsəns) *n. Physics.* **a.** the emission of light at low temperatures by any process other than incandescence, such as phosphorescence or chemiluminescence. **b.** the light emitted by such a process. [C19: from Latin *lūmen* light] —ˌ**lumiˈnescent** *adj.*
luminosity (ˌluːmɪˈnɒsɪtɪ) *n., pl.* **-ties. 1.** the condition of being luminous. **2.** something that is luminous. **3.** *Astronomy.* a measure of the amount of light emitted by a star. **4.** *Physics.* the attribute of an object or colour enabling the extent to which an object emits light to be observed. Former name: **brightness.** See also **colour.**
luminous (ˈluːmɪnəs) *adj.* **1.** radiating or reflecting light; shining; glowing: *luminous colours.* **2.** (*not in technical use*) exhibit-

ing luminescence: *luminous paint.* **3.** full of light; well-lit. **4.** (of a physical quantity in photometry) evaluated according to the visual sensation produced in an observer rather than by absolute energy measurements: *luminous flux; luminous intensity.* Compare **radiant. 5.** easily understood; lucid; clear. **6.** enlightening or wise. [C15: from Latin *lūminōsus* full of light, from *lūmen* light] —**'luminously** *adv.* —**'luminousness** *n.*

luminous efficacy *n.* **1.** the quotient of the luminous flux of a radiation and its corresponding radiant flux. Symbol: *K* **2.** the quotient of the luminous flux emitted by a source of radiation and the power it consumes. It is measured in lumens per watt. Symbol: η_v, Φ_v

luminous efficiency *n.* the efficiency of polychromatic radiation in producing a visual sensation. It is the radiant flux weighed according to the spectral luminous efficiencies of its constituent wavelengths divided by the corresponding radiant flux. Symbol: *V*

luminous energy *n.* energy emitted or propagated in the form of light; the product of a luminous flux and its duration, measured in lumen seconds. Symbol: Q_v

luminous exitance *n.* the ability of a surface to emit light expressed as the luminous flux per unit area at a specified point on the surface. Symbol: M_v

luminous flux *n.* a measure of the rate of flow of luminous energy, evaluated according to its ability to produce a visual sensation. For a monochromatic light it is the radiant flux multiplied by the spectral luminous efficiency of the light. It is measured in lumens. Symbol: Φ_v

luminous intensity *n.* a measure of the amount of light that a point source radiates in a given direction. It is expressed by the luminous flux leaving the source in that direction per unit of solid angle. Symbol: I_v

lumisterol (luːˈmɪstəˌrɒl) *n. Biochem.* a steroid compound produced when ergosterol is exposed to ultraviolet radiation. Formula: $C_{28}H_{44}O$. [C20: from Latin *lumin-, lūmen* light + STEROL]

lumme *or* **lummy** (ˈlʌmɪ) *interj. Brit.* an exclamation of surprise or dismay. [C19: alteration of *Lord love me*]

lummox (ˈlʌməks) *n. Informal.* a clumsy or stupid person. [C19: origin unknown]

lump[1] (lʌmp) *n.* **1.** a small solid mass without definite shape. **2.** *Pathol.* any small swelling or tumour. **3.** a collection of things; aggregate. **4.** *Informal.* an awkward, heavy, or stupid person. **5.** *(pl.) U.S. informal.* punishment, defeat, or reverses: *he took his lumps.* **6. the lump.** *Brit.* **a.** self-employed workers in the building trade considered collectively, esp. with reference to tax and national insurance evasion. **b.** (*as modifier*): *lump labour.* **7.** (*modifier*) in the form of a lump or lumps: *lump sugar.* **8. a lump in one's throat.** a tight dry feeling in one's throat, usually caused by great emotion. **9. in the lump.** collectively; en masse. ~*vb.* **10.** (*tr.*; often foll. by *together*) to collect into a mass or group. **11.** (*intr.*) to grow into lumps or become lumpy. **12.** (*tr.*) to consider as a single group, often without justification. **13.** (*tr.*) to make or cause lumps in or on. **14.** (*intr.*; often foll. by *along*) to move or proceed in a heavy manner. [C13: probably related to early Dutch *lompe* piece, Scandinavian dialect *lump* block, Middle High German *lumpe* rag]

lump[2] (lʌmp) *vb.* (*tr.*) *Informal.* to tolerate or put up with; endure (in the phrase **lump it**). [C16: origin uncertain]

lumpectomy (lʌmˈpɛktəmɪ) *n., pl.* **-mies.** the surgical removal of a tumour in a breast. [C20: from LUMP[1] + -ECTOMY]

lumpen (ˈlʌmpᵊn) *adj. Informal.* stupid or unthinking. [from German *Lump* vagabond, influenced in meaning by *Lumpen* rag, as in LUMPENPROLETARIAT]

lumpenproletariat (ˌlʌmpənˌprəʊlɪˈtɛərɪət) *n.* (esp. in Marxist theory) the amorphous urban social group below the proletariat, consisting of criminals, tramps, etc. [German, literally: ragged proletariat]

lumper (ˈlʌmpə) *n. U.S.* a stevedore; docker.

lumpfish (ˈlʌmpˌfɪʃ) *n., pl.* **-fish** *or* **-fishes. 1.** a North Atlantic scorpaenoid fish, *Cyclopterus lumpus,* having a globular body covered with tubercles, pelvic fins fused into a sucker, and an edible roe: family *Cyclopteridae.* **2.** any other fish of the family *Cyclopteridae.* ~Also called: **lumpsucker.** [C16: *lump* (now obsolete) lumpfish, from Middle Dutch *lumpe,* perhaps related to LUMP[1]]

lumpish (ˈlʌmpɪʃ) *adj.* **1.** resembling a lump. **2.** stupid, clumsy, or heavy. —**'lumpishly** *adv.* —**'lumpishness** *n.*

lumpsucker (ˈlʌmpˌsʌkə) *n.* See **lumpfish.**

lump sum *n.* a relatively large sum of money, paid at one time, esp. in cash.

lumpy (ˈlʌmpɪ) *adj.* **lumpier, lumpiest. 1.** full of or having lumps. **2.** (esp. of the sea) rough. **3.** (of a person) heavy or bulky. —**'lumpily** *adv.* —**'lumpiness** *n.*

lumpy jaw *n. Vet. science.* a nontechnical name for **actinomycosis.**

luna (ˈluːnə) *n.* the alchemical name for **silver.** [from Latin: moon]

lunacy (ˈluːnəsɪ) *n., pl.* **-cies. 1.** (formerly) any severe mental illness. **2.** foolishness or a foolish act.

luna moth *n.* a large American saturniid moth, *Tropaea* (or *Actias*) *luna,* having light green wings with a yellow crescent-shaped marking on each forewing. [C19: so named from the markings on its wings]

lunar (ˈluːnə) *adj.* **1.** of or relating to the moon. **2.** occurring on, used on, or designed to land on the surface of the moon: *lunar module.* **3.** relating to, caused by, or measured by the position or orbital motion of the moon. **4.** of or containing silver. [C17: from Latin *lūnāris,* from *lūna* the moon]

lunar caustic *n.* silver nitrate fused into sticks, which were formerly used in cauterizing.

lunar eclipse *n.* See under **eclipse** (sense 1).

lunarian (luːˈnɛərɪən) *n.* **1.** an archaic word for **selenographer. 2.** *Myth.* an inhabitant of the moon.

lunar module *n.* the module used to carry two of the three astronauts on an Apollo spacecraft to the surface of the moon and back to the spacecraft.

lunar month *n.* another name for **synodic month.** See **month** (sense 6).

lunar year *n.* See under **year** (sense 6).

lunate (ˈluːneɪt) *or* **lunated** *adj.* **1.** *Anatomy, botany.* shaped like a crescent. ~*n.* **2.** a crescent-shaped bone forming part of the wrist. [C18: from Latin *lūnātus,* crescent-shaped, from *lūnāre,* from *lūna* moon]

lunatic (ˈluːnətɪk) *adj. also* (*rare*) **lunatical** (luːˈnætɪkᵊl). **1.** an archaic word for **insane. 2.** foolish; eccentric; crazy. ~*n.* **3.** a person who is insane. [C13 (adj.) via Old French from Late Latin *lūnāticus* crazy, moonstruck, from Latin *lūna* moon] —**luˈnatically** *adv.*

lunatic asylum *n.* another name, usually regarded as offensive, for **mental home.**

lunatic fringe *n.* the members of a society or group who adopt or support views regarded as extreme or fanatical.

lunation (luːˈneɪʃən) *n.* another name for **synodic month.** See **month** (sense 6).

lunch (lʌntʃ) *n.* **1.** a meal eaten during the middle of the day. **2.** *Caribbean.* (among older people) mid-afternoon tea. Compare **breakfast** (sense 1), **tea** (sense 5). ~*vb.* **3.** (*intr.*) to eat lunch. **4.** (*tr.*) to provide or buy lunch for. [C16: probably short form of LUNCHEON] —**'luncher** *n.*

luncheon (ˈlʌntʃən) *n.* a lunch, esp. a formal one. [C16: probably variant of *nuncheon,* from Middle English *noneschench,* from *none* NOON + *schench* drink]

luncheon club *n.* **1.** *Social welfare.* (in Britain) an arrangement or organization for serving hot midday meals for a small charge to old people in clubs or daycentres. **2.** a society or group of people who meet regularly for an organized lunch: *a ladies' luncheon club.*

luncheonette (ˌlʌntʃəˈnɛt) *n. U.S. and Canadian.* a café or small informal restaurant where light meals and snacks are served.

luncheon meat *n.* a ground mixture of meat (often pork) and cereal, usually tinned.

luncheon voucher *n.* a voucher worth a specified amount issued to employees and redeemable at a restaurant for food. Abbrev.: **LV.** U.S. equivalent: **meal ticket.**

lunch hour *n.* **1.** Also called: **lunch break.** a break in the middle of the working day, usually of one hour, during which lunch may be eaten. **2.** Also called: **lunch time.** the time at which lunch is usually eaten.

lunchroom (ˈlʌntʃˌruːm, -ˌrʊm) *n. U.S. and Canadian.* a room where lunch is served or where students, employees, etc., may eat lunches they bring.

lune[1] (luːn) *n.* **1. a.** a section of the surface of a sphere enclosed between two semicircles that intersect at opposite points on the sphere. **b.** a crescent-shaped figure formed on a plane surface by the intersection of the arcs of two circles. **2.** something shaped like a crescent. **3.** *R.C. Church.* another word for **lunette** (sense 6). [C18: from Latin *lūna* moon]

lune[2] (luːn) *n. Falconry.* a leash for hawks or falcons. [C14 *loigne,* from Old French, from Medieval Latin *longia, longea,* from Latin *longus* LONG[1]]

lunette (luːˈnɛt) *n.* **1.** anything that is shaped like a crescent. **2.** an oval or circular opening to admit light in a dome. **3.** a semicircular panel containing a window, mural, or sculpture. **4.** a ring attached to a vehicle, into which a hook is inserted so that it can be towed. **5.** a type of fortification like a detached bastion. **6.** Also called: **lune.** *R.C. Church.* a case fitted with a bracket to hold the consecrated host. [C16: from French: crescent, from *lune* moon, from Latin *lūna*]

lung (lʌŋ) *n.* **1.** either one of a pair of spongy saclike respiratory organs within the thorax of higher vertebrates, which oxygenate the blood and remove its carbon dioxide. **2.** any similar or analogous organ in other vertebrates or in invertebrates. **3. at the top of one's lungs.** in one's loudest voice; yelling. [Old English *lungen;* related to Old High German *lungun* lung. Compare LIGHTS[2]]

lungan (ˈlʌŋgən) *n.* another name for **longan.**

lunge[1] (lʌndʒ) *n.* **1.** a sudden forward motion. **2.** *Fencing.* a thrust made by advancing the front foot and straightening the back leg, extending the sword arm forwards. ~*vb.* **3.** to move or cause to move with a lunge. **4.** (*intr.*) *Fencing.* to make a lunge. [C18: shortened form of obsolete C17 *allonge,* from French *allonger* to stretch out (one's arm), from Late Latin *ēlongāre* to lengthen. Compare ELONGATE] —**'lunger** *n.*

lunge[2] (lʌndʒ) *n.* **1.** a rope used in training or exercising a horse. ~*vb.* **2.** to exercise or train (a horse) on a lunge. [C17: from Old

French *longe*, shortened from *allonge*, ultimately from Latin *longus* LONG; related to LUNGE[1]]

lungfish ('lʌŋ,fɪʃ) *n., pl.* **-fish** *or* **-fishes.** any freshwater bony fish of the subclass *Dipnoi*, having an air-breathing lung, fleshy paired fins, and an elongated body. The only living species are those of the genera *Lepidosiren* of South America, *Protopterus* of Africa, and *Neoceratodus* of Australia.

lungi *or* **lungee** ('lʊŋgiː) *n.* a long piece of cotton cloth worn as a loincloth, sash, or turban by Indian men or as a skirt. [C17: Hindi, from Persian]

lungworm ('lʌŋ,wɜːm) *n.* **1.** any parasitic nematode worm of the family *Metastrongylidae*, occurring in the lungs of mammals, esp. *Metastrongylus apri* which infects pigs. **2.** any of certain other nematodes that are parasitic in the lungs.

lungwort ('lʌŋ,wɜːt) *n.* **1.** any of several Eurasian plants of the boraginaceous genus *Pulmonaria*, esp. *P. officinalis*, which has spotted leaves and clusters of blue or purple flowers: formerly used to treat lung diseases. **2.** any of various boraginaceous plants of the N temperate genus *Mertensia*, such as *Mertensia maritima* (sea lungwort), having drooping clusters of tubular usually blue flowers.

lunisolar (,luːnɪ'səʊlə) *adj.* resulting from, relating to, or based on the combined gravitational attraction of the sun and moon. [C17: from Latin *lūna* moon + SOLAR]

lunitidal (,luːnɪ'taɪdᵊl) *adj.* of or relating to tidal phenomena as produced by the moon. [C19: from Latin *lūna* moon + TIDAL]

lunitidal interval *n.* the difference in time between the moon crossing a meridian and the following high tide at that meridian.

lunula ('luːnjʊlə) *or* **lunule** ('luːnjuːl) *n., pl.* **-nulae** (-njʊ,liː) *or* **-nules.** the white crescent-shaped area at the base of the human fingernail. Nontechnical name: **half-moon.** [C16: from Latin: small moon, from *lūna*]

lunulate ('luːnjʊ,leɪt) *or* **lunulated** *adj.* **1.** having markings shaped like crescents: *lunulate patterns on an insect.* **2.** Also: **lunular.** shaped like a crescent.

Luo (lə'wəʊ, 'luːəʊ) *n.* **1.** (*pl.* **Luo** *or* **Luos**) a member of a cattle-herding Nilotic people living chiefly east of Lake Victoria in Kenya. **2.** the language of this people, belonging to the Nilotic group of the Nilo-Saharan family.

Lupercalia (,luːpɜː'keɪlɪə) *n., pl.* **-lia** *or* **-lias.** an ancient Roman festival of fertility, celebrated annually on Feb. 15. See also **Saint Valentine's Day.** [Latin, from *Lupercālis* belonging to *Lupercus*, a Roman god of the flocks] —,**Luper'calian** *adj.*

lupin *or U.S.* **lupine** ('luːpɪn) *n.* any papilionaceous plant of the genus *Lupinus*, of North America, Europe, and Africa, with large spikes of brightly coloured flowers and flattened pods. [C14: from Latin *lupīnus* wolfish (see LUPINE); from the belief that the plant ravenously exhausted the soil]

lupine ('luːpaɪn) *adj.* of, relating to, or resembling a wolf. [C17: from Latin *lupīnus*, from *lupus* wolf]

lupulin ('luːpjʊlɪn) *n.* a resinous powder extracted from the female flowers of the hop plant and used as a sedative. [C19: from New Latin *lupulus*, diminutive of *lupus* the hop plant]

lupus ('luːpəs) *n.* any of various ulcerative skin diseases. [C16: via Medieval Latin from Latin: wolf; said to be so called because it rapidly eats away the affected part]

▷**Usage.** In current usage the word *lupus* alone is generally understood to signify lupus vulgaris, lupus erythematosus being normally referred to in full or by the abbreviation LE.

Lupus ('luːpəs) *n., Latin genitive* **Lupi** ('luːpaɪ). a constellation in the S hemisphere lying between Centaurus and Ara.

lupus erythematosus (,ɛrɪ,θiːmə'təʊsəs) *n.* either of two inflammatory diseases of the connective tissue. **Discoid lupus erythematosus** is characterized by a scaly rash over the cheeks and bridge of the nose; **disseminated** or **systemic lupus erythematosus** affects the joints, lungs, kidneys, or skin. Abbrev.: **LE.**

lupus vulgaris (vʌl'gɛərɪs) *n.* tuberculosis of the skin, esp. of the face, with the formation of raised translucent nodules. Sometimes shortened to **lupus.**

lur *or* **lure** (lʊə) *n., pl.* **lures** ('lʊərɪz). a large bronze musical horn found in Danish peat bogs and probably dating to the Bronze Age. [from Danish (and Swedish and Norwegian) *lur*, from Old Norse *lūthr* trumpet]

lurch[1] (lɜːtʃ) *vb. (intr.)* **1.** to lean or pitch suddenly to one side. **2.** to stagger or sway. ~*n.* **3.** the act or an instance of lurching. [C19: origin unknown] —'**lurching** *adj.*

lurch[2] (lɜːtʃ) *n.* **1. leave (someone) in the lurch.** to desert (someone) in trouble. **2.** *Cribbage.* the state of a losing player with less than 30 points at the end of a game (esp. in the phrase **in the lurch**). [C16: from French *lourche* a game similar to backgammon, apparently from *lourche* (adj.) deceived, probably of Germanic origin]

lurch[3] (lɜːtʃ) *vb. (intr.) Archaic or dialect.* to prowl or steal about suspiciously. [C15: perhaps a variant of LURK]

lurcher ('lɜːtʃə) *n.* **1.** a crossbred hunting dog, usually a greyhound cross with a collie, esp. one trained to hunt silently. **2.** *Archaic.* a person who prowls or lurks. [C16: from LURCH[3]]

lurdan ('lɜːdᵊn) *Archaic.* ~*n.* **1.** a stupid or dull person. ~*adj.* **2.** dull or stupid. [C14: from Old French *lourdin*, Old French *lourd* heavy, from Latin *lūridus* LURID]

lure (lʊə) *vb. (tr.)* **1.** (sometimes foll. by *away* or *into*) to tempt or attract by the promise of some type of reward. **2.** *Falconry.* to entice (a hawk or falcon) from the air to the falconer by a lure. ~*n.* **3.** a person or thing that lures. **4.** *Angling.* any of various types of brightly-coloured artificial spinning baits, usually consisting of a plastic or metal body mounted with hooks and trimmed with feathers, etc. See **jig, plug, spoon. 5.** *Falconry.* a feathered decoy to which small pieces of meat can be attached and which is equipped with a long thong. [C14: from Old French *loirre* falconer's lure, from Germanic; related to Old English *lathian* to invite] —'**lurer** *n.*

Lurex ('lʊərɛks) *n.* **1.** *Trademark.* a thin metallic thread coated with plastic. **2.** fabric containing such thread, which gives it a glittering appearance.

lurid ('lʊərɪd) *adj.* **1.** vivid in shocking detail; sensational. **2.** horrible in savagery or violence. **3.** pallid in colour; wan. **4.** glowing with an unnatural glare. [C17: from Latin *lūridus* pale yellow; probably related to *lūtum* a yellow vegetable dye] —'**luridly** *adv.* —'**luridness** *n.*

lurk (lɜːk) *vb. (intr.)* **1.** to move stealthily or be concealed, esp. for evil purposes. **2.** to be present in an unobtrusive way; go unnoticed. ~*n.* **3.** *Austral. and N.Z. slang.* a scheme or stratagem for success. [C13: probably frequentative of LOUR; compare Middle Dutch *loeren* to lie in wait] —'**lurker** *n.*

lurking ('lɜːkɪŋ) *adj.* **1.** lingering and persistent, though unsuspected or unacknowledged: *a lurking suspicion.* **2.** dimly perceived: *a lurking shape half concealed in the shadows.*

Lusatian (luː'seɪʃɪən) *adj.* **1.** of or relating to Lusatia, a region of central Europe now in E Germany and SW Poland, or to its people, or their language. ~*n.* **2.** a native or inhabitant of Lusatia; a Sorb. **3.** the Sorbian language.

luscious ('lʌʃəs) *adj.* **1.** extremely pleasurable, esp. to the taste or smell. **2.** very attractive. **3.** *Archaic.* cloying. [C15 *lucius, licius*, perhaps a shortened form of DELICIOUS] —'**lusciously** *adv.* —'**lusciousness** *n.*

lush[1] (lʌʃ) *adj.* **1.** (of vegetation) abounding in lavish growth. **2.** (esp. of fruits) succulent and fleshy. **3.** luxurious, elaborate, or opulent. [C15: probably from Old French *lasche* lax, lazy, from Latin *laxus* loose; perhaps related to Old English *lǣc*, Old Norse *lakr* weak, German *lasch* loose] —'**lushly** *adv.* —'**lushness** *n.*

lush[2] (lʌʃ) *Slang.* ~*n.* **1.** a heavy drinker, esp. an alcoholic. **2.** alcoholic drink. ~*vb.* **3.** *U.S. and Canadian.* to drink (alcohol) to excess. [C19: origin unknown]

Lusitanian (,luːsɪ'teɪnɪən) *adj.* **1.** *Chiefly poetic.* of or relating to the ancient region of Lusitania, corresponding roughly to present-day Portugal. **2.** *Biology.* denoting flora or fauna characteristically found only in the warm, moist, west-facing coastal regions of Portugal, Spain, France, and the west and southwest coasts of Great Britain and Ireland.

Luso- *combining form.* indicating Portugal or Portuguese. [from Portuguese *lusitano*, from Latin, from *Lusitania*]

lust (lʌst) *n.* **1.** a strong desire for sexual gratification. **2.** a strong desire or drive. ~*vb.* **3.** (*intr.*; often foll. by *after* or *for*) to have a lust (for). [Old English; related to Old High German *lust* desire, Old Norse *losti* sexual desire, Latin *lascīvus* playful, wanton, lustful. Compare LISTLESS]

lustful ('lʌstfʊl) *adj.* **1.** driven by lust. **2.** *Archaic.* vigorous or lusty. —'**lustfully** *adv.* —'**lustfulness** *n.*

lustral ('lʌstrəl) *adj.* **1.** of or relating to a ceremony of purification. **2.** taking place at intervals of five years; quinquennial. [C16: from Latin *lūstrālis* adj. from LUSTRUM]

lustrate ('lʌstreɪt) *vb. (tr.)* to purify by means of religious rituals or ceremonies. [C17: from Latin *lūstrāre* to brighten] —**lus'tration** *n.* —**lustrative** ('lʌstrətɪv) *adj.*

lustre *or U.S.* **luster** ('lʌstə) *n.* **1.** reflected light; sheen; gloss. **2.** radiance or brilliance of light. **3.** great splendour of accomplishment, beauty, etc. **4.** a substance used to polish or put a gloss on a surface. **5.** a vase or chandelier from which hang cut-glass drops. **6.** a drop-shaped piece of cut glass or crystal used as a decoration on a chandelier, vase, etc. **7. a.** a shiny metallic surface on some pottery and porcelain. **b.** (*as modifier*): *lustre decoration.* **8.** *Mineralogy.* the way in which light is reflected from the surface of a mineral. It is one of the properties by which minerals are defined. ~*vb.* **9.** to make, be, or become lustrous. [C16: from Old French, from Old Italian *lustro*, from Latin *lustrāre* to make bright; related to LUSTRUM] —'**lustreless** *or U.S.* '**lusterless** *adj.* —'**lustrous** *adj.*

lustreware *or U.S.* **lusterware** ('lʌstə,wɛə) *n.* pottery or porcelain ware with lustre decoration.

lustring ('lʌstrɪŋ) *or* **lutestring** ('luːt,strɪŋ) *n.* a glossy silk cloth, formerly used for clothing, upholstery, etc. [C17: from Italian *lustrino*, from *lustro* LUSTRE]

lustrum ('lʌstrəm) *or* **lustre** *n., pl.* **-trums** *or* **-tra** (-trə). a period of five years. [C16: from Latin: ceremony of purification, from *lustrāre* to brighten, purify]

lusty ('lʌstɪ) *adj.* **lustier, lustiest. 1.** having or characterized by robust health. **2.** strong or invigorating: *a lusty brew.* —'**lustily** *adv.* —'**lustiness** *n.*

lusus naturae ('luːsʊs næ'tʊəriː) *n.* a freak, mutant, or monster. [C17: Latin: whim of nature]

lutanist ('luːtənɪst) *n.* a variant spelling of **lutenist.**

lute[1] (luːt) *n.* an ancient plucked stringed instrument, consisting of a long fingerboard with frets and gut strings, and a body shaped like a sliced pear. [C14: from Old French *lut*, via Old Provençal from Arabic *al 'ūd*, literally: the wood]

lute[2] (luːt) *n.* **1.** Also called: **luting.** a mixture of cement and clay used to seal the joints between pipes, etc. **2.** *Dentistry.* a thin layer of cement used to fix a crown or inlay in place on a tooth. ~*vb.* **3.** (*tr.*) to seal (a joint or surface) with lute. [C14: via Old French ultimately from Latin *lutum* clay]

luteal (ˈluːtɪəl) *adj.* relating to or characterized by the development of the corpus luteum: *the luteal phase of the oestrous cycle.* [C20: from Latin *lūteus* yellow, relating to *lūtum* a yellow weed]

lutein (ˈluːtɪɪn) *n.* a xanthophyll pigment, occurring in plants, that has a light-absorbing function in photosynthesis. [C20: from Latin *lūteus* yellow + -IN]

luteinizing hormone (ˈluːtɪɪˌnaɪzɪŋ) *n.* a gonadotrophic hormone secreted by the anterior lobe of the pituitary gland. In female vertebrates it stimulates ovulation, and in mammals it also induces the conversion of the ruptured follicle into the corpus luteum. In male vertebrates it promotes maturation of the interstitial cells of the testes and stimulates androgen secretion. Abbrev.: **LH.** Also called: **interstitial cell-stimulating hormone.** See also **follicle-stimulating hormone, prolactin.** [C19: from Latin *lūteum* egg yolk, from *lūteus* yellow]

luteinizing hormone-releasing hormone *n.* a hypothalamic peptide that stimulates the pituitary gland to release luteinizing hormone. Abbrev.: **LH-RH.**

lutenist (ˈluːtənɪst) *or U.S. and Canadian* (*sometimes*) **lutist** (ˈluːtɪst) *n.* a person who plays the lute. [C17: from Medieval Latin *lūtānista,* from *lūtāna,* apparently from Old French *lut* LUTE[1]]

luteolin (ˈluːtɪəlɪn) *n.* a yellow crystalline compound found, in the form of its glycoside, in many plants. Formula: $C_{15}H_{10}O_6$. [C19: via French from New Latin *reseda lūteola,* dyer's rocket, from which this substance is obtained; *lūteola* from Latin *lūteus* yellow]

luteotrophin (ˌluːtɪəʊˈtrəʊfɪn), **luteotrophic hormone,** *or esp. U.S.* **luteotropin, luteotropic hormone** *n.* other names for **prolactin.**

luteous (ˈluːtɪəs) *adj.* of a light to moderate greenish-yellow colour. [C17: from Latin *lūteus* yellow]

lutestring (ˈluːtˌstrɪŋ) *n. Textiles.* a variant of **lustring.**

lutetium *or* **lutecium** (luˈtiːʃɪəm) *n.* a silvery-white metallic element of the lanthanide series, occurring in monazite and used as a catalyst in cracking, alkylation, and polymerization. Symbol: Lu; atomic no.: 71; atomic wt.: 174.97; valency: 3; relative density: 9.835; melting pt.: 1656°C; boiling pt.: 3315°C. [C19: New Latin, from Latin *Lūtētia* ancient name of Paris, home of G. Urbain (1872–1938), French chemist, who discovered it]

Luth. *abbrev. for* Lutheran.

Lutheran (ˈluːθərən) *n.* **1.** a follower of Martin Luther (1483–1546), German leader of the Protestant Reformation, or a member of a Lutheran Church. ~*adj.* **2.** of or relating to Luther or his doctrines, the most important being justification by faith alone, consubstantiation, and the supreme authority of the Bible. **3.** of or denoting any of the Protestant Churches that follow Luther's doctrines. —ˈ**Lutheranism** *n.*

luthern (ˈluːθən) *n.* another name for **dormer.** [C17: probably from LUCARNE, perhaps influenced by LUTHERAN]

Lutine bell (ˈluːtiːn, luːˈtiːn) *n.* a bell, taken from the ship *Lutine,* kept at Lloyd's in London and rung before important announcements, esp. the loss of a vessel.

luting (ˈluːtɪŋ) *n.* **1.** another name for **lute**[2] (sense 1). **2.** Also called: **luting paste.** a strip of pastry placed around the dish to seal the lid of a pie.

lutist (ˈluːtɪst) *n.* **1.** *U.S. and Canadian.* another word for **lutenist.** **2.** a person who makes lutes.

lutite (ˈluːtaɪt) *n.* another name for **pelite.** [C20: from Latin *lutum* mud + -ITE[1]]

lutz (luːts) *n. Skating.* a jump in which the skater takes off from the back outside edge of one skate, makes one, two, or three turns in the air, and lands on the back outside edge of the other skate. [C20: of uncertain origin]

lux (lʌks) *n., pl.* **lux.** the derived SI unit of illumination equal to a luminous flux of 1 lumen per square metre. 1 lux is equivalent to 0.0929 foot-candle. Symbol: lx [C19: from Latin: light]

Lux. *abbrev. for* Luxembourg.

luxate (ˈlʌkseɪt) *vb.* (*tr.*) *Pathol.* to put (a shoulder, knee, etc.) out of joint; dislocate. [C17: from Latin *luxāre* to displace, from *luxus* dislocated; related to Greek *loxos* oblique] —**luxˈation** *n.*

luxe (lʌks, lʊks; *French* lyks) *n.* See **de luxe.** [C16: from French from Latin *luxus* extravagance, LUXURY]

luxulianite *or* **luxullianite** (lʌkˈsuːljəˌnaɪt) *n.* a rare variety of granite containing tourmaline embedded in quartz and feldspar. [C19: named after *Luxulyan,* a village in Cornwall near which it was first found]

luxuriant (lʌgˈzjʊərɪənt) *adj.* **1.** rich and abundant; lush. **2.** very elaborate or ornate. **3.** extremely productive or fertile. [C16: from Latin *luxuriāns,* present participle of *luxuriāre* to abound to excess] —**luxˈuriance** *n.* —**luxˈuriantly** *adv.*

luxuriate (lʌgˈzjʊərɪˌeɪt) *vb.* (*intr.*) **1.** (foll. by *in*) to take voluptuous pleasure; revel. **2.** to flourish extensively or profusely. **3.** to live in a sumptuous way. [C17: from Latin *luxuriāre*] —**luxˌuriˈation** *n.*

luxurious (lʌgˈzjʊərɪəs) *adj.* **1.** characterized by luxury. **2.** enjoying or devoted to luxury. **3.** an archaic word for **lecherous.** [C14: via Old French from Latin *luxuriōsus* excessive] —**luxˈuriously** *adv.* —**luxˈuriousness** *n.*

luxury (ˈlʌkʃərɪ) *n., pl.* **-ries. 1.** indulgence in and enjoyment of rich, comfortable, and sumptuous living. **2.** (*sometimes pl.*) something that is considered an indulgence rather than a necessity. **3.** something pleasant and satisfying: *the luxury of independence.* **4.** (*modifier*) relating to, indicating, or supplying luxury: *a luxury liner.* [C14 (in the sense: lechery): via Old French from Latin *luxuria* excess, from *luxus* extravagance]

Lv *Currency. abbrev. for* lev(a).

LV (in Britain) *abbrev. for* luncheon voucher.

lv. *abbrev. for* leave (of absence, as from military duty).

Lw *the former chemical symbol for* lawrencium (now superseded by Lr).

LW *abbrev. for:* **1.** *Radio.* long wave. **2.** low water.

lwl *or* **LWL** *abbrev. for* length waterline; the length of a vessel at the waterline, taken at the centre axis.

LWM *or* **lwm** *abbrev. for* low water mark.

lx *Physics. symbol for* lux.

LXX *symbol for* Septuagint.

-ly[1] *suffix forming adjectives.* **1.** having the nature or qualities of: *brotherly; godly.* **2.** occurring at certain intervals; every: *daily; yearly.* [Old English *-lic*]

-ly[2] *suffix forming adverbs.* in a certain manner; to a certain degree: *quickly; recently; chiefly.* [Old English *-lice,* from *-lic* -LY[1]]

lyase (ˈlaɪeɪz) *n.* any enzyme that catalyses the separation of two parts of a molecule by the formation of a double bond between them. [C20: from Greek *lusis* a loosening + -ASE]

lycanthrope (ˈlaɪkənˌθrəʊp, laɪˈkænθrəʊp) *n.* **1.** a werewolf. **2.** *Psychiatry.* a person who believes that he is a wolf. [C17: via New Latin, from Greek *lukanthrōpos,* from *lukos* wolf + *anthrōpos* man]

lycanthropy (laɪˈkænθrəpɪ) *n.* **1.** the supposed magical transformation of a human being into a wolf. **2.** *Psychiatry.* a delusion in which a person believes that he is a wolf. [C16: from Greek *lukānthropia,* from *lukos* wolf + *anthrōpos* man] —**lycanthropic** (ˌlaɪkənˈθrɒpɪk) *adj.*

lycée (ˈliːseɪ) *n., pl.* **-cées** (-seɪz). *Chiefly French.* a secondary school. [C19: French, from Latin: LYCEUM]

lyceum (laɪˈsɪəm) *n.* (now chiefly in the names of buildings) **1.** a public building for concerts, lectures, etc. **2.** *U.S.* a cultural organization responsible for presenting concerts, lectures, etc. **3.** another word for **lycée.**

Lyceum (laɪˈsɪəm) *n.* the Aristotelian school of philosophy. [named after the Athenian school and sports ground where Aristotle lectured, from Greek *Lukeion,* named after a temple nearby dedicated to *Apollo Lukeios,* an epithet of unknown origin]

lychee (ˌlaɪˈtʃiː) *n.* a variant spelling of **litchi.**

lych gate (lɪtʃ) *n.* a variant spelling of **lich gate.**

lychnis (ˈlɪknɪs) *n.* any caryophyllaceous plant of the genus *Lychnis,* having red, pink, or white five-petalled flowers. See also **ragged robin.** [C17: New Latin, via Latin, from Greek *lukhnis* a red flower; related to *lukhnos* lamp]

Lycian (ˈlɪsɪən) *adj.* **1.** of or relating to ancient Lycia, on the coast of SW Asia Minor, or to its inhabitants or their language. ~*n.* **2.** an inhabitant of Lycia. **3.** the extinct language of the Lycians, belonging to the Anatolian group or family.

lycopod (ˈlaɪkəˌpɒd) *n.* another name for a **club moss,** esp. one of the genus *Lycopodium.*

lycopodium (ˌlaɪkəˈpəʊdɪəm) *n.* any club moss of the genus *Lycopodium,* resembling moss but having woody tissue and spore-bearing cones: family *Lycopodiaceae.* See also **ground pine** (sense 2). [C18: New Latin, from Greek, from *lukos* wolf + *pous* foot]

Lycra (ˈlaɪkrə) *n. Trademark.* a type of synthetic elastic fabric and fibre used for tight-fitting garments, such as swimming costumes.

lyddite (ˈlɪdaɪt) *n.* **1.** an explosive consisting chiefly of fused picric acid. **2.** a dense black variety of chert, formerly used as a touchstone. [C19: (sense 1) named after *Lydd,* a town in Kent near which the first tests were made]

Lydian (ˈlɪdɪən) *adj.* **1.** of or relating to Lydia, an ancient region on the coast of W Asia Minor, or to its inhabitants or their language. **2.** *Music.* of or relating to an authentic mode represented by the ascending natural diatonic scale from F to F. See also **Hypo-.** Compare **Hypolydian.** ~*n.* **3.** an inhabitant of Lydia. **4.** the extinct language of the Lydians, thought to belong to the Anatolian group or family.

lye (laɪ) *n.* **1.** any solution obtained by leaching, such as the caustic solution obtained by leaching wood ash. **2.** a concentrated solution of sodium hydroxide or potassium hydroxide. [Old English *lēag;* related to Middle Dutch *lōghe,* Old Norse *laug* bath, Latin *lavāre* to wash]

lying[1] (ˈlaɪɪŋ) *vb.* the present participle and gerund of **lie**[1].

lying[2] (ˈlaɪɪŋ) *vb.* the present participle and gerund of **lie**[2].

lying-in *n., pl.* **lyings-in. a.** confinement in childbirth. **b.** (*as modifier*): *a lying-in hospital.*

lyke-wake (ˈlaɪkˌweɪk) *n. Brit.* a watch held over a dead person, often with festivities. [C16: perhaps from Old Norse; see LICH GATE, WAKE[1]]

Lyme disease (laɪm) *n.* a disease of domestic animals and humans, caused by the spirochaete *Borrelia burghdorferi* and transmitted by ticks, and variously affecting the joints, heart, and brain. [C20: named after *Lyme*, Connecticut, the town where it was first identified in humans]

lyme grass (laɪm) *n.* a N temperate perennial dune grass, *Elymus arenarius*, with a creeping stem and rough bluish leaves. [C18: probably a respelling (influenced by its genus name, *Elymus*) of LIME[1], referring to its stabilizing effect (like lime in mortar)]

lymph (lɪmf) *n.* the almost colourless fluid, containing chiefly white blood cells, that is collected from the tissues of the body and transported in the lymphatic system. [C17: from Latin *lympha* water, from earlier *limpa* influenced in form by Greek *numphē* nymph]

lymphadenitis (lɪmˌfædɪˈnaɪtɪs, ˌlɪmfæd-) *n.* inflammation of a lymph node. [C19: New Latin. See LYMPH, ADENITIS]

lymphadenopathy (lɪmˌfædɪˈnɒpəθɪ, ˌlɪmfæd-) *n.* a swelling of the lymph nodes, usually caused by inflammation associated with a viral infection such as rubella.

lymphangial (lɪmˈfændʒɪəl) *adj.* of or relating to a lymphatic vessel.

lymphangitis (ˌlɪmfænˈdʒaɪtɪs) *n., pl.* **-gitides** (-ˈdʒɪtɪˌdiːz). inflammation of one or more of the lymphatic vessels. [C19: see LYMPH, ANGIO-, -ITIS] —**lymphangitic** (ˌlɪmfænˈdʒɪtɪk) *adj.*

lymphatic (lɪmˈfætɪk) *adj.* **1.** of, relating to, or containing lymph: *the lymphatic vessels.* **2.** of or relating to the lymphatic system. **3.** sluggish or lacking vigour. ~*n.* **4.** a lymphatic vessel. [C17 (meaning: mad): from Latin *lymphāticus*. Original meaning perhaps arose from a confusion between *nymph* and LYMPH; compare Greek *numphaleptos* frenzied] —**lymˈphatically** *adv.*

lymphatic system *n.* an extensive network of capillary vessels that transports the interstitial fluid of the body as lymph to the venous blood circulation.

lymphatic tissue *n.* tissue, such as the lymph nodes, tonsils, spleen, and thymus, that produces lymphocytes. Also called: **lymphoid tissue.**

lymph cell *n.* another name for **lymphocyte.**

lymph gland *n.* a former name for **lymph node.**

lymph node *n.* any of numerous bean-shaped masses of tissue, situated along the course of lymphatic vessels, that help to protect against infection by killing bacteria and neutralizing toxins and are the source of lymphocytes.

lympho- *or before a vowel* **lymph-** *combining form.* indicating lymph or the lymphatic system: *lymphogranuloma.*

lymphoblast (ˈlɪmfəʊˌblɑːst) *n.* an abnormal cell consisting of a large nucleus and small cytoplasm that was once thought to be an immature lymphocyte and is now associated with a type of leukaemia (**lymphoblastic leukaemia**). —**lymphoblastic** (ˌlɪmfəʊˈblæstɪk) *adj.*

lymphocyte (ˈlɪmfəʊˌsaɪt) *n.* a type of white blood cell formed in lymphoid tissue. See also **B-lymphocyte, T-lymphocyte.** —**lymphocytic** (ˌlɪmfəʊˈsɪtɪk) *adj.*

lymphocytopenia (ˌlɪmfəʊˌsaɪtəʊˈpiːnɪə) *n. Pathol.* an abnormally low level of lymphocytes in the blood. Also called: **lymphopenia.**

lymphocytosis (ˌlɪmfəʊsaɪˈtəʊsɪs) *n.* an abnormally large number of lymphocytes in the blood: often found in diseases such as glandular fever and smallpox. —**lymphocytotic** (ˌlɪmfəʊsaɪˈtɒtɪk) *adj.*

lymphoid (ˈlɪmfɔɪd) *adj.* of or resembling lymph, or relating to the lymphatic system.

lymphoid tissue *n.* another name for **lymphatic tissue.**

lymphokine (ˈlɪmfəʊˌkaɪn) *n. Immunol.* a protein, released by lymphocytes, that affects other cells involved in the immune response.

lymphoma (lɪmˈfəʊmə) *n., pl.* **-mata** (-mətə) *or* **-mas.** any form of cancer of the lymph nodes. Also called: **lymphosarcoma** (ˌlɪmfəʊsɑːˈkəʊmə). —**lymˈphomatous** *or* **lymˈphomaˌtoid** *adj.*

lymphopoiesis (ˌlɪmfəʊpɔɪˈiːsɪs) *n., pl.* **-ses** (-siːz). the formation of lymphatic tissue or lymphocytes. —**lymphopoietic** (ˌlɪmfəʊpɔɪˈɛtɪk) *adj.*

lyncean (lɪnˈsiːən) *adj.* **1.** of or resembling a lynx. **2.** *Rare.* having keen sight. [C17: probably via Latin, from Greek *Lunkeios* concerning *Lunkeos*, an Argonaut renowned for his sharpsightedness, from *lunx* lynx]

lynch (lɪntʃ) *vb.* (*tr.*) (of a mob) to punish (a person) for some supposed offence by hanging without a trial. [probably after Charles *Lynch* (1736–96), Virginia justice of the peace, who presided over extralegal trials of Tories during the American War of Independence] —ˈ**lyncher** *n.* —ˈ**lynching** *n.*

lynchet (ˈlɪntʃɪt) *n.* a terrace or ridge formed in prehistoric or medieval times by ploughing a hillside. [Old English *hlinc* ridge]

lynch law *n.* the practice of condemning and punishing a person by mob action without a proper trial.

lynx (lɪŋks) *n., pl.* **lynxes** *or* **lynx.** **1.** a feline mammal, *Felis lynx* (or *canadensis*), of Europe and North America, with grey-brown mottled fur, tufted ears, and a short tail. **2.** the fur of this animal. **3. bay lynx.** another name for **bobcat.** **4. desert lynx.** another name for **caracal.** **5.** Also called: **Polish lynx.** a large fancy pigeon from Poland, with spangled or laced markings. [C14: via Latin from Greek *lunx*; related to Old English *lox*, German *Luchs*] —ˈ**lynxˌlike** *adj.*

Lynx (lɪŋks) *n., Latin genitive* **Lyncis** (ˈlɪnsɪs). a faint constellation in the N hemisphere lying between Ursa Major and Cancer.

lynx-eyed *adj.* having keen sight.

lyo- *combining form.* indicating dispersion or dissolution: *lyophilic; lyophilize; lyophobic.* [from Greek *luein* to loose]

lyolysis (laɪˈɒlɪsɪs) *n. Chem.* the formation of an acid and a base from the interaction of a salt with a solvent.

Lyon King of Arms (ˈlaɪən) *n.* the chief herald of Scotland. Also called: **Lord Lyon.** [C14: archaic spelling of LION, referring to the figure on the royal shield]

lyonnaise (ˌlaɪəˈneɪz; *French* ljɔnɛz) *adj.* (of food) cooked or garnished with onions, usually fried. [from French: of *Lyonnais* (former province of E central France)]

lyophilic (ˌlaɪəʊˈfɪlɪk) *adj. Chem.* (of a colloid) having a dispersed phase with a high affinity for the continuous phase: *a lyophilic sol.* Compare **lyophobic.**

lyophilize *or* **lyophilise** (laɪˈɒfɪˌlaɪz) *vb.* (*tr.*) to dry (blood, serum, tissue, etc.) by freezing in a high vacuum.

lyophobic (ˌlaɪəʊˈfəʊbɪk) *adj. Chem.* (of a colloid) having a dispersed phase with little or no affinity for the continuous phase: *a lyophobic sol.* Compare **lyophilic.**

lyosorption (ˌlaɪəʊˈsɔːpʃən) *n. Chem.* the adsorption of a liquid on a solid surface, esp. of a solvent on suspended particles.

Lyra (ˈlaɪərə) *n., Latin genitive* **Lyrae** (ˈlaɪəriː). a small constellation in the N hemisphere lying near Cygnus and Draco and containing the star Vega, an eclipsing binary (**Beta Lyrae**), a planetary nebula (the **Ring Nebula**), and a variable star, **RR Lyrae.**

lyrate (ˈlaɪərɪt) *or* **lyrated** *adj.* **1.** shaped like a lyre. **2.** (of leaves) having a large terminal lobe and smaller lateral lobes. [C18: from New Latin *lyrātus*, Latin from *lyra* LYRE] —ˈ**lyrately** *adv.*

lyra viol (ˈlaɪərə) *n.* a lutelike musical instrument popular in the 16th and 17th centuries: the forerunner of the mandolin.

lyre (laɪə) *n.* **1.** an ancient Greek stringed instrument consisting of a resonating tortoise shell to which a crossbar was attached by two projecting arms. It was plucked with a plectrum and used for accompanying songs. **2.** any ancient instrument of similar design. **3.** a medieval bowed instrument of the violin family. [C13: via Old French from Latin *lyra*, from Greek *lura*]

lyrebird (ˈlaɪəˌbɜːd) *n.* either of two pheasant-like Australian birds, *Menura superba* and *M. alberti*, constituting the family *Menuridae:* during courtship displays, the male spreads its tail into the shape of a lyre.

lyric (ˈlɪrɪk) *adj.* **1.** (of poetry) **a.** expressing the writer's personal feelings and thoughts. **b.** having the form and manner of a song. **2.** of or relating to such poetry. **3.** (of a singing voice) having a light quality and tone. **4.** intended for singing, esp. (in classical Greece) to the accompaniment of the lyre. ~*n.* **5.** a short poem of songlike quality. **6.** (*pl.*) the words of a popular song. ~Also (for senses 1–3): **lyrical.** [C16: from Latin *lyricus*, from Greek *lurikos*, from *lura* LYRE] —ˈ**lyrically** *adv.* —ˈ**lyricalness** *n.*

lyrical (ˈlɪrɪkəl) *adj.* **1.** another word for **lyric** (senses 1–3). **2.** enthusiastic; effusive (esp. in the phrase **to wax lyrical**).

lyricism (ˈlɪrɪˌsɪzəm) *n.* **1.** the quality or style of lyric poetry. **2.** emotional or enthusiastic outpouring.

lyricist (ˈlɪrɪsɪst) *n.* **1.** a person who writes the words for a song, opera, or musical play. **2.** Also called: **lyrist.** a lyric poet.

lyrism (ˈlɪrɪzəm) *n.* **1.** the art or technique of playing the lyre. **2.** a less common word for **lyricism.**

lyrist *n.* **1.** (ˈlaɪərɪst). a person who plays the lyre. **2.** (ˈlɪrɪst). another word for **lyricist** (sense 2).

lys- *combining form.* a variant of **lyso-** before a vowel.

lyse (laɪs, laɪz) *vb.* to undergo or cause to undergo lysis.

Lysenkoism (lɪˈsɛŋkəʊˌɪzəm) *n.* a form of Neo-Lamarckism advocated by T. D. Lysenko (1898–1976), Soviet biologist, emphasizing the importance of the inheritance of acquired characteristics.

lysergic acid (lɪˈsɜːdʒɪk, laɪ-) *n.* a crystalline compound with a polycyclic molecular structure: used in medical research. Formula $C_{16}H_{16}N_2O_2$. [C20: from (HYDRO)LYS(IS) + ERG(OT) + -IC]

lysergic acid diethylamide (daɪˌɛθɪlˈeɪmaɪd, -ˌiːθaɪl-) *n.* See **LSD.**

lysimeter (laɪˈsɪmɪtə) *n.* an instrument for determining solubility, esp. the amount of water-soluble matter in soil. [C20: from *lysi-* (variant of LYSO-) + -METER]

lysin (ˈlaɪsɪn) *n.* any of a group of antibodies or other agents that cause dissolution of cells against which they are directed.

lysine (ˈlaɪsiːn, -sɪn) *n.* an essential amino acid that occurs in proteins.

lysis (ˈlaɪsɪs) *n., pl.* **-ses** (-siːz). **1.** the destruction or dissolution of cells by the action of a particular lysin. **2.** *Med.* the gradual reduction in severity of the symptoms of a disease. [C19: New Latin, from Greek, from *luein* to release]

-lysis *n. combining form.* indicating a loosening, decomposition, or breaking down: *electrolysis; paralysis.* [from Greek, from *lusis* a loosening; see LYSIS]

lyso- *or before a vowel* **lys-** *combining form.* indicating a dissolving or loosening: *lysozyme.* [from Greek *lusis* a loosening]

lysogeny (laɪˈsɒdʒənɪ) *n.* the relationship between a bacteriophage and a bacterium in which the virus does not destroy the bacterial cell, its nucleic acid becoming incorporated with that of its host. —**lysogenic** (ˌlaɪsəʊˈdʒɛnɪk) *adj.*

Lysol (ˈlaɪsɒl) *n. Trademark.* a solution containing a mixture of cresols in water, used as an antiseptic and disinfectant.

lysosome (ˈlaɪsəˌsəʊm) *n.* any of numerous small particles, containing digestive enzymes, that are present in the cytoplasm of most cells. —ˌ**lysoˈsomal** *adj.*
lysozyme (ˈlaɪsəˌzaɪm) *n.* an enzyme occurring in tears, certain body tissues, and egg white: destroys bacteria by hydrolysing polysaccharides in their cell walls. [C20: from LYSO- + (EN)ZYME]
lyssa (ˈlɪsə) *n. Pathol.* a less common word for **rabies.**
-lyte *n. combining form.* indicating a substance that can be decomposed or broken down: *electrolyte.* [from Greek *lutos* soluble, from *luein* to loose]
lythraceous (lɪˈθreɪʃəs, laɪˈθreɪ-) *adj.* of, relating to, or belonging to the *Lythraceae,* a mostly tropical American family of herbaceous plants, shrubs, and trees that includes purple loosestrife and crape myrtle. [C19: from New Latin Lythrum type genus, from Greek *luthron* blood, from the red flowers]
lytic (ˈlɪtɪk) *adj.* **1.** relating to, causing, or resulting from lysis. **2.** of or relating to a lysin. [C19: Greek *lutikos* capable of loosing]
-lytic *adj. combining form.* indicating a loosening or dissolving: *paralytic.* [from Greek, from *lusis;* see -LYSIS]
lytta (ˈlɪtə) *n., pl.* **-tas** *or* **-tae** (-tiː). a rodlike mass of cartilage beneath the tongue in the dog and other carnivores. [C17: New Latin, from Greek *lussa* madness; in dogs, it was believed to be a cause of rabies]

M

m *or* **M** (ɛm) *n., pl.* **m's, M's,** *or* **Ms. 1.** the 13th letter and tenth consonant of the modern English alphabet. **2.** a speech sound represented by this letter, usually a bilabial nasal, as in *mat.*

m *symbol for:* **1.** metre(s). **2.** mile(s). **3.** milli-. **4.** minute(s). **5.** mutual inductance.

M *symbol for:* **1.** *Printing.* em. **2.** mach. **3.** medium (size). **4.** mega-. **5.** *Currency.* mark(s). **6.** million. **7.** *Astronomy.* Messier catalogue; a catalogue published in 1784, in which 103 nebulae and clusters are listed using a numerical system: *M13 is the globular cluster in Hercules.* **8.** Middle. **9.** *Physics.* modulus. **10.** (in Britain) motorway: *the M1 runs from London to Leeds.* **11.** (in Australia) **a.** mature audience (used to describe a category of film certified as suitable for viewing by anyone over the age of 15). **b.** (*as modifier*): *an M film.* **12.** *Logic.* the middle term of a syllogism. **13.** *Physics.* mutual inductance. **14.** *Chem.* molar. ~**15.** *the Roman numeral for* 1000. See **Roman numerals.** ~**16.** *international car registration for* Malta.

m. *abbrev. for:* **1.** *Cricket.* maiden (over). **2.** male. **3.** mare. **4.** married. **5.** masculine. **6.** medicine. **7.** meridian. **8.** month.

M. *abbrev. for:* **1.** Majesty. **2.** Manitoba. **3.** marquis. **4.** Master. **5.** Medieval. **6.** (in titles) Member. **7.** Middle. **8.** million. **9.** Monday. **10.** (*pl.* **MM.** *or* **MM**) Also: **M** *French.* Monsieur. [French equivalent of *Mr*] **11.** mountain.

m- *prefix.* short for **meta-** (sense 4).

M'- *prefix.* a variant of **Mac-.**

'm *contraction of:* **1.** (*vb.*) am. **2.** (*n.*) madam: *yes'm.*

M0 *Symbol for* the amount of money in circulation in notes and coin, plus the banks' till money and the banks' balances at the Bank of England. Informal name: **narrow money.**

M1 *symbol for* the amount of money in circulation in notes, coin, current accounts, and deposit accounts transferable by cheque.

M-1 rifle *n.* a semiautomatic .30 calibre rifle: the basic infantry weapon of the U.S. Army in World War II and the Korean War. Also called: **Garand rifle.**

M2 *symbol for* the amount of money in circulation in notes and coin plus non-interest-bearing bank deposits, building-society deposits, and National Savings accounts.

M3 *symbol for* the amount of money in circulation given by M1 plus all private-sector bank deposits and certificates of deposit. Former symbol: **£M3** (sterling M3).

M3c *symbol for* the amount of money in circulation given by M3 plus foreign currency bank deposits. Former symbol: **M3.** Informal name: **broad money.**

M4 *symbol for* the amount of money in circulation given by M1 plus most private-sector bank deposits and holdings of money-market instruments. Also called: **PSL1.**

M5 *symbol for* the amount of money in circulation given by M4 plus building-society deposits. Also called: **PSL2.**

ma (mɑː) *n.* an informal word for **mother**[1].

MA *abbrev. for:* **1.** Massachusetts. **2.** Master of Arts. **3.** *Psychol.* mental age. **4.** Military Academy. ~**5.** *international car registration for* Morocco. [from French *Maroc*]

ma'am (mæm, mɑːm; *unstressed* məm) *n.* short for **madam:** used as a title of respect, esp. for female royalty.

maar (mɑː) *n., pl.* **maars** *or* **maare** (ˈmɑːrə). (*sometimes cap.*) a coneless volcanic crater that has been formed by a single explosion. [C19: from German]

Ma'ariv *Hebrew.* (*Hebrew* mɑɑˈriv; *Yiddish* ˈmɑɪriv) *n. Judaism.* the evening service.

mabela (mɑːˈbɛlə) *n. S. African.* ground kaffir corn used for making porridge. [from Zulu *amabele* kaffir corn]

mac *or* **mack** (mæk) *n. Brit. informal.* short for **mackintosh** (senses 1, 3).

Mac (mæk) *n. Chiefly U.S. and Canadian.* an informal term of address to a man. [C20: abstracted from MAC-, prefix of Scottish surnames]

MAC *abbrev. for* multiplexed analogue component: a transmission coding system for colour television using satellite broadcasting.

Mac. *abbrev. for* Maccabees (books of the Apocrypha).

Mac-, Mc-, *or* **M'-** *prefix.* (in surnames of Scottish or Irish Gaelic origin) son of: *MacDonald; MacNeice.* [from Goidelic *mac* son of; compare Welsh *mab,* Cornish *mab*]

macabre (məˈkɑːbə, -brə) *adj.* **1.** gruesome; ghastly; grim. **2.** resembling or associated with the danse macabre. [C15: from Old French *danse macabre* dance of death, probably from *macabé* relating to the Maccabees, a Jewish family of patriots who were associated with death because of the doctrines and prayers for the dead in II Macc. (12:43–46)] —**maˈcabrely** *adv.*

macaco (məˈkɑːkəʊ, -ˈkeɪ-) *n., pl.* **-cos.** any of various lemurs, esp. *Lemur macaco,* the males of which are usually black and the females brown. [C18: from French *mococo,* of unknown origin]

macadam (məˈkædəm) *n.* a road surface made of compressed layers of small broken stones, esp. one that is bound together with tar or asphalt. [C19: named after John *McAdam* (1756–1836), Scottish engineer, the inventor]

macadamia (ˌmækəˈdeɪmɪə) *n.* **1.** any tree of the Australian proteaceous genus *Macadamia,* esp. *M. ternifolia,* having clusters of small white flowers and edible nutlike seeds. **2. macadamia nut.** the seed of this tree. [C19: New Latin, named after John *Macadam* (died 1865), Australian chemist]

macadamize *or* **macadamise** (məˈkædəˌmaɪz) *vb.* (*tr.*) to construct or surface (a road) with macadam. —**macˌadamiˈzation** *or* **macˌadamiˈsation** *n.* —**macˈadamˌizer** *or* **macˈadamˌiser** *n.*

macaque (məˈkɑːk) *n.* any of various Old World monkeys of the genus *Macaca,* inhabiting wooded or rocky regions of Asia and Africa. Typically the tail is short or absent and cheek pouches are present. [C17: from French, from Portuguese *macaco,* from Fiot (a W African language) *makaku,* from *kaku* monkey]

macaroni *or* **maccaroni** (ˌmækəˈrəʊnɪ) *n., pl.* **-nis** *or* **-nies. 1.** pasta tubes made from wheat flour. **2.** (in 18th-century Britain) a dandy who affected foreign manners and style. [C16: from Italian (Neapolitan dialect) *maccarone,* probably from Greek *makaria* food made from barley]

macaronic (ˌmækəˈrɒnɪk) *adj.* **1.** (of verse) characterized by a mixture of vernacular words jumbled together with Latin words or Latinized words or with words from one or more other foreign languages. ~*n.* **2.** (*often pl.*) macaronic verse. [C17: from New Latin *macarōnicus,* literally: resembling macaroni (in lack of sophistication); see MACARONI] —ˌ**macaˈronically** *adv.*

macaroni cheese *n.* a dish of macaroni with a cheese sauce.

macaroon (ˌmækəˈruːn) *n.* a kind of sweet biscuit made of ground almonds, sugar, and egg whites. [C17: via French *macaron* from Italian *maccarone* MACARONI]

Macassar oil (məˈkæsə) *n.* an oily preparation formerly put on the hair to make it smooth and shiny. [C19: so called because its ingredients were originally claimed to have come from *Makasar* in central Indonesia]

macaw (məˈkɔː) *n.* any large tropical American parrot of the genera *Ara* and *Anodorhynchus,* having a long tail and brilliant plumage. [C17: from Portuguese *macau,* of unknown origin]

Macc. *abbrev. for* Maccabees (books of the Apocrypha).

Maccabean (ˌmækəˈbiːən) *adj.* of or relating to Judas Maccabaeus, Jewish leader who led a revolt (166–161 B.C.) to recapture Jerusalem, or to the Maccabees, the dynasty founded by him in Jerusalem.

maccaboy, maccoboy (ˈmækəˌbɔɪ), *or* **maccabaw** (ˈmækəˌbɔː) *n.* a dark rose-scented snuff. [C18: from French *macouba,* from the name of the district of the Caribbean island of Martinique where it is made]

maccaroni (ˌmækəˈrəʊnɪ) *n., pl.* **-nis** *or* **-nies.** a variant spelling of **macaroni.**

McCarthyism (məˈkɑːθɪˌɪzəm) *n. Chiefly U.S.* **1.** the practice of making unsubstantiated accusations of disloyalty or Communist leanings. **2.** the use of unsupported accusations for any purpose. [C20: after Senator Joseph *McCarthy* (1908–57)] —**McˈCarthyist** *n., adj.*

McCoy (məˈkɔɪ) *n. Slang.* the genuine person or thing (esp. in the phrase **the real McCoy**). [C20: perhaps after Kid *McCoy,* professional name of Norman Selby (1873–1940), American boxer, who was called "the real McCoy" to distinguish him from another boxer of that name]

mace[1] (meɪs) *n.* **1.** a club, usually having a spiked metal head, used esp. in the Middle Ages. **2.** a ceremonial staff of office carried by certain officials. **3.** See **macebearer. 4.** an early form of billiard cue. [C13: from Old French, probably from Vulgar Latin *mattea* (unattested); apparently related to Latin *mateola* mallet]

mace[2] (meɪs) *n.* a spice made from the dried aril round the nutmeg seed. [C14: formed as a singular from Old French *macis* (wrongly assumed to be plural), from Latin *macir* an oriental spice]

Mace (meɪs) *U.S.* ~*n.* **1.** *Trademark.* a liquid causing tears and nausea, used as a spray for riot control, etc. ~*vb.* **2.** (*tr.*) (*sometimes not cap.*) to use Mace on.

macebearer (ˈmeɪsˌbɛərə) *n.* a person who carries a mace in processions or ceremonies.

macedoine (ˌmæsɪˈdwɑːn) *n.* **1.** a hot or cold mixture of diced vegetables. **2.** a mixture of fruit served in a syrup or in jelly. **3.** any mixture; medley. [C19: from French, literally: Macedonian, alluding to the mixture of nationalities in Macedonia]

Macedonian (ˌmæsɪˈdəʊnɪən) *adj.* **1.** of or relating to Macedonia, a region in the S Balkans now divided between Greece, Bulgaria, and Yugoslavia, or to its inhabitants or any of their languages or dialects. ~*n.* **2.** a native or inhabitant of Macedonia. **3.** the language of modern Macedonia, belonging to the south Slavonic branch of the Indo-European family. **4.** an extinct language spoken in ancient Macedonia.

macer ('meɪsə) *n.* a macebearer, esp. (in Scotland) an official who acts as usher in a court of law. [C14: from Old French *massier,* from *masse* MACE[1]]

maceral ('mæsərəl) *n. Geology.* any of the organic units that constitute coal: equivalent to any of the mineral constituents of a rock. [C20: from Latin *mācerāre* to MACERATE]

macerate ('mæsəˌreɪt) *vb.* **1.** to soften or separate or be softened or separated as a result of soaking. **2.** to break up or cause to break up by soaking: *macerated peaches.* **3.** to become or cause to become thin. [C16: from Latin *mācerāre* to soften] —**'macerˌater** *or* **'macerˌator** *n.* —**'macerative** *adj.* —**ˌmacer'ation** *n.*

MacGuffin (mə'gʌfɪn) *n.* an object or event in a book or a film that serves as the impetus for the plot. [C20: coined (c. 1935) by Sir Alfred Hitchcock (1899–1980), British film director]

Mach[1] (mæk) *n.* short for **Mach number.**

mach. *abbrev. for:* **1.** machine. **2.** machinery. **3.** machinist.

machair ('mæxər) *n. Scot.* (in the western Highlands of Scotland) a strip of sandy, grassy, often lime-rich land just above the high-water mark at a sandy shore: used as grazing or arable land. [C17: from Scottish Gaelic]

machan (mə'tʃɑːn) *n.* (in India) a raised platform used in tiger hunting. [C19: from Hindi]

macher ('mɑxər) *n. Yiddish.* an important or influential person: often used ironically. [Yiddish, from German, literally: doer]

machete (mə'ʃɛtɪ, -'tʃeɪ-) *or* **matchet** *n.* a broad heavy knife used for cutting or as a weapon, esp. in parts of Central and South America. [C16 *macheto,* from Spanish *machete,* from *macho* club, perhaps from Vulgar Latin *mattea* (unattested) club]

Machiavellian *or* **Machiavelian** (ˌmækɪə'vɛlɪən) *adj.* (*sometimes not cap.*) **1.** of or relating to the alleged political principles of Niccolò Machiavelli (1469–1527), Florentine statesman; cunning, amoral, and opportunist. ~*n.* **2.** a cunning, amoral, and opportunist person, esp. a politician. —**ˌMachia'vellianism** *or* **ˌMachia'vellism** *n.* —**ˌMachia'vellist** *adj., n.*

machicolate (mə'tʃɪkəʊˌleɪt) *vb.* (*tr.*) to construct machicolations at the top of (a wall). [C18: from Old French *machicoller,* ultimately from Provençal *machacol,* from *macar* to crush + *col* neck]

machicolation (məˌtʃɪkəʊ'leɪʃən) *n.* **1.** (esp. in medieval castles) a projecting gallery or parapet supported on corbels having openings through which missiles could be dropped. **2.** any such opening.

machinate ('mækɪˌneɪt, 'mæʃ-) *vb.* (*usually tr.*) to contrive, plan, or devise (schemes, plots, etc.). [C17: from Latin *māchinārī* to plan, from *māchina* MACHINE] —**'machiˌnator** *n.*

machination (ˌmækɪ'neɪʃən, ˌmæʃ-) *n.* **1.** an intrigue, plot, or scheme. **2.** the act of devising plots or schemes.

machine (mə'ʃiːn) *n.* **1.** an assembly of interconnected components arranged to transmit or modify force in order to perform useful work. **2.** Also called: **simple machine.** a device for altering the magnitude or direction of a force, esp. a lever, screw, wedge, or pulley. **3.** a mechanically operated device or means of transport, such as a car, aircraft, etc. **4.** any mechanical or electrical device that automatically performs tasks or assists in performing tasks. **5. a.** (*modifier*) denoting a firearm that is fully automatic as distinguished from semiautomatic. **b.** (*in combination*): *machine pistol; machine gun.* **6.** any intricate structure or agency: *the war machine.* **7.** a mechanically efficient, rigid, or obedient person. **8.** an organized body of people that controls activities, policies, etc. **9.** (esp. in the classical theatre) a device such as a pulley to provide spectacular entrances and exits for supernatural characters. **10.** an event, etc., introduced into a literary work for special effect. ~*vb.* **11.** (*tr.*) to shape, cut, or remove (excess material) from (a workpiece) using a machine tool. **12.** to use a machine to carry out a process on (something). [C16: via French from Latin *māchina* machine, engine, from Doric Greek *makhana* pulley; related to *makhos* device, contrivance] —**ma'chinable** *or* **ma'chineable** *adj.* —**maˌchina'bility** *n.* —**ma'chineless** *adj.* —**ma'chine-ˌlike** *adj.*

machine bolt *n.* a fastening bolt with a machine-cut thread.

machine code *or* **language** *n.* instructions for the processing of data in a binary, octal, or hexadecimal code that can be understood and executed by a computer.

machine gun *n.* **1. a.** a rapid-firing automatic gun, usually mounted, from which small-arms ammunition is discharged. **b.** (*as modifier*): *machine-gun fire.* ~*vb.* **machine-gun, -guns, -gunning, -gunned.** **2.** (*tr.*) to shoot or fire at with a machine gun. —**machine gunner** *n.*

machine head *n.* a metal peg-and-gear mechanism for tuning a string on an instrument such as a guitar.

machine intelligence *n. Brit., now rare.* another term for **artificial intelligence.**

machine learning *n.* a branch of artificial intelligence in which a computer generates rules underlying or based on raw data that has been fed into it.

machine moulding *n. Engineering.* the process of making moulds and cores for castings by mechanical means, usually by compacting the moulding sand by vibration instead of by ramming down by hand.

machine readable *adj.* (of data) in a form in which it can be fed into a computer.

machinery (mə'ʃiːnərɪ) *n., pl.* **-eries.** **1.** machines, machine parts, or machine systems collectively. **2.** a particular machine system or set of machines. **3.** a system similar to a machine: *the machinery of government.* **4.** literary devices used for effect in epic poetry.

machine screw *n.* a fastening screw with a machine-cut thread throughout the length of its shank.

machine shop *n.* a workshop in which machine tools are operated.

machine tool *n.* a power-driven machine, such as a lathe, miller, or grinder, for cutting, shaping, and finishing metals or other materials. —**ma'chine-ˌtooled** *adj.*

machine translation *n.* the production of text in one natural language from that in another by means of computer procedures.

machinist (mə'ʃiːnɪst) *n.* **1.** a person who operates machines to cut or process materials. **2.** a maker or repairer of machines.

machismo (mæ'kɪzməʊ, -'tʃɪz-) *n.* strong or exaggerated masculine pride or masculinity. [Mexican Spanish, from Spanish *macho* male, from Latin *masculus* MASCULINE]

Machmeter ('mækˌmiːtə) *n.* an instrument for measuring the Mach number of an aircraft in flight.

Mach number (mæk) *n.* (*often not cap.*) the ratio of the speed of a body in a particular medium to the speed of sound in that medium. Mach number 1 corresponds to the speed of sound. Often shortened to **Mach.** [C19: named after Ernst *Mach* (1838–1916), Austrian physicist and philosopher]

macho ('mætʃəʊ) *adj.* **1.** denoting or exhibiting pride in characteristics believed to be typically masculine, such as physical strength, sexual appetite, etc. ~*n., pl.* **machos.** **2.** a man who displays such characteristics. [C20: from Spanish: male; see MACHISMO]

machree (mə'kriː) *adj.* (*postpositive*) *Irish.* my dear: *mother machree.* [from Irish *mo croidhe*]

machtpolitik ('mɑːxtˌpɒlɪtiːk) *n.* power politics. [from German]

machzor *or* ***mahzor*** *Hebrew.* (max'zɔr; *English* mɑːk'zɔː) *n., pl.* *-zorim* (-zɔ'riːm; *English* -zə'riːm). a Jewish prayer book containing prescribed holiday rituals. [literally: cycle]

macintosh ('mækɪnˌtɒʃ) *n.* a variant spelling of **mackintosh.**

mack[1] (mæk) *n. Brit. informal.* a variant spelling of **mac,** short for **mackintosh** (senses 1, 3).

mack[2] (mæk) *n. Slang.* a pimp. [C19: shortened from obsolete *mackerel,* from Old French, of uncertain origin]

mackerel ('mækrəl) *n., pl.* **-rel** *or* **-rels.** **1.** a spiny-finned food fish, *Scomber scombrus,* occurring in northern coastal regions of the Atlantic and in the Mediterranean: family *Scombridae.* It has a deeply forked tail and a greenish-blue body marked with wavy dark bands on the back. Compare **Spanish mackerel** (sense 1). **2.** any of various other fishes of the family *Scombridae,* such as *Scomber colias* (**Spanish mackerel**) and *S. japonicus* (**Pacific mackerel**). ~Compare **horse mackerel.** [C13: from Anglo-French, from Old French *maquerel,* of unknown origin]

mackerel breeze *n.* a strong breeze. [C18: so named because the ruffling of the water by the wind creates good conditions for mackerel fishing]

mackerel shark *n.* another name for **porbeagle.**

mackerel sky *n.* a sky patterned with cirrocumulus or small altocumulus clouds. [from the similarity to the pattern on a mackerel's back]

Mackinaw coat ('mækɪˌnɔː) *n. Chiefly U.S. and Canadian.* a thick short double-breasted plaid coat. Also called: **mackinaw.** [C19: named after *Mackinaw,* variant of *Mackinac* (island in N Michigan)]

mackintosh *or* **macintosh** ('mækɪnˌtɒʃ) *n.* **1.** a waterproof raincoat made of rubberized cloth. **2.** such cloth. **3.** any raincoat. [C19: named after Charles *Macintosh* (1760–1843), who invented it]

mackle ('mækᵊl) *or* **macule** ('mækjuːl) *n. Printing.* a double or blurred impression caused by shifting paper or type. [C16: via French from Latin *macula* spot, stain]

Maclaurin's series (mə'klɔːrɪnz) *n. Maths.* an infinite sum giving the value of a function $f(x)$ in terms of the derivatives of the function evaluated at zero: $f(x) = f(0) + (f'(0)x)/1! + (f''(0)x^2)/2! + \ldots$. Also called: **Maclaurin series.** [C18: named after Colin *Maclaurin* (1698–1746), British mathematician who formulated it]

macle ('mækᵊl) *n.* another name for **chiastolite** and **twin** (sense 3). [C19: via French from Latin *macula* spot, stain]

McNaughten Rules *or* **McNaghten Rules** (mək'nɔːtᵊn) *pl. n.* (in English law) a set of rules established by the case of Regina v. McNaughten (1843) by which legal proof of insanity in the commission of a crime depends upon whether or not the accused can show either that he did not know what he was doing or that he is incapable of realizing that what he was doing was wrong.

Mâcon (*French* mɑkɔ̃) *n.* a red or white wine from the Mâcon area in central France, heavier than the other burgundies.

macramé (mə'krɑːmɪ) *n.* a type of ornamental work made by knotting and weaving coarse thread into a pattern. [C19: via French and Italian from Turkish *makrama* towel, from Arabic *migramah* striped cloth]

macrencephaly (ˌmækrɛn'sɛfəlɪ) *or* (*less commonly*) **macrencephalia** (ˌmækrənsɪ'feɪlɪə) *n.* the condition of having an abnormally large brain.

macro *or* **macro instruction** ('mækrəʊ) *n., pl.* **macros.** a single computer instruction that initiates a set of instructions to perform a specific task.

macro- *or before a vowel* **macr-** *combining form.* **1.** large, long, or great in size or duration: *macroscopic.* **2.** (in pathology) indicating abnormal enlargement or overdevelopment: *macrocyte.* Compare **micro-** (sense 4). [from Greek *makros* large; compare Latin *macer* MEAGRE]

macrobiotics (ˌmækrəʊbaɪ'ɒtɪks) *n.* (*functioning as sing.*) a dietary system in which foods are classified according to the principles of Yin and Yang. It advocates diets of whole grains and vegetables grown without chemical additives. [C20: from MACRO- + Greek *biotos* life + -ICS] —ˌ**macrobi'otic** *adj., n.*

macrocarpa (ˌmækrəʊ'kɑːpə) *n.* a large coniferous tree of New Zealand, *Cupressus macrocarpa,* used for shelter belts on farms and for rough timber. Also called: **Monterey cypress.** [C19: from New Latin, from Greek MACRO- + *karpos* fruit]

macrocephaly (ˌmækrəʊ'sɛfəlɪ) *or* (*less commonly*) **macrocephalia** (ˌmækrəʊsɪ'feɪlɪə) *n.* the condition of having an abnormally large head or skull. —**macrocephalic** (ˌmækrəʊsɪ'fælɪk) *or* ˌ**macro'cephalous** *adj.*

macroclimate ('mækrəʊˌklaɪmɪt) *n.* the prevailing climate of a large area. —**macroclimatic** (ˌmækrəʊklaɪ'mætɪk) *adj.* —ˌ**macrocli'matically** *adv.*

macrocosm ('mækrəˌkɒzəm) *n.* **1.** a complex structure, such as the universe or society, regarded as an entirety, as opposed to microcosms, which have a similar structure and are contained within it. **2.** any complex entity regarded as a complete system in itself. ~Compare **microcosm.** [C16: via French and Latin from Greek *makros kosmos* great world] —ˌ**macro'cosmic** *adj.* —ˌ**macro'cosmically** *adv.*

macrocyst ('mækrəʊˌsɪst) *n.* **1.** an unusually large cyst. **2.** (in slime moulds) an encysted resting protoplasmic mass. See **plasmodium** (sense 1).

macrocyte ('mækrəʊˌsaɪt) *n. Pathol.* an abnormally large red blood cell, over 10 μm in diameter. —**macrocytic** (ˌmækrəʊ'sɪtɪk) *adj.*

macrocytosis (ˌmækrəʊsaɪ'təʊsɪs) *n. Pathol.* the presence in the blood of macrocytes.

macroeconomics (ˌmækrəʊˌiːkə'nɒmɪks, -ˌɛk-) *n.* (*functioning as sing.*) the branch of economics concerned with aggregates, such as national income, consumption, and investment. Compare **microeconomics.** —ˌ**macroˌeco'nomic** *adj.*

macroevolution (ˌmækrəʊˌiːvə'luːʃən) *n. Biology.* the evolution of large taxonomic groups such as genera and families. —ˌ**macroˌevo'lutionary** *adj.*

macrogamete (ˌmækrəʊ'gæmiːt) *or* **megagamete** (ˌmɛgə'gæmiːt) *n.* the larger and apparently female of two gametes in conjugating protozoans. Compare **microgamete.**

macroglia (ˌmækrəʊ'glɪə) *n.* one of the two types of non-nervous tissue (glia) found in the central nervous system: includes astrocytes. Compare **microglia.**

macroglobulin (ˌmækrəʊ'glɒbjʊlɪn) *n. Immunol.* **1.** an immunoglobulin of unusually high relative molecular mass, observed in the blood in some diseases. **2.** Also called: **immunoglobulin M.** the normal form of this immunoglobulin.

macrograph ('mækrəʊˌgrɑːf, -ˌgræf) *n.* a photograph, drawing, etc., in which an object appears as large as or several times larger than the original. —**macrographic** (ˌmækrəʊ'græfɪk) *adj.*

macro lens *n.* a camera lens used for close-up photography (2–10 cm).

macrolepidoptera (ˌmækrəʊˌlɛpɪ'dɒptərə) *pl. n.* a collector's name for that part of the lepidoptera that comprises the butterflies and the larger moths (noctuids, geometrids, bombycids, springtails, etc.): a term without taxonomic significance. Compare **microlepidoptera.**

macromere ('mækrəʊˌmɪə) *n. Embryol.* any of the large yolk-filled cells formed by unequal cleavage of a fertilized ovum.

macromolecule (ˌmækrəʊ'mɒlɪˌkjuːl) *n.* any very large molecule, such as a protein or synthetic polymer. —**macromolecular** (ˌmækrəʊmə'lɛkjʊlə) *adj.*

macron ('mækrɒn) *n.* a diacritical mark (¯) placed over a letter, used in prosody, in the orthography of some languages, and in several types of phonetic respelling systems, to represent a long vowel. [C19: from Greek *makron* something long, from *makros* long]

macronucleus (ˌmækrəʊ'njuːklɪəs) *n., pl.* **-clei** (-klɪˌaɪ). the larger of the two nuclei in ciliated protozoans, involved in feeding and similar processes. Compare **micronucleus.**

macronutrient (ˌmækrəʊ'njuːtrɪənt) *n.* any substance, such as carbon, hydrogen, or oxygen, that is required in large amounts for healthy growth and development.

macrophage ('mækrəʊˌfeɪdʒ) *n.* any large phagocytic cell occurring in the blood, lymph, and connective tissue of vertebrates. See also **histiocyte.** —**macrophagic** (ˌmækrəʊ'fædʒɪk) *adj.*

macrophagous (mə'krɒfəgəs) *adj. Zoology.* (of an animal) feeding on relatively large particles of food.

macrophotography (ˌmækrəʊfə'tɒgrəfɪ) *n.* extremely close-up photography in which the image on the film is as large as, or larger than, the object.

macrophysics (ˌmækrəʊ'fɪzɪks) *n.* (*functioning as sing.*) the branch of physics concerned with macroscopic systems and objects.

macropsia (mə'krɒpsɪə) *n.* the condition of seeing everything in the field of view as larger than it really is, which can occur in diseases of the retina or in some brain disorders.

macropterous (mə'krɒptərəs) *adj.* (of certain animals, esp. some types of ant) having large wings.

macroscopic (ˌmækrəʊ'skɒpɪk) *adj.* **1.** large enough to be visible to the naked eye. Compare **microscopic.** **2.** comprehensive; concerned with large units. **3.** having astronomical dimensions. **4.** *Physics.* capable of being described by the statistical properties of a large number of parts. ~Also: **megascopic.** —ˌ**macro'scopically** *adv.*

macrosociology (ˌmækrəʊˌsəʊsɪ'ɒlədʒɪ) *n.* the branch of sociology concerned with the study of human societies on a wide scale. —ˌ**macroˌsocio'logical** *adj.*

macrosporangium (ˌmækrəʊspɔː'rændʒɪəm) *n., pl.* **-gia** (-dʒɪə). another name for **megasporangium.**

macrospore ('mækrəʊˌspɔː) *n.* another name for **megaspore** (sense 1).

macrotous (mə'krəʊtəs) *adj. Zoology.* having large ears. [from MACRO- + Greek *ous* ear]

macruran (mə'kruərən) *n.* **1.** any decapod crustacean of the group (formerly suborder) *Macrura,* which includes the lobsters, prawns, and crayfish. ~*adj. also* **macrurous, macrural,** *or* **macruroid.** **2.** of, relating to, or belonging to the *Macrura.* [C19: via New Latin, from Greek *makros* long + *oura* tail]

macula ('mækjʊlə) *or* **macule** ('mækjuːl) *n., pl.* **-ulae** (-jʊˌliː) *or* **-ules.** *Anatomy.* **1.** a small spot or area of distinct colour, esp. the macula lutea. **2.** any small discoloured spot or blemish on the skin, such as a freckle. [C14: from Latin] —'**macular** *adj.*

macula lutea ('luːtɪə) *n., pl.* **maculae luteae** ('luːtɪˌiː). a small yellowish oval-shaped spot, rich in cones, near the centre of the retina of the eye, where vision is especially sharp. See also **fovea centralis.** [New Latin, literally: yellow spot]

maculate *Archaic or literary.* ~*vb.* ('mækjʊˌleɪt). **1.** (*tr.*) to spot, stain, or pollute. ~*adj.* ('mækjʊlɪt). **2.** spotted or polluted. [C15: from Latin *maculāre* to stain]

maculation (ˌmækjʊ'leɪʃən) *n.* **1.** a pattern of spots, as on certain animals and plants. **2.** *Archaic.* the act of maculating or the state of being maculated.

macule ('mækjuːl) *n.* **1.** *Anatomy.* another name for **macula.** **2.** *Printing.* another name for **mackle.** [C15: from Latin *macula* spot]

Macumba *Portuguese.* (ma'kumba) *n.* a religious cult in Brazil that combines Christian and voodoo elements.

mad (mæd) *adj.* **madder, maddest.** **1.** mentally deranged; insane. **2.** senseless; foolish: *a mad idea.* **3.** (often foll. by *at*) *Informal.* angry; resentful. **4.** (foll. by *about, on,* or *over;* often postpositive) wildly enthusiastic (about) or fond (of): *mad about football; football-mad.* **5.** extremely excited or confused; frantic: *a mad rush.* **6.** wildly gay; boisterous: *a mad party.* **7.** temporarily overpowered by violent reactions, emotions, etc.: *mad with grief.* **8.** (of animals) **a.** unusually ferocious: *a mad buffalo.* **b.** afflicted with rabies. **9. like mad.** *Informal.* with great energy, enthusiasm, or haste; wildly. **10. mad as a hatter.** crazily eccentric. ~*vb.* **mads, madding, madded.** **11.** *U.S. or archaic.* to make or become mad; act or cause to act as if mad. [Old English *gemǣded,* past participle of *gemǣdan* to render insane; related to *gemād* insane, and to Old High German *gimeit* silly, crazy, Old Norse *meitha* to hurt, damage] —'**maddish** *adj.*

MAD (mæd) *n. U.S. acronym for* mutual assured destruction: a theory of nuclear deterrence whereby each side in a conflict has the capacity to destroy the other in retaliation for a nuclear attack.

madafu (ma'dafuː) *n. E African.* coconut milk. [C19: from Swahili]

Madagascan (ˌmædə'gæskən) *adj.* **1.** of, relating to, or denoting Madagascar, an island republic in the Indian Ocean, off the E coast of Africa, or its people. ~*n.* **2.** a native or inhabitant of Madagascar.

Madagascar aquamarine (ˌmædə'gæskə) *n.* a form of blue beryl from Madagascar, used as a gemstone.

madam ('mædəm) *n., pl.* **madams,** *or* (for sense 1) **mesdames** ('meɪˌdæm). **1.** a polite term of address for a woman, esp. one considered to be of relatively high social status. **2.** a woman who runs a brothel. **3.** *Brit. informal.* a precocious or pompous little girl. [C13: from Old French *ma dame* my lady]

madame ('mædəm; *French* madam) *n., pl.* **mesdames** ('meɪˌdæm; *French* medam). a married Frenchwoman: usually used as a title equivalent to *Mrs,* and sometimes extended to older unmarried women to show respect and to women of other nationalities. [C17: from French. See MADAM]

madcap ('mædˌkæp) *adj.* **1.** impulsive, reckless, or lively. ~*n.* **2.** an impulsive, reckless, or lively person. [C16: from MAD + *cap* (in the figurative sense: head)]

mad cow disease *n.* an informal name for **BSE.**

madden ('mædᵊn) *vb.* to make or become mad or angry.

maddening ('mædᵊnɪŋ) *adj.* **1.** serving to send mad. **2.** extremely irritating or annoying; exasperating. —'**maddeningly** *adv.* —'**maddeningness** *n.*

madder[1] ('mædə) *n.* **1.** any of several rubiaceous plants of the genus *Rubia,* esp. the Eurasian *R. tinctoria,* which has small yellow flowers and a red fleshy root. **2.** the root of this plant. **3.** a dark reddish-purple dye formerly obtained by fermentation of this root; identical to the synthetic dye, alizarin. **4.** a red lake obtained from alizarin and an inorganic base; used as a pigment in inks and paints. [Old English *mædere;* related to Middle Dutch *mēde,* Old Norse *mathra*]

madder[2] ('mædə) *adj.* the comparative of **mad.**

madding ('mædɪŋ) *adj. Archaic.* **1.** acting or behaving as if mad: *the madding crowd.* **2.** making mad; maddening. —'**maddingly** *adv.*

made (meɪd) *vb.* **1.** the past tense and past participle of **make**[1]. *~adj.* **2.** artificially produced. **3.** (*in combination*) produced or shaped as specified: *handmade.* **4. get** *or* **have it made.** *Informal.* to be assured of success. **5. made of money.** very rich.

made dish *n. Cooking.* a dish consisting of a number of different ingredients cooked together.

Madeira (mə'dɪərə) *n.* a rich strong fortified white wine made on the islands of Madeira in the N Atlantic.

Madeira cake *n. Brit.* a kind of rich sponge cake.

madeleine ('mædəlɪn, -ˌleɪn) *n.* a small fancy sponge cake usually coated with jam and coconut. [C19: perhaps after *Madeleine* Paulmier, French pastry cook]

mademoiselle (ˌmædmwə'zɛl; *French* madmwazɛl) *n., pl.* **mesdemoiselles** (ˌmeɪdmwə'zɛl; *French* medmwazɛl). **1.** a young unmarried French girl or woman: usually used as a title equivalent to *Miss.* **2.** a French teacher or governess. [C15: French, from *ma* my + *demoiselle* DAMSEL]

made-up *adj.* **1.** invented; fictional: *a made-up story.* **2.** wearing make-up: *a well made-up woman.* **3.** put together; assembled. **4.** (of a road) surfaced with tarmac, concrete, etc.

madhouse ('mædˌhaʊs) *n. Informal.* **1.** a mental hospital or asylum. **2.** a state of uproar or confusion.

madly ('mædlɪ) *adv.* **1.** in an insane or foolish manner. **2.** with great speed and energy. **3.** *Informal.* extremely or excessively: *I love you madly.*

madman ('mædmən) *or* (*fem.*) **madwoman** *n., pl.* **-men** *or* **-women.** a person who is insane, esp. one who behaves violently; lunatic.

madness ('mædnɪs) *n.* **1.** insanity; lunacy. **2.** extreme anger, excitement, or foolishness. **3.** a nontechnical word for **rabies.**

Madonna (mə'dɒnə) *n.* **1.** *Chiefly R.C. Church.* a designation of the Virgin Mary. **2.** (*sometimes not cap.*) a picture or statue of the Virgin Mary. [C16: Italian, from *ma* my + *donna* lady]

Madonna lily *n.* a perennial widely cultivated Mediterranean lily plant, *Lilium candidum,* with white trumpetshaped flowers. Also called: **Annunciation lily.**

madras ('mædrəs, mə'dræs, -'drɑːs) *n.* **1. a.** a strong fine cotton or silk fabric, usually with a woven stripe. **b.** (*as modifier*): *madras cotton.* **2.** something made of this, esp. a scarf. [C19: so named because the material originated in the *Madras* area of SE India]

madrepore (ˌmædrɪ'pɔː) *n.* any coral of the genus *Madrepora,* many of which occur in tropical seas and form large coral reefs: order *Zoantharia.* [C18: via French from Italian *madrepora* mother-stone, from *madre* mother + *-pora,* from Latin *porus* or Greek *poros* calcareous stone, stalactite] —ˌ**madre'poral, madreporic** (ˌmædrɪ'pɒrɪk), **madreporitic** (ˌmædrɪpə'rɪtɪk), *or* ˌ**madre'porian** *adj.*

madrigal ('mædrɪgᵊl) *n.* **1.** *Music.* a type of 16th- or 17th-century part song for unaccompanied voices with an amatory or pastoral text. Compare **glee** (sense 2). **2.** a 14th-century Italian song, related to a pastoral stanzaic verse form. [C16: from Italian, from Medieval Latin *mātricāle* primitive, apparently from Latin *mātrīcālis* of the womb, from *matrīx* womb] —'**madrigalˌesque** *adj.* —**madrigalian** (ˌmædrɪ'gælɪən, -'geɪ-) *adj.* —'**madrigalist** *n.*

madrilène ('mædrɪˌlɛn, -ˌleɪn; *French* madrilɛn) *n.* a cold consommé flavoured with tomato juice. [shortened from French (*consommé*) *madrilène* from Spanish *madrileño* of Madrid]

madroña (mə'drəʊnjə), **madroño** (mə'drəʊnjəʊ), *or* **madrone** (mə'drəʊnə) *n., pl.* **-ñas, -ños,** *or* **-nes.** an ericaceous North American evergreen tree or shrub, *Arbutus menziesii,* with white flowers and red berry-like fruits. See also **strawberry tree.** [C19: from Spanish]

maduro (mə'dʊərəʊ) *adj.* **1.** (of cigars) dark and strong. *~n., pl.* **-ros. 2.** a cigar of this type. [Spanish, literally: ripe, from Latin *mātūrus* ripe, MATURE]

madwort ('mædˌwɜːt) *n.* **1.** a low-growing Eurasian boraginaceous plant, *Asperugo procumbens,* with small blue flowers. **2.** any of certain other plants, such as alyssum. [C16: once alleged to be a cure for madness]

madzoon (mɑːd'zuːn) *n.* a variant of **matzoon.**

Maecenas (miː'siːnæs) *n.* a wealthy patron of the arts. [named after Gaius *Maecenas* (?70–8 B.C.), Roman statesman and patron]

maelstrom ('meɪlstrəʊm) *n.* **1.** a large powerful whirlpool. **2.** any turbulent confusion. [C17: from obsolete Dutch *maelstroom,* from *malen* to grind, whirl round + *stroom* STREAM]

maenad *or* **menad** ('miːnæd) *n.* **1.** *Classical myth.* a woman participant in the orgiastic rites of Dionysus; bacchante. **2.** a frenzied woman. [C16: from Latin *Maenas,* from Greek *mainas* madwoman] —**mae'nadic** *adj.* —**mae'nadically** *adv.* —'**maenadism** *n.*

maestoso (maɪ'stəʊsəʊ) *Music.* *~adj., adv.* **1.** to be performed majestically. *~n.* **2.** a piece or passage directed to be played in this way. [C18: Italian: majestic, from Latin *māiestās* MAJESTY]

maestro ('maɪstrəʊ) *n., pl.* **-tri** (-trɪ) *or* **-tros. 1.** a distinguished music teacher, conductor, or musician. **2.** any man regarded as the master of an art: often used as a term of address. **3.** See **maestro di cappella.** [C18: Italian: master]

maestro di cappella (dɪ kə'pɛlə) *n.* a person in charge of an orchestra, esp. a private one attached to the palace of a prince in Italy during the baroque period. See **kapellmeister.** [Italian: master of the chapel]

mae west (meɪ) *n. Slang.* an inflatable life jacket, esp. as issued to the U.S. armed forces for emergency use. [C20: after *Mae West,* 1892–1980, American actress, renowned for her generous bust]

MAFF (in Britain) *abbrev. for* Ministry of Agriculture, Fisheries, and Food.

maffick ('mæfɪk) *vb.* (*intr.*) *Brit., archaic.* to celebrate extravagantly and publicly. [C20: back formation from *Mafeking,* town in South Africa, from the rejoicings at the relief of the siege there in 1900] —'**mafficker** *n.*

Mafia *or* **Maffia** ('mæfɪə) *n.* **1. the.** an international secret organization founded in Sicily, probably in opposition to tyranny. It developed into a criminal organization and in the late 19th century was carried to the U.S. by Italian immigrants. **2.** any group considered to resemble the Mafia. [C19: from Sicilian dialect of Italian, literally hostility to the law, boldness, perhaps from Arabic *mahyah* bragging]

mafioso (ˌmæfɪ'əʊsəʊ; *Italian* mafi'oso) *n., pl.* **-sos** *or* **-si** (*Italian* -si). a person belonging to the Mafia.

maftir ('mɑftir) *n. Judaism.* **1.** the final section of the weekly Torah reading. **2.** the person to whom it is read, who also reads the Haftarah.

mag[1] (mæg) *n. Informal.* See **magazine.**

mag[2] (mæg) *Informal, now chiefly Austral.* *~vb.* **mags, magging, magged.** (*intr.*) **1.** to talk; chatter. *~n.* **2.** talk; chatter. [C18: from *Mag,* see MAGPIE]

mag. *abbrev. for:* **1.** magazine. **2.** magnesium. **3.** magnetic. **4.** magnetism. **5.** magnets. **6.** magnitude.

magainin (mə'geɪnɪn) *n.* any of a series of related substances with antibiotic properties, derived from the skins of frogs. [C20: from Hebrew *magain* a shield]

magazine (ˌmægə'ziːn) *n.* **1.** a periodical paperback publication containing articles, fiction, photographs, etc. **2.** a metal case holding several cartridges used in some kinds of automatic firearms; it is removed and replaced when empty. **3.** a building or compartment for storing weapons, explosives, military provisions, etc. **4.** a stock of ammunition. **5.** a device for continuously recharging a stove or boiler with solid fuel. **6.** *Photog.* another name for **cartridge** (sense 5). **7.** a rack for automatically feeding a number of slides through a projector. **8.** a TV or radio programme made up of a series of short nonfiction items. [C16: via French *magasin* from Italian *magazzino,* from Arabic *makhāzin,* plural of *makhzan* storehouse, from *khazana* to store away]

magdalen ('mægdəlɪn) *or* **magdalene** ('mægdəˌliːn, ˌmægdə'liːnɪ) *n.* **1.** *Literary.* a reformed prostitute. **2.** *Rare.* a reformatory for prostitutes. [from Mary *Magdalene,* in the New Testament (Luke 7:36–50)]

Magdalenian (ˌmægdə'liːnɪən) *adj.* **1.** of or relating to the latest Palaeolithic culture in Europe, which ended about 10 000 years ago. *~n.* **2.** the Magdalenian culture. [C19: from French *magdalénien,* after *La Madeleine,* village in Dordogne, France, near which artefacts of the culture were found]

mage (meɪdʒ) *n.* an archaic word for **magician.** [C14: from MAGUS]

Magellanic Cloud (ˌmægɪ'lænɪk) *n.* either of two small irregular galaxies, the **Large Magellanic Cloud** (Nubecula Major) and the **Small Magellanic Cloud** (Nubecula Minor), situated near the S celestial pole at a distance of 160 000 light years and classified as satellites of the Galaxy. [named after Ferdinand *Magellan* (?1480–1521), Portuguese navigator]

Magen David *or* **Mogen David** ('mɔːgən 'deɪvɪd) *n. Judaism.* another name for the **Star of David.** [C20: from Hebrew *māghēn Dāwīdh* shield of David]

magenta (mə'dʒɛntə) *n.* **1. a.** a deep purplish red that is the complementary colour of green and, with yellow and cyan, forms a set of primary colours. **b.** (*as adj.*): *a magenta filter.* **2.** another name for **fuchsin.** [C19: named after *Magenta,* Italy, alluding to the blood shed in a battle there (1859)]

maggie ('mægɪ) *n. Slang.* a magpie.

maggot ('mægət) *n.* **1.** the soft limbless larva of dipterous insects, esp. the housefly and blowfly, occurring in decaying organic matter. **2.** *Rare.* a fancy or whim. [C14: from earlier *mathek;* related to Old Norse *mathkr* worm, Old English *matha,* Old High German *mado* grub]

maggoty ('mægətɪ) *adj.* **1.** relating to, resembling, or ridden with maggots. **2.** *Slang.* very drunk. **3.** *Austral. slang.* annoyed, angry.

Maghrebi *or* **Maghribi** (mæˌgrɪbɪ) *adj.* **1.** of or relating to the people or countries of NW Africa (Maghreb), including Morocco,

Algeria, Tunisia, and sometimes Libya. ~*n.* 2. a native of Maghreb. [from Arabic, literally: the West]

magi ('meɪdʒaɪ) *n.* the plural of **magus.**

magic ('mædʒɪk) *n.* 1. the art that, by use of spells, supposedly invokes supernatural powers to influence events; sorcery. 2. the practice of this art. 3. the practice of illusory tricks to entertain other people; conjuring. 4. any mysterious or extraordinary quality or power: *the magic of springtime.* 5. **like magic.** very quickly. ~*adj. also* **magical.** 6. of or relating to magic: *a magic spell.* 7. possessing or considered to possess mysterious powers: *a magic wand.* 8. unaccountably enchanting: *magic beauty.* 9. *Informal.* wonderful; marvellous; exciting. ~*vb.* **-ics, -icking, -icked.** (*tr.*) 10. to transform or produce by or as if by magic. 11. (foll. by *away*) to cause to disappear by or as if by magic. [C14: via Old French *magique,* from Greek *magikē* witchcraft, from *magos* MAGUS] —'**magical** *adj.* —'**magically** *adv.*

magic carpet *n.* (in fairy stories) a carpet capable of transporting people through the air.

magic eye *n.* a miniature cathode-ray tube in some radio receivers, on the screen of which a pattern is displayed in order to assist tuning.

magician (mə'dʒɪʃən) *n.* 1. another term for **conjurer.** 2. a person who practises magic. 3. a person who has extraordinary skill, influence, or qualities.

magic lantern *n.* an early type of slide projector. Sometimes shortened to **lantern.**

magic mushroom *n. Informal.* any of various types of fungi that contain a hallucinogenic substance, esp. *Psilocybe mexicana,* which contains psilocybin.

magic number *n.* 1. *Physics.* any of the numbers 2, 8, 20, 28, 50, 82, and 126. Nuclides with these numbers of nucleons appear to have greater stability than other nuclides. 2. *Chem.* a number of atoms that is particularly stable in certain types of compound that have clusters of the same type of atom.

magic realism *or* **magical realism** *n.* a style of painting or writing that depicts images or scenes of surreal fantasy in a representational or realistic way. —**magic realist** *or* **magical realist** *n.*

magic square *n.* a square array of rows of integers arranged so that the sum of the integers is the same when taken vertically, horizontally, or diagonally.

magilp (mə'gɪlp) *n. Arts.* a variant spelling of **megilp.**

Maginot line ('mæʒɪˌnəʊ) *n.* any line of defence in which blind confidence is placed. [named after the ineffective line of fortifications along the French–German border whose construction was authorized (1929) by André *Maginot* (1877–1932), French minister of war]

magisterial (ˌmædʒɪ'stɪərɪəl) *adj.* 1. commanding; authoritative. 2. domineering; dictatorial. 3. of or relating to a teacher or person of similar status. 4. of or relating to a magistrate. [C17: from Late Latin *magisteriālis,* from *magister* master] —ˌ**magis'terially** *adv.* —ˌ**magis'terialness** *n.*

magisterium (ˌmædʒɪ'stɪərɪəm) *n.* the teaching authority or function of the Roman Catholic Church. [C19: see MAGISTERY]

magistery ('mædʒɪstərɪ, -trɪ) *n., pl.* **-teries.** *Alchemy.* 1. an agency or substance, such as the philosopher's stone, believed to transmute other substances. 2. any substance capable of healing. [C16: from Medieval Latin *magisterium,* from Latin: mastery, from *magister* master]

magistracy ('mædʒɪstrəsɪ) *or* **magistrature** ('mædʒɪstrəˌtjʊə) *n., pl.* **-cies** *or* **-tures.** 1. the office or function of a magistrate. 2. magistrates collectively. 3. the district under the jurisdiction of a magistrate.

magistral (mə'dʒɪstrəl) *adj.* 1. of, relating to, or characteristic of a master. 2. *Pharmacol.* made up according to a special prescription. Compare **officinal.** 3. *Fortifications.* determining the location of other fortifications: *the magistral line.* ~*n.* 4. a fortification in a determining position. [C16: from Latin *magistrālis* concerning a master, from *magister* master] —**magistrality** (ˌmædʒɪ'strælɪtɪ) *n.* —**magistratically** (ˌmædʒɪ'strætɪkəlɪ) *adv.*

magistrate ('mædʒɪˌstreɪt, -strɪt) *n.* 1. a public officer concerned with the administration of law. 2. another name for **justice of the peace.** 3. *N.Z.* the former name for **district court judge.** [C17: from Latin *magistrātus,* from *magister* master] —'**magisˌtrateship** *n.*

magistrates' court *n.* (in England) a court of summary jurisdiction held before two or more justices of the peace or a stipendiary magistrate to deal with minor crimes, certain civil actions, and preliminary hearings.

Maglemosian *or* **Maglemosean** (ˌmæglə'məʊzɪən) *n.* 1. the first Mesolithic culture of N Europe, dating from 8000 B.C. to about 5000 B.C.: important for the rare wooden objects that have been preserved, such as dugout canoes. ~*adj.* 2. designating or relating to this culture. [C20: named after the site at *Maglemose,* Denmark, where the culture was first classified]

maglev ('mægˌlɛv) *n.* a type of high-speed train that runs on magnets supported by a magnetic field generated around the track. [C20: from *mag(netic) lev(itation)*]

magma ('mægmə) *n., pl.* **-mas** *or* **-mata** (-mətə). 1. a paste or suspension consisting of a finely divided solid dispersed in a liquid. 2. hot molten rock, usually formed in the earth's upper mantle, some of which finds its way into the crust and onto the earth's surface, where it solidifies to form igneous rock. [C15, from Latin: dregs (of an ointment), from Greek: salve made by kneading, from *massein* to knead] —**magmatic** (mæg'mætɪk) *adj.* —'**magmatism** *n.*

magma chamber *n.* a reservoir of magma in the earth's upper crust where the magma may reside temporarily on its way from the upper mantle to the earth's surface.

magna cum laude ('mægnə kʊm 'laʊdeɪ) *Chiefly U.S.* with great praise: the second of three designations for above-average achievement in examinations. [Latin]

magnanimity (ˌmægnə'nɪmɪtɪ) *n., pl.* **-ties.** generosity. [C14: via Old French from Latin *magnanimitās,* from *magnus* great + *animus* soul]

magnanimous (mæg'nænɪməs) *adj.* generous and noble. [C16: from Latin *magnanimus* great-souled] —**mag'nanimously** *adv.* —**mag'nanimousness** *n.*

magnate ('mægneɪt, -nɪt) *n.* 1. a person of power and rank in any sphere, esp. in industry. 2. *History.* a great nobleman. 3. (formerly) a member of the upper chamber in certain European parliaments, as in Hungary. [C15: back formation from earlier *magnates* from Late Latin: great men, plural of *magnās,* from Latin *magnus* great] —'**magnateˌship** *n.*

magnesia (mæg'niːʃə) *n.* another name for **magnesium oxide.** [C14: via Medieval Latin from Greek *Magnēsia,* of *Magnēs* ancient mineral-rich region] —**mag'nesian, magnesic** (mæg'niːsɪk), *or* **mag'nesial** *adj.*

magnesite ('mægnɪˌsaɪt) *n.* a white, colourless, or lightly tinted mineral consisting of naturally occurring magnesium carbonate in hexagonal crystalline form: a source of magnesium and also used in the manufacture of refractory bricks. Formula: $MgCO_3$. [C19: from MAGNESIUM + -ITE[1]]

magnesium (mæg'niːzɪəm) *n.* a light silvery-white metallic element of the alkaline earth series that burns with an intense white flame, occurring principally in magnesite, dolomite, and carnallite: used in light structural alloys, flashbulbs, flares, and fireworks. Symbol: Mg; atomic no.: 12; atomic wt.: 24.312; valency: 2; relative density: 1.738; melting pt.: 651°C; boiling pt.: 1107°C. [C19: New Latin, from MAGNESIA]

magnesium oxide *n.* a white tasteless substance occurring naturally as periclase: used as an antacid and laxative and in refractory materials, such as crucibles and fire bricks. Formula: MgO. Also called: **magnesia.**

magnet ('mægnɪt) *n.* 1. a body that can attract certain substances, such as iron or steel, as a result of a magnetic field; a piece of ferromagnetic substance. See also **electromagnet.** 2. a person or thing that exerts a great attraction. [C15: via Latin from Greek *magnēs,* shortened from *ho Magnēs lithos* the Magnesian stone. See MAGNESIA]

magnetic (mæg'nɛtɪk) *adj.* 1. of, producing, or operated by means of magnetism. 2. of or concerned with a magnet. 3. of or concerned with the magnetism of the earth: *the magnetic equator.* 4. capable of being magnetized. 5. exerting a powerful attraction: *a magnetic personality.* —**mag'netically** *adv.*

magnetic bottle *n.* a configuration of magnetic fields for containing the plasma in controlled thermonuclear reactions.

magnetic bubble *n. Physics.* a small round magnetic domain induced by a magnetic field in a thin film of magnetic material, used in certain types of computer memories.

magnetic character reader *n.* a device that automatically scans and interprets characters printed with magnetic ink. It operates by the process of **magnetic character recognition.**

magnetic circuit *n.* a closed path described by magnetic flux, analogous to a circuit through which an electric current flows.

magnetic compass *n.* a compass containing a magnetic needle pivoted in a horizontal plane, that indicates the direction of magnetic north at points on the earth's surface.

magnetic confinement *n.* another name for **containment** (sense 3).

magnetic constant *n.* the permeability of free space, which has the value $4\pi \times 10^{-7}$ henry per metre. Symbol: μ_0 Also called: **absolute permeability.**

magnetic course *n.* an aircraft's course in relation to the magnetic north. Also called: **magnetic heading.**

magnetic declination *n.* the angle that a compass needle makes with the direction of the geographical north pole at any given point on the earth's surface. Also called: **declination, magnetic variation.**

magnetic dip *or* **inclination** *n.* another name for **dip** (sense 27).

magnetic dipole moment *n.* a measure of the magnetic strength of a magnet or current-carrying coil, expressed as the torque produced when the magnet or coil is set with its axis perpendicular to unit magnetic field. Symbol: m, j Also called: **magnetic moment.** Compare **electromagnetic moment.**

magnetic disk *n. Computer technol.* another name for **disk** (sense 2).

magnetic epoch *n. Geology.* a geologically long period of time during which the magnetic field of the earth retains the same polarity. The magnetic field may reverse during such a period for a geologically short period of time (a **magnetic event**).

magnetic equator *n.* an imaginary line on the earth's surface, near the equator, at all points on which there is no magnetic dip. Also called: **aclinic line.**

magnetic field *n.* a field of force surrounding a permanent magnet or a moving charged particle, in which another permanent magnet or moving charge experiences a force. Compare **electric field.**

magnetic flux *n.* **1.** a measure of the strength of a magnetic field over a given area, equal to the product of the area and the magnetic flux density through it. Symbol: ϕ **2.** a magnetic field.

magnetic flux density *n.* a measure of the strength of a magnetic field at a given point, expressed by the force per unit length on a conductor carrying unit current at that point. Symbol: B Also called: **magnetic induction.**

magnetic induction *n.* another name for **magnetic flux density.**

magnetic ink *n.* ink containing particles of a magnetic material used for printing characters for magnetic character recognition.

magnetic ink character recognition *n.* the process of reading characters printed in magnetic ink. Abbrev.: **MICR.**

magnetic lens *n.* a set of magnets, esp. electromagnets, used to focus or defocus a beam of charged particles in an electron microscope, particle accelerator, or similar device.

magnetic meridian *n.* a continuous imaginary line around the surface of the earth passing through both magnetic poles.

magnetic mine *n.* a mine designed to activate when a magnetic field such as that generated by the metal of a ship's hull is detected.

magnetic mirror *n. Physics.* a configuration of magnetic fields used to confine charged particles, as in a magnetic bottle.

magnetic moment *n.* short for **magnetic dipole moment** or **electromagnetic moment.**

magnetic monopole *n.* another name for **monopole** (sense 2).

magnetic needle *n.* a slender magnetized rod used in certain instruments, such as the magnetic compass, for indicating the direction of a magnetic field.

magnetic north *n.* the direction in which a compass needle points, at an angle (the declination) from the direction of true (geographic) north.

magnetic particle inspection *n. Engineering.* a method of testing for cracks and other defects in a magnetic material, such as steel, by covering it with a magnetic powder and magnetizing it: any variation in the concentration of the powder indicates a flaw in the material.

magnetic pick-up *n.* a type of record player pick-up in which the stylus moves an iron core in a coil, causing a changing magnetic field that produces the current.

magnetic pole *n.* **1.** either of two regions in a magnet where the magnetic induction is concentrated. **2.** either of two variable points on the earth's surface towards which a magnetic needle points, where the lines of force of the earth's magnetic field are vertical.

magnetic resonance *n.* the response by atoms, molecules, or nuclei subjected to a magnetic field to radio waves or other forms of energy: used in medicine for scanning (**magnetic resonance imaging**).

magnetics (mæɡˈnɛtɪks) *n.* (*functioning as sing.*) the branch of physics concerned with magnetism.

magnetic storm *n.* a sudden severe disturbance of the earth's magnetic field, caused by emission of charged particles from the sun.

magnetic stripe *n.* (across the back of various types of cheque card, credit card, etc.) a dark stripe of magnetic material consisting of several tracks onto which information may be coded and which may be read or written to electronically.

magnetic tape *n.* a long narrow plastic or metal strip coated or impregnated with a ferromagnetic material such as iron oxide, used to record sound or video signals or to store information in computers. Sometimes (informally) shortened to **mag tape.**

magnetic tape unit *or* **drive** *n.* a computer device that moves reels of magnetic tape past read-write heads so that data can be transferred to or from the computer.

magnetic variation *n.* another name for **magnetic declination.**

magnetism (ˈmæɡnɪˌtɪzəm) *n.* **1.** the property of attraction displayed by magnets. **2.** any of a class of phenomena in which a field of force is caused by a moving electric charge. See also **electromagnetism, ferromagnetism, diamagnetism, paramagnetism.** **3.** the branch of physics concerned with magnetic phenomena. **4.** powerful attraction. —**ˈmagnetist** *n.*

magnetite (ˈmæɡnɪˌtaɪt) *n.* a black magnetic mineral, found in igneous and metamorphic rocks and as a separate deposit. It is a source of iron. Composition: iron oxide. Formula: Fe_3O_4. Crystal structure: cubic. —**magnetitic** (ˌmæɡnɪˈtɪtɪk) *adj.*

magnetize *or* **magnetise** (ˈmæɡnɪˌtaɪz) *vb.* (*tr.*) **1.** to make (a substance or object) magnetic. **2.** to attract strongly. **3.** an obsolete word for **mesmerize.** —ˌ**magnetˈizable** *or* ˌ**magnetˈisable** *adj.* —ˌ**magnetiˈzation** *or* ˌ**magnetiˈsation** *n.* —ˈ**magnetˌizer** *or* ˈ**magnetˌiser** *n.*

magneto (mæɡˈniːtəʊ) *n., pl.* **-tos.** a small electric generator in which the magnetic field is produced by a permanent magnet, esp. one for providing the spark in an internal-combustion engine. [C19: short for *magnetoelectric generator*]

magneto- *combining form.* indicating magnetism or magnetic properties: *magnetosphere.*

magnetochemistry (mæɡˌniːtəʊˈkɛmɪstrɪ) *n.* the branch of chemistry concerned with the relationship between magnetic and chemical properties. —**magˌnetoˈchemical** *adj.*

magnetoelectricity (mæɡˌniːtəʊɪlɛkˈtrɪsɪtɪ) *n.* electricity produced by the action of magnetic fields. —**magˌnetoeˈlectric** *or* **magˌnetoeˈlectrical** *adj.*

magnetograph (mæɡˈniːtəʊˌɡrɑːf, -ˌɡræf) *n.* a recording magnetometer, usually used for studying variations in the earth's magnetic field.

magnetohydrodynamics (mæɡˌniːtəʊˌhaɪdrəʊdaɪˈnæmɪks) *n.* (*functioning as sing.*) **1.** the study of the behaviour of conducting fluids, such as liquid metals or plasmas, in magnetic fields. **2.** the generation of electricity by subjecting a plasma to a magnetic field and collecting the deflected free electrons. ~Abbrev.: **MHD.** —**magˌnetoˌhydrodynamic** *adj.*

magnetometer (ˌmæɡnɪˈtɒmɪtə) *n.* any instrument for measuring the intensity or direction of a magnetic field, esp. the earth's field. —**magnetometric** (ˌmæɡnɪtəʊˈmɛtrɪk) *adj.* —ˌ**magneˈtometry** *n.*

magnetomotive (mæɡˌniːtəʊˈməʊtɪv) *adj.* causing a magnetic flux.

magnetomotive force *n.* the agency producing a magnetic flux, considered analogous to the electromotive force in an electric circuit; equal to the circular integral of the magnetic field strength. Symbol: F

magneton (ˈmæɡnɪˌtɒn, mæɡˈniːtɒn) *n.* **1.** Also called: **Bohr magneton.** a unit of magnetic moment equal to $eh/4\pi m$ where e and m are the charge and mass of an electron and h is the Planck constant. It has the value $9.274\ 096 \times 10^{-24}$ joule per tesla. Symbol: β or m_B **2.** Also called: **nuclear magneton.** a similar unit equal to $\beta m/M$ where M is the mass of the proton. [C20: from MAGNET + (ELECTR)ON]

magnetosphere (mæɡˈniːtəʊˌsfɪə) *n.* the region surrounding the earth in which the behaviour of charged particles is dominated by the earth's magnetic field. —**magnetospheric** (mæɡˌniːtəʊˈsfɛrɪk) *adj.*

magnetostatics (mæɡˌniːtəʊˈstætɪks) *n.* (*functioning as sing.*). *Physics.* the study of steady-state magnetic fields.

magnetostriction (mæɡˌniːtəʊˈstrɪkʃən) *n.* a change in dimensions of a ferromagnetic material that is subjected to a magnetic field. [C19: from MAGNETO- + CONSTRICTION] —**magˌnetoˈstrictive** *adj.*

magnetron (ˈmæɡnɪˌtrɒn) *n.* a two-electrode electronic valve used with an applied magnetic field to generate high-power microwave oscillations, esp. for use in radar. [C20: from MAGNET + ELECTRON]

magnet school *n.* a school that provides a focus on one subject area throughout its curriculum in order to attract, often from an early age, pupils who wish to specialize in this subject.

magnet steel *n. Engineering.* steel used for the manufacture of permanent magnets, often having a high cobalt content and smaller amounts of nickel, aluminium, or copper.

magnific (mæɡˈnɪfɪk) *or* **magnifical** *adj. Archaic.* magnificent, grandiose, or pompous. [C15: via Old French from Latin *magnificus* great in deeds, from *magnus* great + *facere* to do] —**magˈnifically** *adv.*

Magnificat (mæɡˈnɪfɪˌkæt) *n. Christianity.* the hymn of the Virgin Mary (Luke 1:46-55), used as a canticle. [from the opening phrase in the Latin version, *Magnificat anima mea Dominum* (my soul doth magnify the Lord)]

magnification (ˌmæɡnɪfɪˈkeɪʃən) *n.* **1.** the act of magnifying or the state of being magnified. **2.** the degree to which something is magnified. **3.** a copy, photograph, drawing, etc., of something magnified. **4.** a measure of the ability of a lens or other optical instrument to magnify, expressed as the ratio of the size of the image to that of the object.

magnificence (mæɡˈnɪfɪsəns) *n.* the quality of being magnificent. [C14: via French from Latin *magnificentia*]

magnificent (mæɡˈnɪfɪsᵊnt) *adj.* **1.** splendid or impressive in appearance. **2.** superb or very fine. **3.** (esp. of ideas) noble or elevated. **4.** *Archaic.* great or exalted in rank or action. [C16: from Latin *magnificentio* more splendid; irregular comparative of *magnificus* great in deeds; see MAGNIFIC] —**magˈnificently** *adv.* —**magˈnificentness** *n.*

magnifico (mæɡˈnɪfɪˌkəʊ) *n., pl.* **-coes.** a magnate; grandee. [C16: Italian from Latin *magnificus*; see MAGNIFIC]

magnify (ˈmæɡnɪˌfaɪ) *vb.* **-fies, -fying, -fied.** **1.** to increase, cause to increase, or be increased in apparent size, as through the action of a lens, microscope, etc. **2.** to exaggerate or become exaggerated in importance: *don't magnify your troubles.* **3.** (*tr.*) *Rare.* to increase in actual size. **4.** (*tr.*) *Archaic.* to glorify. [C14: via Old French from Latin *magnificāre* to praise; see MAGNIFIC] —ˈ**magniˌfiable** *adj.*

magnifying glass *or* **magnifier** *n.* a convex lens used to produce an enlarged image of an object.

magniloquent (mæɡˈnɪləkwənt) *adj.* (of speech) lofty in style; grandiloquent. [C17: from Latin *magnus* great + *loquī* to speak] —**magˈniloquence** *n.* —**magˈniloquently** *adv.*

magnitude (ˈmæɡnɪˌtjuːd) *n.* **1.** relative importance or significance: *a problem of the first magnitude.* **2.** relative size or extent: *the magnitude of the explosion.* **3.** *Maths.* a number assigned to a quantity, such as weight, and used as a basis of comparison for the measurement of similar quantities. **4.** Also called: **apparent magnitude.** *Astronomy.* the apparent brightness of a celestial body expressed on a numerical scale on which bright stars have a low value. Values range from –27 (the sun) to +23 measured either by eye (**visual magnitude**) or by photographic methods (**photographic magnitude**). Each integral value represents a brightness 2.512 times greater than the next highest integral value. See also **absolute magnitude. 5.** Also called: **earthquake magnitude.** *Geology.* a measure of the size of an earthquake based on the quantity of energy released: specified on the Richter scale. See **Richter scale.** [C14: from Latin *magnitūdō* size, from *magnus* great] —ˌ**magniˈtudinous** *adj.*

magnolia (mægˈnəʊlɪə) *n.* **1.** any tree or shrub of the magnoliaceous genus *Magnolia* of Asia and North America: cultivated for their white, pink, purple, or yellow showy flowers. **2.** the flower of any of these plants. **3.** a very pale pinkish-white or purplish-white colour. [C18: New Latin, named after Pierre *Magnol* (1638–1715), French botanist]

magnoliaceous (mægˌnəʊlɪˈeɪʃəs) *adj.* of, relating to, or belonging to the *Magnoliaceae,* a family of trees and shrubs, including magnolias and the tulip tree, having large showy flowers.

magnolia metal *n. Engineering.* an alloy used for bearings, consisting largely of lead (up to 80 per cent) and antimony, with the addition of smaller quantities of iron and tin.

magnox (ˈmægnɒks) *n.* an alloy consisting mostly of magnesium with small amounts of aluminium and other metals, used in fuel elements of nuclear reactors. [C20: from *mag(nesium) n(o) ox(idation)*]

magnox reactor *n.* a nuclear reactor using carbon dioxide as the coolant, graphite as the moderator, and uranium cased in magnox as the fuel.

magnum (ˈmægnəm) *n., pl.* **-nums.** a wine bottle holding the equivalent of two normal bottles (approximately 52 fluid ounces). [C18: from Latin: a big thing, from *magnus* large]

magnum opus *n.* a great work of art or literature, esp. the greatest single work of an artist. [Latin]

magnus hitch (ˈmægnəs) *n.* a knot similar to a clove hitch but having one more turn. [C19 *magnus,* of unknown origin]

magot (mɑːˈgəʊ, ˈmægət) *n.* **1.** a Chinese or Japanese figurine in a crouching position, usually grotesque. **2.** a less common name for **Barbary ape.** [C17: from French: grotesque figure, after the Biblical giant *Magog*]

magpie (ˈmægˌpaɪ) *n.* **1.** any of various passerine birds of the genus *Pica,* esp. *P. pica,* having a black-and-white plumage, long tail, and a chattering call: family *Corvidae* (crows, etc.). **2.** any of various similar birds of the Australian family *Cracticidae.* See also **butcherbird** (sense 2). **3.** any of various other similar or related birds. **4.** (*often cap.*) a variety of domestic fancy pigeon typically having black-and-white markings. **5.** *Brit.* a person who hoards small objects. **6.** a person who chatters. **7. a.** the outmost ring but one on a target. **b.** a shot that hits this ring. [C17: from *Mag* diminutive of *Margaret,* used to signify a chatterbox + PIE[2]]

magpie goose *n.* a large black-and-white goose, *Anseranas semipalmata,* of N Australia and adjacent islands.

magpie lark *n.* a common black-and-white bird of Australia, *Grallina cyanoleuca,* that builds a mud nest. Also called: **peewee.**

magpie moth *n.* **1.** a geometrid moth, *Abraxas grossulariata,* showing variable patterning in black on white or yellow, whose looper larvae attack currant and gooseberry bushes. The paler **clouded magpie** is *A. sylvata.* **2. small magpie.** an unrelated micro, *Eurrhypara hortulata.*

MAgr *abbrev. for* Master of Agriculture.

mag tape *n. Informal.* short for **magnetic tape.**

maguey (ˈmægweɪ) *n.* **1.** any of various tropical American agave plants of the genera *Agave* or *Furcraea,* esp. one that yields a fibre or is used in making an alcoholic beverage. **2.** the fibre from any of these plants, used esp. for rope. [C16: Spanish, from Taino]

magus (ˈmeɪgəs) *n., pl.* **magi** (ˈmeɪdʒaɪ). **1.** a Zoroastrian priest. **2.** an astrologer, sorcerer, or magician of ancient times. [C14: from Latin, from Greek *magos,* from Old Persian *magus* magician]

Magyar (ˈmægjɑː) *n.* **1.** (*pl.* **-yars**) a member of the predominant ethnic group of Hungary, also found in NW Siberia. **2.** the Hungarian language. ~*adj.* **3.** of or relating to the Magyars or their language. **4.** *Sewing.* of or relating to a style of sleeve cut in one piece with the bodice.

Mahabharata (məˌhɑːˈbɑːrətə), **Mahabharatam,** *or* **Mahabharatum** (məˌhɑːˈbɑːrətəm) *n.* an epic Sanskrit poem of India, dealing chiefly with the struggle between two rival families. It contains many separate episodes, the most notable of which is the *Bhagavad-Gita.* [Sanskrit, from *mahā* great + *bhārata* story]

maharajah *or* **maharaja** (ˌmɑːhəˈrɑːdʒə) *n.* any of various Indian princes, esp. any of the rulers of the former native states. [C17: Hindi, from *mahā* great + RAJAH]

maharani *or* **maharanee** (ˌmɑːhəˈrɑːniː) *n.* **1.** the wife of a maharajah. **2.** a woman holding the rank of maharajah. [C19: from Hindi, from *mahā* great + RANI]

maharishi (ˌmɑːhɑːˈriːʃɪ, məˈhɑːriːʃɪ) *n. Hinduism.* a Hindu teacher of religious and mystical knowledge. [from Hindi, from *mahā* great + *rishi* sage, saint]

mahatma (məˈhɑːtmə, -ˈhæt-) *n.* (*sometimes cap.*) **1.** *Hinduism.* a Brahman sage. **2.** *Theosophy.* an adept or sage. [C19: from Sanskrit *mahātman,* from *mahā* great + *ātman* soul] —**maˈhatmaism** *n.*

Mahayana (ˌmɑːhəˈjɑːnə) *n.* **a.** a liberal Buddhist school of Tibet, China, and Japan, whose adherents aim to disseminate Buddhist doctrines, seeking enlightenment not for themselves alone, but for all sentient beings. **b.** (*as modifier*): *Mahayana Buddhism.* [from Sanskrit, from *mahā* great + *yāna* vehicle] —ˌ**Mahaˈyanist** *n.*

Mahdi (ˈmɑːdɪ) *n. Islam.* any of a number of Muslim messiahs expected to forcibly convert all mankind to Islam. [Arabic *mahdīy* one who is guided, from *madā* to guide aright] —ˈ**Mahdism** *n.* —ˈ**Mahdist** *n., adj.*

mahewu (maˈhewʊ, -ˈxe-) *n.* (in South Africa) fermented liquid mealie-meal porridge, used as a stimulant by Black Africans. [from Xhosa *amarewu*]

Mahican (məˈhiːkən) *or* **Mohican** (ˈməʊɪkən, məʊˈhiːkən) *n.* **1.** (*pl.* **-cans** *or* **-can**) a member of a North American Indian people formerly living along the Hudson river and east of it, in New York state. **2.** the language of this people, belonging to the Algonquian family.

mahjong *or* **mah-jongg** (ˌmɑːˈdʒɒŋ) *n.* a game of Chinese origin, usually played by four people, in which tiles bearing various designs are drawn and discarded until one player has an entire hand of winning combinations. [from Chinese, literally: sparrows]

mahlstick (ˈmɔːlˌstɪk) *n.* a variant spelling of **maulstick.**

mahogany (məˈhɒgənɪ) *n., pl.* **-nies. 1.** any of various tropical American trees of the meliaceous genus *Swietenia,* esp. *S. mahagoni* and *S. macrophylla,* valued for their hard reddish-brown wood. **2.** any of several trees with similar wood, such as African mahogany (genus *Khaya*) and Philippine mahogany (genus *Shorea*). **3. a.** the wood of any of these trees. See also **acajou** (sense 1). **b.** (*as modifier*): *a mahogany table.* **4.** a reddish-brown colour. [C17: origin obscure]

Mahometan (məˈhɒmɪtᵊn) *n., adj.* a former word for **Muslim.** —**Maˈhometanism** *n.*

mahonia (məˈhəʊnɪə) *n.* any evergreen berberidaceous shrub of the Asian and American genus *Mahonia,* esp. *M. aquifolium:* cultivated for their ornamental spiny divided leaves and clusters of small yellow flowers. [C19: New Latin, named after Bernard *McMahon* (died 1816), American botanist]

mahout (məˈhaʊt) *n.* (in India and the East Indies) an elephant driver or keeper. [C17: Hindi *mahāut,* from Sanskrit *mahāmātra* of great measure, originally a title]

Mahratta (məˈrɑːtə) *n.* a variant spelling of **Maratha.** —**Mahˈratti** *n., adj.*

mahseer (ˈmɑːsɪə) *n.* any of various large freshwater Indian cyprinid fishes, such as *Barbus tor.* [from Hindi]

mahzor *Hebrew.* (maxˈzɔr; *English* mɑːkˈzɔː) *n., pl.* ***-zorim*** (-zɔˈriːm; *English* -zəˈriːm). a variant spelling of **machzor.**

maid (meɪd) *n.* **1.** *Archaic or literary.* a young unmarried girl; maiden. **2. a.** a female servant. **b.** (*in combination*): *a housemaid.* **3.** a spinster. [C12: shortened form of MAIDEN] —ˈ**maidish** *adj.* —ˈ**maidishness** *n.*

maidan (mæˈdɑːn) *n.* (in Pakistan, India, etc.) an open space used for meetings, sports, etc. [Urdu, from Arabic]

maiden (ˈmeɪdᵊn) *n.* **1.** *Archaic or literary.* **a.** a young unmarried girl, esp. when a virgin. **b.** (*as modifier*): *a maiden blush.* **2.** *Horse racing.* **a.** a horse that has never won a race. **b.** (*as modifier*): *a maiden race.* **3.** *Cricket.* See **maiden over. 4.** Also called: **clothes maiden.** *Northern English dialect.* a frame on which clothes are hung to dry; clothes horse. **5.** (*modifier*) of or relating to an older unmarried woman: *a maiden aunt.* **6.** (*modifier*) of or involving an initial experience or attempt: *a maiden voyage; maiden speech.* **7.** (*modifier*) (of a person or thing) untried; unused. **8.** (*modifier*) (of a place) never trodden, penetrated, or captured. [Old English *mægden;* related to Old High German *magad,* Old Norse *mogr* young man, Old Irish *mug* slave] —ˈ**maidenish** *adj.* —ˈ**maidenˌlike** *adj.*

maidenhair fern *or* **maidenhair** (ˈmeɪdᵊnˌhɛə) *n.* any fern of the genus *Adiantum,* esp. *A. capillis-veneris,* of tropical and warm regions, having delicate fan-shaped fronds with small pale-green leaflets: family *Polypodiaceae.* [C15: so called from the hairlike appearance of its fine fronds]

maidenhair tree *n.* another name for **ginkgo.**

maidenhead (ˈmeɪdᵊnˌhɛd) *n.* **1.** a nontechnical word for the **hymen. 2.** virginity; maidenhood. [C13: from *maiden* + *-hed,* variant of -HOOD]

maidenhood (ˈmeɪdᵊnˌhʊd) *n.* **1.** the time during which a woman is a maiden or a virgin. **2.** the condition of being a maiden or virgin.

maidenly (ˈmeɪdᵊnlɪ) *adj.* of or befitting a maiden. —ˈ**maidenliness** *n.*

maiden name *n.* a woman's surname before marriage.

maiden over *n. Cricket.* an over in which no runs are scored.

maiden voyage *n. Nautical.* the first voyage of a vessel.

maid of all work *n.* **1.** a maid who does all types of housework. **2.** a general factotum.

maid of honour *n.* **1.** *U.S. and Canadian.* the principal unmarried attendant of a bride. Compare **bridesmaid, matron of**

honour. 2. *Brit.* a small tart with an almond-flavoured filling. 3. an unmarried lady attending a queen or princess.

maidservant ('meɪd,sɜːvənt) *n.* a female servant.

maieutic (meɪ'juːtɪk) *or* **maieutical** *adj. Philosophy.* of or relating to the Socratic method of eliciting knowledge by a series of questions and answers. [C17: from Greek *maieutikos* relating to midwifery (used figuratively by Socrates), from *maia* midwife]

maigre ('meɪgə) *adj. R.C. Church.* **1.** not containing flesh, and so permissible as food on days of religious abstinence: *maigre food.* **2.** of or designating such a day. [C17: from French: thin; see MEAGRE]

maihem ('meɪhɛm) *n.* a variant spelling of **mayhem.**

maik (mek) *n. Scot.* an old halfpenny. Also called **meck.** [of obscure origin]

mail[1] (meɪl) *n.* **1.** Also called (esp. Brit.): **post.** letters, packages, etc., that are transported and delivered by the post office. **2.** the postal system. **3.** a single collection or delivery of mail. **4.** a train, ship, or aircraft that carries mail. **5.** short for **electronic mail.** **6.** (*modifier*) of, involving, or used to convey mail: *a mail train.* ~*vb.* **7.** (*tr.*) *Chiefly U.S. and Canadian.* to send by mail. Usual Brit. word: **post.** [C13: from Old French *male* bag, probably from Old High German *malha* wallet] —'**mailable** *adj.*

mail[2] (meɪl) *n.* **1.** a type of flexible armour consisting of riveted metal rings or links. **2.** the hard protective shell of such animals as the turtle and lobster. ~*vb.* **3.** (*tr.*) to clothe or arm with mail: *a mailed glove.* [C14: from Old French *maille* mesh, from Latin *macula* spot] —'**mail-less** *adj.*

mail[3] (meɪl) *n. Archaic, chiefly Scot.* a monetary payment, esp. of rent or taxes. [Old English *māl* terms, from Old Norse *māl* agreement]

mail[4] (meɪl) *n. Austral. informal.* a rumour or report, esp. a racing tip.

mailbag ('meɪl,bæg), **mailsack,** *or U.S.* (*sometimes*) **mailpouch** *n.* a large bag used for transporting or delivering mail.

mailbox ('meɪl,bɒks) *n.* another name (esp. U.S. and Canadian) for **letter box.**

mailcoach ('meɪl,kəʊtʃ) *or U.S. and Canadian* **mailcar** *n.* a railway coach specially constructed for the transportation of mail.

mail drop *n. Chiefly U.S. and Canadian.* a receptacle or chute for mail.

mailer ('meɪlə) *n.* **1.** a person who addresses or mails letters, etc. **2.** *U.S. and Canadian.* a machine used for stamping and addressing mail.

mailing list *n.* a register of names and addresses to which advertising matter, etc., is sent by post.

maillot (mæ'jəʊ) *n.* **1.** tights worn for ballet, gymnastics, etc. **2.** a woman's swimsuit. **3.** a jersey. [from French]

mailman ('meɪl,mæn) *n., pl.* **-men.** *Chiefly U.S. and Canadian.* another name for **postman.**

mail merging *n. Computer technol.* a software facility that can produce a large number of personalized letters by combining a file containing a list of names and addresses with one containing a single standard document.

mail order *n.* **1.** an order for merchandise sent by post. **2.** **a.** a system of buying and selling merchandise through the post. **b.** (*as modifier*): *a mail-order firm.*

mailsack ('meɪl,sæk) *n.* another name for a **mailbag.**

mailshot ('meɪl,ʃɒt) *n.* a circular, leaflet, or other advertising material sent by post, or the posting of such material to a large group of people at one time.

maim (meɪm) *vb.* (*tr.*) **1.** to mutilate, cripple, or disable a part of the body of (a person or animal). **2.** to make defective. ~*n.* **3.** *Obsolete.* an injury or defect. [C14: from Old French *mahaignier* to wound, probably of Germanic origin] —**maimedness** ('meɪmɪdnɪs) *n.* —'**maimer** *n.*

mai mai ('maɪ maɪ) *n. N.Z.* a duck-shooter's shelter; hide. [Maori]

main[1] (meɪn) *adj.* (*prenominal*) **1.** chief or principal in rank, importance, size, etc. **2.** sheer or utmost (esp. in the phrase **by main force**). **3.** *Nautical.* of, relating to, or denoting any gear, such as a stay or sail, belonging to the mainmast. **4.** *Obsolete.* significant or important. ~*n.* **5.** a principal pipe, conduit, duct, or line in a system used to distribute water, electricity, etc. **6.** (*pl.*) **a.** the main distribution network for water, gas, or electricity. **b.** (*as modifier*): *mains voltage.* **7.** the chief or most important part or consideration. **8.** great strength or force (now chiefly in the phrase **(with) might and main**). **9.** *Literary.* the open ocean. 10. *Archaic.* short for **mainland.** **11.** **in** (*or* **for**) **the main.** on the whole; for the most part. [C13: from Old English *mægen* strength]

main[2] (meɪn) *n.* **1.** a throw of the dice in dice games. **2.** a cockfighting contest. **3.** a match in archery, boxing, etc. [C16: of unknown origin]

mainbrace ('meɪn,breɪs) *n. Nautical.* a brace attached to the main yard.

main clause *n. Grammar.* a clause that can stand alone as a sentence. Compare **subordinate clause.**

main course *n.* **1.** the principal dish of a meal. **2.** *Nautical.* a square mainsail.

main deck *n.* the uppermost sheltered deck that runs the entire length of a vessel.

mainframe ('meɪn,freɪm) *n.* **1.** **a.** a high-speed general-purpose computer, usually with a large store capacity. **b.** (*as modifier*): *mainframe systems.* **2.** the central processing unit of a computer.

mainland ('meɪnlənd) *n.* **1.** the main part of a land mass as opposed to an island or peninsula. **2.** **the mainland.** a particular landmass as viewed from a nearby island with which it has close links, such as Great Britain as viewed from Northern Ireland or continental Australia as viewed from Tasmania. —'**mainlander** *n.*

main line *n.* **1.** *Railways.* **a.** the trunk route between two points, usually fed by branch lines. **b.** (*as modifier*): *a main-line station.* **2.** *U.S.* a main road. ~*vb.* **mainline.** **3.** (*intr.*) *Slang.* to inject a drug into a vein. ~*adj.* **mainline.** **4.** having an important position, esp. having responsibility for the main areas of activity. —'**main,liner** *n.*

mainly ('meɪnlɪ) *adv.* **1.** for the most part; to the greatest extent; principally. **2.** *Obsolete.* strongly; very much.

main market *n.* the market for trading in the listed securities of companies on the London Stock Exchange. Compare **Third Market, unlisted securities market.**

mainmast ('meɪn,mɑːst) *n. Nautical.* the chief mast of a sailing vessel with two or more masts, being the foremast of a yawl, ketch, or dandy and the second mast from the bow of most others.

main memory *n.* the central memory-storage facility in a computer.

main plane *n.* **a.** one of the principal supporting surfaces of an aircraft, esp. either of the wings. **b.** both wings considered together.

mainsail ('meɪn,seɪl; *Nautical* 'meɪnsᵊl) *n. Nautical.* the largest and lowermost sail on the mainmast.

main sequence *n. Astronomy.* **a.** a stellar grouping consisting of the vast majority of stars of population I, graphically represented on the Hertzsprung-Russell diagram as a diagonal band. **b.** (*as modifier*): *a main-sequence star.*

mainsheet ('meɪn,ʃiːt) *n. Nautical.* the line used to control the angle of the mainsail to the wind.

mainspring ('meɪn,sprɪŋ) *n.* **1.** the principal spring of a mechanism, esp. in a watch or clock. **2.** the chief cause or motive of something.

mainstay ('meɪn,steɪ) *n.* **1.** *Nautical.* the forestay that braces the mainmast. **2.** a chief support.

main store *n. Computer technol.* another name for **memory** (sense 7).

mainstream ('meɪn,striːm) *n.* **1.** **a.** the main current (of a river, cultural trend, etc.): *in the mainstream of modern literature.* **b.** (*as modifier*): *mainstream politics.* ~*adj.* **2.** of or relating to the style of jazz that lies between the traditional and the modern.

mainstream corporation tax *n.* (in Britain) the balance of the corporation tax paid by a company for an accounting period after the advance corporation tax has been deducted.

mainstreeting ('meɪn,striːtɪŋ) *n. Canadian.* the practice of a politician walking about the streets of a town or city to gain votes and greet supporters.

maintain (meɪn'teɪn) *vb.* (*tr.*) **1.** to continue or retain; keep in existence. **2.** to keep in proper or good condition: *to maintain a building.* **3.** to support a style of living: *the money maintained us for a month.* **4.** (*takes a clause as object*) to state or assert: *he maintained that Talbot was wrong.* **5.** to defend against contradiction; uphold: *she maintained her innocence.* **6.** to defend against physical attack. [C13: from Old French *maintenir,* ultimately from Latin *manū tenēre* to hold in the hand] —**main'tainable** *adj.* —**main'tainer** *n.*

maintained school *n.* a school financially supported by the state.

maintenance ('meɪntɪnəns) *n.* **1.** the act of maintaining or the state of being maintained. **2.** a means of support; livelihood. **3.** (*modifier*) of or relating to the maintaining of buildings, machinery, etc.: *maintenance man.* **4.** *Law.* (formerly unlawful) the interference in a legal action by a person having no interest in it, as by providing funds to continue the action. See also **champerty.** **5.** *Law.* a provision ordered to be made by way of periodical payments or a lump sum, as after a divorce for a spouse. **6.** *Computer technol.* **a.** the correction or prevention of faults in hardware by a programme of inspection and the replacement of parts. **b.** the removal of existing faults and the modification of software in response to changes in specification or environment. [C14: from Old French; see MAINTAIN]

maintop ('meɪn,tɒp) *n.* a top or platform at the head of the mainmast.

main-topmast *n. Nautical.* the mast immediately above the mainmast.

maintopsail (,meɪn'tɒpseɪl; *Nautical* ,meɪn'tɒpsᵊl) *n. Nautical.* a topsail set on the mainmast.

main yard *n. Nautical.* a yard for a square mainsail.

maiolica (mə'jɒlɪkə) *n.* a variant of **majolica.**

maisonette *or* **maisonnette** (,meɪzə'nɛt) *n.* self-contained living accommodation often occupying two floors of a larger house and having its own outside entrance. [C19: from French, diminutive of *maison* house]

maist (mest) *determiner.* a Scot. word for **most.**

maître d'hôtel (,mɛtrə dəʊ'tɛl; *French* mɛtrə dotɛl) *n., pl.* **maîtres d'hôtel.** **1.** a head waiter or steward. **2.** the manager or owner of a hotel. [C16: from French: master of (the) hotel]

maître d'hôtel butter *n.* melted butter mixed with parsley and lemon juice.

maize (meɪz) *n.* **1.** Also called: **Indian corn. a.** a tall annual grass, *Zea mays,* cultivated for its yellow edible grains, which develop on a spike. **b.** the grain of this plant, used for food, fodder, and as a source of oil. Usual U.S. and Canadian name: **corn.** See also **sweet corn. 2.** a yellow colour. [C16: from Spanish *maíz,* from Taino *mahiz*]

Maj. *abbrev. for* Major.

majestic (məˈdʒɛstɪk) *or (less commonly)* **majestical** *adj.* having or displaying majesty or great dignity; grand; lofty. —**maˈjestically** *adv.*

majesty (ˈmædʒɪstɪ) *n.* **1.** great dignity of bearing; loftiness; grandeur. **2.** supreme power or authority. **3.** an archaic word for **royalty.** [C13: from Old French, from Latin *mājestās;* related to Latin *major,* comparative of *magnus* great]

Majesty (ˈmædʒɪstɪ) *n., pl.* **-ties.** (preceded by *Your, His, Her,* or *Their*) a title used to address or refer to a sovereign or the wife or widow of a sovereign.

Maj. Gen. *abbrev. for* Major General.

Majlis (ˈmædʒlɪs) *n.* **1.** the parliament of Iran. **2.** (in various N African and Middle Eastern countries) an assembly; council. [from Persian: assembly]

majolica (məˈdʒɒlɪkə, məˈjɒl-) *or* **maiolica** *n.* a type of porous pottery glazed with bright metallic oxides that was originally imported into Italy via the island of Majorca and was extensively made in Italy during the Renaissance. [C16: from Italian, from Late Latin *Mājorica* Majorca]

major (ˈmeɪdʒə) *n.* **1.** *Military.* an officer immediately junior to a lieutenant colonel. **2.** a person who is superior in a group or class. **3.** (often preceded by *the*) *Music.* a major key, chord, mode, or scale. **4.** *U.S., Canadian, Austral., and N.Z.* **a.** the principal field of study of a student at a university, etc.: *his major is sociology.* **b.** a student who is studying a particular subject as his principal field: *a sociology major.* **5.** a person who has reached the age of legal majority. **6.** *Logic.* a major term or premise. **7.** (*pl.*) **the.** *U.S. and Canadian.* the major leagues. ~*adj.* **8.** larger in extent, number, etc.: *the major part.* **9.** of greater importance or priority. **10.** very serious or significant: *a major disaster.* **11.** main, chief, or principal. **12.** of, involving, or making up a majority. **13.** *Music.* **a.** (of a scale or mode) having notes separated by the interval of a whole tone, except for the third and fourth degrees, and seventh and eighth degrees, which are separated by a semitone. **b.** relating to or employing notes from the major scale: *a major key.* **c.** (*postpositive*) denoting a specified key or scale as being major: *C major.* **d.** denoting a chord or triad having a major third above the root. **e.** (in jazz) denoting a major chord with a major seventh added above the root. **14.** *Logic.* constituting the major term or major premise of a syllogism. **15.** *Chiefly U.S., Canadian, Austral., and N.Z.* of or relating to a student's principal field of study at a university, etc. **16.** *Brit.* the elder: used after a schoolboy's surname if he has one or more younger brothers in the same school: *Price major.* **17.** of full legal age. **18.** (*postpositive*) *Change-ringing.* of, relating to, or denoting a method rung on eight bells. ~*vb.* **19.** (*intr.;* usually foll. by *in*) *U.S., Canadian, Austral., and N.Z.* to do one's principal study (in a particular subject): *to major in English literature.* [C15 (adj.): from Latin, comparative of *magnus* great; C17 (n., in military sense): from French, short for SERGEANT MAJOR] —**ˈmajorship** *n.*

▷**Usage.** The overuse of *major* in examples like *the major reason, the major differences, a major factor,* where a comparative is not really implied, is avoided by careful writers and speakers of English.

major axis *n.* the longer or longest axis of an ellipse or ellipsoid.

major-domo (ˌmeɪdʒəˈdəʊməʊ) *n., pl.* **-mos. 1.** the chief steward or butler of a great household. **2.** *Facetious.* a steward or butler. [C16: from Spanish *mayordomo,* from Medieval Latin *mājor domūs* head of the household]

majorette (ˌmeɪdʒəˈrɛt) *n.* See **drum majorette.**

major general *n. Military.* an officer immediately junior to a lieutenant general. —**ˈmajor-ˈgeneralship** *or* **ˈmajor-ˈgeneralcy** *n.*

majority (məˈdʒɒrɪtɪ) *n., pl.* **-ties. 1.** the greater number or part of something: *the majority of the constituents.* **2.** (in an election) the number of votes or seats by which the strongest party or candidate beats the combined opposition or the runner-up. See **relative majority, absolute majority. 3.** the largest party or group that votes together in a legislative or deliberative assembly. **4.** the time of reaching or state of having reached full legal age, when a person is held competent to manage his own affairs, exercise civil rights and duties, etc. **5.** the rank, office, or commission of major. **6.** *Euphemistic.* the dead (esp. in the phrases **join the majority, go** *or* **pass over to the majority). 7.** *Obsolete.* the quality or state of being greater; superiority. **8.** (*modifier*) of, involving, or being a majority: *a majority decision; a majority verdict.* **9. in the majority.** forming or part of the greater number of something. [C16: from Medieval Latin *mājoritās,* from MAJOR (adj.)]

majority carrier *n.* the entity responsible for carrying the greater part of the current in a semiconductor. In n-type semiconductors the majority carriers are electrons; in p-type semiconductors they are positively charged holes. Compare **minority carrier.**

major league *n. U.S. and Canadian.* a league of highest classification in baseball, football, hockey, etc.

Major Mitchell (ˈmɪtʃəl) *n.* an Australian cockatoo, *Kakatoe leadbeateri,* with a white-and-pink plumage. [C19: named after Major (later Sir) Thomas *Mitchell* (1792–1855), Australian explorer]

major orders *pl. n. R.C. Church.* the three higher degrees of holy orders: bishop, priest, and deacon.

major planet *n.* a planet of the solar system, as opposed to an asteroid (minor planet).

major premise *n. Logic.* the premise of a syllogism containing the predicate of its conclusion.

major seventh chord *n.* a chord much used in modern music, esp. jazz and pop, consisting of a major triad with an added major seventh above the root. Compare **minor seventh chord.** Often shortened to **major seventh.**

major suit *n. Bridge.* hearts or spades. Compare **minor suit.**

major term *n. Logic.* the predicate of the conclusion of a syllogism, also occurring as the subject or predicate in the major premise.

majuscule (ˈmædʒəˌskjuːl) *n.* **1.** a large letter, either capital or uncial, used in printing or writing. ~*adj.* **2.** relating to, printed, or written in such letters. Compare **minuscule.** [C18: via French from Latin *mājusculus,* diminutive of *mājor* bigger, MAJOR] —**majuscular** (məˈdʒʌskjʊlə) *adj.*

mak (mæk) *vb.* a Scot. word for **make**[1].

makar (ˈmækər) *n. Scot.* a creative artist, esp. a poet. [a Scot. variant of *maker*]

make[1] (meɪk) *vb.* **makes, making, made.** (*mainly tr.*) **1.** to bring into being by shaping, changing, or combining materials, ideas, etc.; form or fashion; create: *to make a chair from bits of wood; make a poem.* **2.** to draw up, establish, or form: *to make a decision; make one's will.* **3.** to cause to exist, bring about, or produce: *don't make a noise.* **4.** to cause, compel, or induce: *please make him go away.* **5.** to appoint or assign, as to a rank or position: *they made him chairman.* **6.** to constitute: *one swallow doesn't make a summer.* **7.** (*also intr.*) to come or cause to come into a specified state or condition: *to make merry; make someone happy.* **8.** (*copula*) to be or become through development: *he will make a good teacher.* **9.** to cause or ensure the success of: *your news has made my day.* **10.** to amount to: *twelve inches make a foot.* **11.** to be part of or a member of: *did she make one of the party?* **12.** to serve as or be suitable for: *that piece of cloth will make a coat.* **13.** to prepare or put into a fit condition for use: *to make a bed.* **14.** to be the essential element in or part of: *charm makes a good salesman.* **15.** to carry out, effect, or do: *to make a gesture.* **16.** (*intr.;* foll. by *to, as if to,* or *as though to*) to act with the intention or with a show of doing something: *they made to go out; he made as if to hit her.* **17.** to use for a specified purpose: *I will make this town my base.* **18.** to deliver or pronounce: *to make a speech.* **19.** to judge, reckon, or give one's own opinion or information as to: *what time do you make it?* **20.** to cause to seem or represent as being: *that furniture makes the room look dark.* **21.** to earn, acquire, or win for oneself: *to make friends; make a fortune.* **22.** to engage in: *make love not war.* **23.** to traverse or cover (distance) by travelling: *we can make a hundred miles by nightfall.* **24.** to arrive in time for: *he didn't make the first act of the play.* **25.** *Cards.* **a.** to win a trick with (a specified card). **b.** to shuffle (the cards). **c.** *Bridge.* to fulfil (a contract) by winning the necessary number of tricks. **26.** *Cricket.* to score (runs). **27.** *Electronics.* to close (a circuit) permitting a flow of current. Compare **break** (sense 44). **28.** (*intr.*) to increase in depth: *the water in the hold was making a foot a minute.* **29.** (*intr.*) (of hay) to dry and mature. **30.** *Informal.* to gain a place or position on or in: *to make the headlines; make the first team.* **31.** *Informal, chiefly U.S.* to achieve the rank of. **32.** *Taboo slang.* to seduce. **33. make a book.** to take bets on a race or other contest. **34. make a day, night,** etc., **of it.** to cause an activity to last a day, night, etc. **35. make do.** See **do**[1] (sense 36). **36. make eyes at.** to flirt with or ogle. **37. make good.** See **good** (sense 44). **38. make heavy weather (of). a.** *Nautical.* to roll and pitch in heavy seas. **b.** *Informal.* to carry out with great difficulty or unnecessarily great effort. **39. make it. a.** *Informal.* to be successful in doing something. **b.** (foll. by *with*) *Taboo slang.* to have sexual intercourse. **c.** *Slang.* to inject a narcotic drug. **40. make like.** *Slang, chiefly U.S. and Canadian.* to imitate. **41. make love (to). a.** to have sexual intercourse (with). **b.** *Now archaic.* to engage in courtship (with). **42. make time.** See **time** (sense 45). **43. make water. a.** another term for **urinate. b.** (of a boat, hull, etc.) to let in water. ~*n.* **44.** brand, type, or style: *what make of car is that?* **45.** the manner or way in which something is made. **46.** disposition or character; make-up. **47.** the act or process of making. **48.** the amount or number made. **49.** *Bridge.* the contract to be played. **50.** *Cards.* a player's turn to shuffle. **51. on the make. a.** *Informal.* out for profit or conquest. **b.** *Slang.* in search of a sexual partner. ~See also **make after, make away, make for, make of, make off, make out, make over, make-up, make with.** [Old English *macian;* related to Old Frisian *makia* to construct, Dutch *maken,* German *machen* to make] —**ˈmakable** *adj.*

make[2] (meɪk) *n. Archaic.* **1.** a peer or consort. **2.** a mate or spouse. [Old English *gemaca* mate; related to MATCH[1]] —'**makeless** *adj.*

make after *vb. (intr., prep.) Archaic.* to set off in pursuit of; chase.

make away *vb. (intr., adv.)* **1.** to depart in haste. **2. make away with. a.** to steal or abduct. **b.** to kill, destroy, or get rid of.

make believe *vb.* **1.** to pretend or enact a fantasy: *the children made believe they were nurses and doctors.* ~*n.* **make-believe. 2. a.** a fantasy, pretence, or unreality. **b.** *(as modifier): a make-believe world.* **3.** a person who pretends.

makefast ('meɪk,fɑːst) *n.* a strong support to which a vessel is secured.

make for *vb. (intr., prep.)* **1.** to head towards, esp. in haste. **2.** to prepare to attack. **3.** to help to bring about: *your cooperation will make for the success of our project.*

make of *vb. (tr., prep.)* **1.** to interpret as the meaning of: *what do you make of this news?* **2.** to produce or construct from: *houses made of brick.* **3. make little, nothing,** etc., **of. a.** not to understand. **b.** to attribute little, no, etc., importance to. **c.** to gain little or no benefit from. **4. make much, a lot,** etc., **of. a.** *(used with a negative)* to make sense of: *he couldn't make much of her babble.* **b.** to give importance to. **c.** to gain benefit from. **d.** to pay flattering attention to: *the reporters made much of the film star.*

make off *vb.* **1.** *(intr., adv.)* to go or run away in haste. **2. make off with.** to steal or abduct.

make out *vb. (adv.)* **1.** *(tr.)* to discern or perceive: *can you make out that house in the distance?* **2.** *(tr.)* to understand or comprehend: *I can't make out this letter.* **3.** *(tr.)* to write out: *he made out a cheque.* **4.** *(tr.)* to attempt to establish or prove: *he made out a case for her innocence; he made me out to be a liar.* **5.** *(intr.)* to pretend: *he made out that he could cook.* **6.** *(intr.)* to manage or fare: *how did you make out in the contest?* **7.** *(intr.;* often foll. by *with) Informal, chiefly U.S. and Canadian.* to engage in necking or petting: *Alan is making out with Jane.*

make over *vb. (tr., adv.)* **1.** to transfer the title or possession of (property, etc.). **2.** to renovate or remodel: *she made over the dress to fit her sister.* ~*n.* **makeover** ('meɪk,əʊvə). **3.** a complete remodelling.

maker ('meɪkə) *n.* **1.** a person who makes (something); fabricator; constructor. **2.** a person who executes a legal document, esp. one who signs a promissory note. **3.** *Archaic, Scot.* Also called (esp. Scot.): **makar.** a poet.

Maker ('meɪkə) *n.* **1.** a title given to **God** (as Creator). **2. (go to) meet one's Maker.** to die.

make-ready *n. Printing.* the process of preparing the forme and the cylinder or platen packing to achieve the correct impression all over the forme.

makeshift ('meɪk,ʃɪft) *adj.* **1.** serving as a temporary or expedient means, esp. during an emergency. ~*n.* **2.** something serving in this capacity.

make-up *n.* **1.** cosmetics, such as powder, lipstick, etc., applied to the face to improve its appearance. **2. a.** the cosmetics, false hair, etc., used by an actor to highlight his features or adapt his appearance. **b.** the art or result of applying such cosmetics. **3.** the manner of arrangement of the parts or qualities of someone or something. **4.** the arrangement of type matter and illustrations on a page or in a book. **5.** mental or physical constitution. ~*vb.* **make up.** *(adv.)* **6.** *(tr.)* to form or constitute: *these arguments make up the case for the defence.* **7.** *(tr.)* to devise, construct, or compose, sometimes with the intent to deceive: *to make up a song; to make up an excuse.* **8.** *(tr.)* to supply what is lacking or deficient in; complete: *these extra people will make up our total.* **9.** *(tr.)* to put in order, arrange, or prepare: *to make up a bed.* **10.** *(intr.;* foll. by *for)* to compensate or atone (for): *his kindness now makes up for his rudeness yesterday.* **11.** to settle (differences) amicably (often in the phrase **make it up**). **12.** to apply cosmetics to (the face) to enhance one's appearance or so as to alter the appearance for a theatrical role. **13.** to assemble (type and illustrations) into (columns or pages). **14.** *(tr.)* to surface (a road) with tarmac, concrete, etc. **15.** *(tr.)* **a.** to set in order and balance (accounts). **b.** to draw up (accounting statements). **16. make up one's mind.** to decide (about something or to do something): *he made up his mind to take vengeance.* **17. make up to.** *Informal.* **a.** to make friendly overtures to. **b.** to flirt with.

makeweight ('meɪk,weɪt) *n.* **1.** something put on a scale to make up a required weight. **2.** an unimportant person or thing added to make up a lack.

make with *vb. (intr., prep.) Slang, chiefly U.S.* to proceed with the doing, showing, etc., of: *make with the music.*

making ('meɪkɪŋ) *n.* **1. a.** the act of a person or thing that makes or the process of being made. **b.** *(in combination): watchmaking.* **2. be the making of.** to cause the success of. **3. in the making.** in the process of becoming or being made: *a politician in the making.* **4.** something made or the quantity of something made at one time. **5.** make-up; composition.

makings ('meɪkɪŋz) *pl. n.* **1.** potentials, qualities, or materials: *he had the makings of a leader.* **2.** Also called: **rollings.** *Slang.* the tobacco and cigarette paper used for rolling a cigarette. **3.** profits; earnings.

mako[1] ('mɑːkəʊ) *n., pl.* **-kos. 1.** any shark of the genus *Isurus,* esp. *I. glaucus* of Indo-Pacific and Australian seas: family *Isuridae.* **2.** *N.Z.* the teeth of the mako worn as a decoration by early Maoris. [from Maori]

mako[2] ('mɑːkəʊ) *or* **mako-mako** ('mɑːkəʊ,mɑːkəʊ) *n., pl.* **-kos. 1.** Also called: **wineberry.** a small evergreen New Zealand tree, *Aristotelia serrata:* family *Elaeocarpaceae.* **2.** *N.Z.* another name for the **bellbird,** *Anthornis melanura.* [from Maori]

makuta (mɑː'kuːtɑː) *n.* the plural of **likuta.**

MAL *international car registration for* Malaysia.

Mal. *abbrev. for:* **1.** *Bible.* Malachi. **2.** Malay(an).

mal- *combining form.* bad or badly; wrong or wrongly; imperfect or defective: *maladjusted; malfunction.* [Old French, from Latin *malus* bad, *male* badly]

malabsorption (mæləb'sɔːpʃən) *n.* a failure of absorption, esp. by the small intestine in coeliac disease, cystic fibrosis, etc.

malacca *or* **malacca cane** (mə'lækə) *n.* **1.** the stem of the rattan palm. **2.** a walking stick made from this stem. [from *Malacca* in SW Peninsular Malaysia]

malachite ('mælə,kaɪt) *n.* a bright green mineral, found in veins and in association with copper deposits. It is a source of copper and is used as an ornamental stone. Composition: hydrated copper carbonate. Formula: $Cu_2CO_3(OH)_2$. Crystal structure: monoclinic. [C16: via Old French from Latin *molochītēs,* from Greek *molokhitis* mallow-green stone, from *molokhē* mallow]

malacia (mə'leɪʃɪə) *n.* the pathological softening of an organ or tissue, such as bone.

malaco- *or before a vowel* **malac-** *combining form.* denoting softness: *malacology; malacostracan.* [from Greek *malakos*]

malacology (,mælə'kɒlədʒɪ) *n.* the branch of zoology concerned with the study of molluscs. —**malacological** (,mæləkə'lɒdʒɪkᵊl) *adj.* —,**mala'cologist** *n.*

malacophily (,mælə'kɒfɪlɪ) *n. Botany.* pollination of plants by snails. —,**mala'cophilous** *adj.*

malacophyllous (,mælə'kɒfɪləs) *adj.* (of plants living in dry regions) having fleshy leaves in which water is stored.

malacopterygian (,mælə,kɒptə'rɪdʒɪən) *adj.* **1.** of, relating to, or belonging to the *Malacopterygii,* a group of teleost fishes, including herrings and salmon, having soft fin rays. ~*n.* **2.** any malacopterygian fish; a soft-finned fish. ~Compare **acanthopterygian.** [C19: from New Latin *Malacopterygii,* from MALACO- + Greek *pterux* wing, fin]

malacostracan (,mælə'kɒstrəkᵊn) *n.* **1.** any crustacean of the subclass or group *Malacostraca,* including lobsters, crabs, woodlice, sand hoppers, and opossum shrimps. ~*adj. also* **malacostracous. 2.** of, relating to, or belonging to the *Malacostraca.* [C19: from New Latin, from Greek *malakōstrakos,* from MALACO- + *ostrakon* shell]

maladaptive (,mælə'dæptɪv) *adj.* **1.** unsuitably adapted or adapting poorly to (a situation, purpose, etc.). **2.** not encouraging adaptation. —,**mala'dapted** *adj.* —,**mala'daptively** *adv.*

maladdress (,mælə'drɛs) *n.* awkwardness; tactlessness.

maladjusted (,mælə'dʒʌstɪd) *adj.* **1.** *Psychol.* suffering from maladjustment. **2.** badly adjusted.

maladjustment (,mælə'dʒʌstmənt) *n.* **1.** *Psychol.* a failure to meet the demands of society, such as coping with problems and social relationships: usually reflected in emotional instability. **2.** faulty or bad adjustment.

maladminister (,mæləd'mɪnɪstə) *vb. (tr.)* to administer badly, inefficiently, or dishonestly. —,**malad,minis'tration** *n.* —,**malad'minis,trator** *n.*

maladroit (,mælə'drɔɪt) *adj.* **1.** showing or characterized by clumsiness; not dexterous. **2.** tactless and insensitive in behaviour or speech. [C17: from French, from *mal* badly + ADROIT] —,**mala'droitly** *adv.* —,**mala'droitness** *n.*

malady ('mælədɪ) *n., pl.* **-dies. 1.** any disease or illness. **2.** any unhealthy, morbid, or desperate condition: *a malady of the spirit.* [C13: from Old French, from Vulgar Latin *male habitus* (unattested) in poor condition, from Latin *male* badly + *habitus,* from *habēre* to have]

mala fide ('mælə 'faɪdɪ) *adj.* undertaken in bad faith. [from Latin]

Málaga ('mæləgə) *n.* a sweet fortified dessert wine from Málaga, a port in S Spain.

Malagasy (,mælə'gæzɪ) *n.* **1.** *(pl.* **-gasy** *or* **-gasies)** a native or inhabitant of Madagascar; Madagascan. **2.** the official language of Madagascar belonging to the Malayo-Polynesian family. ~*adj.* **3.** of or relating to Madagascar, its people, or their language.

malagueña (,mælə'geɪnjə) *n.* a Spanish dance similar to the fandango. [Spanish: of *Málaga*]

malaise (mæ'leɪz) *n.* a feeling of unease, mild sickness, or depression. [C18: from Old French, from *mal* bad + *aise* EASE]

malam ('mælæm, -əm) *n.* a variant spelling of **mallam.**

malamute *or* **malemute** ('mælə,muːt) *n.* an Alaskan Eskimo dog of the spitz type, having a dense usually greyish coat. [from the name of an Eskimo tribe]

malanders, mallanders, *or* **mallenders** ('mæləndəz) *pl. n. (functioning as sing.)* a disease of horses characterized by an eczematous inflammation behind the knee. [C15: via Old French from Latin *malandria* sore on the neck of a horse]

malapert ('mælə,pɜːt) *Archaic or literary.* ~*adj.* **1.** saucy or impudent. ~*n.* **2.** a saucy or impudent person. [C15: from Old French: unskilful (see MAL-, EXPERT); meaning in English influenced by *apert* frank, from Latin *apertus* open] —'**mala,pertly** *adv.* —'**mala,pertness** *n.*

malapropism ('mæləprɒp,ɪzəm) *n.* **1.** the unintentional misuse of a word by confusion with one of similar sound, esp. when creating a ridiculous effect, as in *I am not under the affluence of alcohol.* **2.** the habit of misusing words in this manner. [C18: after Mrs *Malaprop* in Sheridan's play *The Rivals* (1775), a character who misused words, from MALAPROPOS] —'**malaprop** *or* ,**mala'propian** *adj.*

malapropos (,mælæprə'pəʊ) *adj.* **1.** of an inappropriate or misapplied nature or kind. ~*adv.* **2.** in an inappropriate way or manner. ~*n.* **3.** something inopportune or inappropriate. [C17: from French *mal à propos* not to the purpose]

malar ('meɪlə) *adj.* **1.** of or relating to the cheek or cheekbone. ~*n.* **2.** Also called: **malar bone.** another name for **zygomatic bone.** [C18: from New Latin *mālāris,* from Latin *māla* jaw]

malaria (mə'lɛərɪə) *n.* an infectious disease characterized by recurring attacks of chills and fever, caused by the bite of an anopheles mosquito infected with any of four protozoans of the genus *Plasmodium* (*P. vivax, P. falciparum, P. malariae,* or *P. ovale*). [C18: from Italian *mala aria* bad air, from the belief that the disease was caused by the unwholesome air in swampy districts] —**ma'larial, ma'larian,** *or* **ma'larious** *adj.*

malariology (mə,lɛərɪ'ɒlədʒɪ) *n.* the study of malaria. —**ma,lari'ologist** *n.*

malarkey *or* **malarky** (mə'lɑːkɪ) *n. Slang.* nonsense; rubbish. [C20: of unknown origin]

malassimilation (,mælə,sɪmɪ'leɪʃən) *n. Pathol.* defective assimilation of nutrients.

malate ('mæleɪt, 'meɪ-) *n.* any salt or ester of malic acid. [C18: from MALIC ACID]

Malathion (,mælə'θaɪɒn) *n. Trademark.* a yellow organophosphorus insecticide used as a dust or mist for the control of house flies and garden pests. Formula: $C_{10}H_{19}O_6PS_2$. [C20: from (*diethyl*) MAL(EATE) + THIO- + -ON]

Malay (mə'leɪ) *n.* **1.** a member of a people living chiefly in Malaysia and Indonesia, in SE Asia, who are descendants of Mongoloid immigrants. **2.** the language of this people, belonging to the Malayo-Polynesian family. ~*adj.* **3.** of or relating to the Malays or their language.

Malayalam *or* **Malayalaam** (,mælɪ'ɑːləm) *n.* a language of SW India, belonging to the Dravidian family and closely related to Tamil: the state language of Kerala.

Malayan (mə'leɪən) *adj.* **1.** of or relating to the Malay Peninsula in SE Asia or its people. ~*n.* **2.** a native or inhabitant of the Malay Peninsula, esp. one who is a citizen of Malaysia.

Malayo-Polynesian *n.* **1.** Also called: **Austronesian.** a family of languages extending from Madagascar to the central Pacific, including Malagasy, Malay, Indonesian, Tagalog, and Polynesian. See also **Austro-Asiatic.** ~*adj.* **2.** of or relating to this family of languages.

Malaysian (mə'leɪzɪən) *adj.* **1.** of or relating to Malaysia, a country in SE Asia consisting of part of the Malay Peninsula and the states of Sabah and Sarawak in N Borneo. ~*n.* **2.** a native or inhabitant of Malaysia.

malcontent ('mælkən,tɛnt) *adj.* **1.** disgusted or discontented. ~*n.* **2.** a person who is malcontent. [C16: from Old French]

mal de mer *French.* (mal də mɛr) *n.* seasickness.

maldistribution (,mældɪstrɪ'bjuːʃən) *n.* faulty, unequal, or unfair distribution (as of wealth, business, etc.).

male (meɪl) *adj.* **1.** of, relating to, or designating the sex producing gametes (spermatozoa) that can fertilize female gametes (ova). **2.** of, relating to, or characteristic of a man; masculine. **3.** for or composed of men or boys: *a male choir.* **4.** (of gametes) capable of fertilizing an egg cell in sexual reproduction. **5.** (of reproductive organs, such as a testis or stamen) capable of producing male gametes. **6.** (of flowers) bearing stamens but lacking a functional pistil. **7.** *Electronics, mechanical engineering.* having a projecting part or parts that fit into a female counterpart: *a male plug.* ~*n.* **8.** a male person, animal, or plant. [C14: via Old French from Latin *masculus* MASCULINE] —'**maleness** *n.*

maleate ('mælɪ,eɪt) *n.* any salt or ester of maleic acid. [C19: from MALE(IC ACID) + -ATE[1]]

male chauvinism *n.* the belief, held or alleged to be held by certain men, that men are inherently superior to women. —**male chauvinist** *n., adj.*

male chauvinist pig *n. Informal, derogatory.* a man who exhibits male chauvinism. Abbrev.: **MCP.**

maledict ('mælɪdɪkt) *vb.* **1.** (*tr.*) *Literary.* to utter a curse against. ~*adj.* **2.** *Archaic.* cursed or detestable.

malediction (,mælɪ'dɪkʃən) *n.* **1.** the utterance of a curse against someone or something. **2.** slanderous accusation or comment. [C15: from Latin *maledictiō* a reviling, from *male* ill + *dīcere* to speak] —,**male'dictive** *or* ,**male'dictory** *adj.*

malefactor ('mælɪ,fæktə) *n.* a criminal; wrongdoer. [C15: via Old French from Latin, from *malefacere* to do evil] —'**male,faction** *n.* —'**male,factress** *fem. n.*

male fern *n.* a fern, *Dryopteris filix-mas,* having scaly stalks and pinnate fronds with kidney-shaped spore-producing bodies on the underside: family *Polypodiaceae.* [C16: so called because it was formerly believed to be the male of the lady fern]

maleficent (mə'lɛfɪsənt) *adj.* causing or capable of producing evil or mischief; harmful or baleful. [C17: from Latin *maleficent-,* from *maleficus* wicked, prone to evil, from *malum* evil] —**ma'lefic** *adj.* —**ma'leficence** *n.*

maleic acid (mə'leɪɪk) *n.* a colourless soluble crystalline substance used to synthesize other compounds. Formula: HOOCCH:CHCOOH. Systematic name: ***cis*-butanedioic acid.** [C19: from French *maléique,* altered form of *malique;* see MALIC ACID]

male menopause *n.* a period in a man's later middle age in which he may experience an identity crisis as he feels age overtake his sexual powers.

malemute ('mælə,muːt) *n.* a variant spelling of **malamute.**

malevolent (mə'lɛvələnt) *adj.* **1.** wishing or appearing to wish evil to others; malicious. **2.** *Astrology.* having an evil influence. [C16: from Latin *malevolens,* from *male* ill + *volens,* present participle of *velle* to wish] —**ma'levolence** *n.* —**ma'levolently** *adv.*

malfeasance (mæl'fiːzᵊns) *n. Law.* the doing of a wrongful or illegal act, esp. by a public official. Compare **misfeasance, nonfeasance.** [C17: from Old French *mal faisant,* from *mal* evil + *faisant* doing, from *faire* to do, from Latin *facere*] —**mal'feasant** *n., adj.*

malformation (,mælfɔː'meɪʃən) *n.* **1.** the condition of being faulty or abnormal in form or shape. **2.** *Pathol.* a deformity in the shape or structure of a part, esp. when congenital. —**mal'formed** *adj.*

malfunction (mæl'fʌŋkʃən) *vb.* **1.** (*intr.*) to function imperfectly or irregularly or fail to function. ~*n.* **2.** failure to function or defective functioning.

malgré lui *French.* (malgre lwi) *adv.* in spite of himself.

Malibu board ('mælɪbuː) *n.* a lightweight surfboard, usually having a fin. [C20: named after *Malibu* beach, California]

malic acid ('mælɪk, 'meɪ-) *n.* a colourless crystalline compound occurring in apples and other fruits. Formula: $HOOCCH_2$-CH(OH)COOH. [C18 *malic,* via French *malique* from Latin *mālum* apple]

malice ('mælɪs) *n.* **1.** the desire to do harm or mischief. **2.** evil intent. **3.** *Law.* the state of mind with which an act is committed and from which the intent to do wrong may be inferred. See also **malice aforethought.** [C13: via Old French from Latin *malitia,* from *malus* evil]

malice aforethought *n. Criminal law.* **1.** the predetermination to do an unlawful act, esp. to kill or seriously injure. **2.** the intent with which an unlawful killing is effected, which must be proved for the crime to constitute murder. See also **murder, manslaughter.**

malicious (mə'lɪʃəs) *adj.* **1.** characterized by malice. **2.** motivated by wrongful, vicious, or mischievous purposes. —**ma'liciously** *adv.* —**ma'liciousness** *n.*

malign (mə'laɪn) *adj.* **1.** evil in influence, intention, or effect. ~*vb.* **2.** (*tr.*) to slander or defame. [C14: via Old French from Latin *malīgnus* spiteful, from *malus* evil] —**ma'ligner** *n.* —**ma'lignly** *adv.*

malignancy (mə'lɪgnənsɪ) *n., pl.* **-cies.** **1.** the state or quality of being malignant. **2.** *Pathol.* a cancerous growth.

malignant (mə'lɪgnənt) *adj.* **1.** having or showing desire to harm others. **2.** tending to cause great harm; injurious. **3.** *Pathol.* (of a tumour) uncontrollable or resistant to therapy; rapidly spreading. ~*n.* **4.** *History.* (in the English Civil War) a Parliamentarian term for a **royalist.** [C16: from Late Latin *malīgnāre* to behave spitefully, from Latin *malīgnus* MALIGN] —**ma'lignantly** *adv.*

malignity (mə'lɪgnɪtɪ) *n., pl.* **-ties.** **1.** the condition or quality of being malign, malevolent, or deadly. **2.** (*often pl.*) a malign or malicious act or feeling.

malihini (,mɑːlɪ'hiːnɪ) *n., pl.* **-nis.** (in Hawaii) a foreigner or stranger. [from Hawaiian]

malimprinted (,mælɪm'prɪntɪd) *adj.* (of an animal or person) suffering from a defect in the behavioural process of imprinting, resulting in attraction to members of other species, fetishism, etc. —,**malim'printing** *n.*

malines (mə'liːn) *n.* **1.** a type of silk net used in dressmaking. **2.** another name for **Mechlin lace.** [C19: from French *Malines* (Mechelen) in Belgium, where this lace was traditionally made]

malinger (mə'lɪŋgə) *vb.* (*intr.*) to pretend or exaggerate illness, esp. to avoid work. [C19: from French *malingre* sickly, perhaps from *mal* badly + Old French *haingre* feeble] —**ma'lingerer** *n.*

Malinke (mə'lɪŋkɪ) *or* **Maninke** *n.* **1.** (*pl.* **-ke** *or* **-kes**) a member of a Negroid people of W Africa, living chiefly in Guinea and Mali, noted for their use of cowry shells as currency. **2.** the language of this people, belonging to the Mande branch of the Niger-Congo family.

malison ('mælɪzᵊn, -sᵊn) *n.* an archaic or poetic word for **curse.** [C13: via Old French from Latin *maledictiō* MALEDICTION]

malkin ('mɔːkɪn, 'mɔːl-, 'mæl-) *n.* **1.** an archaic or dialect name for a **cat**[1]. Compare **grimalkin.** **2.** a variant of **mawkin.** [C13: diminutive of *Maud*]

mall (mæl, mɔːl) *n.* **1.** a shaded avenue, esp. one that is open to the public. **2.** *U.S., Canadian, Austral., and N.Z.* short for **shopping mall.** [C17: after *The Mall,* in St James's Park, London. See PALL-MALL]

mallam *or* **malam** (ˈmælæm, -əm) *n. W African.* **1.** (in Islamic W Africa) a man learned in Koranic studies. **2.** (in N Nigeria) a title and form of address for a learned or educated man. [C20: from Hausa]
mallanders (ˈmæləndəz) *n.* a variant spelling of **malanders.**
mallard (ˈmælɑːd) *n., pl.* **-lard** *or* **-lards.** a duck, *Anas platyrhynchos,* common over most of the N hemisphere, the male of which has a dark green head and reddish-brown breast: the ancestor of all domestic breeds of duck. [C14: from Old French *mallart,* perhaps from *maslart* (unattested); see MALE, -ARD]
malleable (ˈmælɪəbᵊl) *adj.* **1.** (esp. of metal) able to be worked, hammered, or shaped under pressure or blows without breaking. **2.** able to be influenced; pliable or tractable. [C14: via Old French from Medieval Latin *malleābilis,* from Latin *malleus* hammer] —ˌ**mallea'bility** *or (less commonly)* ˈ**malleableness** *n.* —ˈ**malleably** *adv.*
malleable iron *n.* **1.** Also called: **malleable cast iron.** cast iron that has been toughened by gradual heating or slow cooling. **2.** a less common name for **wrought iron.**
mallee (ˈmæliː) *n.* **1.** any of several low shrubby eucalyptus trees that flourish in desert regions of Australia. **2.** (usually preceded by *the*) *Austral.* another name for the **bush** (sense 4). **3.** See **mallee root.** [C19: native Australian name]
mallee fowl *n.* an Australian megapode, *Leipoa ocellata,* that allows its eggs to incubate naturally in a sandy mound.
mallee root *n. Austral.* the rootstock (rhizome) of a mallee tree, often used as fuel.
mallemuck (ˈmælɪˌmʌk) *n.* any of various sea birds, such as the albatross, fulmar, or shearwater. [C17: from Dutch *mallemok* from *mal* silly + *mok* gull]
mallenders (ˈmæləndəz) *n.* a less common spelling of **malanders.**
malleolus (məˈliːələs) *n., pl.* **-li** (-ˌlaɪ). either of two rounded bony projections of the tibia and fibula on the sides of each ankle joint. [C17: diminutive of Latin *malleus* hammer] —**mal'leolar** *adj.*
mallet (ˈmælɪt) *n.* **1.** a tool resembling a hammer but having a large head of wood, copper, lead, leather, etc., used for driving chisels, beating sheet metal, etc. **2.** a long stick with a head like a hammer used to strike the ball in croquet or polo. **3.** *Chiefly U.S.* a very large powerful steam locomotive with a conventional boiler but with two separate articulated engine units. [C15: from Old French *maillet* wooden hammer, diminutive of *mail* MAUL (n.)]
malleus (ˈmælɪəs) *n., pl.* **-lei** (-lɪˌaɪ). the outermost and largest of the three small bones in the middle ear of mammals. Nontechnical name: **hammer.** See also **incus, stapes.** [C17: from Latin: hammer]
mallow (ˈmæləʊ) *n.* **1.** any plant of the malvaceous genus *Malva,* esp. *M. sylvestris* of Europe, having purple, pink, or white flowers. See also **dwarf mallow, musk mallow. 2.** any of various related plants, such as the marsh mallow, rose mallow, Indian mallow, and tree mallow. [Old English *mealuwe,* from Latin *malva;* probably related to Greek *malakhē* mallow]
malm (mɑːm) *n.* **1.** a soft greyish limestone that crumbles easily. **2.** a chalky soil formed from this limestone. **3.** an artificial mixture of clay and chalk used to make bricks. [Old English *mealm-* (in compound words); related to Old Norse *malmr* ore, Gothic *malma* sand]
malmsey (ˈmɑːmzɪ) *n.* a sweet Madeira wine. [C15: from Medieval Latin *Malmasia,* corruption of Greek *Monembasia,* Greek port from which the wine was shipped]
malnourished (mælˈnʌrɪʃt) *adj.* undernourished.
malnutrition (ˌmælnjuːˈtrɪʃən) *n.* lack of adequate nutrition resulting from insufficient food, unbalanced diet, or defective assimilation.
malocclusion (ˌmæləˈkluːʒən) *n. Dentistry.* a defect in the normal position of the upper and lower teeth when the mouth is closed, as from abnormal development of the jaw. —ˌ**maloc'cluded** *adj.*
malodorous (mælˈəʊdərəs) *adj.* having a bad smell. —**mal'odorously** *adv.* —**mal'odorousness** *n.*
malonic acid (məˈləʊnɪk, -ˈlɒn-) *n.* another name for **propanedioic acid.** [C19: from French *malonique,* altered form of *malique;* see MALIC ACID]
malonylurea (ˌmælənɪljʊˈrɪə, -ˈjʊərɪə, -niːl-) *n.* another name for **barbituric acid.**
malpighiaceous (mælˌpɪgɪˈeɪʃəs) *adj.* of, relating to, or belonging to the *Malpighiaceae,* a family of tropical plants many of which are lianas. [C19: from New Latin *Malpighia,* after Marcello *Malpighi* (1628–94), Italian physiologist]
Malpighian corpuscle *or* **body** (mælˈpɪgɪən) *n. Anatomy.* an encapsulated cluster of capillaries at the end of each urine-secreting tubule of the kidney. [named after Marcello *Malpighi*]
Malpighian layer *n. Anatomy.* the innermost layer of the epidermis.
Malpighian tubules *or* **tubes** *pl. n.* organs of excretion in insects and many other arthropods: narrow tubules opening into the anterior part of the hindgut.
malposition (ˌmælpəˈzɪʃən) *n.* abnormal position of a bodily part. —**malposed** (mælˈpəʊzd) *adj.*
malpractice (mælˈpræktɪs) *n.* **1.** immoral, illegal, or unethical professional conduct or neglect of professional duty. **2.** any instance of improper professional conduct. —**malpractitioner** (ˌmælprækˈtɪʃənə) *n.*
malt (mɔːlt) *n.* **1.** cereal grain, such as barley, that is kiln-dried after it has germinated by soaking in water. **2.** See **malt liquor. 3.** short for **malt whisky.** ~*vb.* **4.** to make into or become malt. **5.** to make (something, esp. liquor) with malt. [Old English *mealt;* related to Dutch *mout,* Old Norse *malt;* see also MELT]
Malta fever (ˈmɔːltə) *n.* another name for **brucellosis.**
maltase (ˈmɔːlteɪz) *n.* an enzyme that hydrolyses maltose and similar glucosides (α-glucosides) to glucose. Also called: **α-glu'cosiˌdase.** [C19: from MALT + -ASE]
malted milk *n.* **1.** a soluble powder made from dehydrated milk and malted cereals. **2.** a drink made from this powder.
Maltese (mɔːlˈtiːz) *adj.* **1.** of or relating to Malta, a republic in the Mediterranean, or to its inhabitants or their language. ~*n.* **2.** (*pl.* **-tese**) a native or inhabitant of Malta. **3.** the official language of Malta, a form of Arabic with borrowings from Italian, etc. **4.** a breed of toy dog having a very long straight silky white coat. **5.** a domestic fancy pigeon having long legs and a long neck.
Maltese cross *n.* **1.** a cross with triangular arms that taper towards the centre, sometimes having indented outer sides: formerly worn by the Knights of Malta. **2.** (in a film projector) a cam mechanism of this shape that produces intermittent motion.
malt extract *n.* a sticky substance obtained from an infusion of malt.
maltha (ˈmælθə) *n.* **1.** another name for **mineral tar. 2.** any of various naturally occurring mixtures of hydrocarbons, such as ozocerite. [C15: via Latin from Greek: a mixture of wax and pitch]
Malthusian (mælˈθjuːzɪən) *adj.* **1.** of or relating to the theory of Thomas Robert Malthus (1766–1834), British economist, stating that increases in population tend to exceed increases in the means of subsistence and that therefore sexual restraint should be exercised. ~*n.* **2.** a supporter of this theory. —**Mal'thusianism** *n.*
malting (ˈmɔːltɪŋ) *n.* a building in which malt is made or stored. Also called: **malt house.**
malt liquor *n.* any alcoholic drink brewed from malt.
maltose (ˈmɔːltəʊz) *n.* a disaccharide of glucose formed by the enzymic hydrolysis of starch: used in bacteriological culture media and as a nutrient in infant feeding. Formula: $C_{12}H_{22}O_{11}$. [C19: from MALT + -OSE[2]]
maltreat (mælˈtriːt) *vb.* (*tr.*) to treat badly, cruelly, or inconsiderately. [C18: from French *maltraiter*] —**mal'treater** *n.* —**mal'treatment** *n.*
maltster (ˈmɔːltstə) *n.* a person who makes or deals in malt.
malt whisky *n.* whisky made from malted barley.
malty (ˈmɔːltɪ) *adj.* **maltier, maltiest.** of, like, or containing malt. —ˈ**maltiness** *n.*
malvaceous (mælˈveɪʃəs) *adj.* of, relating to, or belonging to the *Malvaceae,* a family of plants that includes mallow, cotton, okra, althaea, and abutilon. [C17: from Latin *malvāceus,* from *malva* MALLOW]
malvasia (ˌmælvəˈsɪə) *n.* **1.** another word for **malmsey. 2.** the type of grape used to make malmsey. [C19: from Italian, from Greek *Monembasia;* see MALMSEY] —ˌ**malva'sian** *adj.*
malversation (ˌmælvɜːˈseɪʃən) *n. Rare.* professional or public misconduct. [C16: from French, from *malverser* to behave badly, from Latin *male versārī*]
malvoisie (ˈmælvɔɪzɪ, -və-) *n.* an amber dessert wine made in France, similar to malmsey. [C14: via Old French from Italian *Malvasia,* from Greek *Monembasia;* see MALMSEY]
malwa (ˈmalwa) *n.* a Ugandan drink brewed from millet. [from Rutooro, a language of W Uganda]
mam (mæm) *n. Informal or dialect.* another word for **mother[1].**
mama (məˈmɑː) *n. Old-fashioned.* an informal word for **mother[1].**
mamaguy (ˈmɑːməˌgaɪ) *Caribbean.* ~*vb.* **1.** (*tr.*) to deceive or tease, either in jest or by deceitful flattery. ~*n.* **2.** an instance of such deception or flattery. [from Spanish *mamar el gallo,* literally: to feed the cock]
mamba (ˈmæmbə) *n.* any aggressive partly arboreal tropical African venomous elapid snake of the genus *Dendroaspis,* esp. *D. angusticeps* (**green** and **black mambas**). [from Zulu *im-amba*]
mambo (ˈmæmbəʊ) *n., pl.* **-bos. 1.** a modern Latin American dance, resembling the rumba, derived from the ritual dance of voodoo. ~*vb.* **2.** (*intr.*) to perform this dance. [American Spanish, probably from Haitian Creole: voodoo priestess]
mamelon (ˈmæmələn) *n.* a small rounded hillock. [C19: from French: nipple]
Mameluke *or* **Mamaluke** (ˈmæmɪˌluːk) *n.* **1.** a member of a military class, originally of Turkish slaves, ruling in Egypt from about 1250 to 1517 and remaining powerful until crushed in 1811. **2.** (in Muslim countries) a slave. [C16: via French, ultimately from Arabic *mamlūk* slave, from *malaka* to possess]
mamey, mammee, *or* **mammee apple** (mæˈmiː) *n.* **1.** a tropical American tree, *Mammea americana,* cultivated for its large edible fruits: family *Guttiferae.* **2.** the fruit of this tree, having yellow pulp and a red skin. **3.** another name for the **marmalade tree.** [C16: from Spanish *mamey,* from Haitian]
mamilla *or U.S.* **mammilla** (mæˈmɪlə) *n., pl.* **-lae** (-liː). **1.** a nipple or teat. **2.** any nipple-shaped part or prominence. [C17: from

Latin, diminutive of *mamma* breast] —'**mamillary** *or U.S.* '**mammillary** *adj.*

mamillate ('mæmɪˌleɪt), **mamillated** *or U.S.* **mammillate, mammillated** *adj.* having nipples or nipple-like protuberances.

mamma[1] *n. Chiefly U.S.* **1.** ('mɑːmə, mə'mɑː). Also: **momma.** another word for **mother**[1]. **2.** ('mɑːmə). *Informal.* a buxom and voluptuous woman. [C16: reduplication of childish syllable *ma;* compare Welsh *mam,* French *maman,* Russian *mama*]

mamma[2] ('mæmə) *n., pl.* **-mae** (-miː). **1.** the milk-secreting organ of female mammals: the breast in women, the udder in cows, sheep, etc. **2.** (*functioning as pl.*) breast-shaped protuberances, esp. from the base of cumulonimbus clouds. [C17: from Latin: breast]

mammal ('mæməl) *n.* any animal of the *Mammalia,* a large class of warm-blooded vertebrates having mammary glands in the female, a thoracic diaphragm, and a four-chambered heart. The class includes the whales, carnivores, rodents, bats, primates, etc. [C19: via New Latin from Latin *mamma* breast] —**mammalian** (mæ'meɪlɪən) *adj., n.* —'**mammalˌlike** *adj.*

mammalogy (mæ'mælədʒɪ) *n.* the branch of zoology concerned with the study of mammals. —**mammalogical** (ˌmæmə'lɒdʒɪkᵊl) *adj.* —**mam'malogist** *n.*

mammary ('mæmərɪ) *adj.* of, relating to, or like a mamma or breast.

mammary gland *n.* any of the milk-producing glands in mammals. In higher mammals each gland consists of a network of tubes and cavities connected to the exterior by a nipple.

mammee (mæ'miː) *n.* a variant spelling of **mamey.**

mammet ('mæmɪt) *n.* another word for **maumet.**

mammiferous (mæ'mɪfərəs) *adj.* having breasts or mammae.

mammilla (mæ'mɪlə) *n., pl.* **-lae** (-liː). the U.S. spelling of **mamilla.** —'**mammillary** *adj.*

mammillate ('mæmɪˌleɪt) *or* **mammillated** *adj.* the U.S. spellings of **mamillate, mamillated.**

mammock ('mæmək) *Dialect.* ~*n.* **1.** a fragment. ~*vb.* **2.** (*tr.*) to tear or shred. [C16: of unknown origin]

mammography (mæ'mɒgrəfɪ) *n.* the technique of using x-rays to examine the breast in the early detection of cancer. —'**mammoˌgraph** *or* '**mammoˌgram** *n.*

mammon ('mæmən) *n.* **1.** riches or wealth regarded as a source of evil and corruption. **2.** avarice or greed. [C14: via Late Latin from New Testament Greek *mammōnas,* from Aramaic *māmōnā* wealth] —'**mammonish** *adj.* —'**mammonism** *n.* —'**mammonist** *or* '**mammonite** *n.* —ˌ**mammon'istic** *adj.*

Mammon ('mæmən) *n. New Testament.* the personification of riches and greed in the form of a false god.

mammoth ('mæməθ) *n.* **1.** any large extinct elephant of the Pleistocene genus *Mammuthus* (or *Elephas*), such as *M. primigenius* (**woolly mammoth**), having a hairy coat and long curved tusks. ~*adj.* **2.** of gigantic size or importance. [C18: from Russian *mamot,* from Tartar *mamont,* perhaps from *mamma* earth, because of a belief that the animal made burrows]

mammy *or* **mammie** ('mæmɪ) *n., pl.* **-mies. 1.** a child's word for **mother**[1]. **2.** *Chiefly southern U.S.* a Negro woman employed as a nurse or servant to a White family.

mammy wagon *n.* a W African vehicle built on a lorry chassis, capable of carrying both passengers and goods.

mampara (mam'pɑːrə) *n. S. African informal.* a clumsy Black African. [of unknown origin]

mampoer (məm'pʊə) *n. S. African.* a home-distilled brandy made from peaches, prickly pears, etc. [of uncertain origin]

mamzer ('mɑmzə) *n.* **1.** a Yiddish slang word for **bastard. 2.** *Judaism.* a child of an incestuous or adulterous union. [from Hebrew]

man (mæn) *n., pl.* **men** (mɛn). **1.** an adult male human being, as distinguished from a woman. **2.** (*modifier*) male; masculine: *a man child.* **3.** a human being regardless of sex or age, considered as a representative of mankind; a person. **4.** (*sometimes cap.*) human beings collectively; mankind: *the development of man.* **5.** Also called: **modern man. a.** a member of any of the living races of *Homo sapiens,* characterized by erect bipedal posture, a highly developed brain, and powers of articulate speech, abstract reasoning, and imagination. **b.** any extinct member of the species *Homo sapiens,* such as Cro-Magnon man. **6.** a member of any of the extinct species of the genus *Homo,* such as Java man, Heidelberg man, and Solo man. **7.** an adult male human being with qualities associated with the male, such as courage or virility: *be a man.* **8.** manly qualities or virtues: *the man in him was outraged.* **9. a.** a subordinate, servant, or employee contrasted with an employer or manager. **b.** (*in combination*): *the number of man-days required to complete a job.* **10.** (*usually pl.*) a member of the armed forces who does not hold commissioned, warrant, or noncommissioned rank (as in the phrase **officers and men**). **11.** a member of a group, team, etc. **12.** a husband, boyfriend, etc.: *man and wife.* **13.** an expression used parenthetically to indicate an informal relationship between speaker and hearer. **14.** a movable piece in various games, such as draughts. **15.** a vassal of a feudal lord. **16. as one man.** with unanimous action or response. **17. be one's own man.** to be independent or free. **18. he's your man.** he's the person needed (for a particular task, role, job, etc.). **19. man and boy.** from childhood. **20. sort out** *or* **separate the men from the boys.** to separate the experienced from the inexperienced. **21. to a man. a.** unanimously. **b.** without exception: *they were slaughtered to a man.* ~*interj.* **22.** *Informal.* an exclamation or expletive, often indicating surprise or pleasure. ~*vb.* **mans, manning, manned.** (*tr.*) **23.** to provide with sufficient men for operation, defence, etc.: *to man a ship.* **24.** to take one's place at or near in readiness for action. **25.** *Falconry.* to induce (a hawk or falcon) to endure the presence of and handling by man, esp. strangers. [Old English *mann;* related to Old Frisian *man,* Old High German *man,* Dutch *man,* Icelandic *mathr*] —'**manless** *adj.*

Man (mæn) *n.* **the.** (*sometimes not cap.*) *U.S.* **1.** *Black slang.* a White man or White men collectively, esp. when in authority, in the police, or held in contempt. **2.** *Slang.* a drug peddler.

Man. *abbrev. for:* **1.** Manila (paper). **2.** Manitoba.

-man *n. combining form.* indicating a person who has a role, works in a place, or operates equipment as specified: *salesman, barman, cameraman.*

▷**Usage.** The use of words ending in *-man* is avoided as implying a male in job advertisements, where sexual discrimination is illegal, and in many other contexts where a term that is not gender-specific is available, such as *salesperson, barperson, camera operator.*

mana ('mɑːnə) *n. Anthropol.* **1.** (in Polynesia, Melanesia, etc.) a concept of a life force, believed to be seated in the head, and associated with high social status and ritual power. **2.** any power achieved by ritual means; prestige; authority. [from Polynesian]

man about town *n.* a fashionable sophisticate, esp. one in a big city.

manacle ('mænəkᵊl) *n.* **1.** (*usually pl.*) a shackle, handcuff, or fetter, used to secure the hands of a prisoner, convict, etc. ~*vb.* (*tr.*) **2.** to put manacles on. **3.** to confine or constrain. [C14: via Old French from Latin *manicula,* diminutive of *manus* hand]

manage ('mænɪdʒ) *vb.* (*mainly tr.*) **1.** (*also intr.*) to be in charge (of); administer: *to manage one's affairs; to manage a shop.* **2.** to succeed in being able (to do something) despite obstacles; contrive: *did you manage to go to sleep?* **3.** to have room, time, etc., for: *can you manage dinner tomorrow?* **4.** to exercise control or domination over, often in a tactful or guileful manner. **5.** (*intr.*) to contrive to carry on despite difficulties, esp. financial ones: *he managed quite well on very little money.* **6.** to wield or handle (a weapon). **7.** *Rare.* to be frugal in the use of. ~*n.* **8.** an archaic word for **manège.** [C16: from Italian *maneggiare* to control, train (esp. horses), ultimately from Latin *manus* hand]

manageable ('mænɪdʒəbᵊl) *adj.* able to be managed or controlled. —ˌ**manageaˈbility** *or* (*less commonly*) '**manageableness** *n.* —'**manageably** *adv.*

managed bonds *pl. n.* investment in a combination of fixed interest securities, equities, gilts, and property, in which an investment manager, acting on a client's behalf, varies the amount invested in each according to the returns expected.

managed currency *n.* a currency that is subject to governmental control with respect to the amount in circulation and the rate of exchange with other currencies.

management ('mænɪdʒmənt) *n.* **1.** the members of the executive or administration of an organization or business. See also **line management, middle management, top management. 2.** managers or employers collectively. **3.** the technique, practice, or science of managing or controlling. **4.** the skilful or resourceful use of materials, time, etc. **5.** the specific treatment of a disease, disorder, etc.

management accounting *n.* another name for **cost accounting.**

management buyout *n.* the purchase of a company by its managers, usually with outside backing from a bank or other institution.

management company *n.* a company that manages a unit trust.

management information system *n.* an arrangement of equipment and procedures, often computerized, that is designed to provide managers with information.

management union *n.* a union that represents managers in negotiations with their employers concerning terms and conditions of employment.

manager ('mænɪdʒə) *n.* **1.** a person who directs or manages an organization, industry, shop, etc. **2.** a person who controls the business affairs of an actor, entertainer, etc. **3.** a person who controls the training of a sportsman or team. **4.** a person who has a talent for managing efficiently. **5.** *Law.* a person appointed by a court to carry on a business during receivership. **6.** (in Britain) a member of either House of Parliament appointed to arrange a matter in which both Houses are concerned. —'**managerˌship** *n.*

manageress (ˌmænɪdʒə'rɛs, 'mænɪdʒəˌrɛs) *n.* a woman who is in charge of a shop, department, canteen, etc.

managerial (ˌmænɪ'dʒɪərɪəl) *adj.* of or relating to a manager or to the functions, responsibilities, or position of management. —ˌ**mana'gerially** *adv.*

managerialism (ˌmænɪ'dʒɪərɪəˌlɪzəm) *n.* the application of managerial techniques of businesses to the running of other organizations, such as the civil service or local authorities. —ˌ**mana'gerialist** *n.*

managing (ˈmænɪdʒɪŋ) *adj.* having administrative control or authority: *a managing director.*

manakin (ˈmænəkɪn) *n.* **1.** any small South American passerine bird of the family *Pipridae,* having a colourful plumage, short bill, and elaborate courtship behaviour. **2.** a variant of **manikin.**

mañana *Spanish.* (maˈɲana; *English* məˈnjɑːnə) *n., adv.* **a.** tomorrow. **b.** some other and later time.

man-at-arms *n., pl.* **men-at-arms.** a soldier, esp. a heavily armed mounted soldier in medieval times.

manatee (ˌmænəˈtiː) *n.* any sirenian mammal of the genus *Trichechus,* occurring in tropical coastal waters of America, the West Indies, and Africa: family *Trichechidae.* They resemble whales and have a prehensile upper lip and a broad flattened tail. [C16: via Spanish from Carib *Manattouï*] —**ˈmanaˌtoid** *adj.*

manchester (ˈmæntʃɪstə) *n. Austral. and N.Z.* **1.** household linen or cotton goods, such as sheets and towels. **2.** Also called: **manchester department.** a section of a store where such goods are sold. [from *Manchester,* a textile centre in NW England]

Manchester terrier *n.* a breed of terrier with a glossy black-and-tan coat. Also called (less commonly): **black-and-tan terrier.**

manchineel (ˌmæntʃɪˈniːl) *n.* a tropical American euphorbiaceous tree, *Hippomane mancinella,* having fruit and milky highly caustic poisonous sap, which causes skin blisters. [C17: via French from Spanish MANZANILLA]

Manchu (mænˈtʃuː) *n.* **1.** (*pl.* **-chus** *or* **-chu**) a member of a Mongoloid people of Manchuria who conquered China in the 17th century, establishing an imperial dynasty that lasted until 1912. **2.** the language of this people, belonging to the Tungusic branch of the Altaic family. *~adj.* **3.** Also: **Ching.** of or relating to the dynasty of the Manchus. [from Manchu, literally: pure]

Manchurian (mænˈtʃʊərɪən) *adj.* **1.** of or relating to Manchuria, a region of NE China, or its people. *~n.* **2.** a native or inhabitant of Manchuria.

manciple (ˈmænsɪpᵊl) *n.* a steward who buys provisions, esp. in a college, Inn of Court, or monastery. [C13: via Old French from Latin *mancipium* purchase, from *manceps* purchaser, from *manus* hand + *capere* to take]

Mancunian (mæŋˈkjuːnɪən) *n.* **1.** a native or inhabitant of Manchester, a city in NW England. *~adj.* **2.** of or relating to Manchester. [from Medieval Latin *Mancunium* Manchester]

-mancy *n. combining form.* indicating divination of a particular kind: *chiromancy.* [from Old French *-mancie,* from Latin *-mantia,* from Greek *manteia* soothsaying] —**-mantic** *adj. combining form.*

Mandaean *or* **Mandean** (mænˈdiːən) *n.* **1.** a member of a Gnostic sect of Iraq. **2.** the form of Aramaic used by this sect. *~adj.* **3.** of or relating to this sect. [C19: from Aramaic *mandaya* Gnostics, from *mandā* knowledge] —**Manˈdaeanism** *or* **Manˈdeanism** *n.*

mandala (ˈmændələ, mænˈdɑːlə) *n.* **1.** *Hindu and Buddhist art.* any of various designs symbolizing the universe, usually circular. **2.** *Psychol.* such a symbol expressing a person's striving for unity of the self. [Sanskrit: circle]

mandamus (mænˈdeɪməs) *n., pl.* **-muses.** *Law.* formerly a writ from, now an order of, a superior court commanding an inferior tribunal, public official, corporation, etc., to carry out a public duty. [C16: Latin, literally: we command, from *mandāre* to command]

mandarin (ˈmændərɪn) *n.* **1.** (in the Chinese Empire) a member of any of the nine senior grades of the bureaucracy, entered by examinations. **2.** a high-ranking official whose powers are extensive and thought to be outside political control. **3.** a person of standing and influence, as in literary or intellectual circles. **4. a.** a small citrus tree, *Citrus nobilis,* cultivated for its edible fruit. **b.** the fruit of this tree, resembling the tangerine. [C16: from Portuguese *mandarim,* via Malay *menteri* from Sanskrit *mantrin* counsellor, from *mantra* counsel] —**ˈmandarinate** *n.*

Mandarin Chinese *or* **Mandarin** *n.* the official language of China since 1917; the form of Chinese spoken by about two thirds of the population and taught in schools throughout China. See also **Chinese, Pekingese.**

Mandarin collar *n.* a high stiff round collar.

mandarin duck *n.* an Asian duck, *Aix galericulata,* the male of which has a distinctive brightly coloured and patterned plumage and crest.

mandate *n.* (ˈmændeɪt, -dɪt). **1.** an official or authoritative instruction or command. **2.** *Politics.* the support or commission given to a government and its policies or an elected representative and his policies through an electoral victory. **3.** (*often cap.*) Also called: **mandated territory.** (formerly) any of the territories under the trusteeship of the League of Nations administered by one of its member states. **4. a.** *Roman law.* a contract by which one person commissions another to act for him gratuitously and the other accepts the commission. **b.** *Contract law.* a contract of bailment under which the party entrusted with goods undertakes to perform gratuitously some service in respect of such goods. **c.** *Scots Law.* a contract by which a person is engaged to act in the management of the affairs of another. *~vb.* (ˈmændeɪt). (*tr.*) **5.** *International law.* to assign (territory) to a nation under a mandate. **6.** to delegate authority to. **7.** *Obsolete.* to give a command to. [C16: from Latin *mandātum* something commanded, from *mandāre* to command, perhaps from *manus* hand + *dāre* to give] —**ˈmanˌdator** *n.*

mandatory (ˈmændətərɪ, -trɪ) *adj.* **1.** having the nature or powers of a mandate. **2.** obligatory; compulsory. **3.** (of a state) having received a mandate over some territory. *~n., pl.* **-ries.** **4.** Also called: **mandatary.** a person or state holding a mandate. —**ˈmandatorily** *adv.*

Mande (ˈmɑːndeɪ) *n., pl.* **-de** *or* **-des.** **1.** a group of African languages, a branch of the Niger-Congo family, spoken chiefly in Mali, Guinea, and Sierra Leone. *~adj.* **2.** of or relating to this group of languages.

Mandelbrot set (ˈmændəlˌbrɒt) *n. Maths.* a set of points in the complex plane that is self-replicating according to some predetermined rule such that the boundary of the set has fractal dimensions, used in the study of fractal geometry and in producing patterns in computer graphics. [C20: after Benoît *Mandelbrot* (born 1924), French mathematician]

mandi (ˈmʌndɪ) *n.* (in India) a big market. [Hindi]

mandible (ˈmændɪbᵊl) *n.* **1.** the lower jawbone in vertebrates. See **jaw** (sense 1). **2.** either of a pair of mouthparts in insects and other arthropods that are usually used for biting and crushing food. **3.** *Ornithol.* either the upper or the lower part of the bill, esp. the lower part. [C16: via Old French from Late Latin *mandibula* jaw, from *mandere* to chew] —**mandibular** (mænˈdɪbjʊlə) *adj.* —**mandibulate** (mænˈdɪbjʊlɪt, -ˌleɪt) *n., adj.*

Mandingo (mænˈdɪŋgəʊ) *n., pl.* **-gos** *or* **-goes.** a former name for **Mande** or **Malinke.**

mandir (ˈmʌndɪə) *n.* a Hindu or Jain temple. [Hindi, from Sanskrit *mandira*]

mandola (ˈmændələ) *n.* an early type of mandolin. [from Italian]

mandolin *or* **mandoline** (ˌmændəˈlɪn) *n.* a plucked stringed instrument related to the lute, having four pairs of strings tuned in ascending fifths stretched over a small light body with a fretted fingerboard. It is usually played with a plectrum, long notes being sustained by the tremolo. [C18: via French from Italian *mandolino,* diminutive of *mandora* lute, ultimately from Greek *pandoura* musical instrument with three strings] —**ˌmandoˈlinist** *n.*

mandorla (mænˈdɔːlə) *n.* (in painting, sculpture, etc.) an almond-shaped area of light, usually surrounding the resurrected Christ or the Virgin at the Assumption. Also called: **vesica.** [from Italian, literally: almond, from Late Latin *amandula;* see ALMOND]

mandrake (ˈmændreɪk) *or* **mandragora** (mænˈdrægərə) *n.* **1.** a Eurasian solanaceous plant, *Mandragora officinarum,* with purplish flowers and a forked root. It was formerly thought to have magic powers and a narcotic was prepared from its root. **2.** another name for the **May apple.** [C14: probably via Middle Dutch from Latin *mandragoras* (whence Old English *mandragora*), from Greek. The form *mandrake* was probably adopted through folk etymology, because of the allegedly human appearance of the root and because *drake* (dragon) suggested magical powers]

mandrel *or* **mandril** (ˈmændrəl) *n.* **1.** a spindle on which a workpiece is supported during machining operations. **2.** a shaft or arbor on which a machining tool is mounted. **3.** the driving spindle in the headstock of a lathe. **4.** *Brit.* a miner's pick. [C16: perhaps related to French *mandrin* lathe]

mandrill (ˈmændrɪl) *n.* an Old World monkey, *Mandrillus sphinx,* of W Africa. It has a short tail and brown hair, and the ridged muzzle, nose, and hindquarters are red and blue. [C18: from MAN + DRILL[4]]

manducate (ˈmændjʊˌkeɪt) *vb.* (*tr.*) *Literary.* to eat or chew. [C17: from Latin *mandūcāre* to chew] —**ˌmanduˈcation** *n.* —**ˌmanduˈcatory** *adj.*

mane (meɪn) *n.* **1.** the long coarse hair that grows from the crest of the neck in such mammals as the lion and horse. **2.** long thick human hair. [Old English *manu;* related to Old High German *mana,* Old Norse *mön,* and perhaps to Old English *mene* and Old High German *menni* necklace] —**maned** *adj.* —**ˈmaneless** *adj.*

man-eater *n.* **1.** an animal, such as a tiger, that has become accustomed to eating human flesh. **2.** any of various sharks that feed on human flesh, esp. the great white shark (*Carcharodon carcharias*). **3.** a human cannibal. **4.** *Informal.* a woman with many lovers. —**ˈman-ˌeating** *adj.*

manège *or* **manege** (mæˈneɪʒ) *n.* **1.** the art of training horses and riders. Compare **dressage.** **2.** a riding school. [C17: via French from Italian *maneggio,* from *maneggiare* to MANAGE]

manes (ˈmɑːneɪz; *Latin* ˈmɑːnɛs) *pl. n.* (*sometimes cap.*) (in Roman legend) **1.** the spirits of the dead, often revered as minor deities. **2.** (*functioning as sing.*) the shade of a dead person. [C14: from Latin, probably: the good ones, from Old Latin *mānus* good]

maneuver (məˈnuːvə) *n., vb.* the usual U.S. spelling of **manoeuvre.** —**maˈneuverable** *adj.* —**maˌneuveraˈbility** *n.* —**maˈneuverer** *n.*

man Friday *n.* a loyal male servant or assistant. [after the native in Daniel Defoe's novel *Robinson Crusoe* (1719)]

manful (ˈmænfʊl) *adj.* a less common word for **manly.** —**ˈmanfully** *adv.* —**ˈmanfulness** *n.*

mangabey (ˈmæŋgəˌbeɪ) *n.* any of several large agile arboreal Old World monkeys of the genus *Cercocebus,* of central Africa, having long limbs and tail and white upper eyelids. [C18: after the name of a region in Madagascar]

manganate (ˈmæŋɡəˌneɪt) *n.* a salt of manganic acid.

manganese (ˈmæŋɡəˌniːz) *n.* a brittle greyish-white metallic element that exists in four allotropic forms, occurring principally in pyrolusite and rhodonite: used in making steel and ferromagnetic alloys. Symbol: Mn; atomic no.: 25; atomic wt.: 54.938; valency: 1, 2 ,3, 4, 6, or 7. [C17: via French from Italian *manganese,* probably altered form of Medieval Latin MAGNESIA]

manganese bronze *n.* any of various alloys containing copper (55–60 per cent), zinc (35–42 per cent), and manganese (about 3.5 per cent).

manganese nodule *n. Geology.* a small irregular concretion found on deep ocean floors having high concentrations of certain metals, esp. manganese.

manganese steel *n.* any very hard steel containing manganese (11–14 per cent), used in dredger buckets, rock-crushers, railway points, etc.

manganic (mænˈɡænɪk) *adj.* of or containing manganese in the trivalent state.

manganic acid *n.* a hypothetical dibasic acid known only in solution and in the form of manganate salts. Formula: H_2MnO_4.

Manganin (ˈmæŋɡənɪn) *n. Trademark.* an alloy of copper containing manganese (13–18 per cent) and nickel (1–4 per cent): it has a high electrical resistance that does not vary greatly with temperature and is used in resistors.

manganite (ˈmæŋɡəˌnaɪt) *n.* a blackish mineral consisting of basic manganese oxide in monoclinic crystalline form: a source of manganese. Formula: MnO(OH).

manganous (ˈmæŋɡənəs, mænˈɡænəs) *adj.* of or containing manganese in the divalent state.

mange (meɪndʒ) *n.* an infectious disorder mainly affecting domestic animals, characterized by itching, formation of papules and vesicles, and loss of hair: caused by parasitic mites. [C14: from Old French *mangeue* itch, literally: eating, from *mangier* to eat]

mangelwurzel (ˈmæŋɡəlˌwɜːzəl) *or* **mangoldwurzel** (ˈmæŋɡəʊldˌwɜːzəl) *n.* a Eurasian variety of the beet plant, *Beta vulgaris,* cultivated as a cattle food, having a large yellowish root. Often shortened to **mangel, mangold.** [C18: from German *Mangoldwurzel,* from *Mangold* beet + *Wurzel* root]

manger (ˈmeɪndʒə) *n.* **1.** a trough or box in a stable, barn, etc., from which horses or cattle feed. **2.** *Nautical.* a basin-like construction in the bows of a vessel for catching water draining from an anchor rode or coming in through the hawseholes. [C14: from Old French *maingeure* food trough, from *mangier* to eat, ultimately from Latin *mandūcāre* to chew]

mangetout (ˈmɑ̃ʒˈtuː) *n.* a variety of garden pea in which the pod is also edible. Also called: **sugar pea.** [C20: from French: eat all]

mangey (ˈmeɪndʒɪ) *adj.* **-gier, -giest.** a variant spelling of **mangy.**

mangle[1] (ˈmæŋɡəl) *vb.* *(tr.)* **1.** to mutilate, disfigure, or destroy by cutting, crushing, or tearing. **2.** to ruin, spoil, or mar. [C14: from Norman French *mangler,* probably from Old French *mahaignier* to maim] —ˈ**mangler** *n.* —ˈ**mangled** *adj.*

mangle[2] (ˈmæŋɡəl) *n.* **1.** Also called: **wringer.** a machine for pressing or drying wet textiles, clothes, etc., consisting of two heavy rollers between which the cloth is passed. ~*vb.* *(tr.)* **2.** to press or dry in a mangle. [C18: from Dutch *mangel,* ultimately from Late Latin *manganum.* See MANGONEL]

mango (ˈmæŋɡəʊ) *n., pl.* **-goes** *or* **-gos. 1.** a tropical Asian anacardiaceous evergreen tree, *Mangifera indica,* cultivated in the tropics for its fruit. **2.** the ovoid edible fruit of this tree, having a smooth rind and sweet juicy orange-yellow flesh. [C16: via Portuguese from Malay *manggā,* from Tamil *mānkāy* from *mān* mango tree + *kāy* fruit]

mangonel (ˈmæŋɡəˌnel) *n. History.* a war engine for hurling stones. [C13: via Old French from Medieval Latin *manganellus,* ultimately from Greek *manganon*]

mangosteen (ˈmæŋɡəʊˌstiːn) *n.* **1.** an East Indian tree, *Garcinia mangostana,* with thick leathery leaves and edible fruit: family *Guttiferae.* **2.** the fruit of this tree, having a sweet juicy pulp and a hard skin. [C16: from Malay *mangustan*]

mangrove (ˈmæŋɡrəʊv, ˈmæn-) *n.* **1. a.** any tropical evergreen tree or shrub of the genus *Rhizophora,* having stiltlike intertwining aerial roots and forming dense thickets along coasts: family *Rhizophoraceae.* **b.** *(as modifier)*: *mangrove swamp.* **2.** any of various similar trees or shrubs of the genus *Avicennia:* family *Avicenniaceae.* [C17 *mangrow* (changed through influence of *grove*), from Portuguese *mangue,* ultimately from Taino]

mangy *or* **mangey** (ˈmeɪndʒɪ) *adj.* **-gier, -giest. 1.** having or caused by mange: *a mangy dog.* **2.** scruffy or shabby: *a mangy carpet.* **3.** *Irish informal.* stingy or miserly: *a mangy reward.* —ˈ**mangily** *adv.* —ˈ**manginess** *n.*

manhandle (ˈmænˌhændəl, ˌmænˈhændəl) *vb.* *(tr.)* **1.** to handle or push (someone) about roughly. **2.** to move or do by manpower rather than by machinery. [C19: from MAN + HANDLE; sense 1 perhaps also influenced by Devon dialect *manangle* to mangle]

Manhattan (mænˈhætən, mən-) *n.* a mixed drink consisting of four parts whisky, one part vermouth, and a dash of bitters. [after *Manhattan,* a borough of New York City]

manhole (ˈmænˌhəʊl) *n.* **1.** Also called: **inspection chamber.** a shaft with a removable cover that leads down to a sewer or drain. **2.** a hole, usually with a detachable cover, through which a man can enter a boiler, tank, etc.

manhood (ˈmænhʊd) *n.* **1.** the state or quality of being a man or being manly. **2.** men collectively. **3.** the state of being human.

manhood suffrage *n.* the right of adult male citizens to vote.

man-hour *n.* a unit for measuring work in industry, equal to the work done by one man in one hour.

manhunt (ˈmænˌhʌnt) *n.* an organized search, usually by police, for a wanted man or fugitive. —ˈ**manˌhunter** *n.*

mania (ˈmeɪnɪə) *n.* **1.** a mental disorder characterized by great excitement and occasionally violent behaviour. See also **manic-depressive. 2.** an obsessional enthusiasm or partiality: *a mania for mushrooms.* [C14: via Late Latin from Greek: madness]

-mania *n. combining form.* indicating extreme desire or pleasure of a specified kind or an abnormal excitement aroused by something: *kleptomania; nymphomania; pyromania.* [from MANIA] —**-maniac** *n. and adj. combining form.*

maniac (ˈmeɪnɪˌæk) *n.* **1.** a wild disorderly person. **2.** a person who has a great craving or enthusiasm for something: *a football maniac.* **3.** *Psychiatry, obsolete.* a person afflicted with mania. [C17: from Late Latin *maniacus* belonging to madness, from Greek]

maniacal (məˈnaɪəkəl) *or* **maniac** (ˈmeɪnɪæk) *adj.* **1.** affected with or characteristic of mania. **2.** characteristic of or befitting a maniac: *maniacal laughter.* —**maˈniacally** *adv.*

manic (ˈmænɪk) *adj.* **1.** characterizing, denoting, or affected by mania. ~*n.* **2.** a person afflicted with mania. [C19: from Greek, from MANIA]

manic-depressive *Psychiatry.* ~*adj.* **1.** denoting a mental disorder characterized either by an alternation between extreme euphoria and deep depression (bipolar manic-depressive disorder or syndrome) or by depression on its own or (rarely) by elation on its own (unipolar disorder). ~*n.* **2.** a person afflicted with this disorder. Compare **cyclothymia.**

Manichaeism *or* **Manicheism** (ˈmænɪkiːˌɪzəm) *n.* **1.** the system of religious doctrines, including elements of Gnosticism, Zoroastrianism, Christianity, Buddhism, etc., taught by the Persian prophet Mani about the 3rd century A.D. It was based on a supposed primordial conflict between light and darkness or goodness and evil. **2.** *Chiefly R.C. Church.* any similar heretical philosophy involving a radical dualism. [C14: from Late Latin *Manichaeus,* from Late Greek *Manikhaios* of Mani] —ˌ**Maniˈchaean** *or* ˌ**Maniˈchean** *adj., n.* —ˈ**Manichee** *n.*

manicotti (ˌmænɪˈkɒtɪ) *pl. n.* large tubular noodles, usually stuffed with ricotta cheese and baked in a tomato sauce. [Italian: sleeves, plural of *manicotto,* diminutive of *manica* sleeve]

manicure (ˈmænɪˌkjʊə) *n.* **1.** care of the hands and fingernails, involving shaping the nails, removing cuticles, etc. **2.** another word for **manicurist.** ~*vb.* **3.** to care for (the hands and fingernails) in this way. **4.** *(tr.)* to trim neatly. [C19: from French, from Latin *manus* hand + *cūra* care]

manicurist (ˈmænɪˌkjʊərɪst) *n.* a person who gives manicures, esp. as a profession.

manifest (ˈmænɪˌfest) *adj.* **1.** easily noticed or perceived; obvious; plain. **2.** *Psychoanal.* of or relating to the ostensible elements of a dream: *manifest content.* Compare **latent** (sense 5). ~*vb.* **3.** *(tr.)* to show plainly; reveal or display: *to manifest great emotion.* **4.** *(tr.)* to prove beyond doubt. **5.** *(intr.)* (of a disembodied spirit) to appear in visible form. **6.** *(tr.)* to list in a ship's manifest. ~*n.* **7.** a customs document containing particulars of a ship, its cargo, and its destination. **8. a.** a list of cargo, passengers, etc., on an aeroplane. **b.** a list of railway trucks or their cargo. **c.** *Chiefly U.S. and Canadian.* a fast freight train carrying perishables. [C14: from Latin *manifestus* plain, literally: struck with the hand, from *manū* with the hand + *-festus* struck] —ˈ**maniˌfestable** *adj.* —ˈ**maniˌfestly** *adv.* —ˈ**maniˌfestness** *n.*

manifestation (ˌmænɪfeˈsteɪʃən) *n.* **1.** the act of demonstrating; display: *a manifestation of solidarity.* **2.** the state of being manifested. **3.** an indication or sign. **4.** a public demonstration of feeling. **5.** the materialization of a disembodied spirit. —ˌ**manifesˈtational** *adj.* —ˌ**maniˈfestative** *adj.*

manifesto (ˌmænɪˈfestəʊ) *n., pl.* **-toes** *or* **-tos.** a public declaration of intent, policy, aims, etc., as issued by a political party, government, or movement. [C17: from Italian, from *manifestare* to MANIFEST]

manifold (ˈmænɪˌfəʊld) *adj. Formal.* **1.** of several different kinds; multiple: *manifold reasons.* **2.** having many different forms, features, or elements: *manifold breeds of dog.* ~*n.* **3.** something having many varied parts, forms, or features. **4.** a copy of a page, book, etc. **5.** a chamber or pipe with a number of inlets or outlets used to collect or distribute a fluid. In an internal-combustion engine the **inlet manifold** carries the vaporized fuel from the carburettor to the inlet ports and the **exhaust manifold** carries the exhaust gases away. **6.** *Maths.* **a.** a collection of objects or a set. **b.** a topological space having specific properties. **7.** (in Kantian philosophy) the totality of the separate elements of sensation which are then organized by the active mind and conceptualized as a perception of an external object. ~*vb.* **8.** *(tr.)* to duplicate (a page, book, etc.). **9.** to make manifold; multiply. [Old English *manigfeald.* See MANY, -FOLD] —ˈ**maniˌfolder** *n.* —ˈ**maniˌfoldly** *adv.* —ˈ**maniˌfoldness** *n.*

manikin, mannikin (ˈmænɪkɪn) *or* *(formerly)* **manakin** *n.* **1.** a little man; dwarf or child. **2. a.** an anatomical model of the body or a part of the body, esp. for use in medical or art instruction. **b.** Also called: **phantom.** an anatomical model of a fully developed fetus, for use in teaching midwifery or obstetrics. **3.** variant spellings of **mannequin.** [C17: from Dutch *manneken*, diminutive of MAN]

Manila (məˈnɪlə) *n.* **1.** a type of cigar made in Manila, chief port of the Philippines. **2.** short for **Manila hemp, Manila paper.**

Manila hemp *or* **Manilla hemp** *n.* a fibre obtained from the plant abaca, used for rope, paper, etc.

Manila paper *or* **Manilla paper** *n.* a strong usually brown paper made from Manila hemp or similar fibres.

Manila rope *or* **Manilla rope** *n.* rope of Manila hemp.

manilla (məˈnɪlə) *n.* an early form of currency in W Africa in the pattern of a small bracelet. [from Spanish: bracelet, diminutive of *mano* hand, from Latin *manus*]

manille (mæˈnɪl) *n.* (in ombre and quadrille) the second best trump. [C17: from French, from Spanish *malilla*, diminutive of *mala* bad]

Maninke (məˈnɪŋkə) *n., pl.* **-ke** *or* **-kes.** a variant of **Malinke.**

man in the moon *n.* **1.** the moon when considered to resemble the face of a man. **2.** (in folklore and nursery rhyme) a character dwelling in the moon.

man in the street *n.* the typical or ordinary person, esp. as a hypothetical unit in statistics.

manioc (ˈmænɪˌɒk) *or* **manioca** (ˌmænɪˈəʊkə) *n.* another name for **cassava** (sense 1). [C16: from Tupi *mandioca;* earlier form *manihot* from French, from Guarani *mandio*]

maniple (ˈmænɪpᵊl) *n.* **1.** (in ancient Rome) a unit of 120 to 200 foot soldiers. **2.** *Christianity.* an ornamental band formerly worn on the left arm by the celebrant at the Eucharist. [C16: from Medieval Latin *manipulus* (the Eucharistic vestment), from Latin, literally: a handful, from *manus* hand]

manipular (məˈnɪpjʊlə) *adj.* **1.** of or relating to an ancient Roman maniple. **2.** of or relating to manipulation.

manipulate (məˈnɪpjʊˌleɪt) *vb.* **1.** (*tr.*) to handle or use, esp. with some skill, in a process or action: *to manipulate a pair of scissors.* **2.** to negotiate, control, or influence (something or someone) cleverly, skilfully, or deviously. **3.** to falsify (a bill, accounts, etc.) for one's own advantage. **4.** (in physiotherapy) to examine or treat manually, as in loosening a joint. [C19: back formation from *manipulation*, from Latin *manipulus* handful] —**manipulability** (məˌnɪpjʊləˈbɪlɪtɪ) *n.* —**maˈnipuˌlatable** *or* **maˈnipulable** *adj.* —**maˌnipuˈlation** *n.* —**maˈnipulative** *adj.* —**maˈnipulatively** *adv.* —**maˈnipuˌlator** *n.* —**maˈnipulatory** *adj.*

manitou, manitu (ˈmænɪˌtuː), *or* **manito** (ˈmænɪˌtəʊ) *n., pl.* **-tous, -tus, -tos** *or* **-tou, -tu, -to.** (among the Algonquian Indians) a deified spirit or force. [C17: from Algonquian; related to Ojibwa *manito* spirit]

man jack *n. Informal.* a single individual (in the phrases **every man jack, no man jack**).

mankind (ˌmænˈkaɪnd) *n.* **1.** human beings collectively; humanity. **2.** men collectively, as opposed to womankind.

manky (ˈmæŋkɪ) *adj.* **mankier, mankiest.** *Slang.* **1.** worthless, rotten, or in bad taste. **2.** dirty, filthy, or bad. [via Polari from Italian *mancare* to be lacking]

manlike (ˈmænˌlaɪk) *adj.* resembling or befitting a man.

man lock *n. Civil engineering.* an airlock that allows workmen to pass in and out of spaces with differing air pressures without pressure losses.

manly (ˈmænlɪ) *adj.* **-lier, -liest.** **1.** possessing qualities, such as vigour or courage, generally regarded as appropriate to or typical of a man; masculine. **2.** characteristic of or befitting a man: *a manly sport.* ~*adv.* **3.** *Archaic.* in a manly manner. —ˈ**manliness** *n.*

man-made *adj.* made or produced by man; artificial.

manna (ˈmænə) *n.* **1.** *Old Testament.* the miraculous food which sustained the Israelites in the wilderness (Exodus 16:14–36). **2.** any spiritual or divine nourishment. **3.** a windfall; an unexpected gift (esp. in the phrase **manna from heaven**). **4.** a sweet substance obtained from various plants, esp. from an ash tree, *Fraxinus ornus* (**manna** or **flowering ash**) of S Europe, used as a mild laxative. [Old English via Late Latin from Greek, from Hebrew *mān*]

manned (mænd) *adj.* **1.** supplied or equipped with men, esp. soldiers. **2.** (of spacecraft, aircraft, etc.) having a human crew.

mannequin (ˈmænɪkɪn) *n.* **1.** a woman who wears the clothes displayed at a fashion show; model. **2.** a life-size dummy of the human body used to fit or display clothes. **3.** *Arts.* another name for **lay figure.** [C18: via French from Dutch *manneken* MANIKIN]

manner (ˈmænə) *n.* **1.** a way of doing or being. **2.** a person's bearing and behaviour: *she had a cool manner.* **3.** the style or customary way of doing or accomplishing something: *sculpture in the Greek manner.* **4.** type or kind: *what manner of man is this?* **5.** mannered style, as in art; mannerism. **6. by all manner of means.** certainly; of course. **7. by no manner of means.** definitely not: *he was by no manner of means a cruel man.* **8. in a manner of speaking.** in a way; so to speak. **9. to the manner born.** naturally fitted to a specified role or activity. ~See also **manners.** [C12: via Norman French from Old French *maniere*, from Vulgar Latin *manuāria* (unattested) a way of handling something, noun use of Latin *manuārius* belonging to the hand, from *manus* hand]

mannered (ˈmænəd) *adj.* **1.** having idiosyncrasies or mannerisms; affected: *mannered gestures.* **2.** of or having mannerisms of style, as in art or literature. **3.** (*in combination*) having manners as specified: *ill-mannered.*

mannerism (ˈmænəˌrɪzəm) *n.* **1.** a distinctive and individual gesture or trait; idiosyncrasy. **2.** (*often cap.*) a principally Italian movement in art and architecture between the High Renaissance and Baroque periods (1520–1600) that sought to represent an ideal of beauty rather than natural images of it, using characteristic distortion and exaggeration of human proportions, perspective, etc. **3.** adherence to a distinctive or affected manner, esp. in art or literature. —ˈ**mannerist** *n.* —ˌ**mannerˈistic** *or* ˌ**mannerˈistical** *adj.* —ˌ**mannerˈistically** *adv.*

mannerless (ˈmænəlɪs) *adj.* having bad manners; boorish. —ˈ**mannerlessness** *n.*

mannerly (ˈmænəlɪ) *adj.* **1.** well-mannered; polite; courteous. ~*adv.* **2.** *Now rare.* with good manners; politely; courteously. —ˈ**mannerliness** *n.*

manners (ˈmænəz) *pl. n.* **1.** social conduct: *he has the manners of a pig.* **2.** a socially acceptable way of behaving.

mannikin (ˈmænɪkɪn) *n.* a variant spelling of **manikin.**

mannish (ˈmænɪʃ) *adj.* **1.** (of a woman) having or displaying qualities regarded as typical of a man. **2.** of or resembling a man. —ˈ**mannishly** *adv.* —ˈ**mannishness** *n.*

mannitol (ˈmænɪˌtɒl) *or* **mannite** (ˈmænaɪt) *n.* a white crystalline water-soluble sweet-tasting alcohol, found in plants and used in dietetic sweets and as a dietary supplement (**E421**). Formula: $C_6H_8(OH)_6$. [from MANNOSE + -ITE[2] + -OL[1]] —**mannitic** (məˈnɪtɪk) *adj.*

mannose (ˈmænəʊs, -nəʊz) *n.* a hexose sugar occurring in mannitol and many polysaccharides. Formula: $C_6H_{12}O_6$. [C20: from MANNA + -OSE[2]]

Mann-Whitney test (ˈmænˈwɪtnɪ) *n.* a statistical test of the difference between the distributions of data collected in two experimental conditions applied to unmatched groups of subjects but comparing the distributions of the ranks of the scores. Also called: **Wilcoxon Mann-Whitney test.**

manoeuvre *or U.S.* **maneuver** (məˈnuːvə) *n.* **1.** a contrived, complicated, and possibly deceptive plan or action: *political manoeuvres.* **2.** a movement or action requiring dexterity and skill. **3. a.** a tactic or movement of one or a number of military or naval units. **b.** (*pl.*) tactical exercises, usually on a large scale. **4.** a planned movement of an aircraft in flight. **5.** any change from the straight steady course of a ship. ~*vb.* **6.** (*tr.*) to contrive or accomplish with skill or cunning. **7.** (*intr.*) to manipulate situations, etc., in order to gain some end: *to manoeuvre for the leadership.* **8.** (*intr.*) to perform a manoeuvre or manoeuvres. **9.** to move or deploy or be moved or deployed, as military units, etc. [C15: from French, from Medieval Latin *manuopera* manual work, from Latin *manū operāre* to work with the hand] —**maˈnoeuvrable** *or U.S.* **maˈneuverable** *adj.* —**maˌnoeuvraˈbility** *or U.S.* **maˌneuveraˈbility** *n.* —**maˈnoeuvrer** *or U.S.* **maˈneuverer** *n.*

man of God *n.* **1.** a saint or prophet. **2.** a clergyman.

man of straw *n.* **1.** a person of little substance. **2.** Also called: **straw man.** *Chiefly U.S.* a person used as a cover for some dubious plan or enterprise; front.

man-of-war *or* **man o' war** *n., pl.* **men-of-war, men o' war.** **1.** a warship. **2.** See **Portuguese man-of-war.**

man-of-war bird *or* **man-o'-war bird** *n.* another name for **frigate bird.**

manometer (məˈnɒmɪtə) *n.* an instrument for comparing pressures; typically a glass U-tube containing mercury, in which pressure is indicated by the difference in levels in the two arms of the tube. [C18: from French *manomètre*, from Greek *manos* sparse + *metron* measure] —**manometric** (ˌmænəʊˈmɛtrɪk) *or* ˌ**manoˈmetrical** *adj.* —ˌ**manoˈmetrically** *adv.* —**maˈnometry** *n.*

manor (ˈmænə) *n.* **1.** (in medieval Europe) the manor house of a lord and the lands attached to it. **2.** (before 1776 in some North American colonies) a tract of land granted with rights of inheritance by royal charter. **3.** a manor house. **4.** a landed estate. **5.** *Brit. slang.* a police district. [C13: from Old French *manoir* dwelling, from *maneir* to dwell, from Latin *manēre* to remain] —**manorial** (məˈnɔːrɪəl) *adj.*

man orchid *n.* an orchid, *Aceras anthropophorum*, having greenish or reddish flowers in a loose spike, with a deeply lobed dark brown lip thought to resemble the silhouette of a man.

manor house *n.* (esp. formerly) the house of the lord of a manor.

manoscopy (məˈnɒskəpɪ) *n. Chem.* the measurement of the densities of gases.

manpower (ˈmænˌpaʊə) *n.* **1.** power supplied by men. **2.** a unit of power based on the rate at which a man can work; approximately 75 watts. **3.** available or suitable power: *the manpower of a battalion.*

manpower planning *n.* a procedure used in organizations to balance future requirements for all levels of employee with the availability of such employees.

manqué *French.* (mɑ̃ke; *English* ˈmɒŋkeɪ) *adj.* (*postpositive*) unfulfilled; potential; would-be: *the manager is an actor manqué.* [C19: literally: having missed]

manrope (ˈmænˌrəʊp) *n. Nautical.* a rope railing.
mansard (ˈmænsɑːd, -səd) *n.* **1.** Also called: **mansard roof.** a roof having two slopes on both sides and both ends, the lower slopes being steeper than the upper. Compare **gambrel roof. 2.** an attic having such a roof. [C18: from French *mansarde,* after François *Mansart* (1598–1666), French architect]
manse (mæns) *n.* **1.** (in certain religious denominations) the house provided for a minister. **2.** *Archaic.* a large house. [C15: from Medieval Latin *mansus* dwelling, from the past participle of Latin *manēre* to stay]
manservant (ˈmænˌsɜːvənt) *n., pl.* **menservants.** a male servant, esp. a valet.
mansion (ˈmænʃən) *n.* **1.** Also called: **mansion house.** a large and imposing house. **2.** a less common word for **manor house. 3.** *Archaic.* any residence. **4.** *Brit.* (*pl.*) a block of flats. **5.** *Astrology.* any of 28 divisions of the zodiac each occupied on successive days by the moon. [C14: via Old French from Latin *mansio* a remaining, from *mansus;* see MANSE]
man-sized *adj.* **1.** of a size appropriate for or convenient for a man. **2.** *Informal.* big; large.
manslaughter (ˈmænˌslɔːtə) *n.* **1.** *Law.* the unlawful killing of one human being by another without malice aforethought. Compare **murder.** See also **homicide, malice aforethought. 2.** (loosely) the killing of a human being.
mansuetude (ˈmænswɪˌtjuːd) *n. Archaic.* gentleness or mildness. [C14: from Latin *mansuētūdō,* from *mansuētus,* past participle of *mansuēscere* to make tame by handling, from *manus* hand + *suescēre* to train]
manta (ˈmæntə; *Spanish* ˈmanta) *n.* **1.** Also called: **manta ray, devilfish, devil ray.** any large ray (fish) of the family *Mobulidae,* having very wide winglike pectoral fins and feeding on plankton. **2.** a rough cotton cloth made in Spain and Spanish America. **3.** a piece of this used as a blanket or shawl. **4.** another word for **mantelet** (sense 2). [Spanish: cloak, from Vulgar Latin; see MANTLE. The manta ray is so called because it is caught in a trap resembling a blanket]
manteau (ˈmæntəʊ; *French* mɑ̃to) *n., pl.* **-teaus** (-təʊz) *or* **-teaux** (*French* -to). a cloak or mantle. [C17: via French from Latin *mantellum* MANTLE]
mantel *or (less commonly)* **mantle** (ˈmæntᵊl) *n.* **1.** a wooden or stone frame around the opening of a fireplace, together with its decorative facing. **2.** Also called: **mantel shelf.** a shelf above this frame. [C15: from French, variant of MANTLE]
mantelet (ˈmæntᵊˌlɛt) *or* **mantlet** *n.* **1.** a woman's short mantle, often lace-trimmed, worn in the mid-19th century. **2.** a portable bulletproof screen or shelter. [C14: from Old French, diminutive of *mantel* MANTLE]
mantelletta (ˌmæntɪˈlɛtə) *n. R.C. Church.* a sleeveless knee-length vestment, worn by cardinals, bishops, etc. [Italian, from Old French *mantelet* or Medieval Latin *mantelletum,* diminutive of Latin *mantellum* MANTLE]
mantelpiece (ˈmæntᵊlˌpiːs) *n.* **1.** Also called: **mantel shelf, chimneypiece.** a shelf above a fireplace often forming part of the mantel. **2.** another word for **mantel** (sense 1).
manteltree *or* **mantletree** (ˈmæntᵊlˌtriː) *n.* a beam made of stone or wood that forms the lintel over a fireplace.
mantic (ˈmæntɪk) *adj.* **1.** of or relating to divination and prophecy. **2.** having divining or prophetic powers. [C19: from Greek *mantikos* prophetic, from *mantis* seer] —ˈ**mantically** *adv.*
-mantic *adj. combining form.* forming adjectives corresponding to nouns ending in **-mancy**: *necromantic.*
mantilla (mænˈtɪlə) *n.* **1.** a woman's lace or silk scarf covering the shoulders and head, often worn over a comb in the hair, esp. in Spain. **2.** a similar covering for the shoulders only. [C18: Spanish, diminutive of *manta* cloak]
mantis (ˈmæntɪs) *n., pl.* **-tises** *or* **-tes** (-tiːz). any carnivorous typically green insect of the family *Mantidae,* of warm and tropical regions, having a long body and large eyes and resting with the first pair of legs raised as if in prayer: order *Dictyoptera.* Also called: **praying mantis.** See also **cockroach.** [C17: New Latin, from Greek: prophet, alluding to its praying posture]
mantissa (mænˈtɪsə) *n.* the fractional part of a common logarithm representing the digits of the associated number but not its magnitude: *the mantissa of 2.4771 is .4771.* Compare **characteristic** (sense 2a.). [C17: from Latin: something added, of Etruscan origin]
mantis shrimp *or* **crab** *n.* any of various borrowing marine shrimplike crustaceans of the order *Stomatopoda* that have a pair of large grasping appendages: subclass *Malacostraca.* See also **squilla.**
mantle (ˈmæntᵊl) *n.* **1.** *Archaic.* a loose wrap or cloak. **2.** such a garment regarded as a symbol of someone's power or authority: *he assumed his father's mantle.* **3.** anything that covers completely or envelops: *a mantle of snow.* **4.** a small dome-shaped or cylindrical mesh impregnated with cerium or thorium nitrates, used to increase illumination in a gas or oil lamp. **5.** Also called: **pallium.** *Zoology.* **a.** a protective layer of epidermis in molluscs that secretes a substance forming the shell. **b.** a similar structure in brachiopods. **6.** *Ornithol.* the feathers of the folded wings and back, esp. when these are of a different colour from the remaining feathers. **7.** *Geology.* the part of the earth between the crust and the core, accounting for more than 82% of the earth's volume (but only 68% of its mass) and thought to be composed largely of peridotite. See also **asthenosphere. 8.** a less common spelling of **mantel. 9.** *Anatomy.* another word for **pallium** (sense 3). **10.** a clay mould formed around a wax model which is subsequently melted out. ~*vb.* **11.** (*tr.*) to envelop or supply with a mantle. **12.** to spread over or become spread over: *the trees were mantled with snow.* **13.** (*tr.*) (of the face, cheeks) to become suffused with blood; flush. **14.** (*intr.*) *Falconry.* (of a hawk or falcon) to spread the wings and tail over food. [C13: via Old French from Latin *mantellum,* diminutive of *mantum* cloak]
mantling (ˈmæntlɪŋ) *n. Heraldry.* the drapery or scrollwork around a shield. [C16: from MANTLE]
man-to-man *adj.* characterized by directness or candour: *a man-to-man discussion.*
Mantoux test (mænˈtuː; *French* mɑ̃tu) *n. Med.* a test for determining the presence of a tubercular infection by injecting tuberculin into the skin. [C19: named after C. *Mantoux,* French physician (1877–1956)]
mantra (ˈmæntrə, ˈmʌn-) *n.* **1.** *Hinduism.* any of those parts of the Vedic literature which consist of the metrical psalms of praise. **2.** *Hinduism, Buddhism.* any sacred word or syllable used as an object of concentration and embodying some aspect of spiritual power. [C19: from Sanskrit, literally: speech, instrument of thought, from *man* to think]
mantrap (ˈmænˌtræp) *n.* a snare for catching men, esp. trespassers.
mantua (ˈmæntjʊə) *n.* a loose gown of the 17th and 18th centuries, worn open in front to show the underskirt. [C17: changed from MANTEAU, through the influence of *Mantua,* city in N Italy]
manual (ˈmænjʊəl) *adj.* **1.** of or relating to a hand or hands. **2.** operated or done by hand: *manual controls.* **3.** physical, as opposed to mental or mechanical: *manual labour.* **4.** by human labour rather than automatic or computer-aided means. **5.** of, relating to, or resembling a manual. ~*n.* **6.** a book, esp. of instructions or information: *a car manual.* **7.** *Music.* one of the keyboards played by hand on an organ. **8.** *Military.* the prescribed drill with small arms. [C15: via Old French from Latin *manuālis,* from *manus* hand] —ˈ**manually** *adv.*
manubrium (məˈnjuːbrɪəm) *n., pl.* **-bria** (-brɪə) *or* **-briums. 1.** *Anatomy.* any handle-shaped part, esp. the upper part of the sternum. **2.** *Zoology.* the tubular mouth that hangs down from the centre of a coelenterate medusa such as a jellyfish. [C17: from New Latin, from Latin: handle, from *manus* hand] —**maˈnubrial** *adj.*
manuf. *or* **manufac.** *abbrev. for:* **1.** manufacture. **2.** manufactured. **3.** manufacturer. **4.** manufacturing.
manufactory (ˌmænjʊˈfæktərɪ, -trɪ) *n., pl.* **-ries.** an obsolete word for **factory.** [C17: from obsolete *manufact;* see MANUFACTURE]
manufacture (ˌmænjʊˈfæktʃə) *vb.* **1.** to process or make (a product) from a raw material, esp. as a large-scale operation using machinery. **2.** (*tr.*) to invent or concoct: *to manufacture an excuse.* ~*n.* **3.** the production of goods, esp. by industrial processes. **4.** a manufactured product. **5.** the creation or production of anything. [C16: from obsolete *manufact* hand-made, from Late Latin *manūfactus,* from Latin *manus* hand + *facere* to make] —ˌ**manuˈfacturable** *adj.* —ˌ**manuˈfacturing** *n., adj.*
manufacturer (ˌmænjʊˈfæktʃərə) *n.* a person or business concern that manufactures goods or owns a factory.
manuka (ˈmɑːnuːkə) *n.* a New Zealand myrtaceous tree, *Leptospermum scoparium,* with strong elastic wood and aromatic leaves. Also called: **tea tree.**
manumit (ˌmænjʊˈmɪt) *vb.* **-mits, -mitting, -mitted.** (*tr.*) to free from slavery, servitude, etc.; emancipate. [C15: from Latin *manūmittere* to release, from *manū* from one's hand + *ēmittere* to send away] —**manumission** (ˌmænjʊˈmɪʃən) *n.* —ˌ**manuˈmitter** *n.*
manure (məˈnjʊə) *n.* **1.** animal excreta, usually with straw, used to fertilize land. **2.** *Chiefly Brit.* any material, esp. chemical fertilizer, used to fertilize land. ~*vb.* **3.** (*tr.*) to spread manure upon (fields or soil). [C14: from Medieval Latin *manuopera;* manual work; see MANOEUVRE] —**maˈnurer** *n.*
manus (ˈmeɪnəs) *n., pl.* **-nus. 1.** *Anatomy.* the wrist and hand. **2.** the corresponding part in other vertebrates. **3.** *Roman law.* the authority of a husband over his wife. **4.** *English law.* (formerly) an oath or the person taking an oath. [C19: Latin: hand]
manuscript (ˈmænjʊˌskrɪpt) *n.* **1.** a book or other document written by hand. **2.** the original handwritten or typed version of a book, article, etc., as submitted by an author for publication. **3. a.** handwriting, as opposed to printing. **b.** (*as modifier*): *a manuscript document.* [C16: from Medieval Latin *manūscriptus,* from Latin *manus* hand + *scribere* to write]
Manx (mæŋks) *adj.* **1.** of, relating to, or characteristic of the Isle of Man in the Irish Sea, its inhabitants, their language, or their dialect of English. ~*n.* **2.** an almost extinct language of the Isle of Man, belonging to the N Celtic branch of the Indo-European family and closely related to Scottish Gaelic. **3.** (*functioning as pl.*) the people of the Isle of Man. [C16: earlier *Maniske,* from Scandinavian, from *Mana* Isle of Man + *-iske* -ISH]
Manx cat *n.* a short-haired tailless variety of cat, believed to originate on the Isle of Man.
Manxman (ˈmæŋksmən) *or* (*fem.*) **Manxwoman** (ˈmæŋkswʊmən) *n., pl.* **-men** *or* **-women.** a native or inhabitant of the Isle of Man.

Manx shearwater *n.* a European oceanic bird, *Puffinus puffinus,* with long slender wings and black-and-white plumage: family *Procellariidae* (shearwaters).

many ('mɛnɪ) *determiner.* **1.** (sometimes preceded by *a great* or *a good*) **a.** a large number of: *many coaches; many times.* **b.** (*as pronoun; functioning as pl.*): *many are seated already.* **2.** (foll. by *a, an,* or *another,* and a sing. noun) each of a considerable number of: *many a man.* **3.** (preceded by *as, too, that,* etc.) **a.** a great number of: *as many apples as you like; too many clouds to see.* **b.** (*as pronoun; functioning as pl.*): *I have as many as you.* ~*n.* **4. the many.** the majority of mankind, esp. the common people: *the many are kept in ignorance while the few prosper.* Compare **few** (sense 7). ~See also **more, most.** [Old English *manig;* related to Old Frisian *manich,* Middle Dutch *menech,* Old High German *manag*]

many-one *adj. Maths, logic.* (of a function) associating a single element of a range with more than one member of the domain.

manyplies ('mɛnɪˌplaɪz) *n.* (*functioning as sing.*) another name for **psalterium.** [C18: from the large number of plies or folds of its membrane]

many-sided *adj.* having many sides, aspects, etc.: *a many-sided personality.* —ˌ**many-'sidedness** *n.*

many-valued logic *n.* **a.** the study of logical systems in which the truth-values that a proposition may have are not restricted to two, representing only truth and falsity. **b.** such a logical system.

manzanilla (ˌmænzə'nɪlə) *n.* a very dry pale sherry. [C19: from Spanish: camomile (referring to its bouquet)]

Maoism ('maʊɪzəm) *n.* **1.** Marxism-Leninism as interpreted by Mao Tse-tung (1893–1976), Chinese Communist leader: distinguished by its theory of guerrilla warfare and its emphasis on the revolutionary potential of the peasantry. **2.** adherence to or reverence for Mao Tse-tung and his teachings. —'**Maoist** *n., adj.*

Maori ('maʊrɪ) *n.* **1.** (*pl.* **-ris** *or* **-ri**) a member of the people living in New Zealand and the Cook Islands since before the arrival of European settlers. They are descended from Polynesian voyagers who migrated in successive waves from the 16th century onwards. **2.** the language of this people, belonging to the Malayo-Polynesian family. ~*adj.* **3.** of or relating to this people or their language.

Maori bug *n.* a large shining black wingless cockroach of New Zealand, *Platyzosteria novae-zelandiae.*

Maori bunk *n. N.Z.* a raised sleeping platform.

Maori hen *n. N.Z.* another name for **weka.**

Maori oven *n.* another name for **hangi** (sense 1).

Maori rat *n.* a small brown rat, *Rattus exulans* Peale, native to New Zealand.

Maoritanga ('maʊrɪˌtʌŋə) *n. N.Z.* the Maori culture; Maori way of life. [Maori]

Maori warden *n.* a person appointed to exercise advisory and minor disciplinary powers in Maori communities.

Mao suit (maʊ) *n.* a simple style of clothing, traditionally made of cotton and commonly worn in Communist China, consisting of loose trousers and a straight jacket with a close-fitting stand-up collar. [C20: named after *Mao* Tse-tung (1893–1976), Chinese leader who popularized the style]

map (mæp) *n.* **1.** a diagrammatic representation of the earth's surface or part of it, showing the geographical distributions, positions, etc., of natural or artificial features such as roads, towns, relief, rainfall, etc. **2.** a diagrammatic representation of the distribution of stars or of the surface of a celestial body: *a lunar map.* **3.** a maplike drawing of anything. **4.** *Maths.* another name for **function** (sense 4). **5.** a slang word for **face** (sense 1). **6. off the map.** no longer important or in existence (esp. in the phrase **wipe off the map**). **7. put on the map.** to make (a town, company, etc.) well-known. ~*vb.* **maps, mapping, mapped.** (*tr.*) **8.** to make a map of. **9.** *Maths.* to represent or transform (a function, figure, set, etc.). [C16: from Medieval Latin *mappa* (*mundi*) map (of the world), from Latin *mappa* cloth] —'**mappable** *adj.* —'**mapless** *adj.* —'**mapper** *n.*

maple ('meɪpᵊl) *n.* **1.** any tree or shrub of the N temperate genus *Acer,* having winged seeds borne in pairs and lobed leaves: family *Aceraceae.* **2.** the hard close-grained wood of any of these trees, used for furniture and flooring. **3.** the flavour of the sap of the sugar maple. ~See also **sugar maple, silver maple, Norway maple, sycamore.** [C14: from Old English *mapel-,* as in *mapeltrēow* maple tree]

maple sugar *n. U.S. and Canadian.* sugar made from the sap of the sugar maple.

maple syrup *n. Chiefly U.S. and Canadian.* a very sweet syrup made from the sap of the sugar maple.

map out *vb.* (*tr., adv.*) to plan or design: *to map out a route.*

mapping ('mæpɪŋ) *n. Maths.* another name for **function** (sense 4).

map projection *n.* a means of representing or a representation of the globe or celestial sphere or part of it on a flat map, using a grid of lines of latitude and longitude.

maquette (mæ'kɛt) *n.* a sculptor's small preliminary model or sketch. [C20: from French, from Italian *macchietta* a little sketch, from *macchia,* from *macchiare,* from Latin *maculāre* to stain, from *macula* spot, blemish]

maquillage *French.* (makijaʒ) *n.* **1.** make-up; cosmetics. **2.** the application of make-up. [from *maquiller* to make up]

maquis (mɑː'kiː) *n., pl.* **-quis** (-'kiː). **1.** shrubby mostly evergreen vegetation found in coastal regions of the Mediterranean: includes myrtles, heaths, arbutus, cork oak, and ilex. **2.** (*often cap.*) **a.** the French underground movement that fought against the German occupying forces in World War II. **b.** a member of this movement. [C20: from French, from Italian *macchia* thicket, from Latin *macula* spot]

mar (mɑː) *vb.* **mars, marring, marred.** **1.** (*tr.*) to cause harm to; spoil or impair. ~*n.* **2.** a disfiguring mark; blemish. [Old English *merran;* compare Old Saxon *merrian* to hinder, Old Norse *merja* to bruise] —'**marrer** *n.*

mar. *abbrev. for:* **1.** maritime. **2.** married.

Mar. *abbrev. for* March.

mara (mə'rɑː) *n.* a harelike South American rodent, *Dolichotis patagonum,* inhabiting the pampas of Argentina: family *Caviidae* (cavies). [from American Spanish *mará,* perhaps of Araucanian origin]

marabou ('mærəˌbuː) *n.* **1.** a large black-and-white African carrion-eating stork, *Leptoptilos crumeniferus,* with a very short naked neck and a straight heavy bill. See also **adjutant bird.** **2.** a down feather of this bird, used to trim garments. **3. a.** a fine white raw silk. **b.** fabric made of this. [C19: from French, from Arabic *murābit* MARABOUT, so called because the stork is considered a holy bird in Islam]

marabout ('mærəˌbuː) *n.* **1.** a Muslim holy man or hermit of North Africa. **2.** a shrine of the grave of a marabout. [C17: via French and Portuguese *marabuto,* from Arabic *murābit*]

marabunta ('mærəˌbʌntə) *n. Caribbean.* **1.** any of several social wasps. **2.** *Slang.* an ill-tempered woman. [C19: perhaps of W African origin]

maraca (mə'rækə) *n.* a percussion instrument, usually one of a pair, consisting of a gourd or plastic shell filled with dried seeds, pebbles, etc. It is used chiefly in Latin American music. [C20: Brazilian Portuguese, from Tupi]

marae (mə'raɪ) *n. N.Z.* a traditional Maori tribal meeting place, originally one in the open air, now frequently a purpose-built building. [Maori]

maraging steel ('mɑːˌreɪdʒɪŋ) *n.* a strong low-carbon steel containing nickel and small amounts of titanium, aluminium, and niobium, produced by transforming to a martensitic structure and heating at 500°C. [C20 *maraging,* from MAR(TENSITE) + *aging*]

maranta (mə'ræntə) *n.* any plant of the tropical American rhizomatous genus *Maranta,* some species of which are grown as pot plants for their showy leaves in variegated shades of green: family *Marantaceae.* [named after Bartolomea *Maranti,* died 1571, Venetian botanist]

marari ('mɑːrɑːriː) *n. N.Z.* a Maori name for **butterfish** (sense 2).

marasca (mə'ræskə) *n.* a European cherry tree, *Prunus cerasus marasca,* with red acid-tasting fruit from which maraschino is made. [C19: from Italian, variant of *amarasca* from *amaro,* from Latin *amārus* bitter]

maraschino (ˌmærə'skiːnəʊ, -'ʃiːnəʊ) *n.* a liqueur made from marasca cherries and flavoured with the kernels, having a taste like bitter almonds. [C18: from Italian; see MARASCA]

maraschino cherry *n.* a cherry preserved in maraschino or an imitation of this liqueur, used as a garnish.

marasmus (mə'ræzməs) *n. Pathol.* general emaciation and wasting, esp. of infants, thought to be associated with severe malnutrition or impaired utilization of nutrients. [C17: from New Latin, from Greek *marasmos,* from *marainein* to waste] —**ma'rasmic** *adj.*

Maratha *or* **Mahratta** (mə'rɑːtə) *n.* a member of a people of India living chiefly in Maharashtra in W central India.

Marathi *or* **Mahratti** (mə'rɑːtɪ) *adj.* **1.** of or relating to Maharashtra state in W central India, its people, or their language. ~*n.* **2.** the state language of Maharashtra, belonging to the Indic branch of the Indo-European family.

marathon ('mærəθən) *n.* **1.** a race on foot of 26 miles 385 yards (42.195 kilometres): an event in the modern Olympics. **2. a.** any long or arduous task, assignment, etc. **b.** (*as modifier*): *a marathon effort.* [referring to the feat of the messenger who ran more than 20 miles from the plain of *Marathon* to Athens to bring the news of victory over the Persians in 490 B.C.]

marathon group *n.* (in psychotherapy) an encounter group that lasts for many hours or days.

maraud (mə'rɔːd) *vb.* **1.** to wander or raid in search of plunder. ~*n.* **2.** an archaic word for **foray.** [C18: from French *marauder* to prowl, from *maraud* vagabond] —**ma'rauder** *n.* —**ma'rauding** *adj.*

maravedi (ˌmærə'veɪdɪ) *n., pl.* **-dis.** any of various Spanish coins of copper or gold. [C15: from Spanish, from Arabic *Murābitīn* (plural of *murābit* MARABOUT), the Moorish dynasty in Córdoba, 1087–1147]

marble ('mɑːbᵊl) *n.* **1. a.** a hard crystalline metamorphic rock resulting from the recrystallization of a limestone: takes a high polish and is used for building and sculpture. **b.** (*as modifier*): *a marble bust.* **2.** a block or work of art of marble. **3.** a small round glass or stone ball used in playing marbles. **4. make one's marble good.** *Austral. and N.Z. informal.* to succeed or do the right thing. **5. pass in one's marble.** *Austral. informal.* to die. ~*vb.* **6.** (*tr.*) to mottle with variegated streaks in imitation of marble. ~*adj.* **7.** cold, hard, or unresponsive. **8.** white like some kinds of marble. ~See also **marbles.** [C12: via Old French from Latin *marmor,* from Greek *marmaros,* related to Greek *marmairein* to gleam] —'**marbled** *adj.* —'**marbler** *n.* —'**marbly** *adj.*

marble cake *n.* a cake with a marbled appearance obtained by incompletely mixing dark and light mixtures.

marbled white *n.* any butterfly of the satyrid genus *Melanargia,* with panelled black-and-white wings, but technically a brown butterfly; found in grassland.

marbles ('mɑːbᵊlz) *n.* **1.** (*functioning as sing.*) a game in which marbles are rolled at one another, similar to bowls. **2.** (*functioning as pl.*) *Informal.* wits: *to lose one's marbles.*

marblewood ('mɑːbᵊlˌwʊd) *n.* **1.** a Malaysian tree, *Diospyros marmorata*: family *Ebenaceae.* **2.** the distinctively marked wood of this tree, having black bands on a lighter background.

marbling ('mɑːblɪŋ) *n.* **1.** a mottled effect or pattern resembling marble. **2.** such an effect obtained by transferring floating colours from a bath of gum solution. **3.** the streaks of fat in lean meat.

Marburg disease ('mɑːˌbɜːg) *n.* a severe, sometimes fatal, viral disease of the green monkey, which may be transmitted to humans. Symptoms include fever, vomiting, and internal bleeding. Also called: **green monkey disease.** [named after *Marburg,* city in W Germany where the first human cases were recorded]

marc (mɑːk; *French* mar) *n.* **1.** the remains of grapes or other fruit that have been pressed for wine-making. **2.** a brandy distilled from these. [C17: from French, from Old French *marchier* to trample (grapes), MARCH[1]]

marcasite ('mɑːkəˌsaɪt) *n.* **1.** a metallic pale yellow mineral consisting of iron pyrites in orthorhombic crystalline form used in jewellery. **2.** a cut and polished form of steel or any white metal used for making jewellery. [C15: from Medieval Latin *marcasīta,* from Arabic *marqashītā,* perhaps from Persian] —**marcasitical** (ˌmɑːkə'sɪtɪkᵊl) *adj.*

marcato (mɑː'kɑːtəʊ) *Music.* ~*adj.* **1.** (of notes) heavily accented. ~*adv.* **2.** with each note heavily accented. [C19: from Italian: marked]

marcel (mɑː'sɛl) *n.* **1.** Also called: **marcel wave.** a hairstyle characterized by repeated regular waves, popular in the 1920s. ~*vb.* **-cels, -celling, -celled. 2.** (*tr.*) to make such waves in (the hair) with special hot irons. [C20: after *Marcel* Grateau (1852–1936), French hairdresser] —**mar'celler** *n.*

marcescent (mɑː'sɛsᵊnt) *adj.* (of the parts of certain plants) remaining attached to the plant when withered. [C18: from Latin *marcescere* to grow weak, from *marcēre* to wither] —**mar'cescence** *n.*

march[1] (mɑːtʃ) *vb.* **1.** (*intr.*) to walk or proceed with stately or regular steps, usually in a procession or military formation. **2.** (*tr.*) to make (a person or group) proceed: *he marched his army to the town.* **3.** (*tr.*) to traverse or cover by marching: *to march a route.* ~*n.* **4.** the act or an instance of marching. **5.** a regular stride: *a slow march.* **6.** a long or exhausting walk. **7.** advance; progression (of time, etc.). **8.** a distance or route covered by marching. **9.** a piece of music, usually in four beats to the bar, having a strongly accented rhythm. **10. steal a march on.** to gain an advantage over, esp. by a secret or underhand enterprise. [C16: from Old French *marchier* to tread, probably of Germanic origin; compare Old English *mearcian* to MARK[1]] —'**marcher** *n.*

march[2] (mɑːtʃ) *n.* **1.** Also called: **marchland.** a frontier, border, or boundary or the land lying along it, often of disputed ownership. ~*vb.* **2.** (*intr.*; often foll. by *upon* or *with*) to share a common border (with). [C13: from Old French *marche,* from Germanic; related to MARK[1]]

March (mɑːtʃ) *n.* the third month of the year, consisting of 31 days. [from Old French, from Latin *Martius* (month) of Mars, god of war]

MArch *abbrev. for* Master of Architecture.

March. *abbrev. for* Marchioness.

march brown *n.* an angler's name for the dun and spinner of various mayflies or an artificial fly imitating one of these.

marcher ('mɑːtʃə) *n.* **1.** an inhabitant of any of the Marches, the border areas between England and Wales or Scotland. **2.** (formerly) **a.** a lord governing and defending such a borderland. **b.** (*as modifier*): *the marcher lords.*

marchesa *Italian.* (mar'keːza) *n., pl.* **-se** (-ze). (in Italy) the wife or widow of a marchese; marchioness.

marchese *Italian.* (mar'keːze) *n., pl.* **-si** (-zi). (in Italy) a nobleman ranking below a prince and above a count; marquis.

Marcheshvan *Hebrew.* (marxɛʃ'van) *n.* another word for ***Cheshvan.*** [from Hebrew *mar* bitter (because it contains no festivals) + CHESHVAN]

March hare *n.* a hare during its breeding season in March, noted for its wild and excitable behaviour (esp. in the phrase **mad as a March hare**).

marching girl *n.* (*often pl.*) *Austral. and N.Z.* one of a team of girls dressed in fancy uniform who perform marching formations.

marching orders *pl. n.* **1.** military orders, esp. to infantry, giving instructions about a march, its destination, etc. **2.** *Informal.* notice of dismissal, esp. from employment. **3.** *Informal.* the instruction to proceed with a task.

marchioness ('mɑːʃənɪs, ˌmɑːʃə'nɛs) *n.* **1.** the wife or widow of a marquis. **2.** a woman who holds the rank of marquis. [C16: from Medieval Latin *marchionissa,* feminine of *marchiō* MARQUIS]

marchland ('mɑːtʃˌlænd, -lənd) *n.* a less common word for **borderland** *or* **march**[2].

marchpane ('mɑːtʃˌpeɪn) *n.* an archaic word for **marzipan.** [C15: from French]

march past *n.* the marching of troops on parade past a person who is reviewing them.

Marcionism ('mɑːʃəˌnɪzəm) *n.* a Gnostic movement of the 2nd and 3rd centuries A.D. [C16: after *Marcion* of Sinope, 2nd-century Gnostic]

Marconi rig (mɑː'kəʊnɪ) *n. Nautical.* a fore-and-aft sailing boat rig with triangular sails. [C20: named after Guglielmo *Marconi* (1874–1937), Italian physicist, from its resemblance to some types of radio aerial] —**Mar'coni-ˌrigged** *adj.*

Mardi Gras ('mɑːdɪ 'grɑː) *n.* the festival of Shrove Tuesday, celebrated in some cities with great revelry. [French: fat Tuesday]

mardy ('mɑːdɪ) *adj. Dialect.* **1.** (of a child) spoilt. **2.** irritable. [from *marred,* past participle of MAR]

mare[1] (mɛə) *n.* the adult female of a horse or zebra. [C12: from Old English, of Germanic origin; related to Old High German *mariha,* Old Norse *merr* mare]

mare[2] ('mɑːreɪ, -rɪ) *n., pl.* **maria** ('mɑːrɪə). **1.** (*cap. when part of a name*) any of a large number of huge dry plains on the surface of the moon, visible as dark markings and once thought to be seas: *Mare Imbrium* (*Sea of Showers*). **2.** a similar area on the surface of Mars, such as *Mare Sirenum.* [from Latin: sea]

mare clausum ('mɑːreɪ 'klaʊsʊm) *n. Law.* a sea coming under the jurisdiction of one nation and closed to all others. Compare **mare liberum.** [Latin: closed sea]

mare liberum ('mɑːreɪ 'liːbərʊm) *n. Law.* a sea open to navigation by shipping of all nations. Compare **mare clausum.** [Latin: free sea]

maremma (mə'rɛmə) *n., pl.* **-me** (-miː). a marshy unhealthy region near the shore, esp. in Italy. [C19: from Italian, from Latin *maritima* MARITIME]

Marengo (mə'rɛŋgəʊ) *adj.* (*postpositive*) browned in oil and cooked with tomatoes, mushrooms, garlic, wine, etc.: *chicken Marengo.* [C19: after a dish prepared for Napoleon after his victory (1800) in the battle of *Marengo* in NW Italy]

mare's-nest *n.* **1.** a discovery imagined to be important but proving worthless. **2.** a disordered situation.

mare's-tail *n.* **1.** a wisp of trailing cirrus cloud, indicating strong winds at high levels. **2.** an erect pond plant, *Hippuris vulgaris,* with minute flowers and crowded whorls of narrow leaves: family *Hippuridaceae.*

Mareva injunction (mə'riːvə) *n. Law.* an order enabling the court to freeze the assets of a defendant, esp. to prevent him from taking them abroad. [C20: named after *Mareva Companai Naviera SA,* the plaintiff in an early case (1975) in which such an order was made]

marg (mɑːdʒ) *n. Brit. informal.* short for **margarine.**

marg. *abbrev. for* margin(al).

margaric (mɑː'gærɪk) *or* **margaritic** *adj.* of or resembling pearl. [C19: from Greek *margaron* pearl]

margaric acid *n.* another name for **heptadecanoic acid.**

margarine (ˌmɑːdʒə'riːn, ˌmɑːgə-) *n.* a substitute for butter, prepared from vegetable and animal fats by emulsifying them with water and adding small amounts of milk, salt, vitamins, colouring matter, etc. [C19: from MARGARIC]

margarita (ˌmɑːgə'riːtə) *n.* a mixed drink consisting of tequila and lemon juice. [C20: from the woman's name]

margarite ('mɑːgəˌraɪt) *n.* **1.** a pink pearly micaceous mineral consisting of hydrated calcium aluminium silicate. Formula: $CaAl_4Si_2O_{10}(OH)_2$. **2.** an aggregate of minute beadlike masses occurring in some glassy igneous rocks. [C19: via German from Greek *margaron* pearl]

Margaux (*French* margo) *n.* a red wine produced in the region around the village of Margaux near Bordeaux.

margay ('mɑːˌgeɪ) *n.* a feline mammal, *Felis wiedi,* of Central and South America, having a dark-striped coat. [C18: from French, from Tupi *mbaracaiá*]

marge[1] (mɑːdʒ) *n. Brit. informal.* short for **margarine.**

marge[2] (mɑːdʒ) *n. Archaic.* a margin. [C16: from French]

margin ('mɑːdʒɪn) *n.* **1.** an edge or rim, and the area immediately adjacent to it; border. **2.** the blank space surrounding the text on a page. **3.** a vertical line on a page, esp. one on the left-hand side, delineating this space. **4.** an additional amount or one beyond the minimum necessary: *a margin of error.* **5.** *Chiefly Austral.* a payment made in addition to a basic wage, esp. for special skill or responsibility. **6.** a bound or limit. **7.** the amount by which one thing differs from another: *a large margin separated the parties.* **8.** *Commerce.* the profit on a transaction. **9.** *Economics.* the minimum return below which an enterprise becomes unprofitable. **10.** *Finance.* **a.** collateral deposited by a client with a broker as security. **b.** the excess of the value of a loan's collateral over the value of the loan. ~Also (archaic): **margent** ('mɑːdʒənt). ~*vb.* (*tr.*) **11.** to provide with a margin; border. **12.** *Finance.* to deposit a margin upon. [C14: from Latin *margō* border; related to MARCH[2], MARK[1]]

marginal (ˈmɑːdʒɪnᵊl) *adj.* **1.** of, in, on, or constituting a margin. **2.** close to a limit, esp. a lower limit: *marginal legal ability.* **3.** not considered central or important; insignificant, minor, small. **4.** *Economics.* relating to goods or services produced and sold at the margin of profitability: *marginal cost.* **5.** *Politics, chiefly Brit. and N.Z.* of or designating a constituency in which elections tend to be won by small margins: *a marginal seat.* **6.** designating agricultural land on the margin of cultivated zones. **7.** *Economics.* relating to a small change in something, such as total cost, revenue, or consumer satisfaction. —**marginality** (ˌmɑːdʒɪˈnælɪtɪ) *n.* —ˈ**marginally** *adv.*

marginalia (ˌmɑːdʒɪˈneɪlɪə) *pl. n.* notes in the margin of a book, manuscript, or letter. [C19: New Latin, noun (neuter plural) from *marginālis* marginal]

marginalize *or* **marginalise** (ˈmɑːdʒɪnᵊˌlaɪz) *vb.* (*tr.*) to relegate to the fringes, out of the mainstream; make seem unimportant: *various economic assumptions marginalize women.* —ˌ**marginaliˈzation** *or* ˌ**marginaliˈsation** *n.*

marginal probability *n. Statistics.* (in a multivariate distribution) the probability of one variable taking a specific value irrespective of the values of the others.

marginate (ˈmɑːdʒɪˌneɪt) *vb.* **1.** (*tr.*) to provide with a margin or margins. ~*adj.* **2.** *Biology.* having a margin of a distinct colour or form: *marginate leaves.* [C18: from Latin *margināre*] —ˌ**marginˈation** *n.*

margravate (ˈmɑːgrəvɪt) *or* **margraviate** (mɑːˈgreɪvɪɪt) *n.* the domain of a margrave.

margrave (ˈmɑːˌgreɪv) *n.* a German nobleman ranking above a count. Margraves were originally counts appointed to govern frontier provinces, but all had become princes of the Holy Roman Empire by the 12th century. [C16: from Middle Dutch *markgrave,* literally: count of the MARCH[2]]

margravine (ˈmɑːgrəˌviːn) *n.* **1.** the wife or widow of a margrave. **2.** a woman who holds the rank of margrave. [C17: from Middle Dutch, feminine of MARGRAVE]

marguerite (ˌmɑːgəˈriːt) *n.* **1.** a cultivated garden plant, *Chrysanthemum frutescens,* whose flower heads have white or pale yellow rays around a yellow disc: family *Compositae* (composites). **2.** any of various related plants with daisy-like flowers, esp. *C. leucanthemum.* [C19: from French: daisy, pearl, from Latin *margarīta,* from Greek *margaritēs,* from *margaron*]

Marheshvan *or* ***Marcheshvan*** *Hebrew.* (marxɛʃˈvan) *n.* another word for ***Cheshvan.***

Mari (ˈmɑːrɪ) *n., pl.* **Mari** *or* **Maris.** another name for **Cheremiss.**

maria (ˈmɑːrɪə) *n.* the plural of **mare**[2].

mariachi (ˌmɑːrɪˈɑːtʃɪ) *n.* a small ensemble of street musicians in Mexico. [C20: from Mexican Spanish]

mariage blanc *French* (marjaʒ blɑ̃) *n., pl.* ***mariages blancs*** (marjaʒ blɑ̃). unconsummated marriage. [C20: literally: white marriage]

mariage de convenance *French.* (marjaʒ də kɔ̃vənɑ̃s) *n., pl.* ***mariages de convenance.*** another term for **marriage of convenience.**

Marian (ˈmɛərɪən) *adj.* **1.** of or relating to the Virgin Mary. **2.** of or relating to some other Mary, such as Mary Queen of Scots or Mary I of England. ~*n.* **3.** a person who has a special devotion to the Virgin Mary. **4.** a supporter of some other Mary.

Marianne (*French* marjan) *n.* a female figure personifying the French republic after the Revolution (1789).

mariculture (ˈmærɪˌkʌltʃə) *n.* the cultivation of marine plants and animals in their natural environment. [C20: from Latin *mari-, mare* sea + CULTURE]

marigold (ˈmærɪˌgəʊld) *n.* **1.** any of various tropical American plants of the genus *Tagetes,* esp. *T. erecta* **(African marigold)** and *T. patula* **(French marigold),** cultivated for their yellow or orange flower heads and strongly scented foliage: family *Compositae* (composites). **2.** any of various similar or related plants, such as the marsh marigold, pot marigold, bur marigold, and fig marigold. [C14: from *Mary* (the Virgin) + GOLD]

marigram (ˈmærɪˌgræm) *n.* a graphic record of the tide levels at a particular coastal station. [from Latin *mare* sea + -GRAM]

marigraph (ˈmærɪˌgræf, -ˌgrɑːf) *n.* a gauge for recording the levels of the tides. [from Latin *mare* sea + -GRAPH]

marijuana *or* **marihuana** (ˌmærɪˈhwɑːnə) *n.* **1.** the dried leaves and flowers of the hemp plant, used for its euphoric effects, esp. in the form of cigarettes. See also **cannabis. 2.** another name for **hemp** (the plant). [C19: from Mexican Spanish]

marimba (məˈrɪmbə) *n.* a Latin American percussion instrument consisting of a set of hardwood plates placed over tuned metal resonators, played with two soft-headed sticks in each hand. [C18: of West African origin]

marina (məˈriːnə) *n.* an elaborate docking facility for yachts and other pleasure boats. [C19: via Italian and Spanish from Latin: MARINE]

marinade *n.* (ˌmærɪˈneɪd). **1.** a spiced liquid mixture of oil, wine, vinegar, herbs, etc., in which meat or fish is soaked before cooking. **2.** meat or fish soaked in this liquid. ~*vb.* (ˈmærɪˌneɪd). **3.** a variant of **marinate.** [C17: from French, from Spanish *marinada,* from *marinar* to pickle in brine, MARINATE]

marinate (ˈmærɪˌneɪt) *vb.* to soak in marinade. [C17: probably from Italian *marinato,* from *marinare* to pickle, ultimately from Latin *marīnus* MARINE] —ˌ**mariˈnation** *n.*

marine (məˈriːn) *adj.* (*usually prenominal*) **1.** of, found in, or relating to the sea. **2.** of or relating to shipping, navigation, etc. **3.** of or relating to a body of seagoing troops: *marine corps.* **4.** of or relating to a government department concerned with maritime affairs. **5.** used or adapted for use at sea: *a marine camera.* ~*n.* **6.** shipping and navigation in general: *the merchant marine.* **7.** (*cap. when part of a name*) a member of a marine corps or similar body. **8.** a picture of a ship, seascape, etc. **9. tell it to the marines.** *Informal.* an expression of disbelief. [C15: from Old French *marin,* from Latin *marīnus,* from *mare* sea]

marine borer *n.* any mollusc or crustacean that lives usually in warm seas and destroys wood by boring into and eating it. The gribble and shipworm are the best known since they penetrate any wood in favourable water. See also **piddock.**

marine engineer *n.* an engineer responsible for all heavy machinery on a ship or an offshore structure.

marine insurance *n.* insurance covering damage to or loss of ship, passengers, or cargo caused by the sea.

mariner (ˈmærɪnə) *n.* a formal or literary word for **seaman.** [C13: from Anglo-French, ultimately from Latin *marīnus* MARINE]

Mariner (ˈmærɪnə) *n.* any of a series of U.S. space probes launched between 1962 and 1971 that sent back photographs and information concerning the surface of Mars and Venus and also studied interplanetary matter.

marine railway *n.* another term for **slipway** (sense 2).

Mariolatry *or* **Maryolatry** (ˌmɛərɪˈɒlətrɪ) *n. Derogatory.* exaggerated veneration of the Virgin Mary. —ˌ**Mariˈolater** *or* ˌ**Maryˈolater** *n.* —ˌ**Mariˈolatrous** *or* ˌ**Maryˈolatrous** *adj.*

Mariology *or* **Maryology** (ˌmɛərɪˈɒlədʒɪ) *n. R.C. Church.* the study of the traditions and doctrines concerning the Virgin Mary. —ˌ**Mariˈologist** *or* ˌ**Maryˈologist** *n.*

marionette (ˌmærɪəˈnɛt) *n.* an articulated puppet or doll whose jointed limbs are moved by strings. [C17: from French, from *Marion,* diminutive of *Marie* Mary + -ETTE]

mariposa (ˌmærɪˈpəʊzə, -sə) *n.* any of several liliaceous plants of the genus *Calochortus,* of the southwestern U.S. and Mexico, having brightly coloured tulip-like flowers. Also called: **mariposa lily** *or* **tulip.** [C19: from Spanish: butterfly; from the likeness of the blooms to butterflies]

marish (ˈmærɪʃ) *adj. Obsolete.* marshy; swampy. [C14: from Old French *marais* MARSH]

Marist (ˈmɛərɪst) *R.C. Church.* ~*n.* **1.** a member of the Society of Mary, a religious congregation founded in 1824. **2.** *N.Z.* a teacher or pupil in a school belonging to the Marist Order. ~*adj.* **3.** of a Marist. [C19: from French *Mariste,* from *Marie* Mary (the virgin)]

maritage (ˈmærɪtɪdʒ) *n. Feudal history.* **1.** the right of a lord to choose the spouses of his wards. **2.** a sum paid to a lord in lieu of his exercising this right. [C16: from Medieval Latin *marītāgium,* a Latinized form of French *mariage* marriage]

marital (ˈmærɪtᵊl) *adj.* **1.** of or relating to marriage: *marital status.* **2.** of or relating to a husband. [C17: from Latin *marītālis,* from *marītus* married (adj.), husband (n.); related to *mās* male] —ˈ**maritally** *adv.*

maritime (ˈmærɪˌtaɪm) *adj.* **1.** of or relating to navigation, shipping, etc.; seafaring. **2.** of, relating to, near, or living near the sea. **3.** (of a climate) having small temperature differences between summer and winter; equable. [C16: from Latin *maritimus* from *mare* sea]

Maritimer (ˈmærɪˌtaɪmə) *n.* a native or inhabitant of the Maritime Provinces of Canada.

marjoram (ˈmɑːdʒərəm) *n.* **1.** Also called: **sweet marjoram.** an aromatic Mediterranean plant, *Origanum* (or *Marjorana*) *hortensis,* with small pale purple flowers and sweet-scented leaves, used for seasoning food and in salads: family *Labiatae* (labiates). **2.** Also called: **wild marjoram, pot marjoram, origan.** a similar and related European plant, *Origanum vulgare.* See also **oregano, origanum.** [C14: via Old French *majorane,* from Medieval Latin *marjorana*]

mark[1] (mɑːk) *n.* **1.** a visible impression, stain, etc., on a surface, such as a spot or scratch. **2** a sign, symbol, or other indication that distinguishes something: *an owner's mark.* **3.** a cross or other symbol made instead of a signature. **4.** a written or printed sign or symbol, as for punctuation: *a question mark.* **5.** a letter, number, or percentage used to grade academic work. **6.** a thing that indicates position or directs; marker. **7.** a desired or recognized standard: *he is not up to the mark.* **8.** an indication of some quality, feature, or prowess: *he has the mark of an athlete.* **9.** quality or importance; note: *a person of little mark.* **10.** a target or goal. **11.** impression or influence: *he left his mark on German literature.* **12.** *Slang.* a suitable victim, esp. for swindling. **13.** (*often cap.*) (in trade names) **a.** model, brand, or type: *the car is a Mark 4.* **b.** a variation on a particular model: *a Mark 3 Cortina.* **14.** *Nautical.* one of the intervals distinctively marked on a sounding lead. Compare **deep** (sense 21). **15.** *Bowls.* another name for the **jack. 16.** *Rugby Union.* an action in which a player standing inside his own 22m line with both feet on the ground catches a forward kick, throw, or knock by an opponent and shouts "mark", entitling himself to a free kick. **17.** *Australian Rules football.* a catch of the ball from a kick of at least 10 yards, after which a free kick is taken. **18. the mark.** *Boxing.* the middle of the stomach at or above the line made by the boxer's trunks. **19.** (in medieval England and Germany) a piece of land held in common by the free men of a community. **20.** an obsolete word for **frontier. 21.** *Statistics.* See **class mark. 22. beside the mark.** irrelevant or off the point. **23. make one's mark.** to succeed or achieve recognition. **24. on your mark** *or* **marks.** a command given to runners in a race to prepare themselves at the starting line. *~vb.* **25.** to make or receive (a visible impression, trace, or stain) on (a surface). **26.** (*tr.*) to characterize or distinguish: *his face was marked by anger.* **27.** (often foll. by *off* or *out*) to set boundaries or limits (on): *to mark out an area for negotiation.* **28.** (*tr.*) to select, designate, or doom by or as if by a mark: *to mark someone as a criminal.* **29.** (*tr.*) to put identifying or designating labels, stamps, etc., on, esp. to indicate price: *to mark the book at one pound.* **30.** (*tr.*) to pay heed or attention to: *mark my words.* **31.** to observe; notice. **32.** to grade or evaluate (scholastic work): *she marks fairly.* **33.** *Brit., football, etc.* to stay close to (an opponent) to hamper his play. **34.** to keep (score) in some games. **35. mark time. a.** to move the feet alternately as in marching but without advancing. **b.** to act in a mechanical and routine way. **c.** to halt progress temporarily, while awaiting developments. *~interj.* **36.** *Rugby Union.* the shout given by a player when calling for a mark. ~See also **markdown, mark-up.** [Old English *mearc* mark; related to Old Norse *mörk* boundary land, Old High German *marha* boundary, Latin *margō* MARGIN]

mark[2] (mɑːk) *n.* **1.** See **Deutschmark, markka, Reichsmark, ostmark. 2.** a former monetary unit and coin in England and Scotland worth two thirds of a pound sterling. **3.** a silver coin of Germany until 1924. [Old English *marc* unit of weight of precious metal, perhaps from the marks on metal bars; apparently of Germanic origin and related to MARK[1]]

markdown (ˈmɑːkˌdaʊn) *n.* **1.** a price reduction. *~vb.* **mark down. 2.** (*tr., adv.*) to reduce in price.

marked (mɑːkt) *adj.* **1.** obvious, evident, or noticeable. **2.** singled out, esp. for punishment, killing, etc.: *a marked man.* **3.** *Linguistics.* distinguished by a specific feature, as in phonology. For example, of the two phonemes /t/ and /d/, the /d/ is marked because it exhibits the feature of voice. —**markedly** (ˈmɑːkɪdlɪ) *adv.* —ˈ**markedness** *n.*

marker (ˈmɑːkə) *n.* **1. a.** something used for distinguishing or marking. **b.** (*as modifier*): *a marker buoy.* **2.** a person or thing that marks. **3.** a person or object that keeps or shows scores in a game.

market (ˈmɑːkɪt) *n.* **1. a.** an event or occasion, usually held at regular intervals, at which people meet for the purpose of buying and selling merchandise. **b.** (*as modifier*): *market day.* **2.** a place, such as an open space in a town, at which a market is held. **3.** a shop that sells a particular merchandise: *an antique market.* **4. the market.** business or trade in a commodity as specified: *the sugar market.* **5.** the trading or selling opportunities provided by a particular group of people: *the foreign market.* **6.** demand for a particular product or commodity: *there is no market for furs here.* **7.** See **stock market. 8.** See **market price, market value. 9. at market.** at the current price. **10. be in the market for.** to wish to buy or acquire. **11. on the market.** available for purchase. **12. play the market. a.** to speculate on a stock exchange. **b.** to act aggressively or unscrupulously in one's own commercial interests. **13. seller's** (*or* **buyer's**) **market.** a market characterized by excess demand (or supply) and thus favourable to sellers (or buyers). *~vb.* **-kets, -keting, -keted. 14.** (*tr.*) to offer or produce for sale. **15.** (*intr.*) to buy or deal in a market. [C12: from Latin *mercātus;* from *mercāri* to trade, from *merx* merchandise] —ˈ**marketer** *n.*

marketable (ˈmɑːkɪtəbᵊl) *adj.* **1.** (of commodities, assets, etc.) **a.** being in good demand; saleable. **b.** suitable for sale. **2.** of or relating to buying or selling on a market: *marketable value.* —ˌ**marketaˈbility** *or* ˈ**marketableness** *n.* —ˈ**marketably** *adv.*

market garden *n. Chiefly Brit.* an establishment where fruit and vegetables are grown for sale. —**market gardener** *n.*

market gardening *n. Chiefly Brit.* the business of growing fruit and vegetables on a commercial scale. Also called (in the U.S. and Canada): **truck farming, trucking.**

marketing (ˈmɑːkɪtɪŋ) *n.* the provision of goods or services to meet consumer needs.

marketing mix *n.* the variables, such as price, promotion, and service, managed by an organization to influence demand for a product or service.

market maker *n.* a dealer in securities on the London Stock Exchange who buys and sells as a principal and since 1986 can also deal with the public as a broker.

market mammy *n.* a W African woman trader.

market order *n.* an instruction to a broker to sell or buy at the best price currently obtainable on the market.

marketplace (ˈmɑːkɪtˌpleɪs) *n.* **1.** a place where a public market is held. **2.** any centre where ideas, opinions, etc., are exchanged. **3.** the commercial world of buying and selling.

market price *n.* the prevailing price, as determined by supply and demand, at which goods, services, etc., may be bought or sold.

market rent *n.* (in Britain) the rent chargeable for accommodation, allowing for the scarcity of that kind of property and the willingness of tenants to pay.

market research *n.* the study of influences upon customer behaviour and the analysis of market characteristics and trends.

market share *n.* the percentage of a total market, in terms of either value or volume, accounted for by the sales of a specific brand.

market town *n. Chiefly Brit.* a town that holds a market, esp. an agricultural centre in a rural area.

market value *n.* the amount obtainable on the open market for the sale of property, financial assets, or goods and services. Compare **par value, book value.**

markhor (ˈmɑːkɔː) *or* **markhoor** (ˈmɑːkʊə) *n., pl.* **-khors, -khor** *or* **-khoors, -khoor.** a large wild Himalayan goat, *Capra falconeri,* with a reddish-brown coat and large spiralled horns. [C19: from Persian, literally: snake-eater, from *mār* snake + *-khōr* eating]

marking (ˈmɑːkɪŋ) *n.* **1.** a mark or series of marks. **2.** the arrangement of colours on an animal, plant, etc. **3.** assessment and correction of school children's or students' written work by teaching staff.

marking ink *n.* indelible ink used for marking linen, clothes, etc.

markka (ˈmɑːkɑː, -kə) *n., pl.* **-kaa** (-kɑː). the standard monetary unit of Finland, divided into 100 pennia. [Finnish. See MARK[2]]

Markov chain (ˈmɑːkɒf) *n. Statistics.* a sequence of events the probability for each of which is dependent only on the event immediately preceding it. [C20: named after Andrei *Markov* (1856–1922), Russian mathematician]

marksman (ˈmɑːksmən) *n., pl.* **-men. 1.** a person skilled in shooting. **2.** a serviceman selected for his skill in shooting, esp. for a minor engagement. **3.** a qualification awarded in certain armed services for skill in shooting. —ˈ**marksmanˌship** *n.* —ˈ**marksˌwoman** *fem. n.*

mark-up *n.* **1.** a percentage or amount added to the cost of a commodity to provide the seller with a profit and to cover overheads, costs, etc. **2. a.** an increase in the price of a commodity. **b.** the amount of this increase. *~vb.* **mark up.** (*tr., adv.*) **3.** to add a percentage for profit, overheads, etc., to the cost of (a commodity). **4.** to increase the price of.

marl[1] (mɑːl) *n.* **1.** a fine-grained sedimentary rock consisting of clay minerals, calcite or aragonite, and silt: used as a fertilizer. *~vb.* **2.** (*tr.*) to fertilize (land) with marl. [C14: via Old French, from Late Latin *margila,* diminutive of Latin *marga*] —**marlacious** (mɑːˈleɪʃəs) *or* ˈ**marly** *adj.*

marl[2] (mɑːl) *vb. Nautical.* to seize (a rope) with marline, using a hitch at each turn. [C15 *marlyn* to bind; related to Dutch *marlen* to tie, Old English *mārels* cable]

marlin (ˈmɑːlɪn) *n., pl.* **-lin** *or* **-lins.** any of several large scombroid food and game fishes of the genera *Makaira, Istiompax,* and *Tetrapturus,* of warm and tropical seas, having a very long upper jaw: family *Istiophoridae.* Also called: **spearfish.** [C20: from MARLINESPIKE; with allusion to the shape of the beak]

marline, marlin (ˈmɑːlɪn), *or* (*less commonly*) **marling** (ˈmɑːlɪŋ) *n. Nautical.* a light rope, usually tarred, made of two strands laid left-handed. [C15: from Dutch *marlijn,* from *marren* to tie + *lijn* line]

marlinespike, marlinspike (ˈmɑːlɪnˌspaɪk), *or* (*less commonly*) **marlingspike** (ˈmɑːlɪŋˌspaɪk) *n. Nautical.* a pointed metal tool used as a fid, spike, and for various other purposes.

marlite (ˈmɑːlaɪt) *or* **marlstone** (ˈmɑːlˌstəʊn) *n.* a type of marl that contains clay and calcium carbonate and is resistant to the decomposing action of air.

marmalade (ˈmɑːməˌleɪd) *n.* **1.** a preserve made by boiling the pulp and rind of citrus fruits, esp. oranges, with sugar. *~adj.* **2.** (of cats) streaked orange or yellow and brown. [C16: via French from Portuguese *marmelada,* from *marmelo* quince, from Latin, from Greek *melimēlon,* from *meli* honey + *mēlon* apple]

marmalade tree *n.* a tropical American sapotaceous tree, *Calocarpum sapota,* with durable wood: its fruit is used to make preserves. Also called: **mamey.**

marmite (ˈmɑːmaɪt) *n.* **1.** a large cooking pot. **2.** soup cooked in such a pot. **3.** an individual covered casserole for serving soup. [from French: pot]

Marmite (ˈmɑːmaɪt) *n. Brit. trademark.* a yeast and vegetable extract used as a spread, flavouring, etc.

marmoreal (mɑːˈmɔːrɪəl) *or* (*less commonly*) **marmorean** *adj.* of, relating to, or resembling marble: *a marmoreal complexion.* [C18: from Latin *marmoreus,* from *marmor* marble] —**marˈmoreally** *adv.*

marmoset (ˈmɑːməˌzɛt) *n.* **1.** any small South American monkey of the genus *Callithrix* and related genera, having long hairy tails, clawed digits, and tufts of hair around the head and ears: family *Callithricidae.* **2. pygmy marmoset.** a related form, *Cebuella pygmaea:* the smallest monkey, inhabiting tropical forests of the Amazon. [C14: from Old French *marmouset* grotesque figure, of obscure origin]

marmot (ˈmɑːmət) *n.* **1.** any burrowing sciurine rodent of the genus *Marmota,* of Europe, Asia, and North America. They are heavily built, having short legs, a short furry tail, and coarse fur. **2. prairie marmot.** another name for **prairie dog.** [C17: from French *marmotte,* perhaps ultimately from Latin *mūr-* (stem of *mūs*) mouse + *montis* of the mountain]

marocain (ˈmærəˌkeɪn) *n.* **1.** a fabric of ribbed crepe. **2.** a garment made from this fabric. [C20: from French *maroquin* Moroccan]

Maronite (ˈmærəˌnaɪt) *n. Christianity.* a member of a body of Uniats of Syrian origin, now living chiefly in Lebanon. [C16: from Late Latin *Marōnīta,* after *Maro,* 5th-century Syrian monk]

maroon[1] (məˈruːn) *vb.* (*tr.*) **1.** to leave ashore and abandon, esp. on an island. **2.** to isolate without resources. ~*n.* **3.** a descendant of a group of runaway slaves living in the remoter areas of the West Indies or Guyana. [C17 (applied to fugitive slaves): from American Spanish *cimarrón* wild, literally: dwelling on peaks, from Spanish *cima* summit]

maroon[2] (məˈruːn) *n.* **1. a.** a dark red to purplish-red colour. **b.** (*as adj.*): *a maroon carpet.* **2.** an exploding firework, esp. one used as a warning signal. [C18: from French, literally: chestnut, MARRON]

maroquin (ˌmærəˈkiːn; ˈmærəkɪn, -kwɪn) *n. Tanning.* morocco leather. [C16: from French: Moroccan]

Marq. *abbrev. for* Marquis.

marque (mɑːk) *n.* **1.** a brand of product, esp. of a car. **2.** an emblem or nameplate used to identify a product, esp. a car. **3.** See **letter of marque.** [from French, from *marquer* to MARK]

marquee (mɑːˈkiː) *n.* **1.** a large tent used for entertainment, exhibition, etc. **2.** Also called: **marquise.** *Chiefly U.S. and Canadian.* a canopy over the entrance to a theatre, hotel, etc. [C17 (originally an officer's tent): invented singular form of MARQUISE, erroneously taken to be plural]

Marquesan (mɑːˈkeɪzᵊn, -sᵊn) *adj.* **1.** of or relating to the Marquesas Islands in the S Pacific or their inhabitants. ~*n.* **2.** a native or inhabitant of the Marquesas Islands.

marquess (ˈmɑːkwɪs) *n.* **1.** (in the British Isles) a nobleman ranking between a duke and an earl. **2.** See **marquis.**

marquessate (ˈmɑːkwɪzɪt) *n.* (in the British Isles) the dignity, rank, or position of a marquess; marquisate.

marquetry *or* **marqueterie** (ˈmɑːkɪtrɪ) *n., pl.* **-quetries** *or* **-queteries.** a pattern of inlaid veneers of wood, brass, ivory, etc., fitted together to form a picture or design, used chiefly as ornamentation in furniture. Compare **parquetry.** [C16: from Old French, from *marqueter* to inlay, from *marque* MARK[1]]

marquis (ˈmɑːkwɪs, mɑːˈkiː; *French* marki) *n., pl.* **-quises** *or* **-quis.** (in various countries) a nobleman ranking above a count, corresponding to a British marquess. The title of marquis is often used in place of that of marquess. [C14: from Old French *marchis,* literally: count of the march, from *marche* MARCH[2]]

marquisate (ˈmɑːkwɪzɪt) *n.* **1.** the rank or dignity of a marquis. **2.** the domain of a marquis.

marquise (mɑːˈkiːz; *French* markiz) *n.* **1.** (in various countries) another word for **marchioness. 2. a.** a gemstone, esp. a diamond, cut in a pointed oval shape and usually faceted. **b.** a piece of jewellery, esp. a ring, set with such a stone or with an oval cluster of stones. **3.** another name for **marquee** (sense 2). [C18: from French, feminine of MARQUIS]

marquisette (ˌmɑːkɪˈzɛt, -kwɪ-) *n.* a leno-weave fabric of cotton, silk, etc. [C20: from French, diminutive of MARQUISE]

marram grass (ˈmærəm) *n.* any of several grasses of the genus *Ammophila* (or *Psamma*), esp. *A. arenaria,* that grow on sandy shores and can withstand drying: often planted to stabilize sand dunes. [C17 *marram,* from Old Norse *marálmr,* from *marr* sea + *hálmr* HAULM]

Marrano (məˈrɑːnəʊ) *n., pl.* **-nos.** a Spanish or Portuguese Jew of the late Middle Ages who was converted to Christianity, esp. one forcibly converted but secretly adhering to Judaism. [from Spanish, literally: pig, with reference to the Jewish prohibition against eating pig meat]

marri (ˈmærɪ) *n., pl.* **-ris.** a species of eucalyptus, *Eucalyptus calophylla,* of Western Australia, widely cultivated for its coloured flowers. [C19: from a native Australian language]

marriage (ˈmærɪdʒ) *n.* **1.** the state or relationship of being husband and wife. **2. a.** the legal union or contract made by a man and woman to live as husband and wife. **b.** (*as modifier*): *marriage licence; marriage certificate.* **3.** the religious or legal ceremony formalizing this union; wedding. **4.** a close or intimate union, relationship, etc.: *a marriage of ideas.* **5.** (in certain card games, such as bezique, pinochle) the king and queen of the same suit. [C13: from Old French; see MARRY[1], -AGE]

marriageable (ˈmærɪdʒəbᵊl) *adj.* (esp. of women) suitable for marriage, usually with reference to age. —ˌ**marriageaˈbility** *or* ˈ**marriageableness** *n.*

marriage bureau *n.* an agency that provides introductions to single people seeking a marriage partner.

marriage guidance *n.* **a.** advice given to couples who have problems in their married life. **b.** (*as modifier*): *a marriage guidance counsellor.*

marriage of convenience *n.* a marriage based on expediency rather than on love.

married (ˈmærɪd) *adj.* **1.** having a husband or wife. **2.** joined in marriage: *a married couple.* **3.** of or involving marriage or married persons. **4.** closely or intimately united. ~*n.* **5.** (*usually pl.*) a married person (esp. in the phrase **young marrieds**).

marron[1] (ˈmærən; *French* marɔ̃) *n.* a large edible sweet chestnut. [from French, of obscure origin]

marron[2] (ˈmærən) *n.* a large freshwater crayfish of Western Australia, *Cherax tenuimanus.* [from a native Australian language]

marrons glacés *French.* (marɔ̃ glase) *pl. n.* chestnuts cooked in syrup and glazed.

marrow[1] (ˈmærəʊ) *n.* **1.** the fatty network of connective tissue that fills the cavities of bones. **2.** the vital part; essence. **3.** vitality. **4.** rich food. **5.** *Brit.* short for **vegetable marrow.** [Old English *mærg;* related to Old Frisian *merg,* Old Norse *mergr*] —ˈ**marrowy** *adj.*

marrow[2] (ˈmærəʊ, -rə) *n. Northeastern English dialect, chiefly Durham.* a companion, esp. a workmate. [C15 *marwe* fellow worker, perhaps of Scandinavian origin; compare Icelandic *margr* friendly]

marrowbone (ˈmærəʊˌbəʊn) *n.* **a.** a bone containing edible marrow. **b.** (*as modifier*): *marrowbone jelly.*

marrowbones (ˈmærəʊˌbəʊnz) *pl. n.* **1.** *Facetious.* the knees. **2.** a rare word for **crossbones.**

marrowfat (ˈmærəʊˌfæt) *or* **marrow pea** *n.* **1.** any of several varieties of pea plant that have large seeds. **2.** the seed of such a plant.

marrow squash *n. U.S. and Canadian.* any of several oblong squashes that have a hard smooth rind, esp. the vegetable marrow.

marry[1] (ˈmærɪ) *vb.* **-ries, -rying, -ried. 1.** to take (someone as one's husband or wife) in marriage. **2.** (*tr.*) to join or give in marriage. **3.** (*tr.*) to acquire (something) by marriage: *marry money.* **4.** to unite closely or intimately. **5.** (*tr.;* sometimes foll. by *up*) to fit together or align (two things); join. **6.** (*tr.*) *Nautical.* **a.** to match up (the strands) of unlaid ropes before splicing. **b.** to seize (two ropes) together at intervals along their lengths. [C13: from Old French *marier,* from Latin *marītāre,* from *marītus* married (man), perhaps from *mās* male] —ˈ**marrier** *n.*

marry[2] (ˈmærɪ) *interj. Archaic.* an exclamation of surprise, anger, etc. [C14: euphemistic for the Virgin *Mary*]

marry into *vb.* (*intr., prep.*) to become a member of (a family) by marriage.

marry off *vb.* (*tr., adv.*) to find a husband or wife for (a person, esp. one's son or daughter).

Mars (mɑːz) *n.* **1.** Also called: the **Red Planet.** the fourth planet from the sun, having a reddish-orange surface with numerous dark patches and two white polar caps. The surface ranges in temperature from about –70°C at night to –40°C during the day. The planet has two tiny satellites, Phobos and Deimos. Mean distance from sun: 228 million km; period of revolution around sun: 686.98 days; period of axial rotation: 24.6225 hours; diameter and mass: 53.2 and 10.7 per cent that of earth respectively. **2.** the alchemical name for **iron.**

Marseillaise (ˌmɑːsəˈleɪz; *French* marsɛjɛz) *n.* **the.** the French national anthem. Words and music were composed in 1792 by C. J. Rouget de Lisle as a war song for the Rhine army of revolutionary France. [C18: from French (*chanson*) *Marseillaise* song of Marseilles (it was first sung in Paris by the battalion of Marseilles)]

marseille (mɑːˈseɪl) *or* **marseilles** (mɑːˈseɪlz) *n.* a strong cotton fabric with a raised pattern, used for bedspreads, etc. [C18: from *Marseille quilting,* made in Marseilles in SE France]

marsh (mɑːʃ) *n.* low poorly drained land that is sometimes flooded and often lies at the edge of lakes, streams, etc. Related adj.: **paludal.** Compare **swamp** (sense 1). [Old English *merisc;* related to German *Marsch,* Dutch *marsk;* related to MERE[2]] —ˈ**marsh,like** *adj.*

marshal (ˈmɑːʃəl) *n.* **1.** (in some armies and air forces) an officer of the highest rank. **2.** (in England) an officer, usually a junior barrister, who accompanies a judge on circuit and performs miscellaneous secretarial duties. **3.** (in the U.S.) **a.** a Federal court officer assigned to a judicial district whose functions are similar to those of a sheriff. **b.** (in some states) the chief police or fire officer. **4.** an officer who organizes or conducts ceremonies, parades, etc. **5.** Also called: **knight marshal.** (formerly in England) an officer of the royal family or court, esp. one in charge of protocol. **6.** an obsolete word for **ostler.** ~*vb.* **-shals, -shalling, -shalled** *or U.S.* **-shals, -shaling, -shaled.** (*tr.*) **7.** to arrange in order: *to marshal the facts.* **8.** to assemble and organize (troops, vehicles, etc.) prior to onward movement. **9.** to arrange (assets, mortgages, etc.) in order of priority. **10.** to guide or lead, esp. in a ceremonious way. **11.** to combine (two or more coats of arms) on one shield. [C13: from Old French *mareschal;* related to Old High German *marahscalc* groom, from *marah* horse + *scalc* servant] —ˈ**marshalcy** *or* ˈ**marshalˌship** *n.* —ˈ**marshaller** *or U.S.* ˈ**marshaler** *n.*

marshalling yard *n. Railways.* a place or depot where railway wagons are shunted and made up into trains and where engines, carriages, etc., are kept when not in use.

Marshal of the Royal Air Force *n.* a rank in the Royal Air Force comparable to that of Field Marshal in the British army.

marsh andromeda *n.* a low-growing pink-flowered ericaceous evergreen shrub, *Andromeda polifolia,* that grows in peaty bogs of northern regions. Also called: **moorwort.**

marshbuck (ˈmɑːʃˌbʌk) *n.* an antelope of the central African swamplands, *Strepsiceros spekei,* with spreading hoofs adapted to boggy ground; an important vector of the tsetse fly. Also called: **sitatunga.**

marsh elder *n.* any of several North American shrubs of the genus *Iva,* growing in salt marshes: family *Compositae* (composites). Compare **elder**[2].

marsh fern *n.* a fern of marshy woodlands, *Thelypteris palustris,* having pale green pinnate leaves and an underground rootstock.

marsh fever *n.* another name for **malaria.**

marsh gas *n.* a hydrocarbon gas largely composed of methane formed when organic material decays in the absence of air.

marsh harrier *n.* **1.** a European harrier, *Circus aeruginosus,* that frequents marshy regions. **2.** a U.S. and Canadian name for **hen harrier.**

marsh hawk *n.* the usual U.S. and Canadian name for the **hen harrier.**

marsh hen *n.* any bird that frequents marshes and swamps, esp. a rail, coot, or gallinule.

marshland (ˈmɑːʃlənd) *n.* land consisting of marshes.

marshmallow (ˌmɑːʃˈmæləʊ) *n.* **1.** a sweet of a spongy texture containing gum arabic or gelatin, sugar, etc. **2.** a sweetened paste or confection made from the root of the marsh mallow. —ˌ**marshˈmallowy** *adj.*

marsh mallow *n.* **1.** a malvaceous plant, *Althaea officinalis,* that grows in salt marshes and has pale pink flowers. The roots yield a mucilage formerly used to make marshmallows. **2.** *U.S. and Canadian.* another name for **rose mallow** (sense 1).

marsh marigold *n.* a yellow-flowered ranunculaceous plant, *Caltha palustris,* that grows in swampy places. Also called: **kingcup, May blobs,** and (U.S.) **cowslip.**

marsh orchid *n.* any of various orchids of the genus *Dactylorchis,* growing in damp places and having mostly purplish flowers.

marsh tit *n.* a small European songbird, *Parus palustris,* with a black head and greyish-brown body: family *Paridae* (tits).

marshwort (ˈmɑːʃˌwɜːt) *n.* a prostrate creeping aquatic perennial umbelliferous plant, *Apium inundatum,* having small white flowers: related to wild celery.

marshy (ˈmɑːʃɪ) *adj.* **marshier, marshiest.** of, involving, or like a marsh. —ˈ**marshiness** *n.*

marsipobranch (ˈmɑːsɪpəʊˌbræŋk) *n., adj.* another word for **cyclostome.** [C19: from New Latin *Marsipobranchia,* from Greek *marsipos* pouch + *branchia* gills]

marsupial (mɑːˈsjuːpɪəl, -ˈsuː-) *n.* **1.** any mammal of the order *Marsupialia,* in which the young are born in an immature state and continue development in the marsupium. The order occurs mainly in Australia and South and Central America and includes the opossums, bandicoots, koala, wombats, and kangaroos. ~*adj.* **2.** of, relating to, or belonging to the *Marsupialia.* **3.** of or relating to a marsupium. [C17: see MARSUPIUM] —**marsupialian** (mɑːˌsjuːpɪˈeɪlɪən, -ˌsuː-) *or* **marˈsupian** *n., adj.*

marsupial mole *n.* any molelike marsupial of the family *Notoryctidae.*

marsupial mouse *n.* any mouselike insectivorous marsupial of the subfamily *Phascogalinae:* family *Dasyuridae.*

marsupium (mɑːˈsjuːpɪəm, -ˈsuː-) *n., pl.* **-pia** (-pɪə). an external pouch in most female marsupials within which the newly born offspring are suckled and complete their development. [C17: New Latin, from Latin: purse, from Greek *marsupion,* diminutive of *marsipos*]

mart (mɑːt) *n.* a market or trading centre. [C15: from Middle Dutch *mart* MARKET]

martagon *or* **martagon lily** (ˈmɑːtəgən) *n.* a Eurasian lily plant, *Lilium martagon,* cultivated for its mottled purplish-red flowers with reflexed petals. Also called: **Turk's-cap lily.** [C15: from French, from Turkish *martagān* a type of turban]

martellato (ˌmɑːtəˈlɑːtəʊ) *or* **martellando** *n.* (in string playing) the practice of bowing the string with a succession of short sharp blows. [Italian: hammered]

Martello tower *or* **Martello** (mɑːˈtɛləʊ) *n.* a small circular tower for coastal defence, formerly much used in Europe. [C18: after Cape *Mortella* in Corsica, where the British navy captured a tower of this type in 1794]

marten (ˈmɑːtɪn) *n., pl.* **-tens** *or* **-ten. 1.** any of several agile arboreal musteline mammals of the genus *Martes,* of Europe, Asia, and North America, having bushy tails and golden brown to blackish fur. See also **pine marten. 2.** the highly valued fur of these animals, esp. that of *M. americana.* ~See also **sable** (sense 1). [C15: from Middle Dutch *martren,* from Old French *(peau) martrine* skin of a marten, from *martre,* probably of Germanic origin]

martensite (ˈmɑːtɪnˌzaɪt) *n.* a constituent formed in steels by rapid quenching, consisting of a supersaturated solid solution of carbon in iron. It is formed by the breakdown of austenite when the rate of cooling is large enough to prevent pearlite forming. [C20: named after Adolf *Martens* (died 1914), German metallurgist] —**martensitic** (ˌmɑːtɪnˈzɪtɪk) *adj.*

martial (ˈmɑːʃəl) *adj.* of, relating to, or characteristic of war, soldiers, or the military life. [C14: from Latin *martiālis* of *Mars,* Roman god of war] —ˈ**martialism** *n.* —ˈ**martialist** *n.* —ˈ**martially** *adv.* —ˈ**martialness** *n.*

martial art *n.* any of various philosophies of self-defence and techniques of single combat, such as judo or karate, originating in the Far East.

martial law *n.* the rule of law established and maintained by the military in the absence of civil law.

Martian (ˈmɑːʃən) *adj.* **1.** of, occurring on, or relating to the planet Mars. ~*n.* **2.** an inhabitant of Mars, esp. in science fiction.

martin (ˈmɑːtɪn) *n.* any of various swallows of the genera *Progne, Delichon, Riparia,* etc., having a square or slightly forked tail. See also **house martin.** [C15: perhaps from St *Martin,* French patron saint, because the birds were believed to migrate at the time of Martinmas]

martinet (ˌmɑːtɪˈnɛt) *n.* a person who maintains strict discipline, esp. in a military force. [C17: from French, from the name of General *Martinet,* drillmaster under Louis XIV] —ˌ**martiˈnetish** *adj.* —ˌ**martiˈnetism** *n.*

martingale (ˈmɑːtɪnˌgeɪl) *n.* **1.** a strap from the reins to the girth of a horse preventing it from carrying its head too high. **2.** any gambling system in which the stakes are raised, usually doubled, after each loss. **3.** Also called: **martingale boom.** *Nautical.* **a.** a chain or cable running from a jib boom to the dolphin striker, serving to counteract strain. **b.** another term for **dolphin striker.** [C16: from French, of uncertain origin]

martini (mɑːˈtiːnɪ) *n., pl.* **-nis. 1.** *(often cap.) Trademark.* an Italian vermouth. **2.** a cocktail of gin and vermouth. [C19 (sense 2): perhaps from the name of the inventor]

Martinmas (ˈmɑːtɪnməs) *n.* the feast of St Martin, a patron saint of France, celebrated on Nov. 11; one of the four quarter days in Scotland.

martlet (ˈmɑːtlɪt) *n.* **1.** an archaic name for a **martin. 2.** *Heraldry.* a footless bird often found in coats of arms, standing for either a martin or a swallow. [C16: from French *martelet,* variant of *martinet,* diminutive of MARTIN]

martyr (ˈmɑːtə) *n.* **1.** a person who suffers death rather than renounce his religious beliefs. **2.** a person who suffers greatly or dies for a cause, belief, etc. **3.** a person who suffers from poor health, misfortune, etc.: *he's a martyr to rheumatism.* **4.** *Facetious or derogatory.* a person who feigns suffering to gain sympathy, help, etc. ~*vb. also* ˈ**martyrˌize** *or* ˈ**martyrˌise.** *(tr.)* **5.** to kill as a martyr. **6.** to make a martyr of. [Old English *martir,* from Church Latin *martyr,* from Late Greek *martur-, martus* witness] —ˌ**martyriˈzation** *or* ˌ**martyriˈsation** *n.*

martyrdom (ˈmɑːtədəm) *n.* **1.** the sufferings or death of a martyr. **2.** great suffering or torment.

martyrology (ˌmɑːtəˈrɒlədʒɪ) *n., pl.* **-gies. 1.** an official list of martyrs. **2.** *Christianity.* the study of the lives of the martyrs. **3.** a historical account of the lives of martyrs. —**martyrological** (ˌmɑːtərəˈlɒdʒɪkᵊl) *or* ˌ**martyroˈlogic** *adj.* —ˌ**martyrˈologist** *n.*

martyry (ˈmɑːtərɪ) *n., pl.* **-tyries.** a shrine or chapel erected in honour of a martyr.

MARV (mɑːv) *n. acronym for* manoeuvrable re-entry vehicle: a missile that has one or more warheads that may be controlled so as to avoid enemy defences.

marvel (ˈmɑːvᵊl) *vb.* **-vels, -velling, -velled** *or U.S.* **-vels, -veling, -veled. 1.** (when *intr.,* often foll. by *at* or *about;* when *tr., takes a clause as object*) to be filled with surprise or wonder. ~*n.* **2.** something that causes wonder. **3.** *Archaic.* astonishment. [C13: from Old French *merveille,* from Late Latin *mīrābilia,* from Latin *mīrābilis,* from *mīrārī* to wonder at]

marvellous *or U.S.* **marvelous** (ˈmɑːvᵊləs) *adj.* **1.** causing great wonder, surprise, etc.; extraordinary. **2.** improbable or incredible. **3.** excellent; splendid. —ˈ**marvellously** *or U.S.* ˈ**marvelously** *adv.* —ˈ**marvellousness** *or U.S.* ˈ**marvelousness** *n.*

marvel-of-Peru *n., pl.* **marvels-of-Peru.** another name for **four-o'clock** (the plant). [C16: first found in Peru]

Marxian (ˈmɑːksɪən) *adj.* of or relating to Karl Marx and his theories. See **Marxism.** —ˈ**Marxianism** *n.*

Marxism (ˈmɑːksɪzəm) *n.* the economic and political theory and practice originated by Karl Marx (1818–83) and Friedrich Engels (1820–95), German political philosophers. It holds that actions and human institutions are economically determined, that the class struggle is the basic agency of historical change, and that capitalism will ultimately be superseded by communism.

Marxism-Leninism *n.* the modification of Marxism by Lenin (1870–1924), Soviet statesman, stressing that imperialism is the highest form of capitalism. —ˈ**Marxist-**ˈ**Leninist** *n., adj.*

Marxist (ˈmɑːksɪst) *n.* **1.** a follower of Marxism. ~*adj.* **2.** (of an economic or political theory) analogous to or derived from the doctrines of Marx. **3.** of or relating to Marx, Marxism, or Marxists and their theories.

Mary (ˈmɛərɪ) *n., pl.* **Maries.** *Austral. slang.* an Aboriginal woman or girl.

mary jane *n. U.S. and Canadian.* a slang term for **marijuana.**

Maryolatry (ˌmɛərɪˈɒlətrɪ) *n.* a variant spelling of **Mariolatry.**

Maryology (ˌmɛərɪˈɒlədʒɪ) *n.* a variant spelling of **Mariology.**

marzipan (ˈmɑːzɪˌpæn) *n.* **1.** a paste made from ground almonds, sugar, and egg whites, used to coat fruit cakes or moulded into sweets. Also called (esp. formerly): **marchpane.** ~*modifier.* **2.** *Informal.* of or relating to the stratum of middle managers in a financial institution or other business: *marzipan layer job losses.* [C19: via German from Italian *marzapane.* See MARCHPANE]

-mas *n. combining form.* indicating a Christian festival: *Christmas; Michaelmas.* [from MASS]

Masai (ˈmɑːsaɪ, mɑːˈsaɪ, ˈmæsaɪ) *n.* **1.** (*pl.* **-sais** *or* **-sai**) a member of a Nilotic people, formerly noted as warriors, living chiefly in Kenya and Tanzania. **2.** the language of this people, belonging to the Nilotic group of the Nilo-Saharan family.

masc. *abbrev. for* masculine.

mascara (mæˈskɑːrə) *n.* a cosmetic substance for darkening, colouring, and thickening the eyelashes, applied with a brush or rod. [C20: from Spanish: mask]

mascle (ˈmɑːskᵊl) *n. Heraldry.* a charge consisting of a lozenge with a lozenge-shaped hole in the middle. Also called: **voided**

lozenge. [C14: from Old French *macle,* perhaps from Latin *macula* spot]

mascon ('mæskɒn) *n.* any of several lunar regions of high gravity. [C20: from MAS(S) + CON(CENTRATION)]

mascot ('mæskət) *n.* a person, animal, or thing considered to bring good luck. [C19: from French *mascotte,* from Provençal *mascotto* charm, from *masco* witch]

masculine ('mæskjʊlɪn) *adj.* **1.** possessing qualities or characteristics considered typical of or appropriate to a man; manly. **2.** unwomanly. **3.** *Grammar.* **a.** denoting a gender of nouns, occurring in many inflected languages, that includes all kinds of referents as well as some male animate referents. **b.** (*as n.*): *German "Weg" is a masculine.* [C14: via French from Latin *masculīnus,* from *masculus* male, from *mās* a male] —'**masculinely** *adv.* —,**mascu'linity** *or* (*less commonly*) '**masculineness** *n.*

masculine ending *n. Prosody.* a stressed syllable at the end of a line of verse. Compare **feminine ending.**

masculine rhyme *n. Prosody.* a rhyme between stressed monosyllables or between the final stressed syllables of polysyllabic words: *book, cook; collect, direct.* Compare **feminine rhyme.**

masculinize *or* **masculinise** ('mæskjʊlɪn,aɪz) *vb.* to make or become masculine, esp. to cause (a woman) to show male secondary sexual characteristics as a result of taking steroids. —,**masculini'zation** *or* ,**masculini'sation** *n.*

maser ('meɪzə) *n.* a device for amplifying microwaves, working on the same principle as a laser. [C20: *m*(*icrowave*) *a*(*mplification by*) *s*(*timulated*) *e*(*mission of*) *r*(*adiation*)]

mash (mæʃ) *n.* **1.** a soft pulpy mass or consistency. **2.** *Agriculture.* a feed of bran, meal, or malt mixed with water and fed to horses, cattle, or poultry. **3.** (esp. in brewing) a mixture of mashed malt grains and hot water, from which malt is extracted. **4.** *Brit., informal.* mashed potatoes. **5.** *Northern English dialect.* a brew of tea. ~*vb.* (*tr.*) **6.** to beat or crush into a mash. **7.** to steep (malt grains) in hot water in order to extract malt, esp. for making malt liquors. **8.** *Northern English dialect.* to brew (tea). **9.** *Archaic.* to flirt with. [Old English *mǣsc-* (in compound words); related to Middle Low German *mēsch*] —**mashed** *adj.* —'**masher** *n.*

MASH *n.* (in the U.S.) *acronym for* Mobile Army Surgical Hospital.

Masham ('mæsəm) *n.* a crossbreed of large sheep having a black and white face and a long curly fleece: kept for lamb production. [C20: named after *Masham,* town in N Yorkshire]

mashiach (mə'ʃiɑx) *n. Judaism.* the messiah. [Hebrew, literally: anointed; compare MESSIAH]

mashie *or* **mashy** ('mæʃɪ) *n., pl.* **mashies.** *Golf.* (formerly) an iron for lofting shots, usually No. 5. [C19: perhaps from French *massue* club, ultimately from Latin *mateola* mallet]

Mashona (mə'ʃəʊnə) *n., pl.* **-na** *or* **-nas.** another name for the **Shona** (sense 1).

masjid *or* **musjid** ('mʌsdʒɪd) *n.* a mosque in an Arab country. [Arabic; see MOSQUE]

mask (mɑːsk) *n.* **1.** any covering for the whole or a part of the face worn for amusement, protection, disguise, etc. **2.** a fact, action, etc., that conceals something: *his talk was a mask for his ignorance.* **3.** another name for **masquerade. 4.** a likeness of a face or head, either sculpted or moulded, such as a death mask. **5.** an image of a face worn by an actor, esp. in ancient Greek and Roman drama, in order to symbolize the character being portrayed. **6.** a variant spelling of **masque. 7.** *Surgery.* a sterile gauze covering for the nose and mouth worn esp. during operations to minimize the spread of germs. **8.** *Sport.* a protective covering for the face worn for fencing, ice hockey, etc. **9.** a carving in the form of a face or head, used as an ornament. **10.** a natural land feature or artificial object which conceals troops, etc., from view. **11.** a device placed over the nose and mouth to facilitate or prevent inhalation of a gas. **12.** *Photog.* a shield of paper, paint, etc., placed over an area of unexposed photographic surface to stop light falling on it. **13.** *Electronics.* a thin sheet of material from which a pattern has been cut, placed over a semiconductor chip so that an integrated circuit can be formed on the exposed areas. **14.** *Computer technol.* a bit pattern which, by convolution with a second pattern in a logical operation, can be used to isolate a specific subset of the second pattern for examination. **15.** *Entomol.* a large prehensile mouthpart (labium) of the dragonfly larva. **16.** the face or head of an animal, such as a fox, or the dark coloration of the face of some animals, such as Siamese cats and certain dogs. **17.** another word for **face pack. 18.** *Now rare.* a person wearing a mask. ~*vb.* **19.** to cover with or put on a mask. **20.** (*tr.*) to conceal; disguise: *to mask an odour.* **21.** (*tr.*) *Photog.* to shield a particular area of (an unexposed photographic surface) in order to prevent or reduce the action of light there. **22.** (*tr.*) to shield a particular area of (a surface to be painted) with masking tape. **23.** (*tr.*) to cover (cooked food, esp. meat) with a savoury sauce or glaze. [C16: from Italian *maschera,* ultimately from Arabic *maskharah* clown, from *sakhira* mockery] —'**mask,like** *adj.*

maskanonge ('mæskə,nɒndʒ), **maskinonge** ('mæskɪ,nɒndʒ), *or* **maskalonge** ('mæskə,lɒndʒ) *n., pl.* **-nonges, -nonge** *or* **-longes, -longe.** variants of **muskellunge.**

masked (mɑːskt) *adj.* **1.** disguised or covered by or as if by a mask. **2.** *Botany.* another word for **personate**[2].

masked ball *n.* a ball at which masks are worn.

masker *or* **masquer** ('mɑːskə) *n.* a person who wears a mask or takes part in a masque.

masking ('mɑːskɪŋ) *n.* **1.** the act or practice of masking. **2.** *Psychol.* the process by which a stimulus (usually visual or auditory) is obscured by the presence of another almost simultaneous stimulus.

masking tape *n.* an adhesive tape used to mask and protect surfaces surrounding an area to be painted.

masochism ('mæsə,kɪzəm) *n.* **1.** *Psychiatry.* an abnormal condition in which pleasure, esp. sexual pleasure, is derived from pain or from humiliation, domination, etc., by another person. **2.** *Psychoanal.* the directing towards oneself of any destructive tendencies. **3.** a tendency to take pleasure from one's own suffering. Compare **sadism.** [C19: named after Leopold von Sacher *Masoch* (1836–95), Austrian novelist, who described it] —'**masochist** *n., adj.* —,**maso'chistic** *adj.* —,**maso'chistically** *adv.*

mason ('meɪsᵊn) *n.* **1.** a person skilled in building with stone. **2.** a person who dresses stone. ~*vb.* **3.** (*tr.*) to construct or strengthen with masonry. [C13: from Old French *masson,* of Frankish origin; perhaps related to Old English *macian* to make]

Mason ('meɪsᵊn) *n.* short for **Freemason.**

mason bee *n.* any bee of the family *Megachilidae* that builds a hard domelike nest of sand, clay, etc., held together with saliva.

masonic (mə'sɒnɪk) *adj.* **1.** (*often cap.*) of, characteristic of, or relating to Freemasons or Freemasonry. **2.** of or relating to masons or masonry. —**ma'sonically** *adv.*

Masonite ('meɪsə,naɪt) *n. Austral. and N.Z. trademark.* a kind of dark brown hardboard used for partitions, lining, etc.

masonry ('meɪsənrɪ) *n., pl.* **-ries. 1.** the craft of a mason. **2.** work that is built by a mason; stonework or brickwork. **3.** (*often cap.*) short for **Freemasonry.**

mason wasp *n.* a solitary wasp of the genus *Odynerus* that excavates its nest in sand or the mortar of old walls.

Masora, Masorah, Massora, *or* **Massorah** (mə'sɔːrə) *n.* **1.** the text of the Hebrew Bible as officially revised by the Masoretes from the 6th to the 10th centuries A.D., with critical notes and commentary. **2.** the collection of these notes, commentaries, etc. [C17: from Hebrew: tradition]

Masorete, Massorete ('mæsə,riːt), *or* **Masorite** ('mæsə,raɪt) *n.* **1.** a member of the school of rabbis that produced the Masora. **2.** a Hebrew scholar who is expert in the Masora. [C16: from Hebrew *māsōreth* MASORA]

Masoretic, Massoretic (,mæsə'rɛtɪk) *or* **Masoretical, Massoretical** *adj.* of or relating to the Masora, the Masoretes, or the system of textual criticism and explanation evolved by them.

masque *or* **mask** (mɑːsk) *n.* **1.** a dramatic entertainment of the 16th to 17th centuries in England, consisting of pantomime, dancing, dialogue, and song, often performed at court. **2.** the words and music written for a masque. **3.** short for **masquerade.** [C16: variant of MASK]

masquer ('mɑːskə) *n.* a variant spelling of **masker.**

masquerade (,mæskə'reɪd) *n.* **1.** a party or other gathering to which the guests wear masks and costumes. **2.** the disguise worn at such a function. **3.** a pretence or disguise. ~*vb.* (*intr.*) **4.** to participate in a masquerade; disguise oneself. **5.** to dissemble. [C16: from Spanish *mascarada,* from *mascara* MASK] —,**masquer'ader** *n.*

mass (mæs) *n.* **1.** a large coherent body of matter without a definite shape. **2.** a collection of the component parts of something. **3.** a large amount or number, such as a great body of people. **4.** the main part or majority: *the mass of the people voted against the government's policy.* **5. in the mass.** in the main; collectively. **6.** the size of a body; bulk. **7.** *Physics.* a physical quantity expressing the amount of matter in a body. It is a measure of a body's resistance to changes in velocity (**inertial mass**) and also of the force experienced in a gravitational field (**gravitational mass**): according to the theory of relativity, inertial and gravitational masses are equal. **8.** (in painting, drawing, etc.) an area of unified colour, shade, or intensity, usually denoting a solid form or plane. **9.** *Pharmacol.* a pastelike composition of drugs from which pills are made. **10.** *Mining.* an irregular deposit of ore not occurring in veins. ~(*modifier*) **11.** done or occurring on a large scale: *mass hysteria; mass radiography.* **12.** consisting of a mass or large number, esp. of people: *a mass meeting.* ~*vb.* **13.** to form (people or things) or (of people or things) to join together into a mass: *the crowd massed outside the embassy.* ~See also **masses, mass in.** [C14: from Old French *masse,* from Latin *massa* that which forms a lump, from Greek *maza* barley cake; perhaps related to Greek *massein* to knead] —**massed** *adj.* —**massedly** ('mæsɪdlɪ, 'mæstlɪ) *adv.*

Mass (mæs, mɑːs) *n.* **1.** (in the Roman Catholic Church and certain Protestant Churches) the celebration of the Eucharist. See also **High Mass, Low Mass. 2.** a musical setting of those parts of the Eucharistic service sung by choir or congregation. [Old English *mæsse,* from Church Latin *missa,* ultimately from Latin *mittere* to send away; perhaps derived from the concluding dismissal in the Roman Mass, *Ite, missa est,* Go, it is the dismissal]

Mass. *abbrev. for* Massachusetts.

Massachuset (,mæsə'tʃuːsɪt) *or* **Massachusetts** *n.* **1.** (*pl.* **-sets, -set,** *or* **-setts**) a member of a North American Indian people formerly living around Massachusetts Bay in NE U.S. **2.** the language of this people, belonging to the Algonquian family. [probably from Algonquian, literally: at the big hill]

massacre ('mæsəkə) *n.* **1.** the wanton or savage killing of large numbers of people, as in battle. **2.** *Informal.* an overwhelming defeat, as in a game. ~*vb.* (*tr.*) **3.** to kill indiscriminately or in large numbers. **4.** *Informal.* to defeat overwhelmingly. [C16: from Old French, of unknown origin] —**massacrer** ('mæsəkrə) *n.*

massage ('mæsɑːʒ, -sɑːdʒ) *n.* **1.** the act of kneading, rubbing, etc., parts of the body to promote circulation, suppleness, or relaxation. ~*vb.* (*tr.*) **2.** to give a massage to. **3.** to treat (stiffness, aches, etc.) by a massage. **4.** to manipulate (statistics, data, etc.) so that they appear to support a particular interpretation or to be better than they are; doctor. **5. massage (someone's) ego.** to boost (someone's) sense of self-esteem by flattery. [C19: from French, from *masser* to rub; see MASS] —'**massager** *or* '**massagist** *n.*

massage parlour *n.* **1.** a business providing massage services. **2.** *Euphemistic.* a brothel.

massasauga (ˌmæsə'sɔːgə) *n.* a North American venomous snake, *Sistrurus catenatus,* that has a horny rattle at the end of the tail: family *Crotalidae* (pit vipers). [C19: named after the *Missisauga* River, Ontario, Canada, where it was first found]

mass defect *n. Physics.* the amount by which the mass of a particular nucleus is less than the total mass of its constituent particles. See also **binding energy.**

massé *or* **massé shot** ('mæsɪ) *n. Billiards.* a stroke made by hitting the cue ball off centre with the cue held nearly vertically, esp. so as to make the ball move in a curve around another ball before hitting the object ball. [C19: from French, from *masser* to hit from above with a hammer, from *masse* sledgehammer, from Old French *mace* MACE[1]]

massed practice *n. Psychol.* learning with no intervals or short intervals between successive bouts of learning. Compare **distributed practice.**

mass-energy *n.* mass and energy considered as equivalent and interconvertible, according to the theory of relativity.

masses ('mæsɪz) *pl. n.* **1.** (preceded by *the*) the body of common people. **2.** (often foll. by *of*) *Informal, chiefly Brit.* great numbers or quantities: *masses of food.*

masseter (mæ'siːtə) *n. Anatomy.* a muscle of the cheek used in moving the jaw, esp. in chewing. [C17: from New Latin from Greek *masētēr* one who chews, from *masāsthai* to chew] —**masseteric** (ˌmæsɪ'tɛrɪk) *adj.*

masseur (mæ'sɜː) *or* (*fem.*) **masseuse** (mæ'sɜːz) *n.* a person who gives massages, esp. as a profession. [C19: from French *masser* to MASSAGE]

massicot ('mæsɪˌkɒt) *n.* a yellow earthy secondary mineral consisting of lead oxide. Formula: PbO. [C15: via French from Italian *marzacotto* ointment, perhaps from Arabic *shabb qubti* Egyptian alum]

massif ('mæsiːf; *French* masif) *n.* **1.** a mass of rock or a series of connected masses forming the peaks of a mountain range. **2.** a part of the earth's crust that is bounded by faults and may be shifted by tectonic movements. [C19: from French, noun use of *massif* MASSIVE]

mass in *vb.* (*adv.*) to fill or block in (the areas of unified colour, shade, etc.) in a painting or drawing.

massive ('mæsɪv) *adj.* **1.** (of objects) large in mass; bulky, heavy, and usually solid. **2.** impressive or imposing in quality, degree, or scope: *massive grief.* **3.** relatively intensive or large; considerable: *a massive dose.* **4.** *Pathol.* affecting a large area of the body: *a massive cancer.* **5.** *Geology.* **a.** (of igneous rocks) having no stratification, cleavage, etc.; homogeneous. **b.** (of sedimentary rocks) arranged in thick poorly defined strata. **6.** *Mineralogy.* without obvious crystalline structure. [C15: from French *massif,* from *masse* MASS] —'**massively** *adv.* —'**massiveness** *n.*

mass leave *n.* (in India) leave taken by a large number of employees at the same time, as a form of protest.

mass-market *adj.* of, for, or appealing to a large number of people; popular: *mass-market paperbacks.*

mass media *pl. n.* the means of communication that reach large numbers of people in a short time, such as television, newspapers, magazines, and radio.

mass noun *n.* a noun that refers to an extended substance rather than to each of a set of isolable objects, as, for example, *water* as opposed to *lake.* In English when used indefinitely they are characteristically preceded by *some* rather than *a* or *an;* they do not have normal plural forms. Compare **count noun.**

mass number *n.* the total number of neutrons and protons in the nucleus of a particular atom. Symbol: *A* Also called: **nucleon number.**

mass observation *n. Chiefly Brit.* (*sometimes caps.*) the study of the social habits of people through observation, interviews, etc.

Massorete ('mæsəˌriːt) *n.* a variant spelling of **Masorete.**

massotherapy (ˌmæsəʊ'θɛrəpɪ) *n.* medical treatment by massage. [C20: from MASS(AGE) + THERAPY] —**massotherapeutic** (ˌmæsəʊˌθɛrə'pjuːtɪk) *adj.* —ˌ**masso'therapist** *n.*

mass-produce *vb.* (*tr.*) to manufacture (goods) to a standardized pattern on a large scale by means of extensive mechanization and division of labour. —ˌ**mass-pro'duced** *adj.* —ˌ**mass-pro'ducer** *n.* —**mass production** *n.*

mass ratio *n.* the ratio of the mass of a fully-fuelled rocket at liftoff to the mass of the rocket without fuel.

mass spectrograph *n.* a mass spectrometer that produces a photographic record of the mass spectrum.

mass spectrometer *or* **spectroscope** *n.* an analytical instrument in which ions, produced from a sample, are separated by electric or magnetic fields according to their ratios of charge to mass. A record is produced (**mass spectrum**) of the types of ion present and their relative amounts.

massy ('mæsɪ) *adj.* **massier, massiest.** a literary word for **massive.** —'**massiness** *n.*

mast[1] (mɑːst) *n.* **1.** *Nautical.* any vertical spar for supporting sails, rigging, flags, etc., above the deck of a vessel or any components of such a composite spar. **2.** any sturdy upright pole used as a support. **3.** Also called: **captain's mast.** *Nautical.* a hearing conducted by the captain of a vessel into minor offences of the crew. **4. before the mast.** *Nautical.* as an apprentice seaman. ~*vb.* **5.** (*tr.*) *Nautical.* to equip with a mast or masts. [Old English *mæst;* related to Middle Dutch *mast* and Latin *mālus* pole] —'**mastless** *adj.* —'**mast**ˌ**like** *adj.*

mast[2] (mɑːst) *n.* the fruit of forest trees, such as beech, oak, etc., used as food for pigs. [Old English *mæst;* related to Old High German *mast* food, and perhaps to MEAT]

mast- *combining form.* a variant of **masto-** before a vowel.

mastaba *or* **mastabah** ('mæstəbə) *n.* a mudbrick superstructure above tombs in ancient Egypt from which the pyramid developed. [from Arabic: bench]

mast cell *n.* a type of granular basophil cell in connective tissue that releases heperin, histamine, and serotonin during inflammation and allergic reactions. [C19: from MAST[2], on the model of German *Mastzelle*]

mastectomy (mæ'stɛktəmɪ) *n., pl.* **-mies.** the surgical removal of a breast.

-masted *adj.* (*in combination*) *Nautical.* having a mast or masts of a specified kind or number: *three-masted; tall-masted.*

master ('mɑːstə) *n.* **1.** the man in authority, such as the head of a household, the employer of servants, or the owner of slaves or animals. **2. a.** a person with exceptional skill at a certain thing: *a master of the violin.* **b.** (*as modifier*): *a master thief.* **3.** (*often cap.*) a great artist, esp. an anonymous but influential artist. **4. a.** a person who has complete control of a situation. **b.** an abstract thing regarded as having power or influence: *they regarded fate as the master of their lives.* **5. a.** a workman or craftsman fully qualified to practise his trade and to train others in it. **b.** (*as modifier*): *master carpenter.* **6. a.** an original copy, stencil, tape, etc., from which duplicates are made. **b.** (*as modifier*): *master copy.* **7.** a player of a game, esp. chess or bridge, who has won a specified number of tournament games. **8.** the principal of some colleges. **9.** a highly regarded teacher or leader whose religion or philosophy is accepted by followers. **10.** a graduate holding a master's degree. **11.** the chief executive officer aboard a merchant ship. **12.** a person presiding over a function, organization, or institution. **13.** *Chiefly Brit.* a male teacher. **14.** an officer of the Supreme Court of Judicature subordinate to a judge. **15.** the superior person or side in a contest. **16.** a machine or device that operates to control a similar one. **17.** (*often cap.*) the heir apparent of a Scottish viscount or baron. ~(*modifier*) **18.** overall or controlling: *master plan.* **19.** designating a device or mechanism that controls others: *master switch.* **20.** main; principal: *master bedroom.* ~*vb.* (*tr.*) **21.** to become thoroughly proficient in: *to master the art of driving.* **22.** to overcome; defeat: *to master your emotions.* **23.** to rule or control as master. [Old English *magister* teacher, from Latin; related to Latin *magis* more, to a greater extent] —'**masterdom** *n.* —'**master**ˌ**hood** *n.* —'**masterless** *adj.* —'**mastership** *n.*

Master ('mɑːstə) *n.* **1.** a title of address placed before the first name or surname of a boy. **2.** a respectful term of address, esp. as used by disciples when addressing or referring to a religious teacher. **3.** an archaic equivalent of **Mr.**

master aircrew *n.* a warrant rank in the Royal Air Force, equal to but before a warrant officer.

master-at-arms *n., pl.* **masters-at-arms.** the senior rating, of Chief Petty Officer rank, in a naval unit responsible for discipline, administration, and police duties.

master builder *n.* **1.** a person skilled in the design and construction of buildings, esp. before the foundation of the profession of architecture. **2.** a self-employed builder who employs labour.

master class *n.* a class for trained musicians, either in private or on television, conducted by a virtuoso player.

master corporal *n.* a noncommissioned officer in the Canadian forces senior to a corporal and junior to a sergeant.

master cylinder *n.* a large cylinder in a hydraulic system in which the working fluid is compressed by a piston. See also **slave cylinder.**

masterful ('mɑːstəful) *adj.* **1.** having or showing mastery. **2.** fond of playing the master; imperious. —'**masterfully** *adv.* —'**masterfulness** *n.*

master key *n.* a key that opens all the locks of a set, the individual keys of which are not interchangeable. Also called: **pass key.**

masterly (ˈmɑːstəlɪ) *adj.* of the skill befitting a master: *a masterly performance.* —ˈ**masterliness** *n.*

mastermind (ˈmɑːstəˌmaɪnd) *vb.* **1.** (*tr.*) to plan and direct (a complex undertaking): *he masterminded the robbery.* ~*n.* **2.** a person of great intelligence or executive talent, esp. one who directs an undertaking.

Master of Arts *n.* a degree, usually postgraduate and in a nonscientific subject, or the holder of this degree. Abbrev.: **MA.**

master of ceremonies *n.* a person who presides over a public ceremony, formal dinner, or entertainment, introducing the events, performers, etc. Abbrev.: **MC.**

master of foxhounds *n.* a person responsible for the maintenance of a pack of foxhounds and the associated staff, equipment, hunting arrangements, etc. Abbrev.: **MFH.**

Master of Science *n.* a postgraduate degree, usually in science, or the holder of this degree. Abbrev.: **MSc.**

Master of the Horse *n.* (in England) the third official of the royal household.

Master of the Queen's Music *n.* (in Britain when the sovereign is female) a court post dating from the reign of Charles I. It is an honorary title and normally held by an established English composer. Also called (when the sovereign is male): **Master of the King's Music.**

Master of the Rolls *n.* (in England) a judge of the court of appeal: the senior civil judge in the country and the Keeper of the Records at the Public Record Office.

masterpiece (ˈmɑːstəˌpiːs) *or* (*less commonly*) **masterwork** (ˈmɑːstəˌwɜːk) *n.* **1.** an outstanding work, achievement, or performance. **2.** the most outstanding piece of work of a creative artist, craftsman, etc. [C17: compare Dutch *meesterstuk,* German *Meisterstück,* a sample of work submitted to a guild by a craftsman in order to qualify for the rank of master]

master race *n.* a race, nation, or group, such as the Germans or Nazis as viewed by Hitler, believed to be superior to other races. German name: **Herrenvolk.**

master sergeant *n.* a senior noncommissioned officer in the U.S. Army, Air Force, and Marine Corps and certain other military forces, ranking immediately below the most senior noncommissioned rank.

mastersinger (ˈmɑːstəˌsɪŋə) *n.* an English spelling of **Meistersinger.**

masterstroke (ˈmɑːstəˌstrəʊk) *n.* an outstanding piece of strategy, skill, talent, etc.: *your idea is a masterstroke.*

master warrant officer *n.* a noncommissioned officer in the Canadian forces junior to a chief warrant officer.

mastery (ˈmɑːstərɪ) *n., pl.* **-teries. 1.** full command or understanding of a subject. **2.** outstanding skill; expertise. **3.** the power of command; control. **4.** victory or superiority.

masthead (ˈmɑːstˌhɛd) *n.* **1.** *Nautical.* **a.** the head of a mast. **b.** (*as modifier*): *masthead sail.* **2.** Also called: **flag.** the name of a newspaper or periodical, its proprietors, staff, etc., printed in large type at the top of the front page. ~*vb.* (*tr.*) **3.** to send (a sailor) to the masthead as a punishment. **4.** to raise (a sail) to the masthead.

mastic (ˈmæstɪk) *n.* **1.** an aromatic resin obtained from the mastic tree and used as an astringent and to make varnishes and lacquers. **2. mastic tree. a.** a small Mediterranean anacardiaceous evergreen tree, *Pistacia lentiscus,* that yields the resin mastic. **b.** any of various similar trees, such as the pepper tree. **3.** any of several sticky putty-like substances used as a filler, adhesive, or seal in wood, plaster, or masonry. **4.** a liquor flavoured with mastic gum. [C14: via Old French from Late Latin *mastichum,* from Latin, from Greek *mastikhē* resin used as chewing gum; from *mastikhan* to grind the teeth]

masticate (ˈmæstɪˌkeɪt) *vb.* **1.** to chew (food). **2.** to reduce (materials such as rubber) to a pulp by crushing, grinding, or kneading. [C17: from Late Latin *masticāre,* from Greek *mastikhan* to grind the teeth] —ˈ**masticable** *adj.* —ˌ**mastiˈcation** *n.* —ˈ**mastiˌcator** *n.*

masticatory (ˈmæstɪkətərɪ, -trɪ) *adj.* **1.** of, relating to, or adapted to chewing. ~*n., pl.* **-tories. 2.** a medicinal substance chewed to increase the secretion of saliva.

mastiff (ˈmæstɪf) *n.* an old breed of large powerful short-haired dog, usually fawn or brindle with a dark mask. [C14: from Old French, ultimately from Latin *mansuētus* tame; see MANSUETUDE]

mastigophoran (ˌmæstɪˈgɒfərən) *n. also* **mastigophore** (ˈmæstɪgəˌfɔː). **1.** any protozoan of the class *Mastigophora* (or *Flagellata*), having one or more flagella. ~*adj. also* **mastigophorous. 2.** of, relating to, or belonging to the *Mastigophora.* ~Also: **flagellate.** [C19 *mastigophore* whip-bearer, from Greek *mastigophoros,* from *mastix* whip + *-phoros* -PHORE]

mastitis (mæˈstaɪtɪs) *n.* inflammation of a breast or an udder.

masto- *or before a vowel* **mast-** *combining form.* indicating the breast, mammary glands, or something resembling a breast or nipple: *mastodon; mastoid.* [from Greek *mastos* breast]

mastodon (ˈmæstəˌdɒn) *n.* any extinct elephant-like proboscidean mammal of the genus *Mammut* (or *Mastodon*), common in Pliocene times. [C19: from New Latin, literally: breast-tooth, referring to the nipple-shaped projections on the teeth] —ˌ**mastoˈdontic** *adj.*

mastoid (ˈmæstɔɪd) *adj.* **1.** shaped like a nipple or breast. **2.** designating or relating to a nipple-like process of the temporal bone behind the ear. ~*n.* **3.** the mastoid process. **4.** *Informal.* mastoiditis.

mastoidectomy (ˌmæstɔɪˈdɛktəmɪ) *n., pl.* **-mies.** surgical removal of the mastoid process.

mastoiditis (ˌmæstɔɪˈdaɪtɪs) *n.* inflammation of the mastoid process.

masturbate (ˈmæstəˌbeɪt) *vb.* to stimulate the genital organs of (oneself or another) to achieve sexual pleasure. [C19: from Latin *masturbārī,* of unknown origin; formerly thought to be derived from *manus* hand + *stuprāre* to defile] —ˌ**masturˈbation** *n.* —ˈ**masturˌbator** *n.* —**masturbatory** (ˈmæstəˌbeɪtərɪ) *adj.*

masurium (məˈsʊərɪəm) *n.* the former name for **technetium.** [C20: New Latin, after *Masuria* in Poland, where it was discovered]

mat[1] (mæt) *n.* **1.** a thick flat piece of fabric used as a floor covering, a place to wipe one's shoes, etc. **2.** a smaller pad of material used to protect a surface from the heat, scratches, etc., of an object placed upon it. **3.** a large piece of thick padded material put on the floor as a surface for wrestling, judo, or gymnastic sports. **4.** *N.Z.* a Maori cloak. **5. go back to the mat.** *N.Z.* to abandon urban civilization. **6.** any surface or mass that is densely interwoven or tangled: *a mat of grass and weeds.* **7.** the solid part of a lace design. **8.** a heavy net of cable or rope laid over a blasting site to prevent the scatter of debris. **9.** *Civil engineering.* short for **mattress** (sense 3). ~*vb.* **mats, matting, matted. 10.** to tangle or weave or become tangled or woven into a dense mass. **11.** (*tr.*) to cover with a mat or mats. [Old English *matte;* related to Old High German *matta*] —ˈ**matless** *adj.*

mat[2] (mæt) *n.* **1.** a border of cardboard, cloth, etc., placed around a picture to act as a frame or as a contrast between picture and frame. **2.** a surface, as on metal or paint. ~*adj.* **3.** having a dull, lustreless, or roughened surface. ~*vb.* **mats, matting, matted.** (*tr.*) **4.** to furnish (a picture) with a mat. **5.** to give (a surface) a mat finish. ~Also (for senses 2, 3, 5): **matt.** [C17: from French, literally: dead; see CHECKMATE]

mat[3] (mæt) *n. Printing, informal.* short for **matrix** (sense 5).

mat. *abbrev. for* matinée.

Matabele (ˌmætəˈbiːlɪ, -ˈbɛlɪ) *n.* **1.** (*pl.* **-les** *or* **-le**) a member of a formerly warlike people of southern Africa, now living in Zimbabwe: driven out of the Transvaal by the Boers in 1837. Now known as **Ndebele. 2.** the language of this people, belonging to the Bantu group of the Niger-Congo family.

matador (ˈmætədɔː) *n.* **1.** the principal bullfighter who is appointed to kill the bull. **2.** (in some card games such as skat) one of the highest ranking cards. **3.** a game played with dominoes in which the dots on adjacent halves must total seven. [C17: from Spanish, from *matar* to kill]

matagouri (ˌmætəˈguːrɪ) *n., pl.* **-ris.** a thorny bush of New Zealand, *Discaria toumatou,* that forms thickets in open country. Also called: **wild Irishman,** (Maori) **tumatakuru.** [from Maori *tumatakuru*]

matai (ˈmɑːtaɪ) *n., pl.* **-tais.** a coniferous evergreen tree of New Zealand, *Podocarpus spicatus,* having a bluish bark and small linear leaves arranged in two rows: timber used for flooring and weatherboards. Also called: **black pine.** [Maori]

mata-mata (ˈmataˈmata) *n.* (in Malaysia) a former name for **police.** [from Malay, reduplicated plural of *mata* eye]

match[1] (mætʃ) *n.* **1.** a formal game or sports event in which people, teams, etc., compete to win. **2.** a person or thing able to provide competition for another: *she's met her match in talking ability.* **3.** a person or thing that resembles, harmonizes with, or is equivalent to another in a specified respect: *that coat is a good match for your hat.* **4.** a person or thing that is an exact copy or equal of another. **5. a.** a partnership between a man and a woman, as in marriage. **b.** an arrangement for such a partnership. **6.** a person regarded as a possible partner, as in marriage. ~*vb.* (*mainly tr.*) **7.** to fit (parts) together: *to match the tongue and groove of boards.* **8.** (*also intr.;* sometimes foll. by *up*) to resemble, harmonize with, correspond to, or equal (one another or something else): *the skirt matches your shoes well.* **9.** (sometimes foll. by *with* or *against*) to compare in order to determine which is the superior: *they matched wits.* **10.** (often foll. by *to* or *with*) to adapt so as to correspond with: *to match hope with reality.* **11.** (often foll. by *with* or *against*) to arrange a competition between. **12.** to find a match for. **13.** *Electronics.* to connect (two circuits) so that their impedances are equal or are equalized by a coupling device, to produce a maximum transfer of energy. [Old English *gemæcca* spouse; related to Old High German *gimmaha* wife, Old Norse *maki* mate] —ˈ**matchable** *adj.* —ˈ**matcher** *n.* —ˈ**matching** *adj.*

match[2] (mætʃ) *n.* **1.** a thin strip of wood or cardboard tipped with a chemical that ignites by friction when rubbed on a rough surface or a surface coated with a suitable chemical (see **safety match**). **2.** a length of cord or wick impregnated with a chemical so that it burns slowly. It is used to fire cannons, explosives, etc. [C14: from Old French *meiche,* perhaps from Latin *myxa* wick, from Greek *muxa* lamp nozzle]

matchboard (ˈmætʃˌbɔːd) *n.* a long thin board with a tongue along one edge and a corresponding groove along the other, used with similar boards to line walls, ceilings, etc.

matchbox (ˈmætʃˌbɒks) *n.* a small box for holding matches.

matched-pairs design *n.* (*modifier*) *Statistics.* (of an experiment) concerned with measuring the values of the dependent variables for pairs of subjects that have been matched to eliminate individual differences and that are respectively subjected to the control and the experimental condition. Compare **between-subjects design, within-subjects design.**

matched sample *n. Statistics.* a sample in which the individuals selected for analysis share all properties except that under investigation.

matchet ('mætʃət) *n.* an earlier name for **machete.**

matchless ('mætʃlɪs) *adj.* unequalled; incomparable; peerless. —'**matchlessly** *adv.* —'**matchlessness** *n.*

matchlock ('mætʃˌlɒk) *n.* **1.** an obsolete type of gunlock igniting the powder by means of a slow match. **2.** a gun having such a lock.

matchmaker[1] ('mætʃˌmeɪkə) *n.* **1.** a person who brings together suitable partners for marriage. **2.** a person who arranges competitive matches. —'**matchˌmaking** *n., adj.*

matchmaker[2] ('mætʃˌmeɪkə) *n.* a person who makes matches (for igniting). —'**matchˌmaking** *n., adj.*

matchmark ('mætʃˌmɑːk) *n.* **1.** a mark made on mating components of an engine, machine, etc., to ensure that the components are assembled in the correct relative positions. ~*vb.* **2.** (*tr.*) to stamp (an object) with matchmarks.

match play *n. Golf.* **a.** scoring according to the number of holes won and lost. **b.** (*as modifier*): *a matchplay tournament.* ~Compare **stroke play.** —**match player** *n.*

match point *n.* **1.** *Tennis, squash, etc.* the final point needed to win a match. **2.** *Bridge.* the unit used for scoring in tournaments.

matchstick ('mætʃˌstɪk) *n.* **1.** the wooden part of a match. ~*adj.* **2.** made with or as if with matchsticks: *a matchstick model.* **3.** (esp. of figures drawn with single strokes) thin and straight: *matchstick men.*

matchwood ('mætʃˌwʊd) *n.* **1.** wood suitable for making matches. **2.** splinters or fragments: *the bomb blew the house to matchwood.*

mate[1] (meɪt) *n.* **1.** the sexual partner of an animal. **2.** a marriage partner. **3. a.** *Informal, chiefly Brit., Austral., and N.Z.* a friend, usually of the same sex: often used to any male in direct address. **b.** (*in combination*) an associate, colleague, fellow sharer, etc.: *a classmate; a flatmate.* **4.** one of a pair of matching items. **5.** *Nautical.* **a.** short for **first mate. b.** any officer below the master on a commercial ship. **c.** a warrant officer's assistant on a ship. **6.** (in some trades) an assistant: *a plumber's mate.* **7.** *Archaic.* a suitable associate. ~*vb.* **8.** to pair (a male and female animal) or (of animals) to pair for reproduction. **9.** to marry or join in marriage. **10.** (*tr.*) to join as a pair; match. [C14: from Middle Low German; related to Old English *gemetta* table-guest, from *mete* MEAT] —'**mateless** *adj.*

mate[2] (meɪt) *n., vb. Chess.* See **checkmate.**

maté *or* **mate** ('mɑːteɪ, 'mæteɪ) *n.* **1.** an evergreen tree, *Ilex paraguariensis,* cultivated in South America for its leaves, which contain caffeine: family *Aquifoliaceae.* **2.** a stimulating milky beverage made from the dried leaves of this tree. ~Also called: **Paraguay tea, yerba, yerba maté.** [C18: from American Spanish (originally referring to the vessel in which the drink was brewed), from Quechua *máti* gourd]

matelassé (mæt'læseɪ) *adj.* (in textiles) having a raised design, as quilting; embossed. [C19: from French *matelasser* to quilt, from *matelas* MATTRESS]

matelot, matlo, *or* **matlow** ('mætləʊ) *n. Slang, chiefly Brit.* a sailor. [C20: from French]

matelote *or* **matelotte** ('mætᵊˌləʊt; *French* matlɔt) *n.* fish served with a sauce of wine, onions, seasonings, and fish stock. [C18: from French, feminine of *matelot* sailor]

mater ('meɪtə) *n. Brit. public school slang.* a word for **mother**[1]: often used facetiously. [C16: from Latin]

mater dolorosa (ˌdɒlə'rəʊsə) *n.* the Virgin Mary sorrowing for the dead Christ, esp. as depicted in art. [Latin: sorrowful mother]

materfamilias (ˌmeɪtəfə'mɪlɪˌæs) *n., pl.* **matresfamilias** (ˌmeɪtreɪzfə'mɪlɪˌæs) the mother of a family or the female head of a family. [C18: from Latin]

material (mə'tɪərɪəl) *n.* **1.** the substance of which a thing is made or composed; component or constituent matter: *raw material.* **2.** facts, notes, etc., that a finished work may be based on or derived from: *enough material for a book.* **3.** cloth or fabric. **4.** a person who has qualities suitable for a given occupation, training, etc.: *that boy is not university material.* ~*adj.* **5.** of, relating to, or composed of physical substance; corporeal. **6.** *Philosophy.* composed of or relating to physical as opposed to mental or spiritual substance: *the material world.* **7.** of, relating to, or affecting economic or physical wellbeing: *material ease.* **8.** of or concerned with physical rather than spiritual interests. **9.** of great import or consequence: *of material benefit to the workers.* **10.** (often foll. by *to*) relevant. **11.** *Philosophy.* of or relating to matter as opposed to form. **12.** *Law.* relevant to the issue before court: applied esp. to facts or testimony of much significance: *a material witness.* ~See also **materials.** [C14: via French from Late Latin *māteriālis,* from Latin *māteria* MATTER] —**ma'terialness** *n.*

material implication *n. Logic.* **1.** the truth-functional connective that forms a compound sentence from two given sentences and assigns the value false to it only when its antecedent is true and its consequent false, without consideration of relevance; loosely corresponds to the English *if ... then.* **2.** a compound sentence formed with this connective.

materialism (mə'tɪərɪəˌlɪzəm) *n.* **1.** interest in and desire for money, possessions, etc., rather than spiritual or ethical values. **2.** *Philosophy.* the monist doctrine that matter is the only reality and that the mind, the emotions, etc., are merely functions of it. Compare **idealism** (sense 3), **dualism** (sense 2). See also **identity theory. 3.** *Ethics.* the rejection of any religious or supernatural account of things. —**ma'terialist** *n., adj.* —**maˌterial'istic** *adj.* —**maˌterial'istically** *adv.*

materiality (məˌtɪərɪ'ælɪtɪ) *n.* **1.** the state or quality of being physical or material. **2.** substance; matter.

materialize *or* **materialise** (mə'tɪərɪəˌlaɪz) *vb.* **1.** (*intr.*) to become fact; actually happen: *our hopes never materialized.* **2.** to invest or become invested with a physical shape or form. **3.** to cause (a spirit, as of a dead person) to appear in material form or (of a spirit) to appear in such form. **4.** (*intr.*) to take shape; become tangible: *after hours of discussion, the project finally began to materialize.* **5.** *Physics.* to form (material particles) from energy, as in pair production. —**maˌteriali'zation** *or* **maˌteriali'sation** *n.* —**ma'terialˌizer** *or* **ma'terialˌiser** *n.*

materially (mə'tɪərɪəlɪ) *adv.* **1.** to a significant extent; considerably: *his death alters the situation materially.* **2.** with respect to material objects. **3.** *Philosophy.* with respect to substance as distinct from form.

material mode *n. Philosophy.* the normal use of language that refers to extra-linguistic subjects without explicit mention of the words themselves. *Fido is a dog* is in the material mode, while *"Fido" is a dog's name* is in the formal mode. See also **use** (sense 18).

materials (mə'tɪərɪəlz) *pl. n.* the equipment necessary for a particular activity.

materia medica (mə'tɪərɪə 'mɛdɪkə) *n.* **1.** the branch of medical science concerned with the study of drugs used in the treatment of disease: includes pharmacy, pharmacology, and the history and physical and chemical properties of drugs. **2.** the drugs used in the treatment of disease. [C17: from Medieval Latin: medical matter]

materiel *or* **matériel** (məˌtɪərɪ'ɛl) *n.* the materials and equipment of an organization, esp. of a military force. Compare **personnel.** [C19: from French: MATERIAL]

maternal (mə'tɜːnᵊl) *adj.* **1.** of, relating to, derived from, or characteristic of a mother. **2.** related through the mother's side of the family: *his maternal uncle.* [C15: from Medieval Latin *māternālis,* from Latin *māternus,* from *māter* mother] —**ma'ternalism** *n.* —**maˌternal'istic** *adj.* —**ma'ternally** *adv.*

maternity (mə'tɜːnɪtɪ) *n.* **1.** motherhood. **2.** the characteristics associated with motherhood; motherliness. **3.** (*modifier*) relating to pregnant women or women at the time of childbirth: *a maternity ward.*

maternity benefit *n.* (in the British National Insurance scheme) a payment (**maternity allowance**) made to a woman having a child, normally from 11 weeks before confinement for a period of 18 weeks, in addition to a flat-rate benefit (**maternity grant**).

maternity leave *n.* a period of paid absence from work, in Britain currently six months, to which a woman is legally entitled during the months immediately before and after childbirth.

mateship ('meɪtʃɪp) *n. Austral.* the comradeship of friends, usually male, viewed as an institution.

mate's rates *pl. n. N.Z. informal.* preferential rates of payment offered to a friend.

matey *or* **maty** ('meɪtɪ) *Brit. informal.* ~*adj.* **1.** friendly or intimate; on good terms. ~*n.* **2.** friend or fellow: usually used in direct address. —'**mateyness** *or* '**matiness** *n.*

mat grass *n.* a widespread perennial European grass, *Nardus stricta,* with dense tufts of bristly leaves, characteristic of peaty moors.

math (mæθ) *n. U.S. and Canadian informal.* short for **mathematics.** Brit. equivalent: **maths.**

math. *U.S. and Canadian abbrev. for* mathematics.

mathematical (ˌmæθə'mætɪkᵊl, ˌmæθ'mæt-) *or* (*less commonly*) **mathematic** *adj.* **1.** of, used in, or relating to mathematics. **2.** characterized by or using the precision of mathematics; exact. **3.** using, determined by, or in accordance with the principles of mathematics. —ˌ**mathe'matically** *adv.*

mathematical expectation *n. Statistics.* another name for **expected value.**

mathematical logic *n.* symbolic logic, esp. that branch concerned with the foundations of mathematics.

mathematical probability *n. Statistics.* **1.** the probability of an event consisting of *n* out of *m* possible equally likely occurrences, defined to be $^{n}/_{m}$. See also **principle of indifference. 2.** the study of such probabilities. ~Also called: **classical probability.**

mathematician (ˌmæθəmə'tɪʃən, ˌmæθmə-) *n.* an expert or specialist in mathematics.

mathematics (ˌmæθə'mætɪks, ˌmæθ'mæt-) *n.* **1.** (*functioning as sing.*) a group of related sciences, including algebra, geometry, and calculus, concerned with the study of number, quantity, shape, and space and their interrelationships by using a specialized notation. **2.** (*functioning as sing. or pl.*) mathematical operations and processes involved in the solution of a problem or study of some scientific field. [C14 *mathematik* (n.), via Latin from Greek (adj.), from *mathēma* a science, *mathēmatikos* (adj.); related to *manthanein* to learn]

maths (mæθs) *n. (functioning as sing.) Brit. informal.* short for **mathematics.** U.S. and Canadian equivalent: **math.**

maths. *Brit. abbrev. for* mathematics.

Matilda (məˈtɪldə) *n. Austral. informal.* **1.** a bushman's swag. **2. walk** *or* **waltz Matilda.** to travel the road carrying one's swag. [C20: from the Christian name]

matin, mattin (ˈmætɪn), *or* **matinal** *adj.* of or relating to matins. [C14: see MATINS]

matinée (ˈmætɪˌneɪ) *n.* **1.** a daytime, esp. afternoon, performance of a play, concert, etc. **2.** *Austral. slang.* sexual intercourse in the daytime. [C19: from French; see MATINS]

matinée coat *or* **jacket** *n.* a short coat for a baby.

matinée idol *n.* (esp. in the 1930s and 1940s) an actor popular as a romantic figure among women.

matins *or* **mattins** (ˈmætɪnz) *n. (functioning as sing. or pl.)* **1. a.** *Chiefly R.C. Church.* the first of the seven canonical hours of prayer, originally observed at night but now often recited with lauds at daybreak. **b.** the service of morning prayer in the Church of England. **2.** *Literary.* a morning song, esp. of birds. [C13: from Old French, ultimately from Latin *mātūtīnus* of the morning, from *Mātūta* goddess of dawn]

matlo *or* **matlow** (ˈmætləʊ) *n.* variant spellings of **matelot.**

matoke (maˈtɔkɛ) *n.* (in Uganda) the flesh of bananas, boiled and mashed as a food. [C20: from Luganda]

matrass *or* **mattrass** (ˈmætrəs) *n. Chem., obsolete.* a long-necked glass flask, used for distilling, dissolving substances, etc. [C17: from French, perhaps related to Latin *mētiri* to measure]

matri- *combining form.* mother or motherhood: *matriarchy.* [from Latin *māter* mother]

matriarch (ˈmeɪtrɪˌɑːk) *n.* **1.** a woman who dominates an organization, community, etc. **2.** the female head of a tribe or family, esp. in a matriarchy. **3.** a very old or venerable woman. [C17: from MATRI- + -ARCH, by false analogy with PATRIARCH] —ˈ**maˈtriˌarchal** *or (less commonly)* ˈ**matriˌarchic** *adj.* —ˌ**matriˈarchalism** *n.*

matriarchate (ˈmeɪtrɪˌɑːkɪt, -keɪt) *n. Rare.* a family or people under female domination or government.

matriarchy (ˈmeɪtrɪˌɑːkɪ) *n., pl.* **-chies. 1.** a form of social organization in which a female is head of the family or society, and descent and kinship are traced through the female line. **2.** any society dominated by women.

matric (məˈtrɪk) *n. Brit.* short for **matriculation** (sense 2).

matrices (ˈmeɪtrɪˌsiːz, ˈmæ-) *n.* a plural of **matrix.**

matricide (ˈmætrɪˌsaɪd, ˈmeɪ-) *n.* **1.** the act of killing one's own mother. **2.** a person who kills his mother. [C16: from Latin *mātrīcīdium* (the act), *mātrīcīda* (the agent). See MATRI-, -CIDE] —ˌ**matriˈcidal** *adj.*

matriclinous (ˌmætrɪˈklaɪnəs), **matroclinous,** *or* **matroclinal** *adj.* (of an animal or plant) showing the characters of the female parent. Compare **patriclinous.** [C20: from MATRI- + Greek *klīnein* to lean]

matriculate *vb.* (məˈtrɪkjʊˌleɪt). **1.** to enrol or be enrolled in an institution, esp. a college or university. **2.** *(intr.)* to attain the academic standard required for a course at such an institution. ~*n.* (məˈtrɪkjʊlɪt). **3.** Also called: **maˈtriculant.** a person who has matriculated. [C16: from Medieval Latin *mātrīculāre* to register, from *mātrīcula*, diminutive of *matrix* list, MATRIX] —**maˈtricuˌlator** *n.*

matriculation (məˌtrɪkjʊˈleɪʃən) *n.* **1.** the process of matriculating. **2.** (in Britain, except Scotland) a former school examination, which was replaced by the General Certificate of Education (Ordinary Level).

matrilineal (ˌmætrɪˈlɪnɪəl, ˌmeɪ-) *adj.* relating to descent or kinship through the female line. —ˌ**matriˈlineally** *adv.*

matrilocal (ˈmætrɪˌləʊkᵊl, ˈmeɪ-) *adj.* denoting, having, or relating to a marriage pattern in which the couple live with the wife's family. —**matrilocality** (ˌmætrɪləʊˈkælɪtɪ, ˌmeɪ-) *n.* —ˌ**matriˈlocally** *adv.*

matrimonial (ˌmætrɪˈməʊnɪəl) *adj.* relating to marriage: *matrimonial troubles.* —ˌ**matriˈmonially** *adv.*

matrimony (ˈmætrɪmənɪ) *n., pl.* **-nies. 1.** the state or condition of being married. **2.** the ceremony or sacrament of marriage. **3. a.** a card game in which the king and queen together are a winning combination. **b.** such a combination. [C14: via Norman French from Latin *mātrimōnium* wedlock, from *māter* mother]

matrimony vine *n.* any of various shrubs of the solanaceous genus *Lycium,* cultivated for their purple flowers and colourful berries. Also called: **boxthorn.**

matrix (ˈmeɪtrɪks, ˈmæ-) *n., pl.* **matrices** (ˈmeɪtrɪˌsiːz, ˈmæ-) *or* **matrixes. 1.** a substance, situation, or environment in which something has its origin, takes form, or is enclosed. **2.** *Anatomy.* the thick tissue at the base of a nail from which a fingernail or toenail develops. **3.** the intercellular substance of bone, cartilage, connective tissue, etc. **4. a.** the rock material in which fossils, pebbles, etc., are embedded. **b.** the material in which a mineral is embedded; gangue. **5.** *Printing.* **a.** a metal mould for casting type. **b.** a papier-mâché or plastic mould impressed from the forme and used for stereotyping. Sometimes shortened to **mat. 6.** a mould used in the production of gramophone records. It is obtained by electrodeposition onto the master. **7.** a bed of perforated material placed beneath a workpiece in a press or stamping machine against which the punch operates. **8.** *Metallurgy.* **a.** the shaped cathode used in electroforming. **b.** the metal constituting the major part of an alloy. **c.** the soft metal in a plain bearing in which the hard particles of surface metal are embedded. **9.** *Maths.* a rectangular array of elements set out in rows and columns, used to facilitate the solution of problems, such as the transformation of coordinates. Usually indicated by parentheses: $\binom{a_d\ b_e\ c_f}{}$. Compare **determinant** (sense 3). **10.** *Linguistics.* the main clause of a complex sentence. **11.** *Computer technol.* a rectangular array of circuit elements usually used to generate one set of signals from another. **12.** *Obsolete.* the womb. [C16: from Latin: womb, female animal used for breeding, from *māter* mother]

matroclinous (ˌmætrəˈklaɪnəs) *adj.* a variant of **matriclinous.**

matron (ˈmeɪtrən) *n.* **1.** a married woman regarded as staid or dignified, esp. a middle-aged woman with children. **2.** a woman in charge of the domestic or medical arrangements in an institution. **3.** *U.S.* a wardress in a prison. **4.** Official name: **nursing officer.** *Brit.* the administrative head of the nursing staff in a hospital. [C14: via Old French from Latin *mātrōna,* from *māter* mother] —ˈ**matronal** *adj.* —ˈ**matronˌhood** *or* ˈ**matronˌship** *n.* —ˈ**matron-ˌlike** *adj.*

matronage (ˈmeɪtrənɪdʒ) *n.* **1.** the state of being a matron. **2.** supervision or care by a matron. **3.** matrons collectively.

matronly (ˈmeɪtrənlɪ) *adj.* of, characteristic of, or suitable for a matron; staid and dignified in a manner associated with a middle-aged, usually plump, woman. —ˈ**matronliness** *n.*

matron of honour *n., pl.* **matrons of honour. 1.** a married woman serving as chief attendant to a bride. Compare **bridesmaid, maid of honour. 2.** a married woman, usually a member of the nobility, who attends a queen or princess.

matronymic (ˌmætrəˈnɪmɪk) *adj., n.* a less common word for **metronymic.**

matt *or* **matte** (mæt) *adj., n., vb.* variant spellings of **mat**[2] (senses 2, 3, 5).

Matt. *Bible. abbrev. for* Matthew.

mattamore (ˈmætəˌmɔː) *n.* a subterranean storehouse or dwelling. [C17: from French, from Arabic *matmura,* from *tamara* to store, bury]

matte[1] (mæt) *n.* an impure fused material consisting of metal sulphides produced during the smelting of a sulphide ore. [C19: from French]

matte[2] (mæt) *n. Films, television.* a mask used to blank out part of an image so that another image can be superimposed.

matted (ˈmætɪd) *adj.* **1.** tangled into a thick mass: *matted hair.* **2.** covered with or formed of matting.

matter (ˈmætə) *n.* **1.** that which makes up something, esp. a physical object; material. **2.** substance that occupies space and has mass, as distinguished from substance that is mental, spiritual, etc. **3.** substance of a specified type: *vegetable matter; reading matter.* **4.** (sometimes foll. by *of* or *for*) thing; affair; concern; question: *a matter of taste; several matters to attend to; no laughing matter.* **5.** a quantity or amount: *a matter of a few pence.* **6.** the content of written or verbal material as distinct from its style or form. **7.** *(used with a negative)* importance; consequence. **8.** *Philosophy.* (in the writings of Aristotle and the Scholastics) that which is itself formless but can receive form and become substance. **9.** *Philosophy.* (in the Cartesian tradition) one of two basic modes of existence, the other being **mind:** matter being extended in space as well as time. **10.** *Printing.* **a.** type set up, either standing or for use. **b.** copy to be set in type. **11.** a secretion or discharge, such as pus. **12.** *Law.* **a.** something to be proved. **b.** statements or allegations to be considered by a court. **13. for that matter.** as regards that. **14.** See **grey matter. 15. no matter. a.** regardless of; irrespective of: *no matter what the excuse, you must not be late.* **b.** *(sentence substitute)* it is unimportant. **16. the matter.** wrong; the trouble: *there's nothing the matter.* ~*vb. (intr.)* **17.** to be of consequence or importance. **18.** to form and discharge pus. [C13 (n.), C16 (vb.): from Latin *māteria* cause, substance, esp. wood, or a substance that produces something else; related to *māter* mother]

matter of course *n.* **1.** an event or result that is natural or inevitable. ~*adj.* **matter-of-course. 2.** *(usually postpositive)* occurring as a matter of course. **3.** accepting things as inevitable or natural: *a matter-of-course attitude.*

matter of fact *n.* **1.** a fact that is undeniably true. **2.** *Law.* a statement of facts the truth of which the court must determine on the basis of the evidence before it: contrasted with **matter of law, matter of opinion. 3.** *Philosophy.* a proposition that is amenable to empirical testing, as contrasted with the truths of logic or mathematics. **4. as a matter of fact.** actually; in fact. ~*adj.* **matter-of-fact. 5.** unimaginative or emotionless: *he gave a matter-of-fact account of the murder.*

matter of opinion *n.* a point open to question; a debatable statement.

matter waves *pl. n.* See **de Broglie waves.**

mattery (ˈmætərɪ) *adj.* discharging pus.

Matthew Walker (ˈmæθjuː ˈwɔːkə) *n.* a knot made at the end of a rope by unlaying the strands and passing them up through the loops formed in the next two strands. [C19: probably named after the man who introduced it]

matting[1] ('mætɪŋ) *n.* **1.** a coarsely woven fabric, usually made of a natural fibre such as straw or hemp and used as a floor covering, packing material, etc. **2.** the act or process of making mats. **3.** material for mats.

matting[2] ('mætɪŋ) *n.* **1.** another word for **mat**[2] (sense 1). **2.** the process of producing a mat finish.

mattins ('mætɪnz) *n.* a variant spelling of **matins.**

mattock ('mætək) *n.* a type of large pick that has one end of its blade shaped like an adze, used for loosening soil, cutting roots, etc. [Old English *mattuc,* of unknown origin; related to Latin *mateola* club, mallet]

mattoid ('mætɔɪd) *n. Rare.* a person displaying eccentric behaviour and mental characteristics that approach the psychotic. [C19: from Italian, from *matto* insane]

mattrass ('mætrəs) *n.* a variant spelling of **matrass.**

mattress ('mætrɪs) *n.* **1.** a large flat pad with a strong cover, filled with straw, foam rubber, etc., and often incorporating coiled springs, used as a bed or as part of a bed. **2.** Also called: **Dutch mattress.** a woven mat of brushwood, poles, etc., used to protect an embankment, dyke, etc., from scour. **3.** a concrete or steel raft or slab used as a foundation or footing. Sometimes shortened to **mat. 4.** a network of reinforcing rods or expanded metal sheeting, used in reinforced concrete. **5.** *Civil engineering.* another name for **blinding** (sense 3). [C13: via Old French from Italian *materasso,* from Arabic *almatrah* place where something is thrown]

maturate ('mætjʊˌreɪt, 'mætʃʊ-) *vb.* **1.** to mature or bring to maturity. **2.** a less common word for **suppurate.** —**maturative** (mə'tjʊərətɪv, mə'tʃʊə-) *adj.*

maturation (ˌmætjʊ'reɪʃən, ˌmætʃʊ-) *n.* **1.** the process of maturing or ripening. **2.** *Zoology.* the development of ova and spermatozoa from precursor cells in the ovary and testis, involving meiosis. **3.** a less common word for **suppuration.** —ˌ**matu'rational** *adj.*

mature (mə'tjʊə, -'tʃʊə) *adj.* **1.** relatively advanced physically, mentally, emotionally, etc.; grown-up. **2.** (of plans, theories, etc.) fully considered; perfected. **3.** due or payable: *a mature debenture.* **4.** *Biology.* **a.** fully developed or differentiated: *a mature cell.* **b.** fully grown; adult: *a mature animal.* **5.** (of fruit, wine, cheese, etc.) ripe or fully aged. **6.** (of a river valley or land surface) in the middle stage of the cycle of erosion, characterized by meanders, maximum relief, etc. See also **youthful** (sense 4), **old** (sense 18). ~*vb.* **7.** to make or become mature. **8.** (*intr.*) (of notes, bonds, etc.) to become due for payment or repayment. [C15: from Latin *mātūrus* early, developed] —**ma'turely** *adv.* —**ma'tureness** *n.*

mature student *n.* a student at a college or university who has passed the usual age for formal education.

maturity (mə'tjʊərɪtɪ, -'tʃʊə-) *n.* **1.** the state or quality of being mature; full development. **2.** *Finance.* **a.** the date upon which a bill of exchange, bond, note, etc., becomes due for repayment. **b.** the state of a bill, note, etc., when due.

matutinal (ˌmætjʊ'taɪnᵊl) *adj.* of, occurring in, or during the morning. [C17: from Late Latin *mātūtīnālis,* from Latin *mātūtīnus,* from *Mātūta* goddess of the dawn] —ˌ**matu'tinally** *adv.*

maty ('meɪtɪ) *n., adj.* **matier, matiest.** a variant of **matey.**

matzo, matzoh ('mæt'səʊ) *or* **matza, matzah** ('mætsə) *n., pl.* **matzos, matzohs, matzas, matzahs,** *or* **matzoth** (*Hebrew* ma'tsɔt). a brittle very thin biscuit of unleavened bread, traditionally eaten during Passover. [from Hebrew *matsāh*]

matzoon (mɑːt'suːn) *or* **madzoon** (mɑːd'zuːn) *n.* a fermented milk product similar to yoghurt. [from Armenian *madzun*]

mauby ('mɑːbɪ, 'mɔː-) *n., pl.* **-bies.** (in the E Caribbean) a bittersweet drink made from the bark of a rhamnaceous tree. [C20: of uncertain origin]

maud (mɔːd) *n.* a shawl or rug of grey wool plaid formerly worn in Scotland. [C18: of unknown origin]

maudlin ('mɔːdlɪn) *adj.* foolishly tearful or sentimental, as when drunk. [C17: from Middle English *Maudelen* Mary Magdalene, typically portrayed as a tearful penitent] —'**maudlinism** *n.* —'**maudlinly** *adv.* —'**maudlinness** *n.*

maugre *or* **mauger** ('mɔːgə) *prep. Obsolete.* in spite of. [C13 (meaning: ill will): from Old French *maugre,* literally: bad pleasure]

maul (mɔːl) *vb.* (*tr.*) **1.** to handle clumsily; paw. **2.** to batter or lacerate. ~*n.* **3.** a heavy two-handed hammer suitable for driving piles, wedges, etc. **4.** *Rugby.* a loose scrum that forms around a player who is holding the ball and on his feet. [C13: from Old French *mail,* from Latin *malleus* hammer. See MALLET] —'**mauler** *n.*

Maulana (mɔː'lɑːnɑː) *n.* (in Pakistan, India, etc.) a title used for a scholar of Persian and Arabic. [Urdu, from Arabic *mawlānā*]

maulers ('mɔːləz) *pl. n. Brit. slang.* the hands.

maulstick *or* **mahlstick** ('mɔːlˌstɪk) *n.* a long stick used by artists to steady the hand holding the brush. [C17: partial translation of Dutch *maalstok,* from obsolete *malen* to paint + *stok* STICK]

Mau Mau ('maʊ ˌmaʊ) *n., pl.* **Mau Maus** *or* **Mau Mau.** *E African slang.* a Ugandan motorcycle policeman who directs traffic. [named after the secret political society founded (1952) in Kenya to drive out European settlers by acts of terrorism]

maumet ('mɔːmɪt) *or* **mammet** ('mæmɪt) *n. Obsolete.* a false god; idol. [C13: from Old French *mahomet* idol, literally: the prophet *Mohammed,* from the belief that his image was worshipped] —'**maumetry** *n.*

maun, man (mɑːn, mɔːn), *or* **mun** (mʌn) *vb.* a dialect word for **must**[1]. [C14: from Old Norse *man* must, will]

maund (mɔːnd) *n.* a unit of weight used in Asia, esp. India, having different values in different localities. A common value in India is 82 pounds or 37 kilograms. [C17: from Hindi *man,* from Sanskrit *manā*]

maunder ('mɔːndə) *vb.* (*intr.*) to move, talk, or act aimlessly or idly. [C17: perhaps from obsolete *maunder* to beg, from Latin *mendīcāre;* see MENDICANT] —'**maunderer** *n.* —'**maundering** *adj.*

maundy ('mɔːndɪ) *n., pl.* **maundies.** *Christianity.* the ceremonial washing of the feet of poor persons in commemoration of Jesus' washing of his disciples' feet (John 13:4–34) re-enacted in some churches on Maundy Thursday. [C13: from Old French *mandé* something commanded, from Latin *mandatum* commandment, from the words of Christ: *Mandātum novum dō vōbīs* A new commandment give I unto you]

Maundy money *n.* specially minted coins distributed by the British sovereign on Maundy Thursday.

Maundy Thursday *n. Christianity.* the Thursday before Easter observed as a commemoration of the Last Supper.

maungy ('mɔːndʒɪ) *adj.* **-gier, -giest.** *West Yorkshire dialect.* (esp. of a child) sulky, bad-tempered, or peevish. [variant of MANGY, in extended sense: restless, dissatisfied]

Maurist ('maʊrɪst) *n.* a member of a congregation of French Benedictine monks founded in 1621 and noted for its scholarly work. [C19: named after *St Maurus,* 6th-century disciple of St Benedict]

Mauritanian (ˌmɒrɪ'teɪnɪən) *adj.* **1.** of or relating to Mauritania, a republic in NW Africa on the Atlantic. ~*n.* **2.** a native or inhabitant of Mauritania.

Mauritian (mə'rɪʃən) *adj.* **1.** of or relating to Mauritius, an island and state in the Indian Ocean. ~*n.* **2.** a native or inhabitant of Mauritius.

Mauser ('maʊzə) *n. Trademark.* **1.** a high-velocity magazine rifle. **2.** a type of automatic pistol. [C19: named after P. P. von *Mauser* (1838–1914), German firearms inventor]

mausoleum (ˌmɔːsə'lɪəm) *n., pl.* **-leums** *or* **-lea** (-'lɪə). a large stately tomb. [C16: via Latin from Greek *mausōleion,* the tomb of *Mausolus,* king of Caria; built at Halicarnassus in the 4th century B.C.] —ˌ**mauso'lean** *adj.*

mauvaise foi *French.* (movɛz fwa) *n. Philosophy.* the expression usually rendered as *bad faith:* see **bad faith** (sense 2).

mauvais pas ('məʊvɛ 'pɑː) *n., pl.* **mauvais pas** (-'pɑː, -'pɑːz). *Mountaineering.* a place that presents a particular difficulty on a climb or walk. [C19: from French: bad step]

mauvais quart d'heure *French.* (movɛ kar dœr) *n. Brit.* a brief unpleasant experience. [literally: (a) bad quarter of an hour]

mauve (məʊv) *n.* **1. a.** any of various pale to moderate pinkish-purple or bluish-purple colours. **b.** (*as adj.*): *a mauve flower.* **2.** Also called: **Perkin's mauve, mauveine** ('məʊviːn, -vɪn). a reddish-purple aniline dye. [C19: from French, from Latin *malva* MALLOW]

maven *or* **mavin** ('meɪvən) *n. U.S.* an expert or connoisseur. [C20: from Yiddish, from Hebrew *mevin* understanding]

maverick ('mævərɪk) *n.* **1.** (in U.S. and Canadian cattle-raising regions) an unbranded animal, esp. a stray calf. **2. a.** a person of independent or unorthodox views. **b.** (*as modifier*): *a maverick politician.* [C19: after Samuel A. *Maverick* (1803–70), Texas rancher, who did not brand his cattle]

mavis ('meɪvɪs) *n.* a popular name for the **song thrush.** [C14: from Old French *mauvis* thrush; origin obscure]

mavourneen *or* **mavournin** (mə'vʊəniːn) *n. Irish.* my darling. [C18: from Irish, from *mo* my + *muirnīn* love]

maw (mɔː) *n.* **1.** the mouth, throat, crop, or stomach of an animal, esp. of a voracious animal. **2.** *Informal.* the mouth or stomach of a greedy person. [Old English *maga;* related to Middle Dutch *maghe,* Old Norse *magi*]

mawger ('mɔːgə) *adj. Caribbean.* (of persons or animals) thin or lean. [from Dutch *mager* thin, MEAGRE]

mawkin ('mɔːkɪn) *n.* **1.** a variant of **malkin. 2.** *Brit. dialect.* **a.** a slovenly woman. **b.** a scarecrow.

mawkish ('mɔːkɪʃ) *adj.* **1.** falsely sentimental, esp. in a weak or maudlin way. **2.** nauseating or insipid in flavour, smell, etc. [C17: from obsolete *mawk* MAGGOT + -ISH] —'**mawkishly** *adv.* —'**mawkishness** *n.*

mawsie ('mɔːzɪ) *n. Northeast Scot. dialect.* a woollen jersey, cardigan, or vest. [perhaps a special use of MARSEILLE]

max. *abbrev. for* maximum.

maxi ('mæksɪ) *adj.* **1. a.** (of a garment) reaching the ankle. **b.** (*as n.*): *she wore a maxi.* **c.** (*in combination*): *a maxidress.* **2.** large or considerable in size for its type: *a maxi saving on fuel.* [C20: shortened from MAXIMUM]

maxilla (mæk'sɪlə) *n., pl.* **-lae** (-liː). **1.** the upper jawbone in vertebrates. See **jaw** (sense 1). **2.** any member of one or two pairs of mouthparts in insects and other arthropods used as accessory jaws. [C17: New Latin, from Latin: jaw] —**maxillar** (mæk'sɪlə) *or* **max'illary** *adj.*

maxilliped (mæk'sɪlɪˌpɛd) *n.* any member of three pairs of appendages in crustaceans, behind the maxillae: specialized for feeding. [C19: *maxilli-*, from MAXILLA + -PED] —**max,illi'ped-ary** *adj.*

maxillofacial (mæk,sɪləʊ'feɪʃəl, ,mæksɪləʊ-) *adj.* of, relating to, or affecting the upper jawbone and face: *maxillofacial surgery.* [C20: from MAXILLA + -O- + FACIAL]

maxim ('mæksɪm) *n.* a brief expression of a general truth, principle, or rule of conduct. [C15: via French from Medieval Latin, from *maxima*, in the phrase *maxima prōpositio* basic axiom (literally: greatest proposition); see MAXIMUM]

maxima ('mæksɪmə) *n.* a plural of **maximum.**

maximal ('mæksɪməl) *adj.* **1.** of, relating to, or achieving a maximum; being the greatest or best possible. **2.** *Maths.* (of a member of an ordered set) being preceded, in order, by all other members of the set. —'**maximally** *adv.*

maximalist ('mæksɪməlɪst) *n.* a person who favours direct action to achieve all his goals and rejects compromise.

Maximalist ('mæksɪməlɪst) *n.* (in early 20th-century Russia) **1.** a member of the radical faction of Social Revolutionaries that supported terrorism against the tsarist regime and advocated a short period of postrevolutionary working-class dictatorship. **2.** a less common name for a **Bolshevik.** ~Compare **Minimalist.** [C20: from French, a translation of Russian; see BOLSHEVIK]

Maxim gun ('mæksɪm) *n.* an obsolete water-cooled machine gun having a single barrel and utilizing the recoil force of each shot to maintain automatic fire. [C19: named after Sir Hiram *Maxim* (1840–1916), British inventor]

maximin ('mæksɪ,mɪn) *n.* **1.** *Maths.* the highest of a set of minimum values. **2.** (in game theory, etc.) the procedure of choosing the strategy that most benefits the least advantaged member of a group. Compare **minimax.** [C20: from MAXI(MUM) + MIN(IMUM)]

maximize *or* **maximise** ('mæksɪ,maɪz) *vb.* **1.** (*tr.*) to make as high or great as possible; increase to a maximum: *to maximize output.* **2.** *Maths.* to find the maximum of (a function). —,**maximi'zation,** ,**maximi'sation,** *or* ,**maxi'mation** *n.* —'**maxi,mizer** *or* '**maxi,miser** *n.*

maximum ('mæksɪməm) *n., pl.* **-mums** *or* **-ma** (-mə). **1.** the greatest possible amount, degree, etc. **2.** the highest value of a variable quantity. **3.** *Maths.* **a.** a value of a function that is greater than any neighbouring value. **b.** a stationary point on a curve at which the tangent changes from a positive value on the left of this point to a negative value on the right. Compare **minimum** (sense 4). **c.** the largest number in a set. **4.** *Astronomy.* **a.** the time at which the brightness of a variable star has its greatest value. **b.** the magnitude of the star at that time. ~*adj.* **5.** of, being, or showing a maximum or maximums. ~Abbrev.: **max.** [C18: from Latin: greatest (the neuter form used as noun), from *magnus* great]

maximum likelihood *n. Statistics.* **1.** the probability of randomly drawing a given sample from a population maximized over the possible values of the population parameters. **2.** the non-Bayesian rule that, given an experimental observation, one should utilize as point estimates of parameters of a distribution those values which give the highest conditional probability to that observation, irrespective of the prior probability assigned to the parameters.

maximum-minimum thermometer *n.* a thermometer that records the highest and lowest temperatures since it was last set.

maximus ('mæksɪməs) *n. Change-ringing.* a method rung on twelve bells. [from Latin: superlative of *magnus* great]

maxisingle ('mæksɪ,sɪŋgᵊl) *n.* an EP or small LP.

maxixe (mə'ʃi:ʃ, mæk'si:ks, mə'ʃi:ʃeɪ) *n.* a Brazilian dance in duple time, a precursor of the tango. [from Brazilian Portuguese]

maxwell ('mækswəl) *n.* the cgs unit of magnetic flux equal to the flux through one square centimetre normal to a field of one gauss. It is equivalent to 10^{-8} weber. Symbol: Mx [C20: named after James Clerk *Maxwell* (1831–79), Scottish physicist]

Maxwell's equations ('mækswəlz) *pl. n.* the set of equations upon which classical electromagnetic theory is based. [C20: named after James Clerk *Maxwell*]

may[1] (meɪ) *vb. past* **might.** (takes an infinitive without *to* or an implied infinitive) used as an auxiliary **1.** to indicate that permission is requested by or granted to someone: *he may go to the park tomorrow if he behaves himself.* **2.** (often foll. by *well*) to indicate possibility: *the rope may break; he may well be a spy.* **3.** to indicate ability or capacity, esp. in questions: *may I help you?* **4.** to express a strong wish: *long may she reign.* **5.** to indicate result or purpose: used only in clauses introduced by *that* or *so that: he writes so that the average reader may understand.* **6.** another word for **might**[1]. **7.** to express courtesy in a question: *whose child may this little girl be?* **8. be that as it may.** in spite of that: a sentence connector conceding the possible truth of a previous statement and introducing an adversative clause: *be that as it may, I still think he should come.* **9. come what may.** whatever happens. **10. that's as may be.** (foll. by a clause introduced by *but*) that may be so. [Old English *mæg*, from *magan:* compare Old High German *mag*, Old Norse *mā*]

▷**Usage.** In careful written usage, *may* is used rather than *can* when reference is made to permission rather than to capability. *He may do it* is, for this reason, more appropriate than *he can do it* when the desired sense is *he is allowed to do it.* In spoken English, however, *can* is often used where the correct use of *may* results in forms that are considered to be awkward. *Can't I?* is preferred on this ground to *mayn't I?* in speech. The difference between *may* and *might* is one of emphasis: *he might be coming* usually indicates less certainty than *he may be coming.* Similarly, *might I have it?* is felt to be more hesitant than *may I have it?* Careful writers and speakers avoid the use of *may* as a subjunctive. *Your analysis may have been more credible if...*, although frequently encountered, is regarded as less acceptable than *Your analysis might have been more credible if....*

may[2] (meɪ) *n.* an archaic word for **maiden.** [Old English *mæg;* related to Old High German *māg* kinsman, Old Norse *māgr* a relative by marriage]

may[3] (meɪ) *n.* **1.** Also: **may tree.** a Brit. name for **hawthorn. 2.** short for **may blossom.** [C16: from the month of MAY, when it flowers]

May (meɪ) *n.* the fifth month of the year, consisting of 31 days. [from Old French, from Latin *Maius* (month) of *Maia*, Roman goddess, identified with the Greek goddess *Maia*]

maya ('maɪə, 'mɑ:jə, 'mɑ:jɑ:) *n. Hinduism.* illusion, esp. the material world of the senses regarded as illusory. [C19: from Sanskrit] —'**mayan** *adj.*

Maya ('maɪə) *n.* **1.** (*pl.* **-ya** *or* **-yas**) Also called: **Mayan.** a member of an American Indian people of Yucatan, Belize, and N Guatemala, having an ancient culture once characterized by outstanding achievements in architecture, astronomy, chronology, painting, and pottery. **2.** the language of this people. See also **Mayan.**

Mayan ('maɪən) *adj.* **1.** of, relating to, or characteristic of the Maya or any of their languages. ~*n.* **2.** a family of Central American Indian languages, including Maya, possibly a member of the Penutian phylum. **3.** another name for a **Maya.**

May apple *n.* **1.** an American plant, *Podophyllum peltatum*, with edible yellowish egg-shaped fruit: family *Podophyllaceae.* **2.** the fruit of this plant.

maybe ('meɪ,bi:) *adv.* **1. a.** perhaps. **b.** (*as sentence modifier*): *maybe I'll come tomorrow.* ~*sentence substitute.* **2.** possibly; neither yes nor no.

May beetle *or* **bug** *n.* another name for **cockchafer** and **June bug.**

May blobs *n.* (*functioning as sing.*) another name for **marsh marigold.**

may blossom *or* **may** *n.* the blossom of the may tree or hawthorn.

Mayday ('meɪ,deɪ) *n.* the international radiotelephone distress signal. [C20: phonetic spelling of French *m'aidez* help me]

May Day *n.* **a.** the first day of May, traditionally a celebration of the coming of spring: in some countries now observed as a holiday in honour of workers. **b.** (*as modifier*): *May-Day celebrations.*

mayest ('meɪɪst) *vb.* a variant of **mayst.**

mayflower ('meɪ,flaʊə) *n.* **1.** any of various plants that bloom in May. **2.** *U.S. and Canadian.* another name for **trailing arbutus. 3.** *Brit.* another name for **hawthorn, cowslip,** or **marsh marigold.**

mayfly ('meɪ,flaɪ) *n., pl.* **-flies. 1.** Also called: **dayfly.** any insect of the order *Ephemeroptera* (or *Ephemerida*). The short-lived adults, found near water, have long tail appendages and large transparent wings; the larvae are aquatic. **2.** *Angling.* an artificial fly resembling this.

mayhap ('meɪ,hæp) *adv.* an archaic word for **perhaps.** [C16: shortened from *it may hap*]

mayhem *or* **maihem** ('meɪhɛm) *n.* **1.** *Law.* the wilful and unlawful infliction of injury upon a person, esp. (formerly) the injuring or removing of a limb rendering him less capable of defending himself against attack. **2.** any violent destruction or confusion. [C15: from Anglo-French *mahem* injury, from Germanic; related to Icelandic *meitha* to hurt. See MAIM]

Maying ('meɪɪŋ) *n.* the traditional celebration of May Day.

mayn't ('meɪənt, meɪnt) *vb. contraction of* may not.

mayonnaise (,meɪə'neɪz) *n.* a thick creamy sauce made from egg yolks, oil, and vinegar or lemon juice, eaten with salads, eggs, etc. [C19: from French, perhaps from *Mahonnais* of *Mahón*, a port in Minorca]

mayor (mɛə) *n.* the chairman and civic head of a municipal corporation in many countries. Scottish equivalent: **provost.** [C13: from Old French *maire*, from Latin *maior* greater. See MAJOR] —'**mayoral** *adj.* —'**mayor,ship** *n.*

mayoralty ('mɛərəltɪ) *n., pl.* **-ties.** the office or term of office of a mayor. [C14: from Old French *mairalté*]

mayoress ('mɛərɪs) *n.* **1.** *Chiefly Brit.* the wife of a mayor. **2.** a female mayor.

maypole ('meɪ,pəʊl) *n.* a tall pole fixed upright in an open space during May-Day celebrations, around which people dance holding streamers attached at its head.

May queen *n.* a girl chosen, esp. for her beauty, to preside over May-Day celebrations.

mayst (meɪst) *or* **mayest** *vb. Archaic or dialect.* (used with the pronoun *thou* or its relative equivalent) a singular form of the present tense of **may.**

may tree *n.* a Brit. name for **hawthorn.**

mayweed ('meɪ,wi:d) *n.* **1.** Also called: **dog fennel, stinking mayweed.** a widespread Eurasian weedy plant, *Anthemis cotula*, having evil-smelling leaves and daisy-like flower heads: family *Compositae* (composites). **2. scentless mayweed.** a similar and related plant, *Tripleurospermum maritimum*, with scentless leaves. [C16: changed from Old English *mægtha* mayweed + WEED[1]]

mazard *or* **mazzard** ('mæzəd) *n.* **1.** an obsolete word for the **head** or **skull. 2.** another word for **mazer.** [C17: altered from MAZER]

Mazdaism *or* **Mazdeism** ('mæzdəˌɪzəm) *n.* another word for **Zoroastrianism.**

maze (meɪz) *n.* **1.** a complex network of paths or passages, esp. one with high hedges in a garden, designed to puzzle those walking through it. Compare **labyrinth** (sense 1). **2.** a similar system represented diagrammatically as a pattern of lines. **3.** any confusing network of streets, pathways, etc.: *a maze of paths.* **4.** a state of confusion. *~vb.* **5** . an archaic or dialect word for **amaze.** [C13: see AMAZE] —'**mazeˌlike** *adj.* —'**mazement** *n.*

mazer ('meɪzə), **mazard,** *or* **mazzard** ('mæzəd) *n. Obsolete.* a large hardwood drinking bowl. [C12: from Old French *masere,* of Germanic origin; compare Old Norse *mösurr* maple]

mazuma (mə'zuːmə) *n. Slang, chiefly U.S.* money. [C20: from Yiddish]

mazurka *or* **mazourka** (mə'zɜːkə) *n.* **1.** a Polish national dance in triple time. **2.** a piece of music composed for this dance. [C19: from Polish: (dance) of *Mazur* (Mazovia) province in Poland]

mazy ('meɪzɪ) *adj.* **mazier, maziest.** of or like a maze; perplexing or confused. —'**mazily** *adv.* —'**maziness** *n.*

mazzard *or* **mazard** ('mæzəd) *n.* a wild sweet cherry tree, *Prunus avium,* often used as a grafting stock for cultivated cherries. [C16: perhaps related to MAZER]

mb *symbol for* millibar.

MB *abbrev. for:* **1.** Bachelor of Medicine. **2.** maternity benefit. **3.** Manitoba. **4.** (in Canada) Medal of Bravery. **5.** *Computer technol.* megabyte.

MBA *abbrev. for* Master of Business Administration.

mbaqanga (ᵊmbɑː'kæŋgə) *n.* a style of Black popular music of urban South Africa. [C20: perhaps from Zulu *umbaqanga* mixture]

MBE *abbrev. for* Member of the Order of the British Empire (a Brit. title).

mbira (ᵊm'biːrə) *n.* an African musical instrument consisting of tuned metal strips attached to a resonating box, which are plucked with the thumbs. Also called: **thumb piano.** [Shona]

mbyte *Computer technol. abbrev. for* megabyte.

MC *abbrev. for:* **1.** Master of Ceremonies. **2.** *Astrology.* Medium Coeli. [Latin: Midheaven]. **3.** (in the U.S.) Member of Congress. **4.** (in Britain) Military Cross. *~***5.** *international car registration for* Monaco.

Mc- *prefix.* a variant of **Mac-.** For names beginning with this prefix, see under **Mac-.**

MCB *abbrev. for* miniature circuit breaker; a small trip switch operated by an overload and used to protect an electric circuit, esp. a domestic circuit as an alternative to a fuse.

MCC (in Britain) *abbrev. for* Marylebone Cricket Club.

MCh *abbrev. for* Master of Surgery. [Latin *Magister Chirurgiae*]

MCom *abbrev. for* Master of Commerce.

MCP *Informal. abbrev. for* male chauvinist pig.

MCPS *abbrev. for* Mechanical Copyright Protection Society.

Md *the chemical symbol for* mendelevium.

MD *abbrev. for:* **1.** Doctor of Medicine. [from Latin *Medicinae Doctor*] **2.** Maryland. **3.** Medical Department. **4.** mentally deficient. **5.** Managing Director.

MDS *abbrev. for* Master of Dental Surgery.

mdse *abbrev. for* merchandise.

me[1] (miː; *unstressed* mɪ) *pron.* (*objective*) **1.** refers to the speaker or writer: *that shocks me; he gave me the glass.* **2.** *Chiefly U.S.* a dialect word for **myself** when used as an indirect object: *I want to get me a car.* *~n.* **3.** *Informal.* the personality of the speaker or writer or something that expresses it: *the real me comes out when I'm happy.* [Old English *mē* (dative); compare Dutch, German *mir,* Latin *mē* (accusative), *mihi* (dative)]

▷**Usage.** Although the nominative case is traditionally required after the verb *to be,* even careful speakers say *it is me* (or *him, her,* etc.) rather than *it is I* in informal contexts. The use of *me,* etc., before an *-ing* form of the verb (*he disapproved of me coming*) is common, but careful speakers and writers use the possessive form: *he disapproved of my coming.*

me[2] (miː) *n.* a variant spelling of **mi.**

Me *chemical symbol for* the methyl group.

ME *abbrev. for:* **1.** Maine. **2.** Marine Engineer. **3.** Mechanical Engineer. **4.** Methodist Episcopal. **5.** Mining Engineer. **6.** Middle English. **7.** (in titles) Most Excellent. **8.** myalgic encephalomyelitis.

Me. *abbrev. for:* **1.** Maine. **2.** Maître.

mea culpa *Latin.* ('meɪɑː 'kʊlpɑː) an acknowledgment of guilt. [literally: my fault]

mead[1] (miːd) *n.* a wine made by fermenting a solution of honey, often with spices added. [Old English *meodu;* related to Old High German *metu,* Greek *methu,* Welsh *medd*]

mead[2] (miːd) *n.* an archaic or poetic word for **meadow.** [Old English *mǣd*]

meadow ('mɛdəʊ) *n.* **1.** an area of grassland, often used for hay or for grazing of animals. **2.** a low-lying piece of grassland, often boggy and near a river. [Old English *mǣdwe,* from *mǣd* MEAD[2]; related to *māwan* to MOW[1]] —'**meadowy** *adj.*

meadow fescue *n.* an erect Eurasian perennial grass, *Festuca pratensis,* with lustrous leaves and stem bases surrounded by dark brown sheaths.

meadow grass *n.* a perennial grass, *Poa pratensis,* that has erect hairless leaves and grows in meadows and similar places in N temperate regions.

meadowlark ('mɛdəʊˌlɑːk) *n.* either of two North American yellow-breasted songbirds, *Sturnella magna* (**eastern meadowlark**) or *S. neglecta* (**western meadowlark**): family *Icteridae* (American orioles).

meadow lily *n.* another name for **Canada lily.**

meadow mouse *n. U.S.* another name for **vole**[1].

meadow mushroom *n.* a saprophytic agaricaceous edible fungus, *Agaricus* (or *Psalliota*) *campestris,* having a white cap with pink or brown gills on the underside.

meadow pipit *n.* a common European songbird, *Anthus pratensis,* with a pale brown speckled plumage: family *Motacillidae* (pipits and wagtails).

meadow rue *n.* any ranunculaceous plant of the N temperate genus *Thalictrum,* esp. *T. flavum,* having clusters of small yellowish-green, white, or purple flowers.

meadow saffron *n.* another name for **autumn crocus.**

meadowsweet ('mɛdəʊˌswiːt) *n.* **1.** a Eurasian rosaceous plant, *Filipendula ulmaria,* with dense heads of small fragrant cream-coloured flowers. See also **dropwort** (sense 1). **2.** any of several North American rosaceous plants of the genus *Spiraea,* having pyramid-shaped sprays of small flowers.

meagre *or U.S.* **meager** ('miːgə) *adj.* **1.** deficient in amount, quality, or extent. **2.** thin or emaciated. **3.** lacking in richness or strength. [C14: from Old French *maigre,* from Latin *macer* lean, poor] —'**meagrely** *or U.S.* '**meagerly** *adv.* —'**meagreness** *or U.S.* '**meagerness** *n.*

meal[1] (miːl) *n.* **1. a.** any of the regular occasions, such as breakfast, lunch, dinner, etc., when food is served and eaten. **b.** (*in combination*): *mealtime.* Related adj.: **prandial. 2.** the food served and eaten. **3. make a meal of.** *Informal.* to perform (a task) with unnecessarily great effort. [Old English *mǣl* measure, set time, meal; related to Old High German *māl* mealtime]

meal[2] (miːl) *n.* **1.** the edible part of a grain or pulse (excluding wheat) ground to a coarse powder, used chiefly as animal food. **2.** *Scot.* oatmeal. **3.** *Chiefly U.S.* maize flour. [Old English *melu;* compare Dutch *meel,* Old High German *melo,* Old Norse *mjöl*] —'**mealless** *adj.*

mealie ('miːlɪ) *n. S. African.* an ear of maize. See also **mealies.** [C19: from Afrikaans *milie,* from Portuguese *milho,* from Latin *milium* millet]

mealie meal *n. S. African.* finely ground maize.

mealie pap *n. S. African.* mealie porridge. [Afrikaans]

mealies ('miːlɪz) *n.* (*functioning as sing.*) a South African word for **maize.**

meal moth *n.* a small pyralid moth, *Pyralis farinalis,* whose larvae are an important pest of stored cereals. The **Indian meal moth** (*Plodia interpunctella*) and the **Mediterranean flour moth** (*Ephestia kuehniella*) are other pyralids with similar habits.

meals on wheels *or* **meals-on-wheels** *n.* (*functioning as sing.*) *Social welfare, Brit.* a service, usually subsidized, and run by a social services department or voluntary body, which delivers hot meals to elderly or housebound people who might otherwise be unable to have them.

meal ticket *n. Slang.* a person, situation, etc., providing a source of livelihood or income. [from original U.S. sense of ticket entitling holder to a meal]

mealworm ('miːlˌwɜːm) *n.* the larva of various beetles of the genus *Tenebrio,* esp. *T. molitor,* feeding on meal, flour, and similar stored foods: family *Tenebrionidae.*

mealy ('miːlɪ) *adj.* **mealier, mealiest. 1.** resembling meal; powdery. **2.** containing or consisting of meal or grain. **3.** sprinkled or covered with meal or similar granules. **4.** (esp. of horses) spotted; mottled. **5.** pale in complexion. **6.** short for **mealy-mouthed.** —'**mealiness** *n.*

mealy bug *n.* any plant-eating homopterous insect of the genus *Pseudococcus* and related genera, coated with a powdery waxy secretion: some species are pests of citrus fruits and greenhouse plants: family *Pseudococcidae.*

mealy-mouthed *adj.* hesitant or afraid to speak plainly; not outspoken. [C16: from MEALY (in the sense: soft, soft-spoken)] —ˌ**mealy-'mouthedness** *n.*

mean[1] (miːn) *vb.* **means, meaning, meant.** (*mainly tr.*) **1.** (*may take a clause as object or an infinitive*) to intend to convey or express. **2.** (*may take a clause as object or an infinitive*) intend: *she didn't mean to hurt it.* **3.** (*may take a clause as object*) to say or do in all seriousness: *the boss means what he says about strikes.* **4.** (*often passive;* often foll. by *for*) to destine or design (for a certain person or purpose): *she was meant for greater things.* **5.** (*may take a clause as object*) to denote or connote; signify; represent: *examples help show exactly what a word means.* **6.** (*may take a clause as object*) to produce; cause: *the weather will mean long traffic delays.* **7.** (*may take a clause as object*) to foretell; portend: *those dark clouds mean rain.* **8.** to have the importance of: *money means nothing to him.* **9.** (*intr.*) to have the intention of behaving or acting (esp. in the phrases **mean well** *or* **mean ill**). **10. mean business.** to be in earnest. [Old English *mænan;* compare Old Saxon *mēnian* to intend, Dutch *meenen*]

mean[2] (miːn) *adj.* **1.** *Chiefly Brit.* miserly, ungenerous, or petty. **2.** humble, obscure, or lowly: *he rose from mean origins to high office.* **3.** despicable, ignoble, or callous: *a mean action.* **4.** poor or shabby: *mean clothing; a mean abode.* **5.** *Informal, chiefly U.S. and Canadian.* bad-tempered; vicious. **6.** *Informal.* ashamed: *he felt mean about not letting the children go to the zoo.* **7.** *Informal, chiefly U.S.* unwell; in low spirits. **8.** *Slang.* excellent; skilful: *he plays a mean trombone.* **9. no mean. a.** of high quality: *no mean performer.* **b.** difficult: *no mean feat.* [C12: from Old English *gemǣne* common; related to Old High German *gimeini,* Latin *communis* common, at first with no pejorative sense] —ˈ**meanly** *adv.* —ˈ**meanness** *n.*

mean[3] (miːn) *n.* **1.** the middle point, state, or course between limits or extremes. **2.** moderation. **3.** *Maths.* **a.** the second and third terms of a proportion, as *b* and *c* in $a/b = c/d$. **b.** another name for **average** (sense 2). See also **geometric mean. 4.** *Statistics.* a statistic obtained by multiplying each possible value of a variable by its probability and then taking the sum or integral over the range of the variable. ~*adj.* **5.** intermediate or medium in size, quantity, etc. **6.** occurring halfway between extremes or limits; average. ~See also **means.** [C14: via Anglo-Norman from Old French *moien,* from Late Latin *mediānus* MEDIAN]

meander (mɪˈændə) *vb.* (*intr.*) **1.** to follow a winding course. **2.** to wander without definite aim or direction. ~*n.* **3.** (*often pl.*) a curve or bend, as in a river. **4.** (*often pl.*) a winding course or movement. **5.** an ornamental pattern, esp. as used in ancient Greek architecture. [C16: from Latin *maeander,* from Greek *Maiandros* the River *Maeander* (Menderes) in SW Turkey] —**meˈanderer** *n.* —**meˈandering** *adj.* —**meˈanderingly** *adv.* —**meˈandrous** *adj.*

mean deviation *n. Statistics.* **1.** the difference between an observed value of a variable and its mean. **2.** Also called: **mean deviation from the mean** (*or* **median**), **average deviation.** a measure of dispersion derived by computing the mean of the absolute values of the differences between observed values of a variable and the variable's mean.

mean distance *n.* the average of the greatest and least distances of a celestial body from its primary.

mean free path *n.* the average distance travelled by a particle, atom, etc., between collisions.

meanie *or* **meany** (ˈmiːnɪ) *n., pl.* **meanies.** *Informal.* **1.** *Chiefly Brit.* a miserly or stingy person. **2.** *Chiefly U.S.* a nasty ill-tempered person.

meaning (ˈmiːnɪŋ) *n.* **1.** the sense or significance of a word, sentence, symbol, etc.; import; semantic or lexical content. **2.** the purpose underlying or intended by speech, action, etc. **3.** the inner, symbolic, or true interpretation, value, or message: *the meaning of a dream.* **4.** valid content; efficacy: *a law with little or no meaning.* **5.** *Philosophy.* **a.** the sense of an expression; its connotation. **b.** the reference of an expression; its denotation. In recent philosophical writings meaning can be used in both the above senses. See also **sense** (sense 13). ~*adj.* **6.** expressive of some sense, intention, criticism, etc.: *a meaning look.* ~See also **well-meaning.**

meaningful (ˈmiːnɪŋfʊl) *adj.* **1.** having great meaning or validity. **2.** eloquent, expressive: *a meaningful silence.* —ˈ**meaningfully** *adv.* —ˈ**meaningfulness** *n.*

meaningless (ˈmiːnɪŋlɪs) *adj.* futile or empty of meaning. —ˈ**meaninglessly** *adv.* —ˈ**meaninglessness** *n.*

mean lethal dose *n.* another term for **median lethal dose.**

mean life *n. Physics.* the average time of existence of an unstable or reactive entity, such as a nucleus, elementary particle, charge carrier, etc.; lifetime. It is equal to the half-life divided by 0.693 15. Symbol: τ

means (miːnz) *n.* **1.** (*functioning as sing. or pl.*) the medium, method, or instrument used to obtain a result or achieve an end: *a means of communication.* **2.** (*functioning as pl.*) resources or income. **3.** (*functioning as pl.*) considerable wealth or income: *a man of means.* **4. by all means.** without hesitation or doubt; certainly: *come with us by all means.* **5. by means of.** with the use or help of. **6. by no manner of means.** definitely not: *he was by no manner of means a cruel man.* **7. by no** (*or* **not by any**) **means.** on no account; in no way: *by no means come!*

mean sea level *n.* (in the UK) the sea level used by the Ordnance Survey as a datum level, determined at Newlyn in Cornwall. See **sea level.**

means of production *pl. n.* (in Marxist theory) the raw materials and means of labour (tools, machines, etc.) employed in the production process.

mean solar day *n.* the time between two successive passages of the mean sun across the meridian at noon. It is the standard for the 24-hour day.

means test *n.* a test involving the checking of a person's income to determine whether he qualifies for financial or social aid from a government. Compare **needs test.**

mean sun *n.* an imaginary sun moving along the celestial equator at a constant speed and completing its annual course in the same time as the sun takes to move round the ecliptic at a varying speed. It is used in the measurement of mean solar time.

meant (mɛnt) *vb.* the past tense and past participle of **mean**[1].

mean time *or* **mean solar time** *n.* the times, at a particular place, measured in terms of the passage of the mean sun, giving 24-hour days (mean solar days) throughout a year.

meantime (ˈmiːnˌtaɪm) *n.* **1.** the intervening time or period, as between events (esp. in the phrase **in the meantime**). ~*adv.* **2.** another word for **meanwhile.**

mean-tone tuning *n.* See **temperament** (sense 4).

meanwhile (ˈmiːnˌwaɪl) *adv.* **1.** during the intervening time or period. **2.** at the same time, esp. in another place. ~*n.* **3.** another word for **meantime.**

meany (ˈmiːnɪ) *n. Informal.* a variant spelling of **meanie.**

meas. *abbrev. for* measure.

measled (ˈmiːzəld) *adj.* (of cattle, sheep, or pigs) infested with tapeworm larvae; measly.

measles (ˈmiːzəlz) *n.* (*functioning as sing. or pl.*) **1.** a highly contagious viral disease common in children, characterized by fever, profuse nasal discharge of mucus, conjunctivitis, and a rash of small red spots spreading from the forehead down to the limbs. Technical names: **morbilli, rubeola.** See also **German measles. 2.** a disease of cattle, sheep, and pigs, caused by infestation with tapeworm larvae. [C14: from Middle Low German *masele* spot on the skin; influenced by Middle English *mesel* leper, from Latin *misellus,* diminutive of *miser* wretched]

measly (ˈmiːzlɪ) *adj.* **-slier, -sliest. 1.** *Informal.* meagre in quality or quantity. **2.** (of meat) measled. **3.** having or relating to measles. [C17: see MEASLES]

measurable (ˈmɛʒərəbᵊl, ˈmɛʒrə-) *adj.* able to be measured; perceptible or significant. —ˌ**measuraˈbility** *or* ˈ**measurableness** *n.* —ˈ**measurably** *adv.*

measure (ˈmɛʒə) *n.* **1.** the extent, quantity, amount, or degree of something, as determined by measurement or calculation. **2.** a device for measuring distance, volume, etc., such as a graduated scale or container. **3.** a system of measurement: *give the size in metric measure.* **4.** a standard used in a system of measurements: *the international prototype kilogram is the measure of mass in SI units.* **5.** a specific or standard amount of something: *a measure of grain; short measure; full measure.* **6.** a basis or standard for comparison: *his work was the measure of all subsequent attempts.* **7.** reasonable or permissible limit or bounds: *we must keep it within measure.* **8.** degree or extent (often in phrases such as **in some measure, in a measure,** etc.): *they gave him a measure of freedom.* **9.** (*often pl.*) a particular action intended to achieve an effect: *they took measures to prevent his leaving.* **10.** a legislative bill, act, or resolution: *to bring in a measure.* **11.** *Music.* another word for **bar**[1] (sense 15a). **12.** *Prosody.* poetic rhythm or cadence; metre. **13.** a metrical foot. **14.** *Poetic.* a melody or tune. **15.** the act of measuring; measurement. **16.** *Archaic.* a dance. **17.** *Printing.* the width of a page or column of type. **18. for good measure.** as an extra precaution or beyond requirements. **19. get the measure of** *or* **get someone's measure.** to assess the nature, character, quality, etc., of someone or something. **20. made to measure.** (of clothes) made to fit an individual purchaser. ~*vb.* **21.** (*tr.;* often foll. by *up*) to determine the size, amount, etc., of by measurement. **22.** (*intr.*) to make a measurement or measurements. **23.** (*tr.*) to estimate or determine: *I measured his strength to be greater than mine.* **24.** (*tr.*) to function as a measurement of: *the ohm measures electrical resistance.* **25.** (*tr.*) to bring into competition or conflict: *he measured his strength against that of his opponent.* **26.** (*intr.*) to be as specified in extent, amount, etc.: *the room measures six feet.* **27.** (*tr.*) to travel or move over as if measuring. **28.** (*tr.*) to adjust or choose: *he measured his approach to suit the character of his client.* **29.** (*intr.*) to allow or yield to measurement. **30. measure one's length.** to fall flat. ~See also **measure off, measure out, measures, measure up.** [C13: from Old French, from Latin *mēnsūra* measure, from *mēnsus,* past participle of *mētīrī* to measure] —ˈ**measurer** *n.*

measured (ˈmɛʒəd) *adj.* **1.** determined by measurement. **2.** slow, stately, or leisurely. **3.** carefully considered; deliberate. —ˈ**measuredly** *adv.* —ˈ**measuredness** *n.*

measured daywork (ˈdeɪˌwɜːk) *n.* a system of wage payment, usually determined by work-study techniques, whereby the wage of an employee is fixed on the understanding that a specific level of work performance will be maintained.

measureless (ˈmɛʒəlɪs) *adj.* limitless, vast, or infinite. —ˈ**measurelessly** *adv.* —ˈ**measurelessness** *n.*

measurement (ˈmɛʒəmənt) *n.* **1.** the act or process of measuring. **2.** an amount, extent, or size determined by measuring. **3.** a system of measures based on a particular standard.

measurement ton *n.* the full name for **ton**[1] (sense 5).

measure off *or* **out** *vb.* (*tr., adv.*) to determine the limits of; mark out: *to measure off an area.*

measure out *vb.* (*tr., adv.*) **1.** to pour or dole out: *they measure out a pint of fluid.* **2.** to administer; mete out: *they measured out harsh punishments.*

measures (ˈmɛʒəz) *pl. n.* rock strata that are characterized by a particular type of sediment or deposit: *coal measures.*

measure up *vb.* **1.** (*adv.*) to determine the size of (something) by measurement. **2. measure up to.** to fulfil (expectations, standards, etc.).

measuring jug *n.* a graduated jug used in cooking to measure ingredients.

measuring worm *n.* the larva of a geometrid moth: it has legs on its front and rear segments only and moves in a series of loops. Also called: **looper, inchworm.**

meat (miːt) *n.* **1.** the flesh of mammals used as food, as distinguished from that of birds and fish. **2.** anything edible, esp. flesh with the texture of meat: *crab meat.* **3.** food, as opposed to drink. **4.** the essence or gist. **5.** an archaic word for **meal**[1]. **6. meat and drink.** a source of pleasure. **7. have one's meat and one's manners.** *Irish informal.* to lose nothing because one's offer is not accepted. [Old English *mete;* related to Old High German *maz* food, Old Saxon *meti,* Gothic *mats*] —**'meatless** *adj.*

meataxe ('miːt,æks) *n.* **1.** a cleaver. **2. mad as a meataxe.** *Austral. and N.Z. informal.* raving.

meatball ('miːt,bɔːl) *n.* **1.** minced beef, shaped into a ball before cooking. **2.** *U.S. and Canadian slang.* a stupid or boring person.

meatus (mɪ'eɪtəs) *n., pl.* **-tuses** *or* **-tus.** *Anatomy.* a natural opening or channel, such as the canal leading from the outer ear to the eardrum. [C17: from Latin: passage, from *meāre* to pass]

meaty ('miːtɪ) *adj.* **meatier, meatiest. 1.** of, relating to, or full of meat: *a meaty stew.* **2.** heavily built; fleshy or brawny. **3.** full of import or interest: *a meaty discussion.* **4.** *Judaism.* another word for **fleishik.** —**'meatily** *adv.* —**'meatiness** *n.*

mecamylamine (,mɛkə'mɪlə,miːn) *n.* a drug administered orally to lower high blood pressure. Formula: $C_{11}H_{21}N.HCl$. [C20: from ME(THYL)+*cam(phane)* (a former name of bornane) + -YL + AMINE]

Mecca ('mɛkə) *n.* (*sometimes not cap.*) a place that attracts many visitors: *Athens is a Mecca for tourists.* [after *Mecca* in W Saudi Arabia, holiest city of Islam and pilgrimage centre]

Meccano (mɪ'kɑːnəʊ) *n. Trademark.* a construction set consisting of miniature metal or plastic parts from which mechanical models can be made.

mech. *abbrev. for:* **1.** mechanical. **2.** mechanics. **3.** mechanism.

mechanic (mɪ'kænɪk) *n.* **1.** a person skilled in maintaining or operating machinery, motors, etc. **2.** *Archaic.* a common labourer. [C14: from Latin *mēchanicus,* from Greek *mēkhanikos,* from *mēkhanē* MACHINE]

mechanical (mɪ'kænɪkᵊl) *adj.* **1.** made, performed, or operated by or as if by a machine or machinery: *a mechanical process.* **2.** concerned with machines or machinery. **3.** relating to or controlled or operated by physical forces. **4.** of or concerned with mechanics. **5.** (of a gesture, etc.) automatic; lacking thought, feeling, etc. **6.** *Philosophy.* accounting for phenomena by physically determining forces. **7.** (of paper, such as newsprint) made from pulp that has been mechanically ground and contains impurities. ~*n.* **8.** *Printing.* another name for **camera-ready copy. 9.** *Archaic.* another word for **mechanic** (sense 2). —**me'chanicalism** *n.* —**me'chanically** *adv.* —**me'chanicalness** *n.*

mechanical advantage *n.* the ratio of the working force exerted by a mechanism to the applied effort.

mechanical drawing *n.* a drawing to scale of a machine, machine component, architectural plan, etc., from which dimensions can be taken.

mechanical engineering *n.* the branch of engineering concerned with the design, construction, and operation of machines and machinery. —**mechanical engineer** *n.*

mechanical equivalent of heat *n. Physics.* a factor for converting units of energy into heat units. It has the value 4.1855 joules per calorie. Symbol: *J*

mechanical instrument *n.* a musical instrument, such as a barrel organ or music box, that plays a preselected piece of music by mechanical means.

mechanician (,mɛkə'nɪʃən) *or* **mechanist** *n.* a person skilled in making machinery and tools; technician.

mechanics (mɪ'kænɪks) *n.* **1.** (*functioning as sing.*) the branch of science, divided into statics, dynamics, and kinematics, concerned with the equilibrium or motion of bodies in a particular frame of reference. See also **quantum mechanics, wave mechanics, statistical mechanics. 2.** (*functioning as sing.*) the science of designing, constructing, and operating machines. **3.** the working parts of a machine. **4.** the technical aspects of something: *the mechanics of poetic style.*

mechanism ('mɛkə,nɪzəm) *n.* **1.** a system or structure of moving parts that performs some function, esp. in a machine. **2.** something resembling a machine in the arrangement and working of its parts: *the mechanism of the ear.* **3.** any form of mechanical device or any part of such a device. **4.** a process or technique, esp. of execution: *the mechanism of novel writing.* **5.** *Philosophy.* **a.** the doctrine that human action can be explained in purely physical terms, whether mechanical or biological. **b.** the explanation of phenomena in causal rather than teleological or essentialist terms. **c.** the view that the task of science is to seek such explanations. **d.** strict determinism. ~Compare **dynamism, vitalism. 6.** *Psychoanal.* **a.** the ways in which psychological forces interact and operate. **b.** a structure having an influence on the behaviour of a person, such as a defence mechanism.

mechanist ('mɛkənɪst) *n.* **1.** a person who accepts a mechanistic philosophy. **2.** another name for a **mechanician.**

mechanistic (,mɛkə'nɪstɪk) *adj.* **1.** *Philosophy.* of or relating to the theory of mechanism. **2.** *Maths.* of or relating to mechanics. —,**mecha'nistically** *adv.*

mechanize *or* **mechanise** ('mɛkə,naɪz) *vb.* (*tr.*) **1.** to equip (a factory, industry, etc.) with machinery. **2.** to make mechanical, automatic, or monotonous. **3.** to equip (an army, etc.) with motorized or armoured vehicles. —,**mechani'zation** *or* ,**mechani'sation** *n.* —**'mecha,nizer** *or* **'mecha,niser** *n.*

mechanoreceptor (,mɛkənəʊrɪ'sɛptə) *n. Physiol.* a sensory receptor, as in the skin, that is sensitive to a mechanical stimulus, such as pressure.

mechanotherapy (,mɛkənəʊ'θɛrəpɪ) *n.* the treatment of disorders or injuries by means of mechanical devices, esp. devices that provide exercise for bodily parts.

Mechlin lace ('mɛklɪn) *n.* bobbin lace made at Mechlin in N Belgium, characterized by patterns outlined by a heavier flat thread. Also called: **malines.**

meck (mɛk) *n. Northeastern Scot. dialect.* a variant of **maik.**

MEcon *abbrev. for* Master of Economics.

meconium (mɪ'kəʊnɪəm) *n.* **1.** the dark green mucoid material that forms the first faeces of a newborn infant. **2.** opium or the juice from the opium poppy. [C17: from New Latin, from Latin: poppy juice (used also of infant's excrement because of similarity in colour), from Greek *mēkōneion,* from *mēkōn* poppy]

meconopsis (,mɛkə'nɒpsɪs) *n.* any plant of the mostly Asiatic papaveraceous genus *Meconopsis,* esp. *M. betonicifolia* (the Tibetan or blue poppy), grown for its showy sky-blue flowers. *M. cambrica* is the Welsh poppy. [New Latin, from Greek *mekon* poppy + -OPSIS]

MEd *abbrev. for* Master of Education.

MED (in New Zealand) *abbrev. for* Municipal Electricity Department.

med. *abbrev. for:* **1.** medical. **2.** medicine. **3.** medieval. **4.** medium.

médaillons (mɛdaɪ'jɔ̃) *pl. n. Cookery.* small round thin pieces of meat, fish, vegetables, etc. Also called: **medallions.** [C20: French: medallions]

medal ('mɛdᵊl) *n.* **1.** a small flat piece of metal bearing an inscription or image, given as an award or commemoration of some outstanding action, event, etc. ~*vb.* **-als, -alling, -alled** *or U.S.* **-als, -aling, -aled. 2.** (*tr.*) to honour with a medal. [C16: from French *médaille,* probably from Italian *medaglia,* ultimately from Latin *metallum* METAL] —**medallic** (mɪ'dælɪk) *adj.*

medallion (mɪ'dæljən) *n.* **1.** a large medal. **2.** an oval or circular decorative device resembling a medal, usually bearing a portrait or relief moulding, used in architecture and textile design. [C17: from French, from Italian *medaglione,* from *medaglia* MEDAL]

medallist *or U.S.* **medalist** ('mɛdᵊlɪst) *n.* **1.** a designer, maker, or collector of medals. **2.** *Chiefly sport.* a winner or recipient of a medal or medals.

Medal of Bravery *n.* a Canadian award for courage. Abbrev.: **MB.**

Medal of Honor *n.* the highest U.S. military decoration, awarded by Congress for conspicuous bravery in action: instituted in 1861 (Navy), 1862 (Army).

medal play *n. Golf.* another name for **stroke play.**

meddle ('mɛdᵊl) *vb.* (*intr.*) **1.** (usually foll. by *with*) to interfere officiously or annoyingly. **2.** (usually foll. by *in*) to involve oneself unwarrantedly: *to meddle in someone's private affairs.* [C14: from Old French *medler,* ultimately from Latin *miscēre* to mix] —**'meddler** *n.* —**'meddling** *adj.* —**'meddlingly** *adv.*

meddlesome ('mɛdᵊlsəm) *adj.* intrusive or meddling. —**'meddlesomely** *adv.* —**'meddlesomeness** *n.*

Mede (miːd) *n.* a member of an Indo-European people of West Iranian speech who established an empire in SW Asia in the 7th and 6th centuries B.C. —**'Median** *n., adj.*

medevac ('mɛdə,væk) *n. Military.* the evacuation of casualties from forward areas to the nearest hospital or base. [C20: from *med(ical) evac(uation)*]

media[1] ('miːdɪə) *n.* **1.** a plural of **medium. 2.** the mass media collectively.

media[2] ('mɛdɪə) *n., pl.* **-diae** (-dɪ,iː). **1.** the middle layer of the wall of a blood or lymph vessel. **2.** one of the main veins in the wing of an insect. **3.** *Phonetics.* **a.** a consonant whose articulation lies midway between that of a voiced and breathed speech sound. **b.** a consonant pronounced with weak voice, as *c* in French *second.* [C19: from Latin *medius* middle]

mediacy ('miːdɪəsɪ) *n.* **1.** the quality or state of being mediate. **2.** a less common word for **mediation.**

mediad ('miːdɪæd) *adj. Anatomy, zoology.* situated near the median line or plane of an organism.

mediaeval (,mɛdɪ'iːvᵊl) *adj.* a variant spelling of **medieval.**

media event *n.* an event that is staged for or exploited by the mass media, whose attention lends it an apparent importance.

medial ('miːdɪəl) *adj.* **1.** of or situated in the middle. **2.** ordinary or average in size. **3.** *Maths.* relating to an average. **4.** another word for **median** (senses 1, 2, 3). **5.** *Zoology.* of or relating to a media. ~*n.* **6.** *Phonetics.* a speech sound between being fortis and lenis; media. [C16: from Late Latin *mediālis,* from *medius* middle] —**'medially** *adv.*

median ('miːdɪən) *adj.* **1.** of, relating to, situated in, or directed towards the middle. **2.** *Biology.* of or relating to the plane that divides an organism or organ into symmetrical parts. **3.** *Statistics.* of or relating to the median. ~*n.* **4.** a middle point, plane, or part. **5.** *Geometry.* **a.** a straight line joining one vertex of a triangle to the midpoint of the opposite side. See also **centroid.** **b.** a straight line joining the midpoints of the nonparallel sides of a trapezium. **6.** *Statistics.* the middle value in a frequency distribution, below and above which lie values with equal total frequencies. **7.** *Statistics.* the middle number or average of the two middle numbers in an ordered sequence of numbers: *7 is the median of both 1, 7, 31 and 2, 5, 9, 16.* **8.** the Canadian word for **central reserve.** [C16: from Latin *mediānus,* from *medius* middle] —'**medianly** *adv.*

median lethal dose *or* **mean lethal dose** *n.* **1.** the amount of a drug or other substance that, when administered to a group of experimental animals, will kill 50 per cent of the group in a specified time. **2.** the amount of ionizing radiation that will kill 50 per cent of a population in a specified time. ~Abbrev.: $\mathbf{LD_{50}}$.

median strip *n.* the U.S. term for **central reserve.**

mediant ('miːdɪənt) *n. Music.* **a.** the third degree of a major or minor scale. **b.** (*as modifier*): *a mediant chord.* [C18: from Italian *mediante,* from Late Latin *mediāre* to be in the middle]

mediastinum (ˌmiːdɪə'staɪnəm) *n., pl.* **-na** (-nə). *Anatomy.* **1.** a membrane between two parts of an organ or cavity such as the pleural tissue between the two lungs. **2.** the part of the thoracic cavity that lies between the lungs, containing the heart, trachea, etc. [C16: from medical Latin, neuter of Medieval Latin *mediastīnus* median, from Latin: low grade of servant, from *medius* mean] —ˌ**medias'tinal** *adj.*

mediate *vb.* ('miːdɪˌeɪt). **1.** (*intr.;* usually foll. by *between* or *in*) to intervene (between parties or in a dispute) in order to bring about agreement. **2.** to bring about (an agreement). **3.** to bring about (an agreement) between parties in a dispute. **4.** to resolve (differences) by mediation. **5.** (*intr.*) to be in a middle or intermediate position. **6.** (*tr.*) to serve as a medium for causing (a result) or transferring (objects, information, etc.). ~*adj.* ('miːdɪɪt). **7.** occurring as a result of or dependent upon mediation. **8.** a rare word for **intermediate. 9.** *Logic.* (of an inference) having more than one premise, esp., being syllogistic in form. [C16: from Late Latin *mediāre* to be in the middle] —'**mediately** *adv.* —'**mediateness** *n.* —'**mediative,** '**mediatory,** *or* ˌ**media'torial** *adj.* —'**mediˌator** *n.* —ˌ**media'torially** *adv.*

mediation (ˌmiːdɪ'eɪʃən) *n.* **1.** the act of mediating; intercession. **2.** *International law.* an attempt to reconcile disputed matters arising between states, esp. by the friendly intervention of a neutral power. **3.** a method of resolving an industrial dispute whereby a third party consults with those involved and recommends a solution which is not, however, binding on the parties.

mediatize *or* **mediatise** ('miːdɪəˌtaɪz) *vb.* (*tr.*) to annex (a state) to another state, allowing the former ruler to retain his title and some authority. [C19: from French *médiatiser;* see MEDIATE, -IZE] —ˌ**mediati'zation** *or* ˌ**mediati'sation** *n.*

medic[1] ('mɛdɪk) *n. Informal.* a doctor, medical orderly, or medical student. [C17: from MEDICAL]

medic[2] ('mɛdɪk) *n.* the usual U.S. spelling of **medick.**

medicable ('mɛdɪkəbəl) *adj.* potentially able to be treated or cured medically. —'**medicably** *adv.*

Medicaid ('mɛdɪˌkeɪd) *n. U.S.* a health assistance programme financed by federal, state, and local taxes to help pay hospital and medical costs for persons of low income. [C20: MEDIC(AL) + AID]

medical ('mɛdɪkəl) *adj.* **1.** of or relating to the science of medicine or to the treatment of patients by drugs, etc., as opposed to surgery. **2.** a less common word for **medicinal.** ~*n.* **3.** *Informal.* a medical examination. [C17: from Medieval Latin *medicālis,* from Latin *medicus* physician, surgeon, from *medērī* to heal] —'**medically** *adv.*

medical certificate *n.* **1.** a document stating the result of a satisfactory medical examination. **2.** a doctor's certificate giving evidence of a person's unfitness for work.

medical examination *n.* an examination carried out to determine the physical fitness of an applicant for a job, life insurance, etc.

medical examiner *n.* **1.** *Chiefly U.S.* a medical expert, usually a physician, employed by a state or local government to determine the cause of sudden death in cases of suspected violence, suicide, etc. Compare **coroner. 2.** a physician who carries out medical examinations.

medical jurisprudence *n.* another name for **forensic medicine.**

medicament (mɪ'dɪkəmənt, 'mɛdɪ-) *n.* a medicine or remedy. [C16: via French from Latin *medicāmentum* from *medicāre* to cure] —**medicamental** (ˌmɛdɪkə'mɛntəl) *or* ˌ**medica'mentary** *adj.*

Medicare ('mɛdɪˌkɛə) *n.* **1.** (in the U.S.) a federally sponsored health insurance programme for persons of 65 or older. **2.** (*often not cap.*) (in Canada) a similar programme covering all citizens. **3.** (in Australia) a government-controlled general health-insurance scheme. [C20: MEDI(CAL) + CARE]

medicate ('mɛdɪˌkeɪt) *vb.* (*tr.*) **1.** to cover or impregnate (a wound, etc.) with an ointment, cream, etc. **2.** to treat (a patient) with a medicine. **3.** to add a medication to (a bandage, shampoo, etc.). [C17: from Latin *medicāre* to heal] —'**mediˌcated** *adj.* —'**medicative** *adj.*

medication (ˌmɛdɪ'keɪʃən) *n.* **1.** treatment with drugs or remedies. **2.** a drug or remedy.

Medicean (ˌmɛdɪ'siːən, -'tʃiː-) *adj.* of, relating to, or characteristic of the Medici, an Italian family of bankers, merchants, and rulers of Florence and Tuscany, prominent in Italian political and cultural history in the 15th, 16th, and 17th centuries.

medicinal (mɛ'dɪsɪnəl) *adj.* **1.** relating to or having therapeutic properties. ~*n.* **2.** a medicinal substance. —**me'dicinally** *adv.*

medicinal leech *n.* a large European freshwater leech, *Hirudo medicinalis,* formerly used in medical bloodletting.

medicine ('mɛdɪsɪn, 'mɛdsɪn) *n.* **1.** any drug or remedy for use in treating, preventing, or alleviating the symptoms of disease. **2.** the science of preventing, diagnosing, alleviating, or curing disease. **3.** any nonsurgical branch of medical science. **4.** the practice or profession of medicine: *he's in medicine.* **5.** something regarded by primitive people as having magical or remedial properties. **6. take one's medicine.** to accept a deserved punishment. **7. a taste** (*or* **dose**) **of one's own medicine.** an unpleasant experience in retaliation for and by similar methods to an unkind or aggressive act. [C13: via Old French from Latin *medicīna* (*ars*) (art of) healing, from *medicus* doctor, from *medērī* to heal]

medicine ball *n.* a heavy ball used for physical training.

medicine chest *n.* a small chest or cupboard for storing medicines, bandages, etc.

medicine lodge *n.* a wooden structure used for magical and religious ceremonies among certain North American Indian peoples.

medicine man *n.* (among certain peoples, esp. North American Indians) a person believed to have supernatural powers of healing; a magician or sorcerer.

medicine shop *n.* (in Malaysia) a Chinese chemist's shop where traditional herbs are sold as well as modern drugs. It is not, however, a dispensary for prescribed medicines.

medick *or U.S.* **medic** ('mɛdɪk) *n.* any small papilionaceous plant of the genus *Medicago,* such as black medick or sickle medick, having yellow or purple flowers and trifoliate leaves. [C15: from Latin *mēdica,* from Greek *mēdikē* (*poa*) Median (grass), a type of clover]

medico ('mɛdɪˌkəʊ) *n., pl.* **-cos.** *Informal.* a doctor or medical student. [C17: via Italian from Latin *medicus*]

medico- *combining form.* medical: *medicolegal.*

medieval *or* **mediaeval** (ˌmɛdɪ'iːvəl) *adj.* **1.** of, relating to, or in the style of the Middle Ages. **2.** *Informal.* old-fashioned; primitive. [C19: from New Latin *medium aevum* the middle age. See MEDIUM, AGE] —ˌ**medi'evally** *or* ˌ**medi'aevally** *adv.*

Medieval Greek *n.* the Greek language from the 7th century A.D. to shortly after the sacking of Constantinople in 1204. Also called: **Middle Greek, Byzantine Greek.** Compare **Koine, Late Greek, Ancient Greek.**

medievalism *or* **mediaevalism** (ˌmɛdɪ'iːvəˌlɪzəm) *n.* **1.** the beliefs, life, or style of the Middle Ages or devotion to those. **2.** a belief, custom, or point of style copied or surviving from the Middle Ages.

medievalist *or* **mediaevalist** (ˌmɛdɪ'iːvəlɪst) *n.* a student or devotee of the Middle Ages. —ˌ**mediˌeval'istic** *or* ˌ**mediˌaeval'istic** *adj.*

Medieval Latin *n.* the Latin language as used throughout Europe in the Middle Ages. It had many local forms incorporating Latinized words from other languages.

medina (mɛ'diːnə) *n.* (*sometimes cap.*) the ancient quarter of any of various North African cities. Compare **kasbah.** [C20: Arabic, literally: town]

mediocre (ˌmiːdɪ'əʊkə, 'miːdɪˌəʊkə) *adj. Often derogatory.* average or ordinary in quality: *a mediocre book.* [C16: via French from Latin *mediocris* moderate, literally: halfway up the mountain, from *medius* middle + *ocris* stony mountain]

mediocrity (ˌmiːdɪ'ɒkrɪtɪ, ˌmɛd-) *n., pl.* **-ties. 1.** the state or quality of being mediocre. **2.** a mediocre person or thing.

meditate ('mɛdɪˌteɪt) *vb.* **1.** (*intr.;* foll. by *on* or *upon*) to think about something deeply. **2.** (*intr.*) to reflect deeply on spiritual matters, esp. as a religious act. **3.** (*tr.*) to plan, consider, or think of doing (something). [C16: from Latin *meditārī* to reflect upon] —'**meditative** *adj.* —'**meditatively** *adv.* —'**meditativeness** *n.* —'**mediˌtator** *n.*

meditation (ˌmɛdɪ'teɪʃən) *n.* **1.** the act of meditating; contemplation; reflection. **2.** contemplation of spiritual matters, esp. as a religious practice.

Mediterranean (ˌmɛdɪtə'reɪnɪən) *adj.* **1.** of, relating to, situated or dwelling on or near the Mediterranean Sea, the inland sea between S Europe, N Africa, and SW Asia. **2.** denoting a postulated subdivision of the Caucasoid race, characterized by slender build and dark complexion. **3.** *Meteorol.* (of a climate) characterized by hot summers and relatively warm winters when most of the annual rainfall occurs. **4.** (*often not cap.*) *Obsolete.* situated in the middle of a landmass; inland. ~*n.* **5.** a native or inhabitant of a Mediterranean country. [C16: from Latin *mediterrāneus,* from *medius* middle + *-terrāneus,* from *terra* land, earth]

Mediterranean fever *n.* another name for **brucellosis.**

Mediterranean fruit fly *n.* a species of dipterous fly, *Ceratitis capitata,* having marbled wings, whose maggots tunnel into fruits such as citrus, peach, and vine in the Mediterranean area, South Africa, and elsewhere: family *Trypetidae.* Also called: **Medfly.**

medium (ˈmiːdɪəm) *adj.* **1.** midway between extremes; average: *a medium size.* **2.** (of a colour) reflecting or transmitting a moderate amount of light: *a medium red.* Compare **light**[1] (sense 28), **dark** (sense 2). ~*n., pl.* **-dia** (-dɪə) *or* **-diums. 3.** an intermediate or middle state, degree, or condition; mean: *the happy medium.* **4.** an intervening substance or agency for transmitting or producing an effect; vehicle: *air is a medium for sound.* **5.** a means or agency for communicating or diffusing information, news, etc., to the public: *television is a powerful medium.* **6.** a person supposedly used as a spiritual intermediary between the dead and the living. **7.** the substance in which specimens of animals and plants are preserved or displayed. **8.** *Biology.* short for **culture medium. 9.** the substance or surroundings in which an organism naturally lives or grows. **10.** *Art.* **a.** the category of a work of art, as determined by its materials and methods of production: *the medium of wood engraving.* **b.** the materials used in a work of art. **11.** any solvent in which pigments are mixed and thinned. **12.** any one of various sizes of writing or printing paper, esp. 18½ by 23½ inches or 17½ by 22 inches (**small medium**). ~See also **mediums.** [C16: from Latin: neuter singular of *medius* middle]

▷**Usage.** Careful writers and speakers do not use *media* as a singular noun when referring to a medium of mass communication, although this use is common: *television is a valuable medium* (not *media*) *for advertising.*

medium-dated *adj.* (of a gilt-edged security) having between five and fifteen years to run before redemption. Compare **long-dated, short-dated.**

medium frequency *n.* a radio-frequency band or radio frequency lying between 3000 and 300 kilohertz. Abbrev.: **MF.**

medium of exchange *n.* anything acceptable as a measure of value and a standard of exchange for goods and services in a particular country, region, etc.

medium-range ballistic missile *n.* a missile that can carry a nuclear weapon with a range of 800 to 2400 km. Abbrev.: **MRBM.**

mediums (ˈmiːdɪəmz) *pl. n.* medium-dated gilt-edged securities.

medium wave *n.* **a.** a radio wave with a wavelength between 100 and 1000 metres. **b.** (*as modifier*): *a medium-wave broadcast.*

medlar (ˈmɛdlə) *n.* **1.** a small Eurasian rosaceous tree, *Mespilus germanica.* **2.** the fruit of this tree, which resembles the crab apple and is not edible until it has begun to decay. **3.** any of several other rosaceous trees or their fruits. [C14: from Old French *medlier,* from Latin *mespilum* medlar fruit, from Greek *mespilon*]

medley (ˈmɛdlɪ) *n.* **1.** a mixture of various types or elements. **2.** a musical composition consisting of various tunes arranged as a continuous whole. **3.** Also called: **medley relay. a.** *Swimming.* a race in which a different stroke is used for each length. **b.** *Athletics.* a relay race in which each leg has a different distance. **4.** an archaic word for **melee.** ~*adj.* **5.** of, being, or relating to a mixture or variety. [C14: from Old French *medlee,* from *medler* to mix, quarrel]

Médoc (meɪˈdɒk, ˈmɛdɒk; *French* medɔk) *n.* a fine red wine from Médoc district of SW France

medulla (mɪˈdʌlə) *n., pl.* **-las** *or* **-lae** (-liː). **1.** *Anatomy.* **a.** the innermost part of an organ or structure. **b.** short for **medulla oblongata. 2.** *Botany.* another name for **pith** (sense 4). [C17: from Latin: marrow, pith, probably from *medius* middle] —**meˈdullary** *or* **meˈdullar** *adj.*

medulla oblongata (ˌɒblɒŋˈgɑːtə) *n., pl.* **medulla oblongatas** *or* **medullae oblongatae** (mɪˈdʌliː ˌɒblɒŋˈgɑːtiː). the lower stalklike section of the brain, continuous with the spinal cord, containing control centres for the heart and lungs. [C17: New Latin: oblong-shaped medulla]

medullary ray *n.* any of the sheets of conducting tissue that run radially through the vascular tissue of some higher plants.

medullary sheath *n.* **1.** *Anatomy.* a myelin layer surrounding and insulating certain nerve fibres. **2.** a layer of thick-walled cells surrounding the pith of the stems of some higher plants.

medullated (ˈmɛdəˌleɪtɪd, mɪˈdʌl-) *adj.* **1.** *Anatomy.* encased in a myelin sheath. **2.** having a medulla.

medulloblastoma (mɪˌdʌləʊblæsˈtəʊmə) *n.* a rapidly growing brain tumour that develops in children and is responsive to radiotherapy.

medusa (mɪˈdjuːzə) *n., pl.* **-sas** *or* **-sae** (-ziː). **1.** another name for **jellyfish** (senses 1, 2). **2.** one of the two forms in which a coelenterate exists. It has a jelly-like umbrella-shaped body, is free swimming, and produces gametes. Also called: **medusoid, medusan.** Compare **polyp.** [C18: from the likeness of its tentacles to the snaky locks of *Medusa,* one of the three Gorgons of Greek mythology] —**meˈdusan** *adj.*

medusoid (mɪˈdjuːzɔɪd) *adj.* **1.** of, relating to, or resembling a medusa. ~*n.* **2.** another name for **medusa** (sense 2).

mee (miː) *n.* (in Malaysia) noodles or a dish containing noodles. [from Chinese (Cantonese) *mien* noodles]

meed (miːd) *n. Archaic.* a recompense; reward. [Old English: wages; compare Old High German *mēta* pay]

meek (miːk) *adj.* **1.** patient, long-suffering, or submissive in disposition or nature; humble. **2.** spineless or spiritless; compliant. **3.** an obsolete word for **gentle.** [C12: related to Old Norse *mjūkr* amenable; compare Welsh *mwytho* to soften] —ˈ**meekly** *adv.* —ˈ**meekness** *n.*

meerkat (ˈmɪəˌkæt) *n.* any of several South African mongooses, esp. *Suricata suricatta* (**slender-tailed meerkat** or **suricate**), which has a lemur-like face and four-toed feet. [C19: from Dutch: sea-cat]

meerschaum (ˈmɪəʃəm) *n.* **1.** Also called: **sepiolite.** a white, yellowish, or pink compact earthy mineral consisting of hydrated magnesium silicate: used to make tobacco pipes and as a building stone. Formula: $Mg_2Si_3O_6(OH)_4$. **2.** a tobacco pipe having a bowl made of this mineral. [C18: German, literally: sea foam]

meet[1] (miːt) *vb.* **meets, meeting, met. 1.** (sometimes foll. by *up* or (*U.S.*) *with*) to come together (with), either by design or by accident; encounter: *I met him unexpectedly; we met at the station.* **2.** to come into or be in conjunction or contact with (something or each other): *the roads meet in the town; the sea meets the sky.* **3.** (*tr.*) to come to or be at the place of arrival of: *to meet a train.* **4.** to make the acquaintance of or be introduced to (someone or each other): *have you two met?* **5.** to gather in the company of (someone or each other): *the board of directors meets on Tuesday.* **6.** to come into the presence of (someone or each other) as opponents: *Joe meets Fred in the boxing match.* **7.** (*tr.*) to cope with effectively; satisfy: *to meet someone's demands.* **8.** (*tr.*) to be apparent to (esp. in the phrase **meet the eye**). **9.** (*tr.*) to return or counter: *to meet a blow with another.* **10.** to agree with (someone or each other): *we met him on the price he suggested.* **11.** (*tr.;* sometimes foll. by *with*) to experience; suffer: *he met his death in a road accident.* **12.** to occur together: *courage and kindliness met in him.* **13.** (*tr.*) *Caribbean.* to find (a person, situation, etc.) in a specified condition: *I met the door open.* ~*n.* **14.** the assembly of hounds, huntsmen, etc., prior to a hunt. **15.** a meeting, esp. a sports meeting. **16.** *U.S.* the place where the paths of two railway trains meet or cross. [Old English *mētan;* related to Old Norse *mœta,* Old Saxon *mōtian*] —ˈ**meeter** *n.*

meet[2] (miːt) *adj. Archaic.* proper, fitting, or correct. [C13: from variant of Old English *gemǣte;* related to Old High German *māza* suitability, Old Norse *mætr* valuable] —ˈ**meetly** *adv.*

meeting (ˈmiːtɪŋ) *n.* **1.** an act of coming together; encounter. **2.** an assembly or gathering. **3.** a conjunction or union. **4.** a sporting competition, as of athletes, or of horse racing.

meeting house *n.* **1.** the place in which certain religious groups, esp. Quakers, hold their meetings for worship. **2.** Also called: **wharepuni.** *N.Z.* a large Maori tribal hall.

mega (ˈmɛgə) *adj. Slang.* extremely good, great, or successful. [C20: probably independent use of MEGA-]

mega- *combining form.* **1.** denoting 10^6: *megawatt.* Symbol: M **2.** (in computer technology) denoting 2^{20} (1 048 576): *megabyte.* **3.** large or great: *megalith.* **4.** *Informal.* greatest: *megastar.* [from Greek *megas* huge, powerful]

megabit (ˈmɛgəˌbɪt) *n. Computer technol.* **1.** one million bits. **2.** 2^{20} bits.

megabuck (ˈmɛgəˌbʌk) *n. U.S. and Canadian slang.* **a.** a million dollars. **b.** (*as modifier*): *a megabuck movie.*

megabyte (ˈmɛgəˌbaɪt) *n. Computer technol.* 2^{20} or 1 048 576 bytes. Abbrevs.: **MB, mbyte.** See also **mega-** (sense 2).

megacephaly (ˌmɛgəˈsɛfəlɪ) *or* **megalocephaly** *n.* the condition of having an unusually large head or cranial capacity. It can be of congenital origin or result from an abnormal overgrowth of the facial bones. Compare **microcephaly.** —**megacephalic** (ˌmɛgəsɪˈfælɪk), ˌ**megaˈcephalous,** ˌ**megaloceˈphalic,** *or* ˌ**megaloˈcephalous** *adj.*

megadeath (ˈmɛgəˌdɛθ) *n.* the death of a million people, esp. in a nuclear war or attack.

megadose (ˈmɛgəˌdəʊs) *n.* a very large dose, as of a medicine, vitamin, etc.

megafauna (ˈmɛgəˌfɔːnə) *n.* the component of the fauna of a region or period that comprises the larger terrestrial animals.

megaflop (ˈmɛgəˌflɒp) *n. Computer technol.* a measure of processing speed, consisting of a million floating-point operations a second. [C20: from MEGA- + *flo(ating) p(oint)*]

megagamete (ˌmɛgəgæˈmiːt) *n.* another name for **macrogamete.**

megahertz (ˈmɛgəˌhɜːts) *n., pl.* **-hertz.** one million hertz; one million cycles per second. Symbol: **MHz.** Former name: **megacycle.**

megalith (ˈmɛgəlɪθ) *n.* a stone of great size, esp. one forming part of a prehistoric monument. See also **alignment** (sense 6), **circle** (sense 11). —ˌ**megaˈlithic** *adj.*

megalithic tomb *n.* a burial chamber constructed of large stones, either underground or covered by a mound and usually consisting of long transepted corridors (**gallery graves**) or of a distinct chamber and passage (**passage graves**). The tombs may date from the 4th millennium B.C.

megalo- *or before a vowel* **megal-** *combining form.* indicating greatness, or abnormal size: *megalopolis; megaloblast.* [from Greek *megas* great]

megaloblast (ˈmɛgələʊˌblɑːst) *n.* an abnormally large red blood cell present in certain types of anaemia. —**megaloblastic** (ˌmɛgələʊˈblæstɪk) *adj.*

megaloblastic anaemia *n.* any form of anaemia, esp. pernicious anaemia, characterized by the presence of megaloblasts in the blood or bone marrow.

megalocardia (ˌmɛgələʊˈkɑːdɪə) *n. Pathol.* abnormal increase in the size of the heart. Also called: **cardiomegaly.**

megalocephaly (ˌmɛgələʊˈsɛfəlɪ) *n.* another word for **megacephaly.**

megalomania (ˌmɛgələʊˈmeɪnɪə) *n.* **1.** a mental illness characterized by delusions of grandeur, power, wealth, etc. **2.** *Informal.* a lust or craving for power. —ˌ**megaloˈmaniac** *adj., n.* —**megalomaniacal** (ˌmɛgələʊməˈnaɪəkᵊl) *adj.*

megalopolis (ˌmɛgəˈlɒpəlɪs) *n.* an urban complex, usually comprising several large towns. [C20: MEGALO- + Greek *polis* city] —**megalopolitan** (ˌmɛgələˈpɒlɪtᵊn) *adj., n.*

megalosaur (ˈmɛgələʊˌsɔː) *n.* any very large Jurassic or Cretaceous bipedal carnivorous dinosaur of the genus *Megalosaurus,* common in Europe: suborder *Theropoda* (theropods). [C19: from New Latin *megalosaurus,* from MEGALO- + Greek *sauros* lizard] —ˌ**megaloˈsaurian** *adj., n.*

megaphanerophyte (ˌmɛgəˈfænərəʊˌfaɪt) *n. Botany.* any tree with a height over 30 metres.

megaphone (ˈmɛgəˌfəʊn) *n.* a funnel-shaped instrument used to amplify the voice. See also **loud-hailer.** —**megaphonic** (ˌmɛgəˈfɒnɪk) *adj.* —ˌ**megaˈphonically** *adv.*

megaphyll (ˈmɛgəfɪl) *n. Botany.* the relatively large type of leaf produced by ferns and seed plants. Compare **microphyll.**

megapode (ˈmɛgəˌpəʊd) *n.* any ground-living gallinaceous bird of the family *Megapodiidae,* of Australia, New Guinea, and adjacent islands. Their eggs incubate in mounds of sand, rotting vegetation, etc., by natural heat. Also called: **mound-builder.** See also **brush turkey, mallee fowl.**

megaron (ˈmɛgəˌrɒn) *n., pl.* **-ra** (-rə). a tripartite rectangular room containing a central hearth surrounded by four pillars, found in Bronze Age Greece and Asia Minor. [from Greek, literally: hall, from *megas* large]

megascopic (ˌmɛgəˈskɒpɪk) *adj.* another word for **macroscopic.**

megasporangium (ˌmɛgəspɔːˈrændʒɪəm) *n., pl.* **-gia** (-dʒɪə). the structure in certain ferns in which the megaspores are formed: corresponds to the ovule in seed plants. Compare **microsporangium.**

megaspore (ˈmɛgəˌspɔː) *n.* **1.** Also called: **macrospore.** the larger of the two types of spore produced by some ferns, which develops into the female gametophyte. Compare **microspore** (sense 1). **2.** the embryo sac of flowering plants. —ˌ**megaˈsporic** *adj.*

megasporophyll (ˌmɛgəˈspɔːrəfɪl) *n.* a leaf on which the megaspores are formed: corresponds to the carpel of a flowering plant. Compare **microsporophyll.** [C20: from MEGA- + SPOROPHYLL]

megass *or* **megasse** (məˈgæs) *n.* another name for **bagasse** (sense 2). [C19: of obscure origin]

megastar (ˈmɛgəˌstɑː) *n.* a very well-known personality in the entertainment business.

megathere (ˈmɛgəˌθɪə) *n.* any of various gigantic extinct American sloths of the genus *Megatherium* and related genera, common in late Cenozoic times. [C19: from New Latin *megathērium,* from MEGA- + *-there,* from Greek *thērion* wild beast] —ˌ**megaˈtherian** *adj.*

megaton (ˈmɛgəˌtʌn) *n.* **1.** one million tons. **2.** an explosive power, esp. of a nuclear weapon, equal to the power of one million tons of TNT. Abbrev.: **mt.** —**megatonic** (ˌmɛgəˈtɒnɪk) *adj.*

megavolt (ˈmɛgəˌvɒlt) *n.* one million volts. Symbol: MV

megawatt (ˈmɛgəˌwɒt) *n.* one million watts. Symbol: MW

Me generation *n.* the generation, originally in the 1970s, characterized by self-absorption; latterly, in the 1980s, characterized by material greed.

Megger (ˈmɛgə) *n. Trademark.* an instrument that generates a high voltage in order to test the resistance of insulation, etc.

megillah (məˈgɪlə; *Hebrew* migiˈla) *n., pl.* **-lahs** *or* **-loth** (*Hebrew* -ˈlɔt). *Judaism.* **1.** a scroll of the Book of Esther, read on the festival of Purim. **2.** *Slang.* anything, such as a story or letter, that is too long or unduly drawn out. [Hebrew: scroll, from *galal* to roll]

megilp *or* **magilp** (məˈgɪlp) *n.* an oil-painting medium of linseed oil mixed with mastic varnish or turpentine. [C18: of unknown origin]

megohm (ˈmɛgˌəʊm) *n.* one million ohms. Symbol: MΩ

megrim[1] (ˈmiːgrɪm) *n. Archaic.* **1.** (*often pl.*) a caprice. **2.** a migraine. [C14: see MIGRAINE]

megrim[2] (ˈmiːgrɪm) *n.* a flatfish, *Lepidorhombus whiffiagonis,* of the turbot family, having a yellowish translucent body up to 50 cm (20 in.) in length, found in European waters, and caught for food. [C19: of uncertain origin]

megrims (ˈmiːgrɪmz) *n.* (*functioning as sing.*) **1.** *Now rare.* a fit of depression. **2.** a disease of horses and cattle; staggers.

meibomian cyst (maɪˈbəʊmɪən) *n.* another name for **chalazion.** [C19: named after H. *Meibom* (1638–1700), German anatomist]

meibomian gland *n.* any of the small sebaceous glands in the eyelid, beneath the conjunctiva.

meiny *or* **meinie** (ˈmeɪnɪ) *n., pl.* **meinies.** *Obsolete.* **1.** a retinue or household. **2.** *Scot.* a crowd. [C13: from Old French *mesnie,* from Vulgar Latin *mansiōnāta* (unattested), from Latin *mansiō* a lodging; see MANSION]

meiocyte (ˈmaɪəʊˌsaɪt) *n. Botany.* a cell that divides by meiosis to produce four haploid spores (**meiospores**).

meiofauna (ˈmaɪəʊˌfɔːnə) *n.* the component of the fauna of a sea or lake bed comprising small (but not microscopic) animals, such as tiny worms and crustaceans. [C20: from Greek *meiōn* less + FAUNA] —ˌ**meioˈfaunal** *adj.*

meiosis (maɪˈəʊsɪs) *n., pl.* **-ses** (-ˌsiːz). **1.** a type of cell division in which a nucleus divides into four daughter nuclei, each containing half the chromosome number of the parent nucleus: occurs in all sexually reproducing organisms in which haploid gametes or spores are produced. Compare **mitosis.** See also **prophase** (sense 2). **2.** *Rhetoric.* another word for **litotes. 3.** *Rare.* any division or splitting. [C16: via New Latin from Greek: a lessening, from *meioun* to diminish, from *meiōn* less] —**meiotic** (maɪˈɒtɪk) *adj.* —**meiˈotically** *adv.*

Meissner effect (ˈmaɪsnə) *n. Physics.* the phenomenon in which magnetic flux is excluded from a substance when it is in a superconducting state, except for a thin layer at the surface. [C20: named after Fritz Walther *Meissner* (1882–1974), German physicist]

Meistersinger (ˈmaɪstəˌsɪŋə) *n., pl.* **-singer** *or* **-singers.** a member of one of the various German guilds of workers or craftsmen organized to compose and perform poetry and music. These flourished in the 15th and 16th centuries. [C19: German: master singer]

mel (mɛl) *n. Pharmacol.* a pure form of honey used in pharmaceutical products. [from Latin]

melaleuca (ˌmɛləˈluːkə) *n.* any shrub or tree of the mostly Australian myrtaceous genus *Melaleuca,* found in sandy or swampy regions. [C19: New Latin, from Greek *melas* black + *leukos* white, from its black trunk and white branches]

melamine (ˈmɛləˌmiːn) *n.* **1.** a colourless crystalline compound used in making synthetic resins; 2,4,6-triamino-1,3,5-triazine. Formula: $C_3H_6N_6$. **2.** melamine resin or a material made from this resin. [C19: from German *Melamin,* from *Melam* distillate of ammonium thiocyanate, with *-am* representing *ammonia*]

melamine resin *n.* a thermosetting amino resin, stable to heat and light, produced from melamine and used for moulded products, adhesives, and surface coatings.

melancholia (ˌmɛlənˈkəʊlɪə) *n.* a former name for **depression.** —ˌ**melanˈcholiˌac** *adj., n.*

melancholic (ˌmɛlənˈkɒlɪk) *adj.* **1.** relating to or suffering from melancholy or melancholia. ~*n.* **2.** a person who suffers from melancholia. —ˌ**melanˈcholically** *adv.*

melancholy (ˈmɛlənkəlɪ) *n., pl.* **-cholies. 1.** a constitutional tendency to gloominess or depression. **2.** a sad thoughtful state of mind; pensiveness. **3.** *Archaic.* **a.** a gloomy character, thought to be caused by too much black bile. **b.** one of the four bodily humours; black bile. See **humour** (sense 8). ~*adj.* **4.** characterized by, causing, or expressing sadness, dejection, etc. [C14: via Old French from Late Latin *melancholia,* from Greek *melankholia,* from *melas* black + *kholē* bile] —**melancholily** (ˈmɛlənˌkɒlɪlɪ) *adv.* —ˈ**melanˌcholiness** *n.*

Melanesian (ˌmɛləˈniːzɪən) *adj.* **1.** of or relating to the Pacific islands of Melanesia, their people, or their languages. ~*n.* **2.** a native or inhabitant of Melanesia: generally Negroid with frizzy hair and small stature. **3.** a group or branch of languages spoken in Melanesia, belonging to the Malayo-Polynesian family. **4.** See also **Neo-Melanesian.**

melange *or* **mélange** (meɪˈlɑːnʒ) *n.* **1.** a mixture; confusion. **2.** *Geology.* a totally disordered mixture of rocks of different shapes, sizes, ages, and origins. [C17: from French *mêler* to mix. See MEDLEY]

melanic (məˈlænɪk) *adj.* relating to melanism or melanosis.

melanin (ˈmɛlənɪn) *n.* any of a group of black or dark brown pigments present in the hair, skin, and eyes of man and animals: produced in excess in certain skin diseases and in melanomas.

melanism (ˈmɛləˌnɪzəm) *n.* **1.** the condition in man and animals of having dark-coloured or black skin, feathers, etc. **Industrial melanism** is the occurrence of dark varieties of animals, esp. moths, in smoke-blackened industrial regions, in which they are well camouflaged. **2.** another name for **melanosis.** —ˌ**melaˈnistic** *adj.*

melanite (ˈmɛləˌnaɪt) *n.* a black variety of andradite garnet.

melano- *or before a vowel* **melan-** *combining form.* black or dark: *melanin; melanism; melanocyte; melanoma.* [from Greek *melas* black]

Melanochroi (ˌmɛləˈnɒkrəʊˌaɪ) *pl. n.* a postulated subdivision of the Caucasoid race, characterized by dark hair and pale complexion. [C19: New Latin from Greek, from *melas* dark + *ōchros* pale] —**Melanochroid** (ˌmɛləˈnɒkrɔɪd) *adj.*

melanocyte (ˈmɛlənəʊˌsaɪt) *n. Anatomy, zoology.* a cell, usually in the epidermis, that contains melanin.

melanoid (ˈmɛləˌnɔɪd) *adj.* **1.** resembling melanin; dark coloured. **2.** characterized by or resembling melanosis.

melanoma (ˌmɛləˈnəʊmə) *n., pl.* **-mas** *or* **-mata** (-mətə). *Pathol.* a malignant tumour composed of melanocytes, occurring esp. in the skin, often as a result of excessive exposure to sunlight.

melanosis (ˌmɛləˈnəʊsɪs) *or* **melanism** (ˈmɛləˌnɪzəm) *n. Pathol.* a skin condition characterized by excessive deposits of melanin. —**melanotic** (ˌmɛləˈnɒtɪk) *adj.*

melanous (ˈmɛlənəs) *adj.* having a dark complexion and black hair. —**melanosity** (ˌmɛləˈnɒsɪtɪ) *n.*

melaphyre (ˈmɛləˌfaɪə) *n. Geology, obsolete.* a type of weathered amygdaloidal basalt or andesite. [C19: via French from Greek *melas* black + (*por*)*phura* purple]

melatonin (ˌmɛlə'təʊnɪn) *n.* the hormone-like secretion of the pineal gland, causing skin colour changes in some animals and thought to be involved in reproductive function. [C20: probably from MELA(NOCYTE) + (SERO)TONIN]

Melba ('mɛlbə) *n.* **do a Melba.** *Austral slang.* to make repeated farewell appearances. [after Dame Nellie *Melba* (1861–1931), Australian opera singer]

Melba sauce *n.* a sweet sauce made from fresh raspberries and served with peach melba, fruit sundaes, etc. [C20: named after Dame Nellie *Melba*]

Melba toast *n.* very thin crisp toast. [C20: named after Dame Nellie *Melba*]

Melchite ('mɛlkaɪt) *Eastern Churches.* ~*adj.* **1.** of or relating to the Uniat Greek Catholic Church in Syria, Egypt, and Israel. ~*n.* **2.** a member of this Church. [C17: from Church Latin *Melchīta,* from Medieval Greek *Melkhītēs,* literally: royalist, from Syriac *malkā* king]

meld[1] (mɛld) *vb.* **1.** (in some card games) to declare or lay down (cards), which then score points. ~*n.* **2.** the act of melding. **3.** a set of cards for melding. [C19: from German *melden* to announce; related to Old English *meldian*]

meld[2] (mɛld) *vb.* to blend or become blended; combine. [C20: blend of MELT + WELD[1]]

melee *or* **mêlée** ('mɛleɪ) *n.* a noisy riotous fight or brawl. [C17: from French *mêlée.* See MEDLEY]

meliaceous (ˌmiːlɪ'eɪʃɪəs) *adj.* of, relating to, or belonging to the *Meliaceae,* a family of tropical and subtropical trees, including mahogany, some of which yield valuable timber. [C19: from New Latin *Melia* type genus, from Greek: ash]

melic ('mɛlɪk) *adj.* (of poetry, esp. ancient Greek lyric poems) intended to be sung. [C17: via Latin from Greek *melikos,* from *melos* song]

melick ('mɛlɪk) *n.* either of two pale green perennial grasses of the genus *Melica,* related to fescue, esp. **wood melick** (*M. uniflora*) having branching flower heads, that are common in woodlands. [New Latin *melica,* of unknown origin]

melilot ('mɛlɪˌlɒt) *n.* any papilionaceous plant of the Old World genus *Melilotus,* having narrow clusters of small white or yellow fragrant flowers. Also called: **sweet clover.** [C15: via Old French from Latin *melilōtos,* from Greek: sweet clover, from *meli* honey + *lōtos* LOTUS]

melinite ('mɛlɪˌnaɪt) *n.* a high explosive made from picric acid. [C19: via French from Greek *mēlinos* (colour) of a quince, from *mēlon* fruit, quince]

meliorate ('miːlɪəˌreɪt) *vb.* a variant of **ameliorate.** —'**meliorable** *adj.* —**meliorative** ('miːlɪərətɪv) *adj., n.* —'**melioˌrator** *n.*

melioration (ˌmiːlɪə'reɪʃən) *n.* the act or an instance of improving or the state of being improved.

meliorism ('miːlɪəˌrɪzəm) *n.* the notion that the world can be improved by human effort. [C19: from Latin *melior* better] —'**meliorist** *adj., n.* —ˌ**melio'ristic** *adj.*

melisma (mɪ'lɪzmə) *n., pl.* **-mata** (-mətə) *or* **-mas.** *Music.* an expressive vocal phrase or passage consisting of several notes sung to one syllable. [C19: from Greek: melody] —**melismatic** (ˌmɛlɪz'mætɪk) *adj.*

melliferous (mɪ'lɪfərəs) *or* **mellific** (mɪ'lɪfɪk) *adj.* forming or producing honey. [C17: from Latin *mellifer,* from *mel* honey + *ferre* to bear]

mellifluous (mɪ'lɪfluəs) *or* **mellifluent** *adj.* (of sounds or utterances) smooth or honeyed; sweet. [C15: from Late Latin *mellifluus* flowing with honey, from Latin *mel* honey + *fluere* to flow] —**mel'lifluously** *or* **mel'lifluently** *adv.* —**mel'lifluousness** *or* **mel'lifluence** *n.*

melliphagous (mɪ'lɪfəgəs) *or* **mellivorous** (mɪ'lɪvərəs) *adj. Zoology.* (of an animal) feeding on honey. [C19: from Latin *mel* honey + Greek *-phagos,* from *phagein* to consume]

mellophone ('mɛləˌfəʊn) *n. Music.* a brass band instrument similar in tone to a French horn. [C20: from MELLOW + -PHONE]

mellow ('mɛləʊ) *adj.* **1.** (esp. of fruits) full-flavoured; sweet; ripe. **2.** (esp. of wines) well-matured. **3.** (esp. of colours or sounds) soft or rich. **4.** kind-hearted, esp. through maturity or old age. **5.** genial, as through the effects of alcohol. **6.** (of soil) soft and loamy. ~*vb.* **7.** to make or become mellow; soften; mature. [C15: perhaps from Old English *meru* soft (as through ripeness)] —'**mellowly** *adv.* —'**mellowness** *n.*

melodeon *or* **melodion** (mɪ'ləʊdɪən) *n. Music.* **1.** a type of small accordion. **2.** a type of keyboard instrument similar to the harmonium. [C19: from German, from *Melodie* melody]

melodic (mɪ'lɒdɪk) *adj.* **1.** of or relating to melody. **2.** of or relating to a part in a piece of music. **3.** tuneful or melodious. —**me'lodically** *adv.*

melodic minor scale *n. Music.* a minor scale modified from the natural by the sharpening of the sixth and seventh when taken in ascending order and the restoration of their original pitches when taken in descending order. See **minor** (sense 4a). Compare **harmonic minor scale.**

melodious (mɪ'ləʊdɪəs) *adj.* **1.** having a tune that is pleasant to the ear. **2.** of or relating to melody; melodic. —**me'lodiously** *adv.* —**me'lodiousness** *n.*

melodist ('mɛlədɪst) *n.* **1.** a composer of melodies. **2.** a singer.

melodize *or* **melodise** ('mɛləˌdaɪz) *vb.* **1.** (*tr.*) to provide with a melody. **2.** (*tr.*) to make melodious. **3.** (*intr.*) to sing or play melodies. —'**meloˌdizer** *or* '**meloˌdiser** *n.*

melodrama ('mɛləˌdrɑːmə) *n.* **1.** a play, film, etc., characterized by extravagant action and emotion. **2.** (formerly) a romantic drama characterized by sensational incident, music, and song. **3.** overdramatic emotion or behaviour. **4.** a poem or part of a play or opera spoken to a musical accompaniment. [C19: from French *mélodrame,* from Greek *melos* song + *drame* DRAMA] —**melodramatist** (ˌmɛlə'dræmətɪst) *n.* —**melodramatic** (ˌmɛlədrə'mætɪk) *adj.* —ˌ**melodra'matically** *adv.*

melodramatize *or* **melodramatise** (ˌmɛləʊ'dræməˌtaɪz) *vb.* (*tr.*) to make melodramatic.

melody ('mɛlədɪ) *n., pl.* **-dies.** **1.** *Music.* **a.** a succession of notes forming a distinctive sequence; tune. **b.** the horizontally represented aspect of the structure of a piece of music. Compare **harmony** (sense 4b.). **2.** sounds that are pleasant because of tone or arrangement, esp. words of poetry. [C13: from Old French, from Late Latin *melōdia,* from Greek *melōidia* singing, from *melos* song + *-ōidia,* from *aoidein* to sing]

meloid ('mɛlɔɪd) *n.* **1.** any long-legged beetle of the family *Meloidae,* which includes the blister beetles and oil beetles. ~*adj.* **2.** of, relating to, or belonging to the *Meloidae.* [C19: from New Latin *Meloē* name of genus]

melon ('mɛlən) *n.* **1.** any of several varieties of two cucurbitaceous vines (see **muskmelon, watermelon**), cultivated for their edible fruit. **2.** the fruit of any of these plants, which has a hard rind and juicy flesh. **3. cut a melon.** *U.S. and Canadian slang.* to declare an abnormally high dividend to shareholders. [C14: via Old French from Late Latin *mēlo,* shortened form of *mēlopepō,* from Greek *mēlopepōn,* from *mēlon* apple + *pepōn* gourd]

melt (mɛlt) *vb.* **melts, melting, melted; melted** *or* **molten** ('məʊltən). **1.** to liquefy (a solid) or (of a solid) to become liquefied, as a result of the action of heat. **2.** to become or make liquid; dissolve: *cakes that melt in the mouth.* **3.** (often foll. by *away*) to disappear; fade. **4.** (foll. by *down*) to melt (metal scrap) for reuse. **5.** (often foll. by *into*) to blend or cause to blend gradually. **6.** to make or become emotional or sentimental; soften. ~*n.* **7.** the act or process of melting. **8.** something melted or an amount melted. [Old English *meltan* to digest; related to Old Norse *melta* to malt (beer), digest, Greek *meldein* to melt] —'**meltable** *adj.* —ˌ**melta'bility** *n.* —'**melter** *n.* —'**meltingly** *adv.* —'**meltingness** *n.*

meltage ('mɛltɪdʒ) *n.* the process or result of melting or the amount melted: *rapid meltage of ice.*

meltdown ('mɛltˌdaʊn) *n.* **1.** (in a nuclear reactor) the melting of the fuel rods as a result of a defect in the cooling system, with the possible escape of radiation into the environment. **2.** *Informal.* a sudden disastrous failure with potential for widespread harm, as a stock-exchange crash.

meltemi (mɛl'tɛmɪ) *n.* a northerly wind in the northeast Mediterranean; etesian wind. [C20: from Modern Greek, from Turkish *meltem*]

melting point *n.* the temperature at which a solid turns into a liquid. It is equal to the freezing point.

melting pot *n.* **1.** a pot in which metals or other substances are melted, esp. in order to mix them. **2.** an area in which many races, ideas, etc., are mixed.

melton ('mɛltən) *n.* a heavy smooth woollen fabric with a short nap, used esp. for overcoats. Also called: **melton cloth.** [C19: from *Melton* Mowbray, Leicestershire, a former centre for making this cloth]

meltwater ('mɛltˌwɔːtə) *n.* melted snow or ice.

melungeon (mə'lʌndʒən) *n.* any of a dark-skinned group of people of the Appalachians in E Tennessee, of mixed Indian, White, and Negro ancestry. [C20: of unknown origin]

mem (mɛm) *n.* the 13th letter in the Hebrew alphabet (מ or, at the end of a word, ם), transliterated as *m.* [Hebrew, literally: water]

mem. *abbrev. for:* **1.** member. **2.** memoir. **3.** memorandum. **4.** memorial.

member ('mɛmbə) *n.* **1.** a person who belongs to a club, political party, etc. **2.** any individual plant or animal in a taxonomic group: *a member of the species.* **3.** any part of an animal body, such as a limb. **4.** another word for **penis.** **5.** any part of a plant, such as a petal, root, etc. **6.** *Maths.* any individual object belonging to a set or logical class. **7.** a distinct part of a whole, such as a proposition in a syllogism. **8.** a component part of a building or construction. [C13: from Latin *membrum* limb, part] —'**memberless** *adj.*

Member ('mɛmbə) *n.* (*sometimes not cap.*) **1.** short for **Member of Parliament.** **2.** a member of some other legislative body.

Member of Parliament *n.* a member of the House of Commons or similar legislative body, as in many Commonwealth countries. Abbrev.: **MP.**

membership ('mɛmbəˌʃɪp) *n.* **1.** the members of an organization collectively. **2.** the state of being a member.

membrane ('mɛmbreɪn) *n.* **1.** any thin pliable sheet of material. **2.** a pliable sheetlike usually fibrous tissue that covers, lines, or connects plant and animal organs or cells. **3.** *Biology.* a double layer of lipid, containing some proteins, that surrounds biological cells and some of their internal structures. **4.** *Physics.* a two-dimensional entity postulated as a fundamental constituent

of matter in some theories of particle physics. **5.** a skin of parchment forming part of a roll. [C16: from Latin *membrāna* skin covering a part of the body, from *membrum* MEMBER]
membrane bone *n.* any bone that develops within membranous tissue, such as the clavicle and bones of the skull, without cartilage formation. Compare **cartilage bone.**
membrane transport *n.* the process by which physiologically important substances, such as calcium ions, sugars, etc., are conveyed across a biological membrane.
membranous ('mɛmbrənəs, mɛm'breɪnəs), **membraneous** (mɛm'breɪnɪəs), *or* **membranaceous** (ˌmɛmbrə'neɪʃəs) *adj.* of or relating to a membrane. —'**membranously** *adv.*
memento (mɪ'mɛntəʊ) *n., pl.* **-tos** *or* **-toes. 1.** something that reminds one of past events; souvenir. **2.** *R.C. Church.* either of two prayers occurring during the Mass. [C15: from Latin, imperative of *meminisse* to remember]
memento mori ('mɔːriː) *n.* an object, such as a skull, intended to remind people of the inevitability of death. [C16: Latin: remember you must die]
memo ('mɛməʊ, 'miːməʊ) *n., pl.* **memos.** short for **memorandum.**
memoir ('mɛmwɑː) *n.* **1.** a biography or historical account, esp. one based on personal knowledge. **2.** an essay or monograph, as on a specialized topic. **3.** *Obsolete.* a memorandum. [C16: from French, from Latin *memoria* MEMORY] —'**memoirist** *n.*
memoirs ('mɛmwɑːz) *pl. n.* **1.** a collection of reminiscences about a period, series of events, etc., written from personal experience or special sources. **2.** an autobiographical record. **3.** a collection or record, as of transactions of a society, etc.
memorabilia (ˌmɛmərə'bɪlɪə) *pl. n., sing.* **-rabile** (-'ræbɪlɪ). **1.** memorable events or things. **2.** objects connected with famous people or events. [C17: from Latin, from *memorābilis* MEMORABLE]
memorable ('mɛmərəbᵊl, 'mɛmrə-) *adj.* worth remembering or easily remembered; noteworthy. [C15: from Latin *memorābilis,* from *memorāre* to recall, from *memor* mindful] —ˌ**memora'bility** *or* '**memorableness** *n.* —'**memorably** *adv.*
memorandum (ˌmɛmə'rændəm) *n., pl.* **-dums** *or* **-da** (-də). **1.** a written statement, record, or communication such as within an office. **2.** a note of things to be remembered. **3.** an informal diplomatic communication, often unsigned: often summarizing the point of view of a government. **4.** *Law.* a short written summary of the terms of a transaction. ~Often (esp. for senses 1 and 2) shortened to **memo.** [C15: from Latin: (something) to be remembered]
memorial (mɪ'mɔːrɪəl) *adj.* **1.** serving to preserve the memory of the dead or a past event. **2.** of or involving memory. ~*n.* **3.** something serving as a remembrance. **4.** a written statement of facts submitted to a government, authority, etc., in conjunction with a petition. **5.** an informal diplomatic paper. [C14: from Late Latin *memoriāle* a reminder, neuter of *memoriālis* belonging to remembrance] —**me'morially** *adv.*
Memorial Day *n.* a holiday in the United States, May 30th in most states, commemorating the servicemen killed in all American wars.
memorialist (mɪ'mɔːrɪəlɪst) *n.* **1.** a person who writes or presents a memorial. **2.** a writer of a memoir or memoirs.
memorialize *or* **memorialise** (mɪ'mɔːrɪəˌlaɪz) *vb. (tr.)* **1.** to honour or commemorate. **2.** to present or address a memorial to. —**meˌmoriali'zation** *or* **meˌmoriali'sation** *n.* —**me'morialˌizer** *or* **me'morialˌiser** *n.*
memoria technica (mɪ'mɔːrɪə 'tɛknɪkə) *n.* a method or device for assisting the memory. [C18: New Latin: artificial memory]
memorize *or* **memorise** ('mɛməˌraɪz) *vb. (tr.)* to commit to memory; learn so as to remember. —'**memoˌrizable** *or* '**memoˌrisable** *adj.* —ˌ**memori'zation** *or* ˌ**memori'sation** *n.* —'**memoˌrizer** *or* '**memoˌriser** *n.*
memory ('mɛmərɪ) *n., pl.* **-ries. 1. a.** the ability of the mind to store and recall past sensations, thoughts, knowledge, etc.: *he can do it from memory.* **b.** the part of the brain that appears to have this function. **2.** the sum of everything retained by the mind. **3.** a particular recollection of an event, person, etc. **4.** the time over which recollection extends: *within his memory.* **5.** commemoration or remembrance: *in memory of our leader.* **6.** the state of being remembered, as after death. **7.** Also called: **memory bank, core store, main store, store.** a part of a computer in which information is stored for immediate use by the central processing unit. See also **virtual storage. 8.** the tendency for a material, system, etc., to show effects that depend on its past treatment or history. **9.** the ability of a material, etc., to return to a former state after a constraint has been removed. [C14: from Old French *memorie,* from Latin *memoria,* from *memor* mindful]
memory bank *n.* another name for **data bank.**
memory mapping *n.* a technique whereby computer peripherals may be addressed as though they formed part of the main memory of the computer.
memory span *n. Psychol.* the capacity of short-term memory, usually between 5 and 10 items.
memory trace *n. Psychol.* the hypothetical structural alteration in brain cells following learning. See also **engram.**
memsahib ('mɛmˌsɑːɪb, -hɪb) *n.* (formerly in India) a term of respect used of a European married woman. [C19: from MA'AM + SAHIB]
men (mɛn) *n.* the plural of **man.**
menace ('mɛnɪs) *vb.* **1.** to threaten with violence, danger, etc. ~*n.* **2.** *Literary.* a threat or the act of threatening. **3.** something menacing; a source of danger. **4.** *Informal.* a nuisance. [C13: ultimately related to Latin *minax* threatening, from *mināri* to threaten] —'**menacer** *n.* —'**menacing** *adj.* —'**menacingly** *adv.*
menad ('miːnæd) *n.* a variant spelling of **maenad.**
menadione (ˌmɛnə'daɪəʊn) *n.* a yellow crystalline compound used in fungicides and as an additive to animal feeds. Also called: **vitamin K_3.** Formula: $C_{11}H_8O_2$. [C20: from ME(THYL) + NA(PHTHA) + DI-[1] + -ONE]
ménage (meɪ'nɑːʒ; *French* menaʒ) *n.* the persons of a household. [C17: from French, from Vulgar Latin *mansiōnāticum* (unattested) household; see MANSION]
ménage à trois *French.* (menaʒ a trwɑ) *n., pl.* ***ménages à trois*** (menaʒ a trwɑ). a sexual arrangement involving a married couple and the lover of one of them. [literally: household of three]
menagerie (mɪ'nædʒərɪ) *n.* **1.** a collection of wild animals kept for exhibition. **2.** the place where such animals are housed. [C18: from French: household management, which formerly included care of domestic animals. See MÉNAGE]
menaquinone (ˌmɛnəkwɪ'nəʊn) *n.* a form of vitamin K synthesized by bacteria in the intestine or in putrefying organic matter. Also called: **vitamin K_2.** [C20: from *me(thyl)-na(phtho)quinone*]
menarche (mɛ'nɑːkɪ) *n.* the first occurrence of menstruation in a woman's life. [C20: New Latin, from Greek *mēn* month + *arkhē* beginning] —**men'archeal** *or* **men'archial** *adj.*
mend (mɛnd) *vb.* **1.** *(tr.)* to repair (something broken or unserviceable). **2.** to improve or undergo improvement; reform (often in the phrase **mend one's ways**). **3.** *(intr.)* to heal or recover. **4.** (of conditions) to improve; become better. ~*n.* **5.** the act of repairing. **6.** a mended area, esp. on a garment. **7. on the mend.** becoming better, esp. in health. [C12: shortened from AMEND] —'**mendable** *adj.* —'**mender** *n.*
mendacity (mɛn'dæsɪtɪ) *n., pl.* **-ties. 1.** the tendency to be untruthful. **2.** a falsehood. [C17: from Late Latin *mendācitās,* from Latin *mendāx* untruthful] —**mendacious** (mɛn'deɪʃəs) *adj.* —**men'daciously** *adv.* —**men'daciousness** *n.*
mendelevium (ˌmɛndɪ'liːvɪəm) *n.* a transuranic element artificially produced by bombardment of einsteinium. Symbol: Md; atomic no.: 101; half-life of most stable isotope, ^{258}Md: 60 days (approx.). [C20: named after D. I. *Mendeleyev* (1834–1907), Russian chemist]
Mendelian (mɛn'diːlɪən) *adj.* of or relating to Mendel's laws.
Mendelism ('mɛndəˌlɪzəm) *or* **Mendelianism** (mɛn'diːlɪəˌnɪzəm) *n.* the science of heredity based on Mendel's laws with some modifications in the light of more recent knowledge.
Mendel's laws ('mɛndᵊlz) *pl. n.* the principles of heredity proposed by Gregor Mendel (1822–84), Austrian monk and botanist. The **Law of Segregation** states that every somatic cell of an individual carries a pair of hereditary units for each character: the pairs separate during meiosis so that each gamete carries only one unit of each pair. The **Law of Independent Assortment** states that the separation of the units of each pair is not influenced by that of any other pair.
mendicant ('mɛndɪkənt) *adj.* **1.** begging. **2.** (of a member of a religious order) dependent on alms for sustenance: *mendicant friars.* **3.** characteristic of a beggar. ~*n.* **4.** a mendicant friar. **5.** a less common word for **beggar.** [C16: from Latin *mendīcāre* to beg, from *mendīcus* beggar, from *mendus* flaw] —'**mendicancy** *or* **mendicity** (mɛn'dɪsɪtɪ) *n.*
mending ('mɛndɪŋ) *n.* something to be mended, esp. clothes.
meneer (mə'nɪə) *n.* a South African title of address equivalent to *sir* when used alone or *Mr* when placed before a name. [Afrikaans]
menfolk ('mɛnˌfəʊk) *or U.S. (sometimes)* **menfolks** *pl. n.* men collectively, esp. the men of a particular family.
menhaden (mɛn'heɪdᵊn) *n., pl.* **-den.** a marine North American fish, *Brevoortia tyrannus:* source of fish meal, fertilizer, and oil: family *Clupeidae* (herrings, etc.). [C18: from Algonquian; probably related to Narragansett *munnawhatteaûg* fertilizer, menhaden]
menhir ('mɛnhɪə) *n.* a single standing stone, often carved, dating from the middle Bronze Age in the British Isles and from the late Neolithic Age in W Europe. [C19: from Breton *men* stone + *hir* long]
menial ('miːnɪəl) *adj.* **1.** consisting of or occupied with work requiring little skill, esp. domestic duties such as cleaning. **2.** of, involving, or befitting servants. **3.** servile. ~*n.* **4.** a domestic servant. **5.** a servile person. [C14: from Anglo-Norman *meignial,* from Old French *meinie* household. See MEINY] —'**menially** *adv.*
Ménière's syndrome *or* **disease** (meɪn'jɛəz) *n.* a disorder of the inner ear characterized by a ringing or buzzing in the ear, dizziness, and impaired hearing. [C19: named after Prosper *Ménière* (1799–1862), French physician]
menilite ('mɛnɪˌlaɪt) *n.* another name for **liver opal,** esp. a brown or grey variety.
meninges (mɪ'nɪndʒiːz) *pl. n., sing.* **meninx** ('miːnɪŋks). the three membranes **(dura mater, arachnoid, pia mater)** that

envelop the brain and spinal cord. [C17: from Greek, pl. of *meninx* membrane] —**meningeal** (mɪˈnɪndʒɪəl) *adj.*

meningitis (ˌmɛnɪnˈdʒaɪtɪs) *n.* inflammation of the membranes that surround the brain or spinal cord, caused by infection. —**meningitic** (ˌmɛnɪnˈdʒɪtɪk) *adj.*

meningocele (mɛˈnɪŋgəʊˌsiːl) *n. Pathol.* protrusion of the meninges through the skull or backbone. [C19: from *meningo-* (see MENINGES) + -CELE]

meningococcus (mɛˌnɪŋgəʊˈkɒkəs) *n., pl.* **-cocci** (-ˈkɒksaɪ). the bacterium that causes cerebrospinal meningitis. —**meˌningoˈcoccal** *adj.*

meniscus (mɪˈnɪskəs) *n., pl.* **-nisci** (-ˈnɪsaɪ) *or* **-niscuses.** 1. the curved upper surface of a liquid standing in a tube, produced by the surface tension. 2. a crescent or half-moon-shaped body or design. 3. a crescent-shaped fibrous cartilage between the bones at certain joints, esp. at the knee. 4. a crescent-shaped lens; a concavo-convex or convexo-concave lens. [C17: from New Latin, from Greek *mēniskos* crescent, diminutive of *mēnē* moon] —**meˈniscoid** *adj.*

menispermaceous (ˌmɛnɪspɜːˈmeɪʃəs) *adj.* of, relating to, or belonging to the *Menispermaceae,* a family of mainly tropical and subtropical plants, most of which are woody climbers with small flowers. [C19: from New Latin *Mēnispermum* name of genus, from Greek *mēnē* moon + *sperma* seed]

Mennonite (ˈmɛnəˌnaɪt) *n.* a member of a Protestant sect that rejects infant baptism, Church organization, and the doctrine of transubstantiation and in most cases refuses military service, public office, and the taking of oaths. [C16: from German *Mennonit,* after *Menno* Simons (1496–1561), Frisian religious leader] —**ˈMennoˌnitism** *n.*

meno (ˈmɛnəʊ) *adv. Music.* 1. (esp. preceding a dynamic or tempo marking) to be played less quickly, less softly, etc. 2. short for **meno mosso.** [from Italian, from Latin *minus* less]

meno- *combining form.* menstruation: *menorrhagia.* [from Greek *mēn* month]

menology (mɪˈnɒlədʒɪ) *n., pl.* **-gies.** 1. an ecclesiastical calendar of the months. 2. *Eastern Churches.* a liturgical book containing the lives of the saints arranged by months. [C17: from New Latin *mēnologium,* from Late Greek *mēnologion,* from Greek *mēn* month + *logos* word, account]

Menomini *or* **Menominee** (məˈnɒmənɪ) *n.* 1. (*pl.* **-ni, -nis** *or* **-nee, -nees**) a member of a North American Indian people formerly living between Lake Michigan and Lake Superior. 2. the language of this people, belonging to the Algonquian family.

meno mosso (ˈmɛnəʊ ˈmɒsəʊ) *adv. Music.* to be played at reduced speed. Often shortened to **meno.** [Italian: less rapid]

menopause (ˈmɛnəʊˌpɔːz) *n.* the period during which a woman's menstrual cycle ceases, normally occurring at an age of 45 to 50. Nontechnical name: **change of life.** [C19: from French, from Greek *mēn* month + *pausis* halt] —ˌ**menoˈpausal** *or* (*rarely*) ˌ**menoˈpausic** *adj.*

menorah (mɪˈnɔːrə; *Hebrew* məˈnɑʊrɔ) *n. Judaism.* 1. a seven-branched candelabrum used in the Temple and now an emblem of Judaism and the badge of the state of Israel. 2. a candelabrum having eight branches and a shammes that is lit during the festival of Chanukah. [from Hebrew: candlestick]

menorrhagia (ˌmɛnɔːˈreɪdʒɪə) *n.* excessive bleeding during menstruation. —**menorrhagic** (ˌmɛnəˈrædʒɪk) *adj.*

menorrhoea (ˌmɛnəˈrɪə) *n.* normal bleeding in menstruation.

Mensa (ˈmɛnsə) *n., Latin genitive* **Mensae** (ˈmɛnsiː). a faint constellation in the S hemisphere lying between Hydrus and Volans and containing part of the Large Magellanic Cloud. [Latin, literally: the table]

mensal[1] (ˈmɛnsᵊl) *adj. Rare.* monthly. [C15: from Latin *mensis* month]

mensal[2] (ˈmɛnsᵊl) *adj. Rare.* relating to or used at the table. [C15: from Latin *mensālis,* from *mensa* table]

mens sana in corpore sano *Latin.* (mɛnz ˈsænə ɪn ˈkɔːpɔːreɪ ˈsænəʊ) *n.* a sound mind in a sound body. [Latin]

menses (ˈmɛnsiːz) *n., pl.* **menses.** 1. another name for **menstruation.** 2. the period of time, usually from three to five days, during which menstruation occurs. 3. the matter discharged during menstruation. [C16: from Latin, pl. of *mensis* month]

Menshevik (ˈmɛnʃɪvɪk) *or* **Menshevist** *n.* a member of the moderate wing of the Russian Social Democratic Party, advocating gradual reform to achieve socialism. Compare **Bolshevik.** [C20: from Russian, literally: minority, from *menshe* less, from *malo* few] —**ˈMenshevism** *n.*

mens rea (ˈmɛnz ˈreɪə) *n. Law.* a criminal intention or knowledge that an act is wrong. It is assumed to be an ingredient of all criminal offences although some minor statutory offences are punishable irrespective of it. [Latin, literally: guilty mind]

men's room *n. Chiefly U.S. and Canadian.* a public lavatory for men.

menstrual (ˈmɛnstrʊəl) *adj.* of or relating to menstruation or the menses.

menstruate (ˈmɛnstrʊˌeɪt) *vb.* (*intr.*) to undergo menstruation. [C17: from Latin *menstruāre,* from *mensis* month]

menstruation (ˌmɛnstrʊˈeɪʃən) *n.* the approximately monthly discharge of blood and cellular debris from the uterus by nonpregnant women from puberty to the menopause. Also called: **menses.** Nontechnical name: **period.** —**menstruous** (ˈmɛnstrʊəs) *adj.*

menstruum (ˈmɛnstrʊəm) *n., pl.* **-struums** *or* **-strua** (-strʊə). a solvent, esp. one used in the preparation of a drug. [C17 (meaning: solvent), C14 (menstrual discharge): from Medieval Latin, from Latin *mēnstruus* monthly, from *mēnsis* month; from an alchemical comparison between a base metal being transmuted into gold and the supposed action of the menses]

mensurable (ˈmɛnsjʊrəbᵊl, -ʃə-) *adj.* a less common word for **measurable.** [C17: from Late Latin *mēnsūrābilis,* from *mēnsūra* MEASURE] —ˌ**mensuraˈbility** *n.*

mensural (ˈmɛnʃərəl) *adj.* 1. of or involving measure. 2. *Music.* of or relating to music in which notes have fixed values in relation to each other. [C17: from Late Latin *mēnsūrālis,* from *mēnsūra* MEASURE]

mensuration (ˌmɛnʃəˈreɪʃən) *n.* 1. the study of the measurement of geometric magnitudes such as length. 2. the act or process of measuring; measurement. —ˌ**mensuˈrational** *adj.* —**mensurative** (ˈmɛnʃərətɪv) *adj.*

menswear (ˈmɛnzˌwɛə) *n.* clothing for men.

-ment *suffix forming nouns, esp. from verbs.* 1. indicating state, condition, or quality: *enjoyment.* 2. indicating the result or product of an action: *embankment.* 3. indicating process or action: *management.* [from French, from Latin *-mentum*]

mental[1] (ˈmɛntᵊl) *adj.* 1. of or involving the mind or an intellectual process. 2. occurring only in the mind: *mental calculations.* 3. affected by mental illness: *a mental patient.* 4. concerned with care for persons with mental illness: *a mental hospital.* 5. *Slang.* insane. [C15: from Late Latin *mentālis,* from Latin *mēns* mind] —**ˈmentally** *adv.*

mental[2] (ˈmɛntᵊl) *adj. Anatomy.* of or relating to the chin. Also: **genial.** [C18: from Latin *mentum* chin]

mental age *n. Psychol.* the mental ability of a child, expressed in years and based on a comparison of his test performance with the performance of children with a range of chronological ages. See also **intelligence quotient.**

mental block *n.* See **block** (sense 23).

mental cruelty *n.* behaviour that causes distress to another person but that does not involve physical assault.

mental deficiency *n. Psychiatry.* a less common term for **mental retardation.**

mental disorder *n. Law.* (in England, according to the Mental Health Act 1983) mental illness, arrested or incomplete development of mind, psychopathic disorder, or any other disorder or disability of the mind. —**mentally disordered** *adj.*

mental handicap *n.* a general or specific intellectual disability, resulting directly or indirectly from injury to the brain or from abnormal neurological development. —**mentally handicapped** *adj.*

mental healing *n.* the healing of a disorder by mental concentration or suggestion. —**mental healer** *n.*

mental home, hospital, *or* **institution** *n.* a home, hospital, or institution for people who are mentally ill.

mental impairment *n. Law.* (in England, according to the Mental Health Act 1983) a state of arrested or incomplete development of mind, which includes significant impairment of intelligence and social functioning and is associated with abnormally aggressive or seriously irresponsible conduct. —**mentally impaired** *adj.*

mentalism (ˈmɛntᵊˌlɪzəm) *n. Philosophy.* the doctrine that mind is the fundamental reality and that objects of knowledge exist only as aspects of the subject's consciousness. Compare **physicalism, idealism** (sense 3). See also **monism** (sense 1), **materialism** (sense 2). —**ˈmentalist** *n.* —ˌ**mentalˈistic** *adj.* —ˌ**mentalˈistically** *adv.*

mentality (mɛnˈtælɪtɪ) *n., pl.* **-ties.** 1. the state or quality of mental or intellectual ability. 2. a way of thinking; mental inclination or character: *his weird mentality.*

mental lexicon *n.* the store of words in a person's mind.

mental reservation *n.* a tacit withholding of full assent or an unexpressed qualification made when one is taking an oath, making a statement, etc.

mental retardation *n. Psychiatry.* the condition of having a low intelligence quotient (below 70).

mentation (mɛnˈteɪʃən) *n.* the process or result of mental activity.

menthaceous (mɛnˈθeɪʃɪəs) *adj.* of, relating to, or belonging to the labiate plant genus *Mentha* (mints, etc.) the members of which have scented leaves. [from New Latin, from Latin *mentha* MINT[1]]

menthol (ˈmɛnθɒl) *n.* an optically active organic compound found in peppermint oil and used as an antiseptic, in inhalants, and as an analgesic. Formula: $C_{10}H_{20}O$. [C19: from German, from Latin *mentha* MINT[1]]

mentholated (ˈmɛnθəˌleɪtɪd) *adj.* containing, treated, or impregnated with menthol.

mention (ˈmɛnʃən) *vb.* (*tr.*) 1. to refer to or speak about briefly or incidentally. 2. to acknowledge or honour. 3. **not to mention (something).** to say nothing of (something too obvious to mention). ~*n.* 4. a recognition or acknowledgment. 5. a slight reference or allusion: *he only got a mention in the article; the author makes no mention of that.* 6. the act of mentioning. 7. *Philosophy, logic, linguistics.* the occurrence (of an expression) in such a context that it is itself referred to rather than performing its own linguistic function. In *"Fido" names Fido,* the word *Fido* is first mentioned and then used to refer to the dog. Compare **use** (sense 18). See also **formal mode.** [C14: via Old

French from Latin *mentiō* a calling to mind, naming, from *mēns* mind] —ˈ**mentionable** *adj.* —ˈ**mentioner** *n.*

mentor (ˈmɛntɔː) *n.* a wise or trusted adviser or guide. [C18: from *Mentor*, adviser of Odysseus' son Telemachus in Odysseus' absence] —**men'torial** *adj.*

mentoring (ˈmɛntərɪŋ) *n.* (in business) the practice of assigning a junior member of staff to the care of a more experienced person who assists him in his career.

menu (ˈmɛnjuː) *n.* **1.** a list of dishes served at a meal or that can be ordered in a restaurant. **2.** a list of options displayed on a visual display unit from which the operator selects an action to be carried out by positioning the cursor or by depressing the appropriate key. [C19: from French *menu* small, detailed (list), from Latin *minūtus* MINUTE[2]]

menu-driven *adj.* (of a computer system) operated through menus.

menura (məˈnjuːrə) *n. Austral.* the lyrebird. [Latin, from Greek *mēnē* crescent moon + *oura* tail]

meow, miaou, miaow (mɪˈaʊ, mjaʊ), *or* **miaul** (mɪˈaʊl, mjaʊl) *vb.* **1.** (*intr.*) (of a cat) to make a characteristic crying sound. ~*interj.* **2.** an imitation of this sound.

MEP (in Britain) *abbrev. for* Member of the European Parliament.

mepacrine (ˈmɛpəkrɪn) *n. Brit.* a drug, mepacrine dihydrochloride, one of the first synthetic substitutes for quinine, formerly widely used to treat malaria but now largely replaced by chloroquine. Formula: $C_{23}H_{30}ClN_3O.2HCl.2H_2O$. U.S. name: **quinacrine.** [C20: from ME(THYL) + PA(LUDISM + A)CR(ID)INE]

meperidine (məˈpɛrɪˌdiːn, -dɪn) *n.* a white crystalline water-soluble drug used as an analgesic. Formula: $C_{15}H_{21}NO_2.HCl$. Also called: **meperidine hydrochloride.** [C20: from METHYL + PIPERIDINE]

Mephistophelean *or* **Mephistophelian** (ˌmɛfɪstəˈfiːlɪən) *adj.* of, relating to, or characteristic of Mephistopheles, a devil in medieval mythology.

mephitic (mɪˈfɪtɪk) *or* **mephitical** *adj.* **1.** poisonous; foul. **2.** foul-smelling; putrid. [C17: from Late Latin *mephīticus* pestilential. See MEPHITIS] —**me'phitically** *adv.*

mephitis (mɪˈfaɪtɪs) *n.* **1.** a foul or poisonous stench. **2.** a poisonous or unpleasant gas emitted from the earth. [C18: from Latin: unwholesome smell, origin obscure]

meprobamate (məˈprəʊbəˌmeɪt, ˌmɛprəʊˈbæmeɪt) *n.* a white bitter powder used as a tranquillizer. Formula: $C_9H_{18}N_2O_4$. [ME(THYL) + PRO(PYL + CAR)BAMATE]

mer. *abbrev. for* meridian.

-mer *suffix forming nouns. Chem.* denoting a substance of a particular class: *monomer; polymer.* [from Greek *meros* part]

meranti (mɪˈræntɪ) *n.* wood from any of several Malaysian trees of the dipterocarpaceous genus *Shorea.* [C18: from Malay]

merbromin (məˈbrəʊmɪn) *n.* a green iridescent crystalline compound that forms a red solution in water: used in medicine as an antiseptic. Formula: $C_{20}H_8Br_2HgNa_2O_6$. See also **Mercurochrome.** [C20: blend of MERCURIC + *dibromofluorescein*]

Mercalli scale (mɜːˈkælɪ) *n.* a 12-point scale for expressing the intensity of an earthquake, ranging from 1 (not felt, except by few under favourable circumstances) to 12 (total destruction). Compare **Richter scale.** See also **intensity** (sense 4). [C20: named after Giuseppe *Mercalli* (1850–1914), Italian volcanologist and seismologist]

mercantile (ˈmɜːkənˌtaɪl) *adj.* **1.** of, relating to, or characteristic of trade or traders; commercial. **2.** of or relating to mercantilism. [C17: from French, from Italian, from *mercante* MERCHANT]

mercantile agency *n.* an enterprise that collects and supplies information about the financial credit standing of individuals and enterprises.

mercantile paper *n.* another name for **commercial paper.**

mercantilism (ˈmɜːkəntɪˌlɪzəm) *n.* **1.** Also called: **mercantile system.** *Economics.* a theory prevalent in Europe during the 17th and 18th centuries asserting that the wealth of a nation depends on its possession of precious metals and therefore that the government of a nation must maximize the foreign trade surplus, and foster national commercial interests, a merchant marine, the establishment of colonies, etc. **2.** a rare word for **commercialism** (sense 1). —ˈ**mercanˌtilist** *n., adj.*

mercaptan (mɜːˈkæptæn) *n.* another name (not in technical usage) for **thiol.** [C19: from German, from Medieval Latin *mercurium captans,* literally: seizing quicksilver]

mercaptide (məˈkæptaɪd, mɜː-) *n.* a salt of a mercaptan, containing the ion RS^-, where R is an alkyl or aryl group.

mercapto- (mɜːˈkæptəʊ) *combining form.* (in chemical compounds) indicating the presence of an HS- group.

mercaptopurine (məˌkæptəˈpjʊəriːn) *n.* a drug used in the treatment of leukaemia. Formula: $C_5H_4N_4S$.

mercat (ˈmɛrkət) *n.* a Scot. word for **market.**

Mercator projection *n.* an orthomorphic map projection on which parallels and meridians form a rectangular grid, scale being exaggerated with increasing distance from the equator. Also called: **Mercator's projection.** [C17: named after Gerardus *Mercator* (1512–94), Flemish cartographer and mathematician]

mercenary (ˈmɜːsɪnərɪ, -sɪnrɪ) *adj.* **1.** influenced by greed or desire for gain. **2.** of or relating to a mercenary or mercenaries. ~*n., pl.* **-naries. 3.** a man hired to fight for a foreign army, etc. **4.** *Rare.* any person who works solely for pay. [C16: from Latin *mercēnārius,* from *mercēs* wages] —ˈ**mercenarily** *adv.* —ˈ**mercenariness** *n.*

mercer (ˈmɜːsə) *n. Brit.* a dealer in textile fabrics and fine cloth. [C13: from Old French *mercier* dealer, from Vulgar Latin *merciārius* (unattested), from Latin *merx* goods, wares] —ˈ**mercery** *n.*

mercerize *or* **mercerise** (ˈmɜːsəˌraɪz) *vb.* (*tr.*) to treat (cotton yarn) with an alkali to increase its strength and reception to dye and impart a lustrous silky appearance. [C19: named after John *Mercer* (1791–1866), English maker of textiles] —ˌ**merceri'zation** *or* ˌ**merceri'sation** *n.*

merchandise *n.* (ˈmɜːtʃənˌdaɪs, -ˌdaɪz). **1.** commercial goods; commodities. ~*vb.* (ˈmɜːtʃənˌdaɪz). **2.** to engage in the commercial purchase and sale of (goods or services); trade. [C13: from Old French. See MERCHANT] —ˈ**merchanˌdiser** *n.*

merchandising (ˈmɜːtʃənˌdaɪzɪŋ) *n.* **1.** the selection and display of goods in a retail outlet. **2.** commercial goods, esp. ones issued to exploit the popularity of a pop group, sporting event, etc.

merchant (ˈmɜːtʃənt) *n.* **1.** a person engaged in the purchase and sale of commodities for profit, esp. on international markets; trader. **2.** *Chiefly U.S. and Canadian.* a person engaged in retail trade. **3.** (esp. in historical contexts) any trader. **4.** *Derogatory.* a person dealing or involved in something undesirable: *a gossip merchant.* **5.** (*modifier*) **a.** of the merchant navy: *a merchant sailor.* **b.** of or concerned with trade: *a merchant ship.* ~*vb.* **6.** (*tr.*) to conduct trade in; deal in. [C13: from Old French, probably from Vulgar Latin *mercātāre* (unattested), from Latin *mercārī* to trade, from *merx* goods, wares] —ˈ**merchant-ˌlike** *adj.*

merchantable (ˈmɜːtʃəntəbᵊl) *adj.* suitable for trading.

merchant bank *n.* (in Britain) a financial institution engaged primarily in accepting foreign bills, advising companies on flotations and takeovers, underwriting new issues, hire-purchase finance, making long-term loans to companies, and managing investment portfolios, funds, and trusts. —**merchant banker** *n.*

merchantman (ˈmɜːtʃəntmən) *n., pl.* **-men.** a merchant ship.

merchant navy *or* **marine** *n.* the ships or crew engaged in a nation's commercial shipping.

merchant prince *n.* a very wealthy merchant.

merchet (ˈmɜːtʃɪt) *n.* (in feudal England) a fine paid by a tenant, esp. a villein, to his lord for allowing the marriage of his daughter. [C13: from Anglo-French, literally: MARKET]

Mercian (ˈmɜːʃɪən) *adj.* **1.** of or relating to Mercia, an Anglo-Saxon kingdom and earldom of central and S England, or the dialect spoken there. ~*n.* **2.** the dialect of Old and Middle English spoken in the Midlands of England south of the River Humber. See also **Anglian, Northumbrian.**

merciful (ˈmɜːsɪfʊl) *adj.* showing or giving mercy; compassionate. —ˈ**mercifully** *adv.* —ˈ**mercifulness** *n.*

merciless (ˈmɜːsɪlɪs) *adj.* without mercy; pitiless, cruel, or heartless. —ˈ**mercilessly** *adv.* —ˈ**mercilessness** *n.*

mercurate (ˈmɜːkjʊˌreɪt) *vb.* **1.** (*tr.*) to treat or mix with mercury. **2.** to undergo or cause to undergo a chemical reaction in which a mercury atom is added to a compound. —ˌ**mercu'ration** *n.*

mercurial (mɜːˈkjʊərɪəl) *adj.* **1.** of, like, containing, or relating to mercury. **2.** volatile; lively: *a mercurial temperament.* **3.** (*sometimes cap.*) of, like, or relating to the god or the planet Mercury. ~*n.* **4.** *Med.* any salt of mercury for use as a medicine. [C14: from Latin *mercuriālis*] —**mer'curially** *adv.* —**mer'curialness** *or* **merˌcuri'ality** *n.*

mercurialism (mɜːˈkjʊərɪəˌlɪzᵊm) *n.* poisoning caused by chronic ingestion of mercury.

mercurialize *or* **mercurialise** (mɜːˈkjʊərɪəˌlaɪz) *vb.* (*tr.*) **1.** to make mercurial. **2.** to treat with mercury or a mercury compound. —**merˌcuriali'zation** *or* **merˌcuriali'sation** *n.*

mercuric (mɜːˈkjʊərɪk) *adj.* of or containing mercury in the divalent state; denoting a mercury(II) compound.

mercuric chloride *n.* a white poisonous soluble crystalline substance used as a pesticide, antiseptic, and preservative for wood. Formula: $HgCl_2$. Systematic name: **mercury(II) chloride.** Also called: **bichloride of mercury, corrosive sublimate.**

mercuric oxide *n.* a soluble poisonous substance existing in red and yellow powdered forms: used as pigments. Formula: HgO. Systematic name: **mercury(II) oxide.**

mercuric sulphide *n.* a compound of mercury, usually existing as a black solid (**metacinnabarite**) or a red solid (**cinnabar** or **vermilion**), which is used as a pigment. Formula: HgS. Systematic name: **mercury(II) sulphide.**

Mercurochrome (məˈkjʊərəˌkrəʊm) *n. Trademark.* a solution of merbromin, used as tropical antibacterial agent.

mercurous (ˈmɜːkjʊrəs) *adj.* of or containing mercury in the monovalent state; denoting a mercury(I) compound. Mercurous salts contain the divalent ion Hg_2^{2+}.

mercurous chloride *n.* a white tasteless insoluble powder used as a fungicide and formerly as a medical antiseptic, cathartic, and diuretic. Formula: Hg_2Cl_2. Systematic name: **mercury(I) chloride.** Also called: **calomel.**

mercury (ˈmɜːkjʊrɪ) *n., pl.* **-ries. 1.** Also called: **quicksilver, hydrargyrum.** a heavy silvery-white toxic liquid metallic element occurring principally in cinnabar: used in thermometers, barometers, mercury-vapour lamps, and dental amalgams. Symbol: Hg; atomic no.: 80; atomic wt.: 200.59; valency: 1 or 2; relative density: 13.546; melting pt.: –38.87°C; boiling pt.: 356.58°C.

2. any plant of the euphorbiaceous genus *Mercurialis*. See **dog's mercury.** 3. *Archaic.* a messenger or courier. [C14: from Latin *Mercurius* messenger of Jupiter, god of commerce; related to *merx* merchandise]

Mercury ('mɜːkjʊrɪ) *n.* the smallest planet and the nearest to the sun. Mean distance from sun: 57.9 million km; period of revolution around sun: 88 days; period of axial rotation: 59 days; diameter and mass: 38 and 5.4 per cent that of earth respectively.

mercury arc *n.* **a.** an electric discharge through ionized mercury vapour, producing a brilliant bluish-green light containing ultraviolet radiation. **b.** (*as modifier*): *a mercury-arc rectifier.* See also **ignitron.**

mercury chloride *n.* See **mercurous chloride, mercuric chloride.**

mercury switch *n. Electrical engineering.* a switch in which a circuit is completed between two terminals by liquid mercury when the switch is tilted.

mercury-vapour lamp *n.* a lamp in which an electric discharge through a low pressure of mercury vapour is used to produce a greenish-blue light. It is used for street lighting and is also a source of ultraviolet radiation.

mercy ('mɜːsɪ) *n., pl.* **-cies. 1.** compassionate treatment of or attitude towards an offender, adversary, etc., who is in one's power or care; clemency; pity. **2.** the power to show mercy: *to throw oneself on someone's mercy.* **3.** a relieving or welcome occurrence or state of affairs: *his death was a mercy after weeks of pain.* **4. at the mercy of.** in the power of. [C12: from Old French, from Latin *mercēs* wages, recompense, price, from *merx* goods]

mercy flight *n.* an aircraft flight to bring a seriously ill or injured person to hospital from an isolated community.

mercy killing *n.* another term for **euthanasia.**

mercy seat *n.* **1.** *Old Testament.* the gold platform covering the Ark of the Covenant and regarded as the throne of God where he accepted sacrifices and gave commandments (Exodus 25:17, 22). **2.** *Christianity.* the throne of God.

mere[1] (mɪə) *adj. superlative* **merest.** being nothing more than something specified: *she is a mere child.* [C15: from Latin *merus* pure, unmixed] —'**merely** *adv.*

mere[2] (mɪə) *n.* **1.** *Dialect or archaic.* a lake or marsh. **2.** *Obsolete.* the sea or an inlet of it. [Old English *mere* sea, lake; related to Old Saxon *meri* sea, Old Norse *marr,* Old High German *mari;* compare Latin *mare*]

mere[3] (mɪə) *n. Archaic.* a boundary or boundary marker. [Old English *gemǣre*]

mere[4] ('mɛrɪ) *n. N.Z.* a short flat striking weapon. [Maori]

-mere *n. combining form.* indicating a part or division: *blastomere.* [from Greek *meros* part, portion] —**-meric** *adj. combining form.*

merengue (mə'rɛŋgeɪ) *n.* **1.** a type of lively dance music originating in the Dominican Republic in the West Indies, which combines African and Spanish elements. **2.** a Caribbean dance in duple time with syncopated rhythm performed to such music. [from American Spanish and Haitian Creole]

mereology (ˌmiːrɪ'ɒlədʒɪ) *n.* the formal study of the logical properties of the relation of part and whole. [C20: via French from Greek *meros* part + -LOGY] —ˌ**mereo'logical** *adj.*

meretricious (ˌmɛrɪ'trɪʃəs) *adj.* **1.** superficially or garishly attractive. **2.** insincere: *meretricious praise.* **3.** *Archaic.* of, like, or relating to a prostitute. [C17: from Latin *merētrīcius,* from *merētrix* prostitute, from *merēre* to earn money] —ˌ**mere'triciously** *adv.* —ˌ**mere'triciousness** *n.*

merganser (mɜː'gænsə) *n., pl.* **-sers** *or* **-ser.** any of several typically crested large marine diving ducks of the genus *Mergus,* having a long slender hooked bill with serrated edges. Also called: **sawbill.** See also **goosander.** [C18: from New Latin, from Latin *mergus* waterfowl, from *mergere* to plunge + *anser* goose]

merge (mɜːdʒ) *vb.* **1.** to meet and join or cause to meet and join. **2.** to blend or cause to blend; fuse. [C17: from Latin *mergere* to plunge] —'**mergence** *n.*

merger ('mɜːdʒə) *n.* **1.** *Commerce.* the combination of two or more companies, either by the creation of a new organization or by absorption by one of the others. Often called (Brit.): **amalgamation. 2.** *Law.* the extinguishment of an estate, interest, contract, right, offence, etc., by its absorption into a greater one. **3.** the act of merging or the state of being merged.

meridian (mə'rɪdɪən) *n.* **1. a.** one of the imaginary lines joining the north and south poles at right angles to the equator, designated by degrees of longitude from 0° at Greenwich to 180°. **b.** the great circle running through both poles. See **prime meridian. 2.** *Astronomy.* **a.** the great circle on the celestial sphere passing through the north and south celestial poles and the zenith and nadir of the observer. **b.** (*as modifier*): *a meridian instrument.* **3.** Also called: **meridian section.** *Maths.* a section of a surface of revolution, such as a paraboloid, that contains the axis of revolution. **4.** the peak; zenith: *the meridian of his achievements.* **5.** *Obsolete.* noon. ~*adj.* **6.** along or relating to a meridian. **7.** of or happening at noon. **8.** relating to the peak of something. [C14: from Latin *merīdiānus* of midday, from *merīdiēs* midday, from *medius* MID[1] + *diēs* day]

meridian circle *n.* an instrument used in astronomy for determining the declination and right ascension of stars. It consists of a telescope attached to a graduated circle.

meridional (mə'rɪdɪənᵊl) *adj.* **1.** along, relating to, or resembling a meridian. **2.** characteristic of or located in the south, esp. of Europe. ~*n.* **3.** an inhabitant of the south, esp. of France. [C14: from Late Latin *merīdiōnālis* southern; see MERIDIAN; for form, compare *septentriōnālis* SEPTENTRIONAL] —**me'ridionally** *adv.*

mering ('mɪərɪŋ) *n. Chiefly Irish.* **a.** another word for **mere**[3]. **b.** (*as modifier*): *the mering wall.* [C16: from MERE[3]]

meringue (mə'ræŋ) *n.* **1.** stiffly beaten egg whites mixed with sugar and baked, often as a topping for pies, cakes, etc. **2.** a small cake or shell of this mixture, often filled with cream. [C18: from French, origin obscure]

merino (mə'riːnəʊ) *n., pl.* **-nos. 1.** a breed of sheep, originating in Spain. **2.** the long fine wool of this sheep. **3.** the yarn made from this wool, often mixed with cotton. **4. pure merino.** *Austral. informal.* **a.** an affluent and socially prominent person. **b.** (*as modifier*): *a pure merino cricketer.* ~*adj.* **5.** made from merino wool. [C18: from Spanish, origin uncertain]

meristem ('mɛrɪˌstɛm) *n.* a plant tissue responsible for growth, whose cells divide and differentiate to form the tissues and organs of the plant. Meristems occur within the stem (see **cambium**) and leaves and at the tips of stems and roots. [C19: from Greek *meristos* divided, from *merizein* to divide, from *meris* portion] —**meristematic** (ˌmɛrɪstɪ'mætɪk) *adj.*

meristic (mə'rɪstɪk) *adj. Biology.* **1.** of or relating to the number of organs or parts in an animal or plant body: *meristic variation.* **2.** segmented: *meristic worms.*

merit ('mɛrɪt) *n.* **1.** worth or superior quality; excellence: *work of great merit.* **2.** (*often pl.*) a deserving or commendable quality or act: *judge him on his merits.* **3.** *Christianity.* spiritual credit granted or received for good works. **4.** the fact or state of deserving; desert. **5.** an obsolete word for **reward.** ~*vb.* **-its, -iting, -ited. 6.** (*tr.*) to be worthy of; deserve: *he merits promotion.* ~See also **merits.** [C13: via Old French from Latin *meritum* reward, desert, from *merēre* to deserve] —'**merited** *adj.* —'**meritless** *adj.*

meritocracy (ˌmɛrɪ'tɒkrəsɪ) *n., pl.* **-cies. 1.** rule by persons chosen not because of birth or wealth, but for their superior talents or intellect. **2.** the persons constituting such a group. **3.** a social system formed on such a basis. —**meritocratic** (ˌmɛrɪtə'krætɪk) *adj.*

meritorious (ˌmɛrɪ'tɔːrɪəs) *adj.* praiseworthy; showing merit. [C15: from Latin *meritōrius* earning money] —ˌ**meri'toriously** *adv.* —ˌ**meri'toriousness** *n.*

merits ('mɛrɪts) *pl. n.* **1.** the actual and intrinsic rights and wrongs of an issue, esp. in a law case, as distinct from extraneous matters and technicalities. **2. on its (his, her,** etc.) **merits.** on the intrinsic qualities or virtues.

merit system *n. U.S.* the system of employing and promoting civil servants solely on the basis of ability rather than patronage. Compare **spoils system.**

merkin ('mɜːkɪn) *n.* **1.** an artificial hairpiece for the pudendum; a pubic wig. **2.** *Obsolete.* the pudendum itself. [C16: of unknown origin]

merle[1] *or* **merl** (mɜːl; *Scot.* mɛrl) *n. Scot.* another name for the (European) **blackbird.** [C15: via Old French from Latin *merula*]

merle[2] (mɜːl) *adj.* (of a dog, esp. a collie) having a bluish-grey coat with speckles or streaks of black. Often **blue merle.** [C20: from dialect *mirlet, mirly* speckled]

merlin ('mɜːlɪn) *n.* a small falcon, *Falco columbarius,* that has a dark plumage with a black-barred tail: used in falconry. See also **pigeon hawk.** [C14: from Old French *esmerillon,* from *esmeril,* of Germanic origin]

merlon ('mɜːlən) *n. Fortifications.* the solid upright section in a crenellated battlement. [C18: from French, from Italian *merlone,* from *merlo* battlement]

mermaid ('mɜːˌmeɪd) *n.* an imaginary sea creature fabled to have a woman's head and upper body and a fish's tail. [C14: from *mere* lake, inlet + MAID]

mermaid's purse *n.* another name for **sea purse.**

merman ('mɜːˌmæn) *n., pl.* **-men.** a male counterpart of the mermaid. [C17: see MERMAID]

mero- *combining form.* part or partial: *merocrine.* [from Greek *meros* part, share]

meroblastic (ˌmɛrəʊ'blæstɪk) *adj. Embryol.* of or showing cleavage of only the nonyolky part of the zygote, as in birds' eggs. Compare **holoblastic.** —ˌ**mero'blastically** *adv.*

merocrine ('mɛrəˌkraɪn, -krɪn) *adj.* (of the secretion of glands) characterized by formation of the product without undergoing disintegration. Compare **holocrine, apocrine.** [C20: from MERO- + Greek *krinein* to separate]

meroplankton (ˌmɛrəʊ'plæŋktən) *n.* plankton consisting of organisms at a certain stage of their life cycles, esp. larvae, the other stages not being spent as part of the plankton community. Compare **holoplankton.**

-merous *adj. combining form.* (in biology) having a certain number or kind of parts: *dimerous.* [from Greek *meros* part, division]

Merovingian (ˌmɛrəʊ'vɪndʒɪən) *adj.* **1.** of or relating to a Frankish dynasty that ruled Gaul and W Germany from about 500 to 751

A.D. ~*n.* **2.** a member or supporter of this dynasty. [C17: from French, from Medieval Latin *Merovingi* offspring of *Merovaeus,* Latin form of *Merowig,* traditional founder of the line]

merozoite (ˌmɛrəʊˈzəʊaɪt) *n.* any of the cells formed by fission of a schizont during the life cycle of sporozoan protozoans, such as the malaria parasite. Compare **trophozoite.** [C20: from MERO- + ZO(O) + -ITE[1]]

merriment (ˈmɛrɪmənt) *n.* gaiety, fun, or mirth.

merry (ˈmɛrɪ) *adj.* **-rier, -riest. 1.** cheerful; jolly. **2.** very funny; hilarious. **3.** *Brit. informal.* slightly drunk. **4.** *Archaic.* delightful. **5. make merry.** to revel; be festive. **6. play merry hell with.** *Informal.* to disturb greatly; disrupt. [Old English *merige* agreeable] —ˈ**merrily** *adv.* —ˈ**merriness** *n.*

merry-andrew *n.* a joker, clown, or buffoon. [C17: original reference of *Andrew* unexplained]

merry dancers *pl. n. Scot.* the aurora borealis.

merry-go-round *n.* **1.** another name for **roundabout** (sense 1). **2.** a whirl of activity or events: *the merry-go-round of the fashion world.*

merrymaking (ˈmɛrɪˌmeɪkɪŋ) *n.* fun, revelry, or festivity. —ˈ**merry**ˌ**maker** *n.*

merry men *pl. n. Facetious.* a person's assistants or followers. [C19: originally, the companions of a knight, outlaw, etc.]

merrythought (ˈmɛrɪˌθɔːt) *n. Brit.* a less common word for **wishbone.**

merse (mɜːs; *Scot.* mɛrs) *n. Scot.* **1.** low level ground by a river or shore, often alluvial and fertile. **2.** a marsh. [Old English *merse* marsh]

Mersey beat (ˈmɜːzɪ) *n.* **a.** the characteristic pop music of the Beatles and other groups from Liverpool in the 1960s. **b.** (*as modifier*): *the Merseybeat years.* [C20: named after the river *Mersey* on whose estuary Liverpool is situated]

mes- *combining form.* a variant of **meso-** before a vowel: *mesarch; mesencephalon; mesenteron.*

mesa (ˈmeɪsə) *n.* a flat tableland with steep edges, common in the southwestern U.S. [from Spanish: table]

mésalliance (meˈzælɪəns; *French* mezaljɑ̃s) *n.* marriage with a person of lower social status. [C18: from French: MISALLIANCE]

mesarch (ˈmɛsɑːk) *adj. Botany.* (of a xylem strand) having the first-formed xylem surrounded by that formed later, as in fern stems. Compare **exarch**[2]**, endarch.** [C19: from MES(O)- + Greek *arkhē* beginning]

mescal (mɛˈskæl) *n.* **1.** Also called: **peyote.** a spineless globe-shaped cactus, *Lophophora williamsii,* of Mexico and the southwestern U.S. Its button-like tubercles (**mescal buttons**) contain mescaline and are chewed by certain Indian tribes for their hallucinogenic effects. **2.** a colourless alcoholic spirit distilled from the fermented juice of certain agave plants. [C19: from American Spanish, from Nahuatl *mexcalli* the liquor, from *metl* MAGUEY + *ixcalli* stew]

mescaline *or* **mescalin** (ˈmɛskəˌliːn, -lɪn) *n.* a hallucinogenic drug derived from mescal buttons. Formula: $C_{11}H_{17}NO_3$.

mesdames (ˈmeɪˌdæm; *French* medam) *n.* the plural of **madame** and **madam** (sense 1).

mesdemoiselles (ˌmeɪdmwəˈzɛl; *French* medmwazɛl) *n.* the plural of **mademoiselle.**

meseems (mɪˈsiːmz) *vb. past* **meseemed.** (*tr.; takes a clause as object*) *Archaic.* it seems to me.

mesembryanthemum (mɪzˌɛmbrɪˈænθɪməm) *n.* any plant of a South African genus (*Mesembryanthemum*) of succulent-leaved prostrate or erect plants widely grown in gardens and greenhouses: family *Aizoaceae.* See **fig marigold, ice plant, Livingstone daisy.** [C18: New Latin, from Greek *mesēmbria* noon + *anthemon* flower]

mesencephalon (ˌmɛsɛnˈsɛfəˌlɒn) *n.* the part of the brain that develops from the middle portion of the embryonic neural tube. Compare **prosencephalon, rhombencephalon.** Nontechnical name: **midbrain.** —**mesencephalic** (ˌmɛsɛnsɪˈfælɪk) *adj.*

mesenchyme (ˈmɛsɛŋˌkaɪm) *n. Embryol.* the part of the mesoderm that develops into connective tissue, cartilage, lymph, blood, etc. [C19: New Latin, from MESO- + -ENCHYMA] —**mesenchymal** (mɛsˈɛŋkɪməl) *or* **mesenchymatous** (ˌmɛsɛŋˈkɪmətəs) *adj.*

mesenteritis (mɛsˌɛntəˈraɪtɪs) *n.* inflammation of the mesentery.

mesenteron (mɛsˈɛntəˌrɒn) *n., pl.* **-tera** (-tərə). a former name for **midgut** (sense 1). —**mes**ˌ**enter**ˈ**onic** *adj.*

mesentery (ˈmɛsəntərɪ, ˈmɛz-) *n., pl.* **-teries.** the double layer of peritoneum that is attached to the back wall of the abdominal cavity and supports most of the small intestine. [C16: from New Latin *mesenterium;* see MESO- + ENTERON] —ˌ**mesen**ˈ**teric** *adj.*

mesh (mɛʃ) *n.* **1.** a network; net. **2.** an open space between the strands of a network. **3.** (*often pl.*) the strands surrounding these spaces. **4.** anything that ensnares, or holds like a net: *the mesh of the secret police.* **5.** the engagement of teeth on interacting gearwheels: *the gears are in mesh.* **6.** a measure of spacing of the strands of a mesh or grid, expressed as the distance between strands for coarse meshes or a number of strands per unit length for fine meshes. ~*vb.* **7.** to entangle or become entangled. **8.** (of gear teeth) to engage or cause to engage. **9.** (*intr.;* often foll. by *with*) to coordinate (with): *to mesh with a policy.* **10.** to work or cause to work in harmony. [C16: probably from Dutch *maesche;* related to Old English *masc,* Old High German *masca*] —ˈ**meshy** *adj.*

mesh connection *n. Electrical engineering.* (in a polyphase system) an arrangement in which the end of each phase is connected to the beginning of the next, forming a ring, each junction being connected to a terminal. See also **delta connection, star connection.**

meshuga (mɪˈʃʊgə) *adj. Yiddish.* crazy. [from Hebrew]

mesiad (ˈmiːzɪæd) *adj. Anatomy, zoology.* relating to or situated at the middle or centre.

mesial (ˈmiːzɪəl) *adj. Anatomy.* another word for **medial** (sense 1). [C19: from MESO- + -IAL] —ˈ**mesially** *adv.*

mesic (ˈmiːzɪk) *adj.* **1.** of, relating to, or growing in conditions of medium water supply: *mesic plants.* **2.** of or relating to a meson. —ˈ**mesically** *adv.*

mesitylene (mɪˈsɪtɪˌliːn, ˈmɛsɪtɪˌliːn) *n.* a colourless liquid that occurs in crude petroleum; 1,3,5-trimethylbenzene. Formula: $C_6H_3(CH_3)_3$. [C19: from *mesityl,* from *mesite,* from New Latin *mesita,* from Greek *mesitēs* mediator + -ENE]

mesmerism (ˈmɛzməˌrɪzəm) *n. Psychol.* **1.** a hypnotic state induced by the operator's imposition of his will on that of the patient. **2.** an early doctrine concerning this. [C19: named after F. A. *Mesmer* (1734–1815), Austrian physician] —**mesmeric** (mɛzˈmɛrɪk) *adj.* —**mes**ˈ**merically** *adv.* —ˈ**mesmerist** *n.*

mesmerize *or* **mesmerise** (ˈmɛzməˌraɪz) *vb.* (*tr.*) **1.** a former word for **hypnotize. 2.** to hold (someone) as if spellbound. —ˌ**mesmeri**ˈ**zation** *or* ˌ**mesmeri**ˈ**sation** *n.* —ˈ**mesmer**ˌ**izer** *or* ˈ**mesmer**ˌ**iser** *n.*

mesnalty (ˈmiːnəltɪ) *n., pl.* **-ties.** *History.* the lands of a mesne lord. [C16: from legal French, from MESNE]

mesne (miːn) *adj. Law.* **1.** intermediate or intervening: used esp. of any assignment of property before the last: *a mesne assignment.* **2. mesne profits.** rents or profits accruing during the rightful owner's exclusion from his land. [C15: from legal French *meien* in the middle, MEAN[3]]

mesne lord *n.* (in feudal society) a lord who held land from a superior lord and kept his own tenants on it.

meso- *or before a vowel* **mes-** *combining form.* middle or intermediate: *mesomorph.* [from Greek *misos* middle]

mesobenthos (ˌmɛzəˈbɛnθəs, ˌmɛsə-) *n.* flora and fauna living at the bottom of seas 182 to 914 metres deep. [from MESO- + Greek *benthos* depth of the sea]

mesoblast (ˈmɛsəʊˌblæst) *n.* another name for **mesoderm.** —ˌ**meso**ˈ**blastic** *adj.*

mesocarp (ˈmɛsəʊˌkɑːp) *n.* the middle layer of the pericarp of a fruit, such as the flesh of a peach.

mesocephalic (ˌmɛsəʊsɪˈfælɪk) *Anatomy.* ~*adj.* **1.** having a medium-sized head, esp. one with a cephalic index between 75 and 80. ~*n.* **2.** an individual with such a head. ~Compare **brachycephalic, dolichocephalic.** —**mesocephaly** (ˌmɛsəʊˈsɛfəlɪ) *n.*

mesocratic (ˌmɛsəˈkrætɪk) *adj.* (of igneous rocks) containing 30–60 per cent of ferromagnesian minerals. [C20: from MESO- + -CRAT, with allusion to the moderately dark colour of the rock. Compare LEUCOCRATIC]

mesoderm (ˈmɛsəʊˌdɜːm) *n.* the middle germ layer of an animal embryo, giving rise to muscle, blood, bone, connective tissue, etc. See also **ectoderm, endoderm.** —ˌ**meso**ˈ**dermal** *or* ˌ**meso**ˈ**dermic** *adj.*

mesogastrium (ˌmɛsəʊˈgæstrɪəm) *n.* the mesentery supporting the embryonic stomach. —ˌ**meso**ˈ**gastric** *adj.*

mesoglea *or* **mesogloea** (ˌmɛsəʊˈgliːə) *n.* the gelatinous material between the outer and inner cellular layers of jellyfish and other coelenterates. [C19: New Latin, from MESO- + Greek *gloia* glue]

mesognathous (mɪˈsɒgnəθəs) *adj. Anthropol.* having slightly projecting jaws. —**me**ˈ**sognathism** *or* **me**ˈ**sognathy** *n.*

mesokurtic (ˌmɛsəʊˈkɜːtɪk) *adj. Statistics.* (of a distribution) having kurtosis $B_2 = 3$, concentrated around its mean like a normal distribution. Compare **leptokurtic, platykurtic.** [C20: from MESO- + Greek *kurtos* arched, bulging + -IC]

Mesolithic (ˌmɛsəʊˈlɪθɪk) *n.* **1.** the period between the Palaeolithic and the Neolithic, in Europe from about 12 000 to 3000 B.C., characterized by the appearance of microliths. ~*adj.* **2.** of or relating to the Mesolithic.

mesomorph (ˈmɛsəʊˌmɔːf) *n.* a person with a muscular body build: said to be correlated with somatotonia. Compare **ectomorph, endomorph (sense 1).**

mesomorphic (ˌmɛsəʊˈmɔːfɪk) *adj.* also **mesomorphous. 1.** *Chem.* existing in or concerned with an intermediate state of matter between a true liquid and a true solid. See also **liquid crystal, smectic, nematic. 2.** relating to or being a mesomorph. —ˌ**meso**ˈ**morphism** *n.* —ˈ**meso**ˌ**morphy** *n.*

meson (ˈmiːzɒn) *n.* any of a group of elementary particles, such as a pion or kaon, that has a rest mass between those of an electron and a proton, and an integral spin. They are responsible for the force between nucleons in the atomic nucleus. Former name: **mesotron.** See also **muon.** [C20: from MESO- + -ON] —**me**ˈ**sonic** *or* ˈ**mesic** *adj.*

mesonephros (ˌmɛsəʊˈnɛfrɒs) *n.* the middle part of the embryonic kidney in vertebrates, becoming the adult kidney in fishes and amphibians and the epididymis in reptiles, birds, and mammals. See also **pronephros, metanephros.** [C19: New Latin, from MESO- + Greek *nephros* kidney] —ˌ**meso**ˈ**nephric** *adj.*

mesopause (ˈmɛsəʊˌpɔːz) *n. Meteorol.* the zone of minimum temperature between the mesosphere and the thermosphere.

mesopelagic (ˌmɛsəʊpəˈlædʒɪk) *adj.* of, relating to, or inhabiting the intermediate depths of the ocean between approximately 100 and 1000 metres.
mesophilic (ˌmɛsəʊˈfɪlɪk) *adj. Biology.* (esp. of bacteria) having an ideal growth temperature of 20–45°C. —**mesophile** (ˈmɛsəʊˌfaɪl) *n.*
mesophyll (ˈmɛsəʊˌfɪl) *n.* the soft chlorophyll-containing tissue of a leaf between the upper and lower layers of epidermis: involved in photosynthesis. —ˌ**mesoˈphyllic** *or* ˌ**mesoˈphyllous** *adj.*
mesophyte (ˈmɛsəʊˌfaɪt) *n.* any plant that grows in surroundings receiving an average supply of water. —**mesophytic** (ˌmɛsəʊˈfɪtɪk) *adj.*
Mesopotamian (ˌmɛsəpəˈteɪmɪən) *adj.* **1.** of or relating to Mesopotamia, a region of SW Asia between the lower and middle reaches of the Tigris and Euphrates rivers, or its ancient civilizations. ~*n.* **2.** a person from Mesopotamia. [Latin from Greek *mesopotamia* (*khora*) (the land) between rivers]
mesosphere (ˈmɛsəʊˌsfɪə) *n.* **1.** the atmospheric layer lying between the stratosphere and the thermosphere, characterized by a rapid decrease in temperature with height. **2.** the solid part of the earth's mantle lying between the asthenosphere and the core. —**mesospheric** (ˌmɛsəʊˈsfɛrɪk) *adj.*
mesothelioma (ˌmɛzəʊˌθiːlɪˈəʊmə) *n., pl.* **-mata** (-mətə) *or* **-mas.** a tumour of the epithelium lining the lungs, abdomen, or heart: often associated with exposure to asbestos dust. [C20: from MESOTHELI(UM) + -OMA]
mesothelium (ˌmɛsəʊˈθiːlɪəm) *n., pl.* **-liums** *or* **-lia** (-lɪə). epithelium, derived from embryonic mesoderm lining body cavities. [from New Latin, from MESO- + (EPI)THELIUM] —ˌ**mesoˈthelial** *adj.*
mesothorax (ˌmɛsəʊˈθɔːræks) *n., pl.* **-raxes** *or* **-races** (-rəˌsiːz). the middle segment of the thorax of an insect, bearing the second pair of walking legs and the first pair of wings. See also **prothorax, metathorax.** —**mesothoracic** (ˌmɛsəʊθɔːˈræsɪk) *adj.*
mesothorium (ˌmɛsəʊˈθɔːrɪəm) *n. Physics, obsolete.* either of two radioactive elements. **Mesothorium I** is now called radium-228. **Mesothorium II** is now called actinium-228.
mesotron (ˈmɛsəˌtrɒn) *n.* a former name for **meson.**
Mesozoic (ˌmɛsəʊˈzəʊɪk) *adj.* **1.** of, denoting, or relating to an era of geological time that began 225 000 000 years ago with the Triassic period and lasted about 155 000 000 years until the end of the Cretaceous period. ~*n.* **2. the.** the Mesozoic era.
mesquite *or* **mesquit** (mɛˈskiːt, ˈmɛskiːt) *n.* any small mimosaceous tree of the genus *Prosopis,* esp. the tropical American *P. juliflora,* whose sugary pods (**mesquite beans**) are used as animal fodder. Also called: **algarroba, honey locust, honey mesquite.** [C19: from Mexican Spanish, from Nahuatl *mizquitl*]
mess (mɛs) *n.* **1.** a state of confusion or untidiness, esp. if dirty or unpleasant: *the house was in a mess.* **2.** a chaotic or troublesome state of affairs; muddle: *his life was a mess.* **3.** *Informal.* a dirty or untidy person or thing. **4.** *Archaic.* a portion of food, esp. soft or semiliquid food. **5.** a place where service personnel eat or take recreation: *an officers' mess.* **6.** a group of people, usually servicemen, who eat together. **7.** the meal so taken. **8. mess of pottage.** a material gain involving the sacrifice of a higher value. ~*vb.* **9.** (*tr.;* often foll. by *up*) to muddle or dirty. **10.** (*intr.*) to make a mess. **11.** (*intr.*) (often foll. by *with*) to interfere; meddle. **12.** (*intr.*) (often foll. by *with* or *together*) *Military.* to group together, esp. for eating. [C13: from Old French *mes* dish of food, from Late Latin *missus* course (at table), from Latin *mittere* to send forth, set out]
mess about *or* **around** *vb.* (*adv.*) **1.** (*intr.*) to occupy oneself trivially; potter. **2.** (when *intr.,* often foll. by *with*) to interfere or meddle (with). **3.** (*intr.;* sometimes foll. by *with*) *Chiefly U.S.* to engage in adultery.
message (ˈmɛsɪdʒ) *n.* **1.** a communication, usually brief, from one person or group to another. **2.** an implicit meaning or moral, as in a work of art. **3.** a formal communiqué. **4.** an inspired communication of a prophet or religious leader. **5.** a mission; errand. **6.** (*pl.*) *Scot.* shopping: *going for the messages.* **7. get the message.** *Informal.* to understand what is meant. ~*vb.* **8.** (*tr.*) to send as a message, esp. to signal (a plan, etc.). [C13: from Old French, from Vulgar Latin *missāticum* (unattested) something sent, from Latin *missus,* past participle of *mittere* to send]
message stick *n.* a stick bearing carved symbols, carried by an Australian Aborigine as identification.
message switching *n. Computer technol.* the maintenance of a telecommunication link between two devices for the duration of a message.
messaline (ˌmɛsəˈliːn, ˈmɛsəˌliːn) *n.* a light lustrous twilled-silk fabric. [C20: from French, origin obscure]
Messapian (məˈseɪpɪən) *or* **Messapic** (məˈseɪpɪk, -ˈsæpɪk) *n.* a scantily recorded language of an ancient people of Calabria (the **Messapii**), thought by some to be related to ancient Illyrian.
Messeigneurs *French.* (mesɛɲœr) *n.* the plural of **Monseigneur.**
messenger (ˈmɛsɪndʒə) *n.* **1.** a person who takes messages from one person or group to another or others. **2.** a person who runs errands or is employed to run errands. **3.** a carrier of official dispatches; courier. **4.** *Nautical.* **a.** a light line used to haul in a heavy rope. **b.** an endless belt of chain, rope, or cable, used on a powered winch to take off power. **5.** *Archaic.* a herald. [C13: from Old French *messagier,* from MESSAGE]
messenger RNA *n. Biochem.* a form of RNA, transcribed from a single strand of DNA, that carries genetic information required for protein synthesis from DNA to the ribosomes. Sometimes shortened to **m-RNA.** See also **transfer RNA, genetic code.**
Messerschmitt (*German* ˈmɛsərˌʃmɪt) *n.* any of various German military planes designed by Willy Messerschmidt (1898–1978), aeronautical engineer. They figured prominently in World War II, including the Me-262, the first jet fighter.
mess hall *n.* a military dining room, usually large.
Messiah (mɪˈsaɪə) *n.* **1.** *Judaism.* the awaited king of the Jews, to be sent by God to free them. **2.** Jesus Christ, when regarded in this role. **3.** an exceptional or hoped for liberator of a country or people. [C14: from Old French *Messie,* ultimately from Hebrew *māshīach* anointed] —**Mesˈsiahˌship** *n.*
messianic (ˌmɛsɪˈænɪk) *adj.* **1.** (*sometimes cap.*) *Bible.* **a.** of or relating to the Messiah, his awaited deliverance of the Jews, or the new age of peace expected to follow this. **b.** of or relating to Jesus Christ or the salvation believed to have been brought by him. **2. a.** of or relating to any popular leader promising deliverance or an ideal era of peace and prosperity. **b.** of or relating to promises of this kind or to an ideal era of this kind. —ˌ**mesˈsiˈanically** *adv.* —**messianism** (mɛˈsaɪənɪzəm) *n.*
Messidor *French.* (mesidɔr) *n.* the month of harvest: the tenth month of the French revolutionary calendar, extending from June 20 to July 19. [C19: from French, from Latin *messis* harvest + Greek *dōron* gift]
Messier catalogue (ˈmɛsɪeɪ) *n. Astronomy.* a catalogue of 103 nonstellar objects, such as nebulae and galaxies, prepared in 1781–86. An object is referred to by its number in this catalogue, for example the Andromeda Galaxy is referred to as *M*31. [C18: named after Charles *Messier* (1730–1817), French astronomer]
messieurs (ˈmɛsəz; *French* mesjø) *n.* the plural of **monsieur.**
mess jacket *n.* a waist-length jacket tapering to a point at the back, worn by officers in the mess for formal dinners.
mess kit *n. Military.* **1.** *Brit.* formal evening wear for officers. **2.** Also called: **mess gear.** eating utensils used esp. in the field.
messmate (ˈmɛsˌmeɪt) *n.* **1.** a person with whom one shares meals in a mess, esp. in the army. **2.** *Austral.* any of various eucalyptus trees that grow amongst other species.
Messrs (ˈmɛsəz) *n.* the plural of **Mr.** [C18: abbreviation from French *messieurs*]
messuage (ˈmɛswɪdʒ) *n. Property law.* a dwelling house together with its outbuildings, curtilage, and the adjacent land appropriated to its use. [C14: from Norman French: household, perhaps through misspelling of Old French *mesnage* MÉNAGE]
messy (ˈmɛsɪ) *adj.* **messier, messiest.** dirty, confused, or untidy. —ˈ**messily** *adv.* —ˈ**messiness** *n.*
mestee (mɛˈstiː) *n.* a variant of **mustee.**
mester (ˈmɛstə) *n. South Yorkshire dialect.* **1.** master: used as a term of address for a man who is the head of a house. **2. bad mester.** a term for the devil, used when speaking to children.
mestizo (mɛˈstiːzəʊ, mɪ-) *n., pl.* **-zos** *or* **-zoes.** a person of mixed parentage, esp. the offspring of a Spanish American and an American Indian. [C16: from Spanish, ultimately from Latin *miscēre* to mix] —**mestiza** (mɛˈstiːzə) *fem. n.*
mestome (ˈmɛstəʊm) *or* **mestom** *n. Botany.* **a.** conducting tissue associated with parenchyma. **b.** (*as modifier*): *a mestome sheath.* [C19: from Greek *mestōma* filling up]
mestranol (ˈmɛstrəˌnɒl, -ˌnəʊl) *n.* a synthetic oestrogen used in combination with progesterones as an oral contraceptive. Formula: $C_{21}H_{26}O_2$. [C20: from M(ETHYL) + (O)ESTR(OGEN) + (*pregn*)*an*(*e*) ($C_{21}H_{36}$) + -OL]
met (mɛt) *vb.* the past tense and past participle of **meet.**
met. *abbrev. for:* **1.** metaphor. **2.** metaphysics. **3.** meteorological: *the met. office weather report.* **4.** meteorology. **5.** metropolitan.
meta- *or sometimes before a vowel* **met-** *prefix.* **1.** indicating change, alteration, or alternation: *metabolism; metamorphosis.* **2.** (of an academic discipline, esp. philosophy) concerned with the concepts and results of the named discipline: *metamathematics; meta-ethics.* See also **metatheory. 3.** occurring or situated behind or after: *metaphase.* **4.** (*often in italics*) denoting that an organic compound contains a benzene ring with substituents in the 1,3-positions: *metadinitrobenzene; meta*-cresol. Abbrev.: *m*-. Compare **ortho-** (sense 4), **para-**[1] (sense 6). **5.** denoting an isomer, polymer, or compound related to a specified compound (often differing from similar compounds that are prefixed by *para-*): *metaldehyde.* **6.** denoting an oxyacid that is a lower hydrated form of the anhydride or a salt of such an acid: *metaphosphoric acid.* Compare **ortho-** (sense 5). [Greek, from *meta* with, after, between, among. Compare Old English *mid, mith* with, Old Norse *meth* with, between]
metabolic pathway *n.* any of the sequences of biochemical reactions, catalysed by enzymes, that occur in all living cells: concerned mainly with the exchange of energy and chemicals. See also **Krebs cycle.**
metabolism (mɪˈtæbəˌlɪzəm) *n.* **1.** the sum total of the chemical processes that occur in living organisms, resulting in growth, production of energy, elimination of waste material, etc. See **anabolism, basal metabolism, catabolism. 2.** the sum total of the chemical processes affecting a particular substance in the body: *carbohydrate metabolism; iodine metabolism.* [C19: from

Greek *metabolē* change, from *metaballein* to change, from META- + *ballein* to throw] —**metabolic** (ˌmɛtəˈbɒlɪk) *adj.* —ˌ**metaˈbolically** *adv.*

metabolite (mɪˈtæbəˌlaɪt) *n.* a substance produced during or taking part in metabolism. [C19: METABOL(ISM) + -ITE[1]]

metabolize *or* **metabolise** (mɪˈtæbəˌlaɪz) *vb.* to produce or be produced by metabolism. —**meˈtaboˌlizable** *or* **meˈtaboˌlisable** *adj.*

metaboly (mɪˈtæbəlɪ) *n. Zoology.* the ability of some cells, esp. protozoans, to alter their shape.

metacarpal (ˌmɛtəˈkɑːpᵊl) *Anatomy.* ~*adj.* **1.** of or relating to the metacarpus. ~*n.* **2.** a metacarpal bone.

metacarpus (ˌmɛtəˈkɑːpəs) *n., pl.* **-pi** (-paɪ). **1.** the skeleton of the hand between the wrist and the fingers, consisting of five long bones. **2.** the corresponding bones in other vertebrates.

metacentre *or U.S.* **metacenter** (ˈmɛtəˌsɛntə) *n.* the intersection of a vertical line through the centre of buoyancy of a floating body at equilibrium with a vertical line through the centre of buoyancy when the body is tilted. —ˌ**metaˈcentric** *adj.*

metachromatic (ˌmɛtəkrəʊˈmætɪk) *adj.* **1.** (of tissues and cells stained for microscopical examination) taking a colour different from that of the dye solution. **2.** (of dyes) capable of staining tissues or cells a colour different from that of the dye solution. **3.** of or relating to metachromatism.

metachromatism (ˌmɛtəˈkrəʊməˌtɪzəm) *n.* a change in colour, esp. when caused by a change in temperature. [C19: from META- + CHROMATO- + -ISM]

metachrosis (ˌmɛtəˈkrəʊsɪs) *n. Zoology.* the ability of some animals, such as chameleons, to change their colour. [C19: from META- + Greek *khrōs* colour]

metacinnabarite (ˌmɛtəsɪˈnæbəˌraɪt) *n.* the black solid form of mercuric sulphide.

metacognition (ˌmɛtəkɒgˈnɪʃən) *n. Psychol.* thinking about one's own mental processes.

meta-ethics *n.* (*functioning as sing.*) the philosophical study of questions about the nature of ethical judgment as distinct from questions of normative ethics, for example, whether ethical judgments state facts or express attitudes, whether there are objective standards of morality, and how moral judgments can be justified. —ˌ**meta-ˈethical** *adj.*

metafemale (ˌmɛtəˈfiːmeɪl) *n. Genetics.* a sterile female organism, esp. a fruit fly (*Drosophila*) that has three X chromosomes. Former name: **superfemale.**

metagalaxy (ˌmɛtəˈgæləksɪ) *n., pl.* **-axies.** the total system of galaxies and intergalactic space making up the universe. —**metagalactic** (ˌmɛtəgəˈlæktɪk) *adj.*

metage (ˈmiːtɪdʒ) *n.* **1.** the official measuring of weight or contents. **2.** a charge for this. [C16: from METE[1]]

metagenesis (ˌmɛtəˈdʒɛnɪsɪs) *n.* another name for **alternation of generations.** —**metagenetic** (ˌmɛtədʒɪˈnɛtɪk) *or* ˌ**metaˈgenic** *adj.* —ˌ**metageˈnetically** *adv.*

metagnathous (mɪˈtægnəθəs) *adj.* (of the beaks of birds such as the crossbill) having crossed tips. [C19: from META- + -GNATHOUS] —**meˈtagnaˌthism** *n.*

metal (ˈmɛtᵊl) *n.* **1. a.** any of a number of chemical elements, such as iron or copper, that are often lustrous ductile solids, have basic oxides, form positive ions, and are good conductors of heat and electricity. **b.** an alloy, such as brass or steel, containing one or more of these elements. **2.** *Printing.* type made of metal. **3.** the substance of glass in a molten state or as the finished product. **4.** short for **road metal. 5.** *Informal.* short for **heavy metal** (sense 1). **6.** *Navy.* **a.** the total weight of projectiles that can be shot by a ship's guns at any one time. **b.** the total weight or number of a ship's guns. **7.** *Heraldry.* gold or silver. **8.** (*pl.*) the rails of a railway. ~*adj.* **9.** made of metal. ~*vb.* **-als, -alling, -alled** *or U.S.* **-als, -aling, -aled.** (*tr.*) **10.** to fit or cover with metal. **11.** to make or mend (a road) with **road metal.** [C13: from Latin *metallum* mine, product of a mine, from Greek *metallon*] —ˈ**metalled** *adj.* —ˈ**metal-ˌlike** *adj.*

metal. *or* **metall.** *abbrev. for:* **1.** metallurgical. **2.** metallurgy.

metalanguage (ˈmɛtəˌlæŋgwɪdʒ) *n.* a language or system of symbols used to discuss another language or system. See also **formal language, natural language.** Compare **object language.**

metal detector *n.* a device that gives an audible or visual signal when its search head comes close to a metallic object embedded in food, buried in the ground, etc.

metallic (mɪˈtælɪk) *adj.* **1.** of, concerned with, or consisting of metal or a metal. **2.** suggestive of a metal: *a metallic click; metallic lustre.* **3.** *Chem.* (of a metal element) existing in the free state rather than in combination: *metallic copper.* —**meˈtallically** *adv.*

metallic bond *n. Chem.* the covalent bonding between atoms in metals, in which the valence electrons are free to move through the crystal.

metallic lens *n.* an arrangement of louvres used to direct and focus electromagnetic or sound waves.

metallic soap *n.* any one of a number of colloidal stearates, palmitates, or oleates of various metals, including aluminium, calcium, magnesium, iron, and zinc. They are used as bases for ointments, fungicides, fireproofing and waterproofing agents, and dryers for paints and varnishes.

metalliferous (ˌmɛtᵊˈlɪfərəs) *adj.* containing a metallic element: *a metalliferous ore.* [C17: from Latin *metallifer* yielding metal, from *metallum* metal + *ferre* to bear]

metalline (ˈmɛtəˌlaɪn) *adj.* **1.** of, resembling, or relating to metals. **2.** containing metals or metal ions.

metallist *or U.S.* **metalist** (ˈmɛtᵊlɪst) *n.* **1.** a person who works with metals. **2.** a person who advocates a system of currency based on a metal, such as gold or silver.

metallize, metallise, *or U.S.* **metalize** (ˈmɛtəˌlaɪz) *vb.* (*tr.*) to make metallic or to coat or treat with metal. —ˌ**metalliˈzation,** ˌ**metalliˈsation,** *or U.S.* ˌ**metaliˈzation** *n.*

metallo- *combining form.* denoting metal: *metallography; metalloid; metallurgy.* [from Greek *metallon*]

metallocene (mɪˈtæləʊˌsiːn) *n. Chem.* any one of a class of organometallic sandwich compounds of the general formula $M(C_5H_5)_2$, where M is a metal atom. See **ferrocene.** [C20: from METALLO- + *-cene*, as in FERROCENE]

metallography (ˌmɛtəˈlɒgrəfɪ) *n.* **1.** the branch of metallurgy concerned with the composition and structure of metals and alloys. **2.** a lithographic process using metal plates instead of stone; metal lithography. —ˌ**metalˈlographer** *or* ˌ**metalˈlographist** *n.* —**metallographic** (mɪˌtæləˈgræfɪk) *adj.* —**meˌtalloˈgraphically** *adv.*

metalloid (ˈmɛtəˌlɔɪd) *n.* **1.** a nonmetallic element, such as arsenic or silicon, that has some of the properties of a metal. ~*adj.* *also* **metalloidal** (ˌmɛtəˈlɔɪdᵊl). **2.** of or being a metalloid. **3.** resembling a metal.

metallophone (mɛˈtæləˌfəʊn) *n.* any of various musical instruments consisting of tuned metal bars struck with a hammer, such as the glockenspiel.

metallurgy (mɛˈtælədʒɪ; *U.S.* ˈmɛtᵊˌlɜːdʒɪ) *n.* the scientific study of the extraction, refining, alloying, and fabrication of metals and of their structure and properties. —ˌ**metalˈlurgic** *or* ˌ**metalˈlurgical** *adj.* —ˌ**metalˈlurgically** *adv.* —**metallurgist** (mɛˈtælədʒɪst, ˈmɛtəˌlɜːdʒɪst) *n.*

metal spraying *n.* a process in which a layer of one metal is sprayed onto another in the molten state.

metal tape *n.* a magnetic recording tape coated with pure iron rather than iron oxide or chromedioxide: it gives enhanced recording quality.

metalwork (ˈmɛtᵊlˌwɜːk) *n.* **1.** the craft of working in metal. **2.** work in metal or articles made from metal.

metalworking (ˈmɛtᵊlˌwɜːkɪŋ) *n.* the processing of metal to change its shape, size, etc., as by rolling, forging, etc., or by making metal articles. —ˈ**metalˌworker** *n.*

metamale (ˈmɛtəˌmeɪl) *n. Genetics.* a sterile male organism, esp. a fruit fly (*Drosophila*) that has one X chromosome and three sets of autosomes. Former name: **supermale.**

metamathematics (ˌmɛtəˌmæθɪˈmætɪks) *n.* (*functioning as sing.*) the logical analysis of the reasoning, principles, and rules that control the use and combination of mathematical symbols, numbers, etc. —ˌ**metaˌmatheˈmatical** *adj.* —ˌ**metaˌmathemaˈtician** *n.*

metamer (ˈmɛtəmə) *n.* any of two or more isomeric compounds exhibiting metamerism.

metamere (ˈmɛtəˌmɪə) *n.* one of the similar body segments into which earthworms, crayfish, and similar animals are divided longitudinally. Also called: **somite.** [C19: from META- + -MERE] —**metameral** (mɪˈtæmərəl) *adj.*

metameric (ˌmɛtəˈmɛrɪk) *adj.* **1.** divided into or consisting of metameres. See also **metamerism** (sense 1). **2.** of or concerned with metamerism. —ˌ**metaˈmerically** *adv.*

metamerism (mɪˈtæməˌrɪzəm) *n.* **1.** Also called: **(metameric) segmentation.** the division of an animal into similar segments (metameres). In many vertebrates it is confined to the embryonic nervous and muscular systems. **2.** *Chem.* a type of isomerism in which molecular structures differ by the attachment of different groups to the same atom, as in $CH_3OC_3H_7$ and $C_2H_5OC_2H_5$.

metamict (ˈmɛtəˌmɪkt) *adj.* of or denoting the amorphous state of a substance that has lost its crystalline structure as a result of the radioactivity of uranium or thorium within it: *metamict minerals.* [C19: from Danish *metamikt* from META- + Greek *miktos* mixed] —ˌ**metamictiˈzation** *or* ˌ**metamictiˈsation** *n.*

metamorphic (ˌmɛtəˈmɔːfɪk) *or* **metamorphous** *adj.* **1.** relating to or resulting from metamorphosis or metamorphism. **2.** (of rocks) altered considerably from the original structure and composition by pressure and heat. Compare **igneous, sedimentary.**

metamorphism (ˌmɛtəˈmɔːfɪzəm) *n.* **1.** the process by which metamorphic rocks are formed. **2.** a variant of **metamorphosis.**

metamorphose (ˌmɛtəˈmɔːfəʊz) *vb.* to undergo or cause to undergo metamorphosis or metamorphism.

metamorphosis (ˌmɛtəˈmɔːfəsɪs) *n., pl.* **-ses** (-ˌsiːz). **1.** a complete change of physical form or substance. **2.** a complete change of character, appearance, etc. **3.** a person or thing that has undergone metamorphosis. **4.** *Zoology.* the rapid transformation of a larva into an adult that occurs in certain animals, for example the stage between tadpole and frog or between chrysalis and butterfly. [C16: via Latin from Greek: transformation, from META- + *morphē* form]

metanephros (ˌmɛtəˈnɛfrɒs) *n., pl.* **-roi** (-rɔɪ). the last-formed posterior part of the embryonic kidney in reptiles, birds, and mammals, which remains functional in the adult. See also **pronephros, mesonephros.** [C19: New Latin, from META- + Greek *nephros* kidney]

metaph. *abbrev. for:* **1.** metaphor(ical). **2.** metaphysics.

metaphase (ˈmɛtəˌfeɪz) *n.* **1.** *Biology.* the second stage of mitosis during which a body of longitudinally arranged threads (see **spindle** (sense 7)) is formed within the cell. See also **prophase** (sense 1), **anaphase** (sense 1), **telophase** (sense 1). **2.** the corresponding stage of the first division of meiosis.

metaphor (ˈmɛtəfə, -ˌfɔː) *n.* a figure of speech in which a word or phrase is applied to an object or action that it does not literally denote in order to imply a resemblance, for example *he is a lion in battle.* Compare **simile.** [C16: from Latin, from Greek *metaphora,* from *metapherein* to transfer, from META- + *pherein* to bear] —**metaphoric** (ˌmɛtəˈfɒrɪk) *or* ˌ**metaˈphorical** *adj.* —ˌ**metaˈphorically** *adv.* —ˌ**metaˈphoricalness** *n.*

metaphosphate (ˌmɛtəˈfɒsfeɪt) *n.* any salt of metaphosphoric acid.

metaphosphoric acid (ˌmɛtəfɒsˈfɒrɪk) *n.* a glassy deliquescent highly polymeric solid, used as a dehydrating agent. Formula: $(HPO_3)_x$. See also **polyphosphoric acid.**

metaphrase (ˈmɛtəˌfreɪz) *n.* **1.** a literal translation. Compare **paraphrase.** ~*vb.* (*tr.*) **2.** to alter or manipulate the wording of. **3.** to translate literally. [C17: from Greek *metaphrazein* to translate]

metaphrast (ˈmɛtəˌfræst) *n.* a person who metaphrases, esp. one who changes the form of a text, as by rendering verse into prose. [C17: from Medieval Greek *metaphrastēs* translator] —ˌ**metaˈphrastic** *or* ˌ**metaˈphrastical** *adj.* —ˌ**metaˈphrastically** *adv.*

metaphysic (ˌmɛtəˈfɪzɪk) *n.* **1.** the system of first principles and assumptions underlying an enquiry or philosophical theory. **2.** an obsolete word for **metaphysician.** ~*adj.* **3.** *Rare.* another word for **metaphysical.**

metaphysical (ˌmɛtəˈfɪzɪkəl) *adj.* **1.** relating to or concerned with metaphysics. **2.** (of a statement or theory) having the form of an empirical hypothesis, but in fact immune from empirical testing and therefore (in the view of the logical positivists) literally meaningless. **3.** (popularly) abstract, abstruse, or unduly theoretical. **4.** incorporeal; supernatural. —ˌ**metaˈphysically** *adv.*

Metaphysical (ˌmɛtəˈfɪzɪkəl) *adj.* **1.** denoting or relating to certain 17th-century poets who combined intense feeling with ingenious thought and often used elaborate imagery and conceits. ~*n.* **2.** a poet of this group.

metaphysicize *or* **metaphysicise** (ˌmɛtəˈfɪzɪˌsaɪz) *vb.* **1.** (*intr.*) to think, write, etc., metaphysically. **2.** (*tr.*) to treat (a subject) metaphysically.

metaphysics (ˌmɛtəˈfɪzɪks) *n.* (*functioning as sing.*) **1.** the branch of philosophy that deals with first principles, esp. of being and knowing. **2.** the philosophical study of the nature of reality, concerned with such questions as the existence of God, the external world, etc. **3.** See **descriptive metaphysics. 4.** (popularly) abstract or subtle discussion or reasoning. [C16: from Medieval Latin, from Greek *ta meta ta phusika* the things after the physics, from the arrangement of the subjects treated in the works of Aristotle (384–322 B.C.)] —**metaphysician** (ˌmɛtəfɪˈzɪʃən) *or* **metaphysicist** (ˌmɛtəˈfɪzɪsɪst) *n.*

metaplasia (ˌmɛtəˈpleɪzɪə) *n.* the transformation of one kind of tissue into a different kind.

metaplasm (ˈmɛtəˌplæzəm) *n.* the nonliving constituents, such as starch and pigment granules, of the cytoplasm of a cell. —ˌ**metaˈplasmic** *adj.*

metapolitics (ˌmɛtəˈpɒlɪtɪks) *n.* (*functioning as sing.*) political theory (often used derogatorily). —**metapolitical** (ˌmɛtəpəˈlɪtɪkəl) *adj.*

metapsychology (ˌmɛtəsaɪˈkɒlədʒɪ) *n. Psychol.* **1.** the study of philosophical questions, such as the relation between mind and body, that go beyond the laws of experimental psychology. **2.** any attempt to state the general laws of psychology. **3.** another word for **parapsychology.** —**metapsychological** (ˌmɛtəˌsaɪkəˈlɒdʒɪkəl) *adj.*

metarchon (mɪˈtɑːkɒn) *n.* a nontoxic substance, such as a chemical to mask pheromones, that reduces the persistence of a pest.

metasoma (ˌmɛtəˈsəʊmə) *n. Zoology.* the posterior part of an arachnid's abdomen (opisthosoma) that never carries appendages.

metasomatism (ˌmɛtəˈsəʊməˌtɪzəm) *or* **metasomatosis** (ˌmɛtəˌsəʊməˈtəʊsɪs) *n.* change in the composition of a rock or mineral by the addition or replacement of chemicals. [C19: from New Latin; see META-, SOMATO-]

metastable (ˌmɛtəˈsteɪbəl) *Physics.* ~*adj.* **1.** (of a body or system) having a state of apparent equilibrium although capable of changing to a more stable state. **2.** (of an atom, molecule, ion, or atomic nucleus) existing in an excited state with a relatively long lifetime. ~*n.* **3.** a metastable atom, ion, molecule, or nucleus. —ˌ**metastaˈbility** *n.*

metastasis (mɪˈtæstəsɪs) *n., pl.* **-ses** (-ˌsiːz). **1.** *Pathol.* the spreading of a disease, esp. cancer cells, from one part of the body to another. **2.** a transformation or change, as in rhetoric, from one point to another. **3.** a rare word for **metabolism.** [C16: via Latin from Greek: transition] —**metastatic** (ˌmɛtəˈstætɪk) *adj.* —ˌ**metaˈstatically** *adv.*

metastasize *or* **metastasise** (mɪˈtæstəˌsaɪz) *vb.* (*intr.*) *Pathol.* (esp. of cancer cells) to spread to a new site in the body via blood or lymph vessels.

metatarsal (ˌmɛtəˈtɑːsəl) *Anatomy.* ~*adj.* **1.** of or relating to the metatarsus. ~*n.* **2.** any bone of the metatarsus.

metatarsus (ˌmɛtəˈtɑːsəs) *n., pl.* **-si** (-saɪ). **1.** the skeleton of the human foot between the toes and the tarsus, consisting of five long bones. **2.** the corresponding skeletal part in other vertebrates.

metatheory (ˈmɛtəˌθɪərɪ) *n.* **1.** philosophical discussion of the foundations, structure, or results of some theory, such as metamathematics. **2.** a formal system that describes the structure of some other system. See also **metalanguage.** —**metatheoretical** (ˌmɛtəθɪəˈrɛtɪkəl) *adj.*

metatherian (ˌmɛtəˈθɪərɪən) *adj.* **1.** of, relating to, or belonging to the *Metatheria,* a subclass of mammals comprising the marsupials. ~*n.* **2.** any metatherian mammal; a marsupial. ~Compare **eutherian, prototherian.** [C19: from New Latin, from META- + Greek *thērion* animal]

metathesis (mɪˈtæθəsɪs) *n., pl.* **-ses** (-ˌsiːz). **1.** the transposition of two sounds or letters in a word. **2.** *Chem.* another name for **double decomposition.** [C16: from Late Latin, from Greek, from *metatithenai* to transpose] —**metathetic** (ˌmɛtəˈθɛtɪk) *or* ˌ**metaˈthetical** *adj.*

metathesize *or* **metathesise** (mɪˈtæθɪˌsaɪz) *vb.* to change or cause to change by metathesis.

metathorax (ˌmɛtəˈθɔːræks) *n., pl.* **-raxes** *or* **-races** (-rəˌsiːz). the third and last segment of an insect's thorax, which bears the third pair of walking legs and the second pair of wings. See also **prothorax, mesothorax.** —**metathoracic** (ˌmɛtəθɔːˈræsɪk) *adj.*

metaxylem (ˌmɛtəˈzaɪlɛm) *n.* xylem tissue that consists of rigid thick-walled cells and occurs in parts of the plant that have finished growing. Compare **protoxylem.**

metazoan (ˌmɛtəˈzəʊən) *n.* **1.** any animal of the group *Metazoa,* in which the body is composed of many cells: includes all animals except sponges and protozoans. ~*adj. also* **metazoic. 2.** of, relating to, or belonging to the *Metazoa.* [C19: from New Latin *Metazoa;* see META-, -ZOA]

mete[1] (miːt) *vb.* (*tr.*) **1.** (usually foll. by *out*) *Formal.* to distribute or allot (something, often unpleasant). ~*vb., n.* **2.** *Poetic, dialect.* (to) measure. [Old English *metan;* compare Old Saxon *metan,* Old Norse *meta,* German *messen* to measure]

mete[2] (miːt) *n. Rare.* a mark, limit, or boundary (esp. in the phrase **metes and bounds**). [C15: from Old French, from Latin *mēta* goal, turning post (in race)]

metecdysis (ˌmɛtɛkˈdaɪsɪs) *n., pl.* **-ses.** the period following the moult (ecdysis) of an arthropod, when the new cuticle is forming.

metempirical (ˌmɛtɛmˈpɪrɪkəl) *or* **metempiric** *adj.* **1.** beyond the realm of experience. **2.** of or relating to metempirics. —ˌ**metemˈpirically** *adv.*

metempirics (ˌmɛtɛmˈpɪrɪks) *n.* (*functioning as sing.*) the branch of philosophy that deals with things existing beyond the realm of experience. —ˌ**metemˈpiricist** *n.*

metempsychosis (ˌmɛtəmsaɪˈkəʊsɪs) *n., pl.* **-ses** (-siːz). **1.** the migration of a soul from one body to another. **2.** the entering of a soul after death upon a new cycle of existence in a new body either of human or animal form. [C16: via Late Latin from Greek, from *metempsukhousthai,* from META- + *-em-* in + *psukhē* soul] —ˌ**metempsyˈchosist** *n.*

metencephalon (ˌmɛtɛnˈsɛfəˌlɒn) *n., pl.* **-lons** *or* **-la** (-lə). the part of the embryonic hindbrain that develops into the cerebellum and pons Varolii. —**metencephalic** (ˌmɛtɛnsɪˈfælɪk) *adj.*

meteor (ˈmiːtɪə) *n.* **1.** a very small meteoroid that has entered the earth's atmosphere. Such objects have speeds approaching 70 kilometres per second. **2.** Also called: **shooting star, falling star.** the bright streak of light appearing in the sky due to the incandescence of such a body heated by friction at its surface. [C15: from Medieval Latin *meteōrum,* from Greek *meteōron* something aloft, from *meteōros* lofty, from *meta-* (intensifier) + *aeirein* to raise]

meteoric (ˌmiːtɪˈɒrɪk) *adj.* **1.** of, formed by, or relating to meteors. **2.** like a meteor in brilliance, speed, or transience. **3.** *Rare.* of or relating to the weather; meteorological. —ˌ**meteˈorically** *adv.*

meteoric water *n. Geology.* ground water that has recently originated from the atmosphere.

meteorism (ˈmiːtɪəˌrɪzəm) *n. Med.* another name for **tympanites.**

meteorite (ˈmiːtɪəˌraɪt) *n.* a rocklike object consisting of the remains of a meteoroid that has fallen on earth. It may be stony (see **aerolite**) or metallic (see **siderite**). —**meteoritic** (ˌmiːtɪəˈrɪtɪk) *adj.*

meteoritics (ˌmiːtɪəˈrɪtɪks) *n.* (*functioning as sing.*) the branch of science concerned with meteors and meteorites. —ˌ**meteorˈiticist** *n.*

meteorograph (ˈmiːtɪərəˌgrɑːf, -ˌgræf) *n.* an instrument that records various meteorological conditions. —ˌ**meteoroˈgraphic** *or* ˌ**meteoroˈgraphical** *adj.*

meteoroid (ˈmiːtɪəˌrɔɪd) *n.* any of the small celestial bodies that are thought to orbit the sun, possibly as the remains of comets.

When they enter the earth's atmosphere, they become visible as meteors. —ˌmeteor'oidal *adj.*

meteorol. or **meteor.** *abbrev. for:* **1.** meteorological. **2.** meteorology.

meteorology (ˌmiːtɪə'rɒlədʒɪ) *n.* the study of the earth's atmosphere, esp. of weather-forming processes and weather forecasting. [C17: from Greek *meteorologia*, from *meteōron* something aloft + *-logia* -LOGY. See METEOR] —**meteorological** (ˌmiːtɪərə'lɒdʒɪkᵊl) *or* ˌ**meteoro'logic** *adj.* —ˌ**meteoro'logically** *adv.* —ˌ**meteor'ologist** *n.*

meteor shower *n.* a transient rain of meteors, such as the Perseids, occurring at regular intervals and coming from a particular region in the sky. It is caused by the earth passing through a large number of meteoroids (a **meteor swarm**).

meter[1] ('miːtə) *n.* the U.S. spelling of **metre**[1].

meter[2] ('miːtə) *n.* the U.S. spelling of **metre**[2].

meter[3] ('miːtə) *n.* **1.** any device that measures and records the quantity of a substance, such as gas, that has passed through it during a specified period. **2.** any device that measures and sometimes records an electrical or magnetic quantity, such as current, voltage, etc. **3.** See **parking meter.** ~*vb.* (*tr.*) **4.** to measure (a rate of flow) with a meter. **5.** to print with stamps by means of a postage meter. [C19: see METE[1]]

-meter *n. combining form.* **1.** indicating an instrument for measuring: *barometer.* **2.** *Prosody.* indicating a verse having a specified number of feet: *pentameter.* [from Greek *metron* measure]

metered mail *n.* mail franked privately, under licence, with a machine bearing special markings (**meter marks**).

meter maid *n. Informal.* a female traffic warden.

metestrus (mɛt'ɛstrəs, -'iːstrəs) *n.* the U.S. spelling of **metoestrus.** —**met'estrous** *adj.*

Meth. *abbrev. for* Methodist.

meth- *combining form.* indicating a chemical compound derived from methane or containing methyl groups: *methacrylate resin.*

methacrylate (mɛθ'ækrɪˌleɪt) *n.* **1.** any ester of methacrylic acid. **2.** See **methacrylate resin.**

methacrylate resin *n.* any acrylic resin derived from methacrylic acid.

methacrylic acid (ˌmɛθə'krɪlɪk) *n.* a colourless crystalline water-soluble substance used in the manufacture of acrylic resins; 2-methylpropenoic acid. Formula: CH_2:C(CH_3)COOH.

methadone ('mɛθəˌdəʊn) *or* **methadon** ('mɛθəˌdɒn) *n.* a narcotic analgesic drug similar to morphine and formerly thought to be less habit-forming. Formula: $C_{21}H_{27}NO$. [C20: from (*di*)*meth*(*yl*) + A(MINO) + D(IPHENYL) + -ONE]

methaemoglobin (mɛtˌhiːmə'gləʊbɪn, mɛˌθiːmə-) *n.* a brown compound of oxygen and haemoglobin formed in the blood by the action of certain drugs.

methamphetamine (ˌmɛθæm'fɛtəmɪn) *n.* a variety of amphetamine used for its stimulant action. [C20: from METH- + AMPHETAMINE]

methanal ('mɛθəˌnæl) *n.* the systematic name for **formaldehyde.**

methane ('miːθeɪn) *n.* a colourless odourless flammable gas, the simplest alkane and the main constituent of natural gas: used as a fuel. Formula: CH_4. See also **marsh gas, firedamp.** [C19: from METH(YL) + -ANE]

methane series *n.* another name for the **alkane series.** See **alkane.**

methanoic acid ('mɛθəˌnəʊɪk) *n.* the systematic name for **formic acid.**

methanol ('mɛθəˌnɒl) *n.* a colourless volatile poisonous liquid compound used as a solvent and fuel. Formula: CH_3OH. Also called: **methyl alcohol, wood alcohol.** [C20: from METHANE + -OL[1]]

metheglin (mə'θɛglɪn) *n.* (esp. formerly) spiced or medicated mead. [C16: from Welsh *meddyglyn*, from *meddyg* healer (from Latin *medicus* MEDICAL) + *llyn* liquor]

methenamine (mɛ'θiːnəˌmiːn, -ˌmaɪn) *n.* another name for **hexamethylenetetramine.** [C20: METH- + -ENE + AMINE]

methinks (mɪ'θɪŋks) *vb. past* **methought.** (*tr.*) (*takes a clause as object*) *Archaic.* it seems to me.

methionine (mɛ'θaɪəˌniːn, -ˌnaɪn) *n.* an essential amino acid containing sulphur, which occurs in many proteins: important in methylating reactions. [C20: METH- + THIONINE]

metho ('mɛθəʊ) *n. Austral.* an informal name for **methylated spirits.**

method ('mɛθəd) *n.* **1.** a way of proceeding or doing something, esp. a systematic or regular one. **2.** orderliness of thought, action, etc. **3.** (*often pl.*) the techniques or arrangement of work for a particular field or subject. **4.** *Bell-ringing.* any of several traditional sets of changes. See **major** (sense 18), **minor** (sense 8). [C16: via French from Latin *methodus*, from Greek *methodos*, literally: a going after, from *meta-* after + *hodos* way]

Method ('mɛθəd) *n.* (*sometimes not cap.*) **a.** a technique of acting in which the actor bases his role on the inner motivation of the character he plays. **b.** (*as modifier*): *a Method actor.*

methodical (mɪ'θɒdɪkᵊl) *or* (*less commonly*) **methodic** *adj.* characterized by method or orderliness; systematic. —**me'thodically** *adv.* —**me'thodicalness** *n.*

Methodism ('mɛθədɪzəm) *n.* the system and practices of the Methodist church.

Methodist ('mɛθədɪst) *n.* **1.** a member of any of the Nonconformist denominations that derive from the system of faith and practice initiated by John Wesley (1703–91), British preacher, and his followers. ~*adj. also* **Methodistic** *or* **Methodistical. 2.** of or relating to Methodism or the Church embodying it (the **Methodist Church**). —ˌ**Method'istically** *adv.*

methodize *or* **methodise** ('mɛθəˌdaɪz) *vb.* (*tr.*) to organize according to a method; systematize. —ˌ**methodi'zation** *or* ˌ**methodi'sation** *n.* —'**methodˌizer** *or* '**methodˌiser** *n.*

methodology (ˌmɛθə'dɒlədʒɪ) *n., pl.* **-gies. 1.** the system of methods and principles used in a particular discipline. **2.** the branch of philosophy concerned with the science of method and procedure. —**methodological** (ˌmɛθədə'lɒdʒɪkᵊl) *adj.* —ˌ**methodo'logically** *adv.* —ˌ**method'ologist** *n.*

methotrexate (ˌmɛθəʊ'trɛkseɪt, ˌmiːθəʊ-) *n.* a drug used in the treatment of certain cancers. Formula: $C_{20}H_{22}N_8O_5$.

methought (mɪ'θɔːt) *vb. Archaic.* the past tense of **methinks.**

methoxide (mɛθ'ɒksaɪd) *n.* a saltlike compound in which the hydrogen atom in the hydroxyl group of methanol has been replaced by a metal atom, usually an alkali metal atom as in sodium methoxide, $NaOCH_3$. Also called: **methylate.**

meths (mɛθs) *n. Chiefly Brit., Austral., and N.Z.* an informal name for **methylated spirits.**

Methuselah (mə'θjuːzələ) *n.* a wine bottle holding the equivalent of eight normal bottles.

methyl ('miːθaɪl, 'mɛθɪl) *n.* **1.** (*modifier*) of, consisting of, or containing the monovalent group of atoms CH_3. **2.** an organometallic compound in which methyl groups are bound directly to a metal atom. [C19: from French *méthyle*, back formation from METHYLENE] —**methylic** (mə'θɪlɪk) *adj.*

methyl acetate *n.* a colourless volatile flammable liquid ester with a fragrant odour, used as a solvent, esp. in paint removers. Formula: CH_3COOCH_3.

methylal ('mɛθɪˌlæl) *n.* a colourless volatile flammable liquid with an odour resembling that of chloroform, used as a solvent and in the manufacture of perfumes and adhesives. Formula: $(CH_3O)_2CH_2$. Also called: **formal.**

methyl alcohol *n.* another name for **methanol.**

methylamine (miː'θaɪləˌmiːn) *n.* a colourless flammable water-soluble gas, used in the manufacture of herbicides, dyes, and drugs. Formula: CH_3NH_2.

methylate ('mɛθɪˌleɪt) *vb.* **1.** (*tr.*) to mix with methanol. **2.** to undergo or cause to undergo a chemical reaction in which a methyl group is introduced into a molecule. ~*n.* **3.** another name for **methoxide.** —ˌ**methyl'ation** *n.* —'**methylˌator** *n.*

methylated spirits *or* **spirit** *n.* (*functioning as sing. or pl.*) alcohol that has been denatured by the addition of methanol and pyridine and a violet dye. Also called: **metho, meths.**

methyl bromide *n.* a colourless poisonous gas or volatile liquid with an odour resembling that of chloroform, used as a solvent, and extinguishant. Formula: CH_3Br.

methyl chloride *n.* a colourless gas with an ether-like odour, used as a refrigerant and anaesthetic. Formula: CH_3Cl. Systematic name: **chloromethane.**

methyl chloroform *n.* the traditional name for **trichloroethane.**

methyldopa (ˌmiːθaɪl'dəʊpə) *n.* a catecholamine drug used to treat hypertension. Formula: $C_{10}H_{13}NO_4$. [C20: from *methyl* + *d*(*ihydr*)*o*(*xy*)*p*(*henyl*)*a*(*lanine*)]

methylene ('mɛθɪˌliːn) *n.* (*modifier*) of, consisting of, or containing the divalent group of atoms $=CH_2$: *a methylene group or radical.* [C19: from French *méthylène*, from Greek *methu* wine + *hulē* wood + -ENE: originally referring to a substance distilled from wood]

methylene blue *n.* a dark-green crystalline compound forming a blue aqueous solution, used as a mild antiseptic and biological stain. Formula: $C_{16}H_{18}N_3SCl.3H_2O$. Also called: **methylthionine chloride.**

methylene chloride *n.* another name for **dichloromethane.**

methyl ethyl ketone *n.* another name for **butanone.**

methyl isobutyl ketone (ˌaɪsəʊ'bjuːtaɪl, -tɪl) *n.* a colourless insoluble liquid ketone used as a solvent for organic compounds, esp. nitrocellulose; 4-methylpentan-2-one. Formula: $CH_3COC_4H_9$. Also called: **hexone.**

methyl methacrylate *n.* a colourless liquid compound, used in the manufacture of certain methacrylate resins. Formula: $CH_2C(CH_3)COOCH_3$.

methylnaphthalene (ˌmiːθaɪl'næpθəˌliːn) *n.* either of two isomeric derivatives of naphthalene: a liquid (1-methylnaphthalene), used in standardizing diesel fuels, or a solid (2-methylnaphthalene), an insecticide.

methylthionine chloride (ˌmiːθaɪl'θaɪəˌniːn) *n.* another name for **methylene blue.**

metic ('mɛtɪk) *n.* (in ancient Greece) an alien having some rights of citizenship in the city in which he lives. [C19: from Greek *metoikos*, from META- (indicating change) + *-oikos* dwelling]

meticulous (mɪ'tɪkjʊləs) *adj.* very precise about details, even trivial ones; painstaking. [C16 (meaning: timid): from Latin *meticulōsus* fearful, from *metus* fear] —**me'ticulously** *adv.* —**me'ticulousness** *n.*

métier ('mɛtɪeɪ) *n.* **1.** a profession or trade, esp. that to which one is well suited. **2.** a person's strong point or speciality. [C18: from French, ultimately from Latin *ministerium* service]

Métis (mɛ'tiːs) *n., pl.* **-tis** (-'tiːs, -'tiːz). **1.** a person of mixed parentage. **2.** *Canadian.* **a.** the offspring or a descendant of a French Canadian and a North American Indian. **b.** a member or descendant of a group of such people, who established themselves in Manitoba and Saskatchewan as a distinct political and cultural force during the nineteenth century. **3.** *U.S.* a person having one eighth Negro ancestry; octoroon. [C19: from French, from Vulgar Latin *mixtīcius* (unattested) of mixed race; compare MESTIZO] —**Métisse** (mɛ'tiːs) *fem. n.*

metoestrus (mɛt'iːstrəs, -'ɛstrəs) *or U.S.* **metestrus** *n. Zoology.* the period in the oestrous cycle following oestrus, characterized by lack of sexual activity. —**met'oestrous** *or U.S.* **met'estrous** *adj.*

metol ('miːtɒl) *n.* a colourless soluble organic substance used, in the form of its sulphate, as a photographic developer; *p*-methylaminophenol. See also **aminophenol.** [C20: from German, an arbitrary coinage]

Metonic cycle (mɪ'tɒnɪk) *n.* a cycle of 235 synodic months after which the phases of the moon recur on the same day of the month. See also **golden number.** [C17: named after *Meton*, 5th-century B.C. Athenian astronomer]

metonym ('mɛtənɪm) *n.* a word used in a metonymy. For example *the bottle* is a metonym for *alcoholic drink*.

metonymy (mɪ'tɒnɪmɪ) *n., pl.* **-mies.** the substitution of a word referring to an attribute for the thing that is meant, as for example the use of *the crown* to refer to a monarch. Compare **synecdoche.** [C16: from Late Latin from Greek: a changing of name, from *meta-* (indicating change) + *onoma* name] —**metonymical** (ˌmɛtə'nɪmɪkᵊl) *or* ˌ**meto'nymic** *adj.* —ˌ**meto'nymically** *adv.*

metope ('mɛtəʊp, 'mɛtəpɪ) *n. Architect.* a square space between two triglyphs in a Doric frieze. [C16: via Latin from Greek *metopē*, from *meta* between + *opē* one of the holes for the beam-ends]

metopic (mɪ'tɒpɪk) *adj.* of or relating to the forehead.

metralgia (mɪ'trældʒɪə) *n.* pain in the uterus. [C20: from METRO-[1] + -ALGIA]

metre[1] *or U.S.* **meter** ('miːtə) *n.* **1.** a metric unit of length equal to approximately 1.094 yards. **2.** the basic SI unit of length; the length of the path travelled by light in free space during a time interval of 1/299 792 458 of a second. In 1983 this definition replaced the previous one based on krypton-86, which in turn had replaced the definition based on the platinum-iridium metre bar kept in Paris. Symbol: m [C18: from French; see METRE[2]]

metre[2] *or U.S.* **meter** ('miːtə) *n.* **1.** *Prosody.* the rhythmic arrangement of syllables in verse, usually according to the number and kind of feet in a line. **2.** *Music.* another word (esp. U.S.) for **time** (sense 22). [C14: from Latin *metrum*, from Greek *metron* measure]

metre-kilogram-second *n.* See **mks units.**

metric ('mɛtrɪk) *adj.* **1.** of or relating to the metre or metric system. **2.** *Maths.* denoting or relating to a set containing pairs of points for each of which a non-negative real number $\rho(x, y)$ (the distance) can be defined, satisfying specific conditions. ~*n.* **3.** *Maths.* the function $\rho(x, y)$ satisfying the conditions of membership of such a set (a **metric space**).

metrical ('mɛtrɪkᵊl) *or* **metric** ('mɛtrɪk) *adj.* **1.** of or relating to measurement. **2.** of or in poetic metre. —'**metrically** *adv.*

metrical psalm *n.* a translation of one of the psalms into rhyming strict-metre verse usually sung as a hymn.

metricate ('mɛtrɪˌkeɪt) *vb.* to convert (a measuring system, instrument, etc.) from nonmetric to metric units. —ˌ**metri'cation** *n.*

metric hundredweight *n.* See **hundredweight** (sense 3).

metrics ('mɛtrɪks) *n.* (*functioning as sing.*) *Prosody.* the art of using poetic metre.

metric system *n.* any decimal system of units based on the metre. For scientific purposes the Système International d'Unités (SI units) is used.

metric ton *n.* another name (not in technical use) for **tonne.**

metrify ('mɛtrɪˌfaɪ) *vb.* **-fies, -fying, -fied.** (*tr.*) *Prosody.* to render into poetic metre. —'**metriˌfier** *n.*

metrist ('mɛtrɪst) *n. Prosody.* a person skilled in the use of poetic metre.

metritis (mɪ'traɪtɪs) *n.* inflammation of the uterus.

metro ('mɛtrəʊ) *or* **métro** (*French* metro) *n., pl.* **-ros.** an underground, or largely underground, railway system in certain cities, esp. in Europe, such as that in Paris. [C20: from French, short for *chemin de fer métropolitain* metropolitan railway]

metro-[1] *or before a vowel* **metr-** *combining form.* indicating the uterus: *metrorrhagia.* [from Greek *mētra* womb]

metro-[2] *combining form.* indicating a measure: *metronome.* [from Greek *metron* measure]

metrology (mɪ'trɒlədʒɪ) *n., pl.* **-gies.** **1.** the science of weights and measures; the study of units of measurement. **2.** a particular system of units. [C19: from Greek *metron* measure] —**metrological** (ˌmɛtrə'lɒdʒɪkᵊl) *adj.* —ˌ**metro'logically** *adv.* —**me'trologist** *n.*

metronidazole (ˌmɛtrə'naɪdəˌzəʊl) *n.* a pale yellow crystalline compound used to treat vaginal trichomoniasis. Formula: $C_6H_9N_3O_3$. [C20: from ME(THYL) + (NI)TRO- + *-n-* + (IM)ID(E) + AZOLE]

metronome ('mɛtrəˌnəʊm) *n.* a mechanical device which indicates the exact tempo of a piece of music by producing a clicking sound from a pendulum with an adjustable period of swing. [C19: from Greek *metron* measure + *nomos* rule, law] —**metronomic** (ˌmɛtrə'nɒmɪk) *adj.*

metronymic (ˌmɛtrə'nɪmɪk) *or* (*less commonly*) **matronymic** *adj.* **1.** (of a name) derived from the name of its bearer's mother or another female ancestor. ~*n.* **2.** a metronymic name. [C19: from Greek *mētronumikos*, from *mētēr* mother + *onoma* name]

metropolis (mɪ'trɒpəlɪs) *n., pl.* **-lises.** **1.** the main city, esp. of a country or region; capital. **2.** a centre of activity. **3.** the chief see in an ecclesiastical province. [C16: from Late Latin from Greek: mother city or state, from *mētēr* mother + *polis* city]

metropolitan (ˌmɛtrə'pɒlɪtən) *adj.* **1.** of or characteristic of a metropolis. **2.** constituting a city and its suburbs: *the metropolitan area.* **3.** of, relating to, or designating an ecclesiastical metropolis. **4.** of or belonging to the home territories of a country, as opposed to overseas territories: *metropolitan France.* ~*n.* **5. a.** *Eastern Churches.* the head of an ecclesiastical province, ranking between archbishop and patriarch. **b.** *Church of England.* an archbishop. **c.** *R.C. Church.* an archbishop or bishop having authority in certain matters over the dioceses in his province. —ˌ**metro'politanism** *n.*

metropolitan county *n.* (in England 1974–86) any of the six conurbations established as units in the new local government system, with elected councils possessing powers resembling those of counties.

metropolitan district *n.* any of the districts, formerly making up metropolitan counties, now forming the sole principal tier of local government. Each metropolitan district has an elected council responsible for education, social services, etc. See also **district** (sense 4).

metrorrhagia (ˌmiːtrɔː'reɪdʒɪə, ˌmɛt-) *n.* abnormal bleeding from the uterus.

-metry *n. combining form.* indicating the process or science of measuring: *anthropometry; geometry.* [from Old French *-metrie*, from Latin *-metria*, from Greek, from *metron* measure] —**-metric** *adj. combining form.*

mettle ('mɛtᵊl) *n.* **1.** courage; spirit. **2.** inherent character. **3. on one's mettle.** roused to putting forth one's best efforts. [C16: originally variant spelling of METAL]

mettled ('mɛtᵊld) *or* **mettlesome** ('mɛtᵊlsəm) *adj.* spirited, courageous, or valiant.

meu (mjuː) *n.* another name for **spignel.** [C16: from Latin *mēum*, from Greek *mēon*]

meum et tuum *Latin.* ('meɪʊm ɛt 'tuːʊm) mine and thine: used to express rights to property. [C16: neuter of *mēus* mine and *tuus* yours]

meunière (mən'jɛə; *French* mønjɛr) *adj.* (of fish) dredged with flour, fried in butter, and served with butter, lemon juice, and parsley. [French, literally: miller's wife]

MeV *symbol for* million electronvolts (10^6 electronvolts).

mevrou (mə'frəʊ) *n.* a South African title of address equivalent to *Mrs* when placed before a surname or *madam* when used alone. [Afrikaans]

mew[1] (mjuː) *vb.* **1.** (*intr.*) (esp. of a cat) to make a characteristic high-pitched cry. ~*n.* **2.** such a sound. [C14: imitative]

mew[2] (mjuː) *n.* any seagull, esp. the common gull, *Larus canus.* Also called: **mew gull, sea mew.** [Old English *mǣw*; compare Old Saxon *mēu*, Middle Dutch *mēwe*]

mew[3] (mjuː) *n.* **1.** a room or cage for hawks, esp. while moulting. ~*vb.* **2.** (*tr.*; often foll. by *up*) to confine (hawks or falcons) in a shelter, cage, etc., usually by tethering them to a perch. **3.** to confine, conceal. [C14: from Old French *mue*, from *muer* to moult, from Latin *mūtāre* to change]

mew[4] (mjuː) *vb.* **1.** (*intr.*) (of hawks or falcons) to moult. **2.** (*tr.*) *Obsolete.* to shed (one's covering, clothes, etc.). [C14: from Old French *muer* to moult, from Latin *mūtāre* to change]

mewl (mjuːl) *vb.* **1.** (*intr.*) (esp. of a baby) to cry weakly; whimper (often in the phrase **mewl and puke**). ~*n.* **2.** such a cry. [C17: imitative] —'**mewler** *n.*

mews (mjuːz) *n.* (*functioning as sing. or pl.*) *Chiefly Brit.* **1.** a yard or street lined by buildings originally used as stables but now often converted into dwellings. **2.** the buildings around a mews. **3.** *Informal.* an individual residence in a mews. [C14: pl. of MEW[3], originally referring to royal stables built on the site of hawks' mews at Charing Cross in London]

MEX *international car registration for* Mexico.

Mex. *abbrev. for:* **1.** Mexican. **2.** Mexico.

Mexican ('mɛksɪkən) *adj.* **1.** of or relating to Mexico, a republic in North America on the Gulf of Mexico and the Pacific, or its people. ~*n.* **2.** a native or inhabitant of Mexico.

Mexican hairless *n.* a breed of small hairless dog with mottled skin.

Mexican wave *n.* the rippling effect produced when the spectators in successive sections of a sports stadium stand up while raising their arms and then sit down. [C20: so called because it was first demonstrated at the World Cup in Mexico in 1986]

MEZ *abbrev. for* Central European Time. [from German *Mitteleuropäische Zeit*]

mezcal (mɛ'skæl) *n.* a variant spelling of **mescal.**

mezcaline ('mɛskəˌliːn) *n.* a variant spelling of **mescaline.**

meze ('mɛzɛ) *n.* a type of hors d'oeuvre eaten esp. with an apéritif or other drink in Greece and the Near East. [C20: from Turkish *meze* snack, appetizer]

mezereon (mɛˈzɪərɪən) *n.* **1.** a Eurasian thymelaeaceous shrub, *Daphne mezereum,* with fragrant early-blooming purplish-pink flowers and small scarlet fruits. **2.** another name for **mezereum.** [C15: via Medieval Latin from Arabic *māzaryūn*]

mezereum (mɪˈzɪərɪəm) *or* **mezereon** *n.* the dried bark of certain shrubs of the genus *Daphne,* esp. mezereon, formerly used as a vesicant and to treat arthritis.

mezuzah (məˈzʊzə, -ˈzuː-; *Hebrew* məzuˈzɑ; *Yiddish* məˈzʊzə) *n., pl.* **-zuzahs** *or* **-zuzoth** (*Hebrew* -zuˈzɔt). *Judaism.* **1.** a piece of parchment inscribed with biblical passages and fixed to the doorpost of the rooms of a Jewish house. **2.** a metal case for such a parchment, sometimes worn as an ornament. [from Hebrew, literally: doorpost]

mezzanine (ˈmɛzəˌniːn, ˈmɛtsəˌniːn) *n.* **1.** Also called: **mezzanine floor, entresol.** an intermediate storey, esp. a low one between the ground and first floor of a building. **2.** *Theatre, U.S. and Canadian.* the first balcony. **3.** *Theatre, Brit.* a room or floor beneath the stage. ~*adj.* **4.** often shortened to **mezz.** of or relating to an intermediate stage in a financial process: *mezzanine funding.* [C18: from French, from Italian, diminutive of *mezzano* middle, from Latin *mediānus* MEDIAN]

mezza voce (ˈmɛtsə ˈvəʊtʃɪ; *Italian* ˈmɛddza ˈvotʃe) *adv. Music.* (in singing) softly; quietly. [Italian, literally: half voice]

mezzo (ˈmɛtsəʊ) *Music.* ~*adv.* **1.** moderately; quite: *mezzo forte; mezzo piano.* ~*n., pl.* **-zos.** **2.** See **mezzo-soprano** (sense 1). [C19: from Italian, literally: half, from Latin *medius* middle]

mezzo-relievo *or* **mezzo-rilievo** (ˌmɛtsəʊrɪˈliːvəʊ) *n.* carving in which the depth of the relief is halfway between that of high relief and low relief. [from Italian: half relief]

mezzo-soprano *n., pl.* **-nos.** **1.** a female voice intermediate between a soprano and contralto and having a range from the A below middle C to the F an eleventh above it. Sometimes shortened to **mezzo.** **2.** a singer with such a voice.

mezzotint (ˈmɛtsəʊˌtɪnt) *n.* **1.** a method of engraving a copper plate by scraping and burnishing the roughened surface. **2.** a print made from a plate so treated. ~*vb.* **3.** (*tr.*) to engrave (a copper plate) in this fashion. [C18: from Italian *mezzotinto* half tint] —ˈ**mezzoˌtinter** *n.*

mf *Music. abbrev. for* mezzo forte. [Italian: moderately loud]

MF *abbrev. for:* **1.** *Radio.* medium frequency. **2.** Middle French.

mfd *abbrev. for* manufactured.

mfg *abbrev. for* manufacturing.

MFH *Hunting. abbrev. for* Master of Foxhounds.

mfr *abbrev. for:* **1.** manufacture. **2.** manufacturer.

mg *symbol for* milligram.

Mg *the chemical symbol for* magnesium.

MG *abbrev. for* machine gun.

MGB *abbrev. for* Ministry of State Security; the Soviet secret police from 1946 to 1954. [from Russian *Ministerstvo gosudarstvennoi bezopasnosti*]

M. Glam *abbrev. for* Mid Glamorgan.

Mgr *abbrev. for:* **1.** manager. **2.** Monseigneur. **3.** Monsignor.

MHA (in Australia and Newfoundland, Canada) *abbrev. for* Member of the House of Assembly.

MHD *abbrev. for* magnetohydrodynamics.

MHG *abbrev. for* Middle High German.

mho (məʊ) *n., pl.* **mhos.** the former name for **siemens.** [C19: formed by reversing the letters of OHM]

MHR (in the U.S. and Australia) *abbrev. for* Member of the House of Representatives.

MHz *symbol for* megahertz.

mi *or* **me** (miː) *n. Music.* (in tonic sol-fa) the third degree of any major scale; mediant. [C16: see GAMUT]

MI *abbrev. for:* **1.** Michigan. **2.** Military Intelligence.

mi. *abbrev. for* mile.

MI5 *abbrev. for* Military Intelligence, section five; a former official and present-day popular name for the counterintelligence agency of the British Government.

MI6 *abbrev. for* Military Intelligence, section six; a former official and present-day popular name for the intelligence and espionage agency of the British Government.

MIA (in Australia) *abbrev. for* Murrumbidgee Irrigation Area.

mia mia (ˈmiːə ˈmiːə) *n.* an Australian Aborigine's hut. [from a native Australian language]

miaou *or* **miaow** (mɪˈaʊ, mjaʊ) *vb., interj.* variant spellings of **meow.**

miasma (mɪˈæzmə) *n., pl.* **-mata** (-mətə) *or* **-mas.** **1.** an unwholesome or foreboding atmosphere. **2.** pollution in the atmosphere, esp. noxious vapours from decomposing organic matter. [C17: New Latin, from Greek: defilement, from *miainein* to defile] —**miˈasmal, miasmatic** (ˌmiːəzˈmætɪk), ˌ**miasˈmatical,** *or* **miˈasmic** *adj.*

miaul (mɪˈaʊl) *vb.* (*intr.*) another word for **meow.**

Mic. *Bible abbrev. for* Micah.

mica (ˈmaɪkə) *n.* any of a group of lustrous rock-forming minerals consisting of hydrous silicates of aluminium, potassium, etc., in monoclinic crystalline form, occurring in igneous and metamorphic rock. Because of their resistance to electricity and heat they are used as dielectrics, in heating elements, etc. Also called: **isinglass.** [C18: from Latin: grain, morsel] —**micaceous** (maɪˈkeɪʃəs) *adj.*

Micawber (mɪˈkɔːbə) *n.* a person who idles and trusts to fortune. [C19: after a character in Charles Dickens' novel *David Copperfield*] —**Miˈcawberish** *adj.* —**Miˈcawberism** *n.*

mice (maɪs) *n.* the plural of **mouse.**

micelle, micell (mɪˈsɛl), *or* **micella** (mɪˈsɛlə) *n. Chem.* **a.** a charged aggregate of molecules of colloidal size in a solution. **b.** any molecular aggregate of colloidal size, such as a particle found in coal. [C19: from New Latin *micella,* diminutive of Latin *mīca* crumb] —**miˈcellar** *adj.*

mich (mɪtʃ) *vb.* (*intr.*) a variant spelling of **mitch.**

Mich. *abbrev. for:* **1.** Michaelmas. **2.** Michigan.

Michaelmas (ˈmɪkəlməs) *n.* Sept. 29, the feast of St Michael the archangel; in England, Ireland, and Wales, one of the four quarter days.

Michaelmas daisy *n. Brit.* any of various plants of the genus *Aster* that have small autumn-blooming purple, pink, or white flowers: family *Compositae* (composites).

Michaelmas term *n.* the autumn term at Oxford and Cambridge Universities, the Inns of Court, and some other educational establishments.

Michelson-Morley experiment (ˈmaɪkəlsənˈmɔːlɪ) *n.* an experiment first performed in 1887 by U.S. scientists A. A. Michelson (1852–1931) and E. W. Morley (1838–1923), in which an interferometer was used to attempt to detect a difference in the velocities of light in directions parallel and perpendicular to the earth's motion. The negative result was explained by the special theory of relativity.

michigan (ˈmɪʃɪgən) *n.* the U.S. name for **newmarket** (sense 2).

micht (mɪxt) *vb., n.* a Scot. word for **might**[1] and **might**[2].

Mick (mɪk) *or* **Mickey** (ˈmɪkɪ) *n.* (*sometimes not cap.*) *Derogatory.* a slang name for an Irishman or a Roman Catholic. [C19: from the nickname for *Michael*]

mickery (ˈmɪkərɪ) *n., pl.* **-eries.** *Austral.* a pool or soakage in a riverbed.

mickey[1] *or* **micky** (ˈmɪkɪ) *n.* **take the mickey (out of).** *Informal.* to tease. [C20: of unknown origin]

mickey[2] *or* **micky** (ˈmɪkɪ) *n. Austral. informal.* a young bull, esp. one that is wild and unbranded.

Mickey Finn *n. Slang.* **a.** a drink containing a drug to make the drinker unconscious, usually formed by the combination of chloral hydrate and alcohol. It can be poisonous. **b.** the drug itself. ~Often shortened to **Mickey.** [C20: of unknown origin]

Mickey Mouse *adj.* (*sometimes not caps.*) *Slang.* **1.** ineffective; trivial; insignificant: *he settled for a Mickey Mouse job instead of something challenging.* **2.** *Chiefly U.S. and Canadian.* (of music, esp. that of dance bands) mechanical or spiritless. [C20: from the name of a cartoon character created by Walt Disney, known for his simple-minded attitudes]

mickle (ˈmɪkəl) *or* **muckle** (ˈmʌkəl) *Archaic or Scot. and northern English dialect.* ~*adj.* **1.** great or abundant. ~*adv.* **2.** much; greatly. ~*n.* **3.** a great amount, esp. in the proverb, *mony a little makes a mickle.* **4.** *Scot.* a small amount, esp. in the proverb, *many a mickle maks a muckle.* [C13 *mikel,* from Old Norse *mikell,* replacing Old English *micel* MUCH]

Micmac (ˈmɪkmæk) *n.* **1.** (*pl.* **-macs** *or* **-mac**) a member of a North American Indian people formerly living in the Maritime Provinces of Canada. **2.** the language of this people, belonging to the Algonquian family.

MICR *abbrev. for* magnetic ink character recognition.

micra (ˈmaɪkrə) *n.* a plural of **micron.**

micro (ˈmaɪkrəʊ) *adj.* **1.** very small. ~*n., pl.* **-cros.** **2.** short for **microcomputer, microlepidoptera, microprocessor, microwave oven.**

micro- *or* **micr-** *combining form.* **1.** small or minute: *microspore.* **2.** involving the use of a microscope: *micrography.* **3.** indicating a method or instrument for dealing with small quantities: *micrometer.* **4.** (in pathology) indicating abnormal smallness or underdevelopment: *microcephaly; microcyte.* Compare **macro-** (sense 2). **5.** denoting 10^{-6}: *microsecond.* Symbol: μ [from Greek *mikros* small]

microaerophile (ˌmaɪkrəʊˈɛərəʊˌfaɪl) *n.* an organism, esp. a bacterium, that thrives in an environment low in oxygen. —**microaerophilic** (ˌmaɪkrəʊˌɛərəʊˈfɪlɪk) *adj.*

microanalysis (ˌmaɪkrəʊəˈnælɪsɪs) *n., pl.* **-ses** (-ˌsiːz). the qualitative or quantitative chemical analysis of very small amounts of substances. —**microanalyst** (ˌmaɪkrəʊˈænəlɪst) *n.* —**microanalytic** (ˌmaɪkrəʊˌænəˈlɪtɪk) *or* ˌ**microˌanaˈlytical** *adj.*

microbalance (ˈmaɪkrəʊˌbæləns) *n.* a precision balance designed to weigh quantities between 10^{-6} and 10^{-9} kilogram.

microbarograph (ˌmaɪkrəʊˈbærəˌgrɑːf, -ˌgræf) *n.* a barograph that records minute changes in atmospheric pressure.

microbe (ˈmaɪkrəʊb) *n.* any microscopic organism, esp. a disease-causing bacterium. [C19: from French, from MICRO- + Greek *bios* life] —**miˈcrobial, miˈcrobic,** *or* (*less commonly*) **miˈcrobian** *adj.*

microbiology (ˌmaɪkrəʊbaɪˈɒlədʒɪ) *n.* the branch of biology involving the study of microorganisms and their effects on man. —**microbiological** (ˌmaɪkrəʊˌbaɪəˈlɒdʒɪkəl) *or* ˌ**microˌbioˈlogic** *adj.* —ˌ**microˌbioˈlogically** *adv.* —ˌ**microbiˈologist** *n.*

microburst (ˈmaɪkrəʊˌbɜːst) *n.* another name for **downburst.**

microcephaly (ˌmaɪkrəʊˈsɛfəlɪ) *n.* the condition of having an abnormally small head or cranial capacity. Compare megacephaly. —**microcephalic** (ˌmaɪkrəʊsɪˈfælɪk) *adj., n.* —ˌ**microˈcephalous** *adj.*

microchemistry (ˌmaɪkrəʊˈkɛmɪstrɪ) *n.* chemical experimentation with minute quantities of material. —ˌ**microˈchemical** *adj.*

microchip (ˈmaɪkrəʊˌtʃɪp) *n.* a small piece of semiconductor material carrying many integrated circuits.

microcircuit (ˈmaɪkrəʊˌsɜːkɪt) *n.* a miniature electronic circuit, esp. one in which a number of permanently connected components are contained in one small chip of semiconducting material. See **integrated circuit.** —ˌ**microˈcircuitry** *n.*

microclimate (ˈmaɪkrəʊˌklaɪmɪt) *n. Ecology.* **1.** the atmospheric conditions affecting an individual or a small group of organisms, esp. when they differ from the climate of the rest of the community. **2.** the entire environment of an individual or small group of organisms. —**microclimatic** (ˌmaɪkrəʊklaɪˈmætɪk) *adj.* —ˌ**microcliˈmatically** *adv.*

microclimatology (ˌmaɪkrəʊˌklaɪməˈtɒlədʒɪ) *n.* the study of climate on a small scale, as of a city. —**microclimatologic** (ˌmaɪkrəʊˌklaɪmətəˈlɒdʒɪk) *or* ˌ**microˌclimatoˈlogical** *adj.* —ˌ**microˌclimaˈtologist** *n.*

microcline (ˈmaɪkrəʊˌklaɪn) *n.* a white, creamy yellow, red, or green mineral of the feldspar group, found in igneous, sedimentary, and metamorphic rocks: used in the manufacture of glass and ceramics. Composition: potassium aluminium silicate. Formula: $KAlSi_3O_8$. Crystal structure: triclinic. [C19: from German *mikroklin*, from *mikro-* MICRO- + Greek *klinein* to lean; so called because its cleavage plane is slightly different from 90°]

micrococcus (ˌmaɪkrəʊˈkɒkəs) *n., pl.* **-cocci** (-ˈkɒksaɪ). **1.** any spherical Gram-positive bacterium of the genus *Micrococcus*, causing fermentation of milk: family *Micrococcaceae*. **2.** any other bacterium of the family *Micrococcaceae*.

microcomputer (ˈmaɪkrəʊkəmˌpjuːtə) *n.* a small computer in which the central processing unit is contained in one or more silicon chips. Sometimes shortened to **micro.**

microcopy (ˈmaɪkrəʊˌkɒpɪ) *n., pl.* **-copies.** a greatly reduced photographic copy of a printed page, drawing, etc., on microfilm or microfiche. Sometimes called **microphotograph.**

microcosm (ˈmaɪkrəʊˌkɒzəm) *or* **microcosmos** (ˌmaɪkrəʊˈkɒzmɒs) *n.* **1.** a miniature representation of something, esp. a unit, group, or place regarded as a copy of a larger one. **2.** man regarded as epitomizing the universe. ~Compare **macrocosm.** [C15: via Medieval Latin from Greek *mikros kosmos* little world] —ˌ**microˈcosmic** *or* ˌ**microˈcosmical** *adj.*

microcosmic salt *n.* a white soluble solid obtained from human urine; ammonium sodium hydrogen phosphate. It is used as a flux in bead tests on metal oxides.

microcrystalline (ˌmaɪkrəʊˈkrɪstᵊˌlaɪn) *adj.* (of a solid) composed of microscopic crystals.

microcyte (ˈmaɪkrəʊˌsaɪt) *n.* an unusually small red blood cell. —**microcytic** (ˌmaɪkrəʊˈsɪtɪk) *adj.*

microdetector (ˌmaɪkrəʊdɪˈtɛktə) *n.* any instrument for measuring small quantities or detecting small effects, esp. a sensitive galvanometer.

microdont (ˈmaɪkrəʊˌdɒnt) *or* **microdontous** (ˌmaɪkrəʊˈdɒntəs) *adj.* having unusually small teeth.

microdot (ˈmaɪkrəʊˌdɒt) *n.* **1.** a microcopy about the size of a pinhead, used esp. in espionage. **2.** a tiny tablet containing LSD.

microeconomics (ˌmaɪkrəʊˌiːkəˈnɒmɪks, -ˌɛkə-) *n.* (*functioning as sing.*) the branch of economics concerned with particular commodities, firms, or individuals and the economic relationships between them. Compare **macroeconomics.** —ˌ**microˌecoˈnomic** *adj.*

microelectronics (ˌmaɪkrəʊɪlɛkˈtrɒnɪks) *n.* (*functioning as sing.*) the branch of electronics concerned with microcircuits. —ˌ**microelecˈtronic** *adj.*

microenvironment (ˈmaɪkrəʊɪnˌvaɪrənmənt) *n. Ecology.* the environment of a small area, such as that around a leaf or plant.

microfarad (ˈmaɪkrəʊˌfærəd) *n.* one millionth of a farad; 10^{-6} farad. Symbol: μF

microfiche (ˈmaɪkrəʊˌfiːʃ) *n.* a sheet of film, usually the size of a filing card, on which books, newspapers, documents, etc., can be recorded in miniaturized form. Sometimes shortened to **fiche.** See also **ultrafiche.** [C20: from French, from MICRO- + *fiche* small card, from Old French *fichier* to fix]

microfilament (ˌmaɪkrəʊˈfɪləmənt) *n.* thin filament, composed of the protein actin and associated proteins, that occurs abundantly in muscle and in the cytoplasm of other cells.

microfilaria (ˌmaɪkrəʊfɪˈlɛərɪə) *n., pl.* **-iae** (-ɪˌiː). *Zoology.* the early larval stage of certain parasitic nematodes (filariae), found in the blood of infected individuals.

microfilm (ˈmaɪkrəʊˌfɪlm) *n.* **1.** a strip of film of standard width on which books, newspapers, documents, etc., can be recorded in miniaturized form. ~*vb.* **2.** to photograph (a page, document, etc.) on microfilm. ~See also **microfiche.**

microfilm plotter *n. Computer technol.* a type of incremental plotter that has a film rather than a paper output.

microform (ˈmaɪkrəʊˌfɔːm) *n. Computer technol.* a method of storing symbolic information by using photographic reduction techniques, such as microfilm, microfiche, etc.

microfossil (ˈmaɪkrəʊˌfɒsᵊl) *n.* a fossil generally less than 0.5 millimetre in size, such as a protozoan, bacterium, or pollen grain.

microgamete (ˌmaɪkrəʊˈgæmiːt) *n.* the smaller and apparently male of two gametes in conjugating protozoans. Compare **macrogamete.**

microglia (ˌmaɪkrəʊˈglɪə) *n.* one of the two types of non-nervous tissue (glia) found in the central nervous system, having macrophage activity. Compare **macroglia.**

micrograph (ˈmaɪkrəʊˌgræf, -ˌgrɑːf) *n.* **1.** a photograph or drawing of an object as viewed through a microscope. **2.** an instrument or machine for producing very small writing or engraving.

micrography (maɪˈkrɒgrəfɪ) *n.* **1.** the description, study, drawing, or photography of microscopic objects. **2.** the technique of using a microscope. **3.** the art or practice of writing in minute characters. —**miˈcrographer** *n.* —**micrographic** (ˌmaɪkrəʊˈgræfɪk) *adj.* —ˌ**microˈgraphically** *adv.*

microgravity (ˈmaɪkrəʊˌgrævɪtɪ) *n.* gravitational effects operating, or apparently operating, in a localized region, as in a spacecraft under conditions of weightlessness.

microgroove (ˈmaɪkrəʊˌgruːv) *n.* **a.** the narrow groove in a long-playing gramophone record. **b.** (*as modifier*): *a microgroove record.*

microhabitat (ˌmaɪkrəʊˈhæbɪtæt) *n. Ecology.* the smallest part of the environment that supports a distinct flora and fauna, such as a fallen log in a forest.

microinstruction (ˈmaɪkrəʊɪnˌstrʌkʃən) *n. Computer technol.* an instruction produced within an arithmetic and logic unit in accordance with a microprogram, that activates a particular circuit to perform part of the operation specified by a machine instruction.

microlepidoptera (ˌmaɪkrəʊˌlɛpɪˈdɒptərə) *pl. n.* a collector's name for the smaller moths: a term without taxonomic significance. Compare **macrolepidoptera.**

microlight *or* **microlite** (ˈmaɪkrəʊˌlaɪt) *n.* a small private aircraft carrying no more than two people, with an empty weight of not more than 150 kg and a wing area not less than 10 square metres: used in pleasure flying and racing.

microlith (ˈmaɪkrəʊˌlɪθ) *n. Archaeol.* a small Mesolithic flint tool which was made from a blade and formed part of hafted tools. —ˌ**microˈlithic** *adj.*

micromere (ˈmaɪkrəʊˌmɪə) *n. Embryol.* any of the small cells formed by unequal cleavage of a fertilized ovum.

micrometeorite (ˌmaɪkrəʊˈmiːtɪəˌraɪt) *n.* a tiny meteorite having a diameter of 10–40 micrometres, found esp. in rainwater and seawater, having entered the atmosphere as a **micrometeoroid** (extremely small meteoroid).

micrometeorology (ˌmaɪkrəʊˌmiːtɪəˈrɒlədʒɪ) *n.* the study of the layer of air immediately above the earth and of small-scale meteorological processes.

micrometer (maɪˈkrɒmɪtə) *n.* **1.** any of various instruments or devices for the accurate measurement of distances or angles. **2.** Also called: **micrometer gauge, micrometer calliper.** a type of gauge for the accurate measurement of small distances, thicknesses, diameters, etc. The gap between its measuring faces is adjusted by a fine screw, the rotation of the screw giving a sensitive measure of the distance moved by the face. —**miˈcrometry** *n.* —**micrometric** (ˌmaɪkrəʊˈmɛtrɪk) *or* ˌ**microˈmetrical** *adj.*

micrometer screw *n.* a screw with a fine thread of definite pitch, such as that of a micrometer gauge.

micrometre (ˈmaɪkrəʊˌmiːtə) *n.* a unit of length equal to 10^{-6} metre. Symbol μm Former name: **micron.**

microminiaturization *or* **microminiaturisation** (ˌmaɪkrəʊˌmɪnɪtʃəraɪˈzeɪʃən) *n.* the production and application of very small semiconductor components and the circuits and equipment in which they are used.

micron (ˈmaɪkrɒn) *n., pl.* **-crons** *or* **-cra** (-krə). a unit of length equal to 10^{-6} metre. It is being replaced by the micrometre, the equivalent SI unit. [C19: New Latin, from Greek *mikros* small]

Micronesian (ˌmaɪkrəʊˈniːzɪən) *adj.* **1.** of or relating to the Pacific islands of Micronesia, their inhabitants, or their languages. ~*n.* **2.** a native or inhabitant of Micronesia, more akin to the Polynesians than the Melanesians, but having Mongoloid traces. **3.** a group of languages spoken in Micronesia, belonging to the Malayo-Polynesian family.

micronucleus (ˌmaɪkrəʊˈnjuːklɪəs) *n., pl.* **-clei** (-klɪˌaɪ) *or* **-cleuses.** the smaller of two nuclei in ciliated protozoans, involved in reproduction. Compare **macronucleus.**

micronutrient (ˌmaɪkrəʊˈnjuːtrɪənt) *n.* any substance, such as a vitamin or trace element, essential for healthy growth and development but required only in minute amounts.

microorganism (ˌmaɪkrəʊˈɔːgəˌnɪzəm) *n.* any organism, such as a bacterium, protozoan, or virus, of microscopic size.

micropalaeontology (ˌmaɪkrəʊˌpælɪɒnˈtɒlədʒɪ) *n.* the branch of palaeontology concerned with the study of microscopic fossils. —**micropalaeontological** (ˌmaɪkrəʊˌpælɪɒntəˈlɒdʒɪkᵊl) *or* ˌ**microˌpalaeontoˈlogic** *adj.* —ˌ**microˌpalaeonˈtologist** *n.*

microparasite (ˌmaɪkrəʊˈpærəˌsaɪt) *n.* any parasitic microorganism. —**microparasitic** (ˌmaɪkrəʊˌpærəˈsɪtɪk) *adj.*

microphagous (maɪˈkrɒfəgəs) *adj. Zoology.* (of an animal) feeding on small particles of food.

microphanerophyte (ˌmaɪkrəʊˈfænərəʊˌfaɪt) *n. Botany.* any shrub or tree having a height of 2 to 8 metres.

microphone (ˈmaɪkrəˌfəʊn) *n.* a device that is used in sound-reproduction systems for converting sound into electrical energy, usually by means of a ribbon or diaphragm set into motion by the sound waves. The vibrations are converted into the equivalent audio-frequency electric currents. Informal name: **mike.** See also **carbon microphone.** Compare **loudspeaker.**

microphonic (ˌmaɪkrəˈfɒnɪk) *adj.* **1.** of or relating to microphones. **2.** (of valves or other electronic components) unusually sensitive to incident sound or mechanical shock.

microphotograph (ˌmaɪkrəʊˈfəʊtəˌgrɑːf, -ˌgræf) *n.* **1.** a photograph in which the image is greatly reduced and therefore requires optical enlargement for viewing purposes. **2.** a less common name for **microcopy** or **photomicrograph** (sense 1). —**ˌmicroˌphotoˈgraphic** *adj.* —**microphotography** (ˌmaɪkrəʊfəˈtɒgrəfɪ) *n.*

microphyll (ˈmaɪkrəʊfɪl) *n. Botany.* the relatively small type of leaf produced by some pteridophyte plants, such as club mosses and quillworts. Compare **megaphyll.**

microphysics (ˌmaɪkrəʊˈfɪzɪks) *n.* (*functioning as sing.*) the branch of physics concerned with small objects and systems, such as atoms, molecules, nuclei, and elementary particles. —**ˌmicroˈphysical** *adj.*

microphyte (ˈmaɪkrəʊˌfaɪt) *n.* any microscopic plant, esp. a parasite. —**microphytic** (ˌmaɪkrəʊˈfɪtɪk) *adj.*

microprint (ˈmaɪkrəʊˌprɪnt) *n.* a microphotograph reproduced on paper and read by a magnifying device. It is used in order to reduce the size of large books, etc.

microprism (ˈmaɪkrəʊˌprɪzəm) *n. Photog.* a small prism incorporated in the focusing screen of many single-lens reflex cameras. The prism stops shimmering when the subject is in focus.

microprocessor (ˌmaɪkrəʊˈprəʊsɛsə) *n. Computer technol.* a single integrated circuit performing the basic functions of the central processing unit in a small computer.

microprogram (ˈmaɪkrəʊˌprəʊgræm) *n. Computer technol.* a sequence of microinstructions that controls the operation of an arithmetic and logic unit so that machine code instructions are executed.

micropropagation (ˌmaɪkrəʊˌprɒpəˈgeɪʃən) *n. Botany.* the production of a large number of individual plants from a small piece of plant tissue cultured in a nutrient medium.

micropsia (maɪˈkrɒpsɪə) *n.* a defect of vision in which objects appear to be smaller than they appear to a person with normal vision.

micropterous (maɪˈkrɒptərəs) *adj.* (of certain animals, esp. some types of ant) having small reduced wings.

micropyle (ˈmaɪkrəʊˌpaɪl) *n.* **1.** a small opening in the integuments of a plant ovule through which the male gametes pass. **2.** a small pore in the shell of an insect's eggs through which the sperm passes. [C19: from MICRO- + Greek *pulē* gate] —**ˌmicroˈpylar** *adj.*

micropyrometer (ˌmaɪkrəʊpaɪˈrɒmɪtə) *n.* a pyrometer for measuring the temperature of very small objects.

microreader (ˈmaɪkrəʊˌriːdə) *n.* an apparatus that produces an enlarged image of a microphotograph.

microscope (ˈmaɪkrəˌskəʊp) *n.* **1.** an optical instrument that uses a lens or combination of lenses to produce a magnified image of a small, close object. Modern optical microscopes have magnifications of about 1500 to 2000. See also **simple microscope, compound microscope, ultramicroscope. 2.** any instrument, such as the electron microscope, for producing a magnified visual image of a small object.

microscopic (ˌmaɪkrəˈskɒpɪk) *or* (*less commonly*) **microscopical** *adj.* **1.** not large enough to be seen with the naked eye but visible under a microscope. Compare **macroscopic. 2.** very small; minute. **3.** of, concerned with, or using a microscope. **4.** characterized by or done with great attention to detail. —**ˌmicroˈscopically** *adv.*

Microscopium (ˌmaɪkrəˈskəʊpɪəm) *n., Latin genitive* **Microscopii** (ˌmaɪkrəˈskəʊpɪˌaɪ). a faint constellation in the S hemisphere lying near Sagittarius and Capricornus.

microscopy (maɪˈkrɒskəpɪ) *n.* **1.** the study, design, and manufacture of microscopes. **2.** investigation by use of a microscope. —**microscopist** (maɪˈkrɒskəpɪst) *n.*

microsecond (ˈmaɪkrəʊˌsɛkənd) *n.* one millionth of a second. Symbol: μs

microseism (ˈmaɪkrəʊˌsaɪzəm) *n.* a very slight tremor of the earth's surface, thought not to be caused by an earthquake. —**microseismic** (ˌmaɪkrəʊˈsaɪzmɪk) *or* **ˌmicroˈseismical** *adj.*

microsmatic (ˌmaɪkrɒzˈmætɪk) *adj.* (of humans and certain animals) having a poor sense of smell. [from MICRO- + Greek *osmē* smell]

microsome (ˈmaɪkrəʊˌsəʊm) *n.* any of the small particles consisting of ribosomes and fragments of attached endoplasmic reticulum that can be isolated from cells by centrifugal action. —**ˌmicroˈsomal** *adj.*

microsporangium (ˌmaɪkrəʊspɔːˈrændʒɪəm) *n., pl.* **-gia** (-dʒɪə). the structure in certain ferns in which the microspores are formed: corresponds to the pollen sac in seed plants. Compare **megasporangium.**

microspore (ˈmaɪkrəʊˌspɔː) *n.* **1.** the smaller of two types of spore produced by some ferns, which develops into the male gametophyte. Compare **megaspore** (sense 1). **2.** the pollen grain of seed plants. —**ˌmicroˈsporic** *or* **ˌmicroˈsporous** *adj.*

microsporophyll (ˌmaɪkrəʊˈspɔːrəfɪl) *n.* a leaf on which the microspores are formed: corresponds to the stamen of a flowering plant. Compare **megasporophyll.** [C19: from MICRO- + SPOROPHYLL]

microstomatous (ˌmaɪkrəʊˈstɒmətəs) *or* **microstomous** (maɪˈkrɒstəməs) *adj. Anatomy.* having an unusually small mouth.

microstructure (ˈmaɪkrəʊˌstrʌktʃə) *n.* structure on a microscopic scale, esp. the structure of an alloy as observed by etching, polishing, and observation under a microscope.

microsurgery (ˌmaɪkrəʊˈsɜːdʒərɪ) *n.* intricate surgery performed on cells, tissues, etc., using a specially designed operating microscope and miniature precision instruments. —**ˌmicroˈsurgical** *adj.*

microswitch (ˈmaɪkrəʊˌswɪtʃ) *n. Electrical engineering.* a switch that operates by small movements of a lever.

microtechnology (ˌmaɪkrəʊtɛkˈnɒlədʒɪ) *n.* technology that uses microelectronics.

microtome (ˈmaɪkrəʊˌtəʊm) *n.* an instrument used for cutting thin sections, esp. of biological material, for microscopical examination.

microtomy (maɪˈkrɒtəmɪ) *n., pl.* **-mies.** the cutting of sections with a microtome. —**microtomic** (ˌmaɪkrəʊˈtɒmɪk) *or* **ˌmicroˈtomical** *adj.* —**miˈcrotomist** *n.*

microtone (ˈmaɪkrəʊˌtəʊn) *n.* any musical interval smaller than a semitone. —**ˌmicroˈtonal** *adj.* —**ˌmicrotoˈnality** *n.* —**ˌmicroˈtonally** *adv.*

microtubule (ˌmaɪkrəʊˈtjuːbjuːl) *n. Biology.* a tubular aggregate of protein subunits that forms structures, such as the mitotic spindle or the cilia of animal cells or of protozoans, in which it interacts with other proteins to generate various cellular movements.

microvillus (ˌmaɪkrəʊˈvɪləs) *n., pl.* **-li** (-laɪ). *Physiol.* a thin protuberance present in great abundance at the surface of some epithelial cells, notably in the gut, thus increasing the surface area available for absorption.

microwave (ˈmaɪkrəʊˌweɪv) *n.* **1. a.** electromagnetic radiation in the wavelength range 0.3 to 0.001 metres: used in radar, cooking, etc. **b.** (*as modifier*): *microwave generator.* **2.** short for **microwave oven.** ~*vb.* (*tr.*) **3.** to cook in a microwave oven.

microwave background *n.* a background of microwave electromagnetic radiation discovered in space in 1965, believed to have emanated from the big bang with which the universe began.

microwave detector *n.* a device for recording the speed of a motorist.

microwave oven *n.* an oven in which food is cooked by microwaves. Often shortened to **micro, microwave.**

microwave spectroscopy *n.* a type of spectroscopy in which information is obtained on the structure and chemical bonding of molecules and crystals by measurements of the wavelengths of microwaves emitted or absorbed by the sample. —**microwave spectroscope** *n.*

microwriter (ˈmaɪkrəʊˌraɪtə) *n.* a small device with six keys for creating text that can be printed or displayed on a visual display unit.

micrurgy (ˈmaɪkrɜːdʒɪ) *n. Biology.* the manipulation and examination of single cells under a microscope. [C20: from MICRO- + Greek *-ourgia* work]

micturate (ˈmɪktjʊˌreɪt) *vb.* (*intr.*) a less common word for **urinate.** [C19: from Latin *micturīre* to desire to urinate, from *mingere* to urinate] —**micturition** (ˌmɪktjʊˈrɪʃən) *n.*

mid[1] (mɪd) *adj.* **1.** *Phonetics.* of, relating to, or denoting a vowel whose articulation lies approximately halfway between high and low, such as *e* in English *bet.* ~*n.* **2.** an archaic word for **middle.** [C12 *midre* (inflected form of *midd,* unattested); related to Old Norse *mithr,* Gothic *midjis*]

mid[2] *or* **'mid** (mɪd) *prep.* a poetic word for **amid.**

mid. *abbrev. for* middle.

Mid. *abbrev. for* Midshipman.

mid- *combining form.* indicating a middle part, point, time, or position: *midday; mid-April; mid-Victorian.* [Old English; see MIDDLE, MID[1]]

midair (ˌmɪdˈɛə) *n.* **a.** some point above ground level, in the air. **b.** (*as modifier*): *a midair collision of aircraft.*

Midas (ˈmaɪdəs) *n.* **the Midas touch.** ability to make money. [after king *Midas* of Greek legend who was given the power of turning everything he touched to gold]

MIDAS (ˈmaɪdəs) *n. acronym for* Missile Defence Alarm System.

mid-Atlantic *adj.* characterized by a blend of British and American styles, elements, etc.: *a disc jockey's mid-Atlantic accent.*

midbrain (ˈmɪdˌbreɪn) *n.* the nontechnical name for **mesencephalon.**

midday (ˈmɪdˈdeɪ) *n.* **a.** the middle of the day; noon. **b.** (*as modifier*): *a midday meal.*

midden (ˈmɪdᵊn) *n.* **1. a.** *Archaic or dialect.* a dunghill or pile of refuse. **b.** *Dialect.* a dustbin. **c.** *Northern English dialect.* an earth closet. **2.** See **kitchen midden.** [C14: from Scandinavian; compare Danish *mödding* from *mög* MUCK + *dynge* pile]

middle (ˈmɪdᵊl) *adj.* **1.** equally distant from the ends or periphery of something; central. **2.** intermediate in status, situation, etc. **3.** located between the early and late parts of a series, time sequence, etc. **4.** not extreme, esp. in size; medium. **5.** (esp. in Greek and Sanskrit grammar) denoting a voice of verbs expressing reciprocal or reflexive action. Compare **active** (sense 5), **passive** (sense 5). **6.** (*usually cap.*) (of a language) intermediate between the earliest and the modern forms: *Middle English.* ~*n.*

7. an area or point equal in distance from the ends or periphery or in time between the early and late parts. **8.** an intermediate part or section, such as the waist. **9.** *Grammar.* the middle voice. **10.** *Logic.* See **middle term.** **11.** the ground between rows of growing plants. **12.** a discursive article in a journal, placed between the leading articles and the book reviews. *~vb. (tr.)* **13.** to place in the middle. **14.** *Nautical.* to fold in two. **15.** *Football.* to return (the ball) from the wing to midfield. **16.** *Cricket.* to hit (the ball) with the middle of the bat. [Old English *middel;* compare Old Frisian *middel,* Dutch *middel,* German *mittel*]

middle age *n.* the period of life between youth and old age, usually (in man) considered to occur approximately between the ages of 40 and 60. —ˌ**middle-ˈaged** *adj.*

Middle Ages *n.* **the.** *European history.* **1.** (broadly) the period from the end of classical antiquity (or the deposition of the last W Roman emperor in 476 A.D.) to the Italian Renaissance (or the fall of Constantinople in 1453). **2.** (narrowly) the period from about 1000 A.D. to the 15th century. Compare **Dark Ages.**

Middle America *n.* the U.S. middle class, esp. those groups that are politically conservative. —**Middle American** *adj., n.*

middlebreaker (ˈmɪdᵊlˌbreɪkə) *or* **middlebuster** *n.* a type of plough that cuts a furrow with the soil heaped on each side, often used for sowing. Also called: **lister.**

middlebrow (ˈmɪdᵊlˌbraʊ) *Disparaging.* *~n.* **1.** a person with conventional tastes and limited cultural appreciation. *~adj.* *also* **middlebrowed.** **2.** of or appealing to middlebrows: *middlebrow culture.* —ˈ**middleˌbrowism** *n.*

middle C *n. Music.* the note graphically represented on the first ledger line below the treble staff or the first ledger line above the bass staff and corresponding in pitch to an internationally standardized fundamental frequency of 261.63 hertz.

middle class *n.* **1.** Also called: **bourgeoisie.** a social stratum that is not clearly defined but is positioned between the lower and upper classes. It consists of businessmen, professional people, etc., along with their families, and is marked by bourgeois values. Compare **lower class, upper class, working class.** *~adj.* **middle-class.** **2.** of, relating to, or characteristic of the middle class.

middle common room *n.* (in certain universities and colleges) a common room for the use of postgraduate students. Compare **junior common room, senior common room.**

middle-distance *adj.* **1.** *Athletics.* relating to or denoting races of a length between the sprints and the distance events, esp. the 800 metres and the 1500 metres. *~n.* **middle distance.** **2.** part of a painting, esp. a landscape between the foreground and far distance.

Middle Dutch *n.* the Dutch language from about 1100 to about 1500. Abbrev.: **MD.**

middle ear *n.* the sound-conducting part of the ear, containing the malleus, incus, and stapes.

Middle Eastern *adj.* (loosely) of or relating to the area around the E Mediterranean, esp. Israel and the Arab countries from Turkey to North Africa and eastwards to Iran.

middle eight *n.* the third contrasting eight-bar section of a 32-bar pop song.

Middle English *n.* the English language from about 1100 to about 1450: main dialects are Kentish, Southwestern (West Saxon), East Midland (which replaced West Saxon as the chief literary form and developed into Modern English), West Midland, and Northern (from which the Scots of Lowland Scotland and other modern dialects developed). Compare **Old English, Modern English.** Abbrev.: **ME.**

middle game *n. Chess.* the central phase between the opening and the endgame.

Middle Greek *n.* another name for **Medieval Greek.**

middle ground *n.* **1.** another term for **middle distance.** **2.** a position of compromise between two opposing views, parties, etc.

Middle High German *n.* High German from about 1200 to about 1500. Abbrev.: **MHG.**

Middle Irish *n.* Irish Gaelic from about 1100 to about 1500.

Middle Low German *n.* Low German from about 1200 to about 1500. Abbrev.: **MLG.**

middleman (ˈmɪdᵊlˌmæn) *n., pl.* **-men.** **1.** an independent trader engaged in the distribution of goods from producer to consumer. **2.** an intermediary. **3.** *Theatre.* the interlocutor in minstrel shows.

middle management *n.* a level of management in an organization or business consisting of executives or senior supervisory staff in charge of the detailed running of an organization or business and reporting to top management. Compare **top management.** —**middle manager** *n.*

middlemost (ˈmɪdᵊlˌməʊst) *adj.* another word for **midmost.**

middle name *n.* **1.** a name between a person's first name and surname. **2.** a characteristic quality for which a person is known: *caution is my middle name.*

middle-of-the-road *adj.* **1.** not extreme, esp. in political views; moderate. **2.** of, denoting, or relating to popular music having a wide general appeal. —ˈ**middle-of-the-ˈroader** *n.*

Middle Palaeolithic *n.* **1.** the period between the Lower and the Upper Palaeolithic, usually taken as equivalent to the Mousterian. *~adj.* **2.** of or relating to this period.

middle passage *n.* **the.** *History.* the journey across the Atlantic Ocean from the W coast of Africa to the West Indies: the longest part of the journey of the slave ships sailing to the West Indies or the Americas.

Middle Persian *n.* the classical form of modern Persian, spoken from about 300 A.D. to about 900. See also **Pahlavi.**

middle school *n. Brit.* a school for children aged between 8 or 9 and 12 or 13. Compare **first school.**

middle term *n. Logic.* the term that appears in both the major and minor premises of a syllogism, but not in the conclusion. Also called: **mean, middle.**

middle watch *n. Nautical.* the watch between midnight and 4 a.m.

middleweight (ˈmɪdᵊlˌweɪt) *n.* **1. a.** a professional boxer weighing 154–160 pounds (70–72.5 kg). **b.** an amateur boxer weighing 71–75 kg (157–165 pounds). **c.** (*as modifier*): *a middleweight contest.* **2.** a wrestler in a similar weight category (usually 172–192 pounds (78–87 kg)).

middling (ˈmɪdlɪŋ) *adj.* **1.** mediocre in quality, size, etc.; neither good nor bad, esp. in health (often in the phrase **fair to middling**). *~adv.* **2.** *Informal.* moderately: *middling well.* [C15 (northern English and Scottish): from MID[1] + -LING[2]] —ˈ**middlingly** *adv.*

middlings (ˈmɪdlɪŋz) *pl. n.* **1.** the poorer or coarser part of flour or other products. **2.** commodities of intermediate grade, quality, size, or price. **3.** *Chiefly U.S.* the part of a pig between the ham and shoulder.

Middx *abbrev. for* Middlesex.

middy (ˈmɪdɪ) *n., pl.* **-dies.** **1.** *Informal.* See **midshipman** (sense 1). **2.** See **middy blouse.** **3.** *Austral.* a glass of beer of a specific size, most commonly half a pint.

middy blouse *n.* a blouse with a sailor collar, worn by women and children, esp. formerly.

midfield (ˌmɪdˈfiːld) *n. Soccer.* **a.** the general area between the two opposing defences. **b.** (*as modifier*): *a midfield player.*

midge (mɪdʒ) *n.* **1.** any fragile mosquito-like dipterous insect of the family *Chironomidae,* occurring in dancing swarms, esp. near water. **2.** any similar or related insect, such as the biting midge and gall midge. **3.** a small or diminutive person or animal. [Old English *mycge;* compare Old High German *mucca,* Danish *myg*] —ˈ**midgy** *adj.*

midget (ˈmɪdʒɪt) *n.* **1.** a dwarf whose skeleton and features are of normal proportions. **2. a.** something small of its kind. **b.** (*as modifier*): *a midget car.* [C19: from MIDGE + -ET]

midgut (ˈmɪdˌɡʌt) *n.* **1.** the middle part of the digestive tract of vertebrates, including the small intestine. **2.** the middle part of the digestive tract of arthropods. ~See also **foregut, hindgut.**

Midheaven (ˈmɪdˈhɛvᵊn) *n. Astrology.* **1.** the point on the ecliptic, measured in degrees, that crosses the meridian of a particular place at a particular time. On a person's birth chart it relates to the time of birth. Abbrev.: **MC.** **2.** the sign of the zodiac containing this point. [C16: initials *MC* represent Latin *medium caeli* middle of the sky]

midi (ˈmɪdɪ) *adj.* **a.** (of a skirt, coat, etc.) reaching to below the knee or midcalf. **b.** (*as n.*): *she wore her new midi.* [C20: from MID-; on the model of MAXI and MINI]

MIDI (ˈmɪdɪ) *n.* (*modifier*) a generally accepted specification for the external control of electronic musical instruments: *a MIDI synthesizer; a MIDI system.* [C20: from *m(usical) i(nstrument) d(igital) i(nterface)*]

midinette (ˌmɪdɪˈnɛt; *French* midinɛt) *n., pl.* **-nettes** (-ˈnɛts; *French* -nɛt). a Parisian seamstress or salesgirl in a clothes shop. [C20: from French, from *midi* noon + *dinette* light meal, since the girls had time for no more than a snack at midday]

midiron (ˈmɪdˌaɪən) *n. Golf.* a club, a No. 2 iron, used for approach shots.

midi system *n.* a complete set of hi-fi sound equipment designed as a single unit that is more compact than the standard equipment.

midland (ˈmɪdlənd) *n.* **a.** the central or inland part of a country. **b.** (*as modifier*): *a midland region.*

midlife crisis (ˈmɪdˌlaɪf) *n.* a crisis that may be experienced in middle age involving frustration, panic, and feelings of pointlessness, sometimes resulting in radical and often ill-advised changes of lifestyle.

midmost (ˈmɪdˌməʊst) *adj., adv.* in the middle or midst.

midnight (ˈmɪdˌnaɪt) *n.* **1. a.** the middle of the night; 12 o'clock at night. **b.** (*as modifier*): *the midnight hour.* **2. burn the midnight oil.** to work or study late into the night. —ˈ**midˌnightly** *adj., adv.*

midnight blue *n.* **a.** a very dark blue colour; bluish black. **b.** (*as adj.*): *a midnight-blue suit.*

midnight sun *n.* the sun visible at midnight during the summer inside the Arctic and Antarctic circles.

mid-off *n. Cricket.* **1.** the fielding position on the off side closest to the bowler. **2.** a fielder in this position.

mid-on *n. Cricket.* **1.** the fielding position on the on side closest to the bowler. **2.** a fielder in this position.

midpoint (ˈmɪdˌpɔɪnt) *n.* **1.** the point on a line that is at an equal distance from either end. **2.** a point in time halfway between the beginning and end of an event.

midrash (ˈmɪdræʃ; *Hebrew* miˈdraʃ) *n., pl.* **midrashim** (mɪˈdrɔʃɪm; *Hebrew* midraˈʃim). *Judaism.* **1.** a homily on a scriptural passage derived by traditional Jewish exegetical methods and consisting usually of embellishment of the scriptural narrative. **2.** one of a number of collections of such homilies composed between 400 and 1200 A.D. [C17: from Hebrew: commentary, from *darash* to search] —**midrashic** (mɪdˈræʃɪk) *adj.*

midrib (ˈmɪdˌrɪb) *n.* the main vein of a leaf, running down the centre of the blade.

midriff (ˈmɪdrɪf) *n.* **1. a.** the middle part of the human body, esp. between waist and bust. **b.** (*as modifier*): *midriff bulge.* **2.** *Anatomy.* another name for the **diaphragm** (sense 1). **3.** the part of a woman's garment covering the midriff. **4.** *U.S.* a woman's garment which exposes the midriff. [Old English *midhrif,* from MID[1] + *hrif* belly]

midsection (ˈmɪdˌsɛkʃən) *n.* **1.** the middle of something. **2.** the middle region of the human body; midriff.

midship (ˈmɪdˌʃɪp) *Nautical.* ~*adj.* **1.** in, of, or relating to the middle of a vessel. ~*n.* **2.** the middle of a vessel.

midshipman (ˈmɪdˌʃɪpmən) *n., pl.* **-men. 1.** a probationary rank held by young naval officers under training, or an officer holding such a rank. **2.** any of several American toadfishes of the genus *Porichthys,* having small light-producing organs on the undersurface of their bodies.

midships (ˈmɪdˌʃɪps) *adv., adj. Nautical.* See **amidships.**

midst[1] (mɪdst) *n.* **1. in the midst of.** surrounded or enveloped by; at a point during, esp. a climactic one. **2. in our midst.** among us. **3.** *Archaic.* the centre. [C14: back formation from *amiddes* AMID]

midst[2] (mɪdst) *prep. Poetic.* See **amid.**

midsummer (ˈmɪdˈsʌmə) *n.* **1. a.** the middle or height of the summer. **b.** (*as modifier*): *a midsummer carnival.* **2.** another name for **summer solstice.**

Midsummer Day *or* **Midsummer's Day** *n.* June 24, the feast of St John the Baptist; in England, Ireland, and Wales, one of the four quarter days. See also **summer solstice.**

midsummer madness *n.* foolish or extravagant behaviour, supposed to occur during the summer.

midsummer-men *n.* (*functioning as sing. or pl.*) another name for **rose-root.**

midterm (ˈmɪdˈtɜːm) *n.* **1. a.** the middle of a term in a school, university, etc. **b.** (*as modifier*): *midterm exam.* **2.** *U.S. Politics.* **a.** the middle of a term of office, esp. of a presidential term, when congressional and local elections are held. **b.** (*as modifier*): *midterm elections.* **3. a.** the middle of the gestation period. **b.** (*as modifier*): *midterm checkup.* See **term** (sense 6).

midtown (ˈmɪdˌtaʊn) *n. U.S. and Canadian.* the centre of a town. See also **downtown, uptown.**

mid-Victorian *adj.* **1.** *British history.* of or relating to the middle period of the reign of Queen Victoria (1837–1901). ~*n.* **2.** a person of the mid-Victorian era.

midway (ˈmɪdˌweɪ) *adj., adv.* **1.** in or at the middle of the distance; halfway. ~*n.* **2.** *U.S. and Canadian.* a place in a fair, carnival, etc., where sideshows are located. **3.** *Obsolete.* a middle place, way, etc.

midweek (ˈmɪdˈwiːk) *n.* **a.** the middle of the week. **b.** (*as modifier*): *a midweek holiday.* —ˌ**midˈweekly** *adj.*

Midwestern (ˈmɪdˈwɛstən) *adj.* of or relating to the Midwest, the N central part of the U.S. —ˈ**Midˈwesterner** *n.*

mid-wicket *n. Cricket.* **1.** the fielding position on the on side, approximately midway between square leg and mid-on. **2.** a fielder in this position.

midwife (ˈmɪdˌwaɪf) *n., pl.* **-wives** (-ˌwaɪvz). a woman skilled in aiding in the delivery of babies. [C14: from Old English *mid* with + *wif* woman]

midwifery (ˈmɪdˌwɪfərɪ) *n.* the art or practice of a midwife; obstetrics.

midwife toad *n.* a European toad, *Alytes obstetricans,* the male of which carries the fertilized eggs on its hind legs until they hatch: family *Discoglossidae.*

midwinter (ˈmɪdˈwɪntə) *n.* **1. a.** the middle or depth of the winter. **b.** (*as modifier*): *a midwinter festival.* **2.** another name for **winter solstice.**

midyear (ˈmɪdˈjɪə) *n.* **a.** the middle of the year. **b.** (*as modifier*): *a midyear examination.*

mien (miːn) *n. Literary.* a person's manner, bearing, or appearance, expressing personality or mood: *a noble mien.* [C16: probably variant of obsolete *demean* appearance; related to French *mine* aspect]

miff (mɪf) *Informal.* ~*vb.* **1.** to take offence or offend. ~*n.* **2.** a petulant mood. **3.** a petty quarrel. [C17: perhaps an imitative expression of bad temper]

miffy (ˈmɪfɪ) *adj.* **-fier, -fiest.** *Informal.* easily upset; oversensitive. —ˈ**miffily** *adv.* —ˈ**miffiness** *n.*

MiG (mɪg) *n.* any of various types of USSR fighter aircraft [from Mi(*koyan*) and G (*urevich*), names of designers]

might[1] (maɪt) *vb.* (takes an implied infinitive or an infinitive without *to*) used as an auxiliary: **1.** making the past tense or subjunctive mood of **may**[1]: *he might have come last night.* **2.** (often foll. by *well*) expressing theoretical possibility: *he might well come.* In this sense *might* looks to the future and functions as a weak form of *may.* See **may**[1] (sense 2).

▷**Usage.** See at **may**[1].

might[2] (maɪt) *n.* **1.** power, force, or vigour, esp. of a great or supreme kind. **2.** physical strength. **3.** (**with**) **might and main.** See **main**[1] (sense 8). [Old English *miht;* compare Old High German *maht,* Dutch *macht*]

mightily (ˈmaɪtɪlɪ) *adv.* **1.** to a great extent, amount, or degree. **2.** with might; powerfully or vigorously.

mighty (ˈmaɪtɪ) *adj.* **mightier, mightiest. 1. a.** having or indicating might; powerful or strong. **b.** (*as collective n.;* preceded by *the*): *the mighty.* **2.** very large; vast. **3.** very great in extent, importance, etc. ~*adv.* **4.** *Informal, chiefly U.S. and Canadian.* (intensifier): *he was mighty tired.* —ˈ**mightiness** *n.*

migmatite (ˈmɪgməˌtaɪt) *n.* a composite rock body containing two types of rock that have interacted with each other but are nevertheless still distinguishable. [C20: alteration of Swedish *migmatit,* from Greek *migma* mixture + -ITE[1]]

mignon (ˈmɪnjɒn; *French* miɲɔ̃) *adj.* small and pretty; dainty. [C16: from French, from Old French *mignot* dainty] —**mignonne** (ˈmɪnjɒn; *French* miɲɔn) *fem. n.*

mignonette (ˌmɪnjəˈnɛt) *n.* **1.** any of various mainly Mediterranean plants of the resedaceous genus *Reseda,* such as *R. odorata* (**garden mignonette**), that have spikes of small greenish-white flowers with prominent anthers. **2.** a type of fine pillow lace. ~*adj.* **3.** of a greyish-green colour; reseda. [C18: from French, diminutive of MIGNON]

migraine (ˈmiːgreɪn, ˈmaɪ-) *n.* a throbbing headache usually affecting only one side of the head and commonly accompanied by nausea and visual disturbances. [C18: (earlier form, C14 *mygrame* MEGRIM[1]): from French, from Late Latin *hēmicrānia* pain in half of the head, from Greek *hēmikrania,* from HEMI- + *kranion* CRANIUM] —ˈ**migrainous** *adj.*

migrant (ˈmaɪgrənt) *n.* **1.** a person or animal that moves from one region, place, or country to another. **2.** an itinerant agricultural worker who travels from one district to another. **3.** *Chiefly Austral.* **a.** an immigrant, esp. a recent one. **b.** (*as modifier*): *a migrant hostel.* ~*adj.* **4.** moving from one region, place, or country to another; migratory. [C17: from Latin *migrāre* to change one's abode]

migrate (maɪˈgreɪt) *vb.* (*intr.*) **1.** to go from one region, country, or place of abode to settle in another, esp. in a foreign country. **2.** (of birds, fishes, etc.) to journey between different habitats at specific times of the year. [C17: from Latin *migrāre* to change one's abode] —**miˈgrator** *n.*

migration (maɪˈgreɪʃən) *n.* **1.** the act or an instance of migrating. **2.** a group of people, birds, etc., migrating in a body. **3.** *Chem.* a movement of atoms, ions, or molecules, such as the motion of ions in solution under the influence of electric fields. —**miˈgrational** *adj.*

migratory (ˈmaɪgrətərɪ, -trɪ) *adj.* **1.** of, relating to, or characterized by migration. **2.** nomadic; itinerant.

MIG welding (mɪg) *n.* metal inert gas welding: a method of welding in which the filler metal wire supplies the electric current to maintain the arc, which is shielded from the access of air by an invert gas, usually argon. Compare **TIG welding.**

mihrab (ˈmiːræb, -rəb) *n. Islam.* the niche in a mosque showing the direction of Mecca. [from Arabic]

mikado (mɪˈkɑːdəʊ) *n., pl.* **-dos.** (*often cap.*) *Archaic.* the Japanese emperor. Compare **tenno.** [C18: from Japanese, from *mi-* honourable + *kado* door, palace gate]

mike[1] (maɪk) *n. Informal.* short for **microphone.**

mike[2] (maɪk) *Brit. slang.* ~*vb.* (*intr.*) **1.** to idle; wait about. ~*n.* **2.** an evasion of work: *to do a mike.* [C19: origin unknown]

Mike (maɪk) *n. Communications.* a code word for the letter *m.*

mikvah *or* **mikveh** (mikˈvɑ, ˈmikvə) *n. Judaism.* a pool used esp. by women for ritual purification after their monthly period. [from Hebrew]

mil (mɪl) *n.* **1.** a unit of length equal to one thousandth of an inch. **2.** an obsolete pharmaceutical unit of volume equal to one millilitre. **3.** a unit of angular measure, used in gunnery, equal to one sixty-four-hundredth of a circumference. [C18: short for Latin *millēsimus* thousandth]

mil. *abbrev. for:* **1.** military. **2.** militia.

milady *or* **miladi** (mɪˈleɪdɪ) *n., pl.* **-dies.** (formerly) a continental title used for an English gentlewoman.

milage (ˈmaɪlɪdʒ) *n.* a variant spelling of **mileage.**

milah (miˈlɑː, ˈmilɑ) *n. Judaism.* a Hebrew term usually translated as **circumcision.**

Milanese (ˌmɪləˈniːz) *adj.* **1.** of or relating to the city of Milan in N Italy, its people, culture, etc. **2.** of a fine lightweight knitted fabric of silk, rayon, etc. ~*n.* **3.** the Italian dialect spoken in Milan. **4.** (*pl.* **-ese**) a native or inhabitant of Milan.

milch (mɪltʃ) *n.* **1.** (*modifier*) (esp. of cattle) yielding milk. **2. milch cow.** *Informal.* a source of easy income, esp. a person. [C13: from Old English *-milce* (in compounds); related to Old English *melcan* to milk]

milchik *or* **milchig** (ˈmilxɪk) *adj. Judaism.* containing or used in the preparation of milk products and so not to be used with meat products. Also called: **milky.** Compare **fleishik.** See also **kashruth.** [Yiddish, from *milch* milk, ultimately from Old High German; compare MILCH; see also MILK]

mild (maɪld) *adj.* **1.** (of a taste, sensation, etc.) not powerful or strong; bland: *a mild curry.* **2.** gentle or temperate in character, climate, behaviour, etc. **3.** not extreme; moderate: *a mild rebuke.* **4.** feeble; unassertive. ~*n.* **5.** *Brit.* draught beer, of darker colour than bitter and flavoured with fewer hops. **6. draw it mild.** speak or act moderately. [Old English *milde*; compare Old Saxon *mildi*, Old Norse *mildr*] —'**mildly** *adv.* —'**mildness** *n.*

milden ('maɪldən) *vb.* to make or become mild or milder.

mildew ('mɪlˌdjuː) *n.* **1.** any of various diseases of plants that affect mainly the leaves and are caused by parasitic fungi. See also **downy mildew, powdery mildew. 2.** any fungus causing this kind of disease. **3.** another name for **mould**[2]. *~vb.* **4.** to affect or become affected with mildew. [Old English *mildēaw*, from *mil-* honey (compare Latin *mel*, Greek *meli*) + *dēaw* DEW] —'**milˌdewy** *adj.*

mild steel *n.* any of a class of strong tough steels that contain a low quantity of carbon (0.1–0.25 per cent).

mile (maɪl) *n.* **1.** Also called: **statute mile.** a unit of length used in English-speaking countries, equal to 1760 yards. 1 mile is equivalent to 1.609 34 kilometres. **2.** See **nautical mile. 3.** See **Swedish mile. 4.** any of various units of length used at different times and places, esp. the Roman mile, equivalent to 1620 yards. **5.** (*often pl.*) *Informal.* a great distance; great deal: *he missed by a mile.* **6.** a race extending over a mile. *~adv.* **7. miles.** (intensifier): *he likes his new job miles better.* [Old English *mīl*, from Latin *mīlia* (*passuum*) a thousand (paces)]

mileage *or* **milage** ('maɪlɪdʒ) *n.* **1.** a distance expressed in miles. **2.** the total number of miles that a motor vehicle has travelled. **3.** allowance for travelling expenses, esp. as a fixed rate per mile. **4.** the number of miles a motor vehicle will travel on one gallon of fuel. **5.** *Informal.* use, benefit, or service provided by something: *this scheme has a lot of mileage left.* **6.** *Informal.* grounds, substance, or weight: *there is some mileage in the objectors' arguments.*

mileometer *or* **milometer** (maɪ'lɒmɪtə) *n.* a device that records the number of miles that a bicycle or motor vehicle has travelled. Usual U.S. and Canadian name: **odometer.**

milepost ('maɪlˌpəʊst) *n.* **1.** *Horse racing.* a marking post on a racecourse a mile before the finishing line. **2.** Also called (esp. Brit.): **milestone.** *Chiefly U.S. and Canadian.* a signpost that shows the distance in miles to or from a place.

miler ('maɪlə) *n.* an athlete, horse, etc., that runs or specializes in races of one mile.

miles gloriosus *Latin.* ('miːleɪs ˌglɔːrɪ'əʊsʊs) *n., pl.* ***milites gloriosi*** ('miːlɪˌteɪs ˌglɔːrɪ'əʊsaɪ). a braggart soldier, esp. as a stock figure in comedy. [from the title of a comedy by Plautus (?254–?184 B.C.), Roman dramatist]

Milesian[1] (maɪ'liːzɪən) *adj.* **1.** of or relating to Miletus, an ancient city in Asia Minor and a major Ionian centre of trade and learning. *~n.* **2.** an inhabitant of Miletus. [via Latin from Greek *Milēsios*]

Milesian[2] (maɪ'liːzɪən) *Facetious.* *~adj.* **1.** Irish. *~n.* **2.** an Irishman. [C16: from *Milesius*, a fictitious king of Spain whose sons were supposed to have conquered Ireland]

milestone ('maɪlˌstəʊn) *n.* **1.** a stone pillar that shows the distance in miles to or from a place. **2.** a significant event in life, history, etc.

milfoil ('mɪlˌfɔɪl) *n.* **1.** another name for **yarrow. 2.** See **water milfoil.** [C13: from Old French, from Latin *milifolium*, from *mille* thousand + *folium* leaf]

miliaria (ˌmɪlɪ'ɛərɪə) *n.* an acute itching eruption of the skin, caused by blockage of the sweat glands. Nontechnical names: **heat rash, prickly heat.** [C19: from New Latin, from Latin *miliārius* MILIARY]

miliary ('mɪljərɪ) *adj.* **1.** resembling or relating to millet seeds. **2.** (of a disease or skin eruption) characterized by small lesions resembling millet seeds: *miliary tuberculosis.* [C17: from Latin *miliārius*, from *milium* MILLET]

miliary fever *n.* an acute infectious fever characterized by profuse sweating and the formation on the skin of minute fluid-filled vesicles. Nontechnical name: **sweating sickness.**

milieu ('miːljɜː; *French* miljø) *n., pl.* **-lieus** *or French* **-lieux** (-ljø). surroundings, location, or setting. [C19: from French, from *mi-* MID[1] + *lieu* place]

milit. *abbrev. for* military.

militant ('mɪlɪtənt) *adj.* **1.** aggressive or vigorous, esp. in the support of a cause: *a militant protest.* **2.** warring; engaged in warfare. *~n.* **3.** a militant person. [C15: from Latin *mīlitāre* to be a soldier, from *mīles* soldier] —'**militancy** *or* (*less commonly*) '**militantness** *n.* —'**militantly** *adv.*

Militant ('mɪlɪtənt) *n.* a member of Militant Tendency, a Trotskyite group formerly operating within the British Labour Party.

militaria (ˌmɪlɪ'tɛərɪə) *pl. n.* items of military interest, such as weapons, uniforms, medals, etc., esp. from the past.

militarism ('mɪlɪtəˌrɪzəm) *n.* **1.** military spirit; pursuit of military ideals. **2.** domination by the military in the formulation of policies, ideals, etc., esp. on a political level. **3.** a policy of maintaining a strong military organization in aggressive preparedness for war.

militarist ('mɪlɪtərɪst) *n.* **1.** a supporter of or believer in militarism. **2.** a devotee of military history, strategy, etc. —ˌ**milita'ristic** *adj.* —ˌ**milita'ristically** *adv.*

militarize *or* **militarise** ('mɪlɪtəˌraɪz) *vb.* (*tr.*) **1.** to convert to military use. **2.** to imbue with militarism. —ˌ**militari'zation** *or* ˌ**militari'sation** *n.*

military ('mɪlɪtərɪ, -trɪ) *adj.* **1.** of or relating to the armed forces (esp. the army), warlike matters, etc. **2.** of, characteristic of, or about soldiers. *~n., pl.* **-taries** *or* **-tary. 3.** (preceded by *the*) the armed services (esp. the army). [C16: via French from Latin *mīlitāris*, from *mīles* soldier] —'**militarily** *adv.*

military academy *n.* a training establishment for young officer cadets entering the army.

military engineering *n.* the design, construction, etc., of military fortifications and communications.

military honours *pl. n.* ceremonies performed by troops in honour of royalty, at the burial of an officer, etc.

military-industrial complex *n.* (in the U.S.) the combined interests of the military establishment and industries involved in producing military material considered as exerting influence on U.S. foreign and economic policy.

military law *n.* articles or regulations that apply to those belonging to the armed services. Compare **martial law.**

military orchid *n.* another name for **soldier orchid.**

military pace *n.* the pace of a single step in marching, taken to be 30 inches for quick time (120 paces to the minute) in both the British and U.S. armies.

military police *n.* a corps within an army that performs police and disciplinary duties. —**military policeman** *n.*

militate ('mɪlɪˌteɪt) *vb.* (*intr.*; usually foll. by *against* or *for*) (of facts, actions, etc.) to have influence or effect: *the evidence militated against his release.* [C17: from Latin *mīlitātus*, from *mīlitāre* to be a soldier] —ˌ**mili'tation** *n.*

militia (mɪ'lɪʃə) *n.* **1.** a body of citizen (as opposed to professional) soldiers. **2.** an organization containing men enlisted for service in emergency only. [C16: from Latin: soldiery, from *mīles* soldier]

militiaman (mɪ'lɪʃəmən) *n., pl.* **-men.** a man serving with the militia.

milium ('mɪlɪəm) *n., pl.* **-ia** (-ɪə). *Pathol.* a small whitish nodule on the skin, usually resulting from a clogged sebaceous gland. [C19: from Latin: millet]

milk (mɪlk) *n.* **1. a.** a whitish nutritious fluid produced and secreted by the mammary glands of mature female mammals and used for feeding their young until weaned. **b.** the milk of cows, goats, or other animals used by man as a food or in the production of butter, cheese, etc. **2.** any similar fluid in plants, such as the juice of a coconut. **3.** any of various milklike pharmaceutical preparations, such as milk of magnesia. **4. cry over spilt milk.** to lament something that cannot be altered. *~vb.* **5.** to draw milk from the udder of (a cow, goat, or other animal). **6.** (*intr.*) (of cows, goats, or other animals) to yield milk. **7.** (*tr.*) to draw off or tap in small quantities: *to milk the petty cash.* **8.** (*tr.*) to extract as much money, help, etc., as possible from: *to milk a situation of its news value.* **9.** (*tr.*) to extract venom, sap, etc., from. [Old English *milc*; compare Old Saxon *miluk*, Old High German *miluh*, Old Norse *mjolk*]

milk-and-water *adj.* (**milk and water** *when postpositive*). weak, feeble, or insipid.

milk bar *n.* **1.** a snack bar at which milk drinks and light refreshments are served. **2.** (in Australia) a shop selling, in addition to milk, basic provisions and other items.

milk cap *n.* any of a large genus (*Lactarius*) of basidiomycetous fungi that are brittle to touch and exude a milky liquid when crushed. Some are funnel-shaped and some parasol-shaped, and most, except for *L. deliciosus*, are inedible.

milk chocolate *n.* chocolate that has been made with milk, having a creamy taste. Compare **plain chocolate.**

milker ('mɪlkə) *n.* **1.** a cow, goat, etc., that yields milk, esp. of a specified quality or amount: *a poor milker.* **2.** a person who milks. **3.** another name for **milking machine.**

milk fever *n.* **1.** a fever that sometimes occurs shortly after childbirth, once thought to result from engorgement of the breasts with milk but now thought to be caused by infection. **2.** *Vet. science.* a disease of cows, goats, etc., occurring shortly after parturition, characterized by low blood calcium levels, paralysis, and loss of consciousness.

milkfish ('mɪlkˌfɪʃ) *n., pl.* **-fish** *or* **-fishes.** a large silvery tropical clupeoid food and game fish, *Chanos chanos*: family *Chanidae*.

milk float *n. Brit.* a small motor vehicle used to deliver milk to houses.

milk glass *n.* opaque white glass, originally produced in imitation of Chinese porcelain.

milking machine *n.* an apparatus for milking cows.

milking shed *n.* a building in which a herd of cows is milked. Compare **milking parlour** (see **parlour** (sense 6)).

milking stool *n.* a low three-legged stool.

milk leg *n.* inflammation and thrombosis of the femoral vein following childbirth, characterized by painful swelling of the leg. Also called: **white leg.** Technical name: **phlegmasia alba dolens.**

milkmaid ('mɪlkˌmeɪd) *n.* a girl or woman who milks cows.

milkman ('mɪlkmən) *n., pl.* **-men. 1.** a man who delivers or sells milk. **2.** a man who milks cows; dairyman.

milko ('mɪlkəʊ) *n., pl.* **milkos.** *Austral.* an informal name for **milkman** (sense 1).

milk of magnesia *n.* a suspension of magnesium hydroxide in water, used as an antacid and laxative.

milk pudding *n. Chiefly Brit.* a hot or cold pudding made by boiling or baking milk with a grain, esp. rice.

milk punch *n.* a spiced drink made of milk and spirits.

milk round *n. Brit.* **1.** a route along which a milkman regularly delivers milk. **2. a.** a regular series of visits, esp. as made by recruitment officers from industry to universities. **b.** (*as modifier*): *milk-round recruitment.*

milk run *n. Aeronautics, informal.* a routine and uneventful flight, esp. on a dangerous mission. [C20: referring to the regular and safe routine of a milkman's round]

milk shake *n.* a cold frothy drink made of milk, flavouring, and sometimes ice cream, whisked or beaten together.

milk sickness *n.* **1.** an acute disease characterized by weakness, vomiting, and constipation, caused by ingestion of the flesh or dairy products of cattle affected with trembles. **2.** *Vet. science.* another name for **trembles** (sense 1).

milk snake *n.* a nonvenomous brown-and-grey North American colubrid snake *Lampropeltis doliata,* related to the king snakes.

milksop (ˈmɪlkˌsɒp) *n.* **1.** a feeble or ineffectual man or youth. **2.** *Brit.* a dish of bread soaked in warm milk, given esp. to infants and invalids. —ˈ**milkˌsoppy** *or* ˈ**milkˌsopping** *adj.* —ˈ**milkˌsopism** *n.*

milk stout *n. Brit.* a rich mellow stout lacking a bitter aftertaste. [C20: so called because its ingredients include LACTOSE]

milk sugar *n.* another name for **lactose.**

milk thistle *n.* another name for **sow thistle.**

milk tooth *n.* any of the first teeth to erupt; a deciduous tooth. Also called: **baby tooth.** See also **dentition.**

milk vetch *n.* any of various papilionaceous plants of the genus *Astragalus,* esp. *A. glycyphyllos,* with clusters of purple, white, or yellowish flowers: formerly reputed to increase milk production in goats.

milkweed (ˈmɪlkˌwiːd) *n.* **1.** Also called: **silkweed.** any plant of the mostly North American genus *Asclepias,* having milky sap and pointed pods that split open to release tufted seeds: family *Asclepiadaceae.* See also **asclepias. 2.** any of various other plants having milky sap. **3. orange milkweed.** another name for **butterfly weed. 4.** another name for **monarch** (the butterfly).

milkwort (ˈmɪlkˌwɜːt) *n.* any of several plants of the genus *Polygala,* having small blue, pink, or white flowers with two petal-like sepals: family *Polygalaceae.* They were formerly believed to increase milk production in nursing women. See also **senega.**

milky (ˈmɪlkɪ) *adj.* **milkier, milkiest. 1.** resembling milk, esp. in colour or cloudiness. **2.** of or containing milk. **3.** spiritless or spineless. **4.** *Judaism.* another word for **milchik.** —ˈ**milkily** *adv.* —ˈ**milkiness** *n.*

Milky Way *n.* **the. 1.** the diffuse band of light stretching across the night sky that consists of millions of faint stars, nebulae, etc., and forms part of the Galaxy. **2.** another name for the **Galaxy.** [C14: translation of Latin *via lactea*]

mill[1] (mɪl) *n.* **1.** a building fitted with machinery for processing materials, manufacturing goods, etc.; factory. **2.** a machine that processes materials, manufactures goods, etc., by performing a continuous or repetitive operation, esp. one involving rotary motion, such as a machine to grind flour, pulverize solids, or press fruit. **3.** any of various small hand mills used for grinding pepper, salt, or coffee for domestic purposes. See also **coffee mill, pepper mill. 4.** a machine that tools or polishes metal. **5.** a hard roller for impressing a design, esp. in a textile-printing machine or in a machine for printing banknotes. **6.** a system, institution, etc., that influences people or things in the manner of a factory: *going through the educational mill.* **7.** an unpleasant experience; ordeal (esp. in the phrases **go** *or* **be put through the mill**). **8.** a fist fight. **9. run of the mill.** ordinary or routine. ~*vb.* **10.** (*tr.*) to grind, press, or pulverize in or as if in a mill. **11.** (*tr.*) to process or produce in or with a mill. **12.** to cut or roll (metal) with or as if with a milling machine. **13.** (*tr.*) to groove or flute the edge of (a coin). **14.** (*intr.;* often foll. by *about* or *around*) to move about in a confused manner. **15.** (*usually tr.*) *Now rare.* to beat (chocolate, etc.). **16.** *Archaic slang.* to fight, esp. with the fists. [Old English *mylen* from Late Latin *molīna* a mill, from Latin *mola* mill, millstone, from *molere* to grind] —ˈ**millable** *adj.*

mill[2] (mɪl) *n.* a U.S. and Canadian monetary unit used in calculations, etc., equal to one thousandth of a dollar. [C18: short for Latin *millēsimum* a thousandth (part)]

millboard (ˈmɪlˌbɔːd) *n.* strong pasteboard, used esp. in book covers. [C18: changed from *milled board*]

milldam (ˈmɪlˌdæm) *n.* a dam built in a stream to raise the water level sufficiently for it to turn a millwheel.

milled (mɪld) *adj.* **1.** (of coins, etc.) having a grooved or fluted edge. **2.** made or treated in a mill.

millefeuille *French.* (milfœj) *n. Brit.* a small iced cake made of puff pastry filled with jam and cream. U.S. name: **napoleon.** [literally: thousand leaves]

millefiori (ˌmɪlɪˈfjɔːrɪ) *n.* **a.** decorative glassware in which coloured glass rods are fused and cut to create flower patterns: an ancient technique revived in Venice in the sixteenth century and in France and England in the nineteenth century. **b.** (*as modifier*): *a millefiori paperweight.* [C19: from Italian: thousand flowers]

millefleurs (ˈmiːlˌflɜː) *n.* a design of stylized floral patterns, used in textiles, tapestries, etc. [French: thousand flowers]

millenarian (ˌmɪlɪˈnɛərɪən) *or* **millenary** *adj.* **1.** of or relating to a thousand or to a thousand years. **2.** of or relating to the millennium or millenarianism. ~*n.* **3.** an adherent of millenarianism.

millenarianism (ˌmɪlɪˈnɛərɪəˌnɪzəm) *n.* **1.** *Christianity.* the belief in a future millennium following the Second Coming of Christ during which he will reign on earth in peace: based on Revelation 20:1–5. **2.** any belief in a future period of ideal peace and happiness.

millenary (mɪˈlɛnərɪ) *n., pl.* **-naries. 1.** a sum or aggregate of one thousand, esp. one thousand years. **2.** another word for a **millennium.** ~*adj., n.* **3.** another word for **millenarian.** [C16: from Late Latin *millēnārius* containing a thousand, from Latin *mille* thousand]

millennium (mɪˈlɛnɪəm) *n., pl.* **-niums** *or* **-nia** (-nɪə). **1. the.** *Christianity.* the period of a thousand years of Christ's awaited reign upon earth. **2.** a period or cycle of one thousand years. **3.** a time of peace and happiness, esp. in the distant future. **4.** a thousandth anniversary. [C17: from New Latin, from Latin *mille* thousand + *annus* year; for form, compare QUADRENNIUM] —**milˈlennial** *adj.* —**milˈlennialist** *n.* —**milˈlennially** *adv.*

millepede (ˈmɪlɪˌpiːd) *or* **milleped** (ˈmɪlɪˌpɛd) *n.* variants of **millipede.**

millepore (ˈmɪlɪˌpɔː) *n.* any tropical colonial coral-like medusoid hydrozoan of the order *Milleporina,* esp. of the genus *Millepora,* having a calcareous skeleton. [C18: from New Latin, from Latin *mille* thousand + *porus* hole]

miller (ˈmɪlə) *n.* **1.** a person who keeps, operates, or works in a mill, esp. a corn mill. **2.** another name for **milling machine. 3.** a person who operates a milling machine. **4.** any of various pale coloured or white moths, especially the medium-sized noctuid *Apatele leporina.* **5.** an edible basidiomycetous fungus, *Clitopilus prunulus,* with a white funnel-shaped cap and pinkish spores, often forming rings in grass.

millerite (ˈmɪləˌraɪt) *n.* a yellow mineral consisting of nickel sulphide in hexagonal crystalline form: a minor ore of nickel. Formula: NiS. [C19: named after W. H. *Miller* (1801–1880), English mineralogist]

miller's thumb *n.* any of several small freshwater European fishes of the genus *Cottus,* esp. *C. gobio,* having a flattened body: family *Cottidae* (bullheads, etc.). [C15: from the alleged likeness of the fish's head to a thumb]

millesimal (mɪˈlɛsɪməl) *adj.* **1. a.** denoting a thousandth. **b.** (*as n.*): *a millesimal.* **2.** of, consisting of, or relating to a thousandth. [C18: from Latin *millēsimus*]

millet (ˈmɪlɪt) *n.* **1.** a cereal grass, *Setaria italica,* cultivated for grain and animal fodder. **2. a.** an East Indian annual grass, *Panicum miliaceum,* cultivated for grain and forage, having pale round shiny seeds. **b.** the seed of this plant. **3.** any of various similar or related grasses, such as pearl millet and Indian millet. [C14: via Old French from Latin *milium;* related to Greek *melinē* millet]

milli- *prefix.* denoting 10^{-3}: *millimetre.* Symbol: m [from French, from Latin *mille* thousand, this meaning being maintained in words borrowed from Latin (*millipede*)]

milliard (ˈmɪlɪˌɑːd, ˈmɪljɑːd) *n. Brit.* (no longer in technical use) a thousand million. U.S. and Canadian equivalent: **billion.** [C19: from French]

milliary (ˈmɪljərɪ) *adj.* relating to or marking a distance equal to an ancient Roman mile of a thousand paces. [C17: from Latin *milliārius* containing a thousand, from *mille* thousand]

millibar (ˈmɪlɪˌbɑː) *n.* a cgs unit of atmospheric pressure equal to 10^{-3} bar, 100 newtons per square metre or 0.7500617 millimetre of mercury.

millieme (miːlˈjɛm) *n.* a Tunisian monetary unit worth one thousandth of a dinar. Also called: **millime.** [from French *millième* thousandth]

milligram *or* **milligramme** (ˈmɪlɪˌgræm) *n.* one thousandth of a gram. Symbol: mg [C19: from French]

millilitre *or U.S.* **milliliter** (ˈmɪlɪˌliːtə) *n.* one thousandth of a litre. Symbol: ml

millimetre *or U.S.* **millimeter** (ˈmɪlɪˌmiːtə) *n.* one thousandth of a metre. Symbol: mm

millimicron (ˈmɪlɪˌmaɪkrɒn) *n.* an obsolete name for a nanometre; one millionth of a millimetre.

milline (ˈmɪlˌlaɪn, mɪlˈlaɪn) *n.* **1.** a unit of advertising copy equal to one agate line of one column width appearing in one million copies of a publication. **2.** Also called: **milline rate.** the cost of this unit. [C20: from MILLION + LINE[1]]

milliner (ˈmɪlɪnə) *n.* a person who makes or sells women's hats. [C16: originally *Milaner,* a native of *Milan,* Italy, at that time famous for its fancy goods]

millinery (ˈmɪlɪnərɪ, -nrɪ) *n.* **1.** hats, trimmings, etc., sold by a milliner. **2.** the business or shop of a milliner.

milling (ˈmɪlɪŋ) *n.* **1.** the act or process of grinding, pressing, or crushing in a mill. **2.** the vertical grooves or fluting on the edge of a coin, etc. **3.** (in W North America) a method of halting a stampede of cattle by turning the leaders in a wide arc until the herd turns in upon itself in a tightening spiral.

milling machine *n.* a machine tool in which a horizontal arbor or vertical spindle rotates a cutting tool above a horizontal table.

million (ˈmɪljən) *n., pl.* **-lions** *or* **-lion. 1.** the cardinal number that is the product of 1000 multiplied by 1000. See also **number** (sense 1). **2.** a numeral, 1 000 000, 10^6, $\overline{M}$, etc., representing this number. **3.** (*often pl.*) *Informal.* an extremely large but unspecified number, quantity, or amount: *I have millions of things to do.* ~*determiner.* **4.** (preceded by *a* or by a numeral) **a.** amounting to a million: *a million light years away.* **b.** (*as pronoun*): *I can see a million under the microscope.* ~Related prefix: **mega-**. **5. gone a million.** *Austral. informal.* done for; sunk. **6. the million.** the mass of the population. [C17: via Old French from early Italian *millione,* from *mille* thousand, from Latin]

millionaire *or* **millionnaire** (ˌmɪljəˈnɛə) *n.* a person whose assets are worth at least a million of the standard monetary units of his country. —ˌ**millionˈairess** *or* ˌ**millionˈnairess** *fem. n.*

millionth (ˈmɪljənθ) *n.* **1. a.** one of 1 000 000 approximately equal parts of something. **b.** (*as modifier*): *a millionth part.* **2.** one of 1 000 000 equal divisions of a particular scientific quantity. Related prefix: **micro-**. **3.** the fraction equal to one divided by 1 000 000. ~*adj.* **4.** (*usually prenominal*) **a.** being the ordinal number of 1 000 000 in numbering or counting order, etc. **b.** (*as n.*): *the millionth to be manufactured.*

millipede, millepede (ˈmɪlɪˌpiːd), *or* **milleped** *n.* any terrestrial herbivorous arthropod of the class *Diplopoda,* having a cylindrical body made up of many segments, each of which bears two pairs of walking legs. See also **myriapod.** [C17: from Latin, from *mille* thousand + *pēs* foot]

millisecond (ˈmɪlɪˌsɛkənd) *n.* one thousandth of a second. Symbol: ms

millpond (ˈmɪlˌpɒnd) *n.* **1.** a pool formed by damming a stream to provide water to turn a millwheel. **2.** any expanse of calm water: *the sea was a millpond.*

millrace (ˈmɪlˌreɪs) *or* **millrun** *n.* **1.** the current of water that turns a millwheel. **2.** the channel for this water.

mill-rind *n.* an iron support fitted across an upper millstone.

millrun (ˈmɪlˌrʌn) *n.* **1.** another name for **millrace. 2.** *Mining.* **a.** the process of milling an ore or rock in order to determine the content or quality of the mineral. **b.** the mineral so examined. ~*adj.* **mill-run. 3.** *Chiefly U.S.* (of commodities) taken straight from the production line; unsorted as to quality.

Mills and Boon *n.* **a.** a firm of British publishers specializing in romantic fiction. **b.** (*as modifier*): *a Mills and Boon heroine.*

Mills bomb (mɪlz) *n.* a type of high-explosive hand grenade. [C20: named after Sir William *Mills* (1856–1932), English inventor]

millstone (ˈmɪlˌstəʊn) *n.* **1.** one of a pair of heavy flat disc-shaped stones that are rotated one against the other to grind grain. **2.** a heavy burden, such as a responsibility or obligation: *his debts were a millstone round his neck.*

millstream (ˈmɪlˌstriːm) *n.* a stream of water used to turn a millwheel.

millwheel (ˈmɪlˌwiːl) *n.* a wheel, esp. a waterwheel, that drives a mill.

millwork (ˈmɪlˌwɜːk) *n.* work done in a mill.

millwright (ˈmɪlˌraɪt) *n.* a person who designs, builds, or repairs grain mills or mill machinery.

milo (ˈmaɪləʊ) *n., pl.* **-los.** any of various early-growing cultivated varieties of sorghum with heads of yellow or pinkish seeds resembling millet. [C19: from Sotho *maili*]

milometer (maɪˈlɒmɪtə) *n.* a variant spelling of **mileometer.**

milord (mɪˈlɔːd) *n.* (formerly) a continental title used for an English gentleman. [C19: via French from English *my lord*]

milquetoast (ˈmɪlkˌtəʊst) *n. U.S. and Canadian.* a meek, submissive, or timid person. [C20: from Caspar *Milquetoast,* a cartoon character invented by H. T. Webster (1885–1952)]

milreis (ˈmɪlˌreɪs; *Portuguese* milˈrɛiʃ) *n., pl.* **-reis.** a former monetary and currency unit of Portugal and Brazil, divided into 1000 reis. [C16: from Portuguese, from *mil* thousand + *réis,* pl. of *real* royal]

milt (mɪlt) *n.* **1.** the testis of a fish. **2.** the spermatozoa and seminal fluid produced by a fish. **3.** *Rare.* the spleen of certain animals, esp. fowls and pigs. ~*vb.* **4.** to fertilize (the roe of a female fish) with milt, esp. artificially. [Old English *milte* spleen; in the sense: fish sperm, probably from Middle Dutch *milte*]

milter (ˈmɪltə) *n.* a male fish that is mature and ready to breed.

Miltonic (mɪlˈtɒnɪk) *or* **Miltonian** (mɪlˈtəʊnɪən) *adj.* characteristic of or resembling the literary style of John Milton (1608–74), English poet, esp. in being sublime and majestic.

Milton Work count (ˈmɪltən wɜːk) *n. Bridge.* a system of hand valuation in which aces count 4, kings 3, queens 2, and jacks 1. [C20: named after *Milton Work,* authority on auction bridge]

mim (mɪm) *adj. Dialect.* prim, modest, or demure. [C17: perhaps imitative of lip-pursing]

mime (maɪm) *n.* **1.** the theatrical technique of expressing an idea or mood or portraying a character entirely by gesture and bodily movement without the use of words. **2.** Also called: **mime artist.** a performer specializing in such a technique, esp. a comic actor. **3.** a dramatic presentation using such a technique. **4.** (in the classical theatre) **a.** a comic performance depending for effect largely on exaggerated gesture and physical action. **b.** an actor in such a performance. ~*vb.* **5.** to express (an idea) in actions or gestures without speech. **6.** (of singers or musicians) to perform as if singing (a song) or playing (a piece of music) that is actually prerecorded. [Old English *mīma,* from Latin *mīmus* mimic actor, from Greek *mimos* imitator] —ˈ**mimer** *n.*

Mimeograph (ˈmɪmɪəˌgrɑːf, -ˌgræf) *n.* **1.** *Trademark.* an office machine for printing multiple copies of text or line drawings from an inked drum to which a cut stencil is fixed. **2.** a copy produced by this machine. ~*vb.* **3.** to print copies from (a prepared stencil) using this machine.

mimesis (mɪˈmiːsɪs) *n.* **1.** *Art, literature.* the imitative representation of nature or human behaviour. **2. a.** any disease that shows symptoms of another disease. **b.** a condition in a hysterical patient that mimics an organic disease. **3.** *Biology.* another name for **mimicry** (sense 2). **4.** *Rhetoric.* representation of another person's alleged words in a speech. [C16: from Greek, from *mimeisthai* to imitate]

mimetic (mɪˈmɛtɪk) *adj.* **1.** of, resembling, or relating to mimesis or imitation, as in art, etc. **2.** *Biology.* of or exhibiting mimicry. —**miˈmetically** *adv.*

mimetite (ˈmɪmɪˌtaɪt, ˈmaɪmɪ-) *n.* a rare secondary mineral consisting of a chloride and arsenate of lead in the form of white or yellowish needle-like hexagonal crystals. Formula: $Pb_5Cl(AsO_4)_3$. [C19: from German, from Greek *mimētēs* imitator (of pyromorphite)]

mimic (ˈmɪmɪk) *vb.* **-ics, -icking, -icked.** (*tr.*) **1.** to imitate (a person, a manner, etc.), esp. for satirical effect; ape. **2.** to take on the appearance of; resemble closely: *certain flies mimic wasps.* **3.** to copy closely or in a servile manner. ~*n.* **4.** a person or an animal, such as a parrot, that is clever at mimicking. **5.** an animal that displays mimicry. ~*adj.* **6.** of, relating to, or using mimicry; imitative. **7.** simulated, make-believe, or mock. [C16: from Latin *mīmicus,* from Greek *mimikos,* from *mimos* MIME] —ˈ**mimicker** *n.*

mimic panel *n.* a panel simulating the geographical layout of a television studio, railway points system, traffic interchange, etc., in which small indicator lamps display the selected state of the lighting circuits, signalling, traffic lights, etc.

mimicry (ˈmɪmɪkrɪ) *n., pl.* **-ries. 1.** the act or art of copying or imitating closely; mimicking. **2.** the resemblance shown by one animal species, esp. an insect, to another, which protects it from predators.

MIMinE *abbrev. for* Member of the Institute of Mining Engineers.

miminy-piminy (ˌmɪmɪnɪˈpɪmɪnɪ) *adj.* a variant of **niminy-piminy.**

mimosa (mɪˈməʊsə, -zə) *n.* **1.** any tropical shrubs or trees of the Mimosaceous genus *Mimosa,* having ball-like clusters of typically yellow flowers and compound leaves that are often sensitive to touch or light. See also **sensitive plant. 2.** any similar or related tree. [C18: from New Latin, probably from Latin *mīmus* MIME, because the plant's sensitivity to touch imitates the similar reaction of animals]

mimosaceous (ˌmɪməˈseɪʃəs, ˌmaɪmə-) *adj.* of, relating to, or belonging to the *Mimosaceae,* a family of tropical and temperate leguminous plants with tiny ball-like clusters: includes acacia, mimosa, and the fever tree.

mimulus (ˈmɪmjʊləs) *n.* See **monkey flower.** [New Latin, from Greek *mimō* ape (from the shape of the corolla)]

MIMunE *abbrev. for* Member of the Institution of Municipal Engineers.

min *symbol for* minim (liquid measure).

Min (mɪn) *n.* any of the dialects or forms of Chinese spoken in Fukien province. Also called: **Fukien.**

min. *abbrev. for:* **1.** mineralogy *or* mineralogical. **2.** minimum. **3.** mining. **4.** minute *or* minutes.

Min. *abbrev. for:* **1.** Minister. **2.** Ministry.

mina[1] (ˈmaɪnə) *n., pl.* **-nae** (-niː) *or* **-nas.** an ancient unit of weight and money, used in Asia Minor, equal to one sixtieth of a talent. [C16: via Latin from Greek *mnā,* of Semitic origin; related to Hebrew *māneh* mina]

mina[2] (ˈmaɪnə) *n.* a variant spelling of **myna** (bird). [C18: from Hindi *mainā*]

minacious (mɪˈneɪʃəs) *adj.* threatening. [C17: from Latin *minax,* from *minārī* to threaten] —**miˈnaciously** *adv.* —**minacity** (mɪˈnæsɪtɪ) *n.*

minaret (ˌmɪnəˈrɛt, ˈmɪnəˌrɛt) *n.* **1.** a slender tower of a mosque having one or more balconies from which the muezzin calls the faithful to prayer. **2.** any structure resembling this. [C17: from French, from Turkish, from Arabic *manārat* lamp, from *nār* fire] —ˌ**minaˈreted** *adj.*

minatory (ˈmɪnətərɪ, -trɪ) *or* **minatorial** *adj.* threatening or menacing. [C16: from Late Latin *minātōrius,* from Latin *minārī* to threaten] —**minatorily** *or* ˌ**minaˈtorially** *adv.*

mince (mɪns) *vb.* **1.** (*tr.*) to chop, grind, or cut into very small pieces. **2.** (*tr.*) to soften or moderate, esp. for the sake of convention or politeness: *I didn't mince my words.* **3.** (*intr.*) to walk or speak in an affected dainty manner. ~*n.* **4.** *Chiefly Brit.* minced meat. [C14: from Old French *mincier,* from Vulgar Latin *minūtiāre* (unattested), from Late Latin *minūtia* smallness; see MINUTIAE] —ˈ**mincer** *n.*

mincemeat (ˈmɪnsˌmiːt) *n.* **1.** a mixture of dried fruit, spices, etc., used esp. for filling pies. **2.** minced meat. **3. make mincemeat of.** *Informal.* to defeat completely.

mince pie *n.* a small round pastry tart filled with mincemeat.

Mincha *Hebrew* (*Hebrew* minˈxɑː; *Yiddish* ˈminxa) *n. Judaism.* the afternoon service.

mincing (ˈmɪnsɪŋ) *adj.* (of a person) affectedly elegant in gait, manner, or speech. —ˈ**mincingly** *adv.*

mind (maɪnd) *n.* **1.** the human faculty to which are ascribed thought, feeling, etc.; often regarded as an immaterial part of a person. **2.** intelligence or the intellect, esp. as opposed to feelings or wishes. **3.** recollection or remembrance; memory: *it comes to mind.* **4.** the faculty of original or creative thought; imagination: *it's all in the mind.* **5.** a person considered as an intellectual being: *the great minds of the past.* **6.** opinion or sentiment: *we are of the same mind; to change one's mind; to have a mind of one's own; to know one's mind; to speak one's mind.* **7.** condition, state, or manner of feeling or thought: *no peace of mind; his state of mind.* **8.** an inclination, desire, or purpose: *I have a mind to go.* **9.** attention or thoughts: *keep your mind on your work.* **10.** a sound mental state; sanity (esp. in the phrase **out of one's mind**). **11.** intelligence, as opposed to material things: *the mind of the universe.* **12.** (in Cartesian philosophy) one of two basic modes of existence, the other being matter. **13. blow someone's mind.** *Slang.* **a.** to cause someone to have a psychedelic experience. **b.** to astound or surprise someone. **14. give (someone) a piece of one's mind.** to criticize or censure (someone) frankly or vehemently. **15. in** *or* **of two minds.** undecided; wavering: *he was in two minds about marriage.* **16. make up one's mind.** to decide (something or to do something): *he made up his mind to go.* **17. on one's mind.** in one's thoughts. **18. put (one) in mind of.** to remind (one) of. *~vb.* **19.** (when *tr., may take a clause as object*) to take offence at: *do you mind if I smoke? I don't mind.* **20.** to pay attention to (something); heed; notice: *to mind one's own business.* **21.** (*tr.; takes a clause as object*) to make certain; ensure: *mind you tell her.* **22.** (*tr.*) to take care of; have charge of: *to mind the shop.* **23.** (when *tr., may take a clause as object*) to be cautious or careful about (something): *mind how you go; mind your step.* **24.** (*tr.*) to obey (someone or something); heed: *mind your father!* **25.** to be concerned (about); be troubled (about); *never mind your hat; never mind about your hat; never mind.* **26.** (*tr.*) *Scot. and English dialect.* to remember: *do ye mind his name?* **27.** (*tr.*) *Scot.* to remind: *that minds me of another story.* **28. mind you.** an expression qualifying a previous statement: *Dogs are nice. Mind you, I don't like all dogs.* ~Related adj.: **mental.** ~See also **mind out.** [Old English *gemynd* mind; related to Old High German *gimunt* memory]

mind-bending *adj. Informal.* **1.** very difficult to understand; complex. **2.** altering one's state of consciousness: *mind-bending drugs.* **3.** reaching the limit of credibility: *they offered a mind-bending salary.* ~*n.* **4.** the process of brainwashing.

mind-blowing *adj. Informal.* producing euphoria; psychedelic.

mind-body problem *n.* the traditional philosophical problem concerning the nature of mind, body, and the relationship between them. See **dualism** (sense 2), **interactionism, parallelism** (sense 3), **monism** (sense 1), **idealism** (sense 3), **materialism** (sense 2), **identity theory, behaviourism** (sense 2).

mind-boggling *adj. Informal.* astonishing; bewildering.

minded ('maɪndɪd) *adj.* **1.** having a mind, inclination, intention, etc., as specified: *politically minded.* **2.** (*in combination*): *money-minded.*

Mindel ('mɪndᵊl) *n.* the second major Pleistocene glaciation of Alpine Europe. See also **Günz, Riss, Würm.** [C20: named after the River *Mindel*, in Bavaria, Germany]

minder ('maɪndə) *n.* **1.** someone who looks after someone or something. **2.** short for **child minder.** **3.** *Slang.* an aide to someone in public life, esp. a politician or political candidate, who keeps control of press and public relations. **4.** *Slang.* someone acting as a bodyguard, guard, or assistant, esp. in the criminal underworld.

mind-expanding *adj.* (of a drug such as LSD) causing a sensation of heightened consciousness; psychedelic.

mindful ('maɪndfʊl) *adj.* (usually *postpositive* and foll. by *of*) keeping aware; heedful: *mindful of your duties.* —'**mindfully** *adv.* —'**mindfulness** *n.*

mindless ('maɪndlɪs) *adj.* **1.** stupid or careless. **2.** requiring little or no intellectual effort: *a mindless task.* —'**mindlessly** *adv.* —'**mindlessness** *n.*

mind-numbing *adj.* extremely boring and uninspiring. —'**mind-ˌnumbingly** *adv.*

mind out *vb.* (*intr., adv.*) *Brit.* to be careful or pay attention.

mind-reader *n.* a person seemingly able to discern the thoughts of another. —'**mind-ˌreading** *n.*

mind-set *n.* the ideas and attitudes with which a person approaches a situation, esp. when these are seen as being difficult to alter.

mind's eye *n.* the visual memory or the imagination.

mind-your-own-business *n.* a Mediterranean urticaceous plant, *Helxine soleirolii*, with small dense leaves: used for cover.

mine[1] (maɪn) *pron.* **1.** something or someone belonging to or associated with me: *mine is best.* **2. of mine.** belonging to or associated with me. *~determiner.* **3.** (*preceding a vowel*) an archaic word for **my:** *mine eyes; mine host.* [Old English *mīn;* compare Old High German, Old Norse *mīn*, Dutch *mijn*]

mine[2] (maɪn) *n.* **1.** a system of excavations made for the extraction of minerals, esp. coal, ores, or precious stones. **2.** any deposit of ore or minerals. **3.** a lucrative source or abundant supply: *she was a mine of information.* **4.** a device containing an explosive designed to destroy ships, vehicles, or personnel, usually laid beneath the ground or in water. **5.** a tunnel or sap dug to undermine a fortification. **6.** a groove or tunnel made by certain insects, esp. in a leaf. *~vb.* **7.** to dig into (the earth) for (minerals). **8.** to make (a hole, tunnel, etc.) by digging or boring. **9.** to place explosive mines in position below the surface of (the sea or land). **10.** to undermine (a fortification) by digging mines or saps. **11.** another word for **undermine.** [C13: from Old French, probably of Celtic origin; compare Irish *mein*, Welsh *mwyn* ore, mine] —'**minable** *or* '**mineable** *adj.*

mine detector *n.* an instrument designed to detect explosive mines. —**mine detection** *n.*

mine dump *n. S. African.* a large mound of residue, esp. from gold-mining operations.

minefield ('maɪnˌfiːld) *n.* **1.** an area of ground or water containing explosive mines. **2.** a subject, situation, etc., beset with hidden problems.

minehunter ('maɪnˌhʌntə) *n.* a naval vessel that searches for mines by electronic means.

minelayer ('maɪnˌleɪə) *n.* a warship or aircraft designed for the carrying and laying of mines.

miner ('maɪnə) *n.* **1.** a person who works in a mine. **2.** Also called: **continuous miner.** a large machine for the automatic extraction of minerals, esp. coal, from a mine. **3.** any of various insects or insect larvae that bore into and feed on plant tissues. See also **leaf miner.** **4.** *Austral.* any of several honey-eaters of the genus *Manorina*, esp. *M. melanocephala* (**noisy miner**), of scrub regions.

mineral ('mɪnərəl, 'mɪnrəl) *n.* **1.** any of a class of naturally occurring solid inorganic substances with a characteristic crystalline form and a homogeneous chemical composition. **2.** any inorganic matter. **3.** any substance obtained by mining, esp. a metal ore. **4.** (*often pl.*) *Brit.* short for **mineral water.** **5.** *Brit.* a soft drink containing carbonated water and flavourings. Usual U.S. word: **soda.** *~adj.* **6.** of, relating to, containing, or resembling minerals. [C15: from Medieval Latin *minerāle* (n.), from *minerālis* (adj.); related to *minera* mine, ore, of uncertain origin]

mineral. *abbrev. for* mineralogy *or* mineralogical.

mineralize *or* **mineralise** ('mɪnərəˌlaɪz, 'mɪnrə-) *vb.* (*tr.*) **1. a.** to impregnate (organic matter, water, etc.) with a mineral substance. **b.** to convert (such matter) into a mineral; petrify. **2.** (of gases, vapours, etc., in magma) to transform (a metal) into an ore. —ˌ**mineraliˈzation** *or* ˌ**mineraliˈsation** *n.*

mineralizer *or* **mineraliser** ('mɪnərəˌlaɪzə) *n.* **1.** any of various gases dissolved in magma that affect the crystallization of igneous rocks and the formation of minerals when the magma cools. **2.** an element, such as oxygen, that combines with a metal to form an ore.

mineral jelly *n.* another name for **petrolatum.**

mineral kingdom *n.* all nonliving material, esp. rocks and minerals. Compare **animal kingdom, plant kingdom.**

mineralocorticoid (ˌmɪnərələʊˈkɔːtɪˌkɔɪd) *n.* any corticosteroid that controls electrolyte and water balance, esp. by promoting retention of sodium by the kidney tubules.

mineralogy (ˌmɪnəˈrælədʒɪ) *n.* the branch of geology concerned with the study of minerals. —**mineralogical** (ˌmɪnərəˈlɒdʒɪkᵊl) *or* ˌ**mineralˈogic** *adj.* —ˌ**mineralˈogically** *adv.* —ˌ**minerˈalogist** *n.*

mineral oil *n.* **1.** *Brit.* any oil of mineral origin, esp. petroleum. **2.** a U.S. and Canadian name for **liquid paraffin.**

mineral pitch *n.* another name for **asphalt.**

mineral spring *n.* a spring of water that contains a high proportion of dissolved mineral salts.

mineral tar *n.* a natural black viscous tar intermediate in properties between petroleum and asphalt. Also called: **maltha.**

mineral water *n.* water containing dissolved mineral salts or gases, usually having medicinal properties.

mineral wax *n.* another name for **ozocerite.**

mineral wool *n.* a fibrous material made by blowing steam or air through molten slag and used for packing and insulation. Also called: **rock wool.**

miner's right *n. Austral. and N.Z.* a licence to prospect for minerals, esp. gold. [C19]

minestrone (ˌmɪnɪˈstrəʊnɪ) *n.* a soup made from a variety of vegetables and pasta. [from Italian, from *minestrare* to serve]

minesweeper ('maɪnˌswiːpə) *n.* a naval vessel equipped to detect and clear mines. —'**mineˌsweeping** *n.*

Ming (mɪŋ) *n.* **1.** the imperial dynasty of China from 1368 to 1644. *~adj.* **2.** of or relating to Chinese porcelain produced during the Ming dynasty, characterized by the use of brilliant colours and a fine-quality body.

minge (mɪndʒ) *n. Brit. taboo slang.* **1.** the female genitals. **2.** women collectively considered as sexual objects. [C20: from Romany; of obscure origin]

mingle ('mɪŋgᵊl) *vb.* **1.** to mix or cause to mix. **2.** (*intr.;* often foll. by *with*) to come into close association. [C15: from Old English *mengan* to mix; related to Middle Dutch *mengen*, Old Frisian *mengja*] —'**mingler** *n.*

Mingrelian (mɪŋˈgriːlɪən) *or* **Mingrel** ('mɪŋgrəl) *n.* **1.** a member of a Georgian people of the former Soviet Union living in the mountains northeast of the Black Sea. **2.** the language of this people, belonging to the South Caucasian family and closely related to Georgian. *~adj.* **3.** of or relating to the Mingrelians or their language.

ming tree *n.* an artificial plant resembling a bonsai plant. [perhaps from MING]

mingy ('mɪndʒɪ) *adj.* **-gier, -giest.** *Brit. informal.* miserly, stingy, or niggardly. [C20: probably a blend of MEAN[2] + STINGY[1]]

mini ('mɪnɪ) *adj.* **1.** (of a woman's dress, skirt, etc.) very short; thigh-length. **2.** (*prenominal*) small; miniature. ~*n., pl.* **minis. 3.** something very small of its kind, esp. a small car or a miniskirt.

mini- *combining form.* smaller or shorter than the standard size: *minibus; miniskirt.* [C20: from MINIATURE and MINIMUM]

miniature ('mɪnɪtʃə) *n.* **1.** a model, copy, or similar representation on a very small scale. **2.** anything that is very small of its kind. **3.** a very small painting, esp. a portrait, showing fine detail on ivory or vellum. **4.** an illuminated letter or other decoration in a manuscript. **5. in miniature.** on a small scale: *games are real life in miniature.* ~*adj.* **6.** greatly reduced in size. **7.** on a small scale; minute. [C16: from Italian, from Medieval Latin *miniātūra,* from *miniāre* to paint red, (in illuminating manuscripts); from MINIUM]

miniature camera *n.* a small camera using 35 millimetre film.

miniaturist ('mɪnɪtʃərɪst) *n.* a person who paints miniature portraits.

miniaturize *or* **miniaturise** ('mɪnɪtʃəˌraɪz) *vb.* (*tr.*) to make or construct (something, esp. electronic equipment) on a very small scale; reduce in size. —ˌ**miniaturi'zation** *or* ˌ**miniaturi'sation** *n.*

minibus ('mɪnɪˌbʌs) *n.* a small bus able to carry approximately ten passengers.

minicab ('mɪnɪˌkæb) *n. Brit.* a small saloon car used as a taxi.

minicomputer (ˌmɪnɪkəm'pjuːtə) *n.* a small comparatively cheap digital computer.

minidress ('mɪnɪˌdrɛs) *n.* a very short dress, at least four inches above the knee. Often shortened to **mini.**

Minié ball ('mɪnɪˌeɪ; *French* miɲe) *n.* a conical rifle bullet, used in the 19th century, manufactured with a hollow base designed to expand when fired to fit the rifling. [C19: named after Capt. C. E. *Minié* (1814–1879), French army officer who invented it]

minify ('mɪnɪˌfaɪ) *vb.* **-fies, -fying, -fied.** (*tr.*) *Rare.* to minimize or lessen the size or importance of (something). [C17: from Latin *minus* less; for form, compare MAGNIFY] —**minification** (ˌmɪnɪfɪ'keɪʃən) *n.*

minikin ('mɪnɪkɪn) *Obsolete.* ~*n.* **1.** a small, dainty, or affected person or thing. ~*adj.* **2.** dainty, prim, or affected. [C16: from Dutch *minneken,* diminutive of *minne* love]

minim ('mɪnɪm) *n.* **1.** a unit of fluid measure equal to one sixtieth of a drachm. It is approximately equal to one drop. Symbol: M **2.** *Music.* a note having the time value of half a semibreve. Usual U.S. and Canadian name: **half-note. 3.** a small or insignificant person or thing. **4.** a downward stroke in calligraphy. ~*adj.* **5.** *Rare.* very small; tiny. [C15 (in its musical meaning): from Latin *minimus* smallest]

minima ('mɪnɪmə) *n.* a plural of **minimum.**

minimal ('mɪnɪməl) *adj.* of the least possible; minimum or smallest. —'**minimally** *adv.*

minimal art *n.* abstract painting or sculpture in which expressiveness and illusion are minimized by the use of simple geometric shapes, flat colour, and arrangements of ordinary objects. —**minimal artist** *n.*

minimalism ('mɪnɪməˌlɪzəm) *n.* **1.** another name for **minimal art. 2.** a type of music based on simple elements and avoiding elaboration or embellishment. **3.** design or style in which the simplest and fewest elements are used to create the maximum effect.

minimalist ('mɪnɪməlɪst) *n.* **1.** a person advocating a minimal policy, style, technique, action, etc. **2.** a minimal artist. ~*adj.* **3.** of or relating to minimal art or artists.

Minimalist ('mɪnɪməlɪst) *n.* (in early 20th-century Russia) **1.** a member of the faction of the Social Revolutionaries that advocated immediate postrevolutionary democracy. **2.** a less common name for a **Menshevik.** ~Compare **Maximalist.**

minimal pair *n. Linguistics.* a pair of speech elements in a given language differing in only one respect and thus serving to identify minimum units such as phonemes, morphemes, etc. For example, *tin* and *din* constitute a minimal pair in English.

minimax ('mɪnɪˌmæks) *n.* **1.** *Maths.* the lowest of a set of maximum values. **2.** (in game theory, etc.) the procedure of choosing the strategy that least benefits the most advantaged member of a group. Compare **maximin.** [C20: from MINI(MUM) + MAX(IMUM)]

minimize *or* **minimise** ('mɪnɪˌmaɪz) *vb.* (*tr.*) **1.** to reduce to or estimate at the least possible degree or amount: *to minimize a risk.* **2.** to rank or treat at less than the true worth; belittle: *to minimize someone's achievements.* —ˌ**minimi'zation** *or* ˌ**minimi'sation** *n.* —'**miniˌmizer** *or* '**miniˌmiser** *n.*

minimum ('mɪnɪməm) *n., pl.* **-mums** *or* **-ma** (-mə). **1.** the least possible amount, degree, or quantity. **2.** the least amount recorded, allowed, or reached: *the minimum in our temperature record this month was 50°.* **3.** (*modifier*) being the least possible, recorded, allowed, etc.: *minimum age.* **4.** *Maths.* a value of a function that is less than any neighbouring value. ~*adj.* **5.** of or relating to a minimum or minimums. [C17: from Latin: smallest thing, from *minimus* least]

minimum lending rate *n.* (in Britain) the minimum rate at which the Bank of England would lend to discount houses between 1971 and 1981, after which it was replaced by the less formal base rate. Abbrev.: **MLR.**

minimum wage *n.* the lowest wage that an employer is permitted to pay by law or union contract.

minimus ('mɪnɪməs) *adj.* (*immediately postpositive*) *Brit.* the youngest: sometimes used after the surname of a schoolboy having elder brothers at the same school: *Hunt minimus.*

mining ('maɪnɪŋ) *n.* **1.** the act, process, or industry of extracting coal, ores, etc., from the earth. **2.** *Military.* the process of laying mines.

mining bee *n.* a solitary bee of the genera *Andrena* and *Halictus,* which sometimes resemble honey bees. [named from their burrowing habits]

minion ('mɪnjən) *n.* **1.** a favourite or dependant, esp. a servile or fawning one. **2.** a servile agent: *the minister's minions.* **3.** a size of printer's type, approximately equal to 7 point. ~*adj.* **4.** dainty, pretty, or elegant. [C16: from French *mignon,* from Old French *mignot,* of Gaulish origin]

minipill ('mɪnɪˌpɪl) *n.* a low-dose oral contraceptive containing progesterone only.

miniseries ('mɪnɪˌsɪəriːz) *n.* a television programme in several parts that is shown on consecutive days or weeks for a short period.

miniskirt ('mɪnɪˌskɜːt) *n.* a very short skirt, originally in the 1960s one at least four inches above the knee. Often shortened to **mini.** —'**miniˌskirted** *adj.*

minister ('mɪnɪstə) *n.* **1.** (esp. in Presbyterian and some Nonconformist Churches) a clergyman. **2.** a person appointed to head a government department. **3.** any diplomatic agent accredited to a foreign government or head of state. **4.** short for **minister plenipotentiary** or **envoy extraordinary and minister plenipotentiary** (see **envoy**[1] (sense 1)). **5.** Also called (in full): **minister resident.** a diplomat ranking after an envoy extraordinary and minister plenipotentiary. **6.** a person who attends to the needs of others, esp. in religious matters. **7.** a person who acts as the agent or servant of a person or thing. ~*vb.* **8.** (*intr.;* often foll. by *to*) to attend to the needs (of); take care (of). **9.** (*tr.*) *Archaic.* to provide; supply. [C13: via Old French from Latin: servant; related to *minus* less] —'**ministerˌship** *n.*

ministerial (ˌmɪnɪ'stɪərɪəl) *adj.* **1.** of or relating to a minister of religion or his office. **2.** of or relating to a government minister or ministry: *a ministerial act.* **3.** (*often cap.*) of or supporting the ministry or government against the opposition. **4.** *Law.* relating to or possessing delegated executive authority. **5.** *Law.* (of an office, duty, etc.) requiring the following of instructions, without power to exercise any personal discretion in doing so. **6.** acting as an agent or cause; instrumental. —ˌ**minis'terially** *adv.*

ministerialist (ˌmɪnɪ'stɪərɪəlɪst) *n. Brit.* a supporter of the governing ministry.

ministerium (ˌmɪnɪ'stɪərɪəm) *n., pl.* **-ria** (-rɪə). the body of the Lutheran ministers in a district. [C19: Latin: MINISTRY]

minister of state *n.* **1.** (in the British Parliament) a minister, usually below cabinet rank, appointed to assist a senior minister with heavy responsibilities. **2.** any government minister.

Minister of the Crown *n. Brit.* any Government minister of cabinet rank.

minister plenipotentiary *n., pl.* **ministers plenipotentiary.** See **envoy**[1] (sense 1).

ministrant ('mɪnɪstrənt) *adj.* **1.** ministering or serving as a minister. ~*n.* **2.** a person who ministers. [C17: from Latin *ministrans,* from *ministrāre* to wait upon]

ministration (ˌmɪnɪ'streɪʃən) *n.* **1.** the act or an instance of serving or giving aid. **2.** the act or an instance of ministering religiously. [C14: from Latin *ministrātiō,* from *ministrāre* to wait upon] —**ministrative** ('mɪnɪstrətɪv) *adj.*

ministry ('mɪnɪstrɪ) *n., pl.* **-tries. 1. a.** the profession or duties of a minister of religion. **b.** the performance of these duties. **2.** ministers of religion or government ministers considered collectively. **3.** the tenure of a minister. **4. a.** a government department headed by a minister. **b.** the buildings of such a department. [C14: from Latin *ministerium* service, from *minister* servant; see MINISTER]

Minitrack ('mɪnɪˌtræk) *n. Trademark.* a system for tracking the course of rockets or satellites by radio signals received at ground stations.

minium ('mɪnɪəm) *n.* another name for **red lead.** [C14 (meaning: vermilion): from Latin]

miniver ('mɪnɪvə) *n.* white fur, used in ceremonial costumes. [C13: from Old French *menu vair,* from *menu* small + *vair* variegated fur, VAIR]

minivet ('mɪnɪvɛt) *n.* any brightly coloured tropical Asian cuckoo shrike of the genus *Pericrocotus.* [C19: of unknown origin]

mink (mɪŋk) *n., pl.* **mink** *or* **minks. 1.** any of several semi-aquatic musteline mammals of the genus *Mustela,* of Europe, Asia, and North America, having slightly webbed feet. **2.** the highly valued fur of these animals, esp. that of the American mink (*M. vison*). **3.** a garment made of this, esp. a woman's coat or stole. [C15: from Scandinavian; compare Danish *mink,* Swedish *mänk*]

minke whale ('mɪŋkə) *n.* a type of small whalebone whale or rorqual, *Balaenoptera acutorostrata,* up to 10 metres long. Also called: **minke.** [C20: probably from Norwegian *minkehval,* from *minke* lesser + *hval* whale]

Minkowski space-time (mɪŋˈkɒfskɪ) *n.* a four-dimensional space in which three coordinates specify the position of a point in space and the fourth represents the time at which an event occurred at that point. [C20: named after Hermann *Minkowski* (1864–1909), German mathematician]

min min (mɪn mɪn) *n. Austral.* will-o'-the-wisp. [from a native Australian language]

Minn. *abbrev. for* Minnesota.

minneola (ˌmɪnɪˈəʊlə) *n.* a juicy citrus fruit that is a cross between a tangerine and a grapefruit. [C20: perhaps from *Mineola*, Texas]

minnesinger (ˈmɪnɪˌsɪŋə) *n.* one of the German lyric poets and musicians of the 12th to 14th centuries. [C19: from German: love-singer]

minnow (ˈmɪnəʊ) *n., pl.* **-nows** *or* **-now.** **1.** a small slender European freshwater cyprinid fish, *Phoxinus phoxinus*. **2.** any other small cyprinid. **3.** *Angling.* a spinning lure imitating a minnow. **4.** a small or insignificant person. [C15: related to Old English *myne* minnow; compare Old High German *muniwa* fish]

Minoan (mɪˈnəʊən) *adj.* **1.** denoting the Bronze Age culture of the Mediterranean island of Crete from about 3000 B.C. to about 1100 B.C. Compare **Mycenaean. 2.** of or relating to the linear writing systems used in Crete and later in mainland Greece. See **Linear A, Linear B.** ~*n.* **3.** a Cretan belonging to the Minoan culture. [C19: named after *Minos*, legendary king of Crete, from the excavations at his supposed palace at Knossos]

minor (ˈmaɪnə) *adj.* **1.** lesser or secondary in amount, extent, importance, or degree: *a minor poet; minor burns.* **2.** of or relating to the minority. **3.** below the age of legal majority. **4.** *Music.* **a.** (of a scale) having a semitone between the second and third and fifth and sixth degrees (**natural minor**). See also **harmonic minor scale, melodic minor scale. b.** (of a key) based on the minor scale. **c.** (*postpositive*) denoting a specified key based on the minor scale: *C minor.* **d.** (of an interval) reduced by a semitone from the major. **e.** (of a chord, esp. a triad) having a minor third above the root. **f.** (esp. in jazz) of or relating to a chord built upon a minor triad and containing a minor seventh: *a minor ninth.* See also **minor key, minor mode. 5.** *Logic.* (of a term or premise) having less generality or scope than another term or proposition. **6.** *U.S. education.* of or relating to an additional secondary subject taken by a student. **7.** (*immediately postpositive*) *Brit.* the younger or junior: sometimes used after the surname of a schoolboy if he has an older brother in the same school: *Hunt minor.* **8.** (*postpositive*) *Change-ringing.* of, relating to, or denoting a set of changes rung on six bells: *grandsire minor.* ~*n.* **9.** a person or thing that is lesser or secondary. **10.** a person below the age of legal majority. **11.** *U.S. and Canadian education.* a subsidiary subject in which a college or university student needs fewer credits than in his major. **12.** *Music.* a minor key, chord, mode, or scale. **13.** *Logic.* a minor term or premise. **14.** *Maths.* **a.** a determinant associated with a particular element of a given determinant and formed by removing the row and column containing that element. **b.** Also called: **cofactor, signed minor.** the number equal to this reduced determinant. **15.** (*cap.*) another name for **Minorite.** ~*vb.* **16.** (*intr.;* usually foll. by *in*) *U.S. education.* to take a minor. ~Compare **major.** [C13: from Latin: less, smaller; related to Old High German *minniro* smaller, Gothic *minniza* least, Latin *minuere* to diminish, Greek *meiōn* less]

minor axis *n.* the shorter or shortest axis of an ellipse or ellipsoid.

Minorca (mɪˈnɔːkə) *n.* a breed of light domestic fowl with glossy white, black, or blue plumage. [named after *Minorca*, island in the W Mediterranean]

minor canon *n. Church of England.* a clergyman who is attached to a cathedral to assist at daily services but who is not a member of the chapter.

Minorite (ˈmaɪnəˌraɪt) *n.* a member of the Franciscan Friars Minor. Also called: **Minor.** [C16: from Medieval Latin *frātrēs minōrēs* lesser brethren, name adopted by St Francis of Assissi as a token of humility]

minority (maɪˈnɒrɪtɪ, mɪ-) *n., pl.* **-ties. 1.** the smaller in number of two parts, factions, or groups. **2.** a group that is different racially, politically, etc., from a larger group of which it is a part. **3. a.** the state of being a minor. **b.** the period during which a person is below legal age. ~Compare **majority. 4.** (*modifier*) relating to or being a minority: *a minority interest; a minority opinion.* [C16: from Medieval Latin *minōritās*, from Latin MINOR]

minority carrier *n.* the entity responsible for carrying the lesser part of the current in a semiconductor. Compare **majority carrier.**

minor key *n. Music.* a key based on notes taken from a corresponding minor scale.

minor league *n.* **1.** *U.S. and Canadian.* any professional league in baseball other than a major league. Compare **major league. 2.** (*modifier*) of relatively little importance: *that firm is very minor league.*

minor mode *n. Music.* any arrangement of notes present in or characteristic of a minor scale or key.

minor orders *pl. n. R.C. Church.* the four lower degrees of holy orders, namely porter, exorcist, lector, and acolyte. Compare **major orders.**

minor planet *n.* another name for **asteroid** (sense 1).

minor premise *n. Logic.* the premise of a syllogism containing the subject of its conclusion.

minor seventh chord *n.* a chord consisting of a minor triad with an added minor seventh above the root. Compare **major seventh chord.** Often shortened to **minor seventh.**

minor suit *n. Bridge.* diamonds or clubs. Compare **major suit.**

minor term *n. Logic.* the subject of the conclusion of a syllogism, also occurring as the subject or predicate in the minor premise.

minster (ˈmɪnstə) *n. Brit.* any of certain cathedrals and large churches, usually originally connected to a monastery. [Old English *mynster*, probably from Vulgar Latin *monisterium* (unattested), variant of Church Latin *monastērium* MONASTERY]

minstrel (ˈmɪnstrəl) *n.* **1.** a medieval wandering musician who performed songs or recited poetry with instrumental accompaniment. **2.** a performer in a minstrel show. **3.** *Archaic or poetic.* any poet, musician, or singer. [C13: from Old French *menestral*, from Late Latin *ministeriālis* an official, from Latin MINISTER]

minstrel show *n.* a theatrical entertainment consisting of songs, dances, comic turns, etc., performed by a troupe of actors wearing black face make-up.

minstrelsy (ˈmɪnstrəlsɪ) *n., pl.* **-sies. 1.** the art of a minstrel. **2.** the poems, music, or songs of a minstrel. **3.** a troupe of minstrels.

mint[1] (mɪnt) *n.* **1.** any N temperate plant of the genus *Mentha*, having aromatic leaves and spikes of small typically mauve flowers: family *Labiatae* (labiates). The leaves of some species are used for seasoning and flavouring. See also **peppermint, spearmint, horsemint, water mint. 2. stone mint.** another name for **dittany** (sense 2). **3.** a sweet flavoured with mint. [Old English *minte*, from Latin *mentha*, from Greek *minthē*; compare Old High German *minza*] —ˈ**minty** *adj.*

mint[2] (mɪnt) *n.* **1.** a place where money is coined by governmental authority. **2.** a very large amount of money: *he made a mint in business.* **3. in mint condition.** in perfect condition; as if new. ~*adj.* **4.** (of coins, postage stamps, etc.) in perfect condition as issued. ~*vb.* **5.** to make (coins) by stamping metal. **6.** (*tr.*) to invent (esp. phrases or words). [Old English *mynet* coin, from Latin *monēta* money, mint, from the temple of Juno *Monēta*, used as a mint in ancient Rome] —ˈ**minter** *n.*

mintage (ˈmɪntɪdʒ) *n.* **1.** the process of minting. **2.** money minted. **3.** a fee paid for minting a coin. **4.** an official impression stamped on a coin.

mint bush *n.* an aromatic shrub of the genus *Prostanthera* with a mintlike odour: family *Labiatae* (labiates): native to Australia.

mint julep *n. Chiefly U.S.* a long drink consisting of bourbon whiskey, crushed ice, sugar, and sprigs of mint.

Minton (ˈmɪntən) *n.* **a.** fine-quality porcelain ware produced in Stoke-on-Trent since 1798. **b.** (*as modifier*): *Minton plate.* [C19: named after Thomas *Minton* (1765–1836), English potter]

mint sauce *n.* a sauce made from mint leaves, sugar, and vinegar, usually served with lamb.

minuend (ˈmɪnjʊˌend) *n.* the number from which another number, the **subtrahend,** is to be subtracted. [C18: from Latin *minuendus* (*numerus*) (the number) to be diminished]

minuet (ˌmɪnjʊˈet) *n.* **1.** a stately court dance of the 17th and 18th centuries in triple time. **2.** a piece of music composed for or in the rhythm of this dance, sometimes as a movement in a suite, sonata, or symphony. See also **scherzo.** [C17: from French *menuet* dainty (referring to the dance steps), from *menu* small]

minus (ˈmaɪnəs) *prep.* **1.** reduced by the subtraction of: *four minus two* (written 4 − 2). **2.** *Informal.* deprived of; lacking: *minus the trimmings, that hat would be ordinary.* ~*adj.* **3. a.** indicating or involving subtraction: *a minus sign.* **b.** Also: **negative.** having a value or designating a quantity less than zero: *a minus number.* **4.** on the negative part of a scale or coordinate axis: *a value of minus 40° C.* **5.** involving a disadvantage, harm, etc.: *a minus factor.* **6.** (*postpositive*) *Education.* slightly below the standard of a particular grade: *he received a B minus for his essay.* **7.** *Botany.* designating the strain of a fungus that can only undergo sexual reproduction with a plus strain. **8.** denoting a negative electric charge. ~*n.* **9.** short for **minus sign. 10.** a negative quantity. **11.** a disadvantage, loss, or deficit. **12.** *Informal.* something detrimental or negative. ~Mathematical symbol: − [C15: from Latin, neuter of MINOR]

minuscule (ˈmɪnəˌskjuːl) *n.* **1.** a lower-case letter. **2.** writing using such letters. **3.** a small cursive 7th-century style of lettering derived from the uncial. ~*adj.* **4.** relating to, printed in, or written in small letters. Compare **majuscule. 5.** very small. **6.** (of letters) lower-case. [C18: from French, from Latin (*littera*) *minuscula* very small (letter), diminutive of MINOR] —**minuscular** (mɪˈnʌskjʊlə) *adj.*

minus sign *n.* the symbol −, indicating subtraction or a negative quantity.

minute[1] (ˈmɪnɪt) *n.* **1.** a period of time equal to 60 seconds; one sixtieth of an hour. **2.** a unit of angular measure equal to one sixtieth of a degree. Symbol: ′. Also called: **minute of arc. 3.** any very short period of time; moment. **4.** a short note or memorandum. **5.** the distance that can be travelled in a minute: *it's only two minutes away.* **6. up to the minute (up-to-the-minute** *when prenominal*). very latest or newest. ~*vb.* (*tr.*) **7.** to record in minutes: *to minute a meeting.* **8.** to time in terms of minutes. ~See also **minutes.** [C14: from Old French from Medieval Latin *minūta*, n. use of Latin *minūtus* MINUTE[2]]

minute[2] (maɪˈnjuːt) *adj.* **1.** very small; diminutive; tiny. **2.** unimportant; petty. **3.** precise or detailed: *a minute examination.* [C15: from Latin *minūtus,* past participle of *minuere* to diminish] —**miˈnuteness** *n.*

minute gun (ˈmɪnɪt) *n.* a gun fired at one-minute intervals as a sign of distress or mourning.

minute hand (ˈmɪnɪt) *n.* the pointer on a timepiece that indicates minutes, typically the longer hand of two. Compare **hour hand, second hand.**

minutely[1] (maɪˈnjuːtlɪ) *adv.* in great detail.

minutely[2] (ˈmɪnɪtlɪ) *adj.* **1.** occurring every minute. ~*adv.* **2.** every minute.

Minuteman (ˈmɪnɪtˌmæn) *n., pl.* **-men. 1.** (*sometimes not cap.*) (in the War of American Independence) a colonial militiaman who promised to be ready to fight at one minute's notice. **2.** a U.S. three-stage intercontinental ballistic missile.

minute mark (ˈmɪnɪt) *n.* the symbol ′ used for minutes of arc and linear feet.

minutes (ˈmɪnɪts) *pl. n.* an official record of the proceedings of a meeting, conference, convention, etc.

minute steak (ˈmɪnɪt) *n.* a small thinly-cut piece of steak that can be cooked quickly.

minutiae (mɪˈnjuːʃɪˌiː) *pl. n., sing.* **-tia** (-ʃɪə). small, precise, or trifling details. [C18: pl. of Late Latin *minūtia* smallness, from Latin *minūtus* MINUTE[2]]

minx (mɪŋks) *n.* a bold, flirtatious, or scheming woman. [C16: of unknown origin] —**ˈminxish** *adj.*

minyan *Hebrew.* (minˈjan; *English* ˈmɪnjən) *n., pl.* ***minyanim*** (minjaˈnim) *or* ***minyans.*** the number of persons required by Jewish law to be present for a religious service, namely, at least ten males over thirteen years of age. [literally: number]

Miocene (ˈmaɪəˌsiːn) *adj.* **1.** of, denoting, or formed in the fourth epoch of the Tertiary period, between the Oligocene and Pliocene epochs, which lasted for 14 million years. ~*n.* **2. the.** this epoch or rock series. [C19: from Greek *meiōn* less + -CENE]

miombo (mɪˈɒmbɒ) *n.* (in E Africa) a dry wooded area with sparse deciduous growth. [C19: probably from a Niger-Congo language]

miosis *or* **myosis** (maɪˈəʊsɪs) *n., pl.* **-ses** (-siːz). **1.** excessive contraction of the pupil of the eye, as in response to drugs. **2.** a variant spelling of **meiosis** (sense 1). [C20: from Greek *muein* to shut the eyes + -OSIS] —**miotic** *or* **myotic** (maɪˈɒtɪk) *adj., n.*

MIP *abbrev. for:* **1.** monthly investment plan. **2.** maximum investment plan: an endowment assurance policy designed to produce maximum profits.

MIPS (mɪps) *n. Computer technol. acronym for* million instructions per second.

mir *Russian.* (mir) *n., pl.* ***miri*** (ˈmiri). a peasant commune in prerevolutionary tsarist Russia. [literally: world]

Mir (mɪə) *n.* a Soviet space station launched in February 1986 and designed as a habitable module for a permanently manned scientific station. [C20: Russian: peace]

mirabile dictu *Latin.* (mɪˈræbɪleɪ ˈdɪktuː) wonderful to relate; amazing to say.

Mira Ceti (ˈmaɪrə ˈsiːtaɪ) *n.* a binary star one component of which, a red supergiant, is a long-period variable with an average period of 330 days.

miracidium (ˌmaɪrəˈsɪdɪəm) *n., pl.* **-ia** (-ɪə). the flat ciliated larva of flukes that hatches from the egg and gives rise asexually to other larval forms. [C20: New Latin, via Late Latin *miracidion,* from Greek *meirax* boy, girl] —ˌ**miraˈcidial** *adj.*

miracle (ˈmɪrək^əl) *n.* **1.** an event that is contrary to the established laws of nature and attributed to a supernatural cause. **2.** any amazing or wonderful event. **3.** a person or thing that is a marvellous example of something: *the bridge was a miracle of engineering.* **4.** short for **miracle play. 5.** (*modifier*) being or seeming a miracle: *a miracle cure.* [C12: from Latin *mīrāculum,* from *mīrārī* to wonder at]

miracle play *n.* a medieval play based on a biblical story or the life of a saint. Compare **mystery play.**

miraculous (mɪˈrækjʊləs) *adj.* **1.** of, like, or caused by a miracle; marvellous. **2.** surprising. **3.** having the power to work miracles. —**miˈraculously** *adv.* —**miˈraculousness** *n.*

mirador (ˌmɪrəˈdɔː) *n.* a window, balcony, or turret. [C17: from Spanish, from *mirar* to look]

mirage (mɪˈrɑːʒ) *n.* **1.** an image of a distant object or sheet of water, often inverted or distorted, caused by atmospheric refraction by hot air. **2.** something illusory. [C19: from French, from (*se*) *mirer* to be reflected]

MIRAS (ˈmaɪˌræs) *n.* (in Britain) *acronym for* mortgage interest relief at source.

mire (maɪə) *n.* **1.** a boggy or marshy area. **2.** mud, muck, or dirt. ~*vb.* **3.** to sink or cause to sink in a mire. **4.** (*tr.*) to make dirty or muddy. **5.** (*tr.*) to involve, esp. in difficulties. [C14: from Old Norse *mýrr;* related to MOSS] —**ˈmiriness** *n.* —**ˈmiry** *adj.*

mirepoix (mɪəˈpwɑː) *n.* a mixture of sautéed root vegetables used as a base for braising meat or for various sauces. [French, probably named in honour of C. P. G. F. de Lévis, Duke of *Mirepoix,* 18th-century French general]

mirk (mɜːk) *n.* a variant spelling of **murk.** —**ˈmirky** *adj.* —**ˈmirkily** *adv.* —**ˈmirkiness** *n.*

mirror (ˈmɪrə) *n.* **1.** a surface, such as polished metal or glass coated with a metal film, that reflects light without diffusion and produces an image of an object placed in front of it. **2.** such a reflecting surface mounted in a frame. **3.** any reflecting surface. **4.** a thing that reflects or depicts something else: *the press is a mirror of public opinion.* ~*vb.* **5.** (*tr.*) to reflect, represent, or depict faithfully: *he mirrors his teacher's ideals.* [C13: from Old French from *mirer* to look at, from Latin *mīrārī* to wonder at] —**ˈmirror-ˌlike** *adj.*

mirror ball *n.* a large revolving ball covered with small pieces of mirror glass so that it reflects light in changing patterns: used in discos and ballrooms.

mirror canon *n. Music.* **1.** a canon in which the parts are written as though seen in a mirror placed between them: one part or set of parts is the upside-down image of the other. **2.** sometimes, less accurately, a piece that can be played backwards.

mirror carp *n.* a variety of the common carp (*Cyprinus carpio*) with reduced scales, giving a smooth shiny body surface.

mirror finish *n.* a smooth highly polished surface produced on metal by mechanical or electrolytic polishing or lapping.

mirror image *n.* **1.** an image as observed in a mirror. **2.** an object that corresponds to another object in the same way as it would correspond to its image in a mirror.

mirror lens *n. Photog.* a lens of long focal length in which some of the lens elements are replaced by mirrors in order to shorten its overall length and reduce its weight.

mirror symmetry *n.* symmetry about a plane (**mirror plane**) that divides the object or system into two mutual mirror images.

mirror writing *n.* backward writing that forms a mirror image of normal writing.

mirth (mɜːθ) *n.* laughter, gaiety, or merriment. [Old English *myrgth;* compare MERRY] —**ˈmirthful** *adj.* —**ˈmirthfully** *adv.* —**ˈmirthfulness** *n.* —**ˈmirthless** *adj.* —**ˈmirthlessly** *adv.* —**ˈmirthlessness** *n.*

MIRV (mɜːv) *n. acronym for* multiple independently targeted re-entry vehicle: **a.** a missile that has several warheads, each one being directed to different enemy targets. **b.** any of the warheads.

mirza (ˈmɜːzə, mɪəˈzɑː) *n.* (in Iran) **1.** a title of respect placed before the surname of an official, scholar, or other distinguished man. **2.** a royal prince: used as a title after a name. [C17: from Persian: son of a lord]

mis-[1] *prefix.* **1.** wrong, bad, or erroneous; wrongly, badly, or erroneously: *misunderstanding; misfortune; misspelling; mistreat; mislead.* **2.** lack of; not: *mistrust.* [Old English *mis(se)-;* related to Middle English *mes-,* from Old French *mes-;* compare Old High German *missa-,* Old Norse *mis-*]

mis-[2] *prefix.* a variant of **miso-** before a vowel.

misadventure (ˌmɪsədˈvɛntʃə) *n.* **1.** an unlucky event; misfortune. **2.** *Law.* accidental death not due to crime or negligence.

misalliance (ˌmɪsəˈlaɪəns) *n.* an unsuitable alliance or marriage.

misandry (ˈmɪsændrɪ) *n.* hatred of men. [C20: from Greek, from MISO- + *-andria,* from *anēr* man] —**misˈandrist** *n., adj.* —**misˈandrous** *adj.*

misanthrope (ˈmɪzənˌθrəʊp) *or* **misanthropist** (mɪˈzænθrəpɪst) *n.* a person who dislikes or distrusts other people or mankind in general. [C17: from Greek *mīsanthrōpos,* from *misos* hatred + *anthrōpos* man] —**misanthropic** (ˌmɪzənˈθrɒpɪk) *or* ˌ**misanˈthropical** *adj.* —ˌ**misanˈthropically** *adv.* —**misanthropy** (mɪˈzænθrəpɪ) *n.*

misapply (ˌmɪsəˈplaɪ) *vb.* **-plies, -plying, -plied.** (*tr.*) **1.** to apply wrongly or badly. **2.** another word for **misappropriate.** —**misapplication** (ˌmɪsæplɪˈkeɪʃən) *n.*

misapprehend (ˌmɪsæprɪˈhɛnd) *vb.* (*tr.*) to misunderstand. —**misapprehension** (ˌmɪsæprɪˈhɛnʃən) *n.* —ˌ**misappreˈhensive** *adj.* —ˌ**misappreˈhensively** *adv.* —ˌ**misappreˈhensiveness** *n.*

misappropriate (ˌmɪsəˈprəʊprɪˌeɪt) *vb.* (*tr.*) to appropriate for a wrong or dishonest use; embezzle or steal. —ˌ**misapˌpropriˈation** *n.*

misbecome (ˌmɪsbɪˈkʌm) *vb.* **-comes, -coming, -came.** (*tr.*) to be unbecoming to or unsuitable for.

misbegotten (ˌmɪsbɪˈgɒt^ən) *adj.* **1.** unlawfully obtained: *misbegotten gains.* **2.** badly conceived, planned, or designed: *a misbegotten scheme.* **3.** Also: **misbegot** (ˌmɪsbɪˈgɒt). *Literary and dialect.* illegitimate; bastard.

misbehave (ˌmɪsbɪˈheɪv) *vb.* to behave (oneself) badly. —ˌ**misbeˈhaver** *n.* —**misbehaviour** (ˌmɪsbɪˈheɪvjə) *n.*

misbelief (ˌmɪsbɪˈliːf) *n.* a false or unorthodox belief.

misc. *abbrev. for:* **1.** miscellaneous. **2.** miscellany.

miscalculate (ˌmɪsˈkælkjʊˌleɪt) *vb.* (*tr.*) to calculate wrongly. —ˌ**miscalcuˈlation** *n.* —ˌ**misˈcalcuˌlator** *n.*

ˌ**misaˈdapt** *vb.*
misˈadd *vb.*
ˌ**misadˈdress** *vb.*
ˌ**misadˌminisˈtration** *n.*
ˌ**misaˈlign** *vb.*
ˌ**misaˈlignment** *n.*
ˌ**misappelˈlation** *n.*
ˌ**misapˈpraise** *vb.*
ˌ**misarˈrange** *vb.*
ˌ**misarˈrangement** *n.*
ˌ**misasˈsociˌate** *vb.*
ˌ**misasˌsociˈation** *n.*

miscall (ˌmɪsˈkɔːl) *vb.* (*tr.*) **1.** to call by the wrong name. **2.** *Dialect.* to abuse or malign. —ˌ**misˈcaller** *n.*

miscarriage (mɪsˈkærɪdʒ) *n.* **1.** (*also* ˈmɪskær-). spontaneous expulsion of a fetus from the womb, esp. prior to the 20th week of pregnancy. **2.** an act of mismanagement or failure: *a miscarriage of justice.* **3.** *Brit.* the failure of freight to reach its destination.

miscarry (mɪsˈkærɪ) *vb.* **-ries, -rying, -ried.** (*intr.*) **1.** to expel a fetus prematurely from the womb; abort. **2.** to fail: *all her plans miscarried.* **3.** *Brit.* (of freight, mail, etc.) to fail to reach a destination.

miscast (ˌmɪsˈkɑːst) *vb.* **-casts, -casting, -cast.** (*tr.*) **1.** to cast badly. **2.** (*often passive*) **a.** to cast (a role or the roles) in (a play, film, etc.) inappropriately: *Falstaff was certainly miscast.* **b.** to assign an inappropriate role to: *he was miscast as Othello.*

miscegenation (ˌmɪsɪdʒɪˈneɪʃən) *n.* interbreeding of races, esp. where differences of pigmentation are involved. [C19: from Latin *miscēre* to mingle + *genus* race] —**miscegenetic** (ˌmɪsɪdʒɪˈnɛtɪk) *adj.*

miscellanea (ˌmɪsəˈleɪnɪə) *pl. n.* a collection of miscellaneous items, esp. literary works. [C16: from Latin: neuter pl. of *miscellāneus* MISCELLANEOUS]

miscellaneous (ˌmɪsəˈleɪnɪəs) *adj.* **1.** composed of or containing a variety of things; mixed; varied. **2.** having varied capabilities, sides, etc. [C17: from Latin *miscellāneus,* from *miscellus* mixed, from *miscēre* to mix] —ˌ**miscelˈlaneously** *adv.* —ˌ**miscelˈlaneousness** *n.*

miscellanist (mɪˈsɛlənɪst) *n.* a writer of miscellanies.

miscellany (mɪˈsɛlənɪ; *U.S.* ˈmɪsəˌleɪnɪ) *n., pl.* **-nies.** (*sometimes pl.*) a miscellaneous collection of items, esp. essays, poems, etc., by different authors in one volume. [C16: from French *miscellanées* (pl.) MISCELLANEA]

mischance (mɪsˈtʃɑːns) *n.* **1.** bad luck. **2.** a stroke of bad luck.

mischief (ˈmɪstʃɪf) *n.* **1.** wayward but not malicious behaviour, usually of children, that causes trouble, irritation, etc. **2.** a playful inclination to behave in this way or to tease or disturb. **3.** injury or harm caused by a person or thing. **4.** a person, esp. a child, who is mischievous. **5.** a source of trouble, difficulty, etc.: *floods are a great mischief to the farmer.* [C13: from Old French *meschief* disaster, from *meschever* to meet with calamity; from *mes-* MIS-[1] + *chever* to reach an end, from *chef* end, CHIEF]

mischievous (ˈmɪstʃɪvəs) *adj.* **1.** inclined to acts of mischief. **2.** teasing; slightly malicious: *a mischievous grin.* **3.** causing or intended to cause harm: *a mischievous plot.* —ˈ**mischievously** *adv.* —ˈ**mischievousness** *n.*

misch metal (mɪʃ) *n.* an alloy of cerium and other rare earth metals, used esp. as a flint in cigarette lighters. [C20: from German *Mischmetall,* from *mischen* to mix]

miscible (ˈmɪsɪbᵊl) *adj.* capable of mixing: *alcohol is miscible with water.* [C16: from Medieval Latin *miscibilis,* from Latin *miscēre* to mix] —ˌ**misciˈbility** *n.*

misconceive (ˌmɪskənˈsiːv) *vb.* to have the wrong idea; fail to understand. —ˌ**misconˈceiver** *n.*

misconceived (ˌmɪskənˈsiːvd) *adj.* faultily or wrongly planned or based.

misconception (ˌmɪskənˈsɛpʃən) *n.* a false or mistaken view, opinion, or attitude.

misconduct *n.* (mɪsˈkɒndʌkt). **1.** behaviour, such as adultery or professional negligence, that is regarded as immoral or unethical. ~*vb.* (ˌmɪskənˈdʌkt). (*tr.*) **2.** to conduct (oneself) in such a way. **3.** to manage (something) badly.

misconstruction (ˌmɪskənˈstrʌkʃən) *n.* **1.** a false interpretation of evidence, facts, etc. **2.** a faulty construction, esp. in grammar.

misconstrue (ˌmɪskənˈstruː) *vb.* **-strues, -struing, -strued.** (*tr.*) to interpret mistakenly.

miscount (ˌmɪsˈkaʊnt) *vb.* **1.** to count or calculate incorrectly. ~*n.* **2.** a false count or calculation.

miscreance (ˈmɪskrɪəns) *or* **miscreancy** *n. Archaic.* lack of religious belief or faith.

miscreant (ˈmɪskrɪənt) *n.* **1.** a wrongdoer or villain. **2.** *Archaic.* an unbeliever or heretic. ~*adj.* **3.** evil or villainous. **4.** *Archaic.* unbelieving or heretical. [C14: from Old French *mescreant* unbelieving, from *mes-* MIS-[1] + *creant,* ultimately from Latin *credere* to believe]

miscreate *vb.* (ˌmɪskrɪˈeɪt). **1.** to create (something) badly or incorrectly. ~*adj.* (ˈmɪskrɪɪt, -ˌeɪt). **2.** *Archaic.* badly or unnaturally formed or made. —ˌ**miscreˈation** *n.*

miscue (ˌmɪsˈkjuː) *n.* **1.** *Billiards.* a faulty stroke in which the cue tip slips off the cue ball or misses it altogether. **2.** *Informal.* a blunder or mistake. ~*vb.* **-cues, -cuing, -cued.** **3.** (*intr.*) *Billiards.* to make a miscue. **4.** (*intr.*) *Theatre.* to fail to answer one's own cue or answer the cue of another. **5.** *Radio.* to start (a record or tape) at the wrong point. **6.** (*intr.*) *Informal.* to blunder.

miscue analysis *n. Brit. Education.* analysis of the errors a pupil makes while reading.

misdate (mɪsˈdeɪt) *vb.* (*tr.*) to date (a letter, event, etc.) wrongly.

misdeal (ˌmɪsˈdiːl) *vb.* **-deals, -dealing, -dealt.** **1.** (*intr.*) to deal out cards incorrectly. ~*n.* **2.** a faulty deal. —ˌ**misˈdealer** *n.*

misdeed (ˌmɪsˈdiːd) *n.* an evil or illegal action.

misdemean (ˌmɪsdɪˈmiːn) *vb.* a rare word for **misbehave.**

misdemeanant (ˌmɪsdɪˈmiːnənt) *n. Criminal law.* (formerly) a person who has committed or been convicted of a misdemeanour. Compare **felon**[1].

misdemeanour *or U.S.* **misdemeanor** (ˌmɪsdɪˈmiːnə) *n.* **1.** *Criminal law.* (formerly) an offence generally less heinous than a felony and which until 1967 involved a different form of trial. Compare **felony. 2.** any minor offence or transgression.

misdirect (ˌmɪsdɪˈrɛkt) *vb.* (*tr.*) **1.** to give (a person) wrong directions or instructions. **2.** to address (a letter, parcel, etc.) wrongly. —ˌ**misdiˈrection** *n.*

misdoubt (mɪsˈdaʊt) *vb.* an archaic word for **doubt** or **suspect.**

mise (miːz, maɪz) *n. Law.* **1.** the issue in the obsolete writ of right. **2.** an agreed settlement. [C15: from Old French: action of putting, from *mettre* to put]

mise en scène *French.* (miz ɑ̃ sɛn) *n.* **1. a.** the arrangement of properties, scenery, etc., in a play. **b.** the objects so arranged; stage setting. **2.** the environment of an event.

miser (ˈmaɪzə) *n.* **1.** a person who hoards money or possessions, often living miserably. **2.** selfish person. **3.** *Civil engineering.* a large hand-operated auger used for loose soils. [C16: from Latin: wretched]

miserable (ˈmɪzərəbᵊl, ˈmɪzrə-) *adj.* **1.** unhappy or depressed; wretched. **2.** causing misery, discomfort, etc.: *a miserable life.* **3.** contemptible: *a miserable villain.* **4.** sordid or squalid: *miserable living conditions.* **5.** *Scot., Austral., and N.Z.* mean; stingy. **6.** (pejorative intensifier): *you miserable wretch.* [C16: from Old French, from Latin *miserābilis* worthy of pity, from *miserārī* to pity, from *miser* wretched] —ˈ**miserableness** *n.* —ˈ**miserably** *adv.*

misère (mɪˈzɛə) *n.* **1.** a call in solo whist and other card games declaring a hand that will win no tricks. **2.** a hand that will win no tricks. [C19: from French: misery]

miserere (ˌmɪzəˈrɛərɪ, -ˈrɪərɪ) *n.* another word for **misericord** (sense 1).

Miserere (ˌmɪzəˈrɛərɪ, -ˈrɪərɪ) *n.* the 51st psalm, the Latin version of which begins "Miserere mei, Deus" ("Have mercy on me, O God").

misericord *or* **misericorde** (mɪˈzɛrɪˌkɔːd) *n.* **1.** a ledge projecting from the underside of the hinged seat of a choir stall in a church, on which the occupant can support himself while standing. **2.** *Christianity.* **a.** a relaxation of certain monastic rules for infirm or aged monks or nuns. **b.** a monastery where such relaxations can be enjoyed. **3.** a small medieval dagger used to give the death stroke to a wounded foe. [C14: from Old French, from Latin *misericordia* compassion, from *miserēre* to pity + *cor* heart]

miserly (ˈmaɪzəlɪ) *adj.* of or resembling a miser; avaricious. —ˈ**miserliness** *n.*

misery (ˈmɪzərɪ) *n., pl.* **-eries.** **1.** intense unhappiness, discomfort, or suffering; wretchedness. **2.** a cause of such unhappiness, discomfort, etc. **3.** squalid or poverty-stricken conditions. **4.** *Brit. informal.* a person who is habitually depressed: *he is such a misery.* **5.** *Dialect.* a pain or ailment. [C14: via Anglo-Norman from Latin *miseria,* from *miser* wretched]

misfeasance (mɪsˈfiːzəns) *n. Law.* the improper performance of an act that is lawful in itself. Compare **malfeasance, nonfeasance.** [C16: from Old French *mesfaisance,* from *mesfaire* to perform misdeeds] —**misˈfeasor** *n.*

misfile (ˌmɪsˈfaɪl) *vb.* to file (papers, records, etc.) wrongly.

misfire (ˌmɪsˈfaɪə) *vb.* (*intr.*) **1.** (of a firearm or its projectile) to fail to fire, explode, or ignite as or when expected. **2.** (of a motor engine or vehicle, etc.) to fail to fire at the appropriate time, often causing a backfire. **3.** to fail to operate or occur as intended. ~*n.* **4.** the act or an instance of misfiring.

misfit *n.* (ˈmɪsˌfɪt). **1.** a person not suited in behaviour or attitude to a particular social environment. **2.** something that does not fit or fits badly. ~*vb.* (ˌmɪsˈfɪt), **-fits, -fitting, -fitted.** (*intr.*) **3.** to fail to fit or be fitted.

misfortune (mɪsˈfɔːtʃən) *n.* **1.** evil fortune; bad luck. **2.** an unfortunate or disastrous event; calamity.

misgive (mɪsˈgɪv) *vb.* **-gives, -giving, -gave, -given.** to make or be apprehensive or suspicious.

misgiving (mɪsˈgɪvɪŋ) *n.* (*often pl.*) a feeling of uncertainty, apprehension, or doubt.

misgovern (ˌmɪsˈgʌvən) *vb.* to govern badly. —ˌ**misˈgovernment** *n.* —ˌ**misˈgovernor** *n.*

misguide (ˌmɪsˈgaɪd) *vb.* (*tr.*) to guide or direct wrongly or badly. —ˌ**misˈguidance** *n.* —ˌ**misˈguider** *n.*

misˈcategoˌrize *or* **misˈcategoˌrise** *vb.*
misˈcharacterˌize *or* **misˈcharacterˌise** *vb.*
misˈchoose *vb.,* **-ˈchooses, -ˈchoosing, -ˈchose, -ˈchosen.**
misˈclassiˌfy *vb.,* **-ˌfies, -ˌfying, -ˌfied.**
ˌ**miscompuˈtation** *n.*
ˌ**misconˈjecture** *vb.*
misˈcopy *vb.,* **-ˈcopies, -ˈcopying, -ˈcopied.**
ˌ**misdeˈfine** *vb.*
ˌ**misˈdiagˌnose** *vb.*
ˌ**misdiagˈnosis** *n.*
misˈeduˌcate *vb.*
ˌ**miseduˈcation** *n.*
ˌ**misemˈploy** *vb.*
misˈestiˌmate *vb., n.*
ˌ**misestiˈmation** *n.*
misˈgauge *vb.*

misguided (ˌmɪsˈgaɪdɪd) *adj.* foolish or unreasonable, esp. in action or behaviour. —ˌ**misˈguidedly** *adv.*
mishandle (ˌmɪsˈhændəl) *vb.* (*tr.*) to handle or treat badly or inefficiently.
mishap (ˈmɪshæp) *n.* **1.** an unfortunate accident. **2.** bad luck.
mishear (ˌmɪsˈhɪə) *vb.* **-hears, -hearing, -heard.** to fail to hear correctly.
mishit *Sport.* ~*n.* (ˈmɪsˌhɪt). **1.** a faulty shot or stroke. ~*vb.* (ˌmɪsˈhɪt), **-hits, -hitting, -hit. 2.** to hit (a ball) with a faulty stroke.
mishmash (ˈmɪʃˌmæʃ) *n.* a confused collection or mixture; hotchpotch. [C15: reduplication of MASH]
Mishmi (ˈmɪʃmɪ) *n.* **1.** (*pl.* **-mi** *or* **-mis**) a member of a Mongoloid hill people of the Brahmaputra area of NE India. **2.** the language of this people, belonging to the Tibeto-Burman branch of the Sino-Tibetan family. ~*adj.* **3.** of or relating to this people or their language.
Mishna (ˈmɪʃnə; *Hebrew* miʃˈna) *n., pl.* **Mishnayoth** (mɪʃˈnɑːjəʊt; *Hebrew* miʃnaˈjɔt) *Judaism.* a compilation of precepts passed down as an oral tradition and collected in the late second century A.D. It forms the earlier part of the Talmud. See also **Gemara.** [C17: from Hebrew: instruction by repetition, from *shānāh* to repeat] —**Mishnaic** (mɪʃˈneɪɪk), ˈ**Mishnic,** *or* ˈ**Mishnical** *adj.*
misinform (ˌmɪsɪnˈfɔːm) *vb.* (*tr.*) to give incorrect information to. —ˌ**misinˈformant** *or* ˌ**misinˈformer** *n.* —**misinformation** (ˌmɪsɪnfəˈmeɪʃən) *n.*
misinterpret (ˌmɪsɪnˈtɜːprɪt) *vb.* (*tr.*) to interpret badly, misleadingly, or incorrectly. —ˌ**misinˌterpreˈtation** *n.* —ˌ**misinˈterpreter** *n.*
misjoinder (mɪsˈdʒɔɪndə) *n. Law.* the improper joining of parties as coplaintiffs or codefendants or of different causes of action in one suit. Compare **nonjoinder.**
misjudge (ˌmɪsˈdʒʌdʒ) *vb.* to judge (a person or persons) wrongly or unfairly. —ˌ**misˈjudger** *n.* —ˌ**misˈjudgment** *or* ˌ**misˈjudgement** *n.*
mislay (mɪsˈleɪ) *vb.* **-lays, -laying, -laid.** (*tr.*) **1.** to lose (something) temporarily, esp. by forgetting where it is. **2.** to lay (something) badly. —**misˈlayer** *n.*
mislead (mɪsˈliːd) *vb.* **-leads, -leading, -led.** (*tr.*) **1.** to give false or misleading information to. **2.** to lead or guide in the wrong direction. —**misˈleader** *n.*
misleading (mɪsˈliːdɪŋ) *adj.* tending to confuse or mislead; deceptive. —**misˈleadingly** *adv.*
mislike (mɪsˈlaɪk) *Archaic.* ~*vb.* (*tr.*) **1.** to dislike. ~*n. also* **misliking. 2.** dislike or aversion. —**misˈliker** *n.*
mismanage (ˌmɪsˈmænɪdʒ) *vb.* (*tr.*) to manage badly or wrongly. —ˌ**misˈmanagement** *n.* —ˌ**misˈmanager** *n.*
mismatch (ˌmɪsˈmætʃ) *vb.* **1.** to match badly, esp. in marriage. ~*n.* **2.** a bad or inappropriate match.
misnomer (ˌmɪsˈnəʊmə) *n.* **1.** an incorrect or unsuitable name or term for a person or thing. **2.** the act of referring to a person by the wrong name. [C15: via Anglo-Norman from Old French *mesnommer* to misname, from Latin *nōmināre* to call by name]
miso (ˈmiːsəʊ) *n.* a thick brown salty paste made from soya beans, used to flavour savoury dishes, esp. soups. [from Japanese]
miso- *or before a vowel* **mis-** *combining form.* indicating hatred: *misogyny.* [from Greek *misos* hatred]
misogamy (mɪˈsɒgəmɪ, maɪ-) *n.* hatred of marriage. —**miˈsogamist** *n.*
misogyny (mɪˈsɒdʒɪnɪ, maɪ-) *n.* hatred of women. [C17: from Greek, from MISO- + *gunē* woman] —**miˈsogynist** *n.* —**miˈsogynous** *adj.*
misology (mɪˈsɒlədʒɪ, maɪ-) *n.* hatred of reasoning or reasoned argument. [C19: from Greek *misologia,* from *misos* hatred + *logos* word, reasoning. See LOGOS] —**miˈsologist** *n.*
misoneism (ˌmɪsəʊˈniːˌɪzəm, ˌmaɪ-) *n.* hatred of anything new. [C19: from Italian *misoneismo;* see MISO-, NEO-, -ISM] —ˌ**misoˈneist** *n.* —ˌ**misoneˈistic** *adj.*
mispickel (ˈmɪsˌpɪkəl) *n.* another name for **arsenopyrite.** [C17: from German]
misplace (ˌmɪsˈpleɪs) *vb.* (*tr.*) **1.** to put (something) in the wrong place, esp. to lose (something) temporarily by forgetting where it was placed; mislay. **2.** (*often passive*) to bestow (trust, confidence, affection, etc.) unadvisedly. —ˌ**misˈplacement** *n.*
misplaced modifier *n. Grammar.* a participle intended to modify a noun but having the wrong grammatical relationship to it as for example *having left* in the sentence *Having left Europe for good, Peter's future seemed bleak indeed.* Usual U.S. and Canadian name: **dangling participle.**
misplay (ˌmɪsˈpleɪ) *vb.* **1.** (*tr.*) to play badly or wrongly in games or sports: *the batsman misplayed the ball.* ~*n.* **2.** a wrong or unskilful play.
misplead (mɪsˈpliːd) *vb.* **-pleads, -pleading, -pleaded, -plead** (-ˈplɛd), *or* **-pled.** (*tr.*) to plead incorrectly.
mispleading (mɪsˈpliːdɪŋ) *n. Law.* an error or omission in pleading.
misprint *n.* (ˈmɪsˌprɪnt). **1.** an error in printing, made through damaged type, careless reading, etc. ~*vb.* (ˌmɪsˈprɪnt). **2.** (*tr.*) to print (a letter) incorrectly.
misprision[1] (mɪsˈprɪʒən) *n.* **a.** a failure to inform the proper authorities of the commission of an act of treason. **b.** the deliberate concealment of the commission of a felony. [C15: via Anglo-French from Old French *mesprision* error, from *mesprendre* to mistake, from *mes-* MIS-[1] + *prendre* to take]
misprision[2] (mɪsˈprɪʒən) *n. Archaic.* **1.** contempt. **2.** failure to appreciate the value of something. [C16: from MISPRIZE]
misprize *or* **misprise** (mɪsˈpraɪz) *vb.* to fail to appreciate the value of; undervalue or disparage. [C15: from Old French *mesprisier,* from *mes-* MIS-[1] + *prisier* to PRIZE[2]]
mispronounce (ˌmɪsprəˈnaʊns) *vb.* to pronounce (a word) wrongly. —**mispronunciation** (ˌmɪsprəˌnʌnsɪˈeɪʃən) *n.*
misquote (ˌmɪsˈkwəʊt) *vb.* to quote (a text, speech, etc.) inaccurately. —ˌ**misquoˈtation** *n.*
misread (ˌmɪsˈriːd) *vb.* **-reads, -reading, -read** (-ˈrɛd). (*tr.*) **1.** to read incorrectly. **2.** to misinterpret.
misreport (ˌmɪsrɪˈpɔːt) *vb.* **1.** (*tr.*) to report falsely or inaccurately. ~*n.* **2.** an inaccurate or false report. —ˌ**misreˈporter** *n.*
misrepresent (ˌmɪsrɛprɪˈzɛnt) *vb.* (*tr.*) to represent wrongly or inaccurately. —ˌ**misrepresenˈtation** *n.* —ˌ**misrepreˈsentative** *adj.* —ˌ**misrepreˈsenter** *n.*
misrule (ˌmɪsˈruːl) *vb.* **1.** (*tr.*) to govern inefficiently or without humanity or justice. ~*n.* **2.** inefficient or inhumane government. **3.** disorder.
miss[1] (mɪs) *vb.* **1.** to fail to reach, hit, meet, find, or attain (some specified or implied aim, goal, target, etc.). **2.** (*tr.*) to fail to attend or be present for: *to miss a train; to miss an appointment.* **3.** (*tr.*) to fail to see, hear, understand, or perceive: *to miss a point.* **4.** (*tr.*) to lose, overlook, or fail to take advantage of: *to miss an opportunity.* **5.** (*tr.*) to leave out; omit: *to miss an entry in a list.* **6.** (*tr.*) to discover or regret the loss or absence of: *he missed his watch; she missed him.* **7.** (*tr.*) to escape or avoid (something, esp. a danger), usually narrowly: *he missed death by inches.* **8. miss the boat** *or* **bus.** to lose an opportunity. ~*n.* **9.** a failure to reach, hit, meet, find, etc. **10. give (something) a miss.** *Informal.* to avoid (something): *give the lecture a miss; give the pudding a miss.* ~See also **miss out.** [Old English *missan* (meaning: to fail to hit); related to Old High German *missan,* Old Norse *missa*] —ˈ**missable** *adj.*
miss[2] (mɪs) *n. Informal.* **1.** an unmarried woman or girl, esp. a schoolgirl. **2.** (in the fashion trade) a garment size in young women's clothes. [C17: shortened form of MISTRESS]
Miss (mɪs) *n.* a title of an unmarried woman or girl, usually used before the surname or sometimes alone in direct address. [C17: shortened from MISTRESS]
▷**Usage.** When reference is made to two or more unmarried women with the same surname, *the Misses Smith* is more formal than *the Miss Smiths.*
Miss. *abbrev. for* Mississippi.
missal (ˈmɪsəl) *n. R.C. Church.* a book containing the prayers, rites, etc., of the Masses for a complete year. [C14: from Church Latin *missale* (n.), from *missālis* concerning the MASS]
missel thrush (ˈmɪsəl) *n.* a variant spelling of **mistle thrush.**
misshape *vb.* (ˌmɪsˈʃeɪp). **-shapes, -shaping, -shaped** *or* **-shapen.** (*tr.*) **1.** to shape badly; deform. ~*n.* (ˈmɪsˌʃeɪp). **2.** something that is badly shaped.
misshapen (ˌmɪsˈʃeɪpən) *adj.* badly shaped; deformed. —ˌ**misˈshapenly** *adv.* —ˌ**misˈshapenness** *n.*
missile (ˈmɪsaɪl) *n.* **1.** any object or weapon that is thrown at a target or shot from an engine, gun, etc. **2. a.** a rocket-propelled weapon that flies either in a fixed trajectory (**ballistic missile**) or in a trajectory that can be controlled during flight (**guided missile**). **b.** (*as modifier*): *a missile carrier.* [C17: from Latin: *missilis,* from *mittere* to send]
missilery *or* **missilry** (ˈmɪsaɪlrɪ) *n.* **1.** missiles collectively. **2.** the design, operation, or study of missiles.
missing (ˈmɪsɪŋ) *adj.* **1.** not present; absent or lost. **2.** not able to be traced and not known to be dead: *nine men were missing after the attack.* **3. go missing.** to become lost or disappear.
missing fundamental *n.* a tone, not present in the sound received by the ear, whose pitch is that of the difference between the two tones that are sounded.
missing link *n.* **1.** (*sometimes caps.;* usually preceded by *the*) a hypothetical extinct animal or animal group, formerly thought to be intermediate between the anthropoid apes and man. **2.** any missing section or part in an otherwise complete series.
missiology (ˌmɪsɪˈɒlədʒɪ) *n. Christian theol.* the study of the missionary function of the Christian Church.

ˌ**misiˌdentifiˈcation** *n.*
ˌ**misiˈdentiˌfy** *vb.,* **-ˌfies, -ˌfying, -ˌfied.**
ˌ**misinˈstruct** *vb.*
ˌ**misinˈstruction** *n.*
misˈlabel *vb.,* **-bels, -belling, -belled.**
misˈmarriage *n.*
misˈmeasure *vb.*
misˈname *vb.*
misˈnumber *vb.*
ˌ**misperˈception** *n.*
misˈphrase *vb.*
misˈprincipled *adj.*
ˌ**misproˈportion** *n.*
misˈpunctuˌate *vb.*
ˌ**mispunctuˈation** *n.*
misˈrecogˌnize *or* **misˈrecogˌnise** *vb.*
ˌ**misreˈlate** *vb.*
ˌ**misreˈlation** *n.*
ˌ**misreˈmember** *vb.*
misˈrhymed *adj.*

mission ('mɪʃən) *n.* **1.** a specific task or duty assigned to a person or group of people: *their mission was to irrigate the desert.* **2.** a person's vocation (often in the phrase **mission in life**). **3.** a group of persons representing or working for a particular country, business, etc., in a foreign country. **4. a.** a special embassy sent to a foreign country for a specific purpose. **b.** *U.S.* a permanent legation. **5. a.** a group of people sent by a religious body, esp. a Christian church, to a foreign country to do religious and social work. **b.** the campaign undertaken by such a group. **6. a.** the work or calling of a missionary. **b.** a building or group of buildings in which missionary work is performed. **c.** the area assigned to a particular missionary. **7.** the dispatch of aircraft or spacecraft to achieve a particular task. **8.** a church or chapel that has no incumbent of its own. **9.** a charitable centre that offers shelter, aid, or advice to the destitute or underprivileged. **10.** (*modifier*) of or relating to an ecclesiastical mission: *a mission station.* **11.** (*modifier*) *U.S.* (of furniture) in the style of the early Spanish missions of the southwestern U.S. ~*vb.* **12.** (*tr.*) to direct a mission to or establish a mission in (a given region). [C16: from Latin *missiō*, from *mittere* to send]

missionary ('mɪʃənərɪ) *n., pl.* **-aries. a.** a member of a religious mission. **b.** (*as modifier*): *missionary work.*

missionary position *n. Informal.* a position for sexual intercourse in which the man lies on top of the woman and they are face to face. [C20: from the belief that missionaries advocated this as the proper position to primitive peoples among whom it was unknown]

missioner ('mɪʃənə) *n.* **1.** a less common name for **missionary. 2.** a person heading a parochial mission in a Christian country.

missis *or* **missus** ('mɪsɪz, -ɪs) *n.* **1.** (usually preceded by *the*) *Informal.* one's wife or the wife of the person addressed or referred to. **2.** an informal term of address for a woman. [C19: spoken version of MISTRESS]

Mississippian (ˌmɪsɪ'sɪpɪən) *adj.* **1.** of or relating to the state of Mississippi in the southeastern U.S. or the Mississippi river, forming the state's W border. **2.** (in North America) of, denoting, or formed in the lower of two subdivisions of the Carboniferous period (see also **Pennsylvanian** (sense 2)), which lasted for 50 million years. ~*n.* **3.** an inhabitant or native of the state of Mississippi. **4. the.** the Mississippian period or rock system equivalent to the lower Carboniferous of Europe.

missive ('mɪsɪv) *n.* **1.** a formal or official letter. **2.** a formal word for **letter.** ~*adj.* **3.** *Rare.* sent or intended to be sent. [C15: from Medieval Latin *missivus*, from *mittere* to send]

miss out *vb.* **1.** (*tr., adv.*) to leave out; overlook. **2.** (*intr., adv.;* often foll. by *on*) to fail to experience: *by leaving early you missed out on the celebrations.*

misspell (ˌmɪs'spɛl) *vb.* **-spells, -spelling, -spelt** *or* **-spelled.** to spell (a word or words) wrongly.

misspelling (ˌmɪs'spɛlɪŋ) *n.* a wrong spelling.

misspend (ˌmɪs'spɛnd) *vb.* **-spends, -spending, -spent.** to spend thoughtlessly or wastefully. —ˌ**mis'spender** *n.*

misstate (ˌmɪs'steɪt) *vb.* (*tr.*) to state incorrectly. —ˌ**mis'statement** *n.*

misstep (ˌmɪs'stɛp) *n.* **1.** a false step. **2.** an error.

missus ('mɪsɪz, -ɪs) *n.* a variant spelling of **missis.**

missy ('mɪsɪ) *n., pl.* **missies.** *Informal.* an affectionate or sometimes disparaging form of address to a young girl.

mist (mɪst) *n.* **1.** a thin fog resulting from condensation in the air near the earth's surface. **2.** *Meteorol.* such an atmospheric condition with a horizontal visibility of 1–2 kilometres. **3.** a fine spray of any liquid, such as that produced by an aerosol container. **4.** *Chem.* a colloidal suspension of a liquid in a gas. **5.** condensed water vapour on a surface that blurs the surface. **6.** something that causes haziness or lack of clarity, such as a film of tears. ~*vb.* **7.** to cover or be covered with or as if with mist. [Old English; related to Middle Dutch, Swedish *mist*, Greek *omikhlē* fog]

mistakable *or* **mistakeable** (mɪ'steɪkəbᵊl) *adj.* liable to be mistaken. —**mis'takably** *or* **mis'takeably** *adv.*

mistake (mɪ'steɪk) *n.* **1.** an error or blunder in action, opinion, or judgment. **2.** a misconception or misunderstanding. ~*vb.* **-takes, -taking, -took, -taken. 3.** (*tr.*) to misunderstand; misinterpret: *she mistook his meaning.* **4.** (*tr.;* foll. by *for*) to take (for), interpret (as), or confuse (with): *she mistook his direct manner for honesty.* **5.** (*tr.*) to choose badly or incorrectly: *he mistook his path.* **6.** (*intr.*) to make a mistake in action, opinion, judgment, etc. [C13 (meaning: to do wrong, err): from Old Norse *mistaka* to take erroneously] —**mis'taker** *n.*

mistaken (mɪ'steɪkən) *adj.* **1.** (*usually predicative*) wrong in opinion, judgment, etc.: *she is mistaken.* **2.** arising from error in judgment, opinion, etc.: *a mistaken viewpoint.* —**mis'takenly** *adv.* —**mis'takenness** *n.*

mistal ('mɪstəl) *n. Dialect.* a cow shed; byre. [C17: of uncertain origin]

mister ('mɪstə) (*sometimes cap.*) ~*n.* **1.** an informal form of address for a man. **2.** *Naval.* **a.** the official form of address for subordinate or senior warrant officers. **b.** the official form of address for all officers in a merchant ship, other than the captain. **c.** *U.S. Navy.* the official form of address used by the commanding officer to his officers, esp. to the more junior. **3.** *Brit.* the form of address for a surgeon. **4.** the form of address for officials holding certain positions: *mister chairman.* ~*vb.* **5.** (*tr.*) *Informal.* to call (someone) mister. [C16: variant of MASTER]

Mister ('mɪstə) *n.* the full form of **Mr.**

mistigris ('mɪstɪgriː) *n.* **1.** the joker or a blank card used as a wild card in a variety of draw poker. **2.** the variety of draw poker using this card. [C19: from French *mistigris* jack of clubs, game in which this card was wild]

mistime (ˌmɪs'taɪm) *vb.* (*tr.*) to time (an action, utterance, etc.) wrongly.

mistle thrush *or* **missel thrush** ('mɪsᵊl) *n.* a large European thrush, *Turdus viscivorus*, with a brown back and spotted breast, noted for feeding on mistletoe berries. [C18: from Old English *mistel* MISTLETOE]

mistletoe ('mɪsᵊlˌtəʊ) *n.* **1.** a Eurasian evergreen shrub, *Viscum album*, with leathery leaves, yellowish flowers, and waxy white berries: grows as a partial parasite on various trees: used as a Christmas decoration: family *Loranthaceae.* **2.** any of several similar and related American plants, esp. *Phoradendron flavescens.* **3. mistletoe cactus.** an epiphytic cactus, *Rhipsalis cassytha*, that grows in tropical America. [Old English *misteltān*, from *mistel* mistletoe + *tān* twig; related to Old Norse *mistilteinn*]

mistook (mɪ'stʊk) *vb.* the past tense of **mistake.**

mistral ('mɪstrəl, mɪ'strɑːl) *n.* a strong cold dry wind that blows through the Rhône valley and S France to the Mediterranean coast, mainly in the winter. [C17: via French from Provençal, from Latin *magistrālis* MAGISTRAL, as in *magistrālis ventus* master wind]

mistreat (ˌmɪs'triːt) *vb.* (*tr.*) to treat badly. —ˌ**mis'treatment** *n.*

mistress ('mɪstrɪs) *n.* **1.** a woman who has a continuing extramarital sexual relationship with a man. **2.** a woman in a position of authority, ownership, or control, such as the head of a household. **3.** a woman or female personification having control over something specified: *she was mistress of her own destiny.* **4.** *Chiefly Brit.* short for **schoolmistress. 5.** an archaic or dialect word for **sweetheart.** [C14: from Old French; see MASTER, -ESS]

Mistress ('mɪstrɪs) *n.* an archaic or dialect title equivalent to **Mrs.**

Mistress of the Robes *n.* (in Britain) a lady of high rank in charge of the Queen's wardrobe.

mistrial (mɪs'traɪəl) *n.* **1.** a trial made void because of some error, such as a defect in procedure. **2.** (in the U.S.) an inconclusive trial, as when a jury cannot agree on a verdict.

mistrust (ˌmɪs'trʌst) *vb.* **1.** to have doubts or suspicions about (someone or something). ~*n.* **2.** distrust. —ˌ**mis'truster** *n.* —ˌ**mis'trustful** *adj.* —ˌ**mis'trustfully** *adv.* —ˌ**mis'trustfulness** *n.*

misty ('mɪstɪ) *adj.* **mistier, mistiest. 1.** consisting of or resembling mist. **2.** obscured by or as if by mist. **3.** indistinct; blurred: *the misty past.* —'**mistily** *adv.* —'**mistiness** *n.*

misunderstand (ˌmɪsʌndə'stænd) *vb.* **-stands, -standing, -stood.** to fail to understand properly.

misunderstanding (ˌmɪsʌndə'stændɪŋ) *n.* **1.** a failure to understand properly. **2.** a disagreement.

misunderstood (ˌmɪsʌndə'stʊd) *adj.* not properly or sympathetically understood: *a misunderstood work of art; misunderstood adolescent.*

misuse *n.* (ˌmɪs'juːs), *also* **misusage. 1.** erroneous, improper, or unorthodox use: *misuse of words.* **2.** cruel or inhumane treatment. ~*vb.* (ˌmɪs'juːz). (*tr.*) **3.** to use wrongly. **4.** to treat badly or harshly.

misuser (ˌmɪs'juːzə) *n. Law.* an abuse of some right, privilege, office, etc., such as one that may lead to its forfeiture. [C17: from Old French *mesuser* (infinitive used as noun)]

MIT *abbrev. for* Massachusetts Institute of Technology.

mitch *or* **mich** (mɪtʃ) *vb.* (*intr.*) *Dialect.* to play truant from school. [C13: probably from Old French *muchier, mucier* to hide, lurk]

mite[1] (maɪt) *n.* any of numerous small free-living or parasitic arachnids of the order *Acarina* (or *Acari*) that can occur in terrestrial or aquatic habitats. See also **gall mite, harvest mite, itch mite, spider mite.** Compare **tick**[2]. [Old English *mīte;* compare Old High German *mīza* gnat, Dutch *mijt*]

mite[2] (maɪt) *n.* **1.** a very small particle, creature, or object. **2.** a very small contribution or sum of money. See also **widow's mite. 3.** a former Flemish coin of small value. **4. a mite.** *Informal.* somewhat: *he's a mite foolish.* [C14: from Middle Low German, Middle Dutch *mīte;* compare MITE[1]]

miter ('maɪtə) *n., vb.* the usual U.S. spelling of **mitre.**

miterwort ('maɪtəˌwɜːt) *n.* the U.S. spelling of **mitrewort.**

mither ('mɪðər) *n.* a Scot. word for **mother**[1].

Mithraism ('mɪθreɪˌɪzəm) *or* **Mithraicism** (mɪθ'reɪɪˌsɪzəm) *n.* the ancient Persian religion of Mithras, god of light identified with the sun. It spread to the Roman Empire during the first three centuries A.D. —**Mithraic** (mɪθ'reɪɪk) *or* ˌ**Mithra'istic** *adj.* —'**Mithraist** *n., adj.*

mithridate ('mɪθrɪˌdeɪt) *n. Obsolete.* a substance believed to be an antidote to every poison and a cure for every disease. [C16: from

mis'teach *vb.,* **-'teaches, -'teaching, -'taught.**
mis'term *vb.*
mis'title *vb.*
ˌ**mistrans'late** *vb.*
mis'type *vb.*
mis'value *vb.,* **-ues, -uing, -ued.**

Late Latin *mithradatium,* after *Mithridates* the Great (?132–63 B.C.), king of Pontus (in Asia Minor), alluding to his legendary immunity to poisons]

mithridatism (ˈmɪθrɪdeɪˌtɪzəm) *n.* immunity to large doses of poison by prior ingestion of gradually increased doses. —**mithridatic** (ˌmɪθrɪˈdætɪk, -ˈdeɪ-) *adj.*

miticide (ˈmɪtɪˌsaɪd) *n.* any drug or agent that destroys mites. —ˌ**mitiˈcidal** *adj.*

mitigate (ˈmɪtɪˌgeɪt) *vb.* to make or become less severe or harsh; moderate. [C15: from Latin *mītigāre,* from *mītis* mild + *agere* to make] —**mitigable** (ˈmɪtɪgəbᵊl) *adj.* —ˌ**mitiˈgation** *n.* —ˈ**mitiˌgative** *or* ˈ**mitiˌgatory** *adj.* —ˈ**mitiˌgator** *n.*

mitigating circumstances *pl. n.* circumstances that may be considered to lessen the culpability of an offender.

mitis (ˈmaɪtɪs, ˈmiː-) *or* **mitis metal** *n.* a malleable iron, fluid enough for casting, made by adding a small amount of aluminium to wrought iron. [C19: from Latin: soft]

Mitnaged (ˌmitnɑˈged) *or* **Misnaged** (misˈnɑged) *n., pl.* **Mitnagdim** (ˌmitnɑgˈdim) *or* **Misnagdim** (misˈnɑgdim) *Judaism.* an orthodox opponent of Chassidism. [from Hebrew, literally: opponent]

mitochondrion (ˌmaɪtəʊˈkɒndrɪən) *n., pl.* **-dria** (-drɪə). a small spherical or rodlike body, bounded by a double membrane, in the cytoplasm of most cells: contains enzymes responsible for energy production. Also called: **chondriosome.** [C19: New Latin, from Greek *mitos* thread + *khondrion* small grain] —ˌ**mitoˈchondrial** *adj.*

mitogen (ˈmaɪtədʒən) *n.* any agent that induces mitosis. —**mitogenic** (ˌmaɪtəʊˈdʒenɪk) *adj.*

mitosis (maɪˈtəʊsɪs, mɪ-) *n.* a method of cell division, in which the nucleus divides into daughter nuclei, each containing the same number of chromosomes as the parent nucleus. See **prophase, metaphase, anaphase, telophase.** Compare **meiosis** (sense 1). [C19: from New Latin, from Greek *mitos* thread] —**mitotic** (maɪˈtɒtɪk, mɪ-) *adj.* —**miˈtotically** *adv.*

mitrailleuse (ˌmɪtraɪˈɜːz) *n.* **1.** an early form of breech-loading machine gun having several parallel barrels. **2.** any French machine gun. [C19: from French, from *mitraille* small shot, from Old French *mistraille* pieces of money, from MITE[2]]

mitral (ˈmaɪtrəl) *adj.* **1.** of or like a mitre. **2.** *Anatomy.* of or relating to the mitral valve.

mitral valve *n.* the valve between the left atrium and the left ventricle of the heart, consisting of two membranous flaps, that prevents regurgitation of blood into the atrium. Also called: **bicuspid valve.**

mitre *or U.S.* **miter** (ˈmaɪtə) *n.* **1.** *Christianity.* the liturgical headdress of a bishop or abbot, in most western churches consisting of a tall pointed cleft cap with two bands hanging down at the back. **2.** short for **mitre joint.** **3.** a bevelled surface of a mitre joint. **4.** (in sewing) a diagonal join where the hems along two sides meet at a corner of the fabric. ~*vb. (tr.)* **5.** to make a mitre joint between (two pieces of material, esp. wood). **6.** to make a mitre in (a fabric). **7.** to confer a mitre upon: *a mitred abbot.* [C14: from Old French, from Latin *mitra,* from Greek *mitra* turban]

mitre block *n.* a block of wood with slots for cutting mitre joints with a saw.

mitre box *n.* an open-ended box with sides having narrow slots to guide a saw in cutting mitre joints.

mitre gear *n.* one of a pair of similar bevel gears having a pitch cone angle of 45°.

mitre joint *n.* a corner joint formed between two pieces of material, esp. wood, by cutting bevels of equal angles at the ends of each piece. Sometimes shortened to **mitre.**

mitre square *n.* a tool with two blades that are at a fixed angle to one another, used to bevel a mitre joint.

mitrewort *or U.S.* **miterwort** (ˈmaɪtəˌwɜːt) *n.* any of several Asian and North American saxifragaceous plants of the genus *Mitella,* having clusters of small white flowers and capsules resembling a bishop's mitre. Also called: **bishop's-cap.**

mitt (mɪt) *n.* **1.** any of various glovelike hand coverings, such as one that does not cover the fingers. **2.** short for **mitten** (sense 1). **3.** *Baseball.* a large round thickly padded leather mitten worn by the catcher. See also **glove** (sense 2). **4.** (*often pl.*) a slang word for **hand.** **5.** *Slang.* a boxing glove. [C18: shortened from MITTEN]

mitten (ˈmɪtᵊn) *n.* **1.** a glove having one section for the thumb and a single section for the other fingers. Sometimes shortened to **mitt.** **2.** *Slang.* a boxing glove. [C14: from Old French *mitaine,* of uncertain origin]

mittimus (ˈmɪtɪməs) *n., pl.* **-muses.** *Law.* a warrant of commitment to prison or a command to a jailer directing him to hold someone in prison. [C15: from Latin: we send, the first word of such a command]

Mitty (ˈmɪtɪ) *n.* **Walter.** **a.** a fictional character given to grand and elaborate fantasies; daydreamer. **b.** (*as modifier*): *a Walter Mitty character; a Mitty act.* [C20: from a short story *The Secret Life of Walter Mitty* (1939), by James Thurber (1894–1961), U.S. humorist and illustrator] —ˌ**Mittyˈesque** *or* ˈ**Mitty-ˌlike** *adj.*

mitzvah (ˈmɪtsvə; *Hebrew* mitsˈva) *n., pl.* **-vahs** *or* **-voth** (*Hebrew* -ˈvɔt). *Judaism.* **1.** a commandment or precept, esp. one found in the Bible. **2.** a good deed. [from Hebrew: commandment]

mix (mɪks) *vb.* **1.** (*tr.*) to combine or blend (ingredients, liquids, objects, etc.) together into one mass. **2.** (*intr.*) to become or have the capacity to become combined, joined, etc.: *some chemicals do not mix.* **3.** (*tr.*) to form (something) by combining two or more constituents: *to mix cement.* **4.** (*tr.;* often foll. by *in* or *into*) to add as an additional part or element (to a mass or compound): *to mix flour into a batter.* **5.** (*tr.*) to do at the same time; combine: *to mix study and pleasure.* **6.** (*tr.*) to consume (drinks or foods) in close succession. **7.** to come or cause to come into association socially: *Pauline has never mixed well.* **8.** (*intr.;* often foll. by *with*) to go together; complement. **9.** (*tr.*) to crossbreed (differing strains of plants or breeds of livestock), esp. more or less at random. **10.** (*tr.*) *Electronics.* to combine (two or more signals). **11.** *Music.* **a.** (in sound recording) to balance and adjust (the recorded tracks) on a multitrack tape machine. **b.** (in live performance) to balance and adjust (the output levels from microphones and pick-ups). **12.** (*tr.*) to merge (two lengths of film) so that the effect is imperceptible. **13. mix it.** *Informal.* **a.** to cause mischief or trouble, often for a person named: *she tried to mix it for John.* **b.** to fight. ~*n.* **14.** the act or an instance of mixing. **15.** the result of mixing; mixture. **16.** a mixture of ingredients, esp. one commercially prepared for making a cake, bread, etc. **17.** *Music.* the sound obtained by mixing. **18.** *Building trades, civil engineering.* the proportions of cement, sand, and aggregate in mortar, plaster, or concrete. **19.** *Informal.* a state of confusion, bewilderment. ~See also **mix-up.** [C15: back formation from *mixt* mixed, via Old French from Latin *mixtus,* from *miscēre* to mix] —ˈ**mixable** *adj.* —ˌ**mixaˈbility** *n.*

mixdown (ˈmɪksˌdaʊn) *n.* (in sound recording) the transfer of a multitrack master mix to two-track stereo tape.

mixed (mɪkst) *adj.* **1.** formed or blended together by mixing. **2.** composed of different elements, races, sexes, etc.: *a mixed school.* **3.** consisting of conflicting elements, thoughts, attitudes, etc.: *mixed feelings; mixed motives.* **4.** (of a legal action) **a.** having the nature of both a real and a personal action, such as a demand for the return of wrongfully withheld property as well as for damages to compensate for the loss. **b.** having aspects or issues determinable by different persons or bodies: *a mixed question of law and fact.* **5.** (of an inflorescence) containing cymose and racemose branches. **6.** (of a nerve) containing both motor and sensory nerve fibres. **7.** *Maths.* **a.** (of a number) consisting of the sum of an integer and a fraction, as 5½. **b.** (of a decimal) consisting of the sum of an integer and a decimal fraction, as 17.43. **c.** (of an algebraic expression) consisting of the sum of a polynomial and a rational fraction, such as $2x + 4x^2 + 2/3x$. —**mixedly** (ˈmɪksɪdlɪ) *adv.* —**mixedness** (ˈmɪksɪdnɪs) *n.*

mixed bag *n. Informal.* something composed of diverse elements, characteristics, people, etc.

mixed blessing *n.* an event, situation, etc., having both advantages and disadvantages.

mixed bud *n.* a bud containing both rudimentary flowers and foliage leaves.

mixed crystal *n. Chem.* a crystal consisting of a solid solution of two or more distinct compounds.

mixed doubles *pl. n. Tennis.* a doubles game with a man and a woman as partners on each side.

mixed economy *n.* an economy in which some industries are privately owned and others are publicly owned or nationalized.

mixed farming *n.* combined arable and livestock farming (on **mixed farms**).

mixed-flow turbine *n.* a water turbine in which water flows radially and axially through the rotating vanes.

mixed grill *n.* a dish made of several kinds of grilled meats, often served with grilled tomatoes and mushrooms.

mixed language *n.* any language containing items of vocabulary or other linguistic characteristics borrowed from two or more existing languages. See also **pidgin, creole** (sense 1), **lingua franca.**

mixed marriage *n.* a marriage between persons of different races or religions.

mixed metaphor *n.* a combination of incongruous metaphors, as *when the Nazi jackboots sing their swan song.*

mixed-up *adj.* in a state of mental confusion; perplexed.

mixer (ˈmɪksə) *n.* **1.** a person or thing that mixes. **2.** *Informal.* **a.** a person considered in relation to his ability to mix socially. **b.** a person who creates trouble for others. **3.** a kitchen appliance, usually electrical, used for mixing foods, etc. **4.** a drink such as ginger ale, fruit juice, etc., used in preparing cocktails. **5.** *Electronics.* a device in which two or more input signals are combined to give a single output signal. **6.** short for **sound mixer, vision mixer.**

mixer tap *n.* a tap in which hot and cold water supplies have a joint outlet but are controlled separately.

mixolydian (ˌmɪksəʊˈlɪdɪən) *adj. Music.* of, relating to, or denoting an authentic mode represented by the ascending natural diatonic scale from G to G. See **Hypo-.** [C16: from Greek *mixoludios* half-Lydian]

mixte (ˈmɪkstɪ) *adj.* of or denoting a type of bicycle frame, usually for women, in which angled twin lateral tubes run back to the rear axle. [C20: from French]

Mixtec (ˈmiːstɛk) *n.* **1.** (*pl.* **-tecs** or **-tec**) a member of an American Indian people of Mexico. **2.** the language of this people. —**Mixˈtecan** *adj., n.*

mixter-maxter ('mɪkstər'mækstər) *Scot.* ~*adj.* **1.** chaotic or confused. ~*n.* **2.** a chaotic or confused mixture; jumble. [C19: reduplicated form based on MIX]

mixture ('mɪkstʃə) *n.* **1.** the act of mixing or state of being mixed. **2.** something mixed; a result of mixing. **3.** *Chem.* a substance consisting of two or more substances mixed together without any chemical bonding between them. **4.** *Pharmacol.* a liquid medicine in which an insoluble compound is suspended in the liquid. **5.** *Music.* an organ stop that controls several ranks of pipes sounding the upper notes in a harmonic series. **6.** the mixture of petrol vapour and air in an internal-combustion engine. [C16: from Latin *mixtūra,* from *mixtus,* past participle of *miscēre* to mix]

mix-up *n.* **1.** a confused condition or situation. **2.** *Informal.* a fight. ~*vb.* **mix up.** (*tr., adv.*) **3.** to make into a mixture: *to mix up ingredients.* **4.** to confuse or confound: *Tom mixes John up with Bill.* **5.** (*often passive*) to put (someone) into a state of confusion: *I'm all mixed up.* **6.** (foll. by *in* or *with;* usually passive) to involve (in an activity or group, esp. one that is illegal): *why did you get mixed up in that drugs racket?* **7. mix it up.** *U.S. and Canadian informal.* to fight.

mizzen *or* **mizen** ('mɪzᵊn) *Nautical.* ~*n.* **1.** a sail set on a mizzenmast. **2.** short for **mizzenmast.** ~*adj.* **3.** of or relating to any kind of gear used with a mizzenmast: *a mizzen staysail.* [C15: from French *misaine,* from Italian *mezzana, mezzano* middle]

mizzenmast *or* **mizenmast** ('mɪzᵊnˌmɑːst; *Nautical* 'mɪzᵊnməst) *n. Nautical.* **1.** (on a yawl, ketch, or dandy) the after mast. **2.** (on a vessel with three or more masts) the third mast from the bow.

mizzle[1] ('mɪzᵊl) *vb., n.* a dialect word for **drizzle.** [C15: perhaps from Low German *miseln* to drizzle; compare Dutch dialect *miezelen* to drizzle] —'**mizzly** *adj.*

mizzle[2] ('mɪzᵊl) *vb.* (*intr.*) *Brit. slang.* to decamp. [C18: of unknown origin]

mk *Currency. symbol for:* **1.** mark. **2.** markka.

Mk *abbrev. for* mark (type of car).

MKSA system *n.* another name for **Giorgi system.**

mks units *pl. n.* a metric system of units based on the metre, kilogram, and second as the units of length, mass, and time; it forms the basis of the SI units.

mkt *abbrev. for* market.

ml *symbol for:* **1.** millilitre. **2.** mile.

ML *abbrev. for* Medieval Latin.

MLA *abbrev. for:* **1.** Member of the Legislative Assembly. **2.** Modern Language Association (of America).

MLC (in India and Australia) *abbrev. for* Member of the Legislative Council.

MLD *abbrev. for* minimum lethal dose (the smallest amount of a drug or toxic agent that will kill a laboratory animal).

MLF *abbrev. for* multilateral (nuclear) force.

MLG *abbrev. for* Middle Low German.

MLitt *abbrev. for* Master of Letters. [Latin *Magister Litterarum*]

Mlle *pl.* **Mlles** the French equivalent of **Miss.** [from French *Mademoiselle*]

MLR *abbrev. for* minimum lending rate.

mm **1.** *symbol for* millimetre. **2.** *abbrev. for* mutatis mutandis.

MM **1.** *abbrev. for* Military Medal. **2.** the French equivalent of **Messrs.** [from French *Messieurs*]

MMC (in Britain) *abbrev. for* Monopolies and Mergers Commission.

MMDS *abbrev. for* multipoint microwave distribution system: a radio alternative to cable television. Sometimes shortened to **MDS.**

Mme *pl.* **Mmes** the French equivalent of **Mrs.** [from French *Madame, Mesdames*]

mmf *abbrev. for* magnetomotive force.

mmHg *abbrev. for* millimetre(s) of mercury (a unit of pressure equal to the pressure that can support a column of mercury 1 millimetre high).

MMM (in Canada) *abbrev. for* Member of the Order of Military Merit.

MMR *n.* a combined vaccine against measles, mumps, and rubella, given to young children.

MMus. *abbrev. for* Master of Music.

Mn *the chemical symbol for* manganese.

MN *abbrev. for:* **1.** (in Britain) Merchant Navy. **2.** Minnesota.

MNA (in Canada) *abbrev. for* Member of the National Assembly (of Quebec).

mnemonic (nɪ'mɒnɪk) *adj.* **1.** aiding or meant to aid one's memory. **2.** of or relating to memory or mnemonics. ~*n.* **3.** something, such as a verse, to assist memory. [C18: from Greek *mnēmonikos,* from *mnēmōn* mindful, from *mnasthai* to remember] —**mne'monically** *adv.*

mnemonics (nɪ'mɒnɪks) *n.* (*usually functioning as sing.*) **1.** the art or practice of improving or of aiding the memory. **2.** a system of rules to aid the memory.

mo (məʊ) *n. Informal.* **1.** *Chiefly Brit.* short for **moment** (sense 1) (esp. in the phrase **half a mo**). **2.** *Chiefly Austral.* short for **moustache** (sense 1).

Mo *the chemical symbol for* molybdenum.

MO *abbrev. for:* **1.** Missouri. **2.** Medical Officer.

mo. *pl.* **mos.** *abbrev. for* month.

Mo. *abbrev. for* Missouri.

m.o. *or* **MO** *abbrev. for:* **1.** mail order. **2.** money order.

-mo *suffix forming nouns.* (in bookbinding) indicating book size by specifying the number of leaves formed by folding one sheet of paper: *12mo, twelvemo,* or *duodecimo; 16mo* or *sixteenmo.* [abstracted from DUODECIMO]

moa ('məʊə) *n.* any large flightless bird of the recently extinct order *Dinornithiformes* of New Zealand (see **ratite**). [C19: from Maori]

Moabite ('məʊəˌbaɪt) *adj.* **1.** of or relating to the ancient kingdom of Moab, east of the Dead Sea. ~*n.* **2.** an inhabitant of Moab.

moa hunter *n.* the name given by anthropologists to the early Maori inhabitants of New Zealand.

moan (məʊn) *n.* **1.** a low prolonged mournful sound expressive of suffering or pleading. **2.** any similar mournful sound, esp. that made by the wind. **3.** a grumble or complaint. ~*vb.* **4.** to utter (words) in a low mournful manner. **5.** (*intr.*) to make a sound like a moan. **6.** (*usually intr.*) to grumble or complain (esp. in the phrase **moan and groan**). [C13: related to Old English *mǣnan* to grieve over] —'**moaner** *n.* —'**moanful** *adj.* —'**moaning** *n., adj.* —'**moaningly** *adv.*

moat (məʊt) *n.* **1.** a wide water-filled ditch surrounding a fortified place, such as a castle. ~*vb.* **2.** (*tr.*) to surround with or as if with a moat: *a moated grange.* [C14: from Old French *motte* mound]

mob (mɒb) *n.* **1. a.** a riotous or disorderly crowd of people; rabble. **b.** (*as modifier*): *mob law; mob violence.* **2.** *Often derogatory.* a group or class of people, animals, or things. **3.** *N.Z.* a flock (of sheep) or a herd (of cattle, esp. when droving). **4.** *Often derogatory.* the masses. **5.** *Slang.* a gang of criminals. ~*vb.* **mobs, mobbing, mobbed.** (*tr.*) **6.** to attack in a group resembling a mob. **7.** to surround, esp. in order to acclaim: *they mobbed the film star.* **8.** to crowd into (a building, plaza, etc.). **9.** (of a group of animals of a prey species) to harass (a predator). ~See also **mobs.** [C17: shortened from Latin *mōbile vulgus* the fickle populace; see MOBILE] —'**mobber** *n.* —'**mobbish** *adj.*

mobcap ('mɒbˌkæp) *n.* a woman's large cotton cap with a pouched crown and usually a frill, worn esp. during the 18th century. Often shortened to **mob.** [C18: from obsolete *mob* woman, esp. a loose-living woman, + CAP]

mobile ('məʊbaɪl) *adj.* **1.** having freedom of movement; movable. **2.** changing quickly in expression: *a mobile face.* **3.** *Sociol.* (of individuals or social groups) moving within and between classes, occupations, and localities: *upwardly mobile.* **4.** (of military forces) able to move freely and quickly to any given area. **5.** (*postpositive*) *Informal.* having transport available: *are you mobile tonight?* ~*n.* **6. a.** a sculpture suspended in midair with delicately balanced parts that are set in motion by air currents. **b.** (*as modifier*): *mobile sculpture.* **7.** short for **mobile library.** [C15: via Old French from Latin *mōbilis,* from *movēre* to move]

-mobile (məʊˌbiːl) *suffix forming nouns.* indicating a vehicle designed for a particular person or purpose: *Popemobile.*

mobile home *n.* living quarters mounted on wheels and capable of being towed by a motor vehicle.

mobile library *n.* a vehicle providing lending library facilities. U.S. and Canadian equivalent: **bookmobile.**

mobility (məʊ'bɪlɪtɪ) *n.* **1.** the ability to move physically: *a handicapped person's mobility may be limited; mobility is part of physical education.* **2.** *Sociol.* (of individuals or social groups) moving within or between classes, occupations, and localities. See also **vertical mobility, horizontal mobility.**

mobility housing *n. Social welfare.* houses designed or adapted for people who have difficulty in walking but are not necessarily chairbound. See also **wheelchair housing.**

mobilize *or* **mobilise** ('məʊbɪˌlaɪz) *vb.* **1.** to prepare for war or other emergency by organizing (national resources, the armed services, etc.). **2.** (*tr.*) to organize for a purpose; marshal. **3.** (*tr.*) to put into motion, circulation, or use. —'**mobiˌlizable** *or* '**mobiˌlisable** *adj.* —ˌ**mobili'zation** *or* ˌ**mobili'sation** *n.*

Möbius strip ('mɜːbɪəs; *German* 'møːbiʊs) *n. Maths.* a one-sided continuous surface, formed by twisting a long narrow rectangular strip of material through 180° and joining the ends. [C19: named after August *Möbius* (1790–1868), German mathematician who invented it]

mobocracy (mɒ'bɒkrəsɪ) *n., pl.* **-cies.** **1.** rule or domination by a mob. **2.** the mob that rules. —**mobocrat** ('mɒbəˌkræt) *n.* —ˌ**mobo'cratic** *or* ˌ**mobo'cratical** *adj.*

mobs (mɒbz) *Informal.* ~*pl. n.* **1.** (usually foll. by *of*) great numbers or quantities; lots: *mobs of people.* ~*adv.* **2.** *Austral. and N.Z.* a great deal: *mobs better.*

mobster ('mɒbstə) *n.* a U.S. slang word for **gangster.**

MoC *abbrev. for* mother of the chapel.

moccasin ('mɒkəsɪn) *n.* **1.** a shoe of soft leather, esp. deerskin, worn by North American Indians. **2.** any soft shoe resembling this. **3.** *N.Z.* a sheepshearer's footgear, usually made of sacking. **4.** short for **water moccasin.** [C17: from Algonquian; compare Narraganset *mocussin* shoe]

moccasin flower *n.* any of several North American orchids of the genus *Cypripedium* with a pink solitary flower. See also **lady's-slipper, cypripedium** (sense 1).

moccasin telegraph *n. Canadian informal.* the transmission of rumour or secret information; the grapevine.
mocha ('mɒkə) *n.* **1.** a strongly flavoured dark brown coffee originally imported from the Arabian port of Mocha. **2.** a flavouring made from coffee and chocolate. **3.** a soft glove leather with a suede finish, made from goatskin or sheepskin. **4. a.** a dark brown colour. **b.** (*as adj.*): *mocha shoes.*
mocha stone *n.* another name for **moss agate.**
mock (mɒk) *vb.* **1.** (when *intr.*, often foll. by *at*) to behave with scorn or contempt (towards); show ridicule (for). **2.** (*tr.*) to imitate, esp. in fun; mimic. **3.** (*tr.*) to deceive, disappoint, or delude. **4.** (*tr.*) to defy or frustrate: *the team mocked the visitors' attempt to score.* ~*n.* **5.** the act of mocking. **6.** a person or thing mocked. **7.** a counterfeit; imitation. **8.** (*often pl.*) *Informal.* (in England and Wales) the school examinations taken as practice before public examinations. ~*adj.* (*prenominal*) **9.** sham or counterfeit. **10.** serving as an imitation or substitute, esp. for practice purposes: *a mock battle; mock finals.* ~See also **mock-up.** [C15: from Old French *mocquer*] —'**mockable** *adj.* —'**mocker** *n.* —'**mocking** *n., adj.* —'**mockingly** *adv.*
mocker ('mɒkə) *n. Austral. slang.* **1.** clothing. **2. all mockered up.** dressed up. [of unknown origin]
mockernut ('mɒkəˌnʌt) *n.* **1.** Also called: **black hickory.** a species of smooth-barked hickory, *Carya tomentosa,* with fragrant foliage that turns bright yellow in autumn. **2.** the nut of this tree. [so called because the nut is difficult to extract]
mockers ('mɒkəz) *pl. n. Informal.* **put the mockers on.** to ruin the chances of success of. Also (Austral.): **put the mock** (*or* **mocks) on.** [C20: perhaps from MOCK]
mockery ('mɒkərɪ) *n., pl.* **-eries. 1.** ridicule, contempt, or derision. **2.** a derisive action or comment. **3.** an imitation or pretence, esp. a derisive one. **4.** a person or thing that is mocked. **5.** a person, thing, or action that is inadequate or disappointing.
mock-heroic *adj.* **1.** (of a literary work, esp. a poem) imitating the style of heroic poetry in order to satirize an unheroic subject, as in Pope's *The Rape of the Lock.* ~*n.* **2.** burlesque imitation of the heroic style or a single work in this style.
mockingbird ('mɒkɪŋˌbɜːd) *n.* any American songbird of the family *Mimidae,* having a long tail and grey plumage: noted for their ability to mimic the song of other birds.
mock moon *n.* another name for **paraselene.**
mock orange *n.* **1.** Also called: **syringa.** any shrub of the genus *Philadelphus,* esp. *P. coronarius,* with white fragrant flowers resembling those of the orange: family *Philadelphaceae.* **2.** any other shrub or tree resembling the orange tree.
mock sun *n.* another name for **parhelion.**
mock turtle soup *n.* an imitation turtle soup made from a calf's head.
mock-up *n.* **1.** a working full-scale model of a machine, apparatus, etc., for testing, research, etc. **2.** a layout of printed matter. ~*vb.* **mock up. 3.** (*tr., adv.*) to build or make a mock-up of.
mod[1] (mɒd) *n. Brit.* **a.** a member of a group of teenagers in the mid-1960s, noted for their clothes-consciousness and opposition to the rockers. **b.** a member of a revived group of this type in the late 1970s and early 1980s, noted also for their clothes-consciousness and opposition to the skinheads. **c.** (*as modifier*): *a mod haircut.* [C20: from MODERNIST]
mod[2] (mɒd) *n.* an annual Highland Gaelic meeting with musical and literary competitions. [C19: from Gaelic *mōd* assembly, from Old Norse; related to MOOT]
MOD (in Britain) *abbrev. for* Ministry of Defence.
mod. *abbrev. for:* **1.** moderate. **2.** moderato. **3.** modern.
modal ('məʊdᵊl) *adj.* **1.** of, relating to, or characteristic of mode or manner. **2.** *Grammar.* (of a verb form or auxiliary verb) expressing a distinction of mood, such as that between possibility and actuality. The modal auxiliaries in English include *can, do, may, must, need, ought, shall, should, will,* and *would.* **3.** *Philosophy, logic.* **a.** qualifying or expressing a qualification of the truth of some statement, for example, as necessary or contingent. **b.** relating to analogous qualifications such as that of rules as obligatory or permissive. **4.** *Metaphysics.* of or relating to the form of a thing as opposed to its attributes, substance, etc. **5.** *Music.* of or relating to a mode. **6.** of or relating to a statistical mode. —'**modally** *adv.*
modality (məʊ'dælɪtɪ) *n., pl.* **-ties. 1.** the condition of being modal. **2.** a quality, attribute, or circumstance that denotes mode, mood, or manner. **3.** *Logic.* the property of a statement of being classified under one of the concepts studied by modal logic, esp. necessity or possibility. **4.** any physical or electrical therapeutic method or agency. **5.** any of the five senses.
modal logic *n.* **1.** the logical study of such philosophical concepts as necessity, possibility, contingency, etc. **2.** the logical study of concepts whose formal properties resemble certain moral, epistemological, and psychological concepts. See also **alethic, deontic, epistemic, doxastic. 3.** any formal system capable of being interpreted as a model for the behaviour of such concepts.
mod cons *pl. n. Informal.* modern conveniences; the usual installations of a modern house, such as hot water, heating, etc.
mode (məʊd) *n.* **1.** a manner or way of doing, acting, or existing. **2.** the current fashion or style. **3.** *Music.* **a.** any of the various scales of notes within one octave, esp. any of the twelve natural diatonic scales taken in ascending order used in plainsong, folk song, and art music until 1600. **b.** (in the music of classical Greece) any of the descending diatonic scales from which the liturgical modes evolved. **c.** either of the two main scale systems in music since 1600: *major mode; minor mode.* **4.** *Logic, linguistics.* another name for **modality** (sense 3) or **mood**[2] (sense 2). **5.** *Philosophy.* a complex combination of ideas the realization of which is not determined by the component ideas. **6.** that one of a range of values that has the highest frequency as determined statistically. Compare **mean**[3] (sense 4), **median** (sense 6). **7.** the quantitative mineral composition of an igneous rock. **8.** *Physics.* one of the possible configurations of a travelling or stationary wave. **9.** *Physics.* one of the fundamental vibrations. [C14: from Latin *modus* measure, manner]
model ('mɒdᵊl) *n.* **1. a.** a representation, usually on a smaller scale, of a device, structure, etc. **b.** (*as modifier*): *a model train.* **2. a.** a standard to be imitated: *she was my model for good scholarship.* **b.** (*as modifier*): *a model wife.* **3.** a representative form, style, or pattern. **4.** a person who poses for a sculptor, painter, or photographer. **5.** a person who wears clothes to display them to prospective buyers; mannequin. **6.** a preparatory sculpture in clay, wax, etc., from which the finished work is copied. **7.** a design or style, esp. one of a series of designs of a particular product: *last year's model.* **8.** *Brit.* **a.** an original unique article of clothing. **b.** (*as modifier*): *a model coat.* **9.** a simplified representation or description of a system or complex entity, esp. one designed to facilitate calculations and predictions. **10.** *Logic.* **a.** an interpretation of a formal system under which the theorems derivable in that system are mapped onto truths. **b.** a theory in which a given sentence is true. ~*vb.* **-els, -elling, -elled** *or U.S.* **-els, -eling, -eled. 11.** to make a model of (something or someone). **12.** to form in clay, wax, etc.; mould. **13.** to display (clothing and accessories) as a mannequin. **14.** to plan or create according to a model or models. **15.** to arrange studio lighting so that highlights and shadows emphasize the desired features of a human form or an inanimate object. [C16: from Old French *modelle,* from Italian *modello,* from Latin *modulus,* diminutive of *modus* MODE] —'**modeller** *or U.S.* '**modeler** *n.*
modelling *or U.S.* **modeling** ('mɒdᵊlɪŋ) *n.* **1.** the act or an instance of making a model. **2.** the practice or occupation of a person who models clothes. **3.** a technique in psychotherapy in which the therapist encourages the patient to model his behaviour on his own.
model theory *n.* the branch of logic that deals with the properties of models; the semantic study of formal systems. —ˌ**model-ˌtheo'retic** *adj.*
modem ('məʊdɛm) *n. Computer technol.* a device for connecting two computers by a telephone line, consisting of a modulator that converts computer signals into audio signals and a corresponding demodulator. [C20: from *mo(dulator) dem(odulator)*]
Modena (*Italian* 'mɔːdena) *n.* (*sometimes not cap.*) a popular variety of domestic fancy pigeon originating in Modena, a city in N Italy.
moderate *adj.* ('mɒdərɪt, 'mɒdrɪt). **1.** not extreme or excessive; within due or reasonable limits: *moderate demands.* **2.** not violent; mild or temperate. **3.** of average quality or extent: *moderate success.* ~*n.* ('mɒdərɪt, 'mɒdrɪt). **4.** a person who holds moderate views, esp. in politics. ~*vb.* ('mɒdəˌreɪt). **5.** to become or cause to become less extreme or violent. **6.** (when *intr.*, often foll. by *over*) to preside over a meeting, discussion, etc. **7.** *Brit. and N.Z.* to act as an external moderator of the overall standards and marks for (some types of school examinations). **8.** *Physics.* to slow down (neutrons), esp. by using a moderator. [C14: from Latin *moderātus* observing moderation, from *moderārī* to restrain] —'**moderately** *adv.* —'**moderateness** *n.* —'**moderatism** *n.*
moderate breeze *n.* a wind of force four on the Beaufort scale.
moderate gale *n.* a gale of force seven on the Beaufort scale, capable of swaying trees.
moderation (ˌmɒdə'reɪʃən) *n.* **1.** the state or an instance of being moderate. **2.** the act of moderating. **3. in moderation.** within moderate or reasonable limits.
Moderations (ˌmɒdə'reɪʃənz) *pl. n.* short for **Honour Moderations.**
moderato (ˌmɒdə'rɑːtəʊ) *adv. Music.* **1.** at a moderate tempo. **2.** (preceded by a tempo marking) a direction indicating that the tempo specified is to be used with restraint: *allegro moderato.* [C18: from Italian, from Latin *moderātus;* see MODERATE]
moderator ('mɒdəˌreɪtə) *n.* **1.** a person or thing that moderates. **2.** *Presbyterian Church.* a minister appointed to preside over a Church court, synod, or general assembly. **3.** a presiding officer at a public or legislative assembly. **4.** a material, such as heavy water or graphite, used for slowing down neutrons in the cores of nuclear reactors so that they have more chance of inducing nuclear fission. **5.** an examiner at Oxford or Cambridge Universities in first public examinations. **6.** (in Britain and New Zealand) one who is responsible for consistency of standards in the grading of some public examinations. —'**modeˌratorship** *n.*
modern ('mɒdən) *adj.* **1.** of, involving, or befitting the present or a recent time; contemporary. **2.** of, relating to, or characteristic of contemporary styles or schools of art, literature, music, etc., esp. those of an experimental kind. **3.** belonging or relating to

the period in history from the end of the Middle Ages to the present. ~*n.* **4.** a contemporary person. **5.** *Printing.* a type style that originated around the beginning of the 19th century, characterized chiefly by marked contrast between thick and thin strokes. Compare **old face.** [C16: from Old French, from Late Latin *modernus,* from *modō* (adv.) just recently, from *modus* MODE] —'**modernly** *adv.* —'**modernness** *n.*

modern dance *n.* a style of free and expressive theatrical dancing not bound by the classical rules of ballet.

moderne (mə'dɛən) *adj. Chiefly U.S.* of or relating to the style of architecture and design, prevalent in Europe and the U.S. in the late 1920s and 1930s, typified by the use of straight lines, tubular chromed steel frames, contrasting inlaid woods, etc. Compare **Art Deco.**

Modern English *n.* the English language since about 1450, esp. any of the standard forms developed from the S East Midland dialect of Middle English. See also **English, Middle English, Old English.**

modern greats *pl. n.* (at Oxford University) the Honour School of Philosophy, Politics, and Economics.

Modern Greek *n.* the Greek language since about 1453 A.D. (the fall of Byzantium). Compare **Demotic, Katharevusa.**

Modern Hebrew *n.* the official language of the state of Israel; a revived form of ancient Hebrew.

modernism ('mɒdəˌnɪzəm) *n.* **1.** modern tendencies, characteristics, thoughts, etc., or the support of these. **2.** something typical of contemporary life or thought. **3.** a 20th-century divergence in the arts from previous traditions, esp. in architecture. See **international modernism.** **4.** (*cap.*) *R.C. Church.* the movement at the end of the 19th and beginning of the 20th centuries that sought to adapt doctrine to the supposed requirements of modern thought. —'**modernist** *n., adj.* —ˌ**modern'istic** *adj.* —ˌ**modern'istically** *adv.*

modernity (mɒ'dɜːnɪtɪ) *n., pl.* **-ties.** **1.** the quality or state of being modern. **2.** something modern.

modernize *or* **modernise** ('mɒdəˌnaɪz) *vb.* **1.** (*tr.*) to make modern in appearance or style: *to modernize a room.* **2.** (*intr.*) to adopt modern ways, ideas, etc. —ˌ**moderni'zation** *or* ˌ**moderni'sation** *n.* —'**modernˌizer** *or* '**modernˌiser** *n.*

modern jazz *n.* any of the styles of jazz that evolved between the early 1940s and the later emergence of avant-garde jazz, characterized by a greater harmonic and rhythmic complexity than hitherto.

modern pentathlon *n.* an athletic contest consisting of five different events: horse riding with jumps, fencing with electric épée, freestyle swimming, pistol shooting, and cross-country running.

modern sequence dancing *n.* a form of dancing in which ballroom dance steps are used as the basis of a wide variety of different dances typically performed in a sequence.

modest ('mɒdɪst) *adj.* **1.** having or expressing a humble opinion of oneself or one's accomplishments or abilities. **2.** reserved or shy: *modest behaviour.* **3.** not ostentatious or pretentious. **4.** not extreme or excessive; moderate. **5.** decorous or decent. [C16: via Old French from Latin *modestus* moderate, from *modus* MODE] —'**modestly** *adv.*

modesty ('mɒdɪstɪ) *n., pl.* **-ties.** the quality or condition of being modest.

modge (mɒdʒ) *vb.* (*tr.*) *Midland English dialect.* to do shoddily; make a mess of. [C20: perhaps a variant of *mudge* to crush (hops)]

modicum ('mɒdɪkəm) *n.* a small amount or portion. [C15: from Latin: a little way, from *modicus* moderate]

modification (ˌmɒdɪfɪ'keɪʃən) *n.* **1.** the act of modifying or the condition of being modified. **2.** something modified; the result of a modification. **3.** a small change or adjustment. **4.** *Grammar.* the relation between a modifier and the word or phrase that it modifies. —'**modifiˌcatory** *or* '**modifiˌcative** *adj.*

modifier ('mɒdɪˌfaɪə) *n.* **1.** Also called: **qualifier.** *Grammar.* a word or phrase that qualifies the sense of another word; for example, the noun *alarm* is a modifier of *clock* in *alarm clock* and the phrase *every day* is an adverbial modifier of *walks* in *he walks every day.* **2.** a person or thing that modifies.

▷**Usage.** Nouns are frequently used in English to modify other nouns: *police officer; chicken farm.* They should be used with restraint, however, esp. when the appropriate adjective can be used without awkwardness: *lunar research* (not *moon research*).

modify ('mɒdɪˌfaɪ) *vb.* **-fies, -fying, -fied.** (*mainly tr.*) **1.** to change the structure, character, intent, etc., of. **2.** to make less extreme or uncompromising: *to modify a demand.* **3.** *Grammar.* (of a word or group of words) to bear the relation of modifier to (another word or group of words). **4.** *Linguistics.* to change (a vowel) by umlaut. **5.** (*intr.*) to be or become modified. [C14: from Old French *modifier,* from Latin *modificāre* to limit, control, from *modus* measure + *facere* to make] —'**modiˌfiable** *adj.* —ˌ**modiˌfia'bility** *or* '**modiˌfiableness** *n.*

modillion (mə'dɪljən) *n. Architect.* one of a set of ornamental brackets under a cornice, esp. as used in the Corinthian order. Compare **mutule.** [C16: via French from Italian *modiglione,* probably from Vulgar Latin *mutiliō* (unattested), from Latin *mūtulus* MUTULE]

modiolus (məʊ'daɪəʊləs, mə-) *n., pl.* **-li** (-ˌlaɪ). the central bony pillar of the cochlea. [C19: New Latin, from Latin: hub of a wheel, from *modus* a measure]

modish ('məʊdɪʃ) *adj.* in the current fashion or style; contemporary. —'**modishly** *adv.* —'**modishness** *n.*

modiste (məʊ'diːst) *n.* a fashionable dressmaker or milliner. [C19: from French, from *mode* fashion]

Mods (mɒdz) *n.* (at Oxford University) short for **Honour Moderations.**

modular ('mɒdjʊlə) *adj.* of, consisting of, or resembling a module or modulus. —**modularity** (ˌmɒdjʊ'lærɪtɪ) *n.*

modulate ('mɒdjʊˌleɪt) *vb.* **1.** (*tr.*) to change the tone, pitch, or volume of. **2.** (*tr.*) to adjust or regulate the degree of. **3.** *Music.* **a.** to subject to or undergo modulation in music. **b.** (often foll. by *to*) to make or become in tune (with a pitch, key, etc.). **4.** (*tr.*) *Physics, electronics.* to cause to vary by a process of modulation. [C16: from Latin *modulātus* in due measure, melodious, from *modulārī* to regulate, from *modus* measure] —**modulability** (ˌmɒdjʊlə'bɪlɪtɪ) *n.* —'**modulative** *or* '**modulatory** *adj.* —'**moduˌlator** *n.*

modulation (ˌmɒdjʊ'leɪʃən) *n.* **1.** the act of modulating or the condition of being modulated. **2.** *Music.* the transition from one key to another. **3.** *Grammar.* **a.** another word for **intonation** (sense 1). **b.** the grammatical expression of modality. **4.** *Electrical engineering.* **a.** the act or process of superimposing the amplitude, frequency, phase, etc., of a wave or signal onto another wave or signal or onto an electron beam. See also **amplitude modulation, frequency modulation, phase modulation, velocity modulation.** **b.** the variation of the modulated signal.

module ('mɒdjuːl) *n.* **1.** a standard unit of measure, esp. one used to coordinate the dimensions of buildings and components; in classical architecture, half the diameter of a column at the base of the shaft. **2.** a self-contained unit or item, such as an assembly of electronic components and associated wiring or a segment of computer software, which itself performs a defined task and can be linked with other such units to form a larger system. **3.** a standardized unit designed to be added to or used as part of an arrangement of similar units, as in furniture. **4.** *Astronautics.* any of several self-contained separable units making up a spacecraft or launch vehicle, each of which has one or more specified tasks: *command module; service module.* **5.** *Education.* a short course of study, esp. of a vocational or technical subject, that together with other such completed courses can count towards a particular qualification. [C16: from Latin *modulus,* diminutive of *modus* MODE]

modulus ('mɒdjʊləs) *n., pl.* **-li** (-ˌlaɪ). **1.** *Physics.* a coefficient expressing a specified property of a specified substance. See **bulk modulus, modulus of rigidity, Young's modulus.** **2.** *Maths.* another name for the **absolute value** (sense 2) of a complex number. **3.** *Maths.* the number by which a logarithm to one base is multiplied to give the corresponding logarithm to another base. **4.** *Maths.* an integer that can be divided exactly into the difference between two other integers: *7 is a modulus of 25 and 11.* See also **congruence** (sense 2). [C16: from Latin, diminutive of *modus* measure]

modulus of elasticity *n.* the ratio of the stress applied to a body or substance to the resulting strain within the elastic limit. Also called: **elastic modulus.** See also **Young's modulus, bulk modulus, modulus of rigidity.**

modulus of rigidity *n.* a modulus of elasticity equal to the ratio of the tangential force per unit area to the resulting angular deformation. Symbol: *G*

modus operandi ('məʊdəs ˌɒpə'rændiː, -'rændaɪ) *n., pl.* **modi operandi** ('məʊdiː ˌɒpə'rændiː, 'məʊdaɪ ˌɒpə'rændaɪ). procedure; method of operating. [C17: from Latin]

modus ponens *Latin.* ('məʊdəs 'pəʊˌnɛnz) *n. Logic.* the principle that whenever a conditional statement and its antecedent are given to be true its consequent may be validly inferred, as in *if it's Tuesday this must be Belgium* and *it's Tuesday so this must be Belgium.* [literally: mood that affirms]

modus tollens *Latin.* ('məʊdəs 'tɒlˌɛnz) *n. Logic.* the principle that whenever a conditional statement and the negation of its consequent are given to be true, the negation of its antecedent may be validly inferred, as in *if it's Tuesday this must be Belgium* and *this isn't Belgium so it's not Tuesday.* [literally: mood that denies]

modus vivendi ('məʊdəs vɪ'vɛndiː, -'vɛndaɪ) *n., pl.* **modi vivendi** ('məʊdiː vɪ'vɛndiː, 'məʊdaɪ vɪ'vɛndaɪ). a working arrangement between conflicting interests; practical compromise. [C19: from Latin: way of living]

mofette (məʊ'fɛt) *n.* an opening in a region of nearly extinct volcanic activity, through which carbon dioxide, nitrogen, and other gases pass. [C19: from French, from Neapolitan Italian *mofeta;* compare dialect German *muffezen* to smell fetid]

mog (mɒg) *or* **moggy** ('mɒgɪ) *n., pl.* **mogs** *or* **moggies.** *Brit.* a slang name for **cat**[1] (sense 1). [C20: of dialect origin, originally a pet name for a cow]

Mogadon ('mɒgəˌdɒn) *n. Trademark.* a benzodiazepine drug, a preparation of nitrazepam, used to treat insomnia.

Mogen David ('məʊgən 'deɪvɪd) *n.* another name for the **Star of David.**

mogul[1] ('məʊgʌl, məʊ'gʌl) *n.* **1.** an important or powerful person. **2.** a type of steam locomotive with a wheel arrangement of two leading wheels, six driving wheels, and no trailing wheels. [C18: from MOGUL]

mogul[2] ('məʊgᵊl) *n.* a mound of hard snow on a ski slope. [C20: perhaps from South German dialect *Mugl*]
Mogul ('məʊgʌl, məʊ'gʌl) *n.* **1.** a member of the Muslim dynasty of Indian emperors established in 1526. **2.** a Muslim Indian, Mongol, or Mongolian. ~*adj.* **3.** of or relating to the Moguls or their empire. [C16: from Persian *mughul* Mongol]
MOH (in Britain) *abbrev. for* Medical Officer of Health.
mohair ('məʊˌhɛə) *n.* **1.** Also called: **angora.** the long soft silky hair that makes up the outer coat of the Angora goat. **2. a.** a fabric made from the yarn of this hair and cotton or wool. **b.** (*as modifier*): *a mohair suit.* [C16: variant (influenced by *hair*) of earlier *mocayare,* ultimately from Arabic *mukhayyar,* literally: choice, from *khayyara* to choose]
Moham. *abbrev. for* Mohammedan.
Mohammedan (məʊ'hæmɪdᵊn) *n., adj.* another word, formerly common in Western usage but never used among Muslims, for **Muslim.** [from *Mohammed* (?570–632 A.D.), prophet and founder of Islam, + -AN]
Mohammedanism (məʊ'hæmɪdᵊˌnɪzəm) *n.* a name, formerly common in Western usage but never used among Muslims, for the Muslim religion; Islam. See **Islam.**
Mohammedanize *or* **Mohammedanise** (məʊ'hæmɪdᵊˌnaɪz) *vb.* (*tr.*) to convert or subject to the religious or cultural influence of Islam; Islamize.
Moharram (məʊ'hærəm) *n.* a variant of **Muharram.**
Mohave *or* **Mojave** (məʊ'hɑːvɪ) *n.* **1.** (*pl.* **-ves** *or* **-ve**) a member of a North American Indian people formerly living along the Colorado River in SW North America. **2.** the language of this people, belonging to the Yuman family.
mohawk ('məʊhɔːk) *n. Ice skating.* a half turn from either edge of either skate to the corresponding edge of the other skate. [C19: after MOHAWK]
Mohawk ('məʊhɔːk) *n.* **1.** (*pl.* **-hawks** *or* **-hawk**) a member of a North American Indian people formerly living along the Mohawk River in the northeastern U.S.; one of the Iroquois peoples. **2.** the language of this people, belonging to the Iroquoian family.
mohel ('mɔɛl, mɔɪl) *n. Judaism.* a man qualified to conduct circumcisions. [from Hebrew]
mohican (məʊ'hiːkən) *n.* **1.** a punk hairstyle in which the head is shaved at the sides and the remaining strip of hair is worn stiffly erect and sometimes brightly coloured. **2.** a person wearing such a hairstyle.
Mohican ('məʊɪkən, məʊ'hiːkən) *n., pl.* **-cans** *or* **-can.** a variant of **Mahican.**
Moho ('məʊhəʊ) *n.* short for **Mohorovičić discontinuity.**
Mohock ('məʊhɒk) *n.* (in 18th-century London) one of a group of aristocratic ruffians, who attacked people in the streets at night. [C18: variant of MOHAWK]
Mohole ('məʊˌhəʊl) *n.* an abandoned research project to drill through the earth's crust down to the Mohorovičić discontinuity to obtain samples of mantle rocks. [C20: from *Moho(rovičić)* + HOLE. See MOHOROVIČIĆ DISCONTINUITY]
Mohorovičić discontinuity (ˌməʊhə'rəʊvɪtʃɪtʃ) *n.* the boundary between the earth's crust and mantle, across which there is a sudden change in the velocity of seismic waves. Often shortened to **Moho.** [C20: named after Andrija *Mohorovičić* (1857–1936), Yugoslav geologist]
Mohs scale (məʊz) *n.* a scale for expressing the hardness of solids by comparing them with ten standards ranging from talc, with a value of 0, to diamond, with a value of 10. [C19: named after Friedrich *Mohs* (1773–1839), German mineralogist]
mohur ('məʊhə) *n.* a former Indian gold coin worth 15 rupees. [C17: from Hindi]
MOI *abbrev. for* Ministry of Information (now superseded by **COI**).
moidore ('mɔɪdɔː) *n.* a former Portuguese gold coin. [C18: from Portuguese *moeda de ouro:* money of gold]
moiety ('mɔɪɪtɪ) *n., pl.* **-ties.** **1.** a half. **2.** one of two parts or divisions of something. [C15: from Old French *moitié,* from Latin *mediētās* middle, from *medius*]
moil (mɔɪl) *Archaic or dialect.* ~*vb.* **1.** to moisten or soil or become moist, soiled, etc. **2.** (*intr.*) to toil or drudge (esp. in the phrase **toil and moil**). ~*n.* **3.** toil; drudgery. **4.** confusion; turmoil. [C14 (to moisten; later: to work hard in unpleasantly wet conditions) from Old French *moillier,* ultimately from Latin *mollis* soft] —'**moiler** *n.*
moire (mwɑː) *n.* a fabric, usually silk, having a watered effect. [C17: from French, earlier *mouaire,* from MOHAIR]
moiré ('mwɑːreɪ) *adj.* **1.** having a watered or wavelike pattern. ~*n.* **2.** such a pattern, impressed on fabrics by means of engraved rollers. **3.** any fabric having such a pattern; moire. **4.** Also: **moiré pattern.** a pattern seen when two geometrical patterns, such as grids, are visually superimposed. [C17: from French, from *moire* MOHAIR]
Moism ('məʊɪzəm) *n.* the religious and ethical teaching of the Chinese philosopher Mo-Zi (?470–?391 B.C.) and his followers, emphasizing universal love, ascetic self-discipline, and obedience to the will of Heaven.
moist (mɔɪst) *adj.* **1.** slightly damp or wet. **2.** saturated with or suggestive of moisture. [C14: from Old French, ultimately related to Latin *mūcidus* musty, from *mūcus* MUCUS] —'**moistly** *adv.* —'**moistness** *n.*
moisten ('mɔɪsᵊn) *vb.* to make or become moist. —'**moistener** *n.*
moisture ('mɔɪstʃə) *n.* water or other liquid diffused as vapour or condensed on or in objects. —'**moistureless** *adj.*
moisturize *or* **moisturise** ('mɔɪstʃəˌraɪz) *vb.* (*tr.*) to add or restore moisture to (the air, the skin, etc.). —'**moisturˌizer** *or* '**moisturˌiser** *n.*
moither ('mɔɪðə) *or* **moider** ('mɔɪdə) *vb. Dialect.* **1.** (*tr.; usually passive*) to bother or bewilder. **2.** (*intr.*) to talk in a rambling or confused manner. [C17: of obscure origin]
Mojave (məʊ'hɑːvɪ) *n.* a variant spelling of **Mohave.**
moke (məʊk) *n.* **1.** *Brit.* a slang name for **donkey** (sense 1). **2.** *Austral. slang.* an inferior type of horse. [C19: origin obscure]
moki ('məʊkɪ) *n., pl.* **mokis** *or* **moki.** either of two edible sea fish of New Zealand, the blue cod (*Percis colias*) or the bastard trumpeter (*Latridopsis ciliaris*). [Maori]
moko ('məʊkəʊ) *n., pl.* **mokos.** *N.Z.* a Maori tattoo or tattoo pattern. [Maori]
mol *Chem. symbol for* mole[3].
mol. *abbrev. for:* **1.** molecular. **2.** molecule.
mola ('məʊlə) *n., pl.* **-la** *or* **-las.** another name for **sunfish** (sense 1). [C17: from Latin, literally: millstone]
molal ('məʊləl) *adj. Chem.* of or consisting of a solution containing one mole of solute per thousand grams of solution. [C20: from MOLE[3] + -AL[1]]
molality (mɒ'lælɪtɪ) *n., pl.* **-ties.** (not in technical usage) a measure of concentration equal to the number of moles of solute in a thousand grams of solvent.
molar[1] ('məʊlə) *n.* **1.** any of the 12 broad-faced grinding teeth in man. **2.** a corresponding tooth in other mammals. ~*adj.* **3.** of, relating to, or designating any of these teeth. **4.** used for or capable of grinding. [C16: from Latin *molāris* for grinding, from *mola* millstone]
molar[2] ('məʊlə) *adj.* **1.** (of a physical quantity) per unit amount of substance: *molar volume.* **2.** (not recommended in technical usage) (of a solution) containing one mole of solute per litre of solution. [C19: from Latin *mōlēs* a mass]
molarity (mɒ'lærɪtɪ) *n.* another name (not in technical usage) for **concentration** (sense 4).
molasse (mə'læs) *n.* a soft sediment produced by the erosion of mountain ranges after the final phase of mountain building. [C18: from French, perhaps alteration of *mollasse,* from Latin *mollis* soft]
molasses (mə'læsɪz) *n.* (*functioning as sing.*) **1.** the thick brown uncrystallized bitter syrup obtained from sugar during refining. **2.** the U.S. and Canadian name for **treacle** (sense 1). [C16: from Portuguese *melaço,* from Late Latin *mellāceum* must, from Latin *mel* honey]
mold (məʊld) *n., vb.* the U.S. spelling of **mould.**
Moldavian (mɒl'deɪvɪən) *adj.* **1.** of or relating to the former Soviet republic of Moldavia or its people. ~*n.* **2.** a native or inhabitant of Moldavia.
moldavite ('mɒldəˌvaɪt) *n.* a green tektite found in Czechoslovakia, thought to be the product of an ancient meteorite impact in Germany. [C19: named after *Moldavia,* then a principality in E Europe]
moldboard ('məʊldˌbɔːd) *n.* the U.S. spelling of **mouldboard.**
molder ('məʊldə) *vb., n.* the U.S. spelling of **moulder.**
molding ('məʊldɪŋ) *n.* the U.S. spelling of **moulding.**
moldy ('məʊldɪ) *adj.* **moldier, moldiest.** the U.S. spelling of **mouldy.** —'**moldiness** *n.*
mole[1] (məʊl) *n. Pathol.* a nontechnical name for **naevus.** [Old English *māl;* related to Old High German *meil* spot]
mole[2] (məʊl) *n.* **1.** any small burrowing mammal, of the family *Talpidae,* of Europe, Asia, and North and Central America: order *Insectivora* (insectivores). They have velvety, typically dark fur and forearms specialized for digging. **2. golden mole.** any small African burrowing molelike mammal of the family *Chrysochloridae,* having copper-coloured fur: order *Insectivora* (insectivores). **3.** *Informal.* a spy who has infiltrated an organization and, often over a long period, become a trusted member of it. [C14: from Middle Dutch *mol,* of Germanic origin; compare Middle Low German *mol*]
mole[3] (məʊl) *n.* the basic SI unit of amount of substance; the amount that contains as many elementary entities as there are atoms in 0.012 kilogram of carbon-12. The entity must be specified and may be an atom, a molecule, an ion, a radical, an electron, a photon, etc. Symbol: mol [C20: from German *Mol,* short for *Molekül* MOLECULE]
mole[4] (məʊl) *n.* **1.** a breakwater. **2.** a harbour protected by a breakwater. [C16: from French *môle,* from Latin *mōlēs* mass]
mole[5] (məʊl) *n. Pathol.* a fleshy growth in the uterus formed by the degeneration of fetal tissues. [C17: medical use of Latin *mola* millstone]
mole cricket *n.* any subterranean orthopterous insect of the family *Gryllotalpidae,* of Europe and North America, similar and related to crickets but having the first pair of legs specialized for digging.
molecular (məʊ'lɛkjʊlə, mə-) *adj.* **1.** of or relating to molecules: *molecular hydrogen.* **2.** *Logic.* (of a sentence, formula, etc.) capable of analysis into atomic formulae of the appropriate kind. —**molecularity** (məʊˌlɛkjʊ'lærɪtɪ) *n.* —**mo'lecularly** *adv.*
molecular beam *or* **ray** *n. Physics.* a parallel beam of atoms or molecules that are at low pressure and suffer no interatomic or intermolecular collisions.

molecular biology *n.* the study of the structure and function of biological molecules, esp. nucleic acids and proteins.
molecular distillation *n.* distillation in which a substance is heated under vacuum, the condensing surface being so close to the substance that no intermolecular collisions can occur before condensation.
molecular film *n.* another name for **monolayer.**
molecular formula *n.* a chemical formula indicating the numbers and types of atoms in a molecule: *H_2SO_4 is the molecular formula of sulphuric acid.* Compare **empirical formula, structural formula.**
molecular genetics *n.* (*functioning as sing.*) the study of the molecular constitution of genes and chromosomes.
molecular sieve *n. Chem.* a material that can absorb large amounts of certain compounds while not absorbing others and is thus suitable for use in separating mixtures.
molecular volume *n.* the volume occupied by one mole of a substance. Also called: **molar volume.**
molecular weight *n.* the former name for **relative molecular mass.**
molecule (ˈmɒlɪˌkjuːl) *n.* **1.** the simplest unit of a chemical compound that can exist, consisting of two or more atoms held together by chemical bonds. **2.** a very small particle. [C18: via French from New Latin *mōlēcula,* diminutive of Latin *mōlēs* mass, MOLE[4]]
mole drain *n.* an underground cylindrical drainage channel cut by a special plough to drain heavy agricultural soil.
molehill (ˈməʊlˌhɪl) *n.* **1.** the small mound of earth thrown up by a burrowing mole. **2. make a mountain out of a molehill.** to exaggerate an unimportant matter out of all proportion.
mole rat *n.* **1.** any burrowing molelike African rodent of the family *Bathyergidae.* **2.** any similar rodent, esp. any member of the genus *Spalax,* of Asia and North Africa: family *Spalacidae.* **3.** another name for **bandicoot rat** (see **bandicoot** (sense 2)).
mole run *n.* (*usually pl.*) *Informal.* any part of a system of underground tunnels, rooms, etc., prepared for use in the event of nuclear war.
moleskin (ˈməʊlˌskɪn) *n.* **1.** the dark grey dense velvety pelt of a mole, used as a fur. **2.** a hard-wearing cotton fabric of twill weave used for work clothes, etc. **3.** (*modifier*) made from moleskin: *a moleskin waistcoat.*
moleskins (ˈməʊlˌskɪnz) *pl. n.* clothing of moleskin.
molest (məˈlɛst) *vb.* (*tr.*) **1.** to disturb or annoy by malevolent interference. **2.** to accost or attack, esp. with the intention of assaulting sexually. [C14: from Latin *molestāre* to annoy, from *molestus* troublesome, from *mōlēs* mass] —**molestation** (ˌməʊlɛˈsteɪʃən) *n.* —**moˈlester** *n.*
moline (məˈlaɪn) *adj. Heraldry.* (of a cross) having arms of equal length, forked and curved back at the ends. [C16: probably from Anglo-French *moliné,* from *molin* MILL[1], referring to the arms curved back like the ends of a mill-rind]
Molinism (ˈmɒlɪnɪzəm) *n. R.C. Church.* a doctrine of grace that attempts to reconcile the efficacy of divine grace with human free will in responding to it. [C17: named after *Luis de Molina* (1535–1600), Spanish Jesuit who taught such a doctrine]
moll (mɒl) *n. Slang.* **1.** the female accomplice of a gangster. **2.** a prostitute. [C17: from *Moll,* familiar form of *Mary*]
mollah (ˈmɔːlə) *n.* an older spelling of **mullah.**
mollescent (mɒˈlɛsᵊnt) *adj. Rare.* tending to soften or become soft. [C19: from Latin *mollēscere* to grow soft, from *mollis* soft] —**molˈlescence** *n.*
mollify (ˈmɒlɪˌfaɪ) *vb.* **-fies, -fying, -fied.** (*tr.*) **1.** to pacify; soothe. **2.** to lessen the harshness or severity of. [C15: from Old French *mollifier,* via Late Latin, from Latin *mollis* soft + *facere* to make] —**ˈmolliˌfiable** *adj.* —**ˌmollifiˈcation** *n.* —**ˈmolliˌfier** *n.*
mollusc *or U.S.* **mollusk** (ˈmɒləsk) *n.* any invertebrate of the phylum *Mollusca,* having a soft unsegmented body and often a shell, secreted by a fold of skin (the mantle). The group includes the gastropods (snails, slugs, etc.), bivalves (clams, mussels, etc.), and cephalopods (cuttlefish, octopuses, etc.). [C18: via New Latin from Latin *molluscus,* from *mollis* soft] —**molluscan** *or U.S.* **molluskan** (mɒˈlʌskən) *adj., n.* —**ˈmollusc-ˌlike** *or U.S.* **ˈmollusk-ˌlike** *adj.*
molluscoid (mɒˈlʌskɔɪd) *or* **molluscoidal** (ˌmɒlʌsˈkɔɪdᵊl) *adj.* of, relating to, or belonging to the *Molluscoidea,* a former phylum including the brachiopods and bryozoans now classified separately. [C19: via New Latin from Latin *molluscus* soft]
Mollweide projection (ˈmɒlˌvaɪdə) *n.* an equal-area map projection with the parallels and the central meridian being straight lines and the other meridians curved. It is often used to show world distributions of various phenomena. [C19: named after Karl B. *Mollweide* (1774–1825), German mathematician and astronomer]
molly[1] (ˈmɒlɪ) *n., pl.* **-lies.** any brightly coloured tropical or subtropical American freshwater cyprinodont fish of the genus *Mollienisia.* [C19: from New Latin *Mollienisia,* from Comte F. N. *Mollien* (1758–1850), French statesman]
molly[2] (ˈmɒlɪ) *n., pl.* **-lies.** *Irish informal.* an effeminate, weak, or cowardly boy or man. [C18: perhaps from *Molly,* pet name for *Mary*]
mollycoddle (ˈmɒlɪˌkɒdᵊl) *vb.* **1.** (*tr.*) to treat with indulgent care; pamper. ~*n.* **2.** a pampered person. [C19: from MOLLY[2] + CODDLE] —**ˈmollyˌcoddler** *n.*
mollyhawk (ˈmɒlɪˌhɔːk) *n. N.Z.* the juvenile of the southern black-backed gull (*Larus dominicanus*).
Molly Maguire (ˈmɒlɪ məˈgwaɪə) *n.* **1.** *Irish history.* a member of a secret society that terrorized law officers during the 1840s to prevent evictions. **2.** (in Pennsylvania from about 1865 to 1877) a member of a society of miners that terrorized mine owners and their agents in an effort to obtain better pay. [C19: the name refers to the female disguise adopted by members of these societies]
mollymawk (ˈmɒlɪˌmɔːk) *n. N.Z.* an informal name for **mallemuck.**
moloch (ˈməʊlɒk) *n.* a spiny Australian desert-living lizard, *Moloch horridus,* that feeds on ants: family *Agamidae* (agamas). Also called: **mountain devil, spiny lizard.**
Molotov cocktail (ˈmɒləˌtɒf) *n.* an elementary incendiary weapon, usually a bottle of petrol with a short-delay fuse or wick; petrol bomb. [C20: named after V. M. *Molotov* (1890–1986), Soviet statesman]
molt (məʊlt) *vb., n.* the usual U.S. spelling of **moult.**
molten (ˈməʊltən) *adj.* **1.** liquefied; melted: *molten lead.* **2.** made by having been melted: *molten casts.* ~*vb.* **3.** the past participle of **melt.**
molto (ˈmɒltəʊ) *adv. Music.* (preceded or followed by a musical direction, esp. a tempo marking) very: *allegro molto; molto adagio.* [from Italian, from Latin *multum* (adv.) much]
mol. wt. *abbrev. for* molecular weight.
moly (ˈməʊlɪ) *n., pl.* **-lies.** a liliaceous plant, *Allium moly,* that is native to S Europe and has yellow flowers in a dense cluster. [C16: from Latin *mōly,* from Greek *mōlu*]
molybdate (mɒˈlɪbdeɪt) *n.* a salt or ester of a molybdic acid.
molybdenite (mɒˈlɪbdɪˌnaɪt) *n.* a soft grey mineral consisting of molybdenum sulphide in hexagonal crystalline form with rhenium as an impurity: the main source of molybdenum and rhenium. Formula: MoS_2.
molybdenous (mɒˈlɪbdɪnəs) *adj.* of or containing molybdenum in the divalent state.
molybdenum (mɒˈlɪbdɪnəm) *n.* a very hard ductile silvery-white metallic element occurring principally in molybdenite: used mainly in alloys, esp. to harden and strengthen steels. Symbol: Mo; atomic no.: 42; atomic wt.: 95.94; valency: 2–6; relative density: 10.22; melting pt.: 2610°C; boiling pt.: 5560°C. [C19: from New Latin, from Latin *molybdaena* galena, from Greek *molubdaina,* from *molubdos* lead]
molybdic (mɒˈlɪbdɪk) *adj.* of or containing molybdenum in the trivalent or hexavalent state.
molybdous (mɒˈlɪbdəs) *adj.* of or containing molybdenum, esp. in a low valence state.
mom (mɒm) *n. Chiefly U.S. and Canadian.* an informal word for **mother**[1].
moment (ˈməʊmənt) *n.* **1.** a short indefinite period of time: *he'll be here in a moment.* **2.** a specific instant or point in time: *at that moment the doorbell rang.* **3. the moment.** the present point of time: *at the moment it's fine.* **4.** import, significance, or value: *a man of moment.* **5.** *Physics.* **a.** a tendency to produce motion, esp. rotation about a point or axis. **b.** the product of a physical quantity, such as force or mass, and its distance from a fixed reference point. See also **moment of inertia. 6.** *Statistics.* the mean of a specified power of the deviations of all the values of a variable in its frequency distribution. The power of the deviations indicates the order of the moment and the deviations may be from the origin (giving a **moment about the origin**) or from the mean (giving a **moment about the mean**). [C14: from Old French, from Latin *mōmentum,* from *movēre* to move]
momentarily (ˈməʊməntərəlɪ, -trɪlɪ) *adv.* **1.** for an instant; temporarily. **2.** from moment to moment; every instant. **3.** *U.S. and Canadian.* very soon. ~Also (for senses 1, 2): **momently** (ˈməʊməntlɪ).
momentary (ˈməʊməntərɪ, -trɪ) *adj.* **1.** lasting for only a moment; temporary. **2.** *Rare.* occurring or present at each moment. —**ˈmomentariness** *n.*
moment of inertia *n.* the tendency of a body to resist angular acceleration, expressed as the sum of the products of the mass of each particle in the body and the square of its perpendicular distance from the axis of rotation. Symbol: *I*
moment of truth *n.* **1.** a moment when a person or thing is put to the test. **2.** the point in a bullfight when the matador is about to kill the bull.
momentous (məʊˈmɛntəs) *adj.* of great significance. —**moˈmentously** *adv.* —**moˈmentousness** *n.*
momentum (məʊˈmɛntəm) *n., pl.* **-ta** (-tə) *or* **-tums.** **1.** *Physics.* the product of a body's mass and its velocity. Symbol: *p* See also **angular momentum. 2.** the impetus of a body resulting from its motion. **3.** driving power or strength. [C17: from Latin: movement; see MOMENT]
momma (ˈmɒmə) *n.* a variant (esp. U.S. and Canadian) of **mamma**[1].
Momus (ˈməʊməs) *n., pl.* **-muses** *or* **-mi** (-maɪ). a cavilling critic. [after *Momus,* Greek god of blame and mockery]
Mon (məʊn) *n.* **1.** (*pl.* **Mon** *or* **Mons**) a member of a people of Burma and Thailand related to the Khmer of Cambodia. **2.** the

language of this people, belonging to the Mon-Khmer family. ~Also called: **Talaing.**

mon. *abbrev. for* monetary.

Mon. *abbrev. for* Monday.

mon- *combining form.* a variant of **mono-** before a vowel.

mona ('məʊnə) *n.* a W African guenon monkey, *Cercopithecus mona,* with dark fur on the back and white or yellow underparts. [C18: from Spanish or Portuguese: monkey]

monachal ('mɒnəkᵊl) *adj.* a less common word for **monastic.** [C16: from Old French, from Church Latin *monachālis,* from *monachus* MONK] —'**monachism** *n.* —'**monachist** *adj., n.*

monacid (mɒn'æsɪd) *or* **monacidic** (ˌmɒnə'sɪdɪk) *adj.* variants of **monoacid.**

Monacan ('mɒnəkən, mə'nɑ:-) *n., adj.* another word for **Monegasque.**

monad ('mɒnæd, 'məʊ-) *n.* **1.** (*pl.* **-ads** *or* **-ades** (-əˌdi:z)) *Philosophy.* **a.** any fundamental singular metaphysical entity, esp. if autonomous. **b.** (in the metaphysics of Leibnitz) a simple indestructible nonspatial element regarded as the unit of which reality consists. **c.** (in pantheistic philosophy) a fundamental metaphysical unit that is spatially extended and psychically aware. **2.** a single-celled organism, esp. a flagellate protozoan. **3.** an atom, ion, or radical with a valency of one. ~Also called (for senses 1, 2): **monas.** [C17: from Late Latin *monas,* from Greek: unit, from *monos* alone] —**mo'nadical** *adj.* —**mo'nadically** *adv.*

monadelphous (ˌmɒnə'dɛlfəs) *adj.* **1.** (of stamens) having united filaments forming a tube around the style. **2.** (of flowers) having monadelphous stamens. [C19: from MONO- + Greek *adelphos* brother, twin + -OUS]

monadic (mɒ'nædɪk) *adj.* **1.** being or relating to a monad. **2.** *Logic, maths.* (of an operator, predicate, etc.) having only a single argument place.

monadism ('mɒnəˌdɪzəm, 'məʊ-) *or* **monadology** (ˌmɒnə'dɒlədʒɪ, ˌməʊ-) *n.* (esp. in the writings of Leibnitz) the philosophical doctrine that monads are the ultimate units of reality. —ˌ**monad'istic** *adj.*

monadnock (mə'nædnɒk) *n.* a residual hill that consists of hard rock in an otherwise eroded area. [C19: named after Mount *Monadnock,* in New Hampshire]

monal *or* **monaul** ('mɒnɔ:l) *n.* any of several S Asian pheasants of the genus *Lophophorus,* the males of which have a brilliantly coloured plumage. [C18: from Hindi]

monandrous (mɒ'nændrəs) *adj.* **1.** having or preferring only one male sexual partner over a period of time. **2.** (of plants) having flowers with only one stamen. **3.** (of flowers) having only one stamen. [C19: from MONO- + -ANDROUS] —**mo'nandry** *n.*

monanthous (mɒ'nænθəs) *adj.* (of certain plants) having or producing only one flower. [C19: from MONO- + Greek *anthos* flower]

monarch ('mɒnək) *n.* **1.** a sovereign head of state, esp. a king, queen, or emperor, who rules usually by hereditary right. **2.** a supremely powerful or pre-eminent person or thing. **3.** Also called: **milkweed.** a large migratory butterfly, *Danaus plexippus,* that has orange-and-black wings and feeds on the milkweed plant: family *Danaidae.* [C15: from Late Latin *monarcha,* from Greek; see MONO-, -ARCH] —**monarchal** (mɒ'nɑ:kᵊl) *or* **monarchial** (mɒ'nɑ:kɪəl) *adj.* —**mo'narchally** *adv.* —**mo'narchical** *or* **mo'narchic** *adj.* —**mo'narchically** *adv.* —'**monarchism** *n.* —'**monarchist** *n., adj.* —ˌ**monar'chistic** *adj.*

monarchy ('mɒnəkɪ) *n., pl.* **-chies.** **1.** a form of government in which supreme authority is vested in a single and usually hereditary figure, such as a king, and whose powers can vary from those of an absolute despot to those of a figurehead. **2.** a country reigned over by a king, prince, or other monarch.

monarda (mɒ'nɑ:də) *n.* any mintlike North American plant of the genus *Monarda:* family *Labiatae* (labiates). See also **horsemint** (sense 2), **bergamot** (sense 4). [C19: from New Latin, named after N. *Monardés* (1493–1588), Spanish botanist]

monas ('mɒnæs, 'məʊ-) *n., pl.* **monades** ('mɒnəˌdi:z). another word for **monad** (senses 1, 2).

monastery ('mɒnəstərɪ, -strɪ) *n., pl.* **-teries.** the residence of a religious community, esp. of monks, living in seclusion from secular society and bound by religious vows. [C15: from Church Latin *monastērium,* from Late Greek *monastērion,* from Greek *monázein* to live alone, from *monos* alone] —**monasterial** (ˌmɒnə'stɪərɪəl) *adj.*

monastic (mə'næstɪk) *adj. also* (*less commonly*) **monastical.** **1.** of or relating to monasteries or monks, nuns, etc. **2.** resembling this sort of life; reclusive. ~*n.* **3.** a person who is committed to this way of life, esp. a monk. —**mo'nastically** *adv.*

monasticism (mə'næstɪˌsɪzəm) *n.* the monastic system, movement, or way of life.

Monastral (mə'næstrəl) *adj. Trademark.* denoting certain fast pigments used in paints and inks, derived from phthalocyanine.

monatomic (ˌmɒnə'tɒmɪk) *or* **monoatomic** (ˌmɒnəʊə'tɒmɪk) *adj. Chem.* **1.** (of an element) having or consisting of single atoms: *argon is a monatomic gas.* **2.** (of a compound or molecule) having only one atom or group that can be replaced in a chemical reaction. **3.** a less common word for **monovalent.**

monaul ('mɒnɔ:l) *n.* a variant spelling of **monal.**

monaural (mɒ'nɔ:rəl) *adj.* **1.** relating to, having, or hearing with only one ear. **2.** another word for **monophonic.** —**mon'aurally** *adv.*

monaxial (mɒ'næksɪəl) *adj.* another word for **uniaxial.**

monazite ('mɒnəˌzaɪt) *n.* a yellow to reddish-brown mineral consisting of a phosphate of thorium, cerium, and lanthanum in monoclinic crystalline form. [C19: from German, from Greek *monazein* to live alone, so called because of its rarity]

mondaine (*French* mɔ̃dɛn) *or* (*masc.*) **mondain** (*French* mɔ̃dɛ̃) *n.* **1.** a woman or man who moves in fashionable society. ~*adj.* **2.** characteristic of fashionable society; worldly. [C19: from French; see MUNDANE]

Monday ('mʌndɪ) *n.* the second day of the week; first day of the working week. [Old English *mōnandæg* moon's day, translation of Late Latin *lūnae diēs*]

Mondayize *or* **Mondayise** ('mʌndɪˌaɪz) *vb.* (*tr.*) *N.Z.* to move (a statutory holiday, such as the Queen's birthday) to the nearest Monday in order to secure a long weekend. —ˌ**Mondayi'zation** *or* ˌ**Mondayi'sation** *n.*

mondial ('mɒndɪəl) *adj.* of or involving the whole world. [C20: from French, ultimately from Latin *mundus*]

Mond process (mɒnd; *German* mɔnt) *n.* a process for obtaining nickel by heating the ore in carbon monoxide to produce nickel carbonyl vapour, which is then decomposed at a higher temperature to yield the metal. [C19: named after Ludwig *Mond* (1839–1909), German chemist and industrialist]

monecious (mɒ'ni:ʃəs) *adj.* a variant spelling of **monoecious.** —**mo'neciously** *adv.*

Monegasque (ˌmɒnə'gæsk) *n.* **1.** a native or inhabitant of Monaco, a principality in SW Europe. ~*adj.* **2.** of or relating to Monaco or its inhabitants. ~Also: **Monacan.** [from French, from Provençal *mounegasc,* from *Mounegue* Monaco]

Monel metal *or* **Monell metal** (mɒ'nɛl) *n. Trademark.* any of various silvery corrosion-resistant alloys containing copper (28 per cent), nickel (67 per cent), and smaller quantities of such metals as iron, manganese, and aluminium. [C20: named after A. Monell (died 1921), president of the International Nickel Co., New York, which introduced the alloys]

moneme ('məʊni:m) *n. Linguistics.* a less common word for **morpheme.** [C20: from MONO- + -EME]

monetarism ('mʌnɪtəˌrɪzəm) *n.* **1.** the theory that inflation is caused by an excess quantity of money in an economy. **2.** an economic policy based on this theory and on a belief in the efficiency of free market forces, that gives priority to achieving price stability by monetary control, balanced budgets, etc., and maintains that unemployment results from excessive real wage rates and cannot be controlled by Keynesian demand management. —'**monetarist** *n., adj.*

monetary ('mʌnɪtərɪ, -trɪ) *adj.* **1.** of or relating to money or currency. **2.** of or relating to monetarism: *a monetary policy.* [C19: from Late Latin *monētārius,* from Latin *monēta* MONEY] —'**monetarily** *adv.*

monetary unit *n.* a unit of value and money of a country, esp. the major or standard unit.

monetize *or* **monetise** ('mʌnɪˌtaɪz) *vb.* (*tr.*) **1.** to establish as the legal tender of a country. **2.** to give a legal value to (a coin). —ˌ**moneti'zation** *or* ˌ**moneti'sation** *n.*

money ('mʌnɪ) *n.* **1.** a medium of exchange that functions as legal tender. **2.** the official currency, in the form of banknotes, coins, etc., issued by a government or other authority. **3.** a particular denomination or form of currency: *silver money.* **4.** property or assets with reference to their realizable value. **5.** (*Law or archaic pl.* **moneys** *or* **monies**) a pecuniary sum or income. **6.** an unspecified amount of paper currency or coins: *money to lend.* **7. for one's money.** in one's opinion. **8. in the money.** *Informal.* well-off; rich. **9. one's money's worth.** full value for the money one has paid for something. **10. put money into.** to invest money in. **11. put money on.** to place a bet on. **12. put one's money where one's mouth is.** See **mouth** (sense 19). ~Related adj.: **pecuniary.** [C13: from Old French *moneie,* from Latin *monēta* coinage; see MINT[2]]

moneybags ('mʌnɪˌbægz) *n.* (*functioning as sing.*) *Informal.* a very rich person.

moneychanger ('mʌnɪˌtʃeɪndʒə) *n.* **1.** a person engaged in the business of exchanging currencies or money. **2.** *Chiefly U.S.* a machine for dispensing coins.

money cowry *n.* **1.** a tropical marine gastropod, *Cypraea moneta.* **2.** the shell of this mollusc, used as money in some parts of Africa and S Asia.

moneyed *or* **monied** ('mʌnɪd) *adj.* **1.** having a great deal of money; rich. **2.** arising from or characterized by money.

moneyer ('mʌnɪə) *n.* **1.** *Archaic.* a person who coins money. **2.** an obsolete word for **banker**[1].

money-grubbing *adj. Informal.* seeking greedily to obtain money at every opportunity. —'**money-ˌgrubber** *n.*

moneylender ('mʌnɪˌlɛndə) *n.* a person who lends money at interest as a living. —'**moneyˌlending** *adj., n.*

moneymaker ('mʌnɪˌmeɪkə) *n.* **1.** a person who is intent on accumulating money. **2.** a person or thing that is or might be profitable. —'**moneyˌmaking** *adj., n.*

money market *n. Finance.* the financial institutions dealing with short-term loans and capital and with foreign exchange. Compare **capital market.**

money of account *n.* another name (esp. U.S. and Canadian) for **unit of account.**
money order *n.* another name (esp. U.S. and Canadian) for **postal order.**
money spider *n.* any of certain small shiny brownish spiders of the family *Linyphiidae.*
money-spinner *n. Informal.* an enterprise, idea, person, or thing that is a source of wealth.
money supply *n.* the total amount of money in a country's economy at a given time. See also **M0, M1, M2, M3, M3c, M4, M5.**
money wages *pl. n. Economics.* wages evaluated with reference to the money paid rather than the equivalent purchasing power. Also called: **nominal wages.** Compare **real wages.**
moneywort ('mʌnɪˌwɜːt) *n.* a European and North American creeping primulaceous plant, *Lysimachia nummularia,* with round leaves and yellow flowers. Also called: **creeping Jennie.**
mong (mʌŋ) *n. Austral. informal.* short for **mongrel.**
monger ('mʌŋgə) *n.* **1.** (*in combination except in archaic use*) a trader or dealer: *ironmonger.* **2.** (*in combination*) a promoter of something unpleasant: *warmonger.* [Old English *mangere,* ultimately from Latin *mangō* dealer; compare Old High German *mangari*] —'**mongering** *n., adj.*
mongo[1] *or* **mongoe**[1] ('mɒŋgəʊ) *n., pl.* **-gos** *or* **-goes.** a Mongolian monetary unit worth one hundredth of a tugrik.
mongo[2] *or* **mongoe**[2] ('mɒŋgəʊ) *n.* variants of **mungo.**
mongol ('mɒŋgᵊl) *n.* (not in technical use) a person affected by Down's syndrome.
Mongol ('mɒŋgɒl, -gᵊl) *n.* **1.** a native or inhabitant of Mongolia in central Asia, esp. a nomad. **2.** the Mongolian language.
mongolian (mɒŋ'gəʊlɪən) *adj.* (not in technical use) of, relating to, or affected by Down's syndrome.
Mongolian (mɒŋ'gəʊlɪən) *adj.* **1.** of or relating to Mongolia, a region of central Asia, its people, or their language. ~*n.* **2.** (*pl.* **-lians**) a native of Mongolia. **3.** the language of Mongolia: see **Khalkha.**
Mongolic (mɒŋ'gɒlɪk) *n.* **1.** a branch or subfamily of the Altaic family of languages, including Mongolian, Kalmuck, and Buryat. **2.** another word for **Mongoloid.**
mongolism ('mɒŋgəˌlɪzəm) *n. Pathol.* a former name (not in technical use) for **Down's syndrome.** [C20: so named because Down's syndrome produces facial features similar to those of the Mongoloid peoples]
mongoloid ('mɒŋgəˌlɔɪd) (not in technical use) *adj.* **1.** relating to or characterized by Down's syndrome. ~*n.* **2.** a person affected by Down's syndrome.
Mongoloid ('mɒŋgəˌlɔɪd) *adj.* **1.** denoting, relating to, or belonging to one of the major racial groups of mankind, characterized by yellowish complexion, straight black hair, slanting eyes, short nose, and scanty facial hair, including most of the peoples of Asia, the Eskimos, and the North American Indians. ~*n.* **2.** a member of this group.
mongoose ('mɒŋˌguːs) *n., pl.* **-gooses.** any small predatory viverrine mammal of the genus *Herpestes* and related genera, occurring in Africa and from S Europe to SE Asia, typically having a long tail and brindled coat. [C17: from Marathi *mangūs,* of Dravidian origin]
mongrel ('mʌŋgrəl) *n.* **1.** a plant or animal, esp. a dog, of mixed or unknown breeding; a crossbreed or hybrid. **2.** *Derogatory.* a person of mixed race. ~*adj.* **3.** of mixed origin, breeding, character, etc. [C15: from obsolete *mong* mixture; compare Old English *gemong* a mingling] —'**mongrelism** *n.* —'**mongrelly** *adj.*
mongrelize *or* **mongrelise** ('mʌŋgrəˌlaɪz) *vb.* (*tr.*) to make mixed or mongrel in breed, race, character, kind, etc. —ˌ**mongreli'zation** *or* ˌ**mongreli'sation** *n.* —'**mongrelˌizer** *or* '**mongrelˌiser** *n.*
'mongst (mʌŋst) *prep. Poetic.* short for **amongst.**
monied ('mʌnɪd) *adj.* a less common spelling of **moneyed.**
monies ('mʌnɪz) *n. Law, archaic.* a plural of **money.**
moniker *or* **monicker** ('mɒnɪkə) *n. Slang.* a person's name or nickname. [C19: from Shelta *munnik,* altered from Irish *ainm* name]
monilial (mə'nɪlɪəl) *adj. Pathol.* denoting a thrush infection, caused by the fungus *Candida* (formerly *Monilia*) *albicans.* [C20: from New Latin *monilia* from Latin *monīle* necklace (referring to the beadlike form of the fungus)]
moniliform (mɒ'nɪlɪˌfɔːm) *adj. Biology.* shaped like a string of beads: *moniliform fungi.* [C19: from New Latin *monīliformis,* from Latin *monīle* necklace + *forma* shape]
monism ('mɒnɪzəm) *n.* **1.** *Philosophy.* the doctrine that the person consists of only a single substance, or that there is no crucial difference between mental and physical events or properties. Compare **dualism** (sense 2). See also **materialism** (sense 2), **idealism** (sense 3). **2.** *Philosophy.* the doctrine that reality consists of an unchanging whole in which change is mere illusion. Compare **pluralism** (sense 5). **3.** the epistemological theory that the object and datum of consciousness are identical. **4.** the attempt to explain anything in terms of one principle only. [C19: from Greek *monos* single + -ISM] —'**monist** *n., adj.* —**mo'nistic** *adj.* —**mo'nistically** *adv.*
monition (məʊ'nɪʃən) *n.* **1.** a warning or caution; admonition. **2.** *Christianity.* a formal notice from a bishop or ecclesiastical court requiring a person to refrain from committing a specific offence. [C14: via Old French from Latin *monitiō,* from *monēre* to warn]
monitor ('mɒnɪtə) *n.* **1.** a person or piece of equipment that warns, checks, controls, or keeps a continuous record of something. **2.** *Education.* **a.** a senior pupil with various supervisory duties. **b.** a pupil assisting a teacher in classroom organization, etc. **3.** a television set used in a studio for viewing or checking a programme being transmitted. **4. a.** a loudspeaker used in a recording studio control room to determine quality or balance. **b.** a loudspeaker used on stage to enable musicians to hear themselves. **5.** a device for controlling the direction of a water jet in fire fighting. **6.** any large predatory lizard of the genus *Varanus* and family *Varanidae,* inhabiting warm regions of Africa, Asia, and Australia. See also **Komodo dragon. 7.** Also called: **giant.** *Mining.* a nozzle for directing a high-pressure jet of water at the material to be excavated. **8.** (formerly) a small heavily armoured shallow-draught warship used for coastal assault. ~*vb.* (*tr.*) **9.** to act as a monitor of. **10.** to observe or record (the activity or performance) of (an engine or other device). **11.** to check (the technical quality of) (a radio or television broadcast). [C16: from Latin, from *monēre* to advise] —**monitorial** (ˌmɒnɪ'tɔːrɪəl) *adj.* —ˌ**moni'torially** *adv.* —'**monitorˌship** *n.* —'**monitress** *fem. n.*
monitory ('mɒnɪtərɪ, -trɪ) *adj. also* **monitorial. 1.** warning or admonishing: *a monitory look.* ~*n., pl.* **-ries. 2.** *Rare.* a letter containing a monition.
monk (mʌŋk) *n.* **1.** a male member of a religious community bound by vows of poverty, chastity, and obedience. Related adj.: **monastic. 2.** (*sometimes cap.*) a fancy pigeon having a bald pate and often large feathered feet. [Old English *munuc,* from Late Latin *monachus,* from Late Greek: solitary (man), from Greek *monos* alone]
monkery ('mʌŋkərɪ) *n., pl.* **-eries.** *Derogatory.* **1.** monastic life or practices. **2.** a monastery or monks collectively.
monkey ('mʌŋkɪ) *n.* **1.** any of numerous long-tailed primates excluding the prosimians (lemurs, tarsiers, etc.): comprise the families *Cercopithecidae* (see **Old World monkey**), *Cebidae* (see **New World monkey**), and *Callithricidae* (marmosets). **2.** any primate except man. **3.** a naughty or mischievous person, esp. a child. **4.** the head of a pile-driver (**monkey engine**) or of some similar mechanical device. **5.** (*modifier*) *Nautical.* denoting a small light structure or piece of equipment contrived to suit an immediate purpose: *a monkey foresail; a monkey bridge.* **6.** *U.S. and Canadian slang.* an addict's dependence on a drug (esp. in the phrase **have a monkey on one's back). 7.** *Slang.* a butt of derision; someone made to look a fool (esp. in the phrase **make a monkey of). 8.** *Slang.* (esp. in bookmaking) £500. **9.** *U.S. and Canadian slang.* $500. **10.** *Austral. slang.* a sheep. ~*vb.* **11.** (*intr.;* usually foll. by *around, with,* etc.) to meddle, fool, or tinker. **12.** (*tr.*) *Rare.* to imitate; ape. [C16: perhaps from Low German; compare Middle Low German *Moneke* name of the ape's son in the tale of Reynard the Fox]
monkey bread *n.* **1.** the gourdlike fruit of the baobab tree. **2. monkey bread tree.** another name for **baobab.**
monkey business *n. Informal.* mischievous, suspect, dishonest, or meddlesome behaviour or acts.
monkey climb *n.* a wrestling throw in which a contestant seizes his opponent's arms or neck, places his feet on his opponent's stomach, and falls backwards, straightening his legs and throwing the opponent over his head.
monkey flower *n.* any of various scrophulariaceous plants of the genus *Mimulus,* cultivated for their yellow or red flowers. See also **musk** (sense 3).
monkey jacket *n.* a short close-fitting jacket, esp. a waist-length jacket similar to a mess jacket.
monkey nut *n. Brit.* another name for a **peanut** (sense 1).
monkey orchid *n.* a European orchid, *Orchis simia,* rare in Britain, having a short dense flower spike that opens from the top downwards. The flowers are white streaked with pink or violet and have five spurs thought to resemble a monkey's arms, legs, and tail.
monkeypot ('mʌŋkɪˌpɒt) *n.* **1.** any of various tropical trees of the genus *Lecythis:* family *Lecythidaceae.* **2.** the large urn-shaped pod of any of these trees, formerly used to catch monkeys by baiting it with sugar. **3.** a melting pot used in making flint glass.
monkey puzzle *n.* a South American coniferous tree, *Araucaria araucana,* having branches shaped like a candelabrum and stiff sharp leaves: family *Araucariaceae.* Also called: **Chile pine.** [so called because monkeys allegedly have difficulty climbing them]
monkey suit *n. U.S. slang.* a man's evening dress.
monkey's wedding *n. S. African informal.* a combination of sunshine and light rain.
monkey tricks *or U.S.* **monkey shines** *pl. n. Informal.* mischievous behaviour or acts, such as practical jokes.
monkey wrench *n.* a wrench with adjustable jaws.
monkfish ('mʌŋkˌfɪʃ) *n., pl.* **-fish** *or* **-fishes. 1.** Also called (U.S.): **goosefish.** any of various anglers of the genus *Lophius.* **2.** another name for the **angel shark.**
Mon-Khmer *n.* **1.** a family of languages spoken chiefly in Cambodia, Burma, and Assam; probably a member of the

Austro-Asiatic phylum. ~*adj.* **2.** of or belonging to this family of languages.
monkhood ('mʌŋkhʊd) *n.* **1.** the condition of being a monk. **2.** monks collectively.
monkish ('mʌŋkɪʃ) *adj.* of, relating to, or resembling a monk or monks. —'**monkishly** *adv.* —'**monkishness** *n.*
monk's cloth *n.* a heavy cotton fabric of basket weave, used mainly for bedspreads. [C19: so called because a similar material was used for making monks' habits]
monkshood ('mʌŋkshʊd) *n.* any of several poisonous N temperate plants of the ranunculaceous genus *Aconitum,* esp. *A. napellus,* that have hooded blue-purple flowers.
mono ('mɒnəʊ) *adj.* **1.** short for **monophonic.** ~*n.* **2.** monophonic sound; monophony.
mono- *or before a vowel* **mon-** *combining form.* **1.** one; single: *monochrome; monorail.* **2.** indicating that a chemical compound contains a single specified atom or group: *monoxide.* [from Greek *monos*]
monoacid (ˌmɒnəʊ'æsɪd), **monacid, monoacidic** (ˌmɒnəʊə'sɪdɪk), *or* **monacidic** *adj. Chem.* (of a base) capable of reacting with only one molecule of a monobasic acid; having only one hydroxide ion per molecule.
monoamine (ˌmɒnəʊ'eɪmiːn) *n.* a substance, such as adrenaline, noradrenaline, or serotonin, that contains a single amine group.
monoamine oxidase *n. Biochem.* an enzyme present in nerve tissue that is responsible for the inactivation of neurotransmitters.
monoamine oxidase inhibitor *n. Biochem.* an agent that inhibits the action of monoamine oxidase. Such inhibitors are used in the treatment of depression.
monoatomic (ˌmɒnəʊə'tɒmɪk) *adj.* a variant of **monatomic.**
monobasic (ˌmɒnəʊ'beɪsɪk) *adj. Chem.* (of an acid, such as hydrogen chloride) having only one replaceable hydrogen atom per molecule.
monocarp ('mɒnəʊˌkɑːp) *n.* a plant that is monocarpic.
monocarpellary (ˌmɒnəʊ'kɑːpɪlərɪ) *or* **monocarpous** (ˌmɒnəʊ'kɑːpəs) *adj.* **1.** (of flowers) having only one carpel. **2.** (of a plant gynoecium) consisting of one carpel.
monocarpic (ˌmɒnəʊ'kɑːpɪk) *or* **monocarpous** *adj.* (of some flowering plants) producing fruit only once before dying. Also: **hapaxanthic.**
Monoceros (mə'nɒsərəs) *n., Latin genitive* **Monocerotis** (məˌnɒsə'rəʊtɪs). a faint constellation on the celestial equator crossed by the Milky Way and lying close to Orion and Canis Major. [C14: via Old French from Latin: unicorn, from Greek *monokeros* with a single horn, from MONO- + *keras* horn]
monochasium (ˌmɒnəʊ'keɪzɪəm) *n., pl.* **-sia** (-zɪə). *Botany.* a cymose inflorescence in which each branch gives rise to one other branch only, as in the forget-me-not and buttercup. Compare **dichasium.** [C19: MONO- + *-chasium* as in DICHASIUM] —ˌ**mono'chasial** *adj.*
monochlamydeous (ˌmɒnəʊklə'mɪdɪəs) *adj.* (of a flower) having a perianth of one whorl of members; not having a separate calyx and corolla. [C19: from Greek, from MONO- + *khlamus* a cloak + -EOUS]
monochloride (ˌmɒnə'klɔːraɪd) *n.* a chloride containing one atom of chlorine per molecule.
monochord ('mɒnəʊˌkɔːd) *n.* an instrument employed in acoustic analysis or investigation, consisting usually of one string stretched over a resonator of wood. Also called: **sonometer** (sə'nɒmɪtə). [C15: from Old French, from Late Latin, from Greek *monokhordon,* from MONO- + *khordē* string]
monochromat (ˌmɒnəʊ'krəʊmæt) *or* **monochromate** (ˌmɒnəʊ'krəʊmeɪt) *n.* a person who perceives all colours as a single hue.
monochromatic (ˌmɒnəʊkrəʊ'mætɪk) *or* **monochroic** (ˌmɒnəʊ'krəʊɪk) *adj.* **1.** Also: **homochromatic.** (of light or other electromagnetic radiation) having only one wavelength. **2.** *Physics.* (of moving particles) having only one kinetic energy. **3.** of or relating to monochromatism. ~*n.* **4.** a person who is totally colour-blind. —ˌ**monochro'matically** *adv.*
monochromatism (ˌmɒnəʊ'krəʊməˌtɪzəm) *n.* a visual defect in which all colours appear as variations of a single hue.
monochromator (ˌmɒnəʊ'krəʊmeɪtə) *n. Physics.* a device that isolates a single wavelength of radiation.
monochrome ('mɒnəˌkrəʊm) *n.* **1.** a black-and-white photograph or transparency. **2.** *Photog.* black and white. **3. a.** a painting, drawing, etc., done in a range of tones of a single colour. **b.** the technique or art of this. **4.** (*modifier*) executed in or resembling monochrome: *a monochrome print.* ~*adj.* **5.** devoid of any distinctive or stimulating characteristics. ~Also called (for senses 3, 4): **monotint.** [C17: via Medieval Latin from Greek *monokhrōmos* of one colour] —ˌ**mono'chromic** *or* ˌ**mono'chromical** *adj.* —'**monoˌchromist** *n.*
monocle ('mɒnək^{ə}l) *n.* a lens for correcting defective vision of one eye, held in position by the facial muscles. [C19: from French, from Late Latin *monoculus* one-eyed, from MONO- + *oculus* eye] —'**monocled** *adj.*
monocline ('mɒnəʊˌklaɪn) *n.* a fold in stratified rocks in which the strata are inclined in the same direction from the horizontal. [C19: from MONO- + Greek *klīnein* to lean] —ˌ**mono'clinal** *adj., n.* —ˌ**mono'clinally** *adv.*
monoclinic (ˌmɒnəʊ'klɪnɪk) *adj. Crystallog.* relating to or belonging to the crystal system characterized by three unequal axes, one pair of which are not at right angles to each other. [C19: from MONO- + Greek *klīnein* to lean + -IC]
monoclinous (ˌmɒnəʊ'klaɪnəs, 'mɒnəʊˌklaɪnəs) *adj.* (of flowering plants) having the male and female reproductive organs on the same flower. Compare **diclinous.** [C19: from MONO- + Greek *klīnē* bed + -OUS] —'**monoˌclinism** *n.*
monoclonal antibody (ˌmɒnəʊ'kləʊn^{ə}l) *n.* an antibody, produced by a single clone of cells grown in culture, that is both pure and specific and is capable of proliferating indefinitely to produce unlimited quantities of identical antibodies: used in diagnosis, therapy, and biotechnology.
monocoque ('mɒnəˌkɒk) *n.* **1.** a type of aircraft fuselage, car body, etc., in which all or most of the loads are taken by the skin. **2.** a type of racing-car design with no separate chassis and body. ~*adj.* **3.** of or relating to the design characteristic of a monocoque. [C20: from French, from MONO- + *coque* shell]
monocotyledon (ˌmɒnəʊˌkɒtɪ'liːd^{ə}n) *n.* any flowering plant of the group *Monocotyledonae,* having a single embryonic seed leaf, leaves with parallel veins, and flowers with parts in threes: includes grasses, lilies, palms, and orchids. Often shortened to **monocot.** Compare **dicotyledon.** —ˌ**monoˌcoty'ledonous** *adj.*
monocracy (mɒ'nɒkrəsɪ) *n., pl.* **-cies.** government by one person. —**monocrat** ('mɒnəˌkræt) *n.* —ˌ**mono'cratic** *adj.*
monocular (mɒ'nɒkjʊlə) *adj.* **1.** having to do with or using only one eye. ~*n.* **2.** a device for use with one eye, such as a field glass. [C17: from Late Latin *monoculus* one-eyed] —**mo'nocularly** *adv.*
monoculture ('mɒnəʊˌkʌltʃə) *n.* the continuous growing of one type of crop.
monocycle ('mɒnəˌsaɪk^{ə}l) *n.* another name for **unicycle.**
monocyclic (ˌmɒnəʊ'saɪklɪk) *adj.* **1.** Also: **mononuclear.** (of a chemical compound) containing only one ring of atoms. **2.** (of sepals, petals, or stamens) arranged in a single whorl. **3.** (of a plant) having a life cycle that is completed in one year.
monocyte ('mɒnəʊˌsaɪt) *n.* a large phagocytic leucocyte with a spherical nucleus and clear cytoplasm. —**monocytic** (ˌmɒnə'sɪtɪk) *adj.* —ˌ**mono'cytoid** *adj.*
monodactylous (ˌmɒnəʊ'dæktɪləs) *adj.* (of certain animals) having a single functional digit.
monodisperse (ˌmɒnəʊdɪs'pɜːs) *adj. Chem.* (of a colloidal system) having particles of similar size.
monodont ('mɒnəʊˌdɒnt) *adj.* (of certain animals, esp. the male narwhal) having a single tooth throughout life.
monodrama ('mɒnəʊˌdrɑːmə) *n.* a play or other dramatic piece for a single performer. —ˌ**monodra'matic** *adj.*
monody ('mɒnədɪ) *n., pl.* **-dies.** **1.** (in Greek tragedy) an ode sung by a single actor. **2.** any poem of lament for someone's death. **3.** *Music.* a style of composition consisting of a single vocal part, usually with accompaniment. [C17: via Late Latin from Greek *monōidia,* from MONO- + *aeidein* to sing] —**monodic** (mɒ'nɒdɪk) *or* **mo'nodical** *adj.* —**mo'nodically** *adv.* —'**monodist** *n.*
monoecious, monecious (mɒ'niːʃəs), *or* **monoicous** (mɒ'nɔɪkəs) *adj.* **1.** (of some flowering plants) having the male and female reproductive organs in separate flowers on the same plant. **2.** (of some animals and lower plants) hermaphrodite. ~Compare **dioecious.** [C18: from New Latin *monoecia,* from MONO- + Greek *oikos* house] —**mo'noeciously** *or* **mo'neciously** *adv.*
monofilament (ˌmɒnə'fɪləmənt) *or* **monofil** ('mɒnəfɪl) *n.* **1.** synthetic thread or yarn composed of a single strand rather than twisted fibres. **2.** a fishing line made of monofilaments.
monogamist (mɒ'nɒgəmɪst) *n.* a person who advocates or practises monogamy. —**moˌnoga'mistic** *adj.*
monogamy (mɒ'nɒgəmɪ) *n.* **1.** the state or practice of having only one husband or wife over a period of time. Compare **bigamy, polygamy** (sense 1), **digamy.** **2.** *Zoology.* the practice of having only one mate. [C17: via French from Late Latin *monogamia,* from Greek; see MONO- + -GAMY] —**mo'nogamous** *adj.* —**mo'nogamously** *adv.* —**mo'nogamousness** *n.*
monogenesis (ˌmɒnəʊ'dʒɛnɪsɪs) *or* **monogeny** (mɒ'nɒdʒɪnɪ) *n.* **1.** the hypothetical descent of all organisms from a single cell or organism. **2.** asexual reproduction in animals. **3.** the direct development of an ovum into an organism resembling the adult. **4.** the hypothetical descent of all human beings from a single pair of ancestors. ~Compare **polygenesis.**
monogenetic (ˌmɒnəʊdʒɪ'nɛtɪk) *or* **monogenous** (mɒ'nɒdʒənəs) *adj.* **1.** of, relating to, or showing monogenesis. **2.** of or relating to animals, such as some flukes, that complete their life cycle on only one host. **3.** (of rocks and rock formations) formed from one source or by one process.
monogenic (ˌmɒnəʊ'dʒɛnɪk) *adj.* **1.** *Genetics.* of or relating to an inherited character difference that is controlled by one pair of genes. **2.** (of animals) producing offspring of one sex.
monogram ('mɒnəˌgræm) *n.* a design of one or more letters, esp. initials, embroidered on clothing, printed on stationery, etc. [C17: from Late Latin *monogramma,* from Greek; see MONO-, -GRAM] —**monogrammatic** (ˌmɒnəgrə'mætɪk) *adj.*
monograph ('mɒnəˌgrɑːf, -ˌgræf) *n.* **1.** a paper, book, or other work concerned with a single subject or aspect of a subject. ~*vb.* (*tr.*) **2.** to write a monograph on. —**monographer** (mɒ'nɒgrəfə) *or* **mo'nographist** *n.* —ˌ**mono'graphic** *adj.* —ˌ**mono'graphically** *adv.*

monogyny (mɒˈnɒdʒɪnɪ) *n.* the custom of having only one female sexual partner over a period of time. —**moˈnogynist** *n.* —**moˈnogynous** *adj.*
monohull (ˈmɒnəʊˌhʌl) *n.* a sailing vessel with a single hull. Compare **multihull.**
monohybrid (ˌmɒnəʊˈhaɪbrɪd) *n. Genetics.* the offspring of two individuals that differ with respect to one pair of genes.
monohydrate (ˌmɒnəʊˈhaɪdreɪt) *n.* a hydrate, such as ferrous sulphate monohydrate, $FeSO_4.H_2O$, containing one molecule of water per molecule of the compound. —ˌ**monoˈhydrated** *adj.*
monohydric (ˌmɒnəʊˈhaɪdrɪk) *adj.* another word for **monohydroxy,** esp. when applied to alcohols.
monohydroxy (ˌmɒnəʊhaɪˈdrɒksɪ) *adj.* (of a chemical compound) containing one hydroxyl group per molecule. Also: **monohydric.**
monoicous (mɒˈnɔɪkəs) *adj.* a variant of **monoecious.** —**moˈnoicously** *adv.*
monolatry (mɒˈnɒlətrɪ) *n.* the exclusive worship of one god without excluding the existence of others. —**monolater** (mɒˈnɒlətə) *or* **moˈnolatrist** *n.* —**moˈnolatrous** *adj.*
monolayer (ˈmɒnəʊˌleɪə) *n.* a single layer of atoms or molecules adsorbed on a surface. Also called: **molecular film.**
monolingual (ˌmɒnəʊˈlɪŋgwəl) *adj.* **1.** knowing or expressed in only one language. ~*n.* **2.** a monolingual person. ~Compare **bilingual, multilingual.**
monolith (ˈmɒnəlɪθ) *n.* **1.** a large block of stone or anything that resembles one in appearance, intractability, etc. **2.** a statue, obelisk, column, etc., cut from one block of stone. **3.** a large hollow foundation piece sunk as a caisson and having a number of compartments that are filled with concrete when it has reached its correct position. [C19: via French from Greek *monolithos* made from a single stone]
monolithic (ˌmɒnəˈlɪθɪk) *adj.* **1.** of, relating to, or like a monolith. **2.** characterized by hugeness, impenetrability, or intractability: *a monolithic government.* **3.** *Electronics.* (of an integrated circuit) having all components manufactured into or on top of a single chip of silicon. Compare **hybrid** (sense 6). —ˌ**monoˈlithically** *adv.*
monologue (ˈmɒnəˌlɒg) *n.* **1.** a long speech made by one actor in a play, film, etc., esp. when alone. **2.** a dramatic piece for a single performer. **3.** any long speech by one person, esp. when interfering with conversation. [C17: via French from Greek *monologos* speaking alone] —**monologic** (ˌmɒnəˈlɒdʒɪk) *or* ˌ**monoˈlogical** *adj.* —**monologist** (ˈmɒnəˌlɒgɪst, məˈnɒləgɪst) *n.* —**monology** (mɒˈnɒlədʒɪ) *n.*
monomania (ˌmɒnəʊˈmeɪnɪə) *n.* an excessive mental preoccupation with one thing, idea, etc. —ˌ**monoˈmaniˌac** *n., adj.* —**monomaniacal** (ˌmɒnəʊməˈnaɪəkᵊl) *adj.*
monomark (ˈmɒnəmɑːk) *n. Brit.* a series of letters or figures to identify goods, personal articles, etc.
monomer (ˈmɒnəmə) *n. Chem.* a compound whose molecules can join together to form a polymer. —**monomeric** (ˌmɒnəˈmɛrɪk) *adj.*
monomerous (mɒˈnɒmərəs) *adj.* (of flowers) having whorls consisting of only one member. [C19: from Greek *monomerēs* of one part; see MONO-, -MERE]
monometallic (ˌmɒnəʊmɪˈtælɪk) *adj.* **1.** (esp. of coins) consisting of one metal only. **2.** relating to monometallism.
monometallism (ˌmɒnəʊˈmɛtᵊˌlɪzəm) *n.* **1.** the use of one metal, esp. gold or silver, as the sole standard of value and currency. **2.** the economic policies supporting a monometallic standard. —ˌ**monoˈmetallist** *n.*
monometer (mɒˈnɒmɪtə) *n. Prosody.* a line of verse consisting of one metrical foot. —**monometrical** (ˌmɒnəʊˈmɛtrɪkᵊl) *or* ˌ**monoˈmetric** *adj.*
monomial (mɒˈnəʊmɪəl) *n.* **1.** *Maths.* an expression consisting of a single term, such as $5ax$. ~*adj.* **2.** consisting of a single algebraic term. **3.** *Biology.* of, relating to, or denoting a taxonomic name that consists of a single term. [C18: MONO- + (BIN)OMIAL]
monomode (ˈmɒnəʊˌməʊd) *adj.* denoting or relating to a type of optical fibre with a core less than 10 micrometres in diameter.
monomolecular (ˌmɒnəʊməˈlɛkjʊlə) *adj.* of, concerned with, or involving single molecules: *a monomolecular layer.*
monomorphic (ˌmɒnəʊˈmɔːfɪk) *or* **monomorphous** *adj.* **1.** (of an individual organism) showing little or no change in structure during the entire life history. **2.** (of a species) existing or having parts that exist in only one form. **3.** (of a chemical compound) having only one crystalline form. —ˌ**monoˈmorphism** *n.*
mononuclear (ˌmɒnəʊˈnjuːklɪə) *adj.* **1.** (of a cell) having only one nucleus. **2.** another word for **monocyclic** (sense 1).
mononucleosis (ˌmɒnəʊˌnjuːklɪˈəʊsɪs) *n.* **1.** *Pathol.* the presence of a large number of monocytes in the blood. **2.** See **infectious mononucleosis.**
monopetalous (ˌmɒnəʊˈpɛtᵊləs) *adj.* **1.** another word for **gamopetalous. 2.** (of flowers) having only one petal.
monophagous (məˈnɒfəgəs) *adj.* feeding on only one type of food: *monophagous insects.* —**moˈnophagy** *n.*
monophobia (ˌmɒnəʊˈfəʊbɪə) *n.* a strong fear of being alone. —ˌ**monoˈphobic** *adj.*
monophonic (ˌmɒnəʊˈfɒnɪk) *adj.* **1.** Also: **monaural.** (of a system of broadcasting, recording, or reproducing sound) using only one channel between source and loudspeaker. Sometimes shortened to **mono.** Compare **stereophonic. 2.** *Music.* of or relating to a style of musical composition consisting of a single melodic line. See also **monody** (sense 3). —**monophony** (mɒˈnɒfənɪ) *n.*
monophthong (ˈmɒnəfˌθɒŋ) *n.* a simple or pure vowel. [C17: from Greek *monophthongos,* from MONO- + *thongos* sound] —**monophthongal** (ˌmɒnəfˈθɒŋgᵊl) *adj.*
monophyletic (ˌmɒnəʊfaɪˈlɛtɪk) *adj.* **1.** relating to or characterized by descent from a single ancestral group of animals or plants. **2.** (of animals or plants) of or belonging to a single stock.
monophyllous (ˌmɒnəʊˈfɪləs) *adj. Botany.* having or consisting of only one leaf or leaflike part.
Monophysite (mɒˈnɒfɪˌsaɪt) *Christianity.* ~*n.* **1.** a person who holds that there is only one nature in the person of Christ, which is primarily divine with human attributes. ~*adj.* **2.** of or relating to this belief. [C17: via Church Latin from Late Greek, from MONO- + *phusis* nature] —**Monophysitic** (ˌmɒnəʊfɪˈsɪtɪk) *adj.* —**Moˈnophyˌsitism** *n.*
monoplane (ˈmɒnəʊˌpleɪn) *n.* an aeroplane with only one pair of wings. Compare **biplane.**
monoplegia (ˌmɒnəʊˈpliːdʒɪə) *n. Pathol.* paralysis limited to one limb or a single group of muscles. —**monoplegic** (ˌmɒnəʊˈpliːdʒɪk) *adj.*
monoploid (ˈmɒnəˌplɔɪd) *adj., n.* a less common word for **haploid.**
monopode (ˈmɒnəˌpəʊd) *n.* **1.** a member of a legendary one-legged race of Africa. **2.** another word for **monopodium.** [C19: from Late Latin *monopodius*]
monopodium (ˌmɒnəˈpəʊdɪəm) *n., pl.* **-dia** (-dɪə). the main axis of growth in the pine tree and similar plants: the main stem, which elongates from the tip and gives rise to lateral branches. Compare **sympodium.** [C19: New Latin, from Greek *monopous,* from MONO- + *pous* foot] —ˌ**monoˈpodial** *adj.* —ˌ**monoˈpodially** *adv.*
monopole (ˈmɒnəˌpəʊl) *n. Physics.* **1.** an electric charge or magnetic pole considered in isolation. **2.** Also called: **magnetic monopole.** a hypothetical elementary particle postulated in certain theories of particle physics to exist as an isolated north or south magnetic pole.
monopolistic competition *n. Economics.* the form of imperfect competition that exists when there are many producers or sellers of similar but differentiated goods or services.
monopolize *or* **monopolise** (məˈnɒpəˌlaɪz) *vb.* (*tr.*) **1.** to have, control, or make use of fully, excluding others. **2.** to obtain, maintain, or exploit a monopoly of (a market, commodity, etc.). —**moˌnopoliˈzation** *or* **moˌnopoliˈsation** *n.* —**moˈnopoˌlizer** *or* **moˈnopoˌliser** *n.*
monopoly (məˈnɒpəlɪ) *n., pl.* **-lies. 1.** exclusive control of the market supply of a product or service. **2. a.** an enterprise exercising this control. **b.** the product or service so controlled. **3.** *Law.* the exclusive right or privilege granted to a person, company, etc., by the state to purchase, manufacture, use, or sell some commodity or to carry on trade in a specified country or area. **4.** exclusive control, possession, or use of something. [C16: from Late Latin, from Greek *monopōlion,* from MONO- + *pōlein* to sell] —**moˈnopolism** *n.* —**moˈnopolist** *n.* —**moˌnopoˈlistic** *adj.* —**moˌnopoˈlistically** *adv.*
Monopoly (məˈnɒpəlɪ) *n. Trademark.* a board game for two to six players who throw dice to advance their tokens around a board, the object being to acquire the property on which their tokens land.
monopropellant (ˌmɒnəʊprəˈpɛlənt) *n.* a solid or liquid rocket propellant containing both the fuel and the oxidizer.
monopsony (məˈnɒpsənɪ) *n., pl.* **-nies.** a situation in which the entire market demand for a product or service consists of only one buyer. [C20: MONO- + Greek *opsōnia* purchase, from *opsōnein* to buy] —**moˌnopsoˈnistic** *adj.*
monopteros (mɒnˈɒptəˌrɒs) *or* **monopteron** *n., pl.* **-teroi** (-təˌrɔɪ) *or* **-tera** (-tərə). a circular classical building, esp. a temple, that has a single ring of columns surrounding it. [C18: Late Latin from Greek, from MONO- + *pteron* a wing] —**monˈopteral** *adj.*
monorail (ˈmɒnəʊˌreɪl) *n.* a single-rail railway, often elevated and with suspended cars.
monosaccharide (ˌmɒnəʊˈsækəˌraɪd, -rɪd) *n.* a simple sugar, such as glucose or fructose, that does not hydrolyse to yield other sugars.
monosemy (ˈmɒnəʊˌsiːmɪ) *n.* the fact of having only a single meaning; absence of ambiguity in a word. Compare **polysemy.** [C20: from MONO- + (POLY)SEMY]
monosepalous (ˌmɒnəʊˈsɛpələs) *adj.* **1.** another word for **gamosepalous. 2.** (of flowers) having only one sepal.
monoski (ˈmɒnəʊˌskiː) *n.* a wide ski on which the skier stands with both feet. —ˈ**monoˌskier** *n.* —ˈ**monoˌskiing** *n.*
monosodium glutamate (ˌmɒnəʊˈsəʊdɪəm) *n.* a white crystalline substance, the sodium salt of glutamic acid, that has little flavour itself but enhances the flavour of proteins either by increasing the amount of saliva produced in the mouth or by stimulating the taste buds: used as a food additive, esp. in Chinese foods. Formula: $NaC_5H_8O_4$. Also called: **sodium glutamate.** Abbrev.: **MSG.**

monosome ('mɒnəˌsəʊm) *n.* an unpaired chromosome, esp. an X-chromosome in an otherwise diploid cell. —**monosomic** (ˌmɒnə'səʊmɪk) *adj.*
monospermous (ˌmɒnəʊ'spɜːməs) *or* **monospermal** *adj.* (of certain plants) producing only one seed.
monostable (ˌmɒnəʊ'steɪbᵊl) *adj. Physics.* (of an electronic circuit) having only one stable state but able to pass into a second state in response to an input pulse.
monostich ('mɒnəˌstɪk) *n.* a poem of a single line. [C16: via Late Latin from Greek; see MONO-, STICH] —ˌ**mono'stichic** *adj.*
monostichous (ˌmɒnəʊ'staɪkəs) *adj. Botany.* (of parts) forming one row.
monostome ('mɒnəˌstəʊm) *or* **monostomous** (mɒ'nɒstəməs) *adj. Zoology, botany.* having only one mouth, pore, or similar opening.
monostrophe (mɒ'nɒstrəfɪ, 'mɒnəˌstrəʊf) *n.* a poem in which all the stanzas or strophes are written in the same metre. —**monostrophic** (ˌmɒnə'strɒfɪk) *adj.*
monostylous (ˌmɒnəʊ'staɪləs) *adj. Botany.* having only one style.
monosyllabic (ˌmɒnəsɪ'læbɪk) *adj.* **1.** (of a word) containing only one syllable. **2.** characterized by monosyllables; curt: *a monosyllabic answer.* —ˌ**monosyl'labically** *adv.*
monosyllable ('mɒnəˌsɪləbᵊl) *n.* a word of one syllable, esp. one used as a sentence. —ˌ**mono'syllaˌbism** *n.*
monosymmetric (ˌmɒnəsɪ'mɛtrɪk) *or* **monosymmetrical** *adj.* **1.** *Crystallog.* variants of **monoclinic.** **2.** *Biology.* variants of **zygomorphic.** —ˌ**monosym'metrically** *adv.* —**monosymmetry** (ˌmɒnə'sɪmɪtrɪ) *n.*
monotheism ('mɒnəʊθɪˌɪzəm) *n.* the belief or doctrine that there is only one God. —'**monoˌtheist** *n., adj.* —ˌ**monothe'istic** *adj.* —ˌ**monothe'istically** *adv.*
monotint ('mɒnəˌtɪnt) *n.* another word for **monochrome** (senses 3, 4).
monotocous (mə'nɒtəkəs) *adj.* (of certain animals) producing a single offspring at a birth. [from MONO- + Greek *tokos* birth]
monotone ('mɒnəˌtəʊn) *n.* **1.** a single unvaried pitch level in speech, sound, etc. **2.** utterance, etc., without change of pitch. **3.** lack of variety in style, expression. etc. ~*adj.* **4.** unvarying or monotonous. **5.** Also: **monotonic** (ˌmɒnə'tɒnɪk). *Maths.* (of a sequence or function) consistently increasing or decreasing in value.
monotonize *or* **monotonise** (mə'nɒtəˌnaɪz) *vb.* (*tr.*) to make monotonous.
monotonous (mə'nɒtənəs) *adj.* **1.** dull and tedious, esp. because of repetition. **2.** unvarying in pitch or cadence. —**mo'notonously** *adv.* —**mo'notonousness** *n.*
monotony (mə'nɒtənɪ) *n., pl.* **-nies.** **1.** wearisome routine; dullness. **2.** lack of variety in pitch or cadence.
monotreme ('mɒnəʊˌtriːm) *n.* any mammal of the primitive order *Monotremata,* of Australia and New Guinea: egg-laying toothless animals with a single opening (cloaca) for the passage of eggs or sperm, faeces, and urine. The group contains only the echidnas and the platypus. [C19: via New Latin from MONO- + Greek *trēma* hole] —**monotrematous** (ˌmɒnəʊ'triːmətəs) *adj.*
monotrichous (mɒ'nɒtrɪkəs) *or* **monotrichic** (ˌmɒnəʊ'trɪkɪk) *adj.* (of bacteria) having a single flagellum.
monotype ('mɒnəˌtaɪp) *n.* **1.** a single print made from a metal or glass plate on which a picture has been painted. **2.** *Biology.* a monotypic genus or species.
Monotype ('mɒnəˌtaɪp) *n.* **1.** *Trademark.* any of various typesetting systems, esp. originally one in which each character was cast individually from hot metal. **2.** type produced by such a system.
monotypic (ˌmɒnəʊ'tɪpɪk) *adj.* **1.** (of a genus or species) consisting of only one type of animal or plant. **2.** of or relating to a monotype.
monounsaturated (ˌmɒnəʊʌn'sætʃəˌreɪtɪd) *adj.* of or relating to a class of vegetable oils, such as olive oil, the molecules of which have long chains of carbon atoms containing only one double bond. See also **polyunsaturated.**
monovalent (ˌmɒnəʊ'veɪlənt) *adj. Chem.* **a.** having a valency of one. **b.** having only one valency. ~Also: **univalent.** —ˌ**mono'valence** *or* ˌ**mono'valency** *n.*
monoxide (mɒ'nɒksaɪd) *n.* an oxide that contains one oxygen atom per molecule: *carbon monoxide, CO.*
Monseigneur *French.* (mɔ̃sɛɲœr) *n., pl.* ***Messeigneurs*** (mesɛɲœr). a title given to French bishops, prelates, and princes. Abbrev.: **Mgr.** [literally: my lord]
monsieur (*French* məsjø; *English* məs'jɜː) *n., pl.* **messieurs** (*French* mesjø; *English* 'mɛsəz). a French title of address equivalent to *sir* when used alone or *Mr* when placed before a name. [literally: my lord]
Monsignor (mɒn'siːnjə; *Italian* monsiɲ'ɲor) *n., pl.* **Monsignors** *or* **Monsignori** (*Italian* monsiɲ'ɲoːri). *R.C. Church.* an ecclesiastical title attached to certain offices or distinctions usually bestowed by the Pope. Abbrevs.: **Mgr, Msgr.** [C17: from Italian, from French MONSEIGNEUR]
monsoon (mɒn'suːn) *n.* **1.** a seasonal wind of S Asia that blows from the southwest in summer, bringing heavy rains, and from the northeast in winter. **2.** the rainy season when the SW monsoon blows, from about April to October. **3.** any wind that changes direction with the seasons. [C16: from obsolete Dutch *monssoen,* from Portuguese *monção,* from Arabic *mawsim* season] —**mon'soonal** *adj.*
mons pubis ('mɒnz 'pjuːbɪs) *n., pl.* **montes pubis** ('mɒntiːz). the fatty cushion of flesh in human males situated over the junction of the pubic bones. Compare **mons veneris.** [C17: New Latin: hill of the pubes]
monster ('mɒnstə) *n.* **1.** an imaginary beast, such as a centaur, usually made up of various animal or human parts. **2.** a person, animal, or plant with a marked structural deformity. **3.** a cruel, wicked, or inhuman person. **4. a.** a very large person, animal, or thing. **b.** (*as modifier*): *a monster cake.* [C13: from Old French *monstre,* from Latin *monstrum* portent, from *monēre* to warn]
monstera (mɒn'stɪərə) *n.* any plant of the tropical climbing genus *Monstera,* some species of which are grown as greenhouse or pot plants for their unusual leathery perforated leaves: family *Araceae. M. deliciosa* is the Swiss cheese plant. [New Latin, perhaps because the leaves were regarded as an aberration]
monstrance ('mɒnstrəns) *n. R.C. Church.* a receptacle, usually of gold or silver, with a transparent container in which the consecrated Host is exposed for adoration. [C16: from Medieval Latin *mōnstrantia,* from Latin *mōnstrāre* to show]
monstrosity (mɒn'strɒsɪtɪ) *n., pl.* **-ties.** **1.** an outrageous or ugly person or thing; monster. **2.** the state or quality of being monstrous.
monstrous ('mɒnstrəs) *adj.* **1.** abnormal, hideous, or unnatural in size, character, etc. **2.** (of plants and animals) abnormal in structure. **3.** outrageous, atrocious, or shocking: *it is monstrous how badly he has been treated.* **4.** huge: *a monstrous audience.* **5.** of, relating to, or resembling a monster. —'**monstrously** *adv.* —'**monstrousness** *n.*
mons veneris ('mɒnz 'vɛnərɪs) *n., pl.* **montes veneris** ('mɒntiːz). the fatty cushion of flesh in human females situated over the junction of the pubic bones. Compare **mons pubis.** [C17: New Latin: hill of Venus, goddess of love]
Mont. *abbrev. for* Montana.
montage (mɒn'tɑːʒ; *French* mɔ̃taʒ) *n.* **1.** the art or process of composing pictures by the superimposition or juxtaposition of miscellaneous elements, such as other pictures or photographs. **2.** such a composition. **3.** a method of film editing involving the juxtaposition or partial superimposition of several shots to form a single image. **4.** a rapidly cut film sequence of this kind. [C20: from French, from *monter* to MOUNT¹]
Montagnard (ˌmɒntən'jɑːd, -'jɑː) *n., pl.* **-gnards** *or* **-gnard.** **1.** a member of a hill people living on the border between Vietnam, Laos, and NE Cambodia. **2.** a member of a North American Indian people living in the N Rocky Mountains. [C19: from French: mountaineer, from *montagne* MOUNTAIN]
Montague grammar ('mɒntəˌgjuː) *n. Logic, linguistics.* a model-theoretic semantic theory for natural language that seeks to encompass indexical expressions and opaque contexts within an extensional theory by constructing set-theoretic representations of the intension of an expression in terms of functions of possible worlds. [named after Richard Merett *Montague* (1930–71), U.S. logician, who devised it]
Montagu's harrier ('mɒntəˌgjuːz) *n.* a brownish European bird of prey, *Circus pygargus,* with long narrow wings and a long tail: family *Accipitridae* (hawks, harriers, etc.). [C19: named after Col. George *Montagu* (1751–1815), British naturalist]
montane ('mɒnteɪn) *adj.* of or inhabiting mountainous regions: *a montane flora.* [C19: from Latin *montānus,* from *mons* MOUNTAIN]
montan wax ('mɒntæn) *n.* a hard wax obtained from lignite and peat, varying in colour from white to dark brown. It is used in polishes and candles. [C20: from Latin *montānus* of a mountain]
montbretia (mɒn'briːʃə) *n.* **1.** any plant of the African iridaceous genus *Montbretia,* with ornamental orange or yellow flowers, grown mostly as pot plants. **2.** See **crocosmia.** [C19: New Latin, named after A. F. E. Coquebert de *Montbret* (1780–1801), French botanist]
mont-de-piété *French.* (mɔ̃dpjete) *n., pl.* ***monts-de-piété*** (mɔ̃dpjete). (formerly) a public pawnshop. [from Italian *monte di pietà* bank of pity]
monte ('mɒntɪ) *n.* **1.** a gambling card game of Spanish origin. **2.** *Austral. informal.* a certainty. [C19: from Spanish: mountain, hence pile of cards]
Monte Carlo method ('mɒntɪ 'kɑːləʊ) *n.* a heuristic mathematical technique for evaluation or estimation of intractable problems by probabilistic simulation and sampling. [C20: named after the casino at Monte Carlo in Monaco, where systems for winning at roulette, etc., are often tried]
monteith (mɒn'tiːθ) *n.* a large ornamental bowl, usually of silver, for cooling wineglasses, which are suspended from the notched rim. [C17: said to be from the name of a Scot who wore a cloak with a scalloped edge]
Monterey pine (ˌmɒntə'reɪ) *n.* another name for **macrocarpa.** [named after *Monterey,* city in California]
montero (mɒn'tɛərəʊ; *Spanish* mon'tero) *n., pl.* **-ros** (-rəʊz; *Spanish* -ros). a round cap with a flap at the back worn by hunters, esp. in Spain in the 17th and 18th centuries. [C17: from Spanish, literally: mountaineer]
Montessori method (ˌmɒntɪ'sɔːrɪ) *n.* a method of nursery education in which children are provided with generous facilities for practical play and allowed to develop at their own pace. [C20:

named after Maria *Montessori* (1870–1952), Italian educational reformer who evolved it]

Montezuma's revenge (ˌmɒntɪˈzuːməz) *n. Informal.* an acute attack of infectious diarrhoea, esp. when experienced in Mexico by tourists. [C20: after *Montezuma* II (1466–1520), Aztec emperor of Mexico killed by the Spanish]

montgolfier (mɒntˈgɒlfɪə; *French* mɔ̃gɔlfje) *n.* a hot-air balloon. [C18: named after the French *Montgolfier* brothers, Jacques (1745–99) and Joseph (1740–1810), who built and ascended in the first practical balloon]

month (mʌnθ) *n.* **1.** one of the twelve divisions (**calendar months**) of the calendar year. **2.** a period of time extending from one date to a corresponding date in the next calendar month. **3.** a period of four weeks or of 30 days. **4.** the period of time (**solar month**) taken by the moon to return to the same longitude after one complete revolution around the earth; 27.321 58 days (approximately 27 days, 7 hours, 43 minutes, 4.5 seconds). **5.** the period of time (**sidereal month**) taken by the moon to make one complete revolution around the earth, measured between two successive conjunctions with a particular star; 27.321 66 days (approximately 27 days, 7 hours, 43 minutes, 11 seconds). **6.** Also called: **lunation.** the period of time (**lunar** or **synodic month**) taken by the moon to make one complete revolution around the earth, measured between two successive new moons; 29.530 59 days (approximately 29 days, 12 hours, 44 minutes, 3 seconds). **7. a month of Sundays.** *Informal.* an extremely long unspecified period of time. [Old English *mōnath;* related to Old High German *mānōd,* Old Norse *mānathr;* compare Gothic *mena* moon]

monthly (ˈmʌnθlɪ) *adj.* **1.** occurring, done, appearing, payable, etc., once every month. **2.** lasting or valid for a month: *a monthly subscription.* ~*adv.* **3.** once a month. ~*n., pl.* **-lies. 4.** a book, periodical, magazine, etc., published once a month. **5.** *Informal.* a menstrual period.

month's mind *n. R.C. Church.* a Mass celebrated in remembrance of a person one month after his death.

monticule (ˈmɒntɪˌkjuːl) *n.* a small hill or mound, such as a secondary volcanic cone. [C18: via French from Late Latin *monticulus,* diminutive of Latin *mons* mountain]

montmorillonite (ˌmɒntməˈrɪləˌnaɪt) *n.* a clay mineral consisting of hydrated aluminium silicate: an important component of bentonite. [C19: named after *Montmorillon,* French town where it was first found, + -ITE[1]]

monument (ˈmɒnjʊmənt) *n.* **1.** an obelisk, statue, building, etc., erected in commemoration of a person or event or in celebration of something. **2.** a notable building or site, esp. one preserved as public property. **3.** a tomb or tombstone. **4.** a literary or artistic work regarded as commemorative of its creator or a particular period. **5.** *U.S.* a boundary marker. **6.** an exceptional example: *his lecture was a monument of tedium.* **7.** an obsolete word for **statue.** [C13: from Latin *monumentum,* from *monēre* to remind, advise]

monumental (ˌmɒnjʊˈmentᵊl) *adj.* **1.** like a monument, esp. in large size, endurance, or importance: *a monumental work of art.* **2.** of, relating to, or being a monument. **3.** *Informal.* (intensifier): *monumental stupidity.* —ˌ**monumenˈtality** *n.* —ˌ**monuˈmentally** *adv.*

mony (ˈmɒnɪ) *determiner.* a Scot. word for **many.**

monzonite (ˈmɒnzəˌnaɪt) *n.* a coarse-grained plutonic igneous rock consisting of equal amounts of plagioclase and orthoclase feldspar, with ferromagnesian minerals. [C19: from German, named after *Monzoni,* Tyrolean mountain where it was found] —**monzonitic** (ˌmɒnzəˈnɪtɪk) *adj.*

moo (muː) *vb.* **1.** (*intr.*) (of a cow, bull, etc.) to make a characteristic deep long sound; low. ~*interj.* **2.** an instance or imitation of this sound.

mooch (muːtʃ) *vb. Slang.* **1.** (*intr.*) (often with *around*) to loiter or walk aimlessly. **2.** (*intr.*) to behave in an apathetic way. **3.** (*intr.*) to sneak or lurk; skulk. **4.** (*tr.*) to cadge **5.** (*tr.*) *Chiefly U.S. and Canadian.* to steal. [C17: perhaps from Old French *muchier* to skulk] —ˈ**moocher** *n.*

mood[1] (muːd) *n.* **1.** a temporary state of mind or temper: *a cheerful mood.* **2.** a sullen or gloomy state of mind, esp. when temporary: *she's in a mood.* **3.** a prevailing atmosphere or feeling. **4. in the mood.** in a favourable state of mind (for something or to do something). [Old English *mōd* mind, feeling; compare Old Norse *mōthr* grief, wrath]

mood[2] (muːd) *n.* **1.** *Grammar.* a category of the verb or verbal inflections that expresses semantic and grammatical differences, including such forms as the indicative, subjunctive, and imperative. **2.** *Logic.* one of the possible arrangements of the syllogism, classified solely by whether the component propositions are universal or particular and affirmative or negative. Compare **figure** (sense 18). ~Also called: **mode.** [C16: from MOOD[1], influenced in meaning by MODE]

moody (ˈmuːdɪ) *adj.* **moodier, moodiest. 1.** sullen, sulky, or gloomy. **2.** temperamental or changeable. —ˈ**moodily** *adv.* —ˈ**moodiness** *n.*

Moog (muːg, məʊg) *n. Music, trademark.* a type of synthesizer. [C20: named after Robert *Moog* (born 1934), U.S. engineer]

mooi (mɔɪ) *adj. S. African slang.* pleasing; nice. [Afrikaans]

moolah (ˈmuːlɑː) *n.* a slang word for **money.**

mooli (ˈmuːlɪ) *n.* a type of large white radish. [E African native name]

moolvie *or* **moolvi** (ˈmuːlviː) *n.* (esp. in India) a Muslim doctor of the law, teacher, or learned man: also used as a title of respect. [C17: from Urdu, from Arabic *mawlawīy;* compare MULLAH]

Moomba (ˈmuːmbə) *n. Austral.* a festival held annually in Melbourne since 1954. [named in the belief that *moomba* was an Aboriginal word meaning "Let's get together and have fun"]

moon (muːn) *n.* **1.** the natural satellite of the earth. Diameter: 3476 km; mass: 7.4×10^{22} kg; mean distance from earth: 384 400 km; periods of rotation and revolution: 27.32 days. **2.** the face of the moon as it is seen during its revolution around the earth, esp. at one of its phases: *new moon; full moon.* **3.** any natural satellite of a planet. **4.** moonlight; moonshine. **5.** something resembling a moon. **6.** a month, esp. a lunar one. **7. once in a blue moon.** very seldom. **8. over the moon.** *Informal.* extremely happy; ecstatic. **9. reach for the moon.** to desire or attempt something unattainable or difficult to obtain. ~*vb.* **10.** (when *tr.,* often foll. by *away;* when *intr.,* often foll. by *around*) to be idle in a listless way, as if in love, or to idle (time) away. **11.** (*intr.*) *Slang.* to expose one's buttocks to passers-by. [Old English *mōna;* compare Old Frisian *mōna,* Old High German *māno*] —ˈ**moonless** *adj.*

Moon (muːn) *n.* a system of embossed alphabetical signs for blind readers, the fourteen basic characters of which can, by rotation, mimic most of the letters of the Roman alphabet, thereby making learning easier for those who learnt to read before going blind. Compare **Braille.** [C19: named after William *Moon* (1818–94), British inventor of the system]

moonbeam (ˈmuːnˌbiːm) *n.* a ray of moonlight.

moon blindness *n.* **1.** *Ophthalmol.* a nontechnical name for **nyctalopia. 2.** Also called: **mooneye.** *Vet. science.* a disorder affecting horses, which causes inflammation of the eyes and sometimes blindness. —ˈ**moon-ˌblind** *adj.*

mooncalf (ˈmuːnˌkɑːf) *n., pl.* **-calves** (-ˌkɑːvz). **1.** a born fool; dolt. **2.** a person who idles time away. **3.** *Obsolete.* a freak or monster.

Moon Child *n.* a euphemistic name for **Cancer** (sense 2b).

mooned (muːnd) *adj.* decorated with a moon.

mooneye (ˈmuːnˌaɪ) *n.* **1.** any of several North American large-eyed freshwater clupeoid fishes of the family *Hiodontidae,* esp. *Hiodon tergisus.* See also **goldeye. 2.** *Vet. science.* another name for **moon blindness** (sense 2).

moon-eyed *adj.* **1.** having the eyes open wide, as in awe. **2.** *Vet. science.* affected with moon blindness.

moon-faced *adj.* having a round face; full-faced.

moonfish (ˈmuːnˌfɪʃ) *n., pl.* **-fishes** *or* **-fish. 1.** any of several deep-bodied silvery carangid fishes, occurring in warm and tropical American coastal waters. **2.** any of various other round silvery fishes, such as the Indo-Pacific *Monodactylus argenteus.* **3.** another name for **opah.**

moonflower (ˈmuːnˌflaʊə) *n.* **1.** any of several night-blooming convolvulaceous plants, esp. the white-flowered *Calonyction* (or *Ipomoea*) *aculeatum.* **2.** Also called: **angels' tears.** a Mexican solanaceous plant, *Datura suaveolens,* planted in the tropics for its white night-blooming flowers.

Moonie (ˈmuːnɪ) *n. Informal.* **1.** a member of the Unification Church. **2.** (*pl.;* preceded by *the*) the Unification Church. [C20: named after the founder Sun Myung *Moon* (born 1920), S Korean industrialist]

moonlight (ˈmuːnˌlaɪt) *n.* **1.** Also called: **moonshine.** light from the sun received on earth after reflection by the moon. **2.** (*modifier*) illuminated by the moon: *a moonlight walk.* ~*vb.* **-lights, -lighting, -lighted. 3.** (*intr.*) *Informal.* to work at a secondary job, esp. at night, and often illegitimately. —ˈ**moonˌlighter** *n.*

moonlight flit *n. Brit. informal.* a hurried departure at night, esp. from rented accommodation to avoid payment of rent owed.

moonlighting (ˈmuːnˌlaɪtɪŋ) *n.* **1.** working at a secondary job. **2.** (in 19th-century Ireland) the carrying out of cattle-maiming, murders, etc., during the night in protest against the land-tenure system.

moonlit (ˈmuːnlɪt) *adj.* illuminated by the moon.

moon pool *n.* (in the oil industry) an open shaft in the centre of the hull of a ship engaged in deep-sea drilling through which drilling takes place.

moonquake (ˈmuːnˌkweɪk) *n.* a light tremor of the moon, detected on the moon's surface.

moonraker (ˈmuːnˌreɪkə) *n. Nautical.* a small square sail set above a skysail.

moon rat *n.* a ratlike SE Asian nocturnal mammal, *Echinosorex gymnurus,* with greyish fur and an elongated snout: family *Erinaceidae* (hedgehogs): the largest living insectivore.

moonrise (ˈmuːnˌraɪz) *n.* the moment when the moon appears above the horizon.

moonscape (ˈmuːnˌskeɪp) *n.* the general surface of the moon or a representation of it.

moonseed (ˈmuːnˌsiːd) *n.* any menispermaceous climbing plant of the genus *Menispermum* and related genera, having red or black fruits with crescent-shaped or ring-shaped seeds.

moonset (ˈmuːnˌsɛt) *n.* the moment when the moon disappears below the horizon.

moonshine (ˈmuːnˌʃaɪn) *n.* **1.** another word for **moonlight** (sense 1). **2.** *U.S. and Canadian.* illegally distilled or smuggled whisky or other spirit. **3.** foolish talk or thought.

moonshiner ('muːnˌʃaɪnə) *n. U.S. and Canadian.* a person who illegally makes or smuggles distilled spirits.
moonshot ('muːnˌʃɒt) *n.* the launching of a spacecraft, rocket, etc., to the moon.
moonstone ('muːnˌstəʊn) *n.* a gem variety of orthoclase or albite that is white and translucent with bluish reflections.
moonstruck ('muːnˌstrʌk) *or* **moonstricken** ('muːnˌstrɪkən) *adj.* deranged or mad.
moonwort ('muːnˌwɜːt) *n.* **1.** Also called (U.S.): **grape fern.** any of various ferns of the genus *Botrychium,* esp. *B. lunaria,* which has crescent-shaped leaflets. **2.** another name for **honesty** (sense 4).
moony ('muːnɪ) *adj.* **moonier, mooniest.** **1.** *Informal.* dreamy or listless. **2.** of or like the moon. **3.** *Brit. slang.* crazy or foolish. —'**moonily** *adv.* —'**mooniness** *n.*
moor[1] (mʊə, mɔː) *n.* a tract of unenclosed ground, usually having peaty soil covered with heather, coarse grass, bracken, and moss. [Old English *mōr;* related to Old Saxon *mōr,* Old High German *muor* swamp] —'**moory** *adj.*
moor[2] (mʊə, mɔː) *vb.* to secure (a ship, boat, etc.) with cables, ropes, or anchors, or (of a ship, boat, etc.) to be secured in this way. [C15: of Germanic origin; related to Old English *mǣrelsrāp* rope for mooring]
Moor (mʊə, mɔː) *n.* a member of a Muslim people of North Africa, of mixed Arab and Berber descent. In the 8th century they were converted to Islam and established power in North Africa and Spain, where they established a civilization (756–1492). [C14: via Old French from Latin *Maurus,* from Greek *Mauros,* possibly from Berber]
moorage ('mʊərɪdʒ, 'mɔːrɪdʒ) *n.* **1.** a place for mooring a vessel. **2.** a charge for mooring. **3.** the act of mooring.
moorburn *or* **muirburn** ('muːrˌbʌrn, 'mʊəˌbɜːn) *n. Scot.* the practice of burning off old growth on a heather moor to encourage new growth for grazing.
moorcock ('mʊəˌkɒk, 'mɔː-) *n.* the male of the red grouse.
Moore ('mʊʊre) *n.* another name for **Mossi.**
moorfowl ('mʊəˌfaʊl, 'mɔː-) *n.* (in Brit. game laws) an archaic name for **red grouse.** Compare **heathfowl.**
moor grass *n.* a grass characteristic of moors, especially **purple moor grass** (*Molinia caerulea*) of heath and fenland and **blue moor grass** (*Sesleria caerulea*) of limestone uplands.
moorhen ('mʊəˌhɛn, 'mɔː-) *n.* **1.** a bird, *Gallinula chloropus,* inhabiting ponds, lakes, etc., having a black plumage, red bill, and a red shield above the bill: family *Rallidae* (rails). **2.** the female of the red grouse.
mooring ('mʊərɪŋ, 'mɔː-) *n.* **1.** a place for mooring a vessel. **2.** a permanent anchor, dropped in the water and equipped with a floating buoy, to which vessels can moor. ~See also **moorings.**
mooring mast *n.* a mast or tower to which a balloon or airship may be moored. Also called: **mooring tower.**
moorings ('mʊərɪŋz, 'mɔː-) *pl. n.* **1.** *Nautical.* the ropes, anchors, etc., used in mooring a vessel. **2.** (*sometimes sing.*) something that provides security or stability.
Moorish ('mʊərɪʃ, 'mɔː-) *adj.* **1.** of or relating to the Moors. **2.** denoting the style of architecture used in Spain from the 13th to 16th century, characterized by the horseshoe arch. ~Also: **Morisco** *or* **Moresco.**
Moorish idol *n.* a tropical marine spiny-finned fish, *Zanclus canescens,* that is common around coral reefs: family *Zanclidae.* It has a deeply compressed body with yellow and black stripes, a beaklike snout, and an elongated dorsal fin.
moorland ('mʊələnd, 'mɔː-) *n. Brit.* an area of moor.
moorwort ('mʊəˌwɜːt, 'mɔː-) *n.* another name for **marsh andromeda.**
moose (muːs) *n., pl.* **moose.** a large North American deer, *Alces alces,* having large flattened palmate antlers: also occurs in Europe and Asia where it is called an elk. [C17: from Algonquian; related to Narraganset *moos,* from *moosu* he strips, alluding to the moose's habit of stripping trees]
moot (muːt) *adj.* **1.** subject or open to debate: *a moot point.* ~*vb.* **2.** (*tr.*) to suggest or bring up for debate. **3.** (*intr.*) to plead or argue theoretical or hypothetical cases, as an academic exercise or as vocational training for law students. ~*n.* **4.** a discussion or debate of a hypothetical case or point, held as an academic activity. **5.** (in Anglo-Saxon England) an assembly, mainly in a shire or hundred, dealing with local legal and administrative affairs. [Old English *gemōt;* compare Old Saxon *mōt,* Middle High German *muoze* meeting] —'**mooter** *n.*
moot court *n.* a mock court trying hypothetical legal cases.
mop[1] (mɒp) *n.* **1.** an implement with a wooden handle and a head made of twists of cotton or a piece of synthetic sponge, used for polishing or washing floors, or washing dishes. **2.** something resembling this, such as a tangle of hair. ~*vb.* **mops, mopping, mopped.** (*tr.*) **3.** (often foll. by *up*) to clean or soak up with or as if with a mop. ~See also **mop up.** [C15 *mappe,* from earlier *mappel,* from Medieval Latin *mappula* cloth, from Latin *mappa* napkin]
mop[2] (mɒp) *Rare.* ~*vb.* **mops, mopping, mopped.** **1.** (*intr.*) to make a grimace or sad expression (esp. in the phrase **mop and mow**). ~*n.* **2.** such a face or expression. [C16: perhaps from Dutch *moppen* to pour; compare Dutch *mop* pug dog]
mop[3] (mɒp) *n.* (in various parts of England) an annual fair at which formerly servants were hired. [C17: from the practice of servants carrying a mop, broom, or flail, etc., to signify the job sought]
mopboard ('mɒpˌbɔːd) *n.* a U.S. word for **skirting board.**
mope (məʊp) *vb.* (*intr.*) **1.** to be gloomy or apathetic. **2.** to move or act in an aimless way. ~*n.* **3.** a gloomy person. ~See also **mopes.** [C16: perhaps from obsolete *mope* fool and related to MOP[2]] —'**moper** *n.* —'**mopy** *adj.*
moped ('məʊpɛd) *n. Brit.* a light motorcycle, not over 50cc. [C20: from MOTOR + PEDAL[1], originally equipped with auxiliary pedals]
mopes (məʊps) *pl. n.* **the.** low spirits.
mopoke ('məʊˌpəʊk) *n.* **1.** Also called (N.Z.): **ruru.** a small spotted owl, *Ninox novaeseelandiae,* of Australia and New Zealand. **2.** (in Australia) a frogmouth, *Podargus strigoides,* with reddish-brown or grey plumage. **3.** *Austral. and N.Z. slang.* a slow or lugubrious person. ~Also called: **morepork.** [C19: imitative of the bird's cry]
moppet ('mɒpɪt) *n.* a less common word for **poppet** (sense 1). [C17: from obsolete *mop* rag doll; of obscure origin]
mop up *vb.* (*tr., adv.*) **1.** to clean with a mop. **2.** *Informal.* to complete (a task, etc.). **3.** *Military.* to clear (remaining enemy forces) after a battle, as by killing, taking prisoner, etc. ~*n.* **mop-up. 4.** the act or an instance of mopping up.
moquette (mɒ'kɛt) *n.* a thick velvety fabric used for carpets, upholstery, etc. [C18: from French; of uncertain origin]
mor (mɔː) *n.* a layer of acidic humus formed in cool moist areas where decomposition is slow. Compare **mull**[4]. [Danish]
MOR *abbrev. for* middle-of-the-road: used esp. in radio programming.
mor. *Bookbinding. abbrev. for* morocco.
Mor. *abbrev. for* Morocco.
mora ('mɔːrə) *n., pl.* **-rae** (-riː) *or* **-ras.** *Prosody.* the quantity of a short syllable in verse represented by the breve (˘). [C16: from Latin: pause]
moraceous (mɔː'reɪʃəs) *adj.* of, relating to, or belonging to the *Moraceae,* a mostly tropical and subtropical family of trees and shrubs, including fig, mulberry, breadfruit, and hop, many of which have latex in the stems and heads enclosed in a fleshy receptacle. [C20: via New Latin from Latin *morus* mulberry tree]
moraine (mɒ'reɪn) *n.* a mass of debris, carried by glaciers and forming ridges and mounds when deposited. [C18: from French, from Savoy dialect *morena,* of obscure origin] —**mo'rainal** *or* **mo'rainic** *adj.*
moral ('mɒrəl) *adj.* **1.** concerned with or relating to human behaviour, esp. the distinction between good and bad or right and wrong behaviour: *moral sense.* **2.** adhering to conventionally accepted standards of conduct. **3.** based on a sense of right and wrong according to conscience: *moral courage; moral law.* **4.** having psychological rather than tangible effects: *moral support.* **5.** having the effects but not the appearance of (victory or defeat): *a moral victory; a moral defeat.* **6.** having a strong probability: *a moral certainty.* **7.** *Law.* (of evidence, etc.) based on a knowledge of the tendencies of human nature. ~*n.* **8.** the lesson to be obtained from a fable or event: *point the moral.* **9.** a concise truth; maxim. **10.** (*pl.*) principles of behaviour in accordance with standards of right and wrong. [C14: from Latin *mōrālis* relating to morals or customs, from *mōs* custom] —'**morally** *adv.*
morale (mɒ'rɑːl) *n.* the degree of mental or moral confidence of a person or group; spirit of optimism. [C18: morals, from French, n. use of MORAL (adj.)]
moral hazard *n. Insurance.* a risk incurred by an insurance company with respect to the possible lack of honesty or prudence among policyholders.
moralism ('mɒrəˌlɪzəm) *n.* **1.** the habit or practice of moralizing. **2.** a moral saying. **3.** the practice of moral principles without reference to religion.
moralist ('mɒrəlɪst) *n.* **1.** a person who seeks to regulate the morals of others or to imbue others with a sense of morality. **2.** a person who lives in accordance with moral principles. **3.** a philosopher who is concerned with casuistic discussions of right action, or who seeks a general characterization of right action, often contrasted with a moral philosopher whose concern is with general philosophical questions about ethics. —ˌ**moral'istic** *adj.* —ˌ**moral'istically** *adv.*
morality (mə'rælɪtɪ) *n., pl.* **-ties.** **1.** the quality of being moral. **2.** conformity, or degree of conformity, to conventional standards of moral conduct. **3.** a system of moral principles. **4.** an instruction or lesson in morals. **5.** short for **morality play.**
morality play *n.* a type of drama written between the 14th and 16th centuries concerned with the conflict between personified virtues and vices.
moralize *or* **moralise** ('mɒrəˌlaɪz) *vb.* **1.** (*intr.*) to make moral pronouncements. **2.** (*tr.*) to interpret or explain in a moral sense. **3.** (*tr.*) to improve the morals of. —ˌ**morali'zation** *or* ˌ**morali'sation** *n.* —'**moralˌizer** *or* '**moralˌiser** *n.*
moral majority *n.* a presumed majority of people believed to be in favour of a stricter code of public morals. [C20: after *Moral Majority,* a right-wing U.S. religious organization, based on SILENT MAJORITY]
moral philosophy *n.* the branch of philosophy dealing with both argument about the content of morality and meta-ethical

discussion of the nature of moral judgment, language, argument, and value.

Moral Rearmament *n.* a worldwide movement for moral and spiritual renewal founded by Frank Buchman in 1938. Also called: **Buchmanism.** Former name: **Oxford Group.**

moral theology *n.* the branch of theology dealing with ethics.

morass (məˈræs) *n.* **1.** a tract of swampy low-lying land. **2.** a disordered or muddled situation or circumstance, esp. one that impedes progress. [C17: from Dutch *moeras,* ultimately from Old French *marais* MARSH]

moratorium (ˌmɒrəˈtɔːrɪəm) *n., pl.* **-ria** (-rɪə) *or* **-riums.** **1.** a legally authorized postponement of the fulfilment of an obligation. **2.** an agreed suspension of activity. [C19: New Latin, from Late Latin *morātōrius* dilatory, from *mora* delay] —**moratory** (ˈmɒrətərɪ, -trɪ) *adj.*

Moravian (məˈreɪvɪən, mɒ-) *adj.* **1.** of or relating to Moravia, a region of central Czechoslovakia, its people, or their dialect of Czech. **2.** of or relating to the Moravian Church. *~n.* **3.** the Moravian dialect. **4.** a native or inhabitant of Moravia. **5.** a member of the Moravian Church. —**Moˈravianism** *n.*

Moravian Church *n.* a Protestant Church originating in Moravia in 1722 as a revival of the sect of Bohemian Brethren. It has close links with the Lutheran Church.

moray (mɒˈreɪ) *n., pl.* **-rays.** any voracious marine coastal eel of the family *Muraenidae,* esp. *Muraena helena,* marked with brilliant patterns and colours. [C17: from Portuguese *moréia,* from Latin *mūrēna,* from Greek *muraina*]

morbid (ˈmɔːbɪd) *adj.* **1.** having an unusual interest in death or unpleasant events. **2.** gruesome. **3.** relating to or characterized by disease; pathologic: *a morbid growth.* [C17: from Latin *morbidus* sickly, from *morbus* illness] —ˈ**morbidly** *adv.* —ˈ**morbidness** *n.*

morbid anatomy *n.* the branch of medical science concerned with the study of the structure of diseased organs and tissues.

morbidity (mɔːˈbɪdɪtɪ) *n.* **1.** the state of being morbid. **2.** Also called: **morbidity rate.** the relative incidence of a particular disease in a specific locality.

morbific (mɔːˈbɪfɪk) *adj.* causing disease; pathogenic. —**morˈbifically** *adv.*

morbilli (mɔːˈbɪlaɪ) *n.* a technical name for **measles.** [C17: from Medieval Latin *morbillus* pustule, diminutive of Latin *morbus* illness]

morceau *French.* (mɔrso) *n., pl.* ***-ceaux*** (-so). **1.** a fragment or morsel. **2.** a short composition, esp. a musical one. [C18: from Old French: MORSEL]

morcha (ˈmɔːtʃɑː) *n.* (in India) a hostile demonstration against the government. [Hindi: entrenchment]

mordacious (mɔːˈdeɪʃəs) *adj.* sarcastic, caustic, or biting. [C17: from Latin *mordax,* from *mordēre* to bite] —**morˈdaciously** *adv.* —**mordacity** (mɔːˈdæsɪtɪ) *or* **morˈdaciousness** *n.*

mordant (ˈmɔːdᵊnt) *adj.* **1.** sarcastic or caustic. **2.** having the properties of a mordant. **3.** pungent. *~n.* **4.** a substance used before the application of a dye, possessing the ability to fix colours in textiles, leather, etc. See also **lake**[2] (sense 1). **5.** an acid or other corrosive fluid used to etch lines on a printing plate. *~vb.* **6.** (*tr.*) to treat (a fabric, yarn, etc.) with a mordant. [C15: from Old French: biting, from *mordre* to bite, from Latin *mordēre*] —ˈ**mordancy** *n.* —ˈ**mordantly** *adv.*

mordent (ˈmɔːdᵊnt) *n. Music.* a melodic ornament consisting of the rapid alternation of a note with a note one degree lower than it. Also called: **lower mordent.** [C19: from German, from Italian *mordente,* from *mordere* to bite]

Mordvin (ˈmɔːdvɪn) *n.* **1.** (*pl.* **-vin** *or* **-vins**) a member of a Finnish people of the middle Volga region, living chiefly in the former Mordvinian (Mordovian) ASSR. **2.** the language of this people, belonging to the Finno-Ugric family.

more (mɔː) *determiner.* **1. a.** the comparative of **much** or **many:** *more joy than you know; more pork sausages.* **b.** (*as pronoun; functioning as sing. or pl.*): *he has more than she has; even more are dying every day.* **2. a.** additional; further: *no more bananas.* **b.** (*as pronoun; functioning as sing. or pl.*): *I can't take any more; more than expected.* **3. more of.** to a greater extent or degree: *we see more of Sue these days; more of a nuisance than it should be.* *~adv.* **4.** used to form the comparative of some adjectives and adverbs: *a more believable story; more quickly.* **5.** the comparative of **much:** *people listen to the radio more now.* **6.** additionally; again: *I'll look at it once more.* **7. more or less. a.** as an estimate; approximately. **b.** to an unspecified extent or degree: *the party was ruined, more or less.* **8. more so.** to a greater extent or degree. **9. neither more nor less than.** simply. **10. think more of.** to have a higher opinion of. **11. what is more.** moreover. [Old English *māra;* compare Old Saxon, Old High German *mēro,* Gothic *maiza.* See also MOST]

▷**Usage.** See at **most.**

moreen (mɒˈriːn) *n.* a heavy, usually watered, fabric of wool or wool and cotton, used esp. in furnishing. [C17: perhaps from MOIRE, influenced by VELVETEEN]

moreish *or* **morish** (ˈmɔːrɪʃ) *adj. Informal.* (of food) causing a desire for more: *these cakes are very moreish.*

morel (mɒˈrel) *n.* any edible saprophytic ascomycetous fungus of the genus *Morchella,* in which the mushroom has a pitted cap: order *Pezizales.* [C17: from French *morille,* probably of Germanic origin; compare Old High German *morhila,* diminutive of *morha* carrot]

morello (məˈreləʊ) *n., pl.* **-los.** a variety of small very dark sour cherry, *Prunus cerasus austera.* [C17: perhaps from Medieval Latin *amārellum* diminutive of Latin *amārus* bitter, but also influenced by Italian *morello* blackish]

moreover (mɔːˈrəʊvə) *sentence connector.* in addition to what has already been said; furthermore.

morepork (ˈmɔːˌpɔːk) *n.* another name (esp. N.Z.) for **mopoke.**

mores (ˈmɔːreɪz) *pl. n. Sociol.* the customs and conventions embodying the fundamental values of a group or society. [C20: from Latin, plural of *mōs* custom]

Moresco (məˈreskəʊ) *n., adj.* a variant of **Morisco.**

Moresque (mɔːˈresk) *adj.* **1.** (esp. of decoration and architecture) of Moorish style. *~n.* **2. a.** Moorish design or decoration. **b.** a specimen of this. [C17: from French, from Italian *moresco,* from *Moro* MOOR]

Moreton Bay fig (ˈmɔːtᵊn) *n.* a large Australian fig tree, *Ficus macrophilla,* having glossy leaves and smooth bark. [named after *Moreton Bay,* Queensland, Australia]

Morgan (ˈmɔːgən) *n.* an American breed of small compact saddle horse. [C19: named after Justin *Morgan,* (1747–98), American owner of the original sire]

morganatic (ˌmɔːgəˈnætɪk) *adj.* of or designating a marriage between a person of high rank and a person of low rank, by which the latter is not elevated to the higher rank and any issue have no rights to the succession of the higher party's titles, property, etc. [C18: from the Medieval Latin phrase *mātrimōnium ad morganāticum* marriage based on the morning-gift (a token present after consummation representing the husband's only liability); *morganātica,* ultimately from Old High German *morgan* morning; compare Old English *morgengiefu* morning-gift] —ˌ**morgaˈnatically** *adv.*

morganite (ˈmɔːgəˌnaɪt) *n.* a pink variety of beryl, used as a gemstone. [C20: named after John Pierpont *Morgan* (1837–1913), U.S. financier, philanthropist, and art collector]

morgen (ˈmɔːgən) *n.* **1.** a South African unit of area, equal to about two acres or 0.8 hectare. **2.** a unit of area, formerly used in Prussia and Scandinavia, equal to about two thirds of an acre. [C17: from Dutch: morning, a morning's ploughing]

morgue (mɔːg) *n.* **1.** another word for **mortuary** (sense 1). **2.** *Informal.* a room or file containing clippings, files, etc., used for reference in a newspaper. [C19: from French *le Morgue,* a Paris mortuary]

morgue *French.* (mɔrg) *n.* superiority; haughtiness.

MORI (ˈmɔːrɪ) *n. acronym for* Market and Opinion Research Institute: *a MORI poll.*

moribund (ˈmɒrɪˌbʌnd) *adj.* **1.** near death. **2.** stagnant; without force or vitality. [C18: from Latin, from *morī* to die] —ˌ**moriˈbundity** *n.* —ˈ**moriˌbundly** *adv.*

morion[1] (ˈmɔːrɪən) *n.* a 16th-century helmet with a brim and wide comb. [C16: via Old French from Spanish *morrión,* perhaps from *morra* crown of the head]

morion[2] (ˈmɔːrɪən) *n.* a smoky brown, grey, or blackish variety of quartz, used as a gemstone. [C18: via French from Latin *mōrion,* a misreading of *mormorion*]

Moriori (ˌmɒrɪˈɔːrɪ) *n.* **1.** an extinct Polynesian people of New Zealand, esp. of the Chatham Islands, who preceded the Maori. **2.** (*pl.* **-ri** *or* **-ris**) a member of this people. **3.** the language of the Moriori, belonging to the Malayo-Polynesian family. *~adj.* **4.** of or relating to the Moriori or their language.

Morisco (məˈrɪskəʊ) *or* **Moresco** (məˈreskəʊ) *n., pl.* **-cos** *or* **-coes.** **1.** a Spanish Moor. **2.** a morris dance. *~adj.* **3.** another word for **Moorish.** [C16: from Spanish, from *Moro* MOOR]

morish (ˈmɔːrɪʃ) *adj.* a variant spelling of **moreish.**

Mormon (ˈmɔːmən) *n.* **1.** a member of the Church of Jesus Christ of Latter-day Saints, founded in 1830 at La Fayette, New York, by Joseph Smith (1805–44) on the basis of supposed revelations by a prophet, Mormon. *~adj.* **2.** of or relating to the Mormons, their Church, or their beliefs. —ˈ**Mormonism** *n.*

morn (mɔːn) *n.* **1.** a poetic word for **morning.** **2. the morn.** *Scot.* tomorrow. **3. the morn's nicht.** *Scot.* tomorrow night. [Old English *morgen;* compare Old High German *morgan,* Old Norse *morginn*]

mornay (ˈmɔːneɪ) *adj.* (*often immediately postpositive*) denoting a cheese sauce used in several dishes: *eggs mornay.* [perhaps named after Philippe de *Mornay* (1549–1623), French Huguenot leader]

morning (ˈmɔːnɪŋ) *n.* **1.** the first part of the day, ending at or around noon. **2.** sunrise; daybreak; dawn. **3.** the beginning or early period: *the morning of the world.* **4. the morning after.** *Informal.* the aftereffects of excess, esp. a hangover. **5.** (*modifier*) of, used, or occurring in the morning: *morning coffee.* ~See also **mornings.** [C13 *morwening,* from MORN, formed on the model of EVENING]

morning-after pill *n.* an oral contraceptive that is effective if taken some hours after intercourse.

morning coat *n.* a cutaway frock coat, part of morning dress. Also called: **tail coat, swallow-tailed coat.**

morning dress *n.* formal day dress for men, comprising a morning coat, usually with grey trousers and top hat.

morning-glory *n., pl.* **-ries.** any of various mainly tropical convolvulaceous plants of the genus *Ipomoea* and related genera, with trumpet-shaped blue, pink, or white flowers, which close in late afternoon.

mornings (ˈmɔːnɪŋz) *adv. Informal.* in the morning, esp. regularly, or during every morning.

morning sickness *n.* nausea occurring shortly after rising: an early symptom of pregnancy.

morning star *n.* a planet, usually Venus, seen just before sunrise during the time that the planet is west of the sun. Also called: **daystar.** Compare **evening star.**

morning tea *n. Austral. and N.Z.* a mid-morning snack with a cup of tea. Brit. equivalent: **elevenses.**

morning watch *n. Nautical.* the watch between 4 and 8 a.m.

Moro (ˈmɔːrəʊ) *n.* **1.** (*pl.* **-ros** *or* **-ro**) a member of a group of predominantly Muslim peoples of the S Philippines: noted for their manufacture of weapons. **2.** the language of these peoples, belonging to the Malayo-Polynesian family. [C19: via Spanish from Latin *Maurus* MOOR]

Moroccan (məˈrɒkən) *adj.* **1.** of or relating to Morocco, a kingdom in NW Africa, or its people. ~*n.* **2.** a native or inhabitant of Morocco.

morocco (məˈrɒkəʊ) *n.* **a.** a fine soft leather made from goatskins, used for bookbinding, shoes, etc. **b.** (*as modifier*): *morocco leather.* [C17: after *Morocco*, where it was originally made]

moron (ˈmɔːrɒn) *n.* **1.** a foolish or stupid person. **2.** a person having an intelligence quotient of between 50 and 70, able to work under supervision. [C20: from Greek *mōros* foolish] —**moronic** (mɒˈrɒnɪk) *adj.* —**moˈronically** *adv.* —ˈ**moronism** *or* **moˈronity** *n.*

morose (məˈrəʊs) *adj.* ill-tempered or gloomy. [C16: from Latin *mōrōsus* peevish, capricious, from *mōs* custom, will, caprice] —**moˈrosely** *adv.* —**moˈroseness** *n.*

morph[1] (mɔːf) *n. Linguistics.* the phonological representation of a morpheme. [C20: shortened form of MORPHEME]

morph[2] (mɔːf) *n. Biology.* any of the different forms of individual found in a polymorphic species. [C20: from Greek *morphē* shape]

morph. *or* **morphol.** *abbrev. for:* **1.** morphological. **2.** morphology.

-morph *n. combining form.* indicating shape, form, or structure of a specified kind: *ectomorph.* [from Greek *-morphos,* from *morphē* shape] —**-morphic** *or* **-morphous** *adj. combining form.* —**-morphy** *n. combining form.*

morphallaxis (ˌmɔːfəˈlæksɪs) *n., pl.* **-laxes** (-ˈlæksiːz). *Zoology.* the transformation of one part into another that sometimes occurs during regeneration of organs in certain animals. [C20: New Latin, from MORPHO- + Greek *allaxis* exchange, from *allassein* to exchange, from *allos* other]

morpheme (ˈmɔːfiːm) *n. Linguistics.* a speech element having a meaning or grammatical function that cannot be subdivided into further such elements. [C20: from French, from Greek *morphē* form, coined on the model of PHONEME; see -EME] —**morˈphemic** *adj.* —**morˈphemically** *adv.*

morphine (ˈmɔːfiːn) *or* **morphia** (ˈmɔːfɪə) *n.* an alkaloid extracted from opium: used in medicine as an anaesthetic and sedative although repeated use causes addiction. Formula: $C_{17}H_{19}NO_3$. [C19: from French, from *Morpheus,* Greek god of sleep and dreams]

morphinism (ˈmɔːfɪˌnɪzəm) *n.* morphine addiction.

morpho- *or before a vowel* **morph-** *combining form.* **1.** indicating form or structure: *morphology.* **2.** morpheme: *morphophonemics.* [from Greek *morphē* form, shape]

morphogenesis (ˌmɔːfəʊˈdʒɛnɪsɪs) *n.* **1.** the development of form and structure in an organism during its growth from embryo to adult. **2.** the evolutionary development of form in an organism or part of an organism. —**morphogenetic** (ˌmɔːfəʊdʒɪˈnɛtɪk) *or* ˌ**morphoˈgenic** *adj.*

morphology (mɔːˈfɒlədʒɪ) *n.* **1.** the branch of biology that is concerned with the form and structure of organisms, esp. their external structure. **2.** the form and structure of words in a language, esp. the consistent patterns of inflection, combination, derivation and change, etc., that may be observed and classified. **3.** the form and structure of anything. —**morphologic** (ˌmɔːfəˈlɒdʒɪk) *or* ˌ**morphoˈlogical** *adj.* —ˌ**morphoˈlogically** *adv.* —**morˈphologist** *n.*

morphophoneme (ˌmɔːfəʊˈfəʊniːm) *n. Linguistics.* the set of phonemes or sequences of phonemes that constitute the various allomorphs of a morpheme. [C20: from MORPHEME + PHONEME]

morphophonemics (ˌmɔːfəʊfəʊˈniːmɪks) *n.* (*functioning as sing.*) *Linguistics.* the study of the phonemic realization of the allomorphs of the morphemes of a language. —ˌ**morphophoˈnemic** *adj.*

morphosis (mɔːˈfəʊsɪs) *n., pl.* **-ses** (-siːz). *Biology.* development in an organism or its parts characterized by structural change. [C17: via New Latin from Greek, from *morphoun* to form, from *morphē* form] —**morphotic** (mɔːˈfɒtɪk) *adj.*

morrell (məˈrɛl) *n.* a tall eucalyptus, *Eucalyptus longicornis,* of SW Australia, having pointed buds. [from a native Australian language]

Morris chair (ˈmɒrɪs) *n.* an armchair with an adjustable back and large cushions. [C19: named after William *Morris* (1834–96), British designer and craftsman]

morris dance (ˈmɒrɪs) *n.* any of various old English folk dances usually performed by men (**morris men**) to the accompaniment of violin, concertina, etc. The dancers are adorned with bells and often represent characters from folk tales. Often shortened to **morris.** [C15 *moreys daunce* Moorish dance. See MOOR] —**morris dancing** *n.*

morro (ˈmɒrəʊ; *Spanish* ˈmorro) *n., pl.* **-ros** (-rəʊz; *Spanish* -ros). a rounded hill or promontory. [from Spanish]

morrow (ˈmɒrəʊ) *n.* (usually preceded by *the*) *Archaic or poetic.* **1.** the next day. **2.** the period following a specified event. **3.** the morning. [C13 *morwe,* from Old English *morgen* morning; see MORN]

morse (mɔːs) *n.* a clasp or fastening on a cope. [C15: from Old French *mors,* from Latin *morsus* clasp, bite, from *mordēre* to bite]

Morse code (mɔːs) *n.* a telegraph code used internationally for transmitting messages. Letters, numbers, etc., are represented by groups of shorter dots and longer dashes, or by groups of the corresponding sounds, *dits* and *dahs,* the groups being separated by spaces. Also called: **international Morse code.** [C19: named after Samuel *Morse* (1791–1872), U.S. inventor]

morsel (ˈmɔːsᵊl) *n.* **1.** a small slice or mouthful of food. **2.** a small piece; bit. **3.** *Irish informal.* a term of endearment for a child. [C13: from Old French, from *mors* a bite, from Latin *morsus,* from *mordēre* to bite]

Morse taper *n. Trademark, engineering.* a taper that is one of a standard series used in the shank of tools to fit a matching taper in the mandrel of a machine tool. [probably named after the *Morse* Twist Drill Co., Massachusetts, U.S.]

mort[1] (mɔːt) *n.* a call blown on a hunting horn to signify the death of the animal hunted. [C16: via Old French from Latin *mors* death]

mort[2] (mɔːt) *n.* a great deal; a great many. [possibly a shortened form of MORTAL used as an intensifier]

mortal (ˈmɔːtᵊl) *adj.* **1.** (of living beings, esp. human beings) subject to death. **2.** of or involving life or the world. **3.** ending in or causing death; fatal: *a mortal blow.* **4.** deadly or unrelenting: *a mortal enemy.* **5.** of or like the fear of death; dire: *mortal terror.* **6.** great or very intense: *mortal pain.* **7.** conceivable or possible: *there was no mortal reason to go.* **8.** *Slang.* long and tedious: *for three mortal hours.* ~*n.* **9.** a mortal being. **10.** *Informal.* a person: *a mean mortal.* [C14: from Latin *mortālis,* from *mors* death] —ˈ**mortally** *adv.*

mortality (mɔːˈtælɪtɪ) *n., pl.* **-ties.** **1.** the condition of being mortal. **2.** great loss of life, as in war or disaster. **3.** the number of deaths in a given period. **4.** mankind; humanity. **5.** an obsolete word for **death.**

mortality rate *n.* another term for **death rate.**

mortality table *n. Insurance.* an actuarial table indicating life expectancy and death frequency for people of a given age, occupation, etc.

mortal sin *n. Christianity.* a sin regarded as involving total loss of grace. Compare **venial sin.**

mortar (ˈmɔːtə) *n.* **1.** a mixture of cement or lime or both with sand and water, used as a bond between bricks or stones or as a covering on a wall. **2.** a muzzle-loading cannon having a short barrel and relatively wide bore that fires low-velocity shells in high trajectories over a short range. **3.** a similar device for firing lifelines, fireworks, etc. **4.** a vessel, usually bowl-shaped, in which substances are pulverized with a pestle. **5.** *Mining.* a cast-iron receptacle in which ore is crushed. ~*vb.* (*tr.*) **6.** to join (bricks or stones) or cover (a wall) with mortar. **7.** to fire on with mortars. [C13: from Latin *mortārium* basin in which mortar is mixed; in some senses, via Old French *mortier* substance mixed inside such a vessel]

mortarboard (ˈmɔːtəˌbɔːd) *n.* **1.** a black tasselled academic cap with a flat square top covered with cloth. **2.** Also called: **hawk.** a small square board with a handle on the underside for carrying mortar.

mortgage (ˈmɔːgɪdʒ) *n.* **1.** a conditional conveyance of property, esp. real property, as security for the repayment of a loan. **2.** the deed effecting such a transaction. **3.** the loan itself. ~*vb.* (*tr.*) **4.** to convey (property) by mortgage. **5.** *Informal.* to pledge. [C14: from Old French, literally: dead pledge, from *mort* dead + *gage* security, GAGE[1]] —ˈ**mortgageable** *adj.*

mortgagee (ˌmɔːgɪˈdʒiː) *n. Law.* **1.** the party to a mortgage who makes the loan. **2.** a person who holds mortgaged property as security for repayment of a loan.

mortgage rate *n.* the level of interest charged by building societies and banks on house-purchase loans.

mortgagor (ˈmɔːgɪdʒə, ˌmɔːgɪˈdʒɔː) *or* **mortgager** *n. Property law.* a person who borrows money by mortgaging his property to the lender as security.

mortician (mɔːˈtɪʃən) *n. Chiefly U.S.* another word for **undertaker.** [C19: from MORTUARY + *-ician,* as in *physician*]

mortification (ˌmɔːtɪfɪˈkeɪʃən) *n.* **1.** a feeling of loss of prestige or self-respect; humiliation. **2.** something causing this. **3.** *Christianity.* the practice of mortifying the senses. **4.** another word for **gangrene.**

mortify (ˈmɔːtɪˌfaɪ) *vb.* **-fies, -fying, -fied.** **1.** (*tr.*) to humiliate or cause to feel shame. **2.** (*tr.*) *Christianity.* to subdue and bring under control by self-denial, disciplinary exercises, etc. **3.** (*intr.*) to undergo tissue death or become gangrenous. [C14: via Old French from Church Latin *mortificāre* to put to death, from

Latin *mors* death + *facere* to do] —'**morti,fier** *n.* —'**morti,fying** *adj.* —'**morti,fyingly** *adv.*

mortise *or* **mortice** ('mɔːtɪs) *n.* **1.** a slot or recess, usually rectangular, cut into a piece of wood, stone, etc., to receive a matching projection (tenon) of another piece, or a mortise lock. **2.** *Printing.* a cavity cut into a letterpress printing plate into which type or another plate is inserted. ~*vb.* (*tr.*) **3.** to cut a slot or recess in (a piece of wood, stone, etc.). **4.** to join (two pieces of wood, stone, etc.) by means of a mortise and tenon. **5.** to cut a cavity in (a letterpress printing plate) for the insertion of type, etc. [C14: from Old French *mortoise,* perhaps from Arabic *murtazza* fastened in position] —'**mortiser** *n.*

mortise lock *n.* a lock set into a mortise in a door so that the mechanism of the lock is enclosed by the door.

mortmain ('mɔːt,meɪn) *n. Law.* the state or condition of lands, buildings, etc., held inalienably, as by an ecclesiastical or other corporation. [C15: from Old French *mortemain,* from Medieval Latin *mortua manus* dead hand, inalienable ownership]

mortuary ('mɔːtʃʊərɪ) *n., pl.* **-aries. 1.** Also called: **morgue.** a building where dead bodies are kept before cremation or burial. ~*adj.* **2.** of or relating to death or burial. [C14 (as n., a funeral gift to a parish priest): via Medieval Latin *mortuārium* (n.) from Latin *mortuārius* of the dead]

morula ('mɒrjʊlə) *n., pl.* **-las** *or* **-lae** (-,liː). *Embryol.* a solid ball of cells resulting from cleavage of a fertilized ovum. [C19: via New Latin, diminutive of Latin *morum* mulberry, from Greek *moron*] —'**morular** *adj.*

morwong ('mɔː,wɒŋ) *n.* a food fish of Australasian coastal waters belonging to the genus *Cheilodactylos:* family *Cirrhitidae* (or *Cheilodactylidae*). [from a native Australian language]

moryah (mɒr'jæ) *interj. Irish.* an exclamation of annoyance, disbelief, etc. [from Irish Gaelic *Mar dhea*]

MOS *Computer technol. abbrev. for* metal oxide semiconductor.

mos. *abbrev. for* months.

mosaic (mə'zeɪɪk) *n.* **1.** a design or decoration made up of small pieces of coloured glass, stone, etc. **2.** the process of making a mosaic. **3. a.** a mottled yellowing that occurs in the leaves of plants affected with any of various virus diseases. **b.** Also called: **mosaic disease.** any of the diseases, such as **tobacco mosaic,** that produce this discoloration. **4.** *Genetics.* another name for **chimera** (sense 4). **5.** an assembly of aerial photographs forming a composite picture of a large area on the ground. **6.** a light-sensitive surface on a television camera tube, consisting of a large number of granules of photoemissive material deposited on an insulating medium. [C16: via French and Italian from Medieval Latin *mōsaicus,* from Late Greek *mouseion* mosaic work, from Greek *mouseios* of the Muses, from *mousa;* see MUSE[2]] —**mosaicist** (mə'zeɪɪsɪst) *n.*

Mosaic (məʊ'zeɪɪk) *or* **Mosaical** *adj.* of or relating to Moses or the laws and traditions ascribed to him.

mosaic disease *n.* a serious viral disease of plants, esp. tobacco, maize, and sugar cane, in which the leaves become mottled by discoloration.

mosaic gold (mə'zeɪɪk) *n.* stannic sulphide, esp. when suspended in lacquer for use in gilding surfaces.

Mosaic law (məʊ'zeɪɪk) *n. Old Testament.* the laws of the Hebrews ascribed to Moses and contained in the Pentateuch.

mosasaur ('məʊsə,sɔː) *or* **mosasaurus** (,məʊsə'sɔːrəs) *n., pl.* **-saurs** *or* **-sauri** (-'sɔːraɪ). any of various extinct Cretaceous giant marine lizards of the genus *Mosasaurus* and related genera, typically having paddle-like limbs. [C18: from Latin *Mosa* the river *Meuse* in W Europe (near which remains were first found) + -SAUR]

moschatel (,mɒskə'tɛl) *n.* a small N temperate plant, *Adoxa moschatellina,* with greenish-white musk-scented flowers: family *Adoxaceae.* Also called: **townhall clock, five-faced bishop.** [C18: via French from Italian *moscatella,* diminutive of *moscato* MUSK]

Moselle (məʊ'zɛl) *n.* (*sometimes not cap.*) a German white wine from the Moselle valley.

Moses basket ('məʊzɪz) *n.* a portable cradle for a baby, often made of straw or wicker. [C20: from *Moses* being left in a cradle of bulrushes (Exodus 2:3)]

mosey ('məʊzɪ) *vb.* (*intr.*) *Informal.* (often foll. by *along* or *on*) to walk in a leisurely manner; amble. [C19: origin unknown]

moshav *Hebrew.* (mɔ'ʃav) *n., pl.* **-shavim** (-ʃa'vim). a cooperative settlement in Israel, consisting of a number of small farms. [C20: from Hebrew *mōshābh* a dwelling]

Moslem ('mɒzləm) *n., pl.* **-lems** *or* **-lem,** *adj.* a variant of **Muslim.** —**Moslemic** (mɒz'lɛmɪk) *adj.* —'**Moslemism** *n.*

Mosotho (mʊ'suːtʊ) *n., pl.* **-tho** *or* **-thos.** a member of the Basotho people. Former name: **Basuto.**

mosque (mɒsk) *n.* a Muslim place of worship, usually having one or more minarets and often decorated with elaborate tracery and texts from the Koran. Also called: **masjid, musjid.** [C14: earlier *mosquee,* from Old French via Italian *moschea,* ultimately from Arabic *masjid* temple]

mosquito (mə'skiːtəʊ) *n., pl.* **-toes** *or* **-tos.** any dipterous insect of the family *Culicidae:* the females have a long proboscis adapted for piercing the skin of man and animals to suck their blood. See also **aedes, anopheles, culex.** [C16: from Spanish, diminutive of *mosca* fly, from Latin *musca*]

mosquito boat *n.* another name for **MTB.**

mosquito hawk *n.* another name for **nighthawk** (sense 1).

mosquito net *or* **netting** *n.* a fine curtain or net put in windows, around beds, etc., to keep mosquitoes out.

moss (mɒs) *n.* **1.** any bryophyte of the class *Musci,* typically growing in dense mats on trees, rocks, moist ground, etc. See also **peat moss. 2.** a clump or growth of any of these plants. **3.** any of various similar but unrelated plants, such as club moss, Spanish moss, Ceylon moss, rose moss, and reindeer moss. **4.** *Scot. and northern English.* a peat bog or marsh. [Old English *mos* swamp; compare Middle Dutch, Old High German *mos* bog, Old Norse *mosi;* compare also Old Norse *mȳrr* MIRE] —'**moss,like** *adj.* —'**mossy** *adj.* —'**mossiness** *n.*

moss agate *n.* a variety of chalcedony with dark greenish mossy markings, used as a gemstone.

mossback ('mɒs,bæk) *n. U.S. and Canadian.* **1.** an old turtle, shellfish, etc., that has a growth of algae on its back. **2.** *Informal.* a provincial or conservative person. —'**moss,backed** *adj.*

Mössbauer effect ('mɒs,baʊə; *German* 'mœsbauər) *n. Physics.* the phenomenon in which an atomic nucleus in a crystal of certain substances emits a gamma ray without any recoil to the atom. The study of the emitted gamma rays (**Mössbauer spectroscopy**) is used to determine the energy levels in a nucleus, the structure of molecules, etc. [C20: named after Rudolf Ludwig *Mössbauer* (born 1929), German physicist]

mossbunker ('mɒs,bʌŋkə) *n. U.S.* another name for **menhaden.** [C18: from Dutch *marsbanker* scad, horse-mackerel]

moss-grown *adj.* covered with moss.

Mossi ('mɒsɪ) *n.* **1.** (*pl.* **-sis** *or* **-si**) a member of a Negroid people of W Africa, living chiefly in Burkina-Faso: noted for their use of cowry shells as currency and for their trading skill. **2.** the language of this people, belonging to the Gur branch of the Niger-Congo family. Also called: **Moore.**

mossie[1] *or* **mozzie** ('mɒzɪ) *n. Austral. and N.Z.* an informal name for **mosquito.**

mossie[2] ('mɒsɪ) *n.* another name for the **Cape sparrow.** [of uncertain origin]

moss layer *n.* See **layer** (sense 2).

mosso ('mɒsəʊ) *adv. Music.* to be performed with rapidity. See also **meno mosso.** [Italian, past participle of *muovere* to MOVE]

moss pink *n.* a North American plant, *Phlox subulata,* forming dense mosslike mats: cultivated for its pink, white, or lavender flowers: family *Polemoniaceae.* Also called: **ground pink.**

moss rose *n.* a variety of rose, *Rosa centifolia muscosa,* that has a mossy stem and calyx and fragrant pink flowers.

moss stitch *n.* a knitting stitch made up of alternate plain and purl stitches.

mosstrooper ('mɒs,truːpə) *n.* a raider in the border country of England and Scotland in the mid-17th century. [C17 *moss,* in northern English dialect sense: bog]

most (məʊst) *determiner.* **1. a.** a great majority of; nearly all: *most people like eggs.* **b.** (*as pronoun; functioning as sing. or pl.*): *most of them don't know; most of it is finished.* **2. the most. a.** the superlative of **many** and **much:** *you have the most money; the most apples.* **b.** (*as pronoun*): *the most he can afford is two pounds.* **3. at (the) most.** at the maximum: *that girl is four at the most.* **4. for the most part.** generally. **5. make the most of.** to use to the best advantage: *she makes the most of her accent.* **6. than most.** than most others: *the leaves are greener than most.* **7. the most.** *Slang, chiefly U.S.* wonderful: *that chick's the most.* ~*adv.* **8. the most.** used to form the superlative of some adjectives and adverbs: *the most beautiful daughter of all.* **9.** the superlative of **much:** *people welcome a drink most after work.* **10.** (intensifier): *a most absurd story.* **11.** *U.S. and Canadian informal or dialect.* almost: *most every town in this state.* [Old English *māst* or *mǣst,* whence Middle English *moste, mēst;* compare Old Frisian *maest,* Old High German *meist,* Old Norse *mestr*]

▷ **Usage.** The meanings of *most* and *mostly* should not be confused. In *she was most affected by the news, most* is equivalent to *very* and is generally acceptable. In *she was mostly affected by the news,* the implication is that there was something else, in addition to the news, which affected her, although less so. *More* and *most* should also be distinguished when used in comparisons. *More* applies to cases involving two persons, objects, etc., *most* to cases involving three or more: *John is the more intelligent of the two; he is the most intelligent of the students.*

-most *suffix. forming the superlative degree of some adjectives and adverbs: hindmost; uppermost.* [Old English *-mǣst, -mest,* originally a superlative suffix, later mistakenly taken as derived from *mǣst* (adv.) most]

Most Honourable *n.* a courtesy title applied to marquesses and members of the Privy Council and the Order of the Bath.

mostly ('məʊstlɪ) *adv.* **1.** almost entirely; chiefly. **2.** on many or most occasions; usually.

Most Reverend *n.* (in Britain) a courtesy title applied to Anglican and Roman Catholic archbishops.

mot[1] (məʊ) *n.* short for **bon mot.** [C16: via French from Vulgar Latin *mottum* (unattested) utterance, from Latin *muttum* a mutter, from *muttīre* to mutter]

mot[2] (mɒt) *n. Dublin slang.* a girl or young woman, esp. one's girlfriend. [perhaps a variant of *mort,* obsolete slang for girl or woman, of unknown origin]

MOT *abbrev. for:* **1.** (in Britain and New Zealand) Ministry of Transport (*Brit.,* now Department of Transport). **2.** (in Britain)

MOT test: a compulsory annual test for all road vehicles over a certain age, which require a valid **MOT certificate.**

mote[1] (məʊt) *n.* a tiny speck. [Old English *mot;* compare Middle Dutch *mot* grit, Norwegian *mutt* speck]

mote[2] (məʊt) *vb. past* **moste** (məʊst). (takes an infinitive without *to*) *Archaic.* may or might. [Old English *mōt,* first person singular present tense of *mōtan* to be allowed]

motel (məʊ'tɛl) *n.* a roadside hotel for motorists, usually having direct access from each room or chalet to a parking space or garage. [C20: from *motor* + *hotel*]

motet (məʊ'tɛt) *n.* a polyphonic choral composition used as an anthem in the Roman Catholic service. [C14: from Old French, diminutive of *mot* word; see MOT[1]]

moth (mɒθ) *n.* any of numerous insects of the order *Lepidoptera* that typically have stout bodies with antennae of various shapes (but not clubbed), including large brightly coloured species, such as hawk moths, and small inconspicuous types, such as the clothes moths. Compare **butterfly** (sense 1). [Old English *moththe;* compare Middle Dutch *motte,* Old Norse *motti*]

mothball ('mɒθ,bɔːl) *n.* **1.** Also called: **camphor ball.** a small ball of camphor or naphthalene used to repel clothes moths in stored clothing, blankets, etc. **2. put in mothballs.** to postpone work on (a project, activity, etc.). ~*vb.* (*tr.*) **3.** to prepare (a ship, aircraft, etc.) for a long period of storage by sealing all openings with plastic to prevent corrosion. **4.** to take (a factory, plant, etc.) out of operation but maintain it so that it can be used in the future. **5.** to postpone work on (a project, activity, etc.).

moth-eaten *adj.* **1.** decayed, decrepit, or outdated. **2.** eaten away by or as if by moths.

mother[1] ('mʌðə) *n.* **1. a.** a female who has given birth to offspring. **b.** (*as modifier*): *a mother bird.* **2.** (*often cap., esp. as a term of address*) a person's own mother. **3.** a female substituting in the function of a mother. **4.** (*often cap.*) *Chiefly archaic.* a term of address for an old woman. **5. a.** motherly qualities, such as maternal affection: *it appealed to the mother in her.* **b.** (*as modifier*): *mother love.* **c.** (*in combination*): *mothercraft.* **6. a.** a female or thing that creates, nurtures, protects, etc., something. **b.** (*as modifier*): *mother church; mother earth.* **7.** a title given to certain members of female religious orders: *mother superior.* **8.** *Christian Science.* God as the eternal Principle. **9.** (*modifier*) native or innate: *mother wit.* **10.** *Offensive taboo slang, chiefly U.S.* short for **motherfucker. 11. be mother.** to pour the tea: *I'll be mother.* ~*vb.* (*tr.*) **12.** to give birth to or produce. **13.** to nurture, protect, etc. as a mother. [Old English *mōdor;* compare Old Saxon *mōdar,* Old High German *muotar,* Latin *māter,* Greek *mētēr*]

mother[2] ('mʌðə) *n.* a stringy slime containing various bacteria that forms on the surface of liquids undergoing acetous fermentation. It can be added to wine, cider, etc. to promote vinegar formation. Also called: **mother of vinegar.** [C16: perhaps from MOTHER[1], but compare Spanish *madre* scum, Dutch *modder* dregs, Middle Low German *modder* decaying object, *mudde* sludge] —'**mothery** *adj.*

motherboard ('mʌðə,bɔːd) *n.* (in an electronic system) a printed circuit board through which signals between all other boards are routed.

Mother Carey's chicken ('kɛərɪ) *n.* another name for **storm petrel.** [origin unknown]

mother country *n.* **1.** the original country of colonists or settlers. **2.** another term for **fatherland.**

motherfucker ('mʌðə,fʌkə) *n. Offensive taboo slang, chiefly U.S.* a person or thing, esp. an exasperating or unpleasant one. Often shortened to **mother.**

motherhood ('mʌðə,hʊd) *n.* **1.** the state of being a mother. **2.** the qualities characteristic of a mother.

Mother Hubbard ('hʌbəd) *n.* (*sometimes not caps.*) a woman's full-length unbelted dress. [C19: after *Mother Hubbard,* a character in a nursery rhyme]

Mothering Sunday ('mʌðərɪŋ) *n. Brit.* the fourth Sunday in Lent, when mothers traditionally receive presents from their children. Also called: **Mother's Day.**

mother-in-law *n., pl.* **mothers-in-law.** the mother of one's wife or husband.

mother-in-law's tongue *n.* See **sansevieria.**

motherland ('mʌðə,lænd) *n.* another word for **fatherland.**

motherless ('mʌðələs) *adj.* **1.** not having a mother. ~*adv.* **2.** (intensifier) *Austral.: motherless broke.*

mother lode *n. Mining.* the principal lode in a system.

motherly ('mʌðəlɪ) *adj.* of or resembling a mother, esp. in warmth, or protectiveness. —'**motherliness** *n.*

Mother of God *n.* a title given to the Virgin Mary.

Mother of Parliaments *n.* **the.** the British Parliament: the model and creator of many other Parliaments. [C19: first used of England in 1865 by John Bright (1811–89), British statesman]

mother-of-pearl *n.* a hard iridescent substance, mostly calcium carbonate, that forms the inner layer of the shells of certain molluscs, such as the oyster. It is used to make buttons, inlay furniture, etc. Also called: **nacre.**

mother-of-pearl moth *n.* a pyralid moth, *Pleuroptya ruralis,* having a pale sheen, that is often seen around nettles, on which its green larvae feed.

mother of the chapel *n.* (in British trade unions in the publishing and printing industries) a woman shop steward. Abbrev.: **MoC.**

mother-of-thousands *n.* **1.** a S European perennial creeping plant, *Linaria cymbalaria,* having small pale blue or lilac flowers. **2.** a saxifragaceous plant, *Saxifraga sarmentosa* or *S. stolonifera,* having white flowers and creeping red runners.

Mother's Day *n.* **1.** *U.S. and Canadian.* the second Sunday in May, observed as a day in honour of mothers. **2.** See **Mothering Sunday.**

mother ship *n.* a ship providing facilities and supplies for a number of small vessels.

Mother Shipton ('ʃɪptᵊn) *n.* a day-flying noctuid moth, *Callistege mi,* mottled brown in colour and named from a fancied resemblance between its darker marking and a haggish profile. [named after *Mother Shipton,* a legendary prophetess in 15th-century Yorkshire]

mother superior *n., pl.* **mother superiors** *or* **mothers superior.** the head of a community of nuns.

mother tongue *n.* **1.** the language first learned by a child. **2.** a language from which another has evolved.

mother wit *n.* native practical intelligence; common sense.

motherwort ('mʌðə,wɜːt) *n.* any of several plants of the Eurasian genus *Leonurus,* esp. *L. cardiaca,* having divided leaves and clusters of small purple or pink flowers: family *Labiatae* (labiates). [C14: so named because it was thought to be beneficial in uterine disorders]

mothproof ('mɒθ,pruːf) *adj.* **1.** (esp. of clothes) chemically treated so as to repel clothes moths. ~*vb.* **2.** (*tr.*) to make (clothes, etc.) mothproof.

mothy ('mɒθɪ) *adj.* **mothier, mothiest. 1.** ragged; moth-eaten. **2.** containing moths; full of moths.

motif (məʊ'tiːf) *n.* **1.** a distinctive idea, esp. a theme elaborated on in a piece of music, literature, etc. **2.** Also: **motive.** a recurring form or shape in a design or pattern. **3.** a single added piece of decoration, such as a symbol or name on a jumper, sweatshirt, etc. [C19: from French. See MOTIVE]

motile ('məʊtaɪl) *adj.* **1.** capable of moving spontaneously and independently. ~*n.* **2.** *Psychol.* a person whose mental imagery strongly reflects movement, esp. his own. [C19: from Latin *mōtus* moved, from *movēre* to move] —**motility** (məʊ'tɪlɪtɪ) *n.*

motion ('məʊʃən) *n.* **1.** the process of continual change in the physical position of an object; movement: *linear motion.* **2.** a movement or action, esp. of part of the human body; a gesture. **3. a.** the capacity for movement. **b.** a manner of movement, esp. walking; gait. **4.** a mental impulse. **5.** a formal proposal to be discussed and voted on in a debate, meeting, etc. **6.** *Law.* an application made to a judge or court for an order or ruling necessary to the conduct of legal proceedings. **7.** *Brit.* **a.** the evacuation of the bowels. **b.** excrement. **8. a.** part of a moving mechanism. **b.** the action of such a part. **9.** *Music.* the upward or downward course followed by a part or melody. Parts whose progressions are in the same direction exhibit **similar motion,** while two parts whose progressions are in opposite directions exhibit **contrary motion.** See also **parallel** (sense 3). **10. go through the motions. a.** to act or perform the task (of doing something) mechanically or without sincerity. **b.** to mimic the action (of something) by gesture. **11. in motion.** operational or functioning (often in the phrases **set in motion, set the wheels in motion**). ~*vb.* **12.** (when *tr., may take a clause as object or an infinitive*) to signal or direct (a person) by a movement or gesture. [C15: from Latin *mōtiō* a moving, from *movēre* to move] —'**motional** *adj.*

motionless ('məʊʃənlɪs) *adj.* not moving; absolutely still. —'**motionlessly** *adv.* —'**motionlessness** *n.*

motion picture *n.* a U.S. and Canadian term for **film** (sense 1).

motion sickness *n.* the state or condition of being dizzy or nauseous from riding in a moving vehicle.

motion study *n.* short for **time and motion study.**

motivate ('məʊtɪ,veɪt) *vb.* (*tr.*) to give incentive to.

motivation (,məʊtɪ'veɪʃən) *n.* **1.** the act or an instance of motivating. **2.** desire to do; interest or drive. **3.** incentive or inducement. **4.** *Psychol.* the process that arouses, sustains and regulates human and animal behaviour. —,**moti'vational** *adj.* —'**moti,vative** *adj.*

motivational research *n.* the application of psychology to the study of consumer behaviour, esp. the planning of advertising and sales campaigns. Also called: **motivation research.**

motive ('məʊtɪv) *n.* **1.** the reason for a certain course of action, whether conscious or unconscious. **2.** a variant of **motif** (sense 2). ~*adj.* **3.** of or causing motion or action: *a motive force.* **4.** of or acting as a motive; motivating. ~*vb.* (*tr.*) **5.** to motivate. [C14: from Old French *motif,* from Late Latin *mōtīvus* (adj.) moving, from Latin *mōtus,* past participle of *movēre* to move] —'**motiveless** *adj.* —'**motivelessly** *adv.* —'**motivelessness** *n.*

motive power *n.* **1.** any source of energy used to produce motion. **2.** the means of supplying power to an engine, vehicle, etc. **3.** any driving force.

motivity (məʊ'tɪvɪtɪ) *n.* the power of moving or of initiating motion.

mot juste *French.* (mo ʒyst) *n., pl.* ***mots justes*** (mo ʒyst). the appropriate word or expression.

motley ('mɒtlɪ) *adj.* **1.** made up of elements of varying type, quality, etc. **2.** multicoloured. ~*n.* **3.** a motley collection or mixture. **4.** the particoloured attire of a jester. **5.** *Obsolete.* a jester. [C14: perhaps from *mot* speck, MOTE[1]]

motmot (ˈmɒtmɒt) *n.* any tropical American bird of the family *Momotidae,* having a long tail and blue and brownish-green plumage: order *Coraciiformes* (kingfishers, etc.). [C19: from American Spanish, imitative of the bird's call]

motocross (ˈməʊtəˌkrɒs) *n.* **1.** a motorcycle race across very rough ground. **2.** another name for **rallycross.** See also **autocross.** [C20: from MOTO(R) + CROSS(-COUNTRY)]

motoneuron (ˌməʊtəʊˈnjʊərɒn) *n. Anatomy.* an efferent nerve cell; motor neuron.

motor (ˈməʊtə) *n.* **1. a.** the engine, esp. an internal-combustion engine, of a vehicle. **b.** (*as modifier*): *a motor scooter.* **2.** Also called: **electric motor.** a machine that converts electrical energy into mechanical energy by means of the forces exerted on a current-carrying coil placed in a magnetic field. **3.** any device that converts another form of energy into mechanical energy to produce motion. **4. a.** *Chiefly Brit.* a car or other motor vehicle. **b.** (*as modifier*): *motor spares.* ~*adj.* **5.** producing or causing motion. **6.** *Physiol.* **a.** of or relating to nerves or neurons that carry impulses that cause muscles to contract. **b.** of or relating to movement or to muscles that induce movement. ~*vb.* **7.** (*intr.*) to travel by car. **8.** (*tr.*) *Brit.* to transport by car. **9.** (*intr.*) *Informal.* to move fast; make good progress. [C16: from Latin *mōtor* a mover, from *movēre* to move]

motorable (ˈməʊtərəbᵊl) *adj.* (of a road) suitable for use by motor vehicles.

motorbicycle (ˈməʊtəˌbaɪsɪkᵊl) *n.* **1.** a motorcycle. **2.** a moped.

motorbike (ˈməʊtəˌbaɪk) *n.* a less formal name for **motorcycle.**

motorboat (ˈməʊtəˌbəʊt) *n.* any boat powered by a motor.

motorbus (ˈməʊtəˌbʌs) *n.* a bus driven by an internal-combustion engine.

motorcade (ˈməʊtəˌkeɪd) *n.* a parade of cars or other motor vehicles. [C20: from MOTOR + CAVALCADE]

motor camp *n. N.Z.* a camp for motorists, tents, and caravans.

motorcar (ˈməʊtəˌkɑː) *n.* **1.** a more formal word for **car** (sense 1). **2.** a self-propelled electric railway car.

motor caravan *n. Brit.* a motor vehicle fitted with equipment for cooking, sleeping, etc., like that of a caravan.

motorcoach (ˈməʊtəˌkəʊtʃ) *n.* a coach driven by an internal-combustion engine.

motorcycle (ˈməʊtəˌsaɪkᵊl) *n.* **1.** Also called: **motorbike.** a two-wheeled vehicle, having a stronger frame than a bicycle, that is driven by a petrol engine, usually with a capacity of between 125 cc and 1000 cc. ~*vb.* (*intr.*) **2.** to ride on a motorcycle. —ˈ**motorˌcyclist** *n.*

motor drive *n. Photog.* a battery-operated motorized system to give fast film advance between exposures. Compare **autowinder.**

-motored *adj.* (*in combination*) having a specified type of motor or number of motors.

motor generator *n.* a generator driven by an electric motor, by means of which the voltage, frequency, or phases of an electrical power supply can be changed.

motorist (ˈməʊtərɪst) *n.* a driver of a car, esp. when considered as a car-owner.

motorize *or* **motorise** (ˈməʊtəˌraɪz) *vb.* (*tr.*) **1.** to equip with a motor. **2.** to provide (military units) with motor vehicles. —ˌ**motoriˈzation** *or* ˌ**motoriˈsation** *n.*

motorman (ˈməʊtəmən) *n., pl.* **-men. 1.** the driver of an electric train. **2.** the operator of a motor.

motor neurone disease *n.* a progressively degenerative disease of the motor system causing muscle weakness and wasting.

motor park *n.* a W African name for **car park.**

motor scooter *n.* a light motorcycle with small wheels and an enclosed engine. Often shortened to **scooter.**

motor vehicle *n.* a road vehicle driven by a motor or engine, esp. an internal-combustion engine.

motor vessel *or* **ship** *n.* a ship whose main propulsion system is a diesel or other internal-combustion engine.

motorway (ˈməʊtəˌweɪ) *n. Brit.* a main road for fast-moving traffic, having limited access, separate carriageways for vehicles travelling in opposite directions, and usually a total of four or six lanes. U.S. names: **superhighway,** (*also Canadian*) **expressway.**

Motown (ˈməʊˌtaʊn) *n. Trademark.* music combining rhythm and blues and pop, or gospel rhythms and modern ballad harmony. [C20: from *Motown Records* of Detroit; from *Mo(tor) Town,* a nickname for Detroit, Michigan, centre of the U.S. car industry]

motser *or* **motza** (ˈmɒtsə) *n. Austral. informal.* a large sum of money, esp. a gambling win. [of uncertain origin; possibly Yiddish]

motte (mɒt) *n. History.* a natural or man-made mound on which a castle was erected. [C14: see MOAT]

MOT test *n.* (in Britain) See **MOT** (sense 2).

mottle (ˈmɒtᵊl) *vb.* **1.** (*tr.*) to colour with streaks or blotches of different shades. ~*n.* **2.** a mottled appearance, as of the surface of marble. **3.** one streak or blotch of colour in a mottled surface. [C17: back formation from MOTLEY]

motto (ˈmɒtəʊ) *n., pl.* **-toes** *or* **-tos. 1.** a short saying expressing the guiding maxim or ideal of a family, organization, etc., esp. when part of a coat of arms. **2.** a short explanatory phrase inscribed on or attached to something. **3.** a verse or maxim contained in a paper cracker. **4.** a quotation prefacing a book or chapter of a book. **5.** a recurring musical phrase. [C16: via Italian from Latin *muttum* utterance]

motty (ˈmɒtɪ) *n. Irish.* the target at which coins are aimed in pitch-and-toss.

Motu (ˈməʊtuː) *n.* **1.** (*pl.* **-tu** *or* **-tus**) a member of an aboriginal people of S Papua. **2.** the language of this people, belonging to the Malayo-Polynesian family. **3.** Also called: **Hiri Motu** *or* (esp. formerly) **Police Motu.** a pidgin version of this language, widely used in Papua New Guinea. Compare **Neo-Melanesian.**

motu proprio (ˈməʊtuː ˈprəʊprɪˌəʊ) *n.* an administrative papal bull. [Latin: of his own accord]

moue *French.* (mu) *n.* a disdainful or pouting look.

mouflon *or* **moufflon** (ˈmuːflɒn) *n.* a wild short-fleeced mountain sheep, *Ovis musimon,* of Corsica and Sardinia. [C18: via French from Corsican *mufrone,* from Late Latin *mufrō*]

mouillé (ˈmwiːeɪ) *adj. Phonetics.* palatalized, as in the sounds represented by Spanish *ll* or *ñ,* Italian *gl* or *gn* (pronounced as (ʎ) and (ɲ) respectively), or French *ll* (representing a (j) sound). [C19: from French, past participle of *mouiller* to moisten, from Latin *mollis* soft]

moujik (ˈmuːʒɪk) *n.* a variant spelling of **muzhik.**

mould[1] *or U.S.* **mold** (məʊld) *n.* **1.** a shaped cavity used to give a definite form to fluid or plastic material. **2.** a frame on which something may be constructed. **3.** something shaped in or made on a mould. **4.** shape, form, design, or pattern. **5.** specific nature, character, or type: *heroic mould.* ~*vb.* (*tr.*) **6.** to make in a mould. **7.** to shape or form, as by using a mould. **8.** to influence or direct: *to mould opinion.* **9.** to cling to: *the skirt moulds her figure.* **10.** *Metallurgy.* to make (a material such as sand) into a mould that is used in casting. [C13 (n.): changed from Old French *modle,* from Latin *modulus* a small measure, MODULE] —ˈ**mouldable** *or U.S.* ˈ**moldable** *adj.* —ˌ**mouldaˈbility** *or U.S.* ˌ**moldaˈbility** *n.*

mould[2] *or U.S.* **mold** (məʊld) *n.* **1.** a coating or discoloration caused by various saprophytic fungi that develop in a damp atmosphere on the surface of stored food, fabrics, wallpaper, etc. **2.** any of the fungi that causes this growth. ~*vb.* **3.** to become or cause to become covered with this growth. ~Also called: **mildew.** [C15: dialect (Northern English) *mowlde* mouldy, from the past participle of *moulen* to become mouldy, probably of Scandinavian origin; compare Old Norse *mugla* mould]

mould[3] *or U.S.* **mold** (məʊld) *n.* **1.** loose soil, esp. when rich in organic matter. **2.** *Poetic.* the earth. [Old English *molde;* related to Old High German *molta* soil, Gothic *mulde*]

mouldboard *or U.S.* **moldboard** (ˈməʊldˌbɔːd) *n.* the curved blade of a plough, which turns over the furrow.

moulder[1] *or U.S.* **molder** (ˈməʊldə) *vb.* (often foll. by *away*) to crumble or cause to crumble, as through decay. [C16: verbal use of MOULD[3]]

moulder[2] *or U.S.* **molder** (ˈməʊldə) *n.* **1.** a person who moulds or makes moulds. **2.** *Printing.* one of the set of electrotypes used for making duplicates.

moulding *or U.S.* **molding** (ˈməʊldɪŋ) *n.* **1.** *Architect.* **a.** a shaped outline, esp. one used on cornices, etc. **b.** a shaped strip made of wood, stone, etc. **2.** something moulded.

moulding board *n.* a board on which dough is kneaded.

mouldwarp (ˈməʊldˌwɔːp) *or* **mouldywarp** (ˈməʊldɪˌwɔːp) *n.* an archaic or dialect name for a **mole**[2] (sense 1). [C14 *moldewarpe;* ultimately from Germanic *moldeworpon* (unattested) earth-thrower, from *moldā* MOULD[3] + *wurp, werp* to throw (both unattested)]

mouldy *or U.S.* **moldy** (ˈməʊldɪ) *adj.* **mouldier, mouldiest** *or U.S.* **moldier, moldiest. 1.** covered with mould. **2.** stale or musty, esp. from age or lack of use. **3.** *Slang.* boring; dull. —ˈ**mouldiness** *or U.S.* ˈ**moldiness** *n.*

mouldy fig *n. Dated slang.* a rigid adherent to older jazz forms.

moulin (ˈmuːlɪn) *n.* a vertical shaft in a glacier, maintained by a constant descending stream of water and debris. [C19: from French: a mill]

moult *or U.S.* **molt** (məʊlt) *vb.* **1.** (of birds, mammals, reptiles, and arthropods) to shed (feathers, hair, skin, or cuticle). ~*n.* **2.** the periodic process of moulting. See also **ecdysis.** [C14 *mouten,* from Old English *mūtian,* as in *bimūtian* to exchange for, from Latin *mūtāre* to change] —ˈ**moulter** *or U.S.* ˈ**molter** *n.*

mound[1] (maʊnd) *n.* **1.** a raised mass of earth, debris, etc. **2.** any heap or pile: *a mound of washing.* **3.** a small natural hill. **4.** *Archaeol.* another word for **barrow**[2]. **5.** an artificial ridge of earth, stone, etc., as used for defence. ~*vb.* **6.** (often foll. by *up*) to gather into a mound; heap. **7.** (*tr.*) to cover or surround with a mound: *to mound a grave.* [C16: earthwork, perhaps from Old English *mund* hand, hence defence: compare Middle Dutch *mond* protection]

mound[2] (maʊnd) *n. Heraldry.* a rare word for **orb** (sense 1). [C13 (meaning: world, C16: orb): from French *monde,* from Latin *mundus* world]

Mound Builder *n.* a member of a group of prehistoric inhabitants of the Mississippi region of the U.S. who built altar-mounds, tumuli, etc.

mound-builder *n.* another name for **megapode.**

mount[1] (maʊnt) *vb.* **1.** to go up (a hill, stairs, etc.); climb. **2.** to get up on (a horse, a platform, etc.). **3.** (*intr.*; often foll. by *up*) to increase; accumulate: *excitement mounted.* **4.** (*tr.*) to fix onto a backing, setting, or support: *to mount a photograph; to mount a* *slide.* **5.** (*tr.*) to provide with a horse for riding, or to place on a horse. **6.** (of male animals) to climb onto (a female animal) for copulation. **7.** (*tr.*) to prepare (a play, musical comedy, etc.) for production. **8.** (*tr.*) to plan and organize (a compaign, an exhibition, etc.) **9.** (*tr.*) *Military.* to prepare or launch (an operation): *the Allies mounted an offensive.* **10.** (*tr.*) to prepare (a skeleton, dead animal, etc.) for exhibition as a specimen. **11.** (*tr.*) to place or carry (weapons) in such a position that they can be fired. **12. mount guard.** See **guard** (sense 26). ~*n.* **13.** a backing, setting, or support onto which something is fixed. **14.** the act or manner of mounting. **15.** a horse for riding. **16.** a slide used in microscopy. **17.** *Philately.* **a.** a small transparent pocket in an album for a postage stamp. **b.** another word (esp. U.S.) for **hinge** (sense 5). [C16: from Old French *munter,* from Vulgar Latin *montāre* (unattested) from Latin *mons* MOUNT[2]] —ˈ**mountable** *adj.* —ˈ**mounter** *n.*

mount[2] (maʊnt) *n.* **1.** a mountain or hill: used in literature and (when cap.) in proper names: *Mount Everest.* **2.** (in palmistry) any of the seven cushions of flesh on the palm of the hand. [Old English *munt,* from Latin *mons* mountain, but influenced in Middle English by Old French *mont*]

mountain (ˈmaʊntɪn) *n.* **1. a.** a natural upward projection of the earth's surface, higher and steeper than a hill and often having a rocky summit. **b.** (*as modifier*): *mountain people; mountain scenery.* **c.** (*in combination*): *a mountaintop.* **2.** a huge heap or mass: *a mountain of papers.* **3.** anything of great quantity or size. **4.** a surplus of a commodity, esp. in the European Community: *the butter mountain.* **5. make a mountain out of a molehill.** See **molehill** (sense 2). [C13: from Old French *montaigne,* from Vulgar Latin *montānea* (unattested) mountainous, from Latin *montānus,* from *mons* mountain]

mountain ash *n.* **1.** any of various trees of the rosaceous genus *Sorbus,* such as *S. aucuparia* (**European mountain ash** or **rowan**), having clusters of small white flowers and bright red berries. **2.** any of several Australian eucalyptus trees, such as *Eucalyptus regnans.*

mountain avens *n.* See **avens** (sense 2).

mountain bike *n.* a type of sturdy bicycle with up to 15 gears, straight handlebars, and heavy-duty tyres.

mountain cat *n.* any of various wild feline mammals, such as the bobcat, lynx, or puma.

mountain chain *n.* a series of ranges of mountains.

mountain devil *n.* another name for **moloch.**

mountaineer (ˌmaʊntɪˈnɪə) *n.* **1.** a person who climbs mountains. **2.** a person living in a mountainous area. ~*vb.* **3.** (*intr.*) to climb mountains. —ˌ**mountainˈeering** *n.*

mountain everlasting *n.* another name for **cat's-foot.**

mountain goat *n.* **1.** short for **Rocky Mountain goat.** **2.** any wild goat inhabiting mountainous regions.

mountain laurel *n.* any of various ericaceous shrubs or trees of the genus *Kalmia,* esp. *K. latifolia* of E North America, which has leathery poisonous leaves and clusters of pink or white flowers. Also called: **calico bush.**

mountain lion *n.* another name for **puma.**

mountainous (ˈmaʊntɪnəs) *adj.* **1.** of or relating to mountains: *a mountainous region.* **2.** resembling a mountain, esp. in size or impressiveness. —ˈ**mountainously** *adv.* —ˈ**mountainousness** *n.*

mountain range *n.* a series of adjoining mountains or of lines of mountains of similar origin.

mountain sheep *n.* **1.** another name for **bighorn.** **2.** any wild sheep inhabiting mountainous regions.

mountain sickness *n.* nausea, headache, and shortness of breath caused by climbing to high altitudes (usually above 12 000 ft.). Also called: **altitude sickness.**

Mountain Standard Time *n.* one of the standard times used in North America, seven hours behind Greenwich Mean Time. Abbrev.: **MST.**

Mount Cook lily *n.* a large white buttercup, *Ranunculus lyallii,* of the South Island alpine country of New Zealand. Also called: **great mountain buttercup.**

mountebank (ˈmaʊntɪˌbæŋk) *n.* **1.** (formerly) a person who sold quack medicines in public places. **2.** a charlatan; fake. ~*vb.* **3.** (*intr.*) to play the mountebank. [C16: from Italian *montambanco* a climber on a bench, from *montare* to MOUNT[1] + *banco* BENCH (see also BANK[1])] —ˌ**mounteˈbankery** *n.*

mounted (ˈmaʊntɪd) *adj.* **1.** equipped with or riding horses: *mounted police.* **2.** provided with a support, backing, etc.

Mountie *or* **Mounty** (ˈmaʊntɪ) *n., pl.* **Mounties.** *Informal.* a member of the Royal Canadian Mounted Police. [nickname evolved from MOUNTED]

mounting (ˈmaʊntɪŋ) *n.* another word for **mount**[1] (sense 13).

mounting-block *n.* a block of stone formerly used to aid a person when mounting a horse.

mourn (mɔːn) *vb.* **1.** to feel or express sadness for the death or loss of (someone or something). **2.** (*intr.*) to observe the customs of mourning, as by wearing black. **3.** (*tr.*) to grieve over (loss or misfortune). [Old English *murnan;* compare Old High German *mornēn* to be troubled, Gothic *maurnan* to grieve, Greek *mermeros* worried]

mourner (ˈmɔːnə) *n.* **1.** a person who mourns, esp. at a funeral. **2.** (at U.S. revivalist meetings) a person who repents publicly.

mournful (ˈmɔːnfʊl) *adj.* **1.** evoking grief; sorrowful. **2.** gloomy; sad. —ˈ**mournfully** *adv.* —ˈ**mournfulness** *n.*

mourning (ˈmɔːnɪŋ) *n.* **1.** the act or feelings of one who mourns; grief. **2.** the conventional symbols of grief, such as the wearing of black. **3.** the period of time during which a death is officially mourned. **4. in mourning.** observing the conventions of mourning. ~*adj.* **5.** of or relating to mourning. —ˈ**mourningly** *adv.*

mourning band *n.* a piece of black material, esp. an armband, worn to indicate that the wearer is in mourning.

mourning cloak *n.* the U.S. name for **Camberwell beauty.**

mourning dove *n.* a brown North American dove, *Zenaidura macroura,* with a plaintive song.

mouse *n.* (maʊs), *pl.* **mice** (maɪs). **1.** any of numerous small long-tailed rodents of the families *Muridae* and *Cricetidae* that are similar to but smaller than rats. See also **fieldmouse, harvest mouse, house mouse.** **2.** any of various related rodents, such as the jumping mouse. **3.** a quiet, timid, or cowardly person. **4.** *Computer technol.* a hand-held device used to control the cursor movement and select computing functions without keying. **5.** *Slang.* a black eye. **6.** *Nautical.* another word for **mousing.** ~*vb.* (maʊz). **7.** to stalk and catch (mice). **8.** (*intr.*) to go about stealthily. **9.** (*tr.*) *Nautical.* to secure (a hook) with mousing. [Old English *mūs;* compare Old Saxon *mūs,* German *maus,* Old Norse *mūs,* Latin *mūs,* Greek *mūs*] —ˈ**mouseˌlike** *adj.*

mousebird (ˈmaʊsˌbɜːd) *n.* another name for **coly.**

mouse deer *n.* another name for **chevrotain.**

mouse-ear *n.* short for **mouse-ear chickweed** (see **chickweed** (sense 2)).

mouser (ˈmaʊzə, ˈmaʊsə) *n.* a cat or other animal that is used to catch mice: usually qualified: *a good mouser.*

mousetail (ˈmaʊsˌteɪl) *n.* any of various N temperate ranunculaceous plants of the genus *Myosurus,* esp. *M. minimus,* with tail-like flower spikes.

mousetrap (ˈmaʊsˌtræp) *n.* **1.** any trap for catching mice, esp. one with a spring-loaded metal bar that is released by the taking of the bait. **2.** *Brit. informal.* cheese of indifferent quality.

mousey (ˈmaʊsɪ) *adj.* **mousier, mousiest.** a variant spelling of **mousy.** —ˈ**mousily** *adv.* —ˈ**mousiness** *n.*

mousing (ˈmaʊzɪŋ) *n. Nautical.* a lashing, shackle, etc., for closing off a hook to prevent a load from slipping off.

moussaka *or* **mousaka** (mʊˈsɑːkə) *n.* a dish originating in the Balkan States, consisting of meat, aubergines, and tomatoes, topped with cheese sauce. [C20: from Modern Greek]

mousse (muːs) *n.* **1.** a light creamy dessert made with eggs, cream, fruit, etc., set with gelatin. **2.** a similar dish made from fish or meat. **3.** short for **styling mousse.** [C19: from French: froth]

mousseline (*French* muslin) *n.* **1.** a fine fabric made of rayon or silk. **2.** a type of fine glass. **3.** short for **mousseline sauce.** [C17: French: MUSLIN]

mousseline de laine *French.* (muslin də lɛn) *n.* a light woollen fabric. [literally: muslin of wool]

mousseline de soie *French.* (muslin də swa) *n.* a thin gauzelike fabric of silk or rayon. [literally: muslin of silk]

mousseline sauce *n.* a light sauce, made by adding whipped cream or egg whites to hollandaise sauce. [from French *mousseline,* literally: muslin]

moustache *or U.S.* **mustache** (məˈstɑːʃ) *n.* **1.** the unshaved growth of hair on the upper lip, and sometimes down the sides of the mouth. **2.** a similar growth of hair or bristles (in animals) or feathers (in birds). **3.** a mark like a moustache. [C16: via French from Italian *mostaccio,* ultimately from Doric Greek *mustax* upper lip] —**mousˈtached** *or U.S.* **musˈtached** *adj.*

moustache cup *n.* a cup with a partial cover to protect a drinker's moustache.

Mousterian (muːˈstɪərɪən) *n.* **1.** a culture characterized by flint flake tools and associated with Neanderthal man, found throughout Europe, North Africa, and the Near East, dating from before 70 000–32 000 B.C. ~*adj.* **2.** of or relating to this culture. [C20: from French *Moustérien* from archaeological finds of the same period in the cave of *Le Moustier,* Dordogne, France]

mousy *or* **mousey** (ˈmaʊsɪ) *adj.* **mousier, mousiest.** **1.** resembling a mouse, esp. in having a light brown or greyish hair colour. **2.** shy or ineffectual: *a mousy little woman.* **3.** infested with mice. —ˈ**mousily** *adv.* —ˈ**mousiness** *n.*

mouth *n.* (maʊθ), *pl.* **mouths** (maʊðz). **1.** the opening through which many animals take in food and issue vocal sounds. **2.** the system of organs surrounding this opening, including the lips, tongue, teeth, etc. **3.** the visible part of the lips on the face. **4.** a person regarded as a consumer of food: *four mouths to feed.* **5.** verbal expression (esp. in the phrase **give mouth to**). **6.** a particular manner of speaking: *a foul mouth.* **7.** *Informal.* boastful, rude, or excessive talk: *he is all mouth.* **8.** the point where a river issues into a sea or lake. **9.** the opening of a container, such as a jar. **10.** the opening of or place leading into a cave, tunnel, volcano, etc. **11.** that part of the inner lip of a horse on which the bit acts, esp. when specified as to sensitivity: *a hard mouth.* **12.** *Music.* the narrow slit in an organ pipe. **13.** the opening between the jaws of a vice or other gripping device. **14.** a pout; grimace. **15. by word of mouth.** orally rather than by written means. **16. down in** *or* **at the mouth.** in low spirits.

17. have a big mouth *or* **open one's big mouth.** *Informal.* to speak indiscreetly, loudly, or excessively. **18. keep one's mouth shut.** to keep a secret. **19. put one's money where one's mouth is.** to take appropriate action to support what one has said. **20. put words into someone's mouth. a.** to represent, often inaccurately, what someone has said. **b.** to tell someone what to say. ~*vb.* (mauð). **21.** to speak or say (something) insincerely, esp. in public. **22.** (*tr.*) to form (words) with movements of the lips but without speaking. **23.** (*tr.*) to accustom (a horse) to wearing a bit. **24.** (*tr.*) to take (something) into the mouth or to move (something) around inside the mouth. **25.** (*intr.*; usually foll. by *at*) to make a grimace. [Old English *mūth;* compare Old Norse *muthr,* Gothic *munths,* Dutch *mond*] —**mouther** ('mauðə) *n.*

mouthbrooder ('mauθ,bruːdə) *or* **mouthbreeder** ('mauθ,briːdə) *n.* any of various African cichlid fishes of the genera *Tilapia* and *Haplochromis* that carry their eggs and young around in the mouth.

mouthful ('mauθ,ful) *n., pl.* **-fuls. 1.** as much as is held in the mouth at one time. **2.** a small quantity, as of food. **3.** a long word or phrase that is difficult to say. **4.** *Brit. informal.* an abusive response. **5.** *Informal, chiefly U.S. and Canadian.* an impressive remark (esp. in the phrase **say a mouthful**).

mouth organ *n.* another name for **harmonica** (sense 1).

mouthpart ('mauθ,pɑːt) *n.* any of the paired appendages in arthropods that surround the mouth and are specialized for feeding.

mouthpiece ('mauθ,piːs) *n.* **1.** the part of a wind instrument into which the player blows. **2.** the part of a telephone receiver into which a person speaks. **3.** the part of a container forming its mouth. **4.** a person who acts as a spokesman, as for an organization. **5.** a publication, esp. a periodical, expressing the official views of an organization. **6.** *Boxing.* another name for **gumshield.**

mouth-to-mouth *adj.* designating a method of artificial respiration involving blowing air rhythmically into the mouth of a person who has stopped breathing, to stimulate return of spontaneous breathing.

mouthwash ('mauθ,wɒʃ) *n.* a medicated aqueous solution, used for gargling and for cleansing the mouth.

mouthwatering ('mauθ,wɔːtərɪŋ) *adj.* whetting the appetite, as from smell, appearance, or description.

mouthy ('mauðɪ) *adj.* **mouthier, mouthiest.** bombastic; excessively talkative.

mouton ('muːtɒn) *n.* sheepskin processed to resemble the fur of another animal, esp. beaver or seal. [from French: sheep. See MUTTON]

movable *or* **moveable** ('muːvəbᵊl) *adj.* **1.** able to be moved or rearranged; not fixed. **2.** (esp. of religious festivals such as Easter) varying in date from year to year. **3.** (usually spelt **moveable**) *Law.* denoting or relating to personal property as opposed to realty. **4.** *Printing.* (of type) cast singly so that each character is on a separate piece of type suitable for composition by hand, as founder's type. ~*n.* **5.** (*often pl.*) a movable article, esp. a piece of furniture. —,**mova'bility** *or* '**movableness** *n.* —'**movably** *adv.*

move (muːv) *vb.* **1.** to go or take from one place to another; change in location or position. **2.** (*usually intr.*) to change (one's dwelling, place of business, etc.). **3.** to be or cause to be in motion; stir. **4.** (*intr.*) (of machines, etc.) to work or operate. **5.** (*tr.*) to cause (to do something); prompt. **6.** (*intr.*) to begin to act: *move soon or we'll lose the order.* **7.** (*intr.*) to associate oneself with a specified social circle: *to move in exalted spheres.* **8.** (*intr.*) to make progress. **9.** (*tr.*) to arouse affection, pity, or compassion in; touch. **10.** (in board games) to change the position of (a piece) or (of a piece) to change position. **11.** (*intr.*) (of merchandise) to be disposed of by being bought. **12.** (when *tr., often takes a clause as object;* when *intr.,* often foll. by *for*) to suggest (a proposal) formally, as in debating or parliamentary procedure. **13.** (*intr.;* usually foll. by *on* or *along*) to go away or to another place; leave. **14.** to cause (the bowels) to evacuate or (of the bowels) to be evacuated. **15.** (*intr.*) *Informal.* to be exciting or active: *the party started moving at twelve.* **16. move heaven and earth.** to take every step possible (to achieve something). ~*n.* **17.** the act of moving; movement. **18.** one of a sequence of actions, usually part of a plan; manoeuvre. **19.** the act of moving one's residence, place of business, etc. **20.** (in board games) **a.** a player's turn to move his piece or take other permitted action. **b.** a permitted manoeuvre of a piece. **21. get a move on.** *Informal.* **a.** to get started. **b.** to hurry up. **22. make a move.** (*usually used with a negative*) *Informal.* to take even the slightest action: *don't make a move without phoning me.* **23. make one's move.** to commit oneself to a position or course of action. **24. on the move. a.** travelling from place to place. **b.** advancing; succeeding. **c.** very active; busy. [C13: from Anglo-French *mover,* from Latin *movēre*]

move in *vb.* (*mainly adv.*) **1.** (*also prep.*) Also (when *prep.*): **move into.** to occupy or take possession of (a new residence, place of business, etc.) or help (someone) to do this. **2.** (*intr.;* often foll. by *on*) *Informal.* to creep close (to), as in preparing to capture. **3.** (*intr.;* often foll. by *on*) *Informal.* to try to gain power or influence (over) or interfere (with).

movement ('muːvmənt) *n.* **1. a.** the act, process, or result of moving. **b.** an instance of moving. **2.** the manner of moving. **3. a.** a group of people with a common ideology, esp. a political or religious one. **b.** the organized action of such a group. **4.** a trend or tendency in a particular sphere. **5.** the driving and regulating mechanism of a watch or clock. **6.** (*often pl.*) a person's location and activities during a specific time. **7. a.** the evacuation of the bowels. **b.** the matter evacuated. **8.** *Music.* a principal self-contained section of a symphony, sonata, etc., usually having its own structure. **9.** tempo or pace, as in music or literature. **10.** *Fine arts.* the appearance of motion in painting, sculpture, etc. **11.** *Prosody.* the rhythmical structure of verse. **12.** a positional change by one or a number of military units. **13.** a change in the market price of a security or commodity.

move out *vb.* (*adv.*) to vacate a residence, place of business, etc., or help (someone) to do this.

mover ('muːvə) *n.* **1.** *Informal.* a person, business, idea, etc., that is advancing or progressing. **2.** a person who moves a proposal, as in a debate. **3.** *U.S. and Canadian.* a removal firm or a person who works for one.

movers and shakers *pl. n. Informal.* the people with power and influence in a particular field of activity. [C20: perhaps from the line "We are the movers and shakers of the world for ever" in 'Ode' by Arthur O'Shaughnessy (1844–81), British poet]

movie ('muːvɪ) *n.* **a.** an informal word for **film** (sense 1). **b.** (*as modifier*): *movie ticket.* [C20: from MOV(ING PICTURE) + -IE]

movie camera *n.* the U.S. and Canadian term for **cine camera.**

movie film *n.* the U.S. and Canadian term for **cine film.**

Movietone ('muːvɪ,təun) *n. U.S. trademark.* the earliest technique of including a soundtrack on film.

moving ('muːvɪŋ) *adj.* **1.** arousing or touching the emotions. **2.** changing or capable of changing position. **3.** causing motion. —'**movingly** *adv.*

moving average *n. Statistics.* (of a sequence of values) a derived sequence of the averages of successive subsequences of a given number of members, often used in time series to even out short-term fluctuations and make a trend clearer: *the 3-term moving average of 4, 6, 8, 7, 9, 8 is 6, 7, 8, 8.*

moving coil *adj.* denoting an electromechanical device in which a suspended coil is free to move in a magnetic field. A current passing through the coil causes it to move, as in loudspeakers and electrical measuring instruments, or movement of the coil gives rise to induced currents, as in microphones and some record-player pick-ups.

moving picture *n.* a U.S. and Canadian name for **film** (sense 1).

moving staircase *or* **stairway** *n.* less common terms for **escalator** (sense 1).

Moviola (,muːvɪ'əulə) *n. Trademark.* a viewing machine used in cutting and editing film.

mow[1] (məu) *vb.* **mows, mowing, mowed, mowed** *or* **mown. 1.** to cut down (grass, crops, etc.) with a hand implement or machine. **2.** (*tr.*) to cut the growing vegetation of (a field, lawn, etc.). [Old English *māwan;* related to Old High German *māen,* Middle Dutch *maeyen* to mow, Latin *metere* to reap, Welsh *medi*] —'**mower** *n.*

mow[2] (mau) *n.* **1.** the part of a barn where hay, straw, etc., is stored. **2.** the hay, straw, etc., stored. [Old English *mūwa;* compare Old Norse *mūgr* heap, Greek *mukōn*]

mow[3] (mau) *n., vb.* an archaic word for **grimace.** [C14: from Old French *moe* a pout, or Middle Dutch *mouwe*]

MOW (in New Zealand) *abbrev. for* Ministry of Works.

mowburnt ('məu,bɜːnt) *adj.* (of hay, straw, etc.) damaged by overheating in a mow.

mowdie ('maudɪ) *or* **mowdiewart** ('maudɪ,wært) *n.* Scot. words for **mole**[2]. [C18: a Scot. variant of MOULDWARP]

mow down *vb.* (*tr., adv.*) to kill in large numbers, esp. by gunfire.

mown (məun) *vb.* a past participle of **mow**[1].

moxa ('mɒksə) *n.* **1.** a downy material obtained from various plants and used in Oriental medicine by being burned on the skin as a cauterizing agent or counterirritant for the skin. **2.** any of various plants yielding this material, such as the wormwood *Artemisia chinensis.* [C17: anglicized version of Japanese *mogusa,* contraction of *moe gusa* burning herb]

moxie ('mɒksɪ) *n. U.S. and Canadian slang.* courage, nerve, or vigour. [from the trademark *Moxie,* a soft drink]

moz *or* **mozz** (mɒz) *n. Austral. slang.* **1.** a hoodoo; hex. **2. put the moz on.** to jinx. [short for MOZZLE]

Mozarab (məu'zærəb) *n.* (formerly) a Christian of Moorish Spain. [C18: via Spanish from Arabic *musta'rib* a would-be Arab] —**Moz'arabic** *adj.*

Mozartean *or* **Mozartian** (məu'tsɑːtɪən) *adj.* of or relating to Wolfgang Amadeus Mozart (1756–91), Austrian composer, or his musical works or style.

mozzarella (,mɒtsə'rɛlə) *n.* a moist white Italian curd cheese made originally from buffalo milk. [from Italian, diminutive of *mozza* a type of cheese, from *mozzare* to cut off]

mozzetta (məu'zɛtə; *Italian* mot'tsetta) *or* **mozetta** *n. R.C. Church.* a short hooded cape worn by the pope, cardinals, etc. [C18: from Italian, shortened from *almozzetta,* from Medieval Latin *almutia* ALMUCE]

mozzie ('mɒzɪ) *n.* a variant spelling of **mossie**[1].

mozzle ('mɒzᵊl) *n. Austral. informal.* luck, esp. bad luck. [from Hebrew *mazzal* luck]

mp *abbrev. for:* **1.** melting point. **2.** *Music.* mezzo piano. [Italian: moderately soft]

MP *abbrev. for:* 1. (in Britain) Member of Parliament. 2. (in Britain) Metropolitan Police. 3. Military Police. 4. Mounted Police.

mpg *abbrev. for* miles per gallon.

MPG (in Britain) *abbrev. for* main professional grade: the basic salary scale for classroom teachers.

mph *abbrev. for* miles per hour.

MPhil *or* **MPh** *abbrev. for* Master of Philosophy.

MPLA *abbrev. for* Movimento Popular de Libertacão de Angola. [Portuguese: Popular Movement for the Liberation of Angola]

MP/M *n. Computer technol.* a multiuser operating system that resembles a CP/M.

MPP (in Canada) *abbrev. for* Member of the Provincial Parliament (of Ontario).

MPS *abbrev. for:* 1. Member of the Pharmaceutical Society. 2. Member of the Philological Society. 3. Member of the Physical Society.

Mr (ˈmɪstə) *n., pl.* **Messrs** (ˈmɛsəz). 1. a title used before a man's name or names or before some office that he holds: *Mr Jones; Mr President.* 2. (in military contexts) a title used in addressing a warrant officer, officer cadet, or junior naval officer. 3. a title placed before the surname of a surgeon. [C17: abbreviation of MISTER]

MR *abbrev. for:* 1. (in Britain) Master of the Rolls. 2. motivation(al) research.

MRA *abbrev. for* Moral Rearmament.

Mr Big *n. Slang, chiefly U.S.* the head of an organization, esp. of a criminal organization.

MRBM *abbrev. for* medium-range ballistic missile.

MRC (in Britain) *abbrev. for* Medical Research Council.

MRCA *abbrev. for* multirole combat aircraft.

MRI *abbrev. for* magnetic resonance imaging.

MRIA *abbrev. for* Member of the Royal Irish Academy.

mridang (mrɪˈdʌŋ) *n.* a drum used in Indian music. [Hindi]

m-RNA *abbrev. for* messenger RNA.

MRP *abbrev. for* manufacturers' recommended price.

Mr Right *n. Informal.* the man considered by a woman to be her perfect marriage partner.

Mrs (ˈmɪsɪz) *n., pl.* **Mrs** *or* **Mesdames.** a title used before the name or names of a married woman. [C17: originally an abbreviation of MISTRESS]

MRSC *abbrev. for* Member of the Royal Society of Chemistry.

Mrs Mop *n. Informal.* a cleaning lady.

Ms (mɪz, məs) *n.* a title substituted for **Mrs** or **Miss** before a woman's name to avoid making a distinction between married and unmarried women.

MS *abbrev. for:* 1. Master of Surgery. 2. (on gravestones) memoriae sacrum. [Latin: sacred to the memory of] 3. Mississippi. 4. motor ship. 5. multiple sclerosis. ~6. *international car registration for* Mauritius.

MS. *or* **ms.** *pl.* **MSS.** *or* **mss.** *abbrev. for* manuscript.

msb *Computer technol. abbrev. for* most significant bit; the bit of binary number with the greatest numerical value or the bit in some other binary pattern which occupies this position.

MSc *abbrev. for* Master of Science.

MS-DOS (ɛmˈɛsˈdɒs) *n. Trademark, computer technol.* a type of disk operating system. [C20: from *M(icro)s(oft),* the company that developed it, + DOS]

MSF (in Britain) *abbrev. for* Manufacturing, Science, Finance (a trade union).

MSG *abbrev. for* monosodium glutamate.

Msgr *abbrev. for* Monsignor.

MSI *Electronics. abbrev. for* medium scale integration.

msl *or* **MSL** *abbrev. for* mean sea level.

MSS *or* **mss** *abbrev. for* manuscripts.

MST *abbrev. for* Mountain Standard Time.

Ms-Th *Physics. symbol for* mesothorium.

Mt *or* **mt** *abbrev. for:* 1. mount: *Mt Everest.* 2. Also: **mtn.** mountain.

MT *abbrev. for* Montana.

mt. *abbrev. for* megaton.

MTB *n. Brit.* a motor torpedo boat.

MTBE *abbrev. for* methyl tertiary-butyl ether: a lead-free antiknock petrol additive.

MTBF *abbrev. for* mean time between failures.

MTech *abbrev. for* Master of Technology.

mtg *abbrev. for* meeting.

mtg. *or* **mtge** *abbrev. for* mortgage.

Mt Rev. *abbrev. for* Most Reverend.

MTV *abbrev. for* music television: a U.S. music channel that operates 24 hours a day.

mu (mjuː) *n.* the 12th letter in the Greek alphabet (Μ, μ), a consonant, transliterated as *m.*

MU *abbrev. for* Musicians' Union.

muc- *combining form.* a variant of **muco-** before a vowel.

much (mʌtʃ) *determiner.* 1. a. (*usually used with a negative*) a great quantity or degree of: *there isn't much honey left.* b. (*as pronoun*): *much has been learned from this.* 2. **a bit much.** *Informal.* rather excessive. 3. **as much.** exactly that: *I suspected as much when I heard.* 4. **make much of.** See **make of** (sense 4). 5. **not much of.** not to any appreciable degree or extent: *he's not much of an actor really.* 6. **not up to much.** *Informal.* of a low standard: *this beer is not up to much.* 7. **think much of.** (*used with a negative*) to have a high opinion of: *I don't think much of his behaviour.* ~*adv.* 8. considerably: *they're much better now.* 9. practically; nearly (esp. in the phrase **much the same).** 10. (*usually used with a negative*) often; a great deal: *it doesn't happen much in this country.* 11. **(as) much as.** even though; although: *much as I'd like to, I can't come.* ~*adj.* 12. (*predicative; usually used with a negative*) impressive or important: *this car isn't much.* ~See also **more, most.** [Old English *mycel;* related to Old English *micel* great, Old Saxon *mikil,* Gothic *mikils;* compare also Latin *magnus,* Greek *megas*]

muchness (ˈmʌtʃnɪs) *n.* 1. *Archaic or informal.* magnitude. 2. **much of a muchness.** *Brit.* very similar.

mucic acid (ˈmjuːsɪk) *n.* a colourless crystalline solid carboxylic acid found in milk sugar and used in the manufacture of pyrrole. Formula: $C_4H_4(OH)_4(COOH)_2$. [C19: *mucic,* from French *mucique;* see MUCUS, -IC]

mucid (ˈmjuːsɪd) *adj. Rare.* mouldy, musty, or slimy. [C17: from Latin *mūcidus,* from *mucēre* to be mouldy] —**muˈcidity** *or* **ˈmucidness** *n.*

mucigen (ˈmjuːsɪdʒən) *n.* a substance present in mucous cells that is converted into mucin.

mucilage (ˈmjuːsɪlɪdʒ) *n.* 1. a sticky preparation, such as gum or glue, used as an adhesive. 2. a complex glutinous carbohydrate secreted by certain plants. [C14: via Old French from Late Latin *mūcilāgo* mouldy juice; see MUCID] —**mucilaginous** (ˌmjuːsɪˈlædʒɪnəs) *adj.* —**ˌmuciˈlaginously** *adv.* —**ˌmuciˈlaginousness** *n.*

mucin (ˈmjuːsɪn) *n. Biochem.* any of a group of nitrogenous mucoproteins occurring in saliva, skin, tendon, etc., that produce a very viscous solution in water. [C19: via French from Latin MUCUS] —**ˈmucinous** *adj.*

muck (mʌk) *n.* 1. farmyard dung or decaying vegetable matter. 2. Also called: **muck soil.** an organic soil rich in humus and used as a fertilizer. 3. dirt or filth. 4. earth, rock material, etc., removed during mining excavations. 5. *Slang, chiefly Brit.* rubbish. 6. See **Lord Muck, Lady Muck.** 7. **make a muck of.** *Slang, chiefly Brit.* to ruin or spoil. ~*vb.* (*tr.*) 8. to spread manure upon (fields, gardens, etc.). 9. to soil or pollute. 10. (often foll. by *out*) to clear muck from. ~See also **muck about, muck in, muck up.** [C13: probably of Scandinavian origin; compare Old Norse *myki* dung, Norwegian *myk*]

muck about *vb. Brit. slang.* 1. (*intr.*) to waste time; misbehave. 2. (when *intr.,* foll. by *with*) to interfere with, annoy, or waste the time of.

muckamuck (ˈmʌkəˌmʌk) *Canadian W coast.* ~*n.* 1. food. ~*vb.* 2. (*intr.*) to consume food; eat. [Chinook Jargon]

mucker (ˈmʌkə) *n.* 1. *Mining.* a person who shifts broken rock or waste. 2. *Brit. slang.* a. a friend; mate. b. a coarse person. —**ˈmuckerish** *adj.*

muck in *vb. (intr., adv.) Brit. slang.* to share something, such as duties, work, etc. (with other people).

muckle (ˈmʌkəl) *Scot.* ~*adj.* 1. large; much. ~*adv.* 2. much; greatly. [dialect variant of MICKLE]

muckrake (ˈmʌkˌreɪk) *n.* 1. an agricultural rake for spreading manure. ~*vb.* 2. (*intr.*) to seek out and expose scandal, esp. concerning public figures. —**ˈmuckˌraker** *n.* —**ˈmuckˌraking** *n.*

mucksweat (ˈmʌkˌswɛt) *n. Brit. informal.* profuse sweat or a state of profuse sweating.

muck up *vb. (adv.) Slang.* 1. (*tr.*) *Brit. and Austral.* to ruin or spoil; make a mess of. 2. (*intr.*) *Austral.* to misbehave.

muck-up day *n. Austral. slang.* the last day of school before the annual examinations, marked by practical jokes and other student pranks.

muckworm (ˈmʌkˌwɜːm) *n.* 1. any larva or worm that lives in mud. 2. *Informal.* a miser.

mucky (ˈmʌkɪ) *adj.* **muckier, muckiest.** 1. dirty. 2. of or like muck. —**ˈmuckily** *adv.* —**ˈmuckiness** *n.*

muco- *or before a vowel* **muc-** *combining form.* mucus or mucous: *mucoprotein; mucin.*

mucoid (ˈmjuːkɔɪd) *or* **mucoidal** *adj.* of the nature of or resembling mucin.

mucopolysaccharide (ˌmjuːkəʊˌpɒlɪˈsækəraɪd) *n. Biochem.* any of a group of complex polysaccharides composed of repeating units of two sugars, one of which contains an amino group.

mucoprotein (ˌmjuːkəʊˈprəʊtiːn) *n.* any of a group of conjugated proteins containing small quantities of mucopolysaccharides; glycoprotein.

mucopurulent (ˌmjuːkəʊˈpjʊərələnt) *adj. Pathol.* composed of or containing both mucus and pus.

mucosa (mjuːˈkəʊsə) *n., pl.* **-sae** (-siː). another word for **mucous membrane.** [C19: New Latin, from Latin *mūcōsus* slimy] —**muˈcosal** *adj.*

mucous (ˈmjuːkəs) *or* **mucose** (ˈmjuːkəʊs, -kəʊz) *adj.* of, resembling, or secreting mucus. [C17: from Latin *mūcōsus* slimy, from MUCUS] —**mucosity** (mjuːˈkɒsɪtɪ) *n.*

mucous membrane *n.* a mucus-secreting membrane that lines body cavities or passages that are open to the external environment. Also called: **mucosa.** —**mucomembranous** (ˌmjuːkəʊˈmɛmbrənəs) *adj.*

mucro ('mju:krəʊ) *n., pl.* **mucrones** (mju:'krəʊni:z). *Biology.* a short pointed projection from certain parts or organs, as from the tip of a leaf. [C17: from Latin *mūcrō* point]

mucronate ('mju:krəʊnɪt, -ˌneɪt) *or* **mucronated** *adj.* terminating in a sharp point. [C18: from Latin *mūcrōnātus* pointed, from MUCRO] —ˌ**mucro'nation** *n.*

mucus ('mju:kəs) *n.* the slimy protective secretion of the mucous membranes, consisting mainly of mucin. [C17: from Latin: nasal secretions; compare *mungere* to blow the nose; related to Greek *muxa* mucus, *muktēr* nose]

mud (mʌd) *n.* **1.** a fine-grained soft wet deposit that occurs on the ground after rain, at the bottom of ponds, lakes, etc. **2.** *Informal.* slander or defamation. **3. clear as mud.** *Informal.* not at all clear. **4. drag (someone's) name in the mud.** to disgrace or defame (someone). **5. here's mud in your eye.** *Informal.* a humorous drinking toast. **6. (someone's) name is mud.** *Informal.* (someone) is disgraced. **7. throw** (*or* **sling**) **mud at.** *Informal.* slander; vilify. ~*vb.* **muds, mudding, mudded. 8.** (*tr.*) to soil or cover with mud. [C14: probably from Middle Low German *mudde;* compare Middle High German *mot* swamp, mud, Swedish *modd* slush]

mud bath *n.* **1.** a medicinal bath in heated mud. **2.** a dirty or muddy occasion, state, etc.

mudcat ('mʌdˌkæt) *n.* any of several large North American catfish living in muddy rivers, esp. in the Mississippi valley.

mud dauber *n.* any of various wasps of the family *Sphecidae,* that construct cells of mud or clay in which they lay their eggs and store live insects as food for the developing larvae. See also **digger wasp.**

muddle ('mʌdᵊl) *vb.* (*tr.*) **1.** (often foll. by *up*) to mix up (objects, items, etc.); jumble. **2.** to confuse. **3.** to make (water) muddy or turbulent. **4.** *U.S.* to mix or stir (alcoholic drinks, etc.). ~*n.* **5.** a state of physical or mental confusion. [C16: perhaps from Middle Dutch *moddelen* to make muddy] —'**muddled** *adj.* —'**muddledness** *or* '**muddlement** *n.* —'**muddling** *adj., n.* —'**muddlingly** *adv.* —'**muddly** *adj.*

muddle along *or* **on** *vb.* (*intr., adv.*) to proceed in a disorganized way.

muddleheaded (ˌmʌdᵊl'hɛdɪd) *adj.* mentally confused or vague. —ˌ**muddle'headedness** *n.*

muddler ('mʌdlə) *n.* **1.** a person who muddles or muddles through. **2.** *U.S.* an instrument for mixing drinks thoroughly.

muddle through *vb.* (*intr., adv.*) *Chiefly Brit.* to succeed in some undertaking in spite of lack of organization.

muddy ('mʌdɪ) *adj.* **-dier, -diest. 1.** covered or filled with mud. **2.** not clear or bright: *muddy colours.* **3.** cloudy: *a muddy liquid.* **4.** (esp. of thoughts) confused or vague. ~*vb.* **-dies, -dying, -died. 5.** to become or cause to become muddy. —'**muddily** *adv.* —'**muddiness** *n.*

Mudéjar *Spanish.* (mu'ðexar) *n., pl.* ***-jares*** (-xares). **1.** *Medieval history.* a Spanish Moor, esp. one permitted to stay in Spain after the Christian reconquest. ~*adj.* **2.** of or relating to a style of architecture orginated by Mudéjares. [from Arabic *mudajjan* one permitted to remain]

mudfish ('mʌdˌfɪʃ) *n., pl.* **-fish** *or* **-fishes.** any of various fishes, such as the bowfin and cichlids, that live at or frequent the muddy bottoms of rivers, lakes, etc.

mud flat *n.* a tract of low muddy land, esp. near an estuary, that is covered at high tide and exposed at low tide.

mudflow ('mʌdˌfləʊ) *n. Geology.* a flow of soil mixed with water down a steep unstable slope.

mudguard ('mʌdˌgɑ:d) *n.* a curved part of a motorcycle, bicycle, etc., attached above the wheels to reduce the amount of water or mud thrown up by them. U.S. and Canadian name: **fender.**

mud hen *n.* any of various birds that frequent marshes or similar places, esp. the coots, rails, etc.

mudir (mu:'dɪə) *n.* a local governor. [C19: via Turkish, from Arabic, from *adāra* to administrate]

mudlark ('mʌdˌlɑ:k) *n.* **1.** *Slang, now rare.* a street urchin. **2.** (formerly) one who made a living by picking up odds and ends in the mud of tidal rivers. **3.** *Austral. slang.* a racehorse that runs well on a wet or muddy course.

mud map *n. Austral.* a map drawn on the ground with a stick.

mudpack ('mʌdˌpæk) *n.* a cosmetic astringent paste containing fuller's earth, used to improve the complexion.

mud pie *n.* a mass of mud moulded into a pie-like shape by a child.

mud puppy *n.* any aquatic North American salamander of the genus *Necturus,* esp. *N. maculosus,* having red feathery external gills and other persistent larval features: family *Proteidae.* See also **neoteny.**

mudra (mə'drɑ:) *n.* any of various ritual hand movements in Hindu religious dancing. [Sanskrit, literally: sign, token]

mudskipper ('mʌdˌskɪpə) *n.* any of various gobies of the genus *Periophthalmus* and related genera that occur in tropical coastal regions of Africa and Asia and can move on land by means of their strong pectoral fins.

mudslinging ('mʌdˌslɪŋɪŋ) *n.* casting malicious slurs on an opponent, esp. in politics. —'**mudˌslinger** *n.*

mudstone ('mʌdˌstəʊn) *n.* a dark grey clay rock similar to shale but with the lamination less well developed.

mud turtle *n.* any of various small turtles of the genus *Kinosternon* and related genera that inhabit muddy rivers in North and Central America: family *Kinosternidae.*

mud volcano *n.* a cone-shaped mound formed from fine mud ejected, with gases and water, from hot springs, geysers, etc., in volcanic regions.

muenster ('mʊnstə) *n.* a whitish-yellow semihard whole milk cheese, often flavoured with caraway or aniseed. [after *Muenster,* Haut-Rhin, France]

muesli ('mju:zlɪ) *n.* a mixture of rolled oats, nuts, fruit, etc., eaten with milk. [Swiss German, from German *Mus* mush, purée + *-li,* diminutive suffix]

muezzin (mu:'ɛzɪn) *n. Islam.* the official of a mosque who calls the faithful to prayer five times a day from the minaret. [C16: changed from Arabic *mu'adhdhin*]

muff[1] (mʌf) *n.* **1.** an open-ended cylinder of fur or cloth into which the hands are placed for warmth. **2.** the tuft on either side of the head of certain fowls. [C16: probably from Dutch *mof,* ultimately from French *mouffle* MUFFLE[1]]

muff[2] (mʌf) *vb.* **1.** to perform (an action) awkwardly. **2.** (*tr.*) to bungle (a shot, catch, etc.) in a game. ~*n.* **3.** any unskilful play in a game, esp. a dropped catch. **4.** any clumsy or bungled action. **5.** a bungler. [C19: of uncertain origin]

muffin ('mʌfɪn) *n.* **1.** *Brit.* a thick round baked yeast roll, usually toasted and served with butter. **2.** *U.S. and Canadian.* a small cup-shaped sweet bread roll, usually eaten hot with butter. [C18: perhaps from Low German *muffen,* cakes]

muffin man *n. Brit.* (formerly) an itinerant seller of muffins.

muffle[1] ('mʌfᵊl) *vb.* (*tr.*) **1.** (often foll. by *up*) to wrap up (the head) in a scarf, cloak, etc., esp. for warmth. **2.** to deaden (a sound or noise), esp. by wrapping. **3.** to prevent (the expression of something) by (someone). ~*n.* **4.** something that muffles. **5.** a kiln with an inner chamber for firing porcelain, enamel, etc., at a low temperature. [C15: probably from Old French; compare Old French *moufle* mitten, *emmouflé* wrapped up]

muffle[2] ('mʌfᵊl) *n.* the fleshy hairless part of the upper lip and nose in ruminants and some rodents. [C17: from French *mufle,* of unknown origin]

muffler ('mʌflə) *n.* **1.** a thick scarf, collar, etc. **2.** the U.S. and Canadian name for **silencer** (sense 1). **3.** something that muffles.

mufti ('mʌftɪ) *n., pl.* **-tis.** civilian dress, esp. as worn by a person who normally wears a military uniform. [C19: perhaps from MUFTI]

Mufti ('mʌftɪ) *n., pl.* **-tis. 1.** a Muslim legal expert and adviser on the law of the Koran. **2.** (in the former Ottoman empire) the leader of the religious community. [C16: from Arabic *muftī,* from *aftā* to give a (legal) decision]

mug[1] (mʌg) *n.* **1.** a drinking vessel with a handle, usually cylindrical and made of earthenware. **2.** Also called: **mugful.** the quantity held by a mug or its contents. [C16: probably from Scandinavian; compare Swedish *mugg*]

mug[2] (mʌg) *n.* **1.** *Slang.* a person's face or mouth: *get your ugly mug out of here!* **2.** *Slang.* a grimace. **3.** *Brit. slang.* a gullible person, esp. one who is swindled easily. **4. a mug's game.** a worthless activity. ~*vb.* **mugs, mugging, mugged. 5.** (*tr.*) *Informal.* to attack or rob (someone) violently. ~See also **mug up.** [C18: perhaps from MUG[1], since drinking vessels were sometimes modelled into the likeness of a face]

mugger[1] ('mʌgə) *n.* **1.** *Informal.* a person who commits robbery with violence, esp. in the street. **2.** *Chiefly U.S. and Canadian.* a person who overacts.

mugger[2], **muggar,** *or* **muggur** ('mʌgə) *n.* a large freshwater crocodile, *Crocodylus niloticus,* inhabiting marshes and pools of India and Ceylon. Also called: **marsh crocodile.** [C19: from Hindi *magar*]

muggins ('mʌgɪnz) *n.* **1.** *Brit. slang.* **a.** a simpleton; silly person. **b.** a title used humorously to refer to oneself. **2.** a variation on the game of dominoes. **3.** a card game. [C19: probably from the surname *Muggins*]

muggy ('mʌgɪ) *adj.* **-gier, -giest.** (of weather, air, etc.) unpleasantly warm and humid. [C18: dialect *mug* drizzle, probably from Scandinavian; compare Old Norse *mugga* mist] —'**muggily** *adv.* —'**mugginess** *n.*

mug up *vb.* (*adv.*) *Brit. slang.* to study (a subject) hard, esp. for an exam. [C19: of unknown origin]

mugwort ('mʌgˌwɜ:t) *n.* **1.** a N temperate perennial herbaceous plant, *Artemisia vulgaris,* with aromatic leaves and clusters of small greenish-white flowers: family *Compositae* (composites). **2.** another name for **crosswort.** [Old English *mucgwyrt,* perhaps from Old English *mycg* MIDGE]

mugwump ('mʌgˌwʌmp) *n.* a neutral or independent person, esp. in politics. [C19: from Algonquian: great chief, from *mogki* great + *-omp* man] —'**mugˌwumpery** *or* '**mugˌwumpism** *n.* —'**mugˌwumpish** *adj.*

Muhammadan *or* **Muhammedan** (mʊ'hæmədᵊn) *n., adj.* another word (not in Muslim use) for **Muslim.**

Muharram (mu:'hærəm) *or* **Moharram** *n.* the first month of the Islamic year. [from Arabic: sacred]

muir (mu:r, mju:r, myr) *n.* **a.** a Scot. word for **moor**[1]. **b.** (*in place names*): *Sheriffmuir.*

muirburn ('mu:rˌbʌrn, 'mju:r-, 'myr-) *n. Scot.* a variant of **moorburn.**

mujaheddin, mujahedeen *or* **mujahideen** ('muːdʒəhə'diːn) *pl. n.* (preceded by *the; sometimes cap.*) (in Afghanistan and Iran) fundamentalist Muslim guerrillas. [C20: from Arabic *mujāhidīn* fighters, ultimately from JIHAD]

mujik ('muːʒɪk) *n.* a variant spelling of **muzhik.**

mukluk ('mʌklʌk) *n.* a soft boot, usually of sealskin, worn by Eskimos. [from Eskimo *muklok* large seal]

mulatto (mjuː'lætəʊ) *n., pl.* **-tos** *or* **-toes. 1.** a person having one Negro and one White parent. *~adj.* **2.** of a light brown colour; tawny. [C16: from Spanish *mulato* young mule, variant of *mulo* MULE[1]]

mulberry ('mʌlbərɪ, -brɪ) *n., pl.* **-ries. 1.** any moraceous tree of the temperate genus *Morus,* having edible blackberry-like fruit, such as *M. alba* (**white mulberry**), the leaves of which are used to feed silkworms. **2.** the fruit of any of these trees. **3.** any of several similar or related trees, such as the paper mulberry and Indian mulberry. **4. a.** a dark purple colour. **b.** (*as adj.*): *a mulberry dress.* [C14: from Latin *mōrum,* from Greek *moron;* related to Old English *mōrberie;* compare Dutch *moerbezie,* Old High German *mūrberi*]

mulch (mʌltʃ) *n.* **1.** half-rotten vegetable matter, peat, etc., used to prevent soil erosion or enrich the soil. *~vb.* **2.** (*tr.*) to cover (the surface of land) with mulch. [C17: from obsolete *mulch* soft; related to Old English *mylisc* mellow; compare dialect German *molsch* soft, Latin *mollis* soft]

mulct (mʌlkt) *vb.* (*tr.*) **1.** to cheat or defraud. **2.** to fine (a person). *~n.* **3.** a fine or penalty. [C15: via French from Latin *multa* a fine]

mule[1] (mjuːl) *n.* **1.** the sterile offspring of a male donkey and a female horse, used as a beast of burden. Compare **hinny**[1]. **2.** any hybrid animal: *a mule canary.* **3.** Also called: **spinning mule.** a machine invented in 1779 that spins cotton into yarn and winds the yarn on spindles. **4.** *Informal.* an obstinate or stubborn person. [C13: from Old French *mul,* from Latin *mūlus* ass, mule]

mule[2] (mjuːl) *n.* a backless shoe or slipper. [C16: from Old French from Latin *mulleus* a magistrate's shoe]

mule deer *n.* a W North American deer, *Odocoileus hemionus,* with long ears and a black-tipped tail.

mules (mjuːlz) *vb.* (*tr.*) *Austral.* to peform the Mules operation on (a sheep).

mule skinner *n. U.S. and Canadian.* an informal term for **muleteer.**

Mules operation (mjuːlz) *n. Austral.* the surgical removal of folds of skin in the breech of a sheep to reduce blowfly strike. [named after J. H. W. *Mules* (died 1946), Australian grazier who first suggested it]

muleta (mjuː'lɛtə) *n.* the small cape attached to a stick used by the matador during the final stages of a bullfight. [Spanish: small mule, crutch, from *mula* MULE[1]]

muleteer (ˌmjuːlɪ'tɪə) *n.* a person who drives mules.

muley ('mjuːlɪ) *or* **mulley** ('mʌlɪ) *adj.* **1.** (of cattle) having no horns. *~n.* **2.** any hornless cow. [C16: variant of dialect *moiley,* from Gaelic *maol,* Welsh *moel* bald]

mulga ('mʌlgə) *n. Austral.* **1.** any of various Australian acacia shrubs, esp. *Acacia aneura,* which grows in the central desert regions and has leaflike leafstalks. **2.** scrub comprised of a dense growth of acacia. **3.** the outback; bush. **4.** an Aboriginal shield. [from a native Australian language]

muliebrity (ˌmjuːlɪ'ɛbrɪtɪ) *n.* **1.** the condition of being a woman. **2.** femininity. [C16: via Late Latin from Latin *muliēbris* womanly, from *mulier* woman]

mulish ('mjuːlɪʃ) *adj.* stubborn; obstinate; headstrong. —'**mulishly** *adv.* —'**mulishness** *n.*

Mulki ('mʊlkɪ) *n.* a native or inhabitant of the former Hyderabad State in India. [Urdu, from *mulk* country]

mull[1] (mʌl) *vb.* (*tr.*) (often foll. by *over*) to study or ponder. [C19: probably from MUDDLE]

mull[2] (mʌl) *vb.* (*tr.*) to heat (wine, ale, etc.) with sugar and spices to make a hot drink. [C17: of unknown origin]

mull[3] (mʌl) *n.* a light muslin fabric of soft texture. [C18: earlier *mulmull,* from Hindi *malmal*]

mull[4] (mʌl) *n.* a layer of nonacidic humus formed in well drained and aerated soils. Compare **mor.** [C20: from Danish *muld;* see MOULD[3]]

mull[5] (mʌl) *n. Scot.* a promontory. [C14: related to Gaelic *maol,* Icelandic *múli*]

mullah, mulla ('mʌlə, 'mʊlə), *or* **mollah** ('mɒlə) *n.* (formerly) a Muslim scholar, teacher, or religious leader: also used as a title of respect. [C17: from Turkish *molla,* Persian and Hindi *mulla,* from Arabic *mawlā* master]

mullein *or* **mullen** ('mʌlɪn) *n.* any of various Mediterranean herbaceous plants of the scrophulariaceous genus *Verbascum,* such as *V. thapsus* (**common mullein** or **Aaron's rod**), typically having tall spikes of yellow flowers and broad hairy leaves. [C15: from Old French *moleine,* probably from Old French *mol* soft, from Latin *mollis*]

muller ('mʌlə) *n.* a flat heavy implement of stone or iron used to grind material against a slab of stone. [C15: probably from *mullen* to grind to powder; compare Old English *myl* dust]

Müllerian mimicry (muː'lɪərɪən) *n. Zoology.* mimicry in which two or more harmful or inedible species resemble each other, so that predators tend to avoid them. [C19: named after J. F. T. *Müller* (1821–97), German zoologist who first described it]

Müller-Lyer illusion ('muːlə'laɪə) *n.* a well-known optical illusion in which a line with inward pointing arrowheads is seen as longer than one of the same length with outward pointing arrowheads. [C19: named after Franz *Müller-Lyer* (1857–1916), German sociologist and psychiatrist]

mullet ('mʌlɪt) *n.* **1.** any of various teleost food fishes belonging to the families *Mugilidae* (see **grey mullet**) or *Mullidae* (see **red mullet**). **2.** the U.S. name for **grey mullet.** [C15: via Old French from Latin *mullus,* from Greek *mullos*]

mulley ('mʌlɪ) *adj., n.* a variant of **muley.**

mulligan ('mʌlɪgən) *n. U.S. and Canadian.* a stew made from odds and ends of food. [C20: perhaps from the surname]

mulligatawny (ˌmʌlɪgə'tɔːnɪ) *n.* a curry-flavoured soup of Anglo-Indian origin, made with meat stock. [C18: from Tamil *milakutanni,* from *milaku* pepper + *tanni* water]

mullion ('mʌlɪən) *n.* **1.** a vertical member between the casements or panes of a window or the panels of a screen. **2.** one of the ribs on a rock face. *~vb.* **3.** (*tr.*) to furnish (a window, screen, etc.) with mullions. [C16: variant of Middle English *munial,* from Old French *moinel,* of unknown origin]

mullite ('mʌlaɪt) *n.* a colourless mineral consisting of aluminium silicate in orthorhombic crystalline form: used as a refractory. Formula: $Al_6Si_2O_{13}$. [from island of *Mull,* off the west coast of Scotland]

mullock ('mʌlək) *n.* **1.** *Austral.* waste material from a mine. **2.** *Dialect.* a mess or muddle. **3. poke mullock at.** *Austral. informal.* to ridicule. [C14: related to Old English *myl* dust, Old Norse *mylja* to crush; see MULLER] —'**mullocky** *adj.*

mulloway ('mʌləˌweɪ) *n.* a large Australian marine sciaenid fish, *Sciaena antarctica,* valued for sport and food. [C19: of unknown origin]

multangular (mʌl'tæŋgjʊlə) *or* **multiangular** *adj.* having many angles.

multeity (mʌl'tiːɪtɪ) *n.* manifoldness. [C19: from Latin *multus* many, perhaps formed by analogy with HAECCEITY]

multi- *combining form.* **1.** many or much: *multiflorous; multimillion.* **2.** more than one: *multiparous; multistorey.* [from Latin *multus* much, many]

multiaccess (ˌmʌltɪ'ækses) *n. Computer technol.* a system in which several users are permitted to have apparently simultaneous access to a computer.

multichannel analyser (ˌmʌltɪ'tʃænᵊl) *n.* an electronic instrument, such as a pulse height analyser, that splits an input waveform into a large number of channels in accordance with a particular parameter of the input.

multicide ('mʌltɪˌsaɪd) *n.* mass murder.

multicollinearity (ˌmʌltɪkəʊˌlɪnɪ'ærɪtɪ) *n. Statistics.* the condition occurring when two or more of the independent variables in a regression equation are correlated.

multicoloured ('mʌltɪˌkʌləd) *adj.* having many colours.

multicultural (ˌmʌltɪ'kʌltʃərəl) *adj.* consisting of, relating to, or designed for the cultures of several different races.

multiculturalism (ˌmʌltɪ'kʌltʃərəˌlɪzəm) *n.* **1.** the state or condition of being multicultural. **2.** the policy of maintaining a diversity of ethnic cultures within a community.

multidisciplinary (ˌmʌltɪ'dɪsɪˌplɪnərɪ) *adj.* of or relating to the study of one topic, involving several subject disciplines.

multiethnic (ˌmʌltɪ'ɛθnɪk) *adj.* consisting of, relating to, or designed for various different races.

multifaceted (ˌmʌltɪ'fæsɪtɪd) *adj.* **1.** (of a gem) having many facets. **2.** having many aspects, abilities, etc.

multifactorial (ˌmʌltɪfæk'tɔːrɪəl) *adj.* **1.** *Genetics.* of or designating inheritance that depends on more than one gene. **2.** involving or including a number of elements or factors.

multifarious (ˌmʌltɪ'fɛərɪəs) *adj.* having many parts of great variety. [C16: from Late Latin *multifārius* manifold, from Latin *multifāriam* on many sides] —ˌ**multi'fariously** *adv.* —ˌ**multi'fariousness** *n.*

multifid ('mʌltɪfɪd) *or* **multifidous** (mʌl'tɪfɪdəs) *adj.* having or divided into many lobes or similar segments: *a multifid leaf.* [C18: from Latin *multifidus,* from *multus* many + *findere* to split] —'**multifidly** *adv.*

multiflora rose (ˌmʌltɪ'flɔːrə) *n.* an Asian climbing shrubby rose, *Rosa multiflora,* having clusters of small fragrant flowers: the source of many cultivated roses.

multifoil ('mʌltɪˌfɔɪl) *n.* an ornamental design having a large number of foils. See also **trefoil** (sense 4), **quatrefoil** (sense 2), **cinquefoil** (sense 2).

multifold ('mʌltɪˌfəʊld) *adj.* many times doubled; manifold.

multifoliate (ˌmʌltɪ'fəʊlɪɪt, -ˌeɪt) *adj. Botany.* having many leaves or leaflets: *a multifoliate compound leaf.*

multiform ('mʌltɪˌfɔːm) *adj.* having many forms or kinds. —**multiformity** (ˌmʌltɪ'fɔːmɪtɪ) *n.*

multigravida (ˌmʌltɪ'grævɪdə) *n.* a woman who is pregnant for at least the third time. Compare **multipara.** [C20: New Latin; see MULTI-, GRAVID]

multigym ('mʌltɪˌdʒɪm) *n.* an exercise apparatus incorporating a variety of weights, used for toning the muscles.

multihull ('mʌltɪˌhʌl) *n.* a sailing vessel with two or more hulls. Compare **monohull.**

multilateral (ˌmʌltɪˈlætərəl, -ˈlætrəl) *adj.* **1.** of or involving more than two nations or parties: *a multilateral pact.* **2.** having many sides. —ˌ**multiˈlaterally** *adv.*
multilingual (ˌmʌltɪˈlɪŋgwəl) *adj.* **1.** able to speak more than two languages. **2.** written or expressed in more than two languages. Compare **bilingual, monolingual.**
multimedia (ˌmʌltɪˈmiːdɪə) *pl. n.* **a.** the combined use of media such as television, slides, etc., esp. in education. **b.** (*as modifier*): *multimedia aids to teaching.*
multimeter (ˈmʌltɪˌmiːtə) *n.* an electrical test instrument offering measurement of several values, usually voltage, current, and resistance.
multimillionaire (ˌmʌltɪˌmɪljəˈnɛə) *n.* a person with a fortune of several million pounds, dollars, etc.
multinational (ˌmʌltɪˈnæʃənᵊl) *adj.* **1.** (of a large business company) operating in several countries. ~*n.* **2.** such a company.
multinomial (ˌmʌltɪˈnəʊmɪəl) *n.* another name for **polynomial** (sense 2b.). [C17: from MULTI- + *-nomial* as in BINOMIAL]
multinuclear (ˌmʌltɪˈnjuːklɪə) *or* **multinucleate** (ˌmʌltɪˈnjuːklɪɪt, -ˌeɪt) *adj.* (of a cell, microorganism, etc.) having more than two nuclei.
multipack (ˈmʌltɪˌpæk) *n.* a form of packaging of foodstuffs, etc., that contains several units and is offered at a price below that of the equivalent number of units.
multipara (mʌlˈtɪpərə) *n., pl.* **-rae** (-ˌriː). a woman who has given birth to more than one viable fetus or living child. Compare **multigravida.** [C19: New Latin, feminine of *multiparus* MULTIPAROUS]
multiparous (mʌlˈtɪpərəs) *adj.* **1.** (of certain species of mammal) producing many offspring at one birth. **2.** of, relating to, or designating a multipara. [C17: from New Latin *multiparus*] —**multiparity** (ˌmʌltɪˈpærɪtɪ) *n.*
multipartite (ˌmʌltɪˈpɑːtaɪt) *adj.* **1.** divided into many parts or sections. **2.** *Government.* a less common word for **multilateral.**
multiparty (ˌmʌltɪˈpɑːtɪ) *adj.* of or relating to a state, political system, etc., in which more than one political party is permitted: *multiparty democracy.*
multipath (ˈmʌltɪˌpɑːθ) *adj.* relating to television or radio signals that travel by more than one route from a transmitter and arrive at slightly different times, causing ghost images or audio distortion.
multiped (ˈmʌltɪˌpɛd) *or* **multipede** (ˈmʌltɪˌpiːd) *Rare.* ~*adj.* **1.** having many feet. ~*n.* **2.** an insect or animal having many feet. [C17: from Latin *multipēs*]
multiphase (ˈmʌltɪˌfeɪz) *adj.* another word for **polyphase** (sense 1).
multiplane (ˈmʌltɪˌpleɪn) *n.* an aircraft that has more than one pair of wings. Compare **monoplane.**
multiple (ˈmʌltɪpᵊl) *adj.* **1.** having or involving more than one part, individual, etc. **2.** *Electronics, U.S. and Canadian.* (of a circuit) having a number of conductors in parallel. ~*n.* **3.** the product of a given number or polynomial and any other one: *6 is a multiple of 2.* **4.** *Telephony.* an electrical circuit accessible at a number of points to any one of which a connection can be made. **5.** short for **multiple store.** [C17: via French from Late Latin *multiplus,* from Latin MULTIPLEX] —ˈ**multiply** *adv.*
multiple alleles *pl. n.* a group of three or more alleles produced by mutation of the gene. Only two of them are present in a normal diploid cell at the same time. —**multiple allelism** *n.*
multiple-choice *adj.* having a number of possible given answers out of which the correct one must be chosen.
multiple factors *pl. n. Genetics.* two or more pairs of genes that act as a unit, producing cumulative effects in the phenotype.
multiple fission *n. Zoology.* asexual reproduction in unicellular organisms, esp. sporozoans, in which the nucleus divides a number of times, followed by division of the cytoplasm, to form daughter cells.
multiple fruit *n.* a fruit, such as a pineapple, formed from the ovaries of individual flowers in an inflorescence.
multiple personality *n. Psychiatry.* a mental disorder in which an individual's personality appears to have become separated into two or more distinct personalities, each with its own complex organization. Nontechnical name: **split personality.**
multiplepoinding (ˌmʌltɪpᵊlˈpɪndɪŋ) *n. Scots Law.* an action to determine the division of a property or fund between several claimants, brought by or on behalf of the present holder.
multiple sclerosis *n.* a chronic progressive disease of the central nervous system characterized by loss of some of the myelin sheath surrounding certain nerve fibres and resulting in speech and visual disorders, tremor, muscular incoordination, partial paralysis, etc. Also called: **disseminated sclerosis.**
multiple star *n.* a system of three or more stars associated by gravitation. See also **binary star.**
multiple store *n.* one of several retail enterprises under the same ownership and management. Also called: **multiple shop.**
multiplet (ˈmʌltɪˌplɛt, -plɪt) *n. Physics.* **1.** a line in a spectrum formed of two or more closely spaced lines, resulting from small differences in energy level of atoms or molecules. **2.** a group of related elementary particles that differ only in electric charge. [from MULTIPLE; on the model of DOUBLET]
multiple voting *n.* the practice of voting in more than one constituency in the same election.
multiplex (ˈmʌltɪˌplɛks) *n.* **1.** *Telecomm.* **a.** the use of a common communications channel for sending two or more messages or signals. In **frequency-division multiplex** the frequency band transmitted by the common channel is split into narrower bands each of which constitutes a distinct channel. In **time-division multiplex** different channels are established by intermittent connections to the common channel. **b.** (*as modifier*): *a multiplex transmitter.* **2. a.** a purpose-built complex containing a number of cinemas and usually a restaurant or bar. **b.** (*as modifier*): *a multiplex cinema.* ~*adj.* **3.** designating a method of map-making using three cameras to produce a stereoscopic effect. **4.** a less common word for **multiple.** ~*vb.* **5.** to send (messages or signals) or (of messages or signals) be sent by multiplex. [C16: from Latin: having many folds, from MULTI- + *plicāre* to fold] —ˈ**multiˌplexer** *n.*
multiplicand (ˌmʌltɪplɪˈkænd) *n.* a number to be multiplied by another number, the **multiplier.** [C16: from Latin *multiplicandus,* gerund of *multiplicāre* to MULTIPLY]
multiplicate (ˈmʌltɪplɪˌkeɪt) *adj. Rare.* manifold.
multiplication (ˌmʌltɪplɪˈkeɪʃən) *n.* **1.** an arithmetical operation, defined initially in terms of repeated addition, usually written $a \times b$, $a.b$, or ab, by which the product of two quantities is calculated: to multiply a by positive integral b is to add a to itself b times. Multiplication by fractions can then be defined in the light of the associative and commutative properties; multiplication by $1/n$ is equivalent to multiplication by 1 followed by division by n: for example $0.3 \times 0.7 = 0.3 \times 7/10 = (0.3 \times 7)/10 = 2.1/10 = 0.21$. **2.** the act of multiplying or state of being multiplied. **3.** the act or process in animals, plants, or people of reproducing or breeding. —ˌ**multipliˈcational** *adj.*
multiplication sign *n.* the symbol ×, placed between numbers to be multiplied, as in $3 \times 4 \times 5 = 60$.
multiplication table *n.* one of a group of tables giving the results of multiplying two numbers together.
multiplicative (ˈmʌltɪplɪˌkeɪtɪv, ˌmʌltɪˈplɪkətɪv) *adj.* **1.** tending or able to multiply. **2.** *Maths.* involving multiplication. —ˈ**multipliˌcatively** *adv.*
multiplicity (ˌmʌltɪˈplɪsɪtɪ) *n., pl.* **-ties. 1.** a large number or great variety. **2.** the state of being multiple. **3.** *Physics.* **a.** the number of levels into which the energy of an atom, molecule, or nucleus splits as a result of coupling between orbital angular momentum and spin angular momentum. **b.** the number of elementary particles in a multiplet.
multiplier (ˈmʌltɪˌplaɪə) *n.* **1.** a person or thing that multiplies. **2.** the number by which another number, the **multiplicand,** is multiplied. **3.** *Physics.* any device or instrument, such as a photomultiplier, for increasing an effect. **4.** *Economics.* **a.** the ratio of the total change in income (resulting from successive rounds of spending) to an initial autonomous change in expenditure. **b.** (*as modifier*): *multiplier effects.*
multiply (ˈmʌltɪˌplaɪ) *vb.* **-plies, -plying, -plied. 1.** to increase or cause to increase in number, quantity, or degree. **2.** (*tr.*) to combine (two numbers or quantities) by multiplication. **3.** (*intr.*) to increase in number by reproduction. [C13: from Old French *multiplier,* from Latin *multiplicāre* to multiply, from *multus* much, many + *plicāre* to fold] —ˈ**multiˌpliable** *or* ˈ**multiˌplicable** *adj.*
multiprocessor (ˌmʌltɪˈprəʊsɛsə) *n. Computer technol.* a number of central processing units linked together to enable parallel processing to take place.
multiprogramming (ˌmʌltɪˈprəʊgræmɪŋ) *n.* a time-sharing technique by which several computer programs are each run for a short period in rotation.
multipurpose (ˌmʌltɪˈpɜːpəs) *adj.* able to be used for many purposes: *a multipurpose gadget.*
multiracial (ˌmʌltɪˈreɪʃəl) *adj.* comprising people of many races. —ˌ**multiˈracialism** *n.*
multirole (ˈmʌltɪˌrəʊl) *adj.* having a number of roles, functions, etc.
multiseriate (ˌmʌltɪˈsɪərɪeɪt) *adj. Botany.* arranged in rows or composed of more than one cell layer.
multiskilling (ˈmʌltɪˌskɪlɪŋ) *n.* the practice of training employees to do a number of different tasks.
multistage (ˈmʌltɪˌsteɪdʒ) *adj.* **1.** (of a rocket or missile) having several stages, each of which can be jettisoned after it has burnt out. **2.** (of a turbine, compressor, or supercharger) having more than one rotor. **3.** (of any process or device) having more than one stage.
multistorey (ˌmʌltɪˈstɔːrɪ) *adj.* **1.** (of a building) having many storeys. ~*n.* **2.** a multistorey car park.
multitasking (ˌmʌltɪˈtɑːskɪŋ) *n. Computer technol.* the execution of various diverse tasks simultaneously.
multitrack (ˈmʌltɪˌtræk) *adj.* (in sound recording) using tape containing two or more tracks, usually four to twenty-four.
multitude (ˈmʌltɪˌtjuːd) *n.* **1.** a large gathering of people. **2. the.** the common people. **3.** a large number. **4.** the state or quality of being numerous. [C14: via Old French from Latin *multitūdō*]
multitudinous (ˌmʌltɪˈtjuːdɪnəs) *adj.* **1.** very numerous. **2.** *Rare.* great in extent, variety, etc. **3.** *Poetic.* crowded. —ˌ**multiˈtudinously** *adv.* —ˌ**multiˈtudinousness** *n.*
multi-user *adj.* (of a computer) capable of being used by several people at once.

multivalent (ˌmʌltɪˈveɪlənt) *adj.* another word for **polyvalent.** —ˌ**multiˈvalency** *n.*
multivariate (ˌmʌltɪˈvɛərɪɪt) *adj. Statistics.* (of a distribution) involving a number of distinct, though not usually independent, random variables.
multiversity (ˌmʌltɪˈvɜːsɪtɪ) *n. Chiefly U.S. and Canadian.* a university with many constituent and affiliated institutions. [C20: MULTI- + UNIVERSITY]
multivibrator (ˌmʌltɪvaɪˈbreɪtə) *n.* an electronic oscillator consisting of two transistors or other electronic devices, coupled so that the input of each is derived from the output of the other.
multivocal (ˌmʌltɪˈvəʊkᵊl) *adj.* having many meanings. [C19: from Latin *multus* many + *vocare* to call; on the model of EQUIVOCAL]
multiwindow (ˌmʌltɪˈwɪndəʊ) *n.* a visual display unit screen that can be divided to show a number of different documents simultaneously.
multum in parvo (ˈmʊltʊm ɪn ˈpɑːvəʊ) much in a small space. [Latin]
multure (ˈmʌltʃə) *n. Archaic or Scot.* **1.** a fee formerly paid to a miller for grinding grain. **2.** the right to receive such a fee. [C13: from Old French *moulture,* from Medieval Latin *molitūra* a grinding, from Latin *molere*]
mum[1] (mʌm) *n.* **1.** *Chiefly Brit.* an informal word for **mother**[1]. **2.** *N.Z. and Austral.* an informal word for **wife** (sense 1). [C19: a child's word]
mum[2] (mʌm) *adj.* **1.** keeping information to oneself; silent. ~*n.* **2. mum's the word.** silence or secrecy is to be observed. [C14: suggestive of closed lips]
mum[3] *or* **mumm** (mʌm) *vb.* **mums, mumming, mummed.** (*intr.*) to act in a mummer's play. [C16: verbal use of MUM[2]]
mum[4] (mʌm) *n. Brit., obsolete.* a type of beer made from cereals, beans, etc. [C17: from German *Mumme,* perhaps from the name of its original brewer]
mumble (ˈmʌmbᵊl) *vb.* **1.** to utter indistinctly, as with the mouth partly closed; mutter. **2.** *Rare.* to chew (food) ineffectually or with difficulty. ~*n.* **3.** an indistinct or low utterance or sound. [C14 *momelen,* from MUM[2]] —ˈ**mumbler** *n.* —ˈ**mumbling** *adj.* —ˈ**mumblingly** *adv.*
mumbo jumbo (ˈmʌmbəʊ) *n., pl.* **mumbo jumbos. 1.** foolish religious reverence, ritual, or incantation. **2.** meaningless or unnecessarily complicated language. **3.** an object of superstitious awe or reverence. [C18: probably from Mandingo *mama dyumbo,* name of a tribal god]
mumchance (ˈmʌmˌtʃɑːns) *adj.* silent; struck dumb. [C16 (masquerade, dumb show): from Middle Low German *mummenschanze* masked serenade; from *mummen* (see MUMMER) + *schanze* CHANCE]
mu meson (mjuː) *n.* a former name for **muon.**
mummer (ˈmʌmə) *n.* **1.** one of a group of masked performers in folk play or mime. **2.** a mime artist. **3.** *Humorous or derogatory.* an actor. [C15: from Old French *momeur,* from *momer* to mime; related to *momon* mask]
Mummerset (ˈmʌməsɪt, -ˌsɛt) *n.* an imitation West Country accent used in drama. [C20: from MUMMER + (*Somer*)*set* (county in SW England)]
mummery (ˈmʌmərɪ) *n., pl.* **-meries. 1.** a performance by mummers. **2.** hypocritical or ostentatious ceremony.
mummify (ˈmʌmɪˌfaɪ) *vb.* **-fies, -fying, -fied. 1.** (*tr.*) to preserve the body of (a human or animal) as a mummy. **2.** (*intr.*) to dry up; shrivel. **3.** (*tr.*) to preserve (an outdated idea, institution, etc.) while making lifeless. —ˌ**mummifiˈcation** *n.*
mummy[1] (ˈmʌmɪ) *n., pl.* **-mies. 1.** an embalmed or preserved body, esp. as prepared for burial in ancient Egypt. **2.** *Obsolete.* the substance of such a body used medicinally. **3.** a mass of pulp. **4.** a dark brown pigment. [C14: from Old French *momie,* from Medieval Latin *mumia,* from Arabic *mūmiyah* asphalt, from Persian *mūm* wax]
mummy[2] (ˈmʌmɪ) *n., pl.* **-mies.** *Chiefly Brit.* a child's word for **mother**[1]. [C19: variant of MUM[1]]
mump[1] (mʌmp) *vb.* (*intr.*) *Archaic.* to be silent. [C16 (to grimace, sulk, be silent): of imitative origin, alluding to the shape of the mouth when mumbling or chewing]
mump[2] (mʌmp) *vb.* (*intr.*) *Archaic.* to beg. [C17: perhaps from Dutch *mompen* to cheat]
mumps (mʌmps) *n.* (*functioning as sing. or pl.*) an acute contagious viral disease of the parotid salivary glands, characterized by swelling of the affected parts, fever, and pain beneath the ear: usually affects children. Also called: **epidemic parotitis.** [C16: from MUMP[1] (to grimace)] —ˈ**mumpish** *adj.*
mumsy (ˈmʌmzɪ) *adj.* **-sier, -siest.** out of fashion; homely or drab.
mun. *abbrev. for* municipal.
munch (mʌntʃ) *vb.* to chew (food) steadily, esp. with a crunching noise. [C14 *monche,* of imitative origin; compare CRUNCH] —ˈ**muncher** *n.*
Münchhausen (*German* ˈmynçhauzən) *n.* **1.** an exaggerated story. **2.** a person who tells such a story. ~*adj.* **3.** denoting or relating to a syndrome in which a patient feigns illness to obtain hospital treatment. [C19: after Baron *Münchhausen,* subject of a series of exaggerated adventure tales written in English by R. E. Raspe (1737–94)]
Munda (ˈmʊndə) *n.* **1.** a family of languages spoken by scattered peoples throughout central India. **2.** (*pl.* **-das**) a member of any of these peoples.
mundane (ˈmʌndeɪn, mʌnˈdeɪn) *adj.* **1.** everyday, ordinary, or banal. **2.** relating to the world or worldly matters. [C15: from French *mondain,* via Late Latin, from Latin *mundus* world] —ˈ**mundanely** *adv.* —ˈ**mundaneness** *n.*
munga (ˈmʌŋgə) *n.* **1.** *N.Z. informal.* an army canteen. **2.** *Austral. and N.Z. slang.* food. [C20: perhaps from French *manger* to eat or from Maori *manga* food remains]
mung bean (mʌŋ) *n.* **1.** an E Asian bean plant, *Phaseolus aureus,* grown for forage and as the source of bean sprouts used in oriental cookery. **2.** the seed of this plant. [C20 *mung,* changed from *mungo,* from Tamil *mūngu,* ultimately from Sanskrit *mudga*]
mungo (ˈmʌŋgəʊ), **mongo,** *or* **mongoe** *n., pl.* **-gos** *or* **-goes.** a cheap felted fabric made from waste wool. [C19: of unknown origin]
municipal (mjuːˈnɪsɪpᵊl) *adj.* of or relating to a town, city, or borough or its local government. [C16: from Latin *mūnicipium* a free town, from *mūniceps* citizen from *mūnia* responsibilities + *capere* to take] —**muˈnicipalism** *n.* —**muˈnicipalist** *n.* —**muˈnicipally** *adv.*
municipality (mjuːˌnɪsɪˈpælɪtɪ) *n., pl.* **-ties. 1.** a city, town, or district enjoying some degree of local self-government. **2.** the governing body of such a unit.
municipalize *or* **municipalise** (mjuːˈnɪsɪpəˌlaɪz) *vb.* (*tr.*) **1.** to bring under municipal ownership or control. **2.** to make a municipality of. —**muˌnicipaliˈzation** *or* **muˌnicipaliˈsation** *n.*
munificent (mjuːˈnɪfɪsənt) *adj.* **1.** (of a person) very generous; bountiful. **2.** (of a gift) generous; liberal. [C16: back formation from Latin *mūnificentia* liberality, from *mūnificus,* from *mūnus* gift + *facere* to make] —**muˈnificence** *or* **muˈnificentness** *n.* —**muˈnificently** *adv.*
muniment (ˈmjuːnɪmənt) *n. Rare.* a means of defence. [C15: via Old French, from Latin *munīre* to defend]
muniments (ˈmjuːnɪmənts) *pl. n.* **1.** *Law.* the title deeds and other documentary evidence relating to the title to land. **2.** *Archaic.* furnishings or supplies.
munition (mjuːˈnɪʃən) *vb.* (*tr.*) to supply with munitions. [C16: via French from Latin *mūnītiō* fortification, from *mūnīre* to fortify. See AMMUNITION] —**muˈnitioner** *n.*
munitions (mjuːˈnɪʃənz) *pl. n.* (*sometimes sing.*) military equipment and stores, esp. ammunition.
munnion (ˈmʌnjən) *n.* an archaic word for **mullion.** [C16: from *monial* mullion]
Munro (mʌnˈrəʊ) *n., pl.* **Munros.** *Mountaineering.* any separate mountain peak over 3000 feet high: originally used of Scotland only but now sometimes extended to other parts of the British Isles. [C20: named after Hugh Thomas *Munro* (1856–1919), who published a list of these in 1891]
Munsell scale (ˈmʌnsᵊl) *n.* a standard chromaticity scale used in specifying colour. It gives approximately equal changes in visual hue. [C20: named after A. H. *Munsell* (1858–1918), U.S. inventor]
münster (ˈmynstə) *n.* a variant of **muenster.**
munt (mʊnt) *n. Zimbabwean slang, derogatory.* a Black African. [from Zulu *umuntu* person]
muntin (ˈmʌntɪn) *n.* another name (esp. U.S.) for **glazing-bar.** [C17: variant of C15 *mountant,* from Old French *montant,* present participle of *monter* to MOUNT[1]]
muntjac *or* **muntjak** (ˈmʌntˌdʒæk) *n.* any small Asian deer of the genus *Muntiacus,* typically having a chestnut-brown coat, small antlers, and a barklike cry. Also called: **barking deer.** [C18: probably changed from Javanese *mindjangan* deer]
Muntz metal (mʌnts) *n.* a type of brass consisting of three parts copper and two parts zinc, used in casting and extrusion. [C19: named after G. F. *Muntz* (1794–1857), British metallurgist]
muon (ˈmjuːɒn) *n.* a positive or negative elementary particle with a mass 207 times that of an electron and spin ½. It was originally called the **mu meson** but is now classified as a lepton. [C20: short for MU MESON] —**muonic** (mjuːˈɒnɪk) *adj.*
muon-catalysed fusion *n. Physics.* an experimental form of nuclear fusion in which hydrogen and deuterium muonic atoms are formed. Because the mass of the muon is much larger than that of the electron, the atoms are smaller, and the nuclei are close enough for fusion to occur.
muonic atom *n. Physics.* an atom in which an orbiting electron has been replaced by a muon.
murage (ˈmjʊərɪdʒ) *n. Brit., archaic.* a tax levied for the construction or maintenance of town walls. [C13: from Old French, ultimately from Latin *mūrus* wall]
mural (ˈmjʊərəl) *n.* **1.** a large painting or picture on a wall. ~*adj.* **2.** of or relating to a wall. [C15: from Latin *mūrālis,* from *mūrus* wall] —ˈ**muralist** *n.*
murdabad (ˈmʊədɑːˌbɑːd) *vb.* (*tr.*) *Indian.* down with; death to: used as part of a slogan in India, Pakistan, etc. Compare **zindabad.** [from Urdu, from Persian *murda* dead]
murder (ˈmɜːdə) *n.* **1.** the unlawful premeditated killing of one human being by another. Compare **manslaughter, homicide. 2.** *Informal.* something dangerous, difficult, or unpleasant: *driving around London is murder.* **3. cry blue murder.** *Informal.*

to make an outcry. **4. get away with murder.** *Informal.* to escape censure; do as one pleases. ~*vb.* (*mainly tr.*) **5.** (*also intr.*) to kill (someone) unlawfully with premeditation or during the commission of a crime. **6.** to kill brutally. **7.** *Informal.* to destroy; ruin: *he murdered her chances of happiness.* **8.** *Informal.* to defeat completely; beat decisively: *the home team murdered their opponents.* ~Also (archaic or dialect): **murther.** [Old English *morthor;* related to Old English *morth,* Old Norse *morth,* Latin *mors* death; compare French *meurtre*] —'**murderer** *n.* —'**murderess** *fem. n.*

murderous ('mɜːdərəs) *adj.* **1.** intending, capable of, or guilty of murder. **2.** *Informal.* very dangerous, difficult, or unpleasant: *a murderous road.* —'**murderously** *adv.* —'**murderousness** *n.*

mure (mjʊə) *vb.* (*tr.*) an archaic or literary word for **immure.** [C14: from Old French *murer,* from Latin *mūrus* wall]

murex ('mjʊəreks) *n., pl.* **murices** ('mjʊərɪˌsiːz). any of various spiny-shelled marine gastropods of the genus *Murex* and related genera: formerly used as a source of the dye Tyrian purple. [C16: from Latin *mūrex* purple fish; related to Greek *muax* sea mussel]

muriate ('mjʊərɪɪt, -ˌeɪt) *n.* an obsolete name for a **chloride.** [C18: back formation from *muriatic;* see MURIATIC ACID]

muriatic acid (ˌmjʊərɪ'ætɪk) *n.* a former name for **hydrochloric acid.** [C17: from Latin *muriāticus* pickled, from *muria* brine]

muricate ('mjʊərɪˌkeɪt) *or* **muricated** *adj. Biology.* having a surface roughened by numerous short points: *muricate stems.* [C17: from Latin *mūricātus* pointed like a MUREX]

murine ('mjʊəraɪn, -rɪn) *adj.* **1.** of, relating to, or belonging to the *Muridae,* an Old World family of rodents, typically having long hairless tails: includes rats and mice. **2.** resembling a mouse or rat. ~*n.* **3.** any animal belonging to the *Muridae.* [C17: from Latin *mūrīnus* of mice, from *mūs* MOUSE]

murk *or* **mirk** (mɜːk) *n.* **1.** gloomy darkness. ~*adj.* **2.** an archaic variant of **murky.** [C13: probably from Old Norse *myrkr* darkness; compare Old English *mirce* dark]

murky *or* **mirky** ('mɜːkɪ) *adj.* **murkier, murkiest** *or* **mirkier, mirkiest. 1.** gloomy or dark. **2.** cloudy or impenetrable as with smoke or fog. —'**murkily** *or* '**mirkily** *adv.* —'**murkiness** *or* '**mirkiness** *n.*

murmur ('mɜːmə) *n.* **1.** a continuous low indistinct sound, as of distant voices. **2.** an indistinct utterance: *a murmur of satisfaction.* **3.** a complaint; grumble: *he made no murmur at my suggestion.* **4.** *Med.* any abnormal soft blowing sound heard within the body, usually over the chest. See also **heart murmur.** ~*vb.* **-murs, -muring, -mured. 5.** to utter (something) in a murmur. **6.** (*intr.*) to complain in a murmur. [C14: as n., from Latin *murmur;* vb. via Old French *murmurer* from Latin *murmurāre* to rumble] —'**murmurer** *n.* —'**murmuring** *n., adj.* —'**murmuringly** *adv.* —'**murmurous** *adj.*

murphy ('mɜːfɪ) *n., pl.* **-phies.** a dialect or informal word for **potato.** [C19: from the common Irish surname *Murphy*]

Murphy bed ('mɜːfɪ) *n. U.S. and Canadian.* a bed designed to be folded or swung into a cabinet when not in use. [C20: named after William *Murphy,* U.S. inventor]

Murphy's Law *n. Informal.* another term for **Sod's law.** [C20: of uncertain origin]

murra ('mʌrə) *n.* See **murrhine** (sense 2).

murragh ('mʌrə) *n.* an angler's name for the **great red sedge,** a large caddis fly, *Phryganea grandis,* of still and running water, esteemed by trout. [of uncertain origin: perhaps from obsolete *murrey* mulberry-coloured, from Old French *moré,* from Latin *morum* mulberry]

murrain ('mʌrɪn) *n.* **1.** any plaguelike disease in cattle. **2.** *Archaic.* a plague. [C14: from Old French *morine,* from *morir* to die, from Latin *morī*]

murre (mɜː) *n. U.S. and Canadian.* any guillemot of the genus *Uria.* [C17: origin unknown]

murree *or* **murri** ('mʌrɪ) *n., pl.* **-rees** *or* **-ris.** *Austral.* an Australian Aborigine. [C19: from a native Australian language]

murrelet ('mɜːlɪt) *n.* any of several small diving birds of the genus *Brachyramphus* and related genera, similar and related to the auks: family *Alcidae,* order *Charadriiformes.* [C19: from MURRE + -LET]

murrey ('mʌrɪ) *adj. Brit., archaic.* mulberry-coloured. [C14: from Old French *moré,* ultimately from Latin *mōrum* mulberry]

murrhine *or* **murrine** ('mʌraɪn, -ɪn) *adj.* **1.** of or relating to an unknown substance used in ancient Rome to make vases, cups, etc. ~*n.* **2.** Also called: **murra.** the substance so used. [C16: from Latin *murr(h)inus* belonging to *murra*]

murrhine glass *n.* a type of Eastern glassware made from fluorspar and decorated with pieces of coloured metal.

murther ('mɜːðə) *n., vb.* an archaic word for **murder.** —'**murtherer** *n.*

mus. *abbrev. for:* **1.** museum. **2.** music. **3.** musical.

musaceous (mjuː'zeɪʃəs) *adj.* of, relating to, or belonging to the *Musaceae,* a family of tropical flowering plants having large leaves and clusters of elongated berry fruits: includes the banana, plantain, and Manila hemp. [C19: from New Latin *Mūsāceae,* from *Mūsa* genus name, from Arabic *mawzah* banana]

Musaf *Hebrew.* (*Hebrew* mʊ'sɑf; *Yiddish* 'mʊsəf) *n. Judaism.* the additional prayers added to the morning service on Sabbaths, festivals, and Rosh Chodesh. [literally: addition]

musar *Hebrew.* (*Hebrew* mʊ'sɑː; *Yiddish* 'mʊsə) *n. Judaism.* **1.** rabbinic literature concerned with ethics, right conduct, etc. **2.** any moralizing speech, esp. one which is critical. [literally: instruction]

MusB *or* **MusBac** *abbrev. for* Bachelor of Music.

Musca ('mʌskə) *n., Latin genitive* **Muscae** ('mʌskiː). a small constellation in the S hemisphere lying between the Southern Cross and Chamaeleon. [Latin: a fly]

muscadel *or* **muscadelle** (ˌmʌskə'dɛl) *n.* another name for **muscatel.**

muscadine ('mʌskədɪn, -ˌdaɪn) *n.* **1.** a woody climbing vitaceous plant, *Vitis rotundifolia,* of the southeastern U.S. **2.** Also called: **scuppernong, bullace grape.** the thick-skinned musk-scented purple grape produced by this plant: used to make wine. [C16: from MUSCADEL]

muscae volitantes ('mʌsiː vɒlɪ'tæntiːz) *pl. n. Pathol.* moving black specks or threads seen before the eyes, caused by opaque fragments floating in the vitreous humour or a defect in the lens. [C18: New Latin: flying flies]

muscarine ('mʌskərɪn, -ˌriːn) *n.* a poisonous alkaloid occurring in certain mushrooms. Formula: $C_8H_{19}NO_3$. [C19: from Latin *muscārius* of flies, from *musca* fly]

muscat ('mʌskət, -kæt) *n.* **1.** any of various grapevines that produce sweet white grapes used for making wine or raisins. **2.** another name for **muscatel** (sense 1). [C16: via Old French from Provençal *muscat,* from *musc* MUSK]

muscatel (ˌmʌskə'tɛl), **muscadel,** *or* **muscadelle** *n.* **1.** Also called: **muscat.** a rich sweet wine made from muscat grapes. **2.** the grape or raisin from a muscat vine. [C14: from Old French *muscadel,* from Old Provençal, from *moscadel,* from *muscat* musky. See MUSK]

muscid ('mʌsɪd) *n.* **1.** any fly of the dipterous family *Muscidae,* including the housefly and tsetse fly. ~*adj.* **2.** of, relating to, or belonging to the *Muscidae.* [C19: via New Latin from Latin *musca* fly]

muscle ('mʌsᵊl) *n.* **1.** a tissue composed of bundles of elongated cells capable of contraction and relaxation to produce movement in an organ or part. **2.** an organ composed of muscle tissue. **3.** strength or force. ~*vb.* **4.** (*intr.;* often foll. by *in, on,* etc.) *Informal.* to force one's way (in). [C16: from medical Latin *musculus* little mouse, from the imagined resemblance of some muscles to mice, from Latin *mūs* mouse] —'**muscly** *adj.*

muscle-bound *adj.* **1.** having overdeveloped and inelastic muscles. **2.** lacking flexibility.

muscle fibre *n.* any of the numerous elongated contractile cells that contain many nuclei and make up striated muscle.

muscleman ('mʌsᵊlˌmæn) *n., pl.* **-men. 1.** a man with highly developed muscles. **2.** a henchman employed by a gangster to intimidate or use violence upon victims.

muscle sense *n.* another name for **kinaesthesia.**

muscovado *or* **muscavado** (ˌmʌskə'vɑːdəʊ) *n.* raw sugar obtained from the juice of sugar cane by evaporating the molasses. [C17: from Portuguese *açúcar mascavado* separated sugar; *mascavado* from *mascavar* to separate, probably from Latin]

muscovite ('mʌskəˌvaɪt) *n.* a pale brown, green, or colourless mineral of the mica group, found in plutonic rocks such as granite and in sedimentary rocks. It is used in the manufacture of lubricants, insulators, paints, and Christmas "snow". Composition: potassium aluminium silicate. Formula: $KAl_2(AlSi_3)O_{10}(OH)_2$. Crystal structure: monoclinic. See also **mica.** [C19: from the phrase *Muscovy glass,* an early name for mica]

Muscovite ('mʌskəˌvaɪt) *n.* **1.** a native or inhabitant of Moscow, capital of Russia. ~*adj.* **2.** an archaic word for **Russian.**

Muscovy duck ('mʌskəvɪ) *or* **musk duck** *n.* a large crested widely domesticated South American duck, *Cairina moschata,* having a greenish-black plumage with white markings and a large red caruncle on the bill. [C17: originally *musk duck,* a name later mistakenly associated with *Muscovy,* an archaic name for Russia]

muscular ('mʌskjʊlə) *adj.* **1.** having well-developed muscles; brawny. **2.** of, relating to, or consisting of muscle. [C17: from New Latin *muscularis,* from *musculus* MUSCLE] —**muscularity** (ˌmʌskjʊ'lærɪtɪ) *n.* —'**muscularly** *adv.*

muscular dystrophy *n.* a genetic disease characterized by progressive deterioration and wasting of muscle fibres, causing difficulty in walking.

musculature ('mʌskjʊlətʃə) *n.* **1.** the arrangement of muscles in an organ or part. **2.** the total muscular system of an organism.

musculocutaneous (ˌmʌskjʊləʊkjuː'teɪnɪəs) *adj.* of, relating to, or supplying the muscles and skin: *musculocutaneous nerve.*

MusD *or* **MusDoc** *abbrev. for* Doctor of Music.

muse[1] (mjuːz) *vb.* **1.** (when *intr.,* often foll. by *on* or *about*) to reflect (about) or ponder (on), usually in silence. **2.** (*intr.*) to gaze thoughtfully. ~*n.* **3.** *Archaic.* a state of abstraction. [C14: from Old French *muser,* perhaps from *mus* snout, from Medieval Latin *mūsus*] —'**muser** *n.* —'**museful** *adj.* —'**musefully** *adv.*

muse[2] (mjuːz) *n.* (often preceded by *the*) a goddess that inspires a creative artist, esp. a poet. [C14: from Old French, from Latin *Mūsa,* from Greek *Mousa* a *Muse* (a Greek patron of a particular art or science]

museology (ˌmjuːzɪ'ɒlədʒɪ) *n.* the science of museum organization. —ˌ**museo'logical** *adj.* —ˌ**muse'ologist** *n.*

musette (mju:ˈzɛt; *French* myzɛt) *n.* **1.** a type of bagpipe with a bellows popular in France during the 17th and 18th centuries. **2.** a dance, with a drone bass originally played by a musette. [C14: from Old French, diminutive of *muse* bagpipe]

musette bag *n. U.S.* an army officer's haversack.

museum (mju:ˈzɪəm) *n.* a place or building where objects of historical, artistic, or scientific interest are exhibited, preserved, or studied. [C17: via Latin from Greek *Mouseion* home of the Muses, from *Mousa*; see **muse**[2]]

museum beetle *n.* See **dermestid.**

museum piece *n.* **1.** an object of sufficient age or interest to be kept in a museum. **2.** *Informal.* a person or thing regarded as antiquated or decrepit.

mush[1] (mʌʃ) *n.* **1.** a soft pulpy mass or consistency. **2.** *U.S.* a thick porridge made from corn meal. **3.** *Informal.* cloying sentimentality. **4.** *Radio.* interference in reception, esp. a hissing noise. [C17: from obsolete *moose* porridge; probably related to MASH; compare Old English *mōs* food]

mush[2] (mʌʃ) *Canadian.* ~*interj.* **1.** an order to dogs in a sled team to start up or go faster. ~*vb.* **2.** to travel by or drive a dog sled. **3.** (*intr.*) to travel on foot, esp. with snowshoes. ~*n.* **4.** a journey with a dogsled. [C19: perhaps from French *marchez* or *marchons,* imperatives of *marcher* to advance] —ˈ**musher** *n.*

mush[3] (mʊʃ) *n. Brit.* a slang word for **face** (sense 1). [C19: from MUSH[1], alluding to the softness of the face]

mush[4] (mʊʃ) *n. Brit. slang.* a familiar or contemptuous term of address. [C19: probably from Gypsy *moosh* a man]

mush area *n.* a region where signals from two or more radio transmitters overlap, causing fading and distortion.

mushroom (ˈmʌʃru:m, -rʊm) *n.* **1. a.** the fleshy spore-producing body of any of various basidiomycetous fungi, typically consisting of a cap (see **pileus**) at the end of a stem arising from an underground mycelium. Some species, such as the field mushroom, are edible. Compare **toadstool. b.** (*as modifier*): *mushroom soup.* **2.** the fungus producing any of these structures. **3. a.** something resembling a mushroom in shape or rapid growth. **b.** (*as modifier*): *mushroom expansion.* ~*vb.* (*intr.*) **4.** to grow rapidly: *demand mushroomed overnight.* **5.** to assume a mushroom-like shape. **6.** to gather mushrooms. [C15: from Old French *mousseron,* from Late Latin *mussiriō,* of obscure origin]

mushroom cloud *n.* the large mushroom-shaped cloud of dust, debris, etc. produced by a nuclear explosion.

mushy (ˈmʌʃɪ) *adj.* **mushier, mushiest. 1.** soft and pulpy. **2.** *Informal.* excessively sentimental or emotional. —ˈ**mushily** *adv.* —ˈ**mushiness** *n.*

music (ˈmju:zɪk) *n.* **1.** an art form consisting of sequences of sounds in time, esp. tones of definite pitch organized melodically, harmonically, rhythmically and according to tone colour. **2.** such an art form characteristic of a particular people, culture, or tradition: *Indian music; rock music; baroque music.* **3.** the sounds so produced, esp. by singing or musical instruments. **4.** written or printed music, such as a score or set of parts. **5.** any sequence of sounds perceived as pleasing or harmonious. **6.** *Rare.* a group of musicians: *the Queen's music.* **7. face the music.** *Informal.* to confront the consequences of one's actions. **8. music to one's ears.** something that is very pleasant to hear: *his news is music to my ears.* [C13: via Old French from Latin *mūsica,* from Greek *mousikē* (*tekhnē*) (art) belonging to the Muses, from *Mousa*; see **muse**[2]]

musical (ˈmju:zɪkᵊl) *adj.* **1.** of, relating to, or used in music: *a musical instrument.* **2.** harmonious; melodious: *musical laughter.* **3.** talented in or fond of music. **4.** involving or set to music: *a musical evening.* ~*n.* **5.** short for **musical comedy.** —ˈ**musically** *adv.* —ˈ**musicalness** *or* ˌ**musiˈcality** *n.*

musical chairs *n.* (*functioning as sing.*) **1.** a party game in which players walk around chairs while music is played, there being one fewer chair than players. Whenever the music stops, the player who fails to find a chair is eliminated. **2.** any situation involving a number of people in a series of interrelated changes.

musical comedy *n.* **1.** a play or film, usually having a light romantic story, that consists of dialogue interspersed with singing and dancing. **2.** such plays and films collectively.

musicale (ˌmju:zɪˈkɑ:l) *n. U.S. and Canadian.* a party or social evening with a musical programme. [C19: shortened from French *soirée musicale* musical evening]

musical glasses *pl. n.* another term for **glass harmonica.**

musicassette (ˌmju:zɪkəˈsɛt) *n.* an audio cassette of prerecorded music.

music box *or* **musical box** *n.* a mechanical instrument that plays tunes by means of pins on a revolving cylinder striking the tuned teeth of a comblike metal plate, contained in a box.

music centre *n.* a single hi-fi unit containing a turntable, amplifier, radio and cassette player.

music drama *n.* **1.** an opera in which the musical and dramatic elements are of equal importance and strongly interfused. **2.** the genre of such operas. [C19: translation of German *Musikdrama,* coined by Richard Wagner (1813–83) to describe his later operas]

music hall *n. Chiefly Brit.* **1. a.** a variety entertainment consisting of songs, comic turns, etc. U.S. and Canadian name: **vaudeville. b.** (*as modifier*): *a music-hall song.* **2.** a theatre at which such entertainments are staged.

musician (mju:ˈzɪʃən) *n.* a person who plays or composes music, esp. as a profession. —**muˈsicianly** *adj.*

musicianship (mju:ˈzɪʃənʃɪp) *n.* skill or artistry in performing music.

music of the spheres *n.* the celestial music supposed by the Greek mathematician Pythagoras (?580–?500 B.C.) to be produced by the regular movements of the stars and planets.

musicology (ˌmju:zɪˈkɒlədʒɪ) *n.* the scholarly study of music. —**musicological** (ˌmju:zɪkəˈlɒdʒɪkᵊl) *adj.* —ˌ**musicoˈlogically** *adv.* —ˌ**musiˈcologist** *n.*

music paper *n.* paper ruled or printed with a stave for writing music.

music roll *n.* a roll of perforated paper for use in a mechanical instrument such as a player piano.

music stand *n.* a frame, usually of wood or metal, upon which a musical score or orchestral part is supported.

musique concrète *French.* (myzik kɔ̃krɛt) *n.* another term for **concrete music.**

musjid (ˈmʌsdʒɪd) *n.* a variant spelling of **masjid.**

musk (mʌsk) *n.* **1.** a strong-smelling glandular secretion of the male musk deer, used in perfumery. **2.** a similar substance produced by certain other animals, such as the civet and otter, or manufactured synthetically. **3.** any of several scrophulariaceous plants of the genus *Mimulus,* esp. the North American *M. moschatus,* which has yellow flowers and was formerly cultivated for its musky scent. See also **monkey flower. 4.** the smell of musk or a similar heady smell. **5.** (*modifier*) containing or resembling musk: *musk oil; a musk flavour.* [C14: from Late Latin *muscus,* from Greek *moskhos,* from Persian *mushk,* probably from Sanskrit *mushká* scrotum (from the appearance of the musk deer's musk bag), diminutive of *mūsh* MOUSE]

musk deer *n.* a small central Asian mountain deer, *Moschus moschiferus.* The male has long tusklike canine teeth and secretes musk.

musk duck *n.* **1.** another name for **Muscovy duck. 2.** a duck, *Biziura lobata,* inhabiting swamps, lakes, and streams in Australia. The male has a leathery pouch beneath the bill and emits a musky odour.

muskeg (ˈmʌsˌkɛg) *n. Chiefly Canadian.* **1.** undrained boggy land characterized by sphagnum moss vegetation: *vast areas of muskeg.* **2.** a bog or swamp of this nature. [C19: from Algonquian: grassy swamp]

muskellunge (ˈmʌskəˌlʌndʒ), **maskalonge** (ˈmæskəˌlɒndʒ), *or* **maskanonge** (ˈmæskəˌnɒndʒ) *n., pl.* **-lunges, -longes, -nonges** *or* **-lunge, -longe, -nonge.** a large North American freshwater game fish, *Esox masquinongy:* family *Esocidae* (pikes, etc.). Often shortened (informally) to **musky** or **muskie.** [C18 *maskinunga,* of Algonquian origin; compare Ojibwa *mashkinonge* big pike]

musket (ˈmʌskɪt) *n.* a long-barrelled muzzle-loading shoulder gun used between the 16th and 18th centuries by infantry soldiers. [C16: from French *mousquet,* from Italian *moschetto* arrow, earlier: sparrow hawk, from *moscha* a fly, from Latin *musca*]

musketeer (ˌmʌskɪˈtɪə) *n.* (formerly) a soldier armed with a musket.

musketry (ˈmʌskɪtrɪ) *n.* **1.** muskets or musketeers collectively. **2.** the technique of using small arms.

muskie (ˈmʌskɪ) *n. Canadian.* an informal name for the **muskellunge.**

musk mallow *n.* **1.** a malvaceous plant, *Malva moschata,* of Europe and N Africa, with purple-spotted stems, pink flowers, and a faint scent of musk. **2.** another name for **abelmosk.**

muskmelon (ˈmʌskˌmɛlən) *n.* **1.** any of several varieties of the melon *Cucumis melo,* such as the cantaloupe and honeydew. **2.** the fruit of any of these melons, having ribbed or warty rind and sweet yellow, white, or green flesh with a musky aroma.

Muskogean *or* **Muskhogean** (mʌsˈkəʊgɪən) *n.* a family of North American Indian languages, probably distantly related to the Algonquian family.

musk orchid *n.* a small Eurasian orchid, *Herminium monorchis,* with dense spikes of musk-scented greenish-yellow flowers.

musk ox *n.* a large bovid mammal, *Ovibos moschatus,* which has a dark shaggy coat, short legs, and widely spaced downward-curving horns and emits a musky smell: now confined to the tundras of Canada and Greenland.

muskrat (ˈmʌskˌræt) *n., pl.* **-rats** *or* **-rat. 1.** a North American beaver-like amphibious rodent, *Ondatra zibethica,* closely related to but larger than the voles: family *Cricetidae.* **2.** the brown fur of this animal. **3.** either of two closely related rodents, *Ondatra obscurus* or *Neofiber alleni* (**round-tailed muskrat**). ~Also called: **musquash.** [C17: by folk etymology, from the same source as MUSQUASH]

musk rose *n.* a prickly shrubby Mediterranean rose, *Rosa moschata,* cultivated for its white musk-scented flowers.

musk turtle *n.* any of several small turtles of the genus *Sternotherus,* esp. *S. odoratus* (**common musk turtle** or **stinkpot**), that emit a strong unpleasant odour: family *Kinosternidae.*

musky[1] (ˈmʌskɪ) *adj.* **muskier, muskiest.** resembling the smell of musk; having a heady or pungent sweet aroma. —ˈ**muskiness** *n.*

musky[2] (ˈmʌskɪ) *n., pl.* **muskies.** an informal name for the **muskellunge.**

Muslim ('mʊzlɪm, 'mʌz-) *or* **Moslem** *n., pl.* **-lims** *or* **-lim.** **1.** a follower of the religion of Islam. ~*adj.* **2.** of or relating to Islam, its doctrines, culture, etc. ~Also (but not in Muslim use): **Muhammadan, Muhammedan, Mohammedan.** [C17: from Arabic, literally: one who surrenders] —'**Muslimism** *or* '**Moslemism** *n.*

muslin ('mʌzlɪn) *n.* a fine plain-weave cotton fabric. [C17: from French *mousseline,* from Italian *mussolina,* from Arabic *mawṣilīy* of Mosul, from *Mawṣil* Mosul, Iraq, where it was first produced]

MusM *abbrev. for* Master of Music.

muso ('mjuːzəʊ) *n., pl.* **musos.** *Slang.* **1.** *Brit. derogatory.* a musician, esp. a pop musician, regarded as being overconcerned with technique rather than musical content or expression. **2.** *Austral.* any musician, esp. a professional one.

musquash ('mʌskwɒʃ) *n.* another name for **muskrat,** esp. the fur. [C17: from Algonquian: compare Natick *musquash,* Abnaki *muskwessu*]

muss (mʌs) *U.S. and Canadian informal.* ~*vb.* **1.** (*tr.;* often foll. by *up*) to make untidy; rumple. ~*n.* **2.** a state of disorder; muddle. [C19: probably a blend of MESS + FUSS] —'**mussy** *adj.* —'**mussily** *adv.* —'**mussiness** *n.*

mussel ('mʌsᵊl) *n.* **1.** any of various marine bivalves of the genus *Mytilus* and related genera, esp. *M. edulis* (**edible mussel**), having a dark slightly elongated shell and living attached to rocks, etc., **2.** any of various freshwater bivalves of the genera *Anodonta, Unio,* etc., attached to rocks, sand, etc. having a flattened oval shell (a source of mother-of-pearl). The **zebra mussel,** *Dreissena polymorpha,* can be a serious nuisance in water mains. [Old English *muscle,* from Vulgar Latin *muscula* (unattested), from Latin *musculus,* diminutive of *mūs* mouse]

Mussulman *or* **Mussalman** ('mʌsᵊlmən) *n., pl.* **-mans.** an archaic word for **Muslim.** [C16: from Persian *Musulmān* (pl.) from Arabic *Muslimūn,* pl. of MUSLIM]

must[1] (mʌst; *unstressed* məst, məs) *vb.* (takes an infinitive without *to* or an implied infinitive) used as an auxiliary: **1.** to express obligation or compulsion: *you must pay your dues.* In this sense, *must* does not form a negative. If used with a negative infinitive it indicates obligatory prohibition. **2.** to indicate necessity: *I must go to the bank tomorrow.* **3.** to indicate the probable correctness of a statement: *he must be there by now.* **4.** to indicate inevitability: *all good things must come to an end.* **5.** to express resolution: **a.** on the part of the speaker when used with *I* or *we: I must finish this.* **b.** on the part of another or others as imputed to them by the speaker, when used with *you, he, she, they,* etc.: *let him get drunk if he must.* **6.** (used emphatically) to express conviction or certainty on the part of the speaker: *he must have reached the town by now, surely; you must be joking.* **7.** (foll. by *away*) used with an implied verb of motion to express compelling haste: *I must away.* ~*n.* **8.** an essential or necessary thing: *strong shoes are a must for hill walking.* [Old English *mōste* past tense of *mōtan* to be allowed, be obliged to; related to Old Saxon *mōtan,* Old High German *muozan,* German *müssen*]

must[2] (mʌst) *n.* the newly pressed juice of grapes or other fruit ready for fermentation. [Old English, from Latin *mustum* new wine, must, from *mustus* (adj.) newborn]

must[3] (mʌst) *n.* mustiness or mould. [C17: back formation from MUSTY]

must[4] (mʌst) *n.* a variant spelling of **musth.**

mustache (mə'stɑːʃ) *n.* the U.S. spelling of **moustache.** —**mus'tached** *adj.*

mustachio (mə'stɑːʃɪˌəʊ) *n., pl.* **-chios.** (*often pl. when considered as two halves*) *Often humorous.* a moustache, esp. when bushy or elaborately shaped. [C16: from Spanish *mostacho* and Italian *mostaccio*] —**mus'tachioed** *adj.*

mustang ('mʌstæŋ) *n.* a small breed of horse, often wild or half wild, found in the southwestern U.S. [C19: from Mexican Spanish *mestengo,* from *mesta* a group of stray animals]

mustard ('mʌstəd) *n.* **1.** any of several Eurasian plants of the cruciferous genus *Brassica,* esp. black mustard and white mustard, having yellow flowers and slender pods: cultivated for their pungent seeds. See also **charlock.** **2.** a paste made from the powdered seeds of any of these plants and used as a condiment. **3. a.** a brownish yellow colour. **b.** (*as adj.*): *a mustard carpet.* **4.** *Slang, chiefly U.S.* zest or enthusiasm. **5. cut the mustard.** *Slang, chiefly U.S.* to come up to expectations. [C13: from Old French *moustarde,* from Latin *mustum* MUST[2], since the original condiment was made by adding must]

mustard and cress *n.* seedlings of white mustard and garden cress, used in salads.

mustard gas *n.* an oily liquid vesicant compound used in chemical warfare. Its vapour causes blindness and burns. Formula: $(ClCH_2CH_2)_2S$.

mustard oil *n.* an oil that is obtained from mustard seeds and used in making soap.

mustard plaster *n. Med.* a mixture of powdered black mustard seeds and an adhesive agent applied to the skin for its relaxing, stimulating, or counterirritant effects.

mustee (mʌ'stiː, 'mʌstiː) *or* **mestee** (mɛ'stiː) *n.* **1.** the offspring of a White and a quadroon. **2.** any person of mixed ancestry. [C17: shortened from MESTIZO]

musteline ('mʌstɪˌlaɪn, -lɪn) *adj.* **1.** of, relating to, or belonging to the *Mustelidae,* a family of typically predatory mammals including weasels, ferrets, minks, polecats, badgers, skunks, and otters: order *Carnivora* (carnivores). ~*n.* **2.** any musteline animal. [C17: from Latin *mustēlīnus,* from *mustēla* weasel, from *mūs* mouse + *-tēla,* of unknown origin]

muster ('mʌstə) *vb.* **1.** to call together (numbers of men) for duty, inspection, etc., or (of men) to assemble in this way. **2. muster in** *or* **out.** *U.S.* to enlist into or discharge from military service. **3.** (*tr.*) *Austral. and N.Z.* to round up (livestock). **4.** (*tr.;* sometimes foll. by *up*) to summon or gather: *to muster one's arguments; to muster up courage.* ~*n.* **5.** an assembly of military personnel for duty, inspection, etc. **6.** a collection, assembly, or gathering. **7.** *Austral. and N.Z.* the rounding up of livestock. **8.** a flock of peacocks. **9. pass muster.** to be acceptable. [C14: from old French *moustrer,* from Latin *monstrāre* to show, from *monstrum* portent, omen]

muster roll *n.* a list of the officers and men in a regiment, ship's company, etc.

musth *or* **must** (mʌst) *n.* (often preceded by *in*) a state of frenzied sexual excitement in the males of certain large mammals, esp. elephants, associated with discharge from a gland between the ear and eye. [C19: from Urdu *mast,* from Persian: drunk]

musty ('mʌstɪ) *adj.* **-tier, -tiest.** **1.** smelling or tasting old, stale, or mouldy. **2.** old-fashioned, dull, or hackneyed: *musty ideas.* [C16: perhaps a variant of obsolete *moisty,* influenced by MUST[3]] —'**mustily** *adv.* —'**mustiness** *n.*

mut (mʌt) *n. Printing.* another word for **em** (sense 1). [C20: shortened from MUTTON]

mutable ('mjuːtəbᵊl) *adj.* **1.** able to or tending to change. **2.** *Astrology.* of or relating to four of the signs of the zodiac, Gemini, Virgo, Sagittarius, and Pisces, which are associated with the quality of adaptability. Compare **cardinal** (sense 9), **fixed** (sense 10). [C14: from Latin *mūtābilis* fickle, from *mūtāre* to change] —ˌ**muta'bility** *or* (*less commonly*) '**mutableness** *n.* —'**mutably** *adv.*

mutagen ('mjuːtədʒən) *n.* a substance or agent that can induce genetic mutation. [C20: from MUTATION + -GEN] —**mutagenic** (ˌmjuːtə'dʒɛnɪk) *adj.* —ˌ**mutagen'icity** *n.*

mutant ('mjuːtᵊnt) *n.* **1.** Also called: **mutation.** an animal, organism, or gene that has undergone mutation. ~*adj.* **2.** of, relating to, undergoing, or resulting from change or mutation. [C20: from Latin *mūtāre* to change]

mutate (mjuː'teɪt) *vb.* to undergo or cause to undergo mutation. [C19: from Latin *mūtātus* changed, from *mūtāre* to change] —**mutative** ('mjuːtətɪv, mjuː'teɪtɪv) *adj.*

mutation (mjuː'teɪʃən) *n.* **1.** the act or process of mutating; change; alteration. **2.** a change or alteration. **3.** a change in the chromosomes or genes of a cell. When this change occurs in the gametes the structure and development of the resultant offspring may be affected. See also **inversion** (sense 11). **4.** another word for **mutant** (sense 1). **5.** a physical characteristic of an individual resulting from this type of chromosomal change. **6.** *Phonetics.* **a.** (in Germanic languages) another name for **umlaut.** **b.** (in Celtic languages) a phonetic change in certain initial consonants caused by a preceding word. —**mu'tational** *adj.* —**mu'tationally** *adv.*

mutation stop *n.* an organ pipe sounding the harmonic of the note normally produced.

mutatis mutandis *Latin.* (muː'tɑːtɪs muː'tændɪs) the necessary changes having been made.

Mutazilite (muː'tɑːzɪˌlaɪt) *n.* a member of an 8th-century liberal Muslim sect, later merged into the Shiahs. [from Arabic *mu'tazilah* body of seceders + -ITE[1]]

mutch[1] (mʌtʃ) *n.* a close-fitting linen cap formerly worn by women and children in Scotland. [C15: from Middle Dutch *mutse* cap, from Medieval Latin *almucia* ALMUCE]

mutch[2] (mʌtʃ) *vb. Dialect.* **1.** (*tr.*) to cadge; beg. **2.** (*intr.*) another word for **mitch.**

mutchkin ('mʌtʃkɪn) *n.* a Scottish unit of liquid measure equal to slightly less than one pint. [C15: from Middle Dutch *mudseken,* from Latin *modius* measure for grain]

mute[1] (mjuːt) *adj.* **1.** not giving out sound or speech; silent. **2.** unable to speak; dumb. **3.** unspoken or unexpressed: *mute dislike.* **4.** *Law.* (of a person arraigned on indictment) refusing to answer a charge. **5.** *Phonetics.* another word for **plosive.** **6.** (of a letter in a word) silent. ~*n.* **7.** a person who is unable to speak. **8.** *Law.* a person who refuses to plead when arraigned on indictment for an offence. **9.** any of various devices used to soften the tone of stringed or brass instruments. **10.** *Phonetics.* a plosive consonant; stop. **11.** a silent letter. **12.** an actor in a dumb show. **13.** a hired mourner at a funeral. ~*vb.* (*tr.*) **14.** to reduce the volume of (a musical instrument) by means of a mute, soft pedal, etc. **15.** to subdue the strength of (a colour, tone, lighting, etc.). [C14 *muwet* from Old French *mu,* from Latin *mūtus* silent] —'**mutely** *adv.* —'**muteness** *n.*

mute[2] (mjuːt) *Archaic.* ~*vb.* **1.** (of birds) to discharge (faeces). ~*n.* **2.** birds' faeces. [C15: from Old French *meutir,* variant of *esmeltir,* of Germanic origin; probably related to SMELT[1] and MELT]

mute swan *n.* a Eurasian swan, *Cygnus olor,* with a pure white plumage, an orange-red bill with a black base, and a curved neck. Compare **whistling swan.**

muti ('mʊtɪ) *n. S. African.* medicine, esp. herbal medicine. [from Zulu *umuthi*]

muticous (ˈmjuːtɪkəs) *adj. Botany.* lacking an awn, spine, or point. Also: **muticate.** [C19: from Latin *muticus* awnless, curtailed]
mutilate (ˈmjuːtɪˌleɪt) *vb.* (*tr.*) **1.** to deprive of a limb, essential part, etc.; maim; dismember. **2.** to mar, expurgate, or damage (a text, book, etc). [C16: from Latin *mutilāre* to cut off; related to *mutilus* maimed] —ˌ**mutiˈlation** *n.* —ˈ**mutiˌlative** *adj.* —ˈ**mutiˌlator** *n.*
mutineer (ˌmjuːtɪˈnɪə) *n.* a person who mutinies.
mutinous (ˈmjuːtɪnəs) *adj.* **1.** openly rebellious or disobedient: *a mutinous child.* **2.** characteristic or indicative of mutiny. —ˈ**mutinously** *adv.* —ˈ**mutinousness** *n.*
mutiny (ˈmjuːtɪnɪ) *n., pl.* **-nies. 1.** open rebellion against constituted authority, esp. by seamen or soldiers against their officers. ~*vb.* **-nies, -nying, -nied. 2.** (*intr.*) to engage in mutiny. [C16: from obsolete *mutine*, from Old French *mutin* rebellious, from *meute* mutiny, ultimately from Latin *movēre* to move]
mutism (ˈmjuːtɪzəm) *n.* **1.** the state of being mute. **2.** *Psychiatry.* **a.** a refusal to speak although the mechanism of speech is not damaged. **b.** the lack of development of speech, due usually to early deafness.
mutt (mʌt) *n. Slang.* **1.** an inept, ignorant, or stupid person. **2.** a mongrel dog; cur. [C20: shortened from MUTTONHEAD]
mutter (ˈmʌtə) *vb.* **1.** to utter (something) in a low and indistinct tone. **2.** (*intr.*) to grumble or complain. **3.** (*intr.*) to make a low continuous murmuring sound. ~*n.* **4.** a muttered sound or complaint. [C14 *moteren*; related to Norwegian (dialect) *mutra*, Old High German *mutilōn*; compare Old English *mōtian* to speak] —ˈ**mutterer** *n.* —ˈ**muttering** *n., adj.* —ˈ**mutteringly** *adv.*
mutton (ˈmʌtᵊn) *n.* **1.** the flesh of sheep, esp. of mature sheep, used as food. **2. mutton dressed (up) as lamb.** an older person, thing, or idea dressed up to look young or new. **3.** *Printing.* another word for **em** (sense 1). Compare **nut** (sense 12). [C13 *moton* sheep, from Old French, from Medieval Latin *multō*, of Celtic origin; the term was adopted in printing to distinguish the pronunciation of *em quad* from *en quad*] —ˈ**muttony** *adj.*
mutton bird *n.* any of several shearwaters, having a dark plumage with greyish underparts, esp. the sooty shearwater (*Puffinus griseus*) of New Zealand, which is collected for food by Maoris, or the short-tailed shearwater (*Puffinus tenuirostris*), which inhabits the Pacific Ocean and in summer nests in Australia. [C19: so named because their cooked flesh is claimed to taste like mutton]
mutton-birder *n. N.Z.* a person who hunts mutton birds.
mutton chop *n.* a piece of mutton from the loin.
muttonchops (ˈmʌtᵊnˌtʃɒps) *pl. n.* side whiskers trimmed in the shape of chops, widening out from the temples.
muttonhead (ˈmʌtᵊnˌhɛd) *n. Slang.* a stupid or ignorant person; fool. —ˈ**muttonˌheaded** *adj.*
mutual (ˈmjuːtʃʊəl) *adj.* **1.** experienced or expressed by each of two or more people or groups about the other; reciprocal: *mutual distrust.* **2.** common to or shared by both or all of two or more parties: *a mutual friend; mutual interests.* **3.** denoting an insurance company, etc., in which the policyholders share the profits and expenses and there are no shareholders. [C15: from Old French *mutuel*, from Latin *mūtuus* reciprocal (originally: borrowed); related to *mūtāre* to change] —**mutuality** (ˌmjuːtjʊˈælɪtɪ) *or* ˈ**mutualness** *n.* —ˈ**mutually** *adv.*
mutual fund *n.* the U.S. and Canadian name for **unit trust.**
mutual inductance *n.* a measure of the mutual induction between two magnetically linked circuits, given as the ratio of the induced electromotive force to the rate of change of current producing it. It is usually measured in henries. Symbol: *M* or L_{12} Also called: **coefficient of mutual induction.**
mutual induction *n.* the production of an electromotive force in a circuit by a current change in a second circuit magnetically linked to the first. See also **mutual inductance.** Compare **self-induction.**
mutual insurance *n.* a system of insurance by which all policyholders become company members under contract to pay premiums into a common fund out of which claims are paid. See also **mutual** (sense 3).
mutualism (ˈmjuːtʃʊəˌlɪzəm) *n.* another name for **symbiosis.** —ˈ**mutualist** *n., adj.* —ˌ**mutualˈistic** *adj.*
mutualize *or* **mutualise** (ˈmjuːtʃʊəˌlaɪz) *vb.* **1.** to make or become mutual. **2.** (*tr.*) *U.S.* to organize or convert (a business enterprise) so that customers or employees own a majority of shares. —ˌ**mutualiˈzation** *or* ˌ**mutualiˈsation** *n.*
mutual savings bank *n. Chiefly U.S.* a savings bank having no subscribed capital stock and distributing all available net profit to depositors who, however, remain creditors without voting power.
mutuel (ˈmjuːtjʊəl) *n.* short for **pari-mutuel.**
mutule (ˈmjuːtjuːl) *n. Architect.* one of a set of flat blocks below the corona of a Doric cornice. Compare **modillion.** [C16: via French from Latin *mūtulus* modillion]
muu-muu (ˈmuːˌmuː) *n.* a loose brightly-coloured dress worn by women in Hawaii. [from Hawaiian]
Muzak (ˈmjuːzæk) *n. Trademark.* recorded light music played in shops, restaurants, factories, etc., to entertain, increase sales or production, etc.
muzhik, moujik, *or* **mujik** (ˈmuːʒɪk) *n.* a Russian peasant, esp. under the tsars. [C16: from Russian: peasant]
muzz (mʌz) *vb.* (*tr.*) *Brit. informal.* to make (something) muzzy.
muzzle (ˈmʌzᵊl) *n.* **1.** the projecting part of the face, usually the jaws and nose, of animals such as the dog and horse. **2.** a guard or strap fitted over an animal's nose and jaws to prevent it biting or eating. **3.** the front end of a gun barrel. ~*vb.* (*tr.*) **4.** to prevent from being heard or noticed: *to muzzle the press.* **5.** to put a muzzle on (an animal). **6.** to take in (a sail). [C15 *mosel*, from Old French *musel*, diminutive of *muse* snout, from Medieval Latin *mūsus*, of unknown origin] —ˈ**muzzler** *n.*
muzzle-loader *n.* a firearm receiving its ammunition through the muzzle. —ˈ**muzzle-ˌloading** *adj.*
muzzle velocity *n.* the velocity of a projectile as it leaves a firearm's muzzle.
muzzy (ˈmʌzɪ) *adj.* **-zier, -ziest. 1.** blurred, indistinct, or hazy. **2.** confused, muddled, or befuddled. [C18: origin obscure] —ˈ**muzzily** *adv.* —ˈ**muzziness** *n.*
mv *Music. abbrev. for* mezzo voce.
MV *abbrev. for:* **1.** motor vessel. **2.** muzzle velocity. ~**3.** *symbol for* megavolt.
MVD *abbrev. for* Ministry of Internal Affairs; the Soviet police organization since 1946. [from Russian *Ministerstvo vnutrennikh del*]
MVO (in Britain) *abbrev. for* Member of the Royal Victorian Order.
MVS *abbrev. for* Master of Veterinary Surgery.
MVSc *abbrev. for* Master of Veterinary Science.
MW **1.** *symbol for* megawatt. **2.** *Radio. abbrev. for* medium wave. **3.** *international car registration for* Malawi.
mwalimu (mwɑːˈliːmuː) *n. E African.* a teacher. [Swahili]
Mx *Physics. symbol for* maxwell.
MX *U.S. abbrev. for* missile-experimental: an intercontinental ballistic missile with up to ten nuclear warheads.
my (maɪ) *determiner.* **1.** of, belonging to, or associated with the speaker or writer (me): *my own ideas; do you mind my smoking?* **2.** used in various forms of address: *my lord; my dear boy.* **3.** used in various exclamations: *my goodness!* ~*interj.* **4.** an exclamation of surprise, awe, etc.: *my, how you've grown!* [C12 *mī*, variant of Old English *mīn* when preceding a word beginning with a consonant]
MY *abbrev. for* motor yacht.
my- *combining form.* a variant of **myo-** before a vowel.
myalgia (maɪˈældʒɪə) *n.* pain in a muscle or a group of muscles. [C19: from MYO- + -ALGIA] —**myˈalgic** *adj.*
myalgic encephalomyelitis (maɪˈældʒɪk ɛnˌsɛfələʊˌmaɪɪˈlaɪtɪs) *n.* a condition involving painful muscles and general weakness, sometimes persisting long after a viral illness. Also called: **postviral syndrome.** Abbrev.: **ME.**
myalism (ˈmaɪəˌlɪzəm) *n.* a kind of witchcraft, similar to obi, practised esp. in the West Indies. [C19: from *myal*, probably of West African origin] —ˈ**myalist** *n.*
myall (ˈmaɪəl) *n.* **1.** any of several Australian acacias, esp. *Acacia pendula*, having hard scented wood used for fences. **2.** an Australian Aborigine living independently of society. [C19: from a native Australian name]
myasthenia (ˌmaɪəsˈθiːnɪə) *n.* **1.** any muscular weakness. **2.** short for **myasthenia gravis.** [C19: from MYO- + ASTHENIA] —**myasthenic** (ˌmaɪəsˈθɛnɪk) *adj.*
myasthenia gravis (ˈgrɑːvɪs) *n.* a chronic progressive disease in which the muscles, esp. those of the head and face, become weak and easily fatigued.
myc- *combining form.* a variant of **myco-** before a vowel.
mycelium (maɪˈsiːlɪəm) *n., pl.* **-lia** (-lɪə). the vegetative body of fungi: a mass of branching filaments (hyphae) that spread throughout the nutrient substratum. [C19 (literally: nail of fungus): from MYCO- + Greek *hēlos* nail] —**myˈcelial** *adj.* —**myceloid** (ˈmaɪsɪˌlɔɪd) *adj.*
mycella (maɪˈsɛlə) *n.* a blue-veined Danish cream cheese, less strongly flavoured than Danish blue. [C20: New Latin, from Greek *mukēs* fungus]
Mycenaean (ˌmaɪsɪˈniːən) *adj.* **1.** of or relating to the ancient Greek city of Mycenae or its inhabitants. **2.** of or relating to the Aegean civilization of Mycenae (1400 to 1100 B.C.).
-mycete *n. combining form.* indicating a member of a class of fungi: *myxomycete.* [from New Latin *-mycetes*, from Greek *mukētes*, plural of *mukēs* fungus]
myceto- *or before a vowel* **mycet-** *combining form.* fungus: *mycetozoan.* [from Greek *mukēs* fungus]
mycetoma (ˌmaɪsɪˈtəʊmə) *n., pl.* **-mas** *or* **-mata** (-mətə). a chronic fungal infection, esp. of the foot, characterized by swelling, usually resulting from a wound.
mycetophagous (ˌmaɪsɪˈtɒfəgəs) *adj. Zoology.* feeding on fungi.
mycetozoan (maɪˌsiːtəʊˈzəʊən) *n.* another name for **myxomycete.**
-mycin *n. combining form.* indicating an antibiotic compound derived from a fungus: *streptomycin.* [from Greek *mukēs* fungus + -IN]
myco- *or before a vowel* **myc-** *combining form.* indicating fungus: *mycology.* [from Greek *mukēs* fungus]
mycobacterium (ˌmaɪkəʊbækˈtɪərɪəm) *n., pl.* **-ria** (-rɪə). any rod-shaped Gram-positive bacterium of the genus *Mycobacterium*, esp. the tubercle bacillus: family *Mycobacteriaceae.*
mycobiont (ˌmaɪkəʊˈbaɪɒnt) *n. Botany.* the fungal constituent of a lichen. Compare **phycobiont.**
mycol. *abbrev. for:* **1.** mycological. **2.** mycology.

mycology (maɪˈkɒlədʒɪ) *n.* **1.** the branch of botany concerned with the study of fungi. **2.** the fungi of a particular region. —**mycological** (ˌmaɪkəˈlɒdʒɪkᵊl) *or* ˌ**mycoˈlogic** *adj.* —**myˈcologist** *n.*

mycoplasma (ˌmaɪkəʊˈplæzmə) *n.* any prokaryotic microorganism of the genus *Mycoplasma,* some species of which cause disease (**mycoplasmosis**) in animals and humans.

mycorrhiza *or* **mycorhiza** (ˌmaɪkəˈraɪzə) *n., pl.* **-zae** (-ziː) *or* **-zas.** an association of a fungus and a higher plant in which the fungus lives within or on the outside of the roots forming a symbiotic or parasitic relationship. See **ectotrophic, endotrophic.** [C19: from MYCO- + Greek *rhiza* root] —ˌ**mycorˈrhizal** *or* ˌ**mycoˈrhizal** *adj.*

mycosis (maɪˈkəʊsɪs) *n.* any infection or disease caused by fungus. —**mycotic** (maɪˈkɒtɪk) *adj.*

Mycostatin (ˌmaɪkəʊˈstætɪn) *n. Trademark.* a brand of **nystatin.**

mycotoxin (ˌmaɪkəˈtɒksɪn) *n.* any of various toxic substances produced by fungi some of which may affect food and others of which are alleged to have been used in warfare. See also **aflatoxin, yellow rain.** —ˌ**mycotoxˈology** *n.*

mycotrophic (ˌmaɪkəʊˈtrɒfɪk) *adj. Botany.* (of a plant) symbiotic with a fungus, esp. a mycorrhizal fungus.

mydriasis (mɪˈdraɪəsɪs, maɪ-) *n.* abnormal dilation of the pupil of the eye, produced by drugs, coma, etc. [C17: via Late Latin from Greek; origin obscure]

mydriatic (ˌmɪdrɪˈætɪk) *adj.* **1.** relating to or causing mydriasis. ~*n.* **2.** a mydriatic drug.

myel- *or before a consonant* **myelo-** *combining form.* the spinal cord or bone marrow: *myeloid.* [from Greek *muelos* marrow, spinal cord, from *mus* muscle]

myelencephalon (ˌmaɪɪlɛnˈsɛfəˌlɒn) *n., pl.* **-lons** *or* **-la** (-lə). the part of the embryonic hindbrain that develops into the medulla oblongata. Nontechnical name: **afterbrain.** —**myelencephalic** (ˌmaɪɪlɛnsəˈfælɪk) *adj.*

myelin (ˈmaɪɪlɪn) *or* **myeline** (ˈmaɪɪˌliːn) *n.* a white tissue forming an insulating sheath (**myelin sheath**) around certain nerve fibres. Damage to the myelin sheath causes neurological disease, as in multiple sclerosis. —ˌ**myeˈlinic** *adj.*

myelinated (ˈmaɪɪlɪˌneɪtɪd) *adj.* (of a nerve fibre) having a myelin sheath.

myelitis (ˌmaɪɪˈlaɪtɪs) *n.* inflammation of the spinal cord or of the bone marrow.

myeloblast (ˈmaɪələʊˌblɑːst) *n.* a cell that gives rise to a granulocyte, normally occurring in the bone marrow but detected in the blood in certain diseases, esp. leukaemia. —**myeloblastic** (ˌmaɪələʊˈblæstɪk) *adj.*

myelocyte (ˈmaɪələʊˌsaɪt) *n.* an immature granulocyte, normally occurring in the bone marrow but detected in the blood in certain diseases. —**myelocytic** (ˌmaɪələʊˈsɪtɪk) *adj.*

myelogram (maɪˈɛləˌgræm) *n.* an x-ray of the spinal cord, after injection with a radio-opaque medium. —ˌ**myeˈlography** *n.*

myeloid (ˈmaɪɪˌlɔɪd) *adj.* of or relating to the spinal cord or the bone marrow.

myeloma (ˌmaɪɪˈləʊmə) *n., pl.* **-mas** *or* **-mata** (-mətə). a usually malignant tumour of the bone marrow or composed of cells normally found in bone marrow. —ˌ**myeˈlomaˌtoid** *adj.*

myiasis (ˈmaɪəsɪs) *n., pl.* **-ses** (-ˌsiːz). **1.** infestation of the body by the larvae of flies. **2.** any disease resulting from such infestation. [C19: New Latin, from Greek *muia* a fly]

mylonite (ˈmaɪləˌnaɪt, ˈmɪlə-) *n.* a fine-grained metamorphic rock, often showing banding and micaceous fracture, formed by the crushing, grinding, or rolling of the original structure. [C19: from Greek *mulōn* mill]

myna, mynah, *or* **mina** (ˈmaɪnə) *n.* any of various tropical Asian starlings of the genera *Acridotheres, Gracula,* etc., esp. *G. religiosa* (see **hill myna**), some of which can mimic human speech. [C18: from Hindi *mainā,* from Sanskrit *madana*]

Mynheer (məˈnɪə) *n.* a Dutch title of address equivalent to *Sir* when used alone or to *Mr* when placed before a name. [C17: from Dutch *mijnheer,* my lord]

myo- *or before a vowel* **my-** *combining form.* muscle: *myocardium.* [from Greek *mus* MUSCLE]

myocardial infarction *n.* destruction of an area of heart muscle as the result of occlusion of a coronary artery. Compare **coronary thrombosis.**

myocardiograph (ˌmaɪəʊˈkɑːdɪəˌgræf, -ˌgrɑːf) *n.* an instrument for recording the movements of heart muscle.

myocarditis (ˌmaɪəʊkɑːˈdaɪtɪs) *n.* inflammation of the heart muscle.

myocardium (ˌmaɪəʊˈkɑːdɪəm) *n., pl.* **-dia** (-dɪə). the muscular tissue of the heart. [C19: *myo-* + *cardium,* from Greek *kardia* heart] —ˌ**myoˈcardial** *adj.*

myoelectric (ˌmaɪəʊɪˈlɛktrɪk) *adj.* denoting a type of powered artificial hand or limb that detects electrical changes in the muscles of the stump and converts these into movements.

myogenic (ˌmaɪəˈdʒɛnɪk) *adj.* originating in or forming muscle tissue.

myoglobin (ˌmaɪəʊˈgləʊbɪn) *n.* a protein that is the main oxygen-carrier of muscle.

myograph (ˈmaɪəˌgræf, -ˌgrɑːf) *n.* an instrument for recording tracings (**myograms**) of muscular contractions. —ˌ**myoˈgraphic** *adj.* —ˌ**myoˈgraphically** *adv.* —**myography** (maɪˈɒgrəfɪ) *n.*

myology (maɪˈɒlədʒɪ) *n.* the branch of medical science concerned with the structure and diseases of muscles. —**myologic** (ˌmaɪəˈlɒdʒɪk) *or* ˌ**myoˈlogical** *adj.* —**myˈologist** *n.*

myoma (maɪˈəʊmə) *n., pl.* **-mas** *or* **-mata** (-mətə). a benign tumour composed of muscle tissue. —**myˈomatous** *adj.*

myopathy (maɪˈɒpəθɪ) *n.* any disease affecting muscles or muscle tissue.

myope (ˈmaɪəʊp) *n.* any person afflicted with myopia. [C18: via French from Greek *muōps;* see MYOPIA]

myophily *or* **myiophily** (maɪˈɒfɪlɪ) *n.* pollination of plants by flies. [from Greek *muia* fly + *philos* loving] —**myˈophilous** or **myiˈophilous** *adj.*

myopia (maɪˈəʊpɪə) *n.* inability to see distant objects clearly because the images are focused in front of the retina; short-sightedness. [C18: via New Latin from Greek *muōps* short-sighted, from *muein* to close (the eyes), blink + *ōps* eye] —**myopic** (maɪˈɒpɪk) *adj.* —**myˈopically** *adv.*

myosin (ˈmaɪəsɪn) *n.* the chief protein of muscle that interacts with actin to form actomyosin during muscle contraction; it is also present in many other cell types. [C19: from MYO- + -OSE[2] + -IN]

myosis (maɪˈəʊsɪs) *n., pl.* **-ses** (-siːz). a variant spelling of **miosis.**

myosotis (ˌmaɪəˈsəʊtɪs) *or* **myosote** (ˈmaɪəˌsəʊt) *n.* any plant of the boraginaceous genus *Myosotis.* See **forget-me-not.** [C18: New Latin from Greek *muosōtis* mouse-ear (referring to its furry leaves), from *muos,* genitive of *mus* mouse + *-ōt-,* stem of *ous* ear]

myotome (ˈmaɪəˌtəʊm) *n.* **1.** any segment of embryonic mesoderm that develops into skeletal muscle in the adult. **2.** any of the segmentally arranged blocks of muscle in lower vertebrates such as fishes.

myotonia (ˌmaɪəˈtəʊnɪə) *n.* lack of muscle tone, frequently including muscle spasm or rigidity. Also called: **amyotonia.** —**myotonic** (ˌmaɪəˈtɒnɪk) *adj.*

myria- *combining form.* indicating a very great number: *myriapod.* [from Greek *murios* countless]

myriad (ˈmɪrɪəd) *adj.* **1.** innumerable. ~*n.* **2.** (*also used in pl.*) a large indefinite number. **3.** *Archaic.* ten thousand. [C16: via Late Latin from Greek *murias* ten thousand]

myriapod (ˈmɪrɪəˌpɒd) *n.* **1.** any terrestrial arthropod of the group *Myriapoda,* having a long segmented body and many walking limbs: includes the centipedes and millipedes. ~*adj.* **2.** of, relating to, or belonging to the *Myriapoda.* [C19: from New Latin *Myriapoda.* See MYRIAD, -POD] —**myriapodan** (ˌmɪrɪˈæpədᵊn) *adj.* —ˌ**myriˈapodous** *adj.*

myrica (mɪˈraɪkə) *n.* the dried root bark of the wax myrtle, used as a tonic and to treat diarrhoea. [C18: via Latin from Greek *murikē* the tamarisk]

myrmeco- *combining form.* ant: *myrmecology; myrmecophile.* [from Greek *murmēx*]

myrmecochory (ˌmɜːmɪkəʊˈkɔːrɪ) *n.* the dispersal of fruits and seeds by ants.

myrmecology (ˌmɜːmɪˈkɒlədʒɪ) *n.* the branch of zoology concerned with the study of ants. —**myrmecological** (ˌmɜːmɪkəˈlɒdʒɪkᵊl) *adj.* —ˌ**myrmeˈcologist** *n.*

myrmecophagous (ˌmɜːmɪˈkɒfəgəs) *adj.* **1.** (of jaws) specialized for feeding on ants. **2.** feeding on ants.

myrmecophile (ˈmɜːmɪkəʊˌfaɪl) *n.* an animal that lives in a colony of ants. —**myrmecophilous** (ˌmɜːmɪˈkɒfɪləs) *adj.*

myrmecophily (ˌmɜːmɪˈkɒfɪlɪ) *n. Biology.* **1.** symbiosis with ants. **2.** pollination of plants by ants.

Myrmidon (ˈmɜːmɪˌdɒn, -dᵊn) *n., pl.* **Myrmidons** *or* **Myrmidones** (mɜːˈmɪdᵊˌniːz). (*often not cap.*) a follower or henchman. [after the *Myrmidons,* a race of people in Greek mythology who were led against Troy by Achilles]

myrobalan (maɪˈrɒbələn, mɪ-) *n.* **1.** the dried plumlike fruit of various tropical trees of the genus *Terminalia,* used in dyeing, tanning, ink, and medicine. **2.** a dye extracted from this fruit. **3.** another name for **cherry plum.** [C16: via Latin from Greek *murobalanos,* from *muron* ointment + *balanos* acorn]

myrrh (mɜː) *n.* **1.** any of several burseraceous trees and shrubs of the African and S Asian genus *Commiphora,* esp. *C. myrrha,* that exude an aromatic resin. Compare **balm of Gilead** (sense 1). **2.** the resin obtained from such a plant, used in perfume, incense, and medicine. **3.** another name for **sweet cicely** (sense 1). [Old English *myrre,* via Latin from Greek *murrha,* ultimately from Akkadian *murrū;* compare Hebrew *mōr,* Arabic *murr*]

myrtaceous (mɜːˈteɪʃəs) *adj.* of, relating to, or belonging to the *Myrtaceae,* a family of mostly tropical and subtropical trees and shrubs having oil glands in the leaves: includes eucalyptus, clove, myrtle, and guava. [C19: via New Latin from Latin *myrtus* myrtle, from Greek *murtos*]

myrtle (ˈmɜːtᵊl) *n.* **1.** any evergreen shrub or tree of the myrtaceous genus *Myrtus,* esp. *M. communis,* a S European shrub with pink or white flowers and aromatic blue-black berries. **2.** short for **crape myrtle.** **3. creeping** *or* **trailing myrtle.** *U.S. and Canadian.* another name for **periwinkle** (the plant). [C16: from Medieval Latin *myrtilla,* from Latin *myrtus,* from Greek *murtos*]

myself (maɪˈsɛlf) *pron.* **1. a.** the reflexive form of *I* or *me.* **b.** (intensifier): *I myself know of no answer.* **2.** (*preceded by a copula*) my usual self: *I'm not myself today.* **3.** *Not standard.* used instead of *I* or *me* in compound noun phrases: *John and myself are voting together.*

▷**Usage.** The use of *myself* for *I* or *me* is often the result of an attempt to be elegant or correct. However, careful users of English only employ *myself* when it follows *I* or *me* in the same clause: *I cut myself,* but *he gave it to me* (not *myself*). The same is true of the other reflexives. This rule does permit constructions such as *he wrote it himself* (unassisted) and *he himself wrote it* (without an intermediary), but these are only to be used to reinforce a previous reference to the same individual.

mystagogue ('mɪstəˌgɒg) *n.* (in Mediterranean mystery religions) a person who instructs those who are preparing for initiation into the mysteries. [C16: via Latin from Greek *mustagōgos,* from *mustēs* candidate for initiation + *agein* to lead. See MYSTIC] —**mystagogic** (ˌmɪstə'gɒdʒɪk) *or* ˌ**mysta'gogical** *adj.* —ˌ**mysta'gogically** *adv.* —**mystagogy** ('mɪstəˌgɒdʒɪ) *n.*

mysterious (mɪ'stɪərɪəs) *adj.* **1.** characterized by or indicative of mystery. **2.** puzzling, curious, or enigmatic. —**mys'teriously** *adv.* —**mys'teriousness** *n.*

mystery[1] ('mɪstərɪ, -trɪ) *n., pl.* **-teries. 1.** an unexplained or inexplicable event, phenomenon, etc. **2.** a person or thing that arouses curiosity or suspense because of an unknown, obscure, or enigmatic quality. **3.** the state or quality of being obscure, inexplicable, or enigmatic. **4.** a story, film, etc., which arouses suspense and curiosity because of facts concealed. **5.** *Christianity.* any truth that is divinely revealed but otherwise unknowable. **6.** *Christianity.* a sacramental rite, such as the Eucharist, or (*when pl.*) the consecrated elements of the Eucharist. **7.** (*often pl.*) any of various rites of certain ancient Mediterranean religions. **8.** *Archaic.* symbolic significance. **9.** short for **mystery play.** [C14: via Latin from Greek *mustērion* secret rites. See MYSTIC]

mystery[2] ('mɪstərɪ) *n., pl.* **-teries.** *Archaic.* **1.** a trade, occupation, or craft. **2.** a guild of craftsmen. [C14: from Medieval Latin *misterium,* from Latin *ministerium* occupation, from *minister* official]

mystery play *n.* (in the Middle Ages) a type of drama based on the life of Christ. Compare **miracle play.**

mystery tour *n.* an excursion to an unspecified destination.

mystic ('mɪstɪk) *n.* **1.** a person who achieves mystical experience or an apprehension of divine mysteries. ~*adj.* **2.** another word for **mystical.** [C14: via Latin from Greek *mustikos,* from *mustēs* mystery initiate; related to *muein* to initiate into sacred rites]

mystical ('mɪstɪkᵊl) *adj.* **1.** relating to or characteristic of mysticism. **2.** *Christianity.* having a divine or sacred significance that surpasses natural human apprehension. **3.** having occult or metaphysical significance, nature, or force. **4.** a less common word for **mysterious.** —'**mystically** *adv.* —'**mysticalness** *n.*

mysticism ('mɪstɪˌsɪzəm) *n.* **1.** belief in or experience of a reality surpassing normal human understanding or experience, esp. a reality perceived as essential to the nature of life. **2.** a system of contemplative prayer and spirituality aimed at achieving direct intuitive experience of the divine. **3.** obscure or confused belief or thought.

mystify ('mɪstɪˌfaɪ) *vb.* **-fies, -fying, -fied.** (*tr.*) **1.** to confuse, bewilder, or puzzle. **2.** to make mysterious or obscure. [C19: from French *mystifier,* from *mystère* MYSTERY[1] or *mystique* MYSTIC] —ˌ**mystifi'cation** *n.* —'**mystiˌfier** *n.* —'**mystiˌfying** *adj.* —'**mystiˌfyingly** *adv.*

mystique (mɪ'stiːk) *n.* an aura of mystery, power, and awe that surrounds a person or thing: *the mystique of the theatre; the mystique of computer programming.* [C20: from French (adj.): MYSTIC]

myth (mɪθ) *n.* **1. a.** a story about superhuman beings of an earlier age taken by preliterate society to be a true account, usually of how natural phenomena, social customs, etc., came into existence. **b.** another word for **mythology** (senses 1, 3). **2.** a person or thing whose existence is fictional or unproven. **3.** (in modern literature) a theme or character type embodying an idea: *Hemingway's myth of the male hero.* **4.** *Philosophy.* (esp. in the writings of Plato) an allegory or parable. [C19: via Late Latin from Greek *muthos* fable, word]

myth. *abbrev. for:* **1.** mythological. **2.** mythology.

mythical ('mɪθɪkᵊl) *or* **mythic** ('mɪθɪk) *adj.* **1.** of or relating to myth. **2.** imaginary or fictitious. —'**mythically** *adv.*

mythicize *or* **mythicise** ('mɪθɪˌsaɪz) *vb.* (*tr.*) to make into or treat as a myth. —ˌ**mythici'zation** *or* ˌ**mythici'sation** *n.* —'**mythicist,** '**mythiˌcizer,** *or* '**mythiˌciser** *n.*

mytho- *combining form.* myth: *mythogenesis; mythography.*

mythological (ˌmɪθə'lɒdʒɪkᵊl) *adj.* **1.** of or relating to mythology. **2.** mythical. —ˌ**mytho'logically** *adv.*

mythologist (mɪ'θɒlədʒɪst) *n.* **1.** an expert in or student of mythology. **2.** a writer or editor of myths.

mythologize *or* **mythologise** (mɪ'θɒləˌdʒaɪz) *vb.* **1.** to tell, study, or explain (myths). **2.** (*intr.*) to create or make up myths. **3.** (*tr.*) to convert into a myth. —**myˌthologi'zation** *or* **myˌthologi'sation** *n.* —**my'thologer, my'tholoˌgizer,** *or* **my'tholoˌgiser** *n.*

mythology (mɪ'θɒlədʒɪ) *n., pl.* **-gies. 1.** a body of myths, esp. one associated with a particular culture, institution, person, etc. **2.** a body of stories about a person, institution, etc.: *the mythology of Hollywood.* **3.** myths collectively. **4.** the study or collecting of myths.

mythomania (ˌmɪθəʊ'meɪnɪə) *n. Psychiatry.* the tendency to lie, exaggerate, or relate incredible imaginary adventures as if they had really happened, occurring in some mental disorders. —**mythomaniac** (ˌmɪθəʊ'meɪnɪˌæk) *n., adj.*

mythopoeia (ˌmɪθəʊ'piːə) *or* **mythopoesis** (ˌmɪθəpəʊ'iːsɪs) *n.* the composition or making of myths. [C19: from Greek, from *muthopoiein,* from *muthos* myth + *poiein* to make]

mythopoeic (ˌmɪθəʊ'piːɪk) *adj.* of or relating to the composition of myths; productive of myths. —ˌ**mytho'poeism** *n.* —ˌ**mytho'poeist** *n.*

mythos ('maɪθɒs, 'mɪθɒs) *n., pl.* **-thoi** (-θɔɪ). **1.** the complex of beliefs, values, attitudes, etc., characteristic of a specific group or society. **2.** another word for **myth** or **mythology.**

myxo ('mɪksəʊ) *n. Austral. slang.* short for **myxomatosis.**

myxo- *or before a vowel* **myx-** *combining form.* mucus or slime: *myxomycete.* [from Greek *muxa* slime, mucus]

myxoedema *or U.S.* **myxedema** (ˌmɪksɪ'diːmə) *n.* a disease resulting from underactivity of the thyroid gland characterized by puffy eyes, face, and hands and mental sluggishness. See also **cretinism.** —**myxoedemic** (ˌmɪksɪ'dɛmɪk), **myxoedematous** (ˌmɪksɪ'dɛmətəs, -'diː-) *or U.S.* ˌ**myxe'demic,** ˌ**myxe'dematous** *adj.*

myxoma (mɪk'səʊmə) *n., pl.* **-mas** *or* **-mata** (-mətə). a tumour composed of mucous connective tissue, usually situated in subcutaneous tissue. —**myxomatous** (mɪk'sɒmətəs) *adj.*

myxomatosis (ˌmɪksəmə'təʊsɪs) *n.* an infectious and usually fatal viral disease of rabbits characterized by swelling of the mucous membranes and formation of skin tumours.

myxomycete (ˌmɪksəʊmaɪ'siːt) *n.* any of a group of organisms having a naked mass of protoplasm and characteristics of both plants and animals: usually classified as fungi. Also called: **mycetozoan, slime mould.** —ˌ**myxomy'cetous** *adj.*

myxovirus ('mɪksəʊˌvaɪərəs) *n.* any of a group of viruses that cause influenza, mumps, and certain other diseases.

mzee (ᵊm'zeɪ) *E African.* ~*n.* **1.** an old person. ~*adj.* **2.** advanced in years. [C19: from Swahili]

mzungu (ᵊm'zʊŋguː) *n. E African.* a White person. [C20: from Swahili]

n *or* **N** (ɛn) *n., pl.* **n's, N's,** *or* **Ns.** **1.** the 14th letter and 11th consonant of the modern English alphabet. **2.** a speech sound represented by this letter, usually an alveolar nasal, as in *nail.*

n[1] *symbol for:* **1.** neutron. **2.** *Optics.* index of refraction. **3.** nano-.

n[2] (ɛn) *determiner.* an indefinite number (of): *there are n objects in a box.*

N *symbol for:* **1.** *Printing.* en. **2.** Also: **kt.** *Chess.* knight. **3.** neper. **4.** neutral. **5.** newton(s). **6.** *Chem.* nitrogen. **7.** North. **8.** Avogadro's number. **9.** noun. ~**10.** *international car registration for* Norway.

n. *abbrev. for:* **1.** natus. [Latin: born] **2.** neuter. **3.** new. **4.** nominative. **5.** noon. **6.** note. **7.** noun. **8.** number.

N. *abbrev. for:* **1.** National(ist). **2.** Navy. **3.** New. **4.** Norse.

n- *prefix. Chem.* short for **normal** (sense 6).

na (nɑː) a variant of **nae.**

Na *the chemical symbol for* sodium. [Latin *natrium*]

NA **1.** *abbrev. for* North America. **2.** *international car registration for* Netherlands Antilles.

n/a *abbrev. for* not applicable.

NAACP (in the U.S.) *abbrev. for* National Association for the Advancement of Colored People.

NAAFI *or* **Naafi** (ˈnæfɪ) *n.* **1.** *acronym for* Navy, Army, and Air Force Institutes: an organization providing canteens, shops, etc., for British military personnel at home or overseas. **2.** a canteen, shop, etc., run by this organization.

naan (nɑːn) *n.* another name for **nan bread.**

naartjie (ˈnɑːtʃɪ) *n. S. African.* a tangerine. [Afrikaans]

nab (næb) *vb.* **nabs, nabbing, nabbed.** (*tr.*) *Informal.* **1.** to arrest. **2.** to catch (someone) in wrongdoing. **3.** to seize suddenly; snatch. [C17: perhaps of Scandinavian origin; compare Danish *nappe,* Swedish *nappa* to snatch. See KIDNAP]

Nabataean *or* **Nabatean** (ˌnæbəˈtiːən) *n.* **1.** a member of an Arab trading people who flourished southeast of Palestine, around the ancient city of Petra, in the Hellenistic and Roman periods. **2.** the extinct form of Aramaic spoken by this people.

nabla (ˈnæblə) *n. Maths.* another name for **del.** [C19: from Greek *nabla,* stringed instrument because it is shaped like a harp]

nabob (ˈneɪbɒb) *n.* **1.** *Informal.* a rich, powerful, or important man. **2.** (formerly) a European who made a fortune in the Orient, esp. in India. **3.** another name for a **nawab.** [C17: from Portuguese *nababo,* from Hindi *nawwāb;* see NAWAB] —**nabobery** (ˈneɪbɒbərɪ, neɪˈbɒbərɪ) *or* ˈ**nabobism** *n.* —ˈ**nabobish** *adj.*

NAC *abbrev. for* National Advisory Council.

nacelle (nəˈsɛl) *n.* a streamlined enclosure on an aircraft, not part of the fuselage, to accommodate an engine, passengers, crew, etc. [C20: from French: small boat, from Late Latin *nāvicella,* a diminutive of Latin *nāvis* ship]

NACODS (ˈneɪkɒdz) *n. acronym for* National Association of Colliery Overmen, Deputies, and Shotfirers.

nacre (ˈneɪkə) *n.* the technical name for **mother-of-pearl.** [C16: via French from Old Italian *naccara,* from Arabic *naqqārah* shell, drum] —ˈ**nacred** *adj.*

nacreous (ˈneɪkrɪəs) *adj.* **1.** relating to or consisting of mother-of-pearl. **2.** having the lustre of mother-of-pearl: *nacreous minerals.*

NACRO *or* **Nacro** (ˈnækrəʊ) *n. acronym for* National Association for the Care and Resettlement of Offenders.

NAD *n. Biochem.* nicotinamide adenine dinucleotide; a coenzyme that is a hydrogen carrier in metabolic reactions, esp. in tissue respiration. Former name: **DPN.**

Na-Dene *or* **Na-Déné** (nɑːˈdeɪnɪ, nəˈdiːn) *n.* a phylum of North American Indian languages including Athapascan, Tlingit, and Haida. [from Haida *na* to dwell + Athapascan *dene* people; coined by Edward Sapir (1884–1939), American anthropologist]

NADH *n. Biochem.* the chemically reduced form of NAD.

nadir (ˈneɪdɪə, ˈnæ-) *n.* **1.** the point on the celestial sphere directly below an observer and diametrically opposite the zenith. **2.** the lowest or deepest point; depths: *the nadir of despair.* [C14: from Old French, from Arabic *nazīr as-samt,* literally: opposite the zenith]

NADP *n. Biochem.* nicotinamide adenine dinucleotide phosphate; a coenzyme with functions similar to those of NAD. Former name: **TPN.**

NADPH *n. Biochem.* the chemically reduced form of NADP.

nae (neɪ) *or* **na** (nɑː) a Scot. word for **no** or **not.**

naevus *or U.S.* **nevus** (ˈniːvəs) *n., pl.* **-vi** (-vaɪ). any congenital growth or pigmented blemish on the skin; birthmark or mole. [C19: from Latin; related to *(g)natus* born, produced by nature] —ˈ**naevoid** *or U.S.* ˈ**nevoid** *adj.*

naff (næf) *adj. Brit. slang.* inferior; in poor taste.

naff off *sentence substitute. Brit. slang.* a forceful expression of dismissal or contempt.

NAFTA (ˈnæftə) *n. acronym for* New Zealand and Australia Free Trade Agreement.

nag[1] (næg) *vb.* **nags, nagging, nagged.** **1.** to scold or annoy constantly. **2.** (when *intr.,* often foll. by *at*) to be a constant source of discomfort or worry (to): *toothache nagged him all day.* ~*n.* **3.** a person, esp. a woman, who nags. [C19: of Scandinavian origin; compare Swedish *nagga* to GNAW, irritate, German *nagen*] —ˈ**nagger** *n.* —ˈ**naggingly** *adv.*

nag[2] (næg) *n.* **1.** *Often derogatory.* a horse. **2.** a small riding horse. [C14: of Germanic origin; related to NEIGH]

Naga (ˈnɑːgə) *n.* **1.** (*pl.* **Nagas** *or* **Naga**) a member of a people of NE India and W Burma: until the early 20th century they practised head-hunting. **2.** the language of this people, belonging to the Sino-Tibetan family of languages and having many dialects.

nagana (nəˈgɑːnə) *n.* a disease of hoofed animals of central and southern Africa, that is caused by parasitic protozoa of the genus *Trypanosoma* and is transmitted by tsetse flies. [from Zulu *u-nakane*]

Nagari (ˈnɑːgərɪ) *n.* **1.** a set of scripts, including Devanagari, used as the writing systems for several languages of India. **2.** another word for **Devanagari.**

nagor (ˈneɪgɔː) *n.* another name for **reedbuck.** [C18: from French, arbitrarily named, from earlier *nanguer*]

Nah. *Bible. abbrev. for* Nahum.

nahal (nəˈhɑːl) *n.* (in Israel) an agricultural settlement, esp. in a border area, set up or manned by members of Nahal, a military youth organization. [C20: from *Nahal,* Hebrew acronym for *No'ar Halutzi Lohem* Pioneer and Military Youth]

NAHT (in Britain) *abbrev. for* National Association of Head Teachers.

Nahuatl (ˈnɑːwɑːtᵊl, nɑːˈwɑːtᵊl) *n.* **1.** (*pl.* **-tl** *or* **-tls**) a member of one of a group of Central American and Mexican Indian peoples including the Aztecs. **2.** the language of these peoples, belonging to the Uto-Aztecan family. ~Also: **Naˈhuatlan.**

NAI (in Britain) *abbrev. for* nonaccidental injury.

naiad (ˈnaɪæd) *n., pl.* **-ads** *or* **-ades** (-əˌdiːz). **1.** *Greek myth.* a nymph dwelling in a lake, river, spring, or fountain. **2.** the aquatic larva of the dragonfly, mayfly, and related insects. **3.** Also called: **water nymph.** any monocotyledonous submerged aquatic plant of the genus *Naias* (or *Najas*), having narrow leaves and small flowers: family *Naiadaceae* (or *Najadaceae*). **4.** any of certain freshwater mussels of the genus *Unio.* See **mussel** (sense 2). [C17: via Latin from Greek *nāias* water nymph; related to *náein* to flow]

naïf (nɑːˈiːf) *adj., n.* a less common word for **naive.**

nail (neɪl) *n.* **1.** a fastening device usually made from round or oval wire, having a point at one end and a head at the other. **2.** anything resembling such a fastening device, esp. in function or shape. **3.** the horny plate covering part of the dorsal surface of the fingers or toes. See **fingernail, toenail.** Related adjs.: **ungual, ungular.** **4.** the claw of a mammal, bird, or reptile. **5.** *Slang.* a hypodermic needle, used for injecting drugs. **6.** a unit of length, formerly used for measuring cloth, equal to two and a quarter inches. **7. a nail in one's coffin.** an experience or event that tends to shorten life or hasten the end of something. **8. bite one's nails. a.** to chew off the ends of one's fingernails. **b.** to be worried or apprehensive. **9. hard as nails. a.** in tough physical condition. **b.** without sentiment or feelings. **10. hit the nail on the head.** to do or say something correct or telling. **11. on the nail.** (of payments) at once; on the spot (esp. in the phrase **pay on the nail**). ~*vb.* (*tr.*) **12.** to attach with or as if with nails. **13.** *Informal.* to arrest, catch, or seize. **14.** *Informal.* to hit or bring down, as with a shot: *I nailed the sniper.* **15.** *Informal.* to expose or detect (a lie or liar). **16.** to fix or focus (one's eyes, attention, etc.) on an object. **17.** to stud with nails. ~See also **nail down, nail up.** [Old English *nægl;* related to Old High German *nagal* nail, Latin *unguis* fingernail, claw, Greek *onux*] —ˈ**nailer** *n.* —ˈ**nail-less** *adj.*

nail-biting *n.* **1.** the act or habit of biting one's fingernails. **2. a.** anxiety or tension. **b.** (*as modifier*): *nail-biting suspense.*

nail bomb *n.* an explosive device containing nails, used by terrorists to cause serious injuries in crowded situations.

nailbrush (ˈneɪlˌbrʌʃ) *n.* a small stiff-bristled brush for cleaning the fingernails.

nail down *vb.* (*tr., adv.*) **1.** to fasten down with or as if with nails. **2.** *Informal.* to extort a definite promise or consent from: *I nailed him down on the deadline.* **3.** *Informal.* to settle in a definite way: *they nailed down the agreement.*

nailfile (ˈneɪlˌfaɪl) *n.* a small file, chiefly either of metal or of board coated with emery, used to trim the nails.

nailhead (ˈneɪlˌhɛd) *n.* a decorative device, as on tooled leather, resembling the round head of a nail.

nail polish *or* **varnish** *or esp. U.S.* **enamel** *n.* a quick-drying cosmetic lacquer applied to colour the nails or make them shiny or esp. both.
nail set *or* **punch** *n.* a punch for driving the head of a nail below or flush with the surrounding surface.
nail up *vb.* (*tr., adv.*) to shut in or fasten tightly with or as if with nails.
nainsook ('neɪnsʊk, 'næn-) *n.* a light soft plain-weave cotton fabric, used esp. for babies' wear. [C19: from Hindi *nainsukh,* literally: delight to the eye, from *nain* eye + *sukh* delight, from Sanskrit *sukha*]
naira ('naɪrə) *n.* the standard monetary unit of Nigeria. [C20: altered from *Nigeria*]
NAI register *n. Social welfare.* (in Britain) a list of children deemed to be at risk of abuse or injury from their parents or guardians, compiled and held by a local authority, area health authority, or NSPCC Special Unit. Also called: **child abuse register.**
Naismith's rule ('neɪsmɪθs) *n. Mountaineering.* a rule of thumb for calculating the time needed for a climbing expedition, allowing 1 hour for every 3 miles of distance plus 1 hour for every 2000 feet of height. [C19: named after W. W. *Naismith* (1856–1935), Scottish climber, who formulated it]
naissant ('neɪsᵊnt) *adj. Heraldry.* (of a beast) having only the forepart shown above a horizontal division of a shield. [C16: from Old French, literally: being born. See NASCENT]
naive, naïve (nɑː'iːv, naɪ'iːv), *or* **naïf** *adj.* **1. a.** having or expressing innocence and credulity; ingenuous. **b.** (*as collective n.; preceded by the*): *only the naive believed him.* **2.** artless or unsophisticated. **3.** lacking developed powers of analysis, reasoning, or criticism: *a naive argument.* **4.** another word for **primitive** (sense 5). ~*n.* **5.** *Rare.* a person who is naive, esp. in artistic style. See **primitive** (sense 10). [C17: from French, feminine of *naïf,* from Old French *naif* native, spontaneous, from Latin *nātīvus* NATIVE, from *nasci* to be born] —**na'ively, na'ïvely,** *or* **na'ïfly** *adv.* —**na'iveness, na'ïveness,** *or* **na'ïfness** *n.*
naive realism *n. Philosophy.* the doctrine that in perception of physical objects what is before the mind is the object itself and not a representation of it. Compare **representationalism** (sense 1).
naivety (naɪ'iːvtɪ), **naiveté,** *or* **naïveté** (ˌnɑːiːv'teɪ) *n., pl.* **-ties** *or* **-tés. 1.** the state or quality of being naive; ingenuousness; simplicity. **2.** a naive act or statement.
naked ('neɪkɪd) *adj.* **1.** having the body completely unclothed; undressed. Compare **bare. 2.** having no covering; bare; exposed: *a naked flame.* **3.** with no qualification or concealment; stark; plain: *the naked facts.* **4.** unaided by any optical instrument, such as a telescope or microscope (esp. in the phrase **the naked eye**). **5.** with no defence, protection, or shield. **6.** (usually foll. by *of*) stripped or destitute: *naked of weapons.* **7.** (of the seeds of gymnosperms) not enclosed in a pericarp. **8.** (of flowers) lacking a perianth. **9.** (of stems) lacking leaves and other appendages. **10.** (of animals) lacking hair, feathers, scales, etc. **11.** *Law.* **a.** unsupported by authority or financial or other consideration: *a naked contract.* **b.** lacking some essential condition to render valid; incomplete. [Old English *nacod;* related to Old High German *nackot* (German *nackt*), Old Norse *nokr,* Latin *nudus*] —'**nakedly** *adv.* —'**nakedness** *n.*
naked ladies *n.* (*functioning as sing.*) another name for **autumn crocus.**
naked lady *n.* a leafless pink orchid found in Australia and New Zealand.
naked singularity *n. Astronomy.* a hypothetical location at which there would be a discontinuity in the space-time continuum as a result of the gravitational collapse of a spherical mass. See also **black hole.**
naker ('neɪkə, 'næk-) *n.* one of a pair of small kettledrums used in medieval music. [C14: from Old French *nacre,* via Medieval Greek *anakara,* from Arabic *naqāra*]
NALGO ('nælgəʊ) *n.* (in Britain) *acronym for* National and Local Government Officers' Association.
naloxone (nə'lɒksəʊn) *n.* a chemical substance that counteracts the effects of opiates by binding to opiate receptors on cells. [C20: from *N-al(lylnor)ox(ymorph)one,* the chemical name]
Nama ('nɑːmə) *or* **Namaqua** (nə'mɑːkwə) *n.* **1.** (*pl.* **-ma, -mas** *or* **-qua, -quas**) a member of a Hottentot people living chiefly in Namaqualand, a coastal region of SW Africa. **2.** the Hottentot language spoken by this people, belonging to the Khoisan family. See also **Damara.** —'**Naman** *or* **Na'maquan** *n., adj.*
namas kar (nə'mʌs kɑː) *n.* a salutation used in India. [Sanskrit, from *namas* salutation, bow + *kara* doing]
namby-pamby (ˌnæmbɪ'pæmbɪ) *adj.* **1.** sentimental or prim in a weak insipid way: *namby-pamby manners.* **2.** clinging, feeble, or spineless: *a namby-pamby child.* ~*n., pl.* **-bies. 3.** a person who is namby-pamby. [C18: a nickname of Ambrose Phillips (died 1749), whose pastoral verse was ridiculed for being insipid]
name (neɪm) *n.* **1.** a word or term by which a person or thing is commonly and distinctively known. Related adj.: **nominal. 2.** mere outward appearance or form as opposed to fact (esp. in the phrase **in name**): *he was a ruler in name only.* **3.** a word, title, or phrase descriptive of character, usually abusive or derogatory: *to call a person names.* **4.** reputation, esp., if unspecified, good reputation: *he's made quite a name for himself.* **5. a.** a famous person or thing: *a name in the advertising world.* **b.** *Chiefly U.S. and Canadian.* (*as modifier*): *a name product.* **6. in** *or* **under the name of.** using as a name. **7. in the name of. a.** for the sake of. **b.** by the sanction or authority of. **8. know by name.** to have heard of without having met. **9. name of the game. a.** anything that is essential, significant, or important. **b.** expected or normal conditions, circumstances, etc.: *in gambling, losing money's the name of the game.* **10. to one's name.** belonging to one: *I haven't a penny to my name.* ~*vb.* (*tr.*) **11.** to give a name to; call by a name: *she named the child Edward.* **12.** to refer to by name; cite: *he named three French poets.* **13.** to determine, fix, or specify: *they have named a date for the meeting.* **14.** to appoint to or cite for a particular title, honour, or duty; nominate: *he was named Journalist of the Year.* **15.** to ban (an MP) from the House of Commons by mentioning him formally by name as being guilty of disorderly conduct. **16. name names.** to cite people, esp. in order to blame or accuse them. **17. name the day.** to choose the day for one's wedding. **18. you name it.** whatever you need, mention, etc. [Old English *nama,* related to Latin *nomen,* Greek *noma,* Old High German *namo,* German *namen*] —'**namable** *or* '**nameable** *adj.*
name-calling *n.* verbal abuse, esp. as a crude form of argument.
name day *n.* **1.** *R.C. Church.* the feast day of a saint whose name one bears. **2.** another name for **ticket day.**
name-dropping *n. Informal.* the practice of referring frequently to famous or fashionable people, esp. as though they were intimate friends, in order to impress others. —'**name-ˌdropper** *n.*
nameless ('neɪmlɪs) *adj.* **1.** without a name; anonymous. **2.** incapable of being named; indescribable: *a nameless horror seized him.* **3.** too unpleasant or disturbing to be mentioned: *nameless atrocities.* **4.** having no legal name; illegitimate: *a nameless child.* —'**namelessly** *adv.* —'**namelessness** *n.*
namely ('neɪmlɪ) *adv.* that is to say: *it was another colour, namely green.*
name part *n.* another name for **title role.**
nameplate ('neɪmˌpleɪt) *n.* a small panel on or next to the door of a room or building, bearing the occupant's name and profession.
namesake ('neɪmˌseɪk) *n.* **1.** a person or thing named after another. **2.** a person or thing with the same name as another. [C17: probably a shortening of the phrase describing people connected *for the name's sake*]
nametape ('neɪmˌteɪp) *n.* a narrow cloth tape attached to articles bearing the owner's name.
Namibian (nɑː'mɪbɪən, nə-) *adj.* **1.** of or relating to Namibia, a country in southern Africa bordering on South Africa. ~*n.* **2.** a native or inhabitant of Namibia.
namma hole ('næmə) *n. Austral.* a natural well in a rock. [C19: from a native Australian language]
nan (næn), **nana,** *or* **nanna** ('nænə) *n.* a child's words for **grandmother.** [see NANNY; compare Greek *nanna* aunt, Medieval Latin *nonna* old woman]
nana ('nɑːnə) *n. Austral. slang.* **1.** the head. **2. do one's nana.** to become very angry. **3. off one's nana.** mad; insane. [C19: probably from BANANA]
nan bread *or* **naan** (nɑːn) *n.* (in Indian cookery) a slightly leavened bread in a large flat leaf shape. [from Hindi]
nancy ('nænsɪ) *n., pl.* **-cies. a.** an effeminate or homosexual boy or man. **b.** (*as modifier*): *his nancy ways.* ~Also called: **nancy boy.** [C20: from the girl's name *Nancy*]
NAND circuit *or* **gate** (nænd) *n. Electronics.* a computer logic circuit having two or more input wires and one output wire that has an output signal if one or more of the input signals are at a low voltage. Compare **OR circuit.** [C20: from *not* + AND; see NOT CIRCUIT, AND CIRCUIT]
nane (nen) *pron.* a Scot. word for **none**[1].
nankeen (næŋ'kiːn) *or* **nankin** ('nænkɪn) *n.* **1.** a hard-wearing buff-coloured cotton fabric. **2. a.** a pale greyish-yellow colour. **b.** (*as adj.*): *a nankeen carpet.* [C18: named after *Nanking,* China, where it originated]
nanny ('nænɪ) *n., pl.* **-nies. 1.** a nurse or nursemaid for children. **2. a.** any person or thing regarded as treating people like children, esp. by being patronizing or overprotective. **b.** (*as modifier*): *the nanny state.* **3.** a child's word for **grandmother.** ~*vb.* **nannies, nannying, nannied. 4.** (*intr.*) to nurse or look after someone else's children. **5.** (*tr.*) to be overprotective towards. [C19: child's name for a nurse]
nannygai ('nænɪˌgaɪ) *n., pl.* **-gais.** an edible sea fish, *Centroberyx affinis,* of Australia which is red in colour and has large prominent eyes. Also called: **red fish.** [C19: from a native Australian language]
nanny goat *n.* a female goat. Compare **billy goat.**
nano- *combining form.* **1.** denoting 10^{-9}: *nanosecond.* Symbol: n **2.** indicating extreme smallness: *nanoplankton.* [from Latin *nānus* dwarf, from Greek *nanos*]
nanometre ('nænəʊˌmiːtə) *n.* one thousand-millionth of a metre. Symbol: nm
nanook ('nænuːk) *n. N Canadian.* the polar bear. [from Eskimo *nanug*]
nanoplankton *or* **nannoplankton** ('nænəʊˌplæŋktən) *n.* microscopic organisms in plankton.

nanosecond (ˈnænəʊˌsɛkənd) *n.* one thousand-millionth of a second. Symbol: ns

Nansen bottle (ˈnænsən) *n.* an instrument used by oceanographers for obtaining samples of sea water from a desired depth. [C19: named after Fridtjof *Nansen* (1861–1930), Norwegian arctic explorer, statesman, and scientist]

Nansen passport *n.* a passport issued to stateless persons by the League of Nations after World War I.

naos (ˈneɪɒs) *n., pl.* **naoi** (ˈneɪɔɪ). **1.** *Rare.* an ancient classical temple. **2.** *Architect.* another name for **cella.** [C18: from Greek: inner part of temple]

nap[1] (næp) *vb.* **naps, napping, napped.** (*intr.*) **1.** to sleep for a short while; doze. **2.** to be unaware or inattentive; be off guard (esp. in the phrase **catch someone napping**). ~*n.* **3.** a short light sleep; doze. [Old English *hnappian;* related to Middle High German *napfen*]

nap[2] (næp) *n.* **1. a.** the raised fibres of velvet or similar cloth. **b.** the direction in which these fibres lie when smoothed down. **2.** any similar downy coating. **3.** *Austral. informal.* blankets, bedding. ~*vb.* **naps, napping, napped. 4.** (*tr.*) to raise the nap of (cloth, esp. velvet) by brushing or similar treatment. [C15: probably from Middle Dutch *noppe;* related to Old English *hnoppian* to pluck]

nap[3] (næp) *n.* **1.** Also called: **napoleon.** a card game similar to whist, usually played for stakes. **2.** a call in this card game, undertaking to win all five tricks. **3.** *Horse racing.* a tipster's choice for an almost certain winner. **4. go nap. a.** to undertake to win all five tricks at nap. **b.** to risk everything on one chance. **5. not to go nap on.** *Austral. slang.* to hold in disfavour. **6. nap hand.** a position in which there is a very good chance of success if a risk is taken. ~*vb.* **naps, napping, napped.** (*tr.*) **7.** *Horse racing.* to name (a horse) as likely to win a race. [C19: short for NAPOLEON, the original name of the card game]

napalm (ˈneɪpɑːm, ˈnæ-) *n.* **1.** a thick and highly incendiary liquid, usually consisting of petrol gelled with aluminium soaps, used in firebombs, flame-throwers, etc. ~*vb.* **2.** (*tr.*) to attack with napalm. [C20: from NA(PHTHENE) + PALM(ITATE)]

nape (neɪp) *n.* the back of the neck. [C13: of unknown origin]

napery (ˈneɪpərɪ) *n. Rare.* household linen, esp. table linen. [C14: from Old French *naperie,* from *nape* tablecloth, from Latin *mappa.* See NAPKIN]

naphtha (ˈnæfθə, ˈnæp-) *n.* **1.** a distillation product from coal tar boiling in the approximate range 80–170°C and containing aromatic hydrocarbons. **2.** a distillation product from petroleum boiling in the approximate range 100–200°C and containing aliphatic hydrocarbons: used as a solvent and in petrol. **3.** an obsolete name for **petroleum.** [C16: via Latin from Greek, of Iranian origin; related to Persian *neft* naphtha]

naphthalene, naphthaline (ˈnæfθəˌliːn, ˈnæp-), *or* **naphthalin** (ˈnæfθəlɪn, ˈnæp-) *n.* a white crystalline volatile solid with a characteristic penetrating odour: an aromatic hydrocarbon used in mothballs and in the manufacture of dyes, explosives, etc. Formula: $C_{10}H_8$. [C19: from NAPHTHA + ALCOHOL + -ENE] —**naphthalic** (næfˈθælɪk, næp-) *adj.*

naphthene (ˈnæfθiːn, ˈnæp-) *n.* any of a class of cycloalkanes, mainly derivatives of cyclopentane, found in petroleum. [C20: from NAPHTHA + -ENE]

naphthol (ˈnæfθɒl, ˈnæp-) *n.* a white crystalline solid that has two isomeric forms, **alpha-naphthol,** used in dyes, and **beta-naphthol,** used in dyes and as an antioxidant. Formula: $C_{10}H_7OH$. [C19: from NAPHTHA + -OL[1]]

naphthyl (ˈnæfθaɪl, -θɪl, ˈnæp-) *n.* (*modifier*) of, consisting of, or containing either of two forms of the monovalent group $C_{10}H_7$–. [C19: from NAPHTHA + -YL]

Napierian logarithm (nəˈpɪərɪən, neɪ-) *n.* another name for **natural logarithm.** [named after John *Napier* (1550–1617), Scottish mathematician who invented logarithms]

Napier's bones (ˈneɪpɪəz) *pl. n.* a set of graduated rods formerly used for multiplication and division. [C17: based on a method invented by John *Napier*]

napiform (ˈneɪpɪˌfɔːm) *adj. Botany.* shaped like a turnip. [C19: from Latin *nāpus* turnip]

napkin (ˈnæpkɪn) *n.* **1.** Also called: **table napkin.** a usually square piece of cloth or paper used while eating to protect the clothes, wipe the mouth, etc.; serviette. **2.** *Rare.* a similar piece of cloth used for example as a handkerchief or headscarf. **3.** a more formal name for **nappy**[1]. **4.** a less common term for **sanitary towel.** [C15: from Old French, from *nape* tablecloth, from Latin *mappa* small cloth, towel; see MAP]

Naples yellow (ˈneɪpᵊlz) *n.* **1.** a yellow pigment, used by artists; lead antimonate. **2.** a similar pigment consisting of a mixture of zinc oxide with yellow colouring matter. **3.** the colour of either of these pigments. [named after *Naples,* a port in SW Italy]

napoleon (nəˈpəʊlɪən) *n.* **1.** a former French gold coin worth 20 francs bearing a portrait of either Napoleon I or Napoleon III. **2.** *Cards.* the full name for **nap**[3] (sense 1). **3.** the U.S. name for ***millefeuille.*** [C19: from French *napoléon,* after *Napoleon* Bonaparte (1769–1821)]

Napoleonic (nəˌpəʊlɪˈɒnɪk) *adj.* relating to or characteristic of Napoleon Bonaparte (1769–1821), Emperor of the French (1804–15), or his era.

Napoleonic Code *n.* the English name for the ***Code Napoléon.***

nappa (ˈnæpə) *n.* a soft leather, used in gloves and clothes, made from sheepskin, lambskin, or kid. [C19: named after *Napa,* California, where it was originally made]

nappe (næp) *n.* **1.** a large sheet or mass of rock, originally a recumbent fold, that has been thrust from its original position by earth movements. **2.** the sheet of water that flows over a dam or weir. **3.** *Geometry.* either of the two parts into which a cone (sense 2) is divided by the vertex. [C20: from French: tablecloth]

napper[1] (ˈnæpə) *n.* a person or thing that raises the nap on cloth.

napper[2] (ˈnæpə) *n. Brit.* a slang or dialect word for **head** (sense 1). [C18: from NAP[1]]

nappy[1] (ˈnæpɪ) *n., pl.* **-pies.** *Brit.* a piece of soft material, esp. towelling or a disposable material, wrapped around a baby in order to absorb its excrement. Also called: **napkin.** U.S. and Canadian name: **diaper.** [C20: changed from NAPKIN]

nappy[2] (ˈnæpɪ) *adj.* **-pier, -piest. 1.** having a nap; downy; fuzzy. **2.** (of alcoholic drink, esp. beer) **a.** having a head; frothy. **b.** strong or heady. **3.** *Dialect, chiefly Brit.* slightly intoxicated; tipsy. **4.** (of a horse) jumpy or irritable; nervy. ~*n.* **5.** any strong alcoholic drink, esp. heady beer. —ˈ**nappiness** *n.*

nappy rash *n. Brit.* (in babies) any irritation to the skin around the genitals, anus, or buttocks, usually caused by contact with urine or excrement. Formal name: **napkin rash.** U.S. and Canadian name: **diaper rash.**

narc (nɑːk) *n. U.S. slang.* a narcotics agent.

narceine *or* **narceen** (ˈnɑːsiːn) *n.* a narcotic alkaloid that occurs in opium. Formula: $C_{23}H_{27}O_8N$. [C19: via French from Greek *narkē* numbness]

narcissism (ˈnɑːsɪˌsɪzəm) *or* **narcism** (ˈnɑːˌsɪzəm) *n.* **1.** an exceptional interest in or admiration for oneself, esp. one's physical appearance. **2.** sexual satisfaction derived from contemplation of one's own physical or mental endowments. [C19: from *Narcissus,* a beautiful youth in Greek mythology who fell in love with his reflection in a pool] —ˈ**narcissist** *n.* —ˌ**narcisˈsistic** *adj.*

narcissus (nɑːˈsɪsəs) *n., pl.* **-cissuses** *or* **-cissi** (-ˈsɪsaɪ, -ˈsɪsiː). any amaryllidaceous plant of the Eurasian genus *Narcissus,* esp. *N. poeticus,* whose yellow, orange, or white flowers have a crown surrounded by spreading segments. [C16: via Latin from Greek *nárkissos,* perhaps from *narkē* numbness, because of narcotic properties attributed to species of the plant]

narco- *or sometimes before a vowel* **narc-** *combining form.* **1.** indicating numbness or torpor: *narcolepsy.* **2.** connected with or derived from illicit drug production: *narcoeconomies.* [from Greek *narkē* numbness]

narcoanalysis (ˌnɑːkəʊəˈnælɪsɪs) *n.* psychoanalysis of a patient in a trance induced by a narcotic drug.

narcolepsy (ˈnɑːkəˌlɛpsɪ) *n. Pathol.* a rare condition characterized by sudden and uncontrollable episodes of deep sleep. —ˌ**narcoˈleptic** *adj.*

narcosis (nɑːˈkəʊsɪs) *n.* unconsciousness induced by narcotics or general anaesthetics.

narcotic (nɑːˈkɒtɪk) *n.* **1.** any of a group of drugs, such as opium and morphine, that produce numbness and stupor. They are used medicinally to relieve pain but are sometimes also taken for their pleasant effects; prolonged use may cause addiction. **2.** anything that relieves pain or induces sleep, mental numbness, etc. **3.** any illegal drug. ~*adj.* **4.** of, relating to, or designating narcotics. **5.** of or relating to narcotics addicts or users. **6.** of or relating to narcosis. [C14: via Medieval Latin from Greek *narkōtikós,* from *narkoūn* to render numb, from *narkē* numbness] —**narˈcotically** *adv.*

narcotism (ˈnɑːkəˌtɪzəm) *n.* stupor or addiction induced by narcotic drugs.

narcotize *or* **narcotise** (ˈnɑːkəˌtaɪz) *vb.* (*tr.*) to place under the influence of a narcotic drug. —ˌ**narcotiˈzation** *or* ˌ**narcotiˈsation** *n.*

nard (nɑːd) *n.* **1.** another name for **spikenard** (senses 1, 2). **2.** any of several plants, such as certain valerians, whose aromatic roots were formerly used in medicine. [C14: via Latin from Greek *nárdos,* perhaps ultimately from Sanskrit *nalada* Indian spikenard, perhaps via Semitic (Hebrew *nērd,* Arabic *nārdīn*)]

nardoo (ˈnɑːduː) *n.* **1.** any of certain cloverlike ferns of the genus *Marsilea,* which grow in swampy areas. **2.** the spores of such a plant, used as food in Australia. [C19: from a native Australian language]

nares (ˈnɛəriːz) *pl. n., sing.* **naris** (ˈnɛərɪs). *Anatomy.* the nostrils. [C17: from Latin; related to Old English *nasu,* Latin *nāsus* nose]

narghile, nargile, *or* **nargileh** (ˈnɑːgɪlɪ, -ˌleɪ) *n.* another name for **hookah.** [C19: from French *narguilé,* from Persian *nārgīleh* a pipe having a bowl made of coconut shell, from *nārgīl* coconut]

narial (ˈnɛərɪəl) *or* **narine** (ˈnɛərɪn, -raɪn) *adj. Anatomy.* of or relating to the nares. [C19: from Latin *nāris* nostril]

nark (nɑːk) *Slang.* ~*n.* **1.** *Brit., Austral., and N.Z.* an informer or spy, esp. one working for the police (**copper's nark**). **2.** *Brit.* a person who complains irritatingly: *an old nark.* **3.** *Austral. and N.Z.* a spoilsport. ~*vb.* **4.** *Brit., Austral., and N.Z.* to annoy, upset, or irritate: *he was narked by her indifference.* **5.** (*intr.*) *Brit., Austral., and N.Z.* to inform or spy, esp. for the police. **6.** (*intr.*) *Brit.* to complain irritatingly. **7. nark at (someone).** *N.Z.* to nag (someone). **8. nark it.** *Brit.* stop it! [C19: probably from Romany *nāk* nose]

narky ('nɑːkɪ) *adj.* **narkier, narkiest.** *Slang.* irritable, complaining, or sarcastic.

Narraganset or **Narragansett** (ˌnærə'gænsɪt) *n.* **1.** (*pl.* **-set, -sets** or **-sett, -setts**) a member of a North American Indian people formerly living in Rhode Island in the northeastern U.S. **2.** the language of this people, belonging to the Algonquian family.

narrate (nə'reɪt) *vb.* **1.** to tell (a story); relate. **2.** to speak in accompaniment of (a film, television programme, etc.). [C17: from Latin *narrāre* to recount, from *gnārus* knowing] —**nar'ratable** *adj.* —**nar'rator** *n.*

narration (nə'reɪʃən) *n.* **1.** the act or process of narrating. **2.** a narrated account or story; narrative. **3.** (in traditional rhetoric) the third step in making a speech, the putting forward of the question.

narrative ('nærətɪv) *n.* **1.** an account, report, or story, as of events, experiences, etc. **2.** (sometimes preceded by *the*) the part of a literary work that relates events. **3.** the process or technique of narrating. ~*adj.* **4.** telling a story: *a narrative poem.* **5.** of or relating to narration: *narrative art.* —'**narratively** *adv.*

narrow ('nærəʊ) *adj.* **1.** small in breadth, esp. in comparison to length. **2.** limited in range or extent. **3.** limited in outlook; lacking breadth of vision. **4.** limited in means or resources; meagre: *narrow resources.* **5.** barely adequate or successful (esp. in the phrase **a narrow escape**). **6.** painstakingly thorough; minute: *a narrow scrutiny.* **7.** *Finance.* denoting an assessment of liquidity as including notes and coin in circulation with the public, banks' till money, and banks' balances: *narrow money.* Compare **broad** (sense 14). **8.** *Dialect.* overcareful with money; parsimonious. **9.** *Phonetics.* **a.** another word for **tense**[1] (sense 4). **b.** relating to or denoting a transcription used to represent phonetic rather than phonemic distinctions. **c.** another word for **close**[1] (sense 21). **10.** (of agricultural feeds) especially rich in protein. **11. narrow squeak.** *Informal.* an escape only just managed. ~*vb.* **12.** to make or become narrow; limit; restrict. ~*n.* **13.** a narrow place, esp. a pass or strait. ~See also **narrows.** [Old English *nearu;* related to Old Saxon *naru*] —'**narrowly** *adv.* —'**narrowness** *n.*

narrow boat *n.* a long narrow bargelike boat with a beam of 2.1 metres (7 feet) or less, used on canals.

narrowcast ('nærəʊˌkɑːst) *vb.* **-casts, -casting, -cast** or **-casted.** **1.** (*tr.*) to supply (television programmes) to a small area by cable television. **2.** (*intr.*) (of programmers or advertisers) to target a specialized audience on radio or television. ~Compare **broadcast.** —'**narrowˌcasting** *n.*

narrow gauge *n.* **1.** a railway track with a smaller distance between the lines than the standard gauge of 56½ inches. ~*adj.* **narrow-gauge** or **narrow-gauged.** **2.** of, relating to, or denoting a railway with a narrow gauge.

narrow-minded *adj.* having a biased or illiberal viewpoint; bigoted, intolerant, or prejudiced. —ˌ**narrow-'mindedly** *adv.* —ˌ**narrow-'mindedness** *n.*

narrows ('nærəʊz) *pl. n.* a narrow part of a strait, river, current, etc.

narrow seas *pl. n.* the channels between Great Britain and the Continent and Great Britain and Ireland.

narthex ('nɑːθɛks) *n.* **1.** a portico at the west end of a basilica or church, esp. one that is at right angles to the nave. **2.** a rectangular entrance hall between the porch and nave of a church. [C17: via Latin from Medieval Greek: enclosed porch, enclosure (earlier: box), from Greek *narthēx* giant fennel, the stems of which were used to make boxes]

narwhal, narwal ('nɑːwəl), or **narwhale** ('nɑːˌweɪl) *n.* an arctic toothed whale, *Monodon monoceros,* having a black-spotted whitish skin and, in the male, a long spiral tusk: family *Monodontidae.* [C17: of Scandinavian origin; compare Danish, Norwegian *narhval,* from Old Norse *nāhvalr,* from *nār* corpse + *hvalr* whale, from its white colour, supposed to resemble a human corpse]

nary ('nɛərɪ) *adv. Dialect.* not; never: *nary a man was left.* [C19: variant of *ne'er a* never a]

NASA ('næsə) *n.* (in the U.S.) *acronym for* National Aeronautics and Space Administration.

nasal ('neɪzᵊl) *adj.* **1.** of or relating to the nose. **2.** *Phonetics.* pronounced with the soft palate lowered allowing air to escape via the nasal cavity instead of or as well as through the mouth. ~*n.* **3.** a nasal speech sound, such as English *m, n,* or *ng.* **4.** another word for **nosepiece** (sense 1). [C17: from French from Late Latin *nāsālis,* from Latin *nāsus* nose] —**nasality** (neɪ'zælɪtɪ) *n.* —'**nasally** *adv.*

nasal index *n.* the ratio of the widest part of the nose to its length multiplied by 100.

nasalize or **nasalise** ('neɪzəˌlaɪz) *vb.* (*tr.*) to pronounce nasally. —ˌ**nasali'zation** or ˌ**nasali'sation** *n.*

nascent ('næsᵊnt, 'neɪ-) *adj.* **1.** starting to grow or develop; being born. **2.** *Chem.* (of an element or simple compound, esp. hydrogen) created within the reaction medium in the atomic form and having a high activity. [C17: from Latin *nascēns* present participle of *nāscī* to be born] —'**nascence** or '**nascency** *n.*

naseberry ('neɪzˌbɛrɪ) *n., pl.* **-berries.** another name for **sapodilla.** [C17: from Spanish *néspera* medlar + BERRY]

nashi ('næʃɪ) *n., pl.* **nashi** or **nashis.** another name for **Asian pear.** [Japanese: pear]

Nasho ('næʃəʊ) *n. Obsolete Austral. slang.* **1.** compulsory military training; conscription. **2.** (*pl.* **Nashos**) a conscript. [C20: shortening and alteration of *national service*]

nasi goreng ('nɑːsɪ gə'rɛŋ) *n.* a dish, originating in Malaysia, consisting of rice fried with a selection of other ingredients. [C20: from Malay *nasi* (cooked) rice + *goreng* fry]

nasion ('neɪzɪən) *n.* a craniometric point where the top of the nose meets the ridge of the forehead. [C20: New Latin, from Latin *nāsus* nose] —'**nasial** *adj.*

naso- *combining form.* nose: *nasopharynx.* [from Latin *nāsus* nose]

nasofrontal (ˌneɪzəʊ'frʌntᵊl) *adj. Anatomy.* of or relating to the nasal and frontal bones.

nasogastric (ˌneɪzəʊ'gæstrɪk) *adj. Anatomy.* of or relating to the nose and stomach: *a nasogastric tube.*

nasopharynx (ˌneɪzəʊ'færɪŋks) *n., pl.* **-pharynges** (-fə'rɪndʒiːz) or **-pharynxes.** the part of the pharynx situated above and behind the soft palate. —**nasopharyngeal** (ˌneɪzəʊfə'rɪndʒɪəl, -ˌfærɪn'dʒɪəl) *adj.*

nastic movement ('næstɪk) *n.* a response of plant parts that is independent of the direction of the external stimulus, such as the opening of buds caused by an alteration in light intensity. [C19 *nastic,* from Greek *nastos* close-packed, from *nassein* to press down]

nasturtium (nə'stɜːʃəm) *n.* any of various plants of the genus *Tropaeolum,* esp. *T. major,* having round leaves and yellow, red, or orange trumpet-shaped spurred flowers: family *Tropaeolaceae.* [C17: from Latin: kind of cress, from *nāsus* nose + *tortus* twisted, from *torquēre* to twist, distort; so called because the pungent smell causes one to wrinkle one's nose]

nasty ('nɑːstɪ) *adj.* **-tier, -tiest.** **1.** unpleasant, offensive, or repugnant. **2.** (of an experience, condition, etc.) unpleasant, dangerous, or painful: *a nasty wound.* **3.** spiteful, abusive, or ill-natured. **4.** obscene or indecent. **5. nasty piece of work.** *Brit. informal.* a cruel or mean person. ~*n., pl.* **-ties.** **6.** an offensive or unpleasant person or thing: *a video nasty.* [C14: origin obscure; probably related to Swedish dialect *nasket* and Dutch *nestig* dirty] —'**nastily** *adv.* —'**nastiness** *n.*

-nasty *n. combining form.* indicating a nastic movement to a certain stimulus: *nyctinasty.* [from Greek *nastos* pressed down, close-pressed] —**-nastic** *adj. combining form.*

NAS/UWT (in Britain) *abbrev. for* National Association of Schoolmasters/Union of Women Teachers.

Nat (næt) *n. N.Z. informal.* **1.** a member of the National Party. **2.** a Member of Parliament for the National Party.

nat. *abbrev. for:* **1.** national. **2.** native. **3.** natural.

natal[1] ('neɪtᵊl) *adj.* **1.** of or relating to birth. **2.** a rare word for **native**: *natal instincts.* [C14: from Latin *nātālis* of one's birth, from *nātus,* from *nascī* to be born]

natal[2] ('neɪtᵊl) *adj. Anatomy.* of or relating to the buttocks. [from New Latin *nates* buttocks]

natality (neɪ'tælɪtɪ) *n., pl.* **-ties.** another name (esp. U.S.) for **birth rate.**

natant ('neɪtᵊnt) *adj.* **1.** (of aquatic plants) floating on the water. **2.** *Rare.* floating or swimming. [C18: from Latin *natāns,* present participle of *natāre* to swim]

natation (nə'teɪʃən) *n.* a formal or literary word for **swimming.** [C16: from Latin *natātiō* a swimming, from *natāre* to swim] —**na'tational** *adj.*

natatorium (ˌneɪtə'tɔːrɪəm) *n., pl.* **-riums** or **-ria** (-rɪə). *Rare.* a swimming pool, esp. an indoor pool. [C20: from Late Latin: swimming place, pool]

natatory (nə'teɪtərɪ) or **natatorial** (ˌnætə'tɔːrɪəl) *adj.* of or relating to swimming. [C18: from Late Latin *natātōrius,* from *natāre* to swim]

natch (nætʃ) *sentence substitute. Informal.* short for **naturally** (sense 3).

nates ('neɪtiːz) *pl. n., sing.* **-tis** (-tɪs). a technical word for the **buttocks.** [C17: from Latin; compare Greek *nōton* back, *nosthi* buttocks]

NATFHE *abbrev. for* National Association of Teachers in Further and Higher Education.

natheless ('neɪθlɪs) or **nathless** ('næθlɪs) *Archaic.* ~*sentence connector.* **1.** another word for **nonetheless.** ~*prep.* **2.** notwithstanding; despite. [Old English *nāthylǣs,* from *nā* never + *thȳ* for that + *lǣs* less]

nation ('neɪʃən) *n.* **1.** an aggregation of people or peoples of one or more cultures, races, etc., organized into a single state: *the Australian nation.* **2.** a community of persons not constituting a state but bound by common descent, language, history, etc.: *the French-Canadian nation.* **3. a.** a federation of tribes, esp. American Indians. **b.** the territory occupied by such a federation. [C13: via Old French from Latin *nātiō* birth, tribe, from *nascī* to be born] —'**nationˌhood** *n.* —'**nationless** *adj.*

national ('næʃənᵊl) *adj.* **1.** of, involving, or relating to a nation as a whole. **2.** of, relating to, or characteristic of a particular nation: *the national dress of Poland.* **3.** *Rare.* nationalistic or patriotic. ~*n.* **4.** a citizen or subject. **5.** a national newspaper. —'**nationally** *adv.*

national accounting *n.* another name for **social accounting.**

national agreement *n.* written formal agreements covering rates of pay and other terms and conditions of employment that are the result of collective bargaining at national level between one or more trade unions and employers in a sector of the economy.

national anthem *n.* a patriotic hymn or other song adopted by a nation for use on public or state occasions.

national assistance *n.* (in Britain) formerly a weekly allowance paid to various groups of people by the state to bring their incomes up to minimum levels established by law. Now replaced by **income support.**

national bank *n.* **1.** (in the U.S.) a commercial bank incorporated under a Federal charter and legally required to be a member of the Federal Reserve System. Compare **state bank. 2.** a bank owned and operated by a government.

National Bureau of Standards *n. U.S.* an organization, founded in 1901, whose function is to establish and maintain standards for units of measurements. Compare **British Standards Institution, International Standards Organization.**

national code *n.* another term for **Australian Rules.**

National Covenant *n.* See **Covenant.**

National Curriculum *n.* (in England and Wales) the curriculum of subjects taught in state schools progressively from 1989. There are ten foundation subjects: English, maths, and science (the core subjects); art, design and technology, geography, history, music, physical education, and a foreign language. Pupils are assessed according to specified attainment targets throughout each of four key stages.

national debt *n.* the total outstanding borrowings of a nation's central government. Also called (esp. U.S.): **public debt.**

national grid *n.* **1.** *Brit.* a network of high-voltage power lines connecting major power stations. **2.** a grid of metric coordinates used by the Ordnance Survey in Britain and Ireland and in New Zealand by the New Zealand Lands and Survey Department and printed on their maps.

National Guard *n.* (in the U.S.) a state military force that can be called into federal service by the president.

National Health Service *n.* (in Britain) the system of national medical services since 1948, financed mainly by taxation.

national income *n. Economics.* the total of all incomes accruing over a specified period to residents of a country and consisting of wages, salaries, profits, rent, and interest.

national insurance *n.* (in Britain) state insurance based on weekly contributions from employees and employers and providing payments to the unemployed, the sick, the retired, etc., as well as medical services. See also **social security, supplementary benefit.**

nationalism ('næʃənəˌlɪzəm, 'næʃnə-) *n.* **1.** a sentiment based on common cultural characteristics that binds a population and often produces a policy of national independence or separatism. **2.** loyalty or devotion to one's country; patriotism. **3.** exaggerated, passionate, or fanatical devotion to a national community. See also **chauvinism.** —'**nationalist** *n., adj.* —ˌ**national'istic** *adj.*

nationality (ˌnæʃə'nælɪtɪ) *n., pl.* **-ties. 1.** the state or fact of being a citizen of a particular nation. **2.** a body of people sharing common descent, history, language, etc.; a nation. **3.** a national group: *30 different nationalities are found in this city.* **4.** national character or quality. **5.** the state or fact of being a nation; national status.

nationalize *or* **nationalise** ('næʃənəˌlaɪz, 'næʃnə-) *vb.* (*tr.*) **1.** to put (an industry, resources, etc.) under state control or ownership. **2.** to make national in scope, character, or status. **3.** a less common word for **naturalize.** —ˌ**nationali'zation** *or* ˌ**nationali'sation** *n.*

national park *n.* an area of countryside for public use designated by a national government as being of notable scenic, environmental, or historical importance.

National Savings Bank *n.* (in Britain) a government savings bank, run through the post office, esp. for small savers.

National School *n.* **1.** (in Ireland) a state primary school. **2.** (in England in the 19th century) a school run by the Church of England for the children of the poor.

national service *n. Chiefly Brit.* compulsory military service.

National Socialism *n. German history.* the doctrines and practices of the Nazis, involving the supremacy of Hitler as Führer, anti-Semitism, state control of the economy, and national expansion. Also called: **Nazism, Naziism.** —**National Socialist** *n., adj.*

national superannuation *n. N.Z.* a pension paid to some elderly people by the Department of Social Welfare.

nation-state *n.* an independent state inhabited by all the people of one nation and one nation only.

nationwide ('neɪʃənˌwaɪd) *adj.* covering or available to the whole of a nation; national: *a nationwide survey.*

native ('neɪtɪv) *adj.* **1.** relating or belonging to a person or thing by virtue of conditions existing at the time of birth: *a native language.* **2.** inherent, natural, or innate: *a native strength.* **3.** born in a specified place: *a native Indian.* **4.** (when *postpositive,* foll. by *to*) originating in a specific place or area: *kangaroos are native to Australia.* **5.** characteristic of or relating to the indigenous inhabitants of a country or area: *the native art of the New Guinea Highlands.* **6.** (of chemical elements, esp. metals) found naturally in the elemental form; not chemically combined as in an ore. **7.** unadulterated by civilization, artifice, or adornment; natural. **8.** *Archaic.* related by birth or race. **9. go native.** (of a settler) to adopt the lifestyle of the local population, esp. when it appears less civilized. ~*n.* **10.** (usually foll. by *of*) a person born in a particular place: *a native of Geneva.* **11.** (usually foll. by *of*) a species of animal or plant originating in a particular place or area: *the kangaroo is a native of Australia.* **12.** a member of an indigenous people of a country or area, esp. a non-White people, as opposed to colonial settlers and immigrants. **13.** *Derogatory, rare.* any non-White. [C14: from Latin *nātīvus* innate, natural, from *nascī* to be born] —'**natively** *adv.* —'**nativeness** *n.*

native bear *n.* an Australian name for **koala.**

native-born *adj.* born in the country or area indicated.

native bush *n. N.Z.* indigenous forest.

native companion *n. Austral.* another name for the **brolga.** [C19: so called because the birds were observed in pairs]

native dog *n. Austral.* a dingo.

native oak *n. Austral.* another name for **casuarina.**

native speaker *n.* a person having a specified native language: *a native speaker of Cree.*

nativism ('neɪtɪˌvɪzəm) *n.* **1.** *Chiefly U.S.* the policy of favouring the natives of a country over the immigrants. **2.** *Anthropol.* the policy of protecting and reaffirming native tribal cultures in reaction to acculturation. **3.** the doctrine that the mind and its capacities are innately structured and that much knowledge is innate. —'**nativist** *n., adj.* —ˌ**nativ'istic** *adj.*

nativity (nə'tɪvɪtɪ) *n., pl.* **-ties.** birth or origin, esp. in relation to the circumstances surrounding it. [C14: via Old French from Late Latin *nātīvitas* birth: see NATIVE]

Nativity (nə'tɪvɪtɪ) *n.* **1.** the birth of Jesus Christ. **2.** the feast of Christmas as a commemoration of this. **3. a.** an artistic representation of the circumstances of the birth of Christ. **b.** (*as modifier*): *a Nativity play.*

natl *abbrev. for* national.

NATO *or* **Nato** ('neɪtəʊ) *n. acronym for* North Atlantic Treaty Organization.

natrium ('neɪtrɪəm) *n.* an obsolete name for **sodium.** [C19: New Latin; see NATRON]

natrolite ('nætrəˌlaɪt, 'neɪ-) *n.* a colourless, white, or yellow zeolite mineral consisting of sodium aluminium silicate in the form of needle-like orthorhombic crystals. Formula: $Na_2Al_2Si_3O_{10}.2H_2O$. [C19: from NATRON + -LITE]

natron ('neɪtrən) *n.* a whitish or yellow mineral that consists of hydrated sodium carbonate and occurs in saline deposits and salt lakes. Formula: $Na_2CO_3.10H_2O$. [C17: via French and Spanish from Arabic *natrūn,* from Greek *nitron*]

NATSOPA (næt'səʊpə) *n.* (in Britain) *acronym for* National Society of Operative Printers, Graphical and Media Personnel.

natter ('nætə) *Chiefly Brit.* ~*vb.* **1.** (*intr.*) to talk idly and at length; chatter or gossip. ~*n.* **2.** prolonged idle chatter or gossip. [C19: changed from *gnatter* to grumble, of imitative origin; compare Low German *gnatteren*] —'**natterer** *n.*

natterjack ('nætəˌdʒæk) *n.* a European toad, *Bufo calamita,* of sandy regions, having a greyish-brown body marked with reddish warty processes: family *Bufonidae.* [C18: of unknown origin]

natty ('nætɪ) *adj.* **-tier, -tiest.** *Informal.* smart in appearance or dress; spruce; dapper: *a natty outfit.* [C18: perhaps from obsolete *netty,* from *net* NEAT[1]; compare Old French *net* trim] —'**nattily** *adv.* —'**nattiness** *n.*

natural ('nætʃrəl, -tʃərəl) *adj.* **1.** of, existing in, or produced by nature: *natural science; natural cliffs.* **2.** in accordance with human nature: *it is only natural to want to be liked.* **3.** as is normal or to be expected; ordinary or logical: *the natural course of events.* **4.** not acquired; innate: *a natural gift for sport.* **5.** being so through innate qualities: *a natural leader.* **6.** not supernatural or strange: *natural phenomena.* **7.** not constrained or affected; genuine or spontaneous. **8.** not artificially dyed or coloured: *a natural blonde.* **9.** following or resembling nature or life; lifelike: *she looked more natural without her make-up.* **10.** not affected by man or civilization; uncultivated; wild: *in the natural state this animal is not ferocious.* **11.** illegitimate; born out of wedlock. **12.** not adopted but rather related by blood: *her natural parents.* **13.** *Music.* **a.** not sharp or flat. **b.** (*postpositive*) denoting a note that is neither sharp nor flat: *B natural.* **c.** (of a key or scale) containing no sharps or flats. Compare **flat**[1] (sense 22), **sharp** (sense 12). **14.** *Music.* of or relating to a trumpet, horn, etc., without valves or keys, on which only notes of the harmonic series of the keynote can be obtained. **15.** determined by inborn conviction: *natural justice; natural rights.* **16.** *Cards.* **a.** (of a card) not a joker or wild card. **b.** (of a canasta or sequence) containing no wild cards. **c.** (of a bid in bridge) describing genuine values; not conventional. **17.** based on the principles and findings of human reason and what is to be learned of God from nature rather than on revelation: *natural religion.* ~*n.* **18.** *Informal.* a person or thing regarded as certain to qualify for success, selection, etc.: *the horse was a natural for first place.* **19.** *Music.* **a.** Also called (U.S.): **cancel.** an accidental cancelling a previous sharp or flat. Usual symbol: ♮ **b.** a note affected by this accidental. Compare **flat**[1] (sense 34), **sharp** (sense 19). **20.** *Pontoon.* the combination of an ace with a ten or court card when dealt to a player as his first two cards. **21.** *Obsolete.* an imbecile; idiot. —'**naturally** *adv.* —'**naturalness** *n.*

natural-born *adj.* being as specified through one's birth: *a natural-born Irishman.*

natural childbirth *n.* a method of childbirth characterized by the absence of anaesthetics, in which the expectant mother is given special breathing and relaxing exercises.

natural classification *n. Biology.* classification of organisms according to relationships based on descent from a common ancestor.

natural deduction *n.* a system of formal logic that has no axioms but permits the assumption of premises of an argument. Such a system uses sequents to record which assumptions are operative at any stage. Compare **axiomatic** (sense 3).

natural frequency *n. Physics.* the frequency at which a system vibrates when set in free vibration. Compare **forcing frequency.**

natural gas *n.* a gaseous mixture consisting mainly of methane trapped below ground; used extensively as a fuel.

natural gender *n.* grammatical gender that reflects, as in English, the sex or animacy of the referent of a noun rather than the form or any other feature of the word.

natural history *n.* **1.** the study of animals and plants in the wild state. **2.** the study of all natural phenomena. **3.** the sum of these phenomena in a given place or at a given time: *the natural history of Iran.* —**natural historian** *n.*

natural immunity *n.* immunity with which an individual is born, which has a genetic basis.

naturalism (ˈnætʃrəˌlɪzəm, -tʃərə-) *n.* **1. a.** a movement, esp. in art and literature, advocating detailed realistic and factual description, esp. that in 19th-century France in the writings of Zola, Flaubert, etc. **b.** the characteristics or effects of this movement. **2.** a school of painting or sculpture characterized by the faithful imitation of appearances for their own sake. **3.** the belief that all religious truth is based not on revelation but rather on the study of natural causes and processes. **4.** *Philosophy.* **a.** a scientific account of the world in terms of causes and natural forces that rejects all spiritual, supernatural, or teleological explanations. **b.** the meta-ethical thesis that moral properties are reducible to natural ones, or that ethical judgments are derivable from nonethical ones. See **naturalistic fallacy.** Compare **descriptivism. 5.** action or thought caused by natural desires and instincts. **6.** devotion to that which is natural.

naturalist (ˈnætʃrəlɪst, -tʃərəl-) *n.* **1.** a person who is versed in or interested in botany or zoology. **2.** a person who advocates or practises naturalism, esp. in art or literature.

naturalistic (ˌnætʃrəˈlɪstɪk, -tʃərə-) *adj.* **1.** of, imitating, or reproducing nature in effect or characteristics. **2.** of or characteristic of naturalism, esp. in art or literature. **3.** of or relating to naturalists. **4.** (of an ethical theory) permitting the inference of ethical judgments from statements of nonethical fact. See **Hume's law.** —ˌ**naturalˈistically** *adv.*

naturalistic fallacy *n.* the supposed fallacy of inferring evaluative conclusions from purely factual premises. See **Hume's law.** Compare **non-naturalism.**

naturalize *or* **naturalise** (ˈnætʃrəˌlaɪz, -tʃərə-) *vb.* **1.** (*tr.*) to give citizenship to (a person of foreign birth). **2.** to be or cause to be adopted in another place, as a word, custom, etc. **3.** (*tr.*) to introduce (a plant or animal from another region) and cause it to adapt to local conditions. **4.** (*intr.*) (of a plant or animal) to adapt successfully to a foreign environment. **5.** (*tr.*) to explain (something unusual) with reference to nature, excluding the supernatural. **6.** (*tr.*) to make natural or more lifelike. —ˌ**naturaliˈzation** *or* ˌ**naturaliˈsation** *n.*

natural justice *n.* the principles and procedures that govern the adjudication of disputes between persons or organizations, chief among which are that the adjudication should be unbiased and given in good faith, and that each party should have equal access to the tribunal and should be aware of arguments and documents adduced by the other.

natural language *n.* **1.** a language that has evolved naturally as a means of communication among people. Compare **artificial language, formal language. 2.** languages of this kind considered collectively.

natural law *n.* **1.** an ethical belief or system of beliefs supposed to be inherent in human nature and discoverable by reason rather than revelation. **2.** a nonlogically necessary truth; law of nature. See also **nomological** (sense 2). **3.** the philosophical doctrine that the authority of the legal system or of certain laws derives from their justifiability by reason, and indeed that a legal system which cannot be so justified has no authority.

natural logarithm *n.* a logarithm to the base e (see **e** (sense 1)). Usually written $\log_e$ or ln. Also called: **Napierian logarithm.** Compare **common logarithm.**

naturally (ˈnætʃrəlɪ, -tʃərə-) *adv.* **1.** in a natural or normal way. **2.** through nature; inherently; instinctively. ~*adv., sentence substitute.* **3.** of course; surely.

natural number *n.* any of the positive integers 1,2,3,4,..., which can be defined in terms of the cardinality of a recursively generated sequence of clauses.

natural philosophy *n.* (now only used in Scottish universities) physical science, esp. physics. —**natural philosopher** *n.*

natural resources *pl. n.* naturally occurring materials such as coal, fertile land, etc., that can be used by man.

natural science *n.* **1.** the sciences collectively that are involved in the study of the physical world and its phenomena, including biology, physics, chemistry, and geology, but excluding social sciences, abstract or theoretical sciences, such as mathematics, and applied sciences. **2.** any one of these sciences. —**natural scientist** *n.*

natural selection *n.* a process resulting in the survival of those individuals from a population of animals or plants that are best adapted to the prevailing environmental conditions. The survivors tend to produce more offspring than those less well adapted, so that the composition of the population is changed.

natural slope *n. Civil engineering.* the maximum angle at which soil will lie in a bank without slipping.

natural theology *n.* the attempt to derive theological truth, and esp. the existence of God, from empirical facts by reasoned argument. Compare **revealed religion, fideism, revelation** (sense 3). —**natural theologian** *n.*

natural virtues *pl. n.* (esp. among the scholastics) those virtues of which man is capable without direct help from God, specifically justice, temperance, prudence, and fortitude. Compare **theological virtues.**

natural wastage *n.* another term for **attrition** (sense 3).

nature (ˈneɪtʃə) *n.* **1.** the fundamental qualities of a person or thing; identity or essential character. **2.** (*often cap., esp. when personified*) the whole system of the existence, arrangement, forces, and events of all physical life that are not controlled by man. **3.** all natural phenomena and plant and animal life, as distinct from man and his creations. **4.** a wild primitive state untouched by man or civilization. **5.** natural unspoilt scenery or countryside. **6.** disposition or temperament. **7.** tendencies, desires, or instincts governing behaviour. **8.** the normal biological needs or urges of the body. **9.** sort; kind; character. **10.** the real appearance of a person or thing: *a painting very true to nature.* **11.** accepted standards of basic morality or behaviour. **12.** *Biology.* the complement of genetic material that partly determines the structure of an organism; genotype. Compare **nurture** (sense 3). **13.** *Irish.* sympathy and fondness for one's own people or native place: *she is full of nature.* **14. against nature.** unnatural or immoral. **15. by nature.** essentially or innately. **16. call of nature.** *Informal, euphemistic or humorous.* the need to urinate or defecate. **17. from nature.** using natural models in drawing, painting, etc. **18. in** (*or* **of**) **the nature of.** essentially the same as; by way of. [C13: via Old French from Latin *nātūra*, from *nātus*, past participle of *nascī* to be born]

nature reserve *n.* an area of land that is protected and managed in order to preserve a particular type of habitat and its flora and fauna which are often rare or endangered.

nature strip *n. Austral. informal.* **1.** a grass strip in front of a house between a fence or footpath and a roadway. **2.** (in S Australia) a verge.

nature study *n.* the study of the natural world, esp. animals and plants, by direct observation at an elementary level.

nature trail *n.* a path through countryside designed and usually signposted to draw attention to natural features of interest.

naturism (ˈneɪtʃəˌrɪzəm) *n.* another name for **nudism.** —ˈ**naturist** *n., adj.*

naturopathy (ˌneɪtʃəˈrɒpəθɪ) *n.* a method of treating disorders, involving the use of herbs and other naturally grown foods, sunlight, fresh air, etc. Also called: **nature cure.** —**naturopath** (ˈneɪtʃərəˌpæθ) *n.* —**naturopathic** (ˌneɪtʃərəˈpæθɪk) *adj.*

nauch (nɔːtʃ) *n.* a variant spelling of **nautch.**

naught (nɔːt) *n.* **1.** *Archaic or literary.* nothing or nothingness; ruin or failure. **2.** a variant spelling (esp. U.S.) of **nought. 3. set at naught.** to have disregard or scorn for; disdain. ~*adv.* **4.** *Archaic or literary.* not at all: *it matters naught.* ~*adj.* **5.** *Obsolete.* worthless, ruined, or wicked. [Old English *nāwiht*, from *nā* NO[1] + *wiht* thing, person; see WIGHT[1], WHIT]

naughty (ˈnɔːtɪ) *adj.* **-tier, -tiest. 1.** (esp. of children or their behaviour) mischievous or disobedient; bad. **2.** mildly indecent; titillating. ~*n., pl.* **-ties. 3.** *Austral. and N.Z. slang.* an act of sexual intercourse. [C14 (originally: needy, of poor quality): from NAUGHT] —ˈ**naughtily** *adv.* —ˈ**naughtiness** *n.*

naughty nineties *n.* **the.** (in Britain) the 1890s, considered to be a period of fun loving and laxity, esp. in sexual morals.

naumachia (nɔːˈmeɪkɪə) *or* **naumachy** (ˈnɔːməkɪ) *n., pl.* **-chiae** (-kɪˌiː), **-chias,** *or* **-chies.** (in ancient Rome) **1.** a mock sea fight performed as an entertainment. **2.** an artificial lake used in such a spectacle. [C16: via Latin from Greek *naumakhiā*, from *naus* ship + *makhē* battle]

nauplius (ˈnɔːplɪəs) *n., pl.* **-plii** (-plɪˌaɪ). the larva of many crustaceans, having a rounded unsegmented body with three pairs of limbs. [C19: from Latin: type of shellfish, from Greek *Nauplios*, one of the sons of Poseidon, god of the sea]

nausea (ˈnɔːzɪə, -sɪə) *n.* **1.** the sensation that precedes vomiting. **2.** a feeling of disgust or revulsion. [C16: via Latin from Greek: seasickness, from *naus* ship]

nauseate (ˈnɔːzɪˌeɪt, -sɪ-) *vb.* **1.** (*tr.*) to arouse feelings of disgust or revulsion in. **2.** to feel or cause to feel sick. —ˈ**nauseˌating** *adj.* —ˌ**nauseˈation** *n.*

nauseous (ˈnɔːzɪəs, -sɪəs) *adj.* **1.** causing nausea. **2.** distasteful to the mind or senses; repulsive. —ˈ**nauseously** *adv.* —ˈ**nauseousness** *n.*

naut. *abbrev. for* nautical.
-naut *n. combining form.* indicating a person engaged in the navigation of a vehicle, esp. one used for scientific investigation: *astronaut.*
nautch *or* **nauch** (nɔːtʃ) *n.* **a.** an intricate traditional Indian dance performed by professional dancing girls. **b.** (*as modifier*): *a nautch girl.* [C18: from Hindi *nāc,* from Sanskrit *nṛtya,* from *nṛtyati* he acts or dances]
nautical (ˈnɔːtɪkᵊl) *adj.* of, relating to, or involving ships, navigation, or seamen. [C16: from Latin *nauticus,* from Greek *nautikos,* from *naus* ship] —ˈ**nautically** *adv.*
nautical mile *n.* **1.** Also called: **international nautical mile, air mile.** a unit of length, used esp. in navigation, equal to 1852 metres (6076.103 feet). **2.** a British unit of length, equal to 1853.18 metres (6082 feet). Former name: **geographical mile.** Compare **sea mile.**
nautiloid (ˈnɔːtɪˌlɔɪd) *n.* **1.** any mollusc of the *Nautiloidea,* a group of cephalopods that includes the pearly nautilus and many extinct forms. ~*adj.* **2.** of, relating to, or belonging to the *Nautiloidea.*
nautilus (ˈnɔːtɪləs) *n., pl.* **-luses** *or* **-li** (-ˌlaɪ). **1.** any cephalopod mollusc of the genus *Nautilus,* esp. the pearly nautilus. **2.** short for **paper nautilus.** [C17: via Latin from Greek *nautilos* sailor, from *naus* ship]
NAV *abbrev. for* net asset value.
nav. *abbrev. for:* **1.** naval. **2.** navigable. **3.** navigation. **4.** navigator.
Navaho *or* **Navajo** (ˈnævəˌhəʊ, ˈnɑː-) *n.* **1.** (*pl.* **-ho, -hos, -hoes** *or* **-jo, -jos, -joes**) a member of a North American Indian people of Arizona, New Mexico, and Utah. **2.** the language of this people, belonging to the Athapascan group of the Na-Dene phylum. [C18: from Spanish *Navajó* pueblo, from Tena *Navahu* large planted field]
naval (ˈneɪvᵊl) *adj.* **1.** of, relating to, characteristic of, or having a navy. **2.** of or relating to ships; nautical. [C16: from Latin *nāvālis,* from *nāvis* ship; related to Greek *naus,* Old Norse *nōr* ship, Sanskrit *nau*]
naval architecture *n.* the designing of ships. —**naval architect** *n.*
navar (ˈnævɑː) *n.* a system of air navigation in which a ground radar station relays signals to each aircraft indicating the relative positions of neighbouring aircraft. [C20: from *nav(igational and traffic control rad)ar*]
Navaratri (nævəˈrɑːtrɪ) *n.* an annual Hindu festival celebrated over nine days in September–October. Observed throughout India, it commemorates the slaying of demons by Rama and the goddess Durga; in some places it is dedicated to all female deities. Also called **Durga Puja.** [from Sanskrit *navaratri* nine nights]
navarin (ˈnævərɪn; *French* navarɛ̃) *n.* a stew of mutton or lamb with root vegetables. [from French]
nave[1] (neɪv) *n.* the central space in a church, extending from the narthex to the chancel and often flanked by aisles. [C17: via Medieval Latin from Latin *nāvis* ship, from the similarity of shape]
nave[2] (neɪv) *n.* the central block or hub of a wheel. [Old English *nafu, nafa;* related to Old High German *naba*]
navel (ˈneɪvᵊl) *n.* **1.** the scar in the centre of the abdomen, usually forming a slight depression, where the umbilical cord was attached. Technical name: **umbilicus.** Related adj.: **umbilical. 2.** a central part, location, or point; middle. **3.** short for **navel orange.** [Old English *nafela;* related to Old Frisian *navla,* Old High German *nabulo* (German *Nabel*), Latin *umbilīcus*]
navel orange *n.* a sweet orange that is usually seedless and has at its apex a navel-like depression enclosing an underdeveloped secondary fruit.
navelwort (ˈneɪvᵊlˌwɜːt) *n.* another name for **pennywort** (sense 1).
navew (ˈneɪvjuː) *n.* another name for **turnip** (senses 1, 2). [C16: from Old French *navel,* from Latin *nāpus*]
navicert (ˈnævɪˌsɜːt) *n.* a certificate specifying the contents of a neutral ship's cargo, issued esp. in time of war by a blockading power. [C20: from Latin *nāvi(s)* ship + English CERT(IFICATE)]
navicular (nəˈvɪkjʊlə) *Anatomy.* ~*adj.* **1.** shaped like a boat. ~*n. also* **naviculare** (nəˌvɪkjʊˈlɑːrɪ). **2.** a small boat-shaped bone of the wrist or foot. [C16: from Late Latin *nāviculāris,* from Latin *nāvicula,* diminutive of *nāvis* ship]
navig. *abbrev. for* navigation.
navigable (ˈnævɪgəbᵊl) *adj.* **1.** wide, deep, or safe enough to be sailed on or through: *a navigable channel.* **2.** capable of being steered or controlled: *a navigable raft.* —ˌ**navigaˈbility** *or* ˈ**navigableness** *n.* —ˈ**navigably** *adv.*
navigate (ˈnævɪˌgeɪt) *vb.* **1.** to plan, direct, or plot the path or position of (a ship, an aircraft, etc.). **2.** (*tr.*) to travel over, through, or on (water, air, or land) in a boat, aircraft, etc. **3.** *Informal.* to direct (oneself, one's way, etc.) carefully or safely: *he navigated his way to the bar.* **4.** (*intr.*) (of a passenger in a motor vehicle) to give directions to the driver; point out the route. **5.** (*intr.*) *Rare.* to voyage in a ship; sail. [C16: from Latin *nāvigāre* to sail, from *nāvis* ship + *agere* to drive]
navigation (ˌnævɪˈgeɪʃən) *n.* **1.** the skill or process of plotting a route and directing a ship, aircraft, etc., along it. **2.** the act or practice of navigating: *dredging made navigation of the river possible.* **3.** *U.S., rare.* ship traffic; shipping. **4.** *Midland English dialect.* an inland waterway; canal. —ˌ**naviˈgational** *adj.*
navigator (ˈnævɪˌgeɪtə) *n.* **1.** a person who is skilled in or performs navigation, esp. on a ship or aircraft. **2.** (esp. formerly) a person who explores by ship. **3.** an instrument or device for assisting a pilot to navigate an aircraft.
navvy (ˈnævɪ) *n., pl.* **-vies.** *Brit. informal.* a labourer on a building site, excavations, etc. [C19: shortened from *navigator,* builder of a navigation (sense 4)]
navy (ˈneɪvɪ) *n., pl.* **-vies. 1.** the warships and auxiliary vessels of a nation or ruler. **2.** (*often cap.;* usually preceded by *the*) the branch of a country's armed services comprising such ships, their crews, and all their supporting services and equipment. **3.** short for **navy blue. 4.** *Archaic or literary.* a fleet of ships. **5.** (*as modifier*): *a navy custom.* [C14: via Old French from Vulgar Latin *nāvia* (unattested) ship, from Latin *nāvis* ship]
navy blue *n.* **a.** a dark greyish-blue colour. **b.** (*as adj.*): *a navy-blue suit.* ~Sometimes shortened to **navy.** [C19: from the colour of the British naval uniform]
navy cut *n.* tobacco finely cut from a block.
Navy List *n.* (in Britain) an official list of all serving commissioned officers of the Royal Navy and reserve officers liable for recall.
navy yard *n.* a naval shipyard, esp. in the U.S.
nawab (nəˈwɑːb) *n.* (formerly) a Muslim ruling prince or powerful landowner in India. Also called: **nabob.** [C18: from Hindi *nawwāb,* from Arabic *nuwwāb,* plural of *na'ib* viceroy, governor]
Naxalite (ˈnʌksəˌlaɪt) *n.* a member of an extreme Maoist group in India that originated in 1967 in West Bengal and which employs tactics of agrarian terrorism and direct action. [C20: named after *Naxalbari,* a town in West Bengal where the movement started]
nay (neɪ) *sentence substitute.* **1.** a word for **no**[1]: archaic or dialectal except in voting by voice. ~*n.* **2. a.** a person who votes in the negative. **b.** a negative vote. ~*adv.* **3.** (*sentence modifier*) *Archaic.* an emphatic form of **no**[1]. ~Compare **aye**[1]. [C12: from Old Norse *nei,* from *ne* not + *ei* ever, AY[1]]
Nazarene (ˌnæzəˈriːn) *n. also* **Nazarite. 1.** an early name for a **Christian** (Acts 24:5) or (when preceded by *the*) for **Christ. 2.** a member of one of several groups of Jewish-Christians found principally in Syria. **3.** a member of an association of German artists called the Nazarenes or Brotherhood of St Luke, founded (1809) in Vienna to revive German religious art after the examples of the Middle Ages and early Renaissance. ~*adj.* **4.** of or relating to Nazareth, a town in N Israel and the home of Jesus in his youth, or to the Nazarenes.
Nazarite[1] (ˈnæzəˌraɪt) *n.* another word for **Nazarene** (senses 1, 2).
Nazarite[2] *or* **Nazirite** (ˈnæzəˌraɪt) *n.* a religious ascetic of ancient Israel. [C16: from Latin *Nazaraeus,* from Hebrew *nāzīr,* from *nāzar* to consecrate + -ITE]
Nazi (ˈnɑːtsɪ) *n., pl.* **Nazis. 1.** a member of the fascist National Socialist German Workers' Party, which was founded in 1919 and seized political control in Germany in 1933 under Adolf Hitler. **2.** *Derogatory.* anyone who thinks or acts like a Nazi, esp. showing racism, brutality, etc. ~*adj.* **3.** of, characteristic of, or relating to the Nazis. [C20: from German, phonetic spelling of the first two syllables of *Nationalsozialist* National Socialist] —**Nazism** (ˈnɑːtˌsɪzəm) *or* **Naziism** (ˈnɑːtsɪˌɪzəm) *n.*
Nazify (ˈnɑːtsɪˌfaɪ) *vb.* **-fies, -fying, -fied.** (*tr.*) to make Nazi in character. —ˌ**Nazifiˈcation** *n.*
nb *Cricket. abbrev. for* no ball.
Nb *the chemical symbol for* niobium.
NB *abbrev. for* New Brunswick.
NB, N.B., nb, *or* **n.b.** *abbrev. for* nota bene. [Latin: note well]
NBA *abbrev. for* Net Book Agreement.
NBC *abbrev. for:* **1.** (in the U.S.) National Broadcasting Company. **2.** (of weapons or warfare) nuclear, biological, and chemical.
NBG *Informal. abbrev. for* no bloody good. Also: **nbg.**
NC *or* **N.C.** *abbrev. for:* **1.** North Carolina. **2.** *Brit. education.* National Curriculum.
NCB *abbrev. for* National Coal Board.
NCC (in Britain) *abbrev. for:* **1.** Nature Conservancy Council. **2.** *Brit. education.* National Curriculum Council.
NCCL *abbrev. for* National Council for Civil Liberties.
NCO *abbrev. for* noncommissioned officer.
NCP *Austral. abbrev. for* National Country Party.
NCVO (in Britain) *abbrev. for* National Council for Voluntary Organizations.
nd *abbrev. for* no date.
Nd *the chemical symbol for* neodymium.
ND, N.D., *or* **N. Dak.** *abbrev. for* North Dakota.
NDE *abbrev. for* near-death experience.
Ndebele (ᵊnˈdɛbɛle) *n.* **1.** (*pl.* **Ndebele**) a member of a Negroid people of Zimbabwe. See also **Matabele. 2.** the language of this people, belonging to the Bantu grouping of the Niger-Congo family.
NDP *abbrev. for:* **1.** net domestic product. **2.** (in Canada) New Democratic Party.
NDT *abbrev. for* nondestructive testing.
Ne *the chemical symbol for* neon.
NE **1.** *symbol for* northeast(ern). **2.** *abbrev. for* Nebraska.

NE *or* **N.E.** *abbrev. for* New England.
ne- *combining form.* a variant of **neo-**, esp. before a vowel: *Nearctic.*
Neanderthal (nɪˈændəˌtɑːl) *(sometimes not cap.)* ~*adj.* **1.** relating to or characteristic of Neanderthal man. **2.** primitive; uncivilized. **3.** *Informal.* ultraconservative; reactionary. ~*n.* **4.** a person showing any such characteristics.
Neanderthal man *n.* a type of primitive man, *Homo neanderthalensis,* or *H. sapiens neanderthalensis,* occurring throughout much of Europe in late Palaeolithic times. [C19: from the anthropological findings (1857) in the Neandertal, a valley near Düsseldorf, Germany]
neanic (nɪˈænɪk) *adj. Zoology.* of or relating to the early stages in the life cycle of an organism, esp. the pupal stage of an insect. [C19: from Greek *neanikus* youthful]
neap (niːp) *adj.* **1.** of, relating to, or constituting a neap tide. ~*n.* **2.** short for **neap tide.** [Old English, as in *nēpflōd* neap tide, of uncertain origin]
Neapolitan (ˌnɪəˈpɒlɪtᵊn) *n.* **1.** a native or inhabitant of Naples, a port in SW Italy. ~*adj.* **2.** of or relating to Naples. [C15: from Latin *Neāpolītānus,* ultimately from Greek *Neapolis* new town]
Neapolitan ice cream *n.* ice cream, usually in brick form, with several layers of different colours and flavours.
Neapolitan sixth *n.* (in musical harmony) a chord composed of the subdominant of the key, plus a minor third and a minor sixth. Harmonically it is equivalent to the first inversion of a major chord built upon the flattened supertonic.
neap tide *n.* either of the two tides that occur at the first or last quarter of the moon when the tide-generating forces of the sun and moon oppose each other and produce the smallest rise and fall in tidal level. Compare **spring tide** (sense 1).
near (nɪə) *prep.* **1.** at or to a place or time not far away from; close to. ~*adv.* **2.** at or to a place or time not far away; close by. **3.** **near to.** not far from; near. **4.** short for **nearly** (esp. in phrases such as **damn near**): *I was damn near killed.* ~*adj.* **5.** *(postpositive)* at or in a place not far away. **6.** *(prenominal)* only just successful or only just failing: *a near escape.* **7.** *(postpositive) Informal.* miserly, mean. **8.** *(prenominal)* closely connected or intimate: *a near relation.* ~*vb.* **9.** to come or draw close (to). ~*n.* **10.** Also called: **nearside. a.** the left side of a horse, team of animals, vehicle, etc. **b.** *(as modifier): the near foreleg.* [Old English *nēar* (adv.), comparative of *nēah* close, NIGH; related to Old Frisian *niār,* Old Norse *nǣr,* Old High German *nāhōr*] —ˈ**nearness** *n.*
near- *combining form.* nearly; almost: *a near-perfect landing.*
nearby *adj.* (ˈnɪəˌbaɪ), *adv.* (ˌnɪəˈbaɪ). not far away; close at hand.
Nearctic (nɪˈɑːktɪk) *adj.* of or denoting a zoogeographical region consisting of North America, north of the tropic of Cancer, and Greenland.
near-death experience *n.* an experience, instances of which have been widely reported, in which a person near death is apparently outside his body and aware of it and the attendant circumstances as separate from him. Abbrev.: **NDE.**
near gale *n. Meteorol.* a wind of force seven on the Beaufort scale or from 32–38 mph.
nearly (ˈnɪəlɪ) *adv.* **1.** not quite; almost; practically. **2. not nearly.** nowhere near; not at all: *not nearly enough money.* **3.** closely: *the person most nearly concerned.*
near miss *n.* **1.** a bomb, shell, etc., that does not exactly hit the target. **2.** any attempt or shot that just fails to be successful. **3.** an incident in which two vehicles narrowly avoid collision.
near money *n.* liquid assets that can be converted to cash very quickly, such as a bank deposit or bill of exchange.
near point *n. Optics.* the nearest point to the eye at which an object remains in focus.
near rhyme *n. Prosody.* another term for **half-rhyme.**
nearside (ˈnɪəˌsaɪd) *n.* **1.** (usually preceded by *the*) *Chiefly Brit.* **a.** the side of a vehicle normally nearer the kerb (in Britain, the left side). **b.** *(as modifier): the nearside door.* ~Compare **offside. 2. a.** the left side of an animal, team of horses, etc. **b.** *(as modifier): the nearside flank.*
near-sighted (ˌnɪəˈsaɪtɪd) *adj.* relating to or suffering from myopia. —ˌ**near-ˈsightedly** *adv.* —ˌ**near-ˈsightedness** *n.*
near thing *n. Informal.* an event or action whose outcome is nearly a failure, success, disaster, etc.
nearthrosis (ˌniːɑːˈθrəʊsɪs) *n., pl.* **-ses** (-siːz). another name for **pseudoarthrosis.**
neat[1] (niːt) *adj.* **1.** clean, tidy, and orderly. **2.** liking or insisting on order and cleanliness; fastidious. **3.** smoothly or competently done; efficient: *a neat job.* **4.** pat or slick: *his excuse was suspiciously neat.* **5.** (of alcoholic drinks) without added water, lemonade, etc.; undiluted. **6.** a less common word for **net**[2]: *neat profits.* **7.** *Slang, chiefly U.S. and Canadian.* good; pleasing; admirable. [C16: from Old French *net,* from Latin *nitidus* clean, shining, from *nitēre* to shine; related to Middle Irish *niam* beauty, brightness, Old Persian *naiba-* beautiful] —ˈ**neatly** *adv.* —ˈ**neatness** *n.*
neat[2] (niːt) *n., pl.* **neat.** *Archaic or dialect.* a domestic bovine animal. [Old English *neat*]
neaten (ˈniːtᵊn) *vb. (tr.)* to make neat; tidy.
neath *or* **'neath** (niːθ) *prep. Archaic.* short for **beneath.**
neat's-foot oil *n.* a yellow fixed oil obtained by boiling the feet and shinbones of cattle and used esp. to dress leather.
neb (nɛb) *n. Archaic or dialect.* **1.** *Chiefly Scot. and northern English.* the peak of a cap. **2.** the beak of a bird or the nose or snout of an animal. **3.** a person's mouth or nose. **4.** the projecting part or end of anything. **5. a.** a peak, esp. in N England. **b.** a prominent gritstone overhang. [Old English *nebb;* related to Old Norse *nef,* Old High German *snabul* (German *Schnabel*)]
NEB *abbrev. for:* **1.** New English Bible. **2.** National Enterprise Board.
Nebr. *abbrev. for* Nebraska.
Nebuchadnezzar (ˌnɛbjʊkədˈnɛzə) *n.* a wine bottle, used esp. for display, holding the equivalent of twenty normal bottles (approximately 520 ounces). [C20: named after *Nebuchadnezzar,* Babylonian king, from the custom of naming large wine bottles after Old Testament figures; compare JEROBOAM]
nebula (ˈnɛbjʊlə) *n., pl.* **-lae** (-ˌliː) *or* **-las. 1.** *Astronomy.* a diffuse cloud of particles and gases (mainly hydrogen) that is visible either as a hazy patch of light (**emission nebula**) or an irregular dark region (**dark nebula**). Compare **extragalactic nebula, planetary nebula. 2.** *Pathol.* **a.** opacity of the cornea. **b.** cloudiness of the urine. **3.** any substance for use in an atomizer spray. [C17: from Latin: mist, cloud; related to Greek *nephétē* cloud, Old High German *nebul* cloud, Old Norse *njól* night] —ˈ**nebular** *adj.*
nebular hypothesis *n.* the theory that the solar system evolved from nebular matter.
nebulize *or* **nebulise** (ˈnɛbjʊˌlaɪz) *vb. (tr.)* to convert (a liquid) into a mist or fine spray; atomize. —ˌ**nebuliˈzation** *or* ˌ**nebuliˈsation** *n.* —ˈ**nebuˌlizer** *or* ˈ**nebuˌliser** *n.*
nebulosity (ˌnɛbjʊˈlɒsɪtɪ) *n., pl.* **-ties. 1.** the state or quality of being nebulous. **2.** *Astronomy.* a nebula.
nebulous (ˈnɛbjʊləs) *adj.* **1.** lacking definite form, shape, or content; vague or amorphous: *nebulous reasons.* **2.** of, characteristic of, or resembling a nebula. **3.** *Rare.* misty or hazy. —ˈ**nebulously** *adv.* —ˈ**nebulousness** *n.*
NEC *abbrev. for* National Executive Committee.
necessaries (ˈnɛsɪsərɪz) *pl. n.* **1.** *(sometimes sing.)* what is needed; essential items: *the necessaries of life.* **2.** *Law.* food, clothing, etc., essential for the maintenance of a dependant in the condition of life to which he or she is accustomed.
necessarily (ˈnɛsɪsərɪlɪ, ˌnɛsɪˈsɛrɪlɪ) *adv.* **1.** as an inevitable or natural consequence: *girls do not necessarily like dolls.* **2.** as a certainty: *he won't necessarily come.*
necessary (ˈnɛsɪsərɪ) *adj.* **1.** needed to achieve a certain desired effect or result; required. **2.** resulting from necessity; inevitable: *the necessary consequences of your action.* **3.** *Logic.* **a.** (of a statement, formula, etc.) true under all interpretations or in all possible circumstances. **b.** (of a proposition) determined to be true by its meaning, so that its denial would be self-contradictory. **c.** (of a property) essential, so that without it its subject would not be the entity it is. **d.** (of an inference) always yielding a true conclusion when its premises are true; valid. **e.** (of a condition) entailed by the truth of some statement or the obtaining of some state of affairs. ~Compare **sufficient** (sense 2). **4.** *Philosophy.* (in a nonlogical sense) expressing a law of nature, so that if it is in this sense necessary that all As are B, even although it is not contradictory to conceive of an A which is not B, we are licensed to infer that if something were an A it would have to be B. **5.** *Rare.* compelled, as by necessity or law; not free. ~*n.* **6.** *Informal.* (preceded by *the*) the money required for a particular purpose. **7. do the necessary.** *Informal.* to do something that is necessary in a particular situation. ~See also **necessaries.** [C14: from Latin *necessārius* indispensable, from *necesse* unavoidable]
necessitarianism (nɪˌsɛsɪˈtɛərɪəˌnɪzəm) *or* **necessarianism** (ˌnɛsɪˈsɛərɪəˌnɪzəm) *n. Philosophy.* another word for **determinism.** Compare **libertarian.** —**neˌcessiˈtarian** *or* ˌ**necesˈsarian** *n., adj.*
necessitate (nɪˈsɛsɪˌteɪt) *vb. (tr.)* **1.** to cause as an unavoidable and necessary result. **2.** *(usually passive)* to compel or require (someone to do something). —**neˌcessiˈtation** *n.* —**neˈcessitative** *adj.*
necessitous (nɪˈsɛsɪtəs) *adj.* very needy; destitute; poverty-stricken. —**neˈcessitously** *adv.*
necessity (nɪˈsɛsɪtɪ) *n., pl.* **-ties. 1.** *(sometimes pl.)* something needed for a desired result; prerequisite: *necessities of life.* **2.** a condition or set of circumstances, such as physical laws or social rules, that inevitably requires a certain result: *it is a matter of necessity to wear formal clothes when meeting the Queen.* **3.** the state or quality of being obligatory or unavoidable. **4.** urgent requirement, as in an emergency or misfortune: *in time of necessity we must all work together.* **5.** poverty or want. **6.** *Rare.* compulsion through laws of nature; fate. **7.** *Philosophy.* **a.** a condition, principle, or conclusion that cannot be otherwise. **b.** the constraining force of physical determinants on all aspects of life. Compare **freedom** (sense 8). **8.** *Logic.* **a.** the property of being necessary. **b.** a statement asserting that some property is essential or statement is necessarily true. **c.** the operator that indicates that the expression it modifies is true in all possible worlds. Usual symbol: □ or ∟. **9. of necessity.** inevitably; necessarily.
neck (nɛk) *n.* **1.** the part of an organism connecting the head with the rest of the body. **2.** the part of a garment around or nearest the neck. **3.** something resembling a neck in shape or

position: *the neck of a bottle.* 4. *Anatomy.* a constricted portion of an organ or part, such as the cervix of the uterus. 5. a narrow or elongated projecting strip of land; a peninsula or isthmus. 6. a strait or channel. 7. the part of a violin, cello, etc., that extends from the body to the tuning pegs and supports the fingerboard. 8. a solid block of lava from the opening of an extinct volcano, exposed after erosion of the surrounding rock. 9. *Botany.* the upper, usually tubular, part of the archegonium of mosses, ferns, etc. 10. the length of a horse's head and neck taken as an approximate distance by which one horse beats another in a race: *to win by a neck.* 11. *Informal.* a short distance, amount, or margin: *he is always a neck ahead in new techniques.* 12. *Informal.* impudence; audacity: *he had the neck to ask for a rise.* 13. *Architect.* the narrow band at the top of the shaft of a column between the necking and the capital, esp. as used in the Tuscan order. 14. another name for **beard** (on printer's type). 15. **break one's neck.** *Informal.* to exert oneself greatly, esp. by hurrying, in order to do something. 16. **by the neck.** *Irish and Scot. slang.* (of a bottle of beer) served unpoured: *give me two bottles of stout by the neck.* 17. **get it in the neck.** *Informal.* to be reprimanded or punished severely. 18. **neck and neck.** absolutely level or even in a race or competition. 19. **neck of the woods.** *Informal.* an area or locality: *a quiet neck of the woods.* 20. **neck or nothing.** whatever the risk; at any cost. 21. **risk one's neck.** to take a great risk. 22. **save one's** *or* **someone's neck.** *Informal.* to escape from or help someone else to escape from a difficult or dangerous situation. 23. **stick one's neck out.** *Informal.* to risk criticism, ridicule, failure, etc., by speaking one's mind. 24. **up to one's neck (in).** deeply involved (in). ~*vb.* 25. (*intr.*) *Informal.* to kiss, embrace, or fondle someone or one another passionately. [Old English *hnecca;* related to Old High German *hnack,* Old Irish *cnocc* hill] —**'necker** *n.*

neckband ('nɛk,bænd) *n.* a band around the neck of a garment as finishing, decoration, or a base for a collar.

neckcloth ('nɛk,klɒθ) *n.* a large ornamental usually white cravat worn formerly by men.

neckerchief ('nɛkətʃɪf, -,tʃiːf) *n.* a piece of ornamental cloth, often square, worn around the neck. [C14: from NECK + KERCHIEF]

Necker cube ('nɛkə) *n.* a line drawing showing the 12 edges of a transparent cube, so that it can be seen alternately facing in two different directions: an example of an ambiguous figure. [C19: named after Louis Albert *Necker* (1786–1861), Swiss mineralogist]

necking ('nɛkɪŋ) *n.* 1. *Informal.* the activity of kissing and embracing passionately. 2. Also called: **gorgerin.** *Architect.* one or more mouldings at the top of a column between the shaft and the capital.

necklace ('nɛklɪs) *n.* a chain, band, or cord, often bearing beads, pearls, jewels, etc., worn around the neck as an ornament, esp. by women.

necklet ('nɛklɪt) *n.* an ornament worn round the neck.

neckline ('nɛk,laɪn) *n.* the shape or position of the upper edge of a dress, blouse, etc.: *a plunging neckline.*

neckpiece ('nɛk,piːs) *n.* a piece of fur, cloth, etc., worn around the neck or neckline.

necktie ('nɛk,taɪ) *n.* the U.S. name for **tie** (sense 11).

neckwear ('nɛk,wɛə) *n.* articles of clothing, such as ties, scarves, etc., worn around the neck.

necro- *or before a vowel* **necr-** *combining form.* indicating death, a dead body, or dead tissue: *necrology; necrophagous; necrosis.* [from Greek *nekros* corpse]

necrobiosis (,nɛkrəʊbaɪ'əʊsɪs) *n. Physiol.* the normal degeneration and death of cells. Compare **necrosis.** —**necrobiotic** (,nɛkrəʊbaɪ'ɒtɪk) *adj.*

necrolatry (nɛ'krɒlətrɪ) *n.* the worship of the dead.

necrology (nɛ'krɒlədʒɪ) *n., pl.* **-gies.** 1. a list of people recently dead. 2. a less common word for **obituary.** —**necrological** (,nɛkrə'lɒdʒɪkᵊl) *adj.* —**ne'crologist** *n.*

necromancy ('nɛkrəʊ,mænsɪ) *n.* 1. the art or practice of supposedly conjuring up the dead, esp. in order to obtain from them knowledge of the future. 2. black magic; sorcery. [C13: (as in sense 1) ultimately from Greek *nekromanteia,* from *nekros* corpse; (as in sense 2) from Medieval Latin *nigromantia,* from Latin *niger* black, which replaced *necro-* through folk etymology] —**'necro,mancer** *n.* —**,necro'mantic** *adj.*

necromania (,nɛkrəʊ'meɪnɪə) *n.* another word for **necrophilia.** —**,necro'mani,ac** *n.*

necrophagous (nə'krɒfəgəs) *adj.* (of an animal, bird, etc.) feeding on carrion.

necrophilia (,nɛkrəʊ'fɪlɪə) *n.* sexual attraction for or sexual intercourse with dead bodies. Also called: **necromania, necrophilism.** —**,necro'phili,ac** *or* **necrophile** ('nɛkrəʊ,faɪl) *n.* —**,necro'philic** *adj.*

necrophilism (nɛ'krɒfɪ,lɪzəm) *n.* 1. another word for **necrophilia.** 2. a strong desire to be dead.

necrophobia (,nɛkrəʊ'fəʊbɪə) *n.* an abnormal fear of death or dead bodies. —**'necro,phobe** *n.* —**,necro'phobic** *adj.*

necrophorous (nɪ'krɒfərəs) *adj.* denoting animals, such as certain beetles, that carry away the bodies of dead animals.

necropolis (nɛ'krɒpəlɪs) *n., pl.* **-lises** *or* **-leis** (-,leɪs). a burial site or cemetery. [C19: Greek, from *nekros* dead + *polis* city]

necropsy ('nɛkrɒpsɪ) *or* **necroscopy** (nɛ'krɒskəpɪ) *n., pl.* **-sies** *or* **-pies.** another name for **autopsy.** [C19: from Greek *nekros* dead body + *opsis* sight]

necrose (nɛ'krəʊs, 'nɛkrəʊs) *vb.* (*intr.*) to cause or undergo necrosis. [C19: back formation from NECROSIS]

necrosis (nɛ'krəʊsɪs) *n.* 1. the death of one or more cells in the body, usually within a localized area, as from an interruption of the blood supply to that part. 2. death of plant tissue due to disease, frost, etc. [C17: New Latin from Greek *nekrōsis,* from *nekroun* to kill, from *nekros* corpse] —**necrotic** (nɛ'krɒtɪk) *adj.*

necrotomy (nɛ'krɒtəmɪ) *n., pl.* **-mies.** 1. dissection of a dead body. 2. surgical excision of dead tissue from a living organism.

necrotroph ('nɛkrəʊ,trəʊf) *n.* a parasitic organism that kills the living cells of its host and then feeds on the dead matter. —**necrotrophic** (,nɛkrəʊ'trɒfɪk) *adj.*

nectar ('nɛktə) *n.* 1. a sugary fluid produced in the nectaries of flowers and collected by bees and other insects. 2. *Classical myth.* the drink of the gods. Compare **ambrosia** (sense 1). 3. any delicious drink, esp. a sweet one. 4. something very pleasant or welcome: *your words are nectar to me.* 5. *Chiefly U.S.* **a.** the undiluted juice of a fruit. **b.** a mixture of fruit juices. [C16: via Latin from Greek *néktar,* perhaps *nek-* death (related to *nekros* corpse) + *-tar,* related to Sanskrit *tarati* he overcomes; compare Latin *nex* death and *trans* across] —**nectareous** (nɛk'tɛərɪəs) *or* **'nectarous** *adj.*

nectarine ('nɛktərɪn) *n.* 1. a variety of peach tree, *Prunus persica nectarina.* 2. the fruit of this tree, which has a smooth skin. [C17: apparently from NECTAR]

nectarivorous (,nɛktə'rɪvərəs) *adj. Zoology.* feeding on nectar.

nectary ('nɛktərɪ) *n., pl.* **-ries.** 1. any of various glandular structures secreting nectar that occur in the flowers, leaves, stipules, etc., of a plant. 2. any of the abdominal tubes in aphids through which honeydew is secreted. [C18: from New Latin *nectarium,* from NECTAR] —**nectarial** (nɛk'tɛərɪəl) *adj.*

NEDC *abbrev. for* National Economic Development Council. Also (informal): **Neddy** ('nɛdɪ).

neddy ('nɛdɪ) *n., pl.* **-dies.** 1. a child's word for a **donkey.** 2. *Informal.* a silly person; fool. 3. *Austral. informal.* a horse, esp. a racehorse: *he lost his money on the neddies.* [C18: from *Ned,* pet form of *Edward*]

née *or* **nee** (neɪ) *adj.* indicating the maiden name of a married woman: *Mrs Bloggs née Blandish.* [C19: from French: past participle (fem.) of *naître* to be born, from Latin *nascī*]

need (niːd) *vb.* 1. (*tr.*) to be in want of: *to need money.* 2. (*tr.*) to require or be required of necessity (to be or do something); be obliged: *to need to do more work.* 3. (takes an infinitive without *to*) used as an auxiliary in negative and interrogative sentences to express necessity or obligation and does not add *-s* when used with *he, she, it,* and singular nouns: *need he go?* 4. (*intr.*) *Archaic.* to be essential or necessary to: *there needs no reason for this.* ~*n.* 5. the fact or an instance of feeling the lack of something: *he has need of a new coat.* 6. a requirement: *the need for vengeance.* 7. necessity or obligation resulting from some situation: *no need to be frightened.* 8. distress or extremity: *a friend in need.* 9. extreme poverty or destitution; penury. ~See also **needs.** [Old English *nēad, nied;* related to Old Frisian *nēd,* Old Saxon *nōd,* Old High German *nōt*]

needful ('niːdfʊl) *adj.* 1. necessary; needed; required. 2. *Archaic.* needy; poverty-stricken. ~*n. Informal.* 3. money or funds: *do you have the needful?* 4. **do the needful.** to perform a necessary task. —**'needfully** *adv.* —**'needfulness** *n.*

neediness ('niːdɪnɪs) *n.* the state of being needy; poverty.

needle ('niːdᵊl) *n.* 1. a pointed slender piece of metal, usually steel, with a hole or eye in it through which thread is passed for sewing. 2. a somewhat larger rod with a point at one or each end, used in knitting. 3. a similar instrument with a hook at one end for crocheting. 4. **a.** another name for **stylus** (sense 3). **b.** a small thin pointed device, esp. one made of stainless steel, used to transmit the vibrations from a gramophone record to the pick-up. 5. *Med.* **a.** the long hollow pointed part of a hypodermic syringe, which is inserted into the body. **b.** an informal name for **hypodermic syringe.** 6. *Surgery.* a pointed steel instrument, often curved, for suturing, puncturing, or ligating. 7. a long narrow stiff leaf in which water loss is greatly reduced: *pine needles.* 8. any slender sharp spine, such as the spine of a sea urchin. 9. any slender pointer for indicating the reading on the scale of a measuring instrument. 10. short for **magnetic needle.** 11. a crystal resembling a needle in shape. 12. a sharp pointed metal instrument used in engraving and etching. 13. anything long and pointed, such as an obelisk: *a needle of light.* 14. a short horizontal beam passed through a wall and supported on vertical posts to take the load of the upper part of the wall. 15. *Informal.* **a.** anger or intense rivalry, esp. in a sporting encounter. **b.** (*as modifier*): *a needle match.* 16. **have** *or* **get the needle (to).** *Brit. informal.* to feel dislike, distaste, nervousness, or annoyance (for): *she got the needle after he had refused her invitation.* ~*vb.* 17. (*tr.*) *Informal.* to goad or provoke, as by constant criticism. 18. (*tr.*) to sew, embroider, or prick (fabric) with a needle. 19. (*tr.*) *U.S.* to increase the alcoholic strength of (beer or other beverages). 20. (*intr.*) (of a substance) to form needle-shaped crystals. [Old English *nǣdl;* related to Gothic *nēthla,* German *Nadel*]

needle bearing *n. Engineering.* an antifriction roller bearing in which long rollers of very small diameter fill the race without a cage to provide spacers between them.
needle bush *n.* a small Australian tree, *Hakea leucoptera,* having needle-shaped leaves and soft wood used for veneers: family *Proteaceae.*
needlecord ('niːdᵊlˌkɔːd) *n.* a corduroy fabric with narrow ribs.
needlecraft ('niːdᵊlˌkrɑːft) *n.* the art or practice of needlework.
needlefish ('niːdᵊlˌfɪʃ) *n., pl.* **-fish** *or* **-fishes. 1.** any ferocious teleost fish of the family *Belonidae* of warm and tropical regions, having an elongated body and long toothed jaws. **2.** another name for **pipefish.**
needle fly *n.* a small stonefly of the genus *Leuctra,* whose rolled-up wings at rest give it a slender pointed appearance.
needleful ('niːdᵊlfʊl) *n.* a length of thread cut for use in a needle.
needlepoint ('niːdᵊlˌpɔɪnt) *n.* **1.** embroidery done on canvas with the same stitch throughout so as to resemble tapestry. **2.** another name for **point lace.**
needless ('niːdlɪs) *adj.* not required or desired; unnecessary. —'**needlessly** *adv.* —'**needlessness** *n.*
needle time *n.* the limited time allocated by a radio channel to the broadcasting of music from records.
needle valve *n.* a valve with a needle-like part that can be moved to control the flow of a fluid.
needlewoman ('niːdᵊlˌwʊmən) *n., pl.* **-women.** a woman who does needlework; seamstress.
needlework ('niːdᵊlˌwɜːk) *n.* **1.** work done with a needle, esp. sewing and embroidery. **2.** the result of such work.
needs (niːdz) *adv.* **1.** (preceded or foll. by *must*) of necessity: *we must needs go; we will go, if needs must.* ~*pl. n.* **2.** what is required; necessities: *the needs of the third world; his needs are modest.*
needs test *n. Social welfare.* an examination of a person's physical or social, rather than financial, circumstances, to determine whether he is eligible for a particular welfare benefit or service. Compare **means test.**
needy ('niːdɪ) *adj.* **needier, neediest. a.** in need of practical or emotional support; distressed. **b.** (*as collective n.;* preceded by *the*)*: the needy.*
Néel point *or* **temperature** (niː'ɛl) *n.* the temperature above which an antiferromagnetic substance loses its antiferromagnetism and becomes paramagnetic. [C20: named after Louis *Néel* (born 1904), French physicist]
neem (niːm) *n.* a large tree of India, *Azadirachta indica,* all parts of which are useful to man: the leaves act as a natural pesticide, the fruit and seeds yield a medicinal oil, the bark is used to make a tonic, and the trunk exudes a gum. [C19: from Hindi *nīm,* from Sanskrit *nimba*]
neep (niːp) *n. Brit.* a dialect name for a **turnip.** [Old English *nǣp,* from Latin *nāpus* turnip]
ne'er (nɛə) *adv.* a poetic contraction of **never.**
Ne'erday ('nerde) *n. Scot.* New Year's Day.
ne'er-do-well *n.* **1.** an improvident, irresponsible, or lazy person. ~*adj.* **2.** useless; worthless: *your ne'er-do-well schemes.*
nefarious (nɪ'fɛərɪəs) *adj.* evil; wicked; sinful. [C17: from Latin *nefārius,* from *nefās* unlawful deed, from *nē* not + *fās* divine law] —**ne'fariously** *adv.* —**ne'fariousness** *n.*
NEG (in transformational grammar) *abbrev. for* negative.
neg. *abbrev. for* negative(ly).
negate (nɪ'geɪt) *vb.* (*tr.*) **1.** to make ineffective or void; nullify; invalidate. **2.** to deny or contradict. [C17: from Latin *negāre,* from *neg-,* variant of *nec* not + *aio* I say] —**ne'gator** *or* **ne'gater** *n.*
negation (nɪ'geɪʃən) *n.* **1.** the opposite or absence of something. **2.** a negative thing or condition. **3.** the act or an instance of negating. **4.** *Logic.* **a.** the operator that forms one sentence from another and corresponds to the English *not.* **b.** a sentence so formed. It is usually written $-p$, $\sim p$, $\bar{p}$ or $\neg p$, where p is the given sentence, and is false when the given sentence is true, and true when it is false.
negative ('nɛgətɪv) *adj.* **1.** expressing or meaning a refusal or denial: *a negative answer.* **2.** lacking positive or affirmative qualities, such as enthusiasm, interest, or optimism. **3.** showing or tending towards opposition or resistance. **4. a.** measured in a direction opposite to that regarded as positive. **b.** having the same magnitude but opposite sense to an equivalent positive quantity. **5.** *Biology.* indicating movement or growth away from a particular stimulus: *negative geotropism.* **6.** *Med.* (of the results of a diagnostic test) indicating absence of the disease or condition for which the test was made. **7.** another word for **minus** (senses 3b, 5). **8.** *Physics.* **a.** (of an electric charge) having the same polarity as the charge of an electron. **b.** (of a body, system, ion, etc.) having a negative electric charge; having an excess of electrons. **c.** (of a point in an electric circuit) having a lower electrical potential than some other point with an assigned zero potential. **9.** short for **electronegative. 10.** (of a lens) capable of causing divergence of a parallel beam of light. **11.** of or relating to a photographic negative. **12.** *Logic.* (of a categorial proposition) denying the satisfaction by the subject of the predicate, as in *some men are irrational; no pigs have wings.* **13.** *Astrology.* of, relating to, or governed by the signs of the zodiac of the earth and water classifications, which are thought to be associated with a receptive passive nature. **14.** short for **Rh negative.** ~*n.* **15.** a statement or act of denial, refusal, or negation. **16.** a negative person or thing. **17.** *Photog.* a piece of photographic film or a plate, previously exposed and developed, showing an image that, in black-and-white photography, has a reversal of tones. In colour photography the image is in complementary colours to the subject so that blue sky appears yellow, green grass appears purple, etc. **18.** *Physics.* a negative object, such as a terminal or a plate in a voltaic cell. **19.** a sentence or other linguistic element with a negative meaning, as the English word *not.* **20.** a quantity less than zero or a quantity to be subtracted. **21.** *Logic.* a negative proposition. **22.** *Archaic.* the right of veto. **23. in the negative.** indicating denial or refusal. ~*sentence substitute.* **24.** (esp. in military communications) a signal code word for **no**[1]. ~*vb.* (*tr.*) **25.** to deny or nullify; negate. **26.** to show to be false; disprove. **27.** to refuse consent to or approval of: *the proposal was negatived.* ~Compare **positive, affirmative.** —'**negatively** *adv.* —'**negativeness** *or* ˌ**nega'tivity** *n.*
negative feedback *n.* See **feedback.**
negative hallucination *n. Psychol.* an apparent abnormal inability to perceive an object.
negative polarity *n. Grammar.* the grammatical character of a word or phrase, such as *ever* or *any,* that may normally only be used in a semantically or syntactically negative or interrogative context.
negative-raising *n. Transformational grammar.* a rule that moves a negative element out of the complement clause of certain verbs, such as *think,* into the main clause, as in the derivation of *He doesn't think that he'll finish.*
negative reinforcement *n. Psychol.* the reinforcing of a response by giving an aversive stimulus when the response is not made and omitting the aversive stimulus when the response is made.
negative resistance *n.* a characteristic of certain electronic components in which an increase in the applied voltage increases the resistance, producing a proportional decrease in current.
negative sign *n.* the symbol (–) used to indicate a negative quantity or a subtraction; minus sign.
negative tax *n.* a payment by the State to a person with a low income, the magnitude of the payment increasing as the income decreases. It is regarded as a form of social welfare. Also called: **negative income tax.**
negativism ('nɛgətɪvˌɪzəm) *n.* **1.** a tendency to be or a state of being unconstructively critical. **2.** any sceptical or derisive system of thought. **3.** *Psychiatry.* refusal to do what is expected or suggested or the tendency to do the opposite. —'**negativist** *n., adj.* —ˌ**negativ'istic** *adj.*
negator (nɪ'geɪtə) *n. Electronics.* another name for **NOT circuit.**
negatron ('nɛgəˌtrɒn) *n.* an obsolete word for **electron.** [C20: from NEGA(TIVE + ELEC)TRON]
neglect (nɪ'glɛkt) *vb.* (*tr.*) **1.** to fail to give due care, attention, or time to: *to neglect a child.* **2.** to fail (to do something) through thoughtlessness or carelessness: *he neglected to tell her.* **3.** to ignore or disregard: *she neglected his frantic signals.* ~*n.* **4.** lack of due care or attention; negligence: *the child starved through neglect.* **5.** the act or an instance of neglecting or the state of being neglected. [C16: from Latin *neglegere* to neglect, from *nec* not + *legere* to select] —**ne'glecter** *or* **ne'glector** *n.*
neglectful (nɪ'glɛktfʊl) *adj.* (when *postpositive,* foll. by *of*) not giving due care and attention (to); careless; heedless. —**ne'glectfully** *adv.* —**ne'glectfulness** *n.*
negligee *or* **negligée** ('nɛglɪˌʒeɪ) *n.* **1.** a woman's light dressing gown, esp. one that is lace-trimmed. **2.** any informal attire. [C18: from French *négligée,* past participle (fem.) of *négliger* to NEGLECT]
negligence ('nɛglɪdʒəns) *n.* **1.** the state or quality of being negligent. **2.** a negligent act. **3.** *Law.* a civil wrong whereby the defendant is in breach of a legal duty of care, resulting in injury to the plaintiff.
negligent ('nɛglɪdʒənt) *adj.* **1.** habitually neglecting duties, responsibilities, etc.; lacking attention, care, or concern; neglectful. **2.** careless or nonchalant. —'**negligently** *adv.*
negligible ('nɛglɪdʒəbᵊl) *adj.* so small, unimportant, etc., as to be not worth considering; insignificant. —ˌ**negligi'bility** *or* '**negligibleness** *n.* —'**negligibly** *adv.*
negotiable (nɪ'gəʊʃəbᵊl) *adj.* **1.** able to be negotiated. **2.** (of a bill of exchange, promissory note, etc.) legally transferable in title from one party to another. —**neˌgotia'bility** *n.*
negotiable instrument *n.* a legal document, such as a cheque or bill of exchange, that is freely negotiable.
negotiant (nɪ'gəʊʃɪənt) *n.* a person, nation, organization, etc. involved in a negotiation.
negotiate (nɪ'gəʊʃɪˌeɪt) *vb.* **1.** to work or talk (with others) to achieve (a transaction, an agreement, etc.). **2.** (*tr.*) to succeed in passing through, around, or over: *to negotiate a mountain pass.* **3.** (*tr.*) *Finance.* **a.** to transfer (a negotiable commercial paper) by endorsement to another in return for value received. **b.** to sell (financial assets). **c.** to arrange for (a loan). [C16: from Latin *negōtiārī* to do business, from *negōtium* business, from *nec* not + *ōtium* leisure] —**ne'gotiˌator** *n.*
negotiation (nɪˌgəʊʃɪ'eɪʃən) *n.* **1.** a discussion set up or intended to produce a settlement or agreement. **2.** the act or process of negotiating.

Negress (ˈniːgrɪs) *n.* a female Negro.
Negrillo (nɪˈgrɪləʊ) *n., pl.* **-los** *or* **-loes.** a member of a dwarfish Negro race of central and southern Africa. [C19: from Spanish, diminutive of *negro* black]
Negritic (nɪˈgrɪtɪk) *adj.* relating to the Negroes or the Negritos.
Negrito (nɪˈgriːtəʊ) *n., pl.* **-tos** *or* **-toes.** a member of any of various dwarfish Negroid peoples of SE Asia and Melanesia. [C19: from Spanish, diminutive of *negro* black]
negritude (ˈniːgrɪˌtjuːd, ˈnɛg-) *n.* **1.** the fact of being a Negro. **2.** awareness and cultivation of the Negro heritage, values, and culture. [C20: from French, from *nègre* NEGRO]
Negro (ˈniːgrəʊ) *n., pl.* **-groes.** **1.** a member of any of the dark-skinned indigenous peoples of Africa and their descendants elsewhere. ~*adj.* **2.** relating to or characteristic of Negroes. [C16: from Spanish or Portuguese: black, from Latin *niger* black] —ˈ**Negroˌism** *n.*
Negroid (ˈniːgrɔɪd) *adj.* **1.** denoting, relating to, or belonging to one of the major racial groups of mankind, characterized by brown-black skin, tightly-curled hair, a short nose, and full lips. This group includes the indigenous peoples of Africa south of the Sahara, their descendants elsewhere, and some Melanesian peoples. ~*n.* **2.** a member of this racial group.
Negrophil (ˈniːgrəʊfɪl) *or* **Negrophile** (ˈniːgrəʊˌfaɪl) *n.* a person who admires Negroes and their culture. —**Negrophilism** (niːˈgrɒfɪˌlɪzəm) *n.*
Negrophobe (ˈniːgrəʊˌfəʊb) *n.* a person who dislikes or fears Negroes. —ˌ**Negroˈphobia** *n.* —ˌ**Negroˈphobic** *adj.*
Negro spiritual (ˈniːgrəʊ) *n.* a type of religious song originating among Negro slaves in the American South.
negus (ˈniːgəs) *n., pl.* **-guses.** a hot drink of port and lemon juice, usually spiced and sweetened. [C18: named after Col. Francis *Negus* (died 1732), its English inventor]
Negus (ˈniːgəs) *n., pl.* **-guses.** a title of the emperor of Ethiopia. [from Amharic: king]
Neh. *Bible. abbrev. for* Nehemiah.
neigh (neɪ) *n.* **1.** the high-pitched cry of a horse; whinny. ~*vb.* **2.** (*intr.*) to make a neigh or a similar noise. **3.** (*tr.*) to utter with a sound like a neigh. [Old English *hnǣgan;* related to Old Saxon *hnēgian*]
neighbour *or U.S.* **neighbor** (ˈneɪbə) *n.* **1.** a person who lives near or next to another. **2. a.** a person or thing near or next to another. **b.** (*as modifier*): *neighbour states.* ~*vb.* **3.** (when *intr.*, often foll. by *on*) to be or live close (to a person or thing). [Old English *nēahbūr*, from *nēah* NIGH + *būr, gebūr* dweller; see BOOR] —ˈ**neighbourless** *or U.S.* ˈ**neighborless** *adj.*
neighbourhood *or U.S.* **neighborhood** (ˈneɪbəˌhʊd) *n.* **1.** the immediate environment; surroundings; vicinity. **2.** a district where people live. **3.** the people in a particular area; neighbours. **4.** neighbourly feeling. **5.** *Maths.* the set of all points whose distance from a given point is less than a specified value. **6.** (*modifier*) of or for a neighbourhood: *a neighbourhood community worker.* **7. in the neighbourhood of.** approximately (a given number).
neighbourhood watch *n.* a scheme under which members of a community agree together to take responsibility for keeping an eye on each other's property, as a way of preventing crime.
neighbourly *or U.S.* **neighborly** (ˈneɪbəlɪ) *adj.* kind, friendly, or sociable, as befits a neighbour. —ˈ**neighbourliness** *or U.S.* ˈ**neighborliness** *n.*
neither (ˈnaɪðə, ˈniːðə) *determiner.* **1. a.** not one nor the other (of two); not either: *neither foot is swollen.* **b.** (*as pronoun*): *neither can win.* ~*conj.* **2.** (*coordinating*) **a.** (used preceding alternatives joined by *nor*) not: *neither John nor Mary nor Joe went.* **b.** another word for **nor** (sense 2). ~*adv.* **3.** (*sentence modifier*) *Not standard.* another word for **either** (sense 4). [C13 (literally, *ne either* not either): changed from Old English *nāwther*, from *nāhwæther*, from *nā* not + *hwæther* which of two; see WHETHER]
▷**Usage.** A verb following a compound subject that uses *neither...(nor)* should be in the singular if both subjects are in the singular: *neither Jack nor John has done the work.* Where the subjects are different in number, the verb usually agrees with the subject nearest to it: *neither they nor Jack was able to come.*
nek (nɛk) *n.* (*cap. when part of name*) *S. African.* a mountain pass: *Lundeans Nek.*
nekton (ˈnɛktɒn) *n.* the population of free-swimming animals that inhabits the middle depths of a sea or lake. Compare **plankton.** [C19: via German from Greek *nēkton* a swimming thing, from *nēkhein* to swim] —**nekˈtonic** *adj.*
nelly (ˈnɛlɪ) *n.* **not on your nelly.** (*sentence substitute*). *Brit. slang.* not under any circumstances; certainly not.
nelson (ˈnɛlsən) *n.* any wrestling hold in which a wrestler places his arm or arms under his opponent's arm or arms from behind and exerts pressure with his palms on the back of his opponent's neck. See **full nelson, half-nelson.** [C19: from a proper name]
nelumbo (nɪˈlʌmbəʊ) *n., pl.* **-bos.** either of the two aquatic plants of the genus *Nelumbo:* family *Nelumbonaceae.* See **lotus** (sense 4), **water chinquapin.** [C19: New Latin, from Sinhalese *nelumbu* lotus]
nemathelminth (ˌnɛməˈθɛlmɪnθ) *n.* any unsegmented worm of the group *Nemathelminthes,* including the nematodes, nematomorphs, and acanthocephalans.
nematic (nɪˈmætɪk) *adj. Chem.* (of a substance) existing in or having a mesomorphic state in which a linear orientation of the molecules causes anisotropic properties. Compare **smectic.** See also **liquid crystal.** [C20: NEMAT(O)- (referring to the threadlike chains of molecules in liquid) + -IC]
nemato- *or before a vowel* **nemat-** *combining form.* indicating a threadlike form: *nematocyst.* [from Greek *nēma* thread]
nematocyst (ˈnɛmətəˌsɪst, nɪˈmætə-) *n.* a structure in coelenterates, such as jellyfish, consisting of a capsule containing a hollow coiled thread that can be everted to sting or paralyse prey and enemies. —ˌ**nematoˈcystic** *adj.*
nematode (ˈnɛməˌtəʊd) *n.* any unsegmented worm of the phylum (or class) *Nematoda,* having a tough outer cuticle. The group includes free-living forms and disease-causing parasites, such as the hookworm and filaria. Also called: **nematode worm, roundworm.**
Nembutal (ˈnɛmbjʊˌtɑːl) *n.* a trademark for **pentobarbitone sodium.**
nem. con. *abbrev. for* nemine contradicente. [Latin: no-one contradicting; unanimously]
nemertean (nɪˈmɜːtɪən) *or* **nemertine** (ˈnɛməˌtaɪn) *n.* **1.** Also called: **ribbon worm.** any soft flattened ribbon-like marine worm of the phylum (or class) *Nemertea* (or *Nemertina*), having an eversible threadlike proboscis. ~*adj.* **2.** of, relating to, or belonging to the *Nemertea.* [C19: via New Latin from Greek *Nēmertēs* a Nereid (sea nymph)]
nemesia (nɪˈmiːʒə) *n.* any plant of the southern African scrophulariaceous genus *Nemesia:* cultivated for their brightly coloured (often reddish) flowers. [C19: New Latin, from Greek *nemesion,* name of a plant resembling this]
Nemesis (ˈnɛmɪsɪs) *n., pl.* **-ses** (-ˌsiːz). (*sometimes not cap.*) an agency of retribution and vengeance. [C16: after *Nemesis,* Greek goddess of retribution and vengeance, via Latin from Greek: righteous wrath, from *némein* to distribute what is due]
nemophila (nəˈmɒfɪlə) *n.* any of a genus, *Nemophila,* of low-growing hairy annual plants, esp. *N. menziesii,* grown for its blue or white flowers: family *Hydrophyllaceae.* [New Latin, from Greek *nemos* a grove + *philein* to love]
nene (ˈneɪˌneɪ) *n.* a rare black-and-grey short-winged Hawaiian goose, *Branta sandvicensis,* having partly webbed feet. [from Hawaiian]
neo- *or sometimes before a vowel* **ne-** *combining form.* **1.** (*sometimes cap.*) new, recent, or a new or modern form or development: *neoclassicism; neocolonialism.* **2.** (*usually cap.*) the most recent subdivision of a geological period: *Neogene.* [from Greek *neos* new]
neoanthropic (ˌniːəʊænˈθrɒpɪk) *adj. Anthropol.* of, relating to, or resembling modern man.
neoarsphenamine (ˌniːəʊɑːsˈfɛnəˌmiːn, -fɪˈnæmɪn) *n.* a derivative of arsenic used in treating syphilis.
Neocene (ˈniːəˌsiːn) *adj., n.* a former word for **Neogene.**
neoclassicism (ˌniːəʊˈklæsɪˌsɪzəm) *n.* **1.** a late 18th- and early 19th-century style in architecture, decorative art, and fine art, based on the imitation of surviving classical models and types. **2.** *Music.* a movement of the 1920s that sought to avoid the emotionalism of late romantic music by reviving the use of counterpoint, forms such as the classical suite, and small instrumental ensembles. —**neoclassical** (ˌniːəʊˈklæsɪkᵊl) *or* ˌ**neoˈclassic** *adj.* —ˌ**neoˈclassicist** *n.*
neocolonialism (ˌniːəʊkəˈləʊnɪəˌlɪzəm) *n.* (in the modern world) political control by an outside power of a country that is in theory sovereign and independent, esp. through the domination of its economy. —ˌ**neocoˈlonial** *adj.* —ˌ**neocoˈlonialist** *n.*
Neo-Darwinism (ˌniːəʊˈdɑːwɪnˌɪzəm) *n.* a modern theory of evolution that relates Darwinism to the occurrence of inheritable variation by genetic mutation. —ˌ**Neo-Darˈwinian** *adj., n.*
neodymium (ˌniːəʊˈdɪmɪəm) *n.* a toxic silvery-white metallic element of the lanthanide series, occurring principally in monazite: used in colouring glass. Symbol: Nd; atomic no.: 60; atomic wt.: 144.24; valency: 3; relative density: 6.80 and 7.00 (depending on allotrope); melting pt.: 1024°C; boiling pt.: 3127°C. [C19: New Latin; see NEO- + DIDYMIUM]
Neogene (ˈniːəˌdʒiːn) *adj.* **1.** of, denoting, or formed during the Miocene and Pliocene epochs. ~*n.* **2. the.** the Neogene period or system.
neogothic (ˌnɪəʊˈgɒθɪk) *n.* another name for **Gothic Revival.**
neoimpressionism (ˌniːəʊɪmˈprɛʃəˌnɪzəm) *n.* a movement in French painting initiated in the 1880s and combining vivid colour technique with strictly formal composition. See also **pointillism.** —ˌ**neoimˈpressionist** *n., adj.*
Neo-Lamarckism (ˌniːəʊləˈmɑːkɪzəm) *n.* a modern theory of evolution based on Lamarckism and emphasizing the influence of environmental factors on genetic changes. —ˌ**Neo-LaˈmarckIan** *adj., n.*
Neo-Latin (ˌniːəʊˈlætɪn) *n.* **1.** another term for **New Latin.** ~*adj.* **2.** denoting or relating to New Latin. **3.** denoting or relating to language that developed from Latin; Romance.
neolith (ˈniːəʊlɪθ) *n.* a Neolithic stone implement.
Neolithic (ˌniːəʊˈlɪθɪk) *n.* **1.** the cultural period that lasted in SW Asia from about 9000 to 6000 B.C. and in Europe from about 4000 to 2400 B.C. and was characterized by primitive crop growing and stock rearing and the use of polished stone and flint tools and weapons. ~*adj.* **2.** relating to this period. ~See also **Mesolithic, Palaeolithic.**

neologism (nɪˈɒləˌdʒɪzəm) *or* **neology** *n., pl.* **-gisms** *or* **-gies.** **1.** a newly coined word, or a phrase or familiar word used in a new sense. **2.** the practice of using or introducing neologisms. **3.** *Rare.* a tendency towards adopting new views, esp. rationalist views, in matters of religion. [C18: via French from NEO- + *-logism,* from Greek *logos* word, saying] —**neˈologist** *n.* —**neˌoloˈgistic, neˌoloˈgistical,** *or* **neological** (ˌnɪəˈlɒdʒɪkᵊl) *adj.* —**neˌoloˈgistically** *or* **ˌneoˈlogically** *adv.*
neologize *or* **neologise** (nɪˈɒləˌdʒaɪz) *vb.* (*intr.*) to invent or use neologisms.
Neo-Melanesian *n.* an English-based creole language widely spoken in the SW Pacific, with borrowings from other languages, esp. Motu. Also called: **Beach-la-Mar.**
neomycin (ˌniːəʊˈmaɪsɪn) *n.* an antibiotic obtained from the bacterium *Streptomyces fradiae,* administered locally in the treatment of skin and eye infections or orally for bowel infections. Formula: $C_{12}H_{26}N_4O_6$. [C20: from NEO- + Greek *mukēs* fungus + -IN]
neon (ˈniːɒn) *n.* **1.** a colourless odourless rare gaseous element, an inert gas occurring in trace amounts in the atmosphere: used in illuminated signs and lights. Symbol: Ne; atomic no.: 10; atomic wt.: 20.179; density: 0.8999 kg/m^3; melting pt.: –248.67°C; boiling pt.: –246.05°C. **2.** (*modifier*) of or illuminated by neon or neon lamps: *neon sign.* [C19: via New Latin from Greek *neon* new]
neonate (ˈniːəʊˌneɪt) *n.* a newborn child, esp. in the first week of life and up to four weeks old. —**ˌneoˈnatal** *adj.* —**ˌneoˈnatally** *adv.*
neonatology (ˌniːəʊnəˈtɒlədʒɪ) *n.* the branch of medicine concerned with the development and disorders of newborn babies. —**ˌneonaˈtologist** *n.*
neon lamp *n.* a glass bulb or tube containing neon at low pressure that gives a pink or red glow when a voltage is applied.
neo-orthodoxy (ˌniːəʊˈɔːθəˌdɒksɪ) *n.* a movement in 20th-century Protestantism, reasserting certain older traditional Christian doctrines. —**ˌneo-ˈorthodox** *adj.*
neophilia (ˌniːəʊˈfɪlɪə) *n.* a tendency to like anything new; love of novelty. —**ˈneoˌphiliac** *n.*
neophobia (ˌniːəʊˈfəʊbɪə) *n.* a tendency to dislike anything new; fear of novelty. —**ˈneoˌphobe** *n.* —**ˌneoˈphobic** *adj.*
neophyte (ˈniːəʊˌfaɪt) *n.* **1.** a person newly converted to a religious faith. **2.** *R.C. Church.* a novice in a religious order. **3.** a novice or beginner. [C16: via Church Latin from New Testament Greek *neophutos* recently planted, from *neos* new + *phuton* a plant] —**neophytic** (ˌniːəʊˈfɪtɪk) *adj.*
neoplasm (ˈniːəʊˌplæzəm) *n. Pathol.* any abnormal new growth of tissue; tumour. —**neoplastic** (ˌniːəʊˈplæstɪk) *adj.*
neoplasticism (ˌniːəʊˈplæstɪˌsɪzəm) *n.* a style of abstract painting evolved in the 1920s in the Netherlands, characterized by the use of horizontal and vertical lines and planes and by black, white, grey, and primary colours.
neoplasty (ˈniːəʊˌplæstɪ) *n.* the surgical formation of new tissue structures or repair of damaged structures.
Neo-Platonism *or* **Neoplatonism** (ˌniːəʊˈpleɪtəˌnɪzəm) *n.* a philosophical system which was first developed in the 3rd century A.D. as a synthesis of Platonic, Pythagorean, and Aristotelian elements, and which, although originally opposed to Christianity, later incorporated it. It dominated European thought until the 13th century and re-emerged during the Renaissance. —**Neo-Platonic** (ˌniːəʊpləˈtɒnɪk) *adj.* —**ˌNeoˈPlatonist** *n., adj.*
neoprene (ˈniːəʊˌpriːn) *n.* a synthetic rubber obtained by the polymerization of chloroprene. It is resistant to oil and ageing and is used in waterproof products, such as diving suits, paints, and adhesives. [C20: from NEO- + PR(OPYL) + -ENE]
neorealism (ˌniːəʊˈriːəlɪzəm) *n. Films.* a movement to depict directly the poor in society: originating in postwar Italy. —**ˌneoˈrealist** *n., adj.*
neoteny (nɪˈɒtənɪ) *n.* the persistence of larval or fetal features in the adult form of an animal. For example, the adult axolotl, a salamander, retains larval external gills. See also **paedogenesis.** [C19: from New Latin *neotenia,* from Greek NEO- + *teinein* to stretch] —**neˈotenous** *adj.*
neoteric (ˌniːəʊˈtɛrɪk) *Rare.* ~*adj.* **1.** belonging to a new fashion or trend; modern: *a neoteric genre.* ~*n.* **2.** a new writer or philosopher. [C16: via Late Latin from Greek *neōterikos* young, fresh, from *neoteros* younger, more recent, from *neos* new, recent] —**ˌneoˈterically** *adv.*
Neotropical (ˌniːəʊˈtrɒpɪkᵊl) *adj.* of or denoting a zoogeographical region consisting of South America and North America south of the tropic of Cancer.
neotype (ˈniːəʊˌtaɪp) *n. Biology.* a specimen selected to replace a type specimen that has been lost or destroyed.
Neozoic (ˌniːəʊˈzəʊɪk) *adj.* of or formed at any time after the end of the Mesozoic era.
NEP *abbrev. for* New Economic Policy.
Nepalese (ˌnɛpəˈliːz) *adj.* **1.** of or relating to Nepal, a Hindu kingdom in S Asia, its people, or their language. ~*n.* **2.** a native or inhabitant of Nepal.
Nepali (nɪˈpɔːlɪ) *n.* **1.** the official language of Nepal, also spoken in Sikkim and parts of India. It forms the E group of Pahari and belongs to the Indic branch of Indo-European. **2.** (*pl.* **-pali** *or* **-palis**) a native or inhabitant of Nepal; a Nepalese. ~*adj.* **3.** of or relating to Nepal, its inhabitants, or their language; Nepalese.
nepenthe (nɪˈpɛnθɪ) *n.* **1.** a drug, or the plant providing it, that ancient writers referred to as a means of forgetting grief or trouble. **2.** anything that produces sleep, forgetfulness, or pleasurable dreaminess. [C16: via Latin from Greek *nēpenthes* sedative made from a herb, from *nē-* not + *penthos* grief] —**neˈpenthean** *adj.*
neper (ˈneɪpə, ˈniː-) *n.* a unit expressing the ratio of two quantities, esp. amplitudes in telecommunications, equal to the natural logarithm of the ratio of the two quantities. Symbol: Np, N [C20: named after John Napier (1550–1617), Scottish mathematician; the name was approved in 1928]
nepeta (ˈnɛpətə) *n.* See **catmint.** [Latin: catmint]
nepheline (ˈnɛfɪlɪn, -ˌliːn) *or* **nephelite** (ˈnɛfɪˌlaɪt) *n.* a whitish mineral consisting of sodium potassium aluminium silicate in hexagonal crystalline form: used in the manufacture of glass and ceramics. Formula: $(Na,K)(AlSi)_2O_4$. [C19: from French *néphéline,* from Greek *nephelē* cloud, so called because pieces of it become cloudy if dipped in nitric acid]
nephelinite (ˈnɛfɪlɪˌnaɪt) *n.* a fine-grained basic laval rock consisting of pyroxene and nepheline.
nephelometer (ˌnɛfɪˈlɒmɪtə) *n. Chem.* an instrument for measuring the size or density of particles suspended in a fluid. [C19 (in the sense: an instrument for measuring the cloudiness of the sky): from Greek *nephelē* cloud + -O- + -METER] —**nephelometric** (ˌnɛfɪləʊˈmɛtrɪk) *adj.* —**ˌnepheˈlometry** *n.*
nephew (ˈnɛvjuː, ˈnɛf-) *n.* a son of one's sister or brother. [C13: from Old French *neveu,* from Latin *nepōs;* related to Old English *nefa,* Old High German *nevo* relative]
nepho- *combining form.* concerning cloud or clouds. [from Greek *nephos* cloud]
nephogram (ˈnɛfəˌgræm) *n. Meteorol.* a photograph of a cloud.
nephograph (ˈnɛfəˌgrɑːf, -ˌgræf) *n.* an instrument for photographing clouds.
nephology (nɪˈfɒlədʒɪ) *n.* the study of clouds. —**nephological** (ˌnɛfəˈlɒdʒɪkᵊl) *adj.* —**neˈphologist** *n.*
nephoscope (ˈnɛfəˌskəʊp) *n.* an instrument for measuring the altitude, velocity, and direction of movement of clouds.
nephralgia (nɪˈfrældʒɪə) *n.* pain in a kidney. —**neˈphralgic** *adj.*
nephrectomy (nɪˈfrɛktəmɪ) *n., pl.* **-mies.** surgical removal of a kidney.
nephridium (nɪˈfrɪdɪəm) *n., pl.* **-ia** (-ɪə). a simple excretory organ of many invertebrates, consisting of a tube through which waste products pass to the exterior. [C19: New Latin: little kidney] —**neˈphridial** *adj.*
nephrite (ˈnɛfraɪt) *n.* a tough fibrous amphibole mineral: a variety of jade consisting of calcium magnesium silicate in monoclinic crystalline form. Formula: $Ca_2Mg_5Si_8O_{22}(OH)_2$. Also called: **kidney stone.** [C18: via German *Nephrit* from Greek *nephrós* kidney, so called because it was thought to be beneficial in kidney disorders]
nephritic (nɪˈfrɪtɪk) *adj.* **1.** of or relating to the kidneys. **2.** relating to or affected with nephritis.
nephritis (nɪˈfraɪtɪs) *n.* inflammation of a kidney.
nephro- *or before a vowel* **nephr-** *combining form.* kidney or kidneys: *nephrotomy.* [from Greek *nephros*]
nephrolepis (ˌnɛfrəˈliːpɪs) *n.* any fern of the tropical genus *Nephrolepis,* some species of which are grown as ornamental greenhouse or house plants for their handsome deeply-cut drooping fronds: family *Polypodiaceae.* Also called **ladder fern, Boston fern.** [New Latin, from Greek *nephros* kidney + *lepsis* scale (from the shape of the indusium)]
nephrology (nɪˈfrɒlədgɪ) *n.* the branch of medicine concerned with diseases of the kidney. —**neˈphrologist** *n.*
nephron (ˈnɛfrɒn) *n.* any of the minute urine-secreting tubules that form the functional unit of the kidneys.
nephroscope (ˈnɛfrəˌskəʊp) *n.* a tubular medical instrument inserted through an incision in the skin to enable examination of a kidney. —**nephroscopy** (nɪˈfrɒskəpɪ) *n.*
nephrosis (nɪˈfrəʊsɪs) *n.* any noninflammatory degenerative kidney disease. —**nephrotic** (nɪˈfrɒtɪk) *adj.*
nephrotomy (nɪˈfrɒtəmɪ) *n., pl.* **-mies.** surgical incision into a kidney.
nepionic (ˌnɛpɪˈɒnɪk) *adj. Zoology.* of or relating to the juvenile period in the life cycle of an organism.
nepit (ˈniːpɪt) *n.* another word for **nit**[4].
ne plus ultra *Latin.* (ˈneɪ ˈplʊs ˈʊltrɑː) *n.* the extreme or perfect point or state. [literally: not more beyond (that is, go no further), allegedly a warning to sailors inscribed on the Pillars of Hercules at Gibraltar]
nepotism (ˈnɛpəˌtɪzəm) *n.* favouritism shown to relatives or close friends by those with power or influence. [C17: from Italian *nepotismo,* from *nepote* NEPHEW, from the former papal practice of granting special favours to nephews or other relatives] —**nepotic** (nɪˈpɒtɪk) *or* **ˌnepoˈtistic** *adj.* —**ˈnepotist** *n.*
Neptune (ˈnɛptjuːn) *n.* the eighth planet from the sun, having eight satellites and a faint planar system of rings or ring fragments. Mean distance from sun: 4497 million km; period of revolution around sun: 164.8 years; period of rotation: 14 hours; diameter and mass: 3.5 and 17.46 times that of earth respectively.
Neptunian (nɛpˈtjuːnɪən) *adj.* **1.** of or relating to Neptune, the Roman god of the sea, or to the sea itself. **2.** of, occurring on, or relating to the planet Neptune. **3.** *Geology.* (of sedimentary rock formations such as dykes) formed under water.

neptunium (nɛpˈtjuːnɪəm) *n.* a silvery metallic transuranic element synthesized in the production of plutonium and occurring in trace amounts in uranium ores. Symbol: Np; atomic no.: 93; half-life of most stable isotope, ^{237}Np: 2.14 × 10^6 years; valency: 3, 4, 5, or 6; relative density: 20.25; melting pt.: 640°C; boiling pt.: 3902°C (est.). [C20: from NEPTUNE, the planet beyond Uranus, because neptunium is the element beyond uranium in the periodic table]

neptunium series *n.* a radioactive series that starts with plutonium-241 and ends with bismuth-209. Neptunium-237 is the longest-lived member of the series. The series does not occur in nature.

neral (ˈnɪəræl) *n. Chem.* the *trans-* isomer of citral. [C20: from *nerol* (an alcohol from NEROLI OIL) + -AL[3]]

NERC *abbrev. for* Natural Environment Research Council.

nerd *or* **nurd** (nɜːd) *n. Slang.* a stupid and feeble person. —ˈ**nerdish** *or* ˈ**nurdish** *adj.* —ˈ**nerdy** *or* ˈ**nurdy** *adj.*

nereis (ˈnɪərɪɪs) *n.* any polychaete worm of the genus *Nereis.* See **ragworm.** [C18: via Latin from Greek *Nērēid,* a sea nymph, from *Nereus,* a sea god; compare Latin *nāre* to swim]

nerine (nəˈriːnɪ) *n.* any plant of the bulbous S. African genus *Nerine,* related to the amaryllis; several species are grown as garden or pot plants for their beautiful pink, orange, red, or white flowers. *N. sarniensis* is the pink-flowered Guernsey lily family *Amaryllidaceae.* [Latin, from Greek *nērēis* a sea nymph]

neritic (nɛˈrɪtɪk) *adj.* of or formed in the region of shallow seas near a coastline. [C20: perhaps from Latin *nērīta* sea mussel, from Greek *nēritēs,* from *Nereus,* a sea god]

Nernst heat theorem (nɛənst) *n.* the principle that reactions in crystalline solids involve changes in entropy that tend to zero as the temperature approaches absolute zero. See **law of thermodynamics** (sense 1). [after W. H. *Nernst* (1864–1941), German physical chemist]

neroli oil *or* **neroli** (ˈnɪərəlɪ) *n.* a brown oil distilled from the flowers of various orange trees, esp. the Seville orange: used in perfumery. [C17: named after Anne Marie de la Tremoïlle of *Neroli,* French-born Italian princess believed to have discovered it]

nervate (ˈnɜːveɪt) *adj.* (of leaves) having veins.

nervation (nɜːˈveɪʃən) *or* **nervature** (ˈnɜːvətʃə) *n.* a less common word for **venation.**

nerve (nɜːv) *n.* **1.** any of the cordlike bundles of fibres that conduct sensory or motor impulses between the brain or spinal cord and another part of the body. **2.** courage, bravery, or steadfastness. **3. lose one's nerve.** to become timid, esp. failing to perform some audacious act. **4.** *Informal.* boldness or effrontery; impudence: *he had the nerve to swear at me.* **5.** muscle or sinew (often in the phrase **strain every nerve**). **6.** a large vein in a leaf. **7.** any of the veins of an insect's wing. ~*vb.* (*tr.*) **8.** to give courage to (oneself); steel (oneself). **9.** to provide with nerve or nerves. ~See also **nerves.** [C16: from Latin *nervus;* related to Greek *neuron;* compare Sanskrit *snāvan* sinew]

nerve block *n.* induction of anaesthesia in a specific part of the body by injecting a local anaesthetic close to the sensory nerves that supply it.

nerve cell *n.* another name for **neuron.**

nerve centre *n.* **1.** a group of nerve cells associated with a specific function. **2.** a principal source of control over any complex activity: *Wall Street is the financial nerve centre of America.*

nerve fibre *n.* a threadlike extension of a nerve cell; axon.

nerve gas *n.* (esp. in chemical warfare) any of various poisonous gases that have a paralysing effect on the central nervous system that can be fatal.

nerve impulse *n.* the electrical wave transmitted along a nerve fibre, usually following stimulation of the nerve-cell body. See also **action potential.**

nerveless (ˈnɜːvlɪs) *adj.* **1.** calm and collected. **2.** listless or feeble. —ˈ**nervelessly** *adv.* —ˈ**nervelessness** *n.*

nerve-racking *or* **nerve-wracking** *adj.* very distressing, exhausting, or harrowing.

nerves (nɜːvz) *pl. n. Informal.* **1.** the imagined source of emotional control: *my nerves won't stand it.* **2.** anxiety, tension, or imbalance: *she's all nerves.* **3. bundle of nerves.** a very nervous person. **4. get on one's nerves.** to irritate, annoy, or upset one.

nervine (ˈnɜːviːn) *adj.* **1.** having a soothing or calming effect upon the nerves. ~*n.* **2.** a nervine drug or agent. [C17: from New Latin *nervīnus,* from Latin *nervus* NERVE]

nerving (ˈnɜːvɪŋ) *n. Vet. science.* surgical removal of part of a nerve trunk, usually because of chronic and disabling inflammation.

nervous (ˈnɜːvəs) *adj.* **1.** very excitable or sensitive; highly strung. **2.** (often foll. by *of*) apprehensive or worried: *I'm nervous of traffic.* **3.** of, relating to, or containing nerves; neural: *nervous tissue.* **4.** affecting the nerves or nervous tissue: *a nervous disease.* **5.** *Archaic.* active, vigorous, or forceful. —ˈ**nervously** *adv.* —ˈ**nervousness** *n.*

nervous breakdown *n.* any mental illness not primarily of organic origin, in which the patient ceases to function properly, often accompanied by severely impaired concentration, anxiety, insomnia, and lack of self-esteem; used esp. of episodes of depression.

nervous system *n.* the sensory and control apparatus of all multicellular animals above the level of sponges, consisting of a network of nerve cells (see **neuron**). See also **central nervous system.**

nervure (ˈnɜːvjʊə) *n.* **1.** *Entomol.* any of the stiff chitinous rods that form the supporting framework of an insect's wing; vein. **2.** *Botany.* any of the veins or ribs of a leaf. [C19: from French; see NERVE, -URE]

nervy (ˈnɜːvɪ) *adj.* **nervier, nerviest. 1.** *Brit. informal.* tense or apprehensive. **2.** having or needing bravery or endurance. **3.** *U.S. and Canadian informal.* brash or cheeky. **4.** *Archaic.* muscular; sinewy. —ˈ**nervily** *adv.* —ˈ**nerviness** *n.*

nescience (ˈnɛsɪəns) *n.* **1.** a formal or literary word for **ignorance. 2.** *Rare.* lack of religious belief; agnosticism. [C17: from Late Latin *nescientia,* from Latin *nescīre* to be ignorant of, from *ne* not + *scīre* to know; compare SCIENCE] —ˈ**nescient** *adj.*

nesh (nɛʃ) *adj. Dialect.* **1.** sensitive to the cold. **2.** timid or cowardly. [from Old English *hnesce;* related to Gothic *hnasqus* tender, soft; of obscure origin]

ness (nɛs) *n.* **a.** *Archaic.* a promontory or headland. **b.** (*cap. as part of a name*): *Orford Ness.* [Old English *næs* headland; related to Old Norse *nes,* Old English *nasu* NOSE]

-ness *suffix forming nouns chiefly from adjectives and participles.* indicating state, condition, or quality, or an instance of one of these: *greatness; selfishness; meaninglessness; a kindness.* [Old English *-nes,* of Germanic origin; related to Gothic *-nassus*]

nesselrode (ˈnɛsᵊlˌrəʊd) *n.* a rich frozen pudding, made of chestnuts, eggs, cream, etc. [C19: named after Count *Nesselrode* (1780–1862), Russian diplomat whose chef invented the dish]

nest (nɛst) *n.* **1.** a place or structure in which birds, fishes, insects, reptiles, mice, etc., lay eggs or give birth to young. **2.** a number of animals of the same species and their young occupying a common habitat: *an ants' nest.* **3.** a place fostering something undesirable: *a nest of thievery.* **4.** the people in such a place: *a nest of thieves.* **5.** a cosy or secluded place. **6.** a set of things, usually of graduated sizes, designed to fit together: *a nest of tables.* **7.** *Military.* a weapon emplacement: *a machine-gun nest.* ~*vb.* **8.** (*intr.*) to make or inhabit a nest. **9.** (*intr.*) to hunt for birds' nests. **10.** (*tr.*) to place in a nest. [Old English; related to Latin *nīdus* (nest) and to BENEATH, SIT] —ˈ**nester** *n.* —ˈ**nest**ˌ**like** *adj.*

nest box *or* **nesting box** *n.* **1.** a box in a henhouse in which domestic chickens lay eggs. **2.** a box designed as a nesting place for wild birds and positioned in a garden, park, or reserve to encourage them to breed there.

nest egg *n.* **1.** a fund of money kept in reserve; savings. **2.** a natural or artificial egg left in a nest to induce hens to lay their eggs in it.

nestle (ˈnɛsᵊl) *vb.* **1.** (*intr.;* often foll. by *up* or *down*) to snuggle, settle, or cuddle closely. **2.** (*intr.*) to be in a sheltered or protected position; lie snugly. **3.** (*tr.*) to shelter or place snugly or partly concealed, as in a nest. [Old English *nestlian.* See NEST] —ˈ**nestler** *n.*

nestling (ˈnɛstlɪŋ, ˈnɛslɪŋ) *n.* **1. a.** a young bird not yet fledged. **b.** (*as modifier*): *a nestling thrush.* **2.** any young person or animal. [C14: from NEST + -LING[1]]

Nestor (ˈnɛstɔː) *n.* (*sometimes not cap.*) a wise old man; sage. [named after the oldest and wisest of the Greeks in the Trojan War]

Nestorianism (nɛˈstɔːrɪəˌnɪzəm) *n.* the doctrine that Christ was two distinct persons, divine and human, implying a denial that the Virgin Mary was the mother of God. It is attributed to Nestorius (died ?451 A.D.), Syrian churchman, and survives in the Iraqi Church. —**Nes**ˈ**torian** *n., adj.*

net[1] (nɛt) *n.* **1.** an openwork fabric of string, rope, wire, etc.; mesh. **2.** a device made of net, used to protect or enclose things or to trap animals. **3. a.** a thin light mesh fabric of cotton, nylon, or other fibre, used for curtains, dresses, etc. **b.** (*as modifier*): *net curtains.* **4.** a plan, strategy, etc., intended to trap or ensnare: *the murderer slipped through the police net.* **5.** *Tennis, badminton, etc.* **a.** a strip of net that divides the playing area into two equal parts. **b.** a shot that hits the net, whether or not it goes over. **6.** the goal in soccer, hockey, etc. **7.** (*often pl.*) *Cricket.* **a.** a pitch surrounded by netting, used for practice. **b.** a practice session in a net. **8.** another word for **network** (sense 2). ~*vb.* **nets, netting, netted. 9.** (*tr.*) to catch with or as if with a net; ensnare. **10.** (*tr.*) to shelter or surround with a net. **11.** (*intr.*) *Tennis, badminton, etc.* to hit a shot into the net. **12.** to make a net out of (rope, string, etc.). [Old English *net;* related to Gothic *nati,* Dutch *net*]

net[2] *or* **nett** (nɛt) *adj.* **1.** remaining after all deductions, as for taxes, expenses, losses, etc.: *net profit.* Compare **gross** (sense 2). **2.** (of weight) after deducting tare. **3.** ultimate; final; conclusive (esp. in the phrase **net result**). ~*n.* **4.** net income, profits, weight, etc. ~*vb.* **nets, netting, netted. 5.** (*tr.*) to yield or earn as clear profit. [C14: clean, neat, from French *net* NEAT[1]; related to Dutch *net,* German *nett*]

net asset value *n.* the total value of the assets of an organization less its liabilities and capital charges. Abbrev.: **NAV.**

netball (ˈnɛtˌbɔːl) *n.* a team game similar to basketball, played mainly by women. —ˈ**net**ˌ**baller** *n.*

net domestic product *n. Economics.* the gross domestic product minus an allowance for the depreciation of capital goods. Abbrev.: **NDP.**
Neth. *abbrev. for* Netherlands.
nether ('nɛðə) *adj.* placed or situated below, beneath, or underground: *nether regions; a nether lip.* [Old English *niothera, nithera,* literally: further down, from *nither* down. Related to Old Irish *nitaram,* German *nieder*]
Netherlander ('nɛðəˌlændə) *n.* a native or inhabitant of the Netherlands, a kingdom in NW Europe.
nethermost ('nɛðəˌməʊst) *adj.* **the.** farthest down; lowest.
nether world *n.* **1.** the world after death; the underworld. **2.** hell. ~Also called: **nether regions.**
net national product *n.* gross national product minus an allowance for the depreciation of capital goods. Abbrev.: **NNP.**
net present value *n. Accounting.* an assessment of the long-term profitability of a project made by adding together all the revenue it can be expected to achieve over its whole life and deducting all the costs involved, discounting both future costs and revenue at an appropriate rate. Abbrev.: **NPV.**
net profit *n.* gross profit minus all operating costs not included in the calculation of gross profit, esp. wages, overheads, and depreciation.
net realizable value *n.* the net value of an asset if it were to be sold, taking into account the cost of making the sale and of bringing the asset into a saleable state. Abbrev.: **NRV.**
netsuke ('nɛtsʊkɪ) *n.* (in Japan) a carved toggle, esp. of wood or ivory, originally used to tether a medicine box, purse, etc., worn dangling from the waist. [C19: from Japanese]
nett (nɛt) *adj., n., vb.* a variant spelling of **net**[2].
netting ('nɛtɪŋ) *n.* any netted fabric or structure.
nettle ('nɛtᵊl) *n.* **1.** any weedy plant of the temperate urticaceous genus *Urtica,* such as *U. dioica* (**stinging nettle**), having serrated leaves with stinging hairs and greenish flowers. **2.** any of various other urticaceous plants with stinging hairs or spines. **3.** any of various plants that resemble urticaceous nettles, such as the dead-nettle, hemp nettle, and horse nettle. **4. grasp the nettle.** to attempt or approach something with boldness and courage. ~*vb.* (*tr.*) **5.** to bother; irritate. **6.** to sting as a nettle does. [Old English *netele;* related to Old High German *nazza* (German *Nessel*)] —'**nettle-ˌlike** *adj.* —'**nettly** *adj.*
nettle rash *n.* a nontechnical name for **urticaria.**
nettlesome ('nɛtᵊlsəm) *adj.* causing or susceptible to irritation.
net ton *n.* the full name for **ton**[1] (sense 2).
netty ('nɛtɪ) *n., pl.* **-ties.** *Northeast English dialect.* a lavatory, originally an earth closet. [of obscure origin]
network ('nɛtˌwɜːk) *n.* **1.** an interconnected group or system: *a network of shops.* **2.** Also: **net.** a system of intersecting lines, roads, veins, etc. **3.** another name for **net**[1] (sense 1) or **netting. 4.** *Radio, television.* a group of broadcasting stations that all transmit the same programme simultaneously. **5.** *Electronics, computer technol.* a system of interconnected components or circuits. ~*vb.* **6.** (*tr.*) *Radio, television.* to broadcast on stations throughout the country: *the Scotland-England match was networked.* **7.** *Computer technol.* (of computers, terminals, etc.) to connect or be connected. **8.** (*intr.*) to form business contacts through informal social meetings.
networking ('nɛtˌwɜːkɪŋ) *n.* **1.** *Computer technol.* the interconnection of two or more networks in different places, as in working at home with a link to a central computer in an office. **2.** *Chiefly U.S. and Canadian.* forming business connections and contacts through informal social meetings. ~*adj.* **3.** of or for networking: *networking systems.* —'**netˌworker** *n.*
Neufchâtel (*French* nøʃɑtɛl) *n.* a soft creamy whole milk cheese, similar to cream cheese. [named after *Neufchâtel,* town in N France where it is made]
neuk (njuːk) *n.* a Scot. word for **nook.**
neume *or* **neum** (njuːm) *n. Music.* one of a series of notational symbols used before the 14th century. [C15: from Medieval Latin *neuma* group of notes sung on one breath, from Greek *pneuma* breath] —'**neumic** *adj.*
neural ('njʊərəl) *adj.* of or relating to a nerve or the nervous system. —'**neurally** *adv.*
neural chip *n.* another name for **neurochip.**
neural computer *n.* another name for **neurocomputer.**
neuralgia (njʊ'rældʒə) *n.* severe spasmodic pain caused by damage to or malfunctioning of a nerve and often following the course of the nerve. —**neu'ralgic** *adj.*
neural network *n.* **1.** an interconnected system of neurons, as in the brain or other parts of the nervous system. **2.** Also called: **neural net.** an analogous network of electronic components, esp. one in a computer designed to mimic the operation of the human brain.
neural tube *n.* the structure in mammalian embryos that develops into the brain and spinal cord. Incomplete development results in **neural-tube defects**, such as spina bifida, in a newborn baby.
neurasthenia (ˌnjʊərəs'θiːnɪə) *n.* an obsolete technical term for a neurosis characterized by extreme lassitude and inability to cope with any but the most trivial tasks. —**neurasthenic** (ˌnjʊərəs'θɛnɪk) *adj.* —ˌ**neuras'thenically** *adv.*
neurectomy (njʊ'rɛktəmɪ) *n., pl.* **-mies.** the surgical removal of a nerve segment.
neurilemma (ˌnjʊərɪ'lɛmə) *n.* a variant of **neurolemma.** [C19: from French *névrilème,* from Greek *neuron* nerve + *eilēma* covering, but influenced also by Greek *lemma* husk]
neuritis (njʊ'raɪtɪs) *n.* inflammation of a nerve or nerves, often accompanied by pain and loss of function in the affected part. —**neuritic** (njʊ'rɪtɪk) *adj.*
neuro- *or before a vowel* **neur-** *combining form.* indicating a nerve or the nervous system: *neuroblast; neurology.* [from Greek *neuron* nerve; related to Latin *nervus*]
neuroanatomy (ˌnjʊərəʊə'nætəmɪ) *n.* the study of the structure of the nervous system. —ˌ**neuroa'natomist** *n.*
neuroblast ('njʊərəʊˌblæst) *n.* an embryonic nerve cell.
neurochip ('njʊərəʊˌtʃɪp) *n. Computer technol.* a semiconductor chip designed for use in an electronic neural network. Also called: **neural chip.**
neurocoele ('njʊərəˌsiːl) *n. Embryol.* a cavity in the embryonic brain and spinal cord that develops into the ventricles and central canal respectively. [C19: from NEURO- + Greek *koilos* hollow]
neurocomputer ('njʊərəʊˌkəmpjuːtə) n. a type of computer designed to mimic the action of the human brain by use of an electronic neural network. Also called: **neural computer.**
neuroendocrine (ˌnjʊərəʊ'ɛndəʊˌkraɪn) *adj.* of, relating to, or denoting the dual control of certain body functions by both nervous and hormonal stimulation: *neuroendocrine system.*
neuroendocrinology (ˌnjʊərəʊˌɛndəʊkrɪ'nɒlədʒɪ) *n.* the study of neuroendocrine systems and neurohormones.
neurofibril (ˌnjʊərəʊ'faɪbrɪl) *n.* any of the delicate threads within the body of a nerve cell that extend into the axon and dendrites. —ˌ**neuro'fibrilar,** ˌ**neurofi'brillar,** *or* ˌ**neurofi'brillary** *adj.*
neurogenic (ˌnjʊərəʊ'dʒɛnɪk) *adj.* originating in or stimulated by the nervous system or nerve impulses.
neuroglia (njʊ'rɒglɪə) *n.* another name for **glia.**
neurohormone ('njʊərəʊˌhɔːməʊn) *n.* a hormone, such as noradrenaline, oxytocin, or vasopressin, that is produced by specialized nervous tissue rather than by endocrine glands.
neurohypophysis (ˌnjʊərəʊhaɪ'pɒfɪsɪs) *n., pl.* **-ses** (-ˌsiːz). the posterior lobe of the pituitary gland. Compare **adenohypophysis.**
neurol. *abbrev. for* neurology.
neurolemma (ˌnjʊərəʊ'lɛmə) *n.* the thin membrane that forms a sheath around nerve fibres. Also: **neurilemma.** [C19: New Latin, from NEURO- + Greek *eilēma* covering]
neuroleptic (ˌnjʊərəʊ'lɛptɪk) *adj.* **1.** capable of affecting the brain, esp. by reducing the intensity of nerve function; tranquillizing. ~*n.* **2.** a neuroleptic drug; major tranquillizer: used in the treatment of psychosis.
neurolinguistics (ˌnjʊərəʊlɪŋ'gwɪstɪks) *n.* (*functioning as sing.*) the branch of linguistics that deals with the encoding of the language faculty in the brain.
neurology (njʊ'rɒlədʒɪ) *n.* the study of the anatomy, physiology, and diseases of the nervous system. —**neurological** (ˌnjʊərə'lɒdʒɪkᵊl) *adj.* —**neu'rologist** *n.*
neuroma (njʊ'rəʊmə) *n., pl.* **-mata** (-mətə) *or* **-mas.** any tumour composed of nerve tissue. —**neuromatous** (njʊ'rɒmətəs) *adj.*
neuromuscular (ˌnjʊərəʊ'mʌskjʊlə) *adj.* of, relating to, or affecting nerves and muscles.
neuron ('njʊərɒn) *or* **neurone** ('njʊərəʊn) *n.* a cell specialized to conduct nerve impulses: consists of a cell body, axon, and dendrites. Also called: **nerve cell.** —**neuronic** (njʊ'rɒnɪk) *adj.*
neuropath ('njʊərəʊˌpæθ) *n.* a person suffering from or predisposed to a disorder of the nervous system.
neuropathology (ˌnjʊərəʊpə'θɒlədʒɪ) *n.* the study of diseases of the nervous system. —**neuropathological** (ˌnjʊərəʊˌpæθə'lɒdʒɪkᵊl) *adj.* —ˌ**neuropa'thologist** *n.*
neuropathy (njʊ'rɒpəθɪ) *n.* any disease of the nervous system. —**neuropathic** (ˌnjʊərəʊ'pæθɪk) *adj.* —ˌ**neuro'pathically** *adv.*
neuropeptide (ˌnjʊərəʊ'pɛptaɪd) *n.* a peptide produced by neural tissue, esp. one with hormonal activity.
neurophysiology (ˌnjʊərəʊˌfɪzɪ'ɒlədʒɪ) *n.* the study of the functions of the nervous system. —**neurophysiological** (ˌnjʊərəʊˌfɪzɪə'lɒdʒɪkᵊl) *adj.* —ˌ**neuroˌphysio'logically** *adv.* —ˌ**neuroˌphysi'ologist** *n.*
neuropil ('njʊərəʊpɪl) *n.* a dense network of neurons and glia in the central nervous system. [from NEURO- + Greek *pilos* hair]
neuropsychiatry (ˌnjʊərəʊsaɪ'kaɪətrɪ) *n.* the branch of medicine concerned with neurological and mental disorders. —**neuropsychiatric** (ˌnjʊərəʊˌsaɪkɪ'ætrɪk) *adj.* —ˌ**neuropsy'chiatrist** *n.*
neuropsychology (ˌnjʊərəʊsaɪ'kɒlədʒɪ) *n.* the study of the effects of brain damage on behaviour and the mind. —ˌ**neuropsy'chologist** *n.*
neuropteran *or* **neuropteron** (njʊ'rɒptərən) *n., pl.* **-terans** *or* **-tera** (-tərə). any neuropterous insect.
neuropterous (njʊ'rɒptərəs) *or* **neuropteran** *adj.* of, relating to, or belonging to the *Neuroptera,* an order of insects having two pairs of large much-veined wings and biting mouthparts: includes the lacewings and antlions. [C18: from New Latin *Neuroptera;* see NEURO-, -PTEROUS]
neuroscience ('njʊərəʊˌsaɪəns) *n.* the study of the anatomy, physiology, and biochemistry of the nervous system.
neurosis (njʊ'rəʊsɪs) *n., pl.* **-ses** (-siːz). a relatively mild mental disorder, characterized by symptoms such as hysteria, anxiety,

depression, or obsessive behaviour. Also called: **psychoneurosis.**

neurosurgery (ˌnjʊərəʊˈsɜːdʒərɪ) *n.* the branch of surgery concerned with the nervous system. —ˌ**neuroˈsurgeon** *n.* —ˌ**neuroˈsurgical** *adj.* —ˌ**neuroˈsurgically** *adv.*

neurotic (njʊˈrɒtɪk) *adj.* **1.** of, relating to, or afflicted by neurosis. ~*n.* **2.** a person who is afflicted with a neurosis or who tends to be emotionally unstable or unusually anxious. —**neuˈrotically** *adv.*

neuroticism (njʊˈrɒtɪˌsɪzəm) *n.* a personality trait characterized by instability, anxiety, aggression, etc.

neurotomy (njʊˈrɒtəmɪ) *n., pl.* **-mies.** the surgical cutting of a nerve, esp. to relieve intractable pain. —**neuˈrotomist** *n.*

neurotoxin (ˌnjʊərəʊˈtɒksɪn) *n.* any of several natural substances that interfere with the electrical activities of nerves, thus preventing them from functioning. —ˌ**neuroˈtoxic** *adj.*

neurotransmitter (ˌnjʊərəʊtrænzˈmɪtə) *n.* a chemical by which a nerve cell communicates with another nerve cell or with a muscle.

neurovascular (ˌnʊərəʊˈvæskjʊlə) *adj.* of, relating to, or affecting both the nerves and the blood vessels.

neuston (ˈnjuːstᵊn) *n.* **1.** organisms, similar to plankton, that float on the surface film of open water. **2.** the ecosystem of the surface film of open water in which such organisms as copepods graze on tiny flagellates, bacteria, etc. [C20: via German from Greek *neustos* swimming, from *nein* to swim] —**neusˈtonic** *adj.*

neut. *abbrev. for* neuter.

neuter (ˈnjuːtə) *adj.* **1.** *Grammar.* **a.** denoting or belonging to a gender of nouns which for the most part have inanimate referents or do not specify the sex of their referents. **b.** (*as n.*): *German "Mädchen" (meaning "girl") is a neuter.* **2.** (of animals and plants) having nonfunctional, underdeveloped, or absent reproductive organs. **3.** sexless or giving no indication of sex: *a neuter sort of name.* ~*n.* **4.** a sexually underdeveloped female insect, such as a worker bee. **5.** a castrated animal, esp. a domestic animal. **6.** a flower in which the stamens and pistil are absent or nonfunctional. ~*vb.* **7.** (*tr.*) to castrate (an animal). [C14: from Latin, from *ne* not + *uter* either (of two)]

neutral (ˈnjuːtrəl) *adj.* **1.** not siding with any party to a war or dispute. **2.** of, belonging to, or appropriate to a neutral party, country, etc.: *neutral land.* **3.** of no distinctive quality, characteristics, or type; indifferent. **4.** (of a colour such as white or black) having no hue; achromatic. **5.** (of a colour) dull, but harmonizing with most other colours. **6.** a less common term for **neuter** (sense 2). **7.** *Chem.* neither acidic nor alkaline. **8.** *Physics.* having zero charge or potential. **9.** *Rare.* having no magnetism. **10.** *Phonetics.* (of a vowel) articulated with the tongue relaxed in mid-central position and the lips midway between spread and rounded: *the word "about" begins with a neutral vowel.* ~*n.* **11.** a neutral person, nation, etc. **12.** a citizen of a neutral state. **13.** the position of the controls of a gearbox that leaves the transmission disengaged. [C16: from Latin *neutrālis;* see NEUTER] —ˈ**neutrally** *adv.*

neutral axis *n. Engineering.* the line or plane through the section of a beam or plate which does not suffer extension or compression when the beam or plate bends.

neutralism (ˈnjuːtrəˌlɪzəm) *n.* (in international affairs) the policy, practice, or attitude of neutrality, noninvolvement, or nonalignment with power blocs. —ˈ**neutralist** *n., adj.*

neutrality (njuːˈtrælɪtɪ) *n.* **1.** the state or character of being neutral, esp. in a dispute, contest, etc. **2.** the condition of being chemically or electrically neutral.

neutralize *or* **neutralise** (ˈnjuːtrəˌlaɪz) *vb.* (*mainly tr.*) **1.** (*also intr.*) to render or become ineffective or neutral by counteracting, mixing, etc.; nullify. **2.** (*also intr.*) to make or become electrically or chemically neutral. **3.** to exclude (a country) from the sphere of warfare or alliances by international agreement: *the great powers neutralized Belgium in the 19th century.* **4.** to render (an army) incapable of further military action. —ˌ**neutraliˈzation** *or* ˌ**neutraliˈsation** *n.* —ˈ**neutralˌizer** *or* ˈ**neutralˌiser** *n.*

neutral monism *n.* the philosophical doctrine that mind and body are both constructs of the same elements which cannot themselves be classified either as mental or physical. See also **monism** (sense 1).

neutral spirits *n.* (*functioning as sing. or pl.*) *U.S.* ethanol of more than 190° proof.

neutretto (njuːˈtrɛtəʊ) *n., pl.* **-tos.** *Physics.* **1.** the neutrino associated with the muon. **2.** (formerly) any of various hypothetical neutral particles. [C20: from NEUTR(INO) + diminutive suffix *-etto*]

neutrino (njuːˈtriːnəʊ) *n., pl.* **-nos.** *Physics.* a stable leptonic neutral elementary particle with zero rest mass and spin ½ that travels at the speed of light. Three types exist, associated with the electron, the muon, and the tau particle. [C20: from Italian, diminutive of *neutrone* NEUTRON]

neutrino astronomy *n.* the detection of neutrinos emitted by the sun from which information about the solar interior can be obtained.

neutron (ˈnjuːtrɒn) *n. Physics.* a neutral elementary particle with a rest mass of $1.674\,82 \times 10^{-27}$ kilogram and spin ½; classified as a baryon. In the nucleus of an atom it is stable but when free it decays. [C20: from NEUTRAL, on the model of ELECTRON]

neutron bomb *n.* a type of nuclear weapon designed to provide a high yield of neutrons but to cause little blast or long-lived radioactive contamination. The neutrons destroy all life in the target area, which theoretically can be entered relatively soon after the attack. Technical name: **enhanced radiation weapon.**

neutron gun *n. Physics.* a device used for producing a beam of fast neutrons.

neutron number *n.* the number of neutrons in the nucleus of an atom. Symbol: *N*

neutron poison *n. Physics.* a nonfissionable material used to absorb neutrons and thus to control nuclear reactions.

neutron star *n.* a star that has collapsed under its own gravity. It is composed solely of neutrons, has a mass of between 1.4 and about 3 times that of the sun, and a density in excess of 10^7 kilograms per cubic metre.

neutropenia (ˌnjuːtrəˈpiːnɪə) *n.* an abnormal reduction in the number of neutrophils in the blood, as seen in certain anaemias and leukaemias.

neutrophil (ˈnjuːtrəˌfɪl) *or* **neutrophile** (ˈnjuːtrəˌfaɪl) *n.* **1.** Also called: **polymorph.** a leucocyte having a lobed nucleus and a fine granular cytoplasm, which stains with neutral dyes. ~*adj.* **2.** (of cells and tissues) readily stainable by neutral dyes.

Nev. *abbrev. for* Nevada.

névé (ˈnɛveɪ) *n.* **1.** Also called: **firn.** a mass of porous ice, formed from snow, that has not yet become frozen into glacier ice. **2.** a snowfield at the head of a glacier that becomes transformed to ice. [C19: from Swiss French *névé* glacier, from Late Latin *nivātus* snow-cooled, from *nix* snow]

never (ˈnɛvə) *adv., sentence substitute.* **1.** at no time; not ever. **2.** certainly not; by no means; in no case. ~*interj.* **3.** Also: **well I never!** surely not! [Old English *nǣfre,* from *ne* not + *ǣfre* EVER]

▷**Usage.** In good usage, *never* is not used with simple past tenses to mean *not* (*I was asleep at midnight, so I did not see* (not *never saw*) *her go*).

never-ending *adj.* having or seeming to have no end; interminable.

nevermore (ˌnɛvəˈmɔː) *adv. Literary.* never again.

never-never *Informal.* ~*n.* **1.** *Brit.* the hire-purchase system of buying. **2.** *Austral.* remote desert country, as that of W Queensland and central Australia. ~*adj.* **3.** imaginary; idyllic (esp. in the phrase **never-never land**).

nevertheless (ˌnɛvəðəˈlɛs) *sentence connector.* in spite of that; however; yet.

nevus (ˈniːvəs) *n., pl.* **-vi** (-vaɪ). the usual U.S. spelling of **naevus.**

new (njuː) *adj.* **1. a.** recently made or brought into being: *a new dress; our new baby.* **b.** (*as collective n.;* preceded by *the*): *the new.* **2.** of a kind never before existing; novel: *a new concept in marketing.* **3.** having existed before but only recently discovered: *a new comet.* **4.** markedly different from what was before: *the new liberalism.* **5.** fresh and unused; not second-hand: *a new car.* **6.** (*prenominal*) having just or recently become: *a new bride.* **7.** (often foll. by *to* or *at*) recently introduced (to); inexperienced (in) or unaccustomed (to): *new to this neighbourhood.* **8.** (*cap. in names or titles*) more or most recent of two or more things with the same name: *the New Testament.* **9.** (*prenominal*) fresh; additional: *I'll send some new troops.* **10.** (often foll. by *to*) unknown; novel: *this is new to me.* **11.** (of a cycle) beginning or occurring again: *a new year.* **12.** (*prenominal*) (of crops) harvested early: *new carrots.* **13.** changed, esp. for the better: *she returned a new woman from her holiday.* **14.** up-to-date; fashionable. **15.** (*cap. when part of a name*) (*prenominal*) being the most recent, usually living, form of a language: *New High German.* **16. turn over a new leaf.** to reform; make a fresh start. ~*adv.* (*usually in combination*) **17.** recently, freshly: *new-laid eggs.* **18.** anew; again. ~See also **news.** [Old English *nīowe;* related to Gothic *niujis,* Old Norse *naujas,* Latin *novus*] —ˈ**newness** *n.*

New Age *n.* **1. a.** a late 1980s philosophy characterized by a belief in alternative medicine, astrology, spiritualism, etc. **b.** (*as modifier*): *New Age therapies.* **2.** Also called: **New Age music.** a type of gentle melodic popular music that takes in elements of jazz, folk, and classical music and is played largely on synthesizers and acoustic instruments.

New Australian *n.* an immigrant to Australia, esp. one whose native tongue is not English.

newborn (ˈnjuːˌbɔːn) *adj.* **1. a.** recently or just born. **b.** (*as collective n.;* preceded by *the*): *the newborn.* **2.** (of hope, faith, etc.) reborn.

new broom *n.* a newly appointed person eager to make changes.

new brutalism *n.* another name for **brutalism.**

Newburg (ˈnjuːbɜːg) *adj.* (*immediately postpositive*) (of shellfish, esp. lobster) cooked in a rich sauce of butter, cream, sherry, and egg yolks. [of unknown origin]

Newcastle disease (ˈnjuːkɑːsᵊl) *n.* an acute viral disease of birds, esp. poultry, characterized by pneumonia and inflammation of the central nervous system. [C20: named after *Newcastle* upon Tyne in NE England, where it was recorded in 1926]

new chum *n.* **1.** *Austral. and N.Z. informal.* a recent British immigrant. **2.** *Austral.* a novice in any activity. **3.** *Austral.* (in the 19th century) a new arrival in a hulk.

New Church *n.* another name for the **New Jerusalem Church.**

newcomer (ˈnjuːˌkʌmə) *n.* a person who has recently arrived or started to participate in something.

New Country *n.* a style of country music of the late 1980s characterized by down-to-earth rather than sentimental lyrics.
new criticism *n.* an approach to literary criticism through close analysis of the text. —**new critic** *n.* —**new critical** *adj.*
New Deal *n.* **1.** (in the U.S.) the domestic policies of President Franklin D. Roosevelt for economic and social reform. **2.** the period of the implementation of these policies (1933–40). —**New Dealer** *n.*
newel ('nju:əl) *n.* **1.** the central pillar of a winding staircase, esp. one that is made of stone. **2.** See **newel post.** [C14: from Old French *nouel* knob, from Medieval Latin *nōdellus,* diminutive of *nōdus* NODE]
newel post *n.* the post at the top or bottom of a flight of stairs that supports the handrail. Sometimes shortened to **newel.**
New Englander *n.* a native or inhabitant of the NE part of the U.S., settled originally by English emigrants in the mid-17th century.
New English Bible *n.* a new Modern English version of the Bible and Apocrypha, published in full in 1970.
newfangled ('nju:'fæŋgᵊld) *adj.* **1.** newly come into existence or fashion, esp. excessively modern. **2.** *Rare.* excessively fond of new ideas, fashions, etc. [C14 *newefangel* liking new things, from *new* + *-fangel,* from Old English *fōn* to take] —'**new'fangledness** *n.*
new-fashioned *adj.* of or following a recent design, trend, etc.
Newfie ('nju:fɪ) *n. Informal.* a native or inhabitant of Newfoundland, a province of E Canada. **2.** the province or island of Newfoundland.
Newfoundland ('nju:fəndlənd, -fənlənd, -ˌlænd; nju:'faʊndlənd) *n.* a large heavy breed of dog similar to a Saint Bernard with a flat coarse usually black coat, originating in Newfoundland, E Canada.
New Guinea macrophylum (ˌmækrəʊ'faɪləm) *n.* the older term for **Trans-New Guinea phylum.**
New Guinea Pidgin *n.* the variety of Neo-Melanesian spoken in Papua New Guinea and neighbouring islands in the W Pacific.
newish ('nju:ɪʃ) *adj.* fairly new. —'**newishly** *adv.* —'**newishness** *n.*
new issue *n. Stock Exchange.* an issue of shares being offered to the public for the first time.
New Jerusalem *n. Christianity.* heaven regarded as the prototype of the earthly Jerusalem; the heavenly city.
New Jerusalem Church *n.* a sect founded in 1787 on the teachings of Swedenborg. Often shortened to **New Church.** See **Swedenborgianism.**
New Latin *n.* the form of Latin used since the Renaissance, esp. for scientific nomenclature. Also called: **Neo-Latin.**
New Learning *n.* the classical and Biblical studies of Renaissance Europe in the 15th and 16th centuries.
New Left *n.* **a.** a loose grouping of left-wing radicals, esp. among students, that arose in many countries after 1960. **b.** (*as modifier*): *New Left propaganda.*
New Look *n.* **the.** a fashion in women's clothes introduced in 1947, characterized by long full skirts.
newly ('nju:lɪ) *adv.* **1.** recently; lately or just: *a newly built shelf.* **2.** again; afresh; anew: *newly raised hopes.* **3.** in a new manner; differently: *a newly arranged hairdo.*
Newlyn datum ('nju:lɪn) *n.* another name for **ordnance datum.** [named after *Newlyn,* Cornwall, where the observations were taken]
newlywed ('nju:lɪˌwɛd) *n.* (*often pl.*) a recently married person.
New Man *n.* **the.** a type of modern man who allows the caring side of his nature to show by being supportive and by sharing child care and housework.
newmarket ('nju:ˌmɑ:kɪt) *n.* **1.** a double-breasted waisted coat with a full skirt worn, esp. for riding, in the 19th century. **2.** a simple gambling card game. [after *Newmarket* in W Suffolk, a famous horse-racing centre]
new maths *n.* (*functioning as sing.*) *Brit.* an approach to mathematics in which the basic principles of set theory are introduced at an elementary level.
new moon *n.* **1.** the moon when it appears as a narrow waxing crescent. **2.** the time at which this occurs. **3.** *Astronomy.* one of the four principal phases of the moon, occurring when it lies between the earth and the sun.
New Orleans jazz ('ɔ:li:ənz) *n.* the jazz originating in New Orleans in the southern U.S. from about 1914; traditional jazz.
new penny *n.* another name for **penny** (sense 1).
new planets *pl. n.* the outer planets Uranus, Neptune, and Pluto, only discovered comparatively recently.
news (nju:z) *n.* (*functioning as sing.*) **1.** current events; important or interesting recent happenings. **2.** information about such events, as in the mass media. **3. a. the.** a presentation, such as a radio broadcast, of information of this type: *the news is at six.* **b.** (*in combination*): *a newscaster.* **4.** interesting or important information not previously known or realized: *it's news to me.* **5.** a person, fashion, etc., widely reported in the mass media: *she is no longer news in the film world.* [C15: from Middle English *newes,* plural of *newe* new (*adj.*) on model of Old French *noveles* or Medieval Latin *nova* new things] —'**newsless** *adj.*
news agency *n.* an organization that collects news reports for newspapers, periodicals, etc. Also called: **press agency.**
newsagent ('nju:zˌeɪdʒənt) *or U.S.* **newsdealer** ('nju:zˌdi:lə) *n.* a shopkeeper who sells newspapers, stationery, etc.
newsboy ('nju:zˌbɔɪ) *or* (*fem.*) **newsgirl** ('nju:zˌgɜ:l) *n.* a boy or girl who sells or delivers newspapers.
newscast ('nju:zˌkɑ:st) *n.* a radio or television broadcast of the news. [C20: from NEWS + (BROAD)CAST] —'**newsˌcaster** *n.*
news conference *n.* another name for **press conference.**
newsflash ('nju:zˌflæʃ) *n.* a brief item of important news, often interrupting a radio or television programme.
newshawk ('nju:zˌhɔ:k) *n. U.S. and Canadian informal.* a newspaper reporter. Also called: **newshound** ('nju:zˌhaʊnd).
newsletter ('nju:zˌlɛtə) *n.* **1.** Also called: **news-sheet.** a printed periodical bulletin circulated to members of a group. **2.** *History.* a written or printed account of the news.
newsmonger ('nju:zˌmʌŋgə) *n. Old-fashioned.* a gossip.
newspaper ('nju:zˌpeɪpə) *n.* **1. a.** a weekly or daily publication consisting of folded sheets and containing articles on the news, features, reviews, and advertisements. Often shortened to **paper. b.** (*as modifier*): *a newspaper article.* **2.** a less common name for **newsprint.**
newspaperman ('nju:zˌpeɪpəˌmæn) *or* (*fem.*) **newspaperwoman** *n., pl.* **-men** *or* **-women. 1.** a person who works for a newspaper as a reporter or editor. **2.** the owner or proprietor of a newspaper.
newspeak ('nju:ˌspi:k) *n.* the language of bureaucrats and politicians, regarded as deliberately ambiguous and misleading. [C20: from *1984,* a novel by George Orwell (1903–50), British writer]
newsprint ('nju:zˌprɪnt) *n.* an inexpensive wood-pulp paper used for newspapers.
newsreader ('nju:zˌri:də) *n.* a news announcer on radio or television.
newsreel ('nju:zˌri:l) *n.* a short film with a commentary presenting current events.
newsroom ('nju:zˌru:m, -ˌrʊm) *n.* a room in a newspaper office or television or radio station, where news is received and prepared for publication or broadcasting.
newsstand ('nju:zˌstænd) *n.* a portable stand or stall in the street, from which newspapers are sold.
New Stone Age *n.* (not now in technical use) another term for **Neolithic.**
New Style *n.* the present method of reckoning dates using the Gregorian calendar.
news vendor *n.* a person who sells newspapers.
newsworthy ('nju:zˌwɜ:ðɪ) *adj.* sufficiently interesting to be reported in a news bulletin. —'**newsˌworthiness** *n.*
newsy ('nju:zɪ) *adj.* **newsier, newsiest.** full of news, esp. gossipy or personal news: *a newsy letter.* —'**newsiness** *n.*
newt (nju:t) *n.* **1.** any of various small semiaquatic urodele amphibians, such as *Triturus vulgaris* (**common newt**) of Europe, having a long slender body and tail and short feeble legs. **2.** *Chiefly Brit.* any other urodele amphibian, including the salamanders. [C15: from *a newt,* a mistaken division of *an ewt; ewt,* from Old English *eveta* EFT[1]]
New Test. *abbrev. for* New Testament.
New Testament *n.* the collection of writings consisting of the Gospels, Acts of the Apostles, Pauline and other Epistles, and the book of Revelation, composed soon after Christ's death and added to the Jewish writings of the Old Testament to make up the Christian Bible.
New Thought *n.* a movement interested in spiritual healing and the power of constructive thinking.
newton ('nju:tᵊn) *n.* the derived SI unit of force that imparts an acceleration of 1 metre per second per second to a mass of 1 kilogram; equivalent to 10^5 dynes or 7.233 poundals. Symbol: N [C20: named after Sir Isaac *Newton* (1643–1727), English scientist and mathematician]
Newtonian (nju:'təʊnɪən) *adj.* of, denoting, or in accordance with the work of Sir Isaac Newton, esp. that in mechanics and gravitation; classical.
Newtonian mechanics *n.* (*functioning as sing.*) a system of mechanics based on Newton's laws of motion.
Newtonian telescope *n.* a type of astronomical reflecting telescope in which light is reflected from a large concave mirror, onto a plane mirror, and through a hole in the side of the body of the telescope to form an image.
Newton's cradle ('nju:tᵊnz) *n.* an ornamental toy consisting of a frame in which five metal balls are suspended in such a way that when one is moved it sets all the others in motion in turn.
Newton's law of gravitation *n.* the principle that two particles attract each other with forces directly proportional to the product of their masses divided by the square of the distance between them.
Newton's laws of motion *pl. n.* three laws of mechanics describing the motion of a body. **The first law** states that a body remains at rest or in uniform motion in a straight line unless acted upon by a force. **The second law** states that a body's rate of change of momentum is proportional to the force causing it. **The third law** states that when a force acts on a body an equal and opposite force acts simultaneously on another body.
new town *n.* (in Britain) a town that has been planned as a complete unit and built with government sponsorship, esp. to accommodate overspill population.

new wave *n.* a movement in art, film-making, politics, etc., that consciously breaks with traditional ideas.

New Wave[1] *n.* **the.** a movement in the French cinema of the 1960s characterized by a fluid use of the camera and an abandonment of traditional editing techniques. Also called: **Nouvelle Vague.**

New Wave[2] *n.* rock music of the late 1970s, related to punk but more complex: sometimes used to include punk.

new wool *n.* wool that is being processed or woven for the first time. Usual U.S. term: **virgin wool.**

New World *n.* **a.** the American continent. **b.** (*as modifier*): *New World customs.*

New World monkey *n.* any monkey of the family *Cebidae*, of Central and South America, having widely separated nostrils: many are arboreal and have a prehensile tail. Compare **Old World monkey.**

New Year *n.* the first day or days of the year in various calendars, usually celebrated as a holiday.

New Year's Day *n.* January 1, celebrated as a holiday in many countries. Often shortened to (U.S. and Canadian informal) **New Year's.**

New Year's Eve *n.* the evening of Dec. 31, often celebrated with parties. See also **Hogmanay.**

New Yorker ('jɔːkə) *n.* a native or inhabitant of the city or state of New York in the northeastern U.S.

New Zealander ('ziːləndə) *n.* a native or inhabitant of New Zealand, a country occupying two main islands and a number of minor islands in the SE Pacific.

New Zealand greenstone ('ziːlənd) *n.* a variety of nephrite from New Zealand, used as a gemstone.

next (nɛkst) *adj.* **1.** immediately following: *the next patient to be examined; do it next week.* **2.** immediately adjoining: *the next room.* **3.** closest to in degree: *the tallest boy next to James; the next-best thing.* **4. the next (Sunday) but one.** the (Sunday) after the next. *~adv.* **5.** at a time or on an occasion immediately to follow: *the patient to be examined next; next, he started to unscrew the telephone receiver.* **6. next to. a.** adjacent to; at or on one side of: *the house next to ours.* **b.** following in degree: *next to your mother, who do you love most?* **c.** almost: *next to impossible.* *~prep.* **7.** *Archaic.* next to. [Old English *nēhst*, superlative of *nēah* NIGH; compare NEAR, NEIGHBOUR]

next door *adj.* (**next-door** *when prenominal*), *adv.* at, in, or to the adjacent house, flat, building, etc.: *we live next door to the dentist; the next-door house.*

next friend *n. Law.* a person acting on behalf of an infant or other person under legal disability.

next of kin *n.* a person's closest relative or relatives.

nexus ('nɛksəs) *n., pl.* **nexus. 1.** a means of connection between members of a group or things in a series; link; bond. **2.** a connected group or series. [C17: from Latin: a binding together, from *nectere* to bind]

Nez Percé ('nɛz 'pɜːs; *French* ne pɛrse) *n.* **1.** (*pl.* **Nez Percés** ('pɜːsɪz; *French* pɛrse) *or* **Nez Percé**) a member of a North American Indian people of the Pacific coast, a tribe of the Sahaptino. **2.** the Sahaptin language of this people. [French, literally: pierced nose]

NF *abbrev. for:* **1.** Norman French (language). **2.** (in Britain) National Front.

N/F *or* **NF** *Banking. abbrev. for* no funds.

NFL (in the U.S. and Canada) *abbrev. for* National Football League.

Nfld *or* **NF** *abbrev. for* Newfoundland.

NFS (in Britain) *abbrev. for* National Fire Service.

NFT *abbrev. for* National Film Theatre.

NFU (in Britain) *abbrev. for* National Farmers' Union.

NFWI (in Britain) *abbrev. for* National Federation of Women's Institutes.

NG *abbrev. for:* **1.** (in the U.S.) National Guard. **2.** New Guinea. **3.** Also: **ng** no good.

NGA (in Britain) *abbrev. for* National Graphical Association.

ngaio ('naɪəʊ) *n., pl.* **ngaios.** a small New Zealand tree, *Myoporum laetum*, yielding useful timber: family *Myoporaceae.* [from Maori]

ngati ('nɑːtiː) *n., pl.* **ngati.** *N.Z.* a tribe or clan. [Maori]

NGC *abbrev. for* New General Catalogue of Nebulae and Clusters of Stars; a catalogue in which over 8000 nebulae, galaxies, and clusters are listed numerically.

NGk *abbrev. for* New Greek.

NGL *abbrev. for* natural gas liquids: liquid hydrocarbons derived from natural gas.

NGO *abbrev. for:* **1.** Non-Governmental Organization. **2.** (in India) nongazetted officer.

ngoma (ᵊŋ'gəʊmə, ᵊŋ'gɒm-) *n. E African.* a type of drum. [Swahili]

ngultrum (ᵊŋ'guːltrəm) *n.* a monetary unit of Bhutan since 1974.

Nguni (ᵊŋ'guːnɪ) *n.* a group of Bantu languages of southern Africa, consisting chiefly of Zulu, Xhosa, and Swazi.

ngwee (ᵊŋ'gweɪ) *n.* a Zambian monetary unit worth one hundredth of a kwacha.

NH *or* **N.H.** *abbrev. for* New Hampshire.

NHI (in Britain) *abbrev. for* National Health Insurance.

NHS (in Britain) *abbrev. for* National Health Service.

Ni *the chemical symbol for* nickel.

NI *abbrev. for:* **1.** (in Britain) National Insurance. **2.** Northern Ireland. **3.** *N.Z.* North Island.

niacin ('naɪəsɪn) *n.* another name for **nicotinic acid.** [C20: from NI(COTINIC) AC(ID) + -IN]

nib (nɪb) *n.* **1.** the writing point of a pen, esp. an insertable tapered metal part with a split tip. **2.** a point, tip, or beak. **3.** (*pl.*) crushed cocoa beans. *~vb.* **nibs, nibbing, nibbed.** (*tr.*) **4.** to provide with a nib. **5.** to prepare or sharpen the nib of. [C16 (in the sense: beak): origin obscure; compare Northern German *nibbe* tip. See NEB, NIBBLE] —'**nib,like** *adj.*

nibble ('nɪbᵊl) *vb.* (when *intr.*, often foll. by *at*) **1.** (esp. of animals, such as mice) to take small repeated bites (of). **2.** to take dainty or tentative bites: *to nibble at a cake.* **3.** to bite (at) gently or caressingly. **4.** (*intr.*) to make petty criticisms. **5.** (*intr.*) to consider tentatively or cautiously: *to nibble at an idea.* *~n.* **6.** a small mouthful. **7.** an instance or the act of nibbling. [C15: related to Low German *nibbelen.* Compare NIB, NEB]

nibbler ('nɪblə) *n.* **1.** a person, animal, or thing that nibbles. **2.** *Engineering.* a tool that cuts sheet material by a series of small rapidly reciprocating cuts.

niblick ('nɪblɪk) *n. Golf.* (formerly) a club, a No. 9 iron, giving a great deal of lift. [C19: of unknown origin]

nibs (nɪbz) *pl. n.* **his nibs.** *Slang.* a mock title used of someone in authority. [C19: of unknown origin]

NICAM *abbrev. for* near-instantaneous companding system: a technique for coding audio signals into digital form.

Nicaraguan (,nɪkə'rægjʊən, -gwən) *adj.* **1.** of or relating to Nicaragua, a republic in Central America, or its people. *~n.* **2.** a native or inhabitant of Nicaragua.

niccolite ('nɪkə,laɪt) *n.* a copper-coloured mineral consisting of nickel arsenide in hexagonal crystalline form, occurring associated with copper and silver ores: a source of nickel. Formula: NiAs. [C19: from New Latin *niccolum* NICKEL + -ITE[1]]

nice (naɪs) *adj.* **1.** pleasant or commendable: *a nice day.* **2.** kind or friendly: *a nice gesture of help.* **3.** good or satisfactory: *they made a nice job of it.* **4.** subtle, delicate, or discriminating: *a nice point in the argument.* **5.** precise; skilful: *a nice fit.* **6.** *Now rare.* fastidious; respectable: *he was not too nice about his methods.* **7.** *Obsolete.* **a.** foolish or ignorant. **b.** delicate. **c.** shy; modest. **d.** wanton. **8. nice and.** pleasingly: *it's nice and cool.* [C13 (originally: foolish): from Old French *nice* simple, silly, from Latin *nescius* ignorant, from *nescīre* to be ignorant; see NESCIENCE] —'**nicely** *adv.* —'**niceness** *n.* —'**nicish** *adj.*

nice-looking *adj. Informal.* attractive in appearance; pretty or handsome.

Nicene Creed ('naɪsiːn) *n.* **1.** the formal summary of Christian beliefs promulgated at the first council of Nicaea, an ancient city now in Turkey, in 325 A.D. **2.** a longer formulation of Christian beliefs authorized at the council of Constantinople in 381, and now used in most Christian liturgies.

nicety ('naɪsɪtɪ) *n., pl.* **-ties. 1.** a subtle point of delicacy or distinction: *a nicety of etiquette.* **2.** (*usually pl.*) a refinement or delicacy: *the niceties of first-class travel.* **3.** subtlety, delicacy, or precision. **4.** excessive refinement; fastidiousness. **5. to a nicety.** with precision.

niche (nɪtʃ, niːʃ) *n.* **1.** a recess in a wall, esp. one that contains a statue. **2.** any similar recess, such as one in a rock face. **3.** a position particularly suitable for the person occupying it: *he found his niche in politics.* **4.** (*modifier*) relating to or aimed at a small specialized group or market: *shampoo shops and other niche retailing ventures.* **5.** *Ecology.* the status of a plant or animal within its community, which determines its activities, relationships with other organisms, etc. *~vb.* **6.** (*tr.*) to place (a statue) in a niche; ensconce (oneself). [C17: from French, from Old French *nichier* to nest, from Vulgar Latin *nīdicāre* (unattested) to build a nest, from Latin *nīdus* NEST]

Nichrome ('naɪkrəʊm) *n. Trademark.* any of various alloys containing nickel, iron, and chromium, with smaller amounts of other components. It is used in electrical heating elements, furnaces, etc.

nicht (nɪxt) *n.* a Scot. word for **night.**

nick (nɪk) *n.* **1.** a small notch or indentation on an edge or surface. **2.** a groove on the shank of a printing type, used to orientate type and often to distinguish the fount. **3.** *Brit.* a slang word for **prison** or **police station. 4. in good nick.** *Informal.* in good condition. **5. in the nick of time.** at the last possible moment; at the critical moment. *~vb.* **6.** (*tr.*) to chip or cut. **7.** (*tr.*) *Slang, chiefly Brit.* **a.** to steal. **b.** to take into legal custody; arrest. **8.** (*intr.*; often foll. by *off*) *Informal.* to move or depart rapidly. **9.** to divide and reset (certain of the tail muscles of a horse) to give the tail a high carriage. **10.** (*tr.*) to guess, catch, etc., exactly. **11.** (*intr.*) (of breeding stock) to mate satisfactorily. **12. nick (someone) for.** *U.S. and Canadian slang.* to defraud (someone) to the extent of. [C15: perhaps changed from C14 *nocke* NOCK]

nickel ('nɪkᵊl) *n.* **1.** a malleable ductile silvery-white metallic element that is strong and corrosion-resistant, occurring principally in pentlandite and niccolite: used in alloys, esp. in toughening steel, in electroplating, and as a catalyst in organic synthesis. Symbol: Ni; atomic no.: 28; atomic wt.: 58.71; valency: 1, 2, or 3; relative density: 8.90; melting pt.: 1453°C; boiling pt.: 2732°C. **2.** a U.S. and Canadian coin and monetary unit worth five cents. *~vb.* **-els, -elling, -elled** *or U.S.* **-els, -eling, -eled. 3.** (*tr.*) to

plate with nickel. [C18: shortened form of German *Kupfernickel* NICCOLITE, literally: copper demon, so called by miners because it was mistakenly thought to contain copper]
nickel bloom *n.* another name for **annabergite.**
nickelic (nɪˈkɛlɪk) *adj.* **1.** of or containing metallic nickel. **2.** of or containing nickel in the trivalent state.
nickeliferous (ˌnɪkəˈlɪfərəs) *adj.* containing nickel.
nickelodeon (ˌnɪkəˈləʊdɪən) *n. U.S.* **1.** an early form of jukebox. **2.** (formerly) a cinema charging five cents for admission. **3.** (formerly) a Pianola, esp. one operated by inserting a five-cent piece. [C20: from NICKEL + (MEL)ODEON]
nickelous (ˈnɪkələs) *adj.* of or containing nickel, esp. in the divalent state.
nickel plate *n.* a thin layer of nickel deposited on a surface, usually by electrolysis.
nickel silver *n.* any of various white alloys containing copper (46–63 per cent), zinc (18–36 per cent), and nickel (6–30 per cent): used in making tableware, etc. Also called: **German silver.**
nickel steel *n. Engineering.* steel containing between 0.5 and 6.0 per cent nickel to increase its strength.
nicker[1] (ˈnɪkə) *vb.* *(intr.)* **1.** (of a horse) to neigh softly. **2.** to laugh quietly; snigger. [C18: perhaps from NEIGH]
nicker[2] (ˈnɪkə) *n., pl.* **-er.** *Brit. slang.* a pound sterling. [C20: of unknown origin]
nick-nack (ˈnɪkˌnæk) *n.* a variant spelling of **knick-knack.**
nickname (ˈnɪkˌneɪm) *n.* **1.** a familiar, pet, or derisory name given to a person, animal, or place: *his nickname was Lefty because he was left-handed.* **2.** a shortened or familiar form of a person's name: *Joe is a nickname for Joseph.* ~*vb.* **3.** *(tr.)* to call by a nickname; give a nickname to. [C15 *a nekename,* mistaken division of *an ekename* an additional name, from *eke* addition + NAME]
nickpoint (ˈnɪkˌpɔɪnt) *n.* a variant spelling (esp. U.S.) of **knickpoint.**
nicky-tam (ˈnɪkɪˈtæm) *n. Scot.* a strap or string secured round a trouser leg below the knee, formerly worn esp. by farm workers to keep the trouser bottoms clear of dirt. [C20: from *knicker* + *tam, taum* a fishing line or string]
Nicol prism (ˈnɪkᵊl) *n.* a device composed of two prisms of Iceland spar or calcite cut at specified angles and cemented together with Canada balsam. It is used for producing plane-polarized light. [C19: named after William *Nicol* (?1768–1851), British physicist, its inventor]
nicotiana (nɪˌkəʊʃɪˈɑːnə, -ˈeɪnə) *n.* any solanaceous plant of the American and Australian genus *Nicotiana,* such as tobacco, having white, yellow, or purple fragrant flowers. [C16: see NICOTINE]
nicotinamide (ˌnɪkəˈtɪnəˌmaɪd, -ˈtiːn-) *n.* the amide of nicotinic acid: a component of the vitamin B complex and essential in the diet for the prevention of pellagra. Formula: $C_6H_6ON_2$.
nicotine (ˈnɪkəˌtiːn) *n.* a colourless oily acrid toxic liquid that turns yellowish-brown in air and light: the principal alkaloid in tobacco, used as an agricultural insecticide. Formula: $C_{10}H_{14}N_2$. [C19: from French, from New Latin *herba nicotiana* Nicot's plant, named after J. *Nicot* (1530-1600), French diplomat who introduced tobacco into France] —ˈ**nicoˌtined** *adj.* —**nicotinic** (ˌnɪkəˈtɪnɪk) *adj.*
nicotinic acid *n.* a vitamin of the B complex that occurs in milk, liver, yeast, etc. Lack of it in the diet leads to the disease pellagra. Formula: $(C_5H_4N)COOH$. Also called: **niacin.**
nicotinism (ˈnɪkətiːˌnɪzəm) *n. Pathol.* a toxic condition of the body or a bodily organ or part caused by nicotine.
nictitate (ˈnɪktɪˌteɪt) *or* **nictate** (ˈnɪkteɪt) *vb.* technical words for **blink** (sense 1). [C19: from Medieval Latin *nictitāre* to wink repeatedly, from Latin *nictāre* to wink, from *nicere* to beckon] —ˌ**nictiˈtation** *or* **nicˈtation** *n.*
nictitating membrane *n.* (in reptiles, birds, and some mammals) a thin fold of skin beneath the eyelid that can be drawn across the eye. Also called: **third eyelid, haw.**
nidation (naɪˈdeɪʃən) *n. Physiol.* another name for **implantation** (sense 2). [from Latin *nīdus* nest]
niddering *or* **nidering** (ˈnɪdərɪŋ) *Archaic.* ~*n.* **1.** a coward. ~*adj.* **2.** cowardly. [C16: a mistaken reading of Old English *nithing* coward; related to *nīth* malice]
niddle-noddle (ˈnɪdᵊlˌnɒdᵊl) *adj.* **1.** nodding. ~*vb.* **2.** to nod rapidly or unsteadily. [C18: reduplication of NOD]
nide (naɪd) *n.* another word for **nye.** [C17: from Latin *nīdus* nest]
nidicolous (nɪˈdɪkələs) *adj.* (of young birds) remaining in the nest for some time after hatching. [C19: from Latin *nīdus* nest + *colere* to inhabit]
nidifugous (nɪˈdɪfjʊgəs) *adj.* (of young birds) leaving the nest very soon after hatching. [C19: from Latin *nīdus* nest + *fugere* to flee]
nidify (ˈnɪdɪˌfaɪ) *or* **nidificate** (ˈnɪdɪfɪˌkeɪt) *vb.* **-fies, -fying, -fied.** *(intr.)* (of a bird) to make or build a nest. [C17: from Latin *nīdificāre,* from *nīdus* a nest + *facere* to make] —ˌ**nidifiˈcation** *n.*
nid-nod (ˈnɪdˌnɒd) *vb.* **-nods, -nodding, -nodded.** to nod repeatedly. [C18: reduplication of NOD]
nidus (ˈnaɪdəs) *n., pl.* **-di** (-daɪ). **1.** the nest in which insects or spiders deposit their eggs. **2.** *Pathol.* a focus of infection. **3.** a cavity in which plant spores develop. [C18: from Latin: NEST] —ˈ**nidal** *adj.*
niece (niːs) *n.* a daughter of one's sister or brother. [C13: from Old French: niece, granddaughter, ultimately from Latin *neptis* granddaughter]
niello (nɪˈɛləʊ) *n., pl.* **-li** (-lɪ) *or* **-los.** **1.** a black compound of sulphur and silver, lead, or copper used to incise a design on a metal surface. **2.** the process of decorating surfaces with niello. **3.** a surface or object decorated with niello. ~*vb.* **-los, -loing, -loed.** **4.** *(tr.)* to decorate or treat with niello. [C19: from Italian from Latin *nigellus* blackish, from *niger* black] —**niˈellist** *n.*
Niersteiner (*German* ˈniːrʃtaɪnər) *n.* a white wine from the region around Nierstein, Germany.
Nietzschean (ˈniːtʃɪən) *adj.* **1.** relating to or characteristic of the ideas and doctrines of Friedrich Wilhelm Nietzsche (1844–1900), German philosopher, esp. his concept of the superman and his rejection of traditional Christian values. ~*n.* **2.** a follower or adherent of Nietzschean philosophy. —ˈ**Nietzscheˌism** *or* ˈ**Nietzscheanˌism** *n.*
nieve (niːv) *n. Scot. and northern English dialect.* the closed hand; fist. [C14: from Old Norse *hnefi*]
nife (naɪf, ˈnaɪfɪ) *n.* the earth's core, thought to be composed of nickel and iron. [C20: from the chemical symbols *Ni* (nickel) and *Fe* (iron)]
nifedipine (naɪˈfɛdɪpiːn) *n. Med.* a calcium antagonist used in the treatment of hypertension and angina pectoris.
niff (nɪf) *Brit. slang.* ~*n.* **1.** a bad smell. ~*vb.* *(intr.)* **2.** to smell badly; stink. [C20: perhaps from SNIFF] —ˈ**niffy** *adj.*
nifty (ˈnɪftɪ) *adj.* **-tier, -tiest.** *Informal.* **1.** pleasing, apt, or stylish. **2.** quick, agile: *he's nifty on his feet.* [C19: of uncertain origin] —ˈ**niftily** *adv.* —ˈ**niftiness** *n.*
NIG *international car registration for* Niger.
nigella (naɪˈdʒɛlə) *n.* any plant of the ranunculaceous genus *Nigella,* from the Mediterranean and W Asia, esp. *N. damascena:* see **love-in-a-mist.** [New Latin, diminutive of Latin *niger* black, from the colour of the seeds]
Niger-Congo *n.* **1.** a family of languages of Africa consisting of the Bantu languages together with most of the languages of the coastal regions of West Africa. The chief branches are Benue-Congo (including Bantu), Kwa, Mande, and West Atlantic. ~*adj.* **2.** relating to or belonging to this family of languages.
Nigerian (naɪˈdʒɪərɪən) *adj.* of or relating to Nigeria, a coastal a republic in West Africa, its people, or its culture. ~*n.* **2.** a native or inhabitant of Nigeria.
Niger seed (ˈnaɪdʒə) *n.* another name for **ramtil** (sense 2). [named after *Niger* in W Africa]
niggard (ˈnɪgəd) *n.* **1.** a stingy person. ~*adj.* **2.** *Archaic.* miserly. [C14: perhaps of Scandinavian origin; related to Swedish dialect *nygg* and Old English *hnēaw* stingy]
niggardly (ˈnɪgədlɪ) *adj.* **1.** stingy or ungenerous. **2.** meagre: *a niggardly salary.* ~*adv.* **3.** stingily; grudgingly. —ˈ**niggardliness** *n.*
nigger (ˈnɪgə) *n.* **1.** *Derogatory.* **a.** another name for a Negro. **b.** *(as modifier): nigger minstrels.* **2.** *Derogatory.* a member of any dark-skinned race. **3. nigger in the woodpile.** a hidden snag or hindrance. [C18: from C16 dialect *neeger,* from French *nègre,* from Spanish NEGRO]
niggle (ˈnɪgᵊl) *vb.* **1.** *(intr.)* to find fault continually. **2.** *(intr.)* to be preoccupied with details; fuss. **3.** *(tr.)* to irritate; worry. ~*n.* **4.** a slight or trivial objection or complaint. **5.** a slight feeling as of misgiving, uncertainty, etc. [C16: from Scandinavian; related to Norwegian *nigla.* Compare NIGGARD] —ˈ**niggler** *n.* —ˈ**niggly** *adj.*
niggling (ˈnɪglɪŋ) *adj.* **1.** petty. **2.** fussy. **3.** irritating. **4.** requiring painstaking work. ~*n.* **5.** an act or instance of niggling. —ˈ**nigglingly** *adv.*
nigh (naɪ) *adj., adv., prep.* an archaic, poetic, or dialect word for **near.** [Old English *nēah, nēh;* related to German *nah,* Old Frisian *nei.* Compare NEAR, NEXT]
night (naɪt) *n.* **1.** the period of darkness each 24 hours between sunset and sunrise, as distinct from day. **2.** *(modifier)* of, occurring, working, etc., at night: *a night nurse.* **3.** the occurrence of this period considered as a unit: *four nights later they left.* **4.** the period between sunset and retiring to bed; evening. **5.** the time between bedtime and morning: *she spent the night alone.* **6.** the weather conditions of the night: *a clear night.* **7.** the activity or experience of a person during a night. **8.** *(sometimes cap.)* any evening designated for a special observance or function. **9.** nightfall or dusk. **10.** a state or period of gloom, ignorance, etc. **11. make a night of it.** to go out and celebrate for most of the night. **12. night and day.** continually: *that baby cries night and day.* ~Related adj.: **nocturnal.** [Old English *niht;* compare Dutch *nacht,* Latin *nox,* Greek *nux*] —ˈ**nightless** *adj.* —ˈ**nightˌlike** *adj.*
night blindness *n. Pathol.* a nontechnical term for **nyctalopia.** —ˈ**nightˌblind** *adj.*
night-blooming cereus *n.* any of several cacti of the genera *Hylocereus, Selenicereus,* etc., having large fragrant flowers that open at night.
nightcap (ˈnaɪtˌkæp) *n.* **1.** a bedtime drink, esp. an alcoholic or hot one. **2.** a soft cap formerly worn in bed.
nightclothes (ˈnaɪtˌkləʊðz) *pl. n.* clothes worn in bed.
nightclub (ˈnaɪtˌklʌb) *n.* a place of entertainment open until late at night, usually offering food, drink, a floor show, dancing, etc. —ˈ**nightˌclubber** *n.*

night dancer *n.* (in Uganda) a person believed to employ the help of the dead in destroying other people.

nightdress (ˈnaɪtˌdrɛs) *n. Brit.* a loose dress worn in bed by women. Also called: **nightgown, nightie.**

nightfall (ˈnaɪtˌfɔːl) *n.* the approach of darkness; dusk.

night fighter *n.* an interceptor aircraft used for operations at night.

nightgown (ˈnaɪtˌgaʊn) *n.* **1.** another name for **nightdress. 2.** a man's nightshirt.

nighthawk (ˈnaɪtˌhɔːk) *n.* **1.** Also called: **bullbat, mosquito hawk.** any American nightjar of the genus *Chordeiles* and related genera, having a dark plumage and, in the male, white patches on the wings and tail. **2.** *Informal.* another name for **night owl.**

night heron *n.* any nocturnal heron of the genus *Nycticorax* and related genera, having short legs and neck, a heavy body, and a short heavy bill.

night horse *n. Austral.* a stockhorse specially trained to work at night.

nightie *or* **nighty** (ˈnaɪtɪ) *n., pl.* **nighties.** *Informal.* short for **nightdress.**

nightingale (ˈnaɪtɪŋˌgeɪl) *n.* **1.** a brownish European songbird, *Luscinia megarhynchos,* with a broad reddish-brown tail: well known for its musical song, usually heard at night. **2.** any of various similar or related birds, such as *Luscinia luscinia* (**thrush nightingale**). [Old English *nihtegale,* literally: night-singer, from NIGHT + *galan* to sing]

Nightingale ward (ˈnaɪtɪŋˌgeɪl) *n.* a long hospital ward with beds on either side and the nurses' station in the middle. [named after Florence *Nightingale* (1820–1910), British nurse]

nightjar (ˈnaɪtˌdʒɑː) *n.* any nocturnal bird of the family *Caprimulgidae,* esp. *Caprimulgus europaeus* (**European nightjar**): order *Caprimulgiformes.* They have a cryptic plumage and large eyes and feed on insects. [C17: NIGHT + JAR[2], so called from its discordant cry]

night latch *n.* a door lock that is operated by means of a knob on the inside and a key on the outside.

night letter *n.* (in the U.S. and Canada) a telegram sent for delivery the next day at a cheaper rate than a regular telegram.

nightlife (ˈnaɪtˌlaɪf) *n.* social life or entertainment taking place in the late evening or night, as in nightclubs.

night-light *n.* a dim light burning at night, esp. for children.

nightlong (ˈnaɪtˌlɒŋ) *adj., adv.* throughout the night.

nightly (ˈnaɪtlɪ) *adj.* **1.** happening or relating to each night. **2.** happening at night. ~*adv.* **3.** at night or each night.

nightmare (ˈnaɪtˌmɛə) *n.* **1.** a terrifying or deeply distressing dream. **2. a.** an event or condition resembling a terrifying dream: *the nightmare of shipwreck.* **b.** (*as modifier*): *a nightmare drive.* **3.** a thing that is feared. **4.** (formerly) an evil spirit supposed to harass or suffocate sleeping people. [C13 (meaning: incubus; C16: bad dream): from NIGHT + Old English *mare, mære* evil spirit, from Germanic; compare Old Norse *mara* incubus, Polish *zmora,* French *cauchemar* nightmare] —ˈ**nightˌmarish** *adj.* —ˈ**nightˌmarishly** *adv.* —ˈ**nightˌmarishness** *n.*

night-night *sentence substitute.* an informal word for **good night.**

night nurse *n.* a nurse whose duty is to look after a patient or patients during the night.

night owl *or* **hawk** *n. Informal.* a person who is or prefers to be up and about late at night.

night raven *n. Poetic.* any bird, esp. the night heron, that is most active at night.

nightrider (ˈnaɪtˌraɪdə) *n.* a member of a band of mounted and usually masked Whites in the southern U.S. who carried out acts of revenge and intimidation at night after the Civil War (1861–65). —ˈ**nightˌriding** *n.*

night robe *n.* a U.S. and Canadian name for **nightdress.**

nights (naɪts) *adv. Informal.* at night, esp. regularly: *he works nights.*

night safe *n.* a safe built into the outside wall of a bank, in which customers can deposit money at times when the bank is closed.

night school *n.* an educational institution that holds classes in the evening for those who are not free during the day.

nightshade (ˈnaɪtˌʃeɪd) *n.* **1.** any of various solanaceous plants, such as deadly nightshade, woody nightshade, and black nightshade. **2.** See **enchanter's nightshade.** [Old English *nihtscada,* apparently NIGHT + SHADE, referring to the poisonous or soporific qualities of these plants]

night shift *n.* **1.** a group of workers who work a shift during the night. **2.** the period worked.

nightshirt (ˈnaɪtˌʃɜːt) *n.* a loose knee-length or longer shirtlike garment worn in bed by men.

night soil *n.* human excrement collected at night from cesspools, privies, etc., and sometimes used as a fertilizer.

nightspot (ˈnaɪtˌspɒt) *n.* an informal word for **nightclub.**

night stick *n.* a U.S. and Canadian name for **truncheon.**

night-time *n.* **a.** the time from sunset to sunrise; night as distinct from day. **b.** (*as modifier*): *a night-time prowler.*

night watch *n.* **1.** a watch or guard kept at night, esp. for security. **2.** the period of time the watch is kept. **3.** a person who keeps such a watch; night watchman.

night watchman *n.* **1.** Also called: **night watch.** a person who keeps guard at night on a factory, public building, etc. **2.** *Cricket.* a batsman sent in to bat to play out time when a wicket has fallen near the end of a day's play.

nightwear (ˈnaɪtˌwɛə) *n.* apparel worn in bed or before retiring to bed; pyjamas, nightdress, dressing gown, etc.

nigrescent (naɪˈgrɛsᵊnt) *adj.* blackish; dark. [C18: from Latin *nigrescere* to grow black, from *niger* black; see NEGRO] —**niˈgrescence** *n.*

nigritude (ˈnɪgrɪˌtjuːd) *n. Rare.* blackness; darkness. [C17: from Latin *nigritūdō,* from *niger* black]

nigrosine (ˈnɪgrəˌsiːn, -sɪn) *or* **nigrosin** (ˈnɪgrəsɪn) *n.* any of a class of black pigments and dyes obtained from aniline: used in inks and shoe polishes and for dyeing textiles. [C19: from Latin *niger* black + -OSE[1] + -INE[1]]

NIHE (in Ireland) *abbrev. for* National Institute for Higher Education.

nihil *Latin.* (ˈnaɪhɪl, ˈniːhɪl) *n.* nil; nothing.

nihilism (ˈnaɪɪˌlɪzəm) *n.* **1.** a complete denial of all established authority and institutions. **2.** *Philosophy.* an extreme form of scepticism that systematically rejects all values, belief in existence, the possibility of communication, etc. **3.** a revolutionary doctrine of destruction for its own sake. **4.** the practice or promulgation of terrorism. [C19: from Latin *nihil* nothing + -ISM, on the model of German *Nihilismus*] —ˈ**nihilist** *n., adj.* —ˌ**nihilˈistic** *adj.*

Nihilism (ˈnaɪɪˌlɪzəm) *n.* (in tsarist Russia) any of several revolutionary doctrines that upheld terrorism.

nihility (naɪˈhɪlɪtɪ) *n.* the state or condition of being nothing; nothingness; nullity.

nihil obstat (ˈɒbstæt) the phrase used by a Roman Catholic censor to declare publication inoffensive to faith or morals. [Latin, literally: nothing hinders]

NII (in Britain) *abbrev. for* nuclear installations inspectorate.

-nik *suffix forming nouns.* denoting a person associated with a specified state or quality: *beatnik.* [C20: from Russian *-nik,* as in *Sputnik* (Soviet artificial satellite), and influenced by Yiddish *-nik* (agent suffix)]

nikau *or* **nikau palm** (ˈniːkaʊ) *n.* a palm tree of the genus *Rhopalostylis,* esp. *R. sapida,* native to New Zealand. The leaves were used by the Maoris to build their whares and the top of the stem is sometimes eaten. [Maori]

nil (nɪl) *n.* another word for nothing: used esp. in the scoring of certain games. [C19: from Latin]

nil desperandum (ˈnɪl ˌdɛspəˈrændəm) *sentence substitute.* never despair. [from Latin, literally: nothing to be despaired of]

Nile blue (naɪl) *n.* **a.** a pale greenish-blue colour. **b.** (*as adj.*): *a Nile-blue carpet.* [after the River *Nile* in Africa]

Nile green *n.* **a.** a pale bluish-green colour. **b.** (*as adj.*): *a Nile-green dress.*

nilgai (ˈnɪlgaɪ), **nilghau,** *or* **nylghau** (ˈnɪlgɔː) *n., pl.* **-gai, -gais** *or* **-ghau, -ghaus.** a large Indian antelope, *Boselaphus tragocamelus.* The male is blue-grey with white markings and has small horns; the female is brownish and has no horns. [C19: from Hindi *nīlgāw* blue bull, from Sanskrit *nīla* dark blue + *go* bull]

Nilometer (naɪˈlɒmɪtə) *n.* a graduated pillar by which the rise and fall of the River Nile can be measured.

Nilo-Saharan (ˌnaɪləʊsəˈhɑːrən) *n.* **1.** a family of languages of Africa, spoken chiefly by Nilotic peoples in a region extending from the Sahara to Kenya and Tanzania, including the Chari-Nile, Saharan, Songhai, and other branches. Classification is complicated by the fact that many languages spoken in this region belong to the unrelated Afro-Asiatic, Kordofanian, and Niger-Congo families. ~*adj.* **2.** relating to or belonging to this family of languages.

Nilotic (naɪˈlɒtɪk) *adj.* **1.** of or relating to the River Nile in Africa. **2.** of, relating to, or belonging to a tall Negroid pastoral people inhabiting the S Sudan, parts of Kenya and Uganda, and neighbouring countries. **3.** relating to or belonging to the group of languages spoken by the Nilotic peoples. ~*n.* **4.** a group of languages of E Africa, including Luo, Dinka, and Masai, now generally regarded as belonging to the Chari-Nile branch of the Nilo-Saharan family. [C17: via Latin from Greek *Neilotikós,* from *Neilos* the Nile]

nil return *n.* a reply of zero to a request for a quantified reply.

nim (nɪm) *n.* a game in which two players alternately remove one or more small items, such as matchsticks, from one of several rows or piles, the object being to take (or avoid taking) the last item remaining on the table. [C20: perhaps from archaic *nim* to take, from Old English *niman*]

nimble (ˈnɪmbᵊl) *adj.* **1.** agile, quick, and neat in movement: *nimble fingers.* **2.** alert; acute: *a nimble intellect.* [Old English *nǣmel* quick to grasp, and *numol* quick at seizing, both from *niman* to take] —ˈ**nimbleness** *n.* —ˈ**nimbly** *adv.*

nimblewit (ˈnɪmbəlˌwɪt) *n. Chiefly U.S. and Canadian.* an alert, bright, and clever person. —ˈ**nimbleˌwitted** *adj.*

nimbostratus (ˌnɪmbəʊˈstreɪtəs, -ˈstrɑːtəs) *n., pl.* **-ti** (-taɪ). a dark-coloured rain-bearing stratus cloud.

nimbus (ˈnɪmbəs) *n., pl.* **-bi** (-baɪ) *or* **-buses. 1. a.** a dark grey rain-bearing cloud. **b.** (*in combination*): *cumulonimbus clouds.* **2. a.** an emanation of light surrounding a saint or deity. **b.** a representation of this emanation. **3.** a surrounding aura or atmosphere. [C17: from Latin: cloud, radiance] —ˈ**nimbused** *adj.*

NIMBY ('nɪmbɪ) *n. acronym for* not in my back yard.
nimiety (nɪ'maɪɪtɪ) *n., pl.* **-ties.** a rare word for **excess.** [C16: from Late Latin *nimietās,* from Latin *nimis* too much]
niminy-piminy ('nɪmɪnɪ'pɪmɪnɪ) *adj.* excessively refined; prim. [C19: imitative of a prim affected enunciation]
nimonic alloy (nɪ'mɒnɪk) *n.* any of various nickel-based alloys used at high temperatures, as in gas turbine blades. [C20: from NI(CKEL) + MO(LYBDENUM) + -IC]
n'importe *French.* (nẽpɔrt) no matter.
Nimrod ('nɪmrɒd) *n.* a person who is dedicated to or skilled in hunting. [after the Old Testament hunter *Nimrod*] —**Nim'rod-ian** *or* **Nim'rodic** *adj.*
nincompoop ('nɪnkəm,puːp, 'nɪŋ-) *n.* a stupid person; fool; idiot. [C17: of unknown origin]
nine (naɪn) *n.* **1.** the cardinal number that is the sum of one and eight. See also **number** (sense 1). **2.** a numeral, 9, IX, etc., representing this number. **3.** something representing, represented by, or consisting of nine units, such as a playing card with nine symbols on it. **4.** Also: **nine o'clock.** nine hours after noon or midnight: *the play starts at nine.* **5. dressed (up) to the nines.** *Informal.* elaborately dressed. **6. 999** (in Britain) the telephone number of the emergency services. **7. nine to five.** normal office hours: *he works nine to five; a nine-to-five job.* ~*determiner.* **8. a.** amounting to nine: *nine days.* **b.** (*as pronoun*): *nine of the ten are ready.* ~Related prefix: **nona-.** [Old English *nigon;* related to Gothic *niun,* Latin *novem*]
nine-days wonder *n.* something that arouses great interest, but only for a short period.
ninefold ('naɪn,fəʊld) *adj.* **1.** equal to or having nine times as many or as much. **2.** composed of nine parts. ~*adv.* **3.** by or up to nine times as many or as much.
ninepins ('naɪn,pɪnz) *n.* **1.** (*functioning as sing.*) another name for **skittles. 2.** (*sing.*) one of the pins used in this game.
nineteen (,naɪn'tiːn) *n.* **1.** the cardinal number that is the sum of ten and nine and is a prime number. See also **number** (sense 1). **2.** a numeral, 19, XIX, etc., representing this number. **3.** something represented by, representing, or consisting of 19 units. **4. talk nineteen to the dozen.** to talk incessantly. ~*determiner.* **5. a.** amounting to nineteen: *nineteen pictures.* **b.** (*as pronoun*): *only nineteen voted.* [Old English *nigontīne*]
nineteenth (,naɪn'tiːnθ) *adj.* **1.** (*usually prenominal*) **a.** coming after the eighteenth in numbering or counting order, position, time, etc., being the ordinal number of *nineteen.* Often written: 19th. **b.** (*as n.*): *the nineteenth was rainy.* ~*n.* **2. a.** one of 19 approximately equal parts of something. **b.** (*as modifier*): *a nineteenth part.* **3.** the fraction that is equal to one divided by 19 (1/19).
nineteenth hole *n. Golf, slang.* the bar in a golf clubhouse. [C20: from its being the next objective after a standard 18-hole round]
nineteenth man *n.* **1.** *Australian Rules football.* the first reserve in a team. **2.** any person acting as a reserve or substitute.
ninetieth ('naɪntɪɪθ) *adj.* **1.** (*usually prenominal*) **a.** being the ordinal number of *ninety* in numbering or counting order, position, time, etc. Often written: 90th. **b.** (*as n.*): *the ninetieth in succession.* ~*n.* **2. a.** one of 90 approximately equal parts of something. **b.** (*as modifier*): *a ninetieth part.* **3.** the fraction equal to one divided by 90 (1/90).
ninety ('naɪntɪ) *n., pl.* **-ties. 1.** the cardinal number that is the product of ten and nine. See also **number** (sense 1). **2.** a numeral, 90, XC, etc., representing this number. **3.** something represented by, representing, or consisting of 90 units. ~*determiner.* **4. a.** amounting to ninety: *ninety times out of a hundred.* **b.** (*as pronoun*): *at least ninety are thought to be missing.* [Old English *nigontig*]
ninhydrin (nɪn'haɪdrɪn) *n.* a chemical reagent used for the detection and analysis of primary amines, esp. amino acids, with which it forms a derivative with an intense purple colour. [C20: from the chemical name *triketo hydrindene*]
ninny ('nɪnɪ) *n., pl.* **-nies.** a dull-witted person. [C16: perhaps from *an innocent* simpleton] —**'ninnyish** *adj.*
ninon ('niːnɒn, 'naɪnɒn; *French* ninɔ̃) *n.* a fine strong silky fabric. [C20: from French]
ninth (naɪnθ) *adj.* **1.** (*usually prenominal*) **a.** coming after the eighth in counting order, position, time, etc.; being the ordinal number of *nine.* Often written: 9th. **b.** (*as n.*): *he came on the ninth; ninth in line.* ~*n.* **2. a.** one of nine equal or nearly equal parts of an object, quantity, measurement, etc. **b.** (*as modifier*): *a ninth part.* **3.** the fraction equal to one divided by nine (1/9). **4.** *Music.* **a.** an interval of one octave plus a second. **b.** one of two notes constituting such an interval. **c.** See **ninth chord.** ~*adv.* **5.** Also: **'ninthly.** after the eighth person, position, event, etc. ~*sentence connector.* **6.** Also: **ninthly.** as the ninth point: linking what follows to the previous statement. [Old English *nigotha;* related to Old High German *niunto,* Old Norse *nīundi*]
ninth chord *n.* a chord much used in jazz and pop, consisting of a major or minor triad with the seventh and ninth added above the root. Often shortened to **ninth.**
niobic (naɪ'əʊbɪk, -'ɒbɪk) *adj.* of or containing niobium in the pentavalent state. Also: **columbic.**
niobite ('naɪə,baɪt) *n.* another name for **columbite.** [C19: NIOBIUM + -ITE[1]]
niobium (naɪ'əʊbɪəm) *n.* a ductile white superconductive metallic element that occurs principally in columbite and tantalite: used in steel alloys. Symbol: Nb; atomic no.: 41; atomic wt.: 92.906; valency: 2, 3, or 5; relative density: 8.57; melting pt.: 2468°C; boiling pt.: 4927°C. Former name: **columbium.** [C19: from New Latin, from *Niobe* (daughter of Tantalus of Greek legend), so named because it occurred in TANTALITE]
niobous (naɪ'əʊbəs) *adj.* of or containing niobium in the trivalent state. Also: **columbous.**
nip[1] (nɪp) *vb.* **nips, nipping, nipped.** (*mainly tr.*) **1.** to catch or tightly compress, as between a finger and the thumb; pinch. **2.** (often foll. by *off*) to remove by clipping, biting, etc. **3.** (when *intr.*, often foll. by *at*) to give a small sharp bite (to): *the dog nipped at his heels.* **4.** (esp. of the cold) to affect with a stinging sensation. **5.** to harm through cold: *the frost nipped the young plants.* **6.** to check or destroy the growth of (esp. in the phrase **nip in the bud**). **7.** *Slang.* to steal. **8.** (*intr.;* foll. by *along, up, out,* etc.) *Brit. informal.* to hurry; dart. **9.** *Slang, chiefly U.S. and Canadian.* to snatch. ~*n.* **10.** the act of nipping; a pinch, snip, etc. **11. a.** a frosty or chilly quality. **b.** severe frost or cold: *the first nip of winter.* **12.** a small piece or quantity: *he went out for a nip of fresh air.* **13.** a sharp flavour or tang. **14.** *Archaic.* a taunting remark. **15. nip and tuck.** *Chiefly U.S. and Canadian.* neck and neck. **16. put the nips in.** *Austral. and N.Z. slang.* to exert pressure on someone, esp. in order to extort money. [C14: of Scandinavian origin; compare Old Norse *hnippa* to prod]
nip[2] (nɪp) *n.* **1.** a small drink of spirits; dram. **2.** *Chiefly Brit.* a measure of spirits usually equal to one sixth of a gill. ~*vb.* **nips, nipping, nipped. 3.** to drink (spirits), esp. habitually in small amounts. [C18: shortened from *nipperkin* a vessel holding a half-pint or less, of uncertain origin; compare Dutch *nippen* to sip]
Nip (nɪp) *n. Slang.* a derogatory word for a **Japanese.** [C20: short for *Nipponese*]
nipa ('niːpə, 'naɪ-) *n.* **1.** a palm tree, *Nipa fruticans,* of S and SE Asia, having feathery leaves, used for thatching, and edible fruit. **2.** the fruit or thatch obtained from this tree. **3.** the sap of this tree, used to make a liquor. [C16: from Malay *nīpah*]
nipper ('nɪpə) *n.* **1.** a person or thing that nips. **2.** the large pincer-like claw of a lobster, crab, or similar crustacean. **3.** *Informal, chiefly Brit.* a small child. **4.** *Austral.* a type of small prawn used as bait.
nippers ('nɪpəz) *pl. n.* an instrument or tool, such as a pair of pliers, for snipping, pinching, or squeezing.
nipping ('nɪpɪŋ) *adj.* **1.** sharp and biting: *a nipping wind.* **2.** sarcastic; bitter. —**'nippingly** *adv.*
nipple ('nɪpᵊl) *n.* **1.** Also called: **mamilla, papilla, teat.** the small conical projection in the centre of the areola of each breast, which in women contains the outlet of the milk ducts. **2.** something resembling a nipple in shape or function. **3.** Also called: **grease nipple.** a small drilled bush, usually screwed into a bearing, through which grease is introduced. **4.** *U.S. and Canadian.* an informal word for **dummy** (sense 11). [C16: from earlier *neble, nible,* perhaps from NEB, NIB]
nipplewort ('nɪpᵊl,wɜːt) *n.* an annual Eurasian plant, *Lapsana communis,* with pointed oval leaves and small yellow flower heads: family *Compositae* (composites).
Nipponese (,nɪpə'niːz) *adj.* **1.** Japanese. ~*n.* **2.** a Japanese person. [from Japanese *Nippon* Japan, literally: land of the rising sun]
nippy ('nɪpɪ) *adj.* **-pier, -piest. 1.** (of weather) chilly, keen, or frosty. **2.** *Brit. informal.* **a.** quick; nimble; active. **b.** (of a motor vehicle) small and relatively powerful. **3.** (of the taste of food) biting, sharp, or pungent. **4.** (of a dog) inclined to bite. —**'nippily** *adv.* —**'nippiness** *n.*
NIRC *abbrev. for* National Industrial Relations Court.
NIREX ('naɪrɛks) *n. acronym for* Nuclear Industry Radioactive Waste Executive.
nirvana (nɪə'vɑːnə, nɜː-) *n. Buddhism, Hinduism.* final release from the cycle of reincarnation attained by extinction of all desires and individual existence, culminating (in Buddhism) in absolute blessedness, or (in Hinduism) in absorption into Brahman. [C19: from Sanskrit: extinction, literally: a blowing out, from *nir-* out + *vāti* it blows] —**nir'vanic** *adj.*
Nisan (niː'san) *n.* (in the Jewish calendar) the first month of the year according to biblical reckoning and the seventh month of the civil year, usually falling within March and April. [from Hebrew]
nisi ('naɪsaɪ) *adj.* (*postpositive*) *Law.* (of a court order) coming into effect on a specified date unless cause is shown within a certain period why it should not: *a decree nisi.* [C19: from Latin: unless, if not]
nisi prius ('praɪəs) *n.* **1.** *English legal history.* **a.** a direction that a case be brought up to Westminster for trial before a single judge and a jury. **b.** the writ giving this direction. **c.** trial before the justices taking the assizes. **2.** (in the U.S.) a court where civil actions are tried by a single judge sitting with a jury as distinguished from an appellate court. [C15: from Latin: unless previously]
Nissen hut ('nɪsᵊn) *n.* a military shelter of semicircular cross section, made of corrugated steel sheet. U.S. and Canadian equivalent: **Quonset hut.** [C20: named after Lt Col. Peter *Nissen* (1871–1930), British mining engineer, its inventor]
nisus ('naɪsəs) *n., pl.* **-sus.** an impulse towards or striving after a goal. [C17: from Latin: effort, from *nītī* to strive]

nit[1] (nɪt) *n.* **1.** the egg of a louse, usually adhering to human hair. **2.** the larva of a louse or similar insect. [Old English *hnitu;* related to Dutch *neet,* Old High German *hniz*]

nit[2] (nɪt) *n.* a unit of luminance equal to 1 candela per square metre. [C20: from Latin *nitor* brightness]

nit[3] (nɪt) *n. Informal, chiefly Brit.* short for **nitwit.**

nit[4] (nɪt) *n.* a unit of information equal to 1.44 bits. Also called: **nepit.** [C20: from *N(apierian dig)it*]

nit[5] (nɪt) *n.* **keep nit.** *Austral. informal.* to keep watch, esp. during illegal activity. [C19: from NIX[1]]

niter ('naɪtə) *n.* the usual U.S. spelling of **nitre.**

niterie ('naɪtərɪ, -trɪ) *n. Slang.* a nightclub.

nitid ('nɪtɪd) *adj. Poetic.* bright; glistening. [C17: from Latin *nitidus,* from *nitere* to shine]

niton ('naɪtɒn) *n.* a less common name for **radon.** [C20: from Latin *nitēre* to shine]

nit-picking *Informal.* ~*n.* **1.** a concern with insignificant details, esp. with the intention of finding fault. ~*adj.* **2.** showing such a concern; fussy. [C20: from NIT[1] + PICK[1]] —'**nit-ˌpicker** *n.*

nitramine ('naɪtrəˌmiːn) *n.* another name for **tetryl.**

nitrate ('naɪtreɪt) *n.* **1.** any salt or ester of nitric acid, such as sodium nitrate, $NaNO_3$. **2.** a fertilizer consisting of or containing nitrate salts. ~*vb.* **3.** (*tr.*) to treat with nitric acid or a nitrate. **4.** to convert or be converted into a nitrate. **5.** to undergo or cause to undergo the chemical process in which a nitro group is introduced into a molecule. —**ni'tration** *n.*

nitrazepam (naɪ'treɪzɪˌpæm) *n.* a synthetic chemical compound belonging to the benzodiazepine group of drugs; a minor tranquillizer used mainly in sleeping pills such as Mogadon. Formula $C_{15}H_{11}N_3O_3$. [C20: from NITRO- + *-azepam;* see DIAZEPAM]

nitre *or U.S.* **niter** ('naɪtə) *n.* another name for **potassium nitrate** *or* **sodium nitrate.** [C14: via Old French from Latin *nitrum,* from Greek *nitron* NATRON]

nitric ('naɪtrɪk) *adj.* of or containing nitrogen, esp. in the pentavalent state.

nitric acid *n.* a colourless or yellowish fuming corrosive liquid usually used in aqueous solution. It is an oxidizing agent and a strong monobasic acid: important in the manufacture of fertilizers, explosives, and many other chemicals. Formula: HNO_3. Former name: **aqua fortis.**

nitric bacteria *pl. n.* bacteria that convert nitrites to nitrates in the soil. See also **nitrobacteria.**

nitric oxide *n.* a colourless slightly soluble gas forming red fumes of nitrogen dioxide in air. Formula: NO. Systematic name: **nitrogen monoxide.**

nitride ('naɪtraɪd) *n.* a compound of nitrogen with a more electropositive element, for example magnesium nitride, Mg_3N_2.

nitriding ('naɪtraɪdɪŋ) *n.* a type of case-hardening in which steel is heated for long periods in ammonia vapour so that nitrogen produced by dissociation on the surface enters the steel.

nitrification (ˌnaɪtrɪfɪ'keɪʃən) *n.* **1.** the oxidation of the ammonium compounds in dead organic material into nitrites and nitrates by soil nitrobacteria, making nitrogen available to plants. See also **nitrogen cycle.** **2. a.** the addition of a nitro group to an organic compound. **b.** the substitution of a nitro group for another group in an organic compound.

nitrify ('naɪtrɪˌfaɪ) *vb.* **-fies, -fying, -fied.** (*tr.*) **1.** to treat or cause to react with nitrogen or a nitrogen compound. **2.** to treat (soil) with nitrates. **3.** (of nitrobacteria) to convert (ammonium compounds) into nitrates by oxidation. —'**nitriˌfiable** *adj.*

nitrile ('naɪtrɪl, -traɪl) *n.* any one of a class of organic compounds containing the monovalent group, -CN. Also called (not in technical usage): **cyanide.**

nitrite ('naɪtraɪt) *n.* any salt or ester of nitrous acid.

nitro ('naɪtrəʊ) *n. Slang.* short for **nitroglycerin.**

nitro- *or before a vowel* **nitr-** *combining form.* **1.** indicating that a chemical compound contains a nitro group, $-NO_2$: *nitrobenzene.* **2.** indicating that a chemical compound is a nitrate ester: *nitrocellulose.* [from Greek *nitron* NATRON]

nitrobacteria (ˌnaɪtrəʊbæk'tɪərɪə) *pl. n., sing.* **-terium** (-'tɪərɪəm). soil bacteria of the order *Pseudomonadales* that are involved in nitrification, including species of *Nitrosomonas* and *Nitrobacter.*

nitrobenzene (ˌnaɪtrəʊ'benziːn) *n.* a yellow oily toxic water-insoluble liquid compound, used as a solvent and in the manufacture of aniline. Formula: $C_6H_5NO_2$.

nitrocellulose (ˌnaɪtrəʊ'seljʊˌləʊs) *n.* another name (not in chemical usage) for **cellulose nitrate.**

Nitro-chalk *n. Trademark.* a chemical fertilizer containing calcium carbonate and ammonium nitrate.

nitrochloroform (ˌnaɪtrəʊ'klɒrəˌfɔːm) *n.* another name for **chloropicrin.**

nitro compound ('naɪtrəʊ) *n.* any one of a class of usually organic compounds that contain the monovalent group, $-NO_2$ (**nitro group** or **radical**), linked to a carbon atom. The commonest example is nitrobenzene, $C_6H_5NO_2$.

nitrogen ('naɪtrədʒən) *n.* **a.** a colourless odourless relatively unreactive gaseous element that forms 78 per cent (by volume) of the air, occurs in many compounds, and is an essential constituent of proteins and nucleic acids: used in the manufacture of ammonia and other chemicals and as a refrigerant. Symbol: N; atomic no.: 7; atomic wt.: 14.0067; valency: 3 or 5; density: 1/251 kg/m^3; melting pt.: -209.86°C; boiling pt.: -195.8°C. **b.** (*as modifier*): *nitrogen cycle.*

nitrogen cycle *n.* the natural circulation of nitrogen by living organisms. Nitrates in the soil, derived from dead organic matter by bacterial action (see **nitrification, nitrogen fixation**), are absorbed and synthesized into complex organic compounds by plants and reduced to nitrates again when the plants and the animals feeding on them die and decay.

nitrogen dioxide *n.* a red-brown poisonous irritating gas that, at ordinary temperatures, exists in equilibrium with dinitrogen tetroxide. It is an intermediate in the manufacture of nitric acid, a nitrating agent, and an oxidizer for rocket fuels. Formula: NO_2.

nitrogen fixation *n.* **1.** the conversion of atmospheric nitrogen into nitrogen compounds by soil bacteria, such as *Rhizobium,* in the root nodules of legumes, and by certain blue-green algae. **2.** a process, such as the Haber process, in which atmospheric nitrogen is converted into a nitrogen compound, used esp. for the manufacture of fertilizer. —'**nitrogen-ˌfixing** *adj.*

nitrogenize *or* **nitrogenise** (naɪ'trɒdʒɪˌnaɪz) *vb.* to combine or treat with nitrogen or a nitrogen compound. —**niˌtrogeni'zation** *or* **niˌtrogeni'sation** *n.*

nitrogen monoxide *n.* the systematic name for **nitric oxide.**

nitrogen mustard *n.* any of a class of organic compounds resembling mustard gas in their molecular structure. General formula: $RN(CH_2CH_2Cl)_2$, where R is an organic group: important in the treatment of cancer.

nitrogenous (naɪ'trɒdʒɪnəs) *adj.* containing nitrogen or a nitrogen compound: *a nitrogenous fertilizer.*

nitrogen peroxide *n.* **1.** an obsolete name for **nitrogen dioxide.** **2.** the equilibrium mixture of nitrogen dioxide and dinitrogen tetroxide.

nitrogen tetroxide *n.* **1.** another name for **dinitrogen tetroxide.** **2.** a brown liquefied mixture of nitrogen dioxide and dinitrogen tetroxide, used as a nitrating, bleaching, and oxidizing agent.

nitroglycerin (ˌnaɪtrəʊ'glɪsərɪn) *or* **nitroglycerine** (ˌnaɪtrəʊ'glɪsəˌriːn) *n.* a pale yellow viscous explosive liquid substance made from glycerol and nitric and sulphuric acids and used in explosives and in medicine as a vasodilator. Formula: $CH_2NO_3CHNO_3CH_2NO_3$. Also called: **trinitroglycerin.**

nitrohydrochloric acid (ˌnaɪtrəʊˌhaɪdrəʊ'klɒrɪk) *n.* another name for **aqua regia.**

nitrometer (naɪ'trɒmɪtə) *n.* an instrument for measuring the amount of nitrogen in a substance. —**nitrometric** (ˌnaɪtrəʊ'metrɪk) *adj.*

nitromethane (ˌnaɪtrəʊ'miːθeɪn) *n.* an oily colourless liquid obtained from methane and used as a solvent and rocket fuel and in the manufacture of synthetic resins. Formula: CH_3NO_2.

nitroparaffin (ˌnaɪtrəʊ'pærəfɪn) *n.* any of a class of colourless toxic compounds with the general formula $C_nH_{2n+1}NO_2$.

nitrophilous (naɪ'trɒfɪləs) *adj.* (of plants) growing in soil well supplied with nitrogen.

nitrosamine (ˌnaɪtrəʊsə'miːn, ˌnaɪtrəʊs'æmiːn) *n.* any one of a class of neutral, usually yellow oily compounds containing the divalent group =NNO.

nitroso (naɪ'trəʊsəʊ) *n.* (*modifier*) of, consisting of, or containing the monovalent group O:N-: *a nitroso compound.* [C19: from Latin *nitrōsus* full of natron; see NITRE]

nitrosyl ('naɪtrəsɪl, -ˌsaɪl) *n.* (*modifier*) another word for **nitroso,** esp. when applied to inorganic compounds: *nitrosyl chloride.* [C19: see NITROSO]

nitrous ('naɪtrəs) *adj.* of, derived from, or containing nitrogen, esp. in a low valency state. [C17: from Latin *nitrōsus* full of natron]

nitrous acid *n.* a weak monobasic acid known only in solution and in the form of nitrite salts. Formula: HNO_2. Systematic name: **dioxonitric(III) acid.**

nitrous bacteria *pl. n.* bacteria that convert ammonia to nitrites in the soil. See also **nitrobacteria.**

nitrous oxide *n.* a colourless nonflammable slightly soluble gas with a sweet smell: used as an anaesthetic in dentistry and surgery. Formula: N_2O. Systematic name: **dinitrogen oxide.** Also called: **laughing gas.**

nitty[1] ('nɪtɪ) *adj.* **-tier, -tiest.** infested with nits.

nitty[2] ('nɪtɪ) *adj.* **-tier, -tiest.** *Informal.* foolish; stupid. [C20: from NITWIT]

nitty-gritty ('nɪtɪ'grɪtɪ) *n.* **the.** *Informal.* the basic facts of a matter, situation, etc.; the core. [C20: perhaps rhyming compound formed from GRIT]

nitwit ('nɪtˌwɪt) *n. Informal.* a foolish or dull person. [C20: perhaps from NIT[1] + WIT[1]]

nival ('naɪvəl) *adj.* of or growing in or under snow. [C17: from Latin *nivālis,* from *nix* snow]

nivation (naɪ'veɪʃən) *n.* the weathering of rock around a patch of snow by alternate freezing and thawing. [C19: from Latin *nix,* stem *niv-* snow]

niveous ('nɪvɪəs) *adj.* resembling snow, esp. in colour. [C17: from Latin *niveus,* from *nix* snow]

Nivôse *French.* (nivoz) *n.* the fourth month of the French revolutionary calendar, extending from Dec. 22 to Jan. 20. [C18: via French from Latin *nivōsus* snowy, from *nix* snow]

nix[1] (nɪks) *U.S. and Canadian informal.* ~*sentence substitute.* **1.** another word for **no**[1] (sense 1). **2.** be careful! watch out! ~*n.* **3.** a rejection or refusal. **4.** nothing at all. ~*vb.* **5.** (*tr.*) to veto, deny, reject, or forbid (plans, suggestions, etc.). [C18: from German, colloquial form of *nichts* nothing]

nix[2] (nɪks) *or* (*fem.*) **nixie** ('nɪksɪ) *n. Germanic myth.* a water sprite, usually unfriendly to humans. [C19: from German *Nixe* nymph or water spirit, from Old High German *nihhus;* related to Old English *nicor* sea monster]

nixer ('nɪksə) *n. Dublin dialect.* a spare-time job. [from NIX[1], (in the sense), no (tax or insurance) + -ER[1]]

Nixie tube ('nɪksɪ) *n. Electronics.* another name for **digitron.**

nizam (naɪ'zæm) *n.* (formerly) a Turkish regular soldier. [C18: ultimately from Arabic *nizām* order, arrangement]

Nizam (nɪ'zɑːm) *n.* the title of the ruler of Hyderabad, India, from 1724 to 1948.

NJ *or* **N.J.** *abbrev. for* New Jersey.

NKGB *abbrev. for* People's Commissariat of State Security: the Soviet secret police from 1943 to 1946. [from Russian *Narodny komissariat gosudarstvennoi bezopasnosti*]

NKVD *abbrev.* the Soviet police and secret police from 1934 to 1943: the police from 1943–46. [from Russian *Narodny komissariat vnutrennikh del* People's Commissariat of Internal Affairs]

nl *abbrev. for:* **1.** *Printing.* new line. **2.** non licet. [Latin: it is not permitted] **3.** non liquet. [Latin: it is not clear]

NL *abbrev. for:* **1.** New Latin. **2.** (in Australia) no liability: denoting a public limited company. **3.** *international car registration for* the Netherlands.

NLC *abbrev. for* National Liberal Club.

NLF *abbrev. for* National Liberation Front.

NLLST *abbrev. for* National Lending Library for Science and Technology.

NLS *abbrev. for* National Library of Scotland.

NLW *abbrev. for* National Library of Wales.

nm *abbrev. for* nautical mile.

NM *or* **N. Mex.** *abbrev. for* New Mexico.

NMR *abbrev. for* nuclear magnetic resonance.

NNE *symbol for* north-northeast.

NNP *abbrev. for* net national product.

NNW *symbol for* north-northwest.

no[1] (nəʊ) *sentence substitute.* **1.** used to express denial, disagreement, refusal, disapproval, disbelief, or acknowledgment of negative statements. **2.** used with question intonation to query a previous negative statement, as in disbelief: *Alfred isn't dead yet. No?* ~*n., pl.* **noes** *or* **nos. 3.** an answer or vote of *no.* **4.** (*often pl.*) a person who votes in the negative. **5. the noes have it.** there is a majority of votes in the negative. Compare (for senses 3–5) **aye. 6. not take no for an answer.** to continue in a course of action despite refusals. ~Compare **yes,** (for senses 3–5) **aye.** [Old English *nā,* from *ne* not, no + *ā* ever; see AY[1]]

no[2] (nəʊ) *determiner.* **1.** not any, not a, or not one: *there's no money left; no card in the file.* **2.** not by a long way; not at all: *she's no youngster.* **3.** (foll. by comparative adjectives and adverbs) not: *no less than forty men; no taller than a child; no more quickly than before.* **4. no go.** See **go** (sense 73). [Old English *nā,* changed from *nān* NONE[1]]

No[1] *or* **Noh** (nəʊ) *n., pl.* **No** *or* **Noh.** the stylized classic drama of Japan, developed in the 15th century or earlier, using music, dancing, chanting, elaborate costumes, and themes from religious stories or myths. [from Japanese *nō* talent, from Chinese *neng*]

No[2] *the chemical symbol for* nobelium.

No. *abbrev. for:* **1.** north(ern). **2.** (*pl.* **Nos.** *or* **nos.**) Also: **no.** number. [from French *numéro*]

n.o. *Cricket. abbrev. for* not out.

no' (no, nəʊ) *adv. Scots.* not.

no-account *adj.* **1.** worthless; good-for-nothing. ~*n.* **2.** a worthless person.

Noachian (nəʊ'eɪkɪən) *or* **Noachic** (nəʊ'ækɪk, -'eɪkɪk) *adj. Old Testament.* of or relating to the patriarch Noah, who survived the Flood.

noah ('nəʊə) *n. Austral.* a shark. [from Australian rhyming slang *Noah's Ark*]

nob[1] (nɒb) *n. Cribbage.* **1.** the jack of the suit turned up. **2. one for his nob.** the call made with this jack, scoring one point. [C19: of uncertain origin]

nob[2] (nɒb) *n. Slang, chiefly Brit.* a person of wealth or social distinction. [C19: of uncertain origin] —'**nobby** *adj.* —'**nobbily** *adv.*

nob[3] (nɒb) *n. Slang.* the head. [C17: perhaps a variant of KNOB]

no-ball *n.* **1.** *Cricket.* an illegal ball, as for overstepping the crease, throwing, etc., for which the batting side scores a run unless the batsman hits the ball, in which case he can only be out by being run out. **2.** *Rounders.* an illegal ball, esp. one bowled too high or too low. ~*sentence substitute.* **3.** *Cricket, rounders.* a call by the umpire indicating a no-ball.

nobble ('nɒbᵊl) *vb.* (*tr.*) *Brit. slang.* **1.** to disable (a race-horse), esp. with drugs. **2.** to win over or outwit (a person) by underhand means. **3.** to suborn (a person, esp. a juror) by threats, bribery, etc. **4.** to steal; filch. **5.** to get hold of; grab. **6.** to kidnap. [C19: back formation from *nobbler,* from false division of *an hobbler* (one who hobbles horses) as *a nobbler*] —'**nobbler** *n.*

nobbut ('nɒbət) *adv. Dialect.* nothing but; only. [C14: from NO[2] + BUT[1]]

nobelium (nəʊ'biːlɪəm) *n.* a transuranic element produced artificially from curium. Symbol: No; atomic no.: 102; half-life of most stable isotope, ^{255}No: 180 seconds (approx.). [C20: New Latin, named after *Nobel* Institute, Stockholm, where it was discovered]

Nobel prize (nəʊ'bɛl) *n.* a prize for outstanding contributions to chemistry, physics, physiology or medicine, literature, economics, and peace that may be awarded annually. It was established in 1901 from the bequest of the Swedish chemist and philanthropist Alfred Nobel (1833–96); the prize for economics being added in 1969.

nobiliary (nə'bɪlɪərɪ) *adj.* of or relating to the nobility. [C18: from French *nobiliaire;* see NOBLE, -ARY]

nobiliary particle *n.* a preposition, such as French *de* or German *von,* occurring as part of a title or surname: *Marquis de Sade; Wernher von Braun.*

nobility (nəʊ'bɪlɪtɪ) *n., pl.* **-ties. 1.** a socially or politically privileged class whose titles are conferred by descent or by royal decree. **2.** the state or quality of being morally or spiritually good; dignity: *the nobility of his mind.* **3.** (in the British Isles) the class of people holding the title of dukes, marquesses, earls, viscounts, or barons and their feminine equivalents collectively; peerage.

noble ('nəʊbᵊl) *adj.* **1.** of or relating to a hereditary class with special social or political status, often derived from a feudal period. **2.** of or characterized by high moral qualities; magnanimous: *a noble deed.* **3.** having dignity or eminence; illustrious. **4.** grand or imposing; magnificent: *a noble avenue of trees.* **5.** of superior quality or kind; excellent: *a noble strain of horses.* **6.** *Chem.* **a.** (of certain elements) chemically unreactive. **b.** (of certain metals, esp. copper, silver, and gold) resisting oxidation. **7.** *Falconry.* **a.** designating long-winged falcons that capture their quarry by stooping on it from above. Compare **ignoble. b.** designating the type of quarry appropriate to a particular species of falcon. ~*n.* **8.** a person belonging to a privileged social or political class whose status is usually indicated by a title conferred by sovereign authority or descent. **9.** (in the British Isles) a person holding the title of duke, marquess, earl, viscount, or baron, or a feminine equivalent. **10.** a former Brit. gold coin having the value of one third of a pound. [C13: via Old French from Latin *nōbilis,* originally, capable of being known, hence well-known, noble, from *noscere* to know] —'**nobleness** *n.* —'**nobly** *adv.*

noble art *or* **science** *n.* **the.** boxing.

noble gas *n.* another name for **inert gas** (sense 1).

nobleman ('nəʊbᵊlmən) *or* (*fem.*) **noblewoman** *n., pl.* **-men** *or* **-women.** a person of noble rank, title, or status; peer; aristocrat.

noble savage *n.* (in romanticism) an idealized view of primitive man.

noblesse (nəʊ'blɛs) *n. Literary.* **1.** noble birth or condition. **2.** the noble class. [C13: from Old French; see NOBLE]

noblesse oblige (nəʊ'blɛs əʊ'bliːʒ; *French* nɔblɛs ɔbliʒ) *n. Often ironic.* the supposed obligation of nobility to be honourable and generous. [French, literally: nobility obliges]

nobody ('nəʊbədɪ) *pron.* **1.** no person; no-one. ~*n., pl.* **bodies. 2.** an insignificant person.

▷**Usage.** See at **everyone.**

nociceptive (ˌnəʊsɪ'sɛptɪv) *adj.* causing or reacting to pain. [C20: from Latin *nocēre* to injure + RECEPTIVE]

nocireceptor ('nəʊsɪrɪˌsɛptə) *n. Physiol.* a receptor sensitive to pain.

nock (nɒk) *n.* **1.** a notch on an arrow that fits on the bowstring. **2.** either of the grooves at each end of a bow that hold the bowstring. ~*vb.* (*tr.*) **3.** to fit (an arrow) on a bowstring. **4.** to put a groove or notch in (a bow or arrow). [C14: related to Swedish *nock* tip]

nocking point *n.* a marked part of the bowstring where the arrow is placed.

no-claim bonus *n.* a reduction on an insurance premium, esp. one covering a motor vehicle, if no claims have been made within a specified period. Also called: **no-claims bonus.**

noctambulism (nɒk'tæmbjʊˌlɪzəm) *or* **noctambulation** *n.* another word for **somnambulism.** [C19: from Latin *nox* night + *ambulāre* to walk] —**noc'tambulist** *n.*

nocti- *or before a vowel* **noct-** *combining form.* night: *noctilucent.* [from Latin *nox, noct-*]

noctiluca (ˌnɒktɪ'luːkə) *n., pl.* **-cae** (-siː). any bioluminescent marine dinoflagellate protozoan of the genus *Noctiluca.* [C17: from Latin, from *nox* night + *lūcēre* to shine]

noctilucent (ˌnɒktɪ'luːsᵊnt) *adj.* shining at night, as certain high-altitude clouds, believed to consist of meteor dust that reflects sunlight. —ˌ**nocti'lucence** *n.*

noctuid ('nɒktjʊɪd) *n.* **1.** any nocturnal moth of the family *Noctuidae:* includes the underwings and antler moth. See also **cutworm, army worm.** ~*adj.* **2.** of, relating to, or belonging to the *Noctuidae.* [C19: via New Latin from Latin *noctua* night owl, from *nox* night]

noctule ('nɒktjuːl) *n.* any of several large Old World insectivorous bats of the genus *Nyctalus,* esp. *N. noctula:* family *Ves-*

pertilionidae. [C18: probably from Late Latin *noctula* small owl, from Latin *noctua* night owl]

nocturn ('nɒktɜːn) *n. R.C. Church.* any of the main sections of the office of matins. [C13: from Medieval Latin *nocturna* (n.), from Latin *nocturnus* nocturnal, from *nox* night]

nocturnal (nɒk'tɜːnᵊl) *adj.* **1.** of, used during, occurring in, or relating to the night. **2.** (of animals) active at night. **3.** (of plants) having flowers that open at night and close by day. ~Compare **diurnal.** [C15: from Late Latin *nocturnālis,* from Latin *nox* night] —ˌ**noctur'nality** *n.* —**noc'turnally** *adv.*

nocturne ('nɒktɜːn) *n.* **1.** a short, lyrical piece of music, esp. one for the piano. **2.** a painting or tone poem of a night scene.

nocuous ('nɒkjʊəs) *adj. Rare.* harmful; noxious. [C17: from Latin *nocuus,* from *nocēre* to hurt] —'**nocuously** *adv.* —'**nocuousness** *n.*

nod (nɒd) *vb.* **nods, nodding, nodded. 1.** to lower and raise (the head) briefly, as to indicate agreement, invitation, etc. **2.** (*tr.*) to express or indicate by nodding: *she nodded approval.* **3.** (*tr.*) to bring or direct by nodding: *she nodded me towards the manager's office.* **4.** (*intr.*) (of flowers, trees, etc.) to sway or bend forwards and back. **5.** (*intr.*) to let the head fall forward through drowsiness; be almost asleep: *the old lady sat nodding by the fire.* **6.** (*intr.*) to be momentarily inattentive or careless: *even Homer sometimes nods.* ~*n.* **7.** a quick down-and-up movement of the head, as in assent, command, etc.: *she greeted him with a nod.* **8.** a short sleep; nap. See also **land of Nod. 9.** a swaying motion, as of flowers, etc., in the wind. **10. nodding acquaintance.** a slight, casual, or superficial knowledge (of a subject or a person). **11. on the nod.** *Informal.* **a.** agreed, as in a committee meeting, without any formal procedure. **b.** (formerly) on credit. **12. the nod.** *Boxing, informal.* the award of a contest to a competitor on the basis of points scored. ~See also **nod off, nod out.** [C14 *nodde,* of obscure origin] —'**nodding** *adj., n.*

nodal ('nəʊdᵊl) *adj.* of or like a node. —**no'dality** *n.* —'**nodally** *adv.*

nodding donkey *n. Informal.* (in the oil industry) a type of reciprocating pump used to extract oil from an inland well. [C20: so called from its shape and movement]

noddle[1] ('nɒdᵊl) *n. Informal, chiefly Brit.* the head or brains: *use your noddle!* [C15: origin obscure]

noddle[2] ('nɒdᵊl) *vb. Informal, chiefly Brit.* to nod (the head), as through drowsiness. [C18: from NOD]

noddy[1] ('nɒdɪ) *n., pl.* **-dies. 1.** any of several tropical terns of the genus *Anous,* esp. *A. stolidus* (**common noddy**), typically having a dark plumage. **2.** a fool or dunce. [C16: perhaps noun use of obsolete *noddy* foolish, drowsy, perhaps from NOD (vb.); the bird is so called because it allows itself to be caught by hand]

noddy[2] ('nɒdɪ) *n., pl.* **-dies.** (*usually pl.*) *Television.* film footage of an interviewer's reactions to comments made by an interviewee, used in editing the interview after it has been recorded. [C20: from NOD]

node (nəʊd) *n.* **1.** a knot, swelling, or knob. **2.** the point on a plant stem from which the leaves or lateral branches grow. **3.** *Physics.* a point at which the amplitude of one of the two kinds of displacement in a standing wave has zero or minimum value. Generally the other kind of displacement has its maximum value at this point. See also **standing wave.** Compare **antinode. 4.** Also called: **crunode.** *Maths.* a point at which two branches of a curve intersect, each branch having a distinct tangent. **5.** *Maths, linguistics.* one of the objects of which a graph or a tree consists; vertex. **6.** *Astronomy.* either of the two points at which the orbit of a body intersects the plane of the ecliptic. When the body moves from the south to the north side of the ecliptic it passes the **ascending node** and from the north to the south side it passes the **descending node. 7.** *Anatomy.* **a.** any natural bulge or swelling of a structure or part, such as those that occur along the course of a lymphatic vessel (**lymph node**). **b.** a finger joint or knuckle. [C16: from Latin *nōdus* knot]

node house *n.* a prefabricated shelter used by welders during the construction of an oil rig.

node of Ranvier ('rɑːnvɪˌeɪ) *n.* any of the gaps that occur at regular intervals along the length of the sheath of a myelinated nerve fibre, at which the axon is exposed. [C19: named after Louis-Antoine *Ranvier* (1835–1922), French histologist]

nodical ('nəʊdɪkᵊl, 'nɒdɪ-) *adj.* of or relating to the nodes of a celestial body, esp. of the moon.

nod off *vb.* (*intr., adv.*) *Informal.* to fall asleep.

nodose ('nəʊdəʊs, nəʊ'dəʊs) *or* **nodous** ('nəʊdəs) *adj.* having nodes or knotlike swellings: *nodose stems.* [C18: from Latin *nōdōsus* knotty] —**nodosity** (nəʊ'dɒsɪtɪ) *n.*

nod out *vb.* (*intr., adv.*) *Slang.* to lapse into stupor, esp. on heroin.

nodule ('nɒdjuːl) *n.* **1.** a small knot, lump, or node. **2.** Also called: **root nodule.** any of the knoblike outgrowths on the roots of clover and many other legumes: contain bacteria involved in nitrogen fixation. **3.** *Anatomy.* any small node or knoblike protuberance. **4.** a small rounded lump of rock or mineral substance, esp. in a matrix of different rock material. [C17: from Latin *nōdulus,* from *nōdus* knot] —'**nodular,** '**nodulose,** *or* '**nodulous** *adj.*

nodus ('nəʊdəs) *n., pl.* **-di** (-daɪ). **1.** a problematic idea, situation, etc. **2.** another word for **node.** [C14: from Latin: knot]

Noel *or* **Noël** (nəʊ'ɛl) *n.* **1.** (esp. in carols) another word for **Christmas. 2.** (*often not cap.*) *Rare.* a Christmas carol. [C19: from French, from Latin *nātālis* a birthday; see NATAL]

noesis (nəʊ'iːsɪs) *n.* **1.** *Philosophy.* the exercise of reason, esp. in the apprehension of universal forms. Compare **dianoia. 2.** *Psychol.* the mental process used in thinking and perceiving; the functioning of the intellect. See also **cognition.** [C19: from Greek *noēsis* thought, from *noein* to think]

noetic (nəʊ'ɛtɪk) *adj.* of or relating to the mind, esp. to its rational and intellectual faculties. [C17: from Greek *noētikos,* from *noein* to think, from *nous* the mind]

nog[1] *or* **nogg** (nɒg) *n.* **1.** Also called: **flip.** a drink, esp. an alcoholic one, containing beaten egg. **2.** *East Anglian dialect.* strong local beer. [C17 (originally: a strong beer): of obscure origin]

nog[2] (nɒg) *n.* **1.** a wooden peg or block built into a masonry or brick wall to provide a fixing for nails. **2.** short for **nogging** (sense 1). [C17: origin unknown]

noggin ('nɒgɪn) *n.* **1.** a small quantity of spirits, usually 1 gill. **2.** a small mug or cup. **3.** an informal word for **head** (sense 1). [C17: of obscure origin]

nogging ('nɒgɪŋ) *n.* **1.** Also called: **nog,** (Scot. and N.Z.) **dwang.** a short horizontal timber member used between the studs of a framed partition. **2.** masonry or brickwork between the timber members of a framed construction. **3.** a number of wooden pieces fitted between the timbers of a half-timbered wall.

no-go area *n.* **1.** a district in a town that is barricaded off, usually by a paramilitary organization, within which the police, army, etc., can only enter by force. **2.** an area that is barred to certain individuals, groups, etc.

Noh (nəʊ) *n.* a variant spelling of **No**[1].

no-hoper *n. Informal.* a useless person; failure.

nohow ('nəʊˌhaʊ) *adv. Not standard.* (*in negative constructions*) **a.** under any conditions. **b.** in any manner.

noil (nɔɪl) *n. Textiles.* the short or knotted fibres that are separated from the long fibres, or staple, by combing. [C17: of unknown origin]

noir (nwɑː) *adj.* (of a film) showing characteristics of a *film noir,* in plot or style.

noise (nɔɪz) *n.* **1.** a sound, esp. one that is loud or disturbing. **2.** loud shouting; clamour; din. **3.** any undesired electrical disturbance in a circuit, degrading the useful information in a signal. See also **signal-to-noise ratio. 4.** talk or interest: *noise about strikes.* **5.** (*pl.*) conventional comments or sounds conveying a reaction, attitude, feeling, etc.: *she made sympathetic noises.* **6. make a noise.** to talk a great deal or complain. **7. make noises about.** *Informal.* to give indications of one's intentions: *the government is making noises about new social security arrangements.* **8. noises off.** *Theatre.* sounds made offstage intended for the ears of the audience: used as a stage direction. ~*vb.* **9.** (*tr.;* usually foll. by *abroad* or *about*) to spread (news, gossip, etc.). **10.** (*intr.*) *Rare.* to talk loudly or at length. **11.** (*intr.*) *Rare.* to make a din or outcry; be noisy. [C13: from Old French, from Latin: NAUSEA]

noise generator *n.* a device used in synthesizers to produce high-frequency sound effects.

noiseless ('nɔɪzlɪs) *adj.* making little or no sound; silent. —'**noiselessly** *adv.* —'**noiselessness** *n.*

noisemaker ('nɔɪzˌmeɪkə) *n. U.S. and Canadian.* something, such as a clapper or bell, used to make a loud noise at football matches, celebrations, etc. —'**noiseˌmaking** *n., adj.*

noisette (nwɑː'zɛt) *adj.* **1.** flavoured or made with hazelnuts. ~*n.* **2.** a small round boneless slice of lamb from the fillet or leg. **3.** a chocolate made with hazelnuts. [from French: hazelnut]

noisome ('nɔɪsəm) *adj.* **1.** (esp. of smells) offensive. **2.** harmful or noxious. [C14: from obsolete *noy,* variant of ANNOY + -SOME[1]] —'**noisomely** *adv.* —'**noisomeness** *n.*

noisy ('nɔɪzɪ) *adj.* **noisier, noisiest. 1.** making a loud or constant noise. **2.** full of or characterized by noise. —'**noisily** *adv.* —'**noisiness** *n.*

noisy miner *n.* a honey-eater, *Manorina melanocephala,* of eastern Australia, having a grey-white plumage and brown wings and noted for its raucous cries.

nolens volens *Latin.* ('nəʊlɛnz 'vəʊlɛnz) *adv.* whether willing or unwilling.

noli-me-tangere ('nəʊlɪˌmeɪ'tæŋgərɪ) *n.* **1.** a warning against interfering or against touching a person or thing. **2.** a work of art depicting Christ appearing to Mary Magdalene after His Resurrection. **3.** another name for **touch-me-not. 4.** a cancerous ulcer affecting soft tissue and bone. [from Latin: do not touch me, the words spoken by Christ to Mary Magdalene (Vulgate, John 20:17)]

nolle prosequi ('nɒlɪ 'prɒsɪˌkwaɪ) *n. Law.* an entry made on the court record when the plaintiff in a civil suit or prosecutor in a criminal prosecution undertakes not to continue the action or prosecution. Compare **non prosequitur.** [Latin: do not pursue (prosecute)]

nolo contendere ('nəʊləʊ kɒn'tɛndərɪ) *n. Law, chiefly U.S.* a plea made by a defendant to a criminal charge having the same effect in those proceedings as a plea of guilty but not precluding him from denying the charge in a subsequent action. [Latin: I do not wish to contend]

nol. pros. *or* **nolle pros.** *abbrev. for* nolle prosequi.

nom. *abbrev. for:* **1.** nominal. **2.** nominative.

noma ('nəʊmə) *n.* a gangrenous inflammation of the mouth, esp. one affecting malnourished children. [C19: New Latin, from Latin *nomē* ulcer, from Greek *nomē* feeding; related to Greek *nemein* to feed]

nomad ('nəʊmæd) *n.* **1.** a member of a people or tribe who move from place to place to find pasture and food. **2.** a person who continually moves from place to place; wanderer. [C16: via French from Latin *nomas* wandering shepherd, from Greek; related to *nemein* to feed, pasture] —'**nomadism** *n.*

nomadic (nəʊ'mædɪk) *adj.* relating to or characteristic of nomads or their way of life. —**no'madically** *adv.*

nomadize *or* **nomadise** ('nəʊmæd,aɪz) *vb.* **1.** (*intr.*) to live as nomads. **2.** (*tr.*) to make into nomads. **3.** (*tr.*) to people (a place) with nomads.

no-man's-land *n.* **1.** land between boundaries, esp. an unoccupied zone between opposing forces. **2.** an unowned or unclaimed piece of land. **3.** an ambiguous area of activity or thought.

nomarch ('nɒmɑːk) *n.* **1.** the head of an ancient Egyptian nome. **2.** the senior administrator in a Greek nomarchy. [C17: from Greek *nomarkhēs*]

nomarchy ('nɒmɑːkɪ, -əkɪ) *n., pl.* **-chies.** any of the provinces of modern Greece; nome. [C19: from Greek; see NOME, -ARCHY]

nombles ('nʌmbᵊlz) *pl. n.* a variant spelling of **numbles.**

nombril ('nɒmbrɪl) *n. Heraldry.* a point on a shield between the fesse point and the lowest point. [C16: from French, literally: navel]

nom de guerre ('nɒm də 'gɛə) *n., pl.* **noms de guerre** ('nɒm də 'gɛə). an assumed name; pseudonym. [literally: war name]

nom de plume ('nɒm də 'pluːm) *n., pl.* **noms de plume** ('nɒm də 'pluːm). another term for **pen name.**

nome (nəʊm) *n.* **1.** any of the provinces of modern Greece; nomarchy. **2.** an administrative division of ancient Egypt. [C18: from Greek *nomos* pasture, region]

nomen ('nəʊmɛn) *n., pl.* **nomina** ('nɒmɪnə). an ancient Roman's second name, designating his gens or clan. See also **agnomen, cognomen, praenomen.** [Latin: a name]

nomenclator ('nəʊmɛn,kleɪtə) *n.* a person who invents or assigns names, as in scientific classification. [C16: from Latin, from *nōmen* name + *calāre* to call]

nomenclature (nəʊ'mɛnklətʃə; *U.S.* 'nəʊmən,kleɪtʃər) *n.* the terminology used in a particular science, art, activity, etc. [C17: from Latin *nōmenclātūra* list of names; see NOMENCLATOR]

nominal ('nɒmɪnᵊl) *adj.* **1.** in name only; theoretical: *the nominal leader.* **2.** minimal in comparison with real worth or what is expected; token: *a nominal fee.* **3.** of, relating to, constituting, bearing, or giving a name. **4.** *Grammar.* of or relating to a noun or noun phrase. ~*n.* **5.** *Grammar.* a nominal element; a noun, noun phrase, or syntactically similar structure. **6.** *Bell-ringing.* the harmonic an octave above the strike tone of a bell. [C15: from Latin *nōminālis* of a name, from *nōmen* name] —'**nominally** *adv.*

nominal aphasia *n.* aphasia in which the primary symptom is an inability to recognize words and to speak the right word.

nominalism ('nɒmɪnᵊ,lɪzəm) *n.* the philosophical theory that the variety of objects to which a single general word, such as *dog,* applies have nothing in common but the name. Compare **conceptualism, realism.** —'**nominalist** *n., adj.* —,**nominal'istic** *adj.*

nominal scale *n. Statistics.* a discrete classification of data, in which data are neither measured nor ordered but subjects are merely allocated to distinct categories: *a record of students' course choices constitutes nominal data which could be correlated with school results.* Compare **ordinal scale, interval scale, ratio scale.**

nominal value *n.* another name for **par value.**

nominal wages *pl. n.* another name for **money wages.**

nominate *vb.* ('nɒmɪ,neɪt). (*mainly tr.*) **1.** to propose as a candidate, esp. for an elective office. **2.** to appoint to an office or position. **3.** to name (someone) to act on one's behalf, esp. to conceal one's identity. **4.** (*intr.*) *Austral.* to stand as a candidate in an election. **5.** *Archaic.* to name, entitle, or designate. ~*adj.* ('nɒmɪnɪt). **6.** *Rare.* having a particular name. [C16: from Latin *nōmināre* to call by name, from *nōmen* name] —'**nomi,nator** *n.*

nomination (,nɒmɪ'neɪʃən) *n.* the act of nominating or state of being nominated, esp. as an election candidate.

nominative ('nɒmɪnətɪv, 'nɒmnə-) *adj.* **1.** *Grammar.* denoting a case of nouns and pronouns in inflected languages that is used esp. to identify the subject of a finite verb. See also **subjective** (sense 6). **2.** appointed rather than elected to a position, office, etc. **3.** bearing the name of a person. ~*n.* **4.** *Grammar.* **a.** the nominative case. **b.** a word or speech element in the nominative case. [C14: from Latin *nōminātīvus* belonging to naming, from *nōmen* name] —**nominatival** (,nɒmɪnə'taɪvᵊl, ,nɒmnə-) *adj.* —'**nominatively** *adv.*

nominee (,nɒmɪ'niː) *n.* **1.** a person who is nominated to an office or as a candidate. **2. a.** a person or organization named to act on behalf of someone else, esp. to conceal the identity of the nominator. **b.** (*as modifier*): *nominee shareholder.* [C17: from NOMINATE + -EE]

nomism ('nəʊmɪzəm) *n.* adherence to a law or laws as a primary exercise of religion. [C20: from Greek *nomos* law, custom] —**no'mistic** *adj.*

nomo- *combining form.* indicating law or custom: *nomology.* [from Greek *nomos* law, custom]

nomocracy (nɒ'mɒkrəsɪ, nəʊ-) *n., pl.* **-cies.** government based on the rule of law rather than arbitrary will, terror, etc. [C19: from Greek, from *nomos* law + -CRACY]

nomogram ('nɒmə,græm, 'nəʊmə-) *or* **nomograph** *n.* **1.** an arrangement of two linear or logarithmic scales such that an intersecting straight line enables intermediate values or values on a third scale to be read off. **2.** any graphic representation of numerical relationships. [C20: from Greek *nomos* law + -GRAM, on the model of French *nomogramme*]

nomography (nɒ'mɒgrəfɪ) *n., pl.* **-phies.** the science of constructing nomographs. See **nomogram.** —**no'mographer** *n.* —**nomographic** (,nɒmə'græfɪk) *or* ,**nomo'graphical** *adj.* —,**nomo'graphically** *adv.*

nomological (,nɒmə'lɒdʒɪkᵊl) *adj.* **1.** of or relating to nomology. **2.** stating or relating to a nonlogical necessity or law of nature. The difference between a nomological and a merely universal statement is that from the universal *all As are Bs* one cannot, but from the nomological *all As must be Bs* one can, infer the counterfactual *if this were an A it would (have to) be a B.* —,**nomo'logically** *adv.*

nomology (nəʊ'mɒlədʒɪ) *n.* **1.** the science of law and law-making. **2.** the branch of science concerned with the formulation of laws explaining natural phenomena. —**no'mologist** *n.*

nomothetic (,nɒmə'θɛtɪk) *or* **nomothetical** *adj.* **1.** giving or enacting laws; legislative. **2.** *Psychol.* of or relating to the search for general laws or traits, esp. in personality theory. Compare **idiographic.** [C17: from Greek *nomothetikos,* from *nomothetēs* lawgiver]

-nomy *n. combining form.* indicating a science or the laws governing a certain field of knowledge: *agronomy; economy.* [from Greek *-nomia* law; related to *nemein* to distribute, control] —**-nomic** *adj. combining form.*

non- *prefix.* **1.** indicating negation: *nonexistent.* **2.** indicating refusal or failure: *noncooperation.* **3.** indicating exclusion from a specified class of persons or things: *nonfiction.* **4.** indicating lack or absence, esp. of a quality associated with what is specified: *nonobjective; nonevent.* [from Latin *nōn* not]

nona- *or before a vowel* **non-** *combining form.* nine: *nonagon.* [from Latin *nōnus*]

nonaccidental injury (,nɒnæksɪ'dɛntᵊl) *n. Social welfare.* damage, such as a bruise, burn, or fracture, deliberately inflicted on a child or an old person. Abbrev.: **NAI.** See also **child abuse.**

nonage ('nəʊnɪdʒ) *n.* **1.** *Law.* the state of being under any of various ages at which a person may legally enter into certain transactions, such as the making of binding contracts, marrying, etc. **2.** any period of immaturity.

nonagenarian (,nəʊnədʒɪ'nɛərɪən) *n.* **1.** a person who is from 90 to 99 years old. ~*adj.* **2.** relating to or denoting a nonagenarian. [C19: from Latin *nōnāgēnārius,* from *nōnāginta* ninety]

nonaggression (,nɒnə'grɛʃən) *n.* **a.** restraint of aggression, esp. between states. **b.** (*as modifier*): *a nonaggression pact.*

nonagon ('nɒnə,gɒn) *n.* a polygon having nine sides. Also called: **enneagon.** —**nonagonal** (nɒn'ægənᵊl) *adj.*

nonaligned (,nɒnə'laɪnd) *adj.* (of states) not part of a major alliance or power bloc, esp. not allied to the U.S., the former Soviet Union, or China. —,**nona'lignment** *n.*

nonanoic acid (,nɒnə'nəʊɪk) *n.* a colourless oily fatty acid with a rancid odour: used in making pharmaceuticals, lacquers, and plastics. Formula: $CH_3(CH_2)_7COOH$. Also called: **pelargonic acid.** [C19: from *nonane* a paraffin, ninth in the methane series, from Latin *nōnus* ninth + -ANE]

non-A, non-B hepatitis *n.* a form of viral hepatitis, not caused by the agents responsible for hepatitis A and hepatitis B, that is commonly transmitted by infected blood transfusions.

nonappearance (,nɒnə'pɪərəns) *n.* failure to appear or attend, esp. as a defendant or witness in court.

nonbeing (nɒn'biːɪŋ) *n.* the philosophical problem arising from the fact that the ability to refer appears to presuppose the existence of whatever is referred to, and yet we can talk intelligibly about nonexistent objects. See also **subsistence** (sense 5).

nonce[1] (nɒns) *n.* the present time or occasion (now only in the phrase **for the nonce**). [C12: from the phrase *for the nonce,* a mistaken division of *for then anes,* literally: for the once, from *then* dative singular of *the* + *anes* ONCE]

nonce[2] (nɒns) *n. Prison slang.* a rapist or child molester; a sexual offender. [C20: of unknown origin]

,**nonaca'demic** *adj.*
,**nonac'ceptance** *n.*
,**nonad'dictive** *adj.*
,**nonagri'cultural** *adj.*
,**nonalco'holic** *adj.*
,**nonat'tendance** *n.*
,**nonat'tributable** *adj.*
,**nonat'tributive** *adj.*
,**nonau'thoritative** *adj.*
non'auto,mated *adj.*
,**nonauto'matic** *adj.*
non'basic *adj.*
,**nonbel'ligerent** *adj.*
,**nonbio'logical** *adj.*
non'breakable *adj.*
non'carbo,nated *adj.*
,**noncar'nivorous** *adj.*
non-'Catholic *adj., n.*
,**non-Cau'casian** *adj., n.*
non'causal *adj.*

nonce word *n.* a word coined for a single occasion.

nonchalant (ˈnɒnʃələnt) *adj.* casually unconcerned or indifferent; uninvolved. [C18: from French, from *nonchaloir* to lack warmth, from NON- + *chaloir,* from Latin *calēre* to be warm] —ˈ**nonchalance** *n.* —ˈ**nonchalantly** *adv.*

noncognitivism (nɒnˈkɒgnɪtɪˌvɪzəm) *n. Philosophy.* the semantic meta-ethical thesis that moral judgments do not express facts and so do not have a truth value thus excluding both naturalism and non-naturalism. See **emotivism, prescriptivism.**

non-com (ˈnɒnˌkɒm) *n.* short for **noncommissioned officer.**

noncombatant (nɒnˈkɒmbətənt) *n.* **1.** a civilian in time of war. **2.** a member of the armed forces whose duties do not include fighting, such as a chaplain or surgeon.

noncommissioned officer (ˌnɒnkəˈmɪʃənd) *n.* (in the armed forces) a person, such as a sergeant or corporal, who is appointed from the ranks as a subordinate officer.

noncommittal (ˌnɒnkəˈmɪtᵊl) *adj.* **1.** not involving or revealing commitment to any particular opinion or course of action: *a noncommittal reply.* **2.** *Rare.* having no outstanding quality, meaning, etc.

non compos mentis *Latin.* (ˈnɒn ˈkɒmpəs ˈmɛntɪs) *adj.* mentally incapable of managing one's own affairs; of unsound mind. [Latin: not in control of one's mind]

nonconductor (ˌnɒnkənˈdʌktə) *n.* a substance that is a poor conductor of heat, electricity, or sound.

nonconformist (ˌnɒnkənˈfɔːmɪst) *n.* **1.** a person who does not conform to generally accepted patterns of behaviour or thought. ~*adj.* **2.** of or characterized by behaviour that does not conform to generally accepted patterns. —ˌ**nonconˈformism** *n.*

Nonconformist (ˌnɒnkənˈfɔːmɪst) *n.* **1.** a member of a Protestant denomination that dissents from an Established Church, esp. the Church of England. ~*adj.* **2.** of, relating to, or denoting Nonconformists. —ˌ**Nonconˈformity** *or* ˌ**Nonconˈformism** *n.*

nonconformity (ˌnɒnkənˈfɔːmɪtɪ) *n.* **1.** failure or refusal to conform. **2.** absence of agreement or harmony.

noncontributory (ˌnɒnkənˈtrɪbjʊtərɪ, -trɪ) *adj.* **1. a.** denoting an insurance or pension scheme for employees, the premiums of which are paid entirely by the employer. **b.** (of a state benefit) not dependent on national insurance contributions. **2.** not providing contribution; noncontributing.

noncooperation (ˌnɒnkəʊˌɒpəˈreɪʃən) *n.* **1.** failure or refusal to cooperate. **2.** refusal to pay taxes, obey government decrees, etc., as a protest. —**noncooperative** (ˌnɒnkəʊˈɒpərətɪv) *adj.* —ˌ**noncoˈoperˌator** *n.*

nondescript (ˈnɒndɪˌskrɪpt) *adj.* **1.** lacking distinct or individual characteristics; having no outstanding features. ~*n.* **2.** a nondescript person or thing. [C17 NON- + Latin *dēscriptus,* past participle of *dēscribere* to copy, DESCRIBE]

nondestructive testing (ˌnɒndɪˈstrʌktɪv) *n.* any of several methods of detecting flaws in metals without causing damage. The most common techniques involve the use of x-rays, gamma rays, and ultrasonic vibrations. Abbrev.: **NDT.**

nondirective therapy *n. Psychiatry.* another name for **client-centred therapy.**

nondisjunction (ˌnɒndɪsˈdʒʌŋkʃən) *n.* the failure of paired homologous chromosomes to move to opposite poles of the cell during meiosis.

nondomiciled (nɒnˈdɒmɪsaɪld) *adj.* of, relating to, or denoting a person who is not domiciled in his country of origin.

nondrip (nɒnˈdrɪp) *adj.* (of paint) specially formulated to minimize dripping during application.

none[1] (nʌn) *pron.* (*functioning as sing. or pl.*) **1.** not any of a particular class: *none of my letters has arrived.* **2.** no-one; nobody: *there were none to tell the tale.* **3.** no part (of a whole); not any (of): *none of it looks edible.* **4. none other.** no other person: *none other than the Queen herself.* **5. none the.** (*foll. by a comparative adj.*) in no degree: *she was none the worse for her ordeal.* **6. none too.** not very: *he was none too pleased with his car.* [Old English *nān,* literally: not one]

▷**Usage.** See at **everyone.**

none[2] (nəʊn) *n.* another word for **nones.**

noneffective (ˌnɒnɪˈfɛktɪv) *Chiefly U.S.* ~*adj.* **1.** not effective. **2.** unfit for or incapable of active military service. ~*n.* **3.** *Military.* a noneffective person.

nonego (nɒnˈiːgəʊ, -ˈɛgəʊ) *n. Philosophy.* everything that is outside one's conscious self, such as one's environment.

nonentity (nɒnˈɛntɪtɪ) *n., pl.* **-ties. 1.** an insignificant person or thing. **2.** a nonexistent thing. **3.** the state of not existing; nonexistence.

nonequivalence (ˌnɒnɪˈkwɪvələns) *n.* **1.** the relationship of being unequal or incomparable. **2.** *Logic.* **a.** the relation between two statements only one of which can be true in any circumstances. **b.** a function of two statements that takes the value true only when one but not both of its arguments is true. **c.** a compound statement asserting that just one of its components is true. ~Also called: **exclusive or.**

nones (nəʊnz) *n.* (*functioning as sing. or pl.*) **1.** (in the Roman calendar) the ninth day before the ides of each month: the seventh day of March, May, July, and October, and the fifth of each other month. See also **calends. 2.** *Chiefly R.C. Church.* the fifth of the seven canonical hours of the divine office, originally fixed at the ninth hour of the day, about 3 p.m. [Old English *nōn,* from Latin *nōna hora* ninth hour, from *nōnus* ninth]

nonessential (ˌnɒnɪˈsɛnʃəl) *adj.* **1.** not essential; not necessary. **2.** *Biochem.* (of an amino acid in a particular organism) able to be synthesized from other substances. ~*n.* **3.** a nonessential person or thing.

nonesuch *or* **nonsuch** (ˈnʌnˌsʌtʃ) *n.* **1.** *Archaic.* a matchless person or thing; nonpareil. **2.** another name for **black medick.**

nonet (nɒˈnɛt) *n.* **1.** a piece of music composed for a group of nine instruments. **2.** an instrumental group of nine players. [C19: from Italian *nonetto,* from *nono* ninth, from Latin *nōnus*]

nonetheless (ˌnʌnðəˈlɛs) *sentence connector.* despite that; however; nevertheless.

non-Euclidean geometry *n.* the branch of modern geometry in which certain axioms of Euclidean geometry are restated. It introduces fundamental changes into the concept of space.

nonevent (ˌnɒnɪˈvɛnt) *n.* a disappointing or insignificant occurrence, esp. one predicted to be important.

nonexecutive director *n.* a director of a commercial company who is not a full-time member of the company but is brought in to advise the other directors.

nonfeasance (nɒnˈfiːzᵊns) *n. Law.* a failure to act when under an obligation to do so. Compare **malfeasance, misfeasance.** [C16: from NON- + *feasance* (obsolete) performing or doing, from French *faisance,* from *faire* to do, from Latin *facere*]

nonferrous (nɒnˈfɛrəs) *adj.* **1.** denoting any metal other than iron. **2.** not containing iron: *a nonferrous alloy.*

nonfiction (nɒnˈfɪkʃən) *n.* **1.** writing dealing with facts and events rather than imaginative narration. **2.** (*modifier*) relating to or denoting nonfiction. —**nonˈfictional** *adj.* —**nonˈfictionally** *adv.*

nonflammable (nɒnˈflæməbᵊl) *adj.* incapable of burning or not easily set on fire; not flammable.

ˌ**nonceˈlestial** *adj.*
nonˈcellular *adj.*
nonˈcentral *adj.*
nonˈcerebral *adj.*
nonˈchargeable *adj.*
non-ˈChristian *adj., n.*
nonˈclaim *n.*
nonˈclassic *or* **nonˈclassical** *adj.*
nonˈclassiˌfied *adj.*
nonˈclerical *adj.*
nonˈclinical *adj.*
ˌ**noncoˈaguˌlating** *adj.*
ˌ**noncolˈlegiate** *adj.*
ˌ**noncomˈbining** *adj.*
ˌ**noncomˈmercial** *adj.*
ˌ**noncomˈmissioned** *adj.*
ˌ**noncomˈmunicant** *n.*
ˌ**noncomˈmunicative** *adj.*
nonˈcommunist *adj., n.*
ˌ**noncomˈpetitive** *adj.*
ˌ**noncomˈpliance** *n.*
ˌ**nonconˈciliatory** *adj.*
ˌ**nonconˈclusive** *adj.*
ˌ**nonconˈcurrent** *adj.*
ˌ**nonconˈductive** *adj.*
ˌ**nonconfiˈdential** *adj.*
ˌ**nonconˈflicting** *adj.*
ˌ**nonconˈgenital** *adj.*
ˌ**nonconˈnective** *adj.*
ˌ**nonconˈsecutive** *adj.*
ˌ**nonconˈsenting** *adj.*
ˌ**nonconstiˈtutional** *adj.*
ˌ**nonconˈstraining** *adj.*
ˌ**nonconˈstructive** *adj.*
ˌ**nonconˈtagious** *adj.*
ˌ**nonconˈtemporary** *adj.*
ˌ**nonconˈtributing** *adj.*
ˌ**nonconˈtrollable** *adj.*
ˌ**nonconˈtrolling** *adj.*
ˌ**noncontroˈversial** *adj.*
ˌ**nonconˈventional** *adj.*
ˌ**nonconˈvergent** *adj.*
ˌ**nonconˈversant** *adj.*
ˌ**nonconˈvertible** *adj.*
ˌ**noncorˈroborative** *adj.*
ˌ**noncorˈroding** *adj.*
ˌ**noncreˈative** *adj.*
nonˈcriminal *adj.*
nonˈcritical *adj.*
nonˈcultiˌvated *adj.*
nonˈcurrent *adj.*
ˌ**nondeˈciduous** *adj.*
ˌ**nondeˈductible** *adj.*
ˌ**nondeˈlivery** *n.*
ˌ**nondemoˈcratic** *adj.*
ˌ**nondeˈmonstrable** *adj.*
ˌ**nondeˌnomiˈnational** *adj.*
ˌ**nondepartˈmental** *adj.*
ˌ**nondeˈpendence** *n.*
ˌ**nondeˈtachable** *adj.*
nonˈdetoˌnating *adj.*
ˌ**nondictaˈtorial** *adj.*
ˌ**nondifˈfusing** *adj.*
ˌ**nondiploˈmatic** *adj.*
ˌ**nondiˈrectional** *adj.*
nonˈdisciˌplinary *adj.*
ˌ**nondisˈcrimiˌnating** *adj.*
ˌ**nondisˈtinctive** *adj.*
ˌ**nondiˈvisible** *adj.*
ˌ**nondocˈtrinal** *adj.*
ˌ**nondogˈmatic** *adj.*
ˌ**nondoˈmestiˌcated** *adj.*
ˌ**nondraˈmatic** *adj.*
nonˈdrinker *n.*
nonˈdriver *n.*
nonˈdurable *adj.*
nonˈearning *adj.*
ˌ**nonecoˈnomic** *adj.*
nonˈedible *adj.*
ˌ**noneˈlastic** *adj.*
ˌ**noneˈlection** *n.*
ˌ**noneˈlective** *adj.*
nonˈeligible *adj.*
ˌ**noneˈmotional** *adj.*
nonˈequal *adj.*
ˌ**noneˈquivalent** *adj.*
ˌ**nonesˈtablishment** *adj.*
nonˈethical *adj.*
ˌ**nonexˈchangeable** *adj.*
ˌ**nonexˈclusive** *adj.*
ˌ**nonexˈecutive** *adj.*
ˌ**nonexˈistence** *n.*
ˌ**nonexˈistent** *adj.*
ˌ**nonexˈplosive** *adj.*
nonˈfactual *adj.*
nonˈfatal *adj.*
nonˈfattening *adj.*
nonˈfatty *adj.*
nonˈfederal *adj.*
ˌ**nonficˈtitious** *adj.*
nonˈfinite *adj.*
nonˈflexible *adj.*
nonˈfluid *adj.*
ˌ**nonforˈmation** *n.*
nonˈfreezing *adj.*
ˌ**nonfulˈfilment** *n.*
nonˈfunctional *adj.*
nonˈfusible *adj.*

nong (nɒŋ) *n. Austral. slang.* a stupid or incompetent person. [C19: perhaps alteration of obsolete English dialect *nigmenog* silly fellow, of unknown origin]

nonharmonic (ˌnɒnhɑːˈmɒnɪk) *adj. Music.* not relating to the harmony formed by a chord or chords.

nonillion (nəʊˈnɪljən) *n.* **1.** (in Britain, France, and Germany) the number represented as one followed by 54 zeros (10^{54}). **2.** (in the U.S. and Canada) the number represented as one followed by 30 zeros (10^{30}). Brit. word: **quintillion.** [C17: from French, from Latin *nōnus* ninth, on the model of MILLION] —**noˈnillionth** *adj., n.*

nonintervention (ˌnɒnɪntəˈvɛnʃən) *n.* refusal to intervene, esp. the abstention by a state from intervening in the affairs of other states or in its own internal disputes. —ˌ**noninterˈventional** *adj.* —ˌ**noninterˈventionist** *n., adj.*

noniron (nɒnˈaɪən) *adj.* (of a fabric) composed of any of various man-made fibres that are crease-resistant and do not require ironing.

nonjoinder (nɒnˈdʒɔɪndə) *n. Law.* the failure to join as party to a suit a person who should have been included either as a plaintiff or as a defendant. Compare **misjoinder.**

nonjudgmental *or* **nonjudgemental** (ˌnɒndʒʌdʒˈmɛntᵊl) *adj.* of, relating to, or denoting an attitude, approach, etc., that is open and not incorporating a judgment one way or the other.

nonjuror (nɒnˈdʒʊərə) *n.* a person who refuses to take an oath, as of allegiance.

non licet (ˈnɒn ˈlaɪsɪt) *adj.* not permitted; unlawful. [C17: Latin, literally: it is not allowed]

non liquet (ˈnɒn ˈlaɪkwɪt) *adj. Roman law.* (of a cause, evidence, etc.) not clear. [C17: Latin, literally: it is not clear]

nonmetal (nɒnˈmɛtᵊl) *n.* any of a number of chemical elements that form negative ions, have acidic oxides, and are generally poor conductors of heat and electricity.

nonmetallic (ˌnɒnmɪˈtælɪk) *adj.* **1.** not of metal. **2.** of, concerned with, or being a nonmetal.

nonmoral (nɒnˈmɒrəl) *adj.* not involving or related to morality or ethics; neither moral nor immoral.

non-naturalism *n.* the meta-ethical doctrine that moral properties exist but are not reducible to "natural", empirical, or supernatural ones, and that moral judgments therefore state a special kind of fact. Compare **naturalistic fallacy.** See also **descriptivism.**

Nonne's syndrome (nɒnz) *n.* another name for **cerebellar syndrome.**

nonobjective (ˌnɒnəbˈdʒɛktɪv) *adj.* of or designating an art movement in which things are depicted in an abstract or purely formalized way, not as they appear in reality.

no-nonsense (ˌnəʊˈnɒnsəns) *adj.* sensible, practical, straightforward; without nonsense of any kind: *a businesslike no-nonsense approach; a severe no-nonsense look.*

nonparametric statistics (ˌnɒnpærəˈmɛtrɪk) *n.* (*functioning as sing.*) the branch of statistics that studies data measurable on an ordinal or nominal scale, to which arithmetic operations cannot be applied.

nonpareil (ˈnɒnpərəl, ˌnɒnpəˈreɪl) *n.* **1.** a person or thing that is unsurpassed or unmatched; peerless example. **2.** (formerly) a size of printers' type equal to 6 point. **3.** *U.S.* a small bead of coloured sugar used to decorate cakes, biscuits, etc. **4.** *Chiefly U.S.* a flat round piece of chocolate covered with this sugar. ~*adj.* **5.** having no match or equal; peerless. [C15: from French, from NON- + *pareil* similar]

nonparous (nɒnˈpærəs) *adj.* never having given birth.

nonparticipating (ˌnɒnpɑːˈtɪsɪˌpeɪtɪŋ) *adj.* **1.** not participating. **2.** (of an assurance policy, share, etc.) not carrying the right to share in a company's profit.

nonpartisan *or* **nonpartizan** (ˌnɒnpɑːtɪˈzæn) *adj.* not partisan or aligned, esp. not affiliated to, influenced by, or supporting any one political party. —ˌ**nonpartiˈsanˌship** *or* ˌ**nonpartiˈzanˌship** *n.*

nonparty (nɒnˈpɑːtɪ) *adj.* not connected with any one political party.

nonpersistent (ˌnɒnpəˈsɪstənt) *adj.* (of pesticides) breaking down rapidly after application; not persisting in the environment.

nonplus (nɒnˈplʌs) *vb.* **-plusses, -plussing, -plussed** *or U.S.* **-pluses, -plusing, -plused. 1.** (*tr.*) to put at a loss; confound: *he was nonplussed by the sudden announcement.* ~*n., pl.* **-pluses. 2.** a state of utter perplexity prohibiting action or speech. [C16: from Latin *nōn plūs* no further (that is, nothing further can be said or done)]

nonproductive (ˌnɒnprəˈdʌktɪv) *adj.* **1.** (of workers) not directly responsible for producing goods. **2.** having disappointing results; unproductive. —ˌ**nonproˈductiveness** *n.* —**nonproductivity** (ˌnɒnprɒdʌkˈtɪvɪtɪ) *n.*

non-profit-making *or U.S.* (*often*) **nonprofit** (nɒnˈprɒfɪt) *adj.* not yielding a profit, esp. because organized or established for some other reason: *a non-profit-making organization.*

nonproliferation (ˌnɒnprəˌlɪfəˈreɪʃən) *n.* **1. a.** limitation of the production or spread of something, esp. nuclear or chemical weapons. **b.** (*as modifier*): *a nonproliferation treaty.* **2.** failure or refusal to proliferate.

non pros. *Law. abbrev. for* non prosequitur.

non-pros (ˌnɒnˈprɒs) *n.* **1.** short for **non prosequitur.** ~*vb.* **-prosses, -prossing, -prossed. 2.** (*tr.*) to enter a judgment of non prosequitur against (a plaintiff).

non prosequitur (ˈnɒn prəʊˈsɛkwɪtə) *n. Law.* (formerly) a judgment in favour of a defendant when the plaintiff failed to take the necessary steps in an action within the time allowed. Compare **nolle prosequi.** [Latin, literally: he does not prosecute]

nonreflexive (ˌnɒnrɪˈflɛksɪv) *adj. Logic.* (of a relation) neither reflexive nor irreflexive; holding between some members of its domain and themselves, and failing to hold between others.

nonrepresentational (ˌnɒnrɛprɪzɛnˈteɪʃənᵊl) *adj. Art.* another word for **abstract** (sense 4).

nonresident (nɒnˈrɛzɪdənt) *n.* **1.** a person who is not residing in the place implied or specified: *the hotel restaurant is open to nonresidents.* **2.** a British person employed abroad on a contract for a minimum of one year, who is exempt from UK income tax provided that he does not spend more than 90 days in the UK during that tax year. ~*adj.* **3.** not residing in the place specified. —**nonˈresidence** *or* **nonˈresidency** *n.*

nonresistant (ˌnɒnrɪˈzɪstənt) *adj.* **1.** incapable of resisting something, such as a disease; susceptible. **2.** *History.* (esp. in 17th-century England) practising passive obedience to royal authority even when its commands were unjust. —ˌ**nonreˈsistance** *n.*

nonˈgaseous *adj.*
ˌ**nongovernˈmental** *adj.*
nonˈgreasy *adj.*
nonˈhabitable *adj.*
nonˈhazardous *adj.*
nonˈheritable *adj.*
ˌ**nonhisˈtorical** *adj.*
nonˈhuman *adj.*
ˌ**noniˈdentical** *adj.*
ˌ**nonidioˈmatic** *adj.*
ˌ**noninˈclusion** *n.*
ˌ**nonindeˈpendent** *adj.*
ˌ**noninˈdictable** *adj.*
ˌ**noninˈdustrial** *adj.*
ˌ**noninˈfectious** *adj.*
ˌ**noninˈflammable** *adj.*
ˌ**noninˈflected** *adj.*
ˌ**noninˈformative** *adj.*
ˌ**noninˈherent** *adj.*
ˌ**noninˈheritable** *adj.*
ˌ**noninˈjurious** *adj.*
ˌ**noninˈstinctive** *adj.*
ˌ**noninstiˈtutional** *adj.*
ˌ**nonintelˈlectual** *adj.*
ˌ**noninterˈchangeable** *adj.*
ˌ**noninterˈsecting** *adj.*
ˌ**noninˈtoxiˌcating** *adj.*
ˌ**noninˈtuitive** *adj.*
ˌ**noninˈvasive** *adj.*
ˌ**noninˈvolvement** *n.*
nonˈirritant *adj., n.*
nonˈjury *adj.*
nonˈkosher *adj.*
nonˈlamiˌnated *adj.*
nonˈlethal *adj.*
nonˈlinear *adj.*
nonˈliterary *adj.*
ˌ**nonliˈturgical** *adj.*
nonˈlocal *adj.*
nonˈlogical *adj.*
nonˈluminous *adj.*
ˌ**nonmagˈnetic** *adj.*
ˌ**nonmaˈlignant** *adj.*
nonˈmaritime *adj.*
nonˈmarried *adj.*
ˌ**nonmaˌterialˈistic** *adj.*
ˌ**nonmaˈternal** *adj.*
ˌ**nonmatheˈmatical** *adj.*
nonˈmeasurable *adj.*
ˌ**nonmeˈchanical** *adj.*
nonˈmedical *adj.*
ˌ**nonmeˈdicinal** *adj.*
ˌ**nonmeˈlodic** *adj.*
nonˈmember *n.*
nonˈmemberˌship *n.*
nonˈmetric *adj.*
nonˈmigratory *adj.*
nonˈmilitant *adj.*
ˌ**nonminisˈterial** *adj.*
nonˈmountainous *adj.*
nonˈmystical *adj.*
nonˈmythical *adj.*
non-ˈnational *adj.*
non-ˈnative *adj.*
non-ˈnatural *adj.*
non-ˈnavigable *adj.*
non-neˈgotiable *adj.*
ˌ**non-ˈnervous** *adj.*
non-ˈnuclear *adj.*
ˌ**nonobˈligatory** *adj.*
ˌ**nonobˈservance** *n.*
ˌ**nonocˈcurrence** *n.*
ˌ**nonofˈficial** *adj.*
nonˈoperable *adj.*
ˌ**nonoperˈational** *adj.*
nonˈoperative *adj.*
ˌ**nonorˈganic** *adj.*
nonˈorthoˌdox *adj.*
ˌ**nonosˈtensive** *adj.*
nonˈparalˌlel *adj.*
ˌ**nonparaˈsitic** *adj.*
ˌ**nonpaˈrental** *adj.*
ˌ**nonparliaˈmentary** *adj.*
ˌ**nonpaˈrochial** *adj.*
ˌ**nonpaˈternal** *adj.*
nonˈpaying *adj.*
nonˈpayment *n.*
nonˈpermanent *adj.*
nonˈpermeable *adj.*
ˌ**nonphiloˈsophical** *adj.*
ˌ**nonphoˈnemic** *adj.*
nonˈphysical *adj.*
ˌ**nonphysioˈlogical** *adj.*
nonˈplaying *adj.*
nonˈpoisonous *adj.*
ˌ**nonpoˈlitical** *adj.*
ˌ**nonpolˈluting** *adj.*
nonˈporous *adj.*
ˌ**nonposˈsession** *n.*
nonˈpractical *adj.*
nonˈpractising *adj.*
nonˈprecious *adj.*
nonˈpredatory *adj.*
ˌ**nonpreˈdictable** *adj.*
ˌ**nonprejuˈdicial** *adj.*
ˌ**nonpreˈscriptive** *adj.*
ˌ**nonpreˈservable** *adj.*
ˌ**nonpreserˈvation** *n.*
ˌ**nonproˈfessional** *adj.*
ˌ**nonproˈgressive** *adj.*
ˌ**nonproˈportional** *adj.*
ˌ**nonproˈtective** *adj.*
nonˈpunishable *adj.*
nonˈracial *adj.*
nonˈradical *adj.*
ˌ**nonradioˈactive** *adj.*
nonˈrational *adj.*
nonˈreader *n.*
ˌ**nonrealˈistic** *adj.*
ˌ**nonrecogˈnition** *n.*
ˌ**nonreˈcoverable** *adj.*
ˌ**nonreˈflective** *adj.*
nonˈregiˌmented *adj.*
nonˈregistered *adj.*
ˌ**nonreˈligious** *adj.*
ˌ**nonreˈnewable** *adj.*
ˌ**nonrepreˈsentative** *adj.*
ˌ**nonresiˈdential** *adj.*

nonrestrictive (ˌnɒnrɪˈstrɪktɪv) *adj.* **1.** not restrictive or limiting. **2.** *Grammar.* denoting a relative clause that is not restrictive. Compare **restrictive** (sense 2).

nonreturn (ˌnɒnrɪˈtɜːn) *adj.* denoting a mechanism that permits flow in a pipe, tunnel, etc., in one direction only: *a nonreturn valve.*

nonreturnable (ˌnɒnrɪˈtɜːnəbᵊl) *adj.* denoting a container, esp. a bottle, on which no returnable deposit is paid on purchase of the contents.

nonreturn valve *n.* another name for **check valve.**

nonrhotic (nɒnˈrəʊtɪk) *adj. Phonetics.* denoting or speaking a dialect of English in which preconsonantal *r*s are not pronounced. —ˌ**nonrhoˈticity** *n.*

nonrigid (nɒnˈrɪdʒɪd) *adj.* **1.** not rigid; flexible. **2.** (of the gas envelope of an airship) flexible and held in shape only by the internal gas pressure.

nonscheduled (nɒnˈʃɛdjuːld; *also, esp. U.S.* nɒnˈskɛdʒʊəld) *adj.* **1.** not according to a schedule or plan; unscheduled. **2.** (of an airline) operating without published flight schedules.

nonsense (ˈnɒnsəns) *n.* **1.** something that has or makes no sense; unintelligible language; drivel. **2.** conduct or action that is absurd. **3.** foolish or evasive behaviour or manners: *she'll stand no nonsense.* **4.** See **no-nonsense. 5.** things of little or no value or importance; trash. ~*interj.* **6.** an exclamation of disagreement. —**nonsensical** (nɒnˈsɛnsɪkᵊl) *adj.* —**nonˈsensically** *adv.* —**nonˈsensicalness** *or* **nonˌsensiˈcality** *n.*

nonsense correlation *n. Statistics.* a correlation supported by data but having no basis in reality, as between incidence of the common cold and ownership of televisions.

nonsense syllable *n. Psychol.* a syllable, like *bik,* having no meaning. Lists of such syllables have been used to investigate memory and learning.

nonsense verse *n.* verse in which the sense is nonexistent or absurd.

non seq. *abbrev. for* non sequitur.

non sequitur (ˈnɒn ˈsɛkwɪtə) *n.* **1.** a statement having little or no relevance to what preceded it. **2.** *Logic.* a conclusion that does not follow from the premises. Abbrev.: **non seq.** [Latin, literally: it does not follow]

nonslip (nɒnˈslɪp) *adj.* designed to reduce or prevent slipping.

nonsmoker (nɒnˈsməʊkə) *n.* **1.** a person who does not smoke. **2.** a train compartment in which smoking is forbidden. —**nonˈsmoking** *adj.*

nonspecific urethritis *n.* inflammation of the urethra as a result of a venereal infection that cannot be traced to a specific cause. Abbrev.: **NSU.**

nonspecular reflection (nɒnˈspɛkjʊlə) *n. Physics.* the diffuse reflection of sound or light waves.

nonstandard (nɒnˈstændəd) *adj.* **1.** denoting or characterized by idiom, vocabulary, etc., that is not regarded as correct and acceptable by educated native speakers of a language; not standard. **2.** deviating from a given standard.

nonstarter (nɒnˈstɑːtə) *n.* **1.** a horse that fails to run in a race for which it has been entered. **2.** a person or thing that is useless, has little chance of success, etc.

nonstative (nɒnˈsteɪtɪv) *Grammar.* ~*adj.* **1.** denoting a verb describing an action rather than a state, as for example *throw* or *thank* as opposed to *know* or *hate.* Compare **stative.** ~*n.* **2.** a nonstative verb. ~Also: **active.**

nonstick (ˈnɒnˈstɪk) *adj.* (of saucepans, frying pans, etc.) coated with a substance such as polytetrafluoroethylene (PTFE) that prevents food sticking to them.

nonstoichiometric (nɒnˌstɔɪkɪəˈmɛtrɪk) *adj. Chem.* (of a solid compound) having a composition in which the ratio of the atoms present is not a simple integer. An example is titanium(IV) oxide, $TiO_{1.8}$.

nonstop (ˈnɒnˈstɒp) *adj., adv.* done without pause or interruption: *a nonstop flight.*

nonstriated (nɒnˈstraɪeɪtɪd) *adj.* (esp. of certain muscle fibres) having no striations.

non-striker *n. Cricket.* the batsman who is not facing the bowling.

nonsuch (ˈnʌnˌsʌtʃ) *n.* a variant spelling of **nonesuch.**

nonsuit (nɒnˈsuːt, -ˈsjuːt) *Law.* ~*n.* **1.** an order of a judge dismissing a suit when the plaintiff fails to show he has a good cause of action or fails to produce any evidence. ~*vb.* **2.** (*tr.*) to order the dismissal of the suit of (a person).

nonsymmetric (ˌnɒnsɪˈmɛtrɪk) *adj. Logic, maths.* (of a relation) not symmetric, asymmetric, or antisymmetric; holding between some pairs of arguments x and y and failing to hold for some other pairs when it holds between y and x.

nontransitive (nɒnˈtrænsɪtɪv) *adj. Logic.* (of a relation) neither transitive nor intransitive.

non troppo (ˈnɒn ˈtrɒpəʊ) *adv. Music.* (preceded by a musical direction, esp. a tempo marking) not to be observed too strictly (esp. in the phrases **allegro ma non troppo, adagio ma non troppo**).

non-U (nɒnˈjuː) *adj. Brit. informal.* (esp. of language) not characteristic of or used by the upper class. Compare **U.**

nonunion (nɒnˈjuːnjən) *adj.* **1.** not belonging or related to a trade union: *nonunion workers.* **2.** not favouring or employing union labour: *a nonunion shop.* **3.** not produced by union labour: *nonunion shirts.* ~*n.* **4.** *Pathol.* failure of broken bones or bone fragments to heal.

nonunionism (nɒnˈjuːnjəˌnɪzəm) *n. Chiefly U.S.* opposition to trade unionism. —**nonˈunionist** *n., adj.*

nonverbal communication (nɒnˈvɜːbᵊl) *n. Psychol.* those aspects of communication, such as gestures and facial expressions, that do not involve verbal communication but which may include nonverbal aspects of speech itself (accent, tone of voice, speed of speaking, etc.).

nonviolence (nɒnˈvaɪələns) *n.* abstention from the use of physical force to achieve goals. —**nonˈviolent** *adj.*

nonvoter (nɒnˈvəʊtə) *n.* **1.** a person who does not vote. **2.** a person not eligible to vote.

nonvoting (nɒnˈvəʊtɪŋ) *adj.* **1.** of or relating to a nonvoter. **2.** *Finance.* (of shares) not entitling the holder to vote at company meetings.

non-White *n. Chiefly S. African.* a person not of the Caucasoid or White race.

noodle[1] (ˈnuːdᵊl) *n.* (*often pl.*) a ribbon-like strip of pasta: noodles are often served in soup or with a sauce. [C18: from German *Nudel,* origin obscure]

noodle[2] (ˈnuːdᵊl) *n.* **1.** *U.S. and Canadian.* a slang word for **head** (sense 1). **2.** a simpleton. [C18: perhaps a blend of NODDLE[1] and NOODLE[1]]

noodle[3] (ˈnuːdᵊl) *vb.* (*intr.*) *Slang.* to improvise aimlessly on a musical instrument.

Noogoora burr (nəˈguːrə) *n. Austral.* a European cocklebur, *Xanthium pungens,* that is poisonous to stock. [from *Noogoora* a sheep station in Queensland]

nook (nʊk) *n.* **1.** a corner or narrow recess, as in a room. **2.** a secluded or sheltered place; retreat. [C13: origin obscure; perhaps related to Norwegian dialect *nok* hook]

nooky *or* **nookie** (ˈnʊkɪ) *n., pl.* **nookies.** *Slang.* sexual intercourse. [C20: of uncertain origin; perhaps from NOOK]

noon (nuːn) *n.* **1. a.** the middle of the day; 12 o'clock in the daytime or the time or point at which the sun crosses the local meridian. **b.** (*as modifier*): *the noon sun.* **2.** *Poetic.* the highest, brightest, or most important part; culmination. [Old English *nōn,* from Latin *nōna* (*hōra*) ninth hour (originally 3 p.m., the ninth hour from sunrise)]

noonday (ˈnuːnˌdeɪ) *n.* **a.** the middle of the day; noon. **b.** (*as modifier*): *the noonday sun.*

no-one *or* **no one** *pron.* no person; nobody.
▷**Usage.** See at **everyone.**

nooning (ˈnuːnɪŋ) *n. Dialect, chiefly U.S.* **1.** a midday break for rest or food. **2.** midday; noon.

noontime (ˈnuːnˌtaɪm) *or* **noontide** *n.* **a.** the middle of the day; noon. **b.** (*as modifier*): *a noontime drink.*

noose (nuːs) *n.* **1.** a loop in the end of a rope or cord, such as a lasso, snare, or hangman's halter, usually tied with a slipknot. **2.** something that restrains, binds, or traps. **3. put one's head in a noose.** to bring about one's own downfall. ~*vb.* (*tr.*) **4.** to secure or catch in or as if in a noose. **5.** to make a noose of or in. [C15: perhaps from Provençal *nous,* from Latin *nōdus* NODE]

Nootka (ˈnʊtkə, ˈnuːt-) *n.* **1.** (*pl.* **-ka** *or* **-kas**) a member of a North American Indian people living in W Canada, in British Columbia and Vancouver Island. **2.** the language of this people, belonging to the Wakashan family.

ˌ**nonreˈstricted** *adj.*
ˌ**nonrouˈtine** *adj.*
nonˈrural *adj.*
ˌ**nonscienˈtific** *adj.*
nonˈseasonal *adj.*
ˌ**nonsecˈtarian** *adj.*
nonˈsecular *adj.*
nonˈsegreˌgated *adj.*
ˌ**nonseˈlective** *adj.*
nonˈsensitive *adj.*
nonˈsexist *adj.*
nonˈsexual *adj.*
nonˈshrinkable *adj.*
ˌ**nonsigˈnificant** *adj.*
nonˈsinkable *adj.*
nonˈskilled *adj.*
nonˈsocial *adj.*
nonˈsoluble *adj.*
nonˈspeaking *adj.*
nonˈspecialist *n.*
ˌ**nonspeˈcific** *adj.*
nonˈspeculative *adj.*
nonˈspiritual *adj.*
nonˈsporting *adj.*
nonˈstainable *adj.*
nonˈstaining *adj.*
ˌ**nonstaˈtistical** *adj.*
ˌ**nonstraˈtegic** *adj.*
nonˈstructural *adj.*
ˌ**nonsubˈscriber** *n.*
ˌ**nonsugˈgestive** *adj.*
nonˈsulphurous *adj.*
ˌ**nonsupˈpression** *n.*
nonˈsurgical *adj.*
ˌ**nonsusˈtaining** *adj.*
nonˈswimmer *n.*
ˌ**nonsymˈbolic** *adj.*
ˌ**nonsystemˈatic** *adj.*
nonˈtaxable *adj.*
nonˈteaching *adj.*
nonˈtechnical *adj.*
nonˈtemporal *adj.*
ˌ**nonterriˈtorial** *adj.*
ˌ**nontheˈatrical** *adj.*
nonˈtoxic *adj.*
ˌ**nontraˈditional** *adj.*
ˌ**nontransˈferable** *adj.*
nonˈtropical *adj.*
nonˈtypical *adj.*
nonˈuniˌform *adj.*
nonˈusage *n.*
nonˈuse *n.*
nonˈuser *n.*
nonˈvenomous *adj.*
nonˈverbal *adj.*
nonˈveriˌfiable *adj.*
nonˈvintage *adj.*
nonˈvocal *adj.*
nonˈvolaˌtile *adj.*
nonˈworking *adj.*

nopal (ˈnəʊpᵊl) *n.* **1.** any of various cactuses of the genus *Nopalea,* esp. the red-flowered *N. cochinellifera,* which is a host plant of the cochineal insect. **2.** a cactus, *Opuntia lindheimeri,* having yellow flowers and purple fruits. See also **prickly pear.** [C18: from Spanish, from Nahuatl *nopálli* cactus]

no-par *adj.* (of securities) without a par value.

nope (nəʊp) *sentence substitute.* an informal word for **no**[1]. [C19: originally U.S., a variant of NO[1]]

nor (nɔː; *unstressed* nə) *conj. (coordinating), prep.* **1.** (used to join alternatives, the first of which is preceded by *neither*) and not: *neither measles nor mumps.* **2.** (foll. by an auxiliary verb or *have, do,* or *be* used as main verbs) (and) not...either: *they weren't talented—nor were they particularly funny.* **3.** *Dialect.* than: *better nor me.* **4.** *Poetic.* neither: *nor wind nor rain.* [C13: contraction of Old English *nōther,* from *nāhwæther* NEITHER]

Nor. *abbrev. for:* **1.** Norman. **2.** north. **3.** Norway. **4.** Norwegian.

nor- *combining form.* **1.** indicating that a chemical compound is derived from a specified compound by removal of a group or groups: *noradrenaline.* **2.** indicating that a chemical compound is a normal isomer of a specified compound. [by shortening from NORMAL]

noradrenaline (ˌnɔːrəˈdrɛnəlɪn, -liːn) *or* **noradrenalin** *n.* a hormone secreted by the adrenal medulla, increasing blood pressure and heart rate, and by the endings of sympathetic nerves, when it acts as a neurotransmitter both centrally and peripherally. Formula: $C_8H_{11}NO_3$. U.S. name: **norepinephrine.**

NOR circuit *or* **gate** (nɔː) *n. Computer technol.* a logic circuit having two or more input wires and one output wire that has a high-voltage output signal only if all input signals are at a low voltage. Compare **AND circuit.** [C20: from NOR, so named because the action performed is similar to the operation of the conjunction *nor* in logic]

nordic (ˈnɔːdɪk) *adj. Skiing.* of or relating to competitions in cross-country racing and ski-jumping. Compare **alpine** (sense 4).

Nordic (ˈnɔːdɪk) *adj.* of, relating to, or belonging to a subdivision of the Caucasoid race typified by the tall blond blue-eyed long-headed inhabitants of N Britain, Scandinavia, N Germany, and the Netherlands. [C19: from French *nordique,* from *nord* NORTH]

norepinephrine (ˌnɔːrɛpɪˈnɛfrɪn, -riːn) *n.* the U.S. name for **noradrenaline.**

Norfolk jacket (ˈnɔːfək) *n.* a man's single-breasted belted jacket with one or two chest pockets and a box pleat down the back. [C19: worn in *Norfolk,* a county of E England, for duck shooting]

Norfolk terrier *n.* a small wiry-coated breed of terrier having a short tail and pendent ears.

noria (ˈnɔːrɪə) *n.* a water wheel with buckets attached to its rim for raising water from a stream into irrigation canals: common in Spain and the Orient. [C18: via Spanish from Arabic *nā'ūra,* from *na'ara* to creak]

norite (ˈnɔːraɪt) *n.* a variety of gabbro that has hypersthene as the main ferromagnesian mineral. [C19: from Norwegian *norit,* from *Norge* Norway + *-it* -ITE[1]]

nork (nɔːk) *n. (usually pl.) Austral. slang.* a female breast. [C20: of unknown origin]

norland (ˈnɔːlənd) *n. Archaic.* the north part of a country or the earth. [C17: contraction of NORTH + LAND]

norm (nɔːm) *n.* **1.** an average level of achievement or performance, as of a group or person. **2.** a standard of achievement or behaviour that is required, desired, or designated as normal. **3.** *Sociol.* an established standard of behaviour shared by members of a social group to which each member is expected to conform. **4.** *Maths.* **a.** the length of a vector expressed as the square root of the sum of the square of its components. **b.** another name for **mode** (sense 6). **5.** *Geology.* the theoretical standard mineral composition of an igneous rock. [C19: from Latin *norma* carpenter's rule, square]

Norm (nɔːm) *n.* a stereotype of the unathletic Australian male. [from a cartoon figure in the government-sponsored *Life, Be In It* campaign]

norm. *abbrev. for* normal.

Norm. *abbrev. for* Norman.

Norma (ˈnɔːmə) *n., Latin genitive* **Normae** (ˈnɔːmiː). a constellation in the S hemisphere crossed by the Milky Way lying near Scorpius and Ara.

normal (ˈnɔːmᵊl) *adj.* **1.** usual; regular; common; typical: *the normal way of doing it; the normal level.* **2.** constituting a standard: *if we take this as normal.* **3.** *Psychol.* **a.** being within certain limits of intelligence, educational success or ability, etc. **b.** conforming to the conventions of one's group. **4.** *Biology, med.* (of laboratory animals) maintained in a natural state for purposes of comparison with animals treated with drugs, etc. **5.** *Chem.* (of a solution) containing a number of grams equal to the equivalent weight of the solute in each litre of solvent. Symbol: *N* **6.** *Chem.* denoting a straight-chain hydrocarbon: *a normal alkane.* Prefix: **n-**, e.g. *n*-octane. **7.** *Geometry.* another word for **perpendicular** (sense 1). ~*n.* **8.** the usual, average, or typical state, degree, form, etc. **9.** anything that is normal. **10.** *Geometry.* a line or plane perpendicular to another line or plane or to the tangent of a curved line or plane at the point of contact. [C16: from Latin *normālis* conforming to the carpenter's square, from *norma* NORM] —**normality** (nɔːˈmælɪtɪ) *or esp. U.S.* ˈ**normalcy** *n.*

normal curve *n. Statistics.* a symmetrical bell-shaped curve representing the probability density function of a normal distribution. The area of a vertical section of the curve represents the probability that the random variable lies between the values which delimit the section.

normal distribution *n. Statistics.* a continuous distribution of a random variable with its mean, median, and mode equal, the probability density function of which is given by $[\sigma\sqrt{(2\pi)}]^{-1}.\exp[-(x-\mu)^2/2\sigma^2]$ where μ is the mean and σ^2 the variance. Also called: **Gaussian distribution.**

normalization *or* **normalisation** (ˌnɔːməlaɪˈzeɪʃən) *n.* **1.** the act or process of normalizing. **2.** *Social welfare.* the policy of offering mentally or physically handicapped people patterns, conditions, and experiences of everyday life as close as possible to those of nonhandicapped people, by not segregating them physically, socially, and administratively from the rest of society.

normalize *or* **normalise** (ˈnɔːməˌlaɪz) *vb. (tr.)* **1.** to bring or make into the normal state. **2.** to bring into conformity with a standard. **3.** to heat (steel) above a critical temperature and allow it to cool in air to relieve internal stresses; anneal.

normally (ˈnɔːməlɪ) *adv.* **1.** as a rule; usually; ordinarily. **2.** in a normal manner.

normal matrix *n.* a square matrix A for which $AA^* = A^*A$, where A^* is the Hermitian conjugate of A.

normal school *n.* (in France, and formerly England, the U.S., and Canada) a school or institution for training teachers. [C19: from French *école normale:* the first French school so named was intended as a model for similar institutions]

Norman (ˈnɔːmən) *n.* **1.** (in the Middle Ages) a member of the people of Normandy in N France descended from the 10th-century Scandinavian conquerors of the country and the native French. **2.** a native or inhabitant of Normandy. **3.** another name for **Norman French.** ~*adj.* **4.** of, relating to, or characteristic of the Normans, esp. the Normans in England, or their dialect of French. **5.** of, relating to, or characteristic of Normandy or its inhabitants. **6.** denoting, relating to, or having the style of Romanesque architecture used in Britain from the Norman Conquest in 1066 until the 12th century. It is characterized by the rounded arch, the groin vault, massive masonry walls, etc.

Norman arch *n. Chiefly Brit.* a semicircular arch, esp. one in the Romanesque style of architecture developed by the Normans in England. Also called: **Roman arch.**

Norman English *n.* the dialect of English used by the Norman conquerors of England.

Norman French *n.* the medieval Norman and English dialect of Old French. See also **Anglo-French** (sense 3).

Normanize *or* **Normanise** (ˈnɔːməˌnaɪz) *vb.* to make or become Norman in character, style, customs, etc. —ˌ**Normaniˈzation** *or* ˌ**Normaniˈsation** *n.*

normative (ˈnɔːmətɪv) *adj.* **1.** implying, creating, or prescribing a norm or standard, as in language: *normative grammar.* **2.** expressing value judgments or prescriptions as contrasted with stating facts: *normative economics.* **3.** of, relating to, or based on norms. —ˈ**normatively** *adv.* —ˈ**normativeness** *n.*

normotensive (ˌnɔːməʊˈtɛnsɪv) *adj.* having or denoting normal blood pressure.

Norn (nɔːn) *n.* the medieval Norse language of the Orkneys, Shetlands, and parts of N Scotland. It was extinct by 1750. [C17: from Old Norse *norrœna* Norwegian, from *northr* north]

Norse (nɔːs) *adj.* **1.** of, relating to, or characteristic of ancient and medieval Scandinavia or its inhabitants. **2.** of, relating to, or characteristic of Norway. ~*n.* **3. a.** the N group of Germanic languages, spoken in Scandinavia; Scandinavian. **b.** any one of these languages, esp. in their ancient or medieval forms. See also **Proto-Norse, Old Norse. 4. the Norse.** *(functioning as pl.)* **a.** the Norwegians. **b.** the Vikings.

Norseman (ˈnɔːsmən) *n., pl.* **-men.** another name for a **Viking.**

north (nɔːθ) *n.* **1.** one of the four cardinal points of the compass, at 0° or 360°, that is 90° from east and west and 180° from south. **2.** the direction along a meridian towards the North Pole. **3.** the direction in which a compass needle points; magnetic north. **4. the north.** *(often cap.)* any area lying in or towards the north. Related adjs.: **arctic, boreal. 5.** *Cards. (usually cap.)* the player or position at the table corresponding to north on the compass. ~*adj.* **6.** situated in, moving towards, or facing the north. **7.** (esp. of the wind) from the north. ~*adv.* **8.** in, to, or towards the north. **9.** *Archaic.* (of the wind) from the north. ~Symbol.: **N** [Old English; related to Old Norse *northr,* Dutch *noord,* Old High German *nord*]

North (nɔːθ) *n.* **the. 1.** the northern part of a country, esp. the northern area of England. **2.** the countries of the world that are economically and technically advanced. ~*adj.* **3. a.** of or denoting the northern part of a specified country, area, etc. **b.** *(as part of a name): North Africa.*

North American *adj.* **1.** of, relating to, or denoting the continent of North America, its people, or cultures. ~*n.* **2.** a native or inhabitant of North America.

Northants (nɔːˈθænts) *abbrev. for* Northamptonshire.

North Atlantic Drift *or* **Current** *n.* the warm ocean current flowing northeast, under the influence of prevailing winds, from the Gulf of Mexico towards NW Europe and warming its climate. Also called: **Gulf Stream.**

northbound (ˈnɔːθˌbaʊnd) *adj.* going or leading towards the north.

north by east *n.* **1.** one point on the compass east of north, 11° 15′ clockwise from north. *~adj., adv.* **2.** in, from, or towards this direction.

north by west *n.* **1.** one point on the compass west of north, 348° 45′ clockwise from north. *~adj., adv.* **2.** in, from, or towards this direction.

northcountryman (ˌnɔːθˈkʌntrɪmən) *n., pl.* **-men.** a native or inhabitant of the North of England.

Northd *abbrev. for* Northumberland.

northeast (ˌnɔːθˈiːst; *Nautical* ˌnɔːrˈiːst) *n.* **1.** the point of the compass or direction midway between north and east, 45° clockwise from north. **2.** (*often cap.;* usually preceded by *the*) any area lying in or towards this direction. *~adj. also* **northeastern. 3.** (*sometimes cap.*) of or denoting the northeastern part of a specified country, area, etc.: *northeast Lincolnshire.* **4.** situated in, proceeding towards, or facing the northeast. **5.** (esp. of the wind) from the northeast. *~adv.* **6.** in, to, towards, or (esp. of the wind) from the northeast. ~Symbol: **NE** —ˌ**northˈeasternmost** *adj.*

northeast by east *n.* **1.** one point on the compass east of northeast, 56° 15′ clockwise from north. *~adj., adv.* **2.** in, from, or towards this direction.

northeast by north *n.* **1.** one point on the compass north of northeast, 33° 45′ clockwise from north. *~adj., adv.* **2.** in, from, or towards this direction.

northeaster (ˌnɔːθˈiːstə; *Nautical* ˌnɔːrˈiːstə) *n.* a strong wind or storm from the northeast.

northeasterly (ˌnɔːθˈiːstəlɪ; *Nautical* ˌnɔːrˈiːstəlɪ) *adj., adv.* **1.** in, towards, or (esp. of a wind) from the northeast. *~n., pl.* **-lies. 2.** a wind or storm from the northeast.

northeastward (ˌnɔːθˈiːstwəd; *Nautical* ˌnɔːrˈiːstwəd) *adj.* **1.** towards or (esp. of a wind) from the northeast. *~n.* **2.** a direction towards or area in the northeast. —ˌ**northˈeastwardly** *adj., adv.*

northeastwards (ˌnɔːθˈiːstwədz; *Nautical* ˌnɔːrˈiːstwədz) *or* **northeastward** *adv.* to the northeast.

norther (ˈnɔːðə) *n. Chiefly southern U.S.* a wind or storm from the north.

northerly (ˈnɔːðəlɪ) *adj.* **1.** of, relating to, or situated in the north. *~adv., adj.* **2.** towards or in the direction of the north. **3.** from the north: *a northerly wind.* *~n., pl.* **-lies. 4.** a wind from the north. —ˈ**northerliness** *n.*

northern (ˈnɔːðən) *adj.* **1.** situated in or towards the north: *northern towns.* **2.** directed or proceeding towards the north: *a northern flow of traffic.* **3.** (esp. of winds) proceeding from the north. **4.** (*sometimes cap.*) of, relating to, or characteristic of the north or North. **5.** (*sometimes cap.*) *Astronomy.* north of the celestial equator.

Northern Cross *n.* a group of the five brightest stars that form a large cross in the constellation Cygnus.

Northerner (ˈnɔːðənə) *n.* (*sometimes not cap.*) a native or inhabitant of the north of any specified region, esp. England or the U.S.

northern hemisphere *n.* (*often caps.*) **1.** that half of the globe lying north of the equator. **2.** *Astronomy.* that half of the celestial sphere north of the celestial equator. ~Abbrev.: **N hemisphere.**

northern lights *pl. n.* another name for **aurora borealis.**

northernmost (ˈnɔːðənˌməʊst) *adj.* situated or occurring farthest north.

Northern Sotho *n.* another name for **Pedi** (the language).

North Germanic *n.* a subbranch of the Germanic languages that consists of Danish, Norwegian, Swedish, Icelandic, and their associated dialects. See also **Old Norse.**

northing (ˈnɔːθɪŋ, -ðɪŋ) *n.* **1.** *Navigation.* movement or distance covered in a northerly direction, esp. as expressed in the resulting difference in latitude. **2.** *Astronomy.* a north or positive declination. **3.** *Cartography.* **a.** the distance northwards of a point from a given parallel indicated by the second half of a map grid reference. **b.** a latitudinal grid line. Compare **easting** (sense 2).

Northman (ˈnɔːθmən) *n., pl.* **-men.** another name for a **Viking.**

north-northeast *n.* **1.** the point on the compass or the direction midway between north and northeast, 22° 30′ clockwise from north. *~adj., adv.* **2.** in, from, or towards this direction. ~Symbol: **NNE**

north-northwest *n.* **1.** the point on the compass or the direction midway between northwest and north, 337° 30′ clockwise from north. *~adj., adv.* **2.** in, from, or towards this direction. ~Symbol: **NNW**

North Pole *n.* **1.** the northernmost point on the earth's axis, at a latitude of 90°N, characterized by very low temperatures. **2.** Also called: **north celestial pole.** *Astronomy.* the point of intersection of the earth's extended axis and the northern half of the celestial sphere, lying about 1° from Polaris. **3.** (*usually not caps.*) the pole of a freely suspended magnet, which is attracted to the earth's magnetic North Pole.

North-Sea gas *n.* (in Britain) natural gas obtained from deposits below the North Sea.

North Star *n.* **the.** another name for **Polaris** (sense 1).

Northumbrian (nɔːˈθʌmbrɪən) *adj.* **1.** of or relating to the northernmost English county of Northumberland, its inhabitants, or their dialect of English. **2.** of or relating to ancient Northumbria, which stretched from the Humber estuary to the Firth of Forth, its inhabitants, or their dialect. *~n.* **3. a.** the dialect of Old and Middle English spoken in Northumbria. See also **Anglian, Mercian. b.** the dialect of Modern English spoken in Northumberland.

northward (ˈnɔːθwəd; *Nautical* ˈnɔːðəd) *adj.* **1.** moving, facing, or situated towards the north. *~n.* **2.** the northward part, direction, etc.; the north. *~adv.* **3.** a variant of **northwards.** —ˈ**northwardly** *adj., adv.*

northwards (ˈnɔːθwədz) *or* **northward** *adv.* towards the north.

northwest (ˌnɔːθˈwɛst; *Nautical* ˌnɔːˈwɛst) *n.* **1.** the point of the compass or direction midway between north and west, clockwise 315° from north. **2.** (*often cap.;* usually preceded by *the*) any area lying in or towards this direction. *~adj. also* **northwestern. 3.** (*sometimes cap.*) of or denoting the northwestern part of a specified country, area, etc.: *northwest Greenland.* *~adj., adv.* **4.** in, to, towards, or (esp. of the wind) from the northwest. ~Symbol: **NW** —ˌ**northˈwesternmost** *adj.*

northwest by north *n.* **1.** one point on the compass north of northwest, 326° 15′ clockwise from north. *~adj., adv.* **2.** in, from, or towards this direction.

northwest by west *n.* **1.** one point on the compass south of northwest, 303° 45′ clockwise from north. *~adj., adv.* **2.** in, from, or towards this direction.

northwester (ˌnɔːθˈwɛstə; *Nautical* ˌnɔːˈwɛstə) *n.* a strong wind or storm from the northwest.

northwesterly (ˌnɔːθˈwɛstəlɪ; *Nautical* ˌnɔːˈwɛstəlɪ) *adj., adv.* **1.** in, towards, or (esp. of a wind) from the northwest. *~n., pl.* **-lies. 2.** a wind or storm from the northwest.

northwestward (ˌnɔːθˈwɛstwəd; *Nautical* ˌnɔːˈwɛstwəd) *adj.* **1.** towards or (esp. of a wind) from the northwest. *~n.* **2.** a direction towards or area in the northwest. —ˌ**northˈwestwardly** *adj., adv.*

northwestwards (ˌnɔːθˈwɛstwədz; *Nautical* ˌnɔːˈwɛstwədz) *or* **northwestward** *adv.* towards or (esp. of a wind) from the northwest.

Norw. *abbrev. for:* **1.** Norway. **2.** Norwegian.

Norway lobster (ˈnɔːweɪ) *n.* a European lobster, *Nephrops norvegicus,* fished for food.

Norway maple *n.* a large Eurasian maple tree, *Acer platanoides,* with broad five-lobed pale green leaves.

Norway rat *n.* another name for **brown rat.**

Norway spruce *n.* a European spruce tree, *Picea abies,* planted for timber and ornament, having drooping branches and dark green needle-like leaves.

Norwegian (nɔːˈwiːdʒən) *adj.* **1.** of, relating to, or characteristic of Norway, a Scandinavian kingdom in NW Europe, its language, or its people. *~n.* **2.** any of the various North Germanic languages of Norway. See also **Nynorsk, Bokmål.** Compare **Norse. 3.** a native, citizen, or inhabitant of Norway.

nor'wester (ˌnɔːˈwɛstə) *n.* **1.** a less common name for **sou'wester. 2.** a drink of strong liquor. **3.** a strong northwest wind. **4.** *N.Z.* a hot dry wind from the Southern Alps. [C18 (in the sense: storm from the northwest): a contraction of NORTHWESTER]

Norwich terrier (ˈnɒrɪdʒ) *n.* a small wiry-coated breed of terrier having either erect or pendent ears. [named after *Norwich,* a city in E England]

Nos. *or* **nos.** *abbrev. for* numbers.

nose (nəʊz) *n.* **1.** the organ of smell and entrance to the respiratory tract, consisting of a prominent structure divided into two hair-lined air passages by a median septum. Related adj.: **nasal. 2.** the sense of smell itself: in hounds and other animals, the ability to follow trails by scent (esp. in the phrases **a good nose, a bad nose**). **3.** another word for **bouquet** (sense 2). **4.** instinctive skill or facility, esp. in discovering things (sometimes in the phrase **follow one's nose**): *he had a nose for good news stories.* **5.** any part regarded as resembling a nose in form or function, such as a nozzle or spout. **6.** the forward part of a vehicle, aircraft, etc., esp. the front end of an aircraft. **7.** narrow margin of victory (in the phrase **(win) by a nose**). **8. cut off one's nose to spite one's face.** to carry out a vengeful action that hurts oneself more than another. **9. get up (someone's) nose.** *Informal.* to annoy or irritate (someone). **10. keep one's nose clean.** to stay out of trouble; behave properly. **11. keep one's nose to the grindstone.** to work hard and continuously. **12. lead (someone) by the nose.** to make (someone) do unquestioningly all one wishes; dominate (someone). **13. look down one's nose at.** *Informal.* to be contemptuous or disdainful of. **14. nose to tail.** (of vehicles) moving or standing very close behind one another. **15. on the nose.** *Slang.* **a.** (in horse-race betting) to win only: *I bet twenty pounds on the nose on that horse.* **b.** *Chiefly U.S. and Canadian.* precisely; exactly. **c.** *Austral.* bad or bad-smelling. **16. pay through the nose.** *Informal.* to pay an exorbitant price. **17. poke, stick,** etc., **one's nose into.** *Informal.* to pry into or interfere in. **18. put someone's nose out of joint.** *Informal.* to thwart or offend someone, esp. by supplanting him or gaining something he regards as his. **19. rub someone's nose in it.** *Informal.* to remind someone unkindly of his failing or error. **20. see no further than (the end of) one's nose.** *Informal.* **a.** to be short-sighted; suffer from myopia. **b.** to lack insight or foresight. **21. turn up one's nose (at).** *Informal.* to behave disdainfully (towards). **22. under one's nose. a.** directly in front of one. **b.** without one noticing. **23. with one's nose in the air.** haughtily. ~*vb.* **24.** (*tr.*) (esp. of horses, dogs, etc.) to rub, touch, or sniff with the nose; nuzzle. **25.** to smell or sniff (wine, etc.). **26.** (*intr.*; usually foll. by *after* or *for*) to search (for) by or as if by scent. **27.** to move or cause to move forwards slowly and carefully: *the car nosed along the cliff top; we nosed the car into the garage.* **28.** (*intr.*; foll. by *into, around, about,* etc.) to pry or snoop (into) or meddle (in). ~See also **nose out.** [Old English *nosu;* related to Old Frisian *nose,* Norwegian *nosa* to smell and *nus* smell] —ˈ**noseless** *adj.* —ˈ**nose,like** *adj.*

nosebag (ˈnəʊz,bæg) *n.* a bag, fastened around the head of a horse and covering the nose, in which feed is placed.

noseband (ˈnəʊz,bænd) *n.* the detachable part of a horse's bridle that goes around the nose. Also called: **nosepiece.** —ˈ**nose,banded** *adj.*

nosebleed (ˈnəʊz,bliːd) *n.* bleeding from the nose, as the result of injury, etc. Technical name: **epistaxis.**

nose cone *n.* the conical forward section of a missile, spacecraft, etc., designed to withstand high temperatures, esp. during re-entry into the earth's atmosphere.

nose dive *n.* **1.** a sudden plunge with the nose or front pointing downwards, esp. of an aircraft. **2.** *Informal.* a sudden drop or sharp decline: *prices took a nose dive.* ~*vb.* **nose-dive. 3.** to perform or cause to perform a nose dive. **4.** (*intr.*) *Informal.* to drop suddenly.

nose flute *n.* (esp. in the South Sea Islands) a type of flute blown through the nose.

nosegay (ˈnəʊz,geɪ) *n.* a small bunch of flowers; posy. [C15: from NOSE + archaic *gay* a toy]

nose job *n. Slang.* a surgical remodelling of the nose for cosmetic reasons.

nose out *vb.* (*tr., adv.*) **1.** to discover by smelling. **2.** to discover by cunning or persistence: *the reporter managed to nose out a few facts.* **3.** *Informal.* to beat by a narrow margin: *he was nosed out of first place by the champion.*

nosepiece (ˈnəʊz,piːs) *n.* **1.** Also called: **nasal.** a piece of armour, esp. part of a helmet, that serves to protect the nose. **2.** the connecting part of a pair of spectacles that rests on the nose; bridge. **3.** the part of a microscope to which one or more objective lenses are attached. **4.** a less common word for **noseband.**

nose rag *n. Slang.* a handkerchief.

nose ring *n.* a ring fixed through the nose, as for leading a bull.

nose wheel *n.* a wheel fitted to the forward end of a vehicle, esp. the landing wheel under the nose of an aircraft.

nosey (ˈnəʊzɪ) *adj.* a variant spelling of **nosy.**

nosh (nɒʃ) *Slang.* ~*n.* **1.** food or a meal. ~*vb.* **2.** to eat. [C20: from Yiddish; compare German *naschen* to nibble] —ˈ**nosher** *n.*

no-show *n.* a person who fails to take up a reserved seat, place, etc., without having cancelled it.

nosh-up *n. Brit. slang.* a large and satisfying meal.

no-side *n. Rugby.* the end of a match, signalled by the referee's whistle.

nosing (ˈnəʊzɪŋ) *n.* **1.** the edge of a step or stair tread that projects beyond the riser. **2.** a projecting edge of a moulding, esp. one that is half-round. [C18: from NOSE + -ING[1]]

noso- *or before a vowel* **nos-** *combining form.* disease: *nosology.* [from Greek *nosos*]

nosocomial (,nɒsəˈkəʊmɪəl) *adj. Medicine.* originating in hospital: *nosocomial disease.* [C19: New Latin *nosocomialis,* via Late Latin from Greek, from *nosokomos* one that tends the sick, from *nosos* (see NOSO-) + *komein* to tend]

nosography (nɒˈsɒgrəfɪ) *n.* a written classification and description of various diseases. —**noˈsographer** *n.* —**nosographic** (,nɒsəˈgræfɪk) *adj.*

nosology (nɒˈsɒlədʒɪ) *n.* the branch of medicine concerned with the classification of diseases. —**nosological** (,nɒsəˈlɒdʒɪkᵊl) *adj.* —,**nosoˈlogically** *adv.* —**noˈsologist** *n.*

nosophobia (,nɒsəˈfəʊbɪə) *n.* the morbid dread of contracting disease.

nostalgia (nɒˈstældʒə, -dʒɪə) *n.* **1.** a yearning for the return of past circumstances, events, etc. **2.** the evocation of this emotion, as in a book, film, etc. **3.** longing for home or family; homesickness. [C18: New Latin (translation of German *Heimweh* homesickness), from Greek *nostos* a return home + -ALGIA] —**nosˈtalgic** *adj.* —**nosˈtalgically** *adv.*

nostoc (ˈnɒstɒk) *n.* any blue-green alga of the genus *Nostoc,* occurring in moist places as rounded colonies consisting of coiled filaments in a gelatinous substance. [C17: New Latin, coined by Paracelsus (1493–1541), Swiss physician and alchemist]

nostology (nɒˈstɒlədʒɪ) *n. Med.* another word for **gerontology.** [C20: from Greek *nostos* a return home (with reference to ageing or second childhood) + -LOGY] —**nostologic** (,nɒstəˈlɒdʒɪk) *adj.*

nostril (ˈnɒstrɪl) *n.* either of the two external openings of the nose. Related adjs.: **narial, narine.** [Old English *nosthyrl,* from *nosu* NOSE + *thyrel* hole]

nostro account (ˈnɒstrəʊ) *n.* a bank account conducted by a British bank with a foreign bank, usually in the foreign currency. Compare **vostro account.**

nostrum (ˈnɒstrəm) *n.* **1.** a patent or quack medicine. **2.** a favourite remedy, as for political or social problems. [C17: from Latin: our own (make), from *noster* our]

nosy *or* **nosey** (ˈnəʊzɪ) *adj.* **nosier, nosiest.** *Informal.* prying or inquisitive. —ˈ**nosily** *adv.* —ˈ**nosiness** *n.*

nosy parker *n. Informal.* a prying person. [C20: apparently arbitrary use of surname *Parker*]

not (nɒt) *adv.* **1. a.** used to negate the sentence, phrase, or word that it modifies: *I will not stand for it.* **b.** (*in combination*): *they cannot go.* **2. not that.** (*conj.*) Also (archaic): **not but what.** which is not to say or suppose that: *I expect to lose the game—not that I mind.* ~*sentence substitute.* **3.** used to indicate denial, negation, or refusal: *certainly not.* [C14 *not,* variant of *nought* nothing, from Old English *nāwiht,* from *nā* no +*wiht* creature, thing. See NAUGHT, NOUGHT]

not- *combining form.* a variant of **noto-** before a vowel.

nota (ˈnəʊtə) *n.* the plural of **notum.**

nota bene *Latin.* (ˈnəʊtə ˈbiːnɪ) note well; take note. Abbrevs.: **NB, N.B., nb, n.b.**

notability (,nəʊtəˈbɪlɪtɪ) *n., pl.* **-ties. 1.** the state or quality of being notable. **2.** a distinguished person; notable.

notable (ˈnəʊtəbᵊl) *adj.* **1.** worthy of being noted or remembered; remarkable; distinguished. ~*n.* **2.** a notable person. [C14: via Old French from Latin *notābilis,* from *notāre* to NOTE] —ˈ**notableness** *n.* —ˈ**notably** *adv.*

notarize *or* **notarise** (ˈnəʊtə,raɪz) *vb.* (*tr.*) to attest to or authenticate (a document, contract, etc.), as a notary.

notary (ˈnəʊtərɪ) *n., pl.* **-ries. 1.** a notary public. **2.** (formerly) a clerk licensed to prepare legal documents. **3.** *Archaic.* a clerk or secretary. [C14: from Latin *notārius* clerk, from *nota* a mark, note] —**notarial** (nəʊˈtɛərɪəl) *adj.* —**noˈtarially** *adv.* —ˈ**notaryship** *n.*

notary public *n., pl.* **notaries public.** a public official, usually a solicitor, who is legally authorized to administer oaths, attest and certify certain documents, etc.

notate (nəʊˈteɪt) *vb.* to write (esp. music) in notation. [C20: back formation from NOTATION]

notation (nəʊˈteɪʃən) *n.* **1.** any series of signs or symbols used to represent quantities or elements in a specialized system, such as music or mathematics. **2.** the act or process of notating. **3. a.** the act of noting down. **b.** a note or record. [C16: from Latin *notātiō* a marking, from *notāre* to NOTE] —**noˈtational** *adj.*

notch (nɒtʃ) *n.* **1.** a V-shaped cut or indentation; nick. **2.** a cut or nick made in a tally stick or similar object. **3.** *U.S. and Canadian.* a narrow pass or gorge. **4.** *Informal.* a step or level (esp. in the phrase **a notch above**). ~*vb.* (*tr.*). **5.** to cut or make a notch in. **6.** to record with or as if with a notch. **7.** (usually foll. by *up*) *Informal.* to score or achieve: *the team notched up its fourth win.* [C16: from incorrect division of *an otch* (as *a notch*), from Old French *oche* notch, from Latin *obsecāre* to cut off, from *secāre* to cut] —ˈ**notchy** *adj.*

notch effect *n. Metallurgy, building trades.* the increase in stress in an area of a component near a crack, depression, etc., or a change in section, such as a sharp angle: can be enough to cause failure of the component although the calculated average stress may be quite safe.

NOT circuit *or* **gate** (nɒt) *n. Computer technol.* a logic circuit that has a high-voltage output signal if the input signal is low, and vice versa: used extensively in computers. Also called: **inverter, negator.** [C20: so named because the action performed on electrical signals is similar to the operation of *not* in logical constructions]

note (nəʊt) *n.* **1.** a brief summary or record in writing, esp. a jotting for future reference. **2.** a brief letter, usually of an informal nature. **3.** a formal written communication, esp. from one government to another. **4.** a short written statement giving any kind of information. **5.** a critical comment, explanatory statement, or reference in the text of a book, often preceded by a number. **6.** short for **banknote. 7.** a characteristic element or atmosphere: *a note of sarcasm.* **8.** a distinctive vocal sound, as of a species of bird or animal: *the note of the nightingale.* **9.** any of a series of graphic signs representing a musical sound whose pitch is indicated by position on the stave and whose duration is indicated by the sign's shape. **10.** Also called (esp. U.S. and Canadian): **tone.** a musical sound of definite fundamental frequency or pitch. **11.** a key on a piano, organ, etc. **12.** a sound, as from a musical instrument, used as a signal or warning: *the note to retreat was sounded.* **13.** short for **promissory note. 14.** *Archaic or poetic.* a tune or melody. **15. of note. a.** distinguished or famous: *an athlete of note.* **b.** worth noticing or paying attention to; important: *nothing of note.* **16. strike the right** (*or* **a false**) **note.** to behave appropriately (or inappropriately). **17. take note.** (often foll. by *of*) to observe carefully; pay close attention (to). ~*vb.* (*tr.; may take a clause as object*) **18.** to notice; perceive: *he noted that there was a man in the shadows.* **19.** to pay close attention to; observe: *they noted every movement.* **20.** to make a written note or memorandum of: *she noted the date in her diary.* **21.** to make particular mention of; remark upon: *I note that you do not wear shoes.* **22.** to write down (music, a melody, etc.) in notes. **23.** to take (an unpaid or dishonoured bill of exchange) to a notary public to re-present the bill and if it is still unaccepted or unpaid to note the circumstances in a register. See **protest** (sense 12). **24.** a less common word for **annotate.** ~See also **notes.** [C13: via Old French from Latin *nota* sign, indication] —ˈ**noteless** *adj.*

notebook (ˈnəʊtˌbʊk) *n.* **1.** a book for recording notes or memoranda. **2.** a book for registering promissory notes.

notecase (ˈnəʊtˌkeɪs) *n.* a less common word for **wallet** (sense 1).

noted (ˈnəʊtɪd) *adj.* **1.** distinguished; celebrated; famous. **2.** of special note or significance; noticeable: *a noted increase in the crime rate.* —ˈ**notedly** *adv.*

notelet (ˈnəʊtlɪt) *n.* a folded card with a printed design on the front, for writing a short informal letter.

note of hand *n.* another name for **promissory note.**

notepaper (ˈnəʊtˌpeɪpə) *n.* paper for writing letters; writing paper.

note row (rəʊ) *n. Music.* another name for **tone row.**

notes (nəʊts) *pl. n.* **1.** short descriptive or summarized jottings taken down for future reference. **2.** a record of impressions, reflections, etc., esp. as a literary form.

notes inégales *French.* (nɔts inegal) *pl. n.* **1.** (esp. in French baroque music) notes written down evenly but executed as if they were divided into pairs of long and short notes. **2.** the style of playing in this manner. [literally: unequal notes]

note value *n.* another term for **time value.**

noteworthy (ˈnəʊtˌwɜːðɪ) *adj.* worthy of notice; notable. —ˈ**noteˌworthily** *adv.* —ˈ**noteˌworthiness** *n.*

nothing (ˈnʌθɪŋ) *pron.* **1.** (*indefinite*) no thing; not anything, as of an implied or specified class of things: *I can give you nothing.* **2.** no part or share: *to have nothing to do with this crime.* **3.** a matter of no importance or significance: *it doesn't matter, it's nothing.* **4.** indicating the absence of anything perceptible; nothingness. **5.** indicating the absence of meaning, value, worth, etc.: *to amount to nothing.* **6.** zero quantity; nought. **7. be nothing to. a.** not to concern or be significant to (someone). **b.** to be not nearly as good as. **8. have** *or* **be nothing to do with.** to have no connection with. **9. have (got) nothing on. a.** to have no engagements to keep. **b.** to be undressed or naked. **c.** *Informal.* to compare unfavourably with. **10. in nothing flat.** *Informal.* in almost no time; very quickly or soon. **11. nothing but.** not something other than; only. **12. nothing doing.** *Informal.* an expression of dismissal, disapproval, lack of compliance with a request, etc. **13. nothing if not.** at the very least; certainly. **14. nothing less than** *or* **nothing short of.** downright; truly. **15. (there's) nothing for it.** (there's) no choice; no other course. **16. there's nothing like.** a general expression of praise: *there's nothing like a good cup of tea.* **17. there's nothing to it.** it is very simple, easy, etc. **18. think nothing of. a.** to regard as routine, easy, or natural. **b.** to have no compunction or hesitation about. **c.** to have a very low opinion of. **19. to say nothing of.** as well as; even disregarding: *he was warmly dressed in a shirt and heavy jumper, to say nothing of his thick overcoat.* **20. stop at nothing.** to be prepared to do anything; be unscrupulous or ruthless. ~*adv.* **21.** in no way; not at all: *he looked nothing like his brother.* ~*n.* **22.** *Informal.* a person or thing of no importance or significance. **23. sweet nothings.** words of endearment or affection. [Old English *nāthing, nān thing,* from *nān* NONE[1] + THING]

▷**Usage.** *Nothing* always takes a singular verb in careful usage, although a plural verb is often heard in informal speech in sentences such as *nothing but books were on the shelf.*

nothingness (ˈnʌθɪŋnɪs) *n.* **1.** the state or condition of being nothing; nonexistence. **2.** absence of consciousness or life. **3.** complete insignificance or worthlessness. **4.** something that is worthless or insignificant.

notice (ˈnəʊtɪs) *n.* **1.** the act of perceiving; observation; attention: *to escape notice.* **2. take notice.** to pay attention; attend. **3. take no notice of.** to ignore or disregard. **4.** information about a future event; warning; announcement. **5.** a displayed placard or announcement giving information. **6.** advance notification of intention to end an arrangement, contract, etc., as of renting or employment (esp. in the phrase **give notice**). **7. at short, two hours', etc., notice.** with notification only a little, two hours, etc., in advance. **8.** *Chiefly Brit.* dismissal from employment. **9.** favourable, interested, or polite attention: *she was beneath his notice.* **10.** a theatrical or literary review: *the play received very good notices.* ~*vb.* (*tr.*) **11.** to become conscious or aware of; perceive; note. **12.** to point out or remark upon. **13.** to pay polite or interested attention to. **14.** to recognize or acknowledge (an acquaintance). [C15: via Old French from Latin *notitia* fame, from *nōtus* known, celebrated]

noticeable (ˈnəʊtɪsəbəl) *adj.* easily seen or detected; perceptible: *the stain wasn't noticeable.* —ˌ**noticeaˈbility** *n.* —ˈ**noticeably** *adv.*

notice board *n. Brit.* a board on which notices, advertisements, bulletins, etc., are displayed. U.S. and Canadian name: **bulletin board.**

notifiable (ˈnəʊtɪˌfaɪəbəl) *adj.* **1.** denoting certain infectious diseases of humans, such as smallpox and tuberculosis, outbreaks of which must be reported to the public health authorities. **2.** denoting certain infectious diseases of animals, such as BSE, foot-and-mouth disease, and rabies, outbreaks of which must be reported to the appropriate veterinary authority.

notification (ˌnəʊtɪfɪˈkeɪʃən) *n.* **1.** the act of notifying. **2.** a formal announcement. **3.** something that notifies; a notice.

notify (ˈnəʊtɪˌfaɪ) *vb.* **-fies, -fying, -fied.** (*tr.*) **1.** to inform; tell. **2.** *Chiefly Brit.* to draw attention to; make known; announce. [C14: from Old French *notifier,* from Latin *notificāre* to make known, from *nōtus* known + *facere* to make] —ˈ**notiˌfier** *n.*

no-tillage *n.* a system of farming in which planting is done in a narrow trench, without tillage, and weeds are controlled with herbicide.

notion (ˈnəʊʃən) *n.* **1.** a vague idea; impression. **2.** an idea, concept, or opinion. **3.** an inclination or whim. ~See also **notions.** [C16: from Latin *nōtiō* a becoming acquainted (with), examination (of), from *noscere* to know]

notional (ˈnəʊʃənəl) *adj.* **1.** relating to, expressing, or consisting of notions or ideas. **2.** not evident in reality; hypothetical or imaginary: *a notional tax credit.* **3.** characteristic of a notion or concept, esp. in being speculative or imaginary; abstract. **4.** *Grammar.* **a.** (of a word) having lexical meaning. **b.** another word for **semantic.** —ˈ**notionally** *adv.*

notions (ˈnəʊʃənz) *pl. n. Chiefly U.S. and Canadian.* pins, cotton, ribbon, and similar wares used for sewing; haberdashery.

notitia (nəʊˈtɪʃɪə) *n.* a register or list, esp. of ecclesiastical districts. [C18: Latin, literally: knowledge, from *notus* known]

noto- *or before a vowel* **not-** *combining form.* the back: *notochord.* [from Greek *nōton* the back]

notochord (ˈnəʊtəˌkɔːd) *n.* a fibrous longitudinal rod in all embryo and some adult chordate animals, immediately above the gut, that supports the body. It is replaced in adult vertebrates by the vertebral column. —ˌ**notoˈchordal** *adj.*

notorious (nəʊˈtɔːrɪəs) *adj.* **1.** well-known for some bad or unfavourable quality, deed, etc.; infamous. **2.** *Rare.* generally known or widely acknowledged. [C16: from Medieval Latin *notōrius* well-known, from *nōtus* known, from *noscere* to know] —**notoriety** (ˌnəʊtəˈraɪɪtɪ) *or* **noˈtoriousness** *n.* —**noˈtoriously** *adv.*

notornis (nəʊˈtɔːnɪs) *n.* a rare flightless rail of the genus *Notornis,* of New Zealand. See **takahe.** [C19: New Latin, from Greek *notos* south + *ornis* bird]

nototherium (ˌnəʊtəʊˈθɪərɪəm) *n.* an extinct rhinoceros-sized Pleistocene marsupial of the genus *Nototherium,* related to the wombats. [C19: New Latin, from Greek *notos* south (referring to their discovery in the S hemisphere) + *thērion* beast]

notour (ˈnəʊtə) *adj.* (in Scots Law) short for **notorious.** A **notour bankrupt** is one who has failed to discharge his debts within the days of grace allowed by the court.

not proven (ˈpruːvən) *adj.* (*postpositive*) a third verdict available to Scottish courts, returned when there is evidence against the defendant but insufficient to convict.

no-trump *Bridge.* ~*n. also* **no-trumps. 1.** a bid or contract to play without trumps. ~*adj. also* **no-trumper. 2.** (of a hand) of balanced distribution suitable for playing without trumps.

Nottm *abbrev. for* Nottingham.

Notts (nɒts) *abbrev. for* Nottinghamshire.

notum (ˈnəʊtəm) *n., pl.* **-ta** (-tə). a cuticular plate covering the dorsal surface of a thoracic segment of an insect. [C19: New Latin, from Greek *nōton* back] —ˈ**notal** *adj.*

notwithstanding (ˌnɒtwɪθˈstændɪŋ, -wɪð-) *prep.* **1.** (*often immediately postpositive*) in spite of; despite. ~*conj.* **2.** (*subordinating*) despite the fact that; although. ~*sentence connector.* **3.** in spite of that; nevertheless. [C14: NOT + *withstanding,* from Old English *withstandan,* on the model of Medieval Latin *non obstante,* Old French *non obstant*]

nougat (ˈnuːgɑː, ˈnʌgət) *n.* a hard chewy pink or white sweet containing chopped nuts, cherries, etc. [C19: via French from Provençal *nogat,* from *noga* nut, from Latin *nux* nut]

nought (nɔːt) *n. also* **naught, ought, aught. 1.** another name for **zero:** used esp. in counting or numbering. ~*n., adj., adv.* **2.** a variant spelling of **naught.** [Old English *nōwiht,* from *ne* not, no + *ōwiht* something; see WHIT]

noughts and crosses *n.* (*functioning as sing.*) a game in which two players, one using a nought, "O", the other a cross, "X", alternately mark one square out of nine formed by two pairs of crossed lines, the winner being the first to get three of his symbols in a row. U.S. and Canadian term: **tick-tack-toe,** (U.S.) **crisscross.**

noumenon (ˈnuːmɪnən, ˈnaʊ-) *n., pl.* **-na** (-nə). **1.** (in Kantian philosophy) a thing as it is in itself, not perceived or interpreted, incapable of being known, but only inferred from the nature of experience. Compare **phenomenon** (sense 3). See also **thing-in-itself. 2.** the object of a purely intellectual intuition. [C18: via German from Greek: thing being thought of, from *noein* to think, perceive; related to *nous* mind] —ˈ**noumenal** *adj.* —ˈ**noumenalism** *n.* —ˈ**noumenalist** *n., adj.* —ˌ**noumeˈnality** *n.* —ˈ**noumenally** *adv.*

noun (naʊn) *n.* **a.** a word or group of words that refers to a person, place, or thing or any syntactically similar word. **b.** (*as modifier*): *a noun phrase.* Abbrevs.: **N, n.** Related adj.: **nominal.** [C14: via Anglo-French from Latin *nōmen* NAME] —ˈ**nounal** *adj.* —ˈ**nounally** *adv.* —ˈ**nounless** *adj.*

noun phrase *n. Grammar.* a constituent of a sentence that consists of a noun and any modifiers it may have, a noun clause, or a word, such as a pronoun, that takes the place of a noun. Abbrev.: **NP.**

nourish (ˈnʌrɪʃ) *vb.* (*tr.*) **1.** to provide with the materials necessary for life and growth. **2.** to support or encourage (an idea, feeling, etc.); foster: *to nourish resentment.* [C14: from Old

French *norir*, from Latin *nūtrīre* to feed, care for] —'**nourisher** *n.* —'**nourishing** *adj.* —'**nourishingly** *adv.*
nourishment ('nʌrɪʃmənt) *n.* **1.** the act or state of nourishing. **2.** a substance that nourishes; food; nutriment.
nous (naʊs) *n.* **1.** *Metaphysics.* mind or reason, esp. when regarded as the principle governing all things. **2.** *Brit. slang.* common sense; intelligence. [C17: from Greek, literally: mind]
nouveau *or before a plural noun* **nouveaux** ('nuːvəʊ) *adj.* (*prenominal*) *facetious or derogatory.* having recently become the thing specified: *a nouveau hippie.* [C20: French, literally: new; on the model of NOUVEAU RICHE]
nouveau riche (ˌnuːvəʊ 'riːʃ; *French* nuvo riʃ) *n., pl.* **nouveaux riches** (ˌnuːvəʊ 'riːʃ; *French* nuvo riʃ). **1.** (often *pl.* and preceded by *the*) a person who has acquired wealth recently and is regarded as vulgarly ostentatious or lacking in social graces. ~*adj.* **2.** of or characteristic of the nouveaux riches. [French, literally: new rich]
nouveau roman *French.* (nuvo rɔmɑ̃) *n., pl.* ***nouveaux romans*** (nuvo rɔmɑ̃). another term for **anti-roman.** See **antinovel.** [literally: new novel]
nouvelle cuisine *French.* ('nuːvɛl kɥizin) *n.* a style of preparing and presenting food, often raw or only lightly cooked, with light sauces, and unusual combinations of flavours and garnishes. [C20: literally: new cookery]
Nouvelle Vague *French.* (nuvɛl vag) *n. Films.* another term for **New Wave**[1].
Nov. *abbrev. for* November.
nova ('nəʊvə) *n., pl.* **-vae** (-viː) *or* **-vas.** a faint variable star that undergoes an explosion and fast increase of luminosity, decreasing to its original luminosity in months or years. Compare **supernova.** [C19: New Latin *nova (stella)* new (star), from Latin *novus* new]
novaculite (nəʊ'vækjʊˌlaɪt) *n.* a fine-grained dense hard rock containing quartz and feldspar: used as a whetstone. [C18: from Latin *novācula* sharp knife, razor, from *novāre* to renew]
novation (nəʊ'veɪʃən) *n.* **1.** *Law.* the substitution of a new obligation for an old one by mutual agreement between the parties, esp. of one debtor or creditor for another. **2.** an obsolete word for **innovation.** [C16: from Late Latin *novātio* a renewing, from Latin *novāre* to renew]
novel[1] ('nɒvᵊl) *n.* **1.** an extended work in prose, either fictitious or partly so, dealing with character, action, thought, etc., esp. in the form of a story. **2. the.** the literary genre represented by novels. **3.** (*usually pl.*) *Obsolete.* a short story or novella. [C15: from Old French *novelle,* from Latin *novella (narrātiō)* new (story); see NOVEL[2]]
novel[2] ('nɒvᵊl) *adj.* of a kind not seen before; fresh; new; original: *a novel suggestion.* [C15: from Latin *novellus* new, diminutive of *novus* new]
novel[3] ('nɒvᵊl) *n. Roman law.* a new decree or an amendment to an existing statute.
novelese (ˌnɒvə'liːz) *n. Derogatory.* a style of writing characteristic of poor novels.
novelette (ˌnɒvə'lɛt) *n.* **1.** an extended prose narrative story or short novel. **2.** a novel that is regarded as being slight, trivial, or sentimental. **3.** a short piece of lyrical music, esp. one for the piano.
novelettish (ˌnɒvə'lɛtɪʃ) *adj.* characteristic of a novelette; trite or sentimental.
novelist ('nɒvəlɪst) *n.* a writer of novels.
novelistic (ˌnɒvə'lɪstɪk) *adj.* of or characteristic of novels, esp. in style or method of treatment: *his novelistic account annoyed other historians.*
novelize *or* **novelise** ('nɒvəˌlaɪz) *vb.* to convert (a true story, film, etc.) into a novel. —ˌ**noveli'zation** *or* ˌ**noveli'sation** *n.*
novella (nəʊ'vɛlə) *n., pl.* **-las** *or* **-le** (-leɪ). **1.** (formerly) a short narrative tale, esp. a popular story having a moral or satirical point. **2.** a short novel; novelette. [C20: from Italian; see NOVEL[1]]
novelty ('nɒvᵊltɪ) *n., pl.* **-ties. 1. a.** the quality of being new and fresh and interesting. **b.** (*as modifier*): *novelty value.* **2.** a new or unusual experience or occurrence. **3.** (*often pl.*) a small usually cheap new toy, ornament, or trinket. [C14: from Old French *novelté;* see NOVEL[2]]
November (nəʊ'vɛmbə) *n.* **1.** the eleventh month of the year, consisting of 30 days. **2.** *Communications.* a code word for the letter *n.* [C13: via Old French from Latin: ninth month, from *novem* nine]
novena (nəʊ'viːnə) *n., pl.* **-nae** (-niː). *R.C. Church.* a devotion consisting of prayers or services on nine consecutive days. [C19: from Medieval Latin, from Latin *novem* nine]
novercal (nəʊ'vɜːkᵊl) *adj. Rare.* stepmotherly. [C17: from Latin *novercālis,* from *noverca* stepmother]
novice ('nɒvɪs) *n.* **1.** a person who is new to or inexperienced in a certain task, situation, etc.; beginner; tyro. **2.** a probationer in a religious order. **3.** a sportsman, esp. an oarsman, who has not won a recognized prize, performed to an established level, etc. **4.** a racehorse, esp. a steeplechaser or hurdler, that has not won a specified number of races. [C14: via Old French from Latin *novīcius,* from *novus* new]
novitiate *or* **noviciate** (nəʊ'vɪʃɪɪt, -ˌeɪt) *n.* **1.** the state of being a novice, esp. in a religious order, or the period for which this lasts. **2.** the part of a religious house where the novices live. **3.** a less common word for **novice.** [C17: from French *noviciat,* from Latin *novīcius* NOVICE]
Novocaine ('nəʊvəˌkeɪn) *n.* a trademark for **procaine hydrochloride.** See **procaine.**
now (naʊ) *adv.* **1.** at or for the present time or moment. **2.** at this exact moment; immediately. **3.** in these times; nowadays. **4.** given the present circumstances: *now we'll have to stay to the end.* **5.** (preceded by *just*) very recently: *he left just now.* **6.** (often preceded by *just*) very soon: *he is leaving just now.* **7. (every) now and again** *or* **then.** occasionally; on and off. **8. for now.** for the time being. **9. now now!** (*interj.*) an exclamation used to rebuke or pacify someone. **10. now then. a.** (*sentence connector*) used to preface an important remark, the next step in an argument, etc. **b.** (*interj.*) an expression of mild reproof: *now then, don't tease!* ~*conj.* **11.** (*subordinating;* often foll. by *that*) seeing that; since it has become the case that: *now you're in charge, things will be better.* ~*sentence connector.* **12. a.** used as a transitional particle or hesitation word: *now, I can't really say.* **b.** used for emphasis: *now listen to this.* **c.** used at the end of a command, esp. in dismissal: *run along, now.* ~*n.* **13.** the present moment or time: *now is the time to go.* ~*adj.* **14.** *Informal.* of the moment; fashionable: *the now look is street fashion.* [Old English *nū;* compare Old Saxon *nū,* German *nun,* Latin *nunc,* Greek *nu*]
nowadays ('naʊəˌdeɪz) *adv.* in these times. [C14: from NOW + *adays* from Old English *a* on + *daeges* genitive of day]
noway ('nəʊˌweɪ) *adv.* **1.** Also in the U.S. (not standard): '**noways.** in no manner; not at all; nowise. ~*sentence substitute.* **no way. 2.** used to make an emphatic refusal, denial etc.
Nowel *or* **Nowell** (nəʊ'ɛl) *n.* archaic spellings of **Noel.**
nowhence ('nəʊˌwɛns) *adv. Archaic.* from no place; from nowhere.
nowhere ('nəʊˌwɛə) *adv.* **1.** in, at, or to no place; not anywhere. **2. get nowhere (fast).** *Informal.* to fail completely to make any progress. **3. nowhere near.** far from; not nearly. ~*n.* **4.** a nonexistent or insignificant place. **5. middle of nowhere.** a completely isolated, featureless, or insignificant place.
nowhither ('nəʊˌwɪðə) *adv. Archaic.* to no place; to nowhere. [Old English *nāhwider.* See NEITHER]
nowise ('nəʊˌwaɪz) *adv.* another word for **noway.**
nowt[1] (naʊt) *n. Northern English.* a dialect word for **nothing.** [from NAUGHT]
nowt[2] (naʊt) *n. Scot. and northern English.* a dialect word for **bullock** and **cattle.** [C13: from Old Norse *naut;* see NEAT[2]]
noxious ('nɒkʃəs) *adj.* **1.** poisonous or harmful. **2.** harmful to the mind or morals; corrupting. [C17: from Latin *noxius* harmful, from *noxa* injury] —'**noxiously** *adv.* —'**noxiousness** *n.*
noyade (nwɑː'jɑːd; *French* nwajad) *n. French history.* execution by drowning, esp. as practised during the Reign of Terror at Nantes from 1793 to 1794. [C19: from French, from *noyer* to drown, from Late Latin *necāre* to drown, from Latin: to put to death]
noyau ('nwaɪəʊ) *n.* a liqueur made from brandy flavoured with nut kernels. [C18: from French: kernel, from Latin *nux* nut]
nozzle ('nɒzᵊl) *n.* **1.** a projecting pipe or spout from which fluid is discharged. **2.** Also called: **propelling nozzle.** a pipe or duct, esp. in a jet engine or rocket, that directs the effluent and accelerates or diffuses the flow to generate thrust. **3.** a socket, such as the part of a candlestick that holds the candle. [C17 *nosle, nosel,* diminutive of NOSE]
np *abbrev. for:* **1.** *Printing.* new paragraph. **2.** *Law.* nisi prius. **3.** no place of publication.
Np **1.** *symbol for* neper. **2.** *the chemical symbol for* neptunium.
NP *abbrev. for* **1.** neuropsychiatric. **2.** neuropsychiatry. **3.** Also: **np.** Notary Public. **4.** noun phrase.
NPA *abbrev. for* Newspaper Publishers' Association.
NPD *Commerce. abbrev. for* new product development.
NPL *abbrev. for* National Physical Laboratory.
NPV *abbrev. for:* **1.** net present value. **2.** no par value.
nr *abbrev. for* near.
NRV *abbrev. for* net realizable value.
ns *abbrev. for:* **1.** new series. **2.** not specified.
NS *abbrev. for:* **1.** New Style (method of reckoning dates). **2.** not sufficient *or* not satisfactory. **3.** Nova Scotia. **4.** nuclear ship.
NSAID *abbrev. for* nonsteroidal anti-inflammatory drug: any of a class of drugs, including aspirin and ibuprofen, used for reducing inflammation and pain in rheumatic diseases. Possible adverse effects include gastric ulceration.
NSB *abbrev. for* National Savings Bank.
NSC *abbrev. for* National Safety Council.
NSF *or* **N/S/F** *Banking. abbrev. for* not sufficient funds.
NSG *Brit. education. abbrev. for* nonstatutory guidelines: practical nonmandatory advice and information on the implementation of the National Curriculum.
NSPCC *abbrev. for* National Society for the Prevention of Cruelty to Children.
NSU *abbrev. for* nonspecific urethritis.
NSW *abbrev. for* New South Wales.
NT *abbrev. for:* **1.** National Trust. **2.** New Testament. **3.** Northern Territory. **4.** no-trump. **5.** (in Ireland) National Teacher (teacher in a National School).
-n't *contraction of* not: used as an enclitic after *be* and *have* when they function as main verbs and after auxiliary verbs or verbs

operating syntactically as auxiliaries: *can't; don't; shouldn't; needn't; daren't; isn't.*

nth (ɛnθ) *adj.* **1.** *Maths.* of or representing an unspecified ordinal number, usually the greatest in a series of values: *the nth power.* **2.** *Informal.* being the last, most recent, or most extreme of a long series: *for the nth time, eat your lunch!* **3. to the nth degree.** *Informal.* to the utmost extreme; as much as possible.

Nth *abbrev. for* North.

NTP *abbrev. for* normal temperature and pressure: standard conditions of 0°C temperature and 101.325 kPa (760 mmHg) pressure. Also: **STP.**

NTS *abbrev. for* National Trust for Scotland.

n-tuple *n. Logic, maths.* an ordered set of *n* elements.

nt. wt. *or* **nt wt** *abbrev. for* net weight.

n-type *adj.* **1.** (of a semiconductor) having more conduction electrons than mobile holes. **2.** associated with or resulting from the movement of electrons in a semiconductor: *n-type conductivity.* ~Compare **p-type.**

nu (njuː) *n.* the 13th letter in the Greek alphabet (Ν, ν), a consonant, transliterated as *n.* [from Greek, of Semitic origin; compare NUN[2]]

NUAAW (in Britain) *abbrev. for* National Union of Agricultural and Allied Workers.

nuance (njuːˈɑːns, ˈnjuːɑːns) *n.* a subtle difference in colour, meaning, tone, etc.; a shade or graduation. [C18: from French, from *nuer* to show light and shade, ultimately from Latin *nūbēs* a cloud]

nub (nʌb) *n.* **1.** a small lump or protuberance. **2.** a small piece or chunk. **3.** the point or gist: *the nub of a story.* **4.** a small fibrous knot in yarn. [C16: variant of *knub,* from Middle Low German *knubbe* KNOB] —**ˈnubbly** *or* **ˈnubby** *adj.*

Nuba (ˈnjuːbə) *n.* **1.** (*pl.* **-bas** *or* **-ba**) a member of a formerly warlike Nilotic people living chiefly in the hills of S central Sudan. **2.** the language or group of related dialects spoken by this people, belonging to the Chari-Nile branch of the Nilo-Saharan family.

nubbin (ˈnʌbɪn) *n. U.S. and Canadian.* something small or undeveloped, esp. a fruit or ear of corn. [C19: diminutive of NUB]

nubble (ˈnʌbᵊl) *n.* a small lump. [C19: diminutive of NUB]

Nubian (ˈnjuːbɪən) *adj.* **1.** of or relating to Nubia, an ancient region of NE Africa, on the Nile. ~*n.* **2.** a native or inhabitant of Nubia.

nubile (ˈnjuːbaɪl) *adj.* (of a girl or woman) **1.** ready or suitable for marriage by virtue of age or maturity. **2.** sexually attractive. [C17: from Latin *nūbilis,* from *nūbere* to marry] —**nubility** (njuːˈbɪlɪtɪ) *n.*

nucellus (njuːˈsɛləs) *n., pl.* **-li** (-laɪ). the central part of a plant ovule containing the embryo sac. [C19: New Latin, from Latin *nucella,* from *nux* nut] —**nuˈcellar** *adj.*

nucha (ˈnjuːkə) *n., pl.* **-chae** (-kiː). *Zoology, anatomy.* the back or nape of the neck. [C14: from Medieval Latin, from Arabic *nukhā'* spinal marrow] —**ˈnuchal** *adj.*

nucivorous (njuːˈsɪvərəs) *adj.* (of animals) feeding on nuts. [from Latin *nux* nut + -VOROUS]

nuclear (ˈnjuːklɪə) *adj.* **1.** of, concerned with, or involving the nucleus of an atom: *nuclear fission.* **2.** *Biology.* of, relating to, or contained within the nucleus of a cell: *a nuclear membrane.* **3.** of, relating to, forming, or resembling any other kind of nucleus. **4.** of, concerned with, or operated by energy from fission or fusion of atomic nuclei: *a nuclear weapon.* **5.** involving, concerned with, or possessing nuclear weapons: *nuclear war; a nuclear strike.*

nuclear bomb *n.* a bomb whose force is due to uncontrolled nuclear fusion or nuclear fission.

nuclear chemistry *n.* the branch of chemistry concerned with nuclear reactions.

nuclear energy *n.* energy released during a nuclear reaction as a result of fission or fusion. Also called: **atomic energy.**

nuclear family *n. Sociol., anthropol.* a primary social unit consisting of parents and their offspring. Compare **extended family.**

nuclear fission *n.* the splitting of an atomic nucleus into approximately equal parts, either spontaneously or as a result of the impact of a particle usually with an associated release of energy. Sometimes shortened to **fission.** Compare **nuclear fusion.**

nuclear-free zone *n.* an area barred, esp. by local authorities, to the storage or deployment of nuclear weapons.

nuclear fuel *n.* a fuel that provides nuclear energy, used in nuclear power stations, nuclear submarines, etc.

nuclear fusion *n.* a reaction in which two nuclei combine to form a nucleus with the release of energy. Sometimes shortened to **fusion.** Compare **nuclear fission.** See also **thermonuclear reaction.**

nuclear isomer *n.* the more formal name for **isomer** (sense 2). —**nuclear isomerism** *n.*

nuclear magnetic resonance *n.* a technique for determining the magnetic moments of nuclei by subjecting a substance to high-frequency radiation and a large magnetic field. The technique is used as a method of determining structure. Abbrev.: **NMR.** See also **electron spin resonance.**

nuclear magnetic resonance scanner *n.* a machine for the medical technique in which changes in the constituent atoms of the body under the influence of a powerful electromagnet are used to generate computed images of the internal organs.

nuclear medicine *n.* the branch of medicine concerned with the use of radionuclides in the diagnosis and treatment of disease.

nuclear physics *n.* (*functioning as sing.*) the branch of physics concerned with the structure and behaviour of the nucleus and the particles of which it consists. —**nuclear physicist** *n.*

nuclear power *n.* power, esp. electrical or motive, produced by a nuclear reactor. Also called: **atomic power.**

nuclear reaction *n.* a process in which the structure and energy content of an atomic nucleus is changed by interaction with another nucleus or particle.

nuclear reactor *n.* a device in which a nuclear reaction is maintained and controlled for the production of nuclear energy. Sometimes shortened to **reactor.** Former name: **atomic pile.** See also **fission reactor, fusion reactor.**

nuclear threshold *n.* the point in war at which a combatant brings nuclear weapons into use.

nuclear waste *n.* another name for **radioactive waste.**

nuclear winter *n.* a period of extremely low temperatures and little light that has been suggested would occur as a result of a nuclear war.

nuclease (ˈnjuːklɪˌeɪz) *n.* any of a group of enzymes that hydrolyse nucleic acids to simple nucleotides.

nucleate (ˈnjuːklɪɪt, -ˌeɪt) *adj.* **1.** having a nucleus. ~*vb.* (*intr.*) **2.** to form a nucleus. —ˌ**nucleˈation** *n.* —**ˈnucleˌator** *n.*

nucleating agent *n. Meteorology.* a substance used to seed clouds to control rainfall and fog formation.

nuclei (ˈnjuːklɪˌaɪ) *n.* a plural of **nucleus.**

nucleic acid (njuːˈkliːɪk, -ˈkleɪ-) *n. Biochem.* any of a group of complex compounds with a high molecular weight that are vital constituents of all living cells. See also **RNA, DNA.**

nuclein (ˈnjuːklɪɪn) *n.* any of a group of proteins, containing phosphorus, that occur in the nuclei of living cells.

nucleo- *or before a vowel* **nucle-** *combining form.* **1.** nucleus or nuclear: *nucleoplasm.* **2.** nucleic acid: *nucleoprotein.*

nucleolus (ˌnjuːklɪˈəʊləs) *n., pl.* **-li** (-laɪ). a small rounded body within a resting nucleus that contains RNA and proteins and is involved in protein synthesis. Also called: **ˈnucleole.** [C19: from Latin, diminutive of NUCLEUS] —ˌ**nucleˈolar, ˈnucleoˌlate,** *or* **ˈnucleoˌlated** *adj.*

nucleon (ˈnjuːklɪˌɒn) *n.* a proton or neutron, esp. one present in an atomic nucleus. [C20: from NUCLE(US) + -ON]

nucleonics (ˌnjuːklɪˈɒnɪks) *n.* (*functioning as sing.*) the branch of physics concerned with the applications of nuclear energy. —ˌ**nucleˈonic** *adj.* —ˌ**nucleˈonically** *adv.*

nucleon number *n.* another name for **mass number.**

nucleophilic (ˌnjuːklɪəʊˈfɪlɪk) *adj. Chem.* having or involving an affinity for positive charge. Nucleophilic reagents (**nucleophiles**) are molecules, atoms, and ions that behave as electron donors. Compare **electrophilic.**

nucleoplasm (ˈnjuːklɪəˌplæzəm) *n.* the protoplasm constituting the nucleus of a plant or animal cell. Also called: **karyoplasm.** —ˌ**nucleoˈplasmic** *or* ˌ**nucleoplasˈmatic** *adj.*

nucleoprotein (ˌnjuːklɪəʊˈprəʊtiːn) *n.* a compound within a cell nucleus that consists of a protein bound to a nucleic acid.

nucleoside (ˈnjuːklɪəˌsaɪd) *n. Biochem.* a compound containing a purine or pyrimidine base linked to a sugar (usually ribose or deoxyribose). [C20: from NUCLEO- + -OSE[2] + -IDE]

nucleosome (ˈnjuːklɪəˌsəʊm) *n.* a repeating structural unit of chromatin that contains DNA and histones.

nucleosynthesis (ˌnjuːklɪəʊˈsɪnθɪsɪs) *n. Astronomy.* the formation of heavier elements from lighter elements by nuclear fusion in stars.

nucleotide (ˈnjuːklɪəˌtaɪd) *n. Biochem.* a compound consisting of a nucleoside linked to phosphoric acid. Nucleic acids are made up of long chains (polynucleotides) of such compounds. [C20: from NUCLEO- + *t* (added for ease of pronunciation) + -IDE]

nucleus (ˈnjuːklɪəs) *n., pl.* **-clei** (-klɪˌaɪ) *or* **-cleuses. 1.** a central or fundamental part or thing around which others are grouped; core. **2.** a centre of growth or development; basis; kernel: *the nucleus of an idea.* **3.** *Biology.* the spherical or ovoid compartment of a cell, bounded by a membrane, that contains the chromosomes and associated molecules that control the characteristics and growth of the cell. **4.** *Anatomy.* any of various groups of nerve cells in the central nervous system. **5.** *Astronomy.* the central portion in the head of a comet, consisting of small solid particles of ice and frozen gases, which vaporize on approaching the sun to form the coma and tail. **6.** *Physics.* the positively charged dense region at the centre of an atom, composed of protons and neutrons, about which electrons orbit. **7.** *Chem.* a fundamental group of atoms in a molecule serving as the base structure for related compounds and remaining unchanged during most chemical reactions: *the benzene nucleus.* **8.** *Botany.* **a.** the central point of a starch granule. **b.** a rare name for **nucellus. 9.** *Phonetics.* the most sonorous part of a syllable, usually consisting of a vowel or frictionless continuant. **10.** *Logic.* the largest individual that is a mereological part of every member of a given class. [C18: from Latin: kernel, from *nux* nut]

nuclide (ˈnjuːklaɪd) *n.* a species of atom characterized by its atomic number and its mass number. See also **isotope.** [C20: from NUCLEO- + *-ide,* from Greek *eidos* shape]

nuddy ('nʌdɪ) *n.* **in the nuddy.** *Informal, chiefly Brit. and Austral.* in the nude; naked. [C20: originally Australian, a variant of NUDE]

nude (nju:d) *adj.* **1.** completely unclothed; undressed. **2.** having no covering; bare; exposed. **3.** *Law.* **a.** lacking some essential legal requirement, esp. supporting evidence. **b.** (of a contract, agreement, etc.) made without consideration and void unless under seal. ~*n.* **4.** the state of being naked (esp. in the phrase **in the nude**). **5.** a naked figure, esp. in painting, sculpture, etc. [C16: from Latin *nūdus*] —'**nudely** *adv.* —'**nudeness** *n.*

nudge (nʌdʒ) *vb.* (*tr.*) **1.** to push or poke (someone) gently, esp. with the elbow, to get attention; jog. **2.** to push slowly or lightly: *as I drove out, I just nudged the gatepost.* ~*n.* **3.** a gentle poke or push. [C17: perhaps from Scandinavian; compare Icelandic *nugga* to push] —'**nudger** *n.*

nudi- *combining form.* naked or bare: *nudibranch.* [from Latin *nūdus*]

nudibranch ('nju:dɪˌbræŋk) *n.* any marine gastropod of the order *Nudibranchia,* characterized by a shell-less, often beautifully coloured, body bearing external gills and other appendages. Also called: **sea slug.** [C19: from NUDI- + *branche,* from Latin *branchia* gills]

nudicaudate (ˌnju:dɪ'kɔ:deɪt) *adj.* (of such animals as rats) having a hairless tail.

nudicaul ('nju:dɪˌkɔ:l) *or* **nudicaulous** (ˌnju:dɪ'kɔ:ləs) *adj.* (of plants) having stems without leaves. [C20: from NUDI- + *caul,* from Latin *caulis* stem]

nudism ('nju:dɪzəm) *n.* the practice of nudity, esp. for reasons of health, religion, etc. —'**nudist** *n., adj.*

nudity ('nju:dɪtɪ) *n., pl.* **-ties.** **1.** the state or fact of being nude; nakedness. **2.** *Rare.* a nude figure, esp. in art.

nudum pactum ('nju:dʊm 'pæktʊm) *n. Law.* an agreement made without consideration and void unless made under seal. [Latin: nude (sense 3b) agreement]

nuée ardente ('nʊeɪ ɑ:'dɑ̃t) *n.* a rapidly moving turbulent incandescent cloud of gas, ash, and rock fragments flowing close to the ground after violent ejection from a volcano. See also **ignimbrite.** [C20: from French, literally: burning cloud]

nugatory ('nju:gətərɪ, -trɪ) *adj.* **1.** of little value; trifling. **2.** not valid: *a nugatory law.* [C17: from Latin *nūgātōrius,* from *nūgārī* to jest, from *nūgae* trifles]

nuggar ('nʌgə) *n.* a sailing boat used to carry cargo on the Nile. [from Arabic]

nugget ('nʌgɪt) *n.* **1.** a small piece or lump, esp. of gold in its natural state. **2.** something small but valuable or excellent. **3.** *N.Z. trademark.* shoe polish. ~*vb.* (*tr.*) **4.** *Austral.* to pick out (nuggets) from the surface of rock. **5.** *N.Z. informal.* to shine (shoes). [C19: origin unknown]

nuggety ('nʌgɪtɪ) *adj.* **1.** of or resembling a nugget. **2.** *Austral. and N.Z. informal.* (of a person) thickset; stocky.

nuisance ('nju:səns) *n.* **1. a.** a person or thing that causes annoyance or bother. **b.** (*as modifier*): *nuisance calls.* **2.** *Law.* something unauthorized that is obnoxious or injurious to the community at large (**public nuisance**) or to an individual, esp. in relation to his ownership or occupation of property (**private nuisance**). **3. nuisance value.** the usefulness of a person's or thing's capacity to cause difficulties or irritation. [C15: via Old French from *nuire* to injure, from Latin *nocēre*]

Nuits-Saint-Georges (*French* nɥisɛ̃ʒɔrʒ) *n.* a fine red wine produced near the town of Nuits-Saint-Georges in Burgundy, E France.

NUJ (in Britain) *abbrev. for* National Union of Journalists.

nuke (nju:k) *Slang, chiefly U.S.* ~*vb.* (*tr.*) **1.** to attack or destroy with nuclear weapons. ~*n.* **2.** a nuclear bomb. **3.** a military strike with nuclear weapons. **4.** nuclear power. **5.** a nuclear power plant.

null (nʌl) *adj.* **1.** without legal force; invalid; (esp. in the phrase **null and void**). **2.** without value or consequence; useless. **3.** lacking distinction; characterless: *a null expression.* **4.** nonexistent; amounting to nothing. **5.** *Maths.* **a.** quantitatively zero. **b.** relating to zero. **c.** (of a set) having no members. **d.** (of a sequence) having zero as a limit. **6.** *Physics.* involving measurement in which conditions are adjusted so that an instrument has a zero reading, as with a Wheatstone bridge. [C16: from Latin *nullus* none, from *ne* not + *ullus* any]

nullah ('nʌlɑ:) *n.* a stream or drain. [C18: from Hindi *nālā*]

nulla-nulla (ˌnʌlə'nʌlə) *n. Austral.* a wooden club used by Aborigines. [from a native Australian language]

null hypothesis *n. Statistics.* the residual hypothesis if the alternative hypothesis tested against it fails to achieve a predetermined significance level. See **hypothesis testing.** Compare **alternative hypothesis.**

nullifidian (ˌnʌlɪ'fɪdɪən) *n.* **1.** a person who has no faith or belief; sceptic; disbeliever. ~*adj.* **2.** having no faith or belief. [C16: from Latin, from *nullus* no + *fidēs* faith]

nullify ('nʌlɪˌfaɪ) *vb.* **-fies, -fying, -fied.** (*tr.*) **1.** to render legally void or of no effect. **2.** to render ineffective or useless; cancel out. [C16: from Late Latin *nullificāre* to despise, from Latin *nullus* of no account + *facere* to make] —ˌ**nullifi'cation** *n.* —'**nulliˌfier** *n.*

nullipara (nʌ'lɪpərə) *n., pl.* **-rae** (-ˌri:). a woman who has never borne a child. [C19: New Latin, from *nullus* no, not any + *-para,* from *parere* to bring forth; see -PAROUS] —**nul'liparous** *adj.*

nullipore ('nʌlɪˌpɔ:) *n.* any of several red seaweeds that secrete and become encrusted with calcium carbonate: family *Rhodophyceae.* [C19: from Latin, from *nullus* no + PORE[2]]

nulli secundus *Latin.* ('nʊli: sə'kʊndʊs) *adj.* second to none.

nullity ('nʌlɪtɪ) *n., pl.* **-ties.** **1.** the state of being null. **2.** a null or legally invalid act or instrument. **3.** something null, ineffective, characterless, etc. [C16: from Medieval Latin *nullitās,* from Latin *nullus* no, not any]

NUM (in Britain) *abbrev. for* National Union of Mineworkers.

num. *abbrev. for:* **1.** number. **2.** numeral.

Num. *Bible. abbrev. for* Numbers.

numb (nʌm) *adj.* **1.** deprived of feeling through cold, shock, etc. **2.** unable to move; paralysed. **3.** characteristic of or resembling numbness: *a numb sensation.* ~*vb.* **4.** (*tr.*) to make numb; deaden, shock, or paralyse. [C15 *nomen,* literally: taken (with paralysis), from Old English *niman* to take; related to Old Norse *nema,* Old High German *niman*] —'**numbly** *adv.* —'**numbness** *n.*

numbat ('nʌmˌbæt) *n.* a small Australian marsupial, *Myrmecobius fasciatus,* having a long snout and tongue and strong claws for hunting and feeding on termites: family *Dasyuridae.* Also called: **banded anteater.** [C20: from a native Australian language]

number ('nʌmbə) *n.* **1.** a concept of quantity that is or can be derived from a single unit, the sum of a collection of units, or zero. Every number occupies a unique position in a sequence, enabling it to be used in counting. It can be assigned to one or more sets that can be arranged in a hierarchical classification: every number is a **complex number;** a complex number is either an **imaginary number** or a **real number,** and the latter can be a **rational number** or an **irrational number;** a rational number is either an **integer** or a **fraction,** while an irrational number can be a **transcendental number** or an **algebraic number.** See also **cardinal number, ordinal number.** **2.** the symbol used to represent a number; numeral. **3.** a numeral or string of numerals used to identify a person or thing, esp. in numerical order: *a telephone number.* **4.** the person or thing so identified or designated: *she was number seven in the race.* **5.** the sum or quantity of equal or similar units or things: *a large number of people.* **6.** one of a series, as of a magazine or periodical; issue. **7. a.** a self-contained piece of pop or jazz music. **b.** a self-contained part of an opera or other musical score, esp. one for the stage. **8.** a group or band of people, esp. an exclusive group: *he was not one of our number.* **9.** *Slang.* a person, esp. a woman: *who's that nice little number?* **10.** *Informal.* an admired article, esp. an item of clothing for a woman: *that little number is by Dior.* **11.** *Slang.* a cannabis cigarette: *roll another number.* **12.** a grammatical category for the variation in form of nouns, pronouns, and any words agreeing with them, depending on how many persons or things are referred to, esp. as singular or plural in number and in some languages dual or trial. **13. any number of.** several or many. **14. by numbers.** *Military.* (of a drill procedure, etc.) performed step by step, each move being made on the call of a number. **15. do a number on (someone).** *U.S. slang.* to manipulate or trick (someone). **16. get** *or* **have someone's number.** *Informal.* to discover someone's true character or intentions. **17. in numbers.** in large numbers; numerously. **18. one's number is up.** *Brit. informal.* one is finished; one is ruined or about to die. **19. without** *or* **beyond number.** of too great a quantity to be counted; innumerable. ~*vb.* (*mainly tr.*) **20.** to assign a number to. **21.** to add up to; total. **22.** (*also intr.*) to list (items) one by one; enumerate. **23.** (*also intr.*) to put or be put into a group, category, etc.: *they were numbered among the worst hit.* **24.** to limit the number of: *his days were numbered.* [C13: from Old French *nombre,* from Latin *numerus*]

number crunching *n. Computer technol.* the large-scale processing of numerical data. —**number cruncher** *n.*

numbered account *n. Banking.* an account identified only by a number, esp. one in a Swiss bank that could contain funds illegally obtained.

number eight wire *n. N.Z.* **1.** a standard gauge of fencing wire. **2.** this wire or something similar used for emergency repairs.

numberless ('nʌmbəlɪs) *adj.* **1.** too many to be counted; countless. **2.** not containing or consisting of numbers. —'**numberlessly** *adv.* —'**numberlessness** *n.*

number line *n.* an infinite line on which points are taken to represent the real numbers by their distance from a reference point.

number off *vb.* (*adv.*) to call out or cause to call out one's number or place in a sequence, esp. in a rank of soldiers: *the sergeant numbered his men off from the right.*

number one *n.* **1.** the first in a series or sequence. **2.** an informal phrase for **oneself, myself,** etc.: *to look after number one.* **3.** *Informal.* the most important person; leader, chief: *he's number one in the organization.* **4.** *Informal.* the best-selling pop record in any one week. ~*adj.* **5.** first in importance, urgency, quality, etc.: *number one priority.* **6.** *Informal.* (of a pop record) having reached the top of the charts.

numberplate ('nʌmbəˌpleɪt) *n.* a plate mounted on the front and back of a motor vehicle bearing the registration number. Usual U.S. term: **license plate,** (Canadian) **licence plate.**

numbers game *or* **racket** *n. U.S.* an illegal lottery in which money is wagered on a certain combination of digits appearing at the beginning of a series of numbers published in a newspaper, as in share prices or sports results. Often shortened to **numbers.**

number theory *n.* the study of integers, their properties, and the relationship between integers.

number work *n.* simple arithmetic and similar mathematical procedures as used and studied at primary level. Also called (esp. formerly): **sums.**

numbfish ('nʌmˌfɪʃ) *n., pl.* **-fish** *or* **-fishes.** any of several electric rays, such as *Narcine tasmaniensis* (**Australian numbfish**). [C18: so called because it numbs its victims]

numbles ('nʌmbᵊlz) *pl. n. Archaic.* the heart, lungs, liver, etc., of a deer or other animal, cooked for food. [C14: from Old French *nombles,* plural of *nomble* thigh muscle of a deer, changed from Latin *lumbulus* a little loin, from *lumbus* loin; see HUMBLE PIE]

numbskull ('nʌmˌskʌl) *n.* a variant spelling of **numskull.** [C18: from NUMB + SKULL]

numdah ('nʌmdɑː) *n.* **1.** a coarse felt made esp. in India. **2.** a saddle pad made from this. **3.** an embroidered rug made from this. ~Also called (for senses 1, 2): **numnah.** [C19: from Urdu *namdā*]

numen ('njuːmɛn) *n., pl.* **-mina** (-mɪnə). **1.** (esp. in ancient Roman religion) a deity or spirit presiding over a thing or place. **2.** a guiding principle, force, or spirit. [C17: from Latin: a nod (indicating a command), divine power; compare *nuere* to nod]

numerable ('njuːmərəbᵊl) *adj.* able to be numbered or counted. —'**numerably** *adv.*

numeral ('njuːmərəl) *n.* **1.** a symbol or group of symbols used to express a number: for example, *6* (*Arabic*), *VI* (*Roman*), *110* (*binary*). ~*adj.* **2.** of, consisting of, or denoting a number. [C16: from Late Latin *numerālis* belonging to number, from Latin *numerus* number]

numerary ('njuːmərərɪ) *adj.* of or relating to numbers.

numerate *adj.* ('njuːmərɪt). **1.** able to use numbers, esp. in arithmetical operations. Compare **literate.** ~*vb.* ('njuːməˌreɪt). (*tr.*) **2.** to read (a numerical expression). **3.** a less common word for **enumerate.** [C18 (vb.): from Latin *numerus* number + -ATE[1], by analogy with *literate*] —**numeracy** ('njuːmərəsɪ) *n.*

numeration (ˌnjuːməˈreɪʃən) *n.* **1.** the act or process of writing, reading, or naming numbers. **2.** a system of numbering or counting. —'**numerative** *adj.*

numerator ('njuːməˌreɪtə) *n.* **1.** *Maths.* the dividend of a fraction: *the numerator of 7/8 is 7. Compare* **denominator. 2.** a person or thing that numbers; enumerator.

numerical (njuːˈmɛrɪkᵊl) *or* **numeric** *adj.* **1.** of, relating to, or denoting a number or numbers. **2.** measured or expressed in numbers: *numerical value.* **3.** *Maths.* **a.** containing or using constants, coefficients, terms, or elements represented by numbers: $3x^2 + 4y = 2$ is a numerical equation. Compare **literal** (sense 6). **b.** another word for **absolute** (sense 11a). —**nu'merically** *adv.*

numerical analysis *n.* a branch of mathematics concerned with methods, usually iterative, for obtaining solutions to problems by means of a computer.

numerical control *n. Engineering.* a form of computer control applied to machine tools, by which an operation is directed from numerical data stored on tape or punched on cards.

numerical identity *n. Logic.* the relation that holds between two relata when they are the selfsame entity, that is, when the terms designating them have the same reference. Compare **qualitative identity.** See also **Leibnitz's law.**

numerology (ˌnjuːməˈrɒlədʒɪ) *n.* the study of numbers, such as the figures in a birth date, and of their supposed influence on human affairs. —**numerological** (ˌnjuːmərəˈlɒdʒɪkᵊl) *adj.* —ˌ**numer'ologist** *n.*

numerous ('njuːmərəs) *adj.* **1.** being many. **2.** consisting of many units or parts: *a numerous collection.* —'**numerously** *adv.* —'**numerousness** *n.*

Numidian (njuːˈmɪdɪən) *adj.* **1.** of or relating to Numidia, an ancient country of N Africa, corresponding roughly to present-day Algeria. ~*n.* **2.** a native or inhabitant of Numidia.

Numidian crane *n.* another name for **demoiselle crane** (see **demoiselle** (sense 1)).

numina ('njuːmɪnə) *n.* the plural of **numen.**

numinous ('njuːmɪnəs) *adj.* **1.** denoting, being, or relating to a numen; divine. **2.** arousing spiritual or religious emotions. **3.** mysterious or awe-inspiring. [C17: from Latin *numin-,* NUMEN + -OUS]

numis. *or* **numism.** *abbrev. for* numismatic(s).

numismatics (ˌnjuːmɪzˈmætɪks) *n.* (*functioning as sing.*) the study or collection of coins, medals, etc. Also called: ˌ**numisma'tology.** [C18: from French *numismatique,* from Latin *nomisma,* from Greek: piece of currency, from *nomizein* to have in use, from *nōmos* use] —ˌ**numis'matic** *adj.* —ˌ**numis'matically** *adv.*

numismatist (njuːˈmɪzmətɪst) *or* **numismatologist** (njuːˌmɪzməˈtɒlədʒɪst) *n.* a person who studies or collects coins, medals, etc.

nummary ('nʌmərɪ) *adj.* of or relating to coins. [C17: from Latin *nummārius*]

nummular ('nʌmjʊlə) *adj.* shaped like a coin; disc-shaped; circular. [C19: from Latin *nummulus* a small coin]

nummulite ('nʌmjʊˌlaɪt) *n.* any of various large fossil protozoans of the family *Nummulitidae,* common in Tertiary times: order *Foraminifera* (foraminifers). [C19: from New Latin *Nummulites* genus name, from Latin *nummulus,* from *nummus* coin] —**nummulitic** (ˌnʌmjʊˈlɪtɪk) *adj.*

numnah ('nʌmnɑː) *n.* another word for **numdah** (senses 1, 2).

numskull *or* **numbskull** ('nʌmˌskʌl) *n.* a stupid person; dolt; blockhead.

nun[1] (nʌn) *n.* **1.** a female member of a religious order. **2.** (*sometimes cap.*) a variety of domestic fancy pigeon having a black-and-white plumage with a ridged peak or cowl of short white feathers. [Old English *nunne,* from Church Latin *nonna,* from Late Latin: form of address used for an elderly woman] —'**nunlike** *adj.*

nun[2] (nʊn) *n.* the 14th letter in the Hebrew alphabet (נ or, at the end of a word, ן), transliterated as *n.*

nunatak ('nʌnəˌtæk) *n.* an isolated mountain peak projecting through the surface of surrounding glacial ice and supporting a distinct fauna and flora after recession of the ice. [C19: via Danish from Eskimo]

nun buoy (nʌn) *n. Nautical.* a green buoy, conical at the top, marking the right side of a channel leading into a harbour. Compare **can buoy.** [C18: from obsolete *nun* a child's spinning top + BUOY]

Nunc Dimittis ('nʌŋk dɪˈmɪtɪs, 'nʊŋk) *n.* **1.** the Latin name for the Canticle of Simeon (Luke 2:29–32). **2.** a musical setting of this. [from the opening words (Vulgate): now let depart]

nunciature ('nʌnsɪətʃə) *n.* the office or term of office of a nuncio. [C17: from Italian *nunziatura;* see NUNCIO]

nuncio ('nʌnʃɪˌəʊ, -sɪ-) *n., pl.* **-cios.** *R.C. Church.* a diplomatic representative of the Holy See, ranking above an internuncio and esp. having ambassadorial status. [C16: via Italian from Latin *nuntius* messenger]

nuncle ('nʌŋkᵊl) *n.* an archaic or dialect word for **uncle.** [C16: from division of *mine uncle* as *my nuncle*]

nuncupative ('nʌŋkjʊˌpeɪtɪv, nʌŋˈkjuːpətɪv) *adj.* (of a will) declared orally by the testator and later written down. [C16: from Late Latin *nuncupātīvus* nominal, from Latin *nuncupāre* to name]

nunhood ('nʌnhʊd) *n.* **1.** the condition, practice, or character of a nun. **2.** nuns collectively.

nunnery ('nʌnərɪ) *n., pl.* **-neries.** the convent or religious house of a community of nuns.

nunny bag ('nʌnɪ) *n. Canadian.* a small sealskin haversack, used chiefly in Newfoundland. [C19 *nunny,* probably from Scottish dialect *noony* luncheon, from NOON]

nun's cloth *or* **veiling** (nʌnz) *n.* a thin soft plain-weave silk or worsted fabric used for veils, dresses, etc.

Nupe ('nuːpeɪ) *n.* **1.** (*pl.* **-pe** *or* **-pes**) a member of a Negroid people of Nigeria, noted as fishermen, who live near the confluence of the Niger and Benue Rivers. **2.** the language of this people, belonging to the Kwa branch of the Niger-Congo family.

NUPE ('njuːpɪ) *n.* (in Britain) *acronym for* National Union of Public Employees.

nuptial ('nʌpʃəl, -tʃəl) *adj.* **1.** relating to marriage; conjugal: *nuptial vows.* **2.** *Zoology.* of or relating to mating: *the nuptial flight of a queen bee.* [C15: from Latin *nuptiālis,* from *nuptiae* marriage, from *nubere* to marry] —'**nuptially** *adv.*

nuptials ('nʌpʃəlz, -tʃəlz) *pl. n.* (*sometimes sing.*) a marriage ceremony; wedding.

NUR (in Britain) *abbrev. for* National Union of Railwaymen.

nurd (nɜːd) *n.* a variant spelling of **nerd.**

Nuri ('nʊərɪ) *n.* **1.** (*pl.* **-ris** *or* **-ri**) Also called: **Kafir.** a member of an Indo-European people of Nuristan, in E Afghanistan, and neighbouring parts of Pakistan. **2.** Also called: '**Kafiri.** the Indo-Iranian language of this people.

nurse (nɜːs) *n.* **1.** a person, usually a woman, who tends the sick, injured, or infirm. **2.** short for **nursemaid. 3.** a woman employed to breast-feed another woman's child; wet nurse. **4.** a worker in a colony of social insects that takes care of the larvae. ~*vb.* (*mainly tr.*) **5.** (*also intr.*) to tend (the sick). **6.** (*also intr.*) to feed (a baby) at the breast; suckle. **7.** to try to cure (an ailment). **8.** to clasp carefully or fondly: *she nursed the crying child in her arms.* **9.** (*also intr.*) (of a baby) to suckle at the breast (of). **10.** to look after (a child) as one's employment. **11.** to attend to carefully; foster, cherish: *he nursed the magazine through its first year; having a very small majority he nursed the constituency diligently.* **12.** to harbour; preserve: *to nurse a grudge.* **13.** *Billiards.* to keep (the balls) together for a series of cannons. [C16: from earlier *norice,* Old French *nourice,* from Late Latin *nūtrīcia* nurse, from Latin *nūtrīcius* nourishing, from *nūtrīre* to nourish] —'**nursing** *n., adj.*

nursehound ('nɜːsˌhaʊnd) *n.* a species of European dogfish, *Scyliorrhinus caniculus.* [C20: NURSE (SHARK) + HOUND[1]]

nursemaid ('nɜːsˌmeɪd) *or* **nurserymaid** ('nɜːsrɪˌmeɪd) *n.* a woman or girl employed to look after someone else's children. Often shortened to **nurse.**

nursery ('nɜːsrɪ) *n., pl.* **-ries. 1. a.** a room in a house set apart for use by children. **b.** (*as modifier*): *nursery wallpaper.* **2.** a place where plants, young trees, etc., are grown commercially. **3.** an establishment providing residential or day care for babies and very young children; crèche. **4.** short for **nursery school.** **5.** anywhere serving to foster or nourish new ideas, etc. **6.** Also called: **nursery cannon.** *Billiards.* **a.** a series of cannons with the three balls adjacent to a cushion, esp. near a corner pocket. **b.** a cannon in such a series.

nurseryman ('nɜːsrɪmən) *n., pl.* **-men.** a person who owns or works in a nursery in which plants are grown.

nursery rhyme *n.* a short traditional verse or song for children, such as *Little Jack Horner.*

nursery school *n.* a school for young children, usually from three to five years old.

nursery slopes *pl. n.* gentle slopes used by beginners in skiing.

nursery stakes *pl. n.* a race for two-year-old horses.

nurse shark *n.* any of various sharks of the family *Orectolobidae,* such as *Ginglymostoma cirratum* of the Atlantic Ocean, having an external groove on each side of the head between the mouth and nostril. [C15 *nussefisshe* (later influenced in spelling by NURSE), perhaps from division of obsolete *an huss* shark, dogfish (of uncertain origin) as *a nuss*]

nursing bottle *n.* another term (esp. U.S.) for **feeding bottle.**

nursing father *n.* a biblical name for **foster father.**

nursing home *n.* **1.** a private hospital or residence staffed and equipped to care for aged or infirm persons. **2.** *Brit.* a private maternity home.

nursing mother *n.* **1.** a mother who is breast-feeding her baby. **2.** a biblical name for **foster mother.**

nursing officer *n.* (in Britain) the official name for **matron** (sense 4).

nursling *or* **nurseling** ('nɜːslɪŋ) *n.* a child or young animal that is being suckled, nursed, or fostered.

nurture ('nɜːtʃə) *n.* **1.** the act or process of promoting the development, etc., of a child. **2.** something that nourishes. **3.** *Biology.* the environmental factors that partly determine the structure of an organism. See also **nature** (sense 12). *~vb. (tr.)* **4.** to feed or support. **5.** to educate or train. [C14: from Old French *norriture,* from Latin *nutrīre* to nourish] —**'nurturable** *adj.* —**'nurturer** *n.*

NUS (in Britain) *abbrev. for:* **1.** National Union of Seamen. **2.** National Union of Students.

nut (nʌt) *n.* **1.** a dry one-seeded indehiscent fruit that usually possesses a woody wall. **2.** (*not in technical use*) any similar fruit, such as the walnut, having a hard shell and an edible kernel. **3.** the edible kernel of such a fruit. **4.** *Slang.* **a.** an eccentric person. **b.** a person who is mentally disturbed. **5.** a slang word for **head** (sense 1). **6. do one's nut.** *Brit. slang.* to be extremely angry; go into a rage. **7. off one's nut.** *Slang.* mad, crazy, or foolish. **8.** a person or thing that presents difficulties (esp. in the phrase **a tough** *or* **hard nut to crack**). **9.** the female component of a screwed assembly, having an internal spiral thread into which a rod with a matching external thread is screwed, esp. a small metallic block, usually hexagonal or square, that fits onto a bolt. **10.** *Mountaineering.* a variously shaped small metal block, usually a wedge or hexagonal prism (originally an ordinary engineer's nut) with a wire or rope loop attached, for jamming into a crack to provide security. Also called: **chock.** **11.** Also called (U.S. and Canadian): **frog.** *Music.* **a.** the ledge or ridge at the upper end of the fingerboard of a violin, cello, etc., over which the strings pass to the tuning pegs. **b.** the end of a violin bow that is held by the player. **12.** *Printing.* another word for **en.** **13.** a small usually gingery biscuit. **14.** *Brit.* a small piece of coal. *~vb.* **nuts, nutting, nutted.** **15.** (*intr.*) to gather nuts. **16.** (*tr.*) *Slang.* to butt (someone) with the head. ~See also **nuts.** [Old English *hnutu;* related to Old Norse *hnot,* Old High German *hnuz* (German *Nuss*)] —**'nut,like** *adj.*

NUT (in Britain) *abbrev. for* National Union of Teachers.

nutant ('njuːtᵊnt) *adj. Botany.* having the apex hanging down: *nutant flowers.* [C18: from Latin *nūtāre* to nod]

nutation (njuː'teɪʃən) *n.* **1.** *Astronomy.* a periodic variation in the precession of the earth's axis causing the earth's poles to oscillate about their mean position. **2.** *Physics.* a periodic variation in the precession of the axis of any spinning body, such as a gyroscope, about the horizontal. **3.** the spiral growth of a shoot, tendril, or similar plant organ, caused by variation in the growth rate in different parts. **4.** the act or an instance of nodding the head. [C17: from Latin *nūtātiō,* from *nūtāre* to nod] —**nu'tational** *adj.*

nutbrown ('nʌt'braʊn) *adj.* of a brownish colour, esp. a reddish-brown: *nutbrown hair.*

nutcase ('nʌt,keɪs) *n. Slang.* an insane or very foolish person.

nutcracker ('nʌt,krækə) *n.* **1.** (*often pl.*) a device for cracking the shells of nuts. **2.** either of two birds, *Nucifraga caryocatactes* of the Old World or *N. columbianus* (**Clark's nutcracker**) of North America, having speckled plumage and feeding on nuts, seeds, etc.: family *Corvidae* (crows).

nutgall ('nʌt,gɔːl) *n.* a nut-shaped gall caused by gall wasps on the oak and other trees.

nuthatch ('nʌt,hætʃ) *n.* any songbird of the family *Sittidae,* esp. *Sitta europaea,* having strong feet and bill, and feeding on insects, seeds, and nuts. [C14 *notehache,* from *note* nut + *hache* hatchet, from the bird's habit of splitting nuts; see NUT, HACK[1]]

nuthouse ('nʌt,haʊs) *n. Slang.* a mental hospital or asylum.

nut key *n. Mountaineering.* a tool for extracting a nut, chock, etc., from a crack after use.

nutlet ('nʌtlɪt) *n.* **1.** any of the one-seeded portions of a fruit, such as a labiate fruit, that fragments when mature. **2.** the stone of a drupe, such as a plum. **3.** a small nut.

nutmeg ('nʌtmɛg) *n.* **1.** an East Indian evergreen tree, *Myristica fragrans,* cultivated in the tropics for its hard aromatic seed: family *Myristicaceae.* See also **mace**[2]. **2.** the seed of this tree, used as a spice. **3.** any of several similar trees or their fruit. **4.** a greyish-brown colour. *~vb.* **-megs, -megging, -megged.** (*tr.*) **5.** *Brit. sport informal.* to kick or hit the ball between the legs of (an opposing player). [C13: from Old French *nois muguede,* from Old Provençal *noz muscada* musk-scented nut, from Latin *nux* NUT + *muscus* MUSK]

nut oil *n.* oil obtained from walnuts, hazelnuts, etc., used in paints and varnishes.

nut pine *n.* either of two varieties of the pine tree *Pinus cembroides,* of Mexico, Arizona, and California, having edible nuts.

nutria ('njuːtrɪə) *n.* **1.** another name for **coypu,** esp. the fur. **2.** a brown colour with a grey tinge. [C19: from Spanish: otter, variant of *lutria,* ultimately from Latin *lūtra* otter]

nutrient ('njuːtrɪənt) *n.* **1.** any of the mineral substances that are absorbed by the roots of plants for nourishment. **2.** any substance that nourishes an animal. *~adj.* **3.** providing or contributing to nourishment: *a nutrient solution.* [C17: from Latin *nūtrīre* to nourish]

nutriment ('njuːtrɪmənt) *n.* any material providing nourishment. [C16: from Latin *nūtrīmentum,* from *nūtrīre* to nourish] —**nutrimental** (,njuːtrɪ'mɛntᵊl) *adj.*

nutrition (njuː'trɪʃən) *n.* **1.** a process in animals and plants involving the intake of nutrient materials and their subsequent assimilation into the tissues. **2.** the act or process of nourishing. **3.** the study of nutrition, esp. in humans. [C16: from Late Latin *nūtrītiō,* from *nūtrīre* to nourish] —**nu'tritional** *or* (less commonly) **nu'tritionary** *adj.* —**nu'tritionally** *adv.*

nutritionist (njuː'trɪʃənɪst) *n.* a person who specializes in nutrition and the nutritive value of various foods.

nutritious (njuː'trɪʃəs) *adj.* nourishing, sometimes to a high degree. [C17: from Latin *nūtrīcius* nourishing, from *nūtrix* a NURSE] —**nu'tritiously** *adv.* —**nu'tritiousness** *n.*

nutritive ('njuːtrɪtɪv) *adj.* **1.** providing nourishment. **2.** of, concerning, or promoting nutrition. *~n.* **3.** a nutritious food. —**'nutritively** *adv.*

nuts (nʌts) *adj.* **1.** a slang word for **insane.** **2.** (foll. by *about* or *on*) *Slang.* extremely fond (of) or enthusiastic (about). *~interj.* **3.** *Slang.* an expression of disappointment, contempt, refusal, or defiance. *~pl. n.* **4.** a taboo slang word for **testicles.**

nuts and bolts *pl. n. Informal.* the essential or practical details.

nutshell ('nʌt,ʃɛl) *n.* **1.** the shell around the kernel of a nut. **2. in a nutshell.** in essence; briefly.

nutter ('nʌtə) *n. Brit. slang.* a mad or eccentric person.

nutting ('nʌtɪŋ) *n.* the act or pastime of gathering nuts.

nutty ('nʌtɪ) *adj.* **-tier, -tiest.** **1.** containing or abounding in nuts. **2.** resembling nuts, esp. in taste. **3.** a slang word for **insane.** **4.** (foll. by *over* or *about*) *Informal.* extremely fond (of) or enthusiastic (about). —**'nuttily** *adv.* —**'nuttiness** *n.*

nutwood ('nʌt,wʊd) *n.* **1.** any of various nut-bearing trees, such as walnut. **2.** the wood of any of these trees.

nux vomica ('nʌks 'vɒmɪkə) *n.* **1.** an Indian spiny loganiaceous tree, *Strychnos nux-vomica,* with orange-red berries containing poisonous seeds. **2.** any of the seeds of this tree, which contain strychnine and other poisonous alkaloids. **3.** a medicine manufactured from the seeds of this tree, formerly used as a heart stimulant. [C16: from Medieval Latin: vomiting nut]

nuzzle ('nʌzᵊl) *vb.* **1.** to push or rub gently against the nose or snout. **2.** (*intr.*) to nestle; lie close. **3.** (*tr.*) to dig out with the snout. [C15 *nosele,* from NOSE (n.)]

NV *abbrev. for* Nevada.

NVQ *abbrev. for* National Vocational Qualification.

NW *symbol for* northwest(ern).

NWT *abbrev. for* Northwest Territories (of Canada).

NY *or* **N.Y.** *abbrev. for* New York (city or state).

nyaff (njæf) *n. Scot.* a small or contemptible person. [C19: perhaps imitative of the bark of a small dog]

nyala ('njɑːlə) *n., pl.* **-la** *or* **-las.** **1.** a spiral-horned southern African antelope, *Tragelaphus angasi,* with a fringe of white hairs along the length of the back and neck. **2. mountain nyala.** a similar and related Ethiopian animal, *T. buxtoni,* lacking the white crest. [from Zulu]

Nyanja ('njændʒə) *n.* **1.** (*pl.* **-ja** *or* **-jas**) a member of a Negroid people of central Africa, living chiefly in Malawi. **2.** the language of this people, belonging to the Bantu group of the Niger-Congo family. Nyanja forms the basis of a pidgin used as a lingua franca in central Africa.

nyanza ('njænzə, nɪ'ænzə) *n.* (*cap. when part of a name*) (in E Africa) a lake. [from Bantu]

NYC *abbrev. for* New York City.

nyctaginaceous (,nɪktədʒɪ'neɪʃəs) *adj.* of, relating to, or belonging to the *Nyctaginaceae,* a family of mostly tropical plants, including bougainvillea, having large coloured bracts surrounding each flower. [from New Latin, from *Nyctago* type genus, from Greek *nukt-, nux* night]

nyctalopia (,nɪktə'ləʊpɪə) *n.* inability to see normally in dim light. Nontechnical name: **night blindness.** Compare **hem-**

eralopia. [C17: via Late Latin from Greek *nuktálōps,* from *nux* night + *alaos* blind + ōps eye]

nyctanthous (nɪk'tænθəs) *adj.* (of plants) flowering at night.

nyctinasty ('nɪktɪˌnæstɪ) *n. Botany.* a nastic movement, such as the closing of petals, that occurs in response to the alternation of day and night. [C20: from Greek *nukt-, nux* night + -NASTY] —ˌ**nycti'nastic** *adj.*

nyctitropism (nɪk'tɪtrəˌpɪzəm) *n.* a tendency of some plant parts to assume positions at night that are different from their daytime positions. [C19: *nyct-,* from Greek *nukt-, nux* night + -TROPISM] —**nyctitropic** (ˌnɪktɪ'trɒpɪk) *adj.*

nyctophobia (ˌnɪktəʊ'fəʊbɪə) *n. Psychiatry.* an abnormal dread of night or darkness. [*nyct-,* from Greek *nukt-, nux* night + -PHOBIA] —ˌ**nycto'phobic** *adj.*

nye (naɪ) *n.* a flock of pheasants. Also called: **nide, eye.** [C15: from old French *ni,* from Latin *nīdus* nest]

nylghau ('nɪlgɔː) *n., pl.* **-ghau** *or* **-ghaus.** another name for **nilgai.**

nylon ('naɪlɒn) *n.* **1.** a class of synthetic polyamide materials made by copolymerizing dicarboxylic acids with diamines. They can be moulded into a variety of articles, such as combs and machine parts. Nylon monofilaments are used for bristles, etc., and nylon fibres can be spun into yarn. **2. a.** yarn or cloth made of nylon, used for clothing, stockings, etc. **b.** (*as modifier*): *a nylon dress.* [C20: originally a trademark]

nylons ('naɪlɒnz) *pl. n.* stockings made of nylon or other man-made material.

nymph (nɪmf) *n.* **1.** *Myth.* a spirit of nature envisaged as a beautiful maiden. **2.** *Chiefly poetic.* a beautiful young woman. **3.** the larva of insects such as the dragonfly and mayfly. It resembles the adult, apart from having underdeveloped wings and reproductive organs, and develops into the adult without a pupal stage. [C14: via Old French from Latin, from Greek *numphē* nymph; related to Latin *nūbere* to marry] —'**nymphal** *or* **nymphean** ('nɪmfɪən) *adj.* —'**nymphlike** *adj.*

nympha ('nɪmfə) *n., pl.* **-phae** (-fiː). *Anatomy.* either one of the labia minora. Also called: '**labium** '**minus pu'dendi.** [C17: from Latin: bride, NYMPH]

nymphaeaceous (ˌnɪmfɪ'eɪʃəs) *adj.* of, relating to, or belonging to the *Nymphaeaceae,* a family of plants, including the water lilies, that grow in water or marshes and have typically floating leaves and showy flowers. [from New Latin, from Latin *nymphaea* water lily, ultimately from Greek *numphaios* sacred to nymphs]

nymphalid ('nɪmfəlɪd) *n.* **1.** any butterfly of the family *Nymphalidae,* typically having brightly coloured wings: includes the fritillaries, tortoiseshells, red admirals, and peacock. ~*adj.* **2.** of, relating to, or belonging to the *Nymphalidae.* [C19: from New Latin, from *Nymphālis* genus name, from Latin; see NYMPH]

nymphet ('nɪmfɪt) *n.* a young girl who is sexually precocious and desirable. [C17 (meaning: a young nymph): diminutive of NYMPH]

nympho ('nɪmfəʊ) *n., pl.* **-phos.** *Informal.* a nymphomaniac.

nympholepsy ('nɪmfəˌlɛpsɪ) *n., pl* **-sies.** a state of violent emotion, esp. when associated with a desire for something one cannot have. [C18: from NYMPHOLEPT, on the model of *epilepsy*] —ˌ**nympho'leptic** *adj.*

nympholept ('nɪmfəˌlɛpt) *n.* a person afflicted by nympholepsy. [C19: from Greek *numpholēptos* caught by nymphs, from *numphē* nymph + *lambanein* to seize]

nymphomania (ˌnɪmfə'meɪnɪə) *n.* a neurotic condition in women in which the symptoms are a compulsion to have sexual intercourse with as many men as possible and an inability to have lasting relationships with them. Compare **satyriasis.** [C18: New Latin, from Greek *numphē* nymph + -MANIA] —ˌ**nympho'maniac** *n., adj.* —**nymphomaniacal** (ˌnɪmfəʊmə'naɪəkᵊl) *adj.*

Nynorsk (*Norwegian* 'nyːnɔːsk; *English* 'niːnɔːsk) *n.* one of the two mutually intelligible official forms of written Norwegian: it also exists in spoken form and is derived from the dialect of W and N Norway. Also called: **Landsmål.** Compare **Bokmål.** [Norwegian: new Norse]

Nyoro ('njɔːrəʊ) *n.* **1.** (*pl.* **-ro** *or* **-ros**) a member of a Negroid people of W Uganda. **2.** the language of this people, belonging to the Bantu group of the Niger-Congo family.

nystagmus (nɪ'stægməs) *n.* involuntary movement of the eye comprising a smooth drift followed by a flick back, occurring in several situations, for example after the body has been rotated.

nystatin ('nɪstətɪn) *n.* an antibiotic obtained from the bacterium *Streptomyces noursei:* used in the treatment of infections caused by certain fungi, esp. *Candida albicans.* [C20: from *New York State,* where it was originated + -IN]

NZ *international car registration for* New Zealand.

NZ *or* **N. Zeal.** *abbrev. for* New Zealand.

NZBC *abbrev. for* New Zealand Broadcasting Commission.

NZCER *abbrev. for* New Zealand Council for Educational Research.

NZEF *abbrev. for* New Zealand Expeditionary Force.

NZEFIP *abbrev. for* New Zealand Expeditionary Force in the Pacific.

NZEI *abbrev. for* New Zealand Educational Institute.

NZLR *abbrev. for* New Zealand Law Reports.

NZMA *abbrev. for* New Zealand Medical Association.

NZR *abbrev. for* New Zealand Railways.

NZRFU *abbrev. for* New Zealand Rugby Football Union.

NZRN *abbrev. for* New Zealand Registered Nurse.

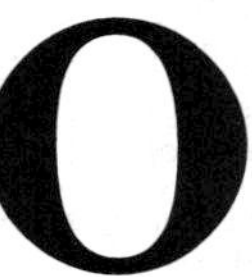

o *or* **O** (əʊ) *n., pl.* **o's, O's,** *or* **Os.** **1.** the 15th letter and fourth vowel of the modern English alphabet. **2.** any of several speech sounds represented by this letter, in English as in *code, pot, cow, move,* or *form.* **3.** another name for **nought.**

O[1] *symbol for:* **1.** *Chem.* oxygen. **2.** a human blood type of the ABO group. See **universal donor. 3.** *Logic.* a particular negative categorial proposition, such as *some men are not married:* often symbolized as **SoP.** Compare **A, E, I**[1]. [from Latin *(neg)o* I deny]

O[2] (əʊ) *interj.* **1.** a variant spelling of **oh. 2.** an exclamation introducing an invocation, entreaty, wish, etc.: *O God! O for the wings of a dove!*

o. *abbrev. for:* **1.** octavo. **2.** old. **3.** only. **4.** order. **5.** *Pharmacol.* pint. [from Latin *octarius*]

O. *abbrev. for:* **1.** Ocean. **2.** octavo. **3.** old.

o- *prefix.* short for **ortho-** (sense 4).

o' (ə) *prep. Informal or archaic.* shortened form of **of:** *a cup o' tea.*

O'- *prefix.* (in surnames of Irish Gaelic origin) descendant of: *O'Corrigan.* [from Irish Gaelic *ó, ua* descendant]

-o *suffix.* forming informal and slang variants and abbreviations, esp. of nouns: *wino; lie doggo; Jacko.* [probably special use of OH]

-o- *connective vowel.* used to connect elements in a compound word: *chromosome; filmography.* Compare **-i-.** [from Greek, stem vowel of many nouns and adjectives in combination]

oaf (əʊf) *n.* a stupid or loutish person. [C17: variant of Old English *ælf* ELF] —**'oafish** *adj.* —**'oafishly** *adv.* —**'oafishness** *n.*

oak (əʊk) *n.* **1.** any deciduous or evergreen tree or shrub of the fagaceous genus *Quercus,* having acorns as fruits and lobed leaves. See also **holm oak, cork oak, red oak, Turkey oak, durmast. 2. a.** the wood of any of these trees, used esp. as building timber and for making furniture. **b.** *(as modifier): an oak table.* **3.** any of various trees that resemble the oak, such as the poison oak, silky oak, and Jerusalem oak. **4. a.** anything made of oak, esp. a heavy outer door to a set of rooms in an Oxford or Cambridge college. **b. sport one's oak.** to shut this door as a sign that one does not want visitors. **5.** the leaves of an oak tree, worn as a garland. **6.** the dark brownish colour of oak wood. **7.** *Austral.* any of various species of casuarina, such as desert oak, swamp oak, or she-oak. [Old English *āc;* related to Old Norse *eik,* Old High German *eih,* Latin *aesculus*]

oak apple *or* **gall** *n.* any of various brownish round galls on oak trees, containing the larva of certain wasps.

Oak-apple Day *n.* (in Britain) May 29, the anniversary of the Restoration (1660), formerly commemorated by the wearing of oak apples or oak leaves, recalling the **Boscobel oak** in which Charles II hid after the battle of Worcester (1651).

oaken (ˈəʊkən) *adj.* made of the wood of the oak.

oak fern *n.* a graceful light green polypody fern, *Thelypteris dryopteris,* having a creeping rhizome, found in acid woodlands of the northern hemisphere.

oak-leaf cluster *n. U.S.* an insignia consisting of oak leaves and acorns awarded to holders of certain military decorations to indicate a further award of the same decoration.

oakum (ˈəʊkəm) *n.* loose fibre obtained by unravelling old rope, used esp. for caulking seams in wooden ships. [Old English *ācuma,* variant of *ācumba,* literally: off-combings, from *ā-* off + *-cumba,* from *cemban* to COMB]

Oamaru stone (ˈɒməruː) *n.* a kind of limestone, of building quality, found at Oamaru on South Island, New Zealand.

O & M *abbrev. for* organization and method (in studies of working methods).

oanshagh (ˈoːnʃəx) *n. Irish.* a foolish girl or woman. [from Irish Gaelic *óinseach*]

OAP (in Britain) *abbrev. for* old age pension *or* pensioner.

OAPEC (əʊˈeɪpɛk) *n. acronym for* Organization of Arab Petroleum Exporting Countries.

oar (ɔː) *n.* **1.** a long shaft of wood for propelling a boat by rowing, having a broad blade that is dipped into and pulled against the water. Oars were also used for steering certain kinds of ancient sailing boats. **2.** short for **oarsman. 3. put one's oar in.** to interfere or interrupt. *~vb.* **4.** to row or propel with or as if with oars: *the two men were oaring their way across the lake.* [Old English *ār,* of Germanic origin; related to Old Norse *ār*] —**'oarless** *adj.* —**'oar,like** *adj.*

oared (ɔːd) *adj.* **1.** equipped with oars. **2.** *(in combination)* having oars as specified: *two-oared.*

oarfish (ˈɔːˌfɪʃ) *n., pl.* **-fish** *or* **-fishes.** a very long ribbonfish, *Regalecus glesne,* with long slender ventral fins. Also called: **king of the herrings.** [C19: referring to the flattened oarlike body]

oarlock (ˈɔːˌlɒk) *n.* the usual U.S. and Canadian word for **rowlock.**

oarsman (ˈɔːzmən) *n., pl.* **-men.** a man who rows, esp. one who rows in a racing boat. —**'oarsman,ship** *n.*

oarweed (ˈɔːˌwiːd) *n.* any of various brown seaweeds, especially a kelp of the genus *Laminaria,* with long broad fronds, common below the low-water mark. [from earlier *oreweed,* from *wore,* from Old English *wár* seaweed + WEED[1]]

OAS *abbrev. for:* **1.** Organization of American States. **2.** (in Algeria) Organisation de l'Armée Secrète. [French: Secret Army Organization]

oasis (əʊˈeɪsɪs) *n., pl.* **-ses** (-siːz). **1.** a fertile patch in a desert occurring where the water table approaches or reaches the ground surface. **2.** a place of peace, safety, or happiness in the midst of trouble or difficulty. [C17: via Latin from Greek, probably of Egyptian origin]

oast (əʊst) *n. Chiefly Brit.* **1.** a kiln for drying hops. **2.** Also called: **oast house.** a building containing such kilns, usually having a conical or pyramidal roof. [Old English *āst;* related to Old Norse *eisa* fire]

oat (əʊt) *n.* **1.** an erect annual grass, *Avena sativa,* grown in temperate regions for its edible seed. **2.** *(usually pl.)* the seeds or fruits of this grass. **3.** any of various other grasses of the genus *Avena,* such as the wild oat. **4.** *Poetic.* a flute made from an oat straw. **5. feel one's oats.** *U.S. and Canadian informal.* **a.** to feel exuberant. **b.** to feel self-important. **6. get one's oats.** *Slang.* to have sexual intercourse. **7. sow one's (wild) oats.** to indulge in adventure or promiscuity during youth. [Old English *āte,* of obscure origin]

oatcake (ˈəʊtˌkeɪk) *n.* a brittle unleavened oatmeal biscuit.

oaten (ˈəʊtᵊn) *adj.* made of oats or oat straw.

oat grass *n.* any of various oatlike grasses, esp. of the genera *Arrhenatherum* and *Danthonia,* of Eurasia and N. Africa.

oath (əʊθ) *n., pl.* **oaths** (əʊðz). **1.** a solemn pronouncement to affirm the truth of a statement or to pledge a person to some course of action, often involving a sacred being or object as witness. **2.** the form of such a pronouncement. **3.** an irreverent or blasphemous expression, esp. one involving the name of a deity; curse. **4. on, upon,** *or* **under oath. a.** under the obligation of an oath. **b.** *Law.* having sworn to tell the truth, usually with one's hand on the Bible. **5. take an oath.** to declare formally with an oath or pledge, esp. before giving evidence. [Old English *āth;* related to Old Saxon, Old Frisian *ēth,* Old High German *eid*]

oatmeal (ˈəʊtˌmiːl) *n.* **1.** meal ground from oats, used for making porridge, oatcakes, etc. **2. a.** a greyish-yellow colour. **b.** *(as adj.): an oatmeal coat.*

OAU *abbrev. for* Organization of African Unity.

OB *Brit. abbrev. for:* **1.** Old Boy. **2.** outside broadcast.

ob. *abbrev. for:* **1.** (on tombstones) obiit. [Latin: he (or she) died] **2.** obiter. [Latin: incidentally; in passing] **3.** oboe.

o.b. *N.Z. abbrev. for* ordinary building (grade) (of timber not from the heart of a log).

ob- *prefix.* inverse or inversely: *obovate.* [from Old French, from Latin *ob.* In compound words of Latin origin, *ob-* (and *oc-, of-, op-*) indicates: to, towards *(object);* against *(oppose);* away from *(obsolete);* before *(obstetric);* down, over *(obtect);* for the sake of *(obsecrate);* and is used as an intensifier *(oblong)*]

oba (ˈɔːbɑː, -bə) *n.* (in W Africa) a Yoruba chief or ruler.

Obad. *Bible. abbrev. for* Obadiah.

obb. *abbrev. for* obbligato.

obbligato *or* **obligato** (ˌɒblɪˈgɑːtəʊ) *Music.* *~adj.* **1.** not to be omitted in performance. *~n., pl.* **-tos** *or* **-ti** (-tiː). **2.** an essential part in a score: *with oboe obbligato.* ~See **ad-lib.** [C18: from Italian, from *obbligare* to OBLIGE]

obconic (ɒbˈkɒnɪk) *or* **obconical** *adj. Botany.* (of a fruit or similar part) shaped like a cone and attached at the pointed end.

obcordate (ɒbˈkɔːdeɪt) *adj. Botany.* heart-shaped and attached at the pointed end: *obcordate leaves.*

obdt *abbrev. for* obedient.

obdurate (ˈɒbdjʊrɪt) *adj.* **1.** not easily moved by feelings or supplication; hardhearted. **2.** impervious to persuasion, esp. to moral persuasion. [C15: from Latin *obdūrāre* to make hard, from *ob-* (intensive) + *dūrus* hard; compare ENDURE] —**'obduracy** *or* **'obdurateness** *n.* —**'obdurately** *adv.*

OBE *abbrev. for* **1.** Officer of the Order of the British Empire (a Brit. title). **2.** out-of-the-body experience.

obeah (ˈəʊbɪə) *n.* another word for **obi**[2].

obedience (əˈbiːdɪəns) *n.* **1.** the condition or quality of being obedient. **2.** the act or an instance of obeying; dutiful or submissive behaviour. **3.** the authority vested in a Church or similar body. **4.** the collective group of persons submitting to this authority. See also **passive obedience.**

obedient (ə'biːdɪənt) *adj.* obeying or willing to obey. [C13: from Old French, from Latin *oboediens,* present participle of *oboedīre* to OBEY] —**o'bediently** *adv.*
obedientiary (əʊˌbiːdɪ'ɛnʃərɪ) *n., pl.* **-ries.** *Christianity.* the holder of any monastic office under the superior. [C18: from Medieval Latin *obedientiarius;* see OBEDIENT, -ARY]
obeisance (əʊ'beɪsəns, əʊ'biː-) *n.* **1.** an attitude of deference or homage. **2.** a gesture expressing obeisance. [C14: from Old French *obéissant,* present participle of *obéir* to OBEY] —**o'beisant** *adj.* —**o'beisantly** *adv.*
obelisk ('ɒbɪlɪsk) *n.* **1.** a stone pillar having a square or rectangular cross section and sides that taper towards a pyramidal top, often used as a monument in ancient Egypt. **2.** *Printing.* another name for **dagger** (sense 2). [C16: via Latin from Greek *obeliskos* a little spit, from *obelos* spit] —ˌ**obe'liscal** *adj.* —ˌ**obe'liskoid** *adj.*
obelize *or* **obelise** ('ɒbɪˌlaɪz) *vb.* (*tr.*) to mark (a word or passage) with an obelus. [C17: from Greek *obelizein*]
obelus ('ɒbɪləs) *n., pl.* **-li** (-ˌlaɪ). **1.** a mark (— or ÷) used in editions of ancient documents to indicate spurious words or passages. **2.** another name for **dagger** (sense 2). [C14: via Late Latin from Greek *obelos* spit]
obese (əʊ'biːs) *adj.* excessively fat or fleshy; corpulent. [C17: from Latin *obēsus,* from *ob-* (intensive) + *edere* to eat] —**o'besity** *or* **o'beseness** *n.*
obey (ə'beɪ) *vb.* **1.** to carry out (instructions or orders); comply with (demands). **2.** to behave or act in accordance with (one's feelings, whims, etc.). [C13: from Old French *obéir,* from Latin *oboedīre,* from *ob-* to, towards + *audīre* to hear] —**o'beyer** *n.*
obfuscate ('ɒbfʌsˌkeɪt) *vb.* (*tr.*) **1.** to obscure or darken. **2.** to perplex or bewilder. [C16: from Latin *ob-* (intensive) + *fuscāre* to blacken, from *fuscus* dark] —ˌ**obfus'cation** *n.* —ˌ**obfus'catory** *adj.*
obi[1] ('əʊbɪ) *n., pl.* **obis** *or* **obi.** **1.** a broad sash tied in a large flat bow at the back, worn by Japanese women and children as part of the national costume. **2.** a narrow sash worn by Japanese men. [C19: from Japanese]
obi[2] ('əʊbɪ) *or* **obeah** *n., pl.* **obis** *or* **obeahs.** **1.** a kind of witchcraft originating in Africa and practised by some West Indians. **2.** a charm or amulet used in this. [of West African origin; compare Edo *obi* poison] —'**obiism** *n.*
obit ('ɒbɪt, 'əʊbɪt) *n. Informal.* **1.** short for **obituary.** **2.** a memorial service.
obiter dictum ('ɒbɪtə 'dɪktəm, 'əʊ-) *n., pl.* **obiter dicta** ('dɪktə). **1.** *Law.* an observation by a judge on some point of law not directly in issue in the case before him and thus neither requiring his decision nor serving as a precedent, but nevertheless of persuasive authority. **2.** any comment, remark, or observation made in passing. [Latin: something said in passing]
obituary (ə'bɪtjʊərɪ) *n., pl.* **-aries.** a published announcement of a death, often accompanied by a short biography of the dead person. [C18: from Medieval Latin *obituārius,* from Latin *obīre* to fall, from *ob-* down + *īre* to go] —**o'bituarist** *n.*
obj. *abbrev. for:* **1.** *Grammar.* object(ive). **2.** objection.
object[1] ('ɒbdʒɪkt) *n.* **1.** a tangible and visible thing. **2.** a person or thing seen as a focus or target for feelings, thought, etc.: *an object of affection.* **3.** an aim, purpose, or objective. **4.** *Informal.* a ridiculous or pitiable person, spectacle, etc. **5.** *Philosophy.* that towards which cognition is directed, as contrasted with the thinking subject; anything regarded as external to the mind, esp. in the external world. **6.** *Grammar.* a noun, pronoun, or noun phrase whose referent is the recipient of the action of a verb. See also **direct object, indirect object.** **7.** *Grammar.* a noun, pronoun, or noun phrase that is governed by a preposition. **8.** **no object.** not a hindrance or obstacle: *money is no object.* [C14: from Late Latin *objectus* something thrown before (the mind), from Latin *obicere;* see OBJECT[2]]
object[2] (əb'dʒɛkt) *vb.* **1.** (*tr.; takes a clause as object*) to state as an objection: *he objected that his motives had been good.* **2.** (*intr.;* often foll. by *to*) to raise or state an objection (to); present an argument (against). [C15: from Latin *obicere,* from *ob-* against + *jacere* to throw]
object ball *n. Billiards, etc.* any ball except the cue ball, esp. one which the striker aims to hit with the cue ball.
object glass *n. Optics.* another name for **objective** (sense 11).
objectify (əb'dʒɛktɪˌfaɪ) *vb.* **-fies, -fying, -fied.** (*tr.*) to represent concretely; present as an object. —**obˌjectifi'cation** *n.*
objection (əb'dʒɛkʃən) *n.* **1.** an expression, statement, or feeling of opposition or dislike. **2.** a cause for such an expression, statement, or feeling. **3.** the act of objecting.
objectionable (əb'dʒɛkʃənəbᵊl) *adj.* unpleasant, offensive, or repugnant. —**obˌjectiona'bility** *or* **ob'jectionableness** *n.* —**ob'jectionably** *adv.*
objective (əb'dʒɛktɪv) *adj.* **1.** existing independently of perception or an individual's conceptions: *are there objective moral values?* **2.** undistorted by emotion or personal bias. **3.** of or relating to actual and external phenomena as opposed to thoughts, feelings, etc. **4.** *Med.* (of disease symptoms) perceptible to persons other than the individual affected. **5.** *Grammar.* denoting a case of nouns and pronouns, esp. in languages having only two cases, that is used to identify the direct object of a finite verb or preposition and for various other purposes. In English the objective case of pronouns is also used in many elliptical constructions (as in *Poor me! Who, him?*), as the subject of a gerund (as in *It was me helping him*), informally as a predicate complement (as in *It's me*), and in nonstandard use as part of a compound subject (as in *John, Larry, and me went fishing*). See also **accusative.** **6.** of, or relating to a goal or aim. ~*n.* **7.** the object of one's endeavours; goal; aim. **8.** Also called: **objective point.** *Military.* a place or position towards which forces are directed. **9.** an actual phenomenon; reality. **10.** *Grammar.* **a.** the objective case. **b.** a word or speech element in the objective case. **11.** Also called: **object glass.** *Optics.* **a.** the lens or combination of lenses nearest to the object in an optical instrument. **b.** the lens or combination of lenses forming the image in a camera or projector. ~Abbrev.: **obj.** Compare **subjective.** —**objectival** (ˌɒbdʒɛk'taɪvəl) *adj.* —**ob'jectively** *adv.* —ˌ**objec'tivity** *or* (*less commonly*) **ob'jectiveness** *n.*
objective danger *n. Mountaineering.* a danger, such as a stone fall or avalanche, to which climbing skill is irrelevant.
objective genitive *n. Grammar.* a use of the genitive case to express an objective relationship, as in Latin *timor mortis* (fear of death).
objective point *n. Military.* another term for **objective** (sense 8).
objective test *n.* a test, such as one using multiple-choice questions, in which the feelings or opinions of the person marking it cannot affect the marks given.
objectivism (əb'dʒɛktɪˌvɪzəm) *n.* **1.** the tendency to stress what is objective. **2.** *Philosophy.* **a.** the meta-ethical doctrine that there are certain moral truths that are independent of the attitudes of any individuals. **b.** the philosophical doctrine that reality is objective, and that sense data correspond with it. —**ob'jectivist** *n., adj.* —**obˌjectiv'istic** *adj.* —**obˌjectiv'istically** *adv.*
object language *n.* a language described by or being investigated by another language. Compare **metalanguage.**
object lesson *n.* **1.** a convincing demonstration of some principle or ideal. **2.** (esp. formerly) a lesson in which a material object forms the basis of the teaching and is available to be inspected.
object program *n.* a computer program translated from the equivalent source program into machine language by the compiler or assembler.
object relations theory *n.* a form of psychoanalytic theory postulating that people relate to others in order to develop themselves.
objet d'art *French.* (ɔbʒɛ dar) *n., pl.* ***objets d'art*** (ɔbʒɛ dar). a small object considered to be of artistic worth. [French: object of art]
objet de vertu (ɒb'ʒeɪ də vɜː'tuː) *n., pl.* **objets de vertu** (ɒb'ʒeɪ də vɜː'tuː). another name for **object of virtu:** see **virtu.** [French, coined by the British as a translation of *object of virtu* but literally meaning only "object of virtue"]
objet trouvé *French.* (ɔbʒɛ truve) *n., pl.* ***objets trouvés*** (ɔbʒɛ truve). any ordinary object considered from an aesthetic viewpoint. [C20: French: found object]
objure (ɒb'dʒʊə) *vb. Rare.* **1.** (*tr.*) to put on oath. **2.** (*intr.*) to swear. [C17: from Latin *objūrāre* to bind by oath] —ˌ**obju'ration** *n.*
objurgate ('ɒbdʒəˌgeɪt) *vb.* (*tr.*) to scold or reprimand. [C17: from Latin *objurgāre,* from *ob-* against + *jurgāre* to scold] —ˌ**objur'gation** *n.* —'**objurˌgator** *n.* —**objurgatory** (ɒb'dʒɜːgətərɪ, -trɪ) *or* **ob'jurgative** *adj.*
obl. *abbrev. for:* **1.** oblique. **2.** oblong.
oblanceolate (ɒb'lɑːnsɪəlɪt, -ˌleɪt) *adj. Botany.* (esp. of leaves) having a broad rounded apex and a tapering base.
oblast ('ɒblɑːst) *n.* an administrative and territorial division in some republics of the former Soviet Union. [from Russian, from Old Slavonic, *vlast* government]
oblate[1] ('ɒbleɪt) *adj.* having an equatorial diameter of greater length than the polar diameter: *the earth is an oblate sphere.* Compare **prolate.** [C18: from New Latin *oblātus* lengthened, from Latin *ob-* towards + *lātus,* past participle of *ferre* to bring] —'**oblately** *adv.*
oblate[2] ('ɒbleɪt) *n.* a person dedicated to a monastic or religious life. [C19: from French *oblat,* from Medieval Latin *oblātus,* from Latin *offerre* to OFFER]
oblation (ɒ'bleɪʃən) *n. Christianity.* **1.** the offering of the bread and wine of the Eucharist to God. **2.** any offering made for religious or charitable purposes. [C15: from Church Latin *oblātiō;* see OBLATE[2]] —**oblatory** ('ɒblətərɪ, -trɪ) *or* **ob'lational** *adj.*
obligate ('ɒblɪˌgeɪt) *vb.* **1.** to compel, constrain, or oblige morally or legally. **2.** (in the U.S.) to bind (property, funds, etc.) as security. ~*adj.* **3.** compelled, bound, or restricted. **4.** *Biology.* able to exist under only one set of environmental conditions: *an obligate parasite cannot live independently of its host.* Compare **facultative** (sense 4). [C16: from Latin *obligāre* to OBLIGE] —'**obligable** *adj.* —**ob'ligative** *adj.* —'**obliˌgator** *n.*
obligation (ˌɒblɪ'geɪʃən) *n.* **1.** a moral or legal requirement; duty. **2.** the act of obligating or the state of being obligated. **3.** *Law.* a legally enforceable agreement to perform some act, esp. to pay money, for the benefit of another party. **4.** *Law.* **a.** a written contract containing a penalty. **b.** an instrument acknowledging indebtedness to secure the repayment of money borrowed. **5.** a person or thing to which one is bound morally or legally. **6.**

something owed in return for a service or favour. 7. a service or favour for which one is indebted. —ˌobliˈgational *adj.*

obligato (ˌɒblɪˈgɑːtəʊ) *adj., n. Music.* a variant spelling of **obbligato.**

obligatory (ɒˈblɪgətərɪ, -trɪ) *adj.* 1. required to be done, obtained, possessed, etc. 2. of the nature of or constituting an obligation. —**obˈligatorily** *adv.*

oblige (əˈblaɪdʒ) *vb.* 1. (*tr.; often passive*) to bind or constrain (someone to do something) by legal, moral, or physical means. 2. (*tr.; usually passive*) to make indebted or grateful (to someone) by doing a favour or service: *we are obliged to you for dinner.* 3. to do a service or favour to (someone): *she obliged the guest with a song.* [C13: from Old French *obliger,* from Latin *obligāre,* from *ob-* to, towards + *ligāre* to bind] —**oˈbliger** *n.*

obligee (ˌɒblɪˈdʒiː) *n.* 1. a person in whose favour an obligation, contract, or bond is created; creditor. 2. a person who receives a bond.

obligement (əˈblaɪdʒmənt) *n. Now chiefly Scot.* a kind helpful action; favour.

obliging (əˈblaɪdʒɪŋ) *adj.* ready to do favours; agreeable; kindly. —**oˈbligingly** *adv.* —**oˈbligingness** *n.*

obligor (ˌɒblɪˈgɔː) *n.* 1. a person who binds himself by contract to perform some obligation; debtor. 2. a person who gives a bond.

oblique (əˈbliːk) *adj.* 1. at an angle; slanting; sloping. 2. *Geometry.* a. (of lines, planes, etc.) neither perpendicular nor parallel to one another or to another line, plane, etc. b. not related to or containing a right angle. 3. indirect or evasive. 4. *Grammar.* denoting any case of nouns, pronouns, etc., other than the nominative and vocative. 5. *Biology.* having asymmetrical sides or planes: *an oblique leaf.* 6. (of a map projection) constituting a type of zenithal projection in which the plane of projection is tangential to the earth's surface at some point between the equator and the poles. ~*n.* 7. something oblique, esp. a line. 8. another name for **solidus** (sense 1). 9. *Navigation.* the act of changing course by less than 90°. 10. an aerial photograph taken at an oblique angle. ~*vb.* (*intr.*) 11. to take or have an oblique direction. 12. (of a military formation) to move forward at an angle. [C15: from Old French, from Latin *oblīquus,* of obscure origin] —**oˈbliquely** *adv.* —**oˈbliqueness** *n.*

oblique angle *n.* an angle that is not a right angle or any multiple of a right angle.

oblique fault *n.* a fault that runs obliquely to, rather than parallel to or perpendicular to, the strike of the affected rocks.

oblique sailing *n.* a ship's movement on a course that is not due north, south, east, or west.

oblique-slip fault *n.* a fault on which the movement is along both the strike and the dip of the fault.

obliquity (əˈblɪkwɪtɪ) *n., pl.* **-ties.** 1. the state or condition of being oblique. 2. a deviation from the perpendicular or horizontal. 3. a moral or mental deviation. 4. Also called: **obliquity of the ecliptic.** *Astronomy.* the angle between the plane of the earth's orbit and that of the celestial equator, equal to approximately 23° 27′ at present. —**oˈbliquitous** *adj.*

obliterate (əˈblɪtəˌreɪt) *vb.* (*tr.*) to destroy every trace of; wipe out completely. [C16: from Latin *oblitterāre* to erase, from *ob-* out + *littera* letter] —**oˌbliteˈration** *n.* —**oˈbliterative** *adj.* —**oˈbliterˌator** *n.*

oblivion (əˈblɪvɪən) *n.* 1. the condition of being forgotten or disregarded. 2. the state of being mentally withdrawn or blank. 3. *Law.* an intentional overlooking, esp. of political offences; amnesty; pardon. [C14: via Old French from Latin *oblīviō* forgetfulness, from *oblīviscī* to forget]

oblivious (əˈblɪvɪəs) *adj.* (usually foll. by *of*) unaware or forgetful. —**obˈliviously** *adv.* —**obˈliviousness** *n.*

oblong (ˈɒbˌlɒŋ) *adj.* 1. having an elongated, esp. rectangular, shape. ~*n.* 2. a figure or object having this shape. [C15: from Latin *oblongus,* from *ob-* (intensive) + *longus* LONG[1]]

obloquy (ˈɒbləkwɪ) *n., pl.* **-quies.** 1. defamatory or censorious statements, esp. when directed against one person. 2. disgrace brought about by public abuse. [C15: from Latin *obloquium* contradiction, from *ob-* against + *loquī* to speak]

obmutescence (ˌɒbmjuːˈtɛsəns) *n. Archaic.* persistent silence. [C17: from Latin *obmūtescere* to become mute] —ˌ**obmuˈtescent** *adj.*

obnoxious (əbˈnɒkʃəs) *adj.* 1. extremely unpleasant. 2. *Obsolete.* exposed to harm, injury, etc. [C16: from Latin *obnoxius,* from *ob-* to + *noxa* injury, from *nocēre* to harm] —**obˈnoxiously** *adv.* —**obˈnoxiousness** *n.*

obnubilate (ɒbˈnjuːbɪˌleɪt) *vb.* (*tr.*) *Literary.* to darken or obscure. [C16: ultimately from Latin *obnūbilāre* to cover with clouds, from *nubes* cloud]

oboe (ˈəʊbəʊ) *n.* 1. a woodwind instrument of the family that includes the bassoon and cor anglais, consisting of a conical tube fitted with a mouthpiece having a double reed. It has a penetrating nasal tone. Range: about two octaves plus a sixth upwards from B flat below middle C. 2. a person who plays this instrument in an orchestra: *second oboe.* ~Archaic form: **hautboy.** [C18: via Italian *oboe,* phonetic approximation to French *haut bois,* literally: high wood (referring to its pitch)] —**ˈoboist** *n.*

oboe da caccia (də ˈkætʃə) *n.* a member of the oboe family; the predecessor of the cor anglais. [Italian: hunting oboe]

oboe d'amore (dɑːˈmɔːreɪ) *n.* a type of oboe pitched a minor third lower than the oboe itself. It is used chiefly in the performance of baroque music.

obolus (ˈɒbələs) *or* **obol** (ˈɒbɒl) *n., pl.* **-li** (-ˌlaɪ) *or* **-ols.** 1. a modern Greek unit of weight equal to one tenth of a gram. 2. a silver coin of ancient Greece worth one sixth of a drachma. [C16: via Latin from Greek *obolos* small coin, nail; related to *obelos* spit, variant of OBELUS]

obovate (ɒbˈəʊveɪt) *adj.* (of a leaf or similar flat part) shaped like the longitudinal section of an egg with the narrower end at the base; inversely ovate.

obovoid (ɒbˈəʊvɔɪd) *adj.* (of a fruit or similar solid part) egg-shaped with the narrower end at the base. Compare **ovoid** (sense 2).

obreption (ɒˈbrɛpʃən) *n. Now rare.* the obtaining of something, such as a gift, in Scots Law esp. a grant from the Crown, by giving false information. Compare **subreption** (sense 1). [C17: from Latin *obreptio,* from *obrepere* to creep up to]

obs. *abbrev. for:* 1. obscure. 2. observation. 3. Also: **Obs.** observatory. 4. obsolete.

obscene (əbˈsiːn) *adj.* 1. offensive or outrageous to accepted standards of decency or modesty. 2. *Law.* (of publications) having a tendency to deprave or corrupt. 3. disgusting; repellent: *an obscene massacre.* [C16: from Latin *obscēnus* inauspicious, perhaps related to *caenum* filth] —**obˈscenely** *adv.*

obscenity (əbˈsɛnɪtɪ) *n., pl.* **-ties.** 1. the state or quality of being obscene. 2. an obscene act, statement, work, etc.

obscurant (əbˈskjʊərənt) *n.* 1. an opposer of reform and enlightenment. ~*adj.* 2. of or relating to an obscurant. 3. causing obscurity. —ˌ**obscuˈrantism** *n.* —ˌ**obscuˈrantist** *n., adj.*

obscure (əbˈskjʊə) *adj.* 1. unclear or abstruse. 2. indistinct, vague, or indefinite. 3. inconspicuous or unimportant. 4. hidden, secret, or remote. 5. (of a vowel) reduced to or transformed into a neutral vowel (ə). 6. gloomy, dark, clouded, or dim. ~*vb.* (*tr.*) 7. to make unclear, vague, or hidden. 8. to cover or cloud over. 9. *Phonetics.* to pronounce (a vowel) with articulation that causes it to become a neutral sound represented by (ə). ~*n.* 10. a rare word for **obscurity.** [C14: via Old French from Latin *obscūrus* dark] —**obscuration** (ˌɒbskjʊˈreɪʃən) *n.* —**obˈscurely** *adv.* —**obˈscureness** *n.*

obscurity (əbˈskjʊərɪtɪ) *n., pl.* **-ties.** 1. the state or quality of being obscure. 2. an obscure person or thing.

obscurum per obscurius (əbˈskjʊərəm pɜː əbˈskjʊərɪəs) *n.* another term for **ignotum per ignotius.** [Latin: the obscure by the more obscure]

obsecrate (ˈɒbsɪˌkreɪt) *vb.* (*tr.*) a rare word for **beseech.** [C16: from Latin *obsecrāre* to entreat (in the name of the gods), from *ob-* for the sake of + *sacrāre* to hold in reverence; see SACRED] —ˌ**obseˈcration** *n.*

obsequent (ˈɒbsɪkwənt) *adj.* (of a river) flowing into a subsequent stream in the opposite direction to the original slope of the land. [C16 (in the obsolete sense: yielding): from Latin *obsequī,* from *sequī* to follow]

obsequies (ˈɒbsɪkwɪz) *pl. n., sing.* **-quy.** funeral rites. [C14: via Anglo-Norman from Medieval Latin *obsequiae* (influenced by Latin *exsequiae*), from *obsequium* compliance] —**obsequial** (ɒbˈsiːkwɪəl) *adj.*

obsequious (əbˈsiːkwɪəs) *adj.* 1. obedient or attentive in an ingratiating or servile manner. 2. *Now rare.* submissive or compliant. [C15: from Latin *obsequiōsus* compliant, from *obsequium* compliance, from *obsequi* to follow, from *ob-* to + *sequi* to follow] —**obˈsequiously** *adv.* —**obˈsequiousness** *n.*

observance (əbˈzɜːvəns) *n.* 1. recognition of or compliance with a law, custom, practice, etc. 2. the act of such recognition. 3. a ritual, ceremony, or practice, esp. of a religion. 4. observation or attention. 5. the degree of strictness of a religious order or community in following its rule. 6. *Archaic.* respectful or deferential attention.

observant (əbˈzɜːvənt) *adj.* 1. paying close attention to detail; watchful or heedful. 2. adhering strictly to rituals, ceremonies, laws, etc. —**obˈservantly** *adv.*

observation (ˌɒbzəˈveɪʃən) *n.* 1. the act of observing or the state of being observed. 2. a comment or remark. 3. detailed examination of phenomena prior to analysis, diagnosis, or interpretation: *the patient was under observation.* 4. the facts learned from observing. 5. an obsolete word for **observance.** 6. *Navigation.* a. a sight taken with an instrument to determine the position of an observer relative to that of a given heavenly body. b. the data so taken. —ˌ**obserˈvational** *adj.* —ˌ**obserˈvationally** *adv.*

observation car *n.* a railway carriage fitted with large expanses of glass to provide a good view of the scenery.

observation post *n. Military.* a position from which observations can be made or from which fire can be directed.

observatory (əbˈzɜːvətərɪ, -trɪ) *n., pl.* **-ries.** 1. an institution or building specially designed and equipped for observing meteorological and astronomical phenomena. 2. any building or structure providing an extensive view of its surroundings.

observe (əbˈzɜːv) *vb.* 1. (*tr.; may take a clause as object*) to see; perceive; notice: *we have observed that you steal.* 2. (when *tr., may take a clause as object*) to watch (something) carefully; pay attention to (something). 3. to make observations of (something), esp. scientific ones. 4. (when *intr.,* usually foll. by *on* or *upon;* when *tr., may take a clause as object*) to make a comment or remark: *the speaker observed that times had changed.* **5.** (*tr.*) to abide by, keep, or follow (a custom, tradition, law, holiday, etc.). [C14: via Old French from Latin *observāre*, from *ob-* to + *servāre* to watch] —**ob'servable** *adj.* —**ob'servableness** *or* **ob,serv-a'bility** *n.* —**ob'servably** *adv.*

observer (əb'zɜːvə) *n.* **1.** a person or thing that observes. **2.** a person who attends a conference solely to note the proceedings. **3.** a person trained to identify aircraft, esp., formerly, a member of an aircrew.

obsess (əb'sɛs) *vb.* (*tr.*; when passive, foll. by *with* or *by*) to preoccupy completely; haunt. [C16: from Latin *obsessus* besieged, past participle of *obsidēre*, from *ob-* in front of + *sedēre* to sit] —**ob'sessive** *adj.* —**ob'sessively** *adv.* —**ob'sessiveness** *n.*

obsession (əb'sɛʃən) *n.* **1.** *Psychiatry.* a persistent idea or impulse that continually forces its way into consciousness, often associated with anxiety and mental illness. **2.** a persistent preoccupation, idea, or feeling. **3.** the act of obsessing or the state of being obsessed. —**ob'sessional** *adj.* —**ob'sessionally** *adv.*

obsessive-compulsive neurosis *n.* *Psychiatry.* a neurosis in which the patient is driven to repeat the same act, such as washing his hands, over and over again, usually for many hours.

obsidian (ɒb'sɪdɪən) *n.* a dark glassy volcanic rock formed by very rapid solidification of lava. Also called: **Iceland agate.** [C17: from Latin *obsidiānus*, erroneous transcription of *obsiānus* (*lapis*) (stone of) *Obsius*, the name (according to the Roman writer Pliny) of the discoverer of a stone resembling obsidian]

obsolesce (,ɒbsə'lɛs) *vb.* (*intr.*) to become obsolete.

obsolescent (,ɒbsə'lɛsᵊnt) *adj.* becoming obsolete or out of date. [C18: from Latin *obsolescere*; see OBSOLETE] —**,obso'lescence** *n.* —**,obso'lescently** *adv.*

obsolete ('ɒbsə,liːt, ,ɒbsə'liːt) *adj.* **1.** out of use or practice; not current. **2.** out of date; unfashionable or outmoded. **3.** *Biology.* (of parts, organs, etc.) vestigial; rudimentary. [C16: from Latin *obsolētus* worn out, past participle of *obsolēre* (unattested), from *ob-* opposite to + *solēre* to be used] —**'obso,letely** *adv.* —**'obso,leteness** *n.*

obstacle ('ɒbstəkᵊl) *n.* **1.** a person or thing that opposes or hinders something. **2.** *Brit.* a fence or hedge used in showjumping. [C14: via Old French from Latin *obstāculum*, from *obstāre*, from *ob-* against + *stāre* to stand]

obstacle race *n.* a race in which competitors have to negotiate various obstacles.

obstet. *abbrev. for* obstetric(s).

obstetric (ɒb'stɛtrɪk) *or* **obstetrical** *adj.* of or relating to childbirth or obstetrics. [C18: via New Latin from Latin *obstetrīcius*, from *obstetrix* a midwife, literally: woman who stands opposite, from *obstāre* to stand in front of; see OBSTACLE] —**ob'stetrically** *adv.*

obstetrician (,ɒbste'trɪʃən) *n.* a physician who specializes in obstetrics.

obstetrics (ɒb'stɛtrɪks) *n.* (*functioning as sing.*) the branch of medicine concerned with childbirth and the treatment of women before and after childbirth.

obstinacy ('ɒbstɪnəsɪ) *n., pl.* **-cies. 1.** the state or quality of being obstinate. **2.** an obstinate act, attitude, etc.

obstinate ('ɒbstɪnɪt) *adj.* **1.** adhering fixedly to a particular opinion, attitude, course of action, etc. **2.** self-willed or headstrong. **3.** difficult to subdue or alleviate; persistent: *an obstinate fever.* [C14: from Latin *obstinātus*, past participle of *obstināre* to persist in, from *ob-* (intensive) + *stin-*, variant of *stare* to stand] —**'obstinately** *adv.*

obstipation (,ɒbstɪ'peɪʃən) *n.* *Pathol.* a severe form of constipation, usually resulting from obstruction of the intestinal tract. [C16: from Latin *obstīpātiō*, from *ob-* (intensive) + *stīpāre* to press together]

obstreperous (əb'strɛpərəs) *adj.* noisy or rough, esp. in resisting restraint or control. [C16: from Latin, from *obstrepere*, from *ob-* against + *strepere* to roar] —**ob'streperously** *adv.* —**ob'streperousness** *n.*

obstruct (əb'strʌkt) *vb.* (*tr.*) **1.** to block (a road, passageway, etc.) with an obstacle. **2.** to make (progress or activity) difficult. **3.** to impede or block a clear view of. [C17: from Latin: built against, past participle of *obstruere*, from *ob-* against + *struere* to build] —**ob'structor** *n.* —**ob'structive** *adj., n.* —**ob'structively** *adv.* —**ob'structiveness** *n.*

obstruction (əb'strʌkʃən) *n.* **1.** a person or thing that obstructs. **2.** the act or an instance of obstructing. **3.** delay of business, esp. in a legislature by means of procedural devices. **4.** *Sport.* the act of unfairly impeding an opposing player. **5.** the state or condition of being obstructed. —**ob'structional** *adj.* —**ob'structionally** *adv.*

obstructionist (əb'strʌkʃənɪst) *n.* **a.** a person who deliberately obstructs business, esp. in a legislature. **b.** (*as modifier*): *obstructionist tactics.* —**ob'structionism** *n.*

obstruent ('ɒbstrʊənt) *Med.* ~*adj.* **1.** causing obstruction, esp. of the intestinal tract. ~*n.* **2.** anything that causes obstruction. [C17: from Latin *obstruere* to OBSTRUCT]

obtain (əb'teɪn) *vb.* **1.** (*tr.*) to gain possession of; acquire; get. **2.** (*intr.*) to be customary, valid, or accepted: *a new law obtains in this case.* **3.** (*tr.*) *Archaic.* to arrive at. **4.** (*intr.*) *Archaic.* to win a victory; succeed. [C15: via Old French from Latin *obtinēre* to take hold of, from *ob-* (intensive) + *tenēre* to hold] —**ob'tainable** *adj.* —**ob,taina'bility** *n.* —**ob'tainer** *n.* —**ob'tainment** *n.*

obtaining by deception *n.* *Law.* the offence of dishonestly obtaining the property of another by some deception or misrepresentation of facts.

obtect (ɒb'tɛkt) *adj.* (of a pupa) encased in a hardened secretion so that the wings, legs, etc., are held immovably to the body, as in butterflies. Also: **ob'tected.** [C19: from Latin *obtectus* covered, past participle of *obtegere*, from *ob-* (intensive) + *tegere* to cover]

obtest (ɒb'tɛst) *vb.* *Rare.* **1.** (*tr.*; *may take a clause as object or an infinitive*) to beg (someone) earnestly. **2.** (when *tr.*, *takes a clause as object*; when *intr.*, may be foll. by *with* or *against*) to object; protest. **3.** (*tr.*) to call (a supernatural power) to witness. [C16: from Latin *obtestārī* to protest, from *ob-* to + *testārī* to bear or call as witness] —**,obtes'tation** *n.*

obtrude (əb'truːd) *vb.* **1.** to push (oneself, one's opinions, etc.) on others in an unwelcome way. **2.** (*tr.*) to push out or forward. [C16: from Latin *obtrūdere*, from *ob-* against + *trūdere* to push forward] —**ob'truder** *n.* —**obtrusion** (əb'truːʒən) *n.*

obtrusive (əb'truːsɪv) *adj.* **1.** obtruding or tending to obtrude. **2.** sticking out; protruding; noticeable. —**ob'trusively** *adv.* —**ob'trusiveness** *n.*

obtund (ɒb'tʌnd) *vb.* (*tr.*) *Rare.* to deaden or dull. [C14: from Latin *obtundere* to beat against, from *ob-* against + *tundere* to belabour] —**ob'tundent** *adj., n.*

obturate ('ɒbtjʊə,reɪt) *vb.* (*tr.*) to stop up (an opening, esp. the breech of a gun). [C17: from Latin *obtūrāre* to block up, of obscure origin] —**,obtu'ration** *n.* —**'obtu,rator** *n.*

obtuse (əb'tjuːs) *adj.* **1.** mentally slow or emotionally insensitive. **2.** *Maths.* **a.** (of an angle) lying between 90° and 180°. **b.** (of a triangle) having one interior angle greater than 90°. **3.** not sharp or pointed. **4.** indistinctly felt, heard, etc.; dull: *obtuse pain.* **5.** (of a leaf or similar flat part) having a rounded or blunt tip. [C16: from Latin *obtūsus* dulled, past participle of *obtundere* to beat down; see OBTUND] —**ob'tusely** *adv.* —**ob'tuseness** *n.*

obverse ('ɒbvɜːs) *adj.* **1.** facing or turned towards the observer. **2.** forming or serving as a counterpart. **3.** (of certain plant leaves) narrower at the base than at the top. ~*n.* **4.** a counterpart or complement. **5.** the side of a coin that bears the main design or device. Compare **reverse** (sense 15). **6.** *Logic.* a categorial proposition derived from another by replacing the original predicate by its negation and changing the proposition from affirmative to negative or vice versa, as *no sum is correct* from *every sum is incorrect.* [C17: from Latin *obversus* turned towards, past participle of *obvertere*, from *ob-* to + *vertere* to turn] —**ob'versely** *adv.*

obvert (ɒb'vɜːt) *vb.* (*tr.*) **1.** *Logic.* to deduce the obverse of (a proposition). **2.** *Rare.* to turn so as to show the main or other side. [C17: from Latin *obvertere* to turn towards; see OBVERSE] —**ob'version** *n.*

obviate ('ɒbvɪ,eɪt) *vb.* (*tr.*) to do away with or counter. [C16: from Late Latin *obviātus* prevented, past participle of *obviāre*; see OBVIOUS] —**,obvi'ation** *n.*

obvious ('ɒbvɪəs) *adj.* **1.** easy to see or understand; evident. **2.** exhibiting motives, feelings, intentions, etc., clearly or without subtlety. **3.** naive or unsubtle: *the play was rather obvious.* **4.** *Obsolete.* being or standing in the way. [C16: from Latin *obvius*, from *obviam* in the way, from *ob-* against + *via* way] —**'obviously** *adv.* —**'obviousness** *n.*

obvolute ('ɒbvə,luːt) *adj.* **1.** (of leaves or petals in the bud) folded so that the margins overlap each other. **2.** turned in or rolled. [C18: from Latin *obvolūtus* past participle of *obvolvere*, from *ob-* to, over + *volvere* to roll] —**,obvo'lution** *n.* —**'obvo,lutive** *adj.*

OC *abbrev. for* Officer Commanding.

Oc. *abbrev. for* Ocean.

o/c *abbrev. for* overcharge.

oca ('əʊkə) *n.* any of various South American herbaceous plants of the genus *Oxalis*, cultivated for their edible tubers: family *Oxalidaceae.* [C20: via Spanish from Quechua *okka*]

OCAM (in Africa) *abbrev. for* Organisation commune africaine et malgache. [French: African and Malagasy Common Organization]

ocarina (,ɒkə'riːnə) *n.* an egg-shaped wind instrument with a protruding mouthpiece and six to eight finger holes, producing an almost pure tone. Also called (U.S. informal): **sweet potato.** [C19: from Italian: little goose, from *oca* goose, ultimately from Latin *avis* bird]

Occam's razor ('ɒkəmz) *n.* a variant spelling of **Ockham's razor.**

occas. *abbrev. for* occasional(ly).

occasion (ə'keɪʒən) *n.* **1.** (sometimes foll. by *of*) the time of a particular happening or event. **2.** (sometimes foll. by *for*) a reason or cause (to do or be something); grounds: *there was no occasion to complain.* **3.** an opportunity (to do something); chance. **4.** a special event, time, or celebration: *the party was quite an occasion.* **5. on occasion.** every so often. **6. rise to the occasion.** to have the courage, wit, etc., to meet the special demands of a situation. **7. take occasion.** to avail oneself of an opportunity (to do something). ~*vb.* **8.** (*tr.*) to bring about, esp. incidentally or by chance. ~See also **occasions.** [C14: from Latin *occāsiō* a falling down, from *occidere*, from *ob-* down + *cadere* to fall]

occasional (əˈkeɪʒənᵊl) *adj.* **1.** taking place from time to time; not frequent or regular. **2.** of, for, or happening on special occasions. **3.** serving as an occasion (for something).
occasionalism (əˈkeɪʒənəˌlɪzəm) *n.* the post-Cartesian theory that the seeming interconnection of mind and matter is effected by God.
occasional licence *n. Brit.* a licence granted to sell alcohol only at specified times.
occasionally (əˈkeɪʒənəlɪ) *adv.* from time to time.
occasional table *n.* a small table with no regular use.
occasions (əˈkeɪʒənz) *pl. n. Archaic.* **1.** (*sometimes sing.*) needs; necessities. **2.** personal or business affairs.
occident (ˈɒksɪdənt) *n.* a literary or formal word for **west.** Compare **orient.** [C14: via Old French from Latin *occidere* to fall, go down (with reference to the setting sun); see OCCASION] —ˌ**occiˈdental** *adj.*
Occident (ˈɒksɪdənt) *n.* (usually preceded by *the*) **1.** the countries of Europe and America. **2.** the western hemisphere. —ˌ**Occiˈdental** *adj., n.* —ˌ**Occiˈdentalism** *n.* —ˌ**Occiˈdentalist** *n., adj.* —ˌ**Occiˈdentally** *adv.*
Occidentalize *or* **Occidentalise** (ˌɒksɪˈdɛntəˌlaɪz) *vb.* to make or become Occidental. —ˌ**Occiˌdentaliˈzation** *or* ˌ**Occiˌdentaliˈsation** *n.*
occipital (ɒkˈsɪpɪtᵊl) *adj.* **1.** of or relating to the back of the head or skull. ~*n.* **2.** short for **occipital bone.**
occipital bone *n.* the saucer-shaped bone that forms the back part of the skull and part of its base.
occipital lobe *n.* the posterior portion of each cerebral hemisphere, concerned with the interpretation of visual sensory impulses.
occiput (ˈɒksɪˌpʌt, -pət) *n., pl.* **occiputs** *or* **occipita** (ɒkˈsɪpɪtə). the back part of the head or skull. [C14: from Latin, from *ob-* at the back of + *caput* head]
occlude (əˈkluːd) *vb.* **1.** (*tr.*) to block or stop up (a passage or opening); obstruct. **2.** (*tr.*) to prevent the passage of. **3.** (*tr.*) *Chem.* (of a solid) to incorporate (a substance) by absorption or adsorption. **4.** *Meteorol.* to form or cause to form an occluded front. **5.** *Dentistry.* to produce or cause to produce occlusion, as in chewing. [C16: from Latin *occlūdere,* from *ob-* (intensive) + *claudere* to close] —**ocˈcludent** *adj.*
occluded front *n. Meteorol.* the line or plane occurring where the cold front of a depression has overtaken the warm front, raising the warm sector from ground level. Also called: **occlusion.**
occlusion (əˈkluːʒən) *n.* **1.** the act or process of occluding or the state of being occluded. **2.** *Meteorol.* another term for **occluded front.** **3.** *Dentistry.* the normal position of the teeth when the jaws are closed. **4.** *Phonetics.* the complete closure of the vocal tract at some point, as in the closure prior to the articulation of a plosive. —**occlusal** (əˈkluːsəl) *adj.*
occlusive (əˈkluːsɪv) *adj.* **1.** of or relating to the act of occlusion. ~*n.* **2.** *Phonetics.* an occlusive speech sound. —**ocˈclusiveness** *n.*
occult *adj.* (ɒˈkʌlt, ˈɒkʌlt). **1. a.** of or characteristic of magical, mystical, or supernatural arts, phenomena, or influences. **b.** (*as n.*): *the occult.* **2.** beyond ordinary human understanding. **3.** secret or esoteric. ~*vb.* (ɒˈkʌlt). **4.** *Astronomy.* (of a celestial body) to hide (another celestial body) from view by occultation or (of a celestial body) to become hidden by occultation. **5.** to hide or become hidden or shut off from view. **6.** (*intr.*) (of lights, esp. in lighthouses) to shut off at regular intervals. [C16: from Latin *occultus,* past participle of *occulere,* from *ob-* over, up + *-culere,* related to *celāre* to conceal] —**ocˈcultly** *adv.* —**ocˈcultness** *n.*
occultation (ˌɒkʌlˈteɪʃən) *n.* **1.** the temporary disappearance of one celestial body as it moves out of sight behind another body. **2.** the act of occulting or the state of being occulted.
occultism (ˈɒkʌlˌtɪzəm) *n.* belief in and the study and practice of magic, astrology, etc. —**ˈoccultist** *n., adj.*
occupancy (ˈɒkjʊpənsɪ) *n., pl.* **-cies. 1.** the act of occupying; possession of a property. **2.** *Law.* the possession and use of property by or without agreement and without any claim to ownership. **3.** *Law.* the act of taking possession of unowned property, esp. land, with the intent of thus acquiring ownership. **4.** the condition or fact of being an occupant, esp. a tenant. **5.** the period of time during which one is an occupant, esp. of property.
occupant (ˈɒkjʊpənt) *n.* **1.** a person, thing, etc., holding a position or place. **2.** *Law.* a person who has possession of something, esp. an estate, house, etc.; tenant. **3.** *Law.* a person who acquires by occupancy the title to something previously without an owner.
occupation (ˌɒkjʊˈpeɪʃən) *n.* **1.** a person's regular work or profession; job or principal activity. **2.** any activity on which time is spent by a person. **3.** the act of occupying or the state of being occupied. **4.** the control of a country by a foreign military power. **5.** the period of time that a nation, place, or position is occupied. **6.** (*modifier*) for the use of the occupier of a particular property: *occupation road; occupation bridge.*
occupational (ˌɒkjʊˈpeɪʃənᵊl) *adj.* of, relating to, or caused by an occupation: *an occupational pension scheme; an occupational disease.* —ˌ**occuˈpationally** *adv.*
occupational pension *n.* a pension derived from a private pension scheme organized by the employer or employers for whom the recipient used to work: distinguished from a state pension financed from national insurance.
occupational pension scheme *n.* a pension scheme provided for the members of a particular occupation or employed by a specific employer or group of employers.
occupational psychology *n. Psychol.* the study of human behaviour at work, including ergonomics, selection procedures, and the effects of stress.
occupational therapy *n. Med.* treatment of people with physical, emotional, or social problems, using purposeful activity to help them overcome or learn to deal with their problems. —**occupational therapist** *n.*
occupation franchise *n. Brit.* the right of a tenant to vote in national and local elections.
occupation groupings *pl. n.* a system of classifying people according to occupation, based originally on information obtained by government census and subsequently developed by market research. The classifications are used by the advertising industry to identify potential markets. The groups are **A, B, C1, C2, D,** and **E.**
occupier (ˈɒkjʊˌpaɪə) *n.* **1.** *Brit.* a person who is in possession or occupation of a house or land. **2.** a person or thing that occupies.
occupy (ˈɒkjʊˌpaɪ) *vb.* **-pies, -pying, -pied.** (*tr.*) **1.** to live or be established in (a house, flat, office, etc.). **2.** (*often passive*) to keep (a person) busy or engrossed; engage the attention of. **3.** (*often passive*) to take up (a certain amount of time or space). **4.** to take and hold possession of, esp. as a demonstration: *students occupied the college buildings.* **5.** to fill or hold (a position or rank). [C14: from Old French *occuper,* from Latin *occupāre* to seize hold of, from *ob-* (intensive) + *capere* to take]
occur (əˈkɜː) *vb.* **-curs, -curring, -curred.** (*intr.*) **1.** to happen; take place; come about. **2.** to be found or be present; exist. **3.** (foll. by *to*) to be realized or thought of (by); suggest itself (to). [C16: from Latin *occurrere* to run up to, from *ob-* to + *currere* to run]
▷**Usage.** In careful English, *occur* and *happen* are not used of prearranged events: *the wedding took place* (not *occurred* or *happened*) *in the afternoon.*
occurrence (əˈkʌrəns) *n.* **1.** something that occurs; a happening; event. **2.** the act or an instance of occurring: *a crime of frequent occurrence.*
occurrent (əˈkʌrənt) *adj. Philosophy.* (of a property) relating to some observable feature of its bearer. Compare **disposition** (sense 4).
ocean (ˈəʊʃən) *n.* **1.** a very large stretch of sea, esp. one of the five oceans of the world, the Atlantic, Pacific, Indian, Arctic, and Antarctic. **2.** the body of salt water covering approximately 70 per cent of the earth's surface. **3.** a huge quantity or expanse: *an ocean of replies.* **4.** *Literary.* the sea. [C13: via Old French from Latin *ōceanus,* from Greek *ōkeanos* Oceanus, a Greek Titan and divinity of the stream believed to flow around the earth]
oceanarium (ˌəʊʃəˈnɛərɪəm) *n., pl.* **-iums** *or* **-ia** (-ɪə). a large saltwater aquarium for marine life.
ocean floor spreading *n.* another term for **seafloor spreading.**
ocean-going *adj.* (of a ship, boat, etc.) suited for travel on the open ocean.
ocean greyhound *n.* a fast ship, esp. a liner.
Oceanian (ˌəʊʃɪˈɑːnɪən) *adj.* **1.** of or relating to Oceania, the islands of the central and S Pacific, including Melanesia, Micronesia, and Polynesia, or to its people, languages, or culture. ~*n.* **2.** a native or inhabitant of Oceania.
oceanic (ˌəʊʃɪˈænɪk) *adj.* **1.** of or relating to the ocean. **2.** living in the depths of the ocean beyond the continental shelf at a depth exceeding 200 metres: *oceanic fauna.* **3.** huge or overwhelming. **4.** (of geological formations) of volcanic origin, arising from the ocean: *oceanic islands.*
Oceanic (ˌəʊʃɪˈænɪk) *n.* **1.** a branch, group, or subfamily of the Malayo-Polynesian family of languages, comprising Polynesian and Melanesian. ~*adj.* **2.** of, relating to, or belonging to this group of languages. **3.** of or relating to Oceania; Oceanian.
oceanic ridge *n.* any section of the narrow, largely continuous range of submarine mountains that extends into all the major oceans and at which new oceanic lithosphere is created by the rise of magma from the earth's interior. See also **seafloor spreading.**
oceanic trench *n.* a long narrow steep-sided depression in the earth's oceanic crust, usually lying above a Benioff zone.
oceanog. *abbrev. for* oceanography.
oceanography (ˌəʊʃəˈnɒɡrəfɪ, ˌəʊʃɪə-) *n.* the branch of science dealing with the physical, chemical, geological, and biological features of the oceans and ocean basins. —ˌ**oceanˈographer** *n.* —**oceanographic** (ˌəʊʃənəˈɡræfɪk, ˌəʊʃɪə-) *or* ˌ**oceanoˈgraphical** *adj.* —ˌ**oceanoˈgraphically** *adv.*
oceanology (ˌəʊʃəˈnɒlədʒɪ, ˌəʊʃɪə-) *n.* the study of the sea, esp. of its economic geography.
ocellus (ɒˈsɛləs) *n., pl.* **-li** (-laɪ). **1.** the simple eye of insects and some other invertebrates, consisting basically of light-sensitive cells. **2.** any eyelike marking in animals, such as the eyespot on the tail feather of a peacock. **3.** *Botany.* **a.** an enlarged discoloured cell in a leaf. **b.** a swelling on the sporangium of certain fungi. [C19: via New Latin from Latin: small eye, from *oculus* eye] —**oˈcellar** *adj.* —**ocellate** (ˈɒsɪˌleɪt) *or* **ocellated** (ˈɒsɪˌleɪtɪd) *adj.* —ˌ**ocelˈlation** *n.*

ocelot ('ɒsɪˌlɒt, 'əʊ-) *n.* a feline mammal, *Felis pardalis,* inhabiting the forests of Central and South America and having a dark-spotted buff-brown coat. [C18: via French from Nahuatl *ocelotl* jaguar]

och (ɒx) *Scot. and Irish.* ~*interj.* **1.** an expression of surprise, contempt, annoyance, impatience, or disagreement. ~*sentence connector.* **2.** an expression used to preface a remark, gain time, etc.: *och, I suppose so.* ~Also: **ach.**

oche ('ɒkɪ) *n. Darts.* the mark or ridge on the floor behind which a player must stand to throw. [of unknown origin; perhaps connected with obsolete *oche* to chop off, from Old French *ocher* to cut a notch in]

ocher ('əʊkə) *n., adj., vb.* the U.S. spelling of **ochre.** —**'ocherous** *or* **'ochery** *adj.* —**ochroid** ('əʊkrɔɪd) *adj.*

ochlocracy (ɒk'lɒkrəsɪ) *n., pl.* **-cies.** rule by the mob; mobocracy. [C16: via French, from Greek *okhlokratia,* from *okhlos* mob + *kratos* power] —**ochlocrat** ('ɒkləˌkræt) *n.* —ˌ**ochlo'cratic** *adj.*

ochlophobia (ˌɒklə'fəʊbɪə) *n. Psychol.* the fear of crowds. [C19: from New Latin, from Greek *okhlos* mob + -PHOBIA]

ochone (ɒ'xəʊn) *interj. Scot. and Irish.* an expression of sorrow or regret. [from Gaelic *ochóin*]

ochre *or U.S.* **ocher** ('əʊkə) *n.* **1.** any of various natural earths containing ferric oxide, silica, and alumina: used as yellow or red pigments. **2. a.** a moderate yellow-orange to orange colour. **b.** (*as adj.*): *an ochre dress.* ~*vb.* **3.** (*tr.*) to colour with ochre. [C15: from Old French *ocre,* from Latin *ōchra,* from Greek *ōkhra,* from *ōkhros* pale yellow] —**ochreous** ('əʊkrɪəs, 'əʊkərəs), **ochrous** ('əʊkrəs), **ochry** ('əʊkərɪ, 'əʊkrɪ) *or U.S.* **'ocherous, 'ochery** *adj.* —**ochroid** ('əʊkrɔɪd) *adj.*

ochrea ('ɒkrɪə) *n., pl.* **-reae** (-rɪˌiː). a variant spelling of **ocrea.**

-ock *suffix forming nouns.* indicating smallness: *hillock.* [Old English *-oc, -uc*]

ocker ('ɒkə) *Austral. slang.* ~*n.* **1.** (*often cap.*) an uncultivated or boorish Australian. ~*adj., adv.* **2.** typical of such a person. [C20: of uncertain origin]

Ockham's razor *or* **Occam's razor** ('ɒkəmz) *n.* a maxim, attributed to William of Ockham (died ?1349), English philosopher, stating that in explaining something assumptions must not be needlessly multiplied. Also called: **the principle of economy.**

o'clock (ə'klɒk) *adv.* **1.** used after a number from one to twelve to indicate the hour of the day or night. **2.** used after a number to indicate direction or position relative to the observer, twelve o'clock being directly ahead or overhead and other positions being obtained by comparisons with a clock face. [C18: abbreviation for *of the clock*]

ocotillo (ˌəʊkə'tiːljəʊ) *n., pl.* **-los.** a cactus-like tree, *Fouquieria splendens,* of Mexico and the southwestern U.S., with scarlet tubular flowers: used for hedges and candlewood: family *Fouquieriaceae.* [Mexican Spanish: diminutive of *ocote* pine, from Nahuatl *ocotl* torch]

OCR *abbrev. for* optical character reader *or* recognition.

ocrea *or* **ochrea** ('ɒkrɪə) *n., pl.* **-reae** (-rɪˌiː). a cup-shaped structure that sheathes the stems of certain plants, formed from united stipules or leaf bases. [C19: from Latin: greave, legging, of obscure origin]

ocreate ('ɒkrɪɪt, -ˌeɪt) *adj.* **1.** *Botany.* possessing an ocrea; sheathed. **2.** *Ornithol.* another word for **booted** (sense 2).

OCS *abbrev. for* Officer Candidate School.

oct. *abbrev. for* octavo.

Oct. *abbrev. for* October.

oct- *combining form.* a variant of **octo-** before a vowel.

octa ('ɒktə) *n.* a variant spelling of **okta.**

octa- *combining form.* a variant of **octo-.**

octachord ('ɒktəˌkɔːd) *n.* **1.** an eight-stringed musical instrument. **2.** a series of eight notes, esp. a scale.

octad ('ɒktæd) *n.* **1.** a group or series of eight. **2.** *Chem.* an element or group with a valency of eight. [C19: from Greek *oktās,* from *oktō* eight] —**oc'tadic** *adj.*

octagon ('ɒktəgən) *or* (*less commonly*) **octangle** *n.* a polygon having eight sides. [C17: via Latin from Greek *oktagōnos,* having eight angles]

octagonal (ɒk'tægənᵊl) *adj.* **1.** having eight sides and eight angles. **2.** of or relating to an octagon. —**oc'tagonally** *adv.*

octahedral (ˌɒktə'hiːdrəl) *adj.* **1.** having eight plane surfaces. **2.** shaped like an octahedron.

octahedrite (ˌɒktə'hiːdraɪt) *n.* another name for **anatase.**

octahedron (ˌɒktə'hiːdrən) *n., pl.* **-drons** *or* **-dra** (-drə). a solid figure having eight plane faces.

octal notation *or* **octal** ('ɒktəl) *n.* a number system having a base 8: often used in computing, one octal digit being equivalent to a group of three bits.

octamerous (ɒk'tæmərəs) *adj.* consisting of eight parts, esp. (of flowers) having the parts arranged in groups of eight.

octameter (ɒk'tæmɪtə) *n. Prosody.* a verse line consisting of eight metrical feet.

octane ('ɒkteɪn) *n.* a liquid alkane hydrocarbon found in petroleum and existing in 18 isomeric forms, esp. the isomer *n*-octane. Formula: C_8H_{18}. See also **isooctane.**

octanedioic acid (ˌɒkteɪndaɪ'əʊɪk) *n.* a colourless crystalline dicarboxylic acid found in suberin and castor oil and used in the manufacture of synthetic resins. Formula: $HOOC(CH_2)_6COOH$. Also called: **suberic acid.** [C20: from OCTANE + DIOL]

octane number *or* **rating** *n.* a measure of the quality of a petrol expressed as the percentage of isooctane in a mixture of isooctane and *n*-heptane that gives a fuel with the same antiknock qualities as the given petrol.

octangle ('ɒktæŋgᵊl) *n.* a less common name for **octagon.**

octangular (ɒk'tæŋgjʊlə) *adj.* having eight angles.

Octans ('ɒktænz) *n., Latin genitive* **Octantis** (ɒk'tæntɪs). a faint constellation in the S hemisphere in which the S celestial pole is situated.

octant ('ɒktənt) *n.* **1.** *Maths.* **a.** any of the eight parts into which the three planes containing the Cartesian coordinate axes divide space. **b.** an eighth part of a circle. **2.** *Astronomy.* the position of a celestial body when it is at an angular distance of 45° from another body. **3.** an instrument used for measuring angles, similar to a sextant but having a graduated arc of 45°. [C17: from Latin *octans* half quadrant, from *octo* eight]

octarchy ('ɒktɑːkɪ) *n., pl.* **-chies.** **1.** government by eight rulers. **2.** a confederacy of eight kingdoms, tribes, etc.

octaroon (ˌɒktə'ruːn) *n.* a variant spelling of **octoroon.**

octavalent (ˌɒktə'veɪlənt) *adj. Chem.* having a valency of eight.

octave ('ɒktɪv) *n.* **1. a.** the interval between two musical notes one of which has twice the pitch of the other and lies eight notes away from it counting inclusively along the diatonic scale. **b.** one of these two notes, esp. the one of higher pitch. **c.** (*as modifier*): *an octave leap.* ~See also **perfect** (sense 9), **diminished** (sense 2), **interval** (sense 5). **2.** *Prosody.* a rhythmic group of eight lines of verse. **3.** ('ɒkteɪv). **a.** a feast day and the seven days following. **b.** the final day of this period. **4.** the eighth of eight basic positions in fencing. **5.** any set or series of eight. ~*adj.* **6.** consisting of eight parts. [C14: (originally: eighth day) via Old French from Medieval Latin *octāva diēs* eighth day (after a festival), from Latin *octo* eight]

octave coupler *n.* a mechanism on an organ and on some harpsichords that enables keys or pedals an octave apart to be played simultaneously.

octavo (ɒk'teɪvəʊ) *n., pl.* **-vos.** **1.** Also called: **eightvo.** a book size resulting from folding a sheet of paper of a specified size to form eight leaves: *demi-octavo.* Often written: **8vo, 8°.** **2.** a book of this size. **3.** (formerly) a size of cut paper 8 inches by 5 inches (20.3 cm by 12.7 cm). [C16: from New Latin phrase *in octavo* in an eighth (of a whole sheet)]

octennial (ɒk'tɛnɪəl) *adj.* **1.** occurring every eight years. **2.** lasting for eight years. [C17: from Latin *octennium* eight years, from *octo* eight + *annus* year] —**oc'tennially** *adv.*

octet (ɒk'tɛt) *n.* **1.** any group of eight, esp. eight singers or musicians. **2.** a piece of music composed for such a group. **3.** *Prosody.* another word for **octave** (sense 2). **4.** *Chem.* a group of eight electrons forming a stable shell in an atom. ~Also (for senses 1, 2, 3): **oc'tette.** [C19: from Latin *octo* eight, on the model of DUET]

octillion (ɒk'tɪljən) *n.* **1.** (in Britain and Germany) the number represented as one followed by 48 zeros (10^{48}). **2.** (in the U.S., Canada, and France) the number represented as one followed by 27 zeros (10^{27}). [C17: from French, on the model of MILLION] —**oc'tillionth** *adj.*

octo-, octa-, *or before a vowel* **oct-** *combining form.* eight: *octosyllabic; octagon.* [from Latin *octo,* Greek *okto*]

October (ɒk'təʊbə) *n.* the tenth month of the year, consisting of 31 days. [Old English, from Latin, from *octo* eight, since it was the eighth month in Roman reckoning]

Octobrist (ɒk'təʊbrɪst) *n.* a member of a Russian political party favouring the constitutional reforms granted in a manifesto issued by tsar Nicholas II in Oct. 1905.

octocentenary (ˌɒktəʊsɛn'tiːnərɪ) *n., pl.* **-naries.** an eight-hundredth anniversary.

octodecimo (ˌɒktəʊ'dɛsɪməʊ) *n., pl.* **-mos.** *Bookbinding.* another word for **eighteenmo.** [C18: from New Latin phrase *in octodecimo* in an eighteenth (of a whole sheet)]

octogenarian (ˌɒktəʊdʒɪ'nɛərɪən) *or* (*less commonly*) **octogenary** (ɒk'tɒdʒɪnərɪ) *n., pl.* **-narians** *or* **-naries.** **1.** a person who is from 80 to 89 years old. ~*adj.* **2.** of or relating to an octogenarian. [C19: from Latin *octōgēnārius* containing eighty, from *octōgēnī* eighty each]

octonary ('ɒktənərɪ) *Rare.* ~*adj.* **1.** relating to or based on the number eight. ~*n., pl.* **-naries.** **2.** *Prosody.* a stanza of eight lines. **3.** a group of eight. [C16: from Latin *octōnārius,* from *octōnī* eight at a time]

octopod ('ɒktəˌpɒd) *n.* **1.** any cephalopod mollusc of the order *Octopoda,* including octopuses and the paper nautilus, having eight tentacles, and lacking an internal shell. ~*adj.* **2.** of, relating to, or belonging to the *Octopoda.*

octopus ('ɒktəpəs) *n., pl.* **-puses.** **1.** any cephalopod mollusc of the genera *Octopus, Eledone,* etc., having a soft oval body with eight long suckered tentacles and occurring at the sea bottom: order *Octopoda* (octopods). **2.** a powerful influential organization with far-reaching effects, esp. harmful ones. **3.** another name for **spider** (sense 8). [C18: via New Latin from Greek *oktōpous* having eight feet]

octoroon *or* **octaroon** (ˌɒktə'ruːn) *n.* a person having one quadroon and one White parent and therefore having one-eighth Negro blood. Compare **quadroon.** [C19: OCTO- + *-roon* as in QUADROON]

octosyllable ('ɒktəˌsɪləbᵊl) *n.* **1.** a line of verse composed of eight syllables. **2.** a word of eight syllables. —**octosyllabic** (ˌɒktəsɪ'læbɪk) *adj.*

octroi ('ɒktrwɑː) *n.* **1.** a duty on various goods brought into certain towns or cities. **2.** the place where such a duty is collected. **3.** the officers responsible for its collection. [C17: from French *octroyer* to concede, from Medieval Latin *auctorizāre* to AUTHORIZE]

octuple ('ɒktjʊpᵊl) *n.* **1.** a quantity or number eight times as great as another. ~*adj.* **2.** eight times as much or as many. **3.** consisting of eight parts. ~*vb.* **4.** (*tr.*) to multiply by eight. [C17: from Latin *octuplus,* from *octo* eight + *-plus* as in *duplus* double]

ocular ('ɒkjʊlə) *adj.* **1.** of or relating to the eye. ~*n.* **2.** another name for **eyepiece.** [C16: from Latin *oculāris* from *oculus* eye] —'**ocularly** *adv.*

ocularist ('ɒkjʊlərɪst) *n.* a person who makes artificial eyes.

oculate ('ɒkjʊˌleɪt) *adj. Zoology.* **1.** possessing eyes. **2.** relating to or resembling eyes: *oculate markings.*

oculist ('ɒkjʊlɪst) *n. Med.* a former term for **ophthalmologist.** [C17: via French from Latin *oculus* eye]

oculo- *or sometimes before a vowel* **ocul-** *combining form.* indicating the eye: *oculomotor.* [from Latin *oculus*]

oculomotor (ˌɒkjʊləʊ'məʊtə) *adj.* relating to or causing eye movements. [C19: from Latin *oculus* eye + MOTOR]

oculomotor nerve *n.* the third cranial nerve, which supplies most of the eye muscles.

od (ɒd, əʊd), **odyl,** *or* **odyle** *n. Archaic.* a hypothetical force formerly thought to be responsible for many natural phenomena, such as magnetism, light, and hypnotism. [C19: coined arbitrarily by Baron Karl von Reichenbach (1788–1869), German scientist] —'**odic** *adj.*

Od, 'Od, *or* **Odd** (ɒd) *n. Euphemistic.* (used in mild oaths) an archaic word for **God.**

OD[1] (ˌəʊ'diː) *Informal.* ~*n.* **1.** an overdose of a drug. ~*vb.* (*intr.*) **OD'ing, OD'd.** **2.** to take an overdose of a drug. [C20: from *o(ver)d(ose)*]

OD[2] *abbrev. for:* **1.** Officer of the Day. **2.** Old Dutch. **3.** ordnance datum. **4.** outside diameter. **5.** Also: **o.d.** *Military.* olive drab. **6.** Also: **O/D.** *Banking.* **a.** on demand. **b.** overdraft. **c.** overdrawn.

ODA (in Britain) *abbrev. for* Overseas Development Administration.

odalisque *or* **odalisk** ('əʊdəlɪsk) *n.* a female slave or concubine. [C17: via French, changed from Turkish *ōdalik,* from *ōdah* room + *-lik* n. suffix]

odd (ɒd) *adj.* **1.** unusual or peculiar in appearance, character, etc. **2.** occasional, incidental, or random: *odd jobs.* **3.** leftover or additional: *odd bits of wool.* **4. a.** not divisible by two. **b.** represented or indicated by a number that is not divisible by two: *graphs are on odd pages.* Compare **even**[1] (sense 7). **5.** being part of a matched pair or set when the other or others are missing: *an odd sock; odd volumes.* **6.** (*in combination*). used to designate an indefinite quantity more than the quantity specified in round numbers: *fifty-odd pounds.* **7.** out-of-the-way or secluded. **8.** *Maths.* (of a function) changing sign but not absolute value when the sign of the independent variable is changed, as in $y=x^3$. Compare **even**[1] (sense 13). **9. odd man out.** a person or thing excluded from others forming a group, unit, etc. ~*n.* **10.** *Golf.* **a.** one stroke more than the score of one's opponent. **b.** an advantage or handicap of one stroke added to or taken away from a player's score. **11.** a thing or person that is odd in sequence or number. ~See also **odds.** [C14: *odde:* from Old Norse *oddi* point, angle, triangle, third or odd number. Compare Old Norse *oddr* point, spot, place; Old English *ord* point, beginning] —'**oddly** *adv.* —'**oddness** *n.*

oddball ('ɒdˌbɔːl) *Informal.* ~*n.* **1.** Also called: **odd bod, odd fish.** a strange or eccentric person. ~*adj.* **2.** strange or peculiar.

Oddfellow ('ɒdˌfɛləʊ) *n.* a member of the **Independent Order of Oddfellows,** a secret benevolent and fraternal association founded in England in the 18th century.

oddity ('ɒdɪtɪ) *n., pl.* **-ties.** **1.** an odd person or thing. **2.** an odd quality or characteristic. **3.** the condition of being odd.

odd-jobman *or* **odd-jobber** *n., pl.* **-men** *or* **-bers.** a person who does casual work, esp. domestic repairs.

odd lot *n.* **1.** a batch of merchandise that contains less than or more than the usual number of units. **2.** *Stock Exchange.* a number of securities less than the standard trading unit of 100.

oddment ('ɒdmənt) *n.* **1.** (*often pl.*) an odd piece or thing; leftover. **2.** *Printing.* any individual part of a book, such as the preface, excluding the main text. **3.** (*pl.*) *N.Z.* pieces of wool, such as belly wool or neck wool, removed from a fleece and sold separately.

odd-pinnate *adj.* (of a plant leaf) pinnate with a single leaflet at the apex.

odds (ɒdz) *pl. n.* **1.** (foll. by *on* or *against*) the probability, expressed as a ratio, that a certain event will take place: *the odds against the outsider are a hundred to one.* **2.** the amount, expressed as a ratio, by which the wager of one better is greater than that of another: *he was offering odds of five to one.* **3.** the likelihood that a certain state of affairs will be found to be so: *the odds are that he is drunk.* **4.** the chances or likelihood of success in a certain undertaking: *their odds were very poor after it rained.* **5.** an equalizing allowance, esp. one given to a weaker side in a contest. **6.** the advantage that one contender is judged to have over another: *the odds are on my team.* **7.** *Brit.* a significant difference (esp. in the phrase **it makes no odds**). **8. at odds.** on bad terms. **9. give** *or* **lay odds.** to offer a bet with favourable odds. **10. take odds.** to accept such a bet. **11. over the odds. a.** more than is expected, necessary, etc.: *he got two pounds over the odds for this job.* **b.** unfair or excessive. **12. what's the odds?** *Brit. informal.* what difference does it make?

odds and ends *pl. n.* miscellaneous items or articles.

odds and sods *pl. n. Brit. informal.* miscellaneous people or things.

odds-on *adj.* **1.** (of a chance, horse, etc.) rated at even money or less to win. **2.** regarded as more or most likely to win, succeed, happen, etc.

ode (əʊd) *n.* **1.** a lyric poem, typically addressed to a particular subject, with lines of varying lengths and complex rhythms. See also **Horatian ode, Pindaric ode.** **2.** (formerly) a poem meant to be sung. [C16: via French from Late Latin *ōda,* from Greek *ōidē,* from *aeidein* to sing]

-ode[1] *n. combining form.* denoting resemblance: *nematode.* [from Greek *-ōdēs,* from *eidos* shape, form]

-ode[2] *n. combining form.* denoting a path or way: *electrode.* [from Greek *-odos,* from *hodos* a way]

odea ('əʊdɪə) *n.* the plural of **odeum.**

odeum ('əʊdɪəm) *n., pl.* **odea** ('əʊdɪə). (esp. in ancient Greece and Rome) a building for musical performances. Also called: '**odeon.** [C17: from Latin, from Greek *ōideion,* from *ōidē* ODE]

odious ('əʊdɪəs) *adj.* offensive; repugnant. [C17: from Latin; see ODIUM] —'**odiously** *adv.* —'**odiousness** *n.*

odium ('əʊdɪəm) *n.* **1.** the dislike accorded to a hated person or thing. **2.** hatred; repugnance. [C17: from Latin; related to *ōdī* I hate, Greek *odussasthai* to be angry]

ODM *abbrev. for* Ministry of Overseas Development.

odometer (ɒ'dɒmɪtə, əʊ-) *n.* the usual U.S. and Canadian name for **mileometer.** [C18 *hodometer,* from Greek *hodos* way + -METER] —**o'dometry** *n.*

-odont *adj. and n. combining form.* having teeth of a certain type; -toothed: *acrodont.* [from Greek *odōn* tooth]

odontalgia (ˌɒdɒn'tældʒɪə) *n.* a technical name for **toothache.** —ˌ**odon'talgic** *adj.*

odonto- *or before a vowel* **odont-** *combining form.* indicating a tooth or teeth: *odontology.* [from Greek *odōn* tooth]

odontoblast (ɒ'dɒntəˌblæst) *n.* any of a layer of cells lining the pulp cavity of a tooth and giving rise to the dentine. —**oˌdonto'blastic** *adj.*

odontoglossum (ɒˌdɒntə'glɒsəm) *n.* any epiphytic orchid of the tropical American genus *Odontoglossum,* having clusters of brightly coloured flowers.

odontoid (ɒ'dɒntɔɪd) *adj.* **1.** toothlike. **2.** of or relating to the odontoid process.

odontoid process *n. Anatomy.* the toothlike upward projection at the back of the second vertebra of the neck.

odontolite (ɒ'dɒntəˌlaɪt) *n.* another name for **bone turquoise.**

odontology (ˌɒdɒn'tɒlədʒɪ) *n.* the branch of science concerned with the anatomy, development, and diseases of teeth and related structures. —**odontological** (ɒˌdɒntə'lɒdʒɪkᵊl) *adj.* —ˌ**odon'tologist** *n.*

odontophore (ɒ'dɒntəˌfɔː) *n.* an oral muscular protrusible structure in molluscs that supports the radula. —**odontophoral** (ˌɒdɒn'tɒfərəl) *or* ˌ**odon'tophorous** *adj.*

odontorhynchous (ɒˌdɒntə'rɪŋkəs) *adj.* (of birds) having toothlike ridges inside the beak. [C19: from ODONTO- + Greek *rhunkhos* snout + -OUS]

odor ('əʊdə) *n.* the U.S. spelling of **odour.** —'**odorless** *adj.*

odoriferous (ˌəʊdə'rɪfərəs) *adj.* having or emitting an odour, esp. a fragrant one. —ˌ**odor'iferously** *adv.* —ˌ**odor'iferousness** *n.*

odorimetry (ˌəʊdə'rɪmɪtrɪ) *n. Chem.* the measurement of the strength and permanence of odours. Also called: **olfactometry.**

odoriphore (əʊ'dɒrɪˌfɔː) *n. Chem.* the group of atoms in an odorous molecule responsible for its odour.

odorous ('əʊdərəs) *adj.* having or emitting a characteristic smell or odour. —'**odorously** *adv.* —'**odorousness** *n.*

odour *or U.S.* **odor** ('əʊdə) *n.* **1.** the property of a substance that gives it a characteristic scent or smell. **2.** a pervasive quality about something: *an odour of dishonesty.* **3.** repute or regard (in the phrases **in good odour, in bad odour**). **4.** *Archaic.* a sweet-smelling fragrance. [C13: from Old French *odur,* from Latin *odor;* related to Latin *olēre* to smell, Greek *ozein*] —'**odourless** *or U.S.* '**odorless** *adj.*

odour of sanctity *n. Derogatory.* sanctimoniousness. [C18: originally, the sweet smell said to be exhaled by the bodies of dead saints]

odyl *or* **odyle** ('ɒdɪl) *n.* other words for **od.**

Odyssey ('ɒdɪsɪ) *n.* (*often not cap.*) any long eventful journey. [after the Greek epic poem, attributed to Homer, describing the ten-year homeward wanderings of the Greek hero Odysseus after the fall of Troy] —**Odyssean** (ˌɒdɪ'siːən) *adj.*

Oe *symbol for* oersted.

OE *abbrev. for* Old English (language).

o.e. *Commerce. abbrev. for* omissions excepted.

OECD *abbrev. for* Organization for Economic Cooperation and Development.
oecology (iːˈkɒlədʒɪ) *n.* a less common spelling of **ecology.** —**oecological** (ˌɛkəˈlɒdʒɪkəl, ˌiː-) *adj.* —ˌ**oecoˈlogically** *adv.* —**oeˈcologist** *n.*
oecumenical (ˌiːkjuˈmɛnɪkəl) *adj.* a less common spelling of **ecumenical.**
OED *abbrev. for* Oxford English Dictionary.
oedema *or* **edema** (ɪˈdiːmə) *n., pl.* **-mata** (-mətə). **1.** *Pathol.* an excessive accumulation of serous fluid in the intercellular spaces of tissue. **2.** *Plant pathol.* an abnormal swelling in a plant caused by a large mass of parenchyma or an accumulation of water in the tissues. [C16: via New Latin from Greek *oidēma,* from *oidein* to swell] —**oedematous, edematous** (ɪˈdɛmətəs) *or* **oeˈdemaˌtose, eˈdemaˌtose** *adj.*
Oedipus complex (ˈiːdɪpəs) *n. Psychoanal.* a group of emotions, usually unconscious, involving the desire of a child, esp. a male child, to possess sexually the parent of the opposite sex while excluding the parent of the same sex. Compare **Electra complex.** [after *Oedipus* of Greek mythology, who killed his father, being unaware of his identity, and unwittingly married his mother] —ˈ**oedipal** *or* ˌ**oediˈpean** *adj.*
oedometer (iːˈdɒmɪtə) *n. Civil engineering.* an instrument for measuring the rate and amount of consolidation of a soil specimen under pressure. [C20: from Greek *oidēma* (see OEDEMA) + -METER]
OEEC (formerly) *abbrev. for* Organization for European Economic Cooperation.
oeil-de-boeuf *French.* (œjdəbœf) *n., pl.* ***oeils-de-boeuf*** (œjdəbœf). a circular window, esp. in 17th- and 18th-century French architecture. [literally: bull's eye]
oeillade (ɜːˈjɑːd; *French* œjad) *n. Literary.* an amorous or suggestive glance; ogle. [C16: from French, from *oeil* eye, from Latin *oculus* + *-ade* as in FUSILLADE]
OEM *abbrev. for* original equipment manufacturer: a computer company whose products are made by customizing basic parts supplied by others.
oenology *or* **enology** (iːˈnɒlədʒɪ) *n.* the study of wine. [C19: from Greek *oinos* wine + -LOGY] —**oenological** *or* **enological** (ˌiːnəˈlɒdʒɪkəl) *adj.* —**oeˈnologist** *or* **eˈnologist** *n.*
oenomel (ˈiːnəˌmɛl) *n.* **1.** a drink made of wine and honey. **2.** *Literary.* a source of strength and sweetness. [C16: via Latin from Greek *oinos* wine + *meli* honey]
oenophile (ˈiːnəˌfaɪl) *n.* a lover or connoisseur of wines. [C20: from Greek *oinos* wine + -PHILE]
oenothera (ˌiːnəˈθɪərə) *n.* any plant of the large taxonomically complicated American genus *Oenothera,* typically having yellow flowers that open in the evening: family *Onagraceae.* See **evening primrose.**
o'er (ɔː, əʊə) *prep., adv.* a poetic contraction of **over.**
oersted (ˈɜːstɛd) *n.* the cgs unit of magnetic field strength; the field strength that would cause a unit magnetic pole to experience a force of 1 dyne in a free space. It is equivalent to 79.58 amperes per metre. Symbol: Oe [C20: named after H. C. *Oersted* (1777–1851), Danish physicist, who discovered electromagnetism]
oesophagoscope *or U.S.* **esophagoscope** (iːˈsɒfəgəʊˌskəʊp) *n. Med.* an instrument for examining the oesophagus. —**oesophagoscopy** (iːˌsɒfəˈgɒskəpɪ) *n.*
oesophagus *or U.S.* **esophagus** (iːˈsɒfəgəs) *n., pl.* **-gi** (-ˌgaɪ). the part of the alimentary canal between the pharynx and the stomach; gullet. [C16: via New Latin from Greek *oisophagos, from oisein,* future infinitive of *pherein* to carry + *-phagos,* from *phagein* to eat] —**oesophageal** *or U.S.* **esophageal** (iːˌsɒfəˈdʒiːəl) *adj.*
oestradiol (ˌiːstrəˈdaɪɒl, ˌɛstrə-) *or U.S.* **estradiol** *n.* the most potent oestrogenic hormone secreted by the mammalian ovary: synthesized and used to treat oestrogen deficiency and cancer of the breast. Formula: $C_{18}H_{24}O_2$. [C20: from New Latin, from OESTRIN + DI-^{1} + -OL^1]
oestrin (ˈiːstrɪn, ˈɛstrɪn) *or U.S.* **estrin** *n.* an obsolete term for **oestrogen.** [C20: from OESTR(US) + -IN]
oestriol (ˈiːstrɪˌɒl, ˈɛstrɪ-) *or U.S.* **estriol** *n.* a weak oestrogenic hormone secreted by the mammalian ovary: a synthetic form is used to treat oestrogen deficiency. Formula: $C_{18}H_{24}O_3$. [C20: from OESTRIN + TRI- + -OL^1]
oestrogen (ˈiːstrədʒən, ˈɛstrə-) *or U.S.* **estrogen** *n.* any of several steroid hormones, that are secreted chiefly by the ovaries and placenta, that induce oestrus, stimulate changes in the female reproductive organs during the oestrous cycle, and promote development of female secondary sexual characteristics. [C20: from OESTRUS + -GEN] —**oestrogenic** (ˌiːstrəˈdʒɛnɪk, ˌɛstrə-) *or U.S.* **estrogenic** (ˌɛstrəˈdʒɛnɪk, ˌiːstrə-) *adj.* —ˌ**oestroˈgenically** *or U.S.* ˌ**estroˈgenically** *adv.*
oestrone (ˈiːstrəʊn, ˈɛstrəʊn) *or U.S.* **estrone** *n.* a weak oestrogenic hormone secreted by the mammalian ovary and having the same medical uses as oestradiol. Formula: $C_{18}H_{22}O_2$. [C20: from OESTR(US) + -ONE]
oestrous cycle *n.* a hormonally controlled cycle of activity of the reproductive organs in many female mammals. The follicular stage (growth of the Graafian follicles, thickening of the lining of the uterus, secretion of oestrogen, and ovulation (see **oestrus**)), is succeeded by the luteal phase (formation of the corpus luteum and secretion of progesterone), followed by regression and a return to the first stage.
oestrus (ˈiːstrəs, ˈɛstrəs) *or U.S.* **estrus, estrum** (ˈiːstrəm, ˈɛstrəm) *n.* a regularly occurring period of sexual receptivity in most female mammals, except humans, during which ovulation occurs and copulation can take place; heat. [C17: from Latin *oestrus* gadfly, hence frenzy, from Greek *oistros*] —ˈ**oestrous,** ˈ**oestral** *or U.S.* ˈ**estrous,** ˈ**estral** *adj.*
oeuvre *French.* (œvrə) *n.* **1.** a work of art, literature, music, etc. **2.** the total output of a writer, painter, etc. [ultimately from Latin *opera,* plural of *opus* work]
of (ɒv; *unstressed* əv) *prep.* **1.** used with a verbal noun or gerund to link it with a following noun that is either the subject or the object of the verb embedded in the gerund: *the breathing of a fine swimmer* (subject); *the breathing of clean air* (object). **2.** used to indicate possession, origin, or association: *the house of my sister; to die of hunger.* **3.** used after words or phrases expressing quantities: *a pint of milk.* **4.** constituted by, containing, or characterized by: *a family of idiots; a rod of iron; a man of some depth.* **5.** used to indicate separation, as in time or space: *within a mile of the town; within ten minutes of the beginning of the concert.* **6.** used to mark apposition: *the city of Naples; a speech on the subject of archaeology.* **7.** about; concerning: *speak to me of love.* **8.** used in passive constructions to indicate the agent: *he was beloved of all.* **9.** *Informal.* used to indicate a day or part of a period of time when some activity habitually occurs: *I go to the pub of an evening.* **10.** *U.S.* before the hour of: *a quarter of nine.* [Old English (as prep. and adv.); related to Old Norse *af,* Old High German *aba,* Latin *ab,* Greek *apo*]
▷**Usage.** See at **off.**
OF *abbrev. for* Old French (language).
ofay (ˈəʊfeɪ) *n. U.S. slang.* a derogatory term for a White person. [C20: origin unknown]
off (ɒf) *prep.* **1.** used to indicate actions in which contact is absent or rendered absent, as between an object and a surface: *to lift a cup off the table.* **2.** used to indicate the removal of something that is or has been appended to or in association with something else: *to take the tax off potatoes.* **3.** out of alignment with: *we are off course.* **4.** situated near to or leading away from: *just off the High Street.* **5.** not inclined towards: *I'm off work; I've gone off you.* ~*adv.* **6.** (*particle*) so as to be deactivated or disengaged: *turn off the radio.* **7.** (*particle*) **a.** so as to get rid of: *sleep off a hangover.* **b.** so as to be removed from, esp. as a reduction: *he took ten per cent off.* **8.** spent away from work or other duties: *take the afternoon off.* **9. a.** on a trip, journey, or race: *I saw her off at the station.* **b.** (*particle*) so as to be completely absent, used up, or exhausted: *this stuff kills off all vermin.* **10.** out from the shore or land: *the ship stood off.* **11. a.** out of contact; at a distance: *the ship was 10 miles off.* **b.** out of the present location: *the girl ran off.* **12.** away in the future: *August is less than a week off.* **13.** (*particle*) so as to be no longer taking place: *the match has been rained off.* **14.** (*particle*) removed from contact with something, as clothing from the body: *the girl took all her clothes off.* **15.** *Commerce.* (used with a preceding number) indicating the number of items required or produced: *please supply 100 off.* **16. off and on** *or* **on and off.** occasionally; intermittently: *he comes here off and on.* **17. off with.** (*interj.*) a command, often peremptory, or an exhortation to remove or cut off (something specified): *off with his head; off with that coat, my dear.* ~*adj.* **18.** not on; no longer operative: *the off position on the dial.* **19.** (*postpositive*) not or no longer taking place; cancelled or postponed: *the meeting is off.* **20.** in a specified condition regarding money, provisions, etc.: *well off; how are you off for bread?* **21.** unsatisfactory or disappointing: *his performance was rather off; an off year for good tennis.* **22.** (*postpositive*) in a condition as specified: *I'd be better off without this job.* **23.** (*postpositive*) no longer on the menu; not being served at the moment: *sorry, love, haddock is off.* **24.** (*postpositive*) (of food or drink) having gone bad, sour, etc.: *this milk is off.* ~*n.* **25.** *Cricket.* **a.** the part of the field on that side of the pitch to which the batsman presents his bat when taking strike: thus for a right-hander, off is on the right-hand side. Compare **leg** (sense 13). **b.** (*in combination*): a fielding position in this part of the field: *mid-off.* **c.** (*as modifier*): *the off stump.* [originally variant of OF; fully distinguished from it in the 17th century]
▷**Usage.** In educated usage, *off* is not followed by *from* or *of*: *he stepped off* (not *off of*) *the platform.* Careful writers also avoid using the word in the place of *from*: *they bought apples from* (rather than *off*) *the man.*
off. *abbrev. for:* **1.** offer. **2.** office. **3.** officer. **4.** official.
off-air *adj., adv.* **1.** obtained by reception of a radiated broadcasting signal rather than by line feed: *an off-air recording.* **2.** connected with a radio or television programme but not broadcast: *an off-air phone-in.*
offal (ˈɒfəl) *n.* **1.** the edible internal parts of an animal, such as the heart, liver, and tongue. **2.** dead or decomposing organic matter. **3.** refuse; rubbish. [C14: from OFF + FALL, referring to parts fallen or cut off; compare German *Abfall* rubbish]
off-balance sheet reserve *n. Accounting.* a sum of money or an asset that should appear on a company's balance but does not; hidden reserve.
offbeat (ˈɒfˌbiːt) *n.* **1.** *Music.* any of the normally unaccented beats in a bar, such as the second and fourth beats in a bar of

four-four time. They are stressed in most rock and some jazz and dance music, such as the bossa nova. ~*adj.* **2. a.** unusual, unconventional, or eccentric. **b.** (*as n.*): *he liked the offbeat in fashion.*

off-Broadway *adj.* **1.** designating the kind of experimental, low-budget, or noncommercial productions associated with theatre outside the Broadway area in New York. **2.** (of theatres) not located in Broadway. ~Compare **off-off-Broadway.**

off-centre *adj.* **1.** displaced from a centre point or axis. **2.** slightly eccentric or unconventional; not completely sound or balanced.

off chance *n.* **1.** a slight possibility. **2. on the off chance.** with the hope: *on the off chance of getting the job.*

off colour *adj.* (**off-colour** *when prenominal*). **1.** *Chiefly Brit.* slightly ill; unwell. **2.** indecent or indelicate; risqué.

offcut (ˈɒfˌkʌt) *n.* a piece of paper, plywood, fabric, etc., remaining after the main pieces have been cut; remnant.

offence *or U.S.* **offense** (əˈfɛns) *n.* **1.** a violation or breach of a law, custom, rule, etc. **2. a.** any public wrong or crime. **b.** a nonindictable crime punishable on summary conviction. **3.** annoyance, displeasure, or resentment. **4. give offence (to).** to cause annoyance or displeasure (to). **5. take offence.** to feel injured, humiliated, or offended. **6.** a source of annoyance, displeasure, or anger. **7.** attack; assault. **8.** *Archaic.* injury or harm. **9.** (ˈɒfɛns). *American football.* (usually preceded by *the*) **a.** the team that has possession of the ball. **b.** the members of a team that play in such circumstances. —**ofˈfenceless** *or U.S.* **ofˈfenseless** *adj.*

offend (əˈfɛnd) *vb.* **1.** to hurt the feelings, sense of dignity, etc., of (a person). **2.** (*tr.*) to be disagreeable to; disgust: *the smell offended him.* **3.** (*intr. except in archaic uses*) to break (a law or laws in general). [C14: via Old French *offendre* to strike against, from Latin *offendere,* from *ob-* against + *fendere* to strike] —**ofˈfender** *n.* —**ofˈfending** *adj.*

offensive (əˈfɛnsɪv) *adj.* **1.** unpleasant or disgusting, as to the senses. **2.** causing anger or annoyance; insulting. **3.** for the purpose of attack rather than defence. ~*n.* **4.** (usually preceded by *the*) an attitude or position of aggression. **5.** an assault, attack, or military initiative, esp. a strategic one. —**ofˈfensively** *adv.* —**ofˈfensiveness** *n.*

offer (ˈɒfə) *vb.* **1.** to present or proffer (something, someone, oneself, etc.) for acceptance or rejection. **2.** (*tr.*) to present as part of a requirement: *she offered English as a second subject.* **3.** (*tr.*) to provide or make accessible: *this stream offers the best fishing.* **4.** (*intr.*) to present itself: *if an opportunity should offer.* **5.** (*tr.*) to show or express willingness or the intention (to do something). **6.** (*tr.*) to put forward (a proposal, opinion, etc.) for consideration. **7.** (*tr.*) to present for sale. **8.** (*tr.*) to propose as payment; bid or tender. **9.** (when *tr.,* often foll. by *up*) to present (a prayer, sacrifice, etc.) as or during an act of worship. **10.** (*tr.*) to show readiness for: *to offer battle.* **11.** (*intr.*) *Archaic.* to make a proposal of marriage. **12.** (*tr.;* sometimes foll. by *up* or *to*) *Engineering.* to bring (a mechanical piece) near to or in contact with another, and often to proceed to fit the pieces together. ~*n.* **13.** something, such as a proposal or bid, that is offered. **14.** the act of offering or the condition of being offered. **15.** *Contract law.* a proposal made by one person that will create a binding contract if accepted unconditionally by the person to whom it is made. See also **acceptance. 16.** a proposal of marriage. **17.** short for **offer price. 18. on offer.** for sale at a reduced price. [Old English, from Latin *offerre* to present, from *ob-* to + *ferre* to bring] —ˈ**offerer** *or* ˈ**offeror** *n.*

offer document *n.* a document sent by a person or firm making a takeover bid to the shareholders of the target company, giving details of the offer that has been made and, usually, reasons for accepting it.

offering (ˈɒfərɪŋ) *n.* **1.** something that is offered. **2.** a contribution to the funds of a religious organization. **3.** a sacrifice, as of an animal, to a deity.

offer price *n. Stock Exchange.* the price at which a market maker is prepared to sell a specific security. Often shortened to **offer.** Compare **bid price.**

offertory (ˈɒfətərɪ) *n., pl.* **-tories.** *Christianity.* **1.** the oblation of the bread and wine at the Eucharist. **2.** the offerings of the worshippers at this service. **3.** the prayers said or sung while the worshippers' offerings are being received. [C14: from Church Latin *offertōrium* place appointed for offerings, from Latin *offerre* to OFFER]

off-glide *n. Phonetics.* a glide caused by the movement of the articulators away from their position in articulating the previous speech sound. Compare **on-glide.**

offhand (ˌɒfˈhænd) *adj. also* **offhanded,** *adv.* **1.** without care, thought, or consideration; sometimes, brusque or ungracious: *an offhand manner.* **2.** without preparation or warning; impromptu. —ˌ**offˈhandedly** *adv.* —ˌ**offˈhandedness** *n.*

office (ˈɒfɪs) *n.* **1. a.** a room or set of rooms in which business, professional duties, clerical work, etc., are carried out. **b.** (*as modifier*): *office furniture; an office boy.* **2.** (*often pl.*) the building or buildings in which the work of an organization, such as a business or government department, is carried out. **3.** a commercial or professional business: *the architect's office approved the plans.* **4.** the group of persons working in an office: *it was a happy office until she came.* **5.** (*cap. when part of a name*) (in Britain) a department of the national government: *the Home Office.* **6.** (*cap. when part of a name*) (in the U.S.) **a.** a governmental agency, esp. of the Federal government. **b.** a subdivision of such an agency or of a department: *Office of Science and Technology.* **7. a.** a position of trust, responsibility, or duty, esp. in a government or organization: *the office of president; to seek office.* **b.** (*in combination*): *an office-holder.* **8.** duty or function: *the office of an administrator.* **9.** (*often pl.*) a minor task or service: *domestic offices.* **10.** (*often pl.*) an action performed for another, usually a beneficial action: *through his good offices.* **11.** a place where tickets, information, etc., can be obtained: *a ticket office.* **12.** *Christianity.* **a.** (*often pl.*) a ceremony or service, prescribed by ecclesiastical authorities, esp. one for the dead. **b.** the order or form of these. **c.** *R.C. Church.* the official daily service. **d.** short for **divine office. 13.** (*pl.*) the parts of a house or estate where work is done, goods are stored, etc. **14.** (*usually pl.*) *Brit., euphemistic.* a lavatory (esp. in the phrase **usual offices**). **15. in** (*or* **out of**) **office.** (of a government) in (or out of) power. **16. the office.** *Slang.* a hint or signal. [C13: via Old French from Latin *officium* service, duty, from *opus* work, service + *facere* to do]

office bearer *n.* a person who holds an office, as in a society, company, club, etc.; official.

office block *n.* a large building designed to provide office accommodation.

office boy *n.* a former name for **office junior.**

office hours *pl. n.* **1.** the hours during which an office is open for business. **2.** the number of hours worked in an office.

office junior *n.* a young person, esp. a school-leaver, employed in an office for running errands and doing other minor jobs.

officer (ˈɒfɪsə) *n.* **1.** a person in the armed services who holds a position of responsibility, authority, and duty, esp. one who holds a commission. **2.** See **police officer. 3.** (on a non-naval ship) any person including the captain and mate, who holds a position of authority and responsibility: *radio officer; engineer officer.* **4.** a person appointed or elected to a position of responsibility or authority in a government, society, etc. **5.** a government official: *a customs officer.* **6.** (in the Order of the British Empire) a member of the grade below commander. ~*vb.* (*tr.*) **7.** to furnish with officers. **8.** to act as an officer over (some section, group, organization, etc.).

officer of arms *n. Heraldry.* a pursuivant or herald.

officer of the day *n.* a military officer whose duty is to take charge of the security of the unit or camp for a day. Also called: **orderly officer.**

officer of the guard *n.* a junior officer whose duty is to command a ceremonial guard. Abbrev.: **OG.**

official (əˈfɪʃəl) *adj.* **1.** of or relating to an office, its administration, or its duration. **2.** sanctioned by, recognized by, or derived from authority: *an official statement.* **3.** appointed by authority, esp. for some special duty. **4.** having a formal ceremonial character: *an official dinner.* ~*n.* **5.** a person who holds a position in an organization, government department, etc., esp. a subordinate position. —**ofˈficially** *adv.*

Official (əˈfɪʃəl) *n.* a member of the Official IRA or Sinn Féin, factions of either of these organizations emphasizing political rather than guerrilla activity. Compare **Provisional.**

officialdom (əˈfɪʃəldəm) *n.* **1.** the outlook or behaviour of officials, esp. those rigidly adhering to regulations; bureaucracy. **2.** officials or bureaucrats collectively.

officialese (əˌfɪʃəˈliːz) *n.* language characteristic of official documents, esp. when verbose or pedantic.

Official Receiver *n.* an officer appointed by the Department of Trade and Industry to receive the income and manage the estate of a bankrupt pending the appointment of a trustee in bankruptcy. See also **receiver** (sense 2).

Official Referee *n. Law.* (in England) a circuit judge attached to the High Court who is empowered to try certain cases, esp. where a detailed examination of accounts or other documents is involved.

Official Solicitor *n.* an officer of the Supreme Court of Judicature with special responsibilities for protecting the interests of persons under disability.

official strike *n.* a collective stoppage of work by part or all of the workforce of an organization with the approval of the trade union concerned. The stoppage may be accompanied by the payment of strike pay by the trade union concerned.

officiant (əˈfɪʃɪənt) *n.* a person who presides and officiates at a religious ceremony.

officiary (əˈfɪʃɪərɪ) *n., pl.* **-aries. 1.** a body of officials. ~*adj.* **2.** of, relating to, or derived from office.

officiate (əˈfɪʃɪˌeɪt) *vb.* (*intr.*) **1.** to hold the position, responsibility, or function of an official. **2.** to conduct a religious or other ceremony. [C17: from Medieval Latin *officiāre,* from Latin *officium;* see OFFICE] —**ofˌficiˈation** *n.* —**ofˈficiˌator** *n.*

officinal (ɒˈfɪsɪnᵊl, ˌɒfɪˈsaɪnᵊl) *Pharmacol., obsolete.* ~*adj.* **1.** (of pharmaceutical products) available without prescription. **2.** (of a plant) having pharmacological properties. ~*n.* **3.** an officinal preparation or plant. [C17: from Medieval Latin *officīnālis,* from Latin *officīna* workshop; see OFFICE] —**ofˈficinally** *adv.*

officious (əˈfɪʃəs) *adj.* **1.** unnecessarily or obtrusively ready to offer advice or services. **2.** marked by such readiness. **3.** *Diplomacy.* informal or unofficial. **4.** *Obsolete.* attentive or obliging.

[C16: from Latin *officiōsus* kindly, from *officium* service; see OFFICE] —**of'ficiously** *adv.* —**of'ficiousness** *n.*
offing ('ɒfɪŋ) *n.* **1.** the part of the sea that can be seen from the shore. **2. in the offing.** likely to occur soon.
offish ('ɒfɪʃ) *adj. Informal.* aloof or distant in manner. —'**offishly** *adv.* —'**offishness** *n.*
off key *adj.* (**off-key** *when prenominal*), *adv.* **1.** *Music.* **a.** not in the correct key. **b.** out of tune. **2.** out of keeping; discordant.
off-licence *n. Brit.* **1.** a shop, or a counter in a pub or hotel, where alcoholic drinks are sold for consumption elsewhere. U.S. equivalents: **package store, liquor store. 2.** a licence permitting such sales.
off limits *adj.* (**off-limits** *when prenominal*). **1.** *U.S., chiefly military.* not to be entered; out of bounds. ~*adv.* **2.** in or into an area forbidden by regulations.
off line *adj.* (**off-line** *when prenominal*). **1.** of, relating to, or concerned with a part of a computer system not connected to the central processing unit but controlled by a computer storage device. Compare **on line. 2.** disconnected from a computer; switched off. **3.** extra to or not involving a continuous sequence of operations, such as a production line. **4.** *Radio, television.* (of processes, such as editing) not carried out on the actual transmission medium.
off-load *vb.* (*tr.*) to get rid of (something unpleasant or burdensome), as by delegation to another.
off-off-Broadway *adj.* of or relating to highly experimental informal small-scale theatrical productions in New York, usually taking place in cafés, small halls, etc. Compare **off-Broadway.**
off-peak *adj.* of or relating to services as used outside periods of intensive use or electricity supplied at cheaper rates during the night.
off-piste *adj.* of or relating to skiing on virgin snow off the regular runs.
offprint ('ɒf,prɪnt) *n.* **1.** Also called (U.S.): **separate.** a separate reprint of an article that originally appeared in a larger publication. ~*vb.* **2.** (*tr.*) to reprint (an article taken from a larger publication) separately.
off-putting *adj. Brit. informal.* disconcerting or disturbing.
off-sales *pl. n. Brit.* sales of alcoholic drink for consumption off the premises by a pub or an off-licence attached to a pub.
offscourings ('ɒf,skaʊərɪŋz) *pl. n.* scum; dregs.
off season *adj.* (**off-season** *when prenominal*). **1.** denoting or occurring during a period of little activity in a trade or business. ~*n.* **2.** such a period. ~*adv.* **3.** in an off-season period.
offset *n.* ('ɒf,sɛt). **1.** something that counterbalances or compensates for something else. **2.** an allowance made to counteract some effect. **3. a.** a printing method in which the impression is made onto an intermediate surface, such as a rubber blanket, which transfers it to the paper. **b.** (*modifier*) relating to, involving, or printed by offset: *offset letterpress; offset lithography.* **4.** another name for **set-off. 5.** *Botany.* **a.** a short runner in certain plants, such as the houseleek, that produces roots and shoots at the tip. **b.** a plant produced from such a runner. **6.** a ridge projecting from a range of hills or mountains. **7.** a narrow horizontal or sloping surface formed where a wall is reduced in thickness towards the top. **8.** a person or group descended collaterally from a particular group or family; offshoot. **9.** *Surveying.* a measurement of distance to a point at right angles to a survey line. ~*vb.* (,ɒf'sɛt), **-sets, -setting, -set. 10.** (*tr.*) to counterbalance or compensate for. **11.** (*tr.*) to print (pictures, text, etc.) using the offset process. **12.** (*tr.*) to construct an offset in (a wall). **13.** (*intr.*) to project or develop as an offset.
offshoot ('ɒf,ʃuːt) *n.* **1.** a shoot or branch growing from the main stem of a plant. **2.** something that develops or derives from a principal source or origin.
offshore (,ɒf'ʃɔː) *adj., adv.* **1.** from, away from, or at some distance from the shore. ~*adj.* **2.** sited or conducted at sea as opposed to on land: *offshore industries.* **3.** based or operating abroad in places where the tax system is more advantageous than that of the home country: *offshore funds.*
offside ('ɒf'saɪd) *adj., adv.* **1.** *Sport.* (in football, hockey, etc.) in a position illegally ahead of the ball or puck when it is played, usually when within one's opponents' half or the attacking zone. ~*n.* **2.** (usually preceded by *the*) *Chiefly Brit.* **a.** the side of a vehicle nearest the centre of the road (in Britain, the right side). **b.** (*as modifier*): *the offside passenger door.* ~Compare **nearside.**
offsider (,ɒf'saɪdə) *n. Austral. and N.Z.* a partner or assistant.
offspring ('ɒf,sprɪŋ) *n.* **1.** the immediate descendant or descendants of a person, animal, etc.; progeny. **2.** a product, outcome, or result.
offstage ('ɒf'steɪdʒ) *adj., adv.* out of the view of the audience; off the stage.
off-street *adj.* located away from a street: *off-street parking.*
off the record *adj.* (**off-the-record** *when prenominal*). **1.** not intended for publication or disclosure; confidential. ~*adv.* **2.** with such an intention; unofficially.
off the shelf *adv.* **1.** from stock and readily available: *you can have this model off the shelf.* ~*adj.* (**off-the-shelf** *when prenominal*). **2.** of or relating to a product that is readily available: *an off-the-shelf model.* **3.** of or denoting a company that has been registered with the Registrar of Companies for the sole purpose of being sold.
off-the-wall *adj.* (**off the wall** *when postpositive*). *Slang.* new or unexpected in an unconventional or eccentric way: *an off-the-wall approach to humour.* [C20: possibly from the use of the phrase in handball and squash to describe a shot that is unexpected]
off-white *n.* **1.** a colour, such as cream or bone, consisting of white mixed with a tinge of grey or with a pale hue. ~*adj.* **2.** of such a colour: *an off-white coat.*
off-year election *n.* (in the U.S.) an election held in a year when a presidential election does not take place.
oflag ('ɒf,lɑːg) *n.* a German prisoner-of-war camp for officers in World War II. [German, short for *Offizierslager* officers' camp]
OFM *abbrev. for* Ordo Fratrum Minorum (the Franciscans). [Latin: Order of Minor Friars]
OFris *abbrev. for* Old Frisian.
OFS *abbrev. for* Orange Free State (in South Africa).
oft (ɒft) *adv.* short for **often** (archaic or poetic except in combinations such as **oft-repeated** and **oft-recurring**). [Old English *oft;* related to Old High German *ofto*]
OFT (in Britain) *abbrev. for* Office of Fair Trading.
OFTEL ('ɒf,tɛl) *n.* (in Britain) *acronym for* Office of Telecommunications.
often ('ɒfᵊn, 'ɒftᵊn) *adv.* **1.** frequently or repeatedly; much of the time. Archaic equivalents: **'often,times, 'oft,times. 2. as often as not.** quite frequently. **3. every so often.** at intervals. **4. more often than not.** in more than half the instances. ~*adj.* **5.** *Archaic.* repeated; frequent. [C14: variant of OFT before vowels and *h*]
OG *abbrev. for:* **1.** Officer of the Guard. **2.** Also: **o.g.** *Philately.* original gum.
o.g. *abbrev. for* own goal.
ogdoad ('ɒgdəʊ,æd) *n.* a group of eight. [C17: via Late Latin from Greek *ogdoas* eighth, from *oktō* eight]
ogee ('əʊdʒiː) *n. Architect.* **1.** Also called: **talon.** a moulding having a cross section in the form of a letter S. **2.** short for **ogee arch.** [C15: probably variant of OGIVE]
ogee arch *n. Architect.* a pointed arch having an S-shaped curve on both sides. Sometimes shortened to **ogee.** Also called: **keel arch.**
Ogen melon ('əʊgɛn) *n.* a variety of small melon having a green skin and sweet pale green flesh. [C20: named after a kibbutz in Israel where it was first developed]
ogham *or* **ogam** ('ɒgəm, ɔːm) *n.* an ancient alphabetical writing system used by the Celts in Britain and Ireland, consisting of straight lines drawn or carved perpendicular to or at an angle to another long straight line. [C17: from Old Irish *ogom,* of uncertain origin but associated with the name *Ogma,* legendary inventor of this alphabet]
ogive ('əʊdʒaɪv, əʊ'dʒaɪv) *n.* **1.** a diagonal rib or groin of a Gothic vault. **2.** another name for **lancet arch. 3.** *Statistics.* a graph the ordinates of which represent cumulative frequencies of the values indicated by the corresponding abscissas. **4.** the conical head of a missile or rocket that protects the payload during its passage through the atmosphere. [C17: from Old French, of uncertain origin] —**o'gival** *adj.*
ogle ('əʊgᵊl) *vb.* **1.** to look at (someone) amorously or lustfully. **2.** (*tr.*) to stare or gape at. ~*n.* **3.** a flirtatious or lewd look. [C17: probably from Low German *oegeln,* from *oegen* to look at] —'**ogler** *n.*
O grade *n.* (in Scotland) **1. a.** the basic level of the Scottish Certificate of Education. **b.** (*as modifier*): *O grade history.* **2.** a pass in a particular subject at O grade: *she has ten O grades.*
ogre ('əʊgə) *n.* **1.** (in folklore) a giant, usually given to eating human flesh. **2.** any monstrous or cruel person. [C18: from French, perhaps from Latin *Orcus* god of the infernal regions] —'**ogreish** *adj.* —'**ogress** *fem. n.*
Ogygian (əʊ'dʒɪdʒɪən) *adj.* of very great age; prehistoric. [C19: from Greek *Ōgugios* relating to *Ogyges,* the most ancient king of Greece, mythical ruler of Boeotia or Attica]
oh (əʊ) *interj.* **1.** an exclamation expressive of surprise, pain, pleasure, etc. ~*sentence connector.* **2.** an expression used to preface a remark, gain time, etc.: *oh, I suppose so.*
OH *abbrev. for* Ohio.
OHG *abbrev. for* Old High German.
ohm (əʊm) *n.* the derived SI unit of electric resistance; the resistance between two points on a conductor when a constant potential difference of 1 volt between them produces a current of 1 ampere. Symbol: Ω [C19: named after Georg Simon *Ohm* (1787–1854), German physicist]
ohmage ('əʊmɪdʒ) *n.* electrical resistance in ohms.
ohmic ('əʊmɪk) *adj.* of or relating to a circuit element, the electrical resistance of which obeys Ohm's law.
ohmmeter ('əʊm,miːtə) *n.* an instrument for measuring electrical resistance.
OHMS (in Britain and the dominions of the Commonwealth) *abbrev. for* On Her (*or* His) Majesty's Service.
Ohm's law (əʊmz) *n.* the principle that the electric current passing through a conductor is directly proportional to the potential difference across it, provided that the temperature remains constant. The constant of proportionality is the resistance of the conductor.
oho (əʊ'həʊ) *interj.* an exclamation expressing surprise, exultation, or derision.

ohv *abbrev. for* overhead valve.
-oid *suffix forming adjectives and associated nouns.* indicating likeness, resemblance, or similarity: *anthropoid.* [from Greek *-oeidēs* resembling form of, from *eidos* form]
-oidea *suffix forming plural proper nouns.* forming the names of zoological classes or superfamilies: *Crinoidea; Canoidea.* [from New Latin, from Latin *-oīdēs* -OID]
oidium (əʊˈɪdɪəm) *n., pl.* **-ia** (-ɪə). *Botany.* any of various fungal spores produced in the form of a chain by the development of septa in a hypha. [New Latin: from OO- + *-idium* diminutive suffix]
oik (ɔɪk) *n. Brit. derogatory, slang.* a person regarded as inferior because ignorant, ill-educated, or lower-class.
oil (ɔɪl) *n.* **1.** any of a number of viscous liquids with a smooth sticky feel. They are usually flammable, insoluble in water, soluble in organic solvents, and are obtained from plants and animals, from mineral deposits, and by synthesis. They are used as lubricants, fuels, perfumes, foodstuffs, and raw materials for chemicals. See also **essential oil, fixed oil. 2. a.** another name for **petroleum. b.** (*as modifier*): *an oil engine; an oil rig.* **3. a.** Also called: **lubricating oil.** any of a number of substances usually derived from petroleum and used for lubrication. **b.** (*in combination*): *an oilcan; an oilstone.* **c.** (*as modifier*): *an oil pump.* **4.** Also called: **fuel oil.** a petroleum product used as a fuel in domestic heating, industrial furnaces, marine engines, etc. **5.** *Brit.* **a.** paraffin, esp. when used as a domestic fuel. **b.** (*as modifier*): *an oil lamp; an oil stove.* **6.** any substance of a consistency resembling that of oil: *oil of vitriol.* **7.** the solvent, usually linseed oil, with which pigments are mixed to make artists' paints. **8. a.** (*often pl.*) oil colour or paint. **b.** (*as modifier*): *an oil painting.* **9.** an oil painting. **10. the good (dinkum) oil.** *Austral. and N.Z. slang.* facts or news. **11. strike oil. a.** to discover petroleum while drilling for it. **b.** *Informal.* to become very rich or successful. ~*vb.* (*tr.*) **12.** to lubricate, smear, polish, etc., with oil or an oily substance. **13.** *Informal.* to bribe (esp. in the phrase **oil someone's palm**). **14. oil one's tongue.** *Informal.* to speak flatteringly or glibly. **15. oil the wheels.** to make things run smoothly. **16.** See **well-oiled.** [C12: from Old French *oile,* from Latin *oleum* (olive) oil, from *olea* olive tree, from Greek *elaia* OLIVE] —ˈ**oil-ˌlike** *adj.*
oil beetle *n.* any of various beetles of the family *Meloidae* that exude an oily evil-smelling blood from their joints, which deters enemies.
oilbird (ˈɔɪlˌbɜːd) *n.* a nocturnal gregarious cave-dwelling bird, *Steatornis caripensis,* of N South America and Trinidad, having a hooked bill and dark plumage: family *Steatornithidae,* order *Caprimulgiformes.* Also called: **guacharo.**
oil cake *n.* stock feed consisting of compressed cubes made from the residue of the crushed seeds of oil-bearing crops such as linseed.
oilcan (ˈɔɪlˌkæn) *n.* a container with a long nozzle for applying lubricating oil to machinery.
oilcloth (ˈɔɪlˌklɒθ) *n.* **1.** waterproof material made by treating one side of a cotton fabric with a drying oil, or a synthetic resin. **2.** another name for **linoleum.**
oil-cooled *adj. Engineering, etc.* (of an engine, apparatus, etc.) having its heat removed by the circulation of oil. —**oil cooler** *n.*
oilcup (ˈɔɪlˌkʌp) *n.* a cup-shaped oil reservoir in a machine providing continuous lubrication for a bearing.
oil drum *n.* a metal drum used to contain or transport oil.
oiled silk *n.* silk treated with oil to make it waterproof.
oiler (ˈɔɪlə) *n.* **1.** a person, device, etc., that lubricates or supplies oil. **2.** an oil tanker. **3.** an oil well.
oilfield (ˈɔɪlˌfiːld) *n.* an area containing reserves of petroleum, esp. one that is already being exploited.
oilfired (ˈɔɪlˌfaɪəd) *adj.* (of central heating) using oil as fuel.
oilgas (ˈɔɪlˌgæs) *n.* a gaseous mixture of hydrocarbons used as a fuel, obtained by the destructive distillation of mineral oils.
oil hardening *n.* a process of hardening high-carbon or alloy steels by heating and cooling in oil. Compare **air hardening.**
oilman (ˈɔɪlmən) *n., pl.* **-men. 1.** a person who owns or operates oil wells. **2.** a person who makes or sells oil.
oil of turpentine *n.* another name for **turpentine** (sense 3).
oil of vitriol *n.* another name for **sulphuric acid.**
oil paint *or* **colour** *n.* paint made of pigment ground in oil, usually linseed oil, used for oil painting.
oil painting *n.* **1.** a picture painted with oil paints. **2.** the art or process of painting with oil paints. **3. he's** *or* **she's no oil painting.** *Informal.* he or she is not good-looking.
oil palm *n.* a tropical African palm tree, *Elaeis guineensis,* the fruits of which yield palm oil.
oil rig *n.* See **rig** (sense 6).
oil sand *n.* a sandstone impregnated with hydrocarbons, esp. such deposits in Alberta, Canada.
oil shale *n.* a fine-grained shale containing oil, which can be extracted by heating.
oilskin (ˈɔɪlˌskɪn) *n.* **1. a.** a cotton fabric treated with oil and pigment to make it waterproof. **b.** (*as modifier*): *an oilskin hat.* **2.** (*often pl.*) a protective outer garment of this fabric.
oil slick *n.* a mass of floating oil covering an area of water, esp. oil that has leaked or been discharged from a ship.
oilstone (ˈɔɪlˌstəʊn) *n.* a stone with a fine grain lubricated with oil and used for sharpening cutting tools. See also **whetstone.**
oil varnish *n.* another name for **varnish** (sense 1).
oil well *n.* a boring into the earth or sea bed for the extraction of petroleum.
oily (ˈɔɪlɪ) *adj.* **oilier, oiliest. 1.** soaked in or smeared with oil or grease. **2.** consisting of, containing, or resembling oil. **3.** flatteringly servile or obsequious. —ˈ**oilily** *adv.* —ˈ**oiliness** *n.*
oink (ɔɪŋk) *interj.* an imitation or representation of the grunt of a pig or the cry of a goose.
ointment (ˈɔɪntmənt) *n.* **1.** a fatty or oily medicated preparation applied to the skin to heal or protect. **2.** a similar substance used as a cosmetic. [C14: from Old French *oignement,* from Latin *unguentum* UNGUENT]
Oireachtas (ˈɛrəkθəs; *Gaelic* ˈɛrəxtəs) *n.* the parliament of the Republic of Ireland, consisting of the president, the Dáil Éireann, and the Seanad Éireann. See also **Dáil Éireann, Seanad Éireann.** [Irish: assembly, from Old Irish *airech* nobleman]
Ojibwa (əʊˈdʒɪbwə) *n.* **1.** (*pl.* **-was** *or* **-wa**) a member of a North American Indian people living in a region west of Lake Superior. **2.** the language of this people, belonging to the Algonquian family. ~Also called: **Chippewa.**
OK *abbrev. for* Oklahoma.
O.K. (ˌəʊˈkeɪ) *Informal.* ~*sentence substitute.* **1.** an expression of approval, agreement, etc. ~*adj.* (*usually postpositive*), *adv.* **2.** in good or satisfactory condition. ~*vb.* **O.K.s, O.K.ing** (ˌəʊˈkeɪɪŋ), **O.K.ed** (ˌəʊˈkeɪd). **3.** (*tr.*) to approve or endorse. ~*n., pl.* **O.K.s. 4.** approval or agreement. ~Also: **OK, o.k., o'kay.** [C19: perhaps from *o(ll) k(orrect),* jocular alteration of *all correct*]
oka (ˈəʊkə) *or* **oke** (əʊk) *n.* **1.** a unit of weight used in Turkey, equal to about 2.75 pounds or 1.24 kilograms. **2.** a unit of liquid measure used in Turkey, equal to about 1.3 pints or 0.75 litres. [C17: from Turkish *ōqah,* from Arabic *ūqiyah,* probably from Greek *ounkia;* perhaps related to Latin *uncia* one twelfth; see OUNCE[1]]
Oka (ˈəʊkə) *n.* a brine-cured Canadian cheese. [named after *Oka,* Quebec, where it is made at a monastery]
Okanagan (ˌəʊkəˈnɑːgən) *or* **Okanogan** (-ˈnəʊgən), **Okinagan** (ˌəʊkɪ-) *n.* **1.** a member of a North American Indian people living in the Okanagan River valley in British Columbia and Washington. **2.** the language of this people, belonging to the Salish people.
okapi (əʊˈkɑːpɪ) *n., pl.* **-pis** *or* **-pi.** a ruminant mammal, *Okapia johnstoni,* of the forests of central Africa, having a reddish-brown coat with horizontal white stripes on the legs and small horns: family *Giraffidae.* [C20: from a Central African word]
okay (ˌəʊˈkeɪ) *sentence substitute, adj., vb., n.* a variant of **O.K.**
oke[1] (əʊk) *n.* another name for **oka.**
oke[2] (əʊk) *adj., adv. Informal.* another term for **O.K.**
okey-doke (ˈəʊkɪˈdəʊk) *or* **okey-dokey** (ˈəʊkɪˈdəʊkɪ) *sentence substitute, adj., adv. Informal.* another term for **O.K.**
Okie (ˈəʊkɪ) *n. U.S. slang, sometimes considered offensive.* **1.** an inhabitant of Oklahoma, U.S. **2.** an impoverished migrant farm worker, esp. one who left Oklahoma during the Depression of the 1930s to work elsewhere in the U.S.
Okla. *abbrev. for* Oklahoma.
okra (ˈəʊkrə) *n.* **1.** Also called: **ladies' fingers.** an annual malvaceous plant, *Hibiscus esculentus,* of the Old World tropics, with yellow-and-red flowers and edible oblong sticky green pods. **2.** the pod of this plant, eaten in soups, stews, etc. See also **gumbo** (sense 1). [C18: of W African origin]
okta *or* **octa** (ˈɒktə) *n.* a unit used in meteorology to measure cloud cover, equivalent to a cloud cover of one eighth of the sky. [C20: from Greek *okta-, oktō* eight]
-ol[1] *suffix forming nouns.* denoting an organic chemical compound containing a hydroxyl group, esp. alcohols and phenols: *ethanol; quinol.* [from ALCOHOL]
-ol[2] *n. combining form.* (*not used systematically*) a variant of **-ole**[1].
old (əʊld) *adj.* **1.** having lived or existed for a relatively long time: *an old man; an old tradition; old wine; an old house; an old country.* **2. a.** of or relating to advanced years or a long life: *old age.* **b.** (*as collective n.;* preceded by *the*): *the old.* **c. old and young.** people of all ages. **3.** decrepit or senile. **4.** worn with age or use: *old clothes; an old car.* **5. a.** (*postpositive*) having lived or existed for a specified period: *a child who is six years old.* **b.** (*in combination*): *a six-year-old child.* **c.** (*as n. in combination*): *a six-year-old.* **6.** (*cap. when part of a name or title*) earlier or earliest of two or more things with the same name: *the old edition; the Old Testament; old Norwich.* **7.** (*cap. when part of a name*) designating the form of a language in which the earliest known records are written: *Old English.* **8.** (*prenominal*) familiar through long acquaintance or repetition: *an old friend; an old excuse.* **9.** practised; hardened: *old in cunning.* **10.** (*prenominal*) (often preceded by *good*) cherished; dear: used as a term of affection or familiarity: *good old George.* **11.** *Informal.* (with any of several nouns) used as a familiar form of address to a person: *old thing; old bean; old stick; old fellow.* **12.** skilled through long experience (esp. in the phrase **an old hand**). **13.** out-of-date; unfashionable. **14.** remote or distant in origin or time of origin: *an old culture.* **15.** (*prenominal*) former; previous: *my old house was small.* **16. a.** (*prenominal*) established for a relatively long time: *an old member.* **b.** (*in combination*): *old-established.* **17.** sensible, wise, or mature: *old beyond one's*

years. **18.** (of a river, valley, or land surface) in the final stage of the cycle of erosion, characterized by flat extensive flood plains and minimum relief. See also **youthful** (sense 4), **mature** (sense 6). **19.** (intensifier) (esp. in phrases such as **a good old time, any old thing, any old how,** etc.). **20.** (of crops) harvested late. **21. good old days.** an earlier period of time regarded as better than the present. **22. little old.** *Informal.* indicating affection, esp. humorous affection: *my little old wife.* **23. the old one** (*or* **gentleman**). *Informal.* a jocular name for **Satan.** ~*n.* **24.** an earlier or past time (esp. in the phrase **of old**): *in days of old.* [Old English *eald;* related to Old Saxon *ald,* Old High German, German *alt,* Latin *altus* high] —**'oldish** *adj.* —**'oldness** *n.*

old age pension *n.* a former name for the state **retirement pension.** —**old age pensioner** *n.*

Old Bill *n. Brit. slang.* **1.** a policeman. **2.** (*functioning as pl; preceded by the*) policemen collectively or in general. [C20: of uncertain origin: perhaps derived from the World War I cartoon of a soldier with a drooping moustache]

old bird *n. Jocular.* a wary and astute person.

old boy *n.* **1.** (*sometimes caps.*) *Brit.* a male ex-pupil of a school. **2.** *Informal, chiefly Brit.* **a.** a familiar name used to refer to a man. **b.** an old man.

old boy network *n. Brit. informal.* the appointment to power of former pupils of the same small group of public schools or universities.

Old Bulgarian *n.* another name for **Old Church Slavonic.**

Old Catholic *adj.* **1.** of or relating to several small national Churches which have broken away from the Roman Catholic Church on matters of doctrine. ~*n.* **2.** a member of one of these Churches.

old chum *n. Austral. informal.* (formerly) **1.** a person who is experienced, esp. in life in colonial Australia. **2.** an experienced convict.

Old Church Slavonic *or* **Slavic** *n.* the oldest recorded Slavonic language: the form of Old Slavonic into which the Bible was translated in the ninth century, preserved as a liturgical language of various Orthodox Churches: belonging to the South Slavonic subbranch of languages.

old clothes man *n.* a person who deals in second-hand clothes.

old country *n.* the country of origin of an immigrant or an immigrant's ancestors.

Old Dart *n.* **the.** *Austral. slang.* England. [C19: of unknown origin]

Old Dutch *n.* the Dutch language up to about 1100, derived from the Low Franconian dialect of Old Low German. See also **Franconian.** Abbrev.: **OD.**

olden ('əʊldᵊn) *adj.* an archaic or poetic word for **old** (often in phrases such as **in olden days** and **in olden times**).

Old English *n.* **1.** Also called: **Anglo-Saxon.** the English language from the time of the earliest settlements in the fifth century A.D. to about 1100. The main dialects were West Saxon (the chief literary form), Kentish, and Anglian. Compare **Middle English, Modern English.** Abbrev.: **OE.** **2.** *Printing.* a Gothic typeface commonly used in England up until the 18th century.

Old English sheepdog *n.* a breed of large bobtailed sheepdog with a profuse shaggy coat.

older ('əʊldə) *adj.* **1.** the comparative of **old.** **2.** Also (of people, esp. members of the same family): **elder.** having lived or existed longer; of greater age.

old-established *adj.* established for a long time.

olde-worlde ('əʊldɪ'wɜːldɪ) *adj. Sometimes facetious.* old-world or quaint.

old face *n. Printing.* a type style that originated in the 18th century, characterized by little contrast between thick and thin strokes. Compare **modern** (sense 5).

oldfangled ('əʊld'fæŋgᵊld) *adj. Derogatory.* out-of-date; old-fashioned. [C20: formed on analogy with NEWFANGLED]

old-fashioned *adj.* **1.** belonging to, characteristic of, or favoured by former times; outdated: *old-fashioned ideas.* **2.** favouring or adopting the dress, manners, fashions, etc., of a former time. **3.** quizzically doubtful or disapproving: *she did not reply, but gave him an old-fashioned look.* **4.** *Scot. and northern English dialect.* old for one's age: *an old-fashioned child.* ~*n.* **5.** a cocktail containing spirit, bitters, fruit, etc. —ˌ**old-'fashionedly** *adv.*

Old French *n.* the French language in its earliest forms, from about the 9th century up to about 1400. Abbrev.: **OF.**

Old Frisian *n.* the Frisian language up to about 1400. Abbrev.: **OFris.**

old girl *n.* **1.** (*sometimes caps.*) *Brit.* a female ex-pupil of a school. **2.** *Informal, chiefly Brit.* **a.** a familiar name used to refer to a woman. **b.** an old woman.

Old Glory *n.* a nickname for the flag of the United States of America.

old gold *n.* **a.** a dark yellow colour, sometimes with a brownish tinge. **b.** (*as adj.*): *an old-gold carpet.*

old guard *n.* **1.** a group that works for a long-established or old-fashioned cause or principle. **2.** the conservative element in a political party or other group. [C19: from *Old Guard,* the French imperial guard created by Napoleon]

old hand *n.* **1.** a person who is skilled at something through long experience. **2.** *Austral. informal.* (in the nineteenth century) an ex-convict. **3.** *Austral. informal.* a person who is long established in a place.

Old Harry *n. Informal.* a jocular name for **Satan.**

old hat *adj.* (*postpositive*) old-fashioned or trite.

Old High German *n.* a group of West Germanic dialects that eventually developed into modern German; High German up to about 1200: spoken in the Middle Ages on the upper Rhine, in Bavaria, Alsace, and elsewhere, including Alemannic, Bavarian, Langobardic, and Upper Franconian. Abbrev.: **OHG.**

Old Icelandic *n.* the dialect of Old Norse spoken and written in Iceland; the Icelandic language up to about 1600.

old identity *n. N.Z.* a person known for a long time in the one locality.

oldie ('əʊldɪ) *n. Informal.* an old person or thing.

Old Irish *n.* the Celtic language of Ireland up to about 900 A.D., introduced to Scotland by Irish settlers about 500 A.D.

old lady *n.* **1.** an informal term for **mother**[1] or **wife** (sense 1). **2.** a large noctuid moth, *Mormo maura,* that has drab patterned wings originally thought to resemble an elderly Victorian lady's shawl.

Old Latin *n.* the Latin language before the classical period, up to about 100 B.C.

old-line *adj.* **1.** *U.S. and Canadian.* conservative; old-fashioned. **2.** well-established; traditional. —ˌ**old-'liner** *n.*

Old Low German *n.* the Saxon and Low Franconian dialects of German up to about 1200; the old form of modern Low German and Dutch. Abbrev.: **OLG.**

old maid *n.* **1.** a woman regarded as unlikely ever to marry; spinster. **2.** *Informal.* a prim, fastidious, or excessively cautious person. **3.** a card game using a pack from which one card has been removed, in which players try to avoid holding the unpaired card at the end of the game. —ˌ**old-'maidish** *adj.*

old man *n.* **1.** an informal term for **father** or **husband** (sense 1). **2.** (*sometimes caps.*) *Informal.* a man in command, such as an employer, foreman, or captain of a ship. **3.** *Sometimes facetious.* an affectionate term used in addressing a man. **4.** another name for **southernwood.** **5.** *Austral. informal.* **a.** an adult male kangaroo. **b.** (*modifier*) very large. **6.** *Christianity.* the unregenerate aspect of human nature.

old man's beard *n.* any of various plants having long trailing parts, esp. traveller's joy and Spanish moss.

old master *n.* **1.** one of the great European painters of the period 1500 to 1800. **2.** a painting by one of these.

old moon *n.* **1.** a phase of the moon lying between last quarter and new moon, when it appears as a waning crescent. **2.** the moon when it appears as a waning crescent. **3.** the time at which this occurs.

Old Nick *n. Informal.* a jocular name for **Satan.**

Old Norse *n.* the language or group of dialects of medieval Scandinavia and Iceland from about 700 to about 1350, forming the North Germanic branch of the Indo-European family of languages. See also **Proto-Norse, Old Icelandic.** Abbrev.: **ON.**

Old North French *n.* any of the dialects of Old French spoken in N France, such as Norman French.

Old Persian *n.* an ancient language belonging to the West Iranian branch of the Indo-European family, recorded in cuneiform inscriptions of the 6th to the 4th centuries B.C. See also **Middle Persian.**

Old Prussian *n.* the former language of the non-German Prussians, belonging to the Baltic branch of the Indo-European family: extinct by 1700.

Old Red Sandstone *n.* **1.** a thick sequence of sedimentary rock (generally, but not always, red) deposited in Britain and NW Europe during the Devonian period. **2.** (in Britain) another term for **Devonian.** ~Abbrev.: **ORS.**

old rose *n.* **a.** a greyish-pink colour. **b.** (*as adj.*): *old-rose gloves.*

Old Saxon *n.* the Saxon dialect of Low German up to about 1200, from which modern Low German is derived. Abbrev.: **OS.**

old school *n.* **1.** *Chiefly Brit.* a school formerly attended by a person. **2.** a group of people favouring traditional ideas or conservative practices.

old school tie *n.* **1.** *Brit.* a distinctive tie that indicates which school the wearer attended. **2.** the attitudes, loyalties, values, etc., associated with British public schools.

Old Slavonic *or* **Slavic** *n.* the South Slavonic language up to about 1400: the language of the Macedonian Slavs that developed into Serbo-Croatian and Bulgarian. See also **Old Church Slavonic.**

old sod *n. Informal.* one's native country: *back to the old sod.*

old soldier *n.* **1.** a former soldier or veteran. **2.** an experienced or practised person.

old squaw *n. U.S. and Canadian.* a long-tailed northern sea duck, *Clangula hyemalis,* having dark wings and a white-and-brown head and body. Also called: **oldwife.**

old stager *n.* a person with experience; old hand.

oldster ('əʊldstə) *n.* **1.** *Informal.* an older person. **2.** *Brit. Navy.* a person who has been a midshipman for four years.

Old Stone Age *n.* (*not now in technical usage*) another term for **Palaeolithic.**

old style *n. Printing.* a type style reviving the characteristics of old face.

Old Style *n.* the former method of reckoning dates using the Julian calendar. Compare **New Style.**
old sweat *n. Brit. informal.* **1.** an old soldier; veteran. **2.** a person who has a great deal of experience in some activity.
old talk *Caribbean.* ~*n.* **1.** superficial chatting. ~*vb.* **old-talk.** **2.** (*intr.*) to indulge in such chatting.
Old Test. *abbrev. for* Old Testament.
Old Testament *n.* the collection of books comprising the sacred Scriptures of the Hebrews and essentially recording the history of the Hebrew people as the chosen people of God; the first part of the Christian Bible.
old-time *adj.* (*prenominal*) of or relating to a former time; old-fashioned: *old-time dancing.*
old-time dance *n. Brit.* a formal or formation dance, such as the lancers. —**old-time dancing** *n.*
old-timer *n.* **1.** a person who has been in a certain place, occupation, etc., for a long time. **2.** *U.S.* an old man.
oldwife ('əʊldˌwaɪf) *n., pl.* **-wives.** **1.** another name for **old squaw.** **2.** any of various fishes, esp. the menhaden or the alewife.
old wives' tale *n.* a belief, usually superstitious or erroneous, passed on by word of mouth as a piece of traditional wisdom.
old woman *n.* **1.** an informal term for **mother**[1] or **wife** (sense 1). **2.** a timid, fussy, or cautious person. —**old womanish** *adj.*
Old World **a.** that part of the world that was known before the discovery of the Americas, comprising Europe, Asia, and Africa. **b.** (*as modifier*): *Old World forests.*
old-world *adj.* of or characteristic of former times, esp., in Europe, quaint or traditional. —ˌ**old-'worldly** *adv.*
Old World monkey *n.* any monkey of the family *Cercopithecidae,* including macaques, baboons, and mandrills. They are more closely related to anthropoid apes than are the New World monkeys, having nostrils that are close together and nonprehensile tails.
olé (əʊ'leɪ) *interj.* **1.** an exclamation of approval or encouragement customary at bullfights, flamenco dancing, and other Spanish or Latin American events. ~*n.* **2.** a cry of olé. [Spanish, from Arabic *wa-llāh,* from *wa* and + *allāh* God]
-ole[1] *or* **-ol** *n. combining form.* **1.** denoting an organic unsaturated compound containing a 5-membered ring: *thiazole.* **2.** denoting an aromatic organic ether: *anisole.* [from Latin *oleum* oil, from Greek *elaion,* from *elaia* olive]
-ole[2] *suffix of nouns.* indicating something small: *arteriole.* [from Latin *-olus,* diminutive suffix]
olea ('əʊlɪə) *n.* a plural of **oleum.**
oleaceous (ˌəʊlɪ'eɪʃəs) *adj.* of, relating to, or belonging to the *Oleaceae,* a family of trees and shrubs, including the ash, jasmine, privet, lilac, and olive. [C19: via New Latin from Latin *olea* OLIVE; see also OIL]
oleaginous (ˌəʊlɪ'ædʒɪnəs) *adj.* **1.** resembling or having the properties of oil. **2.** containing or producing oil. [C17: from Latin *oleāginus,* from *olea* OLIVE; see also OIL]
oleander (ˌəʊlɪ'ændə) *n.* a poisonous evergreen Mediterranean apocynaceous shrub or tree, *Nerium oleander,* with fragrant white, pink, or purple flowers. Also called: **rosebay.** [C16: from Medieval Latin, variant of *arodandrum,* perhaps from Latin RHODODENDRON]
oleaster (ˌəʊlɪ'æstə) *n.* **1.** any of several shrubs of the genus *Elaeagnus,* esp. *E. angustifolia,* of S Europe, Asia, and North America, having silver-white twigs, yellow flowers, and an olive-like fruit: family *Elaeagnaceae.* **2.** Also called: **wild olive.** a wild specimen of the cultivated olive. [Latin: from *olea;* see OLIVE, OIL]
oleate ('əʊlɪˌeɪt) *n.* any salt or ester of oleic acid, containing the ion $C_{17}H_{33}COO^-$ or the group $C_{17}H_{33}COO$-: common components of natural fats.
olecranon (əʊ'lɛkrəˌnɒn, ˌəʊlɪ'kreɪnən) *n. Anatomy.* the bony projection of the ulna behind the elbow joint. [C18: from Greek, shortened from *ōlenokrānon,* from *ōlenē* elbow + *krānion* head] —**olecranal** (əʊ'lɛkrənəl, ˌəʊlɪ'kreɪnəl) *adj.*
olefine *or* **olefin** ('əʊlɪˌfiːn, -fɪn, 'ɒl-) *n.* other names for **alkene.** [C19: from French *oléfiant,* ultimately from Latin *oleum* oil + *facere* to make] —ˌ**ole'finic** *adj.*
oleic acid (əʊ'liːɪk) *n.* a colourless oily liquid unsaturated acid occurring, as the glyceride, in almost all natural fats used in making soaps, ointments, cosmetics, and lubricating oils. Formula: $CH_3(CH_2)_7CH{:}CH(CH_2)_7COOH$. Systematic name: ***cis*-9-octadecenoic acid.** [C19 *oleic,* from Latin *oleum* oil + -IC]
olein ('əʊlɪɪn) *n.* another name for **triolein.** [C19: from French *oléine,* from Latin *oleum* oil + -IN]
oleo- *combining form.* oil: *oleomargarine.* [from Latin *oleum* OIL]
oleograph ('əʊlɪəˌgrɑːf, -ˌgræf) *n.* **1.** a chromolithograph printed in oil colours to imitate the appearance of an oil painting. **2.** the pattern formed by a drop of oil spreading on water. —**oleographic** (ˌəʊlɪə'græfɪk) *adj.* —**oleography** (ˌəʊlɪ'ɒgrəfɪ) *n.*
oleomargarine (ˌəʊlɪəʊˌmɑːdʒə'riːn) *or* **oleomargarin** (ˌəʊlɪəʊ'mɑːdʒərɪn) *n.* other names (esp. U.S.) for **margarine.**
oleo oil ('əʊlɪəʊ) *n.* an oil extracted from beef fat, consisting mainly of a mixture of olein and palmitin. It is used in the manufacture of margarine.
oleoresin (ˌəʊlɪəʊ'rɛzɪn) *n.* **1.** a semisolid mixture of a resin and essential oil, obtained from certain plants. **2.** *Pharmacol.* a liquid preparation of resins and oils, obtained by extraction from plants. —ˌ**oleo'resinous** *adj.*
oleum ('əʊlɪəm) *n., pl.* **olea** ('əʊlɪə) *or* **oleums.** another name for **fuming sulphuric acid.** [from Latin: oil, referring to its oily consistency]
O level *n.* (formerly in Britain) **1. a.** the basic level of the General Certificate of Education, now replaced by **GCSE.** **b.** (*as modifier*): *O level maths.* **2.** a pass in a particular subject at O level: *he has eight O levels.* ~Formal name: **Ordinary level.**
olfaction (ɒl'fækʃən) *n.* **1.** the sense of smell. **2.** the act or function of smelling.
olfactometry (ˌɒlfæk'tɒmɪtrɪ) *n. Chem.* another name for **odorimetry.**
olfactory (ɒl'fæktərɪ, -trɪ) *adj.* **1.** of or relating to the sense of smell. ~*n., pl.* **-ries.** **2.** (*usually pl.*) an organ or nerve concerned with the sense of smell. [C17: from Latin *olfactus,* past participle of *olfacere,* from *olere* to smell + *facere* to make]
olfactory bulb *n.* the anterior and slightly enlarged end of the olfactory tract, from which the cranial nerves concerned with the sense of smell originate.
olfactory nerve *n.* either one of the first pair of cranial nerves, supplying the mucous membrane of the nose.
olfactory tract *n.* a long narrow triangular band of white tissue originating in the olfactory bulb and extending back to the point at which its fibres enter the base of the cerebrum.
OLG *abbrev. for* Old Low German.
olibanum (ɒ'lɪbənəm) *n.* another name for **frankincense.** [C14: from Medieval Latin, from Greek *libanos*]
olid ('ɒlɪd) *adj.* foul-smelling. [C17: from Latin *olidus,* from *olēre* to smell]
oligaemia *or U.S.* **oligemia** (ˌɒlɪ'giːmɪə) *n. Med.* a reduction in the volume of the blood, as occurs after haemorrhage. —ˌ**oli'gaemic** *or U.S.* ˌ**oli'gemic** *adj.*
oligarch ('ɒlɪˌgɑːk) *n.* a member of an oligarchy.
oligarchy ('ɒlɪˌgɑːkɪ) *n., pl.* **-chies.** **1.** government by a small group of people. **2.** a state or organization so governed. **3.** a small body of individuals ruling such a state. **4.** *Chiefly U.S.* a small clique of private citizens who exert a strong influence on government. [C16: via Medieval Latin from Greek *oligarkhia,* from *olígos* few + -ARCHY] —ˌ**oli'garchic** *or* ˌ**oli'garchical** *adj.* —ˌ**oli'garchically** *adv.*
oligo- *or before a vowel* **olig-** *combining form.* indicating a few or little: *oligopoly.* [from Greek *oligos* little, few]
Oligocene ('ɒlɪgəʊˌsiːn, ɒ'lɪg-) *adj.* **1.** of, denoting, or formed in the third epoch of the Tertiary period, which lasted for 15 000 000 years. ~*n.* **2. the.** the Oligocene epoch or rock series. [C19: OLIGO- + -CENE]
oligochaete ('ɒlɪgəʊˌkiːt) *n.* **1.** any freshwater or terrestrial annelid worm of the class *Oligochaeta,* having bristles (chaetae) borne singly along the length of the body: includes the earthworms. ~*adj.* **2.** of, relating to, or belonging to the class *Oligochaeta.* [C19: from New Latin; see OLIGO-, CHAETA]
oligoclase ('ɒlɪgəʊˌkleɪs) *n.* a white, bluish, or reddish-yellow feldspar mineral of the plagioclase series, consisting of aluminium silicates of sodium and calcium. Formula: $NaAlSi_3O_8.CaAl_2Si_2O_8$. [C19: from OLIGO- + -CLASE]
oligomer (ɒ'lɪgəmə) *n.* a compound of relatively low molecular weight containing up to five monomer units. Compare **polymer, copolymer.** [C20: from OLIGO- + *-mer,* as in *polymer*]
oligomerous (ˌɒlɪ'gɒmərəs) *adj. Biology.* having a small number of component parts.
oligonucleotide (ˌɒlɪgəʊ'njuːklɪəˌtaɪd) *n.* a polymer consisting of a small number of nucleotides.
oligopeptide (ˌɒlɪgəʊ'pɛptaɪd) *n. Biochem.* a peptide comprising less than ten amino acids.
oligopoly (ˌɒlɪ'gɒpəlɪ) *n., pl.* **-lies.** *Economics.* a market situation in which control over the supply of a commodity is held by a small number of producers each of whom is able to influence prices and thus directly affect the position of competitors. [C20: from OLIGO- + Greek *pōlein* to sell, on the model of MONOPOLY] —ˌ**oliˌgopo'listic** *adj.*
oligopsony (ˌɒlɪ'gɒpsənɪ) *n., pl.* **-nies.** a market situation in which the demand for a commodity is represented by a small number of purchasers. [C20: from OLIGO- + *-opsony,* from Greek *opsōnia* purchase of food] —ˌ**oliˌgopso'nistic** *adj.*
oligosaccharide (ˌɒlɪgəʊ'sækəˌraɪd, -rɪd) *n.* any one of a class of carbohydrates consisting of a few monosaccharide units linked together. Compare **polysaccharide.**
oligospermia (ˌɒlɪgəʊ'spɜːmɪə) *n.* the condition of having less than the normal number of spermatozoa in the semen: a cause of infertility in men.
oligotrophic (ˌɒlɪgəʊ'trɒfɪk) *adj.* (of lakes and similar habitats) poor in nutrients and plant life and rich in oxygen. Compare **eutrophic.** [C20: from OLIGO- + Greek *trophein* to nourish + -IC] —**oligotrophy** (ˌɒlɪ'gɒtrəfɪ) *n.*
oliguria (ˌɒlɪ'gjʊərɪə) *or* **oliguresis** (ˌɒlɪgjʊ'riːsɪs) *n.* excretion of an abnormally small volume of urine, often as the result of a kidney disorder. Compare **anuria.** [C19: from OLIGO- + -URIA] —**oliguretic** (ˌɒlɪgjʊ'rɛtɪk) *adj.*
olio ('əʊlɪˌəʊ) *n., pl.* **olios.** **1.** a dish of many different ingredients. **2.** a miscellany or potpourri. [C17: from Spanish *olla* stew, from Latin: jar]
olivaceous (ˌɒlɪ'veɪʃəs) *adj.* of an olive colour.

olivary ('ɒlɪvərɪ) *adj.* **1.** shaped like an olive. **2.** *Anatomy.* of or relating to either of two masses of tissue (**olivary bodies**) on the forward portion of the medulla oblongata. [C16: from Latin *olivārius,* from *oliva* OLIVE]

olive ('ɒlɪv) *n.* **1.** an evergreen oleaceous tree, *Olea europaea,* of the Mediterranean region but cultivated elsewhere, having white fragrant flowers, and edible shiny black fruits. **2.** the fruit of this plant, eaten as a relish and used as a source of olive oil. **3.** the wood of the olive tree, used for ornamental work. **4.** any of various trees or shrubs resembling the olive. **5. a.** a yellow-green colour. **b.** (*as adj.*): *an olive coat.* **6.** an angler's name for the dun of various mayflies or an artificial fly in imitation of this. ~*adj.* **7.** of, relating to, or made of the olive tree, its wood, or its fruit. [C13: via Old French from Latin *oliva,* related to Greek *elaia* olive tree; compare Greek *elaion* oil]

olive branch *n.* **1.** a branch of an olive tree used to symbolize peace. **2.** any offering of peace or conciliation.

olive brown *n.* **a.** a dull yellowish-brown to yellowish-green colour. **b.** (*as adj.*): *an olive-brown coat.*

olive crown *n.* (esp. in ancient Greece and Rome) a garland of olive leaves awarded as a token of victory.

olive drab *n. U.S.* **1. a.** a dull but fairly strong greyish-olive colour. **b.** (*as adj.*): *an olive-drab jacket.* **2.** cloth or clothes in this colour, esp. the uniform of the U.S. Army.

olive green *n.* **a.** a colour that is greener, stronger, and brighter than olive; deep yellowish-green. **b.** (*as adj.*): *an olive-green coat.*

olivenite (ɒ'lɪvɪˌnaɪt) *n.* a green to black rare secondary mineral consisting of hydrated basic copper arsenate in orthorhombic crystalline form. Formula: $Cu_2(AsO_4)(OH)$. [C19: from German *Oliven(erz)* olive (ore) + -ITE[1]]

olive oil *n.* a pale yellow oil pressed from ripe olive fruits and used in cooking, medicines, soaps, etc.

olivine ('ɒlɪˌviːn, ˌɒlɪ'viːn) *n.* **1.** an olive-green mineral of the olivine group, found in igneous and metamorphic rocks. The clear-green variety (peridot) is used as a gemstone. Composition: magnesium iron silicate. Formula: $(MgFe)_2SiO_4$. Crystal structure: orthorhombic. **2.** any mineral in the group having the general formula $(Mg,Fe,Mn,Ca)_2SiO_4$. [C18: from German, named after its colour]

olla ('ɒlə; *Spanish* 'oʎa) *n.* **1.** a cooking pot. **2.** short for **olla podrida.** [Spanish, from Latin *olla,* variant of *aulla* pot]

olla podrida (pɒ'driːdə; *Spanish* po'ðriða) *n.* **1.** a Spanish dish, consisting of a stew with beans, sausages, etc. **2.** an assortment; miscellany. [literally: rotten pot]

olm (əʊlm, ɒlm) *n.* a pale blind eel-like salamander, *Proteus anguinus,* of underground streams in SE Europe, that retains its larval form throughout its life: family *Proteidae.* See also **mud puppy.** [C20: from German]

ologoan (ˌʌlə'goːn) *vb.* (*intr.*) *Irish.* to complain loudly without reason: *she's always ologoaning about something.* [from Irish Gaelic *olagón* lament]

ology ('ɒlədʒɪ) *n., pl.* **-gies.** *Informal.* a science or other branch of knowledge. [C19: abstracted from words with this ending, such as *theology, biology,* etc.; see -LOGY]

oloroso (ˌɒlə'rəʊsəʊ) *n.* a full-bodied golden-coloured sweet sherry. [from Spanish: fragrant]

Olympiad (ə'lɪmpɪˌæd) *n.* **1.** a staging of the modern Olympic Games. **2.** the four-year period between consecutive celebrations of the Olympic Games; a unit of ancient Greek chronology dating back to 776 B.C. **3.** an international contest in chess, bridge, etc.

Olympian (ə'lɪmpɪən) *adj.* **1.** of or relating to Mount Olympus, the dwelling place of the classical Greek gods, or to the gods themselves. **2.** majestic or godlike in manner or bearing. **3.** superior to mundane considerations, esp. when impractical. **4.** a less common word for **Olympic** (sense 2). ~*n.* **5.** a god of Olympus. **6.** *Chiefly U.S.* a competitor in the Olympic Games.

Olympic (ə'lɪmpɪk) *adj.* **1.** of or relating to the Olympic Games. **2.** of or relating to ancient Olympia, a plain in the Peloponnese, site of a major sanctuary of the god Zeus and of the original Olympic Games.

Olympic Games *n.* (*functioning as sing. or pl.*) **1.** the greatest Panhellenic festival, held every fourth year in honour of Zeus at ancient Olympia. From 472 B.C., it consisted of five days of games, sacrifices, and festivities. **2.** Also called: **the Olympics.** the modern revival of these games, consisting of international athletic and sporting contests held every four years in a selected country since their inception in Athens in 1896. See also **Winter Olympic Games.**

Om (əʊm) *n. Hinduism.* a sacred syllable typifying the three gods Brahma, Vishnu, and Siva, who are concerned in the threefold operation of integration, maintenance, and disintegration. [from Sanskrit]

OM **1.** *abbrev. for* Order of Merit (a Brit. title). ~**2.** *Currency. symbol for* Ostmark.

Om. *abbrev. for* Ostmark.

-oma *n. combining form.* indicating a tumour: *carcinoma.* [from Greek *-ōma*]

omadhaun ('ɒmədɑːn) *n. Irish.* a foolish man or boy. [C19: from Irish Gaelic *amadán*]

Omani (əʊ'mɑːnɪ) *adj.* **1.** of or relating to Oman, a sultanate in SE Arabia on the Arabian Sea, its people, or its culture. ~*n.* **2.** a native or inhabitant of Oman.

omasum (əʊ'meɪsəm) *n., pl.* **-sa** (-sə). another name for **psalterium.** [C18: from Latin: bullock's tripe]

Omayyad *or* **Ommiad** (əʊ'maɪæd) *n., pl.* **-yads, -yades** (-əˌdiːz) *or* **-ads, -ades** (-əˌdiːz). **1.** a caliph of the dynasty ruling (661–750 A.D.) from its capital at Damascus in Syria. **2.** an emir (756–929 A.D.) or caliph (929–1031 A.D.) of the Omayyad dynasty in Spain.

ombre *or U.S.* **omber** ('ɒmbə) *n.* an 18th-century card game. [C17: from Spanish *hombre* man, referring to the player who attempts to win the stakes]

ombro- *combining form.* indicating rain: *ombrogenous; ombrophilous.* [from Greek *ombros* shower of rain]

ombrogenous (ɒm'brɒdʒɪnəs) *adj.* (of plants) able to flourish in wet conditions.

ombrophilous (ɒm'brɒfɪləs) *adj.* (of plants) tolerant of wet conditions.

ombrophobous (ɒm'brɒfəbəs) *adj.* (of plants) not able to tolerate wet conditions.

ombudsman ('ɒmbʊdzmən) *n., pl.* **-men.** **1.** a commissioner who acts as independent referee between individual citizens and their government or its administration. **2.** (in Britain) an official, without power of sanction or mechanism of appeal, who investigates complaints of maladministration by members of the public against national or local government or its servants. Formal names: **Commissioner for Local Administration, Health Service Commissioner, Parliamentary Commissioner.** See also **Financial Ombudsman.** [C20: from Swedish: commissioner]

-ome *n. combining form.* denoting a mass or part of a specified kind: *rhizome.* [variant of -OMA]

omega ('əʊmɪgə) *n.* **1.** the 24th and last letter of the Greek alphabet (Ω, ω), a long vowel, transliterated as *o* or *ō.* **2.** the ending or last of a series. [C16: from Greek *ō mega* big o; see MEGA-, OMICRON]

omega minus *n.* an unstable negatively charged elementary particle, classified as a baryon, that has a mass 3276 times that of the electron.

omelette *or esp. U.S.* **omelet** ('ɒmlɪt) *n.* a savoury or sweet dish of beaten eggs cooked in fat. [C17: from French *omelette,* changed from *alumette,* from *alumelle* sword blade, changed by mistaken division from *la lemelle,* from Latin (see LAMELLA); apparently from the flat shape of the omelette]

omen ('əʊmən) *n.* **1.** a phenomenon or occurrence regarded as a sign of future happiness or disaster. **2.** prophetic significance. ~*vb.* **3.** (*tr.*) to portend. [C16: from Latin]

omentum (əʊ'mɛntəm) *n., pl.* **-ta** (-tə). *Anatomy.* a double fold of peritoneum connecting the stomach with other abdominal organs. [C16: from Latin: membrane, esp. a caul, of obscure origin]

omer ('əʊmə) *n.* an ancient Hebrew unit of dry measure equal to one tenth of an ephah. [C17: from Hebrew *'ōmer* a measure]

Omer ('əʊmə) *n. Judaism.* a period of seven weeks extending from the second day of Passover to the first day of Shavuoth, and observed as a period of semimourning. [named because sacrifices of an OMER of grain were made]

omertà *Italian.* (omer'ta) *n.* a conspiracy of silence.

omicron (əʊ'maɪkrɒn, 'ɒmɪkrɒn) *n.* the 15th letter in the Greek alphabet (Ο, ο), a short vowel, transliterated as *o.* [from Greek *ō mikron* small o; see MICRO-, OMEGA]

ominous ('ɒmɪnəs) *adj.* **1.** foreboding evil. **2.** serving as or having significance as an omen. [C16: from Latin *ōminōsus,* from OMEN] —'**ominously** *adv.* —'**ominousness** *n.*

omission (əʊ'mɪʃən) *n.* **1.** something that has been omitted or neglected. **2.** the act of omitting or the state of having been omitted. [C14: from Latin *omissiō,* from *omittere* to OMIT] —**o'missive** *adj.* —**o'missiveness** *n.*

omit (əʊ'mɪt) *vb.* **omits, omitting, omitted.** (*tr.*) **1.** to neglect to do or include. **2.** to fail (to do something). [C15: from Latin *omittere,* from *ob-* away + *mittere* to send] —**omissible** (əʊ'mɪsɪbᵊl) *adj.* —**o'mitter** *n.*

OMM (in Canada) *abbrev. for* Officer of the Order of Military Merit.

ommatidium (ˌɒmə'tɪdɪəm) *n., pl.* **-tidia** (-'tɪdɪə). any of the numerous cone-shaped units that make up the compound eyes of some arthropods. [C19: via New Latin from Greek *ommatidion,* from *omma* eye] —ˌ**omma'tidial** *adj.*

ommatophore (ɒ'mætəˌfɔː) *n. Zoology.* a movable stalk or tentacle bearing an eye, occurring in lower animals such as crabs and snails. [C19: from Greek *omma* eye + -PHORE] —**ommatophorous** (ˌɒmə'tɒfərəs) *adj.*

Ommiad (əʊ'maɪæd) *n., pl.* **-ads** *or* **-ades** (-əˌdiːz). a variant spelling of **Omayyad.**

omni- *combining form.* all or everywhere: *omnipresent.* [from Latin *omnis* all]

omnia vincit amor *Latin.* ('ɒmnɪə 'vɪnsɪt 'æmɔː) love conquers all things. [from the Roman poet Virgil's *Eclogues* 10:69]

omnibus ('ɒmnɪˌbʌs, -bəs) *n., pl.* **-buses.** **1.** a less common word for **bus** (sense 1). **2.** Also called: **omnibus volume.** a collection of works by one author or several works on a similar topic, reprinted in one volume. ~*adj.* **3.** (*prenominal*) of, dealing with, or providing for many different things or cases. [C19: from Latin, literally: for all, from *omnis* all]

omnicompetent (ˌɒmnɪ'kɒmpɪtənt) *adj.* able to judge or deal with all matters. —ˌ**omni'competence** *n.*

omnidirectional (ˌɒmnɪdɪˈrɛkʃənᵊl, -daɪ-) *adj.* **1.** (of an antenna) capable of transmitting and receiving radio signals equally in any direction in the horizontal plane. **2.** (of a microphone) equally sensitive in all directions.

omnifarious (ˌɒmnɪˈfɛərɪəs) *adj.* of many or all varieties or forms. [C17: from Late Latin *omnifārius*, from Latin *omnis* all + *-farius* doing, related to *facere* to do] —ˌ**omniˈfariously** *adv.* —ˌ**omniˈfariousness** *n.*

omnific (ɒmˈnɪfɪk) *or* **omnificent** (ɒmˈnɪfɪsᵊnt) *adj. Rare.* creating all things. [C17: via Medieval Latin from Latin *omni-* + *-ficus*, from *facere* to do] —**omˈnificence** *n.*

omnipotent (ɒmˈnɪpətənt) *adj.* **1.** having very great or unlimited power. ~*n.* **2. the Omnipotent.** an epithet for God. [C14: via Old French from Latin *omnipotens* all-powerful, from OMNI- + *potens*, from *posse* to be able] —**omˈnipotence** *n.* —**omˈnipotently** *adv.*

omnipresent (ˌɒmnɪˈprɛzᵊnt) *adj.* (esp. of a deity) present in all places at the same time. —ˌ**omniˈpresence** *n.*

omnirange (ˈɒmnɪˌreɪndʒ) *n.* a very-high-frequency ground radio navigational system to assist a pilot in plotting his exact position.

omniscient (ɒmˈnɪsɪənt) *adj.* **1.** having infinite knowledge or understanding. **2.** having very great or seemingly unlimited knowledge. [C17: from Medieval Latin *omnisciens*, from Latin OMNI- + *scīre* to know] —**omˈniscience** *n.* —**omˈnisciently** *adv.*

omnium-gatherum (ˈɒmnɪəmˈgæðərəm) *n. Often facetious.* a miscellaneous collection; assortment. [C16: from Latin *omnium* of all, from *omnis* all + Latinized form of English *gather*]

omnivore (ˈɒmnɪˌvɔː) *n.* an omnivorous person or animal.

omnivorous (ɒmˈnɪvərəs) *adj.* **1.** eating food of both animal and vegetable origin, or any type of food indiscriminately. **2.** taking in or assimilating everything, esp. with the mind. [C17: from Latin *omnivorus* all-devouring, from OMNI- + *vorāre* to eat greedily] —**omˈnivorously** *adv.* —**omˈnivorousness** *n.*

omophagia (ˌəʊməˈfeɪdʒɪə) *or* **omophagy** (əʊˈmɒfədʒɪ) *n.* the eating of raw food, esp. meat. [C18: via New Latin from Greek *ōmophagia*, from *ōmos* raw + *-phagia*; see -PHAGY] —**omophagic** (ˌəʊməˈfædʒɪk) *or* **omophagous** (əʊˈmɒfəgəs) *adj.*

omphalos (ˈɒmfəˌlɒs) *n.* **1.** (in the ancient world) a sacred conical object, esp. a stone. The most famous omphalos at Delphi was assumed to mark the centre of the earth. **2.** the central point. **3.** *Literary.* another word for **navel.** [Greek: navel]

OMS *abbrev. for* Organisation Mondiale de la Santé. [French: World Health Organization]

on (ɒn) *prep.* **1.** in contact or connection with the surface of; at the upper surface of: *an apple on the ground; a mark on the table cloth.* **2.** attached to: *a puppet on a string.* **3.** carried with: *I've no money on me.* **4.** in the immediate vicinity of; close to or along the side of: *a house on the sea; this verges on the ridiculous!* **5.** within the time limits of a day or date: *he arrived on Thursday.* **6.** being performed upon or relayed through the medium of: *what's on the television?* **7.** at the occasion of: *on his retirement.* **8.** used to indicate support, subsistence, contingency, etc.: *he lives on bread; it depends on what you want.* **9. a.** regularly taking (a drug): *she's on the pill.* **b.** addicted to: *he's on heroin.* **10.** by means of (something considered as a mode of transport) (esp. in such phrases as **on foot, on wheels, on horseback,** etc.). **11.** in the process or course of: *on a journey; on strike.* **12.** concerned with or relating to: *a tax on potatoes; a programme on archaeology.* **13.** used to indicate the basis, grounds, or cause, as of a statement or action: *I have it on good authority.* **14.** against: used to indicate opposition: *they marched on the city at dawn.* **15.** used to indicate a meeting or encounter: *he crept up on her.* **16.** (used with an adj. preceded by *the*) indicating the manner or way in which an action is carried out: *on the sly; on the cheap.* **17.** *Informal or dialect.* to the loss or disadvantage of: *the old car gave out on us.* ~*adv.* (*often used as a particle*) **18.** in the position or state required for the commencement or sustained continuation, as of a mechanical operation: *the radio's been on all night.* **19. a.** attached to, surrounding, or placed in contact with something: *the girl had nothing on.* **b.** taking place: *what's on tonight?* **20.** in a manner indicating continuity, persistence, concentration, etc.: *don't keep on about it; the play went on all afternoon.* **21.** in a direction towards something, esp. forwards; so as to make progress: *we drove on towards London; march on!* **22. on and off** *or* **off and on.** intermittently; from time to time. **23. on and on.** without ceasing; continually. ~*adj.* **24.** functioning; operating: *the on position on a radio control.* **25.** (*postpositive*) *Informal.* **a.** staked or wagered as a bet: *ten pounds on that horse.* **b.** performing, as on stage: *I'm on in five minutes.* **c.** definitely taking place: *the match is on for Friday; their marriage is still on.* **d.** charged to: *the drinks are on me.* **e.** tolerable, practicable, acceptable, etc.: *your plan just isn't on.* **f.** (of a person) willing to do something. **26. on at.** *Informal.* nagging: *she was always on at her husband.* **27. on it.** *Austral. informal.* drinking alcoholic liquor. **28.** *Cricket.* (of a bowler) bowling. ~*n.* **29.** *Cricket.* **a.** (*modifier*) relating to or denoting the leg side of a cricket field or pitch: *the on side; an on drive.* **b.** (*in combination*) used to designate certain fielding positions on the leg side: *long-on; mid-on.* [Old English *an, on;* related to Old Saxon *an,* Old High German, Gothic *ana*]

ON *abbrev. for* **1.** Old Norse. **2.** Ontario.

-on *suffix forming nouns.* **1.** indicating a chemical substance: *interferon; parathion.* **2.** (in physics) indicating an elementary particle or quantum: *electron; photon.* **3.** (in chemistry) indicating an inert gas: *neon; radon.* **4.** (in biochemistry) a molecular unit: *codon; operon.* [from ION]

onager (ˈɒnədʒə) *n., pl.* **-gri** (-ˌgraɪ) *or* **-gers. 1.** a Persian variety of the wild ass, *Equus hemionus.* Compare **kiang. 2.** an ancient war engine for hurling stones. [C14: from Late Latin: military engine for stone throwing, from Latin: wild ass, from Greek *onagros,* from *onos* ass + *agros* field]

onagraceous (ˌɒnəˈgreɪʃəs) *adj.* of, relating to, or belonging to the *Onagraceae,* a family of flowering plants including fuchsia and willowherb. [C19: via New Latin *Onagrāceae,* from Latin *onager;* see ONAGER]

onanism (ˈəʊnəˌnɪzəm) *n.* another name for **masturbation** or **coitus interruptus.** [C18: after *Onan,* son of Judah; see Genesis 38:9] —ˈ**onanist** *n., adj.* —ˌ**onanˈistic** *adj.*

onbeat (ˈɒnˌbiːt) *n. Music.* the first and third beats in a bar of four-four time.

ONC (in Britain) *abbrev. for* Ordinary National Certificate; a qualification recognized by many national technical and professional institutions, roughly equivalent to GCE A Level.

once (wʌns) *adv.* **1.** one time; on one occasion or in one case. **2.** at some past time; formerly: *I could speak French once.* **3.** by one step or degree (of relationship): *a cousin once removed.* **4.** (*in conditional clauses, negatives, etc.*) ever; at all: *if you once forget it.* **5.** multiplied by one. **6. once and away. a.** conclusively. **b.** occasionally. **7. once and for all.** conclusively; for the last time. **8. once in a while.** occasionally; now and then. **9. once or twice** *or* **once and again.** a few times. **10. once upon a time.** used to begin fairy tales and children's stories. ~*conj.* **11.** (*subordinating*) as soon as; if ever or whenever: *once you begin, you'll enjoy it.* ~*n.* **12.** one occasion or case: *you may do it, this once.* **13. all at once. a.** suddenly or without warning. **b.** simultaneously. **14. at once. a.** immediately. **b.** simultaneously. **15. for once.** this time, if (or but) at no other time. [C12 *ones, anes,* adverbial genitive of *on, an* ONE]

once-over *n. Informal.* **1.** a quick examination or appraisal. **2.** a quick but comprehensive piece of work. **3.** a violent beating or thrashing. ~(esp. in the phrase **give (a person** or **thing) the** (or a) **once-over**).

oncer (ˈwʌnsə) *n.* **1.** *Brit. slang.* (formerly) a one-pound note. **2.** *Austral. slang.* a person elected to Parliament who can only expect to serve one term. **3.** *N.Z.* something that happens on only one occasion. [C20: from ONCE]

onchocerciasis (ˌɒŋkəʊsəˈkaɪəsɪs) *n., pl.* **-ses.** a disease found in parts of Africa and tropical America that is caused by a parasitic worm, *Onchocerca volvulus,* and transmitted to humans by various species of black fly. It results in inflammation of the skin and in some cases blindness. Also called: **river blindness.** [C20: from *Onchocerc(a),* the genus of worms + -IASIS]

onco- *combining form.* denoting a tumour: *oncology.* [from Greek *onkos*]

oncogene (ˈɒŋkəʊˌdʒiːn) *n.* any of several genes, first identified in viruses but present in all cells, that when abnormally activated can cause cancer.

oncogenic (ˌɒŋkəʊˈdʒɛnɪk) *or* **oncogenous** (ɒŋˈkɒdʒənəs) *adj.* causing the formation of a tumour: *an oncogenic virus.* —ˌ**oncoˈgenesis** *n.*

oncology (ɒŋˈkɒlədʒɪ) *n.* the branch of medicine concerned with the study, classification, and treatment of tumours. —**oncological** (ˌɒŋkəˈlɒdʒɪkᵊl) *adj.* —**onˈcologist** *n.*

oncoming (ˈɒnˌkʌmɪŋ) *adj.* **1.** coming nearer in space or time; approaching. ~*n.* **2.** the approach or onset: *the oncoming of winter.*

oncost (ˈɒnˌkɒst) *n. Brit.* **1.** another word for **overhead** (sense 7). **2.** (*sometimes pl.*) another word for **overheads.**

OND (in Britain) *abbrev. for* Ordinary National Diploma; a nationally recognized qualification in technical subjects, reached after a two-year full-time or sandwich course.

ondes Martenot (ɔ̃d mɑːtəˈnəʊ) *n. Music.* an electronic keyboard instrument in which the frequency of an oscillator is varied to produce separate musical notes. [C20: French, literally: Martenot waves, invented by Maurice *Martenot* (1898–1980)]

on dit *French* (ɔ̃ di) *n., pl.* ***on dits*** (ɔ̃ di). a rumour; piece of gossip. [literally: it is said, they say]

ondograph (ˈɒndəʊˌgrɑːf, -ˌgræf) *n.* an instrument for producing a graphical recording of an alternating current by measuring the charge imparted to a capacitor at different points in the cycle. [C20: from French, from *onde* wave + -GRAPH]

one (wʌn) *determiner.* **1. a.** single; lone; not two or more: *one car.* **b.** (*as pronoun*): *one is enough for now; one at a time.* **c.** (*in combination*): *one-eyed; one-legged.* **2. a.** distinct from all others; only; unique: *one girl in a million.* **b.** (*as pronoun*): *one of a kind.* **3. a.** a specified (person, item, etc.) as distinct from another or others of its kind: *raise one hand and then the other.* **b.** (*as pronoun*): *which one is correct?* **4.** a certain, indefinite, or unspecified (time); some: *one day you'll be sorry.* **5.** *Informal.* an emphatic word for **a**[1] or **an**[1]: *it was one hell of a fight.* **6.** a certain (person): *one Miss Jones was named.* **7. (all) in one.** combined; united. **8. all one. a.** all the same. **b.** of no consequence: *it's all one to me.* **9. at one.** (often foll. by *with*) in a state of agreement or harmony. **10. be made one.** (of a man and a woman) to become married. **11. many a one.** many people. **12. neither one thing nor the other.** indefinite, undecided, or mixed. **13. never a one.** none. **14. one and all.** everyone, without exception. **15. one by one.** one at a time; individually. **16. one or two.** a few. **17. one way and another.** on balance. **18. one with another.** on average. ~*pron.* **19.** an indefinite person regarded as typical of every person: *one can't say any more than that.* **20.** any indefinite person: used as the subject of a sentence to form an alternative grammatical construction to that of the passive voice: *one can catch fine trout in this stream.* **21.** *Archaic.* an unspecified person: *one came to him.* ~*n.* **22.** the smallest whole number and the first cardinal number; unity. See also **number** (sense 1). **23.** a numeral (1, I, i, etc.) representing this number. **24.** *Music.* the numeral 1 used as the lower figure in a time signature to indicate that the beat is measured in semibreves. **25.** something representing, represented by, or consisting of one unit. **26.** Also called: **one o'clock.** one hour after noon or midnight. **27.** a blow or setback (esp. in the phrase **one in the eye for**). **28. make one.** *Archaic.* to be present as part of a group; attend. **29. the one.** (in Neo-Platonic philosophy) the ultimate being. **30. the Holy One** *or* **the One above.** God. **31. the Evil one.** Satan; the devil. ~Related prefixes: **mono-, uni-.** [Old English *ān,* related to Old French *ān, ēn,* Old High German *ein,* Old Norse *einn,* Latin *unus,* Greek *oinē* ace]

▷**Usage.** Where the pronoun *one* is repeated, as in *one might think one would be unwise to say that, he* is sometimes substituted: *one might think he would be unwise to say that.* Careful writers avoid *one* followed by *he,* however, because of possible ambiguity: *he* in this case could refer either to the same person as *one* or to some other person.

-one *suffix forming nouns.* indicating that a chemical compound is a ketone: *acetone.* [arbitrarily from Greek *-ōnē,* feminine patronymic suffix, but perhaps influenced by *-one* in OZONE]

one another *pron.* the reflexive form of plural pronouns when the action, attribution, etc., is reciprocal: *they kissed one another; knowing one another.* Also: **each other.**

one-armed bandit *n.* a fruit machine operated by pulling down a lever at one side.

one-horse *adj.* **1.** drawn by or using one horse. **2.** (*prenominal*) *Informal.* small or obscure: *a one-horse town.*

Oneida (əʊˈnaɪdə) *n., pl.* **-das** *or* **-da. 1.** (preceded by *the; functioning as pl.*) a North American Indian people formerly living east of Lake Ontario; one of the Iroquois peoples. **2.** a member of this people. **3.** the language of this people, belonging to the Iroquoian family. [from Iroquois *onēyóte',* literally: standing stone]

oneiric (əʊˈnaɪərɪk) *adj. Rare.* of or relating to dreams.

oneiro- *combining form.* indicating a dream: *oneirocritic.* [from Greek *oneiros* dream]

oneirocritic (əʊˌnaɪərəʊˈkrɪtɪk) *n.* a person who interprets dreams. [C17: from Greek *oneirokritikos*] —**oˌneiroˈcritical** *adj.* —**oˌneiroˈcritically** *adv.*

oneiromancy (əʊˈnaɪərəʊˌmænsɪ) *n. Rare.* divination by the interpretation of dreams. [C17: from Greek *oneiros* dream + -MANCY] —**oˈneiroˌmancer** *n.*

one-liner *n. Informal.* a short joke or witty remark or riposte.

one-man *adj.* consisting of or done by or for one man: *a one-man band; a one-man show.*

one-many *adj. Maths, logic.* (of a relation) holding between more than one ordered pair of elements with the same first member.

oneness (ˈwʌnnɪs) *n.* **1.** the state or quality of being one; singleness. **2.** the state of being united; agreement. **3.** uniqueness. **4.** sameness.

one-night stand *n.* **1.** a performance given only once at any one place. **2.** *Informal.* **a.** a sexual encounter lasting only one evening or night. **b.** a person regarded as being only suitable for such an encounter.

one-off *n. Brit.* **a.** something that is carried out or made only once. **b.** (*as modifier*): *a one-off job.* Also: **one-shot.** [See OFF (sense 15)]

one-parent family *n.* a household consisting of at least one dependent child and the mother or father, the other parent being dead or permanently absent. Also called: **single-parent family.**

one-piece *adj.* **1.** (of a garment, esp. a bathing costume) made in one piece. ~*n.* **2.** a garment, esp. a bathing costume, made in one piece.

oner (ˈwʌnə) *n. Brit. informal.* **1.** a single continuous action (esp. in the phrase **down it in a oner**). **2.** an outstanding person or thing. **3.** a heavy blow. [C20: from ONE]

onerous (ˈɒnərəs, ˈəʊ-) *adj.* **1.** laborious or oppressive. **2.** *Law.* (of a contract, lease, etc.) having or involving burdens or obligations that counterbalance or outweigh the advantages. [C14: from Latin *onerōsus* burdensome, from *onus* load] —**ˈonerously** *adv.* —**ˈonerousness** *n.*

oneself (wʌnˈsɛlf) *pron.* **1. a.** the reflexive form of *one.* **b.** (intensifier): *one doesn't do that oneself.* **2.** (*preceded by a copula*) one's normal or usual self: *one doesn't feel oneself after such an experience.*

one-sided *adj.* **1.** considering or favouring only one side of a matter, problem, etc. **2.** having all the advantage on one side. **3.** larger or more developed on one side. **4.** having, existing on, or occurring on one side only. **5.** another term for **unilateral. 6.** denoting a surface on which any two points can be joined without crossing an edge. See **Möbius strip.** —**ˌone-ˈsidedly** *adv.* —**ˌone-ˈsidedness** *n.*

one-step *n.* **1.** an early 20th-century ballroom dance with long quick steps, the precursor of the foxtrot. **2.** a piece of music composed for or in the rhythm of this dance.

one-stop *adj.* having or providing a range of related services or goods in one place: *a one-stop shop.*

one-tailed *adj. Statistics.* (of a significance test) concerned with the hypothesis that an observed value of a sampling statistic either significantly exceeds or falls significantly below a given value, where the error is relevant only in one direction: for instance, in testing whether scales are fair a customer does not regard overweight goods as a relevant error. Compare **two-tailed.**

one-time *adj.* **1.** (*prenominal*) at some time in the past; former. ~*adv.* **2.** *Caribbean informal.* at once.

one-to-one *adj.* **1.** (of two or more things) corresponding exactly. **2.** denoting a relationship or encounter in which someone is involved with only one other person: *one-to-one tuition.* **3.** *Maths.* characterized by or involving the pairing of each member of one set with only one member of another set, without remainder.

one-track *adj.* **1.** *Informal.* obsessed with one idea, subject, etc. **2.** having or consisting of a single track.

one-two *n.* **1.** *Boxing.* a jab with the leading hand followed by a cross with the other hand. **2.** *Soccer.* another term for **wall pass.**

one-up *adj. Informal.* having or having scored an advantage or lead over someone or something.

one-upmanship (wʌnˈʌpmənʃɪp) *n. Informal.* the art or practice of achieving or maintaining an advantage over others, often by slightly unscrupulous means.

one-way *adj.* **1.** moving or allowing travel in one direction only: *one-way traffic; a one-way ticket.* **2.** entailing no reciprocal obligation, action, etc.: *a one-way agreement.*

one-way ticket *n.* the U.S. and Canadian name for **single ticket.**

on-glide *n. Phonetics.* a glide immediately preceding a speech sound, for which the articulators are taking position. Compare **off-glide.**

ongoing (ˈɒnˌgəʊɪŋ) *adj.* **1.** actually in progress: *ongoing projects.* **2.** continually moving forward; developing. **3.** remaining in existence; continuing.

ongoings (ˈɒngoɪŋz) *pl. n.* a Scot. word for **goings-on.**

onie (ˈɒnɪ) *determiner. Scot.* a variant spelling of **ony.**

onion (ˈʌnjən) *n.* **1.** an alliaceous plant, *Allium cepa,* having greenish-white flowers: cultivated for its rounded edible bulb. **2.** the bulb of this plant, consisting of concentric layers of white succulent leaf bases with a pungent odour and taste. **3.** any of several related plants similar to *A. cepa,* such as *A. fistulosum* (Welsh onion). **4. know one's onions.** *Brit. slang.* to be fully acquainted with a subject. [C14: via Anglo-Norman from Old French *oignon,* from Latin *unio* onion, related to UNION] —**ˈoniony** *adj.*

onion dome *n.* a bulb-shaped dome characteristic of Byzantine and Russian church architecture.

onion fly *n.* a small grey dipterous insect, *Delia antiqua,* that is a serious pest of onions. The larvae destroy the bulbs.

onionskin (ˈʌnjənˌskɪn) *n.* a glazed translucent paper.

onion weed *n.* a plant of Australia and New Zealand, *Nuthoscordum inodorum,* having a strong onion-like smell and reproducing from bulbs and seeds.

onium compound *or* **salt** (ˈəʊnɪəm) *n. Chem.* any salt in which the positive ion (**onium ion**) is formed by the attachment of a proton to a neutral compound, as in ammonium, oxonium, and sulphonium compounds. [C20: from (AMM)ONIUM]

on key *adj.* (**on-key** *when prenominal*), *adv.* **1.** in the right key. **2.** in tune.

on line *adj.* (**on-line** *when prenominal*). **1.** of, relating to, or concerned with a peripheral device that is directly connected to and controlled by the central processing unit of a computer. **2.** occurring as part of, or involving, a continuous sequence of operations, such as a production line. ~Compare **off line.**

onlooker (ˈɒnˌlʊkə) *n.* a person who observes without taking part. —**ˈonˌlooking** *adj.*

only (ˈəʊnlɪ) *adj.* (*prenominal*) **1. the.** being single or very few in number: *the only men left in town were too old to bear arms.* **2.** (of a child) having no siblings. **3.** unique by virtue of being superior to anything else; peerless. **4. one and only. a.** (*adj.*) incomparable; unique. **b.** (*as n.*) the object of all one's love: *you are my one and only.* ~*adv.* **5.** without anyone or anything else being included; alone: *you have one choice only; only a genius can do that.* **6.** merely or just: *it's only Henry.* **7.** no more or no greater than: *we met only an hour ago.* **8.** *Irish.* (intensifier): *she was only marvellous; it was only dreadful.* **9.** used in conditional clauses introduced by *if* to emphasize the impossibility of the condition ever being fulfilled: *if I had only known, this would never have happened.* **10.** not earlier than; not...until: *I only found out yesterday.* **11. if only** *or* **if...only.** an expression used to introduce a wish, esp. one felt to be unrealizable. **12. only if.** never...except when. **13. only too. a.** (intensifier): *he was only too pleased to help.* **b.** most regrettably (esp. in the phrase **only too true**). ~*sentence connector.* **14.** but; however: used to introduce an exception or condition: *play outside: only don't go into the street.* [Old English *ānlīc,* from *ān* ONE + *-līc* -LY[2]]

▷**Usage.** In informal English, *only* is often used as a sentence connector: *it would have been possible, only he was not present at the time.* This use is avoided in careful usage, esp. in formal contexts: *it would have been possible had he been present.* In formal speech and writing, *only* is placed directly before the word or words that it modifies: *she could interview only three applicants in the morning.* In all but the most formal contexts, however, it is generally regarded as acceptable to put *only* before the verb: *she could only interview three applicants in the morning.* Care must be taken not to create ambiguity, esp. in written English, in which intonation will not, as it does in speech, help to show to which item in the sentence *only* applies. A sentence such as *she can only see you in the afternoon* is capable of two interpretations and is therefore better rephrased either as *she can see only you in the afternoon* (i.e. nobody else) or as *she can see you only in the afternoon* (i.e. at no other time).

only-begotten *adj. Archaic.* (of a child) being the only offspring of its father.

o.n.o. (*Brit., Austral., and N.Z.* in advertisements) *abbrev. for* or near(est) offer: *£50 o.n.o.*

onomasiology (ˌɒnəʊˌmeɪsɪˈɒlədʒɪ) *n.* **1.** another name for **onomastics** (sense 1). **2.** the branch of semantics concerned with the meanings of and meaning relations between individual words.

onomastic (ˌɒnəˈmæstɪk) *adj.* **1.** of or relating to proper names. **2.** *Law.* denoting a signature in a different handwriting from that to which it is attached. [C17: from Greek *onomastikos,* from *onomazein* to name, from *onoma* NAME]

onomastics (ˌɒnəˈmæstɪks) *n.* **1.** (*functioning as sing.*) the study of proper names, esp. of their origins. **2.** (*functioning as sing. or pl.*) a systematization of the facts about how proper names are formed in a given language.

onomatopoeia (ˌɒnəˌmætəˈpiːə) *n.* **1.** the formation of words whose sound is imitative of the sound of the noise or action designated, such as *hiss, buzz,* and *bang.* **2.** the use of such words for poetic or rhetorical effect. [C16: via Late Latin from Greek *onoma* name + *poiein* to make] —ˌ**onoˌmatoˈpoeic** *or* **onomatopoetic** (ˌɒnəˌmætəpəʊˈɛtɪk) *adj.* —ˌ**onoˌmatoˈpoeically** *or* ˌ**onoˌmatopoˈetically** *adv.*

Onondaga (ˌɒnənˈdɑːgə) *n.* **1.** **1.** (*pl.* **-gas** *or* **-ga**) a member of a North American Indian Iroquois people formerly living between Lake Champlain and the St Lawrence River. **2.** the language of this people, belonging to the Iroquoian family. [from Iroquois *onōtāge',* literally: on the top of the hill (the name of their principal village)] —ˌ**OnonˈDagan** *adj.*

onrush (ˈɒnˌrʌʃ) *n.* a forceful forward rush or flow.

onset (ˈɒnˌsɛt) *n.* **1.** an attack; assault. **2.** a start; beginning.

onshore (ˈɒnˈʃɔː) *adj., adv.* **1.** towards the land: *an onshore gale.* **2.** on land; not at sea.

onside (ˌɒnˈsaɪd) *adj., adv. Football, hockey, etc.* (of a player) in a legal position, as when behind the ball or with a required number of opponents between oneself and the opposing team's goal line. Compare **offside.**

onslaught (ˈɒnˌslɔːt) *n.* a violent attack. [C17: from Middle Dutch *aenslag,* from *aan* ON + *slag* a blow, related to SLAY]

Ont. *abbrev. for* Ontario.

onto *or* **on to** (ˈɒntʊ; *unstressed* ˈɒntə) *prep.* **1.** to a position that is on: *step onto the train as it passes.* **2.** having become aware of (something illicit or secret): *the police are onto us.* **3.** into contact with: *get onto the factory.*

▷**Usage.** *Onto* is now generally accepted as a word in its own right. *On to* is still used, however, where *on* is considered to be part of the verb: *he moved on to the next platform* as contrasted with *he jumped onto the next platform.*

onto- *combining form.* existence or being: *ontogeny; ontology.* [from Late Greek, from *ōn* (stem *ont-*) being, present participle of *einai* to be]

ontogeny (ɒnˈtɒdʒənɪ) *or* **ontogenesis** (ˌɒntəˈdʒɛnɪsɪs) *n.* the entire sequence of events involved in the development of an individual organism. Compare **phylogeny.** —**ontogenic** (ˌɒntəˈdʒɛnɪk) *or* **ontogenetic** (ˌɒntədʒɪˈnɛtɪk) *adj.* —ˌ**ontoˈgenically** *or* ˌ**ontogeˈnetically** *adv.*

ontological argument *n. Philosophy.* **1.** the traditional a priori argument for the existence of God on the grounds that the concept itself necessitates existence. Compare **cosmological argument, teleological argument.** **2.** any analogous argument from the nature of some concept to the existence of whatever instantiates it.

ontology (ɒnˈtɒlədʒɪ) *n.* **1.** *Philosophy.* the branch of metaphysics that deals with the nature of being. **2.** *Logic.* the set of entities presupposed by a theory. —ˌ**ontoˈlogical** *adj.* —ˌ**ontoˈlogically** *adv.*

onus (ˈəʊnəs) *n., pl.* **onuses.** a responsibility, task, or burden. [C17: from Latin: burden]

onus probandi (ˈəʊnəs prəʊˈbændɪ) *n. Law.* the Latin phrase for **burden of proof.**

onward (ˈɒnwəd) *adj.* **1.** directed or moving forwards, onwards, etc. ~*adv.* **2.** a variant of **onwards.**

onwards (ˈɒnwədz) *or* **onward** *adv.* at or towards a point or position ahead, in advance, etc.

ony (ˈɒnɪ) *determiner.* a Scot. word for **any.**

onychophoran (ˌɒnɪˈkɒfərən) *n.* any wormlike invertebrate of the phylum *Onychophora,* having a segmented body, short unjointed limbs, and breathing by means of tracheae: intermediate in structure and evolutionary development between annelids and arthropods. [from New Latin *Onychophora,* from Greek *onukh-* nail, claw + -PHORE]

-onym *n. combining form.* indicating a name or word: *acronym; pseudonym.* [from Greek *-onumon,* from *onuma,* Doric variant of *onoma* name]

onymous (ˈɒnɪməs) *adj.* (of a book) bearing its author's name. [C18: back formation from ANONYMOUS]

onyx (ˈɒnɪks) *n.* **1.** a variety of chalcedony with alternating black and white parallel bands, used as a gemstone. Formula: SiO_2. **2.** a compact variety of calcite used as an ornamental stone; onyx marble. Formula: $CaCO_3$. [C13: from Latin from Greek: fingernail (so called from its veined appearance)]

oo- *or* **oö-** *combining form.* egg or ovum: *oosperm.* [from Greek *ōion* EGG[1]]

oocyte (ˈəʊəˌsaɪt) *n.* an immature female germ cell that gives rise to an ovum after two meiotic divisions.

oodles (ˈuːdᵊlz) *pl. n. Informal.* great quantities: *oodles of money.* [C20: of uncertain origin]

oof (uːf) *n. Slang.* money. [C19: from Yiddish *ooftisch,* from German *auf dem Tische* on the table (referring to gambling stakes)] —ˈ**oofy** *adj.*

oogamy (əʊˈɒgəmɪ) *n.* sexual reproduction involving a small motile male gamete and a large much less motile female gamete: occurs in all higher animals and some plants. —**oˈogamous** *adj.*

oogenesis (ˌəʊəˈdʒɛnɪsɪs) *n.* the formation and maturation of ova from undifferentiated cells in the ovary. See also **oocyte.** —**oogenetic** (ˌəʊədʒɪˈnɛtɪk) *adj.*

oogonium (ˌəʊəˈgəʊnɪəm) *n., pl.* **-nia** (-nɪə) *or* **-niums.** **1.** an immature female germ cell forming oocytes by repeated divisions. **2.** a female sex organ of some algae and fungi producing female gametes (oospheres). —**ooˈgonial** *adj.*

ooh (uː) *interj.* an exclamation of surprise, pleasure, pain, etc.

Ookpik (ˈuːkpɪk) *n. Canadian trademark.* a sealskin doll resembling an owl, first made in 1963 by an Inuit and used abroad as a symbol of Canadian handicrafts. [from Eskimo *ukpik* a snowy owl]

oolite (ˈəʊəˌlaɪt) *n.* any sedimentary rock, esp. limestone, consisting of tiny spherical concentric grains within a fine matrix. [C18: from French from New Latin *oolītēs,* literally: egg stone; probably a translation of German *Rogenstein* roe stone] —**oolitic** (ˌəʊəˈlɪtɪk) *adj.*

oolith (ˈəʊəˌlɪθ) *n.* any of the tiny spherical grains of sedimentary rock of which oolite is composed.

oology (əʊˈɒlədʒɪ) *n.* the branch of ornithology concerned with the study of birds' eggs. —**oological** (ˌəʊəˈlɒdʒɪkᵊl) *adj.* —**oˈologist** *n.*

oolong (ˈuːˌlɒŋ) *n.* a kind of dark tea, grown in China, that is partly fermented before being dried. [C19: from Chinese *wu lung,* from *wu* black + *lung* dragon]

oomiak *or* **oomiac** (ˈuːmɪˌæk) *n.* other words for **umiak.**

oompah (ˈuːmˌpɑː) *n.* a representation of the sound made by a deep brass instrument, esp. in military band music.

oomph (ʊmf) *n. Informal.* **1.** enthusiasm, vigour, or energy. **2.** sex appeal. [C20: perhaps imitative of the bellow of a mating bull]

oont (ʊnt) *n. Anglo-Indian dialect.* a camel. [C19: from Hindi *unt*]

oophorectomy (ˌəʊəfəˈrɛktəmɪ) *n., pl.* **-mies.** surgical removal of an ovary or ovarian tumour. Also called: **ovariectomy.** Compare **ovariotomy.** [C19: from New Latin *ōophoron* ovary, from Greek *ōion* egg + *phoros* bearing, + -ECTOMY]

oophoritis (ˌəʊəfəˈraɪtɪs) *n.* inflammation of an ovary; ovaritis. —**oophoritic** (ˌəʊəfəˈrɪtɪk) *adj.*

oophyte (ˈəʊəˌfaɪt) *n.* the gametophyte in mosses, liverworts, and ferns. —**oophytic** (ˌəʊəˈfɪtɪk) *adj.*

oops (ʊps, uːps) *interj.* an exclamation of surprise or of apology as when someone drops something or makes a mistake.

oose (uːs) *n. Scot. dialect.* dust; fluff. [of unknown origin] —ˈ**oosy** *adj.*

oosperm (ˈəʊəˌspɜːm) *n.* a fertilized ovum; zygote.

oosphere (ˈəʊəˌsfɪə) *n.* a large female gamete produced in the oogonia of algae and fungi.

oospore (ˈəʊəˌspɔː) *n.* a thick-walled sexual spore that develops from a fertilized oosphere in some algae and fungi. —ˌ**ooˈsporic** *or* ˌ**ooˈsporous** *adj.*

ootheca (ˌəʊəˈθiːkə) *n., pl.* **-cae** (-siː). a capsule containing eggs that is produced by some insects and molluscs. [C19: New Latin, from OO- + *thēkē* case] —ˌ**ooˈthecal** *adj.*

oot'd (ˈəʊətɪd) *n. Zoology.* an immature female gamete that develops into an ovum. [C20: from OO- + (SPERMA)TID]

ooze[1] (uːz) *vb.* **1.** (*intr.*) to flow or leak out slowly, as through pores or very small holes. **2.** to exude or emit (moisture, gas, etc.). **3.** (*tr.*) to overflow with: *to ooze charm.* **4.** (*intr.;* often foll. by *away*) to disappear or escape gradually. ~*n.* **5.** a slow flowing or leaking. **6.** an infusion of vegetable matter, such as sumac or oak bark, used in tanning. [Old English *wōs* juice]

ooze[2] (uːz) *n.* **1.** a soft thin mud found at the bottom of lakes and rivers. **2.** a fine-grained calcareous or siliceous marine deposit consisting of the hard parts of planktonic organisms. **3.** muddy ground, esp. of bogs. [Old English *wāse* mud; related to Old French *wāse*, Old Norse *veisa*]

ooze leather *n.* a very soft leather with a suedelike finish. [C19: from OOZE[1] (sense 6)]

oozy[1] ('uːzɪ) *adj.* **oozier, ooziest.** moist or dripping.

oozy[2] ('uːzɪ) *adj.* **oozier, ooziest.** of, resembling, or containing mud; slimy. —'**oozily** *adv.* —'**ooziness** *n.*

OP *abbrev. for:* **1.** *Military.* observation post. **2.** Ordo Praedictatorum (the Dominicans). [Latin: Order of Preachers]

op. *abbrev. for:* **1.** opera. **2.** operation. **3.** opposite. **4.** opus. **5.** operator. **6.** optical.

o.p. *or* **O.P.** *abbrev. for* out of print.

opacity (əʊ'pæsɪtɪ) *n., pl.* **-ties.** **1.** the state or quality of being opaque. **2.** the degree to which something is opaque. **3.** an opaque object or substance. **4.** obscurity of meaning; unintelligibility. **5.** *Physics, photog.* the ratio of the intensity of light incident on a medium, such as a photographic film, to that transmitted through the medium. **6.** *Logic, philosophy.* the property of being an opaque context.

opah ('əʊpə) *n.* a large soft-finned deep-sea teleost fish, *Lampris regius* (or *luna*), of the Atlantic and Pacific Oceans and the Mediterranean Sea, having a deep, brilliantly coloured body: family *Lampridae.* Also called: **moonfish, kingfish.** [C18: of West African origin]

opal ('əʊpᵊl) *n.* an amorphous, usually iridescent, mineral that can be of almost any colour, found in igneous rocks and around hot springs. It is used as a gemstone. Composition: hydrated silica. Formula: $SiO_2.nH_2O$. [C16: from Latin *opalus,* from Greek *opallios,* from Sanskrit *upala* precious stone] —'**opal,like** *adj.*

opalesce (ˌəʊpə'lɛs) *vb.* (*intr.*) to exhibit a milky iridescence.

opalescent (ˌəʊpə'lɛsᵊnt) *adj.* having or emitting an iridescence like that of an opal. —ˌ**opal'escence** *n.*

opal glass *n.* glass that is opalescent or white, made by the addition of fluorides.

opaline ('əʊpəˌlaɪn) *adj.* **1.** opalescent. ~*n.* **2.** an opaque or semiopaque whitish glass.

opaque (əʊ'peɪk) *adj.* **1.** not transmitting light; not transparent or translucent. **2.** not reflecting light; lacking lustre or shine; dull. **3.** not transmitting radiant energy, such as electromagnetic or corpuscular radiation, or sound. **4.** hard to understand; unintelligible. **5.** unintelligent; dense. ~*n.* **6.** *Photog.* an opaque pigment used to block out particular areas on a negative. ~*vb.* **opaques, opaquing, opaqued.** (*tr.*) **7.** to make opaque. **8.** *Photog.* to block out particular areas, such as blemishes, on (a negative), using an opaque. [C15: from Latin *opācus* shady] —**o'paquely** *adv.* —**o'paqueness** *n.*

opaque context *n. Philosophy, logic.* an expression in which the replacement of a term by another with the same reference may change the truth-value of the whole. *John believes that Cicero was a Roman* is opaque, since even though Cicero and Tully are the same person John may know that the given statement is true but not that Tully was a Roman. Compare **transparent context.** See also **intensional, Electra paradox.**

opaque projector *n.* the U.S. and Canadian name for **episcope.**

op art (ɒp) *n.* a style of abstract art chiefly concerned with the exploitation of optical effects such as the illusion of movement. [C20 *op,* short for *optical*]

OPC *or* **opc** *abbrev. for* ordinary Portland cement.

op. cit. (in textual annotations) *abbrev. for* opere citato. [Latin: in the work cited]

ope (əʊp) *vb., adj.* an archaic or poetic word for **open.**

OPEC ('əʊˌpɛk) *n. acronym for* Organization of Petroleum-Exporting Countries.

open ('əʊpᵊn) *adj.* **1.** not closed or barred: *the door is open.* **2.** affording free passage, access, view, etc.; not blocked or obstructed: *the road is open for traffic.* **3.** not sealed, fastened, or wrapped: *an open package.* **4.** having the interior part accessible: *an open drawer.* **5.** extended, expanded, or unfolded: *an open newspaper; an open flower.* **6.** ready for business: *the shops are open.* **7.** able to be obtained; available: *the position advertised last week is no longer open.* **8.** unobstructed by buildings, trees, etc.: *open countryside.* **9.** free to all to join, enter, use, visit, etc.: *an open competition.* **10.** unengaged or unoccupied: *the doctor has an hour open for you to call.* **11.** See **open season.** **12.** not decided or finalized: *an open question.* **13.** ready to entertain new ideas; not biased or prejudiced: *an open mind.* **14.** unreserved or candid: *she was very open in her description.* **15.** liberal or generous: *an open hand.* **16.** extended or eager to receive (esp. in the phrase **with open arms**). **17.** exposed to view; blatant: *open disregard of the law.* **18.** liable or susceptible: *you will leave yourself open to attack if you speak.* **19.** (of climate or seasons) free from frost; mild. **20.** free from navigational hazards, such as ice, sunken ships, etc.: *open water.* **21.** *U.S.* without legal restrictions or enforceable regulations, esp. in relation to gambling, vice, etc.: *an open town.* **22.** without barriers to prevent absconding: *an open prison.* **23.** having large or numerous spacing or apertures: *open ranks.* **24.** full of small openings or gaps; porous: *an open texture.* **25.** *Printing.* (of type matter) generously leaded or widely spaced. **26.** *Music.* **a.** (of a violin or guitar string) not stopped with the finger. **b.** (of a pipe, such as an organ pipe) not closed at either end. **c.** (of a note) played on such a string or pipe. **27.** *Commerce.* **a.** in operation; active: *an open account.* **b.** unrestricted; unlimited: *open credit; open insurance cover.* **28.** See **open cheque.** **29.** (of a return ticket) not specifying a date for travel. **30.** *Sport.* **a.** (of a goal, court, etc.) unguarded or relatively unprotected: *the forward missed an open goal.* **b.** (of a stance, esp. in golf) characterized by the front of the body being turned forward. **31.** (of a wound) exposed to the air. **32.** (esp. of the large intestine) free from obstruction. **33.** undefended and of no military significance: *an open city.* **34.** *Phonetics.* **a.** denoting a vowel pronounced with the lips relatively wide apart. **b.** denoting a syllable that does not end in a consonant, as in *pa.* **35.** *Chess.* (of a file) having no pawns on it. **36.** *Maths.* (of a set) containing points whose neighbourhood consists of other points of the same set: *points inside a circle are an open set.* ~*vb.* **37.** to move or cause to move from a closed or fastened position: *to open a window.* **38.** (when *intr.*, foll. by *on* or *onto*) to render, be, or become accessible or unobstructed: *to open a road; to open a parcel; the door opens into the hall.* **39.** (*intr.*) to come into or appear in view: *the lake opened before us.* **40.** (*tr.*) to puncture (a boil) so as to permit drainage. **41.** to extend or unfold or cause to extend or unfold: *to open a newspaper.* **42.** to disclose or uncover or be disclosed or uncovered: *to open one's heart.* **43.** to cause (the mind) to become receptive or (of the mind) to become receptive. **44.** to operate or cause to operate: *to open a shop.* **45.** (when *intr.*, sometimes foll. by *out*) to make or become less compact or dense in structure: *to open ranks.* **46.** to set or be set in action; start: *to open a discussion; to open the batting.* **47.** (*tr.*) to arrange for (a bank account, savings account, etc.) usually by making an initial deposit. **48.** to turn to a specified point in (a book, magazine, etc.): *open at page one.* **49.** *Law.* to make the opening statement in (a case before a court of law). **50.** (*intr.*) *Cards.* to bet, bid, or lead first on a hand. ~*n.* **51.** (often preceded by *the*) any wide or unobstructed space or expanse, esp. of land or water. **52.** See **open air.** **53.** *Sport.* a competition which all may enter. **54.** **bring** (*or* **come**) **into the open.** to make (or become) evident or public. ~See also **open up.** [Old English; related to Old French *open, epen,* Old Saxon *opan,* Old High German *offan*] —'**openable** *adj.* —'**openly** *adv.* —'**openness** *n.*

open air *n.* **a.** the place or space where the air is unenclosed; the outdoors. **b.** (*as modifier*): *an open-air concert.*

open-and-shut *adj.* easily decided or solved; obvious: *an open-and-shut case.*

open book *n.* a person or thing without secrecy or concealment that can be easily known or interpreted.

opencast mining ('əʊpᵊnˌkɑːst) *n. Brit.* mining by excavating from the surface. Also called: (esp. U.S.) **strip mining,** (Austral. and N.Z.) **open-cut mining.** [C18: from OPEN + archaic *cast* ditch or cutting]

open chain *n.* a chain of atoms in a molecule that is not joined at its ends into the form of a ring.

open cheque *n.* an uncrossed cheque that can be cashed at the drawee bank.

open circuit *n.* an incomplete electrical circuit in which no current flows. Compare **closed circuit.**

open court *n.* a court or trial to which members of the public are freely admitted.

open cut *n. Civil engineering.* an excavation made in the open rather than in a tunnel. See **cut-and-cover.**

open-cut mining *n.* the Austral. and N.Z. name for **opencast mining.**

open day *n.* an occasion on which an institution, such as a school, is open for inspection by the public. Also called: **at-home.** U.S. and Canadian name: **open house.**

open door *n.* **1.** a policy or practice by which a nation grants opportunities for trade to all other nations equally. **2.** free and unrestricted admission. ~*adj.* **open-door.** **3.** open to all; accessible. **4.** (in industrial relations) designating a policy of management being prepared to talk to workers in the office at any time.

open-ended *adj.* **1.** without definite limits, as of duration or amount: *an open-ended contract.* **2.** denoting a question, esp. one on a questionnaire, that cannot be answered "yes", "no", or "don't know".

opener ('əʊpənə) *n.* **1.** an instrument used to open sealed containers such as tins or bottles: *a bottle opener.* **2.** a person who opens, esp. the player who makes the first bid or play. **3.** the first or opening section or episode in a series. **4.** *U.S.* the first song, act, etc., in a variety show. **5.** (*pl.*) a start; beginning (esp. in the phrase **for openers**).

open-eyed *adj.* **1.** with the eyes wide open, as in amazement. **2.** watchful; alert.

open-faced *adj.* **1.** having an ingenuous expression. **2.** (of a watch) having no lid or cover other than the glass.

open-field *adj.* (*prenominal*) *Medieval history.* of or denoting the system in which an arable area was divided into unenclosed strips, esp. cultivated by different tenants.

open game *n. Chess.* a relatively simple game involving open ranks and files, permitting tactical play, and usually following symmetrical development. Compare **closed game.**

open-handed *adj.* generous; liberal. —ˌ**open-'handedly** *adv.* —ˌ**open-'handedness** *n.*

open-hearted *adj.* 1. kindly and warm. 2. disclosing intentions and thoughts clearly; candid. —ˌ**open-ˈheartedly** *adv.* —ˌ**open-ˈheartedness** *n.*

open-hearth furnace *n.* (esp. formerly) a steel-making reverbatory furnace in which pig iron and scrap are contained in a shallow hearth and heated by producer gas.

open-hearth process *n.* a process for making steel using an open-hearth furnace.

open-heart surgery *n.* surgical repair of the heart during which the blood circulation is often maintained mechanically.

open house *n.* 1. a U.S. and Canadian name for **at-home** or **open day.** 2. **keep open house.** to be always ready to provide hospitality. 3. *U.S. and N.Z.* a house available for inspection by prospective buyers.

opening (ˈəupənɪŋ) *n.* 1. the act of making or becoming open. 2. a vacant or unobstructed space, esp. one that will serve as a passageway; gap. 3. *Chiefly U.S.* a tract in a forest in which trees are scattered or absent. 4. the first part or stage of something. 5. **a.** the first performance of something, esp. a theatrical production. **b.** (*as modifier*): *the opening night.* 6. a specific or formal sequence of moves at the start of any of certain games, esp. chess or draughts. 7. an opportunity or chance, esp. for employment or promotion in a business concern. 8. *Law.* the preliminary statement made by counsel to the court or jury before adducing evidence in support of his case.

opening time *n. Brit.* the time at which pubs can legally start selling alcoholic drinks.

open learning *n.* a system of further education on a flexible part-time basis.

open letter *n.* a letter, esp. one of protest, addressed to a person but also made public, as through the press.

open market *n.* a market in which prices are determined by supply and demand, there are no barriers to entry, and trading is not restricted to a specific area.

open market operations *pl. n. Finance.* the purchase and sale on the open market of government securities by the Bank of England for the purpose of regulating the supply of money and credit to the economy.

open marriage *n.* a marriage in which the partners are free to pursue their own social and sexual lives.

open-minded *adj.* having a mind receptive to new ideas, arguments, etc.; unprejudiced. —ˌ**open-ˈmindedly** *adv.* —ˌ**open-ˈmindedness** *n.*

open-mouthed *adj.* 1. having an open mouth, esp. in surprise. 2. greedy or ravenous. 3. clamorous or vociferous.

open order *n. Military.* a formation that allows additional space between the front and near ranks of a guard or inspected unit to allow the inspecting officer to pass.

open-plan *adj.* having no or few dividing walls between areas: *an open-plan office floor.*

open policy *n.* an insurance policy in which the amount payable in the event of a claim is settled after the loss or damage has occurred. Compare **valued policy.**

open position *n. Commerce.* a situation in which a dealer in commodities, securities, or currencies has either unsold stock or uncovered sales.

open primary *n. U.S. government.* a primary in which any registered voter may participate. Compare **closed primary.**

open prison *n.* a penal establishment in which the prisoners are trusted to serve their sentences and so do not need to be locked up, thus extending the range of work and occupation they can safely undertake.

open punctuation *n.* punctuation characterized by sparing use of stops, esp. of the comma. Compare **close punctuation.**

open-reel *adj.* another term for **reel-to-reel.**

open sandwich *n.* a slice of bread covered with a spread or filling but without a top.

open season *n.* a specified period of time in the year when it is legal to hunt or kill game or fish protected at other times by law.

open secret *n.* something that is supposed to be secret but is widely known.

open sentence *n. Logic.* an expression containing a free variable that can be replaced by a name to yield a sentence, as *x is wise.* Also called: **propositional function, sentential function.**

open sesame *n.* a very successful means of achieving a result. [from the magical words used by Ali Baba in the *Arabian Nights* to open the door of the robbers' den]

open set *n. Maths.* 1. a set which is not a closed set. 2. an interval on the real line excluding its end points, as]0, 1[, the set of reals between, but excluding, 0 and 1.

open shop *n.* an establishment in which persons are hired and employed irrespective of their membership or nonmembership of a trade union. Compare **closed shop, union shop.**

open slather *n.* See **slather** (sense 2).

open texture *n. Philosophy.* the failure of natural languages to determine future usage, particularly the ability of predicates to permit the construction of borderline cases.

open up *vb.* (*adv.*) 1. (*intr.*) to start firing a gun or guns. 2. (*intr.*) to speak freely or without restraint. 3. (*intr.*) *Informal.* (of a motor vehicle) to accelerate. 4. (*tr.*) to render accessible: *the motorway opened up the remoter areas.* 5. to make or become more exciting or lively: *the game opened up after half-time.*

open verdict *n.* a finding by a coroner's jury of death without stating the cause.

openwork (ˈəupᵊnˌwɜːk) *n.* ornamental work, as of metal or embroidery, having a pattern of openings or holes.

opera[1] (ˈɒpərə, ˈɒprə) *n.* 1. an extended dramatic work in which music constitutes a dominating feature, either consisting of separate recitatives, arias, and choruses, or having a continuous musical structure. 2. the branch of music or drama represented by such works. 3. the score, libretto, etc., of an opera. 4. a theatre where opera is performed. [C17: via Italian from Latin: work, a work, plural of *opus* work]

opera[2] (ˈɒpərə) *n.* a plural of **opus.**

operable (ˈɒpərəbᵊl, ˈɒprə-) *adj.* 1. capable of being treated by a surgical operation. 2. capable of being operated. 3. capable of being put into practice. —ˌ**operaˈbility** *n.* —ˈ**operably** *adv.*

opéra bouffe (ˈɒpərə ˈbuːf; *French* ɔpera buf) *n., pl.* **opéras bouffes** (*French* ɔpera buf). a type of light or satirical opera common in France during the 19th century. [from French: comic opera]

opera buffa (ˈbuːfə; *Italian* ˈopera ˈbuffa) *n., pl.* **opera buffas** *or* **opere buffe** (*Italian* ˈopere ˈbuffe). comic opera, esp. that originating in Italy during the 18th century. [from Italian: comic opera]

opera cloak *n.* a large cloak worn over evening clothes. Also called: **opera hood.**

opéra comique (kɒˈmiːk; *French* ɔpera kɔmik) *n., pl.* **opéras comiques** (*French* ɔpera kɔmik). a type of opera, not necessarily comic, current in France during the 19th century and characterized by spoken dialogue. It originated in satirical parodies of grand opera.

opera glasses *pl. n.* small low-powered binoculars used by audiences in theatres and opera houses.

opera hat *n.* a collapsible top hat operated by a spring. Also called: **gibus.**

opera house *n.* a theatre designed for opera.

operand (ˈɒpəˌrænd) *n.* a quantity or function upon which a mathematical operation is performed. [C19: from Latin *operandum* (something) to be worked upon, from *operārī* to work]

operant (ˈɒpərənt) *adj.* 1. producing effects; operating. ~*n.* 2. a person or thing that operates. 3. *Psychol.* any response by an organism that is not directly caused by a stimulus.

operant learning *n. Psychol.* another name for **instrumental learning.**

opera seria (ˈsɪərɪə; *Italian* ˈopera ˈsɛːrja) *n., pl.* **opere serie** (*Italian* ˈopere ˈsɛːrje). a type of opera current in 18th century Italy based on a serious plot, esp. a mythological tale. [from Italian: serious opera]

operate (ˈɒpəˌreɪt) *vb.* 1. to function or cause to function. 2. (*tr.*) to control the functioning of: *operate a machine.* 3. to manage, direct, run, or pursue (a business, system, etc.). 4. (*intr.*) to perform a surgical operation (upon a person or animal). 5. (*intr.*) to produce a desired or intended effect. 6. (*tr.*; usually foll. by *on*) to treat or process in a particular or specific way. 7. (*intr.*) to conduct military or naval operations. 8. (*intr.*) to deal in securities on a stock exchange. [C17: from Latin *operārī* to work]

operatic (ˌɒpəˈrætɪk) *adj.* 1. of or relating to opera. 2. histrionic or exaggerated. —ˌ**operˈatically** *adv.*

operating budget *n. Account.* a forecast of the sales revenue, production costs, overheads, cash flow, etc., of an organization, used to monitor its trading activities, usually for one year.

operating system *n.* a program that controls the overall operation of a computer system, typically by performing such tasks as memory allocation, job scheduling, and input/output control.

operating table *n.* the table on which the patient lies during a surgical operation.

operating theatre *n.* a room in which surgical operations are performed.

operation (ˌɒpəˈreɪʃən) *n.* 1. the act, process, or manner of operating. 2. the state of being in effect, in action, or operative (esp. in the phrases **in** *or* **into operation**). 3. a process, method, or series of acts, esp. of a practical or mechanical nature. 4. *Surgery.* any manipulation of the body or one of its organs or parts to repair damage, arrest the progress of a disease, remove foreign matter, etc. 5. **a.** a military or naval action, such as a campaign, manoeuvre, etc. **b.** (*cap. and prenominal when part of a name*): *Operation Crossbow.* 6. *Maths.* **a.** any procedure, such as addition, multiplication, involution, or differentiation, in which one or more numbers or quantities are operated upon according to specific rules. **b.** a function from a set onto itself. 7. a commercial or financial transaction.

operational (ˌɒpəˈreɪʃənᵊl) *adj.* 1. of or relating to an operation or operations. 2. in working order and ready for use. 3. *Military.* capable of, needed in, or actually involved in operations. —ˌ**operˈationally** *adv.*

operational amplifier *n.* a high-gain direct-coupled amplifier, the response of which may be controlled by negative-feedback circuits externally connected.

operationalism (ˌɒpəˈreɪʃənəˌlɪzəm) *or* **operationism** (ˌɒpəˈreɪʃəˌnɪzəm) *n. Philosophy.* the theory that scientific terms are defined by the experimental operations which determine their applicability. —ˌ**operˌationalˈistic** *adj.*

operations research *n.* the analysis of problems in business and industry involving the construction of models and the application of linear programming, critical path analysis, and other quantitative techniques. Also: **operational research.**

operations room *n.* a room from which all the operations of a military, police, or other disciplined activity are controlled.

operative ('ɒpərətɪv) *adj.* **1.** in force, effect, or operation. **2.** exerting force or influence. **3.** producing a desired effect; significant: *the operative word.* **4.** of or relating to a surgical procedure. ~*n.* **5.** a worker, esp. one with a special skill. **6.** *U.S.* a private detective. —'**operatively** *adv.* —'**operativeness** *or* ˌ**opera'tivity** *n.*

operatize *or* **operatise** ('ɒpərəˌtaɪz) *vb.* (*tr.*) to turn (a play, novel, etc.) into an opera.

operator ('ɒpəˌreɪtə) *n.* **1.** a person who operates a machine, instrument, etc., esp., a person who makes connections on a telephone switchboard or at an exchange. **2.** a person who owns or operates an industrial or commercial establishment. **3.** a speculator, esp. one who operates on currency or stock markets. **4.** *Informal.* a person who manipulates affairs and other people. **5.** *Maths.* any symbol, term, letter, etc., used to indicate or express a specific operation or process, such as ∫ (the integral operator), or Δ (the differential operator).

operculum (əʊ'pɜːkjʊləm) *n., pl.* **-la** (-lə) *or* **-lums.** **1.** *Zoology.* **a.** the hard bony flap covering the gill slits in fishes. **b.** the bony plate in certain gastropods covering the opening of the shell when the body is withdrawn. **2.** *Botany.* the covering of the spore-bearing capsule of a moss. **3.** *Biology.* any other covering or lid in various organisms. [C18: via New Latin from Latin: lid, from *operīre* to cover] —**o'percular** *or* **operculate** (əʊ'pɜːkjʊlɪt, -ˌleɪt) *adj.*

operetta (ˌɒpə'rɛtə) *n.* a type of comic or light-hearted opera. [C18: from Italian: a small OPERA[1]] —ˌ**oper'ettist** *n.*

operon ('ɒpəˌrɒn) *n. Genetics.* a group of adjacent genes functioning as a unit under the control of another gene (the **operator gene**). [C20: from OPERATE]

operose ('ɒpəˌrəʊs) *adj. Rare.* **1.** laborious. **2.** industrious; busy. [C17: from Latin *operōsus* painstaking, from *opus* work] —'**operˌosely** *adv.* —'**operˌoseness** *n.*

ophicleide ('ɒfɪˌklaɪd) *n. Music.* an obsolete keyed wind instrument of bass pitch. [C19: from French *ophicléide,* from Greek *ophis* snake + *kleis* key]

ophidian (əʊ'fɪdɪən) *adj.* **1.** snakelike. **2.** of, relating to, or belonging to the *Ophidia,* a suborder of reptiles that comprises the snakes. ~*n.* **3.** any reptile of the suborder *Ophidia;* a snake. [C19: from New Latin *Ophidia* name of suborder, from Greek *ophidion,* from *ophis* snake]

ophiology (ˌɒfɪ'ɒlədʒɪ) *n.* the branch of zoology that is concerned with the study of snakes. [C19: from Greek *ophis* snake + -LOGY] —**ophiological** (ˌɒfɪə'lɒdʒɪkᵊl) *adj.* —ˌ**ophi'ologist** *n.*

ophite ('əʊfaɪt) *n.* any of several greenish mottled rocks with ophitic texture, such as dolerite and diabase. [C17: from Latin *ophītēs,* from Greek, from *ophis* snake: because the mottled appearance resembles the markings of a snake]

ophitic (əʊ'fɪtɪk) *adj.* (of the texture of rocks such as dolerite) having small elongated unorientated feldspar crystals embedded in the ferromagnesian matrix.

Ophiuchus (ɒ'fjuːkəs) *n., Latin genitive* **Ophiuchi** (ɒ'fjuːkaɪ). a large constellation lying on the celestial equator between Hercules and Scorpius and containing the dark nebula, **Ophiuchus Nebula.** [C17: via Latin from Greek *Ophioukhos,* from *ophis* snake + *ekhein* to hold]

ophthalmia (ɒf'θælmɪə) *n.* inflammation of the eye, often including the conjunctiva. [C16: via Late Latin from Greek, from *ophthalmos* eye; see OPTIC]

ophthalmic (ɒf'θælmɪk) *adj.* of or relating to the eye.

ophthalmic optician *n.* See **optician.**

ophthalmitis (ˌɒfθæl'maɪtɪs) *n.* inflammation of the eye.

ophthalmo- *or before a vowel* **ophthalm-** *combining form.* indicating the eye or the eyeball: *ophthalmoscope.* [from Greek *ophthalmos* EYE]

ophthalmol. *or* **ophthal.** *abbrev. for* ophthalmology.

ophthalmologist (ˌɒfθæl'mɒlədʒɪst) *n.* a medical practitioner specializing in the diagnosis and treatment of eye diseases.

ophthalmology (ˌɒfθæl'mɒlədʒɪ) *n.* the branch of medicine concerned with the eye and its diseases. —**ophthalmological** (ɒfˌθælmə'lɒdʒɪkᵊl) *adj.*

ophthalmoscope (ɒf'θælməˌskəʊp) *n.* an instrument for examining the interior of the eye. —**ophthalmoscopic** (ɒfˌθælmə'skɒpɪk) *adj.*

ophthalmoscopy (ˌɒfθæl'mɒskəpɪ) *n.* examination of the interior of the eye with an ophthalmoscope.

-opia *n. combining form.* indicating a visual defect or condition: *myopia.* [from Greek, from *ōps* eye] —**-opic** *adj. combining form.*

opiate *n.* ('əʊpɪɪt). **1.** any of various narcotic drugs containing opium or an alkaloid of opium. **2.** any other narcotic or sedative drug. **3.** something that soothes, deadens, or induces sleep. ~*adj.* ('əʊpɪɪt). **4.** containing or consisting of opium. **5.** inducing relaxation; soporific. ~*vb.* ('əʊpɪˌeɪt). (*tr.*) *Rare.* **6.** to treat with an opiate. **7.** to dull or deaden. [C16: from Medieval Latin *opiātus;* from Latin *opium* poppy juice, OPIUM]

opine (əʊ'paɪn) *vb.* (when *tr., usually takes a clause as object*) to hold or express an opinion: *he opined that it was all a sad mistake.* [C16: from Latin *opīnārī*]

opinion (ə'pɪnjən) *n.* **1.** judgment or belief not founded on certainty or proof. **2.** the prevailing or popular feeling or view: *public opinion.* **3.** evaluation, impression, or estimation of the value or worth of a person or thing. **4.** an evaluation or judgment given by an expert: *a medical opinion.* **5.** the advice given by counsel on a case submitted to him for his view on the legal points involved. **6. a matter of opinion.** a point open to question. **7. be of the opinion (that).** to believe (that). [C13: via Old French from Latin *opīniō* belief, from *opīnārī* to think; see OPINE]

opinionated (ə'pɪnjəˌneɪtɪd) *adj.* holding obstinately and unreasonably to one's own opinions; dogmatic. —**o'pinionˌatedly** *adv.* —**o'pinionˌatedness** *n.*

opinionative (ə'pɪnjənətɪv) *adj. Rare.* **1.** of or relating to opinion. **2.** another word for **opinionated.** —**o'pinionatively** *adv.* —**o'pinionativeness** *n.*

opinion poll *n.* another term for a **poll** (sense 3).

opioid ('əʊpɪˌɔɪd) *n.* any opiate produced naturally in the brain.

opisthobranch (ə'pɪsθəˌbræŋk) *n.* any marine gastropod of the class *Opisthobranchia* (or *Opisthobranchiata*), in which the shell is reduced or absent: includes the pteropods, sea hares, and nudibranchs. [via New Latin from Greek *opisthen* behind + -BRANCH]

opisthognathous (ˌɒpɪs'θɒgnəθəs) *adj.* (of a person or animal) having receding jaws. [C19: from Greek *opisthen* behind + -GNATHOUS] —**opis'thognathism** *n.*

opisthosoma (ɒˌpɪsθə'səʊmə) *n. Zoology.* the abdomen of a spider or other arachnid. [C19: from Greek *opisthen* behind + SOMA[1]]

opium ('əʊpɪəm) *n.* **1.** an addictive narcotic drug extracted from the unripe seed capsules of the opium poppy and containing alkaloids such as morphine and codeine: used in medicine as an analgesic and hypnotic. **2.** something having a tranquillizing or stupefying effect. [C14: from Latin: poppy juice, from Greek *opion,* diminutive of *opos* juice of a plant]

opium den *n.* a place where opium is sold and used.

opiumism ('əʊpɪəˌmɪzəm) *n. Pathol.* addiction to opium or a condition resulting from prolonged use of opium.

opium poppy *n.* a poppy, *Papaver somniferum,* of SW Asia, with greyish-green leaves and typically white or reddish flowers: widely cultivated as a source of opium.

opossum (ə'pɒsəm) *n., pl.* **-sums** *or* **-sum.** **1.** any thick-furred marsupial, esp. *Didelphis marsupialis* (**common opossum**), of the family *Didelphidae* of S North, Central, and South America, having an elongated snout and a hairless prehensile tail. Sometimes (informal) shortened to **possum.** **2.** Also called (Austral. and N.Z.): **possum.** any of various similar animals, esp. the phalanger, *Trichosurus vulpecula,* of the New Zealand bush. [C17: from Algonquian *aposoum;* related to Delaware *apässum,* literally: white beast]

opossum block *n.* (in New Zealand) a block of bush allocated to a licensed opossum trapper.

opossum shrimp *n.* any of various shrimplike crustaceans of the genera *Mysis, Praunus,* etc., of the order *Mysidacea,* in which the females carry the eggs and young around in a ventral brood pouch.

opp. *abbrev. for:* **1.** opposed. **2.** opposite.

oppidan ('ɒpɪdən) *Rare.* ~*adj.* **1.** of a town; urban. ~*n.* **2.** a person living in a town. [C16: from Latin *oppidānus,* from *oppidum* town]

oppilate ('ɒpɪˌleɪt) *vb.* (*tr.*) *Pathol.* to block (the pores, bowels, etc.). [C16: from Latin *oppīlāre,* from *ob-* against + *pīlāre* to pack closely] —ˌ**oppi'lation** *n.*

opponent (ə'pəʊnənt) *n.* **1.** a person who opposes another in a contest, battle, etc. **2.** *Anatomy.* an opponent muscle. ~*adj.* **3.** opposite, as in position. **4.** *Anatomy.* (of a muscle) bringing two parts into opposition. **5.** opposing; contrary. [C16: from Latin *oppōnere* to oppose, from *ob-* against + *pōnere* to place] —**op'ponency** *n.*

opportune ('ɒpəˌtjuːn) *adj.* **1.** occurring at a time that is suitable or advantageous. **2.** fit or suitable for a particular purpose or occurrence. [C15: via Old French from Latin *opportūnus,* from *ob-* to + *portus* harbour (originally: coming to the harbour, obtaining timely protection)] —'**opporˌtunely** *adv.* —'**opporˌtuneness** *n.*

opportunist (ˌɒpə'tjuːnɪst) *n.* **1.** a person who adapts his actions, responses, etc., to take advantage of opportunities, circumstances, etc. ~*adj.* **2.** taking advantage of opportunities and circumstances in this way. —ˌ**oppor'tunism** *n.*

opportunistic (ˌɒpətjʊ'nɪstɪk) *adj.* **1.** of or characterized by opportunism. **2.** *Medicine.* (of an infection) caused by any microorganism that is harmless to a healthy person but debilitates a person whose immune system has been weakened by disease or drug treatment. —ˌ**opportu'nistically** *adv.*

opportunity (ˌɒpə'tjuːnɪtɪ) *n., pl.* **-ties.** **1.** a favourable, appropriate, or advantageous combination of circumstances. **2.** a chance or prospect.

opportunity cost *n. Economics.* cost in terms of the best alternatives foregone.

opportunity shop *n. Austral. and N.Z.* a shop selling second-hand goods for charitable funds.

opposable (ə'pəʊzəbᵊl) *adj.* **1.** capable of being opposed. **2.** Also: **apposable.** (of the thumb of primates, esp. man) capable of being moved into a position facing the other digits so as to be able to touch the ends of each. **3.** capable of being placed opposite something else. —**op'posably** *adv.* —**op,posa'bility** *n.*

oppose (ə'pəuz) *vb.* **1.** (*tr.*) to fight against, counter, or resist strongly. **2.** (*tr.*) to be hostile or antagonistic to; be against. **3.** (*tr.*) to place or set in opposition; contrast or counterbalance. **4.** (*tr.*) to place opposite or facing. **5.** (*intr.*) to be or act in opposition. [C14: via Old French from Latin *oppōnere,* from *ob-* against + *pōnere* to place] —**op'poser** *n.* —**op'posing** *adj.* —**op'posingly** *adv.* —**oppositive** (ə'pɒzɪtɪv) *adj.*

opposed-cylinder *adj.* (of an internal-combustion engine) having cylinders on opposite sides of the crankcase in the same plane.

opposite ('ɒpəzɪt, -sɪt) *adj.* **1.** situated or being on the other side or at each side of something between: *their houses were at opposite ends of the street.* **2.** facing or going in contrary directions: *opposite ways.* **3.** diametrically different in character, tendency, belief, etc.: *opposite views.* **4.** *Botany.* **a.** (of leaves, flowers, etc.) arranged in pairs on either side of the stem. **b.** (of parts of a flower) arranged opposite the middle of another part. **5.** *Maths.* **a.** (of two vertices or sides in an even-sided polygon) separated by the same number of vertices or sides in both a clockwise and anticlockwise direction. **b.** (of a side in a triangle) facing a specified angle. Abbrev.: **opp.** ~*n.* **6.** a person or thing that is opposite; antithesis. **7.** *Maths.* the side facing a specified angle in a right-angled triangle. **8.** a rare word for **opponent.** ~*prep.* **9.** Also: **opposite to.** facing; corresponding to (something on the other side of a division): *the house opposite ours.* **10.** as a co-star with: *she played opposite Olivier in "Hamlet".* ~*adv.* **11.** on opposite sides: *she lives opposite.* —**'oppositely** *adv.* —**'oppositeness** *n.*

opposite number *n.* a person holding an equivalent and corresponding position on another side or situation.

opposite prompt *n. Theatre.* another name for **stage right.** See **prompt.**

opposite sex *n.* **the.** women in relation to men or men in relation to women.

opposition (,ɒpə'zɪʃən) *n.* **1.** the act of opposing or the state of being opposed. **2.** hostility, unfriendliness, or antagonism. **3.** a person or group antagonistic or opposite in aims to another. **4. a.** (usually preceded by *the*) a political party or group opposed to the ruling party or government. **b.** (*cap. as part of a name, esp. in Britain and other Commonwealth countries*): *Her Majesty's Loyal Opposition.* **c. in opposition.** (of a political party) opposing the government. **5.** a position facing or opposite another. **6.** the act of placing something facing or opposite something else. **7.** something that acts as an obstacle to some course or progress. **8.** *Astronomy.* **a.** the position of an outer planet or the moon when it is in line or nearly in line with the earth as seen from the sun and is approximately at its nearest to the earth. **b.** the position of two celestial bodies when they appear to be diametrically opposite each other on the celestial sphere. **9.** *Astrology.* an exact aspect of 180° between two planets, etc., an orb of 8° being allowed. Compare **conjunction** (sense 5), **square** (sense 9), **trine** (sense 1). **10.** *Logic.* **a.** the relation between propositions having the same subject and predicate but differing in quality, quantity, or both, as with *all men are wicked; no men are wicked; some men are not wicked.* **b. square of opposition.** a diagram representing these relations with the contradictory propositions at diagonally opposite corners. **11. the opposition.** *Chess.* a relative position of the kings in the endgame such that the player who has the move is at a disadvantage: *his opponent has the opposition.* —,**oppo'sitional** *adj.* —,**oppo'sitionist** *n.* —,**oppo'sitionless** *adj.*

oppress (ə'prɛs) *vb.* (*tr.*) **1.** to subjugate by cruelty, force, etc. **2.** to afflict or torment. **3.** to lie heavy on (the mind, imagination, etc.). **4.** an obsolete word for **overwhelm.** [C14: via Old French from Medieval Latin *oppressāre,* from Latin *opprimere,* from *ob-* against + *premere* to press] —**op'pressingly** *adv.* —**op'pression** *n.* —**op'pressor** *n.*

oppressive (ə'prɛsɪv) *adj.* **1.** cruel, harsh, or tyrannical. **2.** heavy, constricting, or depressing. —**op'pressively** *adv.* —**op'pressiveness** *n.*

opprobrious (ə'prəubrɪəs) *adj.* **1.** expressing scorn, disgrace, or contempt. **2.** shameful or infamous. —**op'probriously** *adv.* —**op'probriousness** *n.*

opprobrium (ə'prəubrɪəm) *n.* **1.** the state of being abused or scornfully criticized. **2.** reproach or censure. **3.** a cause of disgrace or ignominy. [C17: from Latin *ob-* against + *probrum* a shameful act]

oppugn (ə'pju:n) *vb.* (*tr.*) to call into question; dispute. [C15: from Latin *oppugnāre,* from *ob-* against + *pugnāre* to fight, from *pugnus* clenched fist; see PUGNACIOUS] —**op'pugner** *n.*

oppugnant (ə'pʌgnənt) *adj. Rare.* combative, antagonistic, or contrary. —**op'pugnancy** *n.* —**op'pugnantly** *adv.*

ops. *abbrev. for* operations.

opsimath ('ɒpsɪ,mæθ) *n.* a person who learns late in life. [C19: from Greek *opsimathēs,* from *opse* late + *math-* learn] —**opsimathy** (ɒp'sɪməθɪ) *n.*

opsin ('ɒpsɪn) *n.* the protein that together with retinene makes up the purple visual pigment rhodopsin. [C20: back formation from RHODOPSIN]

-opsis *n. combining form.* indicating a specified appearance or resemblance: *coreopsis.* [from Greek *opsis* sight]

opsitbank ('ɒp,sɪt,bæŋk) *n. S. African.* a two-seater bench originally designed for courting couples. [from Afrikaans *opsit* to sit up + *bank* bench]

opsonic index *n.* the ratio of the number of bacteria destroyed by phagocytes in the blood of a test patient to the number destroyed in the blood of a normal individual.

opsonin ('ɒpsənɪn) *n.* a constituent of blood serum that renders invading bacteria more susceptible to ingestion by phagocytes in the serum. [C20: from Greek *opsōnion* victuals] —**opsonic** (ɒp'sɒnɪk) *adj.*

opsonize, opsonise ('ɒpsə,naɪz), *or* **opsonify** (ɒp'sɒnɪ,faɪ) *vb.* (*tr.*) to subject (bacteria) to the action of opsonins. —,**opsoni'zation,** ,**opsoni'sation,** *or* **op,sonifi'cation** *n.*

opt (ɒpt) *vb.* (when *intr.,* foll. by *for*) to show preference (for) or choose (to do something). See also **opt out.** [C19: from French *opter,* from Latin *optāre* to choose]

opt. *abbrev. for:* **1.** *Grammar.* optative. **2.** optical. **3.** optician. **4.** optics. **5.** optimum. **6.** optional.

optative ('ɒptətɪv) *adj.* **1.** indicating or expressing choice, preference, or wish. **2.** *Grammar.* denoting a mood of verbs in Greek, Sanskrit, etc., expressing a wish. ~*n.* **3.** *Grammar.* **a.** the optative mood. **b.** a verb in this mood. [C16: via French *optatif,* from Late Latin *optātīvus,* from Latin *optāre* to desire]

optic ('ɒptɪk) *adj.* **1.** of or relating to the eye or vision. **2.** a less common word for **optical.** ~*n.* **3.** an informal word for **eye**[1]. **4.** *Brit., trademark.* a device attached to an inverted bottle for dispensing measured quantities of liquid, such as whisky, gin, etc. [C16: from Medieval Latin *opticus,* from Greek *optikos,* from *optos* visible, seen; related to *ōps* eye]

optical ('ɒptɪkᵊl) *adj.* **1.** of, relating to, producing, or involving light. **2.** of or relating to the eye or to the sense of sight; optic. **3.** (esp. of a lens) aiding vision or correcting a visual disorder. —**'optically** *adv.*

optical activity *n.* the ability of substances that are optical isomers to rotate the plane of polarization of a transmitted beam of plane-polarized light.

optical bench *n.* an apparatus for experimentation in optics, typically consisting of an adjustable arrangement of light source, lenses, prisms, etc.

optical character reader *n.* a computer peripheral device enabling letters, numbers, or other characters usually printed on paper to be optically scanned and input to a storage device, such as magnetic tape. The device uses the process of **optical character recognition.** Abbrev. (for both *reader* and *recognition*): **OCR.**

optical crown *n.* an optical glass of low dispersion and relatively low refractive index. It is used in the construction of lenses.

optical density *n. Physics.* the former name for **reflection density** or **transmission density.**

optical disk *n. Computers.* an inflexible disk on which information is stored in digital form by laser technology. Also called: **video disk.**

optical double star *n.* two stars that appear close together when viewed through a telescope but are not physically associated and are often separated by a great distance. Compare **binary star.**

optical fibre *n.* a communications cable consisting of a thin glass fibre in a protective sheath. Light transmitted along the fibre may be modulated with vision, sound, or data signals. See also **fibre optics.**

optical flint *n.* an optical glass of high dispersion and high refractive index containing lead oxide. They are used in the manufacture of lenses, artificial gems, and cut glass. Also called: **flint glass.**

optical glass *n.* any of several types of clear homogeneous glass of known refractive index used in the construction of lenses, etc. See **optical flint, optical crown.**

optical illusion *n.* **1.** an object causing a false visual impression. **2.** an instance of deception by such an object.

optical isomerism *n.* isomerism of chemical compounds in which the two isomers differ only in that their molecules are mirror images of each other. See also **dextrorotation, laevorotatory, racemize.** —**optical isomer** *n.*

optical mark reading *n.* the reading of marks by an optical device whereby the information can be stored in machine-readable form.

optical maser *n.* another name for **laser** (sense 1).

optical pyrometer *n.* See **pyrometer.**

optical rotation *n.* the angle through which plane-polarized light is rotated in its passage through a substance exhibiting optical activity.

optical scanner *n.* a computer peripheral device enabling printed material, including characters and diagrams, to be scanned and converted into a form that can be stored in a computer. See also **optical character reader.**

optical sound *n.* sound recorded in the form of a photographic image on cinematograph films.

optic axis *n.* the direction in a uniaxial crystal or one of the two directions in a biaxial crystal along which a ray of unpolarized light may pass without undergoing double refraction.

optic disc *n.* a small oval-shaped area on the retina marking the site of entrance into the eyeball of the optic nerve. See **blind spot** (sense 1).

optician (ɒpˈtɪʃən) *n.* a general name used to refer to: **a. ophthalmic optician.** Also called: **optometrist.** a person qualified to examine the eyes and prescribe and supply spectacles and contact lenses. **b. dispensing optician.** a person who supplies and fits spectacle frames but is not qualified to prescribe lenses. ~See also **optometrist.** Compare **ophthalmologist.**
optic nerve *n.* the second cranial nerve, which provides a sensory pathway from the retina to the brain.
optics (ˈɒptɪks) *n.* (*functioning as sing.*) the branch of science concerned with vision and the generation, nature, propagation, and behaviour of electromagnetic light.
optic thalamus *n. Anatomy.* an older term for **thalamus** (senses 1, 2).
optimal (ˈɒptɪməl) *adj.* another word for **optimum** (sense 2). —ˌ**optiˈmality** *n.* —ˈ**optimally** *adv.*
optimism (ˈɒptɪˌmɪzəm) *n.* **1.** the tendency to expect the best and see the best in all things. **2.** hopefulness; confidence. **3.** the doctrine of the ultimate triumph of good over evil. **4.** the philosophical doctrine that this is the best of all possible worlds. ~Compare **pessimism.** [C18: from French *optimisme,* from Latin *optimus* best, superlative of *bonus* good] —ˈ**optimist** *n.* —ˌ**optiˈmistic** *or* ˌ**optiˈmistical** *adj.* —ˌ**optiˈmistically** *adv.*
optimize *or* **optimise** (ˈɒptɪˌmaɪz) *vb.* **1.** (*tr.*) to take the full advantage of. **2.** (*tr.*) to plan or carry out (an economic activity) with maximum efficiency. **3.** (*intr.*) to be optimistic. **4.** (*tr.*) to write or modify (a computer program) to achieve maximum efficiency in storage capacity, time, cost, etc. **5.** (*tr.*) to find the best compromise among several often conflicting requirements, as in engineering design. —ˌ**optimiˈzation** *or* ˌ**optimiˈsation** *n.*
optimum (ˈɒptɪməm) *n., pl.* **-ma** (-mə) *or* **-mums. 1.** a condition, degree, amount or compromise that produces the best possible result. ~*adj.* **2.** most favourable or advantageous; best: *optimum conditions.* [C19: from Latin: the best (thing), from *optimus* best; see OPTIMISM]
optimum population *n. Economics.* a population that is sufficiently large to provide an adequate workforce with minimal unemployment.
option (ˈɒpʃən) *n.* **1.** the act or an instance of choosing or deciding. **2.** the power or liberty to choose. **3.** an exclusive opportunity, usually for a limited period, to buy something at a future date: *he has a six month option on the Canadian rights to this book.* **4.** *Commerce.* the right to buy (**call option**) or sell (**put option**) a fixed quantity of a commodity, security, foreign exchange, etc., at a fixed price at a specified date in the future. See also **traded option. 5.** something chosen; choice. **6.** *N.Z.* short for **local option. 7. keep** (*or* **leave**) **one's options open.** not to commit oneself. **8.** See **soft option.** [C17: from Latin *optiō* free choice, from *optāre* to choose]
optional (ˈɒpʃənᵊl) *adj.* possible but not compulsory; left to personal choice. —ˈ**optionally** *adv.*
option money *n. Commerce.* the price paid for buying an option.
optoelectronics (ˌɒptəʊɪlɛkˈtrɒnɪks) *n.* (*functioning as sing.*) the study or use of devices in which an optical input produces an electrical output, or in which electrical stimulation produces visible or infrared output. —ˌ**optoelecˈtronic** *adj.*
optometer (ɒpˈtɒmɪtə) *n.* any of various instruments for measuring the refractive power of the eye.
optometrist (ɒpˈtɒmɪtrɪst) *n.* a person who is qualified to examine the eyes and prescribe and supply spectacles and contact lenses. Also called (esp. Brit.): **ophthalmic optician.** Compare **optician, ophthalmologist.**
optometry (ɒpˈtɒmɪtrɪ) *n.* the science or practice of testing visual acuity and prescribing corrective lenses. —**optometric** (ˌɒptəˈmɛtrɪk) *adj.*
optophone (ˈɒptəˌfəʊn) *n.* a device for blind people that converts printed words into sounds.
opt out *vb.* **1.** (*intr., adv.;* often foll. by *of*) to choose not to be involved (in) or part (of). ~*n.* **opt-out. 2.** the act of opting out, esp. of local-authority administration: *opt-outs by hospitals and schools.*
opulent (ˈɒpjʊlənt) *adj.* **1.** having or indicating wealth. **2.** abundant or plentiful. [C17: from Latin *opulens,* from *opēs* (pl.) wealth] —ˈ**opulence** *or* (*less commonly*) ˈ**opulency** *n.* —ˈ**opulently** *adv.*
opuntia (ɒˈpʌnʃɪə) *n.* any cactus of the genus *Opuntia,* esp. prickly pear, having fleshy branched stems and green, red, or yellow flowers. [C17: New Latin, from Latin *Opuntia* (*herba*) the Opuntian (plant), from *Opus,* ancient town of Locris, Greece]
opus (ˈəʊpəs, ˈɔp-) *n., pl.* **opuses** *or* **opera** (ˈɒpərə). **1.** an artistic composition, esp. a musical work. **2.** (*often cap.*) (usually followed by a number) a musical composition by a particular composer, generally catalogued in order of publication: *Beethoven's opus 61 is his violin concerto.* Abbrev.: **op.** [C18: from Latin: a work; compare Sanskrit *apas* work]
opus anglicanum *Latin.* (ˈəʊpəs æŋglɪˈkɑːnəm) *n.* fine embroidery, esp. of church vestments, produced in England *c.* 1200–*c.*1350; characterized by the rich materials used, esp. silver gilt thread. [literally: English work]
opuscule (ɒˈpʌskjuːl) *n. Rare.* a small or insignificant artistic work. [C17: via French from Latin *opusculum,* from *opus* work] —**oˈpuscular** *adj.*
Opus Dei (ˈəʊpəs ˈdeɪɪ) *n.* another name for **divine office.**
or[1] (ɔː; *unstressed* ə) *conj.* (*coordinating*) **1.** used to join alternatives: *apples or pears; apples or pears or cheese; apples, pears, or cheese.* **2.** used to join rephrasings of the same thing: *to serve in the army, or rather to fight in the army; twelve, or a dozen.* **3.** used to join two alternatives when the first is preceded by *either* or *whether: whether it rains or not we'll be there; either yes or no.* **4. one or two, four or five,** etc. a few. **5. or else.** See **else** (sense 3). **6.** a poetic word for **either** or **whether,** as the first element in correlatives, with *or* also preceding the second alternative. ~See also **exclusive or** and **inclusive or.** [C13: contraction of *other,* used to introduce an alternative, changed (through influence of EITHER) from Old English *oththe;* compare Old High German *odar* (German *oder*)]
▷**Usage.** See at **either** and **neither.**
or[2] (ɔː) *Archaic.* ~*conj.* **1.** (*subordinating;* foll. by *ever* or *ere*) before; when. ~*prep.* **2.** before. [Old English *ār* soon; related to Old Norse *ār* early, Old High German *ēr*]
or[3] (ɔː) *adj.* (*usually postpositive*) *Heraldry.* of the metal gold. [C16: via French from Latin *aurum* gold]
OR *abbrev. for:* **1.** operational research. **2.** Oregon. **3.** *Military.* other ranks.
o.r. *Commerce. abbrev. for* owner's risk.
-or[1] *suffix forming nouns from verbs.* a person or thing that does what is expressed by the verb: *actor; conductor; generator; sailor.* [via Old French *-eur, -eor,* from Latin *-or* or *-ātor*]
-or[2] *suffix forming nouns.* **1.** indicating state, condition, or activity: *terror; error.* **2.** the U.S. spelling of **-our.**
ora (ˈɔːrə) *n.* the plural of **os**[2].
orache *or esp. U.S.* **orach** (ˈɒrɪtʃ) *n.* any of several herbaceous plants or small shrubs of the chenopodiaceous genus *Atriplex,* esp. *A. hortensis* (**garden orache**), which is cultivated as a vegetable. They have typically greyish-green lobed leaves and inconspicuous flowers. [C15: from Old French *arache,* from Latin *atriplex,* from Greek *atraphaxus,* of obscure origin]
oracle (ˈɒrəkᵊl) *n.* **1.** a prophecy, often obscure or allegorical, revealed through the medium of a priest or priestess at the shrine of a god. **2.** a shrine at which an oracular god is consulted. **3.** an agency through which a prophecy is transmitted. **4.** any person or thing believed to indicate future action with infallible authority. **5.** a statement believed to be infallible and authoritative. **6.** *Bible.* **a.** a message from God. **b.** the holy of holies in the Israelite temple. ~See also **oracles.** [C14: via Old French from Latin *ōrāculum,* from *ōrāre* to request]
Oracle (ˈɒrəkᵊl) *n. Trademark.* the Teletext system operated by ITV. See **Teletext.** [C20: acronym of *o(ptional) r(eception of) a(nnouncements by) c(oded) l(ine) e(lectronics)*]
oracles (ˈɒrəkᵊlz) *pl. n.* another term for **Scripture** (sense 1).
oracular (ɒˈrækjʊlə) *adj.* **1.** of or relating to an oracle. **2.** wise and prophetic. **3.** mysterious or ambiguous. —**oˈracularly** *adv.*
oracy (ˈɔːrəsɪ) *n.* the capacity to express oneself in and understand speech. [C20: from Latin *or-, os* mouth, by analogy with *literacy*]
ora et labora *Latin.* (ˈɔːrɑː ɛt ˈlæbɔːˌrɑː) pray and work.
oral (ˈɔːrəl, ˈɒrəl) *adj.* **1.** spoken or verbal: *an oral agreement.* **2.** relating to, affecting, or for use in the mouth: *an oral thermometer.* **3.** of or relating to the surface of an animal, such as a jellyfish, on which the mouth is situated. **4.** denoting a drug to be taken by mouth: *an oral contraceptive.* Compare **parenteral. 5.** of, relating to, or using spoken words. **6.** *Phonetics.* pronounced with the soft palate in a raised position completely closing the nasal cavity and allowing air to pass out only through the mouth. **7.** *Psychoanal.* **a.** relating to a stage of psychosexual development during which the child's interest is concentrated on the mouth. **b.** denoting personality traits, such as dependence, selfishness, and aggression, resulting from fixation at the oral stage. Compare **anal** (sense 2), **genital** (sense 2), **phallic** (sense 2). ~*n.* **8.** an examination in which the questions and answers are spoken rather than written. [C17: from Late Latin *ōrālis,* from Latin *ōs* face] —ˈ**orally** *adv.*
oral eroticism *n. Psychoanal.* libidinal pleasure derived from the lips and mouth, for example by kissing.
oral history *n.* the memories of living people about events or social conditions which they experienced in their earlier lives taped and preserved as historical evidence.
oral hygiene *n.* another name for **dental hygiene.**
oral hygienist *n.* another name for **dental hygienist.**
Oral Law *n. Judaism.* the traditional body of religious law believed to have been revealed to Moses as an interpretation of the Torah and passed on orally until it was codified and recorded, principally in the Mishna and Gemara.
oral society *n.* a society that has not developed literacy.
orang (ɔːˈræŋ, ˈɔːræŋ) *n.* short for **orang-utan.**
orange (ˈɒrɪndʒ) *n.* **1.** any of several citrus trees, esp. *Citrus sinensis* (**sweet orange**) and the Seville orange, cultivated in warm regions for their round edible fruit. See also **tangerine** (sense 1). **2. a.** the fruit of any of these trees, having a yellowish-red bitter rind and segmented juicy flesh. See also **navel orange. b.** (*as modifier*): *orange peel.* **3.** the hard wood of any of these trees. **4.** any of a group of colours, such as that of the skin of an orange, that lie between red and yellow in the visible spectrum in the approximate wavelength range 620–585 nanometres. **5.** a dye or pigment producing these colours. **6.**

orange cloth or clothing: *dressed in orange.* **7.** any of several trees or herbaceous plants that resemble the orange, such as mock orange. *~adj.* **8.** of the colour orange. [C14: via Old French from Old Provençal *auranja,* from Arabic *nāranj,* from Persian *nārang,* from Sanskrit *nāranga,* probably of Dravidian origin]

Orange ('ɒrɪndʒ) *adj.* **1.** of or relating to the Orangemen. **2.** of or relating to the royal dynasty of Orange, since 1815 the reigning house of the Netherlands.

orangeade (ˌɒrɪndʒ'eɪd) *n.* an effervescent or still orange-flavoured drink.

orange blossom *n.* the flowers of the orange tree, traditionally worn by brides.

orange chromide ('krəʊmaɪd) *n.* an Asian cichlid fish, *Etropus maculatus,* with a brownish-orange spotted body.

orange flower water *n.* a distilled infusion of orange blossom, used in cakes, confectionery, etc.

Orangeism ('ɒrɪndʒˌɪzəm) *n.* the practices or principles of Orangemen, esp. Protestant supremacy in Ireland, Northern Ireland, or Canada.

Orangeman ('ɒrɪndʒmən) *n., pl.* **-men.** a member of a society founded as a secret order in Ireland (1795) to uphold the Protestant religion, the Protestant dynasty, and Protestant supremacy against Irish nationalists and Roman Catholics. **Orange Lodges** have since spread to many parts of the former British Empire. [C18: after William, prince of *Orange* (king of England as William III)]

Orangeman's Day *n.* the 12th of July, celebrated by Protestants in Northern Ireland to commemorate the anniversary of the Battle of the Boyne (1690), in which William III defeated the deposed James II.

orange peel *n.* **1.** the thick pitted rind of an orange. **2.** anything resembling this in surface texture, such as skin or porcelain.

orange-peel fungus *n.* See **elf-cup.**

orange pekoe *n.* a superior grade of black tea made from the small leaves at the tips of the plant stems and growing in India and Sri Lanka.

orangery ('ɒrɪndʒərɪ, -dʒrɪ) *n., pl.* **-eries.** a building, such as a greenhouse, in which orange trees are grown.

orange stick *n.* a small stick used to clean the fingernails and cuticles, having one pointed and one rounded end.

orange-tip *n.* a European butterfly, *Anthocharis cardamines,* having whitish wings with orange-tipped forewings: family *Pieridae.*

orangewood ('ɒrɪndʒˌwʊd) *n.* **a.** the hard fine-grained yellowish wood of the orange tree. **b.** (*as modifier*): *an orangewood table.*

orang-utan (ɔːˌræŋuː'tæn, ˌɔːræŋ'uːtæn) *or* **orang-outang** (ɔːˌræŋuː'tæŋ, ˌɔːræŋ'uːtæŋ) *n.* a large anthropoid ape, *Pongo pygmaeus,* of the forests of Sumatra and Borneo, with shaggy reddish-brown hair and strong arms. Sometimes shortened to **orang.** [C17: from Malay *orang hutan,* from *ōrang* man + *hūtan* forest]

ora pro nobis *Latin.* ('ɔːrɑː prəʊ 'nəʊbɪs) *R.C. Church.* a Latin invocation meaning *pray for us.*

orate (ɔː'reɪt) *vb.* (*intr.*) **1.** to make or give an oration. **2.** to speak pompously and lengthily.

oration (ɔː'reɪʃən) *n.* **1.** a formal public declaration or speech. **2.** any rhetorical, lengthy, or pompous speech. **3.** an academic exercise or contest in public speaking. [C14: from Latin *ōrātiō* speech, harangue, from *ōrāre* to plead, pray]

orator ('ɒrətə) *n.* **1.** a public speaker, esp. one versed in rhetoric. **2.** a person given to lengthy or pompous speeches. **3.** *Obsolete.* the plaintiff in a cause of action in chancery.

Oratorian (ˌɒrə'tɔːrɪən) *n.* a member of the religious congregation of the Oratory.

oratorio (ˌɒrə'tɔːrɪəʊ) *n., pl.* **-rios.** a dramatic but unstaged musical composition for soloists, chorus, and orchestra, based on a religious theme. [C18: from Italian, literally: ORATORY[2], referring to the Church of the Oratory at Rome where musical services were held]

oratory[1] ('ɒrətərɪ, -trɪ) *n.* **1.** the art of public speaking. **2.** rhetorical skill or style. [C16: from Latin (*ars*) *ōrātōria* (the art of) public speaking] —ˌ**ora'torical** *adj.* —ˌ**ora'torically** *adv.*

oratory[2] ('ɒrətərɪ, -trɪ) *n., pl.* **-ries.** a small room or secluded place, set apart for private prayer. [C14: from Anglo-Norman, from Church Latin *ōrātōrium* place of prayer, from *ōrāre* to pray]

Oratory ('ɒrətərɪ, -trɪ) *n. R.C. Church.* **1.** Also called: **Congregation of the Oratory.** the religious society of secular priests (**Oratorians**) living in a community founded by St Philip Neri. **2.** any church belonging to this society: *the Brompton Oratory.*

orb (ɔːb) *n.* **1.** (in royal regalia) an ornamental sphere surmounted by a cross, representing the power of a sovereign. **2.** a sphere; globe. **3.** *Poetic.* another word for **eye**[1]. **4.** *Obsolete or poetic.* **a.** a celestial body, esp. the earth or sun. **b.** the orbit of a celestial body. **5.** an archaic word for **circle.** *~vb.* **6.** to make or become circular or spherical. **7.** (*tr.*) an archaic word for **encircle.** [C16: from Latin *orbis* circle, disc]

orbicular (ɔː'bɪkjʊlə), **orbiculate,** *or* **orbiculated** *adj.* **1.** circular or spherical. **2.** (of a leaf or similar flat part) circular or nearly circular. **3.** *Rare.* rounded or total. —**orbicularity** (ɔːˌbɪkjʊ'lærɪtɪ) *n.* —**or'bicularly** *adv.*

orbit ('ɔːbɪt) *n.* **1.** *Astronomy.* the curved path, usually elliptical, followed by a planet, satellite, comet, etc., in its motion around another celestial body under the influence of gravitation. **2.** a range or field of action or influence; sphere: *he is out of my orbit.* **3.** the bony cavity containing the eyeball. Nontechnical name: **eye socket.** **4.** *Zoology.* **a.** the skin surrounding the eye of a bird. **b.** the hollow in which lies the eye or eyestalk of an insect or other arthropod. **5.** *Physics.* the path of an electron in its motion around the nucleus of an atom. *~vb.* **6.** to move around (a body) in a curved path, usually circular or elliptical. **7.** (*tr.*) to send (a satellite, spacecraft, etc.) into orbit. **8.** (*intr.*) to move in or as if in an orbit. [C16: from Latin *orbita* course, from *orbis* circle, ORB] —'**orbitally** *adv.*

orbital ('ɔːbɪtᵊl) *adj.* **1.** of or denoting an orbit. *~n.* **2.** a region surrounding an atomic nucleus in which the distribution of electrons is given by a wave function.

orbital velocity *n.* the velocity required by a spacecraft, satellite, etc., to enter and maintain a given orbit.

orbiter ('ɔːbɪtə) *n.* a spacecraft or satellite designed to orbit a planet or other body without landing on it.

orc (ɔːk) *n.* **1.** any of various whales, such as the killer and grampus. **2.** a mythical monster. [C16: via Latin *orca,* perhaps from Greek *orux* whale]

Orcadian (ɔː'keɪdɪən) *n.* **1.** a native or inhabitant of the Orkneys, islands off the NE coast of Scotland. *~adj.* **2.** of or relating to the Orkneys. [from Latin *Orcades* the Orkney Islands]

orcein ('ɔːsɪɪn) *n.* a brown crystalline material formed by the action of ammonia on orcinol and present in orchil: used as a dye, biological stain, and antiseptic. Formula: $C_{28}H_{24}O_7N_2$. [C19: see ORCINOL]

orch. *abbrev. for:* **1.** orchestra(l). **2.** orchestrated by.

orchard ('ɔːtʃəd) *n.* **1.** an area of land devoted to the cultivation of fruit trees. **2.** a collection of fruit trees especially cultivated. [Old English *orceard, ortigeard,* from *ort-,* from Latin *hortus* garden + *geard* YARD[2]]

orchard bush *n. W African.* open savanna country with occasional trees and scrub, as found north of the W African forest belt.

orchardman ('ɔːtʃədmən) *n., pl.* **-men.** a person who grows and sells orchard fruits.

orchestra ('ɔːkɪstrə) *n.* **1.** a large group of musicians, esp. one whose members play a variety of different instruments. See also **symphony orchestra, string orchestra, chamber orchestra.** **2.** a group of musicians, each playing the same type of instrument: *a balalaika orchestra.* **3.** Also called: **orchestra pit.** the space reserved for musicians in a theatre, immediately in front of or under the stage. **4.** *Chiefly U.S. and Canadian.* the stalls in a theatre. **5.** (in the ancient Greek theatre) the semicircular space in front of the stage. [C17: via Latin from Greek: the space in the theatre reserved for the chorus, from *orkheisthai* to dance] —**orchestral** (ɔː'kestrəl) *adj.* —**or'chestrally** *adv.*

orchestrate ('ɔːkɪˌstreɪt) *vb.* (*tr.*) **1.** to score or arrange (a piece of music) for orchestra. **2.** to arrange, organize, or build up for special or maximum effect. —ˌ**orches'tration** *n.* —'**orchesˌtrator** *n.*

orchestrina (ˌɔːkɪs'triːnə) or **orchestrion** (ɔː'kestrɪən) *n.* any of various types of mechanical musical instrument designed to imitate the sound of an orchestra.

orchid ('ɔːkɪd) *n.* any terrestrial or epiphytic plant of the family *Orchidaceae,* having flowers of unusual shapes and beautiful colours, specialized for pollination by certain insects. See **bee orchid, burnt-tip orchid, fly orchid, frog orchid, lady orchid, lizard orchid, man orchid, monkey orchid, purple-fringed orchid, pyramidal orchid, scented orchid, spider orchid, spotted orchid.** [C19: from New Latin *Orchideae;* see ORCHIS]

orchidaceous (ˌɔːkɪ'deɪʃəs) *adj.* of, relating to, or belonging to the *Orchidaceae,* a family of flowering plants including the orchids.

orchidectomy (ˌɔːkɪ'dektəmɪ) *n., pl.* **-mies.** the surgical removal of one or both testes. [C19: from Greek *orkhis* testicle + -ECTOMY]

orchil ('ɔːkɪl, -tʃɪl) *or* **archil** *n.* **1.** any of various lichens, esp. any of the genera *Roccella, Dendrographa,* and *Lecanora.* **2.** Also called: **cudbear.** a purplish dye obtained by treating these lichens with aqueous ammonia: contains orcinol, orcein, and litmus. [C15: from Old French *orcheil,* of uncertain origin]

orchis ('ɔːkɪs) *n.* **1.** any terrestrial orchid of the N temperate genus *Orchis,* having fleshy tubers and spikes of typically pink flowers. **2.** any of various temperate or tropical orchids of the genus *Habenaria,* such as the fringed orchis. [C16: via Latin from Greek *orkhis* testicle; so called from the shape of its roots]

orchitis (ɔː'kaɪtɪs) *n.* inflammation of one or both testicles. [C18: from New Latin, from Greek *orkhis* testicle + -ITIS] —**orchitic** (ɔː'kɪtɪk) *adj.*

orcinol ('ɔːsɪˌnɒl) *or* **orcin** ('ɔːsɪn) *n.* a colourless crystalline water-soluble solid that occurs in many lichens and from which the dyes found in litmus are derived. Formula: $CH_3C_6H_3(OH)_2$. [C20: from New Latin *orcina,* from Italian *orcello* ORCHIL]

OR circuit *or* **gate** (ɔː) *n. Computer technol.* a logic circuit having two or more input wires and one output wire that gives a high-voltage output signal if one or more input signals are at a high voltage: used extensively as a basic circuit in computers. Compare **AND circuit, NAND circuit.** [C20: so named from its similarity to the function of *or* in logical constructions]

ord. *abbrev. for:* 1. order. 2. ordinal. 3. ordinance. 4. ordnance. 5. ordinary.

ordain (ɔːˈdeɪn) *vb.* (*tr.*) 1. to consecrate (someone) as a priest; confer holy orders upon. 2. (*may take a clause as object*) to decree, appoint, or predestine irrevocably. 3. (*may take a clause as object*) to order, establish, or enact with authority. 4. *Obsolete.* to select for an office. [C13: from Anglo-Norman *ordeiner,* from Late Latin *ordināre,* from Latin *ordo* ORDER] —**orˈdainer** *n.* —**orˈdainment** *n.*

ordeal (ɔːˈdiːl) *n.* 1. a severe or trying experience. 2. *History.* a method of trial in which the guilt or innocence of an accused person was determined by subjecting him to physical danger, esp. by fire or water. The outcome was regarded as an indication of divine judgment. [Old English *ordāl, ordēl;* related to Old Frisian *ordēl,* Old High German *urteili* (German *Urteil*) verdict. See DEAL[1], DOLE[1]]

order (ˈɔːdə) *n.* 1. a state in which all components or elements are arranged logically, comprehensibly, or naturally. 2. an arrangement or disposition of things in succession; sequence: *alphabetical order.* 3. an established or customary method or state, esp. of society. 4. a peaceful or harmonious condition of society: *order reigned in the streets.* 5. (*often pl.*) a class, rank, or hierarchy: *the lower orders.* 6. *Biology.* any of the taxonomic groups into which a class is divided and which contains one or more families. *Carnivora, Primates,* and *Rodentia* are three orders of the class *Mammalia.* 7. an instruction that must be obeyed; command. 8. a decision or direction of a court or judge entered on the court record but not included in the final judgment. 9. a. a commission or instruction to produce or supply something in return for payment. b. the commodity produced or supplied. c. (*as modifier*): *order form.* 10. a procedure followed by an assembly, meeting, etc. 11. (*cap. when part of a name*) a body of people united in a particular aim or purpose. 12. Also called: **religious order.** (*usually cap.*) a group of persons who bind themselves by vows in order to devote themselves to the pursuit of religious aims. 13. *History.* a society of knights constituted as a fraternity, such as the Knights Templars. 14. a. a group of people holding a specific honour for service or merit, conferred on them by a sovereign or state. b. the insignia of such a group. 15. a. any of the five major classical styles of architecture classified by the style of columns and entablatures used. See also **Doric, Ionic, Corinthian, Tuscan, Composite.** b. any style of architecture. 16. *Christianity.* a. the sacrament by which bishops, priests, etc., have their offices conferred upon them. b. any of the degrees into which the ministry is divided. c. the office of an ordained Christian minister. 17. a form of Christian Church service prescribed to be used on specific occasions. 18. *Judaism.* one of the six sections of the Mishna or the corresponding tractates of the Talmud. 19. *Maths.* a. the number of times a function must be differentiated to obtain a given derivative. b. the order of the highest derivative in a differential equation. c. the number of rows or columns in a determinant or square matrix. d. the number of members of a finite group. 20. short for **order of magnitude.** 21. *Military.* (often preceded by *the*) the dress, equipment, or formation directed for a particular purpose or undertaking: *drill order; battle order.* 22. **a tall order.** something difficult, demanding, or exacting. 23. **in order.** a. in sequence. b. properly arranged. c. appropriate or fitting. 24. **in order to.** (*prep.;* foll. by an infinitive) so that it is possible to: *to eat in order to live.* 25. **in order that.** (*conj.*) with the purpose that; so that. 26. **keep order.** to maintain or enforce order. 27. **of** *or* **in the order of.** having an approximately specified size or quantity. 28. **on order.** having been ordered or commissioned but not having been delivered. 29. **out of order.** a. not in sequence. b. not working. c. not following the rules or customary procedure. 30. **to order.** a. according to a buyer's specifications. b. on request or demand. ~*vb.* 31. (*tr.*) to give a command to (a person or animal to do or be something). 32. to request (something) to be supplied or made, esp. in return for payment: *he ordered a hamburger.* 33. (*tr.*) to instruct or command to move, go, etc. (to a specified place): *they ordered her into the house.* 34. (*tr.; may take a clause as object*) to authorize; prescribe: *the doctor ordered a strict diet.* 35. (*tr.*) to arrange, regulate, or dispose (articles) in their proper places. 36. (of fate or the gods) to will; ordain. 37. (*tr.*) *Rare.* to ordain. ~*interj.* 38. an exclamation of protest against an infringement of established procedure. 39. an exclamation demanding that orderly behaviour be restored. ~See also **orders.** [C13: from Old French *ordre,* from Latin *ordō*] —ˈ**orderer** *n.* —ˈ**orderless** *adj.*

order about *or* **around** *vb.* (*tr.*) to bully or domineer.

order arms *interj., n. Military.* the order in drill to hold the rifle close to the right side with the butt resting on the ground.

ordered set *n. Logic, maths.* a sequence of elements that is distinguished from the other sequences of the same element by the order of the elements. Thus <a, b> is not identical with <b, a>.

order in council *n.* (in Britain and various other Commonwealth countries) a decree of the Cabinet, usually made under the authority of a statute: in theory a decree of the sovereign and Privy Council.

ordering (ˈɔːdərɪŋ) *n. Logic.* any of a number of categories of relations that permit at least some members of their domain to be placed in order. A **linear** or **simple ordering** is reflexive, antisymmetric, transitive, and connected, as *less than or equal to* on the integers. A **partial ordering** is reflexive, antisymmetric, and transitive, as set inclusion. Either of these orderings is called *strict* if it is asymmetric instead of reflexive and antisymmetric. It is a *well-ordering* if every nonempty subset has a least member under the relation.

orderly (ˈɔːdəlɪ) *adj.* 1. in order, properly arranged, or tidy. 2. obeying or appreciating method, system, and arrangement. 3. harmonious or peaceful. 4. *Military.* of or relating to orders: *an orderly book.* ~*adv.* 5. *Now rare.* according to custom or rule. ~*n., pl.* **-lies.** 6. *Med.* a male hospital attendant. 7. *Military.* a junior rank detailed to carry orders or perform minor tasks for a more senior officer. —ˈ**orderliness** *n.*

orderly officer *n.* another name for **officer of the day.**

orderly room *n. Military.* a room in the barracks of a battalion or company used for general administrative purposes.

Order of Canada *n.* an order awarded to Canadians for outstanding achievement; established in 1967.

order of magnitude *n.* the approximate size of something, esp. measured in powers of 10: *the order of magnitude of the deficit was as expected; their estimates differ by an order of magnitude.* Also called: **order.**

Order of Merit *n. Brit.* an order conferred on civilians and servicemen for eminence in any field.

Order of Military Merit *n.* an order awarded to members of the Canadian Forces for conspicuous merit; established in 1972.

order of the day *n.* 1. the general directive of a commander in chief or the specific instructions of a commanding officer. 2. *Informal.* the prescribed or only thing offered or available: *prunes were the order of the day.* 3. (in Parliament and similar legislatures) any item of public business ordered to be considered on a specific day. 4. an agenda or programme.

Order of the Garter *n.* the highest order of British knighthood (but see also **Order of the Thistle**) open to women since 1987. It consists of the sovereign, 31 knight companions, and extra members created by statute. Also called: the **Garter.**

Order of the Thistle *n.* an ancient Scottish order of knighthood revived by James VII of Scotland in 1687. It consists of the sovereign, 16 knights brethren, and extra members created by statute. It is the equivalent of the Order of the Garter, and is usually conferred on Scots. Also called: the **Thistle.**

order paper *n.* a list indicating the order in which business is to be conducted, esp. in Parliament.

orders (ˈɔːdəz) *pl. n.* 1. short for **holy orders.** 2. **in (holy) orders.** ordained. 3. **take (holy) orders.** to become ordained. 4. short for **major orders** or **minor orders.**

ordinal (ˈɔːdɪnᵊl) *adj.* 1. denoting a certain position in a sequence of numbers. 2. of, relating to, or characteristic of an order in biological classification. ~*n.* 3. short for **ordinal number.** 4. a book containing the forms of services for the ordination of ministers. 5. *R.C. Church.* a service book. [C14 (in the sense: orderly): from Late Latin *ordinalis* denoting order or place in a series, from Latin *ordō* ORDER]

ordinal number *n.* 1. a number denoting relative position in a sequence, such as *first, second, third.* Sometimes shortened to **ordinal.** 2. *Logic, maths.* a measure of not only the size of a set but also the order of its elements. ~Compare **cardinal number.**

ordinal scale *n. Statistics.* a scale on which data is shown simply in order of magnitude since there is no standard of measurement of differences: for instance, a squash ladder is an ordinal scale since one can say only that one person is better than another, but not by how much. Compare **interval scale, ratio scale, nominal scale.**

ordinance (ˈɔːdɪnəns) *n.* an authoritative regulation, decree, law, or practice. [C14: from Old French *ordenance,* from Latin *ordināre* to set in order]

ordinand (ˈɔːdɪˌnænd) *n. Christianity.* a candidate for ordination.

ordinarily (ˈɔːdᵊnrɪlɪ, ˈɔːdᵊˌnærɪlɪ) *adv.* in ordinary, normal, or usual practice; usually; normally.

ordinary (ˈɔːdᵊnrɪ) *adj.* 1. of common or established type or occurrence. 2. familiar, everyday, or unexceptional. 3. uninteresting or commonplace. 4. having regular or ex officio jurisdiction: *an ordinary judge.* 5. *Maths.* (of a differential equation) containing two variables only and derivatives of one of the variables with respect to the other. ~*n., pl.* **-naries.** 6. a common or average situation, amount, or degree (esp. in the phrase **out of the ordinary**). 7. a normal or commonplace person or thing. 8. *Civil law.* a judge who exercises jurisdiction in his own right. 9. (*usually cap.*) an ecclesiastic, esp. a bishop, holding an office to which certain jurisdictional powers are attached. 10. *R.C. Church.* a. the parts of the Mass that do not vary from day to day. Compare **proper** (sense 13). b. a prescribed form of divine service, esp. the Mass. 11. the U.S. name for **penny-farthing.** 12. *Heraldry.* any of several conventional figures, such as the bend, the fesse, and the cross, commonly charged upon shields. 13. *History.* a clergyman who visited condemned prisoners before their death. 14. *Brit. obsolete.* a. a meal provided regularly at a fixed price. b. the inn providing such meals. 15. **in ordinary.** *Brit.* (used esp. in titles) in regular service or attendance: *physician in ordinary to the sovereign.* [C16 (adj.) and C13 (some n. senses): ultimately from Latin *ordinārius* orderly, from *ordō* order]

Ordinary grade *n.* (in Scotland) the formal name for **O grade.**
ordinary lay *n.* the form of lay found in a cable-laid rope.
Ordinary level *n.* (in Britain) the formal name for **O level.**
ordinary rating *n.* a rank in the Royal Navy comparable to that of a private in the army.
ordinary ray *n.* the plane-polarized ray of light that obeys the laws of refraction in a doubly-refracting crystal. See **double refraction.** Compare **extraordinary ray.**
ordinary seaman *n.* a seaman of the lowest rank, being insufficiently experienced to be an able-bodied seaman.
ordinary shares *pl. n. Brit.* shares representing part of the capital issued by a company and entitling their holders to a dividend that varies according to the prosperity of the company, and to a claim on net assets, after the holders of preference shares have been paid. U.S. equivalent: **common stock.** Compare **preference shares.** See also **A shares.**
ordinate ('ɔːdɪnɪt) *n.* **1.** the vertical or *y*-coordinate of a point in a two-dimensional system of Cartesian coordinates. Compare **abscissa.** ~*adj.* **2.** *Rare.* regular or ordered. [C16: from New Latin phrase (*linea*) *ordināte* (*applicāta*) (line applied) in an orderly manner, from *ordināre* to arrange in order]
ordination (ˌɔːdɪ'neɪʃən) *n.* **1. a.** the act of conferring holy orders. **b.** the reception of holy orders. **2.** the condition of being ordained or regulated. **3.** an arrangement or order.
ordn. *abbrev. for* ordnance.
ordnance ('ɔːdnəns) *n.* **1.** cannon or artillery. **2.** military supplies; munitions. **3. the.** a department of an army or government dealing with military supplies. [C14: variant of ORDINANCE]
ordnance datum *n.* mean sea level calculated from observation taken at Newlyn, Cornwall, and used as the official basis for height calculation on British maps. Abbrev.: **OD.**
Ordnance Survey *n.* the official map-making body of the British or Irish government.
ordonnance ('ɔːdənəns; *French* ɔrdɔnɑ̃s) *n.* **1.** the proper disposition of the elements of a building or an artistic or literary composition. **2.** an ordinance, law, or decree, esp. in French law. [C17: from Old French *ordenance* arrangement, influenced by *ordonner* to order]
Ordovician (ˌɔːdəʊ'vɪʃɪən) *adj.* **1.** of, denoting, or formed in the second period of the Palaeozoic era, between the Cambrian and Silurian periods, which lasted for 60 000 000 years during which marine invertebrates flourished. ~*n.* **2. the.** the Ordovician period or rock system. [C19: from Latin *Ordovices* ancient Celtic tribe in N Wales]
ordure ('ɔːdjʊə) *n.* **1.** excrement; dung. **2.** something regarded as being morally offensive. [C14: via Old French, from *ord* dirty, from Latin *horridus* shaggy]
ore (ɔː) *n.* any naturally occurring mineral or aggregate of minerals from which economically important constituents, esp. metals, can be extracted. [Old English *ār, ōra;* related to Gothic *aiz,* Latin *aes,* Dutch *oer*]
öre ('ørə) *n., pl.* **öre.** a Scandinavian monetary unit worth one hundredth of a Swedish krona and (**øre**) one hundredth of a Danish and Norwegian krone.
oread ('ɔːrɪˌæd) *n. Greek myth.* a mountain nymph. [C16: via Latin from Greek *Oreias,* from *oros* mountain]
orectic (ɒ'rɛktɪk) *adj.* of or relating to the desires. [C18: from Greek *orektikos* causing desire, from *oregein* to desire]
ore dressing *n.* the first stage in the extraction of a metal from an ore in which as much gangue as possible is removed and the ore is prepared for smelting, refining, etc. Also called: **mineral dressing, mineral processing.**
Oreg. *abbrev. for* Oregon.
oregano (ˌɒrɪ'gɑːnəʊ) *n.* **1.** a Mediterranean variety of wild marjoram (*Origanum vulgare*), with pungent leaves. **2.** the dried powdered leaves of this plant, used to season food. ~See also **origanum.** [C18: American Spanish, from Spanish, from Latin *orīganum,* from Greek *origanon* an aromatic herb, perhaps marjoram]
Oregon fir *or* **pine** ('ɒrɪgən) *n.* other names for **Douglas fir.** [after *Oregon,* a state of the northwestern U.S.]
Oregon grape *n.* **1.** an evergreen berberidaceous shrub, *Mahonia aquifolium,* of NW North America, having yellow fragrant flowers and small blue edible berries. **2.** the berry of this shrub.
orfe (ɔːf) *n.* a small slender European cyprinoid fish, *Idus idus,* occurring in two colour varieties, namely the **silver orfe** and the **golden orfe,** popular aquarium fishes. Compare **goldfish.** [C17: from German; related to Latin *orphus,* Greek *orphos* the sea perch]
orfray ('ɔːfrɪ) *n.* a less common spelling of **orphrey.**
org. *abbrev. for:* **1.** organic. **2.** organization. **3.** organized.
organ ('ɔːgən) *n.* **1. a.** Also called: **pipe organ.** a large complex musical keyboard instrument in which sound is produced by means of a number of pipes arranged in sets or stops, supplied with air from a bellows. The largest instruments possess three or more manuals and one pedal keyboard and have the greatest range of any instrument. **b.** (*as modifier*): *organ pipe; organ stop; organ loft.* **2.** any instrument, such as a harmonium, in which sound is produced in this way. See also **reed organ, harmonica. 3.** short for **electric organ** (sense 1a), **electronic organ. 4.** a fully differentiated structural and functional unit, such as a kidney or a root, in an animal or plant. **5.** an agency or medium of communication, esp. a periodical issued by a specialist group or party. **6.** an instrument with which something is done or accomplished. **7.** a euphemistic word for **penis.** [C13: from Old French *organe,* from Latin *organum* implement, from Greek *organon* tool; compare Greek *ergein* to work]
organa ('ɔːgənə) *n.* a plural of **organon** and **organum.**
organdie *or esp. U.S.* **organdy** ('ɔːgəndɪ, ɔː'gæn-) *n., pl.* **-dies.** a fine and slightly stiff cotton fabric used esp. for dresses. [C19: from French *organdi,* of unknown origin]
organelle (ˌɔːgə'nɛl) *n.* a structural and functional unit, such as a mitochondrion, in a cell or unicellular organism. [C20: from New Latin *organella,* from Latin *organum:* see ORGAN]
organ-grinder *n.* a street musician playing a hand organ for money.
organic (ɔː'gænɪk) *adj.* **1.** of, relating to, derived from, or characteristic of living plants and animals. **2.** of or relating to animal or plant constituents or products having a carbon basis. **3.** of or relating to one or more organs of an animal or plant. **4.** of, relating to, or belonging to the class of chemical compounds that are formed from carbon: *an organic compound.* Compare **inorganic** (sense 2). **5.** constitutional in the structure of something; fundamental; integral. **6.** of or characterized by the coordination of integral parts; organized. **7.** of or relating to the essential constitutional laws regulating the government of a state: *organic law.* **8.** of, relating to, or grown with the use of fertilizers or pesticides deriving from animal or vegetable matter. ~*n.* **9.** any substance, such as a fertilizer or pesticide, that is derived from animal or vegetable matter. —**or'ganically** *adv.*
organic chemistry *n.* the branch of chemistry concerned with the compounds of carbon: originally confined to compounds produced by living organisms but now extended to include man-made substances based on carbon, such as plastics. Compare **inorganic chemistry.**
organic disease *n.* any disease in which there is a physical change in the structure of an organ or part. Compare **functional disease.**
organicism (ɔː'gænɪˌsɪzəm) *n.* **1.** the theory that the functioning of living organisms is determined by the working together of all organs as an integrated system. **2.** the theory that all symptoms are caused by organic disease. **3.** the theory that each organ of the body has its own peculiar constitution. —**or'ganicist** *n., adj.* —**orˌgani'cistic** *adj.*
organic psychosis *n.* a severe mental illness produced by damage to the brain, as a result of poisoning, alcoholism, disease, etc. Compare **functional** (sense 4b).
organism ('ɔːgəˌnɪzəm) *n.* **1.** any living animal or plant, including any bacterium or virus. **2.** anything resembling a living creature in structure, behaviour, etc. —ˌ**organ'ismal** *or* ˌ**organ'ismic** *adj.* —ˌ**organ'ismally** *adv.*
organist ('ɔːgənɪst) *n.* a person who plays the organ.
organization *or* **organisation** (ˌɔːgənaɪ'zeɪʃən) *n.* **1.** the act of organizing or the state of being organized. **2.** an organized structure or whole. **3.** a business or administrative concern united and constructed for a particular end. **4.** a body of administrative officials, as of a political party, a government department, etc. **5.** order or system; method. —ˌ**organi'zational** *or* ˌ**organi'sational** *adj.* —ˌ**organi'zationally** *or* ˌ**organi'sationally** *adv.*
organizational psychology *n.* the study of the structure of an organization and of the ways in which the people in it interact, usually undertaken in order to improve the organization.
organization chart *n.* a diagram representing the management structure of a company, showing the responsibilities of each department, the relationships of the departments to each other, and the hierarchy of management.
organization man *n.* **1.** a person who subordinates his personal life to the demands of the organization he works for. **2.** a person who specializes in or is good at organization.
organize *or* **organise** ('ɔːgəˌnaɪz) *vb.* **1.** to form (parts or elements of something) into a structured whole; coordinate. **2.** (*tr.*) to arrange methodically or in order. **3.** (*tr.*) to provide with an organic structure. **4.** (*tr.*) to enlist (the workers) of (a factory, concern, or industry) in a trade union. **5.** (*intr.*) to join or form an organization or trade union. **6.** (*tr.*) *Informal.* to put (oneself) in an alert and responsible frame of mind. [C15: from Medieval Latin *organizare,* from Latin *organum* ORGAN]
organizer *or* **organiser** ('ɔːgəˌnaɪzə) *n.* **1.** a person who organizes or is capable of organizing. **2.** a container with a number of compartments for storage: *hanging organizers to keep your clothes smart.* **3.** *Embryol.* any part of an embryo or any substance produced by it that induces specialization of undifferentiated cells.
organo- *combining form.* **1.** (in biology or medicine) indicating an organ or organs: *organogenesis.* **2.** (in chemistry) indicating a compound containing an organic group: *organometallic; organochlorine; organophosphate.*
organ of Corti ('kɔːtɪ) *n.* the sense organ of the cochlea by which sounds are converted into nerve impulses. [named after Alfonso *Corti* (died 1876), Italian anatomist]
organogenesis (ˌɔːgənəʊ'dʒɛnɪsɪs) *n.* **1.** the formation and development of organs in an animal or plant. **2.** Also called: **organogeny** (ˌɔːgən'ɒdʒənɪ). the study of this process. —**or-**

ganogenetic (ˌɔːgənəʊdʒɪˈnɛtɪk) *adj.* —ˌ**organogeˈnetically** *adv.*

organography (ˌɔːgəˈnɒgrəfɪ) *n.* the description of the organs and major structures of animals and plants. —**organographic** (ˌɔːgənəʊˈgræfɪk) *or* ˌ**organoˈgraphical** *adj.* —ˌ**organˈographist** *n.*

organoleptic (ˌɔːgənəʊˈlɛptɪk) *adj. Physiol.* **1.** able to stimulate an organ, esp. a special sense organ. **2.** able to perceive a sensory stimulus.

organology (ˌɔːgəˈnɒlədʒɪ) *n.* the study of the structure and function of the organs of animals and plants. —**organological** (ˌɔːgənəʊˈlɒdʒɪk^{ə}l) *adj.* —ˌ**organˈologist** *n.*

organometallic (ɔːˌgænəʊmɪˈtælɪk) *adj.* of, concerned with, or being an organic compound with one or more metal atoms in its molecules: *an organometallic compound.*

organon (ˈɔːgəˌnɒn) *or* **organum** *n., pl.* **organa** (ˈɔːgənə), **-nons** *or* **-na, -nums.** *Epistemology.* **1.** a system of logical or scientific rules, esp. that of Aristotle. **2.** *Archaic.* a sense organ, regarded as an instrument for acquiring knowledge. [C16: from Greek: implement; see ORGAN]

organotherapy (ˌɔːgənəʊˈθɛrəpɪ) *n.* the treatment of disease with extracts of animal endocrine glands. —**organotherapeutic** (ˌɔːgənəʊˌθɛrəˈpjuːtɪk) *adj.*

organotin (ˌɔːgænəʊˈtɪn) *adj.* of, concerned with, or being an organic compound with one or more tin atoms in its molecules: used as a pesticide, hitherto considered to decompose safely, now found to be toxic in the food chain.

organ screen *n.* a wooden or stone screen that supports the organ in a cathedral or church and divides the choir from the nave.

organum (ˈɔːgənəm) *n., pl.* **-na** (-nə) *or* **-nums. 1.** a form of polyphonic music originating in the ninth century, consisting of a plainsong melody with parts added at the fourth and fifth. **2.** a variant of **organon.** [C17: via Latin from Greek; see ORGAN]

organza (ɔːˈgænzə) *n.* a thin stiff fabric of silk, cotton, nylon, rayon, etc. [C20: perhaps related to ORGANZINE]

organzine (ˈɔːgənˌziːn, ɔːˈgænziːn) *n.* **1.** a strong thread made of twisted strands of raw silk. **2.** fabric made of such threads. [C17: from French *organsin,* from Italian *organzino,* probably from *Urgench,* a town in central Asia where the fabric was originally produced]

orgasm (ˈɔːgæzəm) *n.* **1.** the most intense point during sexual excitement, characterized by extremely pleasurable sensations and in the male accompanied by ejaculation of semen. **2.** *Rare.* intense or violent excitement. [C17: from New Latin *orgasmus,* from Greek *orgasmos,* from *organ* to mature, swell] —**orˈgasmic** *or* **orˈgastic** *adj.*

orgeat (ˈɔːʒɑː; *French* ɔrʒa) *n.* a drink made from barley or almonds, and orange flower water. [C18: via French, from *orge* barley, from Latin *hordeum*]

orgone (ˈɔːgəʊn) *n.* a substance postulated by the Austrian psychologist Wilhelm Riech (1897–1957), who thought it was present everywhere and needed to be incorporated in people for sexual activity and mental health. [C20: from ORG(ASM) + (HORM)ONE]

orgulous (ˈɔːgjʊləs) *adj. Archaic.* proud. [C13: from Old French, from *orgueil* pride, from Frankish *urgōli* (unattested)]

orgy (ˈɔːdʒɪ) *n., pl.* **-gies. 1.** a wild gathering marked by promiscuous sexual activity, excessive drinking, etc. **2.** an act of immoderate or frenzied indulgence. **3.** (*often pl.*) secret religious rites of the gods Dionysus, Bacchus, etc., marked by drinking, dancing, and songs. [C16: from French *orgies,* from Latin *orgia,* from Greek: nocturnal festival] —ˌ**orgiˈastic** *adj.*

oribi (ˈɒrɪbɪ) *n., pl.* **-bi** *or* **-bis.** a small African antelope, *Ourebia ourebi,* of grasslands and bush south of the Sahara, with fawn-coloured coat and, in the male, ridged spikelike horns. [C18: from Afrikaans, probably from Hottentot *arab*]

oriel (ˈɔːrɪəl) *n.* a bay window, esp. one that is supported by one or more brackets or corbels. Also called: **oriel window.** [C14: from Old French *oriol* gallery, perhaps from Medieval Latin *auleolum* niche]

orient *n.* (ˈɔːrɪənt). **1.** *Poetic.* another word for **east.** Compare **occident. 2.** *Archaic.* the eastern sky or the dawn. **3. a.** the iridescent lustre of a pearl. **b.** (*as modifier*): *orient pearls.* **4.** a pearl of high quality. ~*adj.* (ˈɔːrɪənt). **5.** *Now chiefly poetic.* eastern. **6.** *Archaic.* (of the sun, stars, etc.) rising. ~*vb.* (ˈɔːrɪˌɛnt). **7.** to adjust or align (oneself or something else) according to surroundings or circumstances. **8.** (*tr.*) to position, align, or set (a map, surveying instrument, etc.) with reference to the points of the compass or other specific directions. **9.** (*tr.*) to set or build (a church) in an easterly direction. [C18: via French from Latin *oriēns* rising (sun), from *orīrī* to rise]

▷**Usage.** See at **orientate.**

Orient (ˈɔːrɪənt) *n.* (usually preceded by *the*) **1.** the countries east of the Mediterranean. **2.** the eastern hemisphere.

oriental (ˌɔːrɪˈɛnt^{ə}l) *adj.* another word for **eastern.**

Oriental (ˌɔːrɪˈɛnt^{ə}l) *adj.* **1.** (*sometimes not cap.*) of or relating to the Orient. **2.** of or denoting a zoogeographical region consisting of southeastern Asia from India to Borneo, Java, and the Philippines. ~*n.* **3.** (*sometimes not cap.*) an inhabitant, esp. a native, of the Orient.

Oriental almandine *n.* a variety of corundum resembling almandine in colour and used as a gemstone.

Oriental emerald *n.* a green variety of corundum used as a gemstone.

Orientalism (ˌɔːrɪˈɛntəˌlɪzəm) *n.* **1.** knowledge of or devotion to the Orient. **2.** an Oriental quality, style, or trait. —ˌ**Oriˈentalist** *n.* —ˌ**Oriˌentalˈistic** *adj.*

Orientalize *or* **Orientalise** (ˌɔːrɪˈɛntəˌlaɪz) *vb.* to make, become, or treat as Oriental. —ˌ**Oriˌentaliˈzation** *or* ˌ**Oriˌentaliˈsation** *n.*

Oriental topaz *n.* a variety of corundum resembling topaz in colour and used as a gemstone.

orientate (ˈɔːrɪɛnˌteɪt) *vb.* a variant of **orient.**

▷**Usage.** Careful users avoid *orientate* as an unnecessary back formation from *orientation,* since *orient* has the same range of meanings. Nevertheless, there can be little doubt that either form is acceptable. The excessive use of *orientation* and *orient* (or *orientate*) in such phrases as *orientation course* (preparatory course), *profits-oriented* (or *orientated*) *systems* (those designed to produce high profits), and *student-oriented* (or *orientated*) *lectures* (those prepared with the needs of students in mind) is sometimes frowned on as jargon.

orientation (ˌɔːrɪɛnˈteɪʃən) *n.* **1.** the act or process of orienting or the state of being oriented. **2.** position or positioning with relation to the points of the compass or other specific directions. **3.** the adjustment or alignment of oneself or one's ideas to surroundings or circumstances. **4.** Also called: **orientation course.** *Chiefly U.S. and Canadian.* **a.** a course, programme, lecture, etc., introducing a new situation or environment. **b.** (*as modifier*): *an orientation talk.* **5.** *Psychol.* the knowledge of one's own temporal, social, and practical circumstances in life. **6.** *Biology.* the change in position of the whole or part of an organism in response to a stimulus, such as light. **7.** *Chem.* the relative dispositions of atoms, ions, or groups in molecules or crystals. **8.** the siting of a church on an east-west axis, usually with the altar at the E end. —ˌ**orienˈtational** *adj.*

-oriented *suffix forming adjectives.* designed for, directed towards, motivated by, or concerned with: *computer-oriented courses; managers who are profit-oriented.* See also **usage note** at **orientate.**

orienteer (ˌɔːrɪənˈtɪə) *vb.* (*intr.*) **1.** to take part in orienteering. ~*n.* **2.** a person who takes part in orienteering.

orienteering (ˌɔːrɪɛnˈtɪərɪŋ) *n.* a sport in which contestants race on foot over a course consisting of checkpoints found with the aid of a map and a compass. [C20: from Swedish *orientering;* compare ORIENT]

orifice (ˈɒrɪfɪs) *n. Chiefly technical.* an opening or mouth into a cavity; vent; aperture. [C16: via French from Late Latin *ōrificium,* from Latin *ōs* mouth + *facere* to make]

orifice meter *n. Engineering.* a plate having a central hole that is placed across the flow of a liquid, usually between flanges in a pipeline. The pressure difference generated by the flow velocity through the hole enables the flow quantity to be measured.

oriflamme (ˈɒrɪˌflæm) *n.* a scarlet flag, originally of the abbey of St. Denis in N France, adopted as the national banner of France in the Middle Ages. [C15: via Old French, from Latin *aurum* gold + *flamma* flame]

orig. *abbrev. for:* **1.** origin. **2.** original(ly).

origami (ˌɒrɪˈgɑːmɪ) *n.* the art or process, originally Japanese, of paper folding. [from Japanese, from *ori* a folding + *kami* paper]

origan (ˈɒrɪgən) *n.* another name for **marjoram** (sense 2). [C16: from Latin *orīganum,* from Greek *origanon* an aromatic herb, perhaps marjoram; compare OREGANO]

origanum (əˈrɪgənəm) *n.* any plant of the herbaceous aromatic Mediterranean genus *Origanum:* family *Labiatae.* See **oregano, marjoram, dittany** (sense 1). [New Latin, from Greek *origanon* wild marjoram]

origin (ˈɒrɪdʒɪn) *n.* **1.** a primary source; derivation. **2.** the beginning of something; first stage or part. **3.** (*often pl.*) ancestry or parentage; birth; extraction. **4.** *Anatomy.* **a.** the end of a muscle, opposite its point of insertion. **b.** the beginning of a nerve or blood vessel or the site where it first starts to branch out. **5.** *Maths.* **a.** the point of intersection of coordinate axes or planes. **b.** the point whose coordinates are all zero. See also **pole**^{2} (sense 8). **6.** *Commerce.* the country from which a commodity or product originates: *shipment from origin.* [C16: from French *origine,* from Latin *orīgō* beginning, birth, from *orīrī* to rise, spring from]

original (əˈrɪdʒɪn^{ə}l) *adj.* **1.** of or relating to an origin or beginning. **2.** fresh and unusual; novel. **3.** able to think of or carry out new ideas or concepts. **4.** being that from which a copy, translation, etc., is made. ~*n.* **5.** the first and genuine form of something, from which others are derived. **6.** a person or thing used as a model in art or literature. **7.** a person whose way of thinking is unusual or creative. **8.** an unconventional or strange person. **9.** the first form or occurrence of something. **10.** an archaic word for **originator,** see **originate.**

originality (əˌrɪdʒɪˈnælɪtɪ) *n., pl.* **-ties. 1.** the quality or condition of being original. **2.** the ability to create or innovate. **3.** something original.

originally (əˈrɪdʒɪnəlɪ) *adv.* **1.** in the first place. **2.** in an original way. **3.** with reference to the origin or beginning.

original sin *n.* a state of sin held to be innate in mankind as the descendants of Adam.

originate (əˈrɪdʒɪˌneɪt) *vb.* **1.** to come or bring into being. **2.** (*intr.*) *U.S. and Canadian.* (of a bus, train, etc.) to begin its journey at a specified point. —**o͵rigiˈnation** *n.* —**oˈrigi͵nator** *n.*

orinasal (͵ɔːrɪˈneɪzᵊl) *Phonetics.* ~*adj.* **1.** pronounced with simultaneous oral and nasal articulation. ~*n.* **2.** an orinasal speech sound. [C19: from Latin *ōr-* (from *ōs* mouth) + NASAL] —͵**oriˈnasally** *adv.*

O-ring *n.* a rubber ring used in machinery as a seal against oil, air, etc.

oriole (ˈɔːrɪ͵əʊl) *n.* **1.** any songbird of the mainly tropical Old World family *Oriolidae*, such as *Oriolus oriolus* (**golden oriole**), having a long pointed bill and a mostly yellow-and-black plumage. **2.** any American songbird of the family *Icteridae*, esp. those of the genus *Icterus*, such as the Baltimore oriole, with a typical male plumage of black with either orange or yellow. [C18: from Medieval Latin *oryolus*, from Latin *aureolus*, diminutive of *aureus*, from *aurum* gold]

Orion (əˈraɪən) *n.*, *Latin genitive* **Orionis** (͵ɔːrɪˈəʊnɪs). a conspicuous constellation near Canis Major containing two first magnitude stars (Betelgeuse and Rigel) and a distant low density emission nebula (the **Orion Nebula**).

orison (ˈɒrɪzᵊn) *n. Literary.* another word for **prayer**[1]. [C12: from Old French *oreison*, from Late Latin *ōrātiō*, from Latin: speech, from *ōrāre* to speak]

Oriya (ɒˈriːə) *n.* **1.** (*pl.* **-ya**) a member of a people of India living chiefly in the E state of Orissa and neighbouring states. **2.** the state language of Orissa, belonging to the Indic branch of the Indo-European family.

orle (ɔːl) *n. Heraldry.* a border around a shield. [C16: from French, from *ourler* to hem]

Orleanist (ɔːˈlɪənɪst) *n.* an adherent of the branch of the French Bourbons descended from Louis Philippe Joseph, Duc d'Orléans (1747–93).

Orlon (ˈɔːlɒn) *n. Trademark.* a crease-resistant acrylic fibre or fabric used for clothing, furnishings, etc.

orlop *or* **orlop deck** (ˈɔːlɒp) *n. Nautical.* (in a vessel with four or more decks) the lowest deck. [C15: from Dutch *overloopen* to run over, spill. See OVER, LEAP]

Ormazd *or* **Ormuzd** (ˈɔːməzd) *n. Zoroastrianism.* the creative deity, embodiment of good and opponent of Ahriman. Also called: **Ahura Mazda.** [from Persian, from Avestan *Ahura-Mazda*, from *ahura* spirit + *mazdā* wise]

ormer (ˈɔːmə) *n.* **1.** Also called: **sea-ear.** an edible marine gastropod mollusc, *Haliotis tuberculata*, that has an ear-shaped shell perforated with holes and occurs near the Channel Islands. **2.** any other abalone. [C17: from French (Guernsey dialect), apparently from Latin *auris* ear + *mare* sea]

ormolu (ˈɔːmə͵luː) *n.* **1. a.** a gold-coloured alloy of copper, tin, or zinc used to decorate furniture, mouldings, etc. **b.** (*as modifier*): *an ormolu clock.* **2.** gold prepared to be used for gilding. [C18: from French *or moulu* ground gold]

ornament *n.* (ˈɔːnəmənt). **1.** anything that enhances the appearance of a person or thing. **2.** decorations collectively: *she was totally without ornament.* **3.** a small decorative object. **4.** something regarded as a source of pride or beauty. **5.** *Music.* any of several decorations, such as the trill, mordent, etc., occurring chiefly as improvised embellishments in baroque music. ~*vb.* (ˈɔːnə͵mɛnt). (*tr.*) **6.** to decorate with or as if with ornaments. **7.** to serve as an ornament to. [C14: from Latin *ornāmentum*, from *ornāre* to adorn] —͵**ornamenˈtation** *n.*

ornamental (͵ɔːnəˈmɛntᵊl) *adj.* **1.** of value as an ornament; decorative. **2.** (of a plant) used to decorate houses, gardens, etc. ~*n.* **3.** a plant cultivated for show or decoration. —͵**ornaˈmentally** *adv.*

ornate (ɔːˈneɪt) *adj.* **1.** heavily or elaborately decorated. **2.** (of style in writing) overembellished; flowery. [C15: from Latin *ornāre* to decorate] —**orˈnately** *adv.* —**orˈnateness** *n.*

ornery (ˈɔːnərɪ) *adj. U.S. and Canadian dialect or informal.* **1.** stubborn or vile-tempered. **2.** low; treacherous: *an ornery trick.* **3.** ordinary. [C19: alteration of ORDINARY] —**ˈorneriness** *n.*

ornis (ˈɔːnɪs) *n.* a less common word for **avifauna.** [C19: from Greek: bird]

ornithic (ɔːˈnɪθɪk) *adj.* of or relating to birds or a bird fauna. [C19: from Greek *ornithikos*, from *ornis* bird]

ornithine (ˈɔːnɪ͵θiːn) *n.* an amino acid produced from arginine by hydrolysis: involved in the formation of urea in the liver; diaminopentanoic acid. Formula: $NH_2(CH_2)_3CHNH_2COOH$. [C19: from *ornithuric* (*acid*) secreted in the urine of birds, from ORNITHO- + URIC]

ornithischian (͵ɔːnɪˈθɪskɪən) *adj.* **1.** of, relating to, or belonging to the *Ornithischia*, an order of dinosaurs that included the ornithopods, stegosaurs, ankylosaurs, and triceratops. ~*n.* **2.** any dinosaur of the order *Ornithischia.* [C20: from ORNITHO- + Greek *ischion* hip joint]

ornitho- *or before a vowel* **ornith-** *combining form.* bird or birds: *ornithology; ornithomancy; ornithopter; ornithoscopy; ornithosis.* [from Greek *ornis, ornith-* bird]

ornithol. *or* **ornith.** *abbrev. for:* **1.** ornithological. **2.** ornithology.

ornithology (͵ɔːnɪˈθɒlədʒɪ) *n.* the study of birds, including their physiology, classification, ecology, and behaviour. —**ornithological** (͵ɔːnɪθəˈlɒdʒɪkᵊl) *adj.* —͵**ornithoˈlogically** *adv.* —͵**orniˈthologist** *n.*

ornithomancy (ˈɔːnɪθəʊ͵mænsɪ) *n.* divination from the flight and cries of birds.

ornithophily (͵ɔːnɪˈθɒfɪlɪ) *n.* pollination of flowers by birds. —͵**orniˈthophilous** *adj.*

ornithopod (ˈɔːnɪθə͵pɒd) *n.* any herbivorous typically bipedal ornithischian dinosaur of the suborder *Ornithopoda*, including the iguanodon.

ornithopter (ˈɔːnɪ͵θɒptə) *n.* a heavier-than-air craft sustained in and propelled through the air by flapping wings. Also called: **orthopter.**

ornithorhynchus (͵ɔːnɪθəʊˈrɪŋkəs) *n.* the technical name for **duck-billed platypus.** [C19: New Latin, from ORNITHO- + Greek *rhunkhos* bill]

ornithoscopy (͵ɔːnɪˈθɒskəpɪ) *n.* divination from the observation of birds.

ornithosis (͵ɔːnɪˈθəʊsɪs) *n.* a disease identical to psittacosis that occurs in birds other than parrots and can be transmitted to man.

oro-[1] *combining form.* mountain: *orogeny; orography.* [from Greek *oros*]

oro-[2] *combining form.* oral; mouth: *oromaxillary.* [from Latin, from *ōs*]

orobanchaceous (͵ɔːrəʊbæŋˈkeɪʃəs) *adj.* of, relating to, or belonging to the *Orobanchaceae*, a family of flowering plants all of which are root parasites, including broomrape and toothwort. [via Latin from Greek *orobankhē* broomrape]

orogeny (ɒˈrɒdʒɪnɪ) *or* **orogenesis** (͵ɒrəʊˈdʒɛnɪsɪs) *n.* the formation of mountain ranges by intense upward displacement of the earth's crust. —**orogenic** (͵ɒrəʊˈdʒɛnɪk) *or* **orogenetic** (͵ɒrəʊdʒɪˈnɛtɪk) *adj.* —͵**oroˈgenically** *or* ͵**orogeˈnetically** *adv.*

orography (ɒˈrɒgrəfɪ) *or* **orology** (ɒˈrɒlədʒɪ) *n.* the study or mapping of relief, esp. of mountains. —**oˈrographer** *or* **oˈrologist** *n.* —**orographic** (͵ɒrəʊˈgræfɪk) *or* **orological** (͵ɒrəʊˈlɒdʒɪkᵊl) *adj.* —͵**oroˈgraphically** *or* ͵**oroˈlogically** *adv.*

oroide (ˈɔːrəʊ͵aɪd) *n.* an alloy containing copper, tin, and other metals, used as imitation gold. [C19: from French *or* gold + -OID]

orometer (ɒˈrɒmɪtə) *n.* an aneroid barometer with an altitude scale. [C19: from ORO-[1] (mountain, altitude) + -METER]

oronasal (͵ɔːrəʊˈneɪzᵊl) *adj. Anatomy.* of or relating to the mouth and nose.

orotund (ˈɒrəʊ͵tʌnd) *adj.* **1.** (of the voice) resonant; booming. **2.** (of speech or writing) bombastic; pompous. [C18: from Latin phrase *ore rotundo* with rounded mouth]

orphan (ˈɔːfən) *n.* **1. a.** a child, one or (more commonly) both of whose parents are dead. **b.** (*as modifier*): *an orphan child.* ~*vb.* **2.** (*tr.*) to deprive of one or both parents. [C15: from Late Latin *orphanus*, from Greek *orphanos*; compare Latin *orbus* bereaved]

orphanage (ˈɔːfənɪdʒ) *n.* **1.** an institution for orphans and abandoned children. **2.** the state of being an orphan.

orpharion (ɔːˈfærɪən) *n.* a large lute in use during the 16th and 17th centuries. [C16: from *Orph*(*eus*) + *Arion*, musicians of Greek mythology]

Orphean (ˈɔːfɪən) *adj.* **1.** of or relating to Orpheus, musician and poet of Greek mythology. **2.** melodious or enchanting.

Orphic (ˈɔːfɪk) *adj.* **1.** of or relating to Orpheus or Orphism. **2.** (*sometimes not cap.*) mystical or occult. —**ˈOrphically** *adv.*

Orphism (ˈɔːfɪzəm) *n.* a mystery religion of ancient Greece, widespread from the 6th century onwards, combining pre-Hellenic beliefs, the Thracian cult of Zagreus (Dionysius), etc. [from *Orpheus*, who was credited with the authorship of the poems forming the religion's basis] —**Orˈphistic** *adj.*

orphrey *or* (*less commonly*) **orfray** (ˈɔːfrɪ) *n.* a richly embroidered band or border, esp. on an ecclesiastical vestment. [C13 *orfreis*, from Old French, from Late Latin *aurifrisium, auriphrygium*, from Latin *aurum* gold + *Phrygius* Phrygian]

orpiment (ˈɔːpɪmənt) *n.* a yellow mineral consisting of arsenic trisulphide in monoclinic crystalline form occurring in association with realgar: it is an ore of arsenic. Formula: As_2S_3. [C14: via Old French from Latin *auripigmentum* gold pigment]

orpine (ˈɔːpaɪn) *or* **orpin** (ˈɔːpɪn) *n.* a succulent perennial N temperate crassulaceous plant, *Sedum telephium*, with toothed leaves and heads of small purplish-white flowers. Also called: **livelong** (Brit.), **live-forever** (U.S.). [C14: from Old French, apparently from ORPIMENT (perhaps referring to the yellow flowers of a related species)]

Orpington (ˈɔːpɪŋtən) *n.* **1.** a heavy breed of domestic fowl of various single colours, laying brown eggs. **2.** a breed of brown duck with an orange bill.

orra (ˈɒrə) *adj. Scot.* **1.** odd or unmatched; supernumerary. **2.** occasional or miscellaneous. **3. orra man** *or* **orraman.** an odd-jobman. [C18: of unknown origin]

orrery (ˈɒrərɪ) *n., pl.* **-ries.** a mechanical model of the solar system in which the planets can be moved at the correct relative velocities around the sun. [C18: originally made for Charles Boyle, Earl of *Orrery*]

orris *or* **orrice** (ˈɒrɪs) *n.* **1.** any of various irises, esp. *Iris florentina*, that have fragrant rhizomes. **2.** Also called: **ˈorrisroot.** the rhizome of such a plant, prepared and used as perfume. [C16: variant of IRIS]

ortanique (͵ɔːtəˈniːk) *n.* a hybrid between an orange and a tangerine. [C20: from OR(ANGE) + TAN(GERINE) + (UN)IQUE]

Orth. *abbrev. for* Orthodox (religion).

orthicon (ˈɔːθɪ͵kɒn) *n.* a television camera tube in which an optical image produces a corresponding electrical charge pattern on a mosaic surface that is scanned from behind by an electron beam. The resulting discharge of the mosaic provides the output signal current. See also **image orthicon.** [C20: from ORTHO- + ICON(OSCOPE)]

ortho- *or before a vowel* **orth-** *combining form.* **1.** straight or upright: *orthotropous.* **2.** perpendicular or at right angles: *orthoclastic.* **3.** correct or right: *orthodontics; orthodox; orthography; orthoptics.* **4.** (*often in italics*) denoting an organic compound containing a benzene ring with substituents attached to adjacent carbon atoms (the 1,2- positions): *orthodinitrobenzene.* Abbrev.: *o-*. Compare **para-**[1] (sense 6), **meta-** (sense 4). **5.** denoting an oxyacid regarded as the highest hydrated form of the anhydride or a salt of such an acid: *orthophosphoric acid.* Compare **meta-** (sense 6). **6.** denoting a diatomic substance in which the spins of the two atoms are parallel: *orthohydrogen.* Compare **para-**[1] (sense 8). [from Greek *orthos* straight, right, upright]

orthoboric acid (ˌɔːθəʊˈbɔːrɪk) *n.* the more formal name for **boric acid** (sense 1).

orthocentre *or U.S.* **orthocenter** (ˈɔːθəʊˌsɛntə) *n.* the point of intersection of any two altitudes of a triangle.

orthocephalic (ˌɔːθəʊsɪˈfælɪk) *or* **orthocephalous** (ˌɔːθəʊˈsɛfələs) *adj.* having a skull whose breadth is between 70 and 75 per cent of its length. —ˌ**orthoˈcephaly** *n.*

orthochromatic (ˌɔːθəʊkrəʊˈmætɪk) *adj. Photog.* of or relating to an emulsion giving a rendering of relative light intensities of different colours that corresponds approximately to the colour sensitivity of the eye, esp. one that is insensitive to red light. Sometimes shortened to **ortho.** Compare **panchromatic.** —**orthochromatism** (ˌɔːθəʊˈkrəʊməˌtɪzəm) *n.*

orthoclase (ˈɔːθəʊˌkleɪs, -ˌkleɪz) *n.* a white to pale yellow, red, or green mineral of the feldspar group, found in igneous, sedimentary, and metamorphic rocks. It is used in the manufacture of glass and ceramics. Composition: potassium aluminium silicate. Formula: $KAlSi_3O_8$. Crystal structure: monoclinic.

orthodontics (ˌɔːθəʊˈdɒntɪks) *or* **orthodontia** (ˌɔːθəʊˈdɒntɪə) *n.* (*functioning as sing.*) the branch of dentistry concerned with preventing or correcting irregularities of the teeth. Also called: **dental orthopaedics.** —ˌ**orthoˈdontic** *adj.* —ˌ**orthoˈdontist** *n.*

orthodox (ˈɔːθəˌdɒks) *adj.* **1.** conforming with established or accepted standards, as in religion, behaviour, or attitudes. **2.** conforming to the Christian faith as established by the early Church. [C16: via Church Latin from Greek *orthodoxos,* from *orthos* correct + *doxa* belief] —ˈ**orthoˌdoxly** *adv.*

Orthodox (ˈɔːθəˌdɒks) *adj.* **1.** of or relating to the Orthodox Church of the East. **2.** (*sometimes not cap.*) **a.** of or relating to Orthodox Judaism. **b.** (of an individual Jew) strict in the observance of Talmudic law and in personal devotions.

Orthodox Church *n.* **1.** Also called: **Byzantine Church, Eastern Orthodox Church, Greek Orthodox Church.** the collective body of those Eastern Churches that were separated from the western Church in the 11th century and are in communion with the Greek patriarch of Constantinople. **2.** any of these Churches.

Orthodox Judaism *n.* the form of Judaism characterized by allegiance to the traditional interpretation and to strict observance of the Mosaic Law as interpreted in the Talmud, etc., and regarded as divinely revealed. Compare **Conservative Judaism, Reform Judaism.**

orthodoxy (ˈɔːθəˌdɒksɪ) *n., pl.* **-doxies.** **1.** orthodox belief or practice. **2.** the quality of being orthodox.

orthoepy (ˈɔːθəʊˌɛpɪ) *n.* the study of correct or standard pronunciation. [C17: from Greek *orthoepeia,* from ORTHO- straight + *epos* word] —**orthoepic** (ˌɔːθəʊˈɛpɪk) *adj.* —ˌ**orthoˈepically** *adv.*

orthogenesis (ˌɔːθəʊˈdʒɛnɪsɪs) *n.* **1.** *Biology.* **a.** evolution of a group of organisms in a particular direction, which is generally predetermined. **b.** the theory that proposes such a development. **2.** the theory that there is a series of stages through which all cultures pass in the same order. —**orthogenetic** (ˌɔːθəʊdʒɪˈnɛtɪk) *adj.* —ˌ**orthogeˈnetically** *adv.*

orthogenic (ˌɔːθəʊˈdʒɛnɪk) *adj.* **1.** *Med.* relating to corrective procedures designed to promote healthy development. **2.** of or relating to orthogenesis. —ˌ**orthoˈgenically** *adv.*

orthognathous (ɔːˈθɒgnəθəs) *adj. Anatomy.* having normally aligned jaws. —**orˈthognaˌthism** *or* **orˈthognathy** *n.*

orthogonal (ɔːˈθɒgənᵊl) *adj.* **1.** relating to, consisting of, or involving right angles; perpendicular. **2.** *Maths.* **a.** (of a pair of vectors) having a defined scalar product equal to zero. **b.** (of a pair of functions) having a defined product equal to zero. —**orˈthogonally** *adv.*

orthogonal matrix *n. Maths.* a matrix that is the inverse of its transpose so that any two rows or any two columns are orthogonal vectors. Compare **symmetric matrix.**

orthogonal projection *n. Engineering.* the method used in engineering drawing of projecting views of the object being described, such as plan, elevation, side view, etc., at right angles to each other.

orthographic (ˌɔːθəʊˈgræfɪk) *or* **orthographical** *adj.* of or relating to spelling. —ˌ**orthoˈgraphically** *adv.*

orthographic projection *n.* **1.** a style of engineering drawing in which true dimensions are represented as if projected from infinity on three planes perpendicular to each other, avoiding the effects of perspective. **2.** a type of zenithal map projection in which the area is mapped as if projected from infinity, with resulting distortion of scale away from the centre.

orthography (ɔːˈθɒgrəfɪ) *n., pl.* **-phies.** **1.** a writing system. **2.** **a.** spelling considered to be correct. **b.** the principles underlying spelling. **3.** the study of spelling. **4.** orthographic projection. —**orˈthographer** *or* **orˈthographist** *n.*

orthohydrogen (ˌɔːθəʊˈhaɪdrədʒən) *n. Chem.* the form of molecular hydrogen, constituting about 75 per cent of the total at normal temperatures, in which the nuclei of the atoms spin in the same direction. Compare **parahydrogen.**

orthomorphic (ˌɔːθəʊˈmɔːfɪk) *adj. Geography.* another word for **conformal** (sense 2).

orthopaedics *or U.S.* **orthopedics** (ˌɔːθəʊˈpiːdɪks) *n.* (*functioning as sing.*) **1.** the branch of surgery concerned with disorders of the spine and joints and the repair of deformities of these parts. **2.** **dental orthopaedics.** another name for **orthodontics.** —ˌ**orthoˈpaedic** *or U.S.* ˌ**orthoˈpedic** *adj.* —ˌ**orthoˈpaedist** *or U.S.* ˌ**orthoˈpedist** *n.*

orthophosphate (ˌɔːθəʊˈfɒsfeɪt) *n.* any salt or ester of orthophosphoric acid.

orthophosphoric acid (ˌɔːθəʊfɒsˈfɒrɪk) *n.* a colourless soluble solid tribasic acid used in the manufacture of fertilizers and soaps. Formula: H_3PO_4. Also called: **phosphoric acid.**

orthophosphorous acid (ˌɔːθəʊˈfɒsfərəs) *n.* a white or yellowish hygroscopic crystalline dibasic acid. Formula: H_3PO_3. Also called: **phosphorous acid.**

orthopsychiatry (ˌɔːθəʊsaɪˈkaɪətrɪ) *n.* the study and treatment of mental disorders with emphasis on prevention during childhood. —**orthopsychiatric** (ˌɔːθəʊˌsaɪkɪˈætrɪk) *adj.* —ˌ**orthopsyˈchiatrist** *n.*

orthopter (ˈɔːθɒptə) *n.* another name for **ornithopter.**

orthopteran (ɔːˈθɒptərən) *n., pl.* **-terans.** **1.** Also: **orthopteron** (*pl.* **-tera** (-tərə)) any orthopterous insect. ~*adj.* **2.** another word for **orthopterous.**

orthopterous (ɔːˈθɒptərəs) *or* **orthopteran** *adj.* of, relating to, or belonging to the *Orthoptera,* a large order of insects, including crickets, locusts, and grasshoppers, having leathery forewings and membranous hind wings, hind legs adapted for leaping, and organs of stridulation.

orthoptic (ɔːˈθɒptɪk) *adj.* relating to normal binocular vision.

orthoptics (ɔːˈθɒptɪks) *n.* (*functioning as sing.*) the science or practice of correcting defective vision, as by exercises to strengthen weak eye muscles.

orthoptist (ɔːˈθɒptɪst) *n.* a person who is qualified to practise orthoptics.

orthopyroxene (ˌɔːθəʊpaɪˈrɒksiːn) *n.* a member of the pyroxene group of minerals having an orthorhombic crystal structure, such as enstatite and hypersthene.

orthorhombic (ˌɔːθəʊˈrɒmbɪk) *adj. Crystallog.* relating to the crystal system characterized by three mutually perpendicular unequal axes. Also: **rhombic, trimetric.**

orthoscope (ˈɔːθəʊˌskəʊp) *n. Med., obsolete.* a 19th-century instrument for viewing the fundus of the eye through a layer of water, which eliminates distortion caused by the cornea.

orthoscopic (ˌɔːθəʊˈskɒpɪk) *adj.* **1.** of, relating to, or produced by normal vision. **2.** yielding an undistorted image.

orthostichy (ɔːˈθɒstɪkɪ) *n., pl.* **-chies.** **1.** an imaginary vertical line that connects a row of leaves on a stem. **2.** an arrangement of leaves so connected. ~Compare **parastichy.** [C19: from ORTHO- + Greek *stikhos*] —**orˈthostichous** *adj.*

orthotics (ɔːˈθɒtɪks) *n.* (*functioning as sing.*) the provision and use of artificial or mechanical aids, such as braces, to prevent or assist movement of weak or injured joints or muscles.

orthotist (ɔːˈθɒtɪst) *n.* a person who is qualified to practise orthotics.

orthotone (ˈɔːθəʊˌtəʊn) *adj.* **1.** (of a word) having an independent accent. ~*n.* **2.** an independently accented word.

orthotropic (ˌɔːθəʊˈtrɒpɪk) *adj.* **1.** *Botany.* relating to or showing growth that is in direct line with the stimulus. **2.** (of a material) having different elastic properties in different planes. —**orthotropism** (ɔːˈθɒtrəˌpɪzəm) *n.*

orthotropous (ɔːˈθɒtrəpəs) *adj.* (of a plant ovule) growing straight during development so that the micropyle is at the apex. Compare **anatropous.**

ortolan (ˈɔːtələn) *n.* **1.** Also called: **ortolan bunting.** a brownish Old World bunting, *Emberiza hortulana,* regarded as a delicacy. **2.** any of various other small birds eaten as delicacies, esp. the bobolink. [C17: via French from Latin *hortulānus,* from *hortulus,* diminutive of *hortus* garden]

orts (ɔːts) *pl. n.* (*sometimes sing.*) *Archaic or dialect.* scraps or leavings. [C15: of Germanic origin; related to Dutch *oorete,* from *oor-* remaining + *ete* food]

Orvieto (*Italian* orˈvjɛːto) *n.* a light white wine from the region around the town of Orvieto in central Italy.

Orwellian (ɔːˈwɛlɪən) *adj.* of, relating to, or characteristic of the British writer George Orwell (1903–50) or of his works or social criticism.

-ory[1] *suffix forming nouns.* **1.** indicating a place for: *observatory.* **2.** something having a specified use: *directory.* [via Old French *-orie,* from Latin *-ōrium, -ōria*]

-ory[2] *suffix forming adjectives.* of or relating to; characterized by; having the effect of: *contributory; promissory.* [via Old French *-orie,* from Latin *-ōrius*]
oryx ('ɒrɪks) *n., pl.* **-yxes** *or* **-yx.** any large African antelope of the genus *Oryx,* typically having long straight nearly upright horns. [C14: via Latin from Greek *orux* stonemason's axe, used also of the pointed horns of an antelope]
os[1] (ɒs) *n., pl.* **ossa** ('ɒsə). *Anatomy.* the technical name for **bone.** [C16: from Latin: bone; compare Greek *osteon*]
os[2] (ɒs) *n., pl.* **ora** ('ɔːrə). *Anatomy, zoology.* a mouth or mouthlike part or opening. [C18: from Latin]
os[3] (əʊs) *n., pl.* **osar** ('əʊsɑː). another name for **esker.** [C19 *osar* (pl.), from Swedish *ås* (sing.) ridge]
Os *the chemical symbol for* osmium.
OS *abbrev. for:* **1.** Old School. **2.** Old Style (method of reckoning dates). **3.** Ordinary Seaman. **4.** (in Britain) Ordnance Survey. **5.** outsize. **6.** Old Saxon (language).
o.s. *abbrev. for:* **1.** old series. **2.** only son. **3.** Also: **OS, O/S** out of stock. **4.** Also: **OS, O/S** *Banking.* outstanding.
OSA *abbrev. for* Order of Saint Augustine.
Osage (əʊ'seɪdʒ, 'əʊseɪdʒ) *n.* **1.** (*pl.* **Osages** *or* **Osage**) a member of a North American Indian people formerly living in an area between the Missouri and Arkansas Rivers in the central U.S. **2.** the language of this people, belonging to the Siouan family.
Osage orange *n.* **1.** a North American moraceous tree, *Maclura pomifera,* grown for hedges and ornament. **2.** the warty orange-like fruit of this plant.
OSB *abbrev. for* Order of Saint Benedict.
Oscan ('ɒskən) *n.* **1.** an extinct language of ancient S Italy belonging to the Italic branch of the Indo-European family. See also **Osco-Umbrian. 2.** a speaker of this language; Samnite. *~adj.* **3.** of or relating to this language.
oscar ('ɒskə) *n. Austral. slang.* cash; money. [C20: rhyming slang, from *Oscar* Asche (1871–1936), Australian actor]
Oscar ('ɒskə) *n.* **1.** any of several small gold statuettes awarded annually in the United States by the Academy of Motion Picture Arts and Sciences for outstanding achievements in films. Official name: **Academy Award. 2.** *Communications.* a code word for the letter *o.* [C20: sense 1 said to have been named after a remark made by an official on first seeing the statuette, that it reminded him of his uncle Oscar]
oscillate ('ɒsɪˌleɪt) *vb.* **1.** (*intr.*) to move or swing from side to side regularly. **2.** (*intr.*) to waver between opinions, courses of action, etc. **3.** *Physics.* to undergo or produce or cause to undergo or produce oscillation. [C18: from Latin *oscillāre* to swing, from *oscillum* a swing]
oscillating universe theory *n.* the theory that the universe is oscillating between periods of expansion and contraction.
oscillation (ˌɒsɪ'leɪʃən) *n.* **1.** *Physics, statistics.* **a.** regular fluctuation in value, position, or state about a mean value, such as the variation in an alternating current or the regular swinging of a pendulum. **b.** a single cycle of such a fluctuation. **2.** the act or process of oscillating. **—oscillatory** ('ɒsɪlətərɪ, -trɪ) *adj.*
oscillator ('ɒsɪˌleɪtə) *n.* **1.** a circuit or instrument for producing an alternating current or voltage of a required frequency. **2.** any instrument for producing oscillations. **3.** a person or thing that oscillates.
oscillogram (ɒ'sɪləˌgræm) *n.* the recording obtained from an oscillograph or the trace on an oscilloscope screen.
oscillograph (ɒ'sɪləˌgrɑːf, -ˌgræf) *n.* a device for producing a graphical record of the variation of an oscillating quantity, such as an electric current. **—oscillographic** (ɒˌsɪlə'græfɪk) *adj.* **—oscillography** (ˌɒsɪ'lɒgrəfɪ) *n.*
oscilloscope (ɒ'sɪləˌskəʊp) *n.* an instrument for producing a representation of a rapidly changing quantity on the screen of a cathode-ray tube. The rapid changes are converted into electric signals, which are applied to plates in the cathode-ray tube. Changes in the magnitude of the potential across the plates deflect the electron beam and thus produce a trace on the screen.
oscine ('ɒsaɪn, 'ɒsɪn) *adj.* of, relating to, or belonging to the *Oscines,* a suborder of passerine birds that includes most of the songbirds. [C17: via New Latin from Latin *oscen* singing bird]
oscitancy ('ɒsɪtənsɪ) *or* **oscitance** *n., pl.* **-tancies** *or* **-tances. 1.** the state of being drowsy, lazy, or inattentive. **2.** the act of yawning. ~Also called: ˌ**osci'tation.** [C17: from Latin *oscitāre* to gape, yawn] **—'oscitant** *adj.*
Osco-Umbrian (ˌɒskəʊ'ʌmbrɪən) *n.* **1.** a group of extinct languages of ancient Italy, including Oscan, Umbrian, and Sabellian, which were displaced by Latin. *~adj.* **2.** relating to or belonging to this group of languages.
osculant ('ɒskjʊlənt) *adj.* **1.** *Biology.* (of an organism or group of organisms) possessing some of the characteristics of two different taxonomic groups. **2.** *Zoology.* closely joined or adhering. [C19: from Latin *ōsculārī* to kiss; see OSCULUM]
oscular ('ɒskjʊlə) *adj.* **1.** *Zoology.* of or relating to an osculum. **2.** of or relating to the mouth or to kissing.
osculate ('ɒskjʊˌleɪt) *vb.* **1.** *Usually humorous.* to kiss. **2.** (*intr.*) (of an organism or group of organisms) to be intermediate between two taxonomic groups. **3.** *Geometry.* to touch in osculation. [C17: from Latin *ōsculārī* to kiss; see OSCULUM]
osculation (ˌɒskjʊ'leɪʃən) *n.* **1.** Also called: **tacnode.** *Maths.* a point at which two branches of a curve have a common tangent, each branch extending in both directions of the tangent. **2.** *Rare.* the act or an instance of kissing. **—osculatory** ('ɒskjʊlətərɪ, -trɪ) *adj.*
osculum ('ɒskjʊləm) *n., pl.* **-la** (-lə). *Zoology.* a mouthlike aperture, esp. the opening in a sponge out of which water passes. [C17: from Latin: a kiss, little mouth, diminutive of *ōs* mouth]
OSD *abbrev. for* Order of Saint Dominic.
-ose[1] *suffix forming adjectives.* possessing; resembling: *verbose; grandiose.* [from Latin *-ōsus;* see -OUS]
-ose[2] *suffix forming nouns.* **1.** indicating a carbohydrate, esp. a sugar: *lactose.* **2.** indicating a decomposition product of protein: *albumose.* [from GLUCOSE]
OSF *abbrev. for* Order of Saint Francis.
osier ('əʊzɪə) *n.* **1.** any of various willow trees, esp. *Salix viminalis,* whose flexible branches or twigs are used for making baskets, etc. **2.** a twig or branch from such a tree. **3.** any of several North American dogwoods, esp. the red osier. [C14: from Old French, probably from Medieval Latin *ausēria,* perhaps of Gaulish origin; compare Breton *aoz*]
-osis *suffix forming nouns.* **1.** indicating a process or state: *metamorphosis.* **2.** indicating a diseased condition: *tuberculosis.* Compare **-iasis. 3.** indicating the formation or development of something: *fibrosis.* [from Greek, suffix used to form nouns from verbs with infinitives in *-oein* or *-oun*]
Osmanli (ɒz'mænlɪ) *adj.* **1.** of or relating to the Ottoman Empire. *~n.* **2.** (*pl.* **-lis**) (formerly) a subject of the Ottoman Empire. **3.** the Turkish language, esp. as written in Arabic letters under the Ottoman Empire. [C19: from Turkish, from *Osman* I (1259–1326), Turkish sultan and founder of the Ottoman Empire]
osmic ('ɒzmɪk) *adj.* of or containing osmium in a high valence state, esp. the tetravalent state.
osmious ('ɒzmɪəs) *adj.* another word for **osmous.**
osmiridium (ˌɒzmɪ'rɪdɪəm) *n.* a very hard corrosion-resistant white or grey natural alloy of osmium and iridium in variable proportions, often containing smaller amounts of platinum, ruthenium, and rhodium: used esp. in pen nibs. Also: **iridosmine.** [C19: from OSM(IUM) + IRIDIUM]
osmium ('ɒzmɪəm) *n.* a very hard brittle bluish-white metal, the heaviest known element, occurring with platinum and alloyed with iridium in osmiridium: used to produce platinum alloys, mainly for pen tips and instrument pivots, as a catalyst, and in electric-light filaments. Symbol: Os; atomic no.: 76; atomic wt.: 190.2; valency: 1 to 8; relative density: 22.57; melting pt.: 3045°C (approx.); boiling pt.: 5027°C (approx.). [C19: from Greek *osmē* smell, so called from its penetrating odour]
osmium tetroxide *n.* a yellowish poisonous water-soluble crystalline substance with a penetrating odour, used as a reagent and catalyst in organic synthesis. Formula: OsO_4.
osmometer (ɒz'mɒmɪtə) *n.* an instrument for measuring osmotic pressure. [C20: from OSMO(SIS) + -METER] **—osmometric** (ˌɒzmə'mɛtrɪk) *adj.* **—ˌosmo'metrically** *adv.* **—os'mometry** *n.*
osmoregulation (ˌɒzməʊˌrɛgjʊ'leɪʃən) *n. Zoology.* the adjustment of the osmotic pressure of a cell or organism in relation to the surrounding fluid.
osmose ('ɒzməʊs, -məʊz, 'ɒs-) *vb.* **1.** to undergo or cause to undergo osmosis. *~n.* **2.** a former name for **osmosis.** [C19 (n.): abstracted from the earlier terms *endosmose* and *exosmose;* related to Greek *ōsmos* push]
osmosis (ɒz'məʊsɪs, ɒs-) *n.* **1.** the passage of a solvent through a semipermeable membrane from a less concentrated to a more concentrated solution until both solutions are of the same concentration. **2.** diffusion through any membrane or porous barrier, as in dialysis. **3.** gradual or unconscious assimilation or adoption, as of ideas. [C19: Latinized form from OSMOSE (n.), from Greek *ōsmos* push, thrust] **—osmotic** (ɒz'mɒtɪk, ɒs-) *adj.* **—os'motically** *adv.*
osmotic pressure *n.* the pressure necessary to prevent osmosis into a given solution when the solution is separated from the pure solvent by a semipermeable membrane.
osmous ('ɒzməs) *adj.* of or containing osmium in a low valence state, esp. the divalent state. Also: **osmious.**
osmunda (ɒz'mʌndə) *or* **osmund** ('ɒzmənd) *n.* any fern of the genus *Osmunda,* such as the royal fern, having large spreading fronds: family *Osmundaceae.* [C13: from Old French *osmonde,* of unknown origin]
osnaburg ('ɒznəˌbɜːg) *n.* a coarse plain-woven cotton used for sacks, furnishings, etc. [C16: corruption of *Osnabrück,* NW Germany, where it was originally made]
osprey ('ɒsprɪ, -preɪ) *n.* **1.** a large broad-winged fish-eating diurnal bird of prey, *Pandion haliaetus,* with a dark back and whitish head and underparts: family *Pandioridae.* Often called (U.S. and Canadian): **fish hawk. 2.** any of the feathers of various other birds, used esp. as trimming for hats. [C15: from Old French *ospres,* apparently from Latin *ossifraga,* literally: bone-breaker, from *os* bone + *frangere* to break]
ossa ('ɒsə) *n.* the plural of **os**[1].
ossein ('ɒsɪɪn) *n.* a protein that forms the organic matrix of bone, constituting about 40 per cent of its matter. [C19: from Latin *osseus* bony, from *os* bone]
osseous ('ɒsɪəs) *adj.* consisting of or containing bone, bony. [C17: from Latin *osseus,* from *os* bone] **—'osseously** *adv.*
Osset ('ɒsɪt) *n.* a member of an Iranian people living in the former Soviet Union, chiefly in Ossetia in the Caucasus.

Ossetic (ɒˈsɛtɪk) *or* **Ossetian** (ɒˈsiːʃən) *adj.* **1.** of or relating to the region of Ossetia in the Caucasus, its people, or their language. ~*n.* **2.** the language of the Ossets, belonging to the East Iranian branch of the Indo-European family.

Ossianic (ˈɒsɪənɪk) *adj.* of or relating to Ossian, a legendary Irish hero and bard of the 3rd century A.D.

ossicle (ˈɒsɪkᵊl) *n.* a small bone, esp. one of those in the middle ear. [C16: from Latin *ossiculum*, from *os* bone] —**ossicular** (ɒˈsɪkjʊlə) *adj.*

Ossie (ˈɒzɪ) *adj., n.* a variant spelling of **Aussie.**

ossiferous (ɒˈsɪfərəs) *adj. Geology.* containing or yielding bones: *ossiferous caves.*

ossification (ˌɒsɪfɪˈkeɪʃən) *n.* **1.** the formation of or conversion into bone. **2.** the process of ossifying or the state of being ossified.

ossifrage (ˈɒsɪfrɪdʒ, -ˌfreɪdʒ) *n.* an archaic name for the **lammergeier** and **osprey** (sense 1). [C17: from Latin *ossifraga* sea eagle; see OSPREY]

ossify (ˈɒsɪˌfaɪ) *vb.* **-fies, -fying, -fied.** **1.** to convert or be converted into bone. **2.** (*intr.*) (of habits, attitudes, etc.) to become inflexible. [C18: from French *ossifier*, from Latin *os* bone + *facere* to make] —ˈ**ossiˌfier** *n.*

osso bucco (ˈɒsəʊ ˈbʊkəʊ) *n.* a stew, originally from Italy, made with knuckle of veal, cooked in tomato sauce. [C20: from Italian: marrowbone]

ossuary (ˈɒsjʊərɪ) *n., pl.* **-aries.** any container for the burial of human bones, such as an urn or vault. [C17: from Late Latin *ossuārium*, from Latin *os* bone]

OST (in the U.S.) *abbrev. for* Office of Science and Technology.

osteal (ˈɒstɪəl) *adj.* **1.** of or relating to bone or to the skeleton. **2.** composed of bone; osseous. [C19: from Greek *osteon* bone]

osteitis (ˌɒstɪˈaɪtɪs) *n.* inflammation of a bone. —**osteitic** (ˌɒstɪˈɪtɪk) *adj.*

osteitis deformans (dɪˈfɔːmənz) *n.* another name for **Paget's disease** (sense 1).

ostensible (ɒˈstɛnsɪbᵊl) *adj.* **1.** apparent; seeming. **2.** pretended. [C18: via French from Medieval Latin *ostensibilis*, from Latin *ostendere* to show, from *ob-* before + *tendere* to extend] —**osˌtensiˈbility** *n.* —**osˈtensibly** *adv.*

ostensive (ɒˈstɛnsɪv) *adj.* **1.** obviously or manifestly demonstrative. **2.** a less common word for **ostensible.** **3.** *Philosophy.* (of a definition) given by demonstrative means, esp. by pointing. [C17: from Late Latin *ostentīvus*, from Latin *ostendere* to show; see OSTENSIBLE] —**osˈtensively** *adv.*

ostensory (ɒsˈtɛnsərɪ) *n., pl.* **-sories. R.C. Church.** another word for **monstrance.** [C18: from Medieval Latin *ostensorium*; see OSTENSIBLE]

ostentation (ˌɒstɛnˈteɪʃən) *n.* **1.** pretentious, showy, or vulgar display. **2.** *Archaic.* false appearance. —ˌ**ostenˈtatious** *adj.* —ˌ**ostenˈtatiously** *adv.*

osteo- *or before a vowel* **oste-** *combining form.* indicating bone or bones: *osteopathy.* [from Greek *osteon*]

osteoarthritis (ˌɒstɪəʊɑːˈθraɪtɪs) *n.* chronic inflammation of the joints, esp. those that bear weight, with pain and stiffness. Also called: **degenerative joint disease.** —**osteoarthritic** (ˌɒstɪəʊɑːˈθrɪtɪk) *adj., n.*

osteoblast (ˈɒstɪəʊˌblæst) *n.* a bone-forming cell. —ˌ**osteoˈblastic** *adj.*

osteoclasis (ˌɒstɪˈɒkləsɪs) *n.* **1.** surgical fracture of a bone to correct deformity. **2.** absorption of bone tissue.

osteoclast (ˈɒstɪəʊˌklæst) *n.* **1.** a surgical instrument for fracturing bone. **2.** a large multinuclear cell formed in bone marrow that is associated with the normal absorption of bone. —ˌ**osteoˈclastic** *adj.*

osteogenesis (ˌɒstɪəʊˈdʒɛnɪsɪs) *n.* the formation of bone. —ˌ**osteoˈgenic** *adj.*

osteoid (ˈɒstɪˌɔɪd) *adj.* of or resembling bone; bony.

osteology (ˌɒstɪˈɒlədʒɪ) *n.* the study of the structure and function of bones. —**osteological** (ˌɒstɪəˈlɒdʒɪkᵊl) *adj.* —ˌ**osteoˈlogically** *adv.* —ˌ**osteˈologist** *n.*

osteoma (ˌɒstɪˈəʊmə) *n., pl.* **-mata** (-mətə) *or* **-mas.** a benign tumour composed of bone or bonelike tissue.

osteomalacia (ˌɒstɪəʊməˈleɪʃɪə) *n.* a disease in adults characterized by softening of the bones, resulting from a deficiency of vitamin D and of calcium and phosphorus. [C19: from New Latin, from OSTEO- + Greek *malakia* softness] —ˌ**osteomaˈlacial** *or* **osteomalacic** (ˌɒstɪəʊməˈlæsɪk) *adj.*

osteomyelitis (ˌɒstɪəʊˌmaɪɪˈlaɪtɪs) *n.* inflammation of bone marrow, caused by infection.

osteopath (ˈɒstɪəˌpæθ) *or* (*less commonly*) **osteopathist** (ˌɒstɪˈɒpəθɪst) *n.* a person who practises osteopathy.

osteopathy (ˌɒstɪˈɒpəθɪ) *n.* a system of healing based on the manipulation of bones or other parts of the body. —**osteopathic** (ˌɒstɪəˈpæθɪk) *adj.* —ˌ**osteoˈpathically** *adv.*

osteophyte (ˈɒstɪəˌfaɪt) *n.* a small abnormal bony outgrowth. —**osteophytic** (ˌɒstɪəˈfɪtɪk) *adj.*

osteoplastic (ˌɒstɪəˈplæstɪk) *adj.* **1.** of or relating to osteoplasty. **2.** of or relating to the formation of bone.

osteoplasty (ˈɒstɪəˌplæstɪ) *n., pl.* **-ties.** the branch of surgery concerned with bone repair or bone grafting.

osteoporosis (ˌɒstɪəʊpɔːˈrəʊsɪs) *n.* porosity and brittleness of the bones due to loss of calcium from the bone matrix. [C19: from OSTEO- + PORE² + -OSIS] —ˌ**osteopoˈrotic** *adj.*

osteotome (ˈɒstɪəˌtəʊm) *n.* a surgical instrument for cutting bone, usually a special chisel.

osteotomy (ˌɒstɪˈɒtəmɪ) *n., pl.* **-mies.** the surgical cutting or dividing of bone, usually to correct a deformity.

ostiary (ˈɒstɪərɪ) *n., pl.* **-aries.** *R.C. Church.* another word for **porter²** (sense 4). [C15: from Latin *ostiārius* doorkeeper, from *ostium* door]

ostinato (ˌɒstɪˈnɑːtəʊ) *n.* **a.** a continuously reiterated musical phrase. **b.** (*as modifier*): *an ostinato passage.* [Italian: from Latin *obstinātus* OBSTINATE]

ostiole (ˈɒstɪˌəʊl) *n. Biology.* **1.** the pore in the reproductive bodies of certain algae and fungi through which spores pass. **2.** any small pore. [C19: from Latin *ostiolum*, diminutive of *ostium* door] —**ostiolar** (ˈɒstɪələ) *or* ˈ**ostioˌlate** *adj.*

ostium (ˈɒstɪəm) *n., pl.* **-tia** (-tɪə). *Biology.* **1.** any of the pores in sponges through which water enters the body. **2.** any of the openings in the heart of an arthropod through which blood enters. **3.** any similar opening. [C17: from Latin: door, entrance]

ostler *or* **hostler** (ˈɒslə) *n. Archaic.* a stableman, esp. one at an inn. [C15: variant of *hostler*, from HOSTEL]

Ostmark (ˈɒstˌmɑːk; *German* ˈɔstmark) *n.* (formerly) the standard monetary unit of East Germany, divided into 100 pfennigs. [German, literally: east mark]

ostosis (ɒsˈtəʊsɪs) *n.* the formation of bone; ossification.

ostracize *or* **ostracise** (ˈɒstrəˌsaɪz) *vb.* (*tr.*) **1.** to exclude or banish (a person) from a particular group, society, etc. **2.** (in ancient Greece) to punish by temporary exile. [C17: from Greek *ostrakizein* to select someone for banishment by voting on potsherds; see OSTRACON] —ˈ**ostracism** *n.* —ˈ**ostraˌcizable** *or* ˈ**ostraˌcisable** *adj.* —ˈ**ostraˌcizer** *or* ˈ**ostraˌciser** *n.*

ostracod (ˈɒstrəˌkɒd) *n.* any minute crustacean of the mainly freshwater subclass *Ostracoda*, in which the body is enclosed in a transparent two-valved carapace. [C19: via New Latin from Greek *ostrakōdēs* having a shell, from *ostrakon* shell] —**ostracodan** (ˌɒstrəˈkəʊdən) *or* ˌ**ostraˈcodous** *adj.*

ostracoderm (ˈɒstrəkəˌdɜːm, ɒsˈtrækə-) *n.* any extinct Palaeozoic fishlike jawless vertebrate of the group *Ostracodermi*, characterized by a heavily armoured body. [C19: via New Latin from Greek *ostrakon* shell + -DERM]

ostracon (ˈɒstrəˌkɒn) *n.* (in ancient Greece) a potsherd used for ostracizing. [from Greek]

ostrich (ˈɒstrɪtʃ) *n., pl.* **-triches** *or* **-trich.** **1.** a fast-running flightless African bird, *Struthio camelus*, that is the largest living bird, with stout two-toed feet and dark feathers, except on the naked head, neck, and legs: order *Struthioniformes* (see **ratite**). **2. American ostrich.** another name for **rhea.** **3.** a person who refuses to recognize the truth, reality, etc.: a reference to the ostrich's supposed habit of burying its head in the sand. [C13: from Old French *ostrice*, from Latin *avis* bird + Late Latin *struthio* ostrich, from Greek *strouthion*]

Ostrogoth (ˈɒstrəˌgɒθ) *n.* a member of the eastern group of the Goths, who formed a kingdom in Italy from 493 to 552. [C17: from Late Latin *Ostrogothī*, from *ostro-* east, eastward + GOTH] —ˌ**OstroˈGothic** *adj.*

Ostyak (ˈɒstɪˌæk) *n.* **1.** (*pl.* **-aks** *or* **-ak**) a member of an Ugrian people living in NW Siberia E of the Urals. **2.** the language of this people, belonging to the Finno-Ugric family: related to Hungarian.

OT *abbrev. for:* **1.** occupational therapy. **2.** occupational therapist. **3.** Old Testament. **4.** overtime. **5.** (in Australia) Overland Telegraph (the line from Adelaide to Darwin).

ot- *combining form.* a variant of **oto-** before a vowel: *otalgia.*

otalgia (əʊˈtældʒɪə, -dʒə) *n.* the technical name for **earache.**

OTC *abbrev. for:* **1.** (in Britain) Officers' Training Corps. **2.** *Stock Exchange.* over the counter: denoting dealings between brokers in areas for which no official market prices are quoted. **3.** oxytetracycline.

OTE *abbrev. for* on-target earnings: referring to the salary a salesperson should be able to achieve.

O tempora! O mores! *Latin.* (əʊ ˈtɛmpɔːrɑː əʊ ˈmɔːreɪz) *sentence substitute.* oh the times! oh the customs!: an exclamation at the evil of them.

other (ˈʌðə) *determiner.* **1. a.** (when used before a singular noun, usually preceded by *the*) the remaining (one or ones in a group of which one or some have been specified): *I'll read the other sections of the paper later.* **b. the other.** (*as pronoun; functioning as sing.*): *one walks while the other rides.* **2.** (a) different (one or ones from that or those already specified or understood): *he found some other house; no other man but you; other days were happier.* **3.** additional; further: *there are no other possibilities.* **4.** (preceded by *every*) alternate; two: *it buzzes every other minute.* **5. other than. a.** apart from; besides: *a lady other than his wife.* **b.** different from: *he couldn't be other than what he is.* Archaic form: **other from.** **6. no other.** *Archaic.* nothing else: *I can do no other.* **7. or other.** (preceded by a phrase or word with *some*) used to add vagueness to the preceding pronoun, noun, noun phrase, or adverb: *some dog or other bit him; he's somewhere or other.* **8. other things being equal.** conditions being the same or unchanged. **9. the other day, night,** etc. a few days, nights, etc., ago. **10. the other thing.** an unexpressed alternative. ~*pron.* **11.** another: *show me one other.* **12.** (*pl.*) additional or further ones: *the police have found two and are looking for others.*

13. (*pl.*) other people or things. **14. the others.** the remaining ones (of a group): *take these and leave the others.* **15.** (*pl.*) different ones (from those specified or understood): *they'd rather have others, not these.* See also **each other, one another.** ~*adv.* **16.** (usually used with a negative and foll. by *than*) otherwise; differently: *they couldn't behave other than they do.* [Old English *ōther;* related to Old Saxon *āthar, ōthar,* Old High German *andar*]

other-directed *adj.* guided by values derived from external influences. Compare **inner-directed.**

othergates ('ʌðəˌgeɪts) *Archaic.* ~*adv.* **1.** differently; otherwise. ~*adj.* **2.** different. [C14: from OTHER + GATE[3] + Old English *-s,* adverbial suffix]

otherguess ('ʌðəˌgɛs) *adj. Informal.* another word for **othergates** (sense 2).

otherness ('ʌðənɪs) *n.* the quality of being different or distinct in appearance, character, etc.

other ranks *pl. n.* (*rarely used in sing.*) *Chiefly Brit.* (in the armed forces) all those who do not hold a commissioned rank.

otherwhere ('ʌðəˌwɛə) *adv. Archaic, poetic.* elsewhere.

otherwise ('ʌðəˌwaɪz) *sentence connector.* **1.** or else; if not, then: *go home — otherwise your mother will worry.* ~*adv.* **2.** differently: *I wouldn't have thought otherwise.* **3.** in other respects: *an otherwise hopeless situation.* ~*adj.* **4.** (*predicative*) of an unexpected nature; different: *the facts are otherwise.* ~*pron.* **5.** something different in outcome: *success or otherwise.* [C14: from Old English *on ōthre wīsan* in other manner]

other world *n.* the spirit world or afterlife.

otherworldly (ˌʌðə'wɜːldlɪ) *adj.* **1.** of or relating to the spiritual or imaginative world. **2.** impractical or unworldly. —ˌ**other'worldliness** *n.*

Othman ('ɒθmən, ɒθ'mɑːn) *adj., n.* a variant of **Ottoman.**

otic ('əʊtɪk, 'ɒtɪk) *adj.* of or relating to the ear. [C17: from Greek *ōtikos,* from *ous* ear]

-otic *suffix forming adjectives.* **1.** relating to or affected by: *sclerotic.* **2.** causing: *narcotic.* [from Greek *-ōtikos*]

otiose ('əʊtɪˌəʊs, -ˌəʊz) *adj.* **1.** serving no useful purpose: *otiose language.* **2.** *Rare.* indolent; lazy. [C18: from Latin *ōtiōsus* leisured, from *ōtium* leisure] —**otiosity** (ˌəʊtɪ'ɒsɪtɪ) *or* '**otioseness** *n.*

otitis (əʊ'taɪtɪs) *n.* inflammation of the ear, esp. the middle ear (**otitis media**), with pain, impaired hearing, etc. See also **labyrinthitis.**

oto- *or before a vowel* **ot-** *combining form.* indicating the ear: *otitis; otolith.* [from Greek *ous, ōt-* ear]

otocyst ('əʊtəʊˌsɪst) *n.* **1.** another name for **statocyst. 2.** the embryonic structure in vertebrates that develops into the inner ear in the adult. —ˌ**oto'cystic** *adj.*

otolaryngology (ˌəʊtəʊˌlærɪŋ'gɒlədʒɪ) *n.* the branch of medicine concerned with the ear, nose, and throat and their diseases. Sometimes called: ˌ**otoˌrhinoˌlaryn'gology.** —**otolaryngological** (ˌəʊtəʊləˌrɪŋgə'lɒdʒɪk^əl) *adj.* —ˌ**otoˌlaryn'gologist** *n.*

otolith ('əʊtəʊˌlɪθ) *n.* **1.** any of the granules of calcium carbonate in the inner ear of vertebrates. Movement of otoliths, caused by a change in position of the animal, stimulates sensory hair cells, which convey the information to the brain. **2.** another name for **statolith** (sense 1). —ˌ**oto'lithic** *adj.*

otology (əʊ'tɒlədʒɪ) *n.* the branch of medicine concerned with the ear. —**otological** (ˌəʊtə'lɒdʒɪk^əl) *adj.* —**o'tologist** *n.*

otoscope ('əʊtəʊˌskəʊp) *n.* a medical instrument for examining the external ear. —**otoscopic** (ˌəʊtəʊ'skɒpɪk) *adj.*

OTT *Slang abbrev. for* over the top: see **top**[1] (sense 19b).

ottar ('ɒtə) *n.* a variant of **attar.**

ottava (əʊ'tɑːvə) *n.* an interval of an octave. See **all'ottava.** [Italian: OCTAVE]

ottava rima ('riːmə) *n. Prosody.* a stanza form consisting of eight iambic pentameter lines, rhyming a b a b a b c c. [Italian: eighth rhyme]

otter ('ɒtə) *n., pl.* **-ters** *or* **-ter. 1.** any freshwater carnivorous musteline mammal of the subfamily *Lutrinae,* esp. *Lutra lutra* (**Eurasian otter**), typically having smooth fur, a streamlined body, and webbed feet. **2.** the fur of any of these animals. **3.** Also called: **otter board.** a type of fishing tackle consisting of a weighted board to which hooked and baited lines are attached. ~*vb.* **4.** to fish using an otter. [Old English *otor;* related to Old Norse *otr,* Old High German *ottar*]

otter hound *n.* a dog used for otter hunting, esp. one of a breed, now rare, that stands about 60 cm (24 in.) high and has a harsh thick coat, often greyish with tan markings.

otter shell *n.* See **gaper** (sense 2).

otter shrew *n.* any small otter-like amphibious mammal, esp. *Potamogale velox,* of the family *Potamogalidae* of W and central Africa: order *Insectivora* (insectivores).

otto ('ɒtəʊ) *n.* another name for **attar.**

Otto cycle ('ɒtəʊ) *n.* an engine cycle used on four-stroke petrol engines (**Otto engines**) in which, ideally, combustion and rejection of heat both take place at constant volume. Compare **diesel cycle.** [C19: named after Nikolaus August *Otto* (1832–91), German engineer]

ottoman ('ɒtəmən) *n., pl.* **-mans. 1. a.** a low padded seat, usually armless, sometimes in the form of a chest. **b.** a cushioned footstool. **2.** a corded fabric. [C17: from French *ottomane,* feminine of OTTOMAN]

Ottoman ('ɒtəmən) *or* **Othman** *adj.* **1.** *History.* relating to or denoting the former Turkish empire in Europe, Asia, and Africa, which lasted from the late 13th century until the end of World War I. **2.** denoting or relating to the Turkish language. ~*n., pl.* **-mans. 3.** a Turk of the Ottoman Empire. [C17: from French, via Medieval Latin, from Arabic *Othmānī* Turkish, from Turkish *Othman* Osman I (1259–1326), Turkish sultan and founder of the Ottoman Empire]

ou (əʊ) *n. S. African slang.* a man. [Afrikaans]

OU *abbrev. for:* **1.** the Open University. **2.** Oxford University.

ouabain ('wɑːbɑːɪn) *n.* a poisonous white crystalline glycoside extracted from certain trees and used as a heart stimulant and, by some African tribes, on poison darts. Formula: $C_{29}H_{44}O_{12}.8H_2O$. [C19: from French *ouabaïo,* from Somali *waba yo* native name of tree]

ouananiche (ˌwɑːnə'niːʃ) *n.* a landlocked variety of the Atlantic salmon, *Salmo salar,* found in lakes in SE Canada. [from Canadian French, from Montagnais *wananish,* diminutive of *wanans* salmon]

oubaas ('əʊˌbɑːs) *n. S. African.* a person who is senior in years or rank. [Afrikaans]

oubliette (ˌuːblɪ'ɛt) *n.* a dungeon the only entrance to which is through the top. [C19: from French, from *oublier* to forget]

ouch[1] (aʊtʃ) *interj.* an exclamation of sharp sudden pain.

ouch[2] (aʊtʃ) *n. Archaic.* **1.** a brooch or clasp set with gems. **2.** the setting of a gem. [C15 *an ouch,* mistaken division of C14 *a nouche,* from Old French *nouche,* of Germanic origin; compare Old High German *nusca* buckle]

oud (uːd) *n.* an Arabic stringed musical instrument resembling a lute or mandolin. [from Arabic *al 'ūd,* literally: the wood. Compare LUTE[1]]

ought[1] (ɔːt) *vb.* (foll. by *to; takes an infinitive or implied infinitive*) used as an auxiliary **1.** to indicate duty or obligation: *you ought to pay your dues.* **2.** to express prudent expediency: *you ought to see him.* **3.** (usually with reference to future time) to express probability or expectation: *you ought to finish this work by Friday.* **4.** to express a desire or wish on the part of the speaker: *you ought to come next week.* [Old English *āhte,* past tense of *āgan* to OWE; related to Gothic *aihta*]

▷**Usage.** In careful English, *ought* is not used with *did* or *had. I ought not to do it,* not *I didn't ought to do it; I ought not to have done it,* not *I hadn't ought to have done it.*

ought[2] (ɔːt) *pron., adv.* a variant spelling of **aught**[1].

ought[3] (ɔːt) *n.* a less common word for **nought** (zero). [C19: mistaken division of *a nought* as *an ought;* see NOUGHT]

Ouija ('wiːdʒə) *n. Trademark.* a board on which are marked the letters of the alphabet. Answers to questions are spelt out by a pointer or glass held by the fingertips of the participants, and are supposedly formed by spiritual forces. [C19: from French *oui* yes + German *ja* yes]

ouma ('əʊmɑː) *n. S. African.* **1.** grandmother, esp. in titular use with surname. **2.** *Slang.* any elderly woman. [Afrikaans]

ounce[1] (aʊns) *n.* **1.** a unit of weight equal to one sixteenth of a pound (avoirdupois); 1 ounce is equal to 437.5 grains or 28.349 grams. Abbrev.: **oz. 2.** a unit of weight equal to one twelfth of a Troy or Apothecaries' pound; 1 ounce is equal to 480 grains or 31.103 grams. **3.** short for **fluid ounce. 4.** a small portion or amount. [C14: from Old French *unce,* from Latin *uncia* a twelfth; from *ūnus* one]

ounce[2] (aʊns) *n.* another name for **snow leopard.** [C18: from Old French *once,* by mistaken division of *lonce* as if *l'once,* from Latin LYNX]

oupa ('əʊpɑː) *n. S. African.* **1.** grandfather, esp. in titular use with surname. **2.** *Slang.* any elderly man. [Afrikaans]

our (aʊə) *determiner.* **1.** of, belonging to, or associated in some way with us: *our best vodka; our parents are good to us.* **2.** belonging to or associated with all people or people in general: *our nearest planet is Venus.* **3.** a formal word for *my* used by editors or other writers, and monarchs. **4.** *Informal.* (often sarcastic) used instead of *your: are our feet hurting?* **5.** *Dialect.* belonging to the family of the speaker: *it's our Sandra's birthday tomorrow.* [Old English *ūre* (genitive plural), from US; related to Old French, Old Saxon *ūser,* Old High German *unsēr,* Gothic *unsara*]

-our *suffix forming nouns.* indicating state, condition, or activity: *behaviour; labour.* [in Old French *-eur,* from Latin *-or,* noun suffix]

Our Father *n.* another name for the **Lord's Prayer,** taken from its opening words.

Our Lady *n.* a title given to the Virgin Mary.

ours (aʊəz) *pron.* **1.** something or someone belonging to or associated with us: *ours have blue tags.* **2. of ours.** belonging to or associated with us.

ourself (aʊə'sɛlf) *pron. Archaic.* a variant of **myself,** formerly used by monarchs or editors in formal contexts.

ourselves (aʊə'sɛlvz) *pron.* **1. a.** the reflexive form of *we* or *us.* **b.** (intensifier): *we ourselves will finish it.* **2.** (*preceded by a copula*) our usual selves: *we are ourselves when we're together.* **3.** *Not standard.* used instead of *we* or *us* in compound noun phrases: *other people and ourselves.*

▷**Usage.** See at **myself.**

-ous *suffix forming adjectives.* **1.** having, full of, or characterized by: *dangerous; spacious; languorous.* **2.** (in chemistry) indicating that an element is chemically combined in the lower of two possible valency states: *ferrous; stannous.* Compare **-ic** (sense 2). [from Old French, from Latin *-ōsus* or *-us,* Greek *-os,* adj. suffixes]

ousel (ˈuːzᵊl) *n.* a variant spelling of **ouzel.**

oust (aʊst) *vb. (tr.)* **1.** to force out of a position or place; supplant or expel. **2.** *Property law.* to deprive (a person) of the possession of land. [C16: from Anglo-Norman *ouster,* from Latin *obstāre* to withstand, from *ob-* against + *stāre* to stand]

ouster (ˈaʊstə) *n. Property law.* the act of dispossessing of freehold property; eviction; ejection.

out (aʊt) *adv.* **1.** (*often used as a particle*) at or to a point beyond the limits of some location; outside: *get out at once.* **2.** (*particle*) out of consciousness: *she passed out at the sight of blood.* **3.** (*particle*) used to indicate a burst of activity as indicated by the verb: *fever broke out.* **4.** (*particle*) used to indicate obliteration of an object: *the graffiti were painted out.* **5.** (*particle*) used to indicate an approximate drawing or description: *sketch out; chalk out.* **6.** (*often used as a particle*) away from one's custody or ownership, esp. on hire: *to let out a cottage.* **7.** on sale or on view to the public: *the book is being brought out next May.* **8.** (of a young woman) in or into polite society: *Lucinda had a fabulous party when she came out.* **9.** (of a jury) withdrawn to consider a verdict in private. **10.** (*particle*) used to indicate exhaustion or extinction: *the sugar's run out; put the light out.* **11.** (*particle*) used to indicate a goal or object achieved at the end of the action specified by the verb: *he worked it out; let's fight it out, then!* **12.** (*preceded by a superlative*) existing: *the friendliest dog out.* **13.** an expression in signalling, radio, etc., to indicate the end of a transmission. **14.** *Austral. and N.Z.* in or to Australia or New Zealand: *he came out last year.* **15. out of. a.** at or to a point outside: *out of his reach.* **b.** away from; not in: *stepping out of line; out of focus.* **c.** because of, motivated by: *doing it out of jealousy.* **d.** from (a material or source): *made out of plastic.* **e.** not or no longer having any of (a substance, material, etc.): *we're out of sugar.* ~*adj.* (*postpositive*). **16.** not or not any longer worth considering: *that plan is out because of the weather.* **17.** not allowed: *smoking on duty is out.* **18.** (*also prenominal*) not in vogue; unfashionable: *that sort of dress is out these days.* **19.** (of a fire or light) no longer burning or providing illumination: *the fire is out.* **20.** not working: *the radio's out.* **21.** unconscious: *he was out for two minutes.* **22. out to it.** *Austral. and N.Z. informal.* asleep or unconscious, esp. because drunk. **23.** not in; not at home: *call back later, they're out now.* **24.** desirous of or intent on (something or doing something): *I'm out for as much money as I can get.* **25.** Also: **out on strike.** on strike: *the machine shop is out.* **26.** (in several games and sports) denoting the state in which a player is caused to discontinue active participation, esp. in some specified role. **27.** used up; exhausted: *our supplies are completely out.* **28.** worn into holes: *this sweater is out at the elbows.* **29.** inaccurate, deficient, or discrepant: *out by six pence.* **30.** not in office or authority: *his party will be out at the election.* **31.** completed or concluded, as of time: *before the year is out.* **32.** in flower: *the roses are out now.* **33.** in arms, esp., in rebellion: *one of his ancestors was out in the Forty-Five.* **34.** (*also prenominal*) being out: *the out position on the dial.* ~*prep.* **35.** out of; out through: *he ran out the door.* **36.** *Archaic or dialect.* outside; beyond: *he comes from out our domain.* ~*interj.* **37. a.** an exclamation, usually peremptory, of dismissal, reproach, etc. **b.** (in wireless telegraphy) an expression used to signal that the speaker is signing off. **38. out with it.** a command to make something known immediately, without missing any details. ~*n.* **39.** *Chiefly U.S.* a method of escape from a place, difficult situation, punishment, etc. **40.** *Baseball.* an instance of the putting out of a batter; putout. **41.** *Printing.* **a.** the omission of words from a printed text; lacuna. **b.** the words so omitted. **42. ins and outs.** See **in** (sense 29). ~*vb.* **43.** (*tr.*) to put or throw out. **44.** (*intr.*) to be made known or effective despite efforts to the contrary (esp. in the phrase **will out**): *the truth will out.* **45.** (*tr.*) *Chiefly U.S.* (of homosexuals) to expose (a public figure) as being a fellow homosexual. [Old English *ūt;* related to Old Saxon, Old Norse *ūt,* Old High German *ūz,* German *aus*]

out- *prefix.* **1.** excelling or surpassing in a particular action: *outlast; outlive.* **2.** indicating an external location or situation away from the centre: *outpost; outpatient.* **3.** indicating emergence, an issuing forth, etc.: *outcrop; outgrowth.* **4.** indicating the result of an action: *outcome.*

outage (ˈaʊtɪdʒ) *n.* **1.** a quantity of goods missing or lost after storage or shipment. **2.** a period of power failure, machine stoppage, etc.

out and away *adv.* by far.

out-and-out *adj.* (*prenominal*) thoroughgoing; complete.

out-and-outer *n. Slang.* **1.** a thorough or thoroughgoing person or thing. **2.** a person or thing that is excellent of its kind. **3.** an extremist.

outasight (ˌaʊtəˈsaɪt) *or* **out-of-sight** *adj., interj. Slang.* another term for **far-out.**

outback (ˈaʊtˌbæk) *n.* **a.** the remote bush country of Australia. **b.** (*as modifier*): *outback life.*

outbalance (ˌaʊtˈbæləns) *vb.* another word for **outweigh.**

outbid (ˌaʊtˈbɪd) *vb.* **-bids, -bidding, -bid, -bidden** *or* **-bid.** (*tr.*) to bid higher than; outdo in bidding.

outboard (ˈaʊtˌbɔːd) *adj.* **1.** (of a boat's engine) portable, with its own propeller, and designed to be attached externally to the stern. Compare **inboard** (sense 1). **2.** in a position away from, or further away from, the centre line of a vessel or aircraft, esp. outside the hull or fuselage. ~*adv.* **3.** away from the centre line of a vessel or aircraft, esp. outside the hull or fuselage. ~*n.* **4.** an outboard motor. **5.** a boat fitted with an outboard motor.

outbound (ˈaʊtˌbaʊnd) *adj.* going out; outward bound.

outbrave (ˌaʊtˈbreɪv) *vb. (tr.)* **1.** to surpass in bravery. **2.** to confront defiantly.

outbreak (ˈaʊtˌbreɪk) *n.* a sudden, violent, or spontaneous occurrence, esp. of disease or strife.

outbreed (ˌaʊtˈbriːd) *vb.* **-breeds, -breeding, -bred. 1.** (*intr.*) *Anthropol.* to produce offspring through sexual relations outside a particular family or tribe. **2.** to breed (animals that are not closely related) or (of such animals) to be bred. —ˌ**outˈbreeding** *n.*

outbuilding (ˈaʊtˌbɪldɪŋ) *n.* a building subordinate to but separate from a main building; outhouse.

outburst (ˈaʊtˌbɜːst) *n.* **1.** a sudden and violent expression of emotion. **2.** an explosion or eruption.

outcast (ˈaʊtˌkɑːst) *n.* **1.** a person who is rejected or excluded from a social group. **2.** a vagabond or wanderer. **3.** anything thrown out or rejected. ~*adj.* **4.** rejected, abandoned, or discarded; cast out.

outcaste (ˈaʊtˌkɑːst) *n.* **1.** a person who has been expelled from a caste. **2.** a person having no caste. ~*vb.* **3.** (*tr.*) to cause (someone) to lose his caste.

outclass (ˌaʊtˈklɑːs) *vb. (tr.)* **1.** to surpass in class, quality, etc. **2.** to defeat easily.

outcome (ˈaʊtˌkʌm) *n.* something that follows from an action, dispute, situation, etc.; result; consequence.

outcrop *n.* (ˈaʊtˌkrɒp). **1.** part of a rock formation or mineral vein that appears at the surface of the earth. **2.** an emergence; appearance. ~*vb.* (ˌaʊtˈkrɒp), **-crops, -cropping, -cropped.** (*intr.*) **3.** (of rock strata, mineral veins, etc.) to protrude through the surface of the earth. **4.** another word for **crop out.**

outcross *vb.* (ˌaʊtˈkrɒs). **1.** to breed (animals or plants of the same breed but different strains). ~*n.* (ˈaʊtˌkrɒs). **2.** an animal or plant produced as a result of outcrossing. **3.** an act of outcrossing.

outcry *n.* (ˈaʊtˌkraɪ), *pl.* **-cries. 1.** a widespread or vehement protest. **2.** clamour; uproar. **3.** *Commerce.* a method of trading in which dealers shout out bids and offers at a prearranged meeting: *sale by open outcry.* ~*vb.* (ˌaʊtˈkraɪ), **-cries, -crying, -cried. 4.** (*tr.*) to cry louder or make more noise than (someone or something).

outdate (ˌaʊtˈdeɪt) *vb. (tr.)* (of something new) to cause (something else) to become old-fashioned or obsolete.

outdated (ˌaʊtˈdeɪtɪd) *adj.* old-fashioned or obsolete.

outdistance (ˌaʊtˈdɪstəns) *vb. (tr.)* to leave far behind.

outdo (ˌaʊtˈduː) *vb.* **-does, -doing, -did, -done.** (*tr.*) to surpass or exceed in performance or execution.

outdoor (ˈaʊtˈdɔː) *adj.* (*prenominal*) taking place, existing, or intended for use in the open air: *outdoor games; outdoor clothes.* Also: **out-of-door.**

outdoor relief *n.* another name for **out-relief.**

outdoors (ˌaʊtˈdɔːz) *adv.* **1.** Also: **out-of-doors.** in the open air; outside. ~*n.* **2.** the world outside or far away from human habitation: *the great outdoors.*

outer (ˈaʊtə) *adj.* (*prenominal*) **1.** being or located on the outside; external. **2.** further from the middle or central part. ~*n.* **3.** *Archery.* **a.** the white outermost ring on a target. **b.** a shot that hits this ring. **4.** *Austral.* the unsheltered part of the spectator area at a sports ground. **5. on the outer.** *Austral. and N.Z. informal.* excluded or neglected.

outer bar *n.* (in England) a collective name for junior barristers who plead from outside the bar of the court. Compare **Queen's Counsel.**

outer garments *pl. n.* the garments that are worn over a person's other clothes.

outermost (ˈaʊtəˌməʊst) *adj.* furthest from the centre or middle; outmost.

outer planet *n.* any of the planets Jupiter, Saturn, Uranus, Neptune, and Pluto, whose orbit lies outside the asteroid belt.

outer space *n.* (*not in technical usage*) any region of space beyond the atmosphere of the earth.

outface (ˌaʊtˈfeɪs) *vb. (tr.)* **1.** to face or stare down. **2.** to confront boldly or defiantly.

ˌ**outˈact** *vb.*
ˌ**outˈbargain** *vb.*
ˌ**outˈbluff** *vb.*
ˌ**outˈboast** *vb.*
ˌ**outˈbox** *vb.*
ˌ**outˈdance** *vb.*
ˌ**outˈdare** *vb.*
ˌ**outˈdodge** *vb.*
ˌ**outˈdrink** *vb.,* **-ˈdrinks, -ˈdrinking, -ˈdrank, -ˈdrunk.**
ˌ**outˈeat** *vb.,* **-ˈeats, -ˈeating, -ˈate, -ˈeaten.**

outfall ('aʊtˌfɔːl) *n.* the end of a river, sewer, drain, etc., from which it discharges.
outfield ('aʊtˌfiːld) *n.* **1.** *Cricket.* the area of the field relatively far from the pitch; the deep. Compare **infield** (sense 1). **2.** *Baseball.* **a.** the area of the playing field beyond the lines connecting first, second, and third bases. **b.** the positions of the left fielder, centre fielder, and right fielder taken collectively. Compare **infield** (sense 2). **3.** *Agriculture.* farmland most distant from the farmstead. —**'outˌfielder** *n.*
outfighting ('aʊtˌfaɪtɪŋ) *n.* fighting at a distance and not at close range.
outfit ('aʊtˌfɪt) *n.* **1.** a set of articles or equipment for a particular task, occupation, etc. **2.** a set of clothes, esp. a carefully selected one. **3.** *Informal.* any group or association regarded as a cohesive unit, such as a military company, business house, etc. **4.** the act of fitting out. **5.** *Canadian.* (formerly) the annual shipment of trading goods and supplies sent by a fur company to its trading posts. ~*vb.* **-fits, -fitting, -fitted. 6.** to furnish or be furnished with an outfit, equipment, etc.
outfitter ('aʊtˌfɪtə) *n. Chiefly Brit.* **1.** a shop that sells men's clothes. **2.** a person who provides outfits.
outflank (ˌaʊt'flæŋk) *vb.* (*tr.*) **1.** to go around the flank of (an opposing army). **2.** to get the better of.
outflow ('aʊtˌfləʊ) *n.* **1.** anything that flows out, such as liquid, money, ideas, etc. **2.** the amount that flows out. **3.** the act or process of flowing out.
outfoot (ˌaʊt'fʊt) *vb.* (*tr.*) **1.** (of a boat) to go faster than (another boat). **2.** to surpass in running, dancing, etc.
outfox (ˌaʊt'fɒks) *vb.* (*tr.*) to surpass in guile or cunning.
outgas (ˌaʊt'gæs) *vb.* **-gases** *or* **-gasses, -gassing, -gassed.** to undergo or cause to undergo the removal of adsorbed or absorbed gas from solids, often by heating in free space.
outgeneral (ˌaʊt'dʒɛnərəl) *vb.* **-als, -alling, -alled** *or U.S.* **-als, -aling, -aled.** (*tr.*) to surpass in generalship.
outgo *vb.* (ˌaʊt'gəʊ), **-goes, -going, -went, -gone. 1.** (*tr.*) to exceed or outstrip. ~*n.* ('aʊtˌgəʊ). **2.** cost; outgoings; outlay. **3.** something that goes out; outflow.
outgoing ('aʊtˌgəʊɪŋ) *adj.* **1.** departing; leaving. **2.** leaving or retiring from office: *the outgoing chairman.* **3.** friendly and sociable. ~*n.* **4.** the act of going out.
outgoings ('aʊtˌgəʊɪŋz) *pl. n.* expenditure.
out-group *n. Sociol.* persons excluded from an in-group.
outgrow (ˌaʊt'grəʊ) *vb.* **-grows, -growing, -grew, -grown.** (*tr.*) **1.** to grow too large for (clothes, shoes, etc.). **2.** to lose (a habit, idea, reputation, etc.) in the course of development or time. **3.** to grow larger or faster than.
outgrowth ('aʊtˌgrəʊθ) *n.* **1.** a thing growing out of a main body. **2.** a development, result, or consequence. **3.** the act of growing out.
outgun (ˌaʊt'gʌn) *vb.* (*tr.*) **-guns -gunning, -gunned. 1.** to surpass in fire power. **2.** to surpass in shooting. **3.** *Informal.* to surpass or excel.
outhaul ('aʊtˌhɔːl) *n. Nautical.* a line or cable for tightening the foot of a sail by hauling the clew out along the boom or yard. Also: **'outˌhauler.**
out-Herod (ˌaʊt'hɛrəd) *vb.* (*tr.*) to surpass in evil, excesses, or cruelty. [C17: originally *out-Herod Herod,* from Shakespeare's *Hamlet* (act 3, scene 2), from *Herod* (?73–4 B.C.), king of Judea noted for his cruelty]
outhouse ('aʊtˌhaʊs) *n.* **1.** a building near to, but separate from, a main building; outbuilding. **2.** *U.S.* an outside lavatory.
outing ('aʊtɪŋ) *n.* a short outward and return journey; trip; excursion.
outjockey (ˌaʊt'dʒɒkɪ) *vb.* (*tr.*) to outwit by deception.
outland *adj.* ('aʊtˌlænd, -lənd). **1.** outlying or distant. **2.** *Archaic.* foreign; alien. ~*n.* ('aʊtˌlænd). **3.** (*usually pl.*) the outlying areas of a country or region.
outlander ('aʊtˌlændə) *n.* a foreigner or stranger.
outlandish (aʊt'lændɪʃ) *adj.* **1.** grotesquely unconventional in appearance, habits, etc. **2.** *Archaic.* foreign. —**out'landishly** *adv.* —**out'landishness** *n.*
outlaw ('aʊtˌlɔː) *n.* **1.** (formerly) a person excluded from the law and deprived of its protection. **2.** any fugitive from the law, esp. a habitual transgressor. **3.** a wild or untamed beast. ~*vb.* (*tr.*) **4.** to put (a person) outside the law and deprive of its protection. **5.** (in the U.S.) to deprive (a contract) of legal force. **6.** to ban.
outlawry ('aʊtˌlɔːrɪ) *n., pl.* **-ries. 1.** the act of outlawing or the state of being outlawed. **2.** disregard for the law.
outlay *n.* ('aʊtˌleɪ). **1.** an expenditure of money, effort, etc. ~*vb.* (ˌaʊt'leɪ), **-lays, -laying, -laid. 2.** (*tr.*) to spend (money).
outlet ('aʊtlɛt, -lɪt) *n.* **1.** an opening or vent permitting escape or release. **2.** a means for release or expression of emotion, creative energy, etc. **3. a.** a market for a product or service. **b.** a commercial establishment retailing the goods of a particular producer or wholesaler. **4. a.** a channel that drains a body of water. **b.** the mouth of a river. **5.** a point in a wiring system from which current can be taken to supply electrical devices. **6.** *Anatomy.* the beginning or end of a passage, esp. the lower opening of the pelvis (**pelvic outlet**).
outlier ('aʊtˌlaɪə) *n.* **1.** an outcrop of rocks that is entirely surrounded by older rocks. **2.** a person, thing, or part situated away from a main or related body. **3.** a person who lives away from his place of work, duty, etc. **4.** *Statistics.* a point in a sample widely separated from the main cluster of points in the sample. See **scatter diagram.**
outline ('aʊtˌlaɪn) *n.* **1.** a preliminary or schematic plan, draft, account, etc. **2.** (*usually pl.*) the important features of an argument, theory, work, etc. **3.** the line by which an object or figure is or appears to be bounded. **4. a.** a drawing or manner of drawing consisting only of external lines. **b.** (*as modifier*): *an outline map.* ~*vb.* (*tr.*) **5.** to draw or display the outline of. **6.** to give the main features or general idea of.
outlive (ˌaʊt'lɪv) *vb.* (*tr.*) **1.** to live longer than (someone). **2.** to live beyond (a date or period): *he outlived the century.* **3.** to live through (an experience).
outlook ('aʊtˌlʊk) *n.* **1.** a mental attitude or point of view. **2.** the probable or expected condition or outcome of something: *the weather outlook.* **3.** the view from a place. **4.** view or prospect. **5.** the act or state of looking out.
outlying ('aʊtˌlaɪɪŋ) *adj.* distant or remote from the main body or centre, as of a town or region.
outman (ˌaʊt'mæn) *vb.* **-mans, -manning, -manned.** (*tr.*) **1.** to surpass in manpower. **2.** to surpass in manliness.
outmanoeuvre *or U.S.* **outmaneuver** (ˌaʊtmə'nuːvə) *vb.* (*tr.*) to secure a strategic advantage over by skilful manoeuvre.
outmoded (ˌaʊt'məʊdɪd) *adj.* **1.** no longer fashionable or widely accepted. **2.** no longer practical or usable. —**ˌout'modedly** *adv.* —**ˌout'modedness** *n.*
outmost ('aʊtˌməʊst) *adj.* another word for **outermost.**
outness ('aʊtnɪs) *n.* **1.** the state or quality of being external. **2.** outward expression.
outnumber (ˌaʊt'nʌmbə) *vb.* (*tr.*) to exceed in number.
out of bounds *adj.* (*postpositive*), *adv.* **1.** (often foll. by *to*) not to be entered (by); barred (to): *out of bounds to civilians.* **2.** outside specified or prescribed limits.
out of date *adj.* (**out-of-date** *when prenominal*), *adv.* no longer valid, current, or fashionable; outmoded.
out-of-door *adj.* (*prenominal*) another term for **outdoor.**
out-of-doors *adv., adj.* (*postpositive*) in the open air; outside. Also: **outdoors.**
out of pocket *adj.* (**out-of-pocket** *when prenominal*). **1.** (*postpositive*) having lost money, as in a commercial enterprise. **2.** without money to spend. **3.** (*prenominal*) (of expenses) unbudgeted and paid for in cash.
out-of-the-body experience *n.* a vivid feeling of being detached from one's body, usually involving observing it and its environment from nearby. Abbrev.: **OBE.** Compare **near-death experience.**
out-of-the-way *adj.* (*prenominal*) **1.** distant from more populous areas. **2.** uncommon or unusual.
outpatient ('aʊtˌpeɪʃənt) *n.* a nonresident hospital patient. Compare **inpatient.**
outplacement ('aʊtˌpleɪsmənt) *n.* a service that offers counselling and careers advice, esp. to redundant executives, which is paid for by their previous employer.
outpoint (ˌaʊt'pɔɪnt) *vb.* (*tr.*) **1.** to score more points than. **2.** *Nautical.* to sail closer to the wind (point higher) than (another sailing vessel).
outport ('aʊtˌpɔːt) *n.* **1.** *Chiefly Brit.* a subsidiary port built in deeper water than the original port. **2.** *Canadian.* one of the many isolated fishing villages located in the bays and other indentations of the Newfoundland coast.
outporter ('aʊtˌpɔːtə) *n. Canadian.* an inhabitant or native of a Newfoundland outport.
outpost ('aʊtˌpəʊst) *n.* **1.** *Military.* **a.** a position stationed at a distance from the area occupied by a major formation. **b.** the troops assigned to such a position. **2.** an outlying settlement or position. **3.** a limit or frontier.
outpour *n.* ('aʊtˌpɔː). **1.** the act of flowing or pouring out. **2.** something that pours out. ~*vb.* (ˌaʊt'pɔː). **3.** to pour or cause to pour out freely or rapidly.
outpouring ('aʊtˌpɔːrɪŋ) *n.* **1.** a passionate or exaggerated outburst; effusion. **2.** another word for **outpour** (senses 1, 2).
output ('aʊtˌpʊt) *n.* **1.** the act of production or manufacture. **2.** Also called: **outturn.** the amount produced, as in a given period: *a high weekly output.* **3.** the material produced, manufactured, yielded, etc. **4.** *Electronics.* **a.** the power, voltage, or current delivered by a circuit or component. **b.** the point at which the signal is delivered. **5.** the power, energy, or work produced by an engine or a system. **6.** *Computer technol.* **a.** the information produced by a computer. **b.** the operations and devices involved in producing this information. See also **input/output. 7.**

ˌout'fight *vb.,* **-'fights, -'fighting, -'fought.**
ˌout'fly *vb.,* **-'flies, -'flying, -'flew, -'flown.**
ˌout'guess *vb.*
ˌout'hit *vb.,* **-'hits, -'hitting, -'hit.**
ˌout'jump *vb.*
ˌout'last *vb.*
ˌout'laugh *vb.*
ˌout'leap *vb.,* **-'leaps, -'leaping; -'leapt** *or* **-'leaped.**
ˌout'match *vb.*
ˌout'matched *adj.*
ˌout'pace *vb.*
ˌoutper'form *vb.*
ˌout'play *vb.*
ˌoutpro'duce *vb.*

(*modifier*) of or relating to electronic, computer, or other output: *output signal; output device; output tax.* ~*vb.* **-puts, -putting, -putted** *or* **-put.** (*tr.*) **8.** *Computer technol.* to cause (data) to be emitted as output.

outrage (ˈaʊtˌreɪdʒ) *n.* **1.** a wantonly vicious or cruel act. **2.** a gross violation of decency, morality, honour, etc. **3.** profound indignation, anger, or hurt, caused by such an act. ~*vb.* (*tr.*) **4.** to cause profound indignation, anger, or resentment in. **5.** to offend grossly (feelings, decency, human dignity, etc.). **6.** to commit an act of wanton viciousness, cruelty, or indecency on. **7.** a euphemistic word for **rape**[1]. [C13 (meaning: excess): via French from *outré* beyond, from Latin *ultrā*]

outrageous (aʊtˈreɪdʒəs) *adj.* **1.** being or having the nature of an outrage. **2.** grossly offensive to decency, authority, etc. **3.** violent or unrestrained in behaviour or temperament. **4.** extravagant or immoderate. —**outˈrageously** *adv.* —**outˈrageousness** *n.*

outrank (ˌaʊtˈræŋk) *vb.* (*tr.*) **1.** to be of higher rank than. **2.** to take priority over.

outré (ˈuːtreɪ) *adj.* deviating from what is usual or proper. [C18: from French past participle of *outrer* to pass beyond]

outreach *vb.* (ˌaʊtˈriːtʃ). **1.** (*tr.*) to surpass in reach. **2.** (*tr.*) to go beyond. **3.** to reach or cause to reach out. ~*n.* (ˈaʊtˌriːtʃ). **4.** the act or process of reaching out. **5.** the length or extent of reach. **6.** *Social Welfare.* any systematic effort to provide unsolicited and predefined help to groups or individuals deemed to need it. **7.** (*modifier*) (of welfare work or workers) propagating take-up of a service by seeking out appropriate people and persuading them to accept what is judged good for them. Compare **detached** (sense 3).

out-relief *n. English history.* money given to poor people not living in a workhouse. Also called: **outdoor relief.**

outride *vb.* (ˌaʊtˈraɪd), **-rides, -riding, -rode, -ridden.** (*tr.*) **1.** to outdo by riding faster, farther, or better than. **2.** (of a vessel) to ride out (a storm). ~*n.* (ˈaʊtˌraɪd). **3.** *Prosody, rare.* an extra unstressed syllable within a metrical foot.

outrider (ˈaʊtˌraɪdə) *n.* **1.** a person who goes ahead of a car, group of people, etc., to ensure a clear passage. **2.** a person who goes in advance to investigate, discover a way, etc.; scout. **3.** a person who rides in front of or beside a carriage, esp. as an attendant or guard. **4.** *U.S.* a mounted herdsman.

outrigger (ˈaʊtˌrɪgə) *n.* **1.** a framework for supporting a pontoon outside and parallel to the hull of a boat to provide stability. **2.** a boat equipped with such a framework, esp. one of the canoes of the South Pacific. **3.** any projecting framework attached to a boat, aircraft, building, etc., to act as a support. **4.** *Rowing.* another name for **rigger** (sense 2). [C18: from OUT- + RIG[1] + -ER[1]; perhaps influenced by archaic *outligger* outlier]

outright *adj.* (ˈaʊtˌraɪt). (*prenominal*) **1.** without qualifications or limitations: *outright ownership.* **2.** complete; total: *an outright lie.* **3.** straightforward; direct: *an outright manner.* ~*adv.* (ˌaʊtˈraɪt). **4.** without restrictions: *buy outright.* **5.** without reservation or concealment: *ask outright.* **6.** instantly: *he was killed outright.* **7.** *Obsolete.* straight ahead or out.

outrun (ˌaʊtˈrʌn) *vb.* **-runs, -running, -ran, -run.** (*tr.*) **1.** to run faster, farther, or better than. **2.** to escape from by or as if by running. **3.** to go beyond; exceed.

outrunner (ˈaʊtˌrʌnə) *n.* **1.** an attendant who runs in front of a carriage, etc. **2.** the leading dog in a sled team.

outrush (ˈaʊtˌrʌʃ) *n.* a flowing or rushing out.

outsell (ˌaʊtˈsɛl) *vb.* **-sells, -selling, -sold.** (*tr.*) to sell or be sold in greater quantities than.

outsert (ˈaʊtˌsɜːt) *n.* another word for **wrapround** (sense 5). [C20: based on INSERT]

outset (ˈaʊtˌsɛt) *n.* a start; beginning (esp. in the phrase **from** (*or* **at**) **the outset**).

outshine (ˌaʊtˈʃaɪn) *vb.* **-shines, -shining, -shone.** **1.** (*tr.*) to shine more brightly than. **2.** (*tr.*) to surpass in excellence, beauty, wit, etc. **3.** (*intr.*) *Rare.* to emit light.

outshoot *vb.* (ˌaʊtˈʃuːt), **-shoots, -shooting, -shot.** **1.** (*tr.*) to surpass or excel in shooting. **2.** to go or extend beyond (something). ~*n.* (ˈaʊtˌʃuːt). **3.** a thing that projects or shoots out. **4.** the act or state of shooting out or protruding.

outside *prep.* (ˌaʊtˈsaɪd). **1.** (sometimes foll. by *of*) on or to the exterior of: *outside the house.* **2.** beyond the limits of: *outside human comprehension.* **3.** apart from; other than: *no-one knows outside you and me.* ~*adj.* (ˈaʊtˌsaɪd). **4.** (*prenominal*) situated on the exterior: *an outside lavatory.* **5.** remote; unlikely: *an outside chance.* **6.** not a member of. **7.** the greatest possible or probable (prices, odds, etc.). ~*adv.* (ˌaʊtˈsaɪd). **8.** outside a specified thing or place; out of doors. **9.** *Slang.* not in prison. ~*n.* (ˈaʊtˈsaɪd). **10.** the external side or surface: *the outside of the garage.* **11.** the external appearance or aspect. **12.** the exterior or outer part of something. **13.** (of a path, pavement, etc.) the side nearest the road or away from a wall or building. **14.** *Sport.* an outside player, as in football. **15.** (*pl.*) the outer sheets of a ream of paper. **16.** *Canadian.* (in the north) the settled parts of Canada. **17. at the outside.** *Informal.* at the most or at the greatest extent: *two days at the outside.* **18. outside in.** another term for **inside out.** See **inside** (sense 5).

▷**Usage.** In careful usage, *outside* and *inside* are preferred to *outside of* and *inside of*: *she waits outside* (not *outside of*) *the school.*

outside broadcast *n. Radio, television.* a broadcast not made from a studio.

outside director *n.* a director of a company who is not employed by that company but is often employed by a holding or associated company.

outsider (ˌaʊtˈsaɪdə) *n.* **1.** a person or thing excluded from or not a member of a set, group, etc. **2.** a contestant, esp. a horse, thought unlikely to win in a race. **3.** *Canadian.* (in the north) a person who does not live in the Arctic regions.

outside work *n.* work done off the premises of a business.

out sister *n.* a member of a community of nuns who performs tasks in the outside world on behalf of the community.

outsize (ˈaʊtˌsaɪz) *adj.* **1.** Also: **ˈoutˌsized.** very large or larger than normal: *outsize tomatoes.* ~*n.* **2.** something outsize, such as a garment or person. **3.** (*modifier*) relating to or dealing in outsize clothes: *an outsize shop.*

outskirts (ˈaʊtˌskɜːts) *pl. n.* (*sometimes sing.*) outlying or bordering areas, districts, etc., as of a city.

outsmart (ˌaʊtˈsmɑːt) *vb.* (*tr.*) *Informal.* to get the better of; outwit.

outsole (ˈaʊtˌsəʊl) *n.* the outermost sole of a shoe.

outspan *S. African.* ~*n.* (ˈaʊtˌspæn). **1.** an area on a farm kept available for travellers to rest and refresh animals. **2.** the act of unharnessing or unyoking. ~*vb.* (ˌaʊtˈspæn), **-spans, -spanning, -spanned.** **3.** to unharness or unyoke (animals). [C19: partial translation of Afrikaans *uitspan*, from *uit* out + *spannen* to stretch]

outspoken (ˌaʊtˈspəʊkən) *adj.* **1.** candid or bold in speech. **2.** said or expressed with candour or boldness.

outspread *vb.* (ˌaʊtˈsprɛd), **-spreads, -spreading, -spread.** **1.** to spread out or cause to spread out. ~*adj.* (ˈaʊtˈsprɛd). **2.** spread or stretched out. **3.** scattered or diffused widely. ~*n.* (ˈaʊtˌsprɛd). **4.** a spreading out.

outstand (ˌaʊtˈstænd) *vb.* **-stands, -standing, -stood.** **1.** (*intr.*) to be outstanding or excel. **2.** (*intr.*) *Nautical.* to stand out to sea. **3.** (*tr.*) *Archaic.* to last beyond.

outstanding (ˌaʊtˈstændɪŋ) *adj.* **1.** superior; excellent; distinguished. **2.** prominent, remarkable, or striking. **3.** still in existence; unsettled, unpaid, or unresolved. **4.** (of shares, bonds, etc.) issued and sold. **5.** projecting or jutting upwards or outwards. —**outˈstandingly** *adv.*

outstation (ˈaʊtˌsteɪʃən) *n.* **1.** a station or post in a remote or unsettled region. **2.** in a radio network, any station other than the base station. **3.** *Austral.* a station set up independently of the head station of a large sheep or cattle farm. **4. outstation movement.** *Austral.* the programme to resettle Australian Aborigines on their tribal lands. ~*adv.* **5.** (in Malaysia) away from (the speaker's) town or area.

outstay (ˌaʊtˈsteɪ) *vb.* (*tr.*) **1.** to stay longer than. **2.** to stay beyond (a limit). **3. outstay one's welcome.** See **overstay** (sense 4).

outstretch (ˌaʊtˈstrɛtʃ) *vb.* (*tr.*) **1.** to extend or expand; stretch out. **2.** to stretch or extend beyond.

outstrip (ˌaʊtˈstrɪp) *vb.* **-strips, -stripping, -stripped.** (*tr.*) **1.** to surpass in a sphere of activity, competition, etc. **2.** to be or grow greater than. **3.** to go faster than and leave behind.

outswing (ˈaʊtˌswɪŋ) *n. Cricket.* the movement of a bowled ball from leg to off through the air. Compare **inswing.** —**ˈoutˌswinger** *n.*

outtake (ˈaʊtˌteɪk) *n.* an unreleased take from a recording session, film, or television programme.

outthink (ˌaʊtˈθɪŋk) *vb.* **-thinks, -thinking, -thought.** (*tr.*) **1.** to outdo in thinking. **2.** to outwit.

out tray *n.* (in an office) a tray for outgoing correspondence, documents, etc.

outturn (ˈaʊtˌtɜːn) *n.* **1.** another word for **output** (sense 2). **2.** outcome; result.

outvote (ˌaʊtˈvəʊt) *vb.* (*tr.*) to defeat by a majority of votes.

outward (ˈaʊtwəd) *adj.* **1.** of or relating to what is apparent or superficial. **2.** of or relating to the outside of the body. **3.** belonging or relating to the external, as opposed to the mental, spiritual, or inherent. **4.** of, relating to, or directed towards the outside or exterior. **5.** (of a ship, part of a voyage, etc.) leaving for a particular destination. **6. the outward man. a.** the body as opposed to the soul. **b.** *Facetious.* clothing. ~*adv.* **7.** (of a ship) away from port. **8.** a variant of **outwards.** ~*n.* **9.** the outward part; exterior. —**ˈoutwardness** *n.*

outwardly (ˈaʊtwədlɪ) *adv.* **1.** in outward appearance: *outwardly she looked calm.* **2.** with reference to the outside or outer surface; externally.

ˌoutˈrace *vb.*
ˌoutˈrange *vb.*
ˌoutˈrival *vb.*, **-vals, -valling, -valled.**
ˌoutˈroot *vb.*
ˌoutˈsing *vb.*, **-ˈsings, -ˈsinging, -ˈsang, -ˈsung.**
ˌoutˈsit *vb.*, **-ˈsits, -ˈsitting, -ˈsat.**
ˌoutˈspeak *vb.*, **-ˈspeaks, -ˈspeaking, -ˈspoke, -ˈspoken.**
ˌoutˈsprint *vb.*
ˌoutˈstare *vb.*
ˌoutˈstep *vb.*
ˌoutˈtalk *vb.*
ˌoutˈvalue *vb.*
ˌoutˈwalk *vb.*

outwards ('aʊtwədz) *or* **outward** *adv.* towards the outside; out.

outwash ('aʊt,wɒʃ) *n.* a mass of gravel, sand, etc., carried and deposited by the water derived from melting glaciers.

outwear (,aʊt'wɛə) *vb.* **-wears, -wearing, -wore, -worn.** (*tr.*) **1.** to use up or destroy by wearing. **2.** to last or wear longer than. **3.** to outlive, outgrow, or develop beyond. **4.** to deplete or exhaust in strength, determination, etc.

outweigh (,aʊt'weɪ) *vb.* (*tr.*) **1.** to prevail over; overcome: *his desire outweighed his discretion.* **2.** to be more important or significant than. **3.** to be heavier than.

outwit (,aʊt'wɪt) *vb.* **-wits, -witting, -witted.** (*tr.*) **1.** to get the better of by cunning or ingenuity. **2.** *Archaic.* to be of greater intelligence than.

outwith (,aʊt'wɪθ) *prep. Scot.* outside; beyond.

outwork *n.* ('aʊt,wɜːk). **1.** (*often pl.*) defences which lie outside main defensive works. **2.** work performed away from the factory, office, etc., by which it has been commissioned. ~*vb.* (,aʊt'wɜːk), **-works, -working, -worked** *or* **-wrought.** (*tr.*) **3.** to work better, harder, etc., than. **4.** to work out to completion. —'**out,worker** *n.*

outworn ('aʊtwɔːn, ,aʊt'wɔːn) *adj.* no longer accepted, used, believed, etc.; obsolete or outmoded.

ouzel *or* **ousel** ('uːzᵊl) *n.* **1.** short for **ring ouzel** or **water ouzel** (see **dipper**). **2.** an archaic name for the (European) **blackbird.** [Old English *ōsle,* related to Old High German *amsala* (German *Amsel*), Latin *merula* MERLE[1]]

ouzo ('uːzəʊ) *n.* a strong aniseed-flavoured spirit from Greece. [Modern Greek *ouzon,* of obscure origin]

ova ('əʊvə) *n.* the plural of **ovum.**

oval ('əʊvᵊl) *adj.* **1.** having the shape of an ellipse or ellipsoid. ~*n.* **2.** anything that is oval in shape, such as a sports ground. [C16: from Medieval Latin *ōvālis,* from Latin *ōvum* egg] —'**oval-ly** *adv.* —'**ovalness** *or* **ovality** (əʊ'vælɪtɪ) *n.*

Oval Office *n.* the U.S. presidency. [from the name of the large oval private office of the U.S. president in the White House]

ovals of Cassini (kə'siːnɪ) *pl. n. Maths.* the locus of a point *x,* whose distance from two fixed points, *a* and *b,* is such that $|x-a|\,|x-b|$ is a constant. [C18: named after J. D. *Cassini* (1625–1712), Italian-French astronomer and mathematician]

Ovambo (əʊ'væmbəʊ, ɔː'vambɔː) *n.* **1.** (*pl.* **-bo** *or* **-bos**) a member of a mixed Hottentot and Negroid people of southern Africa, living chiefly in N Namibia: noted for their skill in metal work. **2.** the language of this people, belonging to the Bantu group of the Niger-Congo family.

ovariectomy (əʊ,vɛərɪ'ɛktəmɪ) *n., pl.* **-mies.** *Surgery.* another name for **oophorectomy.**

ovariotomy (əʊ,vɛərɪ'ɒtəmɪ) *n., pl.* **-mies.** surgical incision into an ovary. Compare **oophorectomy.**

ovaritis (,əʊvə'raɪtɪs) *n.* inflammation of an ovary; oophoritis.

ovary ('əʊvərɪ) *n., pl.* **-ries.** **1.** either of the two female reproductive organs, which produce ova and secrete oestrogen hormones. **2.** the corresponding organ in vertebrate and invertebrate animals. **3.** *Botany.* the hollow basal region of a carpel containing one or more ovules. In some plants the carpels are united to form a single compound ovary. [C17: from New Latin *ōvārium,* from Latin *ōvum* egg] —**ovarian** (əʊ'vɛərɪən) *adj.*

ovate ('əʊveɪt) *adj.* **1.** shaped like an egg. **2.** (esp. of a leaf) shaped like the longitudinal section of an egg, with the broader end at the base. Compare **obovate.** [C18: from Latin *ōvātus* egg-shaped; see OVUM] —'**ovately** *adv.*

ovation (əʊ'veɪʃən) *n.* **1.** an enthusiastic reception, esp. one of prolonged applause: *a standing ovation.* **2.** a victory procession less glorious than a triumph awarded to a Roman general. [C16: from Latin *ovātiō* rejoicing, from *ovāre* to exult] —**o'vational** *adj.*

ovel ('ɒvəl) *n. Judaism.* a mourner, esp. during the first seven days after a death. See also **shivah.** [from Hebrew]

oven ('ʌvᵊn) *n.* **1.** an enclosed heated compartment or receptacle for baking or roasting food. **2.** a similar device, usually lined with a refractory material, used for drying substances, firing ceramics, heat-treating, etc. [Old English *ofen;* related to Old High German *ofan,* Old Norse *ofn*] —'**oven-,like** *adj.*

ovenbird ('ʌvᵊn,bɜːd) *n.* **1.** any of numerous small brownish South American passerine birds of the family *Furnariidae* that build oven-shaped clay nests. **2.** a common North American warbler, *Seiurus aurocapillus,* that has an olive-brown striped plumage with an orange crown and builds a cup-shaped nest on the ground.

oven-ready *adj.* (of various foods) bought already prepared so that they are ready to be cooked in the oven.

ovenware ('ʌvᵊn,wɛə) *n.* heat-resistant dishes in which food can be both cooked and served.

over ('əʊvə) *prep.* **1.** directly above; on the top of; via the top or upper surface of: *over one's head.* **2.** on or to the other side of: *over the river.* **3.** during; through, or throughout (a period of time). **4.** in or throughout all parts of: *to travel over England.* **5.** throughout the whole extent of: *over the racecourse.* **6.** above; in preference to: *I like that over everything else.* **7.** by the agency of (an instrument of telecommunication): *we heard it over the radio.* **8.** more than: *over a century ago.* **9.** on the subject of; about: *an argument over nothing.* **10.** while occupied in: *discussing business over golf.* **11.** having recovered from the effects of: *she's not over that last love affair yet.* **12. over and above.** added to; in addition to: *he earns a large amount over and above his salary.* ~*adv.* **13.** in a state, condition, situation, or position that is or has been placed or put over something: *to climb over.* **14.** (*particle*) so as to cause to fall: *knocking over a policeman.* **15.** at or to a point across intervening space, water, etc.: *come over and see us; over in America.* **16.** throughout a whole area: *the world over.* **17.** (*particle*) from beginning to end, usually cursorily: *to read a document over.* **18.** throughout a period of time: *stay over for this week.* **19.** (esp. in signalling and radio) it is now your turn to speak, act, etc. **20.** more than is expected or usual: *not over well.* **21. over again.** once more. **22. over against. a.** opposite to. **b.** contrasting with. **23. over and over.** (often foll. by *again*) repeatedly. **24. over the odds. a.** in addition, esp. when not expected. **b.** unfair or excessive. ~*adj.* **25.** (*postpositive*) finished; no longer in progress: *is the concert over yet?* ~*adv., adj.* **26.** remaining; surplus (often in the phrase **left over).** ~*n.* **27.** *Cricket.* **a.** a series of six balls bowled by a bowler from the same end of the pitch. **b.** the play during this. [Old English *ofer;* related to Old High German *ubir, obar,* Old Norse *yfir,* Latin *super,* Greek *huper*]

over- *prefix.* **1.** excessive or excessively; beyond an agreed or desirable limit: *overcharge; overdue; oversimplify.* **2.** indicating superior rank: *overseer.* **3.** indicating location or movement above: *overhang.* **4.** indicating movement downwards: *overthrow.*

overachieve (,əʊvərə'tʃiːv) *vb.* (*intr.*) to perform (for example, in an examination) better than would be expected on the basis of one's age or talents. —,**overa'chiever** *n.*

overact (,əʊvər'ækt) *vb.* to act or behave in an exaggerated manner, as in a theatrical production. Also: **overplay.**

overage (,əʊvər'eɪdʒ) *adj.* beyond a specified age.

overall *adj.* ('əʊvər,ɔːl) (*prenominal*) **1.** from one end to the other. **2.** including or covering everything: *the overall cost.* ~*adv.* (,əʊvər'ɔːl). **3.** in general; on the whole. ~*n.* ('əʊvər,ɔːl). **4.** *Brit.* a protective work garment usually worn over ordinary clothes. **5.** (*pl.*) hard-wearing work trousers with a bib and shoulder straps or jacket attached.

overarch (,əʊvər'ɑːtʃ) *vb.* (*tr.*) to form an arch over.

overarm ('əʊvər,ɑːm) *adj.* **1.** *Sport, esp. cricket.* bowled, thrown, or performed with the arm raised above the shoulder. ~*adv.* **2.** with the arm raised above the shoulder.

overawe (,əʊvər'ɔː) *vb.* (*tr.*) to subdue, restrain, or overcome by affecting with a feeling of awe.

overbalance *vb.* (,əʊvə'bæləns). **1.** to lose or cause to lose balance. **2.** (*tr.*) another word for **outweigh.** ~*n.* ('əʊvə,bæləns). **3.** excess of weight, value, etc.

overbear (,əʊvə'bɛə) *vb.* **-bears, -bearing, -bore, -borne.** **1.** (*tr.*) to dominate or overcome: *to overbear objections.* **2.** (*tr.*) to press or bear down with weight or physical force. **3.** to produce or bear (fruit, progeny, etc.) excessively.

overbearing (,əʊvə'bɛərɪŋ) *adj.* **1.** domineering or dictatorial in manner or action. **2.** of particular or overriding importance or significance. —,**over'bearingly** *adv.*

overbid *vb.* (,əʊvə'bɪd), **-bids, -bidding, -bid, -bidden** *or* **-bid.** **1.** (*intr.*) *Bridge.* to bid for more tricks than one can expect to win. **2.** to bid more than the value of (something). ~*n.* ('əʊvə,bɪd). **3.** a bid higher than someone else's bid.

overbite ('əʊvə,baɪt) *n. Dentistry.* an extension of the upper front teeth over the lower front teeth when the mouth is closed. Also called: **vertical overlap.**

overblouse ('əʊvə,blaʊz) *n.* a blouse designed to be worn not tucked into trousers or a skirt but to fit loosely over the waist or hips.

overblow (,əʊvə'bləʊ) *vb.* **-blows, -blowing, -blew, -blown.** **1.** *Music.* to blow into (a wind instrument) with greater force than normal in order to obtain the octave above the fundamental in the harmonic series. **2.** to blow (a wind instrument) or (of a wind

,**overa'bound** *vb.*
,**overa'bundance** *n.*
,**overac'centu,ate** *vb.*
,**overac,cumu'lation** *n.*
,**over'active** *adj.*
,**overa'dorned** *adj.*
,**overad'vance** *vb.*
,**overaf'fect** *vb.*
,**overag'gressive** *adj.*
,**overam'bitious** *adj.*
,**overam'bitiously** *adv.*
,**overam'bitiousness** *n.*
,**over'ana,lyse** *vb.*
,**over'angry** *adj.*
,**over'ani,mated** *adj.*
,**over'ani,matedly** *adv.*
,**over,ani'mation** *n.*
,**over'anxious** *adj.*
,**overap,preci'ation** *n.*
,**overap'preciative** *adj.*
,**over,appre'hensive** *adj.*
,**over,appre'hensively** *adv.*
,**over,appre'hensiveness** *n.*
,**over,argu'mentative** *adj.*
,**overas'sert** *vb.*
,**overas'sertion** *n.*
,**overas'sertive** *adj.*
,**overas'sertively** *adv.*
,**overas'sertiveness** *n.*
,**overas'sessment** *n.*
,**overas'sured** *adj.*
,**overat'tached** *adj.*
,**overat'tentive** *adj.*
,**overat'tentively** *adv.*
,**overat'tentiveness** *n.*

instrument) to be blown too hard. 3. to blow over, away, or across.

overblown (ˌəʊvəˈbləʊn) *adj.* 1. overdone or excessive. 2. bombastic; turgid: *overblown prose.* 3. (of flowers, such as the rose) past the stage of full bloom.

overboard (ˈəʊvəˌbɔːd) *adv.* 1. from on board a vessel into the water. 2. **go overboard.** *Informal.* a. to be extremely enthusiastic. b. to go to extremes. 3. **throw overboard.** to reject or abandon.

overboot (ˈəʊvəˌbuːt) *n.* a protective boot worn over an ordinary boot or shoe.

overbuild (ˌəʊvəˈbɪld) *vb.* **-builds, -building, -built.** (*tr.*) 1. to build over or on top of. 2. to erect too many buildings in (an area). 3. to build too large or elaborately.

overburden *vb.* (ˌəʊvəˈbɜːdᵊn). 1. (*tr.*) to load with excessive weight, work, etc. ~*n.* (ˈəʊvəˌbɜːdᵊn). 2. an excessive burden or load. 3. *Geology.* the sedimentary rock material that covers coal seams, mineral veins, etc. —ˌ**overˈburdensome** *adj.*

overcall *Bridge.* ~*n.* (ˈəʊvəˌkɔːl). 1. a bid higher than the preceding one. ~*vb.* (ˌəʊvəˈkɔːl). 2. to bid higher than (an opponent).

overcapitalize *or* **overcapitalise** (ˌəʊvəˈkæpɪtəˌlaɪz) *vb.* (*tr.*) 1. to provide or issue capital for (an enterprise) in excess of profitable investment opportunities. 2. to estimate the capital value of (a company) at an unreasonably or unlawfully high level. 3. to overestimate the market value of (property). —ˌ**overˌcapitaliˈzation** *or* ˌ**overˌcapitaliˈsation** *n.*

overcast *adj.* (ˈəʊvəˌkɑːst). 1. covered over or obscured, esp. by clouds. 2. *Meteorol.* (of the sky) more than 95 per cent cloud-covered. 3. gloomy or melancholy. 4. sewn over by overcasting. ~*vb.* (ˌəʊvəˈkɑːst). 5. to make or become overclouded or gloomy. 6. to sew (an edge, as of a hem) with long stitches passing successively over the edge. ~*n.* (ˈəʊvəˌkɑːst). 7. a covering, as of clouds or mist. 8. *Meteorol.* the state of the sky when more than 95 per cent of it is cloud-covered. 9. *Mining.* a crossing of two passages without an intersection.

overcharge *vb.* (ˌəʊvəˈtʃɑːdʒ). 1. to charge too much. 2. (*tr.*) to fill or load beyond capacity. 3. *Literary.* another word for **exaggerate.** ~*n.* (ˈəʊvəˌtʃɑːdʒ). 4. an excessive price or charge. 5. an excessive load.

overcheck (ˈəʊvəˌtʃɛk) *n.* 1. a thin leather strap attached to a horse's bit to keep its head up. 2. (in textiles) a. a checked pattern laid over another checked pattern. b. a fabric patterned in such a way.

overcloud (ˌəʊvəˈklaʊd) *vb.* 1. to make or become covered with clouds. 2. to make or become dark or dim.

overcoat (ˈəʊvəˌkəʊt) *n.* a warm heavy coat worn over the outer clothes in cold weather.

overcome (ˌəʊvəˈkʌm) *vb.* **-comes, -coming, -came, -come.** 1. (*tr.*) to get the better of in a conflict. 2. (*tr.; often passive*) to render incapable or powerless by laughter, sorrow, exhaustion, etc.: *he was overcome by fumes.* 3. (*tr.*) to surmount (obstacles, objections, etc.). 4. (*intr.*) to be victorious.

overcommit (ˌəʊvəkəˈmɪt) *vb.* **-mits, -mitting, -mitted.** (*tr.*) to promise, undertake, or allocate more than the available resources justify.

overcompensate (ˌəʊvəˈkɒmpɛnˌseɪt) *vb.* 1. to compensate (a person or thing) excessively. 2. (*intr.*) *Psychol.* to engage in overcompensation. —ˌ**overˈcompenˌsatory** *adj.*

overcompensation (ˌəʊvəˌkɒmpɛnˈseɪʃən) *n. Psychol.* an attempt to make up for a character trait by overexaggerating its opposite.

overcrop (ˌəʊvəˈkrɒp) *vb.* **-crops, -cropping, -cropped.** (*tr.*) to exhaust (land) by excessive cultivation.

overdevelop (ˌəʊvədɪˈvɛləp) *vb.* (*tr.*) 1. to develop too much or too far. 2. *Photog.* to process (a film, plate, or print) in developer for more than the required time, at too great a concentration, etc. —ˌ**overdeˈvelopment** *n.*

overdeviate (ˌəʊvəˈdiːvɪˌeɪt) *vb.* to cause (a frequency-modulated radio transmitter) to exceed its specified frequency excursion from the rest frequency.

overdo (ˌəʊvəˈduː) *vb.* **-does, -doing, -did, -done.** (*tr.*) 1. to take or carry too far; do to excess. 2. to exaggerate, overelaborate, or overplay. 3. to cook or bake too long. 4. **overdo it** *or* **things.** to overtax one's strength, capacity, etc.

overdose *n.* (ˈəʊvəˌdəʊs). 1. (esp. of drugs) an excessive dose. ~*vb.* (ˌəʊvəˈdəʊs). 2. to take an excessive dose or give an excessive dose to. —ˌ**overˈdosage** *n.*

overdraft (ˈəʊvəˌdrɑːft) *n.* 1. a draft or withdrawal of money in excess of the credit balance on a bank or building-society cheque account. 2. the amount of money drawn or withdrawn thus.

overdraught (ˈəʊvəˌdrɑːft) *n.* a current of air passed above a fire, as in a furnace.

overdraw (ˌəʊvəˈdrɔː) *vb.* **-draws, -drawing, -drew, -drawn.** 1. to draw on (a bank account) in excess of the credit balance. 2. (*tr.*) to strain or pull (a bow) too far. 3. (*tr.*) to exaggerate in describing or telling.

overdress *vb.* (ˌəʊvəˈdrɛs). 1. to dress (oneself or another) too elaborately or finely. ~*n.* (ˈəʊvəˌdrɛs). 2. a dress that may be worn over a jumper, blouse, etc.

overdrive *n.* (ˈəʊvəˌdraɪv). 1. a very high gear in a motor vehicle used at high speeds to reduce wear and save fuel. ~*vb.* (ˌəʊvəˈdraɪv), **-drives, -driving, -drove, -driven.** 2. (*tr.*) to drive too hard or too far; overwork or overuse.

overdub (in multitrack recording) ~*vb.* (ˌəʊvəˈdʌb), **-dubs, -dubbing, -dubbed.** 1. to add (new sound) on a spare track or tracks. ~*n.* (ˈəʊvəˌdʌb). 2 the addition of new sound to a recording; the blending of various layers of sound in one recording.

overdue (ˌəʊvəˈdjuː) *adj.* past the time specified, required, or preferred for arrival, occurrence, payment, etc.

overdye (ˌəʊvəˈdaɪ) *vb.* (*tr.*) 1. to dye (a fabric, yarn, etc.) excessively. 2. to dye for a second or third time with a different colour.

overestimate *vb.* (ˌəʊvərˈɛstɪˌmeɪt). 1. (*tr.*) to value or estimate too highly. ~*n.* (ˌəʊvərˈɛstɪmɪt). 2. an estimate that is too high. —ˌ**overˌestiˈmation** *n.*

overexpose (ˌəʊvərɪksˈpəʊz) *vb.* (*tr.*) 1. to expose too much or for too long. 2. *Photog.* to expose (a film, plate, or paper) for too long a period or with too bright a light. —ˌ**overexˈposure** *n.*

overfall (ˈəʊvəˌfɔːl) *n.* 1. a turbulent stretch of water caused by marine currents over an underwater ridge. 2. a mechanism that allows excess water to escape from a dam or lock.

overflight (ˈəʊvəˌflaɪt) *n.* the flight of an aircraft over a specific area or territory.

overflow *vb.* (ˌəʊvəˈfləʊ), **-flows, -flowing, -flowed, -flown.** 1. to flow or run over (a limit, brim, bank, etc.). 2. to fill or be filled beyond capacity so as to spill or run over. 3. (*intr.; usually foll. by with*) to be filled with happiness, tears, etc. 4. (*tr.*) to spread or cover over; flood or inundate. ~*n.* (ˈəʊvəˌfləʊ). 5. overflowing matter, esp. liquid. 6. any outlet that enables surplus liquid to be discharged or drained off, esp. one just below the top of a tank or cistern. 7. the amount by which a limit, capacity, etc., is exceeded. 8. *Computer technol.* a condition that occurs when numeric operations produce results too large to store in the register available.

overfly (ˌəʊvəˈflaɪ) *vb.* **-flies, -flying, -flew, -flown.** (*tr.*) to fly over (a territory) or past (a point).

ˌ**overˈbold** *adj.*
ˌ**overˈbook** *vb.*
ˌ**overˈbrave** *adj.*
ˌ**overˈbulky** *adj.*
ˌ**overˈbusy** *adj.*
ˌ**overˈbuy** *vb.*, **-ˈbuys, -ˈbuying, -ˈbought.**
ˌ**overcaˈpacity** *n.*
ˌ**overˈcareful** *adj.*
ˌ**overˈcasual** *adj.*
ˌ**overˈcautious** *adj.*
ˌ**overˌcentraliˈzation** *or* ˌ**overˌcentraliˈsation** *n.*
ˌ**overˈcerebral** *adj.*
ˌ**overˈcivil** *adj.*
ˌ**overˈciviˌlize** *or* ˌ**overˈciviˌlise** *vb.*
ˌ**overˈcommon** *adj.*
ˌ**overcomˈpetitive** *adj.*
ˌ**overcomˈplacency** *n.*
ˌ**overcomˈplacent** *adj.*
ˌ**overˈcomplex** *adj.*
ˌ**overˈcompliˌcate** *vb.*
ˌ**overconˈcern** *n.*
ˌ**overˈconfidence** *n.*
ˌ**overˈconfident** *adj.*
ˌ**overˌconsciˈentious** *adj.*
ˌ**overconˈservative** *adj.*
ˌ**overconˈsiderate** *adj.*
ˌ**overconˈsume** *vb.*
ˌ**overconˈsumption** *n.*
ˌ**overˈcook** *vb.*
ˌ**overˈcool** *vb.*, *adj.*
ˌ**overcorˈrect** *adj.*, *vb.*
ˌ**overcorˈrection** *n.*
ˌ**overˈcostly** *adj.*
ˌ**overˈcritical** *adj.*
ˌ**overˈcritiˌcize** *or* ˌ**overˈcritiˌcise** *vb.*
ˌ**overˈcrowd** *vb.*
ˌ**overˈcultiˌvate** *vb.*
ˌ**overˈcurious** *adj.*
ˌ**overˈdecoˌrate** *vb.*
ˌ**overdeˈfensive** *adj.*
ˌ**overˌdeferˈential** *adj.*
ˌ**overdeˈliberate** *adj.*
ˌ**overˈdelicate** *adj.*
ˌ**overdeˈpendence** *n.*
ˌ**overdeˈpendent** *adj.*
ˌ**overdeˈsirous** *adj.*
ˌ**overˈdetailed** *adj.*
ˌ**overˈdiligent** *adj.*
ˌ**overˈdiligently** *adv.*
ˌ**overdiˈlute** *vb.*
ˌ**overˈdistant** *adj.*
ˌ**overdiˌversifiˈcation** *n.*
ˌ**overdiˈversiˌfy** *vb.*, **-ˌfies, -ˌfying, -ˌfied.**
ˌ**overdiˈversity** *n.*
ˌ**overdraˈmatic** *adj.*
ˌ**overˈdramaˌtize** *or* ˌ**overˈdramaˌtise** *vb.*
ˌ**overˈdrink** *vb.*, **-ˈdrinks, -ˈdrinking, -ˈdrank, -ˈdrunk.**
ˌ**overˈeager** *adj.*
ˌ**overˈearnest** *adj.*
ˌ**overˈeat** *vb.*, **-ˈeats, -ˈeating, -ˈate, -ˈeaten.**
ˌ**overˈeduˌcate** *vb.*
ˌ**overefˈfusive** *adj.*
ˌ**overeˈlaborate** *adj.*, *vb.*
ˌ**overeˌlaboˈration** *n.*
ˌ**overeˈlate** *vb.*
ˌ**overemˈbellish** *vb.*
ˌ**overemˈbroider** *vb.*
ˌ**overeˈmotional** *adj.*
ˌ**overˈemphasis** *n.*
ˌ**overˈemphaˌsize** *or* ˌ**overˈemphaˌsise** *vb.*
ˌ**overemˈphatic** *adj.*
ˌ**overˌemuˈlation** *n.*
ˌ**overenˈthusiˌasm** *n.*
ˌ**overenˌthusiˈastic** *adj.*
ˌ**overexˈacting** *adj.*
ˌ**overexˈcitable** *adj.*
ˌ**overexˈcitably** *adv.*
ˌ**overexˈcite** *vb.*
ˌ**overˈexerˌcise** *vb.*
ˌ**overexˈert** *vb.*
ˌ**overexˈpand** *vb.*
ˌ**overexˈpansion** *n.*
ˌ**overexˈpectant** *adj.*
ˌ**overexˈpenditure** *n.*
ˌ**overexˈplicit** *adj.*
ˌ**overexˈpressive** *adj.*
ˌ**overexˈtend** *vb.*
ˌ**overˈfacile** *adj.*
ˌ**overfaˈmiliar** *adj.*
ˌ**overfaˌmiliˈarity** *n.*
ˌ**overˈfanciful** *adj.*
ˌ**overˈfar** *adj.*, *adv.*
ˌ**overfasˈtidious** *adj.*
ˌ**overˈfearful** *adj.*
ˌ**overˈfeed** *vb.*, **-ˈfeeds, -ˈfeeding, -ˈfed.**
ˌ**overˈfill** *vb.*
ˌ**overˈfish** *vb.*

overfold ('əʊvəˌfəʊld) *n. Geology.* a fold in the form of an anticline in which one limb is more steeply inclined than the other.
overfunding ('əʊvəˌfʌndɪŋ) *n.* (in Britain) a government policy in which it sells more of its securities than would be required to finance public spending, with the object of absorbing surplus funds to curb inflation.
overgarment ('əʊvəˌgɑːmənt) *n.* any garment worn over other clothes, esp. to protect them from wear or dirt.
overglaze ('əʊvəˌgleɪz) *adj.* (of decoration or colours) applied to porcelain or pottery above the glaze.
overgraze (ˌəʊvə'greɪz) *vb.* (*tr.*) to graze (land) beyond its capacity to sustain stock.
overground ('əʊvəˌgraʊnd) *adj.* on or above the surface of the ground: *an overground railway.*
overgrow (ˌəʊvə'grəʊ) *vb.* **-grows, -growing, -grew, -grown. 1.** (*tr.*) to grow over or across (an area, path, etc.). **2.** (*tr.*) to choke or supplant by a stronger growth. **3.** (*tr.*) to grow too large for. **4.** (*intr.*) to grow beyond normal size. —'**overˌgrowth** *n.*
overhand ('əʊvəˌhænd) *adj.* **1.** thrown or performed with the hand raised above the shoulder. **2.** sewn with thread passing over two edges in one direction. ~*adv.* **3.** with the hand above the shoulder; overarm. **4.** with shallow stitches passing over two edges. ~*vb.* **5.** to sew (two edges) overhand.
overhand knot *n.* a knot formed by making a loop in a piece of cord and drawing one end through it. Also called: **thumb knot.**
overhang *vb.* (ˌəʊvə'hæŋ), **-hangs, -hanging, -hung. 1.** to project or extend beyond (a surface, building, etc.). **2.** (*tr.*) to hang or be suspended over. **3.** (*tr.*) to menace, threaten, or dominate. ~*n.* ('əʊvəˌhæŋ). **4.** a formation, object, part of a structure, etc., that extends beyond or hangs over something, such as an outcrop of rock overhanging a mountain face. **5.** the amount or extent of projection. **6.** *Aeronautics.* **a.** half the difference in span of the main supporting surfaces of a biplane or other multiplane. **b.** the distance from the outer supporting strut of a wing to the wing tip.
overhaul *vb.* (ˌəʊvə'hɔːl). (*tr.*) **1.** to examine carefully for faults, necessary repairs, etc. **2.** to make repairs or adjustments to (a car, machine, etc.). **3.** to overtake. ~*n.* ('əʊvəˌhɔːl). **4.** a thorough examination and repair.
overhead *adj.* ('əʊvəˌhɛd). **1.** situated or operating above head height or some other reference level. **2.** (*prenominal*) inclusive: *the overhead price included meals.* ~*adv.* (ˌəʊvə'hɛd). **3.** over or above head height, esp. in the sky. ~*n.* ('əʊvəˌhɛd). **4. a.** a stroke in racket games played from above head height. **b.** (*as modifier*): *an overhead smash.* **5.** *Nautical.* the interior lining above one's head below decks in a vessel. **6.** short for **overhead door. 7.** (*modifier*) of, concerned with, or resulting from overheads: *overhead costs.* ~See also **overheads.**
overhead camshaft *n.* a type of camshaft situated above the cylinder head in an internal-combustion engine. It is usually driven by a chain or a toothed belt from the crankshaft and the cams bear directly onto the valve stems or rocker arms.
overhead door *n.* a door that rotates on a horizontal axis and is supported horizontally when open. Sometimes shortened to **overhead.**
overhead projector *n.* a projector that throws an enlarged image of a transparency onto a surface above and behind the person using it. Alterations and additions can be made to the material on the transparency while the projector is in use.
overheads ('əʊvəˌhɛdz) *pl. n.* business expenses, such as rent, that are not directly attributable to any department or product and can therefore be assigned only arbitrarily. Also called: **burden, fixed costs, indirect costs, oncost.** Compare **prime cost.**
overhead-valve engine *n.* a type of internal-combustion engine in which the inlet and exhaust valves are in the cylinder head above the pistons. U.S. name: **valve-in-head engine.** Compare **side-valve engine.**
overhear (ˌəʊvə'hɪə) *vb.* **-hears, -hearing, -heard.** (*tr.*) to hear (a person, remark, etc.) without the knowledge of the speaker.
overheat (ˌəʊvə'hiːt) *vb.* **1.** to make or become excessively hot. **2.** (*tr.; often passive*) to make very agitated, irritated, etc. **3.** (*intr.*) (of an economy) to tend towards inflation, often as a result of excessive growth in demand. **4.** (*tr.*) to cause (an economy) to tend towards inflation. ~*n.* **5.** the condition of being overheated.
overindulge (ˌəʊvərɪn'dʌldʒ) *vb.* **1.** to indulge (in something, esp. food or drink) immoderately. **2.** (*tr.*) to yield excessively to the wishes of; spoil. —ˌ**overin'dulgence** *n.* —ˌ**overin'dulgent** *adj.*
overissue ('əʊvərˌɪsjuː, -ˌɪʃuː) *vb.* **-sues, -suing, -sued.** (*tr.*) **1.** to issue (shares, banknotes, etc.) in excess of demand or ability to pay. ~*n.* **2.** shares, banknotes, etc., thus issued.
overjoy (ˌəʊvə'dʒɔɪ) *vb.* (*tr.*) to give great delight to. —ˌ**over'joyed** *adj.*
overkill ('əʊvəˌkɪl) *n.* **1.** the capability to deploy more weapons, esp. nuclear weapons, than is necessary to ensure military advantage. **2.** any capacity or treatment that is greater than that required or appropriate.
overland ('əʊvəˌlænd) *adj.* (*prenominal*), *adv.* **1.** over or across land. ~*vb.* **2.** *Austral.* to drive (cattle or sheep) overland. —'**overˌlander** *n.*
overlap *vb.* (ˌəʊvə'læp), **-laps, -lapping, -lapped. 1.** (of two things) to extend or lie partly over (each other). **2.** to cover and extend beyond (something). **3.** (*intr.*) to coincide partly in time, subject, etc. ~*n.* ('əʊvəˌlæp). **4.** a part that overlaps or is overlapped. **5.** the amount, length, etc., overlapping. **6.** the act or fact of overlapping. **7.** a place of overlapping. **8.** *Geology.* the horizontal extension of the lower beds in a series of rock strata beyond the upper beds, usually caused by submergence of the land.
overlay *vb.* (ˌəʊvə'leɪ), **-lays, -laying, -laid.** (*tr.*) **1.** to lay or place something over or upon (something else). **2.** (often foll. by *with*) to cover, overspread, or conceal (with). **3.** (foll. by *with*) to cover (a surface) with an applied decoration: *ebony overlaid with silver.* **4.** to achieve the correct printing pressure all over (a forme or plate) by adding to the appropriate areas of the packing. ~*n.* ('əʊvəˌleɪ). **5.** something that is laid over something else; covering. **6.** an applied decoration or layer, as of gold leaf. **7.** a transparent sheet giving extra details to a map or diagram over which it is designed to be placed. **8.** *Printing.* material, such as paper, used to overlay a forme or plate.
overleaf (ˌəʊvə'liːf) *adv.* on the other side of the page. Also: ˌ**over'page.**
overlie (ˌəʊvə'laɪ) *vb.* **-lies, -lying, -lay, -lain.** (*tr.*) **1.** to lie or rest upon. Compare **overlay. 2.** to kill (a baby or newborn animal) by lying upon it.
overlive (ˌəʊvə'lɪv) *vb.* **1.** to live longer than (another person). **2.** to survive or outlive (an event).
overload *vb.* (ˌəʊvə'ləʊd). **1.** (*tr.*) to put too large a load on or in. ~*n.* ('əʊvəˌləʊd). **2.** an excessive load.
overlong (ˌəʊvə'lɒŋ) *adj., adv.* too or excessively long.
overlook *vb.* (ˌəʊvə'lʊk). (*tr.*) **1.** to fail to notice or take into account. **2.** to disregard deliberately or indulgently. **3.** to look at or over from above: *the garden is overlooked by the prison.* **4.** to afford a view of from above: *the house overlooks the bay.* **5.** to rise above. **6.** to look after. **7.** to look at carefully. **8.** to bewitch or cast the evil eye upon (someone). ~*n.* ('əʊvəˌlʊk). *U.S.* **9.** a high place affording a view. **10.** an act of overlooking.
overlooker ('əʊvəˌlʊkə) *n.* another word (less common) for **overseer** (sense 1).
overlord ('əʊvəˌlɔːd) *n.* a supreme lord or master. —'**overˌlordship** *n.*
overly ('əʊvəlɪ) *adv.* too; excessively.
overman *vb.* (ˌəʊvə'mæn), **-mans, -manning, -manned. 1.** (*tr.*) to supply with an excessive number of men. ~*n.* ('əʊvəˌmæn), *pl.* **-men. 2.** a man who oversees others. **3.** the Nietzschean superman.
overmantel ('əʊvəˌmæntᵊl) *n.* a shelf over a mantelpiece.
overmaster (ˌəʊvə'mɑːstə) *vb.* (*tr.*) to overpower.
overmatch *Chiefly U.S.* ~*vb.* (ˌəʊvə'mætʃ). (*tr.*) **1.** to be more than a match for. **2.** to match with a superior opponent. ~*n.* ('əʊvəˌmætʃ). **3.** a person superior in ability. **4.** a match in which one contestant is superior.
overmatter ('əʊvəˌmætə) *n. Printing.* type that has been set but cannot be used for printing owing to lack of space. Also called: **overset.**
overmuch (ˌəʊvə'mʌtʃ) *adv., adj.* **1.** too much; very much. ~*n.* **2.** an excessive amount.
overnice (ˌəʊvə'naɪs) *adj.* too fastidious, precise, etc.
overnight *adv.* (ˌəʊvə'naɪt). **1.** for the duration of the night: *we stopped overnight.* **2.** in or as if in the course of one night; suddenly: *the situation changed overnight.* ~*adj.* ('əʊvəˌnaɪt). (*usually prenominal*) **3.** done in, occurring in, or lasting the night: *an overnight stop.* **4.** staying for one night: *overnight guests.* **5.** lasting one night: *an overnight trip; an overnight bank*

ˌ**over'fond** *adj.*
ˌ**over'fragile** *adj.*
ˌ**over'full** *adj.*
ˌ**over'furnish** *vb.*
ˌ**overˌgenerali'zation** *or* ˌ**overˌgenerali'sation** *n.*
ˌ**over'generalˌize** *or* ˌ**over'generalˌise** *vb.*
ˌ**over'generous** *adj.*
ˌ**over'hastily** *adv.*
ˌ**over'hastiness** *n.*
ˌ**over'hasty** *adj.*
ˌ**over'hurried** *adj.*
ˌ**overiˌdeal'istic** *adj.*
ˌ**overi'dealˌize** *or* ˌ**overi'dealˌise** *vb.*
ˌ**overim'aginative** *adj.*
ˌ**overim'press** *vb.*
ˌ**overim'pressionable** *adj.*
ˌ**overin'cline** *vb.*
ˌ**overin'dustrialˌize** *or* ˌ**overin'dustrialˌise** *vb.*
ˌ**overin'flate** *vb.*
ˌ**over'influence** *vb.*
ˌ**overˌinflu'ential** *adj.*
ˌ**overin'sistence** *n.*
ˌ**overin'sistent** *adj.*
ˌ**overin'sistently** *adv.*
ˌ**overin'sure** *vb.*
ˌ**overˌintel'lectual** *adj.*
ˌ**overˌintel'lectually** *adv.*
ˌ**overin'tense** *adj.*
ˌ**overin'tensely** *adv.*
ˌ**over'interest** *n.*
ˌ**overin'vest** *vb.*
ˌ**over'laden** *adj.*
ˌ**over'large** *adj.*
ˌ**over'lavish** *adj.*
ˌ**over'leap** *vb.*, **-'leaps, -'leaping; -'leapt** *or* **-'leaped.**
ˌ**over'magniˌfy** *vb.*, **-ˌfies, -ˌfying, -ˌfied.**
ˌ**over'manage** *vb.*
ˌ**over'many** *adj.*
ˌ**over'measure** *n.*
ˌ**over'modest** *adj.*
ˌ**over'modestly** *adv.*
ˌ**over'modiˌfy** *vb.*, **-ˌfies, -ˌfying, -ˌfied.**

loan. **6.** for use during a single night: *overnight clothes.* **7.** occurring in or as if in the course of one night; sudden: *an overnight victory.* ~*vb.* (*intr.*) **8.** to stay the night.

overpage (ˌəʊvəˈpeɪdʒ) *adv.* another word for **overleaf.**

overpass *n.* (ˈəʊvəˌpɑːs). **1.** another name for **flyover** (sense 1). ~*vb.* (ˌəʊvəˈpɑːs), **-passes, -passing, -passed, -past.** (*tr.*) *Now rare.* **2.** to pass over, through, or across. **3.** to exceed. **4.** to get over. **5.** to ignore.

overpay (ˌəʊvəˈpeɪ) *vb.* **-pays, -paying, -paid. 1.** to pay (someone) at too high a rate. **2.** to pay (someone) more than is due, as by an error.

overpersuade (ˌəʊvəpəˈsweɪd) *vb.* (*tr.*) to persuade (someone) against his inclination or judgment.

overpitch (ˌəʊvəˈpɪtʃ) *vb. Cricket.* to bowl (a ball) so that it pitches too close to the stumps.

overplay (ˌəʊvəˈpleɪ) *vb.* **1.** (*tr.*) to exaggerate the importance of. **2.** another word for **overact. 3. overplay one's hand.** to overestimate the worth or strength of one's position.

overplus (ˈəʊvəˌplʌs) *n.* surplus or excess quantity.

overpower (ˌəʊvəˈpaʊə) *vb.* (*tr.*) **1.** to conquer or subdue by superior force. **2.** to have such a strong effect on as to make helpless or ineffective. **3.** to supply with more power than necessary.

overpowering (ˌəʊvəˈpaʊərɪŋ) *adj.* **1.** so strong or intense as to be unbearable. **2.** so powerful as to crush or conquer. —ˌ**over**ˈ**poweringly** *adv.*

overpressure (ˈəʊvəˌprɛʃə) *n.* the blast effect of a nuclear weapon expressed as an amount of pressure greater than normal barometric pressure.

overprint *vb.* (ˌəʊvəˈprɪnt). **1.** (*tr.*) to print (additional matter or another colour) on a sheet of paper. ~*n.* (ˈəʊvəˌprɪnt). **2.** additional matter or another colour printed onto a previously printed sheet. **3.** additional matter, other than a change in face value, applied to a finished postage stamp by printing, stamping, etc. See also **surcharge** (sense 5), **provisional** (sense 2).

overprotect (ˌəʊvəprəˈtɛkt) *vb.* (*tr.*) to protect more than necessary, esp. to shield a child excessively so as to inhibit its development. —ˌ**overpro**ˈ**tective** *adj.*

overqualified (ˌəʊvəˈkwɒlɪˌfaɪd) *adj.* having more managerial experience or academic qualifications than required for a particular job.

overrate (ˌəʊvəˈreɪt) *vb.* (*tr.*) to assess too highly.

overreach (ˌəʊvəˈriːtʃ) *vb.* **1.** (*tr.*) to defeat or thwart (oneself) by attempting to do or gain too much. **2.** (*tr.*) to aim for but miss by going too far or attempting too much. **3.** to get the better of (a person) by trickery. **4.** (*tr.*) to reach or extend beyond or over. **5.** (*intr.*) to reach or go too far. **6.** (*intr.*) (of a horse) to strike the back of a forefoot with the edge of the opposite hind foot.

overreact (ˌəʊvərɪˈækt) *vb.* (*intr.*) to react excessively to something. —ˌ**overre**ˈ**action** *n.*

overrefine (ˌəʊvərɪˈfaɪn) *vb.* **1.** to refine (something) to excess. **2.** (*intr.*) to make excessively fine distinctions. —ˌ**overre**ˈ**finement** *n.*

override (ˌəʊvəˈraɪd) *vb.* **-rides, -riding, -rode, -ridden.** (*tr.*) **1.** to set aside or disregard with superior authority or power. **2.** to supersede or annul. **3.** to dominate or vanquish by or as if by trampling down. **4.** to take manual control of (a system that is usually under automatic control). **5.** to extend or pass over, esp. to overlap. **6.** to ride (a horse) too hard. **7.** to ride over or across. ~*n.* **8.** a device or system that can override an automatic control.

overrider (ˈəʊvəˌraɪdə) *n.* either of two metal or rubber attachments fitted to the bumper of a motor vehicle to prevent the bumpers interlocking with those of another vehicle.

overriding (ˌəʊvəˈraɪdɪŋ) *adj.* taking precedence.

overrule (ˌəʊvəˈruːl) *vb.* (*tr.*) **1.** to disallow the arguments of (a person) by the use of authority. **2.** to rule or decide against (an argument, decision, etc.). **3.** to prevail over, dominate, or influence. **4.** to exercise rule over.

overrun *vb.* (ˌəʊvəˈrʌn), **-runs, -running, -ran, -run. 1.** (*tr.*) to attack or invade and defeat conclusively. **2.** (*tr.*) to swarm or spread over rapidly. **3.** to run over (something); overflow. **4.** to extend or run beyond a limit. **5.** (*intr.*) (of an engine) to run with a closed throttle at a speed dictated by that of the vehicle it drives, as on a decline. **6.** (*tr.*) **a.** to print (a book, journal, etc.) in a greater quantity than ordered. **b.** to print additional copies of (a publication). **7.** (*tr.*) *Printing.* to transfer (set type and other matter) from one column, line, or page, to another. **8.** (*tr.*) *Archaic.* to run faster than. ~*n.* (ˈəʊvəˌrʌn). **9.** the act or an instance of overrunning. **10.** the amount or extent of overrunning. **11.** the number of copies of a publication in excess of the quantity ordered. **12.** the cleared level area at the end of an airport runway.

overrun brake *n.* a brake fitted to a trailer or other towed vehicle that prevents the towed vehicle travelling faster than the towing vehicle when slowing down or descending an incline.

oversaturated (ˌəʊvəˈsætʃəˌreɪtɪd) *adj.* (of igneous rocks) containing excess silica.

overscore (ˌəʊvəˈskɔː) *vb.* (*tr.*) to cancel or cross out by drawing a line or lines over or through.

overseas *adv.* (ˌəʊvəˈsiːz). **1.** beyond the sea; abroad. ~*adj.* (ˈəʊvəˈsiːz). **2.** of, to, in, from, or situated in countries beyond the sea. **3.** Also: **oversea** (ˌəʊvəˈsiː). of or relating to passage over the sea. ~*n.* (ˌəʊvəˈsiːz). **4.** (*functioning as sing.*) *Informal.* a foreign country or foreign countries collectively.

overseas *or* **international telegram** *n. Brit.* another name for **cable** (sense 5).

oversee (ˌəʊvəˈsiː) *vb.* **-sees, -seeing, -saw, -seen.** (*tr.*) **1.** to watch over and direct; supervise. **2.** to watch secretly or accidentally. **3.** *Archaic.* to scrutinize; inspect.

overseer (ˈəʊvəˌsiːə) *n.* **1.** Also called (less commonly): ˌ**over**ˈ**looker.** a person who oversees others, esp. workmen. **2.** *British history.* short for **overseer of the poor;** a minor official of a parish attached to the workhouse or poorhouse.

oversell (ˌəʊvəˈsɛl) *vb.* **-sells, -selling, -sold. 1.** (*tr.*) to sell more of (a commodity) than can be supplied. **2.** to use excessively aggressive methods in selling (commodities). **3.** (*tr.*) to exaggerate the merits of.

overset *vb.* (ˌəʊvəˈsɛt), **-sets, -setting, -set.** (*tr.*) **1.** to disturb or upset. **2.** *Printing.* to set (type or copy) in excess of the space available. ~*n.* (ˈəʊvəˌsɛt). **3.** another name for **overmatter.**

oversew (ˈəʊvəˌsəʊ, ˌəʊvəˈsəʊ) *vb.* **-sews, -sewing, -sewed, -sewn.** to sew (two edges) with close stitches that pass over them both.

oversexed (ˌəʊvəˈsɛkst) *adj.* having an excessive preoccupation with or need for sexual activity.

overshadow (ˌəʊvəˈʃædəʊ) *vb.* (*tr.*) **1.** to render insignificant or less important in comparison. **2.** to cast a shadow or gloom over.

overshoe (ˈəʊvəˌʃuː) *n.* a protective shoe worn over an ordinary shoe.

overshoot (ˌəʊvəˈʃuːt) *vb.* **-shoots, -shooting, -shot. 1.** to shoot or go beyond (a mark or target). **2.** to cause (an aircraft) to fly or taxi too far along (a runway) during landing or taking off, or (of an aircraft) to fly or taxi too far along a runway. **3.** (*tr.*) to pass swiftly over or down over, as water over a wheel. ~*n.* **4.** an act or instance of overshooting. **5.** the extent of such overshooting. **6.** a momentary excessive response of an electrical or mechanical system.

overshot (ˈəʊvəˌʃɒt) *adj.* **1.** having or designating an upper jaw that projects beyond the lower jaw, esp. when considered as an abnormality. **2.** (of a water wheel) driven by a flow of water that passes over the wheel rather than under it. Compare **undershot.**

overside (ˈəʊvəˌsaɪd) *adv.* over the side (of a ship).

oversight (ˈəʊvəˌsaɪt) *n.* **1.** an omission or mistake, esp. one made through failure to notice something. **2.** supervision.

oversimplify (ˌəʊvəˈsɪmplɪˌfaɪ) *vb.* **-fies, -fying, -fied.** to simplify (something) to the point of distortion or error. —ˌ**over**ˌ**simplifi**ˈ**cation** *n.*

oversize *adj.* (ˌəʊvəˈsaɪz). **1.** Also: ˌ**over**ˈ**sized.** larger than the usual size. ~*n.* (ˈəʊvəˌsaɪz). **2.** a size larger than the usual or proper size. **3.** something that is oversize.

overskirt (ˈəʊvəˌskɜːt) *n.* an outer skirt, esp. one that reveals a decorative underskirt.

overslaugh (ˈəʊvəˌslɔː) *n.* **1.** *Military.* the passing over of one duty for another that takes precedence. ~*vb.* **2.** (*tr.*) *U.S.* to pass over; ignore. [C18: from Dutch *overslaan* to pass over]

oversleep (ˌəʊvəˈsliːp) *vb.* **-sleeps, -sleeping, -slept.** (*intr.*) to sleep beyond the intended time for getting up.

oversleeve (ˈəʊvəˌsliːv) *n.* a protective sleeve covering an ordinary sleeve.

overspend *vb.* (ˌəʊvəˈspɛnd). **-spends, -spending, -spent. 1.** to spend in excess of (one's desires or what one can afford or is allocated). **2.** (*tr.; usually passive*) to wear out; exhaust. ~*n.* (ˈəʊvəˌspɛnd). **3.** the amount by which someone or something is overspent.

overspill *n.* (ˈəʊvəˌspɪl). **1. a.** something that spills over or is in excess. **b.** (*as modifier*): *overspill population.* ~*vb.* (ˌəʊvəˈspɪl), **-spills, -spilling, -spilt** *or* **-spilled. 2.** (*intr.*) to overflow.

ˌ**over**ˈ**optiˌmism** *n.*
ˌ**over**ˈ**optimist** *n.*
ˌ**overˌopti**ˈ**mistic** *adj.*
ˌ**overpar**ˈ**ticular** *adj.*
ˌ**over**ˈ**peopled** *adj.*
ˌ**overˌpessi**ˈ**mistic** *adj.*
ˌ**over**ˈ**popuˌlate** *vb.*
ˌ**overˌpopu**ˈ**lation** *n.*
ˌ**over**ˈ**powerful** *adj.*
ˌ**over**ˈ**praise** *vb.*
ˌ**overpre**ˈ**cise** *adj.*
ˌ**over**ˈ**price** *vb.*
ˌ**overpro**ˈ**duce** *vb.*
ˌ**overpro**ˈ**duction** *n.*
ˌ**over**ˈ**prominent** *adj.*
ˌ**over**ˈ**prompt** *adj.*
ˌ**over**ˈ**promptly** *adv.*
ˌ**overpro**ˈ**portion** *vb., n.*
ˌ**over**ˈ**proud** *adj.*
ˌ**over**ˈ**publiˌcize** *or* ˌ**over**ˈ**publiˌcise** *vb.*
ˌ**overre**ˈ**liance** *n.*
ˌ**overre**ˈ**strict** *vb.*
ˌ**overre**ˈ**striction** *n.*
ˌ**over**ˈ**rich** *adj.*
ˌ**over**ˈ**righteous** *adj.*
ˌ**over**ˈ**righteously** *adv.*
ˌ**over**ˈ**righteousness** *n.*
ˌ**over**ˈ**ripe** *adj.*
ˌ**over**ˈ**roast** *vb.*
ˌ**overro**ˈ**mantiˌcize** *or* ˌ**overro**ˈ**mantiˌcise** *vb.*
ˌ**over**ˈ**sceptical** *adj.*
ˌ**over**ˈ**scrupulous** *adj.*
ˌ**over**ˈ**sensitive** *adj.*
ˌ**overse**ˈ**vere** *adj.*
ˌ**over**ˈ**sharp** *adj.*
ˌ**over**ˈ**smart** *adj.*
ˌ**overso**ˈ**licitous** *adj.*
ˌ**overso**ˈ**phistiˌcated** *adj.*
ˌ**over**ˈ**sparing** *adj.*
ˌ**overˌspeciali**ˈ**zation** *or* ˌ**overˌspeciali**ˈ**sation** *n.*
ˌ**over**ˈ**specialˌize** *or* ˌ**over**ˈ**specialˌise** *vb.*

overstaff (ˌəʊvəˈstɑːf) *vb.* (*tr.*) to provide an excessive number of staff for (a factory, hotel, etc.).

overstate (ˌəʊvəˈsteɪt) *vb.* (*tr.*) to state too strongly; exaggerate or overemphasize. —ˌ**overˈstatement** *n.*

overstay (ˌəʊvəˈsteɪ) *vb.* (*tr.*) **1.** to stay beyond the time, limit, or duration of. **2.** *Finance.* to delay a transaction in (a market) until after the point at which the maximum profit would have been made. **3.** *N.Z.* to stay in New Zealand beyond (the period sanctioned by the immigration authorities or the period of a visitor's permit). **4. overstay** *or* **outstay one's welcome.** to stay (at a party, on a visit, etc.), longer than pleases the host or hostess.

overstayer (ˈəʊvəˌsteɪə) *n. N.Z.* an illegal immigrant; a person who remains in New Zealand after the expiry of the period of the permitted visit.

oversteer (ˌəʊvəˈstɪə) *vb.* (*intr.*) (of a vehicle) to turn more sharply, for a particular turn of the steering wheel, than is desirable or anticipated.

overstep (ˌəʊvəˈstɛp) *vb.* **-steps, -stepping, -stepped.** (*tr.*) to go beyond (a certain or proper limit).

overstock (ˌəʊvəˈstɒk) *vb.* (*tr.*) **1.** to hold or supply (a commodity) in excess of requirements. **2.** to run more farm animals on (a piece of land) than it is capable of maintaining.

overstrung (ˌəʊvəˈstrʌŋ) *adj.* **1.** too highly strung; tense. **2.** (of a piano) having two sets of strings crossing each other at an oblique angle.

overstuff (ˌəʊvəˈstʌf) *vb.* (*tr.*) **1.** to force too much into. **2.** to cover (furniture) entirely with upholstery.

oversubscribe (ˌəʊvəsəbˈskraɪb) *vb.* (*tr.; often passive*) to subscribe or apply for in excess of available supply.

overt (ˈəʊvɜːt, əʊˈvɜːt) *adj.* **1.** open to view; observable. **2.** *Law.* open; deliberate. Criminal intent may be inferred from an overt act. [C14: via Old French, from *ovrir* to open, from Latin *aperīre*] —**oˈvertly** *adv.* —**oˈvertness** *n.*

overtake (ˌəʊvəˈteɪk) *vb.* **-takes, -taking, -took, -taken. 1.** *Chiefly Brit.* to move past (another vehicle or person) travelling in the same direction. **2.** (*tr.*) to pass or do better than, after catching up with. **3.** (*tr.*) to come upon suddenly or unexpectedly: *night overtook him.* **4.** (*tr.*) to catch up with; draw level with.

overtask (ˌəʊvəˈtɑːsk) *vb.* (*tr.*) to impose too heavy a task upon.

overtax (ˌəʊvəˈtæks) *vb.* (*tr.*) **1.** to tax too heavily. **2.** to impose too great a strain on.

over-the-counter *adj.* **1. a.** (of securities) not listed or quoted on a stock exchange. **b.** (of a security market) dealing in such securities. **c.** (of security transactions) conducted through a broker's office directly between purchaser and seller and not on a stock exchange. Abbrev.: **OTC. 2.** (of medicinal drugs) able to be sold without a prescription.

overthrow *vb.* (ˌəʊvəˈθrəʊ), **-throws, -throwing, -threw, -thrown. 1.** (*tr.*) to effect the downfall or destruction of (a ruler, institution, etc.), esp. by force. **2.** (*tr.*) to throw or turn over. **3.** to throw (something, esp. a ball) too far. **4.** (*tr.*) *Archaic.* to make mad. ~*n.* (ˈəʊvəˌθrəʊ). **5.** an act of overthrowing. **6.** downfall; destruction. **7.** *Cricket.* **a.** a ball thrown back too far by a fielder. **b.** a run scored because of this.

overthrust (ˈəʊvəˌθrʌst) *n. Geology.* a reverse fault in which the rocks on the upper surface of a fault plane have moved over the rocks on the lower surface. Compare **underthrust.**

overtime *n.* (ˈəʊvəˌtaɪm). **1. a.** work at a regular job done in addition to regular working hours. **b.** (*as modifier*): *overtime pay.* **2.** the rate of pay established for such work. **3.** time in excess of a set period. **4.** *Sport, U.S. and Canadian.* extra time. ~*adv.* (ˈəʊvəˌtaɪm). **5.** beyond the regular or stipulated time. ~*vb.* (ˌəʊvəˈtaɪm). **6.** (*tr.*) to exceed the required time for (a photographic exposure).

overtone (ˈəʊvəˌtəʊn) *n.* **1.** (*often pl.*) additional meaning or nuance: *overtones of despair.* **2.** *Music, acoustics.* any of the tones, with the exception of the fundamental, that constitute a musical sound and contribute to its quality, each having a frequency that is a multiple of the fundamental frequency. See also **harmonic** (sense 7), **partial** (sense 6).

overtop (ˌəʊvəˈtɒp) *vb.* **-tops, -topping, -topped.** (*tr.*) **1.** to exceed in height. **2.** to surpass; excel. **3.** to rise over the top of.

overtrade (ˌəʊvəˈtreɪd) *vb.* (*intr.*) (of an enterprise) to trade in excess of capacity or working capital.

overtrick (ˈəʊvəˌtrɪk) *n. Bridge.* a trick by which a player exceeds his contract.

overtrump (ˌəʊvəˈtrʌmp) *vb. Cards.* to play a trump higher than (one previously played to the trick).

overture (ˈəʊvəˌtjʊə) *n.* **1.** *Music.* **a.** a piece of orchestral music containing contrasting sections that is played at the beginning of an opera or oratorio, often containing the main musical themes of the work. **b.** a similar piece preceding the performance of a play. **c.** Also called: **concert overture.** a one-movement orchestral piece, usually having a descriptive or evocative title. **d.** a short piece in three movements (**French overture** or **Italian overture**) common in the 17th and 18th centuries. **2.** (*often pl.*) a proposal, act, or gesture initiating a relationship, negotiation, etc. **3.** something that introduces what follows. ~*vb.* (*tr.*) **4.** to make or present an overture to. **5.** to introduce with an overture. [C14: via Old French, from Late Latin *apertūra* opening, from Latin *aperīre* to open; see OVERT]

overturn *vb.* (ˌəʊvəˈtɜːn). **1.** to turn or cause to turn from an upright or normal position. **2.** (*tr.*) to overthrow or destroy. **3.** (*tr.*) to invalidate; reverse: *the bill was passed in the Commons but overturned in the Lords.* ~*n.* (ˈəʊvəˌtɜːn). **4.** the act of overturning or the state of being overturned.

over-under *U.S.* ~*adj.* **1.** (of a two-barrelled firearm) having one barrel on top of the other. ~*n.* **2.** an over-under firearm.

overview (ˈəʊvəˌvjuː) *n.* a general survey.

overvoltage (ˈəʊvəˌvəʊltɪdʒ) *n.* a voltage above the normal level.

overwatch (ˌəʊvəˈwɒtʃ) *vb.* (*tr.*) **1.** to watch over. **2.** *Archaic.* to fatigue with long watching or lack of sleep.

overweening (ˌəʊvəˈwiːnɪŋ) *adj.* **1.** (of a person) excessively arrogant or presumptuous. **2.** (of opinions, appetites, etc.) excessive; immoderate. [C14: OVER- + *weening,* from Old English *wēnan:* see WEEN] —ˌ**overˈweeningly** *adv.* —ˌ**overˈweeningness** *n.*

overweigh (ˌəʊvəˈweɪ) *vb.* (*tr.*) **1.** to exceed in weight; overbalance. **2.** to weigh down; oppress.

overweight *adj.* (ˌəʊvəˈweɪt). **1.** weighing more than is usual, allowed, or healthy. ~*n.* (ˈəʊvəˌweɪt). **2.** extra or excess weight. **3.** *Archaic.* greater importance or effect. ~*vb.* (ˌəʊvəˈweɪt). (*tr.*) **4.** to give too much emphasis or consideration to. **5.** to add too much weight to. **6.** to weigh down.

overwhelm (ˌəʊvəˈwɛlm) *vb.* (*tr.*) **1.** to overpower the thoughts, emotions, or senses of. **2.** to overcome with irresistible force. **3.** to overcome, as with a profusion or concentration of something. **4.** to cover over or bury completely. **5.** to weigh or rest upon overpoweringly. **6.** *Archaic.* to overturn.

overwhelming (ˌəʊvəˈwɛlmɪŋ) *adj.* overpowering in effect or force. —ˌ**overˈwhelmingly** *adv.*

overwind (ˌəʊvəˈwaɪnd) *vb.* **-winds, -winding, -wound.** (*tr.*) to wind (a watch) beyond the proper limit.

overwinter (ˌəʊvəˈwɪntə) *vb.* **1.** (*intr.*) to spend winter (in or at a particular place). **2.** (*tr.*) to keep (animals or plants) alive through the winter. **3.** (*intr.*) (of an animal or plant) to remain alive throughout the winter.

overword (ˈəʊvəˌwɜːd) *n.* a repeated word or phrase.

overwork *vb.* (ˌəʊvəˈwɜːk). (*mainly tr.*) **1.** (*also intr.*) to work or cause to work too hard or too long. **2.** to use too much: *to overwork an excuse.* **3.** to decorate the surface of. **4.** to work up. ~*n.* (ˈəʊvəˌwɜːk). **5.** excessive or excessively tiring work. —ˌ**overˈworked** *adj.*

overwrite (ˌəʊvəˈraɪt) *vb.* **-writes, -writing, -wrote, -written. 1.** to write (something) in an excessively ornate or prolix style. **2.** to write too much about (someone or something). **3.** to write on top of (other writing). **4.** to record on a storage medium, such as a magnetic disk, thus destroying what was originally recorded there.

overwrought (ˌəʊvəˈrɔːt) *adj.* **1.** full of nervous tension; agitated. **2.** too elaborate; fussy: *an overwrought style.* **3.** (*often postpositive* and foll. by *with*) with the surface decorated or adorned.

ovi- *or* **ovo-** *combining form.* egg or ovum: *oviform; ovotestis.* [from Latin *ōvum*]

Ovidian (ɒˈvɪdɪən) *adj.* of, relating to, or characteristic of the Roman poet Ovid (43 B.C.–?17 A.D.) or his works.

oviduct (ˈɒvɪˌdʌkt, ˈəʊ-) *n.* the tube through which ova are conveyed from an ovary. Also called (in mammals): **Fallopian tube.** —**oviducal** (ˌɒvɪˈdjuːkᵊl, ˌəʊ-) *or* ˌ**oviˈductal** *adj.*

oviferous (əʊˈvɪfərəs) *or* **ovigerous** (əʊˈvɪdʒərəs) *adj. Zoology.* carrying or producing eggs or ova: *the oviferous legs of certain spiders.*

oviform (ˈəʊvɪˌfɔːm) *adj. Biology.* shaped like an egg.

ovine (ˈəʊvaɪn) *adj.* of, relating to, or resembling a sheep. [C19: from Late Latin *ovīnus,* from Latin *ovis* sheep]

oviparous (əʊˈvɪpərəs) *adj.* (of fishes, reptiles, birds, etc.) producing eggs that hatch outside the body of the mother. Compare **ovoviviparous, viviparous** (sense 1). —**oviparity** (ˌəʊvɪˈpærɪtɪ) *n.* —**oˈviparously** *adv.*

oviposit (ˌəʊvɪˈpɒzɪt) *vb.* (*intr.*) (of insects and fishes) to deposit eggs through an ovipositor. [C19: OVI- + *positus,* past participle of Latin *pōnere* to place] —**oviposition** (ˌəʊvɪpəˈzɪʃən) *n.*

ovipositor (ˌəʊvɪˈpɒzɪtə) *n.* **1.** the egg-laying organ of most female insects, consisting of a pair of specialized appendages at

ˌ**overˈspread** *vb.,* **-ˈspreads, -ˈspreading, -ˈspread.**
ˌ**overˈstimuˌlate** *vb.*
ˌ**overˈstrain** *vb.*
ˌ**overˈstretch** *vb.*
ˌ**overˈstrict** *adj.*
ˌ**overˈstride** *vb.,* **-ˈstrides, -ˈstriding, -ˈstrode, -ˈstridden.**
ˌ**overˈsubtle** *adj.*
ˌ**overˈsubtlety** *n.*
ˌ**oversupˈply** *vb.,* **-ˈplies, -ˈplying, -ˈplied.**
ˌ**oversusˈceptible** *adj.*
ˌ**oversusˈpicious** *adj.*
ˌ**overˌsystemˈatic** *adj.*
ˌ**overˈtask** *vb.*
ˌ**overˈtechnical** *adj.*
ˌ**overˈtire** *vb.*
ˌ**overˈtired** *adj.*
ˌ**overˈtrain** *vb.*
ˌ**overˈuse** *vb., n.*
ˌ**overˈvalue** *vb.,* **-ues, -uing, -ued.**
ˌ**overˈviolent** *adj.*
ˌ**overˈwater** *vb.*
ˌ**overˈwilling** *adj.*
ˌ**overˈwise** *adj.*
ˌ**overˈzealous** *adj.*
ˌ**overˈzealously** *adv.*

the end of the abdomen. **2.** a similar organ in certain female fishes, formed by an extension of the edges of the genital opening.

ovisac ('əʊvɪˌsæk) *n.* a capsule or sac, such as an ootheca, in which egg cells are produced.

ovo- *combining form.* a variant of **ovi-**.

ovoid ('əʊvɔɪd) *adj.* **1.** egg-shaped. **2.** *Botany.* (of a fruit or similar part) egg-shaped with the broader end at the base. Compare **obovoid.** ~*n.* **3.** something that is ovoid.

ovolo ('əʊvəˌləʊ) *n., pl.* **-li** (-ˌlaɪ). *Architect.* a convex moulding having a cross section in the form of a quarter of a circle or ellipse. Also called: **quarter round, thumb.** Compare **congé** (sense 3), **echinus** (sense 1). [C17: from Italian: a little egg, from *ovo* egg, from Latin *ōvum*]

ovotestis (ˌəʊvəʊ'tɛstɪs) *n., pl.* **-tes** (-tiːz). the reproductive organ of snails, which produces both ova and spermatozoa.

ovoviviparous (ˌəʊvəʊvaɪ'vɪpərəs) *adj.* (of certain reptiles, fishes, etc.) producing eggs that hatch within the body of the mother. Compare **oviparous, viviparous** (sense 1). —**ovoviviparity** (ˌəʊvəʊˌvaɪvɪ'pærɪtɪ) *n.*

ovulate ('ɒvjʊˌleɪt) *vb.* (*intr.*) to produce or discharge eggs from an ovary. [C19: from OVULE] —ˌ**ovu'lation** *n.*

ovulation method *n.* another name for **Billings method.**

ovule ('ɒvjuːl) *n.* **1.** a small body in seed-bearing plants that contains the egg cell and develops into the seed after fertilization. **2.** *Zoology.* an immature ovum. [C19: via French from Medieval Latin *ōvulum* a little egg, from Latin *ōvum* egg] —'**ovular** *adj.*

ovum ('əʊvəm) *n., pl.* **ova** ('əʊvə). an unfertilized female gamete; egg cell. [from Latin: egg]

ow (aʊ) *interj.* an exclamation of pain.

owe (əʊ) *vb.* (*mainly tr.*) **1.** to be under an obligation to pay (someone) to the amount of. **2.** (*intr.*) to be in debt: *he still owes for his house.* **3.** (often foll. by *to*) to have as a result (of): *he owes his success to chance.* **4.** to feel the need or obligation to do, give, etc.: *to owe somebody thanks; to owe it to oneself to rest.* **5.** to hold or maintain in the mind or heart (esp. in the phrase **owe a grudge).** [Old English *āgan* to have (C12: to have to); related to Old Saxon *ēgan*, Old High German *eigan*]

owelty ('əʊəltɪ) *n., pl.* **-ties.** *Law.* equality, esp. in financial transactions. [C16: from Anglo-French *owelté*, ultimately from Latin *aequalitas*, from *aequalis* EQUAL]

Owen gun ('əʊɪn) *n.* a type of automatic sub-machine-gun first used by Australian forces in World War II. [named after E. E. *Owen* (1915–49), its Australian inventor]

ower *or* **owre** ('aʊər) *prep., adv., adj.* a Scot. word for **over.**

owing ('əʊɪŋ) *adj.* **1.** (*postpositive*) owed; due. **2. owing to.** (*prep.*) because of or on account of.

▷**Usage.** See at **due.**

owl (aʊl) *n.* **1.** any nocturnal bird of prey of the order *Strigiformes*, having large front-facing eyes, a small hooked bill, soft feathers, and a short neck. **2.** any of various breeds of owl-like fancy domestic pigeon (esp. the **African owl, Chinese owl,** and **English owl**). **3.** a person who looks or behaves like an owl, esp. in having a solemn manner. [Old English *ūle*; related to Dutch *uil*, Old High German *ūwila*, Old Norse *ugla*] —'**owl-**ˌ**like** *adj.*

owlet ('aʊlɪt) *n.* a young or nestling owl.

owlish ('aʊlɪʃ) *adj.* **1.** like an owl. **2.** solemn and wise in appearance. —'**owlishly** *adv.* —'**owlishness** *n.*

own (əʊn) *determiner.* (*preceded by a possessive*) **1. a.** (intensifier): *John's own idea; your own mother.* **b.** (*as pronoun*): *I'll use my own.* **2.** on behalf of oneself or in relation to oneself: *he is his own worst enemy.* **3. come into one's own. a.** to become fulfilled: *she really came into her own when she got divorced.* **4. get one's own back.** *Informal.* to have revenge. **5. hold one's own.** to maintain one's situation or position, esp. in spite of opposition or difficulty. **6. on one's own. a.** without help. **b.** by oneself; alone. ~*vb.* **7.** (*tr.*) to have as one's possession. **8.** (when *intr.*, often foll. by *up, to,* or *up to*) to confess or admit; acknowledge. **9.** (*tr.; takes a clause as object*) *Now rare.* to concede: *I own that you are right.* [Old English *āgen*, originally past participle of *āgan* to have; related to Old Saxon *ēgan*, Old Norse *eiginn*. See OWE]

own brand *n.* **a.** an item packaged and marketed under the brand name of a particular retailer, usually a large supermarket chain, rather than that of the manufacturer. **b.** (*as modifier*): *own-brand products.* ~Also **own label.**

owner ('əʊnə) *n.* a person who owns; legal possessor.

owner-occupier *n. Brit.* a person who owns or is in the process of buying the house or flat he lives in. —ˌ**owner-'occu**ˌ**pied** *adj.* —'**owner-**ˌ**occu'pation** *n.*

ownership ('əʊnəʃɪp) *n.* **1.** the state or fact of being an owner. **2.** legal right of possession; proprietorship.

own goal *n.* **1.** *Soccer.* a goal scored by a player accidentally kicking the ball into his own team's net. Abbrev.: **o.g. 2.** *Informal.* any action that results in disadvantage to the person who took it or to a party, group, etc. with which that person is associated.

owt (aʊt) *pron. Northern English.* a dialect word for **anything.** [a variant of AUGHT[1]]

ox (ɒks) *n., pl.* **oxen** ('ɒksən). **1.** an adult castrated male of any domesticated species of cattle, esp. *Bos taurus*, used for draught work and meat. **2.** any bovine mammal, esp. any of the domestic cattle. [Old English *oxa*; related to Old Saxon, Old High German *ohso*, Old Norse *oxi*]

oxa- *or before a vowel* **ox-** *combining form.* indicating that a chemical compound contains oxygen, used esp. to denote that a heterocyclic compound is derived from a specified compound by replacement of a carbon atom with an oxygen atom: *oxalic acid; oxazine.*

oxalate ('ɒksəˌleɪt) *n.* a salt or ester of oxalic acid.

oxalic acid (ɒk'sælɪk) *n.* a colourless poisonous crystalline dicarboxylic acid found in many plants: used as a bleach and a cleansing agent for metals. Formula: $(COOH)_2$. Systematic name: **ethanedioic acid.** [C18: from French *oxalique*, from Latin *oxalis* garden sorrel; see OXALIS]

oxalis ('ɒksəlɪs, ɒk'sælɪs) *n.* any plant of the genus *Oxalis*, having clover-like leaves which contain oxalic acid and white, pink, red, or yellow flowers: family *Oxalidaceae.* See also **wood sorrel.** [C18: via Latin from Greek: sorrel, sour wine, from *oxus* acid, sharp]

oxazine ('ɒksəˌziːn) *n.* any of 13 heterocyclic compounds with the formula C_4H_5NO. [from OXY-[2] + AZINE]

oxblood ('ɒksˌblʌd) *or* **oxblood red** *adj.* of a dark reddish-brown colour.

oxbow ('ɒksˌbəʊ) *n.* **1.** a U-shaped piece of wood fitted under and around the neck of a harnessed ox and attached to the yoke. **2.** Also called: **oxbow lake, cutoff.** a small curved lake lying on the flood plain of a river and constituting the remnant of a former meander.

Oxbridge ('ɒksˌbrɪdʒ) *n.* **a.** the British universities of Oxford and Cambridge, esp. considered as ancient and prestigious academic institutions, bastions of privilege and superiority, etc. **b.** (*as modifier*): *Oxbridge arrogance.*

oxen ('ɒksən) *n.* the plural of **ox.**

oxeye ('ɒksˌaɪ) *n.* **1.** any Eurasian plant of the genus *Buphthalmum*, having daisy-like flower heads with yellow rays and dark centres: family *Compositae* (composites). **2.** any of various North American plants of the related genus *Heliopsis*, having daisy-like flowers. **3. oxeye daisy.** another name for **daisy** (sense 2).

ox-eyed *adj.* having large round eyes, like those of an ox.

OXFAM *or* **Oxfam** ('ɒksfæm) *n. acronym for* Oxford Committee for Famine Relief.

Oxford ('ɒksfəd) *n.* **1.** Also called: **Oxford Down.** a breed of sheep with short wool and a dark brown face and legs. **2.** a type of stout laced shoe with a low heel. **3.** a lightweight fabric of plain or twill weave used esp. for men's shirts. [after *Oxford*, city in S England]

Oxford accent *n.* the accent associated with Oxford English.

Oxford bags *pl. n.* trousers with very wide baggy legs, originally popular in the 1920s. Often shortened to **bags.**

Oxford blue *n.* **1. a.** a dark blue colour. **b.** (*as adj.*): *an Oxford-blue scarf.* **2.** a person who has been awarded a blue from Oxford University.

Oxford English *n.* that form of the received pronunciation of English supposed to be typical of Oxford University and regarded by many as affected or pretentious.

Oxford frame *n.* a type of picture frame in which the sides of the frame cross each other and project outwards.

Oxford Group *n.* an early name for **Moral Rearmament.**

Oxford Movement *n.* a movement within the Church of England that began at Oxford in 1833, affirmed the continuity of the Church with early Christianity, and strove to restore the High-Church ideals of the 17th century. Its views were publicized in a series of tracts (**Tracts for the Times**) 1833–41. The teaching and practices of the Movement are maintained in the High-Church tradition within the Church of England. Also called: **Tractarianism.**

oxhide ('ɒksˌhaɪd) *n.* leather made from the hide of an ox.

oxidant ('ɒksɪdənt) *n.* a substance that acts or is used as an oxidizing agent. Also called (esp. in rocketry): **oxidizer.**

oxidase ('ɒksɪˌdeɪs, -ˌdeɪz) *n.* any of a group of enzymes that bring about biological oxidation.

oxidate ('ɒksɪˌdeɪt) *vb.* another word for **oxidize.**

oxidation (ˌɒksɪ'deɪʃən) *n.* **a.** the act or process of oxidizing. **b.** (*as modifier*): *an oxidation state; an oxidation potential.* —ˌ**oxi'dational** *adj.* —'**oxi**ˌ**dative** *adj.*

oxidation-reduction *n.* **a.** a reversible chemical process usually involving the transfer of electrons, in which one reaction is an oxidation and the reverse reaction is a reduction. **b.** Also: **redox.** (*as modifier*): *an oxidation-reduction reaction.*

oxidative phosphorylation *n.* the process by which the energy liberated by oxidation of metabolites is used to synthesize the energy-rich molecule ATP.

oxide ('ɒksaɪd) *n.* **1.** any compound of oxygen with another element. **2.** any organic compound in which an oxygen atom is bound to two alkyl or aryl groups; an ether. [C18: from French, from *ox(ygène)* + *(ac)ide*; see OXYGEN, ACID]

oxidimetry (ˌɒksɪ'dɪmɪtrɪ) *n. Chem.* a branch of volumetric analysis in which oxidizing agents are used in titrations. [C20: from OXID(ATION) + -METRY] —**oxidimetric** (ˌɒksɪdɪ'mɛtrɪk) *adj.*

oxidize *or* **oxidise** ('ɒksɪˌdaɪz) *vb.* **1.** to undergo or cause to undergo a chemical reaction with oxygen, as in formation of an oxide. **2.** to form or cause to form a layer of metal oxide, as in rusting. **3.** to lose or cause to lose hydrogen atoms. **4.** to undergo or cause to undergo a decrease in the number of electrons. Compare **reduce** (sense 11c). —ˌ**oxidiˈzation** *or* ˌ**oxidiˈsation** *n.*

oxidizer *or* **oxidiser** (ˈɒksɪˌdaɪzə) *n.* an oxidant, esp. a substance that combines with the fuel in a rocket engine.

oxidizing agent *n. Chem.* a substance that oxidizes another substance, being itself reduced in the process. Common oxidizing agents are oxygen, hydrogen peroxide, and ferric salts. Compare **reducing agent.**

oxime (ˈɒksiːm) *n.* any of a class of compounds with the general formula RR′NOH, where R is an organic group and R′ is either an organic group (**ketoxime**) or hydrogen atom (**aldoxime**): used in the chemical analysis of carbonyl compounds. [C19: from OX(YGEN) + IM(ID)E]

oxlip (ˈɒksˌlɪp) *n.* **1.** Also called: **paigle.** a primulaceous Eurasian woodland plant, *Primula elatior,* with small drooping pale yellow flowers. **2.** a similar and related plant that is a natural hybrid between the cowslip and primrose. [Old English *oxanslyppe,* literally: ox's slippery dropping; see SLIP[3], compare COWSLIP]

Oxo (ˈɒksəʊ) *n. Trademark.* extract of beef in the shape of small cubes which are mixed with boiling water and used for flavouring, as stock, a drink, etc. [C20: from OX + -O]

oxo- *or before a vowel* **ox-** *combining form.* indicating that a chemical compound contains oxygen linked to another atom by a double bond, used esp. to denote that a compound is derived from a specified compound by replacement of a methylene group with a carbonyl group: *oxobutanoic acid.*

oxo acid (ˈɒksəʊ) *n.* another name for **oxyacid.**

Oxon *abbrev. for* Oxfordshire. [from Latin *Oxonia*]

Oxon. (ˈɒksən) *abbrev. for* (in degree titles) of Oxford. [from Latin *Oxoniensis*]

Oxonian (ɒkˈsəʊnɪən) *adj.* **1.** of or relating to the city of Oxford or Oxford University. ~*n.* **2.** a member of Oxford University. **3.** an inhabitant or native of Oxford.

oxonium compound *or* **salt** (ɒkˈsəʊnɪəm) *n. Chem.* any of a class of salts derived from certain organic ethers or alcohols by adding a proton to the oxygen atom and thus producing a positive ion (**oxonium ion**).

oxpecker (ˈɒksˌpɛkə) *n.* either of two African starlings, *Buphagus africanus* or *B. erythrorhynchus,* having flattened bills with which they obtain food from the hides of cattle. Also called: **tick-bird.**

oxtail (ˈɒksˌteɪl) *n.* the skinned tail of an ox, used esp. in soups and stews.

oxter (ˈɒkstə) *n. Scot., Irish, and northern English dialect.* the armpit. [C16: from Old English *oxta;* related to Old High German *Ahsala,* Latin *axilla*]

oxtongue (ˈɒksˌtʌŋ) *n.* **1.** any of various Eurasian plants of the genus *Picris,* having oblong bristly leaves and clusters of dandelion-like flowers: family *Compositae* (composites). **2.** any of various other plants having bristly tongue-shaped leaves, such as alkanet. **3.** the tongue of an ox, braised or boiled as food.

oxy-[1] *combining form.* denoting something sharp; acute: *oxytone.* [from Greek, from *oxus*]

oxy-[2] *combining form.* **1.** containing or using oxygen: *oxyacetylene.* **2.** a former equivalent of **hydroxy-.**

oxyacetylene (ˌɒksɪəˈsɛtɪˌliːn) *n.* **a.** a mixture of oxygen and acetylene; used in a blowpipe for cutting or welding metals at high temperatures. **b.** (*as modifier*): *an oxyacetylene burner.*

oxyacid (ˌɒksɪˈæsɪd) *n.* any acid that contains oxygen. Also called: **oxo acid.**

oxycephaly (ˌɒksɪˈsɛfəlɪ) *n. Pathol.* the condition of having a conical skull. [C20: from Greek *oxys* sharp + -CEPHALY] —**oxycephalic** (ˌɒksɪsɪˈfælɪk) *or* ˌ**oxyˈcephalous** *adj.*

oxygen (ˈɒksɪdʒən) *n.* **a.** a colourless odourless highly reactive gaseous element: the most abundant element in the earth's crust (49.2 per cent). It is essential for aerobic respiration and almost all combustion and is widely used in industry. Symbol: O; atomic no.: 8; atomic wt.: 15.9994; valency: 2; density: 1.429 kg/m^3; melting pt.: –218.4°C; boiling pt.: –182.96°C. **b.** (*as modifier*): *an oxygen mask.* —**oxygenic** (ˌɒksɪˈdʒɛnɪk) *or* **oxygenous** (ɒkˈsɪdʒɪnəs) *adj.*

oxygen acid *n.* another name for **oxyacid.**

oxygenate (ˈɒksɪdʒɪˌneɪt), **oxygenize,** *or* **oxygenise** *vb.* to enrich or be enriched with oxygen: *to oxygenate blood.* —ˌ**oxygenˈation** *n.* —ˈ**oxygeˌnizer** *or* ˈ**oxygeˌniser** *n.*

oxygenator (ˈɒksɪdʒɪˌneɪtə) *n.* an apparatus that oxygenates the blood, esp. while a patient is undergoing an operation.

oxygen effect *n. Biology.* the increased sensitivity to radiation of living organisms, tissues, etc., when they are exposed in the presence of oxygen.

oxygen mask *n.* a device, worn over the nose and mouth, to which oxygen is supplied from a cylinder or other source: used to aid breathing.

oxygen tent *n. Med.* a transparent enclosure covering a bedridden patient, into which oxygen is released to help maintain respiration.

oxygen weed *n. N.Z.* another name for **water hyacinth.**

oxyhaemoglobin *or U.S.* **oxyhemoglobin** (ˌɒksɪˌhiːməʊˈgləʊbɪn, -ˌhɛm-) *n. Biochem.* the bright red product formed when oxygen from the lungs combines with haemoglobin in the blood.

oxyhydrogen (ˌɒksɪˈhaɪdrədʒən) *n.* **a.** a mixture of hydrogen and oxygen used to provide an intense flame for welding. **b.** (*as modifier*): *an oxyhydrogen blowpipe.*

oxymoron (ˌɒksɪˈmɔːrɒn) *n., pl.* **-mora** (-ˈmɔːrə). *Rhetoric.* an epigrammatic effect, by which contradictory terms are used in conjunction: *beautiful tyrant; fiend angelical.* [C17: via New Latin from Greek *oxumōron,* from *oxus* sharp + *mōros* stupid]

oxyntic (ɒkˈsɪntɪk) *adj. Physiol.* secreting acid: *oxyntic cells.* [C19: from Greek *oxunein* to make acid, from *oxus* acid, sharp]

oxysalt (ˌɒksɪˈsɔːlt) *n.* any salt of an oxyacid.

oxysulphide (ˌɒksɪˈsʌlfaɪd) *n. Chem.* a compound containing an element combined with oxygen and sulphur.

oxytetracycline (ˌɒksɪˌtɛtrəˈsaɪklɪn) *n.* a broad-spectrum antibiotic, obtained from the bacterium *Streptomyces rimosus,* used in treating various infections. Formula: $C_{22}H_{24}N_2O_9$. Abbrev.: **OTC.**

oxytocic (ˌɒksɪˈtəʊsɪk) *adj.* **1.** accelerating childbirth by stimulating uterine contractions. ~*n.* **2.** an oxytocic drug or agent. [C19: from Greek, from OXY-[1] + *tokos* childbirth]

oxytocin (ˌɒksɪˈtəʊsɪn) *n.* a polypeptide hormone, secreted by the pituitary gland, that stimulates contractions of the uterus or oviduct and ejection of milk in mammals; alphahypophame: used therapeutically for aiding childbirth. Formula: $C_{43}H_{66}N_{12}O_{12}S_2$. Compare **vasopressin.**

oxytone (ˈɒksɪˌtəʊn) (in the classical Greek language) ~*adj.* **1.** (of a word) having an accent on the final syllable. ~*n.* **2.** an oxytone word. ~Compare **paroxytone, proparoxytone.** [C18: from Greek *oxytonos,* from *oxys* sharp + *tonos* tone]

oyer (ɔɪə) *n.* **1.** *English legal history.* (in the 13th century) an assize. **2.** (formerly) the reading out loud of a document in court. **3.** See **oyer and terminer.**

oyer and terminer (ˈtɜːmɪnə) *n.* **1.** *English law.* (formerly) a commission issued to judges to try cases on assize. It became obsolete with the abolition of assizes and the setting up of crown courts in 1972. **2.** the court in which such a hearing was held. **3.** (in the U.S.) a court exercising higher criminal jurisdiction. [C15: from Anglo-Norman, from *oyer* to hear + *terminer* to judge]

oyez *or* **oyes** (əʊˈjɛs, -ˈjɛz) *interj.* **1.** a cry, usually uttered three times, by a public crier or court official for silence and attention before making a proclamation. ~*n.* **2.** such a cry. [C15: via Anglo-Norman from Old French *oiez!* hear!]

-oyl *suffix of nouns* (in chemistry) indicating an acyl group or radical: *ethanoyl, methanoyl.* [C20: from O(XYGEN) + -YL]

oyster (ˈɔɪstə) *n.* **1. a.** any edible marine bivalve mollusc of the genus *Ostrea,* having a rough irregularly shaped shell and occurring on the sea bed, mostly in coastal waters. **b.** *(as modifier): oyster farm; oyster knife.* **2.** any of various similar and related molluscs, such as the pearl oyster and the **saddle oyster** *(Anomia ephippium).* **3.** the oyster-shaped piece of dark meat in the hollow of the pelvic bone of a fowl. **4.** something from which advantage, delight, profit, etc., may be derived: *the world is his oyster.* **5.** *Informal.* a very uncommunicative person. ~*vb.* **6.** *(intr.)* to dredge for, gather, or raise oysters. [C14 *oistre,* from Old French *uistre,* from Latin *ostrea,* from Greek *ostreon;* related to Greek *osteon* bone, *ostrakon* shell]

oyster bed *n.* a place, esp. on the sea bed, where oysters breed and grow naturally or are cultivated for food or pearls. Also called: **oyster bank, oyster park.**

oystercatcher (ˈɔɪstəˌkætʃə) *n.* any shore bird of the genus *Haematopus* and family *Haematopodidae,* having a black or black-and-white plumage and a long stout laterally compressed red bill.

oyster crab *n.* any of several small soft-bodied crabs of the genus *Pinnotheres,* esp. *P. ostreum,* that live as commensals in the mantles of oysters.

oysterman (ˈɔɪstəmən) *n., pl.* **-men.** *Chiefly U.S.* **1.** a person who gathers, cultivates, or sells oysters. **2.** a boat used in gathering oysters.

oyster pink *n.* **a.** a delicate pinkish-white colour, sometimes with a greyish tinge. **b.** *(as adj.): oyster-pink shoes.*

oyster plant *n.* another name for **salsify** (sense 1) and **sea lungwort** (see **lungwort** (sense 2)).

oyster white *n.* **a.** a greyish-white colour. **b.** *(as adj.): oyster-white walls.*

oz *or* **oz.** *abbrev. for* ounce. [from Italian *onza*]

Oz (ɒz) *n. Austral. slang.* Australia.

Ozalid (ˈɒzəlɪd) *n.* **1.** *Trademark.* a method of duplicating typematter, illustrations, etc., when printed on translucent paper. It is used for proofing. **2.** a reproduction produced by this method. [C20: formed by reversing DIAZO and inserting *l*]

ozocerite *or* **ozokerite** (əʊˈzəʊkəˌraɪt) *n.* a brown or greyish wax that occurs associated with petroleum and is used for making candles and wax paper. Also called: **earth wax, mineral wax.** [C19: from German *ozokerit,* from Greek *ozein* odour + *kēros* beeswax]

ozone (ˈəʊzəʊn, əʊˈzəʊn) *n.* **1.** a colourless gas with a chlorine-like odour, formed by an electric discharge in oxygen: a strong oxidizing agent, used in bleaching, sterilizing water, purifying air, etc. Formula: O_3; density: 2.14 kg/m^3; melting pt.: –192°C; boiling pt.: –110.51. Technical name: **trioxygen.** **2.** *Informal.* clean bracing air, as found at the seaside. [C19: from German *ozon,* from Greek: smell] —**ozonic** (əʊˈzɒnɪk) *or* ˈ**ozonous** *adj.*

ozone-friendly *adj.* not harmful to the ozone layer; using substances that do not produce gases harmful to the ozone layer: *an ozone-friendly refrigerator.*
ozone layer *n.* the region of the stratosphere with the highest concentration of ozone molecules, which by absorbing high-energy solar ultraviolet radiation protects organisms on earth. Also called: **ozonosphere.**
ozonide (əʊˈzəʊnaɪd) *n.* any of a class of unstable explosive compounds produced by the addition of ozone to a double bond in an organic compound.
ozoniferous (ˌəʊzəʊˈnɪfərəs) *adj.* containing ozone.
ozonize *or* **ozonise** (ˈəʊzəʊˌnaɪz) *vb. (tr.)* **1.** to convert (oxygen) into ozone. **2.** to treat (a substance) with ozone —ˌ**ozoniˈzation** *or* ˌ**ozoniˈsation** *n.* —ˈ**ozoˌnizer** *or* ˈ**ozoˌniser** *n.*
ozonolysis (ˌəʊzəʊˈnɒlɪsɪs) *n. Chem.* the process of treating an organic compound with ozone to form an ozonide: used to locate double bonds in molecules.
ozonosphere (əʊˈzəʊnəˌsfɪə, -ˈzɒnə-) *n.* another name for **ozone layer.**
ozs *or* **ozs.** *abbrev. for* ounces.

p *or* **P** (piː) *n., pl.* **p's, P's,** or **Ps.** **1.** the 16th letter and 12th consonant of the modern English alphabet. **2.** a speech sound represented by this letter, usually a voiceless bilabial stop, as in *pig.* **3. mind one's p's and q's.** to be careful to behave correctly and use polite or suitable language.

p *symbol for:* **1.** (in Britain) penny *or* pence. **2.** *Music.* piano: an instruction to play quietly. **3.** pico-. **4.** *Physics.* **a.** momentum. **b.** proton. **c.** pressure.

P *symbol for:* **1.** *Chem.* phosphorus. **2.** *Physics.* **a.** pressure. **b.** power. **c.** parity. **d.** poise. **3.** (on road signs) parking. **4.** *Chess.* pawn. **5.** *Currency.* **a.** peseta. **b.** peso. **c.** pataca. **d.** pula. ~*abbrev. for:* **6.** pharmacy only: used on medicines that can be obtained without a prescription, but only at a shop, such as a chemist's, where there is a pharmacist. ~**7.** *international car registration for* Portugal.

p. *abbrev. for:* **1.** (*pl.* **pp.**) page. **2.** part. **3.** participle. **4.** past. **5.** per. **6.** pint. **7.** pipe. **8.** population. **9.** post [Latin: after] **10.** pro [Latin: in favour of; for]

P. *abbrev. for:* **1.** Pastor. **2.** President. **3.** Priest. **4.** Prince.

p- *prefix.* short for **para-**[1] (sense 6).

pa[1] (pɑː) *n.* an informal word for **father.**

pa[2] *or* **pah** (pɑː) *n. N.Z.* **1.** a Maori village or settlement. **2.** *History.* a Maori defensive position and settlement on a hilltop. **3. go back to the pa.** to abandon city life in favour of rural life. [Maori]

Pa *the chemical symbol for* protactinium.

PA *abbrev. for:* **1.** Pennsylvania. **2.** personal appearance. **3.** personal assistant. **4.** *Military.* Post Adjutant. **5.** power of attorney. **6.** press agent. **7.** Press Association. **8.** *Banking.* private account. **9.** public-address system. **10.** publicity agent. **11.** Publishers Association. **12.** purchasing agent. **13.** *Insurance.* particular average. ~**14.** *international car registration for* Panama.

Pa. *abbrev. for* Pennsylvania.

p.a. *abbrev. for* per annum. [Latin: yearly]

paal (pɑːl) *n. Caribbean.* a stake driven into the ground. [from Dutch: a pile, stake]

PABA ('pɑːbə) *n. acronym for* para-aminobenzoic acid.

pabulum ('pæbjʊləm) *n. Rare.* **1.** food. **2.** food for thought; mental nourishment. [C17: from Latin, from *pascere* to feed]

PABX (in Britain) *abbrev. for* private automatic branch exchange. See also **PBX.**

Pac. *abbrev. for* Pacific.

paca ('pɑːkə, 'pækə) *n.* a large burrowing hystricomorph rodent, *Cuniculus paca,* of Central and South America, having white-spotted brown fur and a large head: family *Dasyproctidae.* [C17: from Spanish, from Tupi]

pace[1] (peɪs) *n.* **1. a.** a single step in walking. **b.** the distance covered by a step. **2.** a measure of length equal to the average length of a stride, approximately 3 feet. See also **Roman pace, geometric pace, military pace.** **3.** speed of movement, esp. of walking or running. **4.** rate or style of proceeding at some activity: *to live at a fast pace.* **5.** manner or action of stepping, walking, etc.; gait. **6.** any of the manners in which a horse or other quadruped walks or runs, the three principal paces being the walk, trot, and canter (or gallop). **7.** a manner of moving, natural to the camel and sometimes developed in the horse, in which the two legs on the same side of the body are moved and put down at the same time. **8.** *Architect.* a step or small raised platform. **9. keep pace with.** to proceed at the same speed as. **10. put (someone) through his paces.** to test the ability of (someone). **11. set the pace.** to determine the rate at which a group runs or walks or proceeds at some other activity. **12. stand** *or* **stay the pace.** to keep up with the speed or rate of others. ~*vb.* **13.** (*tr.*) to set or determine the pace for, as in a race. **14.** (often foll. by *about, up and down,* etc.) to walk with regular slow or fast paces, as in boredom, agitation, etc.: *to pace the room.* **15.** (*tr.;* often foll. by *out*) to measure by paces: *to pace out the distance.* **16.** (*intr.*) to walk with slow regular strides: *to pace along the street.* **17.** (*intr.*) (of a horse) to move at the pace (the specially developed gait). [C13: via Old French from Latin *passūs* step, from *pandere* to spread, unfold, extend (the legs as in walking)]

pace[2] ('peɪsɪ; *Latin* 'pɑːkɛ) *prep.* with due deference to: used to acknowledge politely someone who disagrees with the speaker or writer. [C19: from Latin, from *pāx* peace]

PACE (peɪs) *n.* (in England and Wales) *acronym for* Police and Criminal Evidence Act.

pace bowler *n. Cricket.* a bowler who characteristically delivers the ball rapidly.

pacemaker ('peɪsˌmeɪkə) *n.* **1.** a person, horse, vehicle, etc., used in a race or speed trial to set the pace. **2.** a person, an organization, etc., regarded as being the leader in a particular field of activity. **3.** Also called: **cardiac pacemaker.** a small area of specialized tissue within the wall of the right atrium of the heart whose spontaneous electrical activity initiates and controls the beat of the heart. **4.** Also called: **artificial pacemaker.** an electronic device for use in certain cases of heart disease to assume the functions of the natural cardiac pacemaker.

pacer ('peɪsə) *n.* **1.** a horse trained to move at a special gait, esp. for racing. **2.** another word for **pacemaker** (sense 1).

pacesetter ('peɪsˌsɛtə) *n.* another word for **pacemaker** (senses 1, 2).

paceway ('peɪsˌweɪ) *n. Austral.* a racecourse for trotting and pacing.

pacey *or* **pacy** ('peɪsɪ) *adj.* **pacier, paciest.** fast-moving, quick, lively: *a pacey story.*

pacha ('pɑːʃə, 'pæʃə) *n.* a variant spelling of **pasha.**

pachalic ('pɑːʃəlɪk) *n.* a variant spelling of **pashalik.**

pachisi (pə'tʃiːzɪ, pɑː-) *n.* an Indian game somewhat resembling backgammon, played on a cruciform board using six cowries as dice. [C18: from Hindi *pacīsī,* from *pacīs* twenty-five (the highest score possible in one throw)]

pachouli ('pætʃʊlɪ, pə'tʃuːlɪ) *n.* a variant spelling of **patchouli.**

Pachuco (pə'tʃuːkəʊ) *n., pl.* **-cos.** *U.S.* a young Mexican living in the U.S., esp. one of low social status who belongs to a street gang. [C20: from Mexican Spanish]

pachyderm ('pækɪˌdɜːm) *n.* any very large thick-skinned mammal, such as an elephant, rhinoceros, or hippopotamus. [C19: from French *pachyderme,* from Greek *pakhudermos* thick-skinned, from *pakhus* thick + *derma* skin] —ˌ**pachy'dermatous** *adj.*

pachytene ('pækɪˌtiːn) *n.* the third stage of the prophase of meiosis during which the chromosomes become shorter and thicker and divide into chromatids. [from Greek *pakhus* thick + *tainia* band]

pacific (pə'sɪfɪk) *adj.* **1.** tending or conducive to peace; conciliatory. **2.** not aggressive; opposed to the use of force. **3.** free from conflict; peaceful. [C16: from Old French *pacifique,* from Latin *pācificus,* from *pāx* peace + *facere* to make] —**pa'cifically** *adv.*

Pacific (pə'sɪfɪk) *adj.* of or relating to the Pacific Ocean or its islands.

pacification (ˌpæsɪfɪ'keɪʃən) *n.* the act, process, or policy of pacifying. —'**pacifiˌcatory** *adj.*

Pacific Standard Time *n.* one of the standard times used in North America, based on the local time of the 120° meridian, eight hours behind Greenwich Mean Time. Abbrev.: **PST.**

pacifier ('pæsɪˌfaɪə) *n.* **1.** a person or thing that pacifies. **2.** *U.S. and Canadian.* a baby's dummy or teething ring.

pacifism ('pæsɪˌfɪzəm) *n.* **1.** the belief that violence of any kind is unjustifiable and that one should not participate in war. **2.** the belief that international disputes can be settled by arbitration rather than war.

pacifist ('pæsɪfɪst) *n.* **1.** a person who supports pacifism. **2.** a person who refuses military service. ~*adj.* **3.** advocating, relating to, or characterized by pacifism.

pacify ('pæsɪˌfaɪ) *vb.* **-fies, -fying, -fied.** (*tr.*) **1.** to calm the anger or agitation of; mollify. **2.** to restore to peace or order, esp. by the threat or use of force. [C15: from Old French *pacifier;* see PACIFIC] —'**paciˌfiable** *adj.*

pack[1] (pæk) *n.* **1. a.** a bundle or load, esp. one carried on the back. **b.** (*as modifier*): *a pack animal.* **2.** a collected amount of anything. **3.** a complete set of similar things, esp. a set of 52 playing cards. **4.** a group of animals of the same kind, esp. hunting animals: *a pack of hounds.* **5.** any group or band that associates together, esp. for criminal purposes. **6.** *Rugby.* the forwards of a team or both teams collectively, as in a scrum or in rucking. **7.** the basic organizational unit of Cub Scouts and Brownie Guides. **8. a.** a small package, carton, or container, used to retail commodities, esp. foodstuffs, cigarettes, etc. **b.** (*in combination*): *pack-sealed.* **9.** short for **pack ice.** **10.** the quantity of something, such as food, packaged for preservation. **11.** *Med.* **a.** a sheet or blanket, either damp or dry, for wrapping about the body, esp. for its soothing effect. **b.** a material such as cotton or gauze for temporarily filling a bodily cavity, esp. to control bleeding. **12.** short for **backpack** or **rucksack.** **13.** *Mining.* a roof support, esp. one made of rubble. **14.** short for **face pack.** **15.** a parachute folded and ready for use. **16.** *Computer technol.* another name for **deck** (sense 5). **17. go to the pack.** *Austral. and N.Z. informal.* to fall into a lower state or condition. ~*vb.* **18.** to place or arrange (articles) in (a container), such as clothes in a suitcase. **19.** (*tr.*) to roll up into a bundle. **20.** (when *passive,* often foll. by *out*) to press tightly together; cram: *the audience packed into the foyer; the hall was packed out.* **21.** (*tr.;* foll. by *in* or *into*) to fit (many things, experiences, etc.) into a limited space or time: *she packed a lot of theatre visits into her* *holiday*. **22.** to form (snow, ice, etc.) into a hard compact mass or (of snow, ice, etc.) to become compacted. **23.** (*tr.*) to press in or cover tightly: *to pack a hole with cement*. **24.** (*tr.*) to load (a horse, donkey, etc.) with a burden. **25.** (often foll. by *off* or *away*) to send away or go away, esp. hastily. **26.** (*tr.*) to seal (a joint) by inserting a layer of compressible material between the faces. **27.** (*tr.*) to fill (a bearing or gland) with grease to lubricate it. **28.** (*tr.*) to separate (two adjoining components) so that they have a predetermined gap between them, by introducing shims, washers, plates, etc. **29.** (*tr.*) *Med.* to treat with a pack. **30.** (*tr.*) *Slang.* to be capable of inflicting (a blow): *he packs a mean punch*. **31.** (*tr.*) *U.S. informal.* to carry or wear habitually: *he packs a gun*. **32.** (*intr.*; often foll. by *down*) *Rugby.* to form a scrum. **33.** (*tr.*; often foll. by *into, to,* etc.) *U.S., Canadian, and N.Z.* to carry (goods), esp. on the back: *will you pack your camping equipment into the mountains?* **34. pack one's bags.** *Informal.* to get ready to leave. **35. send packing.** *Informal.* to dismiss peremptorily. ~See also **pack in, pack up.** [C13: related to Middle Low German *pak*, of obscure origin] —ˈ**packable** *adj.*

pack[2] (pæk) *vb.* (*tr.*) to fill (a legislative body, committee, etc.) with one's own supporters: *to pack a jury*. [C16: perhaps changed from PACT]

package (ˈpækɪdʒ) *n.* **1.** any wrapped or boxed object or group of objects. **2. a.** a proposition, offer, or thing for sale in which separate items are offered together as a single or inclusive unit. **b.** (*as modifier*): *a package holiday; a package deal*. **3.** a complete unit consisting of a number of component parts sold separately. **4.** the act or process of packing or packaging. **5.** *Computer technol.* a set of programs designed for a specific type of problem in statistics, production control, etc., making it unnecessary for a separate program to be written for each problem. **6.** the usual U.S. and Canadian word for **packet** (sense 1). ~*vb.* (*tr.*) **7.** to wrap in or put into a package. **8.** to design and produce a package for (retail goods). **9.** to group (separate items) together as a single unit. **10.** to compile (complete books) for a publisher to market.

packager (ˈpækɪdʒə) *n.* an independent firm specializing in design and production, as of illustrated books or television programmes which are sold to publishers or television companies as finished products.

package store *n. U.S.* a store where alcoholic drinks are sold for consumption elsewhere. Canadian name (also sometimes used in the U.S.): **liquor store.** Brit. equivalent: **off-licence.**

packaging (ˈpækɪdʒɪŋ) *n.* **1. a.** the box or wrapping in which a product is offered for sale. **b.** the design of such a box or wrapping, esp. with reference to its ability to attract customers. **2.** the presentation of a person, product, television programme, etc., to the public in a way designed to build up a favourable image. **3.** the work of a packager.

pack animal *n.* an animal, such as a donkey, used to transport goods, equipment, etc.

pack drill *n.* a military punishment by which the offender is made to march about carrying a full pack of equipment.

packed (pækt) *adj.* **1.** completely filled; full: *a packed theatre*. **2.** (of a picnic type of meal) prepared and put in a container or containers beforehand; prepacked: *a packed lunch*.

packer (ˈpækə) *n.* **1.** a person or company whose business is to pack goods, esp. food: *a meat packer*. **2.** a person or machine that packs.

packet (ˈpækɪt) *n.* **1.** a small or medium-sized container of cardboard, paper, etc., often together with its contents: *a packet of biscuits*. Usual U.S. and Canadian word: **package. 2.** a small package; parcel. **3.** Also called: **packet boat.** a boat that transports mail, passengers, goods, etc., on a fixed short route. **4.** *Slang.* a large sum of money: *to cost a packet*. **5. catch, cop,** *or* **get a packet.** *Brit. slang.* to suffer an unpleasant experience or injury, esp. an electric shock. ~*vb.* **6.** (*tr.*) to wrap up in a packet or as a packet. [C16: from Old French *pacquet*, from *pacquer* to pack, from Old Dutch *pak* a pack]

packet switching *n. Computer technol.* the concentration of data into units that are allocated an address prior to transmission.

packframe (ˈpækˌfreɪm) *n. Mountaineering.* a light metal frame with shoulder straps, used for carrying heavy or awkward loads.

packhorse (ˈpækˌhɔːs) *n.* a horse used to transport goods, equipment, etc.

pack ice *n.* a large area of floating ice, usually occurring in polar seas, consisting of separate pieces that have become massed together. Also called: **ice pack.**

pack in *vb.* (*tr., adv.*) **1.** *Brit. and N.Z. informal.* to stop doing (something) (esp. in the phrase **pack it in**). **2.** to carry (something) to base camp, etc. by pack.

packing (ˈpækɪŋ) *n.* **1. a.** material used to cushion packed goods. **b.** (*as modifier*): *a packing needle*. **2.** the packaging of foodstuffs. **3.** *Med.* **a.** the application of a medical pack. **b.** gauze or other absorbent material for packing a wound. **4.** *Printing.* sheets of material, esp. paper, used to cover the platen or impression cylinder of a letterpress machine. **5.** any substance or material used to make watertight or gastight joints, esp. in a stuffing box. **6.** *Engineering.* pieces of material of various thicknesses used to adjust the position of a component or machine before it is secured in its correct position or alignment.

packing box *n.* another name for **stuffing box.**

packing density *n. Computer technol.* a measure of the amount of data that can be held by unit length of a storage medium, such as magnetic tape.

packing fraction *n.* a measure of the stability of a nucleus, equal to the difference between its mass in amu and its mass number, divided by the mass number.

pack of lies *n.* a completely false story, account, etc.

pack rat *n.* any rat of the genus *Neotoma*, of W North America, having a long tail that is furry in some species: family *Cricetidae*. Also called: **wood rat.**

packsack (ˈpækˌsæk) *n.* a U.S. and Canadian word for **knapsack.**

packsaddle (ˈpækˌsædᵊl) *n.* a saddle hung with packs, equipment, etc., used on a pack animal.

packthread (ˈpækˌθrɛd) *n.* a strong twine for sewing or tying up packages.

pack up *vb.* (*adv.*) **1.** to put (things) away in a proper or suitable place. **2.** *Informal.* to give up (an attempt) or stop doing (something): *if you don't do your work better, you might as well pack up*. **3.** (*intr.*) (of an engine, machine, etc.) to fail to operate; break down. **4.** *Engineering.* to use packing to adjust the height of a component or machine before it is secured in its correct position or alignment.

pact (pækt) *n.* an agreement or compact between two or more parties, nations, etc., for mutual advantage. [C15: from Old French *pacte*, from Latin *pactum*, from *pacīscī* to agree]

pacy (ˈpeɪsɪ) *adj.* a variant spelling of **pacey.**

pad[1] (pæd) *n.* **1.** a thick piece of soft material used to make something comfortable, give it shape, or protect it. **2.** a guard made of flexible resilient material worn in various sports to protect parts of the body. **3.** Also called: **stamp pad, ink pad.** a block of firm absorbent material soaked with ink for transferring to a rubber stamp. **4.** Also called: ˈ**notepad, writing pad.** a number of sheets of paper fastened together along one edge. **5.** a flat piece of stiff material used to back a piece of blotting paper. **6. a.** the fleshy cushion-like underpart of the foot of a cat, dog, etc. **b.** any of the parts constituting such a structure. **7.** any of various level surfaces or flat-topped structures, such as a launching pad. **8.** *Entomol.* a nontechnical name for **pulvillus. 9.** the large flat floating leaf of the water lily. **10.** *Electronics.* a resistive attenuator network inserted in the path of a signal to reduce amplitude or to match one circuit to another. **11.** *Slang.* a person's residence. **12.** *Slang.* a bed or bedroom. ~*vb.* **pads, padding, padded.** (*tr.*) **13.** to line, stuff, or fill out with soft material, esp. in order to protect or give shape to. **14.** (often foll. by *out*) to inflate with irrelevant or false information: *to pad out a story*. [C16: origin uncertain; compare Low German *pad* sole of the foot]

pad[2] (pæd) *vb.* **pads, padding, padded. 1.** (*intr.*; often foll. by *along, up,* etc.) to walk with a soft or muffled tread. **2.** (when *intr.*, often foll. by *around*) to travel (a route) on foot, esp. at a slow pace; tramp: *to pad around the country*. ~*n.* **3.** a dull soft sound, esp. of footsteps. **4.** *Archaic.* short for **footpad. 5.** *Archaic or dialect.* a slow-paced horse; nag. **6.** *Dialect and Austral.* a path or track: *a cattle pad*. [C16: perhaps from Middle Dutch *paden*, from *pad* PATH]

padang (ˈpædæŋ) *n.* (in Malaysia) a playing field. [from Malay: plain]

padauk *or* **padouk** (pəˈdaʊk, -ˈdɔːk) *n.* **1.** any of various tropical African or Asian papilionaceous trees of the genus *Pterocarpus* that have reddish wood. **2.** the wood of any of these trees, used in decorative cabinetwork. ~See also **amboyna.** [from a native Burmese word]

padded cell *n.* a room, esp. one in a mental hospital, with padded surfaces in which violent inmates are placed.

padding (ˈpædɪŋ) *n.* **1.** any soft material used to pad clothes, furniture, etc. **2.** superfluous material put into a speech or written work to pad it out; waffle. **3.** inflated or false entries in a financial account, esp. an expense account.

paddle[1] (ˈpædᵊl) *n.* **1.** a short light oar with a flat blade at one or both ends, used without a rowlock to propel a canoe or small boat. **2.** Also called: **float.** a blade of a water wheel or paddle wheel. **3.** a period of paddling: *to go for a paddle upstream*. **4. a.** a paddle wheel used to propel a boat. **b.** (*as modifier*): *a paddle steamer*. **5.** the sliding panel in a lock or sluicegate that regulates the level or flow of water. **6.** any of various instruments shaped like a paddle and used for beating, mixing, etc. **7.** a table-tennis bat. **8.** the flattened limb of a seal, turtle, or similar aquatic animal, specialized for swimming. ~*vb.* **9.** to propel (a canoe, small boat, etc.) with a paddle. **10. paddle one's own canoe. a.** to be self-sufficient. **b.** to mind one's own business. **11.** (*tr.*) to convey by paddling: *we paddled him to the shore*. **12.** (*tr.*) to stir or mix with or as if with a paddle. **13.** to row (a boat) steadily, esp. (of a racing crew) to row firmly but not at full pressure. **14.** (*intr.*) (of steamships) to be propelled by paddle wheels. **15.** (*intr.*) to swim with short rapid strokes, like a dog. **16.** (*tr.*) *U.S. and Canadian informal.* to spank. [C15: of unknown origin] —ˈ**paddler** *n.*

paddle[2] (ˈpædᵊl) *vb.* (*mainly intr.*) **1.** to walk or play barefoot in shallow water, mud, etc. **2.** to dabble the fingers, hands, or feet in water. **3.** to walk unsteadily, like a baby. **4.** (*tr.*) *Archaic.* to fondle with the fingers. ~*n.* **5.** the act of paddling in water. [C16: of uncertain origin] —ˈ**paddler** *n.*

paddlefish ('pædᵊl,fɪʃ) *n., pl.* **-fish** *or* **-fishes.** **1.** a primitive bony fish, *Polyodon spathula,* of the Mississippi River, having a long paddle-like projection to the snout: family *Polyodontidae.* **2.** a similar and related Chinese fish, *Psephurus gladius,* of the Yangtze River.

paddle wheel *n.* a large wheel fitted with paddles, turned by an engine to propel a vessel on the water.

paddle worm *n.* any of a family of green-blue faintly iridescent active marine polychaete worms of the genus *Phyllodoce,* having paddle-shaped swimming lobes, found under stones on the shore.

paddock[1] ('pædək) *n.* **1.** a small enclosed field, usually near a house or stable. **2.** (in horse racing) the enclosure in which horses are paraded and mounted before a race, together with the accompanying rooms. **3.** (in motor racing) an area near the pits where cars are worked on before races. **4.** *Austral. and N.Z.* any area of fenced land. **5.** *Austral. and N.Z.* a playing field. **6. the long paddock.** *Austral.* the stock route. *~vb.* **7.** (*tr.*) to confine (horses, etc.) in a paddock. [C17: variant of dialect *parrock,* from Old English *pearruc* enclosure, of Germanic origin. See PARK]

paddock[2] ('pædək) *n. Archaic or dialect.* a frog or toad. Also called (Scot.): **puddock.** [C12: from *pad* toad, probably from Old Norse *padda;* see -OCK]

paddy[1] ('pædɪ) *n., pl.* **-dies.** **1.** Also called: **paddy field.** a field planted with rice. **2.** rice as a growing crop or when harvested but not yet milled. [from Malay *pādī*]

paddy[2] ('pædɪ) *n., pl.* **-dies.** *Brit. informal.* a fit of temper. [C19: from PADDY]

Paddy ('pædɪ) *n., pl.* **-dies.** (*sometimes not cap.*) an informal, often derogatory, name for an Irishman. [from *Patrick*]

paddy-last *n. Irish.* the last person in a race or competition: *she was paddy-last.*

paddy wagon *n. U.S., Austral., and N.Z.* an informal word for **patrol wagon.**

paddywhack *or* **paddywack** ('pædɪ,wæk) *n. Informal.* **1.** *Brit.* another word for **paddy**[2]. **2.** a spanking or smack.

pademelon *or* **paddymelon** ('pædɪ,mɛlən) *n.* a small wallaby of the genus *Thylogale,* of coastal scrubby regions of Australia. [C19: from a native Australian name]

padlock ('pæd,lɒk) *n.* **1.** a detachable lock having a hinged or sliding shackle, which can be used to secure a door, lid, etc., by passing the shackle through rings or staples. *~vb.* **2.** (*tr.*) to fasten with or as if with a padlock. [C15 *pad,* of obscure origin]

Padma Shri ('pʌdmə 'ʃriː) *n.* (in India) an award for distinguished service in any field. [Hindi: lotus decoration]

padouk (pə'daʊk, -'dɔːk) *n.* a variant spelling of **padauk.**

padre ('pɑːdrɪ) *n. Informal.* (*sometimes cap.*) **1.** father: used to address or refer to a clergyman, esp. a priest. **2.** a chaplain to the armed forces. [via Spanish or Italian from Latin *pater* father]

padrone (pə'drəʊnɪ) *n., pl.* **-nes** *or* **-ni** (-niː). **1.** the owner or proprietor of an inn, esp. in Italy. **2.** *U.S.* an employer who completely controls his workers, esp. a man who exploits Italian immigrants in the U.S. [C17: from Italian; see PATRON[1]]

padsaw ('pæd,sɔː) *n.* a small narrow saw used for cutting curves. [C19: from PAD[1] (in the sense: a handle that can be fitted to various tools) + SAW[1]]

Paduan ('pædjʊən) *adj.* of or relating to Padua, a city in NE Italy. *~n.* **2.** a native or inhabitant of Padua.

paduasoy ('pædjʊə,sɔɪ) *n.* **1.** a rich strong silk fabric used for hangings, vestments, etc. **2.** a garment made of this. [C17: changed (through influence of *Padua* from earlier *poudesoy,* from French *pou-de-soie,* of obscure origin]

paean *or U.S.* (*sometimes*) **pean** ('piːən) *n.* **1.** a hymn sung in ancient Greece in invocation of or thanksgiving to a deity. **2.** any song of praise. **3.** enthusiastic praise: *the film received a paean from the critics.* [C16: via Latin from Greek *paiān* hymn to Apollo, from his title *Paiān,* denoting the physician of the gods]

paederast ('pɛdə,ræst) *n.* a less common spelling of **pederast.** —,**paeder'astic** *adj.* —'**paeder,asty** *n.*

paediatrician *or chiefly U.S.* **pediatrician** (,piːdɪə'trɪʃən) *n.* a medical practitioner who specializes in paediatrics.

paediatrics *or chiefly U.S.* **pediatrics** (,piːdɪ'ætrɪks) *n.* (*functioning as sing.*) the branch of medical science concerned with children and their diseases. —,**paedi'atric** *or chiefly U.S.* ,**pedi'atric** *adj.*

paedo-, *before a vowel* **paed-** *or esp. U.S.* **pedo-, ped-** *combining form.* indicating a child or children: *paedology.* [from Greek *pais, paid-* child]

paedogenesis (,piːdəʊ'dʒɛnɪsɪs) *n.* sexual reproduction in an animal that retains its larval features. See also **neoteny.** —**paedogenetic** (,piːdəʊdʒə'nɛtɪk) *or* ,**paedo'genic** *adj.*

paedology *or U.S.* **pedology** (piː'dɒlədʒɪ) *n.* the study of the character, growth, and development of children. —**paedological** *or U.S.* **pedological** (,piːdᵊ'lɒdʒɪkᵊl) *adj.* —**pae'dologist** *or U.S.* **pe'dologist** *n.*

paedomorphosis (,piːdə'mɔːfəsɪs) *n.* the resemblance of adult animals to the young of their ancestors: seen in the evolution of modern man, who shows resemblances to the young stages of australopithecines.

paedophilia *or esp. U.S.* **pedophilia** (,piːdəʊ'fɪlɪə) *n.* the condition of being sexually attracted to children. —**paedophile** *or esp. U.S.* **pedophile** ('piːdəʊ,faɪl) *or* ,**paedo'phili,ac** *or esp. U.S.* ,**pedo'phili,ac** *n., adj.*

paella (paɪ'ɛlə; *Spanish* pa'eʎa) *n., pl.* **-las** (-ləz; *Spanish* -ʎas). **1.** a Spanish dish made from rice, shellfish, chicken, and vegetables. **2.** the large flat frying pan in which a paella is cooked. [from Catalan, from Old French *paelle,* from Latin *patella* small pan]

paeon ('piːən) *n. Prosody.* a metrical foot of four syllables, with one long one and three short ones in any order. [C17: via Latin *paeon* from Greek *paiōn;* variant of PAEAN] —**pae'onic** *adj.*

paeony ('piːənɪ) *n., pl.* **-nies.** a variant spelling of **peony.**

pagan ('peɪgən) *n.* **1.** a member of a group professing a polytheistic religion or any religion other than Christianity, Judaism, or Islam. **2.** a person without any religion; heathen. *~adj.* **3.** of or relating to pagans or their faith or worship. **4.** heathen; irreligious. [C14: from Church Latin *pāgānus* civilian (hence, not a soldier of Christ), from Latin: countryman, villager, from *pāgus* village] —'**pagandom** *n.* —'**paganish** *adj.* —'**paganism** *n.* —'**paganist** *adj., n.* —,**pagan'istic** *adj.* —,**pagan'istically** *adv.*

paganize *or* **paganise** ('peɪgə,naɪz) *vb.* to become pagan, render pagan, or convert to paganism. —,**pagani'zation** *or* ,**pagani'sation** *n.* —'**pagan,izer** *or* '**pagan,iser** *n.*

page[1] (peɪdʒ) *n.* **1.** one side of one of the leaves of a book, newspaper, letter, etc. or the written or printed matter it bears. Abbrev.: **p.** (*pl.* **pp.**). **2.** such a leaf considered as a unit: *insert a new page.* **3.** an episode, phase, or period: *a glorious page in the revolution.* **4.** *Printing.* the type as set up for printing a page. *~vb.* **5.** another word for **paginate.** **6.** (*intr.;* foll. by *through*) to look through (a book, report, etc.); leaf through. [C15: via Old French from Latin *pāgina*]

page[2] (peɪdʒ) *n.* **1.** a boy employed to run errands, carry messages, etc., for the guests in a hotel, club, etc. **2.** a youth in attendance at official functions or ceremonies, esp. weddings. **3.** *Medieval history.* **a.** a boy in training for knighthood in personal attendance on a knight. **b.** a youth in the personal service of a person of rank, esp. in a royal household: *page of the chamber.* **4.** (in the U.S.) an attendant at Congress or other legislative body. **5.** *Canadian.* a boy or girl employed in the debating chamber of the House of Commons, the Senate, or a legislative assembly to carry messages for members. *~vb.* (*tr.*) **6.** to call out the name of (a person), esp. by a loudspeaker system, so as to give him a message. **7.** to call (a person) by an electronic device, such as a bleep. **8.** to act as a page to or attend as a page. [C13: via Old French from Italian *paggio,* probably from Greek *paidion* boy, from *pais* child]

pageant ('pædʒənt) *n.* **1.** an elaborate colourful parade or display portraying scenes from history, esp. one involving rich costume. **2.** any magnificent or showy display, procession, etc. [C14: from Medieval Latin *pāgina* scene of a play, from Latin: PAGE[1]]

pageantry ('pædʒəntrɪ) *n., pl.* **-ries.** **1.** spectacular display or ceremony. **2.** *Archaic.* pageants collectively.

pageboy ('peɪdʒ,bɔɪ) *n.* **1.** a smooth medium-length hairstyle with the ends of the hair curled under and a long fringe falling onto the forehead from the crown. **2.** a less common word for **page**[2] (sense 1).

Paget's disease ('pædʒɪts) *n.* **1.** Also called: **osteitis deformans.** a chronic disease of the bones characterized by inflammation and deformation. **2.** Also called: **Paget's cancer.** cancer of the nipple and surrounding tissue. [C19: named after Sir James *Paget* (1814–99), British surgeon and pathologist, who described these diseases]

page-turner *n.* an exciting novel, such as a thriller, with a fast-moving story.

paginal ('pædʒɪnᵊl) *adj.* **1.** page-for-page: *paginal facsimile.* **2.** of, like, or consisting of pages. [C17: from Late Latin *pāginālis,* from Latin *pāgina* page]

paginate ('pædʒɪ,neɪt) *vb.* (*tr.*) to number the pages of (a book, manuscript, etc.) in sequence. Compare **foliate.** —,**pagi'nation** *n.*

pagoda (pə'gəʊdə) *n.* an Indian or Far Eastern temple, esp. a tower, usually pyramidal and having many storeys. [C17: from Portuguese *pagode,* ultimately from Sanskrit *bhagavatī* divine]

pagoda tree *n.* a Chinese leguminous tree, *Sophora japonica,* with ornamental white flowers and dark green foliage.

pagurian (pə'gjʊərɪən) *or* **pagurid** (pə'gjʊərɪd, 'pægjʊrɪd) *n.* **1.** any decapod crustacean of the family *Paguridae,* which includes the hermit crabs. *~adj.* **2.** of, relating to, or belonging to the *Paguridae.* [C19: from Latin *pagurus,* from Greek *pagouros* kind of crab]

pah (pɑː) *interj.* an exclamation of disgust, disbelief, etc.

Pahari (pə'hɑːrɪ) *n.* a group of Indo-European languages spoken in the Himalayas, divided into **Eastern Pahari** (Nepali) and **Western Pahari** (consisting of many dialects).

Pahlavi ('pɑːləvɪ) *or* **Pehlevi** *n.* the Middle Persian language, esp. as used in classical Zoroastrian and Manichean literature. [C18: from Persian *pahlavī,* from Old Persian *Parthava* Parthia (ancient Asian country)]

paid (peɪd) *vb.* **1.** the past tense and past participle of **pay**[1]. **2. put paid to.** *Chiefly Brit. and N.Z.* to end or destroy: *breaking his leg put paid to his hopes of running in the Olympics.*

paid-up *adj.* **1.** having paid the due, full, or required fee to be a member of an organization, club, political party, etc. **2.** denoting a security in which all the instalments have been paid; fully paid: *a paid-up share.* 3. denoting all the money that a company has received from its shareholders: *the paid-up capital.* 4. denoting an endowment assurance policy on which the payment of premiums has stopped and the surrender value has been used to purchase a new single-premium policy.

paigle ('peɪgᵊl) *n.* another name for the **cowslip** and **oxlip.** [C16: of uncertain origin]

pail (peɪl) *n.* 1. a bucket, esp. one made of wood or metal. 2. Also called: **'pailful.** the quantity that fills a pail. [Old English *pægel;* compare Catalan *paella* frying pan, PAELLA]

paillasse ('pælɪˌæs, ˌpælɪ'æs) *n.* a variant spelling (esp. U.S.) of **palliasse.**

paillette (pæl'jɛt; *French* pajɛt) *n.* 1. a sequin or spangle sewn onto a costume. 2. a small piece of metal or foil, used in enamelling for decoration. [C19: from French, diminutive of *paille* straw, from Latin *palea*]

pain (peɪn) *n.* 1. the sensation of acute physical hurt or discomfort caused by injury, illness, etc. 2. emotional suffering or mental distress. 3. **on pain of.** subject to the penalty of. 4. Also called: **pain in the neck** *or* (*taboo*) **arse.** *Informal.* a person or thing that is a nuisance. ~*vb.* (*tr.*) 5. to cause (a person) distress, hurt, grief, anxiety, etc. 6. *Informal.* to annoy; irritate. ~See also **pains.** [C13: from Old French *peine,* from Latin *poena* punishment, grief, from Greek *poinē* penalty]

pained (peɪnd) *adj.* having or expressing pain or distress, esp. mental or emotional distress: *a pained expression.*

painful ('peɪnfʊl) *adj.* 1. causing pain; distressing: *a painful duty.* 2. affected with pain: *a painful leg.* 3. tedious or difficult. 4. *Informal.* extremely bad: *a painful performance.* —**'painfully** *adv.* —**'painfulness** *n.*

painkiller ('peɪnˌkɪlə) *n.* 1. an analgesic drug or agent. 2. anything that relieves pain.

painless ('peɪnlɪs) *adj.* 1. not causing pain or distress. 2. not affected by pain. —**'painlessly** *adv.* —**'painlessness** *n.*

pains (peɪnz) *pl. n.* 1. care, trouble, or effort (esp. in the phrases **take pains, be at pains to**). 2. painful sensations experienced during contractions in childbirth; labour pains.

painstaking ('peɪnzˌteɪkɪŋ) *adj.* extremely careful, esp. as to fine detail: *painstaking research.* —**'painsˌtakingly** *adv.* —**'painsˌtakingness** *n.*

paint (peɪnt) *n.* 1. a substance used for decorating or protecting a surface, esp. a mixture consisting of a solid pigment suspended in a liquid, that when applied to a surface dries to form a hard coating. 2. a dry film of paint on a surface. 3. the solid pigment of a paint before it is suspended in liquid. 4. *Informal.* face make-up, such as rouge. 5. short for **greasepaint.** ~*vb.* 6. to make (a picture) of (a figure, landscape, etc.) with paint applied to a surface such as canvas. 7. to coat (a surface) with paint, as in decorating. 8. (*tr.*) to apply (liquid) onto (a surface): *her mother painted the cut with antiseptic.* 9. (*tr.*) to apply make-up onto (the face, lips, etc.). 10. (*tr.*) to describe vividly in words. 11. **paint the town red.** *Informal.* to celebrate uninhibitedly; go on a spree. [C13: from Old French *peint* painted, from *peindre* to paint, from Latin *pingere* to paint, adorn] —**'painty** *adj.*

paintball game ('peɪntˌbɔːl) *n.* a game in which teams of players simulate a military skirmish, shooting each other with paint pellets that explode on impact, marking the players who have been shot.

paintbox ('peɪntˌbɒks) *n.* a box containing a tray of dry watercolour paints.

paintbrush ('peɪntˌbrʌʃ) *n.* a brush used to apply paint.

painted lady *n.* a migratory nymphalid butterfly, *Vanessa cardui,* with pale brownish-red mottled wings.

painted woman *n.* a woman of low moral character.

painter[1] ('peɪntə) *n.* 1. a person who paints surfaces as a trade. 2. an artist who paints pictures.

painter[2] ('peɪntə) *n.* a line attached to the bow of a boat for tying it up. [C15: probably from Old French *penteur* strong rope]

painterly ('peɪntəlɪ) *adj.* 1. having qualities peculiar to painting, esp. the depiction of shapes by means of solid masses of colour, rather than by lines. Compare **linear** (sense 5). 2. of or characteristic of a painter; artistic.

painter's colic *n. Pathol.* another name for **lead colic.** [C19: so called because it frequently affected people who worked with lead-based paints or similar substances]

painting ('peɪntɪŋ) *n.* 1. the art or process of applying paints to a surface such as canvas, to make a picture or other artistic composition. 2. a composition or picture made in this way. 3. the act of applying paint to a surface with a brush.

paint stripper *or* **remover** *n.* a liquid, often caustic, used to remove paint from a surface.

paintwork ('peɪntˌwɜːk) *n.* a surface, such as wood or a car body, that is painted.

pair[1] (pɛə) *n., pl.* **pairs** *or* (*functioning as sing. or pl.*) **pair.** 1. two identical or similar things matched for use together: *a pair of socks.* 2. two persons, animals, things, etc., used or grouped together: *a pair of horses; a pair of scoundrels.* 3. an object considered to be two identical or similar things joined together: *a pair of trousers.* 4. two people joined in love or marriage. 5. a male and a female animal of the same species, esp. such animals kept for breeding purposes. 6. *Parliamentary procedure.* **a.** two opposed members who both agree not to vote on a specified motion or for a specific period of time. **b.** the agreement so made. 7. two playing cards of the same rank or denomination: *a pair of threes.* 8. one member of a matching pair: *I can't find the pair to this glove.* 9. *Rowing.* See **pair-oar.** 10. *Brit. and U.S. dialect.* a group or set of more than two. 11. *Logic, maths.* **a.** a set with two members. **b.** an ordered set with two members. ~*vb.* 12. (often foll. by *off*) to arrange or fall into groups of twos. 13. to group or be grouped in matching pairs: *to pair socks.* 14. to join or be joined in marriage; mate or couple. 15. (when *tr., usually passive*) *Parliamentary procedure.* to form or cause to form a pair: *18 members were paired for the last vote.* ~See also **pairs.** [C13: from Old French *paire,* from Latin *paria* equal (things), from *pār* equal]

▷**Usage.** Like other collective nouns, *pair* takes a singular or a plural verb according to whether it is seen as a unit or as a collection of two things: *the pair of cuff links was gratefully received; that pair* (the two of them) *are on very good terms with each other.*

pair[2] (per) *adj.* a Scot. word for **poor.**

pair bond *n.* the exclusive relationship formed between a male and a female, esp. in some species of animals and birds during courtship and breeding. —**pair bonding** *n.*

pair-oar *n. Rowing.* a racing shell in which two oarsmen sit one behind the other and pull one oar each. Also called: **pair.** Compare **double scull.**

pair production *n.* the production of an electron and a positron from a gamma-ray photon that passes close to an atomic nucleus.

pair royal *n.* (in some card games) a set of three cards of the same denomination.

pairs (pɛəz) *pl. n.* another name for **Pelmanism** (sense 2).

pair trawling *n.* the act or practice of using two boats to trawl for fish.

paisa ('paɪsɑː) *n., pl.* **-se** (-seɪ). a monetary unit of India and Pakistan worth one hundredth of a rupee. [from Hindi]

paisano (paɪ'sɑːnəʊ; *Spanish* pai'sano) *n., pl.* **-nos** (-nəʊz; *Spanish* -nos). *Southwestern U.S.* (often a term of address) 1. *Informal.* a friend; pal. 2. a fellow countryman. [C20: via Spanish from French *paysan* PEASANT]

paisley ('peɪzlɪ) *n.* 1. a pattern of small curving shapes with intricate detailing, usually printed in bright colours. 2. a soft fine wool fabric traditionally printed with this pattern. 3. a garment made of this fabric, esp. a shawl popular in the late 19th century. 4. (*modifier*) of or decorated with this pattern: *a paisley scarf.* [C19: named after *Paisley,* town in SW Scotland where the fabric was manufactured]

paitrick ('petrɪk) *n.* a Scot. word for **partridge.**

Paiute *or* **Piute** ('paɪˌuːt, paɪ'juːt) *n.* 1. (*pl.* **-utes** *or* **-ute**) a member of either of two North American Indian peoples (**Northern Paiute** and **Southern Paiute**) of the Southwestern U.S., related to the Aztecs. 2. the language of either of these peoples, belonging to the Shoshonean subfamily of the Uto-Aztecan family.

pajamas (pə'dʒɑːməz) *pl. n.* the U.S. spelling of **pyjamas.**

PAK *international car registration for* Pakistan.

pakahi ('pɑːkəhiː) *n. N.Z.* **a.** acid land that is unsuitable for cultivation. **b.** (*as modifier*): *pakahi soil.* [C19: from Maori]

pakapoo ('pækəpuː) *n., pl.* **-poos.** *Austral. and N.Z.* 1. a Chinese lottery with betting slips marked with Chinese characters. 2. **like a pakapoo ticket.** untidy, incomprehensible. [C19: from Chinese]

pak-choi cabbage ('pɑːk'tʃɔɪ) *n.* another name for **Chinese cabbage** (sense 2). [from Chinese (Cantonese dialect), literally: white vegetable]

pakeha ('pɑːkɪˌhɑː) *n.* (in New Zealand) a person who is not of Maori ancestry, esp. a White person. [from Maori]

pakeha Maori *n.* (in the 19th century) a European who adopted the Maori way of life.

Paki ('pækɪ) *Brit. slang, derogatory.* ~*n., pl.* **Pakis.** 1. a Pakistani or person of Pakistani descent. 2. (loosely) a person from any part of the Indian subcontinent. ~*adj.* 3. Pakistani or of Pakistani descent. 4. (loosely) denoting a person from the Indian subcontinent.

Paki-bashing *n. Brit. slang.* the activity of making vicious and unprovoked physical assaults upon Pakistani immigrants residing in Britain. —**'Paki-ˌbasher** *n.*

pakirikiri ('pɑːkɪriːˌkɪriː) *n. N.Z.* another name for **blue cod.**

Pakistani (ˌpɑːkɪ'stɑːnɪ, ˌpækɪ-) *n.* 1. (*pl.* **-nis**) a native or inhabitant of Pakistan, a republic in S Asia, or a descendant of one. ~*adj.* 2. of or relating to Pakistan, its people, customs, etc.

pakoko ('pɑːkəʊkəʊ) *n. N.Z.* another name for **bully**[2].

pakora (pə'kɔːrə) *n.* an Indian dish consisting of pieces of vegetable, chicken, etc., dipped in a spiced batter and deep-fried: served with a piquant sauce. [C20: from Hindi]

pal (pæl) *Informal.* ~*n.* 1. a close friend; comrade. 2. an accomplice. ~*vb.* **pals, palling, palled.** 3. (*intr.;* usually foll. by *with* or *about*) to associate as friends. ~See also **pal up.** [C17: from English Gypsy: brother, ultimately from Sanskrit *bhrātar* BROTHER]

PAL (pæl) *n. acronym for* phase alternation line: a colour-television broadcasting system used generally in Europe.

Pal. *abbrev. for* Palestine.

palace ('pælɪs) *n.* (*cap. when part of a name*) 1. the official residence of a reigning monarch or member of a royal family: *Buckingham Palace.* 2. the official residence of various high-ranking church dignitaries or members of the nobility, as of an archbishop. **3.** a large and richly furnished building resembling a royal palace. [C13: from Old French *palais,* from Latin *Palātium* Palatine (one of the seven Hills of Rome) the site of the palace of the emperors]

palace revolution *n.* a coup d'état made by those already in positions of power, usually with little violence.

paladin ('pælədɪn) *n.* **1.** one of the legendary twelve peers of Charlemagne's court. **2.** a knightly champion. [C16: via French from Italian *paladino,* from Latin *palātīnus* imperial official, from *Palātium* Palatine; see PALACE]

palaeanthropic (ˌpælɪæn'θrɒpɪk) *adj.* relating to or denoting the earliest variety of man.

Palaearctic (ˌpælɪ'ɑːktɪk) *adj.* of or denoting a zoogeographical region consisting of Europe, Africa north of the Sahara, and most of Asia north of the Himalayas.

palaeethnology (ˌpælɪɛθ'nɒlədʒɪ) *n.* the study of prehistoric man. —**palaeethnological** (ˌpælɪˌɛθnə'lɒdʒɪkᵊl) *adj.* —ˌ**palaeeth'nologist** *n.*

palaeo-, *before a vowel* **palae-** *or esp. U.S.* **paleo-, pale-** *combining form.* old, ancient, or prehistoric: *palaeography.* [from Greek *palaios* old]

palaeoanthropology (ˌpælɪəʊˌænθrə'pɒlədʒɪ) *n.* the branch of anthropology concerned with primitive man.

palaeobotany (ˌpælɪəʊ'bɒtənɪ) *n.* the study of fossil plants. —**palaeobotanical** (ˌpælɪəʊbə'tænɪkᵊl) *or* ˌ**palaeobo'tanic** *adj.* —ˌ**palaeo'botanist** *n.*

Palaeocene ('pælɪəʊˌsiːn) *adj.* **1.** of, denoting, or formed in the first epoch of the Tertiary period, which lasted for 10 million years. ~*n.* **2. the.** the Palaeocene epoch or rock series. [C19: from French from *paléo-* PALAEO- + Greek *kainos* new, recent]

palaeoclimatology (ˌpælɪəʊˌklaɪmə'tɒlədʒɪ) *n.* the study of climates of the geological past. —ˌ**palaeoˌclima'tologist** *n.*

palaeocurrent ('pælɪəʊˌkʌrənt) *n. Geology.* an ancient current, esp. of water, evidence of which has been preserved in sedimentary rocks as fossilized ripple marks, etc.

palaeoecology (ˌpælɪəʊɪ'kɒlədʒɪ) *n.* the study of fossil animals and plants in order to deduce their ecology and the environmental conditions in which they lived. —ˌ**palaeoˌeco'logical** *adj.* —ˌ**palaeoe'cologist** *n.*

palaeoethnobotany (ˌpælɪəʊˌɛθnəʊ'bɒtənɪ) *n.* the study of fossil seeds and grains to further archaeological knowledge, esp. of the domestication of cereals.

Palaeogene ('pælɪəˌdʒiːn) *adj.* **1.** of or formed in the Palaeocene, Eocene, and Oligocene epochs. ~*n.* **2. the.** the Palaeogene period or system.

palaeogeography (ˌpælɪəʊdʒɪ'ɒgrəfɪ) *n.* the study of geographical features of the geological past. —ˌ**palaeoge'ographer** *n.* —**palaeogeographical** (ˌpælɪəʊˌdʒiːəʊ'græfɪkᵊl) *or* ˌ**palaeoˌgeo'graphic** *adj.* —ˌ**palaeoˌgeo'graphically** *adv.*

palaeography (ˌpælɪ'ɒgrəfɪ) *n.* **1.** the study of the handwritings of the past, and often the manuscripts as well, so that they may be dated, read, etc., and may serve as historical and literary sources. **2.** a handwriting of the past. —**palae'ographer** *n.* —**palaeographic** (ˌpælɪəʊ'græfɪk) *or* ˌ**palaeo'graphical** *adj.*

palaeolith ('pælɪəʊˌlɪθ) *n.* a stone tool dating to the Palaeolithic.

Palaeolithic (ˌpælɪəʊ'lɪθɪk) *n.* **1.** the period of the emergence of primitive man and the manufacture of unpolished chipped stone tools, about 2.5 million to 3 million years ago until about 12 000 B.C. See also **Lower Palaeolithic, Middle Palaeolithic, Upper Palaeolithic.** ~*adj.* **2.** (*sometimes not cap.*) of or relating to this period.

Palaeolithic man *n.* any of various primitive types of man, such as Neanderthal man and Java man, who lived in the Palaeolithic.

palaeomagnetism (ˌpælɪəʊ'mægnɪˌtɪzəm) *n.* the study of the fossil magnetism in rocks, used to determine the past configurations of the continents and to investigate the past shape and magnitude of the earth's magnetic field. —ˌ**palaeomag'netic** *adj.*

palaeontography (ˌpælɪɒn'tɒgrəfɪ) *n.* the branch of palaeontology concerned with the description of fossils. [C19: from PALAEO- + ONTO- + -GRAPHY] —**palaeontographic** (ˌpælɪˌɒntə'græfɪk) *or* ˌ**palaeˌonto'graphical** *adj.*

palaeontol. *abbrev. for* palaeontology.

palaeontology (ˌpælɪɒn'tɒlədʒɪ) *n.* **1.** the study of fossils to determine the structure and evolution of extinct animals and plants and the age and conditions of deposition of the rock strata in which they are found. See also **palaeobotany, palaeozoology. 2.** another name for **palaeozoology.** [C19: from PALAEO- + ONTO- + -LOGY] —**palaeontological** (ˌpælɪˌɒntə'lɒdʒɪkᵊl) *adj.* —ˌ**palaeˌonto'logically** *adv.* —ˌ**palaeon'tologist** *n.*

palaeopathology (ˌpælɪəʊpə'θɒlədʒɪ) *n.* the study of diseases of ancient man. —'**palaeoˌpatho'logical** *adj.* —ˌ**palaeopa'thologist** *n.*

Palaeozoic (ˌpælɪəʊ'zəʊɪk) *adj.* **1.** of, denoting, or relating to an era of geological time that began 600 million years ago with the Cambrian period and lasted about 375 million years until the end of the Permian period. ~*n.* **2. the.** the Palaeozoic era. [C19: from PALAEO- + Greek *zōē* life + -IC]

palaeozoology (ˌpælɪəʊzuː'ɒlədʒɪ) *n.* the study of fossil animals. Also called: **palaeontology.** —**palaeozoological** (ˌpælɪəʊˌzʊə'lɒdʒɪkᵊl) *adj.* —ˌ**palaeozo'ologist** *n.*

palaestra *or esp. U.S.* **palestra** (pə'lɛstrə, -'liː-) *n., pl.* **-tras** *or* **-trae** (-triː). (in ancient Greece or Rome) a public place devoted to the training of athletes. [C16: via Latin from Greek *palaistra,* from *palaiein* to wrestle]

palagi (pə'læŋɪ) *n., pl.* **-gis.** *N.Z.* a Samoan name for a **European.**

palais de danse *French.* (palɛ də dɑ̃s) *n.* a dance hall.

palais glide ('pæleɪ) *n.* a dance with high kicks and gliding steps in which performers link arms in a row. [C20: from PALAIS DE DANSE]

palanquin *or* **palankeen** (ˌpælən'kiːn) *n.* a covered litter, formerly used in the Orient, carried on the shoulders of four men. [C16: from Portuguese *palanquim,* from Prakrit *pallanka,* from Sanskrit *paryanka* couch]

palatable ('pælətəbᵊl) *adj.* **1.** pleasant to taste. **2.** acceptable or satisfactory: *a palatable suggestion.* —ˌ**palata'bility** *or* '**palatableness** *n.* —'**palatably** *adv.*

palatal ('pælətᵊl) *adj.* **1.** Also: **palatine.** of or relating to the palate. **2.** *Phonetics.* of, relating to, or denoting a speech sound articulated with the blade of the tongue touching the hard palate. ~*n.* **3.** Also called: **palatine.** the bony plate that forms the palate. **4.** *Phonetics.* a palatal speech sound, such as the semivowel (j). —'**palatally** *adv.*

palatalize *or* **palatalise** ('pælətəˌlaɪz) *vb.* (*tr.*) to pronounce (a speech sound) with the blade of the tongue touching the palate. —ˌ**palatali'zation** *or* ˌ**palatali'sation** *n.*

palate ('pælɪt) *n.* **1.** the roof of the mouth, separating the oral and nasal cavities. See **hard palate, soft palate. 2.** the sense of taste: *she had no palate for the wine.* **3.** relish or enjoyment. **4.** *Botany.* (in some two-lipped corollas) the projecting part of the lower lip that closes the opening of the corolla. [C14: from Latin *palātum,* perhaps of Etruscan origin]

palatial (pə'leɪʃəl) *adj.* of, resembling, or suitable for a palace; sumptuous. —**pa'latially** *adv.* —**pa'latialness** *n.*

palatinate (pə'lætɪnɪt) *n.* a territory ruled by a palatine prince or noble or count palatine.

palatine[1] ('pæləˌtaɪn) *adj.* **1.** (of an individual) possessing royal prerogatives in a territory. **2.** of, belonging to, characteristic of, or relating to a count palatine, county palatine, palatinate, or palatine. **3.** of or relating to a palace. ~*n.* **4.** *Feudal history.* the lord of a palatinate. **5.** any of various important officials at the late Roman, Merovingian, or Carolingian courts. **6.** (in Colonial America) any of the proprietors of a palatine colony, such as Carolina. [C15: via French from Latin *palātīnus* belonging to the palace, from *palātium;* see PALACE]

palatine[2] ('pæləˌtaɪn) *adj.* **1.** of or relating to the palate. ~*n.* **2.** either of two bones forming the hard palate. [C17: from French *palatin,* from Latin *palātum* palate]

palaver (pə'lɑːvə) *n.* **1.** tedious or time-consuming business, esp. when of a formal nature: *all the palaver of filling in forms.* **2.** loud and confused talk and activity; hubbub. **3.** (often used humorously) a conference. **4.** *Now rare.* talk intended to flatter or persuade. **5.** *W African.* **a.** an argument. **b.** trouble arising from an argument. ~*vb.* **6.** (*intr.*) (often used humorously) to have a conference. **7.** (*intr.*) to talk loudly and confusedly. **8.** (*tr.*) to flatter or cajole. [C18: from Portuguese *palavra* talk, from Latin *parabola* PARABLE]

pale[1] (peɪl) *adj.* **1.** lacking brightness of colour; whitish: *pale morning light.* **2.** (of a colour) whitish; produced by a relatively small quantity of colouring agent. **3.** dim or wan: *the pale stars.* **4.** feeble: *a pale effort.* ~*vb.* **5.** to make or become pale or paler; blanch. **6.** (*intr.; often foll. by before*) to lose superiority or importance (in comparison to): *her beauty paled before that of her hostess.* [C13: from Old French *palle,* from Latin *pallidus* pale, from *pallēre* to look wan] —'**palely** *adv.* —'**paleness** *n.*

pale[2] (peɪl) *n.* **1.** a wooden post or strip used as an upright member in a fence. **2.** an enclosing barrier, esp. a fence made of pales. **3.** an area enclosed by a pale. **4.** a sphere of activity within which certain restrictions are applied. **5.** *Heraldry.* an ordinary consisting of a vertical stripe, usually in the centre of a shield. **6. beyond the pale.** outside the limits of social convention. ~*vb.* **7.** (*tr.*) to enclose with pales. [C14: from Old French *pal,* from Latin *pālus* stake; compare POLE[1]]

palea ('peɪlɪə) *or* **pale** *n., pl.* **paleae** ('peɪlɪˌiː) *or* **pales.** *Botany.* **1.** the scalelike membranous bract that partly encloses a grass flower. **2.** any small membranous bract or scale. [C18: from Latin: straw, chaff; see PALLET[1]] —**paleaceous** (ˌpeɪlɪ'eɪʃəs) *adj.*

paleface ('peɪlˌfeɪs) *n.* a derogatory term for a White person, said to have been used by North American Indians.

paleo- *or before a vowel* **pale-** *combining form.* variants (esp. U.S.) of **palaeo-.**

Palestinian (ˌpælɪ'stɪnɪən) *adj.* **1.** of or relating to Palestine, a historic region in the Middle East now partitioned between Israel and Jordan. ~*n.* **2.** a native or inhabitant of this region or a descendant of one, esp. an Arab now living in Jordan, Lebanon, or Israel, or as a refugee from Israeli-occupied territory.

palestra (pə'lɛstrə, -'liː-) *n., pl.* **-tras** *or* **-trae** (-triː). the usual U.S. spelling of **palaestra.**

paletot ('pæltəʊ) *n.* **1.** a loose outer garment. **2.** a woman's fitted coat often worn over a crinoline or bustle. [C19: from French]

palette ('pælɪt) *n.* **1.** Also: **pallet.** a flat piece of wood, plastic, etc., used by artists as a surface on which to mix their paints. **2.** the range of colours characteristic of a particular artist, painting, or school of painting: *a restricted palette.* **3.** either of the plates of metal attached by a strap to the cuirass in a suit of armour to protect the armpits. [C17: from French, diminutive of *pale* shovel, from Latin *pala* spade]

palette *or* **pallet knife** *n.* **1.** a round-ended spatula with a thin flexible blade used esp. by artists for mixing, applying, and scraping off paint, esp. oil paint. **2.** a knife with a round-ended flexible blade used in cookery for scraping out a mixture from a bowl, spreading icing, etc.

palfrey ('pɔːlfrɪ) *n. Archaic.* a light saddle horse, esp. ridden by women. [C12: from Old French *palefrei,* from Medieval Latin *palafredus,* from Late Latin *paraverēdus,* from Greek *para* beside + Latin *verēdus* light fleet horse, of Celtic origin]

Pali ('pɑːlɪ) *n.* an ancient language of India derived from Sanskrit; the language of the Buddhist scriptures. [C19: from Sanskrit *pāli-bhāsa,* from *pāli* canon + *bhāsa* language, of Dravidian origin]

palikar ('pælɪˌkɑː) *n.* a Greek soldier in the war of independence against Turkey (1821–28). [C19: from Modern Greek *palikari* youth]

palilalia (ˌpælɪ'leɪlɪə) *n.* a speech disorder in which a word or phrase is rapidly repeated. [C20: from Greek *palin* again + *lalein* to babble]

palimony ('pælɪmənɪ) *n. U.S.* alimony awarded to a nonmarried partner after the break-up of a long-term relationship. [C20: from a blend of *pal* + *alimony*]

palimpsest ('pælɪmpˌsɛst) *n.* **1.** a manuscript on which two or more successive texts have been written, each one being erased to make room for the next. ~*adj.* **2.** (of a text) written on a palimpsest. **3.** (of a document) used as a palimpsest. [C17: from Latin *palimpsestus* parchment cleaned for reuse, from Greek *palimpsēstos,* from *palin* again + *psēstos* rubbed smooth, from *psēn* to scrape]

palindrome ('pælɪnˌdrəʊm) *n.* a word or phrase the letters of which, when taken in reverse order, give the same word or phrase, such as *able was I ere I saw Elba.* [C17: from Greek *palindromos* running back again, from *palin* again + -DROME] —**palindromic** (ˌpælɪn'drɒmɪk) *adj.*

paling ('peɪlɪŋ) *n.* **1.** a fence made of pales. **2.** pales collectively. **3.** a single pale. **4.** the act of erecting pales.

palingenesis (ˌpælɪn'dʒɛnɪsɪs) *n., pl.* **-ses** (-ˌsiːz). **1.** *Christianity.* spiritual rebirth through metempsychosis of Christian baptism. **2.** *Biology.* another name for **recapitulation** (sense 2). [C19: from Greek *palin* again + *genesis* birth, GENESIS] —**palingenetic** (ˌpælɪndʒə'nɛtɪk) *adj.* —ˌ**palinge'netically** *adv.*

palinode ('pælɪˌnəʊd) *n.* **1.** a poem in which the poet recants something he has said in a former poem. **2.** *Rare.* a recantation. [C16: from Latin *palinōdia* repetition of a song, from Greek, from *palin* again + *ōidē* song, ODE]

palinopsia (ˌpælɪ'nɒpsɪə) *or* **palinopia** (ˌpælɪ'nəʊpɪə) *n.* a visual disorder in which the patient perceives a prolonged afterimage. [from Greek *palin* again + *ōps* eye]

palisade (ˌpælɪ'seɪd) *n.* **1.** a strong fence made of stakes driven into the ground, esp. for defence. **2.** one of the stakes used in such a fence. **3.** *Botany.* a layer of elongated mesophyll cells containing many chloroplasts, situated below the outer epidermis of a leaf blade. ~*vb.* **4.** (*tr.*) to enclose with a palisade. [C17: via French, from Old Provençal *palissada,* ultimately from Latin *pālus* stake; see PALE[2], POLE[1]]

palisades (ˌpælɪ'seɪdz, 'pælɪˌseɪdz) *pl. n. U.S. and Canadian.* high cliffs in a line, often along a river, resembling a palisade.

palish ('peɪlɪʃ) *adj.* rather pale.

pall[1] (pɔːl) *n.* **1.** a cloth covering, usually black, spread over a coffin or tomb. **2.** a coffin, esp. during the funeral ceremony. **3.** a dark heavy covering; shroud: *the clouds formed a pall over the sky.* **4.** a depressing or oppressive atmosphere: *her bereavement cast a pall on the party.* **5.** *Heraldry.* an ordinary consisting of a Y-shaped bearing. **6.** *Christianity.* **a.** a small square linen cloth with which the chalice is covered at the Eucharist **b.** an archaic word for **pallium** (sense 2). **7.** an obsolete word for **cloak.** ~*vb.* **8.** (*tr.*) to cover or depress with a pall. [Old English *pæll,* from Latin: PALLIUM]

pall[2] (pɔːl) *vb.* **1.** (*intr.;* often foll. by *on*) to become or appear boring, insipid, or tiresome (to): *history classes palled on me.* **2.** to cloy or satiate, or become cloyed or satiated. [C14: variant of APPAL]

Palladian[1] (pə'leɪdɪən) *adj.* denoting, relating to, or having the classical style of architecture created by Andrea Palladio (1508–80), Italian architect. —**Pal'ladianˌism** *n.*

Palladian[2] (pə'leɪdɪən) *adj. Literary.* wise or learned. [C16: from Latin *Palladius,* from Greek *Pallas,* an epithet applied to the goddess Athena, meaning perhaps "(spear) brandisher" or perhaps "virgin"]

palladic (pə'lædɪk, -'leɪ-) *adj.* of or containing palladium in the trivalent or tetravalent state.

palladium[1] (pə'leɪdɪəm) *n.* a ductile malleable silvery-white element of the platinum metal group occurring principally in nickel-bearing ores: used as a hydrogenation catalyst and, alloyed with gold, in jewellery. Symbol: Pd; atomic no.: 46; atomic wt.: 106.4; valency: 2, 3, or 4; relative density: 12.02; melting pt.: 1552°C; boiling pt.: 3140°C. [C19: named after the asteroid *Pallas,* at the time (1803) a recent discovery]

palladium[2] (pə'leɪdɪəm) *n.* something believed to ensure protection; safeguard. [C17: after the *Palladium,* a statue of the goddess *Pallas* Athena on which the safety of the city of Troy depended; see PALLADIAN[2]]

palladous (pə'leɪdəs, 'pælədəs) *adj.* of or containing palladium in the divalent state.

pallbearer ('pɔːlˌbɛərə) *n.* a person who carries or escorts the coffin at a funeral.

pallescent (pæ'lɛsənt) *adj. Botany.* becoming paler in colour with increasing age.

pallet[1] ('pælɪt) *n.* **1.** a straw-filled mattress or bed. **2.** any hard or makeshift bed. [C14: from Anglo-Norman *paillet,* from Old French *paille* straw, from Latin *palea* straw]

pallet[2] ('pælɪt) *n.* **1.** an instrument with a handle and a flat, sometimes flexible, blade used by potters for shaping. **2.** a standard-sized platform of box section open at two ends on which goods may be stacked. The open ends allow the entry of the forks of a lifting truck so that the palletized load can be raised and moved about easily. **3.** *Horology.* the locking lever that engages and disengages alternate end pawls with the escape wheel to give impulses to the balance. **4.** a variant spelling of **palette** (sense 1). **5.** *Music.* a flap valve of wood faced with leather that opens to admit air to the wind chest of an organ. [C16: from Old French *palette* a little shovel, from *pale* spade, from Latin *pala* spade]

palletize *or* **palletise** ('pælɪˌtaɪz) *vb.* (*tr.*) to stack or transport on a pallet or pallets. —ˌ**palleti'zation** *or* ˌ**palleti'sation** *n.*

pallet knife *n.* a variant spelling of **palette knife.**

pallet truck *n.* a powered truck with a mast, sometimes telescopic, on which slides a carriage which can be raised and lowered hydraulically. The carriage has extended forks which can be passed under a palletized load for stacking or moving to a new position. Also called: **stacking truck.**

palliasse *or esp. U.S.* **paillasse** ('pælɪˌæs, ˌpælɪ'æs) *n.* a straw-filled mattress; pallet. [C18: from French *paillasse,* from Italian *pagliaccio,* ultimately from Latin *palea* PALLET[1]]

palliate ('pælɪˌeɪt) *vb.* (*tr.*) **1.** to lessen the severity of (pain, disease, etc.) without curing or removing; alleviate; mitigate. **2.** to cause (an offence) to seem less serious by concealing evidence; extenuate. [C16: from Late Latin *palliāre* to cover up, from Latin *pallium* a cloak, PALLIUM] —ˌ**palli'ation** *n.* —'**palliˌator** *n.*

palliative ('pælɪətɪv) *adj.* **1.** serving to palliate; relieving without curing. ~*n.* **2.** something that palliates, such as a sedative drug or agent. —'**palliatively** *adv.*

pallid ('pælɪd) *adj.* **1.** lacking colour or brightness; wan: *a pallid complexion.* **2.** lacking vigour; vapid: *a pallid performance.* [C17: from Latin *pallidus,* from *pallēre* to be PALE[1]] —'**pallidly** *adv.* —'**pallidness** *or* **pal'lidity** *n.*

pallium ('pælɪəm) *n., pl.* **-lia** (-lɪə) *or* **-liums.** **1.** a garment worn by men in ancient Greece or Rome, made by draping a large rectangular cloth about the body. **2.** *Chiefly R.C. Church.* a woollen vestment consisting of a band encircling the shoulders with two lappets hanging from it front and back: worn by the pope, all archbishops, and (as a mark of special honour) some bishops. **3.** Also called: **mantle.** *Anatomy.* the cerebral cortex and contiguous white matter. **4.** *Zoology.* another name for **mantle** (sense 5). [C16: from Latin: cloak; related to Latin *palla* mantle]

pall-mall ('pæl'mæl) *n. Obsolete.* **1.** a game in which a ball is driven by a mallet along an alley and through an iron ring. **2.** the alley itself. [C17: from obsolete French, from Italian *pallamaglio,* from *palla* ball + *maglio* mallet]

pallor ('pælə) *n.* a pale condition, esp. when unnatural: *fear gave his face a deathly pallor.* [C17: from Latin: whiteness (of the skin), from *pallēre* to be PALE[1]]

pally ('pælɪ) *adj.* **-lier, -liest.** *Informal.* on friendly or familiar terms

palm[1] (pɑːm) *n.* **1.** the inner part of the hand from the wrist to the base of the fingers. **2.** a corresponding part in animals, esp. apes and monkeys. **3.** a linear measure based on the breadth or length of a hand, equal to three to four inches or seven to ten inches respectively. **4.** the part of a glove that covers the palm. **5.** a hard leather shield worn by sailmakers to protect the palm of the hand. **6. a.** the side of the blade of an oar that faces away from the direction of a boat's movement during a stroke. **b.** the face of the fluke of an anchor. **7.** a flattened or expanded part of the antlers of certain deer. **8. in the palm of one's hand.** at one's mercy or command. ~*vb.* (*tr.*) **9.** to conceal in or about the hand, as in sleight-of-hand tricks. **10.** to touch or soothe with the palm of the hand. ~See also **palm off.** [C14 *paume,* via Old French from Latin *palma;* compare Old English *folm* palm of the hand, Greek *palamē*]

palm[2] (pɑːm) *n.* **1.** any treelike plant of the tropical and subtropical monocotyledonous family *Palmaceae* (or *Palmae*), having a straight unbranched trunk crowned with large pinnate or palmate leaves. **2.** a leaf or branch of any of these trees, a symbol of victory, success, etc. **3.** merit or victory. **4.** an emblem or insignia representing a leaf or branch worn on certain military decorations. [Old English, from Latin *palma,* from the likeness of its spreading fronds to a hand; see PALM[1]]

palmaceous (pæl'meɪʃəs) *adj.* of, relating to, or belonging to the palm family, *Palmaceae* (or *Palmae*).

palmar ('pælmə) *adj.* of or relating to the palm of the hand.

palmary ('pælmərɪ) *adj. Rare.* worthy of praise. [C17: from Latin *palmārius* relating to the palm of victory; see PALM[2]]

palmate ('pælmeɪt, -mɪt) *or* **palmated** *adj.* **1.** shaped like an open hand: *palmate antlers.* **2.** *Botany.* having five lobes or segments that spread out from a common point: *palmate leaves.* **3.** (of the feet of most water birds) having three toes connected by a web.

palmation (pæl'meɪʃən) *n.* **1.** the state of being palmate. **2.** a projection or division of a palmate structure.

palm civet *n.* any of various small civet-like arboreal viverrine mammals of the genera *Paradoxurus, Hemigalus,* etc., of Africa and S and SE Asia.

palmer ('pɑːmə) *n.* **1.** (in Medieval Europe) a pilgrim bearing a palm branch as a sign of his visit to the Holy Land. **2.** (in Medieval Europe) an itinerant monk. **3.** (in Medieval Europe) any pilgrim. **4.** any of various artificial angling flies characterized by hackles around the length of the body. [C13: from Old French *palmier,* from Medieval Latin *palmārius,* from Latin *palma* palm]

palmer worm *n.* the hairy black and white caterpillar of the goldtail moth. [C16: originally applied to various destructive caterpillars of migratory habits]

palmette (pæl'mɛt) *n. Archaeol.* an ornament or design resembling the palm leaf. [C19: from French: a little PALM[2]]

palmetto (pæl'mɛtəʊ) *n., pl.* **-tos** *or* **-toes. 1.** any of several small chiefly tropical fan palms, esp. any of the genus *Sabal,* of the southeastern U.S. See also **cabbage palmetto, saw palmetto. 2.** any of various other fan palms such as palms of the genera *Serenoa, Thrinax,* and *Chamaerops.* [C16: from Spanish *palmito* a little PALM[2]]

palmistry ('pɑːmɪstrɪ) *n.* the process or art of interpreting character, telling fortunes, etc., by the configuration of lines, marks, and bumps on a person's hand. Also called: **chiromancy.** [C15 *pawmestry,* from *paume* PALM[1]; the second element is unexplained] —'**palmist** *n.*

palmitate ('pælmɪˌteɪt) *n.* any salt or ester of palmitic acid.

palmitic acid (pæl'mɪtɪk) *n.* a white crystalline solid that is a saturated fatty acid: used in the manufacture of soap and candles. Formula: $(C_{15}H_{31})COOH$. Systematic name: **hexadecanoic acid.** [C19: from French *palmitique;* see PALM[2], -ITE[2], -IC]

palmitin ('pælmɪtɪn) *n.* the colourless glyceride of palmitic acid, occurring in many natural oils and fats. Formula: $(C_{15}H_{31}COO)_3C_3H_5$. Also called: **tripalmitin.** [C19: from French *palmitine,* probably from *palmite* pith of the palm tree; see PALM[2]]

palm off *vb.* (*tr., adv.;* often foll. by *on*) **1.** to offer, sell, or spend fraudulently: *to palm off a counterfeit coin.* **2.** to divert in order to be rid of: *I palmed the unwelcome visitor off on John.*

palm oil *n.* a yellow butter-like oil obtained from the fruit of the oil palm, used as an edible fat and in soap.

palm-oil chop *n.* a W African dish made with meat and palm oil.

palm sugar *n.* sugar obtained from the sap of certain species of palm trees.

Palm Sunday *n.* the Sunday before Easter commemorating Christ's triumphal entry into Jerusalem.

palm vaulting *n.* a less common name for **fan vaulting.**

palm wine *n.* (esp. in W Africa) the sap drawn from the palm tree, esp. when allowed to ferment.

palmy ('pɑːmɪ) *adj.* **palmier, palmiest. 1.** prosperous, flourishing, or luxurious: *a palmy life.* **2.** covered with, relating to, or resembling palms: *a palmy beach.*

palmyra (pæl'maɪrə) *n.* a tall tropical Asian palm, *Borassus flabellifer* with large fan-shaped leaves used for thatching and weaving; grown also for its edible seedlings. [C17: from Portuguese *palmeira* palm tree (see PALM[2]); perhaps influenced by *Palmyra,* city in Syria]

palolo worm (pə'ləʊləʊ) *n.* any of several polychaete worms of the family *Eunicidae,* esp. *Eunice viridis,* of the S Pacific Ocean: reproductive segments are shed from the posterior end of the body when breeding. [C20 *palolo,* from Samoan or Tongan]

palomino (ˌpælə'miːnəʊ) *n., pl.* **-nos.** a golden horse with a cream or white mane and tail. [American Spanish, from Spanish: dovelike, from Latin *palumbīnus,* from *palumbēs* ring dove]

palooka (pə'luːkə) *n. U.S. slang.* a stupid or clumsy boxer or other person. [C20: origin uncertain]

palp (pælp) *or* **palpus** ('pælpəs) *n., pl.* **palps** *or* **palpi** ('pælpaɪ). **1.** either of a pair of sensory appendages that arise from the mouthparts of crustaceans and insects. **2.** either of a pair of tactile organs arising from the head or anterior end of certain annelids and molluscs. [C19: from French, from Latin *palpus* a touching] —'**palpal** *adj.*

palpable ('pælpəbᵊl) *adj.* **1.** (*usually prenominal*) easily perceived by the senses or the mind; obvious: *the excuse was a palpable lie.* **2.** capable of being touched; tangible. **3.** *Med.* capable of being discerned by the sense of touch: *a palpable tumour.* [C14: from Late Latin *palpābilis* that may be touched, from Latin *palpāre* to stroke, touch] —ˌ**palpa'bility** *or* '**palpableness** *n.* —'**palpably** *adv.*

palpate[1] ('pælpeɪt) *vb.* (*tr.*) *Med.* to examine (an area of the body) by the sense of touch and pressure. [C19: from Latin *palpāre* to stroke] —**pal'pation** *n.*

palpate[2] ('pælpeɪt) *adj. Zoology.* of, relating to, or possessing a palp or palps.

palpebral ('pælpɪbrəl) *adj.* of or relating to the eyelid. [C19: from Late Latin *palpebrālis,* from Latin *palpebra* eyelid; probably related to *palpāre* to stroke]

palpebrate *adj.* ('pælpɪbrɪt, -ˌbreɪt). **1.** having eyelids. ~*vb.* ('pælpɪˌbreɪt). **2.** (*intr.*) to wink or blink, esp. repeatedly.

palpitate ('pælpɪˌteɪt) *vb.* (*intr.*) **1.** (of the heart) to beat with abnormal rapidity. **2.** to flutter or tremble. [C17: from Latin *palpitāre* to throb, from *palpāre* to stroke] —'**palpitant** *adj.* —ˌ**palpi'tation** *n.*

palsgrave ('pɔːlzgreɪv) *n. Archaic.* a German count palatine. [C16: from Dutch, from Middle Dutch *paltsgrave,* from *palts* estate of a palatine + *grave* count] —**palsgravine** ('pɔːlzgrəˌviːn) *fem. n.*

palstave ('pɔːlˌsteɪv) *n. Archaeol.* a kind of celt, usually of bronze, made to fit into a split wooden handle rather than having a socket for the handle. [C19: from Danish *paalstav,* from Old Norse, from *páll* spade + *stafr* STAFF[1]]

palsy ('pɔːlzɪ) *Pathol.* ~*n., pl.* **-sies. 1.** paralysis, esp. of a specified type: *cerebral palsy.* ~*vb.* **-sies, -sying, -sied.** (*tr.*) **2.** to paralyse. [C13 *palesi,* from Old French *paralisie,* from Latin PARALYSIS] —'**palsied** *adj.*

palter ('pɔːltə) *vb.* (*intr.*) **1.** to act or talk insincerely. **2.** to haggle. [C16: of unknown origin] —'**palterer** *n.*

paltry ('pɔːltrɪ) *adj.* **-trier, -triest. 1.** insignificant; meagre. **2.** worthless or petty. [C16: from Low Germanic *palter, paltrig* ragged] —'**paltrily** *adv.* —'**paltriness** *n.*

paludal (pə'ljuːdᵊl, 'pæljʊdᵊl) *adj. Rare.* **1.** of, relating to, or produced by marshes. **2.** malarial. [C19: from Latin *palus* marsh; related to Sanskrit *palvala* pond]

paludism ('pæljʊˌdɪzəm) *n. Pathol.* a rare word for **malaria.** [C19: from Latin *palus* marsh]

Paludrine ('pæljʊdrɪn) *n. Trademark.* proguanil hydrochloride, a synthetic antimalarial drug first produced in 1944.

pal up *vb.* (*intr., adv.;* often foll. by *with*) *Informal.* to become friends (with): *he palled up with the other boys.*

paly ('peɪlɪ) *adj.* (*usually postpositive*) *Heraldry.* vertically striped. [C15: from Old French *palé,* from Latin *pālus* stake; see PALE[2]]

palynology (ˌpælɪ'nɒlədʒɪ) *n.* the study of living and fossil pollen grains and plant spores. [C20: from Greek *palunein* to scatter + -LOGY] —**palynological** (ˌpælɪnə'lɒdʒɪkᵊl) *adj.* —ˌ**paly'nologist** *n.*

pam. *or* **pamph.** *abbrev. for* pamphlet.

Pama-Nyungan ('pɑːmə'njuŋgən) *adj.* **1.** of or relating to the largest superfamily of languages within the phylum of languages spoken by the Australian Aborigines. ~*n.* **2.** this phylum.

pampas ('pæmpəz) *n.* (*functioning as sing. or more often pl.*) **a.** the extensive grassy plains of temperate South America, esp. in Argentina. **b.** (*as modifier*): *pampas dwellers.* [C18: from American Spanish *pampa* (sing.), from Quechua *bamba* plain] —**pampean** ('pæmpɪən, pæm'piːən) *adj.*

pampas grass ('pæmpəs, -pəz) *n.* any of various large grasses of the South American genus *Cortaderia* and related genera, widely cultivated for their large feathery silver-coloured flower branches.

pamper ('pæmpə) *vb.* (*tr.*) **1.** to treat with affectionate and usually excessive indulgence; coddle; spoil. **2.** *Archaic.* to feed to excess. [C14: of Germanic origin; compare German dialect *pampfen* to gorge oneself] —'**pamperer** *n.*

pampero (pæm'pɛərəʊ; *Spanish* pam'pero) *n., pl.* **-ros** (-rəʊz; *Spanish* -ros). a dry cold wind in South America blowing across the pampas from the south or southwest. [C19: from American Spanish: (wind) of the PAMPAS]

pamphlet ('pæmflɪt) *n.* **1.** a brief publication generally having a paper cover; booklet. **2.** a brief treatise, often on a subject of current interest, published in pamphlet form. [C14 *pamflet,* from Anglo-Latin *panfletus,* from Medieval Latin *Pamphilus* title of a popular 12th-century amatory poem from Greek *Pamphilos* masculine proper name]

pamphleteer (ˌpæmflɪ'tɪə) *n.* **1.** a person who writes or issues pamphlets, esp. of a controversial nature. ~*vb.* **2.** (*intr.*) to write or issue pamphlets.

pamphrey ('pæmfrɪ) *n. Ulster dialect.* a cabbage. [of unknown origin]

pampootie (ˌpæm'puːtiː) *n.* a rawhide slipper worn by men in the Aran Islands. [C19: of uncertain origin]

pan[1] (pæn) *n.* **1. a.** a wide metal vessel used in cooking. **b.** (*in combination*): *saucepan.* **2.** Also called: '**panful.** the amount such a vessel will hold. **3.** any of various similar vessels used esp. in industry, as for boiling liquids. **4.** a dish used by prospectors, esp. gold prospectors, for separating a valuable mineral from the gravel or earth containing it by washing and agitating. **5.** either of the two dishlike receptacles on a balance. **6.** Also called: **lavatory pan.** *Brit.* the bowl of a lavatory. **7. a.** a natural or artificial depression in the ground where salt can be obtained by the evaporation of brine. **b.** a natural depression containing water or mud. **8.** *Caribbean.* the indented top from an oil drum used as the treble drum in a steel band. **9.** See **hardpan, brainpan. 10.** a small ice floe. **11.** a slang word for **face** (sense 1a). **12.** a small cavity containing priming powder in the locks of old guns. **13.** a hard substratum of soil. **14.** short for **pan loaf.** ~*vb.* **pans, panning, panned. 15.** (when *tr.,* often foll. by *off* or *out*) to wash (gravel) in a pan to separate particles of (valuable minerals) from it. **16.** (*intr.; often foll. by out*) (of gravel) to yield valuable minerals by this process. **17.** (*tr.*) *Informal.* to criticize harshly: *the critics panned his new play.* ~See also **pan out.** [Old English *panne;* related to Old Saxon, Old Norse *panna,* Old High German *pfanna*]

pan[2] (pæn) *n.* **1.** the leaf of the betel tree. **2.** a preparation of this leaf which is chewed, together with betel nuts and lime, in India and the East Indies. [C17: from Hindi, from Sanskrit *parna* feather, wing, leaf]

pan[3] (pæn) *vb.* **pans, panning, panned.** **1.** to move (a film camera) or (of a film camera) to be moved so as to follow a moving object or obtain a panoramic effect. ~*n.* **2. a.** the act of panning. **b.** (*as modifier*): *a pan shot.* [C20: shortened from *panoramic*]

Pan. *abbrev. for* Panama.

pan- *combining form.* **1.** all or every: *panchromatic.* **2.** including or relating to all parts or members: *Pan-African; pantheistic.* [from Greek *pan,* neuter of *pas* all]

panacea (ˌpænəˈsɪə) *n.* a remedy for all diseases or ills. [C16: via Latin from Greek *panakeia* healing everything, from *pan* all + *akēs* remedy] —ˌ**panaˈcean** *adj.*

panache (pəˈnæʃ, -ˈnɑːʃ) *n.* **1.** a dashing manner; style; swagger: *he rides with panache.* **2.** a feathered plume on a helmet. [C16: via French from Old Italian *pennacchio,* from Late Latin *pinnāculum* feather, from Latin *pinna* feather; compare Latin *pinnāculum* PINNACLE]

panada (pəˈnɑːdə) *n.* a mixture of flour, water, etc., or of breadcrumbs soaked in milk, used as a thickening. [C16: from Spanish, from *pan* bread, from Latin *pānis*]

Pan-African *adj.* **1.** of or relating to all African countries or the advocacy of political unity among African countries. ~*n.* **2.** a supporter of the Pan-African movement. —ˈ**Pan-ˈAfricanˌism** *n.*

Panama hat (ˈpænəmɑː) *n.* (*sometimes not cap.*) a hat made of the plaited leaves of the jipijapa plant of Central and South America. Often shortened to **panama** or **Panama.**

Panamanian (ˌpænəˈmeɪnɪən) *adj.* **1.** of or relating to Panama, a republic in Central America, or to its people, customs, etc. ~*n.* **2.** a native or inhabitant of Panama.

Pan-American *adj.* of, relating to, or concerning North, South, and Central America collectively or the advocacy of political or economic unity among American countries. —ˈ**Pan-Aˈmericanˌism** *n.*

pan and tilt head *n. Films, television.* a mounting device on which a camera may be rotated in a horizontal plane (pan) or in a vertical plane (tilt).

Pan-Arabism (ˈærəˌbɪzəm) *n.* the principle of, support for, or the movement towards Arab political union or cooperation. —ˈ**Pan-ˈArab** *adj., n.* —ˈ**Pan-ˈArabic** *adj.*

panatella (ˌpænəˈtelə) *n.* a long slender cigar. [American Spanish *panetela* long slim biscuit, from Italian *panatella* small loaf, from *pane* bread, from Latin *pānis*]

Panathenaea (pæˌnæθɪˈniːə) *n.* (in ancient Athens) a summer festival on the traditional birthday of the goddess Athena.

pancake (ˈpænˌkeɪk) *n.* **1. a.** a thin flat cake made from batter and fried on both sides, often served rolled and filled with a sweet or savoury mixture. **b.** (*as modifier*): *pancake mix.* **2.** a Scot. name for **drop scone.** **3.** a stick or flat cake of compressed make-up. **4.** Also called: **pancake landing.** an aircraft landing made by levelling out a few feet from the ground and then dropping onto it. ~*vb.* **5.** to cause (an aircraft) to make a pancake landing or (of an aircraft) to make a pancake landing.

Pancake Day *n.* another name for **Shrove Tuesday.**

pancake ice *n.* thin slabs of newly formed ice in polar seas.

panchax (ˈpænˌtʃæks) *n.* any of several brightly coloured tropical Asian cyprinodont fishes of the genus *Aplocheilus,* such as *A. panchax* (**blue panchax**). [C19: from New Latin (former generic name), of obscure origin]

panchayat (pənˈtʃɑːjət) *n.* a village council in India. [Hindi, from Sanskrit *panch* five, because such councils originally consisted of five members]

Panchen Lama (ˈpɑːntʃən) *n.* one of the two Grand Lamas of Tibet, ranking below the Dalai Lama. Also called: **Tashi Lama.** [from Tibetan *panchen,* literally: great jewel, from the title of the lama (in full: great jewel among scholars)]

panchromatic (ˌpænkrəʊˈmætɪk) *adj. Photog.* (of an emulsion or film) made sensitive to all colours by the addition of suitable dyes to the emulsion. Compare **orthochromatic.** —**panchromatism** (pænˈkrəʊməˌtɪzəm) *n.*

pancosmism (pænˈkɒzˌmɪzəm) *n.* the philosophical doctrine that the material universe is all that exists. [C19: see PAN-, COSMOS, -ISM]

pancratium (pænˈkreɪʃɪəm) *n., pl.* **-tia** (-ʃɪə). (in ancient Greece) a wrestling and boxing contest. [C17: via Latin from Greek *pankration,* from PAN- + *kratos* strength] —**pancratic** (pænˈkrætɪk) *adj.*

pancreas (ˈpæŋkrɪəs) *n.* a large elongated glandular organ, situated behind the stomach, that secretes insulin and pancreatic juice. [C16: via New Latin from Greek *pankreas,* from *pan-* + *kreas* flesh] —**pancreatic** (ˌpæŋkrɪˈætɪk) *adj.*

pancreatic juice *n.* the clear alkaline secretion of the pancreas that is released into the duodenum and contains several digestive enzymes.

pancreatin (ˈpæŋkrɪətɪn) *n.* the powdered extract of the pancreas of certain animals, such as the pig, used in medicine as an aid to the digestion.

pancreozymin (ˌpæŋkrɪəʊˈzaɪmɪn) *n.* another name for **cholecystokinin.**

panda (ˈpændə) *n.* **1.** Also called: **giant panda.** a large black-and-white herbivorous bearlike mammal, *Ailuropoda melanoleuca,* related to the raccoons and inhabiting the bamboo forests of China: family *Procyonidae.* **2. lesser** *or* **red panda.** a closely related smaller animal resembling a raccoon, *Ailurus fulgens,* of the mountain forests of S Asia, having a reddish-brown coat and ringed tail. [C19: via French from a native Nepalese word]

panda car *n. Brit.* a police patrol car, esp. a blue and white one. [C20: so called because its blue-and-white markings resemble the black-and-white markings of the giant panda]

pandanaceous (ˌpændəˈneɪʃəs) *adj.* of, relating to, or belonging to the *Pandanaceae,* an Old World tropical family of monocotyledonous plants including the screw pines.

pandanus (pænˈdeɪnəs) *n., pl.* **-nuses.** any of various Old World tropical palmlike plants of the genus *Pandanus,* having large aerial prop roots and leaves that yield a fibre used for making mats, etc.: family *Pandanaceae.* See also **screw pine.** [C19: via New Latin from Malay *pandan*]

pandect (ˈpændɛkt) *n.* **1.** a treatise covering all aspects of a particular subject. **2.** (*often pl.*) the complete body of laws of a country; legal code. [C16: via Late Latin from Greek *pandektēs* containing everything, from PAN- + *dektēs* receiver, from *dekhesthai* to receive]

pandemic (pænˈdɛmɪk) *adj.* **1.** (of a disease) affecting persons over a wide geographical area; extensively epidemic. **2.** *Rare.* widespread; general. ~*n.* **3.** a pandemic disease. [C17: from Late Latin *pandēmus,* from Greek *pandēmos* general, from PAN- + *demos* the people]

pandemonium (ˌpændɪˈməʊnɪəm) *n.* **1.** wild confusion; uproar. **2.** a place of uproar and chaos. [C17: coined by John Milton to designate the capital of hell in *Paradise Lost* (1667), from PAN- + Greek *daimōn* DEMON] —ˌ**pandeˈmoniˌac** *or* **pandemonic** (ˌpændɪˈmɒnɪk) *adj.*

pander (ˈpændə) *vb.* **1.** (*intr.;* foll. by *to*) to give gratification (to weaknesses or desires). **2.** (archaic when *tr.*) to act as a go-between in a sexual intrigue (for). ~*n. also* ˈ**panderer.** **3.** a person who caters for vulgar desires, esp. in order to make money. **4.** a person who procures a sexual partner for another; pimp. [C16 (n.): from *Pandare* Pandarus, legendary procurer of Cressida for Troilus]

pandit (ˈpʌndɪt; *spelling pron.* ˈpændɪt) *n. Hinduism.* a variant of **pundit** (sense 3).

P & L *abbrev. for* profit and loss.

P & O *abbrev. for* Peninsular and Oriental (Steamship Company).

pandora (pænˈdɔːrə) *n.* **1.** a handsome red sea bream, *Pagellus erythrinus,* of European coastal waters, caught for food in the Mediterranean. **2.** a marine bivalve mollusc of the genus *Pandora* that lives on the surface of sandy shores and has thin equal valves. [after *Pandora* in Greek mythology, the first woman, from Greek, literally: all-gifted]

pandore (ˈpændɔː) *n. Music.* another word for **bandore.**

pandour (ˈpændʊə) *n.* one of an 18th-century force of Croatian soldiers in the Austrian service, notorious for their brutality. [C18: via French from Hungarian *pandur,* from Croat: guard, probably from Medieval Latin *banderius* summoner, from *bannum* BAN[1]]

pandowdy (pænˈdaʊdɪ) *n., pl.* **-dies.** *U.S.* a deep-dish pie made from fruit, esp. apples, with a cake topping: *apple pandowdy.* [C19: of unknown origin]

p & p *Brit. abbrev. for* postage and packing.

pandurate (ˈpændjʊˌreɪt) *or* **panduriform** (pænˈdjʊərɪˌfɔːm) *adj.* (of plant leaves) shaped like the body of a fiddle. [C19: from Late Latin *pandūra* BANDORE]

pandy (ˈpændɪ) *Chiefly Scot. and Irish.* ~*n., pl.* **-dies.** **1.** (in schools) a stroke on the hand with a strap as a punishment. ~*vb.* **-dies, -dying, -died.** **2.** (*tr.*) to punish with such strokes. [C19: from Latin *pande* (*manum*) stretch out (the hand), from *pandere* to spread or extend]

pane[1] (peɪn) *n.* **1.** a sheet of glass in a window or door. **2.** a panel of a window, door, wall, etc. **3.** a flat section or face, as of a cut diamond. **4.** *Philately.* **a.** any of the rectangular marked divisions of a sheet of stamps made for convenience in selling. **b.** a single page in a stamp booklet. See also **tête-bêche, se tenant.** [C13: from Old French *pan* portion, from Latin *pannus* rag]

pane[2] (peɪn) *n., vb.* a variant of **peen.**

pané *French.* (pane) *adj.* (of fish, meat, etc.) dipped or rolled in breadcrumbs before cooking.

panegyric (ˌpænɪˈdʒɪrɪk) *n.* a formal public commendation; eulogy. [C17: via French and Latin from Greek, from *panēguris* public gathering, from PAN- + *aguris* assembly] —ˌ**paneˈgyrical** *adj.* —ˌ**paneˈgyrically** *adv.* —ˌ**paneˈgyrist** *n.*

panegyrize *or* **panegyrise** (ˈpænɪdʒɪˌraɪz) *vb.* to make a eulogy or eulogies (about).

panel (ˈpænᵊl) *n.* **1.** a flat section of a wall, door, etc. **2.** any distinct section or component of something formed from a sheet of material, esp. of a car body, the spine of a book, etc. **3.** a piece of material inserted in a skirt, dress, etc. **4. a.** a group of persons selected to act as a team in a quiz, to judge a contest, to discuss a topic before an audience, etc. **b.** (*as modifier*): *a panel game.* **5.** a public discussion by such a group: *a panel on public health.* **6.** *Law.* **a.** a list of persons summoned for jury service. **b.** the persons on a specific jury. **7.** *Scots Law.* a person indicted or accused of crime after appearing in court. **8. a.** a thin board used as a surface or backing for an oil painting. **b.** a painting done on such a surface. **9.** any picture with a length much greater than its breadth. **10.** See **instrument panel.** **11.** (in Britain) (formerly) **a.** a list of patients insured under the National Health Insurance Scheme. **b.** a list of medical practitioners within a given area available for consultation by these patients. **12. on the panel.** *Brit. informal.* receiving sickness benefit, esp. from the government. ~*vb.* **-els, -elling, -elled** *or U.S.* **-els, -eling, -eled.** (*tr.*) **13.** to furnish or decorate with panels. **14.** to divide into panels. **15.** *Law.* **a.** to empanel (a jury). **b.** (in Scotland) to bring (a person) to trial; indict. [C13: from Old French: portion, from *pan* piece of cloth, from Latin *pannus;* see PANE[1]]

panel beater *n.* a person who beats out the bodywork of motor vehicles.

panel heating *n.* a system of space heating with panels that contain heating pipes or electrical conductors.

panelling *or U.S.* **paneling** (ˈpænᵊlɪŋ) *n.* **1.** panels collectively, as on a wall or ceiling. **2.** material used for making panels.

panellist *or U.S.* **panelist** (ˈpænᵊlɪst) *n.* a member of a panel, esp. on a radio or television programme.

panel pin *n.* a light slender nail with a narrow head.

panel saw *n.* a saw with a long narrow blade for cutting thin wood.

panel truck *n.* the U.S. and Canadian name for **delivery van.**

panel van *n.* **1.** *Austral.* a small van with two rear doors, esp. one having windows and seats in the rear. **2.** *N.Z.* a small enclosed delivery van.

panettone (pænəˈtəʊnɪ; *Italian* panetˈtoːne) *n., pl.* **-nes** *or* **-ni** (-ni). a kind of Italian spiced brioche containing sultanas: traditionally eaten at Christmas in Italy. [Italian, from *panetto* small loaf, from *pane* bread, from Latin *pānis*]

Pan-European *adj.* of or relating to all European countries or the advocacy of political or economic unity among European countries.

pang (pæŋ) *n.* a sudden brief sharp feeling, as of loneliness, physical pain, or hunger. [C16: variant of earlier *prange,* of Germanic origin]

panga (ˈpæŋgə) *n.* a broad heavy knife of E Africa, used as a tool or weapon. [from a native E African word]

pangenesis (pænˈdʒenɪsɪs) *n.* a former theory of heredity, that each body cell produces hereditary particles that circulate in the blood before collecting in the reproductive cells. See also **blastogenesis** (sense 1). —**pangenetic** (ˌpændʒəˈnetɪk) *adj.* —ˌ**pangeˈnetically** *adv.*

Pan-Germanism *n.* (esp. in the 19th century) the movement for the unification of Germany.

pangolin (pæŋˈgəʊlɪn) *n.* any mammal of the order *Pholidota* found in tropical Africa, S Asia, and Indonesia, having a body covered with overlapping horny scales and a long snout specialized for feeding on ants and termites. Also called: **scaly anteater.** [C18: from Malay *peng-gōling,* from *gōling* to roll over; from its ability to roll into a ball]

panhandle[1] (ˈpænˌhændᵊl) *n.* **1.** (*sometimes cap.*) (in the U.S.) a narrow strip of land that projects from one state into another. **2.** (in a South African city) a plot of land without street frontage.

panhandle[2] (ˈpænˌhændᵊl) *vb. U.S. and Canadian informal.* to accost and beg from (passers-by), esp. on the street. [C19: probably a back formation from *panhandler* a person who begs with a pan] —ˈ**panˌhandler** *n.*

Panhellenic (ˌpænhɛˈlenɪk) *adj.* of or relating to all the Greeks, all Greece, or Panhellenism.

Panhellenism (ˌpænˈhɛlɪˌnɪzəm) *n.* the principle of or support for the union of all Greeks or all Greece. —ˌ**Panˈhellenist** *n.* —ˌ**PanˌhellenˈIstic** *adj.*

panic (ˈpænɪk) *n.* **1.** a sudden overwhelming feeling of terror or anxiety, esp. one affecting a whole group of people. **2.** (*modifier*) of or resulting from such terror: *panic measures.* ~*vb.* **-ics, -icking, -icked.** **3.** to feel or cause to feel panic. [C17: from French *panique,* from New Latin *pānicus,* from Greek *panikos* emanating from *Pan,* Greek god considered as the source of irrational fear] —ˈ**panicky** *adj.*

panic bolt *n.* a bolt on the inside esp. of double doors that is released by pressure on a waist-high bar: used for emergency exits in theatres, shops, etc.

panic button *n.* **1.** a button or switch that operates any of various safety devices, for use in an emergency. **2. hit** *or* **press the panic button.** *Informal.* to react to a situation by demanding emergency action; become excited; panic.

panic buying *n.* the buying up of large quantities of a commodity which, it is feared, is likely to be in short supply.

panic grass *n.* any of various grasses of the genus *Panicum,* such as millet, grown in warm and tropical regions for fodder and grain. [C15 *panic,* from Latin *pānicum,* probably a back formation from *pānicula* PANICLE]

panicle (ˈpænɪkᵊl) *n.* a compound raceme, as in the oat. [C16: from Latin *pānicula* tuft, diminutive of *panus* thread, ultimately from Greek *penos* web; related to *penion* bobbin] —ˈ**panicled** *adj.*

panicmonger (ˈpænɪkˌmʌŋgə) *n.* a person who spreads panic.

panic stations *pl. n. Informal.* a state of alarm; panicky reaction: *when he realized he'd lost the keys it was panic stations.*

panic-stricken *or* **panic-struck** *adj.* affected by panic.

paniculate (pəˈnɪkjʊˌleɪt, -lɪt) *or* **paniculated** *adj. Botany.* growing or arranged in panicles: *a paniculate inflorescence.* —**paˈnicuˌlately** *adv.*

panidiomorphic (pæˌnɪdɪəʊˈmɔːfɪk) *adj.* (of igneous rocks) having well-developed crystals. [C19: from PAN- + IDIOMORPHIC]

Panjabi (pʌnˈdʒɑːbɪ) *n., adj.* a variant spelling of **Punjabi.**

panjandrum (pænˈdʒændrəm) *n.* a pompous self-important official or person of rank. [C18: after a character, the *Grand Panjandrum,* in a nonsense work (1755) by Samuel Foote, English playwright and actor]

pan loaf *n. Irish and Scot. dialect.* a loaf of bread with a light crust all the way round. Often shortened to **pan.** Compare **batch**[1] (sense 4).

panmixia (pænˈmɪksɪə) *or* **panmixis** (pænˈmɪksɪs) *n.* (in population genetics) random mating within an interbreeding population. [C20: from New Latin, from Greek PAN- + *mixis* act of mating]

pannage (ˈpænɪdʒ) *n. Archaic.* **1.** pasturage for pigs, esp. in a forest. **2.** the right to pasture pigs in a forest. **3.** payment for this. **4.** acorns, beech mast, etc., on which pigs feed. [C13: from Old French *pasnage,* ultimately from Latin *pastion-, pastiō* feeding, from *pascere* to feed]

panne (pæn) *n.* a lightweight velvet fabric. [C19: via Old French, from Latin *pinna* wing, feather]

pannier (ˈpænɪə) *n.* **1.** a large basket, esp. one of a pair slung over a beast of burden. **2.** one of a pair of bags slung either side of the back wheel of a motorcycle, bicycle, etc. **3.** (esp. in the 18th century) **a.** a hooped framework to distend a woman's skirt. **b.** one of two puffed-out loops of material worn drawn back onto the hips to reveal the underskirt. [C13: from Old French *panier,* from Latin *pānārium* basket for bread, from *pānis* bread]

pannikin (ˈpænɪkɪn) *n. Chiefly Brit.* a small metal cup or pan. [C19: from PAN[1] + -KIN]

pannikin boss *n. Austral. informal.* a person in charge of a few fellow workers.

panocha (pəˈnəʊtʃə) *or* **penuche** *n.* **1.** a coarse grade of sugar made in Mexico. **2.** (in the U.S.) a sweet made from brown sugar and milk, often with chopped nuts. [Mexican Spanish, diminutive of Spanish *pan* bread, from Latin *pānis*]

panoply (ˈpænəplɪ) *n., pl.* **-plies.** **1.** a complete or magnificent array. **2.** the entire equipment of a warrior. [C17: via French from Greek *panoplia* complete armour, from PAN- + *hopla* armour, pl. of *hoplon* tool] —ˈ**panoplied** *adj.*

panoptic (pænˈɒptɪk) *or* **panoptical** *adj.* taking in all parts, aspects, etc., in a single view; all-embracing: *a panoptic survey.* [C19: from Greek *panoptēs* seeing everything, from PAN- + *optos* visible] —**panˈoptically** *adv.*

panorama (ˌpænəˈrɑːmə) *n.* **1.** an extensive unbroken view, as of a landscape, in all directions. **2.** a wide or comprehensive survey: *a panorama of the week's events.* **3.** a large extended picture or series of pictures of a scene, unrolled before spectators a part at a time so as to appear continuous. **4.** another name for **cyclorama.** [C18: from PAN- + Greek *horāma* view] —**panoramic** (ˌpænəˈræmɪk) *adj.* —ˌ**panoˈramically** *adv.*

panoramic sight *n.* a type of artillery sight with a large field of view.

pan out *vb.* (*intr., adv.*) *Informal.* to work out; turn out; result.

panpipes (ˈpænˌpaɪps) *pl. n.* (*often sing.; often cap.*) a number of reeds or whistles of graduated lengths bound together to form a musical wind instrument. Also called: **pipes of Pan, syrinx.**

pan potentiometer *n.* a control on a stereo sound mixing desk by means of which the relative levels in right- and left-hand channels can be adjusted and hence the apparent position of the recorded or broadcast sound source within the stereo panorama can be controlled. Often shortened to **pan pot.** [C20: from PAN(ORAMIC) + POTENTIOMETER]

panradiometer (ˌpænreɪdɪˈɒmɪtə) *n. Physics.* an instrument used for measuring radiant heat independently of wavelength.

Pan-Slavism *n.* (esp. in the 19th century) the movement for the union of the Slavic peoples, esp. under the hegemony of tsarist Russia. —ˈ**Pan-ˈSlavic** *adj.*

pansophy (ˈpænsəfɪ) *n.* universal knowledge. [C17: from New Latin *pansophia;* see PAN-, -SOPHY] —**pansophic** (pænˈsɒfɪk) *or* **panˈsophical** *adj.* —**panˈsophically** *adv.*

pansy (ˈpænzɪ) *n., pl.* **-sies.** **1.** any violaceous garden plant that is a variety of *Viola tricolor,* having flowers with rounded velvety petals, white, yellow, or purple in colour. See also **wild pansy.** **2.** *Slang.* an effeminate or homosexual man or boy. **3. a.** a strong violet colour. **b.** (*as adj.*): *a pansy carpet.* [C15: from Old French *pensée* thought, from *penser* to think, from Latin *pensāre*]

pant (pænt) *vb.* **1.** to breathe with noisy deep gasps, as when out of breath from exertion or excitement. **2.** to say (something) while breathing thus. **3.** (*intr.; often foll. by for*) to have a frantic desire (for); yearn. **4.** (*intr.*) to pulsate; throb rapidly. ~*n.* **5.** the act or an instance of panting. **6.** a short deep gasping noise; puff. [C15: from Old French *pantaisier,* from Greek *phantasioun* to have visions, from *phantasia* FANTASY]

Pantagruelian (ˌpæntəgruːˈɛlɪən) *adj.* relating to or resembling Pantagruel, a gigantic prince noted for his ironical buffoonery, in Rabelais's satire *Gargantua and Pantagruel* (1534). —ˌ**Pantagruˈelian** *or* ˌ**Pantagruˈelic** *adj.* —ˌ**Pantaˈgruelˌism** *n.* —ˌ**Pantaˈgruelist** *n.*

pantalets *or* **pantalettes** (ˌpæntəˈlɛts) *pl. n.* **1.** long drawers, usually trimmed with ruffles, extending below the skirts: worn during the early and mid 19th century. **2.** a pair of ruffles for the ends of such drawers. [C19: diminutive of PANTALOONS]

pantaloon (ˌpæntəˈluːn) *n. Theatre.* **1.** (in pantomime) an absurd old man, the butt of the clown's tricks. **2.** (*usually cap.*) (in commedia dell'arte) a lecherous old merchant dressed in pantaloons. [C16: from French *Pantalon,* from Italian *Pantalone,* local nickname for a Venetian, probably from *San Pantaleone,* a fourth-century Venetian saint]

pantaloons (ˌpæntəˈluːnz) *pl. n.* **1. a.** *History.* men's tight-fitting trousers, esp. those fastening under the instep worn in the late 18th and early 19th centuries. **b.** children's trousers resembling these. **2.** *Informal or facetious.* any trousers, esp. baggy ones.

pantechnicon (pænˈtɛknɪkən) *n. Brit.* **1.** a large van, esp. one used for furniture removals. **2.** a warehouse where furniture is stored. [C19: from PAN- + Greek *tekhnikon* relating to the arts, from *tekhnē* art; originally the name of a London bazaar, the building later being used as a furniture warehouse]

Pan-Teutonism *n.* another name for **Pan-Germanism.**

pantheism (ˈpænθɪˌɪzəm) *n.* **1.** the doctrine that God is the transcendent reality of which man, nature, and the material universe are manifestations. **2.** any doctrine that regards God as identical with the material universe or the forces of nature. **3.** readiness to worship all or a large number of gods. —ˈ**pantheist** *n.* —ˌ**pantheˈistic** *or* ˌ**pantheˈistical** *adj.* —ˌ**pantheˈistically** *adv.*

pantheon (pænˈθiːən, ˈpænθɪən) *n.* **1.** (esp. in ancient Greece or Rome) a temple to all the gods. **2.** all the gods collectively of a religion. **3.** a monument or building commemorating a nation's dead heroes. [C14: via Latin from Greek *Pantheion,* from PAN- + *-theios* divine, from *theos* god]

panther (ˈpænθə) *n., pl.* **-thers** *or* **-ther. 1.** another name for **leopard** (sense 1), esp. the black variety (**black panther**). **2.** *U.S. and Canadian.* any of various related animals, esp. the puma. [C14: from Old French *pantère,* from Latin *panthēra,* from Greek *panthēr;* perhaps related to Sanskrit *pundarīka* tiger]

panties (ˈpæntɪz) *pl. n.* a pair of women's or children's underpants.

pantihose (ˈpæntɪˌhəʊz) *pl. n.* another name (esp. U.S. and Austral.) for **tights** (sense 1). [C20: from PANTIES + HOSE[2]]

pantile (ˈpænˌtaɪl) *n.* **1.** a roofing tile, with an S-shaped cross section, laid so that the downward curve of one tile overlaps the upward curve of the adjoining tile. **2.** a tapering roofing tile with a semicircular cross section, laid alternately so that the convex side of one tile overlaps the concave side of adjoining tiles. [C17: from PAN[1] + TILE]

pantisocracy (ˌpæntɪˈsɒkrəsɪ) *n.* a community, social group, etc., in which all have rule and everyone is equal. [C18 (coined by Robert *Southey* (1813–43), British poet): from Greek, from PANTO- + *isos* equal + -CRACY]

panto (ˈpæntəʊ) *n., pl.* **-tos.** *Brit. informal.* short for **pantomime** (sense 1).

panto- *or before a vowel* **pant-** *combining form.* all: *pantisocracy; pantofle; pantograph; pantomime.* [from Greek *pant-, pas*]

pantofle, pantoffle (pænˈtɒfᵊl), *or* **pantoufle** (pænˈtuːfᵊl) *n. Archaic.* a kind of slipper. [C15: from French *pantoufle,* from Old Italian *pantofola,* perhaps from Medieval Greek *pantophellos* shoe made of cork, from PANTO- + *phellos* cork]

pantograph (ˈpæntəˌgrɑːf) *n.* **1.** an instrument consisting of pivoted levers for copying drawings, maps, etc., to any desired scale. **2.** a sliding type of current collector, esp. a diamond-shaped frame mounted on a train roof in contact with an overhead wire. **3.** a device consisting of a parallelogram of jointed rods used to suspend a studio lamp so that its height can be adjusted. —**pantographer** (pænˈtɒgrəfə) *n.* —**pantographic** (ˌpæntəˈgræfɪk) *adj.* —ˌ**pantoˈgraphically** *adv.* —**panˈtography** *n.*

pantomime (ˈpæntəˌmaɪm) *n.* **1.** (in Britain) **a.** a kind of play performed at Christmas time characterized by farce, music, lavish sets, stock roles, and topical jokes. Sometimes shortened to **panto. b.** (*as modifier*): *a pantomime horse.* **2.** a theatrical entertainment in which words are replaced by gestures and bodily actions. **3.** action without words as a means of expression. **4.** (in ancient Rome) an actor in a dumb show. **5.** *Informal, chiefly Brit.* a confused or farcical situation. ~*vb.* **6.** another word for **mime** (sense 5). [C17: via Latin from Greek *pantomīmos;* see PANTO-, MIME] —**pantomimic** (ˌpæntəˈmɪmɪk) *adj.* —**pantomimist** (ˈpæntəˌmaɪmɪst) *n.*

pantothenic acid (ˌpæntəˈθɛnɪk) *n.* an oily acid that is a vitamin of the B complex: occurs widely in animal and vegetable foods and is essential for cell growth. Formula: $C_{19}H_{17}NO_5$. [C20: from Greek *pantothen* from every side]

pantoum (pænˈtuːm) *n. Prosody.* a verse form consisting of a series of quatrains in which the second and fourth lines of each verse are repeated as the first and third lines of the next. [C19: via French from Malay *pantun*]

pantry (ˈpæntrɪ) *n., pl.* **-tries.** a small room or cupboard in which provisions, cooking utensils, etc., are kept; larder. [C13: via Anglo-Norman, from Old French *paneterie* store for bread, ultimately from Latin *pānis* bread]

pants (pænts) *pl. n.* **1.** *Brit.* an undergarment reaching from the waist to the thighs or knees. **2.** the usual U.S. and Canadian name for **trousers. 3. bore, scare,** etc., **the pants off.** *Informal.* to bore, scare, etc., extremely. [C19: shortened from *pantaloons;* see PANTALOON]

pantsuit (ˈpæntˌsjuːt, -ˌsuːt) *n.* the U.S. and Canadian term for **trouser suit.**

panty girdle (ˈpæntɪ) *n.* a foundation garment with a crotch, often of lighter material than a girdle.

pantyhose (ˈpæntɪˌhəʊz) *n.* the N.Z. spelling of **pantihose.**

pantywaist (ˈpæntɪˌweɪst) *n. U.S. informal.* a man or boy considered as childish, lacking in courage, etc. [C20: originally a child's garment of trousers buttoned to a jacket at the waist]

panzer (ˈpænzə; *German* ˈpantsər) *n.* **1.** (*modifier*) of, relating to, or characteristic of the fast mechanized armoured units employed by the German army in World War II: *a panzer attack.* **2.** a vehicle belonging to a panzer unit, esp. a tank. **3.** (*pl.*) armoured troops. [C20: from German, from Middle High German, from Old French *panciere* coat of mail, from Latin *pantex* PAUNCH]

pap[1] (pæp) *n.* **1.** any soft or semiliquid food, such as bread softened with milk, esp. for babies or invalids; mash. **2.** *S. African.* porridge made from maize. **3.** worthless or oversimplified ideas; drivel: *intellectual pap.* [C15: from Middle Low German *pappe,* via Medieval Latin from Latin *pappāre* to eat; compare Dutch *pap,* Italian *pappa*]

pap[2] (pæp) *n.* **1.** *Archaic or Scot. and northern English dialect.* a nipple or teat. **2. a.** something resembling a breast or nipple, such as (formerly) one of a pair of rounded hilltops. **b.** (*cap. as part of a name*): *the Pap of Glencoe.* [C12: of Scandinavian origin, imitative of a sucking sound; compare Latin *papilla* nipple, Sanskrit *pippalaka*]

papa[1] (pəˈpɑː) *n. Old-fashioned.* an informal word for **father** (sense 1). [C17: from French, a children's word for father; compare Late Latin *pāpa,* Greek *pappa*]

papa[2] (ˈpɑːpɑː) *n. R.C. Church.* another name for the **pope**[1] (sense 1). [C16: from Italian]

papa[3] (ˈpɑːpa) *n.* a soft blue-grey clay of marine siltstone or sandstone. [Maori]

Papa (ˈpɑːpɑː) *n. Communications.* a code word for the letter *p.*

papacy (ˈpeɪpəsɪ) *n., pl.* **-cies. 1.** the office or term of office of a pope. **2.** the system of government in the Roman Catholic Church that has the pope as its head. [C14: from Medieval Latin *pāpātia,* from *pāpa* POPE[1]]

papain (pəˈpeɪɪn, -ˈpaɪɪn) *n.* a proteolytic enzyme occurring in the unripe fruit of the papaya tree, *Carica papaya:* used as a meat tenderizer and in medicine as an aid to protein digestion. [C19: from PAPAYA]

papal (ˈpeɪpᵊl) *adj.* of or relating to the pope or the papacy. —ˈ**papally** *adv.*

papal cross *n.* a cross with three crosspieces.

Papanicolaou test *or* **smear** (ˌpæpəˈnɪkəluː) *n.* the full name for **Pap test.**

paparazzo (ˌpæpəˈrætsəʊ) *n., pl.* **-razzi** (-ˈrætsiː). a freelance photographer who specializes in candid camera shots of famous people and often invades their privacy to obtain such photographs. [C20: from Italian]

papaveraceous (pəˌpeɪvəˈreɪʃəs) *adj.* of, relating to, or belonging to the *Papaveraceae,* a family of plants having large showy flowers and a cylindrical seed capsule with pores beneath the lid: includes the poppies and greater celandine. [C19: from New Latin, from Latin *papāver* POPPY]

papaverine (pəˈpeɪvəˌriːn, -rɪn) *n.* a white crystalline almost insoluble alkaloid found in opium and used as an antispasmodic to treat coronary spasms and certain types of colic. Formula: $C_{20}H_{21}NO_4$. [C19: from Latin *papāver* POPPY]

papaw (pəˈpɔː) *or* **pawpaw** *n.* **1.** Also called: **custard apple. a.** a bush or small tree, *Asimina triloba,* of central North America, having small fleshy edible fruit: family *Annonaceae.* **b.** the fruit of this tree. **2.** another name for **papaya.** [C16: from Spanish PAPAYA]

papaya (pəˈpaɪə) *n.* **1.** a West Indian evergreen tree, *Carica papaya,* with a crown of large dissected leaves and large green hanging fruit: family *Caricaceae.* **2.** the fruit of this tree, having a yellow sweet edible pulp and small black seeds. ~Also called: **papaw, pawpaw.** [C15 *papaye,* from Spanish *papaya,* from an American Indian language; compare Carib *ababai*] —**paˈpayan** *adj.*

paper (ˈpeɪpə) *n.* **1.** a substance made from cellulose fibres derived from rags, wood, etc., often with other additives, and formed into flat thin sheets suitable for writing on, decorating walls, wrapping, etc. Related adj.: **papyraceous. 2.** a single piece of such material, esp. if written or printed on. **3.** (*usually pl.*) documents for establishing the identity of the bearer; credentials. **4.** (*pl.*) Also called: **ship's papers.** official documents relating to the ownership, cargo, etc., of a ship. **5.** (*pl.*) collected diaries, letters, etc. **6.** See **newspaper** or **wallpaper.** **7.** *Government.* See **white paper, green paper, command paper.** **8.** a lecture or short published treatise on a specific subject. **9.** a short essay, as by a student. **10. a.** a set of written examination questions. **b.** the student's answers. **11.** *Commerce.* See **commercial paper.** **12.** *Theatre slang.* a free ticket. **13. on paper.** in theory, as opposed to fact: *it was a good idea on paper, but failed in practice.* ~*adj.* **14.** made of paper: *paper cups do not last long.* **15.** thin like paper: *paper walls.* **16.** (*prenominal*) existing only as recorded on paper but not yet in practice: *paper profits; paper expenditure.* **17.** taking place in writing: *paper battles.* ~*vb.* **18.** to cover (walls) with wallpaper. **19.** (*tr.*) to cover or furnish with paper. **20.** (*tr.*) *Theatre slang.* to fill (a performance) by giving away free tickets (esp. in the phrase **paper the house**). ~See also **paper over.** [C14: from Latin PAPYRUS] —**'paperer** *n.* —**'papery** *adj.* —**'paperiness** *n.*

paperback ('peɪpəˌbæk) *n.* **1.** a book or edition with covers made of flexible card, sold relatively cheaply. Compare **hardback.** ~*adj. also* **'paperˌbound, soft-cover.** **2.** of or denoting a paperback or publication of paperbacks. ~*vb.* (*tr.*) **3.** to publish in paperback. —**'paperˌbacker** *n.*

paperbark ('peɪpəˌbɑːk) *n.* any of several Australian myrtaceous trees of the genus *Melaleuca,* esp. *M. quinquenervia,* of swampy regions, having spear-shaped leaves and papery bark that can be peeled off in thin layers.

paperboard ('peɪpəˌbɔːd) *n.* **a.** a thick cardboard made of compressed layers of paper pulp; pasteboard. **b.** (*as modifier*): *a paperboard box.*

paperboy ('peɪpəˌbɔɪ) *n.* a boy employed to deliver newspapers, magazines, etc. —**'paperˌgirl** *fem. n.*

paper chase *n.* a cross-country run in which a runner lays a trail of paper for others to follow.

paperclip ('peɪpəˌklɪp) *n.* a clip for holding sheets of paper together, esp. one made of bent wire.

paper-cutter *n.* a machine for cutting paper, usually a blade mounted over a table on which paper can be aligned.

paper filigree *n.* another name for **rolled paperwork.**

paperhanger ('peɪpəˌhæŋə) *n.* **1.** a person who hangs wallpaper as an occupation. **2.** *U.S. slang.* a counterfeiter. —**'paperˌhanging** *n.*

paperknife ('peɪpəˌnaɪf) *n., pl.* **-knives.** a knife with a comparatively blunt blade, esp. one of wood, bone, etc., for opening sealed envelopes.

paperless ('peɪpəlɪs) *adj.* of, relating to, or denoting a means of communication, record keeping, etc., esp. electronic, that does not use paper: *the paperless office.*

paper money *n.* paper currency issued by the government or the central bank as legal tender and which circulates as a substitute for specie.

paper mulberry *n.* a small moraceous E Asian tree, *Broussonetia papyrifera,* the inner bark of which was formerly used for making paper in Japan. See also **tapa.**

paper nautilus *n.* any cephalopod mollusc of the genus *Argonauta,* esp. *A. argo,* of warm and tropical seas, having a papery external spiral shell: order *Octopoda* (octopods). Also called: **argonaut.** Compare **pearly nautilus.**

paper over *vb.* (*tr., adv.*) to conceal (something controversial or unpleasant).

paper tape *n.* a strip of paper used in computers, telex machines, etc., for recording information in the form of rows of either six or eight holes, some or all of which are punched to produce a combination used as a discrete code symbol. U.S. equivalent: **perforated tape.**

paper tiger *n.* a nation, institution, etc., that appears powerful but is in fact weak or insignificant. [C20: translation of a Chinese phrase first applied to the U.S.]

paperweight ('peɪpəˌweɪt) *n.* a small heavy object placed on loose papers to prevent them from scattering.

paperwork ('peɪpəˌwɜːk) *n.* clerical work, such as the completion of forms or the writing of reports or letters.

papeterie ('pæpətrɪ; *French* papetri) *n.* a box or case for papers and other writing materials. [C19: from French, from *papetier* maker of paper, from *papier* PAPER]

Paphian ('peɪfɪən) *adj.* **1.** of or relating to Paphos, a village in SW Cyprus that was the centre of worship of Aphrodite, goddess of love, by ancient Greeks. **2.** *Literary.* of sexual love.

Papiamento (*Spanish* papja'mento) *n.* a creolized Spanish spoken in the Netherlands Antilles. [Spanish, from *papia* talk]

papier collé (*French* papje kɔle) *n.* a type of collage, usually of an abstract design. [French, literally: glued paper]

papier-mâché (ˌpæpjeɪ'mæʃeɪ; *French* papjemaʃe) *n.* **1.** a hard strong substance suitable for painting on, made of paper pulp or layers of paper mixed with paste, size, etc., and moulded when moist. ~*adj.* **2.** made of papier-mâché. [C18: from French, literally: chewed paper]

papilionaceous (pəˌpɪlɪə'neɪʃəs) *adj.* of, relating to, or belonging to the *Papilionaceae,* a family of leguminous plants having irregular flowers: includes peas, beans, clover, alfalfa, gorse, and broom. [C17: from New Latin, from Latin *pāpiliō* butterfly]

papilla (pə'pɪlə) *n., pl.* **-lae** (-liː). **1.** the small projection of tissue at the base of a hair, tooth, or feather. **2.** any other similar protuberance. **3.** any minute blunt hair or process occurring in plants. [C18: from Latin: nipple; related to Latin *papula* pimple] —**pa'pillary, 'papillate,** *or* **'papillose** *adj.*

papilloma (ˌpæpɪ'ləʊmə) *n., pl.* **-mata** (-mətə) *or* **-mas.** *Pathol.* a benign tumour derived from epithelial tissue and forming a rounded or lobulated mass. [C19: from PAPILLA + -OMA] —**ˌpapil'lomatous** *adj.* —**ˌpapilˌloma'tosis** *n.*

papillon ('pæpɪˌlɒn) *n.* a breed of toy spaniel with large ears. [French: butterfly, from Latin *pāpiliō*]

papillote ('pæpɪˌləʊt) *n.* **1.** a paper frill around cutlets, etc. **2. en papillote** (ɑ̃ papijɔt). (of food) cooked in oiled greaseproof paper or foil. [C18: from French PAPILLON]

papist ('peɪpɪst) *n., adj.* (*often cap.*) *Usually disparaging.* another term for **Roman Catholic.** [C16: from French *papiste,* from Church Latin *pāpa* POPE[1]] —**pa'pistical** *or* **pa'pistic** *adj.* —**'papistry** *n.*

papoose *or* **pappoose** (pə'puːs) *n.* an American Indian baby or child. [C17: from Algonquian *papoos*]

pappus ('pæpəs) *n., pl.* **pappi** ('pæpaɪ). a ring of fine feathery hairs surrounding the fruit in composite plants, such as the thistle; aids dispersal of the fruits by the wind. [C18: via New Latin, from Greek *pappos* grandfather, old man, old man's beard, hence: pappus, down] —**'pappose** *or* **'pappous** *adj.*

pappy[1] ('pæpɪ) *adj.* **-pier, -piest.** resembling pap; mushy.

pappy[2] ('pæpɪ) *n., pl.* **-pies.** *U.S.* an informal word for **father.**

paprika ('pæprɪkə, pæ'priː-) *n.* **1.** a mild powdered seasoning made from a sweet variety of red pepper. **2.** the fruit or plant from which this seasoning is obtained. [C19: via Hungarian from Serbian, from *papar* PEPPER]

Pap test *or* **smear** (pæp) *n. Med.* **1.** another name for **cervical smear.** **2.** a similar test for precancerous cells in other organs. ~Also called: **Papanicolaou smear.** [C20: named after George *Papanicolaou* (1883–1962), U.S. anatomist, who devised it]

Papuan ('pæpjʊən) *adj.* **1.** of or relating to Papua New Guinea, a country in the SW Pacific comprising SE New Guinea and adjacent islands, or to any of the languages spoken there. ~*n.* **2.** a native or inhabitant of Papua New Guinea. **3.** any of several languages of Papua New Guinea that apparently do not belong to the Malayo-Polynesian family.

papule ('pæpjuːl) *or* **papula** ('pæpjʊlə) *n., pl.* **-ules** *or* **-ulae** (-jʊˌliː). *Pathol.* a small solid usually round elevation of the skin. [C19: from Latin *papula* pustule, pimple] —**'papular** *adj.* —**ˌpapu'liferous** *adj.*

papyraceous (ˌpæpɪ'reɪʃəs) *adj.* of, relating to, made of, or resembling paper. [C18: from PAPYRUS + -ACEOUS. See PAPER]

papyrology (ˌpæpɪ'rɒlədʒɪ) *n.* the study of ancient papyri. —**papyrological** (ˌpæpɪrə'lɒdʒɪkᵊl) *adj.* —**ˌpapy'rologist** *n.*

papyrus (pə'paɪrəs) *n., pl.* **-ri** (-raɪ) *or* **-ruses.** **1.** a tall aquatic cyperaceous plant, *Cyperus papyrus,* of S Europe and N and central Africa with small green-stalked flowers arranged like umbrella spokes around the stem top. **2.** a kind of paper made from the stem pith of this plant, used by the ancient Egyptians, Greeks, and Romans. **3.** an ancient document written on this paper. [C14: via Latin from Greek *papūros* reed used in making paper]

par (pɑː) *n.* **1.** an accepted level or standard, such as an average (esp. in the phrase **up to par**). **2.** a state of equality (esp. in the phrase **on a par with**). **3.** *Finance.* the established value of the unit of one national currency in terms of the unit of another where both are based on the same metal standard. **4.** *Commerce.* **a.** See **par value.** **b.** the condition of equality between the current market value of a share, bond, etc., and its face value (the **nominal par**). This equality is indicated by **at par,** while **above** (*or* **below**) **par** indicates that the market value is above (or below) face value. **5.** *Golf.* an estimated standard score for a hole or course that a good player should make: *par for the course was 72.* ~*adj.* **6.** average or normal. **7.** (*usually prenominal*) *Commerce.* of or relating to par: *par value.* [C17: from Latin *pār* equal, on a level; see PEER[1]]

par. *abbrev. for:* **1.** paragraph. **2.** parallel. **3.** parenthesis. **4.** parish.

Par. *abbrev. for* Paraguay.

par- *prefix.* a variant of **para-**[1] before a vowel.

para[1] ('pɑːrə) *n., pl.* **-ras** *or* **-ra.** a Yugoslavian monetary unit worth one hundredth of a dinar. [C17: Serbo-Croatian, via Turkish from Persian *pārah* piece, portion]

para[2] ('pærə) *n. Informal.* **1. a.** a soldier in an airborne unit. **b.** an airborne unit. **2.** a paragraph.

para-[1] *or before a vowel* **par-** *prefix.* **1.** beside; near: *parameter; parathyroid.* **2.** beyond: *parapsychology.* **3.** resembling: *paramnesia.* **4.** defective; abnormal: *paraesthesia.* **5.** subsidiary to: *paraphysis.* **6.** (*usually in italics*) denoting that an organic compound contains a benzene ring with substituents attached to atoms that are directly opposite across the ring (the 1,4- positions): *paradinitrobenzene; para*-cresol. Abbrev.: *p-*. Compare **ortho-** (sense 4), **meta-** (sense 4). **7.** denoting an isomer, polymer, or compound related to a specified compound: *paraldehyde; paracasein.* **8.** denoting the form of a diatomic substance in which the spins of the two constituent atoms are antiparallel: *parahydrogen.* Compare **ortho-** (sense 6). [from Greek *para* (prep.) alongside, beyond]

para-[2] *combining form.* indicating an object that acts as a protection against something: *parachute; parasol.* [via French from

Italian *para-*, from *parare* to defend, shield against, ultimately from Latin *parāre* to prepare]

para-aminobenzoic acid *n. Biochem.* an acid present in yeast and liver: used in the manufacture of dyes and pharmaceuticals. Formula: $C_6H_4(NH_2)COOH$.

parabasis (pəˈræbəsɪs) *n., pl.* **-ses** (-ˌsiːz). (in classical Greek comedy) an address from the chorus to the audience. [C19: from Greek, from *parabanein* to step forward]

parabiosis (ˌpærəbaɪˈəʊsɪs) *n.* **1.** the natural union of two individuals, such as Siamese twins, so that they share a common circulation of the blood. **2.** a similar union induced for experimental or therapeutic purposes. [C20: from PARA-¹ + Greek *biōsis* manner of life, from *bios* life] —**parabiotic** (ˌpærəbaɪˈɒtɪk) *adj.*

parablast (ˈpærəˌblæst) *n.* the yolk of an egg, such as a hen's egg, that undergoes meroblastic cleavage. [C19: from PARA-¹ + -BLAST] —ˌ**paraˈblastic** *adj.*

parable (ˈpærəbᵊl) *n.* **1.** a short story that uses familiar events to illustrate a religious or ethical situation. **2.** any of the stories of this kind told by Jesus Christ. [C14: from Old French *parabole*, from Latin *parabola* comparison, from Greek *parabolē* analogy, from *paraballein* to throw alongside, from PARA-¹ + *ballein* to throw] —**parabolist** (pəˈræbəlɪst) *n.*

parabola (pəˈræbələ) *n.* a conic section formed by the intersection of a cone by a plane parallel to its side. Standard equation: $y^2 = 4ax$, where $2a$ is the distance between focus and directrix. [C16: via New Latin from Greek *parabolē* a setting alongside; see PARABLE]

parabolic¹ (ˌpærəˈbɒlɪk) *adj.* **1.** of, relating to, or shaped like a parabola. **2.** shaped like a paraboloid: *a parabolic mirror.*

parabolic² (ˌpærəˈbɒlɪk) *or* **parabolical** *adj.* of or resembling a parable. —ˌ**paraˈbolically** *adv.*

parabolic aerial *n.* a formal name for **dish aerial.**

parabolize¹ *or* **parabolise** (pəˈræbəˌlaɪz) *vb. (tr.)* to explain by a parable.

parabolize² *or* **parabolise** (pəˈræbəˌlaɪz) *vb. (tr.)* to shape like a parabola or paraboloid. —**paˌraboliˈzation** *or* **paˌraboliˈsation** *n.*

paraboloid (pəˈræbəˌlɔɪd) *n.* a geometric surface whose sections parallel to two coordinate planes are parabolic and whose sections parallel to the third plane are either elliptical or hyperbolic. Equations: $x^2/a^2 \pm y^2/b^2 = 2cz$ —**paˌraboˈloidal** *adj.*

parabrake (ˈpærəˌbreɪk) *n.* another name for **brake parachute.**

paracasein (ˌpærəˈkeɪsiɪn, -siːn) *n. U.S.* another name for **casein.**

paracentesis (ˌpærəsɛnˈtiːsɪs) *n. Med.* the surgical puncture of a body cavity in order to draw off excess fluid.

paracetamol (ˌpærəˈsiːtəˌmɒl, -ˈsɛtə-) *n.* a mild analgesic drug used as an alternative to aspirin. [C20: from *para-acetamidophenol*]

parachronism (pəˈrækrəˌnɪzəm) *n.* an error in dating, esp. by giving too late a date. Compare **prochronism.** [C17: from PARA-¹ + *-chronism*, as in ANACHRONISM]

parachute (ˈpærəˌʃuːt) *n.* **1. a.** a device used to retard the fall of a man or package from an aircraft, consisting of a large fabric canopy connected to a harness. **b.** *(as modifier)*: *parachute troops.* Sometimes shortened to **chute.** See also **brake parachute.** ~*vb.* **2.** (of troops, supplies, etc.) to land or cause to land by parachute from an aircraft. **3.** *Canadian.* (in an election) to bring in (a candidate, esp. someone well known) from outside the constituency. [C18: from French, from PARA-² + *chute* fall] —ˈ**paraˌchutist** *n.*

paraclete (ˈpærəˌkliːt) *n. Rare.* a mediator or advocate.

Paraclete (ˈpærəˌkliːt) *n. Christianity.* the Holy Ghost as comforter or advocate. [C15: via Old French from Church Latin *Paraclētus*, from Late Greek *Paraklētos* advocate, from Greek *parakalein* to summon as a helper, from PARA-¹ + *kalein* to call]

parade (pəˈreɪd) *n.* **1.** an ordered, esp. ceremonial, march, assembly, or procession, as of troops being reviewed: *on parade.* **2.** Also called: **parade ground.** a place where military formations regularly assemble. **3.** a visible show or display: *to make a parade of one's grief.* **4.** a public promenade or street of shops. **5.** a successive display of things or people. **6.** the interior area of a fortification. **7.** a parry in fencing. **8. on parade. a.** on display. **b.** showing oneself off. ~*vb.* **9.** (when *intr.*, often foll. by *through* or *along*) to walk or march, esp. in a procession (through): *to parade the streets.* **10.** *(tr.)* to exhibit or flaunt: *he was parading his medals.* **11.** *(tr.)* to cause to assemble in formation, as for a military parade. **12.** *(intr.)* to walk about in a public place. [C17: from French: a making ready, a setting out, a boasting display; compare Italian *parata*, Spanish *parada*, all ultimately from Latin *parāre* to prepare] —**paˈrader** *n.*

paradigm (ˈpærəˌdaɪm) *n.* **1.** *Grammar.* the set of all the inflected forms of a word or a systematic arrangement displaying these forms. **2.** a pattern or model. **3.** a typical or stereotypical example (esp. in the phrase **paradigm case**). **4.** (in the philosophy of science) a very general conception of the nature of scientific endeavour within which a given enquiry is undertaken. [C15: via French and Latin from Greek *paradeigma* pattern, from *paradeiknunai* to compare, from PARA-¹ + *deiknunai* to show] —**paradigmatic** (ˌpærədɪgˈmætɪk) *adj.*

paradise (ˈpærəˌdaɪs) *n.* **1.** heaven as the ultimate abode or state of the righteous. **2.** *Islam.* the sensual garden of delights that the Koran promises the faithful after death. **3.** Also called: **limbo.** (according to some theologians) the intermediate abode or state of the just prior to the Resurrection of Jesus, as in Luke 23:43. **4.** the place or state of happiness enjoyed by Adam before the first sin; the Garden of Eden. **5.** any place or condition that fulfils all one's desires or aspirations. **6.** a park in which foreign animals are kept. [Old English, from Church Latin *paradīsus*, from Greek *paradeisos* garden, of Persian origin; compare Avestan *pairidaēza* enclosed area, from *pairi-* around + *daēza* wall]

paradise duck *n.* a large duck, *Casarca variegata*, of New Zealand, having a brightly coloured plumage.

paradise fish *n.* any of several beautifully coloured labyrinth fishes of the genus *Macropodus*, esp. *M. opercularis*, of S and SE Asia.

paradisiacal (ˌpærədɪˈsaɪəkᵊl), **paradisiac** (ˌpærəˈdɪsɪˌæk), *or* **paradisaical** (ˌpærədɪˈseɪɪkᵊl) *adj.* of, relating to, or resembling paradise. —ˌ**paradiˈsiacally** *or* ˌ**paradiˈsaically** *adv.*

parados (ˈpærəˌdɒs) *n.* a bank behind a trench or other fortification, giving protection from being fired on from the rear. [C19: from French, from PARA-² + *dos* back, from Latin *dorsum*; compare PARASOL, PARAPET]

paradox (ˈpærəˌdɒks) *n.* **1.** a seemingly absurd or self-contradictory statement that is or may be true: *religious truths are often expressed in paradox.* **2.** a self-contradictory proposition, such as *I always tell lies.* **3.** a person or thing exhibiting apparently contradictory characteristics. **4.** an opinion that conflicts with common belief. [C16: from Late Latin *paradoxum*, from Greek *paradoxos* opposed to existing notions, from PARA-¹ + *doxa* opinion] —ˌ**paraˈdoxical** *adj.* —ˌ**paraˈdoxically** *adv.*

paradoxical intention *n.* (in psychotherapy) the deliberate practice of a neurotic habit or thought, undertaken in order to remove it.

paradoxical sleep *n. Physiol.* sleep that appears to be deep but that is characterized by rapid eye movements, heavier breathing, and increased electrical activity of the brain.

paradrop (ˈpærəˌdrɒp) *n.* the delivery of personnel or equipment from an aircraft by parachute.

paraesthesia *or U.S.* **paresthesia** (ˌpærɛsˈθiːzɪə) *n. Pathol.* an abnormal or inappropriate sensation in an organ, part, or area of the skin, as of burning, prickling, tingling, etc. —**paraesthetic** *or U.S.* **paresthetic** (ˌpærɛsˈθɛtɪk) *adj.*

paraffin (ˈpærəfɪn) *or (less commonly)* **paraffine** (ˈpærəˌfiːn) *n.* **1.** Also called: **paraffin oil,** (esp. U.S. and Canadian) **kerosene.** a liquid mixture consisting mainly of alkane hydrocarbons with boiling points in the range 150°–300°C, used as an aircraft fuel, in domestic heaters, and as a solvent. **2.** another name for **alkane. 3.** See **paraffin wax. 4.** See **liquid paraffin.** ~*vb. (tr.)* **5.** to treat with paraffin or paraffin wax. [C19: from German, from Latin *parum* too little + *affinis* adjacent; so called from its chemical inertia]

paraffin wax *n.* a white insoluble odourless waxlike solid consisting mainly of alkane hydrocarbons with melting points in the range 50°-60°C, used in candles, waterproof paper, and as a sealing agent. Also called: **paraffin.**

paraformaldehyde (ˌpærəfɔːˈmældɪˌhaɪd) *or* **paraform** *n.* a white amorphous solid polymeric form of formaldehyde: used as a convenient source of formaldehyde and as a fumigant. Formula: $(CH_2O)n$, where n lies between 6 and 50.

paragenesis (ˌpærəˈdʒɛnɪsɪs) *or* **paragenesia** (ˌpærədʒɪˈniːzɪə) *n.* the order in which the constituent minerals of a rock mass have been formed. —**paragenetic** (ˌpærədʒɪˈnɛtɪk) *adj.* —ˌ**parageˈnetically** *adv.*

paragliding (ˈpærəˌglaɪdɪŋ) *n.* the sport of cross-country gliding using a specially designed parachute shaped like flexible wings. The parachutist glides from an aeroplane to a predetermined landing area. —ˈ**paraˌglider** *n.*

paragnathous (ˌpærəgˈneɪθəs) *adj.* (of certain vertebrates) having the upper and lower jaws of equal length.

paragoge (ˌpærəˈgəʊdʒɪ) *or* **paragogue** (ˈpærəˌgɒg) *n.* the addition of a sound or a syllable to the end of a word, such as *st* in *amongst.* [C17: via Late Latin from Greek *paragōgē* an alteration, ultimately from *paragein* to lead past, change] —**paragogic** (ˌpærəˈgɒdʒɪk) *or* ˌ**paraˈgogical** *adj.* —ˌ**paraˈgogically** *adv.*

paragon (ˈpærəgən) *n.* **1.** a model of excellence; pattern: *a paragon of virtue.* **2.** a size of printer's type, approximately equal to 20 point. ~*vb. (tr.)* **3.** *Archaic.* **a.** to equal or surpass. **b.** to compare. **c.** to regard as a paragon. [C16: via French from Old Italian *paragone* comparison, from Medieval Greek *parakonē* whetstone, from Greek *parakonan* to sharpen against, from PARA-¹ + *akonan* to sharpen, from *akonē* whetstone]

paragraph (ˈpærəˌgrɑːf, -ˌgræf) *n.* **1.** (in a piece of writing) one of a series of subsections each usually devoted to one idea and each usually marked by the beginning of a new line, indentation, increased interlinear space, etc. **2.** *Printing.* the character ¶, used as a reference mark or to indicate the beginning of a new paragraph. **3.** a short article in a newspaper. ~*vb. (tr.)* **4.** to form into paragraphs. **5.** to express or report in a paragraph. [C16: from Medieval Latin *paragraphus*, from Greek *paragraphos* line drawing attention to part of a text, from *paragraphein* to write beside, from PARA-¹ + *graphein* to write] —**paragraphic** (ˌpærəˈgræfɪk) *or* ˌ**paraˈgraphical** *adj.* —ˌ**paraˈgraphically** *adv.*

paragraphia (ˌpærəˈgrɑːfɪə) *n. Psychiatry.* the habitual writing of a different word or letter from the one intended, often the result of a mental disorder or brain injury. [C20: from New Latin; see PARA-[1], -GRAPH]

Paraguayan (ˌpærəˈgwaɪən) *adj.* **1.** of or relating to Paraguay, an inland republic in South America. ~*n.* **2.** a native or inhabitant of Paraguay.

Paraguay tea (ˈpærəˌgwaɪ) *n.* another name for **maté.**

parahydrogen (ˌpærəˈhaɪdrədʒən) *n. Chem.* the form of molecular hydrogen (constituting about 25 per cent of the total at normal temperatures) in which the nuclei of the two atoms in each molecule spin in opposite directions. Compare **orthohydrogen.**

para-influenza virus *n.* any of a group of viruses that cause respiratory infections with influenza-like symptoms, esp. in children.

parakeet *or* **parrakeet** (ˈpærəˌkiːt) *n.* any of numerous small usually brightly coloured long-tailed parrots, such as *Psittacula krameri* (**ring-necked parakeet**), of Africa. [C16: from Spanish *periquito* and Old French *paroquet* parrot, of uncertain origin]

parakelia *or* **parakeelya** (ˌpærəˈkiːljə) *n.* a succulent herb of the genus *Calandrinia*, with purple flowers, that thrives in inland Australia. [from a native Australian language]

paralalia (ˌpærəˈleɪlɪə) *n.* any of various speech disorders, esp. the production of a sound different from that intended.

paralanguage (ˈpærəˌlæŋgwɪdʒ) *n. Linguistics.* nonverbal elements in speech, such as intonation, that may affect the meaning of an utterance.

paraldehyde (pəˈrældɪˌhaɪd) *n.* a colourless liquid substance that is a cyclic trimer of acetaldehyde: used in making dyestuffs and as a hypnotic and anticonvulsant drug. Formula: $(C_2H_4O)_3$.

paralexia (ˌpærəˈlɛksɪə) *n.* a disorder of the ability to read in which words and syllables are meaninglessly transposed. —ˌ**paraˈlexic** *adj.*

paralimnion (ˌpærəˈlɪmnɪɒn) *n. Ecology.* the region of a lake floor between the shoreline or water's edge and the zone of rooted vegetation. [from PARA-[1] + Greek *limnē* lake]

paralinguistics (ˌpærəlɪŋˈgwɪstɪks) *n.* (*functioning as sing.*) the study of paralanguage. —ˌ**paralinˈguistic** *adj.*

paralipomena (ˌpærəlaɪˈpɒmənə) *pl. n.* things added in a supplement to a work. [C14: via late Latin from Greek *paraleipomena,* from PARA- (on one side) + *leipein* to leave]

paralipsis (ˌpærəˈlɪpsɪs) *or* **paraleipsis** (ˌpærəˈlaɪpsɪs) *n., pl.* **-ses** (-siːz). a rhetorical device in which an idea is emphasized by the pretence that it is too obvious to discuss, as in *there are many drawbacks to your plan, not to mention the cost.* [C16: via Late Latin from Greek: neglect, from *paraleipein* to leave aside, from PARA-[1] + *leipein* to leave]

parallax (ˈpærəˌlæks) *n.* **1.** an apparent change in the position of an object resulting from a change in position of the observer. **2.** *Astronomy.* the angle subtended at a celestial body, esp. a star, by the radius of the earth's orbit. **Annual** or **heliocentric parallax** is the apparent displacement of a nearby star resulting from its observation from the earth. **Diurnal** or **geocentric parallax** results from the observation of a planet, the sun, or the moon from the surface of the earth. [C17: via French from New Latin *parallaxis,* from Greek: change, from *parallassein* to change, from PARA-[1] + *allassein* to alter] —**parallactic** (ˌpærəˈlæktɪk) *adj.* —ˌ**paralˈlactically** *adv.*

parallel (ˈpærəˌlɛl) *adj.* (when *postpositive,* usually foll. by *to*) **1.** separated by an equal distance at every point; never touching or intersecting: *parallel walls.* **2.** corresponding; similar: *parallel situations.* **3.** *Music.* **a.** Also: **consecutive.** (of two or more parts or melodies) moving in similar motion but keeping the same interval apart throughout: *parallel fifths.* **b.** denoting successive chords in which the individual notes move in parallel motion. **4.** *Grammar.* denoting syntactic constructions in which the constituents of one construction correspond to those of the other. **5.** *Computer technol.* operating on several items of information, instructions, etc., simultaneously. Compare **serial** (sense 6). ~*n.* **6.** *Maths.* one of a set of parallel lines, planes, etc. **7.** an exact likeness. **8.** a comparison. **9.** Also called: **parallel of latitude.** any of the imaginary lines around the earth parallel to the equator, designated by degrees of latitude ranging from 0° at the equator to 90° at the poles. **10. a.** a configuration of two or more electrical components connected between two points in a circuit so that the same voltage is applied to each (esp. in the phrase **in parallel**). **b.** (*as modifier*): *a parallel circuit.* ~Compare **series** (sense 6). **11.** *Printing.* the character (‖) used as a reference mark. **12.** a trench or line lying in advance of and parallel to other defensive positions. ~*vb.* **-lels, -leling, -leled.** (*tr.*) **13.** to make parallel. **14.** to supply a parallel to. **15.** to be a parallel to or correspond with: *your experience parallels mine.* [C16: via French and Latin from Greek *parallēlos* alongside one another, from PARA-[1] + *allēlos* one another]

parallel bars *pl. n. Gymnastics.* **a.** (*functioning as pl.*) a pair of wooden bars on uprights, sometimes at different heights, for various exercises. **b.** (*functioning as sing.*) an event in a gymnastic competition in which competitors exercise on such bars.

parallelepiped, parallelopiped (ˌpærəˌlɛləˈpaɪpɛd), *or* **parallelepipedon** (ˌpærəˌlɛləˈpaɪpɪdən) *n.* a geometric solid whose six faces are parallelograms. [C16: from Greek *parallēlepipedon;* from *parallēlos* PARALLEL + *epipedon* plane surface, from EPI- + *pedon* ground]

paralleling (ˈpærəˌlɛlɪŋ) *n.* a form of trading in which companies buy highly priced goods in a market in which the prices are low in order to be able to sell them in a market in which the prices are higher.

parallelism (ˈpærəlɛˌlɪzəm) *n.* **1.** the state of being parallel. **2.** *Grammar.* the repetition of a syntactic construction in successive sentences for rhetorical effect. **3.** *Philosophy.* the dualistic doctrine that mental and physical processes are regularly correlated but are not causally connected, so that, for example, pain always accompanies, but is not caused by, a pin-prick. Compare **interactionism, occasionalism.** —ˈ**paralˌlelist** *n., adj.*

parallelogram (ˌpærəˈlɛləˌgræm) *n.* a quadrilateral whose opposite sides are parallel and equal in length. See also **rhombus, rectangle, trapezium, trapezoid.** [C16: via French from Late Latin, from Greek *parallēlogrammon,* from *parallēlos* PARALLEL + *grammē* line, related to *graphein* to write]

parallelogram rule *n. Maths, physics.* a rule for finding the resultant of two vectors by constructing a parallelogram with two adjacent sides representing the magnitudes and directions of the vectors, the diagonal through the point of intersection of the vectors representing their resultant.

parallel processing *n.* the performance by a computer system of two or more simultaneous operations.

parallel resonance *n.* the resonance that results when circuit elements are connected with their inductance and capacitance in parallel, so that the impedance of the combination rises to a maximum at the resonant frequency. Compare **series resonance.**

parallel ruler *n. Engineering.* a drawing instrument in which two parallel edges are connected so that they remain parallel, although the distance between them can be varied.

parallel turn *n. Skiing.* a turn, executed by shifting one's weight, in which the skis stay parallel.

paralogism (pəˈræləˌdʒɪzəm) *n.* **1.** *Logic, psychology.* an argument that is unintentionally invalid. Compare **sophism. 2.** any invalid argument or conclusion. [C16: via Late Latin from Greek *paralogismos,* from *paralogizesthai* to argue fallaciously, from PARA-[1] + *-logizesthai,* ultimately from *logos* word] —**paˈralogist** *n.* —**paˌraloˈgistic** *adj.*

Paralympian (ˌpærəˈlɪmpɪən) *n.* a competitor in the Paralympic Games.

Paralympic (ˌpærəˈlɪmpɪk) *adj.* of or relating to the Paralympic Games.

Paralympic Games *pl. n.* a sporting event, modelled on the Olympic Games, held solely for disabled competitors. Also called: **the Paralympics.** [C20: PARA-[1] + OLYMPIC GAMES]

paralyse *or U.S.* **paralyze** (ˈpærəˌlaɪz) *vb.* (*tr.*) **1.** *Pathol.* to affect with paralysis. **2.** *Med.* to render (a part of the body) insensitive to pain, touch, etc., esp. by injection of an anaesthetic. **3.** to make immobile; transfix. [C19: from French *paralyser,* from *paralysie* PARALYSIS] —ˌ**paralyˈsation** *or U.S.* ˌ**paralyˈzation** *n.* —ˈ**paraˌlyser** *or U.S.* ˈ**paraˌlyzer** *n.*

paralysis (pəˈrælɪsɪs) *n., pl.* **-ses** (-ˌsiːz). **1.** *Pathol.* **a.** impairment or loss of voluntary muscle function or of sensation (**sensory paralysis**) in a part or area of the body, usually caused by a lesion or disorder of the muscles or the nerves supplying them. **b.** a disease characterized by such impairment or loss; palsy. **2.** cessation or impairment of activity: *paralysis of industry by strikes.* [C16: via Latin from Greek *paralusis;* see PARA-[1], -LYSIS]

paralysis agitans (ˈædʒɪˌtænz) *n.* another name for **Parkinson's disease.**

paralytic (ˌpærəˈlɪtɪk) *adj.* **1.** of, relating to, or of the nature of paralysis. **2.** afflicted with or subject to paralysis. **3.** *Brit. informal.* very drunk. ~*n.* **4.** a person afflicted with paralysis. —ˌ**paraˈlytically** *adv.*

paramagnetism (ˌpærəˈmægnɪˌtɪzəm) *n. Physics.* the phenomenon exhibited by substances that have a relative permeability slightly greater than unity and a positive susceptibility. The effect is due to the alignment of unpaired spins of electrons in atoms of the material. Compare **diamagnetism, ferromagnetism.** —**paramagnetic** (ˌpærəmægˈnɛtɪk) *adj.*

paramatta *or* **parramatta** (ˌpærəˈmætə) *n.* a lightweight twill-weave fabric of wool formerly with silk or cotton, used for dresses, etc., now used esp. for rubber-proofed garments. [C19: named after *Parramatta,* New South Wales, Australia, where it was originally produced]

paramecium (ˌpærəˈmiːsɪəm) *n., pl.* **-cia** (-sɪə). any freshwater protozoan of the genus *Paramecium,* having an oval body covered with cilia and a ventral ciliated groove for feeding: class *Ciliata* (ciliates). [C18: New Latin, from Greek *paramēkēs* elongated, from PARA-[1] + *mēkos* length]

paramedic (ˌpærəˈmɛdɪk) *or* **paramedical** *n.* **1.** a person, such as a laboratory technician, who supplements the work of the medical profession. ~*adj.* **2.** of or designating such a person.

parament (ˈpærəmənt) *n., pl.* **paraments** *or* **paramenta** (ˌpærəˈmɛntə). (*often pl.*) an ecclesiastical vestment or decorative hanging. [C14: from Old French *parament,* from Medieval Latin *paramentum,* from Latin *parāre* to prepare]

parameter (pəˈræmɪtə) *n.* **1.** one of a number of auxiliary variables in terms of which all the variables in an implicit functional relationship can be explicitly expressed. See **parametric equa-**

tions. **2.** a variable whose behaviour is not being considered and which may for present purposes be regarded as a constant, as *y* in the partial derivative $\partial f(x,y)/\partial x$. **3.** *Statistics.* a characteristic of the distribution of a population, such as its mean, as distinct from that of a sample. Compare **statistic.** **4.** *Informal.* any constant or limiting factor: *a designer must work within the parameters of budget and practicality.* [C17: from New Latin; see PARA-[1], -METER] —**parametric** (ˌpærəˈmɛtrɪk) *or* ˌ**paraˈmetrical** *adj.*

parametric amplifier *n.* a type of high-frequency amplifier in which energy from a pumping oscillator is transferred to the input signal through a circuit with a varying parameter, usually a varying reactance.

parametric equalizer *n.* an electronic device for cutting or boosting selected frequencies by continuous narrowing or widening of the frequencies to be filtered. Compare **graphic equalizer.**

parametric equations *pl. n.* a set of equations expressing a number of quantities as explicit functions of the same set of independent variables and equivalent to some direct functional relationship of these quantities: *a circle* $x^2 + y^2 = r^2$ *has parametric equations* $x = r \cos \theta$ *and* $y = r \sin \theta$ *in terms of the parameters r and* θ.

parametric statistics *n. (functioning as sing.)* the branch of statistics concerned with data measurable on interval or ratio scales, so that arithmetic operations are applicable to them, enabling parameters such as the mean of the distribution to be defined.

paramilitary (ˌpærəˈmɪlɪtərɪ, -trɪ) *adj.* **1.** denoting or relating to a group of personnel with military structure functioning either as a civil force or in support of military forces. **2.** denoting or relating to a force with military structure conducting armed operations against a ruling or occupying power. ~*n.* **3. a.** a paramilitary force. **b.** a member of such a force.

paramnesia (ˌpæræmˈniːzɪə) *n. Psychiatry.* a disorder of the memory or the faculty of recognition in which dreams may be confused with reality.

paramo (ˈpærəˌməʊ) *n., pl.* **-mos.** a high plateau in the Andes between the tree line and the permanent snow line. [C18: American Spanish, from Spanish: treeless plain]

paramorph (ˈpærəˌmɔːf) *n.* **1.** a mineral that has undergone paramorphism. **2.** a plant or animal that is classified on the basis of inadequate data and differs taxonomically from other members of the species in which it has been placed. —ˌ**paraˈmorphic** *or* ˌ**paraˈmorphous** *adj.*

paramorphine (ˌpærəˈmɔːfiːn) *n.* another name for **thebaine.**

paramorphism (ˌpærəˈmɔːˌfɪzəm) *n.* a process by which the crystalline structure of a mineral alters without any change in its chemical composition.

paramount (ˈpærəˌmaʊnt) *adj.* **1.** of the greatest importance or significance; pre-eminent. ~*n.* **2.** *Rare.* a supreme ruler. [C16: via Anglo-Norman from Old French *paramont,* from *par* by + *-amont* above, from Latin *ad montem* to the mountain] —ˈ**paraˌmountcy** *n.* —ˈ**paraˌmountly** *adv.*

paramour (ˈpærəˌmʊə) *n.* **1.** *Now usually derogatory.* a lover, esp. an adulterous woman. **2.** an archaic word for **beloved** (sense 2). [C13: from Old French, literally: through love]

Paraná pine (pəˈrɑːnə) *n.* **1.** a large pine tree, *Araucaria angustifolia,* of South America yielding softwood timber: family *Pinaceae.* **2.** the wood of this tree.

parang (ˈpɑːræŋ) *n.* a short stout straight-edged knife used by the Dyaks of Borneo. [C19: from Malay]

paranoia (ˌpærəˈnɔɪə) *n.* **1.** a form of schizophrenia characterized by a slowly progressive deterioration of the personality, involving delusions and often hallucinations. **2.** a mental disorder characterized by any of several types of delusions, in which the personality otherwise remains relatively intact. **3.** *Informal.* intense fear or suspicion, esp. when unfounded. [C19: via New Latin from Greek: frenzy, from *paranoos* distraught, from PARA-[1] + *noos* mind] —**paranoiac** (ˌpærəˈnɔɪɪk) *or* **paranoic** (ˌpærəˈnəʊɪk) *adj., n.*

paranoid (ˈpærəˌnɔɪd) *adj.* **1.** of, characterized by, or resembling paranoia. **2.** *Informal.* exhibiting undue suspicion, fear of persecution, etc. ~*n.* **3.** a person who shows the behaviour patterns associated with paranoia.

paranormal (ˌpærəˈnɔːməl) *adj.* **1.** beyond normal explanation. ~*n.* **2. the.** paranormal happenings generally.

paranymph (ˈpærəˌnɪmf) *n. Archaic.* a bridesmaid or best man. [C16: via Late Latin from Greek *paranumphos,* from PARA-[1] + *numphē* bride (literally: person beside the bride)]

paraparesis (ˌpærəpəˈriːsɪs) *n.* muscle weakness, esp. of the legs, allowing limited movement; partial paralysis. —**paraparetic** (ˌpærəpəˈrɛtɪk) *adj.*

parapente (ˈpærəˌpɛntɪ) *n.* **1.** another name for **paraskiing.** **2.** the form of parachute used in this sport.

parapet (ˈpærəpɪt, -ˌpɛt) *n.* **1.** a low wall or railing along the edge of a balcony, roof, etc. **2.** Also called: **breastwork.** a rampart, mound of sandbags, bank, etc., in front of a trench, giving protection from fire from the front. [C16: from Italian *parapetto,* literally: chest-high wall, from PARA-[2] + *petto,* from Latin *pectus* breast]

paraph (ˈpærəf) *n.* a flourish after a signature, originally to prevent forgery. [C14: via French from Medieval Latin *paraphus,* variant of *paragraphus* PARAGRAPH]

paraphasia (ˌpærəˈfeɪzɪə) *n.* a defect of speech in which the normal flow of words is interrupted by inappropriate words and phrases. [C20: from Greek PARA-[1] + *-phasia,* from *phanai* to speak]

paraphernalia (ˌpærəfəˈneɪlɪə) *pl. n.* (*sometimes functioning as sing.*) **1.** miscellaneous articles or equipment. **2.** *Law.* (formerly) articles of personal property given to a married woman by her husband before or during marriage and regarded in law as her possessions over which she has some measure of control. [C17: via Medieval Latin from Latin *parapherna* personal property of a married woman, apart from her dowry, from Greek, from PARA-[1] + *phernē* dowry, from *pherein* to carry]

paraphilia (ˌpærəˈfɪlɪə) *n.* any abnormal sexual behaviour; sexual anomaly or deviation. [C20: from PARA-[1] + *-philia,* from Greek *philos* loving]

paraphrase (ˈpærəˌfreɪz) *n.* **1.** an expression of a statement or text in other words, esp. in order to clarify. **2.** the practice of making paraphrases. ~*vb.* **3.** to put (something) into other words; restate (something). [C16: via French from Latin *paraphrasis,* from Greek, from *paraphrazein* to recount] —**paraphrastic** (ˌpærəˈfræstɪk) *adj.*

paraphysis (pəˈræfɪsɪs) *n., pl.* **-ses** (-ˌsiːz). any of numerous sterile cells occurring between the sex organs of mosses and algae and between the spore-producing bodies of basidiomycetous and ascomycetous fungi. [C19: New Latin from Greek: subsidiary growth, from PARA-[1] + *phusis* growth] —**paˈraphysate** *adj.*

paraplegia (ˌpærəˈpliːdʒə) *n. Pathol.* paralysis of the lower half of the body, usually as the result of disease or injury of the spine. Compare **hemiplegia, quadriplegia.** [C17: via New Latin from Greek: a blow on one side, from PARA-[1] + *plēssein* to strike] —ˌ**paraˈplegic** *adj., n.*

parapodium (ˌpærəˈpəʊdɪəm) *n., pl.* **-dia** (-dɪə). **1.** any of the paired unjointed lateral appendages of polychaete worms, used in locomotion, respiration, etc. **2.** any of various similar appendages of other invertebrates, esp. certain molluscs. [New Latin: from PARA-[1] + -PODIUM]

parapraxis (ˌpærəˈpræksɪs) *n. Psychoanal.* a minor error in action, such as slips of the tongue, supposedly the result of repressed impulses. See also **Freudian slip.** [C20: from PARA-[1] + Greek *praxis* a doing, deed]

parapsychology (ˌpærəsaɪˈkɒlədʒɪ) *n.* the study of mental phenomena, such as telepathy, which are beyond the scope of normal physical explanation. —**parapsychological** (ˌpærəsaɪkəˈlɒdʒɪkəl) *adj.* —ˌ**parapsyˈchologist** *n.*

Paraquat (ˈpærəˌkwɒt) *n. Trademark.* a yellow extremely poisonous soluble solid used in solution as a weedkiller.

Pará rubber (pəˈrɑː, ˈpɑːrə) *n.* a South American rubber obtained from any of various euphorbiaceous trees of the genus *Hevea,* esp. *H. brasiliensis.* See also **rubber tree.** [C19: from *Pará,* a state in N Brazil]

parasailing (ˈpærəˌseɪlɪŋ) *n.* a sport in which a water-skier wearing a parachute is towed by a speedboat, becomes airborne, and sails along in the air.

parasang (ˈpærəˌsæŋ) *n.* a Persian unit of distance equal to about 5.5 km or 3.4 miles. [C16: via Latin and Greek from a Persian word related to modern Persian *farsang*]

parascending (ˈpærəˌsɛndɪŋ) *n.* a sport in which a participant wears a parachute and becomes airborne by being towed by a vehicle into the wind and then descends by parachute.

parascience (ˈpærəˌsaɪəns) *n.* the study of subjects that are outside the scope of traditional science because they cannot be explained by accepted scientific theory or tested by conventional scientific methods.

paraselene (ˌpærəsɪˈliːnɪ) *n., pl.* **-nae** (-niː). *Meteorol.* a bright image of the moon on a lunar halo. Also called: **mock moon.** Compare **parhelion.** [C17: New Latin, from PARA-[1] + Greek *selēnē* moon] —ˌ**paraseˈlenic** *adj.*

Parashah (ˈpærəˌʃɑː; *Hebrew* paraˈʃa) *n., pl.* **-shoth** (-ˌʃəʊt; *Hebrew* -ˈʃɔt). *Judaism.* **1.** any of the sections of the Torah read in the synagogue. **2.** any of the subsections of the weekly lessons read on Sabbaths in the synagogue. ~Also called (Yiddish): **Parsha.** [from Hebrew, from *pārāsh* to divide, separate]

parasite (ˈpærəˌsaɪt) *n.* **1.** an animal or plant that lives in or on another (the host) from which it obtains nourishment. The host does not benefit from the association and is often harmed by it. **2.** a person who habitually lives at the expense of others; sponger. **3.** (formerly) a sycophant. [C16: via Latin from Greek *parasitos* one who lives at another's expense, from PARA-[1] + *sitos* grain] —**parasitic** (ˌpærəˈsɪtɪk) *or* ˌ**paraˈsitical** *adj.* —ˌ**paraˈsitically** *adv.*

parasite drag *n.* the part of the drag on an aircraft that is contributed by nonlifting surfaces, such as fuselage, nacelles, etc. Also called: **parasite resistance.**

parasiticide (ˌpærəˈsɪtɪˌsaɪd) *n.* **1.** any substance capable of destroying parasites. ~*adj.* **2.** destructive to parasites. —ˌ**paraˌsitiˈcidal** *adj.*

parasitic male *n. Zoology.* a male animal that is much smaller than the female and is totally dependent on the female for its nutrition, such as the male of some species of deep-sea angler fish.

parasitic oscillation *n.* (in an electronic circuit) oscillation at any undesired frequency. Sometimes shortened to **parasitic.**

parasitism (ˈpærəsaɪˌtɪzəm) *n.* **1.** the relationship between a parasite and its host. **2.** the state of being infested with parasites. **3.** the state of being a parasite.
parasitize *or* **parasitise** (ˈpærəsɪˌtaɪz, -saɪ-) *vb.* (*tr.*) **1.** to infest or infect with parasites. **2.** to live on (another organism) as a parasite.
parasitoid (ˈpærəsɪˌtɔːd) *n. Zoology.* an animal, esp. an insect, that is parasitic during the larval stage of its life cycle but becomes free-living when adult.
parasitology (ˌpærəsaɪˈtɒlədʒɪ) *n.* the branch of biology that is concerned with the study of parasites. —**parasitological** (ˌpærəˌsaɪtᵊˈlɒdʒɪkᵊl) *adj.* —ˌ**parasitˈologist** *n.*
paraskiing (ˈpærəˌskiːɪŋ) *n.* the sport of jumping off high mountains wearing skis and a light parachute composed of inflatable fabric tubes that form a semirigid wing. Also called: **parapente.**
parasol (ˈpærəˌsɒl) *n.* an umbrella used for protection against the sun; sunshade. [C17: via French from Italian *parasole,* from PARA-[2] + *sole* sun, from Latin *sōl*]
parasol mushroom *n.* any of several fungi of the basidiomycetous genus *Lepiota,* having an umbrella-shaped cap, white gills, and a slender brownish stem with a prominent white ring.
parastichy (pəˈræstɪkɪ) *n., pl.* **-chies. 1.** a hypothetical spiral line connecting the bases of a series of leaves on a stem. **2.** an arrangement of leaves so connected. ~Compare **orthostichy.** [C19: from PARA-[1] + Greek *stikhia,* from *stikhos* row, rank] —**paˈrastichous** *adj.*
parasuicide (ˌpærəˈsuːɪˌsaɪd) *n.* **1.** the deliberate infliction of injury on oneself or the taking of a drug overdose as an attempt at suicide which may not be intended to be successful. **2.** a person who commits such an act.
parasymbiosis (ˌpærəˌsɪmbɪˈəʊsɪs) *n.* the symbiotic relationship that occurs between certain species of fungi and lichens (which are themselves symbiotic associations between a fungus and an alga). —ˌ**paraˈsymbiont** *n.* —ˌ**paraˌsymbiˈotic** *adj.*
parasympathetic (ˌpærəˌsɪmpəˈθɛtɪk) *adj. Anatomy, physiol.* of or relating to the division of the autonomic nervous system that acts in opposition to the sympathetic system by slowing the heartbeat, constricting the bronchi of the lungs, stimulating the smooth muscles of the digestive tract, etc. Compare **sympathetic** (sense 4).
parasynapsis (ˌpærəsɪˈnæpsɪs) *n.* another name for **synapsis** (sense 1). —ˌ**parasynˈaptic** *adj.*
parasynthesis (ˌpærəˈsɪnθɪsɪs) *n.* formation of words by means of compounding a phrase and adding an affix, as for example *light-headed,* which is *light* + *head* with the affix *-ed.* —**parasynthetic** (ˌpærəsɪnˈθɛtɪk) *adj.*
parasyntheton (ˌpærəˈsɪnθətɒn) *n., pl.* **-ta** (-tə). a word formed by parasynthesis; for example, *kind-hearted.* [from Greek]
parataxis (ˌpærəˈtæksɪs) *n.* the juxtaposition of clauses in a sentence without the use of a conjunction, as for example *None of my friends stayed—they all left early.* [C19: New Latin from Greek, from *paratassein,* literally: to arrange side by side, from PARA-[1] + *tassein* to arrange] —**paratactic** (ˌpærəˈtæktɪk) *adj.* —ˌ**paraˈtactically** *adv.*
parathion (ˌpærəˈθaɪɒn) *n.* a slightly water-soluble toxic oil, odourless and colourless when pure, used as an insecticide. Formula: $C_{10}H_{14}NO_5PS$. [C20: from PARA-[1] + THIO- + -ON]
parathyroid (ˌpærəˈθaɪrɔɪd) *adj.* **1.** situated near the thyroid gland. **2.** of or relating to the parathyroid glands. ~*n.* **3.** See **parathyroid gland.**
parathyroid gland *n.* any one of the small egg-shaped endocrine glands situated near or embedded within the thyroid gland: they secrete parathyroid hormone.
parathyroid hormone *n.* the hormone secreted by the parathyroid glands that controls the level of calcium in the blood: a deficiency of the hormone often results in tetany. Also called: **parathormone** (ˌpærəˈθɔːməʊn).
paratonic (ˌpærəˈtɒnɪk) *adj. Botany.* (of a plant movement) occurring in response to an external stimulus.
paratroops (ˈpærəˌtruːps) *pl. n.* troops trained and equipped to be dropped by parachute into a battle area. Also called: ˈ**paratroopers, parachute troops.**
paratyphoid (ˌpærəˈtaɪfɔɪd) *Pathol.* ~*adj.* **1.** resembling typhoid fever or its causative agent. **2.** of or relating to paratyphoid fever. ~*n.* **3.** See **paratyphoid fever.**
paratyphoid fever *n. Pathol.* a disease resembling but less severe than typhoid fever, characterized by chills, headache, nausea, vomiting, and diarrhoea, caused by bacteria of the genus *Salmonella.*
paravane (ˈpærəˌveɪn) *n.* a torpedo-shaped device towed from the bow of a vessel so that the cables will cut the anchors of any moored mines. [C20: from PARA-[2] + VANE]
par avion *French.* (par avjɔ̃) *adv.* by aeroplane: used in labelling mail sent by air.
paraxial (pæˈræksɪəl) *adj. Physics.* (of a light ray) parallel to the axis of an optical system.
parazoan (ˌpærəˈzəʊən) *n., pl.* **-zoa** (-ˈzəʊə). any multicellular invertebrate of the group *Parazoa,* which consists of the sponges (phylum *Porifera*). Compare **metazoan.** [C19: from *parazoa,* formed on the model of *protozoa* and *metazoa,* from PARA-[1] +Greek *zōon* animal]
parboil (ˈpɑːˌbɔɪl) *vb.* (*tr.*) **1.** to boil until partially cooked, often before further cooking. **2.** to subject to uncomfortable heat. [C15: from Old French *parboillir,* from Late Latin *perbullīre* to boil thoroughly (see PER-, BOIL[1]); modern meaning due to confusion of *par-* with *part*]
parbuckle (ˈpɑːˌbʌkᵊl) *n.* **1.** a rope sling for lifting or lowering a heavy cylindrical object, such as a cask or tree trunk. ~*vb.* **2.** (*tr.*) to raise or lower (an object) with such a sling. [C17 *parbunkel:* of uncertain origin]
parcel (ˈpɑːsᵊl) *n.* **1.** something wrapped up; package. **2.** a group of people or things having some common characteristic. **3.** a quantity of some commodity offered for sale; lot. **4.** a distinct portion of land. **5.** an essential part of something (esp. in the phrase **part and parcel**). ~*vb.* **-cels, -celling, -celled** *or U.S.* **-cels, -celing, -celed.** (*tr.*) **6.** (often foll. by *up*) to make a parcel of; wrap up. **7.** (often foll. by *out*) to divide (up) into portions. **8.** *Nautical.* to bind strips of canvas around (a rope). ~*adv.* **9.** an archaic word for **partly.** [C14: from Old French *parcelle,* from Latin *particula* PARTICLE]
parcel-gilt *adj.* partly gilded, esp. (of an item of silverware) having the inner surface gilded. [C15: from *parcel* (in the obsolete adv. sense: partly)+GILT[1]]
parcenary (ˈpɑːsɪnərɪ) *n.* joint heirship. Also called: **coparcenary.** [C16: from Old French *parçonerie,* from *parçon* distribution; see PARCENER]
parcener (ˈpɑːsɪnə) *n.* a person who takes an equal share with another or others; coheir. Also called: **coparcener.** [C13: from Old French *parçonier,* from *parçon* distribution, from Latin *partītiō* a sharing, from *partīre* to divide]
parch (pɑːtʃ) *vb.* **1.** to deprive or be deprived of water; dry up: *the sun parches the fields.* **2.** (*tr.; usually passive*) to make very thirsty: *I was parched after the run.* **3.** (*tr.*) to roast (corn, etc.) lightly. [C14: of obscure origin]
Parcheesi (pɑːˈtʃiːzɪ) *n. Trademark.* a modern board game derived from the ancient game of pachisi.
parchment (ˈpɑːtʃmənt) *n.* **1.** the skin of certain animals, such as sheep, treated to form a durable material, as for bookbinding, or (esp. formerly) manuscripts. **2.** a manuscript, bookbinding, etc., made of or resembling this material. **3.** a type of stiff yellowish paper resembling parchment. [C13: from Old French *parchemin,* via Latin from Greek *pergamēnē,* from *Pergamēnos* of Pergamum (where parchment was made); the form of Old French *parchemin* was influenced by *parche* leather, from Latin *Parthica* (*pellis*) Parthian (leather)] —ˈ**parchmenty** *adj.*
parclose (ˈpɑːˌkləʊz) *n.* a screen or railing in a church separating off an altar, chapel, etc. [C14: from Old French, noun use of past participle of *parclore* to close off; see PER-, CLOSE[1]]
pard[1] (pɑːd) *n. U.S.* short for **pardner.**
pard[2] (pɑːd) *n. Archaic.* a leopard or panther. [C13: via Old French from Latin *pardus,* from Greek *pardos*]
pardalote (ˈpɑːdəˌləʊt) *n.* another name for **diamond bird.** [C19: from New Latin, from Greek *pardalōtos* spotted like a leopard; see PARD[2]]
pardner (ˈpɑːdnə) *n. U.S. dialect.* friend or partner: used as a term of address.
pardon (ˈpɑːdᵊn) *vb.* (*tr.*) **1.** to excuse or forgive (a person) for (an offence, mistake, etc.): *to pardon someone; to pardon a fault.* ~*n.* **2.** forgiveness; allowance. **3. a.** release from punishment for an offence. **b.** the warrant granting such release. **4.** a Roman Catholic indulgence. ~*sentence substitute.* **5.** Also: **pardon me; I beg your pardon. a.** sorry; excuse me. **b.** what did you say? [C13: from Old French, from Medieval Latin *perdōnum,* from *perdōnāre* to forgive freely, from Latin *per* (intensive) + *dōnāre* to grant] —ˈ**pardonable** *adj.* —ˈ**pardonably** *adv.* —ˈ**pardonless** *adj.*
pardoner (ˈpɑːdᵊnə) *n.* (before the Reformation) a person licensed to sell ecclesiastical indulgences.
pare (pɛə) *vb.* (*tr.*) **1.** to peel or cut (the outer layer) from (something). **2.** to cut the edges from (the nails); trim. **3.** to decrease bit by bit. [C13: from Old French *parer* to adorn, from Latin *parāre* to make ready] —ˈ**parer** *n.*
paregoric (ˌpærəˈgɒrɪk) *n.* a medicine consisting of opium, benzoic acid, camphor, and anise oil, formerly widely used to relieve diarrhoea and coughing in children. [C17 (meaning: relieving pain): via Late Latin from Greek *parēgorikos* soothing, from *parēgoros* relating to soothing speech, from PARA-[1] (beside, alongside of) + *-ēgor-,* from *agoreuein* to speak in assembly, from *agora* assembly]
pareira (pəˈrɛərə) *n.* the root of a South American menispermaceous climbing plant, *Chondrodendron tomentosum,* used as a diuretic, tonic, and as a source of curare. [C18: from Portuguese *pareira brava,* literally: wild vine]
paren. *abbrev. for* parenthesis.
parenchyma (pəˈrɛŋkɪmə) *n.* **1.** a soft plant tissue consisting of simple thin-walled cells with intervening air spaces: constitutes the greater part of fruits, stems, roots, etc. **2.** animal tissue that constitutes the essential or specialized part of an organ as distinct from the blood vessels, connective tissue, etc., associated with it. **3.** loosely-packed tissue filling the spaces between the organs in lower animals such as flatworms. [C17: via New Latin from Greek *parenkhuma* something poured in beside, from PARA-[1] + *enkhuma* infusion] —**parenchymatous** (ˌpærɛŋˈkɪmətəs) *adj.*
parent (ˈpɛərənt) *n.* **1.** a father or mother. **2.** a person acting as a father or mother; guardian. **3.** *Rare.* an ancestor. **4.** a source

or cause. **5. a.** an organism or organization that has produced one or more organisms or organizations similar to itself. **b.** (*as modifier*): *a parent organism.* **6.** *Physics, chem.* **a.** a precursor, such as a nucleus or compound, of a derived entity. **b.** (*as modifier*): *a parent nucleus; a parent ion.* [C15: via Old French from Latin *parens* parent, from *parere* to bring forth] —'**parenthood** *n.*

parentage ('pɛərəntɪdʒ) *n.* **1.** ancestry. **2.** derivation from a particular origin. **3.** a less common word for **parenthood.**

parental (pə'rɛntᵊl) *adj.* **1.** of or relating to a parent or parenthood. **2.** *Genetics.* designating the first generation in a line, which gives rise to all succeeding (filial) generations. —**pa'rentally** *adv.*

parent company *n.* a company that owns more than half the shares of another company.

parenteral (pæ'rɛntərəl) *adj. Med.* **1.** (esp. of the route by which a drug is administered) by means other than through the digestive tract, esp. by injection. **2.** designating a drug to be injected. [C20: from PARA-[1] + ENTERO- + -AL[1]] —**par'enterally** *adv.*

parenthesis (pə'rɛnθɪsɪs) *n., pl.* **-ses** (-ˌsiːz). **1.** a phrase, often explanatory or qualifying, inserted into a passage with which it is not grammatically connected, and marked off by brackets, dashes, etc. **2.** Also called: **bracket.** either of a pair of characters, ( ), used to enclose such a phrase or as a sign of aggregation in mathematical or logical expressions. **3.** an intervening occurrence; interlude; interval. **4. in parenthesis.** inserted as a parenthesis. [C16: via Late Latin from Greek: something placed in besides, from *parentithenai,* from PARA-[1] + EN-[2] + *tithenai* to put] —**parenthetic** (ˌpærən'θɛtɪk) *or* ˌ**paren'thetical** *adj.* —ˌ**paren'thetically** *adv.*

parenthesize *or* **parenthesise** (pə'rɛnθɪˌsaɪz) *vb.* (*tr.*) **1.** to place in parentheses. **2.** to insert as a parenthesis. **3.** to intersperse (a speech, writing, etc.) with parentheses.

parenting ('pɛərəntɪŋ) *n.* the care and upbringing of a child.

parent metal *n. Engineering, metallurgy.* the metal of components that are being welded by a molten filler metal.

parent teacher association *n.* a social group of the parents of children at a school and their teachers formed in order to foster better understanding between them and to organize activities on behalf of the school. Abbrev.: **PTA.**

parergon (pə'rɛəgɒn) *n., pl.* **-ga** (-gə). work that is not one's main employment. [C17: from Latin, from Greek, from PARA-[1] + *ergon* work]

paresis (pə'riːsɪs, 'pærɪsɪs) *n., pl.* **-ses** (-ˌsiːz). *Pathol.* **1.** incomplete or slight paralysis of motor functions. **2.** short for **general paresis.** See **general paralysis of the insane.** [C17: via New Latin from Greek: a relaxation, from *parienai* to let go, from PARA-[1] + *hienai* to release] —**paretic** (pə'rɛtɪk) *adj.*

paresthesia (ˌpærɛs'θiːzɪə) *n. Pathol.* the usual U.S. spelling of **paraesthesia.** —**paresthetic** (ˌpærɛs'θɛtɪk) *adj.*

Pareto (pæ'riːtəʊ) *n.* (*modifier*) denoting a law, mathematical formula, etc., originally used by Vilfredo Pareto (1848–1923), Italian sociologist and economist, to express the frequency distribution of incomes in a society.

pareu ('pɑːreɪˌuː) *n.* a rectangle of fabric worn by Polynesians as a skirt or loincloth. [from Tahitian]

parev ('pɑrvə, 'pɑrəv) *or* **parve** *adj. Judaism.* containing neither meat nor milk products and so fit for use with either meat or milk dishes. Compare **milchik, fleishik.** See also **kashruth.**

pareve ('pɑːvə, 'pɑːrəvə) *adj. Judaism.* a variant of **parev.**

par excellence *French.* (par ɛkselɑ̃s; *English* pɑːr 'ɛksələns) *adv.* to a degree of excellence; beyond comparison: *she is the charitable lady par excellence.* [French, literally: by (way of) excellence]

parfait (pɑː'feɪ) *n.* a rich frozen dessert made from eggs and cream with ice cream, fruit, etc. [from French: PERFECT]

parfleche ('pɑːflɛʃ) *n. U.S. and Canadian.* **1.** a sheet of rawhide that has been dried after soaking in lye and water to remove the hair. **2.** an object, such as a case, made of this. [C19: from Canadian French, from French *parer* to ward off, protect + *flèche* arrow]

parget ('pɑːdʒɪt) *n.* **1.** Also called: '**pargeting. a.** plaster, mortar, etc., used to line chimney flues or cover walls. **b.** plasterwork that has incised ornamental patterns. **2.** another name for **gypsum** (esp. when used in building). ~*vb.* (*tr.*) **3.** to cover or decorate with parget. [C14: from Old French *pargeter* to throw over, from *par* PER- + *geter,* from Medieval Latin *jactāre* to throw]

parhelic circle *n. Meteorol.* a luminous band at the same altitude as the sun, parallel to the horizon, caused by reflection of the sun's rays by ice crystals in the atmosphere.

parhelion (pɑː'hiːlɪən) *n., pl.* **-lia** (-lɪə). one of several bright spots on the parhelic circle or solar halo, caused by the diffraction of light by ice crystals in the atmosphere, esp. around sunset. Also called: **mock sun, sundog.** Compare **anthelion.** [C17: via Latin from Greek *parēlion,* from PARA-[1] (beside) + *hēlios* sun] —**parhelic** (pɑː'hiːlɪk, -'hɛlɪk) *or* **parheliacal** (ˌpɑːhɪ'laɪəkᵊl) *adj.*

pari- *combining form.* equal or equally; even (in number): *parisyllabic; paripinnate.* [from Latin *par*]

pariah (pə'raɪə, 'pærɪə) *n.* **1.** a social outcast. **2.** (formerly) a member of a low caste in South India. [C17: from Tamil *paraiyan* drummer, from *parai* drum; so called because members of the caste were the drummers at festivals]

pariah dog *n.* another term for **pye-dog.**

Parian ('pɛərɪən) *adj.* **1.** denoting or relating to a fine white marble mined in classical times in Paros, a Greek island in the S Aegean. **2.** denoting or relating to a fine biscuit porcelain used mainly for statuary. **3.** of or relating to Paros. ~*n.* **4.** a native or inhabitant of Paros. **5.** Parian marble. **6.** Parian porcelain.

paries ('pɛərɪˌiːz) *n., pl.* **parietes** (pə'raɪɪˌtiːz). the wall of an organ or bodily cavity. [C18: from Latin: wall]

parietal (pə'raɪɪtᵊl) *adj.* **1.** *Anatomy, biology.* of, relating to, or forming the walls or part of the walls of a bodily cavity or similar structure: *the parietal bones of the skull.* **2.** of or relating to the side of the skull. **3.** (of plant ovaries) having ovules attached to the walls. **4.** *U.S.* living or having authority within a college. ~*n.* **5.** a parietal bone. [C16: from Late Latin *parietālis,* from Latin *pariēs* wall]

parietal bone *n.* either of the two bones forming part of the roof and sides of the skull.

parietal cell *n.* any one of the cells in the lining of the stomach that produce hydrochloric acid.

parietal lobe *n.* the portion of each cerebral hemisphere concerned with the perception and interpretation of sensations of touch, temperature, and taste and with muscular movements.

pari-mutuel (ˌpærɪ'mjuːtjʊəl) *n., pl.* **pari-mutuels** *or* **paris-mutuels** (ˌpærɪ'mjuːtjʊəlz). **a.** a system of betting in which those who have bet on the winners of a race share in the total amount wagered less a percentage for the management. **b.** (*as modifier*): *the pari-mutuel machine.* [C19: from French, literally: mutual wager]

paring ('pɛərɪŋ) *n.* (*often pl.*) something pared or cut off.

pari passu *Latin.* (ˌpærɪ 'pæsuː, 'pɑːrɪ) *adv. Usually legal.* with equal speed or progress; equably: often used to refer to the right of creditors to receive assets from the same source without one taking precedence.

paripinnate (ˌpærɪ'pɪneɪt) *adj.* (of pinnate leaves) having an even number of leaflets and no terminal leaflet. Compare **imparipinnate.**

Paris green ('pærɪs) *n.* an emerald-green poisonous insoluble substance used as a pigment and insecticide. It is a double salt of copper arsenite and copper acetate. Formula: $3Cu(AsO_2)_2.Cu(C_2H_3O_2)_2$.

parish ('pærɪʃ) *n.* **1.** a subdivision of a diocese, having its own church and a clergyman. Related adj.: **parochial. 2.** the churchgoers of such a subdivision. **3.** (in England and, formerly, Wales) the smallest unit of local government in rural areas. **4.** (in Louisiana) a unit of local government corresponding to a county in other states of the U.S. **5.** the people living in a parish. **6. on the parish.** *History.* receiving parochial relief. [C13: from Old French *paroisse,* from Church Latin *parochia,* from Late Greek *paroikia,* from *paroikos* Christian, sojourner, from Greek: neighbour, from PARA-[1] (beside) + *oikos* house]

Parishad ('pʌrɪʃəd) *n.* (in India) an assembly. [Hindi]

parish clerk *n.* a person designated to assist in various church duties.

parish council *n.* (in England and, formerly, Wales) the administrative body of a parish. See **parish** (sense 3).

parishioner (pə'rɪʃənə) *n.* a member of a particular parish.

parish pump *adj.* of only local interest; parochial.

parish register *n.* a book in which the births, baptisms, marriages, and deaths in a parish are recorded.

Parisian (pə'rɪzɪən) *n.* **1.** a native or inhabitant of Paris, the capital of France. ~*adj.* **2.** of or relating to Paris, its inhabitants, customs, etc.

parison ('pærɪsᵊn) *n.* an unshaped mass of glass before it is moulded into its final form. [C19: from French *paraison,* from *parer* to prepare]

parisyllabic (ˌpærɪsɪ'læbɪk) *adj.* (of a noun or verb, in inflected languages) containing the same number of syllables in all or almost all inflected forms. Compare **imparisyllabic.**

parity[1] ('pærɪtɪ) *n., pl.* **-ties. 1.** equality of rank, pay, etc. **2.** close or exact analogy or equivalence. **3.** *Finance.* **a.** the amount of a foreign currency equivalent at the established exchange rate to a specific sum of domestic currency. **b.** a similar equivalence between different forms of the same national currency, esp. the gold equivalent of a unit of gold-standard currency. **4.** equality between prices of commodities or securities in two separate markets. **5.** *Physics.* **a.** a property of a physical system characterized by the behaviour of the sign of its wave function when reflected in space. The wave function either remains unchanged (**even parity**) or changes in sign (**odd parity**). **b.** a quantum number describing this property, equal to +1 for even parity systems and –1 for odd parity systems. Symbol: *P.* See also **conservation of parity. 6.** *Maths.* a relationship between two integers. If both are odd or both even they have the same parity; if one is odd and one even they have different parity. **7.** (in the U.S.) a system of government support for farm products. [C16: from Late Latin *pāritās;* see PAR]

parity[2] ('pærɪtɪ) *n.* **1.** the condition or fact of having given birth. **2.** the number of children to which a woman has given birth. [C19: from Latin *parere* to bear]

parity check *n.* a check made of computer data to ensure that the total number of bits of value 1 (or 0) in each unit of information remains odd or even after transfer between a peripheral device and the memory or vice versa.

park (pɑːk) *n.* **1.** a large area of land preserved in a natural state for recreational use by the public. See also **national park.** **2.** a piece of open land in a town with public amenities. **3.** *N.Z.* an area, esp. of mountain country, reserved for recreational purposes. **4.** a large area of land forming a private estate. **5.** *English law.* an enclosed tract of land where wild beasts are protected, acquired by a subject by royal grant or prescription. Compare **forest** (sense 5). **6.** an area designed and landscaped to accommodate a group of related enterprises, businesses, research establishments, etc.: *science park.* **7.** *U.S. and Canadian.* See **amusement park.** **8.** *U.S., Canadian, and N.Z.* See **car park.** **9.** *U.S. and Canadian.* a playing field or sports stadium. **10. the park.** *Brit. informal.* a soccer pitch. **11.** a gear selector position on the automatic transmission of a motor vehicle that acts as a parking brake. **12.** the area in which the equipment and supplies of a military formation are assembled. **13.** a high valley surrounded by mountains in the western U.S. ~*vb.* **14.** to stop and leave (a vehicle) temporarily. **15.** to manoeuvre (a motor vehicle) into a space for it to be left: *try to park without hitting the kerb.* **16.** *Stock Exchange.* to register (securities) in the name of another or of nominees in order to conceal their real ownership. **17.** (*tr.*) *Informal.* to leave or put somewhere: *park yourself in front of the fire.* **18.** (*intr.*) *Military.* to arrange equipment in a park. **19.** (*tr.*) to enclose in or as a park. [C13: from Old French *parc,* from Medieval Latin *parricus* enclosure, from Germanic; compare Old High German *pfarrih* pen, Old English *pearruc* PADDOCK[1]] —ˈ**park,like** *adj.*

parka (ˈpɑːkə) *n.* a warm hip-length weatherproof coat with a hood, originally worn by Eskimos. [C19: from Aleutian: skin]

Parker Morris standard (ˈpɑːkə ˈmɒrɪs) *n.* (*often pl.*) (in Britain) a set of minimum criteria for good housing construction, design, and facilities, recommended by the 1961 report of the Central Housing Advisory Committee chaired by Sir Parker Morris. Subsequent governments have urged private and local authority house-builders to achieve these standards.

parkin (ˈpɑːkɪn) *or* **perkin** *n.* (in Britain and New Zealand) a moist spicy ginger cake usually containing oatmeal. [C19: of unknown origin]

parking disc *n.* See **disc** (sense 7).

parking lot *n.* the U.S. and Canadian term for **car park.**

parking meter *n.* a timing device, usually coin-operated, that indicates how long a vehicle may be left parked.

parking orbit *n.* an orbit around the earth or moon in which a spacecraft can be placed temporarily in order to prepare for the next step in its programme.

parking ticket *n.* a summons served for a parking offence.

Parkinson's disease (ˈpɑːkɪnsənz) *n.* a progressive chronic disorder of the central nervous system characterized by impaired muscular coordination and tremor. Often shortened to **Parkinson's.** Also called: ˈ**parkinson,ism, Parkinson's syndrome, paralysis agitans, shaking palsy.** [C19: named after James *Parkinson* (1755–1824), British surgeon, who first described it]

Parkinson's law *n.* the notion, expressed facetiously as a law of economics, that work expands to fill the time available for its completion. [C20: named after C. N. *Parkinson* (born 1909), British historian and writer, who formulated it]

park keeper *n.* (in Britain) an official employed by a local authority to patrol and supervise a public park.

parkland (ˈpɑːk,lænd) *n.* grassland with scattered trees.

park savanna *n.* savanna grassland scattered with trees.

parkway (ˈpɑːk,weɪ) *n.* (in the U.S. and Canada) a wide road planted with trees, turf, etc.

parky (ˈpɑːkɪ) *adj.* **parkier, parkiest.** (*usually postpositive*) *Brit. informal.* (of the weather) chilly; cold. [C19: perhaps from PERKY]

Parl. *abbrev. for:* **1.** Parliament. **2.** Also: **parl.** parliamentary.

parlance (ˈpɑːləns) *n.* **1.** a particular manner of speaking, esp. when specialized; idiom: *political parlance.* **2.** *Archaic.* any discussion, such as a debate. [C16: from Old French, from *parler* to talk, via Medieval Latin from Late Latin *parabola* speech, PARABLE; compare PARLEY]

parlando (pɑːˈlændəʊ) *adj., adv. Music.* to be performed as though speaking. [Italian: speaking, from *parlare* to speak]

parlay (ˈpɑːlɪ) *U.S. and Canadian.* ~*vb.* (*tr.*) **1.** to stake (winnings from one bet) on a subsequent wager. Brit. equivalent: **double up.** **2.** to exploit (one's talent) to achieve worldly success. ~*n.* **3.** a bet in which winnings from one wager are staked on another, or a series of such bets. [C19: variant of *paroli,* via French from Neapolitan Italian *parolo,* from *paro* a pair, from Latin *pār* equal, PAR]

parley (ˈpɑːlɪ) *n.* **1.** a discussion, esp. between enemies under a truce to decide terms of surrender, etc. ~*vb.* **2.** (*intr.*) to discuss, esp. with an enemy under a truce. **3.** (*tr.*) to speak (a foreign language). [C16: from French, from *parler* to talk, from Medieval Latin *parabolāre,* from Late Latin *parabola* speech, PARABLE] —ˈ**parleyer** *n.*

parleyvoo (,pɑːlɪˈvuː) *Informal.* ~*vb.* (*intr.*) **1.** to speak French. ~*n.* **2.** the French language. **3.** a Frenchman. [C20: jocular respelling of *parlez-vous (français)*? do you speak (French)?]

parliament (ˈpɑːləmənt) *n.* **1.** an assembly of the representatives of a political nation or people, often the supreme legislative authority. **2.** any legislative or deliberative assembly, conference, etc. **3.** Also: ˈ**parlement.** (in France before the Revolution) any of several high courts of justice in which royal decrees were registered. [C13: from Anglo-Latin *parliamentum,* from Old French *parlement,* from *parler* to speak; see PARLEY]

Parliament (ˈpɑːləmənt) *n.* **1.** the highest legislative authority in Britain, consisting of the House of Commons, which exercises effective power, the House of Lords, and the sovereign. **2.** a similar legislature in another country. **3.** the two chambers of a Parliament. **4.** the lower chamber of a Parliament. **5.** any of the assemblies of such a body created by a general election and royal summons and dissolved before the next election.

parliamentarian (,pɑːləmɛnˈtɛərɪən) *n.* **1.** an expert in parliamentary procedures, etc. **2.** (*sometimes cap.*) *Brit.* a Member of Parliament. ~*adj.* **3.** of or relating to a parliament or parliaments.

Parliamentarian (,pɑːləmɛnˈtɛərɪən) *n.* **1.** a supporter of Parliament during the English Civil War (1642–51). ~*adj.* **2.** of or relating to Parliament or its supporters during the English Civil War; Parliamentarian.

parliamentarianism (,pɑːləmɛnˈtɛərɪə,nɪzəm) *or* **parliamentarism** (,pɑːləˈmɛntə,rɪzəm) *n.* the system of parliamentary government.

parliamentary (,pɑːləˈmɛntərɪ, -trɪ) *adj.* (*sometimes cap.*) **1.** of or characteristic of a parliament or Parliament. **2.** proceeding from a parliament or Parliament: *a parliamentary decree.* **3.** conforming to or derived from the procedures of a parliament or Parliament: *parliamentary conduct.* **4.** having a parliament or Parliament. **5.** of or relating to Parliament or its supporters during the English Civil War; Parliamentarian.

parliamentary agent *n.* (in Britain) a person who is employed to manage the parliamentary business of a private group.

Parliamentary Commissioner *or in full* **Parliamentary Commissioner for Administration** *n.* (in Britain) the official name for **ombudsman** (sense 2).

parliamentary private secretary *n.* (in Britain) a backbencher in Parliament who assists a minister, esp. in liaison with backbenchers. Abbrev.: **PPS.**

parliamentary secretary *n.* a Member of Parliament appointed, usually as a junior minister, to assist a Minister of the Crown with departmental responsibilities.

parlor car *n.* (in the U.S. and Canada) a comfortable railway coach with individual reserved seats.

parlour *or U.S.* **parlor** (ˈpɑːlə) *n.* **1.** *Old-fashioned.* a living room, esp. one kept tidy for the reception of visitors. **2.** a reception room in a priest's house, convent, etc. **3.** a small room for guests away from the public rooms in an inn, club, etc. **4.** *Chiefly U.S., Canadian, and N.Z.* a room or shop equipped as a place of business: *a billiard parlor.* **5.** *Caribbean.* a small shop, esp. one selling cakes and nonalcoholic drinks. **6.** Also called: **milking parlour.** a building equipped for milking cows in. [C13: from Anglo-Norman *parlur,* from Old French *parleur* room in convent for receiving guests, from *parler* to speak; see PARLEY]

parlour game *n.* an informal indoor game.

parlous (ˈpɑːləs) *Archaic or humorous.* ~*adj.* **1.** dangerous or difficult. **2.** cunning. ~*adv.* **3.** extremely. [C14 *perlous,* variant of PERILOUS] —ˈ**parlously** *adv.* —ˈ**parlousness** *n.*

parl. proc. *abbrev. for* parliamentary procedure.

Parmentier (ˈpɑːmən,tjeɪ; *French* parmɑ̃tje) *adj.* (of soups, etc.) containing or garnished with potatoes. [C19: named after A. *Parmentier* (1737–1813), French horticulturist]

Parmesan *or* **Parmesan cheese** (,pɑːmɪˈzæn, ˈpɑːmɪ,zæn) *n.* a hard dry cheese made from skimmed milk, used grated, esp. on pasta dishes and soups. [C16: from French, from Italian *parmegiano* of *Parma,* a city in N Italy]

Parnassian[1] (pɑːˈnæsɪən) *adj.* of or relating to Mount Parnassus, in Greece, or to poetry.

Parnassian[2] (pɑːˈnæsɪən) *n.* **1.** one of a school of French poets of the late 19th century who wrote verse that emphasized metrical form and restricted emotion. ~*adj.* **2.** of or relating to the Parnassians or their poetry. [C19: from French *parnassien,* from *Parnasse* PARNASSUS; from *Le Parnasse contemporain,* title of an anthology produced by these poets] —**Parˈnassian,ism** *or* **Parˈnas,sism** *n.*

Parnassus (pɑːˈnæsəs) *n.* **1. a.** the world of poetry. **b.** a centre of poetic or other creative activity. **2.** a collection of verse or belles-lettres. [from Mount *Parnassus,* central Greece, in ancient times regarded as the seat of poetry, sacred to Apollo and the Muses]

parochial (pəˈrəʊkɪəl) *adj.* **1.** narrow in outlook or scope; provincial. **2.** of or relating to a parish or parishes. [C14: via Old French from Church Latin *parochiālis;* see PARISH] —**paˈrochial,ism** *n.* —**pa,rochiˈality** *n.* —**paˈrochially** *adv.*

parochial church council *n. Church of England.* an elected body of lay representatives of the members of a parish that administers the affairs of the parish.

parody (ˈpærədɪ) *n., pl.* **-dies.** **1.** a musical, literary, or other composition that mimics the style of another composer, author, etc., in a humorous or satirical way. **2.** mimicry of someone's individual manner in a humorous or satirical way. **3.** something so badly done as to seem an intentional mockery; travesty. ~*vb.* **-dies, -dying, -died.** **4.** (*tr.*) to make a parody of. [C16: via Latin from Greek *paroidiā* satirical poem, from PARA-[1] + *ōidē* song] —**parodic** (pəˈrɒdɪk) *or* **paˈrodical** *adj.* —ˈ**parodist** *n.*

paroicous (pəˈrɔɪkəs) *or* **paroecious** (pəˈriːʃəs) *adj.* (of mosses and related plants) having the male and female reproductive organs at different levels on the same stem. [C19: from Greek *paroikos* living nearby, from PARA-[1] (beside) + *oikos* house; compare PARISH]

parol (ˈpærəl, pəˈrəʊl) *Law.* ~*n.* **1.** (formerly) the pleadings in an action when presented by word of mouth. **2.** an oral statement; word of mouth (now only in the phrase **by parol**). ~*adj.* **3. a.** (of a contract, lease, etc.) made orally or in writing but not under seal. **b.** expressed or given by word of mouth: *parol evidence.* [C15: from Old French *parole* speech; see PAROLE]

parole (pəˈrəʊl) *n.* **1. a.** the freeing of a prisoner before his sentence has expired, on the condition that he is of good behaviour. **b.** the duration of such conditional release. **2.** a promise given by a prisoner, as to be of good behaviour if granted liberty or partial liberty. **3.** a variant spelling of **parol. 4.** *U.S. military.* a password. **5.** *Linguistics.* language as manifested in the individual speech acts of particular speakers. Compare **langue, performance** (sense 7), **competence** (sense 5). **6. on parole. a.** conditionally released from detention. **b.** *Informal.* (of a person) under scrutiny, esp. for a recurrence of an earlier shortcoming. ~*vb.* (*tr.*) **7.** to place (a person) on parole. [C17: from Old French, from the phrase *parole d'honneur* word of honour; *parole* from Late Latin *parabola* speech] —**paˈrolable** *adj.* —**parolee** (pəˌrəʊˈliː) *n.*

paronomasia (ˌpærənəʊˈmeɪzɪə) *n. Rhetoric.* a play on words, esp. a pun. [C16: via Latin from Greek: a play on words, from *paronomazein* to make a change in naming, from PARA-[1] (beside) + *onomazein* to name, from *onoma* a name] —**paronomastic** (ˌpærənəʊˈmæstɪk) *adj.* —**ˌparonoˈmastically** *adv.*

paronym (ˈpærənɪm) *n. Linguistics.* a cognate word. [C19: via Late Latin from Greek *paronumon,* from PARA-[1] (beside) + *onoma* a name] —**ˌparoˈnymic** *or* **paronymous** (pəˈrɒnɪməs) *adj.* —**paˈronymously** *adv.*

parosmia (pæˈrɒzmɪə) *n.* any disorder of the sense of smell. [C19: from PARA- + Greek *osmē* smell]

parotic (pəˈrɒtɪk) *adj.* situated near the ear. [C19: from New Latin *paroticus,* from Greek PARA-[1] (near) + *-oticus,* from *ous* ear]

parotid (pəˈrɒtɪd) *adj.* **1.** relating to or situated near the parotid gland. ~*n.* **2.** See **parotid gland.** [C17: via French, via Latin from Greek *parōtis,* from PARA-[1] (near) + *-ōtis,* from *ous* ear]

parotid gland *n.* a large salivary gland, in man situated in front of and below each ear.

parotitis (ˌpærəˈtaɪtɪs) *or* **parotiditis** (pəˌrɒtɪˈdaɪtɪs) *n.* inflammation of the parotid gland. See also **mumps.** —**parotitic** (ˌpærəˈtɪtɪk) *or* **parotiditic** (pəˌrɒtɪˈdɪtɪk) *adj.*

parotoid (pəˈrɒtɔɪd) *n.* **1.** Also called: **parotoid gland.** any of various warty poison glands on the head and back of certain toads and salamanders. ~*adj.* **2.** resembling a parotid gland. [C19: from Greek *parot(is)* (see PAROTID) + -OID]

-parous *adj. combining form.* giving birth to: *oviparous.* [from Latin *-parus,* from *parere* to bring forth]

parousia (pəˈruːsɪə) *n. Christianity.* another term for the **Second Coming.** [C19: from Greek: presence]

paroxysm (ˈpærəkˌsɪzəm) *n.* **1.** an uncontrollable outburst: *a paroxysm of giggling.* **2.** *Pathol.* **a.** a sudden attack or recurrence of a disease. **b.** any fit or convulsion. [C17: via French from Medieval Latin *paroxysmus* annoyance, from Greek *paroxusmos,* from *paroxunein* to goad, from PARA-[1] (intensifier) + *oxunein* to sharpen, from *oxus* sharp] —**ˌparoxˈysmal** *or* **ˌparoxˈysmic** *adj.* —**ˌparoxˈysmally** *adv.*

paroxytone (pəˈrɒksɪˌtəʊn) *adj.* **1.** (in the classical Greek language) of, relating to, or denoting words having an acute accent on the next to last syllable. ~*n.* **2.** a paroxytone word. ~Compare **oxytone.** [C18: via New Latin from Greek *paroxutonos,* from PARA-[1] (beside) + *-oxutonos* OXYTONE] —**paroxytonic** (ˌpærɒksɪˈtɒnɪk) *adj.*

parpend (ˈpɑːpənd) *or U.S.* **parpen** (ˈpɑːpən) *n.* other names for **perpend**[1].

parquet (ˈpɑːkeɪ, -kɪ) *n.* **1.** a floor covering of pieces of hardwood fitted in a decorative pattern; parquetry. **2.** Also called: **parquet floor.** a floor so covered. **3.** *U.S.* the stalls of a theatre. **4.** the main part of the Paris Bourse, where officially listed securities are traded. Compare **coulisse** (sense 3). **5.** (in France) the department of government responsible for the prosecution of crimes. ~*vb.* (*tr.*) **6.** to cover (a floor) with parquet. [C19: from Old French: small enclosure, from *parc* enclosure; see PARK]

parquet circle *n. U.S.* the seating area of the main floor of a theatre that lies to the rear of the auditorium and underneath the balcony. Also called: **parterre.**

parquetry (ˈpɑːkɪtrɪ) *n.* a geometric pattern of inlaid pieces of wood, often of different kinds, esp. as used to cover a floor or to ornament furniture. Compare **marquetry.**

parr (pɑː) *n., pl.* **parrs** *or* **parr.** a salmon up to two years of age, with dark spots and transverse bands. [C18: of unknown origin]

parrakeet (ˈpærəˌkiːt) *n.* a variant spelling of **parakeet.**

parramatta (ˌpærəˈmætə) *n.* a variant spelling of **paramatta.**

parrel *or* **parral** (ˈpærəl) *n. Nautical.* a ring that holds the jaws of a boom to the mast but lets it slide up and down. [C15: probably from obsolete *aparail* equipment, a variant of APPAREL]

parricide (ˈpærɪˌsaɪd) *n.* **1.** the act of killing either of one's parents. **2.** a person who kills his parent. [C16: from Latin *parricīdium* murder of a parent or relative, and from *parricīda* one who murders a relative, from *parri-* (element related to Greek *pēos* kinsman) + *-cīdium, -cīda* -CIDE] —**ˌparriˈcidal** *adj.*

parritch (ˈpærɪtʃ, ˈpɑːr-) *n.* a Scot. word for **porridge.**

parrot (ˈpærət) *n.* **1.** any bird of the tropical and subtropical order *Psittaciformes,* having a short hooked bill, compact body, bright plumage, and an ability to mimic sounds. Related adj.: **psittacine. 2.** a person who repeats or imitates the words or actions of another unintelligently. **3. sick as a parrot.** *Usually facetious.* extremely disappointed. ~*vb.* **-rots, -roting, -roted. 4.** (*tr.*) to repeat or imitate mechanically without understanding. [C16: probably from French *paroquet;* see PARAKEET] —**ˈparrotry** *n.*

parrot-fashion *adv. Informal.* without regard for meaning; by rote: *she learned it parrot-fashion.*

parrot fever *or* **disease** *n.* another name for **psittacosis.**

parrotfish (ˈpærətˌfɪʃ) *n., pl.* **-fish** *or* **-fishes. 1.** any brightly coloured tropical marine percoid fish of the family *Scaridae,* having parrot-like jaws. **2.** any of various similar fishes.

parrot toadstool *n.* See **wax cap.**

parry (ˈpærɪ) *vb.* **-ries, -rying, -ried. 1.** to ward off (an attack) by blocking or deflecting, as in fencing. **2.** (*tr.*) to evade (questions), esp. adroitly. ~*n., pl.* **-ries. 3.** an act of parrying, esp. (in fencing) using a stroke or circular motion of the blade. **4.** a skilful evasion, as of a question. [C17: from French *parer* to ward off, from Latin *parāre* to prepare]

parse (pɑːz) *vb. Grammar.* **1.** to assign constituent structure to (a sentence or the words in a sentence). **2.** (*intr.*) (of a word or linguistic element) to play a specified role in the structure of a sentence. [C16: from Latin *pars* (*ōrātionis*) part (of speech)] —**ˈparsable** *adj.*

parsec (ˈpɑːˌsɛk) *n.* a unit of astronomical distance equal to the distance from earth at which stellar parallax would be 1 second of arc; equivalent to 3.0857×10^{16} m or 3.262 light years. [C20: from PARALLAX + SECOND[2]]

Parsee *or* **Parsi** (ˈpɑːsiː) *n.* **1.** an adherent of a monotheistic religion of Zoroastrian origin, the practitioners of which were driven out of Persia by the Muslims in the eighth century A.D. It is now found chiefly in western India. ~*adj.* **2.** of or relating to the Parsees or their religion. [C17: from Persian *Pārsī* a Persian, from Old Persian *Pārsa* Persia] —**ˈParseeˌism** *n.*

parser (ˈpɑːzə) *n. Computer technol.* a program or part of a program that interprets input to a computer by recognizing key words or analysing sentence structure.

Parsha (ˈpɑːʃə; *Yiddish* ˈparʃə) *n.* the Yiddish word for **Parashah.**

parsimony (ˈpɑːsɪmənɪ) *n.* extreme care or reluctance in spending; frugality; niggardliness. [C15: from Latin *parcimōnia,* from *parcere* to spare] —**parsimonious** (ˌpɑːsɪˈməʊnɪəs) *adj.* —**ˌparsiˈmoniously** *adv.*

parsley (ˈpɑːslɪ) *n.* **1.** a S European umbelliferous plant, *Petroselinum crispum,* widely cultivated for its curled aromatic leaves, which are used in cooking. **2.** any of various similar and related plants, such as fool's-parsley, stone parsley, and cow parsley. [C14 *persely,* from Old English *petersilie* + Old French *persil, peresil,* both ultimately from Latin *petroselīnum* rock parsley, from Greek *petroselinon,* from *petra* rock + *selinon* parsley]

parsley fern *n.* **1.** any of several plants with crisped foliage, resembling that of parsley. **2.** a small bright green tufted European fern, *Cryptogramma crispa,* that grows on acid scree and rock in uplands.

parsley piert (pɪət) *n.* a small N temperate rosaceous plant, *Aphanes arvensis,* having fan-shaped leaves and small greenish flowers. [C17: from French *perce pierre,* literally: break stone]

parsnip (ˈpɑːsnɪp) *n.* **1.** a strong-scented umbelliferous plant, *Pastinaca sativa,* cultivated for its long whitish root. **2.** the root of this plant, eaten as a vegetable. **3.** any of several similar plants, esp. the cow parsnip. [C14: from Old French *pasnaie,* from Latin *pastināca,* from *pastināre* to dig, from *pastinum* two-pronged tool for digging; also influenced by Middle English *nepe* TURNIP]

parson (ˈpɑːsᵊn) *n.* **1.** a parish priest in the Church of England, formerly applied only to those who held ecclesiastical benefices. **2.** any clergyman. [C13: from Medieval Latin *persōna* parish priest, representative of the parish, from Latin: personage; see PERSON] —**parsonic** (pɑːˈsɒnɪk) *or* **parˈsonical** *adj.*

parsonage (ˈpɑːsᵊnɪdʒ) *n.* the residence of a parson who is not a rector or vicar, as provided by the parish.

parson bird *n.* another name for **tui.** [C19: so called because of its dark plumage with white neck feathers]

parson's nose *n.* the fatty extreme end portion of the tail of a fowl when cooked. Also called: **pope's nose.**

part (pɑːt) *n.* **1.** a piece or portion of a whole. **2.** an integral constituent of something: *dancing is part of what we teach.* **3. a.** an amount less than the whole; bit: *they only recovered part of the money.* **b.** (*as modifier*): *an old car in part exchange for a new one.* **4.** one of several equal or nearly equal divisions: *mix two parts flour to one part water.* **5. a.** an actor's role in a play. **b.** the speech and actions which make up such a role. **c.** a written copy of these. **6.** a person's proper role or duty: *everyone must do his part.* **7.** (*often pl.*) region; area: *you're well known in these parts.* **8.** *Anatomy.* any portion of a larger structure. **9.** a component that can be replaced in a machine, engine, etc.: *spare parts.* **10.** the U.S., Canadian, and Austral. word for **parting** (sense 1). **11.** *Music.* **a.** one of a number of separate melodic lines making up the texture of music. **b.** one of such melodic lines, which is assigned to one or more instrumentalists or singers: *the viola part; the soprano solo part.* **c.** such a line performed from a separately written or printed copy. See **part song. 12. for the most part.** generally. **13. for one's part.** as far as one is concerned. **14. in part.** to some degree; partly. **15. of many parts.** having many different abilities. **16. on the part of.** on behalf of. **17. part and parcel.** an essential ingredient. **18. play a part. a.** to pretend to be what one is not. **b.** (foll. by *in*) to have something to do (with); be instrumental (in): *to play a part in the king's downfall.* **19. take in good part.** to respond to (teasing) with good humour. **20. take part in.** to participate in. **21. take someone's part.** to support someone in an argument. *~vb.* **22.** to divide or separate from one another; take or come apart: *to part the curtains; the seams parted when I washed the dress.* **23.** to go away or cause to go away from one another; stop or cause to stop seeing each other: *the couple parted amicably.* **24.** (*intr.;* foll. by *from*) to leave; say goodbye (to). **25.** (*intr.;* foll. by *with*) to relinquish, esp. reluctantly: *I couldn't part with my teddy bear.* **26.** (*tr.;* foll. by *from*) to cause to relinquish, esp. reluctantly: *he's not easily parted from his cash.* **27.** (*intr.*) to split; separate: *the path parts here.* **28.** (*tr.*) to arrange (the hair) in such a way that a line of scalp is left showing. **29.** (*intr.*) a euphemism for **die**[1] (sense 1). **30.** (*intr.*) *Archaic.* to depart. **31. part company. a.** to end a friendship or association, esp. as a result of a quarrel; separate: *they were in partnership, but parted company last year.* **b.** (foll. by *with*) to leave; go away from; be separated from. *~adv.* **32.** to some extent; partly. ~See also **parts.** [C13: via Old French from Latin *partīre* to divide, from *pars* a part]

part. *abbrev. for:* **1.** participle. **2.** particular.

partake (pɑːˈteɪk) *vb.* **-takes, -taking, -took, -taken.** (*mainly intr.*) **1.** (foll. by *in*) to have a share; participate: *to partake in the excitement.* **2.** (foll. by *of*) to take or receive a portion, esp. of food or drink: *each partook of the food offered to him.* **3.** (foll. by *of*) to suggest or have some of the quality (of): *music partaking of sadness.* **4.** (*tr.*) *Archaic.* to share in. [C16: back formation from *partaker,* earlier *part taker,* based on Latin *particeps* participant; see PART, TAKE] —**parˈtaker** *n.*

partan (ˈpɑːtᵊn; *Scot.* ˈpartᵊn) *n.* a Scots word for **crab**[1] (senses 1 and 2). [C15: of Celtic origin]

parted (ˈpɑːtɪd) *adj.* **1.** *Botany.* divided almost to the base: *parted leaves.* **2.** *Heraldry.* showing two coats of arms divided by a vertical central line.

parterre (pɑːˈtɛə) *n.* **1.** a formally patterned flower garden. **2.** *Brit., Irish.* the pit in a theatre. **3.** *U.S.* another name for **parquet circle.** [C17: from French, from *par* along + *terre* ground]

part exchange *n.* a transaction in which used goods are taken as partial payment for more expensive ones of the same type.

parthenocarpy (pɑːˈθiːnəʊˌkɑːpɪ) *n.* the development of fruit without fertilization or formation of seeds. [C20: from Greek *parthenos* virgin + *karpos* fruit] —**parˌthenoˈcarpic** *or* **parˌthenoˈcarpous** *adj.*

parthenogenesis (ˌpɑːθɪnəʊˈdʒɛnɪsɪs) *n.* **1.** a type of reproduction, occurring in some insects and flowers, in which the unfertilized ovum develops directly into a new individual. **2.** human conception without fertilization by a male; virgin birth. [C19: from Greek *parthenos* virgin + *genesis* birth] —**parthenogenetic** (ˌpɑːθɪˌnəʊdʒɪˈnɛtɪk) *adj.* —**ˌpartheˌnogeˈnetically** *adv.*

parthenospore (pɑːˈθiːnəʊˌspɔː) *n.* another name for **azygospore.**

Parthian shot (ˈpɑːθɪən) *n.* a hostile remark or gesture delivered while departing. [alluding to the custom of archers from *Parthia,* an ancient Asian empire, who shot their arrows backwards while retreating]

partial (ˈpɑːʃəl) *adj.* **1.** relating to only a part; not general or complete: *a partial eclipse.* **2.** biased: *a partial judge.* **3.** (*postpositive;* foll. by *to*) having a particular liking (for). **4.** *Botany.* **a.** constituting part of a larger structure: *a partial umbel.* **b.** used for only part of the life cycle of a plant: *a partial habitat.* **c.** (of a parasite) not exclusively parasitic. **5.** *Maths.* designating or relating to an operation in which only one of a set of independent variables is considered at a time. *~n.* **6.** Also called: **partial tone.** *Music, acoustics.* any of the component tones of a single musical sound, including both those that belong to the harmonic series of the sound and those that do not. **7.** *Maths.* a partial derivative. [C15: from Old French *parcial,* from Late Latin *partiālis* incomplete, from Latin *pars* PART] —**ˈpartially** *adv.* —**ˈpartialness** *n.*

partial derivative *n.* the derivative of a function of two or more variables with respect to one of the variables, the other or others being considered constant. Written $\partial f/\partial x$.

partial eclipse *n.* an eclipse, esp. of the sun, in which the body is only partially hidden. Compare **total eclipse, annular eclipse.**

partial fraction *n. Maths.* one of a set of fractions into which a more complicated fraction can be resolved.

partiality (ˌpɑːʃɪˈælɪtɪ) *n., pl.* **-ties. 1.** favourable prejudice or bias. **2.** (usually foll. by *for*) liking or fondness. **3.** the state or condition of being partial.

partially sighted *adj.* **a.** unable to see properly so that even with corrective aids normal activities are prevented or seriously hindered. **b.** (*as collective n.;* preceded by *the*): *the partially sighted.* —**partial sight** *n.*

partial pressure *n.* the pressure that a gas, in a mixture of gases, would exert if it alone occupied the whole volume occupied by the mixture.

partial product *n.* the result obtained when a number is multiplied by one digit of a multiplier.

partial reinforcement *n. Psychol.* the process of randomly rewarding an organism for making a response on only some of the occasions it makes it.

partible (ˈpɑːtəbᵊl) *adj.* (esp. of property or an inheritance) divisible; separable. [C16: from Late Latin *partibilis,* from *part-, pars* PART]

participate (pɑːˈtɪsɪˌpeɪt) *vb.* (*intr.;* often foll. by *in*) to take part, be or become actively involved, or share (in). [C16: from Latin *participāre,* from *pars* PART + *capere* to take] —**parˈticipant** *adj., n.* —**parˌticiˈpation** *n.* —**parˈticiˌpator** *n.* —**parˈticipatory** *adj.*

participating insurance *n.* a system of insurance by which policyholders receive dividends from the company's profit or surplus.

participle (ˈpɑːtɪsɪpᵊl, pɑːˈtɪsɪpᵊl) *n.* a nonfinite form of verbs, in English and other languages, used adjectivally and in the formation of certain compound tenses. See also **present participle, past participle.** [C14: via Old French from Latin *participium,* from *particeps* partaker, from *pars* PART + *capere* to take] —**participial** (ˌpɑːtɪˈsɪpɪəl) *adj., n.* —ˌ**partiˈcipially** *adv.*

particle (ˈpɑːtɪkᵊl) *n.* **1.** an extremely small piece of matter; speck. **2.** a very tiny amount; iota: *it doesn't make a particle of difference.* **3.** a function word, esp. (in certain languages) a word belonging to an uninflected class having suprasegmental or grammatical function: *the Greek particles "mēn" and "de" are used to express contrast; questions in Japanese are indicated by the particle "ka"; English "up" is sometimes regarded as an adverbial particle.* **4.** a common affix, such as *re-, un-,* or *-ness.* **5.** *Physics.* a body with finite mass that can be treated as having negligible size, and internal structure. **6.** See **elementary particle. 7.** *R.C. Church.* a small piece broken off from the Host at Mass. **8.** *Archaic.* a section or clause of a document. [C14: from Latin *particula* a small part, from *pars* PART]

particle accelerator *n.* a machine for accelerating charged elementary particles to very high energies, used for research in nuclear physics. See also **linear accelerator, cyclotron, betatron, synchrotron, synchrocyclotron.**

particle beam *n.* **1.** a stream of energized particles produced by a particle accelerator. **2.** such a stream emitted by a particle beam weapon.

particle beam weapon *n.* a weapon that fires particle beams into the atmosphere or space.

particle board *n.* the N.Z. name for **chipboard.**

particle physics *n.* the study of fundamental particles and their properties. Also called: **high-energy physics.**

particle separation *n. Transformational grammar.* a rule that moves the particle of a phrasal verb, thus deriving a sentence like *He looked the answer up* from a structure that also underlies *He looked up the answer.*

parti-coloured *or* **party-coloured** (ˈpɑːtɪˌkʌləd) *adj.* having different colours in different parts; variegated. [C16 *parti,* from (obsolete) *party* of more than one colour, from Old French: striped, from Latin *partīre* to divide]

particular (pəˈtɪkjʊlə) *adj.* **1.** (*prenominal*) of or belonging to a single or specific person, thing, category, etc.; specific; special: *the particular demands of the job; no particular reason.* **2.** (*prenominal*) exceptional or marked: *a matter of particular importance.* **3.** (*prenominal*) relating to or providing specific details or circumstances: *a particular account.* **4.** exacting or difficult to please, esp. in details; fussy. **5.** (of the solution of a differential equation) obtained by giving specific values to the arbitrary constants in a general equation. **6.** *Logic.* (of a proposition) affirming or denying something about only some members of a class of objects, as in *some men are not wicked.* Compare **universal** (sense 10). **7.** *Property law.* denoting an estate that precedes the passing of the property into ultimate ownership. See also **remainder** (sense 3), **reversion** (sense 4). *~n.* **8.** a separate distinct item that helps to form a generalization: opposed to *general.* **9.** (*often pl.*) an item of information; detail: *complete in every particular.* **10.** *Logic.* another name for **individual** (sense 7a). **11.** *Philosophy.* an individual object, as contrasted with a universal. See **universal** (sense 12b). **12. in particular.** especially, particularly, or exactly. [C14: from Old French *particuler,* from Late Latin *particulāris* concerning a part, from Latin *particula* PARTICLE] —**parˈticularly** *adv.*

particular average *n. Insurance.* partial damage to or loss of a ship or its cargo affecting only the shipowner or one cargo owner. Abbrev.: **PA.** Compare **general average.**

particularism (pəˈtɪkjʊləˌrɪzəm) *n.* **1.** exclusive attachment to the interests of one group, class, sect, etc., esp. at the expense of the community as a whole. **2.** the principle of permitting each state or minority in a federation the right to further its own interests or retain its own laws, traditions, etc. **3.** *Theol.* the doctrine that divine grace is restricted to the elect. —**parˈticularist** *n., adj.* —**parˌticularˈistic** *adj.*

particularity (pəˌtɪkjʊˈlærɪtɪ) *n., pl.* **-ties. 1.** (*often pl.*) a specific circumstance: *the particularities of the affair.* **2.** great attentiveness to detail; fastidiousness. **3.** the quality of being precise: *a* *description of great particularity.* **4.** the state or quality of being particular as opposed to general; individuality: *the particularity of human situations.*

particularize *or* **particularise** (pə'tɪkjʊlə,raɪz) *vb.* **1.** to treat in detail; give details (about). **2.** (*intr.*) to go into detail. —**par,ticulari'zation** *or* **par,ticulari'sation** *n.* —**par'ticular,izer** *or* **par'ticular,iser** *n.*

Particulars of Claim *pl. n. Law.* (in England) the first reading made by the plaintiff in a county court action, showing the facts upon which he relies in support of his claim and the relief asked for.

particulate (pɑː'tɪkjʊlɪt, -,leɪt) *n.* **1.** a substance consisting of separate particles. ~*adj.* **2.** of or made up of separate particles. **3.** *Genetics.* of, relating to, or designating inheritance of characteristics, esp. with emphasis on the role of genes.

parting ('pɑːtɪŋ) *n.* **1.** *Brit.* the line of scalp showing when sections of hair are combed in opposite directions. U.S., Canadian, and Austral. equivalent: **part.** **2.** the act of separating or the state of being separated. **3. a.** a departure or leave-taking, esp. one causing a final separation. **b.** (*as modifier*): *a parting embrace.* **4.** a place or line of separation or division. **5.** *Chem.* a division of a crystal along a plane that is not a cleavage plane. **6.** a euphemism for **death.** ~*adj.* (*prenominal*) **7.** *Literary.* departing: *the parting day.* **8.** serving to divide or separate.

parting strip *n.* a thin strip of wood, metal, etc., used to separate two adjoining materials.

parti pris *French.* (parti pri) *n.* a preconceived opinion. [C19: literally: side taken]

partisan[1] *or* **partizan**[1] (,pɑːtɪ'zæn, 'pɑːtɪ,zæn) *n.* **1.** an adherent or devotee of a cause, party, etc. **2. a.** a member of an armed resistance group within occupied territory. **b.** (*as modifier*): *partisan forces.* ~*adj.* **3.** of, relating to, or characteristic of a partisan. **4.** relating to or excessively devoted to one party, faction, etc.; one-sided: *partisan control.* [C16: via French, from Old Italian *partigiano,* from *parte* faction, from Latin *pars* PART] —,**parti'sanship** *or* ,**parti'zanship** *n.*

partisan[2] *or* **partizan**[2] ('pɑːtɪzᵊn) *n.* a spear or pike with two opposing axe blades or spikes. [C16: from French *partizane,* from Old Italian *partigiana,* from *partigiano* PARTISAN[1]]

partita (pɑː'tiːtə) *n., pl.* **-te** (-teɪ) *or* **-tas.** *Music.* a type of suite. [Italian: divided (piece), from Latin *partīre* to divide]

partite ('pɑːtaɪt) *adj.* **1.** (*in combination*) composed of or divided into a specified number of parts: *bipartite.* **2.** (esp. of plant leaves) divided almost to the base to form two or more parts. [C16: from Latin *partīre* to divide]

partition (pɑː'tɪʃən) *n.* **1.** a division into parts; separation. **2.** something that separates, such as a large screen dividing a room in two. **3.** a part or share. **4.** a division of a country into two or more separate nations. **5.** *Property law.* a division of property, esp. realty, among joint owners. **6.** *Maths.* any of the ways by which an integer can be expressed as a sum of integers. **7.** *Logic, maths.* **a.** the division of a class into a number of disjoint and exhaustive subclasses. **b.** such a set of subclasses. **8.** *Biology.* a structure that divides or separates. **9.** *Rhetoric.* the second part of a speech where the chief lines of thought are announced. ~*vb.* (*tr.*) **10.** (often foll. by *off*) to separate or apportion into sections: *to partition a room off with a large screen.* **11.** to divide (a country) into two or more separate nations. **12.** *Property law.* to divide (property, esp. realty) among joint owners, by dividing either the property itself or the proceeds of sale. [C15: via Old French from Latin *partītiō,* from *partīre* to divide] —**par'titioner** *or* **par'titionist** *n.*

partition coefficient *n. Chem.* the ratio of the concentrations of a substance in two heterogenous phases in equilibrium with each other.

partitive ('pɑːtɪtɪv) *adj.* **1.** *Grammar.* indicating that a noun involved in a construction refers only to a part or fraction of what it otherwise refers to. The phrase *some of the butter* is a partitive construction; in some inflected languages it would be translated by the genitive case of the noun. **2.** serving to separate or divide into parts. ~*n.* **3.** *Grammar.* a partitive linguistic element or feature. [C16: from Medieval Latin *partītīvus* serving to divide, from Latin *partīre* to divide] —**'partitively** *adv.*

partlet ('pɑːtlɪt) *n.* a woman's garment covering the neck and shoulders, worn esp. during the 16th century. [C14 *Pertelote,* name of the hen in Chaucer's "Nun's Priest's Tale", from Old French, of unknown origin]

partly ('pɑːtlɪ) *adv.* to some extent; not completely.

partner ('pɑːtnə) *n.* **1.** an ally or companion: *a partner in crime.* **2.** a member of a partnership. **3.** one of a pair of dancers or players on the same side in a game: *my bridge partner.* **4.** either member of a couple in a relationship. ~*vb.* **5.** to be or cause to be a partner (of). [C14: variant (influenced by PART) of PARCENER] —**'partnerless** *adj.*

partners ('pɑːtnəz) *pl. n. Nautical.* a wooden construction around an opening in a deck, as to support a mast.

partnership ('pɑːtnəʃɪp) *n.* **1. a.** a contractual relationship between two or more persons carrying on a joint business venture with a view to profit, each incurring liability for losses and the right to share in the profits. **b.** the deed creating such a relationship. **c.** the persons associated in such a relationship. **2.** the state or condition of being a partner.

part-off *n. Caribbean.* a screen used to divide off part of a room, such as the eating place of a parlour.

part of speech *n.* a class of words sharing important syntactic or semantic features; a group of words in a language that may occur in similar positions or fulfil similar functions in a sentence. The chief parts of speech in English are noun, pronoun, adjective, determiner, adverb, verb, preposition, conjunction, and interjection.

parton ('pɑː,tɒn) *n. Physics.* a hypothetical elementary particle postulated as a constituent of neutrons and protons. [from PART + -ON]

partook (pɑː'tʊk) *vb.* the past tense of **partake.**

partridge ('pɑːtrɪdʒ) *n., pl.* **-tridges** *or* **-tridge.** **1.** any of various small Old World gallinaceous game birds of the genera *Perdix, Alectoris,* etc., esp. *P. perdix* (**common** or **European partridge**): family *Phasianidae* (pheasants). **2.** *U.S. and Canadian.* any of various other gallinaceous birds, esp. the bobwhite and ruffed grouse. [C13: from Old French *perdriz,* from Latin *perdix,* from Greek]

partridgeberry ('pɑːtrɪdʒ,bɛrɪ) *n., pl.* **-ries.** **1.** Also called: **boxberry, twinberry.** a creeping woody rubiaceous plant, *Mitchella repens,* of E North America with small white fragrant flowers and scarlet berries. **2.** the berry of the wintergreen. **3.** another name for **wintergreen** (sense 1).

partridge-wood *n.* the dark striped wood of the tropical American papilionaceous tree, *Andira inermis,* used for cabinetwork.

parts (pɑːts) *pl. n.* **1.** personal abilities or talents: *a man of many parts.* **2.** short for **private parts.**

part song *n.* **1.** a song composed in harmonized parts. **2.** (*in more technical usage*) a piece of homophonic choral music in which the topmost part carries the melody.

part-time *adj.* **1.** for less than the entire time appropriate to an activity: *a part-time job; a part-time waitress.* ~*adv.* **part time.** **2.** on a part-time basis: *he works part time.* ~Compare **full-time.** —,**part-'timer** *n.*

parturient (pɑː'tjʊərɪənt) *adj.* **1.** of or relating to childbirth. **2.** giving birth. **3.** producing or about to produce a new idea, etc. [C16: via Latin *parturīre,* from *parere* to bring forth] —**par'turiency** *n.*

parturifacient (pɑː,tjʊərɪ'feɪʃənt) *adj., n.* a medical word for **oxytocic.** [C19: from Latin *parturīre* to be in travail + *facere* to make]

parturition (,pɑːtjʊ'rɪʃən) *n.* the act or process of giving birth. [C17: from Late Latin *parturītiō,* from *parturīre* to be in labour]

partway ('pɑːt,weɪ) *adv.* some of the way; partly: *I stopped reading partway through the chapter.*

part work *n. Brit.* a series of magazines issued as at weekly or monthly intervals, which are designed to be bound together to form a complete course or book.

part-writing *n. Music.* the aspect of composition concerned with the writing of parts, esp. counterpoint.

party ('pɑːtɪ) *n., pl.* **-ties.** **1. a.** a social gathering for pleasure, often held as a celebration. **b.** (*as modifier*): *party spirit.* **c.** (*in combination*): *partygoer.* **2.** a group of people associated in some activity: *a rescue party.* **3. a.** (*often cap.*) a group of people organized together to further a common political aim, such as the election of its candidates to public office. **b.** (*as modifier*): *party politics.* **4.** the practice of taking sides on public issues. **5.** a person, esp. one who participates in some activity such as entering into a contract. **6.** the person or persons taking part in legal proceedings, such as plaintiff or prosecutor: *a party to the action.* **7.** *Informal, humorous.* a person: *he's an odd old party.* ~*vb.* **-ties, -tying, -tied.** (*intr.*) **8.** *Informal.* to celebrate; revel. ~*adj.* **9.** *Heraldry.* (of a shield) divided vertically into two colours, metals, or furs. [C13: from Old French *partie* part, faction, from Latin *partīre* to divide; see PART]

party line *n.* **1.** a telephone line serving two or more subscribers. **2.** the policies or dogma of a political party, to which all members are expected to subscribe. **3.** *Chiefly U.S.* the boundary between adjoining property.

party list *n.* (*modifier*) of or relating to a system of voting in which people vote for a party rather than for a candidate. Parties are assigned the number of seats which reflects their share of the vote. See **proportional representation.**

party man *n.* a loyal member of a political party, esp. one who is slavishly loyal or extremely devoted.

party plan *n.* a method of selling, in which guests at a specially arranged party are invited to buy a range of products.

party politics *pl. n.* politics conducted through, by, or for parties, as opposed to other interests or the public good.

party pooper ('puːpə) *n. Informal.* a person whose behaviour or personality spoils other people's enjoyment. [C20: originally U.S.]

party wall *n. Property law.* a wall separating two properties or pieces of land and over which each of the adjoining owners has certain rights.

parulis (pə'ruːlɪs) *n., pl.* **-lides** (-lɪ,diːz). *Pathol.* another name for **gumboil.** [C19: from PARA-[1] + Greek *oulon* gum]

parure (pə'rʊə) *n.* a set of jewels or other ornaments. [C15: from Old French *pareure* adornment, from *parer* to embellish, from Latin *parāre* to arrange]

par value *n.* the value imprinted on the face of a share certificate or bond and used to assess dividend, capital ownership, or interest. Also called: **face value.** Compare **market value, book value** (sense 2).

parve ('pɑrvə) *adj.* a variant of **parev.**

parvenu *or (fem.)* **parvenue** ('pɑːvəˌnjuː) *n.* **1.** a person who, having risen socially or economically, is considered to be an upstart or to lack the appropriate refinement for his new position. ~*adj.* **2.** of or characteristic of a parvenu. [C19: from French, from *parvenir* to attain, from Latin *pervenīre,* from *per* through + *venīre* to come]

parvifoliate (ˌpɑːvɪ'fəʊlɪˌeɪt) *adj.* (of plants) having small leaves in comparison with the size of the stem.

parvis *or* **parvise** ('pɑːvɪs) *n.* a court or portico in front of a building, esp. a church. [C14: via Old French from Late Latin *paradīsus* PARADISE]

parvovirus ('pɑːvəʊˌvaɪrəs) *n.* any of a group of viruses characterized by their very small size, each of which is specific to a particular species, as for example canine parvovirus. [C20: New Latin from Latin *parvus* little + VIRUS]

pas (pɑː; *French* pɑ) *n., pl.* **pas** (pɑːz; *French* pɑ). **1.** a dance step or movement, esp. in ballet. **2.** *Rare.* the right to precede; precedence. [C18: French, literally: step]

PA's *pl. n. Mountaineering.* a type of rock boot. [C20: named after Pierre Allain, French climber]

pascal ('pæskᵊl) *n.* the derived SI unit of pressure; the pressure exerted on an area of 1 square metre by a force of 1 newton; equivalent to 10 dynes per square centimetre or 1.45×10^{-4} pound per square inch. Symbol: Pa [C20: named after Blaise *Pascal* (1623–62), French philosopher, mathematician, and physicist]

Pascal ('pæsˌkæl, -kᵊl) *n.* a high-level computer programming language developed as a teaching language: used for general-purpose programming. [C20: named after B. *Pascal*]

Pascal's triangle ('pæskᵊlz) *n.* a triangle consisting of rows of numbers; the apex is 1 and each row starts and ends with 1, other numbers being obtained by adding together the two numbers on either side in the row above: used to calculate probabilities.

Pascal's wager *n. Philosophy.* the argument that it is in one's rational self-interest to act as if God exists, since the infinite punishments of hell, provided they have a positive probability, however small, outweigh any countervailing advantage.

Pasch (pɑːsk, pæsk) *n.* an archaic name for **Passover** (sense 1) or **Easter.** [C12: from Old French *pasche,* via Church Latin and Greek from Hebrew *pesakh* PESACH]

paschal ('pæskᵊl) *adj.* **1.** of or relating to Passover. **2.** of or relating to Easter.

paschal flower *n.* another name for **pasqueflower.**

Paschal Lamb *n.* **1.** *(sometimes not caps.) Old Testament.* the lamb killed and eaten on the first day of the Passover. **2.** Christ regarded as this sacrifice.

pas de basque (ˌpɑː də 'bɑːsk; *French* pɑ də bask) *n., pl.* **pas de basque.** a dance step performed usually on the spot, consisting of one long and two short movements during which the weight is transferred from one foot to the other: used esp. in reels and jigs. [from French, literally: Basque step]

pas de chat (*French* pɑdʃa) *n., pl.* **pas de chat.** *Ballet.* a catlike leap. [French: cat's step]

pas de deux (*French* pɑddø) *n., pl.* **pas de deux.** *Ballet.* a sequence for two dancers. [French: step for two]

pase ('pɑːseɪ) *n. Bullfighting.* a movement of the cape or muleta by a matador to attract the bull's attention and guide its attack. [from Spanish, literally: pass]

pash[1] (pæʃ) *n. Slang.* infatuation. [C20: from PASSION]

pash[2] (pæʃ) *Obsolete or dialect.* ~*vb.* **1.** to throw or be thrown and break or be broken to bits; smash. ~*n.* **2.** a crushing blow. [C17 (n.): from earlier *passhen* to throw with violence, probably of imitative origin]

pasha *or* **pacha** ('pɑːʃə, 'pæʃə) *n.* (formerly) a provincial governor or other high official of the Ottoman Empire or the modern Egyptian kingdom: placed after a name when used as a title. [C17: from Turkish *paşa*]

pashalik *or* **pashalic** ('pɑːʃəlɪk) *n.* the province or jurisdiction of a pasha. [C18: from Turkish]

pashka ('pæʃkə) *n.* a rich Russian dessert made of cottage cheese, cream, almonds, currants, etc., set in a special wooden mould and traditionally eaten at Easter.

pashm ('pæʃəm) *n.* the underfur of various Tibetan animals, esp. goats, used for cashmere shawls. [from Persian, literally: wool]

Pashto, Pushto ('pʌʃtəʊ), *or* **Pushtu** *n.* **1.** a language of Afghanistan and NW Pakistan, belonging to the East Iranian branch of the Indo-European family: since 1936 the official language of Afghanistan. **2.** *(pl.* **-to** *or* **-tos, -tu** *or* **tus)** a speaker of the Pashto language; a Pathan. ~*adj.* **3.** denoting or relating to this language or a speaker of it.

paso doble ('pæsəʊ 'dəʊbleɪ; *Spanish* 'paso 'doβle) *n., pl.* **paso dobles** *or* **pasos dobles** (*Spanish* 'pasos 'doβles). **1.** a modern ballroom dance in fast duple time. **2.** a piece of music composed for or in the rhythm of this dance. [Spanish: double step]

pas op ('pɑːs ˌɒp) *interj. S. African.* beware. [Afrikaans]

paspalum (pæs'peɪləm) *n.* any of various grasses of the genus *Paspalum* of Australia and New Zealand having wide leaves.

pasqueflower ('pɑːskˌflaʊə, 'pæsk-) *n.* **1.** a small purple-flowered ranunculaceous plant, *Anemone pulsatilla* (or *Pulsatilla vulgaris*), of N and Central Europe and W Asia. **2.** any of several related North American plants, such as *A. patens.* ~Also called: **paschal flower, pulsatilla.** [C16: from French *passefleur,* from *passer* to excel + *fleur* flower; changed to *pasqueflower* Easter flower, because it blooms at Easter]

pasquinade (ˌpæskwɪ'neɪd) *or* **pasquil** ('pæskwɪl) *n.* **1.** an abusive lampoon or satire, esp. one posted in a public place. ~*vb.* **-ades, -ading, -aded** *or* **-quils, -quilling, -quilled.** **2.** *(tr.)* to ridicule with pasquinade. [C17: from Italian *Pasquino* name given to an ancient Roman statue disinterred in 1501, which was annually posted with satirical verses] —ˌ**pasquin'ader** *n.*

pass (pɑːs) *vb.* **1.** to go onwards or move by or past (a person, thing, etc.). **2.** to run, extend, or lead through, over, or across (a place): *the route passes through the city.* **3.** to go through or cause to go through (an obstacle or barrier): *to pass a needle through cloth.* **4.** to move or cause to move onwards or over: *he passed his hand over her face.* **5.** *(tr.)* to go beyond or exceed: *this victory passes all expectation.* **6.** to gain or cause to gain an adequate or required mark, grade, or rating in (an examination, course, etc.): *the examiner passed them all.* **7.** (often foll. by *away* or *by*) to elapse or allow to elapse: *we passed the time talking.* **8. pass the time of day (with).** to spend time amicably (with), esp. in chatting, with no particular purpose. **9.** *(intr.)* to take place or happen: *what passed at the meeting?* **10.** to speak or exchange or be spoken or exchanged: *angry words passed between them.* **11.** to spread or cause to spread: *we passed the news round the class.* **12.** to transfer or exchange or be transferred or exchanged: *the bomb passed from hand to hand.* **13.** *(intr.)* to undergo change or transition: *to pass from joy to despair.* **14.** (when *tr.,* often foll. by *down*) to transfer or be transferred by inheritance: *the house passed to the younger son.* **15.** to agree to or sanction or to be agreed to or receive the sanction of a legislative body, person of authority, etc.: *the assembly passed 10 resolutions.* **16.** *(tr.)* (of a legislative measure) to undergo (a procedural stage) and be agreed: *the bill passed the committee stage.* **17.** (when *tr.,* often foll. by *on* or *upon*) to pronounce or deliver (judgment, findings, etc.): *the court passed sentence.* **18.** to go or allow to go without comment or censure: *the intended insult passed unnoticed.* **19.** *(intr.)* to opt not to exercise a right, as by not answering a question or not making a bid or a play in card games. **20.** *Physiol.* to discharge (urine, faeces, etc.) from the body. **21. pass water.** to urinate. **22.** *(intr.)* to come to an end or disappear: *his anger soon passed.* **23.** *(intr.;* usually foll. by *for* or *as)* to be likely to be mistaken for or accepted as (someone or something else): *you could easily pass for your sister.* **24.** *(intr.;* foll. by *away, on,* or *over)* a euphemism for **die**[1] (sense 1). **25.** *(tr.) Chiefly U.S.* to fail to declare (a dividend). **26.** *(intr.;* usually foll. by *on* or *upon) Chiefly U.S.* (of a court, jury, etc.) to sit in judgment; adjudicate. **27.** *Sport.* to hit, kick, or throw (the ball) to another player. **28. bring to pass.** *Archaic.* to cause to happen. **29. come to pass.** to happen. ~*n.* **30.** the act of passing. **31. a.** a route through a range of mountains where the summit is lower or where there is a gap between peaks. **b.** *(cap. as part of a name): the Simplon Pass.* **32.** a way through any difficult region. **33.** a permit, licence, or authorization to do something without restriction: *she has a pass to visit the museum on Sundays.* **34. a.** a document allowing entry to and exit from a military installation. **b.** a document authorizing leave of absence. **35.** *Brit.* **a.** the passing of a college or university examination to a satisfactory standard but not as high as honours. **b.** *(as modifier): a pass degree.* ~Compare **honours** (sense 2). **36.** a dive, sweep, or bombing or landing run by an aircraft. **37.** a motion of the hand or of a wand as a prelude to or part of a conjuring trick. **38.** *Informal.* an attempt, in words or action, to invite sexual intimacy. **39.** a state of affairs or condition, esp. a bad or difficult one (esp. in the phrase **a pretty pass).** **40.** *Sport.* the transfer of a ball from one player to another. **41.** *Fencing.* a thrust or lunge with a sword. **42.** *Bridge, etc.* the act of passing (making no bid). **43.** *Bullfighting.* a variant of **pase.** **44.** *Archaic.* a witty sally or remark. ~*interj.* **45.** *Bridge, etc.* a call indicating that a player has no bid to make. ~See also **pass by, pass off, pass out, pass over, pass up.** [C13: from Old French *passer* to pass, surpass, from Latin *passūs* step, PACE[1]]

pass. *abbrev. for:* **1.** passive. **2.** passenger. **3.** passage.

passable ('pɑːsəbᵊl) *adj.* **1.** adequate, fair, or acceptable: *a passable but not outstanding speech.* **2.** (of an obstacle) capable of being passed or crossed. **3.** (of currency) valid for general circulation. **4.** (of a proposed law) able to be ratified or enacted. —'**passableness** *n.*

passably ('pɑːsəblɪ) *adv.* **1.** fairly; somewhat. **2.** acceptably; well enough: *she sings passably.*

passacaglia (ˌpæsə'kɑːljə) *n.* **1.** an old Spanish dance in slow triple time. **2.** a slow instrumental piece characterized by a series of variations on a particular theme played over a repeated bass part. See also **chaconne** (sense 1). [C17: earlier *passacalle,* from Spanish *pasacalle* street dance, from *paso* step + *calle* street; the ending *-alle* was changed to *-aglia* to suggest an Italian origin]

passade (pæ'seɪd) *n. Dressage.* the act of moving back and forth in the same place. [C17: via French from Italian *passata,* from *passare* to PASS]

passage[1] ('pæsɪdʒ) *n.* **1.** a channel, opening, etc., through or by which a person or thing may pass. **2.** *Music.* a section or division of a piece, movement, etc. **3.** a way, as in a hall or lobby. **4.** a section of a written work, speech, etc., esp. one of moderate length. **5.** a journey, esp. by ship: *the outward passage took a* *week.* **6.** the act or process of passing from one place, condition, etc., to another: *passage of a gas through a liquid.* **7.** the permission, right, or freedom to pass: *to be denied passage through a country.* **8.** the enactment of a law or resolution by a legislative or deliberative body. **9.** an evacuation of the bowels. **10.** *Rare.* an exchange or interchange, as of blows, words, etc. (esp. in the phrase **passage of arms**). [C13: from Old French from *passer* to PASS]

passage[2] ('pæsɪdʒ, 'pæsɑːʒ) *Dressage.* ~*n.* **1.** a sideways walk in which diagonal pairs of feet are lifted alternately. **2.** a cadenced lofty trot, the moment of suspension being clearly defined. ~*vb.* **3.** to move or cause to move at a passage. [C18: from French *passager,* variant of *passéger,* from Italian *passeggiare* to take steps, ultimately from Latin *passūs* step, PACE[1]]

passage hawk *or* **passager hawk** ('pæsɪdʒə) *n.* a young hawk or falcon caught while on migration. Compare **eyas, haggard** (sense 4).

passageway ('pæsɪdʒˌweɪ) *n.* a way, esp. one in or between buildings; passage.

passage work *n. Music.* scales, runs, etc., in a piece of music which have no structural significance but provide an opportunity for virtuoso display.

passant ('pæsᵊnt) *adj.* *(usually postpositive) Heraldry.* (of a beast) walking, with the right foreleg raised. [C14: from Old French, present participle of *passer* to PASS]

pass band *n.* the band of frequencies that is transmitted with maximum efficiency through a circuit, filter, etc.

passbook ('pɑːsˌbʊk) *n.* **1.** a book for keeping a record of withdrawals from and payments into a building society. **2.** another name for **bankbook. 3.** a customer's book in which is recorded by a trader a list of credit sales to that customer. **4.** *S. African.* an official document serving to identify the bearer, his race, his residence, and his employment.

pass by *vb.* **1.** (*intr.*) to go or move past. **2.** (*tr., adv.*) to overlook or disregard: *to pass by difficult problems.*

passé ('pɑːseɪ, 'pæseɪ; *French* pɑse) *adj.* **1.** out-of-date: *passé ideas.* **2.** past the prime; faded: *a passé society beauty.* [C18: from French, past participle of *passer* to PASS]

passel ('pæsᵊl) *n. Informal or dialect, chiefly U.S.* a group or quantity of no fixed number. [variant of PARCEL]

passementerie (pæs'mɛntrɪ; *French* pɑsmɑ̃tri) *n.* a decorative trimming of gimp, cord, beads, braid, etc. [C16: from Old French *passement,* from *passer* to trim, PASS]

passenger ('pæsɪndʒə) *n.* **1. a.** a person travelling in a car, train, boat, etc., not driven by him. **b.** (*as modifier*): *a passenger seat.* **2.** *Chiefly Brit.* a member of a group or team who is a burden on the others through not participating fully in the work. **3.** *Archaic.* a wayfarer. [C14: from Old French *passager* passing, from PASSAGE[1]]

passenger pigeon *n.* a gregarious North American pigeon, *Ectopistes migratorius:* became extinct at the beginning of the 20th century.

passe-partout (ˌpæspɑː'tuː; *French* pɑspartu) *n.* **1.** a mounting for a picture in which strips of strong gummed paper are used to bind together the glass, picture, and backing. **2.** the gummed paper used for this. **3.** a mat, often decorated, on which a picture is mounted. **4.** something that secures entry everywhere, esp. a master key. [C17: from French, literally: pass everywhere]

passepied (pɑːs'pjeɪ) *n., pl.* **-pieds** (-'pjeɪ). **1.** a lively minuet of Breton origin, in triple time, popular in the 17th century. **2.** a piece of music composed for or in the rhythm of this dance. [C17: from French: pass the foot]

passer-by *n., pl.* **passers-by.** a person that is passing or going by, esp. on foot.

passerine ('pæsəˌraɪn, -ˌriːn) *adj.* **1.** of, relating to, or belonging to the *Passeriformes,* an order of birds characterized by the perching habit: includes the larks, finches, crows, thrushes, starlings, etc. ~*n.* **2.** any bird belonging to the order *Passeriformes.* [C18: from Latin *passer* sparrow]

pas seul (*French* pɑ sœl) *n., pl.* **pas seuls** (*French.* pɑ sœl). a dance sequence for one person. [French, literally: step on one's own]

passible ('pæsɪbᵊl) *adj.* susceptible to emotion or suffering; able to feel. [C14: from Medieval Latin *passibilis,* from Latin *patī* to suffer; see PASSION] —ˌ**passi'bility** *n.*

passifloraceous (ˌpæsɪflɔː'reɪʃəs) *adj.* of, relating to, or belonging to the *Passifloraceae,* a tropical and subtropical family of climbing plants including the passionflowers: the flowers have five petals and threadlike parts forming a dense mass (corona) around the central disc. [C19: from New Latin *Passiflora,* the type genus (passionflower)]

passim *Latin.* ('pæsɪm) *adv.* here and there; throughout: used to indicate that what is referred to occurs frequently in the work cited.

passing ('pɑːsɪŋ) *adj.* **1.** transitory or momentary: *a passing fancy.* **2.** cursory or casual in action or manner: *a passing reference.* ~*adv., adj.* **3.** *Archaic.* to an extreme degree: *the events were passing strange.* ~*n.* **4.** a place where or means by which one may pass, cross, ford, etc. **5.** a euphemism for **death. 6. in passing.** by the way; incidentally: *he mentioned your visit in passing.*

passing bell *n.* a bell rung to announce a death or a funeral. Also called: **death bell, death knell.**

passing note *or U.S.* **passing tone** *n. Music.* a nonharmonic note through which a melody passes from one harmonic note to the next. Compare **auxiliary note.**

passing shot *n. Tennis.* a winning shot hit outside an opponent's reach.

passion ('pæʃən) *n.* **1.** ardent love or affection. **2.** intense sexual love. **3.** a strong affection or enthusiasm for an object, concept, etc.: *a passion for poetry.* **4.** any strongly felt emotion, such as love, hate, envy, etc. **5.** a state or outburst of extreme anger: *he flew into a passion.* **6.** the object of an intense desire, ardent affection, or enthusiasm. **7.** an outburst expressing intense emotion: *he burst into a passion of sobs.* **8.** *Philosophy.* **a.** any state of the mind in which it is affected by something external, such as perception, desire, etc., as contrasted with action. **b.** feelings, desires or emotions, as contrasted with reason. **9.** the sufferings and death of a Christian martyr. [C12: via French from Church Latin *passiō* suffering, from Latin *patī* to suffer]

Passion ('pæʃən) *n.* **1.** the sufferings of Christ from the Last Supper to his death on the cross. **2.** any of the four Gospel accounts of this. **3.** a musical setting of this: *the St Matthew Passion.*

passional ('pæʃənᵊl) *adj.* **1.** of, relating to, or due to passion or the passions. ~*n.* **2.** a book recounting the sufferings of Christian martyrs or saints.

passionate ('pæʃənɪt) *adj.* **1.** manifesting or exhibiting intense sexual feeling or desire: *a passionate lover.* **2.** capable of, revealing, or characterized by intense emotion: *a passionate plea.* **3.** easily roused to anger; quick-tempered. —'**passionately** *adv.* —'**passionateness** *n.*

passionflower ('pæʃənˌflaʊə) *n.* any passifloraceous plant of the tropical American genus *Passiflora,* cultivated for their red, yellow, greenish, or purple showy flowers: some species have edible fruit. See also **granadilla.** [C17: so called from the alleged resemblance between parts of the flower and the instruments of Christ's crucifixion]

passion fruit *n.* the edible fruit of any of various passionflowers, esp. granadilla.

passionless ('pæʃənlɪs) *adj.* **1.** empty of emotion or feeling: *a passionless marriage.* **2.** calm and detached; dispassionate. —'**passionlessly** *adv.* —'**passionlessness** *n.*

Passion play *n.* a play depicting the Passion of Christ.

Passion Sunday *n.* the fifth Sunday in Lent (the second Sunday before Easter), when Passiontide begins.

Passiontide ('pæʃənˌtaɪd) *n.* the last two weeks of Lent, extending from Passion Sunday to Holy Saturday.

Passion Week *n.* **1.** the week between Passion Sunday and Palm Sunday. **2.** (formerly) Holy Week; the week before Easter.

passivate ('pæsɪˌveɪt) *vb. (tr.)* to render (a metal) less susceptible to corrosion by coating the surface with a substance, such as an oxide.

passive ('pæsɪv) *adj.* **1.** not active or not participating perceptibly in an activity, organization, etc. **2.** unresisting and receptive to external forces; submissive. **3.** not working or operating. **4.** affected or acted upon by an external object or force. **5.** *Grammar.* denoting a voice of verbs in sentences in which the grammatical subject is not the logical subject but rather the recipient of the action described by the verb, as *was broken* in the sentence *The glass was broken by a boy.* Compare **active** (sense 5a). **6.** *Chem.* (of a substance, esp. a metal) apparently chemically unreactive, usually as a result of the formation of a thin protective layer that prevents further reaction. **7.** *Electronics, telecomm.* **a.** containing no source of power and therefore capable only of attenuating a signal: *a passive network.* **b.** not capable of amplifying a signal or controlling a function: *a passive communications satellite.* **8.** *Finance.* (of a bond, share, debt, etc.) yielding no interest. ~*n.* **9.** *Grammar.* **a.** the passive voice. **b.** a passive verb. [C14: from Latin *passīvus* susceptible of suffering, from *patī* to undergo] —'**passively** *adv.* —**pas'sivity** *or* '**passiveness** *n.*

passive obedience *n.* **1.** unquestioning obedience to authority. **2.** the surrender of a person's will to another person.

passive resistance *n.* resistance to a government, law, etc., made without violence, as by fasting, demonstrating peacefully, or refusing to cooperate.

passive smoking *n.* the inhalation of smoke from other people's cigarettes by a nonsmoker. —**passive smoker** *n.*

passive vocabulary *n.* all the words, collectively, that a person can understand. Compare **active vocabulary.**

passivism ('pæsɪˌvɪzəm) *n.* **1.** the theory, belief, or practice of passive resistance. **2.** the quality, characteristics, or fact of being passive. —'**passivist** *n., adj.*

passkey ('pɑːsˌkiː) *n.* **1.** any of various keys, esp. a latchkey. **2.** another term for **master key** or **skeleton key.**

pass law *n.* (in South Africa) a law restricting the movement of Black Africans, esp. from rural to urban areas.

pass off *vb. (adv.)* **1.** to be or cause to be accepted or circulated in a false character or identity: *he passed the fake diamonds off as real.* **2.** (*intr.*) to come to a gradual end; disappear: *eventually the pain passed off.* **3.** to emit (a substance) as a gas or vapour, or (of a substance) to be emitted in this way. **4.** (*intr.*) to take place: *the meeting passed off without disturbance.* **5.** (*tr.*) to set aside or disregard: *I managed to pass off his insult.*

pass out *vb.* (*adv.*) **1.** (*intr.*) *Informal.* to become unconscious; faint. **2.** (*intr.*) *Brit.* (esp. of an officer cadet) to qualify for a military commission; complete a course of training satisfactorily: *General Smith passed out from Sandhurst in 1933.* **3.** (*tr.*) to distribute.

pass over *vb.* **1.** (*tr., adv.*) to take no notice of; disregard: *they passed me over in the last round of promotions.* **2.** (*intr., prep.*) to disregard (something bad or embarrassing): *we shall pass over your former faults.*

Passover ('pɑːsˌəʊvə) *n.* **1.** Also called: **Pesach, Pesah, Feast of the Unleavened Bread.** an eight-day Jewish festival beginning on Nisan 15 and celebrated in commemoration of the passing over or sparing of the Israelites in Egypt, when God smote the firstborn of the Egyptians (Exodus 12). **2.** another term for the **Paschal Lamb.** [C16: from *pass over,* translation of Hebrew *pesah,* from *pāsah* to pass over]

passport ('pɑːspɔːt) *n.* **1.** an official document issued by a government, identifying an individual, granting him permission to travel abroad, and requesting the protection of other governments for him. **2.** a licence granted by a state to a foreigner, allowing the passage of his person or goods through the country. **3.** another word for **sea letter** (sense 1). **4.** a quality, asset, etc., that gains a person admission or acceptance. [C15: from French *passeport,* from *passer* to PASS + PORT[1]]

pass up *vb.* (*tr., adv.*) **1.** *Informal.* to let go by; ignore: *I won't pass up this opportunity.* **2.** to take no notice of (someone).

passus ('pæsəs) *n., pl.* **-sus** *or* **-suses.** (esp. in medieval literature) a division or section of a poem, story, etc. [C16: from Latin. step, PACE[1]]

password ('pɑːsˌwɜːd) *n.* **1.** a secret word, phrase, etc., that ensures admission or acceptance by proving identity, membership, etc. **2.** an action, quality, etc., that gains admission or acceptance.

past (pɑːst) *adj.* **1.** completed, finished, and no longer in existence: *past happiness.* **2.** denoting or belonging to all or a segment of the time that has elapsed at the present moment: *the past history of the world.* **3.** denoting a specific unit of time that immediately precedes the present one: *the past month.* **4.** (*prenominal*) denoting a person who has held and relinquished an office or position; former: *a past president.* **5.** *Grammar.* denoting any of various tenses of verbs that are used in describing actions, events, or states that have been begun or completed at the time of utterance. Compare **aorist, imperfect** (sense 4), **perfect** (sense 8). *~n.* **6. the past.** the period of time or a segment of it that has elapsed: *forget the past.* **7.** the history, experience, or background of a nation, person, etc.: *a soldier with a distinguished past.* **8.** an earlier period of someone's life, esp. one that contains events kept secret or regarded as disreputable. **9.** *Grammar.* **a.** a past tense. **b.** a verb in a past tense. *~adv.* **10.** at a specified or unspecified time before the present; ago: *three years past.* **11.** on or onwards: *I greeted him but he just walked past.* *~prep.* **12.** beyond in time: *it's past midnight.* **13.** beyond in place or position: *the library is past the church.* **14.** moving beyond; in a direction that passes: *he walked past me.* **15.** beyond or above the reach, limit, or scope of: *his foolishness is past comprehension.* **16.** beyond or above in number or amount: *to count past ten.* **17. past it.** *Informal.* unable to perform the tasks one could do when one was younger. **18. not put it past someone.** to consider someone capable of (the action specified). [C14: from *passed,* past participle of PASS]

pasta ('pæstə) *n.* any of several variously shaped edible preparations made from a flour and water dough, such as spaghetti. [Italian, from Late Latin: PASTE[1]]

paste[1] (peɪst) *n.* **1.** a mixture or material of a soft or malleable consistency, such as toothpaste. **2.** an adhesive made from water and flour or starch, used esp. for joining pieces of paper. **3.** a preparation of food, such as meat, that has been powdered to a creamy mass, for spreading on bread, crackers, etc. **4.** any of various sweet doughy confections: *almond paste.* **5.** dough, esp. when prepared with shortening, as for making pastry. **6. a.** Also called: **strass.** a hard shiny glass used for making imitation gems. **b.** an imitation gem made of this glass. **7.** the combined ingredients of porcelain. See also **hard paste, soft paste.** *~vb.* (*tr.*) **8.** (often foll. by *on* or *onto*) to attach by or as if by using paste: *he pasted posters onto the wall.* **9.** (usually foll. by *with*) to cover (a surface) with paper, usually attached with an adhesive: *he pasted the wall with posters.* [C14: via Old French from Late Latin *pasta* dough, from Greek *pastē* barley porridge, from *pastos,* from *passein* to sprinkle]

paste[2] (peɪst) *vb.* (*tr.*) *Slang.* to hit, esp. with the fists; punch or beat soundly. [C19: variant of BASTE[3]]

pasteboard ('peɪstˌbɔːd) *n.* **1. a.** a stiff board formed from layers of paper or pulp pasted together, esp. as used in bookbinding. **b.** (*as modifier*): *a pasteboard book cover.* **2.** *Slang.* a card or ticket. *~adj.* **3.** flimsy; insubstantial. **4.** sham; fake.

pastel ('pæstᵊl, pæ'stɛl) *n.* **1. a.** a substance made of ground pigment bound with gum, used for making sticks for drawing. **b.** a crayon of this. **c.** a drawing done in such crayons. **2.** the medium or technique of pastel drawing. **3.** a pale delicate colour. **4.** a light prose work, esp. a poetic one. **5.** another name for **woad.** *~adj.* **6.** (of a colour) pale; delicate: *pastel blue.* [C17: via French from Italian *pastello,* from Late Latin *pastellus* woad compounded into a paste, diminutive of *pasta* PASTE[1]] —'**pastelist** *or* '**pastellist** *n.*

pastern ('pæstən) *n.* **1.** the part of a horse's foot between the fetlock and the hoof. **2.** Also called: **fetter bone.** either of the two bones that constitute this part. [C14: from Old French *pasturon,* from *pasture* a hobble, from Latin *pāstōrius* of a shepherd, from PASTOR]

paste-up *n.* **1.** Also called (U.S.): **mechanical.** *Printing.* a sheet of paper or board on which are pasted artwork, proofs, etc., for photographing prior to making a plate. **2.** another name for **collage** (senses 1, 2).

pasteurism ('pæstəˌrɪzəm, -stjə-, 'pɑː-) *n. Med.* **1.** a method of securing immunity from rabies in a person who has been bitten by a rabid animal, by daily injections of progressively more virulent suspensions of the infected spinal cord of a rabbit that died of rabies. **2.** a similar method of treating patients with other viral infections by the serial injection of progressively more virulent suspensions of the causative virus. ~Also called: **Pasteur treatment.** [C19: named after Louis *Pasteur* (1822–95), French chemist and bacteriologist]

pasteurization *or* **pasteurisation** (ˌpæstəraɪ'zeɪʃən, -stjə-, ˌpɑː-) *n.* the process of heating beverages, such as milk, beer, wine, or cider, or solid foods, such as cheese or crab meat, to destroy harmful or undesirable microorganisms or to limit the rate of fermentation by the application of controlled heat.

pasteurize *or* **pasteurise** ('pæstəˌraɪz, -stjə-, 'pɑː-) *vb.* (*tr.*) **1.** to subject (milk, beer, etc.) to pasteurization. **2.** *Rare.* to subject (a patient) to pasteurism.

pasteurizer *or* **pasteuriser** ('pæstəˌraɪzə, -stjə-, 'pɑː-) *n.* **1.** an apparatus for pasteurizing substances (esp. milk). **2.** a person who carries out pasteurization.

pastiche (pæ'stiːʃ) *or* **pasticcio** (pæ'stɪtʃəʊ) *n.* **1.** a work of art that mixes styles, materials, etc. **2.** a work of art that imitates the style of another artist or period. [C19: French *pastiche,* Italian *pasticcio,* literally: piecrust (hence, something blended), from Late Latin *pasta* PASTE[1]]

pastille *or* **pastil** ('pæstɪl) *n.* **1.** a small flavoured or medicated lozenge for chewing. **2.** an aromatic substance burnt to fumigate the air. **3.** *Med.* a small coated paper disc formerly used to estimate the dose or intensity of radiation (esp. of x-rays): it changes colour when exposed. **4.** a variant of **pastel** (sense 1). [C17: via French from Latin *pastillus* small loaf, from *pānis* bread]

pastime ('pɑːsˌtaɪm) *n.* an activity or entertainment which makes time pass pleasantly: *golf is my favourite pastime.* [C15: from PASS + TIME, on the model of French *passe-temps*]

pasting ('peɪstɪŋ) *n. Slang.* a thrashing; heavy defeat.

pastis (pæ'stɪs, -'stiːs) *n.* an anise-flavoured alcoholic drink. [from French, of uncertain origin]

pastitsio (pæs'tɪtsɪəʊ) *n.* a Greek dish consisting of minced meat and macaroni topped with béchamel sauce. [C20: from Modern Greek]

past master *n.* **1.** a person with talent for, or experience in, a particular activity: *a past master of tact.* **2.** a person who has held the office of master in a Freemasons' lodge, guild, etc.

pastor ('pɑːstə) *n.* **1.** a clergyman or priest in charge of a congregation. **2.** a person who exercises spiritual guidance over a number of people. **3.** an archaic word for **shepherd** (sense 1). **4.** Also called: **rosy pastor.** a S Asian starling, *Sturnus roseus,* having glossy black head and wings and a pale pink body. [C14: from Latin: shepherd, from *pascere* to feed] —'**pastorˌship** *n.*

pastoral ('pɑːstərəl) *adj.* **1.** of, characterized by, or depicting rural life, scenery, etc. **2.** (of a literary work) dealing with an idealized form of rural existence in a conventional way. **3.** (of land) used for pasture. **4.** denoting or relating to the branch of theology dealing with the duties of a clergyman or priest to his congregation. **5.** of or relating to a clergyman or priest in charge of a congregation or his duties as such. **6.** of or relating to shepherds, their work, etc. *~n.* **7.** a literary work or picture portraying rural life, esp. the lives of shepherds in an idealizing way. See also **eclogue.** **8.** *Music.* a variant of **pastorale.** **9.** *Christianity.* **a.** a letter from a clergyman to the people under his charge. **b.** the letter of a bishop to the clergy or people of his diocese. **c.** Also called: **pastoral staff.** the crosier or staff carried by a bishop as a symbol of his pastoral responsibilities. [C15: from Latin, from PASTOR] —'**pastoralˌism** *n.* —'**pastorally** *adv.*

pastorale (ˌpæstə'rɑːl) *n., pl.* **-rales.** *Music.* **1.** a composition evocative of rural life, characterized by moderate compound duple or quadruple time and sometimes a droning accompaniment. **2.** a musical play based on a rustic story, popular during the 16th century. [C18: Italian, from Latin: PASTORAL]

pastoralist ('pɑːstərəlɪst) *n. Austral.* a grazier or land-holder raising sheep, cattle, etc., on a large scale.

pastorate ('pɑːstərɪt) *n.* **1.** the office or term of office of a pastor. **2.** a body of pastors; pastors collectively.

past participle *n.* a participial form of verbs used to modify a noun that is logically the object of a verb, also used in certain compound tenses and passive forms of the verb in English and other languages.

past perfect *Grammar.* *~adj.* **1.** denoting a tense of verbs used in relating past events where the action had already occurred at the time of the action of a main verb that is itself in a past tense. In English this is a compound tense formed with *had* plus the past participle. ~*n*. **2. a.** the past perfect tense. **b.** a verb in this tense.

pastrami (pəˈstrɑːmɪ) *n*. highly seasoned smoked beef, esp. prepared from a shoulder cut. [from Yiddish, from Romanian *pastramă*, from *păstra* to preserve]

pastry (ˈpeɪstrɪ) *n*., *pl*. **-tries. 1.** a dough of flour, water, shortening, and sometimes other ingredients. **2.** baked foods, such as tarts, made with this dough. **3.** an individual cake or pastry pie. [C16: from PASTE[1]]

pastry cream *n*. a creamy custard, often flavoured, used as a filling for éclairs, flans, etc. Also called: **pastry custard.**

pasturage (ˈpɑːstʃərɪdʒ) *n*. **1.** the right to graze or the business of grazing cattle. **2.** another word for **pasture.**

pasture (ˈpɑːstʃə) *n*. **1.** land covered with grass or herbage and grazed by or suitable for grazing by livestock. **2.** a specific tract of such land. **3.** the grass or herbage growing on it. ~*vb*. **4.** (*tr*.) to cause (livestock) to graze or (of livestock) to graze (a pasture). [C13: via Old French from Late Latin *pā-stūra*, from *pascere* to feed]

pasty[1] (ˈpeɪstɪ) *adj*. **pastier, pastiest. 1.** of or like the colour, texture, etc., of paste. **2.** (esp. of the complexion) pale or unhealthy-looking. ~*n*., *pl*. **pasties. 3.** either one of a pair of small round coverings for the nipples used by striptease dancers. —ˈ**pastily** *adv*. —ˈ**pastiness** *n*.

pasty[2] (ˈpæstɪ) *n*., *pl*. **pasties.** a round of pastry folded over a filling of meat, vegetables, etc.: *Cornish pasty*. [C13: from Old French *pastée*, from Late Latin *pasta* dough]

PA system *n*. See **public-address system.**

pat[1] (pæt) *vb*. **pats, patting, patted. 1.** to hit (something) lightly with the palm of the hand or some other flat surface: *to pat a ball*. **2.** to slap (a person or animal) gently, esp. on the back, as an expression of affection, congratulation, etc. **3.** (*tr*.) to shape, smooth, etc., with a flat instrument or the palm. **4.** (*intr*.) to walk or run with light footsteps. **5. pat (someone) on the back.** *Informal*. to congratulate or encourage (someone). ~*n*. **6.** a light blow with something flat. **7.** a gentle slap. **8.** a small mass of something: *a pat of butter*. **9.** the sound made by a light stroke or light footsteps. **10. pat on the back.** *Informal*. a gesture or word indicating approval or encouragement. [C14: perhaps imitative]

pat[2] (pæt) *adv*. **1.** Also: **off pat.** exactly or fluently memorized or mastered: *he recited it pat*. **2.** opportunely or aptly. **3. stand pat. a.** *Chiefly U.S. and Canadian*. to refuse to abandon a belief, decision, etc. **b.** (in poker, etc.) to play without adding new cards to the hand dealt. ~*adj*. **4.** exactly right for the occasion; apt: *a pat reply*. **5.** too exactly fitting; glib: *a pat answer to a difficult problem*. **6.** exactly right: *a pat hand in poker*. [C17: perhaps adverbial use ("with a light stroke") of PAT[1]]

pat[3] (pæt) *n*. **on one's pat.** *Austral. informal*. alone; on one's own. [C20: rhyming slang, from *Pat* Malone]

Pat (pæt) *n*. an informal name for an Irishman.

pat. *abbrev. for* patent(ed).

patagium (pəˈteɪdʒɪəm) *n*., *pl*. **-gia** (-dʒɪə). **1.** a web of skin between the neck, limbs, and tail in bats and gliding mammals that functions as a wing. **2.** a membranous fold of skin connecting margins of a bird's wing to the shoulder. [C19: New Latin from Latin, from Greek *patageion* gold border on a tunic]

Patagonian (ˌpætəˈgəʊnɪən) *adj*. **1.** of or relating to Patagonia, the southernmost region of South America. ~*n*. **2.** a native or inhabitant of Patagonia.

patch (pætʃ) *n*. **1. a.** a piece of material used to mend a garment or to make patchwork, a sewn-on pocket, etc. **b.** (*as modifier*): *a patch pocket*. **2.** a small piece, area, expanse, etc. **3. a.** a small plot of land. **b.** its produce: *a patch of cabbages*. **4.** a district for which particular officials, such as social workers or policemen, have responsibility: *he's a problem that's on your patch, John*. **5.** *Pathol*. any discoloured area on the skin, mucous membranes, etc., usually being one sign of a specific disorder. **6.** *Med*. **a.** a protective covering for an injured eye. **b.** any protective dressing. **7.** an imitation beauty spot, esp. one made of black or coloured silk, worn by both sexes, esp. in the 18th century. **8.** Also called: **flash.** an identifying piece of fabric worn on the shoulder of a uniform, on a vehicle, etc. **9.** a small contrasting section or stretch: *a patch of cloud in the blue sky*. **10.** a scrap; remnant. **11.** a small set of instructions to correct or improve a computer program. **12. a bad patch.** a difficult or troubled time. **13. not a patch on.** *Informal*. not nearly as good as. ~*vb*. (*tr*.) **14.** to mend or supply (a garment, etc.) with a patch or patches. **15.** to put together or produce with patches. **16.** (of material) to serve as a patch to. **17.** (often foll. by *up*) to mend hurriedly or in a makeshift way. **18.** (often foll. by *up*) to make (up) or settle (a quarrel). **19.** to connect (electric circuits) together temporarily by means of a patch board. **20.** (usually foll. by *through*) to connect (a telephone call) by means of a patch board. **21.** *Computer technol*. to correct or improve (a program) by adding a small set of instructions. [C16 *pacche*, perhaps from French *pieche* PIECE] —ˈ**patchable** *adj*. —ˈ**patcher** *n*.

patch board *or* **panel** *n*. a device with a large number of sockets into which electrical plugs can be inserted to form many different temporary circuits: used in telephone exchanges, computer systems, etc. Also called: **plugboard.**

patchouli, pachouli, *or* **patchouly** (ˈpætʃʊlɪ, pəˈtʃuːlɪ) *n*. **1.** any of several Asiatic trees of the genus *Pogostemon*, the leaves of which yield a heavy fragrant oil: family *Labiatae* (labiates). **2.** the perfume made from this oil. [C19: from Tamil *paccilai*, from *paccu* green + *ilai* leaf]

patch pocket *n*. a pocket on the outside of a garment.

patch quilt *n*. *Irish*. a patchwork quilt.

patch test *n*. *Med*. a test to detect an allergic reaction by applying small amounts of a suspected substance to the skin and then examining the area for signs of irritation.

patchwork (ˈpætʃˌwɜːk) *n*. **1.** needlework done by sewing pieces of different materials together. **2.** something, such as a theory, made up of various parts: *a patchwork of cribbed ideas*.

patchy (ˈpætʃɪ) *adj*. **patchier, patchiest. 1.** irregular in quality, occurrence, intensity, etc.: *a patchy essay*. **2.** having or forming patches. —ˈ**patchily** *adv*. —ˈ**patchiness** *n*.

patd *abbrev. for* patented.

pate (peɪt) *n*. the head, esp. with reference to baldness or (in facetious use) intelligence. [C14: of unknown origin]

pâté (ˈpæteɪ; *French* pɑte) *n*. **1.** a spread of very finely minced liver, poultry, etc., served usually as an hors d'oeuvre. **2.** a savoury pie of meat or fish. [from French: PASTE[1]]

pâté de foie gras (pɑte də fwa grɑ) *n*., *pl*. **pâtés de foie gras** (pɑte də fwa grɑ). a smooth rich paste made from the liver of a specially fattened goose, considered a great delicacy. [French: pâté of fat liver]

patella (pəˈtɛlə) *n*., *pl*. **-lae** (-liː). **1.** *Anatomy*. a small flat triangular bone in front of and protecting the knee joint. Nontechnical name: **kneecap. 2.** *Biology*. a cuplike structure, such as the spore-producing body of certain ascomycetous fungi. **3.** *Archaeol*. a small pan. [C17: from Latin, from *patina* shallow pan] —**paˈtellar** *adj*.

patellate (pəˈtɛlɪt, -leɪt) *adj*. having the shape of a patella. Also: **patelliform** (pəˈtɛlɪˌfɔːm).

paten (ˈpætᵊn), **patin,** *or* **patine** (ˈpætɪn) *n*. a plate, usually made of silver or gold, esp. the plate on which the bread is placed in the Eucharist. [C13: from Old French *patene*, from Medieval Latin, from Latin *patina* pan]

patency (ˈpeɪtᵊnsɪ) *n*. **1.** the condition of being obvious. **2.** the state of a bodily passage, duct, etc., of being open or unobstructed. **3.** *Phonetics*. the degree to which the vocal tract remains unobstructed in the articulation of a speech sound. See also **closure** (sense 6).

patent (ˈpeɪtᵊnt, ˈpætᵊnt) *n*. **1. a.** a government grant to an inventor assuring him the sole right to make, use, and sell his invention for a limited period. **b.** a document conveying such a grant. **2.** an invention, privilege, etc., protected by a patent. **3. a.** an official document granting a right. **b.** any right granted by such a document. **4.** (in the U.S.) **a.** a grant by the government of title to public lands. **b.** the instrument by which such title is granted. **c.** the land so granted. **5.** a sign that one possesses a certain quality. ~*adj*. **6.** open or available for inspection (esp. in the phrases **letters patent, patent writ**). **7.** (ˈpeɪtᵊnt). obvious: *their scorn was patent to everyone*. **8.** concerning protection, appointment, etc., of or by a patent or patents. **9.** proprietary. **10.** (esp. of a bodily passage or duct) being open or unobstructed. **11.** *Biology*. spreading out widely: *patent branches*. **12.** (of plate glass) ground and polished on both sides. ~*vb*. (*tr*.) **13.** to obtain a patent for. **14.** (in the U.S.) to grant (public land or mineral rights) by a patent. **15.** *Metallurgy*. to heat (a metal) above a transformation temperature and cool it at a rate that allows cold working. [C14: via Old French from Latin *patēre* to lie open; n. use, short for *letters patent*, from Medieval Latin *litterae patentes* letters lying open (to public inspection)] —ˈ**patentable** *adj*. —**ˌpatentaˈbility** *n*.

▷ **Usage.** The pronunciation "ˈpætᵊnt" is heard in *letters patent* and *Patent Office* and is the usual U.S. pronunciation for all senses. In Britain "ˈpætᵊnt" is sometimes heard for senses 1, 2 and 3, but "ˈpeɪtᵊnt" is commoner and is regularly used in collocations like *patent leather*.

patentee (ˌpeɪtᵊnˈtiː, ˌpæ-) *n*. a person, group, company, etc., that has been granted a patent.

patent fastener *n*. (in Ireland) another name for **press stud.**

patent leather *n*. leather or imitation leather processed with lacquer to give a hard glossy surface.

patent log *n*. *Nautical*. any of several mechanical devices for measuring the speed of a vessel and the distance travelled, consisting typically of a trailing rotor that registers its rotations on a meter. Compare **chip log.**

patently (ˈpeɪtᵊntlɪ) *adv*. obviously: *he was patently bored*.

patent medicine *n*. a medicine, usually of low potency, protected by a patent and available without a doctor's prescription.

Patent Office (ˈpætᵊnt) *n*. a government department that issues patents. Abbrev.: **Pat. Off.**

patentor (ˌpeɪtᵊnˈtɔː, ˌpæ-) *n*. a person who or official body that grants a patent or patents.

patent right *n*. the exclusive right granted by a patent.

Patent Rolls *pl. n*. (in Britain) the register of patents issued.

patent still *n*. a type of still in which the distillation is continuous. [so called because a still of this type was patented in 1830]

pater (ˈpeɪtə) *n*. *Brit*. a public school slang word for **father:** now chiefly used facetiously. [from Latin]

paterfamilias (ˌpeɪtəfəˈmɪlɪˌæs) *n., pl.* **patresfamilias** (ˌpɑːtreɪzfəˈmɪlɪˌæs). **1.** the male head of a household. **2.** *Roman law.* **a.** the head of a household having authority over its members. **b.** the parental or other authority of another person. [Latin: father of the family]

paternal (pəˈtɜːnᵊl) *adj.* **1.** relating to or characteristic of a father, esp. in showing affection, encouragement, etc.; fatherly. **2.** (*prenominal*) related through the father: *his paternal grandfather.* **3.** inherited or derived from the male parent. [C17: from Late Latin *paternālis,* from Latin *pater* father] —**paˈternally** *adv.*

paternalism (pəˈtɜːnəˌlɪzəm) *n.* the attitude or policy of a government or other authority that manages the affairs of a country, company, community, etc., in the manner of a father, esp. in usurping individual responsibility and the liberty of choice. —**paˈternalist** *n., adj.* —**paˌternalˈistic** *adj.* —**paˌternalˈistically** *adv.*

paternity (pəˈtɜːnɪtɪ) *n.* **1. a.** the fact or state of being a father. **b.** (*as modifier*): *a paternity suit was filed against the man.* **2.** descent or derivation from a father. **3.** authorship or origin: *the paternity of the theory is disputed.* [C15: from Late Latin *paternitās,* from Latin *pater* father]

paternity suit *n. Law.* the U.S. (and in Britain a nontechnical) term for **affiliation proceedings.**

paternoster (ˌpætəˈnɒstə) *n.* **1.** *R.C. Church.* the beads at the ends of each decade of the rosary marking the points at which the Paternoster is recited. **2.** any fixed form of words used as a prayer or charm. **3.** Also called: **paternoster line.** a type of fishing tackle in which short lines and hooks are attached at intervals to the main line. **4.** a type of lift in which platforms are attached to continuous chains. The lift does not stop at each floor but passengers enter while it is moving. [Latin, literally: our father (from the opening of the Lord's Prayer)]

Paternoster (ˌpætəˈnɒstə) *n.* (*sometimes not cap.*) *R.C. Church.* **1.** the Lord's Prayer, esp. in Latin. **2.** the recital of this as an act of devotion. [see PATERNOSTER]

Paterson's curse (ˈpætəsᵊnz) *n.* an Australian name for **viper's bugloss.** [named after A. B. *Paterson* (1864–1941), Australian poet]

path (pɑːθ) *n., pl.* **paths** (pɑːðz). **1.** a road or way, esp. a narrow trodden track. **2.** a surfaced walk, as through a garden. **3.** the course or direction in which something moves: *the path of a whirlwind.* **4.** a course of conduct: *the path of virtue.* [Old English *pæth;* related to Old High German, German *Pfad*] —**ˈpathless** *adj.*

path. (pæθ) *abbrev. for:* **1.** pathological. **2.** pathology.

-path *n. combining form.* **1.** denoting a person suffering from a specified disease or disorder: *neuropath.* **2.** denoting a practitioner of a particular method of treatment: *osteopath.* [back formation from -PATHY]

Pathan (pəˈtɑːn) *n.* a member of the Pashto-speaking people of Afghanistan, NW Pakistan, and elsewhere, most of whom are Muslim in religion. [C17: from Hindi]

pathetic (pəˈθɛtɪk) *adj.* **1.** evoking or expressing pity, sympathy, etc. **2.** distressingly inadequate: *the old man sat huddled in front of a pathetic fire.* **3.** *Brit. informal.* ludicrously or contemptibly uninteresting or worthless: *the standard of goalkeeping in amateur football today is pathetic.* **4.** *Obsolete.* of or affecting the feelings. ~*pl. n.* **5.** pathetic sentiments. [C16: from French *pathétique,* via Late Latin from Greek *pathetikos* sensitive, from *pathos* suffering; see PATHOS] —**paˈthetically** *adv.*

pathetic fallacy *n.* (in literature) the presentation of inanimate objects in nature as possessing human feelings.

pathfinder (ˈpɑːθˌfaɪndə) *n.* **1.** a person who makes or finds a way, esp. through unexplored areas or fields of knowledge. **2.** an aircraft or parachutist who indicates a target area by dropping flares, etc. **3.** a radar device used for navigation or homing onto a target. —**ˈpathˌfinding** *n.*

pathic (ˈpæθɪk) *n.* **1.** a catamite. **2.** a person who suffers; victim. ~*adj.* **3.** of or relating to a catamite. **4.** of or relating to suffering. [C17: via Latin from Greek *pathikos* passive; see PATHOS]

patho- *or before a vowel* **path-** *combining form.* disease: *pathology.* [from Greek *pathos* suffering; see PATHOS]

pathogen (ˈpæθəˌdʒɛn) *or* **pathogene** (ˈpæθəˌdʒiːn) *n.* any agent that can cause disease.

pathogenesis (ˌpæθəˈdʒɛnɪsɪs) *or* **pathogeny** (pəˈθɒdʒɪnɪ) *n.* the origin, development, and resultant effects of a disease. —**pathogenetic** (ˌpæθəʊdʒɪˈnɛtɪk) *adj.*

pathogenic (ˌpæθəˈdʒɛnɪk) *adj.* able to cause or produce disease: *pathogenic bacteria.*

pathognomonic (ˌpæθəgnəˈmɒnɪk) *adj. Pathol.* characteristic or indicative of a particular disease. [C17: from Greek *pathognōmonikos* expert in judging illness, from PATHO- + *gnōmōn* judge] —ˌ**pathognoˈmonically** *adv.*

pathognomy (pəˈθɒgnəmɪ) *n.* study or knowledge of the passions or emotions or their manifestations. [C18: from PATHO- + *-gnomy,* as in PHYSIOGNOMY]

pathol. *abbrev. for:* **1.** pathological. **2.** pathology.

pathological (ˌpæθəˈlɒdʒɪkᵊl) *or* (*less commonly*) **pathologic** *adj.* **1.** of or relating to pathology. **2.** relating to, involving, or caused by disease. **3.** *Informal.* compulsively motivated: *a pathological liar.* —ˌ**pathoˈlogically** *adv.*

pathology (pəˈθɒlədʒɪ) *n., pl.* **-gies. 1.** the branch of medicine concerned with the cause, origin, and nature of disease, including the changes occurring as a result of disease. **2.** the manifestations of disease, esp. changes occurring in tissues or organs. **3.** any variant or deviant condition from normal. —**paˈthologist** *n.*

pathos (ˈpeɪθɒs) *n.* **1.** the quality or power, esp. in literature or speech, of arousing feelings of pity, sorrow, etc. **2.** a feeling of sympathy or pity: *a stab of pathos.* **3.** *Rare or poetic.* a condition of misery. [C17: from Greek: suffering; related to *penthos* sorrow]

pathway (ˈpɑːθˌweɪ) *n.* **1.** another word for **path** (senses 1, 2). **2.** *Biochem.* a chain of reactions associated with a particular metabolic process.

-pathy *n. combining form.* **1.** indicating feeling, sensitivity, or perception: *telepathy.* **2.** indicating disease or a morbid condition: *psychopathy.* **3.** indicating a method of treating disease: *osteopathy.* [from Greek *patheia* suffering; see PATHOS] —**-pathic** *adj. combining form.*

patience (ˈpeɪʃəns) *n.* **1.** tolerant and even-tempered perseverance. **2.** the capacity for calmly enduring pain, trying situations, etc. **3.** *Chiefly Brit.* any of various card games for one player only, in which the cards may be laid out in various combinations as the player tries to use up the whole pack. U.S. equivalent: **solitaire. 4.** *Obsolete.* permission; sufferance. [C13: via Old French from Latin *patientia* endurance, from *patī* to suffer]

patient (ˈpeɪʃənt) *adj.* **1.** enduring trying circumstances with even temper. **2.** tolerant; understanding. **3.** capable of accepting delay with equanimity. **4.** persevering or diligent: *a patient worker.* **5.** *Archaic.* admitting of a certain interpretation. ~*n.* **6.** a person who is receiving medical care. **7.** *Rare.* a person or thing that is the recipient of some action. [C14: see PATIENCE] —**ˈpatiently** *adv.*

patin *or* **patine** (ˈpætɪn) *n.* variants of **paten.**

patina[1] (ˈpætɪnə) *n., pl.* **-nas. 1.** a film of oxide formed on the surface of a metal, esp. the green oxidation of bronze or copper. See also **verdigris** (sense 1). **2.** any fine layer on a surface: *a patina of frost.* **3.** the sheen on a surface that is caused by long handling. [C18: from Italian: coating, from Latin: PATINA[2]]

patina[2] (ˈpætɪnə) *n., pl.* **-nae** (-ˌniː). a broad shallow dish used in ancient Rome. [from Latin, from Greek *patanē* platter]

patio (ˈpætɪˌəʊ) *n., pl.* **-os. 1.** an open inner courtyard, esp. one in a Spanish or Spanish-American house. **2.** an area adjoining a house, esp. one that is paved and used for outdoor activities. [C19: from Spanish: courtyard]

patisserie (pəˈtiːsərɪ) *n.* **1.** a shop where fancy pastries are sold. **2.** such pastries. [C18: French, from *pâtissier* pastry cook, ultimately from Late Latin *pasta* PASTE[1]]

Patna rice (ˈpætnə) *n.* a variety of long-grain rice, used for savoury dishes. [named after *Patna,* a city in NE India]

Pat. Off. *abbrev. for* Patent Office.

patois (ˈpætwɑː; *French* patwa) *n., pl.* **patois** (ˈpætwɑːz; *French* patwa). **1.** an unwritten regional dialect of a language, esp. of French, usually considered substandard. **2.** the jargon of particular group. [C17: from Old French: rustic speech, perhaps from *patoier* to handle awkwardly, from *patte* paw]

pat. pend. *abbrev. for* patent pending.

patri- *combining form.* father: *patricide; patrilocal.* [from Latin *pater,* Greek *patēr* FATHER]

patrial (ˈpeɪtrɪəl) *n.* (in Britain formerly) a person having by statute the right of abode in the United Kingdom, and so not subject to immigration control. [C20: from Latin *patria* native land]

patriarch (ˈpeɪtrɪˌɑːk) *n.* **1.** the male head of a tribe or family. Compare **matriarch** (sense 2). **2.** a very old or venerable man. **3.** *Old Testament.* any of a number of persons regarded as the fathers of the human race, divided into the antediluvian patriarchs, from Adam to Noah, and the postdiluvian, from Noah to Abraham. **4.** *Old Testament.* any of the three ancestors of the Hebrew people: Abraham, Isaac, or Jacob. **5.** *Old Testament.* any of Jacob's twelve sons, regarded as the ancestors of the twelve tribes of Israel. **6.** *Early Christian Church.* the bishop of one of several principal sees, esp. those of Rome, Antioch, and Alexandria. **7.** *Eastern Orthodox Church.* the bishops of the four ancient principal sees of Constantinople, Antioch, Alexandria, and Jerusalem, and also of Russia, Romania, and Serbia, the bishop of Constantinople (the **ecumenical Patriarch**) being highest in dignity among these. **8.** *R.C. Church.* **a.** a title given to the pope. **b.** a title given to a number of bishops, esp. of the Uniat Churches, indicating their rank as immediately below that of the pope. **9.** *Mormon Church.* another word for **Evangelist** (sense 2). **10.** *Eastern Christianity.* the head of the Coptic, Armenian, Syrian Jacobite, or Nestorian Churches, and of certain other non-Orthodox Churches in the East. **11.** the oldest or most venerable member of a group, community, etc.: *the patriarch of steam engines.* **12.** a person regarded as the founder of a community, tradition, etc. [C12: via Old French from Church Latin *patriarcha*] —ˌ**patriˈarchal** *adj.* —ˌ**patriˈarchally** *adv.*

patriarchal cross *n.* a cross with two high horizontal bars, the upper one shorter than the lower.

patriarchate (ˈpeɪtrɪˌɑːkɪt) *n.* **1.** the office, jurisdiction, province, or residence of a patriarch. **2.** a family or people under male domination or government.

patriarchy (ˈpeɪtrɪˌɑːkɪ) *n., pl.* **-chies.** **1.** a form of social organization in which a male is the head of the family and descent, kinship, and title are traced through the male line. **2.** any society governed by such a system.

patrician (pəˈtrɪʃən) *n.* **1.** a member of the hereditary aristocracy of ancient Rome. In the early republic the patricians held almost all the higher offices. Compare **plebs** (sense 2). **2.** a high nonhereditary title awarded by eastern Roman emperors for services to the empire. **3.** (in medieval Europe) **a.** a title borne by numerous princes including several emperors from the 8th to the 12th centuries. **b.** a member of the upper class in numerous Italian republics and German free cities. **4.** an aristocrat. **5.** a person of refined conduct, tastes, etc. ~*adj.* **6.** (esp. in ancient Rome) of, relating to, or composed of patricians. **7.** aristocratic. **8.** oligarchic and often antidemocratic or nonpopular: *patrician political views.* [C15: from Old French *patricien,* from Latin *patricius* noble, from *pater* father]

patriciate (pəˈtrɪʃɪɪt, -ˌeɪt) *n.* **1.** the dignity, position, or rank of a patrician. **2.** the class or order of patricians.

patricide (ˈpætrɪˌsaɪd) *n.* **1.** the act of killing one's father. **2.** a person who kills his father. —ˌ**patriˈcidal** *adj.*

patriclinous (ˌpætrɪˈklaɪnəs), **patroclinous,** *or* **patroclinal** (ˌpætrəˈklaɪnᵊl) *adj.* (of animals and plants) showing the characters of the male parent. Compare **matriclinous.** [C20: from Latin *pater* father + *clīnāre* to incline]

patrilineal (ˌpætrɪˈlɪnɪəl) *or* **patrilinear** *adj.* tracing descent, kinship, or title through the male line. —ˌ**patriˈlineally** *or* ˌ**patriˈlinearly** *adv.*

patrilocal (ˌpætrɪˈləʊkᵊl) *adj.* having or relating to a marriage pattern in which the couple lives with the husband's family. —ˌ**patriˈlocally** *adv.*

patrimony (ˈpætrɪmənɪ) *n., pl.* **-nies.** **1.** an inheritance from one's father or other ancestor. **2.** the endowment of a church. [C14 *patrimoyne,* from Old French, from Latin *patrimonium* paternal inheritance] —**patrimonial** (ˌpætrɪˈməʊnɪəl) *adj.* —ˌ**patriˈmonially** *adv.*

patriot (ˈpeɪtrɪət, ˈpæt-) *n.* a person who vigorously supports his country and its way of life. [C16: via French from Late Latin *patriōta,* from Greek *patriōtēs,* from *patris* native land; related to Greek *patēr* father; compare Latin *pater* father, *patria* fatherland] —**patriotic** (ˌpætrɪˈɒtɪk) *adj.* —ˌ**patriˈotically** *adv.*

patriotism (ˈpætrɪəˌtɪzəm) *n.* devotion to one's own country and concern for its defence. Compare **nationalism.**

patristic (pəˈtrɪstɪk) *or* **patristical** *adj.* of or relating to the Fathers of the Church, their writings, or the study of these. —**paˈtristically** *adv.* —**paˈtristics** *n.* (*functioning as sing.*)

patrol (pəˈtrəʊl) *n.* **1.** the action of going through or around a town, neighbourhood, etc., at regular intervals for purposes of security or observation. **2.** a person or group that carries out such an action. **3.** a military detachment with the mission of security, gathering information, or combat with enemy forces. **4.** a division of a troop of Scouts or Guides. ~*vb.* **-trols, -trolling, -trolled. 5.** to engage in a patrol of (a place). [C17: from French *patrouiller,* from *patouiller* to flounder in mud, from *patte* paw] —**paˈtroller** *n.*

patrol car *n.* a police car with a radio telephone used for patrolling streets and motorways. See also **panda car.**

patrolman (pəˈtrəʊlmən) *n., pl.* **-men.** **1.** *Chiefly U.S.* a man, esp. a policeman, who patrols a certain area. **2.** *Brit.* a man employed to patrol an area to help motorists in difficulty.

patrology (pəˈtrɒlədʒɪ) *n.* **1.** the study of the writings of the Fathers of the Church. **2.** a collection of such writings. [C17: from Greek *patr-, patēr* father + -LOGY] —**patrological** (ˌpætrəˈlɒdʒɪkᵊl) *adj.* —**paˈtrologist** *n.*

patrol wagon *n.* the usual U.S., Austral., and N.Z. term for **Black Maria.** Also called (U.S.): **police wagon.**

patron[1] (ˈpeɪtrən) *n.* **1.** a person who sponsors or aids artists, charities, etc.; protector or benefactor. **2.** a customer of a shop, hotel, etc., esp. a regular one. **3.** See **patron saint.** **4.** (in ancient Rome) the protector of a dependant or client, often the former master of a freedman still retaining certain rights over him. **5.** *Church of England, etc.* a person or body having the right to present a clergyman to a benefice. [C14: via Old French from Latin *patrōnus* protector, from *pater* father] —**patronal** (pəˈtrəʊnᵊl) *adj.* —ˈ**patroness** *fem. n.* —ˈ**patronly** *adj.*

patron[2] (ˈpætərn) *n. Irish.* a variant spelling of **pattern**[2].

patronage (ˈpætrənɪdʒ) *n.* **1. a.** the support given or custom brought by a patron. **b.** the position of a patron. **2.** (in politics) **a.** the practice of making appointments to office, granting contracts, etc. **b.** the favours so distributed. **3. a.** a condescending manner. **b.** any kindness done in a condescending way. **4.** *Church of England, etc.* the right to present a clergyman to a benefice.

patronize *or* **patronise** (ˈpætrəˌnaɪz) *vb.* **1.** to behave or treat in a condescending way. **2.** (*tr.*) to act as a patron by sponsoring or bringing trade to. —ˈ**patronˌizer** *or* ˈ**patronˌiser** *n.*

patronizing *or* **patronising** (ˈpætrəˌnaɪzɪŋ) *adj.* having a superior manner; condescending. —ˈ**patronˌizingly** *or* ˈ**patronˌisingly** *adv.*

patron saint *n.* a saint regarded as the particular guardian of a country, church, trade, person, etc.

patronymic (ˌpætrəˈnɪmɪk) *adj.* **1.** (of a name) derived from the name of its bearer's father or ancestor. In Western cultures, many surnames are patronymic in origin, as for example Irish names beginning with *O'* and English names ending with *-son;* in other cultures, such as Russian, a special patronymic name is used in addition to the surname. ~*n.* **2.** a patronymic name. [C17: via Late Latin from Greek *patronumikos,* from *patēr* father + *onoma* NAME]

patroon (pəˈtruːn) *n.* (in the U.S.) a Dutch land-holder in New Netherland and New York with manorial rights in the colonial era. [C18: from Dutch: PATRON[1]] —**paˈtroonˌship** *n.*

patsy (ˈpætsɪ) *n., pl.* **-sies.** *Slang, chiefly U.S. and Canadian.* a person who is easily cheated, victimized, etc. [C20: of unknown origin]

pattée (ˈpæteɪ, ˈpætɪ) *adj.* (*often postpositive*) (of a cross) having triangular arms widening outwards. [from French *patte* paw]

patten (ˈpætᵊn) *n.* a wooden clog or sandal on a raised wooden platform or metal ring. [C14: from Old French *patin,* probably from *patte* paw]

patter[1] (ˈpætə) *vb.* **1.** (*intr.*) to walk or move with quick soft steps. **2.** to strike with or make a quick succession of light tapping sounds. **3.** (*tr.*) *Rare.* to cause to patter. ~*n.* **4.** a quick succession of light tapping sounds, as of feet: *the patter of mice.* [C17: from PAT[1]]

patter[2] (ˈpætə) *n.* **1.** the glib rapid speech of comedians, salesmen, etc. **2.** quick idle talk; chatter. **3.** the jargon of a particular group; lingo. ~*vb.* **4.** (*intr.*) to speak glibly and rapidly. **5.** to repeat (prayers) in a mechanical or perfunctory manner. [C14: from Latin *pater* in *Pater Noster* Our Father]

pattern[1] (ˈpætᵊn) *n.* **1.** an arrangement of repeated or corresponding parts, decorative motifs, etc.: *although the notes seemed random, a careful listener could detect a pattern.* **2.** a decorative design: *a paisley pattern.* **3.** a style: *various patterns of cutlery.* **4.** a plan or diagram used as a guide in making something: *a paper pattern for a dress.* **5.** a standard way of moving, acting, etc.: *traffic patterns.* **6.** a model worthy of imitation: *a pattern of kindness.* **7.** a representative sample. **8.** a wooden or metal shape or model used in a foundry to make a mould. **9. a.** the arrangement of marks made in a target by bullets. **b.** a diagram displaying such an arrangement. ~*vb.* (*tr.*) **10.** (often foll. by *after* or *on*) to model. **11.** to arrange as or decorate with a pattern. [C14 *patron,* from Medieval Latin *patrōnus* example, from Latin: PATRON[1]]

pattern[2] *or* **patron** (ˈpætərn) *n. Irish.* an outdoor assembly with religious practices, traders' stalls, etc. on the feast day of a patron saint. [C18: variant of PATRON[1]; see PATTERN[1]]

patter song *n. Music.* a humorous song or aria, the text of which consists of rapid strings of words.

patty (ˈpætɪ) *n., pl.* **-ties.** **1.** a small flattened cake of minced food. **2.** a small pie. [C18: from French PÂTÉ]

patu (ˈpɑːtuː) *n., pl.* **patus.** *N.Z.* a short Maori club, now used ceremonially. [Maori]

patulous (ˈpætjʊləs) *adj.* **1.** *Botany.* spreading widely or expanded: *patulous branches.* **2.** *Rare.* gaping. [C17: from Latin *patulus* open, from *patēre* to lie open] —ˈ**patulously** *adv.* —ˈ**patulousness** *n.*

patutuki (ˈpɑːtuːˌtuːkɪ) *n. N.Z.* another name for **blue cod.**

PAU *abbrev. for* Pan American Union.

paua (ˈpɑːʊɑ) *n.* an edible abalone, *Haliotis iris,* of New Zealand, having an iridescent shell used esp. for jewellery. [from Maori]

paucal (ˈpɔːkᵊl) *Grammar.* ~*n.* **1.** a grammatical number occurring in some languages for words in contexts where a few of their referents are described or referred to. ~*adj.* **2.** relating to or inflected for this number. [from Latin *paucus* few]

paucity (ˈpɔːsɪtɪ) *n.* **1.** smallness of quantity; insufficiency; dearth. **2.** smallness of number; fewness. [C15: from Latin *paucitās* scarcity, from *paucus* few]

pauldron (ˈpɔːldrən) *n.* either of two metal plates worn with armour to protect the shoulders. [C15: from French *espauleron,* from *espaule* shoulder; see EPAULETTE]

Pauli exclusion principle (ˈpɔːlɪ, ˈpaʊlɪ) *n. Physics.* the principle that two identical fermions cannot occupy the same quantum state in a body such as an atom; sometimes shortened to **exclusion principle.** [named after Wolfgang *Pauli* (1900–58), U.S. physicist]

Pauline (ˈpɔːlaɪn) *adj.* relating to Saint Paul (died ?67 A.D.) or his doctrines.

Paul Jones (pɔːl dʒəʊnz) *n.* an old-time dance in which partners are exchanged. [C19: named after John Paul *Jones* (1747–92), U.S. naval commander]

paulownia (pɔːˈləʊnɪə) *n.* any scrophulariaceous tree of the Japanese genus *Paulownia,* esp. *P. tomentosa,* having large heart-shaped leaves and clusters of purplish or white flowers. [C19: New Latin, named after Anna *Paulovna,* daughter of Paul I of Russia]

Paul Pry *n.* a nosy person. [C19: from a character in the play *Paul Pry* by John Poole (1825)]

paunch (pɔːntʃ) *n.* **1.** the belly or abdomen, esp. when protruding. **2.** another name for **rumen.** **3.** *Nautical.* a thick mat that prevents chafing. ~*vb.* (*tr.*) **4.** to stab in the stomach; disembowel. [C14: from Anglo-Norman *paunche,* from Old French *pance,* from Latin *panticēs* (pl.) bowels] —'**paunchy** *adj.* —'**paunchiness** *n.*

pauper ('pɔːpə) *n.* **1.** a person who is extremely poor. **2.** (formerly) a destitute person supported by public charity. [C16: from Latin: poor] —'**pauper,ism** *n.*

pauperize *or* **pauperise** ('pɔːpə,raɪz) *vb.* (*tr.*) to make a pauper of; impoverish.

pauropod ('pɔːrə,pɒd) *n.* a member of the *Pauropoda,* a class of minute myriapods less than 2 mm (1/20 in.) in size, having 8 to 10 pairs of legs and branched antennae.

pause (pɔːz) *vb.* (*intr.*) **1.** to cease an action temporarily; stop. **2.** to hesitate; delay: *she replied without pausing.* ~*n.* **3.** a temporary stop or rest, esp. in speech or action; short break. **4.** *Prosody.* another word for **caesura. 5.** Also called: **fermata.** *Music.* a continuation of a note or rest beyond its normal length. Usual symbol: 𝄐 **6. give pause to.** to cause to hesitate. [C15: from Latin *pausa* pause, from Greek *pausis,* from *pauein* to halt] —'**pausal** *adj.* —'**pauser** *n.* —'**pausing** *n., adj.*

pav (pæv) *n. Austral. and N.Z. informal.* short for **pavlova.**

pavage ('peɪvɪdʒ) *n.* **1.** a tax towards paving streets. **2.** the right to levy such a tax. **3.** the act of paving.

pavane *or* **pavan** (pə'vɑːn, -'væn, 'pævᵊn) *n.* **1.** a slow and stately dance of the 16th and 17th centuries. **2.** a piece of music composed for or in the rhythm of this dance, usually characterized by a slow stately triple time. [C16 *pavan,* via French from Spanish *pavana,* from Old Italian *padovana* Paduan (dance), from *Padova* Padua]

pave (peɪv) *vb.* (*tr.*) **1.** to cover (a road, path, etc.) with a firm surface suitable for travel, as with paving stones or concrete. **2.** to serve as the material for a pavement or other hard layer: *bricks paved the causeway.* **3.** (often foll. by *with*) to cover with a hard layer (of): *shelves paved with marble.* **4.** to prepare or make easier (esp. in the phrase **pave the way**): *to pave the way for future development.* [C14: from Old French *paver,* from Latin *pavīre* to ram down] —'**paver** *n.*

pavé ('pæveɪ) *n.* **1.** a paved surface, esp. an uneven one. **2.** a style of setting gems so closely that no metal shows.

pavement ('peɪvmənt) *n.* **1.** a hard-surfaced path for pedestrians alongside and a little higher than a road. U.S. and Canadian word: **sidewalk. 2.** a paved surface, esp. one that is a thoroughfare. **3.** the material used in paving. **4.** *Civil engineering.* the hard layered structure that forms a road carriageway, airfield runway, vehicle park, or other paved areas. **5.** *Geology.* a level area of exposed rock. See **limestone pavement.** [C13: from Latin *pavīmentum* a hard floor, from *pavīre* to beat hard]

pavid ('pævɪd) *adj. Rare.* fearful; timid. [C17: from Latin *pavidus* fearful, from *pavēre* to tremble with fear]

pavilion (pə'vɪljən) *n.* **1.** *Brit.* a building at a sports ground, esp. a cricket pitch, in which players change. **2.** a summerhouse or other decorative shelter. **3.** a building or temporary structure, esp. one that is open and ornamental, for housing exhibitions. **4.** a large ornate tent, esp. one with a peaked top, as used by medieval armies. **5.** one of a set of buildings that together form a hospital or other large institution. **6.** one of four main facets on a brilliant-cut stone between the girdle and the culet. ~*vb.* (*tr.*) *Literary.* **7.** to place or set in or as if in a pavilion: *pavilioned in splendour.* **8.** to provide with a pavilion or pavilions. [C13: from Old French *pavillon* canopied structure, from Latin *pāpiliō* butterfly, tent]

paving ('peɪvɪŋ) *n.* **1.** a paved surface; pavement. **2.** material used for a pavement. ~*adj.* **3.** of or for a paved surface or pavement. **4.** preparatory, facilitating, enabling: *paving legislation.*

paving stone *n.* a concrete or stone slab for paving.

paviour *or U.S.* **pavior** ('peɪvjə) *n.* **1.** a person who lays paving. **2.** a machine for ramming down paving. **3.** material used for paving. [C15: from *paver,* from PAVE]

pavis *or* **pavise** ('pævɪs) *n.* a large square shield, developed in the 15th century, at first portable but later heavy and set up in a permanent position. [C14: from Old French *pavais,* from Italian *pavese* of *Pavia,* Italian city where these shields were originally made]

pavlova (pæv'ləʊvə) *n.* a meringue cake topped with whipped cream and fruit. [C20: named after Anna *Pavlova* (1885–1931), Russian ballerina]

Pavlovian (pæv'ləʊvɪən) *adj.* **1.** of or relating to the work of Ivan Pavlov (1849–1936), Soviet physiologist noted for his studies of conditioned reflexes in dogs. **2.** (of a reaction or response) automatic; involuntary.

Pavo ('pɑːvəʊ) *n., Latin genitive* **Pavonis** (pə'vəʊnɪs). a small constellation near the South Pole lying between Tucana and Ara. [Latin: peacock]

pavonine ('pævə,naɪn) *adj.* of or resembling a peacock or the colours, design, or iridescence of a peacock's tail. [C17: from Latin *pāvōnīnus,* from *pāvō* peacock]

paw (pɔː) *n.* **1.** any of the feet of a four-legged mammal, bearing claws or nails. **2.** *Informal.* a hand, esp. one that is large, clumsy, etc. ~*vb.* **3.** to scrape or contaminate with the paws or feet. **4.** (*tr.*) *Informal.* to touch or caress in a clumsy, rough, or over-familiar manner; maul. [C13: via Old French from Germanic; related to Middle Dutch *pōte,* German *Pfote*]

pawky ('pɔːkɪ) *adj.* **pawkier, pawkiest.** *Dialect or Scot.* having or characterized by a dry wit. [C17: from Scottish *pawk* trick, of unknown origin] —'**pawkily** *adv.* —'**pawkiness** *n.*

pawl (pɔːl) *n.* a pivoted lever shaped to engage with a ratchet wheel to prevent motion in a particular direction. [C17: perhaps from Dutch *pal* pawl]

pawn[1] (pɔːn) *vb.* (*tr.*) **1.** to deposit (an article) as security for the repayment of a loan, esp. from a pawnbroker. **2.** to stake: *to pawn one's honour.* ~*n.* **3.** an article deposited as security. **4.** the condition of being so deposited (esp. in the phrase **in pawn**). **5.** a person or thing that is held as a security, esp. a hostage. **6.** the act of pawning. [C15: from Old French *pan* security, from Latin *pannus* cloth, apparently because clothing was often left as a surety; compare Middle Flemish *paen* pawn, German *Pfand* pledge] —'**pawnage** *n.*

pawn[2] (pɔːn) *n.* **1.** a chessman of the lowest theoretical value, limited to forward moves of one square at a time with the option of two squares on its initial move: it captures with a diagonal move only. Abbrev.: **P.** Compare **piece** (sense 12). **2.** a person, group, etc., manipulated by another. [C14: from Anglo-Norman *poun,* from Old French *pehon,* from Medieval Latin *pedō* infantryman, from Latin *pēs* foot]

pawnbroker ('pɔːn,brəʊkə) *n.* a dealer licensed to lend money at a specified rate of interest on the security of movable personal property, which can be sold if the loan is not repaid within a specified period. —'**pawn,broking** *n.*

Pawnee (pɔː'niː) *n.* **1.** (*pl.* **-nees** *or* **-nee**) a member of a confederacy of related North American Indian peoples, formerly living in Nebraska and Kansas, now chiefly in Oklahoma. **2.** the language of these peoples, belonging to the Caddoan family.

pawnshop ('pɔːn,ʃɒp) *n.* the premises of a pawnbroker.

pawn ticket *n.* a receipt for goods pawned.

pawpaw ('pɔː,pɔː) *n.* a variant of **papaw** or **papaya.**

pax (pæks) *n.* **1.** *Chiefly R.C. Church.* **a.** a greeting signifying Christian love transmitted from one to another of those assisting at the Eucharist; kiss of peace. **b.** a small metal or ivory plate, often with a representation of the Crucifixion, formerly used to convey the kiss of peace from the celebrant at Mass to those attending it, who kissed the plate in turn. ~*interj.* **2.** *Brit. school slang.* a call signalling an end to hostilities or claiming immunity from the rules of a game: usually accompanied by a crossing of the fingers. [Latin: peace]

PAX *abbrev. for* private automatic exchange.

pax vobiscum *Latin.* (pæks vəʊ'bɪskʊm) peace be with you.

paxwax ('pæks,wæks) *n. Dialect.* a strong ligament in the neck of many mammals, which supports the head. [C15: changed from C14 *fax wax,* probably from Old English *feax* hair of the head, *wax* growth]

pay[1] (peɪ) *vb.* **pays, paying, paid. 1.** to discharge (a debt, obligation, etc.) by giving or doing something: *he paid his creditors.* **2.** (when *intr.,* often foll. by *for*) to give (money) to (a person) in return for goods or services: *they pay their workers well; they pay by the hour.* **3.** to give or afford (a person) a profit or benefit: *it pays one to be honest.* **4.** (*tr.*) to give or bestow (a compliment, regards, attention, etc.). **5.** (*tr.*) to make (a visit or call). **6.** (*intr.;* often foll. by *for*) to give compensation or make amends. **7.** (*tr.*) to yield a return of: *the shares pay 15 per cent.* **8.** to give or do (something equivalent) in return; pay back: *he paid for the insult with a blow.* **9.** (*tr.; past tense and past participle* **paid** *or* **payed**) *Nautical.* to allow (a vessel) to make leeway. **10.** *Austral. informal.* to acknowledge or accept (something) as true, just, etc. **11. pay one's way. a.** to contribute one's share of expenses. **b.** to remain solvent without outside help. ~*n.* **12. a.** money given in return for work or services; a salary or wage. **b.** (*as modifier*): *a pay slip; pay claim.* **13.** paid employment (esp. in the phrase **in the pay of**). **14.** *Rare.* a person considered in regard to his ability to pay or promptitude in paying debts, bills, etc. **15.** (*modifier*) requiring the insertion of money or discs before or during use: *a pay phone; a pay toilet.* **16.** (*modifier*) rich enough in minerals to be profitably mined or worked: *pay gravel.* ~See also **pay back, pay down, pay for, pay in, pay off, pay out, pay up.** [C12: from Old French *payer,* from Latin *pācāre* to appease (a creditor), from *pāx* PEACE]

pay[2] (peɪ) *vb.* **pays, paying, payed.** (*tr.*) *Nautical.* to caulk (the seams of a wooden vessel) with pitch or tar. [C17: from Old French *peier,* from Latin *picāre,* from *pix* pitch]

payable ('peɪəbᵊl) *adj.* **1.** (often foll. by *on*) to be paid: *payable on the third of each month.* **2.** that is capable of being paid. **3.** capable of being profitable. **4.** (of a debt) imposing an obligation on the debtor to pay, esp. at once.

pay back *vb.* (*tr., adv.*) **1.** to retaliate against: *to pay someone back for an insult.* **2.** to give or do (something equivalent) in return for a favour, insult, etc. **3.** to repay (a loan). ~*n.* **payback. 4. a.** the return on an investment. **b.** Also called: **payback period.** the time taken for a project to cover its outlay.

pay bed *n.* an informal name for **amenity bed** or **private pay bed.**

payday ('peɪ,deɪ) *n.* the day on which wages or salaries are paid.

pay dirt *n.* **1.** a deposit rich enough in minerals to be worth mining. **2. strike** *or* **hit pay dirt.** *Informal.* to achieve one's objective.

pay down *vb.* (*adv.*) to pay (a sum of money) at the time of purchase as the first of a series of instalments.

PAYE (in Britain and New Zealand) *abbrev. for* pay as you earn; a system by which income tax levied on wage and salary earners is paid by employers directly to the government.

payee (peɪ'iː) *n.* **1.** the person to whom a cheque, money order, etc., is made out. **2.** a person to whom money is paid or due.

payer ('peɪə) *n.* **1.** a person who pays. **2.** the person named in a commercial paper as responsible for its payment on redemption.

pay for *vb.* (*prep.*) **1.** to make payment (of) for. **2.** (*intr.*) to suffer or be punished, as for a mistake, wrong decision, etc.: *in his old age he paid for the laxity of his youth.*

pay in *vb.* (*tr., adv.*) to hand (money, a cheque, etc.) to a cashier for depositing in a bank account.

paying guest *n.* a euphemism for **lodger.** Abbrev.: **PG.**

payload ('peɪˌləʊd) *n.* **1.** that part of a cargo earning revenue. **2. a.** the passengers, cargo, or bombs carried by an aircraft. **b.** the equipment carried by a rocket, satellite, or spacecraft. **3.** the explosive power of a warhead, bomb, etc., carried by a missile or aircraft: *a missile carrying a 50-megaton payload.*

paymaster ('peɪˌmɑːstə) *n.* an official of a government, business, etc., responsible for the payment of wages and salaries.

payment ('peɪmənt) *n.* **1.** the act of paying. **2.** a sum of money paid. **3.** something given in return; punishment or reward.

payment by results *n.* a system of wage payment whereby all or part of the wage varies systematically according to the level of work performance of an employee.

paynim ('peɪnɪm) *n. Archaic.* **1.** a heathen or pagan. **2.** a Muslim. [C13: from Old French *paienime,* from Late Latin *pāgānismus* paganism, from *pāgānus* PAGAN]

pay off *vb.* **1.** (*tr., adv.*) to pay all that is due in wages, etc., and discharge from employment. **2.** (*tr., adv.*) to pay the complete amount of (a debt, bill, etc.). **3.** (*intr., adv.*) to turn out to be profitable, effective, etc.: *the gamble paid off.* **4.** (*tr., adv.* or *intr., prep.*) to take revenge on (a person) or for (a wrong done): *to pay someone off for an insult.* **5.** (*tr., adv.*) *Informal.* to give a bribe to. **6.** (*intr., adv.*) *Nautical.* (of a vessel) to make leeway. ~*n.* **payoff. 7.** the final settlement, esp. in retribution: *the payoff came when the gang besieged the squealer's house.* **8.** *Informal.* the climax, consequence, or outcome of events, a story, etc., esp. when unexpected or improbable. **9.** the final payment of a debt, salary, etc. **10.** the time of such a payment. **11.** *Informal.* a bribe.

payola (peɪ'əʊlə) *n. Informal, chiefly U.S.* **1.** a bribe given to secure special treatment, esp. to a disc jockey to promote a commercial product. **2.** the practice of paying or receiving such bribes. [C20: from PAY[1] + *-ola,* as in *Pianola*]

pay out *vb.* (*adv.*) **1.** to distribute (money); disburse. **2.** (*tr.*) to release (a rope) gradually, hand over hand. **3.** (*tr.*) to retaliate against. ~*n.* **payout. 4.** a sum of money paid out.

payphone ('peɪˌfəʊn) *n.* a public telephone operated by coins or a phonecard.

payroll ('peɪˌrəʊl) *n.* **1.** a list of employees, specifying the salary or wage of each. **2. a.** the total of these amounts or the actual money equivalent. **b.** (*as modifier*): *a payroll tax.*

payt *abbrev. for* payment.

pay television *n.* a system by which television programmes are transmitted in scrambled form, unintelligible except to those who have paid for descrambling equipment. Also called: **subscription television.**

pay up *vb.* (*adv.*) to pay (money) promptly, in full, or on demand.

pazzazz *or* **pazazz** (pə'zæz) *n. Informal.* variants of **pizzazz.**

Pb *the chemical symbol for* lead. [from New Latin *plumbum*]

PB *abbrev. for:* **1.** British Pharmacopoeia. **2.** Prayer Book. **3.** *Athletics.* personal best.

PBX (in Britain) *abbrev. for* private branch exchange; a telephone system that handles the internal and external calls of a building, firm, etc.

pc *abbrev. for:* **1.** per cent. **2.** postcard. **3.** (in prescriptions) post cibum. [Latin: after meals]

PC *abbrev. for:* **1.** personal computer. **2.** Parish Council(lor). **3.** Past Commander. **4.** (in Britain) Police Constable. **5.** Post Commander. **6.** Prince Consort. **7.** (in Britain) Privy Council(lor). **8.** (in Canada) Progressive Conservative.

pc. *abbrev. for:* **1.** (*pl.* **pcs.**) piece. **2.** price.

P/C, p/c, *or* **p.c.** *abbrev. for:* **1.** petty cash. **2.** price current.

PCB *abbrev. for* polychlorinated biphenyl.

pcm *abbrev. for* pulse code modulation.

PCP *n. Trademark.* phencyclidine; a depressant drug used illegally as a hallucinogen. Informal name: **angel dust.**

PCR *abbrev. for* polymerase chain reaction: a technique for rapidly producing many copies of a fragment of DNA for diagnostic or research purposes.

pct *U.S. abbrev. for* per cent.

pd *abbrev. for:* **1.** paid. **2.** Also: **PD.** per diem. **3.** potential difference.

Pd *the chemical symbol for* palladium.

PD (in the U.S.) *abbrev. for* Police Department.

pdq *Slang. abbrev. for* pretty damn quick.

PDR *abbrev. for* price-dividend ratio.

P-D ratio *n.* short for price-dividend ratio.

PDSA (in Britain) *abbrev. for* People's Dispensary for Sick Animals.

pe (peɪ; *Hebrew* pe) *n.* the 17th letter in the Hebrew alphabet (פ or, at the end of a word, ף) transliterated as *p* or, when final, *ph.* [from Hebrew *peh* mouth]

PE *abbrev. for:* **1.** physical education. **2.** potential energy. **3.** Presiding Elder. **4.** Prince Edward Island (Canadian Province). **5.** Also: **p.e.** printer's error. **6.** *Statistics.* probable error. **7.** Protestant Episcopal. ~**8.** *international car registration for* Peru.

pea (piː) *n.* **1.** an annual climbing papilionaceous plant, *Pisum sativum,* with small white flowers and long green pods containing edible green seeds: cultivated in temperate regions. **2. a.** the seed of this plant, eaten as a vegetable. **b.** (*as modifier*): *pea soup.* **3.** any of several other leguminous plants, such as the sweet pea, chickpea, and cowpea. **4. the pea.** *Austral. informal.* the favourite to succeed. [C17: from PEASE (incorrectly assumed to be a plural)] —'**pea,like** *adj.*

peace (piːs) *n.* **1. a.** the state existing during the absence of war. **b.** (*as modifier*): *peace negotiations.* **2.** (*modifier*) denoting a person or thing symbolizing support for international peace: *peace women.* **3.** (*often cap.*) a treaty marking the end of a war. **4.** a state of harmony between people or groups; freedom from strife. **5.** law and order within a state; absence of violence or other disturbance: *a breach of the peace.* **6.** absence of mental anxiety (often in the phrase **peace of mind**). **7.** a state of stillness, silence, or serenity. **8. at peace. a.** in a state of harmony or friendship. **b.** in a state of serenity. **c.** dead: *the old lady is at peace now.* **9. hold** *or* **keep one's peace.** to keep silent. **10. keep the peace.** to maintain or refrain from disturbing law and order. **11. make one's peace with.** to become reconciled with. **12. make peace.** to bring hostilities to an end. ~*vb.* **13.** (*intr.*) *Obsolete except as an imperative.* to be or become silent or still. [C12: from Old French *pais,* from Latin *pāx*]

peaceable ('piːsəbᵊl) *adj.* **1.** inclined towards peace. **2.** tranquil; calm. —'**peaceableness** *n.* —'**peaceably** *adv.*

peaceful ('piːsfʊl) *adj.* **1.** not in a state of war or disagreement. **2.** tranquil; calm. **3.** not involving violence: *peaceful picketing.* **4.** of, relating to, or in accord with a time of peace: *peaceful uses of atomic energy.* **5.** inclined towards peace. —'**peacefully** *adv.* —'**peacefulness** *n.*

peacekeeping ('piːsˌkiːpɪŋ) *n.* **a.** the maintenance of peace, esp. the prevention of further fighting between hostile forces in an area. **b.** (*as modifier*): *a UN peacekeeping force.* —'**peace,keeper** *n.*

peacemaker ('piːsˌmeɪkə) *n.* a person who establishes peace, esp. between others. —'**peace,making** *n.*

peace offering *n.* **1.** something given to an adversary in the hope of procuring or maintaining peace. **2.** *Judaism.* a sacrificial meal shared between the offerer and Jehovah to intensify the union between them.

peace pipe *n.* a long decorated pipe smoked by North American Indians on ceremonial occasions, esp. as a token of peace. Also called: **calumet, pipe of peace.**

peace sign *n.* a gesture made with the palm of the hand outwards and the index and middle fingers raised in a V. See also **V-sign** (sense 2).

peacetime ('piːsˌtaɪm) *n.* **a.** a period without war; time of peace. **b.** (*as modifier*): *a peacetime agreement.*

peach[1] (piːtʃ) *n.* **1.** a small rosaceous tree, *Prunus persica,* with pink flowers and rounded edible fruit: cultivated in temperate regions. See also **nectarine** (sense 1). **2.** the soft juicy fruit of this tree, which has a downy reddish-yellow skin, yellowish-orange sweet flesh, and a single stone. See also **nectarine** (sense 2). **3. a.** a pinkish-yellow to orange colour. **b.** (*as adj.*): *a peach dress.* **4.** *Informal.* a person or thing that is especially pleasing. [C14 *peche,* from Old French, from Medieval Latin *persica,* from Latin *Persicum mālum* Persian apple]

peach[2] (piːtʃ) *vb.* (*intr. except in obsolete uses*) *Slang.* to inform against an accomplice. [C15: variant of earlier *apeche,* from French, from Late Latin *impedicāre* to entangle; see IMPEACH] —'**peacher** *n.*

peach-blow *n.* **1. a.** a delicate purplish-pink colour. **b.** (*as adj.*): *a peach-blow vase.* **2.** a glaze of this colour on Oriental porcelain. [C19: from PEACH[1] + BLOW[3]]

peach brandy *n.* (esp. in S. Africa) a brandy made from fermented peaches.

peach melba *n.* a dessert made of halved peaches, vanilla ice cream, and melba sauce.

peachy ('piːtʃɪ) *adj.* **peachier, peachiest. 1.** of or like a peach, esp. in colour or texture. **2.** *Informal.* excellent; fine. —'**peachily** *adv.* —'**peachiness** *n.*

peacock ('piːˌkɒk) *n., pl.* **-cocks** *or* **-cock. 1.** a male peafowl, having a crested head and a very large fanlike tail marked with blue and green eyelike spots. Related adj.: **pavonine. 2.** another name for **peafowl. 3.** a vain strutting person. ~*vb.* **4.** to display (oneself) proudly. **5.** *Obsolete slang, Austral.* to acquire (the best pieces of land) in such a way that the surrounding land is useless to others. [C14 *pecok, pe-* from Old English *pāwa* (from Latin *pāvō* peacock) + COCK[1]] —'**pea,cockish** *adj.* —'**pea,hen** *fem. n.*

peacock blue *n.* **a.** a greenish-blue colour. **b.** (*as adj.*): *a peacock-blue car.*

peacock butterfly *n.* a European nymphalid butterfly, *Inachis io,* having reddish-brown wings each marked with a purple eye-spot.
peacock ore *n.* another name for **bornite.**
peacock's tail *n.* a handsome brown seaweed, *Padina pavonia* (though coloured yellow-olive, red, and green) whose fan-shaped fronds have concentric bands of iridescent hairs.
pea crab *n.* any of various globular soft-bodied crabs of the genus *Pinnotheres* and related genera that live commensally in the mantles of certain bivalves.
peafowl ('piːˌfaʊl) *n., pl.* **-fowls** *or* **-fowl. 1.** either of two large pheasants, *Pavo cristatus* (**blue peafowl**) of India and Ceylon and *P. muticus* (**green peafowl**) of SE Asia. The males (see **peacock** (sense 1)) have a characteristic bright plumage. **2.** a rare closely related African species, *Afropavo congensis* (**Congo peafowl**), both sexes of which are brightly coloured.
peag *or* **peage** (piːg) *n.* less common words for **wampum.** [shortened from Narraganset *wampompeag* WAMPUM]
pea green *n.* **a.** a yellowish-green colour. **b.** (*as adj.*): *a pea-green teapot.*
pea jacket *or* **peacoat** ('piːˌkəʊt) *n.* a sailor's short heavy double-breasted overcoat of navy wool. [C18: from Dutch *pijjekker,* from *pij* coat of coarse cloth + *jekker* jacket]
peak[1] (piːk) *n.* **1.** a pointed end, edge, or projection: *the peak of a roof.* **2.** the pointed summit of a mountain. **3.** a mountain with a pointed summit. **4.** the point of greatest development, strength, etc.: *the peak of his career.* **5. a.** a sharp increase in a physical quantity followed by a sharp decrease: *a voltage peak.* **b.** the maximum value of this quantity. **c.** (*as modifier*): *peak voltage.* **6.** Also called: **visor.** a projecting piece on the front of some caps. **7. a.** See **widow's peak. b.** the pointed end of a beard. **8.** *Nautical.* **a.** the extreme forward (**forepeak**) or aft (**afterpeak**) part of the hull. **b.** (of a fore-and-aft quadrilateral sail) the after uppermost corner. **c.** the after end of a gaff. ~*vb.* **9.** (*tr.*) *Nautical.* to set (a gaff) or tilt (oars) vertically. **10.** to form or reach or cause to form or reach a peak or maximum. ~*adj.* **11.** of or relating to a period of highest use or demand, as for watching television, commuting, etc.: *peak viewing hours; peak time.* [C16: perhaps from PIKE[2], influenced by BEAK[1]; compare Spanish *pico,* French *pic,* Middle Low German *pēk*] —'**peaky** *adj.*
peak[2] (piːk) *vb.* (*intr.*) to become wan, emaciated, or sickly. [C16: of uncertain origin] —'**peaky** *or* '**peakish** *adj.*
peaked (piːkt) *adj.* having a peak; pointed.
peak load *n.* the maximum load on an electrical power-supply system. Compare **base load.**
peak programme meter *n.* an instrument for assessing the maximum levels of an electrical sound signal. Abbrevs.: **PPM, ppm.**
peal[1] (piːl) *n.* **1.** a loud prolonged usually reverberating sound, as of bells, thunder, or laughter. **2.** *Bell-ringing.* a series of changes rung in accordance with specific rules, consisting of not less than 5000 permutations in a ring of eight bells. **3.** (*not in technical usage*) the set of bells in a belfry. ~*vb.* **4.** (*intr.*) to sound with a peal or peals. **5.** (*tr.*) to give forth loudly and sonorously. **6.** (*tr.*) to ring (bells) in peals. [C14 *pele,* variant of *apele* APPEAL]
peal[2] (piːl) *n.* a dialect name for a grilse or a young sea trout.
pean[1] ('piːən) *n.* a less common U.S. spelling of **paean.**
pean[2] (piːn) *n. Heraldry.* a fur of sable spotted with or. [C16: of uncertain origin]
Peano's axioms (pɪ'ɑːnəʊz) *pl. n.* a set of axioms that yield the arithmetic of the natural numbers. [named after Giuseppe *Peano* (1858–1932), Italian mathematician]
peanut ('piːˌnʌt) *n.* **1.** Also called: **goober, goober pea** and, in Britain, **groundnut, monkey nut. a.** a leguminous plant, *Arachis hypogaea,* of tropical America: widely cultivated for its edible seeds. The seed pods are forced underground where they ripen. See also **hog peanut. b.** the edible nutlike seed of this plant, used for food and as a source of oil. **2.** *U.S. and Canadian slang.* a small or insignificant person. ~See also **peanuts.**
peanut butter *n.* a brownish oily paste made from peanuts.
peanut oil *n.* oil that is made from peanut seeds and used for cooking, in soaps, and in pharmaceutical products.
peanuts ('piːˌnʌts) *n. Slang.* a trifling amount of money.
pear (pɛə) *n.* **1.** a widely cultivated rosaceous tree, *Pyrus communis,* having white flowers and edible fruits. **2.** the sweet gritty-textured juicy fruit of this tree, which has a globular base and tapers towards the apex. **3.** the wood of this tree, used for making furniture. [Old English *pere,* ultimately from Latin *pirum*]
pea rifle *n.* a small rifle.
pearl[1] (pɜːl) *n.* **1.** a hard smooth lustrous typically rounded structure occurring on the inner surface of the shell of a clam or oyster: consists of calcium carbonate secreted in layers around an invading particle such as a sand grain; much valued as a gem. **2.** any artificial gem resembling this. **3.** See **mother-of-pearl. 4.** a person or thing that is like a pearl, esp. in beauty or value. **5.** a pale greyish-white colour, often with a bluish tinge. **6.** a size of printer's type, approximately equal to 5 point. ~*adj.* **7.** of, made of, or set with pearl or mother-of-pearl. **8.** having the shape or colour of a pearl. ~*vb.* **9.** (*tr.*) to set with or as if with pearls. **10.** to shape into or assume a pearl-like form or colour. **11.** (*intr.*) to dive or search for pearls. [C14: from Old French, from Vulgar Latin *pernula* (unattested), from Latin *perna* sea mussel]
pearl[2] (pɜːl) *n., vb.* a variant spelling of **purl**[1] (senses 2, 3, 5).
pearl ash *n.* the granular crystalline form of potassium carbonate.
pearl barley *n.* barley ground into small round grains, used in cooking, esp. in soups and stews.
pearler ('pɜːlə) *n.* **1.** a person who dives for or trades in pearls. **2.** a boat used while searching for pearls. **3.** *Austral. informal.* something outstandingly good.
pearl grey *n.* **a.** a light bluish-grey colour. **b.** (*as adj.*): *pearl-grey shoes.*
pearlite ('pɜːlaɪt) *n.* **1.** the lamellar structure in carbon steels and some cast irons that consists of alternate plates of pure iron and iron carbide. **2.** a variant spelling of **perlite.** —**pearlitic** (pɜː'lɪtɪk) *adj.*
pearlized *or* **pearlised** ('pɜːlaɪzd) *adj.* having or given a pearly lustre: *a pearlized lipstick.*
pearl millet *n.* a tall grass, *Pennisetum glaucum,* cultivated in Africa, E Asia, and the southern U.S. as animal fodder and for its pearly white seeds, which are used as grain.
pearl oyster *n.* any of various tropical marine bivalves of the genus *Pinctada* and related genera: a major source of pearls.
pearlwort ('pɜːlˌwɜːt) *n.* any caryophyllaceous plant of the genus *Sagina,* having small white flowers that are spherical in bud.
pearly ('pɜːlɪ) *adj.* **pearlier, pearliest. 1.** resembling a pearl, esp. in lustre. **2.** of the colour pearl; pale bluish-grey. **3.** decorated with pearls or mother-of-pearl. ~*n., pl.* **pearlies.** (in Britain) **4.** a London costermonger or his wife who wear on ceremonial occasions a traditional dress of dark clothes covered with pearl buttons. **5.** (*pl.*) the clothes or the buttons themselves. —'**pearliness** *n.*
Pearly Gates *pl. n.* **1.** *Informal.* the entrance to heaven. **2.** (*not caps.*) *Brit. slang.* teeth.
pearly king *or* (*fem.*) **pearly queen** *n.* the London costermonger whose ceremonial clothes display the most lavish collection of pearl buttons. See also **pearly** (sense 4).
pearly nautilus *n.* any of several cephalopod molluscs of the genus *Nautilus,* esp. *N. pompilius,* of warm and tropical seas, having a partitioned pale pearly external shell with brown stripes. Also called: **chambered nautilus.** Compare **paper nautilus.**
pearmain ('pɛəˌmeɪn) *n.* any of several varieties of apple having a red skin. [C15: from Old French *permain* a type of pear, perhaps from Latin *Parmēnsis* of Parma]
Pearson's correlation coefficient ('pɪəsənz) *n.* a statistic measuring the linear relationship between two variables in a sample and used as an estimate of the correlation in the whole population, given by $r = Cov\ (X,\ Y)/\sqrt{[(Var(X).Var(Y)]}$. In full: **Pearson's product moment correlation coefficient.** [named after Karl *Pearson* (1857–1936), British mathematician]
peart (pɪət) *adj. Dialect.* lively; spirited; brisk. [C15: variant of PERT] —'**peartly** *adv.* —'**peartness** *n.*
peasant ('pɛzᵊnt) *n.* **1. a.** a member of a class of low social status that depends on either cottage industry or agricultural labour as a means of subsistence. **b.** (*as modifier*): *peasant dress.* **2.** *Informal.* a person who lives in the country; rustic. **3.** *Informal.* an uncouth or uncultured person. [C15: from Anglo-French, from Old French *païsant,* from *païs* country, from Latin *pāgus* rural area; see PAGAN]
peasantry ('pɛzᵊntrɪ) *n.* **1.** peasants as a class. **2.** conduct characteristic of peasants. **3.** the status of a peasant.
pease (piːz) *n., pl.* **pease.** an archaic or dialect word for **pea.** [Old English *peose,* via Late Latin from Latin *pisa* peas, pl. of *pisum,* from Greek *pison*]
pease-brose ('piːz'broz, -'brəʊz) *n. Scot.* brose made from a meal of dried peas.
peasecod *or* **peascod** ('piːzˌkɒd) *n. Archaic.* the pod of a pea plant. [C14: from PEASE + COD[2]]
pease pudding *n.* (esp. in Britain) a dish of split peas that have been soaked and boiled, served with ham or pork.
peashooter ('piːˌʃuːtə) *n.* a tube through which pellets such as dried peas are blown, used as a toy weapon.
peasouper (ˌpiː'suːpə) *n.* **1.** *Informal, chiefly Brit.* dense dirty yellowish fog. **2.** *Canadian.* a disparaging name for a **French Canadian.**
peat[1] (piːt) *n.* **1. a.** a compact brownish deposit of partially decomposed vegetable matter saturated with water: found in uplands and bogs in temperate and cold regions and used as a fuel (when dried) and as a fertilizer. **b.** (*as modifier*): *peat bog.* **2.** a piece of dried peat for use as fuel. [C14: from Anglo-Latin *peta,* perhaps from Celtic; compare Welsh *peth* thing] —'**peaty** *adj.*
peat[2] (piːt) *n.* **1.** *Archaic, derogatory.* a person, esp. a woman. **2.** *Obsolete.* a term of endearment for a girl or woman. [C16: of uncertain origin]
peat moss *n.* any of various mosses, esp. sphagnum, that grow in wet places in dense masses and decay to form peat. Also called: **bog moss.** See also **sphagnum.**
peat reek *n.* **1.** the smoke of a peat fire. **2.** whisky distilled over a peat fire.
peau de soie ('pəʊ də swɑː; *French* po də swa) *n.* a rich reversible silk or rayon fabric. [literally: skin of silk]

peavey *or* **peavy** (ˈpiːvɪ) *n., pl.* **-veys** *or* **-vies.** *U.S. and Canadian.* a wooden lever with a metal pointed end and a hinged hook, used for handling logs. Compare **cant hook.** [C19: named after Joseph *Peavey*, American who invented it]

pebble (ˈpɛbᵊl) *n.* **1. a.** a small smooth rounded stone, esp. one worn by the action of water. **b.** *Geology.* a rock fragment, often rounded, with a diameter of 4–64 mm and thus smaller than a cobble but larger than a granule. **2. a.** a transparent colourless variety of rock crystal, used for making certain lenses. **b.** such a lens. **3.** (*modifier*) *Informal.* (of a lens or of spectacles) thick, with a high degree of magnification or distortion. **4. a.** a grainy irregular surface, esp. on leather. **b.** leather having such a surface. **5.** *Informal, chiefly Austral.* a troublesome or obstinate person or animal. *~vb.* (*tr.*) **6.** to pave, cover, or pelt with pebbles. **7.** to impart a grainy surface to (leather). [Old English *papolstān*, from *papol-* (perhaps of imitative origin) + *stān* stone] —ˈ**pebbly** *adj.*

pebble dash *n. Brit.* a finish for external walls consisting of small stones embedded in plaster.

pebble garden *n. N.Z.* a small ornamental garden mainly composed of an arrangement of pebbles.

pebbling (ˈpɛblɪŋ) *n. Curling.* the act of spraying the rink with drops of hot water to slow down the stone.

pecan (pɪˈkæn, ˈpiːkən) *n.* **1.** a hickory tree, *Carya pecan* (or *C. illinoensis*), of the southern U.S., having deeply furrowed bark and edible nuts. **2.** the smooth oval nut of this tree, which has a sweet oily kernel. [C18: from Algonquian *paccan;* related to Ojibwa *pagân* nut with a hard shell, Cree *pakan*]

peccable (ˈpɛkəbᵊl) *adj.* liable to sin; susceptible to temptation. [C17: via French from Medieval Latin *peccābilis*, from Latin *peccāre* to sin] —ˌ**peccaˈbility** *n.*

peccadillo (ˌpɛkəˈdɪləʊ) *n., pl.* **-los** *or* **-loes.** a petty sin or trifling fault. [C16: from Spanish *pecadillo*, from *pecado* sin, from Latin *peccātum*, from *peccāre* to transgress]

peccant (ˈpɛkənt) *adj. Rare.* **1.** guilty of an offence; corrupt. **2.** violating or disregarding a rule; faulty. **3.** producing disease; morbid. [C17: from Latin *peccans*, from *peccāre* to sin] —ˈ**peccancy** *n.* —ˈ**peccantly** *adv.*

peccary (ˈpɛkərɪ) *n., pl.* **-ries** *or* **-ry.** either of two piglike artiodactyl mammals, *Tayassu tajacu* (**collared peccary**) or *T. albirostris* (**white-lipped peccary**) of forests of southern North America, Central and South America: family *Tayassuidae.* [C17: from Carib]

peccavi (pɛˈkɑːviː) *n., pl.* **-vis.** a confession of guilt. [C16: from Latin, literally: I have sinned, from *peccāre*]

pech (pɛx) *vb., n.* a Scot. word for **pant.** [C15: of imitative origin]

peck[1] (pɛk) *n.* **1.** a unit of dry measure equal to 8 quarts or one quarter of a bushel. **2.** a container used for measuring this quantity. **3.** a large quantity or number. [C13: from Anglo-Norman, of uncertain origin]

peck[2] (pɛk) *vb.* **1.** (when *intr.*, sometimes foll. by *at*) to strike with the beak or with a pointed instrument. **2.** (*tr.;* sometimes foll. by *out*) to dig (a hole) by pecking. **3.** (*tr.*) (of birds) to pick up (corn, worms, etc.) by pecking. **4.** (*intr.;* often foll. by *at*) to nibble or pick (at one's food). **5.** *Informal.* to kiss (a person) quickly and lightly. **6.** (*intr.;* foll. by *at*) to nag. *~n.* **7.** a quick light blow, esp. from a bird's beak. **8.** a mark made by such a blow. **9.** *Informal.* a quick light kiss. [C14: of uncertain origin; compare PICK[1], Middle Low German *pekken* to jab with the beak]

pecker (ˈpɛkə) *n.* **1.** *Brit. slang.* spirits (esp. in the phrase **keep one's pecker up**). **2.** *Informal.* short for **woodpecker. 3.** *U.S. and Canadian slang.* a taboo word for **penis.**

pecking order *n.* **1.** Also called: **peck order.** a natural hierarchy in a group of gregarious birds, such as domestic fowl. **2.** any hierarchical order, as among people in a particular group.

peckish (ˈpɛkɪʃ) *adj. Informal, chiefly Brit.* feeling slightly hungry; having an appetite. [C18: from PECK[2]]

Pecksniffian (pɛkˈsnɪfɪən) *adj.* affecting benevolence or high moral principles. [C19: after Seth *Pecksniff*, character in *Martin Chuzzlewit* (1843), a novel by Charles Dickens]

pectase (ˈpɛkteɪs) *n.* an enzyme occurring in certain ripening fruits: involved in transforming pectin into a soluble form. [C19: from PECTIN + -ASE]

pectate (ˈpɛkteɪt) *n.* a salt or ester of pectic acid. [C19: from PECTIC ACID + -ATE[1]]

pecten (ˈpɛktɪn) *n., pl.* **-tens** *or* **-tines** (-tɪˌniːz). **1.** a comblike structure in the eye of birds and reptiles, consisting of a network of blood vessels projecting inwards from the retina, which it is thought to supply with oxygen. **2.** any other comblike part or organ. **3.** any scallop of the genus *Pecten*, which swim by expelling water from their shell valves in a series of snapping motions. [C18: from Latin: a comb, from *pectere*, related to Greek *pekein* to comb]

pectic acid *n.* a complex acid containing arabinose and galactose that occurs in ripe fruit, beets, and other vegetables. Formula: $C_{35}H_{50}O_{33}$.

pectin (ˈpɛktɪn) *n. Biochem.* any of the acidic hemicelluloses that occur in ripe fruit and vegetables: used in the manufacture of jams because of their ability to solidify to a gel when heated in a sugar solution (may be referred to on food labels as **E440(a)**). [C19: from Greek *pēktos* congealed, from *pegnuein* to set] —ˈ**pectic** *or* ˈ**pectinous** *adj.*

pectinate (ˈpɛktɪˌneɪt) *or* **pectinated** *adj.* shaped like a comb: *pectinate antennae.* [C18: from Latin *pectinātus* combed; see PECTEN] —ˌ**pectiˈnation** *n.*

pectize *or* **pectise** (ˈpɛktaɪz) *vb.* to change into a jelly; gel. [C19: from Greek *pēktos* solidified; see PECTIN] —ˈ**pectizable** *or* ˈ**pectisable** *adj.* —ˌ**pectiˈzation** *or* ˌ**pectiˈsation** *n.*

pectoral (ˈpɛktərəl) *adj.* **1.** of or relating to the chest, breast, or thorax: *pectoral fins.* **2.** worn on the breast or chest: *a pectoral medallion.* **3.** *Rare.* heartfelt or sincere. *~n.* **4.** a pectoral organ or part, esp. a muscle or fin. **5.** a medicine or remedy for disorders of the chest or lungs. **6.** anything worn on the chest or breast for decoration or protection. [C15: from Latin *pectorālis*, from *pectus* breast] —ˈ**pectorally** *adv.*

pectoral fin *n.* either of a pair of fins, situated just behind the head in fishes, that help to control the direction of movement during locomotion.

pectoral girdle *or* **arch** *n.* a skeletal support to which the front or upper limbs of a vertebrate are attached.

pectoral muscle *n.* either of two large chest muscles (**pectoralis major** and **pectoralis minor**), that assist in movements of the shoulder and upper arm.

pectose (ˈpɛkˌtəʊz) *n.* an insoluble carbohydrate found in the cell walls of unripe fruit that is converted to pectin by enzymic processes.

peculate (ˈpɛkjʊˌleɪt) *vb.* to appropriate or embezzle (public money). [C18: from Latin *pecūlārī*, from *pecūlium* private property (originally, cattle); see PECULIAR] —ˌ**peculˈlation** *n.* —ˈ**pecuˌlator** *n.*

peculiar (pɪˈkjuːlɪə) *adj.* **1.** strange or unusual; odd: *a peculiar individual; a peculiar idea.* **2.** distinct from others; special. **3.** (*postpositive;* foll. by *to*) belonging characteristically or exclusively (to): *peculiar to North America.* *~n.* **4.** Also called: **arbitrary.** *Printing.* a special sort, esp. an accented letter. **5.** *Church of England.* a church or parish that is exempt from the jurisdiction of the ordinary in whose diocese it lies. [C15: from Latin *pecūliāris* concerning private property, from *pecūlium*, literally: property in cattle, from *pecus* cattle] —**peˈculiarly** *adv.*

peculiarity (pɪˌkjuːlɪˈærɪtɪ) *n., pl.* **-ties. 1.** a strange or unusual habit or characteristic. **2.** a distinguishing trait, etc. that is characteristic of a particular person; idiosyncrasy. **3.** the state or quality of being peculiar.

peculiar people *pl. n.* **1.** (*sometimes caps.*) a small sect of faith healers founded in London in 1838, having no ministers or external organization. **2.** the Jews considered as God's elect.

peculium (pɪˈkjuːlɪəm) *n. Roman law.* property that a father or master allowed his child or slave to hold as his own. [C17: from Latin; see PECULIAR]

pecuniary (pɪˈkjuːnɪərɪ) *adj.* **1.** consisting of or relating to money. **2.** *Law.* (of an offence) involving a monetary penalty. [C16: from Latin *pecūniāris*, from *pecūnia* money] —**peˈcuniarily** *adv.*

pecuniary advantage *n. Law.* financial advantage that is dishonestly obtained by deception and that constitutes a criminal offence.

ped. *abbrev. for:* **1.** pedal. **2.** pedestal.

ped- *combining form.* a variant (esp. U.S.) of **paedo-.**

-ped *or* **-pede** *n. combining form.* foot or feet: *quadruped; centipede.* [from Latin *pēs, ped-* foot]

pedagogics (ˌpɛdəˈgɒdʒɪks, -ˈgəʊ-) *n.* (*functioning as sing.*) another word for **pedagogy.**

pedagogue *or U.S.* (*sometimes*) **pedagog** (ˈpɛdəˌgɒg) *n.* **1.** a teacher or educator. **2.** a pedantic or dogmatic teacher. [C14: from Latin *paedagōgus*, from Greek *paidagōgos* slave who looked after his master's son, from *pais* boy + *agōgos* leader] —ˌ**pedaˈgogic** *or* ˌ**pedaˈgogical** *adj.* —ˌ**pedaˈgogically** *adv.* —ˈ**pedaˌgogism** *or* ˈ**pedaˌgoguism** *n.*

pedagogy (ˈpɛdəˌgɒgɪ, -ˌgɒdʒɪ, -ˌgəʊdʒɪ) *n.* the principles, practice, or profession of teaching.

pedal[1] (ˈpɛdᵊl) *n.* **1. a.** any foot-operated lever or other device, esp. one of the two levers that drive the chain wheel of a bicycle, the foot brake, clutch control, or accelerator of a car, one of the levers on an organ controlling deep bass notes, or one of the levers on a piano used to create a muted effect or sustain tone. **b.** (*as modifier*): *a pedal cycle; a pianist's pedal technique.* *~vb.* **-als, -alling, -alled** *or U.S.* **-als, -aling, -aled. 2.** to propel (a bicycle, boat, etc.) by operating the pedals. **3.** (*intr.*) to operate the pedals of an organ, piano, etc., esp. in a certain way. **4.** to work (pedals of any kind). [C17: from Latin *pedālis;* see PEDAL[2]]

pedal[2] (ˈpiːdᵊl) *adj.* of or relating to the foot or feet. [C17: from Latin *pedālis*, from *pēs* foot]

pedalfer (pɪˈdælfə) *n.* a type of zonal soil deficient in lime but containing deposits of aluminium and iron, found in wet areas, esp. those with high temperatures. Compare **pedocal.** [C20: PEDO-[2] + ALUM + *-fer*, from Latin *ferrum* iron]

pedalo (ˈpɛdᵊləʊ) *n., pl.* **-los** *or* **-loes.** a pleasure craft driven by pedal-operated paddle wheels. [C20: from PEDAL[1]]

pedal point (ˈpɛdᵊl) *n. Music.* a sustained bass note, over which the other parts move bringing about changing harmonies. Often shortened to **pedal.**

pedal pushers *pl. n.* calf-length trousers or jeans worn by women.

pedal steel guitar *n.* a floor-mounted, multineck, lap steel guitar with each set of strings tuned to a different open chord and foot pedals to raise or lower the pitch.

pedant ('pɛdᵊnt) *n.* 1. a person who relies too much on academic learning or who is concerned chiefly with insignificant detail. 2. *Archaic.* a schoolmaster or teacher. [C16: via Old French from Italian *pedante* teacher; perhaps related to Latin *paedagōgus* PEDAGOGUE] —**pedantic** (pɪ'dæntɪk) *adj.* —**pe'dantically** *adv.*

pedantry ('pɛdᵊntrɪ) *n., pl.* **-ries.** the habit or an instance of being a pedant, esp. in the display of useless knowledge or minute observance of petty rules or details.

pedate ('pɛdeɪt) *adj.* 1. (of a plant leaf) deeply divided into several lobes with the lateral lobes divided into smaller lobes. 2. *Zoology.* having or resembling a foot: *a pedate appendage.* [C18: from Latin *pedātus* equipped with feet, from *pēs* foot] —**'pedately** *adv.*

pedatifid (pɪ'dætɪfɪd, -'deɪ-) *adj.* (of a plant leaf) pedately divided, with the divisions less deep than in a pedate leaf.

peddle ('pɛdᵊl) *vb.* 1. to go from place to place selling (goods, esp. small articles). 2. (*tr.*) to sell (illegal drugs, esp. narcotics). 3. (*tr.*) to advocate (ideas) persistently or importunately: *to peddle a new philosophy.* 4. (*intr.*) *Archaic.* to trifle. [C16: back formation from PEDLAR]

peddler ('pɛdlə) *n.* 1. a person who sells illegal drugs, esp. narcotics. 2. the usual U.S. spelling of **pedlar.**

-pede *n. combining form.* a variant of **-ped.**

pederast *or* (*sometimes*) **paederast** ('pɛdə,ræst) *n.* a man who practises pederasty.

pederasty *or* (*sometimes*) **paederasty** ('pɛdə,ræstɪ) *n.* homosexual relations between men and boys. [C17: from New Latin *paederastia,* from Greek, from *pais* boy + *erastēs* lover, from *eran* to love] —,**peder'astic** *or* (*sometimes*) ,**paeder'astic** *adj.*

pedes ('pɛdiːz) *n.* the plural of **pes.**

pedestal ('pɛdɪstᵊl) *n.* 1. a base that supports a column, statue, etc., as used in classical architecture. 2. a position of eminence or supposed superiority (esp. in the phrases **place, put,** *or* **set on a pedestal**). 3. a. either of a pair of sets of drawers used as supports for a writing surface. b. (*as modifier*): *a pedestal desk.* [C16: from French *piédestal,* from Old Italian *piedestallo,* from *pie* foot + *di* of + *stallo* a stall]

pedestrian (pɪ'dɛstrɪən) *n.* 1. a. a person travelling on foot; walker. b. (*as modifier*): *a pedestrian precinct.* ~*adj.* 2. dull; commonplace: *a pedestrian style of writing.* [C18: from Latin *pedester,* from *pēs* foot]

pedestrian crossing *n. Brit.* a path across a road marked as a crossing for pedestrians. See also **zebra crossing, pelican crossing.** U.S. and Canadian name: **crosswalk.**

pedestrianize *or* **pedestrianise** (pɪ'dɛstrɪə,naɪz) *vb.* (*tr.*) to convert (a street) into an area for the use of pedestrians only, by excluding all motor vehicles. —**pe,destriani'zation** *or* **pe,destriani'sation** *n.*

Pedi ('pɛdɪ) *n.* 1. Also called: **Northern Sotho.** a member of a subgroup of the Sotho people resident in the Transvaal. 2. the dialect of Sotho spoken by this people.

pedi- *combining form.* indicating the foot: *pedicure.* [from Latin *pēs, ped-* foot]

pediatrician (,piːdɪə'trɪʃən) *n.* the U.S. spelling of **paediatrician.**

pediatrics (,piːdɪ'ætrɪks) *n.* the U.S. spelling of **paediatrics.**

pedicab ('pɛdɪ,kæb) *n.* a pedal-operated tricycle, available for hire in some Asian countries, with an attached seat for one or two passengers.

pedicel ('pɛdɪ,sɛl) *n.* 1. the stalk bearing a single flower of an inflorescence. 2. Also called: **peduncle.** *Biology.* any short stalk bearing an organ or organism. 3. the second segment of an insect's antenna. [C17: from New Latin *pedicellus,* from Latin *pedīculus,* from *pēs* foot] —**pedicellate** (pɪ'dɪsɪ,leɪt) *adj.*

pedicle ('pɛdɪkᵊl) *n. Biology.* any small stalk; pedicel; peduncle. [C17: from Latin *pedīculus* small foot; see PEDICEL]

pedicular (pɪ'dɪkjʊlə) *adj.* 1. relating to, infested with, or caused by lice. 2. *Biology.* of or relating to a stem, stalk, or pedicle. [C17: from Latin *pedīculāris,* from *pedīculus,* diminutive of *pedis* louse]

pediculate (pɪ'dɪkjʊlɪt, -,leɪt) *adj.* 1. of, relating to, or belonging to the *Pediculati,* a large order of teleost fishes containing the anglers. ~*n.* 2. any fish belonging to the order *Pediculati.* [C19: from Latin *pedīculus* little foot; see PEDICEL]

pediculosis (pɪ,dɪkjʊ'ləʊsɪs) *n. Pathol.* the state of being infested with lice. [C19: via New Latin from Latin *pedīculus* louse; see PEDICULAR] —**pediculous** (pɪ'dɪkjʊləs) *adj.*

pedicure ('pɛdɪ,kjʊə) *n.* professional treatment of the feet, either by a medical expert or a cosmetician. [C19: via French from Latin *pēs* foot + *curāre* to care for]

pediform ('pɛdɪ,fɔːm) *adj.* shaped like a foot.

pedigree ('pɛdɪ,griː) *n.* 1. a. the line of descent of a purebred animal. b. (*as modifier*): *a pedigree bull.* 2. a document recording this. 3. a genealogical table, esp. one indicating pure ancestry. 4. derivation or background: *the pedigree of an idea.* [C15: from Old French *pie de grue* crane's foot, alluding to the spreading lines used in a genealogical chart] —**'pedi,greed** *adj.*

pediment ('pɛdɪmənt) *n.* 1. a low-pitched gable, esp. one that is triangular, as used in classical architecture. 2. a gently sloping rock surface, formed through denudation under arid conditions. [C16: from obsolete *periment,* perhaps workman's corruption of PYRAMID] —,**pedi'mental** *adj.*

pedipalp ('pɛdɪ,pælp) *n.* either member of the second pair of head appendages of arachnids: specialized for feeding, locomotion, etc. [C19: from New Latin *pedipalpi,* from Latin *pēs* foot + *palpus* palp]

pedlar *or esp. U.S.* **peddler, pedler** ('pɛdlə) *n.* a person who peddles; hawker. [C14: changed from *peder,* from *ped, pedde* basket, of obscure origin]

pedo-[1] *or before a vowel* **ped-** *combining form.* variants (esp. U.S.) of **paedo-.**

pedo-[2] *combining form.* indicating soil: *pedocal.* [from Greek *pedon*]

pedocal ('pɛdə,kæl) *n.* a type of zonal soil that is rich in lime and characteristic of relatively dry areas. Compare **pedalfer.** [from PEDO-[2] + CAL(CIUM)]

pedology[1] (pɪ'dɒlədʒɪ) *n.* a U.S. spelling of **paedology.**

pedology[2] (pɪ'dɒlədʒɪ) *n.* the study of the formation, characteristics, and distribution of soils. —**pedological** (,piːdə'lɒdʒɪkᵊl) *adj.* —**pe'dologist** *n.*

pedometer (pɪ'dɒmɪtə) *n.* a device containing a pivoted weight that records the number of steps taken in walking and hence the distance travelled.

pedophilia (,piːdəʊ'fɪlɪə) *n.* a variant spelling (esp. U.S.) of **paedophilia.**

peduncle (pɪ'dʌŋkᵊl) *n.* 1. the stalk of a plant bearing an inflorescence or solitary flower. 2. *Anatomy.* a stalklike structure, esp. a large bundle of nerve fibres within the brain. 3. *Pathol.* a slender process of tissue by which a polyp or tumour is attached to the body. 4. *Biology.* another name for **pedicel** (sense 2). [C18: from New Latin *pedunculus,* from Latin *pedīculus* little foot; see PEDICLE] —**pe'duncled** *or* **peduncular** (pɪ'dʌŋkjʊlə) *adj.*

pedunculate (pɪ'dʌŋkjʊlɪt, -,leɪt) *or* **pedunculated** *adj.* having, supported on, or growing from a peduncle. —**pe,duncu'lation** *n.*

pedunculate oak *n.* a large deciduous oak tree, *Quercus robur,* of Eurasia, having lobed leaves and stalked acorns. Also called: **common oak.**

pee (piː) *Informal.* ~*vb.* **pees, peeing, peed.** 1. (*intr.*) to urinate. ~*n.* 2. urine. 3. the act of urinating. [C18: a euphemism for PISS, based on the initial letter]

peek (piːk) *vb.* 1. (*intr.*) to glance quickly or furtively; peep. ~*n.* 2. a quick or furtive glance. [C14 *pike,* related to Middle Dutch *kiken* to peek]

peekaboo ('piːkə,buː) *n.* 1. a game for young children, in which one person hides his face and suddenly reveals it and cries "peekaboo." ~*adj.* 2. (of a garment) made of fabric that is almost transparent or patterned with small holes. [C16: from PEEK + BOO]

peel[1] (piːl) *vb.* 1. (*tr.*) to remove (the skin, rind, outer covering, etc.) of (a fruit, egg, etc.). 2. (*intr.*) (of paint, etc.) to be removed from a surface, esp. through weathering. 3. (*intr.*) (of a surface) to lose its outer covering of paint, etc. esp. through weathering. 4. (*intr.*) (of a person or part of the body) to shed skin in flakes or (of skin) to be shed in flakes, esp. as a result of sunburn. 5. *Croquet.* to put (another player's ball) through a hoop or hoops. 6. **keep one's eyes peeled** (*or* **skinned**). to watch vigilantly. ~*n.* 7. the skin or rind of a fruit, etc. ~See also **peel off.** [Old English *pilian* to strip off the outer layer, from Latin *pilāre* to make bald, from *pilus* a hair]

peel[2] (piːl) *n.* a long-handled shovel used by bakers for moving bread, in an oven. [C14 *pele,* from Old French, from Latin *pāla* spade, from *pangere* to drive in; see PALETTE]

peel[3] (piːl) *n.* (in Britain) a fortified tower of the 16th century on the borders between England and Scotland, built to withstand raids. [C14 (fence made of stakes): from Old French *piel* stake, from Latin *pālus;* see PALE[2], PALING]

peeler[1] ('piːlə) *n.* 1. a special knife or mechanical device for peeling vegetables, fruit, etc.: *a potato peeler.* 2. *U.S. slang.* a striptease dancer.

peeler[2] ('piːlə) *n. Irish and obsolete Brit. slang.* another word for **policeman.** [C19: from the founder of the police force, Sir Robert *Peel* (1788–1850), British statesman]

peeling ('piːlɪŋ) *n.* a strip of skin, rind, bark, etc., that has been peeled off: *a potato peeling.*

peel off *vb.* (*adv.*) 1. to remove or be removed by peeling. 2. (*intr.*) *Slang.* to undress. 3. (*intr.*) (of an aircraft) to turn away as by banking, and leave a formation. 4. *Slang.* to go away or cause to go away.

peely-wally *or* **peelie-wallie** ('piːlɪ'wælɪ) *adj. Scot. urban dialect.* off colour; pale and ill-looking: *he's a wee bit peely-wally this morning.* [apparently a reduplicated form of WALLY[2] in the sense: faded]

peen (piːn) *n.* 1. the end of a hammer head opposite the striking face, often rounded or wedge-shaped. ~*vb.* 2. (*tr.*) to strike with the peen of a hammer or with a stream of metal shot in order to bend or shape (a sheet of metal). [C17: variant of *pane,* perhaps from French *panne,* ultimately from Latin *pinna* point]

peep[1] (piːp) *vb.* (*intr.*) 1. to look furtively or secretly, as through a small aperture or from a hidden place. 2. to appear partially or briefly: *the sun peeped through the clouds.* ~*n.* 3. a quick or furtive look. 4. the first appearance: *the peep of dawn.* [C15: variant of PEEK]

peep[2] (piːp) *vb.* (*intr.*) 1. (esp. of young birds) to utter shrill small noises. 2. to speak in a thin shrill voice. ~*n.* 3. a peeping sound. **4.** *U.S.* any of various small sandpipers of the genus *Calidris* (or *Erolia*) and related genera, such as the pectoral sandpiper. [C15: of imitative origin]

peeper ('piːpə) *n.* **1.** a person who peeps. **2.** (*often pl.*) a slang word for **eye**[1] (sense 1).

peephole ('piːpˌhəʊl) *n.* a small aperture, such as one in the door of a flat for observing callers before opening.

Peeping Tom *n.* a man who furtively observes women undressing; voyeur. [C19: after the tailor who, according to legend, peeped at Lady Godiva when she rode naked through Coventry]

peepshow ('piːpˌʃəʊ) *n.* **1.** Also called: **raree show.** a small box with a peephole through which a series of pictures, esp. of erotic poses, can be seen. **2.** a booth from which a viewer can see a live nude model for a fee.

peep sight *n.* an adjustable rear gun sight with a narrow aperture through which the target and the front sight are aligned when aiming.

peepul ('piːpᵊl) *or* **pipal** *n.* an Indian moraceous tree, *Ficus religiosa,* resembling the banyan: regarded as sacred by Buddhists. Also called: **bo tree.** [C18: from Hindi *pīpal,* from Sanskrit *pippala*]

peer[1] (pɪə) *n.* **1.** a member of a nobility; nobleman. **2.** a person who holds any of the five grades of the British nobility: duke, marquess, earl, viscount, and baron. See also **life peer. 3.** a person who is an equal in social standing, rank, age, etc.: *to be tried by one's peers.* **4.** *Archaic.* a companion; mate. [C14 (in sense 3): from Old French *per,* from Latin *pār* equal]

peer[2] (pɪə) *vb. (intr.)* **1.** to look intently with or as if with difficulty: *to peer into the distance.* **2.** to appear partially or dimly: *the sun peered through the fog.* [C16: from Flemish *pieren* to look with narrowed eyes]

peerage ('pɪərɪdʒ) *n.* **1.** the whole body of peers; aristocracy. **2.** the position, rank, or title of a peer. **3.** (esp. in the British Isles) a book listing the peers and giving genealogical and other information about them.

peeress ('pɪərɪs) *n.* **1.** the wife or widow of a peer. **2.** a woman holding the rank of a peer in her own right.

peer group *n.* a social group composed of individuals of approximately the same age.

peerie[1] ('piːrɪ) *n. Scot.* a spinning top. [C19: perhaps from *peir* a Scot. variant of *pear,* alluding to the top's shape]

peerie[2] ('piːrɪ) *adj. Orkney and Shetland dialect.* small. [C19: of uncertain origin; perhaps from Norwegian dialect *piren* niggardly, thin]

peerless ('pɪəlɪs) *adj.* having no equals; matchless.

peer of the realm *n., pl.* **peers of the realm.** (in Great Britain and Northern Ireland) any member of the nobility entitled to sit in the House of Lords.

peetweet ('piːtˌwiːt) *n. U.S.* another name for the **spotted sandpiper.** [C19: imitative of its cry]

peeve (piːv) *Informal.* ~*vb.* **1.** (*tr.*) to irritate; vex; annoy. ~*n.* **2.** something that irritates; vexation: *it was a pet peeve of his.* [C20: back formation from PEEVISH] —**peeved** *adj.*

peevers ('piːvərz) *or* **peever** *n.* (*functioning as sing.*) *Scot. dialect.* hopscotch. [from *peever* (the stone used in the game), of obscure origin]

peevish ('piːvɪʃ) *adj.* **1.** fretful or irritable: *a peevish child.* **2.** *Obsolete.* perverse. [C14: of unknown origin] —'**peevishly** *adv.* —'**peevishness** *n.*

peewee ('piːwiː) *n.* **1.** a variant spelling of **pewee. 2.** a variant (esp. Scot.) of **peewit. 3.** *Austral.* another name for **magpie lark.**

peewit ('piːwɪt) *n.* another name for **lapwing.** [C16: imitative of its call]

peg (pɛg) *n.* **1.** a small cylindrical pin or dowel, sometimes slightly tapered, used to join two parts together. **2.** a pin pushed or driven into a surface: used to mark scores, define limits, support coats, etc. **3.** *Music.* any of several pins passing through the head (**peg box**) of a stringed instrument, which can be turned so as to tune strings wound around them. See also **pin** (sense 11). **4.** Also called: **clothes peg.** *Brit.* a split or hinged pin for fastening wet clothes to a line to dry. U.S. and Canadian equivalent: **clothespin. 5.** *Brit.* a small drink of wine or spirits, esp. of brandy or whisky and soda. **6.** an opportunity or pretext for doing something: *a peg on which to hang a theory.* **7.** a mountaineering piton. **8.** *Croquet.* a post that a player's ball must strike to win the game. **9.** *Angling.* a fishing station allotted to an angler in a competition, marked by a peg in the ground. **10.** *Informal.* a level of self-esteem, importance, etc. (esp. in the phrases **bring** *or* **take down a peg**). **11.** *Informal.* See **peg leg. 12. off the peg.** *Chiefly Brit.* (of clothes) ready to wear, as opposed to tailor-made. ~*vb.* **pegs, pegging, pegged. 13.** (*tr.*) to knock or insert a peg into or pierce with a peg. **14.** (*tr.;* sometimes foll. by *down*) to secure with pegs: *to peg a tent.* **15.** *Mountaineering.* to insert or use pitons. **16.** (*tr.*) to mark (a score) with pegs, as in some card games. **17.** (*tr.*) *Informal.* to aim and throw (missiles) at a target. **18.** (*intr.;* foll. by *away, along,* etc.) *Chiefly Brit.* to work steadily: *he pegged away at his job for years.* **19.** (*tr.*) to stabilize (the price of a commodity, an exchange rate, etc.) by legislation or market operations. ~See also **peg down, peg out.** [C15: from Low Germanic *pegge*]

Pegasus ('pɛgəsəs) *n., Latin genitive* **Pegasi** ('pɛgəˌsaɪ). a constellation in the N hemisphere lying close to Andromeda and Pisces.

pegboard ('pɛgˌbɔːd) *n.* **1.** a board having a pattern of holes into which small pegs can be fitted, used for playing certain games or keeping a score. **2.** another name for **solitaire** (sense 1). **3.** hardboard perforated by a pattern of holes in which articles may be pegged or hung, as for display.

peg climbing *n.* another name for **aid climbing.**

peg down *vb. (tr., adv.)* to make (a person) committed to a course of action or bound to follow rules: *you won't peg him down on any decision.*

pegging ('pɛgɪŋ) *n.* another name for **aid climbing.**

peg leg *n. Informal.* **1.** an artificial leg, esp. one made of wood. **2.** a person with an artificial leg.

pegmatite ('pɛgməˌtaɪt) *n.* any of a class of coarse-grained intrusive igneous rocks consisting chiefly of quartz and feldspar: usually occur as dykes among igneous rocks of finer grain. [C19: from Greek *pegma* something joined together] —**pegmatitic** (ˌpɛgmə'tɪtɪk) *adj.*

peg out *vb. (adv.)* **1.** (*intr.*) *Informal.* to collapse or die. **2.** *Croquet.* **a.** (*intr.*) to win a game by hitting the peg. **b.** (*tr.*) to cause (an opponent's ball) to hit the peg, rendering it out of the game. **3.** (*intr.*) *Cribbage.* to score the point that wins the game. **4.** (*tr.*) to mark or secure with pegs: *to peg out one's claims to a piece of land.*

peg top *n.* a child's spinning top, usually made of wood with a metal centre pin.

peg-top *adj.* (of skirts, trousers, etc.) wide at the hips then tapering off towards the ankle.

Pehlevi ('peɪləvɪ) *n.* a variant of **Pahlavi.**

PEI *abbrev. for* Prince Edward Island.

peignoir ('peɪnwɑː) *n.* a woman's dressing gown or negligee. [C19: from French, from *peigner* to comb, since the garment was worn while the hair was combed]

pejoration (ˌpiːdʒə'reɪʃən) *n.* **1.** *Linguistics.* semantic change whereby a word acquires unfavourable connotations: *the English word "silly" changed its meaning from "holy" or "happy" by pejoration.* Compare **amelioration** (sense 3). **2.** the process of worsening; deterioration.

pejorative (pɪ'dʒɒrətɪv, 'piːdʒər-) *adj.* **1.** (of words, expressions, etc.) having an unpleasant or disparaging connotation. ~*n.* **2.** a pejorative word, expression, etc. [C19: from French *péjoratif,* from Late Latin *pējōrātus,* past participle of *pējōrāre* to make worse, from Latin *pēior* worse] —**pe'joratively** *adv.*

pekan ('pɛkən) *n.* another name for **fisher** (sense 2). [C18: from Canadian French *pékan,* of Algonquian origin; compare Abnaki *pékané*]

peke (piːk) *n. Informal.* a Pekingese dog.

Pekin (piː'kɪn) *n.* a breed of white or cream duck with a bright orange bill. [C18: via French from *Peking,* capital of China]

Pekingese (ˌpiːkɪŋ'iːz) *or* **Pekinese** (ˌpiːkə'niːz) *n.* **1.** (*pl.* **-ese**) a small breed of pet dog with a profuse straight coat, curled plumed tail, and short wrinkled muzzle. **2.** the dialect of Mandarin Chinese spoken in Peking, capital of China, the pronunciation of which serves as a standard for the language. **3.** (*pl.* **-ese**) a native or inhabitant of Peking. ~*adj.* **4.** of or relating to Peking or its inhabitants.

Peking man ('piː'kɪŋ) *n.* an early type of man, *Homo erectus,* remains of which, of the Lower Palaeolithic age, were found in a cave near Peking, China, in 1927.

pekoe ('piːkəʊ) *n.* a high-quality tea made from the downy tips of the young buds of the tea plant. [C18: from Chinese (Amoy) *peh ho,* from *peh* white + *ho* down]

pelage ('pɛlɪdʒ) *n.* the coat of a mammal, consisting of hair, wool, fur, etc. [C19: via French from Old French *pel* animal's coat, from Latin *pilus* hair]

pelagian (pɛ'leɪdʒɪən) *adj.* of or inhabiting the open sea. [C18: from Latin *pelagius,* from Greek *pelagios* of the sea, from *pelagos* sea]

Pelagianism (pɛ'leɪdʒɪəˌnɪzəm) *n. Christianity.* the heretical doctrine first formulated by the British monk Pelagius (?360–?420 A.D.), which rejected the concept of original sin and maintained that the individual takes the initial steps towards salvation by his own efforts and not by the help of divine grace. —**Pe'lagian** *adj., n.*

pelagic (pɛ'lædʒɪk) *adj.* **1.** of or relating to the open sea: *pelagic whaling.* **2.** (of marine life) living or occurring in the upper waters of open sea. **3.** (of geological formations) derived from material that has fallen to the bottom from the upper waters of the sea. [C17: from Latin *pelagicus,* from *pelagus,* from Greek *pelagos* sea]

pelargonic acid (ˌpɛlə'gɒnɪk) *n.* another name for **nonanoic acid.** [C19: so named because it was originally derived from PELARGONIUM leaves]

pelargonium (ˌpɛlə'gəʊnɪəm) *n.* any plant of the chiefly southern African geraniaceous genus *Pelargonium,* having circular or lobed leaves and red, pink, or white aromatic flowers: includes many cultivated geraniums. [C19: via New Latin from Greek *pelargos* stork, on the model of GERANIUM; from the likeness of the seed vessels to a stork's bill]

Pelasgian (pɛ'læzdʒɪən) *n.* **1.** a member of the pre-Hellenic peoples (the **Pelasgi**) who inhabited Greece and the islands and coasts of the Aegean Sea before the arrival of the Bronze Age Greeks. *~adj. also* **Pelasgic. 2.** of or relating to these peoples.

pelecypod (pɪˈlɛsɪˌpɒd) *n., adj.* another word for **bivalve** (senses 1, 2). [C19: from Greek *pelekus* hatchet + -POD]

pelerine (ˈpɛləˌriːn) *n.* a woman's narrow cape with long pointed ends in front. [C18: from French *pèlerine,* feminine of *pèlerin* PILGRIM, that is, a pilgrim's cape]

Pele's hair (ˈpeɪleɪz, ˈpiːliːz) *n.* fine threads of volcanic rock material formed from molten lava by the action of wind, explosion, etc. [C20: translation of Hawaiian *lauoho-o Pele,* from Pele, name of the goddess of volcanoes]

pelf (pɛlf) *n. Contemptuous.* money or wealth, esp. if dishonestly acquired; lucre. [C14: from Old French *pelfre* booty; related to Latin *pilāre* to despoil]

pelham (ˈpɛləm) *n.* a horse's bit for a double bridle, less severe than a curb but more severe than a snaffle. [probably from the proper name *Pelham*]

pelican (ˈpɛlɪkən) *n.* any aquatic bird of the tropical and warm water family *Pelecanidae,* such as *P. onocrotalus* (**white pelican**): order *Pelecaniformes.* They have a long straight flattened bill, with a distensible pouch for engulfing fish. [Old English *pellican,* from Late Latin *pelicānus,* from Greek *pelekān;* perhaps related to Greek *pelekus* axe, perhaps from the shape of the bird's bill; compare Greek *pelekas* woodpecker]

pelican crossing *n.* a type of road crossing marked by black-and-white stripes or by two rows of metal studs and consisting of a pedestrian-operated traffic-light system. [C20: from *pe(destrian) li(ght) con(trolled) crossing,* with *-con* adapted to *-can* of *pelican*]

pelisse (pɛˈliːs) *n.* **1.** a fur-trimmed cloak. **2.** a high-waisted loose coat, usually fur-trimmed, worn esp. by women in the early 19th century. [C18: via Old French from Medieval Latin *pellicia* cloak, from Latin *pellis* skin]

pelite (ˈpiːlaɪt) *n.* any argillaceous rock such as shale. [C19: from Greek *pēlos* mud] —**pelitic** (pɪˈlɪtɪk) *adj.*

pellagra (pəˈleɪgrə, -ˈlæ-) *n. Pathol.* a disease caused by a dietary deficiency of nicotinic acid, characterized by burning or itching often followed by scaling of the skin, inflammation of the mouth, diarrhoea, mental impairment, etc. [C19: via Italian from *pelle* skin + *-agra,* from Greek *agra* paroxysm] —**pelˈlagrous** *adj.*

pellet (ˈpɛlɪt) *n.* **1.** a small round ball, esp. of compressed matter: *a wax pellet.* **2. a.** an imitation bullet used in toy guns. **b.** a piece of small shot. **3.** a stone ball formerly used as a catapult or cannon missile. **4.** Also called: **cast, casting.** *Ornithol.* a mass of undigested food, including bones, fur, feathers, etc., that is regurgitated by certain birds, esp. birds of prey. **5.** a small pill. **6.** a raised area on coins and carved or moulded ornaments. *~vb. (tr.)* **7.** to strike with pellets. **8.** to make or form into pellets. [C14: from Old French *pelote,* from Vulgar Latin *pilota* (unattested), from Latin *pila* ball]

pellicle (ˈpɛlɪkᵊl) *n.* **1.** a thin skin or film. **2.** the hard protective outer layer of certain protozoans, such as those of the genus *Paramecium.* **3.** *Botany.* **a.** the thin outer layer of a mushroom cap. **b.** a growth on the surface of a liquid culture. **4.** *Photog.* the thin layer of emulsion covering a plate, film, or paper. [C16: via French from Latin *pellicula,* from *pellis* skin] —**pellicular** (pɛˈlɪkjʊlə) *adj.*

pellitory (ˈpɛlɪtərɪ, -trɪ) *n., pl.* **-ries. 1.** any of various urticaceous plants of the S and W European genus *Parietaria,* esp. *P. diffusa* (**pellitory-of-the-wall** or **wall pellitory**), that grow in crevices and have long narrow leaves and small pink flowers. **2. pellitory of Spain.** a small Mediterranean plant, *Anacyclus pyrethrum,* the root of which contains an oil formerly used to relieve toothache: family *Compositae* (composites). [C16 *peletre,* from Old French *piretre,* from Latin *pyrethrum,* from Greek *purethron,* from *pur* fire, from the hot pungent taste of the root]

pell-mell (ˈpɛlˈmɛl) *adv.* **1.** in a confused headlong rush: *the hounds ran pell-mell into the yard.* **2.** in a disorderly manner: *the things were piled pell-mell in the room.* *~adj.* **3.** disordered; tumultuous: *a pell-mell rush for the exit.* *~n.* **4.** disorder; confusion. [C16: from Old French *pesle-mesle,* jingle based on *mesler* to MEDDLE]

pellucid (pɛˈluːsɪd) *adj.* **1.** transparent or translucent. **2.** extremely clear in style and meaning; limpid. [C17: from Latin *pellūcidus,* variant of *perlūcidus,* from *perlūcēre* to shine through, from *per* through + *lūcēre* to shine] —**pelˈlucidly** *adv.* —ˌ**pelluˈcidity** *or* **pelˈlucidness** *n.*

Pelmanism (ˈpɛlməˌnɪzəm) *n.* **1.** a system of training to improve the memory. **2.** (*often not cap.*) Also called: **pairs,** (esp. U.S.) **concentration.** a memory card game in which a pack of cards is spread out face down and players try to turn up pairs with the same number. [named after the *Pelman* Institute, founded in London in 1898]

pelmet (ˈpɛlmɪt) *n.* an ornamental drapery or board fixed above a window to conceal the curtain rail. [C19: probably from French *palmette* palm-leaf decoration on cornice moulding; see PALMETTE]

Peloponnesian (ˌpɛləpəˈniːʃən) *adj.* of or relating to the Peloponnese, the S peninsula of Greece.

peloria (pɛˈlɔːrɪə) *n.* the abnormal production of regular flowers in a plant of a species that usually produces irregular flowers. [C19: via New Latin from Greek *pelōros,* from *pelōr* monster] —**peloric** (pɛˈlɔːrɪk, -ˈlɒ-) *adj.*

pelorus (pɪˈlɔːrəs) *n., pl.* **-ruses.** a gyrocompass over which two sight vanes are mounted for measuring the relative bearings of observed points. [of uncertain origin, perhaps from Latin *Pelōrus* a dangerous Sicilian promontory, now called Cape Faro]

pelota (pəˈlɒtə) *n.* any of various games played in Spain, Spanish America, SW France, etc., by two players who use a basket strapped to their wrists or a wooden racket to propel a ball against a specially marked wall. [C19: from Spanish: ball, from Old French *pelote;* see PELLET]

pelt[1] (pɛlt) *vb.* **1.** (*tr.*) to throw (missiles) at (a person). **2.** (*tr.*) to hurl (insults) at (a person). **3.** (*intr.;* foll. by *along, over,* etc.) to move rapidly; hurry. **4.** (*intr.;* often foll. by *down*) to rain heavily. *~n.* **5.** a blow. **6.** speed (esp. in the phrase **at full pelt**). [C15: of uncertain origin, perhaps from PELLET] —ˈ**pelter** *n.*

pelt[2] (pɛlt) *n.* **1.** the skin of a fur-bearing animal, such as a mink, esp. when it has been removed from the carcass. **2.** the hide of an animal, stripped of hair and ready for tanning. [C15: perhaps back formation from PELTRY]

peltast (ˈpɛltæst) *n.* (in ancient Greece) a lightly armed foot soldier. [C17: from Latin *peltasta,* from Greek *peltastēs* soldier equipped with a *pelta,* a small leather shield]

peltate (ˈpɛlteɪt) *adj.* (of leaves) having the stalk attached to the centre of the lower surface. [C18: from Latin *peltātus* equipped with a *pelta,* a small shield; see PELTAST] —ˈ**peltately** *adv.* —**pelˈtation** *n.*

Peltier effect (ˈpɛltɪˌeɪ) *n. Physics.* the production of heat at one junction and the absorption of heat at the other junction of a thermocouple when a current is passed around the thermocouple circuit. The heat produced is additional to the heat arising from the resistance of the wires. Compare **Seebeck effect.** [C19: named after Jean *Peltier* (1785–1845), French physicist, who discovered it]

Peltier element *n.* an electronic device consisting of metal strips between which alternate strips of n-type and p-type semiconductors are connected. Passage of a current causes heat to be absorbed from one set of metallic strips and emitted from the other by the Peltier effect.

Pelton wheel (ˈpɛltən) *n.* a type of impulse turbine in which specially shaped buckets mounted on the perimeter of a wheel are struck by a fast-flowing water jet. [C19: named after L. A. *Pelton* (1829–1908), U.S. engineer who invented it]

peltry (ˈpɛltrɪ) *n., pl.* **-ries.** the pelts of animals collectively. [C15: from Old French *peleterie* collection of pelts, from Latin *pilus* hair]

pelvic (ˈpɛlvɪk) *adj.* of, near, or relating to the pelvis.

pelvic fin *n.* either of a pair of fins attached to the pelvic girdle of fishes that help to control the direction of movement during locomotion.

pelvic girdle *or* **arch** *n.* the skeletal structure supporting the lower limbs in man and the hind limbs or corresponding parts in other vertebrates.

pelvic inflammatory disease *n.* inflammation of a woman's womb, Fallopian tubes, or ovaries as a result of infection with one of a group of bacteria. Abbrev.: **PID.**

pelvimetry (pɛlˈvɪmɪtrɪ) *n. Obstetrics.* measurement of the dimensions of the female pelvis.

pelvis (ˈpɛlvɪs) *n., pl.* **-vises** *or* **-ves** (-viːz). **1.** the large funnel-shaped structure at the lower end of the trunk of most vertebrates: in man it is formed by the hipbones and sacrum. **2.** the bones that form this structure. **3.** any anatomical cavity or structure shaped like a funnel or cup. **4.** short for **renal pelvis.** [C17: from Latin: basin, laver]

pelycosaur (ˈpɛlɪkəʊˌsɔː) *n.* any extinct mammal-like reptile of the order *Pelycosauria,* of Upper Carboniferous to Lower Permian times, from which the therapsids are thought to have evolved. [C19: from New Latin *Pelycosauria,* from Greek *pelyx* bowl, PELVIS, + -SAUR]

Pembroke (ˈpɛmbrʊk) *n.* the smaller variety of corgi, usually having a docked or short tail. [named after *Pembroke* (Pembrokeshire), former Welsh county]

Pembroke table *n.* a small table with drop leaves and often one or more drawers. [perhaps named after Mary Herbert, Countess of *Pembroke* (1561–1621), who originally ordered its design]

pemmican *or* **pemican** (ˈpɛmɪkən) *n.* a small pressed cake of shredded dried meat, pounded into paste with fat and berries or dried fruits, used originally by American Indians and now chiefly for emergency rations. [C19: from Cree *pimikân,* from *pimii* fat, grease]

pemphigus (ˈpɛmfɪgəs, pɛmˈfaɪ-) *n. Pathol.* any of a group of blistering skin diseases, esp. a potentially fatal form (**pemphigus vulgaris**) characterized by large blisters on the skin, mucous membranes of the mouth, genitals, intestines, etc., which eventually rupture and form painful denuded areas from which critical amounts of bodily protein, fluid, and blood may be lost. [C18: via New Latin from Greek *pemphix* bubble]

pen[1] (pɛn) *n.* **1.** an implement for writing or drawing using ink, formerly consisting of a sharpened and split quill, and now of a metal nib attached to a holder. See also **ballpoint, fountain pen. 2.** the writing end of such an implement; nib. **3.** style of writing. **4. the pen. a.** writing as an occupation. **b.** the written word: *the pen is mightier than the sword.* **5.** the long horny internal shell of a squid. ~*vb.* **pens, penning, penned.** **6.** (*tr.*) to write or compose. [Old English *pinne*, from Late Latin *penna* (quill) pen, from Latin: feather]

pen[2] (pɛn) *n.* **1.** an enclosure in which domestic animals are kept: *sheep pen.* **2.** any place of confinement. **3.** a dock for servicing submarines, esp. one having a bombproof roof. ~*vb.* **pens, penning, penned** *or* **pent.** **4.** (*tr.*) to enclose or keep in a pen. [Old English *penn*, perhaps related to PIN]

pen[3] (pɛn) *n. U.S. and Canadian informal.* short for **penitentiary** (sense 1).

pen[4] (pɛn) *n.* a female swan. [C16: of unknown origin]

PEN (pɛn) *n. acronym for* International Association of Poets, Playwrights, Editors, Essayists, and Novelists.

Pen. *abbrev. for* Peninsula.

penal ('piːnᵊl) *adj.* **1.** of, relating to, constituting, or prescribing punishment. **2.** payable as a penalty: *a penal sum.* **3.** used or designated as a place of punishment: *a penal institution.* [C15: from Late Latin *poenālis* concerning punishment, from *poena* penalty] —'**penally** *adv.*

penal code *n.* the codified body of the laws in any legal system that relate to crime and its punishment.

penalize *or* **penalise** ('piːnə,laɪz) *vb.* (*tr.*) **1.** to impose a penalty on (someone), as for breaking a law or rule. **2.** to inflict a handicap or disadvantage on. **3.** *Sport.* to award a free stroke, point, or penalty against (a player or team). **4.** to declare (an act) legally punishable; make subject to a penalty. —,**penali'zation** *or* ,**penali'sation** *n.*

penal servitude *n. English criminal law.* (formerly) the imprisonment of an offender and his subjection to hard labour. It was substituted for transportation in 1853 and abolished in 1948. Compare **hard labour.**

penalty ('pɛnᵊltɪ) *n., pl.* **-ties.** **1.** a legal or official punishment, such as a term of imprisonment. **2.** some other form of punishment, such as a fine or forfeit for not fulfilling a contract. **3.** loss, suffering, or other unfortunate result of one's own action, error, etc. **4.** *Sport, games, etc.* a handicap awarded against a player or team for illegal play, such as a free shot at goal by the opposing team, loss of points, etc. [C16: from Medieval Latin *poenālitās* penalty; see PENAL]

penalty area *n. Soccer.* a rectangular area in front of the goal, within which the goalkeeper may handle the ball and within which a penalty is awarded for a foul by the defending team.

penalty box *n.* **1.** *Soccer.* another name for **penalty area.** **2.** *Ice hockey.* a bench for players serving time penalties.

penalty kick *n.* **1.** *Soccer.* a free kick at the goal from a point (**penalty spot**) within the penalty area and 12 yards (about 11 m) from the goal, with only the goalkeeper allowed to defend it: awarded to the attacking team after a foul within the penalty area by a member of the defending team. **2.** *Rugby Union.* a kick awarded after a serious foul that can be aimed straight at the goal to score three points.

penalty killer *n. Ice hockey.* a good player who, when his team is short-handed because of a penalty, is sent onto the ice to prevent the other side from scoring.

penalty rates *pl. n. Austral. and N.Z.* rates of pay, such as double time, paid to employees working outside normal working hours.

penance ('pɛnəns) *n.* **1.** voluntary self-punishment to atone for a sin, crime, etc. **2.** a feeling of regret for one's wrongdoings. **3.** *Christianity.* **a.** a punishment usually consisting of prayer, fasting, etc., undertaken voluntarily as an expression of penitence for sin. **b.** a punishment of this kind imposed by church authority as a condition of absolution. **4.** *R.C. Church.* a sacrament in which repentant sinners are absolved on condition of confession of their sins to a priest and of performing a penance. ~*vb.* **5.** (*tr.*) (of ecclesiastical authorities) to impose a penance upon (a sinner). [C13: via Old French from Latin *paenitentia* repentance; related to Latin *poena* penalty]

penannular (pɛn'ænjʊlə) *adj.* of or forming an almost complete ring. [C19: from PENE- + ANNULAR]

penates (pə'nɑːtiːz) *pl. n.* See **lares and penates.** [Latin]

pence (pɛns) *n.* a plural of **penny.**

▷**Usage.** Since the decimalization of British currency and the introduction of the abbreviation **p**, as in *10p, 85p*, etc., the abbreviation has tended to replace *pence* in speech, as in *4p* (,fɔː'piː), *12p* (,twɛlv'piː), etc.

pencel, pensel, *or* **pensil** ('pɛnsᵊl) *n.* a small pennon, originally one carried by a knight's squire. [C13: via Anglo-French from Old French *penoncel* a little PENNON]

penchant ('pɒŋʃɒŋ) *n.* a strong inclination or liking; bent or taste. [C17: from French, from *pencher* to incline, from Latin *pendēre* to be suspended]

pencil ('pɛnsᵊl) *n.* **1. a.** a thin cylindrical instrument used for writing, drawing, etc., consisting of a rod of graphite or other marking substance, usually either encased in wood and sharpened or held in a mechanical metal device. **b.** (*as modifier*): *a pencil drawing.* **2.** something similar in shape or function: *a styptic pencil; an eyebrow pencil.* **3.** a narrow set of lines or rays, such as light rays, diverging from or converging to a point. **4.** *Archaic.* an artist's fine paintbrush. **5.** *Rare.* an artist's individual style or technique in drawing. ~*vb.* **-cils, -cilling, -cilled** *or U.S.* **-cils, -ciling, -ciled.** (*tr.*) **6.** to draw, colour, or write with a pencil. **7.** to mark with a pencil. **8. pencil in.** to note, arrange, include, etc. provisionally or tentatively. [C14: from Old French *pincel*, from Latin *pēnicillus* painter's brush, from *pēniculus* a little tail, from *pēnis* tail] —'**penciller** *or U.S.* '**penciler** *n.*

pend (pɛnd) *vb.* (*intr.*) **1.** to await judgment or settlement. **2.** *Dialect.* to hang; depend. ~*n.* **3.** *Scot.* an archway or vaulted passage. [C15: from Latin *pendēre* to hang; related to Latin *pendere* to suspend]

pendant ('pɛndənt) *n.* **1. a.** an ornament that hangs from a piece of jewellery. **b.** a necklace with such an ornament. **2.** a hanging light, esp. a chandelier. **3.** a carved ornament that is suspended from a ceiling or roof. **4.** something that matches or complements something else. **5.** Also called: **pennant.** *Nautical.* a length of wire or rope secured at one end to a mast or spar and having a block or other fitting at the lower end. ~*adj.* **6.** a variant spelling of **pendent.** [C14: from Old French, from *pendre* to hang, from Latin *pendēre* to hang down; related to Latin *pendere* to hang, *pondus* weight, Greek *span* to pull]

pendent ('pɛndənt) *adj.* **1.** dangling. **2.** jutting. **3.** (of a grammatical construction) incomplete: *a pendent nominative is a construction having no verb.* **4.** a less common word for **pending** (senses 2, 3). ~*n.* **5.** a variant spelling of **pendant.** [C15: from Old French *pendant*, from *pendre* to hang; see PENDANT] —'**pendency** *n.* —'**pendently** *adv.*

pendente lite (pɛn'dɛntɪ 'laɪtɪ) *adj. Law.* while a suit is pending. [Latin, literally: with litigation pending]

pendentive (pɛn'dɛntɪv) *n.* any of four triangular sections of vaulting with concave sides, positioned at a corner of a rectangular space to support a circular or polygonal dome. [C18: from French *pendentif*, from Latin *pendens* hanging, from *pendere* to hang]

pending ('pɛndɪŋ) *prep.* **1.** while waiting for or anticipating. ~*adj.* (*postpositive*) **2.** not yet decided, confirmed, or finished: *what are the matters pending?* **3.** imminent: *these developments have been pending for some time.*

pendragon (pɛn'drægən) *n.* a supreme war chief or leader of the ancient Britons. [Welsh, literally: head dragon] —**pen'dragon,ship** *n.*

pendule ('pɒŋdjʊl, 'pɛn-) *n. Mountaineering.* a manoeuvre by which a climber on a rope from above swings in a pendulum-like series of movements to reach another line of ascent. Also called: **pendulum.**

pendulous ('pɛndjʊləs) *adj.* **1.** hanging downwards, esp. so as to swing from side to side. **2.** *Rare.* in a state of indecision; vacillating. [C17: from Latin *pendulus*, from *pendēre* to hang down] —'**pendulously** *adv.* —'**pendulousness** *n.*

pendulum ('pɛndjʊləm) *n.* **1.** a body mounted so that it can swing freely under the influence of gravity. It is either a bob hung on a light thread (**simple pendulum**) or a more complex structure (**compound pendulum**). **2.** such a device used to regulate a clockwork mechanism. **3.** something that changes its position, attitude, etc. fairly regularly: *the pendulum of public opinion.* [C17: from Latin *pendulus* PENDULOUS]

pene- *or before a vowel* **pen-** *prefix.* almost: *peneplain.* [from Latin *paene*]

peneplain *or* **peneplane** ('piːnɪ,pleɪn, ,piːnɪ'pleɪn) *n.* a relatively flat land surface produced by a long period of erosion. [C19: from PENE- + PLAIN[1]] —,**penepla'nation** *n.*

penetralia (,pɛnɪ'treɪlɪə) *pl. n.* **1.** the innermost parts. **2.** secret matters. [C17: from Latin, from *penetrālis* inner, from *penetrāre* to PENETRATE] —,**pene'tralian** *adj.*

penetrance ('pɛnɪtrəns) *n. Genetics.* the percentage frequency with which a gene exhibits its effect. [C20: from PENETR(ANT) + -ANCE, on the model of German *penetranz*]

penetrant ('pɛnɪtrənt) *adj.* **1.** sharp; penetrating. ~*n.* **2.** *Chem.* a substance that lowers the surface tension of a liquid and thus causes it to penetrate or be absorbed more easily. **3.** a person or thing that penetrates.

penetrate ('pɛnɪ,treɪt) *vb.* **1.** to find or force a way into or through (something); pierce; enter. **2.** to diffuse through (a substance); permeate. **3.** (*tr.*) to see through: *their eyes could not penetrate the fog.* **4.** (*tr.*) (of a man) to insert the penis into the vagina of (a woman). **5.** (*tr.*) to grasp the meaning of (a principle, etc.). **6.** (*intr.*) to be understood: *his face lit up as the new idea penetrated.* [C16: from Latin *penetrāre*; related to *penitus* inner, and *penus* the interior of a house] —'**penetrable** *adj.* —,**penetra'bility** *n.* —'**penetrably** *adv.* —'**pene,trator** *n.*

penetrating ('pɛnɪ,treɪtɪŋ) *adj.* tending to or able to penetrate: *a penetrating mind; a penetrating voice.* —'**pene,tratingly** *adv.*

penetration (,pɛnɪ'treɪʃən) *n.* **1.** the act or an instance of penetrating. **2.** the ability or power to penetrate. **3.** keen insight or perception. **4.** *Military.* an offensive manoeuvre that breaks through an enemy's defensive position. **5.** Also called: **market penetration.** the proportion of the total number of potential purchasers of a product or service who either are aware of its existence or actually buy it. **6.** another name for **depth of field.**

penetrometer (,pɛnɪ'trɒmɪtə) *n. Physics.* an instrument used to measure the penetrating power of radiation, such as x-rays.

pen friend *n.* another name for **pen pal.**

pengö ('pɛŋgɜː) *n., pl.* **-gös.** (formerly) the standard monetary unit of Hungary, replaced by the forint in 1946. [from Hungarian, from *pengeni* to sound]

penguin ('pɛŋgwɪn) *n.* **1.** any flightless marine bird, such as *Aptenodytes patagonica* (king penguin) and *Pygoscelis adeliae*

(**Adélie penguin**), of the order *Sphenisciformes* of cool southern, esp. Antarctic, regions: they have wings modified as flippers, webbed feet, and feathers lacking barbs. See also **emperor penguin, king penguin.** 2. an obsolete name for **great auk.** [C16: perhaps from Welsh *pen gwyn*, from *pen* head + *gwyn* white]

penicillate (ˌpɛnɪˈsɪlɪt, -eɪt) *adj. Biology.* having or resembling one or more tufts of fine hairs: *a penicillate caterpillar.* [C19: from Latin *pēnicillus* brush, PENCIL] —ˌ**peniˈcillately** *adv.* —ˌ**peni-cilˈlation** *n.*

penicillin (ˌpɛnɪˈsɪlɪn) *n.* an antibiotic with powerful bacteriostatic action, used to treat pneumonia, gonorrhoea, and infections caused by streptococci and staphylococci: obtained from the fungus *Penicillium*, esp. *P. notatum.* Formula: R-$C_9H_{11}N_2O_4S$ where R is one of several side chains. [C20: from PENICILLIUM]

penicillium (ˌpɛnɪˈsɪlɪəm) *n., pl.* **-cilliums** *or* **-cillia** (-ˈsɪlɪə). any ascomycetous saprophytic fungus of the genus *Penicillium*, which commonly grow as a green or blue mould on stale food: some species are used in cheese-making and others as a source of penicillin. [C19: New Latin, from Latin *pēnicillus* tuft of hairs; named from the tufted appearance of the sporangia of this fungus]

penile (ˈpiːnaɪl) *adj.* of or relating to the penis.

penillion *or* **pennillion** (pɪˈnɪlɪən) *pl. n., sing.* **penill** (pɪˈnɪl). the Welsh art or practice of singing poetry in counterpoint to a traditional melody played on the harp. [from Welsh: verses, plural of *penill* verse, stanza]

peninsula (pɪˈnɪnsjʊlə) *n.* a narrow strip of land projecting into a sea or lake from the mainland. [C16: from Latin, literally: almost an island, from *paene* PENE- + *insula* island] —**penˈinsular** *adj.*

peninsulate (pɪˈnɪnsjʊˌleɪt) *vb.* (*tr.*) to cause (land) to become peninsular.

penis (ˈpiːnɪs) *n., pl.* **-nises** *or* **-nes** (-niːz). the male organ of copulation in higher vertebrates, also used for urine excretion in many mammals. [C17: from Latin]

penis envy *n. Psychoanal.* a Freudian concept in which envy of the penis is postulated as the cause for some of the characteristics found in women.

penitent (ˈpɛnɪtənt) *adj.* 1. feeling regret for one's sins; repentant. ~*n.* 2. a person who is penitent. 3. *Christianity.* **a.** a person who repents his sins and seeks forgiveness for them. **b.** *R.C. Church.* a person who confesses his sins to a priest and submits to a penance imposed by him. [C14: from Church Latin *paenitēns* regretting, from *paenitēre* to repent, of obscure origin] —ˈ**penitence** *n.* —ˈ**penitently** *adv.*

penitential (ˌpɛnɪˈtɛnʃəl) *adj.* 1. of, showing, or constituting penance. ~*n.* 2. *Chiefly R.C. Church.* a book or compilation of instructions for confessors. 3. a less common word for **penitent** (senses 2, 3). —ˌ**peniˈtentially** *adv.*

penitentiary (ˌpɛnɪˈtɛnʃərɪ) *n., pl.* **-ries.** 1. (in the U.S. and Canada) a state or federal prison: in Canada, esp. a federal prison for offenders convicted of serious crimes. Sometimes shortened to **pen.** 2. *R.C. Church.* **a.** a cleric appointed to supervise the administration of the sacrament of penance in a particular area. **b.** a priest who has special faculties to absolve particularly grave sins. **c.** a cardinal who presides over a tribunal that decides all matters affecting the sacrament of penance. **d.** this tribunal itself. ~*adj.* 3. another word for **penitential** (sense 1). 4. *U.S. and Canadian.* (of an offence) punishable by imprisonment in a penitentiary. [C15 (meaning also: an officer dealing with penances): from Medieval Latin *poenitēntiārius*, from Latin *paenitēns* PENITENT]

penknife (ˈpɛnˌnaɪf) *n., pl.* **-knives.** a small knife with one or more blades that fold into the handle; pocketknife. [C15: so called because it was originally used for making and repairing quill pens]

penman (ˈpɛnmən) *n., pl.* **-men.** 1. a person skilled in handwriting. 2. a person who writes by hand in a specified way: *a bad penman.* 3. an author. 4. *Rare.* a scribe.

penmanship (ˈpɛnmənʃɪp) *n.* style or technique of writing by hand. Also called: **calligraphy.**

Penn. *abbrev. for* Pennsylvania.

penna (ˈpɛnə) *n., pl.* **-nae** (-niː). *Ornithol.* any large feather that has a vane and forms part of the main plumage of a bird. [Latin: feather] —**pennaceous** (pɛˈneɪʃəs) *adj.*

pen name *n.* an author's pseudonym. Also called: **nom de plume.**

pennant (ˈpɛnənt) *n.* 1. a type of pennon, esp. one flown from vessels as identification or for signalling. 2. *Chiefly U.S., Canadian, and Austral.* **a.** a flag serving as an emblem of championship in certain sports. **b.** (*as modifier*): *pennant cricket.* 3. *Nautical.* another word for **pendant** (sense 5). [C17: probably a blend of PENDANT and PENNON]

pennate (ˈpɛneɪt) *or* **pennated** *adj. Biology.* 1. having feathers, wings, or winglike structures. 2. another word for **pinnate.** [C19: from Latin *pennātus*, from *penna* wing]

penni (ˈpɛnɪ) *n., pl.* **-nia** (-nɪə) *or* **-nis.** a Finnisn monetary unit worth one hundredth of a markka. [Finnish, from Low German *pennig* PENNY]

penniless (ˈpɛnɪlɪs) *adj.* very poor; almost totally without money. —ˈ**pennilessly** *adv.* —ˈ**pennilessness** *n.*

pennillion (pɪˈnɪlɪən) *n.* a variant spelling of **penillion.**

penninite (ˈpɛnɪˌnaɪt) *n.* a bluish-green variety of chlorite occurring in the form of thick crystals. [C20: from German *Pennin* Pennine (Alps) + -ITE[1]]

pennon (ˈpɛnən) *n.* 1. a long flag, often tapering and rounded, divided, or pointed at the end, originally a knight's personal flag. 2. a small tapering or triangular flag borne on a ship or boat. 3. a poetic word for **wing.** [C14: via Old French ultimately from Latin *penna* feather]

Pennsylvania Dutch (ˌpɛnsɪlˈveɪnɪə) *n.* 1. Also called: **Pennsylvania German.** a dialect of German spoken in E Pennsylvania, the U.S. 2. **the Pennsylvania Dutch.** (*functioning as pl.*) a group of German-speaking people in E Pennsylvania, descended from 18th-century settlers from SW Germany and Switzerland.

Pennsylvanian (ˌpɛnsɪlˈveɪnɪən) *adj.* 1. of the state of Pennsylvania, in the northereastern U.S. 2. (in North America) of, denoting, or formed in the upper of two divisions of the Carboniferous period (see also **Mississippian** (sense 2)), which lasted 30 million years, during which coal measures were formed. ~*n.* 3. an inhabitant or native of the state of Pennsylvania. 4. **the.** the Pennsylvanian period or rock system, equivalent to the Upper Carboniferous of Europe.

penny (ˈpɛnɪ) *n., pl.* **pennies** *or* **pence** (pɛns). 1. Also called (formerly): **new penny.** (in Britain) a bronze coin having a value equal to one hundredth of a pound. Symbol: **p** 2. (in Britain before 1971) a bronze or copper coin having a value equal to one twelfth of a shilling or one two-hundred-and-fortieth of a pound. Abbrev.: **d.** 3. (*pl.* **pennies**). (in the U.S. and Canada) a cent. 4. a coin of similar value, as used in several other countries. 5. (*used with a negative*) *Informal, chiefly Brit.* the least amount of money: *I don't have a penny.* 6. **a bad penny.** *Informal, chiefly Brit.* an objectionable person or thing (esp. in the phrase **turn up like a bad penny**). 7. **a pretty penny.** *Informal.* a considerable sum of money. 8. **spend a penny.** *Brit. informal.* to urinate. 9. **the penny dropped.** *Informal, chiefly Brit.* the explanation of something was finally realized. 10. **two a penny.** plentiful but of little value. [Old English *penig, pening;* related to Old Saxon *penni(n)g*, Old High German *pfeni(n)c*, German *Pfennig*]

penny-a-liner *n. Now rare.* a hack writer or journalist.

penny arcade *n. Chiefly U.S.* a public place with various coin-operated machines for entertainment; amusement arcade.

Penny Black *n.* the first adhesive postage stamp, issued in Britain in 1840; an imperforate stamp bearing the profile of Queen Victoria on a dark background.

pennyboy (ˈpɛnɪˌbɔɪ) *n. Irish slang.* an employee whose duties include menial tasks, such as running errands.

pennycress (ˈpɛnɪˌkrɛs) *n.* any of several cruciferous plants of the genus *Thlaspi* of temperate Eurasia and North America, typically having small white or mauve flowers and rounded or heart-shaped leaves.

penny-dreadful *n., pl.* **-fuls.** *Brit. informal.* a cheap, often lurid or sensational book or magazine.

penny-farthing *n. Brit.* an early type of bicycle with a large front wheel and a small rear wheel, the pedals being attached to the front wheel. U.S. name: **ordinary.** [C20: so called because of the similarity between the relative sizes of the wheels and the relative sizes of the (old) penny and farthing coins]

penny-pincher *n. Informal.* a person who is excessively careful with money. —ˈ**penny-ˌpinching** *n., adj.*

pennyroyal (ˌpɛnɪˈrɔɪəl) *n.* 1. a Eurasian plant, *Mentha pulegium*, with hairy leaves and small mauve flowers, that yields an aromatic oil used in medicine: family *Labiatae* (labiates). 2. Also called: **mock pennyroyal.** a similar and related plant, *Hedeoma pulegioides*, of E North America. [C16: variant of Anglo-Norman *puliol real*, from Old French *pouliol* (from Latin *pūleium* pennyroyal) + *real* ROYAL]

penny shares *pl. n. Stock Exchange.* securities with a low market price, esp. less than 20p, enabling small investors to purchase a large number for a relatively small outlay.

pennyweight (ˈpɛnɪˌweɪt) *n.* a unit of weight equal to 24 grains or one twentieth of an ounce (Troy).

penny whistle *n.* a type of flageolet with six finger holes, esp. a cheap one made of metal. Also called: **tin whistle.**

penny-wise *adj.* 1. greatly concerned with saving small sums of money. 2. **penny-wise and pound-foolish.** careful about trifles but wasteful in large ventures.

pennywort (ˈpɛnɪˌwɜːt) *n.* 1. Also called: **navelwort.** a crassulaceous Eurasian rock plant, *Umbilicus rupestris* (or *Cotyledon umbilicus*), with whitish-green tubular flowers and rounded leaves. 2. a marsh plant, *Hydrocotyle vulgaris*, of Europe and North Africa, having circular leaves and greenish-pink flowers: family *Hydrocotylaceae.* 3. a gentianaceous plant, *Obolaria virginica*, of E North America, with fleshy scalelike leaves and small white or purplish flowers. 4. any of various other plants with rounded penny-like leaves.

pennyworth (ˈpɛnɪˌwɜːθ) *n.* 1. the amount that can be bought for a penny. 2. a small amount: *he hasn't got a pennyworth of sense.*

penology (piːˈnɒlədʒɪ) *n.* 1. the branch of the social sciences concerned with the punishment of crime. 2. the science of prison management. ~Also: **poenology.** [C19: from Greek *poinē* punishment] —**penological** (ˌpiːnəˈlɒdʒɪkəl) *adj.* —ˌ**penoˈlogically** *adv.* —**peˈnologist** *n.*

pen pal *n.* a person with whom one regularly exchanges letters, often a person in another country whom one has not met. Also called: **pen friend.**

penpusher ('pɛn,pʊʃə) *n.* a person who writes a lot, esp. a clerk involved with boring paperwork. —'**pen,pushing** *adj., n.*

pensel *or* **pensil** ('pɛnsᵊl) *n.* variants of **pencel.**

pensile ('pɛnsaɪl) *adj. Ornithol.* designating or building a hanging nest: *pensile birds.* [C17: from Latin *pensilis* hanging down, from *pendēre* to hang] —**pensility** (pɛn'sɪlɪtɪ) *or* '**pensileness** *n.*

pension[1] ('pɛnʃən) *n.* **1.** a regular payment made by the state to people over a certain age to enable them to subsist without having to work. **2.** a regular payment made by an employer to former employees after they retire. **3.** any regular payment made on charitable grounds, by way of patronage, or in recognition of merit, service, etc.: *a pension paid to a disabled soldier.* ~*vb.* **4.** (*tr.*) to grant a pension to. [C14: via Old French from Latin *pēnsiō* a payment, from *pendere* to pay] —'**pensionable** *adj.* —'**pensionless** *adj.*

pension[2] *French.* (pɑ̃sjɔ̃) *n.* (in France and some other countries) **1.** a relatively cheap boarding house. **2.** another name for **full board.** [C17: French; extended meaning of *pension* grant; see PENSION[1]]

pensionary ('pɛnʃənərɪ) *adj.* **1.** constituting a pension. **2.** maintained by or receiving a pension. **3.** *Archaic.* bought with money. ~*n., pl.* **-aries. 4.** a person whose service can be bought; hireling.

pensioneer trustee (,pɛnʃə'nɪə) *n.* (in Britain) a person authorized by the Inland Revenue to oversee the management of a pension fund.

pensioner ('pɛnʃənə) *n.* **1.** a person who is receiving a pension, esp. an old-age pension from the state. **2.** a person dependent on the pay or bounty of another. **3.** *Obsolete, Brit.* another name for **gentleman-at-arms.**

pension mortgage *n.* an arrangement whereby a person takes out a mortgage and pays the capital repayment instalments into a pension fund and the interest to the mortgagee. The loan is repaid out of the tax-free lump sum proceeds of the pension plan on the borrower's retirement.

pension off *vb.* (*tr., adv.*) **1.** to cause to retire from a post and pay a pension to. **2.** to discard, because old and worn: *to pension off submarines.*

pensive ('pɛnsɪv) *adj.* **1.** deeply or seriously thoughtful, often with a tinge of sadness. **2.** expressing or suggesting pensiveness. [C14: from Old French *pensif,* from *penser* to think, from Latin *pensāre* to consider; compare PENSION[1]] —'**pensively** *adv.* —'**pensiveness** *n.*

penstemon (pɛn'stiːmən) *n.* a variant (esp. U.S.) of **pentstemon.**

penstock ('pɛn,stɒk) *n.* **1.** a conduit that supplies water to a hydroelectric power plant. **2.** a channel bringing water from the head gates to a water wheel. **3.** a sluice for controlling water flow. [C17: from PEN[2] + STOCK]

pent (pɛnt) *vb.* a past tense and past participle of **pen**[2].

penta- *combining form.* five: *pentagon; pentameter; pentaprism.* [from Greek *pente* five]

pentachlorophenol (,pɛntə,klɔːrə'fiːnɒl) *n.* a white crystalline water-insoluble compound used as a fungicide, herbicide, and preservative for wood. Formula: C_6Cl_5OH.

pentacle ('pɛntəkᵊl) *n.* another name for **pentagram.** [C16: from Italian *pentacolo* something having five corners; see PENTA-]

pentad ('pɛntæd) *n.* **1.** a group or series of five. **2.** the number or sum of five. **3.** a period of five years. **4.** *Chem.* a pentavalent element, atom, or radical. **5.** *Meteorol.* a period of five days. [C17: from Greek *pentas* group of five]

pentadactyl (,pɛntə'dæktɪl) *adj.* (of the limbs of amphibians, reptiles, birds, and mammals) consisting of an upper arm or thigh, a forearm or shank, and a hand or foot bearing five digits.

pentagon ('pɛntə,gɒn) *n.* a polygon having five sides. —**pentagonal** (pɛn'tægənᵊl) *adj.*

Pentagon ('pɛntə,gɒn) *n.* the military leadership of the U.S. [named after the *Pentagon,* a building in Arlington, Virginia, that houses the U.S. Department of Defense headquarters]

pentagram ('pɛntə,græm) *n.* **1.** a star-shaped figure formed by extending the sides of a regular pentagon to meet at five points. **2.** such a figure used as a magical or symbolic figure by the Pythagoreans, black magicians, etc. ~Also called: **pentacle, pentangle.**

pentahedron (,pɛntə'hiːdrən) *n., pl.* **-drons** *or* **-dra** (-drə). a solid figure having five plane faces. See also **polyhedron.** —,**penta'hedral** *adj.*

pentamerous (pɛn'tæmərəs) *adj.* consisting of five parts, esp. (of flowers) having the petals, sepals, and other parts arranged in groups of five. —**pen'tamer,ism** *n.*

pentameter (pɛn'tæmɪtə) *n.* **1.** a verse line consisting of five metrical feet. **2.** (in classical prosody) a verse line consisting of two dactyls, one stressed syllable, two dactyls, and a final stressed syllable. ~*adj.* **3.** designating a verse line consisting of five metrical feet.

pentamidine (pɛn'tæmɪ,diːn, -dɪn) *n.* a drug used to treat protozoal infections, esp. pneumonia caused by *Pneumocystis carinii* in AIDS patients.

pentane ('pɛnteɪn) *n.* an alkane hydrocarbon having three isomers, esp. the isomer with a straight chain of carbon atoms (*n*-pentane) which is a colourless flammable liquid used as a solvent. Formula: C_5H_{12}.

pentangle ('pɛn,tæŋgᵊl) *n.* another name for **pentagram.**

pentangular (pɛn'tæŋgjʊlə) *adj.* having five angles.

pentanoic acid (,pɛntə'nəʊɪk) *n.* a colourless liquid carboxylic acid with an unpleasant odour, used in making perfumes, flavourings, and pharmaceuticals. Formula: $CH_3(CH_2)_3COOH$. Also called: **valeric acid.** [from PENTANE]

pentaprism ('pɛntə,prɪzəm) *n.* a five-sided prism that deviates light from any direction through an angle of 90°, typically used in single-lens reflex cameras between lens and viewfinder to present the image the right way round.

pentaquine ('pɛntə,kwiːn, -kwɪn) *n.* a synthetic drug used to treat malaria. Formula: $C_{18}H_{27}N_3O$. [C20: from PENTA- + QUINOLINE]

pentarchy ('pɛntɑːkɪ) *n., pl.* **-chies. 1.** government by five rulers. **2.** a ruling body of five. **3.** a union or association of five kingdoms, provinces, etc., each under its own ruler. **4.** a country ruled by a body of five. —**pen'tarchical** *adj.*

pentastich ('pɛntə,stɪk) *n.* a poem, stanza, or strophe that consists of five lines.

Pentateuch ('pɛntə,tjuːk) *n.* the first five books of the Old Testament regarded as a unity. [C16: from Church Latin *pentateuchus,* from Greek PENTA- + *teukhos* tool (in Late Greek: scroll)] —,**Penta'teuchal** *adj.*

pentathlon (pɛn'tæθlən) *n.* an athletic contest consisting of five different events, based on a competition in the ancient Greek Olympics. Compare **decathlon.** [C18: from Greek *pentathlon,* from PENTA- + *athlon* contest] —**pen'tathlete** *n.*

pentatomic (,pɛntə'tɒmɪk) *adj. Chem.* having five atoms in the molecule.

pentatonic scale (,pɛntə'tɒnɪk) *n. Music.* any of several scales consisting of five notes, the most commonly encountered one being composed of the first, second, third, fifth, and sixth degrees of the major diatonic scale.

pentavalent (,pɛntə'veɪlənt) *adj. Chem.* having a valency of five. Also: **quinquevalent.**

pentazocine (pɛn'tæzəʊ,siːn) *n.* a powerful synthetic opiate used in medical practice as an analgesic.

Pentecost ('pɛntɪ,kɒst) *n.* **1.** a Christian festival occurring on Whit Sunday commemorating the descent of the Holy Ghost on the apostles. **2.** Also called: **Feast of Weeks, Shavuot.** *Judaism.* the harvest festival celebrated fifty days after the second day of Passover on the sixth and seventh days of Sivan, and commemorating the giving the Torah on Mount Sinai. [Old English, from Church Latin *pentēcostē,* from Greek *pentēkostē* fiftieth]

Pentecostal (,pɛntɪ'kɒstᵊl) *adj.* **1.** (*usually prenominal*) of or relating to any of various Christian groups that emphasize the charismatic aspects of Christianity and adopt a fundamental attitude to the Bible. **2.** of or relating to Pentecost or the influence of the Holy Ghost. ~*n.* **3.** a member of a Pentecostal Church. —,**Pente'costal,ism** *n.* —,**Pente'costalist** *n., adj.*

pentene ('pɛntiːn) *n.* a colourless flammable liquid alkene having several straight-chained isomeric forms, used in the manufacture of organic compounds. Formula: C_5H_{10}. Also called: **amylene.**

penthouse ('pɛnt,haʊs) *n.* **1.** a flat or maisonette built onto the top floor or roof of a block of flats. **2.** a construction on the roof of a building, esp. one used to house machinery. **3.** a shed built against a building, esp. one that has a sloping roof. **4.** *Real Tennis.* the roofed corridor that runs along three sides of the court. [C14 *pentis* (later *penthouse,* by folk etymology), from Old French *apentis,* from Late Latin *appendicium* appendage, from Latin *appendere* to hang from; see APPENDIX]

pentimento (,pɛntɪ'mɛntəʊ) *n., pl.* **-ti** (-tiː). **1.** the revealing of a painting or part of a painting that has been covered over by a later painting. **2.** the part of a painting thus revealed. [C20: Italian, literally: correction]

pentlandite ('pɛntlən,daɪt) *n.* a brownish-yellow mineral consisting of an iron and nickel sulphide in cubic crystalline form: the principal ore of nickel. Formula: (Fe,Ni)S. [C19: from French; named after J. B. *Pentland* (1797–1873), Irish scientist who discovered it]

pentobarbitone sodium (,pɛntə'bɑːbɪ,təʊn) *n.* a barbiturate drug used in medicine as a sedative and hypnotic. U.S. equivalent: '**sodium ,penta'barbital.** Formula: $C_{11}H_{17}N_2O_3Na$.

pentode ('pɛntəʊd) *n.* **1.** an electronic valve having five electrodes: a cathode, anode, and three grids. **2.** (*modifier*) (of a transistor) having three terminals at the base or gate. [C20: from PENTA- + Greek *hodos* way]

pentomic (pɛn'tɒmɪk) *adj.* denoting or relating to the subdivision of an army division into five battle groups, esp. for nuclear warfare. [C20: from PENTA- + ATOMIC]

pentosan ('pɛntə,sæn) *n. Biochem.* any of a group of polysaccharides, having the general formula $(C_5H_8O_4)_n$: occur in plants, humus, etc. [C20: from PENTOSE + -AN]

pentose ('pɛntəʊs) *n.* any monosaccharide containing five atoms of carbon per molecule: occur mainly in plants and the nucleic acids. [C20: from PENTA- + -OSE[2]]

pentose phosphate pathway *n.* a sequence of metabolic reactions by which NADPH is synthesized, together with ribose phosphate, part of the synthesis of nucleic acids.

Pentothal sodium ('pɛntə,θæl) *n.* a trademark for **thiopentone sodium.**

pentoxide (pɛnt'ɒksaɪd) *n.* an oxide of an element with five atoms of oxygen per molecule.

pentstemon (pɛnt'stiːmən) *or esp. U.S.* **penstemon** *n.* any scrophulariaceous plant of the North American genus *Pentstemon* (or *Penstemon*), having white, pink, red, blue, or purple flowers with five stamens, one of which is bearded and sterile. [C18: New Latin, from PENTA- + Greek *stēmōn* thread (here: stamen)]

pent-up *adj.* (**pent up** *when postpositive*) **1.** not released; repressed: *pent-up emotions.* **2.** kept unwillingly: *I've been pent up in this office for over a year.*

pentyl ('pɛntaɪl, -tɪl) *n.* (*modifier*) of, consisting of, or containing the monovalent group $CH_3CH_2CH_2CH_2CH_2$-: *a pentyl group or radical.*

pentyl acetate *n.* a colourless combustible liquid used as a solvent for paints, in the extraction of penicillin, in photographic film, and as a flavouring. Formula: $CH_3COOC_5H_{11}$. Also called: **amyl acetate.** Nontechnical name: **banana oil.**

pentylenetetrazol (ˌpɛntɪliːn'tɛtrəˌzɒl) *n.* a white crystalline water-soluble substance with a bitter taste, used in medicine to stimulate the central nervous system. Formula: $C_6H_{10}N_4$. [C20: from *penta-methylene-tetrazole*]

penuche (pə'nuːtʃɪ) *n.* a variant of **panocha.**

penuchle *or* **penuckle** ('piːnʌkᵊl) *n.* less common spellings of **pinochle.**

penult ('pɛnʌlt, pɪ'nʌlt) *or* **penultima** (pɪ'nʌltɪmə) *n.* the last syllable but one in a word. [C16: Latin *paenultima syllaba,* from *paene ultima* almost the last]

penultimate (pɪ'nʌltɪmɪt) *adj.* **1.** next to the last. ~*n.* **2.** anything that is next to the last, esp. a penult. [C17: from Latin *paene* almost + ULTIMATE, on the model of Latin *paenultimus*]

penumbra (pɪ'nʌmbrə) *n., pl.* **-brae** (-briː) *or* **-bras. 1.** a fringe region of half shadow resulting from the partial obstruction of light by an opaque object. **2.** *Astronomy.* the lighter and outer region of a sunspot. **3.** *Painting.* the point or area in which light and shade blend. ~Compare **umbra.** [C17: via New Latin from Latin *paene* almost + *umbra* shadow] —**pe'numbral** *or* **pe'numbrous** *adj.*

penurious (pɪ'njʊərɪəs) *adj.* **1.** niggardly with money. **2.** lacking money or means. **3.** yielding little; scanty. —**pe'nuriously** *adv.* —**pe'nuriousness** *n.*

penury ('pɛnjʊrɪ) *n.* **1.** extreme poverty. **2.** extreme scarcity. [C15: from Latin *pēnūria* dearth, of obscure origin]

Penutian (pɪ'njuːtɪən, -ʃən) *n.* **1.** a family of North American Indian languages of the Pacific coast. **2.** a phylum of languages of North and South America, including Araucanian, Chinook, Mayan, and Sahaptin.

peon[1] ('piːən, 'piːɒn) *n.* **1.** a Spanish-American farm labourer or unskilled worker. **2.** (formerly in Spanish America) a debtor compelled to work off his debts. **3.** any very poor person. [C19: from Spanish *peón* peasant, from Medieval Latin *pedō* man who goes on foot, from Latin *pēs* foot; compare Old French *paon* PAWN[2]]

peon[2] (pjuːn, 'piːən, 'piːɒn) *n.* (in India, Sri Lanka, etc., esp. formerly) **1.** a messenger or attendant, esp. in an office. **2.** a native policeman. **3.** a foot soldier. [C17: from Portuguese *peão* orderly; see PEON[1]]

peonage ('piːənɪdʒ) *or* **peonism** ('piːəˌnɪzəm) *n.* **1.** the state of being a peon. **2.** a system in which a debtor must work for his creditor until the debt is paid off.

peony *or* **paeony** ('piːənɪ) *n., pl.* **-nies. 1.** any of various ranunculaceous shrubs and plants of the genus *Paeonia,* of Eurasia and North America, having large pink, red, white, or yellow flowers. **2.** the flower of any of these plants. [Old English *peonie,* from Latin *paeōnia,* from Greek *paiōnia;* related to *paiōnios* healing, from *paiōn* physician]

people ('piːpᵊl) *n.* (*usually functioning as pl.*) **1.** persons collectively or in general. **2.** a group of persons considered together: *blind people.* **3.** (*pl.* **peoples**) the persons living in a country and sharing the same nationality: *the French people.* **4.** one's family: *he took her home to meet his people.* **5.** persons loyal to someone powerful: *the king's people accompanied him in exile.* **6. the people. a.** the mass of persons without special distinction, privileges, etc. **b.** the body of persons in a country, esp. those entitled to vote. ~*vb.* **7.** (*tr.*) to provide with or as if with people or inhabitants. [C13: from Old French *pople,* from Latin *populus;* see POPULACE]

▷**Usage.** See at **person.**

people mover *n.* any of various automated forms of transport for large numbers of passengers over short distances, such as a moving pavement, driverless cars, etc.

people's democracy *n.* (in Communist ideology) a country or form of government in transition from bourgeois democracy to socialism. In this stage there is more than one class, the largest being the proletariat, led by the Communist Party, which is therefore the dominant power.

people's front *n.* a less common term for **popular front.**

pep (pɛp) *n.* **1.** high spirits, energy, or vitality. ~*vb.* **peps, pepping, pepped. 2.** (*tr.;* usually foll. by *up*) to liven by imbuing with new vigour. [C20: short for PEPPER]

PEP *abbrev. for:* **1.** political and economic planning. **2.** personal equity plan: a method of saving in the U.K. with certain tax advantages, in which investments up to a fixed annual value can be purchased.

peperomia (pɛpə'rəʊmɪə) *n.* any plant of the large genus *Peperomia* from tropical and subtropical America with slightly fleshy ornamental leaves, some of which are grown as pot plants: family *Piperaceae.* [New Latin, from Greek *peperi* pepper + *homoios* similar + -IA]

peplos *or* **peplus** ('pɛpləs) *n., pl.* **-loses** *or* **-luses.** (in ancient Greece) the top part of a woman's attire, caught at the shoulders and hanging in folds to the waist. Also called: **peplum.** [C18: from Greek, of obscure origin]

peplum ('pɛpləm) *n., pl.* **-lums** *or* **-la** (-lə). **1.** a flared ruffle attached to the waist of a jacket, bodice, etc. **2.** a variant of **peplos.** [C17: from Latin: full upper garment, from Greek *peplos* shawl]

pepo ('piːpəʊ) *n., pl.* **-pos.** the fruit of any of various cucurbitaceous plants, such as the melon, squash, cucumber, and pumpkin, having a firm rind, fleshy watery pulp, and numerous seeds. [C19: from Latin: pumpkin, from Greek *pepōn* edible gourd, from *peptein* to ripen]

pepper ('pɛpə) *n.* **1.** a woody climbing plant, *Piper nigrum,* of the East Indies, having small black berry-like fruits: family *Piperaceae.* **2.** the dried fruit of this plant, which is ground to produce a sharp hot condiment. See also **black pepper, white pepper. 3.** any of various other plants of the genus *Piper.* See **cubeb, betel, kava. 4.** Also called: **capsicum.** any of various tropical plants of the solanaceous genus *Capsicum,* esp. *C. frutescens,* the fruits of which are used as a vegetable and a condiment. See also **bird pepper, sweet pepper, red pepper, cayenne pepper. 5.** the fruit of any of these capsicums, which has a mild or pungent taste. **6.** the condiment made from the fruits of any of these plants. **7.** any of various similar but unrelated plants, such as water pepper. ~*vb.* (*tr.*) **8.** to season with pepper. **9.** to sprinkle liberally; dot: *his prose was peppered with alliteration.* **10.** to pelt with small missiles. [Old English *piper,* from Latin, from Greek *peperi;* compare French *poivre,* Old Norse *piparr*]

pepper-and-salt *adj.* **1.** (of cloth) marked with a fine mixture of black and white. **2.** (of hair) streaked with grey.

peppercorn ('pɛpəˌkɔːn) *n.* **1.** the small dried berry of the pepper plant (*Piper nigrum*). **2.** something trifling.

peppercorn rent *n.* a rent that is very low or nominal.

peppered moth *n.* a European geometrid moth, *Biston betularia,* occurring in a pale grey speckled form in rural areas and a black form in industrial regions. See also **melanism** (sense 1).

peppergrass ('pɛpəˌgrɑːs) *n.* the usual U.S. and Canadian name for **pepperwort** (sense 2).

pepper mill *n.* a small hand mill used to grind peppercorns.

peppermint ('pɛpəˌmɪnt) *n.* **1.** a temperate mint plant, *Mentha piperita,* with purple or white flowers: cultivated for its downy leaves, which yield a pungent oil. **2.** the oil from this plant, which is used as a flavouring. **3.** a sweet flavoured with peppermint.

pepperoni (ˌpɛpə'rəʊnɪ) *n.* a highly seasoned dry sausage of pork and beef spiced with pepper, used esp. on pizza. [C20: from Italian *peperoni,* plural of *peperone* cayenne pepper]

pepper pot *n.* **1.** a small container with perforations in the top for sprinkling pepper. **2.** a West Indian stew of meat, rice, vegetables, etc., highly seasoned with cassareep.

pepper tree *n.* any of several evergreen anacardiaceous trees of the chiefly South American genus *Schinus,* esp. *S. molle* (also called: **mastic tree**), having yellowish-white flowers and bright red ornamental fruits.

peppertree ('pɛpəˌtriː) *n. N.Z.* another name for **kawakawa.**

pepperwort ('pɛpəˌwɜːt) *n.* **1.** any of various temperate and tropical aquatic or marsh ferns of the genus *Marsilea,* having floating leaves consisting of four leaflets: family *Marsileaceae.* **2.** any of several cruciferous plants of the genus *Lepidium,* esp. *L. campestre,* of dry regions of Eurasia, having small white flowers and pungent seeds. Usual U.S. and Canadian name: **peppergrass.**

peppery ('pɛpərɪ) *adj.* **1.** flavoured with or tasting of pepper. **2.** quick-tempered; irritable. **3.** full of bite and sharpness: *a peppery speech.* —'**pepperiness** *n.*

pep pill *n. Informal.* a tablet containing a stimulant drug.

peppy ('pɛpɪ) *adj.* **-pier, -piest.** *Informal.* full of vitality; bouncy or energetic. —'**peppily** *adv.* —'**peppiness** *n.*

pepsin *or* **pepsine** ('pɛpsɪn) *n.* a proteolytic enzyme produced in the stomach in the inactive form pepsinogen, which, when activated by acid, splits proteins into peptones. [C19: via German from Greek *pepsis,* from *peptein* to digest]

pepsinate ('pɛpsɪˌneɪt) *vb.* (*tr.*) **1.** to treat (a patient) with pepsin. **2.** to mix or infuse (something) with pepsin.

pepsinogen (pɛp'sɪnədʒən) *n.* the inactive precursor of pepsin produced by the stomach.

pep talk *n. Informal.* an enthusiastic talk designed to increase confidence, production, cooperation, etc.

peptic ('pɛptɪk) *adj.* **1.** of, relating to, or promoting digestion. **2.** of, relating to, or caused by pepsin or the action of the digestive juices. [C17: from Greek *peptikos* capable of digesting, from *pepsis* digestion, from *peptein* to digest]

peptic ulcer *n. Pathol.* an ulcer of the mucous membrane lining those parts of the alimentary tract exposed to digestive juices, including the oesophagus, the stomach, the duodenum, and parts of the small intestine.

peptidase ('pɛptɪˌdeɪs, -ˌdeɪz) *n.* any of a group of proteolytic enzymes that hydrolyse peptides to amino acids.

peptide ('pɛptaɪd) *n.* any of a group of compounds consisting of two or more amino acids linked by chemical bonding between their respective carboxyl and amino groups. See also **peptide bond, polypeptide.**

peptide bond *n. Biochem.* a chemical amide linkage, –NH–CO–, formed by the condensation of the amino group of one amino acid with the carboxyl group of another.

peptize *or* **peptise** ('pɛptaɪz) *vb. (tr.) Chem.* to disperse (a substance) into a colloidal state, usually to form a sol. —'**peptizable** *or* '**peptisable** *adj.* —ˌ**pepti'zation** *or* ˌ**pepti'sation** *n.* —'**peptizer** *or* '**peptiser** *n.*

peptone ('pɛptəʊn) *n. Biochem.* any of a group of compounds that form an intermediary group in the digestion of proteins to amino acids. See also **proteose.** [C19: from German *Pepton,* from Greek *pepton* something digested, from *peptein* to digest] —**peptonic** (pɛp'tɒnɪk) *adj.*

peptonize *or* **peptonise** ('pɛptəˌnaɪz) *vb. (tr.)* to hydrolyse (a protein) to peptones by enzymic action, esp. by pepsin or pancreatic extract. —ˌ**peptoni'zation** *or* ˌ**peptoni'sation** *n.* —'**peptoˌnizer** *or* '**peptoˌniser** *n.*

Péquiste (peɪ'kiːst) *n. (sometimes not cap.)* (in Canada) a member or supporter of the Parti Québecois, a political party formed in Quebec and originally advocating Quebec's separation from the rest of Canada. [from the French pronunciation of PQ + *-iste*]

Pequot ('piːkwɒt) *n.* **1.** *(pl.* **-quot** *or* **-quots)** a member of a North American Indian people formerly living in S New England. **2.** the language of this people, belonging to the Algonquian family. [probably based on Narraganset *paquatanog* destroyers]

per (pɜː; *unstressed* pə) *determiner.* **1.** for every: *three pence per pound.* ~*prep.* **2.** (esp. in some Latin phrases) by; through. **3. as per.** according to: *as per specifications.* **4. as per usual.** *Informal.* as usual. [C15: from Latin: by, for each]

PER (in Britain) *abbrev. for* Professional Employment Register.

per. *abbrev. for:* **1.** period. **2.** person.

per- *prefix.* **1.** indicating that a chemical compound contains a high proportion of a specified element: *peroxide; perchloride.* **2.** indicating that a chemical element is in a higher than usual state of oxidation: *permanganate; perchlorate.* **3.** *(not in technical usage)* a variant of **peroxy-:** *persulphuric acid.* [from Latin *per* through. In compound words borrowed from Latin, *per-* indicates: through *(pervade);* throughout *(permanent);* away *(perfidy);* and is used as an intensifier *(permutation)*]

peracid (pɜːr'æsɪd) *n.* **1.** an acid, such as perchloric acid, in which the element forming the acid radical exhibits its highest valency. **2.** *(not in technical usage)* an acid, such as persulphuric acid, that contains the -OOH group. Recommended names: **per'oxo acid, per'oxy acid.** —**peracidity** (ˌpɛrə'sɪdɪtɪ) *n.*

peradventure (pərəd'vɛntʃə, ˌpɜːr-) *Archaic.* ~*adv.* **1.** by chance; perhaps. ~*n.* **2.** chance, uncertainty, or doubt. [C13: from Old French *par aventure* by chance]

perambulate (pə'ræmbjʊˌleɪt) *vb.* **1.** to walk about (a place). **2.** *(tr.)* to walk round in order to inspect. [C16: from Latin *perambulāre* to traverse, from *per* through + *ambulāre* to walk] —**perˌambu'lation** *n.* —**perambulatory** (pə'ræmbjʊlətərɪ, -trɪ) *adj.*

perambulator (pə'ræmbjʊˌleɪtə) *n.* **1.** a formal word for **pram**[1]. **2.** a wheel-like instrument used by surveyors to measure distances.

per annum (pər 'ænəm) *adv.* every year or by the year.

per ardua ad astra *Latin.* (pɜːr 'ɑːdjʊə æd 'æstrə) through difficulties to the stars: the motto of the RAF.

P/E ratio *abbrev. for* **price-earnings ratio.**

perborate (pə'bɔːreɪt) *n.* any of certain salts derived, or apparently derived, from perboric acid. Perborates are used as bleaches in washing powders. See **sodium perborate.**

percale (pə'keɪl, -'kɑːl) *n.* a close-textured woven cotton fabric, plain or printed, used esp. for sheets. [C17: via French from Persian *pargālah* piece of cloth]

percaline ('pɜːkəˌliːn, -lɪn) *n.* a fine light cotton fabric, used esp. for linings. [C19: from French; see PERCALE]

per capita (pə 'kæpɪtə) *adj., adv.* of or for each person. [Latin, literally: according to heads]

perceive (pə'siːv) *vb.* **1.** to become aware of (something) through the senses, esp. the sight; recognize or observe. **2.** *(tr.; may take a clause as object)* to come to comprehend; grasp. [C13: from Old French *perçoivre,* from Latin *percipere* seize entirely, from PER- (thoroughly) + *capere* to grasp] —**per'ceivable** *adj.* —**perˌceiva'bility** *n.* —**per'ceivably** *adv.* —**per'ceiver** *n.*

perceived noise decibel *n.* a unit for measuring perceived levels of noise by comparison with the sound pressure level of a reference sound judged equally noisy by a normal listener. Abbrev.: **PNdB.**

per cent (pə 'sɛnt) *adv.* **1.** Also: **per centum.** in or for every hundred. ~*n. also* **per'cent. 2.** a percentage or proportion. **3.** *(often pl.)* securities yielding a rate of interest as specified: *he bought three percents.* [C16: from Medieval Latin *per centum* out of every hundred]

percentage (pə'sɛntɪdʒ) *n.* **1.** proportion or rate per hundred parts. **2.** *Commerce.* the interest, tax, commission, or allowance on a hundred items. **3.** any proportion in relation to the whole. **4.** *Informal.* profit or advantage.

percentile (pə'sɛntaɪl) *n.* one of 99 actual or notional values of a variable dividing its distribution into 100 groups with equal frequencies; the 90th percentile is the value of a variable such that 90% of the relevant population is below that value. Also called: **centile.**

percept ('pɜːsɛpt) *n.* **1.** a concept that depends on recognition by the senses, such as sight, of some external object or phenomenon. **2.** an object or phenomenon that is perceived. [C19: from Latin *perceptum,* from *percipere* to PERCEIVE]

perceptible (pə'sɛptəbᵊl) *adj.* able to be perceived; noticeable or recognizable. —**perˌcepti'bility** —**per'ceptibly** *adv.*

perception (pə'sɛpʃən) *n.* **1.** the act or the effect of perceiving. **2.** insight or intuition gained by perceiving. **3.** the ability or capacity to perceive. **4.** way of perceiving; awareness or consciousness; view: *advertising affects the customer's perception of a product.* **5.** the process by which an organism detects and interprets information from the external world by means of the sensory receptors. **6.** *Law.* the collection, receipt, or taking into possession of rents, crops, etc. [C15: from Latin *perceptiō* comprehension; see PERCEIVE] —**per'ceptional** *adj.*

perceptive (pə'sɛptɪv) *adj.* **1.** quick at perceiving; observant. **2.** perceptual. **3.** able to perceive. —**per'ceptively** *adv.* —ˌ**percep'tivity** *or* **per'ceptiveness** *n.*

perceptual (pə'sɛptjʊəl) *adj.* of or relating to perception. —**per'ceptually** *adv.*

perceptual defence *n. Psychol.* the process by which it is thought that certain stimuli are either not perceived or are distorted due to their offensive, unpleasant, or threatening nature.

perch[1] (pɜːtʃ) *n.* **1.** a pole, branch, or other resting place above ground on which a bird roosts or alights. **2.** a similar resting place for a person or thing. **3.** another name for **rod** (sense 7). **4.** a solid measure for stone, usually taken as 198 inches by 18 inches by 12 inches. **5.** a pole joining the front and rear axles of a carriage. **6.** a frame on which cloth is placed for inspection. **7.** *Obsolete or dialect.* a pole. ~*vb.* **8.** (usually foll. by *on*) to alight, rest, or cause to rest on or as if on a perch: *the bird perched on the branch; the cap was perched on his head.* **9.** *(tr.)* to inspect (cloth) on a perch. [C13 *perche* stake, from Old French, from Latin *pertica* long staff] —'**percher** *n.*

perch[2] (pɜːtʃ) *n., pl.* **perch** *or* **perches. 1.** any freshwater spiny-finned teleost fish of the family *Percidae,* esp. those of the genus *Perca,* such as *P. fluviatilis* of Europe and *P. flavescens* **(yellow perch)** of North America: valued as food and game fishes. **2.** any of various similar or related fishes. Related adj.: **percoid.** [C13: from Old French *perche,* from Latin *perca,* from Greek *perkē;* compare Greek *perkos* spotted]

perchance (pə'tʃɑːns) *adv. Archaic or poetic.* **1.** perhaps; possibly. **2.** by chance; accidentally. [C14: from Anglo-French *par chance;* see PER, CHANCE]

Percheron ('pɜːʃəˌrɒn) *n.* a compact heavy breed of carthorse, grey or black in colour. [C19: from French, from *le Perche,* region of NW France where the breed originated]

perchlorate (pə'klɔːreɪt) *n.* any salt or ester of perchloric acid. Perchlorate salts contain the ion ClO_4^-.

perchloric acid (pə'klɔːrɪk) *n.* a colourless syrupy oxyacid of chlorine containing a greater proportion of oxygen than chloric acid. It is a powerful oxidizing agent and is used as a laboratory reagent. Formula: $HClO_4$. Systematic name: **chloric(VII) acid.**

perchloride (pə'klɔːraɪd) *n.* a chloride that contains more chlorine than other chlorides of the same element.

perchloroethylene (pəˌklɔːrəʊ'ɛθɪliːn) *or* **perchloroethene** (pəˌklɔːrəʊ'ɛθiːn) *n.* a colourless liquid used as a dry-cleaning solvent. Formula: $CCl_2{:}CCl_2$.

percipient (pə'sɪpɪənt) *adj.* **1.** able to perceive. **2.** perceptive. ~*n.* **3.** a person or thing that perceives. [C17: from Latin *percipiens* observing, from *percipere* to grasp; see PERCEIVE] —**per'cipience** *n.* —**per'cipiently** *adv.*

percoid ('pɜːkɔɪd) *or* **percoidean** (pə'kɔɪdɪən) *adj.* **1.** of, relating to, or belonging to the *Percoidea,* a suborder of spiny-finned teleost fishes including the perches, sea bass, red mullet, cichlids, etc. **2.** of, relating to, or resembling a perch. ~*n.* **3.** any fish belonging to the suborder *Percoidea.* [C19: from Latin *perca* PERCH[2] + -OID]

percolate *vb.* ('pɜːkəˌleɪt). **1.** to cause (a liquid) to pass through a fine mesh, porous substance, etc., or (of a liquid) to pass through a fine mesh, porous substance, etc.; trickle: *rain percolated through the roof.* **2.** to permeate; penetrate gradually: *water percolated the road.* **3.** *(intr.) U.S. informal.* to become active or lively: *she percolated with happiness.* **4.** to make (coffee) or (of coffee) to be made in a percolator. ~*n.* ('pɜːkəlɪt, -ˌleɪt). **5.** a product of percolation. [C17: from Latin *percōlāre,* from PER + *cōlāre* to strain, from *cōlum* a strainer; see COLANDER] —**percolable** ('pɜːkələbᵊl) *adj.* —ˌ**perco'lation** *n.* —'**percolative** *adj.*

percolator ('pɜːkəˌleɪtə) *n.* a kind of coffeepot in which boiling water is forced up through a tube and filters down through the coffee grounds into a container.

per contra ('pɜː 'kɒntrə) *adv.* on the contrary. [from Latin]

percuss (pə'kʌs) *vb. (tr.)* **1.** to strike sharply, rapidly, or suddenly. **2.** *Med.* to tap on (a body surface) with the fingertips or a special hammer to aid diagnosis or for therapeutic purposes. [C16: from Latin *percutere,* from *per-* through + *quatere* to shake] —**per'cussor** *n.*

percussion (pəˈkʌʃən) *n.* **1.** the act, an instance, or an effect of percussing. **2.** *Music.* the family of instruments in which sound arises from the striking of materials with sticks or hammers. **3.** *Music.* **a.** instruments of this family constituting a section of an orchestra, band, etc. **b.** (*as modifier*): *a percussion ensemble.* **4.** *Med.* the act of percussing a body surface. **5.** the act of exploding a percussion cap. [C16: from Latin *percussiō,* from *percutere* to hit; see PERCUSS]

percussion cap *n.* a detonator consisting of a paper or thin metal cap containing material that explodes when struck and formerly used in certain firearms.

percussion instrument *n.* any of various musical instruments that produce a sound when their resonating surfaces are struck directly, as with a stick or mallet, or by leverage action. They may be of definite pitch (as a kettledrum or xylophone), indefinite pitch (as a gong or rattle), or a mixture of both (as various drums).

percussionist (pəˈkʌʃənɪst) *n. Music.* a person who plays any of several percussion instruments, esp. in an orchestra.

percussion lock *n.* a gunlock in which the hammer strikes a percussion cap.

percussion tool *n.* a power driven tool which operates by striking rapid blows: the power may be electricity or compressed air.

percussive (pəˈkʌsɪv) *adj.* of, caused by, or relating to percussion. —**per'cussively** *adv.* —**per'cussiveness** *n.*

percutaneous (ˌpɜːkjuˈteɪnɪəs) *adj. Med.* effected through the skin, as in the absorption of an ointment.

per diem (ˈpɜː ˈdaɪɛm, ˈdiːɛm) *adv.* **1.** every day or by the day. ~*n.* **2. a.** an allowance for daily expenses, usually those incurred while working. **b.** (*as modifier*): *a per-diem allowance.* [from Latin]

perdition (pəˈdɪʃən) *n.* **1.** *Christianity.* **a.** final and irrevocable spiritual ruin. **b.** this state as one that the wicked are said to be destined to endure for ever. **2.** another word for **hell. 3.** *Archaic.* utter disaster, ruin, or destruction. [C14: from Late Latin *perditiō* ruin, from Latin *perdere* to lose, from PER- (away) + *dāre* to give]

perdu *or* **perdue** (ˈpɜːdjuː) *adj.* **1.** *Obsolete.* (of a soldier) placed on hazardous sentry duty. **2.** *Obsolete.* (of a soldier) placed in a hazardous ambush. **3.** (of a person or thing) hidden or concealed. ~*n.* **4.** *Obsolete.* a soldier placed on hazardous sentry duty. **5.** *Obsolete.* a soldier placed in a hazardous ambush. [C16: via French: lost, from *perdre* to lose, from Latin *perdere* to destroy]

perdurable (pəˈdjʊərəbᵊl) *adj. Rare.* extremely durable. [C13: from Late Latin *perdūrābilis,* from Latin *per-* (intensive) + *dūrābilis* long-lasting, from *dūrus* hard] —ˌ**perdura'bility** *n.* —'**perdurably** *adv.*

père *French.* (pɛr; *English* pɛə) *n.* an addition to a French surname to specify the father rather than the son of the same name: *Dumas père.* Compare **fils**[1].

Père David's deer *n.* a large grey deer, *Elaphurus davidianus,* surviving only in captivity as descendants of a herd preserved in the Imperial hunting park near Peking. [C20: named after Father A. *David* (died 1900), French missionary]

peregrinate (ˈpɛrɪgrɪˌneɪt) *vb.* **1.** (*intr.*) to travel or wander about from place to place; voyage. **2.** (*tr.*) to travel through (a place). ~*adj.* **3.** an obsolete word for **foreign.** [C16: from Latin, from *peregrīnārī* to travel; see PEREGRINE] —'**peregriˌnator** *n.*

peregrination (ˌpɛrɪgrɪˈneɪʃən) *n.* **1.** a voyage, esp. an extensive one. **2.** the act or process of travelling.

peregrine (ˈpɛrɪgrɪn) *adj. Archaic.* **1.** coming from abroad. **2.** travelling or migratory; wandering. [C14: from Latin *peregrīnus* foreign, from *pereger* being abroad, from *per* through + *ager* land (that is, beyond one's own land)]

peregrine falcon *n.* a falcon, *Falco peregrinus,* occurring in most parts of the world, having a dark plumage on the back and wings and lighter underparts. See also **duck hawk.**

pereira bark (pəˈrɛərə) *n.* the bark of a South American apocynaceous tree, *Geissospermum vellosii:* source of a substance formerly used for treating malaria. [named after Jonathan *Pereira* (1804–53), English pharmacologist]

peremptory (pəˈrɛmptərɪ) *adj.* **1.** urgent or commanding: *a peremptory ring on the bell.* **2.** not able to be remitted or debated; decisive. **3.** positive or assured in speech, manner, etc.; dogmatic. **4.** *Law.* **a.** admitting of no denial or contradiction; precluding debate. **b.** obligatory rather than permissive. [C16: from Anglo-Norman *peremptorie,* from Latin *peremptōrius* decisive, from *perimere* to take away completely, from PER- (intensive) + *emere* to take] —**per'emptorily** *adv.* —**per'emptoriness** *n.*

Perendale (ˈpɛrənˌdeɪl) *n. N.Z.* a Romney-Cheviot crossbreed of sheep. [C20: named after Sir Geoffrey S. *Peren,* New Zealand agriculturist]

perennate (ˈpɛrɪˌneɪt, pəˈrɛneɪt) *vb.* (*intr.*) (of plants) to live from one growing season to another, usually with a period of reduced activity between seasons. [C17: from Latin *perennātus,* from *perennāre,* from PER- (through) + *annus* year]

perennial (pəˈrɛnɪəl) *adj.* **1.** lasting throughout the year or through many years. **2.** everlasting; perpetual. ~*n.* **3.** a woody or herbaceous plant that continues its growth for at least three years. Compare **annual** (sense 3), **biennial** (sense 3). [C17: from Latin *perennis* continual, from *per* through + *annus* year] —**per'ennially** *adv.*

perentie *or* **perenty** (pəˈrɛntɪ) *n., pl.* **-ties.** a large dark-coloured monitor lizard, *Varanus giganteus,* of central and west Australia which grows to 7 ft. [from a native Australian language]

perestroika (ˌpɛrəˈstrɔɪkə) *n.* the policy of reconstructing the Soviet economy, etc., under the leadership of Mikhail Gorbachov. [C20: Russian, literally: reconstruction]

perf. *abbrev. for:* **1.** perfect. **2.** perforated. **3.** perforation.

perfect *adj.* (ˈpɜːfɪkt). **1.** having all essential elements. **2.** unblemished; faultless: *a perfect gemstone.* **3.** correct or precise: *perfect timing.* **4.** utter or absolute: *a perfect stranger.* **5.** excellent in all respects: *a perfect day.* **6.** *Maths.* exactly divisible into equal integral or polynomial roots: *36 is a perfect square.* **7.** *Botany.* **a.** (of flowers) having functional stamens and pistils. **b.** (of plants) having all parts present. **8.** *Grammar.* denoting a tense of verbs used in describing an action that has been completed by the subject. In English this is a compound tense, formed with *have* or *has* plus the past participle. **9.** *Music.* **a.** of or relating to the intervals of the unison, fourth, fifth, and octave. **b.** (of a cadence) ending on the tonic chord, giving a feeling of conclusion. Also: **full, final.** Compare **imperfect** (sense 6). **10.** *Archaic.* positive certain, or assured. ~*n.* (ˈpɜːfɪkt). **11.** *Grammar.* **a.** the perfect tense. **b.** a verb in this tense. ~*vb.* (pəˈfɛkt). (*tr.*) **12.** to make perfect; improve to one's satisfaction: *he is in Paris to perfect his French.* **13.** to make fully accomplished. **14.** *Printing.* to print the reverse side of (a printed sheet of paper). [C13: from Latin *perfectus,* from *perficere* to perform, from *per* through + *facere* to do] —'**perfectness** *n.* **Usage.** See at **unique.**

perfect competition *n. Economics.* a market situation in which there exists a homogeneous product, freedom of entry, and a large number of buyers and sellers none of whom individually can affect price.

perfect gas *n.* another name for **ideal gas.**

perfectible (pəˈfɛktəbᵊl) *adj.* capable of becoming or being made perfect. —**perˌfecti'bility** *n.*

perfection (pəˈfɛkʃən) *n.* **1.** the act of perfecting or the state or quality of being perfect. **2.** the highest degree of a quality, etc.: *the perfection of faithfulness.* **3.** an embodiment of perfection. [C13: from Latin *perfectiō* a completing, from *perficere* to finish]

perfectionism (pəˈfɛkʃəˌnɪzəm) *n.* **1.** *Philosophy.* the doctrine that man can attain perfection in this life. **2.** the demand for the highest standard of excellence.

perfectionist (pəˈfɛkʃənɪst) *n.* **1.** a person who strives for or demands the highest standards of excellence in work, etc. **2.** a person who believes the doctrine of perfectionism. ~*adj.* **3.** of or relating to perfectionism.

perfective (pəˈfɛktɪv) *adj.* **1.** tending to perfect. **2.** *Grammar.* denoting an aspect of verbs in some languages, including English, used to express that the action or event described by the verb is or was completed: *I lived in London for ten years* is perfective; *I have lived in London for ten years* is imperfective, since the implication is that I still live in London.

perfectly (ˈpɜːfɪktlɪ) *adv.* **1.** completely, utterly, or absolutely. **2.** in a perfect way; extremely well.

perfect number *n.* an integer, such as 28, that is equal to the sum of all its possible factors, excluding itself.

perfecto (pəˈfɛktəʊ) *n., pl.* **-tos.** a large cigar that is tapered from both ends. [Spanish, literally: perfect]

perfector *or* **perfecter** (ˈpɜːfɪktə) *n.* **1.** a person who completes or makes something perfect. **2.** *Printing.* a machine or press capable of printing both sides of the paper in a single operation.

perfect participle *n.* another name for **past participle.**

perfect pitch *n.* another name (not in technical usage) for **absolute pitch** (sense 1).

perfect rhyme *n.* **1.** Also called: **full rhyme.** rhyme between words in which the stressed vowels and any succeeding consonants are identical although the consonants preceding the stressed vowels may be different, as between *part/hart* or *believe/conceive.* **2.** a rhyme between two words that are pronounced the same although differing in meaning, as in *bough/bow.*

perfervid (pɜːˈfɜːvɪd) *adj. Literary.* extremely ardent, enthusiastic, or zealous. [C19: from New Latin *perfervidus,* from Latin *per-* (intensive) + *fervidus* FERVID] —**per'fervidly** *adv.* —**per'fervidness** *n.*

perfidious (pəˈfɪdɪəs) *adj.* guilty, treacherous, or faithless; deceitful. —**per'fidiously** *adv.* —**per'fidiousness** *n.*

perfidy (ˈpɜːfɪdɪ) *n., pl.* **-dies.** a perfidious act. [C16: from Latin *perfidia,* from *perfidus* faithless, from *per* beyond + *fidēs* faith]

perfin (ˈpɜːfɪn) *n. Philately.* the former name for **spif.** [from *perf(orated with) in(itials)*]

perfoliate (pəˈfəʊlɪɪt, -ˌeɪt) *adj.* (of a leaf) having a base that completely encloses the stem, so that the stem appears to pass through it. [C17: from New Latin *perfoliātus,* from Latin *per-* through + *folium* leaf] —**perˌfoli'ation** *n.*

perforate *vb.* (ˈpɜːfəˌreɪt). **1.** to make a hole or holes in (something); penetrate. **2.** (*tr.*) to punch rows of holes between (stamps, coupons, etc.) for ease of separation. ~*adj.* (ˈpɜːfərɪt). **3.** *Biology.* **a.** pierced by small holes: *perforate shells.* **b.** marked with small transparent spots. **4.** *Philately.* another word for **perforated** (sense 2). [C16: from Latin *perforāre,* from *per-* through + *forāre* to pierce] —**perforable** (ˈpɜːfərəbᵊl) *adj.* —ˈ**perforative** *or* ˈ**perforatory** *adj.* —ˈ**perfoˌrator** *n.*

perforated (ˈpɜːfəˌreɪtɪd) *adj.* **1.** pierced with one or more holes. **2.** (esp. of stamps) having perforations. Abbrev.: **perf.**

perforated tape *n.* a U.S. name for **paper tape.**

perforation (ˌpɜːfəˈreɪʃən) *n.* **1.** the act of perforating or the state of being perforated. **2.** a hole or holes made in something. **3. a.** a method of making individual stamps, coupons, etc., easily separable by punching holes along their margins. **b.** the holes punched in this way. Abbrev.: **perf.**

perforation gauge *n.* a graduated scale for measuring perforations and roulettes of postage stamps.

perforce (pəˈfɔːs) *adv.* by necessity; unavoidably. [C14: from Old French *par force;* see PER, FORCE[1]]

perform (pəˈfɔːm) *vb.* **1.** to carry out or do (an action). **2.** (*tr.*) to fulfil or comply with: *to perform someone's request.* **3.** to present or enact (a play, concert, etc.) before or otherwise entertain an audience: *the group performed Hamlet.* **4.** (*intr.*) *Informal.* to accomplish sexual intercourse: *he performed well.* [C14: from Anglo-Norman *perfourmer* (influenced by *forme* FORM), from Old French *parfournir,* from *par-* PER- + *fournir* to provide; see FURNISH] —**perˈformable** *adj.* —**perˈformer** *n.*

performance (pəˈfɔːməns) *n.* **1.** the act, process, or art of performing. **2.** an artistic or dramatic production: *last night's performance was terrible.* **3.** manner or quality of functioning: *a machine's performance.* **4.** *Informal.* mode of conduct or behaviour, esp. when distasteful or irregular: *what did you mean by that performance at the restaurant?* **5.** *Informal.* any tiresome procedure: *what a performance dressing the children to play in the snow!* **6.** any accomplishment. **7.** *Linguistics.* (in transformational grammar) the form of the human language faculty, viewed as concretely embodied in speakers. Compare **competence** (sense 5), **langue, parole** (sense 5).

performance appraisal *n.* the assessment, at regular intervals, of an employee's performance at work.

performance art *n.* a theatrical presentation that incorporates various art forms, such as dance, sculpture, music, etc.

performance test *n. Psychol.* a test designed to assess a person's manual ability.

performative (pəˈfɔːmətɪv) *adj. Linguistics, philosophy.* **1. a.** denoting an utterance that constitutes some act, esp. the act described by the verb. For example, *I confess that I was there* is itself a confession, and so is performative in the narrower sense, while *I'd like you to meet ...* (effecting an introduction) is performative only in the looser sense. See also **locutionary act, illocution, perlocution. b.** (*as n.*)*: that sentence is a performative.* **2. a.** denoting a verb that may be used as the main verb in such an utterance. **b.** (*as n.*)*: "promise" is a performative.* —**perˈformatively** *adv.*

performing (pəˈfɔːmɪŋ) *adj.* (of an animal) trained to perform tricks before an audience, as in a circus.

performing arts *pl. n.* the arts that are primarily performed before an audience, such as dance and drama.

perfume *n.* (ˈpɜːfjuːm). **1.** a mixture of alcohol and fragrant essential oils extracted from flowers, spices, etc., or made synthetically, used esp. to impart a pleasant long-lasting scent to the body, stationery, etc. See also **cologne, toilet water. 2.** a scent or odour, esp. a fragrant one. ~*vb.* (pəˈfjuːm). **3.** (*tr.*) to impart a perfume to. [C16: from French *parfum,* probably from Old Provençal *perfum,* from *perfumar* to make scented, from *per* through (from Latin) + *fumar* to smoke, from Latin *fumāre* to smoke]

perfumer (pəˈfjuːmə) *n.* a person who makes or sells perfume.

perfumery (pəˈfjuːmərɪ) *n., pl.* **-eries. 1.** a place where perfumes are sold. **2.** a factory where perfumes are made. **3.** the process of making perfumes. **4.** perfumes in general.

perfunctory (pəˈfʌŋktərɪ) *adj.* **1.** done superficially, only as a matter of routine; careless or cursory. **2.** dull or indifferent. [C16: from Late Latin *perfunctōrius* negligent, from *perfunctus* dispatched, from *perfungī* to fulfil; see FUNCTION] —**perˈfunctorily** *adv.* —**perˈfunctoriness** *n.*

perfuse (pəˈfjuːz) *vb.* (*tr.*) to suffuse or permeate (a liquid, colour, etc.) through or over (something). [C16: from Latin *perfūsus* wetted, from *perfundere* to pour over, from PER- + *fundere* to pour] —**perˈfusion** *n.* —**perˈfusive** *adj.* —**perˈfused** *adj.*

pergola (ˈpɜːgələ) *n.* a horizontal trellis or framework, supported on posts, that carries climbing plants and may form a covered walk. [C17: via Italian from Latin *pergula* projection from a roof, from *pergere* to go forward]

perhaps (pəˈhæps; *informal* præps) *adv.* **1. a.** possibly; maybe. **b.** (*as sentence modifier*)*: he'll arrive tomorrow, perhaps; perhaps you'll see him tomorrow.* ~*sentence substitute.* **2.** it may happen, be so, etc.; maybe. [C16 *per happes,* from *per* by + *happes* chance, HAP]

peri (ˈpɪərɪ) *n., pl.* **-ris. 1.** (in Persian folklore) one of a race of beautiful supernatural beings. **2.** any beautiful fairy-like creature. [C18: from Persian: fairy, from Avestan *pairikā* witch]

peri- *prefix.* **1.** enclosing, encircling, or around: *pericardium; pericarp; perigon.* **2.** near or adjacent: *perihelion.* [from Greek *peri* around, near, about]

perianth (ˈpɛrɪˌænθ) *n.* the outer part of a flower, consisting of the calyx and corolla. [C18: from French *périanthe,* from New Latin, from PERI- + Greek *anthos* flower]

periapt (ˈpɛrɪˌæpt) *n. Rare.* a charm or amulet. [C16: via French from Greek *periapton,* from PERI- + *haptos* clasped, from *haptein* to fasten]

periastron (ˌpɛrɪˈæstrɒn) *n. Astronomy.* the point in the orbit of a body around a star when it is nearest to the star, esp. applied to double-star systems.

periblem (ˈpɛrɪˌblɛm) *n. Botany.* a layer of meristematic tissue in stems and roots that gives rise to the cortex. [C19: via German from Greek *periblēma* protection, from *periballein* to throw around, from PERI- + *ballein* to throw]

pericarditis (ˌpɛrɪkɑːˈdaɪtɪs) *n.* inflammation of the pericardium. —**pericarditic** (ˌpɛrɪkɑːˈdɪtɪk) *adj.*

pericardium (ˌpɛrɪˈkɑːdɪəm) *n., pl.* **-dia** (-dɪə). the membranous sac enclosing the heart. [C16: via New Latin from Greek *perikardion,* from PERI- + *kardia* heart] —ˌ**periˈcardial** *or* ˌ**periˈcardiˌac** *adj.*

pericarp (ˈpɛrɪˌkɑːp) *n.* **1.** the part of a fruit enclosing the seeds that develops from the wall of the ovary. **2.** a layer of tissue around the reproductive bodies of some algae and fungi. [C18: via French from New Latin *pericarpium*] —ˌ**periˈcarpial** *or* ˌ**periˈcarpic** *adj.*

perichondrium (ˌpɛrɪˈkɒndrɪəm) *n., pl.* **-dria** (-drɪə). the white fibrous membrane that covers the surface of cartilage. [C18: New Latin, from PERI- + Greek *chondros* cartilage] —ˌ**periˈchondrial** *adj.*

periclase (ˈpɛrɪˌkleɪs) *n.* a mineral consisting of magnesium oxide in the form of isometric crystals or grains: occurs in limestone masses. [C19: from New Latin *periclasia,* from Greek *peri* very + *klasis* a breaking, referring to its perfect cleavage] —**periclastic** (ˌpɛrɪˈklæstɪk) *adj.*

Periclean (ˌpɛrɪˈkliːən) *adj.* of or relating to Pericles (?495–429 B.C.), Athenian statesman, or to the period when Athens was the intellectual and artistic leader of the Greek city-states.

periclinal (ˌpɛrɪˈklaɪnᵊl) *adj.* **1.** of or relating to a pericline. **2.** *Botany.* **a.** denoting or relating to cell walls that are parallel to the surface of a plant part, such as a meristem. **b.** (of chimeras) having one component completely enclosed by the other component.

pericline (ˈpɛrɪˌklaɪn) *n.* **1.** a white translucent variety of albite in the form of elongated crystals. **2.** Also called: **dome.** a dome-shaped formation of stratified rock with its slopes following the direction of folding. [C19: from Greek *periklinēs* sloping on all sides, from PERI- + *klinein* to lean]

pericope (pəˈrɪkəpɪ) *n.* a selection from a book, esp. a passage from the Bible read at religious services. [C17: via Late Latin from Greek *perikopē* piece cut out, from PERI- + *kopē* a cutting] —**pericopic** (ˌpɛrɪˈkɒpɪk) *adj.*

pericranium (ˌpɛrɪˈkreɪnɪəm) *n., pl.* **-nia** (-nɪə). the fibrous membrane covering the external surface of the skull. [C16: New Latin, from Greek *perikranion*] —ˌ**periˈcranial** *adj.*

pericycle (ˈpɛrɪˌsaɪkᵊl) *n.* a layer of plant tissue beneath the endodermis: surrounds the conducting tissue in roots and certain stems. [C19: from Greek *perikuklos*] —**pericyclic** (ˌpɛrɪˈsaɪklɪk, -ˈsɪk-) *adj.*

pericynthion (ˌpɛrɪˈsɪnθɪən) *n.* the point at which a spacecraft launched from earth into a lunar orbit is nearest the moon. Compare **perilune, apocynthion.** [C20: from PERI- + *-cynthion,* from *Cynthia,* another name for *Artemis* (Roman name *Diana*), Greek goddess of the hunt and the moon]

periderm (ˈpɛrɪˌdɜːm) *n.* the outer corky protective layer of woody stems and roots, consisting of cork cambium, phelloderm and cork. [C19: from New Latin *peridermis*] —ˌ**periˈdermal** *or* ˌ**periˈdermic** *adj.*

peridium (pəˈrɪdɪəm) *n., pl.* **-ridia** (-ˈrɪdɪə). the distinct outer layer of the spore-bearing organ in many fungi. [C19: from Greek *pēridion* a little wallet, from *pēra* leather bag, of obscure origin]

peridot (ˈpɛrɪˌdɒt) *n.* a pale green transparent variety of the olivine chrysolite, used as a gemstone. [C14: from Old French *peritot,* of unknown origin]

peridotite (ˌpɛrɪˈdəʊtaɪt) *n.* a dark coarse-grained ultrabasic plutonic igneous rock consisting principally of olivine. [C19: from French, from PERIDOT] —**peridotitic** (ˌpɛrɪdəʊˈtɪtɪk) *adj.*

perigee (ˈpɛrɪˌdʒiː) *n.* the point in its orbit around the earth when the moon or an artificial satellite is nearest to the earth. Compare **apogee** (sense 1). [C16: via French from Greek *perigeion,* from PERI- + *gea* earth] —ˌ**periˈgean** *or* ˌ**periˈgeal** *adj.*

periglacial (ˌpɛrɪˈgleɪʃəl) *adj.* relating to a region bordering a glacier: *periglacial climate.*

perigon (ˈpɛrɪgən) *n.* an angle of 360°. Also called: **round angle.** [C19: from PERI- + Greek *gonia* angle]

Perigordian (ˌpɛrɪˈgɔːdɪən) *adj.* **1.** of, relating to, or characteristic of an Upper Palaeolithic culture in Europe, esp. in France. ~*n.* **2. the.** the Perigordian culture. [C20: after *Périgord,* district in France]

perigynous (pəˈrɪdʒɪnəs) *adj.* **1.** (of a flower) having a concave or flat receptacle with a distinct gynoecium surrounded by the other floral parts, as in the rosehip. **2.** of or relating to the parts of a flower arranged in this way. [C19: from New Latin *perigynus;* see PERI-, -GYNOUS] —**peˈrigyny** *n.*

perihelion (ˌpɛrɪˈhiːlɪən) *n., pl.* **-lia** (-lɪə). the point in its orbit when a planet or comet is nearest the sun. Compare **aphelion.** [C17: from New Latin *perihēlium,* from PERI- + Greek *hēlios* sun]

peril (ˈpɛrɪl) *n.* exposure to risk or harm; danger or jeopardy. [C13: via Old French from Latin *perīculum*]

perilous (ˈpɛrɪləs) *adj.* very hazardous or dangerous: *a perilous journey.* —**ˈperilously** *adv.* —**ˈperilousness** *n.*

perilune (ˈpɛrɪˌluːn) *n.* the point in a lunar orbit when a spacecraft launched from the moon is nearest the moon. Compare **apolune, pericynthion.** [C20: from PERI- + *-lune,* from Latin *lūna* moon]

perilymph (ˈpɛrɪˌlɪmf) *n.* the fluid filling the space between the membranous and bony labyrinths of the internal ear.

perimeter (pəˈrɪmɪtə) *n.* **1.** *Maths.* **a.** the curve or line enclosing a plane area. **b.** the length of this curve or line. **2. a.** any boundary around something, such as a field. **b.** (*as modifier*): *a perimeter fence; a perimeter patrol.* **3.** a medical instrument for measuring the limits of the field of vision. [C16: from French *périmètre,* from Latin *perimetros;* see PERI-, -METER] —**perimetric** (ˌpɛrɪˈmɛtrɪk) *or* ˌ**periˈmetrical** *adj.* —ˌ**periˈmetrically** *adv.* —**peˈrimetry** *n.*

perimorph (ˈpɛrɪˌmɔːf) *n.* a mineral that encloses another mineral of a different type. —ˌ**periˈmorphic** *or* ˌ**periˈmorphous** *adj.* —ˌ**periˈmorˌphism** *n.*

perimysium (ˌpɛrɪˈmɪzɪəm) *n., pl.* **-ia** (-ɪə). *Anatomy.* the sheath of fibrous connective tissue surrounding the primary bundles of muscle fibres. [C19: from PERI- + *-mysium,* from Greek *mus* muscle]

perinatal (ˌpɛrɪˈneɪtᵊl) *adj.* of, relating to, or occurring in the period from about three months before to one month after birth.

perineal gland *n. Zoology.* one of a pair of glands that are situated near the anus in some mammals and secrete an odorous substance.

perinephrium (ˌpɛrɪˈnɛfrɪəm) *n., pl.* **-ria** (-rɪə). *Anatomy.* the fatty and connective tissue surrounding the kidney. [C19: from PERI- + *-nephrium,* from Greek *nephros* kidney] —ˌ**periˈnephric** *adj.*

perineum (ˌpɛrɪˈniːəm) *n., pl.* **-nea** (-ˈniːə). **1.** the region of the body between the anus and the genital organs, including some of the underlying structures. **2.** the nearly diamond-shaped surface of the human trunk between the thighs. [C17: from New Latin, from Greek *perinaion,* from PERI- + *inein* to empty out] —ˌ**periˈneal** *adj.*

perineuritis (ˌpɛrɪnjʊˈraɪtɪs) *n.* inflammation of the perineurium. —**perineuritic** (ˌpɛrɪnjʊˈrɪtɪk) *adj.*

perineurium (ˌpɛrɪˈnjʊərɪəm) *n.* the connective tissue forming a sheath around a single bundle of nerve fibres. [C19: from New Latin, from PERI- + Greek *neuron* nerve] —ˌ**periˈneurial** *adj.*

period (ˈpɪərɪəd) *n.* **1.** a portion of time of indefinable length: *he spent a period away from home.* **2. a.** a portion of time specified in some way: *the Arthurian period; Picasso's blue period.* **b.** (*as modifier*): *period costume.* **3.** a nontechnical name for an occurrence of menstruation. **4.** *Geology.* a unit of geological time during which a system of rocks is formed: *the Jurassic period.* **5.** a division of time, esp. of the academic day. **6.** *Physics, maths.* **a.** the time taken to complete one cycle of a regularly recurring phenomenon; the reciprocal of frequency. Symbol: T **b.** an interval in which the values of a periodic function follow a certain pattern that is duplicated over successive intervals: $\sin x = \sin(x + 2\pi)$, *where* 2π *is the period.* **7.** *Astronomy.* **a.** the time required by a body to make one complete rotation on its axis. **b.** the time interval between two successive maxima or minima of light variation of a variable star. **8.** *Chem.* one of the horizontal rows of elements in the periodic table. Each period starts with an alkali metal and ends with a rare gas. Compare **group** (sense 11). **9.** another term (esp. U.S. and Canadian) for **full stop. 10.** a complete sentence, esp. a complex one with several clauses. **11.** *Music.* a passage or division of a piece of music, usually consisting of two or more contrasting or complementary musical phrases and ending on a cadence. Also called: **sentence. 12.** (in classical prosody) a unit consisting of two or more cola. **13.** *Rare.* a completion or end. [C14 *peryod,* from Latin *periodus,* from Greek *periodos* circuit, from PERI- + *hodos* way]

periodate (pɜːˈraɪəˌdeɪt) *n.* any salt or ester of a periodic acid.

periodic (ˌpɪərɪˈɒdɪk) *adj.* **1.** happening or recurring at intervals; intermittent. **2.** of, relating to, or resembling a period. **3.** having or occurring in repeated periods or cycles. —ˌ**periˈodically** *adv.* —**periodicity** (ˌpɪərɪəˈdɪsɪtɪ) *n.*

periodic acid (ˌpɜːraɪˈɒdɪk) *n.* any of various oxyacids of iodine containing a greater proportion of oxygen than iodic acid and differing from each other in water content, esp. either of the crystalline compounds HIO_4 (**metaperiodic acid**) and H_5IO_6 (**paraperiodic acid**). [C19: from PER- + IODIC]

periodical (ˌpɪərɪˈɒdɪkᵊl) *n.* **1.** a publication issued at regular intervals, usually monthly or weekly. ~*adj.* **2.** of or relating to such publications. **3.** published at regular intervals. **4.** periodic or occasional.

periodic function (ˌpɪərɪˈɒdɪk) *n. Maths.* a function, such as sin *x*, whose value is repeated at constant intervals.

periodic law (ˌpɪərɪˈɒdɪk) *n.* the principle that the chemical properties of the elements are periodic functions of their atomic weights (also called: **Mendeleev's law**) or, more accurately, of their atomic numbers.

periodic sentence (ˌpɪərɪˈɒdɪk) *n. Rhetoric.* a sentence in which the completion of the main clause is left to the end, thus creating an effect of suspense.

periodic system (ˌpɪərɪˈɒdɪk) *n.* the classification of the elements based on the periodic law.

periodic table (ˌpɪərɪˈɒdɪk) *n.* a table of the elements, arranged in order of increasing atomic number, based on the periodic law. Elements having similar chemical properties and electronic structures appear in vertical columns (groups).

periodic tenancy *n. Social welfare.* the letting of a dwelling for a repeated short term, as by the week, month, or quarter, with no end date.

periodization *or* **periodisation** (ˌpɪərɪədaɪˈzeɪʃən) *n.* the act or process of dividing history into periods.

period of revolution *n. Astronomy.* the mean time taken for one body, such as a planet, to complete a revolution about another, such as the sun.

periodontal (ˌpɛrɪəˈdɒntᵊl) *adj.* of, denoting, or affecting the gums and other tissues surrounding the teeth: *periodontal disease.*

periodontics (ˌpɛrɪəˈdɒntɪks) *n.* (*functioning as sing.*) the branch of dentistry concerned with diseases affecting the tissues and structures that surround teeth. Also called: **periodontology.** [C19: from PERI- + *-odontics,* from Greek *odōn* tooth] —ˌ**perioˈdontic** *adj.* —ˌ**perioˈdontically** *adv.*

period piece *n.* an object, a piece of music, a play, etc., valued for its quality of evoking a particular historical period: often one regarded as of little except historical interest.

perionychium (ˌpɛrɪəʊˈnɪkɪəm) *n., pl.* **-ia** (-ɪə). the skin that surrounds a fingernail or toenail. [C19: New Latin, from PERI- + Greek *onux* a nail]

periosteum (ˌpɛrɪˈɒstɪəm) *n., pl.* **-tea** (-tɪə). a thick fibrous two-layered membrane covering the surface of bones. [C16: New Latin, from Greek *periosteon,* from PERI- + *osteon* bone] —ˌ**periˈosteal** *adj.*

periostitis (ˌpɛrɪɒˈstaɪtɪs) *n.* inflammation of the periosteum. —**periostitic** (ˌpɛrɪɒˈstɪtɪk) *adj.*

periotic (ˌpɛrɪˈəʊtɪk, -ˈɒtɪk) *adj.* **1.** of or relating to the structures situated around the internal ear. **2.** situated around the ear. [C19: from PERI- + *-otic,* from Greek *ous* ear]

peripatetic (ˌpɛrɪpəˈtɛtɪk) *adj.* **1.** itinerant. **2.** *Brit.* employed in two or more educational establishments and travelling from one to another: *a peripatetic football coach.* ~*n.* **3.** a peripatetic person. [C16: from Latin *peripatēticus,* from Greek *peripatētikos,* from *peripatein* to pace to and fro] —ˌ**peripaˈtetically** *adv.*

Peripatetic (ˌpɛrɪpəˈtɛtɪk) *adj.* **1.** of or relating to the teachings of Aristotle (384–322 B.C.), Greek philosopher, who used to teach while walking about. ~*n.* **2.** a student of Aristotelianism.

peripatus (pəˈrɪpətəs) *n.* any of a genus of wormlike arthropods having a segmented body and short unjointed limbs: belonging to the phylum *Oncychophora.* [from New Latin, from Greek *peripatos* a pacing about; see PERIPATETIC]

peripeteia, peripetia (ˌpɛrɪpɪˈtaɪə, -ˈtɪə), *or* **peripety** (pəˈrɪpətɪ) *n.* (esp. in drama) an abrupt turn of events or reversal of circumstances. [C16: from Greek, from PERI- + *piptein* to fall (to change suddenly, literally: to fall around)] —ˌ**peripeˈteian** *or* ˌ**periˈpeˈtian** *adj.*

peripheral (pəˈrɪfərəl) *adj.* **1.** not relating to the most important part of something; incidental, minor, or superficial. **2.** of, relating to, or of the nature of a periphery. **3.** *Anatomy.* of, relating to, or situated near the surface of the body: *a peripheral nerve.* —**peˈripherally** *adv.*

peripheral device *or* **unit** *n. Computer technol.* any device, such as a card punch, line printer, disk, or magnetic tape unit, concerned with input/output, storage, etc. Often shortened to **peripheral.**

periphery (pəˈrɪfərɪ) *n., pl.* **-eries. 1.** the outermost boundary of an area. **2.** the outside surface of something. **3.** *Anatomy.* the surface or outermost part of the body or one of its organs or parts. [C16: from Late Latin *peripherīa,* from Greek, from PERI- + *pherein* to bear]

periphrasis (pəˈrɪfrəsɪs) *n., pl.* **-rases** (-rəˌsiːz) **1.** a roundabout way of expressing something; circumlocution. **2.** an expression of this kind. [C16: via Latin from Greek, from PERI- + *phrazein* to declare]

periphrastic (ˌpɛrɪˈfræstɪk) *adj.* **1.** employing or involving periphrasis. **2.** expressed in two or more words rather than by an inflected form of one: used esp. of a tense of a verb where the alternative element is an auxiliary verb. For example, *He does go* and *He will go* involve periphrastic tenses. —ˌ**periˈphrastically** *adv.*

periphyton (pəˈrɪfɪˌtɒn) *n.* aquatic organisms, such as certain algae, that live attached to rocks or other surfaces. [C20: from Greek, from PERI- + *phutos,* from *phuein* to grow]

peripteral (pəˈrɪptərəl) *adj.* having a row of columns on all sides. [C19: from PERI- + *-pteral,* from Greek *pteron* wing]

perique (pəˈriːk) *n.* a strong highly-flavoured tobacco cured in its own juices and grown in Louisiana. [C19: apparently from *Périque,* nickname of Pierre Chenet, American tobacco planter who first grew it in Louisiana]

perisarc (ˈpɛrɪˌsɑːk) *n.* the outer chitinous layer secreted by colonial hydrozoan coelenterates, such as species of *Obelia.* [C19:

from PERI- + *-sarc*, from Greek *sarx* flesh] —ˌ**peri'sarcal** *or* ˌ**peri'sarcous** *adj.*

periscope ('pɛrɪˌskəʊp) *n.* any of a number of optical instruments that enable the user to view objects that are not in the direct line of vision, such as one in a submarine for looking above the surface of the water. They have a system of mirrors or prisms to reflect the light and often contain focusing lenses. [C19: from Greek *periskopein* to look around; see PERI-, -SCOPE]

periscopic (ˌpɛrɪ'skɒpɪk) *adj.* (of a lens) having a wide field of view. —ˌ**peri'scopically** *adv.*

perish ('pɛrɪʃ) *vb. (intr.)* **1.** to be destroyed or die, esp. in an untimely way. **2.** to rot: *leather perishes if exposed to bad weather.* **3. perish the thought!** may it never be or happen thus. ~*n.* **4. do a perish.** *Austral. informal.* to die or come near to dying of thirst or starvation. [C13: from Old French *périr*, from Latin *perīre* to pass away entirely, from PER- (away) + *īre* to go]

perishable ('pɛrɪʃəbᵊl) *adj.* **1.** liable to rot or wither. ~*n.* **2.** *(often pl.)* a perishable article, esp. food. —ˌ**perisha'bility** *or* '**perishableness** *n.* —'**perishably** *adv.*

perished ('pɛrɪʃt) *adj. Informal.* (of a person, part of the body, etc.) extremely cold.

perishing ('pɛrɪʃɪŋ) *adj.* **1.** *Informal.* (of weather, etc.) extremely cold. **2.** *Slang.* (intensifier qualifying something undesirable): *it's a perishing nuisance!* —'**perishingly** *adv.*

perisperm ('pɛrɪˌspɜːm) *n.* the nutritive tissue surrounding the embryo in certain seeds, and developing from the nucellus of the ovule. —ˌ**peri'spermal** *adj.*

perispomenon (ˌpɛrɪ'spəʊməˌnɒn) *adj.* **1.** (of a Greek word) bearing a circumflex accent on the last syllable. ~*n.* **2.** a word having such an accent. [from Greek, from PERI- (around) + *spaein* to pull, draw]

perissodactyl (pəˌrɪsəʊ'dæktɪl) *or* **perissodactyle** (pəˌrɪsəʊ'dæktaɪl) *n.* **1.** any placental mammal of the order *Perissodactyla*, having hooves with an odd number of toes: includes horses, tapirs, and rhinoceroses. ~*adj.* **2.** of, relating to, or belonging to the *Perissodactyla*. [C19: from New Latin *perissodactylus*, from Greek *perissos* uneven + *daktulos* digit] —**peˌrisso'dactylous** *adj.*

peristalsis (ˌpɛrɪ'stælsɪs) *n., pl.* **-ses** (-siːz). *Physiol.* the succession of waves of involuntary muscular contraction of various bodily tubes, esp. of the alimentary tract, where it effects transport of food and waste products. [C19: from New Latin, from PERI- + Greek *stalsis* compression, from *stellein* to press together] —ˌ**peri'staltic** *adj.* —ˌ**peri'staltically** *adv.*

peristome ('pɛrɪˌstəʊm) *n.* **1.** a fringe of pointed teeth surrounding the opening of a moss capsule. **2.** any of various parts surrounding the mouth of invertebrates such as echinoderms, earthworms, and protozoans. [C18: from New Latin *peristoma*, from PERI- + Greek *stoma* mouth] —ˌ**peri'stomal** *or* ˌ**peri'stomial** *adj.*

peristyle ('pɛrɪˌstaɪl) *n.* **1.** a colonnade that surrounds a court or building. **2.** an area that is surrounded by a colonnade. [C17: via French from Latin *peristȳlum*, from Greek *peristulon*, from PERI- + *stulos* column] —ˌ**peri'stylar** *adj.*

perithecium (ˌpɛrɪ'θiːsɪəm) *n., pl.* **-cia** (-sɪə). *Botany.* a flask-shaped structure containing asci that are discharged from an apical pore; a type of ascocarp. [C19: from New Latin, from PERI- + Greek *thēkē* case]

peritoneum (ˌpɛrɪtə'niːəm) *n., pl.* **-nea** (-'niːə) *or* **-neums.** a thin translucent serous sac that lines the walls of the abdominal cavity and covers most of the viscera. [C16: via Late Latin from Greek *peritonaion*, from *peritonos* stretched around, from PERI- + *teinein* to stretch] —ˌ**perito'neal** *adj.*

peritonitis (ˌpɛrɪtə'naɪtɪs) *n.* inflammation of the peritoneum. —**peritonitic** (ˌpɛrɪtə'nɪtɪk) *adj.*

peritrack ('pɛrɪˌtræk) *n.* another name for **taxiway.**

peritricha (pə'rɪtrɪkə) *pl. n., sing.* **peritrich** ('pɛrɪˌtrɪk). **1.** ciliate protozoans, of the order *Peritrichida*, in which the cilia are restricted to a spiral around the mouth. **2.** bacteria having the entire cell surface covered with cilia. [C19: from New Latin, from PERI- + Greek *thrix* hair] —**pe'ritrichous** *adj.*

periwig ('pɛrɪˌwɪg) *n.* a wig, such as a peruke. [C16 *perwyke*, changed from French *perruque* wig, PERUKE]

periwinkle[1] ('pɛrɪˌwɪŋkᵊl) *n.* any of various edible marine gastropods of the genus *Littorina*, esp. *L. littorea*, having a spirally coiled shell. Often shortened to **winkle.** [C16: of unknown origin]

periwinkle[2] ('pɛrɪˌwɪŋkᵊl) *n.* **1.** Also called (U.S.): **creeping myrtle, trailing myrtle.** any of several Eurasian apocynaceous evergreen plants of the genus *Vinca*, such as *V. minor* (**lesser periwinkle**) and *V. major* (**greater periwinkle**), having trailing stems and blue flowers. **2. a.** a light purplish-blue colour. **b.** *(as adj.): a periwinkle coat.* [C14 *pervenke*, from Old English *perwince*, from Late Latin *pervinca*]

perjink (pər'dʒɪŋk) *adj. Scot.* prim or finicky. [C19: of unknown origin]

perjure ('pɜːdʒə) *vb. (tr.) Criminal law.* to render (oneself) guilty of perjury. [C15: from Old French *parjurer*, from Latin *perjūrāre*, from PER- + *jūrāre* to make an oath, from *jūs* law] —'**perjurer** *n.*

perjured ('pɜːdʒəd) *adj. Criminal law.* **1. a.** having sworn falsely. **b.** having committed perjury. **2.** involving or characterized by perjury: *perjured evidence.*

perjury ('pɜːdʒərɪ) *n., pl.* **-juries.** *Criminal law.* the offence committed by a witness in judicial proceedings who, having been lawfully sworn or having affirmed, wilfully gives false evidence. [C14: from Anglo-French *parjurie*, from Latin *perjūrium* a false oath; see PERJURE] —**perjurious** (pɜː'dʒʊərɪəs) *adj.* —**per'juriously** *adv.*

perk[1] (pɜːk) *adj.* **1.** pert; brisk; lively. ~*vb.* **2.** See **perk up.** [C16: see PERK UP]

perk[2] (pɜːk) *vb. Informal.* **1.** *(intr.)* (of coffee) to percolate. **2.** *(tr.)* to percolate (coffee).

perk[3] (pɜːk) *n. Brit. informal.* short for **perquisite.**

perkin ('pɜːkɪn) *n.* a variant of **parkin.**

Perkin's mauve ('pɜːkɪnz) *n.* another name for **mauve** (sense 2). [C19: named after Sir William Henry *Perkin* (1838–1907), who first synthesized it]

perk up *vb. (adv.)* **1.** to make or become more cheerful, hopeful, or lively. **2.** to rise or cause to rise briskly: *the dog's ears perked up.* **3.** *(tr.)* to make smarter in appearance: *she perked up her outfit with a bright scarf.* **4.** *(intr.) Austral. slang.* to vomit. [C14 *perk*, perhaps from Norman French *perquer*; see PERCH[1]]

perky ('pɜːkɪ) *adj.* **perkier, perkiest. 1.** jaunty; lively. **2.** confident; spirited. —'**perkily** *adv.* —'**perkiness** *n.*

perlite *or* **pearlite** ('pɜːlaɪt) *n.* a variety of obsidian consisting of masses of small pearly globules: used as a filler, insulator, and soil conditioner. [C19: from French, from *perle* PEARL[1]] —**perlitic** *or* **pearlitic** (pɜː'lɪtɪk) *adj.*

perlocution (ˌpɜːlɒ'kjuːʃən) *n. Philosophy.* the effect that someone has by uttering certain words, such as frightening a person. Also called: **perlocutionary act.** Compare **illocution.** [C16 (in the obsolete sense: the action of speaking): from Medieval or New Latin *perlocūtiō*; see PER-, LOCUTION] —ˌ**perlo'cutionary** *adj.*

perm[1] (pɜːm) *n.* **1.** a hairstyle produced by treatment with heat, chemicals, etc. which gives long-lasting waves, curls, or other shaping. Also called (esp. formerly) **permanent wave. 2.** the act of giving or receiving such a hairstyle. ~*vb. (tr.)* **3.** to give a perm to (hair).

perm[2] (pɜːm) *n.* short for **permutation** (sense 4).

permafrost ('pɜːməˌfrɒst) *n.* ground that is permanently frozen, often to great depths, the surface sometimes thawing in the summer. [C20: from PERMA(NENT) + FROST]

permalloy (pɜːm'ælɔɪ) *n.* any of various alloys containing iron and nickel (45–80 per cent) and sometimes smaller amounts of chromium and molybdenum. [C20: from PERM(EABILITY) + ALLOY]

permanence ('pɜːmənəns) *n.* the state or quality of being permanent.

permanency ('pɜːmənənsɪ) *n., pl.* **-cies. 1.** a person or thing that is permanent. **2.** another word for **permanence.**

permanent ('pɜːmənənt) *adj.* **1.** existing or intended to exist for an indefinite period: *a permanent structure.* **2.** not expected to change for an indefinite time; not temporary: *a permanent condition.* [C15: from Latin *permanens* continuing, from *permanēre* to stay to the end, from *per-* through + *manēre* to remain] —'**permanently** *adv.*

permanent hardness *n. Chem.* hardness of water that cannot be removed by boiling as it results mainly from the presence of calcium and magnesium chlorides and sulphates.

permanent health insurance *n.* a form of insurance that provides up to 75 per cent of a person's salary, until retirement, in case of prolonged illness or disability.

permanent magnet *n.* a magnet, often of steel, that retains its magnetization after the magnetic field producing it has been removed. —**permanent magnetism** *n.*

permanent press *n.* **a.** a chemical treatment for clothing that makes the fabric crease-resistant and sometimes provides a garment with a permanent crease or pleats. **b.** *(as modifier): permanent-press skirts.*

permanent set *n. Engineering.* the change in shape of a material that results when the load to which it is subjected causes the elastic limit to be exceeded and is then removed.

permanent wave *n.* another name (esp. formerly) for **perm**[1] (sense 1).

permanent way *n. Chiefly Brit.* the track of a railway, including the ballast, sleepers, rails, etc.

permanganate (pə'mæŋgəˌneɪt, -nɪt) *n.* a salt of permanganic acid.

permanganic acid (ˌpɜːmæn'gænɪk) *n.* a monobasic acid known only in solution and in the form of permanganate salts. Formula: $HMnO_4$. Systematic name: **manganic(VII) acid.**

permeability (ˌpɜːmɪə'bɪlɪtɪ) *n.* **1.** the state or quality of being permeable. **2.** a measure of the ability of a medium to modify a magnetic field, expressed as the ratio of the magnetic flux density in the medium to the field strength; measured in henries per metre. Symbol: μ See also **relative permeability, magnetic constant. 3.** *Civil engineering.* the rate of diffusion of fluid under pressure through soil. **4.** the rate at which gas diffuses through the surface of a balloon or airship, usually expressed in litres per square metre per day.

permeability coefficient *n.* the volume of an incompressible fluid that will flow in unit time through a unit cube of a porous substance across which a unit pressure difference is maintained.

permeable ('pɜːmɪəbᵊl) *adj.* capable of being permeated, esp. by liquids. [C15: from Late Latin *permeābilis,* from Latin *permeāre* to pervade; see PERMEATE] —'**permeableness** *n.* —'**permeably** *adv.*

permeance ('pɜːmɪəns) *n.* **1.** the act of permeating. **2.** the reciprocal of the reluctance of a magnetic circuit. Symbol: Λ —'**permeant** *adj., n.*

permeate ('pɜːmɪˌeɪt) *vb.* **1.** to penetrate or pervade (a substance, area, etc.): *a lovely smell permeated the room.* **2.** to pass through or cause to pass through by osmosis or diffusion: *to permeate a membrane.* [C17: from Latin *permeāre,* from *per-* through + *meāre* to pass] —ˌ**perme'ation** *n.* —'**permeative** *adj.*

per mensem *Latin.* ('pɜː 'mɛnsəm) *adv.* every month or by the month.

Permian ('pɜːmɪən) *adj.* **1.** of, denoting, or formed in the last period of the Palaeozoic era, between the Carboniferous and Triassic periods, which lasted for 45 000 000 years. ~*n.* **2. the.** the Permian period or rock system. [C19: after *Perm,* a port in Russia]

per mill *or* **mil** (pə 'mɪl) *adv.* by the thousand or in each thousand. [C19: from PER + French or Latin *mille* thousand, on the model of PER CENT]

permissible (pə'mɪsəbᵊl) *adj.* permitted; allowable. —**perˌmissi'bility** *n.* —**per'missibly** *adv.*

permission (pə'mɪʃən) *n.* authorization to do something.

permissive (pə'mɪsɪv) *adj.* **1.** tolerant; lenient: *permissive parents.* **2.** indulgent in matters of sex: *a permissive society.* **3.** granting permission. **4.** *Archaic.* not obligatory. —**per'missively** *adv.* —**per'missiveness** *n.*

permit *vb.* (pə'mɪt), **-mits, -mitting, -mitted. 1.** (*tr.*) to grant permission to do something: *you are permitted to smoke.* **2.** (*tr.*) to consent to or tolerate: *she will not permit him to come.* **3.** (when *intr.*, often foll. by *of;* when *tr.*, often foll. by an infinitive) to allow the possibility (of): *the passage permits of two interpretations; his work permits him to relax nowadays.* ~*n.* ('pɜːmɪt). **4.** an official certificate or document granting authorization; licence. **5.** permission, esp. written permission. [C15: from Latin *permittere,* from *per-* through + *mittere* to send] —**per'mitter** *n.*

permittivity (ˌpɜːmɪ'tɪvɪtɪ) *n., pl.* **-ties.** a measure of the ability of a substance to transmit an electric field, expressed as the ratio of its electric displacement to the applied field strength; measured in farads per metre. Symbol: ε See also **relative permittivity, electric constant.**

permutate ('pɜːmjʊˌteɪt) *vb.* to alter the sequence or arrangement (of); treat by permutation: *endlessly permutating three basic designs.*

permutation (ˌpɜːmjʊ'teɪʃən) *n.* **1.** *Maths.* **a.** an ordered arrangement of the numbers, terms, etc., of a set into specified groups: *the permutations of a, b, and c, taken two at a time, are ab, ba, ac, ca, bc, cb.* **b.** a group formed in this way. The number of permutations of *n* objects taken *r* at a time is $n!/(n-r)!$. Symbol: $_nP_r$. --Compare **combination** (sense 6). **2.** a combination of items made by reordering. **3.** an alteration; transformation. **4.** a fixed combination for selections of results on football pools. Usually shortened to **perm.** [C14: from Latin *permūtātiō,* from *permūtāre* to change thoroughly; see MUTATION] —ˌ**permu'tational** *adj.*

permute (pə'mjuːt) *vb.* (*tr.*) **1.** to change the sequence of. **2.** *Maths.* to subject to permutation. [C14: from Latin *permūtāre,* from PER- + *mūtāre* to change, alter] —**per'mutable** *adj.* —**perˌmuta'bility** *or* **per'mutableness** *n.* —**per'mutably** *adv.*

pernicious (pə'nɪʃəs) *adj.* **1.** wicked or malicious: *pernicious lies.* **2.** causing grave harm; deadly. [C16: from Latin *perniciōsus,* from *perniciēs* ruin, from PER- (intensive) + *nex* death] —**per'niciously** *adv.* —**per'niciousness** *n.*

pernicious anaemia *n.* a form of anaemia characterized by lesions of the spinal cord, weakness, sore tongue, numbness in the arms and legs, diarrhoea, etc.: associated with inadequate absorption of vitamin B_{12}.

pernickety (pə'nɪkɪtɪ) *or U.S.* **persnickety** *adj. Informal.* **1.** excessively precise and attentive to detail; fussy. **2.** (of a task) requiring close attention; exacting. [C19: originally Scottish, of unknown origin] —**per'nicketiness** *or U.S.* **per'snicketiness** *n.*

Pernod ('pɛənəʊ; *French* pɛrno) *n. Trademark.* an aniseed-flavoured apéritif from France.

Peronist (pɛ'rɒnɪst) *n.* **1.** a follower or supporter of Juan Perón (1895–1974), Argentine soldier and statesman. ~*adj.* **2.** of or relating to Juan Perón or to his ideals or policies.

peroneal (ˌpɛrə'niːəl) *adj. Anatomy.* of or relating to the fibula or the outer side of the leg. [C19: from New Latin *peronē* fibula, from Greek: fibula]

perorate ('pɛrəˌreɪt) *vb.* (*intr.*) **1.** to speak at length, esp. in a formal manner. **2.** to conclude a speech or sum up, esp. with a formal recapitulation.

peroration (ˌpɛrə'reɪʃən) *n. Rhetoric.* the conclusion of a speech or discourse, in which points made previously are summed up or recapitulated, esp. with greater emphasis. [C15: from Latin *perōrātiō,* from *perōrāre,* from PER- (thoroughly) + *ōrāre* to speak]

perovskite (pɛ'rɒvskaɪt) *n.* a yellow, brown, or greyish-black mineral form of calcium titanate with some rare-earth elements, which is used in certain high-temperature ceramic superconductors. [C19: named after Count Lev Alekseevich *Perovski* (1792–1856), Russian statesman]

peroxidase (pə'rɒksɪˌdeɪs, -ˌdeɪz) *n.* any of a group of enzymes that catalyse the oxidation of a compound by the decomposition of hydrogen peroxide or an organic peroxide. They generally consist of a protein combined with haem.

peroxidation (pəˌrɒksɪ'deɪʃən) *n.* a type of reaction in which oxygen atoms are formed leading to the production of peroxides. It is stimulated in the body by certain toxins and infections.

peroxide (pə'rɒksaɪd) *n.* **1.** short for **hydrogen peroxide,** esp. when used for bleaching hair. **2.** any of a class of metallic oxides, such as sodium peroxide, Na_2O_2, that contain the divalent ion $^-O\text{-}O^-$. **3.** (*not in technical usage*) any of certain dioxides, such as manganese peroxide, MnO_2, that resemble peroxides in their formula but do not contain the $^-O\text{-}O^-$ ion. **4.** any of a class of organic compounds whose molecules contain two oxygen atoms bound together. They tend to be explosive. **5.** (*modifier*) of, relating to, bleached with, or resembling peroxide. ~*vb.* **6.** (*tr.*) to bleach (the hair) with peroxide.

peroxide blonde *n. Usually disparaging.* a woman having hair that is bleached rather than naturally blonde and that looks harsh or unnatural.

peroxisome (pə'rɒksɪˌsəʊm) *n.* a type of organelle present in most eukaryotic cells that carry out oxidative reactions, such as oxidation of alcohol in the liver.

peroxy- *or esp. for inorganic compounds* **peroxo-** *combining form.* indicating the presence of the peroxide group, -O–O-: *peroxysulphuric acid.* Also (not in technical usage): **per-.**

peroxysulphuric acid (pəˌrɒksɪsʌl'fjʊərɪk) *n.* a white hygroscopic crystalline unstable oxidizing acid. Formula: H_2SO_5. Also called (not in technical usage): **persulphuric acid, Caro's acid.**

perpend[1] ('pɜːpənd) *or* **perpent** *n.* a large stone that passes through a wall from one side to the other. Also called: **parpend, perpend stone.** [C15: from Old French *parpain,* of uncertain origin]

perpend[2] (pə'pɛnd) *vb.* an archaic word for **ponder.** [C16: from Latin *perpendere* to examine, from PER- (thoroughly) + *pendere* to weigh]

perpendicular (ˌpɜːpən'dɪkjʊlə) *adj.* **1.** Also: **normal.** at right angles to a horizontal plane. **2.** denoting, relating to, or having the style of Gothic architecture used in England during the 14th and 15th centuries, characterized by tracery having vertical lines, a four-centred arch, and fan vaulting. **3.** upright; vertical. ~*n.* **4.** *Geometry.* a line or plane perpendicular to another. **5.** any instrument used for indicating the vertical line through a given point. **6.** *Mountaineering.* a nearly vertical face. [C14: from Latin *perpendiculāris,* from *perpendiculum* a plumb line, from *per-* through + *pendēre* to hang] —**perpendicularity** (ˌpɜːpənˌdɪkjʊ'lærɪtɪ) *n.* —ˌ**perpen'dicularly** *adv.*

perpetrate ('pɜːpɪˌtreɪt) *vb.* (*tr.*) to perform or be responsible for (a deception, crime, etc.). [C16: from Latin *perpetrāre,* from *per-* (thoroughly) + *patrāre* to perform, perhaps from *pater* father, leader in the performance of sacred rites] —ˌ**perpe'tration** *n.* —'**perpeˌtrator** *n.*

perpetual (pə'pɛtjʊəl) *adj.* **1.** (*usually prenominal*) eternal; permanent. **2.** (*usually prenominal*) seemingly ceaseless because often repeated: *your perpetual complaints.* **3.** *Horticulture.* blooming throughout the growing season or year. ~*n.* **4.** a plant that blooms throughout the growing season. [C14: via Old French from Latin *perpetuālis* universal, from *perpes* continuous, from *per-* (thoroughly) + *petere* to go towards] —**per'petually** *adv.*

perpetual check *n. Chess.* a consecutive series of checks that the checked player cannot avoid, leading to a drawn game.

perpetual debenture *n.* a bond or debenture that can either never be redeemed or cannot be redeemed on demand.

perpetual motion *n.* **1.** Also called: **perpetual motion of the first kind.** motion of a hypothetical mechanism that continues indefinitely without any external source of energy. It is impossible in practice because of friction. **2.** Also called: **perpetual motion of the second kind.** motion of a hypothetical mechanism that derives its energy from a source at a lower temperature. It is impossible in practice because of the second law of thermodynamics.

perpetuate (pə'pɛtjʊˌeɪt) *vb.* (*tr.*) to cause to continue or prevail: *to perpetuate misconceptions.* [C16: from Latin *perpetuāre* to continue without interruption, from *perpetuus* PERPETUAL] —**perˌpetu'ation** *n.*

perpetuity (ˌpɜːpɪ'tjuːɪtɪ) *n., pl.* **-ties. 1.** eternity. **2.** the state or quality of being perpetual. **3.** *Property law.* a limitation preventing the absolute disposal of an estate for longer than the period allowed by law. **4.** an annuity with no maturity date and payable indefinitely. **5. in perpetuity.** for ever. [C15: from Old French *perpetuite,* from Latin *perpetuitās* continuity; see PERPETUAL]

perplex (pə'plɛks) *vb.* (*tr.*) **1.** to puzzle; bewilder; confuse. **2.** to complicate: *to perplex an issue.* [C15: from obsolete *perplex* (adj.) intricate, from Latin *perplexus* entangled, from *per-* (thoroughly) + *plectere* to entwine]

perplexity (pəˈplɛksɪtɪ) *n., pl.* **-ties.** **1.** the state of being perplexed. **2.** the state of being intricate or complicated. **3.** something that perplexes.

per pro (ˈpɜː ˈprəʊ) *prep.* by delegation to; through the agency of: used when signing documents on behalf of someone else. [Latin: abbreviation of *per prōcūrātiōnem*]

▷**Usage.** In formal correspondence, when Brenda Smith is signing on behalf of Peter Jones, she should write *Peter Jones per pro* (or *pp*) *Brenda Smith,* not the other way about.

perquisite (ˈpɜːkwɪzɪt) *n.* **1.** an incidental benefit gained from a certain type of employment, such as the use of a company car. **2.** a customary benefit received in addition to a regular income. **3.** a customary tip. **4.** something expected or regarded as an exclusive right. ~Often shortened (informal) to **perk.** [C15: from Medieval Latin *perquīsītum* an acquired possession, from Latin *perquīrere* to seek earnestly for something, from *per-* (thoroughly) + *quaerere* to ask for, seek]

Perrier water *or* **Perrier** (ˈpɛrɪeɪ) *n. Trademark.* a sparkling mineral water from the south of France. [C20: named after a spring *Source Perrier,* at Vergèze, France]

perron (ˈpɛrən) *n.* an external flight of steps, esp. one at the front entrance of a building. [C14: from Old French, from *pierre* stone, from Latin *petra*]

perry (ˈpɛrɪ) *n., pl.* **-ries.** wine made of pears, similar in taste to cider. [C14 *pereye,* from Old French *peré,* ultimately from Latin *pirum* pear]

pers. *abbrev. for:* **1.** person. **2.** personal.

Pers. *abbrev. for* Persia(n).

persalt (ˈpɜːˌsɔːlt) *n.* any salt of a peracid.

perse (pɜːs) *n.* **a.** a dark greyish-blue colour. **b.** (*as adj.*): *perse cloth.* [C14: from Old French, from Medieval Latin *persus,* perhaps changed from Latin *Persicus* Persian]

per se (ˈpɜː ˈseɪ) *adv.* by or in itself; intrinsically. [Latin]

persecute (ˈpɜːsɪˌkjuːt) *vb.* (*tr.*) **1.** to oppress, harass, or maltreat, esp. because of race, religion, etc. **2.** to bother persistently. [C15: from Old French *persecuter,* back formation from *persecuteur,* from Late Latin *persecūtor* pursuer, from *persequī* to take vengeance upon] —ˈ**perseˌcutive** *or* ˈ**perseˌcutory** *adj.* —ˈ**perseˌcutor** *n.*

persecution (ˌpɜːsɪˈkjuːʃən) *n.* the act of persecuting or the state of being persecuted.

persecution complex *n. Psychol.* an acute irrational fear that other people are plotting one's downfall and that they are responsible for one's failures.

Perseus (ˈpɜːsɪəs) *n., Latin genitive* **Persei** (ˈpɜːsɪˌaɪ). a conspicuous constellation in the N hemisphere lying between Auriga and Cassiopeia and crossed by the Milky Way. It contains the eclipsing binary, Algol.

perseverance (ˌpɜːsɪˈvɪərəns) *n.* **1.** continued steady belief or efforts, withstanding discouragement or difficulty; persistence. **2.** *Christianity.* persistence in remaining in a state of grace until death. —ˌ**perseˈverant** *adj.*

perseveration (pɜːˌsɛvəˈreɪʃən) *n. Psychol.* **1.** the tendency for an impression, idea, or feeling to dissipate only slowly and to recur during subsequent experiences. **2.** an inability to change one's method of working when transferred from one task to another.

persevere (ˌpɜːsɪˈvɪə) *vb.* (*intr.;* often foll. by *in*) to show perseverance. [C14: from Old French *perseverer,* from Latin *persevērāre,* from *perseverus* very strict; see SEVERE] —ˌ**perseˈvering** *adj.* —ˌ**perseˈveringly** *adv.*

Persian (ˈpɜːʃən) *adj.* **1.** of or relating to ancient Persia or modern Iran, in SW Asia, or to their inhabitants or languages. ~*n.* **2.** a native, citizen, or inhabitant of modern Iran; an Iranian. **3.** a member of an Indo-European people of West Iranian speech who established a great empire in SW Asia in the 6th century B.C. **4.** the language of Iran or Persia in any of its ancient or modern forms, belonging to the West Iranian branch of the Indo-European family. See also **Avestan, Old Persian, Pahlavi, Farsi.**

Persian blinds *pl. n.* another term for **persiennes.**

Persian carpet *or* **rug** *n.* a carpet or rug made in Persia or other countries of the Near East by knotting silk or wool yarn by hand onto a woven backing, characterized by rich colours and flowing or geometric designs.

Persian cat *n.* a long-haired variety of domestic cat with a stocky body, round face, and short thick legs.

Persian greyhound *n.* another name for the **Saluki.**

Persian lamb *n.* **1.** a black loosely curled fur obtained from the skin of the karakul lamb. **2.** a karakul lamb.

Persian melon *n.* another name for **winter melon.**

persicaria (ˌpɜːsɪˈkɛərɪə) *n.* another name for **red shank.**

persiennes (ˌpɜːsɪˈɛnz) *pl. n.* outside window shutters having louvres to keep out the sun while maintaining ventilation. Also called: **Persian blinds.** [C19: from French, from *persien* Persian]

persiflage (ˈpɜːsɪˌflɑːʒ) *n.* light frivolous conversation, style, or treatment; friendly teasing. [C18: via French, from *persifler* to tease, from *per-* (intensive) + *siffler* to whistle, from Latin *sībilāre* to whistle]

persimmon (pɜːˈsɪmən) *n.* **1.** any of several tropical trees of the genus *Diospyros,* typically having hard wood and large orange-red fruit: family *Ebenaceae.* **2.** the sweet fruit of any of these trees, which is edible when completely ripe. ~See also **ebony** (sense 1). [C17: of Algonquian origin; related to Delaware *pasimĕnan* dried fruit]

persist (pəˈsɪst) *vb.* (*intr.*) **1.** (often foll. by *in*) to continue steadfastly or obstinately despite opposition or difficulty. **2.** to continue to exist or occur without interruption: *the rain persisted throughout the night.* [C16: from Latin *persistere,* from *per-* (intensive) + *sistere* to stand steadfast, from *stāre* to stand] —**perˈsister** *n.*

persistence (pəˈsɪstəns) *or* **persistency** *n.* **1.** the quality of persisting; tenacity. **2.** the act of persisting; continued effort or existence. **3.** the continuance of an effect after the cause of it has stopped: *persistence of vision.*

persistent (pəˈsɪstənt) *adj.* **1.** showing persistence. **2.** incessantly repeated; unrelenting: *your persistent questioning.* **3.** (of plant parts) remaining attached to the plant after the normal time of withering: *a fruit surrounded by a persistent perianth.* **4.** *Zoology.* **a.** (of parts normally present only in young stages) present in the adult: *persistent gills in axolotls.* **b.** continuing to grow or develop after the normal period of growth: *persistent teeth.* **5.** (of a chemical, esp. when used as an insecticide) slow to break down; not easily degradable. —**perˈsistently** *adv.*

persistent cruelty *n. Brit. law.* conduct causing fear of danger to the life or health of a spouse (used in matrimonial proceedings before magistrates).

persnickety (pəˈsnɪkɪtɪ) *adj.* the U.S. word for **pernickety.**

person (ˈpɜːsᵊn) *n., pl.* **persons.** **1.** an individual human being. **2.** the body of a human being, sometimes including his or her clothing: *guns hidden on his person.* **3.** a grammatical category into which pronouns and forms of verbs are subdivided depending on whether they refer to the speaker, the person addressed, or some other individual, thing, etc. **4.** a human being or a corporation recognized in law as having certain rights and obligations. **5.** *Philosophy.* a being characterized by consciousness, rationality, and a moral sense, and traditionally thought of as consisting of both a body and a mind or soul. **6.** *Archaic.* a character or role; guise. **7. in person. a.** actually present: *the author will be there in person.* **b.** without the help or intervention of others. [C13: from Old French *persone,* from Latin *persōna* mask, perhaps from Etruscan *phersu* mask]

▷**Usage.** *People* is the word usually used to refer to more than one individual: *there were a hundred people at the reception. Persons* is rarely used, except in official English: *several persons were interviewed.*

Person (ˈpɜːsᵊn) *n. Christianity.* any of the three hypostases existing as distinct in the one God and constituting the Trinity. They are the **First Person,** the Father, the **Second Person,** the Son, and the **Third Person,** the Holy Ghost.

-person *suffix forming nouns.* sometimes used instead of *-man* and *-woman* or *-lady: chairperson; salesperson.*

▷**Usage.** See at **-man.**

persona (pɜːˈsəʊnə) *n., pl.* **-nae** (-niː). **1.** (*often pl.*) a character in a play, novel, etc. **2.** an assumed identity or character. **3.** (in Jungian psychology) the mechanism that conceals a person's true thoughts and feelings, esp. in his adaptation to the outside world. [Latin: mask]

personable (ˈpɜːsənəbᵊl) *adj.* pleasant in appearance and personality. —ˈ**personableness** *n.* —ˈ**personably** *adv.*

personage (ˈpɜːsənɪdʒ) *n.* **1.** an important or distinguished person. **2.** another word for **person** (sense 1): *a strange personage.* **3.** *Rare.* a figure in literature, history, etc.

persona grata *Latin.* (pɜːˈsəʊnə ˈgrɑːtə) *n., pl.* ***personae gratae*** (pɜːˈsəʊniː ˈgrɑːtiː). an acceptable person, esp. a diplomat acceptable to the government of the country to which he is sent.

personal (ˈpɜːsənᵊl) *adj.* **1.** of or relating to the private aspects of a person's life: *personal letters; a personal question.* **2.** (*prenominal*) of or relating to a person's body, its care, or its appearance: *personal hygiene; great personal beauty.* **3.** belonging to or intended for a particular person and no-one else: *as a personal favour; for your personal use.* **4.** (*prenominal*) undertaken by an individual himself: *a personal appearance by a celebrity.* **5.** referring to, concerning, or involving a person's individual personality, intimate affairs, etc., esp. in an offensive way: *personal remarks; don't be so personal.* **6.** having the attributes of an individual conscious being: *a personal God.* **7.** of or arising from the personality: *personal magnetism.* **8.** of, relating to, or denoting grammatical person. **9.** *Law.* of or relating to movable property, such as money. Compare **real**[1] (sense 8). ~*n.* **10.** *Law.* an item of movable property.

personal column *n.* a newspaper column containing personal messages, advertisements by charities, requests for friendship, holiday companions, etc.

personal computer *n.* a small inexpensive computer used in word processing, playing computer games, etc.

personal equation *n.* **1.** the variation or error in observation or judgment caused by individual characteristics. **2.** the allowance made for such variation.

personalism (ˈpɜːsənəˌlɪzəm) *n.* **1.** a philosophical movement that stresses the value of persons. **2.** an idiosyncratic mode of behaviour or expression. —ˌ**personalˈistic** *adj.* —ˈ**personalist** *n., adj.*

personality (ˌpɜːsəˈnælɪtɪ) *n., pl.* **-ties.** **1.** *Psychol.* the sum total of all the behavioural and mental characteristics by means of which an individual is recognized as being unique. **2.** the distinctive character of a person that makes him socially attractive: *a salesman needs a lot of personality.* **3.** a well-known person in a certain field, such as sport or entertainment. **4.** a remarkable person: *the old fellow is a real personality.* **5.** the quality of being a unique person. **6.** the distinctive atmosphere of a place or situation. **7.** (*often pl.*) a personal remark.

personality disorder *n. Psychiatry.* any of a group of mental disorders characterized by a permanent disposition to behave in ways causing suffering to oneself or others.

personality inventory *n. Psychol.* a form of personality test in which the subject answers questions about himself. The results are used to determine dimensions of personality, such as extroversion.

personality type *n. Psychol.* a cluster of personality traits commonly occurring together.

personalize *or* **personalise** (ˈpɜːsənəˌlaɪz) *vb.* (*tr.*) **1.** to endow with personal or individual qualities or characteristics. **2.** to mark (stationery, clothing, etc.) with a person's initials, name, etc. **3.** to take (a remark, etc.) personally. **4.** another word for **personify.** —ˌ**personaliˈzation** *or* ˌ**personaliˈsation** *n.*

personally (ˈpɜːsənəlɪ) *adv.* **1.** without the help or intervention of others: *I'll attend to it personally.* **2.** (*sentence modifier*) in one's own opinion or as regards oneself: *personally, I hate onions.* **3.** as if referring to oneself: *to take the insults personally.* **4.** as a person: *we like him personally, but professionally he's incompetent.*

personal organizer *n.* **1.** a diary that stores personal records, appointments, notes, etc. **2.** a pocket-sized electronic device that performs the same functions.

personal pronoun *n.* a pronoun having a definite person or thing as an antecedent and functioning grammatically in the same way as the noun that it replaces. In English, the personal pronouns include *I, you, he, she, it, we,* and *they,* and are inflected for case.

personal property *n. Law.* movable property, such as furniture or money. Compare **real property.** Also called: **personalty.**

personal stereo *n.* a very small audio cassette player designed to be worn attached to a belt and used with lightweight headphones.

personalty (ˈpɜːsənəltɪ) *n., pl.* **-ties.** *Law.* another word for **personal property.** [C16: from Anglo-French, from Late Latin *persōnālitās* personality]

persona non grata *Latin.* (pɜːˈsəʊnə nɒn ˈgrɑːtə) *n., pl.* ***personae non gratae*** (pɜːˈsəʊniː nɒn ˈgrɑːtiː). **1.** an unacceptable or unwelcome person. **2.** a diplomatic or consular officer who is not acceptable to the government or sovereign to whom he is accredited.

personate[1] (ˈpɜːsəˌneɪt) *vb.* (*tr.*) **1.** to act the part of (a character in a play); portray. **2.** a less common word for **personify. 3.** *Criminal law.* to assume the identity of (another person) with intent to deceive. —ˌ**personˈation** *n.* —ˈ**personative** *adj.* —ˈ**personˌator** *n.*

personate[2] (ˈpɜːsənɪt, -ˌneɪt) *adj.* (of the corollas of certain flowers) having two lips in the form of a face. [C18: from New Latin *persōnātus* masked, from Latin *persōna*; see PERSON]

personification (pɜːˌsɒnɪfɪˈkeɪʃən) *n.* **1.** the attribution of human characteristics to things, abstract ideas, etc., as for literary or artistic effect. **2.** the representation of an abstract quality or idea in the form of a person, creature, etc., as in art and literature. **3.** a person or thing that personifies. **4.** a person or thing regarded as an embodiment of a quality: *he is the personification of optimism.*

personify (pɜːˈsɒnɪˌfaɪ) *vb.* **-fies, -fying, -fied.** (*tr.*) **1.** to attribute human characteristics to (a thing or abstraction). **2.** to represent (an abstract quality) in human or animal form. **3.** (of a person or thing) to represent (an abstract quality), as in art or literature. **4.** to be the embodiment of. —**perˈsoniˌfiable** *adj.* —**perˈsoniˌfier** *n.*

personnel (ˌpɜːsəˈnɛl) *n.* **1.** the people employed in an organization or for a service or undertaking. Compare **materiel. 2. a.** the office or department that interviews, appoints, or keeps records of employees. **b.** (*as modifier*): *a personnel officer.* [C19: from French, ultimately from Late Latin *persōnālis* personal (adj.); see PERSON]

perspective (pəˈspɛktɪv) *n.* **1.** a way of regarding situations, facts, etc., and judging their relative importance. **2.** the proper or accurate point of view or the ability to see it; objectivity: *try to get some perspective on your troubles.* **3.** the theory or art of suggesting three dimensions on a two-dimensional surface, in order to recreate the appearance and spatial relationships that objects or a scene in recession present to the eye. **4.** the appearance of objects, buildings, etc., relative to each other, as determined by their distance from the viewer, or the effects of this distance on their appearance. **5.** a view over some distance in space or time; vista; prospect. **6.** a picture in perspective. [C14: from Medieval Latin *perspectīva ars* the science of optics, from Latin *perspicere* to inspect carefully, from *per-* (intensive) + *specere* to behold] —**perˈspectively** *adv.*

Perspex (ˈpɜːspɛks) *n. Trademark.* any of various clear acrylic resins, used chiefly as a substitute for glass.

perspicacious (ˌpɜːspɪˈkeɪʃəs) *adj.* **1.** acutely perceptive or discerning. **2.** *Archaic.* having keen eyesight. [C17: from Latin *perspicax,* from *perspicere* to look at closely; see PERSPECTIVE] —ˌ**perspiˈcaciously** *adv.* —**perspicacity** (ˌpɜːspɪˈkæsɪtɪ) *or* ˌ**perspiˈcaciousness** *n.*

perspicuity (ˌpɜːspɪˈkjuːɪtɪ) *n.* **1.** the quality of being perspicuous. **2.** another word for **perspicacity.**

perspicuous (pəˈspɪkjʊəs) *adj.* (of speech or writing) easily understood; lucid. [C15: from Latin *perspicuus* transparent, from *perspicere* to explore thoroughly; see PERSPECTIVE] —**perˈspicuously** *adv.* —**perˈspicuousness** *n.*

perspiration (ˌpɜːspəˈreɪʃən) *n.* **1.** the salty fluid secreted by the sweat glands of the skin. **2.** the act or process of secreting this fluid.

perspiratory (pəˈspaɪərətərɪ, -trɪ) *adj.* of, relating to, or stimulating perspiration.

perspire (pəˈspaɪə) *vb.* to secrete or exude (perspiration) through the pores of the skin. [C17: from Latin *perspīrāre* to blow, from *per-* (through) + *spīrare* to breathe; compare INSPIRE] —**perˈspiringly** *adv.*

persuade (pəˈsweɪd) *vb.* (*tr.; may take a clause as object or an infinitive*) **1.** to induce, urge, or prevail upon successfully: *he finally persuaded them to buy it.* **2.** to cause to believe; convince: *even with the evidence, the police were not persuaded.* [C16: from Latin *persuādēre,* from *per-* (intensive) + *suādēre* to urge, advise] —**perˈsuadable** *or* **perˈsuasible** *adj.* —**perˌsuadaˈbility** *or* **perˌsuasiˈbility** *n.* —**perˈsuader** *n.*

persuasion (pəˈsweɪʒən) *n.* **1.** the act of persuading or of trying to persuade. **2.** the power to persuade. **3.** the state of being persuaded; strong belief. **4.** an established creed or belief, esp. a religious one. **5.** a sect, party, or faction. [C14: from Latin *persuāsiō*; see PERSUADE]

persuasive (pəˈsweɪsɪv) *adj.* having the power or ability to persuade; tending to persuade: *a persuasive salesman.* —**perˈsuasively** *adv.* —**perˈsuasiveness** *n.*

persulphuric acid *or U.S.* **persulfuric acid** (ˌpɜːsʌlˈfjʊərɪk) *n.* other names (not in technical usage) for **peroxysulphuric acid.**

pert (pɜːt) *adj.* **1.** saucy, impudent, or forward. **2.** jaunty: *a pert little hat.* **3.** *Obsolete.* clever or brisk. [C13: variant of earlier *apert,* from Latin *apertus* open, from *aperīre* to open; influenced by Old French *aspert,* from Latin *expertus* EXPERT] —ˈ**pertly** *adv.* —ˈ**pertness** *n.*

PERT (pɜːt) *n. acronym for* programme evaluation and review technique.

pert. *abbrev. for* pertaining.

pertain (pəˈteɪn) *vb.* (*intr.;* often foll. by *to*) **1.** to have reference, relation, or relevance. **2.** to be appropriate. **3.** to belong (to) or be a part (of); be an adjunct, attribute, or accessory (of). [C14: from Latin *pertinēre,* from *per-* (intensive) + *tenēre* to hold]

pertinacious (ˌpɜːtɪˈneɪʃəs) *adj.* **1.** doggedly resolute in purpose or belief; unyielding. **2.** stubbornly persistent. [C17: from Latin *pertināx,* from *per-* (intensive) + *tenāx* clinging, from *tenēre* to hold] —ˌ**pertiˈnaciously** *adv.* —**pertinacity** (ˌpɜːtɪˈnæsɪtɪ) *or* ˌ**pertiˈnaciousness** *n.*

pertinent (ˈpɜːtɪnənt) *adj.* relating to the matter at hand; relevant. [C14: from Latin *pertinēns,* from *pertinēre* to PERTAIN] —ˈ**pertinence** *n.* —ˈ**pertinently** *adv.*

perturb (pəˈtɜːb) *vb.* (*tr.; often passive*) **1.** to disturb the composure of; trouble. **2.** to throw into disorder. **3.** *Physics, astronomy.* to cause (a planet, electron, etc.) to undergo a perturbation. [C14: from Old French *pertourber,* from Latin *perturbāre* to confuse, from *per-* (intensive) + *turbāre* to agitate, from *turba* confusion] —**perˈturbable** *adj.* —**perˈturbably** *adv.* —**perˈturbing** *adj.* —**perˈturbingly** *adv.*

perturbation (ˌpɜːtəˈbeɪʃən) *n.* **1.** the act of perturbing or the state of being perturbed. **2.** a cause of disturbance or upset. **3.** *Physics.* a secondary influence on a system that modifies simple behaviour, such as the effect of the other electrons on one electron in an atom. **4.** *Astronomy.* a small continuous deviation in the inclination and eccentricity of the orbit of a planet or comet, due to the attraction of neighbouring planets.

pertussis (pəˈtʌsɪs) *n.* the technical name for **whooping cough.** [C18: New Latin, from Latin *per-* (intensive) + *tussis* cough] —**perˈtussal** *adj.*

Peru Current (pəˈruː) *n.* another name for the **Humboldt Current.**

peruke (pəˈruːk) *n.* a type of wig for men, fashionable in the 17th and 18th centuries. Also called: **periwig.** [C16: from French *perruque,* from Italian *perrucca* wig, of obscure origin]

peruse (pəˈruːz) *vb.* (*tr.*) **1.** to read or examine with care; study. **2.** to browse or read through in a leisurely way. [C15 (meaning: to use up): from PER- (intensive) + USE] —**peˈrusal** *n.* —**peˈruser** *n.*

Peruvian (pəˈruːvɪən) *adj.* **1.** of or relating to Peru, a republic in W South America, or to its people, customs, etc. ~*n.* **2.** a native or inhabitant of Peru.

Peruvian bark *n.* another name for **cinchona** (sense 2).

perv (pɜːv) *Slang.* ~*n.* **1.** a pervert. **2.** *Austral.* an erotic glance or look. ~*vb. also* **perve.** (*intr.*) **3.** *Austral.* to give a person an erotic look.

pervade (pɜːˈveɪd) *vb.* (*tr.*) to spread through or throughout, esp. subtly or gradually; permeate. [C17: from Latin *pervādere,* from *per-* through + *vādere* to go] —**perˈvader** *n.* —**pervasion** (pɜːˈveɪʒən) *n.*

pervasive (pɜːˈveɪsɪv) *adj.* pervading or tending to pervade. [C18: from Latin *pervāsus,* past participle of *pervādere* to PERVADE] —**perˈvasively** *adv.* —**perˈvasiveness** *n.*

perverse (pəˈvɜːs) *adj.* **1.** deliberately deviating from what is regarded as normal, good, or proper. **2.** persistently holding to what is wrong. **3.** wayward or contrary; obstinate; cantankerous. **4.** *Archaic.* perverted. [C14: from Old French *pervers,* from Latin *perversus* turned the wrong way] —**perˈversely** *adv.* —**perˈverseness** *n.*

perversion (pəˈvɜːʃən) *n.* **1.** any abnormal means of obtaining sexual satisfaction. **2.** the act of perverting or the state of being perverted. **3.** a perverted form or usage.

perversity (pəˈvɜːsɪtɪ) *n., pl.* **-ties. 1.** the quality or state of being perverse. **2.** a perverse action, comment, etc.

perversive (pəˈvɜːsɪv) *adj.* perverting or tending to pervert.

pervert *vb.* (pəˈvɜːt). (*tr.*) **1.** to use wrongly or badly. **2.** to interpret wrongly or badly; distort. **3.** to lead into deviant or perverted beliefs or behaviour; corrupt. **4.** to debase. ~*n.* (ˈpɜːvɜːt). **5.** a person who practises sexual perversion. [C14: from Old French *pervertir,* from Latin *pervertere* to turn the wrong way, from *per-* (indicating deviation) + *vertere* to turn] —**perˈverter** *n.* —**perˈvertible** *adj.*

perverted (pəˈvɜːtɪd) *adj.* **1.** deviating greatly from what is regarded as normal or right; distorted. **2.** of or practising sexual perversion. **3.** incorrectly interpreted. —**perˈvertedly** *adv.* —**perˈvertedness** *n.*

pervious (ˈpɜːvɪəs) *adj.* **1.** able to be penetrated; permeable. **2.** receptive to new ideas; open-minded. [C17: from Latin *pervius,* from *per-* (through) + *via* a way] —**ˈperviously** *adv.* —**ˈperviousness** *n.*

pes (peɪz, piːz) *n., pl.* **pedes** (ˈpɛdiːz). **1.** the technical name for the human **foot. 2.** the corresponding part in higher vertebrates. **3.** any footlike part. [C19: New Latin: foot]

Pesach *or* **Pesah** (ˈpeɪsɑːk; *Hebrew* ˈpɛsax) *n.* other words for **Passover** (sense 1). [from Hebrew *pesah;* see PASSOVER]

pesade (pɛˈsɑːd) *n. Dressage.* a position in which the horse stands on the hind legs with the forelegs in the air. [C18: from French, from *posade,* from Italian *posata* a halt, from *posare* to stop, from Latin *pausa* end]

peseta (pəˈseɪtə; *Spanish* peˈseta) *n.* the standard monetary unit of Spain and its dependencies, divided into 100 céntimos. [C19: from Spanish, diminutive of PESO]

pesewa (pɪˈseɪwɑː) *n.* a Ghanaian monetary unit worth one hundredth of a cedi.

Peshitta (pəˈʃiːtə) *or* **Peshito** (pəˈʃiːtəʊ) *n.* the principal Syriac version of the Bible. [C18 *Peshito,* from Syriac]

pesky (ˈpɛskɪ) *adj.* **peskier, peskiest.** *U.S. and Canadian informal.* troublesome: *pesky flies.* [C19: probably changed from *pesty;* see PEST] —**ˈpeskily** *adv.* —**ˈpeskiness** *n.*

peso (ˈpeɪsəʊ; *Spanish* ˈpeso) *n., pl.* **-sos** (-səʊz; *Spanish* -sos). **1.** the standard monetary unit, comprising 100 centavos, of Colombia, Cuba, the Dominican Republic, Mexico, and the Philippines. **2.** the standard monetary unit of Uruguay, divided into 100 centesimos. **3.** a coin or currency note worth a peso. **4.** another name for **piece of eight.** [C16: from Spanish: weight, from Latin *pēnsum* something weighed out, from *pendere* to weigh]

pessary (ˈpɛsərɪ) *n., pl.* **-ries.** *Med.* **1.** a device for inserting into the vagina, either as a support for the uterus or (**diaphragm pessary**) as a contraceptive. **2.** a medicated vaginal suppository. [C14: from Late Latin *pessārium,* from Latin *pessum,* from Greek *pessos* plug]

pessimism (ˈpɛsɪˌmɪzəm) *n.* **1.** the tendency to expect the worst and see the worst in all things. **2.** the doctrine of the ultimate triumph of evil over good. **3.** the doctrine that this world is corrupt and that man's sojourn in it is a preparation for some other existence. [C18: from Latin *pessimus* worst, from *malus* bad] —**ˈpessimist** *n.* —**ˌpessiˈmistic** *or* (*less commonly*) **ˌpessiˈmistical** *adj.* —**ˌpessiˈmistically** *adv.*

pest (pɛst) *n.* **1.** a person or thing that annoys, esp. by imposing itself when it is not wanted; nuisance. **2. a.** any organism that damages crops, injures or irritates livestock or man, or reduces the fertility of land. **b.** (*as modifier*): *pest control.* **3.** *Rare.* an epidemic disease or pestilence. [C16: from Latin *pestis* plague, of obscure origin]

pester (ˈpɛstə) *vb.* (*tr.*) to annoy or nag continually. [C16: from Old French *empestrer* to hobble (a horse), from Vulgar Latin *impāstōriāre* (unattested) to use a hobble, from *pāstōria* (unattested) a hobble, from Latin *pāstōrius* relating to a herdsman, from *pastor* herdsman] —**ˈpesterer** *n.* —**ˈpesteringly** *adv.*

pesthouse (ˈpɛstˌhaʊs) *n. Obsolete.* a hospital for treating persons with infectious diseases. Also called: **lazaretto.**

pesticide (ˈpɛstɪˌsaɪd) *n.* a chemical used for killing pests, esp. insects and rodents. —**ˌpestiˈcidal** *adj.*

pestiferous (pɛˈstɪfərəs) *adj.* **1.** *Informal.* troublesome; irritating. **2.** breeding, carrying, or spreading infectious disease. **3.** corrupting; pernicious. [C16: from Latin *pestifer,* from *pestis* contagious disease, PEST + *ferre* to bring] —**pesˈtiferously** *adv.* —**pesˈtiferousness** *n.*

pestilence (ˈpɛstɪləns) *n.* **1. a.** any epidemic outbreak of a deadly and highly infectious disease, such as the plague. **b.** such a disease. **2.** an evil influence or idea.

pestilent (ˈpɛstɪlənt) *adj.* **1.** annoying; irritating. **2.** highly destructive morally or physically; pernicious. **3.** infected with or likely to cause epidemic or infectious disease. [C15: from Latin *pestilens* unwholesome, from *pestis* plague] —**ˈpestilently** *adv.*

pestilential (ˌpɛstɪˈlɛnʃəl) *adj.* **1.** dangerous or troublesome; harmful or annoying. **2.** of, causing, or resembling pestilence. —**ˌpestiˈlentially** *adv.*

pestle (ˈpɛsᵊl) *n.* **1.** a club-shaped instrument for mixing or grinding substances in a mortar. **2.** a tool for pounding or stamping. ~*vb.* **3.** to pound (a substance or object) with or as if with a pestle. [C14: from Old French *pestel,* from Latin *pistillum;* related to *pinsāre* to crush]

pesto (ˈpɛstəʊ) *n.* a sauce for pasta, consisting of basil leaves, nuts, garlic, oil, and Parmesan cheese, all crushed together. [Italian, shortened form of *pestato,* past participle of *pestare* to pound, crush]

pet[1] (pɛt) *n.* **1.** a tame animal kept in a household for companionship, amusement, etc. **2.** a person who is fondly indulged; favourite: *teacher's pet.* ~*adj.* **3.** kept as a pet: *a pet dog.* **4.** of or for pet animals: *pet food.* **5.** particularly cherished; favourite: *a pet theory; a pet hatred.* **6.** familiar or affectionate: *a pet name.* **7. pet day.** *Scot. and Irish.* a single fine day during a period of bad weather. ~*vb.* **pets, petting, petted. 8.** (*tr.*) to treat (a person, animal, etc.) as a pet; pamper. **9.** (*tr.*) to pat or fondle (an animal, child, etc.). **10.** (*intr.*) *Informal.* (of two people) to caress each other in an erotic manner, as during lovemaking (often in the phrase **heavy petting**). [C16: origin unknown] —**ˈpetter** *n.*

pet[2] (pɛt) *n.* **1.** a fit of sulkiness, esp. at what is felt to be a slight; pique. ~*vb.* **pets, petting, petted. 2.** (*intr.*) to take offence; sulk. [C16: of uncertain origin]

PET *abbrev. for* positron emission tomography.

Pet. *Bible. abbrev. for* Peter.

peta- *prefix.* denoting 10^{15}: *petametres.* Symbol: P [C20: so named because it is the SI prefix after TERA-; on the model of PENTA-, the prefix after TETRA-]

petal (ˈpɛtᵊl) *n.* any of the separate parts of the corolla of a flower: often brightly coloured. [C18: from New Latin *petalum,* from Greek *petalon* leaf; related to *petannunai* to lie open] —**ˈpetaline** *adj.* —**ˈpetal-ˌlike** *adj.* —**ˈpetalled** *adj.*

-petal *adj. combining form.* seeking: *centripetal.* [from New Latin *-petus,* from Latin *petere* to seek]

petaliferous (ˌpɛtəˈlɪfərəs) *or* **petalous** *adj.* bearing or having petals.

petalody (ˈpɛtəˌləʊdɪ) *n.* a condition in certain plants in which stamens or other parts of the flower assume the form and function of petals. [C19: from Greek *petalōdēs* like a leaf, from *petalon* leaf] —**petalodic** (ˌpɛtəˈlɒdɪk) *adj.*

petaloid (ˈpɛtəˌlɔɪd) *adj. Biology.* resembling a petal, esp. in shape: *the petaloid pattern on a sea urchin.*

pétanque (ˌpeɪˈtɑ̃k; *French* petɑ̃k) *n.* another name, esp. in the South of France, for ***boules.*** [French, from Provençal *pèd tanco* foot fixed (to the ground)]

petard (pɪˈtɑːd) *n.* **1.** (formerly) a device containing explosives used to breach a wall, doors, etc. **2. hoist with one's own petard.** being the victim of one's own schemes. **3.** a type of explosive firework. [C16: from French: firework, from *péter* to break wind, from Latin *pēdere*]

petasus (ˈpɛtəsəs) *or* **petasos** (ˈpɛtəsəs, -ˌsɒs) *n.* a broad-brimmed hat worn by the ancient Greeks, such as one with wings on either side as traditionally worn by Mercury. [C16: via Latin from Greek *petasos*]

petaurist (pəˈtɔːrɪst) *n.* another name for **flying phalanger.** [C20: from Latin *petaurista* tightrope walker]

petcock (ˈpɛtˌkɒk) *n.* a small valve for checking the water content of a steam boiler or draining waste from the cylinder of a steam engine. [C19: from PET[1] or perhaps French *pet,* from *péter* to break wind + COCK[1]]

petechia (pɪˈtiːkɪə) *n., pl.* **-chiae** (-kɪˌiː). a minute discoloured spot on the surface of the skin or mucous membrane, caused by an underlying ruptured blood vessel. [C18: via New Latin from Italian *petecchia* freckle, of obscure origin] —**peˈtechial** *adj.*

peter[1] (ˈpiːtə) *vb.* (*intr.;* foll. by *out* or *away*) to fall (off) in volume, intensity, etc., and finally cease: *the cash petered out in three months.* [C19: of unknown origin]

peter[2] (ˈpiːtə) *Bridge, whist. vb.* (*intr.*) **1.** to play a high card before a low one in a suit, usually a conventional signal of a doubleton holding or of strength in that suit. ~*n.* **2.** the act of petering. [C20: perhaps a special use of PETER[1] (to fall off in power)]

peter[3] (ˈpiːtə) *n. Slang.* **1.** a safe, till, or cash box. **2.** a prison cell. **3.** the witness box in a courtroom. **4.** *Chiefly U.S.* a taboo slang word for **penis.** [C17 (meaning a case): from the name *Peter*]

Peterborough (ˈpiːtəbərə, -brə) *n.* a traditional type of wooden canoe formerly made in Peterborough, SE Ontario.

peterman (ˈpiːtəmən) *n., pl.* **-men.** *Slang.* a burglar skilled in safe-breaking. [C19: from PETER[3]]

Peter Pan *n.* a youthful, boyish, or immature man. [C20: after the main character in *Peter Pan* (1904), a play by J. M. *Barrie* (1860–1937), British dramatist and novelist]

Peter Pan collar *n.* a collar on a round neck, having two rounded ends at the front.

Peter Principle *n.* **the.** the theory, usually taken facetiously, that all members in a hierarchy rise to their own level of incompetence. [C20: from the book *The Peter Principle* (1969) by Dr. Lawrence J. *Peter* and Raymond Hull, in which the theory was originally propounded]

petersham ('piːtəʃəm) *n.* **1.** a thick corded ribbon used to stiffen belts, button bands, etc. **2.** a heavy woollen fabric used esp. for coats. **3.** a kind of overcoat made of such fabric. [C19: named after Viscount *Petersham* (died 1851), British army officer]

Peter's pence *or* **Peter pence** *n.* **1.** an annual tax, originally of one penny, formerly levied for the maintenance of the Papal See: abolished by Henry VIII in 1534. **2.** a voluntary contribution made by Roman Catholics in many countries for the same purpose. [C13: referring to St *Peter*, leader of the apostles considered as the first pope]

Peters' projection *n.* a form of modified Mercator's map projection that gives prominence to Third World countries. [C20: named after Arno *Peters*, German historian]

pethidine ('pɛθɪˌdiːn) *n.* another name for **meperidine.** [C20: perhaps a blend of PIPERIDINE + ETHYL]

pétillant *French* (petijɑ̃) *adj.* (of wine) slightly effervescent. [French, from *pétiller* to effervesce]

petiolate ('pɛtɪəˌleɪt) *or* **petiolated** *adj.* (of a plant or leaf) having a leafstalk. Compare **sessile** (sense 1).

petiole ('pɛtɪˌəʊl) *n.* **1.** the stalk by which a leaf is attached to the rest of the plant. **2.** *Zoology.* a slender stalk or stem, such as the connection between the thorax and abdomen of ants. [C18: via French from Latin *petiolus* little foot, from *pēs* foot]

petiolule ('piːtɪəʊlˌjuːl) *n.* the stalk of any of the leaflets making up a compound leaf. [C19: from New Latin *petiolūlus,* diminutive of Latin *petiolus;* see PETIOLE]

petit ('pɛtɪ) *adj.* (*prenominal*) *Chiefly law.* of little or lesser importance; small: *petit jury.* [C14: from Old French: little, of obscure origin]

petit bourgeois ('pɛtɪ 'bʊəʒwɑː; *French* pəti burʒwa) *n., pl.* **petits bourgeois** ('pɛtɪ 'bʊəʒwɑːz; *French* pəti burʒwa). **1.** Also called: **petite bourgeoisie, petty bourgeoisie.** the section of the middle class with the lowest social status, generally composed of shopkeepers, lower clerical staff, etc. **2.** a member of this stratum. *~adj.* **3.** of, relating to, or characteristic of the petit bourgeois, esp. indicating a sense of self-righteousness and a high degree of conformity to established standards of behaviour.

petite (pə'tiːt) *adj.* (of a woman) small, delicate, and dainty. [C18: from French, feminine of *petit* small]

petit four ('pɛtɪ 'fɔː; *French* pəti fur) *n., pl.* **petits fours** ('pɛtɪ 'fɔːz; *French* pəti fur). any of various very small rich sweet cakes and biscuits, usually decorated with fancy icing, marzipan, etc. [French, literally: little oven]

petition (pɪ'tɪʃən) *n.* **1.** a written document signed by a large number of people demanding some form of action from a government or other authority. **2.** any formal request to a higher authority or deity; entreaty. **3.** *Law.* a formal application in writing made to a court asking for some specific judicial action: *a petition for divorce.* **4.** the action of petitioning. *~vb.* **5.** (*tr.*) to address or present a petition to (a person in authority, government, etc.): *to petition Parliament.* **6.** (*intr.; foll. by for*) to seek by petition: *to petition for a change in the law.* [C14: from Latin *petītiō,* from *petere* to seek] —**pe'titionary** *adj.*

petitioner (pɪ'tɪʃənə) *n.* **1.** a person who presents a petition. **2.** *Chiefly Brit.* the plaintiff in a divorce suit.

petitio principii (pɪ'tɪʃɪˌəʊ prɪn'kɪpɪˌaɪ) *n. Logic.* a form of fallacious reasoning in which the conclusion has been assumed in the premises; begging the question. Sometimes shortened to **petitio.** [C16: Latin, translation of Greek *to en arkhei aiteisthai* an assumption at the beginning]

petit jury *n.* a jury of 12 persons empanelled to determine the facts of a case and decide the issue pursuant to the direction of the court on points of law. Also called: **petty jury.** Compare **grand jury.** —**petit juror** *n.*

petit larceny *n.* **1.** (formerly in England) the stealing of property valued at 12 pence or under. Abolished 1827. **2.** (in some states of the U.S.) the theft of property having a value below a certain figure. ~Also called: **petty larceny.** Compare **grand larceny.** —**petit larcenist** *n.*

petit mal ('pɛtɪ 'mæl; *French* pəti mal) *n.* a mild form of epilepsy characterized by periods of impairment or loss of consciousness for up to 30 seconds. Compare **grand mal.** [C19: French: little illness]

petit point ('pɛtɪ 'pɔɪnt; *French* pəti pwɛ̃) *n.* **1.** Also called: **tent stitch.** a small diagonal needlepoint stitch used for fine detail. **2.** work done with such stitches, esp. fine tapestry. ~Compare **gros point.** [French: small point]

petits pois (*French* pəti pwa) *pl. n.* small sweet fresh green peas. [French: small peas]

Petrarchan sonnet ('pɛtrɑːkən) *n.* a sonnet form associated with the Italian poet Petrarch (1304–74), having an octave rhyming a b b a a b b a and a sestet rhyming either c d e c d e or c d c d c d. Also called: **Italian sonnet.**

petrel ('pɛtrəl) *n.* any oceanic bird of the order *Procellariiformes,* having a hooked bill and tubular nostrils: includes albatrosses, storm petrels, and shearwaters. See also **storm petrel.** [C17: variant of earlier *pitteral,* associated by folk etymology with St *Peter,* because the bird appears to walk on water]

Petri dish ('piːtrɪ) *n.* a shallow circular flat-bottomed dish, often with a fitting cover, used in laboratories, esp. for producing cultures of microorganisms. [C19: named after J. R. *Petri* (1852–1921), German bacteriologist]

petrifaction (ˌpɛtrɪ'fækʃən) *or* **petrification** (ˌpɛtrɪfɪ'keɪʃən) *n.* **1.** the act or process of forming petrified organic material. **2.** the state of being petrified.

petrify ('pɛtrɪˌfaɪ) *vb.* **-fies, -fying, -fied. 1.** (*tr.; often passive*) to convert (organic material, esp. plant material) into a fossilized form by impregnation with dissolved minerals so that the original appearance is preserved. **2.** to make or become dull, unresponsive, insensitive, etc.; deaden. **3.** (*tr.; often passive*) to stun or daze with horror, fear, etc. [C16: from French *pétrifier,* ultimately from Greek *petra* stone, rock] —**'petriˌfier** *n.*

Petrine ('piːtraɪn) *adj.* **1.** *New Testament.* of or relating to the apostle St Peter, his position of leadership, or the epistles, etc., attributed to him. **2.** *R.C. Church.* of or relating to the supremacy in the Church that the pope is regarded as having inherited from St Peter: *the Petrine claims.*

petro- *or before a vowel* **petr-** *combining form.* **1.** indicating stone or rock: *petrology.* **2.** indicating petroleum, its products, etc.: *petrochemical.* [from Greek *petra* rock or *petros* stone]

petrochemical (ˌpɛtrəʊ'kɛmɪkᵊl) *n.* **1.** any substance, such as acetone or ethanol, obtained from petroleum or natural gas. *~adj.* **2.** of, concerned with, or obtained from petrochemicals or related to petrochemistry. —ˌ**petro'chemically** *adv.*

petrochemistry (ˌpɛtrəʊ'kɛmɪstrɪ) *n.* **1.** the chemistry of petroleum and its derivatives. **2.** the branch of chemistry concerned with the chemical composition of rocks.

petrodollar ('pɛtrəʊˌdɒlə) *n.* money, paid in dollars, earned by a country for the exporting of petroleum.

petrog. *abbrev. for* petrography.

petroglyph ('pɛtrəˌglɪf) *n.* a drawing or carving on rock, esp. a prehistoric one. [C19: via French from Greek *petra* stone + *gluphē* carving]

petrography (pɛ'trɒgrəfɪ) *n.* the branch of petrology concerned with the description and classification of rocks. Abbrev.: **petrog.** —**pe'trographer** *n.* —**petrographic** (ˌpɛtrə'græfɪk) *or* ˌ**petro'graphical** *adj.* —ˌ**petro'graphically** *adv.*

petrol ('pɛtrəl) *n.* any one of various volatile flammable liquid mixtures of hydrocarbons, mainly hexane, heptane, and octane, obtained from petroleum and used as a solvent and a fuel for internal-combustion engines. Usually petrol also contains additives such as antiknock compounds and corrosion inhibitors. U.S. and Canadian name: **gasoline.** [C16: via French from Medieval Latin PETROLEUM]

petrol. *abbrev. for* petrology.

petrolatum (ˌpɛtrə'leɪtəm) *n.* a translucent gelatinous substance obtained from petroleum; used as a lubricant and in medicine as an ointment base and protective dressing. Also called: **mineral jelly, petroleum jelly.** [C19: from PETROL + Latin *-atum* -ATE[1]]

petrol bomb *n.* **1.** a home-made incendiary device, consisting of a bottle filled with petrol and stoppered with a wick, that is thrown by hand; Molotov cocktail. *~vb.* **petrol-bomb.** (*tr.*) **2.** to attack with petrol bombs. —**petrol bomber** *n.*

petrol engine *n.* an internal-combustion engine that uses petrol as fuel.

petroleum (pə'trəʊlɪəm) *n.* a dark-coloured thick flammable crude oil occurring in sedimentary rocks around the Persian Gulf, in parts of North and South America, and below the North Sea, consisting mainly of hydrocarbons. Fractional distillation separates the crude oil into petrol, paraffin, diesel oil, lubricating oil, etc. Fuel oil, paraffin wax, asphalt, and carbon black are extracted from the residue. [C16: from Medieval Latin, from Latin *petra* stone + *oleum* oil]

petroleum ether *n.* a volatile mixture of the higher alkane hydrocarbons, obtained as a fraction of petroleum and used as a solvent.

petroleum jelly *n.* another name for **petrolatum.**

petrolic (pɛ'trɒlɪk) *adj.* of, relating to, containing, or obtained from petroleum.

petrology (pɛ'trɒlədʒɪ) *n., pl.* **-gies.** the study of the composition, origin, structure, and formation of rocks. Abbrev.: **petrol.** —**petrological** (ˌpɛtrə'lɒdʒɪkᵊl) *adj.* —ˌ**petro'logically** *adv.* —**pe'trologist** *n.*

petrol pump *n.* a device at a filling station that is used to deliver petrol to the tank of a car and which displays the quantity, quality, and usually the cost of the petrol delivered.

petrol station *n. Brit.* another term for **filling station.**

petronel ('pɛtrəˌnɛl) *n.* a firearm of large calibre used in the 16th and early 17th centuries, esp. by cavalry soldiers. [C16: from French, literally: of the breast, from *poitrine* breast, from Latin *pectus*]

petrosal (pɛ'trəʊsᵊl) *adj. Anatomy.* of, relating to, or situated near the dense part of the temporal bone that surrounds the inner ear. [C18: from Latin *petrōsus* full of rocks, from *petra* a rock, from Greek]

petrous ('pɛtrəs, 'piː-) *adj.* **1.** *Anatomy.* denoting the dense part of the temporal bone that surrounds the inner ear. **2.** *Rare.* like rock or stone. [C16: from Latin *petrōsus* full of rocks]

pe-tsai cabbage ('peɪ'tsaɪ) *n.* another name for **Chinese cabbage** (sense 1). [from Chinese (Peking) *pe ts'ai,* literally: white vegetable]

petticoat ('pɛtɪˌkəʊt) *n.* **1.** a woman's light undergarment in the form of an underskirt or including a bodice supported by shoulder straps. **2.** *Informal.* **a.** a humorous or mildly disparaging name for a woman. **b.** (*as modifier*): *petticoat politics.* [C15: see PETTY, COAT]

pettifog ('pɛtɪˌfɒg) *vb.* **-fogs, -fogging, -fogged.** (*intr.*) to be a pettifogger.

pettifogger ('pɛtɪˌfɒgə) *n.* **1.** a lawyer of inferior status who conducts unimportant cases, esp. one who is unscrupulous or resorts to trickery. **2.** any person who quibbles or fusses over details. [C16: from PETTY + *fogger,* of uncertain origin, perhaps from *Fugger,* name of a family (C15–16) of German financiers] —'**pettiˌfoggery** *n.*

pettifogging ('pɛtɪˌfɒgɪŋ) *adj.* **1.** petty: *pettifogging details.* **2.** mean; quibbling: *pettifogging lawyers.*

pettish ('pɛtɪʃ) *adj.* peevish; petulant: *a pettish child.* [C16: from PET[2]] —'**pettishly** *adv.* —'**pettishness** *n.*

pettitoes ('pɛtɪˌtəʊz) *pl. n.* pig's trotters, esp. when used as food. [C16: from Old French *petite oie,* literally: little goose (giblets of a goose)]

petty ('pɛtɪ) *adj.* **-tier, -tiest. 1.** trivial; trifling; inessential: *petty details.* **2.** of a narrow-minded, mean, or small-natured disposition or character: *petty spite.* **3.** minor or subordinate in rank: *petty officialdom.* **4.** *Law.* of lesser importance. [C14: from Old French PETIT] —'**pettily** *adv.* —'**pettiness** *n.*

petty cash *n.* a small cash fund kept on a firm's premises for the payment of minor incidental expenses.

petty jury *n.* a variant spelling of **petit jury.** —**petty juror** *n.*

petty larceny *n.* a variant spelling of **petit larceny.**

petty officer *n.* a noncommissioned officer in a naval service, comparable in rank to a sergeant in an army or marine corps.

petty sessions *n.* (*functioning as sing. or pl.*) another term for **magistrates' court.**

petulant ('pɛtjʊlənt) *adj.* irritable, impatient, or sullen in a peevish or capricious way. [C16: via Old French from Latin *petulāns* bold, from *petulāre* (unattested) to attack playfully, from *petere* to assail] —'**petulance** *or* '**petulancy** *n.* —'**petulantly** *adv.*

petunia (pɪ'tjuːnɪə) *n.* any solanaceous plant of the tropical American genus *Petunia:* cultivated for their white, pink, blue, or purple funnel-shaped flowers. [C19: via New Latin from obsolete French *petun* variety of tobacco, from Tupi *petyn*]

petuntse *or* **petuntze** (pɪ'tʌntsɪ, -'tʊn-) *n.* a fusible feldspathic mineral used in hard-paste porcelain; china stone. [C18: from Chinese (Peking) *pe tun tzu,* from *pe* white + *tun* heap + *tzu* offspring]

pew (pjuː) *n.* **1.** (in a church) **a.** one of several long benchlike seats with backs, used by the congregation. **b.** an enclosed compartment reserved for the use of a family or other small group. **2.** *Brit. informal.* a seat (esp. in the phrase **take a pew**). [C14 *pywe,* from Old French *puye,* from Latin *podium* a balcony, from Greek *podion* supporting structure, from *pous* foot]

pewee *or* **peewee** ('piːwiː) *n.* any of several small North American flycatchers of the genus *Contopus,* having a greenish-brown plumage. [C19: imitative of its cry]

pewit ('piːwɪt) *n.* another name for **lapwing.** [C13: imitative of the bird's cry]

pewter ('pjuːtə) *n.* **1. a.** any of various alloys containing tin (80–90 per cent), lead (10–20 per cent), and sometimes small amounts of other metals, such as copper and antimony. **b.** (*as modifier*): *pewter ware; a pewter tankard.* **2. a.** a bluish-grey colour. **b.** (*as adj.*): *pewter tights.* **3.** plate or kitchen utensils made from pewter. [C14: from Old French *peaultre,* of obscure origin; related to Old Provençal *peltre* pewter] —'**pewterer** *n.*

peyote (peɪ'əʊtɪ, pɪ-) *n.* another name for **mescal** (sense 1). [Mexican Spanish, from Nahuatl *peyotl*]

pF *symbol for* picofarad.

pf. *abbrev for:* **1.** perfect. **2.** Also: **pfg.** pfennig. **3.** preferred.

pfennig ('fɛnɪg; *German* 'pfɛnɪç) *n., pl.* **-nigs** *or* **-nige** (*German* -nɪgə). **1.** a German monetary unit worth one hundredth of a Deutschmark. **2.** (formerly) a monetary unit worth one hundredth of an East German ostmark. [German: PENNY]

PG[1] *symbol for* a film certified for viewing by anyone, but which contains scenes that may be unsuitable for children, for whom parental guidance is necessary. Austral. equivalent: **PGR.** [C20: from abbreviation of *parental guidance*]

PG[2] *abbrev. for:* **1.** paying guest. **2.** postgraduate.

pg. *abbrev. for* page.

Pg. *abbrev. for:* **1.** Portugal. **2.** Portuguese.

PGA *abbrev. for* Professional Golfers' Association.

PGR *abbrev. for:* **1.** psychogalvanic response. **2.** (in Australia) parental guidance recommended. See **PG**[1].

pH *n.* potential of hydrogen; a measure of the acidity or alkalinity of a solution equal to the common logarithm of the reciprocal of the concentration of hydrogen ions in moles per cubic decimetre of solution. Pure water has a pH of 7, acid solutions have a pH less than 7, and alkaline solutions a pH greater than 7.

Ph *chemical symbol for* phenyl group or radical.

ph. *abbrev. for* phase.

phacelia (fə'siːlɪə) *n.* any plant of the mostly annual American genus *Phacelia,* esp. *P. campanularia,* grown for its large, deep blue bell flowers: family *Hydrophyllaceae.* [New Latin, from Greek *phakelos* cluster (from the habit of the flowers) + -IA]

phaeic ('fiːɪk) *adj.* (of animals) having dusky coloration; less dark than melanic. [C19: from Greek *phaiós* dusky] —'**phaeism** *n.*

phaeton ('feɪtᵊn) *n.* a light four-wheeled horse-drawn carriage with or without a top, usually having two seats. [C18: from *Phaëthon* in Greek mythology, the son of Helios (the sun god), who borrowed his father's chariot]

phage (feɪdʒ) *n.* short for **bacteriophage.**

-phage *n. combining form.* indicating something that eats or consumes something specified: *bacteriophage.* [from Greek *-phagos;* see PHAGO-] —**-phagous** *adj. combining form.*

phagedaena *or* **phagedena** (ˌfædʒɪ'diːnə) *n. Pathol.* a rapidly spreading ulcer that destroys tissues as it increases in size. [C17: via Latin from Greek, from *phagein* to eat]

phago- *or before a vowel* **phag-** *combining form.* eating, consuming, or destroying: *phagocyte.* [from Greek *phagein* to consume]

phagocyte ('fægəˌsaɪt) *n.* an amoeboid cell or protozoan that engulfs particles, such as food substances or invading microorganisms. —**phagocytic** (ˌfægə'sɪtɪk) *adj.*

phagocytosis (ˌfægəsaɪ'təʊsɪs) *n.* the process by which a cell, such as a white blood cell, ingests microorganisms, other cells, and foreign particles.

phagomania (ˌfægəʊ'meɪnɪə) *n.* a compulsive desire to eat. —ˌ**phagoˈmaniˌac** *n.*

-phagy *or* **-phagia** *n. combining form.* indicating an eating or devouring: *anthropophagy.* [from Greek *-phagia;* see PHAGO-]

phalange ('fælændʒ) *n., pl.* **phalanges** (fæ'lændʒiːz). *Anatomy.* another name for **phalanx** (sense 5). [C16: via French, ultimately from Greek PHALANX]

phalangeal (fə'lændʒɪəl) *adj. Anatomy.* of or relating to a phalanx or phalanges.

phalanger (fə'lændʒə) *n.* any of various Australasian arboreal marsupials, such as *Trichosurus vulpecula* (**brush-tailed phalanger**), having dense fur and a long tail: family *Phalangeridae.* Also called (Australian and N.Z.): **possum.** See also **flying phalanger.** [C18: via New Latin from Greek *phalaggion* spider's web, referring to its webbed hind toes]

Phalangist (fə'lændʒɪst) *n.* **a.** a member of a Lebanese Christian paramilitary organization founded in 1936 and originally based on similar ideas to the fascist Falange in Spain. **b.** (*as modifier*): *Phalangist leaders.*

phalanstery ('fælənstərɪ, -strɪ) *n., pl.* **-steries. 1.** (in Fourierism) **a.** buildings occupied by a phalanx. **b.** a community represented by a phalanx. **2.** any similar association or the buildings occupied by such an association. [C19: from French *phalanstère,* from *phalange* PHALANX, on the model of *monastère* MONASTERY]

phalanx ('fælæŋks) *n., pl.* **phalanxes** *or* **phalanges** (fæ'lændʒiːz). **1.** an ancient Greek and Macedonian battle formation of hoplites presenting long spears from behind a wall of overlapping shields. **2.** any closely ranked unit or mass of people: *the police formed a phalanx to protect the embassy.* **3.** a number of people united for a common purpose. **4.** (in Fourierism) a group of approximately 1800 persons forming a commune in which all property is collectively owned. **5.** *Anatomy.* any of the bones of the fingers or toes. **6.** *Botany.* a bundle of stamens, joined together by their stalks (filaments). [C16: via Latin from Greek: infantry formation in close ranks, bone of finger or toe]

phalarope ('fæləˌrəʊp) *n.* any aquatic shore bird of the family *Phalaropidae,* such as *Phalaropus fulicarius* (**grey phalarope**), of northern oceans and lakes, having a long slender bill and lobed toes: order *Charadriiformes.* [C18: via French from New Latin *Phalaropus,* from Greek *phalaris* coot + *pous* foot]

phallic ('fælɪk) *adj.* **1.** of, relating to, or resembling a phallus: *a phallic symbol.* **2.** *Psychoanal.* **a.** relating to a stage of psychosexual development during which a male child's interest is concentrated on the genital organs. **b.** designating personality traits, such as conceit and self-assurance, due to fixation at the phallic stage of development. Compare **anal** (sense 2), **oral** (sense 7), **genital** (sense 2). **c.** (in Freudian theory) denoting a phase of early childhood in which there is a belief that both sexes possess a phallus. **3.** of or relating to phallicism.

phallicism ('fælɪˌsɪzəm) *or* **phallism** *n.* the worship or veneration of the phallus. —'**phallicist** *or* '**phallist** *n.*

phalloidin (fə'lɔɪdɪn) *n.* a peptide toxin, responsible for the toxicity of the death cap mushroom, *Amanita phalloides.* [C20: New Latin, from PHALLUS + -OID + -IN]

phallus ('fæləs) *n., pl.* **-li** (-laɪ) *or* **-luses. 1.** another word for **penis. 2.** an image of the male sexual organ, esp. one venerated as a religious symbol of reproductive power. [C17: via Late Latin from Greek *phallos*]

-phane *n. combining form.* indicating something resembling a specified substance: *cellophane.* [from Greek *phainein* to shine, (in passive) appear]

phanerocrystalline (ˌfænərəʊ'krɪstəlɪn, -ˌlaɪn) *adj.* (of igneous and metamorphic rocks) having a crystalline structure in which the crystals are large enough to be seen with the naked eye. [C19: from Greek *phaneros* visible + CRYSTALLINE]

phanerogam ('fænərəʊˌgæm) *n.* any plant of the former major division *Phanerogamae,* which included all seed-bearing plants; a former name for **spermatophyte.** Compare **cryptogam.** [C19: from New Latin *phanerogamus,* from Greek *phaneros* visible + *gamos* marriage] —ˌ**phaneroˈgamic** *or* **phanerogamous** (ˌfænə'rɒgəməs) *adj.*

phanerophyte ('fænərə,faɪt, fə'nɛrə-) *n.* a tree or shrub that bears its perennating buds more than 25 cm above the level of the soil. [C20: from Greek *phanero-* visible + -PHYTE]

Phanerozoic (,fænərə'zəʊɪk) *adj.* **1.** of or relating to that part of geological time represented by rocks in which the evidence of life is abundant, comprising the Palaeozoic, Mesozoic, and Cenozoic eras. ~*n.* **2. the.** the Phanerozoic era. ~Compare **Cryptozoic.**

phantasm ('fæntæzəm) *n.* **1.** a phantom. **2.** an illusory perception of an object, person, etc. **3.** (in the philosophy of Plato) objective reality as distorted by perception. [C13: from Old French *fantasme,* from Latin *phantasma,* from Greek; related to Greek *phantazein* to cause to be seen, from *phainein* to show] —**phan'tasmal** *or* **phan'tasmic** *adj.* —**phan'tasmally** *or* **phan'tasmically** *adv.*

phantasmagoria (,fæntæzmə'gɔːrɪə) *or* **phantasmagory** (fæn'tæzməgərɪ) *n.* **1.** *Psychol.* a shifting medley of real or imagined figures, as in a dream. **2.** *Films.* a sequence of pictures made to vary in size rapidly while remaining in focus. **3.** *Rare.* a shifting scene composed of different elements. [C19: probably from French *fantasmagorie* production of phantasms, from PHANTASM + *-agorie,* perhaps from Greek *ageirein* to gather together] —**phantasmagoric** (,fæntæzmə'gɒrɪk) *or* **,phantasma'gorical** *adj.* —**,phantasma'gorically** *adv.*

phantasy ('fæntəsɪ) *n., pl.* **-sies.** an archaic spelling of **fantasy.**

phantom ('fæntəm) *n.* **1. a.** an apparition or spectre. **b.** (*as modifier*): *a phantom army marching through the sky.* **2.** the visible representation of something abstract, esp. as appearing in a dream or hallucination: *phantoms of evil haunted his sleep.* **3.** something apparently unpleasant or horrific that has no material form. **4.** *Med.* another name for **manikin** (sense 2b). [C13: from Old French *fantosme,* from Latin *phantasma,* PHANTASM]

phantom limb *n.* the illusion that a limb still exists following its amputation, sometimes with the sensation of pain (**phantom limb pain**).

phantom pregnancy *n.* the occurrence of signs of pregnancy, such as enlarged abdomen and absence of menstruation, when no embryo is present, due to hormonal imbalance. Also called: **false pregnancy.** Technical name: **pseudocyesis.**

-phany *n. combining form.* indicating a manifestation: *theophany.* [from Greek *-phania,* from *phainein* to show; see -PHANE] —**-phanous** *adj. combining form.*

phar., Phar., pharm., *or* **Pharm.** *abbrev. for:* **1.** pharmaceutical. **2.** pharmacist. **3.** pharmacopoeia. **4.** pharmacy.

Pharaoh ('fɛərəʊ) *n.* the title of the ancient Egyptian kings. [Old English *Pharaon,* via Latin, Greek, and Hebrew ultimately from Egyptian *pr-'o* great house] —**Pharaonic** (fɛə'rɒnɪk) *adj.*

Pharaoh ant *n.* a small yellowish-red ant, *Monomorium pharaonis,* of warm regions: accidentally introduced into many countries, infesting heated buildings.

Pharisaic (,færɪ'seɪɪk) *or* **Pharisaical** *adj.* **1.** *Judaism.* of, relating to, or characteristic of the Pharisees or Pharisaism. **2.** (*often not cap.*) righteously hypocritical. —**,Phari'saically** *adv.* —**,Phari'saicalness** *n.*

Pharisaism ('færɪseɪ,ɪzəm) *or* **Phariseeism** ('færɪsiː,ɪzəm) *n.* **1.** *Judaism.* the tenets and customs of the Pharisees. **2.** (*often not cap.*) observance of the external forms of religion without genuine belief; hypocrisy.

Pharisee ('færɪ,siː) *n.* **1.** *Judaism.* a member of an ancient Jewish sect that was opposed to the Sadducees, teaching strict observance of Jewish tradition as interpreted rabbinically and believing in life after death and in the coming of the Messiah. **2.** (*often not cap.*) a self-righteous or hypocritical person. [Old English *Farīsēus,* ultimately from Aramaic *perīshāiyā,* pl. of *perīsh* separated]

pharmaceutical (,fɑːmə'sjuːtɪkᵊl) *or* (*less commonly*) **pharmaceutic** *adj.* of or relating to drugs or pharmacy. [C17: from Late Latin *pharmaceuticus,* from Greek *pharmakeus* purveyor of drugs; see PHARMACY] —**,pharma'ceutically** *adv.*

pharmaceutics (,fɑːmə'sjuːtɪks) *n.* **1.** (*functioning as sing.*) another term for **pharmacy** (sense 1). **2.** pharmaceutical remedies.

pharmacist ('fɑːməsɪst) *or* (*less commonly*) **pharmaceutist** (,fɑːmə'sjuːtɪst) *n.* a person qualified to prepare and dispense drugs.

pharmaco- *combining form.* indicating drugs: *pharmacology; pharmacopoeia.* [from Greek *pharmakon* drug, potion]

pharmacodynamics (,fɑːməkəʊdaɪ'næmɪks) *n.* (*functioning as sing.*) the branch of pharmacology concerned with the action of drugs on the physiology of the body. —**,pharmacody'namic** *adj.*

pharmacognosy (,fɑːmə'kɒgnəsɪ) *n.* the branch of pharmacology concerned with the study of crude drugs of plant and animal origin. [C19: from PHARMACO- + *gnosy,* from Greek *gnosis* knowledge] —**,pharma'cognosist** *n.* —**pharmacognostic** (,fɑːməkɒg'nɒstɪk) *adj.*

pharmacol. *abbrev. for* pharmacology.

pharmacology (,fɑːmə'kɒlədʒɪ) *n.* the science or study of drugs, including their characteristics, action, and uses. —**pharmacological** (,fɑːməkə'lɒdʒɪkᵊl) *adj.* —**,pharmaco'logically** *adv.* —**,pharma'cologist** *n.*

pharmacopoeia *or U.S.* (*sometimes*) **pharmacopeia** (,fɑːməkə'piːə) *n.* an authoritative book containing a list of medicinal drugs with their uses, preparation, dosages, formulas, etc. [C17: via New Latin from Greek *pharmakopoiia* art of preparing drugs, from PHARMACO- + *-poiia,* from *poiein* to make] —**,pharmaco'poeial** *or* **,pharmaco'poeic** *adj.* —**,pharmaco'poeist** *n.*

pharmacy ('fɑːməsɪ) *n., pl.* **-cies.** **1.** Also called: **pharmaceutics.** the practice or art of preparing and dispensing drugs. **2.** a dispensary. [C14: from Medieval Latin *pharmacia,* from Greek *pharmakeia* making of drugs, from *pharmakon* drug]

pharyngeal (,færɪn'dʒiːəl) *or* **pharyngal** (fə'rɪŋgᵊl) *adj.* **1.** of, relating to, or situated in or near the pharynx. **2.** *Phonetics.* pronounced or supplemented in pronunciation with an articulation in or constriction of the pharynx. ~*n.* **3.** *Phonetics.* a pharyngeal speech sound. [C19: from New Latin *pharyngeus;* see PHARYNX]

pharyngeal tonsil *n.* the technical name for **adenoids.**

pharyngitis (,færɪn'dʒaɪtɪs) *n.* inflammation of the pharynx.

pharyngo- *or before a vowel* **pharyng-** *combining form.* pharynx: *pharyngoscope.*

pharyngology (,færɪŋ'gɒlədʒɪ) *n.* the branch of medical science concerned with the pharynx and its diseases. —**pharyngological** (,færɪŋgə'lɒdʒɪkᵊl) *adj.* —**,pharyn'gologist** *n.*

pharyngoscope (fə'rɪŋgə,skəʊp) *n.* a medical instrument for examining the pharynx. —**pharyngoscopic** (fə,rɪŋgə'skɒpɪk) *adj.* —**pharyngoscopy** (,færɪŋ'gɒskəpɪ) *n.*

pharyngotomy (,færɪŋ'gɒtəmɪ) *n., pl.* **-mies.** surgical incision into the pharynx.

pharynx ('færɪŋks) *n., pl.* **pharynges** (fæ'rɪndʒiːz) *or* **pharynxes.** the part of the alimentary canal between the mouth and the oesophagus. Compare **nasopharynx.** [C17: via New Latin from Greek *pharunx* throat; related to Greek *pharanx* chasm]

phase (feɪz) *n.* **1.** any distinct or characteristic period or stage in a sequence of events or chain of development: *there were two phases to the resolution; his immaturity was a passing phase.* **2.** *Astronomy.* one of the recurring shapes of the portion of the moon or an inferior planet illuminated by the sun: *the new moon, first quarter, full moon, and last quarter are the four principal phases of the moon.* **3.** *Physics.* **a.** the fraction of a cycle of a periodic quantity that has been completed at a specific reference time, expressed as an angle. **b.** (*as modifier*): *a phase shift.* **4.** *Physics.* a particular stage in a periodic process or phenomenon. **5. in phase.** (of two waveforms) reaching corresponding phases at the same time. **6. out of phase.** (of two waveforms) not in phase. **7.** *Chem.* a distinct state of matter characterized by homogeneous composition and properties and the possession of a clearly defined boundary. **8.** *Zoology.* a variation in the normal form of an animal, esp. a colour variation, brought about by seasonal or geographical change. **9.** *Biology.* (*usually in combination*) a stage in mitosis or meiosis: *prophase; metaphase.* **10.** *Electrical engineering.* one of the circuits in a system in which there are two or more alternating voltages displaced by equal amounts in phase (sense 5). See also **polyphase** (sense 1). **11.** (in systemic grammar) the type of correspondence that exists between the predicators in a clause that has two or more predicators; for example connection by *to,* as in *I managed to do it,* or *-ing,* as in *we heard him singing.* ~*vb.* (*tr.*) **12.** (*often passive*) to execute, arrange, or introduce gradually or in stages: *a phased withdrawal.* **13.** (sometimes foll. by *with*) to cause (a part, process, etc.) to function or coincide with (another part, process, etc.): *he tried to phase the intake and output of the machine; he phased the intake with the output.* **14.** *Chiefly U.S.* to arrange (processes, goods, etc.) to be supplied or executed when required. [C19: from New Latin *phases,* pl. of *phasis,* from Greek: aspect; related to Greek *phainein* to show] —**'phaseless** *adj.* —**'phasic** *or* **'phaseal** *adj.*

phase-contrast microscope *n.* a microscope that makes visible details of colourless transparent objects. It employs a method of illumination such that small differences of refractive index of the materials in the object cause differences of luminous intensity by interference.

phase in *vb.* (*tr., adv.*) to introduce in a gradual or cautious manner: *the legislation was phased in over two years.*

phase modulation *n.* a type of modulation, used in communication systems, in which the phase of a radio carrier wave is varied by an amount proportional to the instantaneous amplitude of the modulating signal.

phase out *vb.* **1.** (*tr., adv.*) to discontinue or withdraw gradually. ~*n.* **phase-out.** **2.** *Chiefly U.S.* the action or an instance of phasing out: *a phase-out of conventional forces.*

phase rule *n.* the principle that in any system in equilibrium the number of degrees of freedom is equal to the number of components less the number of phases plus two. See also **degree of freedom, component** (sense 4).

phase speed *or* **velocity** *n. Physics.* the speed at which the phase of a wave is propagated, the product of the frequency times the wavelength. This is the quantity that is determined by methods using interference. In a dispersive medium it differs from the group speed. Also called: **wave speed, wave velocity.**

-phasia *n. combining form.* indicating speech disorder of a specified kind: *aphasia.* [from Greek, from *phanai* to speak] —**-phasic** *adj. and n. combining form.*

phasing ('feɪzɪŋ) *n. Electrical engineering.* a tonal sweep achieved by varying the phase relationship of two similar audio signals by mechanical or electronic means.
phasmid ('fæzmɪd) *n.* **1.** any plant-eating insect of the mainly tropical order *Phasmida:* includes the leaf insects and stick insects. ~*adj.* **2.** of, relating to, or belonging to the order *Phasmida.* [C19: from New Latin *Phasmida,* from Greek *phasma* spectre]
phasor ('feɪzɔː) *n. Electrical engineering.* a rotating vector representing a quantity, such as an alternating current or voltage, that varies sinusoidally.
phatic ('fætɪk) *adj.* (of speech, esp. of conversational phrases) used to establish social contact and to express sociability rather than specific meaning. [C20: from Greek *phat(os)* spoken + -IC]
PHC *abbrev. for* Pharmaceutical Chemist.
PhD *abbrev. for* Doctor of Philosophy. Also: **DPhil.**
pheasant ('fɛzᵊnt) *n.* **1.** any of various long-tailed gallinaceous birds of the family *Phasianidae,* esp. *Phasianus colchicus* (**ring-necked pheasant**), having a brightly-coloured plumage in the male: native to Asia but introduced elsewhere. **2.** any of various other gallinaceous birds of the family *Phasianidae,* including the quails and partridges. **3.** *U.S. and Canadian.* any of several other gallinaceous birds, esp. the ruffed grouse. [C13: from Old French *fesan,* from Latin *phāsiānus,* from Greek *phasianos ornis* Phasian bird, named after the River *Phasis,* in Colchis]
pheasant's eye *n.* **1.** an annual ranunculaceous plant, *Adonis annua* (or *autumnalis*), with scarlet flowers and finely divided leaves: native to S Europe but naturalized elsewhere. **2.** a type of narcissus, *Narcissus poeticus,* that has white petals and a small red-ringed cup.
phellem ('fɛləm) *n. Botany.* the technical name for **cork** (sense 4). [C20: from Greek *phellos* cork + PHLOEM]
phelloderm ('fɛləʊˌdɜːm) *n.* a layer of thin-walled cells produced by the inner surface of the cork cambium. [C19: from Greek *phellos* cork + -DERM] —**ˌphello'dermal** *adj.*
phellogen ('fɛlədʒən) *n. Botany.* the technical name for **cork cambium.** [C19: from Greek *phellos* cork + -GEN] —**phellogenetic** (ˌfɛləʊdʒɪ'nɛtɪk) *or* **phellogenic** (ˌfɛləʊ'dʒɛnɪk) *adj.*
phenacaine ('fiːnəˌkeɪn, 'fɛn-) *n.* a crystalline basic compound that is the hydrochloride of holocaine: used as a local anaesthetic in ophthalmic medicine. Formula: $C_{18}H_{22}N_2O_2HCl$. [C20: from PHENO- + ACETO- + COCAINE]
phenacetin (fɪ'næsɪtɪn) *n.* a white crystalline solid used in medicine to relieve pain and fever. Formula: $CH_3CONHC_6H_4OC_2H_5$. Also called: **acetophenetidin.** [C19: from PHENETIDINE + ACETYL + -IN]
phenacite ('fɛnəˌsaɪt) *or* **phenakite** ('fɛnəˌkaɪt) *n.* a colourless or white glassy mineral consisting of beryllium silicate in hexagonal crystalline form: occurs in veins in granite. Formula: Be_2SiO_4. [C19: from Greek *phenax* a cheat, because of its deceptive resemblance to quartz]
phenanthrene (fɪ'nænθriːn) *n.* a colourless crystalline aromatic compound isomeric with anthracene: used in the manufacture of dyes, drugs, and explosives. Formula: $C_{14}H_{10}$. [C19: from PHENO- + ANTHRACENE]
phenazine ('fɛnəˌziːn) *n.* a yellow crystalline compound that is the parent compound of many azine dyes and some antibiotics. Formula: $C_6H_4N_2C_6H_4$. [C19: from PHENO- + AZINE]
phencyclidine (fɛn'sɪklɪˌdiːn) *n.* See **PCP.**
phenetics (fɪ'nɛtɪks) *n.* (*functioning as sing.*) *Biology.* a system of classification based on similarities between organisms without regard to their evolutionary relationships. [C20: from PHEN(OTYPE) + (GEN)ETICS] —**phe'netic** *adj.*
phenetidine (fɪ'nɛtɪˌdiːn, -dɪn) *n.* a liquid amine that is a derivative of phenetole, existing in three isomeric forms: used in the manufacture of dyestuffs. Formula: $H_2NC_6H_4OC_2H_5$. [C19: from PHENETOLE + -ID[3] + -INE[2]]
phenetole ('fɛnɪˌtəʊl, -ˌtɒl) *n.* a colourless oily compound; phenyl ethyl ether. Formula: $C_6H_5OC_2H_5$. [C19: from PHENO- + ETHYL + -OLE[1]]
phenformin (fɛn'fɔːmɪn) *n.* a biguanide administered orally in the treatment of diabetes to lower blood levels of glucose. Formula: $C_{10}H_{15}N_5$. [C20: from PHEN(YL) + FORM(ALDEHYDE) + -IN]
phenix ('fiːnɪks) *n.* a U.S. spelling of **phoenix.**
pheno- *or before a vowel* **phen-** *combining form.* **1.** showing or manifesting: *phenotype.* **2.** indicating that a molecule contains benzene rings: *phenobarbitone.* [from Greek *phaino-* shining, from *phainein* to show; its use in a chemical sense is exemplified in *phenol,* so called because originally prepared from illuminating gas]
phenobarbitone (ˌfiːnəʊ'bɑːbɪˌtəʊn) *or* **phenobarbital** (ˌfiːnəʊ'bɑːbɪtᵊl) *n.* a white crystalline derivative of barbituric acid used as a sedative for treating insomnia and epilepsy. Formula: $C_{12}H_{12}N_2O_3$.
phenocopy ('fiːnəʊˌkɒpɪ) *n., pl.* **-copies.** a noninheritable change in an organism that is caused by environmental influence during development but resembles the effects of a genetic mutation.
phenocryst ('fiːnəˌkrɪst, 'fɛn-) *n.* any of several large crystals that are embedded in a mass of smaller crystals in igneous rocks such as porphyry. [C19: from PHENO- (shining) + CRYSTAL]
phenol ('fiːnɒl) *n.* **1.** Also called: **carbolic acid.** a white crystalline soluble poisonous acidic derivative of benzene, used as an antiseptic and disinfectant and in the manufacture of resins, nylon, dyes, explosives, and pharmaceuticals; hydroxybenzene. Formula: C_6H_5OH. **2.** *Chem.* any of a class of weakly acidic organic compounds whose molecules contain one or more hydroxyl groups bound directly to a carbon atom in an aromatic ring.
phenolate ('fiːnəˌleɪt) *vb.* **1.** (*tr.*) Also: **carbolize.** to treat or disinfect with phenol. ~*n.* **2.** another name (not in technical usage) for **phenoxide.**
phenolic (fɪ'nɒlɪk) *adj.* of, containing, or derived from phenol.
phenolic resin *n.* any one of a class of resins derived from phenol, used in paints, adhesives, and as thermosetting plastics. See also **Bakelite.**
phenology (fɪ'nɒlədʒɪ) *n.* the study of recurring phenomena, such as animal migration, esp. as influenced by climatic conditions. [C19: from PHENO(MENON) + -LOGY] —**phenological** (ˌfiːnə'lɒdʒɪkᵊl) *adj.* —**phe'nologist** *n.*
phenolphthalein (ˌfiːnɒl'θeɪliːn, -lɪɪn, -'θæl-) *n.* a colourless crystalline compound used in medicine as a laxative and in chemistry as an indicator. Formula: $C_{20}H_{14}O_4$.
phenomena (fɪ'nɒmɪnə) *n.* a plural of **phenomenon.**
phenomenal (fɪ'nɒmɪnᵊl) *adj.* **1.** of or relating to a phenomenon. **2.** extraordinary; outstanding; remarkable: *a phenomenal achievement.* **3.** *Philosophy.* known or perceived by the senses rather than the mind. —**phe'nomenally** *adv.*
phenomenalism (fɪ'nɒmɪnəˌlɪzəm) *n. Philosophy.* the doctrine that statements about physical objects and the external world can be analysed in terms of possible or actual experiences, and that entities, such as physical objects, are only mental constructions out of phenomenal appearances. Compare **idealism** (sense 3), **realism** (sense 6). —**phe'nomenalist** *n., adj.* —**pheˌnomenal'istically** *adv.*
phenomenology (fɪˌnɒmɪ'nɒlədʒɪ) *n. Philosophy.* **1.** the movement founded by the German philosopher Edmund Husserl (1859–1938), which concentrates on the detailed description of conscious experience, without recourse to explanation, metaphysical assumptions, and traditional philosophical questions. **2.** the science of phenomena as opposed to the science of being. —**phenomenological** (fɪˌnɒmɪnə'lɒdʒɪkᵊl) *adj.* —**pheˌnomeno'logically** *adv.* —**pheˌnome'nologist** *n.*
phenomenon (fɪ'nɒmɪnən) *n., pl.* **-ena** (-ɪnə) *or* **-enons.** **1.** anything that can be perceived as an occurrence or fact by the senses. **2.** any remarkable occurrence or person. **3.** *Philosophy.* **a.** the object of perception, experience, etc. **b.** (in the writings of Kant) a thing as it appears and is interpreted in perception and reflection, as distinguished from its real nature as a thing-in-itself. Compare **noumenon.** [C16: via Late Latin from Greek *phainomenon,* from *phainesthai* to appear, from *phainein* to show]
▷**Usage.** Although *phenomena* is often treated as if it were singular, correct usage is to employ *phenomenon* with a singular construction and *phenomena* with a plural: *that is an interesting phenomenon* (not *phenomena*); *several new phenomena were recorded in his notes.*
phenothiazine (ˌfiːnəʊ'θaɪəziːn) *n.* **1.** a colourless to light yellow insoluble crystalline compound used as an anthelmintic for livestock and in insecticides. Formula: $C_{12}H_9NS$. **2.** any of several drugs derived from phenothiazine and used as strong tranquillizers and in the treatment of schizophrenia.
phenotype ('fiːnəʊˌtaɪp) *n.* the physical constitution of an organism as determined by the interaction of its genetic constitution and the environment. Compare **genotype.** —**phenotypic** (ˌfiːnəʊ'tɪpɪk) *or* ˌ**pheno'typical** *adj.* —ˌ**pheno'typically** *adv.*
phenoxide (fɪ'nɒksaɪd) *n.* any of a class of salts of phenol. They contain the ion $C_6H_5O^-$. Also called: **phenolate.**
phenoxy resin (fɪ'nɒksɪ) *n. Chem.* any of a class of resins derived from polyhydroxy ethers.
phenyl ('fiːnaɪl, 'fɛnɪl) *n.* (*modifier*) of, containing, or consisting of the monovalent group C_6H_5, derived from benzene: *a phenyl group or radical.*
phenylalanine (ˌfiːnaɪl'æləˌniːn, ˌfɛnɪl-) *n.* an aromatic essential amino acid; a component of proteins.
phenylamine (ˌfiːnaɪlə'miːn, ˌfɛnɪl-) *n.* another name for **aniline.**
phenylbutazone (ˌfiːnaɪl'bjuːtəˌzəʊn) *n.* an anti-inflammatory drug used in the treatment of rheumatic diseases. [C20: from *(dioxodi)phenylbut(ylpyr)azo(lidi)ne*]
phenylketonuria (ˌfiːnaɪlˌkiːtə'njʊərɪə) *n.* a congenital metabolic disorder characterized by the abnormal accumulation of phenylalanine in the body fluids, resulting in various degrees of mental deficiency. [C20: New Latin; see PHENYL, KETONE, -URIA]
phenytoin (ˌfɛnɪ'təʊɪn) *n.* an anticonvulsant drug used in the treatment of epilepsy. [C20: from *(di)pheny(lhydan)toin*]
pheromone ('fɛrəˌməʊn) *n.* a chemical substance, secreted externally by certain animals, such as insects, affecting the behaviour or physiology of other animals of the same species. [C20: *phero-,* from Greek *pherein* to bear + (HOR)MONE]
phew (fjuː) *interj.* an exclamation of relief, surprise, disbelief, weariness, etc.
phi (faɪ) *n., pl.* **phis.** the 21st letter in the Greek alphabet, Φ, φ, a consonant, transliterated as *ph* or *f.*
phial ('faɪəl) *n.* a small bottle for liquids; vial. [C14: from Old French *fiole,* from Latin *phiola* saucer, from Greek *phialē* wide shallow vessel]

Phi Beta Kappa ('faɪ 'beɪtə 'kæpə, 'biːtə) *n.* (in the U.S.) **1.** a national honorary society, founded in 1776, membership of which is based on high academic ability. **2.** a member of this society. [from the initials of the Greek motto *philosophia biou kubernētēs* philosophy the guide of life]

phil. *abbrev. for:* **1.** philosophy. **2.** philharmonic.

Phil. *abbrev. for:* **1.** Philippians. **2.** Philippines. **3.** Philadelphia. **4.** Philharmonic.

philadelphus (ˌfɪlə'dɛlfəs) *n.* any shrub of the N temperate genus *Philadelphus,* cultivated for their strongly scented showy flowers: family *Philadelphaceae.* See also **mock orange** (sense 1). [C19: New Latin, from Greek *philadelphon* mock orange, literally: loving one's brother]

philander (fɪ'lændə) *vb.* (*intr.;* often foll. by *with*) (of a man) to flirt with women. [C17: from Greek *philandros* fond of men, from *philos* loving + *anēr* man; used as a name for a lover in literary works] —**phi'landerer** *n.*

philanthropic (ˌfɪlən'θrɒpɪk) *or* **philanthropical** *adj.* showing concern for humanity, esp. by performing charitable actions, donating money, etc. —ˌ**philan'thropically** *adv.*

philanthropy (fɪ'lænθrəpɪ) *n., pl.* **-pies.** **1.** the practice of performing charitable or benevolent actions. **2.** love of mankind in general. [C17: from Late Latin *philanthrōpia,* from Greek: love of mankind, from *philos* loving + *anthrōpos* man] —**phi'lanthropist** *or* **philanthrope** ('fɪlənˌθrəʊp) *n.*

philately (fɪ'lætəlɪ) *n.* the collection and study of postage stamps and all related material concerned with postal history. [C19: from French *philatélie,* from PHILO- + Greek *ateleia* exemption from charges (here referring to stamps), from A-[1] + *telos* tax, payment] —**philatelic** (ˌfɪlə'tɛlɪk) *adj.* —ˌ**phila'telically** *adv.* —**phi'latelist** *n.*

-phile *or* **-phil** *n. combining form.* indicating a person or thing having a fondness or preference for something specified: *bibliophile; Francophile.* [from Greek *philos* loving]

Philem. *Bible. abbrev. for* Philemon.

philharmonic (ˌfɪlhɑː'mɒnɪk, ˌfɪlə-) *adj.* **1.** fond of music. **2.** (*cap. when part of a name*) denoting an orchestra, choir, society, etc., devoted to the performance, appreciation, and study of music. ~*n.* **3.** (*cap. when part of a name*) a specific philharmonic choir, orchestra, or society. [C18: from French *philharmonique,* from Italian *filarmonico* music-loving; see PHILO-, HARMONY]

philhellene (fɪl'hɛliːn) *or* **philhellenist** (fɪl'hɛlɪnɪst) *n.* **1.** a lover of Greece and Greek culture. **2.** *European history.* a supporter of the cause of Greek national independence. —**philhellenic** (ˌfɪlhɛ'liːnɪk) *adj.* —**philhellenism** (fɪl'hɛlɪˌnɪzəm) *n.*

-philia *n. combining form.* **1.** indicating a tendency towards: *haemophilia.* **2.** indicating an abnormal liking for: *necrophilia.* [from Greek *philos* loving] —**-philiac** *n. combining form.* —**-philous** *or* **-philic** *adj. combining form.*

philibeg ('fɪlɪˌbɛg) *n.* a variant spelling of **filibeg.**

philippic (fɪ'lɪpɪk) *n.* a bitter or impassioned speech of denunciation; invective. [C16: after the orations of Demosthenes, 4th-century Athenian orator, against *Philip* of Macedon (382–336 B.C.)]

Philippine ('fɪlɪˌpiːn) *adj.* of or relating to the Phillipines, a republic in SE Asia; Filipino (sense 3)

Philippine mahogany *n.* any of various Philippine hardwood trees of the genus *Shorea* and related genera: family *Dipterocarpaceae.*

Philistine ('fɪlɪˌstaɪn) *n.* **1.** a person who is unreceptive to or hostile towards culture, the arts, etc.; a smug boorish person. **2.** a member of the non-Semitic people who inhabited ancient Philistia on the coast of SW Palestine. ~*adj.* **3.** (*sometimes not cap.*) boorishly uncultured. **4.** of or relating to the ancient Philistines. —**Philistinism** ('fɪlɪstɪˌnɪzəm) *n.*

Phillips curve ('fɪlɪps) *n. Economics.* a curve that purports to plot the relationship between unemployment and inflation on the theory that as inflation falls unemployment rises and vice versa. [C20: named after A. W. H. *Phillips* (1914–75), English economist who formulated the theory]

Phillips screw *n. Trademark.* a screw having a cruciform slot into which a screwdriver with a cruciform point (**Phillips screwdriver** (*Trademark*)) fits.

phillumenist (fɪ'ljuːmənɪst, -'luː-) *n.* a person who collects matchbox labels. [C20: from PHILO- + Latin *lumen* light + -IST] —**phil'lumeny** *n.*

philo- *or before a vowel* **phil-** *combining form.* indicating a love of: *philology; philanthropic.* [from Greek *philos* loving]

philodendron (ˌfɪlə'dɛndrən) *n., pl.* **-drons** *or* **-dra** (-drə). any aroid evergreen climbing plant of the tropical American genus *Philodendron:* cultivated as house plants. [C19: New Latin from Greek: lover of trees]

philogyny (fɪ'lɒdʒɪnɪ) *n. Rare.* fondness for women. Compare **misogyny.** [C17: from Greek *philogunia,* from PHILO- + *gunē* woman] —**phi'logynist** *n.* —**phi'logynous** *adj.*

philol. *abbrev. for:* **1.** philological. **2.** philology.

philology (fɪ'lɒlədʒɪ) *n.* (no longer in scholarly use) **1.** comparative and historical linguistics. **2.** the scientific analysis of written records and literary texts. **3.** the study of literature in general. [C17: from Latin *philologia,* from Greek: love of language] —**philological** (ˌfɪlə'lɒdʒɪkᵊl) *adj.* —ˌ**philo'logically** *adv.* —**phi'lologist** *or* (*less commonly*) **phi'lologer** *n.*

philomel ('fɪləˌmɛl) *or* **philomela** (ˌfɪləʊ'miːlə) *n.* poetic names for a **nightingale.** [C14 *philomene,* via Medieval Latin from Latin *philomēla,* from Greek]

philoprogenitive (ˌfɪləʊprəʊ'dʒɛnɪtɪv) *adj. Rare.* **1.** fond of children. **2.** producing many offspring.

philos. *abbrev. for:* **1.** philosopher. **2.** philosophical.

philosopher (fɪ'lɒsəfə) *n.* **1.** a student, teacher, or devotee of philosophy. **2.** a person of philosophical temperament, esp. one who is patient, wise, and stoical. **3.** (formerly) an alchemist or devotee of occult science. **4.** a person who establishes the ideology of a cult or movement: *the philosopher of the revolution.*

philosopher kings *pl. n.* **1.** (in the political theory of Plato) the elite whose education has given them true knowledge of the Forms and esp. of the Form of the Good, thus enabling them alone to rule justly. **2.** *Informal.* any ideologically motivated elite.

philosopher's stone *n.* a stone or substance thought by alchemists to be capable of transmuting base metals into gold.

philosophical (ˌfɪlə'sɒfɪkᵊl) *or* **philosophic** *adj.* **1.** of or relating to philosophy or philosophers. **2.** reasonable, wise, or learned. **3.** calm and stoical, esp. in the face of difficulties or disappointments. **4.** (formerly) of or relating to science or natural philosophy. —ˌ**philo'sophically** *adv.* —ˌ**philo'sophicalness** *n.*

philosophical logic *n.* the branch of philosophy that studies the relationship between formal logic and ordinary language, esp. the extent to which the former can be held accurately to represent the latter.

philosophize *or* **philosophise** (fɪ'lɒsəˌfaɪz) *vb.* **1.** (*intr.*) to make philosophical pronouncements and speculations. **2.** (*tr.*) to explain philosophically. —**phiˌlosophi'zation** *or* **phiˌlosophi'sation** *n.* —**phi'losoˌphizer** *or* **phi'losoˌphiser** *n.*

philosophy (fɪ'lɒsəfɪ) *n., pl.* **-phies.** **1.** the academic discipline concerned with making explicit the nature and significance of ordinary and scientific beliefs and investigating the intelligibility of concepts by means of rational argument concerning their presuppositions, implications, and interrelationships; in particular, the rational investigation of the nature and structure of reality (metaphysics), the resources and limits of knowledge (epistemology), the principles and import of moral judgment (ethics), and the relationship between language and reality (semantics). **2.** the particular doctrines relating to these issues of some specific individual or school: *the philosophy of Descartes.* **3.** the critical study of the basic principles and concepts of a discipline: *the philosophy of law.* **4.** *Archaic or literary.* the investigation of natural phenomena, esp. alchemy, astrology, and astronomy. **5.** any system of belief, values, or tenets. **6.** a personal outlook or viewpoint. **7.** serenity of temper. [C13: from Old French *filosofie,* from Latin *philosophia,* from Greek, from *philosophos* lover of wisdom]

-philous *or* **-philic** *adj. combining form.* indicating love of or fondness for: *heliophilous.* [from Latin *-philus,* from Greek *-philos;* see -PHILE]

philtre *or U.S.* **philter** ('fɪltə) *n.* a drink supposed to arouse love, desire, etc. [C16: from Latin *philtrum,* from Greek *philtron* love potion, from *philos* loving]

phimosis (faɪ'məʊsɪs) *n.* abnormal tightness of the foreskin, preventing its being retracted over the tip of the penis. [C17: via New Latin from Greek: a muzzling, from *phimos* a muzzle]

phi-phenomenon ('faɪfɪˌnɒmɪnən) *n., pl.* **-na** (-nə). *Psychol.* **1.** the illusion that when two lights are rapidly turned on and off in succession something appears to move backwards and forwards between them while the lights stay stationary. **2.** a similar illusion in which one light appears to move smoothly backwards and forwards. [C20: arbitrary use of Greek *phi*]

phiz (fɪz) *n. Slang, chiefly Brit.* the face or a facial expression: *an ugly phiz.* Also called: **phizog** ('fɪzɒg, fɪ'zɒg). [C17: colloquial shortening of PHYSIOGNOMY]

phlebectomy (flɪ'bɛktəmɪ) *n.* the surgical excision of a vein or part of a vein.

phlebitis (flɪ'baɪtɪs) *n.* inflammation of a vein. [C19: via New Latin from Greek; see PHLEBO-, -ITIS] —**phlebitic** (flɪ'bɪtɪk) *adj.*

phlebo- *or before a vowel* **phleb-** *combining form.* indicating a vein: *phlebotomy.* [from Greek *phleps, phleb-* vein]

phlebography (flɪ'bɒgrəfɪ) *n.* another name for **venography.**

phlebosclerosis (ˌflɛbəʊsklɪ'rəʊsɪs) *n. Pathol.* hardening and loss of elasticity of the veins. Also called: **venosclerosis.**

phlebotomize *or* **phlebotomise** (flɪ'bɒtəˌmaɪz) *vb.* (*tr.*) *Surgery.* to perform phlebotomy on (a patient).

phlebotomy (flɪ'bɒtəmɪ) *n., pl.* **-mies.** surgical incision into a vein. Also called: **venesection.** [C14: from Old French *flebothomie,* from Late Latin *phlebotomia,* from Greek] —**phlebotomic** (ˌflɛbə'tɒmɪk) *or* ˌ**phlebo'tomical** *adj.* —**phle'botomist** *n.*

phlegm (flɛm) *n.* **1.** the viscid mucus secreted by the walls of the respiratory tract. **2.** *Archaic.* one of the four bodily humours. **3.** apathy; stolidity; indifference. **4.** self-possession; imperturbability; coolness. [C14: from Old French *fleume,* from Late Latin *phlegma,* from Greek: inflammation, from *phlegein* to burn] —'**phlegmy** *adj.*

phlegmatic (flɛg'mætɪk) *or* **phlegmatical** *adj.* **1.** having a stolid or unemotional disposition. **2.** not easily excited.

—**phleg'matically** *adv.* —**phleg'maticalness** *or* **phleg'maticness** *n.*
phloem ('fləʊɛm) *n.* tissue in higher plants that conducts synthesized food substances to all parts of the plant. [C19: via German from Greek *phloos* bark]
phlogistic (flɒ'dʒɪstɪk) *adj.* **1.** *Pathol.* of inflammation; inflammatory. **2.** *Chem.* of, concerned with, or containing phlogiston.
phlogiston (flɒ'dʒɪstɒn, -tən) *n. Chem.* a hypothetical substance formerly thought to be present in all combustible materials and to be released during burning. [C18: via New Latin from Greek, from *phlogizein* to set alight; related to *phlegein* to burn]
phlogopite ('flɒgəˌpaɪt) *n.* a brownish mica that consists of a hydrous silicate of potassium, magnesium, and aluminium, occurring principally in marble and dolomite. Formula: $KMg_3Al-Si_3O_{10}(OH)_2$. See also **mica.** [C19: from Greek *phlogōpos* of fiery appearance, from *phlox* flame + *ōps* eye]
phlox (flɒks) *n., pl.* **phlox** *or* **phloxes.** any polemoniaceous plant of the chiefly North American genus *Phlox:* cultivated for their clusters of white, red, or purple flowers. [C18: via Latin from Greek: a plant of glowing colour, literally: flame]
phlyctena *or* **phlyctaena** (flɪk'tiːnə) *n., pl.* **-nae** (-niː). *Pathol.* a small blister, vesicle, or pustule. [C17: via New Latin from Greek *phluktaina,* from *phluzein* to swell]
-phobe *n. combining form.* indicating a person or thing that fears or hates: *Germanophobe; xenophobe.* [from Greek *-phobos* fearing] —**-phobic** *adj. combining form.*
phobia ('fəʊbɪə) *n. Psychiatry.* an abnormal intense and irrational fear of a given situation, organism, or object. [C19: from Greek *phobos* fear]
-phobia *n. combining form.* indicating an extreme abnormal fear of or aversion to: *acrophobia; claustrophobia.* [via Latin from Greek, from *phobos* fear] —**-phobic** *adj. combining form.*
phobic ('fəʊbɪk) *adj.* **1.** of, relating to, or arising from a phobia. ~*n.* **2.** a person suffering from a phobia.
phocine ('fəʊsaɪn) *adj.* **1.** of, relating to, or resembling a seal. **2.** of, relating to, or belonging to the *Phocinae,* a subfamily that includes the harbour seal and grey seal. [C19: ultimately from Greek *phōkē* a seal]
phocomelia (ˌfəʊkəʊ'miːlɪə) *or* **phocomely** (fəʊ'kɒməlɪ) *n.* a congenital deformity resulting from prenatal interference with the development of the fetal limbs, characterized esp. by short stubby hands or feet attached close to the body. [C19: via New Latin from Greek *phōkē* a seal + *melos* a limb] —ˌ**phoco'melic** *adj.*
phoebe ('fiːbɪ) *n.* any of several greyish-brown North American flycatchers of the genus *Sayornis,* such as *S. phoebe* (**eastern phoebe**). [C19: imitative of the bird's call]
Phoenician (fə'nɪʃɪən, -'niːʃən) *n.* **1.** a member of an ancient Semitic people of NW Syria who dominated the trade of the ancient world in the first millennium B.C. and founded colonies throughout the Mediterranean. **2.** the extinct language of this people, belonging to the Canaanitic branch of the Semitic subfamily of the Afro-Asiatic family. ~*adj.* **3.** of or relating to Phoenicia, an ancient E Mediterranean maritime country, the Phoenicians, or their language.
phoenix *or U.S.* **phenix** ('fiːnɪks) *n.* **1.** a legendary Arabian bird said to set fire to itself and rise anew from the ashes every 500 years. **2.** a person or thing of surpassing beauty or quality. [Old English *fenix,* via Latin from Greek *phoinix;* identical in form with Greek *Phoinix* Phoenician, purple]
Phoenix ('fiːnɪks) *n., Latin genitive* **Phoenices** ('fiːnɪˌsiːz). a constellation in the S hemisphere lying between Grus and Eridanus.
phon (fɒn) *n.* a unit of loudness that measures the intensity of a sound by the number of decibels it is above a reference tone having a frequency of 1000 hertz and a root-mean-square sound pressure of 20×10^{-6} pascal. [C20: via German from Greek *phōnē* sound, voice]
phon. *abbrev. for:* **1.** Also: **phonet.** phonetics. **2.** phonology.
phonate (fəʊ'neɪt) *vb. (intr.)* to articulate speech sounds, esp. to cause the vocal cords to vibrate in the execution of a voiced speech sound. [C19: from Greek *phōnē* voice] —**pho'nation** *n.* —**phonatory** ('fəʊnətərɪ, -trɪ) *adj.*
phone[1] (fəʊn) *n., vb.* short for **telephone.**
phone[2] (fəʊn) *n. Phonetics.* a single uncomplicated speech sound. [C19: from Greek *phōnē* sound, voice]
-phone *combining form.* **1.** *(forming nouns)* indicating voice, sound, or a device giving off sound: *microphone; telephone.* **2.** *(forming nouns and adjectives)* (a person) speaking a particular language: *Francophone.* [from Greek *phōnē* voice, sound] —**-phonic** *adj. combining form.*
phonecard ('fəʊnˌkɑːd) *n.* **1.** a public telephone that is operated by a special card instead of coins. **2.** the card used, which operates for the number or duration of calls paid for in the purchase price of the card.
phone-in *n.* **a.** a radio or television programme in which listeners' or viewers' questions, comments, etc., are telephoned to the studio and broadcast live as part of a discussion. **b.** *(as modifier): a phone-in programme.*
phoneme ('fəʊniːm) *n. Linguistics.* one of the set of speech sounds in any given language that serve to distinguish one word from another. A phoneme may consist of several phonetically distinct articulations, which are regarded as identical by native speakers, since one articulation may be substituted for another without any change of meaning. Thus /p/ and /b/ are separate phonemes in English because they distinguish such words as *pet* and *bet,* whereas the light and dark /l/ sounds in *little* are not separate phonemes since they may be transposed without changing meaning. [C20: via French from Greek *phōnēma* sound, speech]
phonemic (fə'niːmɪk) *adj. Linguistics.* **1.** of or relating to the phoneme. **2.** relating to or denoting speech sounds that belong to different phonemes rather than being allophonic variants of the same phoneme. Compare **phonetic** (sense 2). **3.** of or relating to phonemics. —**pho'nemically** *adv.*
phonemics (fə'niːmɪks) *n. (functioning as sing.)* that aspect of linguistics concerned with the classification, analysis, interrelation, and environmental changes of the phonemes of a language. —**pho'nemicist** *n.*
phonendoscope (fə'nɛndəˌskəʊp) *n.* an instrument that amplifies small sounds, esp. within the human body. [C20: from PHONO- + ENDO- + -SCOPE]
phoner ('fəʊnə) *n. Informal.* a person making a telephone call.
phonetic (fə'nɛtɪk) *adj.* **1.** of or relating to phonetics. **2.** denoting any perceptible distinction between one speech sound and another, irrespective of whether the sounds are phonemes or allophones. Compare **phonemic** (sense 2). **3.** conforming to pronunciation: *phonetic spelling.* [C19: from New Latin *phōnēticus,* from Greek *phōnētikos,* from *phōnein* to make sounds, speak] —**pho'netically** *adv.*
phonetic alphabet *n.* a list of the words used in communications to represent the letters of the alphabet, as in E for Echo, T for Tango.
phonetician (ˌfəʊnɪ'tɪʃən) *n.* a person skilled in phonetics or one who employs phonetics in his work.
phonetics (fə'nɛtɪks) *n. (functioning as sing.)* the science concerned with the study of speech processes, including the production, perception, and analysis of speech sounds from both an acoustic and a physiological point of view. This science, though capable of being applied to language studies, technically excludes linguistic considerations. Compare **phonology.**
phonetist ('fəʊnɪtɪst) *n.* **1.** another name for **phonetician. 2.** a person who advocates or uses a system of phonetic spelling.
phoney *or esp. U.S.* **phony** ('fəʊnɪ) *Informal.* ~*adj.* **-nier, -niest. 1.** not genuine; fake. **2.** (of a person) insincere or pretentious. ~*n., pl.* **-neys** *or* **-nies. 3.** an insincere or pretentious person. **4.** something that is not genuine; a fake. [C20: origin uncertain] —'**phoneyness** *or esp. U.S.* '**phoniness** *n.*
phonics ('fɒnɪks) *n. (functioning as sing.)* **1.** an obsolete name for **acoustics** (sense 1). **2.** a method of teaching people to read by training them to associate letters with their phonetic values. —'**phonic** *adj.* —'**phonically** *adv.*
phono- *or before a vowel* **phon-** *combining form.* indicating a sound or voice: *phonograph; phonology.* [from Greek *phōnē* sound, voice]
phonochemistry (ˌfəʊnəʊ'kɛmɪstrɪ) *n.* the branch of chemistry concerned with the chemical effects of sound and ultrasonic waves.
phonogram ('fəʊnəˌgræm) *n.* **1.** any written symbol standing for a sound, syllable, morpheme, or word. **2.** a sequence of written symbols having the same sound in a variety of different words, for example, *ough* in *bought, ought,* and *brought.* —ˌ**phono'gramic** *or* ˌ**phono'grammic** *adj.*
phonograph ('fəʊnəˌgrɑːf, -ˌgræf) *n.* **1.** an early form of gramophone capable of recording and reproducing sound on wax cylinders. **2.** another U.S. and Canadian word for **gramophone** or **record player.**
phonography (fəʊ'nɒgrəfɪ) *n.* **1.** a writing system that represents sounds by individual symbols. Compare **logography. 2.** the employment of such a writing system. —**pho'nographer** *or* **pho'nographist** *n.* —**phonographic** (ˌfəʊnə'græfɪk) *adj.*
phonol. *abbrev. for* phonology.
phonolite ('fəʊnəˌlaɪt) *n.* a fine-grained volcanic igneous rock consisting of alkaline feldspars and nepheline. [C19: via French from German *Phonolith;* see PHONO-, -LITE] —**phonolitic** (ˌfəʊnə'lɪtɪk) *adj.*
phonology (fə'nɒlədʒɪ) *n., pl.* **-gies. 1.** the study of the sound system of a language or of languages in general. Compare **syntax** (senses 1, 2), **semantics. 2.** such a sound system. —**phonological** (ˌfəʊnə'lɒdʒɪkəl, ˌfɒn-) *adj.* —ˌ**phono'logically** *adv.* —**pho'nologist** *n.*
phonometer (fə'nɒmɪtə) *n.* an apparatus that measures the intensity of sound, esp. one calibrated in phons. —**phonometric** (ˌfəʊnə'mɛtrɪk) *or* ˌ**phono'metrical** *adj.*
phonon ('fəʊnɒn) *n. Physics.* a quantum of vibrational energy in the acoustic vibrations of a crystal lattice. [C20: from PHONO- + -ON]
phono plug ('fəʊnəʊ) *n. Electrical engineering.* a type of coaxial connector, used esp. in audio equipment.
phonoscope ('fəʊnəˌskəʊp) *n.* a device that renders visible the vibrations of sound waves.
phonotactics ('fəʊnəʊˌtæktɪks) *n. (functioning as sing.) Linguistics.* the study of the possible arrangement of the sounds of a language in the words of that language. [C20: from PHONO- + *-tactics,* on the model of *syntactic;* see SYNTAX]

phonotype ('fəʊnəˌtaɪp) *n. Printing.* **1.** a type bearing a phonetic symbol. **2.** text printed in phonetic symbols. —**phonotypic** (ˌfəʊnə'tɪpɪk) *or* ˌ**phono'typical** *adj.*

phonotypy ('fəʊnəˌtaɪpɪ) *n.* the transcription of speech into phonetic symbols. —'**phonoˌtypist** *or* '**phonoˌtyper** *n.*

phony ('fəʊnɪ) *adj.* **-nier, -niest,** *n., pl.* **-nies.** a variant spelling (esp. U.S.) of **phoney.** —'**phoniness** *n.*

-phony *n. combining form.* indicating a specified type of sound: *cacophony; euphony.* [from Greek *-phōnia,* from *phōnē* sound] —**-phonic** *adj. combining form.*

phony war *n.* **1.** (in wartime) a period of apparent calm and inactivity, esp. the period at the beginning of World War II. **2.** (in peacetime) a contrived embattled atmosphere; mock war.

phooey ('fu:ɪ) *interj. Informal.* an exclamation of scorn, contempt, disbelief, etc. [C20: probably variant of PHEW]

-phore *n. combining form.* indicating a person or thing that bears or produces: *gonophore; semaphore.* [from New Latin *-phorus,* from Greek *-phoros* bearing, from *pherein* to bear] — **-phorous** *adj. combining form.*

-phoresis *n. combining form.* indicating a transmission: *electrophoresis.* [from Greek *phorēsis* being carried, from *pherein* to bear]

phoresy ('fɒrəsɪ) *n.* an association in which one animal clings to another to ensure movement from place to place, as some mites use some insects. [C20: from New Latin *phoresia,* from Greek *phorēsis,* from *pherein* to carry]

phormium ('fɔ:mɪəm) *n.* any plant of the New Zealand bulbous genus *Phormium,* with leathery evergreen leaves and red or yellow flowers in panicles. [New Latin, from Greek *phormos* a basket (from a use for the fibres)]

phosgene ('fɒzdʒi:n) *n.* a colourless easily liquefied poisonous gas, carbonyl chloride, with an odour resembling that of new-mown hay: used in chemical warfare as a lethal choking agent and in the manufacture of pesticides, dyes, and polyurethane resins. Formula: $COCl_2$. [C19: from Greek *phos* light + *-gene,* variant of -GEN]

phosgenite ('fɒzdʒɪˌnaɪt) *n.* a rare fluorescent secondary mineral consisting of lead chloro-carbonate in the form of greyish tetragonal crystals. Formula: $Pb_2(Cl_2CO_3)$.

phosphatase ('fɒsfəˌteɪs, -ˌteɪz) *n.* any of a group of enzymes that catalyse the hydrolysis of organic phosphates.

phosphate ('fɒsfeɪt) *n.* **1.** any salt or ester of any phosphoric acid, esp. a salt of orthophosphoric acid. **2.** (*often pl.*) any of several chemical fertilizers containing phosphorous compounds. [C18: from French *phosphat;* see PHOSPHORUS, -ATE[1]] —**phosphatic** (fɒs'fætɪk) *adj.*

phosphatide ('fɒsfəˌtaɪd) *n.* another name for **phospholipid.**

phosphatidylcholine (ˌfɒsfətɪdaɪl'kəʊli:n) *n.* the systematic name for **lecithin.**

phosphatidylethanolamine (ˌfɒsfətɪdaɪlˌɛθə'nɒləmi:n) *n.* the systematic name for **cephalin.**

phosphatidylserine (ˌfɒsfətɪdaɪl'sɪəri:n) *n.* any of a class of phospholipids occurring in biological membranes and fats.

phosphatize *or* **phosphatise** ('fɒsfəˌtaɪz) *vb.* **1.** (*tr.*) to treat with a phosphate or phosphates, as by applying a fertilizer. **2.** to change or be changed into a phosphate. —ˌ**phosphati'zation** *or* ˌ**phosphati'sation** *n.*

phosphaturia (ˌfɒsfə'tjʊərɪə) *n. Pathol.* an abnormally large amount of phosphates in the urine. [C19: New Latin, from PHOSPHATE + -URIA] —ˌ**phospha'turic** *adj.*

phosphene ('fɒsfi:n) *n.* the sensation of light caused by pressure on the eyelid of a closed eye or by other mechanical or electrical interference with the visual system. [C19: from Greek *phos* light + *phainein* to show]

phosphide ('fɒsfaɪd) *n.* any compound of phosphorus with another element, esp. a more electropositive element.

phosphine ('fɒsfi:n) *n.* a colourless inflammable gas that is slightly soluble in water and has a strong fishy odour: used as a pesticide. Formula: PH_3.

phosphite ('fɒsfaɪt) *n.* any salt or ester of phosphorous acid.

phospho- *or before a vowel* **phosph-** *combining form.* containing phosphorus: *phosphocreatine.* [from French, from *phosphore* PHOSPHORUS]

phosphocreatine (ˌfɒsfə'kri:əˌti:n) *or* **phosphocreatin** *n.* a compound of phosphoric acid and creatine found in vertebrate muscle.

phospholipid (ˌfɒsfə'lɪpɪd) *n.* any of a group of compounds composed of fatty acids, phosphoric acid, and a nitrogenous base: important constituents of all membranes. Also called: **phosphatide.**

phosphonic acid (fɒs'fɒnɪk) *n.* the systematic name for **phosphorous acid.**

phosphoprotein (ˌfɒsfə'prəʊti:n) *n.* any of a group of conjugated proteins, esp. casein, in which the protein molecule is bound to phosphoric acid.

phosphor ('fɒsfə) *n.* a substance, such as the coating on a cathode-ray tube, capable of emitting light when irradiated with particles of electromagnetic radiation. [C17: from French, ultimately from Greek *phōsphoros* PHOSPHORUS]

phosphorate ('fɒsfəˌreɪt) *vb.* **1.** to treat or combine with phosphorus. **2.** (*tr.*) *Rare.* to cause (a substance) to exhibit phosphorescence.

phosphor bronze *n.* any of various hard corrosion-resistant alloys containing copper, tin (2–8 per cent), and phosphorus (0.1–0.4 per cent): used in gears, bearings, cylinder casings, etc.

phosphoresce (ˌfɒsfə'rɛs) *vb.* (*intr.*) to exhibit phosphorescence.

phosphorescence (ˌfɒsfə'rɛsəns) *n.* **1.** *Physics.* **a.** a fluorescence that persists after the bombarding radiation producing it has stopped. **b.** a fluorescence for which the average lifetime of the excited atoms is greater than 10^{-8} seconds. **2.** the light emitted in phosphorescence. **3.** the emission of light during a chemical reaction, such as bioluminescence, in which insufficient heat is evolved to cause fluorescence. Compare **fluorescence.**

phosphorescent (ˌfɒsfə'rɛsᵊnt) *adj.* exhibiting or having the property of phosphorescence. —ˌ**phospho'rescently** *adv.*

phosphoric (fɒs'fɒrɪk) *adj.* of or containing phosphorus in the pentavalent state.

phosphoric acid *n.* **1.** a colourless solid tribasic acid used in the manufacture of fertilizers and soap. Formula: H_3PO_4. Systematic name: **phosphoric(V) acid.** Also called: **orthophosphoric acid. 2.** any oxyacid of phosphorus produced by reaction between phosphorus pentoxide and water. See also **metaphosphoric acid, pyrophosphoric acid, hypophosphoric acid.**

phosphorism ('fɒsfəˌrɪzəm) *n.* poisoning caused by prolonged exposure to phosphorus.

phosphorite ('fɒsfəˌraɪt) *n.* **1.** a fibrous variety of the mineral apatite. **2.** any of various mineral deposits that consist mainly of calcium phosphate. —**phosphoritic** (ˌfɒsfə'rɪtɪk) *adj.*

phosphoroscope (fɒs'fɒrəˌskəʊp) *n.* an instrument for measuring the duration of phosphorescence after the source of radiation causing it has been removed.

phosphorous ('fɒsfərəs) *adj.* of or containing phosphorus in the trivalent state.

phosphorous acid *n.* **1.** a white or yellowish hygroscopic crystalline dibasic acid. Formula: H_3PO_3. Systematic name: **phosphoric acid.** Also called: **orthophosphorous acid. 2.** any oxyacid of phosphorus containing less oxygen than the corresponding phosphoric acid.

phosphorus ('fɒsfərəs) *n.* **1.** an allotropic nonmetallic element occurring in phosphates and living matter. Ordinary phosphorus is a toxic flammable phosphorescent white solid; the red form is less reactive and nontoxic: used in matches, pesticides, and alloys. The radioisotope **phosphorus-32 (radiophosphorus),** with a half-life of 14.3 days, is used in radiotherapy and as a tracer. Symbol: P; atomic no.: 15; atomic wt.: 30.974; valency: 3 or 5; relative density: 1.82 (white), 2.20 (red); melting pt.: 44.1°C (white); boiling pt.: 280°C (white). **2.** a less common name for a **phosphor.** [C17: via Latin from Greek *phōsphoros* light-bringing, from *phōs* light + *pherein* to bring]

Phosphorus ('fɒsfərəs) *n.* a morning star, esp. Venus.

phosphorus pentoxide *n.* a white odourless solid produced when phosphorus burns: has a strong affinity for water with which it forms phosphoric acids. Formula: P_2O_5 (commonly existing as the dimer P_4O_{10}). Also called: **phosphoric anhydride.**

phosphorylase (fɒs'fɒrɪˌleɪs, -ˌleɪz) *n.* any of a group of enzymes that catalyse the hydrolysis of glycogen to glucose-1-phosphate. [C20: from PHOSPHORUS + -YL + -ASE]

phosphorylation (ˌfɒsfərɪ'leɪʃən) *n.* the chemical or enzymic introduction into a compound of a phosphoryl group (a trivalent radical of phosphorus and oxygen).

phossy jaw ('fɒsɪ) *n.* a gangrenous condition of the lower jawbone caused by prolonged exposure to phosphorus fumes. [C19: *phossy,* colloquial shortening of PHOSPHORUS]

phot (fɒt, fəʊt) *n.* a unit of illumination equal to one lumen per square centimetre. 1 phot is equal to 10 000 lux. [C20: from Greek *phōs* light]

phot. *abbrev. for:* **1.** photograph. **2.** photographic. **3.** photography.

photic ('fəʊtɪk) *adj.* **1.** of or concerned with light. **2.** *Biology.* of or relating to the production of light by organisms. **3.** Also: **photobathic.** designating the zone of the sea where photosynthesis takes place. [C19: from PHOTO- + -IC]

photo ('fəʊtəʊ) *n., pl.* **-tos.** short for **photograph** (sense 1).

photo- *combining form.* **1.** of, relating to, or produced by light: *photosynthesis.* **2.** indicating a photographic process: *photolithography.* [from Greek *phōs, phōt-* light]

photoactinic (ˌfəʊtəʊæk'tɪnɪk) *adj.* emitting actinic radiation.

photoactive (ˌfəʊtəʊ'æktɪv) *adj.* (of a substance) capable of responding to light or other electromagnetic radiation.

photoautotrophic (ˌfəʊtəʊˌɔ:təʊ'trɒfɪk) *adj.* (of plants) capable of using light as the energy source in the synthesis of food from inorganic matter. See also **photosynthesis.**

photobathic (ˌfəʊtəʊ'bæθɪk) *adj.* another word for **photic** (sense 3). [from PHOTO- + Greek *bathus* deep + -IC]

photobiology (ˌfəʊtəʊbaɪ'ɒlədʒɪ) *n.* the branch of biology concerned with the effect of light on living organisms. —**photobiological** (ˌfəʊtəʊˌbaɪə'lɒdʒɪkᵊl) *adj.* —ˌ**photobi'ologist** *n.*

photo call *n.* a time arranged for photographers, esp. press photographers, to take pictures of a celebrity, the cast of a play, etc., usually for publicity purposes.

photocatalysis (ˌfəʊtəʊkə'tælɪsɪs) *n., pl.* **-ses** (-si:z). the alteration of the rate of a chemical reaction by light or other electromagnetic radiation.

photocathode (ˌfəʊtəʊˈkæθəʊd) *n.* a cathode that undergoes or is used for photoemission.

photocell (ˈfəʊtəʊˌsɛl) *n.* a device in which the photoelectric or photovoltaic effect or photoconductivity is used to produce a current or voltage when exposed to light or other electromagnetic radiation. They are used in exposure meters, burglar alarms, etc. Also called: **photoelectric cell, electric eye.**

photochemistry (ˌfəʊtəʊˈkɛmɪstrɪ) *n.* the branch of chemistry concerned with the chemical effects of light and other electromagnetic radiations. Also called: **actinochemistry.** —**photochemical** (ˌfəʊtəʊˈkɛmɪkᵊl) *adj.* —ˌ**photoˈchemically** *adv.* —ˌ**photoˈchemist** *n.*

photochromic (ˌfəʊtəʊˈkrəʊmɪk) *adj.* (of glass) changing colour with the intensity of incident light, used, for example, in sunglasses that darken as the sunlight becomes brighter.

photochronograph (ˌfəʊtəʊˈkrɒnəˌgrɑːf, -ˌgræf) *n. Physics.* an instrument for measuring very small time intervals by the trace made by a beam of light on a moving photographic film. —**photochronography** (ˌfəʊtəʊkrəˈnɒgrəfɪ) *n.*

photocompose (ˌfəʊtəʊkəmˈpəʊz) *vb.* another word (esp. U.S. and Canadian) for **filmset.** —ˌ**photocomˈposer** *n.*

photocomposition (ˌfəʊtəʊˌkɒmpəˈzɪʃən) *n.* another name (esp. U.S. and Canadian) for **filmsetting.**

photoconduction (ˌfəʊtəʊkənˈdʌkʃən) *n.* conduction of electricity resulting from the absorption of light. See **photoconductivity.**

photoconductivity (ˌfəʊtəʊˌkɒndʌkˈtɪvɪtɪ) *n.* the change in the electrical conductivity of certain substances, such as selenium, as a result of the absorption of electromagnetic radiation. —**photoconductive** (ˌfəʊtəʊkənˈdʌktɪv) *adj.* —ˌ**photoconˈductor** *n.*

photocopier (ˈfəʊtəʊˌkɒpɪə) *n.* an instrument that uses a xerographic process to produce instant copies of written, printed, or graphic work.

photocopy (ˈfəʊtəʊˌkɒpɪ) *n., pl.* **-copies.** **1.** a reproduction of written, printed, or graphic work obtained using a photocopier. See also **microcopy.** ~*vb.* **-copies, -copying, -copied.** **2.** to reproduce (written, printed, or graphic work) using a photocopier.

photocurrent (ˈfəʊtəʊˌkʌrənt) *n.* an electric current produced by electromagnetic radiation in the photoelectric effect, photovoltaic effect, or photoconductivity.

photodegradable (ˌfəʊtəʊdɪˈgreɪdəbᵊl) *adj.* (of plastic) capable of being decomposed by prolonged exposure to light.

photodiode (ˌfəʊtəʊˈdaɪəʊd) *n.* a semiconductor diode, the conductivity of which is controlled by incident illumination.

photodisintegration (ˌfəʊtəʊdɪˌsɪntɪˈgreɪʃən) *n.* disintegration of an atomic nucleus as a result of its absorption of a photon, usually a gamma ray.

photodynamic (ˌfəʊtəʊdaɪˈnæmɪk) *adj.* **1.** of or concerned with photodynamics. **2.** involving or producing an adverse or toxic reaction to light, esp. ultraviolet light. **3.** *Med.* denoting a therapy for cancer in which a cytotoxic drug is activated by a laser.

photodynamics (ˌfəʊtəʊdaɪˈnæmɪks) *n.* (*functioning as sing.*) the branch of biology concerned with the effects of light on the actions of plants and animals.

photoelasticity (ˌfəʊtəʊɪlæˈstɪsɪtɪ) *n.* the effects of stress, such as double refraction, on the optical properties of transparent materials.

photoelectric (ˌfəʊtəʊɪˈlɛktrɪk) *or* **photoelectrical** *adj.* of or concerned with electric or electronic effects caused by light or other electromagnetic radiation. —ˌ**photoeˈlectrically** *adv.* —**photoelectricity** (ˌfəʊtəʊɪlɛkˈtrɪsɪtɪ) *n.*

photoelectric cell *n.* another name for **photocell.**

photoelectric effect *n.* **1.** the ejection of electrons from a solid by an incident beam of sufficiently energetic electromagnetic radiation. **2.** any phenomenon involving electricity and electromagnetic radiation, such as photoemission.

photoelectron (ˌfəʊtəʊɪˈlɛktrɒn) *n.* an electron ejected from an atom, molecule, or solid by an incident photon.

photoelectrotype (ˌfəʊtəʊɪˈlɛktrəʊˌtaɪp) *n.* an electrotype mode using photography.

photoemission (ˌfəʊtəʊɪˈmɪʃən) *n.* the emission of electrons due to the impact of electromagnetic radiation, esp. as a result of the photoelectric effect. —ˌ**photoeˈmissive** *adj.*

photoengrave (ˌfəʊtəʊɪnˈgreɪv) *vb.* (*tr.*) to reproduce (an illustration) by photoengraving. —ˌ**photoenˈgraver** *n.*

photoengraving (ˌfəʊtəʊɪnˈgreɪvɪŋ) *n.* **1.** a photomechanical process for producing letterpress printing plates. **2.** a plate made by this process. **3.** a print made from such a plate.

photo finish *n.* **1.** a finish of a race in which contestants are so close that a photograph is needed to decide the result. **2.** any race or competition in which the winners or placed contestants are separated by a very small margin.

Photofit (ˈfəʊtəʊˌfɪt) *n. Trademark.* **a.** a method of combining photographs of facial features, hair, etc., into a composite picture of a face: used by the police to trace suspects from witnesses' descriptions. **b.** (*as modifier*): *a Photofit picture.*

photoflash (ˈfəʊtəʊˌflæʃ) *n.* another name for **flashbulb.**

photoflood (ˈfəʊtəʊˌflʌd) *n.* a highly incandescent tungsten lamp used as an artificial light source for indoor photography, television, etc. The brightness is obtained by operating with higher than normal current.

photofluorography (ˌfəʊtəʊflʊəˈrɒgrəfɪ) *n. Med.* the process of taking a photograph (**photofluorogram**) of a fluoroscopic image: used in diagnostic screening.

photog. *abbrev. for:* **1.** photograph. **2.** photographer. **3.** photographic. **4.** photography.

photogelatin process (ˌfəʊtəʊˈdʒɛlətɪn) *n.* another name for **collotype** (sense 1).

photogene (ˈfəʊtəʊˌdʒiːn) *n.* another name for **afterimage.** [C19: from Greek *phōtogenēs* light-produced. See PHOTO-, -GENE]

photogenic (ˌfəʊtəˈdʒɛnɪk) *adj.* **1.** (esp. of a person) having features, colouring, and a general facial appearance that look attractive in photographs. **2.** *Biology.* producing or emitting light: *photogenic bacteria.* —ˌ**photoˈgenically** *adv.*

photogeology (ˌfəʊtəʊdʒɪˈɒlədʒɪ) *n.* the study and identification of geological phenomena using aerial photographs.

photogram (ˈfəʊtəˌgræm) *n.* **1.** a picture, usually abstract, produced on a photographic material without the use of a camera, as by placing an object on the material and exposing to light. **2.** *Obsolete.* a photograph, often of the more artistic kind rather than a mechanical record.

photogrammetry (ˌfəʊtəʊˈgræmɪtrɪ) *n.* the process of making measurements from photographs, used esp. in the construction of maps from aerial photographs and also in military intelligence, medical and industrial research, etc. —**photogrammetric** (ˌfəʊtəʊgrəˈmɛtrɪk) *adj.* —ˌ**photoˈgrammetrist** *n.*

photograph (ˈfəʊtəˌgrɑːf, -ˌgræf) *n.* **1.** an image of an object, person, scene, etc., in the form of a print or slide recorded by a camera on photosensitive material. Often shortened to **photo.** ~*vb.* **2.** to take a photograph of (an object, person, scene, etc.).

photographer (fəˈtɒgrəfə) *n.* a person who takes photographs, either as a hobby or a profession.

photographic (ˌfəʊtəˈgræfɪk) *adj.* **1.** of or relating to photography: *a photographic society; photographic materials.* **2.** like a photograph in accuracy or detail. **3.** (of a person's memory) able to retain facts, appearances, etc., in precise detail, often after only a very short view of or exposure to them. —ˌ**photoˈgraphically** *adv.*

photographic magnitude *n. Astronomy.* the magnitude of a star as determined from photographic plates. It depends on the colour of the starlight and differs from the **visual magnitude** since an emulsion has a different colour sensitivity from that of the eye.

photography (fəˈtɒgrəfɪ) *n.* **1.** the process of recording images on sensitized material by the action of light, x-rays, etc., and the chemical processing of this material to produce a print, slide, or cine film. **2.** the art, practice, or occupation of taking and printing photographs, making cine films, etc.

photogravure (ˌfəʊtəʊgrəˈvjʊə) *n.* **1.** any of various methods in which an intaglio plate for printing is produced by the use of photography. **2.** matter printed from such a plate. ~Former name: **heliogravure.** [C19: from PHOTO- + French *gravure* engraving]

photojournalism (ˌfəʊtəʊˈdʒɜːnᵊˌlɪzəm) *n.* journalism in which photographs are the predominant feature. —ˌ**photoˈjournalist** *n.* —ˌ**photoˌjournalˈistic** *adj.*

photokinesis (ˌfəʊtəʊkɪˈniːsɪs, -kaɪ-) *n. Biology.* the movement of an organism in response to the stimulus of light. —**photokinetic** (ˌfəʊtəʊkɪˈnɛtɪk, -kaɪ-) *adj.* —ˌ**photokiˈnetically** *adv.*

photolithograph (ˌfəʊtəʊˈlɪθəˌgrɑːf, -ˌgræf) *n.* **1.** a picture printed by photolithography. ~*vb.* **2.** (*tr.*) to reproduce (pictures, text, etc.) by photolithography.

photolithography (ˌfəʊtəʊlɪˈθɒgrəfɪ) *n.* **1.** a lithographic printing process using photographically made plates. Often shortened to **photolitho** (ˌfəʊtəʊˈlaɪθəʊ). **2.** *Electronics.* a process used in the manufacture of semiconductor devices, thin-film circuits, and printed circuits in which a particular pattern is transferred from a photograph onto a substrate, producing a pattern that acts as a mask during an etching or diffusion process. See also **planar process.** —ˌ**photoliˈthographer** *n.* —**photolithographic** (ˌfəʊtəʊˌlɪθəˈgræfɪk) *adj.* —ˌ**photoˌlithoˈgraphically** *adv.*

photoluminescence (ˌfəʊtəʊˌluːmɪˈnɛsəns) *n.* luminescence resulting from the absorption of light or infrared or ultraviolet radiation. —ˌ**photoˌlumiˈnescent** *adj.*

photolysis (fəʊˈtɒlɪsɪs) *n.* chemical decomposition caused by light or other electromagnetic radiation. Compare **radiolysis.** —**photolytic** (ˌfəʊtəʊˈlɪtɪk) *adj.*

photom. *abbrev. for* photometry.

photomap (ˈfəʊtəʊˌmæp) *n.* **1.** a map constructed by adding grid lines, place names, etc., to one or more aerial photographs. ~*vb.* **-maps, -mapping, -mapped.** **2.** (*tr.*) to map (an area) using aerial photography.

photomechanical (ˌfəʊtəʊmɪˈkænɪkᵊl) *adj.* **1.** of or relating to any of various methods by which printing plates are made using photography. ~*n.* **2.** a final paste-up of artwork or typeset matter or both for photographing and processing into a printing plate. Often shortened to **mechanical.** —ˌ**photomeˈchanically** *adv.*

photomechanical transfer *n.* a method of producing photographic prints or offset printing plates from paper negatives by a chemical transfer process rather than by exposure to light.

photometer (fəʊˈtɒmɪtə) *n.* an instrument used in photometry, usually one that compares the illumination produced by a particular light source with that produced by a standard source. See also **spectrophotometer.**

photometry (fəʊˈtɒmɪtrɪ) *n.* **1.** the measurement of the intensity of light. **2.** the branch of physics concerned with such measurements. —**photometric** (ˌfəʊtəˈmɛtrɪk) *adj.* —ˌ**photoˈmetrically** *adv.* —**phoˈtometrist** *n.*

photomicrograph (ˌfəʊtəʊˈmaɪkrəˌgrɑːf, -ˌgræf) *n.* **1.** a photograph of a microscope image. Sometimes called **microphotograph. 2.** a less common name for **microphotograph** (sense 1). —**photomicrographer** (ˌfəʊtəʊmaɪˈkrɒgrəfə) *n.* —**photomicrographic** (ˌfəʊtəʊˌmaɪkrəˈgræfɪk) *adj.* —ˌ**photoˌmicroˈgraphically** *adv.* —ˌ**photomiˈcrography** *n.*

photomontage (ˌfəʊtəʊmɒnˈtɑːʒ) *n.* **1.** the technique of producing a composite picture by combining several photographs: used esp. in advertising. **2.** the composite picture so produced.

photomosaic (ˌfəʊtəʊməˈzeɪɪk) *n.* a large-scale detailed picture made up of many photographs. See also **mosaic** (sense 5).

photomultiplier (ˌfəʊtəʊˈmʌltɪˌplaɪə) *n.* a device sensitive to electromagnetic radiation, consisting of a photocathode, from which electrons are released by incident photons, and an electron multiplier, which amplifies and produces a detectable pulse of current.

photomural (ˌfəʊtəʊˈmjʊərəl) *n.* a decoration covering all or part of a wall consisting of a single enlarged photograph or a montage.

photon (ˈfəʊtɒn) *n.* a quantum of electromagnetic radiation, regarded as a particle with zero rest mass and charge, unit spin, and energy equal to the product of the frequency of the radiation and the Planck constant.

photonasty (ˈfəʊtəʊˌnæstɪ) *n., pl.* **-ties.** *Botany.* a nastic movement in response to a change in light intensity. —ˌ**photoˈnastic** *adj.*

photonegative (ˌfəʊtəʊˈnɛgətɪv) *adj. Physics.* (of a material) having an electrical conductivity that decreases with increasing illumination.

photoneutron (ˌfəʊtəʊˈnjuːtrɒn) *n.* a neutron emitted from a nucleus as a result of photodisintegration.

photonics (fəʊˈtɒnɪks) *n. (functioning as sing.) Computer technol.* the theoretical study of replacing electron transmission by photon transmission in computers to enhance computer speeds.

photonuclear (ˌfəʊtəʊˈnjuːklɪə) *adj. Physics.* of or concerned with a nuclear reaction caused by a photon.

photo-offset *n. Printing.* an offset process in which the plates are produced photomechanically.

photo opportunity *n.* an opportunity, either preplanned or accidental, for the press to photograph a politician, celebrity, or event.

photoperiod (ˌfəʊtəʊˈpɪərɪəd) *n.* the period of daylight in every 24 hours, esp. in relation to its effects on plants and animals. See also **photoperiodism.** —ˌ**photoˌperiˈodic** *adj.* —ˌ**photoˌperiˈodically** *adv.*

photoperiodism (ˌfəʊtəʊˈpɪərɪəˌdɪzəm) *n.* the response of plants and animals by behaviour, growth, etc., to photoperiods.

photophilous (fəʊˈtɒfələs) *adj.* (esp. of plants) growing best in strong light. —**phoˈtophily** *n.*

photophobia (ˌfəʊtəʊˈfəʊbɪə) *n.* **1.** *Pathol.* abnormal sensitivity of the eyes to light, esp. as the result of inflammation. **2.** *Psychiatry.* abnormal fear of or aversion to sunlight or well-lit places. —ˌ**photoˈphobic** *adj.*

photophore (ˈfəʊtəˌfɔː) *n. Zoology.* any light-producing organ in animals, esp. in certain fishes.

photopia (fəʊˈtəʊpɪə) *n.* the normal adaptation of the eye to light; day vision. [C20: New Latin, from PHOTO- + -OPIA] —**photopic** (fəʊˈtɒpɪk, -ˈtəʊ-) *adj.*

photopolymer (ˌfəʊtəʊˈpɒlɪmə) *n.* a polymeric material that is sensitive to light: used in printing plates, microfilms, etc.

photopositive (ˌfəʊtəʊˈpɒzɪtɪv) *adj. Physics.* (of a material) having an electrical conductivity that increases with increasing illumination.

photorealism (ˌfəʊtəʊˈrɪəˌlɪzəm) *n.* a style of painting and sculpture that depicts esp. commonplace urban images with meticulously accurate detail. —ˌ**photoˈrealist** *n., adj.*

photoreceptor (ˌfəʊtəʊrɪˈsɛptə) *n. Zoology, physiol.* a light-sensitive cell or organ that conveys impulses through the sensory neuron connected to it.

photoreconnaissance (ˌfəʊtəʊrɪˈkɒnɪsəns) *n. Chiefly military.* reconnaissance from the air by camera.

photo relief *n.* a method of showing the configuration of the relief of an area by photographing a model of it that is illuminated by a lamp in the northwest corner.

photosensitive (ˌfəʊtəʊˈsɛnsɪtɪv) *adj.* sensitive to electromagnetic radiation, esp. light: *a photosensitive photographic film.* —ˌ**photoˌsensiˈtivity** *n.*

photosensitize *or* **photosensitise** (ˌfəʊtəʊˈsɛnsɪˌtaɪz) *vb.* (*tr.*) to make (an organism or substance) photosensitive. —ˌ**photoˌsensitiˈzation** *or* ˌ**photoˌsensitiˈsation** *n.*

photoset (ˈfəʊtəʊˌsɛt) *vb.* **-sets, -setting, -set.** another word for **filmset.** —ˈ**photoˌsetter** *n.*

photosphere (ˈfəʊtəʊˌsfɪə) *n.* the visible surface of the sun. —**photospheric** (ˌfəʊtəʊˈsfɛrɪk) *adj.*

Photostat (ˈfəʊtəʊˌstæt) *n.* **1.** *Trademark.* a machine or process used to make quick positive or negative photographic copies of written, printed, or graphic matter. **2.** any copy made by such a machine. ~*vb.* **-stats, -statting** *or* **-stating, -statted** *or* **-stated. 3.** to make a Photostat copy (of). —ˌ**photoˈstatic** *adj.*

photosynthate (ˌfəʊtəʊˈsɪnˌθeɪt) *n.* any substance synthesized in photosynthesis, esp. a sugar.

photosynthesis (ˌfəʊtəʊˈsɪnθɪsɪs) *n.* **1.** (in plants) the synthesis of organic compounds from carbon dioxide and water (with the release of oxygen) using light energy absorbed by chlorophyll. **2.** the corresponding process in certain bacteria. —**photosynthetic** (ˌfəʊtəʊsɪnˈθɛtɪk) *adj.* —ˌ**photosynˈthetically** *adv.*

photosynthesize *or* **photosynthesise** (ˌfəʊtəʊˈsɪnθɪˌsaɪz) *vb.* (of plants and some bacteria) to carry out photosynthesis.

photosystem (ˈfəʊtəʊˌsɪstəm) *n. Botany.* either of two pigment-containing systems, photosystem I or II, in which the light-dependent chemical reactions of photosynthesis occur in the chloroplasts of plants.

phototaxis (ˌfəʊtəʊˈtæksɪs) *or* **phototaxy** *n.* the movement of an entire organism in response to light. —**phototactic** (ˌfəʊtəʊˈtæktɪk) *adj.*

phototherapy (ˌfəʊtəʊˈθɛrəpɪ) *or* **phototherapeutics** (ˌfəʊtəʊˌθɛrəˈpjuːtɪks) *n. (functioning as sing.)* the use of light in the treatment of disease. —ˌ**photoˌtheraˈpeutic** *adj.* —ˌ**photoˌtheraˈpeutically** *adv.*

photothermic (ˌfəʊtəʊˈθɜːmɪk) *or* **photothermal** *adj.* of or concerned with light and heat, esp. the production of heat by light. —ˌ**photoˈthermically** *or* ˌ**photoˈthermally** *adv.*

phototonus (fəʊˈtɒtənəs) *n.* the condition of plants that enables them to respond to the stimulus of light. [C19: from PHOTO- + Greek *tonos* TONE] —**phototonic** (ˌfəʊtəʊˈtɒnɪk) *adj.*

phototopography (ˌfəʊtəʊtəˈpɒgrəfɪ) *n.* the preparation of topographic maps from photographs.

phototransistor (ˌfəʊtəʊtrænˈzɪstə) *n.* a junction transistor, whose base signal is generated by illumination of the base. The emitter current, and hence collector current, increases with the intensity of the light.

phototrophic (ˌfəʊtəʊˈtrɒfɪk) *adj.* (of an organism) obtaining energy from sunlight for the synthesis of organic compounds. —**phototroph** (ˈfəʊtəʊˌtrɒf) *n.*

phototropism (ˌfəʊtəʊˈtrəʊpɪzəm) *n.* **1.** the growth response of plant parts to the stimulus of light, producing a bending towards the light source. **2.** the response of animals to light: sometimes used as another word for **phototaxis.** —ˌ**photoˈtropic** *adj.*

phototropy (ˌfəʊtəʊˈtrəʊpɪ) *n. Chem.* **1.** an alteration in the colour of certain substances as a result of being exposed to light of different wavelengths. **2.** the reversible loss of colour of certain dyestuffs when illuminated at a particular wavelength.

phototube (ˈfəʊtəʊˌtjuːb) *n.* a type of photocell in which radiation falling on a photocathode causes electrons to flow to an anode and thus produce an electric current.

phototype (ˈfəʊtəʊˌtaɪp) *Printing.* ~*n.* **1. a.** a printing plate produced by photography. **b.** a print produced from such a plate. ~*vb.* **2.** (*tr.*) to reproduce (an illustration) using a phototype. —**phototypic** (ˌfəʊtəʊˈtɪpɪk) *adj.* —ˌ**photoˈtypically** *adv.*

phototypesetting (ˌfəʊtəʊˈtaɪpˌsɛtɪŋ) *n.* a U.S. and Canadian name for **filmsetting.**

phototypography (ˌfəʊtəʊtaɪˈpɒgrəfɪ) *n.* any printing process involving the use of photography. —**phototypographical** (ˌfəʊtəʊˌtaɪpəˈgræfɪkᵊl) *adj.* —ˌ**photoˌtypoˈgraphically** *adv.*

photovoltaic (ˌfəʊtəʊvɒlˈteɪɪk) *adj.* of, concerned with, or producing electric current or voltage caused by electromagnetic radiation.

photovoltaic effect *n.* the effect observed when electromagnetic radiation falls on a thin film of one solid deposited on the surface of a dissimilar solid producing a difference in potential between the two materials.

photozincography (ˌfəʊtəʊzɪŋˈkɒgrəfɪ) *n.* a photoengraving process using a printing plate made of zinc. —**photozincograph** (ˌfəʊtəʊˈzɪŋkəˌgrɑːf, -ˌgræf) *n.*

phr. *abbrev. for* phrase.

phrasal (ˈfreɪzᵊl) *adj.* of, relating to, or composed of phrases. —ˈ**phrasally** *adv.*

phrasal verb *n.* (in English grammar) a phrase that consists of a verb plus an adverbial or prepositional particle, esp. one the meaning of which cannot be deduced by analysis of the meaning of the constituents: *"take in" meaning "deceive" is a phrasal verb.*

phrase (freɪz) *n.* **1.** a group of words forming an immediate syntactic constituent of a clause. Compare **clause** (sense 1), **noun phrase, verb phrase. 2.** a particular expression, esp. an original one. **3.** *Music.* a small group of notes forming a coherent unit of melody. **4.** (in choreography) a short sequence of dance movements. ~*vb.* (*tr.*) **5.** *Music.* to divide (a melodic line, part, etc.) into musical phrases, esp. in performance. **6.** to express orally or in a phrase. [C16: from Latin *phrasis,* from Greek: speech, from *phrazein* to declare, tell]

phrase book *n.* a book containing frequently used expressions and their equivalents in a foreign language, esp. for the use of tourists.

phrase marker *n. Linguistics.* a representation, esp. one in the form of a tree diagram, of the constituent structure of a sentence.

phraseogram (ˈfreɪzɪəˌgræm) *n.* a symbol representing a phrase, as in shorthand.

phraseograph ('freɪzɪə,grɑːf) *n.* a phrase for which there exists a phraseogram. —**phraseographic** (,freɪzɪə'græfɪk) *adj.* —**phraseography** (,freɪzɪ'ɒgrəfɪ) *n.*

phraseologist (,freɪzɪ'ɒlədʒɪst) *n.* a person who is interested in or collects phrases or who affects a particular phraseology.

phraseology (,freɪzɪ'ɒlədʒɪ) *n., pl.* **-gies.** **1.** the manner in which words or phrases are used. **2.** a set of phrases used by a particular group of people. —**phraseological** (,freɪzɪə'lɒdʒɪkᵊl) *adj.* —**,phraseo'logically** *adv.*

phrase-structure grammar *n.* a grammar in which relations among the words and morphemes of a sentence are described, but not deeper or semantic relations. Abbrev.: **PSG.** Compare **transformational grammar.**

phrase-structure rule *n. Generative grammar.* a rule of the form A → X where A is a syntactic category label, such as *noun phrase* or *sentence,* and X is a sequence of such labels and/or morphemes, expressing the fact that A can be replaced by X in generating the constituent structure of a sentence. Also called: **rewrite rule.** Compare **transformational rule.**

phrasing ('freɪzɪŋ) *n.* **1.** the way in which something is expressed, esp. in writing; wording. **2.** *Music.* the division of a melodic line, part, etc., into musical phrases.

phratry ('freɪtrɪ) *n., pl.* **-tries.** *Anthropol.* a group of people within a tribe who have a common ancestor. [C19: from Greek *phratria* clan, from *phratēr* fellow clansman; compare Latin *frāter* brother] —**'phratric** *adj.*

phreatic (frɪ'ætɪk) *adj. Geography.* of or relating to ground water occurring below the water table. Compare **vadose.** [C19: from Greek *phrear* a well]

phreatophyte (frɪ'ætəfaɪt) *n.* a plant having very long roots that reach down to the water table or the layer above it. [C20: from Greek *phrear* a well + -PHYTE]

phren. *or* **phrenol.** *abbrev. for* phrenology.

phrenetic (frɪ'nɛtɪk) *adj.* an obsolete spelling of **frenetic.** —**phre'netically** *adv.* —**phre'neticness** *n.*

phrenic ('frɛnɪk) *adj.* **1. a.** of or relating to the diaphragm. **b.** (*as n.*): *the phrenic.* **2.** *Obsolete.* of or relating to the mind. [C18: from New Latin *phrenicus,* from Greek *phrēn* mind, diaphragm]

phrenitis (frɪ'naɪtɪs) *n. Rare.* **1.** another name for **encephalitis. 2.** a state of frenzy; delirium. [C17: via Late Latin from Greek: delirium, from *phrēn* mind, diaphragm + -ITIS] —**phrenitic** (frɪ'nɪtɪk) *adj.*

phreno- *or before a vowel* **phren-** *combining form.* **1.** mind or brain: *phrenology.* **2.** of or relating to the diaphragm: *phrenic.* [from Greek *phrēn* mind, diaphragm]

phrenology (frɪ'nɒlədʒɪ) *n.* (formerly) the branch of science concerned with localization of function in the human brain, esp. determination of the strength of the faculties by the shape and size of the skull overlying the parts of the brain thought to be responsible for them. —**phrenological** (,frɛnə'lɒdʒɪkᵊl) *adj.* —**phre'nologist** *n.*

phrensy ('frɛnzɪ) *n., pl.* **-sies,** *vb.* an obsolete spelling of **frenzy.**

Phrygian ('frɪdʒɪən) *adj.* **1.** of or relating to Phrygia, an ancient country in W central Asia Minor, its inhabitants, or their extinct language. **2.** *Music.* of or relating to an authentic mode represented by the natural diatonic scale from E to E. See **Hypo-. 3.** *Music.* (of a cadence) denoting a progression that leads a piece of music out of the major key and ends on the dominant chord of the relative minor key. ~*n.* **4.** a native or inhabitant of ancient Phrygia. **5.** an ancient language of Phrygia, belonging to the Thraco-Phrygian branch of the Indo-European family: recorded in a few inscriptions.

Phrygian cap *n.* a conical cap of soft material worn during ancient times that became a symbol of liberty during the French Revolution.

PHS (in the U.S.) *abbrev. for* Public Health Service.

phthalein ('θeɪliːn, -lɪɪn, 'θæl-, 'fθæl-) *n.* any of a class of organic compounds obtained by the reaction of phthalic anhydride with a phenol and used in dyes. [C19: from *phthal-,* shortened form of NAPHTHALENE + -IN]

phthalic acid ('θælɪk, 'fθæl-) *n.* a soluble colourless crystalline acid used in the synthesis of dyes and perfumes; 1,2-benzenedicarboxylic acid. Formula: $C_6H_4(COOH)_2$. [C19 *phthalic,* from *phthal-* (see PHTHALEIN) + -IC]

phthalic anhydride *n.* a white crystalline substance used mainly in producing dyestuffs. Formula: $C_6H_4(CO)_2O$.

phthalocyanine (,θæləʊ'saɪə,niːn, ,θeɪ-, ,fθæl-) *n.* **1.** a cyclic blue-green organic pigment. Formula: $(C_6H_4C_2N)_4N_4$. **2.** any of a class of compounds derived by coordination of this compound with a metal atom. They are blue or green pigments used in printing inks, plastics, and enamels. [C20: from *phthal-* (see PHTHALEIN) + CYANINE]

phthiriasis (θɪ'raɪəsɪs) *n. Pathol.* the state or condition of being infested with lice; pediculosis. [C16: via Latin from Greek, from *phtheir* louse]

phthisic ('θaɪsɪk, 'fθaɪsɪk, 'taɪsɪk) *Obsolete.* ~*adj.* **1.** relating to or affected with phthisis. ~*n.* **2.** another name for **asthma.** [C14: from Old French *tisike,* from Latin *phthisicus,* from Greek *phthisikos;* see PHTHISIS] —**'phthisical** *adj.*

phthisis ('θaɪsɪs, 'fθaɪ-, 'taɪ-) *n.* any disease that causes wasting of the body, esp. pulmonary tuberculosis. [C16: via Latin from Greek: a wasting away, from *phthinein* to waste away]

phut (fʌt) *Informal.* ~*n.* **1.** a representation of a muffled explosive sound. ~*adv.* **2. go phut.** to break down or collapse. [C19: of imitative origin]

phyco- *combining form.* seaweed: *phycology.* [from Greek *phukos*]

phycobilin (,faɪkəʊ'baɪlɪn) *n. Botany.* any of a class of red or blue-green pigments found in the red and blue-green algae.

phycobiont (,faɪkəʊ'baɪɒnt) *n. Botany.* the algal constituent of a lichen. Compare **mycobiont.**

phycology (faɪ'kɒlədʒɪ) *n.* the study of algae. —**phycological** (,faɪkə'lɒdʒɪkᵊl) *adj.* —**phy'cologist** *n.*

phycomycete (,faɪkəʊ'maɪsiːt) *n.* any filamentous fungus of the class *Phycomycetes,* in which the spores are produced sexually or asexually: includes certain mildews and moulds. —**,phycomy'cetous** *adj.*

phyla ('faɪlə) *n.* the plural of **phylum.**

phylactery (fɪ'læktərɪ) *n., pl.* **-teries. 1.** *Judaism.* (*usually pl.*) Also called: **Tefillah.** either of the pair of blackened square cases containing parchments inscribed with biblical passages, bound by leather thongs to the head and left arm, and worn by Jewish men during weekday morning prayers. **2.** a reminder or aid to remembering. **3.** *Archaic.* an amulet or charm. [C14: from Late Latin *phylactērium,* from Greek *phulaktērion* outpost, from *phulax* a guard]

phyle ('faɪlɪ) *n., pl.* **-lae** (-liː). a tribe or clan of an ancient Greek people such as the Ionians. [C19: from Greek *phulē* tribe, clan] —**'phylic** *adj.*

phyletic (faɪ'lɛtɪk) *or* **phylogenetic** (,faɪləʊdʒɪ'nɛtɪk) *adj.* of or relating to the evolutionary development of organisms. [C19: from Greek *phuletikos* tribal] —**phy'letically** *or* **,phyloge'netically** *adv.*

-phyll *or* **-phyl** *n. combining form.* leaf: *chlorophyll.* [from Greek *phullon*]

phyllid ('fɪlɪd) *n. Botany.* the leaf of a liverwort or moss.

phyllite ('fɪlaɪt) *n.* a compact lustrous metamorphic rock, rich in mica, derived from a clay rock. [C19: from PHYLL(O)- + -ITE[1]] —**phyllitic** (fɪ'lɪtɪk) *adj.*

phyllo ('fɪləʊ) *n.* a variant of **filo.** [C20: from Greek: leaf]

phyllo- *or before a vowel* **phyll-** *combining form.* leaf: *phyllopod.* [from Greek *phullon* leaf]

phylloclade ('fɪləʊ,kleɪd) *or* **phylloclad** ('fɪləʊ,klæd) *n.* other names for **cladode.** [C19: from New Latin *phyllocladium,* from PHYLLO- + Greek *klados* branch]

phyllode ('fɪləʊd) *n.* a flattened leafstalk that resembles and functions as a leaf. [C19: from New Latin *phyllodium,* from Greek *phullōdēs* leaflike] —**phyl'lodial** *adj.*

phylloid ('fɪlɔɪd) *adj.* resembling a leaf.

phyllome ('fɪləʊm) *n.* a leaf or a leaflike organ. —**phyllomic** (fɪ'lɒmɪk, -'ləʊ-) *adj.*

phylloplane ('fɪləʊ,pleɪn) *n. Ecology.* the surface of a leaf considered as a habitat, esp. for microorganisms. Also called: **phyllosphere.**

phylloquinone (,fɪləʊkwɪ'nəʊn) *n.* a viscous fat-soluble liquid occurring in plants: essential for the production of prothrombin, required in blood clotting. Formula: $C_{31}H_{46}O_2$. Also called: **vitamin K_1.**

phyllosilicate (,fɪləʊ'sɪlɪkeɪt) *n.* any of a class of silicate minerals, including talc, consisting of thin sheets.

phyllosphere ('fɪləʊ,sfɪə) *n.* another name for **phylloplane.**

phyllotaxis (,fɪlə'tæksɪs) *or* **phyllotaxy** *n., pl.* **-taxes** (-'tæksiːz) *or* **-taxies. 1.** the arrangement of the leaves on a stem. **2.** the study of this arrangement in different plants. —**,phyllo'tactic** *adj.*

-phyllous *adj. combining form.* having leaves of a specified number or type: *monophyllous.* [from Greek *-phullos* of a leaf]

phylloxera (,fɪlɒk'sɪərə, fɪ'lɒksərə) *n., pl.* **-rae** (-riː) *or* **-ras.** any homopterous insect of the genus *Phylloxera,* such as *P. vitifolia* (or *Viteus vitifolii*) (**vine phylloxera**), typically feeding on plant juices, esp. of vines: family *Phylloxeridae.* [C19: New Latin, from PHYLLO- + *xēros* dry]

phylo- *or before a vowel* **phyl-** *combining form.* tribe; race; phylum: *phylogeny.* [from Greek *phulon* race]

phylogeny (faɪ'lɒdʒɪnɪ) *or* **phylogenesis** (,faɪləʊ'dʒɛnɪsɪs) *n., pl.* **-nies** *or* **-geneses** (-'dʒɛnɪ,siːz). *Biology.* the sequence of events involved in the evolution of a species, genus, etc. Compare **ontogeny.** [C19: from PHYLO- + -GENY] —**phylogenic** (,faɪləʊ'dʒɛnɪk) *or* **phylogenetic** (,faɪləʊdʒɪ'nɛtɪk) *adj.*

phylum ('faɪləm) *n., pl.* **-la** (-lə). **1.** a major taxonomic division of the animals and plants that contain one or more classes. An example is the phylum *Arthropoda* (insects, crustaceans, arachnids, etc., and myriapods). **2.** any analogous group, such as a group of related language families or linguistic stocks. [C19: New Latin, from Greek *phulon* race]

phys. *abbrev. for:* **1.** physical. **2.** physician. **3.** physics. **4.** physiological. **5.** physiology.

physalis (faɪ'seɪlɪs) *n.* See **Chinese lantern, strawberry tomato.** [New Latin, from Greek *physallis* a bladder (from the form of the calyx)]

physiatrics (,fɪzɪ'ætrɪks) *n.* (*functioning as sing.*) *Med., U.S.* another name for **physiotherapy.** [C19: from PHYSIO- + -IATRICS] —**,physi'atric** *or* **,physi'atrical** *adj.*

physic ('fɪzɪk) *n.* **1.** *Rare.* a medicine or drug, esp. a cathartic or purge. **2.** *Archaic.* the art or skill of healing. **3.** an archaic term for **physics** (sense 1). ~*vb.* **-ics, -icking, -icked.** (*tr.*) **4.** *Archaic.* to treat (a patient) with medicine. [C13: from Old French *fisique,* via Latin, from Greek *phusikē,* from *phusis* nature] —'**physicky** *adj.*

physical ('fɪzɪkᵊl) *adj.* **1.** of or relating to the body, as distinguished from the mind or spirit. **2.** of, relating to, or resembling material things or nature: *the physical universe.* **3.** involving or requiring bodily contact: *rugby is a physical sport.* **4.** of or concerned with matter and energy. **5.** of or relating to physics. **6.** perceptible to the senses; apparent: *a physical manifestation.* ~*n.* **7.** short for **physical examination.** ~See also **physicals.** —'**physically** *adv.* —'**physicalness** *n.*

physical anthropology *n.* the branch of anthropology dealing with the genetic aspect of human development and its physical variations.

physical chemistry *n.* the branch of chemistry concerned with the way in which the physical properties of substances depend on and influence their chemical structure, properties, and reactions.

physical education *n.* training and practice in sports, gymnastics, etc., as in schools and colleges. Abbrev.: **PE.**

physical examination *n. Med.* the process of examining the body by means of sight, touch, percussion, or auscultation to diagnose disease or verify fitness.

physical geography *n.* the branch of geography that deals with the natural features of the earth's surface.

physical handicap *n.* loss of or failure to develop a specific bodily function or functions, whether of movement, sensation, coordination, or speech, but excluding mental impairments or disabilities. —**physically handicapped** *adj.*

physicalism ('fɪzɪkᵊˌlɪzəm) *n. Philosophy.* the doctrine that all phenomena can be described in terms of space and time and that all meaningful statements are either analytic, as in logic and mathematics, or can be reduced to empirically verifiable assertions. See also **logical positivism, identity theory.** —'**physicalist** *n., adj.* —ˌ**physical'istic** *adj.*

physical jerks *pl. n. Brit. informal.* See **jerk**[1] (sense 6).

physical medicine *n.* the branch of medicine devoted to the management of physical disabilities, as resulting from rheumatic disease, asthma, poliomyelitis, etc. See also **rehabilitation** (sense 2).

physicals ('fɪzɪkᵊlz) *pl. n. Commerce.* commodities that can be purchased and used, as opposed to those bought and sold in a futures market. Also called: **actuals.**

physical science *n.* any of the sciences concerned with nonliving matter, energy, and the physical properties of the universe, such as physics, chemistry, astronomy, and geology. Compare **life science.**

physical therapy *n.* another term for **physiotherapy.**

physician (fɪ'zɪʃən) *n.* **1.** a person legally qualified to practise medicine, esp. one specializing in areas of treatment other than surgery; doctor of medicine. **2.** *Archaic.* any person who treats diseases; healer. [C13: from Old French *fisicien,* from *fisique* PHYSIC]

physicist ('fɪzɪsɪst) *n.* a person versed in or studying physics.

physicochemical (ˌfɪzɪkəʊ'kɛmɪkᵊl) *adj.* of, concerned with, or relating to physical chemistry or both physics and chemistry. —ˌ**physico'chemically** *adv.*

physics ('fɪzɪks) *n.* (*functioning as sing.*) **1.** the branch of science concerned with the properties of matter and energy and the relationships between them. It is based on mathematics and traditionally includes mechanics, optics, electricity and magnetism, acoustics, and heat. Modern physics, based on quantum theory, includes atomic, nuclear, particle, and solid-state studies. It can also embrace applied fields such as geophysics and meteorology. **2.** physical properties of behaviour: *the physics of the electron.* **3.** *Archaic.* natural science or natural philosophy. [C16: from Latin *physica,* translation of Greek *ta phusika* natural things, from *phusis* nature]

physio ('fɪzɪəʊ) *n. Informal.* short for **physiotherapy.**

physio- *or before a vowel* **phys-** *combining form.* **1.** of or relating to nature or natural functions: *physiology.* **2.** physical: *physiotherapy.* [from Greek *phusio,* from *phusis* nature, from *phuein* to make grow]

physiocrat ('fɪzɪəʊˌkræt) *n.* a follower of Quesnay's doctrines of government, believing that the inherent natural order governing society was based on land and its natural products as the only true form of wealth. [C18: from French *physiocrate;* see PHYSIO-, -CRAT] —**physiocracy** (ˌfɪzɪ'ɒkrəsɪ) *n.* —ˌ**physio'cratic** *adj.*

physiognomy (ˌfɪzɪ'ɒnəmɪ) *n.* **1.** a person's features or characteristic expression considered as an indication of personality. **2.** the art or practice of judging character from facial features. **3.** the outward appearance of something, esp. the physical characteristics of a geographical region. [C14: from Old French *phisonomie,* via Medieval Latin, from Late Greek *phusiognōmia,* erroneous for Greek *phusiognōmonia,* from *phusis* nature + *gnōmōn* judge] —**physiognomic** (ˌfɪzɪə'nɒmɪk) *or* ˌ**physiog'nomical** *adj.* —ˌ**physiog'nomically** *adv.* —ˌ**physi'ognomist** *n.*

physiography (ˌfɪzɪ'ɒgrəfɪ) *n.* another name for **geomorphology** or **physical geography.** —ˌ**physi'ographer** *n.* —**physiographic** (ˌfɪzɪə'græfɪk) *or* ˌ**physio'graphical** *adj.* —ˌ**physio'graphically** *adv.*

physiol. *abbrev. for:* **1.** physiological. **2.** physiology.

physiological (ˌfɪzɪə'lɒdʒɪkᵊl) *adj.* **1.** of or relating to physiology. **2.** of or relating to normal healthful functioning; not pathological. —ˌ**physio'logically** *adv.*

physiological psychology *n.* the branch of psychology concerned with the study and correlation of physiological and psychological events.

physiology (ˌfɪzɪ'ɒlədʒɪ) *n.* **1.** the branch of science concerned with the functioning of organisms. **2.** the processes and functions of all or part of an organism. [C16: from Latin *physiologia,* from Greek] —ˌ**physi'ologist** *n.*

physiotherapy (ˌfɪzɪəʊ'θɛrəpɪ) *n.* the therapeutic use of physical agents or means, such as massage, exercises, etc. Also called: **physical therapy,** (Informal) **physio,** (U.S.) **physiatrics.** —ˌ**physio'therapist** *n.*

physique (fɪ'ziːk) *n.* the general appearance of the body with regard to size, shape, muscular development, etc. [C19: via French, from *physique* (adj.) natural, from Latin *physicus* physical]

physoclistous (ˌfaɪsəʊ'klɪstəs) *adj.* (of fishes) having an air bladder that is not connected to the alimentary canal. Compare **physostomous.** [C19: from Greek *phusa* bladder + *-clistous,* from *kleistos* closed]

physostigmine (ˌfaɪsəʊ'stɪgmiːn) *or* **physostigmin** (ˌfaɪsəʊ'stɪgmɪn) *n.* an alkaloid found in the Calabar bean used esp. in eye drops to reduce pressure inside the eyeball. Formula: $C_{15}H_{21}N_3O_2$. Also called: **eserine.** [C19: from New Latin *Physostigma* genus name, from Greek *phusa* bladder + *stigma* mark]

physostomous (faɪ'sɒstəməs) *adj.* (of fishes) having a duct connecting the air bladder to part of the alimentary canal. Compare **physoclistous.** [C19: from Greek *phusa* bladder + *-stomous,* from *stoma* mouth]

-phyte *n. combining form.* indicating a plant of a specified type or habitat: *lithophyte; thallophyte.* [from Greek *phuton* plant] —**-phytic** *adj. combining form.*

phyto- *or before a vowel* **phyt-** *combining form.* indicating a plant or vegetation: *phytogenesis.* [from Greek *phuton* plant, from *phuein* to make grow]

phytoalexin (ˌfaɪtəʊə'lɛksɪn) *n. Botany.* any of a group of substances produced by plants that inhibit the growth of pathogenic fungi that infect them. [C20: from PHYTO- + Greek *alexein* to ward off]

phytochemistry (ˌfaɪtəʊ'kɛmɪstrɪ) *n.* the branch of chemistry concerned with plants, their chemical composition and processes. —ˌ**phyto'chemist** *n.*

phytochrome ('faɪtəʊˌkrəʊm) *n. Botany.* a blue-green pigment, present in most plants, that mediates many light-dependent processes, including photoperiodism and the greening of leaves.

phytogenesis (ˌfaɪtəʊ'dʒɛnɪsɪs) *or* **phytogeny** (faɪ'tɒdʒənɪ) *n.* the branch of botany concerned with the origin and evolution of plants. —**phytogenetic** (ˌfaɪtəʊdʒɪ'nɛtɪk) *adj.* —ˌ**phytoge'netically** *adv.*

phytogenic (ˌfaɪtəʊ'dʒɛnɪk) *adj.* derived from plants: *coal is a phytogenic substance.*

phytogeography (ˌfaɪtəʊdʒɪ'ɒgrəfɪ) *n.* the branch of botany that is concerned with the geographical distribution of plants. —ˌ**phytoge'ographer** *n.* —ˌ**phytoˌgeo'graphic** *or* ˌ**phytoˌgeo'graphical** *adj.*

phytography (faɪ'tɒgrəfɪ) *n.* the branch of botany that is concerned with the detailed description of plants. —**phytographic** (ˌfaɪtə'græfɪk) *adj.*

phytohormone (ˌfaɪtəʊ'hɔːməʊn) *n.* a hormone-like substance produced by a plant.

phytology (faɪ'tɒlədʒɪ) *n.* a rare name for **botany** (sense 1). —**phytological** (ˌfaɪtə'lɒdʒɪkᵊl) *adj.* —ˌ**phyto'logically** *adv.* —**phy'tologist** *n.*

phyton ('faɪtɒn) *n.* a unit of plant structure, usually considered as the smallest part of the plant that is capable of growth when detached from the parent plant. [C20: from Greek. See -PHYTE]

phytopathology (ˌfaɪtəʊpə'θɒlədʒɪ) *n.* the branch of botany concerned with diseases of plants. —**phytopathological** (ˌfaɪtəʊˌpæθə'lɒdʒɪkᵊl) *adj.* —ˌ**phytopa'thologist** *n.*

phytophagous (faɪ'tɒfəgəs) *adj.* (esp. of insects) feeding on plants. —**phytophagy** (faɪ'tɒfədʒɪ) *n.*

phytoplankton (ˌfaɪtə'plæŋktən) *n.* the plant constituent of plankton, mainly unicellular algae. Compare **zooplankton.** —**phytoplanktonic** (ˌfaɪtəplæŋk'tɒnɪk) *adj.*

phytosociology (ˌfaɪtəʊˌsəʊsɪ'ɒlədʒɪ, -ˌsəʊʃɪ-) *n.* the branch of ecology concerned with the origin, development, etc., of plant communities. —**phytosociological** (ˌfaɪtəʊˌsəʊsɪə'lɒdʒɪkᵊl, -ˌsəʊʃɪə-) *adj.* —ˌ**phytoˌsocio'logically** *adv.* —ˌ**phytoˌsoci'ologist** *n.*

phytotoxin (ˌfaɪtə'tɒksɪn) *n.* a toxin, such as strychnine, that is produced by a plant. Compare **zootoxin.** —ˌ**phyto'toxic** *adj.*

phytotron ('faɪtəʊˌtrɒn) *n.* a building in which plants can be grown on a large scale, under controlled conditions. [C20: from PHYTO- + -TRON, on the model of CYCLOTRON]

pi[1] (paɪ) *n., pl.* **pis.** **1.** the 16th letter in the Greek alphabet (Π, π), a consonant, transliterated as *p.* **2.** *Maths.* a transcendental number, fundamental to mathematics, that is the ratio of the circumference of a circle to its diameter. Approximate value: 3.141 592... ; symbol: π [C18 (mathematical use): representing the first letter of Greek *periphereia* PERIPHERY]

pi[2] *or* **pie** (paɪ) *n., pl.* **pies. 1.** a jumbled pile of printer's type. **2.** a jumbled mixture. *~vb.* **pies, piing, pied** *or* **pies, pieing, pied.** (*tr.*) **3.** to spill and mix (set type) indiscriminately. **4.** to mix up. [C17: of uncertain origin]
pi[3] (paɪ) *adj. Brit. slang.* See **pious** (senses 2, 3).
PI 1. *abbrev. for* Philippine Islands. **2.** *international car registration for* Philippine Islands.
piacular (paɪ'ækjʊlə) *adj.* **1.** making expiation for a sacrilege. **2.** requiring expiation. [C17: from Latin *piāculum* propitiatory sacrifice, from *piāre* to appease]
piaffe (pɪ'æf) *n. Dressage.* a passage done on the spot. [C18: from French, from *piaffer* to strut]
pia mater ('paɪə 'meɪtə) *n.* the innermost of the three membranes (see **meninges**) that cover the brain and spinal cord. [C16: from Medieval Latin, literally: pious mother, intended to translate Arabic *umm raqīqah* tender mother]
pianism ('piːəˌnɪzəm) *n.* technique, skill, or artistry in playing the piano. —ˌ**pia'nistic** *adj.*
pianissimo (pɪə'nɪsɪˌməʊ) *adj., adv. Music.* (to be performed) very quietly. Symbol: *pp* [C18: from Italian, superlative of *piano* soft]
pianist ('pɪənɪst) *n.* a person who plays the piano.
piano[1] (pɪ'ænəʊ) *n., pl.* **-anos.** a musical stringed instrument resembling a harp set in a vertical or horizontal frame, played by depressing keys that cause hammers to strike the strings and produce audible vibrations. See also **grand piano, upright piano.** [C19: short for PIANOFORTE]
piano[2] ('pjɑːnəʊ) *adj., adv. Music.* (to be performed) softly. Symbol: *p* [C17: from Italian, from Latin *plānus* flat; see PLAIN[1]]
piano accordion *n.* an accordion in which the right hand plays a piano-like keyboard. See **accordion.** —**piano accordionist** *n.*
pianoforte (pɪ'ænəʊ'fɔːtɪ) *n.* the full name for **piano**[1]. [C18: from Italian, originally (*gravecembalo col*) *piano e forte* (harpsichord with) soft and loud; see PIANO[2], FORTE[2]]
Pianola (pɪə'nəʊlə) *n. Trademark.* a type of mechanical piano in which the keys are depressed by air pressure from bellows, this air flow being regulated by perforations in a paper roll. Also called: **player piano.**
piano nobile ('pjɑːnəʊ 'nəʊbɪlɪ) *n. Architect.* the main floor of a large house, containing the reception rooms: usually of lofty proportions. [Italian: great floor]
piano player *n.* **1.** another name for **pianist. 2.** any of various devices for playing a piano automatically.
piano roll *n.* a perforated roll of paper actuating the playing mechanism of a Pianola. Also called: **music roll.**
piano stool *n.* a stool on which a pianist sits when playing a piano, esp. one whose height is adjustable.
piano trio *n.* **1.** an instrumental ensemble consisting of a piano, a violin, and a cello. **2.** a piece of music written for such an ensemble, usually having the form and commonest features of a sonata.
piassava (ˌpiːə'sɑːvə) *or* **piassaba** (ˌpiːə'sɑːbə) *n.* **1.** either of two South American palm trees, *Attalea funifera* or *Leopoldinia piassaba.* **2.** the coarse fibre obtained from either of these trees, used to make brushes and rope. [C19: via Portuguese from Tupi *piaçaba*]
piastre *or* **piaster** (pɪ'æstə) *n.* **1.** the standard monetary unit of South Vietnam, divided into 100 cents. **2. a.** a fractional monetary unit of Egypt, Lebanon, the Sudan, and Syria worth one hundredth of a pound. **b.** Also called: **kurus.** a Turkish monetary unit worth one hundredth of a lira. **c.** a Libyan monetary unit worth one hundredth of a dinar. **3.** a rare word for **piece of eight.** [C17: from French *piastre,* from Italian *piastra d'argento* silver plate; related to Italian *piastro* PLASTER]
piazza (pɪ'ætsə, -'ædzə; *Italian* 'pjattsa) *n.* **1.** a large open square in an Italian town. **2.** *Chiefly Brit.* a covered passageway or gallery. [C16: from Italian: marketplace, from Latin *platēa* courtyard, from Greek *plateia;* see PLACE]
pibroch ('piːbrɒk; *Gaelic* 'piːbrɒx) *n.* **1.** a form of music for Scottish bagpipes, consisting of a theme and variations. **2.** a piece of such music. [C18: from Gaelic *piobaireachd,* from *piobair* piper]
pic (pɪk) *n., pl.* **pics** *or* **pix.** *Informal.* a photograph, picture, or illustration. [C20: shortened from PICTURE]
pica[1] ('paɪkə) *n.* **1.** Also called: **em, pica em.** a printer's unit of measurement, equal to 12 points or 0.166 ins. **2.** (formerly) a size of printer's type equal to 12 point. **3.** a typewriter type size having 10 characters to the inch. [C15: from Anglo-Latin *pīca* list of ecclesiastical regulations, apparently from Latin *pīca* magpie, with reference to its habit of making collections of miscellaneous items; the connection between the original sense (ecclesiastical list) and the typography meanings is obscure]
pica[2] ('paɪkə) *n. Pathol.* an abnormal craving to ingest substances such as clay, dirt, or hair, sometimes occurring during pregnancy, in persons with chlorosis, etc. [C16: from medical Latin, from Latin: magpie, being an allusion to its omnivorous feeding habits]
picador ('pɪkəˌdɔː) *n. Bullfighting.* a horseman who pricks the bull with a lance in the early stages of a fight to goad and weaken it. [C18: from Spanish, literally: pricker, from *picar* to prick; see PIQUE[1]]
Picardy third ('pɪkədɪ) *n. Music.* a major chord used in the final chord of a piece of music in the minor mode. Also called: **tierce de Picardie.** [translation of French *tierce de Picardie,* from its use in the church music of *Picardy,* N France]
picaresque (ˌpɪkə'rɛsk) *adj.* **1.** of or relating to a type of fiction in which the hero, a rogue, goes through a series of episodic adventures. It originated in Spain in the 16th century. **2.** of or involving rogues or picaroons. [C19: via French from Spanish *picaresco,* from *pícaro* a rogue]
picaroon *or* **pickaroon** (ˌpɪkə'ruːn) *n. Archaic.* an adventurer or rogue. [C17: from Spanish *picarón,* from *pícaro*]
picayune (ˌpɪkə'juːn) *adj. also* **picayunish.** *U.S. and Canadian informal.* **1.** of small value or importance. **2.** mean; petty. *~n.* **3.** the half real, an old Spanish-American coin. **4.** *U.S.* any coin of little value, esp. a five-cent piece. [C19: from French *picaillon* coin from Piedmont, from Provençal *picaioun,* of unknown origin] —ˌ**pica'yunishly** *adv.* —ˌ**pica'yunishness** *n.*
piccalilli ('pɪkəˌlɪlɪ) *n.* a pickle of mixed vegetables, esp. onions, cauliflower, and cucumber, in a mustard sauce. [C18 *piccalillo,* perhaps a coinage based on PICKLE]
piccanin ('pɪkəˌnɪn, ˌpɪkə'nɪn) *n. S. African informal.* a Black African child. [variant of PICCANINNY]
piccaninny *or esp. U.S.* **pickaninny** (ˌpɪkə'nɪnɪ) *n., pl.* **-nies. 1.** *Offensive.* a small Black or Aboriginal child. **2.** (*modifier*) tiny: *a piccaninny fire won't last long.* [C17: perhaps from Portuguese *pequenino* tiny one, from *pequeno* small]
piccolo ('pɪkəˌləʊ) *n., pl.* **-los.** a woodwind instrument, the smallest member of the flute family, lying an octave above that of the flute. See **flute** (sense 1). [C19: from Italian: small; compare English PETTY, French *petit*]
pice (paɪs) *n., pl.* **pice. 1.** a former Indian coin worth one sixty-fourth of a rupee. **2.** a fractional monetary unit of Nepal worth one hundredth of a rupee. [C17: from Mahratti *paisā*]
piceous ('pɪsɪəs, 'paɪsɪəs) *adj.* of, relating to, or resembling pitch. [C17: from Latin *piceus,* from *pix* PITCH[2]]
pichiciego (ˌpɪtʃɪsɪ'eɪgəʊ) *n., pl.* **-gos. 1.** a very small Argentine armadillo, *Chlamyphorus truncatus,* with white silky hair and pale pink plates on the head and back. **2. greater pichiciego.** a similar but larger armadillo, *Burmeisteria retusa.* [C19: from Spanish, probably from Guarani *pichey* small armadillo + Spanish *ciego* blind]
pick[1] (pɪk) *vb.* **1.** to choose (something) deliberately or carefully, from or as if from a group or number; select. **2.** to pluck or gather (fruit, berries, or crops) from (a tree, bush, field, etc.): *to pick hops; to pick a whole bush.* **3.** (*tr.*) to clean or prepare (fruit, poultry, etc.) by removing the indigestible parts. **4.** (*tr.*) to remove loose particles from (the teeth, the nose, etc.). **5.** (esp. of birds) to nibble or gather (corn, etc.). **6.** (*tr.*) to pierce, dig, or break up (a hard surface) with a pick. **7.** (*tr.*) to form (a hole) in this way. **8.** (when *intr.,* foll. by *at*) to nibble (at) fussily or without appetite. **9.** to separate (strands, fibres, etc.), as in weaving. **10.** (*tr.*) to provoke (an argument, fight, etc.) deliberately. **11.** (*tr.*) to steal (money or valuables) from (a person's pocket). **12.** (*tr.*) to open (a lock) with an instrument other than a key. **13.** to pluck the strings of (a guitar, banjo, etc.). **14.** (*tr.*) to make (one's way) carefully on foot: *they picked their way through the rubble.* **15. pick and choose.** to select fastidiously, fussily, etc. **16. pick someone's brains.** to obtain information or ideas from someone. *~n.* **17.** freedom or right of selection (esp. in the phrase **take one's pick**). **18.** a person, thing, etc., that is chosen first or preferred: *the pick of the bunch.* **19.** the act of picking. **20.** the amount of a crop picked at one period or from one area. **21.** *Printing.* a speck of dirt or metal or a blob of ink on the surface of set type or a printing plate. *~*See also **pick at, pick off, pick on, pick out, pick-up.** [C15: from earlier *piken* to pick, influenced by French *piquer* to pierce; compare Middle Low German *picken,* Dutch *pikken*] —'**pickable** *adj.*
pick[2] (pɪk) *n.* **1.** a tool with a handle carrying a long steel head curved and tapering to a point at one or both ends, used for loosening soil, breaking rocks, etc. **2.** any of various tools used for picking, such as an ice pick or toothpick. **3.** a plectrum. [C14: perhaps variant of PIKE[2]]
pick[3] (pɪk) (in weaving) *~vb.* **1.** (*tr.*) to cast (a shuttle). *~n.* **2.** one casting of a shuttle. **3.** a weft or filling thread. [C14: variant of PITCH[1]]
pickaback ('pɪkəˌbæk) *n., adv., adj., vb.* another word for **piggyback.**
pickaninny (ˌpɪkə'nɪnɪ) *n., pl.* **-nies.** a variant spelling (esp. U.S.) of **piccaninny.**
pickaroon (ˌpɪkə'ruːn) *n.* a variant spelling of **picaroon.**
pick at *vb.* (*intr., prep.*) to make criticisms of in a niggling or petty manner.
pickaxe *or U.S.* **pickax** ('pɪkˌæks) *n.* **1.** a large pick or mattock. *~vb.* **2.** to use a pickaxe on (earth, rocks, etc.). [C15: from earlier *pikois* (but influenced also by AXE), from Old French *picois,* from *pic* PICK[2]; compare also PIQUE[1]]
picker ('pɪkə) *n.* **1.** a person or thing that picks, esp. that gathers fruit, crops, etc. **2.** (in weaving) a person or the part of the loom that casts the shuttle.
pickerel ('pɪkərəl, 'pɪkrəl) *n., pl.* **-el** *or* **-els.** any of several North American freshwater game fishes, such as *Esox americanus* and *E. niger:* family *Esocidae* (pikes, walleye, etc.). [C14: a small pike; diminutive of PIKE[1]]

pickerelweed ('pɪkərəlˌwiːd, 'pɪkrəl-) *n.* any of several North American freshwater plants of the genus *Pontederia*, esp. *P. cordata*, having arrow-shaped leaves and purple flowers: family *Pontederiaceae*.

picket ('pɪkɪt) *n.* **1.** a pointed stake, post, or peg that is driven into the ground to support a fence, provide a marker for surveying, etc. **2.** an individual or group that stands outside an establishment to make a protest, to dissuade or prevent employees or clients from entering, etc. **3.** Also: **picquet.** a small detachment of troops or warships positioned towards the enemy to give early warning of attack. *~vb.* **4.** to post or serve as pickets at (a factory, embassy, etc.): *let's go and picket the shop.* **5.** to guard (a main body or place) by using or acting as a picket. **6.** (*tr.*) to fasten (a horse or other animal) to a picket. **7.** (*tr.*) to fence (an area, boundary, etc.) with pickets. [C18: from French *piquet*, from Old French *piquer* to prick; see PIKE[2]] —'**picketer** *n.*

picket fence *n.* a fence consisting of pickets supported at close regular intervals by being driven into the ground, by interlacing with strong wire, or by nailing to horizontal timbers fixed to posts in the ground.

picket line *n.* a line of people acting as pickets.

pickin ('pɪkɪn) *n. W African.* a small child. [from Portuguese *pequeno*; see PICCANINNY]

pickings ('pɪkɪŋz) *pl. n.* (*sometimes sing.*) money, profits, etc., acquired easily or by more or less dishonest means; spoils.

pickle ('pɪk^əl) *n.* **1.** (*often pl.*) vegetables, such as cauliflowers, onions, etc., preserved in vinegar, brine, etc.. **2.** any food preserved in this way. **3.** a liquid or marinade, such as spiced vinegar, for preserving vegetables, meat, fish, etc. **4.** *Chiefly U.S. and Canadian.* a cucumber that has been preserved and flavoured in a pickling solution, such as brine or vinegar. **5.** *Informal.* an awkward or difficult situation: *to be in a pickle.* **6.** *Brit. informal.* a mischievous child. *~vb.* (*tr.*) **7.** to preserve in a pickling liquid. **8.** to immerse (a metallic object) in a liquid, such as an acid, to remove surface scale. [C14: perhaps from Middle Dutch *pekel*; related to German *Pökel* brine] —'**pickler** *n.*

pickled ('pɪk^əld) *adj.* **1.** preserved in a pickling liquid. **2.** *Informal.* intoxicated; drunk.

picklock ('pɪkˌlɒk) *n.* **1.** a person who picks locks, esp. one who gains unlawful access to premises by this means. **2.** an instrument for picking locks.

pick-me-up *n. Informal.* a tonic or restorative, esp. a special drink taken as a stimulant.

pick off *vb.* (*tr., adv.*) to aim at and shoot one by one.

pick on *vb.* (*intr., prep.*) to select for something unpleasant, esp. in order to bully, blame, or cause to perform a distasteful task.

pick out *vb.* (*tr., adv.*) **1.** to select for use or special consideration, illustration, etc., as from a group. **2.** to distinguish (an object from its surroundings), as in painting: *she picked out the woodwork in white.* **3.** to perceive or recognize (a person or thing previously obscured): *we picked out his face among the crowd.* **4.** to distinguish (sense or meaning) from or as if from a mass of detail or complication. **5.** to play (a tune) tentatively, by or as if by ear.

pickpocket ('pɪkˌpɒkɪt) *n.* a person who steals from the pockets or handbags of others in public places.

pick-up *n.* **1.** Also called: **pick-up arm, tone arm.** the light balanced arm of a record player that carries the wires from the cartridge to the preamplifier. **2.** an electromagnetic transducer that converts the vibrations of the steel strings of an electric guitar or other amplified instrument into electric signals. **3.** another name for **cartridge** (sense 3). **4.** a small truck with an open body and low sides, used for light deliveries. **5.** *Informal, chiefly U.S.* an ability to accelerate rapidly: *this car has good pick-up.* **6.** *Informal.* a casual acquaintance, usually one made with sexual intentions. **7.** *Informal.* **a.** a stop to collect passengers, goods, etc. **b.** the people or things collected. **8.** *Slang.* a free ride in a motor vehicle. **9.** *Informal.* an improvement. **10.** *Slang.* a pick-me-up. *~vb.* **pick up.** (*adv.*) **11.** (*tr.*) to gather up in the hand or hands. **12.** (*tr.*) to acquire, obtain, or purchase casually, incidentally, etc. **13.** (*tr.*) to catch (a disease): *she picked up a bad cold during the weekend.* **14.** (*intr.*) to improve in health, condition, activity, etc.: *the market began to pick up.* **15.** (*reflexive*) to raise (oneself) after a fall or setback. **16.** (*tr.*) to notice or sense: *she picked up a change in his attitude.* **17.** to resume where one left off; return to: *we'll pick up after lunch; they picked up the discussion.* **18.** (*tr.*) to learn gradually or as one goes along. **19.** (*tr.*) to take responsibility for paying (a bill): *he picked up the bill for dinner.* **20.** (*tr.*) *Informal.* to reprimand: *he picked her up on her table manners.* **21.** (*tr.*) to collect or give a lift to (passengers, hitchhikers, goods, etc.). **22.** (*tr.*) *Informal.* to become acquainted with, esp. with a view to having sexual relations. **23.** (*tr.*) *Informal.* to arrest. **24.** to increase (speed): *the cars picked up down the straight.* **25.** (*tr.*) to receive (electrical signals, a radio signal, sounds, etc.), as for transmission or amplification.

Pickwickian (pɪk'wɪkɪən) *adj.* **1.** of, relating to, or resembling Mr Pickwick in Charles Dickens' *The Pickwick Papers* (1837), esp. in being naive or benevolent. **2.** (of the use or meaning of a word, etc.) odd or unusual.

picky ('pɪkɪ) *adj.* **pickier, pickiest.** *Informal.* fussy; finicky; choosy. —'**pickily** *adv.* —'**pickiness** *n.*

picnic ('pɪknɪk) *n.* **1.** a trip or excursion to the country, seaside, etc., on which people bring food to be eaten in the open air. **2. a.** any informal meal eaten outside. **b.** (*as modifier*): *a picnic lunch.* **3.** *Informal.* an easy or agreeable task (esp. in the phrase **it was no picnic**). **4.** *Informal, chiefly Austral.* a troublesome situation or experience. *~vb.* **-nics, -nicking, -nicked. 5.** (*intr.*) to eat a picnic. [C18: from French *piquenique*, of unknown origin] —'**picnicker** *n.*

picnic races *pl. n. Austral.* horse races for amateur riders held in rural areas.

pico- *prefix.* denoting 10^{-12}: *picofarad.* Symbol: p [from Spanish *pico* small quantity, odd number, peak]

picofarad ('piːkəʊˌfærəd, -æd) *n.* a million millionth of a farad; 10^{-12} farad. Symbol: pF

picoline ('pɪkəˌliːn, -lɪn) *n.* a liquid derivative of pyridine found in bone oil and coal tar; methylpyridene. Formula: $C_5H_4N(CH_3)$. [C19: from Latin *pic-*, *pix* PITCH[2] + -OL[2] + -INE[2]] —**picolinic** (ˌpɪkə'lɪnɪk) *adj.*

picong ('pɪkɒŋ) *n. Caribbean.* any teasing or satirical banter, originally a verbal duel in song. [from Spanish *picón* mocking, from *picar* to pierce; compare PICADOR]

picosecond ('piːkəʊˌsɛkənd, 'paɪkəʊ-) *n.* a million millionth of a second; 10^{-12} second.

picot ('piːkəʊ) *n.* any of a pattern of small loops, as on lace. [C19: from French: small point, from *pic* point]

picotee (ˌpɪkə'tiː) *n.* a type of carnation having pale petals edged with a darker colour, usually red. [C18: from French *picoté* marked with points, from PICOT]

picquet ('pɪkɪt) *n.* a variant spelling of **picket** (sense 3).

picrate ('pɪkreɪt) *n.* **1.** any salt or ester of picric acid, such as sodium picrate. **2.** a charge-transfer complex formed by picric acid.

picric acid ('pɪkrɪk) *n.* a toxic sparingly soluble crystalline yellow acid used as a dye, antiseptic, and explosive. Formula: $C_6H_2OH(NO_2)_3$. Systematic name: **2,4,6-trinitrophenol.** See also **lyddite.**

picrite ('pɪkraɪt) *n.* a coarse-grained ultrabasic igneous rock consisting of olivine and augite with small amounts of plagioclase feldspar.

picro- *or before a vowel* **picr-** *combining form.* bitter: *picrotoxin.* [from Greek *pikros*]

picrotoxin (ˌpɪkrə'tɒksɪn) *n.* a bitter poisonous crystalline compound used as an antidote for barbiturate poisoning. Formula: $C_{30}H_{34}O_{13}$.

Pict (pɪkt) *n.* a member of any of the peoples who lived in Britain north of the Forth and Clyde in the first to the fourth centuries A.D.: later applied chiefly to the inhabitants of NE Scotland. Throughout Roman times the Picts carried out border raids. [Old English *Peohtas*; later forms from Late Latin *Pictī* painted men, from *pingere* to paint]

Pictish ('pɪktɪʃ) *n.* **1.** the language of the Picts, of which few records survive. Its origins are much disputed and it was extinct by about 900 A.D. *~adj.* **2.** of or relating to the Picts.

pictogram ('pɪktəˌgræm) *n.* another word for **pictograph.**

pictograph ('pɪktəˌgrɑːf, -ˌgræf) *n.* **1.** a picture or symbol standing for a word or group of words, as in written Chinese. **2.** a chart on which symbols are used to represent values, such as population levels or consumption. [C19: from Latin *pictus*, from *pingere* to paint] —**pictographic** (ˌpɪktə'græfɪk) *adj.* —**pictography** (pɪk'tɒgrəfɪ) *n.*

Pictor ('pɪktə) *n.*, *Latin genitive* **Pictoris** (pɪk'tɔːrɪs). a faint constellation in the S hemisphere lying between Dorado and Carina. [Latin: painter]

pictorial (pɪk'tɔːrɪəl) *adj.* **1.** relating to, consisting of, or expressed by pictures. **2.** (of books, newspapers, etc.) containing pictures. **3.** of or relating to painting or drawing. **4.** (of language, style, etc.) suggesting a picture; vivid; graphic. *~n.* **5. a.** a magazine, newspaper, etc., containing many pictures. **b.** (*cap. when part of a name*): *the Sunday Pictorial.* [C17: from Late Latin *pictōrius*, from Latin *pictor* painter, from *pingere* to paint] —**pic'torially** *adv.*

picture ('pɪktʃə) *n.* **1. a.** a visual representation of something, such as a person or scene, produced on a surface, as in a photograph, painting, etc. **b.** (*as modifier*): *picture gallery; picture postcard.* **2.** a mental image or impression: *a clear picture of events.* **3.** a verbal description, esp. one that is vivid. **4.** a situation considered as an observable scene: *the political picture.* **5.** a person or thing that bears a close resemblance to another: *he was the picture of his father.* **6.** a person, scene, etc., considered as typifying a particular state or quality: *the picture of despair.* **7.** a beautiful person or scene: *you'll look a picture.* **8.** a complete image on a television screen, comprising two interlaced fields. **9. a.** a motion picture; film. **b.** (*as modifier*): *picture theatre.* **10. the pictures.** *Chiefly Brit.* a cinema or film show. **11.** another name for **tableau vivant.** **12. get the picture.** *Informal.* to understand a situation. **13. in the picture.** informed about a given situation. *~vb.* (*tr.*) **14.** to visualize or imagine. **15.** to describe or depict, esp. vividly. **16.** (*often passive*) to put in a picture or make a picture of: *they were pictured sitting on the rocks.* [C15: from Latin *pictūra* painting, from *pingere* to paint]

picture card *n.* another name for **court card.**

picturegoer ('pɪktʃəˌgəʊə) *n. Brit., old-fashioned.* a person that goes to the cinema, esp. frequently.

picture hat *n.* a decorated hat with a very wide brim, esp. as worn by women in paintings by Gainsborough and Reynolds.

picture house *n. Chiefly Brit.* an old-fashioned name for **cinema** (sense 1).

picture moulding *n.* **1.** the edge around a framed picture. **2.** Also called: **picture rail.** the moulding or rail near the top of a wall from which pictures can be hung.

picture palace *n. Brit.* an old-fashioned name for **cinema** (sense 1).

picturesque (ˌpɪktʃəˈrɛsk) *adj.* **1.** visually pleasing, esp. in being striking or vivid: *a picturesque view.* **2.** having a striking or colourful character, nature, etc. **3.** (of language) graphic; vivid. [C18: from French *pittoresque* (but also influenced by PICTURE), from Italian *pittoresco,* from *pittore* painter, from Latin *pictor*] —ˌ**picturˈesquely** *adv.* —ˌ**picturˈesqueness** *n.*

picture tube *n.* another name for **television tube.**

picture window *n.* a large window having a single pane of glass, usually placed so that it overlooks a view.

picture writing *n.* **1.** any writing system that uses pictographs. **2.** a system of artistic expression and communication using pictures or symbolic figures.

picul (ˈpɪkᵊl) *n.* a unit of weight, used in China, Japan, and SE Asia, equal to approximately 60 kilograms or 133 pounds. [C16: from Malay *pīkul* a grown man's load]

PID *abbrev. for* pelvic inflammatory disease.

piddle (ˈpɪdᵊl) *vb.* **1.** (*intr.*) *Informal.* to urinate. **2.** (when *tr.,* often foll. by *away*) to spend (one's time) aimlessly; fritter. [C16: origin unknown] —ˈ**piddler** *n.*

piddling (ˈpɪdlɪŋ) *adj. Informal.* petty; trifling; trivial. —ˈ**piddlingly** *adv.*

piddock (ˈpɪdək) *n.* any marine bivalve of the family *Pholadidae,* boring into rock, clay, or wood by means of sawlike shell valves. See also **shipworm.** [C19: origin uncertain]

pidgin (ˈpɪdʒɪn) *n.* a language made up of elements of two or more other languages and used for contacts, esp. trading contacts, between the speakers of other languages. Unlike creoles, pidgins do not constitute the mother tongue of any speech community. [C19: perhaps from Chinese pronunciation of English *business*]

pidgin English *n.* a pidgin in which one of the languages involved is English.

pi-dog *n.* a variant spelling of **pye-dog.**

pie[1] (paɪ) *n.* **1.** a baked food consisting of a sweet or savoury filling in a pastry-lined dish, often covered with a pastry crust. **2. have a** (*or* **one's**) **finger in the pie. a.** to have an interest in or take part in some activity. **b.** to meddle or interfere. **3. pie in the sky.** illusory hope or promise of some future good; false optimism. [C14: of obscure origin]

pie[2] (paɪ) *n.* an archaic or dialect name for **magpie.** [C13: via Old French from Latin *pīca* magpie; related to Latin *pīcus* woodpecker]

pie[3] (paɪ) *n., vb. Printing.* a variant spelling of **pi**[2].

pie[4] (paɪ) *n.* a very small former Indian coin worth one third of a pice. [C19: from Hindi *pā'ī,* from Sanskrit *pādikā* a fourth]

pie[5] *or* **pye** (paɪ) *n. History.* a book for finding the Church service for any particular day. [C15: from Medieval Latin *pica* almanac; see PICA[1]]

pie[6] (paɪ) *adj.* **be pie on.** *N.Z. informal.* to be keen on. [from Maori *pai ana*]

piebald (ˈpaɪˌbɔːld) *adj.* **1.** marked or spotted in two different colours, esp. black and white: *a piebald horse.* ~*n.* **2.** a black-and-white pied horse. [C16: PIE[2] + BALD; see also PIED]

pie cart *n. N.Z.* a mobile van selling warmed-up food and drinks.

piece (piːs) *n.* **1.** an amount or portion forming a separate mass or structure; bit: *a piece of wood.* **2.** a small part, item, or amount forming part of a whole, esp. when broken off or separated: *a piece of bread.* **3.** a length by which a commodity is sold, esp. cloth, wallpaper, etc. **4.** an instance or occurrence: *a piece of luck.* **5.** *Slang.* a girl or woman regarded as an object of sexual attraction: *a nice piece.* **6.** an example or specimen of a style or type, such as an article of furniture: *a beautiful piece of Dresden china.* **7.** *Informal.* an opinion or point of view: *to state one's piece.* **8.** a literary, musical, or artistic composition. **9.** a coin having a value as specified: *fifty-pence piece.* **10.** a small object, often individually shaped and designed, used in playing certain games, esp. board games: *chess pieces.* **11. a.** a firearm or cannon. **b.** (*in combination*): *fowling-piece.* **12.** any chessman other than a pawn. **13.** *U.S. and Canadian.* a short time or distance: *down the road a piece.* **14.** *Scot. and English dialect.* **a.** a slice of bread or a sandwich. **b.** a packed lunch taken to work, school, etc. **15.** (*usually pl.*) *Austral. and N.Z.* fragments of fleece wool. See also **oddment** (sense 3). **16. give someone a piece of one's mind.** *Informal.* to criticize or censure someone frankly or vehemently. **17. go to pieces. a.** (of a person) to lose control of oneself; have a breakdown. **b.** (of a building, organization, etc.) to disintegrate. **18. nasty piece of work.** *Brit. informal.* a cruel or mean person. **19. of a piece.** of the same kind; alike. **20. piece of cake.** *Informal.* something easily obtained or achieved. ~*vb.* (*tr.*) **21.** (often foll. by *together*) to fit or assemble piece by piece. **22.** (often foll. by *up*) to patch or make up (a garment) by adding pieces. **23.** *Textiles.* to join (broken threads) during spinning. ~See also **piece out.** [C13 *pece,* from Old French, of Gaulish origin; compare Breton *pez* piece, Welsh *peth* portion]

pièce de résistance *French.* (pjɛs də rezistɑ̃s) *n.* **1.** the principal or most outstanding item in a series or creative artist's work. **2.** the main dish of a meal.

piece-dyed *adj.* (of fabric) dyed after weaving. Compare **yarn-dyed.**

piece goods *pl. n.* goods, esp. fabrics, made in standard widths and lengths. Also called: **yard goods.**

piecemeal (ˈpiːsˌmiːl) *adv.* **1.** by degrees; bit by bit; gradually. **2.** in or into pieces or piece from piece: *to tear something piecemeal.* ~*adj.* **3.** fragmentary or unsystematic: *a piecemeal approach.* [C13 *pecemele,* from PIECE + *-mele,* from Old English *mælum* quantity taken at one time]

piece of eight *n., pl.* **pieces of eight.** a former Spanish coin worth eight reals; peso.

piece out *vb.* (*tr., adv.*) **1.** to extend by adding pieces. **2.** to cause to last longer by using only a small amount at a time: *to piece out rations.*

piecer (ˈpiːsə) *n. Textiles.* a person who mends, repairs, or joins something, esp. broken threads on a loom.

piece rate *n.* a fixed rate paid according to the quantity produced.

piecework (ˈpiːsˌwɜːk) *n.* work paid for according to the quantity produced. Compare **timework.**

pie chart *n.* a circular graph divided into sectors proportional to the magnitudes of the quantities represented.

piecrust table (ˈpaɪˌkrʌst) *n.* a round table, ornamented with carved moulding suggestive of a pie crust.

pied (paɪd) *adj.* having markings of two or more colours. [C14: from PIE[2]; an allusion to the magpie's black-and-white colouring]

pied-à-terre (ˌpjeɪtɑːˈtɛə) *n., pl.* **pieds-à-terre** (ˌpjeɪtɑːˈtɛə). a flat, house, or other lodging for secondary or occasional use. [French, literally: foot on (the) ground]

piedmont (ˈpiːdmɒnt) *adj.* (*prenominal*) (of glaciers, plains, etc.) formed or situated at the foot of a mountain or mountain range. [via French from Italian *piémonte,* from *pié,* variant of *piede* foot + *mont* mountain]

piedmontite (ˈpiːdmɒnˌtaɪt, -mən-) *n.* a dark red mineral occurring in metamorphic rocks: a complex hydrated silicate containing calcium, aluminium, iron, and manganese. Formula: $Ca_2(Al,Fe,Mn)_3(SiO_4)_3OH$. [C19: from *Piedmont,* a region of NW Italy]

pie-dog *n.* a variant spelling of **pye-dog.**

Pied Piper *n.* (*sometimes not caps.*) a person who entices others to follow him. [after the legendary *Pied Piper* of Hamelin, who rid the town of Hamelin of rats by luring them away with his piping]

pied-piping *n. Transformational grammar.* the principle that a noun phrase may take with it the rest of a prepositional phrase or a larger noun phrase in which it is contained, when moved in a transformation. For example, when the interrogative pronoun is moved to initial position, other words are moved too, as in *to whom did you speak?*

pied wagtail *n.* a British songbird, *Motacilla alba yarrellii,* with a black throat and back, long black tail, and white underparts and face: family *Motacillidae* (wagtails and pipits).

pie-eater *n. Austral. informal, offensive.* a person of little account or importance.

pie-eyed *adj.* a slang term for **drunk** (sense 1).

pieman (ˈpaɪmən) *n., pl.* **-men.** *Brit., obsolete.* a seller of pies.

pier (pɪə) *n.* **1.** a structure with a deck that is built out over water, and used as a landing place, promenade, etc. **2.** a pillar that bears heavy loads, esp. one of rectangular cross section. **3.** the part of a wall between two adjacent openings. **4.** another name for **buttress** (sense 1). [C12 *per,* from Anglo-Latin *pera* pier supporting a bridge]

pierce (pɪəs) *vb.* (*mainly tr.*) **1.** to form or cut (a hole) in (something) with or as if with a sharp instrument. **2.** to thrust into or penetrate sharply or violently: *the thorn pierced his heel.* **3.** to force (a way, route, etc.) through (something). **4.** (of light) to shine through or penetrate (darkness). **5.** (*also intr.*) to discover or realize (something) suddenly or (of an idea) to become suddenly apparent. **6.** (of sounds or cries) to sound sharply through (the silence). **7.** to move or affect (a person's emotions, bodily feelings, etc.) deeply or sharply: *the cold pierced their bones.* **8.** (*intr.*) to penetrate or be capable of penetrating: *piercing cold.* [C13 *percen,* from Old French *percer,* ultimately from Latin *pertundere,* from *per* through + *tundere* to strike] —ˈ**pierceable** *adj.* —ˈ**piercer** *n.* —ˈ**piercing** *adj.* —ˈ**piercingly** *adv.*

pier glass *n.* a tall narrow mirror, usually one of a pair or set, designed to hang on the wall between windows, usually above a pier table.

Pierian (paɪˈɪərɪən) *adj.* **1.** of or relating to Pieria, a region of ancient Macedonia: the country of the Muses. **2.** of or relating to the Muses or artistic or poetic inspiration.

pieridine (paɪˈɛərɪˌdaɪn) *adj.* of, relating to, or belonging to the *Pieridae,* a family of butterflies including the whites and brimstones.

pieris (ˈpaɪərɪs) *n.* any plant of a genus, *Pieris,* of American and Asiatic shrubs, esp. *P. formosa forestii,* grown for the bright red colour of its young foliage: family *Ericaceae.* [New Latin, from Greek *Pierides,* a name for the Muses]

Pierrot ('pɪərəʊ; *French* pjɛro) *n.* **1.** a male character from French pantomime with a whitened face, white costume, and pointed hat. **2.** (*usually not cap.*) a clown or masquerader so made up.

pier table *n.* a side table designed to stand against a wall between windows.

pietà (pɪɛ'tɑː) *n.* a sculpture, painting, or drawing of the dead Christ, supported by the Virgin Mary. [Italian: pity, from Latin *pietās* PIETY]

pietism ('paɪɪˌtɪzəm) *n.* **1.** a less common word for **piety. 2.** excessive, exaggerated, or affected piety or saintliness. —'**pietist** *n.* —ˌ**pie'tistic** *or* ˌ**pie'tistical** *adj.*

Pietism ('paɪɪˌtɪzəm) *n. History.* a reform movement in the German Lutheran Churches during the 17th and 18th centuries that strove to renew the devotional ideal. —'**Pietist** *n.*

piet-my-vrou ('piːtˌmeɪ'frəʊ) *n. S. African.* a cuckoo, *Notococcyx solitarius,* having a red breast. [from Afrikaans *piet* Peter + *my* my + *vrou* wife: onomatopoeic, based on the bird's three clear notes]

piety ('paɪɪtɪ) *n., pl.* **-ties. 1.** dutiful devotion to God and observance of religious principles. **2.** the quality or characteristic of being pious. **3.** a pious action, saying, etc. **4.** *Now rare.* devotion and obedience to parents or superiors. [C13 *piete,* from Old French, from Latin *pietās* piety, dutifulness, from *pius* PIOUS]

piezo- (paɪ'iːzəʊ-, piː'eɪzəʊ-, 'piːtsəʊ-) *combining form.* pressure: *piezometer.* [from Greek *piezein* to press]

piezochemistry (paɪˌiːzəʊ'kɛmɪstrɪ) *n.* the study of chemical reactions at high pressures.

piezoelectric crystal (paɪˌiːzəʊɪ'lɛktrɪk) *n.* a crystal, such as quartz, that produces a potential difference across its opposite faces when under mechanical stress. See also **piezoelectric effect.**

piezoelectric effect *or* **piezoelectricity** (paɪˌiːzəʊɪlɛk'trɪsɪtɪ) *n. Physics.* **a.** the production of electricity or electric polarity by applying a mechanical stress to certain crystals. **b.** the converse effect in which stress is produced in a crystal as a result of an applied potential difference. —**piˌezoe'lectrically** *adv.*

piezomagnetic effect (paɪˌiːzəʊmæg'nɛtɪk) *or* **piezomagnetism** (paɪˌiːzəʊ'mægnɪtɪzəm) *n. Physics.* **a.** the production of a magnetic field by applying a mechanical stress to certain crystals. **b.** the converse effect in which stress is produced in a crystal as a result of an applied magnetic field. —**piˌezomag'netically** *adj.*

piezometer (ˌpaɪɪ'zɒmɪtə) *n.* any instrument for the measurement of pressure (**piezometry**), esp. very high pressure, or for measuring the compressibility of materials under pressure. —**piezometric** (paɪˌiːzəʊ'mɛtrɪk) *adj.* —**piˌezo'metrically** *adv.*

piffle ('pɪfᵊl) *Informal.* ~*n.* **1.** nonsense: *to talk piffle.* ~*vb.* **2.** (*intr.*) to talk or behave feebly. [C19: origin uncertain]

piffling ('pɪflɪŋ) *adj.* worthless, trivial.

pig (pɪg) *n.* **1.** any artiodactyl mammal of the African and Eurasian family *Suidae,* esp. *Sus scrofa* (**domestic pig**), typically having a long head with a movable snout, a thick bristle-covered skin, and, in wild species, long curved tusks. **2.** a domesticated pig weighing more than 120 pounds (54 kg). **3.** *Informal.* a dirty, greedy, or bad-mannered person. **4.** the meat of swine; pork. **5.** *Derogatory.* a slang word for **policeman. 6. a.** a mass of metal, such as iron, copper, or lead, cast into a simple shape for ease of storing or transportation. **b.** a mould in which such a mass of metal is formed. **7.** *Brit. informal.* something that is difficult or unpleasant. **8. a pig in a poke.** something bought or received without prior sight or knowledge. **9. make a pig of oneself.** *Informal.* to overindulge oneself. **10. on the pig's back.** *Irish and N.Z.* successful; established: *he's on the pig's back now.* ~Related adj. (for senses 1, 2): **porcine.** ~*vb.* **pigs, pigging, pigged. 11.** (*intr.*) (of a sow) to give birth. **12.** (*intr.*) Also: **pig it.** *Informal.* to live in squalor. **13.** (*tr.*) *Informal.* to devour (food) greedily. ~See also **pig out.** [C13 *pigge,* of obscure origin]

pig bed *n.* a bed of sand in which pig iron is cast.

pig dog *n. N.Z.* a dog bred for hunting wild pigs in the bush.

pigeon[1] ('pɪdʒɪn) *n.* **1.** any of numerous birds of the family *Columbidae,* having a heavy body, small head, short legs, and long pointed wings: order *Columbiformes.* See **rock dove. 2.** *Slang.* a victim or dupe. [C14: from Old French *pijon* young dove, from Late Latin *pīpiō* young bird, from *pīpīre* to chirp]

pigeon[2] ('pɪdʒɪn) *n. Brit. informal.* concern or responsibility (often in the phrase **it's his, her,** etc., **pigeon**). [C19: altered from PIDGIN]

pigeon breast *n.* a deformity of the chest characterized by an abnormal protrusion of the breastbone, caused by rickets or by obstructed breathing during infancy. Also called: **chicken breast.**

pigeon hawk *n.* the North American variety of the merlin.

pigeon-hearted *or* **pigeon-livered** *adj.* of a timid or fearful disposition.

pigeonhole ('pɪdʒɪnˌhəʊl) *n.* **1.** a small compartment for papers, letters, etc., as in a bureau. **2.** a hole or recess in a dovecote for pigeons to nest in. **3.** *Informal.* a category or classification. ~*vb.* (*tr.*) **4.** to put aside or defer. **5.** to classify or categorize, esp. in a rigid manner.

pigeon pea *n.* another name for **dhal.**

pigeon-toed *adj.* having the toes turned inwards.

pigeonwing ('pɪdʒɪnˌwɪŋ) *n. Chiefly U.S.* a fancy step in dancing in which the feet are clapped together.

pigface ('pɪgˌfeɪs) *n. Austral.* a creeping succulent plant of the genus *Carpobrotus,* having bright-coloured flowers and red fruits and often grown for ornament: family *Aizoaceae.*

pig fern *n. N.Z.* giant bracken.

pigfish ('pɪgˌfɪʃ) *n., pl.* **-fish** *or* **-fishes. 1.** Also called: **hogfish.** any of several grunts, esp. *Orthopristis chrysopterus,* of the North American Atlantic coast. **2.** any of several wrasses, such as *Achoerodus gouldii* (**giant pigfish**), that occur around the Great Barrier Reef.

piggery ('pɪgərɪ) *n., pl.* **-geries. 1.** a place where pigs are kept and reared. **2.** great greediness; piggishness.

piggin ('pɪgɪn) *n.* a small wooden bucket or tub. Also called: **pipkin.** [C16: origin unknown]

piggish ('pɪgɪʃ) *adj.* **1.** like a pig, esp. in appetite or manners. **2.** *Informal, chiefly Brit.* obstinate or mean. —'**piggishly** *adv.* —'**piggishness** *n.*

piggy ('pɪgɪ) *n., pl.* **-gies. 1.** a child's word for a pig, esp. a piglet. **2.** a child's word for toe or, sometimes, finger. ~*adj.* **-gier, -giest. 3.** another word for **piggish.**

piggyback ('pɪgɪˌbæk) *or* **pickaback** *n.* **1.** a ride on the back and shoulders of another person. **2.** a system whereby a vehicle, aircraft, etc., is transported for part of its journey on another vehicle, such as a flat railway wagon, another aircraft, etc. ~*adv.* **3.** on the back and shoulders of another person. **4.** on or as an addition to something else. ~*adj.* **5.** of or for a piggyback: *a piggyback ride; piggyback lorry trains.* **6.** of or relating to a type of heart transplant in which the transplanted heart functions in conjunction with the patient's own heart. ~*vb.* (*tr.*) **7.** to give (a person) a piggyback on one's back and shoulders. **8.** to transport (one vehicle) on another.

piggy bank *n.* a child's coin bank shaped like a pig with a slot for coins.

pig-headed *adj.* stupidly stubborn. —ˌ**pig-'headedly** *adv.* —ˌ**pig-'headedness** *n.*

pig iron *n.* crude iron produced in a blast furnace and poured into moulds in preparation for making wrought iron, steels, alloys, etc.

pig-jump *vb.* (*intr.*) (of a horse) to jump from all four legs.

Pig Latin *n.* a secret language used by children in which any consonants at the beginning of a word are placed at the end, followed by *-ay;* for example *cathedral* becomes *athedralcay.*

piglet ('pɪglɪt) *n.* a young pig.

pigmeat ('pɪgˌmiːt) *n.* a less common name for **pork, ham**[1] (sense 2), or **bacon** (sense 1).

pigment ('pɪgmənt) *n.* **1.** a substance occurring in plant or animal tissue and producing a characteristic colour, such as chlorophyll in green plants and haemoglobin in red blood. **2.** any substance used to impart colour. **3.** a powder that is mixed with a liquid to give a paint, ink, etc. [C14: from Latin *pigmentum,* from *pingere* to paint] —'**pigmentary** *adj.*

pigmentation (ˌpɪgmən'teɪʃən) *n.* **1.** coloration in plants, animals, or man caused by the presence of pigments. **2.** the deposition of pigment in animals, plants, or man.

Pigmy ('pɪgmɪ) *n., pl.* **-mies.** a variant spelling of **Pygmy.**

pignut ('pɪgˌnʌt) *n.* **1.** Also called: **hognut. a.** the bitter nut of any of several North American hickory trees, esp. *Carya glabra* (**brown hickory**). **b.** any of the trees bearing such a nut. **2.** another name for **earthnut.**

pig out *vb.* (*intr., adv.*) *U.S. and Canadian slang.* to gorge oneself.

pigpen ('pɪgˌpɛn) *n.* a U.S. and Canadian word for **pigsty.**

pig-root *vb.* (*intr.*) *N.Z.* another term for **pig-jump.**

pigs (pɪgz) *interj. Austral. taboo slang.* an expression of derision or disagreement. Also called: **pig's arse, pig's bum.**

pig's ear *n.* **1.** *Cockney rhyming slang.* beer. **2.** something that has been badly or clumsily done; a botched job (esp. in the phrase **make a pig's ear of (something)**).

pig's fry *n.* the heart, liver, lights, and sweetbreads of a pig cooked, esp. fried, together.

pigskin ('pɪgˌskɪn) *n.* **1.** the skin of the domestic pig. **2.** leather made of this skin. **3.** *U.S. and Canadian informal.* a football. ~*adj.* **4.** made of pigskin.

pigstick ('pɪgˌstɪk) *vb.* (*intr.*) (esp. in India) to hunt and spear wild boar, esp. from horseback.

pigsticker ('pɪgˌstɪkə) *n.* **1.** a person that hunts wild boar. **2.** *Slang.* a large sharp hunting knife.

pigsticking ('pɪgˌstɪkɪŋ) *n.* the sport of hunting wild boar.

pigsty ('pɪgˌstaɪ) *or U.S. and Canadian* **pigpen** *n., pl.* **-sties. 1.** a pen for pigs; sty. **2.** *Brit.* a dirty or untidy place.

pigswill ('pɪgˌswɪl) *n.* waste food or other edible matter fed to pigs. Also called: **pig's wash.**

pigtail ('pɪgˌteɪl) *n.* **1.** a bunch of hair or one of two bunches on either side of the face, worn loose or plaited. **2.** a twisted roll of tobacco. —'**pigˌtailed** *adj.*

pigweed ('pɪgˌwiːd) *n.* **1.** Also called: **redroot.** any of several coarse North American amaranthaceous weeds of the genus *Amaranthus,* esp. *A. retroflexus,* having hairy leaves and green flowers. **2.** a U.S. name for **fat hen.**

pika ('paɪkə) *n.* any burrowing lagomorph mammal of the family *Ochotonidae* of mountainous regions of North America and Asia, having short rounded ears, a rounded body, and rudimentary tail. Also called: **cony.** [C19: from Tungusic *piika*]

pikau (ˈpiːkaʊ) *n. N.Z.* a pack, knapsack, or rucksack. [Maori]
pike[1] (paɪk) *n., pl.* **pike** *or* **pikes.** **1.** any of several large predatory freshwater teleost fishes of the genus *Esox,* esp. *E. lucius* (**northern pike**), having a broad flat snout, strong teeth, and an elongated body covered with small scales: family *Esocidae.* **2.** any of various similar fishes. [C14: short for *pikefish,* from Old English *pīc* point, with reference to the shape of its jaw]
pike[2] (paɪk) *n.* **1.** a medieval weapon consisting of an iron or steel spearhead joined to a long pole, the pikestaff. **2.** a point or spike. ~*vb.* **3.** (*tr.*) to stab or pierce using a pike. [Old English *pīc* point, of obscure origin]
pike[3] (paɪk) *n.* short for **turnpike** (senses 1, 2).
pike[4] (paɪk) *n. Northern English dialect.* a pointed or conical hill. [Old English *pīc,* of obscure origin]
pike[5] (paɪk) *or* **piked** (paɪkt) *adj.* (of the body position of a diver) bent at the hips but with the legs straight. [C20: of obscure origin]
pikelet (ˈpaɪklɪt) *n.* a dialect word for a **crumpet** (sense 1). [C18: from Welsh *bara pyglyd* pitchy bread]
pikeman (ˈpaɪkmən) *n., pl.* **-men.** (formerly) a soldier armed with a pike.
pikeperch (ˈpaɪkˌpɜːtʃ) *n., pl.* **-perch** *or* **-perches.** any of various pikelike freshwater teleost fishes of the genera *Stizostedion* (or *Lucioperca*), such as *S. lucioperca* of Europe: family *Percidae* (perches).
piker (ˈpaɪkə) *n. Slang.* **1.** *Austral.* a wild bullock. **2.** *U.S., Austral., and N.Z.* a lazy person; shirker. **3.** a mean person. **4.** *N.Z.* a useless person; failure. [C19: perhaps related to PIKE[3]]
pikestaff (ˈpaɪkˌstɑːf) *n.* the wooden handle of a pike.
pilaster (pɪˈlæstə) *n.* a shallow rectangular column attached to the face of a wall. [C16: from French *pilastre,* from Latin *pīla* pillar] —**piˈlastered** *adj.*
pilau (pɪˈlaʊ), **pilaf, pilaff** (ˈpɪlæf), **pilao** (pɪˈlaʊ), *or* **pilaw** (pɪˈlɔː) *n.* a dish originating from the East, consisting of rice flavoured with spices and cooked in stock, to which meat, poultry, or fish may be added. [C17: from Turkish *pilāw,* from Persian]
pilch (pɪltʃ) *n. Brit., archaic.* **1.** an outer garment, originally one made of skin. **2.** an infant's outer wrapping, worn over the napkin. [C17: from Old English *pylce* a garment made of skin and fur, from Late Latin *pellicia,* from Latin *pellis* fur]
pilchard (ˈpɪltʃəd) *n.* a European food fish, *Sardina* (or *Clupea*) *pilchardus,* with a rounded body covered with large scales: family *Clupeidae* (herrings). [C16 *pylcher,* of obscure origin]
pile[1] (paɪl) *n.* **1.** a collection of objects laid on top of one another or of other material stacked vertically; heap; mound. **2.** *Informal.* a large amount of money (esp. in the phrase **make a pile**). **3.** (*often pl.*) *Informal.* a large amount: *a pile of work.* **4.** a less common word for **pyre. 5.** a large building or group of buildings. **6.** short for **voltaic pile. 7.** *Physics.* a structure of uranium and a moderator used for producing atomic energy; nuclear reactor. **8.** *Metallurgy.* an arrangement of wrought-iron bars that are to be heated and worked into a single bar. **9.** the point of an arrow. ~*vb.* **10.** (often foll. by *up*) to collect or be collected into or as if into a pile: *snow piled up in the drive.* **11.** (*intr.;* foll. by *in, into, off, out,* etc.) to move in a group, esp. in a hurried or disorganized manner: *to pile off the bus.* **12. pile arms.** to prop a number of rifles together, muzzles together and upwards, butts forming the base. **13. pile it on.** *Informal.* to exaggerate. ~See also **pile up.** [C15: via Old French from Latin *pīla* stone pier]
pile[2] (paɪl) *n.* **1.** a long column of timber, concrete, or steel that is driven into the ground to provide a foundation for a structure. **2.** *Heraldry.* an ordinary shaped like a wedge, usually displayed point-downwards. ~*vb.* (*tr.*) **3.** to drive (piles) into the ground. **4.** to provide or support (a structure) with piles. [Old English *pīl,* from Latin *pīlum*]
pile[3] (paɪl) *n.* **1.** *Textiles.* **a.** the yarns in a fabric that stand up or out from the weave, as in carpeting, velvet, etc. **b.** one of these yarns. **2.** soft fine hair, fur, wool, etc. [C15: from Anglo-Norman *pyle,* from Latin *pilus* hair]
pilea (ˈpɪlɪə) *n.* any plant of the tropical annual or perennial genus *Pilea,* esp. *P. muscosa,* the artillery or gunpowder plant, which releases a cloud of pollen when shaken; some others are grown for their ornamental foliage: family *Urticaceae.* [New Latin, from Greek *pilos* cap (from the shape of the segments of the perianth)]
pileate (ˈpaɪlɪɪt, -ˌeɪt, ˈpɪl-) *or* **pileated** (ˈpaɪlɪˌeɪtɪd, ˈpɪl-) *adj.* **1.** (of birds) having a crest. **2.** *Botany.* having a pileus. [C18: from Latin *pīleātus* wearing a felt cap, from PILEUS]
pile-driver *n.* **1.** a machine that drives piles into the ground either by repeatedly allowing a heavy weight to fall on the head of the pile or by using a steam hammer. **2.** *Informal.* a forceful punch or kick.
pileous (ˈpaɪlɪəs, ˈpɪl-) *adj. Biology.* **1.** hairy. **2.** of or relating to hair. [C19: ultimately from Latin *pilus* a hair]
piles (paɪlz) *pl. n.* a nontechnical name for **haemorrhoids.** [C15: from Latin *pilae* balls (referring to the appearance of external piles)]
pile shoe *n.* an iron casting shaped to a point and fitted to a lower end of a wooden or concrete pile. Also called: **shoe.**
pileum (ˈpaɪlɪəm, ˈpɪl-) *n., pl.* **-lea** (-lɪə). the top of a bird's head from the base of the bill to the occiput. [C19: New Latin, from Latin PILEUS]
pile up *vb.* (*adv.*) **1.** to gather or be gathered in a pile; accumulate. **2.** *Informal.* to crash or cause to crash. ~*n.* **pile-up. 3.** *Informal.* a multiple collision of vehicles.
pileus (ˈpaɪlɪəs, ˈpɪl-) *n., pl.* **-lei** (-lɪˌaɪ). the upper cap-shaped part of a mushroom or similar spore-producing body. [C18 (botanical use): New Latin, from Latin: felt cap]
pilewort (ˈpaɪlˌwɜːt) *n.* any of several plants, such as lesser celandine, thought to be effective in treating piles.
pilfer (ˈpɪlfə) *vb.* to steal (minor items), esp. in small quantities. [C14 *pylfre* (n.) from Old French *pelfre* booty; see PELF] —**ˈpilferer** *n.* —**ˈpilfering** *n.*
pilferage (ˈpɪlfərɪdʒ) *n.* **1.** the act or practice of stealing small quantities or articles. **2.** the amount so stolen.
pilgarlic (pɪlˈgɑːlɪk) *n.* **1.** *Obsolete.* a bald head or a man with a bald head. **2.** *Dialect.* a pitiable person. [C16: literally: peeled garlic]
pilgrim (ˈpɪlgrɪm) *n.* **1.** a person who undertakes a journey to a sacred place as an act of religious devotion. **2.** any wayfarer. [C12: from Provençal *pelegrin,* from Latin *peregrīnus* foreign, from *per* through + *ager* field, land; see PEREGRINE]
pilgrimage (ˈpɪlgrɪmɪdʒ) *n.* **1.** a journey to a shrine or other sacred place. **2.** a journey or long search made for exalted or sentimental reasons. ~*vb.* **3.** (*intr.*) to make a pilgrimage.
Pilgrim Fathers *or* **Pilgrims** *pl. n.* **the.** the English Puritans who sailed on the Mayflower to New England, where they founded Plymouth Colony in SE Massachusetts (1620).
pili[1] (pɪˈliː) *n., pl.* **-lis. 1.** a burseraceous Philippine tree, *Canarium ovatum,* with edible seeds resembling almonds. **2.** Also called: **pili nut.** the seed of this tree. [from Tagalog]
pili[2] (ˈpaɪlɪ) *pl. n., sing.* **pilus** (ˈpaɪləs). *Bacteriol.* short curled hairlike processes on the surface of certain bacteria that are involved in conjugation and the attachment of the bacteria to other cells. [C20: from Latin: hairs]
piliferous (paɪˈlɪfərəs) *adj.* **1.** (esp. of plants or their parts) bearing or ending in a hair or hairs. **2.** designating the outer layer of root epidermis, which bears the root hairs. [C19: from Latin *pilus* hair + -FEROUS. Compare PILE[3]]
piliform (ˈpɪlɪˌfɔːm) *adj. Botany.* resembling a long hair.
piling (ˈpaɪlɪŋ) *n.* **1.** the act of driving piles. **2.** a number of piles. **3.** a structure formed of piles.
pill[1] (pɪl) *n.* **1.** a small spherical or ovoid mass of a medicinal substance, intended to be swallowed whole. **2. the.** (*sometimes cap.*) *Informal.* an oral contraceptive. **3.** something unpleasant that must be endured (esp. in the phrase **bitter pill to swallow**). **4.** *Slang.* a ball or disc. **5.** *Slang.* an unpleasant or boring person. ~*vb.* **6.** (*tr.*) to give pills to. **7.** (*tr.*) to make pills of. **8.** (*intr.*) to form into small balls. **9.** (*tr.*) *Slang.* to blackball. ~See also **pills.** [C15: from Middle Flemish *pille,* from Latin *pilula* a little ball, from *pila* ball]
pill[2] (pɪl) *vb.* **1.** *Archaic or dialect.* to peel or skin (something). **2.** *Archaic.* to pillage or plunder (a place). **3.** *Obsolete.* to make or become bald. [Old English *pilian,* from Latin *pilāre* to strip]
pillage (ˈpɪlɪdʒ) *vb.* **1.** to rob (a town, village, etc.) of (booty or spoils), esp. during a war. ~*n.* **2.** the act of pillaging. **3.** something obtained by pillaging; booty. [C14: via Old French from *piller* to despoil, probably from *peille* rag, from Latin *pīleus* felt cap] —**ˈpillager** *n.*
pillar (ˈpɪlə) *n.* **1.** an upright structure of stone, brick, metal, etc., that supports a superstructure or is used for ornamentation. **2.** something resembling this in shape or function: *a pillar of stones; a pillar of smoke.* **3.** a tall, slender, usually sheer rock column, forming a separate top. **4.** a prominent supporter: *a pillar of the Church.* **5. from pillar to post.** from one place to another. ~*vb.* **6.** (*tr.*) to support with or as if with pillars. [C13: from Old French *pilier,* from Latin *pīla;* see PILE[1]]
pillar box *n.* **1.** (in Britain) a red pillar-shaped public letter box situated on a pavement. ~*adj.* **pillar-box. 2.** characteristic of a pillar box (in the phrase **pillar-box red**).
pill beetle *n.* a very common beetle, *Byrrhus pilula,* typical of the family *Byrrhidae,* that can feign death by withdrawing legs and antennae into grooves underneath the oval body.
pillbox (ˈpɪlˌbɒks) *n.* **1.** a box for pills. **2.** a small enclosed fortified emplacement, usually made of reinforced concrete. **3.** a small round hat, now worn esp. by women.
pill bug *n.* any of various woodlice of the genera *Armadillidium* and *Oniscus,* capable of rolling up into a ball when disturbed.
pillion (ˈpɪljən) *n.* **1.** a seat or place behind the rider of a motorcycle, scooter, horse, etc. ~*adv.* **2.** on a pillion: *to ride pillion.* [C16: from Gaelic; compare Scottish *pillean,* Irish *pillīn* couch; related to Latin *pellis* skin]
pilliwinks (ˈpɪlɪˌwɪŋks) *pl. n.* a medieval instrument of torture for the fingers and thumbs. [C14: of uncertain origin]
pillock (ˈpɪlək) *n. Brit. slang.* a stupid or annoying person. [C14: from Scandinavian dialect *pillicock* penis]
pillory (ˈpɪlərɪ) *n., pl.* **-ries. 1.** a wooden framework into which offenders were formerly locked by the neck and wrists and exposed to public abuse and ridicule. **2.** exposure to public scorn or abuse. ~*vb.* **-ries, -rying, -ried.** (*tr.*) **3.** to expose to public scorn or ridicule. **4.** to punish by putting in a pillory. [C13: from Anglo-Latin *pillorium,* from Old French *pilori,* of uncertain origin; related to Provençal *espillori*]
pillow (ˈpɪləʊ) *n.* **1.** a cloth case stuffed with feathers, foam rubber, etc., used to support the head, esp. during sleep. **2.** Also

called: **cushion.** a padded cushion or board on which pillow lace is made. **3.** anything like a pillow in shape or function. ~*vb.* (*tr.*) **4.** to rest (one's head) on or as if on a pillow. **5.** to serve as a pillow for. [Old English *pylwe,* from Latin *pulvīnus* cushion; compare German *Pfühl*]

pillow block *n.* a block, such as a simple journal, that supports a shaft.

pillowcase ('pɪləʊˌkeɪs) *or* **pillowslip** ('pɪləʊˌslɪp) *n.* a removable washable cover of cotton, linen, nylon, etc., for a pillow.

pillow fight *n.* a mock fight in which participants thump each other with pillows.

pillow lace *n.* lace made by winding thread around bobbins on a padded cushion or board. Compare **point lace.**

pillow lava *n.* lava that has solidified under water, having a characteristic structure comprising a series of close-fitting pillow-shaped masses.

pillow sham *n. Chiefly U.S.* a decorative cover for a bed pillow.

pillow talk *n.* intimate conversation in bed.

pills (pɪlz) *pl. n.* a taboo slang word for **testicles.**

pillwort ('pɪlˌwɜːt) *n.* a small Eurasian water fern, *Pilularia globulifera,* with globular spore-producing bodies. [C19: from PILL[1] + WORT]

pilocarpine (ˌpaɪləʊ'kɑːpaɪn, -pɪn) *or* **pilocarpin** (ˌpaɪləʊ'kɑːpɪn) *n.* an alkaloid extracted from the leaves of the jaborandi tree, formerly used to induce sweating. Formula: $C_{11}H_{16}N_2O_2$. [C19: from New Latin *Pilocarpus* genus name, from Greek *pilos* hair + *karpos* fruit]

pilomotor (ˌpaɪləʊ'məʊtə) *adj. Physiol.* causing movement of hairs: *pilomotor nerves.*

pilose ('paɪləʊz) *or* **pilous** *adj. Biology.* covered with fine soft hairs: *pilose leaves.* [C18: from Latin *pilōsus,* from *pilus* hair] —**pilosity** (paɪ'lɒsɪtɪ) *n.*

pilot ('paɪlət) *n.* **1. a.** a person who is qualified to operate an aircraft or spacecraft in flight. **b.** (*as modifier*): *pilot error.* **2. a.** a person who is qualified to steer or guide a ship into or out of a port, river mouth, etc. **b.** (*as modifier*): *a pilot ship.* **3.** a person who steers a ship. **4.** a person who acts as a leader or guide. **5.** *Machinery.* a guide, often consisting of a tongue or dowel, used to assist in joining two mating parts together. **6.** *Machinery.* a plug gauge for measuring an internal diameter. **7.** *Films.* a colour test strip accompanying black-and-white rushes from colour originals. **8.** an experimental programme on radio or television. **9.** See **pilot film. 10.** (*modifier*) used in or serving as a test or trial: *a pilot project.* **11.** (*modifier*) serving as a guide: *a pilot beacon.* ~*vb.* (*tr.*) **12.** to act as pilot of. **13.** to control the course of. **14.** to guide or lead (a project, people, etc.). [C16: from French *pilote,* from Medieval Latin *pilotus,* ultimately from Greek *pēdon* oar; related to Greek *pous* foot]

pilotage ('paɪlətɪdʒ) *n.* **1.** the act of piloting an aircraft or ship. **2.** a pilot's fee. **3.** the navigation of an aircraft by the observation of ground features and use of charts.

pilot balloon *n.* a meteorological balloon used to observe air currents.

pilot bird *n.* a warbler of forest floors in SE Australia, *Pycnoptilus floccosus,* named from its alleged habit of accompanying the superb lyrebird.

pilot biscuit *n.* another term for **hardtack.**

pilot cloth *n.* a type of thick blue cloth used esp. to make sailor's coats.

pilot engine *n.* a locomotive that leads one or more other locomotives at the head of a train of coaches or wagons.

pilot film *n.* a film of short duration serving as a guide to a projected series.

pilot fish *n.* **1.** a small carangid fish, *Naucrates ductor,* of tropical and subtropical seas, marked with dark vertical bands: often accompanies sharks and other large fishes. **2.** any of various similar or related fishes.

pilot house *n. Nautical.* an enclosed structure on the bridge of a vessel from which it can be navigated; wheelhouse.

piloting ('paɪlətɪŋ) *n.* **1.** the navigational handling of a ship near land using buoys, soundings, landmarks, etc., or the finding of a ship's position by such means. **2.** the occupation of a pilot.

pilot lamp *n.* a small light in an electric circuit or device that lights up when the circuit is closed or when certain conditions prevail.

pilot light *n.* **1.** a small auxiliary flame that ignites the main burner of a gas appliance when the control valve opens. **2.** a small electric light used as an indicator.

pilot officer *n.* the most junior commissioned rank in the British Royal Air Force and in certain other air forces.

pilot plant *n.* a small-scale industrial plant in which problems can be identified and solved before the full-scale plant is built.

pilot study *n.* a small-scale experiment or set of observations undertaken to decide how and whether to launch a full-scale project.

pilot whale *n.* any of several black toothed whales of the genus *Globicephala,* such as *G. melaena,* that occur in all seas except polar seas: family *Delphinidae.* Also called: **black whale, blackfish.**

pilous ('paɪləs) *adj.* a variant of **pilose.**

Pils (pɪlz, pɪls) *n.* a type of lager-like beer. [C20: abbrev. of PILSNER]

Pilsner ('pɪlznə) *or* **Pilsener** *n.* a type of pale beer with a strong flavour of hops. [named after *Pilsen* (Plzeň), W Czechoslovakia, where it was originally brewed]

Piltdown man ('pɪltˌdaʊn) *n.* an advanced hominid postulated from fossil bones found in Sussex in 1912, but shown by modern dating methods in 1953 to be a hoax.

pilule ('pɪljuːl) *n.* a small pill. [C16: via French from Latin *pilula* little ball, from *pila* ball] —'**pilular** *adj.*

pimento (pɪ'mɛntəʊ) *n., pl.* **-tos.** another name for **allspice** or **pimiento.** [C17: from Spanish *pimiento* pepper plant, from Medieval Latin *pigmenta* spiced drink, from Latin *pigmentum* PIGMENT]

pi meson *n.* another name for **pion.**

pimiento (pɪ'mjɛntəʊ, -'mɛn-) *n., pl.* **-tos.** a Spanish pepper, *Capsicum annuum,* with a red fruit used raw in salads, cooked as a vegetable, and as a stuffing for green olives. Also called: **pimento.** [variant of PIMENTO]

pimp[1] (pɪmp) *n.* **1.** a man who solicits for a prostitute or brothel and lives off the earnings. **2.** a man who procures sexual gratification for another; procurer; pander. ~*vb.* **3.** (*intr.*) to act as a pimp. [C17: of unknown origin]

pimp[2] (pɪmp) *Slang, chiefly Austral. and N.Z.* ~*n.* **1.** a spy or informer. ~*vb.* **2.** (*intr.*; often foll. by *on*) to inform (on). [of unknown origin]

pimpernel ('pɪmpəˌnɛl, -nᵊl) *n.* **1.** any of several plants of the primulaceous genus *Anagallis,* such as the scarlet pimpernel, typically having small star-shaped flowers. **2.** any of several similar and related plants, such as *Lysimachia nemorum* (**yellow pimpernel**). [C15: from Old French *pimpernelle,* ultimately from Latin *piper* PEPPER; compare Old English *pipeneale*]

pimple ('pɪmpᵊl) *n.* a small round usually inflamed swelling of the skin. [C14: related to Old English *pipilian* to break out in spots; compare Latin *papula* pimple] —'**pimpled** *adj.* —'**pimply** *adj.* —'**pimpliness** *n.*

pin (pɪn) *n.* **1. a.** a short stiff straight piece of wire pointed at one end and either rounded or having a flattened head at the other: used mainly for fastening pieces of cloth, paper, etc., esp. temporarily. **b.** (*in combination*): *pinhole.* **2.** short for **cotter pin, hairpin, panel pin, rolling pin,** or **safety pin. 3.** an ornamental brooch, esp. a narrow one. **4.** a badge worn fastened to the clothing by a pin. **5.** something of little or no importance (esp. in the phrases **not care** *or* **give a pin (for)**). **6.** a peg or dowel. **7.** anything resembling a pin in shape, function, etc. **8.** (in various bowling games) a usually club-shaped wooden object set up in groups as a target. **9.** Also called: **safety pin.** a clip on a hand grenade that prevents its detonation until removed or released. **10.** *Nautical.* **a.** See **belaying pin. b.** the axle of a sheave. **c.** the sliding closure for a shackle. **11.** *Music.* a metal tuning peg on a piano, the end of which is inserted into a detachable key by means of which it is turned. **12.** *Surgery.* a metal rod, esp. of stainless steel, for holding together adjacent ends of fractured bones during healing. **13.** *Chess.* a position in which a piece is pinned against a more valuable piece or the king. **14.** *Golf.* the flagpole marking the hole on a green. **15.** the cylindrical part of a key that enters a lock. **16.** *Wrestling.* a position in which a person is held tight or immobile, esp. with both shoulders touching the ground. **17.** a dovetail tenon used to make a dovetail joint. **18.** (in Britain) a miniature beer cask containing 4½ gallons. **19.** (*usually pl.*) *Informal.* a leg. **20. be put to the pin on one's collar.** *Irish.* to be forced to make an extreme effort. ~*vb.* **pins, pinning, pinned.** (*tr.*) **21.** to attach, hold, or fasten with or as if with a pin or pins. **22.** to transfix with a pin, spear, etc. **23.** (foll. by *on*) *Informal.* to place (the blame for something): *he pinned the charge on his accomplice.* **24.** *Chess.* to cause (an enemy piece) to be effectively immobilized by attacking it with a queen, rook, or bishop so that moving it would reveal a check or expose a more valuable piece to capture. **25.** Also: **underpin.** to support (masonry), as by driving in wedges over a beam. ~See also **pin down.** [Old English *pinn;* related to Old High German *pfinn,* Old Norse *pinni* nail]

PIN (pɪn) *n. acronym for* personal identification number: a number used by a holder of a cash card or credit card used in EFTPOS.

p-i-n *abbrev. for* p-type, intrinsic, n-type: a form of construction of semiconductor devices.

pinaceous (paɪ'neɪʃəs) *adj.* of, relating to, or belonging to the *Pinaceae,* a family of conifers with needle-like leaves: includes pine, spruce, fir, larch, and cedar. [C19: via New Latin from Latin *pīnus* a pine]

piña cloth ('piːnjə) *n.* a fine fabric made from the fibres of the pineapple leaf. [C19: from Spanish *piña* pineapple]

piña colada ('piːnjə kə'lɑːdə) *n.* a drink consisting of pineapple juice, coconut, and rum. [C20: from Spanish, literally: strained pineapple]

pinafore ('pɪnəˌfɔː) *n.* **1.** *Chiefly Brit.* an apron, esp. one with a bib. **2.** *Chiefly Brit.* short for **pinafore dress. 3.** *Chiefly U.S.* an overdress buttoning at the back. [C18: from PIN + AFORE]

pinafore dress *n. Brit.* a sleeveless dress worn over a blouse or sweater. Often shortened to **pinafore.** U.S. and Canadian name: **jumper.**

pinaster (paɪ'næstə, pɪ-) *n.* a Mediterranean pine tree, *Pinus pinaster,* with paired needles and prickly cones. Also called:

maritime (*or* **cluster**) **pinaster.** [C16: from Latin: wild pine, from *pīnus* pine]

pinball ('pɪn,bɔːl) *n.* **a.** a game in which the player shoots a small ball through several hazards on a table, electrically operated machine, etc. **b.** (*as modifier*): *a pinball machine.*

pince-nez ('pæns,neɪ, 'pɪns-; *French* pɛ̃sne) *n., pl.* **pince-nez.** eyeglasses that are held in place only by means of a clip over the bridge of the nose. [C19: French, literally: pinch-nose]

pincer movement ('pɪnsə) *n.* a military tactical movement in which two columns of an army follow a curved route towards each other with the aim of isolating and surrounding an enemy. Also called: **envelopment.**

pincers ('pɪnsəz) *pl. n.* **1.** Also called: **pair of pincers.** a gripping tool consisting of two hinged arms with handles at one end and, at the other, curved bevelled jaws that close on the workpiece: used esp. for extracting nails. **2.** the pair or pairs of jointed grasping appendages in lobsters and certain other arthropods. [C14: from Old French *pinceour,* from Old French *pincier* to PINCH]

pinch (pɪntʃ) *vb.* **1.** to press (something, esp. flesh) tightly between two surfaces, esp. between a finger and the thumb (see **nip**[1]). **2.** to confine, squeeze, or painfully press (toes, fingers, etc.) because of lack of space: *these shoes pinch.* **3.** (*tr.*) to cause stinging pain to: *the cold pinched his face.* **4.** (*tr.*) to make thin or drawn-looking, as from grief, lack of food, etc. **5.** (usually foll. by *on*) to provide (oneself or another person) with meagre allowances, amounts, etc. **6. pinch pennies.** to live frugally because of meanness or to economize. **7.** (*tr.*) *Nautical.* to sail (a sailing vessel) so close to the wind that her sails begin to luff and she loses way. **8.** (*intr.*; sometimes foll. by *out*) (of a vein of ore) to narrow or peter out. **9.** (usually foll. by *off, out,* or *back*) to remove the tips of (buds, shoots, etc.) to correct or encourage growth. **10.** (*tr.*) *Informal.* to steal or take without asking. **11.** (*tr.*) *Informal.* to arrest. ~*n.* **12.** a squeeze or sustained nip. **13.** the quantity of a substance, such as salt, that can be taken between a thumb and finger. **14.** a very small quantity. **15.** a critical situation; predicament; emergency: *if it comes to the pinch we'll have to manage.* **16.** (usually preceded by *the*) sharp, painful, or extreme stress, need, etc.: *feeling the pinch of poverty.* **17.** See **pinch bar. 18.** *Slang.* a robbery. **19.** *Slang.* a police raid or arrest. **20. at a pinch.** if absolutely necessary. **21. with a pinch** *or* **grain of salt.** without wholly believing; sceptically. [C16: probably from Old Norman French *pinchier* (unattested); related to Old French *pincier* to pinch; compare Late Latin *punctiāre* to prick]

pinch bar *n.* a crowbar with a lug formed on it to provide a fulcrum.

pinchbeck ('pɪntʃ,bɛk) *n.* **1.** an alloy of copper and zinc, used as imitation gold. **2.** a spurious or cheap imitation; sham. ~*adj.* **3.** made of pinchbeck. **4.** sham, spurious, or cheap. [C18 (the alloy), C19 (something spurious): after Christopher *Pinchbeck* (?1670–1732), English watchmaker who invented it]

pinchcock ('pɪntʃ,kɒk) *n.* a clamp used to compress a flexible tube to control the flow of fluid through it.

pinch effect *n.* the constriction of a beam of charged particles, caused by a force on each particle due to its motion in the magnetic field generated by the movement of the other particles.

pinch-hit *vb.* **-hits, -hitting, -hit.** (*intr.*) **1.** *Baseball.* to bat as a substitute for the scheduled batter. **2.** *U.S. and Canadian informal.* to act as a substitute. —**pinch hitter** *n.*

pinchpenny ('pɪntʃ,pɛnɪ) *adj.* **1.** niggardly; miserly. ~*n., pl.* **-nies. 2.** a miserly person; niggard.

pin curl *n.* a small section of hair wound in a circle and secured with a hairpin to set it in a curl.

pincushion ('pɪn,kʊʃən) *n.* a small well-padded cushion in which pins are stuck ready for use.

pindan ('pɪn,dæn) *n.* **1.** a desert region of Western Australia. **2.** the vegetation growing in this region. [from a native Australian language]

Pindaric (pɪn'dærɪk) *adj.* **1.** of, relating to, or resembling the style of Pindar (?518–?438 B.C.), Greek lyric poet. **2.** *Prosody.* having a complex metrical structure, either regular or irregular. ~*n.* **3.** See **Pindaric ode.**

Pindaric ode *n.* a form of ode associated with Pindar consisting of a triple unit or groups of triple units, with a strophe and an antistrophe of identical structure followed by an epode of a different structure. Often shortened to **Pindaric.**

pindling ('pɪndlɪŋ) *adj. Dialect.* **1.** *Western Brit.* peevish or fractious. **2.** *U.S.* sickly or puny. [C19: perhaps changed from *spindling*]

pin down *vb.* (*tr., adv.*) **1.** to force (someone) to make a decision or carry out a promise. **2.** to define clearly: *he had a vague suspicion that he couldn't quite pin down.* **3.** to confine to a place: *the fallen tree pinned him down.*

pine[1] (paɪn) *n.* **1.** any evergreen resinous coniferous tree of the genus *Pinus,* of the N hemisphere, with long needle-shaped leaves and brown cones: family *Pinaceae.* See also **longleaf pine, nut pine, pitch pine, Scots pine. 2.** any other tree or shrub of the family *Pinaceae.* **3.** the wood of any of these trees. **4.** any of various similar but unrelated plants, such as ground pine and screw pine. [Old English *pīn,* from Latin *pīnus* pine]

pine[2] (paɪn) *vb.* **1.** (*intr.*; often foll. by *for* or an infinitive) to feel great longing or desire; yearn. **2.** (*intr.*; often foll. by *away*) to become ill, feeble, or thin through worry, longing, etc. **3.** (*tr.*) *Archaic.* to mourn or grieve for. ~*n.* **4.** *Archaic.* a deep longing. [Old English *pīnian* to torture, from *pīn* pain, from Medieval Latin *pēna,* from Latin *poena* PAIN]

pineal ('pɪnɪəl, paɪ'niːəl) *adj.* **1.** resembling a pine cone. **2.** of or relating to the pineal gland. [C17: via French from Latin *pīnea* pine cone]

pineal eye *n.* an outgrowth of the pineal gland that forms an eyelike structure on the top of the head in certain cold-blooded vertebrates.

pineal gland *or* **body** *n.* a pea-sized organ in the brain, situated beneath the posterior part of the corpus callosum, that secretes melatonin into the bloodstream. Technical names: **epiphysis, epiphysis cerebri.**

pineapple ('paɪn,æpᵊl) *n.* **1.** a tropical American bromeliaceous plant, *Ananas comosus,* cultivated in the tropics for its large fleshy edible fruit. **2.** the fruit of this plant, consisting of an inflorescence clustered around a fleshy axis and surmounted by a tuft of leaves. **3.** *Military slang.* a hand grenade. [C14 *pinappel* pine cone; C17: applied to the fruit because of its appearance]

pineapple weed *n.* an Asian plant, *Matricaria matricarioides,* naturalized in Europe and North America, having greenish-yellow flower heads, and smelling of pineapple when crushed: family *Compositae* (composites).

pine cone *n.* the seed-producing structure of a pine tree. See **cone** (sense 3a).

pine end *n. Dialect.* the gable or gable end of a building.

pine marten *n.* a marten, *Martes martes,* of N European and Asian coniferous woods, having dark brown fur with a creamy-yellow patch on the throat. See also **sweet marten.**

pinene ('paɪniːn) *n.* either of two isomeric terpenes, found in many essential oils and constituting the main part of oil of turpentine. The commonest structural isomer (**α-pinene**) is used in the manufacture of camphor, solvents, plastics, and insecticides. Formula: $C_{10}H_{16}$. [C20: from PINE[1] + -ENE]

pine needle *n.* any of the fine pointed leaves of a pine.

pinery ('paɪnərɪ) *n., pl.* **-neries. 1.** a place, esp. a hothouse, where pineapples are grown. **2.** a forest of pine trees, esp. one cultivated for timber.

pine tar *n.* a brown or black semisolid or viscous substance, produced by the destructive distillation of pine wood, used in roofing compositions, paints, medicines, etc.

pinetum (paɪ'niːtəm) *n., pl.* **-ta** (-tə). an area of land where pine trees and other conifers are grown. [C19: from Latin, from *pīnus* PINE[1]]

pin-eyed *adj.* (of flowers, esp. primulas) having the stigma in the mouth of the corolla, on the end of a long style with the stamens lower in the tube. Compare **thrum-eyed.**

pinfall ('pɪn,fɔːl) *n. Wrestling.* another name for **fall** (sense 48).

pinfeather ('pɪn,fɛðə) *n. Ornithol.* a feather emerging from the skin and still enclosed in its horny sheath.

pinfish ('pɪn,fɪʃ) *n., pl.* **-fish** *or* **-fishes.** a small porgy, *Lagodon rhomboides,* occurring off the SE North American coast of the Atlantic. Also called: **sailor's choice.** [so named because it has spines]

pinfold ('pɪn,fəʊld) *n.* **1. a.** a pound for stray cattle. **b.** a fold or pen for sheep or cattle. ~*vb.* **2.** (*tr.*) to gather or confine in or as if in a pinfold. [Old English *pundfald,* from POUND[3] + FOLD[2]]

ping (pɪŋ) *n.* **1.** a short high-pitched resonant sound, as of a bullet striking metal or a sonar echo. ~*vb.* **2.** (*intr.*) to make such a noise. [C19: of imitative origin] —'**pinging** *adj.*

pinger ('pɪŋə) *n.* a device that makes a pinging sound, esp. one that can be preset to ring at a particular time.

pingo ('pɪŋgəʊ) *n., pl.* **-gos.** a mound of earth or gravel formed through pressure from a layer of water trapped between newly frozen ice and underlying permafrost in Arctic regions. [C20: from Eskimo]

Ping-Pong ('pɪŋ,pɒŋ) *n. Trademark.* another name for **table tennis.** Also called: **ping pong.**

pinguid ('pɪŋgwɪd) *adj.* fatty, oily, or greasy; soapy. [C17: from Latin *pinguis* fat, rich] —**pin'guidity** *n.*

pinhead ('pɪn,hɛd) *n.* **1.** the head of a pin. **2.** something very small. **3.** *Informal.* a stupid or contemptible person.

pinheaded ('pɪn,hɛdɪd) *adj. Informal.* stupid or silly. —'**pin,headedness** *n.*

pinhole ('pɪn,həʊl) *n.* **1.** a small hole made with or as if with a pin. **2.** *Archery.* the exact centre of an archery target, in the middle of the gold zone.

pinhole camera *n.* a camera with a pinhole as an aperture instead of a lens.

pinion[1] ('pɪnjən) *n.* **1.** *Chiefly poetic.* a bird's wing. **2.** the part of a bird's wing including the flight feathers. ~*vb.* (*tr.*) **3.** to hold or bind (the arms) of (a person) so as to restrain or immobilize him. **4.** to confine or shackle. **5.** to make (a bird) incapable of flight by removing that part of (the wing) from which the flight feathers grow. [C15: from Old French *pignon* wing, from Latin *pinna* wing]

pinion[2] ('pɪnjən) *n.* a cogwheel that engages with a larger wheel or rack, which it drives or by which it is driven. [C17: from French *pignon* cogwheel, from Old French *peigne* comb, from Latin *pecten* comb; see PECTEN]

pinite ('pɪnaɪt, 'paɪ-) *n.* a greyish-green or brown mineral containing amorphous aluminium and potassium sulphates. [C19: from German *Pinit,* named after the *Pini* mine, Schneeberg, Saxony]
pin joint *n.* a mechanical joint that will transmit axial load but will not transmit torque.
pink[1] (pɪŋk) *n.* **1.** any of a group of colours with a reddish hue that are of low to moderate saturation and can usually reflect or transmit a large amount of light; a pale reddish tint. **2.** pink cloth or clothing: *dressed in pink.* **3.** any of various Old World plants of the caryophyllaceous genus *Dianthus,* such as *D. plumarius* (**garden pink**), cultivated for their fragrant flowers. See also **carnation** (sense 1). **4.** any of various plants of other genera, such as the moss pink. **5.** the flower of any of these plants. **6.** the highest or best degree, condition, etc. (esp. in the phrases **in the pink of health, in the pink**). **7. a.** a huntsman's scarlet coat. **b.** a huntsman who wears a scarlet coat. *~adj.* **8.** of the colour pink. **9.** *Brit. informal.* left-wing. **10.** *U.S. derogatory.* **a.** sympathetic to or influenced by Communism. **b.** leftist or radical, esp. half-heartedly. **11.** (of a huntsman's coat) scarlet or red. *~vb.* **12.** *(intr.)* another word for **knock** (sense 7). [C16 (the flower), C18 (the colour): perhaps a shortening of PINKEYE] —'**pinkish** *adj.* —'**pinkness** *n.* —'**pinky** *adj.*
pink[2] (pɪŋk) *vb. (tr.)* **1.** to prick lightly with a sword or rapier. **2.** to decorate (leather, cloth, etc.) with a perforated or punched pattern. **3.** to cut with pinking shears. **4.** *Austral. and N.Z. informal.* to shear (a sheep) with special care so that the skin shows through. [C14: perhaps of Low German origin; compare Low German *pinken* to peck]
pink[3] (pɪŋk) *n.* a sailing vessel with a narrow overhanging transom. [C15: from Middle Dutch *pinke,* of obscure origin]
pink elephants *pl. n.* a facetious name applied to hallucinations caused by drunkenness.
pinkeye ('pɪŋk,aɪ) *n.* **1.** Also called: **acute conjunctivitis.** an acute contagious inflammation of the conjunctiva of the eye, characterized by redness, discharge, etc.: usually caused by bacterial infection. **2.** Also called: **infectious keratitis.** a similar condition affecting the cornea of horses and cattle. [C16: partial translation of obsolete Dutch *pinck oogen* small eyes]
pink-eye *or* **pink-hi** ('pɪŋk,aɪ) *n. Austral.* a holiday or celebration, esp. among Aboriginals. [C20: from a native Australian language]
pink-footed goose *n.* a Eurasian goose, *Anser brachyrhynchus,* having a reddish-brown head, pink legs, and a pink band on its black beak.
pink gin *n.* a mixture of gin and bitters.
pinkie *or* **pinky** ('pɪŋkɪ) *n., pl.* **-ies.** *Scot., U.S., and Canadian.* the little finger. [C19: from Dutch *pinkje,* diminutive of PINK[1]; compare PINKEYE]
pinking shears *pl. n.* scissors with a serrated edge on one or both blades, producing a wavy edge to material cut, thus preventing fraying.
pink noise *n.* noise containing a mixture of frequencies, but excluding higher frequencies.
pinko ('pɪŋkəʊ) *n., pl.* **-os** *or* **-oes.** *U.S. derogatory.* a person regarded as mildly left-wing.
pinkroot ('pɪŋk,ruːt) *n.* **1.** any of several loganiaceous plants of the genus *Spigelia,* esp. *S. marilandica,* of the southeastern U.S., having red-and-yellow flowers and pink roots. **2.** the powdered root of this plant, used as a vermifuge. **3.** a fungal disease of onions and related plants resulting in stunted growth and shrivelled pink roots.
pink salmon *n.* **1.** any salmon having pale pink flesh, esp. *Oncorhynchus gorbuscha,* of the Pacific Ocean. **2.** the flesh of such a fish.
pink slip *n. U.S. informal.* a notice of redundancy issued to an employee.
pin money *n.* **1.** an allowance by a husband to his wife for personal expenditure. **2.** money saved or earned to be used for incidental expenses.
pinna ('pɪnə) *n., pl.* **-nae** (-niː) *or* **-nas. 1.** any leaflet of a pinnate compound leaf. **2.** *Zoology.* a feather, wing, fin, or similarly shaped part. **3.** another name for **auricle** (sense 2). [C18: via New Latin from Latin: wing, feather, fin]
pinnace ('pɪnɪs) *n.* any of various kinds of ship's tender. [C16: from French *pinace,* apparently from Old Spanish *pinaza,* literally: something made of pine, ultimately from Latin *pīnus* pine]
pinnacle ('pɪnəkᵊl) *n.* **1.** the highest point or level, esp. of fame, success, etc. **2.** a towering peak, as of a mountain. **3.** a slender upright structure in the form of a cone, pyramid, or spire on the top of a buttress, gable, or tower. *~vb. (tr.)* **4.** to set on or as if on a pinnacle. **5.** to furnish with a pinnacle or pinnacles. **6.** to crown with a pinnacle. [C14: via Old French from Late Latin *pinnāculum* a peak, from Latin *pinna* wing]
pinnate ('pɪneɪt, 'pɪnɪt) *or* **pinnated** *adj.* **1.** like a feather in appearance. **2.** (of compound leaves) having the leaflets growing opposite each other in pairs on either side of the stem. [C18: from Latin *pinnātus,* from *pinna* feather] —'**pinnately** *adv.* —**pin'nation** *n.*
pinnati- *combining form.* pinnate or pinnately: *pinnatifid.*
pinnatifid (pɪ'nætɪfɪd) *adj.* (of leaves) pinnately divided into lobes reaching more than halfway to the midrib. —**pin'natifidly** *adv.*
pinnatipartite (pɪ,nætɪ'pɑːtaɪt) *adj.* (of leaves) pinnately divided into lobes reaching just over halfway to the midrib.
pinnatiped (pɪ'nætɪ,pɛd) *adj.* (of birds) having lobate feet.
pinnatisect (pɪ'nætɪ,sɛkt) *adj.* (of leaves) pinnately divided almost to the midrib but not into separate leaflets.
pinner ('pɪnə) *n.* **1.** a person or thing that pins. **2.** a small dainty apron. **3.** a cap with two long flaps pinned on.
pinniped ('pɪnɪ,pɛd) *or* **pinnipedian** (,pɪnɪ'piːdɪən) *adj.* **1.** of, relating to, or belonging to the *Pinnipedia,* an order of aquatic placental mammals having a streamlined body and limbs specialized as flippers: includes seals, sea lions, and the walrus. *~n.* **2.** any pinniped animal. ~Compare **fissiped.** [C19: from New Latin *pinnipēs,* from Latin *pinna* feather, fin + *pēs* foot]
pinnule ('pɪnjuːl) *or* **pinnula** ('pɪnjʊlə) *n., pl.* **pinnules** *or* **pinnulae** ('pɪnjʊ,liː). **1.** any of the lobes of a leaflet of a pinnate compound leaf, which is itself pinnately divided. **2.** *Zoology.* any feather-like part, such as any of the arms of a sea lily. [C16: from Latin *pinnula,* diminutive of *pinna* feather] —'**pinnular** *adj.*
pinny ('pɪnɪ) *n., pl.* **-nies.** a child's or informal name for **pinafore** (sense 1).
pinochle, penuchle, penuckle, *or* **pinocle** ('piːnʌkᵊl) *n.* **1.** a card game for two to four players similar to bezique. **2.** the combination of queen of spades and jack of diamonds in this game. [C19: of unknown origin]
pinole (pɪ'nəʊlɪ) *n.* (in the southwestern United States) flour made of parched ground corn, mesquite beans, sugar, etc. [from American Spanish, from Nahuatl]
pinotage ('pɪnətɑːʒ) *n. N.Z.* a type of red wine made from Pinot Noir grapes.
Pinot Noir (piː'nəʊ nwɑː) *n.* a variety of black grape, grown esp. for wine-making. [French]
pinpoint ('pɪn,pɔɪnt) *vb. (tr.)* **1.** to locate or identify exactly: *to pinpoint a problem; to pinpoint a place on a map.* *~n.* **2.** an insignificant or trifling thing. **3.** the point of a pin. **4.** *(modifier)* exact: *a pinpoint aim.*
pinprick ('pɪn,prɪk) *n.* **1.** a slight puncture made by or as if by a pin. **2.** a small irritation. *~vb.* **3.** *(tr.)* to puncture with or as if with a pin.
pin rail *n. Nautical.* a strong wooden rail or bar containing holes for belaying pins to which lines are fastened on sailing vessels. Compare **fife rail.**
pins and needles *n. (functioning as sing.) Informal.* **1.** a tingling sensation in the fingers, toes, legs, etc., caused by the return of normal blood circulation after its temporary impairment. **2. on pins and needles.** in a state of anxious suspense or nervous anticipation.
pinstripe ('pɪn,straɪp) *n.* (in textiles) **a.** a very narrow stripe in fabric or the fabric itself, used esp. for men's suits. **b.** *(as modifier): a pinstripe suit.*
pint (paɪnt) *n.* **1.** a unit of liquid measure of capacity equal to one eighth of a gallon. 1 Brit. pint is equal to 0.568 litre, 1 U.S. pint to 0.473 litre. **2.** a unit of dry measure of capacity equal to one half of a quart. 1 U.S. dry pint is equal to one sixty-fourth of a U.S. bushel or 0.5506 litre. **3.** a measure having such a capacity. **4.** *Brit. informal.* **a.** a pint of beer. **b.** a drink of beer: *he's gone out for a pint.* [C14: from Old French *pinte,* of uncertain origin; perhaps from Medieval Latin *pincta* marks used in measuring liquids, ultimately from Latin *pingere* to paint; compare Middle Low German, Middle Dutch *pinte*]
pinta[1] ('pɪntə) *n.* a tropical infectious skin disease caused by the bacterium *Treponema carateum* and characterized by the formation of papules and loss of pigmentation in circumscribed areas. Also called: **mal de pinto.** [C19: from American Spanish, from Spanish: spot, ultimately from Latin *pictus* painted, from *pingere* to paint]
pinta[2] ('paɪntə) *n. Informal.* a pint of milk. [C20: phonetic rendering of *pint of*]
pintadera (,pɪntə'dɛərə) *n.* a decorative stamp, usually made of clay, found in the Neolithic of the E Mediterranean and in many American cultures. [from Spanish, literally: an instrument for making decorations on bread, from *pintado* mottled, from *pintar* to PAINT]
pintado petrel (pɪn'tɑːdəʊ) *n.* another name for **Cape pigeon.** [C19: Portuguese: past participle of *pintar* to paint, referring to the mottled coloration]
pintail ('pɪn,teɪl) *n., pl.* **-tails** *or* **-tail.** a greyish-brown duck, *Anas acuta,* with slender pointed wings and a pointed tail.
pintle ('pɪntᵊl) *n.* **1.** a pin or bolt forming the pivot of a hinge. **2.** the link bolt, hook, or pin on a vehicle's towing bracket. **3.** the needle or plunger of the injection valve of an oil engine. [Old English *pintel* penis]
pinto ('pɪntəʊ) *U.S. and Canadian.* *~adj.* **1.** marked with patches of white; piebald. *~n., pl.* **-tos. 2.** a pinto horse. [C19: from American Spanish (originally: painted, spotted), ultimately from Latin *pingere* to paint]
pinto bean *n.* a variety of kidney bean that has mottled seeds and is grown for food and fodder in the southwestern U.S.
pint-size *or* **pint-sized** *adj. Informal.* very small; tiny.
Pintubi ('pɪntəbɪ) *n.* **1.** *(pl.* **-bi** *or* **-bis)** an Aboriginal people of the southern border area of Western Australia and the Northern Territory. **2.** the language of this people.

pin tuck *n.* a narrow ornamental fold used esp. on shirt fronts and dress bodices.

pin-up *n.* **1.** *Informal.* **a.** a picture of a sexually attractive person, esp. when partially or totally undressed. **b.** (*as modifier*): *a pin-up magazine.* **2.** *Slang.* a person who has appeared in such a picture. **3.** a photograph of a famous personality. **4.** (*modifier*) *U.S.* designed to be hung from a wall: *a pin-up lamp.*

pinwheel ('pɪnˌwiːl) *n.* **1.** another name for **Catherine wheel** (sense 1). **2.** a cogwheel whose teeth are formed by small pins projecting either axially or radially from the rim of the wheel. **3.** the U.S. and Canadian name for **windmill** (sense 3).

pinwork ('pɪnˌwɜːk) *n.* (in needlepoint lace) the fine raised stitches.

pinworm ('pɪnˌwɜːm) *n.* a parasitic nematode worm, *Enterobius vermicularis,* infecting the colon, rectum, and anus of humans: family *Oxyuridae.* Also called: **threadworm.**

pin wrench *n.* a wrench fitted with a cylindrical pin that registers in a hole in the part to be rotated, used to improve the application of the turning moment.

pinxit *Latin.* ('pɪŋksɪt) he (or she) painted it: an inscription sometimes found on paintings following the artist's name.

piny ('paɪnɪ) *adj.* **pinier, piniest.** of, resembling, or covered with pine trees.

Pinyin ('pɪn'jɪn) *n.* a system of romanized spelling developed in China in 1958: used to transliterate Chinese characters into the Roman alphabet.

piolet (pjəʊ'leɪ) *n.* a type of ice axe. [C19: from French (Savoy) dialect *piola* axe]

pion ('paɪɒn) *or* **pi meson** *n. Physics.* a meson having a positive or negative charge and a rest mass 273 times that of the electron, or no charge and a rest mass 264 times that of the electron. [C20: from Greek letter PI + ON]

pioneer (ˌpaɪə'nɪə) *n.* **1. a.** a colonist, explorer, or settler of a new land, region, etc. **b.** (*as modifier*): *a pioneer wagon.* **2.** an innovator or developer of something new. **3.** *Military.* a member of an infantry group that digs entrenchments, makes roads, etc. **4.** *Ecology.* the first species of plant or animal to colonize an area of bare ground. ~*vb.* **5.** to be a pioneer (in or of). **6.** (*tr.*) to initiate, prepare, or open up: *to pioneer a medical programme.* [C16: from Old French *paonier* infantryman, from *paon* PAWN[2]; see also PEON[1]]

Pioneer (ˌpaɪə'nɪə) *n. Irish.* a total abstainer from alcoholic drink, esp. a member of the **Pioneer Total Abstinence Association,** a society devoted to abstention.

pious ('paɪəs) *adj.* **1.** having or expressing reverence for a god or gods; religious; devout. **2.** marked by reverence. **3.** marked by false reverence; sanctimonious. **4.** sacred; not secular. **5.** *Archaic.* having or expressing devotion for one's parents or others. [C17: from Latin *pius,* related to *piāre* to expiate] —'**piously** *adv.* —'**piousness** *n.*

pip[1] (pɪp) *n.* **1.** the seed of a fleshy fruit, such as an apple or pear. **2.** any of the segments marking the surface of a pineapple. **3.** a rootstock or flower of the lily of the valley or certain other plants. [C18: short for PIPPIN]

pip[2] (pɪp) *n.* **1.** a short high-pitched sound, a sequence of which can act as a time signal, esp. on radio. **2.** a radar blip. **3. a.** a spot or single device, such as a spade, diamond, heart, or club on a playing card. **b.** any of the spots on dice or dominoes. **4.** *Informal.* the emblem worn on the shoulder by junior officers in the British Army, indicating their rank. ~*vb.* **pips, pipping, pipped.** **5.** (of a young bird) **a.** (*intr.*) to chirp; peep. **b.** to pierce (the shell of its egg) while hatching. **6.** (*intr.*) to make a short high-pitched sound. [C16 (in the sense: spot or speck); C17 (vb.); C20 (in the sense: short high-pitched sound): of obscure, probably imitative origin; senses 1 and 5 are probably related to PEEP[2]]

pip[3] (pɪp) *n.* **1.** a contagious disease of poultry characterized by the secretion of thick mucus in the mouth and throat. **2.** *Facetious slang.* a minor human ailment. **3.** *Brit. slang.* a bad temper or depression (esp. in the phrase **give (someone) the pip**). ~*vb.* **pips, pipping, pipped. 4.** *Brit. slang.* to cause to be annoyed or depressed. [C15: from Middle Dutch *pippe,* ultimately from Latin *pituita* phlegm; see PITUITARY]

pip[4] (pɪp) *vb.* **pips, pipping, pipped.** (*tr.*) *Brit. slang.* **1.** to wound or kill, esp. with a gun. **2.** to defeat (a person), esp. when his success seems certain (often in the phrase **pip at the post**). **3.** to blackball or ostracize. [C19 (originally in the sense: to blackball): probably from PIP[2]]

pipa ('piːpə) *n.* a tongueless South American toad, *Pipa pipa,* that carries its young in pits in the skin of its back. [C18: from Surinam dialect, probably of African origin]

pipage ('paɪpɪdʒ) *n.* **1.** pipes collectively. **2.** conveyance by pipes. **3.** the money charged for such conveyance.

pipal ('paɪpᵊl) *n.* a variant of **peepul.**

pipe[1] (paɪp) *n.* **1.** a long tube of metal, plastic, etc., used to convey water, oil, gas, etc. **2.** a long tube or case. **3. a.** an object made in any of various shapes and sizes, consisting of a small bowl with an attached tubular stem, in which tobacco or other substances are smoked. **b.** (*as modifier*): *a pipe bowl.* **4.** Also called: '**pipeful.** the amount of tobacco that fills the bowl of a pipe. **5.** *Zoology, botany.* any of various hollow organs, such as the respiratory passage of certain animals. **6. a.** any musical instrument whose sound production results from the vibration of an air column in a simple tube. **b.** any of the tubular devices on an organ, in which air is made to vibrate either directly, as in a flue pipe, or by means of a reed. **7.** an obsolete three-holed wind instrument, held in the left hand while played and accompanied by the tabor. See **tabor. 8. the pipes.** See **bagpipes. 9.** a shrill voice or sound, as of a bird. **10. a.** a boatswain's pipe. **b.** the sound it makes. **11.** (*pl.*) *Informal.* the respiratory tract or vocal cords. **12.** *Metallurgy.* a conical hole in the head of an ingot, made by escaping gas as the metal cools. **13.** a cylindrical vein of rich ore, such as one of the vertical diamond-bearing veins at Kimberley, South Africa. **14.** Also called: **volcanic pipe.** a vertical cylindrical passage in a volcano through which molten lava is forced during eruption. **15.** *U.S. slang.* something easy to do, esp. a simple course in college. **16. put that in your pipe and smoke it.** *Informal.* accept that fact if you can. ~*vb.* **17.** to play (music) on a pipe. **18.** (*tr.*) to summon or lead by a pipe: *to pipe the dancers.* **19.** to utter (something) shrilly. **20. a.** to signal orders to (the crew) by a boatswain's pipe. **b.** (*tr.*) to signal the arrival or departure of: *to pipe the admiral aboard.* **21.** (*tr.*) to convey (water, gas, etc.) by a pipe or pipes. **22.** (*tr.*) to provide with pipes. **23.** (*tr.*) to trim (an article, esp. of clothing) with piping. **24.** (*tr.*) to force (cream, icing, etc.) through a shaped nozzle to decorate food. ~See also **pipe down, pipe up.** [Old English *pīpe* (n.), *pīpian* (vb.), ultimately from Latin *pīpāre* to chirp] —'**pipeless** *adj.* —'**pipy** *adj.*

pipe[2] (paɪp) *n.* **1.** a large cask for wine, oil, etc. **2.** a measure of capacity for wine equal to four barrels. 1 pipe is equal to 126 U.S. gallons or 105 Brit. gallons. **3.** a cask holding this quantity with its contents. [C14: via Old French (in the sense: tube, tubular vessel), ultimately from Latin *pīpāre* to chirp; compare PIPE[1]]

pipeclay ('paɪpˌkleɪ) *n.* **1.** a fine white pure clay, used in the manufacture of tobacco pipes and pottery and for whitening leather and similar materials. ~*vb.* **2.** (*tr.*) to whiten with pipeclay.

pipe cleaner *n.* a short length of thin wires twisted so as to hold tiny tufts of yarn: used to clean the stem of a tobacco pipe.

piped music *n.* light popular music prerecorded and played through amplifiers in a shop, restaurant, factory, etc., as background music. See also **Muzak.**

pipe down *vb.* (*intr., adv.*) *Informal.* to stop talking, making noise, etc.

pipe dream *n.* a fanciful or impossible plan or hope. [alluding to dreams produced by smoking an opium pipe]

pipefish ('paɪpˌfɪʃ) *n., pl.* **-fish** *or* **-fishes.** any of various teleost fishes of the genera *Nerophis, Syngnathus,* etc., having a long tubelike snout and an elongated body covered with bony plates: family *Syngnathidae.* Also called: **needlefish.**

pipefitting ('paɪpˌfɪtɪŋ) *n.* **1. a.** the act or process of bending, cutting to length, and joining pipes. **b.** the branch of plumbing involving this. **2.** the threaded gland nuts, unions, adapters, etc., used for joining pipes. —'**pipeˌfitter** *n.*

pipe jacking *n.* a method of laying underground pipelines by assembling the pipes at the foot of an access shaft and pushing them through the ground.

pipeline ('paɪpˌlaɪn) *n.* **1.** a long pipe, esp. underground, used to transport oil, natural gas, etc., over long distances. **2.** a medium of communication, esp. a private one. **3. in the pipeline.** in the process of being completed, delivered, or produced. ~*vb.* (*tr.*) **4.** to convey by pipeline. **5.** to supply with a pipeline.

pipe major *n.* the noncommissioned officer, generally of warrant officer's rank, who is responsible for the training, duty, and discipline of a military or civilian pipe band.

pip-emma ('pɪp'ɛmə) *adv. Old-fashioned.* in the afternoon; p.m. [World War I phonetic alphabet for P, M]

pipe organ *n.* another name for **organ** (the musical instrument). Compare **reed organ.**

piper ('paɪpə) *n.* **1.** a person who plays a pipe or bagpipes. **2. pay the piper and call the tune.** to bear the cost of an undertaking and control it.

piperaceous (ˌpɪpə'reɪʃəs) *adj.* of, relating to, or belonging to the *Piperaceae,* a family of pungent tropical shrubs and climbing flowering plants: includes pepper, betel, and cubeb. [C17: via New Latin from Latin *piper* PEPPER]

piperazine (pɪ'pɛrəˌziːn, -zɪn) *n.* a white crystalline deliquescent heterocyclic nitrogen compound used as an insecticide, corrosion inhibitor, and veterinary anthelmintic. Formula: $C_4H_{10}N_2$.

piperidine (pɪ'pɛrɪˌdiːn, -dɪn) *n.* a colourless liquid heterocyclic compound with a peppery ammoniacal odour: used in making rubbers and curing epoxy resins. Formula: $C_5H_{11}N$.

piperine ('pɪpəˌraɪn, -rɪn) *n.* a crystalline insoluble alkaloid that is the active ingredient of pepper, used as a flavouring and as an insecticide. Formula: $C_{17}H_{19}NO_3$. [C19: from Latin *piper* PEPPER]

pipe roll *n. History.* an annual record of the accounts of a sheriff or other minister of the crown kept at the British Exchequer from the 12th to the 19th centuries. Also called: **the Great Roll of the Exchequer.** [C17: from PIPE[1] and ROLL; perhaps from documents being rolled into a pipe shape]

piperonal ('pɪpərəʊˌnæl) *n.* a white fragrant aldehyde that is used in flavourings, perfumery, and suntan lotions. Formula: $C_6H_3O_2CH_2CHO$. Also called: **heliotropin.**

pipes of Pan *pl. n.* another term for **panpipes.**

pipestone ('paɪpˌstəʊn) *n.* a variety of consolidated red clay used by American Indians to make tobacco pipes.

pipette (pɪˈpɛt) *n.* **1.** a calibrated glass tube drawn to a fine bore at one end, filled by sucking liquid into the bulb, and used to transfer or measure known volumes of liquid. ~*vb.* **2.** (*tr.*) to transfer or measure out (a liquid) using a pipette. [C19: via French: little pipe, from *pipe* PIPE[1]]

pipe up *vb.* (*intr., adv.*) **1.** to commence singing or playing a musical instrument: *the band piped up.* **2.** to speak up, esp. in a shrill voice.

pipewort (ˈpaɪpˌwɜːt) *n.* a perennial plant, *Eriocaulon septangulare,* of wet places in W Ireland, the Scottish Hebrides, and the eastern U.S., having a twisted flower stalk and a greenish-grey scaly flower head: family *Eriocaulaceae.*

pipi (ˈpɪpiː) *n., pl.* **pipi** *or* **pipis.** any of various shellfishes, esp. *Plebidonax deltoides* of Australia or *Mesodesma novae-zelandiae* of New Zealand. [Maori]

piping (ˈpaɪpɪŋ) *n.* **1.** pipes collectively, esp. pipes formed into a connected system, as in the plumbing of a house. **2.** a cord of icing, whipped cream, etc., often used to decorate desserts and cakes. **3.** a thin strip of covered cord or material, used to edge hems, etc. **4.** the sound of a pipe or a set of bagpipes. **5.** the art or technique of playing a pipe or bagpipes. **6.** a shrill voice or sound, esp. a whistling sound. ~*adj.* **7.** making a shrill sound. **8.** *Archaic.* relating to the pipe (associated with peace), as opposed to martial instruments, such as the fife or trumpet. ~*adv.* **9. piping hot.** extremely hot.

pipistrelle (ˌpɪpɪˈstrɛl) *n.* any of numerous small brownish insectivorous bats of the genus *Pipistrellus,* occurring in most parts of the world: family *Vespertilionidae.* [C18: via French from Italian *pipistrello,* from Latin *vespertīliō* a bat, from *vesper* evening, because of its nocturnal habits]

pipit (ˈpɪpɪt) *n.* any of various songbirds of the genus *Anthus* and related genera, having brownish speckled plumage and a long tail: family *Motacillidae.* Also called: **titlark.** [C18: probably of imitative origin]

pipiwharauroa (ˈpiːpiːˌfæræuːˌrɔːə) *n. N.Z.* a Pacific migratory bird with a metallic green-gold plumage.

pipkin (ˈpɪpkɪn) *n.* **1.** a small metal or earthenware vessel. **2.** another name for **piggin.** [C16: perhaps a diminutive of PIPE[2]; see -KIN]

pippin (ˈpɪpɪn) *n.* **1.** any of several varieties of eating apple with a rounded oblate shape. **2.** the seed of any of these fruits. [C13: from Old French *pepin,* of uncertain origin]

pipsissewa (pɪpˈsɪsəwə) *n.* any of several ericaceous plants of the Asian and American genus *Chimaphila,* having jagged evergreen leaves and white or pinkish flowers. Also called: **wintergreen.** [C19: from Cree *pipisisikweu,* literally: it breaks it into pieces, so called because it was believed to be efficacious in treating bladder stones]

pipsqueak (ˈpɪpˌskwiːk) *n. Informal.* a person or thing that is insignificant or contemptible. [C20: from PIP[2] + SQUEAK]

piquant (ˈpiːkənt, -kɑːnt) *adj.* **1.** having an agreeably pungent or tart taste. **2.** lively or stimulating to the mind. **3.** *Archaic.* cutting or severe. [C16: from French (literally: prickling), from *piquer* to prick, goad; see PIQUE[1]] —**ˈpiquancy** *or* (*less commonly*) **ˈpiquantness** *n.* —**ˈpiquantly** *adv.*

pique[1] (piːk) *n.* **1.** a feeling of resentment or irritation, as from having one's pride wounded. ~*vb.* **piques, piquing, piqued.** (*tr.*) **2.** to cause to feel resentment or irritation. **3.** to excite or arouse. **4.** (foll. by *on* or *upon*) to pride or congratulate (oneself). [C16: from French, from *piquer* to prick, sting; see PICK[1]]

pique[2] (piːk) *Piquet.* ~*n.* **1.** a score of 30 points made by a player from a combination of cards held before play begins and from play while his opponent's score is nil. ~*vb.* **2.** to score a pique (against). [C17: from French *pic,* of uncertain origin]

piqué (ˈpiːkeɪ) *n.* a close-textured fabric of cotton, silk, or spun rayon woven with lengthwise ribs. [C19: from French *piqué* pricked, from *piquer* to prick]

piquet (pɪˈkɛt, -ˈkeɪ) *n.* a card game for two people playing with a reduced pack and scoring points for card combinations and tricks won. [C17: from French, of unknown origin; compare PIQUE[2]]

piracy (ˈpaɪrəsɪ) *n., pl.* **-cies.** **1.** *Brit.* robbery on the seas within admiralty jurisdiction. **2.** a felony, such as robbery or hijacking, committed aboard a ship or aircraft. **3.** the unauthorized use or appropriation of patented or copyrighted material, ideas, etc. [C16: from Anglo-Latin *pirātia,* from Late Greek *peirāteia;* see PIRATE]

piragua (pɪˈrɑːgwə, -ˈræg-) *n.* another word for **pirogue.** [C17: via Spanish from Carib: dugout canoe]

piranha *or* **piraña** (pɪˈrɑːnjə) *n.* any of various small freshwater voracious fishes of the genus *Serrasalmus* and related genera, of tropical America, having strong jaws and sharp teeth: family *Characidae* (characins). [C19: via Portuguese from Tupi: fish with teeth, from *pirá* fish + *sainha* tooth]

pirate (ˈpaɪrɪt) *n.* **1.** a person who commits piracy. **2. a.** a vessel used by pirates. **b.** (*as modifier*): *a pirate ship.* **3.** a person who illicitly uses or appropriates someone else's literary, artistic, or other work. **4. a.** a person or group of people who broadcast illegally. **b.** (*as modifier*): *a pirate radio station.* ~*vb.* **5.** (*tr.*) to use, appropriate, or reproduce (artistic work, ideas, etc.) illicitly. [C15: from Latin *pīrāta,* from Greek *peirātēs* one who attacks, from *peira* an attempt, attack] —**piratic** (paɪˈrætɪk) *or* **piˈratical** *adj.* —**piˈratically** *adv.*

piripiri (ˈpɪriːˌpɪriː) *n., pl.* **-ris.** See **biddy-biddy.** [Maori]

pirn (pɜːn; *Scot.* pɪrn) *n. Scot.* **1.** a reel or bobbin. **2.** (in weaving) the spool of a shuttle. **3.** a fishing reel. [C15: of uncertain origin]

pirog (pɪˈrəʊg) *n., pl.* **-rogi** (-ˈrəʊgɪ). a large pie filled with meat, vegetables, etc. [from Russian: pie]

pirogue (pɪˈrəʊg) *or* **piragua** *n.* any of various kinds of dugout canoes. [C17: via French from Spanish PIRAGUA]

pirouette (ˌpɪrʊˈɛt) *n.* **1.** a body spin, esp. in dancing, on the toes or the ball of the foot. ~*vb.* **2.** (*intr.*) to perform a pirouette. [C18: from French, from Old French *pirouet* spinning top; related to Italian *pirolo* little peg]

pirozhki *or* **piroshki** (pɪˈrɒʃkɪ) *pl. n., sing.* **pirozhok** (ˈpɪrəˌʒɒk). small triangular pastries filled with meat, vegetables, etc. [C20: from Russian, from *pirozhók,* diminutive of PIROG]

pis aller *French.* (piz ale) *n.* a last resort; stopgap. [literally: (at) the worst going]

piscary (ˈpɪskərɪ) *n., pl.* **-ries.** **1.** a place where fishing takes place. **2.** the right to fish in certain waters. [C15: from Latin *piscārius* fishing, from *piscis* a fish]

piscatorial (ˌpɪskəˈtɔːrɪəl) *or* **piscatory** (ˈpɪskətərɪ, -trɪ) *adj.* **1.** of or relating to fish, fishing, or fishermen. **2.** devoted to fishing. [C19: from Latin *piscātōrius,* from *piscātor* fisherman] —**ˌpiscaˈtorially** *adv.*

Pisces (ˈpaɪsiːz, ˈpɪ-) *n., Latin genitive* **Piscium** (ˈpaɪsɪəm). **1.** *Astronomy.* a faint extensive zodiacal constellation lying between Aquarius and Aries on the ecliptic. **2.** *Astrology.* **a.** Also called: the **Fishes.** the twelfth sign of the zodiac, symbol ♓, having a mutable water classification and ruled by the planets Jupiter and Neptune. The sun is in this sign between about Feb. 19 and March 20. **b.** a person born when the sun is in this sign. **3. a.** a taxonomic group that comprises all fishes. See **fish** (sense 1). **b.** a taxonomic group that comprises the bony fishes only. See **teleost.** ~*adj.* **4.** *Astrology.* born under or characteristic of Pisces. ~Also (for senses 2b, 4): **Piscean** (ˈpaɪsɪən). [C14: Latin: the fishes]

pisci- *combining form.* fish: *pisciculture.* [from Latin *piscis*]

pisciculture (ˈpɪsɪˌkʌltʃə) *n.* the rearing and breeding of fish under controlled conditions. —**ˌpisciˈcultural** *adj.* —**ˌpisciˈculturally** *adv.* —**ˌpisciˈculturist** *n., adj.*

piscina (pɪˈsiːnə) *n., pl.* **-nae** (-niː) *or* **-nas.** *R.C. Church.* a stone basin, with a drain, in a church or sacristy where water used at Mass is poured away. [C16: from Latin: fish pond, from *piscis* a fish] —**piscinal** (ˈpɪsɪnᵊl) *adj.*

piscine (ˈpɪsaɪn) *adj.* of, relating to, or resembling a fish.

Piscis Austrinus (ˈpɪsɪs ɒˈstraɪnəs, ˈpaɪ-) *n., Latin genitive* **Piscis Austrini** (ɒˈstraɪnaɪ). a small constellation in the S hemisphere lying between Aquarius and Grus and containing the first-magnitude star Fomalhaut. [Latin: the Southern Fish]

piscivorous (pɪˈsɪvərəs) *adj.* feeding on fish: *piscivorous birds.*

pisé (ˈpiːzeɪ) *n.* rammed earth or clay used to make floors or walls. Also called: **pisé de terre.** [C18: French, from past participle of *piser,* from Latin *pisare* to beat, pound]

pish (pʃ, pɪʃ) *interj.* **1.** an exclamation of impatience or contempt. ~*vb.* **2.** to make this exclamation at (someone or something).

pishogue (pɪˈʃəʊg) *n. Irish.* sorcery; witchcraft. [from Irish *piseog, pisreog*]

pisiform (ˈpɪsɪˌfɔːm) *adj.* **1.** *Zoology, botany.* resembling a pea. ~*n.* **2.** a small pealike bone on the ulnar side of the carpus. [C18: via New Latin from Latin *pīsum* pea + *forma* shape]

pismire (ˈpɪsˌmaɪə) *n.* an archaic or dialect word for an **ant.** [C14 (literally: urinating ant, from the odour of formic acid characteristic of an ant hill): from PISS + obsolete *mire* ant, of Scandinavian origin; compare Old Norse *maurr,* Middle Low German *mīre* ant]

pisolite (ˈpaɪsəʊˌlaɪt) *n.* any sedimentary rock consisting of pea-sized concentric formations **(pisoliths)** within a fine matrix. [C18: from New Latin *pisolithus* pea stone, from Greek *pisos* pea + *lithos* -LITE] —**pisolitic** (ˌpaɪsəʊˈlɪtɪk) *adj.*

piss (pɪs) *Slang.* ~*vb.* **1.** (*intr.*) *Taboo.* to urinate. **2.** (*tr.*) *Taboo.* to discharge as or in one's urine: *to piss blood.* ~*n.* **3.** *Taboo.* an act of urinating. **4.** *Taboo.* urine. **5.** *Austral. taboo.* beer. **6. take the piss.** to tease or make fun of someone or something. [C13: from Old French *pisser,* probably of imitative origin] —**ˈpisser** *n.*

piss about *or* **around** *vb.* (*adv.*) *Taboo slang.* **1.** (*intr.*) to behave in a casual or silly way. **2.** (*tr.*) to waste the time of.

piss artist *n. Brit. slang.* **1.** a boastful or incompetent person. **2.** a person who drinks heavily and gets drunk frequently.

pissed (pɪst) *adj. Brit. taboo slang.* intoxicated; drunk.

pisshead (ˈpɪsˌhɛd) *n. Slang.* a drunkard.

piss off *vb.* (*adv.*) *Taboo slang.* **1.** (*tr.; often passive*) to annoy, irritate, or disappoint. **2.** (*intr.*) *Chiefly Brit.* to go away; depart, often used to dismiss a person.

piss-up *n. Slang, chiefly Brit.* a drinking session.

pistachio (pɪˈstɑːʃɪˌəʊ) *n., pl.* **-os.** **1.** an anacardiaceous tree, *Pistacia vera,* of the Mediterranean region and W Asia, with small hard-shelled nuts. **2.** Also called: **pistachio nut.** the nut of this tree, having an edible green kernel. **3.** the sweet flavour of the pistachio nut, used esp. in ice creams. ~*adj.* **4.** of a yellowish-green colour. [C16: via Italian and Latin from Greek *pistakion* pistachio nut, from *pistakē* pistachio tree, from Persian *pistah*]

pistareen (ˌpɪstəˈriːn) *n.* a Spanish coin, used in the U.S. and the West Indies until the 18th century. [C18: perhaps changed from PESETA]

piste (piːst) *n.* **1.** a trail, slope, or course for skiing. **2.** a rectangular area for fencing bouts. [C18: via Old French from Old Italian *pista,* from *pistare* to tread down]

pistil (ˈpɪstɪl) *n.* the female reproductive part of a flower, consisting of one or more separate or fused carpels; gynoecium. [C18: from Latin *pistillum* PESTLE]

pistillate (ˈpɪstɪlɪt, -ˌleɪt) *adj.* (of plants) **1.** having pistils but no anthers. **2.** having or producing pistils.

pistol (ˈpɪst^{ə}l) *n.* **1.** a short-barrelled handgun. **2. hold a pistol to a person's head.** to threaten a person in order to force him to do what one wants. ~*vb.* **-tols, -tolling, -tolled** *or U.S.* **-tols, -toling, -toled. 3.** (*tr.*) to shoot with a pistol. [C16: from French *pistole,* from German, from Czech *pišťala* pistol, pipe; related to Russian *pischal* shepherd's pipes]

pistole (pɪsˈtəʊl) *n.* any of various gold coins of varying value, formerly used in Europe. [C16: from Old French, shortened from *pistolet,* literally: little PISTOL]

pistoleer (ˌpɪstəˈlɪə) *n. Obsolete.* a person, esp. a soldier, who is armed with or fires a pistol.

pistol grip *n.* **a.** a handle shaped like the butt of a pistol. **b.** (*as modifier*): *a pistol-grip camera.*

pistol-whip *vb.* **-whips, -whipping, -whipped.** (*tr.*) *U.S.* to beat or strike with a pistol barrel.

piston (ˈpɪstən) *n.* a disc or cylindrical part that slides to and fro in a hollow cylinder. In an internal-combustion engine it is forced to move by the expanding gases in the cylinder head and is attached by a pivoted connecting rod to a crankshaft or flywheel, thus converting reciprocating motion into rotation. [C18: via French from Old Italian *pistone,* from *pistare* to pound, grind, from Latin *pinsere* to crush, beat]

piston ring *n.* a split ring, usually made of cast iron, that fits into a groove on the rim of a piston to provide a spring-loaded seal against the cylinder wall.

piston rod *n.* **1.** the rod that connects the piston of a reciprocating steam engine to the crosshead. **2.** a less common name for a **connecting rod.**

piston slap *n.* the characteristic sound of a seriously worn piston in a cylinder (usually of the engine of a motor car).

pit[1] (pɪt) *n.* **1.** a large, usually deep opening in the ground. **2. a.** a mine or excavation with a shaft, esp. for coal. **b.** the shaft in a mine. **c.** (*as modifier*): *pit pony; pit prop.* **3.** a concealed danger or difficulty. **4. the pit.** hell. **5.** Also called: **orchestra pit.** the area that is occupied by the orchestra in a theatre, located in front of the stage. **6.** an enclosure for fighting animals or birds, esp. gamecocks. **7.** *Anatomy.* **a.** a small natural depression on the surface of a body, organ, structure, or part; fossa. **b.** the floor of any natural bodily cavity: *the pit of the stomach.* **8.** *Pathol.* a small indented scar at the site of a former pustule; pockmark. **9.** any of various small areas in a plant cell wall that remain unthickened when the rest of the cell becomes lignified. **10.** a working area at the side of a motor-racing track for servicing or refuelling vehicles. **11.** *U.S.* a section on the floor of a commodity exchange devoted to a special line of trading. **12.** a rowdy card game in which players bid for commodities. **13.** an area of sand or other soft material at the end of a long-jump approach, behind the bar of a pole vault, etc., on which an athlete may land safely. **14.** the ground floor of the auditorium of a theatre. **15.** *Brit.* a slang word for **bed** (sense 2) or **bedroom** (sense 1). **16.** another word for **pitfall** (sense 2). **17. dig a pit for.** to try to ensnare or trick. ~*vb.* **pits, pitting, pitted. 18.** (*tr.;* often foll. by *against*) to match in opposition, esp. as antagonists. **19.** to mark or become marked with pits. **20.** (*tr.*) to place or bury in a pit. ~See also **pits.** [Old English *pytt,* from Latin *puteus;* compare Old French *pet,* Old High German *pfuzzi*]

pit[2] (pɪt) *Chiefly U.S. and Canadian.* ~*n.* **1.** the stone of a cherry, plum, etc. ~*vb.* **pits, pitting, pitted. 2.** (*tr.*) to extract the stone from (a fruit). [C19: from Dutch: kernel; compare PITH]

pit[3] (pɪt) *vb.* a Scot. word for **put.**

pita (ˈpiːtə) *n.* **1.** any of several agave plants yielding a strong fibre. See also **istle. 2.** a species of pineapple, *Ananas magdalenae,* the leaves of which yield a white fibre. **3.** Also called: **pita fibre.** the fibre obtained from any of these plants, used in making cordage and paper. [C17: via Spanish from Quechua]

pitapat (ˌpɪtəˈpæt) *adv.* **1.** with quick light taps or beats. ~*vb.* **-pats, -patting, -patted. 2.** (*intr.*) to make quick light taps or beats. ~*n.* **3.** such taps or beats.

pit bull terrier *n.* a dog resembling the Staffordshire bull terrier but somewhat larger: originally developed for dog-fighting; it is not recognized as a breed by kennel clubs. Also called: **American pit bull terrier.**

pitch[1] (pɪtʃ) *vb.* **1.** to hurl or throw (something); cast; fling. **2.** (*usually tr.*) to set up (a camp, tent, etc.). **3.** (*tr.*) to place or thrust (a stake, spear, etc.) into the ground. **4.** (*intr.*) to move vigorously or irregularly to and fro or up and down. **5.** (*tr.*) to set the level, character, or slope of. **6.** (*intr.*) to slope downwards. **7.** (*intr.*) to fall forwards or downwards. **8.** (*intr.*) (of a vessel) to dip and raise its bow and stern alternately. **9.** (*tr.;* foll. by *up*) *Cricket.* to bowl (a ball) so that it bounces near the batsman. **10.** (*intr.*) (of a missile, aircraft, etc.) to deviate from a stable flight attitude by movement of the longitudinal axis about the lateral axis. Compare **yaw** (sense 1), **roll** (sense 14). **11.** (*tr.*) (in golf) to hit (a ball) steeply into the air, esp. with backspin to minimize roll. **12.** (*tr.*) *Music.* **a.** to sing or play accurately (a note, interval, etc.). **b.** (*usually passive*) (of a wind instrument) to specify or indicate its basic key or harmonic series by its size, manufacture, etc. **13.** (*tr.*) *Cards.* to lead (a suit) and so determine trumps for that trick. **14.** *Baseball.* **a.** (*tr.*) to throw (a baseball) to a batter. **b.** (*intr.*) to act as pitcher in a baseball game. **15.** *Southwest English dialect.* (used with *it* as subject) to snow without the settled snow melting. **16. in there pitching.** *U.S. and Canadian informal.* taking part with enthusiasm. **17. pitch a tale** (*or* **yarn**). to tell a story, usually of a fantastic nature. ~*n.* **18.** the degree of elevation or depression. **19. a.** the angle of descent of a downward slope. **b.** such a slope. **20.** the extreme height or depth. **21.** *Mountaineering.* a section of a route between two belay points, sometimes equal to the full length of the rope but often shorter. **22.** the degree of slope of a roof, esp. when expressed as a ratio of height to span. **23.** the distance between corresponding points on adjacent members of a body of regular form, esp. the distance between teeth on a gearwheel or between threads on a screw thread. **24.** the distance between regularly spaced objects such as rivets, bolts, etc. **25.** the pitching motion of a ship, missile, etc. **26. a.** the distance a propeller advances in one revolution, assuming no slip. **b.** the blade angle of a propeller or rotor. **27.** *Music.* **a.** the auditory property of a note that is conditioned by its frequency relative to other notes: *high pitch; low pitch.* **b.** an absolute frequency assigned to a specific note, fixing the relative frequencies of all other notes. The fundamental frequencies of the notes A–G, in accordance with the frequency A = 440 hertz, were internationally standardized and accepted in 1939. See also **concert pitch** (sense 1), **international pitch. 28.** *Cricket.* the rectangular area between the stumps, 22 yards long and 10 feet wide; the wicket. **29.** *Geology.* the inclination of the axis of an anticline or syncline or of a stratum or vein from the horizontal. **30.** another name for **seven-up. 31.** the act or manner of pitching a ball, as in cricket. See also **full pitch. 32.** *Chiefly Brit.* a vendor's station, esp. on a pavement. **33.** *Slang.* a persuasive sales talk, esp. one routinely repeated. **34.** *Chiefly Brit.* (in many sports) the field of play. **35.** Also called: **pitch shot.** *Golf.* an approach shot in which the ball is struck in a high arc. **36. make a pitch for.** *U.S. and Canadian slang.* **a.** to give verbal support to. **b.** to attempt to attract (someone) sexually or romantically. **37. queer someone's pitch.** *Brit. informal.* to upset someone's plans. ~See also **pitch in, pitch into, pitch on.** [C13 *picchen;* possibly related to PICK[1]]

pitch[2] (pɪtʃ) *n.* **1.** any of various heavy dark viscid substances obtained as a residue from the distillation of tars. See also **coal-tar pitch. 2.** any of various similar substances, such as asphalt, occurring as natural deposits. **3.** any of various similar substances obtained by distilling certain organic substances so that they are incompletely carbonized. **4.** crude turpentine obtained as sap from pine trees. ~Related adj.: **piceous.** ~*vb.* **5.** (*tr.*) to apply pitch to (something). [Old English *pic,* from Latin *pix*]

pitch accent *n.* (in languages such as Ancient Greek or modern Swedish) an accent in which emphatic syllables are pronounced on a higher musical pitch relative to other syllables. Also called: **tonic accent.**

pitch-and-toss *n.* a game of skill and chance in which the player who pitches a coin nearest to a mark has the first chance to toss all the coins, winning those that land heads up.

pitchbend (ˈpɪtʃˌbɛnd) *n.* an electronic device that enables a player to bend the pitch of a note being sounded on a synthesizer, usually with a pitch wheel, strip, or lever.

pitch-black *adj.* **1.** extremely dark; unlit: *the room was pitch-black.* **2.** of a deep black colour.

pitchblende (ˈpɪtʃˌblɛnd) *n.* a blackish mineral that is a type of uraninite and occurs in veins, frequently associated with silver: the principal source of uranium and radium. Formula: UO_2. [C18: partial translation of German *Pechblende,* from *Pech* PITCH[2] (from its black colour) + BLENDE]

pitch circle *n.* an imaginary circle passing through the teeth of a gearwheel, concentric with the gearwheel, and having a radius that would enable it to be in contact with a similar circle around a mating gearwheel.

pitch-cone angle *n.* (in a bevel gear) the apex angle of the truncated cone (pitch cone) which forms the reference surface on which the teeth of a bevel gear are cut.

pitch-dark *adj.* extremely or completely dark.

pitched battle *n.* **1.** a battle ensuing from the deliberate choice of time and place, engaging all the planned resources. **2.** any fierce encounter, esp. one with large numbers.

pitcher[1] (ˈpɪtʃə) *n.* **1.** a large jug, usually rounded with a narrow neck and often of earthenware, used mainly for holding water. **2.** *Botany.* any of the urn-shaped leaves of the pitcher plant. [C13: from Old French *pichier,* from Medieval Latin *picārium,* variant of *bicārium* BEAKER]

pitcher[2] (ˈpɪtʃə) *n.* **1.** *Baseball.* the player on the fielding team who pitches the ball to the batter. **2.** Also called: **pitching niblick.** *Golf.* an iron with a steep-angled head, similar to a niblick. **3.** a granite stone used in paving.

pitcher plant *n.* any of various insectivorous plants of the genera *Sarracenia, Nepenthes,* and *Darlingtonia,* having leaves modified to form pitcher-like organs that attract and trap insects, which are then digested. See also **huntsman's-cup.**

pitchfork (ˈpɪtʃˌfɔːk) *n.* **1.** a long-handled fork with two or three long curved tines for lifting, turning, or tossing hay. ~*vb.* (*tr.*) **2.** to use a pitchfork on (something). **3.** to thrust (someone) unwillingly into a position.

pitch in *vb.* (*intr., adv.*) **1.** to cooperate or contribute. **2.** to begin energetically.

pitching tool *n.* a masonry chisel for rough work.

pitch into *vb.* (*intr., prep.*) *Informal.* **1.** to assail physically or verbally. **2.** to get on with doing (something).

pitchman (ˈpɪtʃmən) *n., pl.* **-men.** *U.S. and Canadian.* **1.** an itinerant pedlar of small merchandise who operates from a stand at a fair, etc. **2.** any high-pressure salesman or advertiser.

pitchometer (pɪtʃˈɒmɪtə) *n.* an instrument embodying a clinometer, for measuring the pitch of a ship's propeller.

pitch on *or* **upon** *vb.* (*intr., prep.*) to determine or decide.

pitch pine *n.* **1.** any of various coniferous trees of the genus *Pinus,* esp. *P. rigida,* of North America, having red-brown bark and long lustrous light brown cones: valued as a source of turpentine and pitch. **2.** the wood of any of these trees.

pitch pipe *n.* a small pipe, esp. one having a reed like a harmonica, that sounds a note or notes of standard frequency. It is used for establishing the correct starting note for unaccompanied singing.

pitchstone (ˈpɪtʃˌstəʊn) *n.* a dark glassy acid volcanic rock similar in composition to granite, usually intruded as dykes, sills, etc. [C18: translation of German *Pechstein*]

pitchy (ˈpɪtʃɪ) *adj.* **pitchier, pitchiest. 1.** full of or covered with pitch. **2.** resembling pitch. —ˈ**pitchiness** *n.*

piteous (ˈpɪtɪəs) *adj.* **1.** exciting or deserving pity. **2.** *Archaic.* having or expressing pity. —ˈ**piteously** *adv.* —ˈ**piteousness** *n.*

pitfall (ˈpɪtˌfɔːl) *n.* **1.** an unsuspected difficulty or danger. **2.** a trap in the form of a concealed pit, designed to catch men or wild animals. [Old English *pytt* PIT[1] + *fealle* trap]

pith (pɪθ) *n.* **1.** the soft fibrous tissue lining the inside of the rind in fruits such as the orange and grapefruit. **2.** the essential or important part, point, etc. **3.** weight; substance. **4.** Also called: **medulla.** *Botany.* the central core of unspecialized cells surrounded by conducting tissue in stems. **5.** the soft central part of a bone, feather, etc. ~*vb.* (*tr.*) **6.** to destroy the brain and spinal cord of (a laboratory animal) by piercing or severing. **7.** to kill (animals) by severing the spinal cord. **8.** to remove the pith from (a plant). [Old English *pitha;* compare Middle Low German *pedik,* Middle Dutch *pitt*(*e*)]

pithead (ˈpɪtˌhɛd) *n.* the top of a mine shaft and the buildings, hoisting gear, etc., situated around it.

pithecanthropus (ˌpɪθɪkænˈθrəʊpəs, -ˈkænθrə-) *n., pl.* **-pi** (-ˌpaɪ). any primitive apelike man of the former genus *Pithecanthropus,* now included in the genus *Homo.* See **Java man, Peking man.** [C19: New Latin, from Greek *pithēkos* ape + *anthrōpos* man] —ˌ**pitheˈcanthroˌpine** *or* ˌ**pitheˈcanthroˌpoid** *adj.*

pith helmet *n.* a lightweight hat made of pith that protects the wearer from the sun. Also called: **topee, topi.**

pithos (ˈpɪθɒs, ˈpaɪ-) *n., pl.* **-thoi** (-θɔɪ). a large ceramic container for oil or grain. [from Greek]

pithy (ˈpɪθɪ) *adj.* **pithier, pithiest. 1.** terse and full of meaning or substance. **2.** of, resembling, or full of pith. —ˈ**pithily** *adv.* —ˈ**pithiness** *n.*

pitiable (ˈpɪtɪəbəl) *adj.* exciting or deserving pity or contempt. —ˈ**pitiableness** *n.* —ˈ**pitiably** *adv.*

pitiful (ˈpɪtɪfʊl) *adj.* **1.** arousing or deserving pity. **2.** arousing or deserving contempt. **3.** *Archaic.* full of pity or compassion. —ˈ**pitifully** *adv.* —ˈ**pitifulness** *n.*

pitiless (ˈpɪtɪlɪs) *adj.* having or showing little or no pity or mercy. —ˈ**pitilessly** *adv.* —ˈ**pitilessness** *n.*

Pitjantjatjara (ˌpɪtʃəntʃəˈtʃærə) *or* **Pitjantjara** (ˌpɪtʃənˈdʒærə) *n.* **1.** (*pl.* **-ra** *or* **-ras**) an Aboriginal people of the desert area of South Australia. **2.** the language of this people.

pitman (ˈpɪtmən) *n., pl.* **-men.** *Chiefly Scot. and northern English.* a person who works down a mine, esp. a coal miner.

piton (ˈpiːtɒn; *French* pitɔ̃) *n. Mountaineering.* a metal spike that may be driven into a crevice of rock or into ice and used to secure a rope. [C20: from French: ringbolt]

Pitot-static tube (ˈpiːtəʊˈstætɪk) *n.* combined Pitot and static pressure tubes placed in a fluid flow to measure the total and static pressures. The difference in pressures, as recorded on a manometer or airspeed indicator, indicates the fluid velocity. Also called: **Pitot tube.**

Pitot tube (ˈpiːtəʊ) *n.* **1.** a small tube placed in a fluid with its open end upstream and the other end connected to a manometer. It measures the total pressure of the fluid. **2.** short for **Pitot-static tube,** esp. one fitted to an aircraft. [C18: named after its inventor, Henri *Pitot* (1695–1771), French physicist]

pits (pɪts) *pl. n. Slang.* **the.** the worst possible person, place, or thing. [C20: perhaps shortened from *armpits*]

pitsaw (ˈpɪtˌsɔː) *n.* a large saw formerly used for cutting logs into planks, operated by two men, one standing on top of the log and the other in a pit underneath it.

pit-sawn *adj.* (of timber, esp. formerly) sawn into planks by hand in a saw-pit.

pit stop *n.* **1.** *Motor racing.* a brief stop made at a pit by a racing car for repairs, refuelling, etc. **2.** *Informal.* any stop made during a car journey for refreshment, rest, or refuelling.

pitta bread *or* **pitta** (ˈpɪtə) *n.* a flat rounded slightly leavened bread, originally from the Middle East, with a hollow inside like a pocket, which can be filled with food. Also called: **Arab bread, Greek bread.** [from Modern Greek: a cake]

pittance (ˈpɪtəns) *n.* a small amount or portion, esp. a meagre allowance of money. [C16: from Old French *pietance* ration, ultimately from Latin *pietās* duty]

pitter-patter (ˈpɪtəˌpætə) *n.* **1.** the sound of light rapid taps or pats, as of raindrops. ~*vb.* **2.** (*intr.*) to make such a sound. ~*adv.* **3.** with such a sound: *the rain fell pitter-patter on the window.*

Pitt Street Farmer *n. Austral. slang.* another name for **Collins Street Farmer.** [C20: after a principal business street in Sydney, Australia]

pituitary (pɪˈtjuːɪtərɪ, -trɪ) *n., pl.* **-taries. 1.** See **pituitary gland, pituitary extract.** ~*adj.* **2.** of or relating to the pituitary gland. **3.** *Archaic.* of or relating to phlegm or mucus. [C17: from Late Latin *pītuītārius* slimy, from *pītuīta* phlegm]

pituitary extract *n.* a preparation of the pituitary gland, used in medicine for the therapeutic effects of its hormones.

pituitary gland *or* **body** *n.* the master endocrine gland, attached by a stalk to the base of the brain. Its two lobes (see **adenohypophysis** and **neurohypophysis**) secrete hormones affecting skeletal growth, development of the sex glands, and the functioning of the other endocrine glands. Also called: **hypophysis, hypophysis cerebri.**

pituri (ˈpɪtʃərɪ) *n., pl.* **-ris.** an Australian solanaceous shrub, *Duboisia hopwoodii,* the leaves of which are the source of a narcotic used by the Aborigines. [C19: from a native Australian name]

pit viper *n.* any venomous snake of the New World family *Crotalidae,* having a heat-sensitive organ in a pit on each side of the head: includes the rattlesnakes.

pity (ˈpɪtɪ) *n., pl.* **pities. 1.** sympathy or sorrow felt for the sufferings of another. **2. have** (*or* **take**) **pity on.** to have sympathy or show mercy for. **3.** something that causes regret or pity. **4.** an unfortunate chance: *what a pity you can't come.* **5. more's the pity.** it is highly regrettable (that). ~*vb.* **pities, pitying, pitied.** (*tr.*) **6.** to feel pity for. [C13: from Old French *pité,* from Latin *pietās* duty] —ˈ**pitying** *adj.* —ˈ**pityingly** *adv.*

pityriasis (ˌpɪtəˈraɪəsɪs) *n.* **1.** any of a group of skin diseases characterized by the shedding of dry flakes of skin. **2.** a similar skin disease of certain domestic animals. [C17: via New Latin from Greek *pituriasis* scurfiness, from *pituron* bran]

più (pjuː) *adv. Music.* (*in combination*) more (quickly, softly, etc.): *più allegro, più mosso, più lento.* [Italian, from Latin *plus* more]

piupiu (ˈpiːuːˌpiːuː) *n.* a skirt made from the leaves of the New Zealand flax, worn by Maoris on ceremonial occasions. [Maori]

Piute (ˈpaɪˌuːt, paɪˈjuːt) *n.* a variant spelling of **Paiute.**

pivot (ˈpɪvət) *n.* **1.** a short shaft or pin supporting something that turns; fulcrum. **2.** the end of a shaft or arbor that terminates in a bearing. **3.** a person or thing upon which progress, success, etc., depends. **4.** the person or position from which a military formation takes its reference, as when altering position. ~*vb.* **5.** (*tr.*) to mount on or provide with a pivot or pivots. **6.** (*intr.*) to turn on or as if on a pivot. [C17: from Old French; perhaps related to Old Provençal *pua* tooth of a comb]

pivotal (ˈpɪvətəl) *adj.* **1.** of, involving, or acting as a pivot. **2.** of crucial importance. —ˈ**pivotally** *adv.*

pivot bridge *n.* another name for **swing bridge.**

pivot grammar *n. Psychol.* a loose grammar said to govern two-word utterances by children.

pix[1] (pɪks) *pl. n. Informal.* photographs; prints.

pix[2] (pɪks) *n.* a less common spelling of **pyx.**

pixel (ˈpɪksəl) *n.* any of a number of very small picture elements that make up a picture, as on a visual display unit. [C20: from *pix* pictures + *el*(*ement*)]

pixie *or* **pixy** (ˈpɪksɪ) *n., pl.* **pixies.** (in folklore) a fairy or elf. [C17: of obscure origin]

pixilated *or* **pixillated** (ˈpɪksɪˌleɪtɪd) *adj. Chiefly U.S.* **1.** eccentric or whimsical. **2.** *Slang.* drunk. [C20: from PIXIE + *-lated,* as in *stimulated, titillated,* etc.] —ˌ**pixiˈlation** *or* ˌ**pixilˈlation** *n.*

pize (paɪz) *vb.* (*tr.*) *Yorkshire dialect.* to strike (someone a blow). [of obscure origin]

pizz. *Music. abbrev. for* pizzicato.

pizza (ˈpiːtsə) *n.* a dish of Italian origin consisting of a baked disc of dough covered with cheese and tomatoes, usually with the addition of mushrooms, anchovies, sausage, or ham. [C20: from Italian, perhaps from Vulgar Latin *picea* (unattested), from Latin *piceus* relating to PITCH[2]; perhaps related to Medieval Greek *pitta* cake]

pizzazz *or* **pizazz** (pəˈzæz) *n. Informal.* an attractive combination of energy and style; sparkle, vitality, glamour. Also called: **bezazz, bezzazz, pazzazz, pazazz, pzazz.** [C20: origin obscure]

pizzeria (ˌpiːtsəˈriːə) *n.* a place where pizzas are made, sold, or eaten. [C20: from Italian, from PIZZA + *-eria* -ERY]

pizzicato (ˌpɪtsɪˈkɑːtəʊ) *Music.* ~*adj., adv.* **1.** (in music for the violin family) to be plucked with the finger. ~*n.* **2.** the style or technique of playing a normally bowed stringed instrument in this manner. [C19: from Italian: pinched, from *pizzicare* to twist, twang]

pizzle ('pɪz^{ə}l) *n. Archaic or dialect.* the penis of an animal, esp. a bull. [C16: of Germanic origin; compare Low German *pēsel,* Flemish *pēzel,* Middle Dutch *pēze* sinew]

pk *pl.* **pks** *abbrev. for:* **1.** pack. **2.** park. **3.** peak.

PK *abbrev. for* psychokinesis.

pkg. *pl.* **pkgs.** *abbrev. for* package.

pkt *abbrev. for* packet.

pl *abbrev. for:* **1.** place. **2.** plate. **3.** plural.

PL **1.** (in transformational grammar) *abbrev. for* plural. ~**2.** *international car registration for* Poland.

Pl. (in street names) *abbrev. for* Place.

PL/1 *n.* programming language 1: a high-level computer programming language designed for mathematical and scientific purposes. [C20: *p(rogramming) l(anguage) 1*]

PLA *abbrev. for* Port of London Authority.

plaas (plɑːs) *n. S. African.* a farm. [Afrikaans]

placable ('plækəb^{ə}l) *adj.* easily placated or appeased. [C15: via Old French from Latin *plācābilis,* from *plācāre* to appease; related to *placēre* to please] —ˌ**placa'bility** *or* '**placableness** *n.* —'**placably** *adv.*

placard ('plækɑːd) *n.* **1.** a printed or written notice for public display; poster. **2.** a small plaque or card. ~*vb.* (*tr.*) **3.** to post placards on or in. **4.** to publicize or advertise by placards. **5.** to display as a placard. [C15: from Old French *plaquart,* from *plaquier* to plate, lay flat; see PLAQUE]

placate (plə'keɪt) *vb.* (*tr.*) to pacify or appease. [C17: from Latin *plācāre;* see PLACABLE] —**pla'cation** *n.*

placatory ('plækətərɪ, -trɪ; plə'keɪtərɪ) *or* (*less commonly*) **placative** ('plækətɪv, plə'keɪtɪv) *adj.* placating or intended to placate.

place (pleɪs) *n.* **1.** a particular point or part of space or of a surface, esp. that occupied by a person or thing. **2.** a geographical point, such as a town, city, etc. **3.** a position or rank in a sequence or order. **4. a.** an open square lined with houses of a similar type in a city or town. **b.** (*cap. when part of a street name*): *Grosvenor Place.* **5.** space or room. **6.** a house or living quarters. **7.** a country house with grounds. **8.** any building or area set aside for a specific purpose. **9.** a passage in a book, play, film, etc.: *to lose one's place.* **10.** proper or appropriate position or time: *he still thinks a woman's place is in the home.* **11.** right or original position: *put it back in its place.* **12.** suitable, appropriate, or customary surroundings (esp. in the phrases **out of place, in place**). **13.** right, prerogative, or duty: *it is your place to give a speech.* **14.** appointment, position, or job: *a place at college.* **15.** position, condition, or state: *if I were in your place.* **16. a.** a space or seat, as at a dining table. **b.** (*as modifier*): *place mat.* **17.** *Maths.* the relative position of a digit in a number. See also **decimal place. 18.** any of the best times in a race. **19.** *Horse racing.* **a.** *Brit.* the first, second, or third position at the finish. **b.** *U.S. and Canadian.* the first or usually the second position at the finish. **c.** (*as modifier*): *a place bet.* **20.** *Theatre.* one of the three unities. See **unity** (sense 8). **21.** *Archaic.* an important position, rank, or role. **22. all over the place.** in disorder or disarray. **23. another place.** *Brit., Parliamentary procedure.* **a.** (in the House of Commons) the House of Lords. **b.** (in the House of Lords) the House of Commons. **24. give place (to).** to make room (for) or be superseded (by). **25. go places.** *Informal.* **a.** to travel. **b.** to become successful. **26. in place of. a.** instead of; in lieu of: *go in place of my sister.* **b.** in exchange for: *he gave her it in place of her ring.* **27. know one's place.** to be aware of one's inferior position. **28. pride of place.** the highest or foremost position. **29. put someone in his** (*or* **her**) **place.** to humble someone who is arrogant, conceited, forward, etc. **30. take one's place.** to take up one's usual or specified position. **31. take the place of.** to be a substitute for. **32. take place.** to happen or occur. **33. the other place.** *Facetious.* **a.** (at Oxford University) Cambridge University. **b.** (at Cambridge University) Oxford University. ~*vb.* (*mainly tr.*) **34.** to put or set in a particular or appropriate place. **35.** to find or indicate the place of. **36.** to identify or classify by linking with an appropriate context: *to place a face.* **37.** to regard or view as being: *to place prosperity above sincerity.* **38.** to make (an order, a bet, etc.). **39.** to find a home or job for (someone). **40.** to appoint to an office or position. **41.** (often foll. by *with*) to put under the care (of). **42.** to direct or aim carefully. **43.** (*passive*) *Brit.* to cause (a racehorse, greyhound, athlete, etc.) to arrive in first, second, third, or sometimes fourth place. **44.** (*intr.*) *U.S. and Canadian.* (of a racehorse, greyhound, etc.) to finish among the first three in a contest, esp. in second position. **45.** to invest (funds). **46.** to sing (a note) with accuracy of pitch. **47.** to insert (an advertisement) in a newspaper, journal, etc. [C13: via Old French from Latin *platēa* courtyard, from Greek *plateia,* from *platus* broad; compare French *plat* flat]

placebo (plə'siːbəʊ) *n., pl.* **-bos** *or* **-boes. 1.** *Med.* an inactive substance or other sham form of therapy administered to a patient usually to compare its effects with those of a real drug or treatment, but sometimes for the psychological benefit to the patient through his believing he is receiving treatment. See also **control group, placebo effect. 2.** something said or done to please or humour another. **3.** *R.C. Church.* a traditional name for the vespers of the office for the dead. [C13 (in the ecclesiastical sense): from Latin *Placebo Domino* I shall please the Lord (from the opening of the office for the dead); C19 (in the medical sense)]

placebo effect *n. Med.* a positive therapeutic effect claimed by a patient after receiving a placebo believed by him to be an active drug. See **control group.**

place card *n.* a card placed on a dinner table before a seat, as at a formal dinner, indicating who is to sit there.

place kick *Football.* ~*n.* **1.** a kick in which the ball is placed in position before it is kicked. ~*vb.* **place-kick. 2.** to kick (a ball) using a place kick. ~Compare **drop kick, punt**[2].

placeman ('pleɪsmən) *n., pl.* **-men.** *Brit., derogatory.* a person who holds a public office, esp. for private profit and as a reward for political support.

placement ('pleɪsmənt) *n.* **1.** the act of placing or the state of being placed. **2.** arrangement or position. **3.** the process or business of finding employment.

place name *n.* the name of a geographical location, such as a town or area.

placenta (plə'sɛntə) *n., pl.* **-tas** *or* **-tae** (-tiː). **1.** the vascular organ formed in the uterus of most mammals during pregnancy, consisting of both maternal and embryonic tissues and providing oxygen and nutrients for the fetus and transfer of waste products from the fetal to the maternal blood circulation. See also **afterbirth. 2.** the corresponding organ or part in certain other mammals. **3.** *Botany.* **a.** the part of the ovary of flowering plants to which the ovules are attached. **b.** the mass of tissue in nonflowering plants that bears the sporangia or spores. [C17: via Latin from Greek *plakoeis* flat cake, from *plax* flat]

placental (plə'sɛnt^{ə}l) *or* **placentate** *adj.* (esp. of animals) having a placenta: *placental mammals.* See also **eutherian.**

placentation (ˌplæsɛn'teɪʃən) *n.* **1.** *Botany.* the way in which ovules are attached in the ovary. **2.** *Zoology.* **a.** the way in which the placenta is attached in the uterus. **b.** the process of formation of the placenta.

place of safety order *n. Social welfare, law.* (in Britain) under the Children and Young Persons Act 1969, an order granted by a justice to a person or agency granting authority to detain a child or young person and take him or her to a place of safety for not more than 28 days, because of the child's actual or likely ill-treatment or neglect, etc.

placer ('plæsə) *n.* **a.** surface sediment containing particles of gold or some other valuable mineral. **b.** (*in combination*): *placer-mining.* [C19: from American Spanish: deposit, from Spanish *plaza* PLACE]

place setting *n.* the set of items of cutlery, crockery, and glassware laid for one person at a dining table.

placet ('pleɪsɛt) *n.* a vote or expression of assent by saying the word *placet.* [C16: from Latin, literally: it pleases]

place-value *adj.* denoting a series in which successive digits represent successive powers of the base.

placid ('plæsɪd) *adj.* having a calm appearance or nature. [C17: from Latin *placidus* peaceful; related to *placēre* to please] —**placidity** (plə'sɪdɪtɪ) *or* '**placidness** *n.* —'**placidly** *adv.*

placing ('pleɪsɪŋ) *n. Stock Exchange.* a method of issuing securities to the public using an intermediary, such as a stockbroking firm.

placket ('plækɪt) *n. Dressmaking.* **1.** a piece of cloth sewn in under a closure with buttons, hooks and eyes, zips, etc. **2.** the closure itself. [C16: perhaps from Middle Dutch *plackaet* breastplate, from Medieval Latin *placca* metal plate]

placoderm ('plækəˌdɜːm) *n.* any extinct bony-plated fishlike vertebrate of the class *Placodermi,* of Silurian to Permian times: thought to have been the earliest vertebrates with jaws. [C19: from Greek *plac-, plax* a flat plate + -DERM]

placoid ('plækɔɪd) *adj.* **1.** platelike or flattened. **2.** (of the scales of sharks and other elasmobranchs) toothlike; composed of dentine with an enamel tip and basal pulp cavity. [C19: from Greek *plac-, plax* flat]

plafond (plə'fɒn; *French* plafɔ̃) *n.* **1.** a ceiling, esp. one having ornamentation. **2.** a card game, a precursor of contract bridge. [C17: from French, literally: ceiling, maximum, from *plat* flat + *fond* bottom, from Latin *fundus* bottom]

plagal ('pleɪg^{ə}l) *adj.* **1.** (of a cadence) progressing from the subdominant to the tonic chord, as in the *Amen* of a hymn. **2.** (of a mode) commencing upon the dominant of an authentic mode, but sharing the same final as the authentic mode. Plagal modes are designated by the prefix *Hypo-* before the name of their authentic counterparts: *the Hypodorian mode.* ~Compare **authentic** (sense 5). [C16: from Medieval Latin *plagālis,* from *plaga,* perhaps from Greek *plagos* side]

plage (plɑːʒ) *n.* another name for **flocculus** (sense 1). [French, literally: beach, strand]

plagiarism ('pleɪdʒəˌrɪzəm) *n.* **1.** the act of plagiarizing. **2.** something plagiarized. —'**plagiarist** *n.* —ˌ**plagia'ristic** *adj.*

plagiarize *or* **plagiarise** ('pleɪdʒəˌraɪz) *vb.* to appropriate (ideas, passages, etc.) from (another work or author). —'**plagiaˌrizer** *or* '**plagiaˌriser** *n.*

plagiary ('pleɪdʒərɪ) *n., pl.* **-ries.** *Archaic.* a person who plagiarizes or a piece of plagiarism. [C16: from Latin *plagiārus* plunderer, from *plagium* kidnapping; related to *plaga* snare]

plagio- *combining form.* slanting, inclining, or oblique: *plagiotropism.* [from Greek *plagios,* from *plagos* side]

plagioclase (ˈpleɪdʒɪəʊˌkleɪz) *n.* a series of feldspar minerals consisting of a mixture of sodium and calcium aluminium silicates in triclinic crystalline form: includes albite, oligoclase, and labradorite. —**plagioclastic** (ˌpleɪdʒɪəʊˈklæstɪk) *adj.*

plagioclimax (ˌpleɪdʒɪəʊˈklaɪmæks) *n. Ecology.* the climax stage of a community, influenced by man or some other outside factor.

plagiotropism (ˌpleɪdʒɪəʊˈtrəʊˌpɪzəm) *n.* the growth of a plant at an angle to the vertical in response to a stimulus. —ˌ**plagioˈtropic** *adj.*

plague (pleɪg) *n.* **1.** any widespread and usually highly contagious disease with a high fatality rate. **2.** an infectious disease of rodents, esp. rats, transmitted to man by the bite of the rat flea (*Xenopsylla cheopis*). **3.** See **bubonic plague.** **4.** something that afflicts or harasses. **5.** *Informal.* an annoyance or nuisance. **6.** a pestilence, affliction, or calamity on a large scale, esp. when regarded as sent by God. **7.** *Archaic.* used to express annoyance, disgust, etc.: *a plague on you.* ~*vb.* **plagues, plaguing, plagued.** (*tr.*) **8.** to afflict or harass. **9.** to bring down a plague upon. **10.** *Informal.* to annoy. [C14: from Late Latin *plāga* pestilence, from Latin: a blow; related to Greek *plēgē* a stroke, Latin *plangere* to strike] —ˈ**plaguer** *n.*

plaguy *or* **plaguey** (ˈpleɪgɪ) *Archaic, informal.* ~*adj.* **1.** disagreeable or vexing. ~*adv.* **2.** disagreeably or annoyingly. —ˈ**plaguily** *adv.*

plaice (pleɪs) *n., pl.* **plaice** *or* **plaices.** **1.** a European flatfish, *Pleuronectes platessa,* having an oval brown body marked with red or orange spots and valued as a food fish: family *Pleuronectidae.* **2.** *U.S. and Canadian.* any of various other fishes of the family *Pleuronectidae,* esp. *Hippoglossoides platessoides.* [C13: from Old French *plaïz,* from Late Latin *platessa* flatfish, from Greek *platus* flat]

plaid (plæd, pleɪd) *n.* **1.** a long piece of cloth of a tartan pattern, worn over the shoulder as part of Highland costume. **2. a.** a crisscross weave or cloth. **b.** (*as modifier*): *a plaid scarf.* [C16: from Scottish Gaelic *plaide,* of obscure origin]

plain[1] (pleɪn) *adj.* **1.** flat or smooth; level. **2.** not complicated; clear: *the plain truth.* **3.** not difficult; simple or easy: *a plain task.* **4.** honest or straightforward. **5.** lowly, esp. in social rank or education. **6.** without adornment or show: *a plain coat.* **7.** (of fabric) without pattern or of simple untwilled weave. **8.** not attractive. **9.** not mixed; simple: *plain vodka.* **10.** *Knitting.* of or done in plain. ~*n.* **11.** a level or almost level tract of country, esp. an extensive treeless region. **12.** a simple stitch in knitting made by putting the right needle into a loop on the left needle, passing the wool round the right needle, and pulling it through the loop, thus forming a new loop. **13.** (in billiards) **a.** the unmarked white ball, as distinguished from the spot balls. **b.** the player using this ball. **14.** (in Ireland) short for **plain porter,** a light porter: *two pints of plain, please.* ~*adv.* **15.** (intensifier): *just plain tired.* ~See also **plains.** [C13: from Old French: simple, from Latin *plānus* level, distinct, clear] —ˈ**plainly** *adv.* —ˈ**plainness** *n.*

plain[2] (pleɪn) *vb.* a dialect or poetic word for **complain.** [C14 *pleignen,* from Old French *plaindre* to lament, from Latin *plangere* to beat]

plainchant (ˈpleɪnˌtʃɑːnt) *n.* another name for **plainsong.** [C18: from French, rendering Medieval Latin *cantus plānus;* see PLAIN[1]]

plain chocolate *n.* chocolate with a slightly bitter flavour and dark colour. Compare **milk chocolate.**

plain clothes *pl. n.* **a.** ordinary clothes, as distinguished from uniform, as worn by a police detective on duty. **b.** (*as modifier*): *a plain-clothes policeman.*

plain flour *n.* flour to which no raising agent has been added.

plain-laid *adj.* (of a cable or rope) made of three strands twisted together in the usual right-handed direction.

plains (pleɪnz) *pl. n. Chiefly U.S.* extensive tracts of level or almost level treeless countryside; prairies.

plain sailing *n.* **1.** *Informal.* smooth or easy progress. **2.** *Nautical.* sailing in a body of water that is unobstructed; clear sailing. Compare **plane sailing.**

Plains Indian *n.* a member of any of the North American Indian peoples formerly living in the Great Plains of the U.S. and Canada, east of the Rocky Mountains.

plainsman (ˈpleɪnzmən) *n., pl.* **-men.** a person who lives in a plains region, esp. in the Great Plains of North America.

plainsong (ˈpleɪnˌsɒŋ) *n.* the style of unison unaccompanied vocal music used in the medieval Church, esp. in Gregorian chant. Also called: **plainchant.** [C16: translation of Medieval Latin *cantus plānus*]

plain-spoken *adj.* candid; frank; blunt.

plaint (pleɪnt) *n.* **1.** *Archaic.* a complaint or lamentation. **2.** *Law.* a statement in writing of grounds of complaint made to a court of law and asking for redress of the grievance. [C13: from Old French *plainte,* from Latin *planctus* lamentation, from *plangere* to beat]

plain text *n. Telecomm.* a message set in a directly readable form rather than in coded groups.

plaintiff (ˈpleɪntɪf) *n.* a person who brings a civil action in a court of law. Compare **defendant** (sense 1). [C14: from legal French *plaintif,* from Old French *plaintif* (adj.) complaining, from *plainte* PLAINT]

plaintive (ˈpleɪntɪv) *adj.* expressing melancholy; mournful. [C14: from Old French *plaintif* grieving, from *plainte* PLAINT] —ˈ**plaintively** *adv.* —ˈ**plaintiveness** *n.*

plaister (ˈpleɪstə) *n. Obsolete or Scot.* plaster.

plait (plæt) *n.* **1.** a length of hair, ribbon, etc., that has been plaited. **2.** (in Britain) a loaf of bread of several twisting or intertwining parts. **3.** a rare spelling of **pleat.** ~*vb.* **4.** (*tr.*) to intertwine (strands or strips) in a pattern. [C15 *pleyt,* from Old French *pleit,* from Latin *plicāre* to fold; see PLY[2]]

plan (plæn) *n.* **1.** a detailed scheme, method, etc., for attaining an objective. **2.** (*sometimes pl.*) a proposed, usually tentative idea for doing something. **3.** a drawing to scale of a horizontal section through a building taken at a given level. Compare **ground plan** (sense 1), **elevation** (sense 5). **4.** an outline, sketch, etc. **5.** (in perspective drawing) any of several imaginary planes perpendicular to the line of vision and between the eye and object depicted. ~*vb.* **plans, planning, planned.** **6.** to form a plan (for) or make plans (for). **7.** (*tr.*) to make a plan of (a building). **8.** (*tr.; takes a clause as object or an infinitive*) to have in mind as a purpose; intend. [C18: via French from Latin *plānus* flat; compare PLANE[1], PLAIN[1]]

planar (ˈpleɪnə) *adj.* **1.** of or relating to a plane. **2.** lying in one plane; flat. [C19: from Late Latin *plānāris* on level ground, from Latin *plānus* flat] —**planarity** (pleɪˈnærɪtɪ) *n.*

planarian (pləˈnɛərɪən) *n.* any free-living turbellarian flatworm of the mostly aquatic suborder *Tricladida,* having a three-branched intestine. [C19: from New Latin *Plānāria* type genus, from Late Latin *plānārius* level, flat; see PLANE[1]]

planar process *n.* a method of producing diffused junctions in semiconductor devices. A pattern of holes is etched into an oxide layer formed on a silicon substrate, into which impurities are diffused through the holes.

planation (pleɪˈneɪʃən) *n.* the erosion of a land surface until it is basically flat.

planchet (ˈplɑːntʃɪt) *n.* a piece of metal ready to be stamped as a coin, medal, etc.; flan. [C17: from French: little board, from *planche* PLANK[1]]

planchette (plɑːnˈʃɛt) *n.* a heart-shaped board on wheels with a pencil attached that writes messages under supposed spirit guidance. [C19: from French: little board, from *planche* PLANK[1]]

Planck constant *or* **Planck's constant** (plæŋk) *n.* a fundamental constant equal to the energy of any quantum of radiation divided by its frequency. It has a value of 6.6262×10^{-34} joule seconds. Symbol: *h* See also **Dirac constant.** [named after Max *Planck* (1858–1947), German physicist]

Planck's law *n. Physics.* a law that is the basis of quantum theory, which states that the energy of electromagnetic radiation is confined to indivisible packets (quanta), each of which has an energy equal to the product of the Planck constant and the frequency of the radiation.

plane[1] (pleɪn) *n.* **1.** *Maths.* a flat surface in which a straight line joining any two of its points lies entirely on that surface. **2.** a flat or level surface. **3.** a level of existence, performance, attainment, etc. **4. a.** short for **aeroplane.** **b.** a wing or supporting surface of an aircraft or hydroplane. ~*adj.* **5.** level or flat. **6.** *Maths.* (of a curve, figure, etc.) lying entirely in one plane. ~*vb.* (*intr.*) **7.** to fly without moving wings or using engines; glide. **8.** (of a boat) to rise partly and skim over the water when moving at a certain speed. **9.** to travel by aeroplane. [C17: from Latin *plānum* level surface] —ˈ**planeness** *n.*

plane[2] (pleɪn) *n.* **1.** a tool with an adjustable sharpened steel blade set obliquely in a wooden or iron body, for levelling or smoothing timber surfaces, cutting mouldings or grooves, etc. **2.** a flat tool, usually metal, for smoothing the surface of clay or plaster in a mould. ~*vb.* (*tr.*) **3.** to level, smooth, or cut (timber, wooden articles, etc.) using a plane or similar tool. **4.** (often foll. by *off*) to remove using a plane. [C14: via Old French from Late Latin *plāna* plane, from *plānāre* to level]

plane[3] (pleɪn) *n.* See **plane tree.**

plane angle *n.* an angle between two intersecting lines.

plane chart *n.* a chart used in plane sailing, in which the lines of latitude and longitude are straight and parallel.

plane geometry *n.* the study of the properties of and relationships between plane curves, figures, etc.

plane polarization *n.* a type of polarization in which waves of light or other electromagnetic radiation are restricted to vibration in a single plane.

planer (ˈpleɪnə) *n.* **1.** a machine with a cutting tool that makes repeated horizontal strokes across the surface of a workpiece: used to cut flat surfaces into metal. **2.** a machine for planing wood, esp. one in which the cutting blades are mounted on a rotating drum. **3.** *Printing.* a flat piece of wood used to level type in a chase. **4.** any person or thing that planes.

plane sailing *n. Nautical.* navigation without reference to the earth's curvature. Compare **plain sailing.**

plane surveying *n.* the surveying of areas of limited size, making no corrections for the earth's curvature.

planet (ˈplænɪt) *n.* **1.** Also called: **major planet.** any of the nine celestial bodies, Mercury, Venus, earth, Mars, Jupiter, Saturn, Uranus, Neptune, or Pluto, that revolve around the sun in elliptical orbits and are illuminated by light from the sun. **2.** any celestial body revolving around a star, illuminated by light from that star. **3.** *Astrology.* any of the planets of the solar system, excluding the earth but including the sun and moon, each thought to rule one or sometimes two signs of the zodiac. See also **house** (sense 9). [C12: via Old French from Late Latin *planēta,* from Greek *planētēs* wanderer, from *planaein* to wander]

plane table *n.* **1.** a surveying instrument consisting of a drawing board mounted on adjustable legs, and used in the field for plotting measurements directly. ~*vb.* **plane-table. 2.** to survey (a plot of land) using a plane table.

planetarium (ˌplænɪˈtɛərɪəm) *n., pl.* **-iums** *or* **-ia** (-ɪə). **1.** an instrument for simulating the apparent motions of the sun, moon, and planets against a background of constellations by projecting images of these bodies onto the inside of a domed ceiling. **2.** a building in which such an instrument is housed. **3.** a model of the solar system, sometimes mechanized to show the relative motions of the planets.

planetary (ˈplænɪtərɪ, -trɪ) *adj.* **1.** of or relating to a planet. **2.** mundane; terrestrial. **3.** wandering or erratic. **4.** *Astrology.* under the influence of one of the planets. **5.** (of a gear, esp. an epicyclic gear) having an axis that rotates around that of another gear. **6.** (of an electron) having an orbit around the nucleus of an atom. ~*n., pl.* **-taries. 7.** a train of planetary gears.

planetary nebula *n.* a very faint hot star surrounded by an expanding envelope of tenuous ionized gases, mainly hydrogen, that emit a fluorescent glow because of intense short-wave radiation from the star.

planetesimal hypothesis (ˌplænɪˈtɛsɪməl) *n.* the discredited theory that the close passage of a star to the sun caused many small bodies (**planetesimals**) to be drawn from the sun, eventually coalescing to form the planets. [C20: *planetesimal,* from PLANET + INFINITESIMAL]

planetoid (ˈplænɪˌtɔɪd) *n.* another name for **asteroid** (sense 1). —ˌ**planeˈtoidal** *adj.*

planetology (ˌplænɪˈtɒlədʒɪ) *n. Astronomy.* the study of the origin, composition, and distribution of matter in the planets.

plane tree *or* **plane** *n.* any tree of the genus *Platanus,* having ball-shaped heads of fruits and leaves with pointed lobes: family *Platanaceae.* The hybrid *P.* × *hispanica* (**London plane**) is frequently planted in towns. Also called: **platan.** [C14 *plane,* from Old French, from Latin *platanus,* from Greek *platanos,* from *platos* wide, referring to the leaves]

planet-struck *or* **planet-stricken** *adj. Astrology.* affected by the influence of a planet, esp. malignly.

planet wheel *or* **gear** *n.* any one of the wheels of an epicyclic gear train that orbits the central axis of the train.

planform (ˈplænˌfɔːm) *n.* the outline or silhouette of an object, esp. an aircraft, as seen from above.

plangent (ˈplændʒənt) *adj.* **1.** having a loud deep sound. **2.** resonant and mournful in sound. [C19: from Latin *plangere* to beat (esp. the breast, in grief); see PLAIN[2]] —ˈ**plangency** *n.* —ˈ**plangently** *adv.*

planimeter (plæˈnɪmɪtə) *n.* a mechanical integrating instrument for measuring the area of an irregular plane figure, such as the area under a curve, by moving a point attached to an arm around the perimeter of the figure.

planimetry (plæˈnɪmɪtrɪ) *n.* the measurement of plane areas. —**planimetric** (ˌplænɪˈmɛtrɪk) *or* ˌ**planiˈmetrical** *adj.*

planish (ˈplænɪʃ) *vb. (tr.)* to give a final finish to (metal) by hammering or rolling to produce a smooth surface. [C16: from Old French *planir* to smooth out, from Latin *plānus* flat, PLAIN[1]] —ˈ**planisher** *n.*

planisphere (ˈplænɪˌsfɪə) *n.* a projection or representation of all or part of a sphere on a plane surface, such as a polar projection of the celestial sphere onto a chart. [C14: from Medieval Latin *plānisphaerium,* from Latin *plānus* flat + Greek *sphaira* globe] —**planispheric** (ˌplænɪˈsfɛrɪk) *adj.*

plank[1] (plæŋk) *n.* **1.** a stout length of sawn timber. **2.** something that supports or sustains. **3.** one of the policies in a political party's programme. **4. walk the plank.** to be forced by pirates to walk to one's death off the end of a plank jutting out over the water from the side of a ship. ~*vb. (tr.)* **5.** to cover or provide (an area) with planks. **6.** to beat (meat) to make it tender. **7.** *Chiefly U.S. and Canadian.* to cook or serve (meat or fish) on a special wooden board. [C13: from Old Norman French *planke,* from Late Latin *planca* board, from *plancus* flat-footed; probably related to Greek *plax* flat surface]

plank[2] (plæŋk) *vb. (tr.) Scot.* to hide; cache. [C19: a variant of *plant*]

planking (ˈplæŋkɪŋ) *n.* **1.** a number of planks. **2.** the act of covering or furnishing with planks.

plank-sheer *n. Nautical.* a plank or timber covering the upper ends of the frames of a wooden vessel. [C14 *plancher,* from Old French *planchier,* from *planche* plank, from Latin *planca;* spelling influenced by PLANK[1], SHEER[1]]

plankton (ˈplæŋktən) *n.* the organisms inhabiting the surface layer of a sea or lake, consisting of small drifting plants and animals, such as diatoms. Compare **nekton.** [C19: via German from Greek *planktos* wandering, from *plazesthai* to roam] —**planktonic** (plæŋkˈtɒnɪk) *adj.*

planned economy *n.* another name for **command economy.**

planned obsolescence *n.* the policy of deliberately limiting the life of a product in order to encourage the purchaser to replace it. Also called: **built-in obsolescence.**

planning blight *n.* the harmful effects of uncertainty about likely restrictions on the types and extent of future development in a particular area on the quality of life of its inhabitants and the normal growth of its business and community enterprises.

planning permission *n.* (in Britain) formal permission that must be obtained from a local authority before development or a change of use of land or buildings.

plano- *or sometimes before a vowel* **plan-** *combining form.* indicating flatness or planeness: *plano-concave.* [from Latin *plānus* flat, level]

plano-concave (ˌpleɪnəʊˈkɒnkeɪv) *adj.* (of a lens) having one side concave and the other side plane.

plano-convex (ˌpleɪnəʊˈkɒnvɛks) *adj.* (of a lens) having one side convex and the other side plane.

planogamete (ˈplænəgəˌmiːt) *n.* a motile gamete, such as a spermatozoon. [C19: from Greek *planos* wandering (see PLANET) + GAMETE]

planography (pləˈnɒgrəfɪ) *n. Printing.* any process, such as lithography, for printing from a flat surface. —**planographic** (ˌpleɪnəˈgræfɪk) *adj.* —ˌ**planoˈgraphically** *adv.*

planometer (plæˈnɒmɪtə) *n.* a flat metal plate used for directly testing the flatness of metal surfaces in accurate metalwork. —**planometric** (ˌpleɪnəˈmɛtrɪk) *adj.* —ˌ**planoˈmetrically** *adv.* —**plaˈnometry** *n.*

planosol (ˈpleɪnəˌsɒl) *n.* a type of intrazonal soil of humid or subhumid uplands having a strongly leached upper layer overlying a clay hardpan. [C20: from Latin PLANO- + *solum* soil]

plant[1] (plɑːnt) *n.* **1.** any living organism that typically synthesizes its food from inorganic substances, possesses cellulose cell walls, responds slowly and often permanently to a stimulus, lacks specialized sense organs and nervous system, and has no powers of locomotion. **2.** such an organism that is green, terrestrial, and smaller than a shrub or tree; a herb. **3.** a cutting, seedling, or similar structure, esp. when ready for transplantation. **4.** *Informal.* a thing positioned secretly for discovery by another, esp. in order to incriminate an innocent person. **5.** *Snooker, etc.* a position in which the cue ball can be made to strike an intermediate which then pockets another ball. ~*vb. (tr.)* **6.** (often foll. by *out*) to set (seeds, crops, etc.) into (ground) to grow. **7.** to place firmly in position. **8.** to establish; found. **9.** to implant in the mind. **10.** *Slang.* to deliver (a blow). **11.** *Informal.* to position or hide, esp. in order to deceive or observe. **12.** to place (young fish, oysters, spawn, etc.) in (a lake, river, etc.) in order to stock the water. ~See also **plant out.** [Old English, from Latin *planta* a shoot, cutting] —ˈ**plantable** *adj.* —ˈ**plantˌlike** *adj.*

plant[2] (plɑːnt) *n.* **1. a.** the land, buildings, and equipment used in carrying on an industrial, business, or other undertaking or service. **b.** (*as modifier*): *plant costs.* **2.** a factory or workshop. **3.** mobile mechanical equipment for construction, road-making, etc. [C20: special use of PLANT[1]]

Plantagenet (plænˈtædʒɪnɪt) *n.* **a.** any one of a line of English kings, ruling from the ascent of Henry II (1154) to the death of Richard III (1485). **b.** (*as modifier*) *a Plantagenet ruler.* [C12: from Old French, literally: sprig of broom, with reference to the crest of the Angevin kings, from Latin *planta* sprig + *genista* broom]

plant agreement *n.* a collective agreement at plant level within industry.

plantain[1] (ˈplæntɪn) *n.* any of various N temperate plants of the genus *Plantago,* esp. *P. major* (**great plantain**), which has a rosette of broad leaves and a slender spike of small greenish flowers: family *Plantaginaceae.* See also **ribwort.** [C14 *plauntein,* from Old French *plantein,* from Latin *plantāgō,* from *planta* sole of the foot]

plantain[2] (ˈplæntɪn) *n.* **1.** a large tropical musaceous plant, *Musa paradisiaca.* **2.** the green-skinned banana-like fruit of this plant, eaten as a staple food in many tropical regions. [C16: from Spanish *platano* plantain, PLANE TREE]

plantain-eater *n.* another name for **touraco.**

plantain lily *n.* any of several Asian plants of the liliaceous genus *Hosta,* having broad ribbed leaves and clusters of white, blue, or lilac flowers. Also called: **day lily.**

plantar (ˈplæntə) *adj.* of, relating to, or occurring on the sole of the foot or a corresponding part: *plantar warts.* [C18: from Latin *plantāris,* from *planta* sole of the foot]

plantation (plænˈteɪʃən) *n.* **1.** an estate, esp. in tropical countries, where cash crops such as rubber, oil palm, etc., are grown on a large scale. **2.** a group of cultivated trees or plants. **3.** (formerly) a colony or group of settlers. **4.** *Rare.* the planting of seeds, shoots, etc.

planter (ˈplɑːntə) *n.* **1.** the owner or manager of a plantation. **2.** a machine designed for rapid, uniform, and efficient planting of seeds in the ground. **3.** a colonizer or settler. **4.** a decorative pot or stand for house plants.

planter's punch *n.* a cocktail consisting of rum with lime or lemon juice and sugar.

plantigrade (ˈplæntɪˌgreɪd) *adj.* **1.** walking with the entire sole of the foot touching the ground, as, for example, man and bears. ~*n.* **2.** a plantigrade animal. [C19: via French from New Latin *plantigradus,* from Latin *planta* sole of the foot + *gradus* a step]

plant kingdom *n.* a category of living organisms comprising all plants. Compare **animal kingdom, mineral kingdom.**

plant louse *n.* **1.** another name for an **aphid.** **2. jumping plant louse.** any small active cicada-like insect of the homopterous family *Psyllidae* (or *Chermidae*), having hind legs adapted for leaping, and feeding on plant juices.

plantocracy (plɑːn'tɒkrəsɪ) *n., pl.* **-cies.** a ruling social class composed of planters.

plant out *vb.* (*tr., adv.*) to set (a seedling that has been raised in a greenhouse, frame, or other sheltered place) to grow out in open ground.

planula ('plænjʊlə) *n., pl.* **-lae** (-ˌliː). the ciliated free-swimming larva of hydrozoan coelenterates such as the hydra. [C19: from New Latin: a little plane, from Latin *plānum* level ground] —'**planular** *adj.*

plaque (plæk, plɑːk) *n.* **1.** an ornamental or commemorative inscribed tablet or plate of porcelain, wood, etc. **2.** a small flat brooch or badge, as of a club, etc. **3.** *Pathol.* any small abnormal patch on or within the body, such as the typical lesion of psoriasis. **4.** short for **dental plaque. 5.** *Bacteriol.* a clear area within a bacterial or tissue culture caused by localized destruction of the cells by a bacteriophage or other virus. [C19: from French, from *plaquier* to plate, from Middle Dutch *placken* to beat (metal) into a thin plate]

plash[1] (plæʃ) *vb., n.* a less common word for **splash.** [Old English *plæsc,* probably imitative; compare Dutch *plas*]

plash[2] (plæʃ) *vb.* another word for **pleach.** [C15: from Old French *plassier,* from *plais* hedge, woven fence, from Latin *plectere* to plait; compare PLEACH]

plashy ('plæʃɪ) *adj.* **plashier, plashiest. 1.** wet or marshy. **2.** splashing or splashy.

-plasia *or* **-plasy** *n. combining form.* indicating growth, development, or change: *hypoplasia.* [from New Latin, from Greek *plasis* a moulding, from *plassein* to mould]

plasm ('plæzəm) *n.* **1.** protoplasm of a specified type: *germ plasm.* **2.** a variant of **plasma.**

-plasm *n. combining form.* (in biology) indicating the material forming cells: *protoplasm.* [from Greek *plasma* something moulded; see PLASMA] —**-plasmic** *adj. combining form.*

plasma ('plæzmə) *or* **plasm** *n.* **1.** the clear yellowish fluid portion of blood or lymph in which the corpuscles and cells are suspended. **2.** short for **blood plasma. 3.** a former name for **protoplasm** or **cytoplasm. 4.** *Physics.* **a.** a hot ionized material consisting of nuclei and electrons. It is sometimes regarded as a fourth state of matter and is the material present in the sun, most stars, and fusion reactors. **b.** the ionized gas in an electric discharge or spark, containing positive ions and electrons and a small number of negative ions together with un-ionized material. **5.** a green slightly translucent variety of chalcedony, used as a gemstone. **6.** a less common term for **whey.** [C18: from Late Latin: something moulded, from Greek, from *plassein* to mould] —**plasmatic** (plæz'mætɪk) *or* '**plasmic** *adj.*

plasma engine *n.* an engine that generates thrust by reaction to the emission of a jet of plasma.

plasmagel ('plæzməˌdʒɛl) *n.* another name for **ectoplasm** (sense 1).

plasmagene ('plæzməˌdʒiːn) *n. Biology.* a self-replicating particle occurring in the cytoplasm of a cell and functioning in a way similar to but independent of chromosomal genes. —**plasmagenic** (ˌplæzmə'dʒɛnɪk) *adj.*

plasmalemma (ˌplæzmə'lɛmə) *or* **plasma membrane** *n.* other names for **cell membrane.**

plasmapheresis (ˌplæzmə'fɛrəsəs) *n.* (in blood transfusion) a technique for removing healthy or infected plasma by separating it from the red blood cells by settling or using a centrifuge and retransfusing the red blood cells in a harmless fluid into the donor or patient. [C20: from PLASM + Greek *aphairesis* taking away]

plasmasol ('plæzməˌsɒl) *n.* another name for **endoplasm.**

plasma torch *n.* an electrical device for converting a gas into a plasma, used for melting metal.

plasmid ('plæzmɪd) *n.* a small circle of bacterial DNA that is independent of the main bacterial chromosome. Plasmids often contain genes for drug resistances and can be transmitted between bacteria of the same and different species: used in genetic engineering. [C20: from PLASM + -ID[1]]

plasmin ('plæzmɪn) *n.* a proteolytic enzyme that causes fibrinolysis in blood clots.

plasminogen (plæz'mɪnədʒən) *n. Biochem.* a zymogen found in blood that gives rise to plasmin on activation.

plasmo- *or before a vowel* **plasm-** *combining form.* of, relating to, or resembling plasma: *plasmolysis.* [from Greek *plasma;* see PLASMA]

plasmodesma (ˌplæzmə'dɛzmə) *or* **plasmodesm** ('plæzməˌdɛzəm) *n., pl.* **-desmata** (-'dɛzmətə) *or* **-desms.** *Botany.* any of various very fine cytoplasmic threads connecting the cytoplasm of adjacent cells via minute holes in the cell walls. [C20: from PLASMO- + Greek *desma* bond]

plasmodium (plæz'məʊdɪəm) *n., pl.* **-dia** (-dɪə). **1.** an amoeboid mass of protoplasm, containing many nuclei: a stage in the life cycle of certain organisms, esp. the nonreproductive stage of the slime moulds. **2.** any parasitic sporozoan protozoan of the genus *Plasmodium,* such as *P. falciparum* and *P. vivax,* which cause malaria. [C19: New Latin; see PLASMA, -ODE[1]] —**plas'modial** *adj.*

plasmoid ('plæzˌmɔɪd) *n. Physics.* a section of a plasma having a characteristic shape.

plasmolyse *or U.S.* **plasmolyze** ('plæzməˌlaɪz) *vb.* to subject (a cell) to plasmolysis or (of a cell) to undergo plasmolysis.

plasmolysis (plæz'mɒlɪsɪs) *n.* the shrinkage of protoplasm away from the cell walls that occurs as a result of excessive water loss, esp. in plant cells (see **exosmosis**). —**plasmolytic** (ˌplæzmə'lɪtɪk) *adj.* —ˌ**plasmo'lytically** *adv.*

plasmon ('plæzmɒn) *n. Genetics.* the sum total of plasmagenes in a cell. [C20: from German, from Greek *plasma.* See PLASMA]

plasmosome ('plæzməˌsəʊm) *n.* another name for **nucleolus.**

-plast *n. combining form.* indicating an organized living cell or particle of living matter: *protoplast.* [from Greek *plastos* formed, from *plassein* to form]

plaster ('plɑːstə) *n.* **1.** a mixture of lime, sand, and water, sometimes stiffened with hair or other fibres, that is applied to the surface of a wall or ceiling as a soft paste that hardens when dry. **2.** *Brit.* an adhesive strip of material, usually medicated, for dressing a cut, wound, etc. **3.** short for **mustard plaster** or **plaster of Paris.** ~*vb.* **4.** to coat (a wall, ceiling, etc.) with plaster. **5.** (*tr.*) to apply like plaster: *she plastered make-up on her face.* **6.** (*tr.*) to cause to lie flat or to adhere. **7.** (*tr.*) to apply a plaster cast to. **8.** (*tr.*) *Slang.* to strike or defeat with great force. [Old English, from Medieval Latin *plastrum* medicinal salve, building plaster, via Latin from Greek *emplastron* curative dressing, from EM- + *plassein* to form] —'**plasterer** *n.* —'**plastery** *adj.*

plasterboard ('plɑːstəˌbɔːd) *n.* a thin rigid board, in the form of a layer of plaster compressed between two layers of fibreboard, used to form or cover walls.

plaster cast *n.* **1.** *Surgery.* a cast made of plaster of Paris. See **cast** (sense 40). **2.** a copy or mould of a sculpture or other object cast in plaster of Paris.

plastered ('plɑːstəd) *adj. Slang.* intoxicated; drunk.

plastering ('plɑːstərɪŋ) *n.* a coating or layer of plaster.

plaster of Paris *n.* **1.** a white powder that sets to a hard solid when mixed with water, used for making sculptures and casts, as an additive for lime plasters, and for making casts for setting broken limbs. It is usually the hemihydrate of calcium sulphate, $2CaSO_4.H_2O$. **2.** the hard plaster produced when this powder is mixed with water: a fully hydrated form of calcium sulphate. ~Sometimes shortened to **plaster.** [C15: from Medieval Latin *plastrum parisiense,* originally made from the gypsum of *Paris*]

plastic ('plæstɪk, 'plɑːs-) *n.* **1.** any one of a large number of synthetic usually organic materials that have a polymeric structure and can be moulded when soft and then set, esp. such a material in a finished state containing plasticizer, stabilizer, filler, pigments, etc. Plastics are classified as thermosetting (such as Bakelite) or thermoplastic (such as PVC) and are used in the manufacture of many articles and in coatings, artificial fibres, etc. Compare **resin** (sense 2). **2.** short for **plastic money.** ~*adj.* **3.** made of plastic. **4.** easily influenced; impressionable: *the plastic minds of children.* **5.** capable of being moulded or formed. **6.** *Fine arts.* **a.** of or relating to moulding or modelling: *the plastic arts.* **b.** produced or apparently produced by moulding: *the plastic draperies of Giotto's figures.* **7.** having the power to form or influence: *the plastic forces of the imagination.* **8.** *Biology.* of or relating to any formative process; able to change, develop, or grow: *plastic tissues.* **9.** of or relating to plastic surgery. **10.** *Slang.* superficially attractive yet unoriginal or artificial: *plastic food.* [C17: from Latin *plasticus* relating to moulding, from Greek *plastikos,* from *plassein* to form] —'**plastically** *adv.*

-plastic *adj. combining form.* growing or forming: *neoplastic.* [from Greek *plastikos;* see PLASTIC]

plastic bomb *n.* a bomb consisting of an adhesive jelly-like explosive fitted around a detonator.

plastic bullet *n.* a solid PVC cylinder, 10 cm long and 38 mm in diameter, fired by police in riots to regain control. Formal name: **baton round.**

Plasticine ('plæstɪˌsiːn) *n. Trademark.* a soft coloured material used, esp. by children, for modelling.

plasticity (plæ'stɪsɪtɪ) *n.* **1.** the quality of being plastic or able to be moulded. **2.** (in pictorial art) the quality of depicting space and form so that they appear three-dimensional.

plasticize *or* **plasticise** ('plæstɪˌsaɪz) *vb.* to make or become plastic, as by the addition of a plasticizer. —ˌ**plastici'zation** *or* ˌ**plastici'sation** *n.*

plasticizer *or* **plasticiser** ('plæstɪˌsaɪzə) *n.* any of a number of substances added to materials in order to modify their physical properties. Their uses include softening and improving the flexibility of plastics and preventing dried paint coatings from becoming too brittle.

plastic money *n.* credit cards, used instead of cash. [C20: from the cards being made of plastic]

plastic surgery *n.* the branch of surgery concerned with therapeutic or cosmetic repair or re-formation of missing, injured, or malformed tissues or parts. Also called: **anaplasty.** —**plastic surgeon** *n.*

plastid ('plæstɪd) *n.* any of various small particles in the cytoplasm of the cells of plants and some animals that contain pigments (see **chromoplast**), starch, oil, protein, etc. [C19: via German from Greek *plastēs* sculptor, from *plassein* to form]

plastometer (plæ'stɒmɪtə) *n.* an instrument for measuring plasticity. —**plastometric** (ˌplæstəʊ'mɛtrɪk) *adj.* —**plas'tometry** *n.*

plastron ('plæstrən) *n.* the bony plate forming the ventral part of the shell of a tortoise or turtle. [C16: via French from Italian *piastrone*, from *piastra* breastplate, from Latin *emplastrum* PLASTER] —'**plastral** *adj.*

-plasty *n. combining form.* indicating plastic surgery involving a bodily part, tissue, or a specified process: *rhinoplasty; neoplasty.* [from Greek *-plastia*; see -PLAST]

plat[1] (plæt) *n.* a small area of ground; plot. [C16 (also occurring in Middle English in place names): originally variant of PLOT[2]]

plat[2] (plæt) *n., vb.* **plats, platting, platted.** *Dialect.* a variant spelling of **plait.** [C16: variant of PLAIT]

plat. *abbrev. for:* **1.** plateau. **2.** platoon.

platan ('plætᵊn) *n.* another name for **plane tree.** [C14: from Latin *platanus*, from Greek *platanos*; see PLANE TREE]

plat du jour ('plɑː də 'ʒʊə; *French* pla dy ʒur) *n., pl.* **plats du jour** ('plɑːz də 'ʒʊə; *French* pla dy ʒur). the specially prepared or recommended dish of the day on a restaurant's menu. [French, literally: dish of the day]

plate (pleɪt) *n.* **1. a.** a shallow usually circular dish made of porcelain, earthenware, glass, etc., on which food is served or from which food is eaten. **b.** *(as modifier): a plate rack.* **2. a.** Also called: '**plateful.** the contents of a plate or the amount a plate will hold. **b.** *Austral. and N.Z.* a plate of cakes, sandwiches, etc., brought by a guest to a party: *everyone was asked to bring a plate.* **3.** an entire course of a meal: *a cold plate.* **4.** any shallow or flat receptacle, esp. for receiving a collection in church. **5.** flat metal of uniform thickness obtained by rolling, usually having a thickness greater than about three millimetres. **6.** a thin coating of metal usually on another metal, as produced by electrodeposition, chemical action, etc. **7.** metal or metalware that has been coated in this way, esp. with gold or silver: *Sheffield plate.* **8.** dishes, cutlery, etc., made of gold or silver. **9.** a sheet of metal, plastic, rubber, etc., having a printing surface produced by a process such as stereotyping, moulding, or photographic deposition. **10.** a print taken from such a sheet or from a woodcut, esp. when appearing in a book. **11.** a thin flat sheet of a substance, such as metal or glass. **12.** armour made of overlapping or articulated pieces of thin metal. **13.** *Photog.* **a.** a sheet of glass, or sometimes metal, coated with photographic emulsion on which an image can be formed by exposure to light. **b.** *(as modifier): a plate camera.* **14.** an orthodontic device, esp. one used for straightening children's teeth. **15.** an informal word for **denture** (sense 1). **16.** *Anatomy.* any flat platelike structure or part. **17. a.** a cup or trophy awarded to the winner of a sporting contest, esp. a horse race. **b.** a race or contest for such a prize. **18.** any of the rigid layers of the earth's lithosphere of which there are believed to be at least 15. See also **plate tectonics. 19.** *Electronics.* **a.** *Chiefly U.S.* the anode in an electronic valve. **b.** an electrode in an accumulator or capacitor. **20.** a horizontal timber joist that supports rafters or studs. **21.** a light horseshoe for flat racing. **22.** a thin cut of beef from the brisket. **23.** See **plate rail. 24.** Also called: **Communion plate.** *R.C. Church.* a flat plate held under the chin of a communicant in order to catch any fragments of the consecrated Host. **25.** *Archaic.* a coin, esp. one made of silver. **26. on a plate.** in such a way as to be acquired without further trouble: *he was handed the job on a plate.* **27. on one's plate.** waiting to be done or dealt with: *he has a lot on his plate at the moment.* ~*vb. (tr.)* **28.** to coat (a surface, usually metal) with a thin layer of other metal by electrolysis, chemical reaction, etc. **29.** to cover with metal plates, as for protection. **30.** *Printing.* to make a stereotype or electrotype from (type or another plate). **31.** to form (metal) into plate, esp. by rolling. **32.** to give a glossy finish to (paper) by calendering. **33.** to grow (microorganisms) in a culture medium. [C13: from Old French: thin metal sheet, something flat, from Vulgar Latin *plattus* (unattested); related to Greek *platus* flat]

plate armour *n.* armour made of thin metal plates, which superseded mail during the 14th century.

plateau ('plætəʊ) *n., pl.* **-eaus** *or* **-eaux** (-əʊz). **1.** a wide mainly level area of elevated land. **2.** a relatively long period of stability; levelling off: *the rising prices reached a plateau.* [C18: from French, from Old French *platel* something flat, from *plat* flat; see PLATE]

plated ('pleɪtɪd) *adj.* **1. a.** coated with a layer of metal. **b.** *(in combination): gold-plated.* **2.** (of a fabric) knitted in two different yarns so that one appears on the face and the other on the back.

plate glass *n.* glass formed into a thin sheet by rolling, used for windows.

platelayer ('pleɪtˌleɪə) *n. Brit.* a workman who lays and maintains railway track. U.S. equivalent: **trackman.**

platelet ('pleɪtlɪt) *n.* a minute particle occurring in the blood of vertebrates and involved in clotting of the blood. Formerly called: **thrombocyte.** [C19: a small PLATE]

platemark ('pleɪtˌmɑːk) *n., vb.* another name for **hallmark** (senses 1, 4).

platen ('plætᵊn) *n.* **1.** a flat plate in a printing press that presses the paper against the type. **2.** the roller on a typewriter, against which the keys strike. **3.** the worktable of a machine tool, esp. one that is slotted to enable clamping belts to be used. [C15: from Old French *platine*, from *plat* flat; see PLATE]

plater ('pleɪtə) *n.* **1.** a person or thing that plates. **2.** *Horse racing.* **a.** a mediocre horse entered chiefly for minor races. **b.** a blacksmith who shoes racehorses with the special type of light shoe used for racing.

plate rail *n. Railways.* an early flat rail with an extended flange on its outer edge to retain wheels on the track. Sometimes shortened to **plate.**

plate tectonics *n. (functioning as sing.) Geology.* the study of the structure of the earth's crust with reference to the theory that the earth's lithosphere is divided into large rigid blocks (**plates**) that are floating on semimolten rock and are thus able to interact with each other at their boundaries, and to the associated theories of continental drift and seafloor spreading.

platform ('plætfɔːm) *n.* **1.** a raised floor or other horizontal surface, such as a stage for speakers. **2.** a raised area at a railway station, from which passengers have access to the trains. **3.** See **drilling platform, production platform. 4.** the declared principles, aims, etc., of a political party, an organization, or an individual. **5.** a level raised area of ground. **6. a.** the thick raised sole of some high-heeled shoes. **b.** *(as modifier): platform shoes.* **7.** a vehicle or level place on which weapons are mounted and fired. [C16: from French *plateforme*, from *plat* flat + *forme* form, layout]

platform rocker *n. U.S. and Canadian.* a rocking chair supported on a stationary base.

platform ticket *n.* a ticket for admission to railway platforms but not for travel.

platina ('plætɪnə, plə'tiːnə) *n.* an alloy of platinum and several other metals, including palladium, osmium, and iridium. [C18: from Spanish: silvery element, from *plata* silver, from Provençal: silver plate]

plating ('pleɪtɪŋ) *n.* **1.** a coating or layer of material, esp. metal. **2.** a layer or covering of metal plates.

platinic (plə'tɪnɪk) *adj.* of or containing platinum, esp. in the tetravalent state.

platiniferous (ˌplætɪ'nɪfərəs) *adj.* platinum-bearing.

platiniridium (ˌplætɪnɪ'rɪdɪəm) *n.* any alloy of platinum and iridium: used in jewellery, electrical contacts, and hypodermic needles.

platinize *or* **platinise** ('plætɪˌnaɪz) *vb. (tr.)* to coat with platinum. —ˌ**platini'zation** *or* ˌ**platini'sation** *n.*

platino-, platini-, *or before a vowel* **platin-** *combining form.* of, relating to, containing, or resembling platinum: *platinotype.*

platinocyanic acid (ˌplætɪnəʊsaɪ'ænɪk) *n.* a hypothetical tetrabasic acid known only in the form of platinocyanide salts. Formula: $H_2Pt(CN)_4$.

platinocyanide (ˌplætɪnəʊ'saɪəˌnaɪd, -nɪd) *n.* any salt containing the divalent complex cation $[Pt(CN)_4]^{2-}$.

platinoid ('plætɪˌnɔɪd) *adj.* containing or resembling platinum: *a platinoid metal.*

platinotype ('plætɪnəʊˌtaɪp) *n.* an obsolete process for producing photographic prints using paper coated with an emulsion containing platinum salts, the resulting image in platinum black being more permanent and of a richer tone than the usual silver image.

platinous ('plætɪnəs) *adj.* of or containing platinum, esp. in the divalent state.

platinum ('plætɪnəm) *n.* **1.** a ductile malleable silvery-white metallic element, very resistant to heat and chemicals. It occurs free and in association with other platinum metals, esp. in osmiridium: used in jewellery, laboratory apparatus, electrical contacts, dentistry, electroplating, and as a catalyst. Symbol: Pt; atomic no.: 78; atomic wt.: 195.09; valency: 1–4; relative density: 21.45; melting pt.: 1772°C; boiling pt.: 3827°C (approx.). **2. a.** a medium to light grey colour. **b.** *(as adj.): a platinum carpet.* [C19: New Latin, from PLATINA, on the model of other metals with the suffix *-um*]

platinum black *n. Chem.* a black powder consisting of very finely divided platinum metal. It is used as a catalyst, esp. in hydrogenation reactions.

platinum-blond *or (fem.)* **platinum-blonde** *adj.* **1.** (of hair) of a pale silver-blond colour. **2. a.** having hair of this colour. **b.** *(as n.): she was a platinum blonde.*

platinum disc *n.* **a.** (in Britain) an LP record certified to have sold 300 000 copies or a single certified to have sold 600 000 copies. **b.** (in the U.S.) an LP record or single certified to have sold one million copies.

platinum metal *n.* any of the group of precious metallic elements consisting of ruthenium, rhodium, palladium, osmium, iridium, and platinum.

platitude ('plætɪˌtjuːd) *n.* **1.** a trite, dull, or obvious remark or statement; a commonplace. **2.** staleness or insipidity of thought or language; triteness. [C19: from French, literally: flatness, from *plat* flat] —ˌ**plati'tudinous** *adj.*

platitudinize *or* **platitudinise** (ˌplætɪ'tjuːdɪˌnaɪz) *vb. (intr.)* to speak or write in platitudes. —ˌ**plati'tudiˌnizer** *or* ˌ**plati'tudiˌniser** *n.*

Platonic (plə'tɒnɪk) *adj.* **1.** of or relating to Plato (?427–?347 B.C.), Greek philosopher and one of the founders of western philosophy, or to his teachings. **2.** (*often not cap.*) free from physical desire: *Platonic love.* —**Pla'tonically** *adv.*

Platonic solid *n.* any of the five possible regular polyhedra: cube, tetrahedron, octahedron, icosahedron, and dodecahedron. Also called (esp. formerly): **Platonic body.** [C17: named after *Plato*, who was the first to list them]

Platonism ('pleɪtəˌnɪzəm) *n.* **1.** the teachings of Plato and his followers, esp. the philosophical theory that the meanings of general words are real existing abstract entities (Forms) and that particular objects have properties in common by virtue of their relationship with these Forms. Compare **nominalism, conceptualism, intuitionism.** **2.** the realist doctrine that mathematical entities have real existence and that mathematical truth is independent of human thought. **3.** See **Neo-Platonism.** —'**Platonist** *n.*

platoon (plə'tuːn) *n.* **1.** *Military.* a subunit of a company usually comprising three sections of ten to twelve men: commanded by a lieutenant. **2.** a group or unit of people, esp. one sharing a common activity, characteristic, etc. [C17: from French *peloton* little ball, group of men, from *pelote* ball; see PELLET]

Plattdeutsch (*German* 'platdɔytʃ) *n.* another name for **Low German.** [literally: flat (that is, low) German]

platteland ('platəˌlant) *n.* **the.** (in South Africa) the area outside the cities and chief towns. [C20: from Afrikaans, from Dutch *plat* flat + *land* country]

platter ('plætə) *n.* **1.** a large shallow usually oval dish or plate, used for serving food. **2.** a course of a meal, usually consisting of several different foods served on the same plate: *a seafood platter.* **3.** *U.S. and Canadian slang.* a gramophone record. [C14: from Anglo-Norman *plater,* from *plat* dish, from Old French *plat* flat; see PLATE]

platy[1] ('pleɪtɪ) *adj.* **platier, platiest.** of, relating to, or designating rocks the constituents of which occur in flaky layers: *platy fracture.* [C19: from PLATE + -Y[1]]

platy[2] ('plætɪ) *n., pl.* **platy, platys,** *or* **platies.** any of various small brightly coloured freshwater cyprinodont fishes of the Central American genus *Xiphophorus,* esp. *X. maculatus.* [C20: shortened from New Latin *Platypoecilus* former genus name, from PLATY- + *-poecilus,* from Greek *poikilos* spotted]

platy- *combining form.* indicating something flat: *platyhelminth.* [from Greek *platus* flat]

platyhelminth (ˌplætɪ'hɛlmɪnθ) *n.* any invertebrate of the phylum *Platyhelminthes* (the flatworms). [C19: from New Latin *Platyhelmintha* flatworm, from PLATY- + Greek *helmins* worm] —ˌ**platyhel'minthic** *adj.*

platykurtic (ˌplætɪ'kɜːtɪk) *adj. Statistics.* (of a distribution) having kurtosis B_2 less than 3, less heavily concentrated about the mean than a normal distribution. Compare **leptokurtic, mesokurtic.** [C20: from PLATY- + Greek *kurtos* arched, bulging + -IC]

platypus ('plætɪpəs) *n., pl.* **-puses.** See **duck-billed platypus.** [C18: New Latin, from PLATY- + *-pus,* from Greek *pous* foot]

platyrrhine ('plætɪˌraɪn) *or* **platyrrhinian** (ˌplætɪ'rɪnɪən) *adj.* **1.** (esp. of New World monkeys) having widely separated nostrils opening to the side of the face. **2.** (of humans) having an unusually short wide nose. ~*n.* **3.** an animal or person with this characteristic. ~Compare **catarrhine.** [C19: from New Latin *platyrrhinus,* from PLATY- + *-rrhinus,* from Greek *rhis* nose]

plaudit ('plɔːdɪt) *n.* (*usually pl.*) **1.** an expression of enthusiastic approval or approbation. **2.** a round of applause. [C17: shortened from earlier *plaudite,* from Latin: applaud!, from *plaudere* to APPLAUD]

plausible ('plɔːzəbᵊl) *adj.* **1.** apparently reasonable, valid, truthful, etc.: *a plausible excuse.* **2.** apparently trustworthy or believable: *a plausible speaker.* [C16: from Latin *plausibilis* worthy of applause, from *plaudere* to APPLAUD] —ˌ**plausi'bility** *or* '**plausibleness** *n.* —'**plausibly** *adv.*

plausive ('plɔːsɪv) *adj.* **1.** expressing praise or approval; applauding. **2.** *Obsolete.* plausible.

play (pleɪ) *vb.* **1.** to occupy oneself in (a sport or diversion); amuse oneself in (a game). **2.** (*tr.*) to contend against (an opponent) in a sport or game: *Ed played Tony at chess and lost.* **3.** to fulfil or cause to fulfil (a particular role) in a team game: *he plays defence; he plays in the defence.* **4.** (*tr.*) to address oneself to (a ball) in a game: *play the ball not the man.* **5.** (*intr.;* often foll. by *about* or *around*) to behave carelessly, esp. in a way that is unconsciously cruel or hurtful; trifle or dally (with): *to play about with a young girl's affections.* **6.** (when *intr.,* often foll. by *at*) to perform or act the part (of) in or as in a dramatic production; assume or simulate the role (of): *to play the villain; just what are you playing at?* **7.** to act out or perform (a dramatic production). **8.** to give a performance in (a place) or (of a performance) to be given in a place. **9.** to have the ability to perform on (a musical instrument): *David plays the harp.* **10.** to perform (on a musical instrument) as specified: *he plays out of tune.* **11.** (*tr.*) **a.** to reproduce (a tune, melody, piece of music, note, etc.) on an instrument. **b.** to perform works by (a specific composer): *to play Brahms.* **12.** to discharge or cause to discharge: *he played the water from the hose onto the garden.* **13.** to operate, esp. to cause (a record player, radio, etc.) to emit sound or (of a record player, radio, etc.) to emit (sound): *he played a record; the radio was playing loudly.* **14.** to move or cause to move freely, quickly, or irregularly: *lights played on the scenery.* **15.** (*tr.*) *Stock Exchange.* to speculate or operate aggressively for gain in (a market). **16.** (*tr.*) *Angling.* to attempt to tire (a hooked fish) by alternately letting out and reeling in line and by using the rod's flexibility. **17.** to put (a card, counter, piece, etc.) into play. **18.** to gamble (money) on a game. **19. play ball.** *Informal.* to cooperate. **20. play fair** (*or* **false**). (often foll. by *with*) to prove oneself fair (or unfair) in one's dealings. **21. play by ear.** See **ear**[1] (sense 20). **22. play for time.** to delay the outcome of some activity so as to gain time to one's own advantage. **23. play into the hands of.** to act directly to the advantage of (an opponent). **24. play the fool.** See **fool**[1] (sense 5). **25. play the game.** See **game**[1] (sense 21). ~*n.* **26.** a dramatic composition written for performance by actors on a stage, on television, etc.; drama. **27. a.** the performance of a dramatic composition. **b.** (*in combination*): *playreader.* **28. a.** games, exercise, or other activity undertaken for pleasure, diversion, etc., esp. by children. **b.** (*in combination*): *playroom.* **c.** (*as modifier*): *play dough.* **29.** manner of action, conduct, or playing: *fair play.* **30.** the playing or conduct of a game or the period during which a game is in progress: *rain stopped play.* **31.** *U.S. and Canadian.* a move or manoeuvre in a game: *a brilliant play.* **32.** the situation of a ball that is within the defined area and being played according to the rules (in the phrases **in play, out of play**). **33.** a turn to play: *it's my play.* **34.** the act of playing for stakes; gambling. **35.** action, activity, or operation: *the play of the imagination.* **36.** freedom of or scope or space for movement: *too much play in the rope.* **37.** light, free, or rapidly shifting motion: *the play of light on the water.* **38.** fun, jest, or joking: *I only did it in play.* **39. make a play for.** *Informal.* **a.** to make an obvious attempt to gain. **b.** to attempt to attract or seduce. ~See also **play along, playback, play down, play off, play on, play out, play up, play with.** [Old English *plega* (n.), *plegan* (vb.); related to Middle Dutch *pleyen*] —'**playable** *adj.*

playa ('plɑːjə; *Spanish* 'plaja) *n.* (in the U.S.) a temporary lake, or its dry often salty bed, in a desert basin. [Spanish: shore, from Late Latin *plagia,* from Greek *plagios* slanting, from *plagos* side; compare French *plage* beach]

play-act *vb.* **1.** (*intr.*) to pretend or make believe. **2.** (*intr.*) to behave in an overdramatic or affected manner. **3.** to act in or as in (a play). —'**play-ˌacting** *n.* —'**play-ˌactor** *n.*

play along *vb.* (*adv.*) **1.** (*intr.;* usually foll. by *with*) to cooperate (with), esp. as a temporary measure. **2.** (*tr.*) to manipulate as if in a game, esp. for one's own advantage: *he played the widow along until she gave him her money.*

playback ('pleɪˌbæk) *n.* **1.** the act or process of reproducing a recording, esp. on magnetic tape. **2.** the part of a tape recorder serving to reproduce or used for reproducing recorded material. **3.** (*modifier*) of or relating to the reproduction of signals from a recording: *the playback head of a tape recorder.* ~*vb.* **play back.** (*adv.*) **4.** to reproduce (recorded material) on (a magnetic tape) by means of a tape recorder.

playbill ('pleɪˌbɪl) *n.* **1.** a poster or bill advertising a play. **2.** the programme of a play.

playboy ('pleɪˌbɔɪ) *n.* a man, esp. one of private means, who devotes himself to the pleasures of nightclubs, expensive holiday resorts, female company, etc.

play-centre *n.* the N.Z. name for **playgroup.**

play down *vb.* (*tr., adv.*) to make little or light of; minimize the importance of.

player ('pleɪə) *n.* **1.** a person who participates in or is skilled at some game or sport. **2.** a person who plays a game or sport professionally. **3.** a person who plays a musical instrument. **4.** an actor. **5.** *Informal.* a participant, esp. a powerful one, in a particular field of activity: *a leading city player.* **6.** See **record player.** **7.** the playing mechanism in a Pianola.

player piano *n.* a mechanical piano; Pianola.

playful ('pleɪfʊl) *adj.* **1.** full of high spirits and fun: *a playful kitten.* **2.** good-natured and humorous: *a playful remark.* —'**playfully** *adv.* —'**playfulness** *n.*

playgoer ('pleɪˌgəʊə) *n.* a person who goes to theatre performances, esp. frequently.

playground ('pleɪˌgraʊnd) *n.* **1.** an outdoor area for children's play, esp. one having swings, slides, etc., or adjoining a school. **2.** a place or region particularly popular as a sports or holiday resort. **3.** a sphere of activity: *reading was his private playground.*

playgroup ('pleɪˌgruːp) *n.* a regular meeting of small children arranged by their parents or a welfare agency to give them an opportunity of supervised creative play. See also **preschool, playschool.**

playhouse ('pleɪˌhaʊs) *n.* **1.** a theatre where live dramatic performances are given. **2.** a toy house, small room, etc., for children to play in.

playing card *n.* one of a pack of 52 rectangular pieces of stiff card, used for playing a wide variety of games, each card having one or more symbols of the same kind (diamonds, hearts, clubs, or spades) on the face, but an identical design on the reverse. See also **suit** (sense 4).

playing field *n. Chiefly Brit.* a field or open space used for sport.

playlet ('pleɪlɪt) *n.* a short play.

play-lunch *n. N.Z.* a schoolchild's mid-morning snack.

playmate ('pleɪˌmeɪt) *or* **playfellow** *n.* a friend or partner in play or recreation: *childhood playmates.*

play off *vb.* (*adv.*) **1.** (*tr.*; usually foll. by *against*) to deal with or manipulate as if in playing a game: *to play one person off against another.* **2.** (*intr.*) to take part in a play-off. ~*n.* **play-off. 3.** *Sport.* an extra contest to decide the winner when two or more competitors are tied. **4.** *Chiefly U.S. and Canadian.* a contest or series of games to determine a championship, as between the winners of two competitions.

play on *vb.* (*intr.*) **1.** (*adv.*) to continue to play. **2.** (*prep.*) Also: **play upon.** to exploit or impose upon (the feelings or weakness of another) to one's own advantage. **3.** (*adv.*) *Cricket.* to hit the ball into one's own wicket.

play on words *n.* another term for **pun**[1] (sense 1).

play out *vb.* (*tr., adv.*) **1.** to finish: *let's play the game out if we aren't too late.* **2.** (*often passive*) *Informal.* to use up or exhaust. **3.** to release gradually: *he played the rope out.*

playpen ('pleɪˌpɛn) *n.* a small enclosure, usually portable, in which a young child can be left to play in safety.

playroom ('pleɪˌruːm, -ˌrʊm) *n.* a recreation room, esp. for children.

playschool ('pleɪˌskuːl) *n.* an informal nursery group taking preschool children in half-day sessions. Also called: **playgroup.**

playsuit ('pleɪˌsuːt, -ˌsjuːt) *n.* a woman's or child's outfit, usually comprising shorts and a top.

plaything ('pleɪˌθɪŋ) *n.* **1.** a toy. **2.** a person regarded or treated as a toy: *he thinks she is just his plaything.*

playtime ('pleɪˌtaɪm) *n.* a time for play or recreation, esp. the school break.

play up *vb.* (*adv.*) **1.** (*tr.*) to emphasize or highlight: *to play up one's best features.* **2.** *Brit. informal.* to behave irritatingly (towards). **3.** (*intr.*) *Brit. informal.* (of a machine, car, etc.) to function erratically: *the car is playing up again.* **4.** *Brit. informal.* to hurt; give (one) pain or trouble: *my back's playing me up again.* **5. play up to. a.** to support (another actor) in a performance. **b.** to try to gain favour with by flattery.

play with *vb.* (*intr., prep.*) **1.** to consider without giving deep thought to or coming to a conclusion concerning: *we're playing with the idea of emigrating.* **2.** to behave carelessly with: *to play with a girl's affections.* **3.** to fiddle or mess about with: *he's just playing with his food.*

playwright ('pleɪˌraɪt) *n.* a person who writes plays.

plaza ('plɑːzə; *Spanish* 'plaθa) *n.* **1.** an open space or square, esp. in Spain or a Spanish-speaking country. **2.** *Chiefly U.S. and Canadian.* **a.** a modern complex of shops, buildings, and parking areas. **b.** (*cap. when part of a name*): *Rockefeller Plaza.* [C17: from Spanish, from Latin *platēa* courtyard, from Greek *plateia*; see PLACE]

plc *or* **PLC** *abbrev. for* public limited company. See also **limited** (sense 5).

plea (pliː) *n.* **1.** an earnest entreaty or request: *a plea for help.* **2. a.** *Law.* something alleged or pleaded by or on behalf of a party to legal proceedings in support of his claim or defence. **b.** *Criminal law.* the answer made by an accused to the charge: *a plea of guilty.* **c.** (in Scotland and formerly in England) a suit or action at law. **3.** an excuse, justification, or pretext: *he gave the plea of a previous engagement.* [C13: from Anglo-Norman *plai*, from Old French *plaid* lawsuit, from Medieval Latin *placitum* court order (literally: what is pleasing), from Latin *placēre* to please]

plea bargaining *n.* an agreement between the prosecution and defence, sometimes including the judge, in which the accused agrees to plead guilty to a lesser charge in return for more serious charges being dropped.

pleach (pliːtʃ) *vb. Chiefly Brit.* to construct or repair (a hedge) by interlacing the shoots. Also: **plash.** [C14 *plechen*, from Old North French *plechier*, from Latin *plectere* to weave, plait; compare PLASH[2]]

plead (pliːd) *vb.* **pleads, pleading; pleaded, plead** (plɛd), *or esp. Scot. and U.S.* **pled** (plɛd). **1.** (when *intr.*, often foll. by *with*) to appeal earnestly or humbly (to). **2.** (*tr.*; *may take a clause as object*) to give as an excuse; offer in justification or extenuation: *to plead ignorance; he pleaded that he was insane.* **3.** (*intr.*; often foll. by *for*) to provide an argument or appeal (for): *her beauty pleads for her.* **4.** *Law.* to declare oneself to be (guilty or not guilty) in answer to the charge. **5.** *Law.* to advocate (a case) in a court of law. **6.** (*intr.*) *Law.* **a.** to file pleadings. **b.** to address a court as an advocate. [C13: from Old French *plaidier*, from Medieval Latin *placitāre* to have a lawsuit, from Latin *placēre* to please; see PLEA] —'**pleadable** *adj.* —'**pleader** *n.*

pleading ('pliːdɪŋ) *n. Law.* **1.** the act of presenting a case in court, as by a lawyer on behalf of his client. **2.** the art or science of preparing the formal written statements of the parties to a legal action. See also **pleadings.**

pleadings ('pliːdɪŋz) *pl. n. Law.* the formal written statements presented alternately by the plaintiff and defendant in a lawsuit setting out the respective matters relied upon.

pleasance ('plɛzəns) *n.* **1.** a secluded part of a garden laid out with trees, walks, etc. **2.** *Archaic.* enjoyment or pleasure. [C14 *plesaunce*, from Old French *plaisance*, from *plaisant* pleasant, from *plaisir* to PLEASE]

pleasant ('plɛzᵊnt) *adj.* **1.** giving or affording pleasure; enjoyable. **2.** having pleasing or agreeable manners, appearance, habits, etc. **3.** *Obsolete.* merry and lively. [C14: from Old French *plaisant*, from *plaisir* to PLEASE] —'**pleasantly** *adv.* —'**pleasantness** *n.*

pleasantry ('plɛzᵊntrɪ) *n., pl.* **-ries. 1.** (*often pl.*) an agreeable or amusing remark, often one made in order to be polite: *they exchanged pleasantries.* **2.** an agreeably humorous manner or style. **3.** *Rare.* enjoyment; pleasantness: *a pleasantry of life.* [C17: from French *plaisanterie*, from *plaisant* PLEASANT]

please (pliːz) *vb.* **1.** to give satisfaction, pleasure, or contentment to (a person); make or cause (a person) to be glad. **2.** to be the will of or have the will (to): *if it pleases you; the court pleases.* **3. if you please.** if you will or wish, sometimes used in ironic exclamation. **4. pleased with.** happy because of. **5. please oneself.** to do as one likes. ~*adv.* **6.** (*sentence modifier*) used in making polite requests and in pleading, asking for a favour, etc.: *please don't tell the police where I am.* **7. yes please.** a polite formula for accepting an offer, invitation, etc. [C14 *plese*, from Old French *plaisir*, from Latin *placēre* to please, satisfy] —'**pleasable** *adj.* —**pleased** *adj.* —**pleasedly** ('pliːzɪdlɪ) *adv.* —'**pleaser** *n.*

pleasing ('pliːzɪŋ) *adj.* giving pleasure; likable or gratifying. —'**pleasingly** *adv.* —'**pleasingness** *n.*

pleasurable ('plɛʒərəbᵊl) *adj.* enjoyable, agreeable, or gratifying. —'**pleasurableness** *n.* —'**pleasurably** *adv.*

pleasure ('plɛʒə) *n.* **1.** an agreeable or enjoyable sensation or emotion: *the pleasure of hearing good music.* **2.** something that gives or affords enjoyment or delight: *his garden was his only pleasure.* **3. a.** amusement, recreation, or enjoyment. **b.** (*as modifier*): *a pleasure boat; pleasure ground.* **4.** *Euphemistic.* sexual gratification or enjoyment: *he took his pleasure of her.* **5.** a person's preference or choice. ~*vb.* **6.** (when *intr.*, often foll. by *in*) *Archaic.* to give pleasure to or take pleasure (in). [C14 *plesir*, from Old French; related to Old French *plaisir* to PLEASE] —'**pleasureful** *adj.* —'**pleasureless** *adj.*

pleasure principle *n. Psychoanal.* the idea that psychological processes and actions are governed by the gratification of needs. It is seen as the governing process of the id, whereas the reality principle is the governing process of the ego. See also **hedonism.**

pleat (pliːt) *n.* **1.** any of various types of fold formed by doubling back fabric and pressing, stitching, or steaming into place. See also **box pleat, inverted pleat, kick pleat, knife pleat, sunburst pleats.** ~*vb.* **2.** (*tr.*) to arrange (material, part of a garment, etc.) in pleats. [C16: variant of PLAIT]

pleater ('pliːtə) *n.* an attachment on a sewing machine that makes pleats.

pleb (plɛb) *n.* **1.** short for **plebeian. 2.** *Brit. informal, often derogatory.* a common vulgar person. ~See also **plebs.**

plebby ('plɛbɪ) *adj.* **-bier, -biest.** *Brit. informal, often derogatory.* common or vulgar: *a plebby party.* [C20: shortened from PLEBEIAN]

plebe (pliːb) *n. Informal.* a member of the lowest class at the U.S. Naval Academy or Military Academy; freshman. [C19: shortened from PLEBEIAN]

plebeian (plə'biːən) *adj.* **1.** of, relating to, or characteristic of the common people, esp. those of Rome. **2.** lacking refinement; philistine or vulgar: *plebeian tastes.* ~*n.* **3.** one of the common people, esp. one of the Roman plebs. **4.** a person who is coarse, vulgar, or lacking in refinement or discernment. [C16: from Latin *plēbēius* belonging to the people, from *plēbs* the common people of ancient Rome] —**ple'beianˌism** *n.*

plebiscite ('plɛbɪˌsaɪt, -sɪt) *n.* **1.** a direct vote by the electorate of a state, region, etc., on some question of usually national importance, such as union with another state or acceptance of a government programme. **2.** any expression or determination of public opinion on some matter. ~See also **referendum.** [C16: from Old French *plēbiscite*, from Latin *plēbiscītum* decree of the people, from *plēbs* the populace + *scītum*, from *scīscere* to decree, approve, from *scīre* to know] —**plebiscitary** (plə'bɪsɪtərɪ) *adj.*

plebs (plɛbz) *n.* **1.** (*functioning as pl.*) the common people; the masses. **2.** (*functioning as sing. or pl.*) common people of ancient Rome. Compare **patrician.** [C17: from Latin: the common people of ancient Rome]

plectognath ('plɛktɒgˌnæθ) *n.* **1.** any spiny-finned marine fish of the mainly tropical order *Plectognathi* (or *Tetraodontiformes*), having a small mouth, strong teeth, and small gill openings: includes puffers, triggerfish, trunkfish, sunfish, etc. ~*adj.* **2.** of, relating to, or belonging to the order *Plectognathi.* [C19: via New Latin from Greek *plektos* twisted + *gnathos* jaw]

plectrum ('plɛktrəm) *or* **plectron** ('plɛktrən) *n., pl.* **-tra** (-trə), **-trums** *or* **-tra, -trons.** any implement for plucking a string, such as a small piece of plastic, wood, etc., used to strum a guitar, or the quill that plucks the string of a harpsichord. [C17: from Latin *plēctrum* quill, plectrum, from Greek *plektron*, from *plessein* to strike]

pled (plɛd) *vb. U.S. or* (*esp. in legal usage*) *Scot.* a past tense and past participle of **plead.**

pledge (plɛdʒ) *n.* **1.** a formal or solemn promise or agreement, esp. to do or refrain from doing something. **2. a.** collateral for the payment of a debt or the performance of an obligation. **b.** the condition of being collateral (esp. in the phrase **in pledge**). **3.** a sign, token, or indication: *the gift is a pledge of their sincerity.* **4.** an assurance of support or goodwill, conveyed by drinking to a person, cause, etc.; toast: *we drank a pledge to their success.* **5.** a person who binds himself, as by becoming bail or surety for another. **6. take** *or* **sign the pledge.** to make a vow to abstain from alcoholic drink. ~*vb.* **7.** to promise formally or solemnly: *he pledged allegiance.* **8.** (*tr.*) to bind or secure by or as if by a pledge: *they were pledged to secrecy.* **9.** to give, deposit, or offer (one's word, freedom, property, etc.) as a guarantee, as for the repayment of a loan. **10.** to drink a toast to (a person, cause, etc.). [C14: from Old French *plege,* from Late Latin *plebium* gage, security, from *plebīre* to pledge, of Germanic origin; compare Old High German *pflegan* to look after, care for] —**'pledgable** *adj.*

pledgee (plɛdʒ'iː) *n.* **1.** a person to whom a pledge is given. **2.** a person to whom property is delivered as a pledge.

pledget ('plɛdʒɪt) *n.* a small flattened pad of wool, cotton, etc., esp. for use as a pressure bandage to be applied to wounds or sores. [C16: of unknown origin]

pledgor, pledgeor (plɛdʒ'ɔː), *or* **pledger** ('plɛdʒə) *n.* a person who gives or makes a pledge.

-plegia *n. combining form.* indicating a specified type of paralysis: *paraplegia.* [from Greek, from *plēgē* stroke, from *plēssein* to strike] —**-plegic** *adj. and n. combining form.*

pleiad ('plaɪəd) *n.* a brilliant or talented group, esp. one with seven members. [C16: originally French *Pléiade,* name of a group of French poets, after a group of Alexandrian Greek poets who were called this after the *Pleiades,* the seven daughters of Atlas in Greek mythology]

Pleiades ('plaɪəˌdiːz) *pl. n.* a conspicuous open star cluster in the constellation Taurus, containing several hundred stars only six or seven of which are visible to the naked eye. Compare **Hyades.**

plein-air (ˌpleɪn'ɛə; *French* plɛnɛr) *adj.* of or in the manner of various French 19th-century schools of painting, esp. impressionism, concerned with the observation of light and atmosphere effects outdoors. [C19: from French phrase *en plein air* in the open (literally: full) air] —**plein-airist** (ˌpleɪn'ɛərɪst) *n.*

pleio- *combining form.* a variant of **plio-.**

Pleiocene ('plaɪəʊˌsiːn) *adj., n.* a variant spelling of **Pliocene.**

pleiotropism (plaɪ'ɒtrəˌpɪzəm) *n. Genetics.* the condition of a gene of affecting more than one characteristic of the phenotype.

Pleistocene ('plaɪstəˌsiːn) *adj.* **1.** of, denoting, or formed in the first epoch of the Quaternary period, which lasted for about 990 000 years. It was characterized by extensive glaciations of the N hemisphere and the evolutionary development of man. ~*n.* **2. the.** the Pleistocene epoch or rock series. [C19: from Greek *pleistos* most + *kainos* recent]

plenary ('pliːnərɪ, 'plɛn-) *adj.* **1.** full, unqualified, or complete: *plenary powers; plenary indulgence.* **2.** (of assemblies, councils, etc.) attended by all the members. ~*n., pl.* **-ries. 3.** a book of the gospels or epistles and homilies read at the Eucharist. [C15: from Late Latin *plēnārius,* from Latin *plēnus* full; related to Middle English *plener;* see PLENUM] —**'plenarily** *adv.*

plenipotent (plə'nɪpətənt) *adj.* a less common word for **plenipotentiary.**

plenipotentiary (ˌplɛnɪpə'tɛnʃərɪ) *adj.* **1.** (esp. of a diplomatic envoy) invested with or possessing full power or authority. **2.** conferring full power or authority. **3.** (of power or authority) full; absolute. ~*n., pl.* **-aries. 4.** a person invested with full authority to transact business, esp. a diplomat authorized to represent a country. See also **envoy**[1] (sense 1). [C17: from Medieval Latin *plēnipotentiārius,* from Latin *plēnus* full + *potentia* POWER]

plenish ('plɛnɪʃ) *vb.* (*tr.*) *Archaic or Scot.* to fill, stock, or resupply. [C15: from Old French *pleniss-,* from *plenir,* from Latin *plēnus* full] —**'plenisher** *n.* —**'plenishment** *n.*

plenitude ('plɛnɪˌtjuːd) *n.* **1.** abundance; copiousness. **2.** the condition of being full or complete. [C15: via Old French from Latin *plēnitūdō,* from *plēnus* full]

plenteous ('plɛntɪəs) *adj.* **1.** ample; abundant: *a plenteous supply of food.* **2.** producing or yielding abundantly: *a plenteous grape harvest.* [C13 *plenteus,* from Old French *plentivous,* from *plentif* abundant, from *plenté* PLENTY] —**'plenteously** *adv.* —**'plenteousness** *n.*

plentiful ('plɛntɪfʊl) *adj.* **1.** ample; abundant. **2.** having or yielding an abundance: *a plentiful year.* —**'plentifully** *adv.* —**'plentifulness** *n.*

plenty ('plɛntɪ) *n., pl.* **-ties. 1.** (often foll. by *of*) a great number, amount, or quantity; lots: *plenty of time; there are plenty of cars on display here.* **2.** generous or ample supplies of wealth, produce, or resources: *the age of plenty.* **3. in plenty.** existing in abundance: *food in plenty.* ~*determiner.* **4. a.** very many; ample: *plenty of people believe in ghosts.* **b.** (*as pronoun*): *there's plenty more; that's plenty, thanks.* ~*adv.* **5.** *Not standard, chiefly U.S.* (intensifier): *he was plenty mad.* **6.** *Informal.* more than adequately; abundantly: *the water's plenty hot enough.* [C13: from Old French *plenté,* from Late Latin *plēnitās* fullness, from Latin *plēnus* full]

plenum ('pliːnəm) *n., pl.* **-nums** *or* **-na** (-nə). **1.** an enclosure containing gas at a higher pressure than the surrounding environment. **2.** a fully attended meeting or assembly, esp. of a legislative body. **3.** (esp. in the philosophy of the Stoics) space regarded as filled with matter. Compare **vacuum** (sense 1). **4.** the condition or quality of being full. [C17: from Latin: space filled by matter, from *plēnus* full]

plenum system *n.* a type of air-conditioning system in which air is passed into a room at a pressure greater than atmospheric pressure.

pleo- *combining form.* a variant of **plio-**: *pleochroism; pleomorphism.*

pleochroism (plɪ'ɒkrəʊˌɪzəm) *n.* a property of certain crystals of absorbing light to an extent that depends on the orientation of the electric vector of the light with respect to the optic axes of the crystal. The effect occurs in uniaxial crystals (**dichroism**) and esp. in biaxial crystals (**trichroism**). [C19: PLEO- + *-chroism* from Greek *khrōs* skin colour] —**pleochroic** (ˌpliːə'krəʊɪk) *adj.*

pleomorphism (ˌpliːə'mɔːˌfɪzəm) *or* **pleomorphy** ('pliːəˌmɔːfɪ) *n.* **1.** the occurrence of more than one different form in the life cycle of a plant or animal. **2.** the occurrence of more than one different form of crystal of one chemical compound; polymorphism. —ˌ**pleo'morphic** *adj.*

pleonasm ('pliːəˌnæzəm) *n. Rhetoric.* **1.** the use of more words than necessary or an instance of this, such as *a tiny little child.* **2.** a word or phrase that is superfluous. [C16: from Latin *pleonasmus,* from Greek *pleonasmos* excess, from *pleonazein* to be redundant] —ˌ**pleo'nastic** *adj.* —ˌ**pleo'nastically** *adv.*

pleopod ('pliːəˌpɒd) *n.* another name for **swimmeret.** [C19: from Greek *plein* to swim + *pous* foot]

plesiosaur ('pliːsɪəˌsɔː) *n.* any of various extinct marine reptiles of the order *Sauropterygia,* esp. any of the suborder *Plesiosauria,* of Jurassic and Cretaceous times, having a long neck, short tail, and paddle-like limbs. See also **ichthyosaur.** Compare **dinosaur, pterosaur.** [C19: from New Latin *plēsiosaurus,* from Greek *plēsios* near + *sauros* a lizard]

plessor ('plɛsə) *n.* another name for **plexor.**

plethora ('plɛθərə) *n.* **1.** superfluity or excess; overabundance. **2.** *Pathol., obsolete.* a condition caused by dilation of superficial blood vessels, characterized esp. by a reddish face. [C16: via Medieval Latin from Greek *plēthōrē* fullness, from *plēthein* to grow full] —**plethoric** (plɛ'θɒrɪk) *adj.* —**ple'thorically** *adv.*

plethysmograph (plə'θɪzməˌgrɑːf, -ˌgræf, -'θɪs-) *n.* a device for measuring the fluctuations in volume of a bodily organ or part, such as those caused by variations in the amount of blood it contains. [C19: from Greek *plēthusmos* enlargement + *graphein* to write]

pleugh *or* **pleuch** (pluː, pluːx) *n., vb.* a Scot. word for **plough.**

pleura ('plʊərə) *n., pl.* **pleurae** ('plʊəriː). **1.** the thin transparent serous membrane enveloping the lungs and lining the walls of the thoracic cavity. **2.** the plural of **pleuron.** [C17: via Medieval Latin from Greek: side, rib] —**'pleural** *adj.*

pleurisy ('plʊərɪsɪ) *n.* inflammation of the pleura, characterized by pain that is aggravated by deep breathing or coughing. [C14: from Old French *pleurisie,* from Late Latin *pleurisis,* from Greek *pleuritis,* from *pleura* side] —**pleuritic** (plʊ'rɪtɪk) *adj., n.*

pleurisy root *n.* **1.** the root of the butterfly weed, formerly used as a cure for pleurisy. **2.** another name for **butterfly weed.**

pleuro- *or before a vowel* **pleur-** *combining form.* **1.** of or relating to the side: *pleurodont; pleurodynia.* **2.** indicating the pleura: *pleurotomy.* [from Greek *pleura* side]

pleurocentesis (ˌplʊərəʊsɛn'tiːsɪs) *n.* another name for **thoracentesis.**

pleurodont ('plʊərəʊˌdɒnt) *adj.* **1.** (of the teeth of some reptiles) having no roots and being fused by their lateral sides only to the inner surface of the jawbone. See also **acrodont** (sense 1). **2.** having pleurodont teeth: *pleurodont lizards.* ~*n.* **3.** an animal having pleurodont teeth.

pleurodynia (ˌplʊərəʊ'daɪnɪə) *n.* pain in the muscles between the ribs. [C19: from New Latin, from PLEURO- + Greek *-odynia,* from *odynē* pain]

pleuron ('plʊərɒn) *n., pl.* **pleura** ('plʊərə). the part of the cuticle of arthropods that covers the lateral surface of a body segment. [C18: from Greek: side]

pleuropneumonia (ˌplʊərəʊnjuː'məʊnɪə) *n.* the combined disorder of pleurisy and pneumonia.

pleurotomy (plʊ'rɒtəmɪ) *n., pl.* **-mies.** surgical incision into the pleura, esp. to drain fluid, as in pleurisy.

pleuston ('pluːstən, -stɒn) *n.* a mass of small organisms, esp. algae, floating at the surface of shallow pools. [C20: from Greek *pleusis* sailing, from *plein* to sail; for form, compare PLANKTON]

pleustonic (pluː'stɒnɪk) *adj.* **1.** of or relating to pleuston. **2.** denoting a marine organism held at the surface of the water by a float, such as the Portuguese man-of-war.

plew, plu, *or* **plue** (pluː) *n. Canadian history.* a beaver skin used as a standard unit of value in the fur trade. [from Canadian French *pelu* (adj.) hairy, from French *poilu,* from *poil* hair, from Latin *pilus*]

plexiform ('plɛksɪˌfɔːm) *adj.* like or having the form of a network or plexus; intricate or complex.

Plexiglas ('plɛksɪˌglɑːs) *n. U.S. trademark.* a transparent plastic, polymethylmethacrylate, used for combs, plastic sheeting, etc.

plexor ('plɛksə) *or* **plessor** *n. Med.* a small hammer with a rubber head for use in percussion of the chest and testing reflexes. [C19: from Greek *plēxis* a stroke, from *plēssein* to strike]

plexus ('plɛksəs) *n., pl.* **-uses** *or* **-us. 1.** any complex network of nerves, blood vessels, or lymphatic vessels. **2.** an intricate network or arrangement. [C17: New Latin, from Latin *plectere* to braid, PLAIT]

pliable ('plaɪəbᵊl) *adj.* easily moulded, bent, influenced, or altered. —ˌ**plia'bility** *or* '**pliableness** *n.* —'**pliably** *adv.*
pliant ('plaɪənt) *adj.* **1.** easily bent; supple: *a pliant young tree.* **2.** easily modified; adaptable; flexible: *a pliant system.* **3.** yielding readily to influence; compliant. [C14: from Old French, from *plier* to fold, bend; see PLY²] —'**pliancy** *or* '**pliantness** *n.* —'**pliantly** *adv.*
plica ('plaɪkə) *n., pl.* **plicae** ('plaɪsiː). **1.** Also called: **fold.** *Anatomy.* a folding over of parts, such as a fold of skin, muscle, peritoneum, etc. **2.** *Pathol.* a condition of the hair characterized by matting, filth, and the presence of parasites. [C17: from Medieval Latin: a fold, from Latin *plicāre* to fold; see PLY²] —'**plical** *adj.*
plicate ('plaɪkeɪt) *or* **plicated** *adj.* having or arranged in parallel folds or ridges; pleated: *a plicate leaf; plicate rock strata.* [C18: from Latin *plicātus* folded, from *plicāre* to fold] —'**plicately** *adv.* —'**plicateness** *n.*
plication (plaɪ'keɪʃən) *or* **plicature** ('plɪkətʃə) *n.* **1.** the act of folding or the condition of being folded or plicate. **2.** a folded part or structure, esp. a fold in a series of rock strata. **3.** *Surgery.* the act or process of suturing together the walls of a hollow organ or part to reduce its size.
plié ('pliːeɪ) *n.* a classic ballet practice posture with back erect and knees bent. [French: bent, from *plier* to bend]
plier ('plaɪə) *n.* a person who plies a trade.
pliers ('plaɪəz) *pl. n.* a gripping tool consisting of two hinged arms with usually serrated jaws that close on the workpiece. [C16: from PLY¹]
plight¹ (plaɪt) *n.* a condition of extreme hardship, danger, etc. [C14 *plit,* from Old French *pleit* fold, PLAIT; probably influenced by Old English *pliht* peril, PLIGHT²]
plight² (plaɪt) *vb. (tr.)* **1.** to give or pledge (one's word): *he plighted his word to attempt it.* **2.** to promise formally or pledge (allegiance, support, etc.): *to plight aid.* **3. plight one's troth. a.** to make a promise of marriage. **b.** to give one's solemn promise. ~*n.* **4.** *Archaic or dialect.* a solemn promise, esp. of engagement; pledge. [Old English *pliht* peril; related to Old High German, German *Pflicht* duty] —'**plighter** *n.*
plimsoll *or* **plimsole** ('plɪmsəl) *n. Brit.* a light rubber-soled canvas shoe worn for various sports. Also called: **gym shoe, sandshoe.** [C20: so called because of the resemblance of the rubber sole to a PLIMSOLL LINE]
Plimsoll line ('plɪmsəl) *n.* another name for **load line.** [C19: named after Samuel *Plimsoll* (1824–98), MP, who advocated its adoption]
Plinian ('plɪnɪən) *adj. Geology.* (of a volcanic eruption) characterized by repeated explosions. [C20: named after *Pliny* the Younger (?62–113 A.D.), Roman writer who described such eruptions]
plink (plɪŋk) *n.* **1.** a short sharp often metallic sound as of a string on a musical instrument being plucked or a bullet striking metal. ~*vb.* **2.** *(intr.)* to make such a noise. **3.** to hit (a target, such as a tin can) by shooting or to shoot at such a target. [C20: of imitative origin] —'**plinking** *n., adj.*
plinth (plɪnθ) *n.* **1.** Also called: **socle.** the rectangular slab or block that forms the lowest part of the base of a column, statue, pedestal, or pier. **2.** Also called: **plinth course.** the lowest part of the wall of a building that appears above ground level, esp. one that is formed of a course of stone or brick. **3.** a flat block on either side of a doorframe, where the architrave meets the skirting. **4.** a flat base on which a structure or piece of equipment is placed. [C17: from Latin *plinthus,* from Greek *plinthos* brick, shaped stone]
plio-, pleo-, *or* **pleio-** *combining form.* greater in size, extent, degree, etc.; more: *Pliocene.* [from Greek *pleiōn* more, from *polus* much, many]
Pliocene *or* **Pleiocene** ('plaɪəʊˌsiːn) *adj.* **1.** of, denoting, or formed in the last epoch of the Tertiary period, which lasted for ten million years, during which many modern mammals appeared. ~*n.* **2. the.** the Pliocene epoch or rock series. [C19: PLIO- + *-cene,* from Greek *kainos* recent]
plissé ('pliːseɪ, 'plɪs-) *n.* **1.** fabric with a wrinkled finish, achieved by treatment involving caustic soda: *cotton plissé.* **2.** such a finish on a fabric. [French *plissé* pleated, from *plisser* to pleat; see PLY²]
PLO *abbrev. for* Palestine Liberation Organization.
ploat (pləʊt) *vb. (tr.) Northeastern English dialect.* **1.** to thrash; beat soundly. **2.** to pluck (a fowl). [from Dutch or Flemish *ploten* to pluck the feathers or fur from]
plod (plɒd) *vb.* **plods, plodding, plodded. 1.** to make (one's way) or walk along (a path, road, etc.) with heavy usually slow steps. **2.** *(intr.)* to work slowly and perseveringly. ~*n.* **3.** the act of plodding. **4.** the sound of slow heavy steps. [C16: of imitative origin] —'**plodder** *n.* —'**plodding** *adj.* —'**ploddingly** *adv.* —'**ploddingness** *n.*
plodge (plɒdʒ) *Northeastern English dialect.* ~*vb.* **1.** *(intr.)* to wade in water, esp. the sea. ~*n.* **2.** the act of wading. [of imitative origin; related to PLOD]
-ploid *adj. and n. combining form.* indicating a specific multiple of a single set of chromosomes: *diploid.* [from Greek *-pl(oos)* -fold + -OID] —**ploidy** *n. combining form.*
plonk¹ (plɒŋk) *vb.* **1.** (often foll. by *down*) to drop or be dropped, esp. heavily or suddenly: *he plonked the money on the table.* ~*n.* **2.** the act or sound of plonking. ~*interj.* **3.** an exclamation imitative of this sound.
plonk² (plɒŋk) *n. Brit., Austral., and N.Z. informal.* alcoholic drink, usually wine, esp. of inferior quality. [C20: perhaps from French *blanc* white, as in *vin blanc* white wine]
plonker ('plɒŋkə) *n. Slang.* a stupid person. [C20: from PLONK¹]
plonko ('plɒŋkəʊ) *n., pl.* **plonkos.** *Austral. slang.* an alcoholic, esp. one who drinks wine. [C20: from PLONK²]
plook (plʊk) *n. Scot.* a variant spelling of **plouk.**
plop (plɒp) *n.* **1.** the characteristic sound made by an object dropping into water without a splash. ~*vb.* **plops, plopping, plopped. 2.** to fall or cause to fall with the sound of a plop: *the stone plopped into the water.* ~*interj.* **3.** an exclamation imitative of this sound: *to go plop.* [C19: imitative of the sound]
plosion ('pləʊʒən) *n. Phonetics.* the sound of an abrupt break or closure, esp. the audible release of a stop. Also called: **explosion.**
plosive ('pləʊsɪv) *Phonetics.* ~*adj.* **1.** articulated with or accompanied by plosion. ~*n.* **2.** a plosive consonant; stop. [C20: from French, from *explosif* EXPLOSIVE]
plot¹ (plɒt) *n.* **1.** a secret plan to achieve some purpose, esp. one that is illegal or underhand: *a plot to overthrow the government.* **2.** the story or plan of a play, novel, etc. **3.** *Military.* a graphic representation of an individual or tactical setting that pinpoints an artillery target. **4.** *Chiefly U.S.* a diagram or plan, esp. a surveyor's map. ~*vb.* **plots, plotting, plotted. 5.** to plan secretly (something illegal, revolutionary, etc.); conspire. **6.** *(tr.)* to mark (a course, as of a ship or aircraft) on a map. **7.** *(tr.)* to make a plan or map of. **8. a.** to locate and mark (one or more points) on a graph by means of coordinates. **b.** to draw (a curve) through these points. **9.** *(tr.)* to construct the plot of (a literary work). [C16: from PLOT², influenced in use by COMPLOT]
plot² (plɒt) *n.* **1.** a small piece of land: *a vegetable plot.* ~*vb.* **plots, plotting, plotted. 2.** *(tr.)* to arrange or divide (land) into plots. [Old English: piece of land, plan of an area]
plotter ('plɒtə) *n.* an instrument for plotting lines or angles on a chart.
plough *or esp. U.S.* **plow** (plaʊ) *n.* **1.** an agricultural implement with sharp blades, attached to a horse, tractor, etc., for cutting or turning over the earth. **2.** any of various similar implements, such as a device for clearing snow. **3.** a plane with a narrow blade for cutting grooves in wood. **4.** (in agriculture) ploughed land. **5. put one's hand to the plough.** to begin or undertake a task. ~*vb.* **6.** to till (the soil) with a plough. **7.** to make (furrows or grooves) in (something) with or as if with a plough. **8.** (when *intr.,* usually foll. by *through*) to move (through something) in the manner of a plough: *the ship ploughed the water.* **9.** *(intr.;* foll. by *through*) to work at slowly or perseveringly. **10.** *(intr.;* foll. by *into* or *through*) (of a vehicle) to run uncontrollably into something in its path: *the plane ploughed into the cottage roof.* **11.** *(tr.;* foll. by *in, up, under,* etc.) to turn over (a growing crop, manure, etc.) into the earth with a plough. **12.** *(intr.) Brit. slang.* to fail an examination. [Old English *plōg* plough land; related to Old Norse *plogr,* Old High German *pfluoc*] —'**plougher** *or esp. U.S.* '**plower** *n.*
Plough (plaʊ) *n.* **the.** the group of the seven brightest stars in the constellation Ursa Major. Also called: **Charles's Wain.** Usual U.S. name: the **Big Dipper.**
plough back *vb. (tr., adv.)* to reinvest (the profits of a business) in the same business.
ploughboy *or esp. U.S.* **plowboy** ('plaʊˌbɔɪ) *n.* **1.** a boy who guides the animals drawing a plough. **2.** any country boy.
ploughman *or esp. U.S.* **plowman** ('plaʊmən) *n., pl.* **-men. 1.** a man who ploughs, esp. using horses. **2.** any farm labourer. —'**ploughmanship** *or esp. U.S.* '**plowmanship** *n.*
ploughman's lunch *n.* a snack lunch, served esp. in a pub, consisting of bread and cheese with pickle.
ploughman's spikenard *n.* a European plant, *Inula conyza,* with tubular yellowish flower heads surrounded by purple bracts: family *Compositae* (composites). Also called: **fleawort.**
Plough Monday *n.* the first Monday after Epiphany, which in N and E England used to be celebrated with a procession of ploughmen drawing a plough from house to house.
ploughshare *or esp. U.S.* **plowshare** ('plaʊˌʃɛə) *n.* the horizontal pointed cutting blade of a mouldboard plough.
ploughstaff *or esp. U.S.* **plowstaff** ('plaʊˌstɑːf) *n.* **1.** Also called: '**ploughtail.** one of the handles of a plough. **2.** a spade-shaped tool used to clean the ploughshare and mouldboard.
plouk *or* **plook** (plʊk) *n. Scot.* a pimple. [C15: of uncertain origin] —'**plouky** *or* '**plooky** *adj.*
plover ('plʌvə) *n.* **1.** any shore bird of the family *Charadriidae,* typically having a round head, straight bill, and large pointed wings: order *Charadriiformes.* **2.** any of similar and related birds, such as the Egyptian plover (see **crocodile bird**) and the upland plover. **3. green plover.** another name for **lapwing.** [C14: from Old French *plovier* rainbird, from Latin *pluvia* rain]
plow (plaʊ) *n., vb.* the usual U.S. spelling of **plough.** —'**plower** *n.*
plowter *or* **plouter** ('plaʊtər) *Scot.* ~*vb. (intr.)* **1.** to work or play in water or mud; dabble. **2.** to potter. ~*n.* **3.** the act of plowtering. [C19: of uncertain origin]
ploy (plɔɪ) *n.* **1.** a manoeuvre or tactic in a game, conversation, etc.; stratagem; gambit. **2.** any business, job, hobby, etc., with

which one is occupied: *angling is his latest ploy*. **3.** *Chiefly Brit.* a frolic, escapade, or practical joke. [C18: originally Scot. and northern English, perhaps from obsolete n. sense of EMPLOY meaning an occupation]

PLP (in Britain) *abbrev. for* Parliamentary Labour Party.

PLR *abbrev. for* Public Lending Right.

plu *or* **plue** (pluː) *n.* variant spellings of **plew**.

pluck (plʌk) *vb.* **1.** (*tr.*) to pull off (feathers, fruit, etc.) from (a fowl, tree, etc.). **2.** (when *intr.*, foll. by *at*) to pull or tug. **3.** (*tr.*; foll. by *off, away*, etc.) *Archaic.* to pull (something) forcibly or violently (from something or someone). **4.** (*tr.*) to sound (the strings) of (a musical instrument) with the fingers, a plectrum, etc. **5.** (*tr.*) another word for **strip**[1] (sense 7). **6.** (*tr.*) *Slang.* to fleece or swindle. ~*n.* **7.** courage, usually in the face of difficulties or hardship. **8.** a sudden pull or tug. **9.** the heart, liver, and lungs, esp. of an animal used for food. [Old English *pluccian, plyccan;* related to German *pflücken*] —ˈ**plucker** *n.*

pluck up *vb.* (*tr., adv.*) **1.** to pull out; uproot. **2.** to muster (courage, one's spirits, etc.).

plucky (ˈplʌkɪ) *adj.* **pluckier, pluckiest.** having or showing courage in the face of difficulties, danger, etc. —ˈ**pluckily** *adv.* —ˈ**pluckiness** *n.*

plug (plʌg) *n.* **1.** a piece of wood, cork, or other material, often cylindrical in shape, used to stop up holes and gaps or as a wedge for taking a screw or nail. **2.** such a stopper used esp. to close the waste pipe of a bath, basin, or sink while it is in use and removed to let the water drain away. **3.** a device having one or more pins to which an electric cable is attached: used to make an electrical connection when inserted into a socket. **4.** Also called: **volcanic plug.** a mass of solidified magma filling the neck of an extinct volcano. **5.** See **sparking plug. 6. a.** a cake of pressed or twisted tobacco, esp. for chewing. **b.** a small piece of such a cake. **7.** *Angling.* a weighted artificial lure with one or more sets of hooks attached, used in spinning. **8.** *Informal.* a recommendation or other favourable mention of a product, show, etc., as on television, on radio, or in newspapers. **9.** *Slang.* a shot, blow, or punch (esp. in the phrase **take a plug at**). **10.** *Informal.* the mechanism that releases water to flush a lavatory (esp. in the phrase **pull the plug**). **11.** *Chiefly U.S.* an old horse. ~*vb.* **plugs, plugging, plugged. 12.** (*tr.*) to stop up or secure (a hole, gap, etc.) with or as if with a plug. **13.** (*tr.*) to insert or use (something) as a plug: *to plug a finger into one's ear.* **14.** (*tr.*) *Informal.* to make favourable and often-repeated mentions of (a song, product, show, etc.), esp. on television, on radio, or in newspapers. **15.** (*tr.*) *Slang.* to shoot with a gun: *he plugged six rabbits.* **16.** (*tr.*) *Slang.* to punch or strike. **17.** (*intr.*; foll. by *along, away*, etc.) *Informal.* to work steadily or persistently. [C17: from Middle Dutch *plugge;* related to Middle Low German *plugge,* German *Pflock*] —ˈ**plugger** *n.*

plugboard (ˈplʌg,bɔːd) *n.* another name for **patch board.**

plug compatible *adj. Computer technol.* (of peripheral devices) designed to be plugged into computer systems produced by different manufacturers.

plug gauge *n. Engineering.* an accurately machined plug used for checking the diameter of a hole. Compare **ring gauge.**

plughole (ˈplʌg,həʊl) *n.* a hole, esp. in a bath, basin, or sink, through which waste water drains and which can be closed with a plug.

plug in *vb.* (*tr., adv.*) to connect (an electrical appliance) with a power source by means of an electrical plug.

plug-ugly *adj.* **1.** *Informal.* extremely ugly. ~*n., pl.* **-lies. 2.** *U.S. slang.* a city tough; ruffian. [C19: origin obscure; originally applied to ruffians in New York who attempted to exert political pressure]

plum[1] (plʌm) *n.* **1.** a small rosaceous tree, *Prunus domestica,* with white flowers and an edible oval fruit that is purple, yellow, or green and contains an oval stone. See also **greengage, damson. 2.** the fruit of this tree. **3.** a raisin, as used in a cake or pudding. **4. a.** a dark reddish-purple colour. **b.** (*as adj.*): *a plum carpet.* **5.** *Informal.* **a.** something of a superior or desirable kind, such as a financial bonus. **b.** (*as modifier*): *a plum job.* [Old English *plūme;* related to Latin *prunum,* German *Pflaume*] —ˈ**plum,like** *adj.*

plum[2] (plʌm) *adj., adv.* a variant spelling of **plumb** (senses 3–6).

plumage (ˈpluːmɪdʒ) *n.* the layer of feathers covering the body of a bird. [C15: from Old French, from *plume* feather, from Latin *plūma* down]

plumate (ˈpluːmeɪt, -mɪt) *or* **plumose** *adj. Zoology, botany.* **1.** of, relating to, or possessing one or more feathers or plumes. **2.** resembling a plume; covered with small hairs: *a plumate seed.* [C19: from Latin *plumātus* covered with feathers; see PLUME]

plumb (plʌm) *n.* **1.** a weight, usually of lead, suspended at the end of a line and used to determine water depth or verticality. **2.** the perpendicular position of a freely suspended plumb line (esp. in the phrases **out of plumb, off plumb**). ~*adj. also* **plum. 3.** (*prenominal*) *Informal, chiefly U.S.* (intensifier): *a plumb nuisance.* ~*adv. also* **plum. 4.** in a vertical or perpendicular line. **5.** *Informal, chiefly U.S.* (intensifier): *plumb stupid.* **6.** *Informal.* exactly; precisely (also in the phrase **plumb on**). ~*vb.* **7.** (*tr.*; often foll. by *up*) to test the alignment of or adjust to the vertical with a plumb line. **8.** (*tr.*) to undergo or experience (the worst extremes of misery, sadness, etc.): *to plumb the depths of despair.* **9.** (*tr.*) to understand or master (something obscure): *to plumb a mystery.* **10.** to connect or join (a device such as a tap) to a water pipe or drainage system. [C13: from Old French *plomb* (unattested) lead line, from Old French *plon* lead, from Latin *plumbum* lead] —ˈ**plumbable** *adj.*

plumbaginaceous (plʌm,bædʒɪˈneɪʃəs) *adj.* of, relating to, or belonging to the *Plumbaginaceae,* a family of typically coastal plants having flowers with a brightly coloured calyx and five styles: includes leadwort, thrift, and sea lavender.

plumbago (plʌmˈbeɪgəʊ) *n., pl.* **-gos. 1.** any plumbaginaceous plant of the genus *Plumbago,* of warm regions, having clusters of blue, white, or red flowers. See also **leadwort. 2.** another name for **graphite.** [C17: from Latin: lead ore, leadwort, translation of Greek *polubdaina* lead ore, from *polubdos* lead]

plumb bob *n.* the weight, usually of lead, at the end of a plumb line; plummet.

plumbeous (ˈplʌmbɪəs) *adj.* made of or relating to lead or resembling lead in colour. [C16: from Latin *plumbeus* leaden, from *plumbum* lead]

plumber (ˈplʌmə) *n.* a person who installs and repairs pipes, fixtures, etc., for water, drainage, and gas. [C14: from Old French *plommier* worker in lead, from Late Latin *plumbārius,* from Latin *plumbum* lead]

plumbery (ˈplʌmərɪ) *n., pl.* **-eries. 1.** the workshop of a plumber. **2.** another word for **plumbing** (sense 1).

plumbic (ˈplʌmbɪk) *adj.* of or containing lead in the tetravalent state.

Plumbicon (ˈplʌmbɪ,kɒn) *n. Trademark.* a development of the vidicon television camera tube in which the photosensitive material is lead oxide.

plumbiferous (plʌmˈbɪfərəs) *adj.* (of ores, rocks, etc.) containing or yielding lead.

plumbing (ˈplʌmɪŋ) *n.* **1.** Also called: **plumbery.** the trade or work of a plumber. **2.** the pipes, fixtures, etc., used in a water, drainage, or gas installation. **3.** the act or procedure of using a plumb to gauge depth, a vertical, etc.

plumbism (ˈplʌm,bɪzəm) *n.* chronic lead poisoning. [C19: from Latin *plumbum* lead]

plumb line *n.* **1.** a string with a metal weight at one end that, when suspended, points directly towards the earth's centre of gravity and so is used to determine verticality, the depth of water, etc. **2.** another name for **plumb rule.**

plumbous (ˈplʌmbəs) *adj.* of or containing lead in the divalent state. [C17: from Late Latin *plumbōsus* full of lead, from Latin *plumbum* lead]

plumb rule *n.* a plumb line attached to a narrow board, used by builders, surveyors, etc.

plumbum (ˈplʌmbəm) *n.* an obsolete name for **lead**[2] (the metal). [from Latin]

plume (pluːm) *n.* **1.** a feather, esp. one that is large or ornamental. **2.** a feather or cluster of feathers worn esp. formerly as a badge or ornament in a headband, hat, etc. **3.** *Biology.* any feathery part, such as the structure on certain fruits and seeds that aids dispersal by wind. **4.** something that resembles a plume: *a plume of smoke.* **5.** a token or decoration of honour; prize. ~*vb.* (*tr.*) **6.** to adorn or decorate with feathers or plumes. **7.** (of a bird) to clean or preen (itself or its feathers). **8.** (foll. by *on* or *upon*) to pride or congratulate (oneself). [C14: from Old French, from Latin *plūma* downy feather] —ˈ**plumeless** *adj.* —ˈ**plume,like** *adj.*

plume moth *n.* **1.** one of a family (*Pterophoridae*) of slender-bodied micro moths with narrow wings, each usually divided into two, three, or four "plumes". The type is the white *Pterophorus pentadactylus.* **2. many-plumed moth.** an unrelated species, *Alucita hexadactyla.*

plummet (ˈplʌmɪt) *vb.* **-mets, -meting, -meted. 1.** (*intr.*) to drop down; plunge. ~*n.* **2.** another word for **plumb bob. 3.** a lead plumb used by anglers to determine the depth of water. [C14: from Old French *plommet* ball of lead, from *plomb* lead, from Latin *plumbum*]

plummy (ˈplʌmɪ) *adj.* **-mier, -miest. 1.** of, full of, or resembling plums. **2.** *Brit. informal.* (of speech) having a deep tone and a refined and somewhat drawling articulation. **3.** *Brit. informal.* choice; desirable.

plumose (ˈpluːməʊs, -məʊz) *adj.* another word for **plumate.** [C17: from Latin *plūmōsus* feathery] —ˈ**plumosely** *adv.* —**plumosity** (pluːˈmɒsɪtɪ) *n.*

plump[1] (plʌmp) *adj.* **1.** well filled out or rounded; fleshy or chubby: *a plump turkey.* **2.** bulging, as with contents; full: *a plump wallet.* **3.** (of amounts of money) generous; ample: *a plump cheque.* ~*vb.* **4.** (often foll. by *up* or *out*) to make or become plump: *to plump up a pillow.* [C15 (meaning: dull, rude), C16 (in current senses): perhaps from Middle Dutch *plomp* dull, blunt] —ˈ**plumply** *adv.* —ˈ**plumpness** *n.*

plump[2] (plʌmp) *vb.* **1.** (often foll. by *down, into*, etc.) to drop or fall suddenly and heavily: *to plump down on the sofa.* **2.** (*intr.*; foll. by *for*) to give support (to) or make a choice (of) one out of a group or number. ~*n.* **3.** a heavy abrupt fall or the sound of this. ~*adv.* **4.** suddenly or heavily: *he ran plump into the old lady.* **5.** straight down; directly: *the helicopter landed plump in the middle of the field.* ~*adj., adv.* **6.** in a blunt, direct, or decisive manner. [C14: probably of imitative origin; compare Middle Low German *plumpen,* Middle Dutch *plompen*]

plump[3] (plʌmp) *n. Archaic or dialect.* a group of people, animals, or things; troop; cluster. [C15: of uncertain origin]

plumper (ˈplʌmpə) *n.* a pad carried in the mouth by actors to round out the cheeks.

plum pudding *n.* (in Britain) a dark brown rich boiled or steamed pudding made with flour, suet, sugar, and dried fruit.

plumule (ˈpluːmjuːl) *n.* **1.** the embryonic shoot of seed-bearing plants. **2.** a down feather of young birds that persists in some adults. [C18: from Late Latin *plūmula* a little feather]

plumy (ˈpluːmɪ) *adj.* **plumier, plumiest.** **1.** plumelike; feathery. **2.** consisting of, covered with, or adorned with feathers.

plunder (ˈplʌndə) *vb.* **1.** to steal (valuables, goods, sacred items, etc.) from (a town, church, etc.) by force, esp. in time of war; loot. **2.** (*tr.*) to rob or steal (choice or desirable things) from (a place): *to plunder an orchard.* ~*n.* **3.** anything taken by plundering or theft; booty. **4.** the act of plundering; pillage. [C17: probably from Dutch *plunderen* (originally: to plunder household goods); compare Middle High German *plunder* bedding, household goods] —ˈ**plunderable** *adj.* —ˈ**plunderer** *n.* —ˈ**plunderous** *adj.*

plunderage (ˈplʌndərɪdʒ) *n.* **1.** *Maritime law.* **a.** the embezzlement of goods on board a ship. **b.** the goods embezzled. **2.** the act of plundering.

plunge (plʌndʒ) *vb.* **1.** (usually foll. by *into*) to thrust or throw (something, oneself, etc.): *they plunged into the sea.* **2.** to throw or be thrown into a certain state or condition: *the room was plunged into darkness.* **3.** (usually foll. by *into*) to involve or become involved deeply (in): *he plunged himself into a course of Sanskrit.* **4.** (*intr.*) to move or dash violently or with great speed or impetuosity. **5.** (*intr.*) to descend very suddenly or steeply: *the ship plunged in heavy seas; a plunging neckline.* **6.** (*intr.*) *Informal.* to speculate or gamble recklessly, for high stakes, etc. ~*n.* **7.** a leap or dive as into water. **8.** *Informal.* a swim; dip. **9.** *Chiefly U.S.* a place where one can swim or dive, such as a swimming pool. **10.** a headlong rush: *a plunge for the exit.* **11.** a pitching or tossing motion. **12. take the plunge.** *Informal.* **a.** to resolve to do something dangerous or irrevocable. **b.** to get married. [C14: from Old French *plongier,* from Vulgar Latin *plumbicāre* (unattested) to sound with a plummet, from Latin *plumbum* lead]

plunge bath *n.* a bath large enough to immerse the whole body or to dive into.

plunger (ˈplʌndʒə) *n.* **1.** a rubber suction cup fixed to the end of a rod, used to clear blocked drains. **2.** a device or part of a machine that has a plunging or thrusting motion; piston. **3.** *Informal.* a reckless gambler.

plunk (plʌŋk) *vb.* **1.** to pluck (the strings) of (a banjo, harp, etc.) or (of such an instrument) to give forth a sound when plucked. **2.** (often foll. by *down*) to drop or be dropped, esp. heavily or suddenly. ~*n.* **3.** the act or sound of plunking. **4.** *Informal.* a hard blow. ~*interj.* **5.** an exclamation imitative of the sound of something plunking. ~*adv.* **6.** *Informal.* exactly; squarely: *plunk into his lap.* [C20: imitative]

Plunket baby (ˈplʌŋkət) *n. N.Z. informal.* a baby brought up in infancy under the dietary recommendations of the Royal New Zealand Society for the Health of Women and Children, known as the Plunket Society. [named after Sir William Lee *Plunket* (1864–1920), Governor General of New Zealand at the time of the society's founding (1907)]

Plunket nurse *n. N.Z.* a child-care nurse appointed by the Plunket Society.

pluperfect (pluːˈpɜːfɪkt) *adj., n. Grammar.* another term for **past perfect.** [C16: from the Latin phrase *plūs quam perfectum* more than perfect]

plur. *abbrev. for:* **1.** plural. **2.** plurality.

plural (ˈplʊərəl) *adj.* **1.** containing, involving, or composed of more than one person, thing, item, etc.: *a plural society.* **2.** denoting a word indicating that more than one referent is being referred to or described. ~*n.* **3.** *Grammar.* **a.** the plural number. **b.** a plural form. [C14: from Old French *plurel,* from Late Latin *plūrālis* concerning many, from Latin *plūs* more] —ˈ**plurally** *adv.*

pluralism (ˈplʊərəˌlɪzəm) *n.* **1.** the holding by a single person of more than one ecclesiastical benefice or office. **2.** *Sociol.* a theory of society as several autonomous but interdependent groups having equal power. **3.** the existence in a society of groups having distinctive ethnic origin, cultural forms, religions, etc. **4.** a theory that views the power of employers as being balanced by the power of trade unions in industrial relations such that the interests of both sides can be catered for. **5.** *Philosophy.* **a.** the metaphysical doctrine that reality consists of more than two basic types of substance. Compare **monism** (sense 1), **dualism** (sense 2). **b.** the metaphysical doctrine that reality consists of independent entities rather than one unchanging whole. Compare **monism** (sense 1), **absolutism** (sense 2b). —ˈ**pluralist** *n., adj.* —ˌ**pluralˈistic** *adj.*

plurality (plʊəˈrælɪtɪ) *n., pl.* **-ties.** **1.** the state of being plural or numerous. **2.** *Maths.* a number greater than one. **3.** the U.S. and Canadian term for **relative majority.** **4.** a large number. **5.** the greater number; majority. **6.** another word for **pluralism** (sense 1).

pluralize *or* **pluralise** (ˈplʊərəˌlaɪz) *vb.* **1.** (*intr.*) to hold more than one ecclesiastical benefice or office at the same time. **2.** to make or become plural. —ˌ**pluraliˈzation** *or* ˌ**pluraliˈsation** *n.* —ˈ**pluralˌizer** *or* ˈ**pluralˌiser** *n.*

plural voting *n.* **1.** a system that enables an elector to vote more than once in an election. **2.** (in Britain before 1948) a system enabling certain electors to vote in more than one constituency.

pluri- *combining form.* denoting several: *pluriliteral; pluripresence.* [from Latin *plur-, plus* more, *plures* several]

pluriliteral (ˌplʊrɪˈlɪtərəl) *adj.* (in Hebrew grammar) containing more than three letters in the root.

pluripresence (ˌplʊrɪˈprɛzəns) *n. Theol.* presence in more than one place at the same time.

plus (plʌs) *prep.* **1.** increased by the addition of: *four plus two* (written 4 + 2). **2.** with or with the addition of: *a good job, plus a new car.* ~*adj.* **3.** (*prenominal*) Also: **positive.** indicating or involving addition: *a plus sign.* **4.** another word for **positive** (senses 8, 9). **5.** on the positive part of a scale or coordinate axis: *a value of +x.* **6.** indicating the positive side of an electrical circuit. **7.** involving positive advantage or good: *a plus factor.* **8.** (*postpositive*) *Informal.* having a value above that which is stated or expected: *she had charm plus.* **9.** (*postpositive*) slightly above a specified standard on a particular grade or percentage: *he received a B+ rating on his essay.* **10.** *Botany.* designating the strain of fungus that can only undergo sexual reproduction with a minus strain. ~*n.* **11.** short for **plus sign.** **12.** a positive quantity. **13.** *Informal.* something positive or to the good. **14.** a gain, surplus, or advantage. ~Mathematical symbol: + [C17: from Latin: more; compare Greek *pleiōn,* Old Norse *fleiri* more, German *viel* much]

▷**Usage.** *Plus, together with,* and *along with* do not create compound subjects in the way that *and* does: the number of the verb depends on that of the subject to which *plus, together with,* or *along with* is added: *this task, plus all the others, was* (not *were*) *undertaken by the government; the doctor, together with the nurses, was* (not *were*) *waiting for the patient.*

plus fours *pl. n.* men's baggy knickerbockers reaching below the knee, now only worn for hunting, golf, etc. [C20: so called because the trousers are made with four inches of material to hang over at the knee]

plush (plʌʃ) *n.* **1. a.** a fabric with a cut pile that is longer and softer than velvet. **b.** (*as modifier*): *a plush chair.* ~*adj.* **2.** Also: ˈ**plushy.** *Informal.* lavishly appointed; rich; costly. [C16: from French *pluche,* from Old French *peluchier* to pluck, ultimately from Latin *pilus* a hair, PILE[3]] —ˈ**plushly** *adv.* —ˈ**plushness** *n.*

plus sign *n.* the symbol +, indicating addition or positive quantity.

Pluto (ˈpluːtəʊ) *n.* the second smallest planet and the farthest known from the sun; it has one known satellite, Charon. Its existence was predicted before it was discovered in 1930. Mean distance from sun: 5907 million km; period of revolution around sun: 248.4 years; period of axial rotation: 6.4 days; diameter and mass: 47 and 10 per cent that of earth respectively. [Latin, from Greek *Ploutōn,* literally: the rich one]

PLUTO (ˈpluːtəʊ) *n.* the code name of pipelines laid under the English Channel to supply fuel to the Allied forces landing in Normandy in 1944. [C20: from *p(ipe)l(ine) u(nder) t(he) o(cean)*]

plutocracy (pluːˈtɒkrəsɪ) *n., pl.* **-cies.** **1.** the rule or control of society by the wealthy. **2.** a state or government characterized by the rule of the wealthy. **3.** a class that exercises power by virtue of its wealth. [C17: from Greek *ploutokratia* government by the rich, from *ploutos* wealth + *-kratia* rule, power] —**plutocratic** (ˌpluːtəˈkrætɪk) *or* ˌ**plutoˈcratical** *adj.* —ˌ**plutoˈcratically** *adv.*

plutocrat (ˈpluːtəˌkræt) *n.* a member of a plutocracy.

pluton (ˈpluːtɒn) *n.* any mass of igneous rock that has solidified below the surface of the earth. [C20: back formation from PLUTONIC]

Plutonian (pluːˈtəʊnɪən) *adj.* of or relating to Pluto (Greek god of the underworld) or the underworld; infernal.

plutonic (pluːˈtɒnɪk) *adj.* (of igneous rocks) derived from magma that has cooled and solidified below the surface of the earth. Also: **abyssal.** [C20: named after *Pluto;* see PLUTONIAN]

plutonium (pluːˈtəʊnɪəm) *n.* a highly toxic metallic transuranic element. It occurs in trace amounts in uranium ores and is produced in a nuclear reactor by neutron bombardment of uranium-238. The most stable and important isotope, **plutonium-239,** readily undergoes fission and is used as a reactor fuel in nuclear power stations and in nuclear weapons. Symbol: Pu; atomic no.: 94; half-life of ^{239}Pu: 24 360 years; valency: 3, 4, 5, or 6; melting pt.: 641°C; boiling pt.: 3327°C. [C20: named after the planet *Pluto* because Pluto lies beyond Neptune and plutonium was discovered soon after NEPTUNIUM]

pluvial (ˈpluːvɪəl) *adj.* **1.** of, characterized by, or due to the action of rain; rainy: *pluvial insurance.* ~*n.* **2.** *Geology.* a period of persistent heavy rainfall, esp. one occurring in unglaciated regions during the Pleistocene epoch. [C17: from Latin *pluviālis* rainy, from *pluvia* rain]

pluviometer (ˌpluːvɪˈɒmɪtə) *n.* another word for **rain gauge.** —**pluviometric** (ˌpluːvɪəˈmɛtrɪk) *adj.* —ˌ**pluvioˈmetrically** *adv.* —ˌ**pluviˈometry** *n.*

Pluviôse *French.* (plyvjoz) *n.* the rainy month: the fifth month of the French revolutionary calendar, extending from Jan. 21 to Feb. 19. [C19 *pluviose,* C15 *pluvious;* see PLUVIOUS]

pluvious (ˈpluːvɪəs) *or* **pluviose** *adj.* of or relating to rain; rainy. [C15: from Late Latin *pluviōsus* full of rain, from *pluvia* rain, from *pluere* to rain]

ply[1] (plaɪ) *vb.* **plies, plying, plied.** (*mainly tr.*) **1.** to carry on, pursue, or work at (a job, trade, etc.). **2.** to manipulate or wield (a tool). **3.** to sell (goods, wares, etc.), esp. at a regular place. **4.** (usually foll. by *with*) to provide (with) or subject (to) repeatedly or persistently: *he plied us with drink the whole evening; to ply a horse with a whip; he plied the speaker with questions.* **5.** (*intr.*) to perform or work steadily or diligently: *to ply with a spade.* **6.** (*also intr.*) (esp. of a ship) to travel regularly along (a route) or in (an area): *to ply between Dover and Calais; to ply the trade routes.* [C14 *plye,* short for *aplye* to APPLY]

ply[2] (plaɪ) *n., pl.* **plies. 1. a.** a layer, fold, or thickness, as of cloth, wood, yarn, etc. **b.** (*in combination*): *four-ply.* **2.** a thin sheet of wood glued to other similar sheets to form plywood. **3.** one of the strands twisted together to make rope, yarn, etc. ~*vb.* (*tr.*) **4.** to twist together (two or more single strands) to make yarn. [C15: from Old French *pli* fold, from *plier* to fold, from Latin *plicāre*]

Plymouth Brethren (ˈplɪməθ) *pl. n.* a religious sect founded *c.* 1827, strongly Puritanical in outlook and prohibiting many secular occupations for its members. It combines elements of Calvinism, Pietism, and millenarianism, and has no organized ministry.

Plymouth Rock *n.* a heavy American breed of domestic fowl.

plywood (ˈplaɪˌwʊd) *n.* a structural board consisting of an odd number of thin layers of wood glued together under pressure, with the grain of one layer at right angles to the grain of the adjoining layer.

pm *abbrev. for* premium.

Pm *the chemical symbol for* promethium.

PM *abbrev. for:* **1.** Prime Minister. **2.** Past Master (of a fraternity). **3.** Paymaster. **4.** Postmaster. **5.** *Military.* Provost Marshal.

p.m., P.M., pm, *or* **PM** *abbrev. for:* **1.** (indicating the time period from midday to midnight) post meridiem. Compare **a.m.** [Latin: after noon] **2.** post-mortem (examination).

PMG *abbrev. for:* **1.** Paymaster General. **2.** Postmaster General. **3.** *Military.* Provost Marshal General.

PMS *abbrev. for* premenstrual syndrome.

PMT *abbrev. for:* **1.** photomechanical transfer. **2.** premenstrual tension.

PN, P/N, *or* **pn** *abbrev. for* promissory note.

PNdB *abbrev. for* perceived noise decibel.

pneuma (ˈnjuːmə) *n. Philosophy.* a person's vital spirit, soul, or creative energy. Compare **psyche.** [C19: from Greek: breath, spirit, wind; related to *pnein* to blow, breathe]

pneumatic (njʊˈmætɪk) *adj.* **1.** of or concerned with air, gases, or wind. Compare **hydraulic. 2.** (of a machine or device) operated by compressed air or by a vacuum: *a pneumatic drill; pneumatic brakes.* **3.** containing compressed air: *a pneumatic tyre.* **4.** of or concerned with pneumatics. **5.** *Theol.* **a.** of or relating to the soul or spirit. **b.** of or relating to the Holy Ghost or other spiritual beings. **6.** (of the bones of birds) containing air spaces which reduce their weight as an adaptation to flying. **7.** *Informal.* (of a woman) well rounded, esp. with a large bosom. ~*n.* **8.** short for **pneumatic tyre.** [C17: from Late Latin *pneumaticus* of air or wind, from Greek *pneumatikos* of air or breath, from PNEUMA] —**pneuˈmatically** *adv.*

pneumatic conveyor *n. Engineering.* a tube through which powdered or granular material, such as cement, grain, etc. is transported by a flow of air.

pneumatics (njʊˈmætɪks) *n.* (*functioning as sing.*) the branch of physics concerned with the mechanical properties of gases, esp. air. Also called: **aerometry, pneumodynamics.**

pneumatic trough *n. Chem.* a shallow dishlike vessel filled with a liquid, usually water, and used in collecting gases by displacement of liquid from a filled jar held with its open end under the surface of the liquid.

pneumatic tyre *n.* a rubber tyre filled with air under pressure, used esp. on motor vehicles.

pneumato- *combining form.* air; breath or breathing; spirit: *pneumatophore; pneumatology.* [from Greek *pneuma, pneumat-,* breath; see PNEUMA]

pneumatology (ˌnjuːməˈtɒlədʒɪ) *n.* **1.** the branch of theology concerned with the Holy Ghost and other spiritual beings. **2.** an obsolete name for **psychology** (the science). **3.** an obsolete term for **pneumatics.** —**pneumatological** (ˌnjuːmətəˈlɒdʒɪkᵊl) *adj.* —ˌ**pneumaˈtologist** *n.*

pneumatolysis (ˌnjuːməˈtɒlɪsɪs) *n.* a type of metamorphism in which hot gases from solidifying magma react with surrounding rock.

pneumatometer (ˌnjuːməˈtɒmɪtə) *n.* an instrument for measuring the pressure exerted by air being inhaled or exhaled during a single breath. Compare **spirometer.** —ˌ**pneumaˈtometry** *n.*

pneumatophore (njuːˈmætəʊˌfɔː) *n.* **1.** a specialized root of certain swamp plants, such as the mangrove, that branches upwards and undergoes gaseous exchange with the atmosphere. **2.** a polyp in coelenterates of the order *Siphonophora,* such as the Portuguese man-of-war, that is specialized as a float.

pneumectomy (njuːˈmɛktəmɪ) *n., pl.* **-mies.** *Surgery.* another word for **pneumonectomy.**

pneumo-, pneumono- *or before a vowel* **pneum-, pneumon-** *combining form.* of or related to a lung or the lungs; respiratory: *pneumoconiosis; pneumonitis.* [from Greek *pneumōn* lung or *pneuma* breath]

pneumobacillus (ˌnjuːməʊbəˈsɪləs) *n., pl.* **-li** (-laɪ). a rod-shaped bacterium that occurs in the respiratory tract, esp. the Gram-negative *Klebsiella pneumoniae,* which causes pneumonia.

pneumococcus (ˌnjuːməʊˈkɒkəs) *n., pl.* **-cocci** (-ˈkɒksaɪ). a spherical bacterium that occurs in the respiratory tract, esp. the Gram-positive *Diplococcus pneumoniae,* which causes pneumonia. —ˌ**pneumoˈcoccal** *adj.*

pneumoconiosis (ˌnjuːməʊˌkəʊnɪˈəʊsɪs) *or* **pneumonoconiosis** (ˌnjuːmənəʊˌkəʊnɪˈəʊsɪs) *n.* any disease of the lungs or bronchi caused by the inhalation of metallic or mineral particles: characterized by inflammation, cough, and fibrosis. [C19: shortened from *pneumonoconiosis,* from PNEUMO- + *-coniosis,* from Greek *konis* dust]

pneumocystis (ˌnjuːməʊˈsɪstɪs) *n.* a genus of microorganisms, probably protozoa. *Pneumocystis carinii* is a cause of pneumonia in people whose immune defences have been lowered by drugs or a disease.

pneumodynamics (ˌnjuːməʊdaɪˈnæmɪks) *n.* (*functioning as sing.*) another name for **pneumatics.**

pneumoencephalogram (ˌnjuːməʊɛnˈsɛfələˌgræm) *n.* See **encephalogram.** —**pneumoencephalography** (ˌnjuːməʊɛnˌsɛfəˈlɒgrəfɪ) *n.*

pneumogastric (ˌnjuːməʊˈgæstrɪk) *adj. Anatomy.* **1.** of or relating to the lungs and stomach. **2.** a former term for **vagus.**

pneumograph (ˈnjuːməˌgrɑːf, -ˌgræf) *n. Med.* an instrument for making a record (**pneumogram**) of respiratory movements.

pneumonectomy (ˌnjuːməʊˈnɛktəmɪ) *or* **pneumectomy** (njuːˈmɛktəmɪ) *n., pl.* **-mies.** the surgical removal of a lung or part of a lung. [C20: from Greek *pneumōn* lung + -ECTOMY]

pneumonia (njuːˈməʊnɪə) *n.* inflammation of one or both lungs, in which the air sacs (alveoli) become filled with liquid, which renders them useless for breathing. It is usually caused by bacterial (esp. pneumococcal) or viral infection. [C17: New Latin from Greek from *pneumōn* lung]

pneumonic (njuːˈmɒnɪk) *adj.* **1.** of, relating to, or affecting the lungs; pulmonary. **2.** of or relating to pneumonia. [C17: from New Latin *pneumonicus,* from Greek, from *pneumon* lung]

pneumonitis (ˌnjuːmɒnˈaɪtɪs) *n.* inflammation of the lungs.

pneumothorax (ˌnjuːməʊˈθɔːræks) *n.* **1.** the abnormal presence of air between the lung and the wall of the chest (pleural cavity), resulting in collapse of the lung. **2.** *Med.* the introduction of air into the pleural cavity to collapse the lung: a former treatment for tuberculosis.

p-n junction *n. Electronics.* a boundary between a p-type and n-type semiconductor that functions as a rectifier and is used in diodes and junction transistors.

po (pəʊ) *n., pl.* **pos.** *Brit.* an informal word for **chamber pot.** [C19: from POT[1]]

Po *the chemical symbol for* polonium.

PO *abbrev. for:* **1.** Post Office. **2.** Personnel Officer. **3.** petty officer. **4.** Pilot Officer. **5.** Also: **p.o.** postal order.

poaceous (pəʊˈeɪʃəs) *adj.* (in former botanic classification) of, relating to, or belonging to the plant family *Poaceae* (grasses). [C18: via New Latin from Greek *poa* grass]

poach[1] (pəʊtʃ) *vb.* **1.** to catch (game, fish, etc.) illegally by trespassing on private property. **2.** to encroach on or usurp (another person's rights, duties, etc.) or steal (an idea, employee, etc.). **3.** *Tennis, badminton, etc.* to take or play (shots that should belong to one's partner). **4.** to break up (land) into wet muddy patches, as by riding over it, or (of land) to become broken up in this way. **5.** (*intr.*) (of the feet, shoes, etc.) to sink into heavy wet ground. [C17: from Old French *pocher,* of Germanic origin; compare Middle Dutch *poken* to prod; see POKE[1]]

poach[2] (pəʊtʃ) *vb.* to simmer (eggs, fish, etc.) very gently in water, milk, stock, etc. [C15: from Old French *pochier* to enclose in a bag (as the yolks are enclosed by the whites); compare POKE[2]]

poacher[1] (ˈpəʊtʃə) *n.* a person who illegally hunts game, fish, etc., on someone else's property.

poacher[2] (ˈpəʊtʃə) *n.* a metal pan with individual cups for poaching eggs.

POB *abbrev. for* Post Office Box.

pochard (ˈpəʊtʃəd) *n., pl.* **-chards** *or* **-chard.** any of various diving ducks of the genera *Aythya* and *Netta,* esp. *A. ferina* of Europe, the male of which has a grey-and-black body and a reddish head. [C16: of unknown origin]

pochette (pəˈʃɛt) *n.* an envelope-shaped handbag used by women and men. [C20: from French: little pocket]

pock (pɒk) *n.* **1.** any pustule resulting from an eruptive disease, esp. from smallpox. **2.** another word for **pockmark** (sense 1). [Old English *pocc;* related to Middle Dutch *pocke,* perhaps to Latin *bucca* cheek] —ˈ**pocky** *adj.*

pocket (ˈpɒkɪt) *n.* **1.** a small bag or pouch in a garment for carrying small articles, money, etc. **2.** any bag or pouch or anything resembling this. **3. a.** a cavity or hollow in the earth, etc., such as one containing gold or other ore. **b.** the ore in such a place. **4.** a small enclosed or isolated area: *a pocket of resistance.* **5.** any of the six holes with pouches or nets let into the corners and sides of a billiard table. **6.** a position in a race in which a competitor is hemmed in. **7.** *Australian Rules football.*

a player in one of two side positions at the ends of the ground: *back pocket; forward pocket.* **8.** *S. African.* a bag or sack of vegetables or fruit. **9. in one's pocket.** under one's control. **10. in** *or* **out of pocket.** having made a profit or loss, as after a transaction. **11. line one's pockets.** to make money, esp. by dishonesty when in a position of trust. **12.** (*modifier*) suitable for fitting in a pocket; small: *a pocket edition.* ~*vb.* **-ets, -eting, -eted.** (*tr.*) **13. to put into one's pocket. 14.** to take surreptitiously or unlawfully; steal. **15.** (*usually passive*) to enclose or confine in or as if in a pocket. **16.** to receive (an insult, injury, etc.) without retaliating. **17.** to conceal or keep back (feelings): *he pocketed his pride and accepted help.* **18.** *Billiards, etc.* to drive (a ball) into a pocket. **19.** *U.S.* (esp. of the President) to retain (a bill) without acting on it in order to prevent it from becoming law. See also **pocket veto. 20.** to hem in (an opponent), as in racing. [C15: from Anglo-Norman *poket* a little bag, from *poque* bag, from Middle Dutch *poke* POKE[2], bag; related to French *poche* pocket] —ˈ**pocketable** *adj.* —ˈ**pocketless** *adj.*

pocket battleship *n.* a small heavily armoured and armed battle cruiser specially built to conform with treaty limitations on tonnage and armament, esp. any of those built by Germany in the 1930s.

pocket billiards *n.* (*functioning as sing.*) *Billiards.* **1.** another name for **pool**[2] (sense 5). **2.** any game played on a table in which the object is to pocket the balls, esp. snooker and pool.

pocketbook (ˈpɒkɪtˌbʊk) *n. U.S. and Canadian.* a small bag or case for money, papers, etc., carried by a handle or in the pocket.

pocket borough *n.* (before the Reform Act of 1832) an English borough constituency controlled by one person or family who owned the land. Compare **rotten borough.**

pocketful (ˈpɒkɪtfʊl) *n., pl.* **-fuls. 1.** as much as a pocket will hold. **2.** *Informal.* a large amount: *it cost him a pocketful of money.*

pocket gopher *n.* the full name for **gopher** (sense 1).

pocketknife (ˈpɒkɪtˌnaɪf) *n., pl.* **-knives.** a small knife with one or more blades that fold into the handle; penknife.

pocket money *n.* **1.** *Brit.* a small weekly sum of money given to children by parents as an allowance. **2.** money for day-to-day spending, incidental expenses, etc.

pocket mouse *n.* any small mouselike rodent with cheek pouches, of the genus *Perognathus,* of desert regions of W North America: family *Heteromyidae.*

pocket veto *n. U.S.* **1.** the action of the President in retaining unsigned a bill passed by Congress within the last ten days of a session and thus causing it to die. **2.** any similar action by a state governor or other chief executive.

pockmark (ˈpɒkˌmɑːk) *n.* **1.** Also called: **pock.** a pitted scar left on the skin after the healing of a smallpox or similar pustule. **2.** any pitting of a surface that resembles or suggests such scars. ~*vb.* **3.** (*tr.*) to scar or pit (a surface) with pockmarks.

poco (ˈpəʊkəʊ; *Italian* ˈpɔːko) *or* **un poco** *adj., adv. Music.* (*in combination*) a little; to a small degree: *poco rit.; un poco meno mosso.* [from Italian: little, from Latin *paucus* few, scanty]

poco a poco *adv.* (*in combination*) *Music.* little by little: *poco a poco rall.* [Italian]

pococurante (ˌpəʊkəʊkjʊˈræntɪ) *n.* **1.** a person who is careless or indifferent. ~*adj.* **2.** indifferent or apathetic. [C18: from Italian, from *poco* little + *curante* caring] —ˌ**pococuˈranteism** *or* ˌ**pococuˈrantism** *n.*

pod[1] (pɒd) *n.* **1. a.** the fruit of any leguminous plant, consisting of a long two-valved case that contains several seeds and splits along both sides when ripe. **b.** the seedcase as distinct from the seeds. **2.** any similar fruit. **3.** a streamlined structure attached by a pylon to an aircraft and used to house a jet engine (**podded engine**), fuel tank, armament, etc. ~*vb.* **pods, podding, podded. 4.** (*tr.*) to remove the pod or shell from (peas, beans, etc.). **5.** (*intr.*) (of a plant) to produce pods. [C17: perhaps back formation from earlier *podware* bagged vegetables, probably from *pod,* variant of COD[2] + WARE[1]]

pod[2] (pɒd) *n.* a small group of animals, esp. seals, whales, or birds. [C19: of unknown origin]

pod[3] (pɒd) *n.* **1.** a straight groove along the length of certain augers and bits. **2.** the socket that holds the bit in a boring tool. [C16: of unknown origin]

POD *abbrev. for* pay on delivery.

-pod *or* **-pode** *n. combining form.* indicating a certain type or number of feet: *arthropod; tripod.* [from Greek *-podos* footed, from *pous* foot]

podagra (pəˈdægrə) *n.* gout of the foot or big toe. [C15: via Latin from Greek, from *pous* foot + *agra* a trap] —**poˈdagral, poˈdagric, poˈdagrical,** *or* **poˈdagrous** *adj.*

poddy (ˈpɒdɪ) *Austral.* ~*n., pl.* **-dies. 1.** a handfed calf or lamb. **2.** any creature at an early stage of growth: *poddy mullet.* ~*vb.* **3.** to rear by hand. [perhaps from *poddy* (adj.) fat]

poddy-dodger (ˈpɒdɪˌdɒdʒə) *n. Austral. informal.* a cattle thief who steals unbranded calves.

podesta (pɒˈdɛstə; *Italian* podeˈsta) *n.* **1.** (in modern Italy) a subordinate magistrate in some towns. **2.** (in Fascist Italy) the chief magistrate of a commune. **3.** (in medieval Italy) **a.** any of the governors of the Lombard cities appointed by Frederick Barbarossa. **b.** a chief magistrate in any of various republics, such as Florence. [C16: from Italian: power, from Latin *potestās* ability, power, from *posse* to be able]

podge (pɒdʒ) *or* **pudge** (pʌdʒ) *n. Informal.* a short chubby person.

podgy (ˈpɒdʒɪ) *adj.* **podgier, podgiest.** short and fat; chubby. —ˈ**podgily** *adv.* —ˈ**podginess** *n.*

podiatry (pɒˈdiːətrɪ, -ˈdaɪ-) *n. Chiefly U.S.* another word for **chiropody.** [C20: from Greek *pous* foot] —**poˈdiatrist** *n.*

podium (ˈpəʊdɪəm) *n., pl.* **-diums** *or* **-dia** (-dɪə). **1.** a small raised platform used by lecturers, orchestra conductors, etc.; dais. **2.** a plinth that supports a colonnade or wall. **3.** a low wall surrounding the arena of an ancient amphitheatre. **4.** *Zoology.* **a.** the terminal part of a vertebrate limb. **b.** any footlike organ, such as the tube foot of a starfish. [C18: from Latin: platform, balcony, from Greek *podion* little foot, from *pous* foot]

-podium *n. combining form.* a part resembling a foot: *pseudopodium.* [from New Latin: footlike; see PODIUM]

podophyllin *or* **podophylin resin** (ˌpɒdəʊˈfɪlɪn) *n.* a bitter yellow resin obtained from the dried underground stems of the May apple and mandrake: used as a cathartic and to treat warts. [C19: from New Latin *Podophyllum* genus of herbs including the May apple, from *podo-,* from Greek *pous* foot + *phullon* leaf]

-podous *adj. combining form.* having feet of a certain kind or number: *cephalopodous.*

podzol (ˈpɒdzɒl) *or* **podsol** (ˈpɒdsɒl) *n.* a type of soil characteristic of coniferous forest regions having a greyish-white colour in its upper leached layers. [C20: from Russian: ash ground, from *pod* ground + *zola* ashes] —**podˈzolic** *or* **podˈsolic** *adj.*

podzolization (ˌpɒdzɒlaɪˈzeɪʃən), **podsolization** (ˌpɒdsɒlaɪˈzeɪʃən) *or* **podzolisation, podsolisation** *n.* the process by which the upper layer of a soil becomes acidic through the leaching of bases which are deposited in the lower horizons.

podzolize (ˈpɒdzɒˌlaɪz), **podsolize** (ˈpɒdsɒˌlaɪz) *or* **podzolise, podsolise** *vb.* (*usually passive*) to make into or form a podzol: *podzolized soil.*

POE *abbrev. for:* **1.** *Military.* port of embarkation. **2.** port of entry.

poem (ˈpəʊɪm) *n.* **1.** a composition in verse, usually characterized by concentrated and heightened language in which words are chosen for their sound and suggestive power as well as for their sense, and using such techniques as metre, rhyme, and alliteration. **2.** a literary composition that is not in verse but exhibits the intensity of imagination and language common to it: *a prose poem.* **3.** anything resembling a poem in beauty, effect, etc. [C16: from Latin *poēma,* from Greek, variant of *poiēma* something composed, created, from *poiein* to make]

poenology (piːˈnɒlədʒɪ) *n.* a variant spelling of **penology.**

poesy (ˈpəʊɪzɪ) *n., pl.* **-sies. 1.** an archaic word for **poetry. 2.** *Poetic.* the art of writing poetry. **3.** *Archaic or poetic.* a poem or verse, esp. one used as a motto. [C14: via Old French from Latin *poēsis,* from Greek, from *poiēsis* poetic art, creativity, from *poiein* to make]

poet (ˈpəʊɪt) *or* (*sometimes when fem.*) **poetess** *n.* **1.** a person who writes poetry. **2.** a person with great imagination and creativity. [C13: from Latin *poēta,* from Greek *poiētēs* maker, poet, from *poiein* to make]

poet. *abbrev. for:* **1.** poetic(al). **2.** poetry.

poetaster (ˌpəʊɪˈtæstə, -ˈteɪ-) *n.* a writer of inferior verse. [C16: from Medieval Latin; see POET, -ASTER]

poetic (pəʊˈɛtɪk) *or* **poetical** *adj.* **1.** of or relating to poetry. **2.** characteristic of or befitting poetry, as in being elevated, sublime, etc. **3.** characteristic of a poet. **4.** recounted in verse. —**poˈetically** *adv.*

poeticize (pəʊˈɛtɪˌsaɪz), **poetize** (ˈpəʊɪˌtaɪz) *or* **poeticise, poetise** *vb.* **1.** (*tr.*) to put into poetry or make poetic. **2.** (*intr.*) to speak or write poetically.

poetic justice *n.* fitting retribution; just deserts.

poetic licence *n.* justifiable departure from conventional rules of form, fact, logic, etc., as in poetry.

poetics (pəʊˈɛtɪks) *n.* (*usually functioning as sing.*) **1.** the principles and forms of poetry or the study of these, esp. as a form of literary criticism. **2.** a treatise on poetry.

poet laureate *n., pl.* **poets laureate.** *Brit.* the poet appointed as court poet of Britain who is given a lifetime post as an officer of the Royal Household. The first was Ben Jonson in 1616.

poetry (ˈpəʊɪtrɪ) *n.* **1.** literature in metrical form; verse. **2.** the art or craft of writing verse. **3.** poetic qualities, spirit, or feeling in anything. **4.** anything resembling poetry in rhythm, beauty, etc. [C14: from Medieval Latin *poētria,* from Latin *poēta* POET]

POEU (in Britain) *abbrev. for* Post Office Engineers Union.

po-faced *adj.* (of a person) wearing a disapproving stern expression. [C20: probably changed from *poor-faced*]

pogey *or* **pogy** (ˈpəʊgɪ) *n., pl.* **pogeys** *or* **pogies.** *Canadian slang.* **1.** financial or other relief given to the unemployed by the government; dole. **2.** unemployment insurance. **3. a.** the office distributing relief to the unemployed. **b.** (*as modifier*): *pogey clothes.* [C20: from earlier *pogie* workhouse, of unknown origin]

pogge (pɒg) *n.* **1.** Also called: **armed bullhead.** a European marine scorpaenoid fish, *Agonus cataphractus,* of northern European waters, with a large head, long thin tail, and body completely covered with bony plates: family *Agonidae.* **2.** any other fish of the family *Agonidae.* [C18: of unknown origin]

pogo (ˈpəʊgəʊ) *vb.* **pogos, pogoing, pogoed.** (*intr.*) to jump up and down in one spot, as in a punk dance of the 1970s. [C20: from POGO STICK; from the motion] —ˈ**pogoer** *n.*

pogonia (pəˈɡəʊnɪə) *n.* any orchid of the chiefly American genus *Pogonia,* esp. the snakesmouth, having pink or white fragrant flowers. [C19: New Latin, from Greek *pōgōnias* bearded, from *pōgōn* a beard]
pogo stick *n.* a stout pole with a handle at the top, steps for the feet and a spring at the bottom, so that the user can spring up, down, and along on it. [C20: of uncertain origin]
pogrom (ˈpɒɡrəm) *n.* an organized persecution or extermination of an ethnic group, esp. of Jews. [C20: via Yiddish from Russian: destruction, from *po-* like + *grom* thunder]
pogy (ˈpəʊɡɪ, ˈpɒɡɪ) *n.* **1.** (*pl.* **pogies** *or* **pogy**) another name for the **porgy**. **2.** (*pl.* **pogies**) a variant spelling of **pogey**. [C19: perhaps from Algonquian *pohegan* menhaden]
pohutukawa (pəˌhuːtəˈkɑːwə) *n.* a myrtaceous New Zealand tree, *Metrosideros tomentosa,* with red flowers and hard red wood. [from Maori]
poi[1] (pɔɪ, ˈpəʊɪ) *n.* a Hawaiian dish made of the root of the taro baked, pounded to a paste, and fermented. [C19: from Hawaiian]
poi[2] (pɔɪ) *n. N.Z.* a ball of woven flax swung rhythmically in poi dances. [Maori]
poi dance *n. N.Z.* a women's formation dance that involves singing and manipulating a poi.
-poiesis *n. combining form.* indicating the act of making or producing something specified: *haematopoiesis.* [from Greek, from *poiēsis* a making; see POESY] —**-poietic** *adj. combining form.*
poignant (ˈpɔɪnjənt, -nənt) *adj.* **1.** sharply distressing or painful to the feelings. **2.** to the point; cutting or piercing: *poignant wit.* **3.** keen or pertinent in mental appeal: *a poignant subject.* **4.** pungent in smell. [C14: from Old French, from Latin *pungens* pricking, from *pungere* to sting, pierce, grieve] —ˈ**poignancy** *or* ˈ**poignance** *n.* —ˈ**poignantly** *adv.*
poikilocyte (ˈpɔɪkɪləʊˌsaɪt) *n.* an abnormally shaped red blood cell. [C19: from Greek *poikilos* various + -CYTE]
poikilothermic (ˌpɔɪkɪləʊˈθɜːmɪk) *or* **poikilothermal** (ˌpɔɪkɪləʊˈθɜːməl) *adj.* (of all animals except birds and mammals) having a body temperature that varies with the temperature of the surroundings. Compare **homoiothermic.** [C19: from Greek *poikilos* various + THERMAL] —ˌ**poikiloˈthermism** *or* ˌ**poikiloˈthermy** *n.*
poilu (ˈpwɑːluː; *French* pwaly) *n.* an infantryman in the French Army, esp. one in the front lines in World War I. [C20: from French, literally: hairy (that is, virile), from *poil* hair, from Latin *pilus* a hair]
poinciana (ˌpɔɪnsɪˈɑːnə) *n.* **1.** any tree of the tropical caesalpiniaceous genus *Poinciana,* having large orange or red flowers. **2.** See **royal poinciana.** [C17: New Latin, named after M. de *Poinci,* 17th-century governor of the French Antilles]
poind (pɪnd) *vb.* (*tr.*) *Scots Law.* **1.** to take (property of a debtor) in execution or by way of distress; distrain. **2.** to impound (stray cattle, etc.). [C15: from Scots, variant of Old English *pyndan* to impound]
poinsettia (pɔɪnˈsɛtɪə) *n.* a euphorbiaceous shrub, *Euphorbia* (or *Poinsettia*) *pulcherrima,* of Mexico and Central America, widely cultivated for its showy scarlet bracts, which resemble petals. [C19: New Latin, from the name of J. P. *Poinsett* (1799–1851), U.S. Minister to Mexico, who introduced it to the U.S.]
point (pɔɪnt) *n.* **1.** a dot or tiny mark. **2.** a location, spot, or position. **3.** any dot or mark used in writing or printing, such as a decimal point or a full stop. **4.** short for **vowel point. 5.** the sharp tapered end of a pin, knife, etc. **6.** a pin, needle, or other object having such a point. **7.** *Maths.* **a.** a geometric element having no dimensions and whose position in space is located by means of its coordinates. **b.** a location: *point of inflection.* **8.** a promontory, usually smaller than a cape. **9.** a specific condition or degree. **10.** a moment: *at that point he left the room.* **11.** an important or fundamental reason, aim, etc.: *the point of this exercise is to train new teachers.* **12.** an essential element or thesis in an argument: *you've made your point; I take your point.* **13.** a suggestion or tip. **14.** a detail or item. **15.** an important or outstanding characteristic, physical attribute, etc.: *he has his good points.* **16.** a distinctive characteristic or quality of an animal, esp. one used as a standard in judging livestock. **17.** (*often pl.*) any of the extremities, such as the tail, ears, or feet, of a domestic animal. **18.** *Ballet.* (*often pl.*) the tip of the toes. **19.** a single unit for measuring or counting, as in the scoring of a game. **20.** *Australian Rules football.* an informal name for **behind** (sense 11). **21.** *Printing.* a unit of measurement equal to one twelfth of a pica, or approximately 0.01384 inch. There are approximately 72 points to the inch. **22.** *Finance.* **a.** a unit of value used to quote security and commodity prices and their fluctuations. **b.** a percentage unit sometimes payable by a borrower as a premium on a loan. **23.** *Navigation.* **a.** one of the 32 marks on the circumference of a compass card indicating direction. **b.** the angle of 11°15′ between two adjacent marks. **c.** a point on the horizon indicated by such a mark. **24.** *Cricket.* **a.** a fielding position at right angles to the batsman on the off side and relatively near the pitch. **b.** a fielder in this position. **25.** any of the numbers cast in the first throw in craps with which one neither wins nor loses by throwing them: 4, 5, 6, 8, 9, or 10. **26.** either of the two electrical contacts that make or break the current flow in the distributor of an internal-combustion engine. **27.** *Brit.* (*often pl.*) a junction of railway tracks in which a pair of rails can be moved so that a train can be directed onto either of two lines. U.S. and Canadian equivalent: **switch. 28.** (*often pl.*) a piece of ribbon, cord, etc., with metal tags at the end: used during the 16th and 17th centuries to fasten clothing. **29.** *Backgammon.* a place or position on the board. **30.** *Brit.* **a.** short for **power point. b.** an informal name for **socket** (sense 2). **31.** an aggressive position adopted in bayonet or sword drill. **32.** the position of the body of a pointer or setter when it discovers game. **33.** *Boxing.* a mark awarded for a scoring blow, knockdown, etc. **34.** any diacritic used in a writing system, esp. in a phonetic transcription, to indicate modifications of vowels or consonants. **35.** *Jewellery.* a unit of weight equal to 0.01 carat. **36.** the act of pointing. **37.** *Ice hockey.* the position just inside the opponents' blue line. **38. at** (*or* **on**) **the point of.** at the moment immediately before a specified condition, action, etc., is expected to begin: *on the point of leaving the room.* **39. beside the point.** not pertinent; irrelevant. **40. case in point.** a specific, appropriate, or relevant instance or example. **41. in point of.** in the matter of; regarding. **42. make a point of. a.** to make (something) one's regular habit. **b.** to do (something) because one thinks it important. **43. not to put too fine a point on it.** to speak plainly and bluntly. **44. score points off.** to gain an advantage at someone else's expense. **45. stretch a point. a.** to make a concession or exception not usually made. **b.** to exaggerate. **46. to the point.** pertinent; relevant. **47. up to a point.** not completely. ~*vb.* **48.** (usually foll. by *at* or *to*) to indicate the location or direction of by or as by extending (a finger or other pointed object) towards it: *he pointed to the front door; don't point that gun at me.* **49.** (*intr.*; usually foll. by *at* or *to*) to indicate or identify a specific person or thing among several: *he pointed at the bottle he wanted; all evidence pointed to Donald as the murderer.* **50.** (*tr.*) to direct or cause to go or face in a specific direction or towards a place or goal: *point me in the right direction.* **51.** (*tr.*) to sharpen or taper. **52.** (*intr.*) (of gun dogs) to indicate the place where game is lying by standing rigidly with the muzzle turned in its direction. **53.** (*tr.*) to finish or repair the joints of (brickwork, masonry, etc.) with mortar or cement. **54.** (*tr.*) *Music.* to mark (a psalm text) with vertical lines to indicate the points at which the music changes during chanting. **55.** to steer (a sailing vessel) close to the wind or (of a sailing vessel) to sail close to the wind. **56.** (*tr.*) *Phonetics.* to provide (a letter or letters) with diacritics. **57.** (*tr.*) to provide (a Hebrew or similar text) with vowel points. ~See also **point off, point out, point up.** [C13: from Old French: spot, from Latin *punctum* a point, from *pungere* to pierce; also influenced by Old French *pointe* pointed end, from Latin *pungere*]
point after *n. American football.* a score given for a successful kick between the goalposts and above the crossbar, following a touchdown.
point-blank *adj.* **1. a.** aimed or fired at a target so close that it is unnecessary to make allowance for the drop in the course of the projectile. **b.** permitting such aim or fire without loss of accuracy: *at point-blank range.* **2.** plain or blunt: *a point-blank question.* ~*adv.* **3.** directly or straight. **4.** plainly or bluntly. [C16: from POINT + BLANK (in the sense: centre spot of an archery target)]
point d'appui *French.* (pwɛ̃ dapɥi) *n., pl.* ***points d'appui*** (pwɛ̃ dapɥi). **1.** a support or prop. **2.** (formerly) the base or rallying point for a military unit.
point defect *n.* an imperfection in a crystal, characterized by one unoccupied lattice position or one interstitial atom, molecule, or ion.
point-device *Obsolete.* ~*adj.* **1.** very correct or perfect; precise. ~*adv.* **2.** to perfection; perfectly; precisely. [C14: perhaps from old French *à point devis* to the point arranged]
point duty *n.* **1.** the stationing of a policeman or traffic warden at a road junction to control and direct traffic. **2.** the position at the head of a military patrol, regarded as being the most dangerous.
pointe (pɔɪnt) *n. Ballet.* the tip of the toe (esp. in the phrase **on pointes**). [from French: point]
pointed (ˈpɔɪntɪd) *adj.* **1.** having a point. **2.** cutting or incisive: *a pointed wit.* **3.** obviously directed at or intended for a particular person or aspect: *pointed criticism.* **4.** emphasized or made conspicuous: *pointed ignorance.* **5.** (of an arch or style of architecture employing such an arch) Gothic. **6.** *Music.* (of a psalm text) marked to show changes in chanting. **7.** (of Hebrew text) with vowel points marked. —ˈ**pointedly** *adv.* —ˈ**pointedness** *n.*
pointed arch *n.* another name for **lancet arch.**
pointer (ˈpɔɪntə) *n.* **1.** a person or thing that points. **2.** an indicator on a measuring instrument. **3.** a long rod or cane used by a lecturer to point to parts of a map, blackboard, etc. **4.** one of a breed of large swift smooth-coated dogs, usually white with black, liver, or lemon markings: when on shooting expeditions it points to the bird with its nose, body, and tail in a straight line. **5.** a helpful piece of information or advice.
Pointers (ˈpɔɪntəz) *pl. n.* **the.** the two brightest stars in the Plough, which lie in the direction pointing towards the Pole Star and are therefore used to locate it.
point estimate *n. Statistics.* a specific value assigned to a parameter of a population on the basis of sampling statistics. Compare **interval estimate.**

point group *n. Crystallog.* another term for **crystal class.**
pointillism (ˈpwæntɪˌlɪzəm, -tiːˌɪzəm, ˈpɔɪn-) *n.* the technique of painting elaborated from impressionism, in which dots of unmixed colour are juxtaposed on a white ground so that from a distance they fuse in the viewer's eye into appropriate intermediate tones. Also called: **divisionism.** [C19: from French, from *pointiller* to mark with tiny dots, from *pointille* little point, from Italian *puntiglio,* from *punto* POINT] —ˈ**pointillist** *n., adj.*
pointing (ˈpɔɪntɪŋ) *n.* **1.** the act or process of repairing or finishing joints in brickwork, masonry, etc., with mortar. **2. a.** the insertion of marks to indicate the chanting of a psalm or the vowels in a Hebrew text. **b.** the sequence of marks so inserted.
point lace *n.* lace made by a needle with buttonhole stitch on a paper pattern. Also called: **needlepoint.** Compare **pillow lace.**
pointless (ˈpɔɪntlɪs) *adj.* **1.** without a point. **2.** without meaning, relevance, or force. **3.** *Sport.* without a point scored. —ˈ**pointlessly** *adv.* —ˈ**pointlessness** *n.*
point off *vb. (tr., adv.)* to mark off from the right-hand side (a number of decimal places) in a whole number to create a mixed decimal: *point off three decimal places in 12345 and you get 12.345.*
point of honour *n., pl.* **points of honour.** a circumstance, event, etc., that involves the defence of one's principles, social honour, etc.
point of inflection *n., pl.* **points of inflection.** *Maths.* a stationary point on a curve at which the tangent is horizontal or vertical and where tangents on either side have the same sign.
point of no return *n.* **1.** a point at which an irreversible commitment must be made to an action, progression, etc. **2.** a point in a journey at which, if one continues, supplies will be insufficient for a return to the starting place.
point of order *n., pl.* **points of order.** a question raised in a meeting or deliberative assembly by a member as to whether the rules governing procedures are being breached.
point of sale *n.* (in retail distribution) the place at which a sale is made. Abbrev.: **POS.**
point-of-sale terminal *n.* (in retail distribution) a device used to record and process information relating to sales. Abbrev.: **POST.**
point of view *n., pl.* **points of view. 1.** a position from which someone or something is observed. **2.** a mental viewpoint or attitude. **3.** the mental position from which a story is observed or narrated: *the omniscient point of view.*
point out *vb. (tr., adv.)* to indicate or specify.
pointsman (ˈpɔɪntsˌmæn, -mən) *n., pl.* **-men. 1.** a person who operates railway points. U.S. and Canadian equivalent: **switchman. 2.** a policeman or traffic warden on point duty.
point source *n. Optics.* a source of light or other radiation that can be considered to have negligible dimensions.
points system *n. Brit.* a system used to assess applicants' eligibility for local authority housing, based on (points awarded for) such factors as the length of time the applicant has lived in the area, how many children are in the family, etc.
point system *n.* **1.** *Printing.* a system of measurement using the **point** (see sense 21) as its unit. **2.** a system for evaluation of achievement, as in education or industry, based on awarding points. **3.** any system of writing or printing, such as Braille, that uses protruding dots.
point-to-point *n.* **1.** *Brit.* **a.** a steeplechase organized by a recognized hunt or other body, usually restricted to amateurs riding horses that have been regularly used in hunting. **b.** *(as modifier): a point-to-point race.* ~*adj.* **2.** (of a route) from one place to the next. **3.** (of a radiocommunication link) from one point to another, rather than broadcast.
point up *vb. (tr., adv.)* to emphasize, esp. by identifying: *he pointed up the difficulties we would encounter.*
pointy (ˈpɔɪntɪ) *adj.* **pointier, pointiest.** having a sharp point or points; pointed.
poise[1] (pɔɪz) *n.* **1.** composure or dignity of manner. **2.** physical balance or assurance in movement or bearing. **3.** the state of being balanced or stable; equilibrium; stability. **4.** the position of hovering. **5.** suspense or indecision. ~*vb.* **6.** to be or cause to be balanced or suspended. **7.** *(tr.)* to hold, as in readiness: *to poise a lance.* **8.** *(tr.)* a rare word for **weigh.** [C16: from Old French *pois* weight, from Latin *pēnsum,* from *pendere* to weigh]
poise[2] (pwɑːz, pɔɪz) *n.* the cgs unit of viscosity; the viscosity of a fluid in which a tangential force of 1 dyne per square centimetre maintains a difference in velocity of 1 centimetre per second between two parallel planes 1 centimetre apart. It is equivalent to 0.1 newton second per square metre. Symbol: P [C20: named after Jean Louis Marie *Poiseuille* (1799–1869), French physician]
poised (pɔɪzd) *adj.* **1.** self-possessed; dignified; exhibiting composure. **2.** balanced and prepared for action: *a skier poised at the top of the slope.*
poison (ˈpɔɪzᵊn) *n.* **1.** any substance that can impair function, cause structural damage, or otherwise injure the body. **2.** something that destroys, corrupts, etc.: *the poison of fascism.* **3.** a substance that retards a chemical reaction or destroys or inhibits the activity of a catalyst. **4.** a substance that absorbs neutrons in a nuclear reactor and thus slows down the reaction. It may be added deliberately or formed during fission. **5. what's your poison?** *Informal.* what would you like to drink? ~*vb. (tr.)* **6.** to give poison to (a person or animal) esp. with intent to kill. **7.** to add poison to. **8.** to taint or infect with or as if with poison. **9.** (foll. by *against*) to turn (a person's mind) against: *he poisoned her mind against me.* **10.** to retard or stop (a chemical or nuclear reaction) by the action of a poison. **11.** to inhibit or destroy (the activity of a catalyst) by the action of a poison. [C13: from Old French *puison* potion, from Latin *pōtiō* a drink, esp. a poisonous one, from *pōtāre* to drink] —ˈ**poisoner** *n.*
poison dogwood *or* **elder** *n.* other names for **poison sumach.**
poison gas *n.* a gaseous substance, such as chlorine, phosgene, or lewisite, used in warfare to kill or harm.
poison hemlock *n.* the U.S. name for **hemlock** (sense 1).
poison ivy *n.* any of several North American anacardiaceous shrubs or vines of the genus *Rhus* (or *Toxicodendron*), esp. *R. radicans,* which has small green flowers and whitish berries that cause an itching rash on contact. See also **sumach** (sense 1).
poison oak *n.* **1.** either of two North American anacardiaceous shrubs, *Rhus toxicodendron* or *R. diversiloba,* that are related to the poison ivy and cause a similar rash. See also **sumach** (sense 1). **2.** *(not in technical use)* another name for **poison ivy.**
poisonous (ˈpɔɪzənəs) *adj.* **1.** having the effects or qualities of a poison. **2.** capable of killing or inflicting injury; venomous. **3.** corruptive or malicious. —ˈ**poisonously** *adv.* —ˈ**poisonousness** *n.*
poison-pen letter *n.* a letter written in malice, usually anonymously, and intended to abuse, frighten, or insult the recipient.
poison pill *n. Finance.* a tactic used by a company fearing an unwelcome takeover bid, in which the value of the company is automatically reduced, as by the sale of an issue of shares having an option unfavourable to the bidders, if the bid is successful.
poison sumach *n.* an anacardiaceous swamp shrub, *Rhus* (or *Toxicodendron*) *vernix* of the southeastern U.S., that has greenish-white berries and causes an itching rash on contact with the skin. Also called: **poison dogwood, poison elder.** See also **sumach.**
Poisson distribution (ˈpwɑːsᵊn) *n. Statistics.* a distribution that represents the number of events occurring randomly in a fixed time at an average rate λ; symbol: $P_0(\lambda)$. For large n and small p with $np = \lambda$ it approximates to the binomial distribution $Bi(n,p)$. [C19: named after S. D. *Poisson* (1781–1840), French mathematician]
Poisson's ratio *n.* a measure of the elastic properties of a material expressed as the ratio of the fractional contraction in breadth to the fractional increase in length when the material is stretched. Symbol: μ or ν
poitín (ˈpɒtiːn) *n.* the Irish Gaelic spelling of **poteen.**
poke[1] (pəʊk) *vb.* **1.** *(tr.)* to jab or prod, as with the elbow, the finger, a stick, etc. **2.** *(tr.)* to make (a hole, opening, etc.) by or as by poking. **3.** (when *intr.,* often foll. by *at*) to thrust (at). **4.** *(tr.) Informal.* to hit with the fist; punch. **5.** (usually foll. by *in, out, out of, through,* etc.) to protrude or cause to protrude: *don't poke your arm out of the window.* **6.** *(tr.)* to stir (a fire, pot, etc.) by poking. **7.** *(intr.)* to meddle or intrude. **8.** *(intr.;* often foll. by *about* or *around)* to search or pry. **9.** *(intr.;* often foll. by *along)* to loiter, potter, dawdle, etc. **10.** *(tr.) Taboo slang.* (of a man) to have sexual intercourse with (a woman). **11. poke fun at.** to mock or ridicule. **12. poke one's nose into.** See **nose** (sense 17). ~*n.* **13.** a jab or prod. **14.** short for **slowpoke. 15.** *Informal.* a blow with one's fist; punch. **16.** *Taboo slang.* sexual intercourse. [C14: from Low German and Middle Dutch *poken* to thrust, prod, strike]
poke[2] (pəʊk) *n.* **1.** *Dialect.* a pocket or bag. **2. a pig in a poke.** See **pig** (sense 8). [C13: from Old Northern French *poque,* of Germanic origin; related to Old English *pocca* bag, Old Norse *poki* POUCH, Middle Dutch *poke* bag; compare POACH[2]]
poke[3] (pəʊk) *n.* **1.** Also called: **poke bonnet.** a woman's bonnet with a brim that projects at the front, popular in the 18th and 19th centuries. **2.** the brim itself. [C18: from POKE[1] (in the sense: to thrust out, project)]
poke[4] (pəʊk) *n.* short for **pokeweed.**
pokeberry (ˈpəʊkbərɪ) *n., pl.* **-berries. 1.** Also called: **inkberry.** the berry of the pokeweed. **2.** another name for the **pokeweed.**
pokelogan (ˈpəʊkˌləʊgən) *n. Canadian.* another name for **bogan.** [C19: from Ojibwa *pokenogun*]
poker[1] (ˈpəʊkə) *n.* **1.** a metal rod, usually with a handle, for stirring a fire. **2.** a person or thing that pokes.
poker[2] (ˈpəʊkə) *n.* a card game of bluff and skill in which bets are made on the hands dealt, the highest-ranking hand (containing the most valuable combinations of sequences and sets of cards) winning the pool. [C19: probably from French *poque* similar card game]
poker dice *n.* **1.** a dice marked on its six faces with the pictures of the playing cards from ace to nine. **2.** a gambling game, based on poker hands, played with five such dice.
poker face *n. Informal.* a face without expression, as that of a poker player attempting to conceal the value of his cards. —ˈ**poker-ˌfaced** *adj.*
poker machine *n. Austral. and N.Z.* a fruit machine. Often shortened to **pokie.**
pokerwork (ˈpəʊkəˌwɜːk) *n.* **1.** the art of decorating wood or leather by burning a design with a heated metal point; pyrography. **2.** artefacts decorated in this way.
pokeweed (ˈpəʊkˌwiːd), **pokeberry,** *or* **pokeroot** *n.* a tall North American plant, *Phytolacca americana,* that has small white

flowers, juicy purple berries, and a poisonous purple root used medicinally: family *Phytolaccaceae*. Sometimes shortened to **poke.** Also called: **inkberry.** [C18 *poke,* shortened from Algonquian *puccoon* plant used in dyeing, from *pak* blood]

pokie ('pəʊkɪ) *n. Austral. informal.* short for **poker machine.**

poky *or* **pokey** ('pəʊkɪ) *adj.* **pokier, pokiest.** 1. *Informal, chiefly U.S.* (esp. of rooms) small and cramped. 2. without speed or energy; slow. ~*n., pl.* **pokies** *or* **pokeys.** 3. a U.S. and Canadian slang word for **jail.** [C19: from POKE[1] (in slang sense: to confine)] —'**pokily** *adv.* —'**pokiness** *n.*

POL *Military. abbrev. for* petroleum, oil, and lubricants.

pol. *abbrev. for:* 1. political. 2. politics.

Pol. *abbrev. for:* 1. Poland. 2. Polish.

Polack ('pəʊlæk) *n. Derogatory slang.* a Pole or a person of Polish descent. [C16: from Polish *Polak* Pole]

polacre (pəʊ'lɑːkə) *or* **polacca** (pəʊ'lækə) *n.* a three-masted sailing vessel used in the Mediterranean. [C17: from either French *polacre* or Italian *polacca* Pole or Polish; origin unknown]

polar ('pəʊlə) *adj.* 1. situated at or near, coming from, or relating to either of the earth's poles or the area inside the Arctic or Antarctic Circles: *polar regions.* 2. having or relating to a pole or poles. 3. pivotal or guiding in the manner of the Pole Star. 4. directly opposite, as in tendency or character. 5. *Chem.* **a.** (of a molecule or compound) being or having a molecule in which there is an uneven distribution of electrons and thus a permanent dipole moment: *water has polar molecules.* **b.** (of a crystal or substance) being or having a crystal that is bound by ionic bonds: *sodium chloride forms polar crystals.*

polar axis *n.* the fixed line in a system of polar coordinates from which the polar angle, θ, is measured anticlockwise.

polar bear *n.* a white carnivorous bear, *Thalarctos maritimus,* of coastal regions of the North Pole.

polar body *n. Physiology.* a tiny cell containing little cytoplasm that is produced with the ovum during oogenesis when the oocyte undergoes meiosis.

polar circle *n.* a term for either the **Arctic Circle** or **Antarctic Circle.**

polar coordinates *pl. n.* a pair of coordinates for locating a point in a plane by means of the length of a radius vector, *r,* which pivots about the origin to establish the angle, θ, that the position of the point makes with a fixed line. Usually written (*r*, θ). See also **Cartesian coordinates, spherical coordinates.**

polar distance *n.* the angular distance of a star, planet, etc., from the celestial pole; the complement of the declination. Also called: **codeclination.**

polar equation *n.* an equation in polar coordinates.

polar front *n. Meteorol.* a front dividing cold polar air from warmer temperate or tropical air.

Polari (pə'lɑːrɪ) *or* **Parlyaree** (pɑː'ljɑːrɪ) *n.* an English slang that is derived from the Lingua Franca of Mediterranean ports; brought to England by sailors from the 16th century onwards. A few words survive, esp. in male homosexual slang. [C19: from Italian *parlare* to speak]

polarimeter (ˌpəʊlə'rɪmɪtə) *n.* 1. an instrument for measuring the amount of polarization of light. 2. an instrument for measuring the rotation of the plane of polarization of light as a result of its passage through a liquid or solution. See **optical activity.** —**polarimetric** (ˌpəʊlərɪ'mɛtrɪk) *adj.* —ˌ**polar'imetry** *n.*

Polaris (pə'lɑːrɪs) *n.* Also called: the **Pole Star,** the **North Star.** the brightest star in the constellation Ursa Minor, situated slightly less than 1° from the north celestial pole. It is a Cepheid variable, with a period of four days. Visual magnitude: 2.08–2.17; spectral type: F8. [shortened from Medieval Latin *stella polāris* polar star]

polariscope (pəʊ'lærɪˌskəʊp) *n.* an instrument for detecting polarized light or for observing objects under polarized light, esp. for detecting strain in transparent materials. See **photoelasticity.**

polarity (pəʊ'lærɪtɪ) *n., pl.* **-ties.** 1. the condition of having poles. 2. the condition of a body or system in which it has opposing physical properties at different points, esp. magnetic poles or electric charge. 3. the particular state of a part of a body or system that has polarity: *an electrode with positive polarity.* 4. the state of having or expressing two directly opposite tendencies, opinions, etc.

polarization *or* **polarisation** (ˌpəʊləraɪ'zeɪʃən) *n.* 1. the condition of having or giving polarity. 2. *Physics.* the process or phenomenon in which the waves of light or other electromagnetic radiation are restricted to certain directions of vibration.

polarize *or* **polarise** ('pəʊləˌraɪz) *vb.* 1. to acquire or cause to acquire polarity. 2. to acquire or cause to acquire polarization: *to polarize light.* 3. to cause people to adopt extreme opposing positions: *to polarize opinion.* —'**polarˌizable** *or* '**polarˌisable** *adj.* —'**polarˌizer** *or* '**polarˌiser** *n.*

polar lights *pl. n.* the aurora borealis in the N hemisphere or the aurora australis in the S hemisphere.

polarography (ˌpəʊlə'rɒgrəfɪ) *n.* a technique for analysing and studying ions in solution by using an electrolytic cell with a very small cathode and obtaining a graph (**polarogram**) of the current against the potential to determine the concentration and nature of the ions. Because the cathode is small, polarization occurs and each type of anion is discharged at a different potential. The apparatus (**polarograph**) usually employs a dropping-mercury cathode. —**polarographic** (ˌpəʊlərə'græfɪk) *adj.*

Polaroid ('pəʊləˌrɔɪd) *Trademark.* ~*n.* 1. a type of plastic sheet that can polarize a transmitted beam of normal light because it is composed of long parallel molecules. It only transmits plane-polarized light if these molecules are parallel to the plane of polarization and, since reflected light is partly polarized, it is often used in sunglasses to eliminate glare. 2. **Polaroid Land Camera.** any of several types of camera yielding a finished print by means of a special developing and processing technique that occurs inside the camera and takes only a few seconds to complete. ~*adj.* 3. of, relating to, using, or used in this type of camera: *Polaroid film.*

polar sequence *n. Astronomy.* a series of stars in the vicinity of the N celestial pole whose accurately determined magnitudes serve as the standard for visual and photographic magnitudes of stars.

polar wandering *n. Geology.* the movement of the earth's magnetic poles with respect to the geographic poles.

polder ('pəʊldə, 'pɒl-) *n.* a stretch of land reclaimed from the sea or a lake, esp. in the Netherlands. [C17: from Middle Dutch *polre*]

pole[1] (pəʊl) *n.* 1. a long slender usually round piece of wood, metal, or other material. 2. the piece of timber on each side of which a pair of carriage horses are hitched. 3. another name for **rod** (sense 7). 4. *Horse racing, chiefly U.S. and Canadian.* **a.** the inside lane of a racecourse. **b.** (*as modifier*): *the pole position.* **c.** one of a number of markers placed at intervals of one sixteenth of a mile along the side of a racecourse. 5. *Nautical.* **a.** any light spar. **b.** the part of a mast between the head and the attachment of the uppermost shrouds. 6. **under bare poles.** *Nautical.* (of a sailing vessel) with no sails set. 7. **up the pole.** *Brit., Austral., and N.Z. informal.* **a.** slightly mad. **b.** mistaken; on the wrong track. ~*vb.* 8. (*tr.*) to strike or push with a pole. 9. (*tr.*) **a.** to set out (an area of land or garden) with poles. **b.** to support (a crop, such as hops or beans) on poles. 10. (*tr.*) to deoxidize (a molten metal, esp. copper) by stirring it with green wood. 11. to punt (a boat). 12. (usually foll. by *on*) *Austral. informal.* to scrounge (from) or impose (on). [Old English *pāl,* from Latin *pālus* a stake, prop; see PALE[2]]

pole[2] (pəʊl) *n.* 1. either of the two antipodal points where the earth's axis of rotation meets the earth's surface. See also **North Pole, South Pole.** 2. *Astronomy.* short for **celestial pole.** 3. *Physics.* **a.** either of the two regions at the extremities of a magnet to which the lines of force converge or from which they diverge. **b.** either of two points or regions in a piece of material, system, etc., at which there are opposite electric charges, as at the two terminals of a battery. 4. *Maths.* an isolated singularity of an analytical function. 5. *Biology.* **a.** either end of the axis of a cell, spore, ovum, or similar body. **b.** either end of the spindle formed during the metaphase of mitosis and meiosis. 6. *Physiol.* the point on a neuron from which the axon or dendrites project from the cell body. 7. either of two mutually exclusive or opposite actions, opinions, etc. 8. *Geom.* the origin in a system of polar or spherical coordinates. 9. any fixed point of reference. 10. **poles apart** (*or* **asunder**). having widely divergent opinions, tastes, etc. 11. **from pole to pole.** throughout the entire world. [C14: from Latin *polus* end of an axis, from Greek *polos* pivot, axis, pole; related to Greek *kuklos* circle]

Pole (pəʊl) *n.* a native, inhabitant, or citizen of Poland, a republic in central Europe, or a speaker of Polish.

poleaxe *or U.S.* **poleax** ('pəʊlˌæks) *n.* 1. another term for **battle-axe** (sense 1). 2. a former naval weapon with an axe blade on one side of the handle and a spike on the other. 3. an axe used by butchers to slaughter animals. ~*vb.* 4. (*tr.*) to hit or fell with or as if with a poleaxe. [C14 *pollax* battle-axe, from POLL + AXE]

polecat ('pəʊlˌkæt) *n., pl.* **-cats** *or* **-cat.** 1. Also called (formerly): **foumart.** a dark brown musteline mammal, *Mustela putorius,* of woodlands of Europe, Asia, and N Africa, that is closely related to but larger than the weasel and gives off an unpleasant smell. See also **sweet marten.** 2. any of various related animals, such as the **marbled polecat,** *Vormela peregusna.* 3. *U.S.* a nontechnical name for **skunk** (sense 1). [C14 *polcat,* perhaps from Old French *pol* cock, from Latin *pullus,* + CAT; from its habit of preying on poultry]

pole horse *n.* a horse harnessed alongside the shaft (pole) of a vehicle. Also called: **poler.**

pole house *n. N.Z.* a timber house built on a steep section and supported by heavy debarked logs in long piles.

poleis ('pɒlaɪs) *n.* the plural of **polis**[1].

polemarch ('pɒlɪˌmɑːk) *n.* (in ancient Greece) a civilian official, originally a supreme general. [C16: from Greek *polemarchos,* from *polemos* war + *archos* ruler]

polemic (pə'lɛmɪk) *adj. also* **po'lemical.** 1. of or involving dispute or controversy. ~*n.* 2. an argument or controversy, esp. over a doctrine, belief, etc. 3. a person engaged in such an argument or controversy. [C17: from Medieval Latin *polemicus,* from Greek *polemikos* relating to war, from *polemos* war] —**po'lemically** *adv.* —**polemicist** (pə'lɛmɪsɪst) *or* **polemist** ('pɒlɪmɪst) *n.*

polemics (pəˈlɛmɪks) *n.* (*functioning as sing.*) the art or practice of dispute or argument, as in attacking or defending a doctrine or belief.

polemoniaceous (ˌpɒlɪˌməʊnɪˈeɪʃəs) *adj.* of, relating to, or belonging to the *Polemoniaceae,* a chiefly North American family of plants that includes phlox and Jacob's ladder. [C19: from New Latin *Polemōnium* type genus, from Greek *polemōnion* a plant, perhaps valerian]

polenta (pəʊˈlɛntə) *n.* a thick porridge made in Italy, usually from maize. [C16: via Italian from Latin: pearl barley, perhaps from Greek *palē* pollen]

pole piece *n. Electrical engineering.* a piece of ferromagnetic material forming an extension of the magnetic circuit in an electric motor, etc., used to concentrate the magnetic field where it will be most effective.

pole position *n.* **1.** (in motor racing) the starting position on the inside of the front row, generally considered the best one. **2.** an advantageous starting position.

poler (ˈpəʊlə) *n.* **1.** another name for **pole horse. 2.** a person or thing that poles, esp. a punter. **3.** *Austral. slang.* an idler or sponger.

pole star *n.* a guiding principle, rule, standard, etc.

Pole Star *n.* **the.** the star closest to the N celestial pole at any particular time. At present this is Polaris, but it will eventually be replaced by some other star owing to precession of the earth's axis.

pole vault *n.* **1. the.** a field event in which competitors attempt to clear a high bar with the aid of an extremely flexible long pole. **2.** a single attempt in the pole vault. ~*vb.* **pole-vault. 3.** (*intr.*) to perform a pole vault or compete in the pole vault. —ˈ**pole-ˌvaulter** *n.*

poley (ˈpəʊlɪ) *adj. Austral.* (of cattle) hornless or polled.

poleyn (ˈpəʊleɪn) *n.* a piece of armour for protecting the knee. Also called: **kneecap.** [from Old French *polain*]

police (pəˈliːs) *n.* **1. a.** (often preceded by *the*) the organized civil force of a state, concerned with maintenance of law and order, the detection and prevention of crime, etc. **b.** (*as modifier*): *a police inquiry.* **2.** (*functioning as pl.*) the members of such a force collectively. **3.** any organized body with a similar function: *security police.* **4.** *Archaic.* **a.** the regulation and control of a community, esp. in regard to the enforcement of law, the prevention of crime, etc. **b.** the department of government concerned with this. ~*vb.* (*tr.*) **5.** to regulate, control, or keep in order by means of a police or similar force. **6.** to observe or record the activity or enforcement of: *a committee was set up to police the new agreement on picketing.* **7.** *U.S.* to make or keep (a military camp, etc.) clean and orderly. [C16: via French from Latin *polītīa* administration, government; see POLITY]

police court *n.* **1.** another name for **magistrates' court. 2.** (in Scotland, formerly) a burgh court with limited jurisdiction, presided over by lay magistrates or a stipendiary magistrate: replaced in 1975 by the **district court.**

police dog *n.* a dog, often an Alsatian, trained to help the police, as in tracking.

policeman (pəˈliːsmən) *or* (*fem.*) **policewoman** *n., pl.* **-men** *or* **-women.** a member of a police force, esp. one holding the rank of constable.

policeman's helmet *n.* a Himalayan balsaminaceous plant, *Impatiens glandulifera,* with large purplish-pink flowers, introduced into Britain.

Police Motu *n.* a pidginized version of the Motu language, used as a lingua franca in Papua, originally chiefly by the police. Also called: **Hiri Motu.**

police officer *n.* a member of a police force, esp. a constable; policeman. Often shortened to (esp. as form of address): **officer.**

police state *n.* a state or country in which a repressive government maintains control through the police.

police station *n.* the office or headquarters of the police force of a district.

police wagon *n. U.S.* another term for **patrol wagon.**

policy[1] (ˈpɒlɪsɪ) *n., pl.* **-cies. 1.** a plan of action adopted or pursued by an individual, government, party, business, etc. **2.** wisdom, prudence, shrewdness, or sagacity. **3.** *Scot.* (*often pl.*) the improved grounds surrounding a country house. [C14: from Old French *policie,* from Latin *polītīa* administration, POLITY]

policy[2] (ˈpɒlɪsɪ) *n., pl.* **-cies.** a document containing a contract of insurance. [C16: from Old French *police* certificate, from Old Italian *polizza,* from Latin *apodixis* proof, from Greek *apodeixis* demonstration, proof]

policyholder (ˈpɒlɪsɪˌhəʊldə) *n.* a person or organization in whose name an insurance policy is registered.

policy science *n.* a branch of the social sciences concerned with the formulation and implementation of policy in bureaucracies, etc.

polio (ˈpəʊlɪəʊ) *n.* short for **poliomyelitis.**

poliomyelitis (ˌpəʊlɪəʊˌmaɪəˈlaɪtɪs) *n.* an acute infectious viral disease, esp. affecting children. In its paralytic form (**acute anterior poliomyelitis**) the brain and spinal cord are involved, causing weakness, paralysis, and wasting of muscle. Often shortened to **polio.** Also called: **infantile paralysis.** [C19: New Latin, from Greek *polios* grey + *muelos* marrow]

polis[1] (ˈpɒlɪs) *n., pl.* **poleis** (ˈpɒlaɪs). an ancient Greek city-state. [from Greek: city]

polis[2] (ˈpolɪs) *n. Scot. and Irish.* the police or a police officer. [C19: a variant pronunciation of *police*]

polish (ˈpɒlɪʃ) *vb.* **1.** to make or become smooth and shiny by rubbing, esp. with wax or an abrasive. **2.** (*tr.*) to make perfect or complete. **3.** to make or become elegant or refined. ~*n.* **4.** a finish or gloss. **5.** the act of polishing or the condition of having been polished. **6.** a substance used to produce a smooth and shiny, often protective surface. **7.** elegance or refinement, esp. in style, manner, etc. ~See also **polish off, polish up.** [C13 *polis,* from Old French *polir,* from Latin *polīre* to polish] —ˈ**polishable** *adj.* —ˈ**polisher** *n.*

Polish (ˈpəʊlɪʃ) *adj.* **1.** of, relating to, or characteristic of Poland, a republic in central Europe, or of its people or their language. ~*n.* **2.** the official language of Poland, belonging to the West Slavonic branch of the Indo-European family.

polished (ˈpɒlɪʃt) *adj.* **1.** accomplished: *a polished actor.* **2.** impeccably or professionally done: *a polished performance.* **3.** (of rice) having had the outer husk removed by milling.

Polish notation *n.* a logical notation that dispenses with the need for brackets by writing the logical constants as operators preceding their arguments.

polish off *vb.* (*tr., adv.*) *Informal.* **1.** to finish or process completely. **2.** to dispose of or kill; eliminate.

polish up *vb.* (*adv.*) **1.** to make or become smooth and shiny by polishing. **2.** (when *intr.*, foll. by *on*) to study or practise until adept at; improve: *polish up your spelling; he's polishing up on his German.*

polit. *abbrev. for:* **1.** political. **2.** politics.

Politburo (ˈpɒlɪtˌbjʊərəʊ) *n.* **1.** the executive and policy-making committee of a Communist Party. **2.** the supreme policy-making authority in most Communist countries. [C20: from Russian: contraction of *Politicheskoe Buro* political bureau]

polite (pəˈlaɪt) *adj.* **1.** showing a great regard for others, as in manners, speech, behaviour, etc.; courteous. **2.** cultivated or refined: *polite society.* **3.** elegant or polished: *polite letters.* [C15: from Latin *polītus* polished; see POLISH] —**poˈlitely** *adv.* —**poˈliteness** *n.*

politesse (ˌpɒlɪˈtɛs) *n.* formal or genteel politeness. [C18: via French from Italian *politezza,* ultimately from Latin *polīre* to POLISH]

politic (ˈpɒlɪtɪk) *adj.* **1.** artful or shrewd; ingenious: *a politic manager.* **2.** crafty or unscrupulous; cunning: *a politic old scoundrel.* **3.** sagacious, wise, or prudent, esp. in statesmanship: *a politic choice.* **4.** an archaic word for **political.** ~See also **body politic, politics.** [C15: from Old French *politique,* from Latin *polīticus* concerning civil administration, from Greek *politikos,* from *politēs* citizen, from *polis* city] —ˈ**politicly** *adv.*

political (pəˈlɪtɪkᵊl) *adj.* **1.** of or relating to the state, government, the body politic, public administration, policy-making, etc. **2. a.** of, involved in, or relating to government policy-making as distinguished from administration or law. **b.** of or relating to the civil aspects of government as distinguished from the military. **3.** of, dealing with, or relating to politics: *a political person.* **4.** of, characteristic of, or relating to the parties and the partisan aspects of politics. **5.** organized or ordered with respect to government: *a political unit.* —**poˈlitically** *adv.*

political economy *n.* the former name for **economics** (sense 1).

political prisoner *n.* someone imprisoned for holding, expressing, or acting in accord with particular political beliefs.

political science *n.* (esp. as an academic subject) the study of the state, government, and politics: one of the social sciences. —**political scientist** *n.*

politician (ˌpɒlɪˈtɪʃən) *n.* **1.** a person actively engaged in politics, esp. a full-time professional member of a deliberative assembly. **2.** a person who is experienced or skilled in the art or science of politics, government, or administration; statesman. **3.** *Disparaging, chiefly U.S.* a person who engages in politics out of a wish for personal gain, as realized by holding a public office.

politicize *or* **politicise** (pəˈlɪtɪˌsaɪz) *vb.* **1.** (*tr.*) to render political in tone, interest, or awareness. **2.** (*intr.*) to participate in political discussion or activity. —**poˌliticiˈzation** *or* **poˌliticiˈsation** *n.*

politicking (ˈpɒlɪˌtɪkɪŋ) *n.* political activity, esp. seeking votes.

politico (pəˈlɪtɪˌkəʊ) *n., pl.* **-cos.** *Chiefly U.S.* an informal word for a **politician** (senses 1, 3). [C17: from Italian or Spanish]

politico- *combining form.* denoting political or politics: *politicoeconomic.*

politics (ˈpɒlɪtɪks) *n.* **1.** (*functioning as sing.*) the practice or study of the art and science of forming, directing, and administrating states and other political units; the art and science of government; political science. **2.** (*functioning as sing.*) the complex or aggregate of relationships of people in society, esp. those relationships involving authority or power. **3.** (*functioning as pl.*) political activities or affairs: *party politics.* **4.** (*functioning as sing.*) the business or profession of politics. **5.** (*functioning as sing. or pl.*) any activity concerned with the acquisition of power, gaining one's own ends, etc.: *company politics are frequently vicious.* **6.** (*functioning as pl.*) opinions, principles, sympathies, etc., with respect to politics: *his conservative politics.* **7.** (*functioning as pl.*) **a.** the policy-formulating aspects of government as distinguished from the administrative, or legal. **b.** the civil functions of government as distinguished from the military.

polity ('pɒlɪtɪ) *n., pl.* **-ties.** **1.** a form of government or organization of a state, church, society, etc.; constitution. **2.** a politically organized society, state, city, etc. **3.** the management of public or civil affairs. **4.** political organization. [C16: from Latin *polītīa,* from Greek *politeia* citizenship, civil administration, from *politēs* citizen, from *polis* city]

polje ('pəʊljɛ) *n. Geography.* a large elliptical depression in karst regions, sometimes containing a marsh or small lake. [Serbo-Croatian, literally: field; related to FLOOR]

polka ('pɒlkə) *n., pl.* **-kas.** **1.** a 19th-century Bohemian dance with three steps and a hop, in fast duple time. **2.** a piece of music composed for or in the rhythm of this dance. *~vb.* **-kas, -kaing, -kaed.** **3.** (*intr.*) to dance a polka. [C19: via French from Czech *pulka* half-step, from *pul* half]

polka dot *n.* **1.** one of a pattern of small circular regularly spaced spots on a fabric. **2. a.** a fabric or pattern with such spots. **b.** (*as modifier*): *a polka-dot dress.* [C19: of uncertain origin]

poll (pəʊl) *n.* **1.** the casting, recording, or counting of votes in an election; a voting. **2.** the result or quantity of such a voting: *a heavy poll.* **3.** Also called: **opinion poll. a.** a canvassing of a representative sample of a large group of people on some question in order to determine the general opinion of the group. **b.** the results or record of such a canvassing. **4.** any counting or enumeration: *a poll of the number of men with long hair.* **5.** short for **poll tax. 6.** a list or enumeration of people, esp. for taxation or voting purposes. **7.** the striking face of a hammer. **8.** the occipital or back part of the head of an animal. *~vb.* (*mainly tr.*) **9.** to receive (a vote or quantity of votes): *he polled 10 000 votes.* **10.** to receive, take, or record the votes of: *he polled the whole town.* **11.** to canvass (a person, group, area, etc.) as part of a survey of opinion. **12.** *Chiefly U.S.* to take the vote, verdict, opinion, etc., individually of each member (of a jury, conference, etc.). **13.** (*sometimes intr.*) to cast (a vote) in an election. **14.** *Computer technol.* (in data transmission when several terminals share communications channels) to check each channel rapidly to establish which are free, or to call for data from each terminal in turn. **15.** to clip or shear. **16.** to remove or cut short the horns of (cattle). [C13 (in the sense: a human head) and C17 (in the modern sense: a counting of heads, votes): from Middle Low German *polle* hair of the head, head, top of a tree; compare Swedish *pull* crown of the head]

pollack *or* **pollock** ('pɒlək) *n., pl.* **-lacks, -lack** *or* **-locks, -lock.** a gadoid food fish, *Pollachius pollachius,* that has a dark green back and a projecting lower jaw and occurs in northern seas, esp. the North Atlantic Ocean. [C17: from earlier Scottish *podlok,* of obscure origin]

pollan ('pɒlən) *n.* any of several varieties of the whitefish *Coregonus pollan* that occur in lakes in Northern Ireland. [C18: probably from Irish *poll* lake]

pollard ('pɒləd) *n.* **1.** an animal, such as a sheep or deer, that has either shed its horns or antlers or has had them removed. **2.** a tree that has had its branches cut back to encourage a more bushy growth. *~vb.* **3.** (*tr.*) to convert into a pollard; poll. [C16: hornless animal; see POLL]

polled (pəʊld) *adj.* **1.** (of animals, esp. cattle) having the horns cut off or being naturally hornless. **2.** *Archaic.* shorn of hair; bald.

pollen ('pɒlən) *n.* a fine powdery substance produced by the anthers of seed-bearing plants, consisting of numerous fine grains containing the male gametes. [C16: from Latin: powder; compare Greek *palē* pollen] —**pollinic** (pə'lɪnɪk) *adj.*

pollen analysis *n.* another name for **palynology.**

pollen basket *n.* the part of the hind leg of a bee that is specialized for carrying pollen, typically consisting of a trough bordered by long hairs. Technical name: **corbicula.**

pollen count *n.* a measure of the pollen present in the air over a 24-hour period, often published to enable sufferers from hay fever to predict the severity of their attacks.

pollen tube *n.* a hollow tubular outgrowth that develops from a pollen grain after pollination, grows down the style to the ovule, and conveys male gametes to the egg cell.

pollex ('pɒlɛks) *n., pl.* **-lices** (-lɪˌsiːz). the first digit of the forelimb of amphibians, reptiles, birds, and mammals, such as the thumb of man and other primates. [C19: from Latin: thumb, big toe] —**pollical** ('pɒlɪkᵊl) *adj.*

pollinate ('pɒlɪˌneɪt) *vb.* (*tr.*) to transfer pollen from the anthers to the stigma of (a flower). —ˌ**polli'nation** *n.* —'**polliˌnator** *n.*

polling ('pəʊlɪŋ) *n.* **1. a.** the casting or registering of votes at an election. **b.** (*as modifier*): *polling day.* **2.** the conducting of a public opinion poll. **3.** *Computer technol.* the automatic interrogation of terminals by a central controlling machine to determine if they are ready to receive or transmit messages.

polling booth *n.* a semienclosed space in which a voter stands to mark a ballot paper during an election.

polling station *n.* a building, such as a school, designated as the place to which voters go during an election to cast their votes.

polliniferous *or* **polleniferous** (ˌpɒlɪ'nɪfərəs) *adj.* **1.** producing pollen: *polliniferous plants.* **2.** specialized for carrying pollen: *the polliniferous legs of bees.*

pollinium (pə'lɪnɪəm) *n., pl.* **-ia** (-ɪə). a mass of cohering pollen grains, produced by plants such as orchids and transported as a whole during pollination. [C19: New Latin; see POLLEN]

pollinosis *or* **pollenosis** (ˌpɒlɪ'nəʊsɪs) *n. Pathol.* a technical name for **hay fever.**

polliwog *or* **pollywog** ('pɒlɪˌwɒg) *n.* **1.** *Brit. dialect, U.S., and Canadian.* another name for **tadpole. 2.** *Informal.* a sailor who has not crossed the equator. Compare **shellback.** [C15 *polwygle;* see POLL, WIGGLE]

pollster ('pəʊlstə) *n.* a person who conducts opinion polls.

poll tax *n.* **1.** a tax levied per head of adult population. **2.** an informal name for **community charge.**

pollucite ('pɒljʊˌsaɪt, pə'luːˌsaɪt) *n.* a colourless rare mineral consisting of a hydrated caesium aluminium silicate, often containing some rubidium. It occurs in coarse granite, esp. in Manitoba, and is an important source of caesium. Formula: $CsAlSi_2O_6.½H_2O$. [C19: from Latin *polluc-,* stem of *Pollux* + -ITE[1]; originally called *pollux,* alluding to Castor and Pollux, since it was associated with another mineral called *castor* or *castorite*]

pollutant (pə'luːtᵊnt) *n.* a substance that pollutes, esp. a chemical or similar substance that is produced as a waste product of an industrial process.

pollute (pə'luːt) *vb.* (*tr.*) **1.** to contaminate, as with poisonous or harmful substances. **2.** to make morally corrupt or impure; sully. **3.** to desecrate or defile. [C14 *polute,* from Latin *polluere* to defile] —**pol'luter** *n.* —**pol'lution** *n.*

polluted (pə'luːtɪd) *adj.* **1.** made unclean or impure; contaminated. **2.** *U.S. slang.* intoxicated; drunk.

Pollux ('pɒləks) *n.* the brightest star in the constellation Gemini, lying close to the star **Castor.** Visual magnitude: 1.2; spectral type: K0; distance: 35 light years.

Pollyanna (ˌpɒlɪ'ænə) *n.* a person who is constantly or excessively optimistic. [C20: after the chief character in *Pollyanna* (1913), a novel by Eleanor Porter (1868–1920), U.S. writer]

polo ('pəʊləʊ) *n.* **1.** a game similar to hockey played on horseback using long-handled mallets **(polo sticks)** and a wooden ball. **2.** any of several similar games, such as one played on bicycles. **3.** short for **water polo. 4.** Also called: **polo neck. a.** a collar on a garment, worn rolled over to fit closely round the neck. **b.** a garment, esp. a sweater, with such a collar. [C19: from Balti (dialect of Kashmir): ball, from Tibetan *pulu*]

polonaise (ˌpɒlə'neɪz) *n.* **1.** a ceremonial marchlike dance in three-four time from Poland. **2.** a piece of music composed for or in the rhythm of this dance. **3.** a woman's costume with a tight bodice and an overskirt drawn back to show a decorative underskirt. [C18: from French *danse polonaise* Polish dance]

polonium (pə'ləʊnɪəm) *n.* a very rare radioactive element that occurs in trace amounts in uranium ores. The isotope **polonium-210** is produced artificially and is used as a lightweight power source in satellites and to eliminate static electricity in certain industries. Symbol: Po; atomic no.: 84; half-life of most stable isotope, ^{209}Po: 103 years; valency: 2, 4, or 6; melting pt.: 254°C; boiling pt.: 962°C. [C19: New Latin, from Medieval Latin *Polōnia* Poland; named in honour of the Polish nationality of its discoverer, Marie Curie (1867–1934)]

polony (pə'ləʊnɪ) *n., pl.* **-nies.** *Brit.* another name for **bologna sausage.** [C16: perhaps from *Bologna,* a city in N Italy]

poltergeist ('pɒltəˌgaɪst) *n.* a spirit believed to manifest its presence by rappings and other noises and also by acts of mischief, such as throwing furniture about. [C19: from German, from *poltern* to be noisy + *Geist* GHOST]

poltroon (pɒl'truːn) *n.* **1.** an abject or contemptible coward. *~adj.* **2.** a rare word for **cowardly.** [C16: from Old French *poultron,* from Old Italian *poltrone* lazy good-for-nothing, apparently from *poltrīre* to lie indolently in bed, from *poltro* bed]

poly ('pɒlɪ) *n., pl.* **polys.** *Informal.* short for **polytechnic.**

poly- *combining form.* **1.** more than one; many or much: *polyhedron.* **2.** having an excessive or abnormal number or amount: *polycythaemia.* [from Greek *polus* much, many; related to Old English *fela* many]

polyadelphous (ˌpɒlɪə'dɛlfəs) *adj.* **1.** (of stamens) having united filaments so that they are arranged in three or more groups. **2.** (of flowers) having polyadelphous stamens. [C19: from New Latin, from POLY- + *-adelphous* from Greek *adelphos* brother]

polyadic (ˌpɒlɪ'ædɪk) *adj. Logic, maths.* (of a relation, operation, etc.) having several argument places, as ... *moves ... from ... to ...,* which might be represented as $Mpox_1y_1z_1t_1x_2y_2z_2t_2$ where *p* names a person, *o* an object, and each *t* a time, and each *<x,y,z>* the coordinates of a place. [C20: modelled on MONADIC]

polyamide (ˌpɒlɪ'æmaɪd, -mɪd) *n.* any one of a class of synthetic polymeric materials containing recurring -CONH- groups. See also **nylon.**

polyandry ('pɒlɪˌændrɪ) *n.* **1.** the practice or condition of being married to more than one husband at the same time. Compare **polygamy. 2.** the practice in animals of a female mating with more than one male during one breeding season. **3.** the condition in flowers of having a large indefinite number of stamens. ~Compare **polygyny.** [C18: from Greek *poluandria,* from POLY- + *-andria* from *anēr* man] —ˌ**poly'androus** *adj.*

polyanthus (ˌpɒlɪ'ænθəs) *n., pl.* **-thuses. 1.** any of several hybrid garden primroses, esp. *Primula polyantha,* which has brightly coloured flowers. **2. polyanthus narcissus.** a Eurasian amaryllidaceous plant, *Narcissus tazetta,* having clusters of small yellow or white fragrant flowers. [C18: New Latin, Greek: having many flowers]

polyatomic (ˌpɒlɪəˈtɒmɪk) *adj.* (of a molecule) containing more than two atoms.

polybasic (ˌpɒlɪˈbeɪsɪk) *adj.* (of an acid) having two or more replaceable hydrogen atoms per molecule.

polybasite (ˌpɒlɪˈbeɪsaɪt, pəˈlɪbəˌsaɪt) *n.* a grey to black metallic mineral consisting of a sulphide of silver, antimony, and copper in the form of platelike monoclinic crystals. It occurs in veins of silver ore. Formula: $(Ag,Cu)_{16}Sb_2S_{11}$. [C19: from POLY- + BASE[1] + -ITE[1]]

polycarbonate (ˌpɒlɪˈkɑːbəˌneɪt, -nɪt) *n.* any of a class of strong transparent thermoplastic resins used in moulding materials, laminates, etc.

polycarboxylate (ˌpɒlɪˈkɑːbɒkˌsɪleɪt) *n.* a salt or ester of a polycarboxylic acid. Polycarboxylate esters are used in certain detergents.

polycarboxylic acid (ˌpɒlɪˈkɑːbɒkˌsɪlɪk) *n.* a type of carboxylic acid containing two or more carboxyl groups.

polycarpellary (ˌpɒlɪkɑːˈpɛlərɪ) *adj.* (of a plant gynoecium) having or consisting of many carpels.

polycarpic (ˌpɒlɪˈkɑːpɪk) *or* **polycarpous** *adj.* (of a plant) able to produce flowers and fruit several times in succession. —ˈ**polyˌcarpy** *n.*

polycarpous (ˌpɒlɪˈkɑːpəs) *or* **polycarpic** *adj.* (of plants) having a gynoecium consisting of many distinct carpels.

polycentrism (ˌpɒlɪˈsɛntrɪzəm) *n.* the fact, principle, or advocacy of the existence of more than one guiding or predominant ideological or political centre in a political system, alliance, etc., in the Communist world today.

polychaete (ˈpɒlɪˌkiːt) *n.* **1.** any marine annelid worm of the class *Polychaeta,* having a distinct head and paired fleshy appendages (parapodia) that bear bristles (chaetae or setae) and are used in swimming: includes the lugworms, ragworms, and sea mice. ~*adj. also* **polychaetous. 2.** of, relating to, or belonging to the class *Polychaeta.* [C19: from New Latin, from Greek *polukhaitēs:* having much hair; see CHAETA]

polychasium (ˌpɒlɪˈkeɪzɪəm) *n., pl.* **-sia** (-zɪə). *Botany.* a cymose inflorescence in which three or more branches arise from each node. [C20: from New Latin, from POLY- + *-chasium* as in DICHASIUM]

polychlorinated biphenyl (ˌpɒlɪˈklɔːrɪˌneɪtɪd) *n.* any of a group of compounds in which chlorine atoms replace the hydrogen atoms in biphenyl: used in industry in electrical insulators and in the manufacture of plastics; a toxic pollutant that can become concentrated in animal tissue. Abbrev.: **PCB.**

polychromatic (ˌpɒlɪkrəʊˈmætɪk), **polychromic** (ˌpɒlɪˈkrəʊmɪk), *or* **polychromous** *adj.* **1.** having various or changing colours. **2.** (of light or other electromagnetic radiation) containing radiation with more than one wavelength. —**polychromatism** (ˌpɒlɪˈkrəʊməˌtɪzəm) *n.*

polychrome (ˈpɒlɪˌkrəʊm) *adj.* **1.** having various or changing colours; polychromatic. **2.** made with or decorated in various colours. ~*n.* **3.** a work of art or artefact in many colours.

polychromy (ˈpɒlɪˌkrəʊmɪ) *n.* decoration in many colours, esp. in architecture or sculpture.

polyclinic (ˌpɒlɪˈklɪnɪk) *n.* a hospital or clinic able to treat a wide variety of diseases: general hospital.

polyconic projection (ˌpɒlɪˈkɒnɪk) *n.* a type of conic projection in which the parallels are not concentric and all meridians except the central one are curved lines. It is neither equal-area nor conformal, but is suitable for maps of areas or countries of great longitudinal extent.

polycotyledon (ˌpɒlɪˌkɒtɪˈliːdᵊn) *n.* any of various plants, esp. gymnosperms, that have or appear to have more than two cotyledons. —ˌ**polyˌcotyˈledonous** *adj.*

polycrystal (ˈpɒlɪˌkrɪstᵊl) *n.* an object composed of randomly orient crystals, formed by rapid solidification.

polycyclic (ˌpɒlɪˈsaɪklɪk) *adj.* **1.** (of a molecule or compound) containing or having molecules that contain two or more closed rings of atoms. **2.** *Biology.* having two or more rings or whorls: *polycyclic shells; a polycyclic stele.* ~*n.* **3.** a polycyclic compound: *anthracene is a polycyclic.*

polycystic (ˌpɒlɪˈsɪstɪk) *adj. Med.* containing many cysts: *a polycystic ovary.*

polycythaemia *or esp. U.S.* **polycythemia** (ˌpɒlɪsaɪˈθiːmɪə) *n.* an abnormal condition of the blood characterized by an increase in the number of red blood cells. It can occur as a primary disease of unknown cause (**polycythaemia vera** or **erythraemia**) or in association with respiratory or circulatory diseases. [C19: from POLY- + CYTO- + -HAEMIA]

polydactyl (ˌpɒlɪˈdæktɪl) *adj. also* **polydactylous. 1.** (of man and other vertebrates) having more than the normal number of digits. ~*n.* **2.** a human or other vertebrate having more than the normal number of digits. [C19: via French from Greek *poludaktulos* many-toed; see DACTYL]

polydemic (ˌpɒlɪˈdɛmɪk) *adj. Ecology, rare.* growing in or inhabiting more than two regions. [C20: from POLY- + ENDEMIC]

polydipsia (ˌpɒlɪˈdɪpsɪə) *n. Pathol.* excessive thirst. [C18: New Latin, from POLY- + *-dipsia,* from Greek *dipsa* thirst] —ˌ**polyˈdipsic** *adj.*

polyembryony (ˌpɒlɪˈɛmbrɪənɪ) *n.* the production of more than one embryo from a single fertilized egg cell: occurs in certain plants and parasitic hymenopterous insects. —**polyembryonic** (ˌpɒlɪˌɛmbrɪˈɒnɪk) *adj.*

polyene (ˈpɒlɪˌiːn) *n.* a chemical compound containing a chain of alternating single and double carbon-carbon bonds.

polyester (ˌpɒlɪˈɛstə) *n.* any of a large class of synthetic materials that are polymers containing recurring -COO- groups: used as plastics, textile fibres, and adhesives.

polyethene (ˌpɒlɪˈɛθiːn) *n.* the systematic name for **polythene.**

polyethylene (ˌpɒlɪˈɛθɪˌliːn) *n.* another name for **polythene.**

polygala (pəˈlɪɡələ) *n.* any herbaceous plant or small shrub of the polygalaceous genus *Polygala.* See also **milkwort.** [C18: New Latin, from Greek *polugalon,* from POLY- + *gala* milk]

polygalaceous (ˌpɒlɪɡəˈleɪʃəs, pəˌlɪɡ-) *adj.* of, relating to, or belonging to the *Polygalaceae,* a family of plants having flowers with two large outer petal-like sepals, three small sepals, and three to five petals: includes milkwort.

polygamy (pəˈlɪɡəmɪ) *n.* **1.** the practice of having more than one wife or husband at the same time. Compare **polyandry, polygyny. 2. a.** the condition of having male, female, and hermaphrodite flowers on the same plant. **b.** the condition of having these different types of flower on separate plants of the same species. **3.** the practice in male animals of having more than one mate during one breeding season. [C16: via French from Greek *polugamia* from POLY- + -GAMY] —**poˈlygamist** *n.* —**poˈlygamous** *adj.* —**poˈlygamously** *adv.*

polygene (ˈpɒlɪˌdʒiːn) *n.* any of a group of genes that each produce a small quantitative effect on a particular characteristic of the phenotype, such as height.

polygenesis (ˌpɒlɪˈdʒɛnɪsɪs) *n.* **1.** *Biology.* evolution of a polyphyletic organism or group. **2.** the hypothetical descent of the different races of man from different ultimate ancestors. ~Compare **monogenesis.** —**polygenetic** (ˌpɒlɪdʒɪˈnɛtɪk) *adj.* —ˌ**polygeˈnetically** *adv.*

polyglot (ˈpɒlɪˌɡlɒt) *adj.* **1.** having a command of many languages. **2.** written in, composed of, or containing many languages. ~*n.* **3.** a person with a command of many languages. **4.** a book, esp. a Bible, containing several versions of the same text written in various languages. **5.** a mixture or confusion of languages. [C17: from Greek *poluglōttos* literally: many-tongued, from POLY- + *glōtta* tongue] —ˈ**polyˌglotism** *or* ˈ**polyˌglottism** *n.*

polygon (ˈpɒlɪˌɡɒn) *n.* a closed plane figure bounded by three or more straight sides that meet in pairs in the same number of vertices, and do not intersect other than at these vertices. The sum of the interior angles is $(n-2) \times 180°$ for n sides; the sum of the exterior angles is 360°. A **regular polygon** has all its sides and angles equal. Specific polygons are named according to the number of sides, such as triangle, pentagon, etc. [C16: via Latin from Greek *polugōnon* figure with many angles] —**polygonal** (pəˈlɪɡənᵊl) *adj.* —**poˈlygonally** *adv.*

polygonaceous (ˌpɒlɪɡəˈneɪʃəs, pəˌlɪɡə-) *adj.* of, relating to, or belonging to the *Polygonaceae,* a chiefly N temperate family of plants having a sheathing stipule (ocrea) clasping the stem and small inconspicuous flowers: includes dock, sorrel, buckwheat, knotgrass, and rhubarb.

polygonum (pəˈlɪɡənəm) *n.* any polygonaceous plant of the genus *Polygonum,* having stems with knotlike joints and spikes of small white, green, or pink flowers. See also **knotgrass, bistort, prince's-feather** (sense 2). [C18: New Latin, from Greek *polugonon* knotgrass, from *polu-* POLY- + *-gonon,* from *gonu* knee]

polygraph (ˈpɒlɪˌɡrɑːf, -ˌɡræf) *n.* **1.** an instrument for the simultaneous electrical or mechanical recording of several involuntary physiological activities, including blood pressure, skin resistivity, pulse rate, respiration, and perspiration, used esp. as a lie detector. **2.** a device for producing copies of written, printed, or drawn matter. [C18: from Greek *polugraphos* writing copiously] —**polygraphic** (ˌpɒlɪˈɡræfɪk) *adj.* —ˌ**polyˈgraphically** *adv.*

polygyny (pəˈlɪdʒɪnɪ) *n.* **1.** the practice or condition of being married to more than one wife at the same time. Compare **polygamy. 2.** the practice in animals of a male mating with more than one female during one breeding season. **3.** the condition in flowers of having many styles. ~Compare **polyandry.** [C18: from POLY- + *-gyny,* from Greek *gunē* a woman] —**poˈlygynist** *n.* —**poˈlygynous** *adj.*

polyhedral angle (ˌpɒlɪˈhiːdrəl) *n.* a geometric configuration formed by the intersection of three or more planes, such as the faces of a polyhedron, that have a common vertex. See also **solid angle.**

polyhedron (ˌpɒlɪˈhiːdrən) *n., pl.* **-drons** *or* **-dra** (-drə). a solid figure consisting of four or more plane faces (all polygons), pairs of which meet along an edge, three or more edges meeting at a vertex. In a **regular polyhedron** all the faces are identical regular polygons making equal angles with each other. Specific polyhedrons are named according to the number of faces, such as tetrahedron, icosahedron, etc. [C16: from Greek *poluedron,* from POLY- + *hedron* side, base] —ˌ**polyˈhedral** *adj.*

polyhydric (ˌpɒlɪˈhaɪdrɪk) *adj.* another word for **polyhydroxy,** esp. when applied to alcohols.

polyhydroxy (ˌpɒlɪhaɪˈdrɒksɪ) *adj.* (of a chemical compound) containing two or more hydroxyl groups per molecule. Also: **polyhydric.**

polyisoprene (ˌpɒlɪˈaɪsəˌpriːn) *n.* any of various polymeric forms of isoprene, occurring in rubbers.

polymath (ˈpɒlɪˌmæθ) *n.* a person of great and varied learning. [C17: from Greek *polumathēs* having much knowledge] —ˌ**polyˈmathic** *adj.* —**polymathy** (pəˈlɪməθɪ) *n.*

polymer (ˈpɒlɪmə) *n.* a naturally occurring or synthetic compound, such as starch or Perspex, that has large molecules made up of many relatively simple repeated units. Compare **copolymer, oligomer.** —**polymerism** (pəˈlɪməˌrɪzəm, ˈpɒlɪmə-) *n.*

polymerase (pəˈlɪməreɪz) *n.* any enzyme that catalyses the synthesis of a polymer, esp. the synthesis of DNA or RNA.

polymeric (ˌpɒlɪˈmɛrɪk) *adj.* of, concerned with, or being a polymer: *a polymeric compound.* [C19: from Greek *polumerēs* having many parts]

polymerization *or* **polymerisation** (pəˌlɪməraɪˈzeɪʃən, ˌpɒlɪməraɪ-) *n.* the act or process of forming a polymer or copolymer, esp. a chemical reaction in which a polymer is formed.

polymerize *or* **polymerise** (ˈpɒlɪməˌraɪz, pəˈlɪmə-) *vb.* to react or cause to react to form a polymer.

polymerous (pəˈlɪmərəs) *adj.* **1.** (of flowers) having the petals, sepals, and other parts arranged in whorls of many parts. **2.** *Biology.* having or being composed of many parts.

polymorph (ˈpɒlɪˌmɔːf) *n.* **1.** a species of animal or plant that exhibits polymorphism. **2.** any of the crystalline forms of a chemical compound that exhibits polymorphism. **3.** Also called: **polymorphonuclear leucocyte.** a common type of white blood cell that has a lobed nucleus and granular cytoplasm and functions as a phagocyte. [C19: from Greek *polumorphos* having many forms]

polymorphic function *n. Computer technol.* a function in a computer program that can deal with a number of different types of data.

polymorphism (ˌpɒlɪˈmɔːfɪzəm) *n.* **1.** *Biology.* **a.** the occurrence of more than one form of individual in a single species within an interbreeding population. **b.** the occurrence of more than one form in the individual polyps of a coelenterate colony. **2.** the existence or formation of different types of crystal of the same chemical compound.

polymorphonuclear (ˌpɒlɪˌmɔːfəʊˈnjuːklɪə) *adj.* (of a leucocyte) having a lobed or segmented nucleus. See also **polymorph** (sense 3).

polymorphous (ˌpɒlɪˈmɔːfəs) *or* **polymorphic** *adj.* **1.** having, taking, or passing through many different forms or stages. **2.** (of a substance) exhibiting polymorphism. **3.** (of an animal or plant) displaying or undergoing polymorphism.

polymyxin (ˌpɒlɪˈmɪksɪn) *n.* any of several toxic polypeptide antibiotics active against Gram-negative bacteria, obtained from the soil bacterium *Bacillus polymyxa.* [C20: from New Latin *Bacillus polymyxa;* see POLY-, MYXO-, -IN]

Polynesian (ˌpɒlɪˈniːʒən, -ʒɪən) *adj.* **1.** of or relating to Polynesia, a group of islands in the Pacific Ocean, or to its people or any of their languages. ~*n.* **2.** a member of the people that inhabit Polynesia, generally of Caucasoid features with light skin and wavy hair. **3.** a branch of the Malayo-Polynesian family of languages, including Maori and Hawaiian and a number of other closely related languages of the S and central Pacific.

polyneuritis (ˌpɒlɪnjʊˈraɪtɪs) *n.* inflammation of many nerves at the same time.

polynomial (ˌpɒlɪˈnəʊmɪəl) *adj.* **1.** of, consisting of, or referring to two or more names or terms. ~*n.* **2. a.** a mathematical expression consisting of a sum of terms each of which is the product of a constant and one or more variables raised to a positive or zero integral power. For one variable, x, the general form is given by: $a_0x^n + a_1x^{n-1} + \ldots + a_{n-1}x + a_n$, where a_0, a_1, etc., are real numbers. **b.** Also called: **multinomial.** any mathematical expression consisting of the sum of a number of terms. **3.** *Biology.* a taxonomic name consisting of more than two terms, such as *Parus major minor* in which *minor* designates the subspecies.

polynuclear (ˌpɒlɪˈnjuːklɪə) *or* **polynucleate** *adj.* having many nuclei; multinuclear.

polynucleotide (ˌpɒlɪˈnjuːklɪəˌtaɪd) *n. Biochem.* a molecular chain of nucleotides chemically bonded by a series of ester linkages between the phosphoryl group of one nucleotide and the hydroxyl group of the sugar in the adjacent nucleotide. Nucleic acids consist of long chains of polynucleotides.

polynya (ˈpɒlənˌjɑː) *n.* a stretch of open water surrounded by ice, esp. near the mouths of large rivers, in arctic seas. [C19: from Russian, from *poly* open, hollowed-out]

polyonymous (ˌpɒlɪˈɒnɪməs) *adj.* having or known by several different names.

polyp (ˈpɒlɪp) *n.* **1.** *Zoology.* one of the two forms of individual that occur in coelenterates. It usually has a hollow cylindrical body with a ring of tentacles around the mouth. Compare **medusa** (sense 2). **2.** Also called: **polypus.** *Pathol.* a small vascularized growth arising from the surface of a mucous membrane, having a rounded base or a stalklike projection. [C16 *polip,* from French *polype* nasal polyp, from Latin *pōlypus* sea animal, nasal polyp, from Greek *polupous* having many feet] —ˈ**polypous** *or* ˈ**polypoid** *adj.*

polypary (ˈpɒlɪpərɪ) *or* **polyparium** (ˌpɒlɪˈpɛərɪəm) *n., pl.* **-paries** *or* **-paria** (-ˈpɛərɪə). the common base and connecting tissue of a colony of coelenterate polyps, esp. coral. [C18: from New Latin *polypārium;* see POLYP]

polypeptide (ˌpɒlɪˈpɛptaɪd) *n.* any of a group of natural or synthetic polymers made up of amino acids chemically linked together; this class includes the proteins. See also **peptide.**

polypetalous (ˌpɒlɪˈpɛtələs) *adj.* (of flowers) having many distinct or separate petals. Compare **gamopetalous.**

polyphagia (ˌpɒlɪˈfeɪdʒə) *n.* **1. a.** an abnormal desire to consume excessive amounts of food, esp. as the result of a neurological disorder. **b.** an insatiable appetite. **2.** the habit of certain animals, esp. certain insects, of feeding on many different types of food. [C17: New Latin, from Greek, from *poluphagos* eating much; see POLY-, -PHAGY] —**polyphagous** (pəˈlɪfəgəs) *adj.*

polyphase (ˈpɒlɪˌfeɪz) *adj.* **1.** Also: **multiphase.** (of an electrical system, circuit, or device) having, generating, or using two or more alternating voltages of the same frequency, the phases of which are cyclically displaced by fractions of a period. See also **single-phase, two-phase, three-phase. 2.** having more than one phase.

polyphone (ˈpɒlɪˌfəʊn) *n.* a letter or character having more than one phonetic value, such as English *c,* pronounced (k) before *a, o,* or *u* or (s) before *e* or *i.*

polyphonic (ˌpɒlɪˈfɒnɪk) *adj.* **1.** *Music.* composed of relatively independent melodic lines or parts; contrapuntal. **2.** many-voiced. **3.** *Phonetics.* of, relating to, or denoting a polyphone. —ˌ**polyˈphonically** *adv.*

polyphonic prose *n.* a rhythmically free prose employing poetic devices, such as assonance and alliteration.

polyphony (pəˈlɪfənɪ) *n., pl.* **-nies. 1.** polyphonic style of composition or a piece of music utilizing it. **2.** the use of polyphones in a writing system. [C19: from Greek *poluphōnia* diversity of tones, from POLY- + *phōnē* speech, sound] —**poˈlyphonous** *adj.* —**poˈlyphonously** *adv.*

polyphosphoric acid (ˌpɒlɪfɒsˈfɒrɪk) *n.* **1.** any one of a series of oxyacids of phosphorus with the general formula $H_{n+2}P_nO_{3n+1}$. The first member is pyrophosphoric acid ($n = 2$) and the series includes the highly polymeric metaphosphoric acid. The higher acids exist in an equilibrium mixture. **2.** a glassy or liquid mixture of orthophosphoric and polyphosphoric acids: used industrially as a dehydrating agent, catalyst, and oxidizing agent.

polyphyletic (ˌpɒlɪfaɪˈlɛtɪk) *adj. Biology.* relating to or characterized by descent from more than one ancestral group of animals or plants. [C19: from POLY- + PHYLETIC] —ˌ**polyphyˈletically** *adv.*

polyphyodont (ˌpɒlɪˈfaɪəʊˌdɒnt) *adj.* having many successive sets of teeth, as fishes and other lower vertebrates. Compare **diphyodont.** [C19: from Greek *poluphuēs* manifold (from *polu-* POLY- + *phuē* growth) + -ODONT]

polyploid (ˈpɒlɪˌplɔɪd) *adj.* **1.** (of cells, organisms, etc.) having more than twice the basic (haploid) number of chromosomes. ~*n.* **2.** an individual or cell of this type. —ˌ**polyˈploidal** *or* ˌ**polyˈploidic** *adj.* —ˈ**polyˌploidy** *n.*

polypod (ˈpɒlɪˌpɒd) *adj. also* **polypodous** (pəˈlɪpədəs). **1.** (esp. of insect larvae) having many legs or similar appendages. ~*n.* **2.** an animal of this type.

polypody (ˈpɒlɪˌpəʊdɪ) *n., pl.* **-dies. 1.** any of various ferns of the genus *Polypodium,* esp. *P. vulgare,* having deeply divided leaves and round naked sori: family *Polypodiaceae.* **2.** any fern of the family *Polypodiaceae,* all having opaque leaves and all except the harts-tongue divided leaves. [C15: from Latin *polypodium,* from Greek, from POLY- + *pous* foot]

polypoid (ˈpɒlɪˌpɔɪd) *adj.* **1.** of, relating to, or resembling a polyp. **2.** (of a coelenterate) having the body in the form of a polyp.

polypropylene (ˌpɒlɪˈprəʊpɪˌliːn) *n.* any of various tough flexible synthetic thermoplastic materials made by polymerizing propylene and used for making moulded articles, laminates, bottles, pipes, and fibres for ropes, bristles, upholstery, and carpets. Systematic name: **polypropene.**

polyprotodont (ˌpɒlɪˈprəʊtəʊˌdɒnt) *n.* any marsupial of the group *Polyprotodontia,* characterized by four or more upper incisor teeth on each side of the jaw: includes the opossums and bandicoots. Compare **diprotodont.** [C19: from POLY- + PROTO- + -ODONT]

polyptych (ˈpɒlɪptɪk) *n.* an altarpiece consisting of more than three panels, set with paintings or carvings, and usually hinged for folding. Compare **diptych, triptych.** [C19: via Late Latin from Greek *poluptuchon* something folded many times, from POLY- + *ptuchē* a fold]

polypus (ˈpɒlɪpəs) *n., pl.* **-pi** (-paɪ). *Pathol.* another word for **polyp** (sense 2). [C16: via Latin from Greek: POLYP]

polyrhythm (ˈpɒlɪˌrɪðəm) *n. Music.* a style of composition in which each part exhibits different rhythms. —ˌ**polyˈrhythmic** *adj.*

polyribosome (ˌpɒlɪˈraɪbəˌsəʊm) *n. Biochem.* an assemblage of ribosomes associated with a messenger RNA molecule, involved in peptide synthesis. Also called: **polysome.**

polysaccharide (ˌpɒlɪˈsækəˌraɪd, -rɪd) *or* **polysaccharose** (ˌpɒlɪˈsækəˌrəʊz, -ˌrəʊs) *n.* any one of a class of carbohydrates whose molecules contain linked monosaccharide units: includes starch, inulin, and cellulose. General formula: $(C_6H_{10}O_5)_n$. See also **oligosaccharide.**

polysemy (ˌpɒlɪˈsiːmɪ, pəˈlɪsəmɪ) *n.* the existence of several meanings in a single word. Compare **monosemy.** [C20: from New Latin *polysēmia,* from Greek *polusēmos* having many meanings, from POLY- + *sēma* a sign] —ˌ**polyˈsemous** *adj.*

polysepalous (ˌpɒlɪˈsɛpələs) *adj.* (of flowers) having distinct separate sepals. Compare **gamosepalous.**
polysome (ˈpɒlɪˌsəʊm) *n.* another name for **polyribosome.**
polysomic (ˌpɒlɪˈsəʊmɪk) *adj.* of, relating to, or designating a basically diploid chromosome complement, in which some but not all the chromosomes are represented more than twice. [C20: from POLY- + -SOME[3] + -IC]
polystichous (ˌpɒlɪˈstaɪkəs) *adj.* (of plant parts) arranged in a number of rows.
polystyrene (ˌpɒlɪˈstaɪriːn) *n.* a synthetic thermoplastic material obtained by polymerizing styrene; used as a white rigid foam **(expanded polystyrene)** for insulating and packing and as a glasslike material in light fittings and water tanks.
polysulphide (ˌpɒlɪˈsʌlfaɪd) *n.* any sulphide of a metal containing divalent anions in which there are chains of sulphur atoms, as in the polysulphides of sodium, Na_2S_2, Na_2S_3, Na_2S_4, etc.
polysyllable (ˈpɒlɪˌsɪləbᵊl) *n.* a word consisting of more than two syllables. —**polysyllabic** (ˌpɒlɪsɪˈlæbɪk) *or* ˌ**polysylˈlabical** *adj.* —ˌ**polysylˈlabically** *adv.*
polysyllogism (ˌpɒlɪˈsɪləˌdʒɪzəm) *n.* a chain of syllogisms in which the conclusion of one syllogism serves as a premise for the next.
polysyndeton (ˌpɒlɪˈsɪndɪtən) *n.* **1.** *Rhetoric.* the use of several conjunctions in close succession, esp. where some might be omitted, as in *he ran and jumped and laughed for joy.* **2.** Also called: **syndesis.** *Grammar.* a sentence containing more than two coordinate clauses. [C16: POLY- + -*syndeton,* from Greek *sundetos* bound together]
polysynthetic (ˌpɒlɪsɪnˈθɛtɪk) *adj.* denoting languages, such as Eskimo, in which single words may express the meaning of whole phrases or clauses by virtue of multiple affixes. Compare **synthetic** (sense 3), **analytic** (sense 3), **agglutinative** (sense 2). —**polysynthesis** (ˌpɒlɪˈsɪnθɪsɪs) *n.* —ˌ**polyˈsynthesism** *n.* —ˌ**polysynˈthetically** *adv.*
polytechnic (ˌpɒlɪˈtɛknɪk) *n.* **1.** *Brit.* a college offering advanced full- and part-time courses, esp. vocational courses, in many fields at and below degree standard. ~*adj.* **2.** of or relating to technical instruction and training. [C19: via French from Greek *polutekhnos* skilled in many arts. See TECHNIC]
polytene (ˈpɒlɪˌtiːn) *adj.* denoting a type of giant-size chromosome consisting of many replicated genes in parallel, found esp. in *Drosophila* larvae. [C20: from POLY- + Greek *taenia* band]
polytetrafluoroethylene (ˌpɒlɪˌtɛtrəˌfluərəʊˈɛθɪˌliːn) *n.* a white thermoplastic material with a waxy texture, made by polymerizing tetrafluoroethylene. It is nonflammable, resists chemical action and radiation, and has a high electrical resistance and an extremely low coefficient of friction. It is used for making gaskets, hoses, insulators, bearings, and for coating metal surfaces in chemical plants and in nonstick cooking vessels. Abbrev.: **PTFE.** Also called (trademark): **Teflon.**
polytheism (ˈpɒlɪθiːˌɪzəm, ˌpɒlɪˈθiːɪzəm) *n.* the worship of or belief in more than one god. —ˈ**polyˌtheist** *n.* —ˌ**polytheˈistic** *adj.* —ˌ**polytheˈistically** *adv.*
polythene (ˈpɒlɪˌθiːn) *n.* any one of various light thermoplastic materials made from ethylene with properties depending on the molecular weight of the polymer. The common forms are a waxy flexible plastic (**low-density polythene**) and a tougher rigid more crystalline form (**high-density polythene**). Polythene is used for packaging, moulded articles, pipes and tubing, insulation, textiles, and coatings on metal. Systematic name: **polyethene.** Also called: **polyethylene.**
polytonality (ˌpɒlɪtəʊˈnælɪtɪ) *or* **polytonalism** *n. Music.* the simultaneous use of more than two different keys or tonalities. —ˌ**polyˈtonal** *adj.* —ˌ**polyˈtonally** *adv.* —ˌ**polyˈtonalist** *n.*
polytrophic (ˌpɒlɪˈtrɒfɪk) *adj.* (esp. of bacteria) obtaining food from several different organic sources.
polytypic (ˌpɒlɪˈtɪpɪk) *or* **polytypical** *adj.* **1.** existing in, consisting of, or incorporating several different types or forms. **2.** *Biology.* (of a taxonomic group) having many subdivisions, esp. (of a species) having many subspecies and geographical races.
polyunsaturated (ˌpɒlɪʌnˈsætʃəˌreɪtɪd) *adj.* of or relating to a class of animal and vegetable fats, the molecules of which consist of long carbon chains with many double bonds. Polyunsaturated compounds are less likely to be converted into cholesterol in the body. They are widely used in margarines and in the manufacture of paints and varnishes. See also **monounsaturated.**
polyurethane (ˌpɒlɪˈjʊərəˌθeɪn) *or* **polyurethan** (ˌpɒlɪˈjʊərəˌθæn) *n.* a class of synthetic materials made by copolymerizing an isocyanate and a polyhydric alcohol and commonly used as a foam (**polyurethane foam**) for insulation and packing, as fibres and hard inert coatings, and in a flexible form (**polyurethane rubber**) for diaphragms and seals.
polyuria (ˌpɒlɪˈjʊərɪə) *n. Pathol., physiol.* the state or condition of discharging abnormally large quantities of urine, often accompanied by a need to urinate frequently. —ˌ**polyˈuric** *adj.*
polyvalent (ˌpɒlɪˈveɪlənt, pəˈlɪvələnt) *adj.* **1.** *Chem.* having more than one valency. **2.** (of a vaccine) **a.** effective against several strains of the same disease-producing microorganism, antigen, or toxin. **b.** produced from cultures containing several strains of the same microorganism. —ˌ**polyˈvalency** *n.*
polyvinyl (ˌpɒlɪˈvaɪnɪl, -ˈvaɪnᵊl) *n.* (*modifier*) designating a plastic or resin formed by polymerization of a vinyl derivative.
polyvinyl acetate *n.* a colourless odourless tasteless resin used in emulsion paints, adhesives, sealers, a substitute for chicle in chewing gum, and for sealing porous surfaces. Abbrev.: **PVA.**
polyvinyl chloride *n.* the full name of **PVC.**
polyvinylidene chloride (ˌpɒlɪvaɪˈnɪlɪˌdiːn) *n.* any one of a class of thermoplastic materials formed by the polymerization of vinylidene chloride: used in packaging and for making pipes and fittings for chemical equipment. Also called: **saran.**
polyvinyl resin *n.* any of a class of thermoplastic resins that are made by polymerizing or copolymerizing a vinyl compound. The commonest type is PVC.
polyzoan (ˌpɒlɪˈzəʊən) *n., adj.* another word for **bryozoan.** [C19: from New Latin, *Polyzoa* class name, from POLY- + -*zoan,* from Greek *zoion* an animal]
polyzoarium (ˌpɒlɪzəʊˈɛərɪəm) *n., pl.* **-ia** (-ɪə). a colony of bryozoan animals or its supporting skeletal framework. —ˌ**polyzoˈarial** *adj.*
polyzoic (ˌpɒlɪˈzəʊɪk) *adj. Zoology.* **1.** (of certain colonial animals) having many zooids or similar polyps. **2.** producing or containing many sporozoites.
pom (pɒm) *n. Slang, Austral. and N.Z.* short for **pommy.**
POM *abbrev. for* prescription-only medicine (*or* medication).
pomace (ˈpʌmɪs) *n.* **1.** the pulpy residue of apples or similar fruit after crushing and pressing, as in cider-making. **2.** any pulpy substance left after crushing, mashing, etc. [C16: from Medieval Latin *pōmācium* cider, from Latin *pōmum* apple]
pomaceous (pɒˈmeɪʃəs) *adj.* of, relating to, or bearing pomes, such as the apple, pear, and quince trees. [C18: from New Latin *pōmāceus,* from Latin *pōmum* apple]
pomade (pəˈmɑːd, -ˈmeɪd) *n.* **1.** a perfumed oil or ointment put on the hair, as to make it smooth and shiny. ~*vb.* **2.** (*tr.*) to put pomade on. ~Also: **pomatum** (pəˈmeɪtəm). [C16: from French *pommade,* from Italian *pomato* (originally made partly from apples), from Latin *pōmum* apple]
pomander (pəʊˈmændə) *n.* **1.** a mixture of aromatic substances in a sachet or an orange, formerly carried as scent or as a protection against disease. **2.** a container for such a mixture. [C15: from Old French *pome d'ambre,* from Medieval Latin *pōmum ambrae* apple of amber]
pombe (ˈpɔmbɛ) *n. E African.* any alcoholic drink. [Swahili]
pome (pəʊm) *n.* the fleshy fruit of the apple and related plants, consisting of an enlarged receptacle enclosing the ovary and seeds. [C15: from Old French, from Late Latin *pōma* apple, pl. (assumed to be sing.) of Latin *pōmum* apple]
pomegranate (ˈpɒmɪˌɡrænɪt, ˈpɒmˌɡrænɪt) *n.* **1.** an Asian shrub or small tree, *Punica granatum,* cultivated in semitropical regions for its edible fruit: family *Punicaceae.* **2.** the many-chambered globular fruit of this tree, which has tough reddish rind, juicy red pulp, and many seeds. [C14: from Old French *pome grenate,* from Latin *pōmum* apple + *grenate,* from Latin *grānātum,* from *grānātus* full of seeds]
pomelo (ˈpɒmɪˌləʊ) *n., pl.* **-los. 1.** a tropical rutaceous tree, *Citrus maxima* (or *C. decumana*), grown widely in oriental regions for its large yellow grapefruit-like edible fruit. **2.** the fruit of this tree. **3.** *Chiefly U.S.* another name for **grapefruit.** ~Also called: **shaddock.** [C19: from Dutch *pompelmoes, perhaps from pompoen* big + Portuguese *limão* a lemon]
Pomeranian (ˌpɒməˈreɪnɪən) *adj.* **1.** of or relating to Pomerania, a region of N central Europe, or its inhabitants. ~*n.* **2.** a native or inhabitant of Pomerania, esp. a German. **3.** a breed of toy dog of the spitz type with a long thick straight coat.
pomfret[1] (ˈpʌmfrɪt, ˈpɒm-) *or* **pomfret-cake** *n.* a small black rounded confection of liquorice. Also called: **Pontefract cake.** [C19: from *Pomfret,* earlier form of *Pontefract,* the town in N England where the cake was originally made]
pomfret[2] (ˈpɒmfrɪt) *n.* **1.** any of various fishes of the genus *Stromateidae* of the Indian and Pacific oceans: valued as food fishes. **2.** any of various scombroid fishes, esp. *Brama raii,* of northern oceans: valued as food fishes. [C18: perhaps from a diminutive form of Portuguese *pampo*]
pomiculture (ˈpɒmɪˌkʌltʃə) *n.* the cultivation of fruit. [C19: from Latin *pōmum* apple, fruit + CULTURE]
pomiferous (pɒˈmɪfərəs) *adj.* (of the apple, pear, etc.) producing pomes or pomelike fruits. [C17: from Latin *pomifer* fruit-bearing]
pommel (ˈpʌməl, ˈpɒm-) *n.* **1.** the raised part on the front of a saddle. **2.** a knob at the top of a sword or similar weapon. ~*vb.* **-mels, -melling, -melled** *or U.S.* **-mels, -meling, -meled. 3.** a less common word for **pummel.** [C14: from Old French *pomel* knob, from Vulgar Latin *pōmellum* (unattested) little apple, from Latin *pōmum* apple]
pommy (ˈpɒmɪ) *n., pl.* **-mies.** (*sometimes cap.*) *Slang.* a mildly offensive word used by Australians and New Zealanders for an English person. Sometimes shortened to **pom.** [C20: of uncertain origin. Among a number of explanations are: (1) based on a blend of IMMIGRANT and POMEGRANATE (alluding to the red cheeks of English immigrants); (2) from the abbreviation *POME,* Prisoner of Mother England (referring to convicts)]
pomology (pɒˈmɒlədʒɪ) *n.* the branch of horticulture that is concerned with the study and cultivation of fruit. [C19: from New Latin *pōmologia,* from Latin *pōmum* apple, fruit] —**pomological** (ˌpɒməˈlɒdʒɪkᵊl) *adj.* —ˌ**pomoˈlogically** *adv.* —**pomˈologist** *n.*

pomp (pɒmp) *n.* **1.** stately or magnificent display; ceremonial splendour. **2.** vain display, esp. of dignity or importance. **3.** *Obsolete.* a procession or pageant. [C14: from Old French *pompe,* from Latin *pompa* procession, from Greek *pompē;* related to Greek *pompein* to send]

pompadour ('pɒmpəˌdʊə) *n.* an early 18th-century hairstyle for women, having the front hair arranged over a pad to give it greater height and bulk. [C18: named after the Marquise de *Pompadour,* mistress of Louis XV of France, who originated it]

pompano ('pɒmpəˌnəʊ) *n., pl.* **-no** *or* **-nos. 1.** any of several deep-bodied carangid food fishes of the genus *Trachinotus,* esp. *T. carolinus,* of American coastal regions of the Atlantic. **2.** a spiny-finned food fish, *Palometa simillima,* of North American coastal regions of the Pacific: family *Stromateidae* (butterfish, etc.). [C19: from Spanish *pámpano* type of fish, of uncertain origin]

Pompeiian (pɒm'peɪən, -'piː-) *adj.* of or relating to Pompeii, an ancient city in Italy buried by an eruption of Vesuvius (79 A.D.).

pompilid ('pɒmpɪlɪd) *n.* another name for the **spider-hunting wasp.** [C20: from New Latin *pompilus,* from Greek *pompilos* a fish that accompanies ships, from *pempein* to send, escort]

pom-pom ('pɒmpɒm) *n.* an automatic rapid-firing, small-calibre cannon, esp. a type of antiaircraft cannon used in World War II. Also called: **pompom.** [C19: of imitative origin]

pompon ('pɒmpɒn) *or* **pompom** *n.* **1.** a ball of tufted silk, wool, feathers, etc., worn on a hat for decoration. **2. a.** the small globelike flower head of certain cultivated varieties of dahlia and chrysanthemum. **b.** (*as modifier*): *pompon dahlia.* [C18: from French, from Old French *pompe* knot of ribbons, of uncertain origin]

pomposity (pɒm'pɒsɪtɪ) *n., pl.* **-ties. 1.** vain or ostentatious display of dignity or importance. **2.** the quality of being pompous. **3.** ostentatiously lofty style, language, etc. **4.** a pompous action, remark, etc.

pompous ('pɒmpəs) *adj.* **1.** exaggeratedly or ostentatiously dignified or self-important. **2.** ostentatiously lofty in style: *a pompous speech.* **3.** *Rare.* characterized by ceremonial pomp or splendour. —**'pompously** *adv.* —**'pompousness** *n.*

'pon (pɒn) *prep. Poetic or archaic. contraction of* upon.

ponce (pɒns) *Derogatory slang, chiefly Brit.* ~*n.* **1.** a man given to ostentatious or effeminate display in manners, speech, dress, etc. **2.** another word for **pimp**[1]. ~*vb.* **3.** (*intr.;* often foll. by *around* or *about*) to act like a ponce. [C19: from Polari, from Spanish *pu(n)to* male prostitute or French *pront* prostitute] —**'poncy** *or* **'poncey** *adj.*

poncho ('pɒntʃəʊ) *n., pl.* **-chos.** a cloak of a kind originally worn in South America, made of a rectangular or circular piece of cloth, esp. wool, with a hole in the middle to put the head through. [C18: from American Spanish, from Araucanian *pantho* woollen material]

pond (pɒnd) *n.* **a.** a pool of still water, often artificially created. **b.** (*in combination*): *a fishpond.* [C13 *ponde* enclosure; related to POUND[3]]

ponder ('pɒndə) *vb.* (when *intr.,* sometimes foll. by *on* or *over*) to give thorough or deep consideration (to); meditate (upon). [C14: from Old French *ponderer,* from Latin *ponderāre* to weigh, consider, from *pondus* weight; related to *pendere* to weigh]

ponderable ('pɒndərəbᵊl) *adj.* **1.** able to be evaluated or estimated; appreciable. **2.** capable of being weighed or measured. ~*n.* **3.** (*often pl.*) something that can be evaluated or appreciated; a substantial thing. —ˌ**pondera'bility** *n.* —**'ponderably** *adv.*

ponderous ('pɒndərəs) *adj.* **1.** of great weight; heavy; huge. **2.** (esp. of movement) lacking ease or lightness; awkward, lumbering, or graceless. **3.** dull or laborious: *a ponderous oration.* [C14: from Latin *ponderōsus* of great weight, from *pondus* weight] —**'ponderously** *adv.* —**'ponderousness** *or* **ponderosity** (ˌpɒndə'rɒsɪtɪ) *n.*

pond lily *n.* another name for **water lily.**

Pondo ('pɒndəʊ) *n.* **1.** (*pl.* **-do** *or* **-dos**) a member of a Negro people of southern Africa, living chiefly in Pondoland, part of the Transkei, South Africa. **2.** the language of this people, belonging to the Bantu grouping of the Niger-Congo family, and closely related to Xhosa.

pondokkie (pɒn'dɒkɪ) *or* **pondok** ('pɒndɒk) *n. Derogatory.* (in southern Africa) a crudely made house built of tin sheet, reeds, etc. [C20: from Malay *pondók* leaf house]

pond scum *n.* a greenish layer floating on the surface of stagnant waters, consisting of various freshwater algae.

pond-skater *n.* any of various heteropterous insects of the family *Gerrididae,* esp. *Gerris lacustris* (**common pond-skater**), having a slender hairy body and long hairy legs with which they skim about on the surface of ponds. Also called: **water strider, water skater.**

pond snail *n.* a general term for the freshwater snails: often specifically for the **great pond snail** (*Limnaea stagnalis*) and others of that genus. *L. truncatula* is a host of the liver fluke.

pondweed ('pɒndˌwiːd) *n.* **1.** any of various water plants of the genus *Potamogeton,* which grow in ponds and slow streams: family *Potamogetonaceae.* **2.** Also called: **waterweed.** *Brit.* any of various unrelated water plants, such as Canadian pondweed, mare's-tail, and water milfoil, that have thin or much divided leaves.

pone[1] (pəʊn) *n. Southern U.S.* **1.** Also called: **pone bread, corn pone.** bread made of maize. **2.** a loaf or cake of this. [C17: from Algonquian; compare Delaware *apán* baked]

pone[2] (pəʊn, 'pəʊnɪ) *n. Cards.* the player to the right of the dealer, or the nondealer in two-handed games. [C19: from Latin: put!, that is, play, from *ponere* to put]

pong (pɒŋ) *Brit. informal.* ~*n.* **1.** a disagreeable or offensive smell; stink. ~*vb.* **2.** (*intr.*) to give off an unpleasant smell; stink. [C20: perhaps from Romany *pan* to stink] —**'pongy** *adj.*

ponga ('pɒŋə) *n.* a tall tree fern, *Cyathea dealbata,* of New Zealand, with large leathery leaves. [Maori]

pongee (pɒn'dʒiː, 'pɒndʒiː) *n.* **1.** a thin plain-weave silk fabric from China or India, left in its natural colour. **2.** a cotton or rayon fabric similar to or in imitation of this, but not necessarily in the natural colour. [C18: from Mandarin Chinese (Peking) *pen-chī* woven at home, on one's own loom, from *pen* own + *chi* loom]

pongid ('pɒŋgɪd, 'pɒndʒɪd) *n.* **1.** any primate of the family *Pongidae,* which includes the gibbons and the great apes. ~*adj.* **2.** of, relating to, or belonging to the family *Pongidae.* [from New Latin *Pongo* type genus, from Kongo *mpongi* ape]

pongo ('pɒŋgəʊ) *n., pl.* **-gos. 1.** an anthropoid ape, esp. an orang-utan or (formerly) a gorilla. **2.** *Military slang.* a soldier or marine. [C17: from Kongo *mpongo*]

poniard ('pɒnjəd) *n.* **1.** a small dagger with a slender blade. ~*vb.* **2.** (*tr.*) to stab with a poniard. [C16: from Old French *poignard* dagger, from *poing* fist, from Latin *pugnus;* related to Latin *pugnāre* to fight]

pons (pɒnz) *n., pl.* **pontes** ('pɒntiːz). **1.** a bridge of connecting tissue. **2.** short for **pons Varolii.** [Latin: bridge]

pons asinorum (ˌæsɪ'nɔːrəm) *n.* the geometric proposition that the angles opposite the two equal sides of an isosceles triangle are equal. [Latin: bridge of asses, referring originally to the fifth proposition of the first book of Euclid, which was considered difficult for students to learn]

pons Varolii (və'rəʊlɪˌaɪ) *n., pl.* **pontes Varolii** ('pɒntiːz). a broad white band of connecting nerve fibres that bridges the hemispheres of the cerebellum in mammals. Sometimes shortened to **pons.** [C16: New Latin, literally: bridge of Varoli, after Costanzo *Varoli* (?1543–75), Italian anatomist]

pont (pɒnt) *n.* (in South Africa) a river ferry, esp. one that is guided by a cable from one bank to the other. [C17: from Dutch: ferryboat, PUNT[1]; reintroduced through Afrikaans in 19th or 20th century]

Pontefract cake ('pɒntɪˌfrækt) *n.* another name for **pomfret.**

pontianak (ˌpɒntɪ'ɑːnæk) *n.* (in Malay folklore) a female vampire; the ghost of a woman who has died in childbirth. [from Malay]

pontifex ('pɒntɪˌfɛks) *n., pl.* **pontifices** (pɒn'tɪfɪˌsiːz). (in ancient Rome) any of the senior members of the Pontifical College, presided over by the **Pontifex Maximus.** [C16: from Latin, perhaps from Etruscan but influenced by folk etymology as if meaning literally: bridge-maker, from *pons* bridge + *-fex* from *facere* to make]

pontiff ('pɒntɪf) *n.* a former title of the pagan high priest at Rome, later used of popes and occasionally of other bishops, and now confined exclusively to the pope. [C17: from French *pontife,* from Latin PONTIFEX]

pontifical (pɒn'tɪfɪkᵊl) *adj.* **1.** of, relating to, or characteristic of a pontiff, the pope, or a bishop. **2.** having an excessively authoritative manner; pompous. ~*n.* **3.** *R.C. Church, Church of England.* a book containing the prayers and ritual instructions for ceremonies restricted to a bishop. ~See also **pontificals.** —**pon'tifically** *adv.*

Pontifical Mass *n. R.C. Church, Church of England.* a solemn celebration of Mass by a bishop.

pontificals (pɒn'tɪfɪkᵊlz) *pl. n. Chiefly R.C. Church.* the insignia and special vestments worn by a bishop, esp. when celebrating High Mass.

pontificate *vb.* (pɒn'tɪfɪˌkeɪt). (*intr.*) **1.** Also (*less commonly*): **pontify** ('pɒntɪˌfaɪ). to speak or behave in a pompous or dogmatic manner. **2.** to serve or officiate as a pontiff, esp. in celebrating a Pontifical Mass. ~*n.* (pɒn'tɪfɪkɪt). **3.** the office or term of office of a pontiff, now usually the pope.

pontil ('pɒntɪl) *n.* a less common word for **punty.** [C19: from French, apparently from Italian *puntello;* see PUNTY]

pontine ('pɒntaɪn) *adj.* **1.** of or relating to bridges. **2.** of or relating to the pons Varolii. [C19: from Latin *pons* bridge]

pontonier (ˌpɒntə'nɪə) *n. Military, obsolete.* a person in charge of or involved in building a pontoon bridge. [C19: from French *pontonnier,* from Latin *pontō* ferry boat, PONTOON[1]]

pontoon[1] (pɒn'tuːn) *n.* **1. a.** a watertight float or vessel used where buoyancy is required in water, as in supporting a bridge, in salvage work, or where a temporary or mobile structure is required in military operations. **b.** (*as modifier*): *a pontoon bridge.* **2.** *Nautical.* a float, often inflatable, for raising a vessel in the water. [C17: from French *ponton,* from Latin *pontō* punt, floating bridge, from *pōns* bridge]

pontoon[2] (pɒn'tuːn) *n.* **1.** Also called: **twenty-one** (esp. U.S.), **vingt-et-un.** a gambling game in which players try to obtain card combinations better than the banker's but never worth more than 21 points. **2.** (in this game) the combination of an ace with a ten or court card when dealt to a player as his first two cards.

[C20: probably an alteration of French *vingt-et-un*, literally: twenty-one]

pony ('pəʊnɪ) *n., pl.* **ponies.** **1.** any of various breeds of small horse, usually under 14.2 hands. **2. a.** a small drinking glass, esp. for liqueurs. **b.** the amount held by such a glass. **3.** anything small of its kind. **4.** *Brit. slang.* a sum of £25, esp. in bookmaking. **5.** Also called: **trot.** *U.S. slang.* a literal translation used by students, often illicitly, in preparation for foreign language lessons or examinations; crib. [C17: from Scottish *powney*, perhaps from obsolete French *poulenet* a little colt, from *poulain* colt, from Latin *pullus* young animal, foal]

pony express *n.* (in the American West) a system of mail transport that employed relays of riders and mounts, esp. that operating from Missouri to California in 1860–61.

ponytail ('pəʊnɪˌteɪl) *n.* a hairstyle in which the hair is pulled tightly into a band or ribbon at the back of the head into a loose hanging fall.

pony trekking *n.* the act of riding ponies cross-country, esp. as a pastime.

pooch (puːtʃ) *n. Chiefly U.S. and Canadian.* a slang word for **dog** (sense 1). [of unknown origin]

pood (puːd) *n.* a unit of weight, used in Russia, equal to 36.1 pounds or 16.39 kilograms. [C16: from Russian *pud*, probably from Old Norse *pund* POUND[2]]

poodle ('puːdᵊl) *n.* **1.** a breed of dog, with varieties of different sizes, having curly hair, which is generally clipped from ribs to tail: originally bred to hunt waterfowl. **2.** a person who is servile; lackey. [C19: from German *Pudel*, short for *Pudelhund*, from *pudeln* to splash + *Hund* dog; the dogs were formerly trained as water dogs; see PUDDLE, HOUND[1]]

poodle-faker *n. Slang.* a young man or newly commissioned officer who makes a point of socializing with women; ladies' man.

poof (pʊf, puːf) *or* **poove** *n. Brit. derogatory slang.* a male homosexual. [C20: from French *pouffe* puff]

poofter ('pʊftə, 'puːf-) *n. Derogatory slang.* **1.** a man who is considered effeminate or homosexual. **2.** *N.Z.* a contemptible person. [C20: expanded form of POOF]

pooh (puː) *interj.* **1.** an exclamation of disdain, contempt, or disgust. ~*n., vb.* **2.** a childish word for **faeces** *or* **defecate.**

Pooh-Bah ('puː'bɑː) *n.* a pompous self-important official holding several offices at once and fulfilling none of them. [C19: after the character, the Lord-High-Everything-Else, in *The Mikado* (1885), a light opera by Gilbert and Sullivan]

pooh-pooh ('puː'puː) *vb.* (*tr.*) to express disdain or scorn for; dismiss or belittle.

pool[1] (puːl) *n.* **1.** a small body of still water, usually fresh; small pond. **2.** a small isolated collection of liquid spilt or poured on a surface; puddle: *a pool of blood.* **3.** a deep part of a stream or river where the water runs very slowly. **4.** an underground accumulation of oil or gas, usually forming a reservoir in porous sedimentary rock. **5.** See **swimming pool.** [Old English *pōl;* related to Old Frisian *pōl*, German *Pfuhl*]

pool[2] (puːl) *n.* **1.** any communal combination of resources, funds, etc.: *a typing pool.* **2.** the combined stakes of the betters in many gambling sports or games; kitty. **3.** *Commerce.* a group of producers who conspire to establish and maintain output levels and high prices, each member of the group being allocated a maximum quota; price ring. **4.** *Finance, chiefly U.S.* **a.** a joint fund organized by security-holders for speculative or manipulative purposes on financial markets. **b.** the persons or parties involved in such a combination. **5.** any of various billiard games in which the object is to pot all the balls with the cue ball, esp. that played with 15 coloured and numbered balls, popular in the U.S.; pocket billiards. ~*vb.* (*tr.*) **6.** to combine (investments, money, interests, etc.) into a common fund, as for a joint enterprise. **7.** *Commerce.* to organize a pool of (enterprises). **8.** *Austral. informal.* to inform on or incriminate (someone). ~See also **pools.** [C17: from French *poule*, literally: hen used to signify stakes in a card game, from Medieval Latin *pulla* hen, from Latin *pullus* young animal]

poolroom ('puːlˌruːm, -ˌrʊm) *n. U.S. and Canadian.* a hall or establishment where pool, billiards, etc., are played.

pools (puːlz) *pl. n. Brit.* an organized nationwide principally postal gambling pool betting on the result of football matches. Also called: **football pools.** [C20: from POOL[2] (in the sense: a gambling kitty)]

pool table *n.* a billiard table on which pool is played.

poon[1] (puːn) *n.* **1.** any of several trees of the SE Asian genus *Calophyllum* having lightweight hard wood and shiny leathery leaves: family *Guttiferae.* **2.** the wood of any of these trees, used to make masts and spars. [C17: from Singhalese *pūna*]

poon[2] (puːn) *n. Austral. slang.* a stupid or ineffectual person. [C20: from English dialect]

poonce (puːns) *n. Austral. slang.* **1.** a male homosexual. **2.** a stupid person. ~*vb.* (*intr.*) **3.** to behave effeminately. [C20: perhaps a blend of POOF and PONCE]

poon up *vb.* (*intr., adv.*) *Austral. slang.* to dress flashily: *to get pooned up for the evening.* [C20: from POON[2]]

poop[1] (puːp) *Nautical.* ~*n.* **1.** a raised structure at the stern of a vessel, esp. a sailing ship. **2.** See **poop deck.** ~*vb.* **3.** (*tr.*) (of a wave or sea) to break over the stern of (a vessel). **4.** (*intr.*) (of a vessel) to ship a wave or sea over the stern, esp. repeatedly. [C15: from Old French *pupe*, from Latin *puppis* poop, ship's stern]

poop[2] (puːp) *vb. U.S. and Canadian slang.* **1.** (*tr.; usually passive*) to cause to become exhausted; tire: *he was pooped after the race.* **2.** (*intr.; usually foll. by out*) to give up or fail, esp. through tiredness: *he pooped out of the race.* [C14 *poupen* to blow, make a sudden sound, perhaps of imitative origin]

poop[3] (puːp) *n. U.S. and Canadian slang.* **a.** information; the facts. **b.** (*as modifier*): *a poop sheet.* [of unknown origin]

poop[4] (puːp) *Informal.* ~*vb.* (*intr.*) **1.** to defecate. ~*n.* **2.** faeces; excrement. [perhaps related to POOP[2]]

poop deck *n. Nautical.* the deck on top of the poop.

pooper-scooper *n.* a device used to remove dogs' excrement from public areas. [C20: POOP[4] + -ER[1] + SCOOP]

poor (pʊə, pɔː) *adj.* **1. a.** lacking financial or other means of subsistence; needy. **b.** (*as collective n.; preceded by the*): *the poor.* **2.** characterized by or indicating poverty: *the country had a poor economy.* **3.** deficient in amount; scanty or inadequate: *a poor salary.* **4.** (when *postpositive*, usually foll. by *in*) badly supplied (with resources, materials, etc.): *a region poor in wild flowers.* **5.** lacking in quality; inferior. **6.** giving no pleasure; disappointing or disagreeable: *a poor play.* **7.** (*prenominal*) deserving of pity; unlucky: *poor John is ill again.* **8. poor man's (something).** a (cheaper) substitute for (something). [C13: from Old French *povre*, from Latin *pauper;* see PAUPER, POVERTY] —'**poorness** *n.*

poor box *n.* a box, esp. one in a church, used for the collection of alms or money for the poor.

poorhouse ('pʊəˌhaʊs, 'pɔː-) *n.* (formerly) a publicly maintained institution offering accommodation to the poor.

poor law *n. English history.* a law providing for the relief or support of the poor from public, esp. parish, funds.

poorly ('pʊəlɪ, 'pɔː-) *adv.* **1.** in a poor way or manner; badly. ~*adj.* **2.** (*usually postpositive*) *Informal.* in poor health; rather ill: *she's poorly today.*

poor man's orange *n. N.Z. informal, obsolete.* a grapefruit.

poor mouth *n.* **1.** *Irish.* unjustified complaining, esp. to excite sympathy: *she always has the poor mouth.* ~*vb.* **poor-mouth.** (*tr.*) **2.** *Informal.* to speak of disparagingly; decry.

poor rate *n. English history.* a rate or tax levied by parishes for the relief or support of the poor.

poor relation *n.* a person or thing considered inferior to another or others: *plastic is a poor relation of real leather.*

poort (pʊət) *n.* (in South Africa) a steep narrow mountain pass, usually following a river or stream. [C19: from Afrikaans, from Dutch: gateway; see PORT[4]]

poortith ('puːrˌtɪθ) *n. Scot.* a variant of **puirtith.**

poor White *n. Often offensive.* **a.** a poverty-stricken and underprivileged White person, esp. in the southern U.S. and South Africa. **b.** (*as modifier*): *poor White trash.*

Pooterish ('puːtərɪʃ) *adj.* characteristic of or resembling the fictional character Pooter, esp. in being bourgeois, genteel, or self-important. [C20: from Charles *Pooter*, the hero of *Diary of a Nobody* (1892), by George and Weedon Grossmith]

poove (puːv) *n. Brit. derogatory slang.* a variant of **poof.**

pop[1] (pɒp) *vb.* **pops, popping, popped.** **1.** to make or cause to make a light sharp explosive sound. **2.** to burst open or cause to burst open with such a sound. **3.** (*intr.; often foll. by in, out, etc.*) *Informal.* to come (to) or go (from) rapidly or suddenly; to pay a brief or unexpected visit (to). **4.** (*intr.*) (esp. of the eyes) to protrude: *her eyes popped with amazement.* **5.** to shoot or fire at (a target) with a firearm. **6.** (*tr.*) to place or put with a sudden movement: *she popped some tablets into her mouth.* **7.** (*tr.*) *Informal.* to pawn: *he popped his watch yesterday.* **8.** (*tr.*) *Slang.* to take (a drug) in pill form or as an injection: *pill popping.* **9. pop the question.** *Informal.* to propose marriage. ~*n.* **10.** a light sharp explosive sound; crack. **11.** *Informal.* a flavoured nonalcoholic carbonated beverage. ~*adv.* **12.** with a popping sound. ~*interj.* **13.** an exclamation denoting a sharp explosive sound. ~See also **pop off, pop-up.** [C14: of imitative origin]

pop[2] (pɒp) *n.* **1. a.** music of general appeal, esp. among young people, that originated as a distinctive genre in the 1950s. It is generally characterized by a heavy rhythmic element and the use of electrical amplification. **b.** (*as modifier*): *pop music; a pop record; a pop group.* **2.** *Informal.* a piece of popular or light classical music. ~*adj.* **3.** *Informal.* short for **popular.**

pop[3] (pɒp) *n.* **1.** an informal word for **father.** **2.** *Informal.* a name used in addressing an old or middle-aged man.

POP *abbrev. for* Post Office Preferred (size of envelopes, etc.).

pop. *abbrev. for:* **1.** popular. **2.** popularly. **3.** population.

pop art *n.* a movement in modern art that imitates the methods, styles, and themes of popular culture and mass media, such as comic strips, advertising, and science fiction.

popcorn ('pɒpˌkɔːn) *n.* **1.** a variety of maize having hard pointed kernels that puff up when heated. **2.** the puffed edible kernels of this plant. [C19: so called because of the noise the grains make when they swell up and burst on heating]

pope[1] (pəʊp) *n.* **1.** (*often cap.*) the bishop of Rome as head of the Roman Catholic Church. **2.** *Eastern Orthodox Churches.* **a.** a title sometimes given to a parish priest. **b.** a title sometimes given to the Greek Orthodox patriarch of Alexandria. **3.** a person assuming or having a status or authority resembling that of a pope. [Old English *papa*, from Church Latin: bishop, esp. of

Rome, from Late Greek *papas* father-in-God, from Greek *pappas* father]

pope[2] (pəʊp) *n.* another name for **ruffe** (the fish).

popedom ('pəʊpdəm) *n.* **1.** the office or dignity of a pope. **2.** the tenure of office of a pope. **3.** the dominion of a pope; papal government.

popery ('pəʊpərɪ) *n.* a derogatory name for **Roman Catholicism.**

pope's eye *n.* **1.** (in sheep and cows) a gland in the middle of the thigh surrounded by fat. ~*adj.* **popeseye. 2.** (in Scotland) denoting a cut of steak.

pope's nose *n.* another name for **parson's nose.**

popeyed ('pɒp,aɪd) *adj.* **1.** having bulging prominent eyes. **2.** staring in astonishment; amazed.

popgun ('pɒp,gʌn) *n.* a toy gun that fires a pellet or cork by means of compressed air and makes a popping sound.

popinjay ('pɒpɪn,dʒeɪ) *n.* **1.** a conceited, foppish, or excessively talkative person. **2.** an archaic word for **parrot. 3.** the figure of a parrot used as a target. [C13 *papeniai,* from Old French *papegay* a parrot, from Spanish *papagayo,* from Arabic *babaghā*]

popish ('pəʊpɪʃ) *adj. Derogatory.* belonging to or characteristic of Roman Catholicism. —**'popishly** *adv.*

poplar ('pɒplə) *n.* **1.** any tree of the salicaceous genus *Populus,* of N temperate regions, having triangular leaves, flowers borne in catkins, and light soft wood. See also **aspen, balsam poplar, Lombardy poplar, white poplar. 2.** any of various trees resembling the true poplars, such as the tulip tree. **3.** the wood of any of these trees. [C14: from Old French *poplier,* from *pouple,* from Latin *pōpulus*]

poplin ('pɒplɪn) *n.* **a.** a strong fabric, usually of cotton, in plain weave with fine ribbing, used for dresses, children's wear, etc. **b.** (*as modifier*): *a poplin shirt.* [C18: from French *papeline,* perhaps from *Poperinge,* a centre of textile manufacture in Flanders]

popliteal (pɒp'lɪtɪəl, ,pɒplɪ'ti:əl) *adj.* of, relating to, or near the part of the leg behind the knee. [C18: from New Latin *popliteus* the muscle behind the knee joint, from Latin *poples* the ham of the knee]

popmobility ('pɒpməʊ,bɪlɪtɪ) *n.* a form of exercise that combines aerobics in a continuous dance routine, performed to pop music. [C20: POP[2] + MOBILITY]

pop off *vb.* (*intr., adv.*) *Informal.* **1.** to depart suddenly or unexpectedly. **2.** to die, esp. suddenly or unexpectedly: *he popped off at the age of sixty.* **3.** to speak out angrily or indiscreetly: *he popped off at his boss and got fired.*

popover ('pɒp,əʊvə) *n.* **1.** *Brit.* an individual Yorkshire pudding, often served with roast beef. **2.** *U.S. and Canadian.* a light puffy hollow muffin made from a batter mixture. **3.** a simple garment for women or girls that is put on by being slipped over the head.

poppadom *or* **poppadum** ('pɒpədəm) *n.* a thin round crisp Indian bread, fried or roasted and served with curry, etc. [from Hindi]

popper ('pɒpə) *n.* **1.** a person or thing that pops. **2.** *Brit.* an informal name for **press stud. 3.** *Chiefly U.S. and Canadian.* a container for cooking popcorn in. **4.** *Slang.* an amyl nitrite capsule, which is crushed and its contents inhaled by drug users as a stimulant.

poppet ('pɒpɪt) *n.* **1.** a term of affection for a small child or sweetheart. **2.** Also called: **poppet valve.** a mushroom-shaped valve that is lifted from its seating by applying an axial force to its stem: commonly used as an exhaust or inlet valve in an internal-combustion engine. **3.** *Nautical.* a temporary supporting brace for a vessel hauled on land or in a dry dock. [C14: early variant of PUPPET]

poppet head *n.* the framework above a mining shaft that supports the winding mechanism.

poppied ('pɒpɪd) *adj.* **1.** covered with poppies. **2.** of or relating to the effects of poppies, esp. in inducing drowsiness or sleep.

popping crease *n. Cricket.* a line four feet in front of and parallel with the bowling crease, at or behind which the batsman stands. [C18: from POP[1] (in the obsolete or dialect sense: to hit) + CREASE[1]]

popple ('pɒpᵊl) *vb.* (*intr.*) **1.** (of boiling water or a choppy sea) to heave or toss; bubble. **2.** (often foll. by *along*) (of a stream or river) to move with an irregular tumbling motion: *the small rivulet poppled along over rocks and stones for half a mile.* [C14: of imitative origin; compare Middle Dutch *popelen* to bubble, throb]

poppy ('pɒpɪ) *n., pl.* **-pies. 1.** any of numerous papaveraceous plants of the temperate genus *Papaver,* having red, orange, or white flowers and a milky sap: see **corn poppy, Iceland poppy, opium poppy. 2.** any of several similar or related plants, such as the California poppy, prickly poppy, horned poppy, and Welsh poppy. **3.** any of the drugs, such as opium, that are obtained from these plants. **4. a.** a strong red to reddish-orange colour. **b.** (*as adj.*): *a poppy dress.* **5.** a less common name for **poppyhead** (sense 2). **6.** an artificial red poppy flower worn to mark Remembrance Sunday. [Old English *popæg,* ultimately from Latin *papāver*]

poppycock ('pɒpɪ,kɒk) *n. Informal.* senseless chatter; nonsense. [C19: from Dutch dialect *pappekak,* literally: soft excrement, from *pap* soft + *kak* dung; see PAP[1]]

Poppy Day *n.* an informal name for **Remembrance Sunday.**

poppyhead ('pɒpɪ,hɛd) *n.* **1.** the hard dry seed-containing capsule of a poppy. See also **capsule** (sense 3a). **2.** a carved ornament, esp. one used on the top of the end of a pew or bench in Gothic church architecture.

poppy seed *n.* the small grey seeds of one type of poppy flower, used esp. on loaves and as a cake filling.

pop shop *n.* a slang word for a **pawnshop.**

Popsicle ('pɒpsɪkᵊl) *n. U.S. and Canadian trademark.* an ice lolly.

popsy ('pɒpsɪ) *n., pl.* **-sies.** *Old-fashioned Brit. slang.* an attractive young woman. [C19: diminutive formed from *pop,* shortened from POPPET; originally a nursery term]

populace ('pɒpjʊləs) *n.* (*sometimes functioning as pl.*) **1.** the inhabitants of an area. **2.** the common people; masses. [C16: via French from Italian *popolaccio* the common herd, from *popolo* people, from Latin *populus*]

popular ('pɒpjʊlə) *adj.* **1.** appealing to the general public; widely favoured or admired. **2.** favoured by an individual or limited group: *I'm not very popular with her.* **3.** connected with, representing, or prevailing among the general public; common: *popular discontent.* **4.** appealing to or comprehensible to the layman: *a popular lecture on physics.* ~*n.* **5.** (*usually pl.*) cheap newspapers with mass circulation; the popular press. Also shortened to **pops.** [C15: from Latin *populāris* belonging to the people, democratic, from *populus* people] —**popularity** (,pɒpjʊ'lærɪtɪ) *n.*

popular etymology *n. Linguistics.* another name for **folk etymology.**

popular front *n.* (*often cap.*) any of the left-wing groups or parties that were organized from 1935 onwards to oppose the spread of fascism.

popularize *or* **popularise** ('pɒpjʊlə,raɪz) *vb.* (*tr.*) **1.** to make popular; make attractive to the general public. **2.** to make or cause to become easily understandable or acceptable. —,**populari'zation** *or* ,**populari'sation** *n.* —**'popular,izer** *or* **'popular,iser** *n.*

popularly ('pɒpjʊləlɪ) *adv.* **1.** by the public as a whole; generally or widely. **2.** usually; commonly: *his full name is Robert, but he is popularly known as Bob.* **3.** in a popular manner.

popular music *n.* music having wide appeal, esp. characterized by lightly romantic or sentimental melodies. See also **pop**[2].

popular sovereignty *n.* (in the pre-Civil War U.S.) the doctrine that the inhabitants of a territory should be free from federal interference in determining their own domestic policy, esp. in deciding whether or not to allow slavery.

populate ('pɒpjʊ,leɪt) *vb.* (*tr.*) **1.** (*often passive*) to live in; inhabit. **2.** to provide a population for; colonize or people. [C16: from Medieval Latin *populāre* to provide with inhabitants, from Latin *populus* people]

population (,pɒpjʊ'leɪʃən) *n.* **1.** (*sometimes functioning as pl.*) all the persons inhabiting a country, city, or other specified place. **2.** the number of such inhabitants. **3.** (*sometimes functioning as pl.*) all the people of a particular race or class in a specific area: *the Chinese population of San Francisco.* **4.** the act or process of providing a place with inhabitants; colonization. **5.** *Ecology.* a group of individuals of the same species inhabiting a given area. **6.** *Astronomy.* either of two main groups of stars classified according to age and location. **Population I** consists of hot white stars, many occurring in galactic clusters and forming the arms of spiral galaxies. Stars of **population II** are older, the brightest being red giants, and are found in the centre of spiral and elliptical galaxies in globular clusters. **7.** Also called: **universe.** *Statistics.* the entire finite or infinite aggregate of individuals or items from which samples are drawn.

population control *n.* a policy of attempting to limit the growth in numbers of a population, esp. in poor or densely populated parts of the world, by programmes of contraception or sterilization.

population explosion *n.* a rapid increase in the size of a population caused by such factors as a sudden decline in infant mortality or an increase in life expectancy.

population pyramid *n.* a pyramid-shaped diagram illustrating the age distribution of a population: the youngest are represented by a rectangle at the base, the oldest by one at the apex.

Populist ('pɒpjʊlɪst) *n.* **1.** *U.S. history.* a member of the People's Party, formed largely by agrarian interests to contest the 1892 presidential election. The movement gradually dissolved after the 1904 election. **2.** (*often not cap.*) a politician or other person who claims to support the interests of the ordinary people. ~*adj. also* **Populistic. 3.** of, characteristic of, or relating to the People's Party, the Populists, or any individual or movement with similar aims. —**'Populism** *n.*

populist shop steward *n.* a shop steward who operates in a delegate role, putting the immediate interests of his members before union principles and policies.

populous ('pɒpjʊləs) *adj.* containing many inhabitants; abundantly populated. [C15: from Late Latin *populōsus*] —**'populously** *adv.* —**'populousness** *n.*

pop-up *adj.* **1.** (of an appliance) characterized by or having a mechanism that pops up: *a pop-up toaster.* **2.** (of a book) having pages that rise when opened to simulate a three-dimensional form. ~*vb.* **pop up. 3.** (*intr., adv.*) to appear suddenly from below.

porangi ('pɔ:ræŋɪ) *adj. N.Z. informal.* crazy; mad. [Maori]

porbeagle ('pɔ:,bi:gᵊl) *n.* any of several voracious sharks of the genus *Lamna,* esp. *L. nasus,* of northern seas: family *Isuridae.*

Also called: **mackerel shark.** [C18: from Cornish *porgh-bugel,* of obscure origin]

porcelain (ˈpɔːslɪn, -leɪn, ˈpɔːsə-) *n.* **1.** a more or less translucent ceramic material, the principal ingredients being kaolin and petuntse (hard paste) or other clays, ground glassy substances, soapstone, bone ash, etc. **2.** an object made of this or such objects collectively. **3.** (*modifier*) of, relating to, or made from this material: *a porcelain cup.* [C16: from French *porcelaine,* from Italian *porcellana* cowrie shell, porcelain (from its shell-like finish), literally: relating to a sow (from the resemblance between a cowrie shell and a sow's vulva), from *porcella* little sow, from *porca* sow, from Latin; see PORK] —**porcellaneous** (ˌpɔːsəˈleɪnɪəs) *adj.*

porcelain clay *n.* another name for **kaolin.**

porch (pɔːtʃ) *n.* **1.** a low structure projecting from the doorway of a house and forming a covered entrance. **2.** *U.S. and Canadian.* an exterior roofed gallery, often partly enclosed; veranda. [C13: from French *porche,* from Latin *porticus* portico]

porcine (ˈpɔːsaɪn) *adj.* of, connected with, or characteristic of pigs. [C17: from Latin *porcīnus,* from *porcus* a pig]

porcupine (ˈpɔːkjʊˌpaɪn) *n.* any of various large hystricomorph rodents of the families *Hystricidae,* of Africa, Indonesia, S Europe, and S Asia, and *Erethizontidae,* of the New World. All species have a body covering of protective spines or quills. [C14 *porc despyne* pig with spines, from Old French *porc espin;* see PORK, SPINE] —ˈ**porcuˌpinish** *adj.* —ˈ**porcuˌpiny** *adj.*

porcupine fish *n.* any of various plectognath fishes of the genus *Diodon* and related genera, of temperate and tropical seas, having a body that is covered with sharp spines and can be inflated into a globe: family *Diodontidae.* Also called: **globefish.**

porcupine grass *n. Austral.* another name for **spinifex** (sense 2).

porcupine provisions *pl. n. Finance.* provisions, such as poison pills or staggered directorships, made in the bylaws of a company to deter takeover bids. Also called: **shark repellents.**

pore[1] (pɔː) *vb.* (*intr.*) **1.** (foll. by *over*) to make a close intent examination or study (of a book, map, etc.): *he pored over the documents for several hours.* **2.** (foll. by *over, on,* or *upon*) to think deeply (about): *he pored on the question of their future.* **3.** (foll. by *over, on,* or *upon*) *Rare.* to look earnestly or intently (at); gaze fixedly (upon). [C13 *pouren;* perhaps related to PEER[2]]

pore[2] (pɔː) *n.* **1.** *Anatomy, zoology.* any small opening in the skin or outer surface of an animal. **2.** *Botany.* any small aperture, esp. that of a stoma through which water vapour and gases pass. **3.** any other small hole, such as a space in a rock, soil, etc. [C14: from Late Latin *porus,* from Greek *poros* passage, pore]

porgy (ˈpɔːgɪ) *n., pl.* **-gy** *or* **-gies. 1.** Also called: **pogy.** any of various sparid fishes, many of which occur in American Atlantic waters. See also **scup, sheepshead. 2.** any of various similar or related fishes. [C18: from Spanish *pargo,* from Latin *phager* type of fish, from Greek *phagros* sea bream]

poriferan (pɔːˈrɪfərən) *n.* **1.** any invertebrate of the phylum *Porifera,* which comprises the sponges. ~*adj. also* **poriferous. 2.** of, relating to, or belonging to the phylum *Porifera.* [C19: from New Latin *porifer* bearing pores]

poriferous (pɔːˈrɪfərəs) *adj.* **1.** *Biology.* having many pores. **2.** another word for **poriferan** (sense 2).

porina (pɒˈraɪnə) *n. N.Z.* **a.** the larva of a moth which causes damage to grassland. **b.** (*as modifier*): *porina infestation.* [from New Latin]

porism (ˈpɔːrɪzəm) *n.* a type of mathematical proposition considered by Euclid, the meaning of which is now obscure. It is thought to be a proposition affirming the possibility of finding such conditions as will render a certain problem indeterminate or capable of innumerable solutions. [C14: from Late Latin *porisma,* from Greek: deduction, from *porizein* to deduce, carry; related to Greek *poros* passage] —**porismatic** (ˌpɔːrɪzˈmætɪk) *adj.*

pork (pɔːk) *n.* the flesh of pigs used as food. [C13: from Old French *porc,* from Latin *porcus* pig]

pork barrel *n. U.S. slang.* a bill or project requiring considerable government spending in a locality to the benefit of the legislator's constituents who live there. [C20: term originally applied to the Federal treasury considered as a source of lucrative grants]

porker (ˈpɔːkə) *n.* a pig, esp. a young one weighing between 40 and 67 kg, fattened to provide meat such as pork chops.

pork pie *n.* **1.** a pie filled with minced seasoned pork. **2.** See **porky**[2].

porkpie hat (ˈpɔːkˌpaɪ) *n.* a hat with a round flat crown and a brim that can be turned up or down.

pork pig *n.* a pig, typically of a lean type, bred and used principally for pork.

pork scratchings *pl. n.* small pieces of crisply cooked pork crackling, eaten cold as an appetizer with drinks.

porky[1] (ˈpɔːkɪ) *adj.* **porkier, porkiest. 1.** belonging to or characteristic of pork: *a porky smell.* **2.** *Informal.* fat; obese. —ˈ**porkiness** *n.*

porky[2] (ˈpɔːkɪ) *n., pl.* **porkies.** *Brit. slang.* a lie. Also called: **pork pie.** [from rhyming slang *pork pie* lie]

porn (pɔːn) *or* **porno** (ˈpɔːnəʊ) *n., adj. Informal.* short for **pornography** or **pornographic.**

pornocracy (pɔːˈnɒkrəsɪ) *n.* government or domination of government by whores. [C19: from Greek, from *pornē* a prostitute, harlot + -CRACY]

pornography (pɔːˈnɒgrəfɪ) *n.* **1.** writings, pictures, films, etc., designed to stimulate sexual excitement. **2.** the production of such material. ~Sometimes (informal) shortened to **porn** *or* **porno.** [C19: from Greek *pornographos* writing of harlots, from *pornē* a harlot + *graphein* to write] —**porˈnographer** *n.* —**pornographic** (ˌpɔːnəˈgræfɪk) *adj.* —ˌ**pornoˈgraphically** *adv.*

poromeric (ˌpɔːrəˈmɛrɪk) *adj.* **1.** (of a plastic) permeable to water vapour. ~*n.* **2.** a substance having this characteristic, esp. one based on polyurethane and used in place of leather in making shoe uppers. [C20: from PORO(SITY) + (POLY)MER + -IC]

porosity (pɔːˈrɒsɪtɪ) *n., pl.* **-ties. 1.** the state or condition of being porous. **2.** *Geology.* the ratio of the volume of space to the total volume of a rock. [C14: from Medieval Latin *porōsitās,* from Late Latin *porus* PORE[2]]

porous (ˈpɔːrəs) *adj.* **1.** permeable to water, air, or other fluids. **2.** *Biology, geology.* having pores; poriferous. [C14: from Medieval Latin *porōsus,* from Late Latin *porus* PORE[2]] —ˈ**porously** *adv.* —ˈ**porousness** *n.*

porphyria (pɔːˈfɪrɪə) *n.* a hereditary disease of body metabolism, producing abdominal pain, mental confusion, etc. [C19: from New Latin, from *porphyrin* a purple substance excreted by patients suffering from this condition, from Greek *porphura* purple]

porphyrin (ˈpɔːfɪrɪn) *n.* any of a group of pigments occurring widely in animal and plant tissues and having a heterocyclic structure formed from four pyrrole rings linked by four methylene groups. [C20: from Greek *porphura* purple, referring to its colour]

porphyritic (ˌpɔːfɪˈrɪtɪk) *adj.* **1.** (of rocks) having large crystals in a fine groundmass of minerals. **2.** consisting of porphyry.

porphyrogenite (ˌpɔːfəˈrɒdʒɪˌnaɪt) *n.* (*sometimes cap.*) a prince born after his father has succeeded to the throne. [C17: via Medieval Latin from Late Greek *porphurogennētos* born in the purple, from Greek *porphuros* purple]

porphyroid (ˈpɔːfɪˌrɔɪd) *adj.* **1.** (of metamorphic rocks) having a texture characterized by large crystals set in a finer groundmass. ~*n.* **2.** a metamorphic rock having this texture.

porphyropsin (ˌpɔːfɪˈrɒpsɪn) *n.* a purple pigment occurring in the retina of the eye of certain freshwater fishes. [C20: from Greek *porphura* purple + -OPSIS + -IN, on the model of RHODOPSIN]

porphyry (ˈpɔːfɪrɪ) *n., pl.* **-ries. 1.** a reddish-purple rock consisting of large crystals of feldspar in a finer groundmass of feldspar, hornblende, etc. **2.** any igneous rock with large crystals embedded in a finer groundmass of minerals. [C14 *porfurie,* from Late Latin *porphyrītēs,* from Greek *porphuritēs* (*lithos*) purple (stone), from *porphuros* purple]

porpoise (ˈpɔːpəs) *n., pl.* **-poise** *or* **-poises. 1.** any of various small cetacean mammals of the genus *Phocaena* and related genera, having a blunt snout and many teeth: family *Delphinidae* (or *Phocaenidae*). **2.** (*not in technical use*) any of various related cetaceans, esp. the dolphin. [C14: from French *pourpois,* from Medieval Latin *porcopiscus* (from Latin *porcus* pig + *piscis* fish), replacing Latin *porcus marīnus* sea pig]

porrect (pəˈrɛkt) *adj. Botany.* extended forwards. [C20: from Latin *porrectus,* from *porrigere* to stretch out]

porridge (ˈpɒrɪdʒ) *n.* **1.** a dish made from oatmeal or another cereal, cooked in water or milk to a thick consistency. **2.** *Slang.* a term in prison (esp. in the phrase **do porridge**). [C16: variant (influenced by Middle English *porray* pottage) of POTTAGE]

porringer (ˈpɒrɪndʒə) *n.* a small dish, often with a handle, for soup, porridge, etc. [C16: changed from Middle English *potinger, poteger,* from Old French *potager,* from *potage* soup, contents of a pot; see POTTAGE]

port[1] (pɔːt) *n.* **1.** a town or place alongside navigable water with facilities for the loading and unloading of ships. **2.** See **port of entry.** [Old English, from Latin *portus* harbour, port]

port[2] (pɔːt) *n.* **1.** Also called (formerly): **larboard. a.** the left side of an aircraft or vessel when facing the nose or bow. **b.** (*as modifier*): *the port bow.* Compare **starboard** (sense 1). ~*vb.* **2.** to turn or be turned towards the port. [C17: origin uncertain]

port[3] (pɔːt) *n.* a sweet fortified dessert wine. [C17: after *Oporto,* Portugal, from where it came originally]

port[4] (pɔːt) *n.* **1.** *Nautical.* **a.** an opening in the side of a ship, fitted with a watertight door, for access to the holds. **b.** See **porthole** (sense 1). **2.** a small opening in a wall, armoured vehicle, etc., for firing through. **3.** an aperture, esp. one controlled by a valve, by which fluid enters or leaves the cylinder head of an engine, compressor, etc. **4.** *Electronics.* a logical circuit for the input and ouput of data. **5.** *Chiefly Scot.* a gate or portal in a town or fortress. [Old English, from Latin *porta* gate]

port[5] (pɔːt) *Military.* ~*vb.* **1.** (*tr.*) to carry (a rifle, etc.) in a position diagonally across the body with the muzzle near the left shoulder. ~*n.* **2.** this position. [C14: from Old French, from *porter* to carry, from Latin *portāre*]

port[6] (pɔːt) *n. Austral.* **1.** a travelling bag, such as a suitcase. **2.** any other kind of bag, such as a shopping bag. [C20: shortened from PORTMANTEAU]

Port. *abbrev. for:* **1.** Portugal. **2.** Portuguese.

porta ('pɔːtə) *n. Anatomy.* an aperture in an organ, such as the liver, esp. one providing an opening for blood vessels. [C14: from Latin: gate, entrance]

portable ('pɔːtəbᵊl) *adj.* **1.** able to be carried or moved easily, esp. by hand. **2.** *Archaic.* able to be endured; bearable. ~*n.* **3.** an article designed to be readily carried by hand, such as a television, typewriter, etc. [C14: from Late Latin *portābilis*, from Latin *portāre* to carry] —ˌ**porta'bility** *n.* —'**portably** *adv.*

portage ('pɔːtɪdʒ; *French* pɔrtaʒ) *n.* **1.** the act of carrying; transport. **2.** the cost of carrying or transporting. **3.** the act or process of transporting boats, supplies, etc., overland between navigable waterways. **4.** the route overland used for such transport. ~*vb.* **5.** to transport (boats, supplies, etc.) overland between navigable waterways. [C15: from French, from Old French *porter* to carry]

Portakabin ('pɔːtəˌkæbɪn) *n. Trademark.* a portable building quickly set up for use as a temporary office, etc.

portal ('pɔːtᵊl) *n.* **1.** an entrance, gateway, or doorway, esp. one that is large and impressive. **2.** any entrance or access to a place. ~*adj.* **3.** *Anatomy.* **a.** of or relating to a portal vein: *hepatic portal system.* **b.** of or relating to a porta. [C14: via Old French from Medieval Latin *portāle*, from Latin *porta* gate, entrance]

portal frame *n. Civil engineering, building trades.* a frame, usually of steel, consisting of two uprights and a cross beam at the top: the simplest structural unit in a framed building or a doorway.

portal-to-portal *adj.* of or relating to the period between the actual times workers enter and leave their mine, factory, etc.: *portal-to-portal pay.*

portal vein *n.* any vein connecting two capillary networks, esp. in the liver (**hepatic portal vein**).

portamento (ˌpɔːtə'mɛntəʊ) *n., pl.* **-ti** (-tɪ). *Music.* a smooth slide from one note to another in which intervening notes are not separately discernible. Compare **glissando.** [C18: from Italian: a carrying, from Latin *portāre* to carry]

portative ('pɔːtətɪv) *adj.* **1.** a less common word for **portable. 2.** concerned with the act of carrying. [C14: from French, from Latin *portāre* to carry]

portative organ *n. Music.* a small portable organ with arm-operated bellows popular in medieval times.

portcullis (pɔːt'kʌlɪs) *n.* an iron or wooden grating suspended vertically in grooves in the gateway of a castle or fortified town and able to be lowered so as to bar the entrance. [C14 *port colice*, from Old French *porte coleïce* sliding gate, from *porte* door, entrance + *coleïce*, from *couler* to slide, flow, from Late Latin *cōlāre* to filter]

porte-cochere (ˌpɔːtkɒ'ʃɛə) *n.* **1.** a large covered entrance for vehicles leading into a courtyard. **2.** a large roof projecting over a drive to shelter travellers entering or leaving vehicles. [C17: from French: carriage entrance, from *porte* gateway + *coche* coach]

portend (pɔː'tɛnd) *vb. (tr.)* **1.** to give warning of; predict or foreshadow. **2.** *Obsolete.* to indicate or signify; mean. [C15: from Latin *portendere* to indicate, foretell; related to *prōtendere* to stretch out]

portent ('pɔːtɛnt) *n.* **1.** a sign or indication of a future event, esp. a momentous or calamitous one; omen. **2.** momentous or ominous significance: *a cry of dire portent.* **3.** a miraculous occurrence; marvel. [C16: from Latin *portentum* sign, omen, from *portendere* to PORTEND]

portentous (pɔː'tɛntəs) *adj.* **1.** of momentous or ominous significance. **2.** miraculous, amazing, or awe-inspiring; prodigious. **3.** self-important or pompous. —**por'tentously** *adv.* —**por'tentousness** *n.*

porter[1] ('pɔːtə) *n.* **1.** a person employed to carry luggage, parcels, supplies, etc., esp. at a railway station or hotel. **2.** (in hospitals) a person employed to move patients from place to place. **3.** *U.S. and Canadian.* a railway employee who waits on passengers, esp. in a sleeper. **4.** *E African.* a manual labourer. [C14: from Old French *portour*, from Late Latin *portātōr*, from Latin *portāre* to carry]

porter[2] ('pɔːtə) *n.* **1.** *Chiefly Brit.* a person in charge of a gate or door; doorman or gatekeeper. **2.** a person employed by a university or college as a caretaker and doorkeeper who also answers enquiries. **3.** a person in charge of the maintenance of a building, esp. a block of flats. **4.** Also called: **ostiary.** *R.C. Church.* a person ordained to what was formerly the lowest in rank of the minor orders. [C13: from Old French *portier*, from Late Latin *portārius* doorkeeper, from Latin *porta* door]

porter[3] ('pɔːtə) *n. Brit.* a dark sweet ale brewed from black malt. [C18: shortened from *porter's ale*, apparently because it was a favourite beverage of porters]

porterage ('pɔːtərɪdʒ) *n.* **1.** the work of carrying supplies, goods, etc., done by porters. **2.** the charge made for this.

porterhouse ('pɔːtəˌhaʊs) *n.* **1.** Also called: **porterhouse steak.** a thick choice steak of beef cut from the middle ribs or sirloin. **2.** (formerly) a place in which porter, beer, etc., and sometimes chops and steaks, were served. [C19 (sense 1): said to be named after a porterhouse or chophouse in New York]

portfire ('pɔːtˌfaɪə) *n.* (formerly) a slow-burning fuse used for firing rockets and fireworks and, in mining, for igniting explosives. [C17: from French *porte-feu*, from *porter* to carry + *feu* fire]

portfolio (pɔːt'fəʊlɪəʊ) *n., pl.* **-os. 1.** a flat case, esp. of leather, used for carrying maps, drawings, etc. **2.** the contents of such a case, such as drawings, paintings, or photographs, that demonstrate recent work: *an art student's portfolio.* **3.** such a case used for carrying ministerial or state papers. **4.** the responsibilities or role of the head of a government department: *the portfolio for foreign affairs.* **5. Minister without portfolio.** a cabinet minister who is not responsible for any government department. **6.** the complete investments held by an individual investor or by a financial organization. [C18: from Italian *portafoglio*, from *portāre* to carry + *foglio* leaf, paper, from Latin *folium* leaf]

porthole ('pɔːtˌhəʊl) *n.* **1.** a small aperture in the side of a vessel to admit light and air, usually fitted with a watertight glass or metal cover, or both. Sometimes shortened to **port. 2.** an opening in a wall or parapet through which a gun can be fired; embrasure.

portico ('pɔːtɪkəʊ) *n., pl.* **-coes** *or* **-cos. 1.** a covered entrance to a building; porch. **2.** a covered walkway in the form of a roof supported by columns or pillars, esp. one built on to the exterior of a building. [C17: via Italian from Latin *porticus* PORCH]

portière (ˌpɔːtɪ'ɛə; *French* pɔrtjɛr) *n.* a curtain hung in a doorway. [C19: via French from Medieval Latin *portāria*, from Latin *porta* door] —ˌ**porti'èred** *adj.*

portion ('pɔːʃən) *n.* **1.** a part of a whole; fraction. **2.** a part allotted or belonging to a person or group. **3.** an amount of food served to one person; helping. **4.** *Law.* **a.** a share of property, esp. one coming to a child from the estate of his parents. **b.** the property given by a woman to her husband at marriage; dowry. **5.** a person's lot or destiny. ~*vb. (tr.)* **6.** to divide up; share out. **7.** to give a share to (a person); assign or allocate. **8.** *Law.* to give a dowry or portion to (a person); endow. [C13: via Old French from Latin *portiō* portion, allocation; related to *pars* PART] —'**portionless** *adj.*

Portland cement ('pɔːtlənd) *n.* a cement that hardens under water and is made by heating a slurry of clay and crushed chalk or limestone to clinker in a kiln. [C19: named after the Isle of *Portland*, SW England, because its colour resembles that of the stone quarried there]

portly ('pɔːtlɪ) *adj.* **-lier, -liest. 1.** stout or corpulent. **2.** *Archaic.* stately; impressive. [C16: from PORT[5] (in the sense: deportment, bearing)] —'**portliness** *n.*

portmanteau (pɔːt'mæntəʊ) *n., pl.* **-teaus** *or* **-teaux** (-təʊz). **1.** (formerly) a large travelling case made of stiff leather, esp. one hinged at the back so as to open out into two compartments. **2.** (*modifier*) embodying several uses or qualities: *the heroine is a portmanteau figure of all the virtues.* [C16: from French: cloak carrier, from *porter* to carry + *manteau* cloak MANTLE]

portmanteau word *n.* another name for **blend** (sense 7). [C19: from the idea that two meanings are packed into one word]

port of call *n.* **1.** any port where a ship stops, excluding its home port. **2.** any place visited on a traveller's itinerary.

port of entry *n. Law.* an airport, harbour, etc., where customs officials are stationed to supervise the entry into and exit from a country of persons and merchandise.

portrait ('pɔːtrɪt, -treɪt) *n.* **1. a.** a painting, drawing, sculpture, photograph, or other likeness of an individual, esp. of the face. **b.** (*as modifier*): *a portrait gallery.* **2.** a verbal description or picture, esp. of a person's character. ~*adj.* **3.** *Printing* (of an illustration in a book, magazine, etc.) of greater height than width. Compare **landscape** (sense 5a).

portraitist ('pɔːtrɪtɪst, -treɪ-) *n.* an artist, photographer, etc., who specializes in portraits.

portraiture ('pɔːtrɪtʃə) *n.* **1.** the practice or art of making portraits. **2. a.** another term for **portrait** (sense 1). **b.** portraits collectively. **3.** a verbal description.

portray (pɔː'treɪ) *vb. (tr.)* **1.** to represent in a painting, drawing, sculpture, etc.; make a portrait of. **2.** to make a verbal picture of; depict in words. **3.** to play the part of (a character) in a play or film. [C14: from Old French *portraire* to depict, from Latin *prōtrahere* to drag forth, bring to light, from PRO-[1] + *trahere* to drag] —**por'trayable** *adj.* —**por'trayal** *n.* —**por'trayer** *n.*

portress ('pɔːtrɪs) *n.* a female porter, esp. a doorkeeper.

Port-Salut ('pɔː səˈluː; *French* pɔrsaly) *n.* a mild semihard whole-milk cheese of a round flat shape. Also called: **Port du Salut.** [C19: named after the Trappist monastery at *Port du Salut* in NW France where it was first made]

Portuguese (ˌpɔːtjʊ'giːz) *n.* **1.** the official language of Portugal, a republic in SW Europe, its overseas territories, and Brazil: the native language of approximately 110 million people. It belongs to the Romance group of the Indo-European family and is derived from the Galician dialect of Vulgar Latin. **2.** (*pl.* **-guese**) a native, citizen, or inhabitant of Portugal. ~*adj.* **3.** relating to, denoting, or characteristic of Portugal, its inhabitants, or their language.

Portuguese man-of-war *n.* any of several large complex colonial hydrozoans of the genus *Physalia*, esp. *P. physalis*, having an aerial float and long stinging tentacles: order *Siphonophora.* Sometimes shortened to **man-of-war.**

portulaca (ˌpɔːtjʊ'lækə, -'leɪkə) *n.* any portulacaceous plant of the genus *Portulaca*, such as rose moss and purslane, of tropical and subtropical America, having yellow, pink, or purple showy flowers. [C16: from Latin: PURSLANE]

portulacaceous (ˌpɔːtjʊlə'keɪʃəs) *adj.* of, relating to, or belonging to the *Portulacaceae*, a family of fleshy-leaved flowering plants that are common in the U.S.

POS *abbrev. for* point of sale.

pos. *abbrev. for:* **1.** position. **2.** positive.

posada *Spanish.* (po'saða) *n., pl.* **-das** (-ðas). an inn in a Spanish-speaking country. [literally: place for stopping]

pose[1] (pəʊz) *vb.* **1.** to assume or cause to assume a physical attitude, as for a photograph or painting. **2.** (*intr.*; often foll. by *as*) to pretend to be or present oneself (as something one is not). **3.** (*intr.*) to affect an attitude or play a part in order to impress others. **4.** (*tr.*) to put forward, ask, or assert: *to pose a question.* ~*n.* **5.** a physical attitude, esp. one deliberately adopted for or represented by an artist or photographer. **6.** a mode of behaviour that is adopted for effect. [C14: from Old French *poser* to set in place, from Late Latin *pausāre* to cease, put down (influenced by Latin *pōnere* to place)]

pose[2] (pəʊz) *vb.* (*tr.*) **1.** *Rare.* to puzzle or baffle. **2.** *Archaic.* to question closely. [C16: from obsolete *appose,* from Latin *appōnere* to put to, set against; see OPPOSE]

poser[1] ('pəʊzə) *n.* **1.** a person who poses. **2.** *Informal.* a person who likes to be seen in trendsetting clothes in fashionable bars, discos, etc.

poser[2] ('pəʊzə) *n.* a baffling or insoluble question.

poseur (pəʊ'zɜː) *n.* a person who strikes an attitude or assumes a pose in order to impress others. [C19: from French, from *poser* to POSE[1]]

posey ('pəʊzɪ) *or* **poserish** ('pəʊzərɪʃ) *adj. Informal.* (of a place) for, characteristic of, or full of posers; affectedly trendy.

posh (pɒʃ) *Informal, chiefly Brit.* ~*adj.* **1.** smart, elegant, or fashionable; exclusive: *posh clothes.* **2.** upper-class or genteel. ~*adv.* **3.** in a manner associated with the upper class: *to talk posh.* [C19: often said to be an acronym of the phrase *port out, starboard home,* the most desirable location for a cabin in British ships sailing to and from the East, being the north-facing or shaded side; but more likely to be a development of obsolete slang *posh* a dandy]

posho ('pɔʃɔ) *n. E African.* **1.** corn meal. **2.** payment of workers in foodstuffs rather than money. [from Swahili]

posit ('pɒzɪt) *vb.* (*tr.*) **1.** to assume or put forward as fact or the factual basis for an argument; postulate. **2.** to put in position. ~*n.* **3.** a fact, idea, etc., that is posited; assumption. [C17: from Latin *pōnere* to place, position]

positif ('pɒsɪtɪf) *n.* (on older organs) a manual controlling soft stops. [from French: positive]

position (pə'zɪʃən) *n.* **1.** the place, situation, or location of a person or thing: *he took up a position to the rear.* **2.** the appropriate or customary location: *the telescope is in position for use.* **3.** the arrangement or disposition of the body or a part of the body: *the corpse was found in a sitting position.* **4.** the manner in which a person or thing is placed; arrangement. **5.** *Military.* an area or point occupied for tactical reasons. **6.** mental attitude; point of view; stand: *what's your position on this issue?* **7.** social status or standing, esp. high social standing. **8.** a post of employment; job. **9.** the act of positing a fact or viewpoint. **10.** something posited, such as an idea, proposition, etc. **11.** *Sport.* the part of a field or playing area where a player is placed or where he generally operates. **12.** *Music.* **a.** the vertical spacing or layout of the written notes in a chord. Chords arranged with the three upper voices close together are in **close position.** Chords whose notes are evenly or widely distributed are in **open position.** See also **root position. b.** one of the points on the fingerboard of a stringed instrument, determining where a string is to be stopped. **13.** (in classical prosody) **a.** the situation in which a short vowel may be regarded as long, that is, when it occurs before two or more consonants. **b. make position.** (of a consonant, either on its own or in combination with other consonants, such as x in Latin) to cause a short vowel to become metrically long when placed after it. **14.** *Finance.* the market commitment of a dealer in securities, currencies, or commodities: *a long position; a short position.* **15. in a position.** (foll. by an infinitive) able (to): *I'm not in a position to reveal these figures.* ~*vb.* (*tr.*) **16.** to put in the proper or appropriate place; locate. **17.** *Sport.* to place (oneself or another player) in a particular part of the field or playing area. **18.** *Rare.* to locate or ascertain the position of. [C15: from Late Latin *positiō* a positioning, affirmation, from *pōnere* to place, lay down] —**po'sitional** *adj.*

positional notation *n.* the method of denoting numbers by the use of a finite number of digits, each digit having its value multiplied by its place value, as in 936 = (9 × 100) + (3 × 10) + 6.

position audit *n. Commerce.* a systematic assessment of the current strengths and weaknesses of an organization as a prerequisite for future strategic planning.

position effect *n.* the effect on the phenotype of interacting genes when their relative positions on the chromosome are altered, as by inversion.

positive ('pɒzɪtɪv) *adj.* **1.** characterized by or expressing certainty or affirmation: *a positive answer.* **2.** composed of or possessing actual or specific qualities; real: *a positive benefit.* **3.** tending to emphasize what is good or laudable; constructive: *he takes a very positive attitude when correcting pupils' mistakes.* **4.** tending towards progress or improvement; moving in a beneficial direction. **5.** *Philosophy.* **a.** constructive rather than sceptical. **b.** (of a concept) denoting the presence rather than the absence of some property. **6.** independent of circumstances; absolute or unqualified. **7.** (*prenominal*) *Informal.* (intensifier): *a positive delight.* **8.** *Maths.* **a.** having a value greater than zero: *a positive number.* **b.** designating, consisting of, or graduated in one or more quantities greater than zero: *positive direction.* **9.** *Maths.* **a.** measured in a direction opposite to that regarded as negative. **b.** having the same magnitude as but opposite sense to an equivalent negative quantity. **10.** *Grammar.* denoting the usual form of an adjective as opposed to its comparative or superlative form. **11.** *Biology.* indicating movement or growth towards a particular stimulus. **12.** *Physics.* **a.** (of an electric charge) having an opposite polarity to the charge of an electron and the same polarity as the charge of a proton. **b.** (of a body, system, ion, etc.) having a positive electric charge; having a deficiency of electrons: *a positive ion.* **c.** (of a point in an electric circuit) having a higher electric potential than some other point with an assigned zero potential. **13.** short for **electropositive. 14.** (of a lens) capable of causing convergence of a parallel beam of light. **15.** *Med.* (of the results of an examination or test) indicating the existence or presence of a suspected disorder or pathogenic organism. **16.** *Med.* (of the effect of a drug or therapeutic regimen) beneficial or satisfactory. **17.** short for **Rh positive. 18.** (of a machine part) having precise motion with no hysteresis or backlash. **19.** *Chiefly U.S.* (of a government) directly involved in activities beyond the minimum maintenance of law and order, such as social welfare or the organization of scientific research. **20.** *Economics.* of or denoting an analysis that is free of ethical, political, or value judgments. **21.** *Astrology.* of, relating to, or governed by the group of signs of the zodiac that belong to the air and fire classifications, which are associated with a self-expressive spontaneous nature. ~*n.* **22.** something that is positive. **23.** *Maths.* a quantity greater than zero. **24.** *Photog.* a print or slide showing a photographic image whose colours or tones correspond to those of the original subject. **25.** *Grammar.* the positive degree of an adjective or adverb. **26.** a positive object, such as a terminal or plate in a voltaic cell. **27.** *Music.* **a.** Also called: **positive organ.** a medieval nonportable organ with one manual and no pedals. Compare **portative organ. b.** a variant spelling of **positif.** ~Compare **negative.** [C13: from Late Latin *positīvus* positive, agreed on an arbitrary basis, from *pōnere* to place] —'**positiveness** *n.*

positive discrimination *or* **action** *n.* the provision of special opportunities in employment, training, etc. for a disadvantaged group, such as women, ethnic minorities, etc. U.S. equivalent: **affirmative action.**

positive feedback *n.* See **feedback** (sense 1).

positively ('pɒzɪtɪvlɪ) *adv.* **1.** in a positive manner. **2.** (intensifier): *he disliked her; in fact, he positively hated her.* ~*sentence substitute.* **3.** unquestionably; absolutely.

positive polarity *n. Grammar.* the grammatical characteristic of a word or phrase, such as *delicious* or *rather,* that may normally only be used in a semantically or syntactically positive or affirmative context.

positive vetting *n.* the checking of a person's background, political affiliation, etc., to assess his suitability for a position that may involve national security.

positivism ('pɒzɪtɪˌvɪzəm) *n.* **1.** a strong form of empiricism, esp. as established in the philosophical system of Auguste Comte, that rejects metaphysics and theology as seeking knowledge beyond the scope of experience, and holds that experimental investigation and observation are the only sources of substantial knowledge. See also **logical positivism. 2.** Also called: **legal positivism.** the jurisprudential doctrine that the legitimacy of a law depends on its being enacted in proper form, rather than on its content. Compare **natural law** (sense 3). **3.** the quality of being definite, certain, etc. —'**positivist** *n., adj.* —ˌ**positiv'istic** *adj.* —ˌ**positiv'istically** *adv.*

positron ('pɒzɪˌtrɒn) *n. Physics.* the antiparticle of the electron, having the same mass but an equal and opposite charge. It is produced in certain decay processes and in pair production, annihilation occurring when it collides with an electron. [C20: from *posi(tive + elec)tron*]

positron emission tomography *n.* a technique for assessing brain activity and function by recording the emission of positrons when radioactively labelled glucose, introduced into the brain, is metabolized.

positronium (ˌpɒzɪ'trəʊnɪəm) *n. Physics.* a short-lived entity consisting of a positron and an electron bound together. It decays by annihilation to produce two or three photons. [C20: from POSITRON + -IUM]

posology (pə'sɒlədʒɪ) *n.* the branch of medicine concerned with the determination of appropriate doses of drugs or agents. [C19: from French *posologie,* from Greek *posos* how much] —**posological** (ˌpɒsə'lɒdʒɪkᵊl) *adj.*

poss (pɒs) *vb.* (*tr.*) to wash (clothes) by agitating them with a long rod, pole, etc. [of uncertain origin]

poss. *abbrev. for:* **1.** possession. **2.** possessive. **3.** possible. **4.** possibly.

posse ('pɒsɪ) *n.* **1.** *U.S.* short for **posse comitatus,** the able-bodied men of a district assembled together and forming a group upon whom the sheriff may call for assistance in maintaining law and order. **2.** *Law.* possibility (esp. in the phrase **in posse**). **3.** *Slang.* a Jamaican street gang in the U.S. **4.** *Informal.* a group of friends or associates. [C16: from Medieval Latin (n.): power, strength, from Latin (vb.): to be able, have power]

posse comitatus (ˌkɒmɪˈtɑːtəs) *n.* the formal legal term for **posse** (sense 1). [Medieval Latin: strength (manpower) of the county]

possess (pəˈzɛs) *vb. (tr.)* **1.** to have as one's property; own. **2.** to have as a quality, faculty, characteristic, etc.: *to possess good eyesight.* **3.** to have knowledge or mastery of: *to possess a little French.* **4.** to gain control over or dominate: *whatever possessed you to act so foolishly?* **5.** (foll. by *of*) to cause to be the owner or possessor: *I am possessed of the necessary information.* **6.** (often foll. by *with*) to cause to be influenced or dominated (by): *the news possessed him with anger.* **7.** to have sexual intercourse with. **8.** *Now rare.* to keep control over or maintain (oneself or one's feelings) in a certain state or condition: *possess yourself in patience until I tell you the news.* **9.** *Archaic.* to gain or seize. [C15: from Old French *possesser,* from Latin *possidēre* to own, occupy; related to Latin *sedēre* to sit] —**posˈsessor** *n.*

possessed (pəˈzɛst) *adj.* **1.** (foll. by *of*) owning or having. **2.** (*usually postpositive*) under the influence of a powerful force, such as a spirit or strong emotion. **3.** a less common word for **self-possessed.**

possession (pəˈzɛʃən) *n.* **1.** the act of possessing or state of being possessed: *in possession of the crown.* **2.** anything that is owned or possessed. **3.** (*pl.*) wealth or property. **4.** the state of being controlled or dominated by or as if by evil spirits. **5.** the physical control or occupancy of land, property, etc., whether or not accompanied by ownership: *to take possession of a house.* **6.** a territory subject to a foreign state or to a sovereign prince: *colonial possessions.* **7.** *Sport.* control of the ball, puck, etc., as exercised by a player or team: *he got possession in his own half.*

possession order *n.* (in Britain) a court order that entitles a landlord legally to evict a tenant or squatter and regain possession of the property.

possessive (pəˈzɛsɪv) *adj.* **1.** of or relating to possession or ownership. **2.** having or showing an excessive desire to possess, control, or dominate: *a possessive mother.* **3.** *Grammar.* **a.** another word for **genitive** (sense 1). **b.** denoting an inflected form of a noun or pronoun used to convey the idea of possession, association, etc., as *my* or *Harry's.* ~*n.* **4.** *Grammar.* **a.** the possessive case. **b.** a word or speech element in the possessive case. —**posˈsessively** *adv.* —**posˈsessiveness** *n.*

possessory (pəˈzɛsərɪ) *adj.* **1.** of, relating to, or having possession. **2.** *Law.* arising out of, depending upon, or concerned with possession: *a possessory title.*

posset (ˈpɒsɪt) *n.* a drink of hot milk curdled with ale, beer, etc., flavoured with spices, formerly used as a remedy for colds. [C15 *possoote,* of unknown origin]

possibility (ˌpɒsɪˈbɪlɪtɪ) *n., pl.* **-ties. 1.** the state or condition of being possible. **2.** anything that is possible. **3.** a competitor, candidate, etc., who has a moderately good chance of winning, being chosen, etc. **4.** (*often pl.*) a future prospect or potential: *my new house has great possibilities.*

possible (ˈpɒsɪbᵊl) *adj.* **1.** capable of existing, taking place, or proving true without contravention of any natural law. **2.** capable of being achieved: *it is not possible to finish in three weeks.* **3.** having potential or capabilities for favourable use or development: *the idea is a possible money-spinner.* **4.** that may or may not happen or have happened; feasible but less than probable: *it is possible that man will live on Mars.* **5.** *Logic.* (of a statement, formula, etc.) capable of being true under some interpretation, or in some circumstances. Usual symbol: *Mp* or ◇*p,* where *p* is the given expression. ~*n.* **6.** another word for **possibility** (sense 3). [C14: from Latin *possibilis* that may be, from *posse* to be able, have power]

possible world *n. Logic.* (in modal logic) a semantic device formalizing the notion of what the world might have been like. A statement is necessarily true if and only if it is true in every possible world.

possibly (ˈpɒsɪblɪ) *sentence substitute, adv.* **1. a.** perhaps or maybe. **b.** (*as sentence modifier*): *possibly he'll come.* ~*adv.* **2.** by any chance; at all: *he can't possibly come.*

possie *or* **pozzy** (ˈpɒzɪ) *n. Austral. and N.Z. informal.* a place; position: *if we're early for the film we'll get a good possie at the back.*

possum (ˈpɒsəm) *n.* **1.** an informal name for **opossum** (sense 1). **2.** an Austral. and N.Z. name for **phalanger. 3. play possum.** to pretend to be dead, ignorant, asleep, etc., in order to deceive an opponent.

post¹ (pəʊst) *n.* **1.** a length of wood, metal, etc., fixed upright in the ground to serve as a support, marker, point of attachment, etc. **2.** *Horse racing.* **a.** either of two upright poles marking the beginning (**starting post**) and end (**winning post**) of a racecourse. **b.** the finish of a horse race. **3.** any of the main upright supports of a piece of furniture, such as a four-poster bed. ~*vb. (tr.)* **4.** (sometimes foll. by *up*) to fasten or put up (a notice) in a public place. **5.** to announce by means of or as if by means of a poster: *to post banns.* **6.** to publish (a name) on a list. [Old English, from Latin *postis;* related to Old High German *first* ridgepole, Greek *pastas* colonnade]

post² (pəʊst) *n.* **1.** a position to which a person is appointed or elected; appointment; job. **2.** a position or station to which a person, such as a sentry, is assigned for duty. **3.** a permanent military establishment. **4.** *Brit.* either of two military bugle calls (**first post** and **last post**) ordering or giving notice of the time to retire for the night. **5.** See **trading post** (senses 1, 2). ~*vb.* **6.** (*tr.*) to assign to or station at a particular place or position. **7.** *Chiefly Brit.* to transfer to a different unit or ship on taking up a new appointment, etc. [C16: from French *poste,* from Italian *posto,* ultimately from Latin *pōnere* to place]

post³ (pəʊst) *n.* **1.** *Chiefly Brit.* letters, packages, etc., that are transported and delivered by the Post Office; mail. **2.** *Chiefly Brit.* a single collection or delivery of mail. **3.** *Brit.* an official system of mail delivery. **4.** (formerly) any of a series of stations furnishing relays of men and horses to deliver mail over a fixed route. **5.** a rider who carried mail between such stations. **6.** *Brit.* another word for **pillar box. 7.** *Brit.* short for **post office. 8.** a size of writing or printing paper, 15¼ by 19 inches or 16½ by 21 inches (**large post**). **9.** any of various book sizes, esp. 5¼ by 8¼ inches (**post octavo**) and 8¼ by 10¼ inches (**post quarto**). **10. by return of post.** *Brit.* by the next mail in the opposite direction. ~*vb.* **11.** (*tr.*) *Chiefly Brit.* to send by post. U.S. and Canadian word: **mail. 12.** (*tr.*) *Book-keeping.* **a.** to enter (an item) in a ledger. **b.** (often foll. by *up*) to compile or enter all paper items in (a ledger). **13.** (*tr.*) to inform of the latest news. **14.** (*intr.*) (of a rider) to rise from and reseat oneself in a saddle in time with the motions of a trotting horse; perform a rising trot. **15.** (*intr.*) (formerly) to travel with relays of post horses. **16.** *Archaic.* to travel or dispatch with speed; hasten. ~*adv.* **17.** with speed; rapidly. **18.** by means of post horses. [C16: via French from Italian *poste,* from Latin *posita* something placed, from *pōnere* to put, place]

POST *abbrev. for* point of sales terminal.

post- *prefix.* **1.** after in time or sequence; following; subsequent: *postgraduate.* **2.** behind; posterior to: *postorbital.* [from Latin, from *post* after, behind]

postage (ˈpəʊstɪdʒ) *n.* **a.** the charge for delivering a piece of mail. **b.** (*as modifier*): *postage charges.*

postage due stamp *n.* a stamp affixed by a Post Office to a letter, parcel, etc., indicating that insufficient or no postage has been prepaid and showing the amount to be paid by the addressee on delivery.

postage meter *n. Chiefly U.S. and Canadian.* a postal franking machine. Also called: **postal meter.**

postage stamp *n.* **1.** a printed paper label with a gummed back for attaching to mail as an official indication that the required postage has been paid. **2.** a mark directly printed or embossed on an envelope, postcard, etc., serving the same function.

postal (ˈpəʊstᵊl) *adj.* of or relating to a Post Office or to the mail-delivery service. —ˈ**postally** *adv.*

postal card *n. U.S.* another term for **postcard.**

postal note *n. Austral. and N.Z.* the usual name for **postal order.**

postal order *n.* a written order for the payment of a sum of money, to a named payee, obtainable and payable at a post office.

post-and-rail fence *n.* a fence constructed of upright wooden posts with horizontal timber slotted through it.

post-and-rail tea *n. Austral. informal.* (in the 19th century) a coarse tea in which floating particles resembled a post-and-rail fence.

postaxial (pəʊstˈæksɪəl) *adj. Anatomy.* **1.** situated or occurring behind the axis of the body. **2.** of or relating to the posterior part of a vertebrate limb.

postbag (ˈpəʊstˌbæg) *n.* **1.** *Chiefly Brit.* another name for **mailbag. 2.** the mail received by a magazine, radio programme, public figure, etc.

post-bellum (ˈpəʊstˈbɛləm) *adj.* (*prenominal*) of or during the period after a war, esp. the American Civil War. [C19: Latin *post* after + *bellum* war]

postbox (ˈpəʊstˌbɒks) *n. Chiefly Brit.* a box into which mail is put for collection by the postal service. Also called: **letter box.**

postboy (ˈpəʊstˌbɔɪ) *n.* **1.** a man or boy who brings the post round to offices. **2.** another name for **postilion.**

postbus (ˈpəʊstˌbʌs) *n.* (in Britain, esp. in rural districts) a vehicle carrying the mail that also carries passengers.

post captain *n. History.* (formerly) a naval officer holding a commission as a captain, as distinct from an officer with the courtesy title of captain.

postcard (ˈpəʊstˌkɑːd) *n.* a card, often bearing a photograph, picture, etc., on one side, (**picture postcard**), for sending a message by post without an envelope. Also called (U.S.): **postal card.**

postcava (pəʊstˈkɑːvə, -ˈkeɪvə) *n. Anatomy.* the inferior vena cava. [C19: New Latin; see POST-, VENA CAVA] —**postˈcaval** *adj.*

post chaise *n.* a closed four-wheeled horse-drawn coach used as a rapid means for transporting mail and passengers in the 18th and 19th centuries. [C18: from POST³ + CHAISE]

postcode (ˈpəʊstˌkəʊd) *n. Brit.* a code of letters and digits used as part of a postal address to aid the sorting of mail. Also called: **postal code.** U.S. equivalent: **zip code.**

postˈanal *adj.*
ˌ**post-Aristoˈtelian** *adj.*
ˌ**post-Auˈgustan** *adj.*
post-ˈCambrian *adj.*
ˌ**post-Carbonˈiferous** *adj.*
ˌ**post-Caroˈlingian** *adj.*
ˌ**post-Carˈtesian** *adj.*
postˈclassical *adj.*

post-cyclic *adj. Transformational grammar.* denoting rules that apply only after the transformations of a whole cycle. Compare **cyclic** (sense 6), **last-cyclic.**

postdate (pəʊst'deɪt) *vb. (tr.)* **1.** to write a future date on (a document), as on a cheque to prevent it being paid until then. **2.** to assign a date to (an event, period, etc.) that is later than its previously assigned date of occurrence. **3.** to be or occur at a later date than.

postdiluvian (ˌpəʊstdɪ'lu:vɪən, -daɪ-) *adj. also* **postdiluvial. 1.** existing or occurring after the biblical Flood. ~*n.* **2.** a person or thing existing after the biblical Flood. [C17: from POST- + *diluvian,* from Latin *diluvium* deluge, flood]

postdoctoral (pəʊst'dɒktərəl) *adj.* of, relating to, or designating studies, research, or professional work above the level of a doctorate.

poster ('pəʊstə) *n.* **1.** a large printed picture, used for decoration. **2.** a placard or bill posted in a public place as an advertisement.

poste restante ('pəʊst rɪ'stænt; *French* pɔst rɛstɑ̃t) *n.* **1.** (not in the U.S. and Canada) an address on mail indicating that it should be kept at a specified post office until collected by the addressee. **2.** the mail-delivery service or post-office department that handles mail having this address. ~U.S. and Canadian equivalent: **general delivery.** [French, literally: mail remaining]

posterior (pɒ'stɪərɪə) *adj.* **1.** situated at the back of or behind something. **2.** coming after or following another in a series. **3.** coming after in time. **4.** *Zoology.* (of lower animals) of or near the hind end. **5.** *Botany.* (of a flower) situated nearest to the main stem. **6.** *Anatomy.* dorsal or towards the spine. ~Compare **anterior.** ~*n.* **7.** the buttocks; rump. **8.** *Statistics.* a posterior probability. [C16: from Latin: latter, from *posterus* coming next, from *post* after] —**pos'teriorly** *adv.*

posterior probability *n. Statistics.* the probability assigned to some parameter or to an event on the basis of its observed frequency in a sample, and calculated from a prior probability by Bayes' theorem. Compare **prior probability.** See also **empirical** (sense 5).

posterity (pɒ'stɛrɪtɪ) *n.* **1.** future or succeeding generations. **2.** all of one's descendants. [C14: from French *postérité,* from Latin *posteritās* future generations, from *posterus* coming after, from *post* after]

postern ('pɒstən) *n.* **1.** a back door or gate, esp. one that is for private use. ~*adj.* **2.** situated at the rear or the side. [C13: from Old French *posterne,* from Late Latin *posterula (jānua)* a back (entrance), from *posterus* coming behind; see POSTERIOR, POSTERITY]

poster paint *or* **colour** *n.* a gum-based opaque watercolour paint used for writing posters, etc.

post exchange *n. U.S.* a government-subsidized shop operated mainly for military personnel. Abbrev.: **PX.**

postexilian (ˌpəʊstɪg'zɪlɪən) *or* **postexilic** *adj. Old Testament.* existing or occurring after the Babylonian exile of the Jews (587–539 B.C.).

postfeminist (pəʊst'fɛmɪnɪst) *adj.* **1.** resulting from or including the beliefs and ideas of feminism. **2.** differing from or showing moderation of these beliefs and ideas. ~*n.* **3.** a person who believes in or advocates any of the ideas that have developed from the feminist movement.

postfix *vb.* (pəʊst'fɪks). **1.** *(tr.)* to add or append at the end of something; suffix. ~*n.* ('pəʊstˌfɪks). **2.** a less common word for **suffix.**

post-Fordism (ˌpəʊst'fɔ:dɪzəm) *n.* the idea that modern industrial production has moved away from mass production in huge factories, as pioneered by U.S. car manufacturer Henry Ford (1863–1947), towards specialized markets based on small flexible manufacturing units. —ˌ**post-'Fordist** *adj.*

post-free *adv., adj.* **1.** *Brit.* with the postage prepaid; post-paid. **2.** free of postal charge.

postglacial (pəʊst'gleɪsɪəl) *adj.* formed or occurring after a glacial period, esp. after the Pleistocene epoch.

postgraduate (pəʊst'grædjʊɪt) *n.* **1.** a student who has obtained a degree from a university, etc., and is pursuing studies for a more advanced qualification. **2.** *(modifier)* of or relating to such a student or to his studies. ~Also (U.S. and Canadian): **graduate.**

posthaste ('pəʊst'heɪst) *adv.* **1.** with great haste; as fast as possible. ~*n.* **2.** *Archaic.* great haste.

post hoc ('pəʊst 'hɒk) *n. Logic.* the fallacy of assuming that temporal succession is evidence of causal relation. [from Latin, short for *Post hoc ergo propter hoc* after this, therefore on account of this]

post horn *n.* a simple valveless natural horn consisting of a long tube of brass or copper, either straight or coiled; formerly often used to announce the arrival of a mailcoach.

post horse *n.* (formerly) a horse kept at an inn or post house for use by postriders or for hire to travellers.

post house *n.* (formerly) a house or inn where horses were kept for postriders or for hire to travellers.

posthumous ('pɒstjʊməs) *adj.* **1.** happening or continuing after one's death. **2.** (of a book, etc.) published after the author's death. **3.** (of a child) born after the father's death. [C17: from Latin *postumus* the last, but modified as though from Latin *post* after + *humus* earth, that is, after the burial] —'**posthumously** *adv.*

posthypnotic suggestion (ˌpəʊsthɪp'nɒtɪk) *n.* a suggestion made to the subject while in a hypnotic trance, to be acted upon at some time after emerging from the trance.

postiche (pɒ'sti:ʃ) *adj.* **1.** (of architectural ornament) inappropriately applied; sham. **2.** false or artificial; spurious. ~*n.* **3.** another term for **hairpiece** (sense 2). **4.** an imitation, counterfeit, or substitute. **5.** anything that is false; sham or pretence. [C19: from French, from Italian *apposticcio* (n.), from Late Latin *appositīcius* (adj.); see APPOSITE]

posticous (pɒ'sti:kəs, -'staɪ-) *or* **postical** *adj.* (of the position of plant parts) behind another part; posterior. [C19: from Latin *postīcus* that is behind, from *post* after]

postie ('pəʊstɪ) *n. Scot., Austral., and N.Z. informal.* a postman.

postil ('pɒstɪl) *n.* **1.** a commentary or marginal note, as in a Bible. **2.** a homily or collection of homilies. ~*vb.* **-tils, -tiling, -tiled** *or* **-tils, -tilling, -tilled. 3.** *Obsolete.* to annotate (a biblical passage). [C15 *(postille):* from Old French *postille* from Medieval Latin *postilla,* perhaps from *post illa (verba textus),* after these words in the text, often the opening phrase of such an annotation]

postilion *or* **postillion** (pɒ'stɪljən) *n.* a person who rides the near horse of the leaders in order to guide a team of horses drawing a coach. [C16: from French *postillon,* from Italian *postiglione,* from *posta* POST[3]]

postimpressionism (ˌpəʊstɪm'prɛʃəˌnɪzəm) *n.* a movement in painting in France at the end of the 19th century, begun by Cézanne and exemplified by Gauguin, Van Gogh, and Matisse, which rejected the naturalism and momentary effects of impressionism but adapted its use of pure colour to paint subjects with greater subjective emotion. —ˌ**postim'pressionist** *n., adj.* —ˌ**postimˌpression'istic** *adj.*

postindustrial (ˌpəʊstɪn'dʌstrɪəl) *adj.* characteristic of, relating to, or denoting work or a society that is no longer based on heavy industry.

posting[1] ('pəʊstɪŋ) *n.* a wrestling attack in which the opponent is hurled at the post in one of the corners of the ring.

posting[2] ('pəʊstɪŋ) *n.* an appointment to a position or post.

postliminy (pəʊst'lɪmɪnɪ) *or* **postliminium** (ˌpəʊstlɪ'mɪnɪəm) *n., pl.* **-inies** *or* **-ia** (-ɪə). *International law.* the right by which persons and property seized in war are restored to their former status on recovery. [C19: (in this sense): from Latin *postlīminium* a return behind one's threshold, from *līmen* threshold]

postlude ('pəʊstlu:d) *n.* **1.** *Music.* a final or concluding piece or movement. **2.** a voluntary played at the end of a Church service. [C19: from POST- + *-lude,* from Latin *lūdus* game; compare PRELUDE]

postman ('pəʊstmən) *or (fem.)* **postwoman** *n., pl.* **-men** *or* **-women.** a person who carries and delivers mail as a profession.

postman's knock *n.* a children's party game in which a kiss is exchanged for a pretend letter.

postmark ('pəʊstˌmɑ:k) *n.* **1.** any mark stamped on mail by postal officials, such as a simple obliteration, date mark, or indication of route. See also **cancellation.** ~*vb.* **2.** *(tr.)* to put such a mark on mail.

postmaster ('pəʊstˌmɑ:stə) *or (fem.)* **postmistress** *n.* an official in charge of a local post office.

postmaster general *n., pl.* **postmasters general.** the executive head of the postal service in certain countries.

postmeridian (ˌpəʊstmə'rɪdɪən) *adj.* after noon; in the afternoon or evening. [C17: from Latin *postmerīdiānus* in the afternoon; see POST-, MERIDIAN]

post meridiem ('pəʊst mə'rɪdɪəm) the full form of **p.m.** [C17: Latin: after noon]

post mill *n.* a windmill built round a central post on which the whole mill can be turned so that the sails catch the wind.

postmillennial (ˌpəʊstmɪ'lɛnɪəl) *adj.* existing or taking place after the millennium.

postmillennialism (ˌpəʊstmɪ'lɛnɪəˌlɪzəm) *n.* the doctrine or belief that the Second Coming of Christ will be preceded by the millennium. —ˌ**postmil'lennialist** *n.*

postmodernism (pəʊst'mɒdəˌnɪzəm) *n.* (in the arts, architecture, etc.) a style and school of thought that rejects the dogma and practices of any form of modernism; in architecture it contrasts with international modernism and features elements from several periods, esp. the Classical, often with ironic use of decoration. —**post'modernist** *n., adj.*

post'coital *adj.*
ˌ**postconso'nantal** *adj.*
ˌ**postconva'lescent** *adj.*
ˌ**post-Co'pernican** *adj.*
ˌ**post-Dar'winian** *adj.*
ˌ**postdeˌvelop'mental** *adj.*
ˌ**post-De'vonian** *adj.*
ˌ**postdiag'nostic** *adj.*
ˌ**postdi'gestive** *adj.*
ˌ**poste'lection** *adj.*
post-'Eocene *adj.*
ˌ**posthyp'notic** *adj.*
ˌ**post-Ju'rassic** *adj.*
post-'Kantian *adj.*
post-'Keynesian *adj.*
post-'Marxian *adj.*
ˌ**postmeno'pausal** *adj.*
post'menstrual *adj.*
ˌ**post-Meso'zoic** *adj.*
post-'Mioˌcene *adj.*

postmortem (pəʊst'mɔːtəm) *adj.* **1.** (*prenominal*) occurring after death. ~*n.* **2.** analysis or study of a recently completed event: *a postmortem on a game of chess.* **3.** See **postmortem examination.** [C18: from Latin, literally: after death]

postmortem examination *n.* dissection and examination of a dead body to determine the cause of death. Also called: **autopsy, necropsy.**

postnasal drip (pəʊst'neɪzᵊl) *n. Med.* a mucus secretion from the rear part of the nasal cavity into the nasopharynx, usually as the result of a cold or an allergy.

post-obit (pəʊst'əʊbɪt, -'ɒbɪt) *Chiefly law.* ~*n.* **1.** Also called: **post-obit bond.** a bond given by a borrower, payable after the death of a specified person, esp. one given to a moneylender by an expectant heir promising to repay when his interest falls into possession. ~*adj.* **2.** taking effect after death. [C18: from Latin *post obitum* after death]

post office *n.* a building or room where postage stamps are sold and other postal business is conducted.

Post Office *n.* a government department or authority in many countries responsible for postal services and often telecommunications.

post office box *n.* a private numbered place in a post office, in which letters received are kept until called for.

postoperative (pəʊst'ɒpərətɪv, -'ɒprətɪv) *adj.* of, relating to, or occurring in the period following a surgical operation. —**post'operatively** *adv.*

postorbital (pəʊst'ɔːbɪtᵊl) *adj. Anatomy.* situated behind the eye or the eye socket.

post-paid *adv., adj.* with the postage prepaid.

postpartum (pəʊst'pɑːtəm) *adj. Med.* following childbirth. [Latin: after the act of giving birth]

postpone (pəʊst'pəʊn, pə'spəʊn) *vb.* (*tr.*) **1.** to put off or delay until a future time. **2.** to put behind in order of importance; defer. [C16: from Latin *postpōnere* to put after, neglect, from POST- + *ponere* to place] —**post'ponable** *adj.* —**post'ponement** *n.* —**post'poner** *n.*

postposition (ˌpəʊstpə'zɪʃən) *n.* **1.** placement of a modifier or other speech element after the word that it modifies or to which it is syntactically related. **2.** a word or speech element so placed. —ˌ**postpo'sitional** *adj.* —ˌ**postpo'sitionally** *adv.*

postpositive (pəʊst'pɒzɪtɪv) *adj.* **1.** (of an adjective or other modifier) placed after the word modified, either immediately after, as in *two men abreast,* or as part of a complement, as in *those men are bad.* ~*n.* **2.** a postpositive modifier. —**post'positively** *adv.*

postproduction (ˌpəʊstprə'dʌkʃən) *n.* **a.** the work on a film or a television programme, such as editing, dubbing, etc., that takes place after shooting or videotaping is completed. **b.** (*as modifier*): *postproduction costs.*

postrider ('pəʊstˌraɪdə) *n.* (formerly) a person who delivered post on horseback.

post road *n.* a road or route over which post is carried and along which post houses were formerly sited.

postscript ('pəʊsˌskrɪpt, 'pəʊst-) *n.* **1.** a message added at the end of a letter, after the signature. **2.** any supplement, as to a document or book. [C16: from Late Latin *postscribere* to write after, from POST- + *scribere* to write]

post town *n.* a town having a main Post Office branch.

post-traumatic stress disorder *n.* a psychological condition, characterized by anxiety, withdrawal, and a proneness to physical illness, that may follow a traumatic experience.

postulant ('pɒstjʊlənt) *n.* a person who makes a request or application, esp. a candidate for admission to a religious order. [C18: from Latin *postulāns* asking, from *postulāre* to ask, demand] —'**postulancy** *or* '**postulantˌship** *n.*

postulate *vb.* ('pɒstjʊˌleɪt). (*tr.; may take a clause as object*) **1.** to assume to be true or existent; take for granted. **2.** to ask, demand, or claim. **3.** to nominate (a person) to a post or office subject to approval by a higher authority. ~*n.* ('pɒstjʊlɪt). **4.** something taken as self-evident or assumed as the basis of an argument. **5.** a necessary condition or prerequisite. **6.** a fundamental principle. **7.** *Logic, maths.* an unproved and indemonstrable statement that should be taken for granted: used as an initial premise or underlying hypothesis in a process of reasoning. [C16: from Latin *postulāre* to ask for, require; related to *pōscere* to request] —ˌ**postu'lation** *n.*

postulator ('pɒstjʊˌleɪtə) *n. R.C. Church.* a person, usually a priest, deputed to prepare and present a plea for the beatification or canonization of some deceased person.

posture ('pɒstʃə) *n.* **1.** a position or attitude of the limbs or body. **2.** a characteristic manner of bearing the body; carriage: *to have good posture.* **3.** the disposition of the parts of a visible object. **4.** a mental attitude or frame of mind. **5.** a state, situation, or condition. **6.** a false or affected attitude; pose. ~*vb.* **7.** to assume or cause to assume a bodily position or attitude. **8.** (*intr.*) to assume an affected or unnatural bodily or mental posture; pose. [C17: via French from Italian *postura,* from Latin *positūra,* from *pōnere* to place] —'**postural** *adj.* —'**posturer** *n.*

posturize *or* **posturise** ('pɒstʃəˌraɪz) *vb.* a less common word for **posture** (senses 7, 8).

postviral syndrome (ˌpəʊst'vaɪrəl) *n.* another name for **myalgic encephalomyelitis.** Abbrev.: **PVS.**

postvocalic (ˌpəʊstvə'kælɪk) *adj. Phonetics.* following a vowel.

posy ('pəʊzɪ) *n., pl.* **-sies.** **1.** a small bunch of flowers or a single flower; nosegay. **2.** *Archaic.* a brief motto or inscription, esp. one on a trinket or a ring. [C16: variant of POESY]

pot[1] (pɒt) *n.* **1.** a container made of earthenware, glass, or similar material; usually round and deep, often having a handle and lid, used for cooking and other domestic purposes. **2.** short for **flowerpot, teapot.** **3.** the amount that a pot will hold; potful. **4.** a chamber pot, esp. a small one designed for a baby or toddler. **5.** a handmade piece of pottery. **6.** a large mug or tankard, as for beer. **7.** *Austral.* any of various measures used for serving beer. **8.** *Informal.* a cup or trophy, esp. of silver, awarded as a prize in a competition. **9.** the money or stakes in the pool in gambling games, esp. poker. **10.** (*often pl.*) *Informal.* a large amount, esp. of money. **11.** a wicker trap for catching fish, esp. crustaceans: *a lobster pot.* **12.** *Billiards, etc.* a shot by which a ball is pocketed. **13.** *Chiefly Brit.* short for **chimneypot.** **14.** *U.S. informal.* a joint fund created by a group of individuals or enterprises and drawn upon by them for specified purposes. **15.** *Hunting.* See **pot shot.** **16.** See **potbelly.** **17. go to pot.** to go to ruin; deteriorate. ~*vb.* **pots, potting, potted.** (*mainly tr.*) **18.** to set (a plant) in a flowerpot to grow. **19.** to put or preserve (goods, meat, etc.) in a pot. **20.** to cook (food) in a pot. **21.** to shoot (game) for food rather than for sport. **22.** to shoot (game birds or animals) while they are on the ground or immobile rather than flying or running. **23.** (*also intr.*) to shoot casually or without careful aim at (an animal, etc.). **24.** to sit (a baby or toddler) on a chamber pot. **25.** (*also intr.*) to shape clay as a potter. **26.** *Billiards, etc.* to pocket (a ball). **27.** *Informal.* to capture or win; secure. ~See also **pot on.** [Late Old English *pott,* from Medieval Latin *pottus* (unattested), perhaps from Latin *pōtus* a drink; compare Middle Low German *pot,* Old Norse *pottr*]

pot[2] (pɒt) *n.* **a.** *Scot. and northern English dialect.* a deep hole or pothole. **b.** (*cap. when part of a name*): *Pen-y-Ghent Pot.* [C14: perhaps identical with POT[1] but possibly of Scandinavian origin; compare Swedish dialect *putt* water hole, pit]

pot[3] (pɒt) *n. Slang.* cannabis used as a drug in any form, such as leaves (marijuana or hemp) or resin (hashish). [C20: perhaps shortened from Mexican Indian *potiguaya*]

pot[4] (pɒt) *n. Informal.* short for **potentiometer.**

pot. *abbrev. for* potential.

potable ('pəʊtəbᵊl) *adj.* **1.** a less common word for **drinkable.** ~*n.* **2.** something fit to drink; a beverage. [C16: from Late Latin *pōtābilis* drinkable, from Latin *pōtāre* to drink] —ˌ**pota'bility** *n.*

potae ('pɔtaɪ) *n. N.Z.* a hat. [Maori]

potage *French.* (pɔtaʒ; *English* pəʊ'tɑːʒ) *n.* any thick soup. [C16: from Old French; see POTTAGE]

potamic (pə'tæmɪk) *adj.* of or relating to rivers. [C19: from Greek *potamos* river]

potamology (ˌpɒtə'mɒlədʒɪ) *n.* the scientific study of rivers. [C19: from Greek *potamos* river + -LOGY]

potash ('pɒtˌæʃ) *n.* **1.** another name for **potassium carbonate,** esp. the form obtained by leaching wood ash. **2.** another name for **potassium hydroxide.** **3.** potassium chemically combined in certain compounds: *chloride of potash.* [C17 *pot ashes,* translation of obsolete Dutch *potaschen;* so called because originally obtained by evaporating the lye of wood ashes in pots]

potash alum *n.* the full name for **alum** (sense 1).

potassium (pə'tæsɪəm) *n.* a light silvery element of the alkali metal group that is highly reactive and rapidly oxidizes in air; occurs principally in carnallite and sylvite. It is used when alloyed with sodium as a cooling medium in nuclear reactors and its compounds are widely used, esp. in fertilizers. Symbol: K; atomic no.: 19; atomic wt.: 39.102; valency: 1; relative density: 0.86; melting pt.: 63.65°C; boiling pt.: 774°C. [C19: New Latin *potassa* potash] —**po'tassic** *adj.*

potassium-argon dating *n.* a technique for determining the age of minerals based on the occurrence in natural potassium of a small fixed amount of radioisotope ^{40}K that decays to the stable argon isotope ^{40}Ar with a half-life of 1.28×10^9 years. Measurement of the ratio of these isotopes thus gives the age of the mineral. Compare **radiocarbon dating, rubidium-strontium dating.**

ˌ**post-Mo'saic** *adj.*
ˌ**post-Myce'naean** *adj.*
ˌ**post-Naˌpole'onic** *adj.*
post'nasal *adj.*
post'natal *adj.*
ˌ**post-New'tonian** *adj.*
post'nuptial *adj.*
post-'Oligoˌcene *adj.*
post'oral *adj.*
ˌ**post-Ordo'vician** *adj.*
ˌ**post-Palaeo'zoic** *adj.*
post-'Pauline *adj.*
post-'Permian *adj.*
ˌ**postpi'tuitary** *adj.*
post-'Pleistoˌcene *adj.*
post-'Plioˌcene *adj.*
post'prandial *adj.*
ˌ**post-Refor'mation** *adj.*
ˌ**post-Revo'lutionary** *adj.*
post'season *adj.*
post'seasonal *adj.*
ˌ**post-Si'lurian** *adj.*
ˌ**post-So'cratic** *adj.*
ˌ**post-Tal'mudic** *adj.*
post-'Tertiary *adj.*
ˌ**post-Tri'assic** *adj.*
post-'Vedic *adj.*
ˌ**post-Vic'torian** *adj.*
post'war *adj.*

potassium bitartrate *n.* another name (not in technical usage) for **potassium hydrogen tartrate.**
potassium bromide *n.* a white crystalline soluble substance with a bitter saline taste used in making photographic papers and plates and in medicine as a sedative. Formula: KBr.
potassium carbonate *n.* a white odourless substance used in making glass and soft soap and as an alkaline cleansing agent. Formula: K_2CO_3.
potassium chlorate *n.* a white crystalline soluble substance used in fireworks, matches, and explosives, and as a disinfectant and bleaching agent. Formula: $KClO_3$.
potassium cyanide *n.* a white poisonous granular soluble solid substance used in photography and in extracting gold from its ores. Formula: KCN.
potassium dichromate *n.* an orange-red crystalline soluble solid substance that is a good oxidizing agent and is used in making chrome pigments and as a bleaching agent. Formula: $K_2Cr_2O_7$.
potassium ferricyanide *n.* a bright red soluble crystalline substance used in making dyes, pigments, and light-sensitive paper. Formula: $K_3Fe(CN)_6$. Also called: **red prussiate of potash.**
potassium ferrocyanide *n.* a yellow soluble crystalline compound used in case-hardening steel and making dyes and pigments. Formula: $K_4Fe(CN)_6$. Also called: **yellow prussiate of potash.**
potassium hydrogen tartrate *n.* a colourless or white soluble crystalline salt used in baking powders, soldering fluxes, and laxatives. Formula: $KHC_4H_4O_6$. Also called (not in technical usage): **potassium bitartrate, cream of tartar.**
potassium hydroxide *n.* a white deliquescent alkaline solid used in the manufacture of soap, liquid shampoos, and detergents. Formula: KOH. Also called: **caustic potash.** See also **lye.**
potassium nitrate *n.* a colourless or white crystalline compound used in gunpowders, pyrotechnics, fertilizers, and as a preservative for foods, esp. as a curing salt for ham, sausages, etc. (**E252**). Formula: KNO_3. Also called: **saltpetre, nitre.**
potassium permanganate *n.* a dark purple poisonous odourless soluble crystalline solid, used as a bleach, disinfectant, and antiseptic. Formula: $KMnO_4$. Systematic name: **potassium manganate(V).**
potassium sulphate *n.* a soluble substance usually obtained as colourless crystals of the decahydrate: used in making glass and as a fertilizer. Formula: K_2SO_4.
potation (pəʊˈteɪʃən) *n.* **1.** the act of drinking. **2.** a drink or draught, esp. of alcoholic drink. [C15: from Latin *pōtātiō* a drinking, from *pōtāre* to drink]
potato (pəˈteɪtəʊ) *n., pl.* **-toes. 1.** Also called: **Irish potato, white potato. a.** a solanaceous plant, *Solanum tuberosum,* of South America: widely cultivated for its edible tubers. **b.** the starchy oval tuber of this plant, which has a brown or red skin and is cooked and eaten as a vegetable. **2.** any of various similar plants, esp. the sweet potato. **3. hot potato.** *Slang.* a delicate or awkward matter. [C16: from Spanish *patata* white potato, from Taino *batata* sweet potato]
potato beetle *n.* another name for the **Colorado beetle.**
potato blight *n.* a devastating disease of potatoes produced by the fungus *Phytophthora infestaris* and the cause of the Irish potato famine of the mid 19th century.
potato chip *n.* **1.** (*usually pl.*) another name for **chip** (sense 4). **2.** (*usually pl.*) the U.S. and Canadian term for **crisp** (sense 10).
potato crisp *n.* (*usually pl.*) another name for **crisp** (sense 10).
potatory (ˈpəʊtətərɪ, -trɪ) *adj. Rare.* of, relating to, or given to drinking. [C19: from Late Latin *pōtātōrius* concerning drinking, from Latin *pōtāre* to drink]
pot-au-feu (*French* pɔtofø) *n.* **1.** a traditional French stew of beef and vegetables. **2.** the large earthenware casserole in which this is cooked. [literally: pot on the fire]
potbelly (ˈpɒtˌbɛlɪ) *n., pl.* **-lies. 1.** a protruding or distended belly. **2.** a person having such a belly. **3.** *U.S. and Canadian.* a small bulbous stove in which wood or coal is burned. —ˈ**potˌbellied** *adj.*
potboiler (ˈpɒtˌbɔɪlə) *n. Informal.* a literary or artistic work of little merit produced quickly in order to make money.
pot-bound *adj.* (of a pot plant) having grown to fill all the available root space and therefore lacking room for continued growth.
potboy (ˈpɒtˌbɔɪ) *or* **potman** (ˈpɒtmən) *n., pl.* **-boys** *or* **-men.** *Chiefly Brit.* (esp. formerly) a youth or man employed at a public house to serve beer, etc.
potch (pɒtʃ) *n. Chiefly Austral., slang.* inferior quality opal used in jewellery for mounting precious opals. [C20: of uncertain origin]
pot cheese *n. U.S.* a type of coarse dry cottage cheese.
poteen *or* **poitín** (ˈpɒtiːn) *n.* (in Ireland) illicit spirit, often distilled from potatoes. [C19: from Irish *poitín* little pot, from *pota* pot]
potency (ˈpəʊtᵊnsɪ) *or* **potence** *n., pl.* **-tencies** *or* **-tences. 1.** the state or quality of being potent. **2.** latent or inherent capacity for growth or development. [C16: from Latin *potentia* power, from *posse* to be able]
potent[1] (ˈpəʊtᵊnt) *adj.* **1.** possessing great strength; powerful. **2.** (of arguments, etc.) persuasive or forceful. **3.** influential or authoritative. **4.** tending to produce violent physical or chemical effects: *a potent poison.* **5.** (of a male) capable of having sexual intercourse. [C15: from Latin *potēns* able, from *posse* to be able] —ˈ**potently** *adv.* —ˈ**potentness** *n.*
potent[2] (ˈpəʊtᵊnt) *adj. Heraldry.* (of a cross) having flat bars across the ends of the arms. [C17: from obsolete *potent* a crutch, from Latin *potentia* power]
potentate (ˈpəʊtᵊnˌteɪt) *n.* a man who possesses great power or authority, esp. a ruler or monarch. [C14: from Late Latin *potentātus* ruler, from Latin: rule, command, from *potens* powerful, from *posse* to be able]
potential (pəˈtɛnʃəl) *adj.* **1. a.** possible but not yet actual. **b.** (*prenominal*) capable of being or becoming but not yet in existence; latent. **2.** *Grammar.* (of a verb or form of a verb) expressing possibility, as English *may* and *might.* **3.** an archaic word for **potent**[1]. ~*n.* **4.** latent but unrealized ability or capacity: *Jones has great potential as a sales manager.* **5.** *Grammar.* a potential verb or verb form. **6.** short for **electric potential.** [C14: from Old French *potencial,* from Late Latin *potentiālis,* from Latin *potentia* power] —**poˈtentially** *adv.*
potential difference *n.* the difference in electric potential between two points in an electric field; the work that has to be done in transferring unit positive charge from one point to the other, measured in volts. Abbrev.: **pd.** Symbol: $U, \Delta V,$ or $\Delta\phi$ Compare **electromotive force.**
potential divider *n.* a tapped or variable resistor or a chain of fixed resistors in series, connected across a source of voltage and used to obtain a desired fraction of the total voltage. Also called: **voltage divider.**
potential energy *n.* the energy of a body or system as a result of its position in an electric, magnetic, or gravitational field. It is measured in joules (SI units), electronvolts, ergs, etc. Symbol: $E_p, V, U,$ or ϕ Abbrev.: **PE.**
potentiality (pəˌtɛnʃɪˈælɪtɪ) *n., pl.* **-ties. 1.** latent or inherent capacity or ability for growth, fulfilment, etc. **2.** a person or thing that possesses such a capacity.
potential well *n. Physics.* a localized region in a field of force in which the potential suddenly decreases.
potentiate (pəˈtɛnʃɪˌeɪt) *vb.* (*tr.*) **1.** to cause to be potent. **2.** *Med.* to increase (the individual action or effectiveness) of two drugs by administering them in combination with each other.
potentilla (ˌpəʊtᵊnˈtɪlə) *n.* any rosaceous plant or shrub of the N temperate genus *Potentilla,* having five-petalled flowers. See also **cinquefoil** (sense 1), **silverweed** (sense 1), **tormentil.** [C16: New Latin, from Medieval Latin: garden valerian, from Latin *potēns* powerful, POTENT[1]]
potentiometer (pəˌtɛnʃɪˈɒmɪtə) *n.* **1.** an instrument for determining a potential difference or electromotive force by measuring the fraction of it that balances a standard electromotive force. **2.** a device with three terminals, two of which are connected to a resistance wire and the third to a brush moving along the wire, so that a variable potential can be tapped off: used in electronic circuits, esp. as a volume control. Sometimes shortened to **pot.** —**poˌtentiˈometry** *n.*
potentiometric (pəˌtɛnʃɪəˈmɛtrɪk) *adj. Chem.* (of a titration) having the end point determined by a change in potential of an electrode immersed in the solution.
potful (ˈpɒtfʊl) *n.* the amount held by a pot.
pothead (ˈpɒtˌhɛd) *n. Slang.* a habitual user of cannabis.
pothecary (ˈpɒθɪkərɪ) *n., pl.* **-caries.** an archaic or Brit. dialect variant of **apothecary.**
potheen (ˈpɒtiːn, ˈpɒθiːn) *n.* a rare variant of **poteen.**
pother (ˈpɒðə) *n.* **1.** a commotion, fuss, or disturbance. **2.** a choking cloud of smoke, dust, etc. ~*vb.* **3.** to make or be troubled or upset. [C16: of unknown origin]
potherb (ˈpɒtˌhɜːb) *n.* any plant having leaves, flowers, stems, etc., that are used in cooking for seasoning and flavouring or are eaten as a vegetable.
pothole (ˈpɒtˌhəʊl) *n.* **1.** *Geography.* **a.** a deep hole in limestone areas resulting from action by running water. See also **sinkhole** (sense 1). **b.** a circular hole in the bed of a river produced by abrasion. **2.** a deep hole, esp. one produced in a road surface by wear or weathering.
potholing (ˈpɒtˌhəʊlɪŋ) *n. Brit.* a sport in which participants explore underground caves. —ˈ**potˌholer** *n.*
pothook (ˈpɒtˌhʊk) *n.* **1.** a curved or S-shaped hook used for suspending a pot over a fire. **2.** a long hook used for lifting hot pots, lids, etc. **3.** an S-shaped mark, often made by children when learning to write.
pothouse (ˈpɒtˌhaʊs) *n. Brit.* (formerly) a small tavern or pub.
pothunter (ˈpɒtˌhʌntə) *n.* **1.** a person who hunts for food or for profit without regard to the rules of sport. **2.** *Informal.* a person who enters competitions for the sole purpose of winning prizes. —ˈ**potˌhunting** *n., adj.*
potiche (pɒˈtiːʃ) *n., pl.* **-tiches** (-ˈtiːʃɪz, -ˈtiːʃ). a tall vase or jar, as of porcelain, with a round or polygonal body that narrows towards the neck and a detached lid or cover. [French, from *pot* pot; compare POTTAGE]
potion (ˈpəʊʃən) *n.* **1.** a drink, esp. of medicine, poison, or some supposedly magic beverage. **2.** a rare word for **beverage.** [C13: via Old French from Latin *pōtiō* a drink, especially a poisonous one, from *pōtāre* to drink]

potlatch ('pɒt,lætʃ) *n.* **1.** *Anthropol.* a competitive ceremonial activity among certain North American Indians, esp. the Kwakiutl, involving a lavish distribution of gifts and the destruction of property to emphasize the wealth and status of the chief or clan. **2.** *U.S. and Canadian informal.* a wild party or revel. [C19: from Chinook, from Nootka *patshatl* a giving, present]

pot liquor *n. Chiefly U.S.* the broth in which meat, esp. pork or bacon, and vegetables have been cooked.

potluck ('pɒt'lʌk) *n. Informal.* **1.** whatever food happens to be available without special preparation. **2.** whatever is available (esp. in the phrase **take potluck**).

potman ('pɒtmən) *n., pl.* **-men.** *Chiefly Brit.* another word for **potboy.**

pot marigold *n.* a Central European and Mediterranean plant, *Calendula officinalis,* grown for its rayed orange-and-yellow showy flowers, the petals of which were formerly used to colour food: family *Compositae* (composites). See also **calendula.**

potometer (pə,tɒmɪtə) *n.* an apparatus that measures the rate of water uptake by a plant or plant part. [from Latin *pōtāre* to drink + -METER]

pot on *vb.* (*tr., adv.*) to transfer (a plant) to a larger flowerpot.

potoroo (,pɒtə'ruː) *n.* another name for **kangaroo rat.** [from a native Australian language]

potpie ('pɒt,paɪ) *n.* a meat and vegetable stew with a pie crust on top.

pot plant *n.* a plant grown in a flowerpot, esp. indoors.

potpourri (,pəʊ'pʊərɪ) *n., pl.* **-ris.** **1.** a collection of mixed flower petals dried and preserved in a pot to scent the air. **2.** a collection of unrelated or disparate items; miscellany. **3.** a medley of popular tunes. **4.** a stew of meat and vegetables. [C18: from French, literally: rotten pot, translation of Spanish *olla podrida* miscellany]

pot roast *n.* meat, esp. beef, that is browned and cooked slowly in a covered pot with very little water, often with vegetables added.

potsherd ('pɒt,ʃɜːd) *or* **potshard** ('pɒt,ʃɑːd) *n.* a broken fragment of pottery. [C14: from POT[1] + *schoord* piece of broken crockery; see SHARD]

pot shot *n.* **1.** a chance shot taken casually, hastily, or without careful aim. **2.** a shot fired to kill game in disregard of the rules of sport. **3.** a shot fired at quarry within easy range, often from an ambush.

pot still *n.* a type of still used in distilling whisky in which heat is applied directly to the pot in which the wash is contained.

potstone ('pɒt,stəʊn) *n.* an impure massive variety of soapstone, formerly used for making cooking vessels.

pottage ('pɒtɪdʒ) *n.* a thick meat or vegetable soup. [C13: from Old French *potage* contents of a pot, from *pot* POT[1]]

potted ('pɒtɪd) *adj.* **1.** placed or grown in a pot. **2.** cooked or preserved in a pot: *potted shrimps.* **3.** *Informal.* summarized or abridged: *a potted version of a novel.*

potter[1] ('pɒtə) *n.* a person who makes pottery.

potter[2] ('pɒtə) *or esp. U.S. and Canadian* **putter** *Chiefly Brit.* ~*vb.* **1.** (*intr.;* often foll. by *about* or *around*) to busy oneself in a desultory though agreeable manner. **2.** (*intr.;* often foll. by *along* or *about*) to move with little energy or direction: *to potter about town.* **3.** (*tr.;* usually foll. by *away*) to waste (time): *to potter the day away.* ~*n.* **4.** the act of pottering. [C16 (in the sense: to poke repeatedly): from Old English *potian* to thrust; see PUT] —'**potterer** *or esp. U.S. and Canadian* '**putterer** *n.*

potter's field *n. U.S.* a cemetery where the poor or unidentified are buried at the public expense. [named after the Biblical field bought by the Sanhedrin to be used as a burial place for strangers and the friendless poor (Acts 1:19; Matthew 27:7)]

potter's wheel *n.* a device with a horizontal rotating disc, on which clay is moulded into pots, bowls, etc., by hand.

potter wasp *n.* any of various solitary wasps of the genus *Eumenes,* which construct vaselike cells of mud or clay, in which they lay their eggs: family *Vespidae.*

pottery ('pɒtərɪ) *n., pl.* **-teries.** **1.** articles, vessels, etc., made from earthenware and dried and baked in a kiln. **2.** a place where such articles are made. **3.** the craft or business of making such articles. [C15: from Old French *poterie,* from *potier* potter, from *pot* POT[1]]

potting shed ('pɒtɪŋ) *n.* a building in which plants are set in flowerpots and in which empty pots, potting compost, etc., are stored.

pottle ('pɒt^{ə}l) *n. Archaic.* a liquid measure equal to half a gallon. [C14: *potel,* from Old French: a small POT[1]]

potto ('pɒtəʊ) *n., pl.* **-tos.** **1.** Also called: **kinkajou.** a short-tailed prosimian primate, *Perodicticus potto,* having vertebral spines protruding through the skin in the neck region: family *Lorisidae.* **2. golden potto.** another name for **angwantibo.** **3.** another name for **kinkajou** (sense 1). [C18: of West African origin; compare Wolof *pata* type of tail-less monkey]

Pott's disease (pɒts) *n.* a disease of the spine, usually caused by tubercular infection and characterized by weakening and gradual disintegration of the vertebrae and the intervertebral discs. [C18: named after Percivall *Pott* (1714–88), English surgeon]

Pott's fracture *n.* a fracture of the lower part of the fibula, usually with dislocation of the ankle.

potty[1] ('pɒtɪ) *adj.* **-tier, -tiest.** *Brit. informal.* **1.** foolish or slightly crazy. **2.** trivial or insignificant. **3.** (foll. by *about* or *on*) very keen (about). [C19: perhaps from POT[1]] —'**pottiness** *n.*

potty[2] ('pɒtɪ) *n., pl.* **-ties.** a child's word for **chamber pot.**

pot-walloper *or* **potwaller** ('pɒt,wɒlə) *n.* (in some English boroughs) a man entitled to the franchise before 1832 by virtue of possession of his own fireplace. [C18: from POT[1] + *wallop* to boil furiously, from Old English *weallan* to boil]

pouch (paʊtʃ) *n.* **1.** a small flexible baglike container: *a tobacco pouch.* **2.** a saclike structure in any of various animals, such as the abdominal receptacle marsupium in marsupials or the cheek fold in rodents. **3.** *Anatomy.* any sac, pocket, or pouchlike cavity or space in an organ or part. **4.** another word for **mailbag.** **5.** a Scot. word for **pocket.** ~*vb.* **6.** (*tr.*) to place in or as if in a pouch. **7.** to arrange or become arranged in a pouchlike form. **8.** (*tr.*) (of certain birds and fishes) to swallow. [C14: from Old Norman French *pouche,* from Old French *poche* bag; see POKE[2]] —'**pouchy** *adj.*

pouched (paʊtʃt) *adj.* having a pouch or pouches.

pouf *or* **pouffe** (puːf) *n.* **1.** a large solid cushion, usually cylindrical or cubic in shape, used as a seat. **2. a.** a woman's hair style, fashionable esp. in the 18th century, in which the hair is piled up in rolled puffs. **b.** a pad set in the hair to make such puffs. **3.** a stuffed pad worn under panniers. **4.** (pʊf, puːf). *Brit. derogatory slang.* less common spellings of **poof.** [C19: from French; see PUFF]

Poujadism ('puːʒɑːdɪzəm) *n.* a conservative reactionary movement to protect the business interests of small traders. [C20: named after Pierre *Poujade* (born 1920), French publisher and bookseller who founded such a movement in 1954] —'**Poujadist** *n., adj.*

poulard *or* **poularde** ('puːlɑːd) *n.* a hen that has been spayed for fattening. Compare **capon.** [C18: from Old French *pollarde,* from *polle* hen; see PULLET]

poult[1] (pəʊlt) *n.* the young of a gallinaceous bird, esp. of domestic fowl. [C15: syncopated variant of *poulet* PULLET]

poult[2] (pʊlt) *n.* a fine plain-weave fabric of silk, rayon, nylon, etc., with slight ribs across it. Also called: **poult-de-soie.** [C20: from French; of unknown origin; compare PADUASOY]

poulterer ('pəʊltərə) *n. Brit.* another word for a **poultryman.** [C17: from obsolete *poulter,* from Old French *pouletier,* from *poulet* PULLET]

poultice ('pəʊltɪs) *n.* **1.** Also called: **cataplasm.** *Med.* a local moist and often heated application for the skin consisting of substances such as kaolin, linseed, or mustard, used to improve the circulation, treat inflamed areas, etc. **2.** *Austral. slang.* a large sum of money, esp. a debt. [C16: from earlier *pultes,* from Latin *puls* a thick porridge]

poultry ('pəʊltrɪ) *n.* domestic fowls collectively. [C14: from Old French *pouletrie,* from *pouletier* poultry-dealer]

poultryman ('pəʊltrɪmən) *or* **poulterer** *n., pl.* **-trymen** *or* **-terers.** **1.** Also called: **chicken farmer.** a person who rears domestic fowls, esp. chickens, for their eggs or meat. **2.** a dealer in poultry, esp. one who sells the dressed carcasses.

pounce[1] (paʊns) *vb.* **1.** (*intr.;* often foll. by *on* or *upon*) to spring or swoop, as in capturing prey. ~*n.* **2.** the act of pouncing; a spring or swoop. **3.** the claw of a bird of prey. [C17: apparently from Middle English *punson* pointed tool; see PUNCHEON[2]] —'**pouncer** *n.*

pounce[2] (paʊns) *vb.* (*tr.*) to emboss (metal) by hammering from the reverse side. [C15 *pounsen,* from Old French *poinçonner* to stamp; perhaps the same as POUNCE[1]]

pounce[3] (paʊns) *n.* **1.** a very fine resinous powder, esp. of cuttlefish bone, formerly used to dry ink or sprinkled over parchment or unsized writing paper to stop the ink from running. **2.** a fine powder, esp. of charcoal, that is tapped through perforations in paper corresponding to the main lines of a design in order to transfer the design to another surface. **3.** (*as modifier*): *a pounce box.* ~*vb.* (*tr.*) **4.** to dust (paper) with pounce. **5.** to transfer (a design) by means of pounce. [C18: from Old French *ponce,* from Latin *pūmex* PUMICE] —'**pouncer** *n.*

pouncet box ('paʊnsɪt) *n.* a box with a perforated top used for containing perfume. [C16 *pouncet,* perhaps alteration of *pounced* punched, perforated; see POUNCE[1]]

pound[1] (paʊnd) *vb.* **1.** (when *intr.,* often foll. by *on* or *at*) to strike heavily and often. **2.** (*tr.*) to beat to a pulp; pulverize. **3.** (*tr.*) to instil by constant drilling: *to pound Latin into him.* **4.** (*tr.;* foll. by *out*) to produce, as by typing heavily. **5.** to walk (the pavement, street, etc.) repeatedly: *he pounded the pavement looking for a job.* **6.** (*intr.*) to throb heavily. ~*n.* **7.** a heavy blow; thump. **8.** the act of pounding. [Old English *pūnian;* related to Dutch *puin* rubble] —'**pounder** *n.*

pound[2] (paʊnd) *n.* **1.** an avoirdupois unit of weight that is divided into 16 ounces and is equal to 0.453 592 kilograms. Abbrev.: **lb.** **2.** a troy unit of weight divided into 12 ounces equal to 0.373 242 kilograms. Abbrev.: **lb tr** *or* **lb t.** **3.** an apothecaries' unit of weight, used in the U.S., that is divided into 5760 grains and is equal to one pound troy. **4.** (*not in technical usage*) a unit of force equal to the mass of 1 pound avoirdupois where the acceleration of free fall is 32.174 feet per second per second. Abbrev.: **lbf.** **5. a.** the standard monetary unit of the United Kingdom and its dependencies, divided into 100 pence. Official name: **pound sterling.** **b.** (*as modifier*): *a pound coin.* **6.** the standard monetary unit of the following countries: **a.**

Cyprus: divided into 1000 cents. **b.** Egypt: divided into 100 piastres. **c.** Ireland: divided into 100 pence. **d.** Lebanon: divided into 100 piastres. **e.** Malta: divided into 100 pence. **f.** Sudan: divided into 100 piastres. **g.** Syria: divided into 100 piastres. **7.** another name for **lira** (sense 2). **8.** Also called: **pound Scots.** a former Scottish monetary unit originally worth an English pound but later declining in value to 1 shilling 8 pence. [Old English *pund,* from Latin *pondō* pound; related to German *Pfund* pound, Latin *pondus* weight]

pound[3] (paʊnd) *n.* **1.** an enclosure, esp. one maintained by a public authority, for keeping officially removed vehicles or distrained goods or animals, esp. stray dogs. **2.** a place where people are confined. **3. a.** a trap for animals. **b.** a trap or keepnet for fish. See **pound net.** ~*vb.* **4.** (*tr.*) to confine in or as if in a pound; impound, imprison, or restrain. [C14: from Late Old English *pund-* as in *pundfeald* PINFOLD]

poundage[1] (ˈpaʊndɪdʒ) *n.* **1.** a tax, charge, or other payment of so much per pound of weight. **2.** a tax, charge, or other payment of so much per pound sterling. **3.** a weight expressed in pounds.

poundage[2] (ˈpaʊndɪdʒ) *n. Agriculture.* **a.** confinement of livestock within a pound. **b.** the fee required for freeing a head of livestock from a pound.

poundal (ˈpaʊndᵊl) *n.* the fps unit of force; the force that imparts an acceleration of 1 foot per second per second to a mass of 1 pound. 1 poundal is equivalent to 0.1382 newton or 1.382×10^4 dynes. Abbrev.: **pdl.** [C19: from POUND[2] + QUINTAL]

pound cake *n.* a rich fruit cake originally made with a pound each of butter, sugar, and flour.

pound cost averaging *n. Stock Exchange.* a method of accumulating capital by investing a fixed sum in a particular security at regular intervals, in order to achieve an average purchase price below the arithmetic average of the market prices on the purchase dates.

-pounder (ˈpaʊndə) *n.* (*in combination*) **1.** something weighing a specified number of pounds: *a 200-pounder.* **2.** something worth a specified number of pounds: *a ten-pounder.* **3.** a gun that discharges a shell weighing a specified number of pounds: *a two-pounder.*

pound net *n.* a fishing trap having an arrangement of standing nets directing the fish into an enclosed net.

pound of flesh *n.* something that is one's legal right but is an unreasonable demand (esp. in the phrase **to have one's pound of flesh**). [from Shakespeare's *The Merchant of Venice* (1600), Act IV, scene i]

pound sterling *n.* the official name for the standard monetary unit of the United Kingdom. See **pound**[2] (sense 5).

pour (pɔː) *vb.* **1.** to flow or cause to flow in a stream. **2.** (*tr.*) to issue, emit, etc., in a profuse way. **3.** (*intr.;* often foll. by *down*) Also: **pour with rain.** to rain heavily: *it's pouring down outside.* **4.** (*intr.*) to move together in large numbers; swarm. **5.** (*intr.*) to serve tea, coffee, etc.: *shall I pour?* **6. it never rains but it pours.** events, esp. unfortunate ones, come together or occur in rapid succession. **7. pour cold water on.** *Informal.* to be unenthusiastic about or discourage. **8. pour oil on troubled waters.** to try to calm a quarrel, etc. ~*n.* **9.** a pouring, downpour, etc. [C13: of unknown origin] —ˈ**pourer** *n.*

pourboire *French.* (purbwar) *n.* a tip; gratuity. [literally: for drinking]

pour encourager les autres *French.* (pur ɑ̃kuraʒe lez otrə) in order to encourage the others: often used ironically.

pourparler *French.* (purparle; *English* pʊəˈpɑːleɪ) *n.* an informal or preliminary conference. [literally: for speaking]

pourpoint (ˈpʊəˌpɔɪnt) *n.* a man's stuffed quilted doublet of a kind worn between the Middle Ages and the 17th century. [C15: from Old French, from *pourpoindre* to stick, from *pour-* variant of *par-,* from Latin *per* through + *poindre* to pierce, from Latin *pungere* to puncture]

pour point *n. Chem.* the lowest temperature at which a mineral oil will flow under specified conditions.

pousse-café *French.* (puskafe) *n.* **1.** a drink of liqueurs of different colours in unmixed layers. **2.** any liqueur taken with coffee at the end of a meal. [literally: coffee-pusher]

poussette (puːˈsɛt) *n.* **1.** a figure in country dancing in which couples hold hands and move up or down the set to change positions. ~*vb.* **2.** (*intr.*) to perform such a figure. [C19: from French, from *pousser* to push]

poussin (*French* pusɛ̃) *n.* a young chicken reared for eating. [from French]

pou sto (ˈpuː ˈstəʊ) *n., pl.* **pou stos.** *Literary.* **1.** a place upon which to stand. **2.** a basis of operation. [Greek: where I may stand, from Archimedes' saying that he could move the earth if given a place to stand]

pout[1] (paʊt) *vb.* **1.** to thrust out (the lips), as when sullen, or (of the lips) to be thrust out. **2.** (*intr.*) to swell out; protrude. **3.** (*tr.*) to utter with a pout. ~*n.* **4.** (*sometimes* **the pouts**) a fit of sullenness. **5.** the act or state of pouting. [C14: of uncertain origin; compare Swedish dialect *puta* inflated, Danish *pude* PILLOW] —ˈ**poutingly** *adv.*

pout[2] (paʊt) *n., pl.* **pout** *or* **pouts. 1.** short for **horned pout** or **eelpout. 2.** any of various gadoid food fishes, esp. the bib (also called **whiting pout**). **3.** any of certain other stout-bodied fishes. [Old English *-pūte* as in *ǣlepūte* eelpout; related to Dutch *puit* frog]

pouter (ˈpaʊtə) *n.* **1.** a person or thing that pouts. **2.** a breed of domestic pigeon with a large crop capable of being greatly puffed out.

poverty (ˈpɒvətɪ) *n.* **1.** the condition of being without adequate food, money, etc. **2.** scarcity or dearth: *a poverty of wit.* **3.** a lack of elements conducive to fertility in land or soil. [C12: from Old French *poverté,* from Latin *paupertās* restricted means, from *pauper* POOR]

poverty-stricken *adj.* suffering from extreme poverty.

poverty trap *n.* the situation of being unable to escape poverty because of being dependent on state benefits, which are reduced by the same amount as any extra income gained.

pow[1] (paʊ) *interj.* an exclamation imitative of a collision, explosion, etc.

pow[2] (paʊ) *n. Scot.* the head or a head of hair. [a Scot. variant of POLL]

pow[3] (paʊ) *n. Scot.* a creek or slow stream. [C15: from earlier Scots *poll*]

POW *abbrev. for* prisoner of war.

powan (ˈpaʊən) *n.* **1.** a freshwater whitefish, *Coregonus clupeoides,* occurring in some Scottish lakes. **2.** any of certain similar related fishes, such as the vendace. ~Also called: **lake herring.** [C17: Scottish variant of POLLAN]

powder (ˈpaʊdə) *n.* **1.** a solid substance in the form of tiny loose particles. **2.** any of various preparations in this form, such as gunpowder, face powder, or soap powder. **3.** fresh loose snow, esp. when considered as skiing terrain. **4. take a powder.** *U.S. and Canadian slang.* to run away or disappear. ~*vb.* **5.** to turn into powder; pulverize. **6.** (*tr.*) to cover or sprinkle with or as if with powder. [C13: from Old French *poldre,* from Latin *pulvis* dust] —ˈ**powderer** *n.* —ˈ**powdery** *adj.*

powder blue *n.* **a.** a dusty pale blue colour. **b.** (*as adj.*) *a powder-blue coat.*

powder burn *n.* a superficial burn of the skin caused by a momentary intense explosion, esp. of gunpowder.

powder compact *n.* See **compact**[1] (sense 11).

powder flask *n.* a small flask or case formerly used to carry gunpowder.

powder horn *n.* a powder flask consisting of the hollow horn of an animal.

powder keg *n.* **1.** a small barrel used to hold gunpowder. **2.** *Informal.* a potential source or scene of violence, disaster, etc.

powder metallurgy *n.* the science and technology of producing solid metal components from metal powder by compaction and sintering.

powder monkey *n.* (formerly) a boy who carried powder from the magazine to the guns on warships.

powder puff *n.* a soft pad or ball of fluffy material used for applying cosmetic powder to the skin.

powder room *n. Euphemistic.* a lavatory for women in a restaurant, department store, etc.

powdery mildew *n.* **1.** a plant disease characterized by a superficial white powdery growth on stems and leaves, caused by parasitic ascomycetous fungi of the family *Erysiphaceae:* affects the rose, aster, apple, vine, oak, etc. **2.** any of the fungi causing this disease. ~Compare **downy mildew.**

power (ˈpaʊə) *n.* **1.** ability or capacity to do something. **2.** (*often pl.*) a specific ability, capacity, or faculty. **3.** political, financial, social, etc., force or influence. **4.** control or dominion or a position of control, dominion, or authority. **5.** a state or other political entity with political, industrial, or military strength. **6.** a person who exercises control, influence, or authority: *he's a power in the state.* **7.** a prerogative, privilege, or liberty. **8. a.** legal authority to act, esp. in a specified capacity, for another. **b.** the document conferring such authority. **9. a.** a military force. **b.** military potential. **10.** *Maths.* **a.** the value of a number or quantity raised to some exponent. **b.** another name for **exponent** (sense 4). **11.** *Statistics.* the probability of rejecting the null hypothesis in a test when it is false. The power of a test of a given null depends on the particular alternative hypothesis against which it is tested. **12.** *Physics, engineering.* a measure of the rate of doing work expressed as the work done per unit time. It is measured in watts, horsepower, etc. Symbol: P **13. a.** the rate at which electrical energy is fed into or taken from a device or system. It is expressed, in a direct-current circuit, as the product of current and voltage and, in an alternating-current circuit, as the product of the effective values of the current and voltage and the cosine of the phase angle between them. It is measured in watts. **b.** (*as modifier*): *a power amplifier.* **14.** the ability to perform work. **15. a.** mechanical energy as opposed to manual labour. **b.** (*as modifier*): *a power tool.* **16.** a particular form of energy: *nuclear power.* **17. a.** a measure of the ability of a lens or optical system to magnify an object, equal to the reciprocal of the focal length. It is measured in dioptres. **b.** another word for **magnification. 18.** *Informal.* a large amount or quantity: *a power of good.* **19. in one's power.** (*often foll. by an infinitive*) able or allowed (to). **20. in (someone's) power.** under the control or sway of (someone). **21. the powers that be.** the established authority or administration. ~*vb.* (*tr.*) **22.** to give or provide power to. **23.** to fit (a machine) with a motor or engine. **24.** (*intr.*) *Slang.* to travel with great speed or force. [C13: from Anglo-Norman *poer,* from Vulgar Latin *potēre* (unattested), from Latin *posse* to be able]

power amplifier *n. Electronics.* an amplifier that is usually the final amplification stage in a device and is designed to give the required power output.

powerboat (ˈpaʊəˌbəʊt) *n.* a boat propelled by an inboard or outboard motor.

powerboating (ˈpaʊəˌbəʊtɪŋ) *n.* the sport of driving powerboats in racing competitions.

power cut *n.* a temporary interruption or reduction in the supply of electrical power to a particular area. Sometimes shortened to **cut.**

power dive *n.* **1.** a steep dive by an aircraft with its engines at high power. ~*vb.* **power-dive. 2.** to cause (an aircraft) to perform a power dive or (of an aircraft) to perform a power dive.

power dressing *n.* a style of dressing in severely tailored suits, adopted by some women executives to project an image of efficiency.

power drill *n.* a hand tool with a rotating chuck driven by an electric motor and designed to take an assortment of tools for drilling, grinding, polishing, etc.

power factor *n.* (in an electrical circuit) the ratio of the power dissipated to the product of the input volts times amps.

powerful (ˈpaʊəfʊl) *adj.* **1.** having great power, force, potency, or effect. **2.** extremely effective or efficient in action: *a powerful drug; a powerful lens.* **3.** *Dialect.* large or great: *a powerful amount of trouble.* ~*adv.* **4.** *Dialect.* extremely; very: *he ran powerful fast.* —ˈ**powerfully** *adv.* —ˈ**powerfulness** *n.*

powerhouse (ˈpaʊəˌhaʊs) *n.* **1.** an electrical generating station or plant. **2.** *Informal.* a forceful or powerful person or thing.

powerless (ˈpaʊəlɪs) *adj.* without power or authority. —ˈ**powerlessly** *adv.* —ˈ**powerlessness** *n.*

power line *n.* a set of conductors used to transmit and distribute electrical energy. Sometimes shortened to **line.**

power lunch *n.* a high-powered business meeting conducted over lunch.

power of appointment *n. Property law.* authority to appoint persons either from a particular class (**special power**) or selected by the donee of the power (**general power**) to take an estate or interest in property.

power of attorney *n.* **1.** legal authority to act for another person in certain specified matters. **2.** the document conferring such authority. ~Also called: **letter of attorney.**

power pack *n.* a device for converting the current from a supply into direct or alternating current at the voltage required by a particular electrical or electronic device.

power plant *n.* **1.** the complex, including machinery, associated equipment, and the structure housing it, that is used in the generation of power, esp. electrical power. **2.** the equipment supplying power to a particular machine or for a particular operation or process.

power point *n.* **1.** an electrical socket mounted on or recessed into a wall. **2.** such a socket, esp. one installed before the introduction of 13 ampere ring mains, that is designed to provide a current of up to 15 amperes for supplying heaters, etc., rather than lights.

power politics *n.* (*functioning as sing.*) (in international affairs) the threat or use of force as an instrument of national policy.

power series *n.* a mathematical series whose terms contain ascending positive integral powers of a variable, such as $a_0 + a_1x + a_2x^2 + \dots$

power set *n. Maths, logic.* a set the elements of which are all the subsets of a given set.

power station *n.* an electrical generating station.

power steering *n.* a form of steering used on vehicles, where the torque applied to the steering wheel is augmented by engine power. Also called: **power-assisted steering.**

power structure *n.* **1.** the structure or distribution of power and authority in a community. **2.** the people and groups who are part of such a structure.

powwow (ˈpaʊˌwaʊ) *n.* **1.** a talk, conference, or meeting. **2.** a magical ceremony of certain North American Indians, usually accompanied by feasting and dancing. **3.** (among certain North American Indians) a medicine man. **4.** a meeting of or negotiation with North American Indians. ~*vb.* **5.** (*intr.*) to hold a powwow. [C17: from Algonquian; related to Natick *pauwau* one who practises magic, Narraganset *powwaw*]

pox (pɒks) *n.* **1.** any disease characterized by the formation of pustules on the skin that often leave pockmarks when healed. **2.** (usually preceded by *the*) an informal name for **syphilis. 3. a pox on (someone** *or* **something).** (*interj.*) *Archaic.* an expression of intense disgust or aversion for (someone or something). [C15: changed from *pocks,* plural of POCK]

poxy (ˈpɒksɪ) *adj.* **poxier, poxiest.** *Slang.* **1.** having or having had syphilis. **2.** rotten; lousy; unpleasant.

Poynting theorem (ˈpɔɪntɪŋ) *n.* the theorem that the rate of flow of electromagnetic energy through unit area is equal to the **Poynting vector,** i.e. the cross product of the electric and magnetic field intensities. [C19: named after John Henry *Poynting* (1852–1914), British physicist]

pozzuolana (ˌpɒtswəˈlɑːnə) *or* **pozzolana** (ˌpɒtsəˈlɑːnə) *n.* **1.** a type of porous volcanic ash used in making hydraulic cements. **2.** any of various artificial substitutes for this ash used in cements. ~Also called: **puzzolana.** [C18: from Italian: of *Pozzuoli,* a port in SW Italy in a region of great volcanic activity]

pozzy (ˈpɒzɪ) *n., pl.* **pozzies.** a variant spelling of **possie.**

pp *abbrev. for:* **1.** past participle. **2.** per procurationem. See **per pro. 3.** privately printed. ~**4.** *Music. symbol for* pianissimo: an instruction to play very quietly.

pp *or* **PP** *abbrev. for:* **1.** parcel post. **2.** prepaid. **3.** post-paid. **4.** (in prescriptions) post prandium. [Latin: after a meal]

PP *abbrev. for:* **1.** Parish Priest. **2.** past President.

pp. *abbrev. for* pages.

ppd *abbrev. for:* **1.** post-paid. **2.** prepaid.

PPE *abbrev. for* philosophy, politics, and economics: a university course.

ppm *abbrev. for:* **1.** *Chem.* parts per million. **2.** Also: **PPM.** peak programme meter.

PPP *abbrev. for* purchasing power parity: a rate of exchange between two currencies that gives them equal purchasing powers in their own economies.

ppr *or* **p.pr.** *abbrev. for* present participle.

PPS *abbrev. for:* **1.** parliamentary private secretary. **2.** Also: **pps** post postscriptum. [Latin: after postscript; additional postscript]

PPTA (in New Zealand) *abbrev. for* Post-primary Teachers Association.

pq *abbrev. for* previous question.

PQ (in Canada) *abbrev. for:* **1.** Province of Quebec. **2.** Parti Québecois.

pr *abbrev. for:* **1.** (*pl.* **prs**) pair. **2.** paper. **3.** (in prescriptions) per rectum. [Latin: through the rectum; to be inserted into the anus] **4.** power.

Pr *the chemical symbol for* praseodymium.

PR *abbrev. for:* **1.** proportional representation. **2.** public relations. **3.** Puerto Rico.

pr. *abbrev. for:* **1.** Also: **Pr.** preferred stock. **2.** price. **3.** pronoun.

Pr. *abbrev. for:* **1.** Priest. **2.** Prince.

pracharak (prəˈtʃɑːrək) *n.* (in India) a person appointed to propagate a cause through personal contact, meetings, public lectures, etc. [Hindi]

practicable (ˈpræktɪkəbᵊl) *adj.* **1.** capable of being done; feasible. **2.** usable. [C17: from French *praticable,* from *pratiquer* to practise; see PRACTICAL] —ˌ**practicaˈbility** *or* ˈ**practicableness** *n.* —ˈ**practicably** *adv.*

▷**Usage.** See at **practical.**

practical (ˈpræktɪkᵊl) *adj.* **1.** of, involving, or concerned with experience or actual use; not theoretical. **2.** of or concerned with ordinary affairs, work, etc. **3.** adapted or adaptable for use. **4.** of, involving, or trained by practice. **5.** being such for all useful or general purposes; virtual. ~*n.* **6.** an examination in the practical skills of a subject: *a science practical.* [C17: from earlier *practic,* from French *pratique,* via Late Latin from Greek *praktikos,* from *prassein* to experience, negotiate, perform] —ˌ**practiˈcality** *or* ˈ**practicalness** *n.*

▷**Usage.** In careful usage, a distinction is made between *practical* and *practicable. Practical* refers to a person, idea, project, etc., as being more concerned with or relevant to practice than theory: *he is a very practical person; the idea had no practical application. Practicable* refers to a project or idea as being capable of being done or put into effect: *the plan was expensive, yet practicable.*

practical joke *n.* a prank or trick usually intended to make the victim appear foolish. —**practical joker** *n.*

practically (ˈpræktɪkəlɪ, -klɪ) *adv.* **1.** virtually; almost: *it has rained practically every day.* **2.** in actuality rather than in theory: *what can we do practically to help?*

practical reason *or* **reasoning** *n. Philosophy, logic.* **1.** the faculty by which human beings determine how to act. **2.** reasoning concerning the relative merits of actions. **3.** the principles governing arguments which issue in actions or intentions to act.

practice (ˈpræktɪs) *n.* **1.** a usual or customary action or proceeding: *it was his practice to rise at six; he made a practice of stealing stamps.* **2.** repetition or exercise of an activity in order to achieve mastery and fluency. **3.** the condition of having mastery of a skill or activity through repetition (esp. in the phrases **in practice, out of practice**). **4.** the exercise of a profession: *he set up practice as a lawyer.* **5.** the act of doing something: *he put his plans into practice.* **6.** the established method of conducting proceedings in a court of law. ~*vb.* **7.** the U.S. spelling of **practise.** [C16: from Medieval Latin *practicāre* to practise, from Greek *praktikē* practical science, practical work, from *prattein* to do, act]

practise *or U.S.* **practice** (ˈpræktɪs) *vb.* **1.** to do or cause to do repeatedly in order to gain skill. **2.** (*tr.*) to do (something) habitually or frequently: *they practise ritual murder.* **3.** to observe or pursue (something, such as a religion): *to practise Christianity.* **4.** to work at (a profession, job, etc.): *he practises medicine.* **5.** (foll. by *on* or *upon*) to take advantage of (someone, someone's credulity, etc.). [C15: see PRACTICE]

practised *or U.S.* **practiced** (ˈpræktɪst) *adj.* **1.** expert; skilled; proficient. **2.** acquired or perfected by practice.

practitioner (prækˈtɪʃənə) *n.* **1.** a person who practises a profession or art. **2.** *Christian Science.* a person authorized to practise spiritual healing. [C16: from *practician,* from Old French *praticien,* from *pratiquer* to PRACTISE]

Pradesh (prə'deɪʃ) *n. Indian.* a state, esp. a state in the Union of India. [Hindi]

prae- *prefix.* an archaic variant of **pre-**.

praedial *or* **predial** ('priːdɪəl) *adj.* **1.** of or relating to land, farming, etc. **2.** attached to or occupying land. [C16: from Medieval Latin *praediālis,* from Latin *praedium* farm, estate] —ˌ**praedi'ality** *or* ˌ**predi'ality** *n.*

praefect ('priːfɛkt) *n.* a variant spelling of **prefect** (senses 4–7). —**praefectorial** (ˌpriːfɛk'tɔːrɪəl) *adj.*

praemunire (ˌpriːmjʊ'naɪərɪ) *n. English history.* **1.** a writ charging with the offence of resorting to a foreign jurisdiction, esp. to that of the Pope, in a matter determinable in a royal court. **2.** the statute of Richard II defining this offence. [C14: from the Medieval Latin phrase (in the text of the writ) *praemūnīre faciās,* literally: that you cause (someone) to be warned in advance, from Latin *praemūnīre* to fortify or protect in front, from *prae* in front + *mūnīre* to fortify; in Medieval Latin the verb was confused with Latin *praemonēre* to forewarn]

praenomen (priː'nəʊmɛn) *n., pl.* **-nomina** (-'nɒmɪnə) *or* **-nomens.** an ancient Roman's first or given name. See also **agnomen, cognomen, nomen.** [C18: from Latin, from *prae-* before + *nōmen* NAME] —**praenominal** (priː'nɒmɪnᵊl) *adj.* —**prae'nominally** *adv.*

Praesepe (praɪ'siːpɪ) *n.* an open cluster of several hundred stars in the constellation Cancer, visible to the naked eye as a hazy patch of light.

praesidium (prɪ'sɪdɪəm) *n.* a variant spelling of **presidium.**

praetor *or* **pretor** ('priːtə, -tɔː) *n.* (in ancient Rome) any of several senior magistrates ranking just below the consuls. [C15: from Latin: one who leads the way, probably from *praeīre,* from *prae-* before + *īre* to go] —**prae'torial** *or* **pre'torial** *adj.* —**'praetorship** *or* **'pretorship** *n.*

praetorian *or* **pretorian** (priː'tɔːrɪən) *adj.* **1.** of or relating to a praetor. ~*n.* **2.** a person holding praetorian rank; a praetor or ex-praetor.

Praetorian *or* **Pretorian** (priː'tɔːrɪən) *adj.* **1.** of or relating to the Praetorian Guard, the bodyguard of the Roman emperors from 27 B.C. to 312 A.D. **2.** (*sometimes not cap.*) resembling the Praetorian Guard, esp. in being corrupt. ~*n.* **3.** a member of the Praetorian Guard.

pragmatic (præg'mætɪk) *adj.* **1.** advocating behaviour that is dictated more by practical consequences than by theory or dogma. **2.** *Philosophy.* of or relating to pragmatism. **3.** involving everyday or practical business. **4.** of or concerned with the affairs of a state or community. **5.** *Rare.* interfering or meddlesome; officious. Also (for senses 3, 5): **pragmatical.** [C17: from Late Latin *prāgmaticus,* from Greek *prāgmatikos* from *pragma* act, from *prattein* to do] —**prag'matically** *adv.* —**pragˌmati'cality** *n.*

pragmatics (præg'mætɪks) *n.* (*functioning as sing.*) **1.** the study of those aspects of language that cannot be considered in isolation from its use. **2.** the study of the relation between symbols and those who use them.

pragmatic sanction *n.* an edict, decree, or ordinance issued with the force of fundamental law by a sovereign.

pragmatism ('prægməˌtɪzəm) *n.* **1.** action or policy dictated by consideration of the immediate practical consequences rather than by theory or dogma. **2.** *Philosophy.* **a.** the doctrine that the content of a concept consists only in its practical applicability. **b.** the doctrine that truth consists not in correspondence with the facts but in successful coherence with experience. See also **instrumentalism.** —**'pragmatist** *n., adj.* —ˌ**pragma'tistic** *adj.*

Prairial *French.* (prɛrial) *n.* the month of meadows: the ninth month of the French Revolutionary calendar, extending from May 21 to June 19. [C18: from French *prairie* meadow]

prairie ('prɛərɪ) *n.* (*often pl.*) a treeless grassy plain of the central U.S. and S Canada. Compare **pampas, steppe, savanna.** [C18: from French, from Old French *praierie,* from Latin *prātum* meadow]

prairie chicken, fowl, grouse, *or* **hen** *n.* either of two mottled brown-and-white grouse, *Tympanuchus cupido* or *T. pallidicinctus,* of North America.

prairie dog *n.* any of several gregarious sciurine rodents of the genus *Cynomys,* such as *C. ludovicianus,* that live in large complex burrows in the prairies of North America. Also called: **prairie marmot.**

prairie oyster *n.* **1.** a drink consisting of raw unbeaten egg, vinegar or Worcester sauce (**Worcester oyster**), salt, and pepper: a supposed cure for a hangover. **2.** the testicles of a bull calf cooked and eaten.

prairie schooner *n. Chiefly U.S.* a horse-drawn covered wagon similar to but smaller than a Conestoga wagon, used in the 19th century to cross the prairies of North America.

prairie soil *n.* a soil type occurring in temperate areas formerly under prairie grasses and characterized by a black A horizon, rich in plant foods.

prairie turnip *n.* another name for **breadroot.**

prairie wolf *n.* another name for **coyote** (sense 1).

praise (preɪz) *n.* **1.** the act of expressing commendation, admiration, etc. **2.** the extolling of a deity or the rendering of homage and gratitude to a deity. **3.** the condition of being commended, admired, etc. **4.** *Archaic.* the reason for praise. **5. sing someone's praises.** to commend someone highly. ~*vb.* (*tr.*) **6.** to express commendation, admiration, etc., for. **7.** to proclaim or describe the glorious attributes of (a deity) with homage and thanksgiving. [C13: from Old French *preisier,* from Late Latin *pretiāre* to esteem highly, from Latin *pretium* prize; compare PRIZE², PRECIOUS] —**'praiser** *n.*

praiseworthy ('preɪzˌwɜːðɪ) *adj.* deserving of praise; commendable. —**'praiseˌworthily** *adv.* —**'praiseˌworthiness** *n.*

prajna ('prʊdʒnə, -njɑː) *n.* wisdom or understanding considered as the goal of Buddhist contemplation. [from Sanskrit *prajñā,* from *prajānāti* he knows]

Prakrit ('prɑːkrɪt) *n.* any of the vernacular Indic languages as distinguished from Sanskrit: spoken from about 300 B.C. to the Middle Ages. See also **Pali.** [C18: from Sanskrit *prākṛta* original, from *pra-* before + *kṛ* to do, make + *-ta* indicating a participle] —**Pra'kritic** *adj.*

praline ('prɑːliːn) *n.* **1.** a confection of nuts with caramelized sugar, used in desserts and as a filling for chocolates. **2.** Also called: **sugared almond.** a sweet consisting of an almond encased in sugar. [C18: from French, named after César de Choiseul, comte de Plessis-*Praslin* (1598-1675), French field marshal whose chef first concocted it]

pralltriller ('prɑːlˌtrɪlə) *n.* **1.** an ornament used in 18th-century music consisting of an inverted mordent with an added initial upper note. **2.** another word for **inverted mordent.** [German: bouncing trill]

pram[1] (præm) *n. Brit.* a cotlike four-wheeled carriage for a baby. U.S. and Canadian term: **baby carriage.** [C19: shortened and altered from PERAMBULATOR]

pram[2] (prɑːm) *n. Nautical.* a light tender with a flat bottom and a bow formed from the ends of the side and bottom planks meeting in a small raised transom. [C16: from Middle Dutch *prame;* related to Old Frisian *prām*]

prance (prɑːns) *vb.* **1.** (*intr.*) to swagger or strut. **2.** (*intr.*) to caper, gambol, or dance about. **3.** (*intr.*) **a.** (of a horse) to move with high lively springing steps. **b.** to ride a horse that moves in this way. **4.** (*tr.*) to cause to prance. ~*n.* **5.** the act or an instance of prancing. [C14 *prauncen;* perhaps related to German *prangen* to be in full splendour; compare Danish (dialect) *pransk* lively, spirited, used of a horse] —**'prancer** *n.* —**'prancingly** *adv.*

prandial ('prændɪəl) *adj. Facetious.* of or relating to a meal. [C19: from Latin *prandium* meal, luncheon] —**'prandially** *adv.*

prang (præŋ) *Chiefly Brit. slang.* ~*n.* **1.** an accident or crash in an aircraft, car, etc. **2.** an aircraft bombing raid. **3.** an achievement. ~*vb.* **4.** to crash or damage (an aircraft, car, etc.). **5.** to damage (a town, etc.) by bombing. [C20: possibly imitative of an explosion; perhaps related to Malay *perang* war, fighting]

prank[1] (præŋk) *n.* a mischievous trick or joke, esp. one in which something is done rather than said. [C16: of unknown origin] —**'prankish** *adj.*

prank[2] (præŋk) *vb.* **1.** (*tr.*) to dress or decorate showily or gaudily. **2.** (*intr.*) to make an ostentatious display. [C16: from Middle Dutch *pronken;* related to German *Prunk* splendour, *prangen* to be in full splendour]

prankster ('præŋkstə) *n.* a practical joker.

prase (preɪz) *n.* a light green translucent variety of chalcedony. [C14: from French, from Latin *prasius* a leek-green stone, from Greek *prasios,* from *prason* a leek]

praseodymium (ˌpreɪzɪəʊ'dɪmɪəm) *n.* a malleable ductile silvery-white element of the lanthanide series of metals. It occurs principally in monazite and bastnaesite and is used with other rare earths in carbon-arc lights and as a pigment in glass. Symbol: Pr; atomic no.: 59; atomic wt.: 140.91; valency: 3 or 4; relative density: 6.77; melting pt.: 931°C; boiling pt.: 3212°C. [C20: New Latin, from Greek *prasios* of a leek-green colour + DIDYMIUM]

prat (præt) *n. Slang.* an incompetent or ineffectual person: often used as a term of abuse. [C20: probably special use of C16 *prat* buttocks, of unknown origin]

prate (preɪt) *vb.* **1.** (*intr.*) to talk idly and at length; chatter. **2.** (*tr.*) to utter in an idle or empty way. ~*n.* **3.** idle or trivial talk; prattle; chatter. [C15: of Germanic origin; compare Middle Dutch *prāten,* Icelandic and Norwegian *prata,* Danish *prate*] —**'prater** *n.* —**'pratingly** *adv.*

pratfall ('prætˌfɔːl) *n. U.S. and Canadian slang.* a fall upon one's buttocks. [C20: from C16 *prat* buttocks (of unknown origin) + FALL]

pratincole ('prætɪŋˌkəʊl, 'preɪ-) *n.* any of various swallow-like shore birds of the southern Old World genus *Glareola* and related genera, esp. *G. pratincola,* having long pointed wings, short legs, and a short bill: family *Glareolidae,* order *Charadriiformes.* [C18: from New Latin *pratincola* field-dwelling, from Latin *prātum* meadow + *incola* inhabitant]

pratique ('prætiːk, præ'tiːk) *n.* formal permission given to a vessel to use a foreign port upon satisfying the requirements of local health authorities. [C17: from French, from Medieval Latin *practica* PRACTICE]

prattle ('prætᵊl) *vb.* **1.** (*intr.*) to talk in a foolish or childish way; babble. **2.** (*tr.*) to utter in a foolish or childish way. ~*n.* **3.** foolish or childish talk. [C16: from Middle Low German *pratelen* to chatter; see PRATE] —**'prattler** *n.* —**'prattlingly** *adv.*

prau (praʊ) *n.* another word for **proa.**

prawn (prɔːn) *n.* **1.** any of various small edible marine decapod crustaceans of the genera *Palaemon, Penaeus,* etc., having a slender flattened body with a long tail and two pairs of pincers. **2. come the raw prawn.** *Austral. informal.* to attempt deception. [C15: of obscure origin] —ˈ**prawner** *n.*

prawn cracker *n.* a puffy savoury crisp made from rice flour and prawn flavouring, served with Chinese food.

praxis (ˈpræksɪs) *n., pl.* **praxises** *or* **praxes** (ˈpræksiːz). **1.** the practice and practical side of a profession or field of study, as opposed to the theory. **2.** a practical exercise. **3.** accepted practice or custom. [C16: via Medieval Latin from Greek: deed, action, from *prassein* to do]

pray (preɪ) *vb.* **1.** (when *intr.*, often foll. by *for;* when *tr., usually takes a clause as object*) to utter prayers (to God or other object of worship): *we prayed to God for the sick child.* **2.** (when *tr., usually takes a clause as object or an infinitive*) to make an earnest entreaty (to or for); beg or implore: *she prayed to be allowed to go; leave, I pray you.* **3.** (*tr.*) *Rare.* to accomplish or bring by praying: *to pray a soul into the kingdom.* ~*interj.* **4.** *Archaic.* I beg you; please: *pray, leave us alone.* [C13: from Old French *preier,* from Latin *precārī* to implore, from *prex* an entreaty; related to Old English *fricgan,* Old High German *frāgēn* to ask, Old Norse *fregna* to enquire]

prayer[1] (prɛə) *n.* **1. a.** a personal communication or petition addressed to a deity, esp. in the form of supplication, adoration, praise, contrition, or thanksgiving. **b.** any other form of spiritual communion with a deity. **2.** a similar personal communication that does not involve adoration, addressed to beings venerated as being closely associated with a deity, such as angels or saints. **3.** the practice of praying: *prayer is our solution to human problems.* **4.** (*often pl.*) a form of devotion, either public or private, spent mainly or wholly praying: *morning prayers.* **5.** (*cap. when part of a recognized name*) a form of words used in praying: *the Lord's Prayer.* **6.** an object or benefit prayed for. **7.** an earnest request, petition, or entreaty. **8.** *Law.* a request contained in a petition to a court for the relief sought by the petitioner. **9.** *U.S. slang.* a chance or hope: *she doesn't have a prayer of getting married.* [C13 *preiere,* from Old French, from Medieval Latin *precāria,* from Latin *precārius* obtained by begging, from *prex* prayer] —ˈ**prayerless** *adj.*

prayer[2] (ˈpreɪə) *n.* a person who prays.

prayer beads (prɛə) *pl. n. R.C. Church.* the beads of the rosary.

prayer book (prɛə) *n.* **1.** *Ecclesiast.* a book that contains the prayers used at church services or recommended for private devotions. **2.** *Church of England.* (*often caps.*) another name for **Book of Common Prayer.**

prayerful (ˈprɛəfʊl) *adj.* inclined to or characterized by prayer. —ˈ**prayerfully** *adv.* —ˈ**prayerfulness** *n.*

prayer meeting (prɛə) *n. Chiefly Protestantism.* a religious meeting at which the participants offer up prayers to God.

prayer rug (prɛə) *n.* the small carpet on which a Muslim kneels and prostrates himself while saying his prayers. Also called: **prayer mat.**

prayer shawl (prɛə) *n. Judaism.* another word for **tallith.**

prayer wheel (prɛə) *n. Buddhism.* (esp. in Tibet) a wheel or cylinder inscribed with or containing prayers, each revolution of which is counted as an uttered prayer, so that such prayers can be repeated by turning it.

praying mantis *or* **mantid** *n.* another name for **mantis.**

PRB *abbrev. for* (after the signatures of Pre-Raphaelite painters) Pre-Raphaelite Brotherhood.

pre- *prefix.* before in time, rank, order, position, etc.: *predate; pre-eminent; premeditation; prefrontal; preschool.* [from Latin *prae-*, from *prae* before, beforehand, in front]

preach (priːtʃ) *vb.* **1.** to make known (religious truth) or give religious or moral instruction or exhortation in (sermons). **2.** to advocate (a virtue, action, etc.), esp. in a moralizing way. [C13: from Old French *prechier,* from Church Latin *praedicāre,* from Latin: to proclaim in public; see PREDICATE] —ˈ**preachable** *adj.*

preacher (ˈpriːtʃə) *n.* **1.** a person who has the calling and function of preaching the Christian Gospel, esp. a Protestant clergyman. **2.** a person who preaches.

preachify (ˈpriːtʃɪˌfaɪ) *vb.* **-fies, -fying, -fied.** (*intr.*) *Informal.* to preach or moralize in a tedious manner. —ˈ**preachiˌfying** *n.*

preachment (ˈpriːtʃmənt) *n.* **1.** the act of preaching. **2.** a tedious or pompous sermon or discourse.

preachy (ˈpriːtʃɪ) *adj.* **preachier, preachiest.** *Informal.* inclined to or marked by preaching.

preacquisition profit (ˌpriːækwɪˈzɪʃən) *n.* the retained profit of a company earned before a takeover and therefore not eligible for distribution as a dividend to the shareholders of the acquiring company.

preadamite (priːˈædəˌmaɪt) *n.* **1.** a person who believes that there were people on earth before Adam. **2.** a person assumed to have lived before Adam. ~*adj. also* **preadamic** (ˌpriːəˈdæmɪk). **3.** of or relating to a preadamite.

preadaptation (ˌpriːædəpˈteɪʃən) *n. Biology.* the possession by a species or other group of characteristics that may favour survival in a changed environment, such as the limblike fins of crossopterygian fishes, which are preadaptation to terrestrial life.

preamble (priːˈæmbəl) *n.* **1.** a preliminary or introductory statement, esp. attached to a statute or constitution setting forth its purpose. **2.** a preliminary or introductory conference, event, fact, etc. [C14: from Old French *préambule,* from Late Latin *praeambulum* walking before, from Latin *prae-* before + *ambulāre* to walk]

preamplifier (priːˈæmplɪˌfaɪə) *n.* an electronic amplifier used to improve the signal-to-noise ratio of an electronic device. It boosts a low-level signal to an intermediate level before it is transmitted to the main amplifier. Sometimes shortened to **preamp.**

preaxial (priːˈæksɪəl) *adj. Anatomy.* **1.** situated or occurring in front of the axis of the body. **2.** of or relating to the anterior part of a vertebrate limb. —**preˈaxially** *adv.*

prebend (ˈprɛbənd) *n.* **1.** the stipend assigned by a cathedral or collegiate church to a canon or member of the chapter. **2.** the land, tithe, or other source of such a stipend. **3.** a less common word for **prebendary. 4.** *Church of England.* the office, formerly with an endowment, of a prebendary. [C15: from Old French *prébende,* from Medieval Latin *praebenda* pension, stipend, from Latin *praebēre* to offer, supply, from *prae* forth + *habēre* to have, offer] —**prebendal** (prɪˈbɛndəl) *adj.*

prebendary (ˈprɛbəndərɪ, -drɪ) *n., pl.* **-daries. 1.** a canon or member of the chapter of a cathedral or collegiate church who holds a prebend. **2.** *Church of England.* an honorary canon with the title of prebendary.

prec. *abbrev. for* preceding.

Precambrian *or* **Pre-Cambrian** (priːˈkæmbrɪən) *adj.* **1.** of, denoting, or formed in the earliest geological era, which lasted for about 4 000 000 000 years before the Cambrian period. ~*n.* **2. the.** the Precambrian era. See **Archaeozoic, Proterozoic.**

precancel (priːˈkænsəl) *vb.* **-cels, -celling, -celled** *or U.S.* **-cels, -celing, -celed. 1.** (*tr.*) to cancel (postage stamps) before placing them on mail. ~*n.* **2.** a precancelled stamp. —**preˌcancelˈlation** *n.*

precancerous *adj.* (esp. of cells) displaying characteristics that may develop into cancer.

precarious (prɪˈkɛərɪəs) *adj.* **1.** liable to failure or catastrophe; insecure; perilous. **2.** *Archaic.* dependent on another's will. [C17: from Latin *precārius* obtained by begging (hence, dependent on another's will), from *prex* PRAYER[1]] —**preˈcariously** *adv.* —**preˈcariousness** *n.*

precast *adj.* (ˈpriːˌkɑːst). **1.** (esp. of concrete when employed as a structural element in building) cast in a particular form before being used. ~*vb.* (priːˈkɑːst), **-casts, -casting, -cast. 2.** (*tr.*) to cast (concrete) in a particular form before use.

precatory (ˈprɛkətərɪ, -trɪ) *adj. Rare.* of, involving, or expressing entreaty; supplicatory. Also: **precative** (ˈprɛkətɪv). [C17: from Late Latin *precātōrius* relating to petitions, from Latin *precārī* to beg, PRAY]

precaution (prɪˈkɔːʃən) *n.* **1.** an action taken to avoid a dangerous or undesirable event. **2.** caution practised beforehand; circumspection. [C17: from French, from Late Latin *praecautiō,* from Latin *praecavēre* to guard against, from *prae* before + *cavēre* to beware] —**preˈcautionary** *or* **preˈcautional** *adj.* —**preˈcautious** *adj.*

precede (prɪˈsiːd) *vb.* **1.** to go or be before (someone or something) in time, place, rank, etc. **2.** (*tr.*) to preface or introduce. [C14: via Old French from Latin *praecēdere* to go before, from *prae* before + *cēdere* to move]

precedence (ˈprɛsɪdəns) *or* **precedency** *n.* **1.** the act of preceding or the condition of being precedent. **2.** the ceremonial order or priority to be observed by persons of different stations on formal occasions: *the officers are seated according to precedence.* **3.** a right to preferential treatment: *I take precedence over you.*

precedent *n.* (ˈprɛsɪdənt). **1.** *Law.* a judicial decision that serves as an authority for deciding a later case. **2.** an example or instance used to justify later similar occurrences. ~*adj.* (prɪˈsiːdənt, ˈprɛsɪdənt). **3.** preceding.

precedented (ˈprɛsɪˌdɛntɪd) *adj.* (of a decision, etc.) supported by having a precedent.

precedential (ˌprɛsɪˈdɛnʃəl) *adj.* **1.** of, involving, or serving as a precedent. **2.** having precedence. —ˌ**preceˈdentially** *adv.*

ˌpreabˈsorb *vb.*
ˌpreacˈcept *vb.*
ˌpreacˈcustom *vb.*
ˌpreacˈquaint *vb.*
ˌpreaˈdapt *vb.*
ˌpreadˈdress *vb.*
ˌpreadˈjust *vb.*
ˌpreadoˈlescence *n.*
ˌpreadoˈlescent *n., adj.*
ˌpreaˈdult *adj.*
preˈadverˌtise *vb.*
ˌprealˈlot *vb.*, **-ˈlots, -ˈlotting, -ˈlotted.**
ˌpreanˈnounce *vb.*
ˌpreanˈtiquity *n.*
ˌpreapˈpearance *n.*
ˌpreappliˈcation *n.*
ˌpreapˈpoint *vb.*
preˈarm *vb.*
ˌprearˈrange *vb.*
ˌprearˈranged *adj.*
ˌprearˈrangement *n.*
ˌpreascerˈtain *vb.*
ˌpreasˈsemble *vb.*
ˌpreasˈsign *vb.*
ˌpreasˈsumption *n.*
ˌpreasˈsurance *n.*
ˌpreatˈtune *vb.*
ˌpre-Auˈgustan *adj.*
ˌpre-Babyˈlonian *adj.*
preˈboil *vb.*
pre-ˈBritish *adj.*
pre-ˈBuddhist *adj.*
ˌpre-Byzˈantine *adj.*
ˌprecapitalˈistic *adj.*
ˌpre-Carbonˈiferous *adj.*

preceding (prɪˈsiːdɪŋ) *adj.* (*prenominal*) going or coming before; former.

precentor (prɪˈsɛntə) *n.* **1.** a cleric who directs the choral services in a cathedral. **2.** a person who leads a congregation or choir in the sung parts of church services. [C17: from Late Latin *praecentor* leader of the music, from *prae* before + *canere* to sing] —**precentorial** (ˌpriːsɛnˈtɔːrɪəl) *adj.* —**preˈcentorˌship** *n.*

precept (ˈpriːsɛpt) *n.* **1.** a rule or principle for action. **2.** a guide or rule for morals; maxim. **3.** a direction, esp. for a technical operation. **4.** *Law.* **a.** a writ or warrant. **b.** a written order to a sheriff to arrange an election, the empanelling of a jury, etc. **c.** (in England) an order to collect money under a rate. [C14: from Latin *praeceptum* maxim, injunction, from *praecipere* to admonish, from *prae* before + *capere* to take]

preceptive (prɪˈsɛptɪv) *adj.* **1.** of, resembling, or expressing a precept or precepts. **2.** didactic. —**preˈceptively** *adv.*

preceptor (prɪˈsɛptə) *n.* **1.** *U.S.* a practising physician giving practical training to a medical student. **2.** the head of a preceptory. **3.** *Rare.* a tutor or instructor. —**preˈceptorate** *n.* —**preceptorial** (ˌpriːsɛpˈtɔːrɪəl) *or* **preˈceptoral** *adj.* —**preˈceptorˌship** *n.* —**preˈceptress** *fem. n.*

preceptory (prɪˈsɛptərɪ) *n., pl.* **-ries.** (formerly) a subordinate house or community of the Knights Templars.

precess (prɪˈsɛs) *vb.* to undergo or cause to undergo precession.

precession (prɪˈsɛʃən) *n.* **1.** the act of preceding. **2.** See **precession of the equinoxes.** **3.** the motion of a spinning body, such as a top, gyroscope, or planet, in which it wobbles so that the axis of rotation sweeps out a cone. [C16: from Late Latin *praecessiō* a going in advance, from Latin *praecēdere* to PRECEDE] —**preˈcessional** *adj.* —**preˈcessionally** *adv.*

precession of the equinoxes *n.* the slightly earlier occurrence of the equinoxes each year due to the slow continuous westward shift of the equinoctial points along the ecliptic by 50 seconds of arc per year. It is caused by the precession of the earth's axis.

precinct (ˈpriːsɪŋkt) *n.* **1. a.** an enclosed area or building marked by a fixed boundary such as a wall. **b.** such a boundary. **2.** an area in a town, often closed to traffic, that is designed or reserved for a particular purpose: *a shopping precinct; pedestrian precinct.* **3.** *U.S.* **a.** a district of a city for administrative or police purposes. **b.** the police responsible for such a district. **4.** *U.S.* a polling or electoral district. [C15: from Medieval Latin *praecinctum* (something) surrounded, from Latin *praecingere* to gird around, from *prae* before, around + *cingere* to gird]

precincts (ˈpriːsɪŋkts) *pl. n.* the surrounding region or area.

preciosity (ˌprɛʃɪˈɒsɪtɪ) *n., pl.* **-ties.** fastidiousness or affectation, esp. in speech or manners.

precious (ˈprɛʃəs) *adj.* **1.** beloved; dear; cherished. **2.** very costly or valuable. **3.** held in high esteem, esp. in moral or spiritual matters. **4.** very fastidious or affected, as in speech, manners, etc. **5.** *Informal.* worthless: *you and your precious ideas!* ~*adv.* **6.** *Informal.* (intensifier): *there's precious little left.* [C13: from Old French *precios,* from Latin *pretiōsus* valuable, from *pretium* price, value] —ˈ**preciously** *adv.* —ˈ**preciousness** *n.*

precious coral *n.* another name for **red coral.**

precious metal *n.* any of the metals gold, silver, or platinum.

precious stone *n.* any of certain rare minerals, such as diamond, ruby, sapphire, emerald, or opal, that are highly valued as gemstones.

precipice (ˈprɛsɪpɪs) *n.* **1. a.** the steep sheer face of a cliff or crag. **b.** the cliff or crag itself. **2.** a precarious situation. [C16: from Latin *praecipitium* steep place, from *praeceps* headlong] —ˈ**precipiced** *adj.*

precipitant (prɪˈsɪpɪtənt) *adj.* **1.** hasty or impulsive; rash. **2.** rushing or falling rapidly or without heed. **3.** abrupt or sudden. ~*n.* **4.** *Chem.* a substance or agent that causes a precipitate to form. —**preˈcipitance** *or* **preˈcipitancy** *n.* —**preˈcipitantly** *adv.*

precipitate *vb.* (prɪˈsɪpɪˌteɪt). **1.** (*tr.*) to cause to happen too soon or sooner than expected; bring on. **2.** to throw or fall from or as from a height. **3.** to cause (moisture) to condense and fall as snow, rain, etc., or (of moisture, rain, etc.) to condense and fall thus. **4.** *Chem.* to undergo or cause to undergo a process in which a dissolved substance separates from solution as a fine suspension of solid particles. ~*adj.* (prɪˈsɪpɪtɪt). **5.** rushing ahead. **6.** done rashly or with undue haste. **7.** sudden and brief. ~*n.* (prɪˈsɪpɪtɪt). **8.** *Chem.* a precipitated solid in its suspended form or after settling or filtering. [C16: from Latin *praecipitāre* to throw down headlong, from *praeceps* headlong, steep, from *prae* before, in front + *caput* head] —**preˈcipitable** *adj.* —**preˌcipitaˈbility** *n.* —**preˈcipitately** *adv.* —**preˈcipitateness** *n.* —**preˈcipitative** *adj.* —**preˈcipiˌtator** *n.*

precipitation (prɪˌsɪpɪˈteɪʃən) *n.* **1.** *Meteorol.* **a.** rain, snow, sleet, dew, etc., formed by condensation of water vapour in the atmosphere. **b.** the deposition of these on the earth's surface. **c.** the amount precipitated. **2.** the production or formation of a chemical precipitate. **3.** the act of precipitating or the state of being precipitated. **4.** rash or undue haste. **5.** *Spiritualism.* the appearance of a spirit in bodily form; materialization.

precipitation hardening *n. Metallurgy.* a process in which alloys are strengthened by the formation, in their lattice, of a fine dispersion of one component when the metal is quenched from a high temperature and aged at an intermediate temperature.

precipitin (prɪˈsɪpɪtɪn) *n. Immunol.* an antibody that causes precipitation when mixed with its specific antigen.

precipitous (prɪˈsɪpɪtəs) *adj.* **1.** resembling a precipice or characterized by precipices. **2.** very steep. **3.** hasty or precipitate. —**preˈcipitously** *adv.* —**preˈcipitousness** *n.*

precis *or* **précis** (ˈpreɪsiː) *n., pl.* **precis** *or* **précis** (ˈpreɪsiːz). **1.** a summary of the essentials of a text; abstract. ~*vb.* **2.** (*tr.*) to make a precis of. [C18: from French: PRECISE]

precise (prɪˈsaɪs) *adj.* **1.** strictly correct in amount or value: *a precise sum.* **2.** designating a certain thing and no other; particular: *this precise location.* **3.** using or operating with total accuracy: *precise instruments.* **4.** strict in observance of rules, standards, etc.: *a precise mind.* [C16: from French *précis,* from Latin *praecīdere* to curtail, from *prae* before + *caedere* to cut] —**preˈcisely** *adv.* —**preˈciseness** *n.*

precisian (prɪˈsɪʒən) *n.* a punctilious observer of rules or forms, esp. in the field of religion. —**preˈcisianism** *n.*

precision (prɪˈsɪʒən) *n.* **1.** the quality of being precise; accuracy. **2.** (*modifier*) characterized by or having a high degree of exactness: *precision grinding; a precision instrument.* [C17: from Latin *praecīsiō* a cutting off; see PRECISE] —**preˈcisionism** *n.* —**preˈcisionist** *n.*

preclinical (priːˈklɪnɪkᵊl) *adj. Med.* **1.** of, relating to, or occurring during the early phases of a disease before accurate diagnosis is possible. **2.** of, relating to, or designating an early period of scientific study by a medical student before practical experience with patients. —**preˈclinically** *adv.*

preclude (prɪˈkluːd) *vb.* (*tr.*) **1.** to exclude or debar. **2.** to make impossible, esp. beforehand. [C17: from Latin *praeclūdere* to shut up, from *prae* in front, before + *claudere* to close] —**preˈcludable** *adj.* —**preclusion** (prɪˈkluːʒən) *n.* —**preclusive** (prɪˈkluːsɪv) *adj.* —**preˈclusively** *adv.*

precocial (prɪˈkəʊʃəl) *adj.* **1.** (of the young of some species of birds after hatching) covered with down, having open eyes, and capable of leaving the nest within a few days of hatching. ~*n.* **2.** a precocial bird. ~Compare **altricial.** [C19: see PRECOCIOUS]

precocious (prɪˈkəʊʃəs) *adj.* **1.** ahead in development, such as the mental development of a child. **2.** *Botany.* (of plants, fruit, etc.) flowering or ripening early. [C17: from Latin *praecox* early maturing, from *prae* early + *coquere* to ripen] —**preˈcociously** *adv.* —**preˈcociousness** *or* **precocity** (prɪˈkɒsɪtɪ) *n.*

precognition (ˌpriːkɒgˈnɪʃən) *n. Psychol.* the alleged ability to foresee future events. See also **clairvoyance, clairaudience.** [C17: from Late Latin *praecognitiō* foreknowledge, from *praecognoscere* to foresee, from *prae* before + *cognoscere* to know, ascertain] —**precognitive** (priːˈkɒgnɪtɪv) *adj.*

pre-Columbian *adj.* of or relating to the Americas before they were discovered (1492) by Christopher Columbus (1451–1506).

preconceive (ˌpriːkənˈsiːv) *vb.* (*tr.*) to form an idea of beforehand; conceive of ahead in time.

preconception (ˌpriːkənˈsɛpʃən) *n.* **1.** an idea or opinion formed beforehand. **2.** a bias; prejudice.

precondition (ˌpriːkənˈdɪʃən) *n.* **1.** a necessary or required condition; prerequisite. ~*vb.* **2.** (*tr.*) *Psychol.* to present successively two stimuli to (an organism) without reinforcement so that they become associated; if a response is then conditioned to the second stimulus on its own, the same response will be evoked by the first stimulus.

preconize *or* **preconise** (ˈpriːkəˌnaɪz) *vb.* (*tr.*) **1.** to announce or commend publicly. **2.** to summon publicly. **3.** (of the pope) to approve the appointment of (a nominee) to one of the higher dignities in the Roman Catholic Church. [C15: from Medieval Latin *praecōnīzāre* to make an announcement, from Latin *praecō* herald] —ˌ**preconiˈzation** *or* ˌ**preconiˈsation** *n.*

preconscious (priːˈkɒnʃəs) *adj.* **1.** *Psychol.* prior to the development of consciousness. ~*n.* **2.** *Psychoanal.* mental contents or activity not immediately in consciousness but readily brought there. ~Compare **subconscious, unconscious.** —**preˈconsciously** *adv.* —**preˈconsciousness** *n.*

precontract *n.* (priːˈkɒntrækt). **1.** a contract or arrangement made beforehand, esp. a betrothal. ~*vb.* (ˌpriːkənˈtrækt). **2.** to betroth or enter into a betrothal by previous agreement. **3.** to make (an agreement, etc.) by prior arrangement.

pre-ˈCeltic *adj.*
preˈcensor *vb.*
ˌpre-Chauˈcerian *adj.*
preˈcheck *vb.*
preˈchill *vb.*
ˌpre-Chiˈnese *adj.*
pre-ˈChristian *adj.*
pre-ˈChristmas *adj.*
ˌpreciviliˈzation *or* **ˌpreciviliˈsation** *n.*
preˈclassical *adj.*
preˈclean *vb.*
preˈcogiˌtate *vb.*
preˈcollege *adj.*
ˌprecolˈlegiate *adj.*
ˌpreconˈcert *vb.*
ˌpreconˈcession *n.*
ˌpreconˈdemn *vb.*
ˌprecondemˈnation *n.*
ˌpreconˈjecture *vb.*
ˌpreconˈnection *n.*
ˌpreconˌsiderˈation *n.*
ˌpreconˈsidered *adj.*
ˌpreconˈstruct *vb.*
ˌpreconsulˈtation *n.*

precritical (priː'krɪtɪkəl) *adj.* of, relating to, or occurring during the period preceding a crisis or a critical state or condition: *a precritical phase of a disease.*
precursor (prɪ'kɜːsə) *n.* **1.** a person or thing that precedes and shows or announces someone or something to come; harbinger. **2.** a predecessor or forerunner. **3.** a chemical substance that gives rise to another more important substance. [C16: from Latin *praecursor* one who runs in front, from *praecurrere,* from prae in front + *currere* to run]
precursory (prɪ'kɜːsərɪ) *or* **precursive** *adj.* **1.** serving as a precursor. **2.** preliminary or introductory.
pred. *abbrev. for* predicate.
predacious *or* **predaceous** (prɪ'deɪʃəs) *adj.* **1.** (of animals) habitually hunting and killing other animals for food. **2.** preying on others. [C18: from Latin *praeda* plunder; compare PREDATORY] —**pre'daciousness, pre'daceousness,** *or* **predacity** (prɪ'dæsɪtɪ) *n.*
predate (priː'deɪt) *vb.* (*tr.*) **1.** to affix a date to (a document, paper, etc.) that is earlier than the actual date. **2.** to assign a date to (an event, period, etc.) that is earlier than the actual or previously assigned date of occurrence. **3.** to be or occur at an earlier date than; precede in time.
predation (prɪ'deɪʃən) *n.* a relationship between two species of animal in a community, in which one (the predator) hunts, kills, and eats the other (the prey).
predator ('prɛdətə) *n.* **1.** any carnivorous animal. **2.** a predatory person or thing.
predatory ('prɛdətərɪ, -trɪ) *adj.* **1.** *Zoology.* another word for **predacious** (sense 1). **2.** of, involving, or characterized by plundering, robbing, etc. [C16: from Latin *praedātōrius* rapacious, from *praedārī* to pillage, from *praeda* booty] —**'predatorily** *adv.* —**'predatoriness** *n.*
predatory pricing *n. Commerce.* offering goods or services at such a low price that competitors are forced out of the market.
predecease (ˌpriːdɪ'siːs) *vb.* **1.** to die before (some other person). ~*n.* **2.** *Rare.* earlier death.
predecessor ('priːdɪˌsɛsə) *n.* **1.** a person who precedes another, as in an office. **2.** something that precedes something else. **3.** an ancestor; forefather. [C14: via Old French from Late Latin *praedēcessor,* from *prae* before + *dēcēdere* to go away, from *dē* away + *cēdere* to go]
predella (prɪ'dɛlə; *Italian* pre'dɛlla) *n., pl.* **-le** (-liː; *Italian* -le). **1.** a painting or sculpture or a series of small paintings or sculptures in a long narrow strip forming the lower edge of an altarpiece or the face of an altar step or platform. **2.** a platform in a church upon which the altar stands. [C19: from Italian: stool, step, probably from Old High German *bret* board]
predestinarian (ˌpriːdɛstɪ'nɛərɪən) *Theol.* ~*n.* **1.** a person who believes in divine predestination. ~*adj.* **2.** of or relating to predestination or characterizing those who believe in it. —ˌ**predesti'narianism** *n.*
predestinate *vb.* (priː'dɛstɪˌneɪt). **1.** (*tr.*) another word for **predestine.** ~*adj.* (priː'dɛstɪnɪt, -ˌneɪt). **2.** predestined or foreordained. **3.** *Theol.* subject to predestination; decided by God from all eternity.
predestination (priːˌdɛstɪ'neɪʃən) *n.* **1.** *Theol.* **a.** the act of God foreordaining every event from eternity. **b.** the doctrine or belief, esp. associated with Calvin, that the final salvation of some of mankind is foreordained from eternity by God. **2.** the act of predestining or the state of being predestined.
predestine (priː'dɛstɪn) *or* **predestinate** *vb.* (*tr.*) **1.** to foreordain; determine beforehand. **2.** *Theol.* (of God) to decree from eternity (any event, esp. the final salvation of individuals). [C14: from Latin *praedestināre* to resolve beforehand, from *destināre* to determine, DESTINE] —**pre'destinable** *adj.*
predeterminate (ˌpriːdɪ'tɜːmɪnɪt, -ˌneɪt) *adj.* determined beforehand; predetermined. —ˌ**prede'terminately** *adv.*
predetermine (ˌpriːdɪ'tɜːmɪn) *vb.* (*tr.*) **1.** to determine beforehand. **2.** to influence or incline towards an opinion beforehand; bias. —ˌ**predeˌtermi'nation** *n.* —ˌ**prede'terminative** *adj.* —ˌ**prede'terminer** *n.*
predial ('priːdɪəl) *adj.* a variant spelling of **praedial.**
predicable ('prɛdɪkəbəl) *adj.* **1.** capable of being predicated or asserted. ~*n.* **2.** a quality, attribute, etc., that can be predicated. **3.** *Logic, obsolete.* one of the five Aristotelian classes of predicates (**the five heads of predicables**), namely genus, species, difference, property, and relation. [C16: from Latin *praedicābilis,* from *praedicāre* to assert publicly; see PREDICATE, PREACH] —ˌ**predica'bility** *or* **'predicableness** *n.*
predicament (prɪ'dɪkəmənt) *n.* **1.** a perplexing, embarrassing, or difficult situation. **2.** ('prɛdɪkəmənt). *Logic, obsolete.* one of Aristotle's ten categories of being. **3.** *Archaic.* a specific condition, circumstance, state, position, etc. [C14: from Late Latin *praedicāmentum* what is predicated, from *praedicāre* to announce, assert; see PREDICATE]
predicant ('prɛdɪkənt) *adj.* **1.** of or relating to preaching. ~*n.* **2.** a member of a religious order founded for preaching, esp. a Dominican. **3.** (ˌprɛdɪ'kænt). a variant spelling of **predikant.** [C17: from Latin *praedicāns* preaching, from *praedicāre* to say publicly; see PREDICATE]
predicate *vb.* ('prɛdɪˌkeɪt). (*mainly tr.*) **1.** (*also intr.; when tr., may take a clause as object*) to proclaim, declare, or affirm. **2.** to imply or connote. **3.** (foll. by *on* or *upon*) to base or found (a proposition, argument, etc.). **4.** *Logic.* **a.** to assert or affirm (a property, characteristic, or condition) of the subject of a proposition. **b.** to make (a term, expression, etc.) the predicate of a proposition. ~*n.* ('prɛdɪkɪt). **5.** *Grammar.* **a.** the part of a sentence in which something is asserted or denied of the subject of a sentence; one of the two major components of a sentence, the other being the subject. **b.** (*as modifier*): *a predicate adjective.* **6.** *Logic.* **a.** an expression that is derived from a sentence by the deletion of a name. **b.** a property, characteristic, or attribute that may be affirmed or denied of something. The categorial statement *all men are mortal* relates two predicates, *is a man* and *is mortal.* **c.** the term of a categorial proposition that is affirmed or denied of its subject. In this example *all men* is the subject, and *mortal* is the predicate. **d.** a function from individuals to truth values, the truth set of the function being the extension of the predicate. ~*adj.* ('prɛdɪkɪt). **7.** of or relating to something that has been predicated. [C16: from Latin *praedicāre* to assert publicly, from *prae* in front, in public + *dīcere* to say] —ˌ**predi'cation** *n.*
predicate calculus *n.* the system of symbolic logic concerned not only with relations between propositions as wholes but also with the representation by symbols of individuals and predicates in propositions and with quantification over individuals. Also called: **functional calculus.** See also **propositional calculus.**
predicative (prɪ'dɪkətɪv) *adj.* **1.** *Grammar.* relating to or occurring within the predicate of a sentence: *a predicative adjective.* Compare **attributive. 2.** *Logic.* (of a definition) given in terms that do not require quantification over entities of the same type as that which is thereby defined. Compare **impredicative.** —**pre'dicatively** *adv.*
predicator ('prɛdɪˌkeɪtə) *n.* (in systemic grammar) the part of a sentence or clause containing the verbal group; one of the four or five major components into which clauses can be divided, the others being subject, object, adjunct, and (in some versions of the grammar) complement.
predicatory ('prɛdɪˌkeɪtərɪ, ˌprɛdɪ'keɪtərɪ) *adj.* of, relating to, or characteristic of preaching or a preacher. [C17: from Late Latin *praedicātōrius,* from *praedicāre* to proclaim]
predict (prɪ'dɪkt) *vb.* (*tr.; may take a clause as object*) to state or make a declaration about in advance, esp. on a reasoned basis; foretell. [C17: from Latin *praedīcere* to mention beforehand, from *prae* before + *dīcere* to say] —**pre'dictable** *adj.* —**preˌdicta'bility** *or* **pre'dictableness** *n.* —**pre'dictably** *adv.*
prediction (prɪ'dɪkʃən) *n.* **1.** the act of predicting. **2.** something predicted; a forecast, prophecy, etc. —**pre'dictive** *adj.* —**pre'dictively** *adv.*
predictor (prɪ'dɪktə) *n.* **1.** a person or thing that predicts. **2.** an instrument, used in conjunction with an anti-aircraft gun, that determines the speed, distance, height, and direction of hostile aircraft. **3.** *Statistics.* a more modern term for **independent variable.**
predigest (ˌpriːdaɪ'dʒɛst, -dɪ-) *vb.* (*tr.*) to treat (food) artificially to aid subsequent digestion in the body. —ˌ**predi'gestion** *n.*
predikant *or* **predicant** (ˌprɛdɪ'kænt) *n.* a minister in the Dutch Reformed Church, esp. in South Africa. [from Dutch, from Old French *predicant,* from Late Latin *praedicans* preaching, from *praedicāre* to PREACH]
predilection (ˌpriːdɪ'lɛkʃən) *n.* a predisposition, preference, or bias. [C18: from French *prédilection,* from Medieval Latin *praedīligere* to prefer, from Latin *prae* before + *dīligere* to love]
predispose (ˌpriːdɪ'spəʊz) *vb.* (*tr.*) **1.** (often foll. by *to* or *towards*) to incline or make (someone) susceptible to something beforehand. **2.** *Chiefly law.* to dispose of (property, etc.) beforehand; bequeath. —ˌ**predis'posal** *n.*
predisposition (ˌpriːdɪspə'zɪʃən) *n.* **1.** the condition of being predisposed. **2.** *Med.* susceptibility to a specific disease. Compare **diathesis.**
prednisolone (prɛd'nɪsəˌləʊn) *n.* a steroid drug derived from prednisone and having the same uses as cortisone. [C20: altered from PREDNISONE]
prednisone ('prɛdnɪˌsəʊn) *n.* a steroid drug derived from cortisone and having the same uses. [C20: perhaps from PRE(GNANT) + -D(IE)N(E) + (CORT)ISONE]
predominant (prɪ'dɒmɪnənt) *adj.* **1.** having superiority in power, influence, etc., over others. **2.** prevailing; prominent. —**pre'dominance** *or* **pre'dominancy** *n.* —**pre'dominantly** *adv.*
predominate (prɪ'dɒmɪˌneɪt) *vb.* **1.** (*intr.;* often foll. by *over*) to have power, influence, or control. **2.** (*intr.*) to prevail or preponderate. **3.** (*tr.*) *Rare.* to dominate or have control over. ~*adj.* (prɪ'dɒmɪnɪt). **4.** another word for **predominant.** [C16: from Medieval Latin *praedominārī,* from Latin *prae* before + *dominārī*

ˌ**precon'trive** *vb.*
ˌ**precon'viction** *n.*
pre'cook *vb.*
pre-'Dantean *adj.*
ˌ**pre-Dar'winian** *adj.*
ˌ**prede'sign** *vb.*
pre'desigˌnate *vb.*
ˌ**prede'terminable** *adj.*
ˌ**predis'solve** *vb.*
ˌ**predis'tinguish** *vb.*
ˌ**predi'vide** *vb.*
pre'doom *vb.*

to bear rule, domineer] —**pre'dominately** *adv.* —**pre,domi'nation** *n.* —**pre'domi,nator** *n.*

pre-echo (priː'ɛkəʊ) *n.* **1.** something that has preceded and anticipated something else; precursor. **2.** a fault in an audio recording in which a sound that is to come is heard too early: on tape sometimes caused by print-through.

pre-eclampsia (,priːɪ'klæmpsɪə) *n. Pathol.* a toxic condition of pregnancy characterized by high blood pressure, protein in the urine, abnormal weight gain, and oedema. Compare **eclampsia.**

pre-embryo (priː'ɛmbrɪəʊ) *n.* the structure formed after fertilization of an ovum but before differentiation of embryonic tissue.

preemie *or* **premie** ('priːmɪ) *n. Slang, chiefly U.S. and Canadian.* a premature infant. [C20: altered from PREMATURE]

pre-eminent (prɪ'ɛmɪnənt) *adj.* extremely eminent or distinguished; outstanding. —**pre-'eminence** *n.* —**pre-'eminently** *adv.*

pre-empt (prɪ'ɛmpt) *vb.* **1.** (*tr.*) to acquire in advance of or to the exclusion of others; appropriate. **2.** (*tr.*) *Chiefly U.S.* to occupy (public land) in order to acquire a prior right to purchase. **3.** (*intr.*) *Bridge.* to make a high opening bid, often on a weak hand, to shut out opposition bidding. —**pre-'emptor** *n.* —**pre-'emptory** *adj.*

pre-emption (prɪ'ɛmpʃən) *n.* **1.** *Law.* the purchase of or right to purchase property in advance of or in preference to others. **2.** *International law.* the right of a government to intercept and seize for its own purposes goods or property of the subjects of another state while in transit, esp. in time of war. [C16: from Medieval Latin *praeemptiō*, from *praeemere* to buy beforehand, from *emere* to buy]

pre-emptive (prɪ'ɛmptɪv) *adj.* **1.** of, involving, or capable of pre-emption. **2.** *Bridge.* (of a high bid) made to shut out opposition bidding. **3.** *Military.* designed to reduce or destroy an enemy's attacking strength before it can use it: *a pre-emptive strike.* —**pre-'emptively** *adv.*

preen[1] (priːn) *vb.* **1.** (of birds) to maintain (feathers) in a healthy condition by arrangement, cleaning, and other contact with the bill. **2.** to dress or array (oneself) carefully; primp. **3.** (usually foll. by *on*) to pride or congratulate (oneself). [C14 *preinen*, probably from *prunen* to PRUNE[3], influenced by *prenen* to prick, pin (see PREEN[2]); suggestive of the pricking movement of the bird's beak] —**'preener** *n.*

preen[2] (priːn) *n. Scot.* a pin, esp. a decorative one. [Old English *prēon* a pin; related to Middle High German *pfrieme* awl, Dutch *priem* bodkin]

pre-exilian (,priːɪg'zɪlɪən) *or* **pre-exilic** *adj. Old Testament.* prior to the Babylonian exile of the Jews (587–539 B.C.).

pref. *abbrev. for:* **1.** preface. **2.** prefatory. **3.** preference. **4.** preferred. **5.** prefix.

prefab ('priː,fæb) *n.* **a.** a building that is prefabricated, esp. a small house. **b.** (*as modifier*): *a prefab house.*

prefabricate (priː'fæbrɪ,keɪt) *vb.* (*tr.*) to manufacture sections of (a building), esp. in a factory, so that they can be easily transported to and rapidly assembled on a building site. —**pre,fabri'cation** *n.* —**pre'fabri,cator** *n.*

preface ('prɛfɪs) *n.* **1.** a statement written as an introduction to a literary or other work, typically explaining its scope, intention, method, etc.; foreword. **2.** anything introductory. **3.** *R.C. Church.* a prayer of thanksgiving and exhortation serving as an introduction to the canon of the Mass. ~*vb.* (*tr.*) **4.** to furnish with a preface. **5.** to serve as a preface to. [C14: from Medieval Latin *praefātia*, from Latin *praefātiō* a saying beforehand, from *praefārī* to utter in advance, from *prae* before + *fārī* to say] —**'prefacer** *n.*

prefatory ('prɛfətərɪ, -trɪ) *or* **prefatorial** (,prɛfə'tɔːrɪəl) *adj.* of, involving, or serving as a preface; introductory. [C17: from Latin *praefārī* to say in advance; see PREFACE] —**'prefatorily** *or* **,prefa'torially** *adv.*

prefect ('priːfɛkt) *n.* **1.** (in France, Italy, etc.) the chief administrative officer in a department. **2.** (in France, etc.) the head of a police force. **3.** *Brit.* a schoolchild appointed to a position of limited power over his fellows. **4.** (in ancient Rome) any of several magistrates or military commanders. **5.** Also called: **prefect apostolic.** *R.C. Church.* an official having jurisdiction over a missionary district that has no ordinary. **6.** *R.C. Church.* one of two senior masters in a Jesuit school or college (the **prefect of studies** and the **prefect of discipline** or **first prefect**). **7.** *R.C. Church.* a cardinal in charge of a congregation of the Curia. ~Also (for senses 4–7): **praefect.** [C14: from Latin *praefectus* one put in charge, from *praeficere* to place in authority over, from *prae* before + *facere* to do, make] —**prefectorial** (,priːfɛk'tɔːrɪəl) *adj.*

prefecture ('priːfɛk,tjʊə) *n.* **1.** the office, position, or area of authority of a prefect. **2.** the official residence of a prefect in France, Italy, etc. —**pre'fectural** *adj.*

prefer (prɪ'fɜː) *vb.* **-fers, -ferring, -ferred.** **1.** (when *tr.*, *may take a clause as object or an infinitive*) to like better or value more highly: *I prefer to stand.* **2.** *Law.* to give preference, esp. to one creditor over others. **3.** (esp. of the police) to put (charges) before a court, judge, magistrate, etc., for consideration and judgment. **4.** (*tr.; often passive*) to advance in rank over another or others; promote. [C14: from Latin *praeferre* to carry in front, prefer, from *prae* in front + *ferre* to bear] —**pre'ferrer** *n.*

preferable ('prɛfərəb^{ə}l, 'prɛfrəb^{ə}l) *adj.* preferred or more desirable. —**,prefera'bility** *or* **'preferableness** *n.* —**'preferably** *adv.*

preference ('prɛfərəns, 'prɛfrəns) *n.* **1.** the act of preferring. **2.** something or someone preferred. **3.** *Law.* **a.** the settling of the claims of one or more creditors before or to the exclusion of those of the others. **b.** a prior right to payment, as of a dividend or share in the assets of a company in the event of liquidation. **4.** *International trade.* the granting of favour or precedence to particular foreign countries, as by levying differential tariffs.

preference shares *pl. n. Brit. and Austral.* shares representing part of the capital issued by a company and entitling their holders to priority with respect to both net profit and net assets. Preference shares usually carry a definite rate of dividend that is generally lower than that declared on ordinary shares. U.S. and Canadian name: **preferred stock.** Compare **ordinary shares, preferred ordinary shares.**

preferential (,prɛfə'rɛnʃəl) *adj.* **1.** showing or resulting from preference. **2.** giving, receiving, or originating from preference in international trade. —**preferentiality** (,prɛfə,rɛnʃɪ'ælɪtɪ) *n.* —**,prefer'entially** *adv.*

preferential voting *n.* a system of voting in which the electors signify their choices, as of candidates, in order of preference.

preferment (prɪ'fɜːmənt) *n.* **1.** the act of promoting or advancing to a higher position, office, etc. **2.** the state of being preferred for promotion or social advancement. **3.** the act of preferring.

preferred ordinary shares *pl. n. Brit.* shares issued by a company that rank between preference shares and ordinary shares in the payment of dividends. Compare **preference shares.**

preferred stock *n.* the U.S. and Canadian name for **preference shares.**

prefiguration (,priːfɪgə'reɪʃən) *n.* **1.** the act of prefiguring. **2.** something that prefigures, such as a prototype. —**pre'figurative** *adj.* —**pre'figuratively** *adv.* —**pre'figurativeness** *n.*

prefigure (priː'fɪgə) *vb.* (*tr.*) **1.** to represent or suggest in advance. **2.** to imagine or consider beforehand. —**pre'figurement** *n.*

prefix *n.* ('priːfɪks). **1.** *Grammar.* an affix that precedes the stem to which it is attached, as for example *un-* in *unhappy.* Compare **suffix** (sense 1). **2.** something coming or placed before. ~*vb.* (priː'fɪks, 'priːfɪks). (*tr.*) **3.** to put or place before. **4.** *Grammar.* to add (a morpheme) as a prefix to the beginning of a word. —**prefixal** ('priːfɪksəl, priː'fɪks-) *adj.* —**'prefixally** *adv.* —**prefixion** (priː'fɪkʃən) *n.*

preformation (,priːfɔː'meɪʃən) *n.* **1.** the act of forming in advance; previous formation. **2.** *Biology.* the theory, now discredited, that an individual develops by simple enlargement of a fully differentiated egg cell. Compare **epigenesis** (sense 1).

prefrontal (priː'frʌnt^{ə}l) *adj.* situated in, involving, or relating to the foremost part of the frontal lobe of the brain.

preggers ('prɛgəz) *adj. Chiefly Brit.* an informal word for **pregnant** (sense 1).

preggy ('prɛgɪ) *adj. N.Z.* an informal word for **pregnant** (sense 1).

preglacial (priː'gleɪsɪəl) *adj.* formed or occurring before a glacial period, esp. before the Pleistocene epoch.

pregnable ('prɛgnəb^{ə}l) *adj.* capable of being assailed or captured. [C15 *prenable*, from Old French *prendre* to take, from Latin *prehendere* to lay hold of, catch] —**,pregna'bility** *n.*

pregnancy ('prɛgnənsɪ) *n., pl.* **-cies.** **1.** the state or condition of being pregnant. **2.** the period from conception to childbirth.

pregnant ('prɛgnənt) *adj.* **1.** carrying a fetus or fetuses within the womb. **2.** full of meaning or significance. **3.** inventive or imaginative. **4.** prolific or fruitful. [C16: from Latin *praegnāns* with child, from *prae* before + (*g*)*nascī* to be born] —**'pregnantly** *adv.*

prehensile (prɪ'hɛnsaɪl) *adj.* adapted for grasping, esp. by wrapping around a support: *a prehensile tail.* [C18: from French *préhensile*, from Latin *prehendere* to grasp] —**prehensility** (,priːhɛn'sɪlɪtɪ) *n.*

prehension (prɪ'hɛnʃən) *n.* **1.** the act of grasping. **2.** apprehension by the senses or the mind.

,predy'nastic *adj.*
,pre-e'lect *vb.*
,pre-e'lection *n.*
pre-'Empire *adj.*
,pre-en'gage *vb.*
,pre-en'gagement *n.*
,pre-en'listment *n.*
,pre-es'tablish *vb.*
pre-'esti,mate *vb.*
,pre-ex,ami'nation *adj.*
,pre-ex'amine *vb.*
,pre-ex'ist *vb.*
,pre-ex'istence *n.*
,pre-ex'pose *vb.*
'pre'flight *adj.*
pre'form *vb.*
,prefor'mation *n.*
pre'franked *adj.*
pre'freeze *vb.*, **-'freezes, -'freezing, -'froze, -'frozen.**
,pre-Ger'manic *adj.*
pre-'Gothic *adj.*
pre-'Greek *adj.*
pre'harden *vb.*
pre'heat *vb.*

prehistoric (ˌpriːhɪˈstɒrɪk) *or* **prehistorical** *adj.* of or relating to man's development before the appearance of the written word. —ˌ**prehisˈtorically** *adv.*

prehistory (priːˈhɪstərɪ) *n., pl.* **-ries.** **1.** the prehistoric period. **2.** the study of this period, relying entirely on archaeological evidence. —**prehistorian** (ˌpriːhɪˈstɔːrɪən) *n.*

prehominid (priːˈhɒmɪnɪd) *n.* any of various extinct manlike primates. See **australopithecine.**

pre-ignition (ˌpriːɪgˈnɪʃən) *n.* ignition of all or part of the explosive charge in an internal-combustion engine before the exact instant necessary for correct operation.

prejudge (priːˈdʒʌdʒ) *vb. (tr.)* to judge beforehand, esp. without sufficient evidence. —**preˈjudger** *n.* —**preˈjudgment** *or* **preˈjudgement** *n.*

prejudice (ˈprɛdʒʊdɪs) *n.* **1.** an opinion formed beforehand, esp. an unfavourable one based on inadequate facts. **2.** the act or condition of holding such opinions. **3.** intolerance of or dislike for people of a specific race, religion, etc. **4.** disadvantage or injury resulting from prejudice. **5. in** (*or* **to**) **the prejudice of.** to the detriment of. **6. without prejudice.** *Law.* without dismissing or detracting from an existing right or claim. ~*vb. (tr.)* **7.** to cause to be prejudiced. **8.** to disadvantage or injure by prejudice. [C13: from Old French *préjudice,* from Latin *praejūdicium* a preceding judgment, disadvantage, from *prae* before + *jūdicium* trial, sentence, from *jūdex* a judge]

prejudicial (ˌprɛdʒʊˈdɪʃəl) *adj.* causing prejudice; detrimental or damaging. —ˌ**prejuˈdicially** *adv.*

prelacy (ˈprɛləsɪ) *n., pl.* **-cies. 1.** Also called: **prelature** (ˈprɛlɪtʃə). **a.** the office or status of a prelate. **b.** prelates collectively. **2.** Also called: **prelatism** (ˈprɛləˌtɪzəm). *Often derogatory.* government of the Church by prelates.

prelapsarian (ˌpriːlæpˈsɛərɪən) *adj.* characteristic of or relating to the human state or time before the Fall: *prelapsarian innocence.*

prelate (ˈprɛlɪt) *n.* a Church dignitary of high rank, such as a cardinal, bishop, or abbot. [C13: from Old French *prélat,* from Church Latin *praelātus,* from Latin *praeferre* to hold in special esteem, PREFER] —**prelatic** (prɪˈlætɪk) *or* **preˈlatical** *adj.*

prelatism (ˈprɛləˌtɪzəm) *n.* government of the Church by prelates; episcopacy. —ˈ**prelatist** *n.*

prelect (prɪˈlɛkt) *vb. (intr.) Rare.* to lecture or discourse in public. [C17: from Late Latin *praelegere* to instruct by reading, lecture, from *prae* in front of, in public + *legere* to read, choose] —**preˈlection** *n.* —**preˈlector** *n.*

prelexical (priːˈlɛksɪkəl) *adj. Transformational grammar.* denoting or applicable at a stage in the formation of a sentence at which words and phrases have not yet replaced all of the underlying grammatical and semantic material of that sentence in the speaker's mind.

prelibation (ˌpriːlaɪˈbeɪʃən) *n. Rare.* an advance taste or sample; foretaste. [C16: from Late Latin *praelībātiō* a tasting beforehand, offering of the first fruits, from Latin *prae* before + *lībāre* to taste]

prelim. *abbrev. for* preliminary.

preliminaries (prɪˈlɪmɪnərɪz) *pl. n.* the full word for **prelims.**

preliminary (prɪˈlɪmɪnərɪ) *adj.* **1.** (*usually prenominal*) occurring before or in preparation; introductory. ~*n., pl.* **-naries. 2.** a preliminary event or occurrence. **3.** an eliminating contest held before the main competition. [C17: from New Latin *praelīmināris,* from Latin *prae* before + *līmen* threshold] —**preˈliminarily** *adv.*

prelims (ˈpriːlɪmz, prəˈlɪmz) *pl. n.* **1.** Also called: **front matter.** the pages of a book, such as the title page and contents, before the main text. **2.** the first public examinations taken for the bachelor's degree in some universities. **3.** (in Scotland) the school examinations taken as practice before public examinations. [C19: a contraction of PRELIMINARIES]

prelingually deaf (priːˈlɪŋgwəlɪ) *adj.* **a.** deaf from birth or having acquired deafness before learning to speak. **b.** (*as collective n.;* preceded by *the*): *the prelingually deaf.*

preliterate (priːˈlɪtərɪt) *adj.* relating to a society that has not developed a written language. —**preliteracy** (priːˈlɪtərəsɪ) *n.*

prelude (ˈprɛljuːd) *n.* **1. a.** a piece of music that precedes a fugue, or forms the first movement of a suite, or an introduction to an act in an opera, etc. **b.** (esp. for piano) a self-contained piece of music. **2.** something serving as an introduction or preceding event, occurrence, etc. ~*vb.* **3.** to serve as a prelude to (something). **4.** (*tr.*) to introduce by a prelude. [C16: (n.) from Medieval Latin *praelūdium,* from *prae* before + *-lūdium* entertainment, from Latin *lūdus* play; (vb.) from Late Latin *praelūdere* to play beforehand, rehearse, from *lūdere* to play] —**preluder** (prɪˈljuːdə, ˈprɛljʊdə) *n.* —**preˈludial** *adj.* —**prelusion** (prɪˈljuːʒən) *n.* —**prelusive** (prɪˈljuːsɪv) *or* **prelusory** (prɪˈljuːsərɪ) *adj.* —**preˈlusively** *or* **preˈlusorily** *adv.*

prem (prɛm) *n. Informal.* a premature infant.

prem. *abbrev. for* premium.

premarital (priːˈmærɪtəl) *adj.* (esp. of sexual relations) occurring before marriage. Compare **extramarital.**

premature (ˌprɛməˈtjʊə, ˈprɛməˌtjʊə) *adj.* **1.** occurring or existing before the normal or expected time. **2.** impulsive or hasty: *a premature judgment.* **3.** (of an infant) weighing less than 2500 g (5½ lbs) and usually born before the end of the full period of gestation. [C16: from Latin *praemātūrus,* very early from *prae* in advance + *mātūrus* ripe] —ˌ**premaˈturely** *adv.* —ˌ**premaˈtureness** *or* ˌ**premaˈturity** *n.*

premaxilla (ˌpriːmækˈsɪlə) *n., pl.* **-lae** (-liː). either of two bones situated in the upper jaw between the maxillary bones. —ˌ**preˈmaxˈillary** *adj.*

premed (priːˈmɛd) *Informal.* ~*adj.* **1.** short for **premedical.** ~*n. also* **premedic. 2.** short for **premedication. 3.** a premedical student.

premedical (priːˈmɛdɪkəl) *adj.* **1.** of or relating to a course of study prerequisite for entering medical school. **2.** of or relating to a person engaged in such a course of study: *a premedical student.* —**preˈmedically** *adv.*

premedication (ˌpriːmɛdɪˈkeɪʃən) *n. Surgery.* any drugs administered to sedate and otherwise prepare a patient for general anaesthesia.

premeditate (prɪˈmɛdɪˌteɪt) *vb.* to plan or consider (something, such as a violent crime) beforehand. —**preˈmediˌtatedly** *adv.* —**preˈmediˌtative** *adj.* —**preˈmediˌtator** *n.*

premeditation (prɪˌmɛdɪˈteɪʃən) *n.* **1.** *Law.* prior resolve to do some act or to commit a crime. **2.** the act of premeditating.

premenstrual (priːˈmɛnstrʊəl) *adj.* of or occurring before a menstrual period.

premenstrual tension *or* **syndrome** *n.* any of various symptoms, including esp. nervous tension, that may be experienced as a result of hormonal changes in the days before a menstrual period starts. Abbrevs.: **PMT, PMS.**

premie (ˈpriːmɪ) *n.* a variant spelling of **preemie.**

premier (ˈprɛmjə) *n.* **1.** another name for **prime minister. 2.** any of the heads of governments of the Canadian provinces and the Australian states. **3.** (*pl.*) *Austral.* the winners of a premiership. ~*adj.* (*prenominal*) **4.** first in importance, rank, etc. **5.** first in occurrence; earliest. [C15: from Old French: first, from Latin *prīmārius* principal, from *prīmus* first]

premier danseur *French.* (prəmje dɑ̃sœr) *or* (*fem.*) ***première danseuse*** (prəmjɛr dɑ̃søz) *n., pl.* ***premiers danseurs*** *or* (*fem.*) ***premières danseuses.*** the principal dancer in a ballet company. [C19: literally: first dancer]

premiere (ˈprɛmɪˌɛə, ˈprɛmɪə) *n.* **1.** the first public performance of a film, play, opera, etc. **2.** the leading lady in a theatre company. ~*vb.* **3.** to give or be the first public performance of. [C19: from French, feminine of *premier* first]

premiership (ˈprɛmjəʃɪp) *n.* **1.** the office of premier. **2. a.** *Austral.* a championship competition held among a number of sporting clubs. **b.** a victory in such a championship.

premillenarian (ˌpriːmɪlɪˈnɛərɪən) *n.* **1.** a believer in or upholder of the doctrines of premillennialism. ~*adj.* **2.** of or relating to premillennialism. —ˌ**premilleˈnarianism** *n.*

premillennial (ˌpriːmɪˈlɛnɪəl) *adj.* of or relating to the period preceding the millennium.

premillennialism (ˌpriːmɪˈlɛnɪəˌlɪzəm) *n.* the doctrine or belief that the millennium will be preceded by the Second Coming of Christ. —ˌ**premilˈlennialist** *n.*

premise *n.* (ˈprɛmɪs). **1.** Also: ˈ**premiss.** *Logic.* a statement that is assumed to be true for the purpose of an argument from which a conclusion is drawn. ~*vb.* (prɪˈmaɪz, ˈprɛmɪs). **2.** (when *tr., may take a clause as object*) to state or assume (a proposition) as a premise in an argument, theory, etc. [C14: from Old French *prémisse,* from Medieval Latin *praemissa* sent on before, from Latin *praemittere* to dispatch in advance, from *prae* before + *mittere* to send]

premises (ˈprɛmɪsɪz) *pl. n.* **1.** a piece of land together with its buildings, esp. considered as a place of business. **2.** *Law.* **a.** (in a deed, etc.) the matters referred to previously; the aforesaid; the foregoing. **b.** the introductory part of a grant, conveyance, etc. **3.** *Law.* (in the U.S.) the part of a bill in equity that states the names of the parties, details of the plaintiff's claims, etc.

premium (ˈpriːmɪəm) *n.* **1.** an amount paid in addition to a standard rate, price, wage, etc.; bonus. **2.** the amount paid or payable, usually in regular instalments, for an insurance policy. **3.** the amount above nominal or par value at which something sells. **4. a.** an offer of something free or at a specially reduced price as an inducement to buy a commodity or service. **b.** (*as modifier*): *a premium offer.* **5.** a prize given to the winner of a competition; award. **6.** *U.S.* an amount sometimes charged for a loan of money in addition to the interest. **7.** great value or regard: *to put a premium on someone's services.* **8.** a fee, now rarely required, for instruction or apprenticeship in a profession or trade. **9. at a premium. a.** in great demand or of high value, usually because of scarcity. **b.** above par. [C17: from Latin *praemium* prize, booty, reward]

Premium Savings Bonds *pl. n.* (in Britain) bonds issued by the Treasury since 1956 for purchase by the public. No interest is

ˌ**pre-Hoˈmeric** *adj.*
preˈhuman *adj.*
preˈindiˌcate *vb.*
ˌ**preinˈdustrial** *adj.*
ˌ**preinˈform** *vb.*
ˌ**preinˈstruct** *vb.*
preˈkinderˌgarten *adj.*
ˌ**preloˈcate** *vb.*
pre-ˈMarxian *adj.*
ˌ**pre-Menˈdelian** *adj.*

paid but there is a monthly draw for cash prizes of various sums. Also called: **premium bonds.**

premolar (priːˈməʊlə) *adj.* **1.** situated before a molar tooth. ~*n.* **2.** any one of eight bicuspid teeth in the human adult, two situated on each side of both jaws between the first molar and the canine.

premonish (prɪˈmɒnɪʃ) *vb.* (*tr.*) *Rare.* to admonish beforehand; forewarn.

premonition (ˌprɛməˈnɪʃən) *n.* **1.** an intuition of a future, usually unwelcome, occurrence; foreboding. **2.** an early warning of a future event; forewarning. [C16: from Late Latin *praemonitiō*, from Latin *praemonēre* to admonish beforehand, from *prae* before + *monēre* to warn, advise] —**premonitory** (prɪˈmɒnɪtərɪ, -trɪ) *adj.*

Premonstratensian (ˌpriːˌmɒnstrəˈtɛnsɪən) *n.* **a.** a member of a religious order founded at Prémontré in N France in 1120 by St Norbert (about 1080–1134). **b.** (*as modifier*): *a Premonstratensian canon.* [C17: from Medieval Latin (*locus*) *praemonstrātus* the place foreshown, because it was said to have been prophetically pointed out by St Norbert]

premorse (prɪˈmɔːs) *adj. Biology.* appearing as though the end had been bitten off: *a premorse leaf.* [C18: from Latin *praemorsus* bitten off in front, from *praemordēre*, from *prae* in front + *mordēre* to bite]

premunition (ˌpriːmjʊˈnɪʃən) *n. Med.* a state of immunity acquired as the result of a persistent latent infection. [C15 (in the sense: to protect beforehand): from Latin *praemūnitiō*, from *praemūnīre*, from *prae* before + *mūnīre* to fortify]

prenatal (priːˈneɪtᵊl) *adj.* **1.** occurring or present before birth; during pregnancy. ~*n.* **2.** *Informal.* a prenatal examination. ~Also: **antenatal.** —**preˈnatally** *adv.*

prenomen (priːˈnəʊmɛn) *n., pl.* **-nomina** (-ˈnɒmɪnə) *or* **-nomens.** *U.S.* a less common spelling of **praenomen.**

prenominal (priːˈnɒmɪnᵊl) *adj.* **1.** placed before a noun, esp. (of an adjective or sense of an adjective) used only before a noun. **2.** of or relating to a praenomen.

prenotion (priːˈnəʊʃən) *n.* a rare word for **preconception.**

prentice (ˈprɛntɪs) *n.* an archaic word for **apprentice.**

prenuptial agreement *n.* a contract made between a man and woman before they marry, agreeing on the distribution of their assets in the event of divorce.

preoccupation (priːˌɒkjʊˈpeɪʃən) *or* **preoccupancy** (priːˈɒkjʊpənsɪ) *n.* **1.** the state of being preoccupied, esp. mentally. **2.** something that holds the attention or preoccupies the mind.

preoccupied (priːˈɒkjʊˌpaɪd) *adj.* **1.** engrossed or absorbed in something, esp. one's own thoughts. **2.** already or previously occupied. **3.** *Biology.* (of a taxonomic name) already used to designate a genus, species, etc.

preoccupy (priːˈɒkjʊˌpaɪ) *vb.* **-pies, -pying, -pied.** (*tr.*) **1.** to engross the thoughts or mind of. **2.** to occupy before or in advance of another. [C16: from Latin *praeoccupāre* to capture in advance, from *prae* before + *occupāre* to seize, take possession of]

preordain (ˌpriːɔːˈdeɪn) *vb.* (*tr.*) to ordain, decree, or appoint beforehand. —**preordination** (ˌpriːɔːdɪˈneɪʃən) *n.*

prep (prɛp) *n. Informal.* short for **preparation** (sense 5) or (chiefly U.S.) **preparatory school.**

prep. *abbrev. for:* **1.** preparation. **2.** preparatory. **3.** preposition.

preparation (ˌprɛpəˈreɪʃən) *n.* **1.** the act or process of preparing. **2.** the state of being prepared; readiness. **3.** (*often pl.*) a measure done in order to prepare for something; provision: *to make preparations for something.* **4.** something that is prepared, esp. a medicine. **5.** (esp. in a boarding school) **a.** homework. **b.** the period reserved for this. Usually shortened to **prep.** **6.** *Music.* **a.** the anticipation of a dissonance so that the note producing it in one chord is first heard in the preceding chord as a consonance. **b.** a note so employed. **7.** (*often cap.*) the preliminary prayers at Mass or divine service.

preparative (prɪˈpærətɪv) *adj.* **1.** serving to prepare; preparatory. ~*n.* **2.** something that prepares. —**preˈparatively** *adv.*

preparatory (prɪˈpærətərɪ, -trɪ) *adj.* **1.** serving to prepare. **2.** introductory or preliminary. **3.** occupied in preparation. **4.** **preparatory to.** as a preparation to; before: *a drink preparatory to eating.* —**preˈparatorily** *adv.*

preparatory school *n.* **1.** (in Britain) a private school, usually single-sex and for children between the ages of 6 and 13, generally preparing pupils for public school. **2.** (in the U.S.) a private secondary school preparing pupils for college. ~Often shortened to **prep school.**

prepare (prɪˈpɛə) *vb.* **1.** to make ready or suitable in advance for a particular purpose or for some use, event, etc.: *to prepare a meal; to prepare to go.* **2.** to put together using parts or ingredients; compose or construct. **3.** (*tr.*) to equip or outfit, as for an expedition. **4.** (*tr.*) *Music.* to soften the impact of (a dissonant note) by the use of preparation. **5.** **be prepared.** (*foll. by an infinitive*) to be willing and able (to do something): *I'm not prepared to reveal these figures.* [C15: from Latin *praeparāre*, from *prae* before + *parāre* to make ready] —**preˈparer** *n.*

preparedness (prɪˈpɛərɪdnɪs) *n.* the state of being prepared or ready, esp. militarily ready for war. —**preˈparedly** *adv.*

prepared piano *n.* a piano in which some strings have been damped by having objects placed between them or tuned differently from the rest for specific tonal effect. This process was pioneered by John Cage.

prepay (priːˈpeɪ) *vb.* **-pays, -paying, -paid.** (*tr.*) to pay for in advance. —**preˈpayable** *adj.* —**preˈpayment** *n.*

prepense (prɪˈpɛns) *adj.* (*postpositive*) (usually in legal contexts) arranged in advance; premeditated (esp. in the phrase **malice prepense**). [C18: from Anglo-Norman *purpensé*, from Old French *purpenser* to consider in advance, from *penser* to think, from Latin *pēnsāre* to weigh, consider]

preponderant (prɪˈpɒndərənt) *adj.* greater in weight, force, influence, etc. —**preˈponderance** *or* **preˈponderancy** *n.* —**preˈponderantly** *adv.*

preponderate (prɪˈpɒndəˌreɪt) *vb.* (*intr.*) **1.** (often foll. by *over*) to be more powerful, important, numerous, etc. (than). **2.** to be of greater weight than something else. **3.** *Archaic.* to be weighed down. [C17: from Late Latin *praeponderāre* to be of greater weight, from *pondus* weight] —**preˈponderately** *adv.* —**preˈponderˌating** *adj.* —**preˌponderˈation** *n.*

preposition (ˌprɛpəˈzɪʃən) *n.* a word or group of words used before a noun or pronoun to relate it grammatically or semantically to some other constituent of a sentence. Abbrev.: **prep.** [C14: from Latin *praepositiō* a putting before, from *pōnere* to place] —ˌ**prepoˈsitional** *adj.* —ˌ**prepoˈsitionally** *adv.*

▷**Usage.** The practice of ending a sentence with a preposition (*they are the people I hate talking to*) has been much condemned, but careful users avoid it only where it would be stylistically clumsy.

prepositive (priːˈpɒzɪtɪv) *adj.* **1.** (of a word or speech element) placed before the word governed or modified. ~*n.* **2.** a prepositive element. —**preˈpositively** *adv.*

prepositor (priːˈpɒzɪtə) *or* **prepostor** (priːˈpɒstə) *n. Brit., rare.* a prefect in any of certain public schools. [C16: from Latin *praepositus* placed before]

prepossess (ˌpriːpəˈzɛs) *vb.* (*tr.*) **1.** to preoccupy or engross mentally. **2.** to influence in advance for or against a person or thing; prejudice; bias. **3.** to make a favourable impression on beforehand.

prepossessing (ˌpriːpəˈzɛsɪŋ) *adj.* creating a favourable impression; attractive. —ˌ**preposˈsessingly** *adv.* —ˌ**preposˈsessingness** *n.*

prepossession (ˌpriːpəˈzɛʃən) *n.* **1.** the state or condition of being prepossessed. **2.** a prejudice or bias, esp. a favourable one.

preposterous (prɪˈpɒstərəs) *adj.* contrary to nature, reason, or sense; absurd; ridiculous. [C16: from Latin *praeposterus* reversed, from *prae* in front, before + *posterus* following] —**preˈposterously** *adv.* —**preˈposterousness** *n.*

prepotency (prɪˈpəʊtᵊnsɪ) *n.* **1.** the state or condition of being prepotent. **2.** *Genetics.* the ability of one parent to transmit more characteristics to its offspring than the other parent. **3.** *Botany.* the ability of pollen from one source to bring about fertilization more readily than that from other sources.

prepotent (prɪˈpəʊtᵊnt) *adj.* **1.** greater in power, force, or influence. **2.** *Biology.* showing prepotency. [C15: from Latin *praepotens* very powerful, from *posse* to be able] —**preˈpotently** *adv.*

preppy (ˈprɛpɪ) *Informal.* ~*adj.* **1.** characteristic of or denoting a fashion style of neat, understated, and often expensive clothes; young but classic: suggesting that the wearer is well off, upper class, and conservative. ~*n., pl.* **-pies.** **2.** a person exhibiting such style. [C20: originally U.S., from *preppy* a person who attends or has attended a preparatory school before college]

preproduction (ˌpriːprəˈdʌkʃən) *n.* **1.** preliminary work on or trial production of a play, industrial prototype, etc. ~*adj.* **2.** (of a period, model, etc.) preliminary; trial.

prep school *n. Informal.* See **preparatory school.**

prepuce (ˈpriːpjuːs) *n.* **1.** the retractable fold of skin covering the tip of the penis. Nontechnical name: **foreskin.** **2.** a similar fold of skin covering the tip of the clitoris. [C14: from Latin *praepūtium*] —**preputial** (priːˈpjuːʃəl) *adj.*

prequel (ˈpriːkwəl) *n.* a film that is made about an earlier stage of a story or character's life because the later part of it has already made a successful film. [C20: from PRE- + (*se*)*quel*]

Pre-Raphaelite (ˌpriːˈræfəlaɪt) *n.* **1.** a member of the Pre-Raphaelite Brotherhood, an association of British painters and writers founded in 1848 to combat the shallow conventionalism of academic painting and revive the fidelity to nature and the vivid realistic colour that they considered typical of Italian painting before Raphael (1483–1520). ~*adj.* **2.** of, in the manner of, or relating to Pre-Raphaelite painting and painters. —ˌ**PreˈRaphaelˌitism** *n.*

preˈmix *vb.*
ˌ**pre-Moˈsaic** *adj.*
preˈnuptial *adj.*
preˈpack *vb.*
preˈpackage *vb.*
preˈpacked *adj.*
preˈpalatal *adj.*
preˈplan *vb.*, **-ˈplans, -ˈplanning, -ˈplanned.**
preˈprandial *adj.*
ˌ**prepuˈbescent** *n., adj.*
ˌ**prepubliˈcation** *adj.*
preˈreading *n., adj.*
ˌ**prereˈcord** *vb.*
ˌ**pre-Reforˈmation** *adj.*
preˈregister *vb.*

prerequisite (priːˈrɛkwɪzɪt) *adj.* **1.** required as a prior condition. ~*n.* **2.** something required as a prior condition.

prerogative (prɪˈrɒɡətɪv) *n.* **1.** an exclusive privilege or right exercised by a person or group of people holding a particular office or hereditary rank. **2.** any privilege or right. **3.** a power, privilege, or immunity restricted to a sovereign or sovereign government. **4.** *Archaic.* precedence or pre-eminence. ~*adj.* **5.** having or able to exercise a prerogative. [C14: from Latin *praerogātīva* privilege, earlier: group with the right to vote first, from *prae* before + *rogāre* to ask, beg for]

pres. *abbrev. for:* **1.** present (time). **2.** presidential.

Pres. *abbrev. for* President.

presa (ˈprɛsɑː) *n., pl.* **-se** (-seɪ). *Music.* a sign or symbol used in a canon, round, etc., to indicate the entry of each part. Usual signs: +, :S:, or ⋇ [Italian, literally: a taking up, from *prendere* to take, from Latin *prehendere* to grasp]

presage *n.* (ˈprɛsɪdʒ). **1.** an intimation or warning of something about to happen; portent; omen. **2.** a sense of what is about to happen; foreboding. **3.** *Archaic.* a forecast or prediction. ~*vb.* (ˈprɛsɪdʒ, prɪˈseɪdʒ). **4.** (*tr.*) to have a presentiment of. **5.** (*tr.*) to give a forewarning of; portend. **6.** (*intr.*) to make a prediction. [C14: from Latin *praesāgium* presentiment, from *praesāgīre* to perceive beforehand, from *sāgīre* to perceive acutely] —**preˈsageful** *adj.* —**preˈsagefully** *adv.* —**preˈsager** *n.*

presale (ˈpriːseɪl) *n.* the practice of arranging the sale of a product before it is available.

Presb. *abbrev. for* Presbyterian.

presbyopia (ˌprɛzbɪˈəʊpɪə) *n.* a progressively diminishing ability of the eye to focus, noticeable from middle to old age, caused by loss of elasticity of the crystalline lens. [C18: New Latin, from Greek *presbus* old man + *ōps* eye] —**presbyopic** (ˌprɛzbɪˈɒpɪk) *adj.*

presbyter (ˈprɛzbɪtə) *n.* **1. a.** an elder of a congregation in the early Christian Church. **b.** (in some Churches having episcopal politics) an official who is subordinate to a bishop and has administrative, teaching, and sacerdotal functions. **2.** (in some hierarchical Churches) another name for **priest**. **3.** (in the Presbyterian Church) **a.** a teaching elder. **b.** a ruling elder. [C16: from Late Latin, from Greek *presbuteros* an older man, from *presbus* old man]

presbyterate (prɛzˈbɪtərɪt, -ˌreɪt) *n.* **1.** the status or office of a presbyter. **2.** a group of presbyters.

presbyterial (ˌprɛzbɪˈtɪərɪəl) *adj.* of or relating to a presbyter or presbytery. Also: **presbyteral** (prɛzˈbɪtərəl). —ˌ**presbyˈterially** *adv.*

presbyterian (ˌprɛzbɪˈtɪərɪən) *adj.* **1.** of, relating to, or designating Church government by presbyters or lay elders. ~*n.* **2.** an upholder of this type of Church government. —ˌ**presbyˈterianism** *n.* —ˌ**presbyˌterianˈistic** *adj.*

Presbyterian (ˌprɛzbɪˈtɪərɪən) *adj.* **1.** of or relating to any of various Protestant Churches governed by presbyters or lay elders and adhering to various modified forms of Calvinism. In 1972 the Presbyterian Church of England became part of the United Reformed Church. ~*n.* **2.** a member of a Presbyterian Church. —ˌ**Presbyˈterianism** *n.*

presbytery (ˈprɛzbɪtərɪ, -trɪ) *n., pl.* **-teries. 1.** *Presbyterian Church.* **a.** a local Church court composed of ministers and elders. **b.** the congregations or churches within the jurisdiction of any such court. **2.** the part of a cathedral or church east of the choir, in which the main altar is situated; sanctuary. **3.** presbyters or elders collectively. **4.** government of a church by presbyters or elders. **5.** *R.C. Church.* the residence of a parish priest. [C15: from Old French *presbiterie,* from Church Latin *presbyterium,* from Greek *presbyterion;* see PRESBYTER]

preschool *or* **pre-school** (priːˈskuːl) *adj.* **a.** (of a child) under the age at which compulsory education begins. **b.** (of services) for or relating to preschool children.

prescience (ˈprɛsɪəns) *n.* knowledge of events before they take place; foreknowledge. [C14: from Latin *praescīre* to foreknow, from *prae* before + *scīre* to know] —ˈ**prescient** *adj.* —ˈ**presciently** *adv.*

prescind (prɪˈsɪnd) *vb. Rare.* **1.** (*intr.;* usually foll. by *from*) to withdraw attention (from something). **2.** (*tr.*) to isolate, remove, or separate, as for special consideration. [C17: from Late Latin *praescindere* to cut off in front, from Latin *prae* before + *scindere* to split]

prescribe (prɪˈskraɪb) *vb.* **1.** to lay down as a rule or directive. **2.** *Law.* to claim or acquire (a right, title, etc.) by prescription. **3.** *Law.* to make or become invalid or unenforceable by lapse of time. **4.** *Med.* to recommend or order the use of (a drug or other remedy). [C16: from Latin *praescrībere* to write previously, from *prae* before + *scrībere* to write] —**preˈscriber** *n.*

prescript *n.* (ˈpriːskrɪpt). **1.** something laid down or prescribed. ~*adj.* (prɪˈskrɪpt, ˈpriːskrɪpt). **2.** prescribed as a rule. [C16: from Latin *praescriptum* something written down beforehand, from *praescrībere* to PRESCRIBE]

prescriptible (prɪˈskrɪptəbᵊl) *adj.* **1.** subject to prescription. **2.** depending on or derived from prescription. —**preˌscriptiˈbility** *n.*

prescription (prɪˈskrɪpʃən) *n.* **1. a.** written instructions from a physician, dentist, etc., to a pharmacist stating the form, dosage strength, etc., of a drug to be issued to a specific patient. **b.** the drug or remedy prescribed. **2.** (*modifier*) (of drugs) available legally only with a doctor's prescription. **3. a.** written instructions for an optician on the proper grinding of lenses for spectacles. **b.** (*as modifier*): *prescription glasses.* **4.** the act of prescribing. **5.** something that is prescribed. **6.** a long established custom or a claim based on one. **7.** *Law.* **a.** the uninterrupted possession of property over a stated period of time, after which a right or title is acquired (**positive prescription**). **b.** the barring of adverse claims to property, etc., after a specified period of time has elapsed, allowing the possessor to acquire title (**negative prescription**). **c.** the right or title acquired in either of these ways. [C14: from legal Latin *praescriptiō* an order, prescription; see PRESCRIBE]

prescriptive (prɪˈskrɪptɪv) *adj.* **1.** making or giving directions, rules, or injunctions. **2.** sanctioned by long-standing usage or custom. **3.** derived from or based upon legal prescription: *a prescriptive title.* —**preˈscriptively** *adv.* —**preˈscriptiveness** *n.*

prescriptivism (prɪˈskrɪptɪˌvɪzəm) *n. Ethics.* the theory that moral utterances have no truth value but prescribe attitudes to others and express the conviction of the speaker. Compare **descriptivism, emotivism.**

presell (priːˈsɛl) *vb.* (*tr.*) **-sells, -selling, -sold. 1.** to promote (a product, entertainment, etc.) with publicity in advance of its appearance. **2.** to prepare (the public) for a product, entertainment, etc., with advance publicity. **3.** to agree a sale of (a product) before it is available. **4.** to sell (a book) before its publication date.

presence (ˈprɛzəns) *n.* **1.** the state or fact of being present. **2.** the immediate proximity of a person or thing. **3.** personal appearance or bearing, esp. of a dignified nature. **4.** an imposing or dignified personality. **5.** an invisible spirit felt to be nearby. **6.** *Electronics.* a recording control that boosts midrange frequencies. **7.** (of a recording) a quality that gives the impression that the listener is in the presence of the original source of the sound. **8.** *Obsolete.* assembly or company. **9.** *Obsolete.* short for **presence chamber.** [C14: via Old French from Latin *praesentia* a being before, from *praeesse* to be before, from *prae* before + *esse* to be]

presence chamber *n.* the room in which a great person, such as a monarch, receives guests, assemblies, etc.

presence of mind *n.* the ability to remain calm and act constructively during times of crisis.

presenile dementia (priːˈsiːnaɪl) *n.* a form of dementia, of unknown cause, starting before a person is old.

present[1] (ˈprɛzᵊnt) *adj.* **1.** (*prenominal*) in existence at the moment in time at which an utterance is spoken or written. **2.** (*postpositive*) being in a specified place, thing, etc.: *the murderer is present in this room.* **3.** (*prenominal*) now in consideration or under discussion: *the present topic; the present author.* **4.** *Grammar.* denoting a tense of verbs used when the action or event described is occurring at the time of utterance or when the speaker does not wish to make any explicit temporal reference. **5.** *Archaic.* readily available; instant: *present help is at hand.* **6.** *Archaic.* mentally alert; attentive. ~*n.* **7. the present.** the time being; now. **8.** *Grammar.* **a.** the present tense. **b.** a verb in this tense. **9. at present.** at the moment; now. **10. for the present.** for the time being; temporarily. ~See also **presents.** [C13: from Latin *praesens,* from *praeesse* to be in front of, from *prae-* before, in front + *esse* to be]

present[2] *vb.* (prɪˈzɛnt). (*mainly tr.*) **1.** to introduce (a person) to another, esp. to someone of higher rank. **2.** to introduce to the public: *to present a play.* **3.** to introduce and compere (a radio or television show). **4.** to show; exhibit: *he presented a brave face to the world.* **5.** to put forward; submit: *she presented a proposal for a new book.* **6.** to bring or suggest to the mind: *to present a problem.* **7.** to give or award: *to present a prize.* **8.** to endow with or as if with a gift or award: *to present a university with a foundation scholarship.* **9.** to offer formally: *to present one's compliments.* **10.** to offer or hand over for action or settlement: *to present a bill.* **11.** to represent or depict in a particular manner: *the actor presented Hamlet as a very young man.* **12.** to salute someone with (one's weapon) (usually in the phrase **present arms**). **13.** to aim or point (a weapon). **14.** to nominate (a clergyman) to a bishop for institution to a benefice in his diocese. **15.** to lay (a charge, etc.) before a court, magistrate, etc., for consideration or trial. **16.** to bring a formal charge or accusation against (a person); indict. **17.** *Chiefly U.S.* (of a grand jury) to take notice of (an offence) from personal knowledge or observation, before any bill of indictment has been drawn up. **18.** (*intr.*) *Med., psychol., etc.* to seek treatment for a particular symptom or problem: *she presented with postnatal depression.* **19.** (*intr.*) *Informal.* to produce a favourable, etc. impression: *she*

ˌ**preregisˈtration** *n.*
ˌ**pre-ReˈnaissAnce** *adj.*
ˌ**prereˈtirement** *adj.*
pre-ˈRoman *adj.*
ˌ**pre-RoˈmAntic** *adj.*
ˌ**prescienˈtific** *adj.*
preˈseasonal *adj.*
ˌ**preseˈlect** *vb.*

presents well in public; he presents as harmless but has poisoned his family. **20. present oneself.** to appear, esp. at a specific time and place. ~*n.* ('prɛzᵊnt). **21.** anything that is presented; a gift. **22. make someone a present of something.** to give someone something: *I'll make you a present of a new car.* [C13: from Old French *presenter,* from Latin *praesentāre* to exhibit, offer, from *praesens* PRESENT[1]]

presentable (prɪ'zɛntəbᵊl) *adj.* **1.** fit to be presented or introduced to other people. **2.** fit to be displayed or offered. —**pre'sentableness** *or* **pre,senta'bility** *n.* —**pre'sentably** *adv.*

presentation (,prɛzən'teɪʃən) *n.* **1.** the act of presenting or state of being presented. **2.** the manner of presenting, esp. the organization of visual details to create an overall impression: *the presentation of the project is excellent but the content poor.* **3.** the method of presenting: *his presentation of the facts was muddled.* **4.** a verbal report presented with illustrative material, such as slides, graphs, etc.: *a presentation on the company results.* **5. a.** an offering or bestowal, as of a gift. **b.** (*as modifier*): *a presentation copy of a book.* **6.** a performance or representation, as of a play. **7.** the formal introduction of a person, as into society or at court; debut. **8.** the act or right of nominating a clergyman to a benefice. **9.** *Med.* the position of a baby relative to the birth canal at the time of birth. **10.** *Commerce.* another word for **presentment** (sense 4). **11.** *Television.* linking material between programmes, such as announcements, trailers, or weather reports. **12.** an archaic word for **gift. 13.** *Philosophy.* a sense datum. **14.** (*often cap.*) another name for (feast of) **Candlemas.** —**,presen'tational** *adj.*

presentationism (,prɛzən'teɪʃə,nɪzəm) *n. Philosophy.* the theory that objects are identical with our perceptions of them. Compare **representationalism.** —**,presen'tationist** *n., adj.*

presentative (prɪ'zɛntətɪv) *adj.* **1.** *Philosophy.* **a.** able to be known or perceived immediately. **b.** capable of knowing or perceiving in this way. **2.** subject to or conferring the right of ecclesiastical presentation. —**pre'sentativeness** *n.*

present-day *n.* (*modifier*) of the modern day; current: *I don't like present-day fashions.*

presentee (,prɛzən'tiː) *n.* **1.** a person who is presented, as at court. **2.** a person to whom something is presented.

presenter (prɪ'zɛntə) *n.* **1.** a person who presents something or someone. **2.** *Radio, television.* a person who introduces a show, links items, interviews guests, etc.; compere.

presentient (prɪ'sɛnʃənt, -'zɛn-, priː-) *adj.* characterized by or experiencing a presentiment. [C19: from Latin *praesentiens* present participle of *praesentire,* from *prae-* PRE- + *sentire* to feel]

presentiment (prɪ'zɛntɪmənt) *n.* a sense of something about to happen; premonition. [C18: from obsolete French, from *pressentir* to sense beforehand; see PRE-, SENTIMENT]

presently ('prɛzəntlɪ) *adv.* **1.** in a short while; soon. **2.** at the moment. **3.** an archaic word for **immediately.**

presentment (prɪ'zɛntmənt) *n.* **1.** the act of presenting or state of being presented; presentation. **2.** something presented, such as a picture, play, etc. **3.** *Law, chiefly U.S.* a statement on oath by a grand jury of something within their own knowledge or observation, esp. the commission of an offence when the indictment has been laid before them. **4.** *Commerce.* the presenting of a bill of exchange, promissory note, etc.

present participle *n.* a participial form of verbs used adjectivally when the action it describes is contemporaneous with that of the main verb of a sentence and also used in the formation of certain compound tenses. In English this form ends in *-ing.* Compare **gerund.**

present perfect *adj., n. Grammar.* another term for **perfect** (senses 8, 11).

presents ('prɛzənts) *pl. n. Law.* used in a deed or document to refer to itself: *know all men by these presents.*

present value *n.* the current capital value of a future income or outlay or of a series of such incomes or outlays. It is computed by the process of discounting at a predetermined rate of interest.

preservative (prɪ'zɜːvətɪv) *n.* **1.** something that preserves or tends to preserve, esp. a chemical added to foods to inhibit decomposition. ~*adj.* **2.** tending or intended to preserve.

preserve (prɪ'zɜːv) *vb.* (*mainly tr.*) **1.** to keep safe from danger or harm; protect. **2.** to protect from decay or dissolution; maintain: *to preserve old buildings.* **3.** to maintain possession of; keep up: *to preserve a façade of indifference.* **4.** to prevent from decomposition or chemical change. **5.** to prepare (food), as by freezing, drying, or salting, so that it will resist decomposition. **6.** to make preserves of (fruit, etc.). **7.** to rear and protect (game) in restricted places for hunting or fishing. **8.** (*intr.*) to maintain protection and favourable conditions for game in preserves. ~*n.* **9.** something that preserves or is preserved. **10.** a special area or domain: *archaeology is the preserve of specialists.* **11.** (*usually pl.*) fruit, etc., prepared by cooking with sugar. **12.** areas where game is reared for private hunting or fishing. [C14: via Old French, from Late Latin *praeservāre* literally: to keep safe in advance, from Latin *prae-* before + *servāre* to keep safe] —**pre'servable** *adj.* —**pre,serva'bility** *n.* —**pre'servably** *adv.* —**preservation** (,prɛzə'veɪʃən) *n.* —**pre'server** *n.*

preset (priː'sɛt) *vb.* **-sets, -setting, -set.** (*tr.*) **1.** to set (a timing device) so that something begins to operate at the time specified. ~*n.* **2.** *Electronics.* a control, such as a variable resistor, that is not as accessible as the main controls and is used to set initial conditions.

preshrunk (priː'ʃrʌŋk) *adj.* (of fabrics, garments, etc.) having undergone a shrinking process during manufacture so that further shrinkage will not occur.

preside (prɪ'zaɪd) *vb.* (*intr.*) **1.** to sit in or hold a position of authority, as over a meeting. **2.** to exercise authority; control. **3.** to occupy a position as an instrumentalist: *he presided at the organ.* [C17: via French from Latin *praesidēre* to superintend, from *prae* before + *sedēre* to sit] —**pre'sider** *n.*

presidency ('prɛzɪdənsɪ) *n., pl.* **-cies. 1. a.** the office, dignity, or term of a president. **b.** (*often cap.*) the office of president of a republic, esp. the office of the President of the U.S. **2.** *Mormon Church.* **a.** a local administrative council consisting of a president and two executive members. **b.** (*often cap.*) the supreme administrative body composed of the Prophet and two councillors.

president ('prɛzɪdənt) *n.* **1.** (*often cap.*) the chief executive or head of state of a republic, esp. of the U.S. **2.** (in the U.S.) the chief executive officer of a company, corporation, etc. **3.** a person who presides over an assembly, meeting, etc. **4.** the chief executive officer of certain establishments of higher education. [C14: via Old French from Late Latin *praesidens* ruler; see PRESIDE] —**presidential** (,prɛzɪ'dɛnʃəl) *adj.* —**,presi'dentially** *adv.* —**'president,ship** *n.*

president-elect *n.* a person who has been elected president but has not yet entered office.

presidio (prɪ'sɪdɪ,əʊ; *Spanish* pre'siðjo) *n., pl.* **-sidios** (-'sɪdɪ,əʊz; *Spanish* -'siðjos). a military post or establishment, esp. in countries under Spanish control. [C19: from Spanish: garrison, from Latin *praesidium* a guard, protection; see PRESIDE]

presidium *or* **praesidium** (prɪ'sɪdɪəm) *n., pl.* **-iums** *or* **-ia** (-ɪə). **1.** (*often cap.*) (in Communist countries) a permanent committee of a larger body, such as a legislature, that acts for it when it is in recess. **2.** a collective presidency, esp. of a nongovernmental organization. [C20: from Russian *prezidium,* from Latin *praesidium,* from *praesidēre* to superintend; see PRESIDE]

presignify (priː'sɪgnɪ,faɪ) *vb.* **-fies, -fying, -fied.** (*tr.*) to signify beforehand; foreshadow; foretell.

press[1] (prɛs) *vb.* **1.** to apply or exert weight, force, or steady pressure on: *he pressed the button on the camera.* **2.** (*tr.*) to squeeze or compress so as to alter in shape or form. **3.** to apply heat or pressure to (clothing) so as to smooth out or mark with creases; iron. **4.** to make (objects) from soft material by pressing with a mould, form, etc., esp. to make gramophone records from plastic. **5.** (*tr.*) to hold tightly or clasp, as in an embrace. **6.** (*tr.*) to extract or force out (juice) by pressure (from). **7.** (*tr.*) *Weightlifting.* to lift (a weight) successfully with a press: *he managed to press 280 pounds.* **8.** (*tr.*) to force, constrain, or compel. **9.** to importune or entreat (a person) insistently; urge: *they pressed for an answer.* **10.** to harass or cause harassment. **11.** (*tr.*) to plead or put forward strongly or importunately: *to press a claim.* **12.** (*intr.*) to be urgent. **13.** (*tr.*; usually passive) to have little of: *we're hard pressed for time.* **14.** (when *intr.,* often foll. by *on* or *forward*) to hasten or advance or cause to hasten or advance in a forceful manner. **15.** (*intr.*) to crowd; throng; push. **16.** (*tr.*) (formerly) to put to death or subject to torture by placing heavy weights upon. **17.** (*tr.*) *Archaic.* to trouble or oppress. ~*n.* **18.** any machine that exerts pressure to form, shape, or cut materials or to extract liquids, compress solids, or hold components together while an adhesive joint is formed. **19.** See **printing press. 20.** the art or process of printing. **21. at** *or* **in (the) press.** being printed. **22. to (the) press.** to be printed: *when is this book going to press?* **23. a. the press.** news media and agencies collectively, esp. newspapers. **b.** (*as modifier*): *a press matter; press relations.* **24. the press.** those who work in the news media, esp. newspaper reporters and photographers. **25.** the opinions and reviews in the newspapers, etc.: *the play received a poor press.* **26.** the act of pressing or state of being pressed. **27.** the act of crowding, thronging, or pushing together. **28.** a closely packed throng of people; crowd; multitude. **29.** urgency or hurry in business affairs. **30.** a cupboard, esp. a large one used for storing clothes or linen. **31.** a wood or metal clamp or vice to prevent tennis rackets, etc., from warping when not in use. **32.** *Weightlifting.* a lift in which the weight is raised to shoulder level and then above the head. [C14 *pressen,* from Old French *presser,* from Latin *pressāre,* from *premere* to press]

press[2] (prɛs) *vb.* (*tr.*) **1.** to recruit (men) by forcible measures for military service. **2.** to use for a purpose other than intended, (esp. in the phrase **press into service**). ~*n.* **3.** recruitment into military service by forcible measures, as by a press gang. [C16: back formation from *prest* to recruit soldiers; see PREST[2]; also influenced by PRESS[1]]

press agency *n.* another name for **news agency.**

pre'set *vb.*
pre'shape *vb.*
pre'shrink *vb.*
pre'sift *vb.*
'presoak *n.*
pre'soak *vb.*
,pre-So'cratic *adj.*

press agent *n.* a person employed to obtain favourable publicity, such as notices in newspapers, for an organization, actor, etc. Abbrev.: **PA.**

press box *n.* an area reserved for reporters, as in a sports stadium.

press conference *n.* an interview for press and television reporters given by a politician, film star, etc.

press fit *n. Engineering.* a type of fit for mating parts, usually tighter than a sliding fit, used when the parts do not have to move relative to each other.

press gallery *n.* an area set apart for newspaper reporters, esp. in a legislative assembly.

press gang *n.* **1.** (formerly) a detachment of men used to press civilians for service in the navy or army. ~*vb.* **press-gang.** (*tr.*) **2.** to force (a person) to join the navy or army by a press gang. **3.** to induce (a person) to perform a duty by forceful persuasion: *his friends press-ganged him into joining the committee.*

pressie *or* **prezzie** ('prɛzɪ) *n.* an informal word for **present**[2] (sense 21).

pressing ('prɛsɪŋ) *adj.* **1.** demanding immediate attention. **2.** persistent or importunate. ~*n.* **3.** a large specified number of gramophone records produced at one time from a master record. **4.** a component formed in a press. **5.** *Football.* the tactic of trying to stay very close to the opposition when they are in possession of the ball. —'**pressingly** *adv.* —'**pressingness** *n.*

pressman ('prɛsmən, -ˌmæn) *n., pl.* **-men. 1.** a person who works for the press. **2.** a person who operates a printing press.

pressmark ('prɛsˌmɑːk) *n. Library science.* a location mark on a book indicating a specific bookcase. [C19: from PRESS[1] (in the sense: cupboard) + MARK[1]]

press of sail *n. Nautical.* the most sail a vessel can carry under given conditions. Also called: **press of canvas.**

pressor ('prɛsə, -sɔː) *adj. Physiol.* relating to or producing an increase in blood pressure. [C19: from Latin *premere* to press]

press release *n.* an official announcement or account of a news item circulated to the press.

pressroom ('prɛsˌruːm, -ˌrʊm) *n.* the room in a printing establishment that houses the printing presses.

press stud *n.* a fastening device consisting of one part with a projecting knob that snaps into a hole on another like part, used esp. in closures in clothing. Also called: **popper, snap fastener.**

press-up *n.* an exercise in which the body is alternately raised from and lowered to the floor by the arms only, the trunk being kept straight with the toes and hands resting on the floor. Also called (U.S. and Canadian): **push-up.**

pressure ('prɛʃə) *n.* **1.** the state of pressing or being pressed. **2.** the exertion of force by one body on the surface of another. **3.** a moral force that compels: *to bring pressure to bear.* **4.** an urgent claim or demand or series of urgent claims or demands: *to work under pressure.* **5.** a burdensome condition that is hard to bear: *the pressure of grief.* **6.** the force applied to a unit area of a surface, usually measured in pascals (newtons per square metre), millibars, torr, or atmospheres. Symbol: *p* or *P* **7.** short for **atmospheric pressure** or **blood pressure.** ~*vb.* **8.** (*tr.*) to constrain or compel, as by the application of moral force. **9.** another word for **pressurize.** [C14: from Late Latin *pressūra* a pressing, from Latin *premere* to press] —'**pressureless** *adj.*

pressure cabin *n.* the pressurized cabin of an aircraft or spacecraft.

pressure-cook *vb.* to cook (food) in a pressure cooker.

pressure cooker *n.* **1.** a strong hermetically sealed pot in which food may be cooked quickly under pressure at a temperature above the normal boiling point of water. **2.** *N.Z. informal.* a trainee student attending a shortened qualifying course.

pressure drag *n.* the part of the total drag of a body moving through a gas or liquid caused by the components of the pressures at right angles to the surface of the body.

pressure gauge *n.* any instrument for measuring fluid pressure. See also **Bourdon gauge, manometer.**

pressure gradient *n.* **1.** the change of pressure per unit distance. See **adverse pressure gradient, favourable pressure gradient. 2.** *Meteorol.* the decrease in atmospheric pressure per unit of horizontal distance, shown on a synoptic chart by the spacing of the isobars.

pressure group *n.* a group of people who seek to exert pressure on legislators, public opinion, etc., in order to promote their own ideas or welfare.

pressure head *n. Physics.* a more formal name for **head** (sense 24a).

pressure point *n.* any of several points on the body above an artery that, when firmly pressed, will control bleeding from the artery at a point farther away from the heart.

pressure suit *n.* an inflatable suit worn by a person flying at high altitudes or in space, to provide protection from low pressure.

pressure vessel *n. Engineering.* a vessel designed for containing substances, reactions, etc., at pressures above atmospheric pressure.

pressurize *or* **pressurise** ('prɛʃəˌraɪz) *vb.* (*tr.*) **1.** to increase the pressure in (an enclosure, such as an aircraft cabin) in order to maintain approximately atmospheric pressure when the external pressure is low. **2.** to increase pressure on (a fluid). **3.** to make insistent demands of (someone); coerce. —ˌ**pressuri'zation** *or* ˌ**pressuri'sation** *n.* —'**pressurˌizer** *or* '**pressurˌiser** *n.*

pressurized-water reactor *n.* a nuclear reactor using water as coolant and moderator at a pressure that is too high to allow boiling to take place inside the reactor. The fuel is enriched uranium oxide cased in zirconium. Abbrev.: **PWR.**

presswork ('prɛsˌwɜːk) *n.* **1.** the operation of a printing press. **2.** the matter printed by a printing press.

prest[1] (prɛst) *adj. Obsolete.* prepared for action or use; ready. [C13: via Old French from Late Latin *praestus* ready to hand; see PRESTO]

prest[2] (prɛst) *n. Obsolete.* a loan of money. [C16: originally, loan money offered as an inducement to recruits, from Old French: advance pay in the army, from *prester* to lend, from Latin *praestāre* to provide, from *prae* before + *stāre* to stand]

Prestel ('prɛsˌtɛl) *n. Trademark.* the Viewdata service operated by British Telecom. See **Viewdata.**

prestidigitation (ˌprɛstɪˌdɪdʒɪ'teɪʃən) *n.* another name for **sleight of hand.** [C19: from French: quick-fingeredness, from Latin *praestigiae* feats of juggling, tricks, probably influenced by French *preste* nimble, and Latin *digitus* finger; see PRESTIGE] —ˌ**presti'digiˌtator** *n.*

prestige (prɛ'stiːʒ) *n.* **1.** high status or reputation achieved through success, influence, wealth, etc.; renown. **2. a.** the power to influence or impress; glamour. **b.** (*modifier*): *a prestige car.* [C17: via French from Latin *praestigiae* feats of juggling, tricks; apparently related to Latin *praestringere* to bind tightly, blindfold, from *prae* before + *stringere* to draw tight, bind]

prestigious (prɛ'stɪdʒəs) *adj.* **1.** having status or glamour; impressive or influential. **2.** *Rare.* characterized by or using deceit, cunning, or illusion; fraudulent. —**pres'tigiously** *adv.* —**pres'tigiousness** *n.*

prestissimo (prɛ'stɪsɪˌməʊ) *Music.* ~*adj., adv.* **1.** to be played as fast as possible. ~*n., pl.* **-mos. 2.** a piece or passage directed to be played in this way. [C18: from Italian: very quickly, from *presto* fast]

presto ('prɛstəʊ) *adj., adv.* **1.** *Music.* to be played very fast. ~*adv.* **2.** immediately, suddenly, or at once (esp. in the phrase **hey presto**). ~*n., pl.* **-tos. 3.** *Music.* a movement or passage directed to be played very quickly. [C16: from Italian: fast, from Late Latin *praestus* (adj.) ready to hand, Latin *praestō* (adv.) present]

prestress (ˌpriː'strɛs) *vb.* (*tr.*) to apply tensile stress to (the steel cables, wires, etc., of a precast concrete part) before the load is applied.

prestressed concrete *n.* concrete that contains steel wires, cables, etc., that are prestressed within their elastic limit to counteract the stresses that will occur under load.

presumable (prɪ'zjuːməbᵊl) *adj.* able to be presumed or taken for granted.

presumably (prɪ'zjuːməblɪ) *adv.* (*sentence modifier*) one presumes or supposes that: *presumably he won't see you, if you're leaving tomorrow.*

presume (prɪ'zjuːm) *vb.* **1.** (when *tr., often takes a clause as object*) to take (something) for granted; assume. **2.** (when *tr., often foll. by an infinitive*) to take upon oneself (to do something) without warrant or permission; dare: *do you presume to copy my work?* **3.** (*intr.*; foll. by *on* or *upon*) to rely or depend: *don't presume on his agreement.* **4.** *Law.* to take as proved until contrary evidence is produced. **5.** (*tr.*) *Rare.* to constitute proof of or evidence for. [C14: via Old French from Latin *praesūmere* to take in advance, from *prae* before + *sūmere* to ASSUME] —**presumedly** (prɪ'zjuːmɪdlɪ) *adv.* —**pre'sumer** *n.* —**pre'suming** *adj.* —**pre'sumingly** *adv.*

presumption (prɪ'zʌmpʃən) *n.* **1.** the act of presuming. **2.** bold or insolent behaviour or manners. **3.** a belief or assumption based on reasonable evidence. **4.** a ground or basis on which to presume. **5.** *Law.* an inference of the truth of a fact from other facts proved, admitted, or judicially noticed. [C13: via Old French from Latin *praesumptiō* a using in advance, anticipation, from *praesūmere* to take beforehand; see PRESUME]

presumptive (prɪ'zʌmptɪv) *adj.* **1.** based on presumption or probability. **2.** affording reasonable ground for belief. **3.** of or relating to embryonic tissues that become differentiated into a particular tissue or organ: *presumptive epidermis.* —**pre'sumptively** *adv.* —**pre'sumptiveness** *n.*

presumptuous (prɪ'zʌmptjʊəs) *adj.* **1.** characterized by presumption or tending to presume; bold; forward. **2.** an obsolete word for **presumptive.** —**pre'sumptuously** *adv.* —**pre'sumptuousness** *n.*

presuppose (ˌpriːsə'pəʊz) *vb.* (*tr.*) **1.** to take for granted; assume. **2.** to require or imply as a necessary prior condition. **3.** *Philosophy, logic, linguistics.* to require (a condition) to be satisfied as a precondition for a statement to be either true or false or for a speech act to be felicitous. *Have you stopped beating your wife?* presupposes that the person addressed has a wife and has beaten her. —**presupposition** (ˌpriːsʌpə'zɪʃən) *n.*

pret. *abbrev. for* preterite.

pre'surgical *adj.*

pretence *or U.S.* **pretense** (prɪˈtɛns) *n.* **1.** the act of pretending. **2.** a false display; affectation. **3.** a claim, esp. a false one, to a right, title, or distinction. **4.** make-believe or feigning. **5.** a false claim or allegation; pretext. **6.** a less common word for **pretension** (sense 3).

pretend (prɪˈtɛnd) *vb.* **1.** (when *tr., usually takes a clause as object or an infinitive*) to claim or allege (something untrue). **2.** (*tr.; may take a clause as object or an infinitive*) to make believe, as in a play: *you pretend to be Ophelia.* **3.** (*intr.; foll. by to*) to present a claim, esp. a dubious one: *to pretend to the throne.* **4.** (*intr.; foll. by to*) *Obsolete.* to aspire as a candidate or suitor (for). ~*adj.* **5.** fanciful; make-believe; simulated: *a pretend gun.* [C14: from Latin *praetendere* to stretch forth, feign, from *prae* in front + *tendere* to stretch]

pretender (prɪˈtɛndə) *n.* **1.** a person who pretends or makes false allegations. **2.** a person who mounts a claim, as to a throne or title.

pretension (prɪˈtɛnʃən) *n.* **1.** (*often pl.*) a false or unsupportable claim, esp. to merit, worth, or importance. **2.** a specious or unfounded allegation; pretext. **3.** the state or quality of being pretentious.

pretensive (prɪˈtɛnsɪv) *adj. Caribbean.* pretentious.

pretentious (prɪˈtɛnʃəs) *adj.* **1.** making claim to distinction or importance, esp. undeservedly. **2.** having or creating a deceptive outer appearance of great worth; ostentatious. —**preˈtentiously** *adv.* —**preˈtentiousness** *n.*

preter- *prefix.* beyond, more than, or exceeding: *preternatural.* [from Latin *praeter-*, from *praeter*]

preterhuman (ˌpriːtəˈhjuːmən) *adj. Rare.* beyond what is human.

preterite *or U.S.* **preterit** (ˈprɛtərɪt) *Grammar.* ~*n.* **1.** a tense of verbs used to relate past action, formed in English by inflection of the verb, as *jumped, swam.* **2.** a verb in this tense. ~*adj.* **3.** denoting this tense. [C14: from Late Latin *praeteritum* (*tempus*) past (time, tense), from Latin *praeterīre* to go by, from PRETER- + *īre* to go]

preterition (ˌprɛtəˈrɪʃən) *n.* **1.** the act of passing over or omitting. **2.** *Roman law.* the failure of a testator to name one of his children in his will, thus invalidating it. **3.** (in Calvinist theology) the doctrine that God passed over or left unpredestined those not elected to final salvation. [C17: from Late Latin *praeteritiō* a passing over]

preteritive (prɪˈtɛrɪtɪv) *adj.* (of a verb) having only past tense forms.

preterm (ˌpriːˈtɜːm) *adj.* **1.** (of a baby) born prematurely. ~*adv.* **2.** prematurely.

pretermit (ˌpriːtəˈmɪt) *vb.* **-mits, -mitting, -mitted.** (*tr.*) *Rare.* **1.** to overlook intentionally; disregard. **2.** to fail to do; neglect; omit. [C16: from Latin *praetermittere* to let pass, from PRETER- + *mittere* to send, release] —**pretermission** (ˌpriːtəˈmɪʃən) *n.* —ˌ**preterˈmitter** *n.*

preternatural (ˌpriːtəˈnætʃrəl) *adj.* **1.** beyond what is ordinarily found in nature; abnormal. **2.** another word for **supernatural.** [C16: from Medieval Latin *praeternātūrālis,* from Latin *praeter natūram* beyond the scope of nature] —ˌ**preterˈnaturally** *adv.* —ˌ**preterˈnaturalism** *n.* —ˌ**preterˈnaturalness** *or* ˌ**preterˌnatuˈrality** *n.*

pretext (ˈpriːtɛkst) *n.* **1.** a fictitious reason given in order to conceal the real one. **2.** a specious excuse; pretence. [C16: from Latin *praetextum* disguise, from *praetexere* to weave in front, disguise; see TEXTURE]

pretonic (priːˈtɒnɪk) *adj.* denoting or relating to the syllable before the one bearing the primary stress in a word.

pretor (ˈpriːtə) *n.* a variant spelling of **praetor.**

prettify (ˈprɪtɪˌfaɪ) *vb.* **-fies, -fying, -fied.** (*tr.*) to make pretty, esp. in a trivial fashion; embellish. —ˌ**prettifiˈcation** *n.* —ˈ**prettiˌfier** *n.*

pretty (ˈprɪtɪ) *adj.* **-tier, -tiest. 1.** pleasing or appealing in a delicate or graceful way. **2.** dainty, neat, or charming. **3.** *Informal, often ironical.* excellent, grand, or fine: *here's a pretty mess!* **4.** *Informal.* lacking in masculinity; effeminate; foppish. **5.** *Archaic or Scot.* vigorous or brave. **6.** an archaic word for **elegant. 7. a pretty penny.** *Informal.* a large sum of money. **8. sitting pretty.** *Informal.* well placed or established financially, socially, etc. ~*n., pl.* **-ties. 9.** a pretty person or thing. ~*adv.* **10.** *Informal.* fairly or moderately; somewhat. **11.** *Informal.* quite or very. ~*vb.* **-ties, -tying, -tied. 12.** (*tr.;* often foll. by *up*) to make pretty; adorn. [Old English *prættig* clever; related to Middle Low German *prattich* obstinate, Dutch *prettig* glad, Old Norse *prettugr* cunning] —ˈ**prettily** *adv.* —ˈ**prettiness** *n.*

pretty-pretty *adj. Informal.* excessively or ostentatiously pretty.

pretzel (ˈprɛtsəl) *n.* a brittle savoury biscuit, in the form of a knot or stick, glazed and salted on the outside, eaten esp. in Germany and the U.S. [C19: from German, from Old High German *brezitella;* perhaps related to Medieval Latin *bracellus* bracelet, from Latin *bracchium* arm]

prevail (prɪˈveɪl) *vb.* (*intr.*) **1.** (often foll. by *over* or *against*) to prove superior; gain mastery: *skill will prevail.* **2.** to be or appear as the most important feature; be prevalent. **3.** to exist widely; be in force. **4.** (often foll. by *on* or *upon*) to succeed in persuading or inducing. [C14: from Latin *praevalēre* to be superior in strength, from *prae* beyond + *valēre* to be strong] —**preˈvailer** *n.*

prevailing (prɪˈveɪlɪŋ) *adj.* **1.** generally accepted; widespread: *the prevailing opinion.* **2.** most frequent or conspicuous; predominant: *the prevailing wind is from the north.* —**preˈvailingly** *adv.*

prevalent (ˈprɛvələnt) *adj.* **1.** widespread or current. **2.** superior in force or power; predominant. [C16 (in the sense: powerful): from Latin *praevalens* very strong, from *praevalēre:* see PREVAIL] —ˈ**prevalence** *or* ˈ**prevalentness** *n.* —ˈ**prevalently** *adv.*

prevaricate (prɪˈværɪˌkeɪt) *vb.* (*intr.*) to speak or act falsely or evasively with intent to deceive. [C16: from Latin *praevāricārī* to walk crookedly, from *prae* beyond + *vāricare* to straddle the legs; compare Latin *vārus* bent] —**preˌvariˈcation** *n.* —**preˈvariˌcator** *n.*

prevenient (prɪˈviːnɪənt) *adj.* coming before; anticipating or preceding. [C17: from Latin *praevenīre* to precede, PREVENT] —**preˈveniently** *adv.*

prevent (prɪˈvɛnt) *vb.* **1.** (*tr.*) to keep from happening, esp. by taking precautionary action. **2.** (*tr.;* often foll. by *from*) to keep (someone from doing something); hinder; impede. **3.** (*intr.*) to interpose or act as a hindrance. **4.** (*tr.*) *Archaic.* to anticipate or precede. [C15: from Latin *praevenīre,* from *prae* before + *venīre* to come] —**preˈventable** *or* **preˈventible** *adj.* —**preˌventaˈbility** *or* **preˌventiˈbility** *n.* —**preˈventably** *or* **preˈventibly** *adv.*

preventer (prɪˈvɛntə) *n.* **1.** a person or thing that prevents. **2.** *Nautical.* a rope or other piece of gear rigged to prevent a sail from gybing.

prevention (prɪˈvɛnʃən) *n.* **1.** the act of preventing. **2.** a hindrance, obstacle, or impediment.

preventive (prɪˈvɛntɪv) *adj.* **1.** tending or intended to prevent or hinder. **2.** *Med.* **a.** tending to prevent disease; prophylactic. **b.** of or relating to the branch of medicine concerned with prolonging life and preventing disease. **3.** (in Britain) of, relating to, or belonging to the customs and excise service or the coastguard. ~*n.* **4.** something that serves to prevent or hinder. **5.** *Med.* any drug or agent that tends to prevent or protect against disease. **6.** another name for **contraceptive.** ~Also (except for sense 3): **preventative** (prɪˈvɛntətɪv). —**preˈventively** *adv.* —**preˈventiveness** *n.*

preverbal (ˌpriːˈvɜːbᵊl) *adj.* **1.** being before the development of speech: *preverbal infants.* **2.** *Grammar.* coming before the verb.

preview *or U.S.* **prevue** (ˈpriːvjuː) *n.* **1.** an advance or preliminary view or sight. **2.** an advance showing before public presentation of a film, art exhibition, etc., usually before an invited audience of celebrities and journalists. **3.** a public peformance of a play before the official first night. ~*vb.* **4.** (*tr.*) to view in advance.

preview monitor *n.* (in a television studio control room) a picture monitor used for inspecting a picture source before it is switched to transmission.

previous (ˈpriːvɪəs) *adj.* **1.** (*prenominal*) existing or coming before something else in time or position; prior. **2.** (*postpositive*) *Informal.* taking place or done too soon; premature. **3. previous to.** before; prior to. [C17: from Latin *praevius* leading the way, from *prae* before + *via* way] —ˈ**previously** *adv.* —ˈ**previousness** *n.*

previous question *n.* **1.** (in the House of Commons) a motion to drop the present topic under debate, put in order to prevent a vote. **2.** (in the House of Lords and U.S. legislative bodies) a motion to vote on a bill or other question without delay. ~See also **closure** (sense 4).

previse (prɪˈvaɪz) *vb.* (*tr.*) *Rare.* **1.** to predict or foresee. **2.** to notify in advance. [C16: from Latin *praevidēre* to foresee, from *prae* before + *vidēre* to see]

prevision (prɪˈvɪʒən) *n. Rare.* **1.** the act or power of foreseeing; prescience. **2.** a prophetic vision or prophecy.

prevocalic (ˌpriːvəʊˈkælɪk) *adj.* (of a consonant) coming immediately before a vowel. —ˌ**prevoˈcalically** *adv.*

prewar (ˌpriːˈwɔː, ˈpriːˌwɔː) *adj.* of or occurring in the period before a war, esp. before World War I or II.

prey (preɪ) *n.* **1.** an animal hunted or captured by another for food. **2.** a person or thing that becomes the victim of a hostile person, influence, etc. **3. bird** *or* **beast of prey.** a bird or animal that preys on others for food. **4.** an archaic word for **booty.** ~*vb.* (*intr.;* often foll. by *on* or *upon*) **5.** to hunt or seize food by killing other animals. **6.** to make a victim (of others), as by profiting at their expense. **7.** to exert a depressing or obsessive effect (on the mind, spirits, etc.); weigh heavily (upon). [C13: from Old French *preie,* from Latin *praeda* booty; see PREDATORY] —ˈ**preyer** *n.*

prezzie (ˈprɛzɪ) *n.* a variant of **pressie,** an informal word for **present**[2] (sense 21).

priapic (praɪˈæpɪk, -ˈeɪ-) *or* **priapean** (ˌpraɪəˈpiːən) *adj.* of or relating to the penis or to male sexuality; phallic. [from *Priapus* (Greek god of male procreative power) + -IC]

ˈ**pretest** *n.*
preˈtest *vb.*
preˈwarm *vb.*
ˈ**prewash** *n.*
preˈwash *vb.*

priapism ('praɪəˌpɪzəm) *n. Pathol.* prolonged painful erection of the penis, caused by neurological disorders, obstruction of the penile blood vessels, etc. [C17: from Late Latin *priāpismus,* ultimately from Greek *Priapus*; see PRIAPIC]

price (praɪs) *n.* **1.** the sum in money or goods for which anything is or may be bought or sold. **2.** the cost at which anything is obtained. **3.** the cost of bribing a person. **4.** a sum of money offered or given as a reward for a capture or killing. **5.** value or worth, esp. high worth. **6.** *Gambling.* another word for **odds.** **7. at any price.** whatever the price or cost. **8. at a price.** at a high price. **9. beyond** (*or* **without**) **price.** invaluable or priceless. **10. the price of (one).** *Irish.* what (one) deserves, esp. a fitting punishment: *it's just the price of him.* **11. what price (something)?** what are the chances of (something) happening now? ~*vb.* (*tr.*) **12.** to fix or establish the price of. **13.** to ascertain or discover the price of. **14. price out of the market.** to charge so highly for as to prevent the sale, hire, etc., of. [C13 *pris,* from Old French, from Latin *pretium* price, value, wage] —'**pricer** *n.*

price control *n.* the establishment and maintenance of maximum price levels for basic goods and services by a government, esp. during periods of war or inflation.

price discrimination *n. Economics.* the setting of different prices to be charged to different consumers or in different markets for the same goods or services.

price-dividend ratio *n.* the ratio of the price of a share on a stock exchange to the dividends per share paid in the previous year, used as a measure of a company's potential as an investment. Abbrevs.: **P-D ratio, PDR.**

price-earnings ratio *n.* the ratio of the price of a share on a stock exchange to the earnings per share, used as a measure of a company's future profitability. Abbrev.: **P/E ratio.**

price-fixing *n.* **1.** the setting of prices by agreement among producers and distributors. **2.** another name for **price control** or **resale price maintenance.**

price leadership *n. Marketing.* the setting of the price of a product or service by a dominant firm at a level that competitors can match, in order to avoid a price war.

priceless ('praɪslɪs) *adj.* **1.** of inestimable worth; beyond valuation; invaluable. **2.** *Informal.* extremely amusing or ridiculous. —'**pricelessly** *adv.* —'**pricelessness** *n.*

price ring *n.* a group of traders formed to maintain the prices of their goods.

prices and incomes policy *n.* voluntary or statutory regulation of the level of increases in prices and incomes.

price-sensitive *adj.* likely to affect the price of property, esp. shares and securities: *price-sensitive information.*

price support *n.* government maintenance of specified price levels at a minimum above market equilibrium by subsidy or by purchase of the market surplus at the guaranteed levels.

price tag *n.* **1.** a ticket or label on an article for sale showing its price. **2.** the cost, esp. of something not usually priced: *the price tag on a top footballer.*

price war *n.* a period of intense competition among enterprises, esp. retail enterprises, in the same market, characterized by repeated price reductions rather than advertising, brand promotion, etc.

pricey *or* **pricy** ('praɪsɪ) *adj.* **pricier, priciest.** an informal word for **expensive.**

prick (prɪk) *vb.* (*mainly tr.*) **1. a.** to make (a small hole) in (something) by piercing lightly with a sharp point. **b.** to wound in this manner. **2.** (*intr.*) to cause or have a piercing or stinging sensation. **3.** to cause to feel a sharp emotional pain: *knowledge of such poverty pricked his conscience.* **4.** to puncture or pierce. **5.** to mark, delineate, or outline by dots or punctures. **6.** (*also intr.*; usually foll. by *up*) to rise or raise erect; point: *the dog pricked his ears up at his master's call.* **7.** (usually foll. by *out* or *off*) to transplant (seedlings) into a larger container. **8.** (often foll. by *off*) *Navigation.* to measure or trace (a course, distance, etc.) on a chart with dividers. **9.** *Archaic.* to rouse or impel; urge on. **10.** (*intr.*) *Archaic.* to ride fast on horseback; spur a horse on. **11. prick up one's ears.** to start to listen attentively; become interested. ~*n.* **12.** the act of pricking or the condition or sensation of being pricked. **13.** a mark made by a sharp point; puncture. **14.** a sharp emotional pain resembling the physical pain caused by being pricked: *a prick of conscience.* **15.** a taboo slang word for **penis.** **16.** *Slang, derogatory.* an obnoxious or despicable man. **17.** an instrument or weapon with a sharp point, such as a thorn, goad, bee sting, etc. **18.** the footprint or track of an animal, esp. a hare. **19.** *Obsolete.* a small mark caused by pricking a surface; dot; point. **20. kick against the pricks.** to hurt oneself by struggling against something in vain. [Old English *prica* point, puncture; related to Dutch *prik,* Icelandic *prik* short stick, Swedish *prick* point, stick]

pricker ('prɪkə) *n.* **1.** a person or thing that pricks. **2.** *U.S.* a thorn; prickle.

pricket ('prɪkɪt) *n.* **1.** a male deer in the second year of life having unbranched antlers. **2.** a sharp metal spike on which to stick a candle. **3.** a candlestick having such a spike. [C14 *priket,* from *prik* PRICK]

prickle ('prɪkᵊl) *n.* **1.** *Botany.* a pointed process arising from the outer layer of a stem, leaf, etc., and containing no woody or conducting tissue. Compare **thorn** (sense 1). **2.** a pricking or stinging sensation. ~*vb.* **3.** to feel or cause to feel a stinging sensation. **4.** (*tr.*) to prick, as with a thorn. [Old English *pricel;* related to Middle Low German *prekel,* German *Prickel*]

prickly ('prɪklɪ) *adj.* **-lier, -liest. 1.** having or covered with prickles. **2.** stinging or tingling. **3.** bad-tempered or irritable. **4.** full of difficulties; knotty: *a prickly problem.* —'**prickliness** *n.*

prickly ash *n.* a North American rutaceous shrub or small tree, *Zanthoxylum americanum,* having prickly branches, feathery aromatic leaves, and bark used as a remedy for toothache. Also called: **toothache tree.**

prickly heat *n.* a nontechnical name for **miliaria.**

prickly pear *n.* **1.** any of various tropical cacti of the genus *Opuntia,* having flattened or cylindrical spiny joints and oval fruit that is edible in some species. See also **cholla, nopal** (sense 2). **2.** the fruit of any of these plants.

prickly poppy *n.* an annual papaveraceous plant, *Argemone mexicana,* of tropical America, having prickly stems and leaves and large yellow or white flowers.

prick song *n. Obsolete.* **a.** a piece of written vocal music. **b.** vocal music sung from a copy. [C16: from *pricked song, prickt song,* from PRICK (in the sense: to mark out, notate)]

pride (praɪd) *n.* **1.** a feeling of honour and self-respect; a sense of personal worth. **2.** excessive self-esteem; conceit. **3.** a source of pride. **4.** satisfaction or pleasure taken in one's own or another's success, achievements, etc. (esp. in the phrase **take (a) pride in**). **5.** the better or most superior part of something; flower. **6.** the most flourishing time. **7.** a group (of lions). **8.** the mettle of a horse; courage; spirit. **9.** *Archaic.* sexual desire, esp. in a female animal. **10.** *Archaic.* display, pomp, or splendour. **11. pride of place.** the most important position. ~*vb.* **12.** (*tr.*; foll. by *on* or *upon*) to take pride in (oneself) for. **13.** (*intr.*) to glory or revel (in). [Old English *prȳda;* related to Latin *prodesse* to be useful, Old Norse *prūthr* stately; see PROUD] —'**prideful** *adj.* —'**pridefully** *adv.*

prie-dieu (priːˈdjɜː) *n.* a piece of furniture consisting of a low surface for kneeling upon and a narrow front surmounted by a rest for the elbows or for books, for use when praying. [C18: from French, from *prier* to pray + *Dieu* God]

prier *or* **pryer** ('praɪə) *n.* a person who pries.

priest (priːst) *or* (*fem.*) **priestess** *n.* **1.** *Christianity.* a person ordained to act as a mediator between God and man in administering the sacraments, preaching, blessing, guiding, etc. **2.** (in episcopal Churches) a minister in the second grade of the hierarchy of holy orders, ranking below a bishop but above a deacon. **3.** a minister of any religion. **4.** *Judaism.* a descendant of the family of Aaron who has certain privileges in the synagogue service. **5.** (in some non-Christian religions) an official who offers sacrifice on behalf of the people and performs other religious ceremonies. **6.** (*sometimes cap.*) a variety of fancy pigeon having a bald pate with a crest or peak at the back of the head. **7.** *Angling.* a small club used to kill fish caught. ~*vb.* (*tr.*) **8.** to make a priest; ordain. [Old English *prēost,* apparently from PRESBYTER; related to Old High German *prēster,* Old French *prestre*] —'**priestess** *n.* —'**priest**ˌ**like** *adj.*

priestcraft ('priːstˌkrɑːft) *n.* **1.** the art and skills involved in the work of a priest. **2.** *Derogatory.* the influence of priests upon politics or the use by them of secular power.

priest-hole *or* **priest's hole** *n.* a secret chamber in certain houses in England, built as a hiding place for Roman Catholic priests when they were proscribed in the 16th and 17th centuries.

priesthood ('priːstˌhʊd) *n.* **1.** the state, order, or office of a priest. **2.** priests collectively.

priestly ('priːstlɪ) *adj.* **-lier, -liest.** of, relating to, characteristic of, or befitting a priest. —'**priestliness** *n.*

priest-ridden *adj.* dominated or governed by or excessively under the influence of priests.

prig[1] (prɪg) *n.* a person who is smugly self-righteous and narrow-minded. [C18: of unknown origin] —'**priggery** *or* '**priggishness** *n.* —'**priggish** *adj.* —'**priggishly** *adv.* —'**priggism** *n.*

prig[2] (prɪg) *Brit. slang, archaic.* ~*vb.* **prigs, prigging, prigged. 1.** another word for **steal.** ~*n.* **2.** another word for **thief.** [C16: of unknown origin]

prill (prɪl) *vb.* **1.** (*tr.*) to convert (a material) into a granular free-flowing form. ~*n.* **2.** prilled material. [C18: originally a Cornish copper-mining term, of obscure origin]

prim (prɪm) *adj.* **primmer, primmest. 1.** affectedly proper, precise, or formal. ~*vb.* **prims, primming, primmed. 2.** (*tr.*) to make prim. **3.** to purse (the mouth) primly or (of the mouth) to be so pursed. [C18: of unknown origin] —'**primly** *adv.* —'**primness** *n.*

prim. *abbrev. for:* **1.** primary. **2.** primitive.

prima ballerina ('priːmə) *n.* a leading female ballet dancer. [from Italian, literally: first ballerina]

primacy ('praɪməsɪ) *n., pl.* **-cies. 1.** the state of being first in rank, grade, etc. **2.** *Christianity.* the office, rank, or jurisdiction of a primate or senior bishop or (in the Roman Catholic Church) the pope.

prima donna ('priːmə 'dɒnə) *n., pl.* **prima donnas. 1.** a female operatic star; diva. **2.** *Informal.* a temperamental person. [C19: from Italian: first lady]

primaeval (praɪˈmiːvᵊl) *adj.* a variant spelling of **primeval.**

prima facie ('praɪmə 'feɪʃɪ) at first sight; as it seems at first. [C15: from Latin, from *prīmus* first + *faciēs* FACE]

prima-facie evidence *n. Law.* evidence that is sufficient to establish a fact or to raise a presumption of the truth of a fact unless controverted.

primage ('praɪmɪdʒ) *n. N.Z.* tax added to customs duty.

primal ('praɪməl) *adj.* **1.** first or original. **2.** chief or most important. [C17: from Medieval Latin *prīmālis,* from Latin *prīmus* first]

primal therapy *n. Psychol.* a form of psychotherapy in which patients are encouraged to scream abusively about their parents and agonizingly about their own suffering in infancy. Also called: **primal scream therapy, scream therapy.** [C20: from the book *The Primal Scream* (1970) by Arthur Janov, U.S. psychologist, who originated the treatment]

primaquine ('praɪməˌkwiːn) *n.* a synthetic drug used in the treatment of malaria. Formula: $C_{15}H_{21}N_3O$. [C20: from *prima-,* from Latin *prīmus* first + QUIN(OLIN)E]

primarily ('praɪmərəlɪ) *adv.* **1.** principally; chiefly; mainly. **2.** at first; originally.

primary ('praɪmərɪ) *adj.* **1.** first in importance, degree, rank, etc. **2.** first in position or time, as in a series. **3.** fundamental; basic. **4.** being the first stage; elementary. **5.** (*prenominal*) of or relating to the education of children up to the age of 11. **6.** (of the flight feathers of a bird's wing) growing from the manus. **7. a.** being the part of an electric circuit, such as a transformer or induction coil, in which a changing current induces a current in a neighbouring circuit: *a primary coil.* **b.** (of a current) flowing in such a circuit. Compare **secondary. 8. a.** (of a product) consisting of a natural raw material; unmanufactured. **b.** (of production or industry) involving the extraction or winning of such products. Agriculture, fishing, forestry, hunting, and mining are primary industries. Compare **secondary** (sense 7), **tertiary** (sense 2). **9.** *Chem.* **a.** (of an organic compound) having a functional group attached to a carbon atom that is attached to at least two hydrogen atoms. **b.** (of an amine) having only one organic group attached to the nitrogen atom; containing the group NH_2. **c.** (of a salt) derived from a tribasic acid by replacement of one acidic hydrogen atom with a metal atom or electropositive group. **10.** *Linguistics.* **a.** derived from a word that is not a derivation but the ultimate form itself. *Lovable* is a primary derivative of *love.* **b.** (of Latin, Greek, or Sanskrit tenses) referring to present or future time. Compare **historic** (sense 3). **11.** *Geology, obsolete.* relating to the Palaeozoic or earlier eras. ~*n., pl.* **-ries. 12.** a person or thing that is first in rank, occurrence, etc. **13.** (in the U.S.) **a.** a preliminary election in which the voters of a state or region choose a party's convention delegates, nominees for office, etc. See also **closed primary, direct primary, open primary. b.** a local meeting of voters registered with one party to nominate candidates, select convention delegates, etc. Full name: **primary election. 14.** See **primary colour. 15.** any of the flight feathers growing from the manus of a bird's wing. **16.** a primary coil, winding, inductance, or current in an electric circuit. **17.** *Astronomy.* a celestial body around which one or more specified secondary bodies orbit: *the sun is the primary of the earth.* [C15: from Latin *prīmārius* of the first rank, principal, from *prīmus* first]

primary accent *or* **stress** *n. Linguistics.* the strongest accent in a word or breath group, as that on the first syllable of *agriculture.* Compare **secondary accent.**

primary cell *n.* an electric cell that generates an electromotive force by the direct and usually irreversible conversion of chemical energy into electrical energy. It cannot be recharged efficiently by an electric current. Also called: **voltaic cell.** Compare **secondary cell.**

primary colour *n.* **1.** Also called: **additive primary.** any of three spectral colours (usually red, green, and blue) that can be mixed to match any other colour, including white light but excluding black. **2.** Also called: **subtractive primary.** any one of the spectral colours cyan, magenta, or yellow that can be subtracted from white light to match any other colour. An equal mixture of the three produces a black pigment. **3.** Also called: **psychological primary.** any one of the colours red, yellow, green, or blue. All other colours look like a mixture of two or more of these colours and they play a unique role in the processing of colour by the visual system. ~See also **secondary colour, complementary colour.**

primary effect *n. Psychol.* the process whereby the first few items on a list are learnt more rapidly than the middle items.

primary election *n.* See **primary** (sense 13).

primary processes *pl. n. Psychoanal.* unconscious, irrational thought processes, such as condensation or displacement, governed by the pleasure principle. Compare **secondary processes.**

primary qualities *pl. n.* (in empiricist philosophy) those properties of objects that are directly known by experience, such as size, shape, and number.

primary school *n.* **1.** (in Britain) a school for children below the age of 11. It is usually divided into an infant and a junior section. **2.** (in the U.S. and Canada) a school equivalent to the first three or four grades of elementary school, sometimes including a kindergarten.

primary stress *n. Linguistics.* another term for **primary accent.**

primate[1] ('praɪmeɪt) *n.* **1.** any placental mammal of the order *Primates,* typically having flexible hands and feet with opposable first digits, good eyesight, and, in the higher apes, a highly developed brain: includes lemurs, lorises, monkeys, apes, and man. ~*adj.* **2.** of, relating to, or belonging to the order *Primates.* [C18: from New Latin *primates,* plural of *prīmās* principal, from *prīmus* first] —**primatial** (praɪ'meɪʃəl) *adj.*

primate[2] ('praɪmeɪt) *n.* **1.** another name for **archbishop. 2. Primate of all England.** the Archbishop of Canterbury. **3. Primate of England.** the Archbishop of York. [C13: from Old French, from Latin *prīmās* principal, from *prīmus* first]

primatology (ˌpraɪmə'tɒlədʒɪ) *n.* the branch of zoology that is concerned with the study of primates.

prime (praɪm) *adj.* **1.** (*prenominal*) first in quality or value; first-rate. **2.** (*prenominal*) fundamental; original. **3.** (*prenominal*) first in importance, authority, etc.; chief. **4.** *Maths.* **a.** having no factors except itself or one: $x^2 + x + 3$ *is a prime polynomial.* **b.** (foll. by *to*) having no common factors (with): *20 is prime to 21.* **5.** *Finance.* having the best credit rating: *prime investments.* ~*n.* **6.** the time when a thing is at its best. **7.** a period of power, vigour, etc., usually following youth (esp. in the phrase **the prime of life**). **8.** the beginning of something, such as the spring. **9.** *Maths.* short for **prime number. 10.** *Linguistics.* a semantically indivisible element; minimal component of the sense of a word. **11.** *Music.* **a.** unison. **b.** the tonic of a scale. **12.** *Chiefly R.C. Church.* the second of the seven canonical hours of the divine office, originally fixed for the first hour of the day, at sunrise. **13.** the first of eight basic positions from which a parry or attack can be made in fencing. ~*vb.* **14.** to prepare (something); make ready. **15.** (*tr.*) to apply a primer, such as paint or size, to (a surface). **16.** (*tr.*) to fill (a pump) with its working fluid before starting, in order to improve the sealing of the pump elements and to expel air from it before starting. **17.** (*tr.*) to increase the quantity of fuel in the float chamber of (a carburettor) in order to facilitate the starting of an engine. **18.** (*tr.*) to insert a primer into (a gun, mine, charge, etc.) preparatory to detonation or firing. **19.** (*intr.*) (of a steam engine or boiler) to operate with or produce steam mixed with large amounts of water. **20.** (*tr.*) to provide with facts, information, etc., beforehand; brief. [(adj.) C14: from Latin *prīmus* first; (n.) C13: from Latin *prīma* (*hora*) the first (hour); (vb.) C16: of uncertain origin, probably connected with n.] —'**primely** *adv.* —'**primeness** *n.*

prime cost *n.* the portion of the cost of a commodity that varies directly with the amount of it produced, principally comprising materials and labour. Also called: **variable cost.** Compare **overheads.**

prime meridian *n.* the 0° meridian from which the other meridians or lines of longitude are calculated, usually taken to pass through Greenwich.

prime minister *n.* **1.** the head of a parliamentary government. **2.** the chief minister of a sovereign or a state. —**prime ministership** *or* **prime ministry** *n.*

prime mover *n.* **1.** the original or primary force behind an idea, enterprise, etc. **2. a.** the source of power, such as fuel, wind, electricity, etc., for a machine. **b.** the means of extracting power from such a source, such as a steam engine, electric motor, etc. **3.** (in the philosophy of Aristotle) that which is the cause of all movement.

Prime Mover *n.* (usually preceded by *the*) *Philosophy.* God, esp. when considered as a first cause.

prime number *n.* an integer that cannot be factorized into other integers but is only divisible by itself or 1, such as 2, 3, 7, and 11. Sometimes shortened to **prime.** Compare **composite number.**

primer[1] ('praɪmə) *n.* **1.** an introductory text, such as a school textbook. **2.** *Printing.* See **long primer, great primer.** [C14: via Anglo-Norman from Medieval Latin *primārius* (*liber*) a first (book), from Latin *prīmārius* PRIMARY]

primer[2] ('praɪmə) *n.* **1.** a person or thing that primes. **2.** a device, such as a tube containing explosive, for detonating the main charge in a gun, mine, etc. **3.** a substance, such as paint, applied to a surface as a base, sealer, etc. Also called (for senses 2, 3): **priming.** [C15: see PRIME (vb.)]

prime rate *n.* the lowest commercial interest rate charged by a bank at a particular time.

primero (prɪ'mɛərəʊ) *n. Chiefly Brit.* a 16th- and 17th-century card game. [C16: from Spanish *primera* card game, from *primero* first, from Latin *prīmārius* chief]

primers ('prɪməz) *pl. n. N.Z. informal.* the youngest class in a primary school.

prime time *n.* **1.** the peak viewing time on television, for which advertising rates are the highest. ~*adj.* **primetime. 2.** occurring during or designed for prime time: *a primetime drama.*

primeval *or* **primaeval** (praɪ'miːvəl) *adj.* of or belonging to the first age or ages, esp. of the world. [C17: from Latin *prīmaevus* youthful, from *prīmus* first + *aevum* age] —**pri'mevally** *or* **pri'maevally** *adv.*

prime vertical *n. Astronomy.* the great circle passing through the observer's zenith and meeting the horizon due east and west.

primigravida (ˌpraɪmɪ'grævɪdə) *n., pl.* **-das** *or* **-dae** (-ˌdiː). *Obstetrics.* a woman who is pregnant for the first time. [C19: New Latin, from Latin *prima* first + *gravida* GRAVID (woman)]

primine (ˈpraɪmɪn) *n. Botany.* the integument surrounding an ovule or the outer of two such integuments. Compare **secundine.** [C19: via French from Latin *prīmus* first]

priming (ˈpraɪmɪŋ) *n.* **1.** something used to prime. **2.** a substance, used to ignite an explosive charge.

primipara (praɪˈmɪpərə) *n., pl.* **-ras** *or* **-rae** (-ˌriː). *Obstetrics.* a woman who has borne only one child. Also written: **Para I.** [C19: from Latin, from *prīmus* first + *parere* to bring forth] —**primiparity** (ˌprɪmɪˈpærɪtɪ) *n.* —**priˈmiparous** *adj.*

primitive (ˈprɪmɪtɪv) *adj.* **1.** of or belonging to the first or beginning; original. **2.** characteristic of an early state, esp. in being crude or uncivilized: *a primitive dwelling.* **3.** *Anthropol.* denoting or relating to a preliterate and nonindustrial social system. **4.** *Biology.* **a.** of, relating to, or resembling an early stage in the evolutionary development of a particular group of organisms: *primitive amphibians.* **b.** another word for **primordial** (sense 3). **5.** showing the characteristics of primitive painters; untrained, childlike, or naive. **6.** *Geology.* of, relating to, or denoting rocks formed in or before the Palaeozoic era. **7.** denoting a word from which another word is derived, as for example *hope,* from which *hopeless* is derived. **8.** *Protestant theol.* of, relating to, or associated with a minority group that breaks away from a sect, denomination, or Church in order to return to what is regarded as the original simplicity of the Gospels. ~*n.* **9.** a primitive person or thing. **10. a.** an artist whose work does not conform to traditional, academic, or avant-garde standards of Western painting, such as a painter from an African or Oceanic civilization. **b.** a painter of the pre-Renaissance era in European painting. **c.** a painter of any era whose work appears childlike or untrained. Also called (for a, c): **naive.** **11.** a work by such an artist. **12.** a word or concept from which another word or concept is derived. **13.** *Maths.* a curve, function, or other form from which another is derived. [C14: from Latin *prīmitīvus* earliest of its kind, primitive, from *prīmus* first] —ˈ**primitively** *adv.* —ˈ**primitiveness** *n.*

primitivism (ˈprɪmɪtɪˌvɪzəm) *n.* **1.** the condition of being primitive. **2.** the notion that the value of primitive cultures is superior to that of the modern world. **3.** the principles, characteristics, etc., of primitive art and artists. —ˈ**primitivist** *n., adj.* —ˌ**primitivˈistic** *adj.*

primo (ˈpriːməʊ) *n., pl.* **-mos** *or* **-mi** (-mɪ). *Music.* the upper or right-hand part in a piano duet. Compare **secondo.** [Italian: first, from Latin *prīmus*]

primogenitor (ˌpraɪməʊˈdʒɛnɪtə) *n.* **1.** a forefather; ancestor. **2.** an earliest parent or ancestor, as of a race. [C17: alteration of PROGENITOR after PRIMOGENITURE]

primogeniture (ˌpraɪməʊˈdʒɛnɪtʃə) *n.* **1.** the state of being a first-born. **2.** *Law.* the right of an eldest son to succeed to the estate of his ancestor to the exclusion of all others. Compare **ultimogeniture.** [C17: from Medieval Latin *prīmōgenitūra* birth of a first child, from Latin *prīmō* at first + Late Latin *genitūra* a birth] —**primogenitary** (ˌpraɪməʊˈdʒɛnɪtərɪ, -trɪ) *adj.*

primordial (praɪˈmɔːdɪəl) *adj.* **1.** existing at or from the beginning; earliest; primeval. **2.** constituting an origin; fundamental. **3.** *Biology.* of or relating to an early stage of development: *primordial germ cells.* ~*n.* **4.** an elementary or basic principle. [C14: from Late Latin *prīmōrdiālis* original, from Latin *prīmus* first + *ōrdīrī* to begin] —**priˌmordiˈality** *n.* —**priˈmordially** *adv.*

primordium (praɪˈmɔːdɪəm) *n., pl.* **-dia** (-dɪə). *Biology.* an organ or part in the earliest stage of development.

primp (prɪmp) *vb.* to dress (oneself), esp. in fine clothes; prink. [C19: probably from PRIM]

primrose (ˈprɪmˌrəʊz) *n.* **1.** any of various temperate primulaceous plants of the genus *Primula,* esp. *P. vulgaris* of Europe, which has pale yellow flowers. **2.** short for **evening primrose.** **3.** Also called: **primrose yellow.** a light to moderate yellow, sometimes with a greenish tinge. ~*adj.* **4.** of, relating to, or abounding in primroses. **5.** of the colour primrose. **6.** pleasant or gay. [C15: from Old French *primerose,* from Medieval Latin *prīma rosa* first rose]

primrose path *n.* (often preceded by *the*) a pleasurable way of life.

primula (ˈprɪmjʊlə) *n.* any primulaceous plant of the N temperate genus *Primula,* having white, yellow, pink, or purple funnel-shaped flowers with five spreading petals: includes the primrose, oxlip, cowslip, and polyanthus. [C18: New Latin, from Medieval Latin *prīmula* (*vēris*) little first one (of the spring)]

primulaceous (ˌprɪmjʊˈleɪʃəs) *adj.* of, relating to, or belonging to the *Primulaceae,* a family of plants having funnel-shaped or bell-shaped flowers: includes primrose, moneywort, pimpernel, and loosestrife.

primum mobile *Latin.* (ˈpraɪmʊm ˈməʊbɪlɪ) *n.* **1.** a prime mover. **2.** *Astronomy.* the outermost empty sphere in the Ptolemaic system that was thought to revolve around the earth from east to west in 24 hours carrying with it the inner spheres of the planets, sun, moon, and fixed stars. [C15: from Medieval Latin: first moving (thing)]

primus (ˈpraɪməs) *n. Scottish Episcopal Church.* the presiding bishop in the Synod. [from Latin: first]

Primus (ˈpraɪməs) *n. Trademark.* a portable paraffin cooking stove, used esp. by campers. Also called: **Primus stove.**

primus inter pares *Latin.* (ˈpraɪməs ɪntə ˈpɑːrɪz) first among equals.

prin. *abbrev. for:* **1.** principal. **2.** principle.

prince (prɪns) *n.* **1.** (in Britain) a son of the sovereign or of one of the sovereign's sons. **2.** a nonreigning male member of a sovereign family. **3.** the monarch of a small territory, such as Monaco, usually called a principality, that was at some time subordinate to an emperor or king. **4.** any sovereign; monarch. **5.** a nobleman in various countries, such as Italy and Germany. **6.** an outstanding member of a specified group: *a merchant prince.* **7.** *U.S. and Canadian informal.* a generous and charming man. [C13: via Old French from Latin *princeps* first man, ruler, chief] —ˈ**princeˌlike** *adj.*

Prince Albert (prɪnz ˈælbət) *n.* a man's double-breasted frock coat worn esp. in the early 20th century.

prince consort *n.* the husband of a female sovereign, who is himself a prince.

princedom (ˈprɪnsdəm) *n.* **1.** the dignity, rank, or position of a prince. **2.** a land ruled by a prince; principality.

princeling (ˈprɪnslɪŋ) *n.* **1.** Also called: **princekin.** a young prince. **2.** Also called: **princelet.** the ruler of an insignificant territory; petty or minor prince.

princely (ˈprɪnslɪ) *adj.* **-lier, -liest.** **1.** generous or lavish. **2.** of, belonging to, or characteristic of a prince. ~*adv.* **3.** in a princely manner. —ˈ**princeliness** *n.*

Prince of Darkness *n.* another name for **Satan.**

Prince of Peace *n. Bible.* the future Messiah (Isaiah 9:6): held by Christians to be Christ.

Prince of Wales *n.* the eldest son and heir apparent of the British sovereign.

prince regent *n.* a prince who acts as regent during the minority, disability, or absence of the legal sovereign.

prince royal *n.* the eldest son of a monarch.

prince's-feather *n.* **1.** an amaranthaceous garden plant, *Amaranthus hybridus hypochondriacus,* with spikes of bristly brownish-red flowers. **2.** a tall tropical polygonaceous plant, *Polygonum orientale,* with hanging spikes of pink flowers.

princess (prɪnˈsɛs) *n.* **1.** (in Britain) a daughter of the sovereign or of one of the sovereign's sons. **2.** a nonreigning female member of a sovereign family. **3.** the wife and consort of a prince. **4.** any very attractive or outstanding woman. **5.** *Archaic.* a female sovereign. **6.** Also called: **princess dress, princess line.** a style of dress with a fitted bodice and an A-line skirt that is shaped by seams from shoulder to hem without a seam at the waistline.

princess royal *n.* the eldest daughter of a British or (formerly) a Prussian sovereign: a title not always conferred.

principal (ˈprɪnsɪpᵊl) *adj.* (*prenominal*) **1.** first in importance, rank, value, etc.; chief. **2.** denoting or relating to capital or property as opposed to interest, etc. ~*n.* **3.** a person who is first in importance or directs some event, action, organization, etc. **4.** (in Britain) a civil servant of an executive grade who is in charge of a section. **5.** *Law.* **a.** a person who engages another to act as his agent. **b.** an active participant in a crime. **c.** the person primarily liable to fulfil an obligation. **6.** the head of a school or other educational institution. **7.** (in Scottish schools) a head of department. **8.** *Finance.* **a.** capital or property, as contrasted with the income derived from it. **b.** the original amount of a debt on which interest is calculated. **9.** a main roof truss or rafter. **10.** *Music.* **a.** the chief instrumentalist in a section of the orchestra. **b.** one of the singers in an opera company. **c.** either of two types of open diapason organ stops, one of four-foot length and pitch and the other of eight-foot length and pitch. **11.** the leading performer in a play. [C13: via Old French from Latin *principālis* chief, from *princeps* chief man, PRINCE] —ˈ**principally** *adv.* —ˈ**principalship** *n.*

principal axis *n.* **1.** the line passing through the centres of curvature of the faces of a lens or a curved mirror. **2.** any of three mutually perpendicular axes about which the moment of inertia of a body is maximum.

principal boy *n.* the leading male role in a pantomime, played by a woman.

principal focus *n.* another name for **focal point.**

principalities (ˌprɪnsɪˈpælɪtɪz) *pl. n.* (*often cap.*) the seventh of the nine orders into which the angels are divided in medieval angelology.

principality (ˌprɪnsɪˈpælɪtɪ) *n., pl.* **-ties.** **1. a.** a territory ruled by a prince. **b.** a territory from which a prince draws his title. **2.** the dignity or authority of a prince. [C14 (in the sense: pre-eminence): via Old French from Latin *principālis* PRINCIPAL]

principal nursing officer *n.* a grade of nurse concerned with administration in the British National Health Service.

principal parts *pl. n.* **1.** *Grammar.* the main inflected forms of a verb, from which all other inflections may be deduced. In English they are generally considered to consist of the third person present singular, present participle, past tense, and past participle. **2.** the sides and interior angles of a triangle.

principate (ˈprɪnsɪˌpeɪt) *n.* **1.** a state ruled by a prince. **2.** a form of rule in the early Roman Empire in which some republican forms survived.

principium (prɪnˈsɪpɪəm) *n., pl.* **-ia** (-ɪə). (*usually pl.*) a principle, esp. a fundamental one. [C17: Latin: an origin, beginning]

principle (ˈprɪnsɪpᵊl) *n.* **1.** a standard or rule of personal conduct: *a man of principle.* **2.** (*often pl.*) a set of such moral rules: *he'd stoop to anything; he has no principles.* **3.** adherence to such a moral code; morality: *it's not the money but the principle of the thing; torn between principle and expediency.* **4.** a fundamental or general truth or law: *first principles.* **5.** the essence of something: *the male principle.* **6.** a source or fundamental cause; origin: *principle of life.* **7.** a rule or law concerning a natural phenomenon or the behaviour of a system: *the principle of the conservation of mass.* **8.** an underlying or guiding theory or belief: *the hereditary principle; socialist principles.* **9.** *Chem.* a constituent of a substance that gives the substance its characteristics and behaviour: *bitter principle.* **10. in principle.** in theory or essence. **11. on principle.** because of or in demonstration of a principle. [C14: from Latin *principium* beginning, basic tenet]

Principle (ˈprɪnsɪpᵊl) *n. Christian Science.* another word for **God.**

principled (ˈprɪnsɪpᵊld) *adj.* **a.** having high moral principles. **b.** (*in combination*): *high-principled.*

principle of economy *n.* **the.** another name for **Ockham's razor.**

principle of indifference *n.* the principle that, in the absence of any reason to expect one event rather than another, all the possible events should be assigned the same probability. See **mathematical probability.**

principle of least action *n.* the principle that motion between any two points in a conservative dynamical system is such that the action has a minimum value with respect to all paths between the points that correspond to the same energy. Also called: **Maupertuis principle.**

prink (prɪŋk) *vb.* **1.** to dress (oneself, etc.) finely; deck out. **2.** (*intr.*) to preen oneself. [C16: probably changed from PRANK[2] (to adorn, decorate)] —ˈ**prinker** *n.*

print (prɪnt) *vb.* **1.** to reproduce (text, pictures, etc.), esp. in large numbers, by applying ink to paper or other material by one of various processes. **2.** to produce or reproduce (a manuscript, a book, data, etc.) in print, as for publication. **3.** to write (letters, etc.) in the style of printed matter. **4.** to mark or indent (a surface) by pressing (something) onto it. **5.** to produce a photographic print from (a negative). **6.** (*tr.*) to implant or fix in the mind or memory. **7.** (*tr.*) to make (a mark or indentation) by applying pressure. ~*n.* **8.** printed matter such as newsprint. **9.** a printed publication such as a newspaper or book. **10. in print. a.** in printed or published form. **b.** (of a book, etc.) offered for sale by the publisher. **11. out of print.** no longer available from a publisher. **12.** a design or picture printed from an engraved plate, wood block, or other medium. **13.** printed text, esp. with regard to the typeface used: *small print.* **14.** a positive photographic image in colour or black and white produced, usually on paper, from a negative image on film. Compare **slide** (sense 13). **15. a.** a fabric with a printed design. **b.** (*as modifier*): *a print dress.* **16. a.** a mark or indentation made by pressing something onto a surface. **b.** a stamp, die, etc., that makes such an impression. **c.** the surface subjected to such an impression. **17.** See **fingerprint.** ~See also **print out.** [C13 *priente,* from Old French: something printed, from *preindre* to make an impression, from Latin *premere* to press]

printable (ˈprɪntəbᵊl) *adj.* **1.** capable of being printed or of producing a print. **2.** suitable for publication. —ˌ**printaˈbility** *or* ˈ**printableness** *n.*

printed circuit *n.* an electronic circuit in which certain components and the connections between them are formed by etching a metallic coating or by electrodeposition on one or both sides of a thin insulating board. Also called: **printed circuit board** *or* **card.**

printer (ˈprɪntə) *n.* **1.** a person or business engaged in printing. **2.** a machine or device that prints. **3.** *Computer technol.* an output device for printing results on paper.

printer's devil *n.* an apprentice or errand boy in a printing establishment.

printery (ˈprɪntərɪ) *n., pl.* **-eries. 1.** *Chiefly U.S.* an establishment in which typographic printing is carried out. **2.** an establishment in which fabrics are printed.

printhead (ˈprɪntˌhɛd) *n. Computer technol.* a component in a printer that forms a printed character.

printing (ˈprɪntɪŋ) *n.* **1. a.** the process, business, or art of producing printed matter. **b.** (*as modifier*): *printing ink.* **2.** printed text. **3.** Also called: **impression.** all the copies of a book or other publication printed at one time. **4.** a form of writing in which letters resemble printed letters.

printing press *n.* any of various machines used for printing.

printmaker (ˈprɪntˌmeɪkə) *n.* a person who makes print, esp. a craftsman or artist in this field.

print out *vb.* (*tr., adv.*) **1.** (of a computer output device, such as a line printer) to produce (printed information). ~*n.* **print-out. 2.** such printed information.

print shop *n.* a place in which printing is carried out.

print-through *n.* the unwanted transfer of a recorded magnetic field pattern from one turn of magnetic tape to the preceding or succeeding turn on a reel, causing distortion.

print unions *pl. n.* the trade unions within the printing industry. See **NGA, SOGAT.**

printwheel (ˈprɪntˌwiːl) *n.* another name for **daisywheel.**

prion[1] (ˈpraɪən) *n.* any of various dovelike petrels of the genus *Pachyptila* of the southern oceans that have a serrated bill. [C19: New Latin, from Greek *priōn* a saw]

prion[2] (ˈpraɪɒn) *n.* an infectious protein particle postulated by some to be the cause of scrapie, BSE, and some human encephalopathies.

prior[1] (ˈpraɪə) *adj.* **1.** (*prenominal*) previous; preceding. **2. prior to.** before; until. ~*n.* **3.** *Statistics.* a prior probability. [C18: from Latin: previous]

prior[2] (ˈpraɪə) *n.* **1.** the superior of a house and community in certain religious orders. **2.** the deputy head of a monastery or abbey, ranking immediately below the abbot. **3.** (formerly) a chief magistrate in medieval Florence and other Italian republics. [C11: from Late Latin: head, from Latin (adj.): previous, from Old Latin *pri* before]

priorate (ˈpraɪərɪt) *n.* the office, status, or term of office of a prior.

prioress (ˈpraɪərɪs) *n.* a nun holding an office in her convent corresponding to that of a prior in a male religious order.

prioritize *or* **prioritise** (praɪˈɒrɪˌtaɪz) *vb.* (*tr.*) **1.** to arrange (items to be attended to) in order of their relative importance. **2.** to give priority to or establish as a priority.

priority (praɪˈɒrɪtɪ) *n., pl.* **-ties. 1.** the condition of being prior; antecedence; precedence. **2.** the right of precedence over others. **3.** something given specified attention: *my first priority.*

prior probability *n. Statistics.* the probability assigned to a parameter or to an event in advance of any empirical evidence, often subjectively or on the assumption of the principle of indifference. Compare **posterior probability.**

priory (ˈpraɪərɪ) *n., pl.* **-ories.** a religious house governed by a prior, sometimes being subordinate to an abbey. [C13: from Medieval Latin *priōria;* see PRIOR[2]]

prisage (ˈpraɪzɪdʒ) *n.* a customs duty levied until 1809 upon wine imported into England. [C16: from Anglo-French, from Old French *prise* a taking or requisitioning, duty, from *prendre* to take; see PRISE]

prise *or* **prize** (praɪz) *vb.* (*tr.*) **1.** to force open by levering. **2.** to extract or obtain with difficulty: *they had to prise the news out of him.* ~*n.* **3.** *Rare or dialect.* a tool involving leverage in its use or the leverage so employed. ~U.S. and Canadian equivalent: **pry.** [C17: from Old French *prise* a taking, from *prendre* to take, from Latin *prehendere;* see PRIZE[1]]

prisere (ˈpraɪˌsɪə) *n. Ecology.* a primary sere or succession from bare ground to the community climax. [C20: PRI(MARY) + SERE[2]]

prism (ˈprɪzəm) *n.* **1.** a transparent polygonal solid, often having triangular ends and rectangular sides, for dispersing light into a spectrum or for reflecting and deviating light. They are used in spectroscopes, binoculars, periscopes, etc. **2.** a form of crystal with faces parallel to the vertical axis. **3.** *Maths.* a polyhedron having parallel, polygonal, and congruent bases and sides that are parallelograms. [C16: from Medieval Latin *prisma,* from Greek: something shaped by sawing, from *prizein* to saw]

prismatic (prɪzˈmætɪk) *adj.* **1.** concerned with, containing, or produced by a prism. **2.** exhibiting bright spectral colours: *prismatic light.* **3.** *Crystallog.* another word for **orthorhombic.** —**prisˈmatically** *adv.*

prismatoid (ˈprɪzməˌtɔɪd) *n.* a polyhedron whose vertices lie in either one of two parallel planes. Compare **prism** (sense 3), **prismoid.** [C19: from Greek *prismatoeidēs* shaped like a prism; see PRISM, -OID] —ˌ**prismaˈtoidal** *adj.*

prismoid (ˈprɪzmɔɪd) *n.* a prismatoid having an equal number of vertices in each of the two parallel planes and whose sides are trapeziums or parallelograms. [C18: from French *prismoïde;* see PRISM, -OID] —**prisˈmoidal** *adj.*

prison (ˈprɪzᵊn) *n.* **1.** a public building used to house convicted criminals and accused persons remanded in custody and awaiting trial. See also **jail, penitentiary, reformatory. 2.** any place of confinement or seeming confinement. [C12: from Old French *prisun,* from Latin *prēnsiō* a capturing, from *prehendere* to lay hold of]

prisoner (ˈprɪzənə) *n.* **1.** a person deprived of liberty and kept in prison or some other form of custody as a punishment for a crime, while awaiting trial, or for some other reason. **2.** a person confined by any of various restraints: *we are all prisoners of time.* **3. take (someone) prisoner.** to capture and hold (someone) as a prisoner, esp. as a prisoner of war.

prisoner of war *n.* a person, esp. a serviceman, captured by an enemy in time of war. Abbrev.: **POW.**

prisoner's base *n.* a children's game involving two teams, members of which chase and capture each other to increase the number of children in their own base.

prissy (ˈprɪsɪ) *adj.* **-sier, -siest.** fussy and prim, esp. in a prudish way. [C20: probably from PRIM + SISSY] —ˈ**prissily** *adv.* —ˈ**prissiness** *n.*

pristine (ˈprɪstaɪn, -tiːn) *adj.* **1.** of or involving the earliest period, state, etc.; original. **2.** pure; uncorrupted. [C15: from Latin *pristinus* primitive; related to *prīmus* first, PRIME]

prithee (ˈprɪðɪ) *interj. Archaic.* pray thee; please. [C16: shortened from *I pray thee*]

prittle-prattle (ˈprɪtᵊlˌprætᵊl) *n.* foolish or idle talk; babble. [C16: reduplication of PRATTLE]

priv. *abbrev. for:* **1.** private. **2.** privative.

privacy (ˈpraɪvəsɪ, ˈprɪvəsɪ) *n.* **1.** the condition of being private or withdrawn; seclusion. **2.** the condition of being secret; secrecy. 3. *Philosophy.* the condition of being necessarily restricted to a single person.

Privatdocent (*German* priˈvaːtdoˈtsɛnt) *n.* (esp. in German-speaking countries) a university lecturer who formerly received fees from his students rather than a university salary. [German, from *privat* PRIVATE + *docent* (for *Dozent* lecturer) from Latin *docēre* to teach]

private (ˈpraɪvɪt) *adj.* 1. not widely or publicly known: *they had private reasons for the decision.* 2. confidential; secret: *a private conversation.* 3. not for general or public use: *a private bathroom.* 4. (*prenominal*) individual; special: *my own private recipe.* 5. (*prenominal*) having no public office, rank, etc.: *a private man.* 6. (*prenominal*) denoting a soldier of the lowest military rank: *a private soldier.* 7. of, relating to, or provided by a private individual or organization, rather than by the state or a public body: *the private sector; private housing.* 8. (of a place) retired; sequestered; not overlooked. 9. (of a person) reserved; uncommunicative. **10. in private.** in secret; confidentially. ~*n.* **11.** a soldier of the lowest rank, sometimes separated into qualification grades, in many armies and marine corps: *private first class.* [C14: from Latin *prīvātus* belonging to one individual, withdrawn from public life, from *prīvāre* to deprive, bereave] —ˈ**privately** *adv.*

private bar *n. Brit.* the saloon or lounge bar of a public house. Also called: **the private.** Compare **public bar.**

private bill *n.* a bill presented to Parliament or Congress on behalf of a private individual, corporation, etc.

private company *n.* a limited company that does not issue shares for public subscription and whose owners do not enjoy an unrestricted right to transfer their shareholdings. Compare **public company.**

private detective *n.* an individual privately employed to investigate a crime, keep watch on a suspected person, or make other inquiries. Also called: **private investigator.**

private enterprise *n.* 1. economic activity undertaken by private individuals or organizations under private ownership. Compare **public enterprise.** 2. another name for **capitalism.**

privateer (ˌpraɪvəˈtɪə) *n.* 1. an armed, privately owned vessel commissioned for war service by a government. 2. Also called: **privateersman.** a commander or member of the crew of a privateer. ~*vb.* 3. (*intr.*) to serve as a privateer.

private eye *n. Informal.* a private detective.

private health insurance *n.* insurance against the need for medical treatment as a private patient.

private hotel *n.* 1. a residential hotel or boarding house in which the proprietor has the right to refuse to accept a person as a guest, esp. a person arriving by chance. 2. *Austral. and N.Z.* a hotel not having a licence to sell alcoholic liquor.

private income *n.* an income from sources other than employment, such as investment. Also called: **private means.**

private language *n. Philosophy.* a language that is not merely secret or accidentally limited to one user, but that cannot in principle be communicated to another.

private law *n.* the branch of law that deals with the rights and duties of private individuals and the relations between them. Compare **public law.**

private life *n.* the social or family life or personal relationships of an individual, esp. of a person in the public eye, such as a politician or celebrity.

private member *n.* a member of a legislative assembly, such as the House of Commons, not having an appointment in the government.

private member's bill *n.* a public bill introduced in the House of Commons by a private member.

private parts *or* **privates** (ˈpraɪvɪts) *pl. n.* euphemistic terms for **genitals.**

private patient *n. Brit.* a patient receiving medical treatment not paid for by the National Health Service.

private pay bed *n.* (in Britain) a bed in a National Health Service hospital, reserved for private patients who pay a consultant acting privately for treatment and who are charged by the health service for use of hospital facilities. Often shortened to **pay bed.** Compare **amenity bed.**

private practice *n. Brit.* medical practice that is not part of the National Health Service.

private press *n.* a printing establishment primarily run as a pastime.

private property *n.* land or belongings owned by a person or group and kept for their exclusive use.

private school *n.* a school under the financial and managerial control of a private body or charitable trust, accepting mostly fee-paying pupils.

private secretary *n.* 1. a secretary entrusted with the personal and confidential matters of a business executive. 2. a civil servant who acts as aide to a minister or senior government official. Compare **parliamentary private secretary.**

private sector *n.* the part of a country's economy that consists of privately owned enterprises. Compare **public sector.**

private treaty *n.* a sale of property for a price agreed directly between seller and buyer.

private view *n.* a preview, esp. of an art exhibition, for specially invited guests.

private viewdata *n.* an interactive video text system with restricted access.

privation (praɪˈveɪʃən) *n.* 1. loss or lack of the necessities of life, such as food and shelter. 2. hardship resulting from this. 3. the state of being deprived. 4. *Logic, obsolete.* the absence from an object of what ordinarily or naturally belongs to such objects. [C14: from Latin *prīvātiō* deprivation]

privative (ˈprɪvətɪv) *adj.* 1. causing privation. 2. expressing lack or negation, as for example the English suffix *-less* and prefix *un-*. 3. *Logic, obsolete.* (of a proposition) that predicates a logical privation. [C16: from Latin *prīvātīvus* indicating loss, negative] —ˈ**privatively** *adv.*

privatize *or* **privatise** (ˈpraɪvɪˌtaɪz) *vb.* (*tr.*) to transfer (the production of goods or services) from the public sector of an economy into private ownership and operation. —ˌ**privatiˈzation** *or* ˌ**privatiˈsation** *n.*

privet (ˈprɪvɪt) *n.* **a.** any oleaceous shrub of the genus *Ligustrum,* esp. *L. vulgare,* having oval dark green leaves, white flowers, and purplish-black berries. **b.** (*as modifier*): *a privet hedge.* [C16: of unknown origin]

privet hawk *n.* a hawk moth, *Sphinx ligustri,* with a mauve-and-brown striped body: frequents privets.

privilege (ˈprɪvɪlɪdʒ) *n.* 1. a benefit, immunity, etc., granted under certain conditions. 2. the advantages and immunities enjoyed by a small usually powerful group or class, esp. to the disadvantage of others: *one of the obstacles to social harmony is privilege.* 3. any of the fundamental rights guaranteed to the citizens of a country by its constitution. 4. **a.** the right of a lawyer to refuse to divulge information obtained in confidence from a client. **b.** the right claimed by any of certain other functionaries to refuse to divulge information: *executive privilege.* 5. the rights and immunities enjoyed by members of most legislative bodies, such as freedom of speech, freedom from arrest in civil cases during a session, etc. 6. *U.S. stock exchange.* a speculative contract permitting its purchaser to make optional purchases or sales of securities at a specified time over a limited period of time. See also **call** (sense 58), **put** (sense 20), **spread** (sense 24c.), **straddle** (sense 9). ~*vb.* (*tr.*) 7. to bestow a privilege or privileges upon. 8. (foll. by *from*) to free or exempt. [C12: from Old French *privilēge,* from Latin *prīvilēgium* law relevant to rights of an individual, from *prīvus* an individual + *lēx* law]

privileged (ˈprɪvɪlɪdʒd) *adj.* 1. enjoying or granted as a privilege or privileges. 2. *Law.* **a.** not actionable as a libel or slander. **b.** (of a communication, document, etc.) that a witness cannot be compelled to divulge. 3. *Nautical.* (of a vessel) having the right of way.

privily (ˈprɪvɪlɪ) *adv. Archaic or literary.* in a secret way.

privity (ˈprɪvɪtɪ) *n., pl* **-ties.** 1. a legally recognized relationship existing between two parties, such as that between lessor and lessee and between the parties to a contract: *privity of estate; privity of contract.* 2. secret knowledge that is shared. [C13: from Old French *priveté*]

privy (ˈprɪvɪ) *adj.* **privier, priviest.** 1. (*postpositive;* foll. by *to*) participating in the knowledge of something secret. 2. *Archaic.* secret, hidden, etc. 3. *Archaic.* of or relating to one person only. ~*n., pl.* **privies.** 4. a lavatory, esp. an outside one. 5. *Law.* a person in privity with another. See **privity** (sense 1). [C13: from Old French *privé* something private, from Latin *prīvātus* PRIVATE]

privy chamber *n.* 1. a private apartment inside a royal residence. 2. *Archaic.* a private room reserved for the use of a specific person or group.

privy council *n.* 1. the council of state of a monarch or noble, esp. formerly. 2. *Archaic.* a private or secret council.

Privy Council *n.* the private council of the British sovereign, consisting of all current and former ministers of the Crown and other distinguished subjects, all of whom are appointed for life. —**Privy Councillor** *n.*

privy purse *n.* (*often caps.*) 1. **a.** (in Britain) an allowance voted by Parliament for the private expenses of the monarch: part of the civil list. **b.** (in other countries) a similar sum of money for the monarch. 2. an official of the royal household responsible for dealing with the monarch's private expenses. Full name: **Keeper of the Privy Purse.**

privy seal *n.* (*often caps.*) (in Britain) a seal affixed to certain documents issued by royal authority: of less rank and importance than the great seal.

prix fixe (*French* pri fiks) *n., pl.* **prix fixes** (fiks). a fixed price charged for one of a set number of meals offered on a menu. Compare **à la carte, table d'hôte.**

Prix Goncourt *n.* an annual prize for a work of French fiction. [C20: after the Académie *Goncourt,* founded by the will of Edmond Goncourt (1822–96), French writer]

prize[1] (praɪz) *n.* 1. **a.** a reward or honour for victory or for having won a contest, competition, etc. **b.** (*as modifier*): *prize jockey; prize essay.* 2. something given to the winner of any game of chance, lottery, etc. 3. something striven for. 4. any valuable property captured in time of war, esp. a vessel. [C14: from Old French *prise* a capture, from Latin *prehendere* to seize; influenced also by Middle English *prise* reward; see PRICE]

prize[2] (praɪz) *vb.* (*tr.*) to esteem greatly; value highly. [C15 *prise,* from Old French *preisier* to PRAISE]

prize[3] (praɪz) *vb., n.* a variant spelling of **prise.**

prize court *n. Law.* a court having jurisdiction to determine how property captured at sea in wartime is to be distributed.

prizefight ('praɪz,faɪt) *n.* a boxing match for a prize or purse, esp. one of the fights popular in the 18th and 19th centuries. —'**prize,fighter** *n.* —'**prize,fighting** *n.*

prize money *n.* 1. any money offered, paid, or received as a prize. 2. (formerly) a part of the money realized from the sale of a captured vessel.

prize ring *n.* 1. the enclosed area or ring used by prizefighters. 2. **the prize ring.** the sport of prizefighting.

prizewinner ('praɪz,wɪnə) *n.* a person, animal, or thing that wins a prize. —'**prize,winning** *adj.*

prn (in prescriptions) *abbrev. for* pro re nata. [Latin: as the situation demands; as needed]

pro[1] (prəʊ) *adv.* 1. in favour of a motion, issue, course of action, etc. Compare **anti.** ~*prep.* 2. in favour of. ~*n., pl.* **pros.** 3. (*usually pl.*) an argument or vote in favour of a proposal or motion. See also **pros and cons.** 4. (*usually pl.*) a person who votes in favour of a proposal, motion, etc. ~Compare **con**[2]. [from Latin *prō* (prep.) in favour of]

pro[2] (prəʊ) *n., pl.* **pros,** *adj.* 1. *Informal.* short for **professional.** 2. *Slang.* a prostitute. [C19: by shortening]

PRO *abbrev. for:* 1. Public Records Office. 2. public relations officer.

pro-[1] *prefix.* 1. in favour of; supporting: *pro-Chinese.* 2. acting as a substitute for: *proconsul; pronoun.* [from Latin *prō* (adv. and prep.). In compound words borrowed from Latin, *prō-* indicates: forward, out (*project*); forward and down (*prostrate*); away from a place (*prodigal*); onward in time or space (*proceed*); extension outwards (*propagate*); before in time or place (*provide, protect*); on behalf of (*procure*); acting as a substitute for (*pronominal*); and sometimes intensive force (*promiscuous*)]

pro-[2] *prefix.* before in time or position; anterior; forward: *prophase; procephalic; prognathous.* [from Greek *pro* (prep.) before (in time, position, rank, etc.)]

proa ('prəʊə) *or* **prau** *n.* any of several kinds of canoe-like boats used in the South Pacific, esp. one equipped with an outrigger and sails. [C16: from Malay *parāhū* a boat]

proactive (prəʊ'æktɪv) *adj.* 1. tending to initiate change rather than reacting to events. 2. *Psychol.* of or denoting a mental process that affects a subsequent process. [C20: from PRO-[2] + (RE)ACTIVE]

proactive inhibition *or* **interference** *n. Psychol.* the tendency for earlier memories to interfere with the retrieval of material learned later. Compare **retroactive inhibition.**

pro-am ('prəʊ'æm) *adj.* (of a golf tournament, snooker tournament, etc.) involving both professional and amateur players.

prob. *abbrev. for:* 1. probable. 2. probably. 3. problem.

probabilism ('prɒbəbɪ,lɪzəm) *n.* 1. *Philosophy.* the doctrine that although certainty is impossible, probability is a sufficient basis for belief and action. 2. the principle of Roman Catholic moral theology that in a situation in which authorities differ as to what is the right course of action it is permissible to follow any course which has the support of some authority. —'**probabilist** *n., adj.* —,**probabil'istic** *adj.* —,**probabil'istically** *adv.*

probability (,prɒbə'bɪlɪtɪ) *n., pl.* **-ties.** 1. the condition of being probable. 2. an event or other thing that is probable. 3. *Statistics.* a measure or estimate of the degree of confidence one may have in the occurrence of an event, measured on a scale from zero (impossibility) to one (certainty). It may be defined as the proportion of favourable outcomes to the total number of possibilities if these are indifferent (**mathematical probability**), or the proportion observed in a sample (**empirical probability**), or the limit of this as the sample size tends to infinity (**relative frequency**), or by more subjective criteria (**subjective probability**).

probability density function *n. Statistics.* a function representing the relative distribution of frequency of a continuous random variable from which parameters such as its mean and variance can be derived and having the property that its integral from *a* to *b* is the probability that the variable lies in this interval. Its graph is the limiting case of a histogram as the amount of data increases and the class intervals decrease in size. Also called: **density function.** Compare **cumulative distribution function, frequency distribution.**

probability function *n. Statistics.* the function the values of which are probabilities of the distinct outcomes of a discrete random variable.

probable ('prɒbəbᵊl) *adj.* 1. likely to be or to happen but not necessarily so. 2. most likely: *the probable cause of the accident.* ~*n.* 3. a person who is probably to be chosen for a team, event, etc. [C14: via Old French from Latin *probābilis* that may be proved, from *probāre* to prove]

probable cause *n. Law.* reasonable grounds for holding a belief, esp. such as will justify bringing legal proceedings against a person or will constitute a defence to a charge of malicious prosecution.

probably ('prɒbəblɪ) *adv.* 1. (*sentence modifier; not used with a negative or in a question*) in all likelihood or probability: *I'll probably see you tomorrow.* ~*sentence substitute.* 2. I believe such a thing or situation may be the case.

proband ('prəʊbænd) *n.* another name (esp. U.S.) for **propositus** (sense 2). [C20: from Latin *probandus,* gerundive of *probāre* to test]

probang ('prəʊbæŋ) *n. Surgery.* a long flexible rod, often with a small sponge at one end, for inserting into the oesophagus, as to apply medication. [C17: variant, apparently by association with PROBE, of *provang,* name coined by W. Rumsey (1584–1660), Welsh judge, its inventor; of unknown origin]

probate ('prəʊbɪt, -beɪt) *n.* 1. the act or process of officially proving the authenticity and validity of a will. 2. a. the official certificate stating a will to be genuine and conferring on the executors power to administer the estate. b. the probate copy of a will. 3. (in the U.S.) all matters within the jurisdiction of a probate court. 4. (*modifier*) of, relating to, or concerned with probate: *probate value; a probate court.* ~*vb.* 5. (*tr.*) *Chiefly U.S. and Canadian.* to establish officially the authenticity and validity of (a will). [C15: from Latin *probāre* to inspect]

probation (prə'beɪʃən) *n.* 1. a system of dealing with offenders by placing them under the supervision of a probation officer. 2. **on probation.** a. under the supervision of a probation officer. b. undergoing a test period. 3. a trial period, as for a teacher, religious novitiate, etc. 4. the act of proving or testing. 5. a period during which a new employee may have his employment terminated on the grounds of unsuitability. —**pro'bational** *or* **pro'bationary** *adj.* —**pro'bationally** *adv.*

probationary assistant *n. N.Z.* a teacher in the first probationary years. Abbrev.: **PA.**

probationer (prə'beɪʃənə) *n.* a person on probation.

probation officer *n.* an officer of a court who supervises offenders placed on probation and assists and befriends them.

probative ('prəʊbətɪv) *or* **probatory** ('prəʊbətərɪ, -trɪ) *adj.* 1. serving to test or designed for testing. 2. providing proof or evidence. [C15: from Late Latin *probātīvus* concerning proof] —'**probatively** *adv.*

probe (prəʊb) *vb.* 1. (*tr.*) to search into or question closely. 2. to examine (something) with or as if with a probe. ~*n.* 3. something that probes, examines, or tests. 4. *Surgery.* a slender and usually flexible instrument for exploring a wound, sinus, etc. 5. a thorough inquiry, such as one by a newspaper into corrupt practices. 6. *Electronics.* a lead connecting to or containing a measuring or monitoring circuit used for testing. 7. *Electronics.* a conductor inserted into a waveguide or cavity resonator to provide coupling to an external circuit. 8. any of various devices that provide a coupling link, esp. a flexible tube extended from an aircraft to link it with another so that it can refuel. 9. See **space probe.** [C16: from Medieval Latin *proba* investigation, from Latin *probāre* to test] —'**probeable** *adj.* —'**prober** *n.*

probity ('prəʊbɪtɪ) *n.* confirmed integrity; uprightness. [C16: from Latin *probitās* honesty, from *probus* virtuous]

problem ('prɒbləm) *n.* 1. a. any thing, matter, person, etc., that is difficult to deal with, solve, or overcome. b. (*as modifier*): *a problem child.* 2. a puzzle, question, etc., set for solution. 3. *Maths.* a statement requiring a solution usually by means of one or more operations or geometric constructions. 4. (*modifier*) designating a literary work that deals with difficult moral questions: *a problem play.* [C14: from Late Latin *problēma,* from Greek: something put forward; related to *proballein* to throw forwards, from PRO-[2] + *ballein* to throw]

problematic (,prɒblə'mætɪk) *or* **problematical** *adj.* 1. having the nature or appearance of a problem; questionable. 2. *Logic, obsolete.* (of a proposition) asserting that a property may or may not hold. Compare **apodeictic** (sense 2), **assertoric.** —,**prob-lem'atically** *adv.*

pro bono publico *Latin.* ('prəʊ 'bəʊnəʊ 'pʊblɪkəʊ) for the public good.

proboscidean *or* **proboscidian** (,prəʊbɒ'sɪdɪən) *adj.* 1. of, relating to, or belonging to the *Proboscidea,* an order of massive herbivorous placental mammals having tusks and a long trunk: contains the elephants. ~*n.* 2. any proboscidean animal.

proboscis (prəʊ'bɒsɪs) *n., pl.* **-cises** *or* **-cides** (-sɪ,diːz). 1. a long flexible prehensile trunk or snout, as of an elephant. 2. the elongated mouthparts of certain insects, adapted for piercing or sucking food. 3. any similar part or organ. 4. *Informal, facetious.* a person's nose, esp. if large. [C17: via Latin from Greek *proboskis* trunk of an elephant, from *boskein* to feed]

proboscis monkey *n.* an Old World monkey, *Nasalis larvatus,* of Borneo, with an elongated bulbous nose.

proc. *abbrev. for:* 1. procedure. 2. proceedings. 3. process.

procaine ('prəʊkeɪn, prəʊ'keɪn) *n.* a colourless or white crystalline water-soluble substance used, as the hydrochloride, as a local anaesthetic; 2-diethylaminoethyl-4-amino benzoate. Formula: $NH_2C_6H_4COOC_2H_4N(C_2H_5)_2$. See also **Novocaine.** [C20: from PRO-[1] + (CO)CAINE]

,**proabo'lition** *adj.*
,**proa'mendment** *adj.*
,**pro-A'merican** *adj., n.*
,**proannex'ation** *adj.*
,**proap'proval** *adj.*
,**proarbi'tration** *adj.*
,**proauto'mation** *adj.*
pro'biblical *adj.*
pro-'Bolshevik *adj., n.*
pro-'British *adj.*
pro-'Buddhist *n., adj.*
pro'business *adj.*

procambium (prəʊ'kæmbɪəm) *n.* undifferentiated plant tissue, just behind the growing tip in stems and roots, that develops into conducting tissues. [C19: from PRO-^{2} + CAMBIUM] —**pro'cambial** *adj.*

procarp ('prəʊkɑːp) *n.* a female reproductive organ in red algae. [C19: from New Latin *procarpium,* from PRO-^{2} + *-carpium,* from Greek *karpos* fruit]

procaryote (prəʊ'kærɪɒt) *n.* a variant spelling of **prokaryote.**

procathedral (ˌprəʊkə'θiːdrəl) *n.* a church serving as a cathedral.

procedural agreement *n.* regulations agreed between the parties to collective bargaining, defining the bargaining units, bargaining scope, procedures for collective bargaining, and the facilities to be provided to trade union representatives.

procedure (prə'siːdʒə) *n.* **1.** a way of acting or progressing in a course of action, esp. an established method. **2.** the established mode or form of conducting the business of a legislature, the enforcement of a legal right, etc. **3.** *Computer technol.* another name for **subroutine.** —**pro'cedural** *adj.* —**pro'cedurally** *adv.*

proceed (prə'siːd) *vb.* (*intr.*) **1.** (often foll. by *to*) to advance or carry on, esp. after stopping. **2.** (often foll. by *with*) to undertake and continue (something or to do something): *he proceeded with his reading.* **3.** (often foll. by *against*) to institute or carry on a legal action. **4.** to emerge or originate; arise: *evil proceeds from the heart.* ~See also **proceeds.** [C14: from Latin *prōcēdere* to advance, from PRO-^{1} + *cēdere* to go] —**pro'ceeder** *n.*

proceeding (prə'siːdɪŋ) *n.* **1.** an act or course of action. **2. a.** the institution of a legal action. **b.** any step taken in a legal action. **3.** (*pl.*) the minutes of the meetings of a club, society, etc. **4.** (*pl.*) legal action; litigation. **5.** (*pl.*) the events of an occasion, meeting, etc.

proceeds ('prəʊsiːdz) *pl. n.* **1.** the profit or return derived from a commercial transaction, investment, etc. **2.** the result, esp. the revenue or total sum, accruing from some undertaking or course of action, as in commerce.

proceleusmatic (ˌprɒsɪluːs'mætɪk) *Prosody.* ~*adj.* **1.** denoting or consisting of a metrical foot of four short syllables. ~*n.* **2.** a proceleusmatic metrical foot. [C18: from Late Latin *proceleusmaticus,* from Greek *prokeleusmatikos,* from *prokeleuein* to drive on, from PRO-^{2} + *keleuein* to give orders]

procephalic (ˌprəʊsɪ'fælɪk) *adj. Anatomy.* of or relating to the anterior part of the head.

process^{1} ('prəʊsɛs) *n.* **1.** a series of actions that produce a change or development: *the process of digestion.* **2.** a method of doing or producing something. **3.** a forward movement. **4.** the course of time. **5. a.** a summons, writ, etc., commanding a person to appear in court. **b.** the whole proceedings in an action at law. **6.** a natural outgrowth or projection of a part, organ, or organism. **7.** a distinct subtask of a computer system which can be regarded as proceeding in parallel with other subtasks of the system. **8.** (*modifier*) relating to the general preparation of a printing forme or plate by the use, at some stage, of photography. **9.** (*modifier*) denoting a film, film scene, shot, etc., made by techniques that produce unusual optical effects. ~*vb.* (*tr.*) **10.** to subject to a routine procedure; handle. **11.** to treat or prepare by a special method, esp. to treat (food) in order to preserve it: *to process cheese.* **12. a.** to institute legal proceedings against. **b.** to serve a process on. **13.** *Photog.* **a.** to develop, rinse, fix, wash, and dry (exposed film, etc.). **b.** to produce final prints or slides from (undeveloped film). **14.** *Computer technol.* to perform mathematical and logical operations on (data) according to programmed instructions in order to obtain the required information. **15.** to prepare (food) using a food processor. [C14: from Old French *procès,* from Latin *prōcessus* an advancing, from *prōcēdere* to PROCEED]

process^{2} (prə'sɛs) *vb.* (*intr.*) to proceed in or as if in a procession. [C19: back formation from PROCESSION]

process engineering *n.* the branch of engineering concerned with industrial processes, esp. continuous ones, such as the production of petrochemicals. —**process engineer** *n.*

procession (prə'sɛʃən) *n.* **1.** the act of proceeding in a regular formation. **2.** a group of people or things moving forwards in an orderly, regular, or ceremonial manner. **3.** a hymn, litany, etc., sung in a procession. **4.** *Christianity.* the emanation of the Holy Spirit. ~*vb.* **5.** (*intr.*) *Rare.* to go in procession. [C12: via Old French from Latin *prōcessiō* a marching forwards] —**pro'cessionary** *adj.*

processional (prə'sɛʃənəl) *adj.* **1.** of, relating to, or suitable for a procession. ~*n.* **2.** *Christianity.* **a.** a book containing the prayers, hymns, litanies, and liturgy prescribed for processions. **b.** a hymn, litany, etc., used in a procession. —**pro'cessionally** *adv.*

processionary moth *n.* a moth of the family *Thaumetopoeidae,* esp. the **oak processionary moth** (*Thaumetopoea processionea*), the larvae of which leave the communal shelter nightly for food in a V-shaped procession.

processor ('prəʊsɛsə) *n.* **1.** *Computer technol.* another name for **central processing unit. 2.** a person or thing that carries out a process.

process printing *n.* a method of making reproductions of a coloured picture, usually by using four halftone plates for different coloured inks.

process-server *n.* a sheriff's officer who serves legal documents such as writs for appearance in court.

procès-verbal *French.* (prɔsɛverbal) *n., pl.* ***-baux*** (-bo). a written record of an official proceeding; minutes. [C17: from French: see PROCESS, VERBAL]

pro-choice *adj.* (of an organization, pressure group, etc.) supporting the right of a woman to have an abortion. Compare **pro-life.**

prochronism ('prəʊkrəˌnɪzəm) *n.* an error in dating that places an event earlier than it actually occurred. Compare **parachronism.** [C17: from PRO-^{2} + Greek *khronos* time + -ISM, by analogy with ANACHRONISM]

proclaim (prə'kleɪm) *vb.* (*tr.*) **1.** (*may take a clause as object*) to announce publicly; declare. **2.** (*may take a clause as object*) to show or indicate plainly. **3.** to praise or extol. [C14: from Latin *prōclāmāre* to shout aloud] —**pro'claimer** *n.* —**proclamation** (ˌprɒklə'meɪʃən) *n.* —**proclamatory** (prə'klæmətərɪ, -trɪ) *adj.*

proclitic (prəʊ'klɪtɪk) *adj.* **1. a.** relating to or denoting a monosyllabic word or form having no stress or accent and pronounced as a prefix of the following word, as in English *'t* for *it* in *'twas.* **b.** (in classical Greek) relating to or denoting a word that throws its accent onto the following word. ~*n.* **2.** a proclitic word or form. ~Compare **enclitic.** [C19: from New Latin *proclīticus,* from Greek *proklinein* to lean forwards; formed on the model of ENCLITIC]

proclivity (prə'klɪvɪtɪ) *n., pl.* **-ties.** a tendency or inclination. [C16: from Latin *prōclīvitās,* from *prōclīvis* steep, from PRO-^{1} + *clīvus* a slope]

proconsul (prəʊ'kɒnsᵊl) *n.* **1.** an administrator or governor of a colony, occupied territory, or other dependency. **2.** (in ancient Rome) the governor of a senatorial province. [C14: from Latin, from *prō consule* (someone acting) for the consul. See PRO-^{2}, CONSUL] —**proconsular** (prəʊ'kɒnsjʊlə) *adj.* —**pro'consulate** *or* **pro'consulship** *n.*

procrastinate (prəʊ'kræstɪˌneɪt, prə-) *vb.* (*usually intr.*) to put off or defer (an action) until a later time; delay. [C16: from Latin *prōcrāstināre* to postpone until tomorrow, from PRO-^{1} + *crās* tomorrow] —**proˌcrasti'nation** *n.* —**pro'crastiˌnator** *n.*

procreate ('prəʊkrɪˌeɪt) *vb.* **1.** to beget or engender (offspring). **2.** (*tr.*) to bring into being. [C16: from Latin *prōcreāre,* from PRO-^{1} + *creāre* to create] —'**procreant** *or* '**procreˌative** *adj.* —ˌ**procre'ation** *n.* —'**procreˌator** *n.*

Procrustean (prəʊ'krʌstɪən) *adj.* tending or designed to produce conformity by violent or ruthless methods. [from *Procrustes,* a robber in Greek mythology, who fitted travellers into his bed by stretching or lopping off their limbs]

procryptic (prəʊ'krɪptɪk) *adj.* (of animals) having protective coloration. [C19: from PRO-^{2} + Greek *kruptein* to conceal] —**pro'cryptically** *adv.*

procto- *or before a vowel* **proct-** *combining form.* indicating the anus or rectum: *proctology.* [from Greek *prōktos*]

proctology (prɒk'tɒlədʒɪ) *n.* the branch of medical science concerned with the rectum. —**proctological** (ˌprɒktə'lɒdʒɪkᵊl) *adj.* —**proc'tologist** *n.*

proctor ('prɒktə) *n.* **1.** a member of the teaching staff of any of certain universities having the duties of enforcing discipline. **2.** *U.S.* (in a college or university) a supervisor or monitor who invigilates examinations, enforces discipline, etc. **3.** (formerly) an agent, esp. one engaged to conduct another's case in a court. **4.** (formerly) an agent employed to collect tithes. **5.** *Church of England.* one of the elected representatives of the clergy in Convocation and the General Synod. ~*vb.* **6.** (*tr.*) *U.S.* to invigilate (an examination). [C14: syncopated variant of PROCURATOR] —**proctorial** (prɒk'tɔːrɪəl) *adj.* —**proc'torially** *adv.*

proctoscope ('prɒktəˌskəʊp) *n.* a medical instrument used for examining the rectum. —**proctoscopic** (ˌprɒktə'skɒpɪk) *adj.* —**proctoscopy** (prɒk'tɒskəpɪ) *n.*

procumbent (prəʊ'kʌmbənt) *adj.* **1.** Also: **prostrate.** (of stems) growing along the ground. **2.** leaning forwards or lying on the face. [C17: from Latin *prōcumbere* to fall forwards; compare INCUMBENT]

procuration (ˌprɒkjʊ'reɪʃən) *n.* **1.** the act of procuring. **2.** *Law.* **a.** the appointment of an agent, procurator, or attorney. **b.** the office, function, or authority of such an official. **c.** the formal written authority given to such an official. See also **power of attorney. 3.** *Criminal law.* the offence of procuring women for immoral purposes. **4.** *Archaic.* the management of another person's affairs.

procurator ('prɒkjʊˌreɪtə) *n.* **1.** (in ancient Rome) a civil official of the emperor's administration, often employed as the governor of a minor province or as a financial agent. **2.** *Rare.* a person engaged and authorized by another to manage his affairs. [C13:

pro'capitalist *adj.*
pro-'Catholic *n., adj.*
ˌ**pro-Ca'tholiˌcism** *n.*
ˌ**procentrali'zation** *or* ˌ**procentrali'sation** *adj.*
ˌ**pro-Chi'nese** *adj.*
pro'church *adj.*
pro'clerical *adj.*
pro-'Communˌism *n.*
pro-'Communist *adj., n.*
ˌ**pro-Con'federate** *adj.*
ˌ**procon'scription** *adj.*
ˌ**proconser'vation** *adj.*

from Latin: a manager, from *prōcūrāre* to attend to] —**procuracy** ('prɒkjʊrəsɪ) *or* '**procuˌratorship** *n.* —**procuratorial** (ˌprɒkjʊrə'tɔːrɪəl) *or* **procuratory** ('prɒkjʊrətərɪ, -trɪ) *adj.*

procurator fiscal *n.* (in Scotland) a legal officer who performs the functions of public prosecutor and coroner.

procuratory ('prɒkjʊrətərɪ) *n. Law.* authorization to act on behalf of someone else.

procure (prə'kjʊə) *vb.* **1.** (*tr.*) to obtain or acquire; secure. **2.** to obtain (women or girls) to act as prostitutes. [C13: from Latin *prōcūrāre* to look after, from PRO-[1] + *cūrāre* to care for] —**pro'curable** *adj.* —**pro'curance** *or* **pro'cural** *n.*

procurement (prə'kjʊəmənt) *n.* **1.** the act or an instance of procuring. **2.** *Commerce.* **a.** the act of buying. **b.** (*as modifier*): *procurement cost; procurement budget.*

procurer (prə'kjʊərə) *or* (*fem.*) **procuress** (prə'kjʊərɪs) *n.* a person who procures, esp. one who procures women or girls as prostitutes.

Procyon ('prəʊsɪən) *n.* the brightest star in the constellation Canis Minor, a binary with a very faint companion. Visual magnitude: 0.4; spectral type: F3; distance: 11 light years. [C17: via Latin from Greek *Prokuōn* literally: before the Dog, from PRO-[2] + *kuōn* dog; so named because it rises just before Sirius, the Dog Star]

prod (prɒd) *vb.* **prods, prodding, prodded.** **1.** to poke or jab with or as if with a pointed object. **2.** (*tr.*) to rouse or urge to action. ~*n.* **3.** the act or an instance of prodding. **4.** a sharp or pointed object. **5.** a stimulus or reminder. [C16: of uncertain origin] —'**prodder** *n.*

prod. *abbrev. for:* **1.** produce. **2.** produced. **3.** product.

prodigal ('prɒdɪg(ə)l) *adj.* **1.** recklessly wasteful or extravagant, as in disposing of goods or money. **2.** lavish in giving or yielding: *prodigal of compliments.* ~*n.* **3.** a person who spends lavishly or squanders money. [C16: from Medieval Latin *prōdigālis* wasteful, from Latin *prōdigus* lavish, from *prōdigere* to squander, from PRO-[1] + *agere* to drive] —ˌ**prodi'gality** *n.* —'**prodigally** *adv.*

prodigious (prə'dɪdʒəs) *adj.* **1.** vast in size, extent, power, etc. **2.** wonderful or amazing. **3.** *Obsolete.* threatening. [C16: from Latin *prōdigiōsus* marvellous, from *prōdigium* see PRODIGY] —**pro'digiously** *adv.* —**pro'digiousness** *n.*

prodigy ('prɒdɪdʒɪ) *n., pl.* **-gies.** **1.** a person, esp. a child, of unusual or marvellous talents. **2.** anything that is a cause of wonder and amazement. **3.** something monstrous or abnormal. **4.** an archaic word for **omen.** [C16: from Latin *prōdigium* an unnatural happening, from PRO-[1] + *-igium,* probably from *āio* I say]

prodrome ('prəʊdrəʊm) *n. Med.* any symptom that signals the impending onset of a disease. [C19: via French from New Latin *prodromus,* from Greek *prodromos* forerunner, from PRO-[2] + *dramein* to run] —**pro'dromal** *or* **prodromic** (prəʊ'drɒmɪk) *adj.*

produce *vb.* (prə'djuːs). **1.** to bring (something) into existence; yield. **2.** to bring forth (a product) by mental or physical effort; make: *she produced a delicious dinner for us.* **3.** (*tr.*) to give birth to. **4.** (*tr.*) to manufacture (a commodity): *this firm produces cartons.* **5.** (*tr.*) to give rise to: *her joke produced laughter.* **6.** (*tr.*) to present to view: *to produce evidence.* **7.** to bring before the public: *he produced two plays and a film last year.* **8.** to conceive and create the overall sound of (a record) and supervise its arrangement, recording, and mixing. **9.** (*tr.*) *Geometry.* to extend (a line). ~*n.* ('prɒdjuːs). **10.** anything that is produced; product. **11.** agricultural products regarded collectively: *farm produce.* [C15: from Latin *prōdūcere* to bring forward, from PRO-[1] + *dūcere* to lead] —**pro'ducible** *adj.* —**proˌduci'bility** *n.*

producer (prə'djuːsə) *n.* **1.** a person or thing that produces. **2.** *Brit.* a person responsible for the artistic direction of a play, including interpretation of the script, preparation of the actors, and overall design. **3.** *U.S. and Canadian.* a person who organizes the stage production of a play, including the finance, management, etc. **4.** the person who takes overall administrative responsibility for a film or television programme. Compare **director** (sense 4). **5.** *Economics.* a person or business enterprise that generates goods or services for sale. Compare **consumer** (sense 1). **6.** *Chem.* an apparatus or plant for making producer gas. **7.** (*often pl.*) *Ecology.* an organism, esp. a green plant, that builds up its own tissues from simple inorganic compounds. See also **consumer** (sense 3), **decomposer.**

producer gas *n.* a mixture of carbon monoxide and nitrogen produced by passing air over hot coke, used mainly as a fuel. Also called: **air gas.** See also **water gas.**

producer goods *or* **producer's goods** *pl. n.* other terms for **capital goods.**

product ('prɒdʌkt) *n.* **1.** something produced by effort, or some mechanical or industrial process. **2.** the result of some natural process. **3.** a result or consequence. **4.** a substance formed in a chemical reaction. **5.** *Maths.* **a.** the result of the multiplication of two or more numbers, quantities, etc. **b.** Also called: **set product.** another name for **intersection** (sense 3). **6.** See **Cartesian product.** [C15: from Latin *prōductum* (something) produced, from *prōdūcere* to bring forth]

product differentiation *n. Commerce.* the real or illusory distinction between competing products in a market.

production (prə'dʌkʃən) *n.* **1.** the act of producing. **2.** anything that is produced; product. **3.** the amount produced or the rate at which it is produced. **4.** *Economics.* the creation or manufacture for sale of goods and services with exchange value. **5.** any work created as a result of literary or artistic effort. **6.** the organization and presentation of a film, play, opera, etc. **7.** *Brit.* the artistic direction of a play. **8.** **a.** the supervision of the arrangement, recording, and mixing of a record. **b.** the overall sound quality or character of a recording: *the material is very strong but the production is poor.* **9.** (*modifier*) manufactured by a mass-production process: *a production model of a car.* **10. make a production (out) of.** *Informal.* to make an unnecessary fuss about. —**pro'ductional** *adj.*

production line *n.* a factory system in which parts or components of the end product are transported by a conveyor through a number of different sites at each of which a manual or machine operation is performed on them without interrupting the flow of production.

production platform *n.* (in the oil industry) a platform from which development wells are drilled that also houses a processing plant and other equipment necessary to keep an oilfield in production.

productive (prə'dʌktɪv) *adj.* **1.** producing or having the power to produce; fertile. **2.** yielding favourable or effective results. **3.** *Economics.* **a.** producing or capable of producing goods and services that have monetary or exchange value: *productive assets.* **b.** of or relating to such production: *the productive processes of an industry.* **4.** (*postpositive;* foll. by *of*) resulting in: *productive of good results.* **5.** denoting an affix or combining form used to produce new words. —**pro'ductively** *adv.* —**pro'ductiveness** *n.*

productivity (ˌprɒdʌk'tɪvɪtɪ) *n.* **1.** the output of an industrial concern in relation to the materials, labour, etc., it employs. **2.** the state of being productive.

productivity bargaining *n.* the process of reaching an agreement (**productivity agreement**) through collective bargaining whereby the employees of an organization agree to changes which are intended to improve productivity in return for an increase in pay or other benefits.

product liability *n.* the liability to the public of a manufacturer or trader for selling a faulty product.

product life cycle *n. Marketing.* the four stages (introduction, growth, maturity, and decline) into one of which the sales of a product fall during its market life.

product line *n. Marketing.* a group of related products marketed by the same company.

proem ('prəʊem) *n.* an introduction or preface, such as to a work of literature. [C14: from Latin *prooemium* introduction, from Greek *prooimion,* from PRO-[2] + *hoimē* song] —**proemial** (prəʊ'iːmɪəl) *adj.*

proenzyme (prəʊ'ɛnzaɪm) *n.* the inactive form of an enzyme; zymogen.

proestrus (prəʊ'ɛstrəs, -'iːstrəs) *n.* the usual U.S. spelling of **prooestrus.**

prof (prɒf) *n. Informal.* short for **professor.**

Prof. *abbrev. for* Professor.

profane (prə'feɪn) *adj.* **1.** having or indicating contempt, irreverence, or disrespect for a divinity or something sacred. **2.** not designed or used for religious purposes; secular. **3.** not initiated into the inner mysteries or sacred rites. **4.** vulgar, coarse, or blasphemous: *profane language.* ~*vb.* (*tr.*) **5.** to treat or use (something sacred) with irreverence. **6.** to put to an unworthy or improper use. [C15: from Latin *profānus* outside the temple, from PRO-[1] + *fānum* temple] —**profanation** (ˌprɒfə'neɪʃən) *n.* —**profanatory** (prə'fænətərɪ, -trɪ) *adj.* —**pro'fanely** *adv.* —**pro'faneness** *n.* —**pro'faner** *n.*

profanity (prə'fænɪtɪ) *n., pl.* **-ties.** **1.** the state or quality of being profane. **2.** vulgar or irreverent action, speech, etc.

profess (prə'fɛs) *vb.* **1.** to affirm or announce (something, such as faith); acknowledge: *to profess ignorance; to profess a belief in God.* **2.** (*tr.*) to claim (something, such as a feeling or skill, or to be or do something), often insincerely or falsely: *to profess to be a skilled driver.* **3.** to receive or be received into a religious order, as by taking vows. [C14: from Latin *prōfitērī* to confess openly, from PRO-[1] + *fatērī* to confess]

professed (prə'fɛst) *adj.* (*prenominal*) **1.** avowed or acknowledged. **2.** alleged or pretended. **3.** professing to be qualified as: *a professed philosopher.* **4.** having taken vows of a religious order. —**professedly** (prə'fɛsɪdlɪ) *adv.*

profession (prə'fɛʃən) *n.* **1.** an occupation requiring special training in the liberal arts or sciences, esp. one of the three learned professions, law, theology, or medicine. **2.** the body of people in such an occupation. **3.** the act of professing; avowal; declaration. **4.** **a.** Also called: **profession of faith.** a declara-

ˌ**pro-Dar'winian** *adj., n.*
ˌ**prodemo'cratic** *adj.*
ˌ**prodis'armament** *adj.*
ˌ**prodisso'lution** *adj.*
ˌ**proen'forcement** *adj.*
ˌ**pro-Euro'pean** *adj., n.*
pro'fascist *adj., n.*
ˌ**profeder'ation** *adj.*
pro'feminist *adj., n.*

tion of faith in a religion, esp. as made on entering the Church of that religion or an order belonging to it. **b.** the faith or the religion that is the subject of such a declaration. [C13: from Medieval Latin *professiō* the taking of vows upon entering a religious order, from Latin: public acknowledgment; see PROFESS]

professional (prəˈfɛʃənᵊl) *adj.* **1.** of, relating to, suitable for, or engaged in as a profession. **2.** engaging in an activity for gain or as a means of livelihood. **3.** extremely competent in a job, etc. **4.** undertaken or performed for gain or by people who are paid. ~*n.* **5.** a person who belongs to or engages in one of the professions. **6.** a person who engages for his livelihood in some activity also pursued by amateurs. **7.** a person who engages in an activity with great competence. **8.** an expert player of a game who gives instruction, esp. to members of a club by whom he is hired. —**proˈfessionally** *adv.*

professional association *n.* a body of persons engaged in the same profession, formed usually to control entry into the profession, maintain standards, and represent the profession in discussions with other bodies.

professional foul *n. Football.* a deliberate foul committed as a last-ditch tactic to prevent an opponent from scoring.

professionalism (prəˈfɛʃənəˌlɪzəm) *n.* **1.** the methods, character, status, etc., of a professional. **2.** the pursuit of an activity for gain or livelihood. —**proˈfessionalist** *n., adj.*

professor (prəˈfɛsə) *n.* **1.** the principal lecturer or teacher in a field of learning at a university or college; a holder of a university chair. **2.** *Chiefly U.S. and Canadian.* any teacher in a university or college. See also **associate professor, assistant professor, full professor. 3.** a person who claims skill and instructs others in some sport, occupation, etc. **4.** a person who professes his opinions, beliefs, etc. [C14: from Medieval Latin: one who has made his profession in a religious order, from Latin: a public teacher; see PROFESS] —**professorial** (ˌprɒfɪˈsɔːrɪəl) *adj.* —ˌ**profesˈsorially** *adv.*

professoriate (ˌprɒfɪˈsɔːrɪɪt) *or* **professorate** (prəˈfɛsərɪt) *n.* **1.** a group of professors. **2.** Also called (esp. Brit.): **professorship** (prəˈfɛsəʃɪp). the rank or position of university professor.

proffer (ˈprɒfə) *vb.* **1.** (*tr.*) to offer for acceptance; tender. ~*n.* **2.** the act of proffering. [C13: from Old French *proffrir,* from PRO-¹ + *offrir* to offer] —ˈ**profferer** *n.*

proficient (prəˈfɪʃənt) *adj.* **1.** having great facility (in an art, occupation, etc.); skilled. ~*n.* **2.** an archaic word for an **expert.** [C16: from Latin *prōficere* to make progress, from PRO-¹ + *facere* to make] —**proˈficiency** *n.* —**proˈficiently** *adv.*

profile (ˈprəʊfaɪl) *n.* **1.** a side view, outline, or representation of an object, esp. of a human face or head. **2.** a view or representation of an object, esp. a building, in contour or outline. **3.** a short biographical sketch of a subject. **4.** a graph, table, or list of scores representing the extent to which a person, field, or object exhibits various tested characteristics or tendencies: *a population profile.* **5.** a vertical section of soil from the ground surface to the parent rock showing the different horizons. **6. a.** a vertical section of part of the earth's crust showing the layers of rock. **b.** a representation of such a section. **7.** the outline of the shape of a river valley either from source to mouth (**long profile**) or at right angles to the flow of the river (**cross profile**). ~*vb.* (*tr.*) **8.** to draw, write, or make a profile of. **9.** to cut out a shape from a blank (as of steel) with a cutter. [C17: from Italian *profilo,* from *profilare* to sketch lightly, from PRO-¹ + Latin *fīlum* thread] —ˈ**profiler** *or* **profilist** (ˈprəʊfɪlɪst) *n.*

profile component *n. Brit. Education.* attainment targets in different subjects brought together for the general assessment of a pupil.

profile drag *n.* the sum of the surface friction drag and the form drag for a body moving subsonically through a fluid.

profit (ˈprɒfɪt) *n.* **1.** (*often pl.*) excess of revenues over outlays and expenses in a business enterprise over a given period of time, usually a year. **2.** the monetary gain derived from a transaction. **3. a.** income derived from property or an investment, as contrasted with capital gains. **b.** the ratio of this income to the investment or principal. **4.** *Economics.* **a.** the income or reward accruing to a successful entrepreneur and held to be the motivating factor of all economic activity in a capitalist economy. **b.** (*as modifier*): *the profit motive.* **5.** a gain, benefit, or advantage. ~*vb.* **6.** to gain or cause to gain profit. [C14: from Latin *prōfectus* advance, from *prōficere* to make progress; see PROFICIENT] —ˈ**profiter** *n.* —ˈ**profitless** *adj.*

profitable (ˈprɒfɪtəbᵊl) *adj.* affording gain, benefit, or profit. —ˈ**profitably** *adv.* —ˈ**profitableness** *or* ˌ**profitaˈbility** *n.*

profit and loss *n. Book-keeping.* an account compiled at the end of a financial year showing that year's revenue and expense items and indicating gross and net profit or loss.

profit centre *n.* a unit or department of a company that is responsible for its costs and its profits.

profiteer (ˌprɒfɪˈtɪə) *n.* **1.** a person who makes excessive profits, esp. by charging exorbitant prices for goods in short supply. ~*vb.* **2.** (*intr.*) to make excessive profits.

profiterole (ˌprɒfɪtəˈrəʊl, ˈprɒfɪtəˌrəʊl, prəˈfɪtəˌrəʊl) *n.* a small case of choux pastry with a sweet or savoury filling. [C16: from French, literally: a small profit, (related to the gifts, etc., given to a servant), from *profiter* to PROFIT]

profit-sharing *n.* a system in which a portion of the net profit of a business is distributed to its employees, usually in proportion to their wages or their length of service.

profit taking *n.* selling commodities, securities, etc., at a profit after a rise in market values or before an expected fall in values.

profligate (ˈprɒflɪgɪt) *adj.* **1.** shamelessly immoral or debauched. **2.** wildly extravagant or wasteful. ~*n.* **3.** a profligate person. [C16: from Latin *prōflīgātus* corrupt, from *prōflīgāre* to overthrow, from PRO-¹ + *flīgere* to beat] —**profligacy** (ˈprɒflɪgəsɪ) *n.* —ˈ**profligately** *adv.*

profluent (ˈprɒflʊənt) *adj.* flowing smoothly or abundantly. [C15: from Latin *prōfluere* to flow along]

pro-form *n.* a word having grammatical function but assuming the meaning of an antecedent word or phrase for which it substitutes: *the word "does" is a pro-form for "understands Greek" in "I can't understand Greek but he does."*

pro forma (ˈprəʊ ˈfɔːmə) *adj.* **1.** prescribing a set form or procedure. ~*adv.* **2.** performed in a set manner. [Latin: for form's sake]

pro forma invoice *n.* an invoice issued before an order is placed or before the goods are delivered giving all the details and the cost of the goods.

profound (prəˈfaʊnd) *adj.* **1.** penetrating deeply into subjects or ideas: *a profound mind.* **2.** showing or requiring great knowledge or understanding: *a profound treatise.* **3.** situated at or extending to a great depth. **4.** reaching to or stemming from the depths of one's nature: *profound regret.* **5.** intense or absolute: *profound silence.* **6.** thoroughgoing; extensive: *profound changes.* ~*n.* **7.** *Archaic or literary.* a great depth; abyss. [C14: from Old French *profund,* from Latin *profundus* deep, from PRO-¹ + *fundus* bottom] —**proˈfoundly** *adv.* —**proˈfoundness** *or* **profundity** (prəˈfʌndɪtɪ) *n.*

profuse (prəˈfjuːs) *adj.* **1.** plentiful, copious, or abundant: *profuse compliments.* **2.** (often foll. by *in*) free or generous in the giving (of): *profuse in thanks.* [C15: from Latin *profundere* to pour lavishly] —**proˈfusely** *adv.* —**proˈfuseness** *or* **proˈfusion** *n.*

prog¹ (prɒg) *vb.* **progs, progging, progged. 1.** (*intr.*) *Brit. slang or dialect.* to prowl about for or as if for food or plunder. ~*n.* **2.** *Brit. slang or dialect.* food obtained by begging. **3.** *Canadian dialect.* a Newfoundland word for **food.** [C17: of unknown origin]

prog² (prɒg) *Brit. slang, archaic.* **1.** *n.* short for **proctor** (sense 1). ~*vb.* **progs, progging, progged. 2.** (*tr.*) (of a proctor) to discipline (a student).

prog³ (prɒg) *n. Informal.* short for **programme,** esp. a television programme.

prog. *abbrev. for:* **1.** programme. **2.** progress. **3.** progressive.

Prog. *abbrev. for* Progressive (Party, movement, etc.).

progenitive (prəʊˈdʒɛnɪtɪv) *adj.* capable of bearing offspring. —**proˈgenitiveness** *n.*

progenitor (prəʊˈdʒɛnɪtə) *n.* **1.** a direct ancestor. **2.** an originator or founder of a future development; precursor. [C14: from Latin: ancestor, from PRO-¹ + *genitor* parent, from *gignere* to beget]

progeny (ˈprɒdʒɪnɪ) *n., pl.* **-nies. 1.** the immediate descendant or descendants of a person, animal, etc. **2.** a result or outcome. [C13: from Latin *prōgeniēs* lineage; see PROGENITOR]

progeria (prəʊˈdʒɪərɪə) *n. Med.* premature old age, a rare condition occurring in children and characterized by small stature, absent or greying hair, wrinkled skin, and other signs of old age. [C20: from PRO-² + Greek *gēras* old age]

progestational (ˌprəʊdʒɛˈsteɪʃənᵊl) *adj. Physiol.* **1.** of or relating to the phase of the menstrual cycle, lasting approximately 14 days, during which the uterus is prepared for pregnancy by the secretion of progesterone from the corpus luteum. **2.** preceding gestation; before pregnancy.

progesterone (prəʊˈdʒɛstəˌrəʊn) *n.* a steroid hormone, secreted mainly by the corpus luteum in the ovary, that prepares and maintains the uterus for pregnancy. Formula: $C_{21}H_{30}O_2$. Also called: **corpus luteum hormone.** [C20: from PRO-¹ + GE(STATION) + STER(OL) + -ONE]

progestogen (prəʊˈdʒɛstədʒən) *or* **progestin** (prəˈdʒɛstɪn) *n.* any of a group of steroid hormones that have progesterone-like activity, used in oral contraceptives and in treating gynaecological disorders. [C20: from PROGEST(ERONE) + -IN]

proglottis (prəʊˈglɒtɪs) *or* **proglottid** *n., pl.* **-glottides** (-ˈglɒtɪˌdiːz). any of the segments that make up the body of a tapeworm. Each contains reproductive organs and separates from the worm when filled with fertilized eggs. [C19: from Greek *proglōssis, proglōttis* point of the tongue, from PRO-² + *glōssa, glōtta* (so called because of its shape)] —**proˈglottic** *or* ˌ**proglotˈtidean** *adj.*

prognathous (prɒgˈneɪθəs) *or* **prognathic** (prɒgˈnæθɪk) *adj.* having a projecting lower jaw. [C19: from PRO-² + Greek *gnathos* jaw] —**prognathism** (ˈprɒgnəˌθɪzəm) *n.*

prognosis (prɒgˈnəʊsɪs) *n., pl.* **-noses** (-ˈnəʊsiːz). **1.** *Med.* **a.** a prediction of the course or outcome of a disease or disorder. **b.**

proˈforeign *adj.* **pro-ˈFreudian** *adj., n.* **pro-ˈGentile** *adj., n.* **pro-ˈGerman** *adj.*

the chances of recovery from a disease. **2.** any forecast or prediction. [C17: via Latin from Greek: knowledge beforehand]

prognostic (prɒg'nɒstɪk) *adj.* **1.** of, relating to, or serving as a prognosis. **2.** foretelling or predicting. ~*n.* **3.** *Med.* any symptom or sign used in making a prognosis. **4.** a sign or forecast of some future occurrence. [C15: from Old French *pronostique,* from Latin *prognōsticum,* from Greek *prognōstikon,* from *progignōskein* to know in advance]

prognosticate (prɒg'nɒstɪˌkeɪt) *vb.* **1.** to foretell (future events) according to present signs or indications; prophesy. **2.** (*tr.*) to foreshadow or portend. [C16: from Medieval Latin *prognōsticāre* to predict] —**progˌnosti'cation** *n.* —**prog'nosticative** *adj.* —**prog'nostiˌcator** *n.*

program *or* (*sometimes*) **programme** ('prəʊgræm) *n.* **1.** a sequence of coded instructions fed into a computer, enabling it to perform specified logical and arithmetical operations on data. ~*vb.* **-grams, -gramming, -grammed** *or* **-grammes, -gramming, -grammed. 2.** (*tr.*) to feed a program into (a computer). **3.** (*tr.*) to arrange (data) into a suitable form so that it can be processed by a computer. **4.** (*intr.*) to write a program.

program generator *n.* a computer program that can be used to help to create other computer programs.

programmable *or* **programable** (prəʊ'græməbᵊl) *adj.* (esp. of a device or operation) capable of being programmed for automatic operation or computer processing. —**proˌgramma'bility** *n.*

programmatic (ˌprəʊgrə'mætɪk) *adj.* **1.** of or relating to programme music. **2.** of or relating to a programme.

programme *or U.S.* **program** ('prəʊgræm) *n.* **1.** a written or printed list of the events, performers, etc., in a public performance. **2.** a performance or series of performances, often presented at a scheduled time, esp. on radio or television. **3.** a specially arranged selection of things to be done. *what's the programme for this afternoon?* **4.** a plan, schedule, or procedure. **5.** a syllabus or curriculum. ~*vb.* **-grammes, -gramming, -grammed** *or U.S.* **-grams, -graming, -gramed. 6.** to design or schedule (something) as a programme. ~*n., vb.* **7.** *Computer technol.* a variant spelling of **program.** [C17: from Late Latin *programma,* from Greek: written public notice, from PRO-[2] + *graphein* to write]

programmed camera *n. Photog.* a camera with electronic facilities for setting both aperture and shutter speed automatically on the basis of a through-the-lens light value and a given film speed.

programmed learning *n.* a teaching method in which the material to be learnt is broken down into easily understandable parts on which the pupil is able to test himself .

programme evaluation and review technique *n.* a method of planning, controlling, and checking the times taken to finish important parts of complex operations, such as making aircraft, ships, or bridges. Acronym: **PERT.** Compare **critical path analysis.**

programme music *n.* music that is intended to depict or evoke a scene or idea. Compare **absolute music.**

programme of study *n. Brit. Education.* the prescribed syllabus that pupils must be taught at each key stage in the National Curriculum.

programmer ('prəʊgræmə) *n.* a person who writes a program so that data may be processed by a computer.

programming language *n.* a simple language system designed to facilitate the writing of computer programs. See **high-level language, low-level language, machine code.**

program statement *n.* a single instruction in a computer program.

program trading *n.* trading on international stock exchanges using a computer program to exploit differences between stock index futures and actual share prices on world equity markets.

progress *n.* ('prəʊgrɛs). **1.** movement forwards, esp. towards a place or objective. **2.** satisfactory development, growth, or advance: *she is making progress in maths.* **3.** advance towards completion, maturity, or perfection: *the steady onward march of progress.* **4.** (*modifier*) of or relating to progress: *a progress report.* **5.** *Biology.* increasing complexity, adaptation, etc., during the development of an individual or evolution of a group. **6.** *Brit.* a stately royal journey. **7. in progress.** taking place; under way. ~*vb.* (prə'grɛs). **8.** (*intr.*) to move forwards or onwards, as towards a place or objective. **9.** to move towards or bring nearer to completion, maturity, or perfection. [C15: from Latin *prōgressus* a going forwards, from *prōgredī* to advance, from PRO-[1] + *gradī* to step]

progress chaser *n.* a person employed to make sure at each stage, esp. of a manufacturing process, that a piece of work is on schedule and is delivered to the customer on time. —**progress chasing** *n.*

progression (prə'grɛʃən) *n.* **1.** the act of progressing; advancement. **2.** the act or an instance of moving from one thing or unit in a sequence to the next. **3.** *Maths.* a sequence of numbers in which each term differs from the succeeding term by a constant relation. See also **arithmetic progression, geometric progression, harmonic progression. 4.** *Music.* movement, esp. of a logical kind, from one note to the next (**melodic progression**) or from one chord to the next (**harmonic progression**). **5.** *Astrology.* one of several calculations, based on the movement of the planets, from which it is supposed that one can find the expected developments in a person's birth chart and the probable trends of circumstances for a year in his life. —**pro'gressional** *adj.* —**pro'gressionally** *adv.*

progressionist (prə'grɛʃənɪst) *or* **progressist** (prə'grɛsɪst) *n. Rare.* an advocate of social, political, or economic progress; a member of a progressive political party. —**pro'gressionism** *n.*

progressive (prə'grɛsɪv) *adj.* **1.** of or relating to progress. **2.** proceeding or progressing by steps or degrees. **3.** (*often cap.*) favouring or promoting political or social reform through government action, or even revolution, to improve the lot of the majority: *a progressive policy.* **4.** denoting or relating to an educational system that allows flexibility in learning procedures, based on activities determined by the needs and capacities of the individual child, the aim of which is to integrate academic with social development. **5.** (of a tax or tax system) graduated so that the rate increases relative to the amount taxed. Compare **regressive** (sense 2). **6.** (esp. of a disease) advancing in severity, complexity, or extent. **7.** (of a dance, card game, etc.) involving a regular change of partners after one figure, one game, etc. **8.** denoting an aspect of verbs in some languages, including English, used to express prolonged or continuous activity as opposed to momentary or habitual activity: *a progressive aspect of the verb "to walk" is "is walking."* ~*n.* **9.** a person who advocates progress, as in education, politics, etc. **10. a.** the progressive aspect of a verb. **b.** a verb in this aspect. —**pro'gressively** *adv.* —**pro'gressiveness** *n.* —**pro'gressivism** *n.* —**pro'gressivist** *n.*

Progressive (prə'grɛsɪv) *n.* **1.** a member or supporter of a Progressive Party, any of various political parties advocating reform and progress, or of any other movement with similar aims. **2.** of, relating to, or characteristic of a Progressive Party, Progressive movement, or Progressives.

Progressive Conservative *n.* (in Canada) a member or supporter of the Progressive Conservative Party, a major political party with conservative policies.

progress payment *n.* an instalment of a larger payment made to a contractor for work carried out up to a specified stage of the job.

prohibit (prə'hɪbɪt) *vb.* (*tr.*) **1.** to forbid by law or other authority. **2.** to hinder or prevent. [C15: from Latin *prohibēre* to prevent, from PRO-[1] + *habēre* to hold] —**pro'hibiter** *or* **pro'hibitor** *n.*

prohibition (ˌprəʊɪ'bɪʃən) *n.* **1.** the act of prohibiting or state of being prohibited. **2.** an order or decree that prohibits. **3.** (*sometimes cap.*) (esp. in the U.S.) a policy of legally forbidding the manufacture, transportation, sale, or consumption of alcoholic beverages except for medicinal or scientific purposes. **4.** *Law.* an order of a superior court (in Britain the High Court) forbidding an inferior court to determine a matter outside its jurisdiction. —ˌ**prohi'bitionary** *adj.*

Prohibition (ˌprəʊɪ'bɪʃən) *n.* the period (1920–33) when the manufacture, sale, and transportation of intoxicating liquors was banned by constitutional amendment in the U.S. —ˌ**Prohi'bitionist** *n.*

prohibitionist (ˌprəʊɪ'bɪʃənɪst) *n.* (*sometimes cap.*) a person who favours prohibition, esp. of alcoholic beverages. —ˌ**prohi'bitionism** *n.*

prohibitive (prə'hɪbɪtɪv) *or* (*less commonly*) **prohibitory** (prə'hɪbɪtərɪ, -trɪ) *adj.* **1.** prohibiting or tending to prohibit. **2.** (esp. of prices) tending or designed to discourage sale or purchase. —**pro'hibitively** *adv.* —**pro'hibitiveness** *n.*

project *n.* ('prɒdʒɛkt). **1.** a proposal, scheme, or design. **2. a.** a task requiring considerable or concerted effort, such as one by students. **b.** the subject of such a task. ~*vb.* (prə'dʒɛkt). **3.** (*tr.*) to propose or plan. **4.** (*tr.*) to predict; estimate; extrapolate: *we can project future needs on the basis of the current birth rate.* **5.** (*tr.*) to throw or cast forwards. **6.** to jut or cause to jut out. **7.** (*tr.*) to send forth or transport in the imagination: *to project oneself into the future.* **8.** (*tr.*) to cause (an image) to appear on a surface. **9.** to cause (one's voice) to be heard clearly at a distance. **10.** *Psychol.* **a.** (*intr.*) (esp. of a child) to believe that others share one's subjective mental life. **b.** to impute to others (one's hidden desires and impulses), esp. as a means of defending oneself. Compare **introject. 11.** (*tr.*) *Geometry.* to draw a projection of. **12.** (*intr.*) to communicate effectively, esp. to a large gathering. [C14: from Latin *prōicere* to throw down, from PRO-[1] + *iacere* to throw]

projectile (prə'dʒɛktaɪl) *n.* **1.** an object or body thrown forwards. **2.** any self-propelling missile, esp. one powered by a rocket or the rocket itself. **3.** any object that can be fired from a gun, such as a bullet or shell. ~*adj.* **4.** capable of being or designed to be hurled forwards. **5.** projecting or thrusting forwards. **6.** *Zoology.* another word for **protrusile.** [C17: from New Latin *prōjectilis* jutting forwards]

ˌ**proimmi'gration** *adj.*
ˌ**proinˌdustriali'zation**
or ˌ**proinˌdustriali'sation** *adj.*
pro'industry *adj.*
ˌ**prointe'gration** *adj.*
ˌ**prointer'vention** *adj.*
ˌ**proin'vestment** *adj.*
ˌ**proirri'gation** *adj.*

projection (prəˈdʒɛkʃən) *n.* **1.** the act of projecting or the state of being projected. **2.** an object or part that juts out. **3.** see **map projection. 4.** the representation of a line, figure, or solid on a given plane as it would be seen from a particular direction or in accordance with an accepted set of rules. **5.** a scheme or plan. **6.** a prediction based on known evidence and observations. **7. a.** the process of showing film on a screen. **b.** the image or images shown. **8.** *Psychol.* **a.** the belief, esp. in children, that others share one's subjective mental life. **b.** the process of projecting one's own hidden desires and impulses. See also **defence mechanism. 9.** the mixing by alchemists of powdered philosopher's stone with molten base metals in order to transmute them into gold. —**proˈjectional** *adj.*

projectionist (prəˈdʒɛkʃənɪst) *n.* a person responsible for the operation of film projection machines.

projection room *n.* a small room in a cinema in which the film projectors are operated.

projection television *n.* a television receiver in which a very bright picture on a small cathode-ray tube screen is optically projected onto a large screen.

projective (prəˈdʒɛktɪv) *adj.* relating to or concerned with projection: *projective geometry.* —**proˈjectively** *adv.*

projective geometry *n.* the branch of geometry concerned with the properties of solids that are invariant under projection and section.

projective test *n.* any psychological test, such as the Rorschach test, in which the subject is asked to respond to vague material. It is thought that unconscious ideas are thus projected, which, when the responses are interpreted, reveal hidden aspects of the subject's personality.

projector (prəˈdʒɛktə) *n.* **1.** an optical instrument that projects an enlarged image of individual slides onto a screen or wall. Full name: **slide projector. 2.** an optical instrument in which a strip of film is wound past a lens at a fixed speed so that the frames can be viewed as a continuously moving sequence on a screen or wall. Full name: **film** *or* **cine projector. 3.** a device for projecting a light beam. **4.** a person who devises projects.

projet (ˈprɒʒeɪ) *n. Diplomacy.* a draft of a proposed treaty; plan or proposition. [C19: via French from Latin *prōjectum* something projecting]

prokaryon (prəʊˈkærɪɒn) *n.* the nucleus of a prokaryote.

prokaryote *or* **procaryote** (prəʊˈkærɪɒt) *n.* an organism having cells in each of which the genetic material is in a single filament of DNA, not enclosed in a nucleus. Bacteria and blue-green algae are prokaryotes. Compare **eukaryote.** [from PRO-^{2} + KARYO- + *-ote* as in *zygote*] —**prokaryotic** *or* **procaryotic** (prəʊˌkærɪˈɒtɪk) *adj.*

prolactin (prəʊˈlæktɪn) *n.* a gonadotrophic hormone secreted by the anterior lobe of the pituitary gland. In mammals it stimulates the secretion of progesterone by the corpus luteum and initiates and maintains lactation. Also called: **luteotrophin, luteotrophic hormone.** See also **follicle-stimulating hormone, luteinizing hormone.**

prolamine (ˈprəʊləˌmiːn, -mɪn; prəʊˈlæmiːn) *n.* any of a group of simple plant proteins, including gliadin, hordein, and zein. [C20: from PROL(INE) + AM(MONIA) + -INE^{2}]

prolapse (ˈprəʊlæps, prəʊˈlæps) *Pathol.* ~*n.* **1.** Also called: **prolapsus** (prəʊˈlæpsəs). the sinking or falling down of an organ or part. Compare **proptosis.** ~*vb.* (*intr.*) **2.** (of an organ, etc.) to sink from its normal position. [C17: from Latin *prōlābi* to slide along, from PRO-^{1} + *lābī* to slip]

prolate (ˈprəʊleɪt) *adj.* having a polar diameter of greater length than the equatorial diameter. Compare **oblate**^{1}. [C17: from Latin *prōferre* to enlarge] —ˈ**prolately** *adv.* —ˈ**prolateness** *n.*

prole (prəʊl) *n., adj. Derogatory slang, chiefly Brit.* short for **proletarian.**

proleg (ˈprəʊˌlɛg) *n.* any of the short paired unjointed appendages on each abdominal segment of a caterpillar and any of certain other insect larvae. [C19: from PRO-^{1} + LEG]

prolegomenon (ˌprəʊlɛˈgɒmɪnən) *n., pl.* **-na** (-nə). (*often pl.*) a preliminary discussion, esp. a formal critical introduction to a lengthy text. [C17: from Greek, from *prolegein,* from PRO-^{2} + *legein* to say] —ˌ**proleˈgomenal** *adj.*

prolepsis (prəʊˈlɛpsɪs) *n., pl.* **-ses** (-siːz). **1.** a rhetorical device by which objections are anticipated and answered in advance. **2.** use of a word after a verb in anticipation of its becoming applicable through the action of the verb, as *flat* in *hammer it flat.* [C16: via Late Latin from Greek: anticipation, from *prolambanein* to anticipate, from PRO-^{2} + *lambanein* to take] —**proˈleptic** *adj.*

proletarian (ˌprəʊlɪˈtɛərɪən) *or* (*less commonly*) **proletary** (ˈprəʊlɪtərɪ, -trɪ) *adj.* **1.** of, relating, or belonging to the proletariat. ~*n., pl.* **-tarians** *or* **-taries. 2.** a member of the proletariat. [C17: from Latin *prōlētārius* one whose only contribution to the state was his offspring, from *prōlēs* offspring] —ˌ**proleˈtarianism** *n.* —ˌ**proleˈtarianness** *n.*

proletariat (ˌprəʊlɪˈtɛərɪət) *n.* **1.** all wage-earners collectively. **2.** the lower or working class. **3.** (in Marxist theory) the class of wage-earners, esp. industrial workers, in a capitalist society, whose only possession of significant material value is their labour. **4.** (in ancient Rome) the lowest class of citizens, who had no property. [C19: via French from Latin *prōlētārius* PROLETARIAN]

pro-life *adj.* (of an organization, pressure group, etc.) supporting the right to life of the unborn; against abortion, experiments on embryos, etc. —ˌ**pro-ˈlifer** *n.*

proliferate (prəˈlɪfəˌreɪt) *vb.* **1.** to grow or reproduce (new parts, cells, etc.) rapidly. **2.** to grow or increase or cause to grow or increase rapidly. [C19: from Medieval Latin *prōlifer* having offspring, from Latin *prōlēs* offspring + *ferre* to bear] —**proˌliferˈation** *n.* —**proˈliferative** *adj.*

proliferous (prəˈlɪfərəs) *adj.* **1.** (of plants) producing many side branches or offshoots. **2.** (of plants and certain animals) reproducing by means of buds, offshoots, etc. [C17: from Medieval Latin *prōlifer* having offspring]

prolific (prəˈlɪfɪk) *adj.* **1.** producing fruit, offspring, etc., in abundance. **2.** producing constant or successful results. **3.** (often foll. by *in* or *of*) rich or fruitful. [C17: from Medieval Latin *prōlificus,* from Latin *prōlēs* offspring] —**proˈlifically** *adv.* —**proˈlificness** *or* **proˈlificacy** *n.*

proline (ˈprəʊliːn, -lɪn) *n.* a nonessential amino acid that occurs in protein. [C20: from PYRROLIDINE]

prolix (ˈprəʊlɪks, prəʊˈlɪks) *adj.* **1.** (of a speech, book, etc.) so long as to be boring; verbose. **2.** indulging in prolix speech or writing; long-winded. [C15: from Latin *prōlixus* stretched out widely, from PRO-^{1} + *līquī* to flow] —**proˈlixity** *or* (*less commonly*) **proˈlixness** *n.* —**proˈlixly** *adv.*

prolocutor (prəʊˈlɒkjʊtə) *n.* a chairman, esp. of the lower house of clergy in a convocation of the Anglican Church. [C15: from Latin: advocate, from PRO-^{1} + *loquī* to speak] —**proˈlocutorˌship** *n.*

PROLOG *or* **Prolog** (ˈprəʊlɒg) *n.* a computer programming language based on mathematical logic. [C20: from *pro(gramming in) log(ic)*]

prologue *or U.S.* (*often*) **prolog** (ˈprəʊlɒg) *n.* **1. a.** the prefatory lines introducing a play or speech. **b.** the actor speaking these lines. **2.** a preliminary act or event. **3.** (in early opera) **a.** an introductory scene in which a narrator summarizes the main action of the work. **b.** a brief independent play preceding the opera, esp. one in honour of a patron. ~*vb.* **-logues, -loguing, -logued** *or U.S.* **-logs, -loging, -loged. 4.** (*tr.*) to introduce or preface with or as if with a prologue. [C13: from Latin *prologus,* from Greek *prologos,* from PRO-^{2} + *logos* discourse]

prolong (prəˈlɒŋ) *vb.* (*tr.*) to lengthen in duration or space; extend. [C15: from Late Latin *prōlongāre* to extend, from Latin PRO-^{1} + *longus* long] —**prolongation** (ˌprəʊlɒŋˈgeɪʃən) *n.* —**proˈlonger** *n.* —**proˈlongment** *n.*

prolonge (prəˈlɒndʒ) *n.* (formerly) a specially fitted rope used as part of the towing equipment of a gun carriage. [C19: from French, from *prolonger* to PROLONG]

prolusion (prəˈluːʒən) *n.* **1.** a preliminary written exercise. **2.** an introductory essay, sometimes of a slight or tentative nature. [C17: from Latin *prōlūsiō* preliminary exercise, from *prōlūdere* to practise beforehand, from PRO-^{1} + *lūdere* to play] —**prolusory** (prəˈluːzərɪ) *adj.*

prom (prɒm) *n.* **1.** *Brit.* short for **promenade** (sense 1) or **promenade concert. 2.** *U.S. and Canadian informal.* short for **promenade** (sense 3).

PROM (prɒm) *n. Computer technol. acronym for* Programmable Read Only Memory.

prom. *abbrev. for* promontory.

promenade (ˌprɒməˈnɑːd) *n.* **1.** *Chiefly Brit.* a public walk, esp. at a seaside resort. **2.** a leisurely walk, esp. one in a public place for pleasure or display. **3.** *U.S. and Canadian.* a ball or formal dance at a high school or college. **4.** a marchlike step in dancing. **5.** a marching sequence in a square or country dance. ~*vb.* **6.** to take a promenade in or through (a place). **7.** (*intr.*) *Dancing.* to perform a promenade. **8.** (*tr.*) to display or exhibit (someone or oneself) on or as if on a promenade. [C16: from French, from *promener* to lead out for a walk, from Late Latin *prōmināre* to drive (cattle) along, from PRO-^{1} + *mināre* to drive, probably from *minārī* to threaten] —ˌ**promeˈnader** *n.*

promenade concert *n.* a concert at which some of the audience stand rather than sit. Often shortened to **prom.**

promenade deck *n.* an upper covered deck of a passenger ship for the use of the passengers.

promethazine (prəʊˈmɛθəˌziːn) *n.* an antihistamine drug used to treat allergies and to prevent vomiting, esp. in motion sickness. [C20: from PRO(PYL) + (*di*)*meth*(*ylamine*) + (PHENOTHI)AZINE]

Promethean (prəˈmiːθɪən) *adj.* **1.** of or relating to Prometheus, in Greek myth the Titan who stole fire from Olympus to give to mankind. In punishment he was chained to a rock, where an eagle tore at his liver until Hercules freed him. **2.** creative, original, or life-enhancing. ~*n.* **3.** a person who resembles Prometheus.

promethium (prəˈmiːθɪəm) *n.* a radioactive element of the lanthanide series artificially produced by the fission of uranium. Symbol: Pm; atomic no.: 61; half-life of most stable isotope, ^{145}Pm: 17.7 years; valency: 3; melting pt.: 1080°C (approx.); boiling pt.:

pro-ˈJewish *adj.*

proˈlabour *adj.*

2460°C (approx.). [C20: New Latin from *Prometheus*; see PROMETHEAN]

prominence ('prɒmɪnəns) *n.* **1.** the state or quality of being prominent. **2.** something that is prominent, such as a protuberance. **3.** relative importance or consequence. **4.** *Astronomy.* an eruption of incandescent gas from the sun's surface that can reach an altitude of several hundred thousand kilometres. It is visible during a total eclipse.

prominent ('prɒmɪnənt) *adj.* **1.** jutting or projecting outwards. **2.** standing out from its surroundings; noticeable. **3.** widely known; eminent. [C16: from Latin *prōminēre* to jut out, from PRO-[1] + *ēminēre* to project] —**'prominently** *adv.* —**'prominentness** *n.*

prominent moth *n.* any moth of the family *Notodontidae* characterized by tufts of scales on the back edge of the forewing that stand up prominently at rest and give the group its name. It includes the puss moth and buff-tip as well as those with *prominent* in the name.

promiscuity (ˌprɒmɪ'skjuːɪtɪ) *n.* **1.** promiscuous sexual behaviour. **2.** indiscriminate mingling, mixture, or confusion, as of parts or elements.

promiscuous (prə'mɪskjʊəs) *adj.* **1.** indulging in casual and indiscriminate sexual relationships. **2.** consisting of a number of dissimilar parts or elements mingled in a confused or indiscriminate manner. **3.** indiscriminate in selection. **4.** casual or heedless. [C17: from Latin *prōmiscuus* indiscriminate, from PRO-[1] + *miscēre* to mix] —**pro'miscuously** *adv.* —**pro'miscuousness** *n.*

promise ('prɒmɪs) *vb.* **1.** (often foll. by *to;* when *tr., may take a clause as object or an infinitive*) to give an assurance of (something to someone); undertake (to do something) in the future: *I promise that I will come.* **2.** (*tr.*) to undertake to give (something to someone): *he promised me a car for my birthday.* **3.** (when *tr., takes an infinitive*) to cause one to expect that in the future one is likely (to be or do something): *she promises to be a fine soprano.* **4.** (*usually passive*) to engage to be married; betroth: *I'm promised to Bill.* **5.** (*tr.*) to assure (someone) of the authenticity or inevitability of something (often in the parenthetic phrase **I promise you,** used to emphasize a statement): *there'll be trouble, I promise you.* ~*n.* **6.** an undertaking or assurance given by one person to another agreeing or guaranteeing to do or give something, or not to do or give something, in the future. **7.** indication of forthcoming excellence or goodness: *a writer showing considerable promise.* **8.** the thing of which an assurance is given. [C14: from Latin *prōmissum* a promise, from *prōmittere* to send forth] —**'promiser** *n.*

Promised Land *n.* **1.** heaven, esp. when considered as the goal towards which Christians journey in their earthly lives. **2.** any longed-for place where one expects to find greater happiness or fulfilment. [originally referring to the land of Canaan, promised by God to Abraham and his descendants (Genesis 12:7)]

promisee (ˌprɒmɪ'siː) *n. Contract law.* a person to whom a promise is made. Compare **promisor.**

promising ('prɒmɪsɪŋ) *adj.* showing promise of favourable development or future success. —**'promisingly** *adv.*

promisor (ˌprɒmɪ'sɔː, 'prɒmɪˌsɔː) *n. Contract law.* a person who makes a promise. Compare **promisee.**

promissory ('prɒmɪsərɪ) *adj.* **1.** containing, relating to, or having the nature of a promise. **2.** *Insurance.* stipulating how the provisions of an insurance contract will be fulfilled after it has been signed.

promissory note *n. Chiefly U.S. commerce.* a document, usually negotiable, containing a signed promise to pay a stated sum of money to a specified person at a designated date or on demand. Also called: **note, note of hand.**

promo ('prəʊməʊ) *n., pl.* **-mos.** *Informal.* something that is used to promote a product, esp. a videotape film used to promote a pop record. [C20: shortened from *promotion*]

promontory ('prɒməntərɪ, -trɪ) *n., pl.* **-ries.** **1.** a high point of land, esp. of rocky coast, that juts out into the sea. **2.** *Anatomy.* any of various projecting structures. [C16: from Latin *prōmunturium* headland; related to *prōminēre;* see PROMINENT]

promote (prə'məʊt) *vb.* (*tr.*) **1.** to further or encourage the progress or existence of. **2.** to raise to a higher rank, status, degree, etc. **3.** to advance (a pupil or student) to a higher course, class, etc. **4.** to urge the adoption of; work for: *to promote reform.* **5.** to encourage the sale of (a product) by advertising or securing financial support. **6.** *Chess.* to exchange (a pawn) for any piece other than a king when the pawn reaches the 8th rank. [C14: from Latin *prōmovēre* to push onwards, from PRO-[1] + *movēre* to move] —**pro'motable** *adj.* —**pro'motion** *n.* —**pro'motional** *adj.*

promoter (prə'məʊtə) *n.* **1.** a person or thing that promotes. **2.** a person who helps to organize, develop, or finance an undertaking. **3.** a person who organizes and finances a sporting event, esp. a boxing match. **4.** *Chem.* a substance added in small amounts to a catalyst to increase its activity. **5.** *Genetics.* the site on an operon that must bind with messenger RNA polymerase before transcription of the operon occurs.

promotive (prə'məʊtɪv) *adj.* tending to promote. —**pro'motiveness** *n.*

prompt (prɒmpt) *adj.* **1.** performed or executed without delay. **2.** quick or ready to act or respond. ~*adv.* **3.** *Informal.* punctually. ~*vb.* **4.** (*tr.*) to urge (someone to do something). **5.** to remind (an actor, singer, etc.) of lines forgotten during a performance. **6.** (*tr.*) to refresh the memory of. **7.** (*tr.*) to give rise to by suggestion: *his affairs will prompt discussion.* ~*n.* **8.** *Commerce.* **a.** the time limit allowed for payment of the debt incurred by purchasing goods or services on credit. **b.** the contract specifying this time limit. **c.** Also called: **prompt note.** a memorandum sent to a purchaser to remind him of the time limit and the sum due. **9.** the act of prompting. **10.** anything that serves to remind. **11.** an aid to the operator of a computer in the form of a question or statement that appears on the screen showing that the equipment is ready to proceed and indicating the options available. [C15: from Latin *promptus* evident, from *prōmere* to produce, from PRO-[1] + *emere* to buy] —**'promptly** *adv.* —**'promptness** *n.*

promptbook ('prɒmptˌbʊk) *n.* the production script of a play containing notes, cues, etc.

prompter ('prɒmptə) *n.* **1.** a person offstage who reminds the actors of forgotten lines or cues. **2.** a person, thing, etc., that prompts.

promptitude ('prɒmptɪˌtjuːd) *n.* the quality of being prompt; punctuality.

prompt side *n. Theatre.* the side of the stage where the prompter is, usually to the actor's left in Britain and to his right in the United States.

promulgate ('prɒməlˌgeɪt) *vb.* (*tr.*) **1.** to put into effect (a law, decree, etc.), esp. by formal proclamation. **2.** to announce or declare officially. **3.** to make widespread. ~Also (archaic): **promulge** (prəʊ'mʌldʒ). [C16: from Latin *prōmulgāre* to bring to public knowledge; probably related to *provulgāre* to publicize, from PRO-[1] + *vulgāre* to make common, from *vulgus* the common people] —ˌ**promul'gation** *n.* —**'promulˌgator** *n.*

promycelium (ˌprəʊmaɪ'siːlɪəm) *n., pl.* **-lia** (-lɪə). *Botany.* a short tubular outgrowth from certain germinating fungal spores that produces spores itself and then dies. [C19: New Latin from PRO-[1] + MYCELIUM] —ˌ**promy'celial** *adj.*

pron. *abbrev. for:* **1.** pronominal. **2.** pronoun. **3.** pronounced. **4.** pronunciation.

pronate (prəʊ'neɪt) *vb.* (*tr.*) to turn (the forearm or hand) so that the palmar surface is directed downwards. [C19: from Late Latin *prōnāre* to bend forwards, bow] —**pro'nation** *n.*

pronator (prəʊ'neɪtə) *n.* any muscle that effects pronation.

prone (prəʊn) *adj.* **1.** lying flat or face downwards; prostrate. **2.** sloping or tending downwards. **3.** having an inclination to do something. [C14: from Latin *prōnus* bent forward, from PRO-[1]] —**'pronely** *adv.* —**'proneness** *n.*

-prone *adj. combining form.* liable or disposed to suffer: *accident-prone.*

pronephros (prəʊ'nɛfrɒs) *n., pl.* **-roi** (-rɔɪ) *or* **-ra** (-rə). the first-formed anterior part of the embryonic kidney in vertebrates, which remains functional in the larvae of the lower vertebrates. See also **mesonephros, metanephros.** [C19: New Latin, from PRO-[2] + Greek *nephros* kidney] —**pro'nephric** *adj.*

prong (prɒŋ) *n.* **1.** a sharply pointed end of an instrument, such as on a fork. **2.** any pointed projecting part. ~*vb.* **3.** (*tr.*) to prick or spear with or as if with a prong. [C15: related to Middle Low German *prange* a stake, Gothic *anaprangan* to afflict] —**pronged** *adj.*

pronghorn ('prɒŋˌhɔːn) *n.* a ruminant mammal, *Antilocapra americana,* inhabiting rocky deserts of North America and having small branched horns: family *Antilocapridae.* Also called: **American antelope.**

prong key *n.* a key or spanner with two prongs or projections which engage corresponding holes in the face of a nut or component to be turned for tightening, adjustment, etc.

pronominal (prəʊ'nɒmɪnᵊl) *adj.* relating to or playing the part of a pronoun. [C17: from Late Latin *prōnōminālis,* from *prōnōmen* a PRONOUN] —**pro'nominally** *adv.*

pronominalize *or* **pronominalise** (prəʊ'nɒmɪnəˌlaɪz) *vb.* (*tr.*) to make (a word) into or treat as a pronoun. —**proˌnominali'zation** *or* **proˌnominali'sation** *n.*

pronotum (prəʊ'nəʊtəm) *n.* the notum of the prothorax of an insect. [C19: PRO-[2] + NOTUM]

pronoun ('prəʊˌnaʊn) *n.* one of a class of words that serves to replace a noun phrase that has already been or is about to be mentioned in the sentence or context. Abbrev.: **pron.** [C16: from Latin *prōnōmen,* from PRO-[1] + *nōmen* noun]

pronounce (prə'naʊns) *vb.* **1.** to utter or articulate (a sound or sequence of sounds). **2.** (*tr.*) to utter or articulate (sounds or words) in the correct way. **3.** (*tr.; may take a clause as object*) to proclaim officially and solemnly: *I now pronounce you man and wife.* **4.** (when *tr., may take a clause as object*) to declare as one's judgment: *to pronounce the death sentence upon someone.* **5.** (*tr.*) to make a phonetic transcription of (sounds or words). [C14:

pro'military *adj.*
ˌpromi'nority *adj.*
pro'modern *adj.*
pro'monarchist *adj., n.*
pro-'Muslim *adj., n.*
pro'nationalist *adj., n.*
ˌpronational'istic *adj.*
pro-'Negro *adj.*

from Latin *prōnuntiāre* to announce, from PRO-[1] + *nuntiāre* to announce] —**pro'nounceable** *adj.* —**pro'nouncer** *n.*

pronounced (prə'naʊnst) *adj.* **1.** strongly marked or indicated. **2.** (of a sound) articulated with vibration of the vocal cords; voiced. —**pronouncedly** (prə'naʊnsɪdlɪ) *adv.*

pronouncement (prə'naʊnsmənt) *n.* **1.** an official or authoritative statement or announcement. **2.** the act of pronouncing, declaring, or uttering formally.

pronto ('prɒntəʊ) *adv. Informal.* at once; promptly. [C20: from Spanish: quick, from Latin *promptus* PROMPT]

pronuclear[1] (ˌprəʊ'njuːklɪə) *adj.* in favour of or supporting the use of nuclear power. —ˌ**pro'nuclearist** *n., adj.*

pronuclear[2] (ˌprəʊ'njuːklɪə) *adj.* of or relating to a pronucleus.

pronucleus (ˌprəʊ'njuːklɪəs) *n., pl.* **-clei** (-klɪˌaɪ). the nucleus of a mature ovum or spermatozoan before fertilization.

pronunciamento (prəˌnʌnsɪə'mɛntəʊ) *n., pl.* **-tos.** **1.** an edict, proclamation, or manifesto, esp. one issued by rebels in a Spanish-speaking country. **2.** an authoritarian announcement. [C19: from Spanish: pronouncement]

pronunciation (prəˌnʌnsɪ'eɪʃən) *n.* **1.** the act, instance, or manner of pronouncing sounds. **2.** the supposedly correct manner of pronouncing sounds in a given language. **3.** a phonetic transcription of a word.

pro-oestrus (prəʊ'iːstrəs, -'ɛstrəs) *or U.S.* **proestrus** *n.* the period in the oestrous cycle that immediately precedes oestrus.

proof (pruːf) *n.* **1.** any evidence that establishes or helps to establish the truth, validity, quality, etc., of something. **2.** *Law.* the whole body of evidence upon which the verdict of a court is based. **3.** *Maths, logic.* a sequence of steps or statements that establishes the truth of a proposition. See also **direct** (sense 17), **induction** (senses 4, 8). **4.** the act of testing the truth of something (esp. in the phrase **put to the proof**). **5.** *Scots Law.* trial before a judge without a jury. **6.** *Printing.* a trial impression made from composed type for the correction of errors. **7.** (in engraving, etc.) a print made by an artist or under his supervision for his own satisfaction before he hands the plate over to a professional printer. **8.** *Photog.* a trial print from a negative. **9. a.** the alcoholic strength of proof spirit. **b.** the strength of a beverage or other alcoholic liquor as measured on a scale in which the strength of proof spirit is 100 degrees. ~*adj.* **10.** (*usually postpositive;* foll. by *against*) able to resist; impervious (to): *the roof is proof against rain.* **11.** having the alcoholic strength of proof spirit. **12.** of proved strength or impenetrability: *proof armour.* ~*vb.* **13.** (*tr.*) to take a proof from (type matter, a plate, etc.). **14.** to proofread (text) or inspect (a print, etc.), as for approval. **15.** to render (something) proof, esp. to waterproof. [C13: from Old French *preuve* a test, from Late Latin *proba,* from Latin *probāre* to test]

-proof *adj., vb. combining form.* secure against (damage by); (make) impervious to: *waterproof; mothproof; childproof.* [from PROOF (adj.)]

proofread ('pruːfˌriːd) *vb.* **-reads, -reading, -read** (-ˌrɛd). to read (copy or printer's proofs) to detect and mark errors to be corrected. —'**proofˌreader** *n.*

proof spirit *n.* **1.** (in Britain and Canada) a mixture of alcohol and water or an alcoholic beverage that contains 49.28 per cent of alcohol by weight, 57.1 per cent by volume at 51°F: up until 1980 used as a standard of alcoholic liquids. **2.** (in the U.S.) a similar standard mixture containing 50 per cent of alcohol by volume at 60°F.

proof stress *n. Engineering.* the equivalent of yield stress in materials which have no clearly defined yield point.

proof theory *n.* the branch of logic that studies the syntactic properties of formal theories, esp. the syntactic characterization of deductive validity.

prop[1] (prɒp) *vb.* **props, propping, propped.** (when *tr.,* often foll. by *up*) **1.** (*tr.*) to support with a rigid object, such as a stick. **2.** (*tr.;* usually also foll. by *against*) to place or lean. **3.** (*tr.*) to sustain or support. **4.** (*intr.*) *Austral. and N.Z.* to stop suddenly or unexpectedly. ~*n.* **5.** something that gives rigid support, such as a stick. **6.** a person or thing giving support, as of a moral or spiritual nature. **7.** *Rugby.* either of the forwards at either end of the front row of a scrum. [C15: related to Middle Dutch *proppe* vine prop; compare Old High German *pfropfo* shoot, German *Pfropfen* stopper]

prop[2] (prɒp) *n.* short for **property** (sense 8).

prop[3] (prɒp) *n.* an informal word for **propeller.**

prop. *abbrev. for:* **1.** proper(ly). **2.** property. **3.** proposition. **4.** proprietor.

propaedeutic (ˌprəʊpɪ'djuːtɪk) *n.* **1.** (*often pl.*) preparatory instruction basic to further study of an art or science. ~*adj. also* **propaedeutical.** **2.** of, relating to, or providing such instruction. [C19: from Greek *propaideuein* to teach in advance, from PRO-[2] + *paideuein* to rear]

propagable ('prɒpəgəbəl) *adj.* capable of being propagated. —ˌ**propaga'bility** *or* '**propagableness** *n.*

propaganda (ˌprɒpə'gændə) *n.* **1.** the organized dissemination of information, allegations, etc., to assist or damage the cause of a government, movement, etc. **2.** such information, allegations, etc. [C18: from Italian, use of *propāgandā* in the New Latin title *Sacra Congregatio de Propaganda Fide* Sacred Congregation for Propagating the Faith] —ˌ**propa'gandism** *n.* —ˌ**propa'gandist** *n., adj.*

Propaganda (ˌprɒpə'gændə) *n. R.C. Church.* a congregation responsible for directing the work of the foreign missions and the training of priests for these.

propagandize *or* **propagandise** (ˌprɒpə'gændaɪz) *vb.* **1.** (*tr.*) to spread by propaganda. **2.** (*tr.*) to subject to propaganda. **3.** (*intr.*) to spread or organize propaganda.

propagate ('prɒpəˌgeɪt) *vb.* **1.** *Biology.* to reproduce or cause to reproduce; breed. **2.** (*tr.*) *Horticulture.* to produce (plants) by layering, grafting, cuttings, etc. **3.** (*tr.*) to promulgate; disseminate. **4.** *Physics.* to move through, cause to move through, or transmit, esp. in the form of a wave: *to propagate sound.* **5.** (*tr.*) to transmit (characteristics) from one generation to the next. [C16: from Latin *propāgāre* to increase (plants) by cuttings, from *propāgēs* a cutting, from *pangere* to fasten] —ˌ**propa'gation** *n.* —ˌ**propa'gational** *adj.* —'**propagative** *adj.*

propagator ('prɒpəˌgeɪtə) *n.* **1.** a person or thing that propagates. **2.** a shallow box with a heating element and cover used for germinating seeds or rooting cuttings.

propagule ('prɒpəˌgjuːl) *or* **propagulum** (prəʊ'pægjʊləm) *n.* a plant part, such as a bud, that becomes detached from the rest of the plant and grows into a new plant. [C20: from PROPAG(ATE) + -ULE]

propane ('prəʊpeɪn) *n.* a colourless flammable gaseous alkane found in petroleum and used as a fuel. Formula: $CH_3CH_2CH_3$. [C19: from PROPIONIC ACID + -ANE]

propanedioic acid (ˌprəʊpeɪndaɪ'əʊɪk) *n.* a colourless crystalline compound that occurs in sugar beet. Formula: $CH_2(COOH)_2$. Also called: **malonic acid.** [C20: from PROPANE + DI-[1] + -O- + -IC]

propanoic acid (ˌprəʊpə'nəʊɪk) *n.* a colourless liquid carboxylic acid used in inhibiting the growth of moulds in bread. Formula: CH_3CH_2COOH. Former name: **propionic acid.** [C20: from PROPANE + -O- + -IC]

proparoxytone (ˌprəʊpə'rɒksɪˌtəʊn) *adj.* **1.** (in Ancient Greek) of, relating to, or denoting words having an acute accent on the third syllable from the end. ~*n.* **2.** a proparoxytone word. ~Compare **paroxytone.** [C18: from Greek *proparoxutonos;* see PRO-[2], PAROXYTONE]

pro patria *Latin.* ('prəʊ 'pætrɪˌɑː) for one's country.

propel (prə'pɛl) *vb.* **-pels, -pelling, -pelled.** (*tr.*) to impel, drive, or cause to move forwards. [C15: from Latin *prōpellere* to drive onwards, from PRO-[1] + *pellere* to drive]

propellant *or* **propellent** (prə'pɛlənt) *n.* **1.** something that provides or causes propulsion, such as the explosive charge in a gun or the fuel in a rocket. **2.** the gas used to carry the liquid droplets in an aerosol spray.

propellent (prə'pɛlənt) *adj.* able or tending to propel.

propeller (prə'pɛlə) *n.* **1.** a device having blades radiating from a central hub that is rotated to produce thrust to propel a ship, aircraft, etc. **2.** a person or thing that propels.

propeller shaft *n.* the shaft that transmits power from the gearbox to the differential gear in a motor vehicle or from the engine to the propeller in a ship or aircraft.

propelling pencil *n.* a pencil consisting of a metal or plastic case containing a replaceable lead. As the point is worn away the lead can be extended, usually by turning part of the case.

propend (prəʊ'pɛnd) *vb.* (*intr.*) *Obsolete.* to be inclined or disposed. [C16: from Latin *prōpendēre* to hang forwards]

propene ('prəʊpiːn) *n.* a colourless gaseous alkene obtained by cracking petroleum: used in synthesizing many organic compounds. Formula: $CH_3CH{:}CH_2$. Also called: **propylene.**

propensity (prə'pɛnsɪtɪ) *n., pl.* **-ties.** **1.** a natural tendency or disposition. **2.** *Obsolete.* partiality. [C16: from Latin *prōpensus* inclined to, from *prōpendēre* to PROPEND]

proper ('prɒpə) *adj.* **1.** (*usually prenominal*) appropriate or suited for some purpose: *in its proper place.* **2.** correct in behaviour or conduct. **3.** excessively correct in conduct; vigorously moral. **4.** up to a required or regular standard. **5.** (*immediately postpositive*) (of an object, quality, etc.) referred to or named specifically so as to exclude anything not directly connected with it: *his claim is connected with the deed proper.* **6.** (*postpositive;* foll. by *to*) belonging to or characteristic of a person or thing. **7.** (*prenominal*) *Brit. informal.* (intensifier): *I felt a proper fool.* **8.** (*usually postpositive*) (of heraldic colours) considered correct for the natural colour of the object or emblem depicted: *three martlets proper.* **9.** *Maths, logic.* (of a relation) distinguished from a weaker relation by excluding the case where the relata are identical. For example, every set is a subset of itself, but a **proper subset** must exclude at least one member of the containing set. See also **strict** (sense 6). **10.** *Archaic.* pleasant or good. ~*adv.* **11.** *Brit. dialect.* (intensifier): *he's proper stupid.* **12. good and proper.** *Informal.* thoroughly: *to get drunk good and proper.* ~*n.* **13.** the parts of the Mass that vary according to the particular day or feast on which the Mass is celebrated. Compare **ordinary** (sense 10). [C13: via Old French from Latin *prōprius* special] —'**properly** *adv.* —'**properness** *n.*

properdin ('prəʊpədɪn) *n. Immunol.* a protein present in blood serum that, acting with complement, is involved in the destruction of alien cells, such as bacteria.

proper fraction *n.* a fraction in which the numerator has a lower absolute value than the denominator, as ½ or $x/(3 + x^2)$.

proper motion *n.* the very small continuous change in the direction of motion of a star relative to the sun. It is determined from its radial and tangential motion.

proper noun *or* **name** *n.* the name of a person, place, or object, as for example *Iceland, Patrick,* or *Uranus.* Compare **common noun.**

propertied (ˈprɒpətɪd) *adj.* owning land or property.

property (ˈprɒpətɪ) *n., pl.* **-ties. 1.** something of value, either tangible, such as land, or intangible, such as patents, copyrights, etc. **2.** *Law.* the right to possess, use, and dispose of anything. **3.** possessions collectively or the fact of owning possessions of value. **4. a.** a piece of land or real estate, esp. used for agricultural purposes. **b.** (*as modifier*): *property rights.* **5.** *Chiefly Austral.* a ranch or station esp. a small one. **6.** a quality, attribute, or distinctive feature of anything, esp. a characteristic attribute such as the density or strength of a material. **7.** *Logic, obsolete.* another name for **proprium. 8.** any movable object used on the set of a stage play or film. Usually shortened to **prop.** [C13: from Old French *propriété,* from Latin *proprietās* something personal, from *proprius* one's own]

property bond *n.* a bond issued by a life-assurance company, the premiums for which are invested in a property-owning fund.

property centre *n.* a service for buying and selling property, including conveyancing, provided by a group of local solicitors. In full: **solicitors' property centre.**

property man *n.* a member of the stage crew in charge of the stage properties. Usually shortened to **propman.**

prophage (ˈprəʊfeɪdʒ) *n.* a virus that exists in a bacterial cell and undergoes division with its host without destroying it. Compare **bacteriophage.** [C20: by contraction from French *probactériophage; see* PRO-[2], BACTERIOPHAGE]

prophase (ˈprəʊˌfeɪz) *n.* **1.** the first stage of mitosis, during which the nuclear membrane disappears and the nuclear material resolves itself into chromosomes. See also **metaphase, anaphase, telophase. 2.** the first stage of meiosis, divided into leptotene, zygotene, pachytene, diplotene, and diakinesis phases.

prophecy (ˈprɒfɪsɪ) *n., pl.* **-cies. 1. a.** a message of divine truth revealing God's will. **b.** the act of uttering such a message. **2.** a prediction or guess. **3.** the function, activity, or charismatic endowment of a prophet or prophets. [C13: ultimately from Greek *prophētēs* PROPHET]

prophesy (ˈprɒfɪˌsaɪ) *vb.* **-sies, -sying, -sied. 1.** to reveal or foretell (something, esp. a future event) by or as if by divine inspiration. **2.** (*intr.*) *Archaic.* to give instruction in religious subjects. [C14 *prophecien,* from PROPHECY] —ˈ**propheˌsiable** *adj.* —ˈ**propheˌsier** *n.*

prophet (ˈprɒfɪt) *n.* **1.** a person who supposedly speaks by divine inspiration, esp. one through whom a divinity expresses his will. **2.** a person who predicts the future: *a prophet of doom.* **3.** a spokesman for a movement, doctrine, etc. **4.** *Christian Science.* **a.** a seer in spiritual matters. **b.** the vanishing of material sense to give way to the conscious facts of spiritual truth. [C13: from Old French *prophète,* from Latin *prophēta,* from Greek *prophētēs* one who declares the divine will, from PRO-[2] + *phanai* to speak] —ˈ**prophetess** *fem. n.* —ˈ**prophet-ˌlike** *adj.*

Prophet (ˈprɒfɪt) *n.* **the.** the principal designation of Mohammed (?570–632 A.D.) as the founder of Islam.

prophetic (prəˈfɛtɪk) *adj.* **1.** of or relating to a prophet or prophecy. **2.** containing or of the nature of a prophecy; predictive. —**proˈphetically** *adv.*

prophylactic (ˌprɒfɪˈlæktɪk) *adj.* **1.** protecting from or preventing disease. **2.** protective or preventive. ~*n.* **3.** a prophylactic drug or device. **4.** *Chiefly U.S.* another name for **condom.** [C16: via French from Greek *prophulaktikos,* from *prophulassein* to guard by taking advance measures, from PRO-[2] + *phulax* a guard]

prophylaxis (ˌprɒfɪˈlæksɪs) *n.* the prevention of disease or control of its possible spread.

propinquity (prəˈpɪŋkwɪtɪ) *n.* **1.** nearness in place or time. **2.** nearness in relationship. [C14: from Latin *propinquitās* closeness, from *propinquus* near, from *prope* near by]

propionate (ˈprəʊpɪəˌneɪt) *n.* any ester or salt of propionic acid.

propionic acid (ˌprəʊpɪˈɒnɪk) *n.* the former name for **propanoic acid.** [C19: from Greek *pro-* first + *pionic* from *piōn* fat, because it is first in order of the fatty acids]

propitiate (prəˈpɪʃɪˌeɪt) *vb.* (*tr.*) to appease or make well disposed; conciliate. [C17: from Latin *propitiāre* to appease, from *propitius* gracious] —**proˈpitiable** *adj.* —**proˌpitiˈation** *n.* —**proˌpitiˈatious** *adj.* —**proˈpitiative** *adj.* —**proˈpitiˌator** *n.*

propitiatory (prəˈpɪʃɪətərɪ) *adj.* **1.** designed or intended to propitiate; conciliatory; expiatory. ~*n.* **2.** the mercy seat. —**proˈpitiatorily** *adv.*

propitious (prəˈpɪʃəs) *adj.* **1.** favourable; auguring well. **2.** gracious or favourably inclined. [C15: from Latin *propitius* well disposed, from *prope* close to] —**proˈpitiously** *adv.* —**proˈpitiousness** *n.*

propjet (ˈprɒpˌdʒɛt) *n.* another name for **turboprop.**

propman (ˈprɒpˌmæn) *n., pl.* **-men.** short for **property man.**

propolis (ˈprɒpəlɪs) *n.* a greenish-brown resinous aromatic substance collected by bees from the buds of trees for use in the construction of hives. Also called: **bee glue, hive dross.** [C17: via Latin from Greek: suburb, bee glue, from *pro-* before + *polis* city]

propone (prəˈpon, -ˈpəʊn) *vb. Scot.* to propose or put forward, esp. before a court. [C14: from Latin *prōpōnere* to PROPOSE]

proponent (prəˈpəʊnənt) *n.* **1.** a person who argues in favour of something. **2.** *Law.* a person who seeks probate of a will. [C16: from Latin *prōpōnere* to PROPOSE]

proportion (prəˈpɔːʃən) *n.* **1.** the relationship between different things or parts with respect to comparative size, number, or degree; relative magnitude or extent; ratio. **2.** the correct or desirable relationship between parts of a whole; balance or symmetry. **3.** a part considered with respect to the whole. **4.** (*pl.*) dimensions or size: *a building of vast proportions.* **5.** a share, part, or quota. **6.** *Maths.* a relationship that maintains a constant ratio between two variable quantities: *x increases in direct proportion to y.* **7.** *Maths.* a relationship between four numbers or quantities in which the ratio of the first pair equals the ratio of the second pair. ~*vb.* (*tr.*) **8.** to adjust in relative amount, size, etc. **9.** to cause to be harmonious in relationship of parts. [C14: from Latin *prōportiō* (a translation of Greek *analogia*), from phrase *prō portione,* literally: for (its, his, one's) PORTION] —**proˈportionable** *adj.* —**proˌportionaˈbility** *n.* —**proˈportionably** *adv.* —**proˈportionment** *n.*

proportional (prəˈpɔːʃənᵊl) *adj.* **1.** of, involving, or being in proportion. **2.** *Maths.* having or related by a constant ratio. ~*n.* **3.** *Maths.* an unknown term in a proportion: *in a/b = c/x, x is the fourth proportional.* —**proˌportionˈality** *n.* —**proˈportionally** *adv.*

proportional counter *n.* an instrument for detecting and measuring the intensity of ionizing radiation. It is similar to a Geiger counter but operates at a lower potential difference such that the magnitude of the discharge is directly proportional to the number of gas molecules ionized by the detected particle. This may permit the identification of the particle or the determination of its energy.

proportional representation *n.* representation of parties in an elective body in proportion to the votes they win. Abbrev.: **PR.** Compare **first-past-the-post.** See also **Additional Member System, Alternative Vote, party list, Single Transferable Vote.**

proportional spacing *n.* a feature of some typewriters and other output devices whereby the space allotted to each character is determined by the width of the character.

proportionate *adj.* (prəˈpɔːʃənɪt). **1.** being in proper proportion. ~*vb.* (prəˈpɔːʃəˌneɪt). **2.** (*tr.*) to make proportionate. —**proˈportionately** *adv.* —**proˈportionateness** *n.*

proposal (prəˈpəʊzᵊl) *n.* **1.** the act of proposing. **2.** something proposed, as a plan. **3.** an offer, esp. of marriage.

propose (prəˈpəʊz) *vb.* **1.** (when *tr., may take a clause as object*) to put forward (a plan, motion, etc.) for consideration or action. **2.** (*tr.*) to nominate, as for a position. **3.** (*tr.*) to plan or intend (to do something): *I propose to leave town now.* **4.** (*tr.*) to announce the drinking of (a toast) to (the health of someone, etc.). **5.** (*intr.; often foll. by to*) to make an offer of marriage (to someone). [C14: from Old French *proposer,* from Latin *prōpōnere* to display, from PRO-[1] + *pōnere* to place] —**proˈposable** *adj.* —**proˈposer** *n.*

proposition (ˌprɒpəˈzɪʃən) *n.* **1.** a proposal or topic presented for consideration. **2.** *Philosophy.* **a.** the content of a sentence that affirms or denies something and is capable of being true or false. **b.** the meaning of such a sentence: *I am warm* always expresses the same proposition whoever the speaker is. Compare **statement** (sense 8). **3.** *Maths.* a statement or theorem, usually containing its proof. **4.** *Informal.* a person or matter to be dealt with: *he's a difficult proposition.* **5.** an invitation to engage in sexual intercourse. ~*vb.* **6.** (*tr.*) to propose a plan, deal, etc., to, esp. to engage in sexual intercourse. [C14 *proposicioun,* from Latin *prōpositiō* a setting forth; see PROPOSE] —ˌ**propoˈsitional** *adj.* —ˌ**propoˈsitionally** *adv.*

propositional attitude *n. Logic, philosophy.* a relation between a person and a proposition, such as belief, desire, intention, etc.

propositional calculus *n.* the system of symbolic logic concerned only with the relations between propositions as wholes, taking no account of their internal structure. Compare **predicate calculus.**

propositional function *n.* another name for **open sentence.**

propositus (prəˈpɒzɪtəs) *or (fem.)* **proposita** (prəˈpɒzɪtə) *n., pl.* **-ti** (-ˌtaɪ) *or (fem.)* **-tae** (-tiː). **1.** *Law.* the person from whom a line of descent is traced. **2.** *Med.* Also called (esp. U.S.): **proband.** the first patient to be investigated in a family study, to whom all relationships are referred. [from New Latin, from Latin *prōpōnere* to set forth; see PROPOUND]

propound (prəˈpaʊnd) *vb.* (*tr.*) **1.** to suggest or put forward for consideration. **2.** *English law.* **a.** to produce (a will or similar instrument) to the proper court or authority in order for its validity to be established. **b.** (of an executor) to bring (an action to obtain probate) in solemn form. [C16 *propone,* from Latin *prōpōnere* to set forth from PRO-[1] + *pōnere* to place] —**proˈpounder** *n.*

propr *abbrev. for* proprietor.

propraetor *or* **propretor** (prəʊˈpriːtə) *n.* (in ancient Rome) a citizen, esp. an ex-praetor, granted a praetor's imperium to be exercised outside Rome, esp. in the provinces. [Latin, from *prō praetōre* one who acts for a praetor]

propranolol (prəʊˈprænəˌlɒl) *n.* a drug used in the treatment of angina pectoris, arrhythmia, hypertension, and other forms of heart disease. Formula: $C_{16}H_{21}NO_2$. [C20: from PRO(PYL) + PR(OP)ANOL (from PROPANE + -OL) + -OL]

proprietary (prəˈpraɪtərɪ, -trɪ) *adj.* **1.** of, relating to, or belonging to property or proprietors. **2.** privately owned and controlled. **3.** *Med.* of or denoting a drug or agent manufactured and distributed under a trade name. Compare **ethical** (sense 3). ~*n., pl.* **-taries. 4.** *Med.* a proprietary drug or agent. **5.** a proprietor or proprietors collectively. **6. a.** right to property. **b.** property owned. **7.** Also called: **lord proprietary.** (in Colonial America) an owner, governor, or grantee of a proprietary colony. [C15: from Late Latin *proprietārius* an owner, from *proprius* one's own] —**proˈprietarily** *adv.*

proprietary colony *n. U.S. history.* any of various colonies, granted by the Crown in the 17th century to a person or group of people with full governing rights.

proprietary name *n.* a name that is a trademark.

proprietor (prəˈpraɪətə) *n.* **1.** an owner of an unincorporated business enterprise. **2.** a person enjoying exclusive right of ownership to some property. **3.** *U.S. history.* a governor or body of governors of a proprietary colony. —**proˈprietorship** *n.* —**proprietorial** (prəˌpraɪəˈtɔːrɪəl) *adj.* —**proˈprietress** *or* **proˈprietrix** *fem. n.*

propriety (prəˈpraɪətɪ) *n., pl.* **-ties. 1.** the quality or state of being appropriate or fitting. **2.** conformity to the prevailing standard of behaviour, speech, etc. **3.** (*pl.*) **the proprieties.** the standards of behaviour considered correct by polite society. [C15: from Old French *propriété,* from Latin *proprietās* a peculiarity, from *proprius* one's own]

proprioceptor (ˌprəʊprɪəˈsɛptə) *n. Physiol.* any receptor (as in the gut, blood vessels, muscles, etc.) that supplies information about the state of the body. Compare **exteroceptor, interoceptor.** [C20: from *proprio-,* from Latin *proprius* one's own + RECEPTOR] —ˌ**proprioˈceptive** *adj.*

proprium (ˈprəʊprɪəm) *n. Logic, obsolete.* Also called: **property.** an attribute that is not essential to a species but is common and peculiar to it. [C16: Latin, neuter sing. of *proprius* proper, own]

prop root *n.* a root that grows from and supports the stem above the ground in plants such as mangroves.

proptosis (prɒpˈtəʊsɪs) *n., pl.* **-ses** (-siːz). *Pathol.* the forward displacement of an organ or part, such as the eyeball. See also **exophthalmos.** Compare **prolapse.** [C17: via Late Latin from Greek, from *propiptein* to fall forwards]

propulsion (prəˈpʌlʃən) *n.* **1.** the act of propelling or the state of being propelled. **2.** a propelling force. [C15: from Latin *prōpellere* to PROPEL] —**proˈpulsive** *or* **proˈpulsory** *adj.*

propyl (ˈprəʊpɪl) *n.* (*modifier*) of, consisting of, or containing the monovalent group of atoms C_3H_7-: *a propyl group or radical.* [C19: from PROP(IONIC ACID) + -YL]

propylaeum (ˌprɒpɪˈliːəm) *or* **propylon** (ˈprɒpɪˌlɒn) *n., pl.* **-laea** (-ˈliːə) *or* **-lons, -la.** a portico, esp. one that forms the entrance to a temple. [C18: via Latin from Greek *propulaion* before the gate, from PRO-[2] + *pulē* gate]

propylene (ˈprəʊpɪˌliːn) *n.* another name for **propene.** [C19: from PROPYL + -ENE]

propylene glycol *n.* a colourless viscous hydroscopic sweet-tasting compound used as an antifreeze and brake fluid. Formula: $CH_3CHOHCH_2OH$. Systematic name: **1,2-dihydroxypropane.**

propylite (ˈprɒpɪˌlaɪt) *n. Geology.* an altered andesite or similar rock containing calcite, chlorite, etc., produced by the action of hot water. [C20: from *propylon* (see PROPYLAEUM) + -ITE[1]; so named because it is associated with the start of the Tertiary volcanic era]

pro rata (ˈprəʊ ˈrɑːtə) in proportion. [Medieval Latin]

prorate (prəʊˈreɪt, ˈprəʊreɪt) *vb. Chiefly U.S. and Canadian.* to divide, assess, or distribute (something) proportionately. [C19: from PRO RATA] —**proˈratable** *adj.* —**proˈration** *n.*

prorogue (prəˈrəʊg) *vb.* to discontinue the meetings of (a legislative body) without dissolving it. [C15: from Latin *prorogāre* literally: to ask publicly, from *prō-* in public + *rogāre* to ask] —**prorogation** (ˌprəʊrəˈgeɪʃən) *n.*

pros. *abbrev. for* prosody.

prosaic (prəʊˈzeɪɪk) *adj.* **1.** lacking imagination. **2.** having the characteristics of prose. [C16: from Late Latin *prōsaicus,* from Latin *prōsa* PROSE] —**proˈsaically** *adv.* —**proˈsaicness** *n.*

prosaism (prəʊˈzeɪɪzəm) *or* **prosaicism** (prəʊˈzeɪɪˌsɪzəm) *n.* **1.** prosaic quality or style. **2.** a prosaic expression, thought, etc. —**proˈsaist** *n.*

pros and cons *pl. n.* the various arguments in favour of and against a motion, course of action, etc. [C16: from Latin *prō* for + *con,* from *contrā* against]

proscenium (prəˈsiːnɪəm) *n., pl.* **-nia** (-nɪə) *or* **-niums. 1.** the arch or opening separating the stage from the auditorium together with the area immediately in front of the arch. **2.** (in ancient theatres) the stage itself. [C17: via Latin from Greek *proskēnion,* from *pro-* before + *skēnē* scene]

prosciutto (prəʊˈʃuːtəʊ; *Italian* proˈʃutto) *n.* cured ham from Italy: usually served as an hors d'oeuvre. [Italian, literally: dried beforehand, from *pro-* PRE- + *asciutto* dried]

proscribe (prəʊˈskraɪb) *vb.* (*tr.*) **1.** to condemn or prohibit. **2.** to outlaw; banish; exile. **3.** (in ancient Rome) to outlaw (a citizen) by posting his name in public. [C16: from Latin *prōscrībere* to put up a written public notice, from *prō-* in public + *scrībere* to write] —**proˈscriber** *n.*

proscription (prəʊˈskrɪpʃən) *n.* **1.** the act of proscribing or the state of being proscribed. **2.** denunciation, prohibition, or exclusion. **3.** outlawry or ostracism. [C14: from Latin *prōscriptiō;* see PROSCRIBE] —**proˈscriptive** *adj.* —**proˈscriptively** *adv.* —**proˈscriptiveness** *n.*

prose (prəʊz) *n.* **1.** spoken or written language as in ordinary usage, distinguished from poetry by its lack of a marked metrical structure. **2.** a passage set for translation into a foreign language. **3.** commonplace or dull discourse, expression, etc. **4.** *R.C. Church.* a hymn recited or sung after the gradual at Mass. **5.** (*modifier*) written in prose. **6.** (*modifier*) matter-of-fact. ~*vb.* **7.** to write or say (something) in prose. **8.** (*intr.*) to speak or write in a tedious style. [C14: via Old French from Latin phrase *prōsa ōrātiō* straightforward speech, from *prorsus* prosaic, from *prōvertere* to turn forwards, from PRO-[1] + *vertere* to turn] —ˈ**proseˌlike** *adj.*

prosector (prəʊˈsɛktə) *n.* a person who prepares or dissects anatomical subjects for demonstration. [C19: from Latin, from *prōsecare* to cut up; probably on the model of French *prosecteur*]

prosecute (ˈprɒsɪˌkjuːt) *vb.* **1.** (*tr.*) to bring a criminal action against (a person) for some offence. **2.** (*intr.*) **a.** to seek redress by legal proceedings. **b.** to institute or conduct a prosecution. **3.** (*tr.*) to engage in or practise (a profession or trade). **4.** (*tr.*) to continue to do (a task, etc.). [C15: from Latin *prōsequī* to follow, from *prō-* forward + *sequī* to follow] —ˈ**proseˌcutable** *adj.*

prosecuting attorney *n. U.S. Law.* (in some states) an officer in a judicial district appointed to conduct criminal prosecutions on behalf of the state and people.

prosecution (ˌprɒsɪˈkjuːʃən) *n.* **1.** the act of prosecuting or the state of being prosecuted. **2. a.** the institution and conduct of legal proceedings against a person. **b.** the proceedings brought in the name of the Crown to put an accused on trial. **3.** the lawyers acting for the Crown to put the case against a person. Compare **defence** (sense 6). **4.** the following up or carrying on of something begun, esp. with a view to its accomplishment or completion.

prosecutor (ˈprɒsɪˌkjuːtə) *n.* a person who institutes or conducts legal proceedings, esp. in a criminal court.

proselyte (ˈprɒsɪˌlaɪt) *n.* **1.** a person newly converted to a religious faith or sect; a convert, esp. a gentile converted to Judaism. ~*vb.* **2.** a less common word for **proselytize.** [C14: from Church Latin *prosēlytus,* from Greek *prosēlutos* recent arrival, convert, from *proserchesthai* to draw near] —**proselytism** (ˈprɒsɪlɪˌtɪzəm) *n.* —**proselytic** (ˌprɒsɪˈlɪtɪk) *adj.*

proselytize *or* **proselytise** (ˈprɒsɪlɪˌtaɪz) *vb.* to convert (someone) from one religious faith to another. —ˌ**proselytiˈzation** *or* ˌ**proselytiˈsation** *n.* —ˈ**proselytˌizer** *or* ˈ**proselytˌiser** *n.*

prosencephalon (ˌprɒsɛnˈsɛfəlɒn) *n., pl.* **-la** (-lə). the part of the brain that develops from the anterior portion of the neural tube. Compare **mesencephalon, rhombencephalon.** Nontechnical name: **forebrain.** [C19: from New Latin, from Greek *prosō* forward + *enkephalos* brain] —**prosencephalic** (ˌprɒsɛnsɪˈfælɪk) *adj.*

prosenchyma (prɒsˈɛŋkɪmə) *n.* a plant tissue consisting of long narrow cells with pointed ends: occurs in conducting tissue. [C19: from New Latin, from Greek *pros-* towards + *enkhuma* infusion; compare PARENCHYMA] —**prosenchymatous** (ˌprɒsɛnˈkaɪmətəs) *adj.*

prose poem *n.* a prose composition characterized by a poetic style.

prosimian (prəʊˈsɪmɪən) *n.* **1.** any primate of the primitive suborder *Prosimii,* including lemurs, tree shrews, lorises, and tarsiers. ~*adj.* **2.** of, relating to, or belonging to the *Prosimii.* ~Compare **anthropoid** (sense 4). [C19: via New Latin from PRO-[1] + Latin *sīmia* ape]

prosit German. (ˈproːzɪt) *interj.* good health! cheers! [German, from Latin, literally: may it prove beneficial]

prosody (ˈprɒsədɪ) *n.* **1.** the study of poetic metre and of the art of versification, including rhyme, stanzaic forms, and the quantity and stress of syllables. **2.** a system of versification. **3.** the patterns of stress and intonation in a language. [C15: from Latin *prosōdia* accent of a syllable, from Greek *prosōidia* song set to music, from *pros* towards + *ōidē,* from *aoidē* song; see ODE] —**prosodic** (prəˈsɒdɪk) *adj.* —ˈ**prosodist** *n.*

prosoma (prəʊˈsəʊmə) *n., pl.* **-mas** *or* **-mata** (-mətə). Zoology. the head and thorax of an arachnid.

prosopagnosia (ˌprɒsəpægˈnəʊzɪə) *n.* an inability to recognize faces. [C20: from Greek *prosōpon* face + AGNOSIA]

prosopography (ˌprɒsəˈpɒgrəfɪ) *n.* **1.** a description of a person's life and career. **2.** the study of such descriptions as part of history, esp. Roman history. [C16: from New Latin *prosopographia,* from Greek *prosōpon person* + -GRAPHY] —ˌ**prosoˈpographer** *n.* —**prosopographical** (ˌprɒsəpəˈgræfɪkəl) *adj.* —ˌ**prosopoˈgraphically** *adv.*

pro-ˈProtestant *adj., n.*
ˌ**proreˈform** *adj.*
ˌ**prorestoˈration** *adj.*
ˌ**proreˈvision** *adj.*
ˌ**prorevoˈlutionary** *adj.*
proˈslavery *adj.*

prosopopoeia *or* **prosopopeia** (ˌprɒsəpəˈpiːə) *n.* **1.** *Rhetoric.* another word for **personification. 2.** a figure of speech that represents an imaginary, absent, or dead person speaking or acting. [C16: via Latin from Greek *prosōpopoiia* dramatization, from *prosōpon* face + *poiein* to make] —ˌ**prosopoˈpoeial** *or* ˌ**prosopoˈpeial** *adj.*

prospect *n.* (ˈprɒspɛkt). **1.** (*sometimes pl.*) a probability or chance for future success, esp. as based on present work or aptitude: *a good job with prospects.* **2.** a vision of the future; what is foreseen; expectation: *she was excited at the prospect of living in London; unemployment presents a grim prospect.* **3.** a view or scene, esp. one offering an extended outlook. **4.** a prospective buyer, project, etc. **5.** a survey or observation. **6.** *Mining.* **a.** a known or likely deposit of ore. **b.** the location of a deposit of ore. **c.** a sample of ore for testing. **d.** the yield of mineral obtained from a sample of ore. ~*vb.* (prəˈspɛkt). **7.** (when *intr.*, often foll. by *for*) to explore (a region) for gold or other valuable minerals. **8.** (*tr.*) to work (a mine) to discover its profitability. **9.** (*intr.*; often foll. by *for*) to search (for). [C15: from Latin *prōspectus* distant view, from *prōspicere* to look into the distance, from *prō-* forward + *specere* to look] —ˈ**prospectless** *adj.*

prospective (prəˈspɛktɪv) *adj.* **1.** looking towards the future. **2.** (*prenominal*) anticipated or likely. —**proˈspectively** *adv.*

prospector (prəˈspɛktə) *n.* a person who searches for the natural occurrence of gold, petroleum, etc.

prospectus (prəˈspɛktəs) *n., pl.* **-tuses. 1.** a formal statement giving details of a forthcoming event, such as the publication of a book or an issue of shares. **2.** a pamphlet or brochure giving details of courses, as at a college or school. [C18: Latin, literally: distant view; see PROSPECT]

prosper (ˈprɒspə) *vb.* (*usually intr.*) to thrive, succeed, etc., or cause to thrive, succeed, etc. in a healthy way. [C15: from Latin *prosperāre* to succeed, from *prosperus* fortunate, from PRO-[1] + *spēs* hope]

prosperity (prɒˈspɛrɪtɪ) *n.* the condition of prospering; success or wealth.

prosperous (ˈprɒspərəs) *adj.* **1.** flourishing; prospering. **2.** rich; affluent; wealthy. **3.** favourable or promising. —ˈ**prosperously** *adv.* —ˈ**prosperousness** *n.*

prostaglandin (ˌprɒstəˈglændɪn) *n.* any of a group of potent hormone-like compounds composed of essential fatty acids and found in all mammalian tissues, esp. human semen. Prostaglandins stimulate the muscles of the uterus and affect the blood vessels; they are used to induce abortion or birth. [C20: from *prosta(te) gland* + -IN; it was originally believed to be secreted by the prostate gland]

prostate (ˈprɒsteɪt) *n.* **1.** Also called: **prostate gland.** a gland in male mammals that surrounds the neck of the bladder and urethra and secretes a liquid constituent of the semen. ~*adj.* **2.** Also: **prostatic** (prɒˈstætɪk). of or relating to the prostate gland. [C17: via Medieval Latin from Greek *prostatēs* something standing in front (of the bladder), from *pro-* in front + *histanai* to cause to stand]

prostatectomy (ˌprɒstəˈtɛktəmɪ) *n., pl.* **-mies.** surgical removal of all or a part of the prostate gland.

prostatitis (ˌprɒstəˈtaɪtɪs) *n.* inflammation of the prostate gland.

prosternum (prəʊˈstɜːnəm) *n., pl.* **-na** (-nə) *or* **-nums.** the sternum of the prothorax of an insect.

prosthesis (ˈprɒsθɪsɪs, prɒsˈθiːsɪs) *n., pl.* **-ses** (-ˌsiːz). **1.** *Surgery.* **a.** the replacement of a missing bodily part with an artificial substitute. **b.** an artificial part such as a limb, eye, or tooth. **2.** *Linguistics.* another word for **prothesis.** [C16: via Late Latin from Greek: an addition, from *prostithenai* to add, from *pros* towards + *tithenai* to place] —**prosthetic** (prɒsˈθɛtɪk) *adj.* —**prosˈthetically** *adv.*

prosthetic group *n.* the nonprotein component of a conjugated protein, such as the lipid group in a lipoprotein.

prosthetics (prɒsˈθɛtɪks) *n.* (*functioning as sing.*) the branch of surgery concerned with prosthesis.

prosthodontics (ˌprɒsθəˈdɒntɪks) *n.* (*functioning as sing.*) the branch of dentistry concerned with the artificial replacement of missing teeth. [C20: from PROSTH(ESIS) + -ODONT + -ICS] —ˌ**prosthoˈdontist** *n.*

prostitute (ˈprɒstɪˌtjuːt) *n.* **1.** a woman who engages in sexual intercourse for money. **2.** a man who engages in such activity, esp. in homosexual practices. **3.** a person who offers his talent or work for unworthy purposes. ~*vb.* (*tr.*) **4.** to offer (oneself or another) in sexual intercourse for money. **5.** to offer (a person, esp. oneself, or a person's talent) for unworthy purposes. [C16: from Latin *prōstituere* to expose to prostitution, from *prō-* in public + *statuere* to cause to stand] —ˌ**prostiˈtution** *n.* —ˈ**prostiˌtutor** *n.*

prostomium (prəʊˈstəʊmɪəm) *n., pl.* **-mia** (-mɪə). the lobe at the head end of earthworms and other annelids: bears tentacles, palps, etc., or forms part of a sucker or proboscis. [via New Latin from Greek *prostomion* mouth] —**proˈstomial** *adj.*

prostrate *adj.* (ˈprɒstreɪt). **1.** lying with the face downwards, as in submission. **2.** exhausted physically or emotionally. **3.** helpless or defenceless. **4.** (of a plant) growing closely along the ground. ~*vb.* (prɒˈstreɪt). (*tr.*) **5.** to bow or cast (oneself) down, as in submission. **6.** to lay or throw down flat, as on the ground. **7.** to make helpless or defenceless. **8.** to make exhausted. [C14: from Latin *prōsternere* to throw to the ground, from *prō-* before + *sternere* to lay low] —**prosˈtration** *n.*

prostyle (ˈprəʊstaɪl) *adj.* **1.** (of a building) having a row of columns in front, esp. as in the portico of a Greek temple. ~*n.* **2.** a prostyle building, portico, etc. [C17: from Latin *prostȳlos*, from Greek: with pillars in front, from PRO-[2] + *stulos* pillar]

prosy (ˈprəʊzɪ) *adj.* **prosier, prosiest. 1.** of the nature of or similar to prose. **2.** dull, tedious, or long-winded. —ˈ**prosily** *adv.* —ˈ**prosiness** *n.*

Prot. *abbrev. for:* **1.** Protestant. **2.** Protectorate.

prot- *combining form.* a variant of **proto-** before a vowel.

protactinium (ˌprəʊtækˈtɪnɪəm) *n.* a toxic radioactive metallic element that occurs in uranium ores and is produced by neutron irradiation of thorium. Symbol: Pa; atomic no.: 91; half-life of the most stable isotope, ^{231}Pa: 32 500 years; valency: 4 or 5; relative density: 15.4 (calc.); melting pt.: below 1600°C. Former name: **protoactinium.**

protagonist (prəʊˈtægənɪst) *n.* **1.** the principal character in a play, story, etc. **2.** a supporter, esp. when important or respected, of a cause, political party, etc. [C17: from Greek *prōtagōnistēs*, from *prōtos* first + *agōnistēs* actor] —**proˈtagonism** *n.*

protamine (ˈprəʊtəˌmiːn) *n.* any of a group of basic simple proteins that occur, in association with nucleic acids, in the sperm of some fish. [C19: from German: see PROTO-, AMINE]

protandrous (prəʊˈtændrəs) *adj.* (of plants and hermaphrodite animals) producing male gametes before female gametes. Compare **protogynous.** —**proˈtandry** *n.*

protanopia (ˌprəʊtəˈnəʊpɪə) *n.* a form of colour blindness characterized by a tendency to confuse reds and greens and by a loss of sensitivity to red light. [C20: New Latin, from PROTO- + AN- + -OPIA] —**protanopic** (ˌprəʊtəˈnɒpɪk) *adj.*

protasis (ˈprɒtəsɪs) *n., pl.* **-ses** (-siːz). **1.** *Logic, grammar.* the antecedent of a conditional statement, such as *it rains* in *if it rains the game will be cancelled.* Compare **apodosis. 2.** (in classical drama) the introductory part of a play. [C17: via Latin from Greek: a proposal, from *pro-* before + *teinein* to extend] —**protatic** (prɒˈtætɪk) *adj.*

protea (ˈprəʊtɪə) *n.* any shrub or small tree of the genus *Protea*, of tropical and southern Africa, having flowers with coloured bracts arranged in showy heads: family *Proteaceae.* [C20: from New Latin, from *Proteus* (a Greek sea god capable of changing his shape at will), referring to the large number of different forms of the plant] —**proteaceous** (ˌprəʊtɪˈeɪʃəs) *adj.*

protean (prəʊˈtiːən, ˈprəʊtɪən) *adj.* readily taking on various shapes or forms; variable. [C16: from *Proteus*]

protease (ˈprəʊtɪˌeɪs) *n.* any enzyme involved in proteolysis. [C20: from PROTEIN + -ASE]

protect (prəˈtɛkt) *vb.* (*tr.*) **1.** to defend from trouble, harm, attack, etc. **2.** *Economics.* to assist (domestic industries) by the imposition of protective tariffs on imports. **3.** *Commerce.* to provide funds in advance to guarantee payment of (a note, draft, etc.). [C16: from Latin *prōtegere* to cover before, from PRO-[1] + *tegere* to cover]

protectant (prəˈtɛktənt) *n.* a chemical substance that affords protection, as against frost, rust, insects, etc.

protection (prəˈtɛkʃən) *n.* **1.** the act of protecting or the condition of being protected. **2.** something that protects. **3. a.** the imposition of duties or quotas on imports, designed for the protection of domestic industries against overseas competition, expansion of domestic employment, etc. **b.** Also called: **protectionism.** the system, policy, or theory of such restrictions. Compare **free trade. 4.** a document that grants protection or immunity from arrest or harassment to a person, esp. a traveller. **5.** *Mountaineering.* security on a climb provided by running belays, etc. **6.** *Informal.* **a.** Also called: **protection money.** money demanded by gangsters for freedom from molestation. **b.** freedom from molestation purchased in this way. —**proˈtectionˌism** *n.* —**proˈtectionist** *n., adj.*

protection ratio *n.* the minimum acceptable ratio between the amplitudes of a wanted radio or television broadcast signal and any interfering signal.

protective (prəˈtɛktɪv) *adj.* **1.** giving or capable of giving protection. **2.** *Economics.* of, relating to, or intended for protection of domestic industries. ~*n.* **3.** something that protects. **4.** a condom. —**proˈtectively** *adv.* —**proˈtectiveness** *n.*

protective coloration *n.* the coloration of an animal that enables it to blend with its surroundings and therefore escape the attention of predators.

protective tariff *n.* a tariff levied on imports to protect the domestic economy rather than to raise revenue.

protector (prəˈtɛktə) *n.* **1.** a person or thing that protects. **2.** *History.* a person who exercised royal authority during the minority, absence, or incapacity of the monarch. —**proˈtectoral** *adj.* —**proˈtectress** *fem. n.*

pro-ˈSoviet *adj.* ˌ**prosuperˈvision** *adj.* ˌ**prosurˈrender** *adj.* **proˈsyndicalˌism** *n.*

Protector (prəˈtɛktə) *n.* short for **Lord Protector,** the title borne by Oliver Cromwell (1653–58) and by Richard Cromwell (1658–59) as heads of state during the period known as the **Protectorate.**

protectorate (prəˈtɛktərɪt) *n.* **1. a.** a territory largely controlled by but not annexed to a stronger state. **b.** the relation of a protecting state to its protected territory. **2.** the office or period of office of a protector.

protectory (prəˈtɛktərɪ) *n., pl.* **-ries.** an institution for the care of homeless, delinquent, or destitute children.

protégé *or (fem.)* **protégée** (ˈprəʊtɪˌʒeɪ) *n.* a person who is protected and aided by the patronage of another person. [C18: from French *protéger* to PROTECT]

protein (ˈprəʊtiːn) *n.* any of a large group of nitrogenous compounds of high molecular weight that are essential constituents of all living organisms. They consist of one or more chains of amino acids linked by peptide bonds and are folded into a specific three-dimensional shape maintained by further chemical bonding. [C19: via German from Greek *prōteios* primary, from *protos* first + -IN] —ˌ**proteinˈaceous, proˈteinic,** *or* **proˈteinous** *adj.*

proteinase (ˈprəʊtɪˌneɪs, -ˌneɪz) *n.* another name for **endopeptidase.**

proteinuria (ˌprəʊtɪˈnjʊərɪə) *n. Med.* another name for **albuminuria.**

pro tempore *Latin.* (ˈprəʊ ˈtɛmpərɪ) *adv., adj.* for the time being. Often shortened to **pro tem** (ˈprəʊ ˈtɛm).

proteolysis (ˌprəʊtɪˈɒlɪsɪs) *n.* the hydrolysis of proteins into simpler compounds by the action of enzymes: occurs esp. during digestion. [C19: from New Latin, from *proteo-* (from PROTEIN) + -LYSIS] —**proteolytic** (ˌprəʊtɪəˈlɪtɪk) *adj.*

proteose (ˈprəʊtɪˌəʊs, -ˌəʊz) *n. Now rare.* any of a group of compounds formed during proteolysis that are less complex than metaproteins but more so than peptones. Also called (esp. U.S.): **albumose.** [C20: from PROTEIN + -OSE[2]]

protero- *combining form.* anterior or former in time, place, order, etc.: *proterozoic.* [from Greek *proteros* fore]

Proterozoic (ˌprəʊtərəʊˈzəʊɪk) *n.* **1.** the later of two divisions of the Precambrian era, during which the earliest plants and animals are assumed to have lived. Compare **Archaeozoic.** ~*adj.* **2.** of or formed in the late Precambrian era.

protest *n.* (ˈprəʊtɛst). **1. a.** public, often organized, dissent or manifestation of such dissent. **b.** (*as modifier*): *a protest march.* **2.** a declaration or objection that is formal or solemn. **3.** an expression of disagreement or complaint: *without a squeak of protest.* **4. a.** a formal notarial statement drawn up on behalf of a creditor and declaring that the debtor has dishonoured a bill of exchange or promissory note. **b.** the action of drawing up such a statement. **c.** a formal declaration by a taxpayer disputing the legality or accuracy of his assessment. **5.** a statement made by the master of a vessel attesting to the circumstances in which his vessel was damaged or imperilled. **6.** the act of protesting. **7. under protest.** having voiced objections; unwillingly. ~*vb.* (prəˈtɛst). **8.** (when *intr.,* foll. by *against, at, about,* etc.; when *tr., may take a clause as object*) to make a strong objection (to something, esp. a supposed injustice or offence). **9.** (when *tr., may take a clause as object*) to assert or affirm in a formal or solemn manner. **10.** (when *tr., may take a clause as object*) to put up arguments against; disagree; complain; object: *"I'm okay," she protested; he protested that it was not his turn to wash up.* **11.** (*tr.*) *Chiefly U.S.* to object forcefully to: *leaflets protesting Dr King's murder.* **12.** (*tr.*) to declare formally that (a bill of exchange or promissory note) has been dishonoured. [C14: from Latin *prōtestārī* to make a formal declaration, from *prō-* before + *testārī* to assert] —**proˈtestant** *adj., n.* —**proˈtester** *or* **proˈtestor** *n.* —**proˈtestingly** *adv.*

Protestant (ˈprɒtɪstənt) *n.* **a.** an adherent of Protestantism. **b.** (*as modifier*): *the Protestant Church.*

Protestant Episcopal Church *n.* the full title of the **Episcopal Church.**

Protestantism (ˈprɒtɪstənˌtɪzəm) *n.* **1.** the religion or religious system of any of the Churches of Western Christendom that are separated from the Roman Catholic Church and adhere substantially to principles established by Luther, Calvin, etc., in the Reformation. **2.** the Protestant Churches collectively. **3.** adherence to the principles of the Reformation.

protestation (ˌprəʊtɛsˈteɪʃən) *n.* **1.** the act of protesting. **2.** something protested about. **3.** a strong declaration.

prothalamion (ˌprəʊθəˈleɪmɪən) *or* **prothalamium** *n., pl.* **-mia** (-mɪə). a song or poem in celebration of a marriage. [C16: from Greek *pro-* before + *thalamos* marriage; coined by Edmund Spenser, on the model of EPITHALAMION]

prothallus (prəʊˈθæləs) *or* **prothallium** (prəʊˈθælɪəm) *n., pl.* **-li** (-laɪ) *or* **-lia** (-lɪə). *Botany.* the small flat free-living green disc of tissue that bears the reproductive organs of pteridophytes. [C19: from New Latin, from *pro-* before + Greek *thallus* a young shoot] —**proˈthallic** *or* **proˈthallial** *adj.*

prothesis (ˈprɒθɪsɪs) *n.* **1.** a process in the development of a language by which a phoneme or syllable is prefixed to a word to facilitate pronunciation: *Latin "scala" gives Spanish "escala" by prothesis.* **2.** *Eastern Orthodox Church.* the solemn preparation of the Eucharistic elements before consecration. [C16: via Late Latin from Greek: a setting out in public, from *pro-* forth + *thesis* a placing] —**prothetic** (prəˈθɛtɪk) *adj.* —**proˈthetically** *adv.*

prothonotary (ˌprəʊθəˈnəʊtərɪ, -trɪ, prəʊˈθɒnə-) *or* **protonotary** *n., pl.* **-taries.** (formerly) a chief clerk in certain law courts. [C15: from Medieval Latin *prōthonotārius,* from *prōtho-* PROTO- + Late Latin *notārius* NOTARY] —**prothonotarial** (prəʊˌθɒnəˈtɛərɪəl) *or* **proˌtonoˈtarial** *adj.*

prothorax (prəʊˈθɔːræks) *n., pl.* **-thoraxes** *or* **-thoraces** (-ˈθɔːrəˌsiːz). the first segment of the thorax of an insect, which bears the first pair of walking legs. See also **mesothorax, metathorax.**

prothrombin (prəʊˈθrɒmbɪn) *n. Biochem.* a zymogen found in blood that gives rise to thrombin on activation. See also **phylloquinone.**

protist (ˈprəʊtɪst) *n.* any organism belonging to the kingdom *Protista,* including bacteria, protozoans, unicellular algae and fungi, regarded as distinct from plants and animals. [C19: from New Latin *Protista* most primitive organisms, from Greek *prōtistos* the very first, from *prōtos* first]

protium (ˈprəʊtɪəm) *n.* the most common isotope of hydrogen, having a mass number of 1. [C20: New Latin, from PROTO- + -IUM]

proto- *or sometimes before a vowel* **prot-** *combining form.* **1.** indicating the first in time, order, or rank: *protomartyr.* **2.** primitive, ancestral, or original: *prototype.* **3.** indicating the reconstructed earliest stage of a language: *Proto-Germanic.* **4.** indicating the first in a series of chemical compounds: *protoxide.* **5.** indicating the parent of a chemical compound or an element: *protactinium.* [from Greek *prōtos* first, from *pro* before; see PRO-[2]]

protoactinium (ˌprəʊtəʊækˈtɪnɪəm) *n.* the former name of **protactinium.**

protochordate (ˌprəʊtəʊˈkɔːdeɪt) *n.* **1.** any chordate animal of the subphyla *Hemichordata* (acorn worms), *Urochordata* (tunicates), and *Cephalochordata* (lancelets). ~*adj.* **2.** of or relating to protochordates.

protocol (ˈprəʊtəˌkɒl) *n.* **1.** the formal etiquette and code of behaviour, precedence, and procedure for state and diplomatic ceremonies. **2.** a memorandum or record of an agreement, esp. one reached in international negotiations, a meeting, etc. **3. a.** an amendment to a treaty or convention. **b.** an annexe appended to a treaty to deal with subsidiary matters or to render the treaty more lucid. **c.** a formal international agreement or understanding on some matter. **4.** *Philosophy.* In full: **protocol statement.** a statement that is immediately verifiable by experience. See **logical positivism.** **5.** *Computer technol.* the set form in which data must be presented for handling by a particular computer configuration. [C16: from Medieval Latin *prōtocollum,* from Late Greek *prōtokollon* sheet glued to the front of a manuscript, from PROTO- + *kolla* glue]

protogenic (ˌprəʊtəˈdʒɛnɪk) *adj. Chem.* (of a compound) able to donate a hydrogen ion (proton) in a chemical reaction.

Proto-Germanic *n.* the prehistoric unrecorded language that was the ancestor of all Germanic languages.

protogynous (prəʊˈtɒdʒɪnəs) *adj.* (of plants and hermaphrodite animals) producing female gametes before male ones. Compare **protandrous.** —**proˈtogyny** *n.*

protohistory (ˌprəʊtəʊˈhɪstərɪ, -ˈhɪstrɪ) *n.* the period or stage of human development or of a particular culture immediately prior to the emergence of writing. —**protohistoric** (ˌprəʊtəʊhɪˈstɒrɪk) *adj.*

protohuman (ˌprəʊtəʊˈhjuːmən) *n.* **1.** any of various prehistoric primates that resembled modern man. ~*adj.* **2.** of or relating to any of these primates.

Proto-Indo-European *n.* the prehistoric unrecorded language that was the ancestor of all Indo-European languages.

protolanguage (ˌprəʊtəʊˈlæŋgwɪdʒ) *n.* an extinct and unrecorded language reconstructed by comparison of its recorded or living descendants. Also called: **Ursprache.**

protolithic (ˌprəʊtəʊˈlɪθɪk) *adj.* of or referring to the earliest Stone Age.

protomartyr (ˌprəʊtəʊˈmɑːtə) *n.* **1.** St Stephen as the first Christian martyr. **2.** the first martyr to lay down his life in any cause.

protomorphic (ˌprəʊtəʊˈmɔːfɪk) *adj. Biology.* primitive in structure; primordial.

proton (ˈprəʊtɒn) *n.* a stable, positively charged elementary particle, found in atomic nuclei in numbers equal to the atomic number of the element. It is a baryon with a charge of 1.6022×10^{-19} coulomb, a rest mass of $1.672\,52 \times 10^{-27}$ kilogram, and spin ½. [C20: from Greek *prōtos* first]

protonema (ˌprəʊtəˈniːmə) *n., pl.* **-nemata** (-ˈniːmətə). a branched threadlike structure that grows from a moss spore and eventually develops into the moss plant. [C19: from New Latin, from PROTO- + Greek *nema* thread] —ˌ**protoˈnemal** *or* **protonematal** (ˌprəʊtəˈniːmətᵊl, -ˈnɛmətᵊl) *adj.*

protonic (prəʊˈtɒnɪk) *adj. Chem.* (of a solvent, such as water) able to donate hydrogen ions to solute molecules.

proton microscope *n.* a powerful type of microscope that uses a beam of protons, giving high resolution and sharp contrast.

proton number *n.* another name for **atomic number.** Symbol: *Z*

Proto-Norse *n.* the North Germanic language of Scandinavia up to about 700 A.D. See also **Old Norse.**

protopathic (ˌprəʊtəˈpæθɪk) *adj. Physiol.* **1.** of or relating to a sensory nerve that perceives only coarse stimuli, such as pain.

2. of or relating to such perception. [C20: from PROTO- + Greek *pathos* suffering, disease + -IC] —**protopathy** (prəʊˈtɒpəθɪ) *n.*
protophilic (ˌprəʊtəˈfɪlɪk) *adj. Chem.* having or involving an affinity for hydrogen ions (protons).
protoplasm (ˈprəʊtəˌplæzəm) *n. Biology.* the living contents of a cell: a complex translucent colourless colloidal substance differentiated into cytoplasm and nucleoplasm. [C19: from New Latin, from PROTO- + Greek *plasma* form] —ˌ**protoˈplasmic** *adj.*
protoplast (ˈprəʊtəˌplæst) *n.* a unit consisting of the living parts of a cell, including the protoplasm and cell membrane but not the vacuoles or (in plants) the cell wall. [C16: from Late Latin *prōtoplastus* the first-formed, from Greek *prōtoplastos,* from PROTO- + *plassein* to shape] —ˌ**protoˈplastic** *adj.*
protoporphyrin (ˌprəʊtəʊˈpɔːfɪrɪn) *n.* a type of porphyrin that, when combined with an iron atom, forms haem, the oxygen-bearing prosthetic group of the red blood pigment haemoglobin.
Protosemitic (ˌprəʊtəʊsɪˈmɪtɪk) *n.* the hypothetical parent language of the Semitic group of languages.
protostar (ˈprəʊtəʊˌstɑː) *n.* a condensation, interstellar gas, or dust, from which a star is thought to develop.
protostele (ˈprəʊtəˌstiːl, -ˌstiːlɪ) *n.* a simple type of stele with a central core of xylem surrounded by a cylinder of phloem: occurs in most roots and the stems of ferns, etc. —ˌ**protoˈstelic** *adj.*
prototherian (ˌprəʊtəʊˈθɪərɪən) *adj.* **1.** of, relating to, or belonging to the *Prototheria,* a subclass of mammals that includes the monotremes. ~*n.* **2.** any prototherian mammal; a monotreme. ~Compare **eutherian, metatherian.** [C19: New Latin, from PROTO- + Greek *theria* wild animals]
prototrophic (ˌprəʊtəˈtrɒfɪk) *adj.* **1.** (esp. of bacteria) feeding solely on inorganic matter. **2.** (of cultured bacteria, fungi, etc.) having no specific food requirements.
prototype (ˈprəʊtəˌtaɪp) *n.* **1.** one of the first units manufactured of a product, which is tested so that the design can be changed if necessary before the product is manufactured commercially. **2.** a person or thing that serves as an example of a type. **3.** *Biology.* the ancestral or primitive form of a species or other group; an archetype. —ˌ**protoˈtypal, prototypic** (ˌprəʊtəˈtɪpɪk), *or* ˌ**protoˈtypical** *adj.*
protoxide (prəʊˈtɒksaɪd) *n.* the oxide of an element that contains the smallest amount of oxygen of any of its oxides.
protoxylem (ˌprəʊtəˈzaɪləm) *n.* the first-formed xylem tissue, consisting of extensible thin-walled cells thickened with rings or spirals of lignin. Compare **metaxylem.**
protozoan (ˌprəʊtəˈzəʊən) *n., pl.* **-zoa** (-ˈzəʊə) *or* **-zoans. 1.** Also called: **protozoon** (ˌprəʊtəˈzəʊɒn), *pl.* **-zoa.** any minute invertebrate of the phylum *Protozoa,* including flagellates, ciliates, sporozoans, amoebas, and foraminifers. ~*adj. also* ˌ**protoˈzoic. 2.** of, relating to, or belonging to the *Protozoa.* [C19: via New Latin from Greek PROTO- + *zoion* animal]
protozoology (ˌprəʊtəʊzəʊˈɒlədʒɪ) *n.* the branch of zoology concerned with the study of protozoans. —**protozoological** (ˌprəʊtəʊˌzəʊəˈlɒdʒɪkᵊl) *adj.* —ˌ**protozoˈologist** *n.*
protract (prəˈtrækt) *vb. (tr.)* **1.** to lengthen or extend (a speech, etc.); prolong in time. **2.** (of a muscle) to draw, thrust, or extend (a part, etc.) forwards. **3.** to plot or draw using a protractor and scale. [C16: from Latin *prōtrahere* to prolong, from PRO-¹ + *trahere* to drag] —**proˈtractedly** *adv.* —**proˈtractedness** *n.* —**proˈtractive** *adj.*
protractile (prəˈtræktaɪl) *or (less commonly)* **protractible** *adj.* able to be extended or protruded: *protractile muscle.*
protraction (prəˈtrækʃən) *n.* **1.** the act or process of protracting. **2.** the state or condition of being protracted. **3.** a prolongation or protrusion. **4.** an extension of something in time or space. **5.** something that is extended in time or space. **6.** the irregular lengthening of a syllable that is usually short.
protractor (prəˈtræktə) *n.* **1.** an instrument for measuring or drawing angles on paper, usually a flat semicircular transparent plastic sheet graduated in degrees. **2.** a person or thing that protracts. **3.** a surgical instrument for removing a bullet from the body. **4.** *Anatomy.* a former term for **extensor.**
protrude (prəˈtruːd) *vb.* **1.** to thrust or cause to thrust forwards or outwards. **2.** to project or cause to project from or as if from a surface. [C17: from Latin, from PRO-² + *trudere* to thrust] —**proˈtrudable** *adj.* —**proˈtrudent** *adj.*
protrusile (prəˈtruːsaɪl) *adj. Zoology.* capable of being thrust forwards: *protrusile jaws.* Also: **projectile.**
protrusion (prəˈtruːʒən) *n.* **1.** something that protrudes. **2.** the state or condition of being protruded. **3.** the act or process of protruding.
protrusive (prəˈtruːsɪv) *adj.* **1.** tending to project or jut outwards. **2.** a less common word for **obtrusive. 3.** *Archaic.* causing propulsion. —**proˈtrusively** *adv.* —**proˈtrusiveness** *n.*
protuberant (prəˈtjuːbərənt) *adj.* swelling out from the surrounding surface; bulging. [C17: from Late Latin *prōtūberāre* to swell, from PRO-¹ + *tūber* swelling] —**proˈtuberance** *or* **proˈtuberancy** *n.* —**proˈtuberantly** *adv.*
protuberate (prəˈtjuːbəˌreɪt) *vb. (intr.) Rare.* to swell out or project from the surrounding surface; bulge out.
protyle (ˈprəʊtaɪl) *or* **protyl** (ˈprəʊtɪl) *n.* a hypothetical primitive substance from which the chemical elements were supposed to have been formed. [C19: from Greek *prōt-* PROTO- + *hylē* substance]
proud (praʊd) *adj.* **1.** (foll. by *of,* an infinitive, or a clause) pleased or satisfied, as with oneself, one's possessions, achievements, etc, or with another person, his or her achievements, qualities, etc. **2.** feeling honoured or gratified by or as if by some distinction. **3.** having an inordinately high opinion of oneself; arrogant or haughty. **4.** characterized by or proceeding from a sense of pride: *a proud moment.* **5.** having a proper sense of self-respect. **6.** stately or distinguished. **7.** bold or fearless. **8.** (of a surface, edge, etc.) projecting or protruding from the surrounding area. **9.** (of animals) restive or excited, esp. sexually; in heat. ~*adv.* **10. do (someone) proud. a.** to entertain (someone) on a grand scale: *they did us proud at the hotel.* **b.** to honour or distinguish (a person): *his honesty did him proud.* [Late Old English *prūd,* from Old French *prud, prod* brave, from Late Latin *prōde* useful, from Latin *prōdesse* to be of value, from *prōd-,* variant of *prō-* for + *esse* to be] —ˈ**proudly** *adv.* —ˈ**proudness** *n.*
proud flesh *n.* a nontechnical name for **granulation tissue.** [C14: from PROUD (in the sense: swollen, protruding)]
Proustian (ˈpruːstɪən) *adj.* **1.** of or relating to Marcel Proust (1871–1922), French novelist, or to his works or his style. ~*n.* **2.** an admirer of Marcel Proust's works.
proustite (ˈpruːstaɪt) *n.* a red mineral consisting of silver arsenic sulphide in hexagonal crystalline form. Formula: Ag_3AsS_3. [C19: from French, named after J. L. *Proust* (1754–1826), French chemist]
prov. *abbrev. for:* **1.** province. **2.** provincial. **3.** provisional.
Prov. *abbrev. for:* **1.** Provençal. **2.** *Bible.* Proverbs. **3.** Province. **4.** Provost.
prove (pruːv) *vb.* **proves, proving, proved; proved** *or* **proven.** *(mainly tr.)* **1.** *(may take a clause as object or an infinitive)* to establish or demonstrate the truth or validity of; verify, esp. by using an established sequence of procedures or statements. **2.** to establish the quality of, esp. by experiment or scientific analysis. **3.** *Law.* to establish the validity and genuineness of (a will). **4.** to show (oneself) able or courageous. **5.** *(copula)* to be found or shown (to be): *this has proved useless; he proved to be invaluable.* **6.** *Printing.* to take a trial impression of (type, etc.). **7.** *(intr.)* (of dough) to rise in a warm place before baking. **8.** *Archaic.* to undergo. [C12: from Old French *prover,* from Latin *probāre* to test, from *probus* honest] —ˈ**provable** *adj.* —ˌ**provaˈbility** *n.* —ˈ**provably** *adv.*
proven (ˈpruːvᵊn) *vb.* **1.** a past participle of **prove. 2.** See **not proven.** ~*adj.* **3.** tried; tested: *a proven method.* —ˈ**provenly** *adv.*
provenance (ˈprɒvɪnəns) *or (chiefly U.S.)* **provenience** (prəʊˈviːnɪəns) *n.* a place of origin, esp. that of a work of art or archaeological specimen. [C19: from French, from *provenir,* from Latin *prōvenīre* to originate, from *venīre* to come]
Provençal (ˌprɒvɒnˈsɑːl; *French* prɔvɑ̃sal) *adj.* **1.** relating to, denoting, or characteristic of Provence, a former province of SE France, its inhabitants, their dialect of French, or their Romance language. ~*n.* **2.** a language of Provence, closely related to Catalan, French, and Italian, belonging to the Romance group of the Indo-European family. It was important in the Middle Ages as a literary language, and attempts have been made since the 19th century to revive its literary status. See also **langue d'oc. 3.** a native or inhabitant of Provence.
Provençale (ˌprɒvɒnˈsɑːl; *French* prɔvɑ̃sal) *adj.* (of dishes) prepared with garlic, oil, and often tomatoes.
provender (ˈprɒvɪndə) *n.* **1.** any dry feed or fodder for domestic livestock. **2.** food in general. [C14: from Old French *provendre,* from Late Latin *praebenda* grant, from Latin *praebēre* to proffer; influenced also by Latin *prōvidēre* to look after]
proventriculus (ˌprəʊvɛnˈtrɪkjʊləs) *n., pl.* **-triculi** (-ˈtrɪkjʊˌlaɪ). **1.** the first part of the stomach of birds, the gizzard. **2.** the thick muscular stomach of crustaceans and insects; gizzard. [C19: from New Latin, from Latin PRO-¹ + *ventriculus* little belly, from *venter* belly] —ˌ**provenˈtricular** *adj.*
proverb (ˈprɒvɜːb) *n.* **1.** a short, memorable, and often highly condensed saying embodying, esp. with bold imagery, some commonplace fact of experience. **2.** a person or thing exemplary in respect of a characteristic: *Antarctica is a proverb for extreme cold.* **3.** *Ecclesiast.* a wise saying or admonition providing guidance. ~*vb. (tr.)* **4.** to utter or describe (something) in the form of a proverb. **5.** to make (something) a proverb. [C14: via Old French from Latin *prōverbium,* from *verbum* word]
proverbial (prəˈvɜːbɪəl) *adj.* **1.** *(prenominal)* commonly or traditionally referred to, esp. as being an example of some peculiarity, characteristic, etc. **2.** of, connected with, embodied in, or resembling a proverb. —**proˈverbially** *adv.*
provide (prəˈvaɪd) *vb. (mainly tr.)* **1.** to put at the disposal of; furnish or supply. **2.** to afford; yield: *this meeting provides an opportunity to talk.* **3.** *(intr.;* often foll. by *for* or *against)* to take careful precautions (over): *he provided against financial ruin by wise investment.* **4.** *(intr.;* foll. by *for)* to supply means of support (to), esp. financially: *he provides for his family.* **5.** (in statutes,

documents, etc.) to determine (what is to happen in certain contingencies), esp. by including a proviso condition. **6.** to confer and induct into ecclesiastical offices. **7.** *Now rare.* to have or get in store: *in summer many animals provide their winter food.* [C15: from Latin *prōvidēre* to provide for, from *prō-* beforehand + *vidēre* to see] —**proˈvider** *n.*

providence (ˈprɒvɪdəns) *n.* **1. a.** *Christianity.* God's foreseeing protection and care of his creatures. **b.** such protection and care as manifest by some other force. **2.** a supposed manifestation of such care and guidance. **3.** the foresight or care exercised by a person in the management of his affairs or resources.

Providence (ˈprɒvɪdəns) *n. Christianity.* God, esp. as showing foreseeing care and protection of his creatures. [C14: via French from Latin *prōvidentia,* from *prōvidēre* to provide; see PROVIDE, -ENCE]

provident (ˈprɒvɪdənt) *adj.* **1.** providing for future needs. **2.** exercising foresight in the management of one's affairs or resources. **3.** characterized by or proceeding from foresight. [C15: from Latin *prōvidens* foreseeing, from *prōvidēre* to PROVIDE] —ˈ**providently** *adv.*

provident club *n. Brit.* a hire-purchase system offered by some large retail organizations.

providential (ˌprɒvɪˈdenʃəl) *adj.* relating to, characteristic of, or presumed to proceed from or as if from divine providence. —ˌ**proviˈdentially** *adv.*

provident society *n.* another name for **friendly society.**

providing (prəˈvaɪdɪŋ) *or* **provided** *conj.* (*subordinating;* sometimes foll. by *that*) on the condition or understanding (that): *I'll play, providing you pay me.*

province (ˈprɒvɪns) *n.* **1.** a territory governed as a unit of a country or empire. **2.** a district, territory, or region. **3.** (*pl.;* usually preceded by *the*) those parts of a country lying outside the capital and other large cities and regarded as outside the mainstream of sophisticated culture. **4.** *Ecology.* a subdivision of a region, characterized by a particular fauna and flora. **5.** an area or branch of learning, activity, etc. **6.** the field or extent of a person's activities or office. **7.** *R.C. Church, Church of England.* an ecclesiastical territory, usually consisting of several dioceses, and having an archbishop or metropolitan at its head. **8.** a major administrative and territorial subdivision of a religious order. **9.** *History.* a region of the Roman Empire outside Italy ruled by a governor from Rome. [C14: from Old French, from Latin *prōvincia* conquered territory]

provincewide (ˈprɒvɪnsˌwaɪd) *Canadian.* ~*adj.* **1.** covering or available to the whole of a province: *a provincewide referendum.* ~*adv.* **2.** throughout a province: *an advertising campaign to go provincewide.*

provincial (prəˈvɪnʃəl) *adj.* **1.** of or connected with a province. **2.** characteristic of or connected with the provinces; local. **3.** having attitudes and opinions supposedly common to people living in the provinces; rustic or unsophisticated; limited. **4.** *N.Z.* denoting a football team representing a province, one of the historical administrative areas of New Zealand. ~*n.* **5.** a person lacking the sophistications of city life; rustic or narrow-minded individual. **6.** a person coming from or resident in a province or the provinces. **7.** the head of an ecclesiastical province. **8.** the head of a major territorial subdivision of a religious order. —**provinciality** (prəˌvɪnʃɪˈælɪtɪ) *n.* —**proˈvincially** *adv.*

provincialism (prəˈvɪnʃəˌlɪzəm) *n.* **1.** narrowness of mind or outlook; lack of sophistication. **2.** a word or attitude characteristic of a provincial. **3.** attention to the affairs of one's province rather than the whole nation. **4.** the state or quality of being provincial. ~Also called: **localism.**

proving ground *n.* a place or situation in which something new, such as equipment or a theory, can be tested.

provirus (ˈprəʊˌvaɪrəs) *n.* the inactive form of a virus in a host cell.

provision (prəˈvɪʒən) *n.* **1.** the act of supplying or providing food, etc. **2.** something that is supplied or provided. **3.** preparations made beforehand (esp. in the phrase **make provision for**). **4.** (*pl.*) food and other necessities, esp. for an expedition. **5.** (*pl.*) food obtained for a household. **6.** a demand, condition, or stipulation formally incorporated in a document; proviso. **7.** the conferring of and induction into ecclesiastical offices. ~*vb.* **8.** (*tr.*) to supply with provisions. [C14: from Latin *prōvīsiō* a providing; see PROVIDE] —**proˈvisioner** *n.*

provisional (prəˈvɪʒənᵊl) *or* (*less commonly*) **provisionary** (prəˈvɪʒənərɪ) *adj.* **1.** subject to later alteration; temporary or conditional: *a provisional decision.* ~*n.* **2.** a postage stamp surcharged during an emergency to alter the stamp's denomination or significance until a new or regular issue is printed. —**proˈvisionally** *adv.*

Provisional (prəˈvɪʒənᵊl) *n.* a member of the Provisional IRA or Sinn Féin, factions of either of these organizations following a policy of terrorism to achieve Irish unity. Also called: **Provo.** Compare **Official.**

proviso (prəˈvaɪzəʊ) *n., pl.* **-sos** *or* **-soes. 1.** a clause in a document or contract that embodies a condition or stipulation. **2.** a condition or stipulation. [C15: from Medieval Latin phrase *prōvīsō quod* it being provided that, from Latin *prōvīsus* provided]

provisory (prəˈvaɪzərɪ) *adj.* **1.** containing a proviso; conditional. **2.** another word for **provisional.** —**proˈvisorily** *adv.*

provitamin (prəʊˈvɪtəmɪn) *n.* a substance, such as carotene, that is converted into a vitamin in animal tissues.

Provo (ˈprəʊvəʊ) *n., pl.* **-vos.** another name for a **Provisional.**

provocation (ˌprɒvəˈkeɪʃən) *n.* **1.** the act of provoking or inciting. **2.** something that causes indignation, anger, etc. **3.** *English criminal law.* words or conduct that incite a person to attack another with fatal results.

provocative (prəˈvɒkətɪv) *adj.* acting as a stimulus or incitement, esp. to anger or sexual desire; provoking: *a provocative look; a provocative remark.* —**proˈvocatively** *adv.* —**proˈvocativeness** *n.*

provoke (prəˈvəʊk) *vb.* (*tr.*) **1.** to anger or infuriate. **2.** to cause to act or behave in a certain manner; incite or stimulate. **3.** to promote (certain feelings, esp. anger, indignation, etc.) in a person. **4.** *Obsolete.* to summon. [C15: from Latin *prōvocāre* to call forth, from *vocāre* to call] —**proˈvoking** *adj.* —**proˈvokingly** *adv.*

provolone (ˌprəʊvəˈləʊnɪ) *n.* a mellow, pale yellow, soft, and sometimes smoked cheese, made of cow's milk: usually moulded in the shape of a pear. [Italian, from *provola,* apparently from Medieval Latin *probula* cheese made from buffalo milk]

provost (ˈprɒvəst) *n.* **1.** an appointed person who superintends or presides. **2.** the head of certain university colleges or schools. **3.** (in Scotland) the chairman and civic head of certain district councils or (formerly) of a burgh council. Compare **convener** (sense 2). **4.** *Church of England.* the senior dignitary of one of the more recent cathedral foundations. **5.** *R.C. Church.* **a.** the head of a cathedral chapter in England and some other countries. **b.** (formerly) the member of a monastic community second in authority under the abbot. **6.** (in medieval times) an overseer, steward, or bailiff in a manor. **7.** *Obsolete.* a prison warder. **8.** (prəˈvəʊ). *Brit. and Canadian military.* a military policeman. [Old English *profost,* from Medieval Latin *prōpositus* placed at the head (of), from Latin *praepōnere* to place first, from *prae-* before + *pōnere* to put]

provost court (prəˈvəʊ) *n.* a military court for trying people charged with minor offences in an occupied area.

provost guard (prəˈvəʊ) *n.* (esp. in the U.S.) a detachment under command of the provost marshal.

provost marshal (prəˈvəʊ) *n.* the officer in charge of military police and thus responsible for military discipline in a large camp, area, or city.

prow (praʊ) *n.* the bow of a vessel. [C16: from Old French *proue,* from Latin *prora,* from Greek *prōra;* related to Latin *pro* in front]

prowess (ˈpraʊɪs) *n.* **1.** outstanding or superior skill or ability. **2.** bravery or fearlessness, esp. in battle. [C13: from Old French *proesce,* from *prou* good; see PROUD]

prowl (praʊl) *vb.* **1.** (when *intr.,* often foll. by *around* or *about*) to move stealthily around (a place) as if in search of prey or plunder. ~*n.* **2.** the act of prowling. **3. on the prowl. a.** moving around stealthily. **b.** zealously pursuing members of the opposite sex. [C14 *prollen,* of unknown origin] —ˈ**prowler** *n.*

prox. *abbrev. for* proximo (next month).

proxemics (prɒkˈsiːmɪks) *n.* (*functioning as sing.*) the study of spatial interrelationships in humans or in populations of animals of the same species.

Proxima (ˈprɒksɪmə) *n.* a flare star in the constellation Centaurus that is the nearest star to the sun. It is a red dwarf of very low magnitude. Distance: 4.3 light years. Also called: **Proxima Centauri.** See also **Rigil Kent.**

proximal (ˈprɒksɪməl) *adj.* **1.** *Anatomy.* situated close to the centre, median line, or point of attachment or origin. Compare **distal. 2.** another word for **proximate.** —ˈ**proximally** *adv.*

proximate (ˈprɒksɪmɪt) *or* **proximal** *adj.* **1.** next or nearest in space or time. **2.** very near; close. **3.** immediately preceding or following in a series. **4.** a less common word for **approximate.** [C16: from Late Latin *proximāre* to draw near, from Latin *proximus* next, from *prope* near] —ˈ**proximately** *adv.* —ˈ**proximateness** *n.* —ˌ**proxiˈmation** *n.*

proxime accessit (ˈprɒksɪmɪ ækˈsesɪt) *n.* the person coming next after the winner in a competitive examination or an academic prize giving; runner-up. [Latin: he came next]

proximity (prɒkˈsɪmɪtɪ) *n.* **1.** nearness in space or time. **2.** nearness or closeness in a series. [C15: from Latin *proximitās* closeness; see PROXIMATE]

proximity fuse *n.* an electronically triggered device designed to detonate an explosive charge in a missile, etc., at a predetermined distance from the target.

proximo (ˈprɒksɪməʊ) *adv. Now rare except when abbreviated in formal correspondence.* in or during the next or coming month: *a letter of the seventh proximo.* Abbrev.: **prox.** Compare **instant, ultimo.** [C19: from Latin: in or on the next, from *proximus* next]

proxy (ˈprɒksɪ) *n., pl.* **proxies. 1.** a person authorized to act on behalf of someone else; agent: *to vote by proxy.* **2.** the authority, esp. in the form of a document, given to a person to act on behalf

ˈ**proˈwar** *adj.*

of someone else. [C15 *prokesye,* contraction of *procuracy,* from Latin *prōcūrātiō* procuration; see PROCURE]

prs *abbrev. for* pairs.

PRT *abbrev. for* petroleum revenue tax.

prude (pruːd) *n.* a person who affects or shows an excessively modest, prim, or proper attitude, esp. regarding sex. [C18: from French, from *prudefemme,* from Old French *prode femme* respectable woman; see PROUD] —**'prudish** *adj.* —**'prudishly** *adv.* —**'prudishness** *or* **'prudery** *n.*

prudence ('pruːdəns) *n.* **1.** caution in practical affairs; discretion or circumspection. **2.** care taken in the management of one's resources. **3.** consideration for one's own interests. **4.** the condition or quality of being prudent.

prudent ('pruːdᵊnt) *adj.* **1.** discreet or cautious in managing one's activities; circumspect. **2.** practical and careful in providing for the future. **3.** exercising good judgment or common sense. [C14: from Latin *prūdēns* far-sighted, contraction of *prōvidens* acting with foresight; see PROVIDENT] —**'prudently** *adv.*

prudential (pruː'dɛnʃəl) *adj.* **1.** characterized by or resulting from prudence. **2.** exercising prudence or sound judgment. —**pru'dentially** *adv.*

pruinose ('pruːɪˌnəʊs, -ˌnəʊz) *adj. Botany.* coated with a powdery or waxy bloom. [C19: from Latin *pruīnōsus* frost-covered, from *pruīna* hoarfrost]

prune¹ (pruːn) *n.* **1.** a purplish-black partially dried fruit of any of several varieties of plum tree. **2.** *Slang, chiefly Brit.* a dull, uninteresting, or foolish person. [C14: from Old French *prune,* from Latin *prūnum* plum, from Greek *prounon*]

prune² (pruːn) *vb.* **1.** to remove (dead or superfluous twigs, branches, etc.) from (a tree, shrub, etc.), esp. by cutting off. **2.** to remove (anything undesirable or superfluous) from (a book, etc.). [C15: from Old French *proignier* to clip, probably from *provigner* to prune vines, from *provain* layer (of a plant,) from Latin *propāgo* a cutting] —**'prunable** *adj.* —**'pruner** *n.*

prune³ (pruːn) *vb.* an archaic word for **preen.**

prunella¹ (pruː'nɛlə), **prunelle** (pruː'nɛl), *or* **prunello** (pruː'nɛləʊ) *n.* a strong fabric, esp. a twill-weave worsted, used for gowns and the uppers of some shoes. [C17: perhaps from PRUNELLE, with reference to the colour of the cloth]

prunella² (pruː'nɛlə) *n.* See **selfheal.** [New Latin, altered from *brunella,* from German *Braüne* quinsy, which it was thought to cure]

prunelle (pruː'nɛl) *n.* a green French liqueur made from sloes. [C18: from French: a little plum, from *prune* PRUNE¹]

pruning hook *n.* a tool with a curved steel blade terminating in a hook, used for pruning.

prurient ('prʊərɪənt) *adj.* **1.** unusually or morbidly interested in sexual thoughts or practices. **2.** exciting or encouraging lustfulness; erotic. [C17: from Latin *prūrīre* to itch, to lust after] —**'prurience** *n.* —**'pruriently** *adv.*

prurigo (prʊə'raɪgəʊ) *n.* a chronic inflammatory disease of the skin characterized by the formation of papules and intense itching. [C19: from Latin: an itch] —**pruriginous** (prʊə'rɪdʒɪnəs) *adj.*

pruritus (prʊə'raɪtəs) *n. Pathol.* **1.** any intense sensation of itching. **2.** any of various conditions characterized by intense itching. [C17: from Latin: an itching; see PRURIENT] —**pruritic** (prʊə'rɪtɪk) *adj.*

Prus. *abbrev. for* Prussia(n).

prusik ('prʌsɪk) *n. Mountaineering.* **1.** Also: **prusik knot.** a sliding knot that locks under pressure and can be used to form a loop (**prusik loop**) in which a climber can place his foot in order to stand or ascend a rope. ~*vb.* **-siks, -siking, -siked.** (*intr.*) **2.** to climb (up a standing rope) using prusik loops. [C20: named after Dr *Prusik,* Austrian climber who devised the knot]

Prussian ('prʌʃən) *adj.* **1.** of, relating to, or characteristic of Prussia, a former state in N Germany, or its people, esp. of the Junkers and their formal military tradition. ~*n.* **2.** a German native or inhabitant of Prussia. **3.** a member of a Baltic people formerly inhabiting the coastal area of the SE Baltic. **4.** See **Old Prussian.**

Prussian blue *n.* **1.** any of a number of blue pigments containing ferrocyanide or ferricyanide ions. **2. a.** the blue or deep greenish-blue colour of this pigment. **b.** (*as adj.*): *a Prussian-blue carpet.*

Prussianism ('prʌʃəˌnɪzəm) *n.* the ethos of the Prussian state and aristocracy, esp. militarism and stern discipline.

Prussianize *or* **Prussianise** ('prʌʃəˌnaɪz) *vb.* (*tr.*) to make Prussian in character, esp. with respect to military matters. —**ˌPrussiani'zation** *or* **ˌPrussiani'sation** *n.*

prussiate ('prʌʃɪɪt) *n.* any cyanide, ferrocyanide, or ferricyanide.

prussic acid ('prʌsɪk) *n.* the weakly acidic extremely poisonous aqueous solution of hydrogen cyanide. [C18: from French *acide prussique* Prussian acid, so called because obtained from Prussian blue]

pry¹ (praɪ) *vb.* **pries, prying, pried.** **1.** (*intr.;* often foll. by *into*) to make an impertinent or uninvited inquiry (about a private matter, topic, etc.). ~*n., pl.* **pries.** **2.** the act of prying. **3.** a person who pries. [C14: of unknown origin]

pry² (praɪ) *vb.* **pries, prying, pried.** the U.S. and Canadian word for **prise.** [C14: of unknown origin]

pryer ('praɪə) *n.* a variant spelling of **prier.**

prytaneum (ˌprɪtə'niːəm) *n., pl.* **-nea** (-'niːə). the public hall of a city in ancient Greece. [Latin, from Greek *prutaneion,* from *prutanis, prutaneus*]

Przewalski's horse (ˌpɜːʒə'vælskɪz) *n.* a rare wild horse, *Equus przewalskii,* of W Mongolia, having an erect mane and no forelock. [C19: named after the Russian explorer Nikolai Mikhailovich *Przewalski* (1839–1888), who discovered it]

PS *abbrev. for:* **1.** Passenger Steamer. **2.** phrase structure. **3.** Police Sergeant. **4.** Also: **ps.** postscript. **5.** private secretary. **6.** prompt side.

ps. *abbrev. for* pieces.

Ps. *or* **Psa.** *Bible. abbrev. for* Psalm.

PSA *abbrev. for:* **1.** (in Britain) Property Services Agency. **2.** (in New Zealand) Public Service Association.

psalm (sɑːm) *n.* **1.** (*often cap.*) any of the 150 sacred songs, lyric poems, and prayers that together constitute a book (Psalms) of the Old Testament. **2.** a musical setting of one of these poems. **3.** any sacred song or hymn. [Old English, from Late Latin *psalmus,* from Greek *psalmos* song accompanied on the harp, from *psallein* to play (the harp)] —**'psalmic** *adj.*

psalmist ('sɑːmɪst) *n.* the composer of a psalm or psalms, esp. (when *cap.* and preceded by *the*) David, traditionally regarded as the author of The Book of Psalms.

psalmody ('sɑːmədɪ, 'sæl-) *n., pl.* **-dies.** **1.** the act of singing psalms or hymns. **2.** the art or practice of the setting to music or singing of psalms. [C14: via Late Latin from Greek *psalmōdia* singing accompanied by a harp, from *psalmos* (see PSALM) + *ōidē* ODE] —**'psalmodist** *n.* —**psalmodic** (sɑː'mɒdɪk, sæl-) *adj.*

Psalter ('sɔːltə) *n.* **1.** the Book of Psalms, esp. in the version in the Book of Common Prayer. **2.** a translation, musical, or metrical version of the Psalms. **3.** a devotional or liturgical book containing a version of Psalms, often with a musical setting. [Old English *psaltere,* from Late Latin *psaltērium,* from Greek *psaltērion* stringed instrument, from *psallein* to play a stringed instrument]

psalterium (sɔːl'tɪərɪəm) *n., pl.* **-teria** (-'tɪərɪə). the third compartment of the stomach of ruminants, between the reticulum and abomasum. Also called: **omasum.** [C19: from Latin *psaltērium* PSALTER; from the similarity of its folds to the pages of a book]

psaltery ('sɔːltərɪ) *n., pl.* **-teries.** *Music.* an ancient stringed instrument similar to the lyre, but having a trapezoidal sounding board over which the strings are stretched. [Old English: see PSALTER]

psammite ('sæmaɪt) *n.* a rare name for **sandstone.** [C19: from Greek *psammos* sand] —**psammitic** (sæ'mɪtɪk) *adj.*

p's and q's *pl. n.* behaviour within social conventions; manners (esp. in the phrase **to mind one's p's and q's**). [altered from *p(lea)se and (than)k-you's*]

PSBR (in Britain) *abbrev. for* public sector borrowing requirement: the excess of government expenditure over receipts (mainly from taxation) that has to be financed by borrowing from the banks or the public.

psephite ('siːfaɪt) *n.* any rock, such as a breccia, that consists of large fragments embedded in a finer matrix. [C19: via French from Greek *psēphos* a pebble] —**psephitic** (siː'fɪtɪk) *adj.*

psephology (sɛ'fɒlədʒɪ) *n.* the statistical and sociological study of elections. [C20: from Greek *psephos* pebble, vote + -LOGY, from the ancient Greeks' custom of voting with pebbles] —**psephological** (ˌsɛfə'lɒdʒɪkᵊl) *adj.* —**ˌpsepho'logically** *adv.* —**pse'phologist** *n.*

pseud (sjuːd) *n.* **1.** *Informal.* a false, artificial, or pretentious person. ~*adj.* **2.** another word for **pseudo.**

pseud. *abbrev. for* pseudonym.

pseudaxis (sjuː'dæksɪs) *n. Botany.* another name for **sympodium.**

Pseudepigrapha (ˌsjuːdɪ'pɪgrəfə) *pl. n.* various Jewish writings from the first century B.C. to the first century A.D. that claim to have been divinely revealed but which have been excluded from the Greek canon of the Old Testament. Also called (R.C. Church): **Apocrypha.** [C17: from Greek *pseudepigraphos* falsely entitled, from PSEUDO- + *epigraphein* to inscribe] —**Pseudepigraphic** (ˌsjuːdɛpɪ'græfɪk), **ˌPseudepi'graphical,** *or* **ˌPseude'pigraphous** *adj.*

pseudo ('sjuːdəʊ) *adj. Informal.* not genuine; pretended.

pseudo- *or sometimes before a vowel* **pseud-** *combining form.* **1.** false, pretending, or unauthentic: *pseudo-intellectual.* **2.** having a close resemblance to: *pseudopodium.* [from Greek *pseudēs* false, from *pseudein* to lie]

pseudoarthrosis (ˌsjuːdəʊɑː'θrəʊsɪs) *or* **pseudarthrosis** (ˌsjuːdɑː'θrəʊsɪs) *n., pl.* **-ses** (-siːz). a joint formed by fibrous tissue bridging the gap between the two fragments of bone of an old fracture that have not united. Nontechnical names: **false joint, false ankylosis.** Also called: **nearthrosis.**

ˌpseudoan'tique *adj.*
ˌpseudoar'chaic *adj.*
ˌpseudoˌaristo'cratic *adj.*
ˌpseudoar'tistic *adj.*
ˌpseudoˌbio'graphic *or* **ˌpseudoˌbio'graphical** *adj.*

pseudocarp ('sjuːdəʊˌkɑːp) *n.* a fruit, such as the strawberry and apple, that includes parts other than the ripened ovary. Also called: **false fruit, accessory fruit.** —ˌ**pseudo'carpous** *adj.*
pseudocopulation (ˌsjuːdəʊˌkɒpjʊ'leɪʃən) *n. Botany.* pollination of plants, esp. orchids, by male insects while attempting to mate with flowers that resemble the female insect.
pseudocyesis (ˌsjuːdəʊsaɪ'iːsɪs) *n., pl.* **-ces** (-siːz). the technical name for **phantom pregnancy.**
pseudohermaphroditism (ˌsjuːdəʊhɜː'mæfrədaɪˌtɪzəm) *n.* the congenital condition of having the organs of reproduction of one sex and the external genitalia, usually malformed, of the opposite sex. Compare **hermaphroditism.**
pseudo-intransitive *adj.* denoting an occurrence of a normally transitive verb in which a direct object is not explicitly stated or forms the subject of the sentence, as in *Margaret is cooking* or *these apples cook well.*
pseudomonas (sjuː'dɒmənəs) *n., pl.* **pseudomonades** (ˌsjuːdəʊ'mɒnədiːz). any of a genus of rodlike Gram-negative bacteria that live in soil and decomposing organic matter: many species are pathogenic to plants and a few are pathogenic to man. [C20: from New Latin, from PSEUDO- + Greek *monas* unit]
pseudomorph ('sjuːdəʊˌmɔːf) *n.* a mineral that has an uncharacteristic crystalline form as a result of assuming the shape of another mineral that it has replaced. —ˌ**pseudo'morphic** *or* ˌ**pseudo'morphous** *adj.* —ˌ**pseudo'morphism** *n.*
pseudomutuality (ˌsjuːdəʊˌmjuːtjʊ'ælɪtɪ) *n., pl.* **-ties.** *Psychol.* a relationship between two persons in which conflict of views or opinions is solved by simply ignoring it.
pseudonym ('sjuːdəˌnɪm) *n.* a fictitious name adopted, esp. by an author. [C19: via French from Greek *pseudōnumon*] —ˌ**pseudo'nymity** *n.*
pseudonymous (sjuː'dɒnɪməs) *adj.* **1.** having or using a false or assumed name. **2.** writing or having been written under a pseudonym. —**pseu'donymously** *adv.*
pseudopodium (ˌsjuːdəʊ'pəʊdɪəm) *n., pl.* **-dia** (-dɪə). a temporary projection from the cell of a protozoan, leucocyte, etc., used for feeding and locomotion.
pseudoscalar (ˌsjuːdəʊ'skeɪlə) *n. Maths.* a variable quantity that has magnitude but not direction and is an odd function of the coordinates. Compare **pseudovector, scalar** (sense 1), **tensor** (sense 2), **vector** (sense 1).
pseudovector (ˌsjuːdəʊ'vɛktə) *n. Maths.* a variable quantity, such as angular momentum, that has magnitude and orientation with respect to an axis. The components are even functions of the coordinates. Also called: **axial vector.** Compare **pseudoscalar, scalar** (sense 1), **tensor** (sense 2), **vector** (sense 1).
psf *abbrev. for* pounds per square foot.
PSG *abbrev. for* phrase structure grammar.
pshaw (pʃɔː) *interj. Becoming rare* an exclamation of disgust, impatience, disbelief, etc.
psi[1] *abbrev. for* pounds per square inch.
psi[2] (psaɪ) *n.* **1.** the 23rd letter of the Greek alphabet (Ψ, ψ), a composite consonant, transliterated as *ps.* **2. a.** paranormal or psychic phenomena collectively. **b.** (*as modifier*): *psi powers.*
psia *abbrev. for* pounds per square inch, absolute.
psid *abbrev. for* pounds per square inch, differential.
psig *abbrev. for* pounds per square inch, gauge.
psilocybin (ˌsɪlə'saɪbɪn, ˌsaɪlə-) *n.* a crystalline phosphate ester that is the active principle of the hallucinogenic fungus *Psilocybe mexicana.* Formula: $C_{12}H_{17}N_2O_4P$. [C20: from New Latin *Psilocybe* (from Greek *psilos* bare + *kubē* head) + -IN]
psilomelane (sɪ'lɒmɪˌleɪn) *n.* a common black to grey secondary mineral consisting of hydrated basic oxide of manganese and barium: a source of manganese. Formula: $BaMn_9O_{16}(OH)_4$. [C19: from Greek *psilos* bare + *melas* black]
psi particle *n.* See **J/psi particle.**
psittacine ('sɪtəˌsaɪn, -sɪn) *adj.* of, relating to, or resembling a parrot. [C19: from Late Latin *psittacīnus,* from Latin *psittacus* a parrot]
psittacosis (ˌsɪtə'kəʊsɪs) *n.* a disease of parrots, caused by the bacterium *Chlamydia psittaci,* that can be transmitted to man, in whom it produces inflammation of the lungs and pneumonia. Also called: **parrot fever.** [C19: from New Latin, from Latin *psittacus* a parrot, from Greek *psittakos;* see -OSIS]
PSK *abbrev. for* phase shift keying: a digital data modulation system in which binary data signals switch the phase of a radio frequency carrier.
PSL *abbrev. for* private sector liquidity: a measure of the money supply. See **M4; M5.**
psoas ('səʊəs) *n.* either of two muscles of the loins that aid in flexing and rotating the thigh. [C17: from New Latin, from Greek *psoai* (pl.)]
psoralea (sə'reɪlɪə) *n.* any plant of the tropical and subtropical leguminous genus *Psoralea,* having curly leaves, white or purple flowers, and short one-seeded pods. See **breadroot.** [C19: via New Latin from Greek *psōraleos* mangy, from *psōra* mange, an allusion to the glandular dots of the plant]
psoriasis (sə'raɪəsɪs) *n.* a skin disease characterized by the formation of reddish spots and patches covered with silvery scales: tends to run in families. [C17: via New Latin from Greek: itching disease, from *psōra* itch] —**psoriatic** (ˌsɔːrɪ'ætɪk) *adj.*
PSS *or* **pss.** *abbrev. for* postscripts.
psst (pst) *interj.* an exclamation of beckoning, esp. one made surreptitiously.
PST (in the U.S. and Canada) *abbrev. for* Pacific Standard Time.
PSTN *abbrev. for* public switched telephone network: the conventional message switched telephone network.
PSV *abbrev. for* public service vehicle.
psych *or* **psyche** (saɪk) *vb.* (*tr.*) *Informal.* to psychoanalyse. See also **psych out, psych up.** [C20: shortened from PSYCHOANALYSE]
psych. *abbrev. for:* **1.** psychological. **2.** psychology.
psyche ('saɪkɪ) *n.* the human mind or soul. [C17: from Latin, from Greek *psukhē* breath, soul; related to Greek *psukhein* to breathe]
psychedelia (ˌsaɪkə'dɛlɪə, -'diːlɪə) *n.* (*functioning as sing. or pl.*) psychedelic objects, dress, music, etc.
psychedelic *or* **psychodelic** (ˌsaɪkɪ'dɛlɪk) *adj.* **1.** relating to or denoting new or altered perceptions or sensory experiences, as through the use of hallucinogenic drugs. **2.** denoting any of the drugs, esp. LSD, that produce these effects. **3.** *Informal.* (of painting, fabric design, etc.) having the vivid colours and complex patterns popularly associated with the visual effects of psychedelic states. [C20: from PSYCHE + Greek *delos* visible] —ˌ**psyche'delically** *or* ˌ**psycho'delically** *adv.*
psychiatric social worker *n. Social welfare.* (in Britain) a qualified person who works with mentally disordered people and their families, based in a psychiatric hospital, child guidance clinic, or social services department area team, and who may also be an approved social worker.
psychiatry (saɪ'kaɪətrɪ) *n.* the branch of medicine concerned with the diagnosis and treatment of mental disorders. —**psychiatric** (ˌsaɪkɪ'ætrɪk) *or* ˌ**psychi'atrical** *adj.* —ˌ**psychi'atrically** *adv.* —**psy'chiatrist** *n.*
psychic ('saɪkɪk) *adj.* **1. a.** outside the possibilities defined by natural laws, as mental telepathy. **b.** (of a person) sensitive to forces not recognized by natural laws. **2.** mental as opposed to physical; psychogenic. **3.** *Bridge.* (of a bid) based on less strength than would normally be required to make the bid. ~*n.* **4.** a person who is sensitive to parapsychological forces or influences. [C19: from Greek *psukhikos* of the soul or life] —'**psychical** *adj.* —'**psychically** *adv.*
psychic determinism *n. Psychol.* the assumption, made esp. by Freud, that mental processes do not occur by chance but that a cause can always be found for them.
psycho ('saɪkəʊ) *n., pl.* **-chos,** *adj.* an informal word for **psychopath** or **psychopathic.**
psycho- *or sometimes before a vowel* **psych-** *combining form.* indicating the mind or psychological or mental processes: *psychology; psychogenesis; psychosomatic.* [from Greek *psukhē* spirit, breath]
psychoacoustics (ˌsaɪkəʊə'kuːstɪks) *n.* (*functioning as sing.*) *Psychol.* the study of the relationship between sounds and their physiological and psychological effects.
psychoactive (ˌsaɪkəʊ'æktɪv) *adj.* (of drugs such as LSD, opium, and the barbiturates) capable of affecting mental activity. Also: **psychotropic.**
psychoanal. *abbrev. for* psychoanalysis.
psychoanalyse *or U.S.* **psychoanalyze** (ˌsaɪkəʊ'ænəˌlaɪz) *vb.* (*tr.*) to examine or treat (a person) by psychoanalysis. —ˌ**psycho'anaˌlyser** *or U.S.* ˌ**psycho'anaˌlyzer** *n.*
psychoanalysis (ˌsaɪkəʊə'nælɪsɪs) *n.* a method of studying the mind and treating mental and emotional disorders based on revealing and investigating the role of the unconscious mind. —**psychoanalyst** (ˌsaɪkəʊ'ænəlɪst) *n.* —**psychoanalytic** (ˌsaɪkəʊˌænə'lɪtɪk) *or* ˌ**psychoˌana'lytical** *adj.* —ˌ**psychoˌana'lytically** *adv.*
psychobabble ('saɪkəʊˌbæbᵊl) *n. Informal.* the jargon of psychology, esp. as used and popularized in various types of psychotherapy.
psychobiography (ˌsaɪkəʊbaɪ'ɒgrəfɪ) *n.* a biography that pays particular attention to a person's psychological development. —**psychobiographical** (ˌsaɪkəʊbaɪəʊ'græfɪkᵊl) *adj.*
psychobiology (ˌsaɪkəʊbaɪ'ɒlədʒɪ) *n. Psychol.* the attempt to understand the psychology of organisms in terms of their bio-

ˌ**pseudo-Bo'hemian** *adj.*
ˌ**pseudo'classic** *or* ˌ**pseudo'classical** *adj.*
ˌ**pseudo'classiˌcism** *n.*
ˌ**pseudo'cultiˌvated** *adj.*
ˌ**pseudoˌdemo'cratic** *adj.*
ˌ**pseudo-EˌlizaˈbethanS** *adj.*
ˌ**pseudo-'Georgian** *adj.*
ˌ**pseudo-'Gothic** *adj.*
ˌ**pseudo-'Grecian** *adj.*
ˌ**pseudohis'toric** *or* ˌ**pseudohis'torical** *adj.*
ˌ**pseudo'literary** *adj.*
ˌ**pseudoˌmedi'eval** *adj.*
ˌ**pseudo'modern** *adj.*
ˌ**pseudo'mythical** *adj.*
ˌ**pseudo-ˌori'ental** *adj.*
ˌ**pseudoˌpatri'otic** *adj.*
ˌ**pseudoˌphilo'sophical** *adj.*
ˌ**pseudopro'fessional** *adj.*
ˌ**pseudoˌpsycho'logical** *adj.*
ˌ**pseudo'scholarly** *adj.*
ˌ**pseudo'science** *n.*
ˌ**pseudoˌscien'tific** *adj.*
ˌ**pseudoˌsocial'istic** *adj.*
ˌ**pseudo-Vic'torian** *adj.*

logical functions and structures. —**psychobiological** (ˌsaɪkəʊbaɪəˈlɒdʒɪkᵊl) *adj.* —ˌ**psychobioˈlogically** *adv.* —ˌ**psychobiˈologist** *n.*
psychochemical (ˌsaɪkəʊˈkɛmɪkᵊl) *n.* **1.** any of various chemical compounds whose primary effect is the alteration of the normal state of consciousness. ~*adj.* **2.** of or relating to such chemical compounds.
psychodrama (ˈsaɪkəʊˌdrɑːmə) *n. Psychiatry.* a form of group therapy in which individuals act out, before an audience, situations from their past. —**psychodramatic** (ˌsaɪkəʊdrəˈmætɪk) *adj.*
psychodynamics (ˌsaɪkəʊdaɪˈnæmɪks) *n.* (*functioning as sing.*) *Psychol.* the study of interacting motives and emotions. —ˌ**psychodyˈnamic** *adj.* —ˌ**psychodyˈnamically** *adv.*
psychogalvanic response (ˌsaɪkəʊgælˈvænɪk) *n.* another name for **galvanic skin response.** Abbrev.: **PGR.**
psychogenesis (ˌsaɪkəʊˈdʒɛnɪsɪs) *n. Psychol.* the study of the origin and development of personality, human behaviour, and mental processes. —**psychogenetic** (ˌsaɪkəʊdʒɪˈnɛtɪk) *adj.* —ˌ**psychogeˈnetically** *adv.*
psychogenic (ˌsaɪkəʊˈdʒɛnɪk) *adj. Psychol.* (esp. of disorders or symptoms) of mental, rather than organic, origin. —ˌ**psychoˈgenically** *adv.*
psychogeriatric (ˌsaɪkəʊdʒɛrɪˈætrɪk) *adj.* **1.** *Med.* (of an old person) no longer in touch with everyday realities; exhibiting delusions; mentally incompetent. ~*n.* **2. a.** *Derogatory.* a confused old person. **b.** an impersonal label for a patient, as a unit, requiring institutional services appropriate for a mentally disordered old person. ~See also **confused elderly, geriatric, senile.**
psychogeriatrics (ˌsaɪkəʊdʒɛrɪˈætrɪks) *n.* (*functioning as sing.*) *Med.* the branch of health care concerned with the study, diagnosis, and sometimes treatment of mentally disordered old people. Compare **geriatrics.**
psychognosis (saɪˈkɒgnəsɪs) *n. Psychol.* **1.** the use of hypnosis to study mental phenomena. **2.** the study of personality by observation of outward bodily signs. —**psychognostic** (ˌsaɪkɒgˈnɒstɪk) *adj.*
psychohistory (ˌsaɪkəʊˈhɪstərɪ, -ˈhɪstrɪ) *n., pl.* **-ries.** biography based on psychological theories of personality development.
psychokinesis (ˌsaɪkəʊkɪˈniːsɪs, -kaɪ-) *n.* **1.** (in parapsychology) alteration of the state of an object by mental influence alone, without any physical intervention. **2.** *Psychiatry.* a state of violent uncontrolled motor activity. [C20: from PSYCHO- + Greek *kinēsis* motion] —**psychokinetic** (ˌsaɪkəʊkɪˈnɛtɪk) *adj.*
psychol. *abbrev. for:* **1.** psychological. **2.** psychology.
psycholinguistics (ˌsaɪkəʊlɪŋˈgwɪstɪks) *n.* (*functioning as sing.*) the psychology of language, including language acquisition by children, the mental processes underlying adult comprehension and production of speech, language disorders, etc. —ˌ**psychoˈlinguist** *n.* —ˌ**psycholinˈguistic** *adj.*
psychological (ˌsaɪkəˈlɒdʒɪkᵊl) *adj.* **1.** of or relating to psychology. **2.** of or relating to the mind or mental activity. **3.** having no real or objective basis; arising in the mind: *his backaches are all psychological.* **4.** affecting the mind. —ˌ**psychoˈlogically** *adv.*
psychological block *n.* See **block** (sense 23).
psychological moment *n.* the most appropriate time for producing a desired effect: *he proposed to her at the psychological moment.*
psychological primary *n.* one of a set of perceived colours (red, yellow, blue, green, black, and white) that can be used to characterize all other perceived colours.
psychological warfare *n.* the military application of psychology, esp. to propaganda and attempts to influence the morale of enemy and friendly groups in time of war.
psychologism (saɪˈkɒləˌdʒɪzəm) *n.* **1.** the belief in the importance and relevance of psychology for other sciences. **2.** the belief that psychology is the basis for all other natural and social sciences. —**psyˌcholoˈgistic** *adj.*
psychologize *or* **psychologise** (saɪˈkɒləˌdʒaɪz) *vb.* (*intr.*) **1.** to make interpretations of behaviour and mental processes. **2.** to carry out investigation in the field of psychology.
psychology (saɪˈkɒlədʒɪ) *n., pl.* **-gies. 1.** the scientific study of all forms of human and animal behaviour, sometimes concerned with the methods through which behaviour can be modified. See also **analytic psychology, clinical psychology, comparative psychology, educational psychology, experimental psychology. 2.** *Informal.* the mental make-up or structure of an individual that causes him to think or act in the way he does. —**psyˈchologist** *n.*
psychomachia (ˌsaɪkəʊˈmækɪə) *or* **psychomachy** (ˈsaɪkəʊməkɪ) *n.* conflict of the soul. [C17: from Late Latin *psȳchomachia,* title of a poem by Prudentius (about 400), from Greek *psukhē* spirit + *makhē* battle]
psychometrics (ˌsaɪkəʊˈmɛtrɪks) *n.* (*functioning as sing.*) **1.** the branch of psychology concerned with the design and use of psychological tests. **2.** the application of statistical and mathematical techniques to psychological testing.
psychometry (saɪˈkɒmɪtrɪ) *n. Psychol.* **1.** measurement and testing of mental states and processes. See also **psychometrics. 2.** (in parapsychology) the supposed ability to deduce facts about events by touching objects related to them. —**psychometric** (ˌsaɪkəʊˈmɛtrɪk) *or* ˌ**psychoˈmetrical** *adj.* —ˌ**psychoˈmetrically** *adv.* —**psychometrician** (ˌsaɪkəʊməˈtrɪʃən) *or* **psyˈchometrist** *n.*
psychomotor (ˌsaɪkəʊˈməʊtə) *adj.* of, relating to, or characterizing movements of the body associated with mental activity.
psychoneurosis (ˌsaɪkəʊnjʊˈrəʊsɪs) *n., pl.* **-roses** (-ˈrəʊsiːz). another word for **neurosis.** —**psychoneurotic** (ˌsaɪkəʊnjʊˈrɒtɪk) *adj.*
psychopath (ˈsaɪkəʊˌpæθ) *n.* a person afflicted with a personality disorder characterized by a tendency to commit antisocial and sometimes violent acts and a failure to feel guilt for such acts. Also called: **sociopath.** —ˌ**psychoˈpathic** *adj.* —ˌ**psychoˈpathically** *adv.*
psychopathic disorder *n. Law.* (in England, according to the Mental Health Act 1983) a persistent disorder or disability of mind which results in abnormally aggressive or seriously irresponsible conduct on the part of the person concerned. See also **mental disorder.**
psychopathic personality *n. Psychiatry.* an antisocial personality characterized by the failure to develop any sense of moral responsibility and the capability of performing violent or antisocial acts.
psychopathology (ˌsaɪkəʊpəˈθɒlədʒɪ) *n.* the scientific study of mental disorders. —**psychopathological** (ˌsaɪkəʊˌpæθəˈlɒdʒɪkᵊl) *adj.* —ˌ**psychopaˈthologist** *n.*
psychopathy (saɪˈkɒpəθɪ) *n. Psychiatry.* **1.** another name for **psychopathic personality. 2.** any mental disorder or disease.
psychopharmacology (ˌsaɪkəʊˌfɑːməˈkɒlədʒɪ) *n.* the study of drugs that affect the mind. —**psychopharmacological** (ˌsaɪkəʊˌfɑːməkəˈlɒdʒɪkᵊl) *adj.* —ˌ**psychoˌpharmaˈcologist** *n.*
psychophysics (ˌsaɪkəʊˈfɪzɪks) *n.* (*functioning as sing.*) the branch of psychology concerned with the relationship between physical stimuli and the effects they produce in the mind. —ˌ**psychoˈphysical** *adj.*
psychophysiology (ˌsaɪkəʊˌfɪzɪˈɒlədʒɪ) *n.* the branch of psychology concerned with the physiological basis of mental processes. —**psychophysiological** (ˌsaɪkəʊˌfɪzɪəˈlɒdʒɪkᵊl) *adj.* —ˌ**psychoˌphysiˈologist** *n.*
psychoprophylaxis (ˌsaɪkəʊˌprəʊfɪˈlæksɪs) *n.* a method of preparing women for natural childbirth by means of special breathing and relaxation.
psychosexual (ˌsaɪkəʊˈsɛksjʊəl) *adj.* of or relating to the mental aspects of sex, such as sexual fantasies. —ˌ**psychoˌsexuˈality** *n.* —ˌ**psychoˈsexually** *adv.*
psychosis (saɪˈkəʊsɪs) *n., pl.* **-choses** (-ˈkəʊsiːz). any form of severe mental disorder in which the individual's contact with reality becomes highly distorted. Compare **neurosis.** [C19: New Latin, from PSYCHO- + -OSIS]
psychosocial (ˌsaɪkəʊˈsəʊʃəl) *adj.* of or relating to processes or factors that are both social and psychological in origin.
psychosomatic (ˌsaɪkəʊsəˈmætɪk) *adj.* of or relating to disorders, such as stomach ulcers, thought to be caused or aggravated by psychological factors such as stress.
psychosurgery (ˌsaɪkəʊˈsɜːdʒərɪ) *n.* any surgical procedure on the brain, such as a frontal lobotomy, to relieve serious mental disorders. —**psychosurgical** (ˌsaɪkəʊˈsɜːdʒɪkᵊl) *adj.*
psychotherapy (ˌsaɪkəʊˈθɛrəpɪ) *or* (*less commonly*) **psychotherapeutics** (ˌsaɪkəʊˌθɛrəˈpjuːtɪks) *n.* the treatment of nervous disorders by psychological methods. —ˌ**psychoˌtheraˈpeutic** *adj.* —ˌ**psychoˌtheraˈpeutically** *adv.* —ˌ**psychoˈtherapist** *n.*
psychotic (saɪˈkɒtɪk) *Psychiatry.* ~*adj.* **1.** of, relating to, or characterized by psychosis. ~*n.* **2.** a person suffering from psychosis. —**psyˈchotically** *adv.*
psychotomimetic (saɪˌkɒtəʊmɪˈmɛtɪk) *adj.* (of drugs such as LSD and mescaline) capable of inducing psychotic symptoms.
psychotropic (ˌsaɪkəʊˈtrɒpɪk) *adj.* another word for **psychoactive.**
psych out *vb.* (*mainly tr., adv.*) *Informal.* **1.** to guess correctly the intentions of (another); outguess. **2.** to analyse or solve (a problem, etc.) psychologically. **3.** to intimidate or frighten. **4.** (*intr., adv.*) to lose control psychologically; break down.
psychro- *combining form.* cold: *psychrometer.* [from Greek *psukhros*]
psychrometer (saɪˈkrɒmɪtə) *n.* a type of hygrometer consisting of two thermometers, one of which has a dry bulb and the other a bulb that is kept moist and ventilated. The difference between the readings of the thermometers gives an indication of atmospheric humidity. Also called: **wet-and-dry-bulb thermometer.**
psychrophilic (ˌsaɪkrəʊˈfɪlɪk) *adj.* (esp. of bacteria) showing optimum growth at low temperatures.
psych up *vb.* (*tr., adv.*) *Informal.* to get (oneself or another) into a state of psychological readiness for an action, performance, etc.
psyllid (ˈsɪlɪd) *or* **psylla** (ˈsɪlə) *n.* any homopterous insect of the family *Psyllidae,* which comprises the jumping plant lice. See **plant louse** (sense 2). [C19: from Greek *psulla* flea]
pt *abbrev. for:* **1.** part. **2.** past tense. **3.** patient. **4.** payment. **5.** point. **6.** port. **7.** pro tempore.
Pt *abbrev. for* (in place names): **1.** Point. **2.** Port. ~**3.** *the chemical symbol for* platinum.
PT *abbrev. for:* **1.** physical therapy. **2.** physical training. **3.** postal telegraph. **4.** pupil teacher. **5.** (in Britain, formerly) purchase tax.

pt. *abbrev. for:* **1.** pint. **2.** preterite.
pta *symbol for* peseta.
PTA *abbrev. for:* **1.** Parent-Teacher Association. **2.** (in Britain) Passenger Transport Authority.
ptarmigan ('tɑːmɪɡən) *n., pl.* **-gans** *or* **-gan. 1.** any of several arctic and subarctic grouse of the genus *Lagopus*, esp. *L. mutus*, which has a white winter plumage. **2.** (*sometimes cap.*) a created domestic fancy pigeon with ruffled or curled feathers on the wings and back. [C16: changed (perhaps influenced by Greek *pteron* wing) from Scottish Gaelic *tarmachan*, diminutive of *tarmach*, of obscure origin]
PT boat *n.* patrol torpedo boat, the former U.S. term for an **MTB.**
Pte *Military. abbrev. for* private.
PTE (in Britain) *abbrev. for* Passenger Transport Executive.
pteridology (ˌtɛrɪ'dɒlədʒɪ) *n.* the branch of botany concerned with the study of ferns and related plants. [C19: from *pterido-*, from Greek *pteris* fern + -LOGY] —**pteridological** (ˌtɛrɪdəʊ'lɒdʒɪkᵊl) *adj.* —ˌ**pteri'dologist** *n.*
pteridophyte ('tɛrɪdəʊˌfaɪt) *n.* any plant of the division *Pteridophyta*, reproducing by spores and having vascular tissue, roots, stems, and leaves: includes the ferns, horsetails, and club mosses. [C19: from *pterido-*, from Greek *pteris* fern + -PHYTE] —**pteridophytic** (ˌtɛrɪdəʊ'fɪtɪk) *or* **pteridophytous** (ˌtɛrɪ'dɒfɪtəs) *adj.*
pteridosperm ('tɛrɪdəˌspɜːm) *n.* any extinct seed-producing fernlike plant of the group *Pteridospermae*. Also called: **seed fern.** [C19: from Greek *pteris* a fern + -SPERM]
ptero- *combining form.* wing, feather, or a part resembling a wing: *pterodactyl.* [from Greek *pteron* wing, feather]
pterodactyl (ˌtɛrə'dæktɪl) *n.* any extinct flying reptile of the genus *Pterodactylus* and related genera, having membranous wings supported on an elongated fourth digit. See also **pterosaur.** [C19: from PTERO- + Greek *daktulos* finger]
pteropod ('tɛrəˌpɒd) *n.* any small marine gastropod mollusc of the group or order *Pteropoda*, in which the foot is expanded into two winglike lobes for swimming and the shell is absent or thin-walled. Also called: **sea butterfly.**
pterosaur ('tɛrəˌsɔː) *n.* any extinct flying reptile of the order *Pterosauria*, of Jurassic and Cretaceous times: included the pterodactyls. Compare **dinosaur, plesiosaur.**
-pterous *or* **-pteran** *adj. combining form.* indicating a specified number or type of wings: *dipterous.* [from Greek *-pteros*, from *pteron* wing]
pterygial (tə'rɪdʒɪəl) *adj. Zoology.* of or relating to a fin or wing. [from Greek *pterux* wing]
pterygoid process ('tɛrɪˌɡɔɪd) *n. Anatomy.* either of two long bony plates extending downwards from each side of the sphenoid bone within the skull. [C18 *pterygoid*, from Greek *pterugoeidēs*, from *pterux* wing; see -OID]
pteryla ('tɛrɪlə) *n., pl.* **-lae** (-ˌliː). *Ornithol.* any of the tracts of skin that bear contour feathers, arranged in lines along the body of a bird. [C19: from New Latin, from Greek *pteron* feather + *hulē* wood, forest]
PTFE *abbrev. for* polytetrafluoroethylene.
ptg *abbrev. for* printing.
ptisan (tɪ'zæn) *n.* **1.** grape juice drained off without pressure. **2.** a variant spelling of **tisane.** [C14: from Old French *tisane*, from Latin *ptisana*, from Greek *ptisanē* barley groats]
PTN *abbrev. for* public telephone network: the telephone network provided in Britain by British Telecom.
PTO *or* **pto** *abbrev. for* please turn over.
ptochocracy (təʊ'kɒkrəsɪ) *n., pl.* **-cies.** government by the poor. [C18: from Greek, from *ptochos* poor + -CRACY]
Ptolemaic (ˌtɒlɪ'meɪɪk) *adj.* **1.** of or relating to the 2nd-century Greek astronomer Ptolemy, or to his conception of the universe. **2.** of or relating to the Macedonian dynasty that ruled Egypt from the death of Alexander the Great (323 B.C.) to the death of Cleopatra (30 B.C.).
Ptolemaic system *n.* the theory of planetary motion developed by Ptolemy from the hypotheses of earlier philosophers, stating that the earth lay at the centre of the universe with the sun, the moon, and the known planets revolving around it in complicated orbits. Beyond the largest of these orbits lay a sphere of fixed stars. See also **epicycle** (sense 1). Compare **Copernican system.**
Ptolemaist (ˌtɒlɪ'meɪɪst) *n.* a believer in or adherent of the Ptolemaic system of the universe.
ptomaine *or* **ptomain** ('təʊmeɪn) *n.* any of a group of amines, such as cadaverine or putrescine, formed by decaying organic matter. [C19: from Italian *ptomaina*, from Greek *ptoma* corpse, from *piptein* to fall]
ptomaine poisoning *n.* a popular term for **food poisoning.** Ptomaines were once erroneously thought to be a cause of food poisoning.
ptosis ('təʊsɪs) *n., pl.* **ptoses** ('təʊsiːz). prolapse or drooping of a part, esp. the eyelid. [C18: from Greek: a falling] —**ptotic** ('tɒtɪk) *adj.*
pts *abbrev. for:* **1.** parts. **2.** payments. **3.** points. **4.** ports.
pts. *abbrev. for* pints.
PTT *abbrev. for* Post Telephone and Telegraph Administration; the usually national monopolies used to provide postal, telephonic, and telegraphic communication services.
Pty *Austral., N.Z., and S. African. abbrev. for* proprietary: used to denote a private limited company.
ptyalin ('taɪəlɪn) *n. Biochem.* an amylase secreted in the saliva of man and other animals. [C19: from Greek *ptualon* saliva, from *ptuein* to spit]
ptyalism ('taɪəˌlɪzəm) *n.* excessive secretion of saliva. [C17: from Greek *ptualismos*, from *ptualizein* to produce saliva, from *ptualon* saliva]
p-type *adj.* **1.** (of a semiconductor) having a density of mobile holes in excess of that of conduction electrons. **2.** associated with or resulting from the movement of holes in a semiconductor: *p-type conductivity.* Compare **n-type.**
Pu *the chemical symbol for* plutonium.
pub (pʌb) *n.* **1.** *Chiefly Brit.* a building with a bar and one or more public rooms licensed for the sale and consumption of alcoholic drink, often also providing light meals. Formal name: **public house. 2.** *Austral. and N.Z.* a hotel. ~*vb.* **pubs, pubbing, pubbed. 3.** (*intr.*) *Informal* to visit a pub or pubs (esp. in the phrase **go pubbing**).
pub. *abbrev. for:* **1.** public. **2.** publication. **3.** published. **4.** publisher. **5.** publishing.
pub-crawl *Informal, chiefly Brit.* ~*n.* **1.** a drinking tour of a number of pubs or bars. ~*vb.* **2.** (*intr.*) to make such a tour.
puberty ('pjuːbətɪ) *n.* the period at the beginning of adolescence when the sex glands become functional and the secondary sexual characteristics emerge. Also called: **pubescence.** [C14: from Latin *pūbertās* maturity, from *pūber* adult] —'**pubertal** *adj.*
puberulent (pju'bɛrjʊlənt) *adj. Biology.* covered with very fine down; finely pubescent. [C19: from Latin *pūber*]
pubes ('pjuːbiːz) *n., pl.* **pubes** ('pjuːbiːz). **1.** the region above the external genital organs, covered with hair from the time of puberty. **2.** pubic hair. **3.** the pubic bones. **4.** the plural of **pubis.** [from Latin]
pubescent (pjuː'bɛsᵊnt) *adj.* **1.** arriving or having arrived at puberty. **2.** (of certain plants and animals or their parts) covered with a layer of fine short hairs or down. [C17: from Latin *pūbēscere* to reach manhood, from *pūber* adult] —**pu'bescence** *n.*
pub grub *n. Informal.* food served in a pub.
pubic ('pjuːbɪk) *adj.* of or relating to the pubes or pubis: *pubic hair.*
pubis ('pjuːbɪs) *n., pl.* **-bes** (-biːz). one of the three sections of the hipbone that forms part of the pelvis. [C16: shortened from New Latin *os pūbis* bone of the PUBES]
publ. *abbrev. for:* **1.** publication. **2.** published. **3.** publisher.
public ('pʌblɪk) *adj.* **1.** of, relating to, or concerning the people as a whole. **2.** open or accessible to all: *public gardens.* **3.** performed or made openly or in the view of all: *public proclamation.* **4.** (*prenominal*) well-known or familiar to people in general: *a public figure.* **5.** (*usually prenominal*) maintained at the expense of, serving, or for the use of a community: *a public library.* **6.** open, acknowledged, or notorious: *a public scandal.* **7. go public. a.** (of a private company) to issue shares for subscription by the public. **b.** to reveal publicly hitherto confidential information. ~*n.* **8.** the community or people in general. **9.** a part or section of the community grouped because of a common interest, activity, etc.: *the racing public.* [C15: from Latin *pūblicus*, changed from *pōplicus* of the people, from *populus* people]
public-address system *n.* a system of one or more microphones, amplifiers, and loudspeakers for increasing the sound level of speech or music, used in auditoriums, public gatherings, etc. Sometimes shortened to **PA system.**
publican ('pʌblɪkən) *n.* **1.** (in Britain) a person who keeps a public house. **2.** (in ancient Rome) a public contractor, esp. one who farmed the taxes of a province. [C12: from Old French *publicain*, from Latin *pūblicānus* tax gatherer, from *pūblicum* state revenues]
public assistance *n. U.S.* payment given to individuals by government agencies on the basis of need.
publication (ˌpʌblɪ'keɪʃən) *n.* **1.** the act or process of publishing a printed work. **2.** any printed work offered for sale or distribution. **3.** the act or an instance of making information public. **4.** the act of disseminating defamatory matter, esp. by communicating it to a third person. See **libel, slander.** Archaic word: **publishment.** [C14: via Old French from Latin *pūblicātiō* confiscation of an individual's property, from *pūblicāre* to seize and assign to public use]
public bar *n. Brit.* a bar in a public house usually serving drinks at a cheaper price than in the saloon bar. Also called: **the public.** Compare **private bar.**
public bill *n.* (in Parliament) a bill dealing with public policy that usually applies to the whole country. Compare **private bill, hybrid bill.**
public company *n.* a limited company whose shares may be purchased by the public and traded freely on the open market and whose share capital is not less than a statutory minimum; public limited company. Compare **private company.**
public convenience *n.* a public lavatory, esp. one in a public place.
public corporation *n.* (in Britain) an organization established to run a nationalized industry or state-owned enterprise. The chair-

man and board members are appointed by a government minister, and the government has overall control.
public debt *n. Chiefly U.S.* **1.** the total financial obligations incurred by all governmental bodies of a nation. **2.** another name for **national debt.**
public defender *n.* (in the U.S.) a lawyer engaged at public expense to represent indigent defendants.
public domain *n.* **1.** *U.S.* lands owned by a state or by the federal government. **2.** *U.S. and Canadian.* the status of a published work or invention upon which the copyright or patent has expired or which has not been patented or subject to copyright. It may thus be freely used by the public.
public enemy *n.* a notorious person, such as a criminal, who is regarded as a menace to the public.
public enterprise *n.* economic activity by governmental organizations. Compare **private enterprise** (sense 1).
public expenditure *n.* spending by central government, local authorities, and public corporations.
public footpath *n.* a footpath along which the public has right of way.
public gallery *n.* the gallery in a chamber of Parliament reserved for members of the public who wish to listen to the proceedings. Also called: **strangers' gallery.**
public health inspector *n.* (in Britain) a former name for **Environmental Health Officer.**
public holiday *n.* a holiday observed over the whole country.
public house *n.* **1.** *Brit.* the formal name for **pub.** **2.** *U.S. and Canadian.* an inn, tavern, or small hotel.
publicist ('pʌblɪsɪst) *n.* **1.** a person who publicizes something, esp. a press or publicity agent. **2.** a journalist. **3.** *Rare.* a person learned in public or international law.
publicity (pʌ'blɪsɪtɪ) *n.* **1. a.** the technique or process of attracting public attention to people, products, etc., as by the use of the mass media. **b.** (*as modifier*): *a publicity agent.* **2.** public interest resulting from information supplied by such a technique or process. **3.** information used to draw public attention to people, products, etc. **4.** the state of being public. [C18: via French from Medieval Latin *pūblicitās;* see PUBLIC]
publicize *or* **publicise** ('pʌblɪˌsaɪz) *vb.* (*tr.*) to bring to public notice; advertise.
public law *n.* **1.** a law that applies to the public of a state or nation. **2.** the branch of law that deals with relations between a state and its individual members. Compare **private law.**
Public Lending Right *n.* the right of authors to receive payment when their books are borrowed from public libraries. Abbrev.: **PLR.**
public-liability insurance *n.* (in Britain) a form of insurance, compulsory for any business in contact with the public, which pays compensation to a member of the public suffering injury or damage as a result of the policyholder or his employees failing to take reasonable care.
public limited company *n.* another name for **public company.** Abbrev.: **plc** *or* **PLC.**
publicly ('pʌblɪklɪ) *adv.* **1.** in a public manner; without concealment; openly. **2.** in the name or with the consent of the public.
public nuisance *n.* **1.** *Law.* an illegal act causing harm to members of a particular community rather than to any individual. **2.** *Informal.* a person who is generally considered objectionable.
public opinion *n.* the attitude of the public, esp. as a factor in determining the actions of government.
public ownership *n.* ownership by the state; nationalization.
public prosecutor *n. Law.* an official in charge of prosecuting important cases.
public relations *n.* (*functioning as sing. or pl.*) **1. a.** the practice of creating, promoting, or maintaining goodwill and a favourable image among the public towards an institution, public body, etc. **b.** the methods and techniques employed. **c.** (*as modifier*): *the public relations industry.* **2.** the condition of the relationship between an organization and the public. **3.** the professional staff employed to create, promote, or maintain a favourable relationship between an organization and the public. Abbrev.: **PR.**
public school *n.* **1.** (in England and Wales) a private independent fee-paying secondary school. **2.** any school that is part of a free local educational system.
public sector *n.* the part of an economy that consists of state-owned institutions, including nationalized industries and services provided by local authorities. Compare **private sector.**
public servant *n.* **1.** an elected or appointed holder of a public office. **2.** the Austral. and N.Z. name for **civil servant.**
public service *n.* **1. a.** government employment. **b.** the management and administration of the affairs of a political unit, esp. the civil service. **2. a.** a service provided for the community: *buses provide a public service.* **b.** (*as modifier*): *a public-service announcement.* **3.** the Austral. and N.Z. name for the **civil service.**
public-service corporation *n. U.S.* a private corporation that provides services to the community, such as telephone service, public transport.
public speaking *n.* the art or practice of making speeches to large audiences. —**public speaker** *n.*
public spending *n.* expenditure by central government, local authorities, and public enterprises.
public-spirited *adj.* having or showing active interest in public welfare or the good of the community.
public transport *n.* a system of buses, trains, etc., running on fixed routes, on which the public may travel.
public utility *n.* an enterprise concerned with the provision to the public of essentials, such as electricity or water. Also called (U.S.): **public-service corporation.**
public works *pl. n.* engineering projects and other constructions, financed and undertaken by a government for the community.
publish ('pʌblɪʃ) *vb.* **1.** to produce and issue (printed matter) for distribution and sale. **2.** (*intr.*) to have one's written work issued for publication. **3.** (*tr.*) to announce formally or in public. **4.** (*tr.*) to communicate (defamatory matter) to someone other than the person defamed: *to publish a libel.* [C14: from Old French *puplier,* from Latin *pūblicāre* to make PUBLIC] —'**publishable** *adj.*
publisher ('pʌblɪʃə) *n.* **1.** a company or person engaged in publishing periodicals, books, music, etc. **2.** *U.S. and Canadian.* the proprietor of a newspaper or his representative.
púcán ('puːkɑːn) *n. Irish.* a traditional Connemara open sailing boat. [Irish Gaelic]
puccoon (pə'kuːn) *n.* **1.** Also called: **alkanet.** any of several North American boraginaceous plants of the genus *Lithospermum,* esp. *L. canescens,* that yield a red dye. See also **gromwell.** **2.** any of several other plants that yield a reddish dye, esp. the bloodroot (**red puccoon**). **3.** the dye from any of these plants. [C17: of Algonquian origin; see POKEWEED]
puce (pjuːs) *n.* **a.** a colour varying from deep red to dark purplish-brown. **b.** (*as adj.*): *a puce carpet.* [C18: shortened from French *couleur puce* flea colour, from Latin *pūlex* flea]
puck[1] (pʌk) *n.* **1.** a small disc of hard rubber used in ice hockey. **2.** a stroke at the ball in hurling. **3.** *Irish slang.* a sharp blow. ~*vb.* (*tr.*) **4.** to strike (the ball) in hurling. **5.** *Irish slang.* to strike hard; punch. [C19: of unknown origin]
puck[2] (pʌk) *n.* (*often cap.*) a mischievous or evil spirit. Also called: **Robin Goodfellow.** [Old English *pūca,* of obscure origin] —'**puckish** *adj.*
pucka ('pʌkə) *adj.* a less common spelling of **pukka.**
pucker ('pʌkə) *vb.* **1.** to gather or contract (a soft surface such as the skin of the face) into wrinkles or folds, or (of such a surface) to be so gathered or contracted. ~*n.* **2.** a wrinkle, crease, or irregular fold. [C16: perhaps related to POKE[2], from the creasing into baglike wrinkles]
puckerood (ˌpʌkə'ruːd) *adj. N.Z.* ruined; exhausted. [from Maori *pakaru* to shatter]
pud (pʊd) *n. Brit. informal.* short for **pudding.**
pudding ('pʊdɪŋ) *n.* **1.** a sweetened usually cooked dessert made in many forms and of various ingredients, such as flour, milk, and eggs, with fruit, etc. **2.** a savoury dish, usually soft and consisting partially of pastry or batter: *steak-and-kidney pudding.* **3.** the dessert course in a meal. **4.** a sausage-like mass of seasoned minced meat, oatmeal, etc., stuffed into a prepared skin or bag and boiled. [C13 *poding;* compare Old English *puduc* a wart, Low German *puddek* sausage] —'**puddingy** *adj.*
pudding club *n. Slang.* the state of being pregnant (esp. in the phrase **in the pudding club**).
pudding stone *n.* a conglomerate rock in which there is a difference in colour and composition between the pebbles and the matrix.
puddle ('pʌdᵊl) *n.* **1.** a small pool of water, esp. of rain. **2.** a small pool of any liquid. **3.** a worked mixture of wet clay and sand that is impervious to water and is used to line a pond or canal. **4.** *Rowing.* the patch of eddying water left by the blade of an oar after completion of a stroke. ~*vb.* **5.** (*tr.*) to make (clay, etc.) into puddle. **6.** (*tr.*) to subject (iron) to puddling. **7.** (*intr.*) to dabble or wade in puddles, mud, or shallow water. **8.** (*intr.*) to mess about. [C14 *podel,* diminutive of Old English *pudd* ditch, of obscure origin] —'**puddler** *n.* —'**puddly** *adj.*
puddling ('pʌdlɪŋ) *n.* **1.** a process for converting pig iron into wrought iron by heating it with ferric oxide in a furnace to oxidize the carbon. **2.** *Building.* the process of making a puddle.
puddock ('pʌdək) *n.* a Scot. variant of **paddock**[2].
pudency ('pjuːdᵊnsɪ) *n.* modesty, shame, or prudishness. [C17: from Late Latin *pudentia,* from Latin *pudēre* to feel shame]
pudendum (pjuː'dɛndəm) *n., pl.* **-da** (-də). (*often pl.*) the human external genital organs collectively, esp. of a female. [C17: from Late Latin, from Latin *pudenda* the shameful (parts), from *pudēre* to be ashamed] —**pu'dendal** *or* **pudic** ('pjuːdɪk) *adj.*
pudge (pʌdʒ) *n. Informal.* a variant of **podge.** [C19: of uncertain origin; see PUDGY]
pudgy ('pʌdʒɪ) *adj.* **pudgier, pudgiest.** a variant spelling (esp. U.S.) of **podgy.** [C19: of uncertain origin; compare earlier *pudsy* plump, perhaps from Scottish *pud* stomach, plump child] —'**pudgily** *adv.* —'**pudginess** *n.*
pudu ('puːˌduː) *n.* a diminutive Andean antelope, *Pudu pudu,* some 35 cm (13 to 14 in.) tall at the shoulder, with short straight horns and reddish-brown spotted coat. [C19: its native name]
pueblo ('pwɛbləʊ; *Spanish* 'pweβlo) *n., pl.* **-los** (-ləʊz; *Spanish* -los). **1.** a communal village, built by certain Indians of the southwestern U.S. and parts of Latin America, consisting of one or more flat-roofed stone or adobe houses. **2.** (in Spanish Ameri-

ca) a village or town. **3.** (in the Philippines) a town or township. [C19: from Spanish: people, from Latin *populus*]
Pueblo ('pwɛbləʊ) *n., pl.* **-lo** *or* **-los.** a member of any of the North American Indian peoples who live in pueblos, including the Tanoans, Zuñi, and Hopi.
puerile ('pjʊəraɪl) *adj.* **1.** exhibiting silliness; immature; trivial. **2.** of or characteristic of a child. [C17: from Latin *puerīlis* childish, from *puer* a boy] —'**puerilely** *adv.* —**puerility** (pjʊə'rɪlɪtɪ) *n.*
puerilism ('pjʊərɪˌlɪzəm) *n. Psychiatry.* immature or childish behaviour by an adult.
puerperal (pjuː'ɜːpərəl) *adj.* of, relating to, or occurring during the puerperium. [C18: from New Latin *puerperālis* relating to childbirth; see PUERPERIUM]
puerperal fever *n.* a serious, formerly widespread, form of blood poisoning caused by infection contracted during childbirth.
puerperal psychosis *n.* a mental disorder sometimes occurring in women after childbirth, characterized by deep depression, delusions of the child's death, and homicidal feelings towards the child.
puerperium (pjuə'pɪərɪəm) *n.* the period following childbirth, lasting approximately six weeks, during which the uterus returns to its normal size and shape. [C17: from Latin: childbirth, from *puerperus* relating to a woman in labour, from *puer* boy + *parere* to bear]
Puerto Rican ('pwɜːtəʊ 'riːkən, 'pwɛə-) *adj.* **1.** of or relating to Puerto Rico, an autonomous commonwealth (in association with the U.S.) in the Caribbean, or to its people, customs, etc. ~*n.* **2.** a native or inhabitant of Puerto Rico or a descendant of one, esp. one who has emigrated to the U.S.
puff (pʌf) *n.* **1.** a short quick draught, gust, or emission, as of wind, smoke, air, etc., esp. a forceful one. **2.** the amount of wind, smoke, etc., released in a puff. **3.** the sound made by or associated with a puff. **4.** an instance of inhaling and expelling the breath as in smoking. **5.** a swelling. **6.** a light aerated pastry usually filled with cream, jam, etc. **7.** a powder puff. **8.** exaggerated praise, as of a book, product, etc., esp. through an advertisement. **9.** a piece of clothing fabric gathered up so as to bulge in the centre while being held together at the edges. **10.** a loose piece of hair wound into a cylindrical roll, usually over a pad, and pinned in place in a coiffure. **11.** a less common word for **quilt** (sense 1). **12.** one's breath (esp. in the phrase **out of puff**). **13.** *Derogatory slang.* a male homosexual. **14.** a dialect word for **puffball.** ~*vb.* **15.** to blow or breathe or cause to blow or breathe in short quick draughts or blasts. **16.** (*tr.;* often foll. by *out;* usually passive) to cause to be out of breath. **17.** to take puffs or draws at (a cigarette, cigar, or pipe). **18.** to move with or by the emission of puffs: *the steam train puffed up the incline.* **19.** (often foll. by *up, out,* etc.) to swell, as with air, pride, etc. **20.** (*tr.*) to praise with exaggerated empty words, often in advertising. **21.** (*tr.*) to apply (cosmetic powder) from a powder puff to (the face). **22.** *Auctioneering.* to increase the price of (a lot) artificially by having an accomplice make false bids. [Old English *pyffan;* related to Dutch German *puffen,* Swiss *pfuffen,* Norwegian *puffa,* all of imitative origin]
puff adder *n.* **1.** a large venomous African viper, *Bitis arietans,* that is yellowish-grey with brown markings and inflates its body when alarmed. **2.** another name for **hognose snake.**
puffball ('pʌfˌbɔːl) *n.* any of various basidiomycetous saprophytic fungi of the genera *Calvatia* and *Lycoperdon,* having a round fruiting body that discharges a cloud of brown spores when mature.
puffbird ('pʌfˌbɜːd) *n.* any of various brownish tropical American birds of the family *Bucconidae,* having a large head: order *Piciformes* (woodpeckers, etc.). [C19: so called because of its habit of puffing out its feathers]
puffer ('pʌfə) *n.* **1.** a person or thing that puffs. **2.** Also called: **globefish.** any marine plectognath fish of the family *Tetraodontidae,* having an elongated spiny body that can be inflated to form a globe.
puffery ('pʌfərɪ) *n., pl.* **-eries.** *Informal.* exaggerated praise, esp. in publicity or advertising.
puffin ('pʌfɪn) *n.* any of various northern diving birds of the family Alcidae (auks, etc.), esp. *Fratercula arctica* (**common** or **Atlantic puffin**), having a black-and-white plumage and a brightly coloured vertically flattened bill: order *Charadriiformes.* [C14: perhaps of Cornish origin]
puff pastry *or U.S.* **puff paste** *n.* a dough rolled in thin layers incorporating fat to make a rich flaky pastry for pies, rich pastries, etc.
puff-puff *n. Brit.* a children's name for a steam locomotive or railway train.
puffy ('pʌfɪ) *adj.* **puffier, puffiest. 1.** short of breath. **2.** swollen or bloated: *a puffy face.* **3.** pompous or conceited. **4.** blowing in gusts. —'**puffily** *adv.* —'**puffiness** *n.*
pug[1] (pʌg) *n.* **1.** Also called: **carlin.** a small compact breed of dog with a smooth coat, lightly curled tail, and a short wrinkled nose. **2.** any of several small geometrid moths, mostly of the genus *Eupithecia,* with slim forewings held outstretched at rest. [C16: of uncertain origin] —'**puggish** *adj.*
pug[2] (pʌg) *vb.* **pugs, pugging, pugged.** (*tr.*) **1.** to mix or knead (clay) with water to form a malleable mass or paste, often in a **pug mill. 2.** to fill or stop with clay or a similar substance. **3.** (of cattle) to trample (the ground) into consolidated mud. [C19: of uncertain origin]
pug[3] (pʌg) *n.* a slang name for **boxer** (sense 1). [C20: shortened from PUGILIST]
pugging ('pʌgɪŋ) *n.* material such as clay, mortar, sawdust, sand, etc., inserted between wooden flooring and ceiling to reduce the transmission of sound. Also called: **pug.**
puggree, pugree ('pʌgrɪ) *or* **puggaree, pugaree** ('pʌgərɪ) *n.* **1.** the usual Indian word for **turban. 2.** a scarf, usually pleated, around the crown of some hats, esp. sun helmets. [C17: from Hindi *pagrī,* from Sanskrit *parikara*]
puggy ('pʌgɪ) *adj.* **-gier, -giest.** *Dialect and N.Z.* sticky, claylike. [probably from PUG[2]]
pugilism ('pjuːdʒɪˌlɪzəm) *n.* the art, practice, or profession of fighting with the fists; boxing. [C18: from Latin *pugil* a boxer; related to *pugnus* fist, *pugna* a fight] —'**pugilist** *n.* —ˌ**pugi'listic** *adj.* —ˌ**pugi'listically** *adv.*
pugnacious (pʌg'neɪʃəs) *adj.* readily disposed to fight; belligerent. [C17: from Latin *pugnāx*] —**pug'naciously** *adv.* —**pugnacity** (pʌg'næsɪtɪ) *or* **pug'naciousness** *n.*
pug nose *n.* a short stubby upturned nose. [C18: from PUG[1]] —'**pug-ˌnosed** *adj.*
Pugwash conferences ('pʌgˌwɒʃ) *pl. n.* international peace conferences of scientists held regularly to discuss world problems. [C20: from *Pugwash,* Nova Scotia, where the first conference was held]
puha ('puːhɑː) *n. N.Z.* another name for **sow thistle.** [Maori]
puir (puːr, pyr) *adj.* a Scot. word for **poor.**
puirtith *or* **poortith** ('puːrˌtɪθ, 'pyr-) *n. Scot.* poverty. [C16: from Old French *pouerteit, poverteit;* compare POVERTY]
puisne ('pjuːnɪ) *adj.* (esp. of a subordinate judge) of lower rank. [C16: from Anglo-French, from Old French *puisné* born later, from *puis* at a later date, from Latin *posteā* afterwards + *né* born, from *naistre* to be born, from Latin *nascī*]
puissance ('pjuːɪsᵊns, 'pwiːsɑːns) *n.* **1.** a competition in showjumping that tests a horse's ability to jump a limited number of large obstacles. **2.** *Archaic or poetic.* power. [C15: from Old French; see PUISSANT]
puissant ('pjuːɪsᵊnt) *adj. Archaic or poetic.* powerful. [C15: from Old French, ultimately from Latin *potēns* mighty, from *posse* to have power] —'**puissantly** *adv.*
puke (pjuːk) *Slang.* ~*vb.* **1.** to vomit. ~*n.* **2.** the act of vomiting. **3.** the matter vomited. [C16: probably of imitative origin; compare German *spucken* to spit]
pukeko ('pʊkəkəʊ) *n., pl.* **-kos.** a wading bird, *Porphyrio melanotus,* of New Zealand, with a brightly coloured plumage. [Maori]
pukka *or* **pucka** ('pʌkə) *adj.* (esp. in India) **1.** properly or perfectly done, constructed, etc.: *a pukka road.* **2.** genuine: *pukka sahib.* [C17: from Hindi *pakkā* firm, from Sanskrit *pakva*]
pul (puːl) *n., pl.* **puls** *or* **puli** ('puːlɪ). an Afghan monetary unit worth one hundredth of an afghani. [via Persian from Turkish: small coin, from Late Greek *phollis* bag for money, from Latin *follis* bag]
pulchritude ('pʌlkrɪˌtjuːd) *n. Formal or literary.* physical beauty. [C15: from Latin *pulchritūdō,* from *pulcher* beautiful] —ˌ**pulchri'tudinous** *adj.*
pule (pjuːl) *vb.* (*intr.*) to cry plaintively; whimper. [C16: perhaps of imitative origin] —'**puler** *n.*
puli ('pjuːlɪ, 'pʊlɪ) *n.* a breed of Hungarian sheepdog having a very long dense coat, usually black, that hangs in strands with a ropy or corded appearance. [Hungarian, literally: leader]
Pulitzer prize ('pʊlɪtsə) *n.* one of a group of prizes established by Joseph Pulitzer (1847–1911), U.S. newspaper publisher, and awarded yearly since 1917 for excellence in American journalism, literature, and music.
pull (pʊl) *vb.* (*mainly tr.*) **1.** (*also intr.*) to exert force on (an object) so as to draw it towards the source of the force. **2.** to exert force on so as to remove; extract: *to pull a tooth.* **3.** to strip of feathers, hair, etc.; pluck. **4.** to draw the entrails from (a fowl). **5.** to rend or tear. **6.** to strain (a muscle, ligament, or tendon) injuriously. **7.** (usually foll. by *off*) *Informal.* to perform or bring about: *to pull off a million-pound deal.* **8.** (often foll. by *on*) *Informal.* to draw out (a weapon) for use: *he pulled a knife on his attacker.* **9.** *Informal.* to attract: *the pop group pulled a crowd.* **10.** (*intr.;* usually foll. by *on* or *at*) to drink or inhale deeply: *to pull at one's pipe; pull on a bottle of beer.* **11.** to put on or make (a grimace): *to pull a face.* **12.** (*also intr.;* foll by *away, out, over,* etc.) to move (a vehicle) or (of a vehicle) be moved in a specified manner: *he pulled his car away from the roadside.* **13.** *Printing.* to take (a proof) from type. **14.** *Golf, baseball, etc.* to hit (a ball) so that it veers away from the direction in which the player intended to hit it (to the left for a right-handed player). **15.** *Cricket.* to hit (a ball pitched straight or on the off side) to the leg side. **16.** *Hurling.* to strike (a fast-moving ball) in the same direction as it is already moving. **17.** (*also intr.*) to row (a boat) or take a stroke of (an oar) in rowing. **18.** to be rowed by: *a racing shell pulls one, two, four, or eight oars.* **19.** (of a rider) to restrain (a horse), esp. to prevent it from winning a race. **20.** (*intr.*) (of a horse) to resist strongly the attempts of a rider to rein in or check it. **21. pull a fast one.** *Slang.* to play a sly trick. **22. pull apart** *or* **to pieces.** to criticize harshly. **23. pull your head in.** *Austral. informal.* be quiet!

24. **pull (one's) punches.** **a.** *Informal.* to restrain the force of one's criticisms or actions. **b.** *Boxing.* to restrain the force of one's blows, esp. when deliberately losing after being bribed, etc. **25. pull one's weight.** *Informal.* to do one's fair or proper share of a task. **26. pull strings.** *Informal.* to exercise personal influence, esp. secretly or unofficially. **27. pull (someone's) leg.** *Informal.* to make fun of, fool, or tease (someone). ~*n.* **28.** an act or an instance of pulling or being pulled. **29.** the force or effort used in pulling: *the pull of the moon affects the tides on earth.* **30.** the act or an instance of taking in drink or smoke. **31.** *Printing.* a proof taken from type: *the first pull was smudged.* **32.** something used for pulling, such as a knob or handle. **33.** *Informal.* special advantage or influence: *his uncle is chairman of the company, so he has quite a lot of pull.* **34.** *Informal.* the power to attract attention or support. **35.** a period of rowing. **36.** a single stroke of an oar in rowing. **37.** the act of pulling the ball in golf, cricket, etc. **38.** the act of checking or reining in a horse. **39.** the amount of resistance in a bowstring, trigger, etc. ~See also **pull about, pull back, pull down, pull in, pull off, pull on, pull out, pull through, pull together, pull up.** [Old English *pullian;* related to Icelandic *pūla* to beat] —**'puller** *n.*

pull about *vb.* (*tr., adv.*) to handle roughly: *the thugs pulled the old lady about.*

pull back *vb.* (*adv.*) **1.** to return or be returned to a rearward position by pulling: *the army pulled back.* ~*n.* **pullback. 2.** the act of pulling back. **3.** a device for restraining the motion of a mechanism, etc., or for returning it to its original position.

pull down *vb.* (*tr., adv.*) to destroy or demolish: *the old houses were pulled down.*

pullet ('pʊlɪt) *n.* a young hen of the domestic fowl, less than one year old. [C14: from Old French *poulet* chicken, from Latin *pullus* a young animal or bird]

pulley ('pʊlɪ) *n.* **1.** a wheel with a grooved rim in which a rope, chain, or belt can run in order to change the direction or point of application of a force applied to the rope, etc. **2.** a number of such wheels pivoted in parallel in a block, used to raise heavy loads. **3.** a wheel with a flat, convex, or grooved rim mounted on a shaft and driven by or driving a belt passing around it. [C14 *poley,* from Old French *polie,* from Vulgar Latin *polidium* (unattested), apparently from Late Greek *polidion* (unattested) a little pole, from Greek *polos* axis]

pull in *vb.* (*adv.*) **1.** (*intr.;* often foll. by *to*) to reach a destination: *the train pulled in at the station.* **2.** (*intr.*) Also: **pull over.** (of a motor vehicle, driver, etc.) **a.** to draw in to the side of the road in order to stop or to allow another vehicle to pass. **b.** to stop (at a café, lay-by, etc.). **3.** (*tr.*) to draw or attract: *his appearance will pull in the crowds.* **4.** (*tr.*) *Slang.* to arrest. **5.** (*tr.*) to earn or gain (money). ~*n.* **pull-in. 6.** *Brit.* a roadside café, esp. for lorry drivers.

Pullman ('pʊlmən) *n., pl.* **-mans.** a luxurious railway coach, esp. a sleeping car. Also called: **Pullman car.** [C19: named after George M. *Pullman* (1831–97), the U.S. inventor who first manufactured such coaches]

pull off *vb.* (*tr.*) **1.** to remove (clothing) forcefully. **2.** (*adv.*) to succeed in performing (a difficult feat).

pull on *vb.* (*tr., adv.*) to don (clothing).

pullorum disease (pʊ'lɔːrəm) *n.* an acute serious bacterial disease of very young birds, esp. chickens, characterized by a whitish diarrhoea: caused by *Salmonella pullorum,* transmitted during egg production. Also called: **bacillary white diarrhoea.** [Latin *pullōrum* of chickens, from *pullus* chicken]

pull out *vb.* (*adv.*) **1.** (*tr.*) to extract. **2.** (*intr.*) to depart: *the train pulled out of the station.* **3.** *Military.* to withdraw or escape or be withdrawn or rescued, as from a difficult situation: *the troops were pulled out of the ruined city.* **4.** (*intr.*) (of a motor vehicle, driver, etc.) **a.** to draw away from the side of the road. **b.** to draw out from behind another vehicle to overtake. **5.** (*intr.*) to abandon a position or situation, esp. a dangerous or embarrassing one. **6.** (foll. by *of*) to level out or cause to level out (from a dive). ~*n.* **pull-out. 7.** an extra leaf of a book that folds out. **8.** a removable section of a magazine, etc. **9.** a flight manoeuvre during which an aircraft levels out after a dive. **10.** a withdrawal from a position or situation, esp. a dangerous or embarrassing one.

pullover ('pʊlˌəʊvə) *n.* a garment, esp. a sweater, that is pulled on over the head.

pull through *vb.* **1.** Also: **pull round.** to survive or recover or cause to survive or recover, esp. after a serious illness or crisis. ~*n.* **pull-through. 2.** a weighted cord with a piece of cloth at the end used to clean the bore of a firearm.

pull together *vb.* **1.** (*intr., adv.*) to cooperate or work harmoniously. **2. pull oneself together.** *Informal.* to regain one's self-control or composure.

pullulate ('pʌljʊˌleɪt) *vb.* (*intr.*) **1.** (of animals, etc.) to breed rapidly or abundantly; teem; swarm. **2.** (of plants or plant parts) to sprout, bud, or germinate. [C17: from Latin *pullulāre* to sprout, from *pullulus* a baby animal, from *pullus* young animal] —ˌ**pullu'lation** *n.*

pull up *vb.* (*adv.*) **1.** (*tr.*) to remove by the roots. **2.** (often foll. by *with* or *on*) to move level (with) or ahead (of) or cause to move level (with) or ahead (of), esp. in a race. **3.** to stop: *the car pulled up suddenly.* **4.** (*tr.*) to rebuke. ~*n.* **pull-up. 5.** *Brit.* a roadside café; pull-in.

pullus ('pʊləs) *n.* a technical term for a chick or young bird. [C18: from Latin, from *pullulāre* to sprout]

pulmonary ('pʌlmənərɪ, -mənrɪ, 'pʊl-) *adj.* **1.** of, or relating to or affecting the lungs. **2.** having lungs or lunglike organs. [C18: from Latin *pulmōnārius,* from *pulmō* a lung; related to Greek *pleumōn* a lung]

pulmonary artery *n.* either of the two arteries that convey oxygen-depleted blood from the heart to the lungs.

pulmonary vein *n.* any one of the four veins that convey oxygen-rich blood from the lungs to the heart.

pulmonate ('pʌlmənɪt, 'pʊl-) *adj.* **1.** having lungs or lunglike organs. **2.** of, relating to, or belonging to the *Pulmonata,* a mostly terrestrial subclass or order of gastropod molluscs, including snails and slugs, in which the mantle is adapted as a lung. ~*n.* **3.** any pulmonate mollusc. [C19: from New Latin *pulmōnātus*]

pulmonic (pʌl'mɒnɪk, pʊl-) *adj.* **1.** of or relating to the lungs; pulmonary. ~*n.* **2.** *Rare.* **a.** a person with lung disease. **b.** a drug or remedy for lung disease. [C17: from French *pulmonique,* from Latin *pulmō* a lung; see PULMONARY]

Pulmotor ('pʌlˌməʊtə, 'pʊl-) *n. Trademark.* an apparatus for pumping oxygen into the lungs during artificial respiration.

pulp (pʌlp) *n.* **1.** soft or fleshy plant tissue, such as the succulent part of a fleshy fruit. **2.** a moist mixture of cellulose fibres, as obtained from wood, from which paper is made. **3. a.** a magazine or book containing trite or sensational material, and usually printed on cheap rough paper. **b.** (*as modifier*): *a pulp novel.* **4.** *Dentistry.* the soft innermost part of a tooth, containing nerves and blood vessels. **5.** any soft soggy mass or substance. **6.** *Mining.* pulverized ore, esp. when mixed with water. ~*vb.* **7.** to reduce (a material or solid substance) to pulp or (of a material or solid substance) to be reduced to pulp. **8.** (*tr.*) to remove the pulp from (fruit). [C16: from Latin *pulpa*] —**'pulper** *n.*

pulpit ('pʊlpɪt) *n.* **1.** a raised platform, usually surrounded by a barrier, set up in churches as the appointed place for preaching, leading in prayer, etc. **2.** any similar raised structure, such as a lectern. **3.** a medium for expressing an opinion, such as a column in a newspaper. **4.** (usually preceded by *the*) **a.** the preaching of the Christian message. **b.** the clergy or their message and influence. [C14: from Latin *pulpitum* a platform]

pulpwood ('pʌlpˌwʊd) *n.* pine, spruce, or any other soft wood used to make paper.

pulpy ('pʌlpɪ) *adj.* **pulpier, pulpiest.** having a soft or soggy consistency. —**'pulpily** *adv.* —**'pulpiness** *n.*

pulque ('pʊlkɪ; *Spanish* 'pulke) *n.* a light alcoholic drink from Mexico made from the juice of various agave plants, esp. the maguey. [C17: from Mexican Spanish, apparently from Nahuatl, from *puliuhqui* decomposed, since it will only keep for a day]

pulsar ('pʌlˌsɑː) *n.* any of a number of very small extremely dense stars first discovered in 1967, which rotate very fast emitting regular pulses of polarized radiation, esp. radio waves. They are thought to be neutron stars formed during supernova explosions. [C20: from *puls(ating st)ar,* on the model of QUASAR]

pulsate (pʌl'seɪt) *vb.* (*intr.*) **1.** to expand and contract with a rhythmical beat; throb. **2.** *Physics.* to vary in intensity, magnitude, size, etc.: *the current was pulsating.* **3.** to quiver or vibrate. [C18: from Latin *pulsāre* to push] —**pulsative** ('pʌlsətɪv) *adj.* —**'pulsatively** *adv.*

pulsatile ('pʌlsəˌtaɪl) *adj.* beating rhythmically; pulsating or throbbing. —**pulsatility** (ˌpʌlsə'tɪlɪtɪ) *n.*

pulsatilla (ˌpʌlsə'tɪlə) *n.* another name for **pasqueflower.** [C16: from Medieval Latin, from *pulsāta* beaten (by the wind)]

pulsating star *n.* a type of variable star, the variation in brightness resulting from expansion and subsequent contraction of the star.

pulsation (pʌl'seɪʃən) *n.* **1.** the act of pulsating. **2.** *Physiol.* a rhythmic beating or pulsing esp. of the heart or an artery.

pulsator (pʌl'seɪtə) *n.* **1.** a device that stimulates rhythmic motion of a body; a vibrator. **2.** any pulsating machine, device, or part.

pulsatory ('pʌlsətərɪ, -trɪ) *adj.* **1.** of or relating to pulsation. **2.** throbbing or pulsating.

pulse[1] (pʌls) *n.* **1.** *Physiol.* **a.** the rhythmical contraction and expansion of an artery at each beat of the heart, often discernible to the touch at points such as the wrists. **b.** a single pulsation of the heart or arteries. **2.** *Physics, electronics.* **a.** a transient sharp change in voltage, current, or some other quantity normally constant in a system. **b.** one of a series of such transient disturbances, usually recurring at regular intervals and having a characteristic geometric shape. **c.** (*as modifier*): *a pulse generator.* Less common name: **impulse. 3. a.** a recurrent rhythmical series of beats, waves, vibrations, etc. **b.** any single beat, wave, etc., in such a series. **4.** bustle, vitality, or excitement: *the pulse of a city.* **5.** the feelings or thoughts of a group or society as they can be measured: *the pulse of the voters.* **6. keep one's finger on the pulse.** to be well-informed about current events. ~*vb.* **7.** (*intr.*) to beat, throb, or vibrate. [C14 *pous,* from Latin *pulsus* a beating, from *pellere* to beat] —**'pulseless** *adj.*

pulse[2] (pʌls) *n.* **1.** the edible seeds of any of several papilionaceous plants, such as peas, beans, and lentils. **2.** the plant producing any of these seeds. [C13 *pols,* from Old French, from Latin *puls* pottage of pulse]

pulse code modulation *n. Electronics.* a form of pulse modulation in which the information is carried by coded groups of pulses. Abbrev.: **pcm.**

pulse height analyser *n. Electronics.* a multichannel analyser that sorts pulses into selected amplitude ranges.

pulsejet ('pʌlsˌdʒɛt) *n.* a type of ramjet engine in which air is admitted through movable vanes that are closed by the pressure resulting from each intermittent explosion of the fuel in the combustion chamber, thus causing a pulsating thrust. Also called: **pulsejet engine, pulsojet** ('pʌlsəʊˌdʒɛt).

pulse modulation *n. Electronics.* **1.** a type of modulation in which a train of pulses is used as the carrier wave, one or more of its parameters, such as amplitude, being modulated or modified in order to carry information. **2.** the modulation of a continuous carrier wave by means of pulses.

pulsimeter (pʌl'sɪmɪtə) *n. Med.* an instrument for measuring the strength and rate of the pulse. Also called: **pulsometer.**

pulsometer (pʌl'sɒmɪtə) *n.* **1.** another name for **pulsimeter. 2.** a vacuum pump that operates by steam being condensed and water admitted alternately in two chambers.

pulverable ('pʌlvərəbᵊl) *adj.* able to be pulverized.

pulverize *or* **pulverise** ('pʌlvəˌraɪz) *vb.* **1.** to reduce (a substance) to fine particles, as by crushing or grinding, or (of a substance) to be so reduced. **2.** (*tr.*) to destroy completely; defeat or injure seriously. [C16: from Late Latin *pulverizare* or French *pulvériser,* from Latin *pulverum,* from *pulvis* dust] —'**pulverˌizable** *or* '**pulverˌisable** *adj.* —ˌ**pulveri'zation** *or* ˌ**pulveri'sation** *n.* —'**pulverˌizer** *or* '**pulverˌiser** *n.*

pulverulent (pʌl'vɛrʊlənt) *adj.* consisting of, covered with, or crumbling to dust or fine particles. [C17: from Latin *pulverulentus,* from *pulvis* dust] —**pul'verulence** *n.*

pulvillus (pʌl'vɪləs) *n., pl.* **-li** (-laɪ). a small pad between the claws at the end of an insect's leg. [C18: from Latin, from *pulvīnulus,* diminutive of *pulvīnus* cushion]

pulvinate ('pʌlvɪˌneɪt) *or* **pulvinated** *adj.* **1.** *Architect.* (of a frieze) curved convexly; having a swelling. **2.** *Botany.* **a.** shaped like a cushion. **b.** (of a leafstalk) having a pulvinus. [C19: from Latin *pulvīnātus* cushion-shaped]

pulvinus (pʌl'vaɪnəs) *n., pl.* **-ni** (-naɪ). a swelling at the base of a leafstalk: changes in its turgor pressure cause changes in the position of the leaf. [C19: from Latin: cushion]

puma ('pjuːmə) *n.* a large American feline mammal, *Felis concolor,* that resembles a lion, having a plain greyish-brown coat and long tail. Also called: **cougar, mountain lion.** [C18: via Spanish from Quechuan]

pumice ('pʌmɪs) *n.* **1.** Also called: **pumice stone.** a light porous acid volcanic rock having the composition of rhyolite, used for scouring and, in powdered form, as an abrasive and for polishing. ~*vb.* **2.** (*tr.*) to rub or polish with pumice. [C15 *pomys,* from Old French *pomis,* from Latin *pūmex*] —**pumiceous** (pjuː'mɪʃəs) *adj.*

pumice country *n. N.Z.* volcanic farmland in the North Island.

pummel ('pʌməl) *vb.* **-mels, -melling, -melled** *or U.S.* **-mels, -meling, -meled.** (*tr.*) to strike repeatedly with or as if with the fists. Also (less commonly): **pommel.** [C16: see POMMEL]

pump[1] (pʌmp) *n.* **1.** any device for compressing, driving, raising, or reducing the pressure of a fluid, esp. by means of a piston or set of rotating impellers. **2.** *Biology.* a mechanism for the active transport of ions, such as protons, calcium ions, and sodium ions, across cell membranes: *a sodium pump.* ~*vb.* **3.** (when *tr.,* usually foll. by *from, out, into, away,* etc.) to raise or drive (air, liquid, etc., esp. into or from something) with a pump or similar device. **4.** (*tr.;* usually foll. by *in* or *into*) to supply in large amounts: *to pump capital into a project.* **5.** (*tr.*) to deliver (shots, bullets, etc.) repeatedly with great force. **6.** to operate (something, esp. a handle or lever) in the manner of a pump or (of something) to work in this way: *to pump the pedals of a bicycle.* **7.** (*tr.*) to obtain (information) from (a person) by persistent questioning. **8.** (*intr.;* usually foll. by *from* or *out of*) (of liquids) to flow freely in large spurts: *oil pumped from the fissure.* [C15: from Middle Dutch *pumpe* pipe, probably from Spanish *bomba,* of imitative origin]

pump[2] (pʌmp) *n.* **1.** a low-cut low-heeled shoe without fastenings, worn esp. for dancing. **2.** a type of shoe with a rubber sole, used in games such as tennis; plimsoll. [C16: of unknown origin]

pumped storage *n.* (in hydroelectric systems) a method of using power at a period of low demand to pump water back up to a high storage reservoir so that it can be released to generate electricity at a period of peak demand.

pumpernickel ('pʌmpəˌnɪkᵊl) *n.* a slightly sour black bread, originating in Germany, made of coarse rye flour. [C18: from German, of uncertain origin]

pump gun *n.* a repeating gun operated by a slide-action mechanism feeding ammunition from a magazine under the barrel into the breech.

pump iron *vb.* (*intr.*) *Slang.* to exercise with weights; do bodybuilding exercises.

pumpkin ('pʌmpkɪn) *n.* **1.** any of several creeping cucurbitaceous plants of the genus *Cucurbita,* esp. *C. pepo* of North America and *C. maxima* of Europe. **2. a.** the large round fruit of any of these plants, which has a thick orange rind, pulpy flesh, and numerous seeds. **b.** (*as modifier*): *pumpkin pie.* [C17: from earlier *pumpion,* from Old French *pompon,* from Latin *pepo,* from Greek *pepōn,* from *pepōn* ripe, from *peptein* to ripen]

pumpkinseed ('pʌmpkɪnˌsiːd) *n.* **1.** the seed of the pumpkin. **2.** a common North American freshwater sunfish, *Lepomis gibbosus,* with brightly coloured markings: family *Centrarchidae.*

pump priming *n.* **1.** the act or process of introducing fluid into a pump to improve the sealing of the pump parts on starting and to expel air from it. **2.** *U.S.* government expenditure designed to stimulate economic activity in stagnant or depressed areas. **3.** another term for **deficit financing.**

pump room *n.* a building or room at a spa in which the water from a mineral spring may be drunk.

pun[1] (pʌn) *n.* **1.** the use of words or phrases to exploit ambiguities and innuendoes in their meaning, usually for humorous effect; a play on words. An example is: *"Ben Battle was a soldier bold, And used to war's alarms: But a cannonball took off his legs, So he laid down his arms."* (Thomas Hood). ~*vb.* **puns, punning, punned. 2.** (*intr.*) to make puns. [C17: possibly from Italian *puntiglio* point of detail, wordplay; see PUNCTILIO]

pun[2] (pʌn) *vb.* **puns, punning, punned.** (*tr.*) *Brit.* to pack (earth, rubble, etc.) by pounding. [C16: dialectal variant of POUND[1]] —'**punner** *n.*

puna *Spanish.* ('puna) *n.* **1.** a high cold dry plateau, esp. in the Andes. **2.** another name for **mountain sickness.** [C17: from American Spanish, from Quechuan]

punce (pʌns) *Scot. and northern English dialect.* ~*vb.* (*tr.*) **1.** to kick, beat, or hit. ~*n.* **2.** a kick or punch. [perhaps a blend of PUNCH[1] and POUNCE[1]]

punch[1] (pʌntʃ) *vb.* **1.** to strike blows (at), esp. with a clenched fist. **2.** (*tr.*) *Western U.S.* to herd or drive (cattle), esp. for a living. **3.** (*tr.*) to poke or prod with a stick or similar object. ~*n.* **4.** a blow with the fist. **5.** *Informal.* telling force, point, or vigour: *his arguments lacked punch.* **6. pull (one's) punches.** See at **pull** (sense 24). [C15: perhaps a variant of POUNCE[2]] —'**puncher** *n.*

punch[2] (pʌntʃ) *n.* **1.** a tool or machine for piercing holes in a material. **2.** any of various tools used for knocking a bolt, rivet, etc., out of a hole. **3.** a tool or machine used for stamping a design on something or shaping it by impact. **4.** the solid die of a punching machine for cutting, stamping, or shaping material. **5.** *Computer technol.* a device, such as a card punch or tape punch, used for making holes in a card or paper tape. **6.** see **centre punch.** ~*vb.* **7.** (*tr.*) to pierce, cut, stamp, shape, or drive with a punch. [C14: shortened from *puncheon,* from Old French *ponçon;* see PUNCHEON[2]]

punch[3] (pʌntʃ) *n.* any mixed drink containing fruit juice and, usually, alcoholic liquor, generally hot and spiced. [C17: perhaps from Hindi *pānch,* from Sanskrit *pañca* five; the beverage originally included five ingredients]

Punch (pʌntʃ) *n.* the main character in the traditional children's puppet show **Punch and Judy.**

punchball ('pʌntʃˌbɔːl) *n.* **1.** Also called (U.S. and Canadian): **punching bag.** a stuffed or inflated ball or bag, either suspended or supported by a flexible rod, that is punched for exercise, esp. boxing training. **2.** *U.S.* a game resembling baseball in which a light ball is struck with the fist.

punchboard ('pʌntʃˌbɔːd) *n.* a board full of holes into which numbers on pieces of paper have been pushed, which a player attempts to push out.

punchbowl ('pʌntʃˌbəʊl) *n.* **1.** a large bowl for serving punch, lemonade, etc., usually with a ladle and often having small drinking glasses hooked around the rim. **2.** *Brit.* a bowl-shaped depression in the land.

punch-drunk *adj.* **1.** demonstrating or characteristic of the behaviour of a person who has suffered repeated blows to the head, esp. a professional boxer. **2.** dazed; stupefied.

punched card *or esp. U.S.* **punch card** *n.* a card on which data can be coded in the form of punched holes. In computing, there are usually 80 columns and 12 rows, each column containing a pattern of holes representing one character. Sometimes shortened to **card.**

punched tape *or U.S.* (*sometimes*) **perforated tape** *n.* other terms for **paper tape.**

puncheon[1] ('pʌntʃən) *n.* **1.** a large cask of variable capacity, usually between 70 and 120 gallons. **2.** the volume of such a cask used as a liquid measure. [C15 *poncion,* from Old French *ponchon,* of uncertain origin]

puncheon[2] ('pʌntʃən) *n.* **1.** a short wooden post that is used as a vertical strut. **2.** a less common name for **punch**[2] (sense 1). [C14 *ponson,* from Old French *ponçon,* from Latin *punctiō* a puncture, from *pungere* to prick]

Punchinello (ˌpʌntʃɪ'nɛləʊ) *n., pl.* **-los** *or* **-loes. 1.** a type of clown from Italian burlesque or puppet shows, the prototype of Punch. **2.** (*sometimes not cap.*) any grotesque or absurd character. [C17: from earlier *Polichinello,* from Italian (Neapolitan dialect) *Polecenella,* from Italian *pulcino* chicken, ultimately from Latin *pullus* young animal]

punch line *n.* the culminating part of a joke, funny story, etc., that gives it its humorous or dramatic point.

punch-up *n. Brit. informal.* a fight, brawl, or violent argument.

punchy ('pʌntʃɪ) *adj.* **punchier, punchiest. 1.** an informal word for **punch-drunk. 2.** *Informal.* incisive or forceful: *a punchy article.* —'**punchily** *adv.* —'**punchiness** *n.*

punctate ('pʌŋkteɪt) *or* **punctated** *adj.* having or marked with minute spots, holes, or depressions. [C18: from New Latin *punctātus,* from Latin *punctum* a point] —**punc'tation** *n.*

punctilio (pʌŋk'tɪlɪ,əʊ) *n., pl.* **-os.** 1. strict attention to minute points of etiquette. 2. a petty formality or fine point of etiquette. [C16: from Italian *puntiglio* small point, from *punto* point, from Latin *punctum* point]

punctilious (pʌŋk'tɪlɪəs) *adj.* 1. paying scrupulous attention to correctness in etiquette. 2. attentive to detail. —**punc'tiliously** *adv.* —**punc'tiliousness** *n.*

punctual ('pʌŋktjʊəl) *adj.* 1. arriving or taking place at an arranged time; prompt. 2. (of a person) having the characteristic of always keeping to arranged times, as for appointments, meetings, etc. 3. *Obsolete.* precise; exact; apposite. 4. *Maths.* consisting of or confined to a point in space. [C14: from Medieval Latin *punctuālis* concerning detail, from Latin *punctum* point] —**,punctu'ality** *n.* —**'punctually** *adv.*

punctuate ('pʌŋktjʊ,eɪt) *vb.* (*mainly tr.*) 1. (*also intr.*) to insert punctuation marks into (a written text). 2. to interrupt or insert at frequent intervals: *a meeting punctuated by heckling.* 3. to give emphasis to. [C17: from Medieval Latin *punctuāre* to prick, from Latin *punctum* a prick, from *pungere* to puncture] —**'punctu,ator** *n.*

punctuation (,pʌŋktjʊ'eɪʃən) *n.* 1. the use of symbols not belonging to the alphabet of a writing system to indicate aspects of the intonation and meaning not otherwise conveyed in the written language. 2. the symbols used for this purpose. 3. the act or an instance of punctuating.

punctuation mark *n.* any of the signs used in punctuation, such as a comma or question mark.

puncture ('pʌŋktʃə) *n.* 1. a small hole made by a sharp object. 2. a perforation and loss of pressure in a pneumatic tyre, made by sharp stones, glass, etc. 3. the act of puncturing or perforating. *~vb.* 4. (*tr.*) to pierce (a hole) in (something) with a sharp object. 5. to cause (something pressurized, esp. a tyre) to lose pressure by piercing, or (of a tyre, etc.) to be pierced and collapse in this way. 6. (*tr.*) to depreciate (a person's self-esteem, pomposity, etc.). [C14: from Latin *punctūra,* from *pungere* to prick] —**'puncturable** *adj.* —**'puncturer** *n.*

pundit ('pʌndɪt) *n.* 1. an expert. 2. (formerly) a learned person. 3. Also called: **pandit.** a Brahman learned in Sanskrit and, esp. in Hindu religion, philosophy or law. [C17: from Hindi *pandit,* from Sanskrit *pandita* learned man, from *pandita* learned]

pung (pʌŋ) *n. Eastern U.S. and Canadian.* a horse-drawn sleigh with a boxlike body on runners. [C19: shortened from Algonquian *tom-pung;* compare TOBOGGAN]

punga ('pʌŋə) *n.* a variant spelling of **ponga.**

pungent ('pʌndʒənt) *adj.* 1. having an acrid smell or sharp bitter flavour. 2. (of wit, satire, etc.) biting; caustic. 3. *Biology.* ending in a sharp point: *a pungent leaf.* [C16: from Latin *pungens* piercing, from *pungere* to prick] —**'pungency** *n.* —**'pungently** *adv.*

Punic ('pju:nɪk) *adj.* 1. of or relating to ancient Carthage or the Carthaginians. 2. characteristic of the treachery of the Carthaginians. *~n.* 3. the language of the ancient Carthaginians; a late form of Phoenician. [C15: from Latin *Pūnicus,* variant of *Poenicus* Carthaginian, from Greek *Phoinix*]

punish ('pʌnɪʃ) *vb.* 1. to force (someone) to undergo a penalty or sanction, such as imprisonment, fines, death, etc., for some crime or misdemeanour. 2. (*tr.*) to inflict punishment for (some crime, etc.). 3. (*tr.*) to use or treat harshly or roughly, esp. as by overexertion: *to punish a horse.* 4. (*tr.*) *Informal.* to consume (some commodity) in large quantities: *to punish the bottle.* [C14 *punisse,* from Old French *punir,* from Latin *pūnīre* to punish, from *poena* penalty] —**'punisher** *n.* —**'punishing** *adj.* —**'punishingly** *adv.*

punishable ('pʌnɪʃəbᵊl) *adj.* liable to be punished or deserving of punishment. —**,punisha'bility** *n.*

punishment ('pʌnɪʃmənt) *n.* 1. a penalty or sanction given for any crime or offence. 2. the act of punishing or state of being punished. 3. *Informal.* rough treatment. 4. *Psychol.* any aversive stimulus administered to an organism as part of training.

punitive ('pju:nɪtɪv) *or* (*less commonly*) **punitory** ('pju:nɪtərɪ, -trɪ) *adj.* relating to, involving, or with the intention of inflicting punishment: *a punitive expedition.* [C17: from Medieval Latin *pūnītīvus* concerning punishment, from Latin *pūnīre* to punish] —**'punitively** *adv.* —**'punitiveness** *n.*

Punjabi *or* **Panjabi** (pʌn'dʒɑ:bɪ) *n.* 1. a member of the chief people of the Punjab, NW India. 2. the state language of the Punjab, belonging to the Indic branch of the Indo-European family. *~adj.* 3. of or relating to the Punjab, its people, or their language.

punk[1] (pʌŋk) *n.* 1. a. a youth movement of the late 1970s, characterized by anti-Establishment slogans and outrageous clothes and hairstyles. b. an adherent of punk. c. short for **punk rock.** d. (*as modifier*): *a punk record.* 2. an inferior, rotten, or worthless person or thing. 3. worthless articles collectively. 4. a petty criminal or hoodlum. 5. *Obsolete.* a young male homosexual; catamite. 6. *Obsolete.* a prostitute. *~adj.* 7. inferior, rotten, or worthless. [C16: via Polari from Spanish *pu(n)ta* prostitute, *pu(n)to* male prostitute] —**'punkish** *adj.*

punk[2] (pʌŋk) *n.* 1. dried decayed wood that smoulders when ignited: used as tinder. 2. any of various other substances that smoulder when ignited, esp. one used to light fireworks. [C18: of uncertain origin]

punka *or* **punkah** ('pʌŋkə) *n.* a fan made of a palm leaf or leaves. [C17: from Hindi *pankhā,* from Sanskrit *paksaka* fan, from *paksa* wing]

punk rock *n.* a fast abrasive style of rock music of the late 1970s, characterized by aggressive or offensive lyrics and performance. Sometimes shortened to **punk.** —**punk rocker** *n.*

punnet ('pʌnɪt) *n. Chiefly Brit.* a small basket for fruit, such as strawberries. [C19: perhaps diminutive of dialect *pun* POUND[2]]

punster ('pʌnstə) *n.* a person who is fond of making puns, esp. one who makes a tedious habit of this.

punt[1] (pʌnt) *n.* 1. an open flat-bottomed boat with square ends, propelled by a pole. See **quant.** *~vb.* 2. to propel (a boat, esp. a punt) by pushing with a pole on the bottom of a river, etc. [Old English *punt* shallow boat, from Latin *pontō* punt, PONTOON[1]]

punt[2] (pʌnt) *n.* 1. a kick in certain sports, such as rugby, in which the ball is released and kicked before it hits the ground. *~vb.* 2. to kick (a ball, etc.) using a punt. [C19: perhaps a variant of English dialect *bunt* to push, perhaps a nasalized variant of BUTT[3]]

punt[3] (pʌnt) *Chiefly Brit. ~vb.* 1. (*intr.*) to gamble; bet. *~n.* 2. a gamble or bet, esp. against the bank, as in roulette, or on horses. 3. Also called: **punter.** a person who bets. 4. **take a punt at.** *Austral. and N. Z. informal.* to have an attempt or try at (something). [C18: from French *ponter* to punt, from *ponte* bet laid against the banker, from Spanish *punto* point, from Latin *punctum*]

punt[4] (pʊnt) *n.* the Irish pound. [Irish Gaelic: pound]

punter[1] ('pʌntə) *n.* a person who punts a boat.

punter[2] ('pʌntə) *n.* a person who kicks a ball.

punter[3] ('pʌntə) *n.* 1. a person who places a bet. 2. *Informal.* any member of the public, esp. when a customer: *the punters flock into the sales.* 3. *Slang.* a prostitute's client. 4. *Slang.* a victim of a con man.

punty ('pʌntɪ) *n., pl.* **-ties.** a long iron rod used in the finishing process of glass-blowing. [C17: see PONTIL]

puny ('pju:nɪ) *adj.* **-nier, -niest.** 1. having a small physique or weakly constitution. 2. paltry; insignificant. [C16: from Old French *puisne* PUISNE] —**'punily** *adv.* —**'puniness** *n.*

pup (pʌp) *n.* 1. a. a young dog, esp. when under one year of age; puppy. b. the young of various other animals, such as the seal. 2. **in pup.** (of a bitch) pregnant. 3. *Informal, chiefly Brit., contemptuous.* a conceited young man (esp. in the phrase **young pup**). 4. **sell (someone) a pup.** to swindle (someone) by selling him something worthless. 5. **the night's a pup.** *Austral. slang.* it's early yet. *~vb.* **pups, pupping, pupped.** 6. (of dogs, seals, etc.) to give birth to (young). [C18: back formation from PUPPY]

pupa ('pju:pə) *n., pl.* **-pae** (-pi:) *or* **-pas.** an insect at the immobile nonfeeding stage of development between larva and adult, when many internal changes occur. See **coarctate, exarate, obtect.** [C19: via New Latin, from Latin: a doll, puppet] —**'pupal** *adj.*

puparium (pju:'pɛərɪəm) *n., pl.* **-ia** (-ɪə). a hard barrel-shaped case enclosing the pupae of the housefly and other dipterous insects. —**pu'parial** *adj.*

pupate (pju:'peɪt) *vb.* (*intr.*) (of an insect larva) to develop into a pupa. —**pu'pation** *n.*

pupil[1] ('pju:pᵊl) *n.* 1. a student who is taught by a teacher, esp. a young student. 2. *Civil and Scots Law.* a boy under 14 or a girl under 12 who is in the care of a guardian. [C14: from Latin *pupillus* an orphan, from *pūpus* a child]

pupil[2] ('pju:pᵊl) *n.* the dark circular aperture at the centre of the iris of the eye, through which light enters. [C16: from Latin *pūpilla,* diminutive of *pūpa* girl, puppet; from the tiny reflections in the eye]

pupillage *or U.S.* **pupilage** ('pju:pɪlɪdʒ) *n.* 1. the condition of being a pupil or duration for which one is a pupil. 2. (in England) the period spent by a newly called barrister in the chambers of a member of the bar.

pupillary[1] *or* **pupilary** ('pju:pɪlərɪ) *adj.* of or relating to a pupil or legal ward. [C17: from PUPIL[1] + -ARY] —**,pupil'larity** *or* **,pupi'larity** *n.*

pupillary[2] *or* **pupilary** ('pju:pɪlərɪ) *adj.* of or relating to the pupil of the eye. [C18: from Latin *pūpilla* PUPIL[2]]

pupiparous (pju:'pɪpərəs) *adj.* (of certain dipterous flies) producing young that have already reached the pupa stage at the time of hatching. [C19: from New Latin *pupiparus,* from PUPA + *parere* to bring forth]

puppet ('pʌpɪt) *n.* 1. a. a small doll or figure of a person or animal moved by strings attached to its limbs or by the hand inserted in its cloth body. b. (*as modifier*): *a puppet theatre.* 2. a. a person, group, state, etc., that appears independent but is in fact controlled by another. b. (*as modifier*): *a puppet government.* [C16 *popet,* perhaps from Old French *poupette* little doll, ultimately from Latin *pūpa* girl, doll]

puppeteer (,pʌpɪ'tɪə) *n.* a person who manipulates puppets.

puppetry ('pʌpɪtrɪ) *n.* 1. the art of making and manipulating puppets and presenting puppet shows. 2. unconvincing or specious presentation.

Puppis ('pʌpɪs) *n., Latin genitive* **Puppis.** a constellation in the S hemisphere lying between Vela and Canis Major, a section of which is crossed by the Milky Way. [Latin: the ship, the POOP of a ship]

puppy ('pʌpɪ) *n., pl.* **-pies.** **1.** a young dog; pup. **2.** *Informal, contemptuous.* a brash or conceited young man; pup. [C15 *popi,* from Old French *popée* doll; compare PUPPET] —'**puppy,hood** *n.* —'**puppyish** *adj.*

puppy fat *n.* fatty tissue that develops in childhood or adolescence and usually disappears by maturity.

puppy love *n.* another term for **calf love.**

pup tent *n.* another name for **shelter tent.**

Purana (pʊ'rɑːnə) *n.* any of a class of Sanskrit writings not included in the Vedas, characteristically recounting the birth and deeds of Hindu gods and the creation, destruction, or recreation of the universe. [C17: from Sanskrit: ancient, from *purā* formerly] —**Pu'ranic** *adj.*

Purbeck marble *or* **stone** ('pɜːbɛk) *n.* a fossil-rich limestone that takes a high polish: used for building, etc. [C15: named after *Purbeck,* Dorset, where it is quarried]

purblind ('pɜː,blaɪnd) *adj.* **1.** partly or nearly blind. **2.** lacking in insight or understanding; obtuse. [C13: see PURE, BLIND; compare PARBOIL]

purchasable ('pɜːtʃɪsəbᵊl) *adj.* **1.** able to be bribed or corrupted. **2.** able to be bought. —,**purchasa'bility** *n.*

purchase ('pɜːtʃɪs) *vb. (tr.)* **1.** to obtain (goods, etc.) by payment. **2.** to obtain by effort, sacrifice, etc.: *to purchase one's freedom.* **3.** to draw, haul, or lift (a load) with the aid of mechanical apparatus. **4.** to acquire (an estate) other than by inheritance. ~*n.* **5.** something that is purchased, esp. an article bought with money. **6.** the act of buying. **7.** acquisition of an estate by any lawful means other than inheritance. **8.** a rough measure of the mechanical advantage achieved by a lever. **9.** a firm foothold, grasp, etc., as for climbing or levering something. **10.** a means of achieving some influence, advantage, etc. [C13: from Old French *porchacier* to strive to obtain, from *por-* for + *chacier* to CHASE] —'**purchaser** *n.*

purchase ledger *n. Commerce.* a record of a company's purchases of goods and services showing the amounts paid and due.

purchase tax *n. Brit.* a tax levied on nonessential consumer goods and added to selling prices by retailers.

purdah *or* **purda** ('pɜːdə) *n.* **1.** the custom in some Muslim and Hindu communities of keeping women in seclusion, with clothing that conceals them completely when they go out. **2.** a screen in a Hindu house used to keep the women out of view. **3.** a veil worn by Hindu women of high caste. [C19: from Hindi *parda* veil, from Persian *pardah*]

purdonium (pɜː'dəʊnɪəm) *n.* a type of coal scuttle having a slanted cover that is raised to open it, and an inner removable metal container for the coal. [C19: named after its inventor, a Mr *Purdon*]

pure (pjʊə) *adj.* **1.** not mixed with any extraneous or dissimilar materials, elements, etc.: *pure nitrogen.* **2.** free from tainting or polluting matter; clean; wholesome: *pure water.* **3.** free from moral taint or defilement: *pure love.* **4.** *(prenominal)* (intensifier): *pure stupidity; a pure coincidence.* **5.** (of a subject, etc.) studied in its theoretical aspects rather than for its practical applications: *pure mathematics; pure science.* Compare **applied.** **6.** (of a vowel) pronounced with more or less unvarying quality without any glide; monophthongal. **7.** (of a consonant) not accompanied by another consonant. **8.** of supposedly unmixed racial descent: *a pure Negro.* **9.** *Genetics, biology.* breeding true for one or more characteristics; homozygous. **10.** *Music.* **a.** (of a sound) composed of a single frequency without overtones. **b.** (of intervals in the system of just intonation) mathematically accurate in respect to the ratio of one frequency to another. [C13: from Old French *pur,* from Latin *pūrus* unstained] —'**pureness** *n.*

purebred *adj.* ('pjʊə'brɛd). **1.** denoting a pure strain obtained through many generations of controlled breeding. ~*n.* ('pjʊə,brɛd). **2.** a purebred animal. Compare **grade** (sense 9), **crossbred** (sense 2).

pure culture *n. Bacteriol.* a culture containing a single species of microorganism.

puree *or* **puri** ('puːrɪ) *n.* an unleavened flaky Indian bread, that is deep-fried in ghee and served hot. [Hindi]

purée ('pjʊəreɪ) *n.* **1.** a smooth thick pulp of cooked and sieved fruit, vegetables, meat, or fish. ~*vb.* **-rées, -réeing, -réed.** **2.** *(tr.)* to make (cooked foods) into a purée. [C19: from French *purer* to PURIFY]

pure line *n.* a breed or strain of animals or plants in which certain characters appear in successive generations as a result of inbreeding or self-fertilization.

purely ('pjʊəlɪ) *adv.* **1.** in a pure manner. **2.** entirely: *purely by chance.* **3.** in a chaste or innocent manner.

purfle ('pɜːfᵊl) *n. also* **purfling.** **1.** a ruffled or curved ornamental band, as on clothing, furniture, etc. ~*vb.* **2.** *(tr.)* to decorate with such a band or bands. [C14: from Old French *purfiler* to decorate with a border, from *filer* to spin, from *fil* thread, from Latin *fīlum*]

purgation (pɜː'geɪʃən) *n.* the act of purging or state of being purged; purification.

purgative ('pɜːgətɪv) *Med.* ~*n.* **1.** a drug or agent for purging the bowels. ~*adj.* **2.** causing evacuation of the bowels; cathartic. —'**purgatively** *adv.*

purgatorial (,pɜːgə'tɔːrɪəl) *adj.* **1.** serving to purify from sin. **2.** of, relating to, or like purgatory. —,**purga'torially** *adv.*

purgatory ('pɜːgətərɪ, -trɪ) *n.* **1.** *Chiefly R.C. Church.* a state or place in which the souls of those who have died in a state of grace are believed to undergo a limited amount of suffering to expiate their venial sins and become purified of the remaining effects of mortal sin. **2.** a place or condition of suffering or torment, esp. one that is temporary. [C13: from Old French *purgatoire,* from Medieval Latin *pūrgātōrium,* literally: place of cleansing, from Latin *pūrgāre* to PURGE]

purge (pɜːdʒ) *vb.* **1.** *(tr.)* to rid (something) of (impure or undesirable elements). **2.** *(tr.)* to rid (a state, political party, etc.) of (dissident or troublesome people). **3.** *(tr.)* **a.** to empty (the bowels) by evacuation of faeces. **b.** to cause (a person) to evacuate his bowels. **4. a.** to clear (a person) of a charge. **b.** to free (oneself) of guilt, as by atonement: *to purge contempt.* **5.** *(intr.)* to be cleansed or purified. ~*n.* **6.** the act or process of purging. **7.** the elimination of opponents or dissidents from a state, political party, etc. **8.** a purgative drug or agent; cathartic. [C14: from Old French *purger,* from Latin *pūrgāre* to purify] —'**purger** *n.*

Purification of the Virgin Mary *n.* **the.** *Christianity.* the feast (Feb. 2) commemorating the presentation of Jesus in the Temple after the completion of Mary's purification (Luke 2:22). Also called: **Candlemas.**

purificator ('pjʊərɪfɪ,keɪtə) *n. Christianity.* a small white linen cloth used to wipe the chalice and paten and also the lips and fingers of the celebrant at the Eucharist.

purify ('pjʊərɪ,faɪ) *vb.* **-fies, -fying, -fied.** **1.** to free (something) of extraneous, contaminating, or debasing matter. **2.** *(tr.)* to free (a person, etc.) from sin or guilt. **3.** *(tr.)* to make clean, as in a ritual, esp. the churching of women after childbirth. [C14: from Old French *purifier,* from Late Latin *pūrificāre* to cleanse, from *pūrus* pure + *facere* to make] —,**purifi'cation** *n.* —**purificatory** ('pjʊərɪfɪ,keɪtərɪ) *adj.* —'**puri,fier** *n.*

Purim ('pʊərɪm; *Hebrew* puː'riːm) *n.* a Jewish holiday celebrated on Adar 14, in February or March, and in Adar Sheni in leap years, to commemorate the deliverance of the Jews from the massacre planned for them by Haman (Esther 9). [Hebrew *pūrīm,* plural of *pūr* lot; from the casting of lots by Haman]

purine ('pjʊəriːn) *or* **purin** ('pjʊərɪn) *n.* **1.** a colourless crystalline solid that can be prepared from uric acid. Formula: $C_5H_5N_4$. **2.** Also called: **purine base.** any of a number of nitrogenous bases, such as guanine and adenine, that are derivatives of purine and constituents of nucleic acids and certain coenzymes. [C19: from German *Purin;* see PURE, URIC, -INE[2]]

puriri (puː'riːriː) *n., pl.* **-ris.** a forest tree, *Vitex lucens,* of New Zealand, having red berries and glossy green leaves and yielding a durable dark brown timber.

purism ('pjʊə,rɪzəm) *n.* insistence on traditional canons of correctness of form or purity of style or content, esp. in language, art, or music. —'**purist** *adj., n.* —**pu'ristic** *adj.* —**pu'ristically** *adv.*

puritan ('pjʊərɪtᵊn) *n.* **1.** a person who adheres to strict moral or religious principles, esp. one opposed to luxury and sensual enjoyment. ~*adj.* **2.** characteristic of a puritan. [C16: from Late Latin *pūritās* PURITY] —'**puritan,ism** *n.*

Puritan ('pjʊərɪtᵊn) (in the late 16th and 17th centuries) ~*n.* **1.** any of the more extreme English Protestants, most of whom were Calvinists, who wished to purify the Church of England of most of its ceremony and other aspects that they deemed to be Catholic. ~*adj.* **2.** of, characteristic of, or relating to the Puritans. —'**Puritan,ism** *n.*

puritanical (,pjʊərɪ'tænɪkᵊl) *or (less commonly)* **puritanic** *adj.* **1.** *Usually disparaging.* strict in moral or religious outlook, esp. in shunning sensual pleasures. **2.** *(sometimes cap.)* of or relating to a puritan or the Puritans. —,**puri'tanically** *adv.* —,**puri'tanicalness** *n.*

purity ('pjʊərɪtɪ) *n.* **1.** the state or quality of being pure. **2.** *Physics.* a measure of the amount of a single-frequency colour in a mixture of spectral and achromatic colours.

purl[1] (pɜːl) *n.* **1.** Also called: **purl stitch.** a knitting stitch made by doing a plain stitch backwards. **2.** a decorative border, as of lace. **3.** gold or silver wire thread. ~*vb.* **4.** to knit (a row or garment) in purl stitch. **5.** to edge (something) with a purl. ~Also (for senses 2, 3, 5): **pearl.** [C16: from dialect *pirl* to twist into a cord]

purl[2] (pɜːl) *vb.* **1.** *(intr.)* (of a stream, etc.) to flow with a gentle curling or rippling movement and a murmuring sound. ~*n.* **2.** a curling movement of water; eddy. **3.** a murmuring sound, as of a shallow stream. [C16: related to Norwegian *purla* to bubble]

purler[1] ('pɜːlə) *n. Informal.* a headlong or spectacular fall (esp. in the phrase **come a purler**).

purler[2] ('pɜːlə) *n. Austral. slang.* something outstanding in its class. [of unknown origin]

purlieu ('pɜːljuː) *n.* **1.** *English history.* land on the edge of a forest that was once included within the bounds of the royal forest but was later separated although still subject to some of the forest laws, esp. regarding hunting. **2.** *(usually pl.)* a neighbouring area; outskirts. **3.** *(often pl.)* a place one frequents; haunt. **4.** *Rare.* a district or suburb, esp. one that is poor or squalid. [C15 *purlewe,* from Anglo-French *puralé* a going through (influenced also by Old French *lieu* place), from Old French *puraler* to traverse, from *pur* through + *aler* to go]

purlin *or* **purline** ('pɜːlɪn) *n.* a horizontal beam that provides intermediate support for the common rafters of a roof construction. [C15: of uncertain origin]

purloin (pɜː'lɔɪn) *vb.* to take (something) dishonestly; steal. [C15: from Old French *porloigner* to put at a distance, from *por-* for + *loin* distant, from Latin *longus* long] —**pur'loiner** *n.*

purple ('pɜːpᵊl) *n.* **1.** any of various colours with a hue lying between red and blue and often highly saturated; a nonspectral colour. **2.** a dye or pigment producing such a colour. **3.** cloth of this colour, often used to symbolize royalty or nobility. **4.** (usually preceded by *the*) high rank; nobility. **5. a.** the official robe of a cardinal. **b.** the rank, office, or authority of a cardinal as signified by this. **6. the purple.** bishops collectively. ~*adj.* **7.** of the colour purple. **8.** (of writing) excessively elaborate or full of imagery: *purple prose.* **9.** noble or royal. [Old English, from Latin *purpura* purple dye, from Greek *porphura* the purple fish (*Murex*)] —'**purpleness** *n.* —'**purplish** *adj.* —'**purply** *adj.*

purple emperor *n.* any of several Old World nymphalid butterflies of the genus *Apatura,* esp. *A. iris,* having mottled purple-and-brown wings.

purple-fringed orchid *or* **orchis** *n.* either of two North American orchids, *Habenaria psychodes* or *H. fimbriata,* having purple fringed flowers.

purple gallinule *n.* a long-toed purple aquatic bird, *Porphyrio porphyrio* (or *Porphyrula martinica*), of the southern U.S. and Europe, with red legs and red bill: family *Rallidae* (rails, etc.).

purple heart *n.* **1.** any of several tropical American leguminous trees of the genus *Peltogyne.* **2.** the decorative purple heartwood of any of these trees. **3.** *Informal, chiefly Brit.* a heart-shaped purple tablet consisting mainly of amphetamine.

Purple Heart *n.* a decoration awarded to members of the U.S. Armed Forces for a wound incurred in action.

purple medic *n.* another name for **alfalfa.**

purple patch *n.* 1. Also called: **purple passage.** a section in a piece of writing characterized by rich, fanciful, or ornate language. **2.** *Slang.* a period of success, good fortune, etc.

purport *vb.* (pɜː'pɔːt). (*tr.*) **1.** to claim to be (true, official, etc.) by manner or appearance, esp. falsely. **2.** (esp. of speech or writing) to signify or imply. ~*n.* ('pɜːpɔːt). **3.** meaning; significance; import. **4.** purpose; object; intention. [C15: from Anglo-French: contents, from Old French *porporter* to convey, from *por-* forth + *porter* to carry, from Latin *portāre*]

purported (pɜː'pɔːtɪd) *adj.* alleged; supposed; rumoured: *a purported two million deal.* —**pur'portedly** *adv.*

purpose ('pɜːpəs) *n.* **1.** the reason for which anything is done, created, or exists. **2.** a fixed design, outcome, or idea that is the object of an action or other effort. **3.** fixed intention in doing something; determination: *a man of purpose.* **4.** practical advantage or use: *to work to good purpose.* **5.** that which is relevant or under consideration (esp. in the phrase **to** or **from the purpose**). **6.** *Archaic.* purport. **7. on purpose.** intentionally. ~*vb.* (*tr.*) **8.** to intend or determine to do (something). [C13: from Old French *porpos,* from *porposer* to plan, from Latin *prōpōnere* to PROPOSE]

purpose-built *adj.* made to serve a specific purpose.

purposeful ('pɜːpəsfʊl) *adj.* **1.** having a definite purpose in view. **2.** fixed in one's purpose; determined. —'**purposefully** *adv.* —'**purposefulness** *n.*

purposeless ('pɜːpəslɪs) *adj.* having no fixed plan or intention. —'**purposelessly** *adv.* —'**purposelessness** *n.*

purposely ('pɜːpəslɪ) *adv.* for a definite reason; on purpose.

purposive ('pɜːpəsɪv) *adj.* **1.** relating to, having, or indicating conscious intention. **2.** serving a purpose; useful. —'**purposively** *adv.* —'**purposiveness** *n.*

purpura ('pɜːpjʊrə) *n. Pathol.* any of several blood diseases causing purplish spots or patches due to subcutaneous bleeding. [C18: via Latin from Greek *porphura* a shellfish yielding purple dye] —'**purpuric** *adj.*

purpure ('pɜːpjʊə) *n., adj.* (*usually postpositive*) *Heraldry.* purple. [Old English from Latin *purpura* PURPLE]

purpurin ('pɜːpjʊrɪn) *n.* a red crystalline compound used as a stain for biological specimens; 1,2,4-trihydroxyanthraquinone. Formula: $C_{14}H_5O_2(OH)_3$. [C19: from Latin *purpura* PURPLE + -IN]

purr (pɜː) *vb.* **1.** (*intr.*) (esp. of cats) to make a low vibrant sound, usually considered as expressing pleasure, etc. **2.** (*tr.*) to express (pleasure, etc.) by this sound. ~*n.* **3.** a purring sound. [C17: of imitative origin; compare French *ronronner* to purr, German *schnurren,* Dutch *snorren*]

purse (pɜːs) *n.* **1.** a small bag or pouch, often made of soft leather, for carrying money, esp. coins. **2.** *U.S. and Canadian.* a woman's handbag. **3.** anything resembling a small bag or pouch in form or function. **4.** wealth; funds; resources. **5.** a sum of money that is offered, esp. as a prize. ~*vb.* **6.** (*tr.*) to contract (the mouth, lips, etc.) into a small rounded shape. [Old English *purs,* probably from Late Latin *bursa* bag, ultimately from Greek: leather]

purser ('pɜːsə) *n.* an officer aboard a passenger ship, merchant ship, or aircraft who keeps the accounts and attends to the welfare of the passengers.

purse seine *n.* a large net towed, usually by two boats, that encloses a school of fish and is then closed at the bottom by means of a line resembling the string formerly used to draw shut the neck of a money pouch or purse.

purse strings *pl. n.* control of finance or expenditure (esp. in such phrases as **hold** or **control the purse strings**).

purslane ('pɜːslɪn, -leɪn) *n.* **1.** a weedy portulacaceous plant, *Portulaca oleracea,* with small yellow flowers and fleshy leaves, which are used in salads and as a potherb. **2.** any of various similar or related plants, such as sea purslane and water purslane. [C14 *purcelane,* from Old French *porcelaine,* from Late Latin *porcillāgō,* from Latin *porcillāca,* variant of *portulāca*]

pursuance (pə'sjuːəns) *n.* the carrying out or pursuing of an action, plan, etc.

pursuant (pə'sjuːənt) *adj.* **1.** (*usually postpositive;* often foll. by *to*) *Chiefly law.* in agreement or conformity. **2.** *Archaic.* pursuing. [C17: related to Middle English *poursuivant* following after, from Old French; see PURSUE] —**pur'suantly** *adv.*

pursue (pə'sjuː) *vb.* **-sues, -suing, -sued.** (*mainly tr.*) **1.** (*also intr.*) to follow (a fugitive, etc.) in order to capture or overtake. **2.** (esp. of something bad or unlucky) to follow closely or accompany: *ill health pursued her.* **3.** to seek or strive to attain (some object, desire, etc.). **4.** to follow the precepts of (a plan, policy, etc.). **5.** to apply oneself to (one's studies, hobbies, interests, etc.). **6.** to follow persistently or seek to become acquainted with. **7.** to continue to discuss or argue (a point, subject, etc.). [C13: from Anglo-Norman *pursiwer,* from Old French *poursivre,* from Latin *prōsequī* to follow after] —**pur'suer** *n.*

pursuit (pə'sjuːt) *n.* **1. a.** the act of pursuing, chasing, or striving after. **b.** (*as modifier*): *a pursuit plane.* **2.** an occupation, hobby, or pastime. **3.** (in cycling) a race in which the riders set off at intervals along the track and attempt to overtake each other. [C14: from Old French *poursieute,* from *poursivre* to prosecute, PURSUE]

pursuivant ('pɜːsɪvənt) *n.* **1.** the lowest rank of heraldic officer. **2.** *History.* a state or royal messenger. **3.** *History.* a follower or attendant. [C14: from Old French, from *poursivre* to PURSUE]

pursy ('pɜːsɪ) *adj.* **1.** short-winded. **2.** *Archaic.* fat; over-weight. [C15: alteration of earlier *pursive,* from Anglo-French *porsif,* ultimately from Latin *pulsāre* to PULSATE]

purtenance ('pɜːtɪnəns) *n. Archaic.* the inner organs, viscera. [C14: from Old French *pertinance* something that belongs; see APPURTENANCE]

purulent ('pjʊərʊlənt) *adj.* of, relating to, or containing pus. [C16: from Latin *pūrulentus,* from PUS] —'**purulence** *or* '**purulency** *n.* —'**purulently** *adv.*

purvey (pə'veɪ) *vb.* (*tr.*) **1.** to sell or provide (commodities, esp. foodstuffs) on a large scale. **2.** to publish or make available (lies, scandal, etc.). ~*n.* ('pɜːvɪ). **3.** *Scot.* the food and drink laid on at a wedding reception, etc. [C13: from Old French *porveeir,* from Latin *prōvidēre* to PROVIDE]

purveyance (pə'veɪəns) *n.* **1.** *History.* the collection or requisition of provisions for a sovereign. **2.** *Rare.* the act of purveying. **3.** *Rare.* that which is purveyed.

purveyor (pə'veɪə) *n.* **1.** (*often pl.*) a person, organization, etc., that supplies food and provisions. **2.** a person who spreads, repeats, or sells (information, lies, etc.). **3.** a person or thing that habitually provides or supplies a particular thing or quality: *a purveyor of humour.* **4.** *History.* an officer providing or exacting provisions, lodging, etc., for a sovereign.

purview ('pɜːvjuː) *n.* **1.** the scope of operation or concern of something. **2.** the breadth or range of outlook or understanding. **3.** *Law.* the body of a statute, containing the enacting clauses. [C15: from Anglo-Norman *purveu,* from *porveeir* to furnish; see PURVEY]

pus (pʌs) *n.* the yellow or greenish fluid product of inflammation, composed largely of dead leucocytes, exuded plasma, and liquefied tissue cells. [C16: from Latin *pūs;* related to Greek *puon* pus]

Puseyism ('pjuːzɪˌɪzəm) *n.* a derogatory term for the **Oxford Movement,** used by its contemporary opponents. [C19: after E. B. *Pusey* (1800–82), one of the movement's leaders] —'**Puseyite** *n., adj.*

push (pʊʃ) *vb.* **1.** (when *tr.,* often foll. by *off, away,* etc.) to apply steady force to (something) in order to move it. **2.** to thrust (one's way) through something, such as a crowd, by force. **3.** (when *intr.,* often foll. by *for*) to apply oneself vigorously (to achieving a task, plan, etc.). **4.** (*tr.*) to encourage or urge (a person) to some action, decision, etc. **5.** (when *intr.,* often foll. by *for*) to be an advocate or promoter (of): *to push for acceptance of one's theories.* **6.** (*tr.*) to use one's influence to help (a person): *to push one's own candidate.* **7.** to bear upon (oneself or another person) in order to achieve more effort, better results, etc.: *she was a woman who liked to push her husband.* **8.** (*tr.*) to make too much of (an advantage or opportunity), thus risking failure: *to push one's luck.* **9.** *Tennis, cricket, etc.* to hit (a ball) with a stiff pushing stroke. **10.** (*tr.*) *Informal.* to sell (narcotic drugs) illegally. **11.** (*intr.;* foll. by *out, into,* etc.) (esp. of geographical features) to reach or extend: *the cliffs pushed out to the sea.* **12.** (*tr.*) to overdevelop (a photographic film), usually by the equivalent of up to two stops, to compensate for underexposure or increase contrast. **13. push up (the) daisies.** *Slang.* to be dead and buried. ~*n.* **14.** the act of pushing; thrust. **15.** a part or device that is pressed to operate some mechanism. **16.** *Informal.* ambitious or enterprising drive, energy, etc. **17.** *Informal.* a special effort or attempt to advance, as of an army in a war: *to make a* *push.* **18.** *Informal.* a number of people gathered in one place, such as at a party. **19.** *Austral. slang.* a group or gang, esp. one considered to be a clique. **20.** *Tennis, cricket, etc.* a stiff pushing stroke. **21. at a push.** *Informal.* with difficulty; only just. **22. the push.** *Informal, chiefly Brit.* dismissal, esp. from employment. ~See also **push about, push along, push in, push off, push on, push through.** [C13: from Old French *pousser,* from Latin *pulsāre,* from *pellere* to drive]

push about *or* **around** *vb. (tr., adv.) Slang.* to bully; keep telling (a person) what to do in a bossy manner.

push along *vb. (intr., adv.) Informal.* to go away; leave.

pushball ('pʊʃˌbɔːl) *n. Chiefly U.S. and Canadian.* a game in which two teams try to push a heavy ball towards opposite goals.

push-bike *n. Brit.* an informal name for **bicycle.**

push button *n.* **1.** an electrical switch operated by pressing a button, which closes or opens a circuit. **2.** *(modifier)* **push-button. a.** operated by a push button: *a push-button radio.* **b.** initiated as simply as by pressing a button: *push-button warfare.*

pushcart ('pʊʃˌkɑːt) *n.* another name (esp. U.S. and Canadian) for **barrow**[1] (sense 3).

pushchair ('pʊʃˌtʃɛə) *n. Brit.* a usually collapsible chair-shaped carriage in which a small child may be wheeled. Also called: **baby buggy, buggy.** U.S. and Canadian word: **stroller.** Austral. words: **pusher, stroller.**

pushed (pʊʃt) *adj.* (often foll. by *for*) *Informal.* short (of) or in need (of time, money, etc.).

pusher ('pʊʃə) *n.* **1.** *Informal.* a person who sells illegal drugs, esp. narcotics such as heroin and morphine. **2.** *Informal.* an actively or aggressively ambitious person. **3. a.** a type of aircraft propeller placed behind the engine. **b.** a type of aircraft using such a propeller. **4.** a person or thing that pushes. **5.** *Brit.* a rakelike implement used by small children to push food onto a spoon. **6.** *Austral.* the usual name for **pushchair.**

push fit *n. Engineering.* another name for **sliding fit.**

push in *vb. (intr., adv.)* to force one's way into a group of people, queue, etc.

pushing ('pʊʃɪŋ) *adj.* **1.** enterprising, resourceful, or aggressively ambitious. **2.** impertinently self-assertive. ~*adv.* **3.** almost or nearly (a certain age, speed, etc.): *pushing fifty.* —'**pushingly** *adv.* —'**pushingness** *n.*

push money *n.* a cash inducement provided by a manufacturer or distributor for a retailer or his staff, to reward successful selling.

push off *vb. (adv.)* **1.** Also: **push out.** to move into open water, as by being cast off from a mooring. **2.** *(intr.) Informal.* to go away; leave.

push on *vb. (intr., adv.)* to resume one's course; carry on one's way steadily; press on.

pushover ('pʊʃˌəʊvə) *n. Informal.* **1.** something that is easily achieved or accomplished. **2.** a person, team, etc., that is easily taken advantage of or defeated.

pushpin ('pʊʃˌpɪn) *n. U.S. and Canadian.* a pin with a small ball-shaped head.

push-pull *n. (modifier)* using two similar electronic devices, such as matched valves, made to operate 180° out of phase with each other. The outputs are combined to produce a signal that replicates the input waveform: *a push-pull amplifier.*

pushrod ('pʊʃˌrɒd) *n.* a metal rod transmitting the reciprocating motion that operates the valves of an internal-combustion engine having the camshaft in the crankcase.

push-start *vb. (tr.)* **1.** to start (a motor vehicle) by pushing it while it is in gear, thus turning the engine. ~*n.* **2.** the act or process of starting a vehicle in this way.

push through *vb. (tr.)* to compel to accept: *the bill was pushed through Parliament.*

Pushto ('pʌʃtəʊ) *or* **Pushtu** ('pʌʃtuː) *n., adj.* variant spellings of **Pashto.**

push-up *n.* the U.S. and Canadian term for **press-up.**

pushy ('pʊʃɪ) *adj.* **pushier, pushiest.** *Informal.* **1.** offensively assertive or forceful. **2.** aggressively or ruthlessly ambitious. —'**pushily** *adv.* —'**pushiness** *n.*

pusillanimous (ˌpjuːsɪ'lænɪməs) *adj.* characterized by a lack of courage or determination. [C16: from Late Latin *pusillanimis* from Latin *pusillus* weak + *animus* courage] —**pusillanimity** (ˌpjuːsɪlə'nɪmɪtɪ) *n.* —ˌ**pusil'lanimously** *adv.*

puss[1] (pʊs) *n.* **1.** an informal name for a **cat.** See also **pussy**[1] (sense 1). **2.** *Slang.* a girl or woman. **3.** an informal name for a **hare.** [C16: related to Middle Low German *pūs,* Dutch *poes,* Lithuanian *puz*]

puss[2] (pʊs) *n. Slang.* **1.** the face. **2.** *Irish.* a gloomy or sullen expression. [C17: from Irish *pus*]

puss moth *n.* a large pale prominent moth, *Cerura vinula,* whose larvae feed on willow and poplar, and are bright green with a masklike red head and claspers modified as "tails" that are protruded and raised in a state of alarm: family *Notodontidae.*

pussy[1] ('pʊsɪ) *n., pl.* **pussies. 1.** Also called: **puss, pussycat** ('pʊsɪˌkæt). an informal name for a **cat. 2.** a furry catkin, esp. that of the pussy willow. **3.** a rare word for **tipcat. 4.** *Taboo slang.* the female pudenda. **5.** *Taboo slang.* a woman considered as a sexual object. [C18: from PUSS[1]]

pussy[2] ('pʌsɪ) *adj.* **-sier, -siest.** containing or full of pus.

pussyfoot ('pʊsɪˌfʊt) *Informal.* ~*vb. (intr.)* **1.** to move about stealthily or warily like a cat. **2.** to avoid committing oneself. ~*n., pl.* **-foots. 3.** a person who pussyfoots.

pussy willow ('pʊsɪ) *n.* **1.** an American willow tree, *Salix discolor,* with silvery silky catkins: widely planted for ornament. **2.** any of various similar willows.

pustulant ('pʌstjʊlənt) *adj.* **1.** causing the formation of pustules. ~*n.* **2.** an agent causing such formation.

pustulate *vb.* ('pʌstjʊˌleɪt). **1.** to form or cause to form into pustules. ~*adj.* ('pʌstjʊlɪt, -ˌleɪt). **2.** covered with pustules. —ˌ**pustu'lation** *n.*

pustule ('pʌstjuːl) *n.* **1.** a small inflamed elevated area of skin containing pus. **2.** any small distinct spot resembling a pimple or blister. [C14: from Latin *pustula* a blister, variant of *pūsula;* compare Greek *phusallis* bladder, *phusa* bellows] —**pustular** ('pʌstjʊlə) *adj.*

put (pʊt) *vb.* **puts, putting, put.** *(mainly tr.)* **1.** to cause to be (in a position or place): *to put a book on the table.* **2.** to cause to be (in a state, relation, etc.): *to put one's things in order.* **3.** (foll. by *to*) to cause (a person) to experience the endurance or suffering (of): *to put to death; to put to the sword.* **4.** to set or commit (to an action, task, or duty), esp. by force: *he put him to work.* **5.** to render, transform, or translate: *to put into English.* **6.** to set (words) in a musical form (esp. in the phrase **put to music**). **7.** (foll. by *at*) to estimate: *he put the distance at fifty miles.* **8.** (foll. by *to*) to utilize (for the purpose of): *he put his knowledge to good use.* **9.** (foll. by *to*) to couple a female animal (with a male) for the purpose of breeding: *the farmer put his heifer to the bull.* **10.** to state; express: *to put it bluntly.* **11.** to set or make (an end or limit): *he put an end to the proceedings.* **12.** to present for consideration in anticipation of an answer or vote; propose: *he put the question to the committee; I put it to you that one day you will all die.* **13.** to invest (money) in; give (support) to: *he put five thousand pounds into the project.* **14.** to impart: *to put zest into a party.* **15.** to throw or cast. **16. not know where to put oneself.** to feel awkward or embarrassed. **17. put paid to.** to destroy irrevocably and utterly: *the manager's disfavour put paid to their hopes for promotion.* **18. stay put.** to refuse to leave; keep one's position. ~*n.* **19.** a throw or cast, esp. in putting the shot. **20.** Also called: **put option.** *Stock Exchange.* an option to sell a stated amount of securities at a specified price during a specified limited period. Compare **call** (sense 58). ~See also **put about, put across, put aside, put away, put back, put by, put down, put forth, put forward, put in, put off, put on, put on to, put out, put over, put through, put up, put upon.** [C12 *puten* to push; related to Old English *potian* to push, Norwegian, Icelandic *pota* to poke]

put about *vb. (adv.)* **1.** *Nautical.* to change course or cause to change course: *we put about and headed for home.* **2.** *(tr.)* to make widely known: *he put about the news of the air disaster.* **3.** *(tr.; usually passive)* to disconcert or disturb: *she was quite put about by his appearance.*

put across *vb. (tr.)* **1.** *(adv.)* to communicate in a comprehensible way: *he couldn't put things across very well.* **2. put one across.** *Informal.* to get (someone) to accept or believe a claim, excuse, etc., by deception: *they put one across their teacher.*

putamen (pjuː'teɪmɛn) *n., pl.* **-tamina** (-'tæmɪnə). the hard endocarp or stone of fruits such as the peach, plum, and cherry. [C19: from Latin: clippings, from *putāre* to prune]

put aside *vb. (tr., adv.)* **1.** to move (an object, etc.) to one side, esp. in rejection. **2.** to store up; save: *to put money aside for a rainy day.* **3.** to ignore or disregard: *let us put aside our differences.*

putative ('pjuːtətɪv) *adj.* **1.** *(prenominal)* commonly regarded as being: *the putative father.* **2.** *(prenominal)* considered to exist or have existed; inferred. **3.** *Grammar.* denoting a mood of the verb in some languages used when the speaker does not have direct evidence of what he is asserting, but has inferred it on the basis of something else. [C15: from Late Latin *putātīvus* supposed, from Latin *putāre* to consider] —'**putatively** *adv.*

put away *vb. (tr., adv.)* **1.** to return (something) to the correct or proper place: *he put away his books.* **2.** to save: *to put away money for the future.* **3.** to lock up in a prison, mental institution, etc.: *they put him away for twenty years.* **4.** to eat or drink, esp. in large amounts. **5.** to put to death, because of old age or illness: *the dog had to be put away.*

put back *vb. (tr., adv.)* **1.** to return to its former place. **2.** to move to a later time or date: *the wedding was put back a fortnight.* **3.** to delay or impede the progress of: *the strike put back production severely.*

put by *vb. (tr., adv.)* to set aside (money, goods, etc.) to be kept for the future; store; save.

put down *vb. (tr., adv.)* **1.** to make a written record of. **2.** to repress: *to put down a rebellion.* **3.** to consider; account: *they put him down for an ignoramus.* **4.** to attribute: *I put the mistake down to his inexperience.* **5.** to put to death, because of old age or illness: *the vet put the cat down.* **6.** to table on the agenda: *the MPs put down a motion on the increase in crime.* **7.** to put (a baby) to bed. **8.** to dismiss, reject, or humiliate. ~*n.* **put-down. 9.** a cruelly crushing remark.

put forth *vb. (tr., adv.) Formal.* **1.** to present; propose. **2.** (of a plant) to produce or bear (leaves, branches, shoots, etc.).

put forward *vb. (tr., adv.)* **1.** to propose; suggest. **2.** to offer the name of; nominate.

put in *vb. (adv.)* **1.** *(intr.) Nautical.* to bring a vessel into port, esp. for a brief stay: *we put in for fresh provisions.* **2.** (often foll. by *for*) to apply or cause to apply (for a job, in a competition, etc.). **3.** *(tr.)* to submit: *he put in his claims form.* **4.** to intervene with (a remark) during a conversation. **5.** *(tr.)* to devote (time, effort, etc.) to a task: *he put in three hours overtime last night.* **6.** *(tr.)* to establish or appoint: *he put in a manager.* **7.** *(tr.) Cricket.* to cause (a team, esp. the opposing one) to bat: *England won the toss and put the visitors in to bat.* ~*n.* **put-in. 8.** *Rugby.* the act of throwing the ball into a scrum.

putlog ('pʌtˌlɒg) *or* **putlock** *n.* a short horizontal beam that with others supports the floor planks of a scaffold. [C17: changed (through influence of LOG[1]) from earlier *putlock,* probably from PUT (past participle) + LOCK]

put off *vb.* **1.** *(tr., adv.)* to postpone or delay: *they have put off the dance until tomorrow.* **2.** *(tr., adv.)* to evade (a person) by postponement or delay: *they tried to put him off, but he came anyway.* **3.** *(tr., adv.)* to confuse; disconcert: *he was put off by her appearance.* **4.** *(tr., prep.)* to cause to lose interest in or enjoyment of: *the accident put him off driving.* **5.** *(intr., adv.) Nautical.* to be launched off from shore or from a ship: *we put off in the lifeboat towards the ship.* **6.** *(tr., adv.) Archaic.* to remove (clothes). ~*n.* **putoff. 7.** *Chiefly U.S.* a pretext or delay.

put on *vb. (tr., mainly adv.)* **1.** to clothe oneself in: *to put on a coat.* **2.** *(usually passive)* to adopt (an attitude or feeling) insincerely: *his misery was just put on.* **3.** to present or stage (a play, show, etc.). **4.** to increase or add: *she put on weight; the batsman put on fifty runs before lunch.* **5.** to cause (an electrical device) to function. **6.** *(also prep.)* to wager (money) on a horse race, game, etc.: *he put ten pounds on the favourite.* **7.** *(also prep.)* to impose as a burden or levy: *to put a tax on cars.* **8.** *Cricket.* to cause (a bowler) to bowl. **9. put (someone) on. a.** to connect (a person) by telephone. **b.** *Slang.* to mock or tease. ~*n.* **put-on.** *Slang, chiefly U.S. and Canadian.* **10.** a hoax or piece of mockery. **11.** an affected manner or mode of behaviour.

put on to *vb. (tr., prep.)* **1.** to connect by telephone. **2.** to inform (someone) of (a person's location or activities): *I'll put the police on to you if you don't stop.* **3.** to tell (a person) about (someone or something beneficial): *can you put me on to a cheap supermarket?*

put out *vb. (tr., adv.)* **1.** *(often passive)* **a.** to annoy; anger. **b.** to confound or disturb; confuse. **2.** to extinguish or douse (a fire, light, etc.): *he put out the fire.* **3.** to poke forward: *to put out one's tongue.* **4.** to be or present a source of inconvenience or annoyance to (a person): *I hope I'm not putting you out.* **5.** to issue or publish; broadcast: *the authorities put out a leaflet.* **6.** to render unconscious. **7.** to dislocate: *he put out his shoulder in the accident.* **8.** to show or exert: *the workers put out all their energy in the campaign.* **9.** to pass, give out (work to be done) at different premises. **10.** to lend (money) at interest. **11.** *Cricket.* to dismiss (a player or team). **12.** *Baseball.* to cause (a batter or runner) to be out by a fielding play. ~*n.* **putout. 13.** *Baseball.* a play in which the batter or runner is put out.

put over *vb. (tr., adv.)* **1.** *Informal.* to communicate (facts, information, etc.) comprehensibly: *he puts his thoughts over badly.* **2.** *Chiefly U.S.* to postpone; defer: *the match was put over a week.* Brit. equivalent: **put off. 3. put (a fast) one over on.** *Informal.* to get (someone) to accept or believe a claim, excuse, etc., by deception: *he put one over on his boss.*

put-put ('pʌtˌpʌt) *Informal.* ~*n.* **1.** a light chugging or popping sound, as made by a petrol engine. **2.** a vehicle powered by an engine making such a sound. ~*vb.* **-puts, -putting, -putted. 3.** *(intr.)* to make or travel along with such a sound.

putrefy ('pjuːtrɪˌfaɪ) *vb.* **-fies, -fying, -fied.** (of organic matter) to decompose or rot with an offensive smell. [C15: from Old French *putrefier* + Latin *putrefacere,* from *puter* rotten + *facere* to make] —**putrefaction** (ˌpjuːtrɪ'fækʃən) *n.* —**ˌputre'factive** *or* **putrefacient** (ˌpjuːtrɪ'feɪʃənt) *adj.* —**'putreˌfiable** *adj.* —**'putreˌfier** *n.*

putrescent (pjuː'trɛsᵊnt) *adj.* **1.** becoming putrid; rotting. **2.** characterized by or undergoing putrefaction. [C18: from Latin *putrescere* to become rotten] —**pu'trescence** *n.*

putrescible (pjuː'trɛsɪbᵊl) *adj.* **1.** liable to become putrid. ~*n.* **2.** a putrescible substance. [C18: from Latin *putrescere* to decay] —**puˌtresci'bility** *n.*

putrescine (pjuː'trɛsiːn, -ɪn) *n.* a colourless crystalline amine produced by decaying animal matter; 1,4-diaminobutane. Formula: $H_2N(CH_2)_4NH_2$. [C20: from Latin *putrescere* + -INE[2]]

putrid ('pjuːtrɪd) *adj.* **1.** (of organic matter) in a state of decomposition, usually giving off a foul smell: *putrid meat.* **2.** morally corrupt or worthless. **3.** sickening; foul: *a putrid smell.* **4.** *Informal.* deficient in quality or value: *a putrid film.* [C16: from Latin *putridus* rotten, from *putrēre* to be rotten] —**pu'tridity** *or* **'putridness** *n.* —**'putridly** *adv.*

putsch (pʊtʃ) *n.* a violent and sudden uprising; political revolt, esp. a coup d'état. [C20: from German: from Swiss German: a push, of imitative origin]

putt (pʌt) *Golf.* ~*n.* **1.** a stroke on the green with a putter to roll the ball into or near the hole. ~*vb.* **2.** to strike (the ball) in this way. [C16: of Scottish origin; related to PUT]

puttee *or* **putty** ('pʌtɪ) *n., pl.* **-tees** *or* **-ties.** *(usually pl.)* a strip of cloth worn wound around the legs from the ankle to the knee, esp. as part of a military uniform in World War I. [C19: from Hindi *paṭṭī,* from Sanskrit *paṭṭikā,* from *paṭṭa* cloth]

putter[1] ('pʌtə) *n. Golf.* **1.** a club with a short shaft for putting, usually having a solid metal head. **2.** a golfer who putts: *he is a good putter.*

putter[2] ('pʌtə) *vb.* the usual U.S. and Canadian word for **potter**[2]. —**'putterer** *n.*

putter[3] ('pʊtə) *n.* **1.** a person who puts: *the putter of a question.* **2.** a person who puts the shot.

put through *vb. (tr., mainly adv.)* **1.** to carry out to a conclusion: *he put through his plan.* **2.** *(also prep.)* to organize the processing of: *she put through his application to join the organization.* **3.** to connect by telephone. **4.** to make (a telephone call).

putting green ('pʌtɪŋ) *n.* **1.** (on a golf course) the area of closely mown grass at the end of a fairway where the hole is. **2.** an area of smooth grass with several holes for putting games.

putto ('pʊtəʊ) *n., pl.* **-ti** (-tɪ). a representation of a small boy, a cherub or cupid, esp. in baroque painting or sculpture. See also **amoretto.** [from Italian, from Latin *putus* boy]

putty ('pʌtɪ) *n., pl.* **-ties. 1.** a stiff paste made of whiting and linseed oil that is used to fix glass panes into frames and to fill cracks or holes in woodwork, etc. **2.** any substance with a similar consistency, function, or appearance. **3.** a mixture of lime and water with sand or plaster of Paris used on plaster as a finishing coat. **4.** *(as modifier)*: *a putty knife.* **5.** See **putty powder. 6.** a person who is easily influenced or persuaded: *he's putty in her hands.* **7. a.** a colour varying from a greyish-yellow to a greyish-brown or brownish-grey. **b.** *(as adj.)*: *putty-coloured.* **8. up to putty.** *Austral. informal.* worthless or useless. ~*vb.* **-ties, -tying, -tied. 9.** *(tr.)* to fix, fill, or coat with putty. [C17: from French *potée* a potful]

putty powder *n.* a powder, either tin oxide or tin and lead oxide, used for polishing glassware, metal, etc.

puttyroot ('pʌtɪˌruːt) *n.* a North American orchid, *Aplectrum hyemale,* bearing a single leaf and yellowish-brown or purple flowers. Also called: **adam-and-eve.** [C19: so named because it yields a glutinous material sometimes used to make putty]

put up *vb. (adv., mainly tr.)* **1.** to build; erect: *to put up a statue.* **2.** to accommodate or be accommodated at: *can you put me up for tonight?* **3.** to increase (prices). **4.** to submit or present (a plan, case, etc.). **5.** to offer: *to put a house up for sale.* **6.** to provide or supply; give: *to put up a good fight.* **7.** to provide (money) for; invest in: *they put up five thousand for the new project.* **8.** to preserve or can (jam, etc.). **9.** to pile up (long hair) on the head in any of several styles. **10.** *(also intr.)* to nominate or be nominated as a candidate, esp. for a political or society post: *he put his wife up as secretary; he put up for president.* **11.** *Archaic.* to return (a weapon) to its holder, as a sword to its sheath: *put up your pistol!* **12. put up to. a.** to inform or instruct (a person) about (tasks, duties, etc.). **b.** to urge or goad (a person) on to; incite to. **13. put up with.** *Informal.* to endure; tolerate. ~*adj.* **put-up. 14.** dishonestly or craftily prearranged or conceived (esp. in the phrase **put-up job**).

put upon *vb. (intr., prep., usually passive)* **1.** to presume on (a person's generosity, good nature, etc.); take advantage of: *he's always being put upon.* **2.** to impose hardship on; maltreat: *he was sorely put upon.*

puzzle ('pʌzᵊl) *vb.* **1.** to perplex or be perplexed. **2.** *(intr.;* foll. by *over)* to attempt the solution (of); ponder (about): *he puzzled over her absence.* **3.** *(tr.;* usually foll. by *out)* to solve by mental effort: *he puzzled out the meaning of the inscription.* ~*n.* **4.** a person or thing that puzzles. **5.** a problem that cannot be easily or readily solved. **6.** the state or condition of being puzzled. **7.** a toy, game, or question presenting a problem that requires skill or ingenuity for its solution. See **jigsaw puzzle, Chinese puzzle.** [C16: of unknown origin] —**'puzzling** *adj.*

puzzlement ('pʌzᵊlmənt) *n.* the state or condition of being puzzled; perplexity.

puzzler ('pʌzlə) *n.* a person or thing that puzzles.

puzzolana (ˌputsə'lɑːnə) *n.* a variant of **pozzuolana.**

PVA *abbrev. for* polyvinyl acetate.

PVC *abbrev. for* polyvinyl chloride; a synthetic thermoplastic material made by polymerizing vinyl chloride. The properties depend on the added plasticizer. The flexible forms are used in hosepipes, insulation, shoes, garments, etc. Rigid PVC is used for moulded articles.

PVS *abbrev. for* postviral syndrome.

Pvt. *Military. abbrev. for* private.

PW *abbrev. for* policewoman.

PWD *abbrev. for* Public Works Department.

PWR *abbrev. for* pressurized-water reactor.

pwt *abbrev. for* pennyweight.

PX *U. S. military. abbrev. for* Post Exchange.

PY *international car registration for* Paraguay.

py- *combining form.* variant of **pyo-** before a vowel.

pya (pjɑː, pɪ'ɑː) *n.* a Burmese monetary unit worth one hundredth of a kyat. [from Burmese]

pyaemia *or* **pyemia** (paɪ'iːmɪə) *n.* blood poisoning characterized by pus-forming microorganisms in the blood. [C19: from New Latin, from Greek *puon* pus + *haima* blood] —**py'aemic** *or* **py'emic** *adj.*

pyat, pyot, *or* **pyet** ('paɪət) *Scot.* ~*n.* **1.** the magpie. ~*adj.* **2.** pied. [Middle English *piot,* from PIE[2]]

pycnidium (pɪk'nɪdɪəm) *n., pl.* **-ia** (-ɪə). a small flask-shaped structure containing spores that occurs in ascomycetes and certain other fungi. [C19: from New Latin, from Greek *puknos* thick]

pycno- *or before a vowel* **pycn-** *combining form.* indicating thickness or density: *pycnometer.* [via New Latin from Greek *puknos* thick]

pycnometer (pɪk'nɒmɪtə) *n.* a small glass bottle of known volume for determining the relative density of liquids and solids by weighing. —**pycnometric** (ˌpɪknə'mɛtrɪk) *adj.*

pye (paɪ) *n.* a variant spelling of **pie**[5].

pye-dog, pie-dog *or* **pi-dog** *n.* an ownerless half-wild Asian dog. [C19: Anglo-Indian *pye, paë,* from Hindi *pāhī* outsider]

pyelitis (ˌpaɪə'laɪtɪs) *n.* inflammation of the pelvis of the kidney. Compare **pyelonephritis.** —**pyelitic** (ˌpaɪə'lɪtɪk) *adj.*

pyelo- *or before a vowel* **pyel-** *combining form.* denoting the renal pelvis: *pyelonephritis.* [from Greek *puelos* trough, pan; in the sense: pelvis]

pyelography (ˌpaɪə'lɒgrəfɪ) *n. Med.* the branch of radiology concerned with examination of the kidney and associated structures by means of an x-ray picture called a **pyelogram** ('paɪələʊˌgræm). Also called: **urography.** —**pyelographic** (ˌpaɪələʊ'græfɪk) *adj.*

pyelonephritis (ˌpaɪələʊnɪ'fraɪtɪs) *n.* inflammation of the kidney and renal pelvis. Compare **pyelitis.**

pygidium (paɪ'dʒɪdɪəm, -'gɪd-) *n., pl.* **-ia** (-ɪə). the terminal segment, division, or other structure in certain annelids, arthropods, and other invertebrates. [C19: from New Latin, from Greek *pugē* rump] —**py'gidial** *adj.*

pygmy *or* **pigmy** ('pɪgmɪ) *n., pl.* **-mies. 1.** an abnormally undersized person. **2.** something that is a very small example of its type. **3.** a person of little importance or significance. **4.** (*modifier*) of very small stature or size. [C14 *pigmeis* the Pygmies, from Latin *Pygmaeus* a Pygmy, from Greek *pugmaios* undersized, from *pugmē* fist] —**pygmaean** *or* **pygmean** (pɪg'miːən) *adj.*

Pygmy *or* **Pigmy** ('pɪgmɪ) *n., pl.* **-mies.** a member of one of the dwarf peoples of Equatorial Africa, noted for their hunting and forest culture.

pyinkado (pjɪŋ'kɑːdəʊ) *n.* **1.** a leguminous tree, *Xylia xylocarpa* (or *dolabriformis*), native to India and Burma. **2.** the heavy durable timber of this tree, used for construction. [C19: from Burmese]

pyjama *or U.S.* **pajama** (pə'dʒɑːmə) *n.* (*modifier*) **1.** of or forming part of pyjamas: *pyjama top.* **2.** requiring pyjamas to be worn: *a pyjama party.* ~See also **pyjamas.** [C19: via Persian or Urdu from Persian *pāë, pāy* foot, leg + *jāmah* clothing, garment]

pyjama cricket *n. Austral. informal.* one-day cricket, esp. when played at night in coloured uniforms.

pyjamas *or U.S.* **pajamas** (pə'dʒɑːməz) *pl. n.* **1.** loose-fitting nightclothes comprising a jacket or top and trousers. **2.** full loose-fitting ankle-length trousers worn by either sex in various Eastern countries. **3.** women's flared trousers or trouser suit used esp. for leisure wear.

pyknic ('pɪknɪk) *adj.* (of a physical type) characterized by a broad squat fleshy physique with a large chest and abdomen. [C20: from Greek *puknos* thick]

pylon ('paɪlən) *n.* **1.** a large vertical steel tower-like structure supporting high-tension electrical cables. **2.** a post or tower for guiding pilots or marking a turning point in a race. **3.** a streamlined aircraft structure for attaching an engine pod, external fuel tank, etc., to the main body of the aircraft. **4.** a monumental gateway, such as one at the entrance to an ancient Egyptian temple. **5.** a temporary artificial leg. [C19: from Greek *pulōn* a gateway]

pylorectomy (ˌpaɪlɔː'rɛktəmɪ) *n., pl.* **-mies.** the surgical removal of all or part of the pylorus, often including the adjacent portion of the stomach (**partial gastrectomy**).

pylorus (paɪ'lɔːrəs) *n., pl.* **-ri** (-raɪ). the small circular opening at the base of the stomach through which partially digested food (chyme) passes to the duodenum. [C17: via Late Latin from Greek *pulōrus* gatekeeper, from *pulē* gate + *ouros* guardian] —**py'loric** *adj.*

pyo- *or before a vowel* **py-** *combining form.* denoting pus: *pyosis.* [from Greek *puon*]

pyoderma (ˌpaɪəʊ'dɜːmə) *n. Pathol.* any skin eruption characterized by pustules or the formation of pus.

pyogenesis (ˌpaɪəʊ'dʒɛnɪsɪs) *n. Pathol.* the formation of pus. —ˌ**pyo'genic** *adj.*

pyoid ('paɪɔɪd) *adj.* resembling pus.

pyorrhoea *or esp. U.S.* **pyorrhea** (ˌpaɪə'rɪə) *n.* inflammation of the gums characterized by the discharge of pus and loosening of the teeth; periodontal disease. —ˌ**pyor'rhoeal,** ˌ**pyor'rhoeic** *or esp. U.S.* ˌ**pyor'rheal,** ˌ**pyor'rheic** *adj.*

pyosis (paɪ'əʊsɪs) *n. Pathol.* the formation of pus.

pyr- *combining form.* a variant of **pyro-** before a vowel.

pyracantha (ˌpaɪrə'kænθə) *n.* any rosaceous shrub of the genus *Pyracantha,* esp. the firethorn, widely cultivated for ornament. [C17: from Greek *purakantha* name of a shrub, from PYRO- + *akantha* thorn]

pyralid ('pɪrəlɪd) *n.* **1.** any moth of the mostly tropical family *Pyralidae,* typically having narrow forewings and broad fringed hind wings: includes the bee moths and the corn borer. ~*adj.* **2.** of, relating to, or belonging to the family *Pyralidae.* [C19: via New Latin from Greek *puralis:* a mythical winged insect believed to live in fire, from *pur* fire]

pyramid ('pɪrəmɪd) *n.* **1.** a huge masonry construction that has a square base and, as in the case of the ancient Egyptian royal tombs, four sloping triangular sides. **2.** an object, formation, or structure resembling such a construction. **3.** *Maths.* a solid having a polygonal base and triangular sides that meet in a common vertex. **4.** *Crystallog.* a crystal form in which three planes intersect all three axes of the crystal. **5.** *Anatomy.* any pointed or cone-shaped bodily structure or part. **6.** *Finance.* a group of enterprises containing a series of holding companies structured so that the top holding company controls the entire group with a relatively small proportion of the total capital invested. **7.** *Chiefly U.S.* the series of transactions involved in pyramiding securities. **8.** (*pl.*) a game similar to billiards with fifteen coloured balls. ~*vb.* **9.** to build up or be arranged in the form of a pyramid. **10.** *Chiefly U.S.* to speculate in (securities or property) by increasing purchases on additional margin or collateral derived from paper profits associated with high prices of securities and property in a boom. **11.** *Finance.* to form (companies) into a pyramid. [C16 (earlier *pyramis*): from Latin *pyramis,* from Greek *puramis,* probably from Egyptian] —**pyramidal** (pɪ'ræmɪdᵊl), ˌ**pyra'midical,** *or* ˌ**pyra'midic** *adj.* —**py'ramidally** *or* ˌ**pyra'midically** *adv.*

pyramidal orchid *n.* a chalk-loving orchid, *Anacamptis pyramidalis,* bearing a dense cone-shaped spike of purplish-pink flowers with a long curved spur.

pyramidal peak *n. Geology.* a sharp peak formed where the ridges separating three or more cirques intersect; horn.

pyramid selling *n.* a practice adopted by some manufacturers of advertising for distributors and selling them batches of goods. The first distributors then advertise for more distributors who are sold subdivisions of the original batches at an increased price. This process continues until the final distributors are left with a stock that is unsaleable except at a loss.

pyran ('paɪræn, paɪ'ræn) *n.* an unsaturated heterocyclic compound having a ring containing five carbon atoms and one oxygen atom and two double bonds. It has two isomers depending on the position of the saturated carbon atom relative to the oxygen. [C20: from PYRO- + -AN]

pyranometer (ˌpaɪrə'nɒmɪtə) *n. Physics.* another name for **solarimeter.**

pyrargyrite (paɪ'rɑːdʒɪˌraɪt) *n.* a dark red to black mineral consisting of silver antimony sulphide in hexagonal crystalline form: occurs in silver veins and is an important ore of silver. Formula: Ag_3SbS_3. [C19: from German *Pyrargyrit,* from PYRO- + Greek *arguros* silver]

pyrazole ('paɪrəˌzəʊl) *n.* a crystalline soluble basic heterocyclic compound; 1,2-diazole. Formula: $C_3H_4N_2$. [C19: from German, from PYRROLE + inserted *-az-* (see AZO-)]

pyre (paɪə) *n.* a heap or pile of wood or other combustible material, esp. one used for cremating a corpse. [C17: from Latin *pyra,* from Greek *pura* hearth, from *pur* fire]

pyrene[1] ('paɪriːn) *n.* a solid polynuclear aromatic hydrocarbon extracted from coal tar. Formula: $C_{16}H_{10}$. [C19: from PYRO- + -ENE]

pyrene[2] ('paɪriːn) *n. Botany.* any of several small hard stones that occur in a single fruit and contain a single seed each. [C19: from New Latin *pyrena,* from Greek *purēn*]

Pyrenean (ˌpɪrə'niːən) *adj.* of or relating to the Pyrenees, a mountain range between France and Spain.

Pyrenean mountain dog *n.* a large heavily built dog of an ancient breed originally used to protect sheep from wild animals: it has a long thick white coat with a dense ruff.

pyrenoid ('paɪrəˌnɔɪd) *n.* any of various small protein granules that occur in certain algae, mosses, and protozoans and are involved in the synthesis of starch. [C19: from PYRENE[2] + -OID]

pyrethrin (paɪ'riːθrɪn) *n.* **1.** Also called: **pyrethrin I.** an oily water-insoluble compound used as an insecticide. Formula: $C_{21}H_{28}O_3$. **2.** Also called: **pyrethrin II.** a compound of similar chemical structure and action, also found in pyrethrum. Formula: $C_{22}H_{28}O_5$. [C19: from PYRETHRUM + -IN]

pyrethroid (paɪ'riːθrɔɪd) *n.* **1.** any of various chemical compounds having similar insecticidal properties to pyrethrin. ~*adj.* **2.** of or relating to such compounds.

pyrethrum (paɪ'riːθrəm) *n.* **1.** any of several cultivated Eurasian chrysanthemums, such as *Chrysanthemum coccineum* and *C. roseum,* with white, pink, red, or purple flowers. **2.** any insecticide prepared from the dried flowers of any of these plants, esp. *C. roseum.* [C16: via Latin from Greek *purethron* feverfew, probably from *puretos* fever; see PYRETIC]

pyretic (paɪ'rɛtɪk) *adj. Pathol.* of, relating to, or characterized by fever. Compare **antipyretic.** [C18: from New Latin *pyreticus,* from Greek *puretos* fever, from *pur* fire]

Pyrex ('paɪrɛks) *n. Trademark.* **a.** any of a variety of borosilicate glasses that have low coefficients of expansion, making them suitable for heat-resistant glassware used in cookery and chemical apparatus. **b.** (*as modifier*): *a Pyrex dish.*

pyrexia (paɪˈrɛksɪə) *n.* a technical name for **fever.** [C18: from New Latin, from Greek *purexis,* from *puressein* to be feverish, from *pur* fire] —**py'rexial** *or* **py'rexic** *adj.*

pyrgeometer (ˌpɜːdʒɪˈɒmɪtə) *n. Physics.* an instrument for measuring the loss of heat by radiation from the earth's surface.

pyrheliometer (pəˌhiːlɪˈɒmɪtə) *n.* an instrument for measuring the intensity of the sun's radiant energy. —**pyrheliometric** (pəˌhiːlɪəʊˈmɛtrɪk) *adj.*

pyridine (ˈpɪrɪˌdiːn) *n.* a colourless hygroscopic liquid with a characteristic odour. It is a basic heterocyclic compound containing one nitrogen atom and five carbon atoms in its molecules and is used as a solvent and in preparing other organic chemicals. Formula: C_5H_5N. [C19: from PYRO- + -ID[3] + -INE[2]]

pyridoxal (ˌpɪrɪˈdɒksəl) *n. Biochem.* a naturally occurring derivative of pyridoxine that is a precursor of a coenzyme (**pyridoxal phosphate**) involved in several enzymic reactions. Formula: $(CH_2OH)(CHO)C_5HN(OH)(CH_3)$.

pyridoxamine (ˌpɪrɪˈdɒksəmiːn) *n. Biochem.* a metabolic form of pyridoxine.

pyridoxine (ˌpɪrɪˈdɒksiːn) *n. Biochem.* a derivative of pyridine that is a precursor of the compounds pyridoxal and pyridoxamine. Also called: **vitamin B$_6$.** [C20: from PYRID(INE) + OX(YGEN) + -INE[2]]

pyriform (ˈpɪrɪˌfɔːm) *adj.* (esp. of organs of the body) pear-shaped. [C18: from New Latin *pyriformis,* from *pyri-,* erroneously from Latin *pirum* pear + *-formis* -FORM]

pyrimidine (paɪˈrɪmɪˌdiːn) *n.* **1.** a liquid or crystalline organic compound with a penetrating odour; 1,3-diazine. It is a weakly basic soluble heterocyclic compound and can be prepared from barbituric acid. Formula: $C_4H_4N_2$. **2.** Also called: **pyrimidine base.** any of a number of similar compounds having a basic structure that is derived from pyrimidine, including cytosine, thymine, and uracil, which are constituents of nucleic acids. [C20: variant of PYRIDINE]

pyrite (ˈpaɪraɪt) *n.* a yellow mineral, found in igneous and metamorphic rocks and in veins. It is a source of sulphur and is used in the manufacture of sulphuric acid. Composition: iron sulphide. Formula: FeS_2. Crystal structure: cubic. Also called: **iron pyrites, pyrites.** Nontechnical name: **fool's gold.** [C16: from Latin *pyrites* flint, from Greek *puritēs* (*lithos*) fire (stone), that is, capable of withstanding or striking fire, from *pur* fire] —**pyritic** (paɪˈrɪtɪk) *or* **py'ritous** *adj.*

pyrites (paɪˈraɪtiːz, *in combination* ˈpaɪraɪts) *n., pl.* **-tes. 1.** another name for **pyrite. 2.** any of a number of other disulphides of metals, esp. of copper and tin.

pyro- *or before a vowel* **pyr-** *combining form.* **1.** denoting fire, heat, or high temperature: *pyromania; pyrometer.* **2.** caused or obtained by fire or heat: *pyroelectricity.* **3.** *Chem.* **a.** denoting a new substance obtained by heating another: *pyroboric acid is obtained by heating boric acid.* **b.** denoting an acid or salt with a water content intermediate between that of the ortho- and meta- compounds: *pyro-phosphoric acid.* **4.** *Mineralogy.* **a.** having a property that changes upon the application of heat: *pyromorphite.* **b.** having a flame-coloured appearance: *pyroxylin.*

pyrocatechol (ˌpaɪrəʊˈkætɪˌtʃɒl, -kɒl) *or* **pyrocatechin** (ˌpaɪrəʊˈkætɪkɪn) *n.* another name for **catechol.**

pyrochemical (ˌpaɪrəʊˈkɛmɪkəl) *adj.* of, concerned with, being, producing, or resulting from chemical changes at high temperatures. —ˌ**pyro'chemically** *adv.*

pyroclastic (ˌpaɪrəʊˈklæstɪk) *adj.* (of rocks) formed from the solid fragments ejected during a volcanic eruption.

pyroconductivity (ˌpaɪrəʊˌkɒndʌkˈtɪvɪtɪ) *n.* conductivity that can be induced in certain solids by heating them.

pyroelectric (ˌpaɪrəʊɪˈlɛktrɪk) *adj.* **1.** of, concerned with, or exhibiting pyroelectricity. ~*n.* **2.** a pyroelectric substance.

pyroelectricity (ˌpaɪrəʊɪlɛkˈtrɪsɪtɪ, -ˌiːlɛk-) *n.* the development of opposite charges at the ends of the axis of certain hemihedral crystals, such as tourmaline, as a result of a change in temperature.

pyrogallate (ˌpaɪrəʊˈgæleɪt) *n.* any salt or ester of pyrogallol.

pyrogallol (ˌpaɪrəʊˈgælɒl) *n.* a white lustrous crystalline soluble phenol with weakly acidic properties; 1,2,3-trihydroxybenzene: used as a photographic developer and for absorbing oxygen in gas analysis. Formula: $C_6H_3(OH)_3$. [C20: from PYRO- + GALL(IC)[2] + -OL[1]] —ˌ**pyro'gallic** *adj.*

pyrogen (ˈpaɪrəʊˌdʒɛn) *n.* any of a group of substances that cause a rise in temperature in an animal body.

pyrogenic (ˌpaɪrəʊˈdʒɛnɪk) *or* **pyrogenous** (paɪˈrɒdʒɪnəs) *adj.* **1.** produced by or producing heat. **2.** *Pathol.* causing or resulting from fever. **3.** *Geology.* less common words for **igneous.**

pyrognostics (ˌpaɪrɒgˈnɒstɪks) *pl. n.* the characteristics of a mineral, such as fusibility and flame coloration, that are revealed by the application of heat. [C19: from PYRO- + *-gnostics,* from Greek *gnōsis* knowledge]

pyrography (paɪˈrɒgrəfɪ) *n., pl.* **-phies. 1.** the art or process of burning designs on wood or leather with heated tools or a flame. **2.** a design made by this process. —**py'rographer** *n.* —**pyrographic** (ˌpaɪrəʊˈgræfɪk) *adj.*

pyroligneous (ˌpaɪrəʊˈlɪgnɪəs) *or* **pyrolignic** *adj.* (of a substance) produced by the action of heat on wood, esp. by destructive distillation. [C18: from French *pyroligneux,* from PYRO- + *ligneux* LIGNEOUS]

pyroligneous acid *n.* the crude reddish-brown acidic liquid obtained by the distillation of wood and containing acetic acid, methanol, and acetone. Also called: **wood vinegar.**

pyrolusite (ˌpaɪrəʊˈluːsaɪt) *n.* a blackish fibrous or soft powdery mineral consisting of manganese dioxide in tetragonal crystalline form. It occurs in association with other manganese ores and is an important source of manganese. Formula: MnO_2. [C19: from PYRO- + Greek *lousis* a washing + -ITE[1], from its use in purifying glass]

pyrolyse *or U.S.* **pyrolyze** (ˈpaɪrəʊˌlaɪz) *vb.* (*tr.*) to subject to pyrolysis. —'**pyroˌlyser** *or* '**pyroˌlyzer** *n.*

pyrolysis (paɪˈrɒlɪsɪs) *n.* **1.** the application of heat to chemical compounds in order to cause decomposition. **2.** chemical decomposition of compounds caused by high temperatures. —**pyrolytic** (ˌpaɪrəʊˈlɪtɪk) *adj.*

pyromagnetic (ˌpaɪrəʊmægˈnɛtɪk) *adj.* a former term for **thermomagnetic.**

pyromancy (ˈpaɪrəʊˌmænsɪ) *n.* divination by fire or flames. —'**pyroˌmancer** *n.* —ˌ**pyro'mantic** *adj.*

pyromania (ˌpaɪrəʊˈmeɪnɪə) *n. Psychiatry.* the uncontrollable impulse and practice of setting things on fire. —ˌ**pyro'maniˌac** *n.* —**pyromaniacal** (ˌpaɪrəʊməˈnaɪəkəl) *adj.*

pyrometallurgy (ˌpaɪrəʊmɛˈtælədʒɪ, -ˈmɛtəˌlɜːdʒɪ) *n.* the branch of metallurgy involving processes performed at high temperatures, including sintering, roasting, smelting, casting, refining, alloying, and heat treatment.

pyrometer (paɪˈrɒmɪtə) *n.* an instrument for measuring high temperatures, esp. by measuring the brightness (**optical pyrometer**) or total quantity (**radiation pyrometer**) of the radiation produced by the source. Other types include the resistance thermometer and the thermocouple. —**pyrometric** (ˌpaɪrəʊˈmɛtrɪk) *or* ˌ**pyro'metrical** *adj.* —ˌ**pyro'metrically** *adv.* —**py'rometry** *n.*

pyromorphite (ˌpaɪrəʊˈmɔːfaɪt) *n.* a green, yellow, brown, or grey secondary mineral that consists of lead chloro-phosphate in the form of hexagonal crystals. Formula: $Pb_5Cl(PO_4)_3$. [C19: from German *Pyromorphit,* from PYRO- + Greek *morphē* form + -ITE[1], an allusion to the fact that it assumes a crystalline form when heated]

pyrone (ˈpaɪrəʊn, paɪˈrəʊn) *n.* **1.** either of two heterocyclic compounds that have a ring containing five carbon atoms and one oxygen atom with two double bonds and a second oxygen atom attached to a carbon atom in either the *ortho*-position (**alpha pyrone**) or the *para*-position (**gamma pyrone**). **2.** any one of a class of compounds that are substituted derivatives of a pyrone.

pyrope (ˈpaɪrəʊp) *n.* a deep yellowish-red garnet that consists of magnesium aluminium silicate and is used as a gemstone. Formula: $Mg_3Al_2(SiO_4)_3$. [C14 (used loosely of a red gem; modern sense C19): from Old French *pirope,* from Latin *pyrōpus* bronze, from Greek *purōpus* fiery-eyed, from *pur* fire + *ōps* eye]

pyrophoric (ˌpaɪrəʊˈfɒrɪk) *adj.* **1.** (of a chemical) igniting spontaneously on contact with air. **2.** (of an alloy) producing sparks when struck or scraped: *lighter flints are made of pyrophoric alloy.* [C19: from New Latin *pyrophorus,* from Greek *purophoros* fire-bearing, from *pur* fire + *pherein* to bear]

pyrophosphate (ˌpaɪrəʊˈfɒsfeɪt) *n.* any salt or ester of pyrophosphoric acid.

pyrophosphoric acid (ˌpaɪrəʊfɒsˈfɒrɪk) *n.* a crystalline soluble solid acid formed by the reaction between one molecule of phosphorus pentoxide and two water molecules. Formula: $H_4P_2O_7$. See also **polyphosphoric acid.**

pyrophotometer (ˌpaɪrəʊfəʊˈtɒmɪtə) *n.* a type of pyrometer in which the temperature of an incandescent body is determined by photometric measurement of the light it emits. —ˌ**pyropho'tometry** *n.*

pyrophyllite (ˌpaɪrəʊˈfɪlaɪt) *n.* a white, silvery, or green micaceous mineral that consists of hydrated aluminium silicate in monoclinic crystalline form and occurs in metamorphic rocks. Formula: $Al_2Si_4O_{10}(OH)_2$.

pyrosis (paɪˈrəʊsɪs) *n. Pathol.* a technical name for **heartburn.** [C18: from New Latin, from Greek: a burning, from *puroun* to burn, from *pur* fire]

pyrostat (ˈpaɪrəʊˌstæt) *n.* **1.** a device that activates an alarm or extinguisher in the event of a fire. **2.** a thermostat for use at high temperatures. —ˌ**pyro'static** *adj.*

pyrosulphate (ˌpaɪrəʊˈsʌlfeɪt) *n.* any salt of pyrosulphuric acid. Also called: **disulphate.**

pyrosulphuric acid (ˌpaɪrəʊsʌlˈfjʊərɪk) *n.* a fuming liquid acid made by adding sulphur trioxide to concentrated sulphuric acid. Formula: $H_2S_2O_7$. Also called: **disulphuric acid.** See also **fuming sulphuric acid.**

pyrotechnics (ˌpaɪrəʊˈtɛknɪks) *n.* **1.** (*functioning as sing.*) the art or craft of making fireworks. **2.** (*functioning as sing. or pl.*) a firework display. **3.** (*functioning as sing. or pl.*) brilliance of display, as in the performance of music. ~Also called: '**pyroˌtechny.** —ˌ**pyro'technic** *or* ˌ**pyro'technical** *adj.*

pyroxene (paɪˈrɒksiːn) *n.* any of a group of silicate minerals having the general formula $ABSi_2O_6$, where A is usually calcium, sodium, magnesium, or iron, and B is usually magnesium, iron, chromium, manganese, or aluminium. Pyroxenes occur in basic igneous rocks and some metamorphic rocks, and have colours ranging from white to dark green or black. They may be monoclinic (clinopyroxenes) or orthorhombic (orthopyroxenes) in crystal structure. Examples are augite (the most important pyroxene), diopside, enstatite, hypersthene, and jadeite. [C19: PYRO- + *-xene* from Greek *xenos* foreign, because it was mistakenly thought to have originated elsewhere when found in igneous rocks] —**pyroxenic** (ˌpaɪrɒkˈsɛnɪk) *adj.*

pyroxenite (paɪˈrɒksɪˌnaɪt) *n.* a very dark coarse-grained ultrabasic rock consisting entirely of pyroxene minerals.

pyroxylin (paɪˈrɒksɪlɪn) *n.* a yellow substance obtained by nitrating cellulose with a mixture of nitric and sulphuric acids; guncotton: used to make collodion, plastics, lacquers, and adhesives. [C19: from PYRO- + XYL(O)- + -IN]

pyrrhic[1] (ˈpɪrɪk) *Prosody.* ~*n.* **1.** a metrical foot of two short or unstressed syllables. ~*adj.* **2.** of or relating to such a metrical foot. **3.** (of poetry) composed in pyrrhics. [C16: via Latin, from Greek *purrhikhē*, traditionally said to be named after its inventor *Purrhikhos*]

pyrrhic[2] (ˈpɪrɪk) *n.* **1.** a war dance of ancient Greece. ~*adj.* **2.** of or relating to this dance. [C17: Latin from Greek *purrhikhios* belonging to the *purrhikhē* war dance performed in armour; see PYRRHIC[1]]

Pyrrhic victory (ˈpɪrɪk) *n.* a victory in which the victor's losses are as great as those of the defeated. Also called: **Cadmean victory.** [named after *Pyrrus*, king of Epirus who defeated the Romans at Asculum in 279 B.C. but suffered heavy losses]

pyrrhotite (ˈpɪrəˌtaɪt) *or* **pyrrhotine** (ˈpɪrəˌtiːn, -ˌtaɪn, -tɪn) *n.* a common bronze-coloured magnetic mineral consisting of ferrous sulphide in hexagonal crystalline form. Formula: FeS. [C19: from Greek *purrhotēs* redness, from *purrhos* fiery, from *pur* fire]

pyrrhuloxia (ˌpɪrəˈlɒksɪə) *n.* a grey-and-pink crested bunting, *Pyrrhuloxia sinuata*, of Central and SW North America, with a short parrot-like bill. [from New Latin *Pyrrhula* genus of the finches (from Greek *purrhoulas* a flame-coloured bird, from *purrhos* red, from *pur* fire) + *Loxia* genus of the crossbills, from Greek *loxos* oblique]

pyrrole (ˈpɪrəʊl, pɪˈrəʊl) *n.* a colourless insoluble toxic liquid having a five-membered ring containing one nitrogen atom, found in many naturally occurring compounds, such as chlorophyll. Formula: C_4H_5N. Also called: **azole.** [C19: from Greek *purrhos* red, from *pur* fire + -OLE[1]] —**pyrrolic** (pɪˈrɒlɪk) *adj.*

pyrrolidine (pɪˈrɒlɪˌdiːn) *n.* an almost colourless liquid occurring in tobacco leaves and made commercially by hydrogenating pyrrole. It is a strongly alkaline heterocyclic base with molecules that contain a ring of four carbon atoms and one nitrogen atom. Formula: C_4H_9N.

pyruvic acid (paɪˈruːvɪk) *n.* a colourless pleasant-smelling liquid formed as an intermediate in the metabolism of proteins and carbohydrates, helping to release energy to the body; 2-oxopropanoic acid. Formula: CH_3COCH_2OH. [C19: *pyruvic* from PYRO- + Latin *ūva* grape]

Pythagoras' theorem (paɪˈθægərəs) *n.* the theorem that in a right-angled triangle the square of the length of the hypotenuse equals the sum of the squares of the other two sides. [named after *Pythagoras* (?580–?500 B.C.), Greek mathematician and philosopher]

Pythagorean (paɪˌθægəˈriːən) *adj.* **1.** of or relating to Pythagoras. **2.** *Music.* denoting the diatonic scale of eight notes arrived at by Pythagoras and based on a succession of fifths. ~*n.* **3.** a follower of Pythagoras.

Pythagoreanism (paɪˌθægəˈriːəˌnɪzəm) *n.* the teachings of Pythagoras and his followers, esp. that the universe is essentially a manifestation of mathematical relationships.

Pythian (ˈpɪθɪən) *adj. also* **Pythic. 1.** of or relating to the ancient Greek city of Delphi or its oracle. ~*n.* **2.** an inhabitant of ancient Delphi. [C16: via Latin *Pȳthius* from Greek *Puthios* of Delphi]

Pythian Games *pl. n.* (in ancient Greece) the second most important Panhellenic festival, celebrated in the third year of each Olympiad near Delphi. The four-year period between celebrations was known as a **Pythiad** (ˈpɪθɪˌæd).

python (ˈpaɪθən) *n.* any large nonvenomous snake of the family *Pythonidae* of Africa, S Asia, and Australia, such as *Python reticulatus* (**reticulated python**). They can reach a length of more than 20 feet and kill their prey by constriction. [C16: New Latin, after *Python* (in Greek mythology, a dragon killed by Apollo at Delphi); see PYTHIAN] —**pythonic** (paɪˈθɒnɪk) *adj.*

Pythonesque (ˌpaɪθəˈnɛsk) *adj.* denoting a kind of humour that is absurd and unpredictable; zany; surreal. [C20: named after the British television show *Monty Python's Flying Circus*, first broadcast in 1969]

pythoness (ˈpaɪθəˌnɛs) *n.* (in ancient Greece) **1.** a woman, such as Apollo's priestess at Delphi, believed to be possessed by an oracular spirit. **2.** a female soothsayer. [C14 *phitonesse*, ultimately from Greek *Puthōn* Python; see PYTHON]

pyuria (paɪˈjʊərɪə) *n. Pathol.* any condition characterized by the presence of pus in the urine. [C19: from New Latin, from Greek *puon* pus + *ouron* urine]

pyx *or* (*less commonly*) **pix** (pɪks) *n.* **1.** Also called: **pyx chest.** the chest in which coins from the British mint are placed to be tested for weight, etc. **2.** *Christianity.* any receptacle in which the Eucharistic Host is kept. [C14: from Latin *pyxis* small box, from Greek, from *puxos* box tree]

pyxidium (pɪkˈsɪdɪəm) *or* **pyxis** (ˈpɪksɪs) *n., pl.* **-ia** (-ɪə) *or* **pyxides** (ˈpɪksɪˌdiːz). the dry fruit of such plants as the plantain: a capsule whose upper part falls off when mature so that the seeds are released. [C19: via New Latin from Greek *puxidion* a little box, from *puxis* box, PYX]

pyxie (ˈpɪksɪ) *n.* a creeping evergreen shrub, *Pyxidanthera barbulata*, of the eastern U.S. with small white or pink star-shaped flowers: family *Diapensiaceae*. [C19: shortened from New Latin *Pyxidanthera*, from PYXIS + ANTHER]

pyxis (ˈpɪksɪs) *n., pl.* **pyxides** (ˈpɪksɪˌdiːz). **1.** a small box used by the ancient Greeks and Romans to hold medicines, etc. **2.** a rare word for **pyx. 3.** another name for **pyxidium.** [C14: via Latin from Greek: box]

Pyxis (ˈpɪksɪs) *n., Latin genitive* **Pyxidis** (ˈpɪksɪdɪs). an inconspicuous constellation close to Puppis that was originally considered part of the more extensive constellation Argo.

pzazz (pəˈzæz) *n. Informal.* a variant of **pizzazz.**

Q

q *or* **Q** (kjuː) *n., pl.* **q's, Q's,** *or* **Qs.** **1.** the 17th letter and 13th consonant of the modern English alphabet. **2.** a speech sound represented by this letter, in English usually a voiceless velar stop, as in *unique* and *quick*.

q *symbol for* quintal.

Q *symbol for:* **1.** *Chess.* queen. **2.** question. **3.** *Physics.* heat.

q. *abbrev. for:* **1.** quart. **2.** quarter. **3.** quarterly. **4.** query. **5.** question. **6.** quire.

Q. *abbrev. for:* **1.** quartermaster. **2.** (*pl.* **Qq., qq.**) Also: **q.** quarto. **3.** Quebec. **4.** Queen. **5.** question. **6.** *Electronics.* Q factor.

qadi (ˈkɑːdɪ, ˈkeɪdɪ) *n., pl.* **-dis.** a variant spelling of **cadi.**

QARANC *abbrev. for* Queen Alexandra's Royal Army Nursing Corps.

qawwali (kəˈvɑːlɪ) *n.* an Islamic religious song, esp. in Asia.

QB **1.** *abbrev. for* Queen's Bench. **2.** *Chess. symbol for* queen's bishop.

QBP *Chess. symbol for* queen's bishop's pawn.

QC *abbrev. for* Queen's Counsel.

QCD *abbrev. for* quantum chromodynamics.

q.e. *abbrev. for* quod est. [Latin: which is]

QED *abbrev. for:* **1.** quod erat demonstrandum. [Latin: which was to be shown or proved] **2.** quantum electrodynamics.

QEF *abbrev. for* quod erat faciendum. [Latin: which was to be done]

QF *abbrev. for* quick-firing.

Q factor *n.* **1.** a measure of the relationship between stored energy and rate of energy dissipation in certain electrical components, devices, etc., thus indicating their efficiency. **2.** Also called: **Q value.** the heat released in a nuclear reaction, usually expressed in millions of electronvolts for each individual reaction. ~Symbol: Q [C20: short for *quality factor*]

QFD *abbrev. for* quantum flavourdynamics.

Q fever *n.* an acute disease characterized by fever and pneumonia, transmitted to man by the rickettsia *Coxiella burnetii.* [C20: from *q(uery) fever* (the cause being unknown when it was named)]

qi (tʃiː) *n.* a variant of **chi**^{2}.

qibla (ˈkɪblə) *n.* a variant of **kiblah.**

qintar (kɪnˈtɑː, ˈkɪntɑː) *or* **qindar** (kɪnˈdɑː) *n.* an Albanian monetary unit worth one hundredth of a lek.

QKt *Chess. symbol for* queen's knight.

QKtP *Chess. symbol for* queen's knight's pawn.

ql *abbrev. for* quintal.

q.l. (in prescriptions) *abbrev. for* quantum libet. [Latin: as much as you please]

Qld *or* **QLD** *abbrev. for* Queensland.

qm (in prescriptions) *abbrev. for* quaque mane. [Latin: every morning]

QM *abbrev. for* Quartermaster.

QMC *abbrev. for* Quartermaster Corps.

Q-methodology *n.* a statistical methodology used by psychologists to identify alternative world-views, opinions, interpretations, etc. in terms of statistically independent patterns of response recognized by clustering together individuals whose orderings of items, typically attitude statements, are similar. Compare **R-methodology.**

QMG *abbrev. for* Quartermaster General.

QMS *abbrev. for* Quartermaster Sergeant.

qn (in prescriptions) *abbrev. for* quaque nocte. [Latin: every night]

QN *Chess. symbol for* queen's knight.

QNP *Chess. symbol for* queen's knight's pawn.

qoph (kʊf, kɒf; *Hebrew* kɔf) *n.* a variant of **koph.**

qorma (ˈkɔːmə) *n.* a variant spelling of **korma.**

QP *Chess. symbol for* queen's pawn.

Qq. *or* **qq.** *abbrev. for:* **1.** quartos. **2.** questions.

qqv *abbrev. for* quae vide (denoting a cross reference to more than one item). Compare **qv.** [New Latin: which (words, items, etc.) see]

QR *Chess. symbol for* queen's rook.

qr. *pl.* **qrs.** *abbrev. for:* **1.** quarter. **2.** quarterly. **3.** quire.

QRP *Chess. symbol for* queen's rook's pawn.

qs *abbrev. for:* **1.** (in prescriptions) quantum sufficit. [Latin: as much as will suffice] **2.** quarter section (of land).

QS *abbrev. for* quarter sessions.

Q-ship *n.* a merchant ship with concealed guns, used to decoy enemy ships into the range of its weapons. [named from *q(uery)*]

QSM (in New Zealand) *abbrev. for* Queen's Service Medal.

QSO *abbrev. for:* **1.** *Astronomy.* quasi-stellar object. **2.** (in New Zealand) Queen's Service Order.

Q-sort *n.* a psychological test requiring subjects to sort items relative to one another along a dimension such as "agree"/"disagree" for analysis by Q-methodological statistics.

qt *pl.* **qt** *or* **qts** *abbrev. for* quart.

q.t. *Informal.* **1.** *abbrev. for* quiet. **2. on the q.t.** secretly.

qto *abbrev. for* quarto.

qty *abbrev. for* quantity.

qu. *abbrev. for:* **1.** queen. **2.** query. **3.** question.

qua (kweɪ, kwɑː) *prep.* in the capacity of; by virtue of being. [C17: from Latin, ablative singular (feminine) of *qui* who]

quack^{1} (kwæk) *vb.* (*intr.*) **1.** (of a duck) to utter a harsh guttural sound. **2.** to make a noise like a duck. ~*n.* **3.** the harsh guttural sound made by a duck. [C17: of imitative origin; related to Dutch *kwakken*, German *quacken*]

quack^{2} (kwæk) *n.* **1. a.** an unqualified person who claims medical knowledge or other skills. **b.** (*as modifier*): *a quack doctor.* **2.** *Brit., Austral., and N.Z. informal.* a doctor; physician or surgeon. ~*vb.* **3.** (*intr.*) to act in the manner of a quack. [C17: short for QUACKSALVER] —ˈ**quackish** *adj.*

quackery (ˈkwækərɪ) *n., pl.* **-eries.** the activities or methods of a quack.

quack grass *n.* another name for **couch grass.** [C19: a variant of QUICK GRASS]

quacksalver (ˈkwækˌsælvə) *n.* an archaic word for **quack**^{2}. [C16: from Dutch, from *quack*, apparently: to hawk + *salf* SALVE]

quad^{1} (kwɒd) *n.* short for **quadrangle** (sense 2).

quad^{2} (kwɒd) *n. Printing.* a block of type metal used for spacing. [C19: shortened from QUADRAT]

quad^{3} (kwɒd) *n.* a variant spelling of **quod** (prison).

quad^{4} (kwɒd) *n.* short for **quadruplet** (sense 1).

quad^{5} (kwɒd) *adj., n.* short for **quadraphonic** *or* **quadraphonics.**

quad. *abbrev. for:* **1.** quadrangle. **2.** quadrant. **3.** quadrilateral.

quaddy (ˈkwɒdɪ) *n. Austral.* short for **quadrella.**

quadr- *combining form.* a variant of **quadri-** before a vowel.

quadragenarian (ˌkwɒdrədʒɪˈnɛərɪən) *n.* **1.** a person who is between 40 and 49 years old. ~*adj.* **2.** being from 40 to 49 years old. [C19: from Latin *quadrāgēnārius* consisting of forty, from *quadrāgintā* forty]

Quadragesima (ˌkwɒdrəˈdʒɛsɪmə) *n.* **1.** Also called: **Quadragesima Sunday.** the first Sunday in Lent. **2.** *Obsolete.* the forty days of Lent. [C16: from Medieval Latin *quadrāgēsima dies* the fortieth day]

Quadragesimal (ˌkwɒdrəˈdʒɛsɪməl) *adj.* of, relating to, or characteristic of Lent or the season of Lent.

quadrangle (ˈkwɒdˌræŋɡ^{ə}l) *n.* **1.** *Geometry.* a plane figure consisting of four points connected by four lines. In a **complete quadrangle,** six lines connect all pairs of points. **2.** a rectangular courtyard, esp. one having buildings on all four sides. Often shortened to **quad.** **3.** the building surrounding such a courtyard. [C15: from Late Latin *quadrangulum* figure having four corners] —**quadrangular** (kwɒˈdræŋɡjʊlə) *adj.*

quadrant (ˈkwɒdrənt) *n.* **1.** *Geometry.* **a.** a quarter of the circumference of a circle. **b.** the area enclosed by two perpendicular radii of a circle and its circumference. **c.** any of the four sections into which a plane is divided by two coordinate axes. **2.** a piece of a mechanism in the form of a quarter circle, esp. one used as a cam or a gear sector. **3.** an instrument formerly used in astronomy and navigation for measuring the altitudes of stars, consisting of a graduated arc of 90° and a sighting mechanism attached to a movable arm. [C14: from Latin *quadrāns* a quarter] —**quadrantal** (kwɒˈdrænt^{ə}l) *adj.*

quadraphonics *or* **quadrophonics** (ˌkwɒdrəˈfɒnɪks) *n.* (*functioning as sing.*) a system of sound recording and reproduction that uses four independent loudspeakers to give directional sources of sound. The speakers are fed by four separate amplified signals. —ˌ**quadraˈphonic** *or* ˌ**quadroˈphonic** *adj.* —**quadraphony** *or* **quadrophony** (kwɒˈdrɒfənɪ) *n.*

quadrat (ˈkwɒdrət) *n.* **1.** *Ecology.* an area of vegetation, usually one square metre, selected at random for study of the plants in the surrounding area. **2.** *Printing.* an archaic name for **quad**^{2}. [C14 (meaning "a square"): variant of QUADRATE]

quadrate *n.* (ˈkwɒdrɪt, -reɪt). **1.** a cube, square, or a square or cubelike object. **2.** one of a pair of bones of the upper jaw of fishes, amphibians, reptiles, and birds that articulates with the lower jaw. In mammals it forms the incus. ~*adj.* (ˈkwɒdrɪt, -reɪt). **3.** of or relating to this bone. **4.** square or rectangular. ~*vb.* (kwɒˈdreɪt). **5.** (*tr.*) to make square or rectangular. **6.** (often foll. by *with*) to conform or cause to conform. [C14: from Latin *quadrāre* to make square]

quadratic (kwɒˈdrætɪk) *Maths.* ~*n.* **1.** Also called: **quadratic equation.** an equation containing one or more terms in which the variable is raised to the power of two, but no terms in which it is raised to a higher power. ~*adj.* **2.** of or relating to the second power.

quadratics (kwɒ'drætɪks) *n.* (*functioning as sing.*) the branch of algebra concerned with quadratic equations.

quadrature ('kwɒdrətʃə) *n.* **1.** *Maths.* the process of determining a square having an area equal to that of a given figure or surface. **2.** the process of making square or dividing into squares. **3.** *Astronomy.* a configuration in which two celestial bodies, usually the sun and the moon or a planet, form an angle of 90° with a third body, usually the earth. **4.** *Electronics.* the relationship between two waves that are 90° out of phase.

quadrella (kwɒ'drɛlə) *n. Austral.* four nominated horseraces in which the punter bets on selecting the four winners.

quadrennial (kwɒ'drɛnɪəl) *adj.* **1.** occurring every four years. **2.** relating to or lasting four years. ~*n.* **3.** a period of four years. —**quad'rennially** *adv.*

quadrennium (kwɒ'drɛnɪəm) *n., pl.* **-niums** *or* **-nia** (-nɪə). a period of four years. [C17: from Latin *quadriennium,* from QUADRI- + *annus* year]

quadri- *or before a vowel* **quadr-** *combining form.* four: *quadrilateral; quadrilingual; quadrisyllabic.* [from Latin; compare *quattuor* four]

quadric ('kwɒdrɪk) *Maths.* ~*adj.* **1.** having or characterized by an equation of the second degree, usually in two or three variables. **2.** of the second degree. ~*n.* **3.** a quadric curve, surface, or function.

quadricentennial (ˌkwɒdrɪsɛn'tɛnɪəl) *n.* **1.** a 400th anniversary. ~*adj.* **2.** of, relating to, or celebrating a 400th anniversary.

quadriceps ('kwɒdrɪˌsɛps) *n., pl.* **-cepses** (-ˌsɛpsɪz) *or* **-ceps.** *Anatomy.* a large four-part muscle of the front of the thigh, which extends the leg. [C19: New Latin, from QUADRI- + *-ceps* as in BICEPS] —**quadricipital** (ˌkwɒdrɪ'sɪpɪtᵊl) *adj.*

quadrifid ('kwɒdrɪfɪd) *adj. Botany.* divided into four lobes or other parts: *quadrifid leaves.*

quadriga (kwɒ'driːgə) *n., pl.* **-gas** *or* **-gae** (-dʒiː). (in the classical world) a two-wheeled chariot drawn by four horses abreast. [C18: from Latin, from earlier *quadrijugae* a team of four, from QUADRI- + *jugum* yoke]

quadrilateral (ˌkwɒdrɪ'lætərəl) *adj.* **1.** having or formed by four sides. ~*n.* **2.** Also called: **tetragon.** a polygon having four sides. A **complete quadrilateral** consists of four lines and their six points of intersection.

quadrille[1] (kwɒ'drɪl, kwə-) *n.* **1.** a square dance of five or more figures for four or more couples. **2.** a piece of music for such a dance, alternating between simple duple and compound duple time. [C18: via French from Spanish *cuadrilla,* diminutive of *cuadro* square, from Latin *quadra*]

quadrille[2] (kwɒ'drɪl, kwə-) *n.* an old card game for four players. [C18: from French, from Spanish *cuartillo,* from *cuarto* fourth, from Latin *quartus,* influenced by QUADRILLE[1]]

quadrillion (kwɒ'drɪljən) *n.* **1.** (in Britain, France, and Germany) the number represented as one followed by 24 zeros (10^{24}). U.S. and Canadian word: **septillion. 2.** (in the U.S. and Canada) the number represented as one followed by 15 zeros (10^{15}). ~*determiner.* **3.** (preceded by *a* or a numeral) **a.** amounting to this number: *a quadrillion atoms.* **b.** (*as pronoun*): *a quadrillion.* [C17: from French *quadrillon,* from QUADRI- + *-illion,* on the model of *million*] —**quad'rillionth** *adj.*

quadrinomial (ˌkwɒdrɪ'nəʊmɪəl) *n.* an algebraic expression containing four terms.

quadripartite (ˌkwɒdrɪ'pɑːtaɪt) *adj.* **1.** divided into or composed of four parts. **2.** maintained by or involving four participants or groups of participants.

quadriplegia (ˌkwɒdrɪ'pliːdʒɪə, -dʒə) *n. Pathol.* paralysis of all four limbs, usually as the result of injury to the spine. Also called: **tetraplegia.** Compare **hemiplegia, paraplegia.** [C20: from QUADRI- + Greek *plēgē* a blow, from *plēssein* to strike] —**quadriplegic** (ˌkwɒdrɪ'pliːdʒɪk) *adj., n.*

quadripole ('kwɒdrɪˌpəʊl) *n. Physics.* an electric circuit with two input and two output terminals.

quadrisect ('kwɒdrɪˌsɛkt) *vb.* to divide into four parts, esp. into four equal parts. —ˌ**quadri'section** *n.*

quadrivalent (ˌkwɒdrɪ'veɪlənt) *adj. Chem.* another word for **tetravalent.** —ˌ**quadri'valency** *or* ˌ**quadri'valence** *n.*

quadrivial (kwɒ'drɪvɪəl) *adj.* **1.** having or consisting of four roads meeting at a point. **2.** (of roads or ways) going in four directions. **3.** of or relating to the quadrivium.

quadrivium (kwɒ'drɪvɪəm) *n., pl.* **-ia** (-ɪə) (in medieval learning) the higher division of the seven liberal arts, consisting of arithmetic, geometry, astronomy, and music. Compare **trivium.** [from Medieval Latin, from Latin: crossroads, meeting of four ways, from QUADRI- + *via* way]

quadroon (kwɒ'druːn) *n.* the offspring of a Mulatto and a White; a person who is one-quarter Negro. [C18: from Spanish *cuarterón,* from *cuarto* quarter, from Latin *quartus*]

quadrophonics (ˌkwɒdrə'fɒnɪks) *n.* a variant spelling of **quadraphonics.**

quadrumanous (kwɒ'druːmənəs) *adj.* (of monkeys and apes) having all four feet specialized for use as hands. [C18: from New Latin *quadrumanus,* from QUADRI- + Latin *manus* hand]

quadruped ('kwɒdrʊˌpɛd) *n.* **1.** an animal, esp. a mammal, that has all four limbs specialized for walking. ~*adj.* **2.** having four feet. [C17: from Latin *quadrupēs,* from *quadru-* (see QUADRI-) + *pēs* foot] —**quadrupedal** (kwɒ'druːpɪdᵊl, ˌkwɒdrʊ'pɛdᵊl) *adj.*

quadruple ('kwɒdrʊpᵊl, kwɒ'druːpᵊl) *vb.* **1.** to multiply by four or increase fourfold. ~*adj.* **2.** four times as much or as many; fourfold. **3.** consisting of four parts. ~*n.* **4.** a quantity or number four times as great as another. [C16: via Old French from Latin *quadruplus,* from *quadru-* (see QUADRI-) + *-plus* -fold] —**'quadruply** *adv.*

quadruplet ('kwɒdrʊplɪt, kwɒ'druːplɪt) *n.* **1.** one of four offspring born at one birth. Often shortened to **quad. 2.** a group or set of four similar things. **3.** *Music.* a group of four notes to be played in a time value of three.

quadruple time *n.* musical time in which there are four beats in each bar.

quadruplex ('kwɒdrʊˌplɛks, kwɒ'druːplɛks) *adj.* **1.** consisting of four parts; fourfold. **2.** denoting a type of television video tape recorder having four transversely rotating heads. [C19: from Latin, from *quadru-* (see QUADRI-) + *-plex* -fold] —**quadruplicity** (ˌkwɒdrʊ'plɪsɪtɪ) *n.*

quadruplicate *adj.* (kwɒ'druːplɪkɪt, -ˌkeɪt). **1.** fourfold or quadruple. ~*vb.* (kwɒ'druːplɪˌkeɪt). **2.** to multiply or be multiplied by four. ~*n.* (kwɒ'druːplɪkɪt, -ˌkeɪt). **3.** a group or set of four things. [C17: from Latin *quadruplicāre* to increase fourfold] —**quad**ˌ**rupli'cation** *n.*

quadrupole ('kwɒdrʊˌpəʊl) *n. Physics.* a set of four associated electric charges or two associated magnetic dipoles.

quaere ('kwɪərɪ) *Rare.* ~*n.* **1.** a query or question. ~*interj.* **2.** ask or inquire: used esp. to introduce a question. [C16: Latin, imperative of *quaerere* to inquire]

quaestor ('kwiːstə, -tɔː) *or U.S.* (*sometimes*) **questor** ('kwɛstə) *n.* any of several magistrates of ancient Rome, usually a financial administrator. [C14: from Latin, from *quaerere* to inquire] —**quaestorial** (kwɛ'stɔːrɪəl) *adj.* —**'quaestor**ˌ**ship** *n.*

quaff (kwɒf, kwɑːf) *vb.* to drink heartily or in one draught. [C16: perhaps of imitative origin; compare Middle Low German *quassen* to eat or drink excessively] —**'quaffer** *n.*

quag (kwæg, kwɒg) *n.* another word for **quagmire.** [C16: perhaps related to QUAKE; compare Middle Low German *quabbe*]

quagga ('kwægə) *n., pl.* **-gas** *or* **-ga.** a recently extinct member of the horse family (*Equidae*), *Equus quagga,* of southern Africa: it had a sandy brown colouring with zebra-like stripes on the head and shoulders. [C18: from obsolete Afrikaans, from Hottentot *quăgga;* compare Xhosa *i-qwara* something striped]

quaggy ('kwægɪ, 'kwɒgɪ) *adj.* **-gier, -giest. 1.** resembling a marsh or quagmire; boggy. **2.** yielding, soft, or flabby. —**'quagginess** *n.*

quagmire ('kwægˌmaɪə, 'kwɒg-) *n.* **1.** a soft wet area of land that gives way under the feet; bog. **2.** an awkward, complex, or embarrassing situation. [C16: from QUAG + MIRE]

quahog ('kwɑːˌhɒg) *n.* an edible clam, *Venus* (or *Mercenaria*) *mercenaria,* native to the Atlantic coast of North America, having a large heavy rounded shell. Also called: **hard-shell clam, hard-shell, round clam.** Compare **soft-shell clam.** [C18: from Narraganset, short for *poquauhock,* from *pohkeni* dark + *hogki* shell]

quaich *or* **quaigh** (kwex, kweɪx) *n. Scot.* a small shallow drinking cup, usually with two handles. [from Scottish Gaelic *cuach* cup]

quail[1] (kweɪl) *n., pl.* **quails** *or* **quail. 1.** any small Old World gallinaceous game bird of the genus *Coturnix* and related genera, having a rounded body and small tail: family *Phasianidae* (pheasants). **2.** any of various similar and related American birds, such as the bobwhite. [C14: from Old French *quaille,* from Medieval Latin *quaccula,* probably of imitative origin]

quail[2] (kweɪl) *vb.* (*intr.*) to shrink back with fear; cower. [C15: perhaps from Old French *quailler,* from Latin *coāgulāre* to curdle]

quaint (kweɪnt) *adj.* **1.** attractively unusual, esp. in an old-fashioned style: *a quaint village.* **2.** odd, peculiar, or inappropriate: *a quaint sense of duty.* [C13 (in the sense: clever): from Old French *cointe,* from Latin *cognitus* known, from *cognoscere* to ascertain] —**'quaintly** *adv.* —**'quaintness** *n.*

quair (kwer, kweə) *n. Scot.* a book. [a variant of QUIRE[1]]

quake (kweɪk) *vb.* (*intr.*) **1.** to shake or tremble with or as with fear. **2.** to convulse or quiver, as from instability. ~*n.* **3.** the act or an instance of quaking. **4.** *Informal.* short for **earthquake.** [Old English *cwacian;* related to Old English *cweccan* to shake, Old Irish *bocaim,* German *wackeln*]

Quaker ('kweɪkə) *n.* **1.** a member of the Society of Friends, a Christian sect whose central belief is the doctrine of the Inner Light. Quakers reject sacraments, ritual, and formal ministry, hold meetings at which any member may speak, and have promoted many causes for social reform. ~*adj.* **2.** of, relating to, or designating the Society of Friends or its religious beliefs or practices. [C17: originally a derogatory nickname, alluding either to their alleged ecstatic fits, or to their founder George Fox's injunction to "*quake* at the word of the Lord"] —**'Quakeress** *fem. n.* —**'Quakerish** *adj.* —**'Quakerism** *n.*

Quaker gun *n.* a dummy gun, as of wood. [alluding to the Quakers' traditional pacifism]

quaking ('kweɪkɪŋ) *adj.* unstable or unsafe to walk on, as a bog or quicksand: *a quaking bog; quaking sands.*

quaking grass *n.* any grass of the genus *Briza*, of N temperate regions and South America, having delicate flower branches that shake in the wind.

quaky ('kweɪkɪ) *adj.* **quakier, quakiest.** inclined to quake; shaky; tremulous. —'**quakily** *adv.* —'**quakiness** *n.*

quale ('kwɑːlɪ, 'kweɪ-) *n., pl.* **-lia** (-lɪə). *Philosophy.* an essential property or quality. [C17: Latin, neuter singular of *qualis* of what kind]

qualification (ˌkwɒlɪfɪ'keɪʃən) *n.* **1.** an ability, quality, or attribute, esp. one that fits a person to perform a particular job or task: *he has no qualifications to be a teacher.* **2.** a condition that modifies or limits; restriction. **3.** the act of qualifying or state of being qualified.

qualified ('kwɒlɪˌfaɪd) *adj.* **1.** having the abilities, qualities, attributes, etc., necessary to perform a particular job or task. **2.** limited, modified, or restricted; not absolute.

qualifier ('kwɒlɪˌfaɪə) *n.* **1.** a person or thing that qualifies, esp. a contestant in a competition who wins a preliminary heat or contest and so earns the right to take part in the next round. **2.** a preliminary heat or contest. **3.** *Grammar.* another word for **modifier** (sense 1).

qualify ('kwɒlɪˌfaɪ) *vb.* **-fies, -fying, -fied.** **1.** to provide or be provided with the abilities or attributes necessary for a task, office, duty, etc.: *his degree qualifies him for the job; he qualifies for the job, but would he do it well?* **2.** (*tr.*) to make less strong, harsh, or violent; moderate or restrict. **3.** (*tr.*) to modify or change the strength or flavour of. **4.** (*tr.*) *Grammar.* another word for **modify** (sense 3). **5.** (*tr.*) to attribute a quality to; characterize. **6.** (*intr.*) to progress to the final stages of a competition, as by winning preliminary contests. [C16: from Old French *qualifier*, from Medieval Latin *quālificāre* to characterize, from Latin *quālis* of what kind + *facere* to make] —'**qualiˌfiable** *adj.* —**qualificatory** ('kwɒlɪfɪkətərɪ, -ˌkeɪ-) *adj.*

qualitative ('kwɒlɪtətɪv, -ˌteɪ-) *adj.* involving or relating to distinctions based on quality or qualities. Compare **quantitative.** —'**qualitatively** *adv.*

qualitative analysis *n.* See **analysis** (sense 4).

qualitative identity *n. Logic.* the relation that holds between two relata that have properties in common. This term is used to distinguish many uses of the words *identical* or *same* in ordinary language from strict identity or numerical identity.

quality ('kwɒlɪtɪ) *n., pl.* **-ties.** **1.** a distinguishing characteristic, property, or attribute. **2.** the basic character or nature of something. **3.** a trait or feature of personality. **4.** degree or standard of excellence, esp. a high standard. **5.** (formerly) high social status or the distinction associated with it. **6.** musical tone colour; timbre. **7.** *Logic.* the characteristic of a proposition that is dependent on whether it is affirmative or negative. **8.** *Phonetics.* the distinctive character of a vowel, determined by the configuration of the mouth, tongue, etc., when it is articulated and distinguished from the pitch and stress with which it is uttered. **9.** (*modifier*) having or showing excellence or superiority: *a quality product.* [C13: from Old French *qualité*, from Latin *quālitās* state, nature, from *quālis* of what sort]

quality control *n.* control of the relative quality of a manufactured product, usually by statistical sampling techniques.

quality factor *n.* a property of ionizing radiations that affects their ability to cause biological effects. For weakly ionizing radiations such as gamma rays it has value 1 whilst for alpha rays it is about 20. Former name: **relative biological effectiveness.**

qualm (kwɑːm) *n.* **1.** a sudden feeling of sickness or nausea. **2.** a pang or sudden feeling of doubt, esp. concerning moral conduct; scruple. **3.** a sudden sensation of misgiving or unease. [Old English *cwealm* death or plague; related to Old High German *qualm* despair, Dutch *kwalm* smoke, stench] —'**qualmish** *adj.* —'**qualmishly** *adv.* —'**qualmishness** *n.*

quamash ('kwɒmæʃ, kwə'mæʃ) *n.* another name for **camass** (sense 1).

quandary ('kwɒndrɪ, -dərɪ) *n., pl.* **-ries.** a situation or circumstance that presents problems difficult to solve; predicament; dilemma. [C16: of uncertain origin; perhaps related to Latin *quandō* when]

quandong, quandang ('kwɒnˌdɒŋ), *or* **quantong** ('kwɒnˌtɒŋ) *n.* **1.** Also called: **native peach. a.** a small Australian santalaceous tree, *Eucarya acuminata* (or *Fusanus acuminatus*). **b.** the edible fruit or nut of this tree, used in preserves. **2. silver quandong. a.** an Australian tree, *Elaeocarpus grandis:* family *Elaeocarpaceae.* **b.** the pale easily worked timber of this tree. [from a native Australian language]

quango ('kwæŋgəʊ) *n., pl.* **-gos.** *acronym for* quasi-autonomous nongovernmental *or* (*rarely*) national government organization.

quant[1] (kwɒnt) *n.* **1.** a long pole for propelling a boat, esp. a punt, by pushing on the bottom of a river or lake. ~*vb.* **2.** to propel (a boat) with a quant. [C15: probably from Latin *contus* a pole, from Greek *kontos*]

quant[2] (kwɒnt) *n. Informal.* a highly paid computer specialist with a degree in a quantitative science, employed by a financial house, to predict the future price movements of securities, commodities, currencies, etc. [C20: from QUANTITATIVE]

quanta ('kwɒntə) *n.* the plural of **quantum.**

quantal ('kwɒntəl) *adj.* **1.** of or relating to a quantum or an entity that is quantized. **2.** denoting something that is capable of existing in only one of two states.

quantic ('kwɒntɪk) *n.* a homogeneous function of two or more variables in a rational and integral form, as in $x^2 + 3xy + y^2$. [C19: from Latin *quantus* how great]

quantifier ('kwɒntɪˌfaɪə) *n.* **1.** *Logic.* **a.** a symbol including a variable that indicates the degree of generality of the expression in which that variable occurs, as $(\exists x)$ in $(\exists x)Fx$, rendered "something is an F", (x) in $(x)(Fx \rightarrow Gx)$, rendered "all Fs are Gs". **b.** any other symbol with an analogous interpretation: *the existential quantifier,* $(\exists x)$, *corresponds to the words "there is something, x, such that..."* **2.** *Grammar.* a word or phrase in a natural language having this role, such as *some, all,* or *many* in English.

quantify ('kwɒntɪˌfaɪ) *vb.* **-fies, -fying, -fied.** (*tr.*) **1.** to discover or express the quantity of. **2.** *Logic.* to specify the quantity of (a term) by using a quantifier, such as *all, some,* or *no.* [C19: from Medieval Latin *quantificāre,* from Latin *quantus* how much + *facere* to make] —'**quantifiable** *adj.* —ˌ**quantifi'cation** *n.*

quantitative ('kwɒntɪtətɪv, -ˌteɪ-) *or* **quantitive** *adj.* **1.** involving or relating to considerations of amount or size. Compare **qualitative. 2.** capable of being measured. **3.** *Prosody.* denoting or relating to a metrical system, such as that in Latin and Greek verse, that is based on the relative length rather than stress of syllables. —'**quantitatively** *or* '**quantitively** *adv.*

quantitative analysis *n.* See **analysis** (sense 4).

quantity ('kwɒntɪtɪ) *n., pl.* **-ties.** **1. a.** a specified or definite amount, weight, number, etc. **b.** (*as modifier*): *a quantity estimate.* **2.** the aspect or property of anything that can be measured, weighed, counted, etc. **3.** a large or considerable amount. **4.** *Maths.* an entity having a magnitude that may be denoted by a numerical expression. **5.** *Physics.* a specified magnitude or amount; the product of a number and a unit. **6.** *Logic.* the characteristic of a proposition dependent on whether it is a universal or particular statement, considering all or only part of a class. **7.** *Prosody.* the relative duration of a syllable or the vowel in it. [C14: from Old French *quantité,* from Latin *quantitās* extent, amount, from *quantus* how much]

quantity surveyor *n.* a person who estimates the cost of the materials and labour necessary for a construction job.

quantity theory *n. Economics.* a theory stating that the general price level varies directly with the quantity of money in circulation and the velocity with which it is circulated, and inversely with the volume of production expressed by the total number of money transactions.

quantize *or* **quantise** ('kwɒntaɪz) *vb.* (*tr.*) **1.** *Physics.* to restrict (a physical quantity) to one of a set of values characterized by quantum numbers. **2.** *Maths.* to limit (a variable) to values that are integral multiples of a basic unit. —ˌ**quanti'zation** *or* ˌ**quanti'sation** *n.*

quantometer (kwɑn'tɒmɪtə) *n. Engineering.* a spectroscopic instrument for measuring the percentage of different metals present in a sample.

quantum ('kwɒntəm) *n., pl.* **-ta** (-tə). **1.** *Physics.* **a.** the smallest quantity of some physical property, such as energy, that a system can possess according to the quantum theory. **b.** a particle with such a unit of energy. **2.** amount or quantity, esp. a specific amount. **3.** (*often used with a negative*) the least possible amount that can suffice: *there is not a quantum of evidence for your accusation.* **4.** something that can be quantified or measured. **5.** (*modifier*) loosely, sudden, spectacular, or vitally important: *a quantum improvement.* [C17: from Latin *quantus* (adj.) how much]

quantum chromodynamics *n. Physics.* a theory describing the strong interaction in terms of quarks and gluons, with the colour of quarks used as an analogue of charge and the gluon as an analogue of the photon. Abbrev.: **QCD.** [C20: *chromodynamics* from CHROMO- (referring to quark colour) + DYNAMICS, modelled on QUANTUM ELECTRODYNAMICS]

quantum efficiency *n.* **1.** *Physics.* the number of electrons released by a photocell per photon of incident radiation of a given energy. **2.** *Chem.* the number of chemical species that undergo reaction per photon of absorbed radiation of a given energy.

quantum electrodynamics *n. Physics.* a relativistic quantum mechanical theory concerned with electromagnetic interactions. Abbrev.: **QED.**

quantum electronics *n.* the application of quantum mechanics to the study of the generation and amplification of power at microwave frequencies in solid crystals.

quantum field theory *n. Physics.* quantum mechanical theory concerned with elementary particles, which are represented by fields whose normal modes of oscillation are quantized.

quantum flavourdynamics *n.* a gauge theory of the electromagnetic and weak interactions. Also called: **electroweak theory.** Abbrev.: **QFD.** [C20: *flavourdynamics* from FLAVOUR (referring to quark flavour) + DYNAMICS, modelled on QUANTUM ELECTRODYNAMICS]

quantum gravity *n. Physics.* a theory of the gravitational interaction that involves quantum mechanics to explain the force.

quantum leap *or* **jump** *n.* a sudden highly significant advance; breakthrough. [C20: from its use in physics meaning the sudden jump of an electron, atom, etc. from one energy level to another]

quantum mechanics *n.* (*functioning as sing.*) the branch of mechanics, based on the quantum theory used for interpreting the behaviour of elementary particles and atoms, which do not obey Newtonian mechanics.

quantum meruit *Latin.* (ˈmɛruːɪt) as much as he has earned: denoting a payment for goods or services in partial fulfilment of a contract or for those supplied when no price has been agreed.
quantum number *n. Physics.* one of a set of integers or half-integers characterizing the energy states of a particle or system of particles. A function of the number multiplied by a fixed quantity gives the amount of some specified physical quantity possessed by the system.
quantum state *n. Physics.* a state of a system characterized by a set of quantum numbers and represented by an eigenfunction. Each state has energy which has a value that is precise within the limits imposed by the uncertainty principle but which may be changed by applying a field of force. States that have the same energy are called **degenerate.** See also **energy level.**
quantum statistics *n.* (*functioning as sing.*) *Physics.* statistics concerned with the distribution of a number of identical elementary particles, atoms, ions, or molecules among possible quantum states.
quantum theory *n.* a theory concerning the behaviour of physical systems based on Planck's law, which states that they can only possess certain properties, such as energy and angular momentum, in discrete amounts (quanta). The theory later developed in several equivalent mathematical forms based on the De Broglie wavelength (see **wave mechanics**) and on the Heisenberg uncertainty principle.
quaquaversal (ˌkwɑːkwəˈvɜːsəl) *adj. Geology.* directed outwards in all directions from a common centre: *the quaquaversal dip of a pericline.* [C18: from Latin *quāquā* in every direction + *versus* towards]
quar. *abbrev. for:* **1.** quarter. **2.** quarterly.
quarantine (ˈkwɒrənˌtiːn) *n.* **1.** a period of isolation or detention, esp. of persons or animals arriving from abroad, to prevent the spread of disease, usually consisting of the maximum known incubation period of the suspected disease. **2.** the place or area where such detention is enforced. **3.** any period or state of enforced isolation. ~*vb.* **4.** (*tr.*) to isolate in or as if in quarantine. [C17: from Italian *quarantina* period of forty days, from *quaranta* forty, from Latin *quadrāgintā*]
quarantine flag *n. Nautical.* the yellow signal flag for the letter Q, flown alone from a vessel to indicate that there is no disease aboard and to request pratique or, with a second signal flag, to indicate that there is disease aboard. Also called: **yellow flag, yellow jack.**
quare (kwɛə) *adj. Irish dialect.* **1.** remarkable or strange: *a quare fellow.* **2.** great or good: *you're in a quare mess.* [probably variant of QUEER]
quark[1] (kwɑːk) *n. Physics.* any of a set of at least five hypothetical elementary particles postulated together with their antiparticles to be fundamental units of all baryons and mesons. The magnitude of their charge is either two thirds or one third of that of the electron. [C20: coined by Irish writer James Joyce in the novel *Finnegans Wake* (1939), and given special application in physics]
quark[2] (kwɑːk) *n.* a type of low-fat soft cheese. [from German]
quarrel[1] (ˈkwɒrəl) *n.* **1.** an angry disagreement; argument. **2.** a cause of disagreement or dispute; grievance. ~*vb.* **-rels, -relling, -relled** *or U.S.* **-rels, -reling, -reled.** (*intr.*; often foll. by *with*) **3.** to engage in a disagreement or dispute; argue. **4.** to find fault; complain. [C14: from Old French *querele,* from Latin *querēlla* complaint, from *querī* to complain] —ˈ**quarreller** *or U.S.* ˈ**quarreler** *n.*
quarrel[2] (ˈkwɒrəl) *n.* **1.** an arrow having a four-edged head, fired from a crossbow. **2.** a small square or diamond-shaped pane of glass, usually one of many in a fixed or casement window and framed with lead. [C13: from Old French *quarrel* pane, from Medieval Latin *quadrellus,* diminutive of Latin *quadrus* square]
quarrelsome (ˈkwɒrəlsəm) *adj.* inclined to quarrel or disagree; belligerent. —ˈ**quarrelsomely** *adv.* —ˈ**quarrelsomeness** *n.*
quarrian *or* **quarrion** (ˈkwɒrɪən) *n.* a cockatiel, *Leptolophus hollandicus,* of scrub and woodland regions of inland Australia, that feeds on seeds and grasses. [C20: probably from a native Australian language]
quarrier (ˈkwɒrɪə) *n.* another word for **quarryman.**
quarry[1] (ˈkwɒrɪ) *n., pl.* **-ries. 1.** an open surface excavation for the extraction of building stone, slate, marble, etc., by drilling, blasting, or cutting. **2.** a copious source of something, esp. information. ~*vb.* **-ries, -rying, -ried. 3.** to extract (stone, slate, etc.) from or as if from a quarry. **4.** (*tr.*) to excavate a quarry in. **5.** to obtain (something, esp. information) diligently and laboriously: *he was quarrying away in the reference library.* [C15: from Old French *quarriere,* from *quarre* (unattested) square-shaped stone, from Latin *quadrāre* to make square]
quarry[2] (ˈkwɒrɪ) *n., pl.* **-ries. 1.** an animal, bird, or fish that is hunted, esp. by other animals; prey. **2.** anything pursued or hunted. [C14 *quirre* entrails offered to the hounds, from Old French *cuirée* what is placed on the hide, from *cuir* hide, from Latin *corium* leather; probably also influenced by Old French *coree* entrails, from Latin *cor* heart]
quarry[3] (ˈkwɒrɪ) *n., pl.* **-ries. 1.** a square or diamond shape. **2.** something having this shape. **3.** another word for **quarrel**[2]. [C16: from Old French *quarré;* see QUARREL[2]]
quarryman (ˈkwɒrɪmən) *n., pl.* **-men.** a man who works in or manages a quarry.
quarry tile *n.* a square or diamond-shaped unglazed floor tile. [C20: from QUARRY[3]]
quart[1] (kwɔːt) *n.* **1.** a unit of liquid measure equal to a quarter of a gallon or two pints. 1 U.S. quart (0.946 litre) is equal to 0.8326 U.K. quart. 1 U.K. quart (1.136 litres) is equal to 1.2009 U.S. quarts. **2.** a unit of dry measure equal to 2 pints or one eighth of a peck. [C14: from Old French *quarte,* from Latin *quartus* fourth]
quart[2] *n.* **1.** (kɑːt) *Piquet.* a sequence of four cards in the same suit. **2.** (kart). *Fencing.* a variant spelling of **quarte.** [C17: from French *quarte* fourth]
quart. *abbrev. for:* **1.** quarter. **2.** quarterly.
quartan (ˈkwɔːtᵊn) *adj.* (esp. of a malarial fever) occurring every third day. [C13: from Latin *febris quartāna* fever occurring every fourth day, reckoned inclusively]
quarte *French.* (kart) *n.* the fourth of eight basic positions from which a parry or attack can be made in fencing. [C18: from French, fem. of *quart* a quarter]
quarter (ˈkwɔːtə) *n.* **1.** one of four equal or nearly equal parts of an object, quantity, amount, etc. **2.** Also called: **fourth.** the fraction equal to one divided by four (1/4). **3.** *U.S., Canada, etc.* a quarter of a dollar; 25-cent piece. **4.** a unit of weight equal to a quarter of a hundredweight. 1 U.S. quarter is equal to 25 pounds; 1 Brit. quarter is equal to 28 pounds. **5.** short for **quarter-hour. 6.** a fourth part of a year; three months. **7.** *Astronomy.* **a.** one fourth of the moon's period of revolution around the earth. **b.** either of two phases of the moon, **first quarter** or **last quarter,** when half of the lighted surface is visible from the earth. **8.** *Informal.* a unit of weight equal to a quarter of a pound or 4 ounces. **9.** *Brit.* a unit of capacity for grain, etc., usually equal to 8 U.K. bushels. **10.** *Sport.* one of the four periods into which certain games are divided. **11.** *Nautical.* the part of a vessel's side towards the stern, usually aft of the aftermost mast: *the port quarter.* **12.** *Nautical.* the general direction along the water in the quadrant between the beam of a vessel and its stern: *the wind was from the port quarter.* **13.** a region or district of a town or city: *the Spanish quarter.* **14.** a region, direction, or point of the compass. **15.** (*sometimes pl.*) an unspecified person or group of people: *to get word from the highest quarter.* **16.** mercy or pity, as shown to a defeated opponent (esp. in the phrases **ask for** or **give quarter**). **17.** any of the four limbs, including the adjacent parts, of the carcass of a quadruped or bird: *a hind quarter of beef.* **18.** *Vet. science.* the side part of the wall of a horse's hoof. **19.** the part of a shoe or boot covering the heel and joining the vamp. **20.** *Heraldry.* one of four more or less equal quadrants into which a shield may be divided. **21.** *Military slang.* short for **quartermaster.** ~*vb.* **22.** (*tr.*) to divide into four equal or nearly equal parts. **23.** (*tr.*) to divide into any number of parts. **24.** (*tr.*) (esp. formerly) to dismember (a human body): *to be drawn and quartered.* **25.** to billet or be billeted in lodgings, esp. (of military personnel) in civilian lodgings. **26.** (*intr.*) (of gun dogs or hounds) to range over an area of ground in search of game or the scent of quarry. **27.** (*intr.*) *Nautical.* (of the wind) to blow onto a vessel's quarter: *the wind began to quarter.* **28.** (*tr.*) *Heraldry.* **a.** to divide (a shield) into four separate bearings with a cross. **b.** to place (one set of arms) in diagonally opposite quarters to another. ~*adj.* **29.** being or consisting of one of four equal parts: *a quarter pound of butter.* ~See also **quarters.** [C13: from Old French *quartier,* from Latin *quartārius* a fourth part, from *quartus* fourth]
quarterage (ˈkwɔːtərɪdʒ) *n.* **1.** an allowance or payment made quarterly. **2.** *Rare.* shelter or lodging.
quarterback (ˈkwɔːtəˌbæk) *n. U.S. and Canadian.* **1.** a player in American or Canadian football, positioned usually behind the centre, who directs attacking play. **2. Monday-morning quarterbacking.** wisdom after the event, esp. by spectators.
quarter-bound *adj.* (of a book) having a binding consisting of two types of material, the better type being used on the spine.
quarter crack *n. Vet. science.* a sand crack on the inside of the forefoot of a horse.
quarter day *n.* any of four days in the year when certain payments become due. In England, Wales, and Ireland these are Lady Day, Midsummers Day, Michaelmas, and Christmas. In Scotland they are Candlemas, Whit Sunday, Lammas, and Martinmas.
quarterdeck (ˈkwɔːtəˌdɛk) *n. Nautical.* the after part of the weather deck of a ship, traditionally the deck on a naval vessel for official or ceremonial use.
quartered (ˈkwɔːtəd) *adj.* **1.** *Heraldry.* (of a shield) divided into four sections, each having contrasting arms or having two sets of arms, each repeated in diagonally opposite corners. **2.** (of a log) sawn into four equal parts along two diameters at right angles to each other; quartersawn.
quarterfinal (ˈkwɔːtəˌfaɪnᵊl) *n.* the round before the semifinal in a competition.
quarter grain *n.* the grain of quartersawn timber.
quarter horse *n.* a small powerful breed of horse, originally bred for sprinting in quarter-mile races in Virginia in the late 18th century.
quarter-hour *n.* **1.** a period of 15 minutes. **2.** any of the points on the face of a timepiece that mark 15 minutes before or after

the hour, and sometimes 30 minutes after. —ˌ**quarter-ˈhourly** *adv., adj.*

quartering (ˈkwɔːtərɪŋ) *n.* **1.** *Military.* the allocation of accommodation to service personnel. **2.** *Heraldry.* **a.** the marshalling of several coats of arms on one shield, usually representing intermarriages. **b.** any coat of arms marshalled in this way.

quarterlight (ˈkwɔːtəˌlaɪt) *n. Brit.* a small pivoted window in the door of a car for ventilation.

quarterly (ˈkwɔːtəlɪ) *adj.* **1.** occurring, done, paid, etc., at intervals of three months. **2.** of, relating to, or consisting of a quarter. ~*n., pl.* **-lies.** **3.** a periodical issued every three months. ~*adv.* **4.** once every three months. **5.** *Heraldry.* into or in quarters: *a shield divided quarterly.*

quartermaster (ˈkwɔːtəˌmɑːstə) *n.* **1.** an officer responsible for accommodation, food, and equipment in a military unit. **2.** a rating in the navy, usually a petty officer, with particular responsibility for steering a ship and other navigational duties.

quarter-miler *n.* an athlete who specializes in running the quarter mile.

quartern (ˈkwɔːtən) *n.* **1.** a fourth part of certain weights or measures, such as a peck or a pound. **2.** Also called: **quartern loaf.** *Brit.* **a.** a type of loaf 4 inches square, used esp. for making sandwiches. **b.** any loaf weighing 1600 g when baked. [C13: from Old French *quarteron,* from *quart* a quarter]

quarter note *n.* the usual U.S. and Canadian name for **crotchet** (sense 1).

quarter-phase *adj.* another term for **two-phase.**

quarter plate *n.* a photographic plate measuring 8.3 × 10.8 cm.

quarter round *n. Architect.* another name for **ovolo.**

quarters (ˈkwɔːtəz) *pl. n.* **1.** housing or accommodation, esp. as provided for military personnel and their families. **2.** the stations assigned to military personnel, esp. to each crew member of a warship: *general quarters.* **3.** (in India) housing provided by an employer or by the government. **4.** (*functioning as sing.*) *Military slang.* short for **quartermaster.**

quartersaw (ˈkwɔːtəˌsɔː) *vb.* **-saws, -sawing, -sawed, -sawed** *or* **-sawn.** (*tr.*) to saw (timber) into quarters along two diameters of a log at right angles to each other.

quarter section *n. U.S. and Canadian.* a land measure, used in surveying, with sides half a mile long; 160 acres.

quarter sessions *n.* (*functioning as sing. or pl.*) **1.** (in England and Wales, formerly) a criminal court held four times a year before justices of the peace or a recorder, empowered to try all but the most serious offences and to hear appeals from petty sessions. Replaced in 1972 by **crown courts.** Compare **assizes.** **2.** (in Scotland, formerly) a court held by justices of the peace four times a year, empowered to hear appeals from justice of the peace courts and to deal with some licensing matters: abolished in 1975.

quarterstaff (ˈkwɔːtəˌstɑːf) *n., pl.* **-staves** (-ˌsteɪvz, -ˌstɑːvz). **1.** a stout iron-tipped wooden staff about 6ft. long, formerly used in England as a weapon. **2.** the use of such a staff in fighting, sport, or exercise. [C16: of uncertain origin]

quarter tone *n. Music.* a quarter of a whole tone; a pitch interval corresponding to 50 cents measured on the well-tempered scale.

quartet *or* **quartette** (kwɔːˈtɛt) *n.* **1.** a group of four singers or instrumentalists or a piece of music composed for such a group. See **string quartet.** **2.** any group of four. [C18: from Italian *quartetto,* diminutive of *quarto* fourth]

quartic (ˈkwɔːtɪk) *adj., n.* another word for **biquadratic.** [C19: from Latin *quartus* fourth]

quartile (ˈkwɔːtaɪl) *n.* **1.** *Statistics.* one of three actual or notional values of a variable dividing its distribution into four groups with equal frequencies. ~*adj.* **2.** *Statistics.* denoting or relating to a quartile. **3.** *Astrology.* denoting an aspect of two heavenly bodies when their longitudes differ by 90°. [C16: from Medieval Latin *quartīlis,* from Latin *quartus* fourth]

quarto (ˈkwɔːtəʊ) *n., pl.* **-tos.** **1.** a book size resulting from folding a sheet of paper, usually crown or demy, into four leaves or eight pages, each one quarter the size of the sheet. Often written: **4to, 4°.** **2.** (formerly) a size of cut paper 10 in. by 8 in. (25.4 cm by 20.3 cm). [C16: from New Latin phrase *in quartō* in quarter]

quartz (kwɔːts) *n.* **1.** a colourless mineral often tinted by impurities, found in igneous, sedimentary, and metamorphic rocks. It is used in the manufacture of glass, abrasives, and cement, and also as a gemstone; the violet-purple variety is amethyst, the brown variety is cairngorm, the yellow variety is citrine, and the pink variety is rose quartz. Composition: silicon dioxide. Formula: SiO_2. Crystal structure: hexagonal. **2.** short for **quartz glass.** [C18: from German *Quarz,* of Slavic origin]

quartz clock *or* **watch** *n.* a clock or watch that is operated by the vibrations of a quartz crystal controlled by a microcircuit.

quartz crystal *n.* a thin plate or rod cut in certain directions from a piece of piezoelectric quartz and accurately ground so that it vibrates at a particular frequency.

quartz glass *n.* a colourless glass composed of almost pure silica, resistant to very high temperatures and transparent to near-ultraviolet radiation. Sometimes shortened to **quartz.**

quartziferous (kwɔːtˈsɪfərəs) *adj.* containing or composed of quartz.

quartz-iodine lamp *or* **quartz lamp** *n.* a type of tungsten-halogen lamp containing small amounts of iodine and having a quartz envelope, operating at high temperature and producing an intense light for use in car headlamps, etc.

quartzite (ˈkwɔːtsaɪt) *n.* **1.** a white or grey sandstone composed of quartz. **2.** a very hard metamorphic rock consisting of a mosaic of intergrown quartz crystals.

quasar (ˈkweɪzɑː, -sɑː) *n.* any of a class of quasi-stellar objects, first detected in 1963, that are powerful sources of radio waves and other forms of energy. Many have large red shifts (greater than 1.5), which imply enormous velocities of recession, distances of several thousand million light-years, and luminosities 200 times greater than that of an ordinary galaxy. [C20: *quas(i-stell)ar (radio source)*]

quash (kwɒʃ) *vb.* (*tr.*) **1.** to subdue forcefully and completely; put down; suppress. **2.** to annul or make void (a law, decision, etc.). **3.** to reject (an indictment, writ, etc.) as invalid. [C14: from Old French *quasser,* from Latin *quassāre* to shake]

Quashi *or* **Quashie** (ˈkwɑːʃɪ) *n. Caribbean.* an unsophisticated or gullible male Negro peasant: *I'm not a Quashi that anyone can fool.* [from Twi]

quasi (ˈkweɪzaɪ, -saɪ; ˈkwɑːzɪ) *adv.* as if; as it were. [from Latin, literally: as if]

quasi- *combining form.* **1.** almost but not really; seemingly: *a quasi-religious cult.* **2.** resembling but not actually being; so-called: *a quasi-scholar.*

quasi-contract *n.* an implied contract which arises without the express agreement of the parties.

quasi-judicial *adj.* denoting or relating to powers and functions similar to those of a judge, such as those exercised by an arbitrator, administrative tribunal, etc.

Quasimodo (ˌkwɔːzɪˈməʊdəʊ) *n.* another name for **Low Sunday.** [from the opening words of the Latin introit for that day, *quasi modo geniti infantes* as new-born babies]

quasi-quotation *n. Logic.* a metalinguistic device for referring to the form of an expression containing variables without referring to the symbols for those variables. Thus while *"not p"* refers to the expression consisting of the word *not* followed by the letter *p,* the quasi-quotation ⌜*not p*⌝ refers to the form of any expression consisting of the word *not* followed by any value of the variable *p.* Usual symbol: ⌜⌝ (**corners**).

quasi-stellar object *n.* a member of any of several classes of astronomical bodies, including **quasars** (strong radio sources) and **quasi-stellar galaxies** (no traceable radio emission), both of which have exceptionally large red shifts. Abbrev.: **QSO.**

quass (kvɑːs, kwɑːs) *n.* a variant of **kvass.**

quassia (ˈkwɒʃə) *n.* **1.** any tree of the tropical American simaroubaceous genus *Quassia,* having bitter bark and wood. **2.** the bark and wood of *Quassia amara* and of a related tree, *Picrasma excelsa,* used in furniture making. **3.** a bitter compound extracted from this bark and wood, formerly used as a tonic and anthelmintic, now used in insecticides. [C18: from New Latin, named after Graman *Quassi,* a slave who discovered (1730) the medicinal value of the root]

quatercentenary (ˌkwætəsɛnˈtiːnərɪ) *n., pl.* **-naries.** a 400th anniversary or the year or celebration marking it. [C19: from Latin *quater* four times + CENTENARY] —ˌ**quatercenˈtennial** *adj., n.*

quaternary (kwəˈtɜːnərɪ) *adj.* **1.** consisting of fours or by fours. **2.** fourth in a series. **3.** *Chem.* containing or being an atom bound to four other atoms or groups: *a quaternary ammonium compound.* **4.** *Maths.* having four variables. ~*n., pl.* **-naries.** **5.** the number four or a set of four. [C15: from Latin *quaternārius* each containing four, from *quaternī* by fours, distributive of *quattuor* four]

Quaternary (kwəˈtɜːnərɪ) *adj.* **1.** of, denoting, or formed in the most recent period of geological time, which succeeded the Tertiary period one million years ago. ~*n.* **2.** **the.** the Quaternary period or rock system, divided into Pleistocene and Holocene (Recent) epochs or series.

quaternary ammonium compound *n.* a type of ionic compound that can be regarded as derived from ammonium compounds by replacing the hydrogen atoms with organic groups.

quaternion (kwəˈtɜːnɪən) *n.* **1.** *Maths.* a generalized complex number consisting of four components, $x = x_0 + x_1\mathbf{i} + x_2\mathbf{j} + x_3\mathbf{k}$, where $x, x_0 \ldots x_3$ are real numbers and $\mathbf{i}^2 = \mathbf{j}^2 = \mathbf{k}^2 = -1$, $\mathbf{ij} = -\mathbf{ji} = \mathbf{k}$, etc. **2.** another word for **quaternary** (sense 5). [C14: from Late Latin *quaterniōn,* from Latin *quaternī* four at a time]

quaternity (kwəˈtɜːnɪtɪ) *n., pl.* **-ties.** a group of four, esp. a concept of God as consisting of four persons. [C16: from Late Latin *quaternitās,* from Latin *quaternī* by fours; see QUATERNARY]

quatrain (ˈkwɒtreɪn) *n.* a stanza or poem of four lines, esp. one having alternate rhymes. [C16: from French, from *quatre* four, from Latin *quattuor*]

quatre (ˈkætrə; *French* katrə) *n.* a playing card with four pips. [French: four]

quatrefoil (ˈkætrəˌfɔɪl) *n.* **1.** a leaf, such as that of certain clovers, composed of four leaflets. **2.** *Architect.* a carved ornament having four foils arranged about a common centre, esp. one used in tracery. [C15: from Old French, from *quatre* four + *-foil* leaflet; compare TREFOIL]

quattrocento (ˌkwætrəʊˈtʃɛntəʊ; *Italian* kwattroˈtʃɛnto) *n.* the 15th century, esp. in reference to Renaissance Italian art and literature. [Italian, literally: four hundred (short for fourteen hundred)]

quaver ('kweɪvə) *vb.* **1.** to say or sing (something) with a trembling voice. **2.** (*intr.*) (esp. of the voice) to quiver, tremble, or shake. **3.** (*intr.*) *Rare.* to sing or play quavers or ornamental trills. ~*n.* **4.** *Music.* a note having the time value of an eighth of a semibreve. Usual U.S. and Canadian name: **eighth note.** **5.** a tremulous sound or note. [C15 (in the sense: to vibrate, QUIVER): from *quaven* to tremble, of Germanic origin; compare Low German *quabbeln* to tremble] —'**quaverer** *n.* —'**quavering** *adj.* —'**quaveringly** *adv.* —'**quavery** *adj.*

quay (kiː) *n.* a wharf, typically one built parallel to the shoreline. Compare **pier** (sense 1). [C14 *keye,* from Old French *kai,* of Celtic origin; compare Cornish *kē* hedge, fence, Old Breton *cai* fence]

quayage ('kiːɪdʒ) *n.* **1.** a system of quays. **2.** a charge for the use of a quay.

quayside ('kiːˌsaɪd) *n.* the edge of a quay along the water.

Que. *abbrev. for* Quebec.

quean (kwiːn) *n.* **1.** *Archaic.* **a.** a boisterous, impudent, or disreputable woman. **b.** a prostitute; whore. **2.** *Scot.* a young unmarried woman or girl. [Old English *cwene;* related to Old Saxon, Old High German *quena,* Gothic *qino,* Old Norse *kona,* Greek *gunē* woman. Compare QUEEN]

queasy ('kwiːzɪ) *adj.* **-sier, -siest.** **1.** having the feeling that one is about to vomit; nauseous. **2.** feeling or causing uneasiness: *a queasy conscience.* [C15: of uncertain origin] —'**queasily** *adv.* —'**queasiness** *n.*

Quebec (kwɪ'bɛk, kə-, kɛ-) *n. Communications.* a code word for the letter *q.*

Quebecker *or* **Quebecer** (kwɪ'bɛkə, kə-, kɛ-) *n.* a native or inhabitant of Quebec, a province of E Canada.

Québecois (*French* kebɛkwa) *n., pl.* **-cois** (-kwa). a native or inhabitant of the province of Quebec, esp. a French-speaking one.

quebracho (keɪ'brɑːtʃəʊ; *Spanish* ke'βratʃo) *n., pl.* **-chos** (-tʃəʊz; *Spanish* -tʃos). **1.** either of two anacardiaceous South American trees, *Schinopsis lorentzii* or *S. balansae,* having a tannin-rich hard wood used in tanning and dyeing. **2.** an apocynaceous South American tree, *Aspidosperma quebrachoblanco,* whose bark yields alkaloids used in medicine and tanning. **3.** the wood or bark of any of these trees. **4.** any of various other South American trees having hard wood. [C19: from American Spanish, from *quiebracha,* from *quebrar* to break (from Latin *crepāre* to rattle) + *hacha* axe (from French *hache*)]

Quechua, Kechua ('kɛtʃwə), *or* **Quichua** *n.* **1.** (*pl.* **-uas** *or* **-ua**) a member of any of a group of South American Indian peoples of the Andes, including the Incas. **2.** the language or family of languages spoken by these peoples, possibly distantly related to the Tupi-Guarani family. —'**Quechuan,** '**Kechuan,** *or* '**Quichuan** *adj., n.*

queen (kwiːn) *n.* **1.** a female sovereign who is the official ruler or head of state. **2.** the wife or widow of a king. **3.** a woman or a thing personified as a woman considered the best or most important of her kind: *a beauty queen; the queen of ocean liners.* **4.** *Slang.* an effeminate male homosexual. **5. a.** the only fertile female in a colony of social insects, such as bees, ants, and termites, from the eggs of which the entire colony develops. **b.** (*as modifier*): *a queen bee.* **6.** an adult female cat. **7.** one of four playing cards in a pack, one for each suit, bearing the picture of a queen. **8.** a chess piece, theoretically the most powerful piece, able to move in a straight line in any direction or diagonally, over any number of squares. ~*vb.* **9.** *Chess.* to promote (a pawn) to a queen when it reaches the eighth rank. **10.** (*tr.*) to crown as queen. **11.** (*intr.*) to reign as queen. **12. queen it.** (often foll. by *over*) *Informal.* to behave in an overbearing manner. [Old English *cwēn;* related to Old Saxon *quān* wife, Old Norse *kvæn,* Gothic *qēns* wife]

Queen-Anne ('kwiːn'æn) *n.* **1.** a style of furniture popular in England about 1700–20 and in America about 1720–70, characterized by the use of unencumbered curves, walnut veneer, and the cabriole leg. ~*adj.* **2.** in or of this style. **3.** denoting or relating to a style of architecture popular in England during the early 18th century, characterized by red-brick construction with classical ornamentation.

Queen Anne's Bounty *n. Church of England.* **1.** a fund formed in 1704 for the augmentation of the livings of the poorer Anglican clergy. In 1948 the administrators of the fund were replaced by the Church Commissioners for England. **2.** the office or board administering this fund.

Queen Anne's lace *n.* another name for the **wild carrot.**

queen bee *n.* **1.** the fertile female bee in a hive. **2.** *Informal.* a woman in a position of dominance or ascendancy over her peers or associates.

queencake ('kwiːnˌkeɪk) *n.* a small light cake containing currants.

queen consort *n.* the wife of a reigning king.

queen dowager *n.* the widow of a king.

queenly ('kwiːnlɪ) *adj.* **-lier, -liest.** **1.** resembling or appropriate to a queen. **2.** having the rank of queen. ~*adv.* **3.** in a manner appropriate to a queen. —'**queenliness** *n.*

queen mother *n.* the widow of a former king who is also the mother of the reigning sovereign.

queen of puddings *n.* a pudding made of moist but firm breadcrumb and custard mixture topped with jam and meringue.

queen olive *n.* a variety of olive having large fleshy fruit suitable for pickling, esp. one from around Seville in Spain.

queen post *n.* one of a pair of vertical posts that connect the tie beam of a truss to the principal rafters. Compare **king post.**

queen regent *n.* a queen who acts as regent.

queen regnant *n.* a queen who reigns on her own behalf.

Queen's Award *n.* either of two awards instituted by royal warrant (1976) for a sustained increase in export earnings by a British firm (**Queen's Award for Export Achievement**) or for an advance in technology (**Queen's Award for Technological Achievement**).

Queen's Bench Division *n.* (in England when the sovereign is female) one of the divisions of the High Court of Justice. Also called (when the sovereign is male): **King's Bench.**

Queensberry rules ('kwiːnzbərɪ, -brɪ) *pl. n.* **1.** the code of rules followed in modern boxing, requiring the use of padded gloves, rounds of three minutes, and restrictions on the types of blows allowed. **2.** *Informal.* gentlemanly or polite conduct, esp. in a dispute. [C19: named after the ninth Marquess of *Queensberry,* who originated the rules in 1869]

Queen's Counsel *n.* (in England when the sovereign is female) a barrister appointed Counsel to the Crown on the recommendation of the Lord Chancellor, entitled to sit within the bar of the court and to wear a silk gown. Also called (when the sovereign is male): **King's Counsel.**

queen's English *n.* (when the British sovereign is female) standard Southern British English.

queen's evidence *n. English law.* (when the sovereign is female) evidence given for the Crown against his former associates in crime by an accomplice (esp. in the phrase **turn queen's evidence**). Also called (when the sovereign is male): **king's evidence.** U.S. equivalent: **state's evidence.**

Queen's Guide *n.* (in Britain and the Commonwealth when the sovereign is female) a Guide who has passed the highest tests of proficiency.

queen's highway *n.* (in Britain when the sovereign is female) any public road or right of way.

Queensland blue ('kwiːnzˌlænd, -lənd) *n. Austral.* a pumpkin with a bluish skin. [named after the Australian state of *Queensland*]

Queensland cane toad *n. Austral.* a toad, *Bufo marinus,* introduced into Queensland from Hawaii to control insect pests, becoming a pest itself.

Queensland lungfish *n.* a lungfish, *Neoceratodus forsteri,* reaching a length of six feet: occurs in Queensland rivers but introduced elsewhere.

Queensland nut *n.* another name for **macadamia.**

Queen's proctor *n.* (in England when the sovereign is female) an official empowered to intervene in divorce and certain other cases when it is alleged that material facts are being suppressed.

Queen's Regulations *pl. n.* (in Britain and certain other Commonwealth countries when the sovereign is female) the code of conduct for members of the armed forces.

Queen's Scout *n.* (in Britain and the Commonwealth when the sovereign is female) a Scout who has passed the highest tests of endurance, proficiency, and skill. U.S. equivalent: **Eagle Scout.**

queen's shilling *n.* See **king's shilling.**

Queen's speech *n.* (in Britain and the dominions of the Commonwealth when the sovereign is female) another name for the **speech from the throne.**

Queen Street Farmer *n. N.Z.* a businessman who runs a farm, often for a tax loss. [from *Queen Street,* the main business street in Auckland]

queen substance *n.* a pheromone secreted by queen honeybees and consumed by the workers, in whom it causes suppression of egg-laying.

Queensware ('kwiːnzˌwɛə) *or* **Queen's ware** *n.* a type of light white earthenware with a brilliant glaze developed from creamware by Josiah Wedgwood and named in honour of his patroness, Queen Charlotte (1744–1818).

queer (kwɪə) *adj.* **1.** differing from the normal or usual in a way regarded as odd or strange. **2.** suspicious, dubious, or shady. **3.** faint, giddy, or queasy. **4.** *Informal, derogatory.* homosexual. **5.** *Informal.* odd or unbalanced mentally; eccentric or slightly mad. **6.** *Slang.* worthless or counterfeit. ~*n.* **7.** *Informal, derogatory.* a homosexual, usually a male. ~*vb.* (*tr.*) *Informal.* **8.** to spoil or thwart (esp. in the phrase **queer someone's pitch**). **9.** to put in a difficult or dangerous position. [C16: perhaps from German *quer* oblique, ultimately from Old High German *twërh*] —'**queerish** *adj.* —'**queerly** *adv.* —'**queerness** *n.*

queer-bashing *n. Brit. slang.* the activity of making vicious and unprovoked verbal or physical assaults upon homosexuals or supposed homosexuals. —'**queer-ˌbasher** *n.*

queer fish *n. Brit. informal.* an eccentric or odd person.

queer street *n.* (*sometimes caps.*) *Informal.* a difficult situation, such as debt or bankruptcy (in the phrase **in queer street**).

quell (kwɛl) *vb.* (*tr.*) **1.** to suppress or beat down (rebellion, disorder, etc.); subdue. **2.** to overcome or allay: *to quell pain; to quell grief.* [Old English *cwellan* to kill; related to Old Saxon *quellian,* Old High German *quellen,* Old Norse *kvelja* to torment] —'**queller** *n.*

quelquechose ('kɛlkə'ʃəʊz) *n.* an insignificant thing; mere trifle. [French, literally: something]

quench (kwɛntʃ) *vb. (tr.)* **1.** to satisfy (one's thirst, desires, etc.); slake. **2.** to put out (a fire, flame, etc.); extinguish. **3.** to put down or quell; suppress: *to quench a rebellion.* **4.** to cool (hot metal) by plunging it into cold water. **5.** *Physics.* to reduce the degree of (luminescence or phosphorescence) in (excited molecules or a material) by adding a suitable substance. **6.** *Electronics.* **a.** to suppress (sparking) when the current is cut off in an inductive circuit. **b.** to suppress (an oscillation or discharge) in a component or device. [Old English *ācwencan* to extinguish; related to Old Frisian *quinka* to vanish] —ˈ**quenchable** *adj.* —ˈ**quencher** *n.* —ˈ**quenchless** *adj.*

quenelle (kəˈnɛl) *n.* a finely sieved mixture of cooked meat or fish, shaped into various forms and cooked in stock or fried as croquettes. [C19: from French, from German *Knödel* dumpling, from Old High German *knodo* knot]

quercetin *or* **quercitin** (ˈkwɜːsɪtɪn) *n.* a yellow crystalline pigment found naturally as its glycosides in the rind and bark of many plants. It is used in medicine to treat fragile capillaries. Formula: $C_{15}H_{10}O_7$; melting pt: 316–7°C. Also called: **flavin.** [C19: from Latin *quercētum* an oak forest (from *quercus* an oak) + -IN] —**quercetic** (kwɜːˈsɛtɪk, -ˈsiː-) *adj.*

quercine (ˈkwɜːsaɪn) *adj. Rare.* of or relating to the oak. [C17: from Latin *quercus* an oak]

querist (ˈkwɪərɪst) *n.* a person who makes inquiries or queries; questioner.

quern (kwɜːn) *n.* a stone hand mill for grinding corn. [Old English *cweorn;* related to Old Frisian *quern,* Old High German *kurn,* Old Norse *kverna,* Gothic *quairnus* millstone]

quernstone (ˈkwɜːnˌstəʊn) *n.* **1.** another name for **millstone** (sense 1). **2.** one of the two small circular stones used in a quern.

querulous (ˈkwɛrʊləs, ˈkwɛrjʊ-) *adj.* **1.** inclined to make whining or peevish complaints. **2.** characterized by or proceeding from a complaining fretful attitude or disposition: *a querulous tone.* [C15: from Latin *querulus* from *querī* to complain] —ˈ**querulously** *adv.* —ˈ**querulousness** *n.*

query (ˈkwɪərɪ) *n., pl.* **-ries. 1.** a question, esp. one expressing doubt, uncertainty, or an objection. **2.** a less common name for **question mark.** ~*vb.* **-ries, -rying, -ried.** *(tr.)* **3.** to express uncertainty, doubt, or an objection concerning (something). **4.** to express as a query: *"What's up now?"* she queried. **5.** *U.S.* to put a question to (a person); ask. [C17: from earlier *quere,* from Latin *quaere* ask!, from *quaerere* to seek, inquire]

query language *n. Computer technol.* the instructions and procedures used to retrieve information from a database.

ques. *abbrev. for* question.

quest (kwɛst) *n.* **1.** the act or an instance of looking for or seeking; search: *a quest for diamonds.* **2.** (in medieval romance) an expedition by a knight or company of knights to accomplish some prescribed task, such as finding the Holy Grail. **3.** the object of a search; goal or target: *my quest is the treasure of the king.* **4.** *Rare.* a collection of alms. ~*vb. (mainly intr.)* **5.** (foll. by *for* or *after*) to go in search (of). **6.** to go on a quest. **7.** (of gun dogs or hounds) **a.** to search for game. **b.** to bay when in pursuit of game. **8.** *Rare.* to collect alms. **9.** *(also tr.) Archaic.* to go in search of (a thing); seek or pursue. [C14: from Old French *queste,* from Latin *quaesita* sought, from *quaerere* to seek] —ˈ**quester** *n.* —ˈ**questing** *adj.* —ˈ**questingly** *adv.*

question (ˈkwɛstʃən) *n.* **1.** a form of words addressed to a person in order to elicit information or evoke a response; interrogative sentence. **2.** a point at issue: *it's only a question of time until she dies; the question is how long they can keep up the pressure.* **3.** a difficulty or uncertainty; doubtful point: *a question of money; there's no question about it.* **4. a.** an act of asking. **b.** an investigation into some problem or difficulty. **5.** a motion presented for debate by a deliberative body. **6. put the question.** to require members of a deliberative assembly to vote on a motion presented. **7.** *Law.* a matter submitted to a court or other tribunal for judicial or quasi-judicial decision. **8. question of fact.** (in English law) that part of the issue before a court that is decided by the jury. **9. question of law.** (in English law) that part of the issue before a court that is decided by the judge. **10. beg the question. a.** to avoid giving a direct answer by posing another question. **b.** to assume the truth of that which is intended to be proved. See **petitio principii. 11. beyond (all) question.** beyond (any) dispute or doubt. **12. call in** *or* **into question. a.** to make (something) the subject of disagreement. **b.** to cast doubt upon the validity, truth, etc., of (something). **13. in question.** under discussion: *this is the man in question.* **14. out of the question.** beyond consideration; unthinkable or impossible: *the marriage is out of the question.* **15. pop the question.** *Informal.* to propose marriage. **16. put to the question.** (formerly) to interrogate (a person accused of heresy) by torture. ~*vb. (mainly tr.)* **17.** to put a question or questions to (a person); interrogate. **18.** to make (something) the subject of dispute or disagreement. **19.** to express uncertainty about the validity, truth, etc., of (something); doubt. [C13: via Old French from Latin *quaestiō,* from *quaerere* to seek] —ˈ**questioner** *n.*

questionable (ˈkwɛstʃənəbᵊl) *adj.* **1.** (esp. of a person's morality or honesty) admitting of some doubt; dubious. **2.** of disputable value or authority: *a questionable text.* —ˈ**questionableness** *or* ˌ**questionaˈbility** *n.* —ˈ**questionably** *adv.*

questioning (ˈkwɛstʃənɪŋ) *adj.* **1.** proceeding from or characterized by a feeling of doubt or uncertainty. **2.** enthusiastic or eager for philosophical or other investigations; intellectually stimulated: *an alert and questioning mind.* —ˈ**questioningly** *adv.*

questionless (ˈkwɛstʃənlɪs) *adj.* **1.** blindly adhering, as to a principle or course of action; unquestioning. **2.** a less common word for **unquestionable.** —ˈ**questionlessly** *adv.*

question mark *n.* **1.** the punctuation mark ?, used at the end of questions and in other contexts where doubt or ignorance is implied. **2.** this mark used for any other purpose, as to draw attention to a possible mistake, as in a chess commentary.

question master *n. Brit.* the chairman of a quiz or panel game.

questionnaire (ˌkwɛstʃəˈnɛə, ˌkɛs-) *n.* a set of questions on a form, submitted to a number of people in order to collect statistical information. [C20: from French, from *questionner* to ask questions]

question time *n.* (in parliamentary bodies of the British type) a period of time set aside each day for members to question government ministers.

questor (ˈkwɛstə) *n. U.S.* a variant of **quaestor.** —**questorial** (kwɛˈstɔːrɪəl) *adj.* —ˈ**questorˌship** *n.*

quetzal (ˈkɛtsəl) *or* **quezal** (kɛˈsɑːl) *n., pl.* **-zals** *or* **-zales** (-ˈsɑːlɛs). **1.** Also called: **resplendent trogon.** a crested bird, *Pharomachrus mocinno,* of Central and N South America, which has a brilliant green, red, and white plumage and, in the male, long tail feathers: family *Trogonidae,* order *Trogoniformes* (trogons). **2.** the standard monetary unit of Guatemala, divided into 100 centavos. [via American Spanish from Nahuatl *quetzalli* brightly coloured tail feather]

queue (kjuː) *Chiefly Brit.* ~*n.* **1.** a line of people, vehicles, etc., waiting for something: *a queue at the theatre.* **2.** *Computer technol.* a list in which entries are deleted from one end and inserted at the other. **3.** a pigtail. **4. jump the queue.** See **jump** (sense 26). ~*vb.* **queues, queueing** *or* **queuing, queued. 5.** *(intr.;* often foll. by *up)* to form or remain in a line while waiting. **6.** *Computer technol.* to arrange (a number of programs) in a predetermined order for accessing by a computer. ~U.S. and Canadian word: **line.** [C16 (in the sense: tail); C18 (in the sense: pigtail): via French from Latin *cauda* tail]

queue-jump *vb. (intr.)* **1.** to take a place in a queue ahead of those already queueing; push in. **2.** to obtain prior consideration or some other advantage out of turn or unfairly. ~Also: **jump the queue.** —**queue-jumper** *n.*

quibble (ˈkwɪbᵊl) *vb. (intr.)* **1.** to make trivial objections; prevaricate. **2.** *Archaic.* to play on words; pun. ~*n.* **3.** a trivial objection or equivocation, esp. one used to avoid an issue. **4.** *Archaic.* a pun. [C17: probably from obsolete *quib,* perhaps from Latin *quibus* (from *quī* who, which), as used in legal documents, with reference to their obscure phraseology] —ˈ**quibbler** *n.* —ˈ**quibbling** *adj., n.* —ˈ**quibblingly** *adv.*

quiche (kiːʃ) *n.* an open savoury tart with a rich custard filling to which bacon, onion, cheese, etc., are added: *quiche Lorraine.* [French, from German *Kuchen* cake]

Quichua (ˈkɪtʃwə) *n., pl.* **-uas** *or* **-ua.** a variant of **Quechua.**

quick (kwɪk) *adj.* **1.** (of an action, movement, etc.) performed or occurring during a comparatively short time: *a quick move.* **2.** lasting a comparatively short time; brief: *a quick flight.* **3.** accomplishing something in a time that is shorter than normal: *a quick worker.* **4.** characterized by rapidity of movement; swift or fast: *a quick walker.* **5.** immediate or prompt: *a quick reply.* **6.** *(postpositive)* eager or ready to perform (an action): *quick to criticize.* **7.** responsive to stimulation; perceptive or alert; lively: *a quick eye.* **8.** eager or enthusiastic for learning: *a quick intelligence.* **9.** easily excited or aroused: *a quick temper.* **10.** skilfully swift or nimble in one's movements or actions; deft: *quick fingers.* **11.** *Archaic.* **a.** alive; living. **b.** *(as n.)* living people (esp. in the phrase **the quick and the dead**). **12.** *Archaic or dialect.* lively or eager: *a quick dog.* **13.** (of a fire) burning briskly. **14.** composed of living plants: *a quick hedge.* **15.** *Dialect.* (of sand) lacking firmness through being wet. **16. quick with child.** *Archaic.* pregnant, esp. being in an advanced state of pregnancy, when the movements of the fetus can be felt. ~*n.* **17.** any area of living flesh that is highly sensitive to pain or touch, esp. that under a toenail or fingernail or around a healing wound. **18.** the vital or most important part (of a thing). **19.** short for **quickset** (sense 1). **20. cut (someone) to the quick.** to hurt (someone's) feelings deeply; offend gravely. ~*adv. Informal.* **21.** in a rapid or speedy manner; swiftly. **22.** soon: *I hope he comes quick.* ~*interj.* **23.** a command requiring the hearer to perform an action immediately or in as short a time as possible. [Old English *cwicu* living; related to Old Saxon *quik,* Old High German *queck,* Old Norse *kvikr* alive, Latin *vīvus* alive, Greek *bios* life] —ˈ**quickly** *adv.* —ˈ**quickness** *n.*

quick assets *pl. n. Accounting.* assets readily convertible into cash; liquid current assets.

quick-change artist *n.* an actor or entertainer who undertakes several rapid changes of costume during his performance.

quicken (ˈkwɪkən) *vb.* **1.** to make or become faster; accelerate: *he quickened his walk; her heartbeat quickened with excitement.* **2.** to impart to or receive vigour, enthusiasm, etc.; stimulate or be stimulated: *science quickens man's imagination.* **3.** to make or become alive; revive. **4. a.** (of an unborn fetus) to begin to show signs of life. **b.** (of a pregnant woman) to reach the stage of pregnancy at which movements of the fetus can be felt.

quick fire *n.* **1.** rapid continuous gunfire, esp. at a moving target. *~adj.* **quick-fire. 2.** Also: **quick-firing.** capable of or designed for quick fire. **3.** *Informal.* rapid or following one another in rapid succession: *quick-fire questions.*

quick-freeze *vb.* **-freezes, -freezing, -froze, -frozen.** (*tr.*) to preserve (food) by subjecting it to rapid refrigeration at temperatures of 0°C or lower.

quick grass *n.* another name for **couch grass.** [C17: Scot. and northern English variant of *couch grass,* from the earlier *quick* living; compare QUITCH GRASS]

quickie ('kwɪkɪ) *n. Informal.* **1.** Also called (esp. Brit.): **quick one.** a speedily consumed alcoholic drink. **2.** anything made, done, produced, or consumed rapidly or in haste.

quicklime ('kwɪk,laɪm) *n.* another name for **calcium oxide.** [C15: from QUICK (in the archaic sense: living) + LIME[1]]

quick march *n.* **1.** a march at quick time or the order to proceed at such a pace. *~interj.* **2.** a command to commence such a march.

quicksand ('kwɪk,sænd) *n.* a deep mass of loose wet sand that sucks anything on top of it inextricably into it.

quickset ('kwɪk,set) *Chiefly Brit.~n.* **1. a.** a plant or cutting, esp. of hawthorn, set so as to form a hedge. **b.** such plants or cuttings collectively. **2.** a hedge composed of such plants. *~adj.* **3.** composed of such plants. [C15: from *quick* in the archaic sense live, growing + *set* to plant, set in the ground]

quicksilver ('kwɪk,sɪlvə) *n.* **1.** another name for **mercury** (sense 1). *~adj.* **2.** rapid or unpredictable in movement or change: *a quicksilver temper.* [Old English, from *cwicu* alive (see QUICK) + *seolfer* silver]

quickstep ('kwɪk,stɛp) *n.* **1.** a modern ballroom dance in rapid quadruple time. **2.** a piece of music composed for or in the rhythm of this dance. *~vb.* **-steps, -stepping, -stepped. 3.** (*intr.*) to perform this dance.

quick-tempered *adj.* readily roused to anger; irascible.

quickthorn ('kwɪk,θɔːn) *n.* hawthorn, esp. when planted as a hedge. [C17: probably from *quick* in the sense "fast-growing": compare QUICKSET]

quick time *n. Military.* the normal marching rate of 120 paces to the minute. Compare **double time** (sense 3).

quick trick *n. Bridge.* a high card almost certain to win a trick, usually an ace or a king: the unit in one of the systems of hand valuation.

quick-witted *adj.* having a keenly alert mind, esp. as used to avert danger, make effective reply, etc. —,**quick-'wittedly** *adv.* —,**quick-'wittedness** *n.*

quid[1] (kwɪd) *n.* a piece of tobacco, suitable for chewing. [Old English *cwidu* chewing resin; related to Old High German *quiti* glue, Old Norse *kvātha* resin; see CUD]

quid[2] (kwɪd) *n., pl.* **quid. 1.** *Brit.* a slang word for **pound** (sterling). **2. (be) quids in.** *Brit. slang.* to be in a very favourable or advantageous position. **3. not the full quid.** *Austral. and N.Z. slang.* mentally subnormal. [C17: of obscure origin]

quiddity ('kwɪdɪtɪ) *n., pl.* **-ties. 1.** *Philosophy.* the essential nature of something. Compare **haecceity. 2.** a petty or trifling distinction; quibble. [C16: from Medieval Latin *quidditās,* from Latin *quid* what]

quidnunc ('kwɪd,nʌŋk) *n.* a person eager to learn news and scandal; gossipmonger. [C18: from Latin, literally: what now]

quid pro quo ('kwɪd prəʊ 'kwəʊ) *n., pl.* **quid pro quos. 1.** a reciprocal exchange. **2.** something given in compensation, esp. an advantage or object given in exchange for another. [C16: from Latin: something for something]

quiescent (kwɪ'ɛsᵊnt) *adj.* quiet, inactive, or dormant. [C17: from Latin *quiescere* to rest] —**qui'escence** *or* **qui'escency** *n.* —**qui'escently** *adv.*

quiescent tank *n.* a tank, usually for sewage sludge, in which the sludge is allowed to remain for a time so that sedimentation can occur.

quiet ('kwaɪət) *adj.* **1.** characterized by an absence or near absence of noise: *a quiet street.* **2.** characterized by an absence of turbulent motion or disturbance; peaceful, calm, or tranquil: *a quiet glade; the sea is quiet tonight.* **3.** free from activities, distractions, worries, etc.; untroubled: *a quiet life; a quiet day at work.* **4.** marked by an absence of work, orders, etc.; not busy: *the factory is very quiet at the moment.* **5.** private; not public; secret: *a quiet word with someone.* **6.** free from anger, impatience, or other extreme emotion: *a quiet disposition.* **7.** free from pretentiousness or vain display; modest or reserved: *quiet humour.* **8.** *Astronomy.* (of the sun) exhibiting a very low number of sunspots, solar flares, and other surface phenomena; inactive. Compare **active** (sense 8).*~n.* **9.** the state of being silent, peaceful, or untroubled. **10. on the quiet.** without other people knowing; secretly.*~vb.* **11.** a less common word for **quieten.** [C14: from Latin *quiētus,* past participle of *quiēscere* to rest, from *quiēs* repose, rest] —**'quietness** *n.*

quieten ('kwaɪətᵊn) *vb. Chiefly Brit.* **1.** (often foll. by *down*) to make or become calm, silent, etc.; pacify or become peaceful. **2.** (*tr.*) to allay (fear, doubts, etc.).

quietism ('kwaɪə,tɪzəm) *n.* **1.** a form of religious mysticism originating in Spain in the late 17th century, requiring withdrawal of the spirit from all human effort and complete passivity to God's will. **2.** a state of passivity and calmness of mind towards external events. —**'quietist** *n., adj.*

quietly ('kwaɪətlɪ) *adv.* **1.** in a quiet manner. **2. just quietly.** *Austral.* between you and me; confidentially.

quietude ('kwaɪə,tjuːd) *n.* the state or condition of being quiet, peaceful, calm, or tranquil.

quietus (kwaɪ'iːtəs, -'eɪtəs) *n., pl.* **-tuses. 1.** anything that serves to quash, eliminate, or kill; *to give the quietus to a rumour.* **2.** a release from life; death. **3.** the discharge or settlement of debts, duties, etc. [C16: from Latin *quiētus est,* literally: he is at rest, QUIET]

quiff (kwɪf) *n. Brit.* a prominent tuft of hair, esp. one brushed up above the forehead. [C19: of unknown origin]

quill (kwɪl) *n.* **1. a.** any of the large stiff feathers of the wing or tail of a bird. **b.** the long hollow central part of a bird's feather; calamus. **2.** a bird's feather made into a pen for writing. **3.** any of the stiff hollow spines of a porcupine or hedgehog. **4.** a device, formerly usually made from a crow quill, for plucking a harpsichord string. **5.** *Angling.* a length of feather barb stripped of barbules and used for the body of some artificial flies. **6.** a small roll of bark, esp. one of dried cinnamon. **7.** (in weaving) a bobbin or spindle. **8.** a fluted fold, as in a ruff. **9.** a hollow shaft that rotates upon an inner spindle or concentrically about an internal shaft. *~vb.* (*tr.*) **10.** to wind (thread, yarn, etc.) onto a spool or bobbin. **11.** to make or press fluted folds in (a ruff). [C15 (in the sense: hollow reed or pipe): of uncertain origin; compare Middle Low German *quiele* quill]

quillai (kɪ'laɪ) *n.* another name for **soapbark** (sense 1). [C19: via American Spanish from Araucanian]

quillet ('kwɪlɪt) *n. Archaic.* a quibble or subtlety. [C16: from earlier *quillity,* perhaps an alteration of QUIDDITY]

quilling ('kwɪlɪŋ) *n.* decorative craftwork in which a material such as glass, fabric, or paper is formed into small bands or rolls that form the basis of a design.

quillon (*French* kijɔ̃) *n.* (*often pl.*) either half of the extended crosspiece of a sword or dagger. [C19: from French, diminutive of *quille* bowling pin, ultimately from Old High German *kegil* club, stake]

quill pen *n.* another name for **quill** (sense 2).

quillwort ('kwɪl,wɜːt) *n.* any aquatic pteridophyte plant of the genus *Isoetes,* with quill-like leaves at the bases of which are spore-producing structures: family *Isoetaceae.*

quilt (kwɪlt) *n.* **1.** a thick warm cover for a bed, consisting of a soft filling sewn between two layers of material, usually with crisscross seams. **2.** a bedspread or counterpane. **3.** anything quilted or resembling a quilt. *~vb.* (*tr.*) **4.** to stitch together (two pieces of fabric) with (a thick padding or lining) between them: *to quilt cotton and wool.* **5.** to create (a garment, covering, etc.) in this way. **6.** to pad with material. **7.** *Austral. informal.* to strike; clout. [C13: from Old French *coilte* mattress, from Latin *culcita* stuffed item of bedding] —**'quilter** *n.*

quilting ('kwɪltɪŋ) *n.* **1.** material used for making a quilt. **2.** the act or process of making a quilt. **3.** quilted work.

quim (kwɪm) *n. Brit. taboo.* the female genitals. [C19: of uncertain origin]

quin (kwɪn) *n. Brit.* short for **quintuplet** (sense 2). U.S. and Canadian word: **quint.**

quinacrine ('kwɪnə,kriːn) *n.* **1.** another name for **mepacrine. 2.** *Biochem.* as **quinacrine mustard** used as a stain for chromosomes. [C20: from QUIN(INE) + ACR(ID) + -INE[2]]

quinary ('kwaɪnərɪ) *adj.* **1.** consisting of fives or by fives. **2.** fifth in a series. **3.** (of a number system) having a base of five. *~n., pl.* **-ries. 4.** a set of five. [C17: from Latin *quīnārius* containing five, from *quīnī* five each]

quinate ('kwaɪneɪt) *adj. Botany.* arranged in or composed of five parts: *quinate leaflets.* [C19: from Latin *quīnī* five each]

quince (kwɪns) *n.* **1.** a small widely cultivated Asian rosaceous tree, *Cydonia oblonga,* with pinkish-white flowers and edible pear-shaped fruits. **2.** the acid-tasting fruit of this tree, much used in preserves. [C14 *qwince* plural of *quyn* quince, from Old French *coin,* from Latin *cotōneum,* from Greek *kudōnion* quince, Cydonian (apple)]

quincentenary (,kwɪnsɛn'tiːnərɪ) *n., pl.* **-naries.** a 500th anniversary or the year or celebration marking it. [C19: irregularly from Latin *quinque* five + CENTENARY] —**quincentennial** (,kwɪnsɛn'tɛnɪəl) *adj., n.*

quincuncial (kwɪn'kʌnʃəl) *adj.* **1.** consisting of or having the appearance of a quincunx. **2.** (of the petals or sepals of a five-membered corolla or calyx in the bud) arranged so that two members overlap another two completely and the fifth overlaps on one margin and is itself overlapped on the other. —**quin'cuncially** *adv.*

quincunx ('kwɪnkʌŋks) *n.* **1.** a group of five objects arranged in the shape of a rectangle with one at each of the four corners and the fifth in the centre. **2.** *Botany.* a quincuncial arrangement of sepals or petals in the bud. **3.** *Astrology.* an aspect of 150° between two planets. [C17: from Latin: five twelfths, from *quinque* five + *uncia* twelfth; in ancient Rome, this was a coin worth five twelfths of an AS[2] and marked with five spots]

quindecagon (kwɪn'dɛkəgən) *n.* a geometric figure having 15 sides and 15 angles. [C16: from Latin *quindecim* fifteen + *-agon,* as in *decagon*]

quindecaplet (kwɪn'dɛkə,plɛt) *n.* **1.** a group of 15. **2.** one of a group of 15. [C20: irregularly formed on the models of *quadruplet, quintuplet,* etc.]

quindecennial (ˌkwɪndɪˈsɛnɪəl) *adj.* **1.** occurring once every 15 years or over a period of 15 years. ~*n.* **2.** a 15th anniversary. [C20: from Latin *quindecim* fifteen + *annus* year, on the model of *biennial*]

quine (kwaɪn) *n. Scot.* a variant of **quean** (sense 2).

quinella (kwɪˈnɛlə) *n. Austral. and N.Z.* a form of betting on a horse race in which the punter bets on selecting the first and second place-winners in any order. [from American Spanish *quiniela* a game of chance]

quinic acid (ˈkwɪnɪk) *n.* a white crystalline soluble optically active carboxylic acid, found in cinchona bark, bilberries, coffee beans, and the leaves of certain other plants; 1,3,4,5-tetrahydroxycyclohexanecarboxylic acid. Formula: $C_6H_7(OH)_4COOH$.

quinidine (ˈkwɪnɪˌdiːn) *n.* a crystalline alkaloid drug that is an optically active isomer of quinine: used to treat heart arrhythmias. Formula: $C_{20}H_{24}N_2O_2$.

quinine (kwɪˈniːn; *U.S.* ˈkwaɪnaɪn) *n.* a bitter crystalline alkaloid extracted from cinchona bark, the salts of which are used as a tonic, antipyretic, analgesic, etc., and (usually in combination with chloroquine and similar drugs) in malaria therapy. Formula: $C_{20}H_{24}N_2O_2$. [C19: from Spanish *quina* cinchona bark, from Quechua *kina* bark]

quinnat salmon (ˈkwɪnæt) *n.* another name for **Chinook salmon.** [C19: from Salish *t'kwinnat*]

quino- *or before a vowel* **quin-** *combining form.* indicating cinchona, cinchona bark, or quinic acid: *quinidine; quinol; quinoline.* [see QUININE]

quinol (ˈkwɪnɒl) *n.* another name for **hydroquinone.**

quinoline (ˈkwɪnəˌliːn, -lɪn) *n.* **1.** an oily colourless insoluble basic heterocyclic compound synthesized by heating aniline, nitrobenzene, glycerol, and sulphuric acid: used as a food preservative and in the manufacture of dyes and antiseptics. Formula: C_9H_7N. **2.** any substituted derivative of quinoline.

quinone (kwɪˈnəʊn, ˈkwɪnəʊn) *n.* another name for **benzoquinone.**

quinonoid (ˈkwɪnəˌnɔɪd, kwɪˈnəʊnɔɪd) *or* **quinoid** *adj.* of, resembling, or derived from quinone.

quinquagenarian (ˌkwɪŋkwədʒɪˈnɛərɪən) *n.* **1.** a person between 50 and 59 years old. ~*adj.* **2.** being between 50 and 59 years old. **3.** of or relating to a quinquagenarian. [C16: from Latin *quinquāgēnārius* containing fifty, from *quinquāgēnī* fifty each]

Quinquagesima (ˌkwɪŋkwəˈdʒɛsɪmə) *n.* the Sunday preceding Ash Wednesday, the beginning of Lent. Also called: **Quinquagesima Sunday.** [C14: via Medieval Latin from Latin *quinquāgēsima diēs* fiftieth day]

quinque- *combining form.* five: *quinquevalent.* [from Latin *quinque*]

quinquecentenary (ˌkwɪŋkwɪsɛnˈtiːnərɪ) *n., pl.* **-naries.** another name for **quincentenary.**

quinquefoliate (ˌkwɪŋkwɪˈfəʊlɪɪt, -ˌeɪt) *adj.* (of leaves) having or consisting of five leaflets.

quinquennial (kwɪnˈkwɛnɪəl) *adj.* **1.** occurring once every five years or over a period of five years. ~*n.* **2.** another word for **quinquennium.** **3.** a fifth anniversary. —**quinˈquennially** *adv.*

quinquennium (kwɪnˈkwɛnɪəm) *n., pl.* **-nia** (-nɪə). a period or cycle of five years. [C17: from Latin *quinque* five + *annus* year]

quinquepartite (ˌkwɪŋkwɪˈpɑːtaɪt) *adj.* **1.** divided into or composed of five parts. **2.** maintained by or involving five participants or groups of participants.

quinquereme (ˌkwɪŋkwɪˈriːm) *n.* an ancient Roman galley with five banks of oars on each side. [C16: from Latin *quinquerēmis,* from QUINQUE- + *rēmus* oar]

quinquevalent (ˌkwɪŋkwɪˈveɪlənt, kwɪnˈkwɛvələnt) *adj. Chem.* another word for **pentavalent.** —ˌ**quinqueˈvalency** *or* **quinquevalence** (ˌkwɪŋkwɪˈveɪləns, kwɪnˈkwɛvələns) *n.*

quinsy (ˈkwɪnzɪ) *n.* inflammation of the tonsils and surrounding tissues with the formation of abscesses. [C14: via Old French and Medieval Latin from Greek *kunankhē,* from *kuōn* dog + *ankhein* to strangle]

quint[1] *n.* **1.** (kwɪnt). an organ stop sounding a note a fifth higher than that normally produced by the key depressed. **2.** (kɪnt). *Piquet.* a sequence of five cards in the same suit. [C17: from French *quinte,* from Latin *quintus* fifth]

quint[2] (kwɪnt) *n.* the U.S. and Canadian word for **quin.**

quintain (ˈkwɪntɪn) *n.* (esp. in medieval Europe) **1.** a post or target set up for tilting exercises for mounted knights or foot soldiers. **2.** the exercise of tilting at such a target. [C14: from Old French *quintaine,* from Latin: street in a Roman camp between the fifth and sixth maniples, from *quintus* fifth]

quintal (ˈkwɪntᵊl) *n.* **1.** a unit of weight equal to 100 pounds. **2.** a unit of weight equal to 100 kilograms. [C15: via Old French from Arabic *qintār,* possibly from Latin *centēnārius* consisting of a hundred]

quintan (ˈkwɪntən) *adj.* (of a fever) occurring every fourth day. [C17: from Latin *febris quintāna* fever occurring every fifth day, reckoned inclusively]

quinte *French.* (kɛ̃t) *n.* the fifth of eight basic positions from which a parry or attack can be made in fencing. [C18: French, from Latin *quinta,* fem. of *quintus* fifth, from *quinque* five]

quintessence (kwɪnˈtɛsəns) *n.* **1.** the most typical representation of a quality, state, etc. **2.** an extract of a substance containing its principle in its most concentrated form. **3.** (in ancient and medieval philosophy) ether, the fifth and highest essence or element after earth, water, air, and fire, which was thought to be the constituent matter of the heavenly bodies and latent in all things. [C15: via French from Medieval Latin *quinta essentia* the fifth essence, translation of Greek *pemptē ousia*] —**quintessential** (ˌkwɪntɪˈsɛnʃəl) *adj.* —ˌ**quintesˈsentially** *adv.*

quintet *or* **quintette** (kwɪnˈtɛt) *n.* **1.** a group of five singers or instrumentalists or a piece of music composed for such a group. **2.** any group of five. [C19: from Italian *quintetto,* from *quinto* fifth]

quintic (ˈkwɪntɪk) *adj. Maths.* of or relating to the fifth degree: *a quintic equation.*

quintile (ˈkwɪntaɪl) *n. Astrology.* an aspect of 72° between two heavenly bodies. [C17: from Latin *quintus* fifth]

quintillion (kwɪnˈtɪljən) *n., pl.* **-lions** *or* **-lion. 1.** (in Britain, France, and Germany) the number represented as one followed by 30 zeros (10^{30}). U.S. and Canadian word: **nonillion. 2.** (in the U.S. and Canada) the number represented as one followed by 18 zeros (10^{18}). Brit. word: **trillion.** [C17: from Latin *quintus* fifth + *-illion,* as in MILLION] —**quinˈtillionth** *adj.*

quintuple (ˈkwɪntjʊpᵊl, kwɪnˈtjuːpᵊl) *vb.* **1.** to multiply by five. ~*adj.* **2.** five times as much or as many; fivefold. **3.** consisting of five parts. ~*n.* **4.** a quantity or number five times as great as another. [C16: from French, from Latin *quintus,* on the model of QUADRUPLE]

quintuplet (ˈkwɪntjʊplɪt, kwɪnˈtjuːplɪt) *n.* **1.** a group or set of five similar things. **2.** one of five offspring born at one birth. Often shortened to **quin. 3.** *Music.* a group of five notes to be played in a time value of three, four, or some other value.

quintuplicate *adj.* (kwɪnˈtjuːplɪkɪt). **1.** fivefold or quintuple. ~*vb.* (kwɪnˈtjuːplɪˌkeɪt). **2.** to multiply or be multiplied by five. ~*n.* (kwɪnˈtjuːplɪkɪt). **3.** a group or set of five things. —**quinˌtupliˈcation** *n.*

quinze (*French* kɛ̃z) *n.* a card game with rules similar to those of vingt-et-un, except that the score aimed at is 15 rather than 21. [French: fifteen]

quip (kwɪp) *n.* **1.** a sarcastic or cutting remark; gibe. **2.** a witty or clever saying: *a merry quip.* **3.** *Archaic.* another word for **quibble.** ~*vb.* **quips, quipping, quipped. 4.** (*intr.*) to make a quip. [C16: from earlier *quippy,* probably from Latin *quippe* indeed, to be sure]

quipster (ˈkwɪpstə) *n.* a person inclined to make sarcastic or witty remarks.

quipu *or* **quippu** (ˈkiːpuː, ˈkwɪpuː) *n.* a device of the Incas of Peru used to record information, consisting of an arrangement of variously coloured and knotted cords attached to a base cord. [C17: from Spanish *quipo,* from Quechua *quipu,* literally: knot]

quire[1] (kwaɪə) *n.* **1.** a set of 24 or 25 sheets of paper; a twentieth of a ream. **2. a.** four sheets of paper folded once to form a section of 16 pages. **b.** a section or gathering. **3.** a set of all the sheets in a book. [C15 *quayer,* from Old French *quaier,* from Latin *quaternī* four at a time, from *quater* four times]

quire[2] (kwaɪə) *n.* an obsolete spelling of **choir.**

Quirites (kwɪˈraɪtiːz) *pl. n.* the citizens of ancient Rome. [from Latin: inhabitants of *Cures,* later applied generally to Roman citizens]

quirk (kwɜːk) *n.* **1.** an individual peculiarity of character; mannerism or foible. **2.** an unexpected twist or turn: *a quirk of fate.* **3.** a continuous groove in an architectural moulding. **4.** a flourish, as in handwriting. [C16: of unknown origin] —**ˈquirky** *adj.* —**ˈquirkily** *adv.* —**ˈquirkiness** *n.*

quirt (kwɜːt) *U.S.* ~*n.* **1.** a whip with a leather thong at one end. ~*vb.* (*tr.*) **2.** to strike with a quirt. [C19: from Spanish *cuerda* CORD]

quis custodiet ipsos custodes? *Latin.* (kwɪs kʊsˈtəʊdɪˌɛt ˈɪpsɒs kʊsˈtəʊdiːz) who will guard the guards?

quisling (ˈkwɪzlɪŋ) *n.* a traitor who aids an occupying enemy force; collaborator. [C20: after Major Vidkun *Quisling* (1887–1945), Norwegian collaborator with the Nazis]

quist (kwɪst) *n., pl.* **quists** *or* **quist.** *West Midland and southwestern English dialect.* a wood pigeon. [of obscure origin]

quit (kwɪt) *vb.* **quits, quitting, quitted** *or* (*chiefly U.S.*) **quit. 1.** (*tr.*) to depart from; leave: *he quitted the place hastily.* **2.** to resign; give up (a job): *he quitted his job today.* **3.** (*intr.*) (of a tenant) to give up occupancy of premises and leave them: *they received notice to quit.* **4.** to desist or cease from (something or doing something); break off: *quit laughing.* **5.** (*tr.*) to pay off (a debt); discharge or settle. **6.** (*tr.*) *Archaic.* to conduct or acquit (oneself); comport (oneself): *he quits himself with great dignity.* ~*adj.* **7.** (*usually predicative;* foll. by *of*) free (from); released (from): *he was quit of all responsibility for their safety.* [C13: from Old French *quitter,* from Latin *quiētus* QUIET; see QUIETUS]

quitch grass (kwɪtʃ) *n.* another name for **couch grass.** Sometimes shortened to **quitch.** [Old English *cwice;* perhaps related to *cwicu* living, QUICK (with the implication that the grass cannot be killed); compare Dutch *kweek,* Norwegian *kvike,* German *Queckengras*]

quitclaim (ˈkwɪtˌkleɪm) *Law.* ~*n.* **1.** a formal renunciation of any claim against a person or of a right to land. ~*vb.* **2.** (*tr.*) **a.** to renounce (a claim) formally. **b.** to declare (a person) free from liability. [C14: from Anglo-French *quiteclame,* from *quite* QUIT + *clamer* to declare (from Latin *clamāre* to shout)]

quite (kwaɪt) *adv.* **1.** to the greatest extent; completely or absolutely: *you're quite right; quite the opposite.* **2.** (*not used with a negative*) to a noticeable or partial extent; somewhat: *she's quite pretty.* **3.** in actuality; truly: *he thought the bag was heavy, but it was quite light; it's quite the thing to do.* **4. quite a** *or* **an.** (*not used with a negative*) of an exceptional, considerable, or noticeable kind: *quite a girl; quite a long walk.* **5. quite something.** a remarkable or noteworthy thing or person. ~*sentence substitute.* **6.** Also: **quite so.** an expression used to indicate agreement or assent. [C14: adverbial use of *quite* (adj.) QUIT]
▷**Usage.** See at **very.**

quitrent ('kwɪt,rɛnt) *n.* (formerly) a rent payable by a freeholder or copyholder to his lord that released him from liability to perform services.

quits (kwɪts) *Informal.* ~*adj.* (*postpositive*) **1.** on an equal footing; even: *now we are quits.* **2. call it quits.** to agree to end a dispute, contest, etc., agreeing that honours are even. ~*interj.* **3.** an exclamation indicating willingness to give up.

quittance ('kwɪtᵊns) *n.* **1.** release from debt or other obligation. **2.** a receipt or other document certifying this. [C13: from Old French, from *quitter* to release from obligation; see QUIT]

quitter ('kwɪtə) *n.* a person who gives up easily; defeatist, deserter, or shirker.

quittor ('kwɪtə) *n. Vet. science.* infection of the cartilages on the side of a horse's foot, characterized by inflammation and the formation of pus. [C13: perhaps from Old French *cuiture* a boiling, from Latin *coctūra* a cooking, from *coquere* to cook]

quiver[1] ('kwɪvə) *vb.* **1.** (*intr.*) to shake with a rapid tremulous movement; tremble. ~*n.* **2.** the state, process, or noise of shaking or trembling. [C15: from obsolete *cwiver* quick, nimble; compare QUAVER] —'**quiverer** *n.* —'**quivering** *adj.* —'**quiveringly** *adv.* —'**quivery** *adj.*

quiver[2] ('kwɪvə) *n.* a case for arrows. [C13: from Old French *cuivre;* related to Old English *cocer,* Old Saxon *kokari,* Old High German *kohhari,* Medieval Latin *cucurum*]

quiverful ('kwɪvəfʊl) *n.* **1.** the amount that a quiver can hold. **2.** *Literary.* a fair number or full complement: *a quiverful of children.*

qui vive (,kiː 'viːv) *n.* **on the qui vive.** on the alert; attentive. [C18: from French, literally: long live who?, sentry's challenge (equivalent to "To whose party do you belong?" or "Whose side do you support?")]

quixotic (kwɪk'sɒtɪk) *adj.* preoccupied with an unrealistically optimistic or chivalrous approach to life; impractically idealistic. [C18: after *Don Quixote,* the hero of Cervantes' *Don Quixote de la Mancha*] —**quix'otically** *adv.* —**quixotism** ('kwɪksə,tɪzəm) *n.*

quiz (kwɪz) *n., pl.* **quizzes. 1. a.** an entertainment in which the general or specific knowledge of the players is tested by a series of questions, esp. as a radio or television programme. **b.** (*as modifier*): *a quiz programme.* **2.** any set of quick questions designed to test knowledge. **3.** an investigation by close questioning; interrogation. **4.** *Obsolete.* a practical joke; hoax. **5.** *Obsolete.* a puzzling or eccentric individual. **6.** *Obsolete.* a person who habitually looks quizzically at others, esp. through a small monocle. ~*vb.* **quizzes, quizzing, quizzed.** (*tr.*) **7.** to investigate by close questioning; interrogate. **8.** *U.S. and Canadian informal.* to test or examine the knowledge of (a student or class). **9.** (*tr.*) *Obsolete.* to look quizzically at, esp. through a small monocle. [C18: of unknown origin] —'**quizzer** *n.*

quizmaster ('kwɪz,mɑːstə) *n.* a person who puts questions to contestants on a quiz programme.

quizzical ('kwɪzɪkᵊl) *adj.* questioning and mocking or supercilious: *a quizzical look.* —,**quizzi'cality** *n.* —'**quizzically** *adv.*

quod (kwɒd) *n. Chiefly Brit.* a slang word for **jail.** [C18: of uncertain origin; perhaps changed from *quad,* short for *quadrangle*]

quod erat demonstrandum *Latin.* ('kwɒd 'ɛræt ,dɛmən'strændʊm) (at the conclusion of a proof, esp. of a theorem in Euclidean geometry) which was to be proved. Abbrev.: **QED.**

quodlibet ('kwɒdlɪ,bɛt) *n.* **1.** a light piece of music based on two or more popular tunes. **2.** a subtle argument, esp. one prepared as an exercise on a theological topic. [C14: from Latin, from *quod* what + *libet* pleases, that is, whatever you like] —,**quodli'betical** *adj.* —,**quodli'betically** *adv.*

quoin, coign, *or* **coigne** (kwɔɪn, kɔɪn) *n.* **1.** an external corner of a wall. **2.** Also called: **cornerstone.** a stone forming the external corner of a wall. **3.** another name for **keystone** (sense 1). **4.** *Printing.* a metal or wooden wedge or an expanding mechanical device used to lock type up in a chase. **5.** a wedge used for any of various other purposes, such as (formerly) to adjust elevation in muzzle-loading cannon. [C16: variant of COIN (corner)]

quoin post *n.* the vertical post at the side of a lock gate, about which the gate swings.

quoit (kɔɪt) *n.* **1.** a ring of iron, plastic, rope, etc., used in the game of quoits. **2.** *Austral. slang.* a variant spelling of **coit.** [C15: of unknown origin]

quoits (kɔɪts) *pl. n.* (*usually functioning as sing.*) a game in which quoits are tossed at a stake in the ground in attempts to encircle it.

quokka ('kwɒkə) *n.* a small wallaby, *Setonix brachyurus,* formerly abundant in swampy coastal regions of Western Australia but now rare, occurring mostly on offshore islands. [from a native Australian language]

quondam ('kwɒndæm) *adj.* (*prenominal*) of an earlier time; former: *her quondam lover.* [C16: from Latin adv.: formerly]

Quonset hut ('kwɒnsɪt) *n. Trademark, U.S.* a military shelter made of corrugated steel sheet, having a semicircular cross section. Brit. equivalent: **Nissen hut.**

quorate ('kwɔː,reɪt) *adj. Brit.* constituting or having a quorum.

Quorn (kwɔːn) *n. Trademark.* a vegetable protein developed from a type of fungus and used in cooking as a meat substitute.

quorum ('kwɔːrəm) *n.* a minimum number of members in an assembly, society, board of directors, etc., required to be present before any valid business can be transacted: *the quorum is forty.* [C15: from Latin, literally: of whom, occurring in Latin commissions in the formula *quorum vos...duos* (etc.) *volumus* of whom we wish that you be...two]

quot. *abbrev. for* quotation.

quota ('kwəʊtə) *n.* **1.** the proportional share or part of a whole that is due from, due to, or allocated to a person or group. **2.** a prescribed number or quantity, as of items to be manufactured, imported, or exported, immigrants admitted to a country, or students admitted to a college. [C17: from Latin *quota pars* how big a share?, from *quotus* of what number]

quotable ('kwəʊtəbᵊl) *adj.* apt or suitable for quotation: *his remarks are not quotable in mixed company.* —,**quota'bility** *n.*

quotation (kwəʊ'teɪʃən) *n.* **1.** a phrase or passage from a book, poem, play, etc., remembered and spoken, esp. to illustrate succinctly or support a point or an argument. **2.** the act or habit of quoting from books, plays, poems, etc. **3.** *Commerce.* a statement of the current market price of a security or commodity. **4.** an estimate of costs submitted by a contractor to a prospective client; tender. **5.** *Stock Exchange.* registration granted to a company or governmental body, enabling the shares and other securities of the company or body to be officially listed and traded. **6.** *Printing.* a large quadrat that is less than type-high and is used to fill up spaces.

quotation mark *n.* either of the punctuation marks used to begin or end a quotation, respectively " and " or ' and ' in English printing and writing. When double marks are used, single marks indicate a quotation within a quotation, and vice versa. Also called: **inverted comma.** See also **turned comma.**

quote (kwəʊt) *vb.* **1.** to recite a quotation (from a book, play, poem, etc.), esp. as a means of illustrating or supporting a statement. **2.** (*tr.*) to put quotation marks round (a word, phrase, etc.). **3.** *Stock Exchange.* to state (a current market price) of (a security or commodity). ~*n.* **4.** an informal word for **quotation** (senses 1–4). **5.** (*often pl.*) an informal word for **quotation mark:** *put it in quotes.* ~*interj.* **6.** an expression used parenthetically to indicate that the words that follow it form a quotation: *the president said, quote, I shall not run for office in November, unquote.* [C14: from Medieval Latin *quotāre* to assign reference numbers to passages, from Latin *quot* how many]

quoth (kwəʊθ) *vb. Archaic.* (used with all pronouns except *thou* and *you,* and with nouns) another word for **said**[1] (sense 2). [Old English *cwæth,* third person singular of *cwethan* to say; related to Old Frisian *quetha* to say, Old Saxon, Old High German *quethan;* see BEQUEATH]

quotha ('kwəʊθə) *interj. Archaic.* an expression of mild sarcasm, used in picking up a word or phrase used by someone else: *Art thou mad? Mad, quotha! I am more sane than thou.* [C16: from *quoth a* quoth he]

quotidian (kwəʊ'tɪdɪən) *adj.* **1.** (esp. of attacks of malarial fever) recurring daily. **2.** everyday; commonplace. ~*n.* **3.** a malarial fever characterized by attacks that recur daily. [C14: from Latin *quotīdiānus,* variant of *cottīdiānus* daily]

quotient ('kwəʊʃənt) *n.* **1. a.** the result of the division of one number or quantity by another. **b.** the integral part of the result of division. **2.** a ratio of two numbers or quantities to be divided. [C15: from Latin *quotiens* how often]

quo vadis ('kwəʊ 'vɑːdɪs) whither goest thou? [Latin: from the Vulgate version of John 16:5]

quo warranto ('kwəʊ wɒ'ræntəʊ) *n. Law.* a proceeding initiated to determine or (formerly) a writ demanding by what authority a person claims an office, franchise, or privilege. [from Medieval Latin: by what warrant]

Qur'an (kʊ'rɑːn, -'ræn) *n.* a variant of **Koran.**

qv (denoting a cross reference) *abbrev. for* quod vide. [New Latin: which (word, item, etc.) see]

qwerty *or* **QWERTY keyboard** ('kwɜːtɪ) *n.* the standard English language typewriter keyboard layout with the characters q, w, e, r, t, and y positioned on the top row of alphabetic characters at the left side of the keyboard.

qy *abbrev. for* query.

r *or* **R** (ɑː) *n., pl.* **r's, R's,** *or* **Rs.** **1.** the 18th letter and 14th consonant of the modern English alphabet. **2.** a speech sound represented by this letter, in English usually an alveolar semi-vowel, as in *red.* **3.** See **three Rs, the.**

R *symbol for:* **1.** *Chem.* radical. **2.** *Currency.* **a.** rand. **b.** rupee. **3.** Réaumur (scale). **4.** *Physics, electronics.* resistance. **5.** roentgen *or* röntgen. **6.** *Chess.* rook. **7.** Royal. **8.** *Chem.* gas constant. **9.** (in Australia) **a.** restricted exhibition (used to describe a category of film certified as unsuitable for viewing by anyone under the age of 18). **b.** *(as modifier): an R film.* ~**10.** *international car registration for* Romania.

r. *abbrev. for:* **1.** rare. **2.** recipe. **3.** recto. **4.** Also: **r** rod (unit of length). **5.** ruled. **6.** *Cricket, baseball, etc.* run(s).

R. *abbrev. for:* **1.** rabbi. **2.** rector. **3.** Regiment. **4.** Regina. [Latin: Queen] **5.** Republican. **6.** response (in Christian liturgy). **7.** Rex. [Latin: King] **8.** River. **9.** Royal.

R. *or* **r.** *abbrev. for:* **1.** radius. **2.** railway. **3.** registered (trademark). **4.** right. **5.** river. **6.** road. **7.** rouble.

Ra *the chemical symbol for* radium.

RA *abbrev. for:* **1.** rear admiral. **2.** *Astronomy.* right ascension. **3.** (in Britain) Royal Academician *or* Academy. **4.** (in Britain) Royal Artillery. ~ **5.** *international car registration for* Argentina (officially Argentine Republic).

RAAF *abbrev. for* Royal Australian Air Force.

rabato *or* **rebato** (rəˈbɑːtəʊ) *n., pl.* **-tos.** a wired or starched collar, often of intricate lace, that stood up at the back and sides: worn in the 17th century. [C16: from French *rabat* collar, with the ending *-o* added as if the word were from Italian]

rabbet (ˈræbɪt) *or* **rebate** *n.* **1.** a recess, groove, or step, usually of rectangular section, cut into a surface or along the edge of a piece of timber to receive a mating piece. **2.** a joint made between two pieces of timber using a rabbet. ~*vb.* *(tr.)* **3.** to cut or form a rabbet in (timber). **4.** to join (pieces of timber) using a rabbet. [C15: from Old French *rabattre* to beat down]

rabbi (ˈræbaɪ) *n., pl.* **-bis.** *Judaism.* **1.** (in Orthodox Judaism) a man qualified in accordance with traditional religious law to expound, teach, and rule in accordance with this law. **2.** the religious leader of a congregation; the minister of a synagogue. **3. the Rabbis.** the early Jewish scholars whose teachings are recorded in the Talmud. ~See also **Rav.** [Hebrew, from *rabh* master + *-ī* my]

rabbinate (ˈræbɪnɪt) *n.* **1.** the position, function, or tenure of office of a rabbi. **2.** rabbis collectively.

rabbinic (rəˈbɪnɪk) *or* **rabbinical** *adj.* of or relating to the rabbis, their teachings, writings, views, language, etc. —**rabˈbinically** *adv.*

Rabbinic (rəˈbɪnɪk) *or* **Rabbinical Hebrew** *n.* the form of the Hebrew language used by the rabbis of the Middle Ages.

rabbinics (rəˈbɪnɪks) *n. (functioning as sing.)* the study of rabbinic literature of the post-Talmudic period.

rabbinism (ˈræbɪˌnɪzəm) *n.* the teachings and traditions of the rabbis of the Talmudic period. —**ˈrabbinist** *n., adj.* —**ˌrabbiˈnistic** *adj.*

rabbit (ˈræbɪt) *n., pl.* **-bits** *or* **-bit.** **1.** any of various common gregarious burrowing leporid mammals, esp. *Oryctolagus cuniculus* of Europe and North Africa and the cottontail of America. They are closely related and similar to hares but are smaller and have shorter ears. **2.** the fur of such an animal. **3.** *Brit. informal.* a novice or poor performer at a game or sport. ~*vb. (intr.)* **4.** to hunt or shoot rabbits. **5.** (often foll. by *on* or *away*) *Brit. informal.* to talk inconsequentially; chatter. [C14: perhaps from Walloon *robett,* diminutive of Flemish *robbe* rabbit, of obscure origin: C20 in sense 5, from rhyming slang *rabbit and pork* talk]

rabbiter (ˈræbɪtə) *n. Chiefly Austral.* a person who traps and sells rabbits.

rabbit fever *n. Pathol.* another name for **tularaemia.**

rabbitfish (ˈræbɪtˌfɪʃ) *n., pl.* **-fish** *or* **-fishes.** **1.** a large chimaera, *Chimaera monstrosa,* common in European seas, with separate caudal and anal fins and a long whiplike tail. **2.** any of the spiny-finned tropical marine fishes of the family *Siganidae* of Indo-Pacific waters. They have a rabbit-like snout and spines on the pelvic or ventral fins.

rabbitoh *or* **rabbito** (ˈræbɪtˌəʊ) *n. Austral. informal.* an itinerant seller of rabbits for eating. [C20: from such a seller's cry]

rabbit-proof fence *n.* **a.** a fence through which rabbits are unable to pass. **b.** *Austral. informal.* a boundary between certain Australian states, marked by such a fence.

rabbit punch *n.* a short sharp blow to the back of the neck that can cause loss of consciousness or even death. Austral. name: **rabbit killer.**

rabbitry (ˈræbɪtrɪ) *n., pl.* **-ries.** **1.** a place where tame rabbits are kept and bred. **2.** the rabbits kept in such a place.

rabble[1] (ˈræbᵊl) *n.* **1.** a disorderly crowd; mob. **2. the.** *Contemptuous.* the common people. [C14 (in the sense: a pack of animals): of uncertain origin; perhaps related to Middle Dutch *rabbelen* to chatter, rattle]

rabble[2] (ˈræbᵊl) *n.* **1.** Also called: **ˈrabbler.** an iron tool or mechanical device for stirring, mixing, or skimming a molten charge in a roasting furnace. ~*vb.* **2.** *(tr.)* to stir, mix, or skim (the molten charge) in a roasting furnace. [C17: from French *râble,* from Latin *rutābulum* rake for a furnace, from *ruere* to rake, dig up]

rabble-rouser *n.* a person who manipulates the passions of the mob; demagogue. —**ˈrabble-ˌrousing** *adj., n.*

Rabelaisian (ˌræbəˈleɪzɪən, -ʒən) *adj.* **1.** of, relating to, or resembling the work of the French writer François Rabelais (?1494–1553), esp. by broad, often bawdy humour and sharp satire. ~*n.* **2.** a student or admirer of Rabelais. —**ˌRabeˈlaisianism** *n.*

rabi (ˈrʌbɪ) *n.* (in Pakistan, India, etc.) a crop that is harvested at the end of winter. Compare **kharif.** [Urdu: spring crop, from Arabic *rabīʿ* spring]

Rabia (rəˈbɪə) *n.* either the third or the fourth month of the Muslim year, known as **Rabia I** and **Rabia II** respectively; the Muslim spring.

rabid (ˈræbɪd, ˈreɪ-) *adj.* **1.** relating to or having rabies. **2.** zealous; fanatical; violent; raging. [C17: from Latin *rabidus* frenzied, mad, from *rabere* to be mad] —**rabidity** (rəˈbɪdɪtɪ) *or* **ˈrabidness** *n.* —**ˈrabidly** *adv.*

rabies (ˈreɪbiːz) *n. Pathol.* an acute infectious viral disease of the nervous system transmitted by the saliva of infected animals, esp. dogs. It is characterized by excessive salivation, aversion to water, convulsions, and paralysis. Also called: **hydrophobia, lyssa.** [C17: from Latin: madness, from *rabere* to rave] —**rabic** (ˈræbɪk) *or* **rabietic** (ˌreɪbɪˈɛtɪk) *adj.*

RAC *abbrev. for:* **1.** Royal Automobile Club. **2.** Royal Armoured Corps.

raccoon *or* **racoon** (rəˈkuːn) *n., pl.* **-coons** *or* **-coon.** **1.** any omnivorous mammal of the genus *Procyon,* esp. *P. lotor* (**North American raccoon**), inhabiting forests of North and Central America and the West Indies: family *Procyonidae,* order *Carnivora* (carnivores). Raccoons have a pointed muzzle, long tail, and greyish-black fur with black bands around the tail and across the face. **2.** the fur of the North American raccoon. [C17: from Algonquian *ärähkun,* from *ärähkuněm* he scratches with his hands]

raccoon dog *n.* **1.** a canine mammal, *Nyctereutes procyonoides,* inhabiting woods and forests near rivers in E Asia. It has long yellowish-brown black-tipped hair and facial markings resembling those of a raccoon. **2.** Also called: **coonhound.** an American breed of dog having a short smooth black coat with tan markings, bred to hunt raccoons.

race[1] (reɪs) *n.* **1.** a contest of speed, as in running, swimming, driving, riding, etc. **2.** any competition or rivalry: *the race for the White House.* **3.** rapid or constant onward movement: *the race of time.* **4.** a rapid current of water, esp. one through a narrow channel that has a tidal range greater at one end than the other. **5.** a channel of a stream, esp. one for conducting water to or from a water wheel or other device for utilizing its energy: *a mill race.* **6. a.** a channel or groove that contains ball bearings or roller bearings or that restrains a sliding component. **b.** the inner or outer cylindrical ring in a ball bearing or roller bearing. **7.** *Austral. and N.Z.* a narrow passage or enclosure in a sheep yard through which sheep pass individually, as to a sheep dip. **8.** *Austral.* a wire tunnel through which footballers pass from the changing room onto a football field. **9.** *N.Z.* a line of containers coupled together, used in mining to transport coal. **10.** another name for **slipstream** (sense 1). **11.** *Archaic.* the span or course of life. **12. not in the race.** *Austral. informal.* given or having no chance. ~*vb.* **13.** to engage in a contest of speed with (another). **14.** to engage (oneself or one's representative) in a race, esp. as a profession or pastime: *to race pigeons.* **15.** to move or go as fast as possible. **16.** to run (an engine, shaft, propeller, etc.) or (of an engine, shaft, propeller, etc.) to run at high speed, esp. after reduction of the load or resistance. ~See also **race off, races.** [C13: from Old Norse *rās* running; related to Old English *rǣs* attack]

race[2] (reɪs) *n.* **1.** a group of people of common ancestry, distinguished from others by physical characteristics, such as hair type, colour of eyes and skin, stature, etc. Principal races are Caucasoid, Mongoloid, and Negroid. **2. the human race.** human beings collectively. **3.** a group of animals or plants having common characteristics that distinguish them from other members of the same species, usually forming a geographically isolated group; subspecies. **4.** a group of people sharing the same interests, characteristics, etc.: *the race of authors.* [C16: from French, from Italian *razza,* of uncertain origin]

race[3] (reɪs) *n.* a ginger root. [C15: from Old French *rais,* from Latin *rādīx* a root]

racecard ('reɪsˌkɑːd) *n.* a card or booklet at a race meeting with the times of the races, names of the runners, etc., printed on it.

racecourse ('reɪsˌkɔːs) *n.* a long broad track, usually of grass, enclosed between rails, and with starting and finishing points marked upon it, over which horses are raced. Also called (esp. U.S. and Canada): **racetrack.**

racegoer ('reɪsˌgəʊə) *n.* one who attends a race meeting, esp. a habitual frequenter of race meetings.

racehorse ('reɪsˌhɔːs) *n.* a horse specially bred for racing.

raceme (rə'siːm) *n.* an inflorescence in which the flowers are borne along the main stem, with the oldest flowers at the base. It can be simple, as in the foxglove, or compound (see **panicle**). [C18: from Latin *racēmus* bunch of grapes]

race meeting *n.* a prearranged fixture for racing horses (or sometimes greyhounds) over a set course at set times.

racemic (rə'siːmɪk, -'sɛm-) *adj. Chem.* of, concerned with, or being a mixture of dextrorotatory and laevorotatory isomers in such proportions that the mixture has no optical activity. [C19: from RACEME (as in *racemic acid*) + -IC] —**racemism** ('ræsɪˌmɪzəm, rə'siːmɪzəm) *n.*

racemic acid *n.* the optically inactive form of tartaric acid that is sometimes found in grape juice.

racemize *or* **racemise** ('ræsɪˌmaɪz) *vb.* to change or cause to change into a racemic mixture. —ˌ**racemi'zation** *or* ˌ**racemi'sation** *n.*

racemose ('ræsɪˌməʊs, -ˌməʊz) *or* **racemous** *adj.* being or resembling a raceme. [C17: from Latin *racēmōsus* clustering] —'**raceˌmosely** *or* '**racemously** *adv.*

race off *vb. (tr., adv.) Austral. informal.* to entice (a person) away with a view to seduction.

racer ('reɪsə) *n.* **1.** a person, animal, or machine that races. **2.** a turntable used to traverse a heavy gun. **3.** any of several long slender nonvenomous North American snakes of the colubrid genus *Coluber* and related genera, such as *C. lateralis* (**striped racer**).

race relations *n.* **1.** (*functioning as pl.*) the relations between members of two or more human races, esp. within a single community. **2.** (*functioning as sing.*) the branch of sociology concerned with such relations.

race riot *n.* a riot among members of different races in the same community.

races ('reɪsɪz) *pl. n.* **the.** a series of contests of speed between horses (or sometimes greyhounds) over a set course at prearranged times; a race meeting.

racetrack ('reɪsˌtræk) *n.* **1.** a circuit or course, esp. an oval one, used for motor racing, speedway, etc. **2.** the usual U.S. and Canadian word for a **racecourse.**

raceway ('reɪsˌweɪ) *n.* **1.** another word for **race**[1] (sense 5). **2.** a racetrack, esp. one for banger racing. **3.** another word (esp. U.S.) for **race**[1] (sense 6).

rachiotomy (ˌreɪkɪ'ɒtəmɪ) *n.* another name for **laminectomy.**

rachis *or* **rhachis** ('reɪkɪs) *n., pl.* **rachises, rhachises** *or* **rachides, rhachides** ('rækɪˌdiːz, 'reɪ-). **1.** *Botany.* the main axis or stem of an inflorescence or compound leaf. **2.** *Ornithol.* the shaft of a feather, esp. the part that carries the barbs. **3.** another name for **vertebral column.** [C17: via New Latin from Greek *rhakhis* ridge] —**rachial, rhachial** ('reɪkɪəl) *or* **rachidial, rhachidial** (rə'kɪdɪəl) *adj.*

rachitis (rə'kaɪtɪs) *n. Pathol.* another name for **rickets.** [C18: New Latin, from Greek *rhakitis;* see RACHIS] —**rachitic** (rə'kɪtɪk) *adj.*

Rachmanism ('rækməˌnɪzəm) *n.* extortion or exploitation by a landlord of tenants of dilapidated or slum property, esp. when involving intimidation or use of racial fears to drive out sitting tenants whose rent is fixed at a low rate. [C20: after Perec *Rachman* (1920–62), British property-owner born in Poland]

racial ('reɪʃəl) *adj.* **1.** denoting or relating to the division of the human species into races on grounds of physical characteristics. **2.** characteristic of any such group. **3.** relating to or arising from differences between the races: *racial harmony.* **4.** of or relating to a subspecies. —'**racially** *adv.*

racialism ('reɪʃəˌlɪzəm) *or* **racism** *n.* **1.** the belief that races have distinctive cultural characteristics determined by hereditary factors and that this endows some races with an intrinsic superiority over others. **2.** abusive or aggressive behaviour towards members of another race on the basis of such a belief. —'**racialist** *or* '**racist** *n., adj.*

racial unconscious *n. Psychol.* another term for **collective unconscious.**

racing ('reɪsɪŋ) *adj.* **1.** denoting or associated with horse races: *the racing fraternity; a racing man.* ~*n.* **2.** the practice of engaging horses (or sometimes greyhounds) in contests of speed.

rack[1] (ræk) *n.* **1.** a framework for holding, carrying, or displaying a specific load or object: *a plate rack; a hat rack; a hay rack; a luggage rack.* **2.** a toothed bar designed to engage a pinion to form a mechanism that will interconvert rotary and rectilinear motions. **3.** a framework fixed to an aircraft for carrying bombs, rockets, etc. **4.** (usually preceded by *the*) an instrument of torture that stretched the body of the victim. **5.** a cause or state of mental or bodily stress, suffering, etc.; anguish; torment (esp. in the phrase **on the rack**). **6.** *U.S. and Canadian.* (in pool, snooker, etc.) **a.** the triangular frame used to arrange the balls for the opening shot. **b.** the balls so grouped. Brit. equivalent: **frame.** ~*vb. (tr.)* **7.** to torture on the rack. **8.** to cause great stress or suffering to: *guilt racked his conscience.* **9.** to strain or shake (something) violently, as by great physical force: *the storm racked the town.* **10.** to place or arrange in or on a rack: *to rack bottles of wine.* **11.** to move (parts of machinery or a mechanism) using a toothed rack. **12.** to raise (rents) exorbitantly; rack-rent. **13. rack one's brains.** to strain in mental effort, esp. to remember something or to find the solution to a problem. ~See also **rack up.** [C14 *rekke,* probably from Middle Dutch *rec* framework; related to Old High German *recchen* to stretch, Old Norse *rekja* to spread out] —'**racker** *n.*

rack[2] (ræk) *n.* destruction; wreck (obsolete except in the phrase **go to rack and ruin).** [C16: variant of WRACK[1]]

rack[3] (ræk) *n.* another word for **single-foot,** a gait of the horse. [C16: perhaps based on ROCK[2]]

rack[4] (ræk) *n.* **1.** a group of broken clouds moving in the wind. ~*vb.* **2.** (*intr.*) (of clouds) to be blown along by the wind. [Old English *wrǣc* what is driven; related to Gothic *wraks* persecutor, Swedish *vrak* wreckage]

rack[5] (ræk) *vb. (tr.)* **1.** to clear (wine, beer, etc.) as by siphoning it off from the dregs. **2.** to fill a container with (beer, wine, etc.). [C15: from Old Provençal *arraca,* from *raca* dregs of grapes after pressing]

rack[6] (ræk) *n.* the neck or rib section of mutton, pork, or veal. [Old English *hrace;* related to Old High German *rahho,* Danish *harke,* Swedish *harkla* to clear one's throat]

rack-and-pinion *n.* **1.** a device for converting rotary into linear motion and vice versa, in which a gearwheel (the pinion) engages with a flat toothed bar (the rack). ~*adj.* **2.** (of a type of steering gear in motor vehicles) having a track rod with a rack along part of its length that engages with a pinion attached to the steering column.

racket[1] ('rækɪt) *n.* **1.** a noisy disturbance or loud commotion; clamour; din. **2.** gay or excited revelry, dissipation, etc. **3.** an illegal enterprise carried on for profit, such as extortion, fraud, prostitution, drug peddling, etc. **4.** *Slang.* a business or occupation: *what's your racket?* **5.** *Music.* **a.** a medieval woodwind instrument of deep bass pitch. **b.** a reed stop on an organ of deep bass pitch. ~*vb.* **6.** (*intr.;* often foll. by *about*) *Now rare.* to go about gaily or noisily, in search of pleasure, excitement, etc. [C16: probably of imitative origin; compare RATTLE[1]]

racket[2] *or* **racquet** ('rækɪt) *n.* **1.** a bat consisting of an open network of nylon or other strings stretched in an oval frame with a handle, used to strike the ball in tennis, badminton, etc. **2.** a snowshoe shaped like a tennis racket. ~*vb.* **3.** (*tr.*) to strike (a ball, shuttlecock, etc.) with a racket. ~See also **rackets.** [C16: from French *raquette,* from Arabic *rāhat* palm of the hand]

racketeer (ˌrækɪ'tɪə) *n.* **1.** a person engaged in illegal enterprises for profit. ~*vb.* **2.** (*intr.*) to operate a racket. —ˌ**racket'eering** *n.*

racket press *n.* a device consisting of a frame closed by a spring mechanism, for keeping taut the strings of a tennis racket, squash racket, etc.

rackets ('rækɪts) *n.* (*functioning as sing.*) **a.** a game similar to squash played in a large four-walled court by two or four players using rackets and a small hard ball. **b.** (*as modifier*): *a rackets court; a rackets championship.*

racket-tail *n.* any of several birds with a racket-shaped tail, such as certain hummingbirds and kingfishers.

rackety ('rækɪtɪ) *adj.* **1.** noisy, rowdy, or boisterous. **2.** socially lively and, sometimes, mildly dissolute: *a rackety life.*

rack railway *n.* a steep mountain railway having a middle rail fitted with a rack that engages a pinion on the locomotive to provide traction. Also called: **cog railway.**

rack-rent *n.* **1.** a high rent that annually equals or nearly equals the value of the property upon which it is charged. **2.** any extortionate rent. ~*vb.* **3.** to charge an extortionate rent for (property, land, etc.). [C17: from RACK[1] (sense 12) + RENT[1]] —'**rack-ˌrenter** *n.*

rack saw *n. Building trades.* a wide-toothed saw.

rack up *vb. (tr., adv.)* **1.** to accumulate (points). **2.** Also: **rack down.** to adjust the vertical alignment of (the picture from a film projector or telecine machine) so that the upper or lower edges of the frame do not show.

racon ('reɪkɒn) *n.* another name for **radar beacon.** [C20: from *ra(dar)* + *(bea)con*]

raconteur (ˌrækɒn'tɜː) *n.* a person skilled in telling stories. [C19: French, from *raconter* to tell]

racoon (rə'kuːn) *n., pl.* **-coons** *or* **-coon.** a variant spelling of **raccoon.**

racquet ('rækɪt) *n.* a variant spelling of **racket**[2].

racy ('reɪsɪ) *adj.* **racier, raciest. 1.** (of a person's manner, literary style, etc.) having a distinctively lively and spirited quality; fresh. **2.** having a characteristic or distinctive flavour: *a racy wine.* **3.** suggestive; slightly indecent; risqué: *a racy comedy.* —'**racily** *adv.* —'**raciness** *n.*

rad[1] (ræd) *n.* a former unit of absorbed ionizing radiation dose equivalent to an energy absorption per unit mass of 0.01 joule per kilogram of irradiated material. 1 rad is equivalent to 0.01 gray. [C20: shortened from RADIATION]

rad[2] (ræd) *adj.* **radder, raddest.** *Slang, chiefly U.S.* short for **radical** (sense 5).

rad[3] *symbol for* radian.

rad. *abbrev. for:* **1.** radical. **2.** radius. **3.** radix. **4.** radiator.

RADA ('rɑːdə) *n.* (in Britain) *acronym for* Royal Academy of Dramatic Art.

radar ('reɪdɑː) *n.* **1.** a method for detecting the position and velocity of a distant object, such as an aircraft. A narrow beam of extremely high-frequency radio pulses is transmitted and reflected by the object back to the transmitter, the signal being displayed on a radarscope. The direction of the reflected beam and the time between transmission and reception of a pulse determine the position of the object. Former name: **radiolocation. 2.** the equipment used in such detection. [C20 *ra(dio) d(etecting) a(nd) r(anging)*]

radar astronomy *n.* the use of radar to map the surfaces of the planets, their satellites, and other bodies.

radar beacon *n.* a device for transmitting a coded radar signal in response to a signal from an aircraft or ship. The coded signal is then used by the navigator to determine his position. Also called: **racon.**

radarscope ('reɪdɑːˌskəʊp) *n.* a cathode-ray oscilloscope on which radar signals can be viewed. In a **plan position indicator,** the target is represented by a blip on a radial line that rotates around a point, representing the antenna.

radar trap *n.* See **speed trap.**

raddle[1] ('ræd[ə]l) *vb. (tr.)* another word for **interweave.** [C17: from obsolete n. sense of *raddle* meaning a rod, wattle, or lath, from Old French *redalle* a stick, pole; of obscure origin]

raddle[2] ('ræd[ə]l) *vb.* **1.** *(tr.) Chiefly Brit.* to paint (the face) with rouge. ~*n., vb.* **2.** another word for **ruddle.** [C16: variant of RUDDLE]

raddled ('ræd[ə]ld) *adj.* (esp. of a person) unkempt or run-down in appearance. [C17: from RADDLE[2]]

radial ('reɪdɪəl) *adj.* **1.** (of lines, bars, beams of light, etc.) emanating from a common central point; arranged like the radii of a circle. **2.** of, like, or relating to a radius or ray. **3.** spreading out or developing uniformly on all sides. **4.** of or relating to the arms of a starfish or similar radiating structures. **5.** *Anatomy.* of or relating to the radius or forearm. **6.** *Astronomy.* (of velocity) in a direction along the line of sight of a celestial object and measured by means of the red shift (or blue shift) of the spectral lines of the object. Compare **tangential** (sense 2). ~*n.* **7.** a radial part or section. **8.** *Zoology.* **a.** any of the basal fin rays of most bony fishes. **b.** a radial or radiating structure, such as any of the ossicles supporting the oral disc of a sea star. **9.** short for **radial tyre** or **radial drilling machine.** [C16: from Medieval Latin *radiālis,* from RADIUS] —'**radially** *adv.*

radial drilling machine *n.* a machine in which the drilling head is mounted to slide along a radial arm which can be rotated, raised, or lowered on a vertical mast to adjust the position of the drill above the workpiece. Often shortened to **radial.**

radial engine *n.* an internal-combustion engine having a number of cylinders arranged about a central crankcase.

radial keratotomy (ˌkerə'tɒtəmɪ) *n.* an operation designed to improve short-sightedness in which a number of cuts are made around the cornea to change the shape of it. [C20: from KERATO- + -TOMY]

radial-ply *adj.* (of a motor tyre) having the fabric cords in the outer casing running radially to enable the sidewalls to be flexible. Compare **cross-ply.**

radial symmetry *n.* a type of structure of an organism or part of an organism in which a vertical cut through the axis in any of two or more planes produces two halves that are mirror images of each other. Compare **bilateral symmetry.**

radial tyre *n.* a motor-vehicle tyre having a radial-ply casing. Often shortened to **radial.**

radial velocity *n.* the component of the velocity of an object, esp. a celestial body, directed along a line from the observer to the object.

radian ('reɪdɪən) *n.* an SI unit of plane angle; the angle between two radii of a circle that cut off on the circumference an arc equal in length to the radius. 1 radian is equivalent to 57.296 degrees and $\pi/2$ radians equals a right angle. Symbol: **rad** [C19: from RADIUS]

radiance ('reɪdɪəns) *or* **radiancy** *n., pl.* **-ances** *or* **-ancies. 1.** the quality or state of being radiant. **2.** a measure of the amount of electromagnetic radiation leaving or arriving at a point on a surface. It is the radiant intensity in a given direction of a small element of surface area divided by the orthogonal projection of this area onto a plane at right angles to the direction. Symbol: L_e

radiant ('reɪdɪənt) *adj.* **1.** sending out rays of light; bright; shining. **2.** characterized by health, intense joy, happiness, etc.: *a radiant countenance.* **3.** emitted or propagated by or as radiation; radiated: *radiant heat.* **4.** sending out heat by radiation: *a radiant heater.* **5.** *Physics.* (of a physical quantity in photometry) evaluated by absolute energy measurements: *radiant flux; radiant efficiency.* Compare **luminous.** ~*n.* **6.** a point or object that emits radiation, esp. the part of a heater that gives out heat. **7.** *Astronomy.* the point in space from which a meteor shower appears to emanate. [C15: from Latin *radiāre* to shine, from *radius* ray of light, RADIUS] —'**radiantly** *adv.*

radiant efficiency *n.* the ratio of the power emitted by a source of radiation to the power consumed by it. Symbol: η_e

radiant energy *n.* energy that is emitted or propagated in the form of particles or electromagnetic radiation. It is measured in joules. Symbol: Q_e

radiant exitance *n.* the ability of a surface to emit radiation expressed as the radiant flux emitted per unit area at a specified point on the surface. Symbol: M_e

radiant flux *n.* the rate of flow of energy as radiation. It is measured in watts. Symbol: Φ_e

radiant heat *n.* heat transferred in the form of electromagnetic radiation rather than by conduction or convection; infrared radiation.

radiant heating *n.* a system of heating a building by radiant heat emitted from panels containing electrical conductors, hot water, etc.

radiant intensity *n.* a measure of the amount of radiation emitted from a point expressed as the radiant flux per unit solid angle leaving this source. Symbol: I_e

radiata pine (ˌreɪdɪ'ɑːtə) *n. N.Z.* a pine tree, *Pinus radiata,* grown in Australia and New Zealand to produce building timber. Often shortened to **radiata.** [from New Latin]

radiate *vb.* ('reɪdɪˌeɪt). **1.** Also: **eradiate.** to emit (heat, light, or some other form of radiation) or (of heat, light, etc.) to be emitted as radiation. **2.** *(intr.)* (of lines, beams, etc.) to spread out from a centre or be arranged in a radial pattern. **3.** *(tr.)* (of a person) to show (happiness, health, etc.) to a great degree. ~*adj.* ('reɪdɪɪt, -ˌeɪt). **4.** having rays; radiating. **5.** (of a capitulum) consisting of ray flowers. **6.** (of animals or their parts) showing radial symmetry. **7.** adorned or decorated with rays: *a radiate head on a coin.* [C17: from Latin *radiāre* to emit rays]

radiation (ˌreɪdɪ'eɪʃən) *n.* **1.** *Physics.* **a.** the emission or transfer of radiant energy as particles, electromagnetic waves, sound, etc. **b.** the particles, etc., emitted, esp. the particles and gamma rays emitted in nuclear decay. **2.** Also called: **radiation therapy.** *Med.* treatment using a radioactive substance. **3.** *Anatomy.* a group of nerve fibres that diverge from their common source. **4.** See **adaptive radiation. 5.** the act, state, or process of radiating or being radiated. **6.** *Surveying.* the fixing of points around a central plane table by using an alidade and measuring tape. —**radi'ational** *adj.*

radiation pattern *n.* the graphic representation of the strength and direction of electromagnetic radiation in the vicinity of a transmitting aerial.

radiation pyrometer *n.* See **pyrometer.**

radiation resistance *n.* the resistive component of the impedance of a radio transmitting aerial that arises from the radiation of power.

radiation sickness *n. Pathol.* illness caused by overexposure of the body or a part of the body to ionizing radiations from radioactive material or x-rays. It is characterized by vomiting, diarrhoea, and in severe cases by sterility and cancer.

radiative ('reɪdɪətɪv) *or* **radiatory** ('reɪdɪətərɪ, -trɪ) *adj. Physics.* emitting or causing the emission of radiation: *a radiative collision.*

radiator ('reɪdɪˌeɪtə) *n.* **1.** a device for heating a room, building, etc., consisting of a series of pipes through which hot water or steam passes. **2.** a device for cooling an internal-combustion engine, consisting of thin-walled tubes through which water passes. Heat is transferred from the water through the walls of the tubes to the airstream, which is created either by the motion of the vehicle or by a fan. **3.** *Austral. and N.Z.* an electric fire. **4.** *Electronics.* the part of an aerial or transmission line that radiates electromagnetic waves. **5.** an electric space heater.

radical ('rædɪk[ə]l) *adj.* **1.** of, relating to, or characteristic of the basic or inherent constitution of a person or thing; fundamental: *a radical fault.* **2.** concerned with or tending to concentrate on fundamental aspects of a matter; searching or thoroughgoing: *radical thought; a radical re-examination.* **3.** favouring or tending to produce extreme or fundamental changes in political, economic, or social conditions, institutions, habits of mind, etc.: *a radical party.* **4.** *Med.* (of treatment) aimed at removing the source of a disease: *radical surgery.* **5.** *Slang, chiefly U.S.* very good; excellent. **6.** of, relating to, or arising from the root or the base of the stem of a plant: *radical leaves.* **7.** *Maths.* of, relating to, or containing roots of numbers or quantities. **8.** *Linguistics.* of or relating to the root of a word. ~*n.* **9.** a person who favours extreme or fundamental change in existing institutions or in political, social, or economic conditions. **10.** *Maths.* a root of a number or quantity, such as $\sqrt[3]{5}$, $\sqrt{x}$. **11.** *Chem.* **a.** short for **free radical. b.** another name for **group** (sense 10). **12.** *Linguistics.* another word for **root**[1] (sense 9). **13.** (in logographic writing systems such as that used for Chinese) a character conveying lexical meaning. [C14: from Late Latin *rādīcālis* having roots, from Latin *rādix* a root] —'**radicalness** *n.*

radical axis *n.* a line from any point of which tangents to two given circles are of equal length. It is the line joining the points of intersection of two circles.

radicalism ('rædɪkəˌlɪzəm) *n.* **1.** the principles, desires, or practices of political radicals. **2.** a radical movement, esp. in politics.

3. the state or nature of being radical, esp. in politics. —ˌ**radical'istic** *adj.* —ˌ**radical'istically** *adv.*

radically ('rædɪkəlɪ) *adv.* thoroughly; completely; fundamentally: *to alter radically.*

radical sign *n.* the symbol √ placed before a number or quantity to indicate the extraction of a root, esp. a square root. The value of a higher root is indicated by a raised digit in front of the symbol, as in ³√.

radicand ('rædɪˌkænd, ˌrædɪ'kænd) *n.* a number or quantity from which a root is to be extracted, usually preceded by a radical sign: 3 *is the radicand of* √3. [C20: from Latin *rādīcandum*, literally: that which is to be rooted, from *rādīcāre* to take root, from *rādīx* root]

radicchio (ræ'diːkɪəʊ) *n., pl.* **chios.** an Italian variety of chicory, having purple leaves streaked with white that are eaten raw in salads.

radicel ('rædɪˌsɛl) *n.* a very small root; radicle. [C19: from New Latin *radicella* a little root, from Latin *rādīx* root]

radices ('reɪdɪˌsiːz) *n.* a plural of **radix.**

radicle ('rædɪkᵊl) *n.* **1.** *Botany.* **a.** part of the embryo of seed-bearing plants that develops into the main root. **b.** a very small root or rootlike part. **2.** *Anatomy.* any bodily structure resembling a rootlet, esp. one of the smallest branches of a vein or nerve. **3.** *Chem.* a variant spelling of **radical** (sense 11). [C18: from Latin *rādīcula* a little root, from *rādīx* root]

radii ('reɪdɪˌaɪ) *n.* a plural of **radius.**

radio ('reɪdɪəʊ) *n., pl.* **-os. 1.** the use of electromagnetic waves, lying in the radio-frequency range, for broadcasting, two-way communications, etc. **2.** an electronic device designed to receive, demodulate, and amplify radio signals from sound broadcasting stations, etc. **3.** a similar device permitting both transmission and reception of radio signals for two-way communications. **4.** the broadcasting, content, etc., of sound radio programmes: *he thinks radio is poor these days.* **5. a.** the occupation or profession concerned with any aspect of the broadcasting of sound radio programmes: *he's in radio.* **b.** (*modifier*) relating to, produced for, or transmitted by sound radio: *radio drama.* **6.** short for **radiotelegraph, radiotelegraphy,** or **radiotelephone. 7.** (*modifier*) **a.** of, relating to, employed in, or sent by radio signals: *a radio station.* **b.** of, concerned with, using, or operated by radio frequencies: *radio spectrum.* **8.** (*modifier*) (of a motor vehicle) equipped with a radio for communication: *radio car.* ~*vb.* **-os, -oing, -oed. 9.** to transmit (a message) to (a person, radio station, etc.) by means of radio waves. ~Also called (esp. Brit.): **wireless.** [C20: short for *radiotelegraphy*]

radio- *combining form.* **1.** denoting radio, broadcasting, or radio frequency: *radiogram.* **2.** indicating radioactivity or radiation: *radiochemistry; radiolucent.* **3.** indicating a radioactive isotope or substance: *radioactinium; radiothorium; radioelement.* [from French, from Latin *radius* ray; see RADIUS]

radioactivate (ˌreɪdɪəʊ'æktɪˌveɪt) *vb.* (*tr.*) to make radioactive. —ˌ**radioˌacti'vation** *n.*

radioactive (ˌreɪdɪəʊ'æktɪv) *adj.* exhibiting, using, or concerned with radioactivity. —ˌ**radio'actively** *adv.*

radioactive dating *n.* another term for **radiometric dating.**

radioactive decay *n.* disintegration of a nucleus that occurs spontaneously or as a result of electron capture. One or more different nuclei are formed and usually particles and gamma rays are emitted. Sometimes shortened to **decay.** Also called: **disintegration.**

radioactive series *n. Physics.* a series of nuclides each of which undergoes radioactive decay into the next member of the series, ending with a stable element, usually lead. See **uranium series, neptunium series, thorium series, actinium series.**

radioactive tracer *n. Med.* See **tracer** (sense 3).

radioactive waste *n.* any waste material containing radionuclides. Also called: **nuclear waste.**

radioactivity (ˌreɪdɪəʊæk'tɪvɪtɪ) *n.* the spontaneous emission of radiation from atomic nuclei. The radiation can consist of alpha, beta, and gamma radiation.

radio astronomy *n.* a branch of astronomy in which a radio telescope is used to detect and analyse radio signals received on earth from radio sources in space.

radioautograph (ˌreɪdɪəʊ'ɔːtəˌgrɑːf, -ˌgræf) *n.* another name for **autoradiograph.**

radio beacon *n.* a fixed radio transmitting station that broadcasts a characteristic signal by means of which a vessel or aircraft can determine its bearing or position. Sometimes shortened to **beacon.**

radio beam *n.* a narrow beam of radio signals transmitted by a radio or radar beacon, radio telescope, or some other directional aerial, used for communications, navigation, etc. Sometimes shortened to **beam.**

radiobiology (ˌreɪdɪəʊbaɪ'ɒlədʒɪ) *n.* the branch of biology concerned with the effects of radiation on living organisms and the study of biological processes using radioactive substances as tracers. —**radiobiological** (ˌreɪdɪəʊˌbaɪə'lɒdʒɪkᵊl) *adj.* —ˌ**radioˌbio'logically** *adv.* —ˌ**radiobi'ologist** *n.*

radiocarbon (ˌreɪdɪəʊ'kɑːbᵊn) *n.* a radioactive isotope of carbon, esp. carbon-14. See **carbon** (sense 1).

radiocarbon dating *n.* a technique for determining the age of organic materials, such as wood, based on their content of the radioisotope ^{14}C acquired from the atmosphere when they formed part of a living plant. The ^{14}C decays to the nitrogen isotope ^{14}N with a half-life of 5730 years. Measurement of the amount of radioactive carbon remaining in the material thus gives an estimate of its age. Also called: **carbon-14 dating.**

radiochemistry (ˌreɪdɪəʊ'kɛmɪstrɪ) *n.* the chemistry of radioactive elements and their compounds. —ˌ**radio'chemical** *adj.* —ˌ**radio'chemist** *n.*

radiocommunication (ˌreɪdɪəʊkəˌmjuːnɪ'keɪʃən) *n.* communication by means of radio waves.

radio compass *n.* any navigational device that gives a bearing by determining the direction of incoming radio waves transmitted from a particular radio station or beacon. See also **goniometer** (sense 2).

radio control *n.* remote control by means of radio signals from a transmitter. —'**radio-con'trolled** *adj.*

radioelement (ˌreɪdɪəʊ'ɛlɪmənt) *n.* an element that is naturally radioactive.

radio frequency *n.* **1. a.** a frequency or band of frequencies that lie in the range 10 kilohertz to 300 000 megahertz and can be used for radio communications and broadcasting. Abbrevs.: **rf, RF.** See also **frequency band. b.** (*as modifier*): *a radio-frequency amplifier.* **2.** the frequency transmitted by a particular radio station.

radio galaxy *n.* a galaxy that is a strong emitter of radio waves.

radiogenic (ˌreɪdɪəʊ'dʒɛnɪk) *adj.* produced or caused by radioactive decay: *a radiogenic element; radiogenic heat.*

radiogoniometer (ˌreɪdɪəʊˌgəʊnɪ'ɒmɪtə) *n.* a device used to detect the direction of radio waves, consisting of a coil that is free to rotate within two fixed coils at right angles to each other.

radiogram ('reɪdɪəʊˌgræm) *n.* **1.** *Brit.* a unit comprising a radio and record player. **2.** a message transmitted by radiotelegraphy. **3.** another name for **radiograph.**

radiograph ('reɪdɪəʊˌgrɑːf, -ˌgræf) *n.* an image produced on a specially sensitized photographic film or plate by radiation, usually by x-rays or gamma rays. Also called: **radiogram, shadowgraph.**

radiography (ˌreɪdɪ'ɒgrəfɪ) *n.* the production of radiographs of opaque objects for use in medicine, surgery, industry, etc. —ˌ**radi'ographer** *n.* —**radiographic** (ˌreɪdɪəʊ'græfɪk) *adj.* —ˌ**radio'graphically** *adv.*

radio-immuno-assay ('reɪdɪəʊˌɪmjʊnəʊ'æseɪ) *n.* a sensitive immunological assay, making use of radioactive labelling, for the detection and quantification of biologically important substances, such as hormone levels in the blood.

radio interferometer *n.* a type of radio telescope in which two or more aerials connected to the same receiver produce interference patterns that can be analysed to provide information about the source of the radio waves.

radioisotope (ˌreɪdɪəʊ'aɪsətəʊp) *n.* an isotope that is radioactive. —**radioisotopic** (ˌreɪdɪəʊˌaɪsə'tɒpɪk) *adj.*

radiolarian (ˌreɪdɪəʊ'lɛərɪən) *n.* any of various marine protozoans constituting the order *Radiolaria*, typically having a siliceous shell and stiff radiating pseudopodia: class *Sarcodina* (amoeba, etc.). [C19: from New Latin *Radiolaria*, from Late Latin *radiolus* little sunbeam, from Latin *radius* ray, RADIUS]

radiolocation (ˌreɪdɪəʊləʊ'keɪʃən) *n.* a former name for **radar.** —ˌ**radiolo'cational** *adj.*

radiological (ˌreɪdɪə'lɒdʒɪkᵊl) *adj.* **1.** of, relating to, or concerning radiology or the equipment used in radiology. **2.** of, relating to, or involving radioactive materials: *radiological warfare.* —ˌ**radio'logically** *adv.*

radiology (ˌreɪdɪ'ɒlədʒɪ) *n.* the use of x-rays and radioactive substances in the diagnosis and treatment of disease. —ˌ**radi'ologist** *n.*

radiolucent (ˌreɪdɪəʊ'luːsᵊnt) *adj.* almost transparent to electromagnetic radiation, esp. x-rays.

radioluminescence (ˌreɪdɪəʊˌluːmɪ'nɛsəns) *n. Physics.* luminescence that is induced by radiation from a radioactive material. —ˌ**radioˌlumi'nescent** *adj.*

radiolysis (ˌreɪdɪ'ɒlɪsɪs) *n.* chemical decomposition caused by radiation, such as a beam of electrons or x-rays. —**radiolytic** (ˌreɪdɪəʊ'lɪtɪk) *adj.*

radiometeorograph (ˌreɪdɪəʊ'miːtɪərəˌgrɑːf, -ˌgræf) *n.* another name for **radiosonde.**

radiometer (ˌreɪdɪ'ɒmɪtə) *n.* any instrument for the detection or measurement of radiant energy. —**radiometric** (ˌreɪdɪəʊ'mɛtrɪk) *adj.* —ˌ**radi'ometry** *n.*

radiometric dating *n.* any method of dating material based on the decay of its constituent radioactive atoms, such as potassium-argon dating or rubidium-strontium dating. Also called: **radioactive dating.**

radiomicrometer (ˌreɪdɪəʊmaɪ'krɒmɪtə) *n.* an instrument for detecting and measuring small amounts of radiation, usually by a sensitive thermocouple.

radio microphone *n.* a microphone incorporating a radio transmitter so that the user can move around freely.

radiomimetic (ˌreɪdɪəʊmɪ'mɛtɪk) *adj.* (of drugs) producing effects similar to those produced by x-rays.

radionuclide (ˌreɪdɪəʊ'njuːklaɪd) *n.* a nuclide that is radioactive.

radiopager ('reɪdɪəʊˌpeɪdʒə) *n.* a small radio receiver fitted with a buzzer to alert a person to telephone their home, office, etc., to receive a message. —'**radioˌpaging** *n.*

radiopaque (ˌreɪdɪəʊˈpeɪk) *or* **radio-opaque** *adj.* not permitting x-rays or other radiation to pass through. —**radiopacity** (ˌreɪdɪəʊˈpæsɪtɪ) *or* ˌ**radio-oˈpacity** *n.*
radiophone (ˈreɪdɪəʊˌfəʊn) *n.* another name for **radiotelephone** (sense 1).
radiophonic (ˌreɪdɪəʊˈfɒnɪk) *adj.* denoting or relating to music produced by electronic means. —ˌ**radioˈphonically** *adv.* —**radiophony** (ˌreɪdɪˈɒfənɪ) *n.*
radio receiver *n.* an apparatus that receives incoming modulated radio waves and converts them into sound.
radioresistant (ˌreɪdɪəʊrɪˈsɪstənt) *adj. Med.* resistant to the effects of radiation.
radioscope (ˈreɪdɪəʊˌskəʊp) *n.* an instrument, such as a fluoroscope, capable of detecting radiant energy.
radioscopy (ˌreɪdɪˈɒskəpɪ) *n.* another word for **fluoroscopy.** —**radioscopic** (ˌreɪdɪəʊˈskɒpɪk) *adj.* —ˌ**radioˈscopically** *adv.*
radiosensitive (ˌreɪdɪəʊˈsensɪtɪv) *adj.* affected by or sensitive to radiation. —ˌ**radioˈsensitively** *adv.* —ˌ**radioˌsensiˈtivity** *n.*
radiosonde (ˈreɪdɪəʊˌsɒnd) *n.* an airborne instrument to send meteorological information back to earth by radio. Also called: **radiometeorograph.** [C20: RADIO- + French *sonde* sounding line]
radio source *n.* a celestial object, such as a supernova remnant or quasar, that is a source of radio waves.
radio spectrum *n.* the range of electromagnetic frequencies used in radio transmission, lying between 10 kilohertz and 300 000 megahertz.
radio star *n.* a former name for **radio source.**
radio station *n.* **1.** an installation consisting of one or more transmitters or receivers, etc., used for radiocommunications. **2.** a broadcasting organization.
radiotelegram (ˌreɪdɪəʊˈtɛlɪˌgræm) *n.* a message transmitted by radiotelegraphy. Also called: **radiogram.**
radiotelegraph (ˌreɪdɪəʊˈtɛlɪˌgrɑːf) *vb.* **1.** to send (a message) by radiotelegraphy. ~*n.* **2.** a message sent by radiotelegraphy.
radiotelegraphy (ˌreɪdɪəʊtɪˈlɛgrəfɪ) *n.* a type of telegraphy in which messages (usually in Morse code) are transmitted by radio waves. Also called: **wireless telegraphy.** —**radiotelegraphic** (ˌreɪdɪəʊˌtɛlɪˈgræfɪk) *adj.* —ˌ**radioˌteleˈgraphically** *adv.*
radiotelemetry (ˌreɪdɪəʊtɪˈlɛmɪtrɪ) *n.* the use of radio waves for transmitting information from a distant instrument to a device that indicates or records the measurements. Sometimes shortened to **telemetry.**
radiotelephone (ˌreɪdɪəʊˈtɛlɪˌfəʊn) *n.* **1.** Also called: **radiophone, wireless telephone.** a device for communications by means of radio waves rather than by transmitting along wires or cables. ~*vb.* **2.** to telephone (a person) by radiotelephone. ~Sometimes shortened to **radio.** —**radiotelephonic** (ˌreɪdɪəʊˌtɛlɪˈfɒnɪk) *adj.* —**radiotelephony** (ˌreɪdɪəʊtɪˈlɛfənɪ) *n.*
radio telescope *n.* an instrument used in radio astronomy to pick up and analyse radio waves from space and also to transmit radio waves.
radioteletype (ˌreɪdɪəʊˈtɛlɪˌtaɪp) *n.* **1.** a teleprinter that transmits or receives information by means of radio waves rather than by cable or wire. **2.** a network of such devices widely used for communicating news, messages, information, etc. Abbrevs.: **RTT, RTTY.**
radiotherapy (ˌreɪdɪəʊˈθɛrəpɪ) *n.* the treatment of disease, esp. cancer, by means of alpha or beta particles emitted from an implanted or ingested radioisotope, or by means of a beam of high-energy radiation. Compare **chemotherapy.** —**radiotherapeutic** (ˌreɪdɪəʊˌθɛrəˈpjuːtɪk) *adj.* —ˌ**radioˌtheraˈpeutically** *adv.* —ˌ**radioˈtherapist** *n.*
radiothermy (ˈreɪdɪəʊˌθɜːmɪ) *n. Med.* the treatment of disease by means of heat generated by electromagnetic radiation.
radiotoxic (ˌreɪdɪəʊˈtɒksɪk) *adj.* of or denoting the toxic effects of radiation or radioactive substances.
radio valve *n.* another name for **valve** (sense 3).
radio wave *n.* an electromagnetic wave of radio frequency.
radio window *n.* a gap in ionospheric reflection that allows radio waves, with frequencies in the range 10 000 to 40 000 megahertz, to pass from or into space.
radish (ˈrædɪʃ) *n.* **1.** any of various cruciferous plants of the genus *Raphanus*, esp. *R. sativus* of Europe and Asia, cultivated for its edible root. **2.** the root of this plant, which has a pungent taste and is eaten raw in salads. **3. wild radish.** another name for **white charlock.** See **charlock** (sense 2). [Old English *rǣdīc*, from Latin *rādīx* root]
radium (ˈreɪdɪəm) *n.* **a.** a highly radioactive luminescent white element of the alkaline earth group of metals. It occurs in pitchblende, carnotite, and other uranium ores, and is used in radiotherapy and in luminous paints. Symbol: Ra; atomic no.: 88; half-life of most stable isotope, ^{226}Ra: 1620 years; valency: 2; relative density: 5 (approx.); melting pt.: 700°C; boiling pt.: 1140°C. **b.** (*as modifier*): *radium needle.* [C20: from Latin *radius* ray]
radium therapy *n.* treatment of disease, esp. cancer, by exposing affected tissues to radiation from radium.
radius (ˈreɪdɪəs) *n., pl.* **-dii** (-dɪˌaɪ) *or* **-diuses.** **1.** a straight line joining the centre of a circle or sphere to any point on the circumference or surface. **2.** the length of this line, usually denoted by the symbol *r*. **3.** the distance from the centre of a regular polygon to a vertex (**long radius**) or the perpendicular distance to a side (**short radius**). **4.** *Anatomy.* the outer and slightly shorter of the two bones of the human forearm, extending from the elbow to the wrist. **5.** a corresponding bone in other vertebrates. **6.** any of the veins of an insect's wing. **7.** a group of ray flowers, occurring in such plants as the daisy. **8. a.** any radial or radiating part, such as a spoke. **b.** (*as modifier*): *a radius arm.* **9.** the lateral displacement of a cam or eccentric wheel. **10.** a circular area of a size indicated by the length of its radius: *the police stopped every lorry within a radius of four miles.* **11.** the operational limit of a ship, aircraft, etc. [C16: from Latin: rod, ray, spoke]
radius of action *n. Military.* the maximum distance that a ship, aircraft, or land vehicle can travel from its base and return without refuelling.
radius of curvature *n.* the absolute value of the reciprocal of the curvature of a curve at a given point; the radius of a circle the curvature of which is equal to that of the given curve at that point. See also **centre of curvature.**
radius vector *n.* **1.** *Maths.* a line joining a point in space to the origin of polar or spherical coordinates. **2.** *Astronomy.* an imaginary line joining a satellite to the planet or star around which it is orbiting.
radix (ˈreɪdɪks) *n., pl.* **-dices** (-dɪˌsiːz) *or* **-dixes.** **1.** *Maths.* any number that is the base of a number system or of a system of logarithms: *10 is the radix of the decimal system.* **2.** *Biology.* the root or point of origin of a part or organ. **3.** *Linguistics.* a less common word for **root**[1] (sense 9). [C16: from Latin *rādīx* root; compare Greek *rhadix* small branch, *rhiza* root]
radix point *n.* a point, such as the decimal point in the decimal system, separating the integral part of a number from the fractional part.
radome (ˈreɪdəʊm) *n.* a protective housing for a radar antenna made from a material that is transparent to radio waves. [C20: RA(DAR) + DOME]
radon (ˈreɪdɒn) *n.* a colourless radioactive element of the rare gas group, the most stable isotope of which, radon-222, is a decay product of radium. It is used as an alpha particle source in radiotherapy. Symbol: Rn; atomic no.: 86; half-life of ^{222}Rn: 3.82 days; density: 9.73 kg/m^3; melting pt.: −71°C; boiling pt.: −61.8°C. [C20: from RADIUM + -ON]
radula (ˈrædjʊlə) *n., pl.* **-lae** (-ˌliː). a horny tooth-bearing strip on the tongue of molluscs that is used for rasping food. [C19: from Late Latin: a scraping iron, from Latin *rādere* to scrape] —ˈ**radular** *adj.*
RAE (in Britain) *abbrev. for* Royal Aircraft Establishment.
RAEC *abbrev. for* Royal Army Educational Corps.
RAF (*Not standard* ræf) *abbrev. for* Royal Air Force.
raff (ræf) *n. Archaic or dialect.* **1.** rubbish; refuse. **2.** rabble or riffraff. [C14: perhaps from Old French *rafle* a snatching up; compare RAFFLE, RIFFRAFF]
Rafferty (ˈræfətɪ) *or* **Rafferty's rules** *pl. n. Austral. and N.Z. slang.* no rules at all. [C20: of uncertain origin]
raffia *or* **raphia** (ˈræfɪə) *n.* **1.** Also called: **raffia palm.** a palm tree, *Raphia ruffia,* native to Madagascar, that has large plumelike leaves, the stalks of which yield a useful fibre. **2.** the fibre obtained from this plant, used for tying, weaving, etc. **3.** any of several related palms or the fibre obtained from them. [C19: from Malagasy]
raffinate (ˈræfɪˌneɪt) *n.* the liquid left after a solute has been extracted by solvent extraction. [C20: from French *raffiner* to refine + -ATE[1]]
raffinose (ˈræfɪˌnəʊz, -ˌnəʊs) *n. Biochem.* a trisaccharide of fructose, glucose, and galactose that occurs in sugar beet, cotton seed, certain cereals, etc. Formula: $C_{18}H_{32}O_{16}$. [C19: from French *raffiner* to refine + -OSE[2]]
raffish (ˈræfɪʃ) *adj.* **1.** careless or unconventional in dress, manners, etc.; rakish. **2.** tawdry; flashy; vulgar. [C19: see RAFF] —ˈ**raffishly** *adv.* —ˈ**raffishness** *n.*
raffle (ˈræfᵊl) *n.* **1. a.** a lottery in which the prizes are goods rather than money. **b.** (*as modifier*): *a raffle ticket.* ~*vb.* **2.** (*tr.*; often foll. by *off*) to dispose of (goods) in a raffle. [C14 (a dice game): from Old French, of obscure origin] —ˈ**raffler** *n.*
rafflesia (ræˈfliːzɪə) *n.* any of various tropical Asian parasitic leafless plants constituting the genus *Rafflesia,* esp. *R. arnoldi,* the flowers of which grow up to 45 cm (18 inches) across, smell of putrid meat, and are pollinated by carrion flies: family *Rafflesiaceae.* [C19: New Latin, named after Sir Stamford *Raffles* (1781–1826), British colonial administrator who discovered it]
raft[1] (rɑːft) *n.* **1.** a buoyant platform of logs, planks, etc., used as a vessel or moored platform. **2.** a thick slab of reinforced concrete laid over soft ground to provide a foundation for a building. ~*vb.* **3.** to convey on or travel by raft, or make a raft from. [C15: from Old Norse *raptr* RAFTER]
raft[2] (rɑːft) *n. Informal, chiefly U.S. and Canadian.* a large collection or amount: *a raft of old notebooks discovered in a cupboard.* [C19: from RAFF]
rafter (ˈrɑːftə) *n.* any one of a set of sloping beams that form the framework of a roof. [Old English *ræfter;* related to Old Saxon *rehter,* Old Norse *raptr,* Old High German *rāvo;* see RAFT[1]]
RAFVR *abbrev. for* Royal Air Force Volunteer Reserve.
rag[1] (ræg) *n.* **1. a.** a small piece of cloth, such as one torn from a discarded garment, or such pieces of cloth collectively. **b.** (*as modifier*): *a rag doll; a rag book; rag paper.* **2.** a fragmentary

piece of any material; scrap; shred. **3.** *Informal.* a newspaper or other journal, esp. one considered as worthless, sensational, etc. **4.** *Informal.* an item of clothing. **5.** *Informal.* a handkerchief. **6.** *Brit. slang, esp. naval.* a flag or ensign. **7. chew the rag.** *Slang.* **a.** to argue over a point. **b.** to talk idly; gossip. ~See also **rags.** [C14: probably back formation from RAGGED, from Old English *raggig;* related to Old Norse *rögg* tuft]

rag[2] (ræg) *vb.* **rags, ragging, ragged.** (*tr.*) **1.** to draw attention facetiously and persistently to the shortcomings or alleged shortcomings of (a person). **2.** *Brit.* to play rough practical jokes on. ~*n.* **3.** *Brit.* a boisterous practical joke, esp. one on a fellow student. **4.** (in British universities) **a.** a period, usually a week, in which various events are organized to raise money for charity, including a procession of decorated floats and tableaux. **b.** (*as modifier*): *rag day.* [C18: of uncertain origin]

rag[3] (ræg) *Jazz.* ~*n.* **1.** a piece of ragtime music. ~*vb.* **rags, ragging, ragged. 2.** (*tr.*) to compose or perform in ragtime. [C20: shortened from RAGTIME]

rag[4] (ræg) *n.* a roofing slate that is rough on one side. [C13: of obscure origin]

raga (ˈrɑːgə) *n.* (in Indian music) **1.** any of several conventional patterns of melody and rhythm that form the basis for freely interpreted compositions. Each pattern is associated with different aspects of religious devotion. **2.** a composition based on one of these patterns. [C18: from Sanskrit *rāga* tone, colour]

ragamuffin (ˈrægəˌmʌfɪn) *n.* a ragged unkempt person, esp. a child. [C14 *Ragamoffyn,* name of a demon in the poem *Piers Plowman* (1393); probably based on RAG[1]]

rag-and-bone man *n. Brit.* a man who buys and sells discarded clothing, furniture, etc. Also called: **ˈragˌman, ˈragˌpicker.** U.S. equivalent: **junkman.**

ragbag (ˈrægˌbæg) *n.* **1.** a bag for storing odd rags. **2.** a confused assortment; jumble: *a ragbag of ideas.* **3.** Informal. a scruffy or slovenly person. [C19]

ragbolt (ˈrægˌbəʊlt) *n.* a bolt that has angled projections on it to prevent it working loose once it has been driven home.

rage (reɪdʒ) *n.* **1.** intense anger; fury. **2.** violent movement or action, esp. of the sea, wind, etc. **3.** great intensity of hunger, sexual desire, or other feelings. **4.** a fashion or craze (esp. in the phrase **all the rage**). **5.** *Austral. and N.Z. informal.* a dance or party. ~*vb.* (*intr.*) **6.** to feel or exhibit intense anger. **7.** (esp. of storms, fires, etc.) to move or surge with great violence. **8.** (esp. of a disease or epidemic) to spread rapidly and uncontrollably. [C13: via Old French from Latin *rabiēs* madness]

ragged (ˈrægɪd) *adj.* **1.** (of clothes) worn to rags; tattered. **2.** (of a person) dressed in shabby tattered clothes. **3.** having a neglected or unkempt appearance: *ragged weeds.* **4.** having a loose, rough, or uneven surface or edge; jagged. **5.** uneven or irregular: *a ragged beat; a ragged shout.* [C13: probably from *ragge* RAG[1]] —**ˈraggedly** *adv.* —**ˈraggedness** *n.*

ragged robin *n.* a caryophyllaceous plant, *Lychnis floscuculi,* native to Europe and Asia, that has pink or white flowers with ragged petals. Also called: **cuckooflower.** See also **catchfly.**

ragged school *n.* (in Britian, formerly) a free elementary school for poor children.

raggedy (ˈrægɪdɪ) *adj. Informal, chiefly U.S. and Canadian.* somewhat ragged; tattered: *a raggedy doll.*

raggle (ˈrægᵊl) *n. Chiefly Scot.* a thin groove cut in stone or brickwork, esp. to hold the edge of a roof. [C19: of obscure origin]

raggle-taggle (ˈrægᵊlˈtægᵊl) *adj.* motley or unkempt: *a raggle-taggle Gypsy.* [augmented form of RAGTAG]

ragi, raggee, *or* **raggy** (ˈrægɪ) *n.* a cereal grass, *Eleusine coracana,* cultivated in Africa and Asia for its edible grain. [C18: from Hindi]

raglan (ˈræglən) *n.* **1.** a coat with sleeves that continue to the collar instead of having armhole seams. ~*adj.* **2.** cut in this design: *a raglan sleeve.* [C19: named after Lord *Raglan* (1788–1855), British field marshal]

ragman (ˈrægˌmæn) *n., pl.* **-men.** another name for **rag-and-bone man.**

ragout (ræˈguː) *n.* **1.** a richly seasoned stew of meat or poultry and vegetables. ~*vb.* **-gouts** (-ˈguːz), **-gouting** (-ˈguːɪŋ), **-gouted** (-ˈguːd). **2.** (*tr.*) to make into a ragout. [C17: from French, from *ragoûter* to stimulate the appetite again, from *ra-* RE- + *goûter* from Latin *gustāre* to taste]

rag-rolling *n.* a decorating technique in which paint is applied with a roughly folded cloth in order to create a marbled effect.

rags (rægz) *pl. n.* **1.** torn, old, or shabby clothing. **2.** cotton or linen cloth waste used in the manufacture of rag paper. **3. glad rags.** *Informal.* best clothes; finery.

ragstone (ˈrægˌstəʊn) *n.* a hard sandstone or limestone, esp. when used as building stone. Also called: **rag** *or* **ragg.** [C14: from RAG[4] + STONE]

ragtag (ˈrægˌtæg) *n. Disparaging.* the common people; rabble (esp. in the phrase **ragtag and bobtail**). [C19]

ragtime (ˈrægˌtaɪm) *n.* a style of jazz piano music, developed in the U.S. around 1900, having a two-four rhythm base and a syncopated melody. [C20: probably from RAGGED + TIME]

rag trade *n. Informal.* the clothing business, esp. the aspects concerned with the manufacture and sale of dresses.

ragweed (ˈrægˌwiːd) *n.* any plant of the chiefly North American genus *Ambrosia,* such as *A. artemisiifolia* (**common ragweed**): family *Compositae* (composites). Their green tassel-like flowers produce large amounts of pollen, which causes hay fever. Also called: **ambrosia.**

ragworm (ˈrægˌwɜːm) *n.* any polychaete worm of the genus *Nereis,* living chiefly in burrows in sand or mud and having a flattened body with a row of fleshy parapodia along each side. U.S. name: **clamworm.**

ragwort (ˈrægˌwɜːt) *n.* any of several plants of the genus *Senecio,* esp. *S. jacobaea* of Europe, that have yellow daisy-like flowers: family *Compositae* (composites). See also **groundsel** (sense 1).

rah (rɑː) *interj. Informal, chiefly U.S.* short for **hurrah.**

rah-rah (ˈrɑːˌrɑː) *adj.* **1.** *Informal, chiefly U.S.* like or marked by boisterous and uncritical enthusiasm and excitement. ~*n.* **2.** *Austral. slang.* a devotee of Rugby Union football. [C20: a reduplication of RAH]

RAHS *abbrev. for* Royal Australian Historical Society.

rai (raɪ) *n.* a type of Algerian popular music based on traditional Algerian music influenced by modern Western pop. [C20: Arabic, literally: opinion]

raia (ˈrɑːjə, ˈraɪə) *n.* a less common variant of **rayah.**

raid (reɪd) *n.* **1.** a sudden surprise attack: *an air raid.* **2.** a surprise visit by police searching for criminals or illicit goods: *a fraud-squad raid.* See also **bear raid, dawn raid** ~*vb.* (*tr.*) **3.** to make a raid against (a person, thing, etc.). **4.** to sneak into (a place) in order to take something, steal, etc.: *raiding the larder.* [C15: Scottish dialect, from Old English *rād* military expedition; see ROAD] —**ˈraider** *n.*

rail[1] (reɪl) *n.* **1.** a horizontal bar of wood, metal, etc., supported by vertical posts, functioning as a fence, barrier, handrail, etc. **2.** a horizontal bar fixed to a wall on which to hang things: *a picture rail.* **3.** a horizontal framing member in a door or piece of panelling. Compare **stile**[2]. **4.** short for **railing. 5.** one of a pair of parallel bars laid on a prepared track, roadway, etc., that serve as a guide and running surface for the wheels of a railway train, tramcar, etc. **6. a.** short for **railway. b.** (*as modifier*): *rail transport.* **7.** *Nautical.* a trim for finishing the top of a bulwark. **8. off the rails. a.** into or in a state of dysfunction or disorder. **b.** eccentric or mad. ~*vb.* (*tr.*) **9.** to provide with a rail or railings. **10.** (usually foll. by *in* or *off*) to fence (an area) with rails. [C13: from Old French *raille* rod, from Latin *rēgula* ruler, straight piece of wood] —**ˈrailless** *adj.*

rail[2] (reɪl) *vb.* (*intr.;* foll. by *at* or *against*) to complain bitterly or vehemently: *to rail against fate.* [C15: from Old French *railler* to mock, from Old Provençal *ralhar* to chatter, joke, from Late Latin *ragere* to yell, neigh] —**ˈrailer** *n.*

rail[3] (reɪl) *n.* any of various small wading marsh birds of the genus *Rallus* and related genera: family *Rallidae,* order *Gruiformes* (cranes, etc.). They have short wings and neck, long legs, and dark plumage. [C15: from Old French *raale,* perhaps from Latin *rādere* to scrape]

railcar (ˈreɪlˌkɑː) *n.* a passenger-carrying railway vehicle consisting of a single coach with its own power unit.

railcard (ˈreɪlˌkɑːd) *n. Brit.* an identity card that young people or pensioners in Britain can buy, which allows them to buy train tickets more cheaply.

rail gauge *n.* See **gauge** (sense 11).

railhead (ˈreɪlˌhɛd) *n.* **1.** a terminal of a railway. **2.** the farthest point reached by completed track on an unfinished railway. **3.** *Military.* the point at which materiel and personnel are transferred from rail to another conveyance. **4.** the upper part of a railway rail, on which the traffic wheels run.

railing (ˈreɪlɪŋ) *n.* **1.** (*often pl.*) a fence, balustrade, or barrier that consists of rails supported by posts. **2.** rails collectively or material for making rails.

raillery (ˈreɪlərɪ) *n., pl.* **-leries. 1.** light-hearted satire or ridicule; banter. **2.** an example of this, esp. a bantering remark. [C17: from French, from *railler* to tease, banter; see RAIL[2]]

railroad (ˈreɪlˌrəʊd) *n.* **1.** the usual U.S. word for **railway.** ~*vb.* **2.** (*tr.*) *Informal.* to force (a person) into (an action) with haste or by unfair means.

railway (ˈreɪlˌweɪ) *or U.S.* **railroad** *n.* **1.** a permanent track composed of a line of parallel metal rails fixed to sleepers, for transport of passengers and goods in trains. **2.** any track for the wheels of a vehicle to run on: *a cable railway.* **3.** the entire equipment, rolling stock, buildings, property, and system of tracks used in such a transport system. **4.** the organization responsible for operating a railway network. **5.** (*modifier*) of, relating to, or used on a railway or railways: *a railway engine; a railway strike.*

railwayman (ˈreɪlˌweɪmən) *n., pl.* **-men.** *Brit.* a worker on a railway, esp. one other than a driver.

raiment (ˈreɪmənt) *n. Archaic or poetic.* attire; clothing; garments. [C15: shortened from *arrayment,* from Old French *areement;* see ARRAY]

rain (reɪn) *n.* **1. a.** precipitation from clouds in the form of drops of water, formed by the condensation of water vapour in the atmosphere. **b.** a fall of rain; shower. **c.** (*in combination*): *a raindrop.* **2.** a large quantity of anything falling rapidly or in quick succession: *a rain of abuse.* **3. (come) rain or (come) shine. a.** regardless of the weather. **b.** regardless of circumstances. **4. right as rain.** *Brit. informal.* perfectly all right; perfectly fit. ~*vb.* **5.** (*intr.;* with *it* as subject) to be the case that rain is falling. **6.** (often with *it* as subject) to fall or cause to fall like rain: *the lid flew off and popcorn rained on everyone.* **7.** (*tr.*) to bestow in large measure: *to rain abuse on someone.* **8. rain cats and dogs.** *Informal.* to rain heavily; pour. **9. rained off.** cancelled or postponed on account of rain. U.S. and Canadian term: **rained out.** ~See also **rains.** [Old English *regn;* related to Old Frisian *rein,* Old High German *regan,* Gothic *rign*] —'**rainless** *adj.*

rainband ('reɪnˌbænd) *n.* a dark band in the solar spectrum caused by water in the atmosphere.

rainbird ('reɪnˌbɜːd) *n.* any of various birds, such as (in Britain) the green woodpecker, whose cry is supposed to portend rain.

rainbow ('reɪnˌbəʊ) *n.* **1.** a bow-shaped display in the sky of the colours of the spectrum, caused by the refraction and reflection of the sun's rays through rain or mist. **2. a.** any similar display of bright colours. **b.** (*as modifier*): *a rainbow pattern.* **3.** an illusory hope: *to chase rainbows.* **4.** (*modifier*) of or relating to a political grouping together by several minorities, esp. of different races: *the rainbow coalition.*

rainbow bird *n.* an Australian bee-eater, *Merops ornatus,* with a brightly-coloured plumage. It feeds in flight and nests in sandy burrows.

rainbow quartz *n. Mineralogy.* another name for **iris** (sense 3).

rainbow trout *n.* a freshwater trout of North American origin, *Salmo gairdneri,* having a body marked with many black spots and two longitudinal red stripes.

rain check *n. U.S. and Canadian.* **1.** a ticket stub for a baseball or other game that allows readmission on a future date if the event is cancelled because of rain. **2.** the deferral of acceptance of an offer, esp., a voucher issued to a customer wishing to purchase a sale item that is temporarily out of stock, enabling him to buy it at the special price when next the item is available. **3. take a rain check.** *Informal.* to accept the postponement of an offer.

raincoat ('reɪnˌkəʊt) *n.* a coat made of a waterproof material.

rainfall ('reɪnˌfɔːl) *n.* **1.** precipitation in the form of raindrops. **2.** *Meteorol.* the amount of precipitation in a specified place and time.

rainforest ('reɪnˌfɒrɪst) *n.* dense forest found in tropical areas of heavy rainfall. The trees are broad-leaved and evergreen, and the vegetation tends to grow in three layers (undergrowth, intermediate trees and shrubs, and very tall trees, which form a canopy). Also called: **selva.**

rain gauge *n.* an instrument for measuring rainfall or snowfall, consisting of a cylinder covered by a funnel-like lid. Also called: **pluviometer.**

rainmaker ('reɪnˌmeɪkə) *n.* (among American Indians) a professional practitioner of ritual incantations or other actions intended to cause rain to fall. —'**rainˌmaking** *n.*

rainout ('reɪnˌaʊt) *n.* radioactive fallout or atmospheric pollution carried to the earth by rain.

rainproof ('reɪnˌpruːf) *adj.* **1.** Also: '**rainˌtight.** (of garments, materials, buildings, etc.) impermeable to rainwater. ~*vb.* **2.** (*tr.*) to make rainproof.

rains (reɪnz) *pl. n.* **the.** the season of heavy rainfall, esp. in the tropics.

rain shadow *n.* the relatively dry area on the leeward side of high ground in the path of rain-bearing winds.

rainstorm ('reɪnˌstɔːm) *n.* a storm with heavy rain.

rain tree *n.* a leguminous tree, *Samanea saman,* native to Central America and widely planted in the tropics for ornament. It has red-and-yellow feathery flowers and pinnate leaves whose leaflets close at the approach of rain.

rainwater ('reɪnˌwɔːtə) *n.* pure water from rain (as distinguished from spring water, tap water, etc., which may contain minerals and impurities).

rainwater pipe *n. Brit.* another name for **downpipe.**

rainwear ('reɪnwɛə) *n.* waterproof and water-resistant garments designed to be worn in the rain.

rainy ('reɪnɪ) *adj.* **rainier, rainiest. 1.** characterized by a large rainfall: *a rainy climate.* **2.** wet or showery; bearing rain. —'**rainily** *adv.* —'**raininess** *n.*

rainy day *n.* a future time of need, esp. financial.

raise (reɪz) *vb.* (*mainly tr.*) **1.** to move, cause to move, or elevate to a higher position or level; lift. **2.** to set or place in an upright position. **3.** to construct, build, or erect: *to raise a barn.* **4.** to increase in amount, size, value, etc.: *to raise prices.* **5.** to increase in degree, strength, intensity, etc.: *to raise one's voice.* **6.** to advance in rank or status; promote. **7.** to arouse or awaken from or as if from sleep or death. **8.** to stir up or incite; activate: *to raise a mutiny.* **9. raise Cain** (*or* **the devil, hell, the roof,** etc.). **a.** to create a boisterous disturbance. **b.** to react or protest heatedly. **10.** to give rise to; cause or provoke: *to raise a smile.* **11.** to put forward for consideration: *to raise a question.* **12.** to cause to assemble or gather together; collect: *to raise an army.* **13.** to grow or cause to grow: *to raise a crop.* **14.** to bring up; rear: *to raise a family.* **15.** to cause to be heard or known; utter or express: *to raise a shout; to raise a protest.* **16.** to bring to an end; remove: *to raise a siege; raise a ban.* **17.** to cause (dough, bread, etc.) to rise, as by the addition of yeast. **18.** *Poker.* to bet more than (the previous player). **19.** *Bridge.* to bid (one's partner's suit) at a higher level. **20.** *Nautical.* to cause (something) to seem to rise above the horizon by approaching: *we raised land after 20 days.* **21.** to establish radio communications with: *we managed to raise Moscow last night.* **22.** to obtain (money, funds, capital, etc.). **23.** to bring (a surface, a design, etc.) into relief; cause to project. **24.** to cause (a blister, welt, etc.) to form on the skin. **25.** to expel (phlegm) by coughing. **26.** *Phonetics.* to modify the articulation of (a vowel) by bringing the tongue closer to the roof of the mouth. **27.** *Maths.* to multiply (a number) by itself a specified number of times: *8 is 2 raised to the power 3.* **28. a.** to institute (a suit or action at law). **b.** to draw up (a summons). **29.** *Chiefly U.S. and Canadian.* to increase the amount payable on (a cheque, money order, etc.) fraudulently. **30.** *Curling.* to push (a stone) towards the tee with another stone. **31. raise an eyebrow a.** Also: **raise one's eyebrows.** to look quizzical or surprised. **b.** to give rise to doubt or disapproval. **32. raise one's glass (to).** to drink the health of (someone); drink a toast (to). **33. raise one's hat.** *Old-fashioned.* to take one's hat briefly off one's head as a greeting or mark of respect. ~*n.* **34.** the act or an instance of raising. **35.** *Chiefly U.S. and Canadian.* an increase, esp. in salary, wages, etc.; rise. [C12: from Old Norse *reisa;* related to Old English *rǣran* to REAR] —'**raisable** *or* '**raiseable** *adj.* —'**raiser** *n.*

raised beach *n.* a wave-cut platform raised above the shoreline by a relative fall in the water level.

raised bog *n. Ecology.* a bog of convex shape produced by growth of sphagnum and other bog plants in acid conditions and the subsequent build up of acid peat.

raisin ('reɪzᵊn) *n.* a dried grape. [C13: from Old French: grape, ultimately from Latin *racēmus* cluster of grapes; compare Greek *rhax* berry, grape] —'**raisiny** *adj.*

raising ('reɪzɪŋ) *n. Transformational grammar.* a rule that moves a constituent from an embedded clause into the main clause. See also **subject-raising, negative-raising.**

raison d'être *French.* (rezɔ̃ dɛtrə) *n., pl.* ***raisons d'être*** (rezɔ̃ dɛtrə). reason or justification for existence.

raita ('reɪtə, raɪ'iːtə) *n.* an Indian dish of finely chopped cucumber, peppers, mint, etc., in yoghurt, served with curries. [C20: from Hindi]

raj (rɑːdʒ) *n.* (in India) government; rule. [C19: from Hindi, from Sanskrit *rājya,* from *rājati* he rules]

Raj (rɑːdʒ) *n.* **the.** the British government in India before 1947.

Rajab (rə'dʒæb) *n.* the seventh month of the Muslim year.

rajah *or* **raja** ('rɑːdʒə) *n.* **1.** (in India, formerly) a ruler or landlord: sometimes used as a form of address or as a title preceding a name. **2.** a Malayan or Javanese prince or chieftain. [C16: from Hindi *rājā,* from Sanskrit *rājan* king; see RAJ; compare Latin *rex* king]

raja yoga ('rɑːdʒə) *n.* (*sometimes caps.*) a form of yoga chiefly concerned with controlling and using the energy of the mind by meditation. Compare **hatha yoga.** [C19: from Sanskrit *rājan* king + YOGA]

Rajput *or* **Rajpoot** ('rɑːdʒpʊt) *n. Hinduism.* one of a Hindu military caste claiming descent from the Kshatriya, the original warrior caste. [C16: from Hindi, from Sanskrit *rājan* king; see RAJ]

rake[1] (reɪk) *n.* **1.** a hand implement consisting of a row of teeth set in a headpiece attached to a long shaft and used for gathering hay, straw, leaves, etc., or for smoothing loose earth. **2.** any of several mechanical farm implements equipped with rows of teeth or rotating wheels mounted with tines and used to gather hay, straw, etc. **3.** any of various implements similar in shape or function, such as a tool for drawing out ashes from a furnace. **4.** the act of raking. **5.** *N.Z.* a line of wagons coupled together as one unit, used on railways. ~*vb.* **6.** to scrape, gather, or remove (leaves, refuse, etc.) with or as if with a rake. **7.** to level or prepare (a surface, such as a flower bed) with a rake or similar implement. **8.** (*tr.;* sometimes foll. by *out*) to clear (ashes, clinker, etc.) from (a fire or furnace). **9.** (*tr.;* foll. by *up* or *together*) to gather (items or people) with difficulty, as from a scattered area or limited supply. **10.** (*tr.;* often foll. by *through, over,* etc.) to search or examine carefully. **11.** (when *intr.,* foll. by *against, along,* etc.) to scrape or graze: *the ship raked the side of the quay.* **12.** (*tr.*) to direct (gunfire) along the length of (a target): *machine-guns raked the column.* **13.** (*tr.*) to sweep (one's eyes) along the length of (something); scan. ~See also **rake in, rake-off, rake up.** [Old English *raca;* related to Old Norse *raka,* Old High German *rehho* a rake, Gothic *rikan* to heap up, Latin *rogus* funeral pile] —'**raker** *n.*

rake[2] (reɪk) *n.* a dissolute man, esp. one in fashionable society; roué. [C17: short for RAKEHELL]

rake[3] (reɪk) *vb.* (*mainly intr.*) **1.** to incline from the vertical by a perceptible degree, esp. (of a ship's mast or funnel) towards the stern. **2.** (*tr.*) to construct with a backward slope. ~*n.* **3.** the degree to which an object, such as a ship's mast, inclines from the perpendicular, esp. towards the stern. **4.** *Theatre.* the slope of a stage from the back towards the footlights. **5.** *Aeronautics.* **a.** the angle between the wings of an aircraft and the line of symmetry of the aircraft. **b.** the angle between the line joining the centroids of the section of a propeller blade and a line perpendicular to the axis. **6.** the angle between the working face of a cutting tool and a plane perpendicular to the surface of the workpiece. **7.** a slanting ledge running across a crag in the Lake District. [C17: of uncertain origin; perhaps related to German *ragen* to project, Swedish *raka*]

rake[4] (reɪk) *vb.* (*intr.*) **1.** (of gun dogs or hounds) to hunt with the nose to the ground. **2.** (of hawks) **a.** to pursue quarry in full flight. **b.** (often foll. by *away*) to fly wide of the quarry, esp. beyond the control of the falconer. [Old English *racian* to go forward, of uncertain origin]

rakehell (ˈreɪkˌhɛl) *Archaic.* ~*n.* **1.** a dissolute man; rake. ~*adj.* *also* **rakehelly. 2.** profligate; dissolute. [C16: from RAKE[1] + HELL; but compare Middle English *rakel* rash]

rake in *vb.* (*tr., adv.*) *Informal.* to acquire (money) in large amounts.

rake-off *Slang.* ~*n.* **1.** a share of profits, esp. one that is illegal or given as a bribe. ~*vb.* **rake off. 2.** (*tr., adv.*) to take or receive (such a share of profits).

rake up *vb.* (*tr., adv.*) to revive, discover, or bring to light (something forgotten): *to rake up an old quarrel.*

raki *or* **rakee** (rɑːˈkiː, ˈrækɪ) *n.* a strong spirit distilled in Turkey, Yugoslavia, etc., from grain, usually flavoured with aniseed or other aromatics. [C17: from Turkish *rāqī*]

rakish[1] (ˈreɪkɪʃ) *adj.* dissolute; profligate. [C18: from RAKE[2] + -ISH] —ˈ**rakishly** *adv.* —ˈ**rakishness** *n.*

rakish[2] (ˈreɪkɪʃ) *adj.* **1.** dashing; jaunty: *a hat set at a rakish angle.* **2.** *Nautical.* (of a ship or boat) having lines suggestive of speed. [C19: probably from RAKE[3] (sense 1), with reference to the sloping masts of pirate ships]

rale *or* **râle** (rɑːl) *n. Med.* an abnormal crackling sound heard on auscultation of the chest, usually caused by the accumulation of fluid in the lungs. [C19: from French *râle,* from *râler* to breathe with a rattling sound; compare RAIL[3]]

rall. *Music. abbrev. for* rallentando.

rallentando (ˌrælɛnˈtændəʊ) *adj., adv. Music.* becoming slower. Abbrev.: **rall.** Also: **ritardando, ritenuto.** [C19: Italian, from *rallentare* to slow down]

ralline (ˈrælaɪn, -ɪn) *adj.* of, relating to, or belonging to the *Rallidae,* a family of birds that includes the rails, crakes, and coots. [C19: from New Latin *Rallus* RAIL[3]]

rally[1] (ˈrælɪ) *vb.* **-lies, -lying, -lied. 1.** to bring (a group, unit, etc.) into order, as after dispersal, or (of such a group) to reform and come to order: *the troops rallied for a final assault.* **2.** (when *intr.,* foll. by *to*) to organize (supporters, etc.) for a common cause or (of such people) to come together for a purpose. **3.** to summon up (one's strength, spirits, etc.) or (of a person's health, strength, or spirits) to revive or recover. **4.** (*intr.*) *Stock Exchange.* to increase sharply after a decline: *steels rallied after a bad day.* **5.** (*intr.*) *Tennis, squash, etc.* to engage in a rally. ~*n., pl.* **-lies. 6.** a large gathering of people for a common purpose, esp. for some political cause: *the Nuremberg Rallies.* **7.** a marked recovery of strength or spirits, as during illness. **8.** a return to order after dispersal or rout, as of troops, etc. **9.** *Stock Exchange.* a sharp increase in price or trading activity after a decline. **10.** *Tennis, squash, etc.* an exchange of several shots before one player wins the point. **11.** a type of motoring competition over public and closed roads. [C16: from Old French *rallier,* from RE- + *alier* to write; see ALLY] —ˈ**rallier** *n.*

rally[2] (ˈrælɪ) *vb.* **-lies, -lying, -lied.** to mock or ridicule (someone) in a good-natured way; chaff; tease. [C17: from Old French *railler* to tease; see RAIL[2]]

rallycross (ˈrælɪˌkrɒs) *n.* a form of motor sport in which cars race over a one-mile circuit of rough grass with some hard-surfaced sections. See also **autocross, motocross.**

rally round *vb.* (*intr.*) to come to the aid of (someone); offer moral or practical support.

ram (ræm) *n.* **1.** an uncastrated adult male sheep. **2.** a piston or moving plate, esp. one driven hydraulically or pneumatically. **3.** the falling weight of a pile driver or similar device. **4.** short for **battering ram. 5.** Also called: **rostrum, beak.** a pointed projection in the stem of an ancient warship for puncturing the hull of enemy ships. **6.** a warship equipped with a ram. **7.** *Slang.* a sexually active man. ~*vb.* **rams, ramming, rammed. 8.** (*tr.;* usually foll. by *into*) to force or drive, as by heavy blows: *to ram a post into the ground.* **9.** (of a moving object) to crash with force (against another object) or (of two moving objects) to collide in this way: *the Athenian ships rammed the enemy.* **10.** (*tr.;* often foll. by *in* or *down*) to stuff or cram (something into a hole, etc.). **11.** (*tr.;* foll. by *onto, against,* etc.) to thrust violently: *he rammed the books onto the desk.* **12.** (*tr.*) to present (an idea, argument, etc.) forcefully or aggressively (esp. in the phrase **ram (something) down someone's throat**). **13.** (*tr.*) to drive (a charge) into a firearm. [Old English *ramm;* related to Old High German *ram* ram, Old Norse *ramr* fierce, *rimma* to fight] —ˈ**rammer** *n.*

r.a.m. *abbrev. for* relative atomic mass.

Ram (ræm) *n.* **the.** the constellation Aries, the first sign of the zodiac.

RAM[1] (ræm) *n. Computer technol. acronym for* random access memory: a temporary storage space which can be filled with data by the user but which loses it contents when the computer is switched off.

RAM[2] *abbrev. for* Royal Academy of Music.

Ramadan, Rhamadhan (ˌræməˈdɑːn), *or* **Ramazan** (ˌræməˈzɑːn) *n.* **1.** the ninth month of the Muslim year, lasting 30 days, during which strict fasting is observed from sunrise to sunset. **2.** the fast itself. [C16: from Arabic, literally: the hot month, from *ramad* dryness]

ram-air turbine *n.* a small air-driven turbine fitted to an aircraft to provide power in the event of a failure of the normal systems.

Raman effect (ˈrɑːmən) *n.* the change in wavelength of light that is scattered by electrons within a material. The effect is used in **Raman spectroscopy** for studying the properties of molecules. [C20: named after Sir Chandasekhara *Raman* (1888–1970), Indian physicist]

ramble (ˈræmbᵊl) *vb.* (*intr.*) **1.** to stroll about freely, as for relaxation, with no particular direction. **2.** (of paths, streams, etc.) to follow a winding course; meander. **3.** (of plants) to grow in a random fashion. **4.** (of speech, writing, etc.) to lack organization. ~*n.* **5.** a leisurely stroll, esp. in the countryside. [C17: probably related to Middle Dutch *rammelen* to ROAM (of animals); see RAM]

rambler (ˈræmblə) *n.* **1.** a weak-stemmed plant, esp. any of various cultivated hybrid roses that straggle over other vegetation. **2.** a person who rambles, esp. one who takes country walks. **3.** a person who lacks organization in his speech or writing.

rambling (ˈræmblɪŋ) *adj.* **1.** straggling or sprawling haphazardly; unplanned: *a rambling old house.* **2.** (of speech or writing) lacking a coherent plan; diffuse and disconnected. **3.** (of a plant, esp. a rose) profusely climbing and straggling. **4.** nomadic; wandering.

Ramboesque (ˌræmbəʊˈɛsk) *adj.* looking or behaving like or characteristic of Rambo, a fictional film character noted for his mindless brutality. [C20: after *Rambo, First Blood II,* released in Britain 1985] —ˈ**Ramboˌism** *n.*

Rambouillet (ˈrɒmbʊˌjeɪ, ˈræmbʊˌleɪ; *French* rɑ̃bujɛ) *n.* a fine-woolled merino-like breed of sheep. [C19: from *Rambouillet,* a town in N France]

rambunctious (ræmˈbʌŋkʃəs) *adj. Informal.* boisterous; unruly. [C19: probably from Icelandic *ram-* (intensifying prefix) + *-bunctious,* from BUMPTIOUS] —**ramˈbunctiously** *adv.* —**ramˈbunctiousness** *n.*

rambutan (ræmˈbuːtᵊn) *n.* **1.** a sapindaceous tree, *Nephelium lappaceum,* native to SE Asia, that has bright red edible fruit covered with hairs. **2.** the fruit of this tree. [C18: from Malay, from *rambut* hair]

RAMC *abbrev. for* Royal Army Medical Corps.

ramekin *or* **ramequin** (ˈræmɪkɪn) *n.* **1.** a savoury dish made from a cheese mixture baked in a fireproof container. **2.** the container itself. [C18: French *ramequin,* of Germanic origin]

ramentum (rəˈmɛntəm) *n., pl.* **-ta** (-tə). any of the thin brown scales that cover the stems and leaves of young ferns. [C17: from Latin *rādere* to scrape] —**ramentaceous** (ˌræmɛnˈteɪʃəs) *adj.*

rami (ˈreɪmaɪ) *n.* the plural of **ramus.**

ramie *or* **ramee** (ˈræmɪ) *n.* **1.** a woody urticaceous shrub of Asia, *Boehmeria nivea,* having broad leaves and a stem that yields a flaxlike fibre. **2.** the fibre from this plant, used in making fabrics, cord, etc. [C19: from Malay *rami*]

ramification (ˌræmɪfɪˈkeɪʃən) *n.* **1.** the act or process of ramifying or branching out. **2.** an offshoot or subdivision. **3.** (*often pl.*) a subsidiary consequence, esp. one that complicates. **4.** a structure of branching parts.

ramiform (ˈræmɪˌfɔːm) *adj.* having a branchlike shape. [C19: from Latin *rāmus* branch + -FORM]

ramify (ˈræmɪˌfaɪ) *vb.* **-fies, -fying, -fied. 1.** to divide into branches or branchlike parts. **2.** (*intr.*) to develop complicating consequences; become complex. [C16: from French *ramifier,* from Latin *rāmus* branch + *facere* to make]

ramjet *or* **ramjet engine** (ˈræmˌdʒɛt) *n.* **a.** a type of jet engine in which fuel is burned in a duct using air compressed by the forward speed of the aircraft. **b.** an aircraft powered by such an engine. Also called: **athodyd.**

rammish (ˈræmɪʃ) *adj.* like a ram, esp. in being lustful or foul-smelling. —ˈ**rammishly** *adv.* —ˈ**rammishness** *n.*

rammy (ˈræmɪ) *n., pl.* **-mies.** *Central Scot. urban dialect.* a noisy disturbance or free-for-all. [C20: perhaps from earlier Scot. *rammle* row, uproar]

ramose (ˈreɪməʊs, ræˈməʊs) *or* **ramous** (ˈreɪməs) *adj.* having branches. [C17: from Latin *rāmōsus,* from *rāmus* branch] —ˈ**ramosely** *or* ˈ**ramously** *adv.* —**ramosity** (ræˈmɒsɪtɪ) *n.*

ramp (ræmp) *n.* **1.** a sloping floor, path, etc., that joins two surfaces at different levels. **2.** a movable stairway by which passengers enter and leave an aircraft. **3.** the act of ramping. **4.** *Brit. slang.* a swindle, esp. one involving exorbitant prices. **5.** an N.Z. name for **sleeping policeman.** ~*vb.* (*intr.*) **6.** (often foll. by *about* or *around*) (esp. of animals) to rush around in a wild excited manner. **7.** to act in a violent or threatening manner, as when angry (esp. in the phrase **ramp and rage**). [C18 (n.): from C13 *rampe,* from Old French *ramper* to crawl or rear, probably of Germanic origin; compare Middle Low German *ramp* cramp]

rampage *vb.* (ræmˈpeɪdʒ). **1.** (*intr.*) to rush about in an angry, violent, or agitated fashion. ~*n.* (ˈræmpeɪdʒ, ræmˈpeɪdʒ). **2.** angry or destructive behaviour. **3. on the rampage.** behaving violently or destructively. [C18: from Scottish, of uncertain origin; perhaps based on RAMP] —**ramˈpageous** *adj.* —**ramˈpageously** *adv.* —**ramˈpageousness** *n.* —ˈ**rampager** *n.*

rampant (ˈræmpənt) *adj.* **1.** unrestrained or violent in behaviour, desire, opinions, etc. **2.** growing or developing unchecked. **3.** (*postpositive*) *Heraldry.* (of a beast) standing on the hind legs, the right foreleg raised above the left. **4.** (of an arch) having one abutment higher than the other. [C14: from Old French *ramper* to crawl, rear; see RAMP] —'**rampancy** *n.* —'**rampantly** *adv.*

rampart ('ræmpɑːt) *n.* **1.** the surrounding embankment of a fort, often including any walls, parapets, walks, etc., that are built on the bank. **2.** anything resembling a rampart in form or function, esp. in being a defence or bulwark. ~*vb.* **3.** (*tr.*) to provide with a rampart; fortify. [C16: from Old French, from *remparer*, from RE- + *emparer* to take possession of, from Old Provençal *antparar*, from Latin *ante* before + *parāre* to prepare]

rampion ('ræmpɪən) *n.* **1.** a campanulaceous plant, *Campanula rapunculus*, native to Europe and Asia, that has clusters of bluish flowers and an edible white tuberous root used in salads. **2.** any of several plants of the related genus *Phyteuma* that are native to Europe and Asia and have heads of blue flowers. [C16: probably from Old French *raiponce*, from Old Italian *raponzo*, from *rapa* turnip, from Latin *rāpum* turnip; see RAPE[2]]

ramrod ('ræmˌrɒd) *n.* **1.** a rod for cleaning the barrel of a rifle or other small firearms. **2.** a rod for ramming in the charge of a muzzle-loading firearm.

ramshackle ('ræmˌʃækᵊl) *adj.* (esp. of buildings) badly constructed or maintained; rickety, shaky, or derelict. [C17 *ramshackled*, from obsolete *ransackle* to RANSACK]

ramshorn snail ('ræmzˌhɔːn) *n.* any of various freshwater snails of the genus *Planorbis* that are widely used in aquariums.

ramsons ('ræmzənz, -sənz) *pl. n.* (*usually functioning as sing.*) **1.** a broad-leaved garlic, *Allium ursinum*, native to Europe and Asia. **2.** the bulbous root of this plant, eaten as a relish. [Old English *hramesa*; related to Middle Low German *ramese*, Norwegian *rams*]

ramstam ('ræm'stæm) *Scot.* ~*adv.* **1.** headlong; hastily. ~*adj.* **2.** headlong; precipitate. [C18: perhaps from RAM + dialect *stam* to stamp]

ramtil ('ræmtɪl) *n.* **1.** an African plant, *Guizotia abyssinica*, grown in India: family *Compositae* (composites). **2.** Also called: **Niger seed.** the seed of this plant, used as a source of oil and a bird food. [C19: from Hindi, from Sanskrit *rāma* black + *tila* sesame]

ramulose ('ræmjʊˌləʊs) *or* **ramulous** ('ræmjʊləs) *adj.* (of the parts or organs of animals and plants) having many small branches. [C18: from Latin *rāmulōsus* full of branching veins, from *rāmulus* twig, from *rāmus* branch]

ramus ('reɪməs) *n., pl.* **-mi** (-maɪ). **1.** the barb of a bird's feather. **2.** either of the two parts of the lower jaw of a vertebrate. **3.** any part or organ that branches from another part. [C19: from Latin: branch]

ran (ræn) *vb.* the past tense of **run.**

RAN *abbrev. for* Royal Australian Navy.

rance (rɑːns) *n.* a type of red marble, often with white or blue graining, that comes from Belgium. [C19: apparently from French *ranche* rod, pole]

ranch (rɑːntʃ) *n.* **1.** a large tract of land, esp. one in North America, together with the necessary personnel, buildings, and equipment, for rearing livestock, esp. cattle. **2. a.** any large farm for the rearing of a particular kind of livestock or crop: *a mink ranch.* **b.** the buildings, land, etc., connected with it. ~*vb.* **3.** (*intr.*) to manage or run a ranch. **4.** (*tr.*) to raise (animals) on or as if on a ranch. [C19: from Mexican Spanish *rancho* small farm; see RANCHO]

rancher ('rɑːntʃə) *n.* a person who owns, manages, or works on a ranch.

rancherie ('rɑːntʃərɪ) *n.* (in British Columbia, Canada) a settlement of North American Indians, esp. on a reserve. [from Spanish *ranchería*]

ranchero (rɑːn'tʃɛərəʊ) *n., pl.* **-ros.** *Southwestern U.S.* another word for **rancher.** [C19: from American Spanish]

rancho ('rɑːntʃəʊ) *n., pl.* **-chos.** *Southwestern U.S.* **1.** a hut or group of huts for housing ranch workers. **2.** another word for **ranch.** [C17: from Mexican Spanish: camp, from Old Spanish *ranchar* to be billeted, from Old French *ranger* to place]

rancid ('rænsɪd) *adj.* **1.** (of butter, bacon, etc.) having an unpleasant stale taste or smell as the result of decomposition. **2.** (of a taste or smell) rank or sour; stale. [C17: from Latin *rancidus* rank, from *rancēre* to stink] —'**rancidness** *or* **rancidity** (ræn'sɪdɪtɪ) *n.*

rancour *or U.S.* **rancor** ('ræŋkə) *n.* malicious resentfulness or hostility; spite. [C14: from Old French, from late Latin *rancor* rankness] —'**rancorous** *adj.* —'**rancorously** *adv.* —'**rancorousness** *n.*

rand[1] (rænd, rɒnt) *n.* the standard monetary unit of the Republic of South Africa, divided into 100 cents. [C20: from Afrikaans, shortened from *Witwatersrand* (a ridge in NE South Africa), referring to the gold-mining there; related to RAND[2]]

rand[2] (rænd) *n.* **1.** *Shoemaking.* a leather strip put in the heel of a shoe before the lifts are put on. **2.** *Dialect.* **a.** a strip or margin; border. **b.** a strip of cloth; selvage. [Old English; related to Old High German *rant* border, rim of a shield, Old Norse *rönd* shield, rim]

R & A *abbrev. for* Royal and Ancient (Golf Club, St Andrews).

randan[1] (ræn'dæn, 'rændæn) *n.* a boat rowed by three people, in which the person in the middle uses two oars and the people fore and aft use one oar each. [C19: of uncertain origin]

randan[2] (ˌræn'dæn, 'rænˌdæn) *n.* rowdy behaviour; a spree. [C18: perhaps changed from RANDOM]

R & B *abbrev. for* rhythm and blues.

R & D *abbrev. for* research and development.

randem ('rændɛm) *adv.* **1.** with three horses harnessed together as a team. ~*n.* **2.** a carriage or team of horses so driven. [C19: probably from RANDOM + TANDEM]

random ('rændəm) *adj.* **1.** lacking any definite plan or prearranged order; haphazard: *a random selection.* **2.** *Statistics.* **a.** having a value which cannot be determined but only described probabilistically: *a random variable.* **b.** chosen without regard to any characteristics of the individual members of the population so that each has an equal chance of being selected: *random sampling.* ~*n.* **3.** *Chiefly Brit.* another word for **bank**[3] (sense 3). **4. at random.** in a purposeless fashion; not following any prearranged order. [C14: from Old French *randon*, from *randir* to gallop, of Germanic origin; compare Old High German *rinnan* to run] —'**randomly** *adv.* —'**randomness** *n.*

random access *n.* another name for **direct access.**

randomize *or* **randomise** ('rændəˌmaɪz) *vb.* (*tr.*) to set up (a selection process, sample, etc.) in a deliberately random way in order to enhance the statistical validity of any results obtained. —ˌ**randomi'zation** *or* ˌ**randomi'sation** *n.* —'**randomˌizer** *or* '**randomˌiser** *n.*

random numbers *pl. n.* a sequence of numbers that do not form any progression, used to facilitate unbiased sampling of a population. A **random-number generator** is part of the software of most computers and many calculators.

random rubble *n.* masonry in which untooled stones are set without coursing.

random variable *n. Statistics.* a quantity that may take any of a range of values, either continuous or discrete, which cannot be predicted with certainty but only described probabilistically. Abbrev.: **rv.**

random walk *n.* **1.** a mathematical model used to describe physical processes, such as diffusion, in which a particle moves in straight-line steps of constant length but random direction. **2.** *Statistics.* a route consisting of successive and connected steps in which each step is chosen by a random mechanism uninfluenced by any previous step.

random walk theory *n. Stock Exchange.* the theory that the future movement of share prices does not reflect past movements and therefore will not follow a discernible pattern.

R and R *U.S. military. abbrev. for* rest and recreation.

randy ('rændɪ) *adj.* **randier, randiest.** **1.** *Informal, chiefly Brit.* **a.** sexually excited or aroused. **b.** sexually eager or lustful. **2.** *Chiefly Scot.* lacking any sense of propriety or restraint; reckless. ~*n., pl.* **randies.** **3.** *Chiefly Scot.* **a.** a rude or reckless person. **b.** a coarse rowdy woman. [C17: probably from obsolete *rand* to RANT] —'**randily** *adv.* —'**randiness** *n.*

ranee ('rɑːnɪ) *n.* a variant spelling of **rani.**

Ranfurly Shield (ræn'fɜːlɪ) *n.* (in New Zealand) the premier rugby trophy, competed for annually by provincial teams. [C20: named after the Earl of *Ranfurly* (1856–1933), 15th Governor of New Zealand (1897–1904), who presented it to the New Zealand Rugby Football Union in 1902]

rang (ræŋ) *vb.* the past tense of **ring**[2].

▷**Usage.** See at **ring**[2].

rangatira (ˌrʌŋgə'tɪərə) *n. N.Z.* a Maori chief of either sex. [Maori]

range (reɪndʒ) *n.* **1.** the limits within which a person or thing can function effectively: *the range of vision.* **2.** the limits within which any fluctuation takes place: *a range of values.* **3.** the total products of a manufacturer, designer, or stockist: *the new autumn range.* **4. a.** the maximum effective distance of a projectile fired from a weapon. **b.** the distance between a target and a weapon. **5.** an area set aside for shooting practice or rocket testing. **6.** the total distance which a ship, aircraft, or land vehicle is capable of covering without taking on fresh fuel: *the range of this car is about 160 miles.* **7.** *Physics.* the distance that a particle of ionizing radiation, such as an electron or proton, can travel through a given medium, esp. air, before ceasing to cause ionization. **8.** *Maths, logic.* **a.** (of a function) the set of values that the function takes for all possible arguments. Compare **domain** (sense 7). **b.** (of a variable) the set of values that a variable can take. **c.** (of a quantifier) the set of values that the variable bound by the quantifier can take. **9.** *Statistics.* a measure of dispersion obtained by subtracting the smallest from the largest sample values. **10.** the extent of pitch difference between the highest and lowest notes of a voice, instrument, etc. **11.** *U.S. and Canadian.* **a.** an extensive tract of open land on which livestock can graze. **b.** (*as modifier*): *range cattle.* **12.** the geographical region in which a species of plant or animal normally grows or lives. **13.** a rank, row, or series of items. **14.** a series or chain of mountains. **15.** a large stove with burners and one or more ovens, usually heated by solid fuel. **16.** the act or process of ranging. **17.** *Nautical.* a line of sight taken from the sea along two or more navigational aids that mark a navigable channel. **18.** the extension or direction of a survey line, established by marking two or more points. **19.** a double-faced bookcase, as in a library. **20. range of significance.** *Philosophy, logic.* the set of subjects for which a given predicate is intelligible. ~*vb.* **21.** to establish or be situated in a line, row, or series. **22.** (*tr.; often reflexive,* foll. by *with*) to put into a specific category; classify: *she ranges herself with the angels.* **23.** (foll. by *on*) to aim or point (a telescope, gun, etc.) or (of a gun, telescope, etc.) to be pointed or aimed. **24.** to establish the distance of (a target) from (a weapon). **25.** (*intr.*) (of a gun or missile) to have a specified range. **26.** (when *intr.*; foll. by *over*) to wander about (in) an area; roam (over). **27.** (*intr.*; foll. by *over*) (of an animal or plant) to live or grow in its normal habitat. **28.** (*tr.*) to put (cattle) to graze on a range. **29.** (*intr.*) to fluctuate within specific limits: *their ages range from 18 to 21.* **30.** (*intr.*) to extend or run in a specific direction. **31.** (*tr.*) *Nautical.* to coil (an anchor rope or chain) so that it will pay out smoothly. **32.** (*intr.*) *Nautical.* (of a vessel) to swing back and forth while at anchor. **33.** (*tr.*) to make (lines of printers' type) level or even at the margin. [C13: from Old French: row, from *ranger* to position, from *renc* line]

rangefinder ('reɪndʒˌfaɪndə) *n.* **1.** an instrument for determining the distance of an object from the observer, esp. in order to sight a gun or focus a camera. **2.** another word for **tacheometer.**

rangeland ('reɪndʒˌlænd) *n.* (*often pl.*) land that naturally produces forage plants suitable for grazing but where rainfall is too low or erratic for growing crops.

range light *n. Nautical.* **1.** one of a pattern of navigation lights, usually fixed ashore, used by vessels for manoeuvring in narrow channels at night. **2.** one of a distinctive pattern of lights shown at night on the masts of a powered vessel, such as a tugboat, to aid in identifying its size, number of barges in tow, etc.

ranger ('reɪndʒə) *n.* **1.** (*sometimes cap.*) an official in charge of a forest, park, estate, nature reserve, etc. **2.** *Chiefly U.S.* a person employed to patrol a State or national park or forest. Brit. equivalent: **warden.** **3.** *U.S.* one of a body of armed troops employed to police a State or district: *a Texas ranger.* **4.** (in the U.S. and certain other armies) a commando specially trained in making raids. **5.** a person who wanders about large areas of country; a rover.

Ranger *or* **Ranger Guide** ('reɪndʒə) *n. Brit.* a member of the senior branch of the Guides.

ranging pole *or* **rod** *n.* a pole for marking positions in surveying. Also called: **range pole, rod.**

rangiora (ˌræŋɡɪ'ɔːrə, ˌræŋɪ-) *n.* an evergreen shrub or small tree, *Brachyglottis repanda,* of New Zealand, having large ovate leaves and small greenish-white flowers: family *Compositae* (composites). [Maori]

rangy ('reɪndʒɪ) *adj.* **rangier, rangiest.** **1.** (of animals or people) having long slender limbs. **2.** adapted to wandering or roaming. **3.** allowing considerable freedom of movement; spacious; roomy. [C19: from RANGE + -Y[1]] —'**rangily** *adv.* —'**ranginess** *n.*

rani *or* **ranee** ('rɑːnɪ) *n.* (in oriental countries, esp. India) a queen or princess; the wife of a rajah. [C17: from Hindi: queen, from Sanskrit *rājñī,* feminine of *rājan* RAJAH]

rank[1] (ræŋk) *n.* **1.** a position, esp. an official one, within a social organization, esp. the armed forces: *the rank of captain.* **2.** high social or other standing; status. **3.** a line or row of people or things. **4.** the position of an item in any ordering or sequence. **5.** *Brit.* a place where taxis wait to be hired. **6.** a line of soldiers drawn up abreast of each other. Compare **file**[1] (sense 5). **7.** any of the eight horizontal rows of squares on a chessboard. **8.** (in systemic grammar) one of the units of description of which a grammar is composed. Ranks of English grammar are sentence, clause, group, word, and morpheme. **9.** *Music.* a set of organ pipes controlled by the same stop. **10.** *Maths.* (of a matrix) the largest number of linearly independent rows or columns; the number of rows (or columns) of the nonzero determinant of greatest order that can be extracted from the matrix. **11. break ranks.** *Military.* to fall out of line, esp. when under attack. **12. close ranks.** to maintain discipline or solidarity, esp. in anticipation of attack. **13. pull rank.** to get one's own way by virtue of one's superior position or rank. ~*vb.* **14.** (*tr.*) to arrange (people or things) in rows or lines; range. **15.** to accord or be accorded a specific position in an organization, society, or group. **16.** (*tr.*) to array (a set of objects) as a sequence, esp. in terms of the natural arithmetic ordering of some measure of the elements: *to rank students by their test scores.* **17.** (*intr.*) to be important; rate: *money ranks low in her order of priorities.* **18.** *Chiefly U.S.* to take precedence or surpass in rank: *the colonel ranks at this camp.* [C16: from Old French *ranc* row, rank, of Germanic origin; compare Old High German *hring* circle]

rank[2] (ræŋk) *adj.* **1.** showing vigorous and profuse growth: *rank weeds.* **2.** highly offensive or disagreeable, esp. in smell or taste. **3.** (*prenominal*) complete or absolute; utter: *a rank outsider.* **4.** coarse or vulgar; gross: *his language was rank.* [Old English *ranc* straight, noble; related to Old Norse *rakkr* upright, Dutch, Swedish *rank* tall and thin, weak] —'**rankly** *adv.* —'**rankness** *n.*

rank and file *n.* **1.** the ordinary soldiers of an army, excluding the officers. **2.** the great mass or majority of any group or organization, as opposed to the leadership. **3.** (*modifier*) of, relating to, or characteristic of the rank and file: *rank-and-file opinion; rank-and-file support.* —**rank and filer** *n.*

ranker ('ræŋkə) *n.* **1.** a soldier in the ranks. **2.** a commissioned officer who entered service as a recruit, esp. in the army. **3.** a person who ranks.

Rankine cycle ('ræŋkɪn) *n.* the thermodynamic cycle in steam engines by which water is pumped into a boiler at one end and the steam is condensed at the other. [C19: named after W. J. M. *Rankine* (1820–72), Scottish physicist]

Rankine scale *n.* an absolute scale of temperature in which the unit of temperature is equal to that on the Fahrenheit scale and the zero value of temperature is equal to –459.67° F. Compare **Kelvin scale.**

ranking ('ræŋkɪŋ) *adj.* **1.** *Chiefly U.S. and Canadian.* prominent; high ranking. **2.** *Caribbean slang.* possessed of style; fashionable; exciting. ~*n.* **3.** a position on a scale; rating: *a ranking in a tennis tournament.*

rankle ('ræŋkᵊl) *vb.* (*intr.*) to cause severe and continuous irritation, anger, or bitterness; fester: *his failure to win still rankles.* [C14 *ranclen,* from Old French *draoncler* to fester, from *draoncle* ulcer, from Latin *dracunculus* small serpent, from *dracō* serpent; see DRAGON]

rankshift ('ræŋkˌʃɪft) (in systemic grammar) ~*n.* **1.** a phenomenon in which a unit at one rank in the grammar has the function of a unit at a lower rank, as for example in the phrase *the house on the corner,* where the words *on the corner* shift down from the rank of group to the rank of word. ~*vb.* **2.** to shift or be shifted from one linguistic rank to another.

ransack ('rænsæk) *vb.* (*tr.*) **1.** to search through every part of (a house, box, etc.); examine thoroughly. **2.** to plunder; pillage. [C13: from Old Norse *rann* house + *saka* to search, SEEK] —'**ransacker** *n.*

ransom ('rænsəm) *n.* **1.** the release of captured prisoners, property, etc., on payment of a stipulated price. **2.** the price demanded or stipulated for such a release. **3.** rescue or redemption of any kind. **4. hold to ransom. a.** to keep (prisoners, property, etc.) in confinement until payment for their release is made or received. **b.** to attempt to force (a person or persons) to comply with one's demands. **5. a king's ransom.** a very large amount of money or valuables. ~*vb.* (*tr.*) **6.** to pay a stipulated price and so obtain the release of (prisoners, property, etc.). **7.** to set free (prisoners, property, etc.) upon receiving the payment demanded. **8.** to redeem; rescue: *Christ ransomed men from sin.* [C14: from Old French *ransoun,* from Latin *redemptiō* a buying back, REDEMPTION] —'**ransomer** *n.*

rant (rænt) *vb.* **1.** to utter (something) in loud, violent, or bombastic tones. **2.** (*intr.*) *Chiefly Scot.* to make merry; frolic. ~*n.* **3.** loud, declamatory, or extravagant speech; bombast. **4.** *Chiefly Scot.* a wild revel. **5.** *Scot.* an energetic dance or its tune. [C16: from Dutch *ranten* to rave; related to German *ranzen* to gambol] —'**ranter** *n.* —'**ranting** *adj., n.* —'**rantingly** *adv.*

ranunculaceous (rəˌnʌŋkjʊ'leɪʃəs) *adj.* of, relating to, or belonging to the *Ranunculaceae,* a N temperate family of flowering plants typically having flowers with five petals and numerous anthers and styles. The family includes the buttercup, clematis, hellebore, and columbine.

ranunculus (rə'nʌŋkjʊləs) *n., pl.* **-luses** *or* **-li** (-ˌlaɪ). any ranunculaceous plant of the genus *Ranunculus,* having finely divided leaves and typically yellow five-petalled flowers. The genus includes buttercup, crowfoot, spearwort, and lesser celandine. [C16: from Latin: tadpole, from *rāna* a frog]

RAOC *abbrev. for* Royal Army Ordnance Corps.

rap[1] (ræp) *vb.* **raps, rapping, rapped.** **1.** to strike (a fist, stick, etc.) against (something) with a sharp quick blow; knock: *he rapped at the door.* **2.** (*intr.*) to make a sharp loud sound, esp. by knocking. **3.** (*tr.*) to rebuke or criticize sharply. **4.** (*tr.*; foll. by *out*) to put (forth) in sharp rapid speech; utter in an abrupt fashion: *to rap out orders.* **5.** (*intr.*) *Slang.* to talk, esp. volubly. **6.** (*intr.*) to perform a rhythmic monologue with a musical backing. **7. rap over the knuckles.** to reprimand. ~*n.* **8.** a sharp quick blow or the sound produced by such a blow. **9.** a sharp rebuke or criticism. **10.** *Slang.* voluble talk; chatter: *stop your rap.* **11. a.** a fast, rhythmic monologue over a prerecorded instrumental track. **b.** (*as modifier*): *rap music.* **12.** *Slang.* a legal charge or case. **13. beat the rap.** *U.S. and Canadian slang.* to escape punishment or be acquitted of a crime. **14. take the rap.** *Slang.* to suffer the consequences of a mistake, misdeed, or crime, whether guilty or not. [C14: probably of Scandinavian origin; compare Swedish *rappa* to beat] —'**rapping** *n.*

rap[2] (ræp) *n.* (*used with a negative*) the least amount (esp. in the phrase **not to care a rap**). [C18: probably from *ropaire* counterfeit coin formerly current in Ireland]

rap[3] (ræp) *vb., n. Austral. informal.* a variant spelling of **wrap** (senses 7, 11).

rapacious (rə'peɪʃəs) *adj.* **1.** practising pillage or rapine. **2.** greedy or grasping. **3.** (of animals, esp. birds) subsisting by catching living prey. [C17: from Latin *rapāx* grasping, from *rapere* to seize] —**ra'paciously** *adv.* —**rapacity** (rə'pæsɪtɪ) *or* **ra'paciousness** *n.*

rape[1] (reɪp) *n.* **1.** the offence of forcing a person, esp. a woman, to submit to sexual intercourse against that person's will. See also **statutory rape.** **2.** the act of despoiling a country in warfare; rapine. **3.** any violation or abuse: *the rape of justice.* **4.** *Archaic.* abduction: *the rape of the Sabine women.* ~*vb.* (*mainly tr.*) **5.** to commit rape upon (a person). **6.** (*also intr.*) to plunder or despoil (a place) in war. **7.** *Archaic.* to carry off by force; abduct. [C14: from Latin *rapere* to seize]

rape[2] (reɪp) *n.* a Eurasian cruciferous plant, *Brassica napus,* that is cultivated for its seeds, which yield a useful oil, and as a fodder plant. Also called: **colza, cole.** [C14: from Latin *rāpum* turnip]

rape[3] (reɪp) *n.* (*often pl.*) the skins and stalks of grapes left after wine-making: used in making vinegar. [C17: from French *râpe*, of Germanic origin; compare Old High German *raspōn* to scrape together]

rape oil *n.* oil extracted from rapeseed, used as a lubricant, as a constituent of soaps, etc. Also called: **rapeseed oil, colza oil.**

rapeseed (ˈreɪpˌsiːd) *n.* the seed of the rape plant.

raphe (ˈreɪfɪ) *n., pl.* **-phae** (-fiː). **1.** an elongated ridge of conducting tissue along the side of certain seeds. **2.** a longitudinal groove on the valve of a diatom. **3.** *Anatomy.* a connecting ridge, as that between the two halves of the medulla oblongata. [C18: via New Latin from Greek *rhaphē* a seam, from *rhaptein* to sew together]

raphia (ˈræfɪə) *n.* a variant spelling of **raffia.**

raphide (ˈreɪfaɪd) *or* **raphis** (ˈreɪfɪs) *n., pl.* **raphides** (ˈræfɪˌdiːz). any of numerous needle-shaped crystals, usually of calcium oxalate, that occur in many plant cells as a metabolic product. [C18: from French, from Greek *rhaphis* needle]

rapid (ˈræpɪd) *adj.* **1.** (of an action or movement) performed or occurring during a short interval of time; quick: *a rapid transformation.* **2.** characterized by high speed: *rapid movement.* **3.** acting or moving quickly; fast: *a rapid worker.* ~See also **rapids.** [C17: from Latin *rapidus* tearing away, from *rapere* to seize; see RAPE[1]] —ˈ**rapidly** *adv.* —**rapidity** (rəˈpɪdɪtɪ) *or* ˈ**rapidness** *n.*

rapid eye movement *n.* movement of the eyeballs under closed eyelids during paradoxical sleep, which occurs while the sleeper is dreaming. Abbrev.: **REM.**

rapid fire *n.* **1.** a fast rate of gunfire. ~*adj.* **rapid-fire. 2. a.** firing shots rapidly. **b.** denoting medium-calibre mounted guns designed for rapid fire. **3.** done, delivered, or occurring in rapid succession.

rapids (ˈræpɪdz) *pl. n.* part of a river where the current is very fast and turbulent.

rapid transit chess *n.* the U.S. name for **lightning chess.** [from the name of the New York City underground railway system]

rapier (ˈreɪpɪə) *n.* **1.** a long narrow two-edged sword with a guarded hilt, used as a thrusting weapon, popular in the 16th and 17th centuries. **2.** a smaller single-edged 18th-century sword, used principally in France. [C16: from Old French *espee rapiere*, literally: rasping sword; see RASP[1]] —ˈ**rapierˌlike** *adj.*

rapine (ˈræpaɪn) *n.* the seizure of property by force; pillage. [C15: from Latin *rapīna* plundering, from *rapere* to snatch]

rapist (ˈreɪpɪst) *n.* a person who commits rape.

rapparee (ˌræpəˈriː) *n.* **1.** an Irish irregular soldier of the late 17th century. **2.** *Obsolete.* any plunderer or robber. [C17: from Irish *rapairidhe* pike, probably from English RAPIER]

rappee (ræˈpiː) *n.* a moist English snuff of the 18th and 19th centuries. [C18: from French *tabac râpé*, literally: scraped tobacco, from *râper* to scrape; see RAPE[3], RASP[1]]

rappel (ræˈpel) *vb.* **-pels, -pelling, -pelled,** *n.* **1.** another word for **abseil.** ~*n.* **2.** (formerly) a drumbeat to call soldiers to arms. [C19: from French, from *rappeler* to call back, from Latin *appellāre* to summon]

rapper (ˈræpə) *n.* **1.** something used for rapping, such as a knocker on a door. **2.** a performer of rap music.

rapport (ræˈpɔː) *n.* (often foll. by *with*) a sympathetic relationship or understanding. See also **en rapport.** [C15: from French, from *rapporter* to bring back, from RE- + *aporter*, from Latin *apportāre*, from *ad* to + *portāre* to carry]

rapporteur (ˌræpɔːˈtɜː) *n.* a person appointed by a committee to prepare reports of meetings or carry out an investigation. [C18: from French, literally: recorder, reporter]

rapprochement *French.* (raprɔʃmɑ̃) *n.* a resumption of friendly relations, esp. between two countries. [C19: literally: bringing closer]

rapscallion (ræpˈskæljən) *n.* a disreputable person; rascal or rogue. [C17: from earlier *rascallion*; see RASCAL]

rapt[1] (ræpt) *adj.* **1.** totally absorbed; engrossed; spellbound, esp. through or as if through emotion: *rapt with wonder.* **2.** characterized by or proceeding from rapture: *a rapt smile.* [C14: from Latin *raptus* carried away, from *rapere* to seize; see RAPE[1]] —ˈ**raptly** *adv.*

rapt[2] (ræpt) *adj. Austral. and N.Z. informal.* a variant spelling of **wrapped** (sense 2).

raptor (ˈræptə) *n.* another name for **bird of prey.** [C17: from Latin: plunderer, from *rapere* to take by force]

raptorial (ræpˈtɔːrɪəl) *adj. Zoology.* **1.** (of the feet of birds) adapted for seizing prey. **2.** (esp. of birds) feeding on prey; predatory. **3.** of or relating to birds of prey. [C19: from Latin *raptor* a robber, from *rapere* to snatch]

rapture (ˈræptʃə) *n.* **1.** the state of mind resulting from feelings of high emotion; joyous ecstasy. **2.** (*often pl.*) an expression of ecstatic joy. **3.** *Archaic.* the act of transporting a person from one sphere of existence to another, esp. from earth to heaven. ~*vb.* **4.** (*tr.*) *Archaic or literary.* to entrance; enrapture. [C17: from Medieval Latin *raptūra*, from Latin *raptus* RAPT]

rapturous (ˈræptʃərəs) *adj.* experiencing or manifesting ecstatic joy or delight. —ˈ**rapturously** *adv.* —ˈ**rapturousness** *n.*

RAR *abbrev. for* Royal Australian Regiment.

rara avis (ˈrɛərə ˈeɪvɪs) *n., pl.* **rarae aves** (ˈrɛəriː ˈeɪviːz). an unusual, uncommon, or exceptional person or thing. [Latin: rare bird]

rare[1] (rɛə) *adj.* **1.** not widely known; not frequently used or experienced; uncommon or unusual: *a rare word.* **2.** occurring seldom: *a rare appearance.* **3.** not widely distributed; not generally occurring: *a rare herb.* **4.** (of a gas, esp. the atmosphere at high altitudes) having a low density; thin; rarefied. **5.** uncommonly great; extreme: *kind to a rare degree.* **6.** exhibiting uncommon excellence; superlatively good or fine: *rare skill.* **7.** highly valued because of its uncommonness: *a rare prize.* [C14: from Latin *rārus* sparse] —ˈ**rareness** *n.*

rare[2] (rɛə) *adj.* (of meat, esp. beef) very lightly cooked. [Old English *hrēr*; perhaps related to *hreaw* RAW]

rarebit (ˈrɛəbɪt) *n.* another term for **Welsh rabbit.** [C18: by folk etymology from (WELSH) RABBIT; see RARE[2], BIT[1]]

rare earth *n.* **1.** any oxide of a lanthanide. **2.** Also called: **rare-earth element.** another name for **lanthanide.**

raree show (ˈrɛəriː) *n.* **1.** a street show or carnival. **2.** another name for **peepshow.** [C17: *raree* from RARE[1]]

rarefaction (ˌrɛərɪˈfækʃən) *or* **rarefication** (ˌrɛərɪfɪˈkeɪʃən) *n.* the act or process of making less dense or the state of being less dense. —ˌ**rareˈfactional,** ˌ**rarefiˈcational,** *or* ˌ**rareˈfactive** *adj.*

rarefied (ˈrɛərɪˌfaɪd) *adj.* **1.** exalted in nature or character; lofty: *a rarefied spiritual existence.* **2.** current within only a small group; esoteric or exclusive. **3.** (of a gas, esp. the atmosphere at high altitudes) having a low density; thin.

rarefy (ˈrɛərɪˌfaɪ) *vb.* **-fies, -fying, -fied.** to make or become rarer or less dense; thin out. [C14: from Old French *rarefier*, from Latin *rārēfacere*, from *rārus* RARE[1] + *facere* to make] —ˈ**rareˌfiable** *adj.* —ˈ**rareˌfier** *n.*

rare gas *n.* another name for **inert gas** (sense 1).

rarely (ˈrɛəlɪ) *adv.* **1.** hardly ever; seldom: *I'm rarely in town these days.* **2.** to an unusual degree; exceptionally. **3.** *Dialect.* uncommonly well; excellently: *he did rarely at market yesterday.*

rareripe (ˈrɛəˌraɪp) *U.S.* ~*adj.* **1.** ripening early. ~*n.* **2.** a fruit or vegetable that ripens early. [C18 *rare*, variant of RATHE + RIPE]

raring (ˈrɛərɪŋ) *adj.* ready; willing; enthusiastic (esp. in the phrase **raring to go**). [C20: from *rare*, variant of REAR[2]]

rarity (ˈrɛərɪtɪ) *n., pl.* **-ties. 1.** a rare person or thing, esp. something interesting or valued because it is uncommon. **2.** the state or quality of being rare.

RAS *abbrev. for:* **1.** Royal Agricultural Society. **2.** Royal Astronomical Society.

rasbora (ræzˈbɔːrə) *n.* any of the small cyprinid fishes constituting the genus *Rasbora* of tropical Asia and East Africa. Many species are brightly coloured and are popular aquarium fishes. [from New Latin, from an East Indian language]

RASC *abbrev. for* (the former) Royal Army Service Corps, now called Royal Corps of Transport.

rascal (ˈrɑːskᵊl) *n.* **1.** a disreputable person; villain. **2.** a mischievous or impish rogue. **3.** an affectionate or mildly reproving term for a child or old man: *you little rascal; the wicked old rascal kissed her.* **4.** *Obsolete.* a person of lowly birth. ~*adj.* **5.** (*prenominal*) *Obsolete.* **a.** belonging to the mob or rabble. **b.** dishonest; knavish. [C14: from Old French *rascaille* rabble, perhaps from Old Norman French *rasque* mud, filth]

rascality (rɑːˈskælɪtɪ) *n., pl.* **-ties.** mischievous, disreputable, or dishonest character, behaviour, or action.

rascally (ˈrɑːskəlɪ) *adj.* **1.** dishonest or mean; base. **2.** *Archaic.* (esp. of places) wretchedly unpleasant; miserable. ~*adv.* **3.** in a dishonest or mean fashion.

rase (reɪz) *vb.* a variant spelling of **raze.**

rash[1] (ræʃ) *adj.* **1.** acting without due consideration or thought; impetuous. **2.** characterized by or resulting from excessive haste or impetuosity: *a rash word.* [C14: from Old High German *rasc* hurried, clever; related to Old Norse *roskr* brave] —ˈ**rashly** *adv.* —ˈ**rashness** *n.*

rash[2] (ræʃ) *n.* **1.** *Pathol.* any skin eruption. **2.** a series of unpleasant and unexpected occurrences: *a rash of forest fires.* [C18: from Old French *rasche*, from *raschier* to scratch, from Latin *rādere* to scrape] —ˈ**rashˌlike** *adj.*

rasher (ˈræʃə) *n.* a thin slice of bacon or ham. [C16: of unknown origin]

rasorial (rəˈsɔːrɪəl) *adj.* (of birds such as domestic poultry) adapted for scratching the ground for food. [C19: from New Latin *Rasores* such birds, from Latin *rādere* to scrape]

rasp[1] (rɑːsp) *n.* **1.** a harsh grating noise. **2.** a coarse file with rows of raised teeth. ~*vb.* **3.** (*tr.*) to scrape or rub (something) roughly, esp. with a rasp; abrade. **4.** to utter with or make a harsh grating noise. **5.** to irritate (one's nerves or senses); grate (upon). [C16: from Old French *raspe*, of Germanic origin; compare Old High German *raspōn* to scrape] —ˈ**rasper** *n.* —ˈ**raspish** *adj.*

rasp[2] (rɑːsp) *n.* another name, now Scot. or informal, for **raspberry.**

raspatory (ˈrɑːspətərɪ, -trɪ) *n., pl.* **-ies.** a surgical instrument for abrading; surgeon's rasp. [C16: from Medieval Latin *raspatorium*]

raspberry (ˈrɑːzbərɪ, -brɪ) *n., pl.* **-ries. 1.** any of the prickly shrubs of the rosaceous genus *Rubus*, such as *R. strigosus* of E North America and *R. idaeus* of Europe, that have pinkish-white flowers and typically red berry-like fruits (drupelets). See also **bramble. 2. a.** the fruit of any such plant. **b.** (*as modifier*):

raspberry jelly. **3. black raspberry.** Popular name: **blackcap. a.** a related plant, *Rubus occidentalis,* of E North America, that has black berry-like fruits. **b.** the fruit of this plant. **4. a.** a dark purplish-red colour. **b.** (*as adj.*): *a raspberry dress.* **5.** a spluttering noise made with the tongue and lips to express contempt (esp. in the phrase **blow a raspberry**). [C17: from earlier *raspis* raspberry, of unknown origin + BERRY: C19 in sense 5, from rhyming slang *raspberry tart* fart]

rasping ('rɑːspɪŋ) *or* **raspy** *adj.* (esp. of a noise) harsh or grating; rough.

raspings ('rɑːspɪŋz) *pl. n.* browned breadcrumbs for coating fish and other foods before frying, baking, etc.

rasse ('ræsɪ, ræs) *n.* a small civet, *Viverricula indica,* of S and SE Asia. [C19: from Javanese *rase*]

Rasta ('ræstə) *n., adj.* short for **Rastafarian.**

Rastafarian (ˌræstəˈfɛərɪən) *n.* **1.** a member of an originally Jamaican religion that regards Ras Tafari (Haile Selassie (1892–1975), the former emperor of Ethiopia) as God. ~*adj.* **2.** of, characteristic of, or relating to the Rastafarians.

raster ('ræstə) *n.* a pattern of horizontal scanning lines traced by an electron beam, esp. on a television screen. [C20: via German from Latin: rake, from *rādere* to scrape]

rat (ræt) *n.* **1.** any of numerous long-tailed murine rodents, esp. of the genus *Rattus,* that are similar to but larger than mice and are now distributed all over the world. See also **brown rat, black rat. 2.** *Informal.* a person who deserts his friends or associates, esp. in time of trouble. **3.** *Informal.* a worker who works during a strike; blackleg; scab. **4.** *Slang, chiefly U.S.* an informer; stool pigeon. **5.** *Informal.* a despicable person. **6. smell a rat.** to detect something suspicious. ~*vb.* **rats, ratting, ratted. 7.** (*intr.;* usually foll. by *on*) *Informal.* **a.** to divulge secret information (about); betray the trust (of). **b.** to default (on); abandon: *he ratted on the project at the last minute.* **8.** to hunt and kill rats. ~See also **rats.** [Old English *ræt;* related to Old Saxon *ratta,* Old High German *rato*] —**'ratˌlike** *adj.*

rata ('rɑːtə) *n.* either of two New Zealand myrtaceous forest trees, *Metrosideros robusta* or *M. lucida,* having crimson flowers and hard wood. [C19: from Maori]

ratable *or* **rateable** ('reɪtəbᵊl) *adj.* **1.** able to be rated or evaluated. **2.** *Brit.* (of property) liable to payment of rates. —**ˌrataˈbility, ˌrateaˈbility** *or* **'ratableness, 'rateableness** *n.* —**'ratably** *or* **'rateably** *adv.*

ratable value *or* **rateable value** *n. Brit.* (formerly) a fixed value assigned to a property by a local authority, on the basis of which variable annual rates are charged.

ratafia (ˌrætəˈfɪə) *or* **ratafee** (ˌrætəˈfiː) *n.* **1.** any liqueur made from fruit or from brandy with added fruit. **2.** a flavouring essence made from almonds. **3.** *Chiefly Brit.* Also called: **ratafia biscuit.** a small macaroon flavoured with almonds. [C17: from West Indian Creole French]

ratal ('reɪtᵊl) *Brit.* ~*n.* **1.** the amount on which rates are assessed; ratable value. ~*adj.* **2.** of or relating to rates (local taxation). [C19: see RATE[1]]

ratan (ræˈtæn) *n.* a variant spelling of **rattan.**

ratatat-tat ('rætəˌtætˈtæt) *or* **ratatat** ('rætəˈtæt) *n.* the sound of knocking on a door.

ratatouille (ˌrætəˈtwiː) *n.* a vegetable casserole made of tomatoes, aubergines, peppers, etc., fried in oil and stewed slowly. [C19: from French, from *touiller* to stir, from Latin *tudiculāre,* from *tudes* hammer]

ratbag ('rætˌbæg) *n. Slang.* an eccentric, stupid, or unreliable person. [C20: from RAT + BAG]

ratbaggery ('rætˌbægərɪ) *n. Austral. slang.* nonsense, eccentricity.

ratbite fever *or* **disease** ('rætˌbaɪt) *n. Pathol.* an acute infectious febrile disease caused by the bite of a rat infected with either of two pathogenic bacteria (*Streptobacillus moniliformis* or *Spirillum minus*).

rat-catcher *n.* a person whose job is to destroy or drive away vermin, esp. rats.

ratchet ('rætʃɪt) *n.* **1.** a device in which a toothed rack or wheel is engaged by a pawl to permit motion in one direction only. **2.** the toothed rack or wheel forming part of such a device. [C17: from French *rochet,* from Old French *rocquet* blunt head of a lance, of Germanic origin: compare Old High German *rocko* distaff]

ratchet effect *n. Economics.* an effect that occurs when a price or wage increases as a result of temporary pressure but fails to fall back when the pressure is removed.

rate[1] (reɪt) *n.* **1.** a quantity or amount considered in relation to or measured against another quantity or amount: *a rate of 70 miles an hour.* **2. a.** a price or charge with reference to a standard or scale: *rate of interest; rate of discount.* **b.** (*as modifier*): *a rate card.* **3.** a charge made per unit for a commodity, service, etc. **4.** See **rates. 5.** the relative speed of progress or change of something variable; pace: *he works at a great rate; the rate of production has doubled.* **6. a.** relative quality; class or grade. **b.** (*in combination*): *first-rate ideas.* **7.** *Statistics.* a measure of the frequency of occurrence of a given event, such as births and deaths, usually expressed as the number of times the event occurs for every thousand of the total population considered. **8.** a wage calculated against a unit of time. **9.** the amount of gain or loss of a timepiece. **10. at any rate.** in any case; at all events; anyway. ~*vb.* (*mainly tr.*) **11.** (*also intr.*) to assign or receive a position on a scale of relative values; rank: *he is rated fifth in the world.* **12.** to estimate the value of; evaluate: *we rate your services highly.* **13.** to be worthy of; deserve: *this hotel does not rate four stars.* **14.** to consider; regard: *I rate him among my friends.* **15.** *Brit.* to assess the value of (property) for the purpose of local taxation. **16.** *Slang.* to think highly of: *the clients do not rate the new system.* [C15: from Old French, from Medieval Latin *rata,* from Latin *prō ratā parte* according to a fixed proportion, from *ratus* fixed, from *rērī* to think, decide]

rate[2] (reɪt) *vb.* (*tr.*) to scold or criticize severely; rebuke harshly. [C14: perhaps related to Swedish *rata* to chide]

rateable ('reɪtəbᵊl) *adj.* a variant spelling of **ratable.**

rate-cap ('reɪtˌkæp) *vb.* (*tr.*) **-caps, -capping, -capped.** (formerly in Britain) to impose on (a local authority) an upper limit on the level of the rate it may levy. —**'rate-ˌcapping** *n.*

rateen (ræˈtiːn) *n.* a variant spelling of **ratine.**

ratel ('reɪtᵊl) *n.* a musteline mammal, *Mellivora capensis,* inhabiting wooded regions of Africa and S Asia. It has a massive body, strong claws, and a thick coat that is paler on the back and it feeds on honey and small animals. Also called: **honey badger.** [C18: from Afrikaans]

rate of exchange *n.* See **exchange rate.**

rate of return *n. Finance.* the ratio of the annual income from an investment to the original investment, often expressed as a percentage.

ratepayer ('reɪtˌpeɪə) *n. Brit.* (formerly) a person who paid local rates, esp. a householder.

rates (reɪts) *pl. n. Brit.* a tax formerly levied on property by a local authority now replaced by the community charge.

ratfink ('rætˌfɪŋk) *n. Slang, chiefly U.S. and Canadian.* a contemptible or undesirable person. [C20: from RAT + FINK]

ratfish ('rætˌfɪʃ) *n., pl.* **-fish** *or* **-fishes. 1.** another name for **rabbitfish** (sense 1). **2.** a chimaera, *Hydrolagus colliei,* of the North Pacific Ocean, which has a long narrow tail.

rath (raθ) *n. Irish history.* a circular enclosure surrounded by an earthen wall: used as a dwelling and stronghold in former times. [C16: from Irish Gaelic]

ratha (rʌt) *n.* (in India) a four-wheeled carriage drawn by horses or bullocks; chariot. [Hindi]

rathe (reɪð) *or* **rath** (rɑːθ) *adj. Archaic or literary.* **1.** blossoming or ripening early in the season. **2.** eager or prompt. [Old English *hrathe;* related to Old High German *hrado,* Old Norse *hrathr*]

rather ('rɑːðə) *adv.* (*in senses 1-4, not used with a negative*) **1.** relatively or fairly; somewhat: *it's rather dull.* **2.** to a significant or noticeable extent; quite: *she's rather pretty.* **3.** to a limited extent or degree: *I rather thought that was the case.* **4.** with better or more just cause: *this text is rather to be deleted than rewritten.* **5.** more readily or willingly; sooner: *I would rather not see you tomorrow.* ~*sentence connector.* **6.** on the contrary: *it's not cold. Rather, it's very hot indeed.* ~*sentence substitute.* ('rɑːˈðɜː). **7.** an expression of strong affirmation, often in answer to a question: *Is it worth seeing? Rather!* [Old English *hrathor* comparative of *hrœth* READY, quick; related to Old Norse *hrathr*]

▷**Usage.** Both *would* and *had* are used with *rather* in sentences such as *I would rather* (or *had rather*) *go to the film than to the play. Had rather* is less common and now widely regarded as slightly old-fashioned.

rathouse ('ræthaus) *n. Austral. slang.* a mental hospital.

ratify ('rætɪˌfaɪ) *vb.* **-fies, -fying, -fied.** (*tr.*) to give formal approval or consent to. [C14: via Old French from Latin *ratus* fixed (see RATE[1]) + *facere* to make] —**'ratiˌfiable** *adj.* —**ˌratifiˈcation** *n.* —**'ratiˌfier** *n.*

ratine, rateen, ratteen (ræˈtiːn), *or* **ratiné** ('rætɪˌneɪ) *n.* a coarse loosely woven cloth. [C17: from French, from *ratine,* of obscure origin]

rating[1] ('reɪtɪŋ) *n.* **1.** a classification according to order or grade; ranking. **2.** (in certain navies) a sailor who holds neither commissioned nor warrant rank; an ordinary seaman. **3.** *Sailing.* a handicap assigned to a racing boat based on its dimensions, sail area, weight, draught, etc. **3.** the estimated financial or credit standing of a business enterprise or individual. **4.** *Radio, television, etc.* a figure based on statistical sampling indicating what proportion of the total listening and viewing audience tune in to a specific programme or network.

rating[2] ('reɪtɪŋ) *n.* a sharp scolding or rebuke.

ratio ('reɪʃɪˌəʊ) *n., pl.* **-tios. 1.** a measure of the relative size of two classes expressible as a proportion: *the ratio of boys to girls is 2 to 1.* **2.** *Maths.* a quotient of two numbers or quantities. See also **proportion** (sense 6). [C17: from Latin: a reckoning, from *rērī* to think; see REASON]

ratiocinate (ˌrætɪˈɒsɪˌneɪt) *vb.* (*intr.*) to think or argue logically and methodically; reason. [C17: from Latin *ratiōcinārī* to calculate, from *ratiō* REASON] —**ˌratiˌociˈnation** *n.* —**ˌratiˈocinative** *adj.* —**ˌratiˈociˌnator** *n.*

ration ('ræʃən) *n.* **1. a.** a fixed allowance of food, provisions, etc., esp. a statutory one for civilians in time of scarcity or soldiers in time of war: *a tea ration.* **b.** (*as modifier*): *a ration book.* **2.** a sufficient or adequate amount: *you've had your ration of television for today.* ~*vb.* (*tr.*) **3.** (often foll. by *out*) to distribute (provisions), esp. to an army. **4.** to restrict the distribution or consumption of (a commodity) by (people): *the government has rationed sugar; sugar is short, so I'll have to ration you.* ~See also **rations.** [C18: via French from Latin *ratiō* calculation; see REASON]

rational ('ræʃənᵊl) *adj.* **1.** using reason or logic in thinking out a problem. **2.** in accordance with the principles of logic or reason; reasonable. **3.** of sound mind; sane: *the patient seemed quite rational.* **4.** endowed with the capacity to reason; capable of logical thought: *man is a rational being.* **5.** *Maths.* **a.** expressible as a ratio of two integers: *a rational number.* **b.** (of an expression, equation, etc.) containing no variable either in irreducible radical form or raised to a fractional power. ~*n.* **6.** *Maths.* a rational number. [C14: from Latin *ratiōnālis,* from *ratiō* REASON] —'**rationally** *adv.* —'**rationalness** *n.*

rationale (ˌræʃə'nɑːl) *n.* a reasoned exposition, esp. one defining the fundamental reasons for a course of action, belief, etc. [C17: from New Latin, from Latin *ratiōnālis*]

rationalism ('ræʃənəˌlɪzəm) *n.* **1.** reliance on reason rather than intuition to justify one's beliefs or actions. **2.** *Philosophy.* **a.** the doctrine that knowledge about reality can be obtained by reason alone without recourse to experience. **b.** the doctrine that human knowledge can all be encompassed within a single, usually deductive, system. **c.** the school of philosophy, originally Cartesian, which held both the above doctrines. **3.** the belief that knowledge and truth are ascertained by rational thought and not by divine or supernatural revelation. —'**rationalist** *n.* —ˌ**rational'istic** *adj.* —ˌ**rational'istically** *adv.*

rationality (ˌræʃə'nælɪtɪ) *n., pl.* **-ties. 1.** the state or quality of being rational or logical. **2.** the possession or utilization of reason or logic. **3.** a reasonable or logical opinion. **4.** *Economics.* the assumption that an individual will compare all possible combinations of goods and their prices when making purchases.

rationalize *or* **rationalise** ('ræʃənəˌlaɪz) *vb.* **1.** to justify (one's actions, esp. discreditable actions, or beliefs) with plausible reasons, esp. after the event. **2.** *Psychol.* to indulge, often unchallenged, in excuses for or explanations of (behaviour about which one feels uncomfortable or guilty). **3.** to apply logic or reason to (something). **4.** (*tr.*) to eliminate unnecessary equipment, personnel, or processes from (a group of businesses, factory, etc.), in order to make it more efficient. **5.** (*tr.*) *Maths.* to eliminate one or more radicals without changing the value of (an expression) or the roots of (an equation). —ˌ**rationali'zation** *or* ˌ**rationali'sation** *n.* —'**rationalˌizer** *or* '**rationalˌiser** *n.*

rational number *n.* any real number of the form a/b, where a and b are integers and b is not zero, as 7 or 7/3.

rations ('ræʃənz) *pl. n.* (*sometimes sing.*) a fixed daily allowance of food, esp. to military personnel or when supplies are limited. See also **iron rations.**

ratio scale *n. Statistics.* a scale of measurement of data which permits the comparison of differences of values; a scale having a fixed zero value. The distances travelled by a projectile, for instance, are measured on a ratio scale since it makes sense to talk of one projectile travelling twice as far as another. Compare **ordinal scale, interval scale, nominal scale.**

ratite ('rætaɪt) *adj.* **1.** (of flightless birds) having a breastbone that lacks a keel for the attachment of flight muscles. **2.** of or denoting the flightless birds, formerly classified as a group (the *Ratitae*), that have a flat breastbone, feathers lacking vanes, and reduced wings. ~*n.* **3.** a bird, such as an ostrich, kiwi, or rhea, that belongs to this group; a flightless bird. [C19: from Latin *ratis* raft]

rat kangaroo *n.* any of several ratlike kangaroos of the genera *Bettongia, Potorous, Aepyprymnus,* etc., that occur in Australia and Tasmania.

ratline *or* **ratlin** ('rætlɪn) *n. Nautical.* any of a series of light lines tied across the shrouds of a sailing vessel for climbing aloft. [C15: of unknown origin]

RATO ('reɪtəʊ) *n. acronym for* rocket-assisted takeoff.

ratoon *or* **rattoon** (ræ'tuːn) *n.* **1.** a new shoot that grows from near the root or crown of crop plants, esp. the sugar cane, after the old growth has been cut back. ~*vb.* **2.** to propagate or cause to propagate by such a growth. [C18: from Spanish *retoño* young shoot, from RE- + *otoñar* to sprout in autumn, from *otoño* AUTUMN]

rat race *n.* a continual routine of hectic competitive activity: *working in the City is a real rat race.*

rats (ræts) *interj.* **1.** an exclamation of rejection or disdain. ~*adj.* **2.** *Austral. slang.* deranged; insane.

ratsbane ('rætsˌbeɪn) *n.* rat poison, esp. arsenic oxide.

Ratskeller *German.* ('raːtskɛlər) *n.* **1.** the cellar of a town hall, esp. one used as a beer hall or restaurant. **2.** any similar establishment, esp. in the U.S. [German: from *Rat*(*haus*) town hall + *Keller* cellar]

rat snake *n.* any of various nonvenomous rodent-eating colubrid snakes, such as *Elaphe obsoleta* of North America and *Ptyas mucosus* of Asia.

rat-tail *n.* **1.** another name for **grenadier** (the fish). **2. a.** a horse's tail that has no hairs. **b.** a horse having such a tail. **3.** a style of spoon in which the line of the handle is prolonged in a tapering moulding along the back of the bowl. **4.** a kind of woodworking or metalworking file.

rattan *or* **ratan** (ræ'tæn) *n.* **1.** any of the climbing palms of the genus *Calamus* and related genera, having tough stems used for wickerwork and canes. **2.** the stems of such plants collectively. **3.** a stick made from one of these stems. [C17: from Malay *rōtan*]

rat-tat ('rætˌtæt) *n.* a variant of **ratatat-tat.**

ratteen (ræ'tiːn) *n.* a variant spelling of **ratine.**

ratter ('rætə) *n.* **1.** a dog or cat that catches and kills rats. **2.** another word for **rat** (senses 3, 4).

rattish ('rætɪʃ) *adj.* of, resembling, or infested with rats.

rattle[1] ('rætᵊl) *vb.* **1.** to make or cause to make a rapid succession of short sharp sounds, as of loose pellets colliding when shaken in a container. **2.** to shake or cause to shake with such a sound: *the explosion rattled the windows.* **3.** to send, move, drive, etc., with such a sound: *the car rattled along the country road.* **4.** (*intr.;* foll. by *on*) to chatter idly; talk, esp. at length: *he rattled on about his work.* **5.** (*tr.,* foll. by *off, out,* etc.) to recite perfunctorily or rapidly. **6.** (*tr.*) *Informal.* to disconcert; make frightened or anxious. ~*n.* **7.** a rapid succession of short sharp sounds. **8.** a baby's toy filled with small pellets that rattle when shaken. **9.** a series of loosely connected horny segments on the tail of a rattlesnake, vibrated to produce a rattling sound. **10.** any of various European scrophulariaceous plants having a capsule in which the seeds rattle, such as *Pedicularis palustris* (**red rattle**) and *Rhinanthus minor* (**yellow rattle**). **11.** idle chatter. **12.** an idle chatterer. **13.** *Med.* another name for **rale.** [C14: from Middle Dutch *ratelen;* related to Middle High German *razzen,* of imitative origin]

rattle[2] ('rætᵊl) *vb.* (*tr.;* often foll. by *down*) to fit (a vessel or its rigging) with ratlines. [C18: back formation from *rattling,* variant of RATLINE]

rattlebox ('rætᵊlˌbɒks) *n.* any of various tropical and subtropical leguminous plants that have inflated pods within which the seeds rattle.

rattlebrain ('rætᵊlˌbreɪn), **rattlehead,** *or* **rattlepate** *n. Slang.* a light-minded person, full of idle talk.

rattler ('rætlə) *n.* **1.** something that rattles. **2.** *Chiefly U.S. and Canadian.* an informal name for **rattlesnake.**

rattlesnake ('rætᵊlˌsneɪk) *n.* any of the venomous New World snakes constituting the genera *Crotalus* and *Sistrurus,* such as *C. horridus* (**black** or **timber rattlesnake**): family *Crotalidae* (pit vipers). They have a series of loose horny segments on the tail that are vibrated to produce a buzzing or whirring sound.

rattlesnake plantain *n.* any of various small temperate and tropical orchids of the genus *Goodyera,* having mottled or striped leaves and spikes of yellowish-white flowers.

rattletrap ('rætᵊlˌtræp) *n. Informal.* a broken-down old vehicle, esp. an old car.

rattling ('rætlɪŋ) *adv. Informal.* (intensifier qualifying something good, fine, pleasant, etc.): *a rattling good lunch.*

rattly ('rætlɪ) *adj.* **-tlier, -tliest.** having a rattle; rattling.

rattoon (ræ'tuːn) *n., vb.* a variant spelling of **ratoon.**

rat-trap *n.* **1.** a device for catching rats. **2.** *Informal.* a type of bicycle pedal having serrated steel foot pads and a toe clip.

ratty ('rætɪ) *adj.* **-tier, -tiest. 1.** *Brit. and N.Z. informal.* irritable; annoyed. **2.** *Informal.* (of the hair) straggly, unkempt, or greasy. **3.** *U.S. and Canadian slang.* shabby; dilapidated. **4.** *Austral. slang.* **a.** angry. **b.** mad. **5.** of, like, or full of rats. —'**rattily** *adv.* —'**rattiness** *n.*

raucous ('rɔːkəs) *adj.* (of voices, cries, etc.) harshly or hoarsely loud. [C18: from Latin *raucus* hoarse] —'**raucously** *adv.* —'**raucousness** *or* (*less commonly*) **raucity** ('rɔːsɪtɪ) *n.*

raunch (rɔːntʃ) *n. Slang.* **1.** lack of polish or refinement; crudeness. **2.** *Chiefly U.S.* slovenliness or untidiness.

raunchy ('rɔːntʃɪ) *adj.* **-chier, -chiest.** *Slang.* **1. a.** lecherous, vulgar, or smutty. **b.** openly sexual; lusty; earthy. **2.** *Chiefly U.S.* slovenly or untidy. [C20: of unknown origin] —'**raunchily** *adj.* —'**raunchiness** *n.*

rauriki ('raʊrəkiː) *n., pl.* **-kis.** *N.Z.* another name for **sow thistle.** [Maori]

rauwolfia (rɔː'wʊlfɪə, raʊ-) *n.* **1.** any tropical tree or shrub of the apocynaceous genus *Rauwolfia,* esp. *R. serpentina* of SE Asia. **2.** the powdered root of *R. serpentina:* a source of various drugs, esp. reserpine. [C19: New Latin, named after Leonhard *Rauwolf* (died 1596), German botanist]

Rav (ræv; Hebrew rav) *n. Judaism.* **1.** a rabbi who is a person's religious mentor or teacher, or one to whom questions are addressed for authoritative decision. **2.** the title preferred by many orthodox rabbis to distinguish themselves from the clergy of other brands of Judaism.

ravage ('rævɪdʒ) *vb.* **1.** to cause extensive damage to. ~*n.* **2.** (*often pl.*) destructive action: *the ravages of time.* [C17: from French, from Old French *ravir* to snatch away, RAVISH] —'**ravagement** *n.* —'**ravager** *n.*

RAVC *abbrev. for* Royal Army Veterinary Corps.

rave[1] (reɪv) *vb.* **1.** to utter (something) in a wild or incoherent manner, as when mad or delirious. **2.** (*intr.*) to speak in an angry uncontrolled manner. **3.** (*intr.*) (of the sea, wind, etc.) to rage or roar. **4.** (*intr.;* foll. by *over* or *about*) *Informal.* to write or speak (about) with great enthusiasm. **5.** (*intr.*) *Brit. slang.* to enjoy oneself wildly or uninhibitedly. ~*n.* **6.** *Informal.* **a.** enthusiastic or extravagant praise. **b.** (*as modifier*): *a rave review.* **7.** *Brit. slang.* **a.** Also called: **rave-up.** a party. **b.** another name for **Acid-House party. 8.** *Brit. slang.* a fad or fashion: *the latest rave.* [C14 *raven,* apparently from Old French *resver* to wander]

rave[2] (reɪv) *n.* a vertical sidepiece on a wagon. [C16: modification of dialect *rathe,* of uncertain origin]

ravel ('rævᵊl) *vb.* **-els, -elling, -elled** *or U.S.* **-els, -eling, -eled. 1.** to tangle (threads, fibres, etc.) or (of threads, fibres, etc.) to become entangled. **2.** (often foll. by *out*) to tease or draw out (the fibres of a fabric or garment) or (of a garment or fabric) to fray out in loose ends; unravel. **3.** (*tr.;* usually foll. by *out*) to disentangle or resolve: *to ravel out a complicated story.* **4.** to break up (a road surface) in patches or (of a road surface) to begin to break up; fret; scab. **5.** *Archaic.* to make or become confused or complicated. ~*n.* **6.** a tangle or complication. [C16: from Middle Dutch *ravelen*] —**'raveller** *n.* —**'ravelly** *adj.*

ravelin ('rævlɪn) *n. Fortifications.* an outwork having two embankments at a salient angle. [C16: from Italian *ravellino* a little bank, from *riva* bank, from Latin *rīpa*]

ravelment ('rævəlmənt) *n. Rare.* a ravel or tangle.

raven[1] ('reɪvᵊn) *n.* **1.** a large passerine bird, *Corvus corax,* having a large straight bill, long wedge-shaped tail, and black plumage: family *Corvidae* (crows). It has a hoarse croaking cry. **2. a.** a shiny black colour. **b.** (*as adj.*): *raven hair.* [Old English *hrǣfn;* related to Old High German *hraban,* Old Norse *hrafn*]

raven[2] ('rævᵊn) *vb.* **1.** to seize or seek (plunder, prey, etc.). **2.** to eat (something) voraciously or greedily; be ravenous in eating. [C15: from Old French *raviner* to attack impetuously; see RAVENOUS] —**'ravener** *n.*

ravening ('rævənɪŋ) *adj.* (esp. of animals such as wolves) voracious; predatory. —**'raveningly** *adv.*

ravenous ('rævənəs) *adj.* **1.** famished; starving. **2.** rapacious; voracious. [C16: from Old French *ravineux,* from Latin *rapīna* plunder, from *rapere* to seize] —**'ravenously** *adv.* —**'ravenousness** *n.*

raver ('reɪvə) *n. Brit. slang.* a person who leads a wild or uninhibited social life.

ravin ('rævɪn) *vb.* an archaic spelling of **raven**[2].

ravine (rə'viːn) *n.* a deep narrow steep-sided valley, esp. one formed by the action of running water. [C15: from Old French: torrent, from Latin *rapīna* robbery, influenced by Latin *rapidus* RAPID, both from *rapere* to snatch]

raving ('reɪvɪŋ) *adj.* **1. a.** delirious; frenzied. **b.** (*as adv.*): *raving mad.* **2.** *Informal.* (intensifier): *a raving beauty.* ~*n.* **3.** (*usually pl.*) frenzied, irrational, or wildly extravagant talk or utterances. —**'ravingly** *adv.*

ravioli (ˌrævɪ'əʊlɪ) *n.* small squares of pasta containing a savoury mixture of meat, cheese, etc. [C19: from Italian dialect, literally: little turnips, from Italian *rava* turnip, from Latin *rāpa*]

ravish ('rævɪʃ) *vb.* (*tr.*) **1.** (*often passive*) to give great delight to; enrapture. **2.** to rape. **3.** *Archaic.* to carry off by force. [C13: from Old French *ravir,* from Latin *rapere* to seize] —**'ravisher** *n.* —**'ravishment** *n.*

ravishing ('rævɪʃɪŋ) *adj.* delightful; lovely; entrancing. —**'ravishingly** *adv.*

raw (rɔː) *adj.* **1.** (of food) not cooked: *raw onion.* **2.** (*prenominal*) in an unfinished, natural, or unrefined state; not treated by manufacturing or other processes: *raw materials for making steel; raw brick.* **3.** (of the skin, a wound, etc.) having the surface exposed or abraded, esp. painfully. **4.** ignorant, inexperienced, or immature: *a raw recruit.* **5.** (*prenominal*) not selected or modified: *raw statistics.* **6.** frank or realistic: *a raw picture of the breakdown of a marriage.* **7.** (of spirits) undiluted. **8.** *Chiefly U.S.* coarse, vulgar, or obscene. **9.** *Chiefly U.S.* recently done; fresh: *raw paintwork.* **10.** (of the weather) harshly cold and damp. **11.** *Informal.* unfair; unjust (esp. in the phrase **a raw deal**). ~*n.* **12. the raw.** *Brit. informal.* a sensitive point: *his criticism touched me on the raw.* **13. in the raw. a.** *Informal.* without clothes; naked. **b.** in a natural or unmodified state: *life in the raw.* [Old English *hreaw;* related to Old High German *hrao,* Old Norse *hrār* raw, Latin *cruor* thick blood, Greek *kreas* meat] —**'rawish** *adj.* —**'rawly** *adv.* —**'rawness** *n.*

rawaru ('rɑːwɑːruː) *n. N.Z.* a Maori name for **blue cod.**

rawboned ('rɔː'bəʊnd) *adj.* having a lean bony physique.

rawhide ('rɔːˌhaɪd) *n.* **1.** untanned hide. **2.** a whip or rope made of strips cut from such a hide.

rawhide hammer *n.* a hammer, used to avoid damaging a surface, having a head consisting of a metal tube from each end of which a tight roll of hide protrudes.

rawinsonde ('reɪwɪnˌsɒnd) *n.* a hydrogen balloon carrying meteorological instruments and a radar target, enabling the velocity of winds in the atmosphere to be measured. [C20: blend of *radar* + *wind* + *radiosonde*]

Rawlplug ('rɔːlplʌg) *n. Trademark.* a short fibre or plastic tube used to provide a fixing in a wall for a screw.

raw material *n.* **1.** material on which a particular manufacturing process is carried out. **2.** a person or thing regarded as suitable for some particular purpose: *raw material for the army.*

raw milk *n.* unpasteurized milk.

raw silk *n.* **1.** untreated silk fibres reeled from the cocoon. **2.** fabric woven from such fibres.

rax (ræks) *Scot.* ~*vb.* **1.** (*tr.*) to stretch or extend. **2.** (*intr.*) to reach out. **3.** (*tr.*) to pass or give (something to a person) with the outstretched hand; reach: *rax me the salt.* **4.** (*tr.*) to strain or sprain. ~*n.* **5.** the act of stretching or straining. [Old English *raxan*]

ray[1] (reɪ) *n.* **1.** a narrow beam of light; gleam. **2.** a slight indication, esp. of something anticipated or hoped for: *a ray of solace.* **3.** *Maths.* a straight line extending from a point. **4.** a thin beam of electromagnetic radiation or particles. **5.** any of the bony or cartilaginous spines of the fin of a fish that form the support for the soft part of the fin. **6.** any of the arms or branches of a starfish or other radiate animal. **7.** *Astronomy.* one of a number of bright visible streaks of uncertain origin that radiate from certain lunar craters and extend for hundreds of kilometres, crossing mountain ranges and smaller craters. **8.** *Botany.* any strand of tissue that runs radially through the vascular tissue of some higher plants. See **medullary ray.** ~*vb.* **9.** (of an object) to emit (light) in rays or (of light) to issue in the form of rays. **10.** (*intr.*) (of lines, etc.) to extend in rays or on radiating paths. **11.** (*tr.*) to adorn (an ornament, etc.) with rays or radiating lines. [C14: from Old French *rai,* from Latin *radius* spoke, RADIUS]

ray[2] (reɪ) *n.* any of various marine selachian fishes typically having a flattened body, greatly enlarged winglike pectoral fins, gills on the undersurface of the fins, and a long whiplike tail. They constitute the orders *Torpediniformes* (**electric rays**) and *Rajiformes.* [C14: from Old French *raie,* from Latin *raia*]

ray[3] (reɪ) *n. Music.* (in tonic sol-fa) the second degree of any major scale; supertonic. [C14: see GAMUT]

rayah ('rɑːjə, 'raɪə) *n.* (formerly) a non-Muslim subject of the Ottoman Empire. Also (less common) **raia.** [C19: from Turkish *raiyye,* from Arabic *ra'iyah* herd, flock]

Raybans ('reɪˌbænz) *pl. n. Trademark.* a brand of sunglasses.

ray flower *or* **floret** *n.* any of the small strap-shaped flowers in the flower head of certain composite plants, such as the daisy. Compare **disc flower.**

ray gun *n.* (in science fiction) a gun that emits rays to paralyse, stun, or destroy.

Rayleigh disc ('reɪlɪ) *n.* a small light disc suspended in the path of a sound wave, used to measure the intensity of the sound by analysing the resulting deflection of the disc. [named after Lord *Rayleigh* (1842–1919), British physicist]

Rayleigh scattering *n.* a process in which electromagnetic radiation is elastically deflected by particles of matter, without a change of frequency but with a phase change.

rayless ('reɪlɪs) *adj.* **1.** dark; gloomy. **2.** lacking rays: *a rayless flower.* —**'raylessly** *adv.* —**'raylessness** *n.*

raylet ('reɪlɪt) *n.* a small ray.

Raynaud's disease ('reɪnəʊz) *n.* a disease, mainly affecting women, in which spasms in the blood vessels of the fingers or toes restrict blood flow to the affected part, which becomes pale, numb, and sometimes painful. Often shortened to **Raynaud's.** [named after Maurice *Raynaud* (1834–81), French physician who first described it]

rayon ('reɪɒn) *n.* **1.** any of a number of textile fibres made from wood pulp or other forms of cellulose. **2.** any fabric made from such a fibre. **3.** (*modifier*) consisting of or involving rayon: *a rayon shirt.* [C20: from French, from Old French *rai* RAY[1]]

raze *or* **rase** (reɪz) *vb.* (*tr.*) **1.** to demolish (a town, buildings, etc.) completely; level (esp. in the phrase **raze to the ground**). **2.** to delete; erase. **3.** *Archaic.* to graze. [C16: from Old French *raser* from Latin *rādere* to scrape] —**'razer** *or* **'raser** *n.*

razee (ræ'ziː) *History.* ~*n., pl.* **razees. 1.** a sailing ship that has had its upper deck or decks removed. ~*vb.* **razees, razeeing, razeed.** (*tr.*) **2.** to remove the upper deck or decks of (a sailing ship). [C19: from French *rasée* shaved close, from *raser* to RAZE]

razoo (rə'zuː) *n. Austral. and N.Z. informal.* an imaginary coin: *not a brass razoo; they took every last razoo.* [C20: of uncertain origin]

razor ('reɪzə) *n.* **1.** a sharp implement used esp. by men for shaving the face. **2. on a razor's edge** *or* **razor-edge.** in an acute dilemma. ~*vb.* **3.** (*tr.*) to cut or shave with a razor. [C13: from Old French *raseor,* from *raser* to shave; see RAZE]

razorback ('reɪzəˌbæk) *n.* **1.** Also called: **finback.** another name for the **common rorqual** (see **rorqual**). **2.** a semiwild or wild pig of the southeastern U.S., having a narrow body, long legs, and a ridged back.

razorbill ('reɪzəˌbɪl) *or* **razor-billed auk** *n.* a common auk, *Alca torda,* of the North Atlantic, having a thick laterally compressed bill with white markings.

razor blade *n.* a small rectangular piece of metal sharpened on one or both long edges for use in a razor for shaving.

razor-cut *vb.* **-cuts, -cutting, -cut. 1.** (*tr.*) to trim or shape (the hair) with a razor. ~*n.* **razor cut. 2.** a fluffy hairstyle, usually tapering at the neck, trimmed by a razor.

razor-shell *n.* any of various sand-burrowing bivalve molluscs of the genera *Ensis* and *Solen,* which have a long tubular shell. U.S. name: **razor clam.**

razor wire *n.* strong wire with pieces of sharp metal set across it at close intervals, used to make fences or barriers.

razz (ræz) *U.S. and Canadian slang.* ~*vb.* **1.** (*tr.*) to make fun of; deride. ~*n.* **2.** short for **raspberry** (sense 5).

razzia ('ræzɪə) *n., pl.* **-zias.** *History.* a raid for plunder or slaves, esp. one carried out by Moors in North Africa. [C19: from French, from Arabic *ghaziah* war]

razzle-dazzle ('ræzᵊl'dæzᵊl) *or* **razzmatazz** ('ræzmə'tæz) *n. Slang.* **1.** noisy or showy fuss or activity. **2.** a spree or frolic

(esp. in the phrase **on the razzle-dazzle**). [C19: rhyming compound based on DAZZLE]
Rb *the chemical symbol for* rubidium.
RB *international car registration for* (Republic of) Botswana.
RB- *abbrev. for* reconnaissance bomber: *RB-57.*
RBE *abbrev. for* relative biological effectiveness.
rc *abbrev. for* reinforced concrete.
RC *abbrev. for:* **1.** Red Cross. **2.** Reserve Corps. **3.** Also: **R.C.** Roman Catholic. ~**4.** *international car registration for* (Nationalist Republic of) China.
RCA *abbrev. for:* **1.** (formerly) Radio Corporation of America. **2.** Royal Canadian Academy. **3.** Royal College of Art. ~**4.** *international car registration for* Central African Republic.
RCAF *abbrev. for* Royal Canadian Air Force.
RCB(CG) *international car registration for* (Republic of the) Congo.
rcd *abbrev. for* received.
RCH *international car registration for* Republic of Chile.
RCM *abbrev. for* Royal College of Music.
RCMP *abbrev. for* Royal Canadian Mounted Police.
RCN *abbrev. for:* **1.** Royal Canadian Navy. **2.** Royal College of Nursing.
RCO *abbrev. for* Royal College of Organists.
r-colour *or* **r-colouring** *n. Phonetics.* an (r) quality imparted to certain vowels, usually by retroflexion. —**'r-ˌcoloured** *adj.*
RCP *abbrev. for* Royal College of Physicians.
rcpt *abbrev. for* receipt.
RCS *abbrev. for:* **1.** Royal College of Science. **2.** Royal College of Surgeons. **3.** Royal Corps of Signals.
rct *Military. abbrev. for* recruit.
RCT *abbrev. for* Royal Corps of Transport.
RCVS *abbrev. for* Royal College of Veterinary Surgeons.
rd *abbrev. for:* **1.** rendered. **2.** rod (unit of length). **3.** road. **4.** round. **5.** *Physics.* rutherford.
rd *or* **RD** (on a cheque) *abbrev. for* refer to drawer.
Rd *abbrev. for* Road.
RD (in New Zealand) *abbrev. for* Rural Delivery.
RDC (in Britain, formerly) *abbrev. for* Rural District Council.
RDS *abbrev. for* radio data system: a system in which digital signals are transmitted with normal radio programme to effect automatic tuning of receivers and other functions.
RDX *abbrev. for* Research Department Explosive; another name for **cyclonite.**
re[1] (reɪ, riː) *n. Music.* a variant spelling of **ray**[3].
re[2] (riː) *prep.* with reference to. [C18: from Latin *rē*, ablative case of *rēs* thing]
▷**Usage.** *Re,* in contexts such as *re your letter, your remarks have been noted* or *he spoke to me re your complaint,* is common in business or official correspondence. In general English *with reference to* is preferable in the former case and *about* or *concerning* in the latter. Even in business correspondence, the use of *re* is often restricted to the letter heading.
Re[1] *the chemical symbol for* rhenium.
Re[2] *or* **re** *symbol for* rupee.
RE *abbrev. for:* **1.** Reformed Episcopal. **2.** Religious Education. **3.** Right Excellent. **4.** Royal Engineers.
re- *prefix.* **1.** indicating return to a previous condition, restoration, withdrawal, etc.: *rebuild; renew; retrace; reunite.* **2.** indicating repetition of an action: *recopy; remarry.* [from Latin]
▷**Usage.** Verbs beginning with *re-* indicate repetition or restoration. It is unnecessary to add an adverb such as *back* or *again: This must not occur again* (not *recur again*); *we recounted the votes* (not *recounted the votes again,* which implies that the votes were counted three times, not twice).
're *contraction of* are: *we're, you're, they're.*
reach (riːtʃ) *vb.* **1.** (*tr.*) to arrive at or get to (a place, person, etc.) in the course of movement or action: *to reach the office.* **2.** to extend as far as (a point or place): *to reach the ceiling; can you reach?* **3.** (*tr.*) to come to (a certain condition, stage, or situation): *to reach the point of starvation.* **4.** (*intr.*) to extend in influence or operation: *the Roman conquest reached throughout England.* **5.** (*tr.*) *Informal.* to pass or give (something to a person) with the outstretched hand: *to reach someone a book.* **6.** (*intr.*; foll. by *out, for,* or *after*) to make a movement (towards), as if to grasp or touch: *to reach for something on a shelf.* **7.** (*intr.*; foll. by *for* or *after*) to strive or yearn: *to reach for the impossible.* **8.** (*tr.*) to make contact or communication with (someone): *we tried to reach him all day.* **9.** (*tr.*) to strike, esp. in fencing or boxing. **10.** (*tr.*) to amount to (a certain sum): *to reach the five million mark.* **11.** (*intr.*) *Nautical.* to sail on a tack with the wind on or near abeam. ~*n.* **12.** the act of reaching. **13.** the extent or distance of reaching: *within reach of safety; beyond her reach.* **14.** the range of influence, power, jurisdiction, etc. **15.** an open stretch of water, esp. on a river. **16.** *Nautical.* the direction or distance sailed by a vessel on one tack. **17.** a bar on the rear axle of a vehicle connecting it with some part at the front end. **18.** *Television, radio.* the percentage of the population selecting a broadcast programme or channel for more than a specified time during a day or week. **19.** *Advertising.* the proportion of a market that an advertiser hopes to reach at least once in a campaign. [Old English *rǣcan;* related to Old Frisian *rēka,* Old High German *reihheu*] —**'reachable** *adj.* —**'reacher** *n.*
reach-me-down *n. Informal.* **1. a.** (*often pl.*) a garment that is cheaply ready-made or second-hand. **b.** (*as modifier*): *reach-me-down finery.* **2.** (*pl.*) trousers. **3.** (*modifier*) not original; derivative; stale: *a stock of reach-me-down ideas.*
react (rɪˈækt) *vb.* **1.** (*intr.*; foll. by *to, upon,* etc.) (of a person or thing) to act in response to another person, a stimulus, etc. or (of two people or things) to act together in a certain way. **2.** (*intr.*; foll. by *against*) to act in an opposing or contrary manner. **3.** (*intr.*) *Physics.* to exert an equal force in the opposite direction to an acting force. **4.** *Chem.* to undergo or cause to undergo a chemical reaction. [C17: from Late Latin *reagere,* from RE- + Latin *agere* to drive, do]
re-act (riːˈækt) *vb.* (*tr.*) to act or perform again.
reactance (rɪˈæktəns) *n.* **1.** the opposition to the flow of alternating current by the capacitance or inductance of an electrical circuit; the imaginary part of the impedance Z, $Z = R + iX$, where R is the resistance, $i = \sqrt{-1}$, and X is the reactance. It is expressed in ohms. Compare **resistance** (sense 3). **2.** the opposition to the flow of an acoustic or mechanical vibration, usually due to inertia or stiffness. It is the magnitude of the imaginary part of the acoustic or mechanical impedance.
reactant (rɪˈæktənt) *n.* a substance that participates in a chemical reaction, esp. a substance that is present at the start of the reaction. Compare **product** (sense 4).
reaction (rɪˈækʃən) *n.* **1.** a response to some foregoing action or stimulus. **2.** the reciprocal action of two things acting together. **3.** opposition to change, esp. political change, or a desire to return to a former condition or system. **4.** a response indicating a person's feelings or emotional attitude. **5.** *Med.* **a.** any effect produced by the action of a drug, esp. an adverse effect. Compare **side effect. b.** any effect produced by a substance (allergen) to which a person is allergic. **6.** the simultaneous equal and opposite force that acts on a body whenever it exerts a force on another body. **7.** short for **chemical reaction** or **nuclear reaction. 8.** *Stock Exchange.* a sharp fall in price interrupting a general rise. —**re'actional** *adj.*
reactionary (rɪˈækʃənərɪ, -ʃənrɪ) *or* **reactionist** *adj.* **1.** of, relating to, or characterized by reaction, esp. against radical political or social change. ~*n., pl.* **-aries** *or* **-ists. 2.** a person opposed to radical change. —**re'actionism** *n.*
reaction chamber *n. Engineering.* the chamber in a rocket engine in which the reaction or combustion of fuel occurs.
reaction engine *or* **motor** *n.* an engine, such as a jet or rocket engine, that ejects gas at high velocity and develops its thrust from the ensuing reaction.
reaction formation *n. Psychoanal.* a defence mechanism by which a person at a conscious level condemns a repressed wish: thus, a latent homosexual may denounce homosexuality.
reaction time *n. Physiol.* another name for **latent time.**
reaction turbine *n.* a turbine in which the working fluid is accelerated by expansion in both the static nozzles and the rotor blades. Torque is produced by the momentum changes in the rotor and by reaction from fluid accelerating out of the rotor. Compare **impulse turbine.**
reactivate (rɪˈæktɪˌveɪt) *vb.* (*tr.*) to make (something) active or functional again. —**reˌacti'vation** *n.*
reactive (rɪˈæktɪv) *adj.* **1.** readily partaking in chemical reactions: *sodium is a reactive metal; free radicals are very reactive.* **2.** of, concerned with, or having a reactance. **3.** responsive to stimulus. **4.** (of mental illnesses) precipitated by an external cause: *reactive depression.* —**re'actively** *adv.* —**reactivity** (ˌriːækˈtɪvɪtɪ) *or* **re'activeness** *n.*
reactor (rɪˈæktə) *n.* **1.** *Chem.* a substance, such as a reagent, that undergoes a reaction. **2.** short for **nuclear reactor. 3.** a vessel, esp. one in industrial use, in which a chemical reaction takes place. **4.** a coil of low resistance and high inductance that introduces reactance into a circuit. **5.** *Med.* a person sensitive to a particular drug or agent.
read[1] (riːd) *vb.* **reads, reading, read** (rɛd). **1.** to comprehend the meaning of (something written or printed) by looking at and interpreting the written or printed characters. **2.** to be occupied in such an activity: *he was reading all day.* **3.** (when *tr.,* often foll. by *out*) to look at, interpret, and speak aloud (something written or printed): *he read to us from the Bible.* **4.** (*tr.*) to interpret the significance or meaning of through scrutiny and recognition: *he read the sky and predicted rain; to read a map.* **5.** (*tr.*) to interpret or understand the meaning of (signs, characters, etc.) other than by visual means: *to read Braille.* **6.** (*tr.*) to have sufficient knowledge of (a language) to understand the written or printed word: *do you read German?* **7.** (*tr.*) to discover or make out the true nature or mood of: *to read someone's mind.* **8.** to interpret or understand (something read) in a specified way,

ˌ**reab'sorb** *vb.*
ˌ**reab'sorption** *n.*
ˌ**reac'cede** *vb.*
ˌ**reac'cent** *vb.*
ˌ**reac'cept** *vb.*
ˌ**reac'ceptance** *n.*
ˌ**reac'claim** *vb.*
ˌ**reac'commoˌdate** *vb.*
ˌ**reac'credit** *vb.*
ˌ**reac'custom** *vb.*
ˌ**rea'cidiˌfy** *vb.,* **-ˌfies, -ˌfying, -ˌfied.**
ˌ**reac'quaint** *vb.*
ˌ**reac'quaintance** *n.*
ˌ**reac'quire** *vb.*
ˌ**reacqui'sition** *n.*

or (of something read) to convey a particular meaning or impression: *I read this speech as satire; this book reads well.* **9.** (*tr.*) to adopt as a reading in a particular passage: *for "boon" read "bone".* **10.** (*intr.*) to have or contain a certain form or wording: *the sentence reads as follows.* **11.** to undertake a course of study in (a subject): *to read history; read for the bar.* **12.** to gain knowledge by reading: *he read about the war.* **13.** (*tr.*) to register, indicate, or show: *the meter reads 100.* **14.** (*tr.*) to bring or put into a specified condition by reading: *to read a child to sleep.* **15.** (*tr.*) to hear and understand, esp. when using a two-way radio: *we are reading you loud and clear.* **16.** *Computer technol.* to obtain (data) from a storage device, such as magnetic tape. Compare **write** (sense 16). **17.** (*tr.*) to understand (written or printed music) by interpretation of the notes on the staff and to be able to reproduce the musical sounds represented by these notes. **18.** **read a lesson** (*or* **lecture**). *Informal.* to censure or reprimand, esp. in a long-winded manner. **19. read between the lines.** to perceive or deduce a meaning that is hidden or implied rather than being openly stated. **20. you wouldn't read about it.** *Austral. informal.* an expression of dismay, disgust, or disbelief. ~*n.* **21.** matter suitable for reading: *this new book is a very good read.* **22.** the act of reading. ~See also **read in, read into, read out, read up.** [Old English *rǣdan* to advise, explain; related to Old Frisian *rēda,* Old High German *rātan,* Gothic *garēdan*]

read[2] (red) *vb.* **1.** the past tense and past participle of **read**[1]. ~*adj.* **2.** having knowledge gained from books (esp. in the phrases **widely read, well-read**). **3. take (something) as read.** to take (something) for granted as a fact; understand or presume.

readable ('riːdəbᵊl) *adj.* **1.** (of handwriting, etc.) able to be read or deciphered; legible. **2.** (of style of writing) interesting, easy, or pleasant to read. —ˌ**reada'bility** *or* '**readableness** *n.* —'**readably** *adv.*

reader ('riːdə) *n.* **1.** a person who reads. **2.** a person who is fond of reading. **3. a.** *Chiefly Brit.* at a university, a member of staff having a position between that of a senior lecturer and a professor. **b.** *U.S.* a teaching assistant in a faculty who grades papers, examinations, etc., on behalf of a professor. **4. a.** a book that is part of a planned series for those learning to read. **b.** a standard textbook, esp. for foreign-language learning. **5.** a person who reads aloud in public. **6.** a person who reads and assesses the merit of manuscripts submitted to a publisher. **7.** a person employed to read proofs and indicate errors by comparison with the original copy; proofreader. **8.** short for **lay reader. 9.** *Judaism, chiefly Brit.* another word for **cantor** (sense 1).

readership ('riːdəʃɪp) *n.* **1.** all the readers collectively of a particular publication or author: *a readership of five million; Dickens's readership.* **2.** *Chiefly Brit.* the office, position, or rank of university reader.

readies ('rɛdɪz) *pl. n. Informal.* a variant of **ready** (sense 8): see **ready money.**

readily ('rɛdɪlɪ) *adv.* **1.** promptly; eagerly; willingly. **2.** without difficulty or delay; easily or quickly.

read in (riːd) *vb.* (*adv.*) **1.** to read (data) into a computer memory or storage device. **2. read oneself in.** *Church of England.* to assume possession of a benefice by publicly reading the Thirty-nine Articles.

readiness ('rɛdɪnɪs) *n.* **1.** the state of being ready or prepared, as for use or action. **2. in readiness. a.** prepared and waiting: *all was in readiness for the guests' arrival.* **b.** in preparation for: *he tidied the house in readiness for the guests' arrival.* **3.** willingness or eagerness to do something. **4.** ease or promptness.

reading ('riːdɪŋ) *n.* **1. a.** the act of a person who reads. **b.** (*as modifier*): *a reading room; a reading lamp.* **2. a.** ability to read. **b.** (*as modifier*): *the reading public; a child of reading age.* **3.** any matter that can be read; written or printed text. **4.** a public recital or rendering of a literary work. **5.** the form of a particular word or passage in a given text, esp. where more than one version exists. **6.** an interpretation, as of a piece of music, a situation, or something said or written. **7.** knowledge gained from books: *a person of little reading.* **8.** a measurement indicated by a gauge, dial, scientific instrument, etc. **9.** *Parliamentary procedure.* **a.** the formal recital of the body or title of a bill in a legislative assembly in order to begin one of the stages of its passage. **b.** one of the three stages in the passage of a bill through a legislative assembly. See **first reading, second reading, third reading. 10.** the formal recital of something written, esp. a will.

read into (riːd) *vb.* (*tr., prep.*) to discern in or infer from a statement (meanings not intended by the speaker or writer).

readjust (ˌriːə'dʒʌst) *vb.* to adjust or adapt (oneself or something) again, esp. after an initial failure. —ˌ**read'justable** *adj.* —ˌ**re-ad'juster** *n.* —ˌ**read'justment** *n.*

read out (riːd) *vb.* (*adv.*) **1.** (*tr.*) to read (something) aloud. **2.** to retrieve information from a computer memory or storage device. **3.** (*tr.*) *U.S. and Canadian.* to expel (someone) from a political party or other society. ~*n.* **read-out. 4. a.** the act of retrieving information from a computer memory or storage device. **b.** the information retrieved.

read up (riːd) *vb.* (*adv.*; when *intr.*, often foll. by *on*) to acquire information about (a subject) by reading intensively.

read-write head ('riːd'raɪt) *n. Computer technol.* an electromagnet that can both read and write information on a magnetic medium such as magnetic tape or disk.

ready ('rɛdɪ) *adj.* **readier, readiest. 1.** in a state of completion or preparedness, as for use or action. **2.** willing or eager: *ready helpers.* **3.** prompt or rapid: *a ready response.* **4.** (*prenominal*) quick in perceiving; intelligent: *a ready mind.* **5.** (*postpositive*) (foll. by *to*) on the point (of) or liable (to): *ready to collapse.* **6.** (*postpositive*) conveniently near (esp. in the phrase **ready to hand**). **7. make** *or* **get ready.** to prepare (oneself or something) for use or action. ~*n.* **8.** *Informal.* (often preceded by *the*) short for **ready money. 9. at** *or* **to the ready. a.** poised for use or action: *with pen at the ready.* **b.** (of a rifle) in the position normally adopted immediately prior to aiming and firing. ~*vb.* (*tr.*) **10.** to put in a state of readiness; prepare. [Old English (*ge*)*rǣde;* related to Old Frisian *rēde,* Old High German *reiti,* Old Norse *reithr* ready]

ready-made *adj.* **1.** made for purchase and immediate use by any customer: *a ready-made jacket.* **2.** extremely convenient or ideally suited: *a ready-made solution.* **3.** unoriginal or conventional: *ready-made phrases.* ~*n.* **4.** a ready-made article, esp. a garment.

ready-mix *n.* **1.** (*modifier*) consisting of ingredients blended in advance, esp. of food that is ready to cook or eat after addition of milk or water: *a ready-mix cake.* **2.** concrete that is mixed before or during delivery to a building site.

ready money *or* **cash** *n.* funds for immediate use; cash. Also called: **the ready, the readies.**

ready reckoner *n.* a table of numbers used to facilitate simple calculations, esp. one for applying rates of discount, interest, charging, etc. to different sums.

ready-to-wear *adj.* (**ready to wear** *when postpositive*). **1.** (of clothes) not tailored for the wearer; of a standard size. ~*n.* **2.** an article or suit of such clothes.

ready-witted *adj.* quick to learn or perceive.

reafforest (ˌriːə'fɒrɪst) *or* **reforest** *vb.* (*tr.*) to replant (an area that was formerly forested). —ˌ**reafˌforest'ation** *or* ˌ**refor-est'ation** *n.*

reagent (riː'eɪdʒənt) *n.* a substance for use in a chemical reaction, esp. for use in chemical synthesis and analysis.

reagin ('rɪədʒɪn) *n. Immunol.* a type of antibody that is formed against an allergen and is attached to the cells of a tissue. The antigen–antibody reaction that occurs on subsequent contact with the allergen causes tissue damage, leading to the release of histamine and other substances responsible for an allergic reaction. [C20: from Greek, from *reag-ieren* to react + -IN]

real[1] ('rɪəl) *adj.* **1.** existing or occurring in the physical world; not imaginary, fictitious, or theoretical; actual. **2.** (*prenominal*) true; actual; not false: *the real reason.* **3.** (*prenominal*) deserving the name; rightly so called: *a real friend; a real woman.* **4.** not artificial or simulated; genuine: *real sympathy; real fur.* **5.** (of food, etc.) traditionally made and having a distinct flavour: *real ale; real cheese.* **6.** *Philosophy.* existent or relating to actual existence (as opposed to nonexistent, potential, contingent, or apparent). **7.** (*prenominal*) *Economics.* (of prices, incomes, wages, etc.) considered in terms of purchasing power rather than nominal currency value. **8.** (*prenominal*) denoting or relating to immovable property such as land and tenements: *real property.* Compare **personal. 9.** *Physics.* See **image** (sense 2). **10.** *Maths.* involving or containing real numbers alone; having no imaginary part. **11.** *Music.* **a.** (of the answer in a fugue) preserving the intervals as they appear in the subject. **b.** denoting a fugue as having such an answer. Compare **tonal** (sense 3). **12.** *Informal.* (intensifier): *a real fool; a real genius.* **13. the real thing.** the genuine article, not an inferior or mistaken substitute. ~*n.* **14.** short for **real number. 15. the real.** that which exists in fact; reality. **16. for real.** *Slang.* not as a test or trial; in earnest. [C15: from Old French *réel,* from Late Latin *reālis,* from Latin *rēs* thing] —'**realness** *n.*

real[2] (reɪ'ɑːl; *Spanish* re'al) *n., pl.* **reals** *or* **reales** (*Spanish* re'ales). a former small Spanish or Spanish-American silver coin. [C17: from Spanish, literally: royal, from Latin *rēgālis;* see REGAL[1]]

real[3] (*Portuguese* re'al) *n., pl.* **reis** (rəjʃ). a former coin of Portugal and Brazil. [ultimately from Latin *rēgālis* REGAL[1]]

real ale *or* **beer** *n.* any beer which is allowed to ferment in the cask and which when served is pumped up without using carbon dioxide.

real estate *n.* another term, chiefly U.S. and Canadian, for **real property.**

realgar (rɪ'ælgə) *n.* a rare orange-red soft mineral consisting of arsenic sulphide in monoclinic crystalline form. It occurs in Utah and Romania and as a deposit from hot springs. It is an

ˌ**rea'dapt** *vb.*
ˌ**readap'tation** *n.*
re'add *vb.*
ˌ**read'dress** *vb.*
ˌ**read'journ** *vb.*
ˌ**read'journment** *n.*
ˌ**read'mission** *n.*
ˌ**read'mit** *vb.*, **-'mits, -'mitting, -'mitted.**
ˌ**read'mittance** *n.*
ˌ**rea'dopt** *vb.*
ˌ**reaf'firm** *vb.*
ˌ**reaffir'mation** *n.*

important ore of arsenic and is also used as a pigment. Formula: AsS. [C14: via Medieval Latin from Arabic *rahj al-ghar* powder of the mine]

realia (rɪˈeɪlɪə) *pl. n.* real-life facts and material used in teaching. [C20: from neuter pl. of Late Latin *reālis;* see REAL[1]]

realism (ˈrɪəˌlɪzəm) *n.* **1.** awareness or acceptance of the physical universe, events, etc., as they are, as opposed to the abstract or ideal. **2.** awareness or acceptance of the facts and necessities of life; a practical rather than a moral or dogmatic view of things. **3.** a style of painting and sculpture that seeks to represent the familiar or typical in real life, rather than an idealized, formalized, or romantic interpretation of it. **4.** any similar school or style in other arts, esp. literature. **5.** *Philosophy.* the thesis that general terms such as common nouns refer to entities that have a real existence separate from the individuals which fall under them. See also **universal** (sense 12b). Compare **Platonism, nominalism, conceptualism, naive realism. 6.** *Philosophy.* the theory that physical objects continue to exist whether they are perceived or not. Compare **idealism, phenomenalism. 7.** *Logic, philosophy.* the theory that the sense of a statement is given by a specification of its truth conditions, or that there is a reality independent of the speaker's conception of it that determines the truth or falsehood of every statement.

realist (ˈrɪəlɪst) *n.* **1.** a person who is aware of and accepts the physical universe, events, etc., as they are; pragmatist. **2.** an artist or writer who seeks to represent the familiar or typical in real life rather than an idealized, formalized, or romantic interpretation. **3.** *Philosophy.* a person who accepts realism. **4.** (*modifier*) of, relating to, or characteristic of realism or realists in the arts, philosophy, etc.: *a realist school.*

realistic (ˌrɪəˈlɪstɪk) *adj.* **1.** showing awareness and acceptance of reality. **2.** practical or pragmatic rather than ideal or moral. **3.** (of a book, film, etc.) depicting or emphasizing what is real and actual rather than abstract or ideal. **4.** of or relating to philosophical realism. —ˌ**realˈistically** *adv.*

reality (rɪˈælɪtɪ) *n., pl.* **-ties. 1.** the state of things as they are or appear to be, rather than as one might wish them to be. **2.** something that is real. **3.** the state of being real. **4.** *Philosophy.* **a.** that which exists, independent of human awareness. **b.** the totality of facts as they are independent of human awareness of them. See also **conceptualism.** Compare **appearance** (sense 6). **5. in reality.** actually; in fact.

reality principle *n. Psychoanal.* control of behaviour by the ego to meet the conditions imposed by the external world.

realize *or* **realise** (ˈrɪəˌlaɪz) *vb.* **1.** (*when tr., may take a clause as object*) to become conscious or aware of (something). **2.** (*tr., often passive*) to bring (a plan, ambition, etc.) to fruition; make actual or concrete. **3.** (*tr.*) to give (something, such as a drama or film) the appearance of reality. **4.** (*tr.*) (of goods, property, etc.) to sell for or make (a certain sum): *this table realized £800.* **5.** (*tr.*) to convert (property or goods) into cash. **6.** (*tr.*) (of a musicologist or performer) **a.** to expand or complete (a thorough-bass part in a piece of baroque music) by supplying the harmonies indicated in the figured bass. **b.** to reconstruct (a composition) from an incomplete set of parts. **7.** to sound or utter (a phoneme or other speech sound) in actual speech; articulate. —ˈ**realˌizable** *or* ˈ**realˌisable** *adj.* —ˈ**realˌizably** *or* ˈ**realˌisably** *adv.* —ˌ**realiˈzation** *or* ˌ**realiˈsation** *n.* —ˈ**realˌizer** *or* ˈ**realˌiser** *n.*

real life *n.* **a.** actual human life, as lived by real people, esp. contrasted with the lives of fictional or fantasy characters: *miracles don't happen in real life.* **b.** (*as modifier*): *a real-life mystery.*

really (ˈrɪəlɪ) *adv.* **1.** in reality; in actuality; assuredly: *it's really quite harmless.* **2.** truly; genuinely: *really beautiful.* ~*interj.* **3.** an exclamation of dismay, disapproval, doubt, surprise, etc. **4. not really?** an exclamation of surprise or polite doubt.

▷**Usage.** See at **very.**

realm (rɛlm) *n.* **1.** a royal domain; kingdom (now chiefly in such phrases as **Peer of the Realm**). **2.** a field of interest, study, etc.: *the realm of the occult.* [C13: from Old French *reialme,* from Latin *regimen* rule, influenced by Old French *reial* royal, from Latin *rēgālis* REGAL]

real number *n.* any rational or irrational number. See **number** (sense 1).

real part *n.* the term a in a complex number $a + ib$, where $i = \sqrt{-1}$.

realpolitik (reɪˈɑːlpɒlɪˈtiːk) *n.* a ruthlessly realistic and opportunist approach to statesmanship, rather than a moralistic one, esp. as exemplified by the German statesman Otto von Bismarck (1815–98). [C19: German: politics of realism]

real presence *n.* the doctrine that the body of Christ is actually present in the Eucharist.

real property *n.* immovable property, esp. land and buildings, including proprietary rights over land, such as mineral rights. Compare **personal property.** Also called (chiefly U.S. and Canadian) **real estate.**

real tennis *n.* an ancient form of tennis played in a four-walled indoor court with various openings, a sloping-roofed corridor along three sides, and a buttress on the fourth side. Also called: **royal tennis.**

real-time *adj.* denoting or relating to a data-processing system in which a computer receives constantly changing data, such as information relating to air-traffic control, travel booking systems, etc., and processes it sufficiently rapidly to be able to control the source of the data.

realtor (ˈrɪəltə, -ˌtɔː) *n.* a U.S. and Canadian word for an **estate agent,** esp. an accredited one. [C20: from REALTY + -OR[1]]

realty (ˈrɪəltɪ) *n.* another term for **real property.**

real wages *pl. n. Economics.* wages evaluated with reference to their purchasing power rather than to the money actually paid. Compare **money wages.**

ream[1] (riːm) *n.* **1.** a number of sheets of paper, formerly 480 sheets (**short ream**), now 500 sheets (**long ream**) or 516 sheets (**printer's ream** or **perfect ream**). One ream is equal to 20 quires. **2.** (*often pl.*) *Informal.* a large quantity, esp. of written matter: *he wrote reams.* [C14: from Old French *raime,* from Spanish *rezma,* from Arabic *rizmah* bale]

ream[2] (riːm) *vb.* (*tr.*) **1.** to enlarge (a hole) by use of a reamer. **2.** *U.S.* to extract (juice) from (a citrus fruit) using a reamer. [C19: perhaps from C14 *remen* to open up, from Old English *rȳman* to widen]

reamer (ˈriːmə) *n.* **1.** a steel tool with a cylindrical or tapered shank around which longitudinal teeth are ground, used for smoothing the bores of holes accurately to size. **2.** *U.S.* a utensil with a conical projection used for extracting juice from citrus fruits; lemon squeezer.

rean (riːn) *n.* a variant spelling of **reen.**

reap (riːp) *vb.* **1.** to cut or harvest (a crop), esp. corn, from (a field or tract of land). **2.** (*tr.*) to gain or get (something) as a reward for or result of some action or enterprise. [Old English *riopan;* related to Norwegian *ripa* to scratch, Middle Low German *repen* to card, ripple (flax)] —ˈ**reapable** *adj.*

reaper (ˈriːpə) *n.* **1.** a person who reaps or a machine for reaping. **2. the grim reaper.** death.

rear[1] (rɪə) *n.* **1.** the back or hind part. **2.** the area or position that lies at the back: *a garden at the rear of the house.* **3.** the section of a military force or procession farthest from the front. **4.** an informal word for **buttocks** (see **buttock**). **5. bring up the rear.** to be at the back in a procession, race, etc. **6. in the rear.** at the back. **7.** (*modifier*) of or in the rear: *the rear legs; the rear side.* [C17: probably abstracted from REARWARD or REARGUARD]

rear[2] (rɪə) *vb.* **1.** (*tr.*) to care for and educate (children) until maturity; bring up; raise. **2.** (*tr.*) to breed (animals) or grow (plants). **3.** (*tr.*) to place or lift (a ladder, etc.) upright. **4.** (*tr.*) to erect (a monument, building, etc.); put up. **5.** (*intr.; often foll. by up*) (esp. of horses) to lift the front legs in the air and stand nearly upright. **6.** (*intr.; often foll. by up or over*) (esp. of tall buildings) to rise high; tower. **7.** (*intr.*) to start with anger, resentment, etc. [Old English *rǣran;* related to Old High German *rēren* to distribute, Old Norse *reisa* to RAISE] —ˈ**rearer** *n.*

rear admiral *n.* an officer holding flag rank in any of certain navies, junior to a vice admiral.

rearguard (ˈrɪəˌgɑːd) *n.* **1.** a detachment detailed to protect the rear of a military formation, esp. in retreat. **2.** an entrenched or conservative element, as in a political party. **3.** (*modifier*) of, relating to, or characteristic of a rearguard: *a rearguard action.* [C15: from Old French *rereguarde* (modern French *arrière-garde*), from *rer,* from Latin *retro* back + *guarde* GUARD; compare VANGUARD]

rear light *or* **lamp** *n.* a red light, usually one of a pair, attached to the rear of a motor vehicle. U.S. and Canadian names: **tail-light, tail lamp.**

rearm (riːˈɑːm) *vb.* **1.** to arm again. **2.** (*tr.*) to equip (an army, a nation, etc.) with better weapons. —**reˈarmament** *n.*

rearmost (ˈrɪəˌməʊst) *adj.* nearest the rear; coming last.

rearmouse (ˈrɪəˌmaʊs) *n., pl.* **-mice.** an archaic or dialect word for **bat** (the animal). [See REREMOUSE]

rearrange (ˌriːəˈreɪndʒ) *vb.* (*tr.*) **1.** to put (something) into a new order: *to rearrange the lighting.* **2.** to put (something) back in its original order after it has been displaced. **3.** to fix a new date or time for (something postponed): *to rearrange a match.* —ˌ**rearˈranger** *n.* —ˌ**rearˈrangement** *n.*

rear sight *n.* the sight of a gun nearest to the breech.

rear-view mirror *n.* a mirror on a motor vehicle enabling the driver to see traffic behind him.

rearward (ˈrɪəwəd) *adj., adv.* **1.** Also (for adv. only): **rearwards.** towards or in the rear. ~*n.* **2.** a position in the rear, esp. the

ˌ**reaˈlign** *vb.*
ˌ**reaˈlignment** *n.*
reˈalloˌcate *vb.*
ˌ**realloˈcation** *n.*
ˌ**realˈlot** *vb.*, **-ˈlots, -ˈlotting, -ˈlotted.**
ˌ**realˈlotment** *n.*
reˈalter *vb.*
ˌ**realterˈation** *n.*
reˈanaˌlyse *vb.*
ˌ**reaˈnalysis** *n., pl.* **-ses.**
reˈaniˌmate *vb.*
ˌ**reaniˈmation** *n.*
ˌ**reapˈpear** *vb.*
ˌ**reapˈpearance** *n.*
ˌ**reappliˈcation** *n.*
ˌ**reapˈply** *vb.*, **-ˈplies, -ˈplying, -ˈplied.**
ˌ**reapˈpoint** *vb.*
ˌ**reapˈpointment** *n.*
ˌ**reapˈportion** *vb.*
ˌ**reapˈportionment** *n.*
ˌ**reapˈpraisal** *n.*
ˌ**reapˈpraise** *vb.*
reˈargue *vb.*, **-gues, -guing, -gued.**
ˌ**reaˈrousal** *n.*
ˌ**reaˈrouse** *vb.*
ˌ**rearˈrest** *vb., n.*

rear division of a military formation. [C14 (as a noun: the part of an army positioned behind the main body of troops): from Anglo-French *rerewarde*, variant of *reregarde*; see REARGUARD]

reason ('riːzᵊn) *n.* **1.** the faculty of rational argument, deduction, judgment, etc. **2.** sound mind; sanity. **3.** a cause or motive, as for a belief, action, etc. **4.** an argument in favour of or a justification for something. **5.** *Philosophy.* the intellect regarded as a source of knowledge, as contrasted with experience. **6.** *Logic.* grounds for a belief; a premise of an argument supporting that belief. **7. by reason of.** because of. **8. in** *or* **within reason.** within moderate or justifiable bounds. **9. it stands to reason.** it is logical or obvious: *it stands to reason that he will lose.* **10. listen to reason.** to be persuaded peaceably. **11. reasons of State.** political justifications for an immoral act. ~*vb.* **12.** (when *tr., takes a clause as object*) to think logically or draw (logical conclusions) from facts or premises. **13.** (*intr.*; usually foll. by *with*) to urge or seek to persuade by reasoning. **14.** (*tr.*; often foll. by *out*) to work out or resolve (a problem) by reasoning. [C13: from Old French *reisun*, from Latin *ratiō* reckoning, from *rērī* to think] —**'reasoner** *n.*

▷**Usage.** In both speech and writing careful users of English avoid the expression *the reason is because...* since *the reason is...* and *because* mean the same thing. The word *because* should be replaced by *that*: *the reason is that...*

reasonable ('riːzənəbᵊl) *adj.* **1.** showing reason or sound judgment. **2.** having the ability to reason. **3.** having modest or moderate expectations; not making unfair demands. **4.** moderate in price; not expensive. **5.** fair; average: *reasonable weather.* —**'reasonably** *adv.* —**'reasonableness** *n.*

reasoned ('riːzᵊnd) *adj.* well thought-out or well presented: *a reasoned explanation.* —**'reasonedly** *adv.*

reasoning ('riːzənɪŋ) *n.* **1.** the act or process of drawing conclusions from facts, evidence, etc. **2.** the arguments, proofs, etc., so adduced.

reassure (ˌriːə'ʃʊə) *vb.* (*tr.*) **1.** to relieve (someone) of anxieties; restore confidence to. **2.** another term for **reinsure.** —ˌ**reas'surance** *n.* —ˌ**reas'surer** *n.* —ˌ**reas'suringly** *adv.*

reast (riːst) *vb.* a variant spelling of **reest.**

Réaum. *abbrev. for* Réaumur (scale).

Réaumur ('reɪəˌmjʊə) *adj.* indicating measurement on the Réaumur scale of temperature.

Réaumur scale *n.* a scale of temperature in which the freezing point of water is taken as 0° and the boiling point is 80°. [C18: named after René Antoine Ferchault de *Réaumur* (1683–1757), French physicist, who introduced it]

reave[1] (riːv) *vb.* **reaves, reaving, reaved** *or* **reft** (rɛft). *Archaic.* **1.** to carry off (property, prisoners, etc.) by force. **2.** (*tr.*; foll. by *of*) to deprive; strip. See also **reive.** [Old English *reāfian*; related to Old High German *roubōn* to rob, Old Norse *raufa* to break open]

reave[2] (riːv) *vb.* **reaves, reaving, reaved** *or* **reft** (rɛft). *Archaic.* to break or tear (something) apart; cleave. [C13 *reven*, probably from REAVE[1] and influenced in meaning by RIVE]

reb (rɛb) *n.* (*sometimes cap.*) *U.S. informal.* a Confederate soldier in the American Civil War (1861–65). Also called: **Johnny Reb.** [short for REBEL]

Reb (rɛb) *n. Judaism.* an honorific title, corresponding to *Mr*, for those who do not have rabbinic qualifications: usually followed by the person's forename: *Reb Dovid.* [Yiddish, from Hebrew *rabbī* rabbi, master]

rebarbative (rɪ'bɑːbətɪv) *adj. Rare.* fearsome; forbidding. [C19: from French *rébarbatif*, from Old French *rebarber* to repel (an enemy), to withstand (him) face to face, from RE- + *barbe* beard, from Latin *barba*]

rebate[1] *n.* ('riːbeɪt). **1.** a refund of a fraction of the amount payable or paid, as for goods purchased in quantity; discount. ~*vb.* (rɪ'beɪt). (*tr.*) **2.** to deduct (a part) of a payment from (the total). **3.** *Archaic.* to reduce or diminish (something or the effectiveness of something). [C15: from Old French *rabattre* to beat down, hence reduce, deduct, from RE- + *abatre* to put down; see ABATE] —**re'batable** *or* **re'bateable** *adj.* —**'rebater** *n.*

rebate[2] ('riːbeɪt, 'ræbɪt) *n., vb.* another word for **rabbet.**

rebato (rə'bɑːtəʊ) *n., pl.* **-tos.** a variant spelling of **rabato.**

Rebbe ('rɛbə) *n. Judaism.* **1.** the usually dynastic leader of a Chassidic sect. **2.** an individual's chosen spiritual mentor. [Yiddish, from Hebrew *rabbī* rabbi]

rebbetzin ('rɛbətsən) *n. Judaism.* the wife of a rabbi. [from Yiddish]

rebec *or* **rebeck** ('riːbɛk) *n.* a medieval stringed instrument resembling the violin but having a lute-shaped body. [C16: from Old French *rebebe*, from Arabic *rebāb*; perhaps also influenced by Old French *bec* beak]

rebel *vb.* (rɪ'bɛl), **-bels, -belling, -belled.** (*intr.*; often foll. by *against*) **1.** to resist or rise up against a government or other authority, esp. by force of arms. **2.** to dissent from an accepted moral code or convention of behaviour, dress, etc. **3.** to show repugnance (towards). ~*n.* ('rɛbᵊl). **4. a.** a person who rebels. **b.** (*as modifier*): *a rebel soldier; a rebel leader.* **5.** a person who dissents from some accepted moral code or convention of behaviour, dress, etc. [C13: from Old French *rebelle*, from Latin *rebellis* insurgent, from RE- + *bellum* war] —**'rebeldom** *n.*

rebellion (rɪ'bɛljən) *n.* **1.** organized resistance or opposition to a government or other authority. **2.** dissent from an accepted moral code or convention of behaviour, dress, etc. [C14: via Old French from Latin *rebelliō* revolt (of those conquered); see REBEL]

rebellious (rɪ'bɛljəs) *adj.* **1.** showing a tendency towards rebellion. **2.** (of a problem, etc.) difficult to overcome; refractory. —**re'belliously** *adv.* —**re'belliousness** *n.*

rebellow (rɪ'bɛləʊ) *vb. Archaic or literary.* to re-echo loudly.

rebirth (riː'bɜːθ) *n.* **1.** a revival or renaissance: *the rebirth of learning.* **2.** a second or new birth; reincarnation.

rebore *n.* ('riːˌbɔː). **1.** the process of boring out the cylinders of a worn reciprocating engine and fitting oversize pistons. ~*vb.* (riː'bɔː). **2.** (*tr.*) to carry out this process.

reborn (riː'bɔːn) *adj.* born or as if born again, esp. in having undergone spiritual regeneration.

rebound *vb.* (rɪ'baʊnd). (*intr.*) **1.** to spring back, as from a sudden impact. **2.** to misfire, esp. so as to hurt the perpetrator: *the plan rebounded.* ~*n.* ('riːbaʊnd). **3.** the act or an instance of rebounding. **4. on the rebound. a.** in the act of springing back. **b.** *Informal.* in a state of recovering from rejection, disappointment, etc.: *he married her on the rebound from an unhappy love affair.* [C14: from Old French *rebondir*, from RE- + *bondir* to BOUND[2]]

rebozo (rɪ'bəʊzəʊ; *Spanish* re'βoθo) *n., pl.* **-zos** (-zəʊz; *Spanish* -θos). a long wool or linen scarf covering the shoulders and head, worn by Latin American women. [C19: from Spanish: shawl, from *rebozar* to muffle]

rebuff (rɪ'bʌf) *vb.* (*tr.*) **1.** to snub, reject, or refuse (a person offering help or sympathy, an offer of help, etc.) abruptly or out of hand. **2.** to beat back (an attack); repel. ~*n.* **3.** a blunt refusal or rejection; snub. **4.** any sudden check to progress or action. [C16: from Old French *rebuffer*, from Italian *ribuffare*, from *ribuffo* a reprimand, from *ri-* RE- + *buffo* puff, gust, apparently of imitative origin]

rebuke (rɪ'bjuːk) *vb.* **1.** (*tr.*) to scold or reprimand (someone). ~*n.* **2.** a reprimand or scolding. [C14: from Old Norman French *rebuker*, from RE- + Old French *buchier* to hack down, from *busche* log, of Germanic origin] —**re'bukable** *adj.* —**re'buker** *n.*

rebus ('riːbəs) *n., pl.* **-buses.** **1.** a puzzle consisting of pictures representing syllables and words; in such a puzzle the word *hear* might be represented by H followed by a picture of an ear. **2.** a heraldic emblem or device that is a pictorial representation of or pun on the name of the bearer. [C17: from French *rébus*, from the Latin *rēbus* by things, from RES]

rebut (rɪ'bʌt) *vb.* **-buts, -butting, -butted.** (*tr.*) to refute or disprove, esp. by offering a contrary contention or argument. [C13: from Old French *reboter*, from RE- + *boter* to thrust, BUTT[3]] —**re'buttable** *adj.* —**re'buttal** *n.*

rebutter (rɪ'bʌtə) *n.* **1.** *Law.* a defendant's pleading in reply to a plaintiff's surrejoinder. **2.** a person who rebuts.

rec (rɛk) *n. Informal.* short for **recreation** (ground).

rec. *abbrev. for:* **1.** receipt. **2.** recipe. **3.** record. **4.** recorder.

recalcitrant (rɪ'kælsɪtrənt) *adj.* **1.** not susceptible to control or authority; refractory. ~*n.* **2.** a recalcitrant person. [C19: via French from Latin *recalcitrāre*, from RE- + *calcitrāre* to kick, from *calx* heel] —**re'calcitrance** *n.*

recalesce (ˌriːkə'lɛs) *vb.* (*intr.*) to undergo recalescence.

recalescence (ˌriːkə'lɛsəns) *n.* a sudden spontaneous increase in the temperature of cooling iron resulting from an exothermic change in crystal structure occurring at a particular temperature. [C19: from Latin *recalēscere* to grow warm again, from RE- + *calēscere*, from *calēre* to be hot] —ˌ**reca'lescent** *adj.*

recall (rɪ'kɔːl) *vb.* (*tr.*) **1.** (*may take a clause as object*) to bring back to mind; recollect; remember. **2.** to order to return; call back permanently or temporarily: *to recall an ambassador.* **3.** to revoke or take back. **4.** to cause (one's thoughts, attention, etc.) to return from a reverie or digression. **5.** *Poetic.* to restore or revive. ~*n.* **6.** the act of recalling or state of being recalled.

ˌ**reas'cend** *vb.*
ˌ**reas'cent** *n.*
ˌ**reas'semble** *vb.*
ˌ**reas'sembly** *n., pl.* **-blies.**
ˌ**reas'sert** *vb.*
ˌ**reas'sertion** *n.*
ˌ**reas'sess** *vb.*
ˌ**reas'sessment** *n.*
ˌ**reas'sign** *vb.*
ˌ**reas'signment** *n.*
ˌ**reas'simiˌlate** *vb.*
ˌ**reasˌsimi'lation** *n.*
ˌ**reas'sume** *vb.*
ˌ**reas'sumption** *n.*
ˌ**reat'tach** *vb.*
ˌ**reat'tachment** *n.*
ˌ**reat'tain** *vb.*
ˌ**reat'tainment** *n.*
ˌ**reat'tempt** *vb., n.*
ˌ**rea'waken** *vb.*
re'baptism *n.*
ˌ**rebap'tize** *or* ˌ**rebap'tise** *vb.*
re'bid *vb.*, **-'bids, -'bidding, -'bid.**
re'biddable *adj.*
re'bind *vb.*, **-'binds, -'binding, -'bound.**
re'boil *vb.*
re'broadcast *vb.*, **-casts, -casting, -cast.**
re'build *vb.*, **-'builds, -'building, -'built.**
re'burial *n.*
re'bury *vb.*, **-'buries, -'burying, -'buried.**
re'button *vb.*
re'calcuˌlate *vb.*

7. revocation or cancellation. 8. the ability to remember things; recollection. 9. *Military.* (esp. formerly) a signal to call back troops, etc., usually a bugle call: *to sound the recall.* 10. *U.S.* the process by which elected officials may be deprived of office by popular vote. —re'**callable** *adj.*

recant (rɪ'kænt) *vb.* to repudiate or withdraw (a former belief or statement), esp. formally in public. [C16: from Latin *recantāre* to sing again, from RE- + *cantāre* to sing; see CHANT] —**recantation** (ˌriːkæn'teɪʃən) *n.* —**re'canter** *n.*

recap *vb.* ('riːˌkæp, riː'kæp), **-caps, -capping, -capped,** *n.* ('riːˌkæp). 1. *Informal.* short for **recapitulate** *or* **recapitulation.** ~*n.* ('riːˌkæp). 2. *Austral. and N.Z.* another name for **retread.** —**re'cappable** *adj.*

recapitulate (ˌriːkə'pɪtjʊˌleɪt) *vb.* 1. to restate the main points of (an argument, speech, etc.); summarize. 2. (*tr.*) (of an animal) to repeat (stages of its evolutionary development) during the embryonic stages of its life. 3. to repeat at some point during a piece of music (material used earlier in the same work). [C16: from Late Latin *recapitulāre,* literally: to put back under headings; see CAPITULATE] —ˌ**reca'pitulative** *or* ˌ**reca'pitulatory** *adj.*

recapitulation (ˌriːkəˌpɪtjʊ'leɪʃən) *n.* 1. the act of recapitulating, esp. summing up, as at the end of a speech. 2. Also called: **palingenesis.** *Biology.* the apparent repetition in the embryonic development of an animal of the changes that occurred during its evolutionary history. Compare **caenogenesis.** 3. *Music.* the repeating of earlier themes, esp. when forming the final section of a movement in sonata form.

recaption (riː'kæpʃən) *n. Law.* the process of taking back one's own wife, child, property, etc., without causing a breach of the peace. [C17: from RE- + CAPTION (in the sense: seizure)]

recapture (riː'kæptʃə) *vb.* (*tr.*) 1. to capture or take again. 2. to recover, renew, or repeat (a lost or former ability, sensation, etc.): *she soon recaptured her high spirits.* 3. *U.S.* (of the government) to take lawfully (a proportion of the profits of a public-service undertaking). ~*n.* 4. the act of recapturing or fact of being recaptured. 5. *U.S.* the seizure by the government of a proportion of the profits of a public-service undertaking.

recce ('rɛkɪ) *n., vb.,* **-ces, -ceing, -ced** *or* **-ceed.** a slang word for **reconnaissance** or **reconnoitre.**

recd *or* **rec'd** *abbrev. for* received.

recede (rɪ'siːd) *vb.* (*intr.*) 1. to withdraw from a point or limit; go back: *the tide receded.* 2. to become more distant: *hopes of rescue receded.* 3. to slope backwards: *apes have receding foreheads.* 4. a. (of a man's hair) to cease to grow at the temples and above the forehead. b. (of a man) to start to go bald in this way. 5. to decline in value or character. 6. (usually foll. by *from*) to draw back or retreat, as from a promise. [C15: from Latin *recēdere* to go back, from RE- + *cēdere* to yield, CEDE]

re-cede (riː'siːd) *vb.* (*tr.*) to restore to a former owner.

receipt (rɪ'siːt) *n.* 1. a written acknowledgment by a receiver of money, goods, etc., that payment or delivery has been made. 2. the act of receiving or fact of being received. 3. (*usually pl.*) an amount or article received. 4. *Obsolete or U.S. dialect.* another word for **recipe.** ~*vb.* 5. (*tr.*) to acknowledge payment of (a bill), as by marking it. 6. *Chiefly U.S.* to issue a receipt for (money, goods, etc.). [C14: from Old Norman French *receite,* from Medieval Latin *recepta,* from Latin *recipere* to RECEIVE]

receiptor (rɪ'siːtə) *n. Chiefly U.S.* a person who receipts.

receivable (rɪ'siːvəbᵊl) *adj.* 1. suitable for or capable of being received, esp. as payment or legal tender. 2. (of a bill, etc.) awaiting payment: *accounts receivable.* ~*n.* 3. (*usually pl.*) the part of the assets of a business represented by accounts due for payment.

receive (rɪ'siːv) *vb.* (*mainly tr.*) 1. to take (something offered) into one's hand or possession. 2. to have (an honour, blessing, etc.) bestowed. 3. to accept delivery or transmission of (a letter, telephone call, etc.). 4. to be informed of (news or information). 5. to hear and consent to or acknowledge (an oath, confession, etc.). 6. (of a vessel or container) to take or hold (a substance, commodity, or certain amount). 7. to support or sustain (the weight of something); bear. 8. to apprehend or perceive (ideas, etc.). 9. to experience, undergo, or meet with: *to receive a crack on the skull.* 10. (*also intr.*) to be at home to (visitors). 11. to greet or welcome (visitors or guests), esp. in formal style. 12. to admit (a person) to a place, society, condition, etc.: *he was received into the priesthood.* 13. to accept or acknowledge (a precept or principle) as true or valid. 14. to convert (incoming radio signals) into sounds, pictures, etc., by means of a receiver. 15. (*also intr.*) *Tennis.* to play at the other end from the server; be required to return (service). 16. (*also intr.*) to partake of (the Christian Eucharist). 17. (*intr.*) *Chiefly Brit.* to buy and sell stolen goods. [C13: from Old French *receivre,* from Latin *recipere* to take back, from RE- + *capere* to take]

received (rɪ'siːvd) *adj.* generally accepted or believed: *received wisdom.*

Received Pronunciation *n.* the accent of standard Southern British English. Abbrev.: **RP.**

receiver (rɪ'siːvə) *n.* 1. a person who receives something; recipient. 2. a person appointed by a court to manage property pending the outcome of litigation, during the infancy of the owner, or after the owner(s) has been declared bankrupt or of unsound mind. 3. *Chiefly Brit.* a person who receives stolen goods knowing that they have been stolen. 4. the equipment in a telephone, radio, or television that receives incoming electrical signals or modulated radio waves and converts them into the original audio or video signals. 5. the part of a telephone containing the earpiece and mouthpiece that is held by the telephone user. 6. the equipment in a radar system, radio telescope, etc., that converts incoming radio signals into a useful form, usually displayed on the screen of a cathode-ray oscilloscope. 7. an obsolete word for **receptacle.** 8. *Chem.* a vessel in which the distillate is collected during distillation. 9. *U.S. sport.* a player whose function is to receive the ball, esp. a footballer who catches long passes. 10. the metallic frame situated behind the breech of a gun to guide the round into the chamber.

receivership (rɪ'siːvəʃɪp) *n. Law.* 1. the office or function of a receiver. 2. the condition of being administered by a receiver.

receiving order *n. Brit.* a court order appointing a receiver to manage the property of a debtor or bankrupt.

recency effect ('riːsənsɪ) *n. Psychol.* the phenomenon that when people are asked to recall in any order the items on a list, those that come at the end of the list are more likely to be recalled than the others.

recension (rɪ'sɛnʃən) *n.* 1. a critical revision of a literary work. 2. a text revised in this way. [C17: from Latin *recēnsiō,* from *recēnsēre* to survey, from RE- + *cēnsēre* to assess]

recent ('riːsᵊnt) *adj.* having appeared, happened, or been made not long ago; modern, fresh, or new. [C16: from Latin *recens* fresh; related to Greek *kainos* new] —'**recently** *adv.* —'**recentness** *or* '**recency** *n.*

Recent ('riːsᵊnt) *adj., n. Geology.* another word for **Holocene.**

recept ('riːsɛpt) *n. Psychol.* an idea or image formed in the mind by repeated experience of a particular pattern of sensory stimulation. [C20: from RE- + (CON)CEPT]

receptacle (rɪ'sɛptəkᵊl) *n.* 1. an object that holds something; container. 2. *Botany.* a. the enlarged or modified tip of the flower stalk that bears the parts of the flower. b. the shortened flattened stem bearing the florets of the capitulum of composite flowers such as the daisy. c. the part of lower plants that bears the reproductive organs or spores. [C15: from Latin *receptāculum* a store-place, from *receptāre* to receive again, from *recipere* to RECEIVE]

reception (rɪ'sɛpʃən) *n.* 1. the act of receiving or state of being received. 2. the manner in which something, such as a guest or a new idea, is received: *a cold reception.* 3. a formal party for guests, such as one after a wedding. 4. an area in an office, hotel, etc., where visitors or guests are received and appointments or reservations dealt with. 5. short for **reception room.** 6. the quality or fidelity of a received radio or television broadcast: *the reception was poor.* 7. *Brit.* a. the first class in an infant school. b. a class in a school designed to receive new immigrants, esp. those whose knowledge of English is poor. c. (*as modifier*): *a reception teacher.* [C14: from Latin *receptiō* a receiving, from *recipere* to RECEIVE]

reception centre *n. Social welfare.* (in Britain) 1. a place to which distressed people, such as vagrants, addicts, victims of a disaster, refugees, etc., go pending more permanent arrangements. 2. a local-authority home where children are looked after in a family crisis or where long-term placement is arranged for a child whose family cannot provide a home.

receptionist (rɪ'sɛpʃənɪst) *n.* a person employed in an office, hotel, doctor's surgery, etc., to receive clients, guests, or patients, answer the telephone, and arrange appointments, etc.

reception room *n.* 1. a room in a private house suitable for entertaining guests, esp. a lounge or dining room. 2. a room in a hotel suitable for large parties, receptions, etc.

receptive (rɪ'sɛptɪv) *adj.* 1. able to apprehend quickly. 2. tending to receive new ideas or suggestions favourably. 3. able to hold or receive. —**re'ceptively** *adv.* —**receptivity** (ˌriːsɛp'tɪvɪtɪ) *or* **re'ceptiveness** *n.*

receptor (rɪ'sɛptə) *n.* 1. *Physiol.* a sensory nerve ending that changes specific stimuli into nerve impulses. 2. any of various devices that receive information, signals, etc.

recess *n.* (rɪ'sɛs, 'riːsɛs). 1. a space, such as a niche or alcove, set back or indented. 2. (*often pl.*) a secluded or secret place: *recesses of the mind.* 3. a cessation of business, such as the closure of Parliament during a vacation. 4. *Anatomy.* a small cavity or depression in a bodily organ, part, or structure. 5. *U.S. and Canadian.* a break between classes at a school. ~*vb.* (rɪ'sɛs). 6. (*tr.*) to place or set (something) in a recess. 7. (*tr.*) to build a recess or recesses in (a wall, building, etc.). [C16: from Latin *recessus* a retreat, from *recēdere* to RECEDE]

recession[1] (rɪ'sɛʃən) *n.* 1. a temporary depression in economic activity or prosperity. 2. the withdrawal of the clergy and choir in procession from the chancel at the conclusion of a church

reˌcapitali'zation *or* **reˌcapitali'sation** *n.*
re'capitalˌize *or* **re'capitalˌise** *vb.*
re'cast *vb.,* **-'casts, -'casting, -'cast.**
re'caution *vb.*

service. **3.** the act of receding. **4.** a part of a building, wall, etc., that recedes. [C17: from Latin *recessio;* see RECESS]

recession[2] (riːˈsɛʃən) *n.* the act of restoring possession to a former owner. [C19: from RE- + CESSION]

recessional (rɪˈsɛʃənᵊl) *adj.* **1.** of or relating to recession. ~*n.* **2.** a hymn sung as the clergy and choir withdraw from the chancel at the conclusion of a church service.

recessionary (rɪˈsɛʃənərɪ) *adj.* of, caused by, or undergoing economic recession.

recessive (rɪˈsɛsɪv) *adj.* **1.** tending to recede or go back; receding. **2.** *Genetics.* **a.** (of a gene) capable of producing its characteristic phenotype in the organism only when its allele is identical. **b.** (of a character) controlled by such a gene. Compare **dominant** (sense 4). **3.** *Linguistics.* (of stress) tending to be placed on or near the initial syllable of a polysyllabic word. ~*n.* **4.** *Genetics.* **a.** a recessive gene or character. **b.** an organism having such a gene or character. —**reˈcessively** *adv.* —**reˈcessiveness** *n.*

Rechabite (ˈrɛkəˌbaɪt) *n.* a total abstainer from alcoholic drink, esp. a member of the Independent Order of Rechabites, a society devoted to abstention. [C14: via Medieval Latin from Hebrew *Rēkābīm* descendants of *Rēkāb.* See Jeremiah 35:6]

recharge (ˌriːˈtʃɑːdʒ) *vb.* (*tr.*) **1.** to cause (an accumulator, capacitor, etc.) to take up and store electricity again. **2.** to revive or renew (one's energies) (esp. in **recharge one's batteries**). —**reˈchargeable** *adj.*

réchauffé *French.* (reʃofe) *n.* **1.** warmed-up leftover food. **2.** old, stale, or reworked material. [C19: from French *réchauffer* to reheat, from RE- + *chauffer* to warm; see CHAFE]

recherché (rəˈʃɛəʃeɪ; *French* rəʃɛrʃe) *adj.* **1.** known only to connoisseurs; choice or rare. **2.** studiedly refined or elegant. [C18: from French: past participle of *rechercher* to make a thorough search for; see RESEARCH]

recidivism (rɪˈsɪdɪˌvɪzəm) *n.* habitual relapse into crime. [C19: from Latin *recidīvus* falling back, from RE- + *cadere* to fall] —**reˈcidivist** *n., adj.* —**reˌcidiˈvistic** *or* **reˈcidivous** *adj.*

recipe (ˈrɛsɪpɪ) *n.* **1.** a list of ingredients and directions for making something, esp. a food preparation. **2.** *Med.* (formerly) a medical prescription. **3.** a method for achieving some desired objective: *a recipe for success.* [C14: from Latin, literally: take (it)! from *recipere* to take, RECEIVE]

recipience (rɪˈsɪpɪəns) *n.* **1.** the act of receiving. **2.** the quality of being receptive; receptiveness.

recipient (rɪˈsɪpɪənt) *n.* **1.** a person who or thing that receives. ~*adj.* **2.** a less common word for **receptive.** [C16: via French from Latin *recipiēns,* from *recipere* to RECEIVE]

reciprocal (rɪˈsɪprəkᵊl) *adj.* **1.** of, relating to, or designating something given by each of two people, countries, etc., to the other; mutual: *reciprocal friendship; reciprocal trade.* **2.** given or done in return: *a reciprocal favour.* **3.** (of a pronoun) indicating that action is given and received by each subject; for example, *each other* in the sentence *they started to shout at each other.* **4.** *Maths.* of or relating to a number or quantity divided into one. **5.** *Navigation.* denoting a course or bearing that is 180° from the previous or assumed one. ~*n.* **6.** something that is reciprocal. **7.** Also called: **inverse.** *Maths.* a number or quantity that when multiplied by a given number or quantity gives a product of one: *the reciprocal of 2 is 0.5.* [C16: from Latin *reciprocus* alternating] —**reˌciproˈcality** *n.* —**reˈciprocally** *adv.*

reciprocate (rɪˈsɪprəˌkeɪt) *vb.* **1.** to give or feel in return. **2.** to move or cause to move backwards and forwards. **3.** (*intr.*) to be correspondent or equivalent. [C17: from Latin *reciprocāre,* from *reciprocus* RECIPROCAL] —**reˌciproˈcation** *n.* —**reˈciprocative** *or* **reˈciproˌcatory** *adj.* —**reˈciproˌcator** *n.*

reciprocating engine *n.* an engine in which one or more pistons move backwards and forwards inside a cylinder or cylinders.

reciprocity (ˌrɛsɪˈprɒsɪtɪ) *n., pl.* **-ities. 1.** reciprocal action or relation. **2.** a mutual exchange of commercial or other privileges. [C18: via French from Latin *reciprocus* RECIPROCAL]

reciprocity failure *n. Photog.* a failure of the two exposure variables, light intensity and exposure time, to behave in a reciprocal fashion at very high or very low values.

recision (rɪˈsɪʒən) *n.* the act of cancelling or rescinding; annulment: *the recision of a treaty.* [C17: from Latin *recīsiō,* from *recīdere* to cut back]

recit. *Music. abbrev. for* recitative.

recital (rɪˈsaɪtᵊl) *n.* **1.** a musical performance by a soloist or soloists. Compare **concert** (sense 1). **2.** the act of reciting or repeating something learned or prepared. **3.** an account, narration, or description. **4.** a detailed statement of facts, figures, etc. **5.** (*often pl.*) *Law.* the preliminary statement in a deed showing the reason for its existence and leading up to and explaining the operative part. —**reˈcitalist** *n.*

recitation (ˌrɛsɪˈteɪʃən) *n.* **1.** the act of reciting from memory, or a formal reading of verse before an audience. **2.** something recited.

recitative[1] (ˌrɛsɪtəˈtiːv) *n.* a passage in a musical composition, esp. the narrative parts in an oratorio, set for one voice with either continuo accompaniment only or full accompaniment, reflecting the natural rhythms of speech. [C17: from Italian *recitativo;* see RECITE]

recitative[2] (rɪˈsaɪtətɪv) *adj.* of or relating to recital.

recite (rɪˈsaɪt) *vb.* **1.** to repeat (a poem, passage, etc.) aloud from memory before an audience, teacher, etc. **2.** (*tr.*) to give a detailed account of. **3.** (*tr.*) to enumerate (examples, etc.). [C15: from Latin *recitāre* to cite again, from RE- + *citāre* to summon; see CITE] —**reˈcitable** *adj.* —**reˈciter** *n.*

reck (rɛk) *vb. Archaic.* (*used mainly with a negative*) **1.** to mind or care about (something): *to reck nought.* **2.** (*usually impersonal*) to concern or interest (someone). [Old English *reccan;* related to Old High German *ruohhen* to take care, Old Norse *rœkja,* Gothic *rakjan*]

reckless (ˈrɛklɪs) *adj.* having or showing no regard for danger or consequences; heedless; rash: *a reckless driver; a reckless attempt.* [Old English *recceleās* (see RECK, -LESS); related to Middle Dutch *roekeloos,* Old High German *ruahhalōs*] —ˈ**recklessly** *adv.* —ˈ**recklessness** *n.*

reckon (ˈrɛkən) *vb.* **1.** to calculate or ascertain by calculating; compute. **2.** (*tr.*) to include; count as part of a set or class: *I reckon her with the angels.* **3.** (*usually passive*) to consider or regard: *he is reckoned clever.* **4.** (when *tr., takes a clause as object*) to think or suppose; be of the opinion: *I reckon you don't know where to go next.* **5.** (*intr.;* foll. by *with*) to settle accounts (with). **6.** (*intr.;* foll. by *with* or *without*) to take into account or fail to take into account: *the bully reckoned without John's big brother.* **7.** (*intr.;* foll. by *on* or *upon*) to rely or depend: *I reckon on your support in this crisis.* **8.** (*tr.*) *Slang.* to regard as good: *I don't reckon your chances of success.* **9.** (*tr.*) *Informal.* to have a high opinion of: *she was sensitive to bad reviews, even from people she did not reckon.* **10. to be reckoned with.** of considerable importance or influence. [Old English *(ge)recenian* recount; related to Old Frisian *rekenia,* Old High German *rehhanón* to count]

▷**Usage.** Some senses of *reckon* are considered informal by many writers and speakers. The usage *I reckon on your support* is sometimes avoided in formal contexts, while in the sentence *It will snow tonight, I reckon,* the words *believe, suppose, think,* or *imagine* are preferred to *reckon.*

reckoner (ˈrɛkənə) *n.* any of various devices or tables used to facilitate reckoning, esp. a ready reckoner.

reckoning (ˈrɛkənɪŋ) *n.* **1.** the act of counting or calculating. **2.** settlement of an account or bill. **3.** a bill or account. **4.** retribution for one's actions (esp. in the phrase **day of reckoning**). **5.** *Navigation.* short for **dead reckoning.**

reclaim (rɪˈkleɪm) *vb.* (*tr.*) **1.** to claim back: *to reclaim baggage.* **2.** to convert (desert, marsh, waste ground, etc.) into land suitable for growing crops. **3.** to recover (useful substances) from waste products. **4.** to convert (someone) from sin, folly, vice, etc. **5.** *Falconry.* to render (a hawk or falcon) tame. ~*n.* **6.** the act of reclaiming or state of being reclaimed. [C13: from Old French *réclamer,* from Latin *reclāmāre* to cry out, protest, from RE- + *clāmāre* to shout] —**reˈclaimable** *adj.* —**reˈclaimant** *or* **reˈclaimer** *n.*

reclamation (ˌrɛkləˈmeɪʃən) *n.* **1.** the conversion of desert, marsh, or other waste land into land suitable for cultivation. **2.** the recovery of useful substances from waste products. **3.** the act of reclaiming or state of being reclaimed.

réclame *French.* (reklam) *n.* **1.** public acclaim or attention; publicity. **2.** the capacity for attracting publicity.

reclinate (ˈrɛklɪˌneɪt) *adj.* (esp. of a leaf or stem) naturally curved or bent backwards so that the upper part rests on the ground. [C18: from Latin *reclīnātus* bent back]

recline (rɪˈklaɪn) *vb.* to rest or cause to rest in a leaning position. [C15: from Old French *recliner,* from Latin *reclīnāre* to lean back, from RE- + *clīnāre* to LEAN[1]] —**reˈclinable** *adj.* —**reclination** (ˌrɛklɪˈneɪʃən) *n.*

recliner (rɪˈklaɪnə) *n.* a person or thing that reclines, esp. a type of armchair having a back that can be adjusted to slope at various angles and, usually, a leg rest.

recluse (rɪˈkluːs) *n.* **1.** a person who lives in seclusion. **2.** a person who lives in solitude to devote himself to prayer and religious meditation; a hermit, anchorite, or anchoress. ~*adj.* **3.** solitary; retiring. [C13: from Old French *reclus,* from Late Latin *reclūdere* to shut away, from Latin RE- + *claudere* to close] —**reclusion** (rɪˈkluːʒən) *n.* —**reˈclusive** *adj.*

recognition (ˌrɛkəgˈnɪʃən) *n.* **1.** the act of recognizing or fact of being recognized. **2.** acceptance or acknowledgment of a claim, duty, fact, truth, etc. **3.** a token of thanks or acknowledgment. **4.** formal acknowledgment of a government or of the independence of a country. **5.** *Chiefly U.S. and Canadian.* an instance of a chairman granting a person the right to speak in a deliberative body, debate, etc. [C15: from Latin *recognitiō,* from *recognoscere*

reˈchallenge *vb.*
reˈchart *vb.*
reˈcharter *vb.*
reˈcheck *vb., n.*
reˈchristen *vb.*
reˈcircuˌlate *vb.*
ˌreclassifiˈcation *n.*
reˈclassiˌfy *vb.,* **-ˌfies, -ˌfying, -ˌfied.**
reˈclothe *vb.*
ˌrecodifiˈcation *n.*
reˈcodiˌfy *vb.,* **-ˌfies, -ˌfying, -ˌfied.**

to know again, from RE- + *cognoscere* to know, ascertain] —**re·cognitive** (rɪˈkɒgnɪtɪv) *or* **reˈcognitory** *adj.*

recognizance *or* **recognisance** (rɪˈkɒgnɪzəns) *n.* **1.** *Law.* **a.** a bond entered into before a court or magistrate by which a person binds himself to do a specified act, as to appear in court on a stated day, keep the peace, or pay a debt. **b.** a monetary sum pledged to the performance of such an act. **2.** an obsolete word for **recognition.** [C14: from Old French *reconoissance,* from *reconoistre* to RECOGNIZE] —**reˈcognizant** *or* **reˈcognisant** *adj.*

recognize *or* **recognise** (ˈrɛkəgˌnaɪz) *vb.* (*tr.*) **1.** to perceive (a person, creature, or thing) to be the same as or belong to the same class as something previously seen or known; know again. **2.** to accept or be aware of (a fact, duty, problem, etc.): *to recognize necessity.* **3.** to give formal acknowledgment of the status or legality of (a government, an accredited representative, etc.) **4.** *Chiefly U.S. and Canadian.* to grant (a person) the right to speak in a deliberative body, debate, etc. **5.** to give a token of thanks for (a service rendered, etc.). **6.** to make formal acknowledgment of (a claim, etc.). **7.** to show approval or appreciation of (something good or pleasing). **8.** to acknowledge or greet (a person), as when meeting by chance. **9.** (*intr.*) *Chiefly U.S.* to enter into a recognizance. [C15: from Latin *recognoscere* to know again, from RE- + *cognoscere* to know, ascertain] —**ˈrecogˌnizable** *or* **ˈrecogˌnisable** *adj.* —**ˌrecogˌnizaˈbility** *or* **ˌrecogˌnisaˈbility** *n.* —**ˈrecogˌnizably** *or* **ˈrecogˌnisably** *adv.* —**ˈrecogˌnizer** *or* **ˈrecogˌniser** *n.*

recognizee *or* **recognisee** (rɪˌkɒgnɪˈziː) *n. Law.* the person to whom one entering into a recognizance is bound.

recognizor *or* **recognisor** (rɪˌkɒgnɪˈzɔː) *n. Law.* a person who enters into a recognizance.

recoil *vb.* (rɪˈkɔɪl). (*intr.*) **1.** to jerk back, as from an impact or violent thrust. **2.** (often foll. by *from*) to draw back in fear, horror, or disgust: *to recoil from the sight of blood.* **3.** (foll. by *on* or *upon*) to go wrong, esp. so as to hurt the perpetrator. **4.** (of a nucleus, atom, molecule, or elementary particle) to change momentum as a result of the emission of a photon or particle. ~*n.* (rɪˈkɔɪl, ˈriːkɔɪl). **5. a.** the backward movement of a gun when fired. **b.** the distance moved. **6.** the motion acquired by a particle as a result of its emission of a photon or other particle. **7.** the act of recoiling. [C13: from Old French *reculer,* from RE- + *cul* rump, from Latin *cūlus*] —**reˈcoiler** *n.*

recoilless (rɪˈkɔɪllɪs) *adj.* denoting a gun, esp. an antitank weapon, in which the blast is vented to the rear so as to eliminate or reduce recoil.

recollect (ˌrɛkəˈlɛkt) *vb.* (when *tr., often takes a clause as object*) to recall from memory; remember. [C16: from Latin *recolligere* to gather again, from RE- + *colligere* to COLLECT] —**ˌrecolˈlection** *n.* —**ˌrecolˈlective** *adj.* —**ˌrecolˈlectively** *adv.*

recombinant DNA (riːˈkɒmbɪnənt) *n.* DNA molecules that are extracted from different sources and chemically joined together; for example DNA comprising an animal gene may be recombined with DNA from a bacterium.

recombination (ˌriːkɒmbɪˈneɪʃən) *n.* **1.** *Genetics.* any of several processes by which genetic material of different origins becomes combined. It most commonly occurs between two sets of parental chromosomes during production of germ cells. **2.** *Physics.* the union of free electrons and holes in a semiconductor.

recommend (ˌrɛkəˈmɛnd) *vb.* (*tr.*) **1.** (*may take a clause as object or an infinitive*) to advise as the best course or choice; counsel: *to recommend prudence.* **2.** to praise or commend: *to recommend a new book.* **3.** to make attractive or advisable: *the trip has little to recommend it.* **4.** *Archaic.* to entrust (a person or thing) to someone else's care; commend. [C14: via Medieval Latin from Latin RE- + *commendāre* to COMMEND] —**ˌrecomˈmendable** *adj.* —**ˌrecomˈmender** *n.*

recommendation (ˌrɛkəmɛnˈdeɪʃən) *n.* **1.** the act of recommending. **2.** something that recommends, esp. a letter presenting someone as suitable for a job, etc. **3.** something that is recommended, such as a course of action.

recommendatory (ˌrɛkəˈmɛndətərɪ, -trɪ) *adj.* intended to or serving to recommend.

recommit (ˌriːkəˈmɪt) *vb.* **-mits, -mitting, -mitted.** (*tr.*) **1.** to send (a bill) back to a committee for further consideration. **2.** to commit again. —**ˌrecomˈmitment** *or* **ˌrecomˈmittal** *n.*

recompense (ˈrɛkəmˌpɛns) *vb.* **1.** (*tr.*) to pay or reward for service, work, etc. **2.** (*tr.*) to compensate for loss, injury, etc. ~*n.* **3.** compensation for loss, injury, etc.: *to make recompense.* **4.** reward, remuneration, or repayment. [C15: from Old French *recompenser,* from Latin RE- + *compensāre* to balance in weighing; see COMPENSATE] —**ˈrecomˌpensable** *adj.* —**ˈrecomˌpenser** *n.*

recompose (ˌriːkəmˈpəʊz) *vb.* (*tr.*) **1.** to restore to composure or calmness. **2.** to arrange or compose again; reform. —**recomposition** (ˌriːkɒmpəˈzɪʃən) *n.*

reconcilable (ˈrɛkənˌsaɪləbᵊl, ˌrɛkənˈsaɪ-) *adj.* able or willing to be reconciled. —**ˌreconˌcilaˈbility** *or* **ˈreconˌcilableness** *n.* —**ˈreconˌcilably** *adv.*

reconcile (ˈrɛkənˌsaɪl) *vb.* (*tr.*) **1.** (*often passive;* usually foll. by *to*) to make (oneself or another) no longer opposed; cause to acquiesce in something unpleasant: *she reconciled herself to poverty.* **2.** to become friendly with (someone) after estrangement or to re-establish friendly relations between (two or more people). **3.** to settle (a quarrel or difference). **4.** to make (two apparently conflicting things) compatible or consistent with each other. **5.** to reconsecrate (a desecrated church, etc.). [C14: from Latin *reconciliāre* to bring together again, from RE- + *conciliāre* to make friendly, CONCILIATE] —**ˈreconˌcilement** *n.* —**ˈreconˌciler** *n.* —**reconciliation** (ˌrɛkənˌsɪlɪˈeɪʃən) *n.* —**reconciliatory** (ˌrɛkənˈsɪlɪətərɪ, -trɪ) *adj.*

recondite (rɪˈkɒndaɪt, ˈrɛkənˌdaɪt) *adj.* **1.** requiring special knowledge to be understood; abstruse. **2.** dealing with abstruse or profound subjects. [C17: from Latin *reconditus* hidden away, from RE- + *condere* to conceal] —**reˈconditely** *adv.* —**reˈconditeness** *n.*

recondition (ˌriːkənˈdɪʃən) *vb.* (*tr.*) to restore to good condition or working order: *to recondition an engine.*

reconnaissance *or* **reconnoissance** (rɪˈkɒnɪsəns) *n.* **1.** the act of reconnoitring. **2.** the process of obtaining information about the position, activities, resources, etc., of an enemy or potential enemy. **3.** a preliminary inspection of an area of land before an engineering survey is made. [C18: from French, from Old French *reconoistre* to explore, RECOGNIZE]

reconnoitre *or U.S.* **reconnoiter** (ˌrɛkəˈnɔɪtə) *vb.* **1.** to survey or inspect (an enemy's position, region of land, etc.); make a reconnaissance (of). ~*n.* **2.** the act or process of reconnoitring; a reconnaissance. [C18: from obsolete French *reconnoître* to inspect, explore; see RECOGNIZE] —**ˌreconˈnoitrer** *or U.S.* **ˌreconˈnoiterer** *n.*

reconsider (ˌriːkənˈsɪdə) *vb.* **1.** to consider (something) again, with a view to changing one's policy or course of action. **2.** (in a legislative assembly or similar body) to consider again (a bill or other matter) that has already been voted upon. —**ˌreconˌsiderˈation** *n.*

reconstitute (riːˈkɒnstɪˌtjuːt) *vb.* (*tr.*) **1.** to restore (food, etc.) to its former or natural state or a semblance of it, as by the addition of water to a concentrate: *reconstituted lemon juice.* **2.** to reconstruct; form again. —**reconstituent** (ˌriːkənˈstɪtjʊənt) *adj., n.* —**ˌreconstiˈtution** *n.*

reconstruct (ˌriːkənˈstrʌkt) *vb.* (*tr.*) **1.** to construct or form again; rebuild: *to reconstruct a Greek vase from fragments.* **2.** to form a picture of (a crime, past event, etc.) by piecing together evidence or acting out a version of what might have taken place. —**ˌreconˈstructible** *adj.* —**ˌreconˈstruction** *n.* —**ˌreconˈstructive** *or* **ˌreconˈstructional** *adj.* —**ˌreconˈstructor** *n.*

reconvert (ˌriːkənˈvɜːt) *vb.* (*tr.*) **1.** to change (something) back to a previous state or form. **2.** to bring (someone) back to his former religion. **3.** *Property law.* to convert back (property previously converted) into its original form, as land into money and vice versa. See also **conversion** (sense 5). —**reconversion** (ˌriːkənˈvɜːʃən) *n.*

record *n.* (ˈrɛkɔːd). **1.** an account in permanent form, esp. in writing, preserving knowledge or information about facts or events. **2.** a written account of some transaction that serves as legal evidence of the transaction. **3.** a written official report of the proceedings of a court of justice or legislative body, including the judgments given or enactments made. **4.** anything serving as evidence or as a memorial: *the First World War is a record of human folly.* **5.** (*often pl.*) information or data on a specific subject collected methodically over a long period: *weather records.* **6. a.** the best or most outstanding amount, rate, height, etc., ever attained, as in some field of sport: *an Olympic record; a world record; to break the record for the long jump.* **b.** (*as modifier*): *a record time.* **7.** the sum of one's recognized achievements, career, or performance: *the officer has an excellent record.* **8.** a list of crimes of which an accused person has previously been convicted, which are known to the police but may only be disclosed to a court in certain circumstances. **9. have a record.** to be a known criminal; have a previous conviction or convictions. **10.** Also called: **gramophone record, disc.** a thin disc of a plastic material upon which sound has been recorded. Each side has a spiral groove, which undulates in accordance with the frequency and amplitude of the sound. Records were formerly made from a shellac-based compound but are now usually made

reˈcoin *vb.*
ˌrecoloniˈzation *or* **ˌrecoloniˈsation** *n.*
reˈcoloˌnize *or* **reˈcoloˌnise** *vb.*
reˈcolour *vb.*
ˌrecomˈbine *vb.*
ˌrecomˈmence *vb.*
ˌrecomˈmencement *n.*
ˌrecomˈmitment *n.*
ˌrecomˈparison *n.*
ˌrecomˈpound *vb.*
reˈconcenˌtrate *vb.*
ˌreconcenˈtration *n.*
ˌrecondenˈsation *n.*
ˌreconˈdense *vb.*
ˌreconˈfirm *vb.*
ˌreconfirˈmation *n.*
ˌreconˈnect *vb.*
ˌreconˈnection *n.*
reˈconquer *vb.*
reˈconquest *n.*
reˈconseˌcrate *vb.*
ˌreconseˈcration *n.*
ˌreconˈsign *vb.*
ˌreconˈsignment *n.*
ˌreconˈsolidate *vb.*
ˌreconˌsoliˈdation *n.*
ˌreconˈtest *vb.*
ˌreconˈvene *vb.*
ˌreconˈvey *vb.*
ˌreconˈvict *vb.*
ˌreconˈviction *n.*
reˈcopy *vb.,* **-ˈcopies, -ˈcopying, -ˈcopied.**

from vinyl plastics. **11.** the markings made by a recording instrument such as a seismograph. **12.** *Computer technol.* a group of data or piece of information preserved as a unit in machine-readable form. **13.** (in some computer languages) a data structure designed to allow the handling of groups of related pieces of information as though the group was a single entity. **14. for the record.** for the sake of strict factual accuracy. **15. go on record.** to state one's views publicly. **16.** See **off the record. 17. on record. a.** stated in a public document. **b.** publicly known. **18. set** *or* **put the record straight.** to correct an error or misunderstanding. ~*vb.* (rɪ'kɔːd). (*mainly tr.*) **19.** to set down in some permanent form so as to preserve the true facts of: *to record the minutes of a meeting.* **20.** to contain or serve to relate (facts, information, etc.). **21.** to indicate, show, or register: *his face recorded his disappointment.* **22.** to remain as or afford evidence of: *these ruins record the life of the Romans in Britain.* **23.** (*also intr.*) to make a recording of (music, speech, etc.) for reproduction, esp. on a record player or tape recorder, or for later broadcasting. **24.** (*also intr.*) (of an instrument) to register or indicate (information) on a scale: *the barometer recorded a low pressure.* [C13: from Old French *recorder* to call to mind, from Latin *recordārī* to remember, from RE- + *cor* heart] —re'**cordable** *adj.*

record-changer *n.* a device in a record player for changing records automatically.

recorded delivery *n.* a Post Office service by which an official record of posting and delivery is obtained for a letter or package. Compare **registered post.**

recorder (rɪ'kɔːdə) *n.* **1.** a person who records, such as an official or historian. **2.** something that records, esp. an apparatus that provides a permanent record of experiments, etc. **3.** short for **tape recorder. 4.** *Music.* a wind instrument of the flute family, blown through a fipple in the mouth end, having a reedlike quality of tone. There are four usual sizes: bass, tenor, treble, and descant. **5.** (in England) a barrister or solicitor of at least ten years' standing appointed to sit as a part-time judge in the crown court. [sense 4 probably from *record* (*vb.*) in the archaic sense "to sing"] —**re'corder,ship** *n.*

recording (rɪ'kɔːdɪŋ) *n.* **1. a.** the act or process of making a record, esp. of sound on a gramophone record or magnetic tape. **b.** (*as modifier*): *recording studio; recording head.* **2.** the record or tape so produced. **3.** something that has been recorded, esp. a radio or television programme.

Recording Angel *n.* an angel who supposedly keeps a record of every person's good and bad acts.

record of achievement *n. Brit.* a statement of the personal and educational development of each pupil.

record player *n.* a device for reproducing the sounds stored on a record, consisting of a turntable, usually electrically driven, that rotates the record at a fixed speed of 33, 45, or (esp. formerly) 78 revolutions a minute. A stylus vibrates in accordance with undulations in the groove in the record: these vibrations are converted into electric currents, which, after amplification, are recreated in the form of sound by one or more loudspeakers. See also **monophonic, quadraphonics, stereophonic.**

reco-reco ('rɛkəʊ'rɛkəʊ) *n., pl.* **reco-recos.** a percussion instrument consisting of a ridged gourd or bamboo cane that is scraped with a piece of wood or metal. [C20: from a native Brazilian language]

recount (rɪ'kaʊnt) *vb.* (*tr.*) to tell the story or details of; narrate. [C15: from Old French *reconter,* from RE- + *conter* to tell, relate; see COUNT[1]] —**re'countal** *n.*

re-count *vb.* (riː'kaʊnt). **1.** to count (votes, etc.) again. ~*n.* ('riː,kaʊnt). **2.** a second or further count, esp. of votes in a closely contested election.

recoup (rɪ'kuːp) *vb.* **1.** to regain or make good (a financial or other loss). **2.** (*tr.*) to reimburse or compensate (someone), as for a loss. **3.** *Law.* to keep back (something due), having rightful claim to do so; withhold; deduct. ~*n.* **4.** *Rare.* the act of recouping; recoupment. [C15: from Old French *recouper* to cut back, from RE- + *couper* to cut, from *coper* to behead; see COUP] —**re'coupable** *adj.* —**re'coupment** *n.*

recourse (rɪ'kɔːs) *n.* **1.** the act of resorting to a person, course of action, etc., in difficulty or danger (esp. in the phrase **have recourse to**). **2.** a person, organization, or course of action that is turned to for help, protection, etc. **3.** the right to demand payment, esp. from the drawer or endorser of a bill of exchange or other negotiable instrument when the person accepting it fails to pay. **4. without recourse.** a qualified endorsement on such a negotiable instrument, by which the endorser protects himself from liability to subsequent holders. [C14: from Old French *recours,* from Late Latin *recursus* a running back, from RE- + *currere* to run]

recover (rɪ'kʌvə) *vb.* **1.** (*tr.*) to find again or obtain the return of (something lost). **2.** to regain (loss of money, position, time, etc.); recoup. **3.** (of a person) to regain (health, spirits, composure, etc.), as after illness, a setback, or a shock, etc. **4.** to regain (a former and usually better condition): *industry recovered after the war.* **5.** *Law.* **a.** (*tr.*) to gain (something) by the judgment of a court of law: *to recover damages.* **b.** (*intr.*) to succeed in a lawsuit. **6.** (*tr.*) to obtain (useful substances) from waste. **7.** (*intr.*) (in fencing, swimming, rowing, etc.) to make a recovery. [C14: from Old French *recoverer,* from Latin *recuperāre* RECUPERATE] —**re'coverable** *adj.* —**re,covera'bility** *n.* —**re'coverer** *n.*

re-cover (riː'kʌvə) *vb.* (*tr.*) **1.** to cover again. **2.** to provide (a piece of furniture, book, etc.) with a new cover.

recovery (rɪ'kʌvərɪ) *n., pl.* **-eries. 1.** the act or process of recovering, esp. from sickness, a shock, or a setback; recuperation. **2.** restoration to a former or better condition. **3.** the regaining of something lost. **4.** the extraction of useful substances from waste. **5.** *Law.* **a.** the obtaining of a right, etc., by the judgment of a court. **b.** (in the U.S.) the final judgment or verdict in a case. **6.** *Fencing.* a return to the position of guard after making an attack. **7.** *Swimming, rowing, etc.* the action of bringing the arm, oar, etc., forward for another stroke. **8.** *Golf.* a stroke played from the rough or a bunker to the fairway or green.

recovery stock *n. Stock Exchange.* a security that has fallen in price but is believed to have the ability to recover.

recreant ('rɛkrɪənt) *Archaic.* ~*adj.* **1.** cowardly; faint-hearted. **2.** disloyal. ~*n.* **3.** a disloyal or cowardly person. [C14: from Old French, from *recroire* to surrender, from RE- + Latin *crēdere* to believe; compare MISCREANT] —'**recreance** *or* '**recreancy** *n.* —'**recreantly** *adv.*

recreate ('rɛkrɪ,eɪt) *vb. Rare.* to amuse (oneself or someone else). [C15: from Latin *recreāre* to invigorate, renew, from RE- + *creāre* to CREATE] —'**recreative** *adj.* —'**recreatively** *adv.* —'**recre,ator** *n.*

re-create (,riːkrɪ'eɪt) *vb.* to create anew; reproduce. —,**re-cre'ation** *n.* —,**re-cre'ator** *n.*

recreation (,rɛkrɪ'eɪʃən) *n.* **1.** refreshment of health or spirits by relaxation and enjoyment. **2.** an activity or pastime that promotes this. **3. a.** an interval of free time between school lessons. **b.** (*as modifier*): *recreation period.*

recreational (,rɛkrɪ'eɪʃənᵊl) *adj.* **1.** of, relating to, or used for recreation: *recreational facilities.* **2.** (of a drug) taken for pleasure rather than for medical reasons or because of an addiction.

recreation ground *n.* an open space for public recreation, esp. one in a town, with swings and slides, etc., for children. Often shortened (informal) to: **rec.**

recreation room *n. U.S. and Canadian.* **1.** the full name for **rec room. 2.** a room in a hotel, hospital, etc., for entertainment and social gatherings.

recrement ('rɛkrɪmənt) *n.* **1.** *Physiol.* any substance, such as bile, that is secreted from a part of the body and later reabsorbed instead of being excreted. **2.** waste matter; refuse; dross. [C16: via Old French from Latin *recrēmentum* slag, filth, from RE- + *cernere* to sift] —,**recre'mental** *adj.*

recriminate (rɪ'krɪmɪ,neɪt) *vb.* (*intr.*) to return an accusation against someone or engage in mutual accusations. [C17: from Medieval Latin *recrīmināre,* from Latin *crīminārī* to accuse, from *crīmen* an accusation; see CRIME] —**re'criminative** *or* **re'criminatory** *adj.* —**re'crimi,nator** *n.*

recrimination (rɪ,krɪmɪ'neɪʃən) *n.* **1.** the act or an instance of recriminating. **2.** *Law.* a charge made by an accused against his accuser; countercharge.

rec room *n. U.S. and Canadian.* a room in a house used by the family for relaxation and entertainment. In full: **recreation room.**

recrudesce (,riːkruː'dɛs) *vb.* (*intr.*) (of a disease, trouble, etc.) to break out or appear again after a period of dormancy; recur. [C19: from Latin *recrūdēscere* to become raw again, from RE- + *crūdēscere* to grow worse, from *crūdus* bloody, raw; see CRUDE] —,**recru'descence** *n.* —,**recru'descent** *adj.*

recruit (rɪ'kruːt) *vb.* **1. a.** to enlist (men) for military service. **b.** to raise or strengthen (an army, navy, etc.) by enlistment. **2.** (*tr.*) to enrol or obtain (members, support, etc.). **3.** to furnish or be furnished with a fresh supply; renew. **4.** *Archaic.* to recover (health, strength, spirits, etc.). ~*n.* **5.** a newly joined member of a military service. **6.** any new member or supporter. [C17: from French *recrute* literally: new growth, from *recroître* to grow again, from Latin *recrēscere,* from RE- + *crēscere* to grow] —**re'cruitable** *adj.* —**re'cruiter** *n.* —**re'cruitment** *n.*

recrystallize *or* **recrystallise** (riː'krɪstə,laɪz) *vb.* **1.** *Chem.* to dissolve and subsequently crystallize (a substance) from the solution, as in purifying chemical compounds, or (of a substance) to crystallize in this way. **2.** to undergo or cause to undergo the process in which a deformed metal forms a new set of undeformed crystal grains. —**re,crystalli'zation** *or* **re,crystalli'sation** *n.*

rect *or* **rec't** *abbrev. for* receipt.

Rect. *abbrev. for:* **1.** Rector. **2.** Rectory.

recta ('rɛktə) *n.* a plural of **rectum.**

rectal ('rɛktəl) *adj.* of or relating to the rectum. —'**rectally** *adv.*

rectangle ('rɛk,tæŋgᵊl) *n.* a parallelogram having four right angles. Compare **rhombus.** [C16: from Medieval Latin *rectangulum,* from Latin *rectus* straight + *angulus* angle]

rectangular (rɛk'tæŋgjʊlə) *adj.* **1.** shaped like a rectangle. **2.** having or relating to right angles. **3.** mutually perpendicular:

,**re-cre'ation** *n.* **re'cross** *vb.* **re'crown** *vb.*

rectangular coordinates. **4.** having a base or section shaped like a rectangle. —**rec,tangu'larity** *n.* —**rec'tangularly** *adv.*

rectangular coordinates *pl. n.* the Cartesian coordinates in a system of mutually perpendicular axes.

rectangular hyperbola *n.* a hyperbola with perpendicular asymptotes.

recti ('rɛktaɪ) *n.* the plural of **rectus.**

recti- *or before a vowel* **rect-** *combining form.* straight or right: *rectilinear; rectangle.* [from Latin *rectus*]

rectified spirit *n. Chem.* a constant-boiling mixture of ethanol and water, containing 95.6 per cent ethanol.

rectifier ('rɛktɪ,faɪə) *n.* **1.** an electronic device, such as a semiconductor diode or valve, that converts an alternating current to a direct current by suppression or inversion of alternate half cycles. **2.** *Chem.* an apparatus for condensing a hot vapour to a liquid in distillation; condenser. **3.** a thing or person that rectifies.

rectify ('rɛktɪ,faɪ) *vb.* **-fies, -fying, -fied.** (*tr.*) **1.** to put right; correct; remedy. **2.** to separate (a substance) from a mixture or refine (a substance) by fractional distillation. **3.** to convert (alternating current) into direct current. **4.** *Maths.* to determine the length of (a curve). **5.** to cause (an object) to assume a linear motion or characteristic. [C14: via Old French from Medieval Latin *rectificāre* to adjust, from Latin *rectus* straight + *facere* to make] —**'recti,fiable** *adj.* —**,rectifi'cation** *n.*

rectilinear (,rɛktɪ'lɪnɪə) *or* **rectilineal** *adj.* **1.** in, moving in, or characterized by a straight line or lines: *the rectilinear propagation of light.* **2.** consisting of, bounded by, or formed by a straight line or lines. —**,recti'linearly** *or* **,recti'lineally** *adv.*

rectitude ('rɛktɪ,tjuːd) *n.* **1.** moral or religious correctness. **2.** correctness of judgment. [C15: from Late Latin *rectitūdō*, from Latin *rectus* right, straight, from *regere* to rule]

recto ('rɛktəʊ) *n., pl.* **-tos.** **1.** the front of a sheet of printed paper. **2.** the right-hand pages of a book, bearing the odd numbers. Compare **verso** (sense 1b). [C19: from Latin *rectus* right, in *rectō foliō* on the right-hand page]

rectocele ('rɛktəʊ,siːl) *n. Pathol.* a protrusion or herniation of the rectum into the vagina. [C19: New Latin, from RECTUM + -CELE]

rector ('rɛktə) *n.* **1.** *Church of England.* a clergyman in charge of a parish in which, as its incumbent, he would formerly have been entitled to the whole of the tithes. Compare **vicar.** **2.** *R.C. Church.* a cleric in charge of a college, religious house, or congregation. **3.** *Protestant Episcopal Church.* a clergyman in charge of a parish. **4.** *Chiefly Brit.* the head of certain schools or colleges. **5.** (in Scotland) a high-ranking official in a university: now a public figure elected for three years by the students. [C14: from Latin: director, ruler, from *regere* to rule] —**'rectorate** *n.* —**rectorial** (rɛk'tɔːrɪəl) *adj.* —**'rectorship** *n.*

rectory ('rɛktərɪ) *n., pl.* **-ries.** **1.** the official house of a rector. **2.** *Church of England.* the office and benefice of a rector.

rectrix ('rɛktrɪks) *n., pl.* **rectrices** ('rɛktrɪ,siːz, rɛk'traɪsiːz). any of the large stiff feathers of a bird's tail, used in controlling the direction of flight. [C17: from Late Latin, feminine of *rector* governor, RECTOR] —**rectricial** (rɛk'trɪʃəl) *adj.*

rectum ('rɛktəm) *n., pl.* **-tums** *or* **-ta** (-tə). the lower part of the alimentary canal, between the sigmoid flexure of the colon and the anus. [C16: shortened from New Latin *rectum intestinum* the straight intestine]

rectus ('rɛktəs) *n., pl.* **-ti** (-taɪ). *Anatomy.* a straight muscle, esp. either of two muscles of the anterior abdominal wall (**rectus abdominis**). [C18: from New Latin *rectus musculus*]

recumbent (rɪ'kʌmbənt) *adj.* **1.** lying down; reclining. **2.** (of a part or organ) leaning or resting against another organ or the ground: *a recumbent stem.* **3.** (of a fold in a rock formation) having strata nearly parallel to those of the surrounding formation. [C17: from Latin *recumbere* to lie back, from RE- + *cumbere* to lie] —**re'cumbence** *or* **re'cumbency** *n.* —**re'cumbently** *adv.*

recuperate (rɪ'kuːpə,reɪt, -'kjuː-) *vb.* **1.** (*intr.*) to recover from illness or exhaustion. **2.** to recover (losses of money, etc.). [C16: from Latin *recuperāre* to recover, from RE- + *capere* to gain, take] —**re,cuper'ation** *n.* —**re'cuperative** *adj.*

recuperator (rɪ'kuːpə,reɪtə, -'kjuː-) *n.* **1.** a person that recuperates. **2.** a device employing springs or pneumatic power to return a gun to the firing position after the recoil. **3.** *Chemical engineering.* a system of flues that transfers heat from the hot gases leaving a furnace to the incoming air.

recur (rɪ'kɜː) *vb.* **-curs, -curring, -curred.** (*intr.*) **1.** to happen again, esp. at regular intervals. **2.** (of a thought, idea, etc.) to come back to the mind. **3.** (of a problem, etc.) to come up again. **4.** *Maths.* (of a digit or group of digits) to be repeated an infinite number of times at the end of a decimal fraction. [C15: from Latin *recurrere,* from RE- + *currere* to run] —**re'curring** *adj.* —**re'curringly** *adv.*

recurrent (rɪ'kʌrənt) *adj.* **1.** happening or tending to happen again or repeatedly. **2.** *Anatomy.* (of certain nerves, branches of vessels, etc.) turning back, so as to run in the opposite direction. —**re'currently** *adv.* —**re'currence** *n.*

recurrent fever *n.* another name for **relapsing fever.**

recurring decimal *n.* a rational number that contains a pattern of digits repeated indefinitely after the decimal point. Also called: **circulating decimal, repeating decimal.**

recursion (rɪ'kɜːʃən) *n.* **1.** the act or process of returning or running back. **2.** *Logic, maths.* the application of a function to its own values to generate an infinite sequence of values. The **recursion formula** or **clause** of a definition specifies the progression from one term to the next, as given the base clause $f(0) = 0$, $f(n + 1) = f(n) + 3$ specifies the successive terms of the sequence $f(n) = 3n$. [C17: from Latin *recursio,* from *recurrere* RECUR] —**re'cursive** *adj.*

recursive function *n. Logic, maths.* a function defined in terms of the repeated application of a number of simpler functions to their own values, by specifying a base clause and a recursion formula.

recursive subroutine *n. Computer technol.* a subroutine that can call itself as part of its execution.

recurvate (rɪ'kɜːvɪt, -veɪt) *adj. Rare.* bent back.

recurve (rɪ'kɜːv) *vb.* to curve or bend (something) back or down or (of something) to be so curved or bent. [C16: from Latin *recurvāre* from RE- + *curvāre* to CURVE]

recusant ('rɛkjʊzənt) *n.* **1.** (in 16th to 18th century England) a Roman Catholic who did not attend the services of the Church of England, as was required by law. **2.** any person who refuses to submit to authority. ~*adj.* **3.** (formerly, of Catholics) refusing to attend services of the Church of England. **4.** refusing to submit to authority. [C16: from Latin *recūsāns* refusing, from *recūsāre* from RE- + *causārī* to dispute, from *causa* a CAUSE] —**'recusance** *or* **'recusancy** *n.*

recycle (riː'saɪkᵊl) *vb.* (*tr.*) **1.** to pass (a substance) through a system again for further treatment or use. **2.** to reclaim (packaging or products with a limited useful life) for further use. **3.** to institute a different cycle of processes or events in (a machine, system, etc.). **4.** to repeat (a series of operations). ~*n.* **5.** the repetition of a fixed sequence of events. —**re'cyclable** *or* **re'cycleable** *adj.*

red[1] (rɛd) *n.* **1.** any of a group of colours, such as that of a ripe tomato or fresh blood, that lie at one end of the visible spectrum, next to orange, and are perceived by the eye when light in the approximate wavelength range 740–620 nanometres falls on the retina. Red is the complementary colour of cyan and forms a set of primary colours with blue and green. **2.** a pigment or dye of or producing these colours. **3.** red cloth or clothing: *dressed in red.* **4.** a red ball in snooker, billiards, etc. **5.** (in roulette and other gambling games) one of two colours on which players may place even bets, the other being black. **6.** Also called: **inner.** *Archery.* a red ring on a target, between the blue and the gold, scoring seven points. **7. in the red.** *Informal.* in debit; owing money. **8. see red.** *Informal.* to become very angry. ~*adj.* **redder, reddest.** **9.** of the colour red. **10.** reddish in colour or having parts or marks that are reddish: *red hair; red deer.* **11.** having the face temporarily suffused with blood, being a sign of anger, shame, etc. **12.** (of the complexion) rosy; florid. **13.** (of the eyes) bloodshot. **14.** (of the hands) stained with blood, as after committing murder. **15.** bloody or violent: *red revolution.* **16.** (of wine) made from black grapes and coloured by their skins. **17.** denoting the highest degree of urgency in an emergency; used by the police and the army and informally (esp. in the phrase **red alert**). ~*vb.* **reds, redding, redded.** **18.** another word for **redden.** [Old English *rēad;* compare Old High German *rōt,* Gothic *rauths,* Latin *ruber,* Greek *eruthros,* Sanskrit *rohita*] —**'redly** *adv.* —**'redness** *n.*

red[2] (rɛd) *vb.* **reds, redding, red** *or* **redded.** (*tr.*) a variant spelling of **redd**[1].

Red (rɛd) *Informal.* ~*adj.* **1.** Communist, Socialist, or Soviet. **2.** radical, leftist, or revolutionary. ~*n.* **3.** a member or supporter of a Communist or Socialist Party or a national of a state having such a government. **4.** a radical, leftist, or revolutionary. [C19: from the colour chosen to symbolize revolutionary socialism]

red. *abbrev. for* reduce(d).

redact (rɪ'dækt) *vb.* (*tr.*) **1.** to compose or draft (an edict, proclamation, etc.). **2.** to put (a literary work, etc.) into appropriate form for publication; edit. [C15: from Latin *redigere* to bring back, from *red-* RE- + *agere* to drive] —**re'daction** *n.* —**re'dactional** *adj.* —**re'dactor** *n.*

red admiral *n.* a nymphalid butterfly, *Vanessa atalanta,* of temperate Europe and Asia, having black wings with red and white markings. See also **white admiral.**

red algae *pl. n.* the numerous algae that constitute the family *Rhodophyceae,* which contain a red pigment in addition to chlorophyll. The group includes carrageen, dulse, and laver. Also called: **red seaweed.**

redan (rɪ'dæn) *n.* a fortification of two parapets at a salient angle. [C17: from French, from earlier *redent* notching of a saw edge, from RE- + *dent* tooth, from Latin *dēns*]

red-backed shrike *n.* a common Eurasian shrike, *Lanius collurio,* the male of which has a grey crown and rump, brown wings and back, and a black-and-white face.

redback spider *n.* a small venomous Australian spider, *Latrodectus hasselti,* having long thin legs and, in the female, a red stripe on the back of its globular abdomen.

red bag *n.* (in Britain) a fabric bag for a barrister's robes, presented by a Queen's Counsel to a junior in appreciation of good work in a case. See also **blue bag.**

red bark *n.* a kind of cinchona containing a high proportion of alkaloids.
red beds *pl. n.* sequences of red sedimentary rocks, usually sandstones or shales, coloured by the oxidization of the iron in them.
red biddy *n. Informal.* cheap red wine fortified with methylated spirits.
red blood cell *or* **corpuscle** *n.* another name for **erythrocyte.**
red-blooded *adj. Informal.* vigorous; virile. —ˌ**red-ˈbloodedness** *n.*
redbreast (ˈrɛdˌbrɛst) *n.* any of various birds having a red breast, esp. the Old World robin (see **robin** (sense 1)).
redbrick (ˈrɛdˌbrɪk) *n.* (*modifier*) denoting, relating to, or characteristic of a provincial British university of relatively recent foundation, esp. as distinguished from Oxford and Cambridge.
redbud (ˈrɛdˌbʌd) *n.* an American leguminous tree, *Cercis canadensis,* that has heart-shaped leaves and small budlike pink flowers. Also called: **American Judas tree.**
redbug (ˈrɛdˌbʌg) *n. U.S.* another name for **chigger** (sense 1).
redcap (ˈrɛdˌkæp) *n.* **1.** *Brit. informal.* a military policeman. **2.** *U.S. and Canadian.* a porter at an airport or station.
red card *n. Soccer.* a card of a red colour displayed by a referee to indicate that a player has been sent off.
red carpet *n.* **1.** a strip of red carpeting laid for important dignitaries to walk on when arriving or departing. **2. a.** deferential treatment accorded to a person of importance. **b.** (*as modifier*): *the returning hero had a red-carpet reception.*
red cedar *n.* **1.** any of several North American coniferous trees, esp. *Juniperus virginiana,* a juniper that has fragrant reddish wood used for making pencils, and *Thuja plicata,* an arbor vitae. **2.** the wood of any of these trees.
red cent *n.* (*used with a negative*) *Informal, chiefly U.S.* a cent considered as a trivial amount of money (esp. in the phrases **not have a red cent, not worth a red cent,** etc.).
red clover *n.* a papilionaceous plant, *Trifolium pratense,* native to Europe and Asia, frequently planted as a forage crop. It has fragrant red flowers and three-lobed compound leaves.
redcoat (ˈrɛdˌkəʊt) *n.* (formerly) a British soldier.
red cod *n.* a deep-sea fish, *Physiculus bachus,* of Australia and New Zealand, with a grey-and-pink body that turns red when it is removed from water.
red coral *n.* any of several corals of the genus *Corallium,* the skeletons of which are pinkish red in colour and used to make ornaments, etc. Also called: **precious coral.**
red corpuscle *or* **blood cell** *n.* another name for **erythrocyte.**
Red Crescent *n.* a national branch of or the emblem of the Red Cross Society in a Muslim country.
Red Cross *n.* **1.** an international humanitarian organization (**Red Cross Society**) formally established by the Geneva Convention of 1864. It was originally limited to providing medical care for war casualties but its services now include liaison between prisoners of war and their families, relief to victims of natural disasters, etc. **2.** any national branch of this organization. **3.** the emblem of this organization, consisting of a red cross on a white background.
redcurrant (ˈrɛdˈkʌrənt) *n.* **1.** a N temperate shrub, *Ribes rubrum,* having greenish flowers and small edible rounded red berries: family *Grossulariaceae.* **2. a.** the fruit of this shrub. **b.** (*as modifier*): *redcurrant jelly.*
redd[1] *or* **red** (rɛd) *Scot. and northern English dialect.* ~*vb.* **redds, redding, redd** *or* **redded. 1.** (*tr.;* often foll. by *up*) to bring order to; tidy (up). ~*n.* **2.** the act or an instance of redding. [C15 *redden* to clear, perhaps a variant of RID] —ˈ**redder** *n.*
redd[2] (rɛd) *n.* a hollow in sand or gravel on a river bed, scooped out as a spawning place by salmon, trout, or other fish. [C17 (originally: spawn): of obscure origin]
red deer *n.* a large deer, *Cervus elaphus,* formerly widely distributed in the woodlands of Europe and Asia. The coat is reddish brown in summer and the short tail is surrounded by a patch of light-coloured hair.
redden (ˈrɛdᵊn) *vb.* **1.** to make or become red. **2.** (*intr.*) to flush with embarrassment, anger, etc.; blush.
reddish (ˈrɛdɪʃ) *adj.* somewhat red. —ˈ**reddishly** *adv.* —ˈ**reddishness** *n.*
reddle (ˈrɛdᵊl) *n., vb.* a variant spelling of **ruddle.**
red duster *n. Brit.* an informal name for the **Red Ensign.**
red dwarf *n.* one of a class of small cool main-sequence stars.
rede (riːd) *Archaic.* ~*n.* **1.** advice or counsel. **2.** an explanation. ~*vb.* (*tr.*) **3.** to advise; counsel. **4.** to explain. [Old English *rǣdan* to rule; see READ[1]]
red earth *n.* a clayey zonal soil of tropical savanna lands, formed by extensive chemical weathering, coloured by iron compounds, and less strongly leached than laterite.
redeem (rɪˈdiːm) *vb.* (*tr.*) **1.** to recover possession or ownership of by payment of a price or service; regain. **2.** to convert (bonds, shares, etc.) into cash. **3.** to pay off (a promissory note, loan, etc.). **4.** to recover (something pledged, mortgaged, or pawned). **5.** to convert (paper money) into bullion or specie. **6.** to fulfil (a promise, pledge, etc.). **7.** to exchange (trading stamps, coupons, etc.) for goods. **8.** to reinstate in someone's estimation or good opinion; restore to favour: *he redeemed himself by his altruistic action.* **9.** to make amends for. **10.** to recover from captivity, esp. by a money payment. **11.** *Christianity.* (of Christ as Saviour) to free (men) from sin by his death on the Cross. [C15: from Old French *redimer,* from Latin *redimere* to buy back, from *red-* RE- + *emere* to buy] —**reˈdeemer** *n.*
redeemable (rɪˈdiːməbᵊl) *or* **redemptible** (rɪˈdɛmptəbᵊl) *adj.* (of bonds, shares, etc.) **1.** subject to cancellation by repayment at a specified date or under specified conditions. **2.** payable in or convertible into cash. —**reˌdeemaˈbility** *n.* —**reˈdeemably** *adv.*
Redeemer (rɪˈdiːmə) *n.* **The.** Jesus Christ as having brought redemption to mankind.
redeeming (rɪˈdiːmɪŋ) *adj.* serving to compensate for faults or deficiencies in quality, etc.: *one redeeming feature.*
redemption (rɪˈdɛmpʃən) *n.* **1.** the act or process of redeeming. **2.** the state of being redeemed. **3.** *Christianity.* **a.** deliverance from sin through the incarnation, sufferings, and death of Christ. **b.** atonement for guilt. **4.** conversion of paper money into bullion or specie. **5. a.** removal of a financial obligation by paying off a note, bond, etc. **b.** (*as modifier*): *redemption date.* [C14: via Old French from Latin *redemptiō* a buying back; see REDEEM] —**reˈdemptional, reˈdemptive,** *or* **reˈdemptory** *adj.* —**reˈdemptively** *adv.*
redemptioner (rɪˈdɛmpʃənə) *n. History.* an emigrant to Colonial America who paid for his passage by becoming an indentured servant.
redemption yield *n. Stock Exchange.* the yield produced by a redeemable gilt-edged security taking into account the annual interest it pays and an annualized amount to account for any profit or loss when it is redeemed.
Redemptorist (rɪˈdɛmptərɪst) *n. R.C. Church.* a member of a religious congregation founded in 1732 to do missionary work among the poor. [C19: from French *redemptoriste,* from Old French or Latin *redemptor,* from Latin *redimere,* see REDEEM]
Red Ensign *n.* the ensign of the British Merchant Navy, having the Union Jack on a red background at the upper corner of the vertical edge alongside the hoist. Compare **White Ensign, Blue Ensign.**
redeploy (ˌriːdɪˈplɔɪ) *vb.* to assign new positions or tasks to (labour, troops, etc.). —ˌ**redeˈployment** *n.*
redevelop (ˌriːdɪˈvɛləp) *vb.* (*tr.*) **1.** to rebuild or replan (a building, area, etc.). **2.** *Photog.* to develop (a negative or print) for a second time, in order to improve the contrast, colour, etc. **3.** to develop (something) again. —ˌ**redeˈveloper** *n.* —ˌ**redeˈvelopment** *n.*
redevelopment area *n.* an urban area in which all or most of the buildings are demolished and rebuilt.
redeye (ˈrɛdˌaɪ) *n.* **1.** *U.S. slang.* inferior whiskey. **2.** *Canadian slang.* a drink incorporating beer and tomato juice. **3.** another name for **rudd. 4.** *U.S. and Canadian slang.* **a.** an aeroplane flight leaving late at night or arriving early in the morning. **b.** (*as modifier*): *a redeye flight.*
red eye *n. Photog.* an undesirable effect that sometimes appears in flashlight portraits when light from the flash enters the eye and is reflected from the retina on to the film, producing a red colour.
red-faced *adj.* **1.** flushed with embarrassment or anger. **2.** having a florid complexion. —**red-facedly** (ˌrɛdˈfeɪsɪdlɪ, -ˈfeɪstlɪ) *adv.*
redfin (ˈrɛdˌfɪn) *n.* any of various small cyprinid fishes of the genus *Notropis,* esp. *N. cornutus.* They have reddish fins and are popular aquarium fishes.
red fir *n.* **1.** a North American coniferous tree, *Abies magnifica,* having reddish wood valued as timber: family *Pinaceae.* **2.** any of various other pinaceous trees that have reddish wood. **3.** the wood of any of these trees.
red fire *n.* any combustible material that burns with a bright red flame: used in flares and fireworks. The colour is usually produced by strontium salts.
redfish (ˈrɛdˌfɪʃ) *n., pl.* **-fish** *or* **-fishes. 1.** a male salmon that has recently spawned. Compare **blackfish** (sense 2). **2.** any of several red European scorpaenid fishes of the genus *Sebastes,* esp. *S. marinus,* valued as a food fish.
red flag *n.* **1.** a symbol of socialism, communism, or revolution. **2.** a warning of danger or a signal to stop.
red fox *n.* the common fox, *Vulpes vulpes,* which has a reddish-brown coat: family *Canidae,* order *Carnivora* (carnivores).
red giant *n.* a giant star that emits red light (spectral type M).
red grouse *n.* a reddish-brown grouse, *Lagopus scoticus,* of upland moors of Great Britain: an important game bird.

reˈdecoˌrate *vb.*
reˌdecoˈration *n.*
reˈdediˌcate *vb.*
reˌdediˈcation *n.*
ˌ**redeˈfine** *vb.*
ˌ**redeˈfy** *vb.,* **-ˈfies, -ˈfying, -ˈfied.**
ˌ**redeˌliberˈation** *n.*
ˌ**redeˈliver** *vb.*
ˌ**redeˈlivery** *n.*
ˌ**redeˈmand** *vb.*
reˈdemonˌstrate *vb.*
reˌdemonˈstration *n.*
ˌ**redeˈposit** *vb., n.*
ˌ**redeˈscend** *vb.*
ˌ**redeˈscribe** *vb.*
ˌ**redeˈsign** *vb.*
ˌ**redeˈtermine** *vb.*

Red Guard *n.* a member of a Chinese youth movement that attempted to effect the Cultural Revolution (1965–71) in China, initiated to destroy the power of the bureaucrats and revolutionize attitudes and behaviour of the people.

red gum *n.* **1.** any of several Australian myrtaceous trees of the genus *Eucalyptus,* esp. *E. camaldulensis,* which has reddish wood. See also **blue gum. 2.** the hard red wood from this tree, used for making railway sleepers, posts, etc. **3.** another name for **sweet gum.**

red-handed *adj.* (*postpositive*) in the act of committing a crime or doing something wrong or shameful (esp. in the phrase **catch red-handed**). [C19 (earlier, C15 *red hand*)] —ˌ**red-ˈhandedly** *adv.* —ˌ**red-ˈhandedness** *n.*

red hat *n.* **1.** the broad-brimmed crimson hat given to cardinals as the symbol of their rank and office. **2.** the rank and office of a cardinal.

redhead (ˈrɛdˌhɛd) *n.* **1.** a person with red hair. **2.** a diving duck, *Aythya americana,* of North America, the male of which has a grey-and-black body and a reddish-brown head.

red-headed *adj.* **1.** (of a person) having red hair. **2.** (of an animal) having a red head.

red heat *n.* **1.** the temperature at which a substance is red-hot. **2.** the state or condition of being red-hot.

red herring *n.* **1.** anything that diverts attention from a topic or line of inquiry. **2.** a herring cured by salting and smoking.

red-hot *adj.* **1.** (esp. of metal) heated to the temperature at which it glows red: *iron is red-hot at about 500° C.* **2.** extremely hot: *the stove is red-hot, so don't touch it.* **3.** keen, excited, or eager; enthusiastic. **4.** furious; violent: *red-hot anger.* **5.** very recent or topical: *red-hot information.* **6.** *Austral. slang.* extreme, unreasonable, or unfair: *the charges are red-hot.*

red-hot poker *n.* See **kniphofia.**

redia (ˈriːdɪə) *n., pl.* **diae** (-dɪˌiː). a parasitic larva of flukes that has simple locomotory organs, pharynx, and intestine and gives rise either to other rediae or to a different larva (the cercaria). [C19: from New Latin, named after Francesco *Redi* (1629–97), Italian naturalist]

Rediffusion (ˌriːdɪˈfjuːʒən) *n. Brit. trademark.* a system by which radio or television programmes are relayed to subscribers from a receiver via cables.

Red Indian *n., adj.* another name, now considered offensive, for **American Indian.** [see REDSKIN]

redingote (ˈrɛdɪŋˌgəʊt) *n.* **1.** a woman's coat with a close-fitting top and a full skirt. **2.** a man's or woman's full-skirted outer coat of the 18th and 19th centuries. **3.** a woman's light dress or coat of the 18th century, with an open-fronted skirt, revealing a decorative underskirt. [C19: from French, from English *riding coat*]

redintegrate (rɛˈdɪntɪˌgreɪt) *vb.* **1.** (*tr.*) to make whole or complete again; restore to a perfect state; renew. **2.** (*intr.*) *Psychol.* to engage in the process of redintegration. [C15: from Latin *redintegrāre* to renew, from *red-* RE- + *integer* complete] —**red-ˈinteˌgrative** *adj.*

redintegration (rɛˌdɪntɪˈgreɪʃən) *n.* **1.** the act or process of making whole again; renewal. **2.** *Psychol.* the process of responding to a part of a situation in the same manner as one has responded to the whole situation, as in the case of a souvenir reminding one of a holiday.

redivivus (ˌrɛdɪˈvaɪvəs) *adj. Rare.* returned to life; revived. [C17: from Late Latin, from Latin *red-* RE- + *vīvus* alive]

red kowhai *n.* another name for **kaka beak.**

red lead (lɛd) *n.* a bright-red poisonous insoluble oxide of lead usually obtained as a powder by heating litharge in air. It is used as a pigment in paints. Formula: Pb_3O_4. Also called: **minium.**

red-lead ore (ˈrɛdˈlɛd) *n.* another name for **crocoite.**

redleg (ˈrɛdˌlɛg) *n. Caribbean, derogatory.* a poor White.

red-legged partridge *n.* a partridge, *Alectoris rufa,* having a reddish tail, red legs and bill, and flanks barred with chestnut, black, and white: common on farmlands and heaths in SW Europe, including Britain.

red-letter day *n.* a memorably important or happy occasion. [C18: from the red letters used in ecclesiastical calendars to indicate saints' days and feasts]

red light *n.* **1.** a signal to stop, esp. a red traffic signal in a system of traffic lights. **2.** a danger signal. **3.** an instruction to stop or discontinue. **4. a.** a red lamp in a window of or outside a house indicating that it is a brothel. **b.** (*as modifier*): *a red-light district.*

redline (ˈrɛdˌlaɪn) *vb.* (*tr.*) (esp. of a bank or group of banks) to refuse a loan to (a person or country) because of the presumed risks involved.

red man *n. Archaic.* a North American Indian. [C18: see REDSKIN]

red meat *n.* any meat that is dark in colour, esp. beef and lamb. Compare **white meat.**

red mullet *n.* any of the marine percoid fishes constituting the family *Mullidae,* esp. *Mullus surmuletus,* a food fish of European waters. They have a pair of long barbels beneath the chin and a reddish coloration. U.S. name: **goatfish.**

redneck (ˈrɛdˌnɛk) *n. Disparaging.* **1.** (in the southwestern U.S.) a poor uneducated White farm worker. **2.** a person or institution that is extremely reactionary. ~*adj.* **3.** reactionary and bigoted: *redneck laws.*

red ned (nɛd) *n. Austral. slang.* any cheap red wine.

redo (riːˈduː) *vb.* **-does, -doing, -did, -done.** (*tr.*) **1.** to do over again. **2.** *Informal.* to redecorate, esp. thoroughly: *we redid the house last summer.*

red oak *n.* **1.** any of several deciduous oak trees, esp. *Quercus borealis,* native to North America, having bristly leaves with triangular lobes and acorns with small cups. **2.** the hard cross-grained reddish wood of this tree.

red ochre *n.* any of various natural red earths containing ferric oxide: used as pigments.

redolent (ˈrɛdəʊlənt) *adj.* **1.** having a pleasant smell; fragrant. **2.** (*postpositive;* foll. by *of* or *with*) having the odour or smell (of); scented (with): *a room redolent of country flowers.* **3.** (*postpositive;* foll. by *of* or *with*) reminiscent or suggestive (of): *a picture redolent of the 18th century.* [C14: from Latin *redolens* smelling (of), from *redolēre* to give off an odour, from *red-* RE- + *olēre* to smell] —ˈ**redolence** *or* (*less commonly*) ˈ**redolency** *n.* —ˈ**redolently** *adv.*

red osier *n.* any of several willow trees that have red twigs used for basketwork.

red-osier dogwood *n.* a North American shrub, *Cornus stolonifera,* having bright or dark red wood, white flowers, and whitish fruit.

redouble (rɪˈdʌbᵊl) *vb.* **1.** to make or become much greater in intensity, number, etc.: *to redouble one's efforts.* **2.** to send back (sounds) or (of sounds) to be sent back; echo or re-echo. **3.** *Bridge.* to double (an opponent's double). ~*n.* **4.** the act of redoubling.

redoubt (rɪˈdaʊt) *n.* **1.** an outwork or detached fieldwork defending a pass, hilltop, etc. **2.** a temporary defence work built inside a fortification as a last defensive position. [C17: via French from obsolete Italian *ridotta,* from Medieval Latin *reductus* shelter, from Latin *redūcere* to withdraw, from RE- + *dūcere* to lead]

redoubtable (rɪˈdaʊtəbᵊl) *adj.* **1.** to be feared; formidable. **2.** worthy of respect. [C14: from Old French, from *redouter* to dread, from RE- + *douter* to be afraid, DOUBT] —**reˈdoubtableness** *n.* —**reˈdoubtably** *adv.*

redound (rɪˈdaʊnd) *vb.* **1.** (*intr.;* foll. by *to*) to have an advantageous or disadvantageous effect (on): *brave deeds redound to your credit.* **2.** (*intr.;* foll. by *on* or *upon*) to recoil or rebound. **3.** (*intr.*) *Archaic.* to arise; accrue: *wealth redounding from wise investment.* **4.** (*tr.*) *Archaic.* to reflect; bring: *his actions redound dishonour upon him.* [C14: from Old French *redonder,* from Latin *redundāre* to stream over, from *red-* RE- + *undāre* to rise in waves, from *unda* a wave]

redowa (ˈrɛdəvə, -wə) *n.* a Bohemian folk dance similar to the waltz. [C19: via French and German from Czech *rejdovák,* from *rejdovati* to guide around]

redox (ˈriːdɒks) *n.* (*modifier*) another term for **oxidation-reduction.** [C20: from RED(UCTION) + OX(IDATION)]

red packet *n.* (in Hong Kong, Malaysia, etc.) **1.** a sum of money folded inside red paper and given at the Chinese New Year to unmarried younger relatives. **2.** such a gift given at Chinese weddings by the parents to the bride and groom and by the bride and groom to unmarried younger relatives.

red-pencil *vb.* **-cils, -cilling, -cilled** *or U.S.* **-cils, -ciling, -ciled.** (*tr.*) to revise or correct (a book, manuscript, etc.).

red pepper *n.* **1.** any of several varieties of the pepper plant *Capsicum frutescens,* cultivated for their hot pungent red podlike fruits. **2.** the fruit of any of these plants. **3.** the ripe red fruit of the sweet pepper. **4.** another name for **cayenne pepper.**

red pine *n.* a coniferous tree, *Dacrydium cupressinum,* of New Zealand, having narrow sharp pointed leaves: family *Taxaceae.* Also called: **rimu.**

Red Planet *n.* **the.** an informal name for **Mars.**

redpoll (ˈrɛdˌpɒl) *n.* either of two widely distributed finches, *Acanthis flammea* or *A. hornemanni* (**arctic** *or* **hoary redpoll**), having a greyish-brown plumage with a red crown and pink breast.

Red Poll *or* **Polled** *n.* a red hornless short-haired breed of beef and dairy cattle.

redraft *n.* (ˈriːˌdrɑːft). **1.** a second draft. **2.** a bill of exchange drawn on the drawer or endorser of a protested bill by the holder for the amount of the protested bill plus costs and charges. **3.** a re-exported commodity. ~*vb.* (riːˈdrɑːft). (*tr.*) **4.** to make a second copy of; draft again: *to redraft proposals for a project.*

red rag *n.* a provocation; something that infuriates. [so called because red objects supposedly infuriate bulls]

red rattle *n.* See **rattle** (sense 10).

reˈdial *vb.,* **-ˈdials, -ˈdialling, -ˈdialled.**
ˌ**rediˈgest** *vb.*
ˌ**rediˈgestion** *n.*
ˌ**rediˈrect** *vb.*
ˌ**rediˈrection** *n.*
reˈdiscount *vb., n.*
ˌ**redisˈcover** *vb.*
ˌ**redisˈcovery** *n., pl.* **-eries.**
ˌ**redisˈsolve** *vb.*
ˌ**redisˈtribute** *vb.*
ˌ**redistriˈbution** *n.*
ˌ**redisˈtributive** *adj.*
ˌ**rediˈvide** *vb.*
ˌ**rediˈvision** *n.*
reˈdock *vb.*

redress (rɪˈdrɛs) *vb.* (*tr.*) **1.** to put right (a wrong), esp. by compensation; make reparation for: *to redress a grievance.* **2.** to correct or adjust (esp. in the phrase **redress the balance**). **3.** to make compensation to (a person) for a wrong. ~*n.* **4.** the act or an instance of setting right a wrong; remedy or cure: *to seek redress of grievances.* **5.** compensation, amends, or reparation for a wrong, injury, etc. **6.** relief from poverty or want. [C14: from Old French *redrecier* to set up again, from RE- + *drecier* to straighten; see DRESS] —**reˈdressable** *or* **reˈdressible** *adj.* —**reˈdresser** *or* (*less commonly*) **reˈdressor** *n.*

re-dress (riːˈdrɛs) *vb.* (*tr.*) to dress (something) again.

redroot (ˈrɛdˌruːt) *n.* **1.** a bog plant, *Lachnanthes tinctoria*, of E North America, having woolly yellow flowers and roots that yield a red dye: family *Haemodoraceae.* **2.** another name for **pigweed** (sense 1).

red rose *n. English history.* the emblem of the Lancastrian rulers of England. See also **white rose.**

red salmon *n.* **1.** any salmon having reddish flesh, esp. the sockeye salmon. **2.** the flesh of such a fish, esp. canned.

red seaweed *n.* another term for **red algae.**

red setter *n.* a popular name for **Irish setter.**

redshank (ˈrɛdˌʃæŋk) *n.* either of two large common European sandpipers, *Tringa totanus* or *T. erythropus* (**spotted redshank**), having red legs.

red shank *n.* an annual polygonaceous plant, *Polygonum persicaria*, of N temperate regions, having red stems, narrow leaves, and oblong spikes of pink flowers. Also called: **persicaria, lady's-thumb.**

red shift *n.* a shift in the spectral lines of a stellar spectrum towards the red end of the visible region relative to the wavelength of these lines in the terrestrial spectrum. It is thought to be a result of the Doppler effect caused by the recession of stars.

redskin (ˈrɛdˌskɪn) *n.* an informal name, now considered offensive, for an **American Indian.** [C17: so called because one particular tribe, the now extinct Beothuks of Newfoundland, painted themselves with red ochre]

red snapper *n.* any of various marine percoid food fishes of the genus *Lutjanus*, esp. *L. blackfordi*, having a reddish coloration, common in American coastal regions of the Atlantic: family *Lutjanidae* (snappers).

red spider *n.* short for **red spider mite** (see **spider mite**).

red squirrel *n.* **1.** a reddish-brown squirrel, *Sciurus vulgaris*, inhabiting woodlands of Europe and parts of Asia. **2. American red squirrel.** Also called: **chickaree.** either of two reddish-brown squirrels, *Tamiasciurus hudsonicus* or *T. douglasii*, inhabiting forests of North America.

redstart (ˈrɛdˌstɑːt) *n.* **1.** any European songbird of the genus *Phoenicurus*, esp. *P. phoenicurus*, in which the male has a black throat, orange-brown tail and breast, and grey back: family *Muscicapidae* (thrushes, etc.). **2.** any North American warbler of the genus *Setophaga*, esp. *S. ruticilla.* [Old English *rēad* RED + *steort* tail; compare German *Rotsterz*]

red tape *n.* obstructive official routine or procedure; time-consuming bureaucracy. [C18: from the red tape used to bind official government documents]

red tide *n.* a discoloration of sea water caused by an explosive growth in phytoplankton density: sometimes toxic to fish life and, through accumulation in shellfish, to humans.

reduce (rɪˈdjuːs) *vb.* (*mainly tr.*) **1.** (*also intr.*) to make or become smaller in size, number, extent, degree, intensity, etc. **2.** to bring into a certain state, condition, etc.: *to reduce a forest to ashes; to reduce someone to despair.* **3.** (*also intr.*) to make or become slimmer; lose or cause to lose excess weight. **4.** to impoverish (esp. in the phrase **in reduced circumstances**). **5.** to bring into a state of submission to one's authority; subjugate: *the whole country was reduced after three months.* **6.** to bring down the price of (a commodity): *the shirt was reduced in the sale.* **7.** to lower the rank or status of; demote: *he was reduced from corporal to private; reduced to the ranks.* **8.** to set out systematically as an aid to understanding; simplify: *his theories have been reduced in a popular treatise.* **9.** *Maths.* to modify or simplify the form of (an expression or equation), esp. by substitution of one term by another. **10.** to thin out (paint) by adding oil, turpentine, etc.; dilute. **11.** (*also intr.*) *Chem.* **a.** to undergo or cause to undergo a chemical reaction with hydrogen or formation of a hydride. **b.** to lose or cause to lose oxygen atoms. **c.** to undergo or cause to undergo an increase in the number of electrons. Compare **oxidize.** **12.** *Photog.* to lessen the density of (a negative or print) by converting some of the blackened silver in the emulsion to soluble silver compounds by an oxidation process using a photographic reducer. **13.** *Surgery.* to manipulate or reposition (a broken or displaced bone, organ, or part) back to its normal site. **14.** (*also intr.*) *Biology.* to undergo or cause to undergo meiosis. [C14: from Latin *redūcere* to bring back, from RE- + *dūcere* to lead] —**reˈducible** *adj.* —**reˌduciˈbility** *n.* —**reˈducibly** *adv.*

reduced level *n. Surveying.* calculated elevation in relation to a particular datum.

reducer (rɪˈdjuːsə) *n.* **1.** *Photog.* a chemical solution used to lessen the density of a negative or print by oxidizing some of the blackened silver to soluble silver compounds. Compare **intensifier** (sense 3). **2.** a pipe fitting connecting two pipes of different diameters. **3.** a person or thing that reduces.

reducing agent *n. Chem.* a substance that reduces another substance in a chemical reaction, being itself oxidized in the process. Compare **oxidizing agent.**

reducing glass *n.* a lens or curved mirror that produces an image smaller than the object observed.

reductase (rɪˈdʌkteɪz) *n.* any enzyme that catalyses a biochemical reduction reaction. [C20: from REDUCTION + -ASE]

reductio ad absurdum (rɪˈdʌktɪəʊ æd æbˈsɜːdəm) *n.* **1.** a method of disproving a proposition by showing that its inevitable consequences would be absurd. **2.** a method of indirectly proving a proposition by assuming its negation to be true and showing that this leads to an absurdity. **3.** application of a principle or proposed principle to an instance in which it is absurd. [Latin, literally: reduction to the absurd]

reduction (rɪˈdʌkʃən) *n.* **1.** the act or process or an instance of reducing. **2.** the state or condition of being reduced. **3.** the amount by which something is reduced. **4.** a form of an original resulting from a reducing process, such as a copy on a smaller scale. **5.** a simplified form, such as an orchestral score arranged for piano. **6.** *Maths.* **a.** the process of converting a fraction into its decimal form. **b.** the process of dividing out the common factors in the numerator and denominator of a fraction; cancellation. —**reˈductive** *adj.*

reduction division *n.* another name for **meiosis.**

reduction formula *n. Maths.* a formula, such as $\sin(90° \pm A) = \cos A$, expressing the values of a trigonometric function of any angle greater than 90° in terms of a function of an acute angle.

reductionism (rɪˈdʌkʃəˌnɪzəm) *n.* **1.** the analysis of complex things, data, etc., into less complex constituents. **2.** *Often disparaging.* any theory or method that holds that a complex idea, system, etc., can be completely understood in terms of its simpler parts or components. —**reˈductionist** *n., adj.* —**reˌductionˈistic** *adj.*

redundancy (rɪˈdʌndənsɪ) *n., pl.* **-cies.** **1. a.** the state or condition of being redundant or superfluous, esp. superfluous in one's job. **b.** (*as modifier*): *a redundancy payment.* **2.** excessive proliferation or profusion, esp. of superfluity. **3.** duplication of components in electronic or mechanical equipment so that operations can continue following failure of a part. **4.** repetition of information or inclusion of additional information to reduce errors in telecommunication transmissions and computer processing.

redundancy payment *n.* a sum of money given by an employer to an employee who has been made redundant: usually calculated on the basis of the employee's rate of pay and length of service.

redundant (rɪˈdʌndənt) *adj.* **1.** surplus to requirements; unnecessary or superfluous. **2.** verbose or tautological. **3.** deprived of one's job because it is no longer necessary for efficient operation: *he has been made redundant.* **4.** (of components, information, etc.) duplicated or added as a precaution against failure, error, etc. [C17: from Latin *redundans* overflowing, from *redundāre* to run back, stream over; see REDOUND] —**reˈdundantly** *adv.*

red underwing *n.* a large noctuid moth, *Catocala nupta*, having dull forewings and hind wings coloured red and black.

redupl. *abbrev. for* reduplicate *or* reduplication.

reduplicate *vb.* (rɪˈdjuːplɪˌkeɪt). **1.** to make or become double; repeat. **2.** to repeat (a sound or syllable) in a word or (of a sound or syllable) to be repeated, esp. in forming inflections in certain languages. ~*adj.* (rɪˈdjuːplɪkɪt). **3.** doubled or repeated. **4.** (of petals or sepals) having the margins curving outwards. —**reˈduplicative** *adj.*

reduplication (rɪˌdjuːplɪˈkeɪʃən) *n.* **1.** the process or an instance of redoubling. **2.** the state, condition, or quality of being redoubled. **3.** a thing that has been redoubled. **4.** repetition of a sound or syllable in a word, as in the formation of the Latin perfect *tetigi* from *tangere* "touch".

reduviid (rɪˈdjuːvɪɪd) *n.* **1.** any hemipterous bug of the family *Reduviidae*, which includes the assassin bugs and the wheel bug. ~*adj.* **2.** of, relating to, or belonging to the family *Reduviidae.* [C19: from New Latin *Reduviidae*, from Latin *reduvia* a hangnail]

redware (ˈrɛdˌwɛə) *n.* another name for **kelp** (the seaweed).

red water *n.* **1.** a disease of cattle caused by the protozoan *Babesia* (or *Piroplasma*) *bovis*, which destroys the red blood cells, characterized by the passage of red or blackish urine. **2.** any of various other animal diseases characterized by haematuria.

redwing (ˈrɛdˌwɪŋ) *n.* **1.** a small European thrush, *Turdus iliacus*, having a speckled breast, reddish flanks, and brown back. **2.** a North American oriole, *Agelaius phoeniceus*, the male of which has a black plumage with a red-and-yellow patch on each wing.

redwood (ˈrɛdˌwʊd) *n.* a giant coniferous tree, *Sequoia sempervirens*, of coastal regions of California, having reddish

reˈdraw *vb.*, **-ˈdraws, -ˈdrawing, -ˈdrew, -ˈdrawn.**
reˈdrill *vb.*
reˈdry *vb.*, **-ˈdries, -ˈdrying, -ˈdried.**

fibrous bark and durable timber: family *Taxodiaceae*. The largest specimen is over 120 metres (360 feet) tall. See also **sequoia.**

Redwood seconds ('rɛd,wʊd) *n.* (*functioning as sing.*) a scale of measurement of viscosity based on the time in seconds taken for fluid to flow through a standard orifice: accepted as standard in the U.K. in 1886. See also **Saybolt universal seconds, Engler degrees.** [named after Sir B. *Redwood* (1846–1919), British chemist who proposed it]

reebok ('riːbʌk, -bɒk) *n., pl.* **-boks** *or* **-bok.** a variant spelling of **rhebok.**

re-echo (riː'ɛkəʊ) *vb.* **-oes, -oing, -oed. 1.** to echo (a sound that is already an echo); resound. **2.** (*tr.*) to repeat like an echo.

reed (riːd) *n.* **1.** any of various widely distributed tall grasses of the genus *Phragmites,* esp. *P. communis,* that grow in swamps and shallow water and have jointed hollow stalks. **2.** the stalk, or stalks collectively, of any of these plants, esp. as used for thatching. **3.** *Music.* **a.** a thin piece of cane or metal inserted into the tubes of certain wind instruments, which sets in vibration the air column inside the tube. **b.** a wind instrument or organ pipe that sounds by means of a reed. **4.** one of the several vertical parallel wires on a loom that may be moved upwards to separate the warp threads. **5.** a small semicircular architectural moulding. See also **reeding. 6.** an ancient Hebrew unit of length equal to six cubits. **7.** an archaic word for **arrow. 8. broken reed.** a weak, unreliable, or ineffectual person. ~*vb.* (*tr.*) **9.** to fashion into or supply with reeds or reeding. **10.** to thatch using reeds. [Old English *hreod;* related to Old Saxon *hriod,* Old High German *hriot*]

reedbird ('riːd,bɜːd) *n.* any of several birds that frequent reed beds, esp. (in the U.S. and Canada) the bobolink.

reedbuck ('riːd,bʌk) *n., pl.* **-bucks** *or* **-buck.** any antelope of the genus *Redunca,* of Africa south of the Sahara, having a buff-coloured coat and inward-curving horns.

reed bunting *n.* a common European bunting, *Emberiza schoeniclus,* that occurs near reed beds and has a brown streaked plumage with, in the male, a black head.

reed grass *n.* a tall perennial grass, *Glyceria maxima,* of rivers and ponds of Europe, Asia, and Canada.

reeding ('riːdɪŋ) *n.* **1.** a set of small semicircular architectural mouldings. **2.** the milling on the edges of a coin.

reedling ('riːdlɪŋ) *n.* a titlike Eurasian songbird, *Panurus biarmicus,* common in reed beds: family *Muscicapidae* (Old World flycatchers, etc.). It has a tawny back and tail and, in the male, a grey-and-black head. Also called: **bearded tit.**

reed mace *n.* **1.** Also called: (popularly) **bulrush, false bulrush, cat's-tail.** a tall reedlike marsh plant, *Typha latifolia,* with straplike leaves and flowers in long brown sausage-shaped spikes: family *Typhaceae.* See also **bulrush** (sense 2). **2.** a related and similar plant, *Typha angustifolia.*

reed organ *n.* **1.** a wind instrument, such as the harmonium, accordion, or harmonica, in which the sound is produced by reeds, each reed producing one note only. **2.** a type of pipe organ, such as the regal, in which all the pipes are fitted with reeds.

reed pipe *n.* **1.** a wind instrument, such as a clarinet or oboe, whose sound is produced by a vibrating reed. **2.** an organ pipe sounded by a vibrating reed.

reedsman ('riːdzmən) *or U.S.* **reedman** *n., pl.* **-men.** a jazz musician who plays any of a number of wind instruments with a reed, such as the saxophone or clarinet.

reed stop *n.* an organ stop controlling a rank of reed pipes.

reed warbler *n.* any of various common Old World warblers of the genus *Acrocephalus,* esp. *A. scirpaceus,* that inhabit marshy regions and have a brown plumage.

reedy ('riːdɪ) *adj.* **reedier, reediest. 1.** (of a place, esp. a marsh) abounding in reeds. **2.** of or like a reed. **3.** having a tone like a reed instrument; shrill or piping: *a reedy voice.* —'**reedily** *adv.* —'**reediness** *n.*

reef[1] (riːf) *n.* **1.** a ridge of rock, sand, coral, etc., the top of which lies close to the surface of the sea. **2.** a vein of ore, esp. one of gold-bearing quartz. [C16: from Middle Dutch *ref,* from Old Norse *rif* RIB[1], REEF[2]]

reef[2] (riːf) *Nautical.* ~*n.* **1.** the part gathered in when sail area is reduced, as in a high wind. ~*vb.* **2.** to reduce the area of (sail) by taking in a reef. **3.** (*tr.*) to shorten or bring inboard (a spar). [C14: from Middle Dutch *rif;* related to Old Norse *rif* reef, RIB[1], German *reffen* to reef; see REEF[1]]

reefer[1] ('riːfə) *n.* **1.** *Nautical.* a person who reefs, such as a midshipman. **2.** another name for **reefing jacket. 3.** *Slang.* a hand-rolled cigarette, esp. one containing cannabis. [C19: from REEF[2]; applied to the cigarette because of its resemblance to the rolled reef of a sail]

reefer[2] ('riːfə) *n.* a ship, lorry, or other form of transport designed to carry refrigerated cargo. [C20: shortened and adapted from *refrigerator*]

reefing jacket *n.* a man's short double-breasted jacket of sturdy wool. Also called: **reefer.**

reef knot *n.* a knot consisting of two overhand knots turned opposite ways. Also called: **square knot.**

reef point *n. Nautical.* one of several short lengths of line stitched through a sail for tying a reef.

reek (riːk) *vb.* **1.** (*intr.*) to give off or emit a strong unpleasant odour; smell or stink. **2.** (*intr.;* often foll. by *of*) to be permeated (by); be redolent (of): *the letter reeks of subservience.* **3.** (*tr.*) to treat with smoke; fumigate. **4.** (*tr.*) *Chiefly dialect.* to give off or emit (smoke, fumes, vapour, etc.). ~*n.* **5.** a strong offensive smell; stink. **6.** *Chiefly dialect.* smoke or steam; vapour. [Old English *rēocan;* related to Old Frisian *riāka* to smoke, Old High German *rouhhan,* Old Norse *rjūka* to smoke, steam] —'**reeking** *adj.* —'**reekingly** *adv.* —'**reeky** *adj.*

reel[1] (riːl, rɪəl) *n.* **1.** any of various cylindrical objects or frames that turn on an axis and onto which film, magnetic tape, paper tape, wire, thread, etc., may be wound. U.S. equivalent: **spool. 2.** *Angling.* a device for winding, casting, etc., consisting of a revolving spool with a handle, attached to a fishing rod. **3.** a roll of celluloid exhibiting a sequence of photographs to be projected. ~*vb.* (*tr.*) **4.** to wind (cotton, thread, etc.) onto a reel. **5.** (foll. by *in, out,* etc.) to wind or draw with a reel: *to reel in a fish.* [Old English *hrēol;* related to Old Norse *hræll* weaver's rod, Greek *krekein* to weave] —'**reelable** *adj.* —'**reeler** *n.*

reel[2] (riːl, rɪəl) *vb.* (*mainly intr.*) **1.** to sway, esp. under the shock of a blow or through dizziness or drunkenness. **2.** to whirl about or have the feeling of whirling about: *his brain reeled.* ~*n.* **3.** a staggering or swaying motion or sensation. [C14 *relen,* probably from REEL[1]]

reel[3] (riːl, rɪəl) *n.* **1.** any of various lively Scottish dances, such as the **eightsome reel** and **foursome reel,** for a fixed number of couples who combine in square and circular formations. **2.** a piece of music having eight quavers to the bar composed for or in the rhythm of this dance. [C18: from REEL[2]]

reel-fed *adj. Printing.* involving or printing on a web of paper: *a reel-fed press.* Compare **sheet-fed.**

reel man *n. Austral. and N.Z.* the member of a beach life-saving team who controls the reel on which the line is wound.

reel off *vb.* (*tr., adv.*) to recite or write fluently and without apparent effort: *to reel off items on a list.*

reel of three *n.* (in Scottish country dancing) a figure-of-eight movement danced by three people.

reel-to-reel *adj.* **1.** (of magnetic tape) wound from one reel to another in use. **2.** (of a tape recorder) using magnetic tape wound from one reel to another, as opposed to cassettes.

reen *or* **rean** (riːn) *n. Southwest English dialect.* a ditch, esp. a drainage channel. [from earlier *rhine,* from Old English *ryne*]

re-entering angle *n.* an interior angle of a polygon that is greater than 180°. Also called: **re-entrant angle.**

re-entrant (riː'ɛntrənt) *adj.* **1.** (of an angle, esp. in fortifications) pointing inwards. Compare **salient** (sense 2). **2.** *Maths.* (of an angle in a polygon) greater than 180° and thus pointing inwards. ~*n.* **3.** an angle or part that points inwards.

re-entry (riː'ɛntrɪ) *n., pl.* **-tries. 1.** the act of retaking possession of land, etc., under a right reserved in an earlier transfer of the property, such as a lease. **2.** the return of a spacecraft into the earth's atmosphere.

re-entry vehicle *n.* the portion of a ballistic missile that carries a nuclear warhead and re-enters the earth's atmosphere.

reest *or* **reast** (riːst) *vb.* (*intr.*) *Northern English dialect.* (esp. of horses) to be noisily uncooperative. [probably from Scottish *arreest* ARREST; perhaps related to RESTIVE]

reeve[1] (riːv) *n.* **1.** *English history.* the local representative of the king in a shire (under the ealdorman) until the early 11th century. Compare **sheriff. 2.** (in medieval England) a manorial steward who supervised the daily affairs of the manor: often a villein elected by his fellows. **3.** *Canadian government.* (in certain provinces) a president of a local council, esp. in a rural area. **4.** (formerly) a minor local official in any of several parts of England and the U.S. [Old English *gerēva;* related to Old High German *ruova* number, array]

reeve[2] (riːv) *vb.* **reeves, reeving; reeved** *or* **rove** (rəʊv). (*tr.*) *Nautical.* **1.** to pass (a rope or cable) through an eye or other narrow opening. **2.** to fasten by passing through or around something. [C17: perhaps from Dutch *rēven* REEF[2]]

reeve[3] (riːv) *n.* the female of the ruff (the bird). [C17: of uncertain origin]

re'dye *vb.*
re-'edit *vb.*
re-'edu,cate *vb.*
re-,edu'cation *n.*
,re-e'lect *vb.*
,re-e'lection *n.*
re-'eligible *adj.*
,re-em'bark *vb.*
,re-e'merge *vb.*
,re-e'mergence *n.*
,re-e'mergent *adj.*
re-'empha,size *or* re-'empha,sise *vb.*
,re-em'ploy *vb.*
,re-em'ployment *n.*
,re-en'act *vb.*
,re-en'actment *n.*
,re-en'close *vb.*
,re-en'dow *vb.*
,re-en'force *vb.*
,re-en'forcement *n.*
,re-en'forcer *n.*
,re-en'gage *vb.*
,re-en'large *vb.*
,re-en'largement *n.*
,re-en'lighten *vb.*
,re-en'slave *vb.*
re-'enter *vb.*
re-'entrance *n.*
,re-e'quip *vb.,* -'quips, -'quipping, -'quipped.
,re-e'rect *vb.*
,re-es'tablish *vb.*
,re-es'tablishment *n.*
,re-e'valu,ate *vb.*
,re-e,valu'ation *n.*

re-examine (ˌriːɪɡˈzæmɪn) *vb.* (*tr.*) **1.** to examine again. **2.** *Law.* to examine (one's own witness) again upon matters arising out of his cross-examination. —ˌ**re-exˈaminable** *adj.* —ˌ**re-exˌamiˈnation** *n.* —ˌ**re-exˈaminer** *n.*

re-export *vb.* (ˌriːɪkˈspɔːt, riːˈɛkspɔːt). **1.** to export (imported goods, esp. after processing). ~*n.* (riːˈɛkspɔːt). **2.** the act of re-exporting. **3.** a re-exported commodity. —ˌ**re-exporˈtation** *n.* —ˌ**re-exˈporter** *n.*

ref (rɛf) *n. Informal.* short for **referee.**

ref. *abbrev. for:* **1.** referee. **2.** reference. **3.** reformed.

reface (riːˈfeɪs) *vb.* (*tr.*) **1.** to repair or renew the facing of (a wall). **2.** to put a new facing on (a garment).

Ref. Ch. *abbrev. for* Reformed Church.

refection (rɪˈfɛkʃən) *n.* refreshment with food and drink. [C14: from Latin *refectiō* a restoring, from *reficere* to remake, from RE- + *facere* to make]

refectory (rɪˈfɛktərɪ, -trɪ) *n., pl.* **-tories.** a communal dining hall in a religious, academic, or other institution. [C15: from Late Latin *refectōrium,* from Latin *refectus* refreshed]

refectory table *n.* a long narrow dining table supported by two trestles joined by a stretcher or set into a base.

refer (rɪˈfɜː) *vb.* **-fers, -ferring, -ferred.** (often foll. by *to*). **1.** (*intr.*) to make mention (of). **2.** (*tr.*) to direct the attention of (someone) for information, facts, etc.: *the reader is referred to Chomsky, 1965.* **3.** (*intr.*) to seek information (from): *I referred to Directory Enquiries; he referred to his notes.* **4.** (*intr.*) to be relevant (to); pertain or relate (to): *this song refers to an incident in the Civil War.* **5.** (*tr.*) to assign or attribute: *Cromwell referred his victories to God.* **6.** (*tr.*) to hand over for consideration, reconsideration, or decision: *to refer a complaint to another department.* **7.** (*tr.*) to hand back to the originator as unacceptable or unusable. **8.** (*tr.*) *Brit.* to fail (a student) in an examination. **9.** (*tr.*) *Brit.* to send back (a thesis) to a student for improvement. **10. refer to drawer.** a request by a bank that the payee consult the drawer concerning a cheque payable by that bank (usually because the drawer has insufficient funds in his account), payment being suspended in the meantime. **11.** (*tr.*) to direct (a patient) for treatment to another doctor, usually a specialist. **12.** (*tr.*) *Social welfare.* to direct (a client) to another agency or professional for a service. [C14: from Latin *referre* to carry back, from RE- + *ferre* to BEAR[1]] —**referable** (ˈrɛfərəbᵊl) *or* **referrable** (rɪˈfɜːrəbᵊl) *adj.* —**reˈferral** *n.* —**reˈferrer** *n.*

▷**Usage.** The common practice of adding *back* to *refer* is tautologous, since this meaning is already contained in the *re-* of *refer: this refers to* (not *back to*) *what has already been said.* However, when *refer* is used in the sense of passing a document or question for further consideration to the person from whom it was received, it may be appropriate to say *he referred the matter back.*

referee (ˌrɛfəˈriː) *n.* **1.** a person to whom reference is made, esp. for an opinion, information, or a decision. **2.** the umpire or judge in any of various sports, esp. football and boxing, responsible for ensuring fair play according to the rules. **3.** a person who is willing to testify to the character or capabilities of someone. **4.** *Law.* See **Official Referee.** ~*vb.* **-ees, -eeing, -eed. 5.** to act as a referee (in); preside (over).

reference (ˈrɛfərəns, ˈrɛfrəns) *n.* **1.** the act or an instance of referring. **2.** something referred, esp. proceedings submitted to a referee in law. **3.** a direction of the attention to a passage elsewhere or to another book, document, etc. **4.** a book or passage referred to. **5.** a mention or allusion: *this book contains several references to the Civil War.* **6.** *Philosophy.* **a.** the relation between a word, phrase, or symbol and the object or idea to which it refers. **b.** the object referred to by an expression. Compare **sense** (sense 13). **7. a.** a source of information or facts. **b.** (*as modifier*): *a reference book; a reference library.* **8.** a written testimonial regarding one's character or capabilities. **9.** a person referred to for such a testimonial. **10. a.** (foll. by *to*) relation or delimitation, esp. to or by membership of a specific class or group; respect or regard: *all people, without reference to sex or age.* **b.** (*as modifier*): *a reference group.* **11. terms of reference.** the specific limits of responsibility that determine the activities of an investigating body, etc. **12. point of reference.** a fact forming the basis of an evaluation or assessment; criterion. ~*vb.* (*tr.*) **13.** to furnish or compile a list of references for (an academic thesis, publication, etc.). **14.** to make a reference to; refer to: *he referenced Chomsky 1956.* ~*prep.* **15.** *Business jargon.* with reference to: *reference your letter of the 9th inst.* Abbrev.: **re.** —ˈ**referencer** *n.* —**referential** (ˌrɛfəˈrɛnʃəl) *adj.*

reference book *n.* **1.** a book, such as an encyclopedia, dictionary, etc., from which information may be obtained. **2.** *S. African.* another name for **passbook** (sense 4).

referendum (ˌrɛfəˈrɛndəm) *n., pl.* **-dums** *or* **-da** (-də). **1.** submission of an issue of public importance to the direct vote of the electorate. **2.** a vote on such a measure. **3.** a poll of the members of a club, union, or other group to determine their views on some matter. **4.** a diplomatic official's note to his government requesting instructions. ~See also (for senses 1, 2) **plebiscite.** [C19: from Latin: something to be carried back, from *referre* to REFER]

referent (ˈrɛfərənt) *n.* the object or idea to which a word or phrase refers. Compare **sense** (sense 13). [C19: from Latin *referens,* from *referre* to REFER]

referred pain *n. Psychol.* pain felt in the body at some place other than its actual place of origin.

reffo (ˈrɛfəʊ) *n., pl.* **reffos.** *Austral. slang.* an offensive name for a European refugee after World War II.

refill *vb.* (riːˈfɪl). **1.** to fill (something) again. ~*n.* (ˈriːfɪl). **2.** a replacement for a consumable substance in a permanent container. **3.** a second or subsequent filling: *a refill at the petrol station.* **4.** *Informal.* another drink to replace one already drunk. —**reˈfillable** *adj.*

refinancing (ˌriːfɪˈnænsɪŋ) *n.* a method of paying a debt by borrowing additional money thus creating a second debt in order to pay the first.

refine (rɪˈfaɪn) *vb.* **1.** to make or become free from impurities, sediment, or other foreign matter; purify. **2.** (*tr.*) to separate (a mixture) into pure constituents, as in an oil refinery. **3.** to make or become free from coarse characteristics; make or become elegant or polished. **4.** (*tr.;* often foll. by *out*) to remove (something impure or extraneous). **5.** (*intr.;* often foll. by *on* or *upon*) to enlarge or improve (upon) by making subtle or fine distinctions. **6.** (*tr.*) to make (language) more subtle or polished. [C16: from RE- + FINE[1]] —**reˈfinable** *adj.* —**reˈfiner** *n.*

refined (rɪˈfaɪnd) *adj.* **1.** not coarse or vulgar; genteel, elegant, or polite. **2.** subtle; discriminating. **3.** freed from impurities; purified.

refinement (rɪˈfaɪnmənt) *n.* **1.** the act of refining or the state of being refined. **2.** a fine or delicate point, distinction, or expression; a subtlety. **3.** fineness or precision of thought, expression, manners, etc.; polish or cultivation. **4.** a device, change, adaptation, etc., designed to improve performance or increase efficiency.

refinery (rɪˈfaɪnərɪ) *n., pl.* **-eries.** a factory for the purification of some crude material, such as ore, sugar, oil, etc.

refit *vb.* (riːˈfɪt), **-fits, -fitting, -fitted. 1.** to make or be made ready for use again by repairing, re-equipping, or resupplying. ~*n.* (ˈriːˌfɪt). **2.** a repair or re-equipping, as of a ship, for further use. —**reˈfitment** *n.*

refl. *abbrev. for:* **1.** reflection. **2.** reflective. **3.** reflex(ive).

reflate (riːˈfleɪt) *vb.* to inflate or be inflated again. [C20: back formation from REFLATION]

reflation (riːˈfleɪʃən) *n.* **1.** an increase in economic activity. **2.** an increase in the supply of money and credit designed to cause such an increase. ~Compare **inflation** (sense 2). [C20: from RE- + *-flation,* as in INFLATION or DEFLATION]

reflect (rɪˈflɛkt) *vb.* **1.** to undergo or cause to undergo a process in which light, other electromagnetic radiation, sound, particles, etc., are thrown back after impinging on a surface. **2.** (of a mirror, etc.) to form an image of (something) by reflection. **3.** (*tr.*) to show or express: *his tactics reflect his desire for power.* **4.** (*tr.*) to bring as a consequence: *the success of the project reflected great credit on all the staff.* **5.** (*intr.;* foll. by *on* or *upon*) to cause to be regarded in a specified way: *her behaviour reflects well on her.* **6.** (*intr.;* foll. by *on* or *upon*) to cast dishonour, discredit, etc. (on): *his conduct reflects on his parents.* **7.** (*intr.;* usually foll. by *on*) to think, meditate, or ponder. [C15: from Latin *reflectere* to bend back, from RE- + *flectere* to bend; see FLEX]

reflectance (rɪˈflɛktəns) *or* **reflection factor** *n.* a measure of the ability of a surface to reflect light or other electromagnetic radiation, equal to the ratio of the reflected flux to the incident flux. Symbol: ρ Compare **transmittance, absorptance.**

reflecting telescope *n.* a type of telescope in which the initial image is formed by a concave mirror. Also called: **reflector.** Compare **refracting telescope.**

reflection *or* (*less commonly*) **reflexion** (rɪˈflɛkʃən) *n.* **1.** the act of reflecting or the state of being reflected. **2.** something reflected or the image so produced, as by a mirror. **3.** careful or long consideration or thought. **4.** implicit or explicit attribution of discredit or blame. **5.** *Maths.* a transformation in which the direction of one axis is reversed or changes the polarity of one of the variables. **6.** *Anatomy.* the bending back of a structure or part upon itself. —**reˈflectional** *or* **reˈflexional** *adj.*

reflection density *n. Physics.* a measure of the extent to which a surface reflects light or other electromagnetic radiation, equal to the logarithm to base ten of the reciprocal of the reflectance. Symbol: *D* Former name: **optical density.**

reflective (rɪˈflɛktɪv) *adj.* **1.** characterized by quiet thought or contemplation. **2.** capable of reflecting: *a reflective surface.* **3.** produced by reflection. —**reˈflectively** *adv.*

reflectivity (ˌriːflɛkˈtɪvɪtɪ) *n.* **1.** *Physics.* a measure of the ability of a surface to reflect radiation, equal to the reflectance of a layer of material sufficiently thick for the reflectance not to depend on the thickness. **2.** Also called: **reflectiveness.** the quality or capability of being reflective.

ˌ**re-exˈhibit** *vb.*
ˌ**re-exˈperience** *vb.*
reˈfashion *vb.*
reˈfasten *vb.*
reˈfile *vb.*
reˈfilm *vb.*
reˈfilter *vb.*
reˈfinish *vb.*
reˈfinisher *n.*
reˈfire *vb.*

reflectometer (ˌriːflɛkˈtɒmɪtə) *n. Physics.* an instrument for measuring the ratio of the energy of a reflected wave to the incident wave in a system.
reflector (rɪˈflɛktə) *n.* **1.** a person or thing that reflects. **2.** a surface or object that reflects light, sound, heat, etc. **3.** a small translucent red disc, strip, etc., with a reflecting backing on the rear of a road vehicle, which reflects the light of the headlights of a following vehicle. **4.** another name for **reflecting telescope. 5.** part of an aerial placed so as to increase the forward radiation of the radiator and decrease the backward radiation.
reflet (rəˈfleɪ) *n.* an iridescent glow or lustre, as on ceramic ware. [C19: from French: a reflection, from Italian *riflesso,* from Latin *reflexus,* from *reflectere* to REFLECT]
reflex *n.* (ˈriːflɛks). **1. a.** an immediate involuntary response, esp. one that is innate, such as coughing or removal of the hand from a hot surface, evoked by a given stimulus. **b.** (*as modifier*): *a reflex action.* See also **reflex arc. 2. a.** a mechanical response to a particular situation, involving no conscious decision. **b.** (*as modifier*): *a reflex response.* **3.** a reflection; an image produced by or as if by reflection. **4.** a speech element derived from a corresponding form in an earlier state of the language: *"sorrow" is a reflex of Middle English "sorwe."* ~*adj.* (ˈriːflɛks). **5.** *Maths.* (of an angle) between 180° and 360°. **6.** (*prenominal*) turned, reflected, or bent backwards. ~*vb.* (rɪˈflɛks). **7.** (*tr.*) to bend, turn, or reflect backwards. [C16: from Latin *reflexus* bent back, from *reflectere* to reflect] —**reˈflexible** *adj.* —**reˌflexiˈbility** *n.*
reflex arc *n. Physiol.* the neural pathway over which impulses travel to produce a reflex action, consisting of at least one afferent (receptor) and one efferent (effector) neuron.
reflex camera *n.* a camera in which the image is composed and focused on a large ground-glass viewfinder screen. In a **single-lens reflex** the light enters through the camera lens and falls on the film when the viewfinder mirror is retracted. In a **twin-lens reflex** the light enters through a separate lens and is deflected onto the viewfinder screen.
reflexion (rɪˈflɛkʃən) *n. Brit.* a less common spelling of **reflection.** —**reˈflexional** *adj.*
reflexive (rɪˈflɛksɪv) *adj.* **1.** denoting a class of pronouns that refer back to the subject of a sentence or clause. Thus, in the sentence *that man thinks a great deal of himself,* the pronoun *himself* is reflexive. **2.** denoting a verb used transitively with the reflexive pronoun as its direct object, as the French *se lever* "to get up" (literally "to raise oneself") or English *to dress oneself.* **3.** *Physiol.* of or relating to a reflex. **4.** *Logic, maths.* (of a relation) holding between any member of its domain and itself: *"... is a member of the same family as ..." is reflexive.* Compare **irreflexive, nonreflexive.** ~*n.* **5.** a reflexive pronoun or verb. —**reˈflexively** *adv.* —**reˈflexiveness** *or* **reflexivity** (ˌriːflɛkˈsɪvɪtɪ) *n.*
reflexology (ˌriːflɛkˈsɒlədʒɪ) *n.* **1.** a form of therapy practised as a treatment in alternative medicine in which the soles of the feet are massaged: designed to stimulate the blood supply and nerves and thus relieve tension. **2.** *Psychol.* the belief that behaviour can be understood in terms of combinations of reflexes. —ˌ**reflexˈologist** *n.*
refluent (ˈrɛflʊənt) *adj. Rare.* flowing back; ebbing. [C18: from Latin *refluere* to flow back] —ˈ**refluence** *n.*
reflux (ˈriːflʌks) *vb.* **1.** *Chem.* to boil or be boiled in a vessel attached to a condenser, so that the vapour condenses and flows back into the vessel. ~*n.* **2.** *Chem.* **a.** an act of refluxing. **b.** (*as modifier*): *a reflux condenser.* **3.** the act or an instance of flowing back; ebb. [C15: from Medieval Latin *refluxus,* from Latin *refluere* to flow back]
reforest (riːˈfɒrɪst) *vb.* (*tr.*) another word for **reafforest.**
reform (rɪˈfɔːm) *vb.* **1.** (*tr.*) to improve (an existing institution, law, practice, etc.) by alteration or correction of abuses. **2.** to give up or cause to give up a reprehensible habit or immoral way of life. **3.** *Chem.* to change the molecular structure of (a hydrocarbon) to make it suitable for use as petrol by heat, pressure, and the action of catalysts. ~*n.* **4.** an improvement or change for the better, esp. as a result of correction of legal or political abuses or malpractices. **5.** a principle, campaign, or measure aimed at achieving such change. **6.** improvement of morals or behaviour, esp. by giving up some vice. [C14: via Old French from Latin *reformāre* to form again] —**reˈformable** *adj.* —**reˈformative** *adj.* —**reˈformer** *n.*
re-form (riːˈfɔːm) *vb.* to form anew. —ˌ**re-forˈmation** *n.*
reformation (ˌrɛfəˈmeɪʃən) *n.* the act or an instance of reforming or the state of being reformed. —ˌ**reforˈmational** *adj.*
Reformation (ˌrɛfəˈmeɪʃən) *n.* a religious and political movement of 16th-century Europe that began as an attempt to reform the Roman Catholic Church and resulted in the establishment of the Protestant Churches.
reformatory (rɪˈfɔːmətərɪ, -trɪ) *n., pl.* **-ries. 1.** Also called: **reform school.** (formerly) a place of instruction where young offenders were sent for corrective training. Compare **approved school.** ~*adj.* **2.** having the purpose or function of reforming.
Reformed (rɪˈfɔːmd) *adj.* **1.** of or designating a Protestant Church, esp. the Calvinist as distinct from the Lutheran. **2.** of or designating Reform Judaism.
reformism (rɪˈfɔːmɪzəm) *n.* a doctrine or movement advocating reform, esp. political or religious reform, rather than abolition. —**reˈformist** *n., adj.*
Reform Judaism *n.* a movement in Judaism originating in the 19th century, which does not require strict observance of the law, but adapts the historical forms of Judaism to the contemporary world. Compare **Orthodox Judaism, Conservative Judaism.**
refract (rɪˈfrækt) *vb.* (*tr.*) **1.** to cause to undergo refraction. **2.** to measure the refractive capabilities of (the eye, a lens, etc.). [C17: from Latin *refractus* broken up, from *refringere,* from RE- + *frangere* to break] —**reˈfractable** *adj.*
refracting telescope *n.* a type of telescope in which the image is formed by a set of lenses. Also called: **refractor.** Compare **reflecting telescope.**
refraction (rɪˈfrækʃən) *n.* **1.** *Physics.* the change in direction of a propagating wave, such as light or sound, in passing from one medium to another in which it has a different velocity. **2.** the amount by which a wave is refracted. **3.** the ability of the eye to refract light. **4.** the determination of the refractive condition of the eye. **5.** *Astronomy.* the apparent elevation in position of a celestial body resulting from the refraction of light by the earth's atmosphere.
refractive (rɪˈfræktɪv) *adj.* **1.** of or concerned with refraction. **2.** (of a material or substance) capable of causing refraction. —**reˈfractively** *adv.* —**reˈfractiveness** *or* **refractivity** (ˌriːfrækˈtɪvɪtɪ) *n.*
refractive index *n. Physics.* a measure of the extent to which radiation is refracted on passing through the interface between two media. It is the ratio of the sine of the angle of incidence to the sine of the angle of refraction, which can be shown to be equal to the ratio of the phase speed in the first medium to that in the second. In the case of electromagnetic radiation, esp. light, it is usual to give values of the **absolute refractive index** of a medium, that is for radiation entering the medium from free space. Symbol: ν, μ
refractometer (ˌriːfrækˈtɒmɪtə) *n.* any instrument for determining the refractive index of a substance. —**refractometric** (rɪˌfræktəˈmɛtrɪk) *adj.* —ˌ**refracˈtometry** *n.*
refractor (rɪˈfræktə) *n.* **1.** an object or material that refracts. **2.** another name for **refracting telescope.**
refractory (rɪˈfræktərɪ) *adj.* **1.** unmanageable or obstinate. **2.** *Med.* not responding to treatment. **3.** *Physiol.* (of a nerve or muscle) incapable of responding to stimulation, esp. during the period (**refractory period**) immediately following a previous stimulation. **4.** (of a material) able to withstand high temperatures without fusion or decomposition. ~*n., pl.* **-ries. 5.** a material, such as fireclay or alumina, that is able to withstand high temperatures: used to line furnaces, kilns, etc. [C17: variant of obsolete *refractary;* see REFRACT] —**reˈfractorily** *adv.* —**reˈfractoriness** *n.*
refrain[1] (rɪˈfreɪn) *vb.* (*intr.;* usually foll. by *from*) to abstain (from action); forbear. [C14: from Latin *refrēnāre* to check with a bridle, from RE- + *frēnum* a bridle] —**reˈfrainer** *n.* —**reˈfrainment** *n.*
refrain[2] (rɪˈfreɪn) *n.* **1.** a regularly recurring melody, such as the chorus of a song. **2.** a much repeated saying or idea. [C14: via Old French, ultimately from Latin *refringere* to break into pieces]
refrangible (rɪˈfrændʒɪbᵊl) *adj.* capable of being refracted. [C17: from Latin *refringere* to break up, from RE- + *frangere* to break] —**reˌfrangiˈbility** *or* **reˈfrangibleness** *n.*
refresh (rɪˈfrɛʃ) *vb.* **1.** (*usually tr. or reflexive*) to make or become fresh or vigorous, as through rest, drink, or food; revive or reinvigorate. **2.** (*tr.*) to enliven (something worn or faded), as by adding new decorations. **3.** (*tr.*) to stimulate (the memory). **4.** (*tr.*) to replenish, as with new equipment or stores. [C14: from Old French *refreschir;* see RE-, FRESH] —**reˈfreshful** *adj.*
refresher (rɪˈfrɛʃə) *n.* **1.** something that refreshes, such as a cold drink. **2.** *English law.* a fee, additional to that marked on the brief, paid to counsel in a case that lasts more than a day.
refresher course *n.* a short educational course for people to review their subject and developments in it.
refreshing (rɪˈfrɛʃɪŋ) *adj.* **1.** able to or tending to refresh; invigorating. **2.** pleasantly different or novel. —**reˈfreshingly** *adv.*
refreshment (rɪˈfrɛʃmənt) *n.* **1.** the act of refreshing or the state of being refreshed. **2.** (*pl.*) snacks and drinks served as a light meal.
refrigerant (rɪˈfrɪdʒərənt) *n.* **1.** a fluid capable of changes of phase at low temperatures: used as the working fluid of a refrigerator. **2.** a cooling substance, such as ice or solid carbon diox-

reˈfloat *vb.*
reˈflood *vb.*
reˈflower *vb.*
reˈfocus *vb.,* **-cuses, -cusing, -cused** *or* **-cusses, -cussing, -cussed.**
reˈfold *vb.*
reˈforge *vb.*
reˈformuˌlate *vb.*
ˌ**reformuˈlation** *n.*
reˈfortiˌfy *vb.,* **-ˌfies, -ˌfying, -ˌfied.**
reˈframe *vb.*
reˈfreeze *vb.,* **-ˈfreezes, -ˈfreezing, -ˈfroze, -ˈfrozen.**

ide. 3. *Med.* an agent that provides a sensation of coolness or reduces fever. ~*adj.* 4. causing cooling or freezing.

refrigerate (rɪˈfrɪdʒəˌreɪt) *vb.* to make or become frozen or cold, esp. for preservative purposes; chill or freeze. [C16: from Latin *refrīgerāre* to make cold, from RE- + *frīgus* cold] —**reˌfrigerˈation** *n.* —**reˈfrigerative** *adj.* —**reˈfrigeratory** *adj., n.*

refrigerator (rɪˈfrɪdʒəˌreɪtə) *n.* a chamber in which food, drink, etc., are kept cool. Informal word: **fridge.**

refringent (rɪˈfrɪndʒənt) *adj. Physics.* of, concerned with, or causing refraction; refractive. [C18: from Latin *refringere* to break up; see REFRACT] —**reˈfringency** *or* **reˈfringence** *n.*

reft (rɛft) *vb.* a past tense and past participle of **reave.**

refuel (riːˈfjuːəl) *vb.* **-els, -elling, -elled** *or U.S.* **-els, -eling, -eled.** to supply or be supplied with fresh fuel.

refuge (ˈrɛfjuːdʒ) *n.* 1. shelter or protection, as from the weather or danger. 2. any place, person, action, or thing that offers or appears to offer protection, help, or relief: *accused of incompetence, he took refuge in lying.* 3. another name for a traffic island. See **island** (sense 2). ~*vb.* 4. *Archaic.* to take refuge or give refuge to. [C14: via Old French from Latin *refugium,* from *refugere* to flee away, from RE- + *fugere* to escape]

refugee (ˌrɛfjʊˈdʒiː) *n.* **a.** a person who has fled from some danger or problem, esp. political persecution. **b.** (*as modifier*): *a refugee camp; a refugee problem.* —ˌ**refuˈgeeism** *n.*

refugee capital *n. Finance.* money from abroad invested, esp. for a short term, in the country offering the highest interest rate.

refugium (rɪˈfjuːdʒɪəm) *n., pl.* **-gia** (-dʒɪə). a geographical region that has remained unaltered by a climatic change affecting surrounding regions and that therefore forms a haven for relict fauna and flora. [C20: Latin: refuge]

refulgent (rɪˈfʌldʒənt) *adj. Literary.* shining, brilliant, or radiant. [C16: from Latin *refulgēre* to shine brightly, from RE- + *fulgēre* to shine] —**reˈfulgence** *or* (*less commonly*) **reˈfulgency** *n.* —**reˈfulgently** *adv.*

refund *vb.* (rɪˈfʌnd). (*tr.*) 1. to give back (money), as when an article purchased is unsatisfactory. 2. to reimburse (a person). ~*n.* (ˈriːˌfʌnd). 3. return of money to a purchaser or the amount so returned. [C14: from Latin *refundere* to pour back, from RE- + *fundere* to pour] —**reˈfundable** *adj.* —**reˈfunder** *n.*

re-fund (riːˈfʌnd) *vb.* (*tr.*) *Finance.* 1. to discharge (an old or matured debt) by new borrowing, as by a new bond issue. 2. to replace (an existing bond issue) with a new one. [C20: from RE- + FUND]

refurbish (riːˈfɜːbɪʃ) *vb.* (*tr.*) to make neat, clean, or complete, as by renovating, re-equipping, or restoring. —**reˈfurbishing** *or* **reˈfurbishment** *n.*

refusal (rɪˈfjuːzᵊl) *n.* 1. the act or an instance of refusing. 2. the opportunity to reject or accept; option.

refuse[1] (rɪˈfjuːz) *vb.* 1. (*tr.*) to decline to accept (something offered): *to refuse a present; to refuse promotion.* 2. to decline to give or grant (something) to (a person, organization, etc.). 3. (when *tr., takes an infinitive*) to express determination not (to do something); decline: *he refuses to talk about it.* 4. (of a horse) to be unwilling to take (a jump), as by swerving or stopping. 5. (*tr.*) (of a woman) to declare one's unwillingness to accept (a suitor) as a husband. [C14: from Old French *refuser,* from Latin *refundere* to pour back; see REFUND] —**reˈfusable** *adj.* —**reˈfuser** *n.*

refuse[2] (ˈrɛfjuːs) *n.* **a.** anything thrown away; waste; rubbish. **b.** (*as modifier*): *a refuse collection.* [C15: from Old French *refuser* to REFUSE[1]]

refusenik *or* **refusnik** (rɪˈfjuːznɪk) *n.* 1. a Jew in the former Soviet Union who was refused permission to emigrate. 2. a person who refuses to cooperate with a system or comply with a law because of a moral conviction. [C20: from REFUSE[1] + -NIK]

refutation (ˌrɛfjʊˈteɪʃən) *n.* 1. the act or process of refuting. 2. something that refutes; disproof.

refute (rɪˈfjuːt) *vb.* (*tr.*) to prove (a statement, theory, charge, etc.) of (a person) to be false or incorrect; disprove. [C16: from Latin *refūtāre* to rebut] —**refutable** (ˈrɛfjʊtəbᵊl, rɪˈfjuː-) *adj.* —**refutability** (ˌrɛfjʊtəˈbɪlɪtɪ, rɪˌfjuː-) *n.* —**ˈrefutably** *adv.* —**reˈfuter** *n.*

▷**Usage.** *Refute* is often used incorrectly as a synonym of *deny.* In careful usage, however, to *deny* something is to state that it is untrue; to *refute* something is to assemble evidence in order to prove it untrue: *all he could do was deny the allegations since he was unable to refute them.*

reg. *abbrev. for:* 1. regiment. 2. register(ed). 3. registrar. 4. registry. 5. regular(ly). 6. regulation. 7. regulator.

Reg. *abbrev. for:* 1. Regent. 2. Regina.

regain (rɪˈgeɪn) *vb.* (*tr.*) 1. to take or get back; recover. 2. to reach again. —**reˈgainable** *adj.* —**reˈgainer** *n.*

regal[1] (ˈriːgᵊl) *adj.* of, relating to, or befitting a king or queen; royal. [C14: from Latin *rēgālis,* from *rēx* king] —**ˈregally** *adv.*

regal[2] (ˈriːgᵊl) *n.* (*sometimes pl.*) a portable organ equipped only with small reed pipes, popular from the 15th century and recently revived for modern performance. [C16: from French *régale;* of obscure origin]

regale (rɪˈgeɪl) *vb.* (*tr.;* usually foll. by *with*) 1. to give delight or amusement to: *he regaled them with stories of his youth.* 2. to provide with choice or abundant food or drink. ~*n.* 3. *Archaic.* **a.** a feast. **b.** a delicacy of food or drink. [C17: from French *régaler,* from *gale* pleasure; related to Middle Dutch *wale* riches; see also GALA] —**reˈgalement** *n.*

regalia (rɪˈgeɪlɪə) *pl. n.* (*sometimes functioning as sing.*) 1. the ceremonial emblems or robes of royalty, high office, an order, etc. 2. any splendid or special clothes; finery. [C16: from Medieval Latin: royal privileges, from Latin *rēgālis* REGAL]

regality (riːˈgælɪtɪ) *n., pl.* **-ties.** 1. the state or condition of being royal; kingship or queenship; royalty. 2. the rights or privileges of royalty. 3. *Scot. history.* **a.** jurisdiction conferred by the sovereign on a powerful subject. **b.** a territory under such jurisdiction.

regard (rɪˈgɑːd) *vb.* 1. to look closely or attentively at (something or someone); observe steadily. 2. (*tr.*) to hold (a person or thing) in respect, admiration, or affection: *we regard your work very highly.* 3. (*tr.*) to look upon or consider in a specified way: *she regarded her brother as her responsibility.* 4. (*tr.*) to relate to; concern; have a bearing on. 5. to take notice of or pay attention to (something); heed: *he has never regarded the conventions.* 6. **as regards.** (*prep.*) in respect of; concerning. ~*n.* 7. a gaze; look. 8. attention; heed: *he spends without regard to his bank balance.* 9. esteem, affection, or respect. 10. reference, relation, or connection (esp. in the phrases **with regard to** *or* **in regard to**). 11. (*pl.*) good wishes or greetings (esp. in the phrase **with kind regards,** used at the close of a letter). 12. **in this regard.** on this point. [C14: from Old French *regarder* to look at, care about, from RE- + *garder* to GUARD] —**reˈgardable** *adj.*

regardant (rɪˈgɑːdᵊnt) *adj.* (*usually postpositive*) *Heraldry.* (of a beast) shown looking backwards over its shoulder. [C15: from Old French; see REGARD]

regardful (rɪˈgɑːdfʊl) *adj.* 1. (often foll. by *of*) showing regard (for); heedful (of). 2. showing regard, respect, or consideration. —**reˈgardfully** *adv.* —**reˈgardfulness** *n.*

regarding (rɪˈgɑːdɪŋ) *prep.* in respect of; on the subject of.

regardless (rɪˈgɑːdlɪs) *adj.* 1. (usually foll. by *of*) taking no regard or heed; heedless. ~*adv.* 2. in spite of everything; disregarding drawbacks: *to carry on regardless.* —**reˈgardlessly** *adv.* —**reˈgardlessness** *n.*

regatta (rɪˈgætə) *n.* an organized series of races of yachts, rowing boats, etc. [C17: from obsolete Italian (Venetian dialect) *rigatta* contest, of obscure origin]

regd *abbrev. for* registered.

regelate (ˈriːdʒɪˌleɪt) *vb. Physics.* to undergo or cause to undergo regelation. [C19: from RE- + stem of participle of Latin *gelāre* to freeze]

regelation (ˌriːdʒɪˈleɪʃən) *n.* the rejoining together of two pieces of ice as a result of melting under pressure at the interface between them and subsequent refreezing.

regency (ˈriːdʒənsɪ) *n., pl.* **-cies.** 1. government by a regent or a body of regents. 2. the office of a regent or body of regents. 3. a territory under the jurisdiction of a regent or body of regents. 4. *Rare.* the use or exercise of authority; rule or government. [C15: from Medieval Latin *regentia,* from Latin *regere* to rule]

Regency (ˈriːdʒənsɪ) *adj.* characteristic of or relating to the period of the regency of the Prince of Wales in Britain (1811–20) or of Philip, Duke of Orleans, in France (1715–23) or to the styles of architecture, furniture, art, literature, etc., produced in either of them.

regenerate *vb.* (rɪˈdʒɛnəˌreɪt). 1. to undergo or cause to undergo moral, spiritual, or physical renewal or invigoration. 2. to form or be formed again; come or bring into existence once again. 3. to replace (lost or damaged tissues or organs) by new growth, or to cause (such tissues) to be replaced. 4. *Chem.* to restore or be restored to an original physical or chemical state. 5. (*tr.*) *Electronics.* (in a digital system) to reshape (distorted incoming pulses) for onward transmission. ~*adj.* (rɪˈdʒɛnərɪt). 6. morally, spiritually, or physically renewed or reborn; restored or refreshed. —**reˈgenerable** *adj.* —**reˈgeneracy** *n.* —**reˈgenerative** *adj.* —**reˈgeneratively** *adv.* —**reˈgenerˌator** *n.*

regeneration (rɪˌdʒɛnəˈreɪʃən) *n.* 1. the act or process of regenerating or the state of being regenerated; rebirth or renewal. 2. the regrowth by an animal or plant of an organ, tissue, or part that has been lost or destroyed. 3. *Electronics.* the use of positive feedback to increase the amplification of a radio frequency stage.

regenerative cooling *n.* the process of cooling the walls of the combustion chamber of a rocket by circulating the propellant around the chamber before combustion.

regent (ˈriːdʒənt) *n.* 1. the ruler or administrator of a country during the minority, absence, or incapacity of its monarch. 2. (formerly) a senior teacher or administrator in any of certain universities. 3. *U.S. and Canadian.* a member of the governing board of certain schools and colleges. 4. *Rare.* any person who governs or rules. ~*adj.* 5. (*usually postpositive*) acting or functioning as a regent: *a queen regent.* 6. *Rare.* governing, ruling, or controlling. [C14: from Latin *regēns* ruling, from *regere* to rule] —**ˈregental** *adj.* —**ˈregentship** *n.*

reˈfry *vb.,* -ˈ**fries,** -ˈ**frying,** -ˈ**fried.**
reˈfurnish *vb.*
reˈgalvaˌnize *or* reˈgalvaˌnise *vb.*
reˈgather *vb.*
reˈgauge *vb.*
reˈgenesis *n.*

regent-bird *n.* an Australian bower bird, *Sericulus chrysocephalus,* the male of which has a showy yellow and velvety-black plumage. [after the *Prince Regent* (later George IV)]

reggae ('rɛgeɪ) *n.* a type of West Indian popular music having four beats to the bar, the upbeat being strongly accented. [C20: of West Indian origin]

regicide ('rɛdʒɪˌsaɪd) *n.* 1. the killing of a king. 2. a person who kills a king. [C16: from Latin *rēx* king + -CIDE] —ˌ**regi'cidal** *adj.*

regime *or* **régime** (reɪ'ʒiːm) *n.* 1. a system of government or a particular administration: *a fascist regime; the regime of Fidel Castro.* 2. a social system or order. 3. *Med.* another word for **regimen** (sense 1). [C18: from French, from Latin *regimen* guidance, from *regere* to rule]

regimen ('rɛdʒɪˌmɛn) *n.* 1. Also called: **regime.** *Med.* a systematic course of therapy, often including a recommended diet. 2. administration or rule. [C14: from Latin: guidance]

regiment *n.* ('rɛdʒɪmənt). 1. a military formation varying in size from a battalion to a number of battalions. 2. a large number in regular or organized groups: *regiments of beer bottles.* ~*vb.* ('rɛdʒɪˌmɛnt). (*tr.*) 3. to force discipline or order on, esp. in a domineering manner. 4. to organize into a regiment or regiments. 5. to form into organized groups. 6. to assign to a regiment. [C14: via Old French from Late Latin *regimentum* government, from Latin *regere* to rule] —ˌ**regi'mental** *adj.* —ˌ**regi'mentally** *adv.* —ˌ**regimen'tation** *n.*

regimentals (ˌrɛdʒɪ'mɛntᵊlz) *pl. n.* 1. the uniform and insignia of a regiment. 2. military dress.

regimental sergeant major *n. Military.* the senior Warrant Officer I in a British or Commonwealth regiment or battalion, responsible under the adjutant for all aspects of duty and discipline of the warrant officers, NCOs, and men. Abbrev.: **RSM.** Compare **company sergeant major.** See also **warrant officer.**

Regina (rɪ'dʒaɪnə) *n.* queen: now used chiefly in documents, inscriptions, etc. Compare **Rex.**

region ('riːdʒən) *n.* 1. any large, indefinite, and continuous part of a surface or space. 2. an area considered as a unit for geographical, functional, social, or cultural reasons. 3. an administrative division of a country: *Tuscany is one of the regions of the Italian Republic.* 4. a realm or sphere of activity or interest. 5. range, area, or scope: *in what region is the price likely to be?* 6. (in Scotland since 1975) any of the nine territorial divisions into which the mainland of Scotland is divided for purposes of local government. See also **islands council.** [C14: from Latin *regiō,* from *regere* to govern]

regional ('riːdʒənᵊl) *adj.* of, characteristic of, or limited to a region: *the regional dialects of English.* —'**regionally** *adv.*

regional enteritis *n.* another name for **Crohn's disease.**

regionalism ('riːdʒənəˌlɪzəm) *n.* 1. division of a country into administrative regions having partial autonomy. 2. advocacy of such division. 3. loyalty to one's home region; regional patriotism. 4. the common interests of national groups, people, etc., living in the same part of the world. 5. a word, custom, accent, or other characteristic associated with a specific region. —'**regionalist** *n., adj.*

régisseur *French.* (reʒisœr) *n.* an official in a dance company with varying duties, usually including directing productions. [French, from *régir* to manage]

register ('rɛdʒɪstə) *n.* 1. an official or formal list recording names, events, or transactions. 2. the book in which such a list is written. 3. an entry in such a list. 4. a recording device that accumulates data, totals sums of money, etc.: *a cash register.* 5. a movable plate that controls the flow of air into a furnace, chimney, room, etc. 6. *Computer technol.* a location in a storage device that can hold one or more words, esp. one designed for a specific function. 7. *Music.* a. the timbre characteristic of a certain manner of voice production. See **head voice, chest voice.** b. any of the stops on an organ as classified in respect of its tonal quality: *the flute register.* 8. *Printing.* a. the correct alignment of the separate plates in colour printing. b. the exact correspondence of lines of type, columns, etc., on the two sides of a printed sheet of paper. 9. a form of a language associated with a particular social situation or subject matter, such as obscene slang, legal language, or journalese. 10. the act or an instance of registering. ~*vb.* 11. (*tr.*) to enter or cause someone to enter (an event, person's name, ownership, etc.) on a register; formally record. 12. to show or be shown on a scale or other measuring instrument: *the current didn't register on the meter.* 13. to show or be shown in a person's face, bearing, etc.: *his face registered surprise.* 14. (*intr.*) to have an effect; make an impression: *the news of her uncle's death just did not register.* 15. to send (a letter, package, etc.) by registered post. 16. (*tr.*) *Printing.* to adjust (a printing press, forme, etc.) to ensure that the printed matter is in register. 17. (*intr.*; often foll. by *with*) (of a mechanical part) to align (with another part). 18. *Military.* to bring (a gun) to bear on its target by adjustment according to the accuracy of observed single rounds. [C14: from Medieval Latin *registrum,* from Latin *regerere* to transcribe, from RE- + *gerere* to bear] —'**registerer** *n.* —'**registrable** *adj.*

registered disabled *adj. Social welfare.* (in Britain) 1. (of a handicapped person) on a local authority register under the Chronically Sick and Disabled Persons Act 1970. 2. on a register kept by the Manpower Services Commission for employment purposes, and holding a green identity card, thus qualifying for special services. ~Also called: **registered handicapped.** See also **green card** (sense 2), **handicap register.**

Registered General Nurse *n.* (in Britain) a nurse who has completed a three-year training course in all aspects of nursing care, enabling registration with the United Kingdom Central Council for Nursing, Midwifery, and Health Visiting. Abbrev.: **RGN.**

registered post *n.* 1. a Post Office service by which compensation is paid for loss or damage to mail for which a registration fee has been paid. Compare **recorded delivery.** 2. mail sent by this service.

Registered Trademark *n.* See **trademark** (sense 1).

register office *n. Brit.* a government office where civil marriages are performed and births, marriages, and deaths are recorded. Often called: **registry office.**

register ton *n.* the full name for **ton**[1] (sense 7).

registrant ('rɛdʒɪstrənt) *n.* a person who registers a trademark or patent.

registrar (ˌrɛdʒɪ'strɑː, 'rɛdʒɪˌstrɑː) *n.* 1. a person who keeps official records. 2. an administrative official responsible for student records, enrolment procedure, etc., in a school, college, or university. 3. *Brit. and N.Z.* a hospital doctor senior to a houseman but junior to a consultant, specializing in either medicine (**medical registrar**) or surgery (**surgical registrar**). 4. *Chiefly U.S.* a person employed by a company to maintain a register of its security issues. —'**registrarship** *n.*

registration (ˌrɛdʒɪ'streɪʃən) *n.* 1. a. the act of registering or state of being registered. b. (*as modifier*): *a registration number.* 2. an entry in a register. 3. a group of people, such as students, who register at a particular time. 4. a combination of organ or harpsichord stops used in the performance of a piece of music. —ˌ**regis'trational** *adj.*

registration document *n. Brit.* a document giving identification details of a motor vehicle, including its manufacturer, date of registration, engine and chassis numbers, and owner's name. Compare **logbook** (sense 2).

registration number *n.* a sequence of letters and numbers assigned to a motor vehicle when it is registered, usually indicating the year and place of registration, displayed on numberplates at the front and rear of the vehicle, and by which the vehicle may be identified.

registration plate *n.* the Australian and N.Z. name for **numberplate.**

registry ('rɛdʒɪstrɪ) *n., pl.* **-tries.** 1. a place where registers are kept, such as the part of a church where the bride and groom sign a register after a wedding. 2. the registration of a ship's country of origin: *a ship of Liberian registry.* 3. another word for **registration.**

registry office *n. Brit.* a name often used for a **register office.**

Regius professor ('riːdʒɪəs) *n. Brit.* a person appointed by the Crown to a university chair founded by a royal patron. [C17: *regius,* from Latin: royal, from *rex* king]

reglet ('rɛglɪt) *n.* 1. a flat narrow architectural moulding. 2. *Printing.* a strip of oiled wood used for spacing between lines. Compare **lead**[2] (sense 7). [C16: from Old French, literally: a little rule, from *regle* rule, from Latin *rēgula*]

regmaker ('rɛxˌmɑːkə) *n. S. African.* a drink taken to relieve the symptoms of a hangover; a pick-me-up. [Afrikaans]

regnal ('rɛgnəl) *adj.* 1. of a sovereign, reign, or kingdom. 2. designating a year of a sovereign's reign calculated from the date of his or her accession. [C17: from Medieval Latin *rēgnālis,* from Latin *rēgnum* sovereignty; see REIGN]

regnant ('rɛgnənt) *adj.* 1. (*postpositive*) reigning. 2. prevalent; current. [C17: from Latin *regnāre* to REIGN] —'**regnancy** *n.*

rego ('rɛdʒəʊ) *n. Austral. slang.* a. the registration of a motor vehicle. b. a fee paid for this.

regolith ('rɛgəlɪθ) *n.* the layer of loose material covering the bedrock of the earth and moon, etc., comprising soil, sand, rock fragments, volcanic ash, glacial drift, etc. [C20: from Greek *rhēgos* covering, blanket + *lithos* stone]

regorge (rɪ'gɔːdʒ) *vb.* 1. (*tr.*) to vomit up; disgorge. 2. (*intr.*) (esp. of water) to flow or run back. [C17: from French *regorger;* see GORGE]

regosol ('rɛgəˌsɒl) *n.* a type of azonal soil consisting of unconsolidated material derived from freshly deposited alluvium or sands. [C20: from Greek *rhēgos* covering, blanket + Latin *solum* soil]

Reg. prof. *abbrev. for* Regius professor.

regrate (rɪ'greɪt) *vb.* (*tr.*) 1. to buy up (commodities) in advance so as to raise their price for profitable resale. 2. to resell (commodities so purchased); retail. 3. *Building trades.* to redress the surface of (hewn stonework). [C15: from Old French *regrater* perhaps from RE- + *grater* to scratch] —**re'grater** *n.*

regress *vb.* (rɪ'grɛs). 1. (*intr.*) to return or revert, as to a former place, condition, or mode of behaviour. 2. (*tr.*) *Statistics.* to

re'germiˌnate *vb.*
ˌregermi'nation *n.*
re'gild *vb.*
re'glaze *vb.*
re'glue *vb.,* **-'glues, -'gluing, -'glued.**
re'grade *vb.*

measure the extent to which (a dependent variable) is associated with one or more independent variables. ~*n.* ('riːgrɛs). **3.** the act of regressing. **4.** movement in a backward direction; retrogression. **5.** *Logic.* a supposed explanation each stage of which requires to be similarly explained, as saying that knowledge requires a justification in terms of propositions themselves known to be true. [C14: from Latin *regressus* a retreat, from *regredī* to go back, from RE- + *gradī* to go] —**re'gressor** *n.*

regression (rɪ'grɛʃən) *n.* **1.** *Psychol.* the adoption by an adult or adolescent of behaviour more appropriate to a child, esp. as a defence mechanism to avoid anxiety. **2.** *Statistics.* **a.** the analysis or measure of the association between one variable (the dependent variable) and one or more other variables (the independent variables), usually formulated in an equation in which the independent variables have parametric coefficients, which may enable future values of the dependent variable to be predicted. **b.** (*as modifer*): *regression curve.* **3.** *Astronomy.* the slow movement around the ecliptic of the two points at which the moon's orbit intersects the ecliptic. One complete revolution occurs about every 19 years. **4.** *Geology.* the retreat of the sea from the land. **5.** the act of regressing.

regressive (rɪ'grɛsɪv) *adj.* **1.** regressing or tending to regress. **2.** (of a tax or tax system) levied or graduated so that the rate decreases as the amount taxed increases. Compare **progressive** (sense 5). **3.** of, relating to, or characteristic of regression. —**re'gressively** *adv.* —**re'gressiveness** *n.*

regret (rɪ'grɛt) *vb.* **-grets, -gretting, -gretted.** (*tr.*) **1.** (*may take a clause as object or an infinitive*) to feel sorry, repentant, or upset about. **2.** to bemoan or grieve the death or loss of. ~*n.* **3.** a sense of repentance, guilt, or sorrow, as over some wrong done or an unfulfilled ambition. **4.** a sense of loss or grief. **5.** (*pl.*) a polite expression of sadness, esp. in a formal refusal of an invitation. [C14: from Old French *regreter,* of Scandinavian origin; compare Old Norse *grāta* to weep] —**re'gretful** *adj.* —**re'gretfully** *adv.* —**re'gretfulness** *n.* —**re'grettable** *adj.* —**re'grettably** *adv.* —**re'gretter** *n.*

regroup (riː'gruːp) *vb.* **1.** to reorganize (military forces), esp. after an attack or a defeat. **2.** (*tr.*) to rearrange into a new grouping or groupings.

Regt *abbrev. for:* **1.** Regent. **2.** Regiment.

regulable ('rɛgjʊləbᵊl) *adj.* able to be regulated.

regular ('rɛgjʊlə) *adj.* **1.** normal, customary, or usual. **2.** according to a uniform principle, arrangement, or order: *trees planted at regular intervals.* **3.** occurring at fixed or prearranged intervals: *to make a regular call on a customer.* **4.** following a set rule or normal practice; methodical or orderly. **5.** symmetrical in appearance or form; even: *regular features.* **6.** (*prenominal*) organized, elected, conducted, etc., in a proper or officially prescribed manner. **7.** (*prenominal*) officially qualified or recognized: *he's not a regular doctor.* **8.** (*prenominal*) (intensifier): *a regular fool.* **9.** *U.S. and Canadian informal.* likable, dependable, or nice (esp. in the phrase **a regular guy**). **10.** denoting or relating to the personnel or units of the permanent military services: *a regular soldier; the regular army.* **11.** (of flowers) having any of their parts, esp. petals, alike in size, shape, arrangement, etc.; symmetrical. **12.** (of the formation, inflections, etc., of a word) following the usual pattern of formation in a language. **13.** *Maths.* **a.** (of a polygon) equilateral and equiangular. **b.** (of a polyhedron) having identical regular polygons as faces that make identical angles with each other. **c.** (of a prism) having regular polygons as bases. **d.** (of a pyramid) having a regular polygon as a base and the altitude passing through the centre of the base. **e.** another name for **analytic** (sense 5). **14.** *Botany.* another word for **actinomorphic. 15.** (*postpositive*) subject to the rule of an established religious order or community: *canons regular.* **15.** *U.S. politics.* of, selected by, or loyal to the leadership or platform of a political party: *a regular candidate; regular policies.* **16.** *Crystallog.* another word for **cubic** (sense 4). ~*n.* **17.** a professional long-term serviceman in a military unit. **18.** *Informal.* a person who does something regularly, such as attending a theatre or patronizing a shop. **19.** a member of a religious order or congregation, as contrasted with a secular. **20.** *U.S. politics.* a party member loyal to the leadership, organization, platform, etc., of his party. [C14: from Old French *reguler,* from Latin *rēgulāris* of a bar of wood or metal, from *rēgula* ruler, model] —ˌ**regu'larity** *n.* —**'regularly** *adv.*

regularize *or* **regularise** ('rɛgjʊləˌraɪz) *vb.* (*tr.*) to make regular; cause to conform. —ˌ**regulari'zation** *or* ˌ**regulari'sation** *n.*

regulate ('rɛgjʊˌleɪt) *vb.* (*tr.*) **1.** to adjust (the amount of heat, sound, etc., of something) as required; control. **2.** to adjust (an instrument or appliance) so that it operates correctly. **3.** to bring into conformity with a rule, principle, or usage. [C17: from Late Latin *rēgulāre* to control, from Latin *rēgula* a ruler] —**'regulative** *or* **'regulatory** *adj.* —**'regulatively** *adv.*

regulated tenancy *n. Social welfare.* (in Britain) the letting of a dwelling by a nonresident private landlord, usually at a registered fair rent, from which the landlord cannot evict the tenant without a possession order from a court. Compare **assured tenancy.**

regulation (ˌrɛgjʊ'leɪʃən) *n.* **1.** the act or process of regulating. **2.** a rule, principle, or condition that governs procedure or behaviour. **3.** a governmental or ministerial order having the force of law. **4.** *Embryol.* the ability of an animal embryo to develop normally after its structure has been altered or damaged in some way. **5.** (*modifier*) as required by official rules or procedure: *regulation uniform.* **6.** (*modifier*) normal; usual; conforming to accepted standards: *a regulation haircut.* **7.** *Electrical engineering.* the change in voltage occurring when a load is connected across a power supply, caused by internal resistance (for direct current) or internal impedance (alternating current).

regulator ('rɛgjʊˌleɪtə) *n.* **1.** a person or thing that regulates. **2.** the mechanism, including the hairspring and the balance wheel, by which the speed of a timepiece is regulated. **3.** a timepiece, known to be accurate, by which others are timed and regulated. **4.** any of various mechanisms or devices, such as a governor valve, for controlling fluid flow, pressure, temperature, voltage, etc. **5.** Also called: **regulator gene.** a gene the product of which controls the synthesis of a product from another gene.

regulo ('rɛgjʊləʊ) *n.* any of a number of temperatures to which a gas oven may be set: *cook at regulo 4 for 40 minutes.* [C20: from *Regulo,* trademark for a type of thermostatic control on gas ovens]

regulus ('rɛgjʊləs) *n., pl.* **-luses** *or* **-li** (-ˌlaɪ). impure metal forming beneath the slag during the smelting of ores. [C16: from Latin: a petty king, from *rēx* king; formerly used for *antimony,* because it combines readily with gold, thought of as the king of metals] —**'reguline** *adj.*

Regulus ('rɛgjʊləs) *n.* the brightest star in the constellation Leo. Visual magnitude: 1.3; spectral type: B8; distance: 85 light years.

regurgitate (rɪ'gɜːdʒɪˌteɪt) *vb.* **1.** to vomit forth (partially digested food). **2.** (of some birds and certain other animals) to bring back to the mouth (undigested or partly digested food with which to feed the young). **3.** (*intr.*) to be cast up or out, esp. from the mouth. **4.** (*intr.*) *Med.* (of blood) to flow backwards, in a direction opposite to the normal one, esp. through a defective heart valve. [C17: from Medieval Latin *regurgitāre,* from RE- + *gurgitāre* to flood, from Latin *gurges* gulf, whirlpool] —**re'gurgitant** *n., adj.* —**reˌgurgi'tation** *n.*

rehab ('riːhæb) *n.* short for **rehabilitation.**

rehabilitate (ˌriːə'bɪlɪˌteɪt) *vb.* (*tr.*) **1.** to help (a person who is physically or mentally disabled or has just been released from prison) to readapt to society or a new job, as by vocational guidance, retraining, or therapy. **2.** to restore to a former position or rank. **3.** to restore the good reputation of. [C16: from Medieval Latin *rehabilitāre* to restore, from RE- + Latin *habilitās* skill, ABILITY] —ˌ**reha'bilitative** *adj.*

rehabilitation (ˌriːəˌbɪlɪ'teɪʃən) *n.* **1.** the act or process of rehabilitating. **2.** *Med.* **a.** the treatment of physical disabilities by massage, electrotherapy, and exercises. **b.** (*as modifier*): *rehabilitation centre.*

rehash (riː'hæʃ) *vb.* **1.** (*tr.*) to rework, reuse, or make over (old or already used material). ~*n.* **2.** something consisting of old, reworked, or reused material. [C19: from RE- + HASH[1] (to chop into pieces)]

rehearsal (rɪ'hɜːsᵊl) *n.* **1.** a session of practising a play, concert, speech etc., in preparation for public performance. **2.** the act of going through or recounting; recital: *rehearsal of his own virtues was his usual occupation.* **3. in rehearsal.** being prepared for public performance.

rehearse (rɪ'hɜːs) *vb.* **1.** to practise (a play, concert, etc.), in preparation for public performance. **2.** (*tr.*) to run through; recount; recite: *the official rehearsed the grievances of the committee.* **3.** (*tr.*) to train or drill (a person or animal) for the public performance of a part in a play, show, etc. [C16: from Anglo-Norman *rehearser,* from Old French *rehercier* to harrow a second time, from RE- + *herce* harrow] —**re'hearser** *n.*

reheat *vb.* (riː'hiːt). **1.** to heat or be heated again: *to reheat yesterday's soup.* **2.** (*tr.*) to add fuel to (the exhaust gases of an aircraft jet engine) to produce additional heat and thrust. ~*n.* ('riːhiːt), *also* **reheating. 3.** *Aeronautics.* another name (esp. Brit.) for **afterburning** (sense 1). —**re'heater** *n.*

rehoboam (ˌriːə'bəʊəm) *n.* a wine bottle holding the equivalent of six normal bottles (approximately 156 ounces). [C19: named after *Rehoboam,* a son of King Solomon, from Hebrew, literally: the nation is enlarged]

Reich (raɪk; *German* raiç) *n.* (in Germany) **1.** the Holy Roman Empire from 962 to 1806 (**First Reich**). **2.** the Hohenzollern empire from 1871 to 1919 (**Second Reich**). **3.** the Weimar Republic from 1919 to 1933. **4.** the Nazi dictatorship from 1933 to 1945 (**Third Reich**). [German: kingdom]

re'grow *vb.*, **-'grows, -'growing, -'grew, -'grown.**
re'growth *n.*
re'handle *vb.*
re'hang *vb.*, **-'hangs, -'hanging, -'hung.**
re'harden *vb.*
re'harness *vb.*
re'hear *vb.*
re'heel *vb.*
re'hem *vb.*, **-'hems, -'hemming, -'hemmed.**
re'hinge *vb.*
re'hire *vb.*
re'house *vb.*
re'humanˌize *or* **re'humanˌise** *vb.*

Reichsmark (ˈraɪksˌmɑːk; *German* ˈraiçsmark) *n., pl.* **-marks** *or* **-mark.** the standard monetary unit of Germany between 1924 and 1948, divided into 100 **Reichspfennigs.**

Reichstag (ˈraɪksˌtɑːg; *German* ˈraiçstak) *n.* **1.** Also called: **diet.** (in medieval Germany) the estates or a meeting of the estates. **2.** the legislative assembly representing the people in the North German Confederation (1867–71) and in the German empire (1871–1919). **3.** the sovereign assembly of the Weimar Republic (1919–33).

reify (ˈriːɪˌfaɪ) *vb.* **-fies, -fying, -fied.** (*tr.*) to consider or make (an abstract idea or concept) real or concrete. [C19: from Latin *rēs* thing; compare DEIFY] —ˌ**reifiˈcation** *n.* —ˌ**reifiˈcatory** *adj.* —ˈ**reiˌfier** *n.*

reign (reɪn) *n.* **1.** the period during which a monarch is the official ruler of a country. **2.** a period during which a person or thing is dominant, influential, or powerful: *the reign of violence is over.* ~*vb.* (*intr.*) **3.** to exercise the power and authority of a sovereign. **4.** to be accorded the rank and title of a sovereign without having ruling authority, as in a constitutional monarchy. **5.** to predominate; prevail: *a land where darkness reigns.* **6.** (*usually present participle*) to be the most recent winner of a competition, contest, etc.: *the reigning heavyweight champion.* [C13: from Old French *reigne,* from Latin *rēgnum* kingdom, from *rēx* king]

reimburse (ˌriːɪmˈbɜːs) *vb.* (*tr.*) to repay or compensate (someone) for (money already spent, losses, damages, etc.): *your fare will be reimbursed after your interview.* [C17: from RE- + *imburse,* from Medieval Latin *imbursāre* to put in a moneybag, from *bursa* PURSE] —ˌ**reimˈbursable** *adj.* —ˌ**reimˈbursement** *n.* —ˌ**reimˈburser** *n.*

reimport *vb.* (ˌriːɪmˈpɔːt, riːˈɪmpɔːt). **1.** (*tr.*) to import (goods manufactured from exported raw materials). ~*n.* (riːˈɪmpɔːt). **2.** the act of reimporting. **3.** a reimported commodity. —ˌ**reimporˈtation** *n.* —ˌ**reimˈporter** *n.*

reimpression (ˌriːɪmˈprɛʃən) *n.* a reprinting of a book without editorial changes or additions.

rein (reɪn) *n.* **1.** (*often pl.*) one of a pair of long straps, usually connected together and made of leather, used to control a horse, running from the side of the bit or the headstall to the hand of the rider, driver, or trainer. **2.** a similar device used to control a very young child. **3.** any form or means of control: *to take up the reins of government.* **4.** the direction in which a rider turns (in phrases such as **on a left** (*or* **right**) **rein, change the rein**). **5.** something that restrains, controls, or guides. **6. give (a) free rein.** to allow considerable freedom; remove restraints. **7. keep a tight rein on.** to control carefully; limit: *we have to keep a tight rein on expenditure.* **8. on a long rein.** with the reins held loosely so that the horse is relatively unconstrained. **9. shorten the reins.** to take up the reins so that the distance between hand and bit is lessened, in order that the horse may be more collected. ~*vb.* **10.** (*tr.*) to check, restrain, hold back, or halt with or as if with reins. **11.** to control or guide (a horse) with a rein or reins: *they reined left.* ~See also **rein in.** [C13: from Old French *resne,* from Latin *retinēre* to hold back, from RE- + *tenēre* to hold; see RESTRAIN]

reincarnate *vb.* (riːˈɪnkɑːneɪt) (*tr.; often passive*). **1.** to cause to undergo reincarnation; be born again. ~*adj.* (ˌriːɪnˈkɑːnɪt). **2.** born again in a new body.

reincarnation (ˌriːɪnkɑːˈneɪʃən) *n.* **1.** the belief that on the death of the body the soul transmigrates to or is born again in another body. **2.** the incarnation or embodiment of a soul in a new body after it has left the old one at physical death. **3.** embodiment again in a new form, as of a principle or idea. —ˌ**reincarˈnationist** *n., adj.*

reindeer (ˈreɪnˌdɪə) *n., pl.* **-deer** *or* **-deers.** a large deer, *Rangifer tarandus,* having large branched antlers in the male and female and inhabiting the arctic regions of Greenland, Europe, and Asia. It also occurs in North America, where it is known as a caribou. [C14: from Old Norse *hreindýri,* from *hreinn* reindeer + *dyr* animal; related to Dutch *rendier,* German *Renntier;* see DEER]

reindeer moss *n.* any of various lichens of the genus *Cladonia,* esp. *C. rangiferina,* which occur in arctic and subarctic regions, providing food for reindeer.

reinforce (ˌriːɪnˈfɔːs) *vb.* (*tr.*) **1.** to give added strength or support to. **2.** to give added emphasis to; stress, support, or increase: *his rudeness reinforced my determination.* **3.** to give added support to (a military force) by providing more men, supplies, etc. **4.** *Psychol.* to reward an action or response of (a human or animal) so that it becomes more likely to occur again. [C17: from obsolete *renforce,* from French *renforcer;* see RE- + *inforce* ENFORCE] —ˌ**reinˈforcement** *n.*

reinforced concrete *n.* concrete with steel bars, mesh, etc., embedded in it to enable it to withstand tensile and shear stresses.

reinforced plastic *n.* plastic with fibrous matter, such as carbon fibre, embedded in it to confer additional strength.

rein in *vb.* (*adv.*) to stop (a horse) by pulling on the reins.

reins (reɪnz) *pl. n. Archaic.* the kidneys or loins. [C14: from Old French, from Latin *rēnēs* the kidneys]

reinsman (ˈreɪnzmən) *n., pl.* **-men.** *Austral. and N.Z.* the driver in a trotting race.

reinstate (ˌriːɪnˈsteɪt) *vb.* (*tr.*) to restore to a former rank or condition. —ˌ**reinˈstatement** *n.* —ˌ**reinˈstator** *n.*

reinsure (ˌriːɪnˈʃʊə, -ˈʃɔː) *vb.* (*tr.*) **1.** to insure again. **2.** (of an insurer) to obtain partial or complete insurance coverage from another insurer for (a risk on which a policy has already been issued). —ˌ**reinˈsurance** *n.* —ˌ**reinˈsurer** *n.*

reinvent (ˌriːɪnˈvent) *vb.* (*tr.*) **1.** to replace (a product, etc.) with an entirely new version. **2.** to duplicate (something that already exists) in what is therefore a wasted effort (esp. in the phrase **reinvent the wheel**).

reis (*Portuguese* rəjʃ) *n.* the plural of **real**[3] (the coin).

reiterate (riːˈɪtəˌreɪt) *vb.* (*tr.; may take a clause as object*) to say or do again or repeatedly. [C16: from Latin *reiterāre* to repeat, from RE- + *iterāre* to do again, from *iterum* again] —**reˈiterant** *adj.* —**reˌiterˈation** *n.* —**reˈiterative** *adj.* —**reˈiteratively** *adv.*

reive (riːv) *vb.* (*intr.*) *Scot. and northern English dialect.* to go on a plundering raid. [variant of REAVE] —ˈ**reiver** *n.*

reject *vb.* (rɪˈdʒɛkt). (*tr.*) **1.** to refuse to accept, acknowledge, use, believe, etc. **2.** to throw out as useless or worthless; discard. **3.** to rebuff (a person). **4.** (of an organism) to fail to accept (a foreign tissue graft or organ transplant) because of immunological incompatibility. ~*n.* (ˈriːdʒɛkt). **5.** something rejected as imperfect, unsatisfactory, or useless. [C15: from Latin *rēicere* to throw back, from RE- + *jacere* to hurl] —**reˈjectable** *adj.* —**reˈjecter** *or* **reˈjector** *n.* —**reˈjection** *n.* —**reˈjective** *adj.*

rejig (riːˈdʒɪg) *vb.* **-jigs, -jigging, -jigged.** (*tr.*) **1.** to re-equip (a factory or plant). **2.** to rearrange, alter, or manipulate, sometimes in a slightly unscrupulous way. ~*n.* **3.** the act or process of rejigging. —**reˈjigger** *n.*

rejoice (rɪˈdʒɔɪs) *vb.* **1.** (when *tr., takes a clause as object or an infinitive;* when *intr.,* often foll. by *in*) to feel or express great joy or happiness. **2.** (*tr.*) *Archaic.* to cause to feel joy. [C14: from Old French *resjoir,* from RE- + *joir* to be glad, from Latin *gaudēre* to rejoice] —**reˈjoicer** *n.* —**reˈjoicing** *n.*

rejoin[1] (riːˈdʒɔɪn) *vb.* **1.** to come again into company with (someone or something). **2.** (*tr.*) to put or join together again; reunite.

rejoin[2] (rɪˈdʒɔɪn) *vb.* (*tr.*) **1.** to say (something) in reply; answer, reply, or retort. **2.** *Law.* to answer (a plaintiff's reply). [C15: from Old French *rejoign-,* stem of *rejoindre;* see RE-, JOIN]

rejoinder (rɪˈdʒɔɪndə) *n.* **1.** a reply or response to a question or remark, esp. a quick witty one; retort. **2.** *Law.* (in pleading) the answer made by a defendant to the plaintiff's reply. [C15: from Old French *rejoindre* to REJOIN[2]]

rejuvenate (rɪˈdʒuːvɪˌneɪt) *vb.* (*tr.*) **1.** to give new youth, restored vitality, or youthful appearance to. **2.** (*usually passive*) *Geography.* **a.** to cause (a river) to begin eroding more vigorously to a new lower base level, usually because of uplift of the land. **b.** to cause (a land surface) to develop youthful features. [C19: from RE- + Latin *juvenis* young] —**reˌjuveˈnation** *n.* —**reˈjuveˌnator** *n.*

rejuvenesce (rɪˌdʒuːvəˈnɛs) *vb.* **1.** to make or become youthful or restored to vitality. **2.** *Biology.* to convert (cells) or (of cells) to be converted into a more active form. —**reˌjuveˈnescence** *n.* —**reˌjuveˈnescent** *adj.*

rel. *abbrev. for:* **1.** relating. **2.** relative(ly). **3.** released. **4.** religion. **5.** religious.

relapse (rɪˈlæps) *vb.* (*intr.*) **1.** to lapse back into a former state or condition, esp. one involving bad habits. **2.** to become ill again after apparent recovery. ~*n.* **3.** the act or an instance of relapsing. **4.** the return of ill health after an apparent or partial recovery. [C16: from Latin *relabī* to slip back, from RE- + *labī* to slip, slide] —**reˈlapser** *n.*

ˌ**reigˈnite** *vb.*
ˌ**reimˈpose** *vb.*
ˌ**reimpoˈsition** *n.*
ˌ**reimˈprison** *vb.*
ˌ**reinˈcorpoˌrate** *vb.*
ˌ**reincorpoˈration** *n.*
ˌ**reinˈcur** *vb.,* **-ˈcurs, -ˈcurring, -ˈcurred.**
ˌ**reinˈduce** *vb.*
ˌ**reinˈduction** *n.*
ˌ**reinˈfect** *vb.*
ˌ**reinˈfection** *n.*
ˌ**reinˈfest** *vb.*
ˌ**reinfesˈtation** *n.*
ˌ**reinˈflame** *vb.*
ˌ**reinˈform** *vb.*
ˌ**reinˈfuse** *vb.*
ˌ**reinˈfusion** *n.*
ˌ**reinˈocuˌlate** *vb.*
ˌ**reinˌocuˈlation** *n.*
ˌ**reinˈsert** *vb.*
ˌ**reinˈsertion** *n.*
ˌ**reinˈspect** *vb.*
ˌ**reinˈspection** *n.*
ˌ**reinˈstall** *or* ˌ**reinˈstal** *vb.*
ˌ**reinstalˈlation** *n.*
ˌ**reinˈstruct** *vb.*
ˌ**reinˈstruction** *n.*
reˈinteˌgrate *vb.*
ˌ**reinteˈgration** *n.*
ˌ**reinˈter** *vb.,* **-ˈters, -ˈterring, -ˈterred.**
ˌ**reinˈterment** *n.*
ˌ**reinˈterpret** *vb.*
ˌ**reinˌterpreˈtation** *n.*
ˌ**reinˈterroˌgate** *vb.*
ˌ**reinˌterroˈgation** *n.*
ˌ**reintroˈduce** *vb.*
ˌ**reintroˈduction** *n.*
ˌ**reinˈvade** *vb.*
ˌ**reinˈvasion** *n.*
ˌ**reinˈvestiˌgate** *vb.*
ˌ**reinˌvestiˈgation** *n.*
ˌ**reinˈvigorˌate** *vb.*
ˌ**reinˌvigorˈation** *n.*
ˌ**reinˈvite** *vb.*
ˌ**reinˈvoke** *vb.*
ˌ**reinˈvolve** *vb.*
ˌ**reinˈvolvement** *n.*
reˈjudge *vb.*
reˈkey *vb.*
reˈkeyboard *vb.*
reˈkindle *vb.*
reˈlabel *vb.,* **-bels, -belling, -belled.**

relapsing fever *n.* any of various infectious diseases characterized by recurring fever, caused by the bite of body lice or ticks infected with spirochaetes of the genus *Borrelia*. Also called: **recurrent fever.**

relata (rɪˈleɪtə) *n.* the plural of **relatum.**

relate (rɪˈleɪt) *vb.* **1.** (*tr.*) to tell or narrate (a story, information, etc.). **2.** (often foll. by *to*) to establish association (between two or more things) or (of something) to have relation or reference (to something else). **3.** (*intr.*; often foll. by *to*) to form a sympathetic or significant relationship (with other people, things, etc.). [C16: from Latin *relātus* brought back, from *referre* to carry back, from RE- + *ferre* to bear; see REFER] —**reˈlatable** *adj.* —**reˈlater** *n.*

▷**Usage.** *Relate* is frequently applied to personal relationships, as in sense 3, but this usage is vague and is avoided by careful speakers and writers.

related (rɪˈleɪtɪd) *adj.* **1.** connected; associated. **2.** connected by kinship or marriage. **3.** (in diatonic music) denoting or relating to a key that has notes in common with another key or keys. —**reˈlatedness** *n.*

relation (rɪˈleɪʃən) *n.* **1.** the state or condition of being related or the manner in which things are related. **2.** connection by blood or marriage; kinship. **3.** a person who is connected by blood or marriage; relative; kinsman. **4.** reference or regard (esp. in the phrase **in** *or* **with relation to).** **5.** the position, association, connection, or status of one person or thing with regard to another or others. **6.** the act of relating or narrating. **7.** an account or narrative. **8.** *Law.* the principle by which an act done at one time is regarded in law as having been done antecedently. **9.** *Law.* the statement of grounds of complaint made by a relator. **10.** *Logic, maths.* **a.** an association between ordered pairs of objects, numbers, etc., such as ... *is greater than* .... **b.** the set of ordered pairs whose members have such an association. **11.** *Philosophy.* **a. internal relation.** a relation that necessarily holds between its relata, as *4 is greater than 2.* **b. external relation.** a relation that does not so hold. ~See also **relations.** [C14: from Latin *relātiō* a narration, a relation (between philosophical concepts)]

relational (rɪˈleɪʃənəl) *adj.* **1.** *Grammar.* indicating or expressing syntactic relation, as for example the case endings in Latin. **2.** having relation or being related.

relations (rɪˈleɪʃənz) *pl. n.* **1.** social, political, or personal connections or dealings between or among individuals, groups, nations, etc.: *to enjoy good relations.* **2.** family or relatives. **3.** *Euphemistic.* sexual intercourse.

relationship (rɪˈleɪʃənʃɪp) *n.* **1.** the state of being connected or related. **2.** association by blood or marriage; kinship. **3.** the mutual dealings, connections, or feelings that exist between two parties, countries, people, etc.: *a business relationship.* **4.** an emotional or sexual affair or liaison. **5.** *Logic, maths.* another name for **relation** (sense 10).

relative (ˈrɛlətɪv) *adj.* **1.** having meaning or significance only in relation to something else; not absolute: *a relative value.* **2.** (*prenominal*) (of a scientific quantity) being measured or stated relative to some other substance or measurement: *relative humidity; relative density.* Compare **absolute** (sense 10). **3.** (*prenominal*) comparative or respective: *the relative qualities of speed and accuracy.* **4.** (*postpositive*; foll. by *to*) in proportion (to); corresponding (to): *earnings relative to production.* **5.** having reference (to); pertinent (to): *matters not relative to the topic under discussion.* **6.** *Grammar.* denoting or belonging to a class of words that function as subordinating conjunctions in introducing relative clauses. In English, relative pronouns and determiners include *who, which,* and *that.* Compare **demonstrative** (sense 5), **interrogative** (sense 3). **7.** *Grammar.* denoting or relating to a clause (**relative clause**) that modifies a noun or pronoun occurring earlier in the sentence. **8.** (of a musical key or scale) having the same key signature as another key or scale: *C major is the relative major of A minor.* ~*n.* **9.** a person who is related by blood or marriage; relation. **10.** a relative pronoun, clause, or grammatical construction. [C16: from Late Latin *relātīvus* referring] —**ˈrelatively** *adv.* —**ˈrelativeness** *n.*

relative aperture *n. Photog.* the ratio of the equivalent focal length of a lens to the effective aperture of the lens; written as *f/n, f:n,* or *fn,* where *n* is the numerical value of this ratio and is equivalent to the f-number.

relative atomic mass *n.* the ratio of the average mass per atom of the naturally occurring form of an element to one-twelfth the mass of an atom of carbon-12. Symbol: A_r Abbrev.: **r.a.m.** Former name: **atomic weight.**

relative density *n.* the ratio of the density of a substance to the density of a standard substance under specified conditions. For liquids and solids the standard is usually water at 4°C or some other specified temperature. For gases the standard is often air or hydrogen at the same temperature and pressure as the substance. Symbol: *d* See also **specific gravity, vapour density.**

relative frequency *n.* **a.** the ratio of the actual number of favourable events to the total possible number of events; often taken as an estimate of probability. **b.** the proportion of the range of a random variable taking a given value or lying in a given interval.

relative humidity *n.* the mass of water vapour present in the air expressed as a percentage of the mass that would be present in an equal volume of saturated air at the same temperature. Compare **absolute humidity.**

relative majority *n. Brit.* the excess of votes or seats won by the winner of an election over the runner-up when no candidate or party has more than 50 per cent. Compare **absolute majority.**

relative molecular mass *n.* the sum of all the relative atomic masses of the atoms in a molecule; the ratio of the average mass per molecule of a specified isotopic composition of a substance to one-twelfth the mass of an atom of carbon-12. Symbol: M_r Abbrev.: **r.m.m.** Former name: **molecular weight.**

relative permeability *n.* the ratio of the permeability of a medium to that of free space. Symbol: μ_r

relative permittivity *n.* the ratio of the permittivity of a substance to that of free space. Symbol: ε_r Also called: **dielectric constant.**

relativism (ˈrɛlətɪˌvɪzəm) *n.* any theory holding that truth or moral or aesthetic value, etc., is not universal or absolute but may differ between individuals or cultures. See also **historicism.** —ˈ**relativist** *n., adj.*

relativistic (ˌrɛlətɪˈvɪstɪk) *adj.* **1.** *Physics.* having or involving a speed close to that of light so that the behaviour is described by the theory of relativity rather than by Newtonian mechanics: *a relativistic electron; a relativistic velocity.* **2.** *Physics.* of, concerned with, or involving relativity. **3.** of or relating to relativism. —ˌ**relativˈistically** *adv.*

relativity (ˌrɛləˈtɪvɪtɪ) *n.* **1.** either of two theories developed by Albert Einstein (1879–1955), the **special theory of relativity,** which requires that the laws of physics shall be the same as seen by any two different observers in uniform relative motion, and the **general theory of relativity,** which considers observers with relative acceleration and leads to a theory of gravitation. **2.** *Philosophy.* dependence upon some variable factor such as the psychological, social, or environmental context. See **relativism.** **3.** the state or quality of being relative.

relativize *or* **relativise** (ˈrɛlətɪvaɪz) *vb.* **1.** to make or become relative. **2.** (*tr.*) to apply the theory of relativity to. —ˌ**relativiˈzation** *or* ˌ**relativiˈsation** *n.*

relator (rɪˈleɪtə) *n.* **1.** a person who relates a story; narrator. **2.** *English law.* a person who gives information upon which the attorney general brings an action. **3.** *U.S. law.* a person who institutes proceedings by criminal information or quo warranto.

relatum (rɪˈleɪtəm) *n., pl.* **-ta** (-tə). *Logic.* one of the objects between which a relation is said to hold.

relax (rɪˈlæks) *vb.* **1.** to make (muscles, a grip, etc.) less tense or rigid or (of muscles, a grip, etc.) to become looser or less rigid. **2.** (*intr.*) to take rest or recreation, as from work or effort: *on Sundays, she just relaxes; she relaxes by playing golf.* **3.** to lessen the force of (effort, concentration, etc.) or (of effort) to become diminished. **4.** to make (rules or discipline) less rigid or strict or (of rules, etc.) to diminish in severity. **5.** (*intr.*) (of a person) to become less formal; unbend. [C15: from Latin *relaxāre* to loosen, from RE- + *laxāre* to loosen, from *laxus* loose, LAX] —**reˈlaxable** *adj.* —**reˈlaxed** *adj.* —**relaxedly** (rɪˈlæksɪdlɪ) *adv.* —**reˈlaxer** *n.*

relaxant (rɪˈlæksənt) *n.* **1.** *Med.* a drug or agent that relaxes, esp. one that relaxes tense muscles. ~*adj.* **2.** of, relating to, or tending to produce relaxation.

relaxation (ˌriːlækˈseɪʃən) *n.* **1.** rest or refreshment, as after work or effort; recreation. **2.** a form of rest or recreation: *his relaxation is cricket.* **3.** a partial lessening of a punishment, duty, etc. **4.** the act of relaxing or state of being relaxed. **5.** *Physics.* the return of a system to equilibrium after a displacement from this state. **6.** *Maths.* a method by which errors resulting from an approximation are reduced by using new approximations.

relaxation oscillator *n. Electronics.* a nonsinusoidal oscillator, the timing of which is controlled by the charge and discharge time constants of resistance and capacitance components.

relaxin (rɪˈlæksɪn) *n.* **1.** a mammalian polypeptide hormone secreted by the corpus luteum during pregnancy, which relaxes the pelvic ligaments. **2.** a preparation of this hormone, used to facilitate childbirth. [C20: from RELAX + -IN]

relay *n.* (ˈriːleɪ). **1.** a person or team of people relieving others, as on a shift. **2.** a fresh team of horses, dogs, etc., posted at intervals along a route to relieve others. **3.** the act of relaying or process of being relayed. **4. a.** short for **relay race. b.** one of the sections of a relay race. **5.** an automatic device that controls the setting of a valve, switch, etc., by means of an electric motor, solenoid, or pneumatic mechanism. **6.** *Electronics.* an electrical device in which a small change in current or voltage controls the switching on or off of circuits or other devices. **7.** *Radio.* **a.** a combination of a receiver and transmitter designed to receive radio signals and retransmit them, in order to extend their range. **b.** (*as modifier*): *a relay station.* ~*vb.* (rɪˈleɪ). (*tr.*) **8.** to carry or spread (something, such as news or information) by relays. **9.** to supply or replace with relays. **10.** to retransmit (a signal) by means of a relay. **11.** *Brit.* to broadcast (a performance) by sending out signals through a transmitting station: *this concert is being relayed from the Albert Hall.* [C15 *relaien,* from Old French *relaier* to leave behind, from RE- + *laier* to leave, ultimately from Latin *laxāre* to loosen; see RELAX]

relay fast *n.* (esp. in India) a form of protest in which a number of persons go without food by turns. Also called: **relay hunger strike.**

relay race *n.* a race between two or more teams of contestants in which each contestant covers a specified portion of the distance.

release (rɪˈliːs) *vb.* (*tr.*) **1.** to free (a person, animal, etc.) from captivity or imprisonment. **2.** to free (someone) from obligation or duty. **3.** to free (something) from (one's grip); let go or fall. **4.** to issue (a record, film, book, etc.) for sale or circulation. **5.** to make (news or information) known or allow (news, information, etc.) to be made known: *to release details of an agreement.* **6.** *Law.* to relinquish (a right, claim, title, etc.) in favour of someone else. **7.** *Ethology.* to evoke (a response) through the presentation of a stimulus that produces the response innately. ~*n.* **8.** the act of freeing or state of being freed, as from captivity, imprisonment, duty, pain, life, etc. **9.** the act of issuing for sale or publication. **10.** something issued for sale or public showing, esp. a film or a record: *a new release from Bob Dylan.* **11.** a news item, document, etc., made available for publication, broadcasting, etc. **12.** *Law.* the surrender of a claim, right, title, etc., in favour of someone else. **13.** a control mechanism for starting or stopping an engine. **14. a.** the opening of the exhaust valve of a steam engine near the end of the piston stroke. **b.** the moment at which this valve opens. **15.** the electronic control regulating how long a note sounds after a synthesizer key has been released. **16.** the control mechanism for the shutter in a camera. [C13: from Old French *relesser,* from Latin *relaxāre* to slacken; see RELAX] —**reˈleaser** *n.*

relegate (ˈrɛlɪˌgeɪt) *vb.* (*tr.*) **1.** to move to a position of less authority, importance, etc.; demote. **2.** (*usually passive*) *Chiefly Brit.* to demote (a football team, etc.) to a lower division. **3.** to assign or refer (a matter) to another or others, as for action or decision. **4.** (foll. by *to*) to banish or exile. **5.** to assign (something) to a particular group or category. [C16: from Latin *relēgāre* to send away, from RE- + *lēgāre* to send] —**ˈreleˌgatable** *adj.* —**ˌreleˈgation** *n.*

relent (rɪˈlɛnt) *vb.* (*intr.*) **1.** to change one's mind about some decided course, esp. a harsh one; become more mild or amenable. **2.** (of the pace or intensity of something) to slacken. **3.** (of the weather) to become more mild. [C14: from RE- + Latin *lentāre* to bend, from *lentus* flexible, tenacious]

relentless (rɪˈlɛntlɪs) *adj.* **1.** (of an enemy, hostile attitude, etc.) implacable; inflexible; inexorable. **2.** (of pace or intensity) sustained; unremitting. —**reˈlentlessly** *adv.* —**reˈlentlessness** *n.*

relevant (ˈrɛlɪvənt) *adj.* **1.** having direct bearing on the matter in hand; pertinent. **2.** *Linguistics.* another word for **distinctive** (sense 2). [C16: from Medieval Latin *relevans,* from Latin *relevāre* to lighten, from RE- + *levāre* to raise, RELIEVE] —**ˈrelevance** *or* **ˈrelevancy** *n.* —**ˈrelevantly** *adv.*

reliable (rɪˈlaɪəbᵊl) *adj.* able to be trusted; predictable or dependable. —**reˌliaˈbility** *or* (*less commonly*) **reˈliableness** *n.* —**reˈliably** *adv.*

reliance (rɪˈlaɪəns) *n.* **1.** dependence, confidence, or trust. **2.** something or someone upon which one relies. —**reˈliant** *adj.* —**reˈliantly** *adv.*

relic (ˈrɛlɪk) *n.* **1.** something that has survived from the past, such as an object or custom. **2.** something kept as a remembrance or treasured for its past associations; keepsake. **3.** (*usually pl.*) a remaining part or fragment. **4.** *R.C. Church, Eastern Church.* part of the body of a saint or something supposedly used by or associated with a saint, venerated as holy. **5.** *Informal.* an old or old-fashioned person or thing. **6.** (*pl.*) *Archaic.* the remains of a dead person; corpse. **7.** *Ecology.* a less common term for **relict** (sense 1). [C13: from Old French *relique,* from Latin *reliquiae* remains, from *relinquere* to leave behind, RELINQUISH]

relict (ˈrɛlɪkt) *n.* **1.** *Ecology.* **a.** a group of animals or plants that exists as a remnant of a formerly widely distributed group in an environment different from that in which it originated. **b.** (*as modifier*): *a relict fauna.* **2.** *Geology.* **a.** a mountain, lake, glacier, etc., that is a remnant of a pre-existing formation after a destructive process has occurred. **b.** a mineral that remains unaltered after metamorphism of the rock in which it occurs. **3.** an archaic word for **widow** (sense 1). **4.** an archaic word for **relic** (sense 6). [C16: from Latin *relictus* left behind, from *relinquere* to RELINQUISH]

relief (rɪˈliːf) *n.* **1.** a feeling of cheerfulness or optimism that follows the removal of anxiety, pain, or distress. **2.** deliverance from or alleviation of anxiety, pain, distress, etc. **3. a.** help or assistance, as to the poor, needy, or distressed. **b.** (*as modifier*): *relief work.* **4.** something that affords a diversion from monotony. **5.** a person who replaces or relieves another at some task or duty. **6.** a bus, shuttle plane, etc., that carries additional passengers when a scheduled service is full. **7.** a road (**relief road**) carrying traffic round an urban area; bypass. **8. a.** the act of freeing a beleaguered town, fortress, etc.: *the relief of Mafeking.* **b.** (*as modifier*): *a relief column.* **9.** Also called: **relievo, rilievo.** *Sculpture, architecture, etc.* **a.** the projection of forms or figures from a flat ground, so that they are partly or wholly free of it. **b.** a piece of work of this kind. **10.** a printing process, such as engraving, letterpress, etc., that employs raised surfaces from which ink is transferred to the paper. **11.** any vivid effect resulting from contrast: *comic relief.* **12.** variation in altitude in an area; difference between highest and lowest level: *a region of low relief.* **13.** *Mechanical engineering.* the removal of the surface material of a bearing area to allow the access of lubricating fluid. **14.** *Law.* redress of a grievance or hardship: *to seek relief through the courts.* **15.** *European history.* a payment made to his lord by the heir to a fief: the size of the relief was determined by the lord within bounds set by custom. **16. on relief.** *U.S. and Canadian.* (of people) in receipt of government aid because of personal need. [C14: from Old French, from *relever* to raise up; see RELIEVE]

relief map *n.* a map that shows the configuration and height of the land surface, usually by means of contours.

relieve (rɪˈliːv) *vb.* (*tr.*) **1.** to bring alleviation of (pain, distress, etc.) to (someone). **2.** to bring aid or assistance to (someone in need, a disaster area, etc.). **3.** to take over the duties or watch of (someone). **4.** to bring aid or a relieving force to (a besieged town, city, etc.). **5.** to free (someone) from an obligation. **6.** to make (something) less unpleasant, arduous, or monotonous. **7.** to bring into relief or prominence, as by contrast. **8.** (foll. by *of*) *Informal.* to take from: *the thief relieved him of his watch.* **9. relieve oneself.** to urinate or defecate. [C14: from Old French *relever,* from Latin *relevāre* to lift up, relieve, from RE- + *levāre* to lighten] —**reˈlievable** *adj.* —**reˈliever** *n.*

relieved (rɪˈliːvd) *adj.* **1.** (*postpositive;* often foll. by *at, about,* etc.) experiencing relief, esp. from worry or anxiety. **2.** *Mechanical engineering.* having part of the surface cut away to avoid friction or wear.

relievo (rɪlˈjeɪvəʊ, rɪˈliːvəʊ) *n., pl.* **-vos.** another name for **relief** (sense 9). [from Italian, literally: raised work]

religieuse *French.* (rəliʒjøz) *n.* a nun. [C18: feminine of RELIGIEUX]

religieux *French.* (rəliʒjø) *n., pl.* ***-gieux*** (-ʒjø). a member of a monastic order or clerical body. [C17: from Latin *religiōsus* religious]

religion (rɪˈlɪdʒən) *n.* **1.** belief in, worship of, or obedience to a supernatural power or powers considered to be divine or to have control of human destiny. **2.** any formal or institutionalized expression of such belief: *the Christian religion.* **3.** the attitude and feeling of one who believes in a transcendent controlling power or powers. **4.** *Chiefly R.C. Church.* the way of life determined by the vows of poverty, chastity, and obedience entered upon by monks, friars, and nuns: *to enter religion.* **5.** something of overwhelming importance to a person: *football is his religion.* **6.** *Archaic.* **a.** the practice of sacred ritual observances. **b.** sacred rites and ceremonies. [C12: via Old French from Latin *religiō* fear of the supernatural, piety, probably from *religāre* to tie up, from RE- + *ligāre* to bind]

religionism (rɪˈlɪdʒəˌnɪzəm) *n.* extreme religious fervour. —**reˈligionist** *n., adj.*

religiose (rɪˈlɪdʒɪˌəʊs) *adj.* affectedly or extremely pious; sanctimoniously religious. —**reˈligiˌosely** *adv.* —**religiosity** (rɪˌlɪdʒɪˈɒsɪtɪ) *n.*

religious (rɪˈlɪdʒəs) *adj.* **1.** of, relating to, or concerned with religion. **2. a.** pious; devout; godly. **b.** (*as collective n.;* preceded by *the*): *the religious.* **3.** appropriate to or in accordance with the principles of a religion. **4.** scrupulous, exact, or conscientious. **5.** *Christianity.* of or relating to a way of life dedicated to religion by the vows of poverty, chastity, and obedience, and defined by a monastic rule. ~*n.* **6.** *Christianity.* a member of an order or congregation living by such a rule; a monk, friar, or nun. —**reˈligiously** *adv.* —**reˈligiousness** *n.*

relinquish (rɪˈlɪŋkwɪʃ) *vb.* (*tr.*) **1.** to give up (a task, struggle, etc.); abandon. **2.** to surrender or renounce (a claim, right, etc.). **3.** to release; let go. [C15: from French *relinquir,* from Latin *relinquere* to leave behind, from RE- + *linquere* to leave] —**reˈlinquisher** *n.* —**reˈlinquishment** *n.*

reliquary (ˈrɛlɪkwərɪ) *n., pl.* **-quaries.** a receptacle or repository for relics, esp. relics of saints. [C17: from Old French *reliquaire,* from *relique* RELIC]

relique (rəˈliːk, ˈrɛlɪk) *n.* an archaic spelling of **relic.**

reliquiae (rɪˈlɪkwɪˌiː) *pl. n.* fossil remains of animals or plants. [C19: from Latin: remains]

relish (ˈrɛlɪʃ) *vb.* (*tr.*) **1.** to savour or enjoy (an experience) to the full. **2.** to anticipate eagerly; look forward to. **3.** to enjoy the taste or flavour of (food, etc.); savour. **4.** to give appetizing taste or flavour to (food), by or as if by the addition of pickles or spices. ~*n.* **5.** liking or enjoyment, as of something eaten or experienced (esp. in the phrase **with relish**). **6.** pleasurable anticipation: *he didn't have much relish for the idea.* **7.** an appetizing or spicy food added to a main dish to enhance its flavour. **8.** an appetizing taste or flavour. **9.** a zestful trace or touch: *there was a certain relish in all his writing.* **10.** *Music.* (in English lute,

reˈlay *vb.,* **-ˈlays, -ˈlaying, -ˈlaid.**
reˈlearn *vb.*
reˈlet *vb.,* **-ˈlets, -ˈletting, -ˈlet.**
reˈlicense *vb.*
reˈlight *vb.,* **-ˈlights, -ˈlighting; -ˈlighted** *or* **-ˈlit.**
reˈline *vb.*

viol, and keyboard music of the 16th and 17th centuries) a trilling ornament, used esp. at cadences. [C16: from earlier *reles* aftertaste, from Old French: something remaining, from *relaisser* to leave behind; see RELEASE] —'**relishable** *adj.*

relive (riːˈlɪv) *vb.* (*tr.*) to experience (a sensation, event, etc.) again, esp. in the imagination. —**re'livable** *adj.*

relocate (ˌriːləʊˈkeɪt) *vb.* **1.** to move or be moved to a new place, esp. (of an employee, a business, etc.) to a new area or place of employment. **2.** (*intr.*) (of an employee, a business, etc.) to move for reasons of business to a new area or place of employment. —ˌ**relo'cation** *n.*

relocation costs *or* **expenses** *pl. n.* payment made by an employer or a government agency to cover removal expenses and other costs incurred by an employee who is required to take up employment elsewhere.

relucent (rɪˈluːsᵊnt) *adj. Archaic.* bright; shining. [C16: from Latin *relūcēre* to shine out, from RE- + *lūcēre* to shine, from *lūx* light]

reluct (rɪˈlʌkt) *vb.* (*intr.*) *Archaic.* **1.** (often foll. by *against*) to struggle or rebel. **2.** to object; show reluctance. [C16: from Latin *reluctārī* to resist, from RE- + *luctārī* to struggle]

reluctance (rɪˈlʌktəns) *or* (*less commonly*) **reluctancy** *n.* **1.** lack of eagerness or willingness; disinclination. **2.** *Physics.* a measure of the resistance of a closed magnetic circuit to a magnetic flux, equal to the ratio of the magnetomotive force to the magnetic flux.

reluctant (rɪˈlʌktənt) *adj.* **1.** not eager; unwilling; disinclined. **2.** *Archaic.* offering resistance or opposition. [C17: from Latin *reluctārī* to resist; see RELUCT] —**re'luctantly** *adv.*

reluctivity (ˌrɛlʌkˈtɪvɪtɪ) *n., pl.* **-ties.** *Physics.* a specific or relative reluctance of a magnetic material. [C19: RELUCT + *-ivity* on the model of *conductivity*]

relume (rɪˈluːm) *or* **relumine** (rɪˈluːmɪn) *vb.* (*tr.*) *Archaic.* to light or brighten again; rekindle. [C17: from Late Latin *relūmināre,* from Latin RE- + *illūmināre* to ILLUMINE]

rely (rɪˈlaɪ) *vb.* **-lies, -lying, -lied.** (*intr.*; foll. by *on* or *upon*) **1.** to be dependent (on): *he relies on his charm.* **2.** to have trust or confidence (in): *you can rely on us.* [C14: from Old French *relier* to fasten together, repair, from Latin *religāre* to tie back, from RE- + *ligāre* to tie]

REM[1] *abbrev. for* rapid eye movement.

REM[2] *or* **rem** (rɛm) *n. acronym for* roentgen equivalent man.

remain (rɪˈmeɪn) *vb.* (*mainly intr.*) **1.** to stay behind or in the same place: *to remain at home; only Tom remained.* **2.** (*copula*) to continue to be: *to remain cheerful.* **3.** to be left, as after use, consumption, the passage of time, etc.: *a little wine still remained in the bottle.* **4.** to be left to be done, said, etc.: *it remains to be pointed out.* ~See also **remains.** [C14: from Old French *remanoir,* from Latin *remanēre* to be left, from RE- + *manēre* to stay]

remainder (rɪˈmeɪndə) *n.* **1.** a part or portion that is left, as after use, subtraction, expenditure, the passage of time, etc.: *the remainder of the milk; the remainder of the day.* **2.** *Maths.* **a.** the amount left over when one quantity cannot be exactly divided by another: *for 10 ÷ 3, the remainder is 1.* **b.** another name for **difference** (sense 7b). **3.** *Property law.* a future interest in property; an interest in a particular estate that will pass to one at some future date, as on the death of the current possessor. **4.** a number of copies of a book left unsold when demand slows or ceases, which are sold at a reduced price by the publisher. ~*vb.* **5.** (*tr.*) to sell (copies of a book) as a remainder. [C15: from Anglo-French, from Old French *remaindre* (infinitive used as noun), variant of *remanoir;* see REMAIN]

remainderman (rɪˈmeɪndəˌmæn) *n., pl.* **-men.** *Property law.* the person entitled to receive a particular estate on its determination. Compare **reversioner.**

remains (rɪˈmeɪnz) *pl. n.* **1.** any pieces, scraps, fragments, etc., that are left unused or still extant, as after use, consumption, the passage of time, etc.: *the remains of a meal; archaeological remains.* **2.** the body of a dead person; corpse. **3.** Also called: **literary remains.** the unpublished writings of an author at the time of his death.

remake *n.* (ˈriːˌmeɪk). **1.** something that is made again, esp. a new version of an old film. **2.** the act of making again or anew. ~*vb.* (riːˈmeɪk), **-makes, -making, -made. 3.** (*tr.*) to make again or anew.

remand (rɪˈmɑːnd) *vb.* (*tr.*) **1.** *Law.* (of a court or magistrate) to send (a prisoner or accused person) back into custody or admit him to bail, esp. on adjourning a case for further inquiries to be made. **2.** to send back. ~*n.* **3.** the sending of a prisoner or accused person back into custody (or sometimes admitting him to bail) to await trial or continuation of his trial. **4.** the act of remanding or state of being remanded. **5. on remand.** in custody or on bail awaiting trial or completion of one's trial. [C15: from Medieval Latin *remandāre* to send back word, from Latin RE- + *mandāre* to command, confine; see MANDATE] —**re'mandment** *n.*

remand centre *n.* (in Britain) an institution to which accused persons are sent for detention while awaiting appearance before a court. Until 1967 remand centres were for young people between 14 and 21 years of age.

remand home *n.* (no longer in technical use) an institution to which juvenile offenders between 8 and 14 years may be remanded or committed for detention. See also **community home.**

remanence (ˈrɛmənəns) *n. Physics.* the ability of a material to retain magnetization, equal to the magnetic flux density of the material after the removal of the magnetizing field. Also called: **retentivity.** [C17: from Latin *remanēre* to stay behind, REMAIN]

remanent (ˈrɛmənənt) *adj. Rare.* remaining or left over.

remark (rɪˈmɑːk) *vb.* **1.** (when *intr.,* often foll. by *on* or *upon;* when *tr., may take a clause as object*) to pass a casual comment (about); reflect in informal speech or writing. **2.** (*tr.; may take a clause as object*) to perceive; observe; notice. ~*n.* **3.** a brief casually expressed thought or opinion; observation. **4.** notice, comment, or observation: *the event passed without remark.* **5.** *Engraving.* a variant spelling of **remarque.** [C17: from Old French *remarquer* to observe, from RE- + *marquer* to note, MARK] —**re'marker** *n.*

remarkable (rɪˈmɑːkəbᵊl) *adj.* **1.** worthy of note or attention: *a remarkable achievement.* **2.** unusual, striking, or extraordinary: *a remarkable sight.* —**re'markableness** *or* **reˌmarka'bility** *n.* —**re'markably** *adv.*

remarque *or* **remark** (rɪˈmɑːk) *n.* **1.** a mark in the margin of an engraved plate to indicate the stage of production of the plate. It is removed before the plate is finished. **2.** a plate so marked. **3.** a print or proof from a plate so marked. [C19: from French; see REMARK]

remaster (riːˈmɑːstə) *vb.* (*tr.*) to make a new master audio recording, now usually digital, from (an earlier recording), to produce compact discs or stereo records with improved sound reproduction.

rematch *n.* (ˈriːˌmætʃ). **1.** *Sport.* a second or return match between contestants. ~*vb.* (riːˈmætʃ). **2.** (*tr.*) to match (two contestants) again.

remblai (*French* rɑ̃blɛ) *n.* earth used for an embankment or rampart. [C18: from French, from *remblayer* to embank, from *emblayer* to pile up]

Rembrandtesque (ˈrɛmbrænˈtɛsk) *adj.* characteristic or in the style of the Dutch painter Rembrandt (1606–69), esp. in the handling of shade and light.

REME (ˈriːmiː) *n. acronym for* Royal Electrical and Mechanical Engineers.

remedial (rɪˈmiːdɪəl) *adj.* **1.** affording a remedy; curative. **2.** denoting or relating to special teaching, teaching methods, or material for backward and slow learners: *remedial education.* —**re'medially** *adv.*

remedy (ˈrɛmɪdɪ) *n., pl.* **-dies. 1.** (usually foll. by *for* or *against*) any drug or agent that cures a disease or controls its symptoms. **2.** (usually foll. by *for* or *against*) anything that serves to put a fault to rights, cure defects, improve conditions, etc.: *a remedy for industrial disputes.* **3.** the legally permitted variation from the standard weight or quality of coins; tolerance. ~*vb.* (*tr.*) **4.** to relieve or cure (a disease, illness, etc.) by or as if by a remedy. **5.** to put to rights (a fault, error, etc.); correct. [C13: from Anglo-Norman *remedie,* from Latin *remedium* a cure, from *remedērī* to heal again, from RE- + *medērī* to heal; see MEDICAL] —**remediable** (rɪˈmiːdɪəbᵊl) *adj.* —**re'mediably** *adv.* —'**remediless** *adj.*

remember (rɪˈmɛmbə) *vb.* **1.** to become aware of (something forgotten) again; bring back to one's consciousness; recall. **2.** to retain (an idea, intention, etc.) in one's conscious mind: *to remember Pythagoras' theorem; remember to do one's shopping.* **3.** (*tr.*) to give money, etc., to (someone), as in a will or in tipping. **4.** (*tr.;* foll. by *to*) to mention (a person's name) to another person, as by way of greeting or friendship: *remember me to your mother.* **5.** (*tr.*) to mention (a person) favourably, as in prayer. **6.** (*tr.*) to commemorate (a person, event, etc.): *to remember the dead of the wars.* **7. remember oneself.** to recover one's good manners after a lapse; stop behaving badly. [C14: from Old French *remembrer,* from Late Latin *rememorārī* to recall to mind, from Latin RE- + *memor* mindful; see MEMORY] —**re'memberer** *n.*

remembrance (rɪˈmɛmbrəns) *n.* **1.** the act of remembering or state of being remembered. **2.** something that is remembered; reminiscence. **3.** a memento or keepsake. **4.** the extent in time of one's power of recollection. **5. a.** the act of honouring some past event, person, etc. **b.** (*as modifier*): *a remembrance service.*

remembrancer (rɪˈmɛmbrənsə) *n. Archaic.* a reminder, memento, or keepsake.

Remembrancer (rɪˈmɛmbrənsə) *n.* (in Britain) **1.** any of several officials of the Exchequer, esp. one (**Queen's** *or* **King's Remembrancer**) whose duties include collecting debts due to the Crown. **2.** an official (**City Remembrancer**) appointed by the Corporation of the City of London to represent its interests to Parliament and elsewhere.

re'list *vb.*
re'load *vb.*
re'loan *n., vb.*
re'mail *vb.*
re'man *vb.,* **-'mans, -'manning, -'manned.**
ˌ**remanu'facture** *vb.*
re'marriage *n.*
re'marry *vb.,* **-ries, -rying, -ried.**
re'measure *vb.*
re'measurement *n.*
re'melt *vb.*

Remembrance Sunday *n. Brit.* the second Sunday in November, which is the Sunday closest to November 11, the anniversary of the armistice of 1918 that ended World War I, on which the dead of both World Wars are commemorated. Also called: **Remembrance Day.**

remex ('riːmɛks) *n., pl.* **remiges** ('rɛmɪˌdʒiːz). any of the large flight feathers of a bird's wing. [C18: from Latin: a rower, from *rēmus* oar] —**remigial** (rɪ'mɪdʒɪəl) *adj.*

remind (rɪ'maɪnd) *vb.* (*tr.; usually foll. by of; may take a clause as object or an infinitive*) to cause (a person) to remember (something or to do something); make (someone) aware (of something he may have forgotten): *remind me to phone home; flowers remind me of holidays.* —**re'minder** *n.*

remindful (rɪ'maɪndfʊl) *adj.* **1.** serving to remind. **2.** (*postpositive*) bearing in mind; mindful.

reminisce (ˌrɛmɪ'nɪs) *vb.* (*intr.*) to talk or write about old times, past experiences, etc.

reminiscence (ˌrɛmɪ'nɪsəns) *n.* **1.** the act of recalling or narrating past experiences. **2.** (*often pl.*) some past experience, event, etc., that is recalled or narrated; anecdote. **3.** an event, phenomenon, or experience that reminds one of something else. **4.** (in Platonic philosophy) the doctrine that perception and recognition of particulars is possible because the mind has seen the universal forms of all things in a previous disembodied existence. **5.** *Psychol.* the ability to perform a task better when tested some time after the task has been learnt than when tested immediately after learning it.

reminiscent (ˌrɛmɪ'nɪsᵊnt) *adj.* **1.** (*postpositive;* foll. by *of*) stimulating memories (of) or comparisons (with). **2.** characterized by reminiscence. **3.** (of a person) given to reminiscing. [C18: from Latin *reminiscī* to call to mind, from RE- + *mēns* mind] —ˌ**remi'niscently** *adv.*

remise (rɪ'maɪz) *vb.* **1.** (*tr.*) *Law.* to give up or relinquish (a right, claim, etc.); surrender. **2.** *Fencing.* to make a renewed thrust on the same lunge after the first has missed. ~*n.* **3.** *Fencing.* a second thrust made on the same lunge after the first has missed. **4.** *Obsolete.* a hired carriage. **5.** *Obsolete.* a coach house. [C17: from French *remettre* to put back, from Latin *remittere* to send back, from RE- + *mittere* to send]

remiss (rɪ'mɪs) *adj.* (*postpositive*) **1.** lacking in care or attention to duty; negligent. **2.** lacking in energy; dilatory. [C15: from Latin *remissus, from remittere* to release, from RE- + *mittere* to send] —**re'missly** *adv.* —**re'missness** *n.*

remissible (rɪ'mɪsəbᵊl) *adj.* able to be remitted. [C16: from Latin *remissibilis;* see REMIT] —**reˌmissi'bility** *or* **re'missibleness** *n.*

remission (rɪ'mɪʃən) *or* (*less commonly*) **remittal** (rɪ'mɪtᵊl) *n.* **1.** the act of remitting or state of being remitted. **2.** a reduction of the term of a sentence of imprisonment, as for good conduct: *he got three years' remission.* **3.** forgiveness for sin. **4.** discharge or release from penalty, obligation, etc. **5.** lessening of intensity; abatement, as in the severity of symptoms of a disease. **6.** *Rare.* the act of sending a remittance; payment. —**re'missive** *adj.* —**re'missively** *adv.*

remit *vb.* (rɪ'mɪt). **-mits, -mitting, -mitted.** (*mainly tr.*) **1.** (*also intr.*) to send (money, payment, etc.), as for goods or service, esp. by post. **2.** *Law.* (esp. of an appeal court) to send back (a case or proceeding) to an inferior court for further consideration or action. **3.** to cancel or refrain from exacting (a penalty or punishment). **4.** (*also intr.*) to relax (pace, intensity, etc.) or (of pace or the like) to slacken or abate. **5.** to postpone; defer. **6.** *Archaic.* to pardon or forgive (crime, sins, etc.). ~*n.* ('riːmɪt, rɪ'mɪt). **7.** the area of authority or responsibility of an individual or a group: *by taking that action, the committee has exceeded its remit.* **8.** *Law.* the transfer of a case from one court or jurisdiction to another, esp. from an appeal court to an inferior tribunal. **9.** the act of remitting. **10.** something remitted. **11.** *N.Z.* a proposal from a branch of an organization put forward for discussion at the annual general meeting. [C14: from Latin *remittere* to send back, release, RE- + *mittere* to send] —**re'mittable** *adj.* —**re'mittal** *n.*

remittance (rɪ'mɪtəns) *n.* **1.** payment for goods or services received or as an allowance, esp. when sent by post. **2.** the act of remitting.

remittance man *n.* a man living abroad on money sent from home, esp. in the days of the British Empire.

remittee (rɪˌmɪt'iː) *n.* the recipient of a remittance; one to whom payment is sent.

remittent (rɪ'mɪtᵊnt) *adj.* (of a fever or the symptoms of a disease) characterized by periods of diminished severity. —**re'mittence** *or* **re'mittency** *n.* —**re'mittently** *adv.*

remitter (rɪ'mɪtə) *n.* **1.** Also called: **remittor.** a person who remits. **2.** *Property law.* the principle by which a person out of possession of land to which he had a good title is adjudged to regain this when he again enters into possession of the land.

remix *vb.* (riː'mɪks). **1.** to change the balance and separation of (a recording), usually to emphasize the rhythm section. ~*n.* ('riːmɪks). **2.** a remixed version of a recording.

remnant ('rɛmnənt) *n.* **1.** (*often pl.*) a part left over after use, processing, etc. **2.** a surviving trace or vestige, as of a former era: *a remnant of imperialism.* **3.** a piece of material from the end of a roll, sold at a lower price. ~*adj.* **4.** remaining; left over. [C14: from Old French *remenant* remaining, from *remanoir* to REMAIN]

remonetize *or* **remonetise** (riː'mʌnɪˌtaɪz) *vb.* (*tr.*) to reinstate as legal tender: *to remonetize silver.* —**reˌmoneti'zation** *or* **reˌmoneti'sation** *n.*

remonstrance (rɪ'mɒnstrəns) *n.* **1.** the act of remonstrating; protestation. **2.** a protest or reproof, esp. a petition presented in protest against something.

remonstrant (rɪ'mɒnstrənt) *n.* **1.** a person who remonstrates, esp. one who signs a remonstrance. ~*adj.* **2.** *Rare.* remonstrating or protesting.

remonstrate ('rɛmənˌstreɪt) *vb.* (*intr.*) **1.** (usually foll. by *with, against,* etc.) to argue in protest or objection: *to remonstrate with the government.* **2.** *Archaic.* to show or point out. [C16: from Medieval Latin *remonstrāre* to point out (errors), from Latin RE- + *monstrāre* to show] —ˌ**remon'stration** *n.* —**remonstrative** (rɪ'mɒnstrətɪv) *adj.* —'**remonˌstrator** *n.*

remontant (rɪ'mɒntənt) *adj.* **1.** (esp. of cultivated roses) flowering more than once in a single season. ~*n.* **2.** a rose having such a growth. [C19: from French: coming up again, from *remonter;* see REMOUNT]

remontoir *or* **remontoire** (ˌrɛmən'twɑː) *n.* any of various devices used in watches, clocks, etc., to compensate for errors arising from the changes in the force driving the escapement. [C19: from French: winding mechanism, from *remonter* to wind; see REMOUNT]

remora ('rɛmərə) *n.* any of the marine spiny-finned fishes constituting the family *Echeneidae.* They have a flattened elongated body and attach themselves to larger fish, rocks, etc., by a sucking disc on the top of the head. [C16: from Latin, from RE- + *mora* delay; an allusion to its alleged habit of delaying ships]

remorse (rɪ'mɔːs) *n.* **1.** a sense of deep regret and guilt for some misdeed. **2.** compunction; pity; compassion. [C14: from Medieval Latin *remorsus* a gnawing, from Latin *remordēre* to bite again, from RE- + *mordēre* to bite] —**re'morseful** *adj.* —**re'morsefully** *adv.* —**re'morsefulness** *n.*

remorseless (rɪ'mɔːslɪs) *adj.* **1.** without compunction, pity, or compassion. **2.** not abating in intensity; relentless: *a remorseless wind.* —**re'morselessly** *adv.* —**re'morselessness** *n.*

remote (rɪ'məʊt) *adj.* **1.** located far away; distant. **2.** far from any centre of population, society, or civilization; out-of-the-way. **3.** distant in time. **4.** distantly related or connected: *a remote cousin.* **5.** removed, as from the source or point of action. **6.** slight or faint (esp. in the phrases **not the remotest idea, a remote chance**). **7.** (of a person's manner) aloof or abstracted. **8.** operated from a distance; remote-controlled: *a remote monitor.* [C15: from Latin *remōtus* far removed, from *removēre,* from RE- + *movēre* to move] —**re'motely** *adv.* —**re'moteness** *n.*

remote access *n. Computer technol.* access to a computer from a physically separate terminal.

remote control *n.* control of a system or activity by a person at a different place, usually by means of radio or ultrasonic signals or by electrical signals transmitted by wire. —**re'mote-con'trolled** *adj.*

remote sensor *n.* any instrument, such as a radar device or camera, that scans the earth or another planet from space in order to collect data about some aspect of it. —**remote-sensing** *adj., n.*

rémoulade (ˌrɛmə'leɪd; *French* remulad) *n.* a mayonnaise sauce flavoured with herbs, mustard, and capers, served with salads, cold meat, etc. [C19: from French, from Picard dialect *ramolas* horseradish, from Latin *armoracea*]

remould *vb.* (ˌriː'məʊld). (*tr.*) **1.** to mould again. **2.** to bond a new tread onto the casing of (a worn pneumatic tyre). ~*n.* ('riːˌməʊld). **3.** a tyre made by this process. ~Also (for senses 2, 3): **retread.**

remount *vb.* (riː'maʊnt). **1.** to get on (a horse, bicycle, etc.) again. **2.** (*tr.*) to mount (a picture, jewel, exhibit, etc.) again. ~*n.* ('riːmaʊnt). **3.** a fresh horse, esp. (formerly) to replace one killed or injured in battle.

removal (rɪ'muːvᵊl) *n.* **1.** the act of removing or state of being removed. **2. a.** a change of residence. **b.** (*as modifier*): *a removal company.* **3.** dismissal from office.

removalist (rɪ'muːvəlɪst) *n. Austral.* a person or company that transports household effects to a new home.

remove (rɪ'muːv) *vb.* (*mainly tr.*) **1.** to take away and place elsewhere. **2.** to displace (someone) from office; dismiss. **3.** to do away with (a grievance, cause of anxiety, etc.); abolish. **4.** to cause (dirt, stains, or anything unwanted) to disappear; get rid of. **5.** *Euphemistic.* to assassinate; kill. **6.** (*intr.*) *Formal.* to change

re'mend *vb.*
ˌremi'grate *vb.*
ˌremilitari'zation *or* ˌremilitari'sation *n.*
re'militaˌrize *or* re'militaˌrise *vb.*
re'mint *vb.*
re'mix *vb., n.*
re'model *vb.,* -els, -elling, -elled.
re'modeller *n.*
ˌremodifi'cation *n.*
re'modiˌfy *vb.,* -ˌfies, -ˌfying, -ˌfied.
re'moduˌlate *vb.*
re'mortgage *vb.*

the location of one's home or place of business: *the publishers have removed to Mayfair.* ~*n.* **7.** the act of removing, esp. (formal) a removal of one's residence or place of work. **8.** the degree of difference separating one person, thing, or condition from another: *only one remove from madness.* **9.** *Brit.* (in certain schools) a class or form, esp. one for children of about 14 years. **10.** (at a formal dinner, formerly) a dish to be changed while the rest of the course remains on the table. [C14: from Old French *removoir,* from Latin *removēre;* see MOVE] —**re'movable** *adj.* —**re,mova'bility** *or* **re'movableness** *n.* —**re'movably** *adv.* —**re'mover** *n.*

removed (rɪ'muːvd) *adj.* **1.** separated by distance or abstract distinction. **2.** (*postpositive*) separated by a degree of descent or kinship: *the child of a person's first cousin is his first cousin once removed.* —**removedness** (rɪ'muːvɪdnɪs) *n.*

remunerate (rɪ'mjuːnə,reɪt) *vb.* (*tr.*) to reward or pay for work, service, etc. [C16: from Latin *remūnerārī* to reward, from RE- + *mūnerāre* to give, from *mūnus* a gift; see MUNIFICENT] —**re,munera'bility** *n.* —**re'munerable** *adj.* —**re'munerative** *adj.* —**re'muneratively** *adv.* —**re'munerativeness** *n.* —**re'mune,rator** *n.*

remuneration (rɪ,mjuːnə'reɪʃən) *n.* **1.** the act of remunerating. **2.** pay; recompense.

renaissance (rə'neɪsəns; *U.S. also* 'rɛnə,sɒns) *or* **renascence** *n.* a revival or rebirth, esp. of culture and learning. [C19: from French, from Latin RE- + *nascī* to be born]

Renaissance (rə'neɪsəns; *U.S. also* 'rɛnə,sɒns) *n.* **1. the.** the period of European history marking the waning of the Middle Ages and the rise of the modern world: usually considered as beginning in Italy in the 14th century. **2. a.** the spirit, culture, art, science, and thought of this period. Characteristics of the Renaissance are usually considered to include intensified classical scholarship, scientific and geographical discovery, a sense of individual human potentialities, and the assertion of the active and secular over the religious and contemplative life. **b.** (*as modifier*): *Renaissance writers.* See also **High Renaissance.** ~*adj.* **3.** of, characteristic of, or relating to the Renaissance, its culture, etc.

Renaissance man *n.* a man of any period who has a broad range of intellectual interests.

renal ('riːnᵊl) *adj.* of, relating to, resembling, or situated near the kidney. [C17: from French, from Late Latin *rēnālis,* from Latin *rēnēs* kidneys, of obscure origin]

renal pelvis *n.* a small funnel-shaped cavity of the kidney into which urine is discharged before passing into the ureter.

renascence (rɪ'næsəns, -'neɪ-) *n.* a variant of **renaissance.**

renascent (rɪ'næsᵊnt, -'neɪ-) *adj.* becoming active or vigorous again; reviving: *renascent nationalism.* [C18: from Latin *renascī* to be born again]

rencounter (rɛn'kaʊntə) *Archaic.* ~*n. also* **rencontre** (rɛn'kɒntə). **1.** an unexpected meeting. **2.** a hostile clash, as of two armies, adversaries, etc.; skirmish. ~*vb.* **3.** to meet (someone) unexpectedly. [C16: from French *rencontre,* from *rencontrer;* see ENCOUNTER]

rend (rɛnd) *vb.* **rends, rending, rent. 1.** to tear with violent force or to be torn in this way; rip. **2.** (*tr.*) to tear or pull (one's clothes, etc.), esp. as a manifestation of rage or grief. **3.** (*tr.*) (of a noise or cry) to disturb (the air, silence, etc.) with a shrill or piercing tone. **4.** (*tr.*) to pain or distress (the heart, conscience, etc.). [Old English *rendan;* related to Old Frisian *renda*] —**'rendible** *adj.*

render ('rɛndə) *vb.* (*tr.*) **1.** to present or submit (accounts, etc.) for payment, approval, or action. **2.** to give or provide (aid, charity, a service, etc.). **3.** to show (obedience), as due or expected. **4.** to give or exchange, as by way of return or requital: *to render blow for blow.* **5.** to cause to become: *grief had rendered him simple-minded.* **6.** to deliver (a verdict or opinion) formally. **7.** to portray or depict (something), as in painting, music, or acting. **8.** to translate (something) into another language or form. **9.** (sometimes foll. by *up*) to yield or give: *the tomb rendered up its secret.* **10.** (often foll. by *back*) to return (something); give back. **11.** to cover the surface of (brickwork, stone, etc.) with a coat of plaster. **12.** (often foll. by *down*) to extract (fat) from (meat) by melting. **13.** *Nautical.* **a.** to reeve (a line). **b.** to slacken (a rope, etc.). **14.** *History.* (of a feudal tenant) to make (payment) in money, goods, or services to one's overlord. ~*n.* **15.** a first thin coat of plaster applied to a surface. **16.** *History.* a payment in money, goods, or services made by a feudal tenant to his lord. [C14: from Old French *rendre,* from Latin *reddere* to give back (influenced by Latin *prendere* to grasp), from RE- + *dare* to give] —**'renderable** *adj.* —**'renderer** *n.*

rendering ('rɛndərɪŋ) *n.* **1.** the act or an instance of performing a play, piece of music, etc. **2.** a translation of a text from a foreign language. **3.** Also called: **rendering coat, render.** a coat of plaster or cement mortar applied to a surface. **4.** a perspective drawing showing an architect's idea of a finished building, interior, etc.

rendezvous ('rɒndɪ,vuː) *n., pl.* **-vous** (-,vuːz). **1.** a meeting or appointment to meet at a specified time and place. **2.** a place where people meet. ~*vb.* **3.** to meet or cause to meet at a specified time or place. [C16: from French, from *rendez-vous!* present yourselves! from *se rendre* to present oneself; see RENDER]

rendition (rɛn'dɪʃən) *n.* **1.** a performance of a musical composition, dramatic role, etc. **2.** a translation of a text. **3.** the act of rendering. **4.** *Archaic.* surrender. [C17: from obsolete French, from Late Latin *redditiō;* see RENDER]

rendzina (rɛn'dziːnə) *n.* a dark interzonal type of soil found in grassy or formerly grassy areas of moderate rainfall, esp. on chalklands. [C20: from Polish]

renegade ('rɛnɪ,geɪd) *n.* **1. a.** a person who deserts his cause or faith for another; apostate; traitor. **b.** (*as modifier*): *a renegade priest.* **2.** any outlaw or rebel. [C16: from Spanish *renegado,* from Medieval Latin *renegāre* to renounce, from Latin RE- + *negāre* to deny]

renegado (,rɛnɪ'gɑːdəʊ) *n., pl.* **-dos.** an archaic word for **renegade.**

renege *or* **renegue** (rɪ'niːg, -'neɪg) *vb.* **1.** (*intr.;* often foll. by *on*) to go back (on one's promise, etc.). ~*vb., n.* **2.** *Cards.* other words for **revoke.** [C16 (in the sense: to deny, renounce): from Medieval Latin *renegāre* to renounce; see RENEGADE] —**re'neger** *or* **re'neguer** *n.*

renew (rɪ'njuː) *vb.* (*mainly tr.*) **1.** to take up again. **2.** (*also intr.*) to begin (an activity) again; recommence: *to renew an attempt.* **3.** to restate or reaffirm (a promise, etc.). **4.** (*also intr.*) to make (a lease, licence, or contract) valid or effective for a further period. **5.** to extend the period of loan of (a library book). **6.** to regain or recover (vigour, strength, activity, etc.). **7.** to restore to a new or fresh condition. **8.** to replace (an old or worn-out part or piece). **9.** to replenish (a supply, etc.). —**re'newable** *adj.* —**re,newa'bility** *n.* —**re'newer** *n.*

renewable energy *n.* another name for **alternative energy.**

renewal (rɪ'njuːəl) *n.* **1.** the act of renewing or state of being renewed. **2.** something that is renewed.

reni- *combining form.* kidney or kidneys: *reniform.* [from Latin *rēnēs*]

reniform ('rɛnɪ,fɔːm) *adj.* having the shape or profile of a kidney: *a reniform leaf; a reniform mass of haematite.*

renin ('riːnɪn) *n.* a proteolytic enzyme secreted by the kidneys, which plays an important part in the maintenance of blood pressure. [C20: from RENI- + -IN]

renitent (rɪ'naɪtᵊnt, 'rɛnɪtənt) *adj. Rare.* **1.** reluctant; recalcitrant. **2.** not flexible. [C18: from Latin *renītī* to strive afresh, from RE- + *nītī* to endeavour] —**re'nitence** *or* **re'nitency** *n.*

rennet ('rɛnɪt) *n.* **1. a.** the membrane lining the fourth stomach (abomasum) of a young calf. **b.** the stomach of certain other young animals. **2.** a substance, containing the enzyme rennin, prepared esp. from the stomachs of calves and used for curdling milk in making cheese and junket. [C15: related to Old English *gerinnan* to curdle, RUN]

rennin ('rɛnɪn) *n.* an enzyme that occurs in gastric juice and is an active constituent of rennet. It coagulates milk by converting caseinogen to casein. Also called: **chymosin.** [C20: from RENNET + -IN]

renounce (rɪ'naʊns) *vb.* **1.** (*tr.*) to give up (a claim or right), esp. by formal announcement: *to renounce a title.* **2.** (*tr.*) to repudiate: *to renounce Christianity.* **3.** (*tr.*) to give up (some habit, pursuit, etc.) voluntarily: *to renounce one's old ways.* **4.** (*intr.*) *Cards.* to fail to follow suit because one has no more cards of the suit led. ~*n.* **5.** *Rare.* a failure to follow suit in a card game. [C14: from Old French *renoncer,* from Latin *renuntiāre* to disclaim, from RE- + *nuntiāre* to announce, from *nuntius* messenger] —**re'nouncement** *n.* —**re'nouncer** *n.*

renovate ('rɛnə,veɪt) *vb.* (*tr.*) **1.** to restore (something) to good condition: *to renovate paintings.* **2.** to revive or refresh (one's spirits, health, etc.). [C16: from Latin *renovāre,* from RE- + *novāre* to make new, from *novus* NEW] —**,reno'vation** *n.* —**'reno,vative** *adj.* —**'reno,vator** *n.*

renown (rɪ'naʊn) *n.* widespread reputation, esp. of a good kind; fame. [C14: from Anglo-Norman *renoun,* from Old French *renom,* from *renomer* to celebrate, from RE- + *nomer* to name, from Latin *nōmināre*] —**re'nowned** *adj.*

rensselaerite ('rɛnsələ,raɪt, ,rɛnsə'lɛəraɪt) *n.* a white or yellow compact variety of talc, used for ornaments. [C19: named after Stephen Van *Rensselaer* (1764–1839), American army officer and politician]

rent[1] (rɛnt) *n.* **1.** a payment made periodically by a tenant to a landlord or owner for the occupation or use of land, buildings, or other property, such as a telephone. **2.** *Economics.* **a.** that portion of the national income accruing to owners of land and real property. **b.** the return derived from the cultivation of land in excess of production costs. **c.** See **economic rent. 3. for rent.** *Chiefly U.S. and Canadian.* available for use and occupation subject to the payment of rent. ~*vb.* **4.** (*tr.*) to grant (a person) the right to use one's property in return for periodic payments.

re'name *vb.*
,rene'gotiable *adj.*
,rene'goti,ate *vb.*
,renegoti'ation *n.*
re'nomi,nate *vb.*
,renomi'nation *n.*
,renotifi'cation *n.*
re'noti,fy *vb.,* **-,fies, -,fying, -,fied.**

5. (*tr.*) to occupy or use (property) in return for periodic payments. 6. (*intr.; often* foll. by *at*) to be let or rented (for a specified rental). [C12: from Old French *rente* revenue, from Vulgar Latin *rendere* (unattested) to yield; see RENDER] —ˌ**rent-aˈbility** *n.* —ˈ**rentable** *adj.*

rent[2] (rɛnt) *n.* 1. a slit or opening made by tearing or rending; tear. 2. a breach or division, as in relations. *~vb.* 3. the past tense and past participle of **rend.**

rent-a- *prefix.* 1. denoting a rental service. 2. *Derogatory or facetious.* denoting a person or group that performs a function as if hired from a rental service: *rent-a-mob.*

rental (ˈrɛntᵊl) *n.* 1. a. the amount paid by a tenant as rent. b. an income derived from rents received. 2. property available for renting. 3. a less common name for **rent-roll.** *~adj.* 4. of or relating to rent.

rent boy *n.* a young male prostitute.

rent control *n.* regulation by law of the rent a landlord can charge for domestic accommodation and of his right to evict tenants.

rente *French.* (rɑ̃t) *n.* 1. annual income from capital investment; annuity. 2. government securities of certain countries, esp. France. 3. the interest on such securities.

renter (ˈrɛntə) *n.* 1. a person who lets his property in return for rent, esp. a landlord. 2. a person who rents property from another; tenant. 3. a distributor of films to cinemas for commercial showing.

rent-free *adj., adv.* without payment of rent.

rentier *French.* (rɑ̃tje) *n.* a. a person whose income consists primarily of fixed unearned amounts, such as rent or bond interest. b. (*as modifier*): *the rentier class.* [from *rente;* see RENT[1]]

rent-roll *n.* 1. a register of lands and buildings owned by a person, company, etc., showing the rent due and total amount received from each tenant. 2. the total income arising from rented property.

renunciation (rɪˌnʌnsɪˈeɪʃən) *n.* 1. the act or an instance of renouncing. 2. a formal declaration renouncing something. 3. *Stock Exchange.* the surrender to another of the rights to buy new shares in a rights issue. [C14: fromLatin *renunciātiō* a declaration, from *renuntiāre* to report, RENOUNCE] —**reˈnunciative** *or* **reˈnunciatory** *adj.*

renvoi (rɛnˈvɔɪ) *n.* the referring of a dispute or other legal question to a jurisdiction other than that in which it arose. [C17: from French: a sending back, from *renvoyer,* from RE- + *envoyer* to send; see ENVOY]

rep[1] *or* **repp** (rɛp) *n.* a silk, wool, rayon, or cotton fabric with a transversely corded surface. [C19: from French *reps,* perhaps from English *ribs;* see RIB[1]] —**repped** *adj.*

rep[2] (rɛp) *n. Theatre.* short for **repertory (company).**

rep[3] (rɛp) *n.* short for **representative** (senses 2, 5).

rep[4] (rɛp) *n. U.S. informal.* short for **reputation.**

rep. *abbrev. for:* 1. report. 2. reported. 3. reporter. 4. representative. 5. reprint.

Rep. *abbrev. for:* 1. *U.S.* Representative. 2. *U.S.* Republican. 3. Republic.

repair[1] (rɪˈpɛə) *vb.* (*tr.*) 1. to restore (something damaged or broken) to good condition or working order. 2. to heal (a breach or division) in (something): *to repair a broken marriage.* 3. to make good or make amends for (a mistake, injury, etc.). *~n.* 4. the act, task, or process of repairing. 5. a part that has been repaired. 6. state or condition: *in good repair.* [C14: from Old French *reparer,* from Latin *reparāre,* from RE- + *parāre* to make ready] —**reˈpairable** *adj.* —**reˈpairer** *n.*

repair[2] (rɪˈpɛə) *vb.* (*intr.*) 1. (usually foll. by *to*) to go (to a place): *to repair to the country.* 2. (usually foll. by *to*) to have recourse (to) for help, etc.: *to repair to one's lawyer.* 3. (usually foll. by *from*) *Archaic.* to come back; return. *~n. Archaic.* 4. the act of going or returning. 5. a haunt or resort. [C14: from Old French *repairier,* from Late Latin *repatriāre* to return to one's native land, from Latin RE- + *patria* fatherland; compare REPATRIATE]

repairman (rɪˈpɛəˌmæn) *n., pl.* **-men.** a man whose job it is to repair machines, appliances, etc.

repand (rɪˈpænd) *adj. Botany.* having a wavy margin: *a repand leaf.* [C18: from Latin *repandus* bent backwards, from RE- + *pandus* curved] —**reˈpandly** *adv.*

reparable (ˈrɛpərəbᵊl, ˈrɛprə-) *adj.* able to be repaired, recovered, or remedied: *a reparable loss.* [C16: from Latin *reparābilis,* from *reparāre* to REPAIR[1]] —ˌ**reparaˈbility** *n.* —ˈ**reparably** *adv.*

reparation (ˌrɛpəˈreɪʃən) *n.* 1. the act or process of making amends: *an injury admitting of no reparation.* 2. (*usually pl.*) compensation exacted as an indemnity from a defeated nation by the victors: esp. the compensation demanded of Germany by the Treaty of Versailles after World War I. 3. the act or process of repairing or state of having been repaired. [C14 *reparacioun,* ultimately from Latin *reparāre* to REPAIR[1]] —**reparative** (rɪˈpærətɪv) *or* **reˈparatory** *adj.*

repartee (ˌrɛpɑːˈtiː) *n.* 1. a sharp, witty, or aphoristic remark made as a reply. 2. terse rapid conversation consisting of such remarks. 3. skill in making sharp witty replies or conversation. [C17: from French *repartie,* from *repartir* to retort, from RE- + *partir* to go away]

repartition (ˌriːpɑːˈtɪʃən) *n.* 1. distribution or allotment. 2. the act or process of distributing afresh. *~vb.* 3. (*tr.*) to divide up again; reapportion or reallocate.

repast (rɪˈpɑːst) *n.* 1. a meal or the food provided at a meal: *a light repast.* 2. *Archaic.* a. food in general; nourishment. b. the act of taking food or refreshment. *~vb.* 3. (*intr.*) *Archaic.* to feed (on). [C14: from Old French, from *repaistre* to feed, from Late Latin *repāscere* to nourish again, from Latin RE- + *pāscere* to feed, pasture (of animals)]

repat (ˈriːpæt) *adj. Austral. informal.* of or denoting the administrative arm of the Repatriation Commission, which provides assistance to ex-servicemen returning to civilian life and to the widows and dependants of servicemen killed in the line of duty: *he was on repat pension.*

repatriate *vb.* (*tr.*) (riːˈpætrɪˌeɪt). 1. to send back (a refugee, prisoner of war, etc.) to the country of his birth or citizenship. 2. to send back (a sum of money previously invested abroad) to its country of origin. *~n.* (riːˈpætrɪɪt). 3. a person who has been repatriated. [C17: from Late Latin *repatriāre,* from Latin RE- + *patria* fatherland; compare REPAIR[2]] —**reˌpatriˈation** *n.*

repay (rɪˈpeɪ) *vb.* **-pays, -paying, -paid.** 1. to pay back (money) to (a person); refund or reimburse. 2. to make a return for (something) by way of compensation: *to repay kindness.* —**reˈpayable** *adj.* —**reˈpayment** *n.*

repeal (rɪˈpiːl) *vb.* (*tr.*) 1. to annul or rescind officially (something previously ordered); revoke: *these laws were repealed.* 2. *Obsolete.* to call back (a person) from exile. *~n.* 3. an instance or the process of repealing; annulment. [C14: from Old French *repeler,* from RE- + *apeler* to call, APPEAL] —**reˈpealable** *adj.* —**reˈpealer** *n.*

repeat (rɪˈpiːt) *vb.* 1. (when *tr., may take a clause as object*) to say or write (something) again, either once or several times; restate or reiterate. 2. to do or experience (something) again once or several times. 3. (*intr.*) to occur more than once: *the last figure repeats.* 4. (*tr.; may take a clause as object*) to reproduce (the words, sounds, etc.) uttered by someone else; echo. 5. (*tr.*) to utter (a poem, speech, etc.) from memory; recite. 6. (*intr.*) a. (of food) to be tasted again after ingestion as the result of belching or slight regurgitation. b. to belch. 7. (*tr.; may take a clause as object*) to tell to another person (the words, esp. secrets, imparted to one by someone else). 8. (*intr.*) (of a clock) to strike the hour or quarter-hour just past, when a spring is pressed. 9. (*intr.*) *U.S.* to vote (illegally) more than once in a single election. 10. **repeat oneself.** to say or do the same thing more than once, esp. so as to be tedious. *~n.* 11. a. the act or an instance of repeating. b. (*as modifier*): *a repeat performance.* 12. a word, action, etc., that is repeated. 13. an order made out for goods, provisions, etc., that duplicates a previous order. 14. a duplicate copy of something; reproduction. 15. *Radio, television.* a second broadcast of a programme, film, etc., which has already been broadcast before. 16. *Music.* a passage that is an exact restatement of the passage preceding it. [C14: from Old French *repeter,* from Latin *repetere* to seek again, from RE- + *petere* to seek] —**reˌpeataˈbility** *n.* —**reˈpeatable** *adj.*

repeated (rɪˈpiːtɪd) *adj.* done, made, or said again and again; continual or incessant. —**reˈpeatedly** *adv.*

repeater (rɪˈpiːtə) *n.* 1. a person or thing that repeats. 2. Also called: **repeating firearm.** a firearm capable of discharging several shots without reloading. 3. a timepiece having a mechanism enabling it to strike the hour or quarter-hour just past, when a spring is pressed. 4. *Electrical engineering.* a device that amplifies or augments incoming electrical signals and retransmits them, thus compensating for transmission losses. 5. Also called: **substitute.** *Nautical.* one of three signal flags hoisted with others to indicate that one of the top three is to be repeated.

repeating decimal *n.* another name for **recurring decimal.**

repechage (ˌrɛpɪˈʃɑːʒ) *n.* a heat of a competition, esp. in rowing or fencing, in which eliminated contestants have another chance to qualify for the next round or the final. [C19: from French *repêchage* literally: fishing out again, from RE- + *pêcher* to fish + -AGE]

repel (rɪˈpɛl) *vb.* **-pels, -pelling, -pelled.** (*mainly tr.*) 1. to force or drive back (something or somebody, esp. an attacker). 2. (*also intr.*) to produce a feeling of aversion or distaste in (someone or something); be disgusting (to). 3. to push aside; dismiss: *he repelled the suggestion as wrong and impossible.* 4. to be effective in keeping away, controlling, or resisting: *an aerosol spray*

reˈnumber *vb.*
ˌ**reobˈtainable** *adj.*
ˌ**reoccuˈpation** *n.*
reˈoccuˌpy *vb.,* **-ˌpies, -ˌpying, -ˌpied.**
ˌ**reocˈcur** *vb.,* **-ˈcurs, -ˈcurring, -ˈcurred.**
ˌ**reocˈcurrence** *n.*
reˈoil *vb.*
reˈopen *vb.*
reˈorder *vb.*
ˌ**reorganiˌzation** *or* ˌ**reorganiˈsation** *n.*
reˈorganˌize *or* **reˈorganˌise** *vb.*
reˈorganˌizer *or* **reˈorganˌiser** *n.*
reˈoriˌent *vb.*
ˌ**reorienˈtation** *n.*
reˈpack *vb.*
reˈpackage *vb.*
reˈpaint *vb., n.*
reˈpaper *vb.*
reˈpass *vb.*
reˈpave *vb.*

that repels flies. **5.** to have no affinity for; fail to mix with or absorb: *water and oil repel each other.* **6.** to disdain to accept (something); turn away from or spurn: *she repelled his advances.* **7.** (*also intr.*) to exert an opposing force on (something): *an electric charge repels another charge of the same sign.* [C15: from Latin *repellere,* from RE- + *pellere* to push, drive] —**re'peller** *n.*

repellent (rɪ'pɛlənt) *adj.* **1.** giving rise to disgust or aversion; distasteful or repulsive. **2.** driving or forcing away or back; repelling. ~*n. also* **repellant. 3.** something, esp. a chemical substance, that repels: *insect repellent.* **4.** a substance with which fabrics are treated to increase their resistance to water. —**re'pellence** *or* **re'pellency** *n.* —**re'pellently** *adv.*

repent[1] (rɪ'pɛnt) *vb.* to feel remorse (for); be contrite (about); show penitence (for): *he repents of his extravagance; he repented his words.* [C13: from Old French *repentir,* from RE- + *pentir* to be contrite, from Latin *paenitēre* to repent] —**re'penter** *n.*

repent[2] ('riːpᵊnt) *adj. Botany.* lying or creeping along the ground; reptant: *repent stems.* [C17: from Latin *rēpere* to creep]

repentance (rɪ'pɛntəns) *n.* **1.** remorse or contrition for one's past actions or sins. **2.** an act or the process of being repentant; penitence.

repentant (rɪ'pɛntənt) *adj.* **1.** reproaching oneself for one's past actions or sins; contrite. **2.** characterized by or proceeding from a sense of contrition: *a repentant heart; his repentant words.* —**re'pentantly** *adv.*

repercussion (ˌriːpə'kʌʃən) *n.* **1.** (*often pl.*) a result or consequence, esp. one that is somewhat removed from the action or event which precipitated it: *the repercussions of the war are still keenly felt.* **2.** a recoil after impact; a rebound. **3.** a reflection, esp. of sound; echo or reverberation. **4.** *Music.* the reappearance of a fugal subject and answer after an episode. [C16: from Latin *repercussiō,* from *repercutere* to strike back; see PERCUSSION] —ˌ**reper'cussive** *adj.*

repertoire ('rɛpəˌtwɑː) *n.* **1.** all the plays, songs, operas, or other works collectively that a company, actor, singer, dancer, etc., has prepared and is competent to perform. **2.** the entire stock of things available in a field or of a kind: *the comedian's repertoire of jokes was becoming stale.* **3. in repertoire.** denoting the performance of two or more plays, ballets, etc., by the same company in the same venue on different evenings over a period of time: *"Nutcracker" returns to Covent Garden over Christmas in repertoire with "Giselle".* [C19: from French, from Late Latin *repertōrium* inventory; see REPERTORY]

repertory ('rɛpətərɪ, -trɪ) *n., pl.* **-ries. 1.** the entire stock of things available in a field or of a kind; repertoire. **2.** a building or place where a stock of things is kept; repository. **3.** short for **repertory company.** [C16: from Late Latin *repertōrium* storehouse, from Latin *reperīre* to obtain, from RE- + *parere* to bring forth] —ˌ**reper'torial** *adj.*

repertory company *n.* a theatrical company that performs plays from a repertoire, esp. at its own theatre. U.S. name: **stock company.**

repertory society *n. N.Z.* a group that supports amateur performances of plays by its members.

repetend ('rɛpɪˌtɛnd, ˌrɛpɪ'tɛnd) *n.* **1.** *Maths.* the digit or series of digits in a recurring decimal that repeats itself. **2.** anything repeated. [C18: from Latin *repetendum* what is to be repeated, from *repetere* to REPEAT]

répétiteur *French.* (repetitœr) *n.* a member of an opera company who accompanies rehearsals on the piano and coaches the singers. —***répétiteuse*** (repetitœz) *fem. n.*

repetition (ˌrɛpɪ'tɪʃən) *n.* **1.** the act or an instance of repeating; reiteration. **2.** a thing, word, action, etc., that is repeated. **3.** a replica or copy. **4.** *Civil and Scots Law.* the recovery or repayment of money paid or received by mistake, as when the same bill has been paid twice.

repetitious (ˌrɛpɪ'tɪʃəs) *adj.* characterized by unnecessary repetition. —ˌ**repe'titiously** *adv.* —ˌ**repe'titiousness** *n.*

repetitive (rɪ'pɛtɪtɪv) *adj.* characterized by or given to unnecessary repetition; boring: *dull, repetitive work.* —**re'petitively** *adv.* —**re'petitiveness** *n.*

repetitive strain *or* **stress injury** *n.* the full name for **RSI.**

rephrase (riː'freɪz) *vb.* (*tr.*) to phrase again, esp. so as to express more clearly.

repine (rɪ'paɪn) *vb.* (*intr.*) to be fretful or low-spirited through discontent. [C16: from RE- + PINE[2]]

repique (rɪ'piːk) *Piquet.* ~*n.* **1.** a score of 30 points made from the cards held by a player before play begins. ~*vb.* **2.** to score a repique against (someone). [from French *repiq*]

replace (rɪ'pleɪs) *vb.* (*tr.*) **1.** to take the place of; supersede: *the manual worker is being replaced by the machine.* **2.** to substitute a person or thing for (another which has ceased to fulfil its function); put in place of: *to replace an old pair of shoes.* **3.** to put back or return; restore to its rightful place. —**re'placeable** *adj.* —**reˌplacea'bility** *n.* —**re'placer** *n.*

replacement (rɪ'pleɪsmənt) *n.* **1.** the act or process of replacing. **2.** a person or thing that replaces another. **3.** *Geology.* the growth of a mineral within another of different chemical composition by gradual simultaneous deposition and removal.

replant (riː'plɑːnt) *vb.* (*tr.*) **1.** to plant again: *she replanted the bulbs that the dog had dug up.* **2.** to reattach (a severed limb or part) by surgery.

replantation (ˌriːplæn'teɪʃən) *n.* the reattachment of (severed limbs or parts) by surgery.

replay *n.* ('riːˌpleɪ). **1.** Also called: **action replay.** *Television.* a showing again of a sequence of action, esp. of part of a sporting contest immediately after it happens either in slow motion (a **slow-motion replay**) or at normal speed. **2.** a rematch. ~*vb.* (riː'pleɪ). **3.** to play again (a record, television sequence, sporting contest, etc.).

replenish (rɪ'plɛnɪʃ) *vb.* (*tr.*) **1.** to make full or complete again by supplying what has been used up or is lacking. **2.** to put fresh fuel on (a fire). [C14: from Old French *replenir,* from RE- + *plenir* to fill, from Latin *plēnus* full] —**re'plenisher** *n.* —**re'plenishment** *n.*

replete (rɪ'pliːt) *adj.* (*usually postpositive*) **1.** (often foll. by *with*) copiously supplied (with); abounding (in). **2.** having one's appetite completely or excessively satisfied by food and drink; stuffed; gorged; satiated. [C14: from Latin *replētus,* from *replēre* to refill, from RE- + *plēre* to fill] —**re'pletely** *adv.* —**re'pleteness** *n.*

repletion (rɪ'pliːʃən) *n.* **1.** the state or condition of being replete; fullness, esp. excessive fullness due to overeating. **2.** the satisfaction of a need or desire.

replevin (rɪ'plɛvɪn) *Law.* ~*n.* **1.** the recovery of goods unlawfully taken, made subject to establishing the validity of the recovery in a legal action and returning the goods if the decision is adverse. **2.** (formerly) a writ of replevin. ~*vb.* **3.** another word for **replevy.** [C15: from Anglo-French, from Old French *replevir* to give security for, from RE- + *plevir* to PLEDGE]

replevy (rɪ'plɛvɪ) *Law.* ~*vb.* **-plevies, -plevying, -plevied.** (*tr.*) **1.** to recover possession of (goods) by replevin. ~*n., pl.* **-plevies. 2.** another word for **replevin.** [C15: from Old French *replevir;* see REPLEVIN] —**re'pleviable** *or* **re'plevisable** *adj.*

replica ('rɛplɪkə) *n.* an exact copy or reproduction, esp. on a smaller scale. [C19: from Italian, literally: a reply, from *replicare* to repeat, from Latin: to bend back, repeat]

replicate *vb.* ('rɛplɪˌkeɪt). (*mainly tr.*) **1.** (*also intr.*) to make or be a copy of; reproduce. **2.** to fold (something) over on itself; bend back. **3.** to reply to. ~*adj.* ('rɛplɪkɪt). **4.** folded back on itself: *a replicate leaf.* [C19: from Latin *replicātus* bent back; see REPLICA] —'**replicative** *adj.*

replication (ˌrɛplɪ'keɪʃən) *n.* **1.** a reply or response. **2.** *Law.* (formerly) the plaintiff's reply to a defendant's answer or plea. **3.** *Biology.* the production of exact copies of complex molecules, such as DNA molecules, that occurs during growth of living tissue. **4.** repetition of a procedure, such as a scientific experiment, in order to reduce errors. **5.** a less common word for **replica.** [C14: via Old French from Latin *replicātiō* a folding back, from *replicāre* to unroll; see REPLY]

replicon ('rɛplɪˌkɒn) *n. Genetics.* a region of a DNA molecule that is replicated from a single origin.

reply (rɪ'plaɪ) *vb.* **-plies, -plying, -plied.** (*mainly intr.*) **1.** to make answer (to) in words or writing or by an action; respond: *he replied with an unexpected move.* **2.** (*tr.; takes a clause as object*) to say (something) in answer: *he replied that he didn't want to come.* **3.** *Law.* to answer a defendant's plea. **4.** to return (a sound); echo. ~*n., pl.* **-plies. 5.** an answer made in words or writing or through an action; response. **6.** the answer made by a plaintiff or petitioner to a defendant's case. [C14: from Old French *replier* to fold again, reply, from Latin *replicāre* to fold back, from RE- + *plicāre* to fold] —**re'plier** *n.*

repoint (ˌriː'pɔɪnt) *vb.* (*tr.*) to repair the joints of (brickwork, masonry, etc.) with mortar or cement.

repone (rɪ'pəʊn) *vb.* (*tr.*) *Scots Law.* to restore (someone) to his former status, office, etc.; rehabilitate. [C16: from Latin *repōnere* to put back, replace]

report (rɪ'pɔːt) *n.* **1.** an account prepared for the benefit of others, esp. one that provides information obtained through investigation and published in a newspaper or broadcast. **2.** a statement made widely known; rumour: *according to report, he is not dead.* **3.** an account of the deliberations of a committee, body, etc.: *a report of parliamentary proceedings.* **4.** *Brit.* a statement on the progress, academic achievement, etc., of each child in a school, written by teachers and sent to the parents or guardian annually or each term. **5.** a written account of a case decided at law, giving the main points of the argument on each side, the court's findings, and the decision reached. **6.** comment on a person's character or actions; reputation: *he is of good report here.* **7.** a sharp loud noise, esp. one made by a gun. ~*vb.* (when *tr., may take a clause as object;* when *intr.,* often foll. by *on*) **8.** to give an account (of); describe. **9.** to give an account of the results of an investigation (into): *to report on housing conditions.* **10.** (of a committee, legislative body, etc.) to make a formal report on (a bill). **11.** (*tr.*) to complain about (a person), esp. to a superior: *I'll report you to the teacher.* **12.** (*tr.*) to reveal information about (a fugitive, escaped prisoner, etc.) esp. concerning his whereabouts. **13.** (*intr.*) to present oneself or be present at an appointed place or for a specific purpose: *report to the manager's*

re'people *vb.*
re'photoˌgraph *vb.*
re'pin *vb.,* **-'pins, -'pinning, -'pinned.**
re'plan *vb.,* **-'plans, -'planning, -'planned.**
re'polish *vb.*
re'popuˌlate *vb.*

office. **14.** (*intr.*) to say or show that one is (in a certain state): *to report fit.* **15.** (*intr.*; foll. by *to*) to be responsible to and under the authority of: *the plant manager reports to the production controller.* **16.** (*intr.*) to act as a reporter for a newspaper or for radio or television. **17.** *Law.* to take down in writing details of (the proceedings of a court of law) as a record or for publication. [C14: from Old French, from *reporter* to carry back, from Latin *reportāre,* from RE- + *portāre* to carry] —**re'portable** *adj.*

reportage (rɪˈpɔːtɪdʒ, ˌrɛpɔːˈtɑːʒ) *n.* **1.** the act or process of reporting news or other events of general interest. **2.** a journalist's style of reporting. **3.** a technique of documentary film or photo journalism that tells a story entirely through pictures.

reported clause *n. Grammar.* a bound clause that reports what someone has said or thought, bound to a main clause that contains a verb of saying or thinking.

reportedly (rɪˈpɔːtɪdlɪ) *adv.* according to rumour or report: *he is reportedly living in Australia.*

reported speech *n.* another term for **indirect speech.**

reporter (rɪˈpɔːtə) *n.* **1.** a person who reports, esp. one employed to gather news for a newspaper, news agency, or broadcasting organization. **2.** a person, esp. a barrister, authorized to write official accounts of judicial proceedings. **3.** a person authorized to report the proceedings of a legislature. **4.** (in Scotland) *Social welfare.* an official who arranges and conducts children's panel hearings and who may investigate cases and decide on the action to be taken.

reportorial (ˌrɛpɔːˈtɔːrɪəl) *adj. Chiefly U.S.* of or relating to a newspaper reporter. [C20: from REPORTER, influenced by EDITORIAL] —**repor'torially** *adv.*

report stage *n.* the stage preceding the third reading in the passage of a bill through Parliament, at which the bill, as amended in committee, is reported back to the chamber considering it.

repose[1] (rɪˈpəʊz) *n.* **1.** a state of quiet restfulness; peace or tranquillity. **2.** dignified calmness of manner; composure. ~*vb.* **3.** to place (oneself or one's body) in a state of quiet relaxation; lie or lay down at rest. **4.** (*intr.*) to lie when dead, as in the grave. **5.** (*intr.*; foll. by *on, in,* etc.) *Formal.* to take support (from) or be based (on): *your plan reposes on a fallacy.* [C15: from Old French *reposer,* from Late Latin *repausāre,* from RE- + *pausāre* to stop; see PAUSE] —**re'posal** *n.* —**re'poser** *n.* —**re'poseful** *adj.* —**re'posefully** *adv.* —**re'posefulness** *n.*

repose[2] (rɪˈpəʊz) *vb.* (*tr.*) **1.** to put (trust or confidence) in a person or thing. **2.** to place or put (an object) somewhere. [C15: from Latin *repōnere* to store up, from RE- + *pōnere* to put] —**re'posal** *n.*

reposit (rɪˈpɒzɪt) *vb.* (*tr.*) to put away, deposit, or store up. [C17: from Latin *repositus* replaced, from *repōnere;* see REPOSE[2], POSIT]

reposition (ˌriːpəˈzɪʃən) *n.* **1.** the act or process of depositing or storing. **2.** *Surgery.* the return of a broken or displaced organ, or part to its normal site. **3.** *Archaic.* the reinstatement of a person in a post or office. ~*vb.* **4.** (*tr.*) to place in a new position.

repository (rɪˈpɒzɪtərɪ, -trɪ) *n., pl.* **-ries. 1.** a place or container in which things can be stored for safety. **2.** a place where things are kept for exhibition; museum. **3.** a place where commodities are kept before being sold; warehouse. **4.** a place of burial; sepulchre. **5.** a receptacle containing the relics of the dead. **6.** a person to whom a secret is entrusted; confidant. [C15: from Latin *repositōrium,* from *repōnere* to place]

repossess (ˌriːpəˈzɛs) *vb.* (*tr.*) **1.** to take back possession of (property), esp. for nonpayment of money due under a hire-purchase agreement. **2.** to restore ownership of (something) to someone. —**repossession** (ˌriːpəˈzɛʃən) *n.* —ˌ**repos'sessor** *n.*

repot (riːˈpɒt) *vb.* **-pots, -potting, -potted.** (*tr.*) to put (a house plant) into a new usually larger pot.

repoussé (rəˈpuːseɪ) *adj.* **1.** raised in relief, as a design on a thin piece of metal hammered through from the underside. **2.** decorated with such designs. ~*n.* **3.** a design or surface made in this way. **4.** the technique of hammering designs in this way. [C19: from French, from *repousser* to push back, from RE- + *pousser* to PUSH]

repp (rɛp) *n.* a variant spelling of **rep**[1].

repr. *abbrev. for:* **1.** represented. **2.** representing. **3.** reprint(ed).

reprehend (ˌrɛprɪˈhɛnd) *vb.* (*tr.*) to find fault with; criticize. [C14: from Latin *reprehendere* to hold fast, rebuke, from RE- + *prendere* to grasp] —ˌ**repre'hendable** *adj.* —ˌ**repre'hender** *n.*

reprehensible (ˌrɛprɪˈhɛnsəbᵊl) *adj.* open to criticism or rebuke; blameworthy. [C14: from Late Latin *reprehensibilis,* from Latin *reprehendere* to hold back, reprove; see REPREHEND] —ˌ**repreˌhensi'bility** *or* ˌ**repre'hensibleness** *n.* —ˌ**repre'hensibly** *adv.*

reprehension (ˌrɛprɪˈhɛnʃən) *n.* the act or an instance of reprehending; reproof or rebuke. —ˌ**repre'hensive** *or* (*rarely*) ˌ**repre'hensory** *adj.* —ˌ**repre'hensively** *adv.*

represent (ˌrɛprɪˈzɛnt) *vb.* (*tr.*) **1.** to stand as an equivalent of; correspond to: *our tent represents home to us when we go camping.* **2.** to act as a substitute or proxy (for). **3.** to act as or be the authorized delegate or agent for (a person, country, etc.): *an MP represents his constituency.* **4.** to serve or use as a means of expressing: *letters represent the sounds of speech.* **5.** to exhibit the characteristics of; exemplify; typify: *romanticism in music is represented by Beethoven.* **6.** to present an image of through the medium of a picture or sculpture; portray. **7.** to bring clearly before the mind. **8.** to set forth in words; state or explain. **9.** to describe as having a specified character or quality; make out to be: *he represented her as a saint.* **10.** to act out the part of on stage; portray. **11.** to perform or produce (a play); stage. [C14: from Latin *repraesentāre* to exhibit, from RE- + *praesentāre* to PRESENT[2]] —ˌ**repre'sentable** *adj.* —ˌ**repreˌsenta'bility** *n.*

re-present (ˌriːprɪˈzɛnt) *vb.* (*tr.*) to present again. —**re-presentation** (ˌriːprɛzənˈteɪʃən) *n.*

representation (ˌrɛprɪzɛnˈteɪʃən) *n.* **1.** the act or an instance of representing or the state of being represented. **2.** anything that represents, such as a verbal or pictorial portrait. **3.** anything that is represented, such as an image brought clearly to mind. **4.** the principle by which delegates act for a constituency. **5.** a body of representatives. **6.** *Contract law.* an assertion of fact made by one party to induce another to enter into a contract. **7.** an instance of acting for another, on his authority, in a particular capacity, such as executor or administrator. **8.** a dramatic production or performance. **9.** (*often pl.*) a statement of facts, true or alleged, esp. one set forth by way of remonstrance or expostulation. **10.** *Linguistics.* an analysis of a word, sentence, etc., into its constituents: *phonetic representation.*

representational (ˌrɛprɪzɛnˈteɪʃənᵊl) *adj.* **1.** *Fine art.* depicting or attempting to depict objects, scenes, figures, etc., directly as seen; naturalistic. **2.** of or relating to representation.

representationalism (ˌrɛprɪzɛnˈteɪʃənəˌlɪzəm) *or* **representationism** *n.* **1.** *Philosophy.* the doctrine that in perceptions of objects what is before the mind is not the object but a representation of it. Compare **presentationism, naive realism.** See also **barrier of ideas. 2.** *Fine art.* the practice or advocacy of attempting to depict objects, scenes, figures, etc., directly as seen. —ˌ**represenˌtational'istic** *adj.* —ˌ**represen'tationist** *n., adj.*

representative (ˌrɛprɪˈzɛntətɪv) *n.* **1.** a person or thing that represents another or others. **2.** a person who represents and tries to sell the products or services of a firm, esp. a travelling salesman. Often shortened to **rep. 3.** a typical example. **4.** a person representing a constituency in a deliberative, legislative, or executive body, esp. (*cap.*) a member of the U.S. House of Representatives (the lower house of Congress). **5.** *N.Z.* a rugby player, football player, etc., chosen to represent a province in interprovincial sports. ~*adj.* **6.** serving to represent; symbolic. **7. a.** exemplifying a class or kind; typical: *a representative example of the species.* **b.** containing or including examples of all the interests, types, etc., in a group: *a representative collection.* **8.** acting as deputy or proxy for another or others. **9.** acting for or representing a constituency or the whole people in the process of government: *a representative council.* **10.** of, characterized by, or relating to the political principle of representation of the people: *representative government.* **11.** of or relating to a mental picture or representation. —ˌ**repre'sentatively** *adv.* —ˌ**repre'sentativeness** *n.*

repress (rɪˈprɛs) *vb.* (*tr.*) **1.** to keep (feelings, etc.) under control; suppress or restrain: *to repress a desire.* **2.** to put into a state of subjugation: *to repress a people.* **3.** *Psychol.* to banish (thoughts and impulses that conflict with conventional standards of conduct) from one's conscious mind. [C14: from Latin *reprimere* to press back, from RE- + *premere* to PRESS[1]] —**re'presser** *n.* —**re'pressible** *adj.* —**re'pression** *n.* —**re'pressive** *adj.* —**re'pressively** *adv.* —**re'pressiveness** *n.*

re-press (riːˈprɛs) *vb.* (*tr.*) to press again, esp. to reproduce more copies of a gramophone record by a second pressing.

repressed (rɪˈprɛst) *adj.* (of a person) repressing feelings, instincts, desires, etc.

repressor (rɪˈprɛsə) *n. Biochem.* a protein synthesized under the control of a repressor gene, which has the capacity to bind to the operator gene and thereby shut off the expression of the structural genes of the operon.

reprieve (rɪˈpriːv) *vb.* (*tr.*) **1.** to postpone or remit the punishment of (a person, esp. one condemned to death). **2.** to give temporary relief to (a person or thing), esp. from otherwise irrevocable harm: *the government has reprieved the company with a huge loan.* ~*n.* **3.** a postponement or remission of punishment, esp. of a person condemned to death. **4.** a warrant granting a postponement. **5.** a temporary relief from pain or harm; respite. **6.** the act of reprieving or the state of being reprieved. [C16: from Old French *repris* (something) taken back, from *reprendre* to take back, from Latin *reprehendere;* perhaps also influenced by obsolete English *repreve* to reprove] —**re'prievable** *adj.* —**re'priever** *n.*

reprimand (ˈrɛprɪˌmɑːnd) *n.* **1.** a reproof or formal admonition; rebuke. ~*vb.* **2.** (*tr.*) to admonish or rebuke, esp. formally; reprove. [C17: from French *réprimande,* from Latin *reprimenda* (things) to be repressed; see REPRESS]

reprint *n.* (ˈriːˌprɪnt). **1.** a reproduction in print of any matter already published; offprint. **2.** a reissue of a printed work using the same type, plates, etc., as the original. ~*vb.* (riːˈprɪnt). **3.** (*tr.*) to print again. —**re'printer** *n.*

re'price *vb.*

reprisal (rɪˈpraɪzᵊl) *n.* **1.** (*often pl.*) retaliatory action against an enemy in wartime, such as the execution of prisoners of war, destruction of property, etc. **2.** the act or an instance of retaliation in any form. **3.** (formerly) the forcible seizure of the property or subjects of one nation by another. [C15: from Old French *reprisaille,* from Old Italian *ripresaglia,* from *riprendere* to recapture, from Latin *reprehendere* to hold fast; see REPREHEND]

reprise (rɪˈpriːz) *Music.* ~*n.* **1.** the repeating of an earlier theme. ~*vb.* **2.** to repeat (an earlier theme). [C14: from Old French, from *reprendre* to take back, from Latin *reprehendere;* see REPREHEND]

repro (ˈriːprəʊ) *n., pl.* **-pros. 1.** short for **reproduction** (sense 2): *repro furniture.* **2.** short for **reproduction proof.**

reproach (rɪˈprəʊtʃ) *vb.* (*tr.*) **1.** to impute blame to (a person) for an action or fault; rebuke. **2.** *Archaic.* to bring disgrace or shame upon. ~*n.* **3.** the act of reproaching. **4.** rebuke or censure; reproof: *words of reproach.* **5.** disgrace or shame: *to bring reproach upon one's family.* **6.** something that causes or merits blame, rebuke, or disgrace. **7. above** *or* **beyond reproach.** perfect; beyond criticism. [C15: from Old French *reprochier,* from Latin RE- + *prope* near] —**reˈproachable** *adj.* —**reˈproachableness** *n.* —**reˈproachably** *adv.* —**reˈproacher** *n.*

reproachful (rɪˈprəʊtʃfʊl) *adj.* **1.** full of or expressing reproach. **2.** *Archaic.* deserving of reproach; disgraceful. —**reˈproachfully** *adv.* —**reˈproachfulness** *n.*

reprobate (ˈrɛprəʊˌbeɪt) *adj.* **1.** morally unprincipled; depraved. **2.** *Christianity.* destined or condemned to eternal punishment in hell. ~*n.* **3.** an unprincipled, depraved, or damned person. **4.** a disreputable or roguish person: *the old reprobate.* ~*vb.* (*tr.*) **5.** to disapprove of; condemn. **6.** (of God) to destine, consign, or condemn to eternal punishment in hell. [C16: from Late Latin *reprobātus* held in disfavour, from Latin RE- + *probāre* to APPROVE] —**reprobacy** (ˈrɛprəbəsɪ) *n.* —**ˈreproˌbater** *n.*

reprobation (ˌrɛprəʊˈbeɪʃən) *n.* **1.** disapproval, blame, or censure. **2.** *Christianity.* condemnation to eternal punishment in hell; rejection by God. —**reprobative** (ˈrɛprəbətɪv) *or* **ˌreproˈbationary** *adj.* —**ˈreprobatively** *adv.*

reproduce (ˌriːprəˈdjuːs) *vb.* (*mainly tr.*) **1.** to make a copy, representation, or imitation of; duplicate. **2.** (*also intr.*) *Biology.* to undergo or cause to undergo a process of reproduction. **3.** to produce or exhibit again. **4.** to bring back into existence again; re-create. **5.** to bring before the mind again (a scene, event, etc.) through memory or imagination. **6.** (*intr.*) to come out (well, badly, etc.), when copied. **7.** to replace (damaged parts or organs) by a process of natural growth; regenerate. **8.** to cause (a sound or television recording) to be heard or seen. —**ˌreproˈducible** *adj.* —**ˌreproˈducibly** *adv.* —**ˌreproˌduciˈbility** *n.*

reproducer (ˌriːprəˈdjuːsə) *n.* **1.** a person or thing that makes reproductions. **2.** a complete sound reproduction system. **3.** another name for **loudspeaker.**

reproduction (ˌriːprəˈdʌkʃən) *n.* **1.** *Biology.* any of various processes, either sexual or asexual, by which an animal or plant produces one or more individuals similar to itself. **2. a.** an imitation or facsimile of a work of art, esp. of a picture made by photoengraving. **b.** (*as modifier*): *a reproduction portrait.* Sometimes shortened to **repro. 3.** the quality of sound from an audio system: *this amplifier gives excellent reproduction.* **4.** the act or process of reproducing. **5.** the state of being reproduced. **6.** a revival of an earlier production, as of a play.

reproduction proof *n. Printing.* a proof of very good quality used for photographic reproduction to make a printing plate. Sometimes shortened to **repro** or **repro proof.**

reproductive (ˌriːprəˈdʌktɪv) *adj.* of, relating to, characteristic of, or taking part in reproduction. —**ˌreproˈductively** *adv.* —**ˌreproˈductiveness** *n.*

reprography (rɪˈprɒgrəfɪ) *n.* the art or process of copying, reprinting, or reproducing printed material. —**reprographic** (ˌrɛprəˈgræfɪk) *adj.* —**ˌreproˈgraphically** *adv.*

reproof (rɪˈpruːf) *n.* an act or expression of rebuke or censure. Also called: **reproval** (rɪˈpruːvᵊl). [C14 *reproffe,* from Old French *reprove,* from Late Latin *reprobāre* to disapprove of; see REPROBATE]

re-proof (riːˈpruːf) *vb.* (*tr.*) **1.** to treat (a coat, jacket, etc.) so as to renew its texture, waterproof qualities, etc. **2.** to provide a new proof of (a book, galley, etc.)

reprove (rɪˈpruːv) *vb.* (*tr.*) to speak disapprovingly to (a person); rebuke or scold. [C14: from Old French *reprover,* from Late Latin *reprobāre,* from Latin RE- + *probāre* to examine, APPROVE] —**reˈprovable** *adj.* —**reˈprover** *n.* —**reˈproving** *adj.* —**reˈprovingly** *adv.*

rept *abbrev. for:* **1.** receipt. **2.** report.

reptant (ˈrɛptənt) *adj. Biology.* creeping, crawling, or lying along the ground. Also: **repent.** [C17: from Latin *reptāre* to creep]

reptile (ˈrɛptaɪl) *n.* **1.** any of the cold-blooded vertebrates constituting the class *Reptilia,* characterized by lungs, an outer covering of horny scales or plates, and young produced in amniotic eggs. The class today includes the tortoises, turtles, snakes, lizards, and crocodiles; in Mesozoic times it was the dominant group, containing the dinosaurs and related forms. **2.** a grovelling insignificant person: *you miserable little reptile!* ~*adj.* **3.** creeping, crawling, or squirming. **4.** grovelling or insignificant; mean; contemptible. [C14: from Late Latin *reptilis* creeping, from Latin *rēpere* to crawl]

reptilian (rɛpˈtɪlɪən) *adj.* **1.** of, relating to, resembling, or characteristic of reptiles. **2.** mean or treacherous; contemptible: *reptilian behaviour.* ~*n.* **3.** a less common name for **reptile.**

Repub. *abbrev. for:* **1.** Republic. **2.** Republican.

republic (rɪˈpʌblɪk) *n.* **1.** a form of government in which the people or their elected representatives possess the supreme power. **2.** a political or national unit possessing such a form of government. **3.** a constitutional form in which the head of state is an elected or nominated president. **4.** any community or group that resembles a political republic in that its members or elements exhibit a general equality, shared interests, etc.: *the republic of letters.* [C17: from French *république,* from Latin *rēspublica* literally: the public thing, from *rēs* thing + *publica* PUBLIC]

republican (rɪˈpʌblɪkən) *adj.* **1.** of, resembling, or relating to a republic. **2.** supporting or advocating a republic. ~*n.* **3.** a supporter or advocate of a republic.

Republican (rɪˈpʌblɪkən) *adj.* **1.** of, belonging to, or relating to a Republican Party, esp. in the U.S. **2.** of, belonging to, or relating to the Irish Republican Army (IRA), a militant organization of Irish nationalists. ~*n.* **3.** a member or supporter of a Republican Party. **4.** a member or supporter of the IRA.

republicanism (rɪˈpʌblɪkəˌnɪzəm) *n.* **1.** the principles or theory of republican government. **2.** support for a republic. **3.** (*often cap.*) support for a Republican Party or for the IRA.

republicanize *or* **republicanise** (rɪˈpʌblɪkəˌnaɪz) *vb.* (*tr.*) to make republican. —**reˌpublicaniˈzation** *or* **reˌpublicaniˈsation** *n.*

repudiate (rɪˈpjuːdɪˌeɪt) *vb.* (*tr.*) **1.** to reject the authority or validity of; refuse to accept or ratify: *Congress repudiated the treaty that the President had negotiated.* **2.** to refuse to acknowledge or pay (a debt). **3.** to cast off or disown (a son, lover, etc.). [C16: from Latin *repudiāre* to put away, from *repudium* a separation, divorce, from RE- + *pudēre* to be ashamed] —**reˈpudiable** *adj.* —**reˌpudiˈation** *n.* —**reˈpudiative** *adj.* —**reˈpudiˌator** *n.*

repugn (rɪˈpjuːn) *vb. Archaic.* to oppose or conflict (with). [C14: from Old French *repugner,* from Latin *repugnāre* to fight against, from RE- + *pugnāre* to fight]

repugnant (rɪˈpʌgnənt) *adj.* **1.** repellent to the senses; causing aversion. **2.** distasteful; offensive; disgusting. **3.** contradictory; inconsistent or incompatible. [C14: from Latin *repugnāns* resisting; see REPUGN] —**reˈpugnance** *or* (*now rare*) **reˈpugnancy** *n.* —**reˈpugnantly** *adv.*

repulse (rɪˈpʌls) *vb.* (*tr.*) **1.** to drive back or ward off (an attacking force); repel; rebuff. **2.** to reject with coldness or discourtesy: *she repulsed his advances.* ~*n.* **3.** the act or an instance of driving back or warding off; rebuff. **4.** a cold discourteous rejection or refusal. [C16: from Latin *repellere* to drive back, REPEL] —**reˈpulser** *n.*

▷**Usage.** The verbs *repulse* and *repel* share a common meaning of physically driving back or away, but they can be carefully distinguished in other senses. Although the related adjective *repulsive* has the meaning of causing feelings of disgust, *repulse* does not mean to drive away by arousing disgust. Instead, *repel* is normally used in this sense, and *repulse* is used when the required meaning is to reject coldly or drive away with discourtesy.

repulsion (rɪˈpʌlʃən) *n.* **1.** a feeling of disgust or aversion. **2.** *Physics.* a force tending to separate two objects, such as the force between two like electric charges or magnetic poles.

repulsive (rɪˈpʌlsɪv) *adj.* **1.** causing or occasioning repugnance; loathsome; disgusting or distasteful: *a repulsive sight.* **2.** tending to repel, esp. by coldness and discourtesy. **3.** *Physics.* concerned with, producing, or being a repulsion. —**reˈpulsively** *adv.* —**reˈpulsiveness** *n.*

reputable (ˈrɛpjʊtəbᵊl) *adj.* **1.** having a good reputation; honoured, trustworthy, or respectable. **2.** (of words) acceptable as good usage; standard. —**ˌreputaˈbility** *n.* —**ˈreputably** *adv.*

reputation (ˌrɛpjʊˈteɪʃən) *n.* **1.** the estimation in which a person or thing is generally held; opinion. **2.** a high opinion generally held about a person or thing; esteem. **3.** notoriety or fame, esp. for some specified characteristic. **4. have a reputation.** to be known or notorious, esp. for promiscuity, excessive drinking, or the like. [C14: from Latin *reputātiō* a reckoning, from *reputāre* to calculate, meditate; see REPUTE] —**ˌrepuˈtationless** *adj.*

repute (rɪˈpjuːt) *vb.* **1.** (*tr.; usually passive*) to consider (a person or thing) to be as specified: *he is reputed to be intelligent.* ~*n.* **2.** public estimation; reputation: *a writer of little repute.* [C15: from Old French *reputer,* from Latin *reputāre* to think over, from RE- + *putāre* to think]

reputed (rɪˈpjuːtɪd) *adj.* (*prenominal*) generally reckoned or considered; supposed or alleged: *he is the reputed writer of two epic poems.* —**reˈputedly** *adv.*

req. *abbrev. for:* **1.** request. **2.** required. **3.** requisition.

reˈprocess *vb.*
reˈprocessing *adj.*
ˌreproˈgrammable *or*
ˌreproˈgramable *adj.*
ˌreproˈvision *vb.*
ˌrepubliˈcation *n.*
reˈpublish *vb.*
reˈpurchase *vb., n.*
reˈpuriˌfy *vb.,* **-ˌfies, -ˌfying, -ˌfied.**

request (rɪˈkwɛst) *vb.* (*tr.*) **1.** to express a desire for, esp. politely; ask for or demand: *to request a bottle of wine.* ~*n.* **2. a.** the act or an instance of requesting, esp. in the form of a written statement; petition or solicitation: *a request for a song.* **b.** (*as modifier*): *a request programme.* **3. at the request of.** in accordance with the specific demand or wish of (someone). **4. by request.** in accordance with someone's desire. **5. in request.** in demand; popular: *he is in request in concert halls all over the world.* **6. on request.** on the occasion of a demand or request: *application forms are available on request.* [C14: from Old French *requeste,* from Vulgar Latin *requaerere* (unattested) to seek after; see REQUIRE, QUEST] —reˈ**quester** *n.*

request stop *n.* a point on a route at which a bus will stop only if signalled to do so. U.S. equivalent: **flag stop.**

Requiem (ˈrɛkwɪˌɛm) *n.* **1.** *R.C. Church.* a Mass celebrated for the dead. **2.** a musical setting of this Mass. **3.** any piece of music composed or performed as a memorial to a dead person or persons. [C14: from Latin *requiēs* rest, from the opening of the introit, *Requiem aeternam dona eis* Rest eternal grant unto them]

requiem shark *n.* any shark of the family *Carcharhinidae,* occurring mostly in tropical seas and characterized by a nictitating membrane and a heterocercal tail. The family includes the tiger shark and the soupfin. [C17: French *requiem* probably assimilated from a native name]

requiescat (ˌrɛkwɪˈɛskæt) *n.* a prayer for the repose of the souls of the dead. [Latin, from *requiescat in pace* may he rest in peace]

require (rɪˈkwaɪə) *vb.* (*mainly tr.; may take a clause as object or an infinitive*) **1.** to have need of; depend upon; want. **2.** to impose as a necessity; make necessary: *this work requires precision.* **3.** (*also intr.*) to make formal request (for); insist upon or demand, esp. as an obligation. **4.** to call upon or oblige (a person) authoritatively; order or command: *to require someone to account for his actions.* [C14: from Old French *requerre,* from Vulgar Latin *requaerere* (unattested) to seek after, from Latin *requīrere* to seek to know, but also influenced by *quaerere* to seek] —reˈ**quirable** *adj.* —reˈ**quirer** *n.*

requirement (rɪˈkwaɪəmənt) *n.* **1.** something demanded or imposed as an obligation: *Latin is no longer a requirement for entry to university.* **2.** a thing desired or needed. **3.** the act or an instance of requiring.

requisite (ˈrɛkwɪzɪt) *adj.* **1.** absolutely essential; indispensable. ~*n.* **2.** something indispensable; necessity. [C15: from Latin *requīsītus* sought after, from *requīrere* to seek for, REQUIRE] —ˈ**requisitely** *adv.* —ˈ**requisiteness** *n.*

requisition (ˌrɛkwɪˈzɪʃən) *n.* **1.** a request or demand, esp. an authoritative or formal one. **2.** an official form on which such a demand is made. **3.** the act of taking something over, esp. temporarily for military or public use in time of emergency. **4.** a necessary or essential condition; requisite. **5.** a formal request by one government to another for the surrender of a fugitive from justice. ~*vb.* (*tr.*) **6.** to demand and take for use or service, esp. by military or public authority. **7.** (*may take an infinitive*) to require (someone) formally to do (something): *to requisition a soldier to drive a staff officer's car.* —ˌ**requiˈsitionary** *adj.*

requital (rɪˈkwaɪtᵊl) *n.* **1.** the act or an instance of requiting. **2.** a return or compensation for a good or bad action.

requite (rɪˈkwaɪt) *vb.* (*tr.*) to make return to (a person for a kindness or injury); repay with a similar action. [C16: RE- + obsolete *quite* to discharge, repay; see QUIT] —reˈ**quitable** *adj.* —reˈ**quitement** *n.* —reˈ**quiter** *n.*

reradiation (ˌriːreɪdɪˈeɪʃən) *n.* radiation resulting from the previous absorption of primary radiation.

reredorter (ˈrɪəˌdɔːtə) *n. History.* a privy at the back of a monastic dormitory.

reredos (ˈrɪədɒs) *n.* **1.** a screen or wall decoration at the back of an altar, in the form of a hanging, tapestry, painting, or piece of metalwork or sculpture. **2.** another word for **fireback** (sense 1). [C14: from Old French *areredos,* from *arere* behind + *dos* back, from Latin *dorsum*]

reremouse *or* **rearmouse** (ˈrɪəˌmaʊs) *n., pl.* **-mice.** an archaic or dialect word for **bat** (the animal). [Old English *hrēremūs,* probably from *hrēran* to move + *mūs* MOUSE]

rerun *vb.* (riːˈrʌn), **-runs, -running, -ran.** (*tr.*) **1.** to broadcast or put on (a film, play, series, etc.) again. **2.** to run (a race, etc.) again. ~*n.* (ˈriːˌrʌn). **3.** a film, play, series, etc., that is broadcast or put on again; repeat. **4.** a race that is run again. **5.** *Computer technol.* the repeat of a part of a computer program.

res (reɪs) *n., pl.* **res.** *Latin.* a thing, matter, or object.

res. *abbrev. for:* **1.** research. **2.** reserve. **3.** residence. **4.** resides. **5.** resigned. **6.** resolution.

res adjudicata (ˈreɪs əˌdʒuːdɪˈkɑːtə) *n.* another term for **res judicata.**

resale (ˈriːˌseɪl, riːˈseɪl) *n.* the selling again of something purchased. —reˈ**salable** *or* reˈ**saleable** *adj.*

resale price maintenance *n.* the practice by which a manufacturer establishes a fixed or minimum price for the resale of a brand product by retailers or other distributors. U.S. equivalent: **fair trade.** Abbrev.: **rpm.**

rescind (rɪˈsɪnd) *vb.* (*tr.*) to annul or repeal. [C17: from Latin *rēscindere* to cut off, from *re-* (intensive) + *scindere* to cut] —reˈ**scindable** *adj.* —reˈ**scinder** *n.* —reˈ**scindment** *n.*

rescissible (rɪˈsɪsəbᵊl) *adj.* able to be rescinded.

rescission (rɪˈsɪʒən) *n.* the act of rescinding.

rescissory (rɪˈsɪsərɪ) *adj.* having the power to rescind.

rescript (ˈriːˌskrɪpt) *n.* **1.** (in ancient Rome) an ordinance taking the form of a reply by the emperor to a question on a point of law. **2.** any official announcement or edict; a decree. **3.** something rewritten. **4.** the act or process of rewriting. [C16: from Latin *rēscriptum* a reply, from *rēscribere* to write back]

rescue (ˈrɛskjuː) *vb.* **-cues, -cuing, -cued.** (*tr.*) **1.** to bring (someone or something) out of danger, attack, harm, etc.; deliver or save. **2.** to free (a person) from legal custody by force. **3.** *Law.* to seize (goods or property) by force. ~*n.* **4. a.** the act or an instance of rescuing. **b.** (*as modifier*): *a rescue party.* **5.** the forcible removal of a person from legal custody. **6.** *Law.* the forcible seizure of goods or property. [C14: *rescowen,* from Old French *rescourre,* from RE- + *escourre* to pull away, from Latin *excutere* to shake off, from *quatere* to shake] —ˈ**rescuable** *adj.* —ˈ**rescuer** *n.*

research (rɪˈsɜːtʃ) *n.* **1.** systematic investigation to establish facts or principles or to collect information on a subject. ~*vb.* **2.** to carry out investigations into (a subject, problem, etc.). [C16: from Old French *recercher* to seek, search again, from RE- + *cercher* to SEARCH] —reˈ**searchable** *adj.* —reˈ**searcher** *n.*

research and development *n.* the part of a commercial company's activity concerned with applying the results of scientific research to develop new products and improve existing ones. Abbrev.: **R & D.**

reseat (riːˈsiːt) *vb.* (*tr.*) **1.** to show (a person) to a new seat. **2.** to put a new seat on (a chair, etc.). **3.** to provide new seats for (a hall, theatre, etc.). **4.** to re-form the seating of (a valve).

reseau (ˈrɛzəʊ) *n., pl.* **-seaux** (-zəʊ, -zəʊz) *or* **-seaus. 1.** a mesh background to a lace or other pattern. **2.** *Astronomy.* a network of fine lines cut into a glass plate used as a reference grid on star photographs. **3.** *Photog.* a screen covered in a regular pattern of minute coloured dots or lines, formerly used in colour photography. [C19: from French, from Old French *resel* a little net, from *rais* net, from Latin *rēte*]

resect (rɪˈsɛkt) *vb.* (*tr.*) *Surgery.* to cut out part of (a bone, an organ, or other structure or part). [C17: from Latin *resecāre* to cut away, from RE- + *secāre* to cut]

resection (rɪˈsɛkʃən) *n.* **1.** *Surgery.* excision of part of a bone, organ, or other part. **2.** *Surveying.* a method of fixing the position of a point by making angular observations to three fixed points. —reˈ**sectional** *adj.*

reseda (ˈrɛsɪdə) *n.* **1.** any plant of the genus *Reseda,* of the Mediterranean region, including mignonette and dyer's rocket, which has small spikes of grey-green flowers. ~*adj.* **2.** of a greyish-green colour; mignonette. [C18: from New Latin, from Latin: heal! from *resēdāre* to assuage, from RE- + *sēdāre* to soothe; see SEDATE[2]]

reselect (ˌriːsɪˈlɛkt) *vb.* (*tr.*) to choose (someone or something) again, esp. to choose an existing office-holder as candidate for re-election. —ˌ**reseˈlection** *n.*

resemblance (rɪˈzɛmbləns) *n.* **1.** the state or quality of resembling; likeness or similarity in nature, appearance, etc. **2.** the degree or extent to which or the respect in which a likeness exists. **3.** something resembling something else; semblance; likeness. —reˈ**semblant** *adj.*

resemble (rɪˈzɛmbᵊl) *vb.* (*tr.*) to possess some similarity to; be like. [C14: from Old French *resembler,* from RE- + *sembler* to look like, from Latin *similis* like] —reˈ**sembler** *n.*

resent (rɪˈzɛnt) *vb.* (*tr.*) to feel bitter, indignant, or aggrieved at. [C17: from French *ressentir,* from RE- + *sentir* to feel, from Latin *sentīre* to perceive; see SENSE]

resentful (rɪˈzɛntful) *adj.* feeling or characterized by resentment. —reˈ**sentfully** *adv.* —reˈ**sentfulness** *n.*

resentment (rɪˈzɛntmənt) *n.* anger, bitterness, or ill will.

reserpine (ˈrɛsəpɪn) *n.* an insoluble alkaloid, extracted from the roots of the plant *Rauwolfia serpentina,* used medicinally to lower blood pressure and as a sedative and tranquillizer. Formula: $C_{33}H_{40}N_2O_9$; melting pt.: 264–5°C. [C20: from German *Reserpin,* probably from the New Latin name of the plant]

reservation (ˌrɛzəˈveɪʃən) *n.* **1.** the act or an instance of reserving. **2.** something reserved, esp. hotel accommodation, a seat on an aeroplane, in a theatre, etc. **3.** (*often pl.*) a stated or unstated qualification of opinion that prevents one's wholehearted acceptance of a proposal, claim, statement, etc. **4.** an area of land set aside, esp. (in the U.S. and Canada) for American Indian peoples. **5.** *Brit.* the strip of land between the two carriageways of a dual carriageway. **6.** the act or process of keeping back, esp. for oneself; withholding. **7.** *Law.* a right or interest retained by the

reˈ**quicken** *vb.*
reˈ**read** *vb.,* **-ˈreads, -ˈreading, -ˈread.**
ˌ**rereˈcord** *vb.*
ˌ**rereˈcording** *n.*
reˈ**roof** *vb.*
reˈ**route** *vb.*
reˈ**schedule** *vb.*
reˈ**seal** *vb.*
reˈ**sealable** *adj.*
re-ˈ**search** *vb.*
reˈ**sell** *vb.,* **-ˈsells, -ˈselling, -ˈsold.**

grantor in property granted, conveyed, leased, etc., to another: *a reservation of rent.*

reserve (rɪˈzɜːv) *vb.* (*tr.*) **1.** to keep back or set aside, esp for future use or contingency; withhold. **2.** to keep for oneself; retain: *I reserve the right to question these men later.* **3.** to obtain or secure by advance arrangement: *I have reserved two tickets for tonight's show.* **4.** to delay delivery of (a judgment), esp. in order to allow time for full consideration of the issues involved. ~*n.* **5. a.** something kept back or set aside, esp. for future use or contingency. **b.** (*as modifier*): *a reserve stock.* **6.** the state or condition of being reserved: *I have plenty in reserve.* **7.** a tract of land set aside for the protection and conservation of wild animals, flowers, etc.: *a nature reserve.* **8.** the usual Canadian name for **(Indian) reservation** (sense 4). **9.** *Austral. and N.Z.* an area of publicly owned land set aside for sport, recreation, etc. **10.** the act of reserving; reservation. **11.** a member of a team who only plays if a playing member drops out; a substitute. **12.** (*often pl.*) **a.** a part of an army or formation not committed to immediate action in a military engagement. **b.** that part of a nation's armed services not in active service. **13.** coolness or formality of manner; restraint, silence, or reticence. **14.** *Finance.* **a.** a portion of capital not invested (a **capital reserve**) or a portion of profits not distributed (a **revenue** or **general reserve**) by a bank or business enterprise and held to meet legal requirements, future liabilities, or contingencies. **b.** (*often pl.*) liquid assets held by an organization, government, etc., to meet expenses and liabilities. **15. without reserve.** without reservations; fully; wholeheartedly. [C14: from Old French *reserver,* from Latin *reservāre* to save up, from RE- + *servāre* to keep] —**reˈservable** *adj.* —**reˈserver** *n.*

re-serve (riːˈsɜːv) *vb.* (*tr.*) to serve again.

reserve bank *n.* one of the twelve banks forming part of the U.S. Federal Reserve System.

reserve currency *n.* foreign currency that is acceptable as a medium of international payments and that is therefore held in reserve by many countries.

reserved (rɪˈzɜːvd) *adj.* **1.** set aside for use by a particular person or people: *this table is reserved.* **2.** cool or formal in manner; restrained, silent, or reticent. **3.** destined; fated: *a man reserved for great things.* —**reservedly** (rɪˈzɜːvɪdlɪ) *adv.* —**reˈservedness** *n.*

reserved list *n. Brit.* a list of retired naval, army, or air-force officers available for recall to active service in an emergency.

reserved occupation *n. Brit.* in time of war, an occupation from which one will not be called up for military service.

reserved word *n.* a word in a programming language or computer system that has a fixed meaning and therefore cannot be redefined by a programmer.

reserve-grade *adj. Austral.* denoting a sporting team of the second rank in a club.

reserve price *n. Brit.* the minimum price acceptable to the owner of property being auctioned or sold. Also called (esp. Scot. and U.S.): **upset price.**

reserve tranche *n.* the quota of 25 per cent to which a member of the IMF has unconditional access. Prior to 1978 it was paid in gold and known as the **gold tranche.**

reservist (rɪˈzɜːvɪst) *n.* one who serves in the reserve formations of a nation's armed forces.

reservoir (ˈrɛzəˌvwɑː) *n.* **1.** a natural or artificial lake or large tank used for collecting and storing water, esp. for community water supplies or irrigation. **2.** a receptacle for storing gas, esp. one attached to a stove. **3.** *Biology.* a vacuole or cavity in an organism, containing a secretion or some other fluid. **4.** *Anatomy.* another name for **cisterna.** **5.** a place where a great stock of anything is accumulated. **6.** a large supply of something; reserve: *a reservoir of talent.* [C17: from French *réservoir,* from *réserver* to RESERVE]

reset[1] *vb.* (riːˈsɛt), **-sets, -setting, -set.** (*tr.*) **1.** to set again (a broken bone, matter in type, a gemstone, etc.). **2.** to restore (a gauge, dial, etc.) to zero. **3.** Also: **clear.** to restore (the contents of a register or similar device) in a computer system to zero. ~*n.* (ˈriːˌsɛt). **4.** the act or an instance of setting again. **5.** a thing that is set again. **6.** a plant that has been recently transplanted. **7.** a device for resetting instruments, controls, etc. —**reˈsetter** *n.*

reset[2] *Scot.* ~*vb.* (riːˈsɛt). **-sets, -setting, -set.** **1.** to receive or handle goods knowing they have been stolen. ~*n.* (ˈriːsɛt). **2.** the receiving of stolen goods. [C14: from Old French *receter,* from Latin *receptāre,* from *recipere* to receive] —**reˈsetter** *n.*

res gestae (ˈreɪs ˈdʒɛstiː) *pl. n.* **1.** things done or accomplished; achievements. **2.** *Law.* incidental facts and circumstances that are admissible in evidence because they introduce or explain the matter in issue. [Latin]

resh (reɪʃ; *Hebrew* reʃ) *n.* the 20th letter in the Hebrew alphabet (ר), transliterated as *r.* [from Hebrew, from *rōsh* head]

reshuffle (riːˈʃʌfəl) *n.* **1.** an act of shuffling again. **2.** a reorganization, esp. of jobs within a government or cabinet. ~*vb.* **3.** to carry out a reshuffle (on).

reside (rɪˈzaɪd) *vb.* (*intr.*) *Formal.* **1.** to live permanently or for a considerable time (in a place); have one's home (in): *he now resides in London.* **2.** (of things, qualities, etc.) to be inherently present (in); be vested (in): *political power resides in military strength.* [C15: from Latin *residēre* to sit back, from RE- + *sedēre* to sit] —**reˈsider** *n.*

residence (ˈrɛzɪdəns) *n.* **1.** the place in which one resides; abode or home. **2.** a large imposing house; mansion. **3.** the fact of residing in a place or a period of residing. **4.** the official house of the governor of any of various countries. **5.** the state of being officially present. **6. in residence. a.** actually resident: *the royal standard indicates that the Queen is in residence.* **b.** designating a creative artist resident for a set period at a university, college, etc., whose role is to stimulate an active interest in the subject: *composer in residence.* **7.** the seat of some inherent quality, characteristic, etc.

residency (ˈrɛzɪdənsɪ) *n., pl.* **-cies.** **1.** a variant of **residence.** **2.** a regular series of concerts by a band or singer at one venue. **3.** *U.S. and Canadian.* the period, following internship, during which a physician undergoes further clinical training, usually in one medical speciality. **4.** (in India, formerly) the official house of the governor general at the court of a native prince.

resident (ˈrɛzɪdənt) *n.* **1.** a person who resides in a place. **2.** *Social welfare.* an occupant of a welfare agency home. Former name: **inmate.** **3.** (esp. formerly) a representative of the British government in a British protectorate. **4.** (esp. in the 17th century) a diplomatic representative ranking below an ambassador. **5.** (in India, formerly) a representative of the British governor general at the court of a native prince. **6.** a bird or other animal that does not migrate. **7.** *U.S. and Canadian.* a physician who lives in the hospital where he works while undergoing specialist training after completing his internship. Compare **house physician.** **8.** *Brit. and N.Z.* a junior doctor who lives in the hospital where he works. ~*adj.* **9.** living in a place; residing. **10.** living or staying at a place in order to discharge a duty, etc. **11.** (of qualities, characteristics, etc.) existing or inherent (in). **12.** (of birds and other animals) not in the habit of migrating. —ˈ**residentˌship** *n.*

resident commissioner *n.* the representative of Puerto Rico in the U.S. House of Representatives. He may speak but has no vote.

residential (ˌrɛzɪˈdɛnʃəl) *adj.* **1.** suitable for or allocated for residence: *a residential area.* **2.** relating to or having residence. —ˌ**resiˈdentially** *adv.*

residential care *n. Social welfare.* the provision by a welfare agency of a home with social-work supervision for people who need more than just housing accommodation, such as children in care or mentally handicapped adults.

residential school *n.* (in Canada) a boarding school maintained by the Canadian government for Indian and Inuit children from sparsely populated settlements.

residentiary (ˌrɛzɪˈdɛnʃərɪ) *adj.* **1.** residing in a place, esp. officially; resident. **2.** subject to an obligation to reside in an official residence: *a residentiary benefice.* ~*n., pl.* **-tiaries.** **3.** a clergyman obliged to reside in the place of his official appointment.

residents association *n.* an organization composed of voluntary members living in a particular neighbourhood, which aims to improve the social and communal facilities of the neighbourhood and to conserve or improve its environmental advantages. See also **community association, tenants association.**

residual (rɪˈzɪdjʊəl) *adj.* **1.** of, relating to, or designating a residue or remainder; remaining; left over. **2.** (of deposits, soils, etc.) formed by the weathering of pre-existing rocks and the removal of disintegrated material. **3.** of or relating to the payment of residuals. ~*n.* **4.** something left over as a residue; remainder. **5.** *Statistics.* **a.** the difference between the mean of a set of observations and one particular observation. **b.** the difference between the numerical value of one particular observation and the theoretical result. **6.** (*often pl.*) payment made to an actor, actress, musician, etc., for subsequent use of film in which the person appears. —**reˈsidually** *adv.*

residual unemployment *n.* the unemployment that remains in periods of full employment, as a result of those mentally, physically, or emotionally unfit to work.

residuary (rɪˈzɪdjʊərɪ) *adj.* **1.** of, relating to, or constituting a residue; residual. **2.** *Law.* entitled to the residue of an estate after payment of debts and distribution of specific gifts.

residue (ˈrɛzɪˌdjuː) *n.* **1.** matter remaining after something has been removed. **2.** *Law.* what is left of an estate after the discharge of debts and distribution of specific gifts. [C14: from Old French *residu,* from Latin *residuus* remaining over, from *residēre* to stay behind, RESIDE]

residuum (rɪˈzɪdjʊəm) *n., pl.* **-ua** (-jʊə). a more formal word for **residue.**

resign (rɪˈzaɪn) *vb.* **1.** (when *intr.*, often foll. by *from*) to give up tenure of (a job, office, etc.). **2.** (*tr.*) to reconcile (oneself) to; yield: *to resign oneself to death.* **3.** (*tr.*) to give up (a right, claim, etc.); relinquish: *he resigned his claim to the throne.* [C14: from

reˈsettle *vb.*
reˈsettlement *n.*
reˈshape *vb.*
reˈsharpen *vb.*
reˈship *vb.*, **-ˈships, -ˈshipping, -ˈshipped.**
reˈshoe *vb.*, **-ˈshoes, -ˈshoeing, -ˈshod.**

Old French *resigner,* from Latin *resignāre* to unseal, invalidate, destroy, from RE- + *signāre* to seal; see SIGN] —**re'signer** *n.*
re-sign (riː'saɪn) *vb.* to sign (a document, etc.) again.
resignation (ˌrɛzɪg'neɪʃən) *n.* **1.** the act of resigning. **2.** a formal document stating one's intention to resign. **3.** a submissive unresisting attitude; passive acquiescence.
resigned (rɪ'zaɪnd) *adj.* characteristic of or proceeding from an attitude of resignation; acquiescent or submissive. —**resignedly** (rɪ'zaɪnɪdlɪ) *adv.* —**re'signedness** *n.*
resile (rɪ'zaɪl) *vb.* (*intr.*) to spring or shrink back; recoil or resume original shape. [C16: from Old French *resilir,* from Latin *resilīre* to jump back, from RE- + *salīre* to jump] —**re'silement** *n.*
resilience (rɪ'zɪlɪəns) *n.* **1.** Also called: **resiliency.** the state or quality of being resilient. **2.** *Ecology.* the ability of an ecosystem to return to its original state after being disturbed. **3.** *Physics.* the amount of potential energy stored in an elastic material when deformed.
resilient (rɪ'zɪlɪənt) *adj.* **1.** (of an object or material) capable of regaining its original shape or position after bending, stretching, compression, or other deformation; elastic. **2.** (of a person) recovering easily and quickly from shock, illness, hardship, etc.; irrepressible. —**re'siliently** *adv.*
resin ('rɛzɪn) *n.* **1.** Also called: **rosin.** any of a group of solid or semisolid amorphous compounds that are obtained directly from certain plants as exudations. They are used in medicine and in varnishes. **2.** any of a large number of synthetic, usually organic, materials that have a polymeric structure, esp. such a substance in a raw state before it is moulded or treated with plasticizer, stabilizer, filler, etc. Compare **plastic** (sense 1). ~*vb.* **3.** (*tr.*) to treat or coat with resin. [C14: from Old French *resine,* from Latin *rēsīna,* from Greek *rhētinē* resin from a pine] —'**resinous** *adj.* —'**resinously** *adv.* —'**resinousness** *n.*
resinate ('rɛzɪˌneɪt) *vb.* (*tr.*) to impregnate with resin.
resiniferous (ˌrɛzɪ'nɪfərəs) *adj.* yielding or producing resin.
resinoid ('rɛzɪˌnɔɪd) *adj.* **1.** resembling, characteristic of, or containing resin. ~*n.* **2.** any resinoid substance, esp. a synthetic compound.
resipiscence (ˌrɛsɪ'pɪsəns) *n. Literary.* acknowledgment that one has been mistaken. [C16: from Late Latin *resipiscentia,* from *resipiscere* to recover one's senses, from Latin *sapere* to know] —ˌ**resi'piscent** *adj.*
res ipsa loquitur (reɪs ˌɪpsɑː 'lɒkwɪtə) *Law.* the thing or matter speaks for itself. [Latin]
resist (rɪ'zɪst) *vb.* **1.** to stand firm (against); not yield (to); fight (against). **2.** (*tr.*) to withstand the deleterious action of; be proof against: *to resist corrosion.* **3.** (*tr.*) to oppose; refuse to accept or comply with: *to resist arrest; resist the introduction of new technology.* **4.** (*tr.*) to refrain from, esp. in spite of temptation (esp. in the phrases **cannot** *or* **could not resist** (**something**)). ~*n.* **5.** a substance used to protect something, esp. a coating that prevents corrosion. [C14: from Latin *resistere* to stand still, oppose, from RE- + *sistere* to stand firm] —**re'sister** *n.* —**re'sistible** *adj.* —**reˌsisti'bility** *n.* —**re'sistibly** *adv.*
resistance (rɪ'zɪstəns) *n.* **1.** the act or an instance of resisting. **2.** the capacity to withstand something, esp. the body's natural capacity to withstand disease. **3. a.** the opposition to a flow of electric current through a circuit component, medium, or substance. It is the magnitude of the real part of the impedance and is measured in ohms. Symbol: *R* Compare **reactance** (sense 1). **b.** (*as modifier*): *resistance coupling; a resistance thermometer.* **4.** any force that tends to retard or oppose motion: *air resistance; wind resistance.* **5.** (in psychoanalytical theory) the tendency of a person to prevent the translation of repressed thoughts and ideas from the unconscious to the conscious and esp. to resist the analyst's attempt to bring this about. **6.** *Physics.* the magnitude of the real part of the acoustic or mechanical impedance. **7. line of least resistance.** the easiest, but not necessarily the best or most honourable, course of action. **8.** See **passive resistance.**
Resistance (rɪ'zɪstəns) *n.* (*modifier*) of or relating to an illegal organization fighting for national liberty in a country under enemy occupation, esp. in France during World War II: *a Resistance operation.*
resistance thermometer *n.* an accurate type of thermometer in which temperature is calculated from the resistance of a coil of wire (usually of platinum) or of a semiconductor placed at the point at which the temperature is to be measured.
resistance welding *n.* a welding technique in which the parts to be joined are held together under pressure and heat is produced by passing a current through the contact resistance formed between the two surfaces.
resistant (rɪ'zɪstənt) *adj.* **1.** characterized by or showing resistance; resisting. **2. a.** impervious to the action of corrosive substances, heat, etc.: *a highly resistant surface.* **b.** (*in combination*): *a heat-resistant surface.* ~*n.* **3.** a person or thing that resists.
resistive (rɪ'zɪstɪv) *adj.* **1.** another word for **resistant. 2.** exhibiting electrical resistance.
resistivity (ˌriːzɪs'tɪvɪtɪ) *n.* **1.** the electrical property of a material that determines the resistance of a piece of given dimensions. It is equal to *RA/l,* where *R* is the resistance, *A* the cross-sectional area, and *l* the length, and is the reciprocal of conductivity. It is measured in ohms. Symbol: ρ Former name: **specific resistance. 2.** the power or capacity to resist; resistance.
resistless (rɪ'zɪstlɪs) *adj. Archaic.* **1.** unresisting. **2.** irresistible. —**re'sistlessly** *adv.*
resistor (rɪ'zɪstə) *n.* an electrical component designed to introduce a known value of resistance into a circuit.
resit *vb.* (riː'sɪt), **-sits, -sitting, -sat.** (*tr.*) **1.** to sit (an examination) again. ~*n.* ('riːsɪt). **2.** an examination taken again by a person who has not been successful in a previous attempt.
res judicata ('reɪs ˌdʒuːdɪ'kɑːtə) *or* **res adjudicata** *n. Law.* a matter already adjudicated upon that cannot be raised again. [Latin]
resnatron ('rɛznəˌtrɒn) *n.* a tetrode used to generate high power at high frequencies. [C20: from RESONATOR + -TRON]
resoluble (rɪ'zɒljʊbᵊl, 'rɛzəl-) *or* **resolvable** *adj.* able to be resolved or analysed. [C17: from Late Latin *resolubilis,* from Latin *resolvere* to reveal; see RESOLVE] —**reˌsolu'bility, reˌsolva'bility** *or* **re'solubleness, re'solvableness** *n.*
re-soluble (riː'sɒljʊbᵊl) *adj.* capable of being dissolved again. —**re-'solubleness** *or* **re-ˌsolu'bility** *n.* —**re-'solubly** *adv.*
resolute ('rɛzəˌluːt) *adj.* **1.** firm in purpose or belief; steadfast. **2.** characterized by resolution; determined: *a resolute answer.* [C16: from Latin *resolutus,* from *resolvere* to RESOLVE] —'**resoˌlutely** *adv.* —'**resoˌluteness** *n.*
resolution (ˌrɛzə'luːʃən) *n.* **1.** the act or an instance of resolving. **2.** the condition or quality of being resolute; firmness or determination. **3.** something resolved or determined; decision. **4.** a formal expression of opinion by a meeting, esp. one agreed by a vote. **5.** a judicial decision on some matter; verdict; judgment. **6.** the act or process of separating something into its constituent parts or elements. **7.** *Med.* **a.** return from a pathological to a normal condition. **b.** subsidence of the symptoms of a disease, esp. the disappearance of inflammation without the formation of pus. **8.** *Music.* the process in harmony whereby a dissonant note or chord is followed by a consonant one. **9.** the ability of a television or film image to reproduce fine detail. **10.** *Physics.* another word for **resolving power.** —ˌ**reso'lutioner** *or* ˌ**reso'lutionist** *n.*
resolutive (rɪ'zɒljʊtɪv) *adj.* **1.** capable of dissolving; causing disintegration. **2.** *Law.* denoting a condition the fulfilment of which terminates a contract or other legal obligation.
resolvable (rɪ'zɒlvəbᵊl) *adj.* another word for **resoluble.**
resolve (rɪ'zɒlv) *vb.* (*mainly tr.*) **1.** (*takes a clause as object or an infinitive*) to decide or determine firmly. **2.** to express (an opinion) formally, esp. (of a public meeting) one agreed by a vote. **3.** (*also intr.;* usually foll. by *into*) to separate or cause to separate (into) (constituent parts or elements). **4.** (*usually reflexive*) to change, alter, or appear to change or alter: *the ghost resolved itself into a tree.* **5.** to make up the mind of; cause to decide: *the tempest resolved him to stay at home.* **6.** to find the answer or solution to; solve: *to resolve a problem.* **7.** to explain away or dispel: *to resolve a doubt.* **8.** to bring to an end; conclude: *to resolve an argument.* **9.** *Med.* to cause (a swelling or inflammation) to subside, esp. without the formation of pus. **10.** (*also intr.*) to follow (a dissonant note or chord) or (of a dissonant note or chord) to be followed by one producing a consonance. **11.** *Chem.* to separate (a racemic mixture) into its optically active constituents. **12.** *Physics.* **a.** to distinguish between (separate parts) of (an image) as in a microscope, telescope, or other optical instrument. **b.** to separate (two adjacent peaks) in a spectrum by means of a spectrometer. **13.** *Maths.* to split (a vector) into its components in specified directions. **14.** an obsolete word for **dissolve.** ~*n.* **15.** something determined or decided; resolution: *he had made a resolve to work all day.* **16.** firmness of purpose; determination: *nothing can break his resolve.* [C14: from Latin *resolvere* to unfasten, reveal, from RE- + *solvere* to loosen; see SOLVE] —**re'solver** *n.*
resolved (rɪ'zɒlvd) *adj.* fixed in purpose or intention; determined. —**resolvedly** (rɪ'zɒlvɪdlɪ) *adv.* —**re'solvedness** *n.*
resolvent (rɪ'zɒlvənt) *adj.* **1.** serving to dissolve or separate something into its elements; resolving. ~*n.* **2.** something that resolves; solvent. **3.** a drug or agent able to reduce swelling or inflammation.
resolving power *n.* **1.** Also called: **resolution.** *Physics.* **a.** the ability of a microscope, telescope, or other optical instrument to produce separate images of closely placed objects. **b.** the ability of a spectrometer to separate two adjacent peaks in a spectrum. **2.** *Photog.* the ability of an emulsion to show up fine detail in an image.
resonance ('rɛzənəns) *n.* **1.** the condition or quality of being resonant. **2.** sound produced by a body vibrating in sympathy with a neighbouring source of sound. **3.** the condition of a body or system when it is subjected to a periodic disturbance of the same frequency as the natural frequency of the body or system. At this frequency the system displays an enhanced oscillation or vibration. **4.** amplification of speech sounds by sympathetic vibration in the bone structure of the head and chest, resounding

in the cavities of the nose, mouth, and pharynx. **5.** *Electronics.* the condition of an electrical circuit when the frequency is such that the capacitive and inductive reactances are equal in magnitude. In a series circuit there is then maximum alternating current whilst in a parallel circuit there is minimum alternating current. **6.** *Med.* the sound heard when tapping a hollow bodily structure, esp. the chest or abdomen. Change in the quality of the sound often indicates an underlying disease or disorder. **7.** *Chem.* the phenomenon in which the electronic structure of a molecule can be represented by two or more hypothetical structures involving single, double, and triple chemical bonds. The true structure is considered to be an average of these theoretical structures. **8.** *Physics.* **a.** the condition of a system in which there is a sharp maximum probability for the absorption of electromagnetic radiation or capture of particles. **b.** a type of elementary particle of extremely short lifetime. Resonances are regarded as excited states of more stable particles. [C16: from Latin *resonāre* to RESOUND]

resonant (ˈrɛzənənt) *adj.* **1.** (of sound) resounding or re-echoing. **2.** producing or enhancing resonance, as by sympathetic vibration. **3.** characterized by resonance. —**ˈresonantly** *adv.*

resonant cavity *n.* another name for **cavity resonator.**

resonate (ˈrɛzəˌneɪt) *vb.* **1.** to resound or cause to resound; reverberate. **2.** (of a mechanical system, electrical circuit, chemical compound, etc.) to exhibit or cause to exhibit resonance. [C19: from Latin *resonāre*] —ˌ**resoˈnation** *n.*

resonator (ˈrɛzəˌneɪtə) *n.* any body or system that displays resonance, esp. a tuned electrical circuit or a conducting cavity in which microwaves are generated by a resonant current.

resorb (rɪˈsɔːb) *vb.* (*tr.*) to absorb again. [C17: from Latin *resorbēre*, from RE- + *sorbēre* to suck in; see ABSORB] —**reˈsorbent** *adj.* —**reˈsorptive** *adj.*

resorcinol (rɪˈzɔːsɪˌnɒl) *n.* a colourless crystalline phenol with a sweet taste, used in making dyes, drugs, resins, and adhesives. Formula: $C_6H_4(OH)_2$; relative density: 1.27; melting pt.: 111°C; boiling pt. at 1 atm.: 276 °C. [C19: New Latin, from RESIN + ORCINOL] —**reˈsorcinal** *adj.*

resorption (rɪˈsɔːpʃən) *n.* **1.** the process of resorbing or the state of being resorbed. **2.** *Geology.* the remelting of a mineral by magma, resulting in a new crystal form being produced.

resort (rɪˈzɔːt) *vb.* (*intr.*) **1.** (usually foll. by *to*) to have recourse (to) for help, use, etc.: *to resort to violence.* **2.** to go, esp. often or habitually; repair: *to resort to the beach.* ~*n.* **3.** a place to which many people go for recreation, rest, etc.: *a holiday resort.* **4.** the use of something as a means, help, or recourse. **5.** the act of going to a place, esp. for recreation, rest, etc. **6. last resort.** the last possible course of action open to one. [C14: from Old French *resortir* to come out again, from RE- + *sortir* to emerge] —**reˈsorter** *n.*

re-sort (riːˈsɔːt) *vb.* (*tr.*) to sort again.

resound (rɪˈzaʊnd) *vb.* (*intr.*) **1.** to ring or echo with sound; reverberate: *the hall resounded with laughter.* **2.** to make a prolonged echoing noise: *the trumpet resounded.* **3.** (of sounds) to echo or ring. **4.** to be widely famous: *his achievements resounded throughout India.* [C14: from Old French *resoner*, from Latin *resonāre* to sound again]

re-sound (riːˈsaʊnd) *vb.* to sound or cause to sound again.

resounding (rɪˈzaʊndɪŋ) *adj.* **1.** clear and emphatic; unmistakable: *a resounding vote of confidence.* **2.** full of or characterized by resonance; reverberating: *a resounding slap.* —**reˈsoundingly** *adv.*

resource (rɪˈzɔːs, -ˈsɔːs) *n.* **1.** capability, ingenuity, and initiative; quick-wittedness: *a man of resource.* **2.** (*often pl.*) a source of economic wealth, esp. of a country (mineral, land, labour, etc.) or business enterprise (capital, equipment, personnel, etc.). **3.** a supply or source of aid or support; something resorted to in time of need. **4.** a means of doing something; expedient. [C17: from Old French *ressourse* relief, from *resourdre* to rise again, from Latin *resurgere*, from RE- + *surgere* to rise] —**reˈsourceless** *adj.* —**reˈsourcelessness** *n.*

resourceful (rɪˈzɔːsfʊl, -ˈsɔːs-) *adj.* ingenious, capable, and full of initiative, esp. in dealing with difficult situations. —**reˈsourcefully** *adv.* —**reˈsourcefulness** *n.*

resp. *abbrev. for:* **1.** respective(ly). **2.** respondent.

respect (rɪˈspɛkt) *n.* **1.** an attitude of deference, admiration, or esteem; regard. **2.** the state of being honoured or esteemed. **3.** a detail, point, or characteristic; particular: *he differs in some respects from his son.* **4.** reference or relation (esp. in the phrases **in respect of, with respect to**). **5.** polite or kind regard; consideration: *respect for people's feelings.* **6.** (*often pl.*) an expression of esteem or regard (esp. in the phrase **pay one's respects**). ~*vb.* (*tr.*) **7.** to have an attitude of esteem towards; show or have respect for: *to respect one's elders.* **8.** to pay proper attention to; not violate: *to respect Swiss neutrality.* **9.** to show consideration for; treat courteously or kindly. **10.** *Archaic.* to concern or refer to. [C14: from Latin *rēspicere* to look back, pay attention to, from RE- + *specere* to look]

respectable (rɪˈspɛktəbᵊl) *adj.* **1.** having or deserving the respect of other people; estimable; worthy. **2.** having good social standing or reputation. **3.** having socially or conventionally acceptable morals, standards, etc.: *a respectable woman.* **4.** relatively or fairly good; considerable: *a respectable salary.* **5.** fit to be seen by other people; presentable. —**reˌspectaˈbility** *or* (*less commonly*) **reˈspectableness** *n.* —**reˈspectably** *adv.*

respecter (rɪˈspɛktə) *n.* **1.** a person who respects someone or something. **2. no respecter of persons.** a person whose attitude and behaviour is uninfluenced by consideration of another's rank, power, wealth, etc.

respectful (rɪˈspɛktfʊl) *adj.* full of, showing, or giving respect. —**reˈspectfully** *adv.* —**reˈspectfulness** *n.*

respecting (rɪˈspɛktɪŋ) *prep.* concerning; regarding.

respective (rɪˈspɛktɪv) *adj.* **1.** belonging or relating separately to each of several people or things; several: *we took our respective ways home.* **2.** an archaic word for **respectful.** —**reˈspectiveness** *n.*

respectively (rɪˈspɛktɪvlɪ) *adv.* (in listing a number of items or attributes that refer to another list) separately in the order given: *he gave Janet and John a cake and a chocolate respectively.*

respirable (ˈrɛspɪrəbᵊl) *adj.* **1.** able to be breathed. **2.** suitable or fit for breathing. —ˌ**respiraˈbility** *n.*

respiration (ˌrɛspəˈreɪʃən) *n.* **1.** the process in living organisms of taking in oxygen from the surroundings and giving out carbon dioxide (**external respiration**). In terrestrial animals this is effected by breathing air. **2.** the chemical breakdown of complex organic substances, such as carbohydrates and fats, that takes place in the cells and tissues of animals and plants, during which energy is released and carbon dioxide produced (**internal respiration**). —**respiratory** (ˈrɛspərətərɪ, -trɪ) *or* (*rarely*) ˌ**resˈpiˈrational** *adj.*

respirator (ˈrɛspəˌreɪtə) *n.* **1.** an apparatus for providing long-term artificial respiration. **2.** Also called: **gas mask.** a device worn over the mouth and nose to prevent inhalation of noxious fumes or to warm cold air before it is breathed.

respiratory failure *n.* a condition in which the respiratory system is unable to provide an adequate supply of oxygen or to remove carbon dioxide efficiently.

respiratory quotient *n.* *Biology.* the ratio of the volume of carbon dioxide expired to the volume of oxygen consumed by an organism, tissue, or cell in a given time.

respiratory system *n.* the specialized organs, collectively, concerned with external respiration: in humans and other mammals it includes the trachea, bronchi, bronchioles, lungs, and diaphragm.

respire (rɪˈspaɪə) *vb.* **1.** to inhale and exhale (air); breathe. **2.** (*intr.*) to undergo the process of respiration. **3.** *Literary.* to breathe again in a relaxed or easy manner, as after stress or exertion. [C14: from Latin *rēspīrāre* to exhale, from RE- + *spīrāre* to breathe; see SPIRIT]

respite (ˈrɛspɪt, -paɪt) *n.* **1.** a pause from exertion; interval of rest. **2.** a temporary delay. **3.** a temporary stay of execution; reprieve. ~*vb.* **4.** (*tr.*) to grant a respite to; reprieve. [C13: from Old French *respit*, from Latin *respectus* a looking back; see RESPECT] —**ˈrespiteless** *adj.*

respite care *n.* *Social welfare.* occasional usually planned residential care for dependent old or handicapped people, to provide relief for their permanent carers.

resplendent (rɪˈsplɛndənt) *adj.* having a brilliant or splendid appearance. [C15: from *rēsplendēre* to shine brightly, from RE- + *splendēre* to shine; see SPLENDOUR] —**reˈsplendence** *or* **reˈsplendency** *n.* —**reˈsplendently** *adv.*

respond (rɪˈspɒnd) *vb.* **1.** to state or utter (something) in reply. **2.** (*intr.*) to act in reply; react: *to respond by issuing an invitation.* **3.** (*intr.*; foll. by *to*) to react favourably: *this patient will respond to treatment.* **4.** an archaic word for **correspond.** ~*n.* **5.** *Architect.* a pilaster or an engaged column that supports an arch or a lintel. **6.** *Christianity.* a choral anthem chanted in response to a lesson read at a church service. [C14: from Old French *respondre*, from Latin *rēspondēre* to return like for like, from RE- + *spondēre* to pledge; see SPOUSE, SPONSOR] —**reˈspondence** *or* **reˈspondency** *n.* —**reˈsponder** *n.*

respondent (rɪˈspɒndənt) *n.* **1.** *Law.* a person against whom a petition, esp. in a divorce suit, or appeal is brought. ~*adj.* **2.** a less common word for **responsive.**

responsa (rɪˈspɒnsə) *n.* *Judaism.* **1.** the plural of **responsum.** **2.** that part of rabbinic literature concerned with written rulings in answer to questions.

response (rɪˈspɒns) *n.* **1.** the act of responding; reply or reaction. **2.** *Bridge.* a bid replying to a partner's bid or double. **3.** (*usually pl.*) *Christianity.* a short sentence or phrase recited or sung by the choir or congregation in reply to the officiant at a church service. **4.** *Electronics.* the ratio of the output to the input level, at a particular frequency, of a transmission line or electrical device. **5.** any pattern of glandular, muscular, or electrical reactions that arises from stimulation of the nervous system. [C14: from Latin *rēsponsum* answer, from *rēspondēre* to RESPOND] —**reˈsponseless** *adj.*

responser *or* **responsor** (rɪˈspɒnsə) *n.* a radio or radar receiver used in conjunction with an interrogator to receive and display signals from a transponder.

response time *n.* *Computer technol.* the length of time taken by a system to respond to an instruction.

response variable *n.* *Statistics.* a more modern term for **dependent variable** (sense 2).

responsibility (rɪˌspɒnsəˈbɪlɪtɪ) *n., pl.* **-ties.** **1.** the state or position of being responsible. **2.** a person or thing for which one is responsible. 3. the ability or authority to act or decide on one's own, without supervision.

responsible (rɪ'spɒnsəbᵊl) *adj.* **1.** (*postpositive;* usually foll. by *for*) having control or authority (over). **2.** (*postpositive;* foll. by *to*) being accountable for one's actions and decisions (to): *to be responsible to one's commanding officer.* **3.** (of a position, duty, etc.) involving decision and accountability. **4.** (often foll. by *for*) being the agent or cause (of some action): *to be responsible for a mistake.* **5.** able to take rational decisions without supervision; accountable for one's own actions: *a responsible adult.* **6.** able to meet financial obligations; of sound credit. [C16: from Latin *rēsponsus,* from *rēspondēre* to RESPOND] —**re'sponsibleness** *n.* —**re'sponsibly** *adv.*

responsive (rɪ'spɒnsɪv) *adj.* **1.** reacting or replying quickly or favourably, as to a suggestion, initiative, etc. **2.** (of an organism) reacting to a stimulus. —**re'sponsively** *adv.* —**re'sponsiveness** *n.*

responsory (rɪ'spɒnsərɪ) *n., pl.* **-ries.** *Christianity.* an anthem or chant consisting of versicles and responses and recited or sung after a lesson in a church service. [C15: from Late Latin *rēsponsōrium,* from Latin *rēspondēre* to answer]

responsum (rɪ'spɒnsəm) *n., pl.* **-sa** (-sə). *Judaism.* a written answer from a rabbinic authority to a question submitted. [Latin, literally: reply, RESPONSE]

res publica ('reɪs 'pʊblɪˌkɑː) *n.* the state, republic, or commonwealth. [Latin, literally: the public thing]

rest[1] (rɛst) *n.* **1. a.** relaxation from exertion or labour. **b.** (*as modifier*): *a rest period.* **2.** repose; sleep. **3.** any relief or refreshment, as from worry or something troublesome. **4.** calm; tranquillity. **5.** death regarded as repose: *eternal rest.* **6.** cessation from motion. **7. at rest. a.** not moving; still. **b.** calm; tranquil. **c.** dead. **d.** asleep. **8.** a pause or interval. **9.** a mark in a musical score indicating a pause of specific duration. **10.** *Prosody.* a pause in or at the end of a line; caesura. **11.** a shelter or lodging: *a seaman's rest.* **12.** a thing or place on which to put something for support or to steady it; prop. **13.** *Billiards, snooker.* any of various special poles used as supports for the cue in shots that cannot be made using the hand as a support. **14. come to rest.** to slow down and stop. **15. lay to rest.** to bury (a dead person). **16. set (someone's mind) at rest.** to reassure (someone) or settle (someone's mind). ~*vb.* **17.** to take or give rest, as by sleeping, lying down, etc. **18.** to place or position (oneself, etc.) for rest or relaxation. **19.** (*tr.*) to place or position for support or steadying: *to rest one's elbows on the table.* **20.** (*intr.*) to be at ease; be calm. **21.** to cease or cause to cease from motion or exertion; halt. **22.** to lie dead and buried. **23.** (*intr.*) to remain without further attention or action: *let the matter rest.* **24.** to direct (one's eyes) or (of one's eyes) to be directed: *her eyes rested on the sleeping child.* **25.** to depend or cause to depend; base; rely: *the whole argument rests on one crucial fact.* **26.** to place or be placed, as blame, censure, etc. **27.** (*intr.;* foll. by *with, on, upon,* etc.) to be a responsibility (of): *it rests with us to apportion blame.* **28.** *Law.* to finish the introduction of evidence in (a case). **29. rest on one's laurels.** See **laurel** (sense 9). **30. rest on one's oars. a.** to stop rowing for a time. **b.** to stop doing anything for a time. [Old English *ræst, reste,* of Germanic origin; related to Gothic *rasta* a mile, Old Norse *röst* mile] —**'rester** *n.*

rest[2] (rɛst) *n.* (usually preceded by *the*) **1.** something left or remaining; remainder. **2.** the others: *the rest of the world.* ~*vb.* **3.** (*copula*) to continue to be (as specified); remain: *rest assured.* [C15: from Old French *rester* to remain, from Latin *rēstāre,* from RE- + *stāre* to STAND]

rest area *n. Austral. and N.Z.* a motorists' stopping place, usually off a highway, equipped with tables, seats, etc.

restate (riː'steɪt) *vb.* (*tr.*) to state or affirm again or in a new way. —**re'statement** *n.*

restaurant ('rɛstəˌrɒŋ, 'rɛstrɒŋ, -rɒnt) *n.* a commercial establishment where meals are prepared and served to customers. [C19: from French, from *restaurer* to RESTORE]

restaurant car *n. Brit.* a railway coach in which meals are served. Also called: **dining car.**

restaurateur (ˌrɛstərə'tɜː) *n.* a person who owns or runs a restaurant. [C18: via French from Late Latin *restaurātor* one who restores, from Latin *restaurāre* to RESTORE]

rest-cure *n.* **1.** a rest taken as part of a course of medical treatment, as for stress, anxiety, etc. **2.** an easy undemanding time or assignment: usually used with a negative: *it's no rest-cure, I can assure you.*

restful ('rɛstfʊl) *adj.* **1.** giving or conducive to rest. **2.** being at rest; tranquil; calm. —**'restfully** *adv.* —**'restfulness** *n.*

restharrow ('rɛstˌhærəʊ) *n.* any of several Eurasian papilionaceous plants of the genus *Ononis,* such as *O. repens* and *O. spinosa,* with tough woody stems and roots. [C16: from *rest,* variant of ARREST (to hinder, stop) + HARROW[1]]

rest-home *n.* an old people's home.

restiform ('rɛstɪˌfɔːm) *adj.* (esp. of bundles of nerve fibres) shaped like a cord or rope; cordlike. [C19: from New Latin *restiformis,* from Latin *restis* a rope + *forma* shape]

resting ('rɛstɪŋ) *adj.* **1.** not moving or working; at rest. **2.** *Euphemistic.* (of an actor) out of work. **3.** (esp. of plant spores) undergoing a period of dormancy before germination. **4.** (of cells) not undergoing mitosis.

resting place *n.* a place where someone or something rests, esp. (**last resting place**) the grave.

restitution (ˌrɛstɪ'tjuːʃən) *n.* **1.** the act of giving back something that has been lost or stolen. **2.** *Law.* the act of compensating for loss or injury by reverting as far as possible to the position before such injury occurred. **3.** the return of an object or system to its original state, esp. a restoration of shape after elastic deformation. [C13: from Latin *rēstitūtiō,* from *rēstituere* to rebuild, from RE- + *statuere* to set up] —**'restiˌtutive** *or* **ˌresti'tutory** *adj.*

restive ('rɛstɪv) *adj.* **1.** restless, nervous, or uneasy. **2.** impatient of control or authority. [C16: from Old French *restif* balky, from *rester* to remain] —**'restively** *adv.* —**'restiveness** *n.*

restless ('rɛstlɪs) *adj.* **1.** unable to stay still or quiet. **2.** ceaselessly active or moving: *the restless wind.* **3.** worried; anxious; uneasy. **4.** not restful; without repose: *a restless night.* —**'restlessly** *adv.* —**'restlessness** *n.*

rest mass *n.* the mass of an object that is at rest relative to an observer. It is the mass used in Newtonian mechanics.

restoration (ˌrɛstə'reɪʃən) *n.* **1.** the act of restoring or state of being restored, as to a former or original condition, place, etc. **2.** the replacement or giving back of something lost, stolen, etc. **3.** something restored, replaced, or reconstructed. **4.** a model or representation of an extinct animal, landscape of a former geological age, etc.

Restoration (ˌrɛstə'reɪʃən) *adj.* relating to or characteristic of the reign of Charles II (1660–85) in England, following the re-establishment of the monarchy: *Restoration drama.*

restorationism (ˌrɛstə'reɪʃəˌnɪzəm) *n.* belief in a future life in which men will be restored to a state of perfection and happiness. —**ˌresto'rationist** *n., adj.*

restorative (rɪ'stɒrətɪv) *adj.* **1.** tending to revive or renew health, spirits, etc. ~*n.* **2.** anything that restores or revives, esp. a drug or agent that promotes health or strength.

restore (rɪ'stɔː) *vb.* (*tr.*) **1.** to return (something, esp. a work of art or building) to an original or former condition. **2.** to bring back to health, good spirits, etc. **3.** to return (something lost, stolen, etc.) to its owner. **4.** to reintroduce or re-enforce: *to restore discipline.* **5.** to reconstruct (an extinct animal, former landscape, etc.). [C13: from Old French, from Latin *rēstaurāre* to rebuild, from RE- + *-staurāre,* as in *instaurāre* to renew] —**re'storable** *adj.* —**re'storableness** *n.* —**re'storer** *n.*

restrain (rɪ'streɪn) *vb.* (*tr.*) **1.** to hold (someone) back from some action, esp. by force. **2.** to deprive (someone) of liberty, as by imprisonment. **3.** to limit or restrict. [C14 *restreyne,* from Old French *rēstreindre,* from Latin *rēstringere* to draw back tightly, from RE- + *stringere* to draw, bind; see STRAIN[1]] —**re'strainable** *adj.* —**re'strained** *adj.* —**restrainedly** (rɪ'streɪnɪdlɪ) *adv.*

restrainer (rɪ'streɪnə) *n.* **1.** a person who restrains. **2.** a chemical, such as potassium bromide, added to a photographic developer in order to reduce the amount of fog on a film and to retard the development.

restraint (rɪ'streɪnt) *n.* **1.** the ability to control or moderate one's impulses, passions, etc.: *to show restraint.* **2.** the act of restraining or the state of being restrained. **3.** something that restrains; restriction. [C15: from Old French *restreinte,* from *restreindre* to RESTRAIN]

restraint of trade *n.* action tending to interfere with the freedom to compete in business.

restrict (rɪ'strɪkt) *vb.* (often foll. by *to*) to confine or keep within certain often specified limits or selected bounds: *to restrict one's drinking to the evening.* [C16: from Latin *rēstrictus* bound up, from *rēstringere;* see RESTRAIN]

restricted (rɪ'strɪktɪd) *adj.* **1.** limited or confined. **2.** not accessible to the general public or (*esp. U.S.*) out of bounds to military personnel. **3.** *Brit.* denoting or in a zone in which a speed limit or waiting restrictions for vehicles apply. —**re'strictedly** *adv.* —**re'strictedness** *n.*

restricted users group *n.* a group of people who, with knowledge of a secret password, or by some other method, have access to restricted information stored in a computer. Abbrev.: **RUG.**

restriction (rɪ'strɪkʃən) *n.* **1.** something that restricts; a restrictive measure, law, etc. **2.** the act of restricting or the state of being restricted. **3.** *Logic, maths.* a condition that imposes a constraint on the possible values of a variable or on the domain of arguments of a function. —**re'strictionist** *n., adj.*

restriction enzyme *n.* any of several enzymes produced by bacteria as a defence against viral infection and commonly used to cut DNA for genetic manipulation or diagnosis.

restriction fragment *n. Genetics.* a fragment of a DNA molecule cleaved by a restriction enzyme. See also **RFLP.**

restrictive (rɪ'strɪktɪv) *adj.* **1.** restricting or tending to restrict. **2.** *Grammar.* denoting a relative clause or phrase that restricts the number of possible referents of its antecedent. The relative clause in *Americans who live in New York* is restrictive; the

re'spray *vb., n.*
re'stack *vb.*
re'staff *vb.*
re'stage *vb.*
re'start *vb., n.*
re'stock *vb.*
re'straighten *vb.*

relative clause in *Americans, who are generally extrovert,* is nonrestrictive. —**re'strictively** *adv.* —**re'strictiveness** *n.*

restrictive covenant *n. Law.* a covenant imposing a restriction on the use of land for the purpose of preserving the enjoyment or value of adjoining land.

restrictive practice *n. Brit.* **1.** a trading agreement against the public interest. **2.** a practice of a union or other group tending to limit the freedom of other workers or employers.

rest room *n.* a room in a public building having lavatories, washing facilities, and sometimes couches.

rest stop *n.* the U.S. name for **lay-by** (sense 1).

result (rɪ'zʌlt) *n.* **1.** something that ensues from an action, policy, course of events, etc.; outcome; consequence. **2.** a number, quantity, or value obtained by solving a mathematical problem. **3.** *U.S.* a decision of a legislative body. **4.** (*often pl.*) the final score or outcome of a sporting contest. **5.** a favourable result, esp. a victory or success. ~*vb.* (*intr.*) **6.** (often foll. by *from*) to be the outcome or consequence (of). **7.** (foll. by *in*) to issue or terminate (in a specified way, state, etc.); end: *to result in tragedy.* **8.** *Property law.* (of an undisposed or partially disposed of interest in land) to revert to a former owner when the prior interests come to an end. [C15: from Latin *resultāre* to rebound, spring from, from RE- + *saltāre* to leap]

resultant (rɪ'zʌltənt) *adj.* **1.** that results; resulting. ~*n.* **2.** *Maths, physics.* a single vector that is the vector sum of two or more other vectors.

resultant tone *n.* a musical sound sometimes heard when two loud notes are sounded together, either lower in pitch than either (**differential tone**) or higher (**summational tone**).

resume (rɪ'zjuːm) *vb.* **1.** to begin again or go on with (something adjourned or interrupted). **2.** (*tr.*) to occupy again, take back, or recover: *to resume one's seat; resume possession.* **3.** (*tr.*) to assume (a title, office, etc.) again: *to resume the presidency.* **4.** *Archaic.* to summarize; make a résumé of. [C15: from Latin *resūmere* to take up again, from RE- + *sūmere* to take up] —**re'sumable** *adj.* —**re'sumer** *n.*

résumé ('rɛzjʊˌmeɪ) *n.* **1.** a short descriptive summary, as of events. **2.** *U.S. and Canadian.* another name for **curriculum vitae.** [C19: from French, from *résumer* to RESUME]

resumption (rɪ'zʌmpʃən) *n.* the act of resuming or beginning again. [C15: via Old French from Late Latin *resumptiō,* from Latin *resūmere* to RESUME] —**re'sumptive** *adj.* —**re'sumptively** *adv.*

resupinate (rɪ'sjuːpɪnɪt) *adj. Botany.* (of plant parts) reversed or inverted in position, so as to appear to be upside down. [C18: from Latin *resupīnātus* bent back, from *resupīnāre,* from RE- + *supīnāre* to place on the back; see SUPINE] —**reˌsupi'nation** *n.*

resupine (rɪ'sjuːpaɪn) *adj. Rare.* lying on the back; supine. [C17: from Latin *resupīnus* lying on the back]

resurge (rɪ'sɜːdʒ) *vb.* (*intr.*) *Rare.* to rise again from or as if from the dead. [C16: from Latin *resurgere* to rise again, reappear, from RE- + *surgere* to lift, arise, SURGE]

resurgent (rɪ'sɜːdʒənt) *adj.* rising again, as to new life, vigour, etc.: *resurgent nationalism.* —**re'surgence** *n.*

resurrect (ˌrɛzə'rɛkt) *vb.* **1.** to rise or raise from the dead; bring or be brought back to life. **2.** (*tr.*) to bring back into use or activity; revive: *to resurrect an ancient law.* **3.** (*tr.*) to renew (one's hopes, etc.). **4.** (*tr.*) *Facetious.* (formerly) to exhume and steal (a body) from its grave, esp. in order to sell it.

resurrection (ˌrɛzə'rɛkʃən) *n.* **1.** a supposed act or instance of a dead person coming back to life. **2.** belief in the possibility of this as part of a religious or mystical system. **3.** the condition of those who have risen from the dead: *we shall all live in the resurrection.* [C13: via Old French from Late Latin *resurrectiō,* from Latin *resurgere* to rise again; see RESURGE] —ˌ**resur'rectional** *or* ˌ**resur'rectionary** *adj.*

Resurrection (ˌrɛzə'rɛkʃən) *n. Christian theol.* **1.** the rising again of Christ from the tomb three days after his death. **2.** the rising again from the dead of all men at the Last Judgment.

resurrectionism (ˌrɛzə'rɛkʃəˌnɪzəm) *n.* **1.** belief that men will rise again from the dead, esp. the Christian doctrine of the Resurrection of Christ and of all men at the Last Judgment. **2.** *Facetious.* (formerly) body snatching.

resurrectionist (ˌrɛzə'rɛkʃənɪst) *n.* **1.** *Facetious.* (formerly) a body snatcher. **2.** a member of an Anglican religious community founded in 1892. **3.** a person who believes in the Resurrection.

resurrection plant *n.* any of several unrelated desert plants that form a tight ball when dry and unfold and bloom when moistened. The best-known examples are the cruciferous *Anastatica hierochuntica,* club mosses of the genus *Selaginella,* and the composite *Asteriscus pygmoeus.* Also called: **rose of Jericho.**

resuscitate (rɪ'sʌsɪˌteɪt) *vb.* (*tr.*) to restore to consciousness; revive. [C16: from Latin *resuscitāre,* from RE- + *suscitāre* to raise, from *sub-* up from below + *citāre* to rouse, from *citus* quick] —**re'suscitable** *adj.* —**reˌsusci'tation** *n.* —**re'suscitative** *adj.*

resuscitator (rɪ'sʌsɪˌteɪtə) *n.* **1.** an apparatus for forcing oxygen or a mixture containing oxygen into the lungs. **2.** a person who resuscitates.

ret (rɛt) *vb.* **rets, retting, retted.** (*tr.*) to moisten or soak (flax, hemp, jute, etc.) to promote bacterial action in order to facilitate separation of the fibres from the woody tissue by beating. [C15: of Germanic origin; related to Middle Dutch *reeten,* Swedish *röta,* German *rösten;* see ROT]

ret. *abbrev. for:* **1.** retain. **2.** retired. **3.** return(ed).

retable (rɪ'teɪbᵊl) *n.* an ornamental screenlike structure above and behind an altar, esp. one used as a setting for a religious picture or carving. [C19: from French, from Spanish *retablo,* from Latin *retrō* behind + *tabula* board; see REAR[1], TABLE]

retail ('riːteɪl) *n.* **1.** the sale of goods individually or in small quantities to consumers. Compare **wholesale** (sense 1). ~*adj.* **2.** of, relating to, or engaged in such selling: *retail prices.* ~*adv.* **3.** in small amounts or at a retail price. ~*vb.* **4.** to sell or be sold in small quantities to consumers. **5.** (rɪ'teɪl). (*tr.*) to relate (gossip, scandal, etc.) in detail, esp. persistently. [C14: from Old French *retaillier* to cut off, from RE- + *taillier* to cut; see TAILOR] —'**retailer** *n.*

retail price index *n.* (in Britain) a list, based on government figures and usually published monthly, that shows the extent of change in the prices of a range of goods selected as being essential items in the budget of a normal household. Abbrev.: **RPI.**

retain (rɪ'teɪn) *vb.* (*tr.*) **1.** to keep in one's possession. **2.** to be able to hold or contain: *soil that retains water.* **3.** (of a person) to be able to remember (information, facts, etc.) without difficulty. **4.** to hold in position. **5.** to keep for one's future use, as by paying a retainer or nominal charge: *to retain one's rooms for the holidays.* **6.** *Law.* to engage the services of (a barrister) by payment of a preliminary fee. **7.** (in selling races) to buy back a winner that one owns when it is auctioned after the race. **8.** (of racehorse trainers) to pay an advance fee to (a jockey) so as to have prior or exclusive claims upon his services throughout the season. [C14: from Old French *retenir,* from Latin *retinēre* to hold back, from RE- + *tenēre* to hold] —**re'tainable** *adj.* —**re'tainment** *n.*

retained object *n. Grammar.* a direct or indirect object of a passive verb. The phrase *the drawings* in the sentence *Harry was given the drawings* is a retained object.

retainer (rɪ'teɪnə) *n.* **1.** *History.* a supporter or dependant of a person of rank, esp. a soldier. **2.** a servant, esp. one who has been with a family for a long time. **3.** a clip, frame, or similar device that prevents a part of a machine, engine, etc., from moving. **4.** a dental appliance for holding a loose tooth or prosthetic device in position. **5.** a fee paid in advance to secure first option on the services of a barrister, jockey, etc. **6.** a reduced rent paid for a flat, room, etc., during absence to reserve it for future use.

retaining ring *n.* another name for **circlip.**

retaining wall *n.* a wall constructed to hold back earth, loose rock, etc. Also called: **revetment.**

retake *vb.* (riː'teɪk), **-takes, -taking, -took, -taken.** (*tr.*) **1.** to take back or capture again: *to retake a fortress.* **2.** *Films.* to shoot again (a shot or scene). **3.** to tape again (a recording). ~*n.* ('riːˌteɪk). **4.** *Films.* a rephotographed shot or scene. **5.** a retaped recording. —**re'taker** *n.*

retaliate (rɪ'tælɪˌeɪt) *vb.* **1.** (*intr.*) to take retributory action, esp. by returning some injury or wrong in kind. **2.** (*tr.*) *Rare.* to avenge (an injury, wrong, etc.). [C17: from Late Latin *retāliāre,* from Latin RE- + *tālis* of such kind] —**reˌtali'ation** *n.* —**re'taliative** *or* **re'taliatory** *adj.* —**re'taliˌator** *n.*

retard (rɪ'tɑːd) *vb.* (*tr.*) to delay or slow down (the progress, speed, or development) of (something). [C15: from Old French *retarder,* from Latin *retardāre,* from RE- + *tardāre* to make slow, from *tardus* sluggish; see TARDY]

retardant (rɪ'tɑːdᵊnt) *n.* **1.** a substance that reduces the rate of a chemical reaction. ~*adj.* **2.** having a slowing effect.

retardate (rɪ'tɑːdeɪt) *n. Psychol.* a person who is retarded.

retardation (ˌriːtɑː'deɪʃən) *or* (*less commonly*) **retardment** (rɪ'tɑːdmənt) *n.* **1.** the act of retarding or the state of being retarded. **2.** something that retards; hindrance. **3.** the rate of deceleration. **4.** *Psychiatry.* the slowing down of mental functioning and bodily movement. —**re'tardative** *or* **re'tardatory** *adj.*

retarded (rɪ'tɑːdɪd) *adj.* underdeveloped, esp. mentally and esp. having an IQ of 70 to 85. See also **ESN, mental handicap, subnormal** (sense 2).

retarder (rɪ'tɑːdə) *n.* **1.** a person or thing that retards. **2.** a substance added to slow down the rate of a chemical change, such as one added to cement to delay its setting.

retch (rɛtʃ, riːtʃ) *vb.* **1.** (*intr.*) to undergo an involuntary spasm of ineffectual vomiting; heave. **2.** to vomit. ~*n.* **3.** an involuntary spasm of ineffectual vomiting. [Old English *hrǣcan;* related to Old Norse *hrǣkja* to spit]

retd *abbrev. for:* **1.** retired. **2.** retained. **3.** returned.

re'string *vb.*, -'strings, -'stringing, -'strung.
re'structure *vb.*
re'style *vb.*
ˌresub'mit *vb.*, -'mits, -'mitting, -'mitted.
ˌresub'scribe *vb.*
re'summon *vb.*
ˌresup'ply *vb.*, -'plies, -'plying, -'plied.
re'surface *vb.*
ˌresur'vey *vb., n.*

rete ('ri:tɪ) *n., pl.* **retia** ('ri:ʃɪə, -tɪə). *Anatomy.* any network of nerves or blood vessels; plexus. [C14 (referring to a metal network used with an astrolabe): from Latin *rēte* net] —'**retial** *adj.*

retene ('ri:ti:n, 'rɛt-) *n.* a yellow crystalline hydrocarbon found in tar oils from pine wood and in certain fossil resins. Formula: $C_{18}H_{18}$. [C19: from Greek *rhētinē* resin]

retention (rɪ'tɛnʃən) *n.* **1.** the act of retaining or state of being retained. **2.** the capacity to hold or retain liquid. **3.** the capacity to remember. **4.** *Pathol.* the abnormal holding within the body of urine, faeces, etc., that are normally excreted. **5.** *Commerce.* a sum of money owed to a contractor but not paid for an agreed period as a safeguard against any faults found in the work carried out. **6.** *(pl.) Account.* profits earned by a company but not distributed as dividends; retained earnings. [C14: from Latin *retentiō*, from *retinēre* to RETAIN]

retentionist (rɪ'tɛnʃənɪst) *n.* a person who advocates the retention of something, esp. capital punishment.

retentive (rɪ'tɛntɪv) *adj.* having the capacity to retain or remember. —**re'tentively** *adv.* —**re'tentiveness** *n.*

retentivity (ˌri:tɛn'tɪvɪtɪ) *n.* **1.** the state or quality of being retentive. **2.** *Physics.* another name for **remanence.**

rethink *vb.* (ri:'θɪŋk), **-thinks, -thinking, -thought. 1.** to think about (something) again, esp. with a view to changing one's tactics or opinions. ~*n.* ('ri:ˌθɪŋk). **2.** the act or an instance of thinking again.

retiarius (ˌri:tɪ'ɛərɪəs, ˌri:ʃɪ-) *n., pl.* **-arii** (-'ɛərɪˌaɪ). (in ancient Rome) a gladiator armed with a net and trident. [Latin, from *rēte* net]

retiary ('ri:tɪərɪ, -ʃɪə-) *adj. Rare.* of, relating to, or resembling a net or web. [C17: from Latin RETIARIUS]

reticent ('rɛtɪsənt) *adj.* not open or communicative; not saying all that one knows; taciturn; reserved. [C19: from Latin *reticēre* to keep silent, from RE- + *tacēre* to be silent] —'**reticence** *n.* —'**reticently** *adv.*

reticle ('rɛtɪkᵊl) *or (less commonly)* **reticule** *n.* a network of fine lines, wires, etc., placed in the focal plane of an optical instrument to assist measurement of the size or position of objects under observation. Also called: **graticule.** [C17: from Latin *rēticulum* a little net, from *rēte* net]

reticulate *adj.* (rɪ'tɪkjʊlɪt), *also* **reticular** (rɪ'tɪkjʊlə). **1.** in the form of a network or having a network of parts: *a reticulate leaf.* **2.** resembling, covered with, or having the form of a net. ~*vb.* (rɪ'tɪkjʊˌleɪt). **3.** to form or be formed into a net. [C17: from Late Latin *rēticulātus* made like a net] —**re'ticulately** *adv.* —**reˌticu'lation** *n.*

reticule ('rɛtɪˌkju:l) *n.* **1.** (in the 18th and 19th centuries) a woman's small bag or purse, usually in the form of a pouch with a drawstring and made of net, beading, brocade, etc. **2.** a variant of **reticle.** [C18: from French *réticule*, from Latin *rēticulum* RETICLE]

reticulocyte (rɪ'tɪkjʊləˌsaɪt) *n.* an immature red blood cell containing a network of granules or filaments. [C20: from RETICULUM + -CYTE]

reticuloendothelial (rɪˌtɪkjʊləʊˌɛndəʊ'θi:lɪəl) *adj. Physiol.* denoting or relating to a bodily system that consists of all the cells able to ingest bacteria, colloidal particles, etc., with the exception of the leucocytes. See also **macrophage.** [C20: from RETICULUM + ENDOTHELIAL]

reticulum (rɪ'tɪkjʊləm) *n., pl.* **-la** (-lə). **1.** any fine network, esp. one in the body composed of cells, fibres, etc. **2.** the second compartment of the stomach of ruminants, situated between the rumen and psalterium. [C17: from Latin: little net, from *rēte* net]

Reticulum (rɪ'tɪkjʊləm) *n., Latin genitive* **Reticuli** (rɪ'tɪkjʊˌlaɪ). a small constellation in the S hemisphere lying between Dorado and Hydrus.

retiform ('ri:tɪˌfɔ:m, 'rɛt-) *adj. Rare.* netlike; reticulate. [C17: from Latin *rēte* net + *forma* shape]

retina ('rɛtɪnə) *n., pl.* **-nas** *or* **-nae** (-ˌni:). the light-sensitive membrane forming the inner lining of the posterior wall of the eyeball, composed largely of a specialized terminal expansion of the optic nerve. Images focused here by the lens of the eye are transmitted to the brain as nerve impulses. [C14: from Medieval Latin, perhaps from Latin *rēte* net] —'**retinal** *adj.*

retinaculum (ˌrɛtɪ'nækjʊləm) *n., pl.* **-la** (-lə). **1.** connection or retention or something that connects or retains. **2.** *Zoology.* a small hook that joins the forewing and hind wing of a moth during flight. [C18 (a surgical instrument used in castration): Latin, from *rētinēre* to hold back] —ˌ**reti'nacular** *adj.*

retinal rivalry *n. Psychol.* another name for **binocular rivalry.**

retinene ('rɛtɪˌni:n) *or* **retinal** ('rɛtɪnəl) *n.* the aldehyde form of the polyene, retinol (vitamin A), that associates with the protein, opsin, to form the visual purple pigment, rhodopsin. [C20: from RETINA + -ENE]

retinite ('rɛtɪˌnaɪt) *n.* any of various resins of fossil origin, esp. one derived from lignite. [C19: from French *rétinite*, from Greek *rhētinē* resin + -ITE[1]]

retinitis (ˌrɛtɪ'naɪtɪs) *n.* inflammation of the retina. [C20: from New Latin, from RETINA + -ITIS]

retinol ('rɛtɪˌnɒl) *n.* another name for **vitamin A** and **rosin oil.** [C19: from Greek *rhētinē* resin + -OL[1]]

retinoscopy (ˌrɛtɪ'nɒskəpɪ) *n. Ophthalmol.* a procedure for detecting errors of refraction in the eye by means of an instrument (**retinoscope**) that reflects a beam of light from a mirror into the eye. Diagnosis is made by observing the areas of shadow and the direction in which the light moves when the mirror is rotated. Also called: **skiascopy, shadow test.** —**retinoscopic** (ˌrɛtɪnə'skɒpɪk) *adj.* —ˌ**retino'scopically** *adv.* —ˌ**reti'noscopist** *n.*

retinue ('rɛtɪˌnju:) *n.* a body of aides and retainers attending an important person, royalty, etc. [C14: from Old French *retenue*, from *retenir* to RETAIN] —'**retiˌnued** *adj.*

retiral (rɪ'taɪərᵊl) *n. Scot.* the act of retiring from office, one's work, etc.; retirement.

retire (rɪ'taɪə) *vb. (mainly intr.)* **1.** *(also tr.)* to give up or to cause (a person) to give up his work, a post, etc., esp. on reaching pensionable age (in Britain and Australia usually 65 for men, 60 for women). **2.** to go away, as into seclusion, for recuperation, etc. **3.** to go to bed. **4.** to recede or disappear: *the sun retired behind the clouds.* **5.** to withdraw from a sporting contest, esp. because of injury. **6.** *(also tr.)* to pull back (troops, etc.) from battle or an exposed position or (of troops, etc.) to fall back. **7.** *(tr.)* **a.** to remove (bills, bonds, shares, etc.) from circulation by taking them up and paying for them. **b.** to remove (money) from circulation. [C16: from French *retirer*, from Old French RE- + *tirer* to pull, draw] —**re'tirer** *n.*

retired (rɪ'taɪəd) *adj.* **1. a.** having given up one's work, office, etc., esp. on completion of the normal period of service: *a retired headmistress.* **b.** *(as collective n.; preceded by the): the retired.* **2.** withdrawn; secluded: *a retired life; a retired cottage in the woods.*

retiree (rɪ'taɪəˌri:) *n. Chiefly U.S.* a person who has retired from work.

retirement (rɪ'taɪəmənt) *n.* **1. a.** the act of retiring from one's work, office, etc. **b.** *(as modifier): retirement age.* **2.** the period of being retired from work: *she had many plans for her retirement.* **3.** seclusion from the world; privacy. **4.** the act of going away or retreating.

retirement pension *n.* a pension given to a person who has retired from regular employment, either one paid by the state or one arising from the person's former employment.

retirement relief *n.* (in Britain) relief from capital-gains tax given to persons over 60 when disposing of business assets.

retiring (rɪ'taɪərɪŋ) *adj.* shunning contact with others; shy; reserved. —**re'tiringly** *adv.*

retool (ri:'tu:l) *vb.* **1.** to replace, re-equip, or rearrange the tools in (a factory, etc.). **2.** *Chiefly U.S. and Canadian.* to revise or reorganize.

retorsion (rɪ'tɔ:ʃən) *n. Rare.* retaliatory action taken by a state whose citizens have been mistreated by a foreign power by treating the subjects of that power similarly; reprisal. [C17: from French; see RETORT[1]]

retort[1] (rɪ'tɔ:t) *vb.* **1.** (when *tr., takes a clause as object*) to utter (something) quickly, sharply, wittily, or angrily, in response. **2.** to use (an argument) against its originator; turn the tables by saying (something). ~*n.* **3.** a sharp, angry, or witty reply. **4.** an argument used against its originator. [C16: from Latin *retorquēre* to twist back, from RE- + *torquēre* to twist, wrench] —**re'torter** *n.*

retort[2] (rɪ'tɔ:t) *n.* **1.** a glass vessel with a round bulb and long tapering neck that is bent down, used esp. in a laboratory for distillation. **2.** a vessel in which large quantities of material may be heated, esp. one used for heating ores in the production of metals or heating coal to produce gas. ~*vb.* **3.** *(tr.)* to heat in a retort. [C17: from French *retorte*, from Medieval Latin *retorta*, from Latin *retorquēre* to twist back; see RETORT[1]]

retortion (rɪ'tɔ:ʃən) *n.* **1.** the act of retorting. **2.** a variant spelling of **retorsion.**

retouch (ri:'tʌtʃ) *vb. (tr.)* **1.** to restore, correct, or improve (a painting, make-up, etc.) with new touches. **2.** *Photog.* to alter (a negative or print) by painting over blemishes or adding details. **3.** to make small finishing improvements to. **4.** *Archaeol.* to detach small flakes from (a blank) in order to make a tool. ~*n.* **5.** the art or practice of retouching. **6.** a detail that is the result of retouching. **7.** a photograph, painting, etc., that has been retouched. **8.** *Archaeol.* fine percussion to shape flakes of stone into usable tools. —**re'touchable** *adj.* —**re'toucher** *n.*

retrace (rɪ'treɪs) *vb. (tr.)* **1.** to go back over (one's steps, a route, etc.) again: *we retraced the route we took last summer.* **2.** to go over (a past event) in the mind; recall. **3.** to go over (a story, account, etc.) from the beginning. —**re'traceable** *adj.* —**re'tracement** *n.*

re-trace (ri:'treɪs) *vb. (tr.)* to trace (a map, drawing, etc.) again.

retract (rɪ'trækt) *vb.* **1.** *(tr.)* to draw in (a part or appendage): *a snail can retract its horns; to retract the landing gear of an aircraft.* **2.** to withdraw (a statement, opinion, charge, etc.) as invalid or unjustified. **3.** to go back on (a promise or agreement). **4.** *(intr.)* to shrink back, as in fear. **5.** *Phonetics.* to modify the

re'teach *vb.*, -'**teaches**, -'**teaching**, -'**taught.**
re'tell *vb.*, -'**tells**, -'**telling**, -'**told.**
re'test *vb.*
re'testiˌfy *vb.*, -ˌ**fies**, -ˌ**fying**, -**fied.**
re'thread *vb.*
re'tie *vb.*, -'**ties**, -'**tying**, -'**tied.**
re'title *vb.*

articulation of (a vowel) by bringing the tongue back away from the lips. [C16: from Latin *retractāre* to withdraw, from *tractāre* to pull, from *trahere* to drag] —**re'tractable** or **re'tractible** *adj.* —**re,tracta'bility** or **re,tracti'bility** *n.* —**retractation** (,riːtræk'teɪʃən) *n.* —**re'tractive** *adj.*

retractile (rɪ'træktaɪl) *adj.* capable of being drawn in: *the retractile claws of a cat.* —**retractility** (,riːtræk'tɪlɪtɪ) *n.*

retraction (rɪ'trækʃən) *n.* **1.** the act of retracting or state of being retracted. **2.** the withdrawal of a statement, charge, etc.

retractor (rɪ'træktə) *n.* **1.** *Anatomy.* any of various muscles that retract an organ or part. **2.** *Surgery.* an instrument for holding back the edges of a surgical incision or organ or part. **3.** a person or thing that retracts.

retral ('riːtrəl, 'rɛtrəl) *adj. Rare.* at, near, or towards the back. [C19: from Latin *retrō* backwards] —**'retrally** *adv.*

retread *vb.* (riː'trɛd), **-treads, -treading, -treaded. 1.** (*tr.*) another word for **remould** (sense 2). ~*n.* ('riː,trɛd). **2.** another word for **remould** (sense 3). **3.** *N.Z. informal.* a pensioner who has resumed employment, esp. in a former profession.

re-tread (riː'trɛd) *vb.* **-treads, -treading, -trod, -trodden** or **-trod.** (*tr.*) to tread or walk over (one's steps) again.

retreat (rɪ'triːt) *vb.* (*mainly intr.*) **1.** *Military.* to withdraw or retire in the face of or from action with an enemy, either due to defeat or in order to adopt a more favourable position. **2.** to retire or withdraw, as to seclusion or shelter. **3.** (of a person's features) to slope back; recede. **4.** (*tr.*) *Chess.* to move (a piece) back. ~*n.* **5.** the act of retreating or withdrawing. **6.** *Military.* **a.** a withdrawal or retirement in the face of the enemy. **b.** a bugle call signifying withdrawal or retirement, esp. (formerly) to within a defended fortification. **7.** retirement or seclusion. **8.** a place, such as a sanatorium or monastery, to which one may retire for refuge, quiet, etc. **9.** an institution, esp. a private one, for the care and treatment of the mentally ill, infirm, elderly, etc. [C14: from Old French *retret,* from *retraire* to withdraw, from Latin *retrahere* to pull back; see RETRACT]

retrench (rɪ'trɛntʃ) *vb.* **1.** to reduce or curtail (costs); economize. **2.** (*tr.*) to shorten, delete, or abridge. **3.** (*tr.*) to protect by a retrenchment. [C17: from Old French *retrenchier,* from RE- + *trenchier* to cut, from Latin *truncāre* to lop; see TRENCH] —**re'trenchable** *adj.*

retrenchment (rɪ'trɛntʃmənt) *n.* **1.** the act of reducing expenditure in order to improve financial stability. **2.** an extra interior fortification to reinforce outer walls.

retrial (riː'traɪəl) *n.* a second or new trial, esp. of a case that has already been adjudicated upon.

retribution (,rɛtrɪ'bjuːʃən) *n.* **1.** the act of punishing or taking vengeance for wrongdoing, sin, or injury. **2.** punishment or vengeance. [C14: via Old French from Church Latin *retribūtiō,* from Latin *retribuere* to repay, from RE- + *tribuere* to pay; see TRIBUTE] —**retributive** (rɪ'trɪbjʊtɪv) or (*less commonly*) **re'tributory** *adj.* —**re'tributively** *adv.*

retrieval (rɪ'triːvᵊl) *n.* **1.** the act or process of retrieving. **2.** the possibility of recovery, restoration, or rectification (esp. in the phrase **beyond retrieval**). **3.** a computer filing operation that recalls records or other data from a file.

retrieve (rɪ'triːv) *vb.* (*mainly tr.*) **1.** to get or fetch back again; recover: *he retrieved his papers from various people's drawers.* **2.** to bring back to a more satisfactory state; revive. **3.** to extricate from trouble or danger; rescue or save. **4.** to recover or make newly available (stored information) from a computer system. **5.** (*also intr.*) (of dogs) to find and fetch (shot game). **6.** *Tennis, badminton, etc.* to return successfully (a shot difficult to reach). **7.** to recall; remember. ~*n.* **8.** the act of retrieving. **9.** the chance of being retrieved. [C15: from Old French *retrover,* from RE- + *trouver* to find, perhaps from Vulgar Latin *tropāre* (unattested) to compose; see TROVER, TROUBADOUR] —**re'trievable** *adj.* —**re,trieva'bility** *n.* —**re'trievably** *adv.*

retriever (rɪ'triːvə) *n.* **1.** one of a breed of large gun dogs that can be trained to retrieve game: see **golden retriever, labrador retriever. 2.** any dog used to retrieve shot game. **3.** a person or thing that retrieves.

retro ('rɛtrəʊ) *n., pl.* **-ros. 1.** short for **retrorocket.** ~*adj.* **2.** denoting something associated with or revived from the past: *retro dressing; retro fashion.*

retro- *prefix.* **1.** back or backwards: *retroactive.* **2.** located behind: *retrolental.* [from Latin *retrō* behind, backwards]

retroact ('rɛtrəʊ,ækt) *vb.* (*intr.*) **1.** to act in opposition. **2.** to influence or have reference to past events.

retroaction (,rɛtrəʊ'ækʃən) *n.* **1.** an action contrary or reciprocal to a preceding action. **2.** a retrospective action, esp. a law affecting events prior to its enactment.

retroactive (,rɛtrəʊ'æktɪv) *adj.* **1.** applying or referring to the past: *retroactive legislation.* **2.** effective or operative from a date or for a period in the past. —**,retro'actively** *adv.* —**,retro'activeness** or **,retroac'tivity** *n.*

retroactive inhibition or **interference** *n. Psychol.* the tendency for the retention of learned material or skills to be impaired by subsequent learning, esp. by learning of a similar kind. Compare **proactive inhibition.**

retrocede (,rɛtrəʊ'siːd) *vb.* **1.** (*tr.*) to give back; return. **2.** (*intr.*) to go back or retire; recede. —**retrocession** (,rɛtrəʊ'sɛʃən) or **,retro'cedence** *n.* —**,retro'cessive** or **,retro'cedent** *adj.*

retrochoir ('rɛtrəʊ,kwaɪə) *n.* the space in a large church or cathedral behind the high altar.

retrofire ('rɛtrəʊ,faɪə) *n.* **1.** *Phonetics.* the act of firing a retrorocket. **2.** the moment at which it is fired.

retrofit ('rɛtrəʊ,fɪt) *vb.* **-fits, -fitting, -fitted.** (*tr.*) to equip (a vehicle, piece of equipment, etc.) with new parts, safety devices, etc., after manufacture.

retroflex ('rɛtrəʊ,flɛks) or **retroflexed** *adj.* **1.** bent or curved backwards. **2.** *Phonetics.* of, relating to, or involving retroflexion. [C18: from Latin *retrōflexus,* from *retrōflectere,* from RETRO- + *flectere* to bend]

retroflexion or **retroflection** (,rɛtrəʊ'flɛkʃən) *n.* **1.** the act or condition of bending or being bent backwards. **2.** *Phonetics.* the act of turning the tip of the tongue upwards and backwards towards the hard palate in the articulation of a vowel or a consonant.

retrograde ('rɛtrəʊ,greɪd) *adj.* **1.** moving or bending backwards. **2.** (esp. of order) reverse or inverse. **3.** tending towards an earlier worse condition; declining or deteriorating. **4.** *Astronomy.* **a.** occurring or orbiting in a direction opposite to that of the earth's motion around the sun. Compare **direct** (sense 18). **b.** occurring or orbiting in a direction around a planet opposite to the planet's rotational direction: *the retrograde motion of the satellite Phoebe around Saturn.* **c.** appearing to move in a clockwise direction due to the rotational period exceeding the period of revolution around the sun: *Venus has retrograde rotation.* **5.** *Biology.* tending to retrogress; degenerate. **6.** *Music.* of, concerning, or denoting a melody or part that is played backwards. **7.** *Obsolete.* opposed, contrary, or repugnant to. ~*vb.* (*intr.*) **8.** to move in a retrograde direction; retrogress. **9.** *U.S. military.* another word for **retreat** (sense 1). [C14: from Latin *retrōgradī* to go backwards, from *gradi* to walk, go] —**,retrogra'dation** *n.* —**'retro,gradely** *adv.*

retrograde amnesia *n.* amnesia caused by a trauma such as concussion, in which the memory loss relates to material learnt before the trauma. Compare **anterograde amnesia.**

retrogress (,rɛtrəʊ'grɛs) *vb.* (*intr.*) **1.** to go back to an earlier, esp. worse, condition; degenerate or deteriorate. **2.** to move backwards; recede. **3.** *Biology.* to develop characteristics or features of lower or simpler organisms; degenerate. [C19: from Latin *retrōgressus* having moved backwards, from *retrōgradī;* see RETROGRADE] —**,retro'gression** *n.* —**,retro'gressive** *adj.* —**,retro'gressively** *adv.*

retroject (,rɛtrəʊ'dʒɛkt) *vb.* (*tr.*) to throw backwards (opposed to *project*). [C19: from RETRO- + *-ject* as in PROJECT] —**,retro'jection** *n.*

retrolental (,rɛtrəʊ'lɛntᵊl) *adj.* behind a lens, esp. of the eye. [C20: from RETRO- + *-lental,* from New Latin: LENS]

retro-operative *adj.* affecting or operating on past events; retroactive.

retropack ('rɛtrəʊ,pæk) *n.* a system of retrorockets on a spacecraft.

retropulsion (,rɛtrəʊ'pʌlʃən) *n. Med.* an abnormal tendency to walk backwards: a symptom of Parkinson's disease.

retrorocket ('rɛtrəʊ,rɒkɪt) *n.* a small auxiliary rocket engine on a larger rocket, missile, or spacecraft, that produces thrust in the opposite direction to the direction of flight in order to decelerate the vehicle or make it move backwards. Often shortened to **retro.**

retrorse (rɪ'trɔːs) *adj.* (esp. of plant parts) pointing backwards or in a direction opposite to normal. [C19: from Latin *retrōrsus,* shortened form of *retrōversus* turned back, from RETRO- + *vertere* to turn] —**re'trorsely** *adv.*

retrospect ('rɛtrəʊ,spɛkt) *n.* **1.** the act of surveying things past (often in the phrase **in retrospect**). ~*vb. Archaic.* **2.** to contemplate (anything past); look back on (something). **3.** (*intr.;* often foll. by *to*) to refer. [C17: from Latin *retrōspicere* to look back, from RETRO- + *specere* to look]

retrospection (,rɛtrəʊ'spɛkʃən) *n.* the act of recalling things past, esp. in one's personal experience.

retrospective (,rɛtrəʊ'spɛktɪv) *adj.* **1.** looking or directed backwards, esp. in time; characterized by retrospection. **2.** applying to the past; retroactive. ~*n.* **3.** an exhibition of an artist's life's work or a representative selection of it. —**,retro'spectively** *adv.* —**,retro'spectiveness** *n.*

retroussé (rə'truːseɪ; *French* rətruse) *adj.* (of a nose) turned up. [C19: from French *retrousser* to tuck up; see TRUSS]

retroversion (,rɛtrəʊ'vɜːʃən) *n.* **1.** the act of turning or condition of being turned backwards. **2.** the condition of a part or organ, esp. the uterus, that is turned or tilted backwards. —**'retro,verse** *adj.* —**'retro,verted** *adj.*

Retrovir ('rɛtrəʊ,vɪə) *n. Trademark.* a preparation of the drug zidovudine.

re'train *vb.*
,retrans'fer *vb.* **-'fers, -'ferring, -'ferred.**
,retrans'late *vb.*
,retrans'lation *n.*
,retrans'mission *n.*
,retrans'mit *vb.,* **-'mits, -'mitting, -'mitted.**
re'trim *vb.,* **-'trims, -'trimming, -'trimmed.**

retrovirus ('rɛtrəʊˌvaɪrəs) *n.* any of several viruses whose genetic specification is encoded in RNA rather than DNA and that are able to reverse the normal flow of genetic information from DNA to RNA by transcribing RNA into DNA: many retroviruses are known to cause cancer in animals.

retry (riː'traɪ) *vb.* **-tries, -trying, -tried.** (*tr.*) to try again (a case already determined); give a new trial to.

retsina (rɛt'siːnə, 'rɛtsɪnə) *n.* a Greek wine flavoured with resin. [Modern Greek, from Italian *resina* RESIN]

return (rɪ'tɜːn) *vb.* **1.** (*intr.*) to come back to a former place or state. **2.** (*tr.*) to give, take, or carry back; replace or restore. **3.** (*tr.*) to repay or recompense, esp. with something of equivalent value: *return the compliment.* **4.** (*tr.*) to earn or yield (profit or interest) as an income from an investment or venture. **5.** (*intr.*) to come back or revert in thought or speech: *I'll return to that later.* **6.** (*intr.*) to recur or reappear: *the symptoms have returned.* **7.** to answer or reply. **8.** (*tr.*) to vote into office; elect. **9.** (*tr.*) *Law.* (of a jury) to deliver or render (a verdict). **10.** (*tr.*) to send back or reflect (light or sound): *the canyon returned my shout.* **11.** (*tr.*) to submit (a report, etc.) about (someone or something) to someone in authority. **12.** (*tr.*) *Cards.* to lead back (the suit led by one's partner). **13.** (*tr.*) *Ball games.* to hit, throw, or play (a ball) back. **14.** (*tr.*) *Architect.* to turn (a part, decorative moulding, etc.) away from its original direction. **15. return thanks.** (of Christians) to say grace before a meal. ~*n.* **16.** the act or an instance of coming back. **17.** something that is given or sent back, esp. unsatisfactory merchandise returned to the maker or supplier or a theatre ticket sent back by a purchaser for resale. **18.** the act or an instance of putting, sending, or carrying back; replacement or restoration. **19.** (*often pl.*) the yield, revenue, or profit accruing from an investment, transaction, or venture. **20.** the act or an instance of reciprocation or repayment (esp. in the phrase **in return for**). **21.** a recurrence or reappearance. **22.** an official report, esp. of the financial condition of a company. **23. a.** a form (a **tax return**) on which a statement concerning one's taxable income is made. **b.** the statement itself. **24.** (*often pl.*) a statement of the votes counted at an election or poll. **25.** an answer or reply. **26.** *Brit.* short for **return ticket. 27.** *N.Z. informal.* a second helping of food served at a table. **28.** *Architect.* **a.** a part of a building that forms an angle with the façade. **b.** any part of an architectural feature that forms an angle with the main part. **29.** *Law.* a report by a bailiff or other officer on the outcome of a formal document such as a writ, summons, etc., issued by a court. **30.** *Cards.* a lead of a card in the suit that one's partner has previously led. **31.** *Ball games.* the act of playing or throwing a ball back. **32. by return (of post).** *Brit.* by the next post back to the sender. **33. many happy returns (of the day).** a conventional greeting to someone on his or her birthday. **34. the point of no return.** the point at which a person's commitment is irrevocable. ~*adj.* **35.** of, relating to, or characterized by a return: *a return visit; a return performance.* **36.** denoting a second, reciprocated occasion: *a return match.* [C14: from Old French *retorner;* see RE-, TURN]

returnable (rɪ'tɜːnəbᵊl) *adj.* **1.** able to be taken, given, or sent back. **2.** required to be returned by law, as a writ to the court from which it issued. —**reˌturna'bility** *n.*

return crease *n. Cricket.* one of two lines marked at right-angles to each bowling crease, from inside which a bowler must deliver the ball.

returned soldier *n. Austral. and N.Z.* a soldier who has served abroad. Also (Austral.): **returned man.**

returnee (rɪˌtɜːˌniː) *n. Chiefly U.S. and Canadian.* a person who returns to his native country, esp. after war service.

returner (rɪ'tɜːnə) *n.* **1.** a person or thing that returns. **2.** a person who goes back to work after a break, esp. a woman who has had children.

returning officer *n.* (in Britain, Canada, Australia, etc.) an official in charge of conducting an election in a constituency or electoral district, who supervises the counting of votes and announces the results.

return ticket *n. Brit.* a ticket entitling a passenger to travel to his destination and back again. U.S. and Canadian equivalent: **round-trip ticket.**

retuse (rɪ'tjuːs) *adj. Botany.* having a rounded apex and a central depression: *retuse leaves.* [C18: from Latin *retundere* to make blunt, from RE- + *tundere* to pound]

reunify (riː'juːnɪˌfaɪ) *vb.* **-fies, -fying, -fied.** (*tr.*) to bring together again (something, esp. a country previously divided). —**ˌreunifi'cation** *n.*

reunion (riː'juːnjən) *n.* **1.** the act or process of coming together again. **2.** the state or condition of having been brought together again. **3.** a gathering of relatives, friends, or former associates.

reunionist (riː'juːnjənɪst) *n.* a person who desires or works for reunion between the Roman Catholic Church and the Church of England. —**re'unionism** *n.* —**reˌunion'istic** *adj.*

reunite (ˌriːjuː'naɪt) *vb.* to bring or come together again. —**ˌreu'nitable** *adj.* —**ˌreu'niter** *n.*

rev (rɛv) *Informal.* ~*n.* **1.** revolution per minute: *the engine was doing 5000 revs.* ~*vb.* **revs, revving, revved. 2.** (often foll. by *up*) to increase the speed of revolution of (an engine).

rev. *abbrev. for:* **1.** revenue. **2.** reverse(d). **3.** review. **4.** revise(d). **5.** revision. **6.** revolution. **7.** revolving.

Rev. *abbrev. for:* **1.** *Bible.* Revelation. **2.** Reverend.

revalorize *or* **revalorise** (riː'vælәraɪz) *vb.* (*tr.*) **1.** to change the valuation of (assets). **2.** to replace (a currency unit) by another. —**reˌvalori'zation** *or* **reˌvalori'sation** *n.*

revalue (riː'væljuː) *or U.S.* **revaluate** *vb.* **1.** to adjust the exchange value of (a currency), esp. upwards. Compare **devalue. 2.** (*tr.*) to make a fresh valuation or appraisal of. —**reˌvalu'ation** *n.*

revamp (riː'væmp) *vb.* (*tr.*) **1.** to patch up or renovate; repair or restore. ~*n.* **2.** something that has been renovated or revamped. **3.** the act or process of revamping. [C19: from RE- + VAMP[2]] —**re'vamper** *n.* —**re'vamping** *n.*

revanchism (rɪ'væntʃɪzəm) *n.* **1.** a foreign policy aimed at revenge or the regaining of lost territories. **2.** desire or support for such a policy. [C20: from French *revanche* REVENGE] —**re'vanchist** *n., adj.*

rev counter *n. Brit.* an informal name for **tachometer.**

Revd *abbrev. for* Reverend.

reveal (rɪ'viːl) *vb.* (*tr.*) **1.** (*may take a clause as object or an infinitive*) to disclose (a secret); divulge. **2.** to expose to view or show (something concealed). **3.** (of God) to disclose (divine truths) either directly or through the medium of prophets, etc. ~*n.* **4.** *Architect.* the vertical side of an opening in a wall, esp. the side of a window or door between the frame and the front of the wall. [C14: from Old French *reveler,* from Latin *revēlāre* to unveil, from RE- + *vēlum* a VEIL] —**re'vealable** *adj.* —**reˌveala'bility** *n.* —**re'vealer** *n.* —**re'vealment** *n.*

revealed religion *n.* **1.** religion based on the revelation by God to man of ideas that he would not have arrived at by his natural reason alone. **2.** religion in which the existence of God depends on revelation.

revealing (rɪ'viːlɪŋ) *adj.* **1.** of significance or import: *a very revealing experience.* **2.** showing or designed to show more of the body than is usual or conventional: *a revealing costume.* —**re'vealingly** *adv.* —**re'vealingness** *n.*

revegetate (riː'vɛdʒɪˌteɪt) *vb.* (*intr.*) (of plants) to grow again and produce new tissue. —**reˌvege'tation** *n.*

reveille (rɪ'vælɪ) *n.* **1.** a signal, given by a bugle, drum, etc., to awaken soldiers or sailors in the morning. **2.** the hour at which this takes place. ~Also called (esp. U.S.): **rouse.** [C17: from French *réveillez!* awake! from RE- + Old French *esveillier* to be wakeful, ultimately from Latin *vigilāre* to keep watch; see VIGIL]

revel ('rɛvᵊl) *vb.* **-els, -elling, -elled** *or U.S.* **-els, -eling, -eled.** (*intr.*) **1.** (foll. by *in*) to take pleasure or wallow: *to revel in success.* **2.** to take part in noisy festivities; make merry. ~*n.* **3.** (*often pl.*) an occasion of noisy merrymaking. **4.** a less common word for **revelry.** [C14: from Old French *reveler* to be merry, noisy, from Latin *rebellāre* to revolt, REBEL] —**'reveller** *n.* —**'revelment** *n.*

revelation (ˌrɛvə'leɪʃən) *n.* **1.** the act or process of disclosing something previously secret or obscure, esp. something true. **2.** a fact disclosed or revealed, esp. in a dramatic or surprising way. **3.** *Christianity.* **a.** God's disclosure of his own nature and his purpose for mankind, esp. through the words of human intermediaries. **b.** something in which such a divine disclosure is contained, such as the Bible. [C14: from Church Latin *revēlātiō,* from Latin *revēlāre* to REVEAL] —**ˌreve'lational** *adj.*

revelationist (ˌrɛvə'leɪʃənɪst) *n.* a person who believes that God has revealed certain truths to man.

revelry ('rɛvᵊlrɪ) *n., pl.* **-ries.** noisy or unrestrained merrymaking.

revenant ('rɛvɪnənt) *n.* something, esp. a ghost, that returns. [C19: from French: ghost, from *revenir* to come back, from Latin *revenīre,* from RE- + *venīre* to come]

revenge (rɪ'vɛndʒ) *n.* **1.** the act of retaliating for wrongs or injury received; vengeance. **2.** something done as a means of vengeance. **3.** the desire to take vengeance or retaliate. **4.** a return match, regarded as a loser's opportunity to even the score. ~*vb.* (*tr.*) **5.** to inflict equivalent injury or damage for (injury received); retaliate in return for. **6.** to take vengeance for (oneself or another); avenge. [C14: from Old French *revenger,* from Late Latin *revindicāre,* from RE- + *vindicāre* to VINDICATE] —**re'vengeless** *adj.* —**re'venger** *n.* —**re'venging** *adj.* —**re'vengingly** *adv.*

revengeful (rɪ'vɛndʒfʊl) *adj.* full of or characterized by desire for vengeance; vindictive. —**re'vengefully** *adv.* —**re'vengefulness** *n.*

revenue ('rɛvɪˌnjuː) *n.* **1.** the income accruing from taxation to a government during a specified period of time, usually a year. **2. a.** a government department responsible for the collection of government revenue. **b.** (*as modifier*): *revenue men.* **3.** the gross income from a business enterprise, investment, property,

re'turf *vb.*
re'twist *vb.*
re'type *vb.*
ˌreup'holster *vb.*
ˌreusa'bility *n.*
re'usable *adj.*
re'usableness *n.*
re'usably *adv.*
re'use *vb., n.*
ˌreutili'zation *or* **ˌreutili'sation** *n.*
re'utiˌlize *or*
re'utiˌlise *vb.*
re'vacciˌnate *vb.*
ˌrevacci'nation *n.*
re'varnish *vb.*

etc. **4.** a particular item of income. **5.** something that yields a regular financial return; source of income. [C16: from Old French, from *revenir* to return, from Latin *revenīre;* see REVENANT] —'**reve,nued** *adj.*

revenue cutter *n.* a small lightly armed boat used to enforce customs regulations and catch smugglers.

revenuer ('rɛvɪˌnjuːə) *n. U.S. slang.* a revenue officer or cutter.

revenue tariff *n.* a tariff for the purpose of producing public revenue. Compare **protective tariff.**

reverb (rɪ'vɜːb) *n.* an electronic device that creates artificial acoustics.

reverberate (rɪ'vɜːbəˌreɪt) *vb.* **1.** (*intr.*) to resound or re-echo: *the explosion reverberated through the castle.* **2.** to reflect or be reflected many times. **3.** (*intr.*) to rebound or recoil. **4.** (*intr.*) (of the flame or heat in a reverberatory furnace) to be deflected onto the metal or ore on the hearth. **5.** (*tr.*) to heat, melt, or refine (a metal or ore) in a reverberatory furnace. [C16: from Latin *reverberāre* to strike back, from RE- + *verberāre* to beat, from *verber* a lash] —**re'verberant** *or* (*less commonly*) **re'verberative** *adj.* —**re'verberantly** *adv.* —**re'verber'ation** *n.*

reverberation time *n.* a measure of the acoustic properties of a room, equal to the time taken for a sound to fall in intensity by 60 decibels. It is usually measured in seconds.

reverberator (rɪ'vɜːbəˌreɪtə) *n.* **1.** anything that produces or undergoes reverberation. **2.** another name for **reverberatory furnace.**

reverberatory (rɪ'vɜːbərətərɪ, -trɪ) *adj.* **1.** characterized by, utilizing, or produced by reverberation. ~*n., pl.* **-ries. 2.** short for **reverberatory furnace.**

reverberatory furnace *n.* a metallurgical furnace having a curved roof that deflects heat onto the charge so that the fuel is not in direct contact with the ore.

revere (rɪ'vɪə) *vb.* (*tr.*) to be in awe of and respect deeply; venerate. [C17: from Latin *reverērī,* from RE- + *verērī* to fear, be in awe of] —**re'verable** *adj.* —**re'verer** *n.*

reverence ('rɛvərəns) *n.* **1.** a feeling or attitude of profound respect, usually reserved for the sacred or divine; devoted veneration. **2.** an outward manifestation of this feeling, esp. a bow or act of obeisance. **3.** the state of being revered or commanding profound respect. **4. saving your reverence.** *Archaic.* a form of apology for using an obscene or taboo expression. ~*vb.* **5.** (*tr.*) to revere or venerate. —'**reverencer** *n.*

Reverence ('rɛvərəns) *n.* (preceded by *Your* or *His*) a title sometimes used to address or refer to a Roman Catholic priest.

reverend ('rɛvərənd) *adj.* **1.** worthy of reverence. **2.** relating to or designating a clergyman or the clergy. ~*n.* **3.** *Informal.* a clergyman. [C15: from Latin *reverendus* fit to be revered; see REVERE]

Reverend ('rɛvərənd) *adj.* a title of respect for a clergyman. Abbrevs.: **Rev., Revd.** See also **Very Reverend, Right Reverend, Most Reverend.**

▷**Usage.** *Reverend* with a surname alone (*Reverend Smith*), as a term of address (*"Yes, Reverend"*), or in the salutation of a letter (*Dear Rev. Mr Smith*) are all generally considered to be wrong usage. Preferred are (*the*) *Reverend John Smith* or *Reverend Mr Smith* and *Dear Mr Smith.*

Reverend Mother *n.* a title of respect or form of address for the Mother Superior of a convent.

reverent ('rɛvərənt, 'rɛvrənt) *adj.* feeling, expressing, or characterized by reverence. [C14: from Latin *reverēns* respectful] —'**reverently** *adv.* —'**reverentness** *n.*

reverential (ˌrɛvə'rɛnʃəl) *adj.* resulting from or showing reverence: *a pilgrimage is a reverential act, performed by reverent people.* —ˌ**rever'entially** *adv.*

reverie *or* **revery** ('rɛvərɪ) *n., pl.* **-eries. 1.** an act or state of absent-minded daydreaming: *to fall into a reverie.* **2.** a piece of instrumental music suggestive of a daydream. **3.** *Archaic.* a fanciful or visionary notion; daydream. [C14: from Old French *resverie* wildness, from *resver* to behave wildly, of uncertain origin; see RAVE]

revers (rɪ'vɪə) *n., pl.* **-vers** (-'vɪəz). (*usually pl.*) the turned-back lining of part of a garment, esp. of a lapel or cuff. [C19: from French, literally: REVERSE]

reversal (rɪ'vɜːsᵊl) *n.* **1.** the act or an instance of reversing. **2.** a change for the worse; reverse: *a reversal of fortune.* **3.** the state of being reversed. **4.** the annulment of a judicial decision, esp. by an appeal court on grounds of error or irregularity.

reversal film *n.* photographic film that can be processed to produce a positive transparent image for direct projection, rather than a negative for printing.

reverse (rɪ'vɜːs) *vb.* (*mainly tr.*) **1.** to turn or set in an opposite direction, order, or position. **2.** to change into something different or contrary; alter completely: *reverse one's policy.* **3.** (*also intr.*) to move or cause to move backwards or in an opposite direction: *to reverse a car.* **4.** to run (machinery, etc.) in the opposite direction to normal. **5.** to turn inside out. **6.** *Law.* to revoke or set aside (a judgment, decree, etc.); annul. **7.** (often foll. by *out*) to print from plates so made that white lettering or design of (a page, text, display, etc.) appears on a black or coloured background. **8. reverse arms.** *Military.* to turn one's arms upside down, esp. as a token of mourning. **9. reverse the charge(s).** to make a telephone call at the recipient's expense. ~*n.* **10.** the opposite or contrary of something. **11.** the back or rear side of something. **12.** a change to an opposite position, state, or direction. **13.** a change for the worse; setback or defeat. **14. a.** the mechanism or gears by which machinery, a vehicle, etc., can be made to reverse its direction. **b.** (*as modifier*): *reverse gear.* **15.** the side of a coin bearing a secondary design. Compare **obverse** (sense 5). **16. a.** printed matter in which normally black or coloured areas, esp. lettering, appear white, and vice versa. **b.** (*as modifier*): *reverse plates.* **17. in reverse.** in an opposite or backward direction. **18. the reverse of.** emphatically not; not at all: *he was the reverse of polite when I called.* ~*adj.* **19.** opposite or contrary in direction, position, order, nature, etc.; turned backwards. **20.** back to front; inverted. **21.** operating or moving in a manner contrary to that which is usual. **22.** denoting or relating to a mirror image. [C14: from Old French, from Latin *reversus,* from *revertere* to turn back] —**re'versely** *adv.* —**re'verser** *n.*

reverse-charge *adj.* (*prenominal*) (of a telephone call) made at the recipient's expense. U.S. equivalent: **collect.**

reverse takeover *n. Finance.* the purchase of a larger company by a smaller company, esp. of a public company by a private company.

reverse transcriptase (træn'skrɪpteɪz) *n.* an enzyme present in retroviruses that copies RNA into DNA, thus reversing the usual flow of genetic information in which DNA is copied into RNA.

reverse video *n. Computer technol.* a highlighting feature achieved by reversing the colours of normal characters and background on a visual display unit.

reversi (rɪ'vɜːsɪ) *n.* a game played on a draughtboard with 64 pieces, black on one side and white on the other. When pieces are captured they are turned over to join the capturing player's forces; the winner is the player who fills the board with pieces of his colour. [C19: from French; see REVERSE]

reversible (rɪ'vɜːsəbᵊl) *adj.* **1.** capable of being reversed: *a reversible decision.* **2.** capable of returning to an original condition. **3.** *Chem., physics.* capable of assuming or producing either of two possible states and changing from one to the other: *a reversible reaction.* **4.** *Thermodynamics.* (of a change, process, etc.) occurring through a number of intermediate states that are all in thermodynamic equilibrium. **5.** (of a fabric or garment) woven, printed, or finished so that either side may be used as the outer side. ~*n.* **6.** a reversible garment, esp. a coat. —**reˌvers'i'bility** —**re'versibly** *adv.*

reversing light *n.* a light on the rear of a motor vehicle to provide illumination when the vehicle is being reversed.

reversion (rɪ'vɜːʃən) *n.* **1.** a return to or towards an earlier condition, practice, or belief; act of reverting. **2.** the act of reversing or the state of being reversed; reversal. **3.** *Biology.* **a.** the return of individuals, organs, etc., to a more primitive condition or type. **b.** the reappearance of primitive characteristics in an individual or group. **4.** *Property law.* **a.** an interest in an estate that reverts to the grantor or his heirs at the end of a period, esp. at the end of the life of a grantee. **b.** an estate so reverting. **c.** the right to succeed to such an estate. **5.** the benefit payable on the death of a life-insurance policyholder. —**re'versionally** *adv.* —**re'versionary** *or* **re'versional** *adj.*

reversionary bonus *n. Insurance.* a bonus added to the sum payable on death or at the maturity of a with-profits assurance policy.

reversioner (rɪ'vɜːʃənə) *n. Property law.* a person entitled to an estate in reversion. Compare **remainderman.**

reverso (rɪ'vɜːsəʊ) *n., pl.* **-sos.** another name for **verso.**

revert *vb.* (rɪ'vɜːt). (*intr.;* foll. by *to*). **1.** to go back to a former practice, condition, belief, etc.: *she reverted to her old wicked ways.* **2.** to take up again or come back to a former topic. **3.** *Biology.* (of individuals, organs, etc.) to return to a more primitive, earlier, or simpler condition or type. **4.** *Property law.* (of an estate or interest in land) to return to its former owner or his heirs when a grant, esp. a grant for the lifetime of the grantee, comes to an end. **5. revert to type.** to resume characteristics that were thought to have disappeared. ~*n.* ('riːˌvɜːt). **6.** a person who, having been converted, has returned to his former beliefs or Church. [C13: from Latin *revertere* to return, from RE- + *vertere* to turn] —**re'verter** *n.* —**re'vertible** *adj.*

revest (riː'vɛst) *vb.* (often foll. by *in*) to restore (former power, authority, status, etc., to a person) or (of power, authority, etc.) to be restored. [C16: from Old French *revestir* to clothe again, from Latin RE- + *vestīre* to clothe; see VEST]

revet (rɪ'vɛt) *vb.* **-vets, -vetting, -vetted.** to face (a wall or embankment) with stones. [C19: from French *revêt,* from Old French *revestir* to reclothe; see REVEST]

revetment (rɪ'vɛtmənt) *n.* **1.** a facing of stones, sandbags, etc., to protect a wall, embankment, or earthworks. **2.** another name for **retaining wall.** [C18: from French *revêtement* literally, a reclothing, from *revêtir;* see REVEST]

ˌreverifi'cation *n.*
re'veriˌfy *vb.,* **-ˌfies, -ˌfying, -ˌfied.**

re'victual *vb.,* **-uals, -ualling, -ualled.**

review (rɪˈvjuː) *vb.* (*mainly tr.*) **1.** to look at or examine again: *to review a situation.* **2.** to look back upon (a period of time, sequence of events, etc.); remember: *he reviewed his achievements with pride.* **3.** to inspect, esp. formally or officially: *the general reviewed his troops.* **4.** to read through or go over in order to correct. **5.** *Law.* to re-examine (a decision) judicially. **6.** to write a critical assessment of (a book, film, play, concert, etc.), esp. as a profession. ~*n.* **7.** Also called: **reviewal.** the act or an instance of reviewing. **8.** a general survey or report: *a review of the political situation.* **9.** a critical assessment of a book, film, play, concert, etc., esp. one printed in a newspaper or periodical. **10. a.** a publication containing such articles. **b.** (*cap. when part of a name*): *the Saturday Review.* **11.** a second consideration; re-examination. **12.** a retrospective survey. **13.** a formal or official inspection. **14.** a U.S. and Canadian word for **revision** (sense 2). **15.** *Law.* judicial re-examination of a case, esp. by a superior court. **16.** a less common spelling of **revue.** [C16: from French, from *revoir* to see again, from Latin *re-* RE- + *vidēre* to see] —**re'viewable** *adj.* —**re'viewer** *n.*

review copy *n.* a copy of a book sent by a publisher to a journal, newspaper, etc., to enable it to be reviewed.

revile (rɪˈvaɪl) *vb.* to use abusive or scornful language against (someone or something). [C14: from Old French *reviler,* from RE- + *vil* VILE] —**re'vilement** *n.* —**re'viler** *n.*

revise (rɪˈvaɪz) *vb.* **1.** (*tr.*) to change, alter, or amend: *to revise one's opinion.* **2.** *Brit.* to reread (a subject or notes on it) so as to memorize it, esp. in preparation for an examination. **3.** (*tr.*) to prepare a new version or edition of (a previously printed work). ~*n.* **4.** the act, process, or result of revising; revision. [C16: from Latin *revīsere* to look back at, from RE- + *vīsere* to inspect, from *vidēre* to see; see REVIEW, VISIT] —**re'visable** *adj.* —**re'visal** *n.* —**re'viser** *n.*

Revised Standard Version *n.* a revision by American scholars of the American Standard Version of the Bible. The New Testament was published in 1946 and the entire Bible in 1953.

Revised Version *n.* a revision of the Authorized Version of the Bible prepared by two committees of British scholars, the New Testament being published in 1881 and the Old in 1885.

revision (rɪˈvɪʒən) *n.* **1.** the act or process of revising. **2.** *Brit.* the process of rereading a subject or notes on it, esp. in preparation for an examination. **3.** a corrected or new version of a book, article, etc. —**re'visionary** *adj.*

revisionism (rɪˈvɪʒəˌnɪzəm) *n.* **1.** (*sometimes cap.*) **a.** a moderate, nonrevolutionary version of Marxism developed in Germany around 1900. **b.** (in Marxist-Leninist ideology) any dangerous departure from the true interpretation of Marx's teachings. **2.** the advocacy of revision of some political theory, religious doctrine, historical or critical interpretation, etc. **3.** (*usually cap.*) a militant Zionist ideology whose adherents formed the Herut party in Israel. —**re'visionist** *n., adj.*

revisit (riːˈvɪzɪt) *vb.* (*tr.*) **1.** to visit again. **2.** (used in the past participle) to re-examine (a topic or theme) after an interval, with a view to making a fresh appraisal: *Hitchcock revisited.*

revisory (rɪˈvaɪzərɪ) *adj.* of, relating to, or having the power to revise.

revitalize *or* **revitalise** (riːˈvaɪtᵊˌlaɪz) *vb.* (*tr.*) to restore vitality or animation to. —**reˌvitali'zation** *or* **reˌvitali'sation** *n.*

revival (rɪˈvaɪvᵊl) *n.* **1.** the act or an instance of reviving or the state of being revived. **2.** an instance of returning to life or consciousness; restoration of vigour or vitality. **3.** a renewed use, acceptance of, or interest in (past customs, styles, etc.): *a revival of learning; the Gothic revival.* **4.** a new production of a play that has not been recently performed. **5.** a reawakening of faith or renewal of commitment to religion. **6.** an evangelistic meeting or service intended to effect such a reawakening in those present. **7.** the re-establishment of legal validity, as of a judgment, contract, etc.

revivalism (rɪˈvaɪvəˌlɪzəm) *n.* **1.** a movement, esp. an evangelical Christian one, that seeks to reawaken faith. **2.** the tendency or desire to revive former customs, styles, etc.

revivalist (rɪˈvaɪvəlɪst) *n.* **1.** a person who holds, promotes, or presides over religious revivals. **2.** a person who revives customs, institutions, ideas, etc. ~*adj.* **3.** of, relating to, or characterizing revivalism or religious revivals: *a revivalist meeting.* —**reˌvival'istic** *adj.*

revive (rɪˈvaɪv) *vb.* **1.** to bring or be brought back to life, consciousness, or strength; resuscitate or be resuscitated: *revived by a drop of whisky.* **2.** to give or assume new vitality; flourish again or cause to flourish again. **3.** to make or become operative or active again: *the youth movement was revived.* **4.** to bring or come into use or currency again: *to revive a language.* **5.** (*tr.*) to take up again: *he revived his old hobby.* **6.** to bring or come back to mind. **7.** (*tr.*) *Theatre.* to mount a new production of (an old play). [C15: from Old French *revivre* to live again, from Latin *revīvere,* from RE- + *vīvere* to live; see VIVID] —**re'vivable** *adj.* —**reˌviva'bility** *n.* —**re'vivably** *adv.* —**re'viver** *n.* —**re'viving** *adj.* —**re'vivingly** *adv.*

revivify (rɪˈvɪvɪˌfaɪ) *vb.* **-fies, -fying, -fied.** (*tr.*) to give new life or spirit to; revive. —**reˌvivifi'cation** *n.*

reviviscence (ˌrɛvɪˈvɪsəns, rɪˈvɪvɪsəns) *n. Rare.* restoration to life or animation; revival. [C17: from Latin, from *revīviscere* come back to life, related to *vīvere* to live; see REVIVE] —**ˌrevi'viscent** *adj.*

revocable (ˈrɛvəkəbᵊl) *or* **revokable** (rɪˈvəʊkəbᵊl) *adj.* capable of being revoked; able to be cancelled. —**ˌrevoca'bility,** *or* **reˌvoka'bility** *n.* —**'revocably** *or* **re'vokably** *adv.*

revocation (ˌrɛvəˈkeɪʃən) *n.* **1.** the act of revoking or state of being revoked; cancellation. **2. a.** the cancellation or annulment of a legal instrument, esp. a will. **b.** the withdrawal of an offer, power of attorney, etc. —**revocatory** (ˈrɛvəkətərɪ, -trɪ) *adj.*

revoice (riːˈvɔɪs) *vb.* (*intr.*) **1.** to utter again; echo. **2.** to adjust the design of (an organ pipe or wind instrument) as after disuse or to conform with modern pitch.

revoke (rɪˈvəʊk) *vb.* **1.** (*tr.*) to take back or withdraw; cancel; rescind: *to revoke a law.* **2.** (*intr.*) *Cards.* to break a rule of play by failing to follow suit when able to do so; renege. ~*n.* **3.** *Cards.* the act of revoking; a renege. [C14: from Latin *revocāre* to call back, withdraw, from RE- + *vocāre* to call] —**re'voker** *n.*

revolt (rɪˈvəʊlt) *n.* **1.** a rebellion or uprising against authority. **2. in revolt.** in the process or state of rebelling. ~*vb.* **2.** (*intr.*) to rise up in rebellion against authority. **3.** (*usually passive*) to feel or cause to feel revulsion, disgust, or abhorrence. [C16: from French *révolter* to revolt, from Old Italian *rivoltare* to overturn, ultimately from Latin *revolvere* to roll back, REVOLVE] —**re'volter** *n.*

revolting (rɪˈvəʊltɪŋ) *adj.* **1.** causing revulsion; nauseating, disgusting, or repulsive. **2.** *Informal.* unpleasant or nasty: *that dress is revolting.* —**re'voltingly** *adv.*

revolute (ˈrɛvəˌluːt) *adj.* (esp. of the margins of a leaf) rolled backwards and downwards. [C18: from Latin *revolūtus* rolled back; see REVOLVE]

revolution (ˌrɛvəˈluːʃən) *n.* **1.** the overthrow or repudiation of a regime or political system by the governed. **2.** (in Marxist theory) the violent and historically necessary transition from one system of production in a society to the next, as from feudalism to capitalism. **3.** a far-reaching and drastic change, esp. in ideas, methods, etc. **4. a.** movement in or as if in a circle. **b.** one complete turn in such a circle: *a turntable rotating at 33 revolutions per minute.* **5. a.** the orbital motion of one body, such as a planet or satellite, around another. Compare **rotation** (sense 5a). **b.** one complete turn in such motion. **6.** a cycle of successive events or changes. **7.** *Geology.* a profound change in conditions over a large part of the earth's surface, esp. one characterized by mountain building: *an orogenic revolution.* [C14: via Old French from Late Latin *revolūtiō,* from Latin *revolvere* to REVOLVE]

revolutionary (ˌrɛvəˈluːʃənərɪ) *n., pl.* **-aries. 1.** a person who advocates or engages in revolution. ~*adj.* **2.** relating to or characteristic of a revolution. **3.** advocating or engaged in revolution. **4.** radically new or different: *a revolutionary method of making plastics.* **5.** rotating or revolving. —**ˌrevo'lutionarily** *adv.*

Revolutionary (ˌrɛvəˈluːʃənərɪ) *adj.* **1.** *Chiefly U.S.* of or relating to the conflict or period of the War of American Independence (1775–83). **2.** of or relating to any of various other revolutions, esp. the Russian Revolution (1917) or the French Revolution (1789).

Revolutionary calendar *n.* the calendar adopted in France in 1793 and abandoned in 1805. Dates were calculated from Sept. 22, 1792. The months were called Vendémiaire, Brumaire, Frimaire, Nivôse, Pluviôse, Ventôse, Germinal, Floréal, Prairial, Messidor, Thermidor, and Fructidor.

revolutionist (ˌrɛvəˈluːʃənɪst) *n.* **1.** a less common word for a **revolutionary.** ~*adj.* **2.** of, characteristic of, or relating to revolution or revolutionaries.

revolutionize *or* **revolutionise** (ˌrɛvəˈluːʃəˌnaɪz) *vb.* (*tr.*) **1.** to bring about a radical change in: *science has revolutionized civilization.* **2.** to inspire or infect with revolutionary ideas: *they revolutionized the common soldiers.* **3.** to cause a revolution in (a country, etc.). —**ˌrevo'lutionˌizer** *or* **ˌrevo'lutionˌiser** *n.*

revolve (rɪˈvɒlv) *vb.* **1.** to move or cause to move around a centre or axis; rotate. **2.** (*intr.*) to occur periodically or in cycles. **3.** to consider or be considered. **4.** (*intr.;* foll. by *around* or *about*) to be centred or focused (upon): *Juliet's thoughts revolved around Romeo.* ~*n.* **5.** *Theatre.* a circular section of a stage that can be rotated by electric power to provide a scene change. [C14: from Latin *revolvere,* from RE- + *volvere* to roll, wind] —**re'volvable** *adj.* —**re'volvably** *adv.*

revolver (rɪˈvɒlvə) *n.* a pistol having a revolving multichambered cylinder that allows several shots to be discharged without reloading.

revolving (rɪˈvɒlvɪŋ) *adj.* denoting or relating to an engine, such as a radial aero engine, in which the cylinders revolve about a fixed shaft. —**re'volvingly** *adv.*

revolving credit *n.* a letter of credit for a fixed sum, specifying that the beneficiary may make repeated use of the credit provided that the fixed sum is never exceeded.

re'vioˌlate *vb.* **ˌrevio'lation** *n.*

revolving door *n.* a door that rotates about a central vertical axis, esp. one with four leaves arranged at right angles to each other, thereby excluding draughts.

revolving fund *n.* a fund set up for a specific purpose and constantly added to by fresh appropriations or by income from the investments it finances.

revue *or* (*less commonly*) **review** (rɪˈvjuː) *n.* a form of light entertainment consisting of a series of topical sketches, songs, dancing, comic turns, etc. [C20: from French; see REVIEW]

revulsion (rɪˈvʌlʃən) *n.* **1.** a sudden and unpleasant violent reaction in feeling, esp. one of extreme loathing. **2.** the act or an instance of drawing back or recoiling from something. **3.** the diversion of disease or congestion from one part of the body to another by cupping, counterirritants, etc. [C16: from Latin *revulsiō* a pulling away, from *revellere*, from RE- + *vellere* to pull, tear] —**reˈvulsionary** *adj.*

revulsive (rɪˈvʌlsɪv) *adj.* **1.** of or causing revulsion. ~*n.* **2.** *Med.* a counterirritant. —**reˈvulsively** *adv.*

Rev. Ver. *abbrev. for* Revised Version (of the Bible).

reward (rɪˈwɔːd) *n.* **1.** something given or received in return for a deed or service rendered. **2.** a sum of money offered, esp. for help in finding a criminal or for the return of lost or stolen property. **3.** profit or return. **4.** something received in return for good or evil; deserts. **5.** *Psychol.* any pleasant event that follows a response and therefore increases the likelihood of the response recurring in the future. ~*vb.* **6.** (*tr.*) to give (something) to (someone), esp. in gratitude for a service rendered; recompense. [C14: from Old Norman French *rewarder* to regard, from RE- + *warder* to care for, guard, of Germanic origin; see WARD] —**reˈwardable** *adj.* —**reˈwarder** *n.* —**reˈwardless** *adj.*

reward claim *n. Austral. history.* a claim granted to a miner who discovered gold in a new area.

rewarding (rɪˈwɔːdɪŋ) *adj.* giving personal satisfaction; gratifying: *caring for the elderly is rewarding.*

rewa-rewa (ˈreɪwəˈreɪwə) *n.* a tall proteaceous tree of New Zealand, *Knightia excelsa*, yielding a beautiful reddish timber. [C19: from Maori]

rewind *vb.* (riːˈwaɪnd), **-winds, -winding, -wound.** **1.** (*tr.*) to wind back, esp. a film or tape onto the original reel. ~*n.* (ˈriːˌwaɪnd, riːˈwaɪnd). **2.** something rewound. **3.** the act of rewinding. —**reˈwinder** *n.*

rewire (riːˈwaɪə) *vb.* (*tr.*) to provide (a house, engine, etc.) with new wiring. —**reˈwirable** *adj.*

reword (riːˈwɜːd) *vb.* (*tr.*) to alter the wording of; express differently.

rework (riːˈwɜːk) *vb.* (*tr.*) **1.** to use again in altered form: *the theme was reworked in countless poems.* **2.** to rewrite or revise. **3.** to reprocess for use again.

rewrite *vb.* (riːˈraɪt), **-writes, -writing, -wrote, -written.** (*tr.*) **1.** to write (written material) again, esp. changing the words or form. **2.** *Computer technol.* to return (data) to a store when it has been erased during reading. ~*n.* (ˈriːˌraɪt). **3.** something rewritten.

rewrite rule *n. Generative grammar.* another name for **phrase-structure rule.**

Rex (rɛks) *n.* king: part of the official title of a king, now used chiefly in documents, legal proceedings, inscriptions on coins, etc. Compare **Regina.** [Latin]

Rexine (ˈrɛksiːn) *n. Trademark.* a form of artificial leather.

Reye's syndrome (raɪz, reɪz) *n.* a rare metabolic disease in children that can be fatal, involving damage to the brain, liver, and kidneys. [C20: named after R. D. K. *Reye* (1912–78) Australian paediatrician]

Reynard (ˈrɛnəd, ˈrɛnɑːd, ˈreɪnəd, ˈreɪnɑːd) *n.* a name for a fox, used in medieval tales, fables, etc. [from earlier *Renard, Renart*, hero of the French bestiary *Roman de Renart:* ultimately from the Old High German name *Reginhart*, literally, strong in counsel]

Reynolds number (ˈrɛnəldz) *n.* a number, $v\rho l/\eta$, where v is the fluid velocity, ρ the density, η the viscosity, and l a dimension of the system. The value of the number indicates the type of fluid flow. [C19: named after Osborne *Reynolds* (1842–1912), British physicist]

rf *Music. abbrev. for* rinforzando. Also: **rfz.**

Rf *the chemical symbol for* rutherfordium.

RF *abbrev. for* radio frequency.

RF- (in the U.S. Air Force) *abbrev. for* reconnaissance fighter: *RF-4E.*

RFC *abbrev. for:* **1.** Rugby Football Club. **2.** Royal Flying Corps.

RFLP *abbrev. for* restriction fragment length polymorphism: any variation in DNA between individuals revealed by restriction enzymes that cut DNA into fragments of different lengths in consequence of such variations. It is used forensically and in the diagnosis of hereditary disease.

RGN (in Britain) *abbrev. for* Registered General Nurse.

RGS *abbrev. for* Royal Geographical Society.

Rgt *abbrev. for* regiment.

rh *or* **RH** *abbrev. for* right hand.

Rh **1.** *the chemical symbol for* rhodium. ~**2.** *abbrev. for* rhesus (esp. in **Rh factor**).

RH **1.** *abbrev. for* Royal Highness. ~**2.** *international car registration for* (Republic of) Haiti.

RHA *abbrev. for* Royal Horse Artillery.

rhabdomancy (ˈræbdəˌmænsɪ) *n.* divination for water or mineral ore by means of a rod or wand; dowsing; divining. [C17: via Late Latin from Late Greek *rhabdomanteia*, from *rhabdos* a rod + *manteia* divination] —**ˈrhabdoˌmantist** *or* **ˈrhabdoˌmancer** *n.*

rhabdomyoma (ˌræbdəʊmaɪˈəʊmə) *n., pl.* **-mas** *or* **-mata** (-mətə). *Pathol.* a benign tumour of striated muscle. [C19: from New Latin, from Greek *rhabdos* a rod + MYOMA]

rhachis (ˈreɪkɪs) *n., pl.* **rhachises** *or* **rhachides** (ˈrækɪˌdiːz, ˈreɪ-). a variant spelling of **rachis.**

Rhaetian (ˈriːʃən) *n.* **1.** Also called: **Rhaeto-Romanic** (ˈriːtəʊrəʊˈmænɪk). a group of Romance languages or dialects spoken in certain valleys of the Alps, including Romansch, Ladin, and Friulian. ~*adj.* **2.** denoting or relating to this group of languages. **3.** of or relating to Rhaetia, an Alpine province of ancient Rome.

Rhaetic *or* **Rhetic** (ˈriːtɪk) *adj.* **1.** of or relating to a series of rocks formed between the Triassic and Jurassic periods. ~*n.* **2.** **the.** the Rhaetic series.

Rhamadhan (ˌræməˈdɑːn) *n.* a variant spelling of **Ramadan.**

rhamnaceous (ræmˈneɪʃəs) *adj.* of, relating to, or belonging to the *Rhamnaceae*, a widely distributed family of trees and shrubs having small inconspicuous flowers. The family includes the buckthorns. [C19: from New Latin *Rhamnaceae*, from Greek *rhamnos* a thorn]

rhapsodic (ræpˈsɒdɪk) *adj.* **1.** of or like a rhapsody. **2.** lyrical or romantic. —**rhapˈsodically** *adv.*

rhapsodist (ˈræpsədɪst) *n.* **1.** a person who speaks or writes rhapsodies. **2.** a person who speaks with extravagant enthusiasm. **3.** Also called: **rhapsode** (ˈræpsəʊd). (in ancient Greece) a professional reciter of poetry, esp. of Homer. —**ˌrhapsoˈdistic** *adj.*

rhapsodize *or* **rhapsodise** (ˈræpsəˌdaɪz) *vb.* **1.** to speak or write (something) with extravagant enthusiasm. **2.** (*intr.*) to recite or write rhapsodies.

rhapsody (ˈræpsədɪ) *n., pl.* **-dies.** **1.** *Music.* a composition free in structure and highly emotional in character. **2.** an expression of ecstatic enthusiasm. **3.** (in ancient Greece) an epic poem or part of an epic recited by a rhapsodist. **4.** a literary work composed in an intense or exalted style. **5.** rapturous delight or ecstasy. **6.** *Obsolete.* a medley. [C16: via Latin from Greek *rhapsōidia*, from *rhaptein* to sew together + *ōidē* song]

rhatany (ˈrætənɪ) *n., pl.* **-nies.** **1.** either of two South American leguminous shrubs, *Krameria triandra* or *K. argentea*, that have thick fleshy roots. **2.** the dried roots of such shrubs for use as an astringent. ~Also called: **krameria.** [C19: from New Latin *rhatānia*, ultimately from Quechua *ratánya*]

rhd *abbrev. for* right-hand drive.

rhea (ˈrɪə) *n.* either of two large fast-running flightless birds, *Rhea americana* or *Pterocnemia pennata*, inhabiting the open plains of S South America: order *Rheiformes* (see **ratite**). They are similar to but smaller than the ostrich, having three-toed feet and a completely feathered body. [C19: New Latin; arbitrarily named after *Rhea*, a primordial Greek goddess]

rhebok *or* **reebok** (ˈriːbʌk, -bɒk) *n., pl.* **-boks** *or* **-bok.** an antelope, *Pelea capreolus*, of southern Africa, having woolly brownish-grey hair. [C18: Afrikaans, from Dutch *reebok* ROEBUCK]

rheme (riːm) *n. Linguistics.* the constituent of a sentence that adds most new information, in addition to what has already been said in the discourse. The rheme is usually, but not always, associated with the subject. Compare **theme** (sense 5). [C20: from Greek *rhēma* that which is said]

Rhemish (ˈriːmɪʃ) *adj.* of, relating to, or originating in Reims, a city in NE France.

Rhenish (ˈrɛnɪʃ, ˈriː-) *adj.* **1.** of or relating to the River Rhine or the lands adjacent to it, esp. the Rhineland-Palatinate in Germany. ~*n.* **2.** another word for **hock** (the wine).

rhenium (ˈriːnɪəm) *n.* a dense silvery-white metallic element that has a high melting point. It occurs principally in gadolinite and molybdenite and is used, alloyed with tungsten or molybdenum, in high-temperature thermocouples. Symbol: Re; atomic no.: 75; atomic wt.: 186.2; valency: 1–7; relative density: 21.0; melting pt.: 3180°C; boiling pt.: 5627°C (est.). [C19: New Latin, from *Rhēnus* the River Rhine]

rheo. *abbrev. for* rheostat.

rheo- *combining form.* indicating stream, flow, or current: *rheometer; rheoscope.* [from Greek *rheos* stream, anything flowing, from *rhein* to flow]

rheobase (ˈriːəʊˌbeɪs) *n. Physiol.* the minimum nerve impulse required to elicit a response from a tissue.

reˈwake *vb.*, **-ˈwakes, -ˈwaking; -ˈwaked** *or* **-ˈwoke.**
reˈwaken *vb.*
reˈwarm *vb.*
reˈwash *vb.*
reˈweigh *vb.*
reˈweld *vb.*
reˈwiden *vb.*
reˈwrap *vb.*, **-ˈwraps, -ˈwrapping, -ˈwrapped.**
reˈzone *vb.*

rheology (rɪˈɒlədʒɪ) *n.* the branch of physics concerned with the flow and change of shape of matter, esp. the viscosity of liquids. —**rheological** (ˌriːəˈlɒdʒɪkᵊl) *adj.* —**rheˈologist** *n.*

rheometer (rɪˈɒmɪtə) *n.* **1.** *Med.* an instrument for measuring the velocity of the blood flow. **2.** another word for **galvanometer.** —**rheometric** (ˌriːəˈmɛtrɪk) *adj.* —**rheˈometry** *n.*

rheomorphism (ˌriːəˈmɔːfɪzəm) *n. Geology.* the liquefaction of rock, which results in its flowing and intruding into surrounding rocks. —ˌ**rheoˈmorphic** *adj.*

rheoreceptor (ˈriːərɪˌsɛptə) *n. Zoology.* a receptor in fish and some amphibians that responds to water currents.

rheostat (ˈriːəˌstæt) *n.* a variable resistance, usually consisting of a coil of wire with a terminal at one end and a sliding contact that moves along the coil to tap off the current. —ˌ**rheoˈstatic** *adj.*

rheotaxis (ˌriːəˈtæksɪs) *n.* movement of an organism towards or away from a current of water. —**rheotactic** (ˌriːəˈtæktɪk) *adj.*

rheotropism (rɪˈɒtrəˌpɪzəm) *n.* growth of a plant or sessile animal in the direction of a current of water. —**rheotropic** (ˌriːəˈtrɒpɪk) *adj.*

rhesus baby (ˈriːsəs) *n.* a baby suffering from haemolytic disease at birth as its red blood cells (which are Rh positive) have been attacked in the womb by antibodies from its Rh negative mother. [C20: see RH FACTOR]

rhesus factor *n.* See **Rh factor.**

rhesus monkey *n.* a macaque monkey, *Macaca mulatta,* of S Asia: used extensively in medical research. [C19: New Latin, arbitrarily from Greek *Rhesos* Rhēsus, mythological Thracian king]

rhet. *abbrev. for* rhetoric(al).

Rhetic (ˈriːtɪk) *adj., n.* a variant spelling of **Rhaetic.**

rhetor (ˈriːtə) *n.* **1.** a teacher of rhetoric. **2.** (in ancient Greece) an orator. [C14: via Latin from Greek *rhētōr;* related to *rhēma* word]

rhetoric (ˈrɛtərɪk) *n.* **1.** the study of the technique of using language effectively. **2.** the art of using speech to persuade, influence, or please; oratory. **3.** excessive use of ornamentation and contrivance in spoken or written discourse; bombast. **4.** speech or discourse that pretends to significance but lacks true meaning: *all the politician says is mere rhetoric.* [C14: via Latin from Greek *rhētorikē* (*tekhnē*) (the art of) rhetoric, from *rhētōr* RHETOR]

rhetorical (rɪˈtɒrɪkᵊl) *adj.* **1.** concerned with effect or style rather than content or meaning; bombastic. **2.** of or relating to rhetoric or oratory. —**rheˈtorically** *adv.*

rhetorical question *n.* a question to which no answer is required: used esp. for dramatic effect. An example is *Who knows?* (with the implication *Nobody knows*).

rhetorician (ˌrɛtəˈrɪʃən) *n.* **1.** a teacher of the art of rhetoric. **2.** a stylish or eloquent writer or speaker. **3.** a person whose speech is pompous or extravagant.

rheum (ruːm) *n.* a watery discharge from the eyes or nose. [C14: from Old French *reume,* ultimately from Greek *rheuma* bodily humour, stream, from *rhein* to flow]

rheumatic (ruːˈmætɪk) *adj.* **1.** of, relating to, or afflicted with rheumatism. ~*n.* **2.** a person afflicted with rheumatism. [C14: ultimately from Greek *rheumatikos,* from *rheuma* a flow; see RHEUM] —**rheuˈmatically** *adv.*

rheumatic fever *n.* a disease characterized by sore throat, fever, inflammation, and pain in the joints.

rheumatics (ruːˈmætɪks) *n.* (*functioning as sing.*) *Informal.* rheumatism.

rheumatism (ˈruːməˌtɪzəm) *n.* any painful disorder of joints, muscles, or connective tissue. Compare **arthritis, fibrositis.** [C17: from Latin *rheumatismus* catarrh, from Greek *rheumatismos;* see RHEUM]

rheumatoid (ˈruːməˌtɔɪd) *adj.* (of the symptoms of a disease) resembling rheumatism. —ˌ**rheumaˈtoidally** *adv.*

rheumatoid arthritis *n.* a chronic disease of the musculoskeletal system, characterized by inflammation and swelling of joints (esp. joints in the hands, wrists, knees, and feet), muscle weakness, and fatigue.

rheumatology (ˌruːməˈtɒlədʒɪ) *n.* the branch of medicine concerned with the study of rheumatic diseases. —**rheumatological** (ˌruːmətəˈlɒdʒɪkᵊl) *adj.* —ˌ**rheumaˈtologist** *n.*

rheumy (ˈruːmɪ) *adj.* **1.** of the nature of rheum. **2.** *Literary.* damp and unhealthy: *the rheumy air.*

rhexis (ˈrɛksɪs) *n. Med.* the rupture of an organ or blood vessel. [C17: from Greek *rhēxis* a bursting]

Rh factor *n.* an agglutinogen commonly found in human blood: it may cause a haemolytic reaction, esp. during pregnancy or following transfusion of blood that does not contain this agglutinogen. Full name: **rhesus factor.** See also **Rh positive, Rh negative.** [C20: named after the rhesus monkey, in which it was first discovered]

RHG *abbrev. for* Royal Horse Guards.

rhigolene (ˈrɪgəʊˌliːn) *n.* a volatile liquid obtained from petroleum and used as a local anaesthetic. [C19: from Greek *rhigos* cold; see -OLE, -ENE]

rhinal (ˈraɪnᵊl) *adj.* of or relating to the nose; nasal. [C19: from Greek *rhis, rhin*]

rhinencephalon (ˌraɪnɛnˈsɛfəˌlɒn) *n., pl.* **-lons** *or* **-la** (-lə). *Anatomy.* the part of the brain that contains the olfactory bulb and tract and is concerned with the sense of smell. [C19: from RHINO- + ENCEPHALON] —**rhinencephalic** (ˌraɪnɛnsɪˈfælɪk) *adj.*

rhinestone (ˈraɪnˌstəʊn) *n.* an imitation gem made of paste. [C19: translation of French *caillou du Rhin,* referring to Strasbourg, a French city on the Rhine where such gems were made]

Rhine wine (raɪn) *n.* any of several wines produced along the banks of the Rhine, characteristically a white table wine such as riesling.

rhinitis (raɪˈnaɪtɪs) *n.* inflammation of the mucous membrane that lines the nose. —**rhinitic** (raɪˈnɪtɪk) *adj.*

rhino[1] (ˈraɪnəʊ) *n., pl.* **-nos** *or* **-no.** short for **rhinoceros.**

rhino[2] (ˈraɪnəʊ) *n. Brit.* a slang word for **money.** [C17: of unknown origin]

rhino- *or before a vowel* **rhin-** *combining form.* indicating the nose or nasal: *rhinology.* [from Greek *rhis, rhin*]

rhinoceros (raɪˈnɒsərəs, -ˈnɒsrəs) *n., pl.* **-oses** *or* **-os.** any of several perissodactyl mammals constituting the family *Rhinocerotidae* of SE Asia and Africa and having either one horn on the nose, like the **Indian rhinoceros** (*Rhinoceros unicornis*), or two horns, like the African **white rhinoceros** (*Diceros simus*). They have a very thick skin, massive body, and three digits on each foot. [C13: via Latin from Greek *rhinokerōs,* from *rhis* nose + *keras* horn] —**rhinocerotic** (ˌraɪnəʊsɪˈrɒtɪk) *adj.*

rhinoceros beetle *n.* any of various scarabaeid beetles having one or more horns on the head, esp. *Oryctes rhinoceros,* a serious pest on coconut plantations.

rhinoceros bird *n.* another name for the **oxpecker.**

rhinology (raɪˈnɒlədʒɪ) *n.* the branch of medical science concerned with the nose and its diseases. —**rhinological** (ˌraɪnᵊˈlɒdʒɪkᵊl) *adj.* —**rhiˈnologist** *n.*

rhinoplasty (ˈraɪnəʊˌplæstɪ) *n.* plastic surgery of the nose. —ˌ**rhinoˈplastic** *adj.*

rhinoscopy (raɪˈnɒskəpɪ) *n. Med.* examination of the nasal passages, esp. with a special instrument called a **rhinoscope** (ˈraɪnəʊˌskəʊp). —**rhinoscopic** (ˌraɪnəʊˈskɒpɪk) *adj.*

rhizo- *or before a vowel* **rhiz-** *combining form.* root: *rhizomorphous.* [from Greek *rhiza*]

rhizobium (raɪˈzəʊbɪəm) *n., pl.* **-bia** (-bɪə). any rod-shaped bacterium of the genus *Rhizobium,* typically occurring in the root nodules of leguminous plants and able to fix atmospheric nitrogen. See also **nitrogen fixation.** [C20: from RHIZO- + Greek *bios* life]

rhizocarpous (ˌraɪzəʊˈkɑːpəs) *adj.* **1.** (of plants) producing subterranean flowers and fruit. **2.** (of perennial plants) having roots that persist throughout the year but stems and leaves that wither at the end of the growing season.

rhizocephalan (ˌraɪzəʊˈsɛfələn) *n.* **1.** any parasitic crustacean of the order *Rhizocephala,* esp. *Sacculina carcini,* which has a saclike body and sends out absorptive processes into the body of its host, the crab: subclass *Cirripedia* (barnacles). ~*adj. also* **rhizocephalous. 2.** of, relating to, or belonging to the order *Rhizocephala.* [C19: from New Latin *Rhizocephala* (literally: root-headed), from RHIZO- + *-cephala* from Greek *kephalē* head]

rhizogenic (ˌraɪzəʊˈdʒɛnɪk), **rhizogenetic** (ˌraɪzəʊdʒəˈnɛtɪk), *or* **rhizogenous** (raɪˈzɒdʒənəs) *adj.* (of cells and tissues) giving rise to roots.

rhizoid (ˈraɪzɔɪd) *n.* any of various slender hairlike structures that function as roots in mosses, ferns, fungi, and related plants. —**rhiˈzoidal** *adj.*

rhizome (ˈraɪzəʊm) *n.* a thick horizontal underground stem of plants such as the mint and iris whose buds develop into new plants. Also called: **rootstock, rootstalk.** [C19: from New Latin *rhizoma,* from Greek, from *rhiza* a root] —**rhizomatous** (raɪˈzɒmətəs, -ˈzəʊ-) *adj.*

rhizomorph (ˈraɪzəʊˌmɔːf) *n.* a rootlike structure of certain fungi, such as the honey fungus *Armillaria mellea,* consisting of a dense mass of hyphae.

rhizomorphous (ˌraɪzəʊˈmɔːfəs) *adj. Botany.* having the appearance of a root.

rhizopod (ˈraɪzəʊˌpɒd) *n.* **1.** any protozoan of the subclass *Rhizopoda,* characterized by naked protoplasmic processes (pseudopodia): class *Sarcodina.* The group includes the amoebas and foraminifers. ~*adj.* **2.** of, relating to, or belonging to the *Rhizopoda.* —**rhizopodan** (raɪˈzɒpədən) *adj., n.* —**rhiˈzopodous** *adj.*

rhizopus (ˈraɪzəʊpəs) *n.* any phycomycetous fungus of the genus *Rhizopus,* esp. *R. nigricans,* a bread mould. [C19: New Latin, from RHIZO- + Greek *pous* foot]

rhizosphere (ˈraɪzəʊˌsfɪə) *n.* the region of the soil in contact with the roots of a plant. It contains many microorganisms and its composition is affected by root activities.

rhizotomy (raɪˈzɒtəmɪ) *n., pl.* **-mies.** surgical incision into the roots of spinal nerves, esp. for the relief of pain.

Rh negative *n.* **1.** blood that does not contain the Rh factor. **2.** a person having such blood.

rho (rəʊ) *n., pl.* **rhos.** the 17th letter in the Greek alphabet (Ρ, ρ), a consonant transliterated as *r* or *rh.*

rhodamine (ˈrəʊdəˌmiːn, -mɪn) *n.* any one of a group of synthetic red or pink basic dyestuffs used for wool and silk. They are made from phthalic anhydride and aminophenols. [C20: from RHODO- + AMINE]

Rhode Island Red (rəʊd) *n.* a breed of domestic fowl, originating in America, characterized by a dark reddish-brown plumage and the production of brown eggs.
Rhodes grass (rəʊdz) *n.* a perennial grass, *Chloris gayana,* native to Africa but widely cultivated in dry regions for forage. [C19: named after Cecil *Rhodes* (1853–1902), British colonial financier and statesman in South Africa]
Rhodesian man (rəʊ'diːʃən, -ʒɪən) *n.* a type of early man, *Homo rhodesiensis* (or *H. sapiens rhodesiensis*), occurring in Africa in late Pleistocene times and resembling Neanderthal man in many features. [from *Rhodesia* (now Zimbabwe), in SE Africa]
Rhodesian ridgeback ('rɪdʒˌbæk) *n.* a large short-haired breed of dog characterized by a ridge of hair growing along the back in the opposite direction to the rest of the coat.
Rhodesoid (rəʊ'diːzɔɪd) *adj.* relating to or resembling Rhodesian man.
Rhodes scholarship *n.* one of 72 scholarships founded by Cecil Rhodes, awarded annually on merit to Commonwealth and U.S. students to study for two or sometimes three years at Oxford University. —**Rhodes scholar** *n.*
Rhodian ('rəʊdɪən) *adj.* **1.** of or relating to the Greek island of Rhodes. ~*n.* **2.** a native or inhabitant of Rhodes.
rhodic ('rəʊdɪk) *adj.* of or containing rhodium, esp. in the tetravalent state.
rhodinal ('rəʊdɪˌnæl) *n.* another name for **citronellal.**
rhodium ('rəʊdɪəm) *n.* a hard corrosion-resistant silvery-white element of the platinum metal group, occurring free with other platinum metals in alluvial deposits and in nickel ores. It is used as an alloying agent to harden platinum and palladium. Symbol: Rh; atomic no.: 45; atomic wt.: 102.90; valency: 1–6; relative density: 12.4; melting pt.: 1966°C; boiling pt.: 3727°C (approx.). [C19: New Latin, from Greek *rhodon* rose, from the pink colour of its compounds]
rhodo- *or before a vowel* **rhod-** *combining form.* rose or rose-coloured: *rhododendron; rhodolite.* [from Greek *rhodon* rose]
rhodochrosite (ˌrəʊdəʊ'krəʊsaɪt) *n.* a pink, grey, or brown mineral that consists of manganese carbonate in hexagonal crystalline form and occurs in ore veins. Formula: $MnCO_3$. [C19: from Greek *rhodokhrōs* of a rosy colour, from *rhodon* rose + *khrōs* colour]
rhododendron (ˌrəʊdə'dɛndrən) *n.* any ericaceous shrub of the genus *Rhododendron,* native to S Asia but widely cultivated in N temperate regions. They are mostly evergreen and have clusters of showy red, purple, pink, or white flowers. Also called (U.S.): **rosebay.** See also **azalea.** [C17: from Latin: oleander, from Greek, from *rhodon* rose + *dendron* tree]
rhododendron bug *n.* See **lace bug.**
rhodolite ('rɒdəˌlaɪt) *n.* a pale violet or red variety of garnet, used as a gemstone.
rhodonite ('rɒdəˌnaɪt) *n.* a brownish translucent mineral consisting of manganese silicate in triclinic crystalline form with calcium, iron, or magnesium sometimes replacing the manganese. It occurs in metamorphic rocks, esp. in New Jersey (U.S.) and Russia, and is used as an ornamental stone, glaze, and pigment. Formula: $MnSiO_3$. [C19: from German *Rhodonit,* from Greek *rhodon* rose + -ITE[1]]
rhodopsin (rəʊ'dɒpsɪn) *n.* a red pigment in the rods of the retina in vertebrates. It is dissociated by light into retinene, the light energy being converted into nerve signals, and is re-formed in the dark. Also called: **visual purple.** See also **iodopsin.** [C20: from RHODO- + -OPSIS + -IN]
rhoicissus (ˌrəʊɪ'sɪsəs) *n.* any plant of the climbing genus *Rhoicissus,* related to and resembling cissus, esp. *R. rhomboidea* (grape ivy), grown for its shiny evergreen foliage: family *Vitaceae.* [New Latin, from Greek *rhoia* pomegranate + CISSUS]
rhomb (rɒm) *n.* another name for **rhombus.**
rhombencephalon (ˌrɒmbɛn'sɛfəˌlɒn) *n.* the part of the brain that develops from the posterior portion of the embryonic neural tube. Compare **mesencephalon, prosencephalon.** Nontechnical name: **hindbrain.** [C20: from RHOMBUS + ENCEPHALON]
rhombic ('rɒmbɪk) *adj.* **1.** relating to or having the shape of a rhombus. **2.** *Crystallog.* another word for **orthorhombic.**
rhombic aerial *n.* a directional travelling-wave aerial, usually horizontal, consisting of two conductors each forming a pair of adjacent sides of a rhombus.
rhombohedral (ˌrɒmbəʊ'hiːdrəl) *adj.* **1.** of or relating to a rhombohedron. **2.** *Crystallog.* another term for **trigonal** (sense 2).
rhombohedron (ˌrɒmbəʊ'hiːdrən) *n.* a six-sided prism whose sides are parallelograms. [C19: from RHOMBUS + -HEDRON]
rhomboid ('rɒmbɔɪd) *n.* **1.** a parallelogram having adjacent sides of unequal length. ~*adj. also* **rhom'boidal.** **2.** having such a shape. [C16: from Late Latin *rhomboides,* from Greek *rhomboeidēs* shaped like a RHOMBUS]
rhomboideus (rɒm'bɔɪdɪəs) *n., pl.* **-dei** (-dɪˌaɪ). *Anatomy.* either of two muscles that connect the spinal vertebrae to the scapulae. [C19: New Latin, from Late Latin *rhomboides:* see RHOMBOID]
rhombus ('rɒmbəs) *n., pl.* **-buses** *or* **-bi** (-baɪ). an oblique-angled parallelogram having four equal sides. Also called: **rhomb.** Compare **square** (sense 1). [C16: from Greek *rhombos* something that spins; related to *rhembein* to whirl]
rhonchus ('rɒŋkəs) *n., pl.* **-chi** (-kaɪ). a rattling or whistling respiratory sound resembling snoring, caused by secretions in the trachea or bronchi. [C19: from Latin, from Greek *rhenkhos* snoring] —'**rhonchal** *or* '**rhonchial** *adj.*
rhotacism ('rəʊtəˌsɪzəm) *n.* excessive use or idiosyncratic pronunciation of *r.* [C19: from New Latin *rhōtacismus,* from Greek *rhōtakizein* (verb) from the letter *rho*] —'**rhotacist** *n.* —ˌ**rhota'cistic** *adj.*
rhotic ('rəʊtɪk) *adj. Phonetics.* denoting or speaking a dialect of English in which postvocalic *r*s are pronounced. [from Greek *rho,* the letter *r*] —**rhoticity** (rəʊ'tɪsɪtɪ) *n.*
Rh positive *n.* **1.** blood containing the Rh factor. **2.** a person having such blood.
RHS *abbrev. for:* **1.** Royal Historical Society. **2.** Royal Horticultural Society. **3.** Royal Humane Society.
rhubarb ('ruːbɑːb) *n.* **1.** any of several temperate and subtropical plants of the polygonaceous genus *Rheum,* esp. *R. rhaponticum* (**common garden rhubarb**), which has long green and red acid-tasting edible leafstalks, usually eaten sweetened and cooked. **2.** the leafstalks of this plant. **3.** a related plant, *Rheum officinale,* of central Asia, having a bitter-tasting underground stem that can be dried and used medicinally as a laxative or astringent. **4.** *U.S. and Canadian slang.* a heated discussion or quarrel. ~*interj., n., vb.* **5.** the noise made by actors to simulate conversation, esp. by repeating the word *rhubarb* at random. [C14: from Old French *reubarbe,* from Medieval Latin *reubarbum,* probably a variant of *rha barbarum* barbarian rhubarb, from *rha* rhubarb (from Greek, perhaps from *Rha* ancient name of the River Volga) + Latin *barbarus* barbarian]
rhumb (rʌm) *n.* short for **rhumb line.**
rhumba ('rʌmbə, 'rʊm-) *n., pl.* **-bas.** a variant spelling of **rumba.**
rhumbatron ('rʌmbəˌtrɒn) *n.* another name for **cavity resonator.** [C20: from RHUMBA + -TRON, from the rhythmic variation of the waves]
rhumb line *n.* **1.** an imaginary line on the surface of a sphere, such as the earth, that intersects all meridians at the same angle. **2.** the course navigated by a vessel or aircraft that maintains a uniform compass heading. ~Often shortened to **rhumb.** [C16: from Old Spanish *rumbo,* apparently from Middle Dutch *ruum* space, ship's hold, but also influenced by Latin RHOMBUS]
rhyme *or* (*Archaic*) **rime** (raɪm) *n.* **1.** identity of the terminal sounds in lines of verse or in words. **2.** a word that is identical to another in its terminal sound: *"while" is a rhyme for "mile".* **3.** a verse or piece of poetry having corresponding sounds at the ends of the lines: *the boy made up a rhyme about his teacher.* **4.** any verse or piece of poetry. **5. rhyme or reason.** sense, logic, or meaning: *this proposal has no rhyme or reason.* ~*vb.* **6.** to use (a word) or (of a word) to be used so as to form a rhyme; be or make identical in sound. **7.** to render (a subject) into rhyme. **8.** to compose (verse) in a metrical structure. ~See also **masculine rhyme, feminine rhyme, eye rhyme.** [C12: from Old French *rime,* from *rimer* to rhyme, from Old High German *rīm* a number; spelling influenced by RHYTHM] —'**rhymeless** *or* '**rimeless** *adj.*
rhyme royal *n. Prosody.* a stanzaic form introduced into English verse by Chaucer, consisting of seven lines of iambic pentameter rhyming a b a b b c c.
rhymester, rimester ('raɪmstə), **rhymer,** *or* **rimer** *n.* a poet, esp. one considered to be mediocre or mechanical in diction; poetaster or versifier.
rhyming slang *n.* slang in which a word is replaced by another word or phrase that rhymes with it; for example, *apples and pears* meaning *stairs.*
rhynchocephalian (ˌrɪŋkəʊsɪ'fælɪən) *adj.* **1.** of, relating to, or belonging to the *Rhyncocephalia,* an order of lizard-like reptiles common in the Mesozoic era but today represented only by the tuatara. ~*n.* **2.** any reptile belonging to the order *Rhyncocephalia.* [C19: from New Latin *Rhynchocephalia,* from Greek *rhunkhos* a snout + *kephalē* head]
rhynchophore ('rɪŋkəˌfɔː) *n.* a member of the *Rhynchophora,* a former name for the superfamily of beetles (*Curculionoidea*) that comprises the weevils and bark beetles. [C19: New Latin *rhyncophora,* from Greek *rhunkhos* a snout + *-phoros* bearing]
rhyolite ('raɪəˌlaɪt) *n.* a fine-grained igneous rock consisting of quartz, feldspars, and mica or amphibole. It is the volcanic equivalent of granite. [C19: *rhyo-* from Greek *rhuax* a stream of lava + -LITE] —**rhyolitic** (ˌraɪə'lɪtɪk) *adj.*
rhythm ('rɪðəm) *n.* **1. a.** the arrangement of the relative durations of and accents on the notes of a melody, usually laid out into regular groups (**bars**) of beats, the first beat of each bar carrying the stress. **b.** any specific arrangement of such groupings; time: *quadruple rhythm.* **2.** (in poetry) **a.** the arrangement of words into a more or less regular sequence of stressed and unstressed or long and short syllables. **b.** any specific such arrangement; metre. **3.** (in painting, sculpture, architecture, etc.) a harmonious sequence or pattern of masses alternating with voids, of light alternating with shade, of alternating colours, etc. **4.** any sequence of regularly recurring functions or events, such as the regular recurrence of certain physiological functions of the body. [C16: from Latin *rhythmus,* from Greek *rhuthmos;* related to *rhein* to flow] —'**rhythmless** *adj.*
rhythm and blues *n.* (*functioning as sing.*) any of various kinds of popular music derived from or influenced by the blues. Abbrev.: **R & B.**
rhythmical ('rɪðmɪkᵊl) *or* **rhythmic** *adj.* of, relating to, or characterized by rhythm, as in movement or sound; metrical, peri-

odic, or regularly recurring. —'**rhythmically** *adv.* —**rhythmicity** (rɪð'mɪsɪtɪ) *n.*

rhythmic gymnastics *n.* (*functioning as sing. or pl.*) a form of gymnastics involving movements using hand apparatus such as balls, hoops, and ribbons.

rhythmics ('rɪðmɪks) *n.* (*functioning as sing.*) the study of rhythmical movement.

rhythmist ('rɪðmɪst) *n. Rare.* a person who has a good sense of rhythm.

rhythm method *n.* a method of controlling conception without the aid of a contraceptive device, by restricting sexual intercourse to those days in a woman's menstrual cycle on which conception is considered least likely to occur. See also **safe period.**

rhythm section *n.* those instruments in a band or group (usually piano, double bass, and drums) whose prime function is to supply the rhythm.

rhyton ('raɪtɒn) *n., pl.* **-ta** (-tə). (in ancient Greece) a horn-shaped drinking vessel with a hole in the pointed end through which to drink. [C19: from Greek *rhuton,* from *rhutos* flowing; related to *rhein* to flow]

RI *abbrev. for:* **1.** Regina et Imperatrix. [Latin: Queen and Empress] **2.** Rex et Imperator. [Latin: King and Emperor] **3.** Rhode Island. **4.** Royal Institution. **5.** religious instruction. ~**6.** *international car registration for* (Republic of) Indonesia.

ria ('rɪə) *n.* a long narrow inlet of the seacoast, being a former valley that was submerged by a rise in the level of the sea. Rias are found esp. on the coasts of SW Ireland and NW Spain. [C19: from Spanish, from *rio* river]

RIA *abbrev. for* Royal Irish Academy.

RIAA curve *n. Electronics.* a graphical representation, adopted as a worldwide standard, of the amplitude in relation to frequency response required for correct reproduction of microgroove disc recordings, compensating for the characteristics of the recording process. [C20: *R*ecord *I*ndustry *A*ssociation of *A*merica]

rial ('raɪəl) *n.* **1.** the standard monetary and currency unit of Iran, divided into 100 dinars. **2.** the standard monetary and currency unit of Oman. **3.** another name for **riyal.** [C14: from Persian, from Arabic *riyāl* RIYAL]

rialto (rɪ'æltəʊ) *n., pl.* **-tos.** a market or exchange. [C19: after the *Rialto* the business centre of medieval and renaissance Venice]

riant ('raɪənt) *adj. Rare.* laughing; smiling; cheerful. [C16: from French, from *rire* to laugh, from Latin *rīdēre*] —'**riantly** *adv.*

rib[1] (rɪb) *n.* **1.** any of the 24 curved elastic arches of bone that together form the chest wall in man. All are attached behind to the thoracic part of the spinal column. Technical name: **costa.** Compare **true rib, false ribs, floating rib. 2.** the corresponding bone in other vertebrates. **3.** a cut of meat including one or more ribs. **4.** a part or element similar in function or appearance to a rib, esp. a structural or supporting member or a raised strip or ridge. **5.** a structural member in a wing that extends from the leading edge to the trailing edge and maintains the shape of the wing surface. **6.** a projecting moulding or band on the underside of a vault or ceiling, which may be structural or ornamental. **7.** one of a series of raised rows in knitted fabric. See also **ribbing** (sense 3). **8.** a raised ornamental line on the spine of a book where the stitching runs across it. **9.** any of the transverse stiffening timbers or joists forming the frame of a ship's hull. **10.** any of the larger veins of a leaf. **11.** a metal strip running along the top of the barrel of a shotgun or handgun and guiding the alignment of the sights. **12.** a vein of ore in rock. **13.** a projecting ridge of a mountain; spur. ~*vb.* **ribs, ribbing, ribbed.** (*tr.*) **14.** to furnish or support with a rib or ribs. **15.** to mark with or form into ribs or ridges. **16.** to knit plain and purl stitches alternately in order to make raised rows in (knitting). **17.** *Archaic.* to enclose with or as if with ribs. [Old English *ribb;* related to Old High German *rippi,* Old Norse *rif* REEF[1]] —'**ribless** *adj.* —'**rib,like** *adj.*

rib[2] (rɪb) *Informal.* ~*vb.* **ribs, ribbing, ribbed. 1.** (*tr.*) to tease or ridicule. ~*n.* **2.** a joke or hoax. [C20: short for *rib-tickle* (vb.)]

RIBA *abbrev. for* Royal Institute of British Architects.

ribald ('rɪbᵊld) *adj.* **1.** coarse, obscene, or licentious, usually in a humorous or mocking way. ~*n.* **2.** a ribald person. [C13: from Old French *ribauld,* from *riber* to live licentiously, of Germanic origin] —'**ribaldly** *adv.*

ribaldry ('rɪbᵊldrɪ) *n.* ribald language or behaviour.

riband *or* **ribband** ('rɪbənd) *n.* **1.** a ribbon, esp. one awarded for some achievement. See also **blue riband. 2.** a flat rail attached to posts in a palisade. [C14: variant of RIBBON]

ribbed and smoked sheet *n.* another name for **smoked rubber.**

ribbing ('rɪbɪŋ) *n.* **1.** a framework or structure of ribs. **2.** ribs collectively. **3.** a raised pattern in woven or knitted material, made in knitting by doing purl and plain stitches alternately.

ribbon ('rɪbᵊn) *n.* **1.** a narrow strip of fine material, esp. silk, used for trimming, tying, etc. **2.** something resembling a ribbon; a long strip: *a ribbon of land.* **3.** a long thin flexible band of metal used as a graduated measure, spring, etc. **4.** a long narrow strip of ink-impregnated cloth for making the impression of type characters on paper in a typewriter or similar device. **5.** (*pl.*) ragged strips or shreds (esp. in the phrase **torn to ribbons**). **6.** a small strip of coloured cloth signifying membership of an order or award of military decoration, prize, or other distinction. ~*vb.* (*tr.*) **7.** to adorn with a ribbon or ribbons. **8.** to mark with narrow ribbon-like marks. **9.** to reduce to ribbons; tear into strips. [C14 *ryban,* from Old French *riban,* apparently of Germanic origin; probably related to RING, BAND[2]] —'**ribbon,like** *or* '**ribbony** *adj.*

ribbon development *n. Brit.* the building of houses in a continuous row along a main road: common in England between the two World Wars.

ribbonfish ('rɪbᵊn,fɪʃ) *n., pl.* **-fish** *or* **-fishes.** any of various soft-finned deep-sea teleost fishes, esp. *Regalecus glesne* (see **oarfish**), that have an elongated compressed body. They are related to the opah and dealfishes.

ribbon microphone *n.* a type of microphone in which the conductor is a thin ribbon of aluminium alloy moving perpendicularly in a magnetic field. It is strongly directional and can be used to reduce unwanted side noise.

ribbon strip *n.* another name for **ledger board** (sense 2).

ribbonwood ('rɪbən,wʊd) *n.* a small evergreen malvaceous tree, *Hoheria populnea,* of New Zealand. Its wood is used in furniture making and the tough bark for making cord. Also called: **lacebark.**

ribbon worm *n.* another name for **nemertean** (sense 1).

ribcage ('rɪb,keɪdʒ) *n.* the bony structure consisting of the ribs and their connective tissue that encloses and protects the lungs, heart, etc.

ribgrass ('rɪb,grɑːs) *n.* another name for **ribwort.**

riboflavin *or* **riboflavine** (,raɪbəʊ'fleɪvɪn) *n.* a yellow water-soluble vitamin of the B complex that occurs in green vegetables, germinating seeds, and in milk, fish, egg yolk, liver, and kidney. It is essential for the carbohydrate metabolism of cells. It is used as a permitted food colour, yellow or orange-yellow (**E101**). Formula: $C_{17}H_{20}N_4O_6$. Also called: **vitamin B_2, lactoflavin.** [C20: from RIBOSE + FLAVIN]

ribonuclease (,raɪbəʊ'njuːklɪ,eɪs, -,eɪz) *n.* any of a group of enzymes that catalyse the hydrolysis of RNA. [C20: from RIBONUCLE(IC ACID) + -ASE]

ribonucleic acid (,raɪbəʊnjuː'kliːɪk, -'kleɪ-) *n.* the full name of **RNA.** [C20: from RIBO(SE) + NUCLEIC ACID]

ribose ('raɪbəʊz, -bəʊs) *n. Biochem.* a pentose sugar that is an isomeric form of arabinose and that occurs in RNA and riboflavin. Formula: $CH_2OH(CHOH)_3CHO$. [C20: changed from ARABINOSE]

ribosomal RNA *n. Biochem.* a type of RNA thought to be transcribed from DNA in the nucleoli of cell nuclei, subsequently forming the component of ribosomes on which the translation of messenger RNA into protein chains is accomplished. Sometimes shortened to **r-RNA.**

ribosome ('raɪbə,səʊm) *n.* any of numerous minute particles in the cytoplasm of cells, either free or attached to the endoplasmic reticulum, that contain RNA and protein and are the site of protein synthesis. [C20: from RIBO(NUCLEIC ACID) + -SOME[3]] —,**ribo'somal** *adj.*

ribozyme ('raɪbəʊ,zaɪm) *n.* an RNA molecule capable of catalysing a chemical reaction, usually the cleavage of another RNA molecule. [C20: from RIBO(NUCLEIC ACID) + (EN)ZYME]

rib-tickler *n.* a very amusing joke or story. —'**rib-,tickling** *adj.*

ribwort ('rɪb,wɜːt) *n.* a Eurasian plant, *Plantago lanceolata,* that has lancelike ribbed leaves, which form a rosette close to the ground, and a dense spike of small white flowers: family *Plantaginaceae.* Also called: **ribgrass.** See also **plantain**[1].

RIC *abbrev. for* Royal Institute of Chemistry.

rice (raɪs) *n.* **1.** an erect grass, *Oryza sativa,* that grows in East Asia on wet ground and has drooping flower spikes and yellow oblong edible grains that become white when polished. **2.** the grain of this plant. ~*vb.* **3.** (*tr.*) *U.S. and Canadian.* to sieve (potatoes or other vegetables) to a coarse mashed consistency, esp. with a ricer. ~See also **Indian rice.** [C13 *rys,* via French, Italian, and Latin from Greek *orūza,* of Oriental origin]

ricebird ('raɪs,bɜːd) *n.* any of various birds frequenting rice fields, esp. the bobolink.

rice bowl *n.* **1.** a small bowl for eating rice out of, esp. a decorative one made of china or porcelain. **2.** a fertile rice-producing region.

rice grass *n.* another name for **cord grass.**

rice paper *n.* **1.** a thin semitransparent edible paper made from the straw of rice, on which macaroons and similar cakes are baked. **2.** a thin delicate Chinese paper made from an araliaceous plant, *Tetrapanax papyriferum* (**rice-paper plant**) of Taiwan, the pith of which is pared and flattened into sheets.

ricer ('raɪsə) *n. U.S. and Canadian.* a kitchen utensil with small holes through which cooked potatoes and similar soft foods are pressed to form a coarse mash.

ricercare (,riːtʃə'kɑːreɪ) *or* **ricercar** ('riːtʃə,kɑː) *n., pl.* **-cari** ('kɑːriː) *or* **-cars.** (in music of the 16th and 17th centuries) **1.** an elaborate polyphonic composition making extensive use of contrapuntal imitation and usually very slow in tempo. **2.** an instructive composition to illustrate instrumental technique; étude. [Italian, literally: to seek again]

rich (rɪtʃ) *adj.* **1. a.** well supplied with wealth, property, etc.; owning much. **b.** (*as collective n.;* preceded by *the*): *the rich.* **2.** (when *postpositive,* usually foll. by *in*) having an abundance of natural resources, minerals, etc.: *a land rich in metals.* **3.** producing abundantly; fertile: *rich soil.* **4.** (when *postpositive,* foll. by *in* or *with*) well supplied (with desirable qualities); abundant (in): *a country rich with cultural interest.* **5.** of great worth or quality; valuable: *a rich collection of antiques.* **6.** luxuriant or prolific: *a rich growth of weeds.* **7.** expensively elegant, elaborate, or fine; costly: *a rich display.* **8.** (of food) having a large proportion of flavoursome or fatty ingredients, such as spices, butter, or cream. **9.** having a full-bodied flavour: *a rich ruby port.* **10.** (of a smell) pungent or fragrant. **11.** (of colour) intense or vivid; deep: *a rich red.* **12.** (of sound or a voice) full, mellow, or resonant. **13.** (of a fuel-air mixture) containing a relatively high proportion of fuel. Compare **weak** (sense 12). **14.** very amusing, laughable, or ridiculous: *a rich joke; a rich situation.* ~*n.* **15.** See **riches.** [Old English *rīce* (originally of persons: great, mighty), of Germanic origin, ultimately from Celtic (compare Old Irish *rī* king)]

riches (ˈrɪtʃɪz) *pl. n.* wealth; an abundance of money, valuable possessions, or property.

richly (ˈrɪtʃlɪ) *adv.* **1.** in a rich or elaborate manner: *a richly decorated carving.* **2.** fully and appropriately: *he was richly rewarded for his service.*

richness (ˈrɪtʃˌnɪs) *n.* **1.** the state or quality of being rich. **2.** *Ecology.* the number of individuals of a species in a given area.

rich rhyme *n. Prosody.* another term for **rime riche.**

richt (rɪxt) *adj., adv., n.* a Scot. word for **right.**

Richter scale (ˈrɪxtə) *n.* a scale for expressing the magnitude of an earthquake by the quantity of energy released, ranging from 0 to over 8. Compare **Mercalli scale.** See also **magnitude** (sense 5). [C20: named after Charles *Richter* (1900–85) U.S. seismologist]

ricin (ˈraɪsɪn, ˈrɪs-) *n. Biochem.* a highly toxic protein, a lectin, derived from castor-oil seeds: used in experimental cancer therapy. [C19: from New Latin *Ricinus* genus name, from Latin: the castor-oil plant]

ricinoleic acid (ˌrɪsɪnəʊˈliːɪk, -ˈnəʊlɪɪk) *n.* **1.** an oily unsaturated carboxylic acid found, as the glyceride, in castor oil and used in the manufacture of soap and in finishing textiles; 12-hydroxy-9-octadecanoic acid. Formula: $C_{18}H_{34}O_3$. **2.** the mixture of fatty acids obtained by hydrolysing castor oil. [C19: from RICIN + OLEIC ACID]

rick[1] (rɪk) *n.* **1.** a large stack of hay, corn, peas, etc., built in the open in a regular-shaped pile, esp. one with a thatched top. ~*vb.* **2.** (*tr.*) to stack or pile into ricks. [Old English *hrēac;* related to Old Norse *hraukr*]

rick[2] (rɪk) *n.* **1.** a wrench or sprain, as of the back. ~*vb.* **2.** (*tr.*) to wrench or sprain (a joint, a limb, the back, etc.). [C18: see WRICK]

ricker (ˈrɪkə) *n.* a young kauri tree of New Zealand. [from earlier use of the trunks as ships' rigging]

rickets (ˈrɪkɪts) *n.* (*functioning as sing. or pl.*) *Pathol.* a disease mainly of children, characterized by softening of developing bone, and hence bow legs, malnutrition, and enlargement of the liver and spleen, caused by a deficiency of vitamin D. [C17: of unknown origin]

rickettsia (rɪˈkɛtsɪə) *n., pl.* **-siae** (-sɪˌiː) *or* **-sias.** any of a group of parasitic microorganisms, intermediate in structure between bacteria and viruses, that live in the tissues of ticks, mites, and other arthropods, and cause disease when transmitted to man. [C20: named after Howard T. *Ricketts* (1871–1910), U.S. pathologist] —**rickˈettsial** *adj.*

rickettsial disease *n.* any of several acute infectious diseases caused by ticks, mites, or body lice infected with rickettsiae. The main types include typhus, spotted fever, Q fever, trench fever, and tsutsugamushi disease.

rickety (ˈrɪkɪtɪ) *adj.* **1.** (of a structure, piece of furniture, etc.) likely to collapse or break; shaky. **2.** feeble with age or illness; infirm. **3.** relating to, resembling, or afflicted with rickets. [C17: from RICKETS] —**ˈricketiness** *n.*

rickey (ˈrɪkɪ) *n.* a cocktail consisting of gin or vodka, lime juice, and soda water, served iced (esp. in the phrase **a gin rickey**). [C19: of uncertain origin]

rickle (ˈrɪkᵊl) *n. Scot.* **1.** an unsteady or shaky structure, esp. a dilapidated building. **2.** a loose or disorganized heap. [C16: perhaps of Scandinavian origin]

rickrack *or* **ricrac** (ˈrɪkˌræk) *n.* a zigzag braid used for trimming. [C20: dissimilated reduplication of RACK[1]]

rickshaw (ˈrɪkʃɔː) *or* **ricksha** (ˈrɪkʃə) *n.* **1.** Also called: **jinrikisha.** a small two-wheeled passenger vehicle drawn by one or two men, used in parts of Asia. **2.** Also called: **trishaw.** a similar vehicle with three wheels, propelled by a man pedalling as on a tricycle. ~See also **autorickshaw.** [C19: shortened from JINRIKISHA]

ricochet (ˈrɪkəˌʃeɪ, ˈrɪkəˌʃɛt) *vb.* **-chets, -cheting** (-ˌʃeɪɪŋ), **-cheted** (-ˌʃeɪd) *or* **-chets, -chetting** (-ˌʃɛtɪŋ), **-chetted** (-ˌʃɛtɪd). **1.** (*intr.*) (esp. of a bullet) to rebound from a surface or surfaces, usually with a characteristic whining or zipping sound. ~*n.* **2.** the motion or sound of a rebounding object, esp. a bullet. **3.** an object, esp. a bullet, that ricochets. [C18: from French, of unknown origin]

ricotta (rɪˈkɒtə) *n.* a soft white unsalted cheese made from sheep's milk, used esp. in making ravioli and gnocchi. [C19: Italian, from Latin *recocta* recooked, from *recoquere,* from RE- + *coquere* to COOK]

RICS *abbrev. for* Royal Institution of Chartered Surveyors.

rictus (ˈrɪktəs) *n., pl.* **-tus** *or* **-tuses.** **1.** the gap or cleft of an open mouth or beak. **2.** a fixed or unnatural grin or grimace, as in horror or death. [C18: from Latin, from *ringī* to gape] —**ˈrictal** *adj.*

rid (rɪd) *vb.* **rids, ridding, rid** *or* **ridded.** (*tr.*) **1.** (foll. by *of*) to relieve or deliver from something disagreeable or undesirable; make free (of): *to rid a house of mice.* **2. get rid of.** to relieve or free oneself of (something or someone unpleasant or undesirable). [C13 (meaning: to clear land): from Old Norse *rythja;* related to Old High German *riutan* to clear land] —**ˈridder** *n.*

riddance (ˈrɪdᵊns) *n.* the act of getting rid of something undesirable or unpleasant; deliverance or removal (esp. in the phrase **good riddance**).

ridden (ˈrɪdᵊn) *vb.* **1.** the past participle of **ride.** ~*adj.* **2.** (*in combination*) afflicted, affected, or dominated by something specified: *damp-ridden; disease-ridden.*

riddle[1] (ˈrɪdᵊl) *n.* **1.** a question, puzzle, or verse so phrased that ingenuity is required for elucidation of the answer or meaning; conundrum. **2.** a person or thing that puzzles, perplexes, or confuses; enigma. ~*vb.* **3.** to solve, explain, or interpret (a riddle or riddles). **4.** (*intr.*) to speak in riddles. [Old English *rǣdelle, rǣdelse,* from *rǣd* counsel; related to Old Saxon *rādislo,* German *Rätsel*] —**ˈriddler** *n.*

riddle[2] (ˈrɪdᵊl) *vb.* (*tr.*) **1.** (usually foll. by *with*) to pierce or perforate with numerous holes: *riddled with bullets.* **2.** to damage or impair. **3.** to put through a sieve; sift. ~*n.* **4.** a sieve, esp. a coarse one used for sand, grain, etc. [Old English *hriddel* a sieve, variant of *hridder;* related to Latin *crībrum* sieve] —**ˈriddler** *n.*

ride (raɪd) *vb.* **rides, riding, rode, ridden.** **1.** to sit on and control the movements of (a horse or other animal). **2.** (*tr.*) to sit on and propel (a bicycle or similar vehicle). **3.** (*intr.;* often foll. by *on* or *in*) to be carried along or travel on or in a vehicle: *she rides to work on the bus.* **4.** (*tr.*) to travel over or traverse: *they rode the countryside in search of shelter.* **5.** (*tr.*) to take part in by riding: *to ride a race.* **6.** to travel through or be carried across (sea, sky, etc.): *the small boat rode the waves; the moon was riding high.* **7.** (*tr.*) *U.S. and Canadian.* to cause to be carried: *to ride someone out of town.* **8.** (*intr.*) to be supported as if floating: *the candidate rode to victory on his new policies.* **9.** (*intr.*) (of a vessel) to lie at anchor. **10.** (*tr.*) (of a vessel) to be attached to (an anchor). **11.** (esp. of a bone) to overlap or lie over (another structure or part). **12.** *S. African informal.* **a.** (*intr.*) to drive a car. **b.** (*tr.*) to transport (goods, farm produce, etc.) by motor vehicle or cart. **13.** (*tr.*) (esp. of a male animal) to copulate with; mount. **14.** (*tr.; usually passive*) to tyrannize over or dominate: *ridden by fear.* **15.** (*tr.*) *Informal.* to persecute, esp. by constant or petty criticism: *don't ride me so hard over my failure.* **16.** (*intr.*) *Informal.* to continue undisturbed: *I wanted to change something, but let it ride.* **17.** (*tr.*) to endure successfully; ride out. **18.** (*tr.*) to yield slightly to (a blow or punch) in order to lessen its impact. **19.** (*intr.;* often foll. by *on*) (of a bet) to remain placed: *let your winnings ride on the same number.* **20.** (*intr.*) *Jazz.* to play well, esp. in freely improvising at perfect tempo. **21. ride roughshod over.** to domineer over or act with complete disregard for. **22. ride to hounds.** to take part in a fox hunt on horseback. **23. ride for a fall.** to act in such a way as to invite disaster. **24. ride again.** *Informal.* to return to a former activity or scene of activity. **25. riding high.** confident, popular, and successful. ~*n.* **26.** a journey or outing on horseback or in a vehicle. **27.** a path specially made for riding on horseback. **28.** transport in a vehicle, esp. when given freely to a pedestrian; lift: *can you give me a ride to the station?* **29.** a device or structure, such as a roller coaster at a fairground, in which people ride for pleasure or entertainment. **30. take for a ride.** *Informal.* **a.** to cheat, swindle, or deceive. **b.** to take (someone) away in a car and murder him. ~See also **ride down, ride out, ride up.** [Old English *rīdan,* related to Old High German *rītan,* Old Norse *rītha*] —**ˈridable** *or* **ˈrideable** *adj.*

ride down *vb.* (*tr., adv.*) **1.** to trample under the hooves of a horse. **2.** to catch up with or overtake by riding.

rident (ˈraɪdᵊnt) *adj. Rare.* laughing, smiling, or gay. [C17: from Latin *rīdēre* to laugh; see RIANT]

ride out *vb.* (*tr., adv.*) to endure successfully; survive (esp. in the phrase **ride out the storm**).

rider (ˈraɪdə) *n.* **1.** a person or thing that rides, esp. a person who rides a horse, a bicycle, or a motorcycle. **2.** an additional clause, amendment, or stipulation added to a legal or other document, esp. (in Britain) a legislative bill at its third reading. **3.** *Brit.* a statement made by a jury in addition to its verdict, such as a recommendation for mercy. **4.** any of various objects or devices resting on, surmounting, or strengthening something else. **5.** a small weight that can be slid along one arm of a chemical balance to make fine adjustments during weighing. **6.** *Geology.* a thin seam, esp. of coal or mineral ore, overlying a thicker seam. —**ˈriderless** *adj.*

ride up *vb.* (*intr., adv.*) to move or work away from the proper place or position: *her new skirt rode up uncomfortably.*

ridge (rɪdʒ) *n.* **1.** a long narrow raised land formation with sloping sides esp. one formed by the meeting of two faces of a mountain or of a mountain buttress or spur. **2.** any long narrow raised strip or elevation, as on a fabric or in ploughed land. **3.**

Anatomy. any elongated raised margin or border on a bone, tooth, tissue membrane, etc. **4. a.** the top of a roof at the junction of two sloping sides. **b.** (*as modifier*): *a ridge tile.* **5.** the back or backbone of an animal, esp. a whale. **6.** *Meteorol.* an elongated area of high pressure, esp. an extension of an anticyclone. Compare **trough** (sense 4). ~*vb.* **7.** to form into a ridge or ridges. [Old English *hrycg;* related to Old High German *hrucki,* Old Norse *hryggr*] —'**ridge,like** *adj.* —'**ridgy** *adj.*

ridgeling, ridgling ('rɪdʒlɪŋ), *or* **ridgel** ('rɪdʒəl) *n.* **1.** a domestic male animal with one or both testicles undescended, esp. a horse. **2.** an imperfectly castrated male domestic animal. [C16: perhaps from RIDGE, from the belief that the undescended testicles were near the animal's ridge or back]

ridgepole ('rɪdʒ,pəʊl) *n.* **1.** a timber laid along the ridge of a roof, to which the upper ends of the rafters are attached. **2.** the horizontal pole at the apex of a tent.

ridgetree ('rɪdʒ,triː) *n.* another name for **ridgepole** (sense 1).

ridgeway ('rɪdʒ,weɪ) *n. Brit.* a road or track along a ridge, esp. one of great antiquity.

ridicule ('rɪdɪ,kjuːl) *n.* **1.** language or behaviour intended to humiliate or mock; derision. ~*vb.* **2.** (*tr.*) to make fun of, mock, or deride. [C17: from French, from Latin *rīdiculus,* from *rīdēre* to laugh] —'**ridi,culer** *n.*

ridiculous (rɪ'dɪkjʊləs) *adj.* worthy of or exciting ridicule; absurd, preposterous, laughable, or contemptible. [C16: from Latin *rīdiculōsus,* from *rīdēre* to laugh] —**ri'diculously** *adv.* —**ri'diculousness** *n.*

riding[1] ('raɪdɪŋ) *n.* **a.** the art or practice of horsemanship. **b.** (*as modifier*): *a riding school; riding techniques.*

riding[2] ('raɪdɪŋ) *n.* **1.** (*cap. when part of a name*) any of the three former administrative divisions of Yorkshire. **2.** (in Canada) a parliamentary constituency. **3.** (in New Zealand) a rural electorate for local government. [from Old English *thriding,* from Old Norse *thrithjungr* a third. The *th-* was lost by assimilation to the *-t* or *-th* that preceded it, as in *west thriding,* etc.]

riding breeches *pl. n.* tough breeches with a large baggy seat and padding inside the knees, worn for riding horses.

riding crop *n.* a short whip with a thong at one end and a handle for opening gates at the other.

riding habit *n.* a woman's dress worn for riding, usually with a full or a divided skirt.

riding lamp *or* **light** *n.* a light on a boat or ship showing that it is at anchor.

ridotto (rɪ'dɒtəʊ) *n., pl.* **-tos.** an entertainment with music and dancing, often in masquerade: popular in 18th-century England. [C18: from Italian: retreat, from Latin *reductus,* from *redūcere* to lead back]

riel ('riːəl) *n.* the standard monetary and currency unit of Cambodia, divided into 100 sen.

Riemannian geometry (riː'mɑːnjən) *n.* a branch of non-Euclidean geometry in which a line may have many parallels through a given point. It has a model on the surface of a sphere, with lines represented by great circles. Also called: **elliptic geometry.** [named after G. F. B. *Riemann* (1826–66), German mathematician who formulated it]

riempie ('rɪmpɪ) *n. S. African.* a leather thong or lace used mainly to make chair seats. [C19 (earlier *riem*): from Afrikaans, diminutive of *riem,* from Dutch: RIM]

riesling ('riːzlɪŋ, 'raɪz-) *n.* **1.** a white wine from the Rhine valley in Germany and from certain districts in other countries. **2.** the grape used to make this wine. [C19: from German, from earlier *Rüssling,* of obscure origin]

Rif, Riff (rɪf), *or* **Rifi** ('rɪfɪ) *n.* **1.** (*pl.* **Rifs, Riffs, Rifis** *or* **Rif, Riff, Rifi**) a member of a Berber people, inhabiting the Atlas Mountains in Morocco. **2.** Also called: **Rifian, Riffian** ('rɪfɪən). the dialect of Berber spoken by this people.

rifampicin (rɪ'fæmpɪsɪn) *or U.S.* **rifampin** (rɪ'fæmpɪn) *n.* a drug used in the treatment of tuberculosis, meningitis, and leprosy. [C20: from *rifam(y)cin,* from Italian *riformare* to reform + -MYCIN, + inserted PI(PERAZINE)]

rife (raɪf) *adj.* (*postpositive*) **1.** of widespread occurrence; prevalent or current: *rumour was rife in the village.* **2.** very plentiful; abundant. **3.** (foll. by *with*) abounding (in): *a land rife with poverty.* [Old English *rīfe;* related to Old Norse *rīfr* generous, Middle Dutch *rīve*] —'**rifely** *adv.* —'**rifeness** *n.*

riff (rɪf) *Jazz, rock.* ~*n.* **1.** an ostinato played over changing harmonies. ~*vb.* **2.** (*intr.*) to play or perform riffs. [C20: probably altered and shortened from REFRAIN]

riffle ('rɪfᵊl) *vb.* **1.** (when *intr.,* often foll. by *through*) to flick rapidly through (the pages of a book, magazine, etc.), esp. in a desultory manner. **2.** to shuffle (playing cards) by halving the pack and flicking the adjacent corners together. **3.** to make or become a riffle. ~*n.* **4.** *U.S. and Canadian.* **a.** a rapid in a stream. **b.** a rocky shoal causing a rapid. **c.** a ripple on water. **5.** *Mining.* a contrivance on the bottom of a sluice, containing transverse grooves for trapping particles of gold. **6.** the act or an instance of riffling. [C18: probably from RUFFLE[1], influenced by RIPPLE[1]]

riffler ('rɪflə) *n.* a file with a curved face for filing concave surfaces. [C18: from French *rifloir,* from *rifler* to scratch]

riffraff ('rɪf,ræf) *n.* (*sometimes functioning as pl.*) **1.** worthless people, esp. collectively; rabble. **2.** *Dialect.* worthless rubbish. [C15 *rif and raf,* from Old French *rif et raf;* related to *rifler* to plunder, and *rafle* a sweeping up; see RIFLE[2], RAFFLE]

rifle[1] ('raɪfᵊl) *n.* **1. a.** a firearm having a long barrel with a spirally grooved interior, which imparts to the bullet spinning motion and thus greater accuracy over a longer range. **b.** (*as modifier*): *rifle fire.* **2.** (formerly) a large cannon with a rifled bore. **3.** one of the grooves in a rifled bore. **4.** (*pl.*) **a.** a unit of soldiers equipped with rifles. **b.** (*cap. when part of a name*): *the King's Own Rifles.* ~*vb.* (*tr.*) **5.** to cut or mould spiral grooves inside the barrel of (a gun). **6.** to throw or hit (a ball) with great speed. [C18: from Old French *rifler* to scratch; related to Low German *rifeln* from *riefe* groove, furrow]

rifle[2] ('raɪfᵊl) *vb.* (*tr.*) **1.** to search (a house, safe, etc.) and steal from it; ransack. **2.** to steal and carry off: *to rifle goods from a shop.* [C14: from Old French *rifler* to plunder, scratch, of Germanic origin] —'**rifler** *n.*

riflebird ('raɪfᵊl,bɜːd) *n.* any of various birds of paradise of the genera *Ptiloris* and *Craspedophora,* such as *C. magnifica* (**magnificent riflebird**).

rifle green *n. Brit.* **a.** a dark olive green, as in the uniforms of certain rifle regiments. **b.** (*as adj.*): *rifle-green cloth.*

rifle grenade *n.* a grenade fired from a rifle.

rifleman ('raɪfᵊlmən) *n., pl.* **-men. 1.** a person skilled in the use of a rifle, esp. a soldier. **2.** a wren, *Acanthisitta chloris,* of New Zealand: family *Xenicidae.* See also **bush wren.**

rifle range *n.* an area used for target practice with rifles.

riflery ('raɪfᵊlrɪ) *n. U.S.* **1.** rifle shots. **2.** the practice or skill of rifle marksmanship.

rifling ('raɪflɪŋ) *n.* **1.** the cutting of spiral grooves on the inside of a firearm's barrel. **2.** the series of grooves so cut.

rift[1] (rɪft) *n.* **1.** a gap or space made by cleaving or splitting; fissure. **2.** *Geology.* a fault produced by tension on either side of the fault plane. **3.** a gap between two cloud masses; break or chink: *he saw the sun through a rift in the clouds.* **4.** a break in friendly relations between people, nations, etc. ~*vb.* **5.** to burst or cause to burst open; split. [C13: from Old Norse; related to Danish *rift* cleft, Icelandic *ript* breach of contract]

rift[2] (rɪft) *n. U.S.* **1.** a shallow or rocky part in a stream. **2.** the backwash from a wave that has just broken. [C14: from Old Norse *rypta;* related to Icelandic *ropa* to belch]

rift valley *n.* a long narrow valley resulting from the subsidence of land between two parallel faults.

rig[1] (rɪg) *vb.* **rigs, rigging, rigged.** (*tr.*) **1.** *Nautical.* to equip (a vessel, mast, etc.) with (sails, rigging, etc.). **2.** *Nautical.* to set up or prepare ready for use. **3.** to put the components of (an aircraft, etc.) into their correct positions. **4.** to manipulate in a fraudulent manner, esp. for profit: *to rig prices; to rig an election.* ~*n.* **5.** *Nautical.* the distinctive arrangement of the sails, masts, and other spars of a vessel. **6.** in full: **drilling rig.** the installation used in drilling for and exploiting natural oil and gas deposits: *an oil rig.* **7.** apparatus or equipment; gear. **8.** an amateur radio operator's transmitting and receiving set. **9.** *U.S. and Canadian.* a carriage together with one or more horses. **10.** *U.S. and Canadian.* an articulated lorry. ~See also **rig down, rig out, rig up.** [C15: from Scandinavian; related to Norwegian *rigga* to wrap]

rig[2] (rɪg) *n. Scot. and northern English dialect.* a ridge or raised strip of unploughed land in a ploughed field. [a variant of RIDGE]

rigadoon (,rɪgə'duːn) *or* **rigaudon** (*French* rigodɔ̃) *n.* **1.** an old Provençal couple dance, light and graceful, in lively duple time. **2.** a piece of music for or in the rhythm of this dance. [C17: from French, allegedly from its inventor *Rigaud,* a dancing master at Marseille in SE France]

rigamarole ('rɪgəmə,rəʊl) *n.* a variant of **rigmarole.**

rigatoni (,rɪgə'təʊnɪ) *n.* macaroni in the form of short ridged often slightly curved pieces. [C20: Italian, plural of *rigato,* from *rigare* to draw lines, make stripes, from *riga* a line, of Germanic origin]

rig down *vb.* (*adv.*) *Nautical.* to disassemble and stow.

Rigel ('raɪdʒəl, 'raɪgᵊl) *n.* the brightest star, Beta Orionis, in the constellation Orion: a remote blue-white giant and a visual binary. Visual magnitude: 0.2; spectral type: B8. [C16: from Arabic *rijl* foot; from its position in Orion's foot]

-rigged *adj.* (*in combination*) (of a sailing vessel) having a rig of a certain kind: *ketch-rigged; schooner-rigged.*

rigger ('rɪgə) *n.* **1.** a workman who rigs vessels, etc. **2.** *Rowing.* a bracket on a racing shell or other boat to support a projecting rowlock. **3.** a person skilled in the use of pulleys, lifting gear, cranes, etc.

rigging ('rɪgɪŋ) *n.* **1.** the shrouds, stays, halyards, etc., of a vessel. **2.** the bracing wires, struts, and lines of a biplane, balloon, etc. **3.** any form of lifting gear, tackle, etc.

rigging loft *n.* **1.** a loft or gallery in a boatbuilder's yard from which rigging can be fitted. **2.** a loft in a theatre from which scenery, etc., is raised and lowered.

right (raɪt) *adj.* **1.** in accordance with accepted standards of moral or legal behaviour, justice, etc.: *right conduct.* **2.** in accordance with fact, reason, or truth; correct or true: *the right answer.* **3.** appropriate, suitable, fitting, or proper: *the right man for the job.* **4.** most favourable or convenient; preferred: *the right time to act.* **5.** in a satisfactory condition; orderly: *things are right again now.* **6.** indicating or designating the correct time:

the clock is right. **7.** correct in opinion or judgment. **8.** sound in mind or body; healthy or sane. **9.** (*usually prenominal*) of, designating, or located near the side of something or someone that faces east when the front is turned towards the north. **10.** (*usually prenominal*) worn on a right hand, foot, etc. **11.** (*sometimes cap.*) of, designating, supporting, belonging to, or relating to the political or intellectual right (see sense 39). **12.** (*sometimes cap.*) conservative or reactionary: *the right wing of the party.* **13.** *Geometry.* **a.** formed by or containing a line or plane perpendicular to another line or plane. **b.** having the axis perpendicular to the base: *a right circular cone.* **c.** straight: *a right line.* **14.** relating to or designating the side of cloth worn or facing outwards. **15.** *Informal.* (intensifier): *a right idiot.* **16. in one's right mind.** sane. **17. the right side of. a.** in favour with: *you'd better stay on the right side of him.* **b.** younger than: *she's still on the right side of fifty.* ~*adv.* **18.** in accordance with correctness or truth; accurately: *to guess right.* **19.** in the appropriate manner; properly: *do it right next time!* **20.** in a straight line; directly: *right to the top.* **21.** in the direction of the east from the point of view of a person or thing facing north. **22.** absolutely or completely; utterly: *he went right through the floor.* **23.** all the way: *the bus goes right to the city centre.* **24.** without delay; immediately or promptly: *I'll be right over.* **25.** exactly or precisely: *right here.* **26.** in a manner consistent with a legal or moral code; justly or righteously: *do right by me.* **27.** in accordance with propriety; fittingly or suitably: *it serves you right.* **28.** to good or favourable advantage; well: *it all came out right in the end.* **29.** (esp. in religious titles) most or very: *right reverend.* **30.** *Informal or dialect.* (intensifier): *I'm right glad to see you.* **31. right, left, and centre.** on all sides; from every direction. **32. she'll be right.** *Austral. and N.Z. informal.* that's all right; not to worry. **33. right off the bat.** as the first in a series; to begin with. ~*n.* **34.** any claim, title, etc., that is morally just or legally granted as allowable or due to a person: *I know my rights.* **35.** anything that accords with the principles of legal or moral justice. **36.** the fact or state of being in accordance with reason, truth, or accepted standards (esp. in the phrase **in the right**). **37.** *Irish.* an obligation or duty: *you had a right to lock the door.* **38.** the right side, direction, position, area, or part: *the right of the army; look to the right.* **39.** (*often cap.* and preceded by *the*) the supporters or advocates of social, political, or economic conservatism or reaction, based generally on a belief that things are better left unchanged (opposed to *radical* or *left*). **40.** *Boxing.* **a.** a punch with the right hand. **b.** the right hand. **41.** *Finance.* **a.** (*often pl.*) the privilege of a company's shareholders to subscribe for new issues of the company's shares on advantageous terms. **b.** the negotiable certificate signifying this privilege. **42. by right** (*or* **rights**). properly; justly: *by rights you should be in bed.* **43. in one's own right.** having a claim or title oneself rather than through marriage or other connection: *a peeress in her own right.* **44. too right.** *Austral. and N.Z. informal.* an exclamation of agreement. **45. to rights.** consistent with justice, correctness, or orderly arrangement: *he put the matter to rights.* ~*vb.* (*mainly tr.*) **46.** (*also intr.*) to restore to or attain a normal, esp. an upright, position: *the raft righted in a few seconds.* **47.** to make (something) accord with truth or facts; correct. **48.** to restore to an orderly state or condition; put right. **49.** to make reparation for; compensate for or redress (esp. in the phrase **right a wrong**). ~*sentence substitute.* **50. a.** indicating that a statement has been understood. **b.** asking whether a statement has been understood. **c.** indicating a subdividing point within a discourse. ~*interj.* **51.** an expression of agreement or compliance. [Old English *riht, reoht;* related to Old High German *reht*, Gothic *raihts*, Latin *rēctus*] —ˈ**righter** *n.*

rightable (ˈraɪtəbᵊl) *adj.* capable of being righted. —ˈ**rightably** *adv.* —ˈ**rightableness** *n.*

right about *n.* **1.** a turn executed through 180°. ~*adj., adv.* **2.** in the opposite direction.

right angle *n.* **1.** the angle between two radii of a circle that cut off on the circumference an arc equal in length to one quarter of the circumference; an angle of 90° or $\pi/2$ radians. **2. at right angles.** perpendicular or perpendicularly. —ˈ**right-ˌangled** *adj.*

right-angled triangle *n.* a triangle one angle of which is a right angle. U.S. and Canadian name: **right triangle.**

right ascension *n. Astronomy.* the angular distance measured eastwards along the celestial equator from the vernal equinox to the point at which the celestial equator intersects a great circle passing through the celestial pole and the heavenly object in question. Symbol: α Compare **declination** (sense 1).

right away *adv.* without delay; immediately or promptly.

right-down *adv., adj.* a variant of **downright.**

righten (ˈraɪtᵊn) *vb.* **1.** (*tr.*) to set right. **2.** to restore to or attain a normal or upright position.

righteous (ˈraɪtʃəs) *adj.* **1. a.** characterized by, proceeding from, or in accordance with accepted standards of morality, justice, or uprightness; virtuous: *a righteous man.* **b.** (*as collective n.;* preceded by *the*): *the righteous.* **2.** morally justifiable or right, esp. from one's own point of view: *righteous indignation.* [Old English *rīhtwīs*, from RIGHT + WISE[2]] —ˈ**righteously** *adv.* —ˈ**righteousness** *n.*

right-footer *n.* (esp. in Ireland) a Protestant.

rightful (ˈraɪtfʊl) *adj.* **1.** in accordance with what is right; proper or just. **2.** (*prenominal*) having a legally or morally just claim: *the rightful owner.* **3.** (*prenominal*) held by virtue of a legal or just claim: *my rightful property.* —ˈ**rightfully** *adv.* —ˈ**rightfulness** *n.*

right-hand *adj.* (*prenominal*) **1.** of, relating to, located on, or moving towards the right: *a right-hand bend; this car has right-hand drive.* **2.** for use by the right hand; right-handed. **3. right-hand man.** one's most valuable assistant or supporter.

right-handed *adj.* **1.** using the right hand with greater skill or ease than the left. **2.** performed with the right hand: *right-handed writing.* **3.** made for use by the right hand. **4.** worn on the right hand. **5.** turning from left to right; clockwise. —ˌ**right-ˈhandedly** *adv.* —ˌ**right-ˈhandedness** *n.*

right-hander *n.* **1.** a blow with the right hand. **2.** a person who is right-handed.

Right Honourable *adj.* **1.** (in Britain and certain Commonwealth countries) a title of respect for a Privy Councillor or an appeal-court judge. **2.** (in Britain) a title of respect for an earl, a viscount, a baron, or the Lord Mayor or Lord Provost of any of certain cities.

rightish (ˈraɪtɪʃ) *adj.* somewhat right, esp. politically.

rightist (ˈraɪtɪst) *adj.* **1.** of, tending towards, or relating to the political right or its principles; conservative, traditionalist, or reactionary. ~*n.* **2.** a person who supports or belongs to the political right. —ˈ**rightism** *n.*

rightly (ˈraɪtlɪ) *adv.* **1.** in accordance with the true facts; correctly. **2.** in accordance with principles of justice or morality. **3.** with good reason; justifiably: *he was rightly annoyed with her.* **4.** properly or suitably; appropriately: *rightly dressed for a wedding.* **5.** (*used with a negative*) *Informal.* with certainty; positively or precisely (usually in the phrases **I don't rightly know; I can't rightly say**).

right-minded *adj.* holding opinions or principles that accord with what is right or with the opinions of the speaker. —ˌ**right-ˈmindedly** *adv.* —ˌ**right-ˈmindedness** *n.*

rightness (ˈraɪtnɪs) *n.* the state or quality of being right.

righto *or* **right oh** (ˈraɪtˈəʊ) *sentence substitute. Brit. informal.* an expression of agreement or compliance.

right off *adv.* immediately; right away.

right of search *n.* the right of a belligerent to stop and search neutral merchant ships on the high seas in wartime.

right of way *n., pl.* **rights of way. 1.** the right of one vehicle or vessel to take precedence over another, as laid down by law or custom. **2. a.** the legal right of someone to pass over another's land, acquired by grant or by long usage. **b.** the path or road used by this right. **3.** *U.S.* the strip of land over which a power line, railway line, road, etc., extends.

right on *interj.* **1.** *Slang, chiefly U.S. and Canadian.* an exclamation of full agreement, concurrence, or compliance with the wishes, words, or actions of another. ~*adj.* **2.** *Informal.* modern, trendy, and socially aware or relevant: *a suitably right-on title like 'The workers control the means of production'.*

Right Reverend *adj.* (in Britain) a title of respect for an Anglican or Roman Catholic bishop.

rights issue *n. Stock Exchange.* an issue of new shares offered by a company to its existing shareholders on favourable terms. Also called: **capitalization issue.**

right-thinking (ˈraɪtˌθɪŋkɪŋ) *adj.* possessing reasonable and generally acceptable opinions.

right triangle *n.* U.S. and Canadian name for **right-angled triangle.**

rightward (ˈraɪtwəd) *adj.* **1.** situated on or directed towards the right. ~*adv.* **2.** a variant of **rightwards.**

rightwards (ˈraɪtwədz) *or* **rightward** *adv.* towards or on the right.

right whale *n.* any large whalebone whale of the family *Balaenidae.* They are grey or black, have a large head, and, in most, no dorsal fin, and are hunted as a source of whalebone and oil. See also **bowhead.** [C19: perhaps so named because it was *right* for hunting]

right wing *n.* **1.** (*often caps.*) the conservative faction of an assembly, party, etc. **2.** the part of an army or field of battle on the right from the point of view of one facing the enemy. **3. a.** the right-hand side of the field of play from the point of view of a team facing its opponent's goal. **b.** a player positioned in this area in any of various games. **c.** the position occupied by such a player. ~*adj.* **right-wing. 4.** of, belonging to, or relating to the right wing. —ˈ**right-ˈwinger** *n.*

rigid (ˈrɪdʒɪd) *adj.* **1.** not bending; physically inflexible or stiff: *a rigid piece of plastic.* **2.** unbending; rigorously strict; severe: *rigid rules.* ~*adv.* **3.** completely or excessively: *the lecture bored him rigid.* [C16: from Latin *rigidus*, from *rigēre* to be stiff] —ˈ**rigidly** *adv.* —**riˈgidity** *or* ˈ**rigidness** *n.*

rigid designator *n. Logic.* an expression that identifies the same individual in every possible world: for example, "Shakespeare" is a rigid designator since it is possible that Shakespeare might not have been a playwright but not that he might not have been Shakespeare.

rigidify (rɪˈdʒɪdɪˌfaɪ) *vb.* **-fies, -fying, -fied.** to make or become rigid.

Rigil Kent ('raɪdʒɪl 'kɛnt) *n. Astronomy.* the star Alpha Centauri. Often shortened to **Rigil.** [from *Rigil Kentaurus,* from Arabic *al Rigil al Kentaurus* the Centaur's foot]

rigmarole ('rɪgməˌrəʊl) *or* **rigamarole** *n.* **1.** any long complicated procedure. **2.** a set of incoherent or pointless statements; garbled nonsense. [C18: from earlier *ragman roll* a list, probably a roll used in a medieval game, wherein various characters were described in verse, beginning with *Ragemon le bon* Ragman the good]

rigor ('raɪgɔː, 'rɪgə) *n.* **1.** *Med.* a sudden feeling of chilliness, often accompanied by shivering: it sometimes precedes a fever. **2.** ('rɪgə). *Pathol.* rigidity of a muscle; muscular cramp. **3.** a state of rigidity assumed by some animals in reaction to sudden shock. **4.** the inertia assumed by some plants in conditions unfavourable to growth. [see RIGOUR]

rigorism ('rɪgəˌrɪzəm) *n.* **1.** strictness in judgment or conduct. **2.** the religious cult of extreme self-denial. **3.** *R.C. Theol.* the doctrine that in cases of doubt in moral matters the stricter course must always be followed. —'**rigorist** *n.* —ˌ**rigor'istic** *adj.*

rigor mortis ('rɪgə 'mɔːtɪs) *n. Pathol.* the stiffness of joints and muscular rigidity of a dead body, caused by depletion of ATP in the tissues. It begins two to four hours after death and lasts up to about four days, after which the muscles and joints relax. [C19: Latin, literally: rigidity of death]

rigorous ('rɪgərəs) *adj.* **1.** characterized by or proceeding from rigour; harsh, strict, or severe: *rigorous discipline.* **2.** severely accurate; scrupulous: *rigorous book-keeping.* **3.** (esp. of weather) extreme or harsh. **4.** *Maths, logic.* (of a proof) making the validity of the successive steps completely explicit. —'**rigorously** *adv.* —'**rigorousness** *n.*

rigour *or U.S.* **rigor** ('rɪgə) *n.* **1.** harsh but just treatment or action. **2.** a severe or cruel circumstance; hardship: *the rigours of famine.* **3.** strictness, harshness, or severity of character. **4.** strictness in judgment or conduct; rigorism. **5.** *Maths, logic.* logical validity or accuracy. **6.** *Obsolete.* rigidity. [C14: from Latin *rigor*]

rig out *vb.* **1.** (*tr., adv.;* often foll. by *with*) to equip or fit out (with): *his car is rigged out with gadgets.* **2.** to dress or be dressed: *rigged out smartly.* ~*n.* **rigout. 3.** *Informal.* a person's clothing or costume, esp. a bizarre outfit.

rigsdaler ('rɪgzˌdɑːlə) *n.* another word for **rix-dollar.**

rig up *vb.* (*tr., adv.*) to erect or construct, esp. as a temporary measure: *cameras were rigged up to televise the event.*

rijksdaaler ('raɪksˌdɑːlə) *n.* a variant of **rix-dollar.**

rijsttafel ('raɪsˌtɑːfəl) *n.* an Indonesian food consisting of a selection of rice dishes to which are added small pieces of a variety of other foods, such as meat, fish, fruit, pickles, and curry. [from Dutch *rijst* rice + *tafel* table]

Riksmål *Norwegian.* ('riksmɔl) *n.* a former name for **Bokmål.** [literally: language of the kingdom]

rile (raɪl) *vb.* (*tr.*) **1.** to annoy or anger; irritate. **2.** *U.S. and Canadian.* to stir up or agitate (water, etc.); roil or make turbid. [C19: variant of ROIL]

Riley ('raɪlɪ) *n.* **the life of Riley.** a luxurious and carefree existence. [C20: origin unknown]

rilievo *Italian.* (ri'ljevo; *English* ˌrɪlɪ'eɪvəʊ) *n., pl.* **-vi** (-vi; *English* -viː). another name for **relief** (sense 9).

rill (rɪl) *n.* **1.** a brook or stream; rivulet. **2.** a small channel or gulley, such as one formed during soil erosion. **3.** Also: **rille.** one of many winding cracks on the moon. [C15: from Low German *rille;* related to Dutch *ril*]

rillet ('rɪlɪt) *n.* a little rill.

rim (rɪm) *n.* **1.** the raised edge of an object, esp. of something more or less circular such as a cup or crater. **2.** the peripheral part of a wheel, to which the tyre is attached. **3.** *Basketball.* the hoop from which the net is suspended. ~*vb.* **rims, rimming, rimmed.** (*tr.*) **4.** to put a rim on (a pot, cup, wheel, etc.). **5.** *Slang.* to lick, kiss, or suck the anus of (one's sexual partner). **6.** *Ball games.* (of a ball) to run around the edge of (a hole, basket, etc.). [Old English *rima;* related to Old Saxon *rimi,* Old Norse *rimi* ridge]

RIM *international car registration for* (Islamic Republic of) Mauritania.

rimaye (rɪ'meɪ) *n.* another name for **bergschrund.** [C20: French, from Latin *rima* cleft]

rime[1] (raɪm) *n.* **1.** frost formed by the freezing of supercooled water droplets in fog onto solid objects. ~*vb.* **2.** (*tr.*) to cover with rime or something resembling rime. [Old English *hrīm;* related to Dutch *rijm,* Middle High German *rīmeln* to coat with frost]

rime[2] (raɪm) *n., vb.* an archaic spelling of **rhyme.**

rimer ('raɪmə) *n.* another name for **rhymester.**

rime riche ('riːm 'riːʃ) *n., pl.* **rimes riches** ('riːm 'riːʃ). rhyme between words or syllables that are identical in sound, as in *command/demand, pair/pear.* [French, literally: rich rhyme]

rimester ('raɪmstə) *n.* a variant spelling of **rhymester.**

rim-fire *adj.* **1.** (of a cartridge) having the primer in the rim of the base. **2.** (of a firearm) adapted for such cartridges. ~Compare **centre-fire.**

rimose (raɪ'məʊs, -'məʊz) *adj.* (esp. of plant parts) having the surface marked by a network of intersecting cracks. [C18: from Latin *rīmōsus,* from *rīma* a split, crack] —'**rimosely** *adv.* —**rimosity** (raɪ'mɒsɪtɪ) *n.*

rimrock ('rɪmˌrɒk) *n.* rock forming the boundaries of a sandy or gravelly alluvial deposit.

rimu ('riːmuː) *n.* another name for **red pine.** [from Maori]

rimy ('raɪmɪ) *adj.* **rimier, rimiest.** coated with rime.

rind (raɪnd) *n.* **1.** a hard outer layer or skin on bacon, cheese, etc. **2.** the outer layer of a fruit or of the spore-producing body of certain fungi. **3.** the outer layer of the bark of a tree. [Old English *rinde;* Old High German *rinta,* German *Rinde*]

rinderpest ('rɪndəˌpɛst) *n.* an acute contagious viral disease of cattle, characterized by severe inflammation of the intestinal tract and diarrhoea. [C19: German: cattle pest]

rinforzando (ˌriːnfɔː'tsændəʊ) a less common term for **sforzando.** [Italian, literally: reinforcing]

ring[1] (rɪŋ) *n.* **1.** a circular band usually of a precious metal, esp. gold, often set with gems and worn upon the finger as an adornment or as a token of engagement or marriage. **2.** any object or mark that is circular in shape. **3.** a circular path or course: *to run around in a ring.* **4.** a group of people or things standing or arranged so as to form a circle: *a ring of spectators.* **5.** an enclosed space, usually circular in shape, where circus acts are performed. **6.** a square apron or raised platform, marked off by ropes, in which contestants box or wrestle. **7. the ring.** the sport of boxing. **8.** the field of competition or rivalry. **9. throw one's hat in the ring.** to announce one's intention to be a candidate or contestant. **10.** a group of people usually operating illegally and covertly: *a drug ring; a paedophile ring; a ring of antique dealers.* **11.** (esp. at country fairs) an enclosure, often circular, where horses, cattle, and other livestock are paraded and auctioned. **12.** an area reserved for betting at a racecourse. **13.** a circular strip of bark cut from a tree or branch, esp. in order to kill it. **14.** a single turn in a spiral. **15.** *Geometry.* the area of space lying between two concentric circles. **16.** *Maths.* a set that is subject to two binary operations, addition and multiplication, such that the set is an Abelian group under addition and is closed under multiplication, this latter operation being associative. **17.** *Botany.* short for **annual ring. 18.** Also called: **closed chain.** *Chem.* a closed loop of atoms in a molecule. **19.** one of the system of planar circular bands orbiting the planet Saturn. See also **Saturn** (sense 1). **20. run rings around.** *Informal.* to be greatly superior to; outclass completely. ~*vb.* **rings, ringing, ringed.** (*tr.*) **21.** to surround with or as if with or form a ring; encircle. **22.** to mark (a bird) with a ring or clip for subsequent identification. **23.** to fit a ring in the nose of (a bull, pig, etc.) so that it can be led easily. **24.** Also: **ringbark a.** to cut away a circular strip of bark from (a tree or branch) in order to kill it. **b.** to cut a narrow or partial ring from (the trunk of a tree) in order to check or prevent vigorous growth. **25.** *Austral. and N.Z.* to be the fastest shearer in a shearing shed (esp. in the phrase **ring the shed**). [Old English *hring;* related to Old Norse *hringr*]

ring[2] (rɪŋ) *vb.* **rings, ringing, rang, rung. 1.** to emit or cause to emit a sonorous or resonant sound, characteristic of certain metals when struck. **2.** to cause (a bell) to emit a ringing sound by striking it once or repeatedly or (of a bell) to emit such a sound. **3. a.** (*tr.*) to cause (a large bell, esp. a church bell) to emit a ringing sound by pulling on a rope that is attached to a wheel on which the bell swings back and forth, being sounded by a clapper inside it. Compare **chime**[1] (sense 6). **b.** (*intr.*) (of a bell) to sound by being swung in this way. **4.** (*intr.*) (of a building, place, etc.) to be filled with sound; echo: *the church rang with singing.* **5.** (*intr.;* foll. by *for*) to call by means of a bell, buzzer, etc.: *to ring for the butler.* **6.** Also: **ring up.** *Chiefly Brit.* to call (a person) by telephone. **7.** (*tr.*) to strike or tap (a coin) in order to assess its genuineness by the sound produced. **8.** (*intr.*) (of the ears) to have or give the sensation of humming or ringing. **9.** (*intr.*) *Electronics.* (of an electric circuit) to produce a damped oscillatory wave after the application of a sharp input transition. **10. ring a bell.** to sound familiar; remind one of something, esp. indistinctly. **11. ring down the curtain. a.** to lower the curtain at the end of a theatrical performance. **b.** (foll. by *on*) to put an end (to). **12. ring false.** to give the impression of being false. **13. ring the bell. a.** to do, say, or be the right thing. **b.** to reach the pinnacle of success or happiness. **14. ring the changes.** to vary the manner or performance of an action that is often repeated. **15. ring true.** to give the impression of being true: *that story doesn't ring true.* ~*n.* **16.** the act of or a sound made by ringing. **17.** a sound produced by or suggestive of a bell. **18.** any resonant or metallic sound, esp. one sustained or re-echoed: *the ring of trumpets.* **19.** *Informal, chiefly Brit.* a telephone call: *he gave her a ring last night.* **20.** the complete set of bells in a tower or belfry: *a ring of eight bells.* See **peal**[1] (sense 3). **21.** an inherent quality or characteristic: *his explanation has the ring of sincerity.* **22.** *Electronics.* the damped oscillatory wave produced by a circuit that rings. ~See also **ring back, ring in, ring off, ring out, ring up.** [Old English *hringan;* related to Old High German *hringen,* Old Norse *hringja*]

▷**Usage.** *Rang* and *sang* are the correct forms of the past tenses of *ring* and *sing,* although *rung* and *sung* are still heard informally and dialectally: *he rung (rang) the bell.*

ring back *vb.* (*adv.*) to return a telephone call (to).

ringbark ('rɪŋˌbɑːk) *vb.* another term for **ring**[1] (sense 24).

ring binder *n.* a loose-leaf binder fitted with metal rings that can be opened to allow perforated paper to be inserted.

ringbolt ('rɪŋˌbəʊlt) *n.* a bolt with a ring fitted through an eye attached to the bolt head.

ringbone ('rɪŋˌbəʊn) *n.* an abnormal bony growth affecting the pastern of a horse, often causing lameness.

ring circuit *n.* an electrical system in which distribution points are connected to the main supply in a continuous closed circuit.

ringdove ('rɪŋˌdʌv) *n.* **1.** another name for **wood pigeon. 2.** an Old World turtledove, *Streptopelia risoria,* having a greyish plumage with a black band around the neck.

ring-dyke *n.* a dyke having an approximately circular outcrop of rock.

ringed (rɪŋd) *adj.* **1.** displaying ringlike markings. **2.** having or wearing a ring. **3.** formed by rings; annular.

ringed plover *n.* a European shorebird, *Charadrius hiaticula,* with a greyish-brown back, white underparts with a black throat band, and orange legs: family *Charadriidae* (plovers).

ringent ('rɪndʒənt) *adj.* (of the corolla of plants such as the snapdragon) consisting of two distinct gaping lips. [C18: from Latin *ringī* to open the mouth wide]

ringer ('rɪŋə) *n.* **1.** a person or thing that rings a bell. **2.** Also called: **dead ringer.** *Slang.* a person or thing that is almost identical to another. **3.** *U.S.* a contestant, esp. a horse, entered in a competition under false representations of identity, record, or ability. **4.** *Austral. and N.Z.* the fastest shearer in a shed. **5.** *Austral. informal.* the fastest or best at anything. **6.** a quoit thrown so as to encircle a peg. **7.** such a throw. **8.** *Austral.* the keeper of the ring in two-up, who supervises play.

Ringer's solution ('rɪŋəz) *n.* a solution containing the chlorides of sodium, potassium, and calcium, used to correct dehydration and, in physiological experiments, as a medium for in vitro preparations. [named after Sydney *Ringer* (1834–1910), British physician]

ring-fence *vb.* **1.** to assign (money, a grant, fund, etc.) to one particular purpose, so as to restrict its use: *to ring-fence a financial allowance.* **2.** to oblige (a person or organization) to use money for a particular purpose: *to ring-fence a local authority.* ~*n.* **ring fence. 3.** an agreement, contract, etc., in which the use of money is restricted to a particular purpose.

ring finger *n.* the third finger, esp. of the left hand, on which a wedding ring is traditionally worn.

ring flash *n. Photog.* a type of electronic flash in which the light source is arranged in a ring around the lens in order to produce a light without shadows.

ring gauge *n. Engineering.* a ring having an internal diameter of a specified size used for checking the diameter of a cylindrical object or part. Compare **plug gauge.**

ringgit ('rɪŋgɪt) *n.* the standard monetary unit of Malaysia, divided into 100 sens. [from Malay]

ringhals ('rɪŋˌhæls) *n., pl.* **-hals** *or* **-halses.** a venomous elapid snake, *Hemachatus hemachatus,* of southern Africa, which spits venom at its enemies from a distance. Also called: **spitting snake.** [Afrikaans, literally: ring neck]

ring in *vb. (adv.)* **1.** *(intr.) Chiefly Brit.* to report to someone by telephone. **2.** *(tr.)* to accompany the arrival of with bells (esp. in the phrase **ring in the new year**). **3.** *(tr.) Austral.* to substitute (a horse) fraudulently for another horse in a race. **4.** *(tr.) Austral. and N.Z.* to recruit or include (a person). ~*n.* **ring-in. 5.** *Austral.* a horse that serves as a substitute. **6.** *Austral. and N.Z.* a person or thing that is not normally a member of a particular group; outsider.

ringing tone *n. Brit.* a sequence of pairs of tones heard by the dialler on a telephone when the number dialled is ringing. Compare **engaged tone, dialling tone.**

ringleader ('rɪŋˌliːdə) *n.* a person who leads others in any kind of unlawful or mischievous activity.

ringlet ('rɪŋlɪt) *n.* **1.** a lock of hair hanging down in a spiral curl. **2.** any of numerous butterflies of the genus *Erebia,* most of which occur in S Europe and have dark brown wings marked with small black-and-white eyespots: family *Satyridae.* —'**ringleted** *adj.*

ring main *n.* a domestic electrical supply in which outlet sockets are connected to the mains supply through a ring circuit.

ringmaster ('rɪŋˌmɑːstə) *n.* the master of ceremonies in a circus.

ring-necked *adj.* (of animals, esp. certain birds and snakes) having a band of distinctive colour around the neck.

ring-necked pheasant *n.* a common pheasant, *Phasianus colchicus,* originating in Asia. The male has a bright plumage with a band of white around the neck and the female is mottled brown.

ring off *vb. (intr., adv.) Chiefly Brit.* to terminate a telephone conversation by replacing the receiver; hang up.

ring out *vb. (adv.)* **1.** *(tr.)* to accompany the departure of with bells (esp. in the phrase **ring out the old year**). **2.** *(intr.)* to send forth a loud resounding noise.

ring ouzel *n.* a European thrush, *Turdus torquatus,* common in rocky areas. The male has a blackish plumage with a white band around the neck and the female is brown.

ring road *n.* a main road that bypasses a town or town centre. U.S. names: **belt, beltway.**

ring-shout *n.* a West African circle dance that has influenced jazz, surviving in the Black churches of the southern U.S.

ringside ('rɪŋˌsaɪd) *n.* **1.** the area immediately surrounding an arena, esp. the row of seats nearest a boxing or wrestling ring. **2. a.** any place affording a close uninterrupted view. **b.** *(as modifier): a ringside seat.*

ringster ('rɪŋstə) *n.* a member of a ring controlling a market in antiques, art treasures, etc.

ringtail ('rɪŋˌteɪl) *n.* **1.** Also called: **ring-tailed cat.** another name for **cacomistle. 2.** *Austral.* any of several possums having curling prehensile tails used to grasp branches while climbing. **3.** *Austral. and N.Z.* another name for **ring-in** (sense 6).

ring-tailed *adj.* (of an animal) having a tail marked with rings of a distinctive colour.

ring taw *n.* a game of marbles in which players attempt to knock other players' marbles out of a ring.

ring up *vb. (adv.)* **1.** *Chiefly Brit.* to make a telephone call (to). **2.** *(tr.)* to record on a cash register. **3.** *(tr.)* to chronicle; record: *to ring up another success.* **4. ring up the curtain. a.** to begin a theatrical performance. **b.** (often foll. by *on*) to make a start (on).

ringworm ('rɪŋˌwɜːm) *n.* any of various fungal infections of the skin (esp. the scalp) or nails, often appearing as itching circular patches. Also called: **tinea.**

rink (rɪŋk) *n.* **1.** an expanse of ice for skating on, esp. one that is artificially prepared and under cover. **2.** an area for roller skating on. **3.** a building or enclosure for ice skating or roller skating. **4.** *Bowls.* a strip of the green, usually about 5–7 metres wide, on which a game is played. **5.** *Curling.* the strip of ice on which the game is played, usually 41 by 4 metres. **6.** (in bowls and curling) the players on one side in a game. [C14 (Scots): from Old French *renc* row, RANK[1]]

rinse (rɪns) *vb. (tr.)* **1.** to remove soap from (clothes, etc.) by applying clean water in the final stage in washing. **2.** to wash lightly, esp. without using soap: *to rinse one's hands.* **3.** to give a light tint to (hair). ~*n.* **4.** the act or an instance of rinsing. **5.** *Hairdressing.* a liquid preparation put on the hair when wet to give a tint to it: *a blue rinse.* [C14: from Old French *rincer,* from Latin *recens* fresh, new] —'**rinsable** *or* '**rinsible** *adj.* —ˌ**rinsa'bility** *or* ˌ**rinsi'bility** *n.* —'**rinser** *n.*

rioja (riː'əʊxə) *n.* a red or white wine, with a distinctive vanilla bouquet and flavour, produced around the Ebro river in central N Spain. [C20: from *La Rioja,* the area where it is produced]

riot ('raɪət) *n.* **1. a.** a disturbance made by an unruly mob or (in law) three or more persons; tumult or uproar. **b.** *(as modifier): a riot gun; riot police; a riot shield.* **2.** boisterous activity; unrestrained revelry. **3.** an occasion of boisterous merriment. **4.** *Slang.* a person who occasions boisterous merriment. **5.** a dazzling or arresting display: *a riot of colour.* **6.** *Hunting.* the indiscriminate following of any scent by hounds. **7.** *Archaic.* wanton lasciviousness. **8. run riot. a.** to behave wildly and without restraint. **b.** (of plants) to grow rankly or profusely. ~*vb.* **9.** *(intr.)* to take part in a riot. **10.** *(intr.)* to indulge in unrestrained revelry or merriment. **11.** *(tr.;* foll. by *away)* to spend (time or money) in wanton or loose living: *he has rioted away his life.* [C13: from Old French *riote* dispute, from *ruihoter* to quarrel, probably from *ruir* to make a commotion, from Latin *rugīre* to roar] —'**rioter** *n.*

riot act *n.* **read the riot act (to).** to warn or reprimand severely. [referring to the former practice in England of reading the *Riot Act* (1715) to rioters]

riotous ('raɪətəs) *adj.* **1.** proceeding from or of the nature of riots or rioting. **2.** inciting to riot. **3.** characterized by wanton or lascivious revelry: *riotous living.* **4.** characterized by boisterous or unrestrained merriment: *riotous laughter.* —'**riotously** *adv.* —'**riotousness** *n.*

riot shield *n.* a large oblong curved transparent shield used by police controlling crowds.

rip[1] (rɪp) *vb.* **rips, ripping, ripped. 1.** to tear or be torn violently or roughly; split or be rent. **2.** *(tr.;* foll. by *off* or *out)* to remove hastily, carelessly, or roughly: *they ripped out all the old kitchen units.* **3.** *(intr.) Informal.* to move violently or precipitously; rush headlong. **4.** *(intr.;* foll. by *into) Informal.* to pour violent abuse (on); make a verbal attack (on). **5.** *(tr.)* to saw or split (wood) in the direction of the grain. **6. let rip.** to act or speak without restraint. ~*n.* **7.** the place where something is torn; a tear or split. **8.** short for **ripsaw.** ~See also **rip off, rip up.** [C15: perhaps from Flemish *rippen;* compare Middle Dutch *rippen* to pull] —'**rippable** *adj.*

rip[2] (rɪp) *n.* short for **riptide** (sense 1). [C18: perhaps from RIP[1]]

rip[3] (rɪp) *n. Informal, archaic.* **1.** something or someone of little or no value. **2.** an old worn-out horse. **3.** a dissolute character; reprobate. [C18: perhaps altered from *rep,* shortened from REPROBATE]

RIP *abbrev. for* requiescat *or* requiescant in pace. [Latin: may he, she, *or* they rest in peace]

riparian (raɪ'pɛərɪən) *adj.* **1.** of, inhabiting, or situated on the bank of a river. **2.** denoting or relating to the legal rights of the owner of land on a river bank, such as fishing or irrigation. ~*n.* **3.** *Property law.* a person who owns land on a river bank. [C19: from Latin *rīpārius,* from *rīpa* a river bank]

ripcord ('rɪpˌkɔːd) *n.* **1.** a cord that when pulled opens a parachute from its pack. **2.** a cord on the gas bag of a balloon that when pulled opens a panel, enabling gas to escape and the balloon to descend.

ripe (raɪp) *adj.* **1.** (of fruit, grain, etc.) mature and ready to be eaten or used; fully developed. **2.** mature enough to be eaten or used: *ripe cheese.* **3.** fully developed in mind or body. **4.** resembling ripe fruit, esp. in redness or fullness: *a ripe complexion.* **5.** (*postpositive;* foll. by *for*) ready or eager (to undertake or undergo an action). **6.** (*postpositive;* foll. by *for*) suitable; right or opportune: *the time is not yet ripe.* **7.** mature in judgment or knowledge. **8.** advanced but healthy (esp. in the phrase **a ripe old age**). **9.** *Slang.* **a.** complete; thorough. **b.** excessive; exorbitant. **10.** *Slang.* slightly indecent; risqué. [Old English *rīpe;* related to Old Saxon *rīpi,* Old High German *rīfi,* German *reif*] —'**ripely** *adv.* —'**ripeness** *n.*

ripen ('raɪpᵊn) *vb.* to make or become ripe. —'**ripener** *n.*

ripieno (rɪ'pjɛnəʊ; *Italian* ri'pjeːno) *n., pl.* **-ni** (-niː) *or* **-nos.** (in baroque concertos and concerti grossi) the full orchestra, as opposed to the instrumental soloists. Also called: **concerto.** Compare **concertino** (sense 1). [C18: from Italian: from *ri-* RE- + *pieno,* from Latin *plēnus* full]

rip off *vb.* **1.** (*tr.*) to tear violently or roughly (from). **2.** (*adv.*) *Slang.* to steal from or cheat (someone). ~*n.* **rip-off. 3.** *Slang.* an article or articles stolen. **4.** *Slang.* a grossly overpriced article. **5.** *Slang.* the act of stealing or cheating.

riposte *or* **ripost** (rɪ'pɒst, rɪ'pəʊst) *n.* **1.** a swift sharp reply in speech or action. **2.** *Fencing.* a counterattack made immediately after a successful parry. ~*vb.* **3.** (*intr.*) to make a riposte. [C18: from French, from Italian *risposta,* from *rispondere* to reply, RESPOND]

ripper ('rɪpə) *n.* **1.** a person who rips. **2.** a murderer who dissects or mutilates his victims' bodies. **3.** *Slang, chiefly Austral. and N.Z.* a fine or excellent person or thing.

ripping ('rɪpɪŋ) *adj. Archaic Brit. slang.* excellent; splendid. —'**rippingly** *adv.*

ripple[1] ('rɪpᵊl) *n.* **1.** a slight wave or undulation on the surface of water. **2.** a small wave or undulation in fabric, hair, etc. **3.** a sound reminiscent of water flowing quietly in ripples: *a ripple of laughter.* **4.** *Electronics.* an oscillation of small amplitude superimposed on a steady value. **5.** *U.S. and Canadian.* another word for **riffle** (sense 4). **6.** another word for **ripple mark.** ~*vb.* **7.** (*intr.*) to form ripples or flow with a rippling or undulating motion. **8.** (*tr.*) to stir up (water) so as to form ripples. **9.** (*tr.*) to make ripple marks. **10.** (*intr.*) (of sounds) to rise and fall gently: *her laughter rippled through the air.* [C17: perhaps from RIP[1]] —'**rippler** *n.* —'**rippling** *adj.* —'**ripplingly** *adv.* —'**ripply** *adj.*

ripple[2] ('rɪpᵊl) *n.* **1.** a special kind of comb designed to separate the seed from the stalks in flax, hemp, or broomcorn. ~*vb.* **2.** (*tr.*) to comb with this tool. [C14: of Germanic origin; compare Middle Dutch *repelen,* Middle High German *reffen* to ripple] —'**rippler** *n.*

ripple control *n.* the remote control of a switch by electrical impulses.

ripple effect *n.* the repercussions of an event or situation experienced far beyond its immediate location.

ripple mark *n.* one of a series of small wavy ridges of sand formed by waves on a beach, by a current in a sandy riverbed, or by wind on land: sometimes found fossilized on bedding planes of sedimentary rock.

ripplet ('rɪplɪt) *n.* a tiny ripple.

rip-rap *n. Civil engineering.* broken stones loosely deposited in water or on a soft bottom to provide a foundation and protect a riverbed or river banks from scour: used for revetments, embankments, breakwaters, etc. [C19: reduplication of RAP[1]]

rip-roaring *adj. Informal.* characterized by excitement, intensity, or boisterous behaviour.

ripsaw ('rɪp,sɔː) *n.* a handsaw for cutting along the grain of timber.

ripsnorter ('rɪp,snɔːtə) *n. Slang.* a person or thing noted for intensity or excellence. [C19: from RIP[1] + SNORTER] —'**rip,snorting** *adj.*

riptide ('rɪp,taɪd) *n.* **1.** Also called: **rip, tide-rip.** a stretch of turbulent water in the sea, caused by the meeting of currents or abrupt changes in depth. **2.** Also called: **rip current.** a strong current, esp. one flowing outwards from the shore, causing disturbance on the surface.

Ripuarian (,rɪpju'ɛərɪən) *adj.* **1. a.** of or relating to the group of Franks who lived during the 4th century near Cologne along the Rhine. **b.** of or designating their code of laws. ~*n.* **2.** a Ripuarian Frank. [C18: from Medieval Latin *Ripuārius,* perhaps from Latin *rīpa* a river bank]

rip up *vb.* (*tr., adv.*) **1.** to tear (paper) into small pieces. **2.** to annul, cancel, or unilaterally disregard. **3.** to dig up, dig into, or remove (a surface): *they are ripping up the street.*

Rip Van Winkle ('rɪp væn 'wɪŋkᵊl) *n. Informal.* **1.** a person who is oblivious to changes, esp. in social attitudes or thought. **2.** a person who sleeps a lot. [C19: from a character who slept for 20 years, in a story (1819) by U.S. writer Washington Irving]

riroriro ('riːrəʊ,riːrəʊ) *n., pl.* **-ros.** another name for the **grey warbler.** [Maori]

rise (raɪz) *vb.* **rises, rising, rose** (rəʊz), **risen** ('rɪzᵊn). (*mainly intr.*) **1.** to get up from a lying, sitting, kneeling, or prone position. **2.** to get out of bed, esp. to begin one's day: *he always rises early.* **3.** to move from a lower to a higher position or place; ascend. **4.** to ascend or appear above the horizon: *the sun is rising.* **5.** to increase in height or level: *the water rose above the normal level.* **6.** to attain higher rank, status, or reputation: *he will rise in the world.* **7.** to be built or erected: *those blocks of flats are rising fast.* **8.** to become apparent; appear: *new troubles rose to afflict her.* **9.** to increase in strength, degree, intensity, etc.: *her spirits rose; the wind is rising.* **10.** to increase in amount or value: *house prices are always rising.* **11.** to swell up: *dough rises.* **12.** to become erect, stiff, or rigid: *the hairs on his neck rose in fear.* **13.** (of one's stomach or gorge) to manifest or feel nausea; retch. **14.** to become actively rebellious; revolt: *the people rose against their oppressors.* **15.** to slope upwards: *the ground rises beyond the lake.* **16.** to return from the dead; be resurrected. **17.** to originate; come into existence: *that river rises in the mountains.* **18.** (of a session of a court, legislative assembly, etc.) to come to an end; adjourn. **19.** *Angling.* (of fish) to come to the surface of the water, as when taking flies. **20.** (*tr.*) *Nautical.* another term for **raise** (sense 20). **21.** (often foll. by *to*) *Informal.* to respond (to teasing, etc.) or fall into a trap prepared for one. ~*n.* **22.** the act or an instance of rising; ascent. **23.** an increase in height; elevation. **24.** an increase in rank, status, or position. **25.** an increase in amount, cost, or value. **26.** an increase in degree or intensity. **27.** *Brit.* an increase in salary or wages. U.S. and Canadian word: **raise. 28.** a piece of rising ground. **29.** an upward slope or incline. **30.** the appearance of the sun, moon, or other celestial body above the horizon. **31.** the vertical height of a step or of a flight of stairs. **32.** the vertical height of a roof above the walls or columns. **33.** the height of an arch above the impost level. **34.** *Angling.* the act or instance of fish coming to the surface of the water to take flies, etc. **35.** the beginning, origin, or source; derivation. **36.** *Taboo slang.* an erection of the penis. **37. get** *or* **take a rise out of.** to provoke an angry or petulant reaction from. **38. give rise to.** to cause the development of; produce. [Old English *rīsan;* related to Old Saxon *rīsan,* Gothic *reisan*]

rise above *vb.* (*intr., prep.*) to overcome or be unaffected by (something mean or contemptible).

risen ('rɪzᵊn) *vb.* **1.** the past participle of **rise.** ~*adj.* **2.** restored from death; ascended into glory: *the risen Christ.*

riser ('raɪzə) *n.* **1.** a person who rises, esp. from bed: *an early riser.* **2.** the vertical part of a stair or step. **3.** a vertical pipe, esp. one within a building.

rise to *vb.* (*intr., prep.*) to respond adequately to (the demands of something, esp. a testing challenge).

risibility (,rɪzɪ'bɪlɪtɪ) *n., pl.* **-ties. 1.** a tendency to laugh. **2.** hilarity; laughter.

risible ('rɪzɪbᵊl) *adj.* **1.** having a tendency to laugh. **2.** causing laughter; ridiculous. [C16: from Late Latin *rīsibilis,* from Latin *rīdēre* to laugh] —'**risibly** *adv.*

rising ('raɪzɪŋ) *n.* **1.** an insurrection or rebellion; revolt. **2.** the yeast or leaven used to make dough rise in baking. ~*adj.* (*prenominal*) **3.** increasing in rank, status, or reputation: *a rising young politician.* **4.** increasing in maturity; growing up to adulthood: *the rising generation.* ~*adv.* **5.** *Informal.* approaching the age of; nearly: *she's rising 40.*

rising damp *n.* capillary movement of moisture from the ground into the walls of buildings. It results in structural damage up to a level of three feet.

rising trot *n.* a horse's trot in which the rider rises from the saddle every second beat. Compare **sitting trot.**

risk (rɪsk) *n.* **1.** the possibility of incurring misfortune or loss; hazard. **2.** *Insurance.* **a.** chance of a loss or other event on which a claim may be filed. **b.** the type of such an event, such as fire or theft. **c.** the amount of the claim should such an event occur. **d.** a person or thing considered with respect to the characteristics that may cause an insured event to occur. **3. at risk. a.** vulnerable; likely to be lost or damaged. **b.** *Social welfare.* vulnerable to personal damage, to the extent that a welfare agency might take protective responsibility. **4. no risk.** *Austral. informal.* an expression of assent. **5. take** *or* **run a risk.** to proceed in an action without regard to the possibility of danger involved in it. ~*vb.* (*tr.*) **6.** to expose to danger or loss; hazard. **7.** to act in spite of the possibility of (injury or loss): *to risk a fall in climbing.* [C17: from French *risque,* from Italian *risco,* from *rischiare* to be in peril, from Greek *rhiza* cliff (from the hazards of sailing along rocky coasts)] —'**risker** *n.*

risk capital *n. Chiefly Brit.* capital invested in an issue of ordinary shares, esp. of a speculative enterprise. Also called: **venture capital.**

risk factor *n. Med.* a factor, such as a habit or an environmental condition, that predisposes an individual to develop a particular disease.

risky ('rɪskɪ) *adj.* **riskier, riskiest.** involving danger; perilous. —'**riskily** *adv.* —'**riskiness** *n.*

risotto (rɪ'zɒtəʊ) *n., pl.* **-tos.** a dish of rice cooked in stock and served variously with tomatoes, cheese, chicken, etc. [C19: from Italian, from *riso* RICE]

risqué ('rɪskeɪ) *adj.* bordering on impropriety or indecency: *a risqué joke.* [C19: from French *risquer* to hazard, RISK]

Riss (rɪs) *n.* the third major Pleistocene glaciation in Alpine Europe. See also **Günz, Mindel, Würm.** [C20: named after the river *Riss,* a tributary of the Danube in Germany]

rissole ('rɪsəʊl) *n.* a mixture of minced cooked meat coated in egg and breadcrumbs and fried. Compare **croquette.** [C18: from French, probably ultimately from Latin *russus* red; see RUSSET]

risus sardonicus ('riːsəs sɑː'dɒnɪkəs) *n. Pathol.* fixed contraction of the facial muscles resulting in a peculiar distorted grin, caused esp. by tetanus. Also called: **trismus cynicus** ('trɪzməs 'sɪnɪkəs). [C17: New Latin, literally: sardonic laugh]

rit. *Music. abbrev. for:* **1.** ritardando. **2.** ritenuto.

ritardando (ˌrɪtɑː'dændəʊ) *adj., adv.* another term for **rallentando.** Abbrev.: **rit.** [C19: from Italian, from *ritardare* to slow down]

rite (raɪt) *n.* **1.** a formal act or procedure prescribed or customary in religious ceremonies: *fertility rites; the rite of baptism.* **2.** a particular body of such acts or procedures, esp. of a particular Christian Church: *the Latin rite.* **3.** a Christian Church: *the Greek rite.* [C14: from Latin *rītus* religious ceremony]

ritenuto (ˌrɪtə'nuːtəʊ) *adj., adv. Music.* **1.** held back momentarily. **2.** another term for **rallentando.** Abbrev.: **rit.** [C19: from Italian, from past participle of *ritenere,* from Latin *retinēre* to hold back]

rite of passage *or* **rite de passage** (*French* rit də pɑsaʒ) *n.* a ceremony performed in some cultures at times when an individual changes his status, as at puberty and marriage.

ritornello (ˌrɪtə'nɛləʊ) *n., pl.* **-los** *or* **-li** (-liː). *Music.* **1.** an orchestral passage between verses of an aria or song. **2.** a ripieno passage in a concerto grosso. [C17: from Italian, literally: a little return, from *ritorno* a RETURN]

ritual ('rɪtjʊəl) *n.* **1.** the prescribed or established form of a religious or other ceremony. **2.** such prescribed forms in general or collectively. **3.** stereotyped activity or behaviour. **4.** *Psychol.* any repetitive behaviour, such as hand-washing, performed by a person with a compulsive personality disorder. **5.** any formal act, institution, or procedure that is followed consistently: *the ritual of the law.* ~*adj.* **6.** of, relating to, or characteristic of religious, social, or other rituals. [C16: from Latin *rītuālis,* from *rītus* RITE] —'**ritually** *adv.*

ritualism ('rɪtjʊəˌlɪzəm) *n.* **1.** emphasis, esp. exaggerated emphasis, on the importance of rites and ceremonies. **2.** the study of rites and ceremonies, esp. magical or religious ones. —'**ritualist** *n.* —ˌ**ritual'istic** *adj.* —ˌ**ritual'istically** *adv.*

ritualize *or* **ritualise** ('rɪtjʊəˌlaɪz) *vb.* **1.** (*intr.*) to engage in ritualism or devise rituals. **2.** (*tr.*) to make (something) into a ritual.

Ritz (rɪts) *n.* **1.** any very luxurious and expensive establishment: usually used with a negative: *this isn't the Ritz, you know.* **2. put on the Ritz.** (*sometimes not cap.*) to assume a superior air or make an ostentatious display. [from the luxury hotels created by the Swiss César *Ritz* (1850–1918)]

ritzy ('rɪtsɪ) *adj.* **ritzier, ritziest.** *Slang.* luxurious or elegant. —'**ritzily** *adv.* —'**ritziness** *n.*

riv. *abbrev. for* river.

rivage ('rɪvɪdʒ) *n. Archaic.* a bank, shore, or coast. [C14: from Old French, from *rive* river bank, from Latin *rīpa*]

rival ('raɪvᵊl) *n.* **1. a.** a person, organization, team, etc., that competes with another for the same object or in the same field. **b.** (*as modifier*): *rival suitors; a rival company.* **2.** a person or thing that is considered the equal of another or others: *she is without rival in the field of economics.* ~*vb.* **-vals, -valling, -valled** *or U.S.* **-vals, -valing, -valed.** (*tr.*) **3.** to be the equal or near equal of: *an empire that rivalled Rome.* **4.** to try to equal or surpass; compete with in rivalry. [C16: from Latin *rīvālis,* literally: one who shares the same brook, from *rīvus* a brook]

rivalry ('raɪvəlrɪ) *n., pl.* **-ries.** **1.** the act of rivalling; competition. **2.** the state of being a rival or rivals. —'**rivalrous** *adj.*

rive (raɪv) *vb.* **rives, riving, rived, rived** *or* **riven** ('rɪvᵊn). (*usually passive*) **1.** to split asunder: *a tree riven by lightning.* **2.** to tear apart: *riven to shreds.* **3.** *Archaic.* to break (the heart) or (of the heart) to be broken. [C13: from Old Norse *rīfa;* related to Old Frisian *rīva*]

river ('rɪvə) *n.* **1. a.** a large natural stream of fresh water flowing along a definite course, usually into the sea, being fed by tributary streams. **b.** (*as modifier*): *river traffic; a river basin.* **c.** (*in combination*): *riverside; riverbed.* Related adj.: **fluvial.** **2.** any abundant stream or flow: *a river of blood.* **3. sell down the river.** *Informal.* to deceive or betray. [C13: from Old French *riviere,* from Latin *rīpārius* of a river bank, from *rīpa* bank] —'**riverless** *adj.*

river blindness *n.* another name for **onchocerciasis.**

river horse *n.* an informal name for the **hippopotamus.**

riverine ('rɪvəˌraɪn) *adj.* **1.** of, like, relating to, or produced by a river. **2.** located or dwelling near a river; riparian.

rivet ('rɪvɪt) *n.* **1.** a short metal pin for fastening two or more pieces together, having a head at one end, the other end being hammered flat after being passed through holes in the pieces. ~*vb.* **-ets, -eting, -eted.** (*tr.*) **2.** to join by riveting. **3.** to hammer in order to form into a head. **4.** (*often passive*) to cause to be fixed or held firmly, as in fascinated attention, horror, etc.: *to be riveted to the spot.* [C14: from Old French, from *river* to fasten, fix, of unknown origin] —'**riveter** *n.*

riveting ('rɪvətɪŋ) *adj.* absolutely fascinating; enthralling.

riviera (ˌrɪvɪ'ɛərə) *n.* a coastal region reminiscent of the Mediterranean coast of France and N Italy. [C20: from Italian *Riviera,* literally: shore, ultimately from Latin *rīpa* bank, shore]

rivière (ˌrɪvɪ'ɛə) *n.* a necklace the diamonds or other precious stones of which gradually increase in size up to a large centre stone. [C19: from French: brook, RIVER]

rivulet ('rɪvjʊlɪt) *n.* a small stream. [C16: from Italian *rivoletto,* from Latin *rīvulus,* from *rīvus* stream]

rix-dollar ('rɪksˌdɒlə) *n.* any of various former Scandinavian or Dutch small silver coins. Also called: **rijksdaaler, rigsdaler.** [C16: partial translation of obsolete Dutch *rijksdaler; rijk* realm, kingdom]

riyal (rɪ'jɑːl) *n.* the standard monetary and currency unit of Saudi Arabia or Yemen. [from Arabic *riyāl,* from Spanish *real* REAL[2]]

RL **1.** *abbrev. for* Rugby League. ~**2.** *international car registration for* (Republic of) Lebanon.

rly *abbrev. for* railway.

rm *abbrev. for:* **1.** ream. **2.** room.

RM *abbrev. for:* **1.** Royal Mail. **2.** Royal Marines. ~ **3.** *international car registration for* Malagasy Republic.

RMA *abbrev. for* Royal Military Academy (Sandhurst).

R-methodology *n.* any statistical methodology in psychology that is contrasted with Q-methodology.

RMM *international car registration for* (Republic of) Mali.

r.m.m. *abbrev. for* relative molecular mass.

rms *abbrev. for* root mean square.

RMS *abbrev. for:* **1.** Royal Mail Service. **2.** Royal Mail Steamer.

Rn *the chemical symbol for* radon.

RN *abbrev. for* Royal Navy.

RNA *n. Biochem.* ribonucleic acid; any of a group of nucleic acids, present in all living cells, that play an essential role in the synthesis of proteins. On hydrolysis they yield the pentose sugar ribose, the purine bases adenine and guanine, the pyrimidine bases cytosine and uracil, and phosphoric acid. See also **messenger RNA, transfer RNA, ribosomal RNA, DNA.**

RNAS *abbrev. for:* **1.** Royal Naval Air Service(s). **2.** Royal Naval Air Station.

RNIB *Brit. abbrev. for* Royal National Institute for the Blind.

RNLI *abbrev. for* Royal National Lifeboat Institution.

RNR *abbrev. for* Royal Naval Reserve.

RNVR *abbrev. for* Royal Naval Volunteer Reserve.

RNWMP (formerly, in Canada) *abbrev. for* Royal Northwest Mounted Police.

RNZAF *abbrev. for* Royal New Zealand Air Force.

RNZN *abbrev. for* Royal New Zealand Navy.

roach[1] (rəʊtʃ) *n., pl.* **roaches** *or* **roach.** **1.** a European freshwater cyprinid food fish, *Rutilus rutilus,* having a deep compressed body and reddish ventral and tail fins. **2.** any of various similar fishes. [C14: from Old French *roche,* of obscure origin]

roach[2] (rəʊtʃ) *n.* **1.** short for **cockroach.** **2.** *Slang.* the butt of a cannabis cigarette.

roach[3] (rəʊtʃ) *n. Nautical.* **1.** the amount by which the leech of a fore-and-aft sail projects beyond an imaginary straight line between the clew and the head. **2.** the curve at the foot of a square sail. [C18: of unknown origin]

roached (rəʊtʃt) *adj.* arched convexly, as the back of certain breeds of dog, such as the whippet. [C19: from ROACH[3] or *roach* (vb.) to cut (a sail) into a roach]

road (rəʊd) *n.* **1. a.** an open way, usually surfaced with tarmac or concrete, providing passage from one place to another. **b.** (*as modifier*): *road traffic; a road map; a road sign.* **c.** (*in combination*): *the roadside.* **2. a.** a street. **b.** (*cap. when part of a name*): *London Road.* **3. a.** *U.S.* short for **railroad.** **b.** *Brit.* one of the tracks of a railway. **4.** a way, path, or course: *the road to fame.* **5.** (*often pl.*) Also called: **roadstead.** *Nautical.* a partly sheltered anchorage. **6.** a drift or tunnel in a mine, esp. a level one. **7. hit the road.** *Slang.* to start or resume travelling. **8. on the road. a.** travelling, esp. as a salesman. **b.** (of a theatre company, pop group, etc.) on tour. **c.** leading a wandering life. **9. take (to) the road.** to begin a journey or tour. **10. one for the road.** *Informal.* a last alcoholic drink before leaving. [Old English *rād;* related to *rīdan* to RIDE, and to Old Saxon *rēda,* Old Norse *reith*] —'**roadless** *adj.*

road agent *n. U.S.* (formerly) a bandit who robbed stagecoaches; highwayman.

roadbed ('rəʊdˌbɛd) *n.* **1.** the material used to make a road. **2.** a layer of ballast that supports the sleepers of a railway track.

roadblock ('rəʊdˌblɒk) *n.* a barrier set up across a road by the police or military, in order to stop a fugitive, inspect traffic, etc.

road book *n.* a book of maps, sometimes including a gazetteer.

road-fund licence *n. Brit.* a licence showing that the tax payable in respect of a motor vehicle has been paid. [C20: from the former *road fund* for the maintenance of public highways]

road hog *n. Informal.* a selfish or aggressive driver.

roadholding ('rəʊdˌhəʊldɪŋ) *n.* the extent to which a motor vehicle is stable and does not skid, esp. at high speeds, or on sharp bends or wet roads.

roadhouse ('rəʊdˌhaʊs) *n.* a pub, restaurant, etc., that is situated at the side of a road, esp. a country road.

road hump *n.* the official name for **sleeping policeman.**

roadie ('rəʊdɪ) *n. Informal.* a person who transports and sets up equipment for a band or group.

road metal *n.* crushed rock, broken stone, etc., used to construct a road.

road movie *n.* a genre of film in which the chief character is on the run or travelling in search of, or to escape from, himself.

roadroller ('rəʊd,rəʊlə) *n.* a motor vehicle with heavy rollers for compressing road surfaces during road-making.

roadrunner ('rəʊd,rʌnə) *n.* a terrestrial crested bird, *Geococcyx californianus,* of Central and S North America, having a streaked plumage and long tail: family *Cuculidae* (cuckoos). Also called: **chaparral cock.**

road show *n.* **1. a.** a radio show broadcast live from one of a number of towns or venues being visited by a disc jockey who is touring an area. **b.** the touring disc jockey and the personnel and equipment needed to present such a show: *the Radio 1 road show will be in Brighton next week.* **2.** a group of entertainers, esp. pop musicians, on tour. **3.** any occasion when an organization attracts publicity while touring or visiting: *an antiques roadshow; a royal roadshow.*

roadstead ('rəʊd,stɛd) *n. Nautical.* another word for **road** (sense 5).

roadster ('rəʊdstə) *n.* **1.** *Archaic.* an open car, esp. one seating only two. **2.** a kind of bicycle.

road tax *n.* a tax paid, usually annually, on motor vehicles in use on the roads.

road test *n.* **1.** a test to ensure that a vehicle is roadworthy, esp. after repair or servicing, by driving it on roads. **2.** a test of something in actual use. ~*vb.* **road-test.** (*tr.*) **3.** to test (a vehicle) in this way.

road train *n. Austral.* a line of linked trailers pulled by a truck, used for transporting stock, etc.

roadway ('rəʊd,weɪ) *n.* **1.** the surface of a road. **2.** the part of a road that is used by vehicles.

roadwork ('rəʊd,wɜːk) *n.* sports training by running along roads.

road works *pl. n.* repairs to a road or cable under a road, esp. when forming a hazard or obstruction to traffic.

roadworthy ('rəʊd,wɜːðɪ) *adj.* (of a motor vehicle) mechanically sound; fit for use on the roads. —**'road,worthiness** *n.*

roam (rəʊm) *vb.* **1.** to travel or walk about with no fixed purpose or direction; wander. ~*n.* **2.** the act of roaming. [C13: origin unknown] —**'roamer** *n.*

roan (rəʊn) *adj.* **1.** (of a horse) having a bay (**red roan**), chestnut (**strawberry roan**), or black (**blue roan**) coat sprinkled with white hairs. ~*n.* **2.** a horse having such a coat. **3.** a soft unsplit sheepskin leather with a close tough grain, used in bookbinding, etc. [C16: from Old French, from Spanish *roano,* probably from Gothic *rauths* red]

roar (rɔː) *vb.* (*mainly intr.*) **1.** (of lions and other animals) to utter characteristic loud growling cries. **2.** (*also tr.*) (of people) to utter (something) with a loud deep cry, as in anger or triumph. **3.** to laugh in a loud hearty unrestrained manner. **4.** (of horses) to breathe with laboured rasping sounds. See **roaring** (sense 6). **5.** (of the wind, waves, etc.) to blow or break loudly and violently, as during a storm. **6.** (of a fire) to burn fiercely with a roaring sound. **7.** (of a machine, gun, etc.) to operate or move with a loud harsh noise. **8.** (*tr.*) to bring (oneself) into a certain condition by roaring: *to roar oneself hoarse.* ~*n.* **9.** a loud deep cry, uttered by a person or crowd, esp. in anger or triumph. **10.** a prolonged loud cry of certain animals, esp. lions. **11.** any similar noise made by a fire, the wind, waves, artillery, an engine, etc. [Old English *rārian;* related to Old High German *rērēn,* Middle Dutch *reren*] —**'roarer** *n.*

roaring ('rɔːrɪŋ) *adj.* **1.** *Informal.* very brisk and profitable (esp. in the phrase **a roaring trade**). **2. the roaring days.** *Austral.* the period of the Australian goldrushes. **3.** *Irish, derogatory informal.* (intensifier): *a roaring communist.* ~*adv.* **4.** noisily or boisterously (esp. in the phrase **roaring drunk**). ~*n.* **5.** a loud prolonged cry. **6.** a debilitating breathing defect of horses characterized by rasping sounds with each breath: caused by inflammation of the respiratory tract or obstruction of the larynx. Compare **whistling.** —**'roaringly** *adv.*

Roaring Forties *pl. n.* **the.** *Nautical.* the areas of ocean between 40° and 50° latitude in the S Hemisphere, noted for gale-force winds.

roar up *vb.* (*tr., adv.*) *Austral. informal.* to rebuke or reprimand (a person).

roast (rəʊst) *vb.* (*mainly tr.*) **1.** to cook (meat or other food) by dry heat, usually with added fat and esp. in an oven. **2.** to brown or dry (coffee, etc.) by exposure to heat. **3.** *Metallurgy.* to heat (an ore) in order to produce a concentrate that is easier to smelt. **4.** to heat (oneself or something) to an extreme degree, as when sunbathing, sitting before the fire, etc. **5.** (*intr.*) to be excessively and uncomfortably hot. **6.** *Informal.* to criticize severely. ~*n.* **7.** something that has been roasted, esp. meat. [C13: from Old French *rostir,* of Germanic origin; compare Middle Dutch *roosten* to roast] —**'roaster** *n.*

roasting ('rəʊstɪŋ) *Informal.* ~*adj.* **1.** extremely hot. ~*n.* **2.** severe criticism.

rob (rɒb) *vb.* **robs, robbing, robbed. 1.** to take something from (someone) illegally, as by force or threat of violence. **2.** (*tr.*) to plunder (a house, shop, etc.). **3.** (*tr.*) to deprive unjustly: *to be robbed of an opportunity.* [C13: from Old French *rober,* of Germanic origin; compare Old High German *roubōn* to rob] —**'robber** *n.*

robalo ('rɒbə,ləʊ, 'rəʊ-) *n., pl.* **-los** *or* **-lo.** any percoid fish of the family *Centropomidae,* occurring in warm and tropical (mostly marine) waters. Some of the larger species, such as the snooks, are important food fishes and many of the smaller ones are aquarium fishes. [Spanish, probably changed from *lobaro* (unattested), from *lobo* wolf, from Latin *lupus*]

roband ('rɒbənd, 'rəʊbənd) *or* **robbin** *n. Nautical.* a piece of marline used for fastening a sail to a spar. [C18: probably related to Middle Dutch *rabant,* from *ra* sailyard + *bant* band]

robber crab *n.* a terrestrial crab, *Birgus latro,* of the Indo-Pacific region, known for its habit of climbing coconut palms to feed on the nuts.

robber fly *n.* any of the predatory dipterous flies constituting the family *Asilidae,* which have a strong bristly body with piercing mouthparts and which prey on other insects. Also called: **bee killer, assassin fly.**

robber trench *n. Archaeol.* a trench that originally contained the foundations of a wall, the stones of which have been taken away.

robbery ('rɒbərɪ) *n., pl.* **-beries. 1.** *Criminal law.* the stealing of property from a person by using or threatening to use force. **2.** the act or an instance of robbing.

robbin ('rɒbɪn) *n. Nautical.* another word for **roband.**

robe (rəʊb) *n.* **1.** any loose flowing garment, esp. the official vestment of a peer, judge, or academic. **2.** a dressing gown or bathrobe. **3.** *Austral. slang.* a wardrobe. ~*vb.* **4.** to put a robe, etc., on (oneself or someone else); dress. [C13: from Old French: of Germanic origin; compare Old French *rober* to ROB, Old High German *roub* booty]

robe-de-chambre *French.* (rɔbdəʃɑ̃brə) *n., pl.* ***robes-de-chambre*** (rɔbdəʃɑ̃brə). a dressing gown or bathrobe.

robin ('rɒbɪn) *n.* **1.** Also called: **robin redbreast.** a small Old World songbird, *Erithacus rubecula,* related to the thrushes: family *Muscicapidae.* The male has a brown back, orange-red breast and face, and grey underparts. **2.** a North American thrush, *Turdus migratorius,* similar to but larger than the Old World robin. **3.** any of various similar birds having a reddish breast. [C16: arbitrary use of given name]

robing room *n.* a room in a palace, court, legislature, etc., where official robes of office are put on.

robinia (rə'bɪnɪə) *n.* any tree of the leguminous genus *Robinia,* esp. the locust tree (see **locust** (sense 2)).

robin's-egg blue *n. Chiefly U.S.* **a.** a light greenish-blue colour. **b.** (*as adj.*): *a robin's-egg-blue dress.*

roble ('rəʊbleɪ) *n.* **1.** Also called: **white oak.** an oak tree, *Quercus lobata,* of California, having leathery leaves and slender pointed acorns. **2.** any of several similar or related trees. [C19: from Spanish: from Latin *rōbur* oak, strength]

roborant ('rəʊbərənt, 'rɒb-) *adj.* **1.** tending to fortify or increase strength. ~*n.* **2.** a drug or agent that increases strength. [C17: from Latin *rōborāre* to strengthen, from *rōbur* an oak]

robot ('rəʊbɒt) *n.* **1.** any automated machine programmed to perform specific mechanical functions in the manner of a man. **2.** (*modifier*) not controlled by man; automatic: *a robot pilot.* **3.** a person who works or behaves like a machine; automaton. **4.** *S. African.* a set of traffic lights. [C20: (used in *R.U.R.,* a play by Karel Čapek (1890–1938), Czech dramatist) from Czech *robota* work; related to Old Slavonic *rabota* servitude, German *Arbeit* work] —**ro'botic** *adj.* —**'robotism** *or* **'robotry** *n.* —**'robot,like** *adj.*

robot bomb *n.* another name for the **V-1.**

robot dancing, robotics, *or* **robotic dancing** *n.* a dance of the 1980s characterized by jerky mechanical movements.

robotics (rəʊ'bɒtɪks) *n.* (*functioning as sing.*) **1.** the science or technology of designing, building, and using robots. **2.** another name for **robot dancing.**

robotize *or* **robotise** ('rəʊbə,taɪz) *vb.* (*tr.*) **1.** *Chiefly U.S.* to automate: *robotized assembly lines.* **2.** to cause (a person) to be or become mechanical and lifeless, like a robot.

robust (rəʊ'bʌst, 'rəʊbʌst) *adj.* **1.** strong in constitution; hardy; vigorous. **2.** sturdily built: *a robust shelter.* **3.** requiring or suited to physical strength: *a robust sport.* **4.** (esp. of wines) having a rich full-bodied flavour. **5.** rough or boisterous. **6.** (of thought, intellect, etc.) straightforward and imbued with common sense. [C16: from Latin *rōbustus,* from *rōbur* an oak, strength] —**ro'bustly** *adv.*

robustious (rəʊ'bʌstʃəs) *adj. Archaic.* **1.** rough; boisterous. **2.** strong, robust, or stout. —**ro'bustiously** *adv.* —**ro'bustiousness** *n.*

robustness (rəʊ'bʌstnɪs) *n.* **1.** the quality of being robust. **2.** *Computer technol.* the ability of a computer system to cope with errors during execution.

roc (rɒk) *n.* (in Arabian legend) a bird of enormous size and power. [C16: from Arabic *rukhkh,* from Persian *rukh*]

ROC *abbrev. for* Royal Observer Corps.

rocaille (rɒ'kaɪ) *n.* decorative rock or shell work, esp. as ornamentation in a rococo fountain, grotto, or interior. [from French, from *roc* ROCK[1]]

rocambole ('rɒkəm,bəʊl) *n.* a variety of sand leek whose garlic-like bulb is used for seasoning. [C17: from French, from German *Rockenbolle,* literally: distaff bulb (with reference to its shape)]

Roche limit (rɒʃ) *n. Astronomy.* the distance from the centre of a body, such as a planet, at which the tidal forces are stronger than the mutual gravitational attraction between two adjacent orbiting objects. [C19: named after E. A. *Roche* (1820–83), French mathematician]

Rochelle powder (rɒ'ʃel) *n.* another name for **Seidlitz powder.** [C18: named after *La Rochelle,* French port]

Rochelle salt *n.* a white crystalline double salt used in Seidlitz powder. Formula: $KNaC_4H_4O_6.4H_2O$.

roche moutonnée ('rəʊʃ ˌmuːtə'neɪ) *n., pl.* **roches moutonnées** ('rəʊʃ ˌmuːtə'neɪz). a rounded mass of rock smoothed and striated by ice that has flowed over it. [C19: French, literally: fleecy rock, from *mouton* sheep]

rochet ('rɒtʃɪt) *n.* a white surplice with tight sleeves, worn by bishops, abbots, and certain other Church dignitaries. [C14: from Old French, from *roc* coat, outer garment, of Germanic origin; compare Old High German *roc* coat]

rock[1] (rɒk) *n.* **1.** *Geology.* any aggregate of minerals that makes up part of the earth's crust. It may be unconsolidated, such as a sand, clay, or mud, or consolidated, such as granite, limestone, or coal. See also **igneous, sedimentary,** and **metamorphic. 2.** any hard mass of consolidated mineral matter, such as a boulder. **3.** *U.S., Canadian and Austral.* a stone. **4.** a person or thing suggesting a rock, esp. in being dependable, unchanging, or providing firm foundation. **5.** *Brit.* a hard sweet, typically a long brightly-coloured peppermint-flavoured stick, sold esp. in holiday resorts. **6.** *Slang.* a jewel, esp. a diamond. **7.** short for **rock salmon. 8.** (*pl.*) *Taboo slang.* the testicles. **9.** *Slang.* another name for **crack** (sense 29). **10. on the rocks. a.** in a state of ruin or destitution. **b.** (of drinks, esp. whisky) served with ice. [C14: from Old French *roche,* of unknown origin]

rock[2] (rɒk) *vb.* **1.** to move or cause to move from side to side or backwards and forwards. **2.** to reel or sway or cause (someone) to reel or sway, as with a violent shock or emotion. **3.** (*tr.*) to shake or move (something) violently. **4.** (*intr.*) to dance in the rock-and-roll style. **5.** *Mining.* to wash (ore) or (of ore) to be washed in a cradle. **6.** (*tr.*) to roughen (a copper plate) with a rocker before engraving a mezzotint. **7. rock the boat.** *Informal.* to create a disturbance in the existing situation. ~*n.* **8.** a rocking motion. **9.** short for **rock and roll. 10.** Also called: **rock music.** any of various styles of pop music having a heavy beat, derived from rock and roll. [Old English *roccian;* related to Middle Dutch, Old High German *rocken,* German *rücken*]

rockabilly ('rɒkəˌbɪlɪ) *n.* **a.** a fast, spare style of White rock music which originated in the mid-1950s in the U.S. South. **b.** (*as modifier*): *a rockabilly number.* [C20: from ROCK (AND ROLL) + (HILL)BILLY]

rock and roll *or* **rock'n'roll** *n.* **1. a.** a type of pop music originating in the 1950s as a blend of rhythm and blues and country and western. It is generally based upon the twelve-bar blues, the first and third beats in each bar being heavily accented. **b.** (*as modifier*): *the rock-and-roll era.* **2.** dancing performed to such music, with exaggerated body movements stressing the beat. ~*vb.* **3.** (*intr.*) to perform this dance. —**rock and roller** *or* **rock'n'roller** *n.*

rockaway ('rɒkəˌweɪ) *n. U.S.* a four-wheeled horse-drawn carriage, usually with two seats and a hard top.

rock bass (bæs) *n.* **1.** a North American freshwater percoid fish, *Ambloplites rupestris:* an important food fish; family *Centrarchidae* (sunfishes, etc.). **2.** any similar or related fish.

rock boot *n.* a tight-fitting rock-climbing boot with a canvas or suede upper and smooth rubber sole, designed to give good grip on small holds.

rock borer *n.* any of various sea creatures that bore into rock, such as some sea urchins, sponges, annelid worms, barnacles, isopods, and molluscs.

rock bottom *n.* **a.** the lowest possible level. **b.** (*as modifier*): *rock-bottom prices.*

rock-bound *adj.* hemmed in or encircled by rocks. Also (poetic): **rock-girt.**

rock brake *n.* any of various ferns of the genera *Pellaea* and *Cryptogramma,* which grow on rocky ground and have sori at the ends of the veins.

rock cake *n.* a small cake containing dried fruit and spice, with a rough surface supposed to resemble a rock.

rock candy *n.* the usual U.S. and Canadian name for **rock**[1] (sense 5).

rock chopper *n. Austral. slang.* a Roman Catholic. [from the initials RC]

rock climb *n.* **1.** an instance of rock climbing or the route followed. ~*vb.* **rock-climb** (*intr.*) **2.** to practise rock climbing.

rock climbing *n.* the technique and sport of climbing on steep rock faces, usually with ropes and other equipment and as part of a team or pair.

rock cod *n. N.Z.* another name for **blue cod.**

rock cress *n.* another name for **arabis.**

rock crystal *n.* a pure transparent colourless quartz, used in electronic and optical equipment. Formula: SiO_2.

rock dove *or* **pigeon** *n.* a common dove, *Columba livia,* from which domestic and feral pigeons are descended. It has a pale grey plumage with black-striped wings.

rocker ('rɒkə) *n.* **1.** any of various devices that transmit or operate with a rocking motion. See also **rocker arm. 2.** another word for **rocking chair. 3.** either of two curved supports on the legs of a chair or other article of furniture on which it may rock. **4.** a steel tool with a curved toothed cage, used to roughen the copper plate in engraving a mezzotint. **5.** *Mining.* another word for **cradle** (sense 9). **6. a.** an ice skate with a curved blade. **b.** the curve itself. **7.** *Skating.* **a.** a figure consisting of three interconnecting circles. **b.** a half turn in which the skater turns through 180°, so facing about while continuing to move in the same direction. **8.** a rock-music performer, fan, or song. **9.** *Brit.* an adherent of a youth movement rooted in the 1950s, characterized by motorcycle trappings. Compare **mod**[1]. **10. off one's rocker.** *Slang.* crazy; demented.

rocker arm *n.* a lever that rocks about a pivot, esp. a lever in an internal-combustion engine that transmits the motion of a pushrod or cam to a valve.

rockery ('rɒkərɪ) *n., pl.* **-eries.** a garden constructed with rocks, esp. one where alpine plants are grown. Also called: **rock garden.**

rocket[1] ('rɒkɪt) *n.* **1.** a self-propelling device, esp. a cylinder containing a mixture of solid explosives, used as a firework, distress signal, line carrier, etc. **2. a.** any vehicle propelled by a rocket engine, esp. one used to carry a warhead, spacecraft, etc. **b.** (*as modifier*): *rocket propulsion; rocket launcher.* **3.** *Brit. and N.Z. informal.* a severe reprimand (esp. in the phrase **get a rocket**). ~*vb.* **-ets, -eting, -eted. 4.** (*tr.*) to propel (a missile, spacecraft, etc.) by means of a rocket. **5.** (*intr.;* foll. by *off, away,* etc.) to move off at high speed. **6.** (*intr.*) to rise rapidly: *he rocketed to the top.* [C17: from Old French *roquette,* from Italian *rochetto* a little distaff, from *rocca* distaff, of Germanic origin]

rocket[2] ('rɒkɪt) *n.* **1.** a Mediterranean cruciferous plant, *Eruca sativa,* having yellowish-white flowers and leaves used as a salad. **2.** any of several plants of the related genus *Sisymbrium,* esp. *S. irio* (**London rocket**), which grow on waste ground and have pale yellow flowers. **3. yellow rocket.** any of several yellow-flowered plants of the related genus *Barbarea,* esp. *B. vulgaris.* **4. sea rocket.** any of several plants of the related genus *Cakile,* esp. *C. maritima,* which grow along the seashores of Europe and North America and have mauve, pink, or white flowers. **5. dame's rocket.** another name for **dame's violet.** ~See also **dyer's rocket, wall rocket.** [C16: from French *roquette,* from Italian *rochetta,* from Latin *ērūca* a caterpillar, hairy plant]

rocketeer (ˌrɒkɪ'tɪə) *n.* an engineer or scientist concerned with the design, operation, or launching of rockets.

rocket engine *n.* a reaction engine in which a fuel and oxidizer are burnt in a combustion chamber, the products of combustion expanding through a nozzle and producing thrust. Also called: **rocket motor.**

rocketry ('rɒkɪtrɪ) *n.* the science and technology of the design, operation, maintenance, and launching of rockets.

rockfish ('rɒkˌfɪʃ) *n., pl.* **-fish** *or* **-fishes. 1.** any of various fishes that live among rocks, esp. scorpaenid fishes of the genus *Sebastodes* and related genera, such as *S. caurinus* (**copper rockfish**) of North American Pacific coastal waters. **2.** *Brit.* any of several coarse fishes when used as food, esp. the dogfish or wolffish. Formerly called: **rock salmon.**

rock flour *n.* very finely powdered rock, produced when rocks are ground together (as along the faces of a moving fault or during the motion of glaciers) and are thus chemically unweathered.

rock garden *n.* a garden featuring rocks or rockeries.

rockhopper ('rɒkˌhɒpə) *n.* **1.** a small penguin, *Eudyptes crestatus,* of Antarctica, the Falkland Islands, and New Zealand, with a yellow crest on each side of its head. **2.** *Austral. informal.* a fisherman that fishes from the rocks on the sea coast.

rocking chair *n.* a chair set on curving supports so that the sitter may rock backwards and forwards.

rocking horse *n.* a toy horse mounted on a pair of rockers on which a child can rock to and fro in a seesaw movement.

rocking stone *n.* a boulder so delicately poised that it can be rocked. Also called: **logan, logan-stone.**

rockling ('rɒklɪŋ) *n., pl.* **-lings** *or* **-ling.** any small gadoid fish of the genera *Gaidropsarus, Ciliata,* etc. (formerly all included in *Motella*), which have an elongated body with barbels around the mouth and occur mainly in the North Atlantic Ocean. [C17: from ROCK[1] + -LING[1]]

rock lobster *n.* another name for the **spiny lobster.**

rock mechanics *n.* (*functioning as sing.*) the study of the mechanical behaviour of rocks, esp. their strength, elasticity, permeability, porosity, density, and reaction to stress.

rock melon *n. U.S., Austral., and N.Z.* another name for **cantaloupe.**

rock'n'roll *n.* a variant spelling of **rock and roll.** —**rock'n'roller** *n.*

rock oil *n.* another name for **petroleum.**

rockoon (rɒ'kuːn) *n.* a rocket carrying scientific equipment for studying the upper atmosphere, fired from a balloon at high altitude. [C20: from ROCKET[1] + BALLOON]

rock pigeon *n.* another name for **rock dove.**

rock plant *n.* any plant that grows on rocks or in rocky ground.

rock rabbit *n. S. African.* another name for the **dassie.**

rockrose ('rɒkˌrəʊz) *n.* any of various cistaceous shrubs or herbaceous plants of the Mediterranean genera *Helianthemum, Tuberaria,* and *Cistus,* cultivated for their yellow-white or reddish roselike flowers.

rock salmon *n. Brit.* (formerly) any of several coarse fishes when used as food, esp. the dogfish or wolffish: now known as **catfish** or **rockfish.**

rock salt *n.* another name for **halite.**

rockshaft ('rɒkˌʃɑːft) *n.* a shaft that rotates backwards and forwards rather than continuously, esp. one used in the valve gear of a steam engine.
rock snake *or* **python** *n.* any large Australasian python of the genus *Liasis.*
rock steady *n.* a type of slow Jamaican dance music of the 1960s.
rock tripe *n. Canadian.* any of various edible lichens, esp. of the genus *Umbilicaria,* that grow on rocks and are used in the North as a survival food.
rockweed ('rɒkˌwiːd) *n.* any of various seaweeds that grow on rocks exposed at low tide.
rock wool *n.* another name for **mineral wool.**
rocky[1] ('rɒkɪ) *adj.* **rockier, rockiest. 1.** consisting of or abounding in rocks: *a rocky shore.* **2.** hard or unyielding: *rocky determination.* **3.** hard like rock: *rocky muscles.* —'**rockily** *adv.* —'**rockiness** *n.*
rocky[2] ('rɒkɪ) *adj.* **rockier, rockiest. 1.** weak, shaky, or unstable. **2.** *Informal.* (of a person) dizzy; sickly; nauseated. —'**rockily** *adv.* —'**rockiness** *n.*
Rocky Mountain goat *n.* a sure-footed goat antelope, *Oreamnos americanus,* inhabiting the Rocky Mountains of W North America. It has thick white hair and black backward-curving horns.
Rocky Mountain spotted fever *n.* an acute rickettsial disease characterized by high fever, chills, pain in muscles and joints, skin rash, etc. It is caused by the bite of a tick infected with the microorganism *Rickettsia rickettsii.*
rococo (rə'kəʊkəʊ) *n.* (*often cap.*) **1.** a style of architecture and decoration that originated in France in the early 18th century, characterized by elaborate but graceful, light, ornamentation, often containing asymmetrical motifs. **2.** an 18th-century style of music characterized by petite prettiness, a decline in the use of counterpoint, and extreme use of ornamentation. **3.** any florid or excessively ornamental style. ~*adj.* **4.** denoting, being in, or relating to the rococo. **5.** florid or excessively elaborate. [C19: from French, from ROCAILLE, from *roc* ROCK[1]]
rod (rɒd) *n.* **1.** a slim cylinder of metal, wood, etc.; stick or shaft. **2.** a switch or bundle of switches used to administer corporal punishment. **3.** any of various staffs of insignia or office. **4.** power, esp. of a tyrannical kind: *a dictator's iron rod.* **5.** a straight slender shoot, stem, or cane of a woody plant. **6.** See **fishing rod. 7.** Also called: **pole, perch. a.** a unit of length equal to 5½ yards. **b.** a unit of square measure equal to 30¼ square yards. **8.** a straight narrow board marked with the dimensions of a piece of joinery, as the spacing of steps on a staircase. **9.** a metal shaft that transmits power in axial reciprocating motion: *piston rod.* Compare **shaft** (sense 5). **10.** *Surveying.* another name (esp. U.S.) for **staff**[1] (sense 8). **11.** Also called: **retinal rod.** any of the elongated cylindrical cells in the retina of the eye, containing the visual purple (rhodopsin), which are sensitive to dim light but not to colour. Compare **cone** (sense 5). **12.** any rod-shaped bacterium. **13.** a slang word for **penis. 14.** *U.S.* a slang name for **pistol** (sense 1). **15.** short for **hot rod.** [Old English *rodd;* related to Old Norse *rudda* club, Norwegian *rudda, rydda* twig] —'**rodˌlike** *adj.*
rode[1] (rəʊd) *vb.* the past tense of **ride.**
rode[2] (rəʊd) *n. Nautical.* an anchor rope or chain. [C17: of unknown origin]
rode[3] (rəʊd) *vb.* (*intr.*) (of the male woodcock) to perform a display flight at dusk during the breeding season. [C18: in the sense "(of birds) to fly homeward in the evening"; of uncertain origin] —'**roding** *n.*
rodent ('rəʊdᵊnt) *n.* **a.** any of the relatively small placental mammals that constitute the order *Rodentia,* having constantly growing incisor teeth specialized for gnawing. The group includes porcupines, rats, mice, squirrels, marmots, etc. **b.** (*as modifier*): *rodent characteristics.* [C19: from Latin *rōdere* to gnaw, corrode] —'**rodent-ˌlike** *adj.*
rodenticide (rəʊ'dɛntɪˌsaɪd) *n.* a substance used for killing rats, mice, and other rodents.
rodent operative *n. Brit.* a name sometimes used for an official (operative) employed by a local authority to destroy vermin.
rodeo ('rəʊdɪˌəʊ) *n., pl.* **-os.** *Chiefly U.S. and Canadian.* **1.** a display of the skills of cowboys, including bareback riding, steer wrangling, etc. **2.** the rounding up of cattle for branding, counting, inspection, etc. **3.** an enclosure for cattle that have been rounded up. [C19: from Spanish, from *rodear* to go around, from *rueda* a wheel, from Latin *rota*]
rodomontade (ˌrɒdəmɒn'teɪd, -'tɑːd) *Literary.* ~*n.* **1. a.** boastful words or behaviour; bragging. **b.** (*as modifier*): *rodomontade behaviour.* ~*vb.* **2.** (*intr.*) to boast, bluster, or rant. [C17: from French, from Italian *rodomonte* a boaster, from *Rodomonte* the name of a braggart king of Algiers in epic poems by Italian poets Boiardo (1434–94) and Ariosto (1474–1533)]
roe[1] (rəʊ) *n.* **1.** Also called: **hard roe.** the ovary of a female fish filled with mature eggs. **2.** Also called: **soft roe.** the testis of a male fish filled with mature sperm. **3.** the ripe ovary of certain crustaceans, such as the lobster. [C15: from Middle Dutch *roge,* from Old High German *roga;* related to Old Norse *hrogn*]
roe[2] (rəʊ) *n., pl.* **roes** *or* **roe.** short for **roe deer.** [Old English *rā(ha),* related to Old High German *rēh(o),* Old Norse *rā*]
roebuck ('rəʊˌbʌk) *n., pl.* **-bucks** *or* **-buck.** the male of the roe deer.
roe deer *n.* a small graceful deer, *Capreolus capreolus,* of woodlands of Europe and Asia. The antlers are small and the summer coat is reddish-brown.
roentgen *or* **röntgen** ('rɒntgən, -tjən, 'rɛnt-) *n.* a unit of dose of electromagnetic radiation equal to the dose that will produce in air a charge of 0.258×10^{-3} coulomb on all ions of one sign, when all the electrons of both signs liberated in a volume of air of mass one kilogram are stopped completely. Symbol: R or r [named after Wilhelm Konrad *Roentgen* (1845–1923), German physicist who discovered x-rays]
roentgen equivalent man *n.* the dose of ionizing radiation that produces the same effect in man as one roentgen of x- or gamma-radiation. Abbrev.: **REM** *or* **rem.**
roentgenize, roentgenise *or* **röntgenize, röntgenise** ('rɒntgəˌnaɪz, -tjə-, 'rɛnt-) *vb.* (*tr.*) to bombard with x-rays. —ˌ**roentgeni'zation,** ˌ**roentgeni'sation** *or* ˌ**röntgeni'zation,** ˌ**röntgeni'sation** *n.*
roentgeno- *or* **röntgeno-** *combining form.* indicating x-rays: *roentgenogram.* [from ROENTGEN]
roentgenogram, röntgenogram ('rɒntgənəˌgræm, -tjə-, 'rɛnt-) *or* **roentgenograph, röntgenograph** *n. Chiefly U.S.* an x-ray.
roentgenology *or* **röntgenology** (ˌrɒntgə'nɒlədʒɪ, -tjə-, ˌrɛnt-) *n.* an obsolete name for **radiology.** —**roentgenological** *or* **röntgenological** (ˌrɒntgənə'lɒdʒɪkᵊl, -tjə-, ˌrɛnt-) *adj.* —ˌ**roentgeno'logically** *or* ˌ**röntgeno'logically** *adv.* —ˌ**roentgen'ologist** *or* ˌ**röntgen'ologist** *n.*
roentgenopaque *or* **röntgenopaque** (ˌrɒntgənəʊ'peɪk, -tjən-, ˌrɛnt-) *adj.* (of a material) not allowing the transmission of x-rays.
roentgenoscope *or* **röntgenoscope** ('rɒntgənəʊˌskəʊp, -tjə-, 'rɛnt-) *n.* a less common name for **fluoroscope.** —**roentgenoscopic** *or* **röntgenoscopic** (ˌrɒntgənəʊ'skɒpɪk, -tjə-, ˌrɛnt-) *adj.* —**roentgenoscopy** *or* **röntgenoscopy** (ˌrɒntgə'nɒskəpɪ, -tjə-, ˌrɛnt-) *n.*
roentgenotherapy *or* **röntgenotherapy** (ˌrɒntgənə'θɛrəpɪ, -tjə-, ˌrɛnt-) *n.* the therapeutic use of x-rays.
roentgen ray *n.* a former name for **x-ray.**
rogallo (rə'gæləʊ) *n., pl.* **-los.** a flexible fabric delta wing, originally designed as a possible satellite retrieval vehicle but actually developed in the 1960s as the first successful hang-glider. [C20: after Francis M. *Rogallo,* the U.S. engineer who designed it]
rogation (rəʊ'geɪʃən) *n.* (*usually pl.*) *Christianity.* a solemn supplication, esp. in a form of ceremony prescribed by the Church. [C14: from Latin *rogātiō,* from *rogāre* to ask, make supplication]
Rogation Days *pl. n.* April 25 (the **Major Rogation**) and the Monday, Tuesday, and Wednesday before Ascension Day, observed by Christians as days of solemn supplication for the harvest and marked by processions, special prayers, and blessing of the crops.
rogatory ('rɒgətərɪ, -trɪ) *adj.* (esp. in legal contexts) seeking or authorized to seek information. [C19: from Medieval Latin *rogātōrius,* from Latin *rogāre* to ask]
roger ('rɒdʒə) *interj.* **1.** (used in signalling, telecommunications, etc.) message received and understood. Compare **wilco. 2.** an expression of agreement. ~*vb.* **3.** *Taboo slang.* (of a man) to copulate (with). [C20: from the name *Roger,* representing *R* for *received*]
rognon *French.* (rɔɲɔ̃) *n. Mountaineering.* an isolated rock outcrop on a glacier. [C20: literally: kidney]
rogue (rəʊg) *n.* **1.** a dishonest or unprincipled person, esp. a man; rascal; scoundrel. **2.** *Often jocular.* a mischievous or wayward person, often a child; scamp. **3.** any inferior or defective specimen, esp. a defective crop plant, or one of a different, unwanted variety. **4.** *Archaic.* a vagrant. **5. a.** an animal of vicious character that has separated from the main herd and leads a solitary life. **b.** (*as modifier*): *a rogue elephant.* ~*vb.* **6. a.** (*tr.*) to rid (a field or crop) of plants that are inferior, diseased, or of an unwanted variety. **b.** to identify and remove such plants. [C16: of unknown origin; perhaps related to Latin *rogāre* to beg]
roguery ('rəʊgərɪ) *n., pl.* **-gueries. 1.** behaviour characteristic of a rogue. **2.** a roguish or mischievous act.
rogues' gallery *n.* **1.** a collection of photographs of known criminals kept by the police for identification purposes. **2.** a group of undesirable people.
roguish ('rəʊgɪʃ) *adj.* **1.** dishonest or unprincipled. **2.** mischievous or arch. —'**roguishly** *adv.* —'**roguishness** *n.*
roil (rɔɪl) *vb.* **1.** (*tr.*) to make (a liquid) cloudy or turbid by stirring up dregs or sediment. **2.** (*intr.*) (esp. of a liquid) to be agitated or disturbed. **3.** (*intr.*) *Dialect.* to be noisy or boisterous. **4.** (*tr.*) another word (now rare) for **rile** (sense 1). [C16: of unknown origin; compare RILE]
roily ('rɔɪlɪ) *adj.* **roilier, roiliest.** *Rare.* cloudy or muddy.
roister ('rɔɪstə) *vb.* (*intr.*) **1.** to engage in noisy or unrestrained merrymaking; revel. **2.** to brag, bluster, or swagger. [C16: from Old French *rustre* lout, from *ruste* uncouth, from Latin *rusticus* rural; see RUSTIC] —'**roisterer** *n.* —'**roisterous** *adj.* —'**roisterously** *adv.*
rojak ('rodʒa) *n.* (in Malaysia) a salad dish served in chilli sauce. [from Malay]
ROK *international car registration for* Republic of Korea.

Roland ('rəʊlənd) *n.* **a Roland for an Oliver.** an effective retort or retaliation. [after two of Charlemagne's legendary peers]

role *or* **rôle** (rəʊl) *n.* **1.** a part or character in a play, film, etc., to be played by an actor or actress. **2.** *Psychol.* the part played by a person in a particular social setting, influenced by his expectation of what is appropriate. **3.** usual or customary function: *what is his role in the organization?* [C17: from French *rôle* ROLL, an actor's script]

role-playing *n. Psychol.* activity in which a person imitates, consciously or unconsciously, a role uncharacteristic of himself. See also **psychodrama.**

roll (rəʊl) *vb.* **1.** to move or cause to move along by turning over and over. **2.** to move or cause to move along on wheels or rollers. **3.** to flow or cause to flow onwards in an undulating movement: *billows of smoke rolled over the ground.* **4.** (*intr.*) to extend in undulations: *the hills roll down to the sea.* **5.** (*intr.;* usually foll. by *around*) to move or occur in cycles. **6.** (*intr.*) (of a planet, the moon, etc.) to revolve in an orbit. **7.** (*intr.;* foll. by *on, by,* etc.) to pass or elapse: *the years roll by.* **8.** to rotate or cause to rotate wholly or partially: *to roll one's eyes.* **9.** to curl, cause to curl, or admit of being curled, so as to form a ball, tube, or cylinder; coil. **10.** to make or form by shaping into a ball, tube, or cylinder: *to roll a cigarette.* **11.** (often foll. by *out*) to spread or cause to spread out flat or smooth under or as if under a roller: *to roll the lawn; to roll pastry.* **12.** to emit, produce, or utter with a deep prolonged reverberating sound: *the thunder rolled continuously.* **13.** to trill or cause to be trilled: *to roll one's r's.* **14.** (*intr.*) (of a vessel, aircraft, rocket, etc.) to turn from side to side around the longitudinal axis. Compare **pitch**[1] (sense 10), **yaw** (sense 1). **15.** to cause (an aircraft) to execute a roll or (of an aircraft) to execute a roll (sense 40). **16.** (*intr.*) to walk with a swaying gait, as when drunk; sway. **17.** (*intr.;* often foll. by *over*) (of an animal, esp. a dog) to lie on its back and wriggle while kicking its legs in the air, without moving along. **18.** (*intr.*) to wallow or envelop oneself (in). **19.** (*tr.*) to apply ink to (type, etc.) with a roller or rollers. **20.** to throw (dice). **21.** (*intr.*) to operate or begin to operate: *the presses rolled.* **22.** (*intr.*) *Informal.* to make progress; move or go ahead: *let the good times roll.* **23.** (*tr.*) *Informal, chiefly U.S. and N.Z.* to rob (a helpless person, such as someone drunk or asleep). **24.** (*tr.*) *Slang.* to have sexual intercourse or foreplay with (a person). **25. start** *or* **set the ball rolling.** to open or initiate (an action, discussion, movement, etc.). ~*n.* **26.** the act or an instance of rolling. **27.** anything rolled up in a cylindrical form: *a roll of newspaper.* **28.** an official list or register, esp. of names: *an electoral roll.* **29.** a rounded mass: *rolls of flesh.* **30.** a strip of material, esp. leather, fitted with pockets or pouches for holding tools, toilet articles, needles and thread, etc. **31.** a cylinder used to flatten something; roller. **32.** a small loaf of bread for one person: eaten plain, with butter, or as a light meal when filled with meat, cheese, etc. **33.** a flat pastry or cake rolled up with a meat (**sausage roll**), jam (**jam roll**), or other filling. See also **swiss roll. 34.** a swell, ripple, or undulation on a surface: *the roll of the hills.* **35.** a swaying, rolling, or unsteady movement or gait. **36.** a deep prolonged reverberating sound: *the roll of thunder.* **37.** a rhythmical cadenced flow of words. **38.** a trilling sound; trill. **39.** a very rapid beating of the sticks on a drum. **40.** a flight manoeuvre in which an aircraft makes one complete rotation about its longitudinal axis without loss of height or change in direction. **41.** the angular displacement of a vessel, rocket, missile, etc., caused by rolling. **42.** a throw of dice. **43.** a bookbinder's tool having a brass wheel, used to impress a line or repeated pattern on the cover of a book. **44.** *Slang.* an act of sexual intercourse or petting (esp. in the phrase **a roll in the hay**). **45.** *U.S. slang.* an amount of money, esp. a wad of paper money. **46. strike off the roll(s). a.** to expel from membership. **b.** to debar (a solicitor) from practising, usually because of dishonesty. ~See also **roll in, roll off, roll on, roll over, roll up.** [C14 *rollen,* from Old French *roler,* from Latin *rotulus* a little wheel, from *rota* a wheel]

rollaway ('rəʊləˌweɪ) *n.* (*modifier*) mounted on rollers so as to be easily moved, esp. to be stored away after use.

rollbar ('rəʊlˌbɑː) *n.* a bar that reinforces the frame of a car, esp. one used for racing, rallying, etc., to protect the driver if the car should turn over.

roll call *n.* **1.** the reading aloud of an official list of names, those present responding when their names are read out. **2.** the time or signal for such a reading.

rolled gold *n.* a metal, such as brass, coated with a thin layer of gold, usually of above 9 carat purity. It is used in inexpensive jewellery. Also called (U.S.): **filled gold.**

rolled paperwork *n.* a form of decoration on small objects, such as boxes, in which a design is made up of tiny rolls of paper cut crossways and laid together: popular in the 18th and 19th centuries. Also called: **curled paperwork, paper filigree.**

rolled-steel joist *n.* a steel beam, esp. one with a cross section in the form of a letter *H* or *I.* Abbrev.: **RSJ.**

roller ('rəʊlə) *n.* **1.** a cylinder having an absorbent surface and a handle, used for spreading paint. **2.** Also called: **garden roller.** a heavy cast-iron cylinder or pair of cylinders on an axle to which a handle is attached; used for flattening lawns. **3.** a long heavy wave of the sea, advancing towards the shore. Compare **breaker**[1] (sense 2). **4.** a hardened cylinder of precision-ground steel that forms one of the rolling components of a roller bearing or of a linked driving chain. **5.** a cylinder fitted on pivots, used to enable heavy objects to be easily moved; castor. **6.** *Printing.* a cylinder, usually of hard rubber, used to ink a forme or plate before impression. **7.** a cylindrical tube or barrel onto which material is rolled for transport or storage. **8.** any of various other cylindrical devices that rotate about a cylinder, used for any of various purposes. **9.** a small cylinder, esp. one that is heated, onto which a woman's hair may be rolled to make it curl. **10.** *Med.* a bandage consisting of a long strip of muslin or cheesecloth rolled tightly into a cylindrical form before application. **11.** a band fastened around a horse's belly to keep a blanket in position. **12.** any of various Old World birds of the family *Coraciidae,* such as *Coracias garrulus* (**European roller**), that have a blue, green, and brown plumage, a slightly hooked bill, and an erratic flight: order *Coraciiformes* (kingfishers, etc.). **13.** (*often cap.*) a variety of tumbler pigeon that performs characteristic backward somersaults in flight. **14.** a breed of canary that has a soft trilling song in which the notes are run together. **15.** a person or thing that rolls. **16.** *Austral.* a man who rolls and trims fleeces after shearing. **17.** short for **roadroller** or **steam-roller. 18.** short for **roller caption.**

rollerball ('rəʊləˌbɔːl) *n.* a pen having a small moving nylon, plastic, or metal ball as a writing point.

roller bearing *n.* a bearing in which a shaft runs on a number of hardened-steel rollers held within a cage.

roller caption *n. Television.* caption lettering that moves progressively up or across the picture, as for showing the credits at the end of a programme. Often shortened to **roller.**

roller chain *n. Engineering.* a chain for transmitting power in which each link consists of two free-moving rollers held in position by pins connected to sideplates.

roller coaster *n.* another term for **big dipper.**

roller derby *n.* a race on roller skates, esp. one involving aggressive tactics.

roller skate *n.* **1.** a device having clamps and straps for fastening to a boot or shoe and four small wheels that enable the wearer to glide swiftly over a floor or other surface. ~*vb.* **roller-skate. 2.** (*intr.*) to move on roller skates. —**roller skater** *n.*

roller towel *n.* **1.** a towel with the two ends sewn together, hung on a roller. **2.** a continuous towel wound inside a roller enabling a clean section to be pulled out when required.

roll film *n.* a length of photographic film backed with opaque paper and rolled on a spool.

rollick ('rɒlɪk) *vb.* **1.** (*intr.*) to behave in a carefree, frolicsome, or boisterous manner. ~*n.* **2.** a boisterous or carefree escapade or event. [C19: of Scottish dialect origin, probably from ROMP + FROLIC]

rollicking[1] ('rɒlɪkɪŋ) *adj.* boisterously carefree and swaggering.

rollicking[2] ('rɒlɪkɪŋ) *n. Brit. informal.* a very severe telling-off; dressing-down. [C20: from ROLLICK (vb.) (in former sense: to be angry, make a fuss); perhaps influenced by BOLLOCKING]

roll in *vb.* (*mainly intr.*) **1.** (*adv.*) to arrive in abundance or in large numbers. **2.** (*adv.*) *Informal.* to arrive at one's destination. **3. be rolling in.** (*prep.*) *Informal.* to abound or luxuriate in (wealth, money, etc.). **4.** (*adv.; also tr.*) *Hockey.* to return (the ball) to play after it has crossed the touchline.

rolling ('rəʊlɪŋ) *adj.* **1.** having gentle rising and falling slopes; undulating: *rolling country.* **2.** progressing or spreading by stages or by occurrences in different places in succession, with continued or increasing effectiveness: *three weeks of rolling strikes disrupted schools.* **3.** subject to regular review and updating: *a rolling plan for overseas development.* **4.** deeply resounding; reverberating: *rolling thunder.* **5.** *Slang.* extremely rich. **6.** that may be turned up or down: *a rolling hat brim.* ~*adv.* **7.** *Slang.* swaying or staggering (in the phrase **rolling drunk**).

rolling bearing *n.* any bearing in which the antifriction action depends on the rolling action of balls or rollers.

rolling friction *n. Engineering.* frictional resistance to rotation or energy losses in rolling bearings. Compare **sliding friction.**

rolling hitch *n.* a knot used for fastening one rope to another or to a spar, being easily released but jamming when the rope is pulled.

rolling launch *n. Marketing.* the process of introducing a new product onto a market gradually. Compare **roll out** (sense 3).

rolling mill *n.* **1.** a mill or factory where ingots of heated metal are passed between rollers to produce sheets or bars of a required cross section and form. **2.** a machine having rollers that may be shaped to reduce ingots, etc., to a required cross section and form.

rolling pin *n.* a cylinder with handles at both ends, often of wood, used for rolling dough, pastry, etc., out flat.

rolling stock *n.* the wheeled vehicles collectively used on a railway, including the locomotives, passenger coaches, freight wagons, guard's vans, etc.

rolling stone *n.* a restless or wandering person.

rollmop ('rəʊlˌmɒp) *n.* a herring fillet rolled, usually around onion slices, and pickled in spiced vinegar. [C20: from German *Rollmops,* from *rollen* to ROLL + *Mops* pug dog]

rollneck ('rəʊlˌnɛk) *adj.* **1.** (of a garment) having a high neck that may be rolled over. ~*n.* **2.** a rollneck sweater or other garment.

roll off *vb. (intr., adv.) Electronics.* to exhibit gradually reduced response at the upper or lower ends of the working frequency range.

roll of honour *n.* a list of those who have died in war for their country, esp. those from a particular locality or organization.

roll on *vb.* **1.** *Brit.* used to express the wish that an eagerly anticipated event or date will come quickly: *roll on Saturday.* ~*adj.* **roll-on. 2.** (of a deodorant, lip gloss, etc.) dispensed by means of a revolving ball fitted into the neck of the container. ~*n.* **roll-on. 3.** a woman's foundation garment, made of elasticized material and having no fastenings. **4.** a liquid cosmetic, esp. a deodorant, packed in a container having an applicator consisting of a revolving ball.

roll-on/roll-off *adj.* denoting a cargo ship or ferry designed so that vehicles can be driven straight on and straight off.

roll out *vb. (tr., adv.)* **1.** to cause (pastry) to become flatter and thinner by pressure with a rolling pin. **2.** to show (a new type of aircraft) to the public for the first time. **3.** to launch (a new film, product, etc.) in a series of stages over an area, each stage involving an increased number of outlets. ~*n.* **roll-out. 4.** a presentation to the public of a new aircraft, product, etc.; a launch.

roll over *vb. (adv.)* **1.** *(intr.)* to overturn. **2.** See **roll** (sense 17). **3.** *(tr.)* to continue (a loan, debt, etc.) in force for a further period ~*n.* **roll-over. 4. a.** an instance of such continuance of a loan, debt, etc. **b.** *(as modifier)*: *roll-over relief provisions.*

Rolls-Royce (ˌrəʊlzˈrɔɪs) *n. Trademark.* **1.** Also called (informal): **Rolls.** a make of very high-quality, luxurious, and prestigious British car. **2.** anything considered to be the very best of its kind. [named after its designers, Charles Stewart *Rolls* (1877–1910), British pioneer motorist and aviator, and Sir (Frederick) Henry *Royce* (1863–1933), British engineer, who founded the Rolls-Royce Company (1906)]

roll-top desk *n.* a desk having a slatted wooden panel that can be pulled down over the writing surface when not in use. Also called: **roll-top.**

roll up *vb. (adv.)* **1.** to form or cause to form a cylindrical shape. **2.** *(tr.)* to wrap (an object) round on itself or on an axis: *to roll up a map.* **3.** *(intr.) Informal.* to arrive, esp. in a vehicle. ~*n.* **roll-up. 4.** *Brit. informal.* a cigarette made by hand from loose tobacco and cigarette paper. **5.** *Austral.* (in the 19th century) a mass meeting of workers on an issue of common concern. **6.** *Austral.* the attendance at any fixture: *they had a good roll-up.*

rollway (ˈrəʊlˌweɪ) *n.* **1.** an incline down which logs are rolled for transportation. **2.** a series of rollers laid parallel to each other, over which heavy loads may be moved.

roll-your-own *n. Informal.* a hand-rolled cigarette.

roly-poly (ˈrəʊlɪˈpəʊlɪ) *adj.* **1.** plump, buxom, or rotund. ~*n., pl.* **-lies. 2.** *Brit.* a strip of suet pastry spread with jam, fruit, or a savoury mixture, rolled up, and baked or steamed as a pudding. **3.** a plump, buxom, or rotund person. **4.** *Austral.* an informal name for **tumbleweed.** [C17: apparently by reduplication from *roly,* from ROLL]

Rom (rɒm) *n., pl.* **Roma** (ˈrɒmə). a male Gypsy. [Romany]

ROM (rɒm) *n. Computer technol. acronym for* read only memory: a storage device that holds data permanently and cannot in normal circumstances be altered by the programmer.

rom. *Printing. abbrev. for* roman (type).

Rom. *abbrev. for:* **1.** Roman. **2.** Romance (languages). **3.** *Bible.* Romans. **4.** Romania(n).

Romaic (rəʊˈmeɪɪk) *Obsolete.* ~*n.* **1.** the modern Greek vernacular, esp. Demotic. ~*adj.* **2.** of or relating to Greek, esp. Demotic. [C19: from Greek *Rhōmaikos* Roman, with reference to the Eastern Roman Empire]

romaine (rəʊˈmeɪn) *n.* the usual U.S. and Canadian name for **cos**[1] (lettuce). [C20: from French, from *romain* Roman]

romaji (ˈrəʊmɑːdʒɪ) *n.* the Roman alphabet as used to write Japanese.

roman[1] (ˈrəʊmən) *adj.* **1.** of, relating to, or denoting a vertical style of printing type: the usual form of type for most printed matter. Compare **italic.** ~*n.* **2.** roman type or print. [C16: so called because the style of letters is that used in ancient Roman inscriptions]

roman[2] *(French* rɔmɑ̃) *n.* a metrical narrative in medieval French literature derived from the *chansons de geste.*

Roman (ˈrəʊmən) *adj.* **1.** of or relating to ancient Rome or to the extensive empire ruled by it until 1453. See **Byzantine** (sense 1). **2.** of or relating to the modern city of Rome or its inhabitants. **3.** of or relating to Roman Catholicism or the Roman Catholic Church. **4.** denoting, relating to, or having the style of architecture used by the ancient Romans, characterized by large-scale masonry domes, barrel vaults, and semicircular arches. ~*n.* **5.** a citizen or inhabitant of ancient or modern Rome. **6.** *Informal.* short for **Roman Catholic.**

roman à clef *French.* (rɔmɑ̃ a kle) *n., pl.* ***romans à clef*** (rɔmɑ̃ a kle). a novel in which real people are depicted under fictitious names. [literally: novel with a key]

Roman alphabet *n.* the alphabet evolved by the ancient Romans for the writing of Latin, based upon an Etruscan form derived from the Greeks and ultimately from the Phoenicians. The alphabet serves for writing most of the languages of W Europe and many other languages.

Roman arch *n.* another name for **Norman arch.**

Roman calendar *n.* the lunar calendar of ancient Rome, replaced in 45 B.C. by the Julian calendar. It originally consisted of 10 months, with a special month intercalated between Feb. 23 and 24.

Roman candle *n.* a firework that produces a continuous shower of sparks punctuated by coloured balls of fire. [C19: so called from its having been originated in Italy]

Roman Catholic *adj.* **1.** of or relating to the Roman Catholic Church. ~*n.* **2.** a member of this Church. ~Often shortened to **Catholic.**

Roman Catholic Church *n.* the Christian Church over which the pope presides, with administrative headquarters in the Vatican palace in Rome. Also called: **Catholic Church, Church of Rome.**

Roman Catholicism *n.* the beliefs, practices, and system of government of the Roman Catholic Church.

romance *n.* (rəˈmæns, ˈrəʊmæns). **1.** a love affair, esp. an intense and happy but short-lived affair involving young people. **2.** love, esp. romantic love idealized for its purity or beauty. **3.** a spirit of or inclination for adventure, excitement, or mystery. **4.** a mysterious, exciting, sentimental, or nostalgic quality, esp. one associated with a place. **5.** a narrative in verse or prose, written in a vernacular language in the Middle Ages, dealing with strange and exciting adventures of chivalrous heroes. **6.** any similar narrative work dealing with events and characters remote from ordinary life. **7.** the literary genre represented by works of these kinds. **8.** (in Spanish literature) a short narrative poem, usually an epic or historical ballad. **9.** a story, novel, film, etc., dealing with love, usually in an idealized or sentimental way. **10.** an extravagant, absurd, or fantastic account or explanation. **11.** a lyrical song or short instrumental composition having a simple melody. ~*vb.* (rəˈmæns). **12.** *(intr.)* to tell, invent, or write extravagant or romantic fictions. **13.** *(intr.)* to tell extravagant or improbable lies. **14.** *(intr.)* to have romantic thoughts. **15.** *(intr.)* (of a couple) to indulge in romantic behaviour. **16.** *(tr.)* to be romantically involved with. [C13: *romauns,* from Old French *romans,* ultimately from Latin *Rōmānicus* Roman] —**roˈmancer** *n.*

Romance (rəˈmæns, ˈrəʊmæns) *adj.* **1.** denoting, relating to, or belonging to the languages derived from Latin, including Italian, Spanish, Portuguese, French, and Romanian. **2.** denoting a word borrowed from a Romance language: *there are many Romance words in English.* ~*n.* **3.** this group of languages; the living languages that belong to the Italic branch of the Indo-European family.

Roman collar *n.* another name for **clerical collar.**

Romanes (ˈrɒmənɪs) *n.* Romany; the language of the Gypsies. [from Romany]

Romanesque (ˌrəʊməˈnɛsk) *adj.* **1.** denoting, relating to, or having the style of architecture used in W and S Europe from the 9th to the 12th century, characterized by the rounded arch, the groin vault, massive-masonry wall construction, and a restrained use of mouldings. See also **Norman** (sense 6). **2.** denoting or relating to a corresponding style in painting, sculpture, etc. [C18: see ROMAN, -ESQUE]

roman-fleuve *French.* (rɔmɑ̃flœv) *n., pl.* ***romans-fleuves*** (rɔmɑ̃flœv). a novel or series of novels dealing with a family or other group over several generations. [literally: stream novel]

Roman holiday *n.* entertainment or pleasure that depends on the suffering of others. [C19: from Byron's poem *Childe Harold* (IV, 141)]

Romani (ˈrɒmənɪ, ˈrəʊ-) *n., pl.* **-nis.** a variant spelling of **Romany.**

Romanian (rəʊˈmeɪnɪən), **Rumanian,** *or* **Roumanian** *n.* **1.** a native or inhabitant of Romania, a republic in SE Europe bordering on the Black Sea. **2.** the official language of Romania, belonging to the Romance group of the Indo-European family. ~*adj.* **3.** relating to, denoting, or characteristic of Romania, its people, or their language.

Romanic (rəʊˈmænɪk) *adj.* another word for **Roman** or **Romance.**

Romanism (ˈrəʊməˌnɪzəm) *n.* Roman Catholicism, esp. when regarded as excessively or superstitiously ritualistic.

Romanist (ˈrəʊmənɪst) *n.* **1.** a member of a Church, esp. the Church of England, who favours or is influenced by Roman Catholicism. **2.** a Roman Catholic. **3.** a student of classical Roman civilization or law. —ˌ**Romanˈistic** *adj.*

Romanize *or* **Romanise** (ˈrəʊməˌnaɪz) *vb.* **1.** *(tr.)* to impart a Roman Catholic character to (a ceremony, practice, etc.). **2.** *(intr.)* to be converted to Roman Catholicism. **3.** *(tr.)* to transcribe or transliterate (a language) into the Roman alphabet. **4.** to make Roman in character, allegiance, style, etc. —ˌ**Romaniˈzation** *or* ˌ**Romaniˈsation** *n.*

Roman law *n.* **1.** the system of jurisprudence of ancient Rome, codified under Justinian and forming the basis of many modern legal systems. **2.** another term for **civil law.**

Roman mile *n.* a unit of length used in ancient Rome, equivalent to about 1620 yards or 1481 metres.

Roman nose *n.* a nose having a high prominent bridge.

Roman numerals *pl. n.* the letters used by the Romans for the representation of cardinal numbers, still used occasionally today. The integers are represented by the following letters: I (= 1), V (= 5), X (= 10), L (= 50), C (= 100), D (= 500), and M (= 1000).

If a numeral is followed by another numeral of lower denomination, the two are added together; if it is preceded by one of lower denomination, the smaller numeral is subtracted from the greater. Thus VI = 6 (V + I), but IV = 4 (V – I). Other examples are XC (= 90), CL (= 150), XXV (= 25), XLIV (= 44). Multiples of a thousand are indicated by a superior bar: thus, $\overline{\text{V}}$ = 5000, $\overline{\text{X}}$ = 10 000, $\overline{\text{XD}}$ = 490 000, etc.

Romano (rəʊˈmɑːnəʊ) *n.* a hard light-coloured sharp-tasting cheese, similar to Parmesan.

Roman pace *n.* an ancient Roman measure of length, equal to 5 Roman feet or about 58 inches (147 centimetres). See also **geometric pace.**

Romansch *or* **Romansh** (rəʊˈmænʃ) *n.* a group of Rhaetian dialects spoken in the Swiss canton of Graubünden; an official language of Switzerland since 1938. See also **Friulian, Ladin.** [C17: from Romansch, literally: Romance language, from Latin *Rōmānicus* ROMANIC]

Roman snail *n.* a large edible European snail, *Helix pomatia,* the usual *escargot* of menus, erroneously thought to have been introduced to northern Europe by the Romans.

romantic (rəʊˈmæntɪk) *adj.* **1.** of, relating to, imbued with, or characterized by romance. **2.** evoking or given to thoughts and feelings of love, esp. idealized or sentimental love: *a romantic woman; a romantic setting.* **3.** impractical, visionary, or idealistic: *a romantic scheme.* **4.** *Often euphemistic.* imaginary or fictitious: *a romantic account of one's war service.* **5.** (*often cap.*) of or relating to a movement in European art, music, and literature in the late 18th and early 19th centuries, characterized by an emphasis on feeling and content rather than order and form, on the sublime, supernatural, and exotic, and the free expression of the passions and individuality. ~*n.* **6.** a person who is romantic, as in being idealistic, amorous, or soulful. **7.** a person whose tastes in art, literature, etc., lie mainly in romanticism; romanticist. **8.** (*often cap.*) a poet, composer, etc., of the romantic period or whose main inspiration or interest is romanticism. [C17: from French *romantique,* from obsolete *romant* story, romance, from Old French *romans* ROMANCE] —**roˈmantically** *adv.*

romanticism (rəʊˈmæntɪˌsɪzəm) *n.* **1.** (*often cap.*) the theory, practice, and style of the romantic art, music, and literature of the late 18th and early 19th centuries, usually opposed to classicism. **2.** romantic attitudes, ideals, or qualities. —**roˈmanticist** *n.*

romanticize *or* **romanticise** (rəʊˈmæntɪˌsaɪz) *vb.* **1.** (*intr.*) to think or act in a romantic way. **2.** (*tr.*) to interpret according to romantic precepts. **3.** to make or become romantic, as in style. —**roˌmanticiˈzation** *or* **roˌmanticiˈsation** *n.*

Romany *or* **Romani** (ˈrɒmənɪ, ˈrəʊ-) *n.* **1.** (*pl.* **-nies** *or* **-nis**) **a.** another name for a **Gypsy. b.** (*as modifier*): *Romany customs.* **2.** the language of the Gypsies, belonging to the Indic branch of the Indo-European family, but incorporating extensive borrowings from local European languages. Most of its 250 000 speakers are bilingual. It is extinct in Britain. [C19: from Romany *romani* (adj.) Gypsy, ultimately from Sanskrit *domba* man of a low caste of musicians, of Dravidian origin]

romanza (rəˈmænzə) *n. Music.* a short instrumental piece of song-like character. [from Italian]

romaunt (rəˈmɔːnt) *n. Archaic.* a verse romance. [C16: from Old French; see ROMANTIC]

Rom. Cath. *abbrev. for* Roman Catholic.

Rome (rəʊm) *n.* the Roman Catholic Church or Roman Catholicism.

Romeo (ˈrəʊmɪəʊ) *n.* **1.** (*pl.* **-os.**) an ardent male lover. **2.** *Communications.* a code word for the letter *r.* [from the hero of Shakespeare's *Romeo and Juliet*]

Romish (ˈrəʊmɪʃ) *adj. Usually derogatory.* of, relating to, or resembling Roman Catholic beliefs or practices.

Romney Marsh (ˈrɒmnɪ, ˈrʌm-) *n.* a type of hardy long-woolled British sheep from Romney Marsh, on the Kent coast, bred for mutton.

romp (rɒmp) *vb.* (*intr.*) **1.** to play or run about wildly, boisterously, or joyfully. **2. romp home** (*or* **in**). to win a race easily. ~*n.* **3.** a noisy or boisterous game or prank. **4.** an instance of sexual activity between two or more people that is entered into light-heartedly and without emotional commitment: *naked sex romps.* **5.** Also called: **romper.** *Archaic.* a playful or boisterous child, esp. a girl. **6.** an easy victory. [C18: probably variant of RAMP, from Old French *ramper* to crawl, climb] —**rompish** *adj.*

rompers (ˈrɒmpəz) *pl. n.* **1.** a one-piece baby garment consisting of trousers and a bib with straps. **2.** *N.Z.* a type of costume worn by schoolgirls for games and gymnastics.

romp through *vb.* (*intr., prep.*) *Informal.* to progress quickly and easily through something: *he romped through the work.*

rondavel (ˈrɒndɑːvəl) *n. S. African.* a circular often thatched building. [of uncertain origin]

rondeau (ˈrɒndəʊ) *n., pl.* **-deaux** (-dəʊ, -dəʊz). a poem consisting of 13 or 10 lines with two rhymes and having the opening words of the first line used as an unrhymed refrain. See also **roundel.** [C16: from Old French, from *rondel* a little round, from *rond* ROUND]

rondel (ˈrɒndᵊl) *n.* **1.** a rondeau consisting of three stanzas of 13 or 14 lines with a two-line refrain appearing twice or three times. **2.** a figure in Scottish country dancing by means of which couples change position in the set. [C14: from Old French, literally: a little circle, from *rond* ROUND]

rondelet (ˈrɒndəˌlet) *n.* a brief rondeau, having five or seven lines and a refrain taken from the first line. [C16: from Old French: a little RONDEL]

rondo (ˈrɒndəʊ) *n., pl.* **-dos.** a piece of music in which a refrain is repeated between episodes: often constitutes the form of the last movement of a sonata or concerto. [C18: from Italian, from French RONDEAU]

rondure (ˈrɒndjʊə) *n. Literary.* **1.** a circle or curve. **2.** roundness or curvature. [C17: from French *rondeur,* from *rond* ROUND]

rone (rəʊn; *Scot.* ron) *or* **ronepipe** (ˈrəʊnˌpaɪp; *Scot.* ˈronˌpəɪp) *n. Scot.* a drainpipe or gutter for carrying rainwater from a roof. [C19: origin unknown]

Roneo (ˈrəʊnɪəʊ) *Trademark.* ~*vb.* **-neos, -neoing, -neoed.** (*tr.*) **1.** to duplicate (a document) from a stencil. ~*n., pl.* **-neos. 2.** a document reproduced by this process.

ronggeng (ˈrɒŋgɛŋ) *n.* a Malay traditional dance. [Malay]

ronin (ˈrəʊnɪn) *n. Japanese history.* **1.** a lordless samurai, esp. one whose feudal lord had been deprived of his territory. **2.** such samurai collectively. [Japanese]

röntgen (ˈrɒntgən, -tjən, ˈrɛnt-) *n.* a variant spelling of **roentgen.**

roo (ruː) *n. Austral. informal.* a kangaroo.

rood (ruːd) *n.* **1. a.** a crucifix, esp. one set on a beam or screen at the entrance to the chancel of a church. **b.** (*as modifier*): *rood beam; rood arch; rood screen.* **2.** the Cross on which Christ was crucified. **3.** a unit of area equal to one quarter of an acre or 0.10117 hectares. **4.** a unit of area equal to one square rod. [Old English *rōd;* related to Old Saxon *rōda,* Old Norse *rōtha*]

rood screen *n.* a partition of stone or wood, often richly carved and decorated, that separates the chancel from the main part of a church: it is surmounted by a crucifix (rood), and was an important feature of medieval churches, though in England many rood screens were destroyed at the Reformation.

roof (ruːf) *n., pl.* **roofs** (ruːfs, ruːvz). **1. a.** a structure that covers or forms the top of a building. **b.** (*in combination*): *the rooftop.* **c.** (*as modifier*): *a roof garden.* **2.** the top covering of a vehicle, oven, or other structure: *the roof of a car.* **3.** *Anatomy.* any structure that covers an organ or part: *the roof of the mouth.* **4.** a highest or topmost point or part: *Mount Everest is the roof of the world.* **5.** a house or other shelter: *a poor man's roof.* **6.** *Mountaineering.* the underside of a projecting overhang. **7. hit** (*or* **go through**) **the roof.** *Informal.* to get extremely angry; become furious. **8. raise the roof. a.** to create a boisterous disturbance. **b.** to react or protest heatedly. ~*vb.* **9.** (*tr.*) to provide or cover with a roof or rooflike part. [Old English *hrōf;* related to Middle Dutch, Old Norse *hrōf*] —**ˈroofer** *n.* —**ˈroofless** *adj.* —**ˈroofˌlike** *adj.*

roof garden *n.* a garden on a flat roof of a building.

roofing (ˈruːfɪŋ) *n.* **1.** material used to construct a roof. **2.** the act of constructing a roof.

roof rack *n.* a rack attached to the roof of a motor vehicle for carrying luggage, skis, etc.

rooftop (ˈruːfˌtɒp) *n.* the outside part of the roof of a building.

rooftree (ˈruːfˌtriː) *n.* another name for **ridgepole.**

rooibos tea (ˈrɔɪbɒs) *n. S. African.* tea prepared from any of several species of *Borbonia* or *Aspalanthus,* believed to have tonic properties. [from Afrikaans *rooi* red + *bos* bush]

rooikat (ˈrɔɪˌkæt) *n.* a South African lynx, *Felis caracal.* [Afrikaans *rooi* red + *kat* cat]

rooinek (ˈrʊɪnɛk, ˈrɔɪ-) *n. S. African.* a facetious name for an Englishman. [C19: Afrikaans, literally: red neck]

rook[1] (rʊk) *n.* **1.** a large Eurasian passerine bird, *Corvus frugilegus,* with a black plumage and a whitish base to its bill: family *Corvidae* (crows). **2.** *Slang.* a swindler or cheat, esp. one who cheats at cards. ~*vb.* **3.** (*tr.*) *Slang.* to overcharge, swindle, or cheat. [Old English *hrōc;* related to Old High German *hruoh,* Old Norse *hrōkr*]

rook[2] (rʊk) *n.* a chesspiece that may move any number of unoccupied squares in a straight line, horizontally or vertically. Also called: **castle.** [C14: from Old French *rok,* ultimately from Arabic *rukhkh*]

rookery (ˈrʊkərɪ) *n., pl.* **-eries. 1.** a group of nesting rooks. **2.** a clump of trees containing rooks' nests. **3. a.** a breeding ground or communal living area of certain other species of gregarious birds or mammals, esp. penguins or seals. **b.** a colony of any such creatures. **4.** *Archaic.* an overcrowded slum tenement building or area of housing.

rookie (ˈrʊkɪ) *n. Informal.* an inexperienced person or newcomer, esp. a raw recruit in the army. [C20: changed from RECRUIT]

rooky (ˈrʊkɪ) *adj.* **rookier, rookiest.** *Literary.* abounding in rooks.

room (ruːm, rʊm) *n.* **1.** space or extent, esp. unoccupied or unobstructed space for a particular purpose: *is there room to pass?* **2.** an area within a building enclosed by a floor, a ceiling, and walls or partitions. **3.** (*functioning as sing. or pl.*) the people present in a room: *the whole room was laughing.* **4.** (foll. by *for*) opportunity or scope: *room for manoeuvre.* **5.** (*pl.*) a part of a house, hotel, etc. that is rented out as separate accommodation; lodgings: *she got rooms quite easily in Dulwich.* **6.** a euphemistic word for **lavatory** (sense 1). ~*vb.* **7.** (*intr.*) *Chiefly U.S.* to occupy or share a room or lodging: *where does he room?* [Old

English *rūm;* related to Gothic, Old High German *rūm*] —ˈ**roomer** *n.*

roomette (ruːˈmɛt, rʊˈmɛt) *n. U.S. and Canadian.* a self-contained compartment in a railway sleeping car.

roomful (ˈruːmfʊl, ˈrʊm-) *n., pl.* **-fuls.** a number or quantity sufficient to fill a room: *a roomful of furniture.*

rooming house *n. U.S. and Canadian.* a house having self-contained furnished rooms or flats for renting.

roommate (ˈruːmˌmeɪt, ˈrʊm-) *n.* a person with whom one shares a room or lodging.

room service *n.* service in a hotel providing meals, drinks, etc., in guests' rooms.

room temperature *n.* the normal temperature of a living room, usually taken as being around 20°C.

roomy (ˈruːmɪ, ˈrʊmɪ) *adj.* **roomier, roomiest.** having ample room; spacious. —ˈ**roomily** *adv.* —ˈ**roominess** *n.*

roorback (ˈrʊəˌbæk) *n. U.S.* a false or distorted report or account, used to obtain political advantage. [C19: after Baron von *Roorback,* invented author of an imaginary *Tour through the Western and Southern States* (1844), which contained a passage defaming James K. Polk (1795–1849), U.S. statesman]

roose (ruːz) *vb. (tr.) Scot. and northern English dialect.* to praise or flatter. [C13 (n.): from Scandinavian; compare Icelandic *hrōsa* to praise] —ˈ**rooser** *n.*

roost (ruːst) *n.* **1.** a place, perch, branch, etc., where birds, esp. domestic fowl, rest or sleep. **2.** a temporary place to rest or stay. **3. rule the roost.** See **rule** (sense 20). ~*vb.* **4.** (*intr.*) to rest or sleep on a roost. **5.** (*intr.*) to settle down or stay. **6. come home to roost.** to have unfavourable repercussions. [Old English *hrōst;* related to Old Saxon *hrost* loft, German *Rost* grid]

Roost (ruːst) *n.* **the.** a powerful current caused by conflicting tides around the Shetland and Orkney Islands. [C16: from Old Norse *röst*]

rooster (ˈruːstə) *n. Chiefly U.S. and Canadian.* the male of the domestic fowl; a cock.

root[1] (ruːt) *n.* **1. a.** the organ of a higher plant that anchors the rest of the plant in the ground, absorbs water and mineral salts from the soil, and does not bear leaves or buds. **b.** (loosely) any of the branches of such an organ. **2.** any plant part, such as a rhizome or tuber, that is similar to a root in structure, function, or appearance. **3. a.** the essential, fundamental, or primary part or nature of something: *your analysis strikes at the root of the problem.* **b.** (*as modifier*): *the root cause of the problem.* **4.** *Anatomy.* the embedded portion of a tooth, nail, hair, etc. **5.** origin or derivation, esp. as a source of growth, vitality, or existence. **6.** (*pl.*) a person's sense of belonging in a community, place, etc., esp. the one in which he was born or brought up. **7.** an ancestor or antecedent. **8.** *Bible.* a descendant. **9.** the form of a word that remains after removal of all affixes; a morpheme with lexical meaning that is not further subdivisible into other morphemes with lexical meaning. Compare **stem**[1] (sense 9). **10.** *Maths.* a number or quantity that when multiplied by itself a certain number of times equals a given number or quantity: *3 is a cube root of 27.* **11.** Also called: **solution.** *Maths.* a number that when substituted for the variable satisfies a given equation: *2 is a root of* $x^3 - 2x - 4 = 0$. **12.** *Music.* (in harmony) the note forming the foundation of a chord. **13.** *Austral. and N.Z. slang.* sexual intercourse. **14. root and branch.** (*adv.*) entirely; completely; utterly. ~Related adj.: **radical.** ~*vb.* **15.** (*intr.*) Also: **take root.** to put forth or establish a root and begin to grow. **16.** (*intr.*) Also: **take root.** to become established, embedded, or effective. **17.** (*tr.*) to fix or embed with or as if with a root or roots. **18.** *Austral. and N.Z. slang.* to have sexual intercourse (with). ~See also **root out, root up.** [Old English *rōt,* from Old Norse; related to Old English *wyrt* WORT] —ˈ**rooter** *n.* —ˈ**rootˌlike** *adj.* —ˈ**rooty** *adj.* —ˈ**rootiness** *n.*

root[2] (ruːt) *vb. (intr.)* **1.** (of a pig) to burrow in or dig up the earth in search of food, using the snout. **2.** (foll. by *about, around, in,* etc.) *Informal.* to search vigorously but unsystematically. [C16: changed (through influence of ROOT[1]) from earlier *wroot,* from Old English *wrōtan;* related to Old English *wrōt* snout, Middle Dutch *wrōte* mole] —ˈ**rooter** *n.*

root[3] *vb. (intr.;* usually foll. by *for) Informal.* to give support to (a contestant, team, etc.), as by cheering. [C19: perhaps a variant of Scottish *rout* to make a loud noise, from Old Norse *rauta* to roar] —ˈ**rooter** *n.*

root beer *n. U.S. and Canadian.* an effervescent drink made from extracts of various roots and herbs.

root canal *n.* the passage in the root of a tooth through which its nerves and blood vessels enter the pulp cavity.

root-canal therapy *n.* another name for **root treatment.**

root cap *n.* a hollow cone of loosely arranged cells that covers the growing tip of a root and protects it during its passage through the soil.

root climber *n.* any of various climbing plants, such as the ivy, that adhere to a supporting structure by means of small roots growing from the side of the stem.

root crop *n.* a crop, as of turnips or beets, cultivated for the food value of its roots.

rooted (ˈruːtɪd) *adj.* **1.** having roots. **2.** deeply felt: *rooted objections.* **3.** *Austral. slang.* tired or defeated. **4. get rooted!** *Austral. taboo slang.* an exclamation of contemptuous anger or annoyance, esp. against another person.

root ginger *n.* the raw underground stem of the ginger plant used finely chopped or grated, esp. in Chinese dishes.

root hair *n.* any of the hollow hairlike outgrowths of the outer cells of a root, just behind the tip, that absorb water and salts from the soil.

rooting compound *n. Horticulture.* a substance, usually a powder, containing auxins in which plant cuttings are dipped in order to promote root growth.

rootle (ˈruːtᵊl) *vb. (intr.) Brit.* another word for **root**[2].

rootless (ˈruːtlɪs) *adj.* having no roots, esp. (of a person) having no ties with a particular place or community.

rootlet (ˈruːtlɪt) *n.* a small root or branch of a root.

root mean square *n.* the square root of the average of the squares of a set of numbers or quantities: *the root mean square of* 1, 2, *and* 4 is $\sqrt{[(1^2 + 2^2 + 4^2)/3]} = \sqrt{7}$. Abbrev: **rms.**

root nodule *n.* a swelling on the root of a leguminous plant, such as the pea or clover, that contains bacteria of the genus *Rhizobium,* capable of nitrogen fixation.

root out *vb. (tr., adv.)* to remove or eliminate completely: *we must root out inefficiency.*

root position *n. Music.* the vertical distribution of the written notes of a chord in which the root of the chord is in the bass. See **position** (sense 12a), **inversion** (sense 5a).

roots music *n.* **1.** another name for **world music. 2.** reggae, esp. when regarded as authentic and uncommercialized.

rootstock (ˈruːtˌstɒk) *n.* **1.** another name for **rhizome. 2.** another name for **stock** (sense 7). **3.** *Biology.* a basic structure from which offshoots have developed.

root treatment *n. Dentistry.* a procedure, used for treating an abscess at the tip of the root of a tooth, in which the pulp is removed and a filling (**root filling**) inserted in the root canal. Also called: **root-canal therapy.**

root up *vb. (tr., adv.)* to tear or dig up by the roots.

ropable *or* **ropeable** (ˈrəʊpəbᵊl) *adj.* **1.** capable of being roped. **2.** *Austral. and N.Z. informal.* **a.** angry. **b.** wild or intractable: *a ropable beast.*

rope (rəʊp) *n.* **1. a.** a fairly thick cord made of twisted and intertwined hemp or other fibres or of wire or other strong material. **b.** (*as modifier*): *a rope bridge; a rope ladder.* **2.** a row of objects fastened or united to form a line: *a rope of pearls; a rope of onions.* **3.** a quantity of material twisted or wound in the form of a cord. **4.** anything in the form of a filament or strand, esp. something viscous or glutinous: *a rope of slime.* **5. the rope. a.** a rope, noose, or halter used for hanging. **b.** death by hanging, strangling, etc. **6. give (someone) enough** (*or* **plenty of**) **rope to hang himself.** to allow (someone) to accomplish his own downfall by his own foolish acts. **7. know the ropes. a.** to have a thorough understanding of a particular sphere of activity. **b.** to be experienced in the ways of the world. **8. on the ropes. a.** *Boxing.* driven against the ropes enclosing the ring by an opponent's attack. **b.** in a defenceless or hopeless position. ~*vb.* **9.** (*tr.*) to bind or fasten with or as if with a rope. **10.** (*tr.;* usually foll. by *off*) to enclose or divide by means of a rope. **11.** (*intr.*) to become extended in a long filament or thread. **12.** (when *intr.,* foll. by *up*) *Mountaineering.* to tie (climbers) together with a rope. [Old English *rāp;* related to Old Saxon *rēp,* Old High German *reif*]

rope dancer *n.* another name for a **tightrope walker.**

rope in *vb. (tr., adv.)* **1.** *Brit.* to persuade to take part in some activity. **2.** *U.S. and Canadian.* to trick or entice into some activity.

rope's end *n.* a short piece of rope, esp. as formerly used for flogging sailors.

ropewalk (ˈrəʊpˌwɔːk) *n.* a long narrow usually covered path or shed where ropes are made.

rope yarn *n.* the natural or synthetic fibres out of which rope is made.

ropy *or* **ropey** (ˈrəʊpɪ) *adj.* **ropier, ropiest. 1.** *Brit. informal.* **a.** inferior or inadequate. **b.** slightly unwell; below par. **2.** (of a viscous or sticky substance) forming strands or filaments. **3.** resembling a rope: *ropy muscles.* —ˈ**ropily** *adv.* —ˈ**ropiness** *n.*

roque (rəʊk) *n. U.S.* a game developed from croquet, played on a hard surface with a resilient surrounding border from which the ball can rebound. [C19: variant of CROQUET]

Roquefort (ˈrɒkfɔː) *n.* a blue-veined cheese with a strong flavour, made from ewe's and goat's milk: matured in caves. [C19: named after *Roquefort,* village in S France]

roquelaure (ˈrɒkəˌlɔː) *n.* a man's hooded knee-length cloak of the 18th and 19th centuries. [C18: from French, named after the Duc de *Roquelaure* (1656–1738), French marshal]

roquet (ˈrəʊkɪ) *Croquet.* ~*vb.* **-quets** (-kɪz), **-queting** (-kɪɪŋ), **-queted** (-kɪd). **1.** to drive one's ball against (another person's ball) in order to be allowed to croquet. ~*n.* **2.** the act of roqueting. [C19: variant of CROQUET]

ro-ro (ˈrəʊrəʊ) *adj. acronym for* **roll-on/roll-off.**

rorqual (ˈrɔːkwəl) *n.* any of several whalebone whales of the genus *Balaenoptera,* esp. *B. physalus:* family *Balaenopteridae.* They have a dorsal fin and a series of grooves along the throat and chest. Also called: **finback.** [C19: from French, from Norwegian *rörhval,* from Old Norse *reytharhvalr,* from *reythr* (from *rauthr* red) + *hvalr* whale]

Rorschach test (ˈrɔːʃɑːk; *German* ˈrɔrʃax) *n. Psychol.* a personality test consisting of a number of unstructured ink blots presented for interpretation. [C20: named after Hermann *Rorschach* (1884–1922), Swiss psychiatrist]

rort (rɔːt) *n. Austral. informal.* **1.** a rowdy party or celebration. **2.** a dishonest scheme. [C20: back formation from *rorty* (in the sense: good, splendid)] —**'rorty** *adj.*

rosace ('rəʊzeɪs) *n.* **1.** another name for **rose window.** **2.** another name for **rosette.** [C19: from French, from Latin *rosăceus* ROSACEOUS]

rosaceous (rəʊ'zeɪʃəs) *adj.* **1.** of, relating to, or belonging to the *Rosaceae,* a family of flowering plants typically having white, yellow, pink, or red five-petalled flowers. The family includes the rose, strawberry, blackberry, and many fruit trees such as apple, cherry, and plum. **2.** of the colour rose; rose-coloured; rosy. [C18: from Latin *rosăceus* composed of roses, from *rosa* ROSE[1]]

rosaniline (rəʊ'zænɪˌliːn, -lɪn) *or* **rosanilin** *n.* a reddish-brown crystalline insoluble derivative of aniline used, in the form of its soluble hydrochloride, as a red dye. See also **fuchsin.** [C19: from ROSE[1] + ANILINE]

rosarian (rəʊ'zɛərɪən) *n.* a person who cultivates roses, esp. professionally.

rosarium (rəʊ'zɛərɪəm) *n., pl.* **-sariums** *or* **-saria** (-'zɛərɪə). a rose garden. [C19: New Latin]

rosary ('rəʊzərɪ) *n., pl.* **-saries.** **1.** *R.C. Church.* **a.** a series of prayers counted on a string of beads, usually consisting of five or 15 decades of Aves, each decade beginning with a Paternoster and ending with a Gloria. **b.** a string of 55 or 165 beads used to count these prayers as they are recited. **2.** (in other religions) a similar string of beads used in praying. **3.** a bed or garden of roses. **4.** an archaic word for a **garland** (of flowers, leaves, etc.). [C14: from Latin *rosārium* rose garden, from *rosārius* of roses, from *rosa* ROSE[1]]

Roscius ('rɒskɪəs, -sɪəs) *n.* an actor. [from the name of a Roman actor (died 62 B.C.)] —**'Roscian** *adj.*

rose[1] (rəʊz) *n.* **1. a.** any shrub or climbing plant of the rosaceous genus *Rosa,* typically having prickly stems, compound leaves, and fragrant flowers. **b.** *(in combination): rosebush; rosetree.* **2.** the flower of any of these plants. **3.** any of various similar plants, such as the rockrose and Christmas rose. **4. a.** a moderate purplish-red colour; purplish pink. **b.** *(as adj.): rose paint.* **5.** a rose, or a representation of one, as the national emblem of England. **6.** *Jewellery.* **a.** a cut for a diamond or other gemstone, having a hemispherical faceted crown and a flat base. **b.** a gem so cut. **7.** a perforated cap fitted to the spout of a watering can or the end of a hose, causing the water to issue in a spray. **8.** a design or decoration shaped like a rose; rosette. **9.** Also called: **ceiling rose.** *Electrical engineering.* a circular boss attached to a ceiling through which the flexible lead of an electric-light fitting passes. **10.** *History.* See **red rose, white rose.** **11. bed of roses.** a situation of comfort or ease. **12. under the rose.** in secret; privately; sub rosa. ~*vb.* **13.** *(tr.)* to make rose-coloured; cause to blush or redden. [Old English, from Latin *rosa,* probably from Greek *rhodon* rose] —**'roseˌlike** *adj.*

rose[2] (rəʊz) *vb.* the past tense of **rise.**

rosé ('rəʊzeɪ) *n.* any pink wine, made either by removing the skins of red grapes after only a little colour has been extracted or by mixing red and white wines. [C19: from French, literally: pink, from Latin *rosa* ROSE[1]]

rose acacia *n.* a leguminous shrub, *Robinia hispida,* of the southern U.S., having prickly branches bearing clusters of red scentless flowers. See also **locust** (sense 2).

rose apple *n.* an ornamental myrtaceous tree, *Eugenia jambos,* of the East Indies, cultivated in the tropics for its edible fruit.

roseate ('rəʊzɪɪt) *adj.* **1.** of the colour rose or pink. **2.** excessively or idealistically optimistic. —**'roseˌately** *adv.*

rosebay ('rəʊzˌbeɪ) *n.* **1.** *U.S.* any of several rhododendrons, esp. *Rhododendron maximum* of E North America. **2. rosebay willowherb.** a perennial onagraceous plant, *Chamaenerion* (formerly *Epilobium*) *angustifolium,* that has spikes of deep pink flowers and is widespread in open places throughout N temperate regions. **3.** another name for **oleander.**

rosebud ('rəʊzˌbʌd) *n.* **1.** the bud of a rose. **2.** *Literary.* a pretty young woman.

rose campion *n.* a European caryophyllaceous plant, *Lychnis coronaria,* widely cultivated for its pink flowers. Its stems and leaves are covered with white woolly down. Also called: **dusty miller.**

rose chafer *or* **beetle** *n.* a British scarabaeid beetle, *Cetonia aurata,* that has a greenish-golden body with a metallic lustre and feeds on plants.

rose-coloured *adj.* **1.** of the colour rose; rosy. **2.** excessively optimistic. **3. see through rose-coloured glasses** (*or* **spectacles**). to view in an excessively optimistic light.

rose-cut *adj.* (of a gemstone) cut with a hemispherical faceted crown and a flat base.

rosefish ('rəʊzˌfɪʃ) *n., pl.* **-fish** *or* **-fishes.** **1.** a red scorpaenid food fish, *Sebastes marinus,* of North Atlantic coastal waters. **2.** any of various other red fishes.

rose geranium *n.* a small geraniaceous shrub, *Pelargonium graveolens,* grown in North America for its pink flowers and fragrant leaves, used for scenting perfumes and cosmetics.

rosehip ('rəʊzˌhɪp) *n.* the berry-like fruit of a rose plant. See **hip**[2].

rosella (rəʊ'zɛlə) *n.* any of various Australian parrots of the genus *Platycercus,* such as *P. elegans* (**crimson rosella**), often kept as cage birds. [C19: probably alteration of *Rose-hiller,* after *Rose Hill,* Parramatta, near Sydney]

rosemaling ('rəʊzəˌmɑːlɪŋ, -sə-) *n.* a type of painted or carved decoration in Scandinavian peasant style consisting of floral motifs. [C20: from Norwegian, literally: rose painting]

rose mallow *n.* **1.** Also called (U.S. and Canadian): **marsh mallow.** any of several malvaceous marsh plants of the genus *Hibiscus,* such as *H. moscheutos,* of E North America, having pink or white flowers and downy leaves. **2.** *U.S.* another name for the **hollyhock.**

rosemary ('rəʊzmərɪ) *n., pl.* **-maries.** an aromatic European shrub, *Rosmarinus officinalis,* widely cultivated for its grey-green evergreen leaves, which are used in cookery for flavouring and yield a fragrant oil used in the manufacture of perfumes: family *Labiatae* (labiates). It is the traditional flower of remembrance. [C15: earlier *rosmarine,* from Latin *rōs* dew + *marīnus* marine; modern form influenced by folk etymology, as if ROSE[1] + (Virgin) *Mary*]

rose moss *n.* a low-growing portulacaceous plant, *Portulaca grandiflora,* native to Brazil but widely cultivated as a garden plant for its brightly coloured flowers.

rose of Jericho ('dʒɛrɪkəʊ) *n.* another name for the **resurrection plant.**

rose of Sharon (ʃærən) *n.* **1.** Also called: **Aaron's beard.** a creeping shrub, *Hypericum calycinum,* native to SE Europe but widely cultivated, having large yellow flowers: family *Hypericaceae.* **2.** Also called: **althaea.** a Syrian malvaceous shrub, *Hibiscus syriacus* (or *Althaea frutex*), cultivated for its red or purplish flowers.

roseola (rəʊ'ziːələ) *n. Pathol.* **1.** any red skin eruption or rash. **2.** another name for **rubeola.** [C19: from New Latin, diminutive of Latin *roseus* rosy] —**ro'seolar** *adj.*

rose quartz *n.* a rose-pink often translucent variety of quartz that is used for ornaments.

rose-root *n.* a Eurasian crassulaceous mountain plant, *Sedum rosea,* with fleshy pink-tipped leaves, a thick fleshy pinkish underground stem, and a cluster of yellow flowers. Also called: **midsummer-men.**

rosery ('rəʊzərɪ) *n., pl.* **-series.** a bed or garden of roses.

rose topaz *n.* a rose-pink form of topaz produced by heating yellow-brown topaz.

Rosetta stone (rəʊ'zɛtə) *n.* a basalt slab discovered in 1799 at Rosetta, N Egypt, dating to the reign of Ptolemy V (196 B.C.) and carved with parallel inscriptions in Egyptian hieroglyphics, demotic characters, and Greek, which provided the key to the decipherment of ancient Egyptian texts.

rosette (rəʊ'zɛt) *n.* **1.** a decoration or pattern resembling a rose, esp. an arrangement of ribbons or strips formed into a rose-shaped design and worn as a badge or presented as a prize. **2.** another name for **rose window.** **3.** a rose-shaped patch of colour, such as one of the clusters of spots marking a leopard's fur. **4.** *Botany.* a circular cluster of leaves growing from the base of a stem. **5.** any of various plant diseases characterized by abnormal leaf growth. [C18: from Old French: a little ROSE[1]]

rose-water *n.* **1. a.** scented water used as a perfume and in cooking, made by the distillation of rose petals or by impregnation with oil of roses. **b.** *(as modifier): rose-water scent.* **2.** *(modifier)* elegant or delicate, esp. excessively so.

rose window *n.* a circular window, esp. one that has ornamental tracery radiating from the centre to form a symmetrical roselike pattern. Also called: **wheel window, rosette.**

rosewood ('rəʊzˌwʊd) *n.* **1.** the hard dark wood of any of various tropical and subtropical leguminous trees, esp. of the genus *Dalbergia.* It has a roselike scent and is used in cabinetwork. **2.** any of the trees yielding this wood.

Rosh Chodesh (rɔʃ 'xɔdəʃ) *n. Judaism.* the first day of a new month, coinciding usually with the new moon, and also the preceding day if the previous month has 30 days, observed as a minor festival. See also **Jewish calendar.** [from Hebrew, literally: the beginning of the new moon]

Rosh Hashanah *or* **Rosh Hashana** ('rɒʃ hə'ʃɑːnə; *Hebrew* 'rɔʃ haʃa'na) *n.* the festival marking the Jewish New Year, celebrated on the first and second days of Tishri, and marked by penitential prayers and by the blowing of the shofar. [from Hebrew *rōsh hasshānāh,* literally: beginning of the year, from *rōsh* head + *hash-shānāh* year]

Rosicrucian (ˌrəʊzɪ'kruːʃən) *n.* **1.** a member of a society professing esoteric religious doctrines, venerating the emblems of the rose and Cross as symbols of Christ's Resurrection and Redemption, and claiming various occult powers. ~*adj.* **2.** of, relating to, or designating the Rosicrucians or Rosicrucianism. [C17: from Latin *Rosae Crucis* Rose of the Cross, translation of the German name Christian *Rosenkreuz,* supposed founder of the society in the 15th century] —ˌ**Rosi'crucianism** *n.*

Rosie Lee ('rəʊzɪ 'liː) *n. Cockney rhyming slang.* tea.

rosin ('rɒzɪn) *n.* **1.** Also called: **colophony.** a translucent brittle amber substance produced in the distillation of crude turpentine oleoresin and used esp. in making varnishes, printing inks, and sealing waxes and for treating the bows of stringed instruments. **2.** another name for **resin** (sense 1). ~*vb.* **3.** *(tr.)* to treat or coat with rosin. [C14: variant of RESIN] —**'rosiny** *adj.*

rosiner ('rɒzənə) *n. Austral. slang.* a strong alcoholic drink. [from English dialect sense of *rosin* to supply with liquor]

rosin oil *n.* a yellowish fluorescent oily liquid obtained from certain resins, used in the manufacture of carbon black, varnishes, and lacquers. Also called: '**rosinol, retinol.**

rosinweed ('rɒzɪn,wi:d) *n.* any of several North American plants of the genus *Silphium* and related genera, esp. the compass plant, having resinous juice, sticky foliage, and a strong smell: family *Compositae* (composites).

ROSPA ('rɒspə) *n.* (in Britain) *acronym for* Royal Society for the Prevention of Accidents.

rostellum (rɒ'stɛləm) *n., pl.* **-la** (-lə). *Biology.* a small beaklike process, such as the hooked projection from the top of the head in tapeworms or the outgrowth from the stigma of an orchid. [C18: from Latin: a little beak, from *rōstrum* a beak] —**ros'tellate** *or* **ros'tellar** *adj.*

roster ('rɒstə) *n.* **1.** a list or register, esp. one showing the order of people enrolled for duty. *~vb.* **2.** (*tr.*) to place on a roster. [C18: from Dutch *rooster* grating or list (the lined paper looking like a grid)]

rostral ('rɒstrəl) *adj.* **1.** *Biology.* of or like a beak or snout. **2.** adorned with the prows of ships: *a rostral column.*

rostrate ('rɒs,treɪt) *adj. Biology.* having a beak or beaklike process.

rostrum ('rɒstrəm) *n., pl.* **-trums** *or* **-tra** (-trə). **1.** any platform, stage, or dais on which public speakers stand to address an audience. **2.** a platform or dais in front of an orchestra on which the conductor stands. **3.** another word for **ram** (sense 5). **4.** the prow or beak of an ancient Roman ship. **5.** *Biology, zoology.* a beak or beaklike part. [C16: from Latin *rōstrum* beak, ship's prow, from *rōdere* to nibble, gnaw; in plural, *rōstra,* orator's platform, because this platform in the Roman forum was adorned with the prows of captured ships]

rosy ('rəʊzɪ) *adj.* **rosier, rosiest.** **1.** of the colour rose or pink. **2.** having a healthy pink complexion: *rosy cheeks.* **3.** optimistic, esp. excessively so: *a rosy view of social improvements.* **4.** full of health, happiness, or joy: *rosy slumbers.* **5.** resembling, consisting of, or abounding in roses. —'**rosily** *adv.* —'**rosiness** *n.*

rosy finch *n.* any of several finches of the genus *Leucosticte,* occurring in mountainous regions of North America and Asia. They have brown or grey plumage with pink patches on the wings, rump, and tail.

rot[1] (rɒt) *vb.* **rots, rotting, rotted.** **1.** to decay or cause to decay as a result of bacterial or fungal action. **2.** (*intr.;* usually foll. by *off* or *away*) to fall or crumble (off) or break (away), as from natural decay, corrosive action, or long use. **3.** (*intr.*) to become weak, debilitated, or depressed through inertia, confinement, etc.; languish: *rotting in prison.* **4.** to become or cause to become morally corrupt or degenerate. **5.** (*tr.*) *Textiles.* another word for **ret.** *~n.* **6.** the process of rotting or the state of being rotten. **7.** something decomposed, disintegrated, or degenerate. Related adj.: **putrid.** **8.** short for **dry rot.** **9.** *Pathol.* any putrefactive decomposition of tissues. **10.** a condition in plants characterized by breakdown and decay of tissues, caused by parasitic bacteria, fungi, etc. **11.** *Vet. science.* a contagious fungal disease of sheep characterized by inflammation, swelling, a foul-smelling discharge, and lameness. **12.** (*also interj.*) nonsense; rubbish. [Old English *rotian* (vb.); related to Old Norse *rotna.* C13 (n.), from Scandinavian]

rot[2] *abbrev. for* rotation (of a mathematical function).

rota ('rəʊtə) *n. Chiefly Brit.* a register of names showing the order in which people take their turn to perform certain duties. [C17: from Latin: a wheel]

rota bed *n. Social welfare.* a bed in an old people's home, reserved for the regular respite care of dependent old people.

rotachute ('rəʊtə,ʃu:t) *n.* a device serving the same purpose as a parachute, in which the canopy is replaced by freely revolving rotor blades, used for the delivery of stores or recovery of missiles.

Rotameter ('rəʊtə,mi:tə) *n. Trademark.* a device used for measuring the flow of a fluid. It consists of a small float supported in a tapering glass by the flow of the fluid, the height of the float indicating the rate of flow.

rotaplane ('rəʊtə,pleɪn) *n.* an aircraft that derives its lift from freely revolving rotor blades.

Rotarian (rəʊ'tɛərɪən) *n.* **1.** a member of a Rotary Club, any of the local groups of professional and business men, forming an international association to promote community service. *~adj.* **2.** of or relating to Rotary Clubs or their members. —**Ro'tarianism** *n.*

rotary ('rəʊtərɪ) *adj.* **1.** of, relating to, or operating by rotation. **2.** turning or able to turn; revolving. *~n., pl.* **-ries.** **3.** a part of a machine that rotates about an axis. **4.** *U.S. and Canadian.* another term for **roundabout** (for traffic). [C18: from Medieval Latin *rotārius,* from Latin *rota* a wheel]

rotary clothesline *or* **clothes dryer** *n.* an apparatus of radiating spokes that support lines on which clothes are hung to dry and are free to rotate around a central pole.

rotary engine *n.* **1.** an internal-combustion engine having radial cylinders that rotate about a fixed crankshaft. **2.** an engine, such as a turbine or wankel engine, in which power is transmitted directly to rotating components.

rotary plough *or* **tiller** *n.* an implement with a series of blades mounted on a power-driven shaft which rotates so as to break up soil or destroy weeds.

rotary press *n.* a machine for printing from a revolving cylindrical forme, usually onto a continuous strip of paper.

rotary pump *n. Engineering.* a pump for liquids consisting of a specially shaped stator and rotor. The liquid is displaced through the shaped stator by the shaped rotor.

rotate *vb.* (rəʊ'teɪt). **1.** to turn or cause to turn around an axis, line, or point; revolve or spin. **2.** to follow or cause to follow a set order or sequence. **3.** to replace one group of personnel with another. *~adj.* ('rəʊteɪt). **4.** *Botany.* designating a corolla the united petals of which radiate from a central point like the spokes of a wheel. —**ro'tatable** *adj.*

rotation (rəʊ'teɪʃən) *n.* **1.** the act of rotating; rotary motion. **2.** a regular cycle of events in a set order or sequence. **3.** a planned sequence of cropping according to which the crops grown in successive seasons on the same land are varied so as to make a balanced demand on its resources of fertility. **4.** *Maths.* **a.** a circular motion of a configuration about a given point or line, without a change in shape. **b.** a transformation in which the coordinate axes are rotated by a fixed angle about the origin. **c.** another name for **curl** (sense 11). Abbrev. (for c.): **rot** **5. a.** the spinning motion of a body, such as a planet, about an internal axis. Compare **revolution** (sense 5a). **b.** one complete turn in such motion. —**ro'tational** *adj.*

rotator (rəʊ'teɪtə) *n.* **1.** a person, device, or part that rotates or causes rotation. **2.** *Anatomy.* any of various muscles that revolve a part on its axis.

rotatory ('rəʊtətərɪ, -trɪ) *or* (*less commonly*) **rotative** ('rəʊtətɪv) *adj.* of, relating to, possessing, or causing rotation. —'**rotatively** *adv.*

rote[1] (rəʊt) *n.* **1.** a habitual or mechanical routine or procedure. **2. by rote.** by repetition; by heart (often in the phrase **learn by rote**). [C14: origin unknown]

rote[2] (rəʊt) *n.* an ancient violin-like musical instrument; crwth. [C13: from Old French *rote,* of Germanic origin; related to Old High German *rotta,* Middle Dutch *rotte*]

rotenone ('rəʊtɪ,nəʊn) *n.* a white odourless crystalline substance extracted from the roots of derris: a powerful insecticide. Formula: $C_{23}H_{22}O_6$; relative density: 1.27; melting pt.: 163°C. [C20: from Japanese *rōten* derris + -ONE]

rotgut ('rɒt,gʌt) *n. Facetious slang.* alcoholic drink, esp. spirits, of inferior quality.

roti ('rəʊtɪ, 'rʊtɪ) *n.* (in the Caribbean) a type of unleavened bread. [from Hindi: bread]

rotifer ('rəʊtɪfə) *n.* any minute aquatic multicellular invertebrate of the phylum *Rotifera,* having a ciliated wheel-like organ used in feeding and locomotion: common constituents of freshwater plankton. Also called: **wheel animalcule.** [C18: from New Latin *Rotifera,* from Latin *rota* wheel + *ferre* to bear] —**rotiferal** (rəʊ'tɪfərəl) *or* **ro'tiferous** *adj.*

rotisserie (rəʊ'tɪsərɪ) *n.* **1.** a rotating spit on which meat, poultry, etc., can be cooked. **2.** a shop or restaurant where meat is roasted to order. [C19: from French, from Old French *rostir* to ROAST]

rotl ('rɒtᵊl) *n., pl.* **rotls** *or* **artal** ('ɑ:tɑ:l). a unit of weight used in Muslim countries, varying in value between about one and five pounds. [C17: from Arabic *ratl,* perhaps from Greek *litra* a pound]

rotogravure (,rəʊtəʊgrə'vjʊə) *n.* **1.** a printing process using copper cylinders etched photomechanically with many small holes, from which ink is transferred to a moving web of paper, plastic, etc., in a rotary press. **2.** printed material produced in this way, esp. magazines. ~Often shortened to **roto.** [C20: from Latin *rota* wheel + GRAVURE]

roton ('rəʊtɒn) *n. Physics.* a quantum of rotational energy.

rotor ('rəʊtə) *n.* **1.** the rotating member of a machine or device, esp. the armature of a motor or generator or the rotating assembly of a turbine. Compare **stator.** **2.** a device having blades radiating from a central hub that is rotated to produce thrust to lift and propel a helicopter. **3.** the revolving arm of the distributor of an internal-combustion engine. [C20: shortened form of ROTATOR]

rotovate *or* **rotavate** ('rəʊtə,veɪt) *vb.* (*tr.*) to break up (the surface of the earth, or an area of ground) using a Rotovator.

Rotovator *or* **Rotavator** ('rəʊtə,veɪtə) *n. Trademark.* a type of machine with rotating blades that will break up soil, as on rough or uncultivated ground, or work surface material into the soil. [C20: original form *Rotavator,* from *rota(ry)* (*culti*)*vator*]

rotten ('rɒtᵊn) *adj.* **1.** affected with rot; decomposing, decaying, or putrid. **2.** breaking up, esp. through age or hard use; disintegrating: *rotten ironwork.* **3.** morally despicable or corrupt. **4.** untrustworthy, disloyal, or treacherous. **5.** *Informal.* unpleasant, unfortunate, or nasty: *rotten luck; rotten weather.* **6.** *Informal.* unsatisfactory or poor: *rotten workmanship.* **7.** *Informal.* miserably unwell. **8.** *Informal.* distressed, uncomfortable, and embarrassed: *I felt rotten when I had to break the bad news to him.* **9.** (of rocks, soils, etc.) soft and crumbling, esp. as a result of weathering. **10.** *Slang, chiefly Austral. and N.Z.* intoxicated; drunk. [C13: from Old Norse *rottin;* related to Old English *rotian* to ROT] —'**rottenly** *adv.* —'**rottenness** *n.*

rotten borough *n.* (before the Reform Act of 1832) any of certain English parliamentary constituencies with only a very few electors. Compare **pocket borough.**

rottenstone (ˈrɒtᵊnˌstəʊn) *n.* a much-weathered limestone, rich in silica: used in powdered form for polishing metal.

rotter (ˈrɒtə) *n. Slang, chiefly Brit.* a worthless, unpleasant, or despicable person.

Rottweiler (ˈrɒtˌvaɪlə) *n.* a breed of large robustly built dog with a smooth coat of black with dark tan markings on the face, chest, and legs, and usually having a docked tail. [German, named after *Rottweil,* German city where the dog was originally bred]

rotund (rəʊˈtʌnd) *adj.* **1.** rounded or spherical in shape. **2.** plump. **3.** sonorous or grandiloquent; full in tone, style of speaking, etc. [C18: from Latin *rotundus* wheel-shaped, round, from *rota* wheel] —**roˈtundity** *or* **roˈtundness** *n.* —**roˈtundly** *adv.*

rotunda (rəʊˈtʌndə) *n.* a building or room having a circular plan, esp. one that has a dome. [C17: from Italian *rotonda,* from Latin *rotundus* round, from *rota* a wheel]

rouble *or* **ruble** (ˈruːbᵊl) *n.* the standard monetary unit of the republics of the former Soviet Union (now independent states), divided into 100 kopecks. [C16: from Russian *rubl* silver bar, from Old Russian *rublĭ* bar, block of wood, from *rubiti* to cut up]

rouche (ruːʃ) *n.* a variant spelling of **ruche.**

roucou (ˈruːˌkuː) *n.* another name for **annatto.** [C17: via French from Tupi *urucú*]

roué (ˈruːeɪ) *n.* a debauched or lecherous man; rake. [C19: from French, literally: one broken on the wheel, from *rouer,* from Latin *rotāre* to revolve, from *rota* a wheel; with reference to the fate deserved by a debauchee]

rouge (ruːʒ) *n.* **1.** a red powder, used as a cosmetic for adding redness to the cheeks. **2.** short for **jeweller's rouge.** ~*vb.* (*tr.*) **3.** to apply rouge to. [C18: from French: red, from Latin *rubeus*]

Rouge Croix (ˌruːʒ ˈkrwɑː) *n.* a pursuivant at the English college of arms.

Rouge Dragon (ˌruːʒ ˈdrægən) *n.* a pursuivant at the English college of arms.

rouge et noir (ˈruːʒ eɪ ˈnwɑː; *French* ruʒ e nwar) *n.* a card game in which the players put their stakes on any of two red and two black diamond-shaped spots marked on the table. Also called: **trente et quarante.** [French, literally: red and black]

rough (rʌf) *adj.* **1.** (of a surface) not smooth; uneven or irregular. **2.** (of ground) covered with scrub, boulders, etc. **3.** denoting or taking place on uncultivated ground: *rough grazing; rough shooting.* **4.** shaggy or hairy. **5.** turbulent; agitated: *a rough sea.* **6.** (of the performance or motion of something) uneven; irregular: *a rough engine.* **7.** (of behaviour or character) rude, coarse, ill mannered, inconsiderate, or violent. **8.** harsh or sharp: *rough words.* **9.** *Informal.* severe or unpleasant: *a rough lesson.* **10.** (of work, a task, etc.) requiring physical rather than mental effort. **11.** *Informal.* ill or physically upset: *he felt rough after an evening of heavy drinking.* **12.** unfair or unjust: *rough luck.* **13.** harsh or grating to the ear. **14.** harsh to the taste. **15.** without refinement, luxury, etc. **16.** not polished or perfected in any detail; rudimentary; not elaborate: *rough workmanship; rough justice.* **17.** not prepared or dressed: *rough gemstones.* **18.** (of a guess, estimate, etc.) approximate. **19.** *Austral. informal.* (of a chance) not good. **20.** having the sound of *h*; aspirated. **21. rough on.** *Informal, chiefly Brit.* **a.** severe towards. **b.** unfortunate for (a person). **22. the rough side of one's tongue.** harsh words; a reprimand, rebuke, or verbal attack. ~*n.* **23.** rough ground. **24.** a sketch or preliminary piece of artwork. **25.** an unfinished or crude state (esp. in the phrase **in the rough**). **26. the rough.** *Golf.* the part of the course bordering the fairways where the grass is untrimmed. **27.** the side of a tennis or squash racket on which the binding strings form an uneven line. **28.** *Informal.* a rough or violent person; thug. **29.** the unpleasant side of something (esp. in the phrase **take the rough with the smooth**). ~*adv.* **30.** in a rough manner; roughly. **31. sleep rough.** to spend the night in the open; be without a home or without shelter. ~*vb.* **32.** (*tr.*) to make rough; roughen. **33.** (*tr.*; foll. by *out, in,* etc.) to prepare (a sketch, report, piece of work, etc.) in preliminary form. **34. rough it.** *Informal.* to live without the usual comforts or conveniences of life. ~See also **rough out, rough up.** [Old English *rūh;* related to Old Norse *ruksa,* Middle Dutch *rūge, rūwe,* German *rauh*] —ˈ**roughness** *n.*

roughage (ˈrʌfɪdʒ) *n.* **1.** the coarse indigestible constituents of food or fodder, which provide bulk to the diet and aid digestion. See also **dietary fibre.** **2.** any rough or coarse material.

rough-and-ready *adj.* **1.** crude, unpolished, or hastily prepared, but sufficient for the purpose. **2.** (of a person) without formality or refinement; rudely vigorous. —ˈ**rough-and-ˈreadiness** *n.*

rough-and-tumble *n.* **1.** a fight or scuffle without rules. ~*adj.* **2.** characterized by roughness, disorderliness, and disregard for rules or conventions.

rough breathing *n.* (in Greek) the sign (ʽ) placed over an initial vowel, indicating that (in ancient Greek) it was pronounced with an *h.* Compare **smooth breathing.**

roughcast (ˈrʌfˌkɑːst) *n.* **1.** a coarse plaster used to cover the surface of an external wall. **2.** any rough or preliminary form, model, etc. ~*adj.* **3.** covered with or denoting roughcast. ~*vb.* **-casts, -casting, -cast.** **4.** to apply roughcast to (a wall, etc.). **5.** to prepare in rough. **6.** (*tr.*) another word for **rough-hew.** —ˈ**roughˌcaster** *n.*

rough collie *n.* a large long-haired collie having a distinctive ruff and a long narrow head without a pronounced stop.

rough-cut *n.* a first edited version of a film with the scenes in sequence and the soundtrack synchronized.

rough diamond *n.* **1.** an unpolished diamond. **2.** an intrinsically trustworthy or good person with uncouth manners or dress.

rough-dry *adj.* **1.** (of clothes or linen) dried ready for pressing. ~*vb.* **-dries, -drying, -dried.** **2.** (*tr.*) to dry (clothes or linen) without smoothing or pressing.

roughen (ˈrʌfᵊn) *vb.* to make or become rough.

rough fish *n.* a fish that is neither a sport fish nor useful as food or bait for sport fish.

rough-hew *vb.* **-hews, -hewing, -hewed; -hewed** *or* **-hewn.** (*tr.*) **1.** to cut or hew (timber, stone, etc.) roughly without finishing the surface. **2.** Also: **roughcast.** to shape roughly or crudely.

roughhouse (ˈrʌfˌhaʊs) *Slang.* ~*n.* **1.** rough, disorderly, or noisy behaviour. ~*vb.* **2.** to treat (someone) in a boisterous or rough way.

roughie (ˈrʌfɪ) *n. Austral. slang.* **1.** something unfair, esp. a trick: *he put a roughie over.* **2.** (in horse racing) an outsider that wins.

roughish (ˈrʌfɪʃ) *adj.* somewhat rough.

rough-legged buzzard *n.* a buzzard, *Buteo lagopus,* of Europe, Asia, and North America, having feathers covering its legs.

roughly (ˈrʌflɪ) *adv.* **1.** without being exact or fully authenticated; approximately: *roughly half the candidates were successful.* **2.** in a clumsy, coarse, or violent manner: *his captors did not treat him roughly.* **3.** in a crude or primitive manner: *a slab of roughly hewn stone.*

rough music *n.* (formerly) a loud cacophony created with tin pans, drums, etc., esp. as a protest or demonstration of indignation outside someone's house.

roughneck (ˈrʌfˌnɛk) *n. Slang.* **1.** a rough or violent person; thug. **2.** a worker in an oil-drilling operation.

rough out *vb.* (*tr., adv.*) **1.** See **rough** (sense 33). **2.** *Engineering.* to machine (a workpiece, such as a casting or forging) with heavy cuts leaving a rough surface to be finished.

rough passage *n.* **1.** a stormy sea journey. **2.** a difficult or testing time.

rough puff pastry *n.* a rich flaky pastry made with butter and used for pie-crusts, flans, etc.

roughrider (ˈrʌfˌraɪdə) *n.* a rider of wild or unbroken horses.

roughshod (ˈrʌfˌʃɒd) *adj.* **1.** (of a horse) shod with rough-bottomed shoes to prevent sliding. ~*adv.* **2. ride roughshod over.** to domineer over or act with complete disregard for.

rough spin *n. N.Z. informal.* hard or unfair treatment.

rough-spoken *adj.* rude or uncouth in speech; blunt.

rough stuff *n. Informal.* violence.

rough trade *n. Slang.* (in homosexual use) a tough or violent sexual partner, esp. a lorry driver, construction worker, or docker, casually picked up.

rough up *vb.* (*tr., adv.*) **1.** *Informal.* to treat violently; beat up. **2.** to cause (feathers, hair, etc.) to stand up by rubbing against the grain.

roulade (ruːˈlɑːd) *n.* **1.** a slice of meat rolled, esp. around a stuffing, and cooked. **2.** an elaborate run in vocal music. [C18: from French, literally: a rolling, from *rouler* to ROLL]

rouleau (ˈruːləʊ) *n., pl.* **-leaux** (-ləʊ, -ləʊz) *or* **-leaus.** **1.** a roll of paper containing coins. **2.** (*often pl.*) a roll of ribbon. [C17: from French, from *role* ROLL]

roulette (ruːˈlɛt) *n.* **1.** a gambling game in which a ball is dropped onto a spinning horizontal wheel divided into 37 or 38 coloured and numbered slots, with players betting on the slot into which the ball will fall. **2. a.** a toothed wheel for making a line of perforations. **b.** a tiny slit made by such a wheel on a sheet of stamps as an aid to tearing it apart. **3.** a curve generated by a point on one curve rolling on another. ~*vb.* (*tr.*) **4.** to use a roulette on (something), as in engraving, making stationery, etc. [C18: from French, from *rouelle* a little wheel, from *roue* a wheel, from Latin *rota*]

Roumanian (ruːˈmeɪnɪən) *n., adj.* a variant of **Romanian.**

round (raʊnd) *adj.* **1.** having a flat circular shape, as a disc or hoop. **2.** having the shape of a sphere or ball. **3.** curved; not angular. **4.** involving or using circular motion. **5.** (*prenominal*) complete; entire: *a round dozen.* **6.** *Maths.* **a.** forming or expressed by an integer or whole number, with no fraction. **b.** expressed to the nearest ten, hundred, or thousand: *in round figures.* **7.** (of a sum of money) considerable; ample. **8.** fully depicted or developed, as a character in a book. **9.** full and plump: *round cheeks.* **10.** (of sound) full and sonorous. **11.** (of pace) brisk; lively. **12.** (*prenominal*) (of speech) candid; straightforward; unmodified: *a round assertion.* **13.** (of a vowel) pronounced with rounded lips. ~*n.* **14.** a round shape or object. **15. in the round. a.** in full detail. **b.** *Theatre.* with the audience all round the stage. **16.** a session, as of a negotiation: *a round of talks.* **17.** a series, cycle, or sequence: *a giddy round of parties.* **18. the daily round.** the usual activities of one's day. **19.** a stage of a competition: *he was eliminated in the first round.* **20.** (*often pl.*) a series of calls, esp. in a set order: *a doctor's rounds; a milkman's round.* **21.** a playing of all the holes on a golf course. **22.** a single turn of play by each player, as in a card game. **23.**

one of a number of periods constituting a boxing, wrestling, or other match, each usually lasting three minutes. **24.** *Archery.* a specified number of arrows shot from a specified distance. **25.** a single discharge by a number of guns or a single gun. **26.** a bullet, blank cartridge, or other charge of ammunition. **27.** a number of drinks bought at one time for a group of people. **28.** a single slice of bread or toast or two slices making a single serving of sandwiches. **29.** a general outburst of applause, cheering, etc. **30.** movement in a circle or around an axis. **31.** *Music.* a part song in which the voices follow each other at equal intervals at the same pitch. **32.** a sequence of bells rung in order of treble to tenor. Compare **change** (sense 29). **33.** a dance in which the dancers move in a circle. **34.** a cut of beef from the thigh between the rump and the shank. **35. go** *or* **make the rounds. a.** to go from place to place, as in making deliveries or social calls. **b.** (of information, rumour, etc.) to be passed around, so as to be generally known. ~*prep.* **36.** surrounding, encircling, or enclosing: *a band round her head.* **37.** on all or most sides of: *to look round one.* **38.** on or outside the circumference or perimeter of: *the stands round the racecourse.* **39.** situated at various points in: *a lot of shelves round the house.* **40.** from place to place in: *driving round Ireland.* **41.** somewhere in or near: *to stay round the house.* **42.** making a circuit or partial circuit about: *the ring road round the town.* **43.** reached by making a partial circuit about something: *the shop round the corner.* **44.** revolving round a centre or axis: *the earth's motion round its axis.* **45.** so as to have a basis in: *the story is built round a good plot.* ~*adv.* **46.** on all or most sides: *the garden is fenced all round; the crowd gathered round.* **47.** on or outside the circumference or perimeter: *the racing track is two miles round.* **48.** in all directions from a point of reference: *he owns the land for ten miles round.* **49.** to all members of a group: *pass the food round.* **50.** in rotation or revolution: *the wheels turn round.* **51.** by a circuitous route: *the road to the farm goes round by the pond.* **52.** to a specific place: *she came round to see me.* **53. all year round.** throughout the year; in every month. ~*vb.* **54.** to make or become round. **55.** (*tr.*) to encircle; surround. **56.** to move or cause to move with circular motion: *to round a bend.* **57.** (*tr.*) **a.** to pronounce (a speech sound) with rounded lips. **b.** to purse (the lips). ~See also **round down, round off, round on, round out, round up.** [C13: from Old French *ront,* from Latin *rotundus* round, from *rota* a wheel] —'**roundness** *n.*

▷**Usage.** See at **around.**

roundabout ('raʊndəˌbaʊt) *n.* **1.** *Brit.* a revolving circular platform provided with wooden animals, seats, etc., on which people ride for amusement; merry-go-round. **2.** a road junction in which traffic streams circulate around a central island. U.S. and Canadian name: **traffic circle.** **3.** an informal name for **boring mill.** ~*adj.* **4.** indirect or circuitous; devious. ~*adv., prep.* **round about.** **5.** on all sides: *spectators standing round about.* **6.** approximately: *at round about 5 o'clock.*

round and round *adv., prep.* following a circuitous or circular course for a comparatively long time, esp. vainly.

round angle *n.* another name for **perigon.**

round-arm *adj., adv. Cricket.* denoting or using bowling with the arm held more or less horizontal.

round clam *n.* another name for the **quahog.**

round dance *n.* **1.** a dance in which the dancers form a circle. **2.** a ballroom dance, such as the waltz, in which couples revolve.

round down *vb.* (*tr., adv.*) to lower (a number) to the nearest whole number or ten, hundred, or thousand below it. Compare **round up** (sense 2).

rounded ('raʊndɪd) *adj.* **1.** round or curved. **2.** having been made round or curved. **3.** full, mature, or complete. **4.** (of the lips) pursed, as in pronouncing the sound (uː). **5.** (of a speech sound) articulated with rounded lips. —'**roundedly** *adv.* —'**roundedness** *n.*

roundel ('raʊndᵊl) *n.* **1.** a form of rondeau consisting of three stanzas each of three lines with a refrain after the first and the third. **2.** a circular identifying mark in national colours on military aircraft. **3.** a small ornamental circular window, panel, medallion, plate, disc, etc. **4.** a round plate of armour used to protect the armpit. **5.** *Heraldry.* a charge in the shape of a circle. **6.** another word for **roundelay** (sense 1). [C13: from Old French *rondel* a little circle; see RONDEL]

roundelay ('raʊndɪˌleɪ) *n.* **1.** Also called: **roundel.** a slow medieval dance performed in a circle. **2.** a song in which a line or phrase is repeated as a refrain. [C16: from Old French *rondelet* a little rondel, from *rondel;* also influenced by LAY[4]]

rounder ('raʊndə) *n.* **1.** a run round all four bases after one hit in rounders. **2.** a tool or machine for rounding edges or surfaces.

rounders ('raʊndəz) *n.* (*functioning as sing.*) *Brit.* a ball game in which players run between posts after hitting the ball, scoring a **rounder** if they run round all four before the ball is retrieved.

round hand *n.* a style of handwriting with large rounded curves. Compare **italic, copperplate** (sense 3).

Roundhead ('raʊndˌhɛd) *n. English history.* a supporter of Parliament during the Civil War; Parliamentarian. Compare **Cavalier.** [referring to their short-cut hair]

roundhouse ('raʊndˌhaʊs) *n.* **1.** a circular building in which railway locomotives are serviced or housed, radial tracks being fed by a central turntable. **2.** *Boxing slang.* **a.** a swinging punch or style of punching. **b.** (*as modifier*): *a roundhouse style.* **3.** *Pinochle, U.S.* a meld of all four kings and queens. **4.** an obsolete word for **jail.** **5.** *Obsolete.* a cabin on the quarterdeck of a sailing ship.

rounding ('raʊndɪŋ) *n. Computer technol.* a process in which a number is approximated as the closest number that can be expressed using the number of bits or digits available.

rounding error *n. Computer technol.* an error introduced into a computation by the need to perform rounding.

roundish ('raʊndɪʃ) *adj.* somewhat round.

roundlet ('raʊndlɪt) *n. Literary.* a small circle. [C14: from Old French *rondelet,* from Old French RONDEL]

roundly ('raʊndlɪ) *adv.* **1.** frankly, bluntly, or thoroughly: *to be roundly criticized.* **2.** in a round manner or so as to be round.

round off *vb.* (*tr., adv.*) **1.** (often foll. by *with*) to bring to a satisfactory conclusion; complete, esp. agreeably: *we rounded off the evening with a brandy.* **2.** to make round or less jagged.

round on *vb.* (*intr., prep.*) to attack or reply to (someone) with sudden irritation or anger.

round out *vb.* (*tr., adv.*) **1.** to make or become bigger or plumper; fill out, esp. so as to be symmetrical. **2.** to round up (a number).

round robin *n.* **1.** a letter, esp. a petition or protest, having the signatures in a circle in order to disguise the order of signing. **2.** any letter or petition signed by a number of people. **3.** *U.S. and Canadian.* a tournament, as in a competitive game or sport, in which each player plays against every other player.

round-shouldered *adj.* denoting a faulty posture characterized by drooping shoulders and a slight forward bending of the back.

roundsman ('raʊndzmən) *n., pl.* **-men.** **1.** *Brit.* a person who makes rounds, as for inspection or to deliver goods. **2.** *Austral. and N.Z.* a reporter covering a particular district or topic.

round table *n.* **a.** a meeting of parties or people on equal terms for discussion. **b.** (*as modifier*): *a round-table conference.*

round-the-clock *adj.* (*or as adv.* **round the clock**) throughout the day and night.

round top *n.* a platform round the masthead of a sailing ship.

round tower *n.* a freestanding circular stone belfry built in Ireland from the 10th century beside a monastery and used as a place of refuge.

round trip *n.* a trip to a place and back again, esp. returning by a different route.

roundtripping ('raʊndˌtrɪpɪŋ) *n. Finance.* a form of trading in which a company borrows a sum of money from one source and takes advantage of a short-term rise in interest rates to make a profit by lending it to another.

round-trip ticket *n.* the usual U.S. and Canadian name for **return ticket.**

round up *vb.* (*tr., adv.*) **1.** to gather (animals, suspects, etc.) together: *to round ponies up.* **2.** to raise (a number) to the nearest whole number or ten, hundred, or thousand above it. Compare **round down.** ~*n.* **roundup.** **3.** the act of gathering together livestock, esp. cattle, so that they may be branded, counted, or sold. **4.** a collection of suspects or criminals by the police, esp. in a raid. **5.** any similar act of collecting or bringing together: *a roundup of today's news.*

roundwood ('raʊndˌwʊd) *n. Forestry.* small pieces of timber (about 5–15 cm, or 2–6 in.) in diameter; small logs.

roundworm ('raʊndˌwɜːm) *n.* any nematode worm, esp. *Ascaris lumbricoides,* a common intestinal parasite of man and pigs.

roup[1] (ruːp) *n. Vet. science.* any of various chronic respiratory diseases of birds, esp. poultry. [C16: of unknown origin] —'**roupy** *adj.*

roup[2] (raʊp) *Scot. and northern English dialect.* ~*vb.* (*tr.*) **1.** to sell by auction. ~*n.* **2.** an auction. [C16 (originally: to shout): of Scandinavian origin; compare Icelandic *raupa* to boast]

rouse[1] (raʊz) *vb.* **1.** to bring (oneself or another person) out of sleep, unconsciousness, etc., or (of a person) to come to consciousness in this way. **2.** (*tr.*) to provoke, stir, or excite: *to rouse someone's anger.* **3. rouse oneself.** to become active or energetic. **4.** *Hunting.* to start or cause to start from cover: *to rouse game birds.* **5.** (*intr.*) *Falconry.* (of hawks) to ruffle the feathers and cause them to stand briefly on end (a sign of contentment). **6.** (*intr.;* foll. by *on*) *Austral.* to speak scoldingly or rebukingly (to). ~*n.* **7.** *Chiefly U.S.* another term for **reveille.** [C15 (in sense 5): origin obscure] —**rousedness** ('raʊzɪdnɪs) *n.* —'**rouser** *n.*

rouse[2] (raʊz) *n. Archaic.* **1.** an alcoholic drink, esp. a full measure. **2.** another word for **carousal.** [C17: probably a variant of CAROUSE (as in the phrase *drink a rouse,* erroneous for *drink carouse*); compare Danish *drikke en rus* to become drunk, German *Rausch* drunkenness]

rouseabout ('raʊzəˌbaʊt) *n. Austral. and N.Z.* an unskilled labourer in a shearing shed. Also called: **roustabout.**

rousing ('raʊzɪŋ) *adj.* tending to rouse or excite; lively, brisk, or vigorous: *a rousing chorus.* —'**rousingly** *adv.*

roust (raʊst) *vb.* (*tr.;* often foll. by *out*) to rout or stir, as out of bed. [C17: perhaps an alteration of ROUSE[1]]

roustabout ('raʊstəˌbaʊt) *n.* **1.** *Chiefly U.S. and Canadian.* an unskilled labourer on an oil rig. **2.** *Austral.* another word for **rouseabout.**

rout[1] (raʊt) *n.* **1.** an overwhelming defeat. **2.** a disorderly retreat. **3.** a noisy rabble. **4.** *Law.* a group of three or more people proceeding to commit an illegal act. **5.** *Archaic.* a large party or social gathering. ~*vb.* **6.** (*tr.*) to defeat and cause to flee in confusion. [C13: from Anglo-Norman *rute,* from Old French: disorderly band, from Latin *ruptus* broken, from *rumpere* to burst; see ROUTE]

rout[2] (raʊt) *vb.* **1.** to dig over or turn up (something), esp. (of an animal) with the snout; root. **2.** (*tr.; usually foll. by out or up*) to get or find by searching. **3.** (*tr.; usually foll. by out*) to force or drive out: *they routed him out of bed at midnight.* **4.** (*tr.; often foll. by out*) to hollow or gouge out. **5.** (*intr.*) to search, poke, or rummage. [C16: variant of ROOT[2]]

route (ruːt) *n.* **1.** the choice of roads taken to get to a place. **2.** a regular journey travelled. **3.** *Mountaineering.* the direction or course taken by a climb. **4.** *Med.* the means (mouth or injection) by which a drug or agent is administered or enters the body: *oral route.* ~*vb.* **routes, routeing, routed.** (*tr.*) **5.** to plan the route of; send by a particular route. [C13: from Old French *rute,* from Vulgar Latin *rupta via* (unattested), literally: a broken (established) way, from Latin *ruptus* broken, from *rumpere* to break, burst]

▷**Usage.** When forming the present participle or verbal noun from the verb *to route* it is preferable to retain the *e* in order to distinguish the word from *routing,* the present participle or verbal noun from *rout*[1], to defeat or *rout*[2], to dig, rummage: *the routeing of buses from the city centre to the suburbs.* The spelling *routing* in this sense is, however, sometimes encountered, esp. in American English.

routemarch (ˈruːtˌmɑːtʃ) *n.* **1.** *Military.* a long training march. **2.** *Informal.* any long exhausting walk. ~*vb.* **3.** to go or send on a routemarch.

router (ˈraʊtə) *n.* any of various tools or machines for hollowing out, cutting grooves, etc.

routh *or* **rowth** (raʊθ) *Scot.* ~*n.* **1.** abundance. ~*adj.* **2.** abundant; plentiful. [C18: of uncertain origin]

routine (ruːˈtiːn) *n.* **1.** a usual or regular method of procedure, esp. one that is unvarying. **2.** *Computer technol.* a program or part of a program performing a specific function: *an input routine; an output routine.* **3.** a set sequence of dance steps. **4.** *Informal.* a hackneyed or insincere speech. ~*adj.* **5.** of, relating to, or characteristic of routine. [C17: from Old French, from *route* a customary way, ROUTE] —**rouˈtinely** *adv.*

roux (ruː) *n.* a mixture of equal amounts of fat and flour, heated, blended, and used as a basis for sauces. [C19: from French: brownish, from Latin *russus* RUSSET]

rove[1] (rəʊv) *vb.* **1.** to wander about (a place) with no fixed direction; roam. **2.** (*intr.*) (of the eyes) to look around; wander. **3. have a roving eye.** to show a widespread amorous interest in the opposite sex. **4.** (*intr.*) *Australian Rules football.* to play as a rover. ~*n.* **5.** the act of roving. [C15 *roven* (in archery) to shoot at a target chosen at random (C16: to wander, stray), from Scandinavian; compare Icelandic *rāfa* to wander]

rove[2] (rəʊv) *vb.* **1.** (*tr.*) to pull out and twist (fibres of wool, cotton, etc.) lightly, as before spinning or in carding. ~*n.* **2.** wool, cotton, etc., thus prepared. [C18: of obscure origin]

rove[3] (rəʊv) *n.* a metal plate through which a rivet is passed and then clenched over. [C15: from Scandinavian; compare Icelandic *ro*]

rove[4] (rəʊv) *vb.* a past tense and past participle of **reeve**[2].

rove beetle *n.* any beetle of the family *Staphylinidae,* characterized by very short elytra and an elongated body: typically they are of carnivorous or scavenging habits.

rove-over *adj. Prosody.* (in sprung rhythm) denoting a metrical foot left incomplete at the end of one line and completed in the next.

rover[1] (ˈrəʊvə) *n.* **1.** a person who roves; wanderer. **2.** *Archery.* a mark selected at random for use as a target. **3.** *Croquet.* a ball that has been driven through all the hoops but has not yet hit the winning peg. **4.** *Australian Rules football.* one of the three players in the ruck, usually smaller than the other two, selected for his agility in play. [C15: from ROVE[1]]

rover[2] (ˈrəʊvə) *n.* a pirate or pirate ship. [C14: probably from Middle Dutch or Middle Low German, from *roven* to rob]

rover[3] (ˈrəʊvə) *n.* a machine for roving wool, cotton, etc., or a person who operates such a machine. [C18: from ROVE[2]]

Rover *or* **Rover Scout** (ˈrəʊvə) *n. Brit.* the former name for **Venture Scout.**

roving commission *n.* authority or power given in a general area, without precisely defined terms of reference.

row[1] (rəʊ) *n.* **1.** an arrangement of persons or things in a line: *a row of chairs.* **2. a.** *Chiefly Brit.* a street, esp. a narrow one lined with identical houses. **b.** (*cap. when part of a street name*): *Church Row.* **3.** a line of seats, as in a cinema, theatre, etc. **4.** *Maths.* a horizontal linear arrangement of numbers, quantities, or terms, esp. in a determinant or matrix. **5.** a horizontal rank of squares on a chessboard or draughtboard. **6. in a row.** in succession; one after the other: *he won two gold medals in a row.* **7. a hard row to hoe.** a difficult task or assignment. [Old English *rāw, rǣw;* related to Old High German *rīga* line, Lithuanian *raiwe* strip]

row[2] (rəʊ) *vb.* **1.** to propel (a boat) by using oars. **2.** (*tr.*) to carry (people, goods, etc.) in a rowing boat. **3.** to be propelled by means of (oars or oarsmen). **4.** (*intr.*) to take part in the racing of rowing boats as a sport, esp. in eights, in which each member of the crew pulls one oar. Compare **scull** (sense 6). **5.** (*tr.*) to race against in a boat propelled by oars: *Oxford row Cambridge every year.* ~*n.* **6.** an act, instance, period, or distance of rowing. **7.** an excursion in a rowing boat. ~See also **row over.** [Old English *rōwan;* related to Middle Dutch *roien,* Middle High German *rüejen,* Old Norse *rōa,* Latin *rēmus* oar] —ˈ**rower** *n.*

row[3] (raʊ) *n.* **1.** a noisy quarrel or dispute. **2.** a noisy disturbance; commotion: *we couldn't hear the music for the row next door.* **3.** a reprimand. **4. give (someone) a row.** *Informal.* to scold (someone); tell off. ~*vb.* **5.** (*intr.; often foll. by with*) to quarrel noisily. **6.** (*tr.*) *Archaic.* to reprimand. [C18: origin unknown]

rowan (ˈrəʊən, ˈraʊ-) *n.* another name for the (European) **mountain ash.** [C16: from Scandinavian; compare Norwegian *rogn, raun,* Old Norse *reynir*]

rowboat (ˈrəʊˌbəʊt) *n.* the usual U.S. and Canadian word for **rowing boat.**

rowdy (ˈraʊdɪ) *adj.* **-dier, -diest. 1.** tending to create noisy disturbances; rough, loud, or disorderly: *a rowdy gang of football supporters.* ~*n., pl.* **-dies. 2.** a person who behaves in a rough disorderly fashion. [C19: originally U.S. slang, perhaps related to ROW[3]] —ˈ**rowdily** *adv.* —ˈ**rowdiness** *n.*

rowdyism (ˈraʊdɪɪzəm) *n.* rowdy behaviour or tendencies or a habitual pattern of rowdy behaviour: *the problem of rowdyism at football matches.*

rowel (ˈraʊəl) *n.* **1.** a small spiked wheel attached to a spur. **2.** *Vet. science.* a piece of leather or other material inserted under the skin of a horse to cause a discharge. ~*vb.* **-els, -elling, -elled** *or U.S.* **-els, -eling, -eled.** (*tr.*) **3.** to goad (a horse) using a rowel. **4.** *Vet. science.* to insert a rowel in (the skin of a horse) to cause a discharge. [C14: from Old French *roel* a little wheel, from *roe* a wheel, from Latin *rota*]

rowen (ˈraʊən) *n.* another word for **aftermath** (sense 2). [C14 *reywayn,* corresponding to Old French *regaïn,* from RE- + *gaïn* rowen, from *gaignier* to till, earn; see GAIN[1]]

row house (rəʊ) *n.* a U.S. and Canadian term for **terraced house.**

rowing boat (ˈrəʊɪŋ) *n. Chiefly Brit.* a small boat propelled by one or more pairs of oars. Usual U.S. and Canadian word: **rowboat.**

rowing machine *n.* a device with oars and a sliding seat resembling a sculling boat, used to provide exercise.

rowlock (ˈrɒlək) *n.* a swivelling device attached to the gunwale of a boat that holds an oar in place and acts as a fulcrum during rowing. Usual U.S. and Canadian word: **oarlock.**

row over (rəʊ) *vb.* (*intr., adv.*) **1.** to win a rowing race unopposed, by rowing the course. ~*n.* **rowover. 2.** the act of doing this.

rowth (raʊθ) *n., adj. Scot.* a variant spelling of **routh.**

Roy (rɔɪ) *n. Austral. slang.* a trendy Australian male.

royal (ˈrɔɪəl) *adj.* **1.** of, relating to, or befitting a king, queen, or other monarch; regal. **2.** (*prenominal; often cap.*) established, chartered by, under the patronage or in the service of royalty: *the Royal Society of St George.* **3.** being a member of a royal family. **4.** above the usual or normal in standing, size, quality, etc. **5.** *Informal.* unusually good or impressive; first-rate. **6.** *Nautical.* just above the topgallant (in the phrase **royal mast**). ~*n.* **7.** (*sometimes cap.*) *Informal.* a member of a royal family. **8.** Also called: **royal stag.** a stag with antlers having 12 or more branches. **9.** *Nautical.* a sail set next above the topgallant, on a royal mast. **10.** a size of printing paper, 20 by 25 inches. **11.** Also called: **small royal.** *Chiefly Brit.* a size of writing paper, 19 by 24 inches. **12.** any of various book sizes, esp. 6¼ by 10 inches (**royal octavo**), 6¾ by 10¼ inches (**super royal octavo**), and (chiefly Brit.) 10 by 12½ inches (**royal quarto**) and 10¼ by 13½ inches (**super royal quarto**). [C14: from Old French *roial,* from Latin *rēgālis,* fit for a king, from *rēx* king; compare REGAL] —ˈ**royally** *adv.*

Royal Air Force *n.* the air force of Great Britain. Abbrev.: **RAF.**

royal assent *n.* (in Britain) the formal signing of an act of Parliament by the sovereign, by which it becomes law.

royal blue *n.* **a.** a deep blue colour. **b.** (*as adj.*): *a royal-blue carpet.*

royal burgh *n.* (in Scotland) a burgh that was established by a royal charter granted directly by the sovereign.

royal duke *n.* a duke who is also a royal prince, being a member of the royal family.

royal fern *n.* a fern, *Osmunda regalis,* of damp regions, having large fronds up to 2 metres (7 feet) in height, some of which are modified for bearing spores: family *Osmundaceae.*

royal flush *n. Poker.* a hand made up of the five top honours of a suit.

Royal Highness *n.* a title of honour used in addressing or referring to a member of a royal family.

royal icing *n. Brit.* a hard white icing made from egg whites and icing sugar, used for coating and decorating cakes, esp. fruit cakes.

royalist (ˈrɔɪəlɪst) *n.* **1.** a supporter of a monarch or monarchy, esp. a supporter of the Stuarts during the English Civil War. **2.** *Informal.* an extreme reactionary or conservative: *an economic royalist.* ~*adj.* also (*less commonly*) **royalistic. 3.** of, characteristic of, or relating to royalists. —ˈ**royalism** *n.*

royal jelly *n.* a substance secreted by the pharyngeal glands of worker bees and fed to all larvae when very young and to larvae destined to become queens throughout their development.

Royal Marines *pl. n. Brit.* a corps of soldiers specially trained in amphibious warfare. Abbrev.: **RM.**

Royal Navy *n.* the navy of Great Britain. Abbrev.: **RN.**

royal palm *n.* any of several palm trees of the genus *Roystonea,* esp. *R. regia,* of tropical America, having a tall trunk with a tuft of feathery pinnate leaves.

royal poinciana *n.* a caesalpiniaceous tree, *Delonix regia,* that is native to Madagascar but widely cultivated elsewhere, having clusters of large scarlet flowers and long pods. Also called: **flamboyant.**

royal purple *n.* **a.** a deep reddish-purple colour, sometimes approaching a strong violet. **b.** (*as adj.*): *a royal-purple dress.*

royal road *n.* an easy or direct way of achieving a desired end: *the royal road to success.*

royal stag *n.* See **royal** (sense 8).

royal standard *n.* a flag bearing the arms of the British sovereign, flown only when she (or he) is present.

royal tennis *n.* another name for **real tennis.**

royalty ('rɔɪəltɪ) *n., pl.* **-ties. 1.** the rank, power, or position of a king or queen. **2. a.** royal persons collectively. **b.** one who belongs to the royal family. **3.** any quality characteristic of a monarch; kingliness or regal dignity. **4.** a percentage of the revenue from the sale of a book, performance of a theatrical work, use of a patented invention or of land, etc., paid to the author, inventor, or proprietor.

Royal Victorian Order *n.* (in Britain) an order of chivalry founded by Queen Victoria in 1896, membership of which is conferred for special services to the sovereign. Abbrev.: **VO.**

royal warrant *n.* an authorization to a tradesman to supply goods to a royal household.

Royal Worcester *n.* Worcester china made after 1862.

rozzer ('rɒzə) *n. Cockney slang.* a policeman. [C19: of unknown origin]

RP *abbrev. for:* **1.** Received Pronunciation. **2.** Reformed Presbyterian. **3.** Regius Professor.

RPC *abbrev. for* Royal Pioneer Corps.

RPG *abbrev. for* report program generator: a business-oriented computer programming language.

RPI (in Britain) *abbrev. for* retail price index.

rpm *abbrev. for:* **1.** revolutions per minute. **2.** resale price maintenance.

rps *abbrev. for* revolutions per second.

RPS (in Britain) *abbrev. for* Royal Photographic Society.

rpt *abbrev. for* report.

RPV *abbrev. for* remotely piloted vehicle.

RQ *abbrev. for* respiratory quotient.

RR *abbrev. for* Right Reverend.

-rrhagia *n. combining form.* (in pathology) an abnormal discharge or flow: *menorrhagia.* [from Greek *-rrhagia* a bursting forth, from *rhēgnunai* to burst, break]

-rrhoea *or esp. U.S.* **-rrhea** *n. combining form.* (in pathology) a discharge or flow: *diarrhoea.* [from New Latin, from Greek *-rrhoia,* from *rhoia* a flowing, from *rhein* to flow]

r-RNA *abbrev. for* ribosomal RNA.

RRP *abbrev. for* recommended retail price.

Rs *symbol for* rupees.

RS (in Britain) *abbrev. for* Royal Society.

RSA *abbrev. for:* **1.** Republic of South Africa. **2.** Royal Scottish Academy. **3.** Royal Scottish Academician. **4.** Royal Society of Arts. **5.** (in New Zealand) Returned Services Association.

RSC *abbrev. for:* **1.** Royal Shakespeare Company. **2.** Royal Society of Chemistry.

RSG (in Britain) *abbrev. for:* **1.** rate support grant. **2.** *Civil Defence.* Regional Seat of Government.

RSGB *abbrev. for* Radio Society of Great Britain (amateur radio operators).

RSI *abbrev. for* repetitive strain *or* stress injury: a physical condition characterized by pain in the arm, affecting those who repeatedly perform awkward head movements, such as computer-terminal operators and violinists.

RSJ *abbrev. for* rolled-steel joist.

RSL *abbrev. for:* **1.** Royal Society of Literature. **2.** (in Australia) Returned Services League.

RSM *abbrev. for:* **1.** regimental sergeant major. **2.** Royal School of Music. **3.** Royal Society of Medicine. ~**4.** *international car registration for* (Republic of) San Marino.

RSNZ *abbrev. for* Royal Society of New Zealand.

RSPB (in Britain) *abbrev. for* Royal Society for the Protection of Birds.

RSPCA (in Britain and Australia) *abbrev. for* Royal Society for the Prevention of Cruelty to Animals.

RSV *abbrev. for* Revised Standard Version (of the Bible).

RSVP *abbrev. for* répondez s'il vous plaît. [French: please reply]

rt *abbrev. for* right.

RT *abbrev. for* radio telegraphy *or* radio telephony.

RTC (in India) *abbrev. for:* **1.** Road Transport Corporation. **2.** Round Table Conference.

RTE *abbrev. for* Radio Telefis Éireann. [Irish Gaelic: Irish Radio and Television]

Rt Hon. *abbrev. for* Right Honourable.

RTL *Electronics. abbrev. for* Resistor Transistor Logic: a stage in the development of electronic logic circuits.

RTR *abbrev. for* Royal Tank Regiment.

Rt Rev. *abbrev. for* Right Reverend.

RTT *or* **RTTY** *abbrev. for* radioteletype.

Ru *the chemical symbol for* ruthenium.

RU 1. *abbrev. for* Rugby Union. ~**2.** *international car registration for* Burundi.

rub (rʌb) *vb.* **rubs, rubbing, rubbed. 1.** to apply pressure and friction to (something) with a circular or backward and forward motion. **2.** to move (something) with pressure along, over, or against (a surface). **3.** to chafe or fray. **4.** (*tr.*) to bring into a certain condition by rubbing: *rub it clean.* **5.** (*tr.*) to spread with pressure, esp. in order to cause to be absorbed: *he rubbed ointment into his back.* **6.** (foll. by *off, out, away,* etc.) to remove or be removed by rubbing: *the mark would not rub off the chair.* **7.** *Bowls.* (of a bowl) to be slowed or deflected by an uneven patch on the green. **8.** (*tr.*; often foll. by *together*) to move against each other with pressure and friction (esp. in the phrases **rub one's hands,** often a sign of glee, keen anticipation, or satisfaction, and **rub noses,** a greeting among Eskimos). **9. rub (someone's) nose in it.** *Informal.* to remind (someone) unkindly of his failing or error. **10. rub (up) the wrong way.** to arouse anger (in); annoy. **11. rub shoulders** (*or* **elbows**) **with.** *Informal.* to mix with socially or associate with. ~*n.* **12.** the act of rubbing. **13.** (preceded by *the*) an obstacle or difficulty (esp. in the phrase **there's the rub**). **14.** something that hurts the feelings or annoys; cut; rebuke. **15.** *Bowls.* an uneven patch in the green. **16.** any roughness or unevenness of surface. ~See also **rub along, rub down, rub in, rub off, rub out, rub up.** [C15: perhaps from Low German *rubben,* of obscure origin]

rubaboo ('rʌbəˌbuː) *n. Canadian.* a soup or stew made by boiling pemmican with, if available, flour and vegetables. [C19: from Canadian French *rababou,* from Algonquian]

rubáiyát ('ruːbaɪˌjæt) *n. Prosody.* (in Persian poetry) a verse form consisting of four-line stanzas. [C19: from Arabic *rubā'īyah,* from *rubā'īy* consisting of four elements]

rub along *vb.* (*intr., adv.*) *Brit.* **1.** to continue in spite of difficulties. **2.** to maintain an amicable relationship; not quarrel.

rubato (ruː'bɑːtəʊ) *Music.* ~*n., pl.* **-tos. 1.** flexibility of tempo in performance. ~*adj., adv.* **2.** to be played with a flexible tempo. [C19: from the Italian phrase *tempo rubato,* literally: stolen time, from *rubare* to ROB]

rubber[1] ('rʌbə) *n.* **1.** Also called: **India rubber, gum elastic, caoutchouc.** a cream to dark brown elastic material obtained by coagulating and drying the latex from certain plants, esp. the tree *Hevea brasiliensis.* **2.** any of a large variety of elastomers produced by improving the properties of natural rubber or by synthetic means. **3.** *Chiefly Brit.* a piece of rubber or felt used for erasing something written, typed, etc.; eraser. **4.** a coarse file. **5.** a cloth, pad, etc., used for polishing or buffing. **6.** a person who rubs something in order to smooth, polish, or massage. **7.** (*often pl.*) *Chiefly U.S. and Canadian.* a rubberized waterproof article, such as a mackintosh or overshoe. **8.** *Slang.* a male contraceptive; condom. **9.** (*modifier*) made of or producing rubber: *a rubber ball; a rubber factory.* [C17: from RUB + -ER[1]; the tree was so named because its product was used for rubbing out writing]

rubber[2] ('rʌbə) *n.* **1.** *Bridge, whist, etc.* **a.** a match of three games. **b.** the deal that wins such a match. **2.** a series of matches or games in any of various sports. [C16: origin unknown]

rubber band *n.* a continuous loop of thin rubber, used to hold papers, etc., together. Also called: **elastic band.**

rubber bridge *n.* a form of bridge in which fresh hands are dealt for each round and the aim is to win a rubber. Compare **duplicate bridge.**

rubber cement *n.* any of a number of adhesives made by dissolving rubber in a solvent such as benzene.

rubber cheque *n. Facetious.* a cheque that bounces.

rubber goods *pl. n. Euphemistic.* contraceptives; condoms.

rubberize *or* **rubberise** ('rʌbəˌraɪz) *vb.* (*tr.*) to coat or impregnate with rubber.

rubberneck ('rʌbəˌnɛk) *Slang.* ~*n.* **1.** a person who stares or gapes inquisitively, esp. in a naive or foolish manner. **2.** a sightseer or tourist. ~*vb.* **3.** (*intr.*) to stare in a naive or foolish manner.

rubber plant *n.* **1.** a moraceous plant, *Ficus elastica,* with glossy leathery leaves: grows as a tall tree in India and Malaya but is cultivated as a house plant in Europe and North America. **2.** any of several tropical trees, the sap of which yields crude rubber. See also **rubber tree.**

rubber stamp *n.* **1.** a device used for imprinting dates or commonly used phrases on forms, invoices, etc. **2.** automatic authorization of a payment, proposal, etc., without challenge. **3.** a person who makes such automatic authorizations; a cipher or person of little account. ~*vb.* **rubber-stamp.** (*tr.*) **4.** to imprint (forms, invoices, etc.) with a rubber stamp. **5.** *Informal.* to approve automatically.

rubber tree *n.* a tropical American euphorbiaceous tree, *Hevea brasiliensis,* cultivated throughout the tropics, esp. in Malaya, for the latex of its stem, which is the major source of commercial rubber. See also **Pará rubber.**

rubbery ('rʌbərɪ) *adj.* having the texture of or resembling rubber, esp. in flexibility or toughness.

rubbing ('rʌbɪŋ) *n.* an impression taken of an incised or raised surface, such as a brass plate on a tomb, by laying paper over it and rubbing with wax, graphite, etc.

rubbing alcohol *n.* a liquid usually consisting of 70 per cent denatured ethyl alcohol, used by external application as an antiseptic or rubefacient.

rubbish ('rʌbɪʃ) *n.* **1.** worthless, useless, or unwanted matter. **2.** discarded or waste matter; refuse. **3.** foolish words or speech; nonsense. ~*vb.* **4.** (*tr.*) *Informal.* to criticize; attack verbally. [C14 *robys,* of uncertain origin] —'**rubbishy** *adj.*

rubbity ('rʌbətɪ) *n., pl.* **-ties.** *Austral. slang.* a pub. [from rhyming slang *rubbity dub*]

rubble ('rʌbᵊl) *n.* **1.** fragments of broken stones, bricks, etc. **2.** any fragmented solid material. **3.** *Quarrying.* the weathered surface layer of rock. **4.** Also called: '**rubble,work.** masonry constructed of broken pieces of rock, stone, etc. [C14 *robyl;* perhaps related to Middle English *rubben* to rub, or to RUBBISH] —'**rubbly** *adj.*

rubby ('rʌbɪ) *n., pl.* **-bies.** *Canadian slang.* **1.** rubbing alcohol, esp. when mixed with cheap wine for drinking. **2.** a person who drinks such mixtures, esp. a derelict alcoholic.

rub down *vb. (adv.)* **1.** to dry or clean (a horse, athlete, oneself, etc.) vigorously, esp. after exercise. **2.** to make or become smooth by rubbing. **3.** (*tr.*) to prepare (a surface) for painting by rubbing it with sandpaper. ~*n.* **rubdown.** **4.** the act of rubbing down. **5.** the Hong Kong term for **dressing-down.**

rube (ruːb) *n. U.S. and Canadian slang.* an unsophisticated countryman. [C20: probably from the name *Reuben*]

rubefy ('ruːbɪ,faɪ) *vb.* **-fies, -fying, -fied.** (*tr.*) to make red, esp. (of a counterirritant) to make the skin go red. [C19: from Latin *rubefacere,* from *rubeus* red + *facere* to make] —**rubefacient** (,ruːbɪ'feɪʃənt) *adj., n.* —**rubefaction** (,ruːbɪ'fækʃən) *n.*

rubella (ruː'bɛlə) *n.* a mild contagious viral disease, somewhat similar to measles, characterized by cough, sore throat, skin rash, and occasionally vomiting. It can cause congenital defects if caught during the first three months of pregnancy. Also called: **German measles.** [C19: from New Latin, from Latin *rubellus* reddish, from *rubeus* red]

rubellite ('ruːbɪ,laɪt, ruː'bɛl-) *n.* a red transparent variety of tourmaline, used as a gemstone. [C18: from Latin *rubellus* reddish]

rubeola (ruː'biːələ) *n.* technical name for **measles.** Compare **rubella.** [C17: from New Latin, from Latin *rubeus* reddish, from *ruber* red] —**ru'beolar** *adj.*

rubescent (ruː'besᵊnt) *adj. Literary.* reddening; blushing. [C18: from Latin *rubescere* to grow red, from *ruber* red] —**ru'bescence** *n.*

rubiaceous (,ruːbɪ'eɪʃəs) *adj.* of, relating to, or belonging to the *Rubiaceae,* a widely distributed family of trees, shrubs, and herbaceous plants that includes the coffee and cinchona trees, gardenia, madder, and bedstraws. [C19: from New Latin *Rubiaceae,* from Latin *rubia* madder, from *rubeus* red]

Rubicon ('ruːbɪkən) *n.* **1.** (*sometimes not cap.*) a point of no return. **2.** a penalty in piquet by which the score of a player who fails to reach 100 points in six hands is added to his opponent's. **3. cross** (*or* **pass**) **the Rubicon.** to commit oneself irrevocably to some course of action. [after a stream in N Italy, the boundary between Italy and Cisalpine Gaul, across which Julius Caesar led his army to Rome in 49 B.C., thereby committing himself to civil war with the senatorial party]

rubicund ('ruːbɪkənd) *adj.* of a reddish colour; ruddy; rosy. [C16: from Latin *rubicundus,* from *rubēre* to be ruddy, from *ruber* red] —**rubicundity** (,ruːbɪ'kʌndɪtɪ) *n.*

rubidium (ruː'bɪdɪəm) *n.* a soft highly reactive radioactive element of the alkali metal group; the 16th most abundant element in the earth's crust (310 parts per million), occurring principally in pollucite, carnallite, and lepidolite. It is used in electronic valves, photocells, and special glass. Symbol: Rb; atomic no.: 37; atomic wt.: 85.47; half-life of ^{87}Rb: 5×10^{11} years; valency: 1; relative density: 1.53 (solid), 1.47 (liquid); melting pt.: 38.89°C; boiling pt.: 688°C. [C19: from New Latin, from Latin *rubidus* dark red, with reference to the two red lines in its spectrum] —**ru'bidic** *adj.*

rubidium-strontium dating *n.* a technique for determining the age of minerals based on the occurrence in natural rubidium of a fixed amount of the radioisotope ^{87}Rb which decays to the stable strontium isotope ^{87}Sr with a half-life of 5×10^{10} years. Measurement of the ratio of these isotopes thus gives the age of a mineral, for ages of up to about 4×10^9 years.

rubiginous (ruː'bɪdʒɪnəs) *adj.* rust-coloured. [C17: from Latin *rūbīginōsus,* from *rūbīgō* rust, from *ruber* red]

Rubik cube ('ruːbɪk) *or* **Rubik's cube** *n.* a puzzle consisting of a cube of six colours, each face of which is made up of nine squares, eight of which are individually rotatable. The aim is to swivel the squares until each face of the cube shows one colour only. [C20: named after Professor Erno *Rubik* (born 1944), its Hungarian inventor]

rub in *vb. (tr., adv.)* **1.** to spread with pressure, esp. in order to cause to be absorbed. **2. rub it in.** *Informal.* to harp on (something distasteful to a person, of which he does not wish to be reminded).

rubious ('ruːbɪəs) *adj. Literary.* of the colour ruby; dark red. [C17: from RUBY + -OUS]

ruble ('ruːbᵊl) *n.* a variant spelling of **rouble.**

rub off *vb.* **1.** to remove or be removed by rubbing. **2.** (*intr.;* often foll. by *on* or *onto*) to have an effect through close association or contact, esp. so as to make similar: *her crude manners have rubbed off on you.*

rub out *vb. (tr., adv.)* **1.** to remove or be removed with a rubber. **2.** *U.S. slang.* to murder. **3.** *Australian Rules football.* to suspend (a player).

rubric ('ruːbrɪk) *n.* **1.** a title, heading, or initial letter in a book, manuscript, or section of a legal code, esp. one printed or painted in red ink or in some similarly distinguishing manner. **2.** a set of rules of conduct or procedure. **3.** a set of directions for the conduct of Christian church services, often printed in red in a prayer book or missal. **4.** instructions to a candidate at the head of the examination paper. **5.** an obsolete name for **red ochre.** ~*adj.* **6.** written, printed, or marked in red. [C15 *rubrike* red ochre, red lettering, from Latin *rubrīca* (*terra*) red (earth), ruddle, from *ruber* red] —'**rubrical** *adj.* —'**rubrically** *adv.*

rubricate ('ruːbrɪ,keɪt) *vb.* (*tr.*) **1.** to print (a book or manuscript) with red titles, headings, etc. **2.** to mark in red. **3.** to supply with or regulate by rubrics. [C16: from Latin *rubricāre* to colour red, from *rubrīca* red earth; see RUBRIC] —,**rubri'cation** *n.* —'**rubri,cator** *n.*

rubrician (ruː'brɪʃən) *n.* an authority on liturgical rubrics.

rubstone ('rʌb,stəʊn) *n.* a stone used for sharpening or smoothing, esp. a whetstone.

rub up *vb. (adv.) Chiefly Brit.* **1.** (when *intr.,* foll. by *on*) to refresh one's memory (of). **2.** (*tr.*) to smooth or polish.

ruby ('ruːbɪ) *n., pl.* **-bies.** **1.** a deep red transparent precious variety of corundum: occurs naturally in Burma and Ceylon but is also synthesized. It is used as a gemstone, in lasers, and for bearings and rollers in watchmaking. Formula: Al_2O_3. **2. a.** the deep-red colour of a ruby. **b.** (*as adj.*): *ruby lips.* **3. a.** something resembling, made of, or containing a ruby. **b.** (*as modifier*): *ruby necklace.* **4.** (*modifier*) denoting a fortieth anniversary: *our ruby wedding.* **5.** (formerly) a size of printer's type approximately equal to 5½ point. [C14: from Old French *rubi,* from Latin *rubeus* reddish, from *ruber* red] —'**ruby-,like** *adj.*

ruby glass *n.* glass that has a deep rich red colour produced from oxides of various minerals, such as lead, copper, and iron.

ruby silver *n.* another name for **proustite** or **pyrargyrite.**

ruby spinel *n.* a red transparent variety of spinel, used as a gemstone.

ruby-tail wasp *n.* any of various brightly coloured wasps of the family *Chrysididae,* having a metallic sheen, which parasitize bees and other solitary wasps.

RUC *abbrev. for* Royal Ulster Constabulary.

ruche *or* **rouche** (ruːʃ) *n.* a strip of pleated or frilled lawn, lace, etc., used to decorate blouses, dresses, etc., or worn around the neck like a small ruff as in the 16th century. [C19: from French, literally: beehive, from Medieval Latin *rūsca* bark of a tree, of Celtic origin]

ruching ('ruːʃɪŋ) *n.* **1.** material used for a ruche. **2.** a ruche or ruches collectively.

ruck[1] (rʌk) *n.* **1.** a large number or quantity; mass, esp. of ordinary or undistinguished people or things. **2.** (in a race) a group of competitors who are well behind the leaders at the finish. **3.** *Rugby.* a loose scrum that forms around the ball when it is on the ground. **4.** *Australian Rules football.* the three players, two ruckmen and a rover, that do not have fixed positions but follow the ball closely. ~*vb.* **5.** (*intr.*) *Rugby.* to try to win the ball by mauling and scrummaging. [C13 (meaning "heap of firewood"): perhaps from Scandinavian; compare Old Norse *hraukr* RICK[1]]

ruck[2] (rʌk) *n.* **1.** a wrinkle, crease, or fold. ~*vb.* **2.** (usually foll. by *up*) to become or make wrinkled, creased, or puckered. [C18: from Scandinavian; related to Old Norse *hrukka*]

ruck[3] (rʌk) *n. Prison slang.* a fight. [C20: short for RUCKUS]

ruckle ('rʌkᵊl) *n., vb. Brit.* another word for **ruck**[2].

rucksack ('rʌk,sæk) *n.* a large bag, usually having two straps and a supporting frame, carried on the back and often used by climbers, campers, etc. U.S. and Canadian name: **backpack.** [C19: from German, literally: back sack]

ruckus ('rʌkəs) *n., pl.* **-uses.** *Informal.* an uproar; ruction. [C20: from RUCTION + RUMPUS]

ruction ('rʌkʃən) *n. Informal.* **1.** an uproar; noisy or quarrelsome disturbance. **2.** (*pl.*) a violent and unpleasant row; trouble: *there'll be ructions when she hears about it.* [C19: perhaps changed from INSURRECTION]

rudaceous (ruː'deɪʃəs) *adj.* (of conglomerate, breccia, and similar rocks) composed of coarse-grained material. Compare **arenaceous** (sense 1), **argillaceous.** [C20: from Latin *rudis* coarse, rough + -ACEOUS]

rudbeckia (rʌd'bɛkɪə) *n.* any plant of the North American genus *Rudbeckia,* cultivated for their showy flowers, which have golden-yellow rays and green or black conical centres: family *Compositae* (composites). See also **coneflower, black-eyed Susan.** [C18: New Latin, named after Olaus *Rudbeck* (1630–1702), Swedish botanist]

rudd (rʌd) *n.* a European freshwater cyprinid fish, *Scardinius erythrophthalmus,* having a compressed dark greenish body and reddish ventral and tail fins. [C17: probably from dialect *rud* red colour, from Old English *rudu* redness]

rudder ('rʌdə) *n.* **1.** *Nautical.* a pivoted vertical vane that projects into the water at the stern of a vessel and can be controlled by a tiller, wheel, or other apparatus to steer the vessel. **2.** a vertical control surface attached to the rear of the fin used to steer an aircraft, in conjunction with the ailerons. **3.** anything that guides or directs. [Old English *rōther;* related to Old French *rōther,* Old High German *ruodar,* Old Norse *rōthr.* See ROW[2]] —'**rudderless** *adj.*

rudderhead ('rʌdə,hɛd) *n. Nautical.* the top of the rudderpost, to which the steering apparatus may be fixed.

rudderpost ('rʌdə,pəʊst) *n. Nautical.* **1.** Also called: **rudderstock** ('rʌdə,stɒk). a postlike member at the forward edge of a rudder. **2.** the part of the stern frame of a vessel to which a rudder is fitted.

ruddle ('rʌdᵊl), **raddle,** *or* **reddle** *n.* **1.** a red ochre, used esp. to mark sheep. ~*vb.* **2.** (*tr.*) to mark (sheep) with ruddle. [C16: diminutive formed from Old English *rudu* redness; see RUDD]

ruddock ('rʌdək) *n. Brit.* a dialect name for the **robin** (sense 1). [Old English *rudduc;* related to *rudu* redness; see RUDD]

ruddy ('rʌdɪ) *adj.* **-dier, -diest.** **1.** (of the complexion) having a healthy reddish colour, usually resulting from an outdoor life. **2.** coloured red or pink: *a ruddy sky.* ~*adv., adj. Informal, chiefly Brit.* **3.** (intensifier) bloody; damned: *a ruddy fool.* [Old English *rudig,* from *rudu* redness (see RUDD); related to Old High German *rot* RED, Swedish *rod,* Old Norse *rythga* to make rusty] —'**ruddily** *adv.* —'**ruddiness** *n.*

ruddy duck *n.* a small duck, *Oxyura jamaicensis,* that inhabits marshes, ponds, etc., in North America and N South America and has a stiff upright tail. The male has a reddish-brown body and blue bill in the breeding season.

rude (ruːd) *adj.* **1.** insulting or uncivil; discourteous; impolite: *he was rude about her hairstyle.* **2.** lacking refinement; coarse or uncouth. **3.** vulgar or obscene: *a rude joke.* **4.** roughly or crudely made: *we made a rude shelter on the island.* **5.** rough or harsh in sound, appearance, or behaviour. **6.** humble or lowly. **7.** (*prenominal*) robust or sturdy: *in rude health.* **8.** (*prenominal*) approximate or imprecise: *a rude estimate.* [C14: via Old French from Latin *rudis* coarse, unformed] —'**rudely** *adv.* —'**rudeness** *or* (*informal*) '**rudery** *n.*

ruderal ('ruːdərəl) *n.* **1.** a plant that grows on waste ground. ~*adj.* **2.** growing in waste places. [C19: from New Latin *rūderālis,* from Latin *rūdus* rubble]

Rudesheimer ('ruːdəs,haɪmə) *n.* a white Rhine wine: named after the town of Rüdesheim on the Rhine.

rudiment ('ruːdɪmənt) *n.* **1.** (*often pl.*) the first principles or elementary stages of a subject. **2.** (*often pl.*) a partially developed version of something. **3.** *Biology.* an organ or part in its earliest recognizable form, esp. one in an embryonic or vestigial state. [C16: from Latin *rudīmentum* a beginning, from *rudis* unformed; see RUDE]

rudimentary (,ruːdɪ'mɛntərɪ) *or* (*less commonly*) **rudimental** *adj.* **1.** basic; fundamental; not elaborated or perfected. **2.** incompletely developed; vestigial: *rudimentary leaves.* —,**rudi'mentarily** *or* (*less commonly*) ,**rudi'mentally** *adv.*

rudish ('ruːdɪʃ) *adj.* somewhat rude.

rue[1] (ruː) *vb.* **rues, ruing, rued.** **1.** to feel sorrow, remorse, or regret for (one's own wrongdoing, past events with unpleasant consequences, etc.). ~*n.* **2.** *Archaic.* sorrow, pity, or regret. [Old English *hrēowan;* related to Old Saxon *hreuwan,* Old High German *hriuwan*] —'**ruer** *n.*

rue[2] (ruː) *n.* any rutaceous plant of the genus *Ruta,* esp. *R. graveolens,* an aromatic Eurasian shrub with small yellow flowers and evergreen leaves which yield an acrid volatile oil, formerly used medicinally as a narcotic and stimulant. Archaic name: **herb of grace.** Compare **goat's-rue, meadow rue, wall rue.** [C14: from Old French, from Latin *rūta,* from Greek *rhutē*]

rueful ('ruːfʊl) *adj.* **1.** feeling or expressing sorrow or repentance: *a rueful face.* **2.** inspiring sorrow or pity. —'**ruefully** *adv.* —'**ruefulness** *n.*

rufescent (ruː'fɛsᵊnt) *adj. Botany.* tinged with red or becoming red. [C19: from Latin *rūfescere* to grow reddish, from *rūfus* red, auburn] —**ru'fescence** *n.*

ruff[1] (rʌf) *n.* **1.** a circular pleated, gathered, or fluted collar of lawn, muslin, etc., often starched or wired, worn by both men and women in the 16th and 17th centuries. **2.** a natural growth of long or coloured hair or feathers around the necks of certain animals or birds. **3. a.** an Old World shore bird, *Philomachus pugnax,* the male of which has a large erectile ruff of feathers in the breeding season: family *Scolopacidae* (sandpipers, etc.), order *Charadriiformes.* **b.** the male of this bird. Compare **reeve**[3]. [C16: back formation from RUFFLE[1]] —'**ruff,like** *adj.*

ruff[2] (rʌf) *n. Cards.* **1.** (*also vb.*) another word for **trump**[1]. **2.** an old card game similar to whist. [C16: from Old French *roffle;* perhaps changed from Italian *trionfa* TRUMP[1]]

ruffe *or* **ruff**[3] (rʌf) *n.* a European freshwater teleost fish, *Acerina cernua,* having a single spiny dorsal fin: family *Percidae* (perches). Also called: **pope.** [C15: perhaps an alteration of ROUGH (referring to its scales)]

ruffed grouse *n.* a large North American grouse, *Bonasa umbellus,* having brown plumage with darker markings around the neck and a black-tipped fan-shaped tail.

ruffian ('rʌfɪən) *n.* a violent or lawless person; hoodlum or villain. [C16: from Old French *rufien,* from Italian *ruffiano,* perhaps related to Langobardic *hruf* scurf, scabbiness] —'**ruffianism** *n.* —'**ruffianly** *adj.*

ruffle[1] ('rʌfᵊl) *vb.* **1.** to make, be, or become irregular or rumpled: *to ruffle a child's hair; a breeze ruffling the water.* **2.** to annoy, irritate, or be annoyed or irritated. **3.** (*tr.*) to make into a ruffle; pleat. **4.** (of a bird) to erect (its feathers) in anger, display, etc. **5.** (*tr.*) to flick (cards, pages, etc.) rapidly with the fingers. ~*n.* **6.** an irregular or disturbed surface. **7.** a strip of pleated material used for decoration or as a trim. **8.** *Zoology.* another name for **ruff**[1] (sense 2). **9.** annoyance or irritation. [C13: of Germanic origin; compare Middle Low German *ruffelen* to crumple, Old Norse *hrufla* to scratch]

ruffle[2] ('rʌfᵊl) *n.* **1.** a low continuous drumbeat. ~*vb.* **2.** (*tr.*) to beat (a drum) with a low repetitive beat. [C18: from earlier *ruff,* of imitative origin]

ruffle[3] ('rʌfᵊl) *vb.* (*intr.*) *Archaic.* to behave riotously or arrogantly; swagger. [C15: of obscure origin]

ruffler ('rʌflə) *n.* **1.** a person or thing that ruffles. **2.** an attachment on a sewing machine used for making frills.

rufiyaa (ruː'fiːjɑː) *n.* the standard monetary unit of the Republic of the Maldives (divided into 100 laari).

rufous ('ruːfəs) *adj.* reddish-brown. [C18: from Latin *rūfus*]

rug (rʌg) *n.* **1.** a floor covering, smaller than a carpet and made of thick wool or of other material, such as an animal skin. **2.** *Chiefly Brit.* a blanket, esp. one used as a wrap or lap robe for travellers. **3. pull the rug out from under.** to betray, expose, or leave defenceless. [C16: from Scandinavian; compare Norwegian *rugga,* Swedish *rugg* coarse hair. See RAG[1]] —'**rug,like** *adj.*

RUG *Computer technol. abbrev. for* restricted users group.

ruga ('ruːgə) *n., pl.* **-gae** (-dʒiː). (*usually pl.*) *Anatomy.* a fold, wrinkle, or crease. [C18: Latin]

rugby *or* **rugby football** ('rʌgbɪ) *n.* **1.** a form of football played with an oval ball in which the handling and carrying of the ball is permitted. Also called: **rugger. 2.** *Canadian.* another name for **Canadian football.** See also **rugby league, rugby union.** [C19: named after the public school at *Rugby* in central England, where it was first played]

rugby league *n.* a form of rugby football played between teams of 13 players, professionalism being allowed.

rugby union *n.* a form of rugby football played only by amateurs, played between teams of 15 players.

rugged ('rʌgɪd) *adj.* **1.** having an uneven or jagged surface. **2.** rocky or steep: *rugged scenery.* **3.** (of the face) strong-featured or furrowed. **4.** rough, severe, or stern in character. **5.** without refinement or culture; rude: *rugged manners.* **6.** involving hardship; harsh: *he leads a rugged life in the mountains.* **7.** difficult or hard: *a rugged test.* **8.** (of equipment, machines, etc.) designed to withstand rough treatment or use in rough conditions: *a handheld rugged computer which can survive being submerged in water.* **9.** *Chiefly U.S. and Canadian.* sturdy or strong; robust. [C14: from Scandinavian; compare Swedish *rugga* to make rough] —'**ruggedly** *adv.* —'**ruggedness** *n.*

ruggedize *or* **ruggedise** ('rʌgɪ,daɪz) *vb.* (*tr.*) to make durable, as for military use.

rugger ('rʌgə) *n. Chiefly Brit.* an informal name for **rugby.**

rugose ('ruːgəʊs, -gəʊz), **rugous,** *or* **rugate** ('ruːgeɪt, -gɪt) *adj.* wrinkled: *rugose leaves.* [C18: from Latin *rūgōsus,* from *rūga* a wrinkle] —'**rugosely** *adv.* —**rugosity** (ruː'gɒsɪtɪ) *n.*

ruin ('ruːɪn) *n.* **1.** destroyed or decayed building or town. **2.** the state or condition of being destroyed or decayed. **3.** loss of wealth, position, etc., or something that causes such loss; downfall. **4.** something that is severely damaged: *his life was a ruin.* **5.** a person who has suffered a downfall, bankruptcy, etc. **6.** loss of value or usefulness. **7.** *Archaic.* loss of her virginity by a woman outside marriage. ~*vb.* **8.** (*tr.*) to bring to ruin; destroy. **9.** (*tr.*) to injure or spoil: *the town has been ruined with tower blocks.* **10.** (*intr.*) *Archaic or poetic.* to fall into ruins; collapse. **11.** (*tr.*) *Archaic.* to seduce and abandon (a woman). [C14: from Old French *ruine,* from Latin *ruīna* a falling down, from *ruere* to fall violently] —'**ruinable** *adj.* —'**ruiner** *n.*

ruination (,ruːɪ'neɪʃən) *n.* **1.** the act of ruining or the state of being ruined. **2.** something that causes ruin.

ruinous ('ruːɪnəs) *adj.* causing, tending to cause, or characterized by ruin or destruction: *a ruinous course of action.* —'**ruinously** *adv.* —'**ruinousness** *n.*

rule (ruːl) *n.* **1.** an authoritative regulation or direction concerning method or procedure, as for a court of law, legislative body, game, or other human institution or activity: *judges' rules; play according to the rules.* **2.** the exercise of governmental authority or control: *the rule of Caesar.* **3.** the period of time in which a monarch or government has power: *his rule lasted 100 days.* **4.** a customary form or procedure; regular course of action: *he made a morning swim his rule.* **5.** (usually preceded by *the*) the common order of things; normal condition: *violence was the rule rather than the exception.* **6.** a prescribed method or procedure for solving a mathematical problem, or one constituting part of a computer program, usually expressed in an appropriate formalism. **7.** a formal expression of a grammatical regularity in a linguistic description of a language. **8.** any of various devices with a straight edge for guiding or measuring; ruler: *a carpenter's* *rule.* **9. a.** a printed or drawn character in the form of a long thin line. **b.** another name for **dash**[1] (sense 13): *en rule; em rule.* **c.** a strip of brass or other metal used to print such a line. **10.** *Christianity.* a systematic body of prescriptions defining the way of life to be followed by members of a religious order. **11.** *Law.* an order by a court or judge. **12. as a rule.** normally or ordinarily. *~vb.* **13.** to exercise governing or controlling authority over (a people, political unit, individual, etc.): *he ruled for 20 years; his passion for her ruled his life.* **14.** (when *tr.*, *often takes a clause as object*) to decide authoritatively; decree: *the chairman ruled against the proposal.* **15.** (*tr.*) to mark with straight parallel lines or make one straight line, as with a ruler: *to rule a margin.* **16.** (*tr.*) to restrain or control: *to rule one's temper.* **17.** (*intr.*) to be customary or prevalent: *chaos rules in this school.* **18.** (*intr.*) to be pre-eminent or superior: *football rules in the field of sport.* **19.** (*tr.*) *Astrology.* (of a planet) to have a strong affinity with certain human attributes, activities, etc., associated with (one or sometimes two signs of the zodiac): *Mars rules Aries.* **20. rule the roost** (*or* **roast**). to be pre-eminent; be in charge. [C13: from Old French *riule*, from Latin *rēgula* a straight edge; see REGULATE] —'**rulable** *adj.*

rule of three *n.* a mathematical rule asserting that the value of one unknown quantity in a proportion is found by multiplying the denominator of each ratio by the numerator of the other.

rule of thumb *n.* **a.** a rough and practical approach, based on experience, rather than a scientific or precise one based on theory. **b.** (*as modifier*): *a rule-of-thumb decision.*

rule out *vb.* (*tr., adv.*) **1.** to dismiss from consideration. **2.** to make impossible; preclude or prevent: *the rain ruled out outdoor games.*

ruler ('ruːlə) *n.* **1.** a person who rules or commands. **2.** Also called: **rule.** a strip of wood, metal, or other material, having straight edges graduated usually in millimetres or inches, used for measuring and drawing straight lines.

Rules (ruːlz) *pl. n.* short for **Australian Rules** (football).

ruling ('ruːlɪŋ) *n.* **1.** a decision of someone in authority, such as a judge. **2.** one or more parallel ruled lines. *~adj.* **3.** controlling or exercising authority: *the ruling classes.* **4.** prevalent or predominant.

rum[1] (rʌm) *n.* spirit made from sugar cane, either coloured brownish by the addition of caramel or by maturation in oak containers, or left white. [C17: perhaps shortened from C16 *rumbullion*, of uncertain origin]

rum[2] (rʌm) *adj.* **rummer, rummest.** *Brit. slang.* strange; peculiar; odd. [C19: perhaps from Romany *rom* man] —'**rumly** *adv.* —'**rumness** *n.*

rum[3] (rʌm) *n.* short for **rummy**[1].

Rumanian (ruː'meɪnɪən) *n., adj.* a variant of **Romanian.**

rumba *or* **rhumba** ('rʌmbə, 'rʊm-) *n.* **1.** a rhythmic and syncopated Cuban dance in duple time. **2.** a ballroom dance derived from this. **3.** a piece of music composed for or in the rhythm of this dance. [C20: from Spanish: lavish display, of uncertain origin]

rumble ('rʌmbᵊl) *vb.* **1.** to make or cause to make a deep resonant sound: *thunder rumbled in the sky.* **2.** to move with such a sound: *the train rumbled along.* **3.** (*tr.*) to utter with a rumbling sound: *he rumbled an order.* **4.** (*tr.*) to tumble (metal components, gemstones, etc.) in a barrel of smooth stone in order to polish them. **5.** (*tr.*) *Brit. informal.* to find out about (someone or something); discover (something): *the police rumbled their plans.* **6.** (*intr.*) *U.S. slang.* to be involved in a gang fight. *~n.* **7.** a deep resonant sound. **8.** a widespread murmur of discontent. **9.** another name for **tumbler** (sense 4). **10.** *U.S. and N.Z. slang.* a gang fight. [C14: perhaps from Middle Dutch *rummelen;* related to German *rummeln, rumpeln*] —'**rumbler** *n.* —'**rumbling** *adj.* —'**rumblingly** *adv.*

rumble seat *n. U.S. and Canadian.* a folding outside seat at the rear of some early cars; dicky.

rumble strip *n.* one of a set of roughly surfaced strips set in a road on the approach to a junction or hazard, to alert drivers by means of a change in tyre noise.

rumbustious (rʌm'bʌstʃəs) *adj.* boisterous or unruly. [C18: probably a variant of ROBUSTIOUS] —**rum'bustiously** *adv.* —**rum'bustiousness** *n.*

rumen ('ruːmɛn) *n., pl.* **-mens** *or* **-mina** (-mɪnə). the first compartment of the stomach of ruminants, behind the reticulum, in which food is partly digested before being regurgitated as cud. [C18: from Latin: throat, gullet]

ruminant ('ruːmɪnənt) *n.* **1.** any artiodactyl mammal of the suborder *Ruminantia*, the members of which chew the cud and have a stomach of four compartments. The group includes deer, antelopes, cattle, sheep, and goats. **2.** any other animal that chews the cud, such as a camel. *~adj.* **3.** of, relating to, or belonging to the suborder *Ruminantia.* **4.** (of members of this suborder and related animals, such as camels) chewing the cud; ruminating. **5.** meditating or contemplating in a slow quiet way.

ruminate ('ruːmɪˌneɪt) *vb.* **1.** (of ruminants) to chew (the cud). **2.** (when *intr.*, often foll. by *upon, on,* etc.) to meditate or ponder (upon). [C16: from Latin *rūmināre* to chew the cud, from RUMEN] —**rumi'nation** *n.* —'**ruminative** *adj.* —'**ruminatively** *adv.* —'**rumiˌnator** *n.*

rummage ('rʌmɪdʒ) *vb.* **1.** (when *intr.*, often foll. by *through*) to search (through) while looking for something, often causing disorder or confusion. *~n.* **2.** an act of rummaging. **3.** a jumble of articles. **4.** *Obsolete.* confusion or bustle. [C14 (in the sense: to pack a cargo): from Old French *arrumage*, from *arrumer* to stow in a ship's hold, probably of Germanic origin] —'**rummager** *n.*

rummage out *or* **up** *vb.* (*tr.*) to find by searching vigorously; turn out.

rummage sale *n.* **1.** the U.S. and Canadian term for **jumble sale.** **2.** *U.S.* a sale of unclaimed property or unsold stock.

rummer ('rʌmə) *n.* a drinking glass, typically having an ovoid bowl on a short stem. [C17: from Dutch *roemer* a glass for drinking toasts, from *roemen* to praise]

rummy[1] ('rʌmɪ) *or* **rum** *n.* a card game based on collecting sets and sequences. [C20: perhaps from RUM[2]]

rummy[2] ('rʌmɪ) *adj.* another word for **rum**[2].

rummy[3] ('rʌmɪ) *n., pl.* **-mies.** **1.** *U.S. and Canadian.* a slang word for **drunkard.** *~adj.* **2.** of or like rum in taste or smell.

rumour *or U.S.* **rumor** ('ruːmə) *n.* **1. a.** information, often a mixture of truth and untruth, passed around verbally. **b.** (*in combination*): *a rumour-monger.* **2.** gossip or hearsay. **3.** *Archaic.* din or clamour. **4.** *Obsolete.* fame or reputation. *~vb.* **5.** (*tr.; usually passive*) to pass around or circulate in the form of a rumour: *it is rumoured that the Queen is coming.* **6.** *Literary.* to make or cause to make a murmuring noise. [C14: via Old French from Latin *rūmor* common talk; related to Old Norse *rymja* to roar, Sanskrit *rāuti* he cries]

rump (rʌmp) *n.* **1.** the hindquarters of a mammal, not including the legs. **2.** the rear part of a bird's back, nearest to the tail. **3.** a person's buttocks. **4.** Also called: **rump steak.** a cut of beef from behind the loin and above the round. **5.** an inferior remnant. [C15: from Scandinavian; compare Danish *rumpe*, Icelandic *rumpr*, German *Rumpf* trunk of the body] —'**rumpless** *adj.*

rumple ('rʌmpᵊl) *vb.* **1.** to make or become wrinkled, crumpled, ruffled, or dishevelled. *~n.* **2.** a wrinkle, fold, or crease. [C17: from Middle Dutch *rompelen;* related to Old English *gerumpen* creased, wrinkled] —'**rumply** *adj.*

rumpus ('rʌmpəs) *n., pl.* **-puses.** a noisy, confused, or disruptive commotion. [C18: of unknown origin]

rumpus room *n. U.S., Canadian, and N.Z.* a room used for noisy activities, such as parties or children's games.

run (rʌn) *vb.* **runs, running, ran, run.** **1.** (*intr.*) **a.** (of a two-legged creature) to move on foot at a rapid pace so that both feet are off the ground together for part of each stride. **b.** (of a four-legged creature) to move at a rapid gait; gallop or canter. **2.** (*tr.*) to pass over (a distance, route, etc.) in running: *to run a mile; run a race.* **3.** (*intr.*) to run in or finish a race as specified, esp. in a particular position: *John is running third.* **4.** (*tr.*) to perform or accomplish by or as if by running: *to run an errand.* **5.** (*intr.*) to flee; run away: *they took to their heels and ran.* **6.** (*tr.*) to bring into a specified state or condition by running: *to run oneself to a standstill.* **7.** (*tr.*) to track down or hunt (an animal): *to run a fox to earth.* **8.** (*intr.*) to move about freely and without restraint: *the children are running in the garden.* **9.** (*intr.; usually foll. by to*) to go or have recourse, as for aid, assistance, etc.: *he's always running to his mother when he's in trouble.* **10.** (*tr.*) to set (animals) loose on (a field or tract of land) so as to graze freely. **11.** (*intr.;* often foll. by *over, round,* or *up*) to make a short trip or brief informal visit: *I'll run over to your house this afternoon.* **12.** to move quickly and easily on wheels by rolling, or in any of certain other ways: *a ball running along the ground; a sledge running over snow.* **13.** to move or cause to move with a specified result or in a specified manner: *to run a ship aground; to run into a tree.* **14.** (often foll. by *over*) to move or pass or cause to move or pass quickly: *to run a sweeper over the carpet; to run one's eyes over a page.* **15.** (*tr.;* foll. by *into, out of, through,* etc.) to force, thrust, or drive: *she ran a needle into her finger.* **16.** (*tr.*) to drive or maintain and operate (a vehicle). **17.** (*tr.*) to give a lift to (someone) in a vehicle; transport: *he ran her to the station.* **18.** to ply or cause to ply between places on a route: *the bus runs from Piccadilly to Golders Green.* **19.** to operate or be operated; function or cause to function: *the engine is running smoothly; to run a program on a computer.* **20.** (*tr.*) to be in charge of; manage: *to run a company.* **21.** to extend or continue or cause to extend or continue in a particular direction, for a particular duration or distance, etc.: *the road runs north; the play ran for two years; the months ran into years.* **22.** (*intr.*) *Law.* **a.** to have legal force or effect: *the lease runs for two more years.* **b.** to accompany; be an integral part of or adjunct to: *an easement runs with the land.* **23.** (*tr.*) to be subjected to, be affected by, or incur: *to run a risk; run a temperature.* **24.** (*intr.;* often foll. by *to*) to be characterized (by); tend or incline: *her taste runs to extravagant hats; to run to fat.* **25.** (*intr.*) to recur persistently or be inherent: *red hair runs in my family.* **26.** to cause or allow (liquids) to flow or (of liquids) to flow, esp. in a manner specified: *water ran from the broken pipe; the well has run dry.* **27.** (*intr.*) to melt and flow: *the wax grew hot and began to run.* **28.** *Metallurgy.* **a.** to melt or fuse. **b.** (*tr.*) to mould or cast (molten metal): *to run lead into ingots.* **29.** (*intr.*) (of waves, tides, rivers, etc.) to rise high, surge, or be at a specified height: *a high sea was running that night.* **30.** (*intr.*) to be diffused: *the colours in my dress ran when I washed it.* **31.** (*intr.*) (of stitches) to unravel or come undone or (of a garment) to have stitches unravel or come undone. **32.** to sew (an article) with continuous stitches. **33.** (*intr.*) (of growing vines, creepers, etc.) to trail, spread, or climb: *ivy running over a cottage wall.* **34.** (*intr.*) to spread or circulate quickly: *a rumour ran through the town.* **35.** (*intr.*) to be stated or reported: *his story runs as follows.* **36.** to publish or print or be published or printed in a newspaper, magazine, etc.: *they ran his story in the next issue.* **37.** (often foll. by *for*) *Chiefly U.S. and Canadian.* to be a candidate or present as a candidate for political or other office: *Jones is running for president.* **38.** (*tr.*) to get past or through; evade: *to run a blockade.* **39.** (*tr.*) to deal in (arms, etc.), esp. by importing illegally: *he runs guns for the rebels.* **40.** *Nautical.* to sail (a vessel, esp. a sailing vessel) or (of such a vessel) to be sailed with the wind coming from astern. **41.** (*intr.*) (of fish) **a.** to migrate upstream from the sea, esp. in order to spawn. **b.** to swim rapidly in any area of water, esp. during migration. **42.** (*tr.*) *Cricket.* to score (a run or number of runs) by hitting the ball and running between the wickets. **43.** (*tr.*) *Billiards, etc.* to make (a number of successful shots) in sequence. **44.** (*tr.*) *Golf.* to hit (the ball) so that it rolls along the ground. **45.** (*tr.*) *Bridge.* to cash (all one's winning cards in a long suit) successively. **46. run a bath.** to turn on the taps to fill a bath with water for bathing oneself. **47. run close.** to compete closely with; present a serious challenge to: *he got the job, but a younger man ran him close.* **48. run for it.** *Informal.* to attempt to escape from arrest, etc., by running. **49. be run off one's feet.** to be extremely busy. ~*n.* **50.** an act, instance, or period of running. **51.** a gait, pace, or motion faster than a walk: *she went off at a run.* **52.** a distance covered by running or a period of running: *a run of ten miles.* **53.** an act, instance, or period of travelling in a vehicle, esp. for pleasure: *to go for a run in the car.* **54.** free and unrestricted access: *we had the run of the house and garden.* **55. a.** a period of time during which a machine, computer, etc., operates. **b.** the amount of work performed in such a period. **56.** a continuous or sustained period: *a run of good luck.* **57.** a continuous sequence of performances: *the play had a good run.* **58.** *Cards.* a sequence of winning cards in one suit, usually more than five: *a run of spades.* **59.** tendency or trend: *the run of the market.* **60.** type, class, or category: *the usual run of graduates.* **61.** (usually foll. by *on*) a continuous and urgent demand: *a run on butter; a run on the dollar.* **62.** a series of unravelled stitches, esp. in stockings or tights; ladder. **63.** the characteristic pattern or direction of something: *the run of the grain on a piece of wood.* **64. a.** a continuous vein or seam of ore, coal, etc. **b.** the direction in which it lies. **65. a.** a period during which water or other liquid flows. **b.** the amount of such a flow. **66.** a pipe, channel, etc., through which water or other liquid flows. **67.** *U.S.* a small stream. **68.** a steeply inclined pathway or course, esp. a snow-covered one used for skiing and bobsleigh racing. **69.** an enclosure for domestic fowls or other animals, in which they have free movement: *a chicken run.* **70.** (esp. in Australia and New Zealand) a tract of land for grazing livestock. **71.** a track or area frequented by animals: *a deer run; a rabbit run.* **72.** a group of animals of the same species moving together. **73.** the migration of fish upstream in order to spawn. **74.** *Nautical.* **a.** the tack of a sailing vessel in which the wind comes from astern. **b.** part of the hull of a vessel near the stern where it curves upwards and inwards. **75.** *Military.* **a.** a mission in a warplane. **b.** short for **bombing run. 76.** the movement of an aircraft along the ground during takeoff or landing. **77.** *Music.* a rapid scalelike passage of notes. **78.** *Cricket.* a score of one, normally achieved by both batsmen running from one end of the wicket to the other after one of them has hit the ball. Compare **extra** (sense 6), **boundary** (sense 2c). **79.** *Baseball.* an instance of a batter touching all four bases safely, thereby scoring. **80.** *Golf.* the distance that a ball rolls after hitting the ground. **81. a run for (one's) money.** *Informal.* **a.** a strong challenge or close competition. **b.** pleasure derived from an activity. **82. in the long run.** as the eventual outcome of a sequence of events, actions, etc.; ultimately. **83. in the short run.** as the immediate outcome of a series of events, etc. **84. on the run. a.** escaping from arrest; fugitive. **b.** in rapid flight; retreating: *the enemy is on the run.* **c.** hurrying from place to place: *she's always on the run.* **85. the runs.** *Slang.* diarrhoea. ~See also **run about, run across, run after, run along, run around, run away, run down, run in, run into, run off, run on, run out, run over, run through, run to, run up.** [Old English *runnen,* past participle of (*ge*)*rinnan;* related to Old French, Old Norse *rinna,* Old Saxon, Gothic, Old High German *rinnan*]

runabout (ˈrʌnəˌbaʊt) *n.* **1.** a small car, esp. one for use in a town. **2.** a light aircraft. **3.** a light motorboat. **4.** a person who moves about constantly or busily. ~*vb.* **run about. 5.** (*intr., adv.*) to move busily from place to place.

run across *vb.* (*intr., prep.*) to meet unexpectedly; encounter by chance.

run after *vb.* (*intr., prep.*) *Informal.* **1.** to pursue (a member of the opposite sex) with persistent attention. **2.** to pursue (anything) persistently. **3.** to care for in an excessively attentive or servile way: *she runs after her three grown sons as if they were babies.*

runagate (ˈrʌnəˌgeɪt) *n. Archaic.* **a.** a vagabond, fugitive, or renegade. **b.** (*as modifier*): *a runagate priest.* [C16: variant (influenced by RUN) of RENEGADE]

run along *vb.* (*intr., adv.*) (often said patronizingly) to go away; leave.

run around *vb.* (*intr., adv.*) *Informal.* **1.** (often foll. by *with*) to associate habitually (with). **2.** to behave in a fickle or promiscuous manner. ~*n.* **run-around. 3.** *Informal.* deceitful or evasive treatment of a person (esp. in the phrase **give** *or* **get the run-around). 4.** *Printing.* an arrangement of printed matter in which the column width is narrowed to accommodate an illustration.

run away *vb.* (*intr., adv.*) **1.** to take flight; escape. **2.** to go away; depart. **3.** (of a horse) to gallop away uncontrollably. **4. run away with. a.** to abscond or elope with: *he ran away with his boss's daughter.* **b.** to make off with; steal. **c.** to escape from the control of: *his enthusiasm ran away with him.* **d.** to win easily or be assured of victory in (a competition): *he ran away with the race.* ~*n.* **runaway. 5. a.** a person or animal that runs away. **b.** (*as modifier*): *a runaway horse.* **6.** the act or an instance of running away. **7.** (*modifier*) occurring as a result of the act of eloping: *a runaway wedding.* **8.** (*modifier*) (of a race, victory, etc.) easily won.

runch (rʌntʃ) *n. Scot. and northern English.* another name for **white charlock.** See **charlock** (sense 2). [C16: of obscure origin]

runcible spoon (ˈrʌnsɪbᵊl) *n.* a forklike utensil with two broad prongs and one sharp curved prong. [*runcible* coined by the British humorist Edward Lear (1812–88) in a nonsense poem (1871)]

runcinate (ˈrʌnsɪnɪt, -ˌneɪt) *adj.* (of a leaf) having a saw-toothed margin with the teeth or lobes pointing backwards. [C18: from New Latin *runcinātus,* from Latin *runcināre* to plane off, from *runcīna* a carpenter's plane]

rundale (ˈrʌnˌdeɪl) *n.* (formerly) the name given, esp. in Ireland and earlier, in Scotland, to the system of land tenure in which each land-holder had several strips of land that were not contiguous. Also called (in Scotland): ˈ**runrig.** [C16 *ryndale,* from RUN (vb.) + *dale,* a northern variant of DOLE[1], in the sense "a portion"]

rundle (ˈrʌndᵊl) *n.* **1.** a rung of a ladder. **2.** a wheel, esp. of a wheelbarrow. [C14: variant of ROUNDEL]

rundlet (ˈrʌndlɪt) *n. Obsolete.* a liquid measure, generally about 15 gallons. [C14: see ROUNDLET]

run down *vb.* (*mainly adv.*) **1.** to cause or allow (an engine, battery, etc.) to lose power gradually and cease to function or (of an engine, battery, etc.) to do this. **2.** to decline or reduce in number or size: *the firm ran down its sales force.* **3.** (*tr., usually passive*) to tire, sap the strength of, or exhaust: *he was thoroughly run down and needed a holiday.* **4.** (*tr.*) to criticize adversely; denigrate; decry. **5.** (*tr.*) to hit and knock to the ground with a moving vehicle. **6.** *Nautical.* **a.** (*tr.*) to collide with and cause to sink. **b.** (*intr., prep.*) to navigate so as to move parallel to (a coast). **7.** (*tr.*) to pursue and find or capture: *to run down a fugitive.* **8.** (*tr.*) to read swiftly or perfunctorily: *he ran down their list of complaints.* ~*adj.* **run-down. 9.** tired; exhausted. **10.** worn-out, shabby, or dilapidated: *a run-down old house.* ~*n.* **rundown. 11.** a brief review, résumé, or summary. **12.** the process of a motor or mechanism coming gradually to a standstill after the source of power is removed. **13.** a reduction in number or size.

rune (ruːn) *n.* **1.** any of the characters of an ancient Germanic alphabet, derived from the Roman alphabet, in use, esp. in Scandinavia, from the 3rd century A.D. to the end of the Middle Ages. Each character was believed to have a magical significance. **2.** any obscure piece of writing using mysterious symbols. **3.** a kind of Finnish poem or a stanza in such a poem. [Old English *rūn,* from Old Norse *rūn* secret; related to Old Saxon, Old High German, Gothic *runa*] —ˈ**runic** *adj.*

rung[1] (rʌŋ) *n.* **1.** one of the bars or rods that form the steps of a ladder. **2.** a crosspiece between the legs of a chair, etc. **3.** *Nautical.* a spoke on a ship's wheel or a handle projecting from the periphery. **4.** *Dialect.* a cudgel or staff. [Old English *hrung;* related to Old High German *runga,* Gothic *hrugga*] —ˈ**rungless** *adj.*

rung[2] (rʌŋ) *vb.* the past participle of **ring**[2].

run in *vb.* (*adv.*) **1.** to run (an engine) gently, usually for a specified period when it is new, in order that the running surfaces may become polished. **2.** (*tr.*) to insert or include. **3.** (*intr.*) (of an aircraft) to approach a point or target. **4.** (*tr.*) *Informal.* to take into custody; arrest: *he was run in for assault.* ~*n.* **run-in. 5.** *Informal.* an argument or quarrel: *he had a run-in with the boss yesterday.* **6.** *Printing.* matter inserted in an existing paragraph.

run into *vb.* (*prep.; mainly intr.*) **1.** (*also tr.*) to collide with or cause to collide with: *her car ran into a tree.* **2.** to encounter unexpectedly. **3.** (*also tr.*) to be beset by or cause to be beset by: *the project ran into financial difficulties.* **4.** to extend to; be of the order of: *debts running into thousands.*

runlet (ˈrʌnlɪt) *n. Archaic.* a cask for wine, beer, etc. [C14: from Old French *rondelet* ROUNDLET]

runnel (ˈrʌnᵊl) *n. Literary.* a small stream. [C16: from Old English *rynele;* related to RUN]

runner (ˈrʌnə) *n.* **1.** a person who runs, esp. an athlete. **2.** a messenger for a bank or brokerage firm. **3.** an employee of an art or antique dealer who visits auctions to bid on desired lots. **4.** a person engaged in the solicitation of business. **5.** a person on the run; fugitive. **6. a.** a person or vessel engaged in smuggling; smuggler. **b.** (*in combination*): *a rum-runner*. **7.** a person who operates, manages, or controls something. **8. a.** either of the strips of metal or wood on which a sledge runs. **b.** the blade of an ice skate. **9.** a roller or guide for a sliding component. **10.** the rotating element of a water turbine. **11.** another name for **running belay. 12.** any of various carangid fishes of temperate and tropical seas, such as *Caranx crysos* (**blue runner**) of American Atlantic waters. **13.** *Botany*. **a.** Also called: **stolon.** a slender horizontal stem, as of the strawberry, that grows along the surface of the soil and propagates by producing roots and shoots at the nodes or tip. **b.** a plant that propagates in this way. **14.** a strip of lace, linen, etc., placed across a table, dressing table, etc. for protection and decoration. **15.** a narrow rug or carpet, as for a passage. **16.** another word for **rocker** (on a rocking chair).

runner bean *n.* another name for **scarlet runner.**

runner-up *n., pl.* **runners-up.** a contestant finishing a race or competition in second place.

running (ˈrʌnɪŋ) *adj.* **1.** maintained continuously; incessant: *a running battle; running commentary*. **2.** (*postpositive*) without interruption; consecutive: *he lectured for two hours running*. **3.** denoting or relating to the scheduled operation of a public vehicle: *the running time of a train*. **4.** accomplished at a run: *a running jump*. **5.** moving or slipping easily, as a rope or a knot. **6.** (of a wound, sore, etc.) discharging pus or a serous fluid. **7.** denoting or relating to operations for maintenance: *running repairs*. **8.** prevalent; current: *running prices*. **9.** repeated or continuous: *a running design*. **10.** (of certain plants, plant stems, etc.) creeping along the ground. **11.** flowing: *running water*. **12.** (of handwriting) having the letters run together. ~*n.* **13.** management or organization: *the running of a company*. **14.** operation or maintenance: *the running of a machine*. **15.** competition or a competitive situation (in the phrases **in the running, out of the running**). **16. make the running.** to set the pace in a competition or race. **17.** *Rare*. the power or ability to run.

running belay *n.* *Mountaineering*. the clipping of the rope through a karabiner attached to a sling, piton, nut, etc., secured to the mountain: used by a leading climber of a team to reduce the length of a possible fall. Also called: **runner.**

running board *n.* a footboard along the side of a vehicle, esp. an early motorcar.

running commentary *n.* a continuous spoken description of an event while it is happening.

running head *or* **title** *n.* *Printing*. a heading printed at the top of every page or every other page of a book.

running light *n.* *Nautical*. one of several white, red, or green lights displayed by vessels operating at night.

running mate *n.* **1.** *U.S.* a candidate for the subordinate of two linked positions, esp. a candidate for the vice-presidency. **2.** a horse that pairs another in a team.

running repairs *pl. n.* repairs, as to a machine or vehicle, that are minor and can be made with little or no interruption in the use of the item.

running rigging *n.* *Nautical*. the wires and ropes used to control the operations of a sailing vessel. Compare **standing rigging.**

running stitch *n.* a simple form of hand stitching, consisting of small stitches that look the same on both sides of the fabric, usually used for gathering. Sometimes called: **gathering stitch.**

runny (ˈrʌnɪ) *adj.* **-nier, -niest. 1.** tending to flow; liquid. **2.** (of the nose or nasal passages) exuding mucus.

run off *vb.* (*adv.*) **1.** (*intr.*) to depart in haste. **2.** (*tr.*) to produce quickly, as copies on a duplicating machine. **3.** to drain (liquid) or (of liquid) to be drained. **4.** (*tr.*) to decide (a race) by a runoff. **5.** (*tr.*) to get rid of (weight, etc.) by running. **6.** (*intr.*) (of a flow of liquid) to begin to dry up; cease to run. **7. run off with. a.** to steal; purloin. **b.** to elope with. ~*n.* **runoff. 8. a.** an extra race to decide the winner after a tie. **b.** a contest or election held after a previous one has failed to produce a clear victory for any one person. **9.** that portion of rainfall that runs into streams as surface water rather than being absorbed by the soil. **10.** the overflow of a liquid from a container. **11.** *N.Z.* grazing land for store cattle.

run-of-paper *adj.* (of a story, advertisement, etc.) placed anywhere in a newspaper, at the discretion of the editor.

run-of-the-mill *adj.* ordinary, average, or undistinguished in quality, character, or nature; not special or excellent.

run on *vb.* (*adv.*) **1.** (*intr.*) to continue without interruption. **2.** to write with linked-up characters. **3.** *Printing*. to compose text matter without indentation or paragraphing. ~*n.* **run-on. 4.** *Printing*. **a.** text matter composed without indenting. **b.** (*as modifier*): *run-on text matter*. **5. a.** a word added at the end of a dictionary entry whose meaning can be easily inferred from the definition of the headword. **b.** (*as modifier*): *a run-on entry*.

run out *vb.* (*adv.*) **1.** (*intr.*; often foll. by *of*) to exhaust (a supply of something) or (of a supply) to become exhausted. **2. run out on.** *Informal*. to desert or abandon. **3.** (*tr.*) *Cricket*. to dismiss (a running batsman) by breaking the wicket with the ball, or with the ball in the hand, while he is out of his ground. ~*n.* **run-out. 4.** *Cricket*. dismissal of a batsman by running him out. **5.** *Mechanical engineering*. an imperfection of a rotating component so that not all parts revolve in the same plane.

run over *vb.* **1.** (*tr., adv.*) to knock down (a person) with a moving vehicle. **2.** (*intr.*) to overflow the capacity of (a container). **3.** (*intr., prep.*) to examine hastily or make a rapid survey of. **4.** (*intr., prep.*) to exceed (a limit): *we've run over our time*.

runt (rʌnt) *n.* **1.** the smallest and weakest young animal in a litter, esp. the smallest piglet in a litter. **2.** *Derogatory*. an undersized or inferior person. **3.** a large pigeon, originally bred for eating. [C16: origin unknown] —ˈ**runtish** *adj.* —ˈ**runty** *adj.* —ˈ**runtiness** *n.*

run through *vb.* **1.** (*tr., adv.*) to transfix with a sword or other weapon. **2.** (*intr., prep.*) to exhaust (money) by wasteful spending; squander. **3.** (*intr., prep.*) to practise or rehearse: *let's run through the plan*. **4.** (*intr., prep.*) to examine hastily. ~*n.* **run-through. 5.** a practice or rehearsal. **6.** a brief survey.

run time *n.* *Computer technol*. the time during which a computer program is executed.

run to *vb.* (*intr., prep.*) to be sufficient for: *my income doesn't run to luxuries*.

run up *vb.* (*tr., adv.*) **1.** to amass or accumulate; incur: *to run up debts*. **2.** to make by sewing together quickly: *to run up a dress*. **3.** to hoist: *to run up a flag*. ~*n.* **run-up. 4.** an approach run by an athlete for a long jump, pole vault, etc. **5.** a preliminary or preparatory period: *the run-up to the election*.

runway (ˈrʌnˌweɪ) *n.* **1.** a hard level roadway or other surface from which aircraft take off and on which they land. **2.** an enclosure for domestic animals; run. **3.** *Forestry, North American*. a chute for sliding logs down. **4.** a narrow ramp extending from the stage into the audience in a theatre, nightclub, etc.

rupee (ruːˈpiː) *n.* the standard monetary unit of India, Pakistan, and Bhutan (divided into 100 paisas), Sri Lanka, the Maldive Islands, Mauritius, and the Seychelles (divided into 100 cents), and of Nepal (divided into 100 pice). [C17: from Hindi *rupaīyā*, from Sanskrit *rūpya* coined silver, from *rūpa* shape, beauty]

rupiah (ruːˈpiːə) *n., pl.* **-ah** *or* **-ahs.** the standard monetary unit of Indonesia, divided into 100 sen. [from Hindi: RUPEE]

rupicolous (ruːˈpɪkələs) *adj.* *Biology*. living or growing on or among rocks. [C19: from Latin *rūp(ēs)* crag + -I- + -COLOUS]

rupture (ˈrʌptʃə) *n.* **1.** the act of breaking or bursting or the state of being broken or burst. **2.** a breach of peaceful or friendly relations. **3.** *Pathol.* **a.** the breaking or tearing of a bodily structure or part. **b.** another word for **hernia.** ~*vb.* **4.** to break or burst or cause to break or burst. **5.** to affect or be affected with a rupture or hernia. **6.** to undergo or cause to undergo a breach in relations or friendship. [C15: from Latin *ruptūra* a breaking, from *rumpere* to burst forth; see ERUPT] —ˈ**rupturable** *adj.*

rural (ˈrʊərəl) *adj.* **1.** of, relating to, or characteristic of the country or country life. **2.** living in or accustomed to the country. **3.** of, relating to, or associated with farming. ~Compare **urban.** [C15: via Old French from Latin *rūrālis*, from *rūs* the country] —ˈ**ruralism** *n.* —ˈ**ruralist** *n.* —**ruˈrality** *n.* —ˈ**rurally** *adv.*

rural dean *n.* *Chiefly Brit.* a clergyman having authority over a group of parishes.

rural delivery *n.* *N.Z.* a mail service in a country area, often run by contractors for the Post Office.

rural district *n.* (in England and Wales from 1888 to 1974 and Northern Ireland from 1898 to 1973) a rural division of a county.

ruralize *or* **ruralise** (ˈrʊərəˌlaɪz) *vb.* **1.** (*tr.*) to make rural in character, appearance, etc. **2.** (*intr.*) to go into the country to live. —ˌ**ruraliˈzation** *or* ˌ**ruraliˈsation** *n.*

rural science *or* **studies** *n.* *Brit.* the study and theory of agriculture, biology, ecology, and associated fields.

Ruritanian (ˌrʊərɪˈteɪnɪən) *adj.* of or denoting a romantic and idealistic setting in which adventure and intrigue occur. [after the imaginary kingdom in central Europe created by British writer Anthony Hope (1863–1933) in *The Prisoner of Zenda*]

ruru (ˈruːruː) *n.* *N.Z.* another name for **mopoke.** [Maori]

Rus. *abbrev. for* Russia(n).

ruse (ruːz) *n.* an action intended to mislead, deceive, or trick; stratagem. [C15: from Old French: trick, esp. to evade capture, from *ruser* to retreat, from Latin *recūsāre* to refuse]

rush[1] (rʌʃ) *vb.* **1.** to hurry or cause to hurry; hasten. **2.** to make a sudden attack upon (a fortress, position, person, etc.). **3.** (when *intr.*, often foll. by *at, in,* or *into*) to proceed or approach in a reckless manner. **4. rush one's fences.** to proceed with precipitate haste. **5.** (*intr.*) to come, flow, swell, etc., quickly or suddenly: *tears rushed to her eyes*. **6.** *Slang*. to cheat, esp. by grossly overcharging. **7.** (*tr.*) *U.S. and Canadian*. to make a concerted effort to secure the agreement, participation, etc., of (a person). **8.** (*tr.*) *Rugby*. (of a pack) to move (the ball) forwards by short kicks and runs. ~*n.* **9.** the act or condition of rushing. **10.** a sudden surge towards someone or something: *a gold rush*. **11.** a sudden surge of sensation, esp. produced by a drug. **12.** a sudden demand. **13.** *Rugby*. the act of rushing the ball. ~*adj.* (*prenominal*) **14.** requiring speed or urgency: *a rush job*. **15.** characterized by much movement, business, etc.: *a rush period*. [C14 *ruschen*, from Old French *ruser* to put to flight, from Latin *recūsāre* to refuse, reject] —ˈ**rusher** *n.*

rush[2] (rʌʃ) *n.* **1.** any annual or perennial plant of the genus *Juncus*, growing in wet places and typically having grasslike cylindrical leaves and small green or brown flowers: family *Juncaceae*. Many species are used to make baskets. **2.** any of various similar or related plants, such as the woodrush, scouring rush, and spike-rush. **3.** something valueless; a trifle; straw: *not worth a rush.* **4.** short for **rush light.** [Old English *risce, rysce;* related to Middle Dutch *risch,* Norwegian *rusk,* Old Slavonic *rozga* twig, rod] —'**rush,like** *adj.*

rushes (rʌʃɪz) *pl. n.* (*sometimes sing.*) (in film-making) the initial prints of a scene or scenes before editing, usually prepared daily.

rush hour *n.* a period at the beginning and end of the working day when large numbers of people are travelling to or from work.

rush light *or* **candle** *n.* a narrow candle, formerly in use, made of the pith of various types of rush dipped in tallow.

rushy ('rʌʃɪ) *adj.* **rushier, rushiest.** abounding in, covered with, or made of rushes. —'**rushiness** *n.*

rus in urbe *Latin.* (rʊs ɪn 'ɜːbɪ) the country in the town.

rusk (rʌsk) *n.* a light bread dough, sweet or plain, baked twice until it is brown, hard, and crisp: often given to babies. [C16: from Spanish or Portuguese *rosca* screw, bread shaped in a twist, of unknown origin]

Russ (rʌs) *n., pl.* **Russ** *or* **Russes,** *adj.* an archaic word for **Russian** (person or language).

Russ. *abbrev. for* Russia(n).

Russell diagram ('rʌsᵊl) *n.* See **Hertzsprung-Russell diagram.**

Russell's paradox *n. Logic.* the paradox that the class of all classes that are not members of themselves is a member of itself only if it is not, and is not only if it is. This undermines the notion of an all-inclusive universal class. [named after Bertrand *Russell* (1872–1970), British philosopher and mathematician who discovered it]

russet ('rʌsɪt) *n.* **1.** brown with a yellowish or reddish tinge. **2. a.** a rough homespun fabric, reddish-brown in colour, formerly in use for clothing. **b.** (*as modifier*): *a russet coat.* **3.** any of various apples with rough brownish-red skins. **4.** abnormal roughness on fruit, caused by parasites, pesticides, or frost. *~adj.* **5.** (of tanned hide leather) dressed ready for staining. **6.** *Archaic.* simple; homely; rustic: *a russet life.* **7.** of the colour russet: *russet hair.* [C13: from Anglo-Norman, from Old French *rosset,* from *rous,* from Latin *russus;* related to Latin *ruber* red] —'**russety** *adj.*

Russia leather ('rʌʃə) *n.* a smooth dyed leather made from calfskin and scented with birch tar oil, originally produced in Russia.

Russian ('rʌʃən) *adj.* **1.** of, relating to, or characteristic of Russia (either the tsarist empire overthrown in 1917 or the Russian Federation, formerly part of the Soviet Union), its people, or their language. **2.** (loosely) of, relating to, or characteristic of the former Soviet Union; Soviet. *~n.* **3.** the official language of the Russian Federation and of the former Soviet Union: an Indo-European language belonging to the East Slavonic branch. **4.** a native or inhabitant of Russia or the former Soviet Union.

Russian dressing *n.* mayonnaise or vinaigrette with chilli sauce, chopped gherkins, etc.

Russianize *or* **Russianise** ('rʌʃə,naɪz) *vb.* to make or become Russian in style, character, etc. —,**Russiani'zation** *or* ,**Russiani'sation** *n.*

Russian Orthodox Church *n.* the national Church of Russia, constituting a branch of the Eastern Church presided over by the Patriarch of Moscow.

Russian roulette *n.* **1.** a game of chance in which each player in turn spins the cylinder of a revolver loaded with only one cartridge and presses the trigger with the barrel against his own head. **2.** any foolish or potentially suicidal undertaking.

Russian salad *n.* a salad of cold diced cooked vegetables mixed with Russian dressing.

Russian wolfhound *n.* a less common name for **borzoi.**

Russify ('rʌsɪ,faɪ) *vb.* **-fies, -fying, -fied.** (*tr.*) to cause to become Russian in character. —,**Russifi'cation** *n.*

Russky *or* **Russki** ('rʌskɪ) *n., pl.* **-kies** *or* **-kis,** *adj. Chiefly U.S.* a slang word for **Russian.** [C20]

Russo- ('rʌsəʊ-) *combining form.* Russia or Russian: *Russo-Japanese.*

Russophile ('rʌsəʊ,faɪl) *or* **Russophil** *n.* **1.** an admirer of Russia or the former Soviet Union, its customs, political system, etc. *~adj.* **2.** marked by or possessing admiration of Russia or the former Soviet Union.

Russophobe ('rʌsəʊ,fəʊb) *n.* a person with an intense and often irrational hatred (**Russophobia**) for the former Soviet Union, its political system, etc. —,**Russo'phobic** *adj.*

russula ('rʌsjʊlə) *n., pl.* **-lae** (-liː) *or* **-las.** any fungus of the large basidiomycetous genus *Russula,* of typical toadstool shape and often brightly coloured, such as the yellow *R. ochroleuca* and *R. lutea,* the green *R. aeruginea,* the violet-pink *R. fragilis,* and the purple *R. atropurpurea.*

rust (rʌst) *n.* **1.** a reddish-brown oxide coating formed on iron or steel by the action of oxygen and moisture. **2.** Also called: **rust fungus.** *Plant pathol.* **a.** any basidiomycetous fungus of the order *Uredinales,* parasitic on cereal plants, conifers, etc. **b.** any of various plant diseases characterized by reddish-brown discoloration of the leaves and stem, esp. that caused by the rust fungi. **3. a.** a strong brown colour, sometimes with a reddish or yellowish tinge. **b.** (*as adj.*): *a rust carpet.* **4.** any corrosive or debilitating influence, esp. lack of use. *~vb.* **5.** to become or cause to become coated with a layer of rust. **6.** to deteriorate or cause to deteriorate through some debilitating influence or lack of use: *he allowed his talent to rust over the years.* [Old English *rūst;* related to Old Saxon, Old High German *rost*] —'**rustless** *adj.*

rust bucket *n. Slang.* a very badly rusted car.

rustic ('rʌstɪk) *adj.* **1.** of, characteristic of, or living in the country; rural. **2.** having qualities ascribed to country life or people; simple; unsophisticated: *rustic pleasures.* **3.** crude, awkward, or uncouth. **4.** made of untrimmed branches: *a rustic seat.* **5.** denoting or characteristic of a style of furniture popular in England in the 18th and 19th centuries, in which the legs and feet of chairs, tables, etc., were made to resemble roots, trunks, and branches of trees. **6.** (of masonry) having a rusticated finish. *~n.* **7.** a person who comes from or lives in the country. **8.** an unsophisticated, simple, or clownish person from the country. **9.** Also called: '**rustic,work.** brick or stone having a rough finish. [C16: from Old French *rustique,* from Latin *rūsticus,* from *rūs* the country] —'**rustically** *adv.* —**rusticity** (rʌ'stɪsɪtɪ) *n.*

rusticate ('rʌstɪ,keɪt) *vb.* **1.** to banish or retire to the country. **2.** to make or become rustic in style, behaviour, etc. **3.** (*tr.*) *Architect.* to finish (an exterior wall) with large blocks of masonry that are separated by deep joints and decorated with a bold, usually textured, design. **4.** (*tr.*) *Brit.* to send down from university for a specified time as a punishment. [C17: from Latin *rūsticārī,* from *rūs* the country] —,**rusti'cation** *n.* —'**rusti,cator** *n.*

rusticating ('rʌstɪ,keɪtɪŋ) *n.* (in New Zealand) a wide type of weatherboarding used in older houses. Also called: **rusticated.**

rustle[1] ('rʌsᵊl) *vb.* **1.** to make or cause to make a low crisp whispering or rubbing sound, as of dry leaves or paper. **2.** to move with such a sound. *~n.* **3.** such a sound or sounds. [Old English *hrūxlian;* related to Gothic *hrukjan* to CROW, Old Norse *hraukr* raven, CROW] —'**rustling** *adj., n.* —'**rustlingly** *adv.*

rustle[2] ('rʌsᵊl) *vb.* **1.** *Chiefly U.S. and Canadian.* to steal (cattle, horses, etc.). **2.** *U.S. and Canadian informal.* to move swiftly and energetically. [C19: probably special use of RUSTLE[1] (in the sense: to move with quiet sound)]

rustler ('rʌslə) *n.* **1.** *Chiefly U.S. and Canadian.* a cattle or horse thief. **2.** *U.S. and Canadian informal.* an energetic or vigorous person.

rustle up *vb.* (*tr., adv.*) *Informal.* **1.** to prepare (a meal, snack, etc.) rapidly, esp. at short notice. **2.** to forage for and obtain.

rustproof ('rʌst,pruːf) *adj.* treated against rusting.

rusty ('rʌstɪ) *adj.* **rustier, rustiest.** **1.** covered with, affected by, or consisting of rust: *a rusty machine; a rusty deposit.* **2.** of the colour rust. **3.** discoloured by age: *a rusty coat.* **4.** (of the voice) tending to croak. **5.** old-fashioned in appearance; seemingly antiquated: *a rusty old gentleman.* **6.** out of practice; impaired in skill or knowledge by inaction or neglect. **7.** (of plants) affected by the rust fungus. —'**rustily** *adv.* —'**rustiness** *n.*

rut[1] (rʌt) *n.* **1.** a groove or furrow in a soft road, caused by wheels. **2.** any deep mark, hole, or groove. **3.** a narrow or predictable way of life, set of attitudes, etc.; dreary or undeviating routine (esp. in the phrase **in a rut**). *~vb.* **ruts, rutting, rutted.** **4.** (*tr.*) to make a rut or ruts in. [C16: probably from French *route* road]

rut[2] (rʌt) *n.* **1.** a recurrent period of sexual excitement and reproductive activity in certain male ruminants, such as the deer, that corresponds to the period of oestrus in females. **2.** another name for **oestrus.** *~vb.* **ruts, rutting, rutted.** **3.** (*intr.*) (of male ruminants) to be in a period of sexual excitement and activity. [C15: from Old French *rut* noise, roar, from Latin *rugītus,* from *rugīre* to roar]

rutabaga (,ruːtə'beɪgə) *n.* the U.S. and Canadian name for **swede.** [C18: from Swedish dialect *rotabagge,* literally: root bag]

rutaceous (ruː'teɪʃəs) *adj.* of, relating to, or belonging to the *Rutaceae,* a family of tropical and temperate flowering plants many of which have aromatic leaves. The family includes rue, citrus trees, and dittany. [C19: from New Latin *Rutaceae,* from Latin *rūta* RUE[2]]

ruth (ruːθ) *n. Archaic.* **1.** pity; compassion. **2.** repentance; remorse. **3.** grief or distress. [C12: from *rewen* to RUE[1]]

Ruthenian (ruː'θiːnɪən) *adj.* **1.** of or relating to Ruthenia, a region of the Ukraine, or to its people or their dialect of Ukrainian. *~n.* **2.** a dialect of Ukrainian. **3.** a native or inhabitant of Ruthenia.

ruthenic (ruː'θenɪk) *adj.* of or containing ruthenium, esp. in a high valency state.

ruthenious (ruː'θiːnɪəs) *adj.* of or containing ruthenium in a divalent state.

ruthenium (ruː'θiːnɪəm) *n.* a hard brittle white element of the platinum metal group. It occurs free with other platinum metals in pentlandite and other ores and is used to harden platinum and palladium. Symbol: Ru; atomic no.: 44; atomic wt.: 101.07; valency: 1–8; relative density: 12.41; melting pt.: 2310°C; boiling pt.: 3900°C. [C19: from Medieval Latin *Ruthenia* Russia, where it was first discovered]

rutherford ('rʌðəfəd) *n.* a unit of activity equal to the quantity of a radioactive nuclide required to produce one million disintegrations per second. Abbrev.: **rd.** [C20: named after Ernest *Rutherford* (1871–1937), New-Zealand born British physicist]

rutherfordium (ˌrʌðəˈfɔːdɪəm) *n.* the U.S. name for the element with the atomic number 104. Also called: **kurchatovium.** Symbol: Rf [C20: named after Ernest *Rutherford*]

ruthful (ˈruːθfʊl) *adj. Archaic.* full of or causing sorrow or pity. —ˈ**ruthfully** *adv.* —ˈ**ruthfulness** *n.*

ruthless (ˈruːθlɪs) *adj.* feeling or showing no mercy; hardhearted. —ˈ**ruthlessly** *adv.* —ˈ**ruthlessness** *n.*

rutilant (ˈruːtɪlənt) *adj. Rare.* of a reddish colour or glow. [C15: from Latin *rutilāns* having a red glow, from *rutilāre,* from *rutilus* ruddy, red]

rutilated (ˈruːtɪˌleɪtɪd) *adj.* (of minerals, esp. quartz) containing needles of rutile.

rutile (ˈruːtaɪl) *n.* a black, yellowish, or reddish-brown mineral, found in igneous rocks, metamorphosed limestones, and quartz veins. It is a source of titanium. Composition: titanium dioxide. Formula: TiO_2. Crystal structure: tetragonal. [C19: via French from German *Rutil,* from Latin *rutilus* red, glowing]

ruttish (ˈrʌtɪʃ) *adj.* **1.** (of an animal) in a condition of rut. **2.** lascivious or salacious. —ˈ**ruttishly** *adv.* —ˈ**ruttishness** *n.*

rutty (ˈrʌtɪ) *adj.* **-tier, -tiest.** full of ruts or holes: *a rutty track.* —ˈ**ruttily** *adv.* —ˈ**ruttiness** *n.*

rv *Statistics. abbrev. for* random variable.

RV *abbrev. for* Revised Version (of the Bible).

RW *abbrev. for:* **1.** Right Worshipful. **2.** Right Worthy.

RWA *international car registration for* Rwanda.

Rwanda (rʊˈændə) *n.* the official language of Rwanda, a republic in central Africa, belonging to the Bantu group of the Niger-Congo family and closely related to Kirundi.

rwd *abbrev. for* rear-wheel drive.

Rwy *or* **Ry** *abbrev. for* railway.

-ry *suffix forming nouns.* a variant of **-ery:** *dentistry.*

Ryder Cup (raɪdə) *n.* **the.** the trophy awarded in a professional golfing competition between teams representing Britain and Europe and the U.S. [C20: named after Samuel *Ryder* (1859–1936), British businessman and golf patron]

rye[1] (raɪ) *n.* **1.** a tall hardy widely cultivated annual grass, *Secale cereale,* having soft bluish-green leaves, bristly flower spikes, and light brown grain. See also **wild rye. 2.** the grain of this grass, used in making flour and whiskey, and as a livestock food. **3.** Also called: **rye whiskey.** whiskey distilled from rye. U.S. whiskey must by law contain not less than 51 per cent rye. **4.** *U.S.* short for **rye bread.** [Old English *ryge;* related to Old Norse *rugr,* Old French *rogga,* Old Saxon *roggo*]

rye[2] (raɪ) *n. Gypsy dialect.* a gentleman. [from Romany *rai,* from Sanskrit *rājan* king; see RAJAH]

rye bread *n.* any of various breads made entirely or partly from rye flour, often with caraway seeds.

rye-brome *n.* a grass, *Bromus secalinus,* native to Europe and Asia, having rough leaves and wheatlike ears. U.S. names: **cheat, chess.**

rye-grass *n.* any of various grasses of the genus *Lolium,* esp. *L. perenne,* native to Europe, N Africa, and Asia and widely cultivated as forage crops. They have a flattened flower spike and hairless leaves.

Ryobu Shinto (riːˈəʊbuː) *n.* a fusion of Shinto and Buddhism, which flourished in Japan in the 13th century. [from Japanese *ryō bu,* literally: two parts]

ryokan (rɪˈəʊkən) *n.* a traditional Japanese inn. [Japanese]

ryot (ˈraɪət) *n.* (in India) a peasant or tenant farmer. [C17: from Hindi *ra'īyat,* from Arabic *ra'īyah* flock, peasants, from *ra'ā* pasture]

s *or* **S** (ɛs) *n., pl.* **s's, S's,** *or* **Ss.** **1.** the 19th letter and 15th consonant of the modern English alphabet. **2.** a speech sound represented by this letter, usually an alveolar fricative, either voiceless, as in *sit,* or voiced, as in *dogs.* **3. a.** something shaped like an S. **b.** (*in combination*): *an S-bend in a road.*
s *symbol for* second (of time).
S *symbol for:* **1.** satisfactory. **2.** Society. **3.** small (size). **4.** South. **5.** *Chem.* sulphur. **6.** *Physics.* **a.** entropy. **b.** siemens. **c.** strangeness. **7.** *Currency.* **a.** schilling. **b.** sol. **c.** sucre. ~ **8.** *international car registration for* Sweden.
s. *abbrev. for:* **1.** section. **2.** see. **3.** semi-. **4.** shilling. **5.** sign(ed). **6.** singular. **7.** sire. **8.** son. **9.** substantive. **10.** succeeded.
S. *abbrev. for:* **1.** sabbath. **2.** (*pl.* **SS.**) Saint. **3.** Saturday. **4.** Saxon. **5.** school. **6.** Sea. **7.** senate. **8.** September. **9.** Signor. **10.** Socialist. **11.** Society. **12.** Sunday. **13.** (in titles) Fellow. [Latin *socius*]
-s[1] *or* **-es** *suffix.* forming the plural of most nouns: *boys; boxes.* [from Old English *-as,* plural nominative and accusative ending of some masculine nouns]
-s[2] *or* **-es** *suffix.* forming the third person singular present indicative tense of verbs: *he runs; she washes.* [from Old English (northern dialect) *-es, -s,* originally the ending of the second person singular]
-s[3] *suffix of nouns.* forming nicknames and names expressing affection or familiarity: *Fats; Fingers; ducks.* [special use of -s[1]]
-'s *suffix.* **1.** forming the possessive singular of nouns and some pronouns: *man's; one's.* **2.** forming the possessive plural of nouns whose plurals do not end in *-s: children's.* **3.** forming the plural of numbers, letters, or symbols: *20's; p's and q's.* **4.** *Informal.* contraction of *is* or *has: he's here; John's coming; it's gone.* **5.** *Informal.* contraction of *us* with *let: let's.* **6.** *Informal.* contraction of *does* in some questions: *where's he live? what's he do?* [senses 1, 2: assimilated contraction from Middle English *-es,* from Old English, masculine and neuter genitive singular; sense 3, equivalent to -s[1]]
-s' *suffix.* forming the possessive of plural nouns ending in the sound *s* or *z* and of some singular nouns: *girls'; for goodness' sake.*
Sa *a former chemical symbol for* samarium.
SA *abbrev. for:* **1.** Salvation Army. **2.** Sociedad Anónima. [Spanish: limited company] **3.** Société anonyme. [French: limited company] **4.** South Africa. **5.** South America. **6.** South Australia. **7.** (in Nazi Germany) Sturmabteilung. [German: storm troopers]
s.a. *abbrev. for:* **1.** semiannual. **2.** sex appeal. **3.** sine anno. [Latin: without date]
Sab. *abbrev. for* Sabbath.
sabadilla (ˌsæbəˈdɪlə) *n.* **1.** a tropical American liliaceous plant, *Schoenocaulon officinale.* **2.** the bitter brown seeds of this plant, which contain the alkaloids veratrine and veratridine and are used in insecticides. [C19: from Spanish *cebadilla,* diminutive of *cebada* barley, from Latin *cibāre* to feed, from *cibus* food]
Sabaean *or* **Sabean** (səˈbiːən) *n.* **1.** an inhabitant or native of ancient Saba (Sheba), a kingdom in the SW corner of the Arabian peninsula. **2.** the ancient Semitic language of Saba. ~*adj.* **3.** of or relating to ancient Saba, its inhabitants, or their language. [C16: from Latin *Sabaeus,* from Greek *Sabaios* belonging to Saba (Sheba)]
sabayon (ˌsæbaɪˈjɒn; *French* sabajɔ̃) *n.* a dessert or sweet sauce made with egg yolks, sugar, and wine beaten together over heat till thick: served either hot or cold. [C20: from French, alteration of Italian *zabione* ZABAGLIONE]
sabbat (ˈsæbæt, -ət) *n.* another word for **Sabbath** (sense 4).
Sabbatarian (ˌsæbəˈtɛərɪən) *n.* **1.** a person advocating the strict religious observance of Sunday. **2.** a person who observes Saturday as the Sabbath. ~*adj.* **3.** of or relating to the Sabbath or its observance. [C17: from Late Latin *sabbatārius* a Sabbath-keeper] —ˌ**Sabbaˈtarianism** *n.*
Sabbath (ˈsæbəθ) *n.* **1.** the seventh day of the week, Saturday, devoted to worship and rest from work in Judaism and in certain Christian Churches. **2.** Sunday, observed by Christians as the day of worship and rest from work in commemoration of Christ's Resurrection. **3.** (*not cap.*) a period of rest. **4.** Also called: **sabbat, witches' Sabbath.** a midnight meeting or secret rendezvous for practitioners of witchcraft, sorcery, or devil worship. [Old English *sabbat,* from Latin *sabbatum,* from Greek *sabbaton,* from Hebrew *shabbāth,* from *shābath* to rest]
sabbath school *n.* (*sometimes caps.*) *Chiefly U.S.* a school for religious instruction held on the Sabbath.
sabbatical (səˈbætɪkᵊl) *adj.* **1.** denoting a period of leave granted to university staff, teachers, etc., esp. approximately every seventh year: *a sabbatical year; sabbatical leave.* **2.** denoting a post that renders the holder eligible for such leave. ~*n.* **3.** any sabbatical period. [C16: from Greek *sabbatikos;* see SABBATH]
Sabbatical (səˈbætɪkᵊl) *adj. also* **Sabbatic. 1.** of, relating to, or appropriate to the Sabbath as a day of rest and religious observance. ~*n.* **2.** short for **sabbatical year.**
sabbatical year *n.* (*often caps.*) *Bible.* a year during which the land was to be left uncultivated, debts annulled, etc., supposed to be observed every seventh year by the ancient Israelites according to Leviticus 25.
SABC *abbrev. for* South African Broadcasting Corporation.
Sabellian (səˈbɛlɪən) *n.* **1.** an extinct language or group of languages of ancient Italy, surviving only in a few inscriptions belonging to the Osco-Umbrian group. **2.** a member of any of the ancient peoples speaking this language, including the Sabines. ~*adj.* **3.** of or relating to this language or its speakers. [C17: from Latin *Sabellī* group of Italian tribes]
saber (ˈseɪbə) *n., vb.* the U.S. spelling of **sabre.**
sabin (ˈsæbɪn, ˈseɪ-) *n. Physics.* a unit of acoustic absorption equal to the absorption resulting from one square foot of a perfectly absorbing surface. [C20: introduced by Wallace C. *Sabine* (1868–1919), U.S. physicist]
Sabine (ˈsæbaɪn) *n.* **1.** a member of an ancient Oscan-speaking people who lived in central Italy northeast of Rome. ~*adj.* **2.** of, characteristic of, or relating to this people or their language.
sabkha (ˈsæbxə, -kə) *n.* a flat coastal plain with a salt crust, common in Arabia. [C19: from Arabic]
sable (ˈseɪbᵊl) *n., pl.* **-bles** *or* **-ble. 1.** a marten, *Martes zibellina,* of N Asian forests, with dark brown luxuriant fur. **2. a.** the highly valued fur of this animal. **b.** (*as modifier*): *a sable coat.* **3. American sable.** the brown, slightly less valuable fur of the American marten, *Martes americana.* **4.** the colour of sable fur: a dark brown to yellowish-brown colour. ~*adj.* **5.** of the colour of sable fur. **6.** black; dark; gloomy. **7.** (*usually postpositive*) *Heraldry.* of the colour black. [C15: from Old French, from Old High German *zobel,* of Slavic origin; related to Russian *sobol',* Polish *sobol*]
sable antelope *n.* a large black E African antelope, *Hippotragus niger,* with long backward-curving horns.
sabot (ˈsæbəʊ; *French* sabo) *n.* **1.** a shoe made from a single block of wood. **2.** a shoe with a wooden sole and a leather or cloth upper. **3.** a lightweight sleeve in which a subcalibre round is enclosed in order to make it fit the rifling of a firearm. After firing the sabot drops away. **4.** *Austral.* a small sailing boat with a shortened bow. [C17: from French, probably from Old French *savate* an old shoe, also influenced by *bot* BOOT[1]; related to Italian *ciabatta* old shoe, Old Provençal *sabata*]
sabotage (ˈsæbəˌtɑːʒ) *n.* **1.** the deliberate destruction, disruption, or damage of equipment, a public service, etc., as by enemy agents, dissatisfied employees, etc. **2.** any similar action or behaviour. ~*vb.* **3.** (*tr.*) to destroy, damage, or disrupt, esp. by secret means. [C20: from French, from *saboter* to spoil through clumsiness (literally: to clatter in sabots)]
saboteur (ˌsæbəˈtɜː) *n.* a person who commits sabotage. [C20: from French; see SABOTAGE]
sabra (ˈsɑːbrə) *n.* a native-born Israeli Jew. [from Hebrew *Sabēr* prickly pear, common plant in the coastal areas of the country]
sabre *or U.S.* **saber** (ˈseɪbə) *n.* **1.** a stout single-edged cavalry sword, having a curved blade. **2.** a sword used in fencing, having a narrow V-shaped blade, a semicircular guard, and a slightly curved hand. **3.** a cavalry soldier. ~*vb.* **4.** (*tr.*) to injure or kill with a sabre. [C17: via French from German (dialect) *Sabel,* from Middle High German *sebel,* perhaps from Magyar *szablya;* compare Russian *sablya* sabre]
sabre-rattling *n., adj. Informal.* seeking to intimidate by an aggressive display of military power.
sabretache (ˈsæbəˌtæʃ) *n.* a leather case suspended from a cavalryman's saddle. [C19: via French from German *Säbeltasche* sabre pocket]
sabre-toothed tiger *or* **cat** *n.* any of various extinct Tertiary felines of the genus *Smilodon* and related genera, with long curved upper canine teeth.
sabulous (ˈsæbjʊləs) *or* **sabulose** (ˈsæbjʊləʊs) *adj.* **1.** like sand in texture; gritty. **2.** Also: **sabuline** (ˈsæbjʊliːn). (of plants) growing in sand. [C17: from Latin *sabulōsus,* from *sabulum* SAND] —**sabulosity** (ˌsæbjʊˈlɒsɪtɪ) *n.*
sac (sæk) *n.* a pouch, bag, or pouchlike part in an animal or plant. [C18: from French, from Latin *saccus;* see SACK[1]] —ˈ**sac**ˌ**like** *adj.*
sacaton (ˌsækəˈtəʊn) *n.* a coarse grass, *Sporobolus wrightii,* of the southwestern U.S. and Mexico, grown for hay and pasture. [American Spanish *zacatón,* from *zacate* coarse grass, from Nahuatl *zacatl*]
saccade (səˈkɑːd, -ˈkeɪd) *n.* **1.** the movement of the eye when it makes a sudden change of fixation, as in reading. **2.** a sudden

check given to a horse. [C18: from French: a jerk on the reins of a horse]

saccate ('sækeɪt) *adj. Botany.* in the form of a sac; pouched. [C19: from New Latin *saccatus,* from *saccus:* see SACK[1]]

saccharase ('sækəˌreɪs) *n.* another name for **invertase.**

saccharate ('sækəˌreɪt) *n.* any salt or ester of saccharic acid.

saccharic acid (sæ'kærɪk) *n.* a white soluble solid dicarboxylic acid obtained by the oxidation of cane sugar or starch; 2,3,4,5-tetrahydroxyhexanedioic acid. Formula: $COOH(CHOH)_4COOH$.

saccharide ('sækəˌraɪd, -rɪd) *n.* any sugar or other carbohydrate, esp. a simple sugar.

saccharify (sæ'kærɪˌfaɪ), **saccharize,** *or* **saccharise** ('sækəˌraɪz) *vb.* **-fies, -fying, -fied** *(tr.)* to convert (starch) into sugar. —**sacˌcharifiˈcation, ˌsacchariˈzation,** *or* **ˌsacchariˈsation** *n.*

saccharimeter (ˌsækə'rɪmɪtə) *n.* any instrument for measuring the strength of sugar solutions, esp. a type of polarimeter for determining the concentration from the extent to which the solution rotates the plane of polarized light. —**ˌsacchaˈrimetry** *n.*

saccharin ('sækərɪn) *n.* a very sweet white crystalline slightly soluble powder used as a nonfattening sweetener. Formula: $C_7H_5NO_3S$. [C19: from SACCHARO- + -IN]

saccharine ('sækəˌraɪn, -ˌriːn) *adj.* **1.** excessively sweet; sugary: *a saccharine smile.* **2.** of, relating to, of the nature of, or containing sugar or saccharin. —**'saccharinely** *adv.* —**saccharinity** (ˌsækə'rɪnɪtɪ) *n.*

saccharo- *or before a vowel* **sacchar-** *combining form.* sugar: *saccharomycete.* [via Latin from Greek *sakkharon,* ultimately from Sanskrit *śarkarā* sugar]

saccharoid ('sækəˌrɔɪd) *adj.* **1.** Also: **ˌsacchaˈroidal.** *Geology.* having or designating a texture resembling that of loaf sugar: *saccharoid marble.* ~*n.* **2.** *Biochem.* any of a group of polysaccharides that remotely resemble sugars, but are not sweet and are often insoluble.

saccharometer (ˌsækə'rɒmɪtə) *n.* a hydrometer used to measure the strengths of sugar solutions. It is usually calibrated directly to give a reading of concentration.

saccharose ('sækəˌrəʊz, -ˌrəʊs) *n.* a technical name for **sugar** (sense 1).

saccular ('sækjʊlə) *adj.* of or resembling a sac.

sacculate ('sækjʊlɪt, -ˌleɪt) *or* **sacculated** *adj.* of, relating to, or possessing a saccule, saccules, or a sacculus. —**ˌsaccuˈlation** *n.*

saccule ('sækjuːl) *or* **sacculus** ('sækjʊləs) *n., pl.* **-cules** *or* **-li** (liː). **1.** a small sac. **2.** the smaller of the two parts of the membranous labyrinth of the internal ear. Compare **utricle** (sense 1). [C19: from Latin *sacculus* diminutive of *saccus* SACK[1]]

sacculiform (sæ'kjʊlɪˌfɔːm) *adj. Biology.* (of plant parts, etc.) shaped like a small sac.

sacerdotal (ˌsæsə'dəʊtᵊl) *adj.* of, relating to, or characteristic of priests. [C14: from Latin *sacerdōtālis,* from *sacerdōs* priest, from *sacer* sacred] —**ˌsacerˈdotally** *adv.*

sacerdotalism (ˌsæsə'dəʊtᵊˌlɪzəm) *n.* **1.** the principles, methods, etc., of the priesthood. **2.** the belief that ordained priests are endowed with sacramental and sacrificial powers. **3.** exaggerated respect for priests. **4.** *Derogatory.* power over people's opinions and actions achieved by priests through sophistry or guile. —**ˌsacerˈdotalist** *n.*

sachem ('seɪtʃəm) *n.* **1.** *U.S.* a leader of a political party or organization, esp. of Tammany Hall. **2.** another name for **sagamore.** [C17: from Narraganset *sâchim* chief] —**sachemic** (seɪ'tʃɛmɪk, 'seɪtʃə-) *adj.*

sachet ('sæʃeɪ) *n.* **1.** a small sealed envelope, usually made of plastic or waxed paper, for containing cream, shampoo, etc. **2. a.** a small soft bag containing perfumed powder, placed in drawers to scent clothing. **b.** the powder contained in such a bag. [C19: from Old French: a little bag, from *sac* bag; see SACK[1]]

sack[1] (sæk) *n.* **1.** a large bag made of coarse cloth, thick paper, etc., used as a container. **2.** Also called: **'sackˌful.** the amount contained in a sack, sometimes used as a unit of measurement. **3. a.** a woman's loose tube-shaped dress. **b.** Also called: **sacque.** a woman's full loose hip-length jacket, worn in the 18th and mid-20th centuries. **4.** short for **rucksack. 5.** *Cricket.* the Australian word for **bye. 6. the sack.** *Informal.* dismissal from employment. **7.** a slang word for **bed. 8.** *American football.* a tackle on a quarterback which brings him down before he has passed the ball. **9. hit the sack.** *Slang.* to go to bed. **10. rough as sacks.** *N.Z.* uncouth. ~*vb. (tr.)* **11.** *Informal.* to dismiss from employment. **12.** to put into a sack or sacks. **13.** *American football.* to tackle and bring down a quarterback before he has passed the ball. [Old English *sacc,* from Latin *saccus* bag, from Greek *sakkos;* related to Hebrew *saq*] —**'sackˌlike** *adj.*

sack[2] (sæk) *n.* **1.** the plundering of a place by an army or mob, usually involving destruction, slaughter, etc. ~*vb.* **2.** *(tr.)* to plunder and partially destroy (a place). [C16: from French phrase *mettre à sac,* literally: to put (loot) in a sack, from Latin *saccus* SACK[1]] —**'sacker** *n.*

sack[3] (sæk) *n. Archaic except in trademarks.* any dry white wine formerly imported into Britain from SW Europe. [C16 *wyne seck,* from French *vin sec* dry wine, from Latin *siccus* dry]

sackbut ('sækˌbʌt) *n.* a medieval form of trombone. [C16: from French *saqueboute,* from Old French *saquer* to pull + *bouter* to push; see BUTT[3]: used in the Bible (Daniel 3) as a mistranslation of Aramaic *sabb'ka* stringed instrument]

sackcloth ('sækˌklɒθ) *n.* **1.** coarse cloth such as sacking. **2.** garments made of such cloth, worn formerly to indicate mourning or penitence. **3. sackcloth and ashes.** a public display of extreme grief, remorse, or repentance.

sacking ('sækɪŋ) *n.* coarse cloth used for making sacks, woven from flax, hemp, jute, etc.

sack race *n.* a race in which the competitors' legs and often bodies are enclosed in sacks. —**sack racing** *n.*

sacral[1] ('seɪkrəl) *adj.* of, relating to, or associated with sacred rites. [C19: from Latin *sacrum* sacred object]

sacral[2] ('seɪkrəl) *adj.* of or relating to the sacrum. [C18: from New Latin *sacrālis* of the SACRUM]

sacrament ('sækrəmənt) *n.* **1.** an outward sign combined with a prescribed form of words and regarded as conferring some specific grace upon those who receive it. The Protestant sacraments are baptism and the Lord's Supper. In the Roman Catholic and Eastern Churches they are baptism, penance, confirmation, the Eucharist, holy orders, matrimony, and the anointing of the sick (formerly extreme unction). **2.** *(often cap.)* the Eucharist. **3.** the consecrated elements of the Eucharist, esp. the bread. **4.** something regarded as possessing a sacred or mysterious significance. **5.** a symbol; pledge. [C12: from Church Latin *sacrāmentum* vow, from Latin *sacrāre* to consecrate]

sacramental (ˌsækrə'mɛntᵊl) *adj.* **1.** of, relating to, or having the nature of a sacrament. **2.** bound by or as if by a sacrament. ~*n.* **3.** *R.C. Church.* a sacrament-like ritual action, such as the sign of the cross or the use of holy water. —**ˌsacraˈmentally** *adv.* —**sacramentality** (ˌsækrəmɛn'tælɪtɪ) *or* **ˌsacraˈmentalness** *n.*

sacramentalism (ˌsækrə'mɛntᵊˌlɪzəm) *n.* belief in or special emphasis upon the efficacy of the sacraments for conferring grace. —**ˌsacraˈmentalist** *n.*

Sacramentarian (ˌsækrəmɛn'tɛərɪən) *n.* **1.** any Protestant theologian who maintained that the bread and wine of the Eucharist were the body and blood of Christ only in a figurative sense and denied his real presence in these elements. **2.** one who believes in sacramentalism. ~*adj.* **3.** of or relating to Sacramentarians. **4.** *(not cap.)* of or relating to sacraments. —**ˌSacramenˈtarianism** *n.*

sacrarium (sæ'krɛərɪəm) *n., pl.* **-craria** (-'krɛərɪə). **1.** the sanctuary of a church. **2.** *R.C. Church.* a place near the altar of a church, similar in function to the piscina, where materials used in the sacred rites are deposited or poured away. [C18: from Latin *sacrārium,* from *sacer* SACRED]

sacred ('seɪkrɪd) *adj.* **1.** exclusively devoted to a deity or to some religious ceremony or use; holy; consecrated. **2.** worthy of or regarded with reverence, awe, or respect. **3.** protected by superstition or piety from irreligious actions. **4.** connected with or intended for religious use: *sacred music.* **5. sacred to.** dedicated to; in honour of. [C14: from Latin *sacrāre* to set apart as holy, from *sacer* holy] —**'sacredly** *adv.* —**'sacredness** *n.*

Sacred College *n.* the collective body of the cardinals of the Roman Catholic Church.

sacred cow *n. Informal.* a person, institution, custom, etc., unreasonably held to be beyond criticism. [alluding to the Hindu belief that cattle are sacred]

Sacred Heart *n. R.C. Church.* **1.** the heart of Jesus Christ, a symbol of His love and sacrifice. **2.** a representation of this, usually bleeding, as an aid to devotion.

sacred mushroom *n.* **1.** any of various hallucinogenic mushrooms, esp. species of *Psilocybe* and *Amanita,* that have been eaten in rituals in various parts of the world. **2.** a mescal button, used in a similar way.

sacrifice ('sækrɪˌfaɪs) *n.* **1.** a surrender of something of value as a means of gaining something more desirable or of preventing some evil. **2.** a ritual killing of a person or animal with the intention of propitiating or pleasing a deity. **3.** a symbolic offering of something to a deity. **4.** the person, animal, or object surrendered, destroyed, killed, or offered. **5.** a religious ceremony involving one or more sacrifices. **6.** loss entailed by giving up or selling something at less than its value. **7.** *Chess.* the act or an instance of sacrificing a piece. ~*vb.* **8.** to make a sacrifice (of); give up, surrender, or destroy (a person, thing, etc.). **9.** *Chess.* to permit or force one's opponent to capture (a piece) freely, as in playing a combination or gambit: *he sacrificed his queen and checkmated his opponent on the next move.* [C13: via Old French from Latin *sacrificium,* from *sacer* holy + *facere* to make] —**'sacriˌficeable** *adj.* —**'sacriˌficer** *n.*

sacrifice paddock *n. N.Z.* a grassed area allowed to be grazed completely, to be cultivated and resown later.

sacrificial (ˌsækrɪ'fɪʃəl) *adj.* used in or connected with a sacrifice. —**ˌsacriˈficially** *adv.*

sacrificial anode *n. Metallurgy.* an electropositive metal, such as zinc, that protects a more important electronegative part by corroding when attacked by electrolytic action.

sacrilege ('sækrɪlɪdʒ) *n.* **1.** the misuse or desecration of anything regarded as sacred or as worthy of extreme respect: *to play Mozart's music on a kazoo is sacrilege.* **2.** the act or an instance of taking anything sacred for secular use. [C13: from Old French *sacrilège,* from Latin *sacrilegium,* from *sacrilegus* temple-robber, from *sacra* sacred things + *legere* to take] —**sacrilegist** (ˌsækrɪˈliːdʒɪst) *n.*

sacrilegious (ˌsækrɪˈlɪdʒəs) *adj.* **1.** of, relating to, or involving sacrilege; impious. **2.** guilty of sacrilege. —ˌ**sacriˈlegiously** *adv.* —ˌ**sacriˈlegiousness** *n.*

sacring (ˈseɪkrɪŋ) *n. Archaic.* the act or ritual of consecration, esp. of the Eucharist or of a bishop. [C13: from obsolete *sacren* to consecrate, from Latin *sacrāre;* see SACRED]

sacring bell *n. Chiefly R.C. Church.* a small bell rung at the elevation of the Host and chalice during Mass.

sacristan (ˈsækrɪstən) *or* **sacrist** (ˈsækrɪst, ˈseɪ-) *n.* **1.** a person who has charge of the contents of a church, esp. the sacred vessels, vestments, etc. **2.** a less common word for **sexton** (sense 1). [C14: from Medieval Latin *sacristānus,* from *sacrista,* from Latin *sacer* holy]

sacristy (ˈsækrɪstɪ) *n., pl.* **-ties.** a room attached to a church or chapel where the sacred vessels, vestments, etc., are kept and where priests attire themselves. [C17: from Medieval Latin *sacristia;* see SACRISTAN]

sacroiliac (ˌseɪkrəʊˈɪlɪˌæk, ˌsæk-) *Anatomy.* ~*adj.* **1.** of or relating to the sacrum and ilium, their articulation, or their associated ligaments. ~*n.* **2.** the joint where these bones meet.

sacrosanct (ˈsækrəʊˌsæŋkt) *adj.* very sacred or holy; inviolable. [C17: from Latin *sacrōsanctus* made holy by sacred rite, from *sacrō* by sacred rite, from *sacer* holy + *sanctus,* from *sancīre* to hallow] —ˌ**sacroˈsanctity** *or* ˈ**sacroˌsanctness** *n.*

sacrum (ˈseɪkrəm, ˈsækrəm) *n., pl.* **-cra** (-krə). **1.** (in man) the large wedge-shaped bone, consisting of five fused vertebrae, in the lower part of the back. **2.** the corresponding part in some other vertebrates. [C18: from Latin *os sacrum* holy bone, because it was used in sacrifices, from *sacer* holy]

sad (sæd) *adj.* **sadder, saddest. 1.** feeling sorrow; unhappy. **2.** causing, suggestive, or expressive of such feelings: *a sad story.* **3.** unfortunate; unsatisfactory; shabby; deplorable: *her clothes were in a sad state.* **4.** (of pastry, cakes, etc.) not having risen fully; heavy. **5.** (of a colour) lacking brightness; dull or dark. **6.** *Archaic.* serious; grave. [Old English *sæd* weary; related to Old Norse *sathr,* Gothic *saths,* Latin *satur, satis* enough] —ˈ**sadly** *adv.* —ˈ**sadness** *n.*

SAD *abbrev. for* seasonal affective disorder.

sadden (ˈsædᵊn) *vb.* to make or become sad.

saddle (ˈsædᵊl) *n.* **1.** a seat for a rider, usually made of leather, placed on a horse's back and secured with a girth under the belly. **2.** a similar seat on a bicycle, tractor, etc., made of leather or steel. **3.** a back pad forming part of the harness of a packhorse. **4.** anything that resembles a saddle in shape, position, or function. **5.** a cut of meat, esp. mutton, consisting of part of the backbone and both loins. **6.** the part of a horse or similar animal on which a saddle is placed. **7.** the part of the back of a domestic chicken that is nearest to the tail. **8.** *Civil engineering.* a block on top of one of the towers of a suspension bridge over which the cables or chains pass. **9.** *Engineering.* the carriage that slides on the bed of a lathe and supports the slide rest, tool post, or turret. **10.** the nontechnical name for **clitellum. 11.** another name for **col** (sense 1). **12.** a raised piece of wood or metal for covering a doorsill. **13. in the saddle.** in a position of control. ~*vb.* **14.** (sometimes foll. by *up*) to put a saddle on (a horse). **15.** (*intr.*) to mount into the saddle. **16.** (*tr.*) to burden; charge: *I didn't ask to be saddled with this job.* [Old English *sadol, sædel;* related to Old Norse *sothull,* Old High German *satul*] —ˈ**saddleless** *adj.* —ˈ**saddle-ˌlike** *adj.*

saddleback (ˈsædᵊlˌbæk) *n.* **1.** a marking resembling a saddle on the backs of various animals. **2.** a rare bird of New Zealand, *Philesturnus carunculatus,* having a chestnut-coloured saddle-shaped marking across its back and wings. **3.** another name for **saddle roof. 4.** another name for **col** (sense 1).

saddle-backed *adj.* **1.** having the back curved in shape or concave like a saddle. **2.** having a saddleback.

saddlebag (ˈsædᵊlˌbæg) *n.* a pouch or small bag attached to the saddle of a horse, bicycle, etc.

saddlebill (ˈsædᵊlˌbɪl) *n.* a large black-and-white stork, *Ephippiorhynchus senegalensis,* of tropical Africa, having a heavy red bill with a black band around the middle and a yellow patch at the base. Also called: **jabiru.** [C19 (as *saddle-bill stork*): so called because of the appearance of its bill]

saddle block *n. Surgery.* a type of spinal anaesthesia producing sensory loss in the buttocks, inner sides of the thighs, and perineum.

saddlebow (ˈsædᵊlˌbəʊ) *n.* the pommel of a saddle.

saddlecloth (ˈsædᵊlˌklɒθ) *n.* a light cloth put under a horse's saddle, so as to prevent rubbing.

saddle horse *n.* a lightweight horse kept for riding only. Compare **carthorse.** Also called: **saddler.**

saddler (ˈsædlə) *n.* a person who makes, deals in, or repairs saddles and other leather equipment for horses.

saddle roof *n.* a roof that has a ridge and two gables. Also called: **saddleback.**

saddlery (ˈsædlərɪ) *n., pl.* **-dleries. 1.** saddles, harness, and other leather equipment for horses collectively. **2.** the business, work, or place of work of a saddler.

saddle soap *n.* a soft soap containing neat's-foot oil used to preserve and clean leather.

saddle-sore *adj.* **1.** sore after riding a horse. **2.** (of a horse or rider) having sores caused by the chafing of the saddle. ~*n.* **saddle sore. 3.** such a sore.

saddletree (ˈsædᵊlˌtriː) *n.* the frame of a saddle.

Sadducee (ˈsædjʊˌsiː) *n. Judaism.* a member of an ancient Jewish sect that was opposed to the Pharisees, denying the resurrection of the dead, the existence of angels, and the validity of oral tradition. [Old English *saddūcēas,* via Latin and Greek from Late Hebrew *ṣāddūqī,* probably from *Ṣadoq* Zadok, high priest and supposed founder of the sect] —ˌ**Sadduˈcean** *adj.* —ˈ**Sadduˌceeism** *n.*

sadhe, sade, *or* **tsade** (ˈsɑːdiː, ˈtsɑːdiː; *Hebrew* ˈtsadiː) *n.* the 18th letter in the Hebrew alphabet (צ or, at the end of a word ץ), transliterated as *s* or *ts* and pronounced more or less like English *s* or *ts* with pharyngeal articulation.

sadhu *or* **saddhu** (ˈsɑːduː) *n.* a Hindu wandering holy man. [Sanskrit, from *sādhu* good]

sadiron (ˈsædˌaɪən) *n.* a heavy iron pointed at both ends, for pressing clothes. [C19: from SAD (in the obsolete sense: heavy) + IRON]

sadism (ˈseɪdɪzəm, ˈsæ-) *n.* the gaining of pleasure or sexual gratification from the infliction of pain and mental suffering on another person. See also **algolagnia.** Compare **masochism.** [C19: from French, named after the Marquis de *Sade* (1740–1814), French soldier and writer] —ˈ**sadist** *n.* —**sadistic** (səˈdɪstɪk) *adj.* —**saˈdistically** *adv.*

sadomasochism (ˌseɪdəʊˈmæsəˌkɪzəm, ˌsædəʊ-) *n.* **1.** the combination of sadistic and masochistic elements in one person, characterized by both aggressive and submissive periods in relationships with others. **2.** sexual practice in which one partner adopts a sadistic role and the other a masochistic one. Abbrev.: **s/m.** Compare **sadism, masochism.** —ˌ**sadomasoˈchistic** *adj.*

sad sack *n. U.S. slang.* an inept person who makes mistakes despite good intentions. [C20: from a cartoon character created by G. Baker, U.S. cartoonist]

sae (se) *adv.* a Scot. word for **so**[1].

SAE (in the U.S.) *abbrev. for* Society of Automotive Engineers.

s.a.e. *abbrev. for* stamped addressed envelope.

Safar *or* **Saphar** (səˈfɑː) *n.* the second month of the Muslim year. [from Arabic]

safari (səˈfɑːrɪ) *n., pl.* **-ris. 1.** an overland journey or hunting expedition, esp. in Africa. **2.** the people, animals, etc., that go on the expedition. [C19: from Swahili: journey, from Arabic *safarīya,* from *safara* to travel]

safari jacket *n.* another name for **bush jacket.**

safari park *n.* an enclosed park in which lions and other wild animals are kept uncaged in the open and can be viewed by the public from cars, etc.

safari suit *n.* an outfit made of tough cotton, denim, etc., consisting of a bush jacket with matching trousers, shorts, or skirt.

safe (seɪf) *adj.* **1.** affording security or protection from harm: *a safe place.* **2.** (*postpositive*) free from danger: *you'll be safe here.* **3.** secure from risk; certain; sound: *a safe investment; a safe bet.* **4.** worthy of trust; prudent: *a safe companion.* **5.** tending to avoid controversy or risk: *a safe player.* **6.** unable to do harm; not dangerous: *a criminal safe behind bars; water safe to drink.* **7. on the safe side.** as a precaution. ~*adv.* **8.** in a safe condition: *the children are safe in bed now.* **9. play safe.** to act in a way least likely to cause danger, controversy, or defeat. ~*n.* **10.** a strong container, usually of metal and provided with a secure lock, for storing money or valuables. **11.** a small ventilated cupboard-like container for storing food. **12.** *U.S. and Canadian.* a slang word for **condom.** [C13: from Old French *salf,* from Latin *salvus;* related to Latin *salus* safety] —ˈ**safely** *adv.* —ˈ**safeness** *n.*

safe-blower *n.* a person who uses explosives to open safes and rob them.

safe-breaker *n.* a person who breaks open and robs safes. Also called: **safe-cracker.**

safe-conduct *n.* **1.** a document giving official permission to travel through a region, esp. in time of war. **2.** the protection afforded by such a document. ~*vb.* (*tr.*) **3.** to conduct (a person) in safety. **4.** to give a safe-conduct to.

safe-deposit *or* **safety-deposit** *n.* **a.** a place or building with facilities for the safe storage of money or valuables. **b.** (*as modifier*): *a safe-deposit box.*

safeguard (ˈseɪfˌgɑːd) *n.* **1.** a person or thing that ensures protection against danger, damage, injury, etc. **2.** a document authorizing safe-conduct. ~*vb.* **3.** (*tr.*) to defend or protect.

safe house *n.* a place used secretly by undercover agents, terrorists, etc., as a meeting place or refuge.

safekeeping (ˈseɪfˈkiːpɪŋ) *n.* the act of keeping or state of being kept in safety.

safelight (ˈseɪfˌlaɪt) *n. Photog.* a light that can be used in a room in which photographic material is handled, transmitting only those colours to which a particular type of film, plate, or paper is relatively insensitive.

safe period *n. Informal.* the period during the menstrual cycle when conception is considered least likely to occur. See also **rhythm method.**

safe seat *n.* a Parliamentary seat that at an election is sure to be held by the same party as held it before.

safe sex *n.* sexual intercourse using physical protection, such as a condom, or nonpenetrative methods to prevent the spread of such diseases as AIDS.

safety ('seɪftɪ) *n., pl.* **-ties.** 1. the quality of being safe. 2. freedom from danger or risk of injury. 3. a contrivance or device designed to prevent injury. 4. *American football.* a. Also called: **'safety,man.** the defensive player furthest back in the field. b. a play in which the offensive team causes the ball to cross its own goal line and then grounds the ball behind that line, scoring two points for the opposing team. Compare **touchback.**

safety belt *n.* 1. another name for **seat belt.** 2. a belt or strap worn by a person working at a great height and attached to a fixed object to prevent him from falling.

safety catch *n.* a device to prevent the accidental operation of a mechanism, e.g. in a firearm or lift.

safety chain *n.* a chain on the fastening of a bracelet, watch, etc., to ensure that it cannot open enough to fall off accidentally. Also called: **guard.**

safety curtain *n.* a curtain made of fireproof material that can be lowered to separate the auditorium and stage in a theatre to prevent the spread of a fire.

safety factor *n.* another name for **factor of safety.**

safety film *n.* photographic film consisting of a nonflammable cellulose acetate or polyester base.

safety fuse *n.* 1. a slow-burning fuse for igniting detonators from a distance. 2. an electrical fuse that protects a circuit from overloading.

safety glass *n.* glass made by sandwiching a layer of plastic or resin between two sheets of glass so that if broken the fragments will not shatter.

safety lamp *n.* an oil-burning miner's lamp in which the flame is surrounded by a metal gauze to prevent it from igniting combustible gas. Also called: **Davy lamp.**

safety match *n.* a match that will light only when struck against a specially prepared surface.

safety net *n.* 1. a net used in a circus to catch high-wire and trapeze artistes if they fall. 2. any means of protection from hardship or loss, such as insurance.

safety pin *n.* 1. a spring wire clasp with a covering catch, made so as to shield the point when closed and to prevent accidental unfastening. 2. another word for **pin** (sense 9).

safety razor *n.* a razor with a guard or guards fitted close to the cutting edge or edges so that deep cuts are prevented and the risk of accidental cuts reduced.

safety valve *n.* 1. a valve in a pressure vessel that allows fluid to escape when a predetermined level of pressure has been reached. 2. a harmless outlet for emotion, energy, etc.

saffian ('sæfɪən) *n.* leather tanned with sumach and usually dyed a bright colour. [C16: via Russian and Turkish from Persian *sakhtiyān* goatskin, from *sakht* hard]

safflower ('sæflaʊə) *n.* 1. a thistle-like Eurasian annual plant, *Carthamus tinctorius,* having large heads of orange-yellow flowers and yielding a dye and an oil used in paints, medicines, etc.: family *Compositae* (composites). 2. a red dye used for cotton and for colouring foods and cosmetics, or a drug obtained from the florets of this plant. ~Also called: **false saffron.** [C16: via Dutch *saffloer* or German *safflor* from Old French *saffleur,* from Early Italian *saffiore,* of uncertain origin. Influenced by SAFFRON, FLOWER]

saffron ('sæfrən) *n.* 1. an Old World crocus, *Crocus sativus,* having purple or white flowers with orange stigmas. 2. the dried stigmas of this plant, used to flavour or colour food. 3. **meadow saffron.** another name for **autumn crocus.** 4. **false saffron.** another name for **safflower.** 5. a. an orange to orange-yellow colour. b. (*as adj.*): *a saffron dress.* [C13: from Old French *safran,* from Medieval Latin *safranum,* from Arabic *za'farān*]

S.Afr. *abbrev. for* South Africa(n).

safranine *or* **safranin** ('sæfrənɪn, -ˌniːn) *n.* any of a class of azine dyes, used for textiles and biological stains. [C19: from French *safran* SAFFRON + -INE²]

safrole ('sæfrəʊl) *n.* a colourless or yellowish oily water-insoluble liquid present in sassafras and camphor oils and used in soaps and perfumes. Formula: $C_3H_5C_6H_3O_2CH_2$. [C19: from (SAS)SAFR(AS) + -OLE¹]

saft (sæft) *adj.* a Scot. word for **soft.**

sag (sæg) *vb.* (*mainly intr.*) **sags, sagging, sagged.** 1. (*also tr.*) to sink or cause to sink in parts, as under weight or pressure: *the bed sags in the middle.* 2. to fall in value: *prices sagged to a new low.* 3. to hang unevenly; droop. 4. (of courage, spirits, etc.) to weaken; flag. ~*n.* 5. the act or an instance of sagging: *a sag in profits.* 6. *Nautical.* the extent to which a vessel's keel sags at the centre. Compare **hog** (sense 7), **hogged.** 7. a. a marshy depression in an area of glacial till, chiefly in the U.S. Middle West. b. (*as modifier*): *sag and swell topography.* [C15: from Scandinavian; compare Swedish *sacka,* Dutch *zakken,* Norwegian dialect *sakka* to subside, Danish *sakke* to lag behind]

saga ('sɑːgə) *n.* 1. any of several medieval prose narratives written in Iceland and recounting the exploits of a hero or a family. 2. any similar heroic narrative. 3. Also called: **saga novel.** a series of novels about several generations or members of a family. 4. any other artistic production said to resemble a saga. 5. *Informal.* a series of events or a story stretching over a long period. [C18: from Old Norse: a narrative; related to Old English *secgan* to SAY]

sagacious (sə'geɪʃəs) *adj.* 1. having or showing sagacity; wise. 2. *Obsolete.* (of hounds) having an acute sense of smell. [C17: from Latin *sagāx,* from *sāgīre* to be astute] —**sa'gaciously** *adv.* —**sa'gaciousness** *n.*

sagacity (sə'gæsɪtɪ) *n.* foresight, discernment, or keen perception; ability to make good judgments.

sagamore ('sægəˌmɔː) *n.* (among some North American Indians) a chief or eminent man. Also called: **sachem.** [C17: from Abnaki *sāgimau,* literally: he overcomes]

sag bag *n.* another name for **bean bag** (sense 2).

sage¹ (seɪdʒ) *n.* 1. a man revered for his profound wisdom. ~*adj.* 2. profoundly wise or prudent. 3. *Obsolete.* solemn. [C13: from Old French, from Latin *sapere* to be sensible; see SAPIENT] —**'sagely** *adv.* —**'sageness** *n.*

sage² (seɪdʒ) *n.* 1. a perennial Mediterranean plant, *Salvia officinalis,* having grey-green leaves and purple, blue, or white flowers: family *Labiatae* (labiates). 2. the leaves of this plant, used in cooking for flavouring. 3. short for **sagebrush.** [C14: from Old French *saulge,* from Latin *salvia,* from *salvus* safe, in good health (from the curative properties attributed to the plant)]

sagebrush ('seɪdʒˌbrʌʃ) *n.* any of several aromatic plants of the genus *Artemisia,* esp. *A. tridentata,* a shrub of W North America, having silver-green leaves and large clusters of small white flowers: family *Compositae* (composites).

sage Derby *n.* See **Derby**² (sense 2).

sage grouse *n.* a large North American grouse, *Centrocercus urophasianus,* the males of which perform elaborate courtship displays. [C19: so named because it lives among, and eats, SAGEBRUSH]

saggar *or* **sagger** ('sægə) *n.* a clay box in which fragile ceramic wares are placed for protection during firing. [C17: perhaps alteration of SAFEGUARD]

Sagitta (sə'gɪtə) *n., Latin genitive* **Sagittae** (sə'gɪtiː). a small constellation in the N hemisphere lying between Cygnus and Aquila and crossed by the Milky Way. [C16: from Latin, literally: an arrow]

sagittal ('sædʒɪtᵊl) *adj.* 1. resembling an arrow; straight. 2. of or relating to the sagittal suture. 3. situated in a plane parallel to the sagittal suture. —**'sagittally** *adv.*

sagittal suture *n.* a serrated line on the top of the skull that marks the junction of the two parietal bones.

Sagittarius (ˌsædʒɪ'tɛərɪəs) *n., Latin genitive* **Sagittarii** (ˌsædʒɪ'tɛərɪˌaɪ). 1. *Astronomy.* a large conspicuous zodiacal constellation in the S hemisphere lying between Scorpius and Capricornus on the ecliptic and crossed by the Milky Way. 2. Also called: the **Archer.** *Astrology.* a. the ninth sign of the zodiac, symbol ♐, having a mutable fire classification and ruled by the planet Jupiter. The sun is in this sign between Nov. 22 and Dec. 21. b. a person born when the sun is in this sign. ~*adj.* 3. *Astrology.* born under or characteristic of Sagittarius. ~Also (for senses 2b, 3): **Sagittarian** (ˌsædʒɪ'tɛərɪən). [C14: from Latin: an archer, from *sagitta* an arrow]

sagittate ('sædʒɪˌteɪt) *or* **sagittiform** (sə'dʒɪtɪˌfɔːm, 'sædʒ-) *adj.* (esp. of leaves) shaped like the head of an arrow. [C18: from New Latin *sagittātus,* from Latin *sagitta* arrow]

sago ('seɪgəʊ) *n.* a starchy cereal obtained from the powdered pith of a sago palm, used for puddings and as a thickening agent. [C16: from Malay *sāgū*]

sago grass *n. Austral.* a tall tough grass, *Paspalidum globoideum,* grown as forage for cattle.

sago palm *n.* 1. any of various tropical Asian palm trees, esp. any of the genera *Metroxylon, Arenga,* and *Caryota,* the trunks of which yield sago. 2. any of several palmlike cycads that yield sago, esp. *Cycas revoluta.*

saguaro (sə'gwɑːrəʊ, sə'wɑː-) *or* **sahuaro** (sə'wɑːrəʊ) *n., pl.* **-ros.** a giant cactus, *Carnegiea gigantea,* of desert regions of Arizona, S California, and Mexico, having white nocturnal flowers and edible red pulpy fruits. [Mexican Spanish, variant of *sahuaro,* an Indian name]

Sahaptin (sɑː'hæptɪn), **Sahaptan** (sɑː'hæptən), *or* **Sahaptian** (sɑː'hæptɪən) *n.* 1. (*pl.* **-tins, -tans, -tians** *or* **-tin, -tan, -tian**) a member of a North American Indian people of Oregon and Washington, including the Nez Percé. 2. the language of this people. ~Also: **Shahaptin** (ʃə'hæptɪn).

Saharan (sə'hɑːrən) *n.* 1. a group of languages spoken in parts of Chad and adjacent countries, now generally regarded as forming a branch of the Nilo-Saharan family. ~*adj.* 2. relating to or belonging to this group of languages. 3. of or relating to the Sahara, a desert in N Africa.

sahib ('sɑːhɪb) *or* **saheb** ('sɑːhɛb) *n.* (in India) a form of address or title placed after a man's name or designation, used as a mark of respect. [C17: from Urdu, from Arabic *çāhib,* literally: friend]

saice (saɪs) *n.* a variant spelling of **syce.**

said¹ (sɛd) *adj.* 1. (*prenominal*) (in contracts, pleadings, etc.) named or mentioned previously; aforesaid. ~*vb.* 2. the past tense and past participle of **say**¹.

said² ('sɑːɪd) *n.* a variant of **sayyid.**

saiga ('saɪgə) *n.* either of two antelopes, *Saiga tatarica* or *S. mongolica,* of the plains of central Asia, having an enlarged slightly elongated nose. [C19: from Russian]

sail (seɪl) *n.* **1.** an area of fabric, usually Terylene or nylon (formerly canvas), with fittings for holding it in any suitable position to catch the wind, used for propelling certain kinds of vessels, esp. over water. **2.** a voyage on such a vessel: *a sail down the river.* **3.** a vessel with sails or such vessels collectively: *to travel by sail; we raised seven sail in the northeast.* **4.** a ship's sails collectively. **5.** something resembling a sail in shape, position, or function, such as the part of a windmill that is turned by the wind or the part of a Portuguese man-of-war that projects above the water. **6.** the conning tower of a submarine. **7. in sail.** having the sail set. **8. make sail. a.** to run up the sail or to run up more sail. **b.** to begin a voyage. **9. set sail. a.** to embark on a voyage by ship. **b.** to hoist sail. **10. under sail. a.** with sail hoisted. **b.** under way. ~*vb.* (*mainly intr.*) **11.** to travel in a boat or ship: *we sailed to Le Havre.* **12.** to begin a voyage; set sail: *we sail at 5 o'clock.* **13.** (of a vessel) to move over the water: *the liner is sailing to the Caribbean.* **14.** (*tr.*) to manoeuvre or navigate a vessel: *he sailed the schooner up the channel.* **15.** (*tr.*) to sail over: *she sailed the Atlantic single-handed.* **16.** (often foll. by *over, through,* etc.) to move fast or effortlessly: *we sailed through customs; the ball sailed over the fence.* **17.** to move along smoothly; glide. **18.** (often foll. by *in* or *into*) *Informal.* **a.** to begin (something) with vigour. **b.** to make an attack (on) violently with words or physical force. [Old English *segl;* related to Old Frisian *seil,* Old Norse *segl,* German *Segel*] —ˈ**sailable** *adj.* —ˈ**sailless** *adj.*

sailboard (ˈseɪlˌbɔːd) *n.* the craft used for windsurfing, consisting of a moulded board like a surfboard, to which a mast bearing a single sail is attached by a swivel joint.

sailboarding (ˈseɪlˌbɔːdɪŋ) *n.* another name for **windsurfing.**

sailcloth (ˈseɪlˌklɒθ) *n.* **1.** any of various fabrics from which sails are made. **2.** a lighter cloth used for clothing, etc.

sailer (ˈseɪlə) *n.* a vessel, esp. one equipped with sails, with specified sailing characteristics: *a good sailer.*

sailfish (ˈseɪlˌfɪʃ) *n., pl.* **-fish** *or* **-fishes. 1.** any of several large scombroid game fishes of the genus *Istiophorus,* such as *I. albicans* (**Atlantic sailfish**), of warm and tropical seas: family *Istiophoridae.* They have an elongated upper jaw and a long sail-like dorsal fin. **2.** another name for **basking shark.**

sailing (ˈseɪlɪŋ) *n.* **1.** the practice, art, or technique of sailing a vessel. **2.** a method of navigating a vessel: *rhumb-line sailing.* **3.** an instance of a vessel's leaving a port: *scheduled for a midnight sailing.*

sailing boat *or esp. U.S. and Canadian* **sailboat** (ˈseɪlˌbəʊt) *n.* a boat propelled chiefly by sail.

sailing ship *n.* a large sailing vessel.

sailor (ˈseɪlə) *n.* **1.** any member of a ship's crew, esp. one below the rank of officer. **2.** a person who sails, esp. with reference to the likelihood of his becoming seasick: *a good sailor.* **3.** short for **sailor hat** or **sailor suit.** —ˈ**sailorly** *adj.*

sailor hat *n.* a hat with a flat round crown and fairly broad brim that is rolled upwards.

sailor's-choice *n.* any of various small percoid fishes of American coastal regions of the Atlantic, esp. the grunt *Haemulon parra* and the pinfish.

sailor suit *n.* a child's suit, usually navy and white, with a collar that is squared off at the back like a sailor's.

sailplane (ˈseɪlˌpleɪn) *n.* a high-performance glider.

sain (seɪn) *vb.* (*tr.*) *Archaic.* to make the sign of the cross over so as to bless or protect from evil or sin. [Old English *segnian,* from Latin *signare* to SIGN (with the cross)]

sainfoin (ˈsænfɔɪn) *n.* a Eurasian perennial papilionaceous plant, *Onobrychis viciifolia,* widely grown as a forage crop, having pale pink flowers and curved pods. [C17: from French, from Medieval Latin *sānum faenum* wholesome hay, referring to its former use as a medicine]

saint (seɪnt; *unstressed* sənt) *n.* **1.** a person who after death is formally recognized by a Christian Church, esp. the Roman Catholic Church, as having attained, through holy deeds or behaviour, a specially exalted place in heaven and the right to veneration. **2.** a person of exceptional holiness or goodness. **3.** (*pl.*) *Bible.* the collective body of those who are righteous in God's sight. ~*vb.* **4.** (*tr.*) to canonize; recognize formally as a saint. [C12: from Old French, from Latin *sanctus* holy, from *sancīre* to hallow] —ˈ**saintdom** *n.* —ˈ**saintless** *adj.* —ˈ**saintlike** *adj.*

Saint Agnes's Eve (ˈægnɪsɪz) *n., usually abbreviated to* **St Agnes's Eve.** the night of Jan. 20, when according to tradition a woman can discover the identity of her future husband by performing certain rites.

Saint Andrew's Cross (ˈændruːz) *n., usually abbreviated to* **St Andrew's Cross. 1.** a diagonal cross with equal arms. **2.** a white diagonal cross on a blue ground. [C18: so called because *Saint Andrew* is reputed to have been crucified on a cross of this shape]

Saint Anthony's Cross (ˈæntənɪz) *n., usually abbreviated to* **St Anthony's Cross.** another name for **tau cross.**

Saint Anthony's fire *n., usually abbreviated to* **St Anthony's fire.** *Pathol.* another name for **ergotism** or **erysipelas.** [C16: so named because praying to *Saint Anthony* was believed to effect a cure]

Saint Bernard (ˈbɜːnəd) *n., usually abbreviated to* **St Bernard.** a large breed of dog with a dense red-and-white coat, formerly used as a rescue dog in mountainous areas. [C19: so called because they were kept by the monks of the hospice at the Great *Saint Bernard* Pass between Italy and Switzerland]

sainted (ˈseɪntɪd) *adj.* **1.** canonized. **2.** like a saint in character or nature. **3.** hallowed or holy.

Saint Elmo's fire (ˈɛlməʊz) *n., usually abbreviated to* **St Elmo's fire.** (not in technical usage) a luminous region that sometimes appears around church spires, the masts of ships, etc. It is a corona discharge in the air caused by atmospheric electricity. Also called: **corposant.** [C16: so called because it was associated with *Saint Elmo* (a corruption, via *Sant'Ermo,* of *Saint Erasmus,* died 303) the patron saint of Mediterranean sailors]

Saint-Émilion (*French* sɛ̃temiljɔ̃) *n.* a full-bodied red wine, similar to a Burgundy, produced around the town of Saint-Émilion in Bordeaux.

Saint George's Cross (ˈdʒɔːdʒɪz) *n., usually abbreviated to* **St George's Cross.** a red Greek cross on a white background.

Saint George's mushroom *n.* an edible whitish basidiomycetous fungus, *Tricholoma gambosum,* with a floury smell. [so named because it appears earlier than most fungi, around *St George's* day (23 April)]

sainthood (ˈseɪnthʊd) *n.* **1.** the state or character of being a saint. **2.** saints collectively.

Saint John's bread (dʒɒnz) *n., usually abbreviated to* **St John's bread.** another name for **carob** (sense 2). [C16: so called because its beans were thought to be the "locusts" that *John* the Baptist ate in the desert]

Saint John's wort *n., usually abbreviated to* **St John's wort.** any of numerous shrubs or herbaceous plants of the temperate genus *Hypericum,* such as *H. perforatum,* having yellow flowers and glandular leaves: family *Hypericaceae.* See also **rose of Sharon** (sense 1), **tutsan.** [C15: so named because it was traditionally gathered on *Saint John's Eve* (June 23rd) as a protection against evil spirits]

Saint Luke's summer (luːks) *n., usually abbreviated to* **St Luke's summer.** a period of unusually warm weather in the autumn. [referring to *St Luke's* feast-day, Oct. 7 in the pre-Gregorian calendar (now Oct. 18)]

saintly (ˈseɪntlɪ) *adj.* **-lier, -liest.** like, relating to, or suitable for a saint. —ˈ**saintlily** *adv.* —ˈ**saintliness** *n.*

Saint Martin's summer (ˈmɑːtɪnz) *n., usually abbreviated to* **St Martin's summer.** a period of unusually warm weather in the late autumn, esp. early November. [referring to *St Martin's* feast-day, Oct. 31 in the pre-Gregorian calendar (now Nov. 11)]

saintpaulia (səntˈpɔːlɪə) *n.* another name for **African violet.** [C20: New Latin, named after Baron W. von *Saint Paul,* German soldier (died 1910), who discovered it]

saint's day *n. Christianity.* a day in the church calendar commemorating a saint.

Saint-Simonianism (səntsɪˈməʊnɪəˌnɪzəm) *or* **Saint-Simonism** (səntˈsaɪmənɪzəm) *n.* the socialist system advocated by the Comte de Saint-Simon (1760–1825), French social philosopher and founder of French socialism. —**Saint-Siˈmonian** *n., adj.*

Saint Swithin's Day (ˈswɪðɪnz) *n., usually abbreviated to* **St Swithin's Day.** July 15, observed as a Church festival commemorating Saint Swithin (died 862 A.D.) It is popularly supposed that if it rains on this day the rain will persist for the next 40 days.

Saint Valentine's Day (ˈvælənˌtaɪnz) *n., usually abbreviated to* **St Valentine's Day.** Feb. 14, the feast-day of Saint Valentine and the day on which valentines are exchanged, originally connected with the pagan festival of Lupercalia.

Saint Vitus's dance (ˈvaɪtəsɪz) *n., usually abbreviated to* **St Vitus's dance.** *Pathol.* a nontechnical name for **Sydenham's chorea.** [C17: so called because sufferers traditionally prayed to *Saint Vitus* (3rd-century child martyr) for relief]

sair (ser) *adj., adv.* a Scot. word for **sore.**

saith (sɛθ) *vb.* (used with *he, she,* or *it*) *Archaic.* a form of the present tense (indicative mood) of **say**[1].

saithe (seɪθ) *n. Brit.* another name for **coalfish.** [C19: from Old Norse *seithr* coalfish; compare Gaelic *saigh, saighean* coalfish, Irish *saoidhean* young of fish]

Saiva (ˈsaɪvə, ˈʃaɪ-) *n.* **1.** a member of a branch of Hinduism devoted to the worship of the god Siva, but rejecting the notion of his incarnations. ~*adj.* **2.** of or relating to Saivism or Saivites. —ˈ**Saivism** *n.* —ˈ**Saivite** *n.*

sakai (ˈsakaɪ) *n.* (in Malaysia) **1.** a Malaysian aborigine. **2.** a wild or uncouth person. [from Malay]

sake[1] (seɪk) *n.* **1.** benefit or interest (esp. in the phrase **for (someone's** *or* **one's own) sake**). **2.** the purpose of obtaining or achieving (esp. in the phrase **for the sake of (something)**). **3.** used in various exclamations of impatience, urgency, etc.: *for heaven's sake; for pete's sake.* [C13 (in the phrase *for the sake of,* probably from legal usage): from Old English *sacu* lawsuit (hence, a cause); related to Old Norse *sok,* German *Sache* matter]

sake[2], **saké,** *or* **saki** (ˈsækɪ) *n.* a Japanese alcoholic drink made from fermented rice. [C17: from Japanese]

saker (ˈseɪkə) *n.* a large falcon, *Falco cherrug,* of E Europe and central Asia: used in falconry. [C14 *sagre,* from Old French *sacre,* from Arabic *saqr*]

saki (ˈsɑːkɪ) *n.* any of several small mostly arboreal New World monkeys of the genera *Pithecia* and *Chiropotes,* having long hair and a long bushy tail. [C20: French, from Tupi *saqi*]

Sakti ('sæktɪ) *or* **Shakti** ('ʃʌktɪ) *n. Hinduism.* **1.** the female principle or organ of reproduction and generative power in general. **2.** this principle manifested in the consorts of the gods. [C19: from Sanskrit *śakti* power]

Sakyamuni (ˌsɑːkjəˈmuːnɪ) *n.* one of the titles of the Buddha, deriving from the name of Sakya where he was born. [Sanskrit, literally: hermit of the *Sākya* tribe]

sal (sæl) *n.* a pharmacological term for **salt** (sense 3). [Latin]

salaam (səˈlɑːm) *n.* **1.** a Muslim form of salutation consisting of a deep bow with the right palm on the forehead. **2.** a salutation signifying peace, used chiefly by Muslims. ~*vb.* **3.** to make a salaam or salute (someone) with a salaam. [C17: from Arabic *salām* peace, from the phrase *assalām 'alaikum* peace be to you]

salable ('seɪləbᵊl) *adj.* the U.S. spelling of **saleable.**

salacious (səˈleɪʃəs) *adj.* **1.** having an excessive interest in sex. **2.** (of books, magazines, etc.) erotic, bawdy, or lewd. [C17: from Latin *salax* fond of leaping, from *salīre* to leap] —**saˈlaciously** *adv.* —**saˈlaciousness** *or* **salacity** (səˈlæsɪtɪ) *n.*

salad ('sæləd) *n.* **1.** a dish of raw vegetables, such as lettuce, tomatoes, cucumber, etc., served as a separate course with cheese, cold meat, eggs, etc., or as part of a main course. **2.** any dish of cold vegetables or fruit served with a dressing: *potato salad; fruit salad.* **3.** any green vegetable or herb used in such a dish, esp. lettuce. [C15: from Old French *salade,* from Old Provençal *salada,* from *salar* to season with salt, from Latin *sal* salt]

salad days *pl. n.* a period of youth and inexperience. [allusion to *Antony and Cleopatra* (1.v.73) by William Shakespeare: "my salad days When I was green in judgment, cold in blood"]

salad dressing *n.* a sauce for salad, such as oil and vinegar or mayonnaise.

salade (səˈlɑːd) *n.* another word for **sallet.**

salade niçoise (sæˈlɑːd niːˈswɑːz) *n.* a cold dish consisting of a variety of ingredients, usually including hard-boiled eggs, anchovy fillets, olives, tomatoes, and sometimes tuna fish. [C20: from French, literally salade of or from *Nice,* S France]

salamander ('sæləˌmændə) *n.* **1.** any of various urodele amphibians, such as *Salamandra salamandra* (**European fire salamander**) of central and S Europe (family *Salamandridae*). They are typically terrestrial, have an elongated body, and only return to water to breed. **2.** *Chiefly U.S. and Canadian.* any urodele amphibian. **3.** a mythical reptilian creature supposed to live in fire. **4.** an elemental fire-inhabiting being. **5.** any person or thing able to exist in fire or great heat. **6.** *Metallurgy.* a residue of metal and slag deposited on the walls of a furnace. **7.** a portable stove used to heat or dry out a building under construction. [C14: from Old French *salamandre,* from Latin *salamandra,* from Greek] —**salamandrine** (ˌsæləˈmændrɪn) *adj.*

salami (səˈlɑːmɪ) *n.* a highly seasoned type of sausage, usually flavoured with garlic. [C19: from Italian, plural of *salame,* from Vulgar Latin *salāre* (unattested) to salt, from Latin *sal* salt]

sal ammoniac *n.* another name for **ammonium chloride.**

salaried ('sælərɪd) *adj.* earning or yielding a salary: *a salaried worker; salaried employment.*

salary ('sælərɪ) *n., pl.* **-ries.** **1.** a fixed regular payment made by an employer, often monthly, for professional or office work as opposed to manual work. Compare **wage** (sense 1). ~*vb.* **-ries, -rying, -ried.** **2.** (*tr.*) to pay a salary to. [C14: from Anglo-Norman *salarie,* from Latin *salārium* the sum given to Roman soldiers to buy salt, from *sal* salt]

salchow ('sɔːlkəʊ) *n. Figure skating.* a jump from the inner backward edge of one foot with one, two, or three full turns in the air, returning to the outer backward edge of the opposite foot. [C20: named after Ulrich *Salchow* (1877–1949), Swedish figure skater, who originated it]

sale (seɪl) *n.* **1.** the exchange of goods, property, or services for an agreed sum of money or credit. **2.** the amount sold. **3.** the opportunity to sell; market: *there was no sale for luxuries.* **4.** the rate of selling or being sold: *a slow sale of synthetic fabrics.* **5. a.** an event at which goods are sold at reduced prices, usually to clear old stocks. **b.** (*as modifier*): *sale bargains.* **6.** an auction. [Old English *sala,* from Old Norse *sala.* See also SELL]

saleable *or U.S.* **salable** ('seɪləbᵊl) *adj.* fit for selling or capable of being sold. —ˌ**saleaˈbility,** ˈ**saleableness** *or U.S.* ˌ**salaˈbility,** ˈ**salableness** *n.* —ˈ**saleably** *or U.S.* ˈ**salably** *adv.*

sale and lease back *n.* a system of raising capital for a business by selling the business property and then renting it from the new owner for an agreed period.

sale of work *n. Brit.* a sale of goods and handicrafts made by the members of a club, church congregation, etc., to raise money.

sale or return *or* **sale and return** *n.* an arrangement by which a retailer pays only for goods sold, returning those that are unsold to the wholesaler or manufacturer.

salep ('sælɛp) *n.* the dried ground starchy tubers of various orchids, used for food and formerly as drugs. [C18: via French and Turkish from Arabic *sahlab,* shortened from *khusy ath-tha'lab,* literally: fox's testicles, name of an orchid]

saleratus (ˌsæləˈreɪtəs) *n.* another name for **sodium bicarbonate,** esp. when used in baking powders. [C19: from New Latin *sal aerātus* aerated salt]

saleroom ('seɪlˌruːm, -ˌrʊm) *n. Chiefly Brit.* a room where objects are displayed for sale, esp. by auction.

salesclerk ('seɪlzˌklɑːk) *n. U.S. and Canadian.* a shop assistant. Sometimes shortened to **clerk.**

sales forecast *n.* a prediction of future sales of a product, either judgmental or based on previous sales patterns.

Salesian (səˈliːzjən, -ʒən) *adj.* **1.** of or relating to St Francis of Sales (1567–1622), French ecclesiastic and theologian, or to the religious orders founded by him or in his name. See also **Visitation** (sense 2). ~*n.* **2.** a member of a Salesian order, esp. a member of the Society of St Francis of Sales founded in Turin (1854) and dedicated to all types of educational work.

salesman ('seɪlzmən) *n., pl.* **-men.** **1.** Also called: (*fem.*) ˈ**sales**ˌ**woman,** ˈ**sales**ˌ**girl,** ˈ**sales**ˌ**lady,** *or* ˈ**sales**ˌ**person.** a person who sells merchandise or services either in a shop or by canvassing in a designated area. **2.** short for **travelling salesman.**

salesmanship ('seɪlzmənʃɪp) *n.* **1.** the technique, skill, or ability of selling. **2.** the work of a salesman.

sales promotion *n.* activities or techniques intended to create consumer demand for a product or service.

sales resistance *n.* opposition of potential customers to selling, esp. aggressive selling.

salesroom ('seɪlzˌruːm, -ˌrʊm) *n.* a room in which merchandise on sale is displayed.

sales talk *or* **pitch** *n.* an argument or other persuasion used in selling.

sales tax *n.* a tax levied on retail sales receipts and added to selling prices by retailers.

sales trader *n. Stock Exchange.* a person employed by a market maker, or his firm, to find clients.

salet ('sælɪt) *n.* a variant spelling of **sallet.**

saleyard ('seɪlˌjɑːd) *n. Austral. and N.Z.* an area with pens for holding animals before auction.

Salian ('seɪlɪən) *adj.* **1.** denoting or relating to a group of Franks (the **Salii**) who settled in the Netherlands in the 4th century A.D. and later conquered large areas of Gaul, esp. in the north. ~*n.* **2.** a member of this group.

salic ('sælɪk, 'seɪ-) *adj.* (of rocks and minerals) having a high content of silica and alumina. [C20: from *s*(*ilica*) + *al*(*umina*) + -IC]

Salic *or* **Salique** ('sælɪk, 'seɪlɪk) *adj.* of or relating to the Salian Franks or the Salic law.

salicaceous (ˌsælɪˈkeɪʃəs) *adj.* of, relating to, or belonging to the *Salicaceae,* a chiefly N temperate family of trees and shrubs having catkins: includes the willows and poplars. [C19: via New Latin from Latin *salix* a willow]

salicin *or* **salicine** ('sælɪsɪn) *n.* a colourless or white crystalline water-soluble glucoside obtained from the bark of poplar trees and used as a medical analgesic. Formula: $C_{13}H_{18}O_7$. [C19: from French *salicine,* from Latin *salix* willow]

salicional (səˈlɪʃənəl) *or* **salicet** ('sælɪˌsɛt) *n.* a soft-toned organ stop with a reedy quality. [C19: from German, from Latin *salix* willow]

Salic law *n. History.* **1. a.** the code of laws of the Salic Franks and other Germanic tribes. **b.** a law within this code excluding females from inheritance. **2.** a law excluding women from succession to the throne in certain countries, such as France and Spain.

salicornia (ˌsælɪˈkɔːnɪə) *n.* any chenopodiaceous plant of the genus *Salicornia,* of seashores and salt marshes: includes glasswort. [C19: from Late Latin, perhaps from Latin *sal* salt + *cornu* a horn]

salicylate (səˈlɪsɪˌleɪt) *n.* any salt or ester of salicylic acid.

salicylic acid (ˌsælɪˈsɪlɪk) *n.* a white crystalline slightly water-soluble substance with a sweet taste and bitter aftertaste, used in the manufacture of aspirin, dyes, and perfumes, and as a fungicide. Formula: $C_6H_4(OH)(COOH)$. [C19: from *salicyl* (via French from Latin *salix* a willow + -YL) + -IC]

salient ('seɪlɪənt) *adj.* **1.** prominent, conspicuous, or striking: *a salient feature.* **2.** (esp. in fortifications) projecting outwards at an angle of less than 180°. Compare **re-entrant** (sense 1). **3.** *Geometry.* (of an angle) pointing outwards from a polygon and hence less than 180°. Compare **re-entrant** (sense 2). **4.** (esp. of animals) leaping. ~*n.* **5.** *Military.* a projection of the forward line into enemy-held territory. **6.** a salient angle. [C16: from Latin *salīre* to leap] —ˈ**salience** *or* ˈ**saliency** *n.* —ˈ**saliently** *adv.*

salientian (ˌseɪlɪˈɛnʃɪən) *n., adj.* another word for **anuran.** [C19: from New Latin *Salientia,* literally: leapers, from Latin *salīre* to leap]

saliferous (sæˈlɪfərəs) *adj.* (esp. of rock strata) containing or producing salt. [C19: from Latin *sal* SALT + *ferre* to bear]

salify ('sælɪˌfaɪ) *vb.* **-fies, -fying, -fied.** (*tr.*) **1.** to treat, mix with, or cause to combine with a salt. **2.** to convert (a substance) into a salt: *to salify ammonia by treatment with hydrochloric acid.* [C18: from French *salifier,* from New Latin *salificāre,* from Latin *sal* salt + *facere* to make] —ˈ**sali**ˌ**fiable** *adj.* —ˌ**salifiˈcation** *n.*

salimeter (sæˈlɪmɪtə) *n.* another word for **salinometer.** —**salimetric** (ˌsælɪˈmɛtrɪk) *adj.* —**salˈimetry** *n.*

salina (səˈlaɪnə) *n.* a salt marsh, lake, or spring. [C17: from Spanish, from Medieval Latin: salt pit, from Late Latin *salīnus* SALINE]

saline ('seɪlaɪn) *adj.* **1.** of, concerned with, consisting of, or containing common salt: *a saline taste.* **2.** *Med.* of or relating to a saline. **3.** of, concerned with, consisting of, or containing any chemical salt, esp. a metallic salt resembling sodium chloride. ~*n.* 4. *Med.* an isotonic solution of sodium chloride and distilled water. [C15: from Late Latin *salīnus,* from Latin *sal* salt] —**salinity** (sə'lɪnɪtɪ) *n.*

salinometer (ˌsælɪ'nɒmɪtə) *n.* a hydrometer for determining the amount of salt in a solution, usually calibrated to measure concentration. Also called: **salimeter.** —**salinometric** (ˌsælɪnə'mɛtrɪk) *adj.* —ˌ**sali'nometry** *n.*

Salique ('sælɪk, 'seɪlɪk) *adj.* a variant spelling of **Salic.**

Salish ('seɪlɪʃ) *or* **Salishan** ('seɪlɪʃən, 'sæl-) *n.* 1. a family of North American Indian languages spoken in the northwestern U.S. and W Canada. 2. **the Salish.** (*functioning as pl.*) the peoples collectively who speak these languages, divided in Canada into the **Coast Salish** and the **Interior Salish.**

saliva (sə'laɪvə) *n.* the secretion of salivary glands, consisting of a clear usually slightly acid aqueous fluid of variable composition. It moistens the oral cavity and prepares food for swallowing. [C17: from Latin, of obscure origin] —**salivary** (sə'laɪvərɪ, 'sælɪvərɪ) *adj.*

salivary gland *n.* any of the glands in mammals that secrete saliva. In man the chief salivary glands are the **parotid, sublingual,** and **submaxillary glands.**

salivate ('sælɪˌveɪt) *vb.* 1. (*intr.*) to secrete saliva, esp. an excessive amount. 2. (*tr.*) to cause (a laboratory animal, etc.) to produce saliva, as by the administration of mercury. —ˌ**sali'vation** *n.*

sallee *or* **sally** ('sælɪ) *n. Austral.* 1. Also called: **snow gum.** a SE Australian eucalyptus tree, *Eucalyptus pauciflora,* with a pale grey bark. 2. any of various acacia trees. [probably of native origin]

sallet, salet ('sælɪt), *or* **salade** *n.* a light round helmet extending over the back of the neck; replaced the basinet in the 15th century. [C15: from French *salade,* probably from Old Italian *celata,* from *celare* to conceal, from Latin]

sallow[1] ('sæləʊ) *adj.* 1. (esp. of human skin) of an unhealthy pale or yellowish colour. ~*vb.* 2. (*tr.*) to make sallow. [Old English *salu;* related to Old Norse *sol* seaweed (Icelandic *sōlr* yellowish), Old High German *salo,* French *sale* dirty] —'**sallowish** *adj.* —'**sallowly** *adv.* —'**sallowness** *n.*

sallow[2] ('sæləʊ) *n.* 1. any of several small willow trees, esp. the Eurasian *Salix cinerea* (**common sallow**), which has large catkins that appear before the leaves. 2. a twig or the wood of any of these trees. [Old English *sealh;* related to Old Norse *selja,* Old High German *salaha,* Middle Low German *salwīde,* Latin *salix*] —'**sallowy** *adj.*

sally[1] ('sælɪ) *n., pl.* **-lies.** 1. a sudden violent excursion, esp. by besieged forces to attack the besiegers; sortie. 2. a sudden outburst or emergence into action, expression, or emotion. 3. an excursion or jaunt. 4. a jocular retort. ~*vb.* **-lies, -lying, -lied.** (*intr.*) 5. to make a sudden violent excursion. 6. (often foll. by *forth*) to go out on an expedition, etc. 7. to come, go, or set out in an energetic manner. 8. to rush out suddenly. [C16: from Old French *saillie,* from *saillir* to dash forwards, from Latin *salīre* to leap] —'**sallier** *n.*

sally[2] ('sælɪ) *n., pl.* **-lies.** *Bell-ringing.* the lower part of a bell rope, where it is caught at handstroke, into which coloured wool is woven to make a grip. [C19: perhaps from an obsolete or dialect sense of SALLY[1] leaping movement]

Sally ('sælɪ) *n., pl.* **-lies.** *Austral. and N.Z. informal.* a member of the Salvation Army.

Sally Army *n. Brit. informal.* short for **Salvation Army.**

Sally Lunn (lʌn) *n.* a flat round cake made from a sweet yeast dough, usually served hot. [C19: said to be named after an 18th-century English baker who invented it]

sallyport ('sælɪˌpɔːt) *n.* an opening in a fortified place from which troops may make a sally.

salmagundi *or* **salmagundy** (ˌsælmə'gʌndɪ) *n.* 1. a mixed salad dish of cooked meats, eggs, beetroot, etc., popular in 18th-century England. 2. a miscellany; potpourri. [C17: from French *salmigondis,* perhaps from Italian *salami conditi* pickled salami]

Salmanazar (ˌsælmə'næzə) *n.* a wine bottle holding the equivalent of twelve normal bottles (approximately 312 ounces). [C19: humorous allusion to an Assyrian king mentioned in the Bible (II Kings 17:3); compare JEROBOAM]

salmi *or* **salmis** ('sælmɪ) *n., pl.* **-mis** (-mɪ). a ragout of game stewed in a rich brown sauce. [C18: from French, shortened form of *salmigondis* SALMAGUNDI]

salmon ('sæmən) *n., pl.* **-ons** *or* **-on.** 1. any soft-finned fish of the family *Salmonidae,* esp. *Salmo salar* of the Atlantic and *Oncorhynchus* species (sockeye, Chinook, etc.) of the Pacific, which are important food fishes. They occur in cold and temperate waters and many species migrate to fresh water to spawn. 2. *Austral.* any of several unrelated fish. 3. short for **salmon pink.** [C13: from Old French *saumon,* from Latin *salmō;* related to Late Latin *salar* trout]

salmonberry ('sæmənbərɪ, -brɪ) *n., pl.* **-ries.** 1. a spineless raspberry bush, *Rubus spectabilis,* of North America, having reddish-purple flowers and large red or yellow edible fruits. 2. the fruit of this plant. [C19: so called from the colour of the berries]

salmonella (ˌsælmə'nɛlə) *n., pl.* **-lae** (-ˌliː). any Gram-negative rod-shaped aerobic bacterium of the genus *Salmonella,* including *S. typhosa,* which causes typhoid fever, and many species (notably *S. enteritidis*) that cause food poisoning (**salmonellosis**): family *Enterobacteriaceae.* [C19: New Latin, named after Daniel E. *Salmon* (1850–1914), U.S. veterinary surgeon]

salmonid ('sælmənɪd) *n.* any fish of the family *Salmonidae.*

salmon ladder *n.* a series of steps in a river designed to enable salmon to bypass a dam and move upstream to their breeding grounds.

salmonoid ('sælməˌnɔɪd) *adj.* 1. of, relating to, or belonging to the *Salmonoidea,* a suborder of soft-finned teleost fishes having a fatty fin between the dorsal and tail fins: includes the salmon, whitefish, grayling, smelt, and char. 2. of, relating to, or resembling a salmon. ~*n.* 3. any fish belonging to the suborder *Salmonoidea,* esp. any of the family *Salmonidae* (salmon, trout, char).

salmon pink *n.* **a.** a yellowish-pink colour, sometimes with an orange tinge. **b.** (*as adj.*): *a salmon-pink hat.* ~Sometimes shortened to **salmon.**

salmon trout *n.* any of various large trout, esp. the sea trout.

salol ('sælɒl) *n.* a white sparingly soluble crystalline compound with a slight aromatic odour, used as a preservative and to absorb light in sun-tan lotions, plastics, etc.; phenyl salicylate. Formula: $C_6H_4(OH)COOC_6H_5$. [C19: from *salicyl* (see SALICYLIC ACID) + -OL]

salon ('sælɒn) *n.* 1. a room in a large house in which guests are received. 2. an assembly of guests in a fashionable household, esp. a gathering of major literary, artistic, and political figures from the 17th to the early 20th centuries. 3. a commercial establishment in which hairdressers, beauticians, etc., carry on their businesses: *beauty salon.* 4. **a.** a hall for exhibiting works of art. **b.** such an exhibition, esp. one showing the work of living artists. [C18: from French, from Italian *salone,* augmented form of *sala* hall, of Germanic origin; compare Old English *sele* hall, Old High German *sal,* Old Norse *salr* hall]

salon music *n. Sometimes derogatory.* light classical music intended esp. for domestic entertaining.

saloon (sə'luːn) *n.* 1. Also called: **saloon bar.** *Brit.* another word for **lounge** (sense 5). 2. a large public room on a passenger ship. 3. any large public room used for a specific purpose: *a dancing saloon.* 4. *Chiefly U.S. and Canadian.* a place where alcoholic drink is sold and consumed. 5. a closed two-door or four-door car with four to six seats. U.S., Canadian, and N.Z. name: **sedan.** 6. an obsolete word for **salon** (sense 1). [C18: from French SALON]

saloop (sə'luːp) *n.* an infusion of aromatic herbs or other plant parts, esp. salep, formerly used as a tonic or cure. [C18: changed from SALEP]

salopettes (ˌsælə'pɛts) *pl. n.* a garment worn for skiing, consisting of quilted trousers reaching to the chest and held up by shoulder straps. [C20: from French]

salpa ('sælpə) *n., pl.* **-pas** *or* **-pae** (-piː). any of various minute floating animals of the genus *Salpa,* of warm oceans, having a transparent barrel-shaped body with openings at either end: class *Thaliacea,* subphylum *Tunicata* (tunicates). [C19: from New Latin, from Latin: variety of stockfish, from Greek *salpē*] —**salpiform** ('sælpɪˌfɔːm) *adj.*

salpicon ('sælpɪkən) *n.* a mixture of chopped fish, meat, or vegetables in a sauce, used as fillings for croquettes, pastries, etc. [C18: from French, from Spanish, from *salpicar* to sprinkle with salt]

salpiglossis (ˌsælpɪ'glɒsɪs) *n.* any solanaceous plant of the Chilean genus *Salpiglossis,* some species of which are cultivated for their bright funnel-shaped flowers. [C19: New Latin, from Greek *salpinx* trumpet + *glōssa* tongue]

salpingectomy (ˌsælpɪn'dʒɛktəmɪ) *n., pl.* **-mies.** surgical removal of a Fallopian tube. [C20: from SALPINX + -ECTOMY]

salpingitis (ˌsælpɪn'dʒaɪtɪs) *n.* inflammation of a Fallopian tube. [C19: from SALPINX + -ITIS] —**salpingitic** (ˌsælpɪn'dʒɪtɪk) *adj.*

salpinx ('sælpɪŋks) *n., pl.* **salpinges** (sæl'pɪndʒiːz). *Anatomy.* another name for the **Fallopian tube** or the **Eustachian tube.** [C19: from Greek: trumpet] —**salpingian** (sæl'pɪndʒɪən) *adj.*

salsa ('sælsə) *n.* 1. a type of Latin American big-band dance music. 2. a dance performed to this kind of music. 3. *Mexican cookery.* a spicy tomato-based sauce. [C20: from Spanish: sauce]

salsify ('sælsɪfɪ) *n., pl.* **-fies.** 1. Also called: **oyster plant, vegetable oyster.** a Mediterranean plant, *Tragopogon porrifolius,* having grasslike leaves, purple flower heads, and a long white edible taproot: family *Compositae* (composites). 2. the root of this plant, which tastes of oysters and is eaten as a vegetable. [C17: from French *salsifis,* from Italian *sassefrica,* from Late Latin *saxifrica,* from Latin *saxum* rock + *fricāre* to rub]

sal soda *n.* the crystalline decahydrate of sodium carbonate.

salt (sɔːlt) *n.* 1. a white powder or colourless crystalline solid, consisting mainly of sodium chloride and used for seasoning and preserving food. 2. (*modifier*) preserved in, flooded with, containing, or growing in salt or salty water: *salt pork; salt marshes.* 3. *Chem.* any of a class of usually crystalline solid compounds that are formed from, or can be regarded as formed from, an acid and a base by replacement of one or more hydrogen atoms in the acid molecules by positive ions from the base. 4. liveliness or pungency: *his wit added salt to the discussion.* 5. dry or laconic wit. 6. a sailor, esp. one who is old and experienced. 7. short for **saltcellar.** 8. **rub salt into someone's wounds.** to make someone's pain, shame, etc., even worse. 9. **salt of the earth.** a person or group of people regarded as the finest of their kind.

10. with a grain (*or* **pinch**) **of salt.** with reservations; sceptically. **11. worth one's salt.** efficient; worthy of one's pay. ~*vb.* (*tr.*) **12.** to season or preserve with salt. **13.** to scatter salt over (an icy road, path, etc.) to melt the ice. **14.** to add zest to. **15.** (often foll. by *down* or *away*) to preserve or cure with salt or saline solution. **16.** *Chem.* to treat with common salt or other chemical salt. **17.** to provide (cattle, etc.) with salt. **18.** to give a false appearance of value to, esp. to introduce valuable ore fraudulently into (a mine, sample, etc.). ~*adj.* **19.** not sour, sweet, or bitter; salty. **20.** *Obsolete.* rank or lascivious (esp. in the phrase **a salt wit**). ~See also **salt away, salt out, salts.** [Old English *sealt;* related to Old Norse, Gothic *salt,* German *Salz,* Lettish *sāls,* Latin *sāl,* Greek *hals*] —'**saltish** *adj.* —'**saltless** *adj.* —'**salt,like** *adj.* —'**saltness** *n.*

SALT (sɔːlt) *n. acronym for* Strategic Arms Limitation Talks *or* Treaty.

saltant ('sæltənt) *adj.* (of an organism) differing from others of its species because of a saltation. [C17: from Latin *saltāns* dancing, from *saltāre,* from *salīre* to spring]

saltarello (ˌsæltə'rɛləʊ) *n., pl.* **-li** (-lɪ) *or* **-los. 1.** a traditional Italian dance, usually in compound duple time. **2.** a piece of music composed for or in the rhythm of this dance. [C18: from Italian, from *saltare* to dance energetically, from Latin; see SALTANT]

saltation (sæl'teɪʃən) *n.* **1.** *Biology.* an abrupt variation in the appearance of an organism, species, etc., usually caused by genetic mutation. **2.** *Geology.* the leaping movement of sand or soil particles carried in water or by the wind. **3.** a sudden abrupt movement or transition. [C17: from Latin *saltātiō* a dance, from *saltāre* to leap about]

saltatorial (ˌsæltə'tɔːrɪəl) *or* **saltatory** *adj.* **1.** *Biology.* specialized for or characterized by jumping: *the saltatorial legs of a grasshopper.* **2.** of or relating to saltation. [C17 *saltatory,* from Latin *saltātōrius* concerning dancing, from *saltātor* a dancer; see SALTANT]

salt away *or* (*less commonly*) **down** *vb.* (*tr., adv.*) to hoard or save (money, valuables, etc.).

salt bath *n. Metallurgy.* a bath of molten salts in which steel can be immersed to soak to a uniform and accurately maintained temperature as part of the process of heat treatment. Different salts are used for different temperatures.

saltbox ('sɔːltˌbɒks) *n.* **1.** a box for salt with a sloping lid. **2.** *U.S.* a house that has two storeys in front and one storey at the back, with a gable roof that extends downwards over the rear.

saltbush ('sɔːltˌbʊʃ) *n.* any of various chenopodiaceous shrubs of the genus *Atriplex* that grow in alkaline desert regions.

salt cake *n.* an impure form of sodium sulphate obtained as a by-product in several industrial processes: used in the manufacture of detergents, glass, and ceramic glazes.

saltcellar ('sɔːltˌsɛlə) *n.* **1.** a small container for salt used at the table. **2.** *Brit. informal.* either of the two hollows formed above the collarbones of very slim people. [changed (through influence of cellar) from C15 *salt saler; saler* from Old French *saliere* container for salt, from Latin *salārius* belonging to salt, from *sal* salt]

saltchuck ('sɔːltˌtʃʌk) *n. Canadian, chiefly W coast.* any body of salt water. [C20: from SALT + CHUCK[4]]

saltchucker ('sɔːltˌtʃʌkə) *n. Canadian W coast informal.* a saltwater angler.

salt dome *or* **plug** *n.* a domelike structure of stratified rocks containing a central core of salt: formed by the upward movement of a salt deposit.

salted ('sɔːltɪd) *adj.* **1.** seasoned, preserved, or treated with salt. **2.** *Informal.* experienced in an occupation.

salter ('sɔːltə) *n.* **1.** a person who deals in or manufactures salt. **2.** a person who treats meat, fish, etc., with salt.

saltern ('sɔːltən) *n.* **1.** another word for **saltworks. 2.** a place where salt is obtained from pools of evaporated sea water. [Old English *saltærn,* from SALT + *ærn* house. Compare BARN[1], RANSACK]

saltfish ('sɔːltfɪʃ) *n. Caribbean.* salted cod.

salt flat *n.* a flat expanse of salt left by the total evaporation of a body of water.

saltigrade ('sæltɪˌgreɪd) *adj.* (of animals) adapted for moving in a series of jumps. [C19: from New Latin *Saltigradae,* name formerly applied to jumping spiders, from Latin *saltus* a leap + *gradī* to move]

salting ('sɔːltɪŋ) *n.* (*often pl.*) an area of low ground regularly inundated with salt water; often taken to include its halophyte vegetation; a salt marsh.

saltire *or* (*less commonly*) **saltier** ('sɔːlˌtaɪə) *n. Heraldry.* an ordinary consisting of a diagonal cross on a shield. [C14 *sawturoure,* from Old French *sauteour* cross-shaped barricade, from *saulter* to jump, from Latin *saltāre*]

salt lake *n.* an inland lake of high salinity resulting from inland drainage in an arid area of high evaporation.

salt lick *n.* **1.** a place where wild animals go to lick naturally occurring salt deposits. **2.** a block of salt or a salt preparation given to domestic animals to lick.

salt marsh *n.* an area of marshy ground that is intermittently inundated with salt water or that retains pools or rivulets of salt or brackish water, together with its characteristic halophytic vegetation.

salt out *vb.* (*adv.*) Chem. to cause (a dissolved substance) to come out of solution by adding an electrolyte.

saltpan ('sɔːltˌpæn) *n.* a shallow basin, usually in a desert region, containing salt, gypsum, etc., that was deposited from an evaporated salt lake.

saltpetre *or U.S.* **saltpeter** (ˌsɔːlt'piːtə) *n.* **1.** another name for **potassium nitrate. 2.** short for **Chile saltpetre.** [C16: from Old French *salpetre,* from Latin *sal petrae* salt of rock]

salt pork *n.* pork, esp. the fat pork taken from the back, sides, and belly, that has been cured with salt.

salts (sɔːlts) *pl. n.* **1.** *Med.* any of various mineral salts, such as magnesium sulphate or sodium sulphate, for use as a cathartic. **2.** short for **smelling salts. 3. like a dose of salts.** *Informal.* very fast.

saltus ('sæltəs) *n., pl.* **-tuses.** a break in the continuity of a sequence, esp. the omission of a necessary step in a logical argument. [Latin: a leap]

saltwater ('sɔːltˌwɔːtə) *adj.* of, relating to, or inhabiting salt water, esp. the sea: *saltwater fishes.*

saltworks ('sɔːltˌwɜːks) *n.* (*functioning as sing.*) a place, building, or factory where salt is produced.

saltwort ('sɔːltˌwɜːt) *n.* **1.** Also called: **glasswort, kali.** any of several chenopodiaceous plants of the genus *Salsola,* esp. *S. kali,* of beaches and salt marshes, which has prickly leaves, striped stems, and small green flowers. See also **barilla. 2.** another name for **sea milkwort.**

salty ('sɔːltɪ) *adj.* **saltier, saltiest. 1.** of, tasting of, or containing salt. **2.** (esp. of humour) sharp; piquant. **3.** relating to life at sea. —'**saltily** *adv.* —'**saltiness** *n.*

salubrious (sə'luːbrɪəs) *adj.* conducive or favourable to health; wholesome. [C16: from Latin *salūbris,* from *salūs* health] —**sa'lubriously** *adv.* —**sa'lubriousness** *or* **salubrity** (sə'luːbrɪtɪ) *n.*

Saluki (sə'luːkɪ) *n.* a tall breed of hound with a smooth coat and long fringes on the ears and tail. Also called: **Persian greyhound.** [C19: from Arabic *salūqīy* of Saluq, name of an ancient Arabian city]

salutary ('sæljʊtərɪ, -trɪ) *adj.* **1.** promoting or intended to promote an improvement or beneficial effect: *a salutary warning.* **2.** promoting or intended to promote health. [C15: from Latin *salūtāris* wholesome, from *salūs* safety] —'**salutarily** *adv.* —'**salutariness** *n.*

salutation (ˌsælju'teɪʃən) *n.* **1.** an act, phrase, gesture, etc., that serves as a greeting. **2.** a form of words used as an opening to a speech or letter, such as *Dear Sir* or *Ladies and Gentlemen.* **3.** the act of saluting. [C14: from Latin *salūtātiō,* from *salūtāre* to greet; see SALUTE]

salutatory (sə'luːtətərɪ, -trɪ) *adj.* of, relating to, or resembling a salutation. —**sa'lutatorily** *adv.*

salute (sə'luːt) *vb.* **1.** (*tr.*) to address or welcome with friendly words or gestures of respect, such as bowing or lifting the hat; greet. **2.** (*tr.*) to acknowledge with praise or honour: *we salute your gallantry.* **3.** *Military.* to pay or receive formal respect, as by presenting arms or raising the right arm. ~*n.* **4.** the act of saluting. **5.** a formal military gesture of respect. [C14: from Latin *salūtāre* to greet, from *salūs* wellbeing] —**sa'luter** *n.*

salvable ('sælvəbᵊl) *adj.* capable of or suitable for being saved or salvaged. [C17: from Late Latin *salvāre* to save, from Latin *salvus* safe] —ˌ**salva'bility** *or* '**salvableness** *n.* —'**salvably** *adv.*

Salvadorian, Salvadorean (ˌsælvə'dɔːrɪən) *or* **Salvadoran** (ˌsælvə'dɔːrən) *n.* **1.** a native or inhabitant of El Salvador, a republic in Central America. ~*adj.* **2.** of or relating to El Salvador, or its people, culture, etc.

salvage ('sælvɪdʒ) *n.* **1.** the act, process, or business of rescuing vessels or their cargoes from loss at sea. **2. a.** the act of saving any goods or property in danger of damage or destruction. **b.** (*as modifier*): *a salvage operation.* **3.** the goods or property so saved. **4.** compensation paid for the salvage of a vessel or its cargo. **5.** the proceeds from the sale of salvaged goods or property. ~*v.* (*tr.*) **6.** to save or rescue (goods or property) from fire, shiwreck, etc. **7.** to gain (something beneficial) from a failure: *she salvaged little from the broken marriage.* [C17: from Old French, from Medieval Latin *salvāgium,* from *salvāre* to SAVE[1]] —'**salvageable** *adj.* —'**salvager** *n.*

salvation (sæl'veɪʃən) *n.* **1.** the act of preserving or the state of being preserved from harm. **2.** a person or thing that is the means of preserving from harm. **3.** *Christianity.* deliverance by redemption from the power of sin and from the penalties ensuing from it. **4.** *Christian Science.* the realization that Life, Truth, and Love are supreme and that they can destroy such illusions as sin, death, etc. [C13: from Old French *sauvacion,* from Late Latin *salvātiō,* from Latin *salvātus* saved, from *salvāre* to SAVE[1]] —**sal'vational** *adj.*

Salvation Army *n.* **a.** a Christian body founded in 1865 by the British religious leader William Booth (1829–1912) and organized on quasi-military lines for evangelism and social work among the poor. **b.** (*as modifier*): *a Salvation Army hostel.*

salvationist (sæl'veɪʃənɪst) *n.* **1.** a member of an evangelical sect emphasizing the doctrine of salvation. **2.** (*often cap.*) a member of the Salvation Army. ~*adj.* **3.** stressing the doctrine of salvation. **4.** (*often cap.*) of or relating to the Salvation Army. —**sal'vationism** *n.*

Salvation Jane (dʒeɪn) *n. Austral.* another name, used in South Australia, for **viper's bugloss.**

salva veritate *Latin.* ('sælvə ˌvɛrɪ'tɑːteɪ) *adv. Philosophy.* without affecting truth-value.

salve[1] (sælv, sɑːv) *n.* **1.** an ointment for wounds, sores, etc. **2.** anything that heals or soothes. ~*vb.* (*tr.*) **3.** to apply salve to (a wound, sore, etc.). **4.** to soothe, comfort, or appease. [Old English *sealf;* related to Old High German *salba,* Greek *elpos* oil, Sanskrit *sarpis* lard]

salve[2] (sælv) *vb.* **1.** a less common word for **salvage. 2.** an archaic word for **save**[1] (sense 3). [C18: from SALVAGE]

salver ('sælvə) *n.* a tray, esp. one of silver, on which food, letters, visiting cards, etc., are presented. [C17: from French *salve,* from Spanish *salva* tray from which the king's taster sampled food, from Latin *salvāre* to SAVE[1]]

salverform ('sælvəˌfɔːm) *adj.* (of the corolla of the phlox and certain other flowers) consisting of a narrow tube with flat spreading terminal petals.

salvia ('sælvɪə) *n.* any herbaceous plant or small shrub of the genus *Salvia,* such as the sage, grown for their medicinal or culinary properties or for ornament: family *Labiatae* (labiates). [C19: from Latin: SAGE[2]]

salvo[1] ('sælvəʊ) *n., pl.* **-vos** *or* **-voes. 1.** a discharge of fire from weapons in unison, esp. on a ceremonial occasion. **2.** concentrated fire from many weapons, as in a naval battle. **3.** an outburst, as of applause. [C17: from Italian *salva,* from Old French *salve,* from Latin *salvē!* greetings! from *salvēre* to be in good health, from *salvus* safe]

salvo[2] ('sælvəʊ) *n., pl.* **-vos.** *Rare.* **1.** an excuse or evasion. **2.** an expedient to save a reputation or soothe hurt feelings. **3.** (in legal documents) a saving clause; reservation. [C17: from such Medieval Latin phrases as *salvō iurē* the right of keeping safe, from Latin *salvus* safe]

Salvo ('sælvəʊ) *n., pl.* **-vos.** *Austral. slang.* a member of the Salvation Army.

sal volatile (vɒ'lætɪlɪ) *n.* **1.** another name for **ammonium carbonate. 2.** Also called: **spirits of ammonia** *or* (archaic) **hartshorn.** a solution of ammonium carbonate in alcohol and aqueous ammonia, often containing aromatic oils, used as smelling salts. [C17: from New Latin: volatile salt]

salvor *or* **salver** ('sælvə) *n.* a person instrumental in salvaging a vessel or its cargo. [C17: from SALVAGE + -OR[1]]

SAM (sæm) *n. acronym for* surface-to-air missile.

Sam. *Bible. abbrev. for* Samuel.

S.Am. *abbrev. for* South America(n).

samara (sə'mɑːrə, 'sæmərə) *n.* a dry indehiscent one-seeded fruit with a winglike extension to aid dispersal: occurs in the ash, maple, etc. Also called: **key fruit.** [C16: from New Latin, from Latin: seed of an elm]

samariform (sə'mɑːrɪˌfɔːm) *adj. Botany.* shaped like a samara; winged.

Samaritan (sə'mærɪtᵊn) *n.* **1.** a native or inhabitant of Samaria, a kingdom in ancient Palestine. **2.** short for **Good Samaritan. 3.** a member of a voluntary organization **(the Samaritans)** whose aim is to help people in distress or despair. **4.** the dialect of Aramaic spoken in Samaria. ~*adj.* **5.** of or relating to Samaria. —**Sa'maritanism** *n.*

samarium (sə'mɛərɪəm) *n.* a silvery metallic element of the lanthanide series occurring chiefly in monazite and bastnaesite and used in carbon-arc lighting, as a doping agent in laser crystals, and as a neutron-absorber. Symbol: Sm; atomic no.: 62; atomic wt.: 150.35; valency: 2 or 3; relative density: 7.5; melting pt.: 1072°C; boiling pt.: 1778°C. [C19: New Latin, from SAMARSKITE + -IUM]

samarskite (sə'mɑːskaɪt) *n.* a velvety black mineral of complex composition occurring in pegmatites: used as a source of uranium and certain rare earth elements. [C19: named after Colonel von *Samarski,* 19th-century Russian inspector of mines]

Sama-Veda ('sɑːmə'veɪdə) *n. Hinduism.* the third Veda containing the rituals for sacrifices. [C18: from Sanskrit *sāman* a chant + VEDA]

samba ('sæmbə) *n., pl.* **-bas. 1.** a lively modern ballroom dance from Brazil in bouncy duple time. **2.** a piece of music composed for or in the rhythm of this dance. ~*vb.* **-bas, -baing, -baed. 3.** (*intr.*) to perform such a dance. [Portuguese, of African origin]

sambar *or* **sambur** ('sæmbə) *n., pl.* **-bars, -bar** *or* **-burs, -bur.** a S Asian deer, *Cervus unicolor,* with three-tined antlers. [C17: from Hindi, from Sanskrit *śambarra,* of obscure origin]

sambo[1] ('sæmbəʊ) *n., pl.* **-bos. 1.** *Slang.* an offensive word for **Negro:** often used as a term of address. **2.** the offspring of a Negro and a member of another race or a mulatto. [C18: from American Spanish *zambo* a person of Negro descent; perhaps related to Bantu *nzambu* monkey]

sambo[2] *or* **sambo wrestling** ('sæmbəʊ) *n.* a type of wrestling using judo techniques that originated in Russia and now features in international competitions. [C20: from Russian *sam(ozashchita) b(ez) o(ruzhiya)* self-defence without weapons] —**sambo wrestler** *n.*

Sam Browne belt ('sæm 'braʊn) *n.* a military officer's wide belt supported by a strap passing from the left side of the belt over the right shoulder. [C20: named after Sir *Samuel J. Browne* (1824–1901), British general, who invented such a belt]

same (seɪm) *adj.* (usually preceded by *the*) **1.** being the very one: *she is wearing the same hat she wore yesterday.* **2. a.** being the one previously referred to; aforesaid. **b.** (*as n.*): *a note received about same.* **3. a.** identical in kind, quantity, etc.: *two girls of the same age.* **b.** (*as n.*): *we'd like the same, please.* **4.** unchanged in character or nature: *his attitude is the same as ever.* **5. all the same. a.** Also: **just the same.** nevertheless; yet. **b.** immaterial: *it's all the same to me.* ~*adv.* **6.** in an identical manner. [C12: from Old Norse *samr;* related to Old English adverbial phrase *swā same* likewise, Gothic *sama,* Latin *similis,* Greek *homos* same]

▷**Usage.** The use of *same* exemplified in *if you send us your order for the materials, we will deliver same tomorrow* is common in business and official English. In general English, however, this use of the word is avoided: *may I borrow your book? I'll return it* (not *same*) *tomorrow.*

samekh ('sɑːmək; *Hebrew* 'samɛx) *n.* the 15th letter in the Hebrew alphabet (ס) transliterated as *s.* [Hebrew, literally: a support]

sameness ('seɪmnɪs) *n.* **1.** the state or quality of being the same. **2.** lack of change; monotony.

samey ('seɪmɪ) *adj. Informal.* monotonous; repetitive; unvaried.

samfoo ('sæmfuː) *n.* a style of casual dress worn by Chinese women, consisting of a waisted blouse and trousers. [from Chinese (Cantonese) *sam* dress + *foo* trousers]

Samian ('seɪmɪən) *adj.* **1.** of or relating to Samos, an island in the E Aegean Sea, or its inhabitants. ~*n.* **2.** a native or inhabitant of Samos.

Samian ware *n.* **1.** a fine earthenware pottery, reddish-brown or black in colour, found in large quantities on Roman sites. **2.** Also called: **Arretine ware.** the earlier pottery from which this developed, an imitation of a type of Greek pottery, made during the first century B.C. at Arretium. [C19: named after the island of *Samos,* source of a reddish-coloured earth resembling terra sigillata, similar to the earth from which the pottery was made]

samiel ('sæmjɛl) *n.* another word for **simoom.** [C17: from Turkish *samyeli,* from *sam* poisonous + *yel* wind]

samisen ('sæmɪˌsɛn) *n.* a Japanese plucked stringed instrument with a long neck, an unfretted fingerboard, and a rectangular soundbox. [Japanese, from Chinese *san-hsien,* from *san* three + *hsien* string]

samite ('sæmaɪt, 'seɪ-) *n.* a heavy fabric of silk, often woven with gold or silver threads, used in the Middle Ages for clothing. [C13: from Old French *samit,* from Medieval Latin *examitum,* from Greek *hexamiton,* from *hexamitos* having six threads, from *hex* six + *mitos* a thread]

samiti *or* **samithi** ('sʌmɪtɪ) *n.* (in India) an association, esp. one formed to organize political activity. [Hindi]

samizdat (*Russian* səmiz'dat) *n.* (in the Soviet Union) **a.** a system of clandestine printing and distribution of banned or dissident literature. **b.** (*as modifier*): *a samizdat publication.* [C20: from Russian, literally: self-published]

sammy ('sæmɪ) *n., pl.* **-mies.** *Informal.* (in South Africa) an Indian fruit and vegetable vendor who goes from house to house. [C20: from the Christian name *Sammy*]

Samnite ('sæmnaɪt) (in ancient Italy) ~*n.* **1.** a member of an Oscan-speaking people of the S Apennines, who clashed repeatedly with Rome between 350 B.C. and 200 B.C. ~*adj.* **2.** of or relating to this people.

Samoan (sə'məʊən) *adj.* **1.** of or relating to Samoa, a group of islands in the S Pacific, or to its people or their language. ~*n.* **2.** a member of the people that inhabit Samoa. **3.** the language of Samoa, belonging to the Polynesian family of languages.

samosa (sə'məʊsə) *n., pl.* **-sas** *or* **-sa.** (in Indian cookery) a small triangular pastry case containing spiced vegetables or meat and served fried. [C20: from Hindi]

samovar ('sæməˌvɑː, ˌsæmə'vɑː) *n.* (esp. in Russia) a metal urn for making tea, in which the water is heated esp. formerly by charcoal held in an inner container or nowadays more usually by electricity. [C19: from Russian, from *samo-* self (related to SAME) + *varit'* to boil]

Samoyed (ˌsæmə'jɛd) *n.* **1.** (*pl.* **-yed** *or* **-yeds**) a member of a group of peoples who migrated along the Russian Arctic coast and now live chiefly in the area of the N Ural Mountains: related to the Finns. **2.** the languages of these peoples, related to Finno-Ugric within the Uralic family. **3.** (sə'mɔɪɛd). a Siberian breed of dog of the spitz type, having a dense white or cream coat with a distinct ruff, and a tightly curled tail. [C17: from Russian *Samoed*] —ˌ**Samo'yedic** *adj.*

samp (sæmp) *n. S. African.* crushed maize used for porridge. [of uncertain origin]

sampan ('sæmpæn) *n.* any small skiff, widely used in the Orient, that is propelled by oars or a scull. [C17: from Chinese *san pan,* from *san* three + *pan* board]

samphire ('sæmˌfaɪə) *n.* **1.** Also called: **rock samphire.** an umbelliferous plant, *Crithmum maritimum,* of Eurasian coasts, having fleshy divided leaves and clusters of small white flowers. **2. golden samphire.** a Eurasian coastal plant, *Inula crithmoides,* with fleshy leaves and yellow flower heads: family *Compositae* (composites). **3. marsh samphire.** another name for **glasswort** (sense 1). **4.** any of several other plants of coastal areas. [C16 *sampiere,* from French *herbe de Saint Pierre* Saint Peter's herb; perhaps influenced by *camphire* CAMPHOR]

sample (ˈsɑːmpᵊl) *n.* **1. a.** a small part of anything, intended as representative of the whole; specimen. **b.** (*as modifier*): *a sample bottle.* **2.** Also called: **sampling.** *Statistics.* **a.** a set of individuals or items selected from a population for analysis to yield estimates of, or to test hypotheses about, parameters of the whole population. A **biased sample** is one in which the items selected share some property which influences their distribution, while a **random sample** is devised to avoid any such interference so that its distribution is affected only by, and so can be held to represent, that of the whole population. See also **matched sample. b.** (*as modifier*): *sample distribution.* ~*vb.* **3.** (*tr.*) to take a sample or samples of. **4.** *Music.* **a.** to take a short extract from (one record) and mix it into a different backing track. **b.** to record (a sound) and feed it into a computerized synthesizer so that it can be reproduced at any pitch. [C13: from Old French *essample,* from Latin *exemplum* EXAMPLE]

sample point *n. Statistics.* a single possible observed value of a variable; a member of the sample space of an experiment.

sampler (ˈsɑːmplə) *n.* **1.** a person who takes samples. **2.** a piece of embroidery executed as an example of the embroiderer's skill in using a variety of stitches: often incorporating numbers, letters, and the name and age of the embroiderer in a decorative panel. **3.** *Music.* a piece of electronic equipment used for sampling.

sample space *n. Statistics.* the set of possible outcomes of an experiment; the range of values of a random variable.

sampling (ˈsɑːmplɪŋ) *n.* **1.** the process of selecting a random sample. **2.** a variant of **sample** (sense 2). **3.** the process of taking a short extract from (a record) and mixing it into a different backing track. **4.** a process in which a continuous electrical signal is approximately represented by a series of discrete values, usually regularly spaced.

sampling frame *n. Statistics.* See **frame** (sense 13).

sampling statistic *n.* any function of observed data, esp. one used to estimate the corresponding parameter of the underlying distribution, such as the sample mean, sample variance, etc. Compare **parameter** (sense 3).

samsara (səmˈsɑːrə) *n.* **1.** *Hinduism.* the endless cycle of birth, death, and rebirth. **2.** *Buddhism.* the transmigration or rebirth of a person. [Sanskrit, literally: a passing through, from *sam* altogether + *sarati* it runs]

samshu (ˈsæmʃuː, -sjuː) *n.* an alcoholic drink from China that is made from fermented rice and resembles sake. [C17: perhaps modification of Chinese *shao chiu* spirits that will burn, from *shao* to burn + *chiu* spirits]

Samson (ˈsæmsən) *n.* any man of outstanding physical strength. [after the Israelite hero who performed herculean feats of strength against the Philistine oppressors (Judges 13–16)]

samurai (ˈsæmʊˌraɪ, ˈsæmjʊ-) *n., pl.* **-rai. 1.** the Japanese warrior caste that provided the administrative and fighting aristocracy from the 11th to the 19th centuries. **2.** a member of this aristocracy. [C19: from Japanese]

samurai bond *n.* a bond issued in Japan and denominated in yen, available for purchase by nonresidents of Japan.

san (sæn) *n. Old-fashioned informal.* short for **sanatorium** (esp. sense 3).

San (sɑːn) *n.* a group of the Khoisan languages, spoken mostly by Bushmen.

sanative (ˈsænətɪv) *adj.* a less common word for **curative.** [C15: from Medieval Latin *sānātīvus,* from Latin *sānāre* to heal, from *sānus* healthy]

sanatorium (ˌsænəˈtɔːrɪəm) *or U.S.* **sanitarium** *n., pl.* **-riums** *or* **-ria** (-rɪə). **1.** an institution for the medical care and recuperation of persons who are chronically ill. **2.** a health resort. **3.** *Brit.* a room in a boarding school where sick pupils may be treated in isolation. [C19: from New Latin, from Latin *sānāre* to heal]

sanbenito (ˌsænbəˈniːtəʊ) *n., pl.* **-tos. 1.** a yellow garment bearing a red cross, worn by penitent heretics in the Inquisition. **2.** a black garment bearing flames and devils, worn by impenitent heretics at an auto-da-fé. [C16: from Spanish *San Benito* Saint Benedict, an ironical allusion to its likeness to the Benedictine scapular]

sanctified (ˈsæŋktɪˌfaɪd) *adj.* **1.** consecrated or made holy. **2.** a less common word for **sanctimonious.**

sanctify (ˈsæŋktɪˌfaɪ) *vb.* **-fies, -fying, -fied.** (*tr.*) **1.** to make holy. **2.** to free from sin; purify. **3.** to sanction (an action or practice) as religiously binding: *to sanctify a marriage.* **4.** to declare or render (something) productive of or conducive to holiness, blessing, or grace. **5.** *Obsolete.* to authorize to be revered. [C14: from Late Latin *sanctificāre,* from Latin *sanctus* holy + *facere* to make] —ˈ**sanctiˌfiable** *adj.* —ˌ**sanctifiˈcation** *n.* —ˈ**sanctiˌfier** *n.*

sanctimonious (ˌsæŋktɪˈməʊnɪəs) *adj.* affecting piety or making a display of holiness. [C17: from Latin *sanctimonia* sanctity, from *sanctus* holy] —ˌ**sanctiˈmoniously** *adv.* —ˌ**sanctiˈmoniousness** *n.* —ˈ**sanctimony** *n.*

sanction (ˈsæŋkʃən) *n.* **1.** final permission; authorization. **2.** aid or encouragement. **3.** something, such as an ethical principle, that imparts binding force to a rule, oath, etc. **4.** the penalty laid down in a law for contravention of its provisions. **5.** (*often pl.*) a coercive measure, esp. one taken by one or more states against another guilty of violating international law. ~*vb.* (*tr.*) **6.** to give authority to; permit. **7.** to make authorized; confirm. [C16: from Latin *sanctiō* the establishment of an inviolable decree, from *sancīre* to decree] —ˈ**sanctionable** *adj.* —ˈ**sanctioner** *n.* —ˈ**sanctionless** *adj.*

sanction mark *n.* a mark on pieces of 19th-century French furniture signifying that the piece met the quality standards required by the Parisian guild of ebonists.

sanctitude (ˈsæŋktɪˌtjuːd) *n.* saintliness; holiness.

sanctity (ˈsæŋktɪtɪ) *n., pl.* **-ties. 1.** the condition of being sanctified; holiness. **2.** anything regarded as sanctified or holy. **3.** the condition of being inviolable; sacredness: *the sanctity of marriage.* [C14: from Old French *saincteté,* from Latin *sanctitās,* from *sanctus* holy]

sanctuary (ˈsæŋktjʊərɪ) *n., pl.* **-aries. 1.** a holy place. **2.** a consecrated building or shrine. **3.** *Old Testament.* **a.** the Israelite temple at Jerusalem, esp. the holy of holies. **b.** the tabernacle in which the Ark was enshrined during the wanderings of the Israelites. **4.** the chancel, or that part of a sacred building surrounding the main altar. **5. a.** a sacred building where fugitives were formerly entitled to immunity from arrest or execution. **b.** the immunity so afforded. **6.** a place of refuge; asylum. **7.** a place, protected by law, where animals, esp. birds, can live and breed without interference. [C14: from Old French *sainctuarie,* from Late Latin *sanctuārium* repository for holy things, from Latin *sanctus* holy]

sanctuary lamp *n. Christianity.* a lamp, usually red, placed in a prominent position in the sanctuary of a church, that when lit indicates the presence of the Blessed Sacrament.

sanctum (ˈsæŋktəm) *n., pl.* **-tums** *or* **-ta** (-tə). **1.** a sacred or holy place. **2.** a room or place of total privacy or inviolability. [C16: from Latin, from *sanctus* holy]

sanctum sanctorum (sæŋkˈtɔːrəm) *n.* **1.** *Bible.* another term for the **holy of holies. 2.** *Often facetious.* an especially private place. [C14: from Latin, literally: holy of holies, rendering Hebrew *qōdesh haqqodāshīm*]

Sanctus (ˈsæŋktəs) *n.* **1.** *Liturgy.* the hymn that occurs immediately after the preface in the celebration of the Eucharist. **2.** a musical setting of this, usually incorporated into the Ordinary of the Roman Catholic Mass. [C14: from the first word of the hymn, *Sanctus sanctus sanctus* Holy, holy, holy, from Latin *sancīre* to consecrate]

Sanctus bell *n. Chiefly R.C. Church.* a bell rung as the opening words of the Sanctus are pronounced and also at other important points during Mass.

sand (sænd) *n.* **1.** loose material consisting of rock or mineral grains, esp. rounded grains of quartz, between 0.2 and 2 mm in diameter. **2.** (*often pl.*) a sandy area, esp. on the seashore or in a desert. **3. a.** a greyish-yellow colour. **b.** (*as adj.*): *sand upholstery.* **4.** the grains of sandlike material in an hourglass. **5.** *U.S. informal.* courage; grit. **6. the sands are running out.** there is not much time left before death or the end. ~*vb.* **7.** (*tr.*) to smooth or polish the surface of with sandpaper or sand: *to sand a floor.* **8.** (*tr.*) to sprinkle or cover with or as if with sand; add sand to. **9.** to fill or cause to fill with sand: *the channel sanded up.* [Old English; related to Old Norse *sandr,* Old High German *sant,* Greek *hamathos*] —ˈ**sandˌlike** *adj.*

sandal (ˈsændᵊl) *n.* **1.** a light shoe consisting of a sole held on the foot by thongs, straps, etc., worn in hot weather or by women for evening wear. **2.** a strap passing over the instep or around the ankle to keep a low shoe on the foot. [C14: from Latin *sandalium,* from Greek *sandalion* a small sandal, from *sandalon* sandal] —ˈ**sandalled** *adj.*

sandalwood (ˈsændᵊlˌwʊd) *or* **sandal** *n.* **1.** any of several evergreen trees of the genus *Santalum,* esp. *S. album* (**white sandalwood**), of S Asia and Australia, having hard light-coloured heartwood: family *Santalaceae.* **2.** the wood of any of these trees, which is used for carving, is burned as incense, and yields an aromatic oil used in perfumery. **3.** any of various similar trees or their wood, esp. *Pterocarpus santalinus* (**red sandalwood**), a leguminous tree of SE Asia having dark red wood used as a dye. [C14 *sandal,* from Medieval Latin *sandalum,* from Late Greek *sandanon,* from Sanskrit *candana* sandalwood]

sandarac *or* **sandarach** (ˈsændəˌræk) *n.* **1.** Also called: **sandarac tree.** a pinaceous tree, *Tetraclinis articulata* (or *Callitris quadrivalvis*), of NW Africa, having hard fragrant dark wood. **2.** a brittle pale yellow transparent resin obtained from the bark of this tree and used in making varnish and incense. **3.** Also called: **citron wood.** the wood of this tree, used in building. [C16 *sandaracha,* from Latin *sandaraca* red pigment, from Greek *sandarakē*]

sandbag (ˈsændˌbæg) *n.* **1.** a sack filled with sand used for protection against gunfire, floodwater, etc., or as ballast in a balloon, ship, etc. **2.** a bag filled with sand and used as a weapon. ~*vb.* **-bags, -bagging, -bagged.** (*tr.*) **3.** to protect or strengthen with sandbags. **4.** to hit with or as if with a sandbag. **5.** *Finance.* to obstruct (an unwelcome takeover bid) by having prolonged talks in the hope that a more acceptable bidder will come forward. —ˈ**sandˌbagger** *n.*

sandbank (ˈsændˌbæŋk) *n.* a submerged bank of sand in a sea or river, that may be exposed at low tide.

sand bar *n.* a ridge of sand in a river or sea, built up by the action of tides, currents, etc., and often exposed at low tide.

sandblast ('sænd,blɑːst) *n.* **1.** a jet of sand or grit blown from a nozzle under air pressure or steam pressure. ~*vb.* (*tr.*) **2.** to clean, grind, or decorate (a surface) with a sandblast. —'**sand-,blaster** *n.*

sand-blind *adj.* not completely blind; partially able to see. Compare **stone-blind.** [C15: changed (through influence of SAND) from Old English *samblind* (unattested), from *sam-* half, SEMI- + BLIND] —'**sand-,blindness** *n.*

sandbox ('sænd,bɒks) *n.* **1.** a container on a railway locomotive from which sand is released onto the rails to assist the traction. **2.** a box with sand shaped for moulding metal. **3.** a container of sand for small children to play in.

sandbox tree *n.* a tropical American euphorbiaceous tree, *Hura crepitans,* having small woody seed capsules, which explode when ripe to scatter the seeds: formerly used to hold sand for blotting ink.

sandboy ('sænd,bɔɪ) *n.* **happy** (*or* **jolly**) **as a sandboy.** very happy; high-spirited.

sand-cast *vb.* **-casts, -casting, -cast.** (*tr.*) to produce (a casting) by pouring molten metal into a mould of sand. —'**sand-,casting** *n.*

sand castle *n.* a mass of sand moulded into a castle-like shape, esp. as made by a child on the seashore.

sand crack *n. Vet. science.* a deep crack or fissure in the wall of a horse's hoof, often causing lameness. See also **toe crack, quarter crack.**

sand dab *n.* any of various small flatfishes of the genus *Citharichthys* that occur in American Pacific coastal waters and are important food fishes.

sand dollar *n.* any of various flattened disclike echinoderms of the order *Clypeasteroida,* of shallow North American coastal waters: class *Echinoidea* (sea urchins).

sand eel *or* **lance** *n.* any silvery eel-like marine spiny-finned fish of the family *Ammodytidae* found burrowing in sand or shingle. Popular name: **launce.**

sander ('sændə) *n.* **1.** a power-driven tool for smoothing surfaces, esp. wood, plastic, etc., by rubbing with an abrasive disc. **2.** a person who uses such a device.

sanderling ('sændəlɪŋ) *n.* a small sandpiper, *Crocethia alba,* that frequents sandy shores. [C17: perhaps from SAND + Old English *erthling, eorthling* EARTHLING]

sand flea *n.* another name for the **chigoe** (sense 1) and **sand hopper.**

sandfly ('sænd,flaɪ) *n., pl.* **-flies. 1.** any of various small mothlike dipterous flies of the genus *Phlebotomus* and related genera: the bloodsucking females transmit diseases including leishmaniasis: family *Psychodidae.* **2.** any of various similar and related flies.

sandglass ('sænd,glɑːs) *n.* a less common word for **hourglass.**

sandgrouse ('sænd,graʊs) *n.* any bird of the family *Pteroclididae,* of dry regions of the Old World, having very short feet, a short bill, and long pointed wings and tail: order *Columbiformes.*

sandhi ('sændɪ) *n., pl.* **-dhis.** *Linguistics.* modification of the form or sound of a word under the influence of an adjacent word. [from Sanskrit *samdhi* a placing together, from *sam* together + *dadhāti* he puts]

sandhog ('sænd,hɒg) *n. Chiefly U.S. and Canadian.* a person who works in underground or underwater construction projects.

sand hopper *n.* any of various small hopping amphipod crustaceans of the genus *Orchestia* and related genera, common in intertidal regions of seashores. Also called: **beach flea, sand flea.**

Sandinista (,sændɪ'niːstə) *n.* (in Nicaragua) **a.** one of a left-wing group of revolutionaries who formed a socialist coalition government in 1979. **b.** (*as modifier*): *Nicaragua's Sandinista government.* [C20: from Spanish, named after Augusto César *Sandino* a Nicaraguan general and rebel leader, murdered in 1933]

sand lance *or* **launce** *n.* another name for the **sand eel.**

sand leek *n.* a Eurasian alliaceous plant, *Allium scorodoprasum,* having reddish-pink flowers, purple bulbils, and a garlic-like bulb. See also **rocambole.**

sand lizard *n.* a small greyish-brown European lizard, *Lacerta agilis,* that has long clawed digits and, in the male, bright green underparts: family *Lacertidae.*

sandman ('sænd,mæn) *n., pl.* **-men.** (in folklore) a magical person supposed to put children to sleep by sprinkling sand in their eyes.

sand martin *n.* a small brown European songbird, *Riparia riparia,* with white underparts: it nests in tunnels bored in sand, river banks, etc.: family *Hirundinidae* (swallows and martins).

sand painting *n.* a type of painting done by American Indians, esp. in the healing ceremonies of the Navaho, using fine coloured sand on a neutral ground.

sandpaper ('sænd,peɪpə) *n.* **1.** (formerly) a strong paper coated with sand for smoothing and polishing. **2.** a common name for **glasspaper.** ~*vb.* **3.** (*tr.*) to polish or grind (a surface) with or as if with sandpaper.

sandpiper ('sænd,paɪpə) *n.* **1.** any of numerous N hemisphere shore birds of the genera *Tringa, Calidris,* etc., typically having a long slender bill and legs and cryptic plumage: family *Scolopacidae,* order *Charadriiformes.* **2.** any other bird of the family *Scolopacidae,* which includes snipes and woodcocks.

sandpit ('sænd,pɪt) *n.* **1.** a shallow pit or container holding sand for children to play in. **2.** a pit from which sand is extracted.

sandshoe ('sænd,ʃuː) *n. Brit. and Austral.* a light canvas shoe with a rubber sole; plimsoll.

sand shrimp *n.* See **shrimp** (sense 4).

sandsoap ('sænd,səʊp) *n.* a gritty general-purpose soap.

sandstone ('sænd,stəʊn) *n.* any of a group of common sedimentary rocks consisting of sand grains consolidated with such materials as quartz, haematite, and clay minerals: used widely in building.

sandstorm ('sænd,stɔːm) *n.* a strong wind that whips up clouds of sand, esp. in a desert.

sand table *n. Military* a surface on which sand can be modelled into a relief map on which to demonstrate tactics.

sand trap *n.* another name (esp. U.S.) for **bunker** (sense 2).

sand viper *n.* **1.** a S European viper, *Vipera ammodytes,* having a yellowish-brown coloration with a zigzag pattern along the back. **2.** another name for **horned viper.**

sand wasp *n.* a solitary wasp of the subfamily *Sphecinae,* a subgroup of the digger wasps most of which nest in sandy ground.

sand wedge *n. Golf.* a club with a face angle of more than 50°, used in bunker shots to cut through sand, get under the ball, and lift it clear; a No. 10 iron.

sandwich ('sænwɪdʒ, -wɪtʃ) *n.* **1.** two or more slices of bread, usually buttered, with a filling of meat, cheese, etc. **2.** anything that resembles a sandwich in arrangement. ~*vb.* (*tr.*) **3.** to insert tightly between two other things. **4.** to put into a sandwich. **5.** to place between two dissimilar things. [C18: named after John Montagu, 4th Earl of *Sandwich* (1718–92), who ate sandwiches rather than leave the gambling table for meals]

sandwich board *n.* one of two connected boards, usually bearing advertisements, that are hung over the shoulders in front of and behind a person.

sandwich cake *n.* a cake that is made up of two or more layers with a jam or other filling. Also called: **layer cake.**

sandwich compound *n. Chem.* any of a class of organometallic compounds whose molecules have a metal atom or ion bound between two plane parallel organic rings. See also **metallocene.**

sandwich course *n.* any of several courses consisting of alternate periods of study and industrial work.

sandwich man *n.* a man who carries sandwich boards.

sandwich tern *n.* a European tern, *Sterna sandvicensis,* that has a yellow-tipped bill, whitish plumage, and white forked tail, and nests in colonies on beaches, etc. [C18: from the town of *Sandwich* in Kent]

sandworm ('sænd,wɜːm) *n.* any of various polychaete worms that live in burrows on sandy shores, esp. the lugworm.

sandwort ('sænd,wɜːt) *n.* **1.** any of numerous caryophyllaceous plants of the genus *Arenaria,* which grow in dense tufts on sandy soil and have white or pink solitary flowers. **2.** any of various related plants.

sandy ('sændɪ) *adj.* **sandier, sandiest. 1.** consisting of, containing, or covered with sand. **2.** (esp. of hair) reddish-yellow. **3.** resembling sand in texture. —'**sandiness** *n.*

sand yacht *n.* a wheeled boat with sails, built to be propelled over sand, esp. beaches, by the wind.

sandy blight *n. Austral.* a nontechnical name for any of various eye inflammations.

sane (seɪn) *adj.* **1.** sound in mind; free from mental disturbance. **2.** having or showing reason, good judgment, or sound sense. **3.** *Obsolete.* healthy. [C17: from Latin *sānus* healthy] —'**sanely** *adv.* —'**saneness** *n.*

Sanforize *or* **Sanforise** ('sænfə,raɪz) *vb.* (*tr.*) *Trademark.* to preshrink (a fabric) using a patented process.

sang[1] (sæŋ) *vb.* the past tense of **sing.**

▷**Usage.** See at **ring**[2].

sang[2] (sæŋ) *n.* a Scot. word for **song.**

sangar ('sʌŋgə) *n. Military.* a breastwork of stone or sods. [C19: from Pashto]

sangaree (,sæŋgə'riː) *n.* a spiced drink similar to sangria. [C18: from Spanish *sangría* a bleeding, from *sangre* blood, from Latin *sanguis;* see SANGUINE]

sang-froid (*French* sɑ̃frwa) *n.* composure; self-possession; calmness. [C18: from French, literally: cold blood]

Sango ('sɑːŋgəʊ) *n.* a language used in Chad, the Central African Republic, N Zaïre, and the Congo, belonging to the Adamawa branch of the Niger-Congo family.

sangoma (sæŋ'gəʊmə) *n. S. African.* a witch doctor or herbalist. [from Zulu *isangoma*]

sangria (sæŋ'griːə) *n.* a Spanish drink of red wine, sugar, orange or lemon juice, and iced soda, sometimes laced with brandy. [Spanish: a bleeding; see SANGAREE]

sanguinaria (,sæŋgwɪ'nɛərɪə) *n.* **1.** the dried rhizome of the bloodroot, used as an emetic. **2.** another name for **bloodroot** (sense 1). [C19: from New Latin *herba sanguināria,* literally: the bloody herb]

sanguinary ('sæŋgwɪnərɪ) *adj.* **1.** accompanied by much bloodshed. **2.** bloodthirsty. **3.** consisting of, flowing, or stained with blood. [C17: from Latin *sanguinārius*] —'**sanguinarily** *adv.* —'**sanguinariness** *n.*

sanguine ('sæŋgwɪn) *adj.* **1.** cheerful and confident; optimistic. **2.** (esp. of the complexion) ruddy in appearance. **3.** blood-red. **4.** an obsolete word for **sanguinary** (sense 2). ~*n.* **5.** Also called: **red chalk.** a red pencil containing ferric oxide, used in drawing. [C14: from Latin *sanguineus* bloody, from *sanguis* blood] —'**sanguinely** *adv.* —'**sanguineness** *or* **san'guinity** *n.*

sanguineous (sæŋ'gwɪnɪəs) *adj.* **1.** of, containing, relating to, or associated with blood. **2.** a less common word for **sanguine** (senses 1–3). —**san'guineousness** *n.*

sanguinolent (sæŋ'gwɪnələnt) *adj.* containing, tinged with, or mixed with blood. [C15: from Latin *sanguinolentus,* from *sanguis* blood] —**san'guinolency** *n.*

Sanhedrin ('sænɪdrɪn) *n. Judaism.* **1.** the supreme judicial, ecclesiastical, and administrative council of the Jews in New Testament times, having 71 members. **2.** a similar tribunal of 23 members having less important functions and authority. [C16: from Late Hebrew, from Greek *sunedrion* council, from *sun-* SYN- + *hedra* seat]

sanicle ('sænɪkᵊl) *n.* any umbelliferous plant of the genus *Sanicula,* of most regions except Australia, having clusters of small white flowers and oval fruits with hooked bristles: formerly thought to have healing powers. [C15: via Old French from Medieval Latin *sānicula,* probably from Latin *sānus* healthy]

sanidine ('sænɪˌdiːn, -dɪn) *n.* an alkali feldspar that is a high-temperature glassy form of orthoclase in flat, tabular crystals, found in lavas and dykes. Formula: $KAlSi_3O_8$. [C19: from German, from Greek *sanis, sanidos* a board]

sanies ('seɪnɪˌiːz) *n. Pathol.* a thin greenish foul-smelling discharge from a wound, ulcer, etc., containing pus and blood. [C16: from Latin, of obscure origin]

sanitarian (ˌsænɪ'tɛərɪən) *adj.* **1.** of or relating to sanitation. ~*n.* **2.** a sanitation expert.

sanitarium (ˌsænɪ'tɛərɪəm) *n., pl.* **-riums** *or* **-ria** (-rɪə). the U.S. spelling of **sanatorium.** [C19: from Latin *sānitās* health]

sanitary ('sænɪtərɪ, -trɪ) *adj.* **1.** of or relating to health and measures for the protection of health. **2.** conducive to or promoting health; free from dirt, germs, etc.; hygienic. [C19: from French *sanitaire,* from Latin *sānitās* health] —'**sanitarily** *adv.* —'**sanitariness** *n.*

sanitary belt *n.* a belt for supporting a sanitary towel.

sanitary engineering *n.* the branch of civil engineering associated with the supply of water, disposal of sewage, and other public health services. —**sanitary engineer** *n.*

sanitary inspector *n.* (in Britain) a former name for **Environmental Health Officer.**

sanitary towel *or esp. U.S.* **napkin** *n.* an absorbent pad worn externally by women during menstruation to absorb the menstrual flow.

sanitation (ˌsænɪ'teɪʃən) *n.* the study and use of practical measures for the preservation of public health.

sanitize *or* **sanitise** ('sænɪˌtaɪz) *vb. (tr.) Chiefly U.S. and Canadian.* to make sanitary or hygienic, as by sterilizing. —ˌ**saniti'zation** *or* ˌ**saniti'sation** *n.*

sanity ('sænɪtɪ) *n.* **1.** the state of being sane. **2.** good sense or soundness of judgment. [C15: from Latin *sānitās* health, from *sānus* healthy]

sanjak ('sændʒæk) *n.* (in the Turkish Empire) a subdivision of a vilayet. [C16: from Turkish *sancàk,* literally: a flag]

San Jose scale (ˌsæn həʊ'zeɪ) *n.* a small E Asian homopterous insect, *Quadraspidiotus perniciosus,* introduced into the U.S. and other countries, where it has become a serious pest of fruit trees: family *Diaspididae.* [C20: from its first being seen in the United States at *San Jose,* California]

sank (sæŋk) *vb.* the past tense of **sink.**

Sankhya ('sæŋkjə) *n.* one of the six orthodox schools of Hindu philosophy, teaching an eternal interaction of spirit and matter. [from Sanskrit *sāmkhya,* literally: based on calculation, from *samkhyāti* he reckons]

sannyasi (sʌn'jɑːsɪ) *or* **sannyasin** (sʌn'jɑːsɪn) *n.* a Brahman who having attained the fourth and last stage of life as a beggar will not be reborn, but will instead be absorbed into the Universal Soul. [from Hindi: abandoning, from Sanskrit *samnyāsin*]

SANROC ('sænˌrɒk) *n. acronym for* South African Non-Racial Olympics Committee.

sans (sænz) *prep.* an archaic word for **without.** [C13: from Old French *sanz,* from Latin *sine* without, but probably also influenced by Latin *absentiā* in the absence of]

Sans. *or* **Sansk.** *abbrev. for* Sanskrit.

sans-culotte (ˌsænzkju'lɒt; *French* sɑ̃kylɔt) *n.* **1.** (during the French Revolution) **a.** (originally) a revolutionary of the poorer class. **b.** (later) any revolutionary, esp. one having extreme republican sympathies. **2.** any revolutionary extremist. [C18: from French, literally: without knee breeches, because the revolutionaries wore pantaloons or trousers rather than knee breeches] —ˌ**sans-cu'lottism** *n.* —ˌ**sans-cu'lottist** *n.*

sansevieria (ˌsænsɪ'vɪərɪə) *n.* any herbaceous perennial plant of the liliaceous genus *Sansevieria,* of Old World tropical regions. Some are cultivated as house plants for their erect bayonet-like fleshy leaves of variegated green (mother-in-law's tongue); others yield useful fibre (bowstring hemp). [New Latin, named after Raimondo di Sangro (1710–1771), Italian scholar and prince of *San Seviero*]

Sanskrit ('sænskrɪt) *n.* an ancient language of India, the language of the Vedas, of Hinduism, and of an extensive philosophical and scientific literature dating from the beginning of the first millennium B.C. It is the oldest recorded member of the Indic branch of the Indo-European family of languages; recognition of the existence of the Indo-European family arose in the 18th century from a comparison of Sanskrit with Greek and Latin. Although it is used only for religious purposes, it is one of the official languages of India. [C17: from Sanskrit *samskrta* perfected, literally: put together] —'**Sanskritist** *n.*

Sanskritic (sæn'skrɪtɪk) *adj.* **1.** of or relating to Sanskrit. **2.** denoting or belonging to those Indic languages that developed directly from Sanskrit, such as Pali, Hindi, Punjabi, and Bengali. ~*n.* **3.** this group of languages.

Sanson-Flamsteed projection ('sænsən'flæmstiːd) *n.* another name for **sinusoidal projection.** [devised by the cartographer *Sanson* in 1650, adapted by *Flamsteed* in 1729]

sans serif *or* **sanserif** (sæn'sɛrɪf) *n.* a style of printer's typeface in which the characters have no serifs.

Santa Gertrudis ('sæntə gə'truːdɪs) *n.* one of a breed of large red beef cattle developed in Texas.

santalaceous (ˌsæntə'leɪʃəs) *adj.* of, relating to, or belonging to the *Santalaceae,* a family of semiparasitic plants of Australia and Malaysia including sandalwood and quandong. [C19: via New Latin from Late Greek *santalon* sandalwood]

santolina (ˌsæntə'liːnə) *n.* any plant of the evergreen Mediterranean genus *Santolina,* esp. *S. chamaecyparissus,* grown for its silvery-grey felted foliage: family *Compositae.* [New Latin, altered from SANTONICA]

santonica (sæn'tɒnɪkə) *n.* **1.** an oriental wormwood plant, *Artemisia cina* (or *maritima*). **2.** the dried flower heads of this plant, formerly used as a vermifuge. ~Also called: **wormseed.** [C17: New Latin, from Late Latin *herba santonica* herb of the *Santones* (probably wormwood), from Latin *Santonī* a people of Aquitania]

santonin ('sæntənɪn) *n.* a white crystalline soluble substance extracted from the dried flower heads of santonica and used in medicine as an anthelmintic. Formula: $C_{15}H_{18}O_3$. [C19: from SANTONICA + -IN]

sap[1] (sæp) *n.* **1.** a solution of mineral salts, sugars, etc., that circulates in a plant. **2.** any vital body fluid. **3.** energy; vigour. **4.** *Slang.* a gullible or foolish person. **5.** another name for **sapwood.** ~*vb.* **saps, sapping, sapped.** *(tr.)* **6.** to drain of sap. [Old English *sæp;* related to Old High German *sapf,* German *Saft* juice, Middle Low German *sapp,* Sanskrit *sabar* milk juice] —'**sapless** *adj.*

sap[2] (sæp) *n.* **1.** a deep and narrow trench used to approach or undermine an enemy position, esp. in siege warfare. ~*vb.* **saps, sapping, sapped. 2.** to undermine (a fortification, etc.) by digging saps. **3.** *(tr.)* to weaken. [C16 *zappe,* from Italian *zappa* spade, of uncertain origin; perhaps from Old Italian (dialect) *zappo* a goat]

sapajou ('sæpəˌdʒuː) *n.* another name for **capuchin** (monkey). [C17: from French, of Tupi origin]

sapanwood ('sæpənˌwʊd) *n.* a variant spelling of **sappanwood.**

sapele (sə'piːlɪ) *n.* **1.** any of several W African meliaceous trees of the genus *Entandrophragma,* esp. *E. cylindricum,* yielding a hard timber resembling mahogany. **2.** the timber obtained from such a tree, used to make furniture. [C20: West African name]

Saphar (sə'fɑː) *n.* a variant spelling of **Safar.**

saphead[1] ('sæpˌhɛd) *n. Slang.* a simpleton, idiot, or fool. —'**sapˌheaded** *adj.*

saphead[2] ('sæpˌhɛd) *n. Military.* the end of a sap nearest to the enemy.

saphena (sə'fiːnə) *n., pl.* **-nae** (-niː). *Anatomy.* either of two large superficial veins of the legs. [C14: via Medieval Latin from Arabic *ṣāfin*] —**sa'phenous** *adj.*

sapid ('sæpɪd) *adj.* **1.** having a pleasant taste. **2.** agreeable or engaging. [C17: from Latin *sapidus,* from *sapere* to taste] —**sapidity** (sə'pɪdɪtɪ) *or* '**sapidness** *n.*

sapient ('seɪpɪənt) *adj. Often used ironically.* wise or sagacious. [C15: from Latin *sapere* to taste] —'**sapience** —'**sapiently** *adv.*

sapiential (ˌseɪpɪ'ɛnʃəl, ˌsæpɪ-) *adj.* showing, having, or providing wisdom. —ˌ**sapi'entially** *adv.*

sapindaceous (ˌsæpɪn'deɪʃəs) *adj.* of, relating to, or belonging to the *Sapindaceae,* a tropical and subtropical family of trees, shrubs, and lianas including the soapberry, litchi, and supplejack. [C19: via New Latin from Latin *sāpō* soap + *Indus* Indian]

Sapir-Whorf hypothesis (sə'pɪə'wɔːf, 'seɪˌpɪə'wɔːf) *n.* the theory that human languages determine the structure of the real world as perceived by human beings, rather than vice versa, and that this structure is different and incommensurable from one language to another. [named after E. *Sapir* (1884–1939) and B. L. *Whorf* (1897–1943), U.S. linguists]

sapling ('sæplɪŋ) *n.* **1.** a young tree. **2.** *Literary.* a youth.

sapodilla (ˌsæpə'dɪlə) *n.* **1.** a large tropical American evergreen tree, *Achras zapota,* the latex of which yields chicle. **2.** Also called: **sapodilla plum.** the edible brown rough-skinned fruit of this tree, which has a sweet yellowish pulp. ~Also called: **naseberry, sapota.** [C17: from Spanish *zapotillo,* diminutive of *zapote* sapodilla fruit, from Nahuatl *tsapotl*]

saponaceous (ˌsæpəʊˈneɪʃəs) *adj.* resembling soap; soapy. [C18: from New Latin *sāpōnāceus,* from Latin *sāpō* SOAP] —ˌ**sapoˈnaceousness** *n.*
saponaria (ˌsæpəˈnɛərɪə) *n.* See **soapwort.** [New Latin, from Late Latin *saponarius* soapy]
saponify (səˈpɒnɪˌfaɪ) *vb.* **-fies, -fying, -fied.** *Chem.* **1.** to undergo or cause to undergo a process in which a fat is converted into a soap by treatment with alkali. **2.** to undergo or cause to undergo a reaction in which an ester is hydrolysed to an acid and an alcohol as a result of treatment with an alkali. [C19: from French *saponifier,* from Latin *sāpō* SOAP] —**saˈponiˌfiable** *adj.* —**saˈponiˌfier** *n.* —**saˌponifiˈcation** *n.*
saponin (ˈsæpənɪn) *n.* any of a group of plant glycosides with a steroid structure that foam when shaken and are used in detergents. [C19: from French *saponine,* from Latin *sāpō* SOAP]
saponite (ˈsæpəˌnaɪt) *n.* a clay mineral consisting of hydrated magnesium aluminium silicate and occurring in metamorphic rocks such as serpentine. [C19: from Swedish *saponit* (a rendering of German *Seifenstein* soapstone), from Latin *sāpō* SOAP]
sapor (ˈseɪpɔː, -pə) *n. Rare.* the quality in a substance that is perceived by the sense of taste; flavour. [C15: from Latin: SAVOUR] —**sapoˈrific** *or* **ˈsaporous** *adj.*
sapota (səˈpəʊtə) *n.* **1.** (in tropical America) any of various different fruits. **2.** another name for **sapodilla.** [C16: from Spanish *zapote,* from Nahuatl *tsapotl;* see SAPODILLA]
sapotaceous (ˌsæpəˈteɪʃəs) *adj.* of, relating to, or belonging to the *Sapotaceae,* a family of leathery-leaved tropical plants: includes the gutta-percha and balata trees, sapodilla, and shea. [C19: from New Latin *sapota* SAPOTA]
sappanwood *or* **sapanwood** (ˈsæpənˌwʊd) *n.* **1.** a small caesalpiniaceous tree, *Caesalpinia sappan,* of S Asia producing wood that yields a red dye. **2.** the wood of this tree. [C16: *sapan,* via Dutch from Malay *sapang*]
sapper (ˈsæpə) *n.* **1.** a soldier who digs trenches. **2.** (in the British Army) a private of the Royal Engineers.
Sapphic (ˈsæfɪk) *adj.* **1.** *Prosody.* denoting a metre associated with Sappho, 6th-century B.C. Greek poetess, consisting generally of a trochaic pentameter line with a dactyl in the third foot. **2.** of or relating to Sappho or her poetry. **3.** lesbian. ~*n.* **4.** *Prosody.* a verse, line, or stanza written in the Sapphic form.
Sapphic ode *n.* another term for **Horatian ode.**
sapphire (ˈsæfaɪə) *n.* **1. a.** any precious corundum gemstone that is not red, esp. the highly valued transparent blue variety. A synthetic form is used in electronics and precision apparatus. Formula: Al_2O_3. **b.** (*as modifier*): *a sapphire ring.* **2. a.** the blue colour of sapphire. **b.** (*as adj.*): *sapphire eyes.* [C13 *safir,* from Old French, from Latin *sapphīrus,* from Greek *sappheiros,* perhaps from Hebrew *sappīr,* ultimately perhaps from Sanskrit *śanipriya,* literally: beloved of the planet Saturn, from *śani* Saturn + *priya* beloved]
sapphirine (ˈsæfəˌriːn, -rɪn) *n.* **1.** a rare blue or bluish-green mineral that consists of magnesium aluminium silicate in monoclinic crystalline form and occurs as small grains in some metamorphic rocks. **2.** a blue variety of spinel. ~*adj.* **3.** relating to or resembling sapphire.
sapphism (ˈsæfɪzəm) *n.* a less common word for **lesbianism.** [C19: after *Sappho,* 6th-century B.C. Greek poetess, who is believed to have been a lesbian]
sappy (ˈsæpɪ) *adj.* **-pier, -piest. 1.** (of plants) full of sap. **2.** full of energy or vitality. **3.** *Slang.* silly or fatuous. —**ˈsappily** *adv.* —**ˈsappiness** *n.*
sapraemia (sæˈpriːmɪə) *n. Pathol.* blood poisoning caused by toxins of putrefactive bacteria. [C19: New Latin, from SAPRO- + -EMIA] —**saˈpraemic** *adj.*
sapro- *or before a vowel* **sapr-** *combining form.* indicating dead or decaying matter: *saprogenic; saprolite.* [from Greek *sapros* rotten]
saprobe (ˈsæprəʊb) *n.* an organism, esp. a plant, that lives in stagnant or foul water. [C20: from Greek, from SAPRO- + *bios* life] —**sapˈrobic** *adj.*
saprogenic (ˌsæprəʊˈdʒɛnɪk) *or* **saprogenous** (sæˈprɒdʒɪnəs) *adj.* **1.** producing or resulting from decay: *saprogenic bacteria.* **2.** growing on decaying matter. —**saprogenicity** (ˌsæprədʒəˈnɪsɪtɪ) *n.*
saprolite (ˈsæprəʊlɪt) *n.* a deposit of earth, clay, silt, etc., formed by decomposition of rocks that has remained in its original site. —ˌ**saproˈlitic** *adj.*
sapropel (ˈsæprəˌpɛl) *n.* an unconsolidated sludge consisting of the decomposed remains of aquatic organisms, esp. algae, that accumulates at the bottoms of lakes and oceans. [C20: from SAPRO- + *-pel* from Greek *pēlos* mud] —ˌ**saproˈpelic** *adj.*
saprophagous (sæˈprɒfəgəs) *adj.* (of certain animals) feeding on dead or decaying organic matter.
saprophyte (ˈsæprəʊˌfaɪt) *n.* any plant, esp. a fungus or bacterium, that lives and feeds on dead organic matter. —**saprophytic** (ˌsæprəʊˈfɪtɪk) *adj.* —ˌ**saproˈphytically** *adv.*
saprozoic (ˌsæprəʊˈzəʊɪk) *adj.* **1.** (of animals or plants) feeding on dead organic matter. **2.** of or relating to nutrition in which the nutrient substances are derived from dead organic matter.
sapsago (ˈsæpsəˌgəʊ) *n.* a hard greenish Swiss cheese made with sour skim milk and coloured and flavoured with clover. [C19: changed from German *Schabziger,* from *schaben* to grate + dialect *Ziger* a kind of cheese]
sapsucker (ˈsæpˌsʌkə) *n.* either of two North American woodpeckers, *Sphyrapicus varius* or *S. thyroideus,* that have white wing patches and feed on the sap from trees.
sapwood (ˈsæpˌwʊd) *n.* the soft wood, just beneath the bark in tree trunks, that consists of living tissue. Compare **heartwood.**
Sar. *abbrev. for* Sardinia(n).
saraband *or* **sarabande** (ˈsærəˌbænd) *n.* **1.** a decorous 17th-century courtly dance. **2.** *Music.* a piece of music composed for or in the rhythm of this dance, in slow triple time, often incorporated into the classical suite. [C17: from French *sarabande,* from Spanish *zarabanda,* of uncertain origin]
Saracen (ˈsærəsᵊn) *n.* **1.** *History.* a member of one of the nomadic Arabic tribes, esp. of the Syrian desert, that harassed the borders of the Roman Empire in that region. **2. a.** a Muslim, esp. one who opposed the crusades. **b.** (in later use) any Arab. ~*adj.* **3.** of or relating to Arabs of either of these periods, regions, or types. **4.** designating, characterizing, or relating to Muslim art or architecture. [C13: from Old French *Sarrazin,* from Late Latin *Saracēnus,* from Late Greek *Sarakēnos,* perhaps from Arabic *sharq* sunrise, from *shāraqa* to rise] —**Saracenic** (ˌsærəˈsɛnɪk) *or* ˌ**Saraˈcenical** *adj.*
saran (səˈræn) *n.* any one of a class of thermoplastic resins based on vinylidene chloride, used in fibres, moulded articles, and coatings. [C20: after *Saran,* trademark coined by the Dow Chemical Co.]
sarangi (sɑːˈrʌŋgɪ) *n. Music.* a stringed instrument of India played with a bow. [Hindi]
sarcasm (ˈsɑːkæzəm) *n.* **1.** mocking, contemptuous, or ironic language intended to convey scorn or insult. **2.** the use or tone of such language. [C16: from Late Latin *sarcasmus,* from Greek *sarkasmos,* from *sarkazein* to rend the flesh, from *sarx* flesh]
sarcastic (sɑːˈkæstɪk) *adj.* **1.** characterized by sarcasm. **2.** given to the use of sarcasm. —**sarˈcastically** *adv.*
sarcenet *or* **sarsenet** (ˈsɑːsnɪt) *n.* a fine soft silk fabric formerly from Italy and used for clothing, ribbons, etc. [C15: from Old French *sarzinet,* from *Sarrazin* SARACEN]
sarco- *or before a vowel* **sarc-** *combining form.* indicating flesh: *sarcoma.* [from Greek *sark-, sarx* flesh]
sarcocarp (ˈsɑːkəʊˌkɑːp) *n. Botany.* **1.** the fleshy mesocarp of such fruits as the peach or plum. **2.** any fleshy fruit.
sarcoid (ˈsɑːkɔɪd) *adj.* **1.** of, relating to, or resembling flesh: *a sarcoid tumour.* ~*n.* **2.** a tumour resembling a sarcoma.
sarcolemma (ˌsɑːkəʊˈlɛmə) *n., pl.* **-mas** *or* **-mata** (-mətə). the membrane covering a muscle fibre.
sarcoma (sɑːˈkəʊmə) *n., pl.* **-mata** (-mətə) *or* **-mas.** *Pathol.* a usually malignant tumour arising from connective tissue. [C17: via New Latin from Greek *sarkōma* fleshy growth; see SARCO-, -OMA] —**sarˈcomaˌtoid** *or* **sarˈcomatous** *adj.*
sarcomatosis (sɑːˌkəʊməˈtəʊsɪs) *n. Pathol.* a condition characterized by the development of several sarcomas at various bodily sites. [C19: see SARCOMA, -OSIS]
sarcomere (ˈsɑːkəʊˌmɪə) *n.* any of the units that together comprise striped muscle.
sarcophagus (sɑːˈkɒfəgəs) *n., pl.* **-gi** (-ˌgaɪ) *or* **-guses.** a stone or marble coffin or tomb, esp. one bearing sculpture or inscriptions. [C17: via Latin from Greek *sarkophagos* flesh-devouring; from the type of stone used, which was believed to destroy the flesh of corpses]
sarcoplasm (ˈsɑːkəʊˌplæzəm) *n.* the cytoplasm of a muscle fibre. —ˌ**sarcoˈplasmic** *adj.*
sarcous (ˈsɑːkəs) *adj.* (of tissue) muscular or fleshy. [C19: from Greek *sarx* flesh]
sard (sɑːd) *or* **sardius** (ˈsɑːdɪəs) *n.* an orange, red, or brown variety of chalcedony, used as a gemstone. Formula: SiO_2. Also called: **sardine.** [C14: from Latin *sarda,* from Greek *sardios* stone from Sardis]
sardar *or* **sirdar** (səˈdɑː) *n.* (in India) **1.** a title used before the name of Sikh men. **2.** a leader. [Hindi, from Persian]
sardine[1] (sɑːˈdiːn) *n., pl.* **-dine** *or* **-dines. 1.** any of various small marine food fishes of the herring family, esp. a young pilchard. See also **sild. 2. like sardines.** very closely crowded together. [C15: via Old French from Latin *sardīna,* diminutive of *sarda* a fish suitable for pickling]
sardine[2] (ˈsɑːdiːn, -dᵊn) *n.* another name for **sard.** [C14: from Late Latin *sardinus,* from Greek *sardinos lithos* Sardian stone, from *Sardeis* Sardis]
Sardinian (sɑːˈdɪnɪən) *adj.* **1.** of or relating to Sardinia, an island in the Mediterranean, or to its inhabitants or their language. ~*n.* **2.** a native or inhabitant of Sardinia. **3.** the spoken language of Sardinia, sometimes regarded as a dialect of Italian but containing many loan words from Spanish.
sardius (ˈsɑːdɪəs) *n.* **1.** *Old Testament.* a precious stone, probably a ruby, set in the breastplate of the high priest. **2.** another name for **sard.** [C14: via Late Latin from Greek *sardios,* from *Sardeis* Sardis]
sardonic (sɑːˈdɒnɪk) *adj.* characterized by irony, mockery, or derision. [C17: from French *sardonique,* from Latin *sardonius,* from Greek *sardonios* derisive, literally: of Sardinia, alteration of Homeric *sardanios* scornful (laughter or smile)] —**sarˈdonically** *adv.* —**sarˈdonicism** *n.*
sardonyx (ˈsɑːdənɪks) *n.* a variety of chalcedony with alternating reddish-brown and white parallel bands, used as a gemstone.

Formula: SiO_2. [C14: via Latin from Greek *sardonux*, perhaps from *sardion* SARDINE[2] + *onux* nail]

sargasso *or* **sargasso weed** (sɑːˈgæsəʊ) *n., pl.* **-sos.** another name for **gulfweed.** [C16: from Portuguese *sargaço*, of unknown origin]

sargassum (sɑːˈgæsəm) *n.* any floating brown seaweed of the genus *Sargassum*, such as gulfweed, of warm seas, having ribbon-like fronds containing air sacs. [C18: from New Latin; see SARGASSO]

sarge (sɑːdʒ) *n. Informal.* sergeant: used esp. as a term of address.

sari *or* **saree** (ˈsɑːrɪ) *n., pl.* **-ris** *or* **-rees.** the traditional dress of women of India, Pakistan, etc., consisting of a very long narrow piece of cloth elaborately swathed around the body. [C18: from Hindi *sārī*, from Sanskrit *śāṭī*]

sarin (ˈsærɪn) *n.* isopropyl methylphosphonofluoridate: used in chemical warfare as a lethal nerve gas producing asphyxia. Formula: $CH_3P(O)(F)OCH(CH_3)_3$. [C20: from German, of unknown origin]

sark (særk) *n. Scot.* a shirt or (formerly) chemise. [Old English *serc*; related to Old Norse *serkr*]

sarking (ˈsɑːkɪŋ, ˈsærkɪŋ) *n. Scot., northern English, and N.Z.* a timber or felt cladding placed over the rafters of a roof before the tiles or slates are fixed in place. [C15: from verbal use of SARK]

sarky (ˈsɑːkɪ) *adj.* **-kier, -kiest.** *Brit. informal.* sarcastic.

sarmentose (sɑːˈmɛntəʊs), **sarmentous** (sɑːˈmɛntəs), *or* **sarmentaceous** (ˌsɑːmənˈteɪʃəs) *adj.* (of plants such as the strawberry) having stems in the form of runners. [C18: from Latin *sarmentōsus* full of twigs, from *sarmentum* brushwood, from *sarpere* to prune]

sarnie (ˈsɑːnɪ) *n. Brit. informal.* a sandwich. [C20: probably from Northern or dialect pronunciation of first syllable of *sandwich*]

sarod (sæˈrəʊd) *n.* an Indian stringed musical instrument that may be played with a bow or plucked. [C19: from Hindi]

sarong (səˈrɒŋ) *n.* **1.** a draped skirtlike garment worn by men and women in the Malay Archipelago, Sri Lanka, the Pacific islands, etc. **2.** a fashionable Western adaptation of this garment. [C19: from Malay, literally: sheath]

saros (ˈseɪrɒs) *n.* a cycle of about 18 years 11 days (6585.32 days) in which eclipses of the sun and moon occur in the same sequence and at the same intervals as in the previous such cycle. [C19: from Greek, from Babylonian *šāru* 3600 (years); modern astronomical use apparently based on mistaken interpretation of *šāru* as a period of 18½ years] —**saronic** (səˈrɒnɪk) *adj.*

sarpanch (səˈpʌntʃ) *n.* the head of a panchayat. [Urdu, from *sar* head + Sanskrit *panch* five; see PANCHAYAT]

sarracenia (ˌsærəˈsiːnɪə) *n.* any American pitcher plant of the genus *Sarracenia*, having single nodding flowers and leaves modified as pitchers that trap and digest insects: family *Sarraceniaceae*. [C18: New Latin, named after D. *Sarrazin*, 17th-century botanist of Quebec]

sarraceniaceous (ˌsærəˌsiːnɪˈeɪʃəs) *adj.* of, relating to, or belonging to the *Sarraceniaceae*, an American family of pitcher plants.

sarrusophone (səˈruːzəˌfəʊn) *n.* a wind instrument resembling the oboe but made of brass. [C19: named after *Sarrus*, French bandmaster, who invented it (1856)]

sarsaparilla (ˌsɑːsəpəˈrɪlə, ˌsɑːspə-) *n.* **1.** any of various prickly climbing plants of the tropical American genus *Smilax* having large aromatic roots and heart-shaped leaves: family *Smilacaceae*. **2.** the dried roots of any of these plants, formerly used in medicine to treat psoriasis. **3.** a nonalcoholic drink prepared from these roots. **4.** any of various plants resembling true sarsaparilla, esp. the araliaceous plant *Aralia nudicaulis* **(wild sarsaparilla)**, of North America. [C16: from Spanish *sarzaparrilla*, from *zarza* a bramble, (from Arabic *šaras*) + *-parrilla*, from Spanish *parra* a climbing plant]

sarsen (ˈsɑːsᵊn) *n.* **1.** *Geology.* a boulder of silicified sandstone, probably of Tertiary age, found in large numbers in S England. **2.** such a stone used in a megalithic monument. Also called: **greywether.** [C17: probably a variant of SARACEN]

sarsenet (ˈsɑːsnɪt) *n.* a variant spelling of **sarcenet.**

sartor (ˈsɑːtə) *n.* a humorous or literary word for **tailor.** [C17: from Latin: a patcher, from *sarcīre* to patch]

sartorial (sɑːˈtɔːrɪəl) *adj.* **1.** of or relating to a tailor or to tailoring. **2.** *Anatomy.* of or relating to the sartorius. [C19: from Late Latin *sartōrius* from SARTOR] —**sarˈtorially** *adv.*

sartorius (sɑːˈtɔːrɪəs) *n., pl.* **-torii** (-ˈtɔːrɪˌaɪ). *Anatomy.* a long ribbon-shaped muscle that aids in flexing the knee. [C18: New Latin, from *sartorius musculus*, literally: tailor's muscle, because it is used when one sits in the cross-legged position in which tailors traditionally sat while sewing]

Sarum use (ˈsɛərəm) *n.* the distinctive local rite or system of rites used at Salisbury cathedral, S England, in late medieval times. [*Sarum*: Medieval Latin, perhaps shortened and altered from Latin *Sarisburia* Salisbury]

Sarvodaya (səˈvəʊdəjə) *n.* (in India) economic and social development and improvement of a community as a whole. [Hindi, from *sarva* all + *udaya* rise]

SAS *abbrev. for* Special Air Service.

sash[1] (sæʃ) *n.* a long piece of ribbon, silk, etc., worn around the waist like a belt or over one shoulder, as a symbol of rank. [C16: from Arabic *shāsh* muslin]

sash[2] (sæʃ) *n.* **1.** a frame that contains the panes of a window or door. ~*vb.* (*tr.*) **2.** to furnish with a sash, sashes, or sash windows. [C17: originally plural *sashes*, variant of *shashes*, from CHASSIS]

sashay (sæˈʃeɪ) *vb.* (*intr.*) *Informal, chiefly U.S. and Canadian.* **1.** to move, walk, or glide along casually. **2.** to move or walk in a showy way; parade. [C19: from an alteration of *chassé*, a gliding dance step]

sash cord *n.* a strong cord connecting a sash weight to a sliding sash.

sashimi (ˈsæʃɪmɪ) *n.* a Japanese dish of thin fillets of raw fish. [C19: from Japanese *sashi* pierce + *mi* flesh]

sash saw *n.* a small tenon saw used for cutting sashes.

sash weight *n.* a weight used to counterbalance the weight of a sliding sash in a sash window and thus hold it in position at any height.

sash window *n.* a window consisting of two sashes placed one above the other so that one or each can be slid over the other to open the window.

sasin (ˈsæsɪn) *n.* another name for the **blackbuck.** [C19: of unknown origin]

sasine (ˈsesɪn, ˈseɪ-) *n. Scots Law.* the granting of legal possession of feudal property. [C17: Scots variant of SEISIN]

Sask. *abbrev. for* Saskatchewan.

saskatoon (ˌsæskəˈtuːn) *n.* a species of serviceberry, *Amelanchier alnifolia*, of W Canada: noted for its succulent purplish berries. [from Cree *misaskwatomin*, from *misaskwat* tree of many branches + *min* fruit]

sasquatch (ˈsæsˌkwætʃ) *n.* (in Canadian folklore) in British Columbia, a hairy beast or manlike monster said to leave huge footprints. [from Salish]

sass (sæs) *U.S. and Canadian informal.* ~*n.* **1.** insolent or impudent talk or behaviour. ~*vb.* (*intr.*) **2.** to talk or answer back in such a way. [C20: back formation from SASSY[1]]

sassaby (ˈsæsəbɪ) *n., pl.* **-bies.** an African antelope, *Damaliscus lunatus* of grasslands and semideserts, having angular curved horns and an elongated muzzle: thought to be the swiftest hoofed mammal. [C19: from Bantu *tshêsêbê*]

sassafras (ˈsæsəˌfræs) *n.* **1.** an aromatic deciduous lauraceous tree, *Sassafras albidum*, of North America, having three-lobed leaves and dark blue fruits. **2.** the aromatic dried root bark of this tree, used as a flavouring, and yielding sassafras oil. **3.** *Austral.* any of several unrelated trees having a similar fragrant bark. [C16: from Spanish *sasafrás*, of uncertain origin]

sassafras oil *n.* a clear volatile oil that is extracted from the root of the sassafras tree and contains camphor, pinene, and safrole.

Sassanid (ˈsæsənɪd) *n., pl.* **Sassanids** *or* **Sassanidae** (sæˈsænɪˌdiː). any member of the native dynasty that built and ruled an empire in Persia from 224 to 636 A.D. —**Saˈssanian** *adj.*

Sassenach (ˈsæsəˌnæk; *Scot.* -næx) *n. Scot. and occasionally Irish.* an English person or a Lowland Scot. [C18: from Scot. Gaelic *Sasunnach*, Irish *Sasanach*, from Late Latin *saxonēs* Saxons]

sassy[1] (ˈsæsɪ) *adj.* **-sier, -siest.** *U.S. informal.* insolent, impertinent. [C19: variant of SAUCY] —**ˈsassily** *adv.* —**ˈsassiness** *n.*

sassy[2] (ˈsæsɪ), **sasswood** (ˈsæsˌwʊd), *or* **sassy wood** *n.* **1.** a W African leguminous tree, *Erythrophleum guineense*, with poisonous bark **(sassy bark)** and hard strong wood. **2.** the bark or wood of this tree or the alkaloid derived from them, which is sometimes used in medicine. [C19: probably from a language of the Kwa family: compare Twi *sese* plane tree, Ewe *sesewu* a kind of timber tree]

sastra (ˈʃɑːstrə) *n.* a variant spelling of **shastra.**

sastruga (səˈstruːgə, sæ-) *or* **zastruga** *n.* one of a series of ridges on snow-covered plains, caused by the action of wind laden with ice particles. [from Russian *zastruga* groove, from *za* by + *struga* deep place]

sat (sæt) *vb.* the past tense and past participle of **sit.**

SAT *abbrev. for* South Australian Time.

Sat. *abbrev. for:* **1.** Saturday. **2.** Saturn.

Satan (ˈseɪtᵊn) *n.* the devil, adversary of God, and tempter of mankind: sometimes identified with Lucifer (Luke 4:5–8). [Old English, from Late Latin, from Greek, from Hebrew: plotter, from *sāṭan* to plot against]

satang (sæˈtæŋ) *n., pl.* **-tang.** a Thai monetary unit worth one hundredth of a baht. [from Thai *satān*]

satanic (səˈtænɪk) *or* (*now rare*) **satanical** *adj.* **1.** of or relating to Satan. **2.** supremely evil or wicked; diabolic. —**saˈtanically** *adv.* —**saˈtanicalness** *n.*

Satanism (ˈseɪtᵊˌnɪzəm) *n.* **1.** the worship of Satan. **2.** a form of such worship which includes blasphemous or obscene parodies of Christian prayers, etc. **3.** a satanic disposition or satanic practices. —**ˈSatanist** *n., adj.*

satay, satai, *or* **saté** (ˈsæteɪ) *n.* barbecued spiced meat cooked on skewers usually made from the stems of coconut leaves. [from Malay]

SATB *abbrev. for* soprano, alto, tenor, bass: a combination of voices in choral music.

satchel (ˈsætʃəl) *n.* a rectangular bag, usually made of leather or cloth and provided with a shoulder strap, used for carrying books, esp. school books. [C14: from Old French *sachel* a little bag, from Late Latin *saccellus*, from Latin *saccus* SACK[1]] —**ˈsatchelled** *adj.*

sate[1] (seɪt) *vb.* (*tr.*) **1.** to satisfy (a desire or appetite) fully. **2.** to supply beyond capacity or desire. [Old English *sadian;* related to Old High German *satōn;* see SAD, SATIATE]
sate[2] (sæt, seɪt) *vb. Archaic.* a past tense and past participle of **sit.**
sateen (sæ'tiːn) *n.* a glossy linen or cotton fabric, woven in such a way that it resembles satin. [C19: changed from SATIN, on the model of VELVETEEN]
satellite ('sætᵊˌlaɪt) *n.* **1.** a celestial body orbiting around a planet or star: *the earth is a satellite of the sun.* **2.** Also called: **artificial satellite.** a man-made device orbiting around the earth, moon, or another planet transmitting to earth scientific information or used for communication. See also **communications satellite. 3.** a person, esp. one who is obsequious, who follows or serves another. **4.** a country or political unit under the domination of a foreign power. **5.** a subordinate area or community that is dependent upon a larger adjacent town or city. **6.** (*modifier*) subordinate to or dependent upon another: *a satellite nation.* **7.** (*modifier*) of, used in, or relating to the transmission of television signals from a satellite to the house: *a satellite dish aerial.* ~*vb.* **8.** (*tr.*) to transmit by communications satellite. [C16: from Latin *satelles* an attendant, probably of Etruscan origin]
satellite broadcasting *n.* the transmission of television or radio programmes from an artificial satellite at a power suitable for direct reception in the home.
satellite dish aerial *n.* a parabolic aerial for reception from or transmission to an artificial satellite. Often shortened to **dish aerial** or **dish.**
satellitium (ˌsætᵊ'lɪtɪəm, -'lɪʃɪəm) *n. Astrology.* a group of three or more planets lying in one sign of the zodiac. [C17: from Latin, literally: bodyguard, retinue, from *satelles* an attendant. See SATELLITE]
satem ('sɑːtəm, 'seɪ-) *adj.* denoting or belonging to the group of Indo-European languages in which original velar stops became palatalized (k > s or ʃ). These languages belong to the Indic, Iranian, Armenian, Slavonic, Baltic, and Albanian branches and are traditionally regarded as the E group. Compare **centum.** [from Avestan *satəm* hundred; chosen to exemplify the variation of initial *s* with initial *k* (as in *centum*) in Indo-European languages]
satiable ('seɪʃɪəbᵊl, 'seɪʃə-) *adj.* capable of being satiated. —ˌ**satia'bility** *n.* —'**satiably** *adv.*
satiate ('seɪʃɪˌeɪt) *vb.* (*tr.*) **1.** to fill or supply beyond capacity or desire, often arousing weariness. **2.** to supply to satisfaction or capacity. [C16: from Latin *satiāre* to satisfy, from *satis* enough] —ˌ**sati'ation** *n.*
Saticon ('sætɪˌkɒn) *n. Trademark.* a high-resolution television camera tube used when high-definition is required. [C20: from S(ELENIUM) + A(RSENIC) + T(ELLURIUM) (used in the tube screen) + ICON(OSCOPE)]
satiety (sə'taɪɪtɪ) *n.* the state of being satiated. [C16: from Latin *satietās,* from *satis* enough]
satin ('sætɪn) *n.* **1.** a fabric of silk, rayon, etc., closely woven to show much of the warp, giving a smooth glossy appearance. **2.** (*modifier*) of or like satin in texture: *a satin finish.* [C14: via Old French from Arabic *zaitūnī* of *Zaytūn,* Arabic rendering of Chinese *Tseutung* (now *Tsinkiang*), port in southern China from which the cloth was probably first exported] —'**satin-ˌlike** *adj.* —'**satiny** *adj.*
satinet *or* **satinette** (ˌsætɪ'nɛt) *n.* a thin or imitation satin. [C18: from French: small satin]
satinflower ('sætɪnˌflaʊə) *n.* another name for **greater stitchwort** (see **stitchwort**).
satinpod ('sætɪnˌpɒd) *n.* another name for **honesty** (the plant).
satin stitch *n.* an embroidery stitch consisting of rows of flat stitches placed close together. [C17: so called from the satin-like appearance of embroidery using this stitch]
satin walnut *n.* the brown heartwood of the sweet gum tree, used for furniture, fittings, and panelling.
satinwood ('sætɪnˌwʊd) *n.* **1.** a tree, *Chloroxylon swietenia,* that occurs in the East Indies and has hard wood with a satiny texture: family *Flindersiaceae.* **2.** the wood of this tree, used in veneering, cabinetwork, marquetry, etc. **3. West Indian satinwood.** another name for **yellowwood** (sense 2).
satire ('sætaɪə) *n.* **1.** a novel, play, entertainment, etc., in which topical issues, folly, or evil are held up to scorn by means of ridicule and irony. **2.** the genre constituted by such works. **3.** the use of ridicule, irony, etc., to create such an effect. [C16: from Latin *satira* a mixture, from *satur* sated, from *satis* enough]
satirical (sə'tɪrɪkᵊl) *or* **satiric** *adj.* **1.** of, relating to, or containing satire. **2.** given to the use of satire. —**sa'tirically** *adv.* —**sa'tiricalness** *n.*
satirist ('sætərɪst) *n.* **1.** a person who writes satire. **2.** a person given to the use of satire.
satirize *or* **satirise** ('sætəˌraɪz) *vb.* to deride (a person or thing) by means of satire. —ˌ**satiri'zation** *or* ˌ**satiri'sation** *n.* —'**satiˌrizer** *or* '**satiˌriser** *n.*
satisfaction (ˌsætɪs'fækʃən) *n.* **1.** the act of satisfying or state of being satisfied. **2.** the fulfilment of a desire. **3.** the pleasure obtained from such fulfilment. **4.** a source of fulfilment. **5.** reparation or compensation for a wrong done or received. **6.** *R.C. Church, Church of England.* the performance by a repentant sinner of a penance. **7.** *Christianity.* the atonement for sin by the death of Christ. [C15: via French from Latin *satisfactionem,* from *satisfacere* to SATISFY]
satisfactory (ˌsætɪs'fæktərɪ, -trɪ) *adj.* **1.** adequate or suitable; acceptable: *a satisfactory answer.* **2.** giving satisfaction. **3.** constituting or involving atonement, recompense, or expiation for sin. —ˌ**satis'factorily** *adv.* —ˌ**satis'factoriness** *n.*
satisfice ('sætɪsˌfaɪs) *vb.* **1.** (*intr.*) to act in such a way as to satisfy the minimum requirements for achieving a particular result. **2.** (*tr.*) *Obsolete.* to satisfy. [C16: altered from SATISFY] —'**satisˌficer** *n.*
satisficing behaviour ('sætɪsˌfaɪsɪŋ) *n. Economics.* the form of behaviour demonstrated by firms who seek satisfactory profits and satisfactory growth rather than maximum profits.
satisfy ('sætɪsˌfaɪ) *vb.* **-fies, -fying, -fied.** (*mainly tr.*) **1.** (*also intr.*) to fulfil the desires or needs of (a person). **2.** to provide amply for (a need or desire). **3.** to relieve of doubt; convince. **4.** to dispel (a doubt). **5.** to make reparation to or for. **6.** to discharge or pay off (a debt) to (a creditor). **7.** to fulfil the requirements of; comply with: *you must satisfy the terms of your lease.* **8.** *Maths, logic.* to fulfil the conditions of (a theorem, assumption, etc.); to yield a truth by substitution of the given value: *$x = 3$ satisfies $x^2 - 4x + 3 = 0$.* [C15: from Old French *satisfier,* from Latin *satisfacere,* from *satis* enough + *facere* to make, do] —'**satisˌfiable** *adj.* —'**satisˌfier** *n.* —'**satisˌfying** *adj.* —'**satisˌfyingly** *adv.*
satori (sə'tɔːrɪ) *n. Zen Buddhism.* the state of sudden indescribable intuitive enlightenment. [from Japanese]
satrap ('sætræp) *n.* **1.** (in ancient Persia) a provincial governor. **2.** a subordinate ruler, esp. a despotic one. [C14: from Latin *satrapa,* from Greek *satrapēs,* from Old Persian *khshathrapāvan,* literally: protector of the land]
satrapy ('sætrəpɪ) *n., pl.* **-trapies.** the province, office, or period of rule of a satrap.
satsuma (sæt'suːmə) *n.* **1.** a small citrus tree, *Citrus nobilis* var. *unshiu,* cultivated, esp. in Japan, for its edible fruit. **2.** the fruit of this tree, which has a loose rind and easily separable segments. [C19: originally from the province of *Satsuma,* SW Japan]
Satsuma ware ('sætsʊmə) *n.* **1.** simple pottery made in Satsuma, Japan, from the late 16th century. **2.** ornamental glazed porcelain ware made in Satsuma, Japan, from the late 18th century.
saturable ('sætʃərəbᵊl) *adj. Chem.* capable of being saturated. —ˌ**satura'bility** *n.*
saturant ('sætʃərənt) *Chem.* ~*n.* **1.** the substance that causes a solution, etc., to be saturated. ~*adj.* **2.** (of a substance) causing saturation. [C18: from Latin *saturāns*]
saturate *vb.* ('sætʃəˌreɪt). **1.** to fill, soak, or imbue totally. **2.** to make (a chemical compound, vapour, solution, magnetic material, etc.) saturated or (of a compound, vapour, etc.) to become saturated. **3.** (*tr.*) *Military.* to bomb or shell heavily. ~*adj.* ('sætʃərɪt, -ˌreɪt). **4.** a less common word for **saturated.** [C16: from Latin *saturāre,* from *satur* sated, from *satis* enough] —ˌ**satu'rater** *or* ˌ**satu'rator** *n.*
saturated ('sætʃəˌreɪtɪd) *adj.* **1.** (of a solution or solvent) containing the maximum amount of solute that can normally be dissolved at a given temperature and pressure. See also **supersaturated. 2.** (of a colour) having a large degree of saturation. **3.** (of a chemical compound) **a.** containing no multiple bonds and thus being incapable of undergoing additional reactions: *a saturated hydrocarbon.* **b.** containing no unpaired valence electrons. **4.** (of a fat, esp. an animal fat) containing a high proportion of fatty acids having single bonds. See also **polyunsaturated, unsaturated. 5.** (of a vapour) containing the equilibrium amount of gaseous material at a given temperature and pressure. See also **supersaturated. 6.** (of a magnetic material) fully magnetized. **7.** extremely wet; soaked.
saturation (ˌsætʃə'reɪʃən) *n.* **1.** the act of saturating or the state of being saturated. **2.** *Chem.* the state of a chemical compound, solution, or vapour when it is saturated. **3.** *Meteorol.* the state of the atmosphere when it can hold no more water vapour at its particular temperature and pressure, the relative humidity then being 100 per cent. **4.** the attribute of a colour that enables an observer to judge its proportion of pure chromatic colour. See also **colour. 5.** *Physics.* the state of a ferromagnetic material in which it is fully magnetized. The magnetic domains are then all fully aligned. **6.** *Electronics.* the state of a valve or semiconductor device that is carrying the maximum current of which it is capable and is therefore unresponsive to further increases of input signal. **7.** the level beyond which demand for a product or service is not expected to increase. ~*modifier.* **8.** denoting the maximum possible intensity of coverage of an area: *saturation bombing; a saturation release of a film.*
saturation diving *n.* a method of diving to great depths in which the diver's blood is saturated with helium, which, unlike the nitrogen of the air, is not absorbed by the blood and therefore does not cause decompression sickness.
saturation point *n.* **1.** the point at which no more (people, things, ideas, etc.) can be absorbed, accommodated, used, etc. **2.** *Chem.* the point at which no more solute can be dissolved in a solution or gaseous material absorbed in a vapour.
Saturday ('sætədɪ) *n.* the seventh and last day of the week: the Jewish Sabbath. [Old English *sæternes dæg,* translation of

Latin *Saturnī diēs* day of Saturn; compare Middle Dutch *saterdach,* Dutch *zaterdag*]

Saturn ('sætɜːn) *n.* **1.** one of the **giant planets,** the sixth planet from the sun, around which revolve planar concentric rings (**Saturn's rings**) consisting of small frozen particles. The planet has at least 22 satellites. Mean distance from sun: 1425 million km; period of revolution around sun: 29.46 years; period of axial rotation: 10.23 hours; diameter and mass: 9.36 and 95.14 times that of the earth, respectively. **2.** the alchemical name for **lead**[2]. —**Saturnian** (sæ'tɜːnɪən) *adj.*

Saturnalia (ˌsætə'neɪlɪə) *n., pl.* **-lia** *or* **-lias. 1.** an ancient Roman festival celebrated in December: renowned for its general merry-making. **2.** (*sometimes not cap.*) a period or occasion of wild revelry. [C16: from Latin *Sāturnālis* relating to *Saturn,* the Roman god of agriculture] —ˌ**Satur'nalian** *adj.*

Saturnian (sæ'tɜːnɪən) *adj.* **1.** of or connected with the Roman god Saturn, whose reign was thought of as a golden age; happy, simple, or pure. **2.** *Prosody.* denoting a very early verse form in Latin in which the accent was one of stress rather than quantity, there being an equal number of main stresses in each line, regardless of the number of unaccented syllables. ~*n.* **3.** a line in Saturnian metre.

saturniid (sæ'tɜːnɪɪd) *n.* **1.** any moth of the mainly tropical family *Saturniidae,* typically having large brightly coloured wings: includes the emperor, cecropia, and luna moths. ~*adj.* **2.** of, relating to, or belonging to the *Saturniidae.*

saturnine ('sætəˌnaɪn) *adj.* **1.** having a gloomy temperament; taciturn. **2.** *Archaic.* **a.** of or relating to lead. **b.** having or symptomatic of lead poisoning. [C15: from French *saturnin,* from Medieval Latin *sāturnīnus* (unattested), from Latin *Sāturnus* Saturn, with reference to the gloomy influence attributed to the planet Saturn] —'**saturˌninely** *adv.* —**saturninity** (ˌsætə'nɪnɪtɪ) *n.*

saturnism ('sætəˌnɪzəm) *n. Pathol.* another name for **lead poisoning.** [C19: from New Latin *sāturnismus;* properties similar to those of lead were attributed to the planet]

satyagraha ('sɔːtjɑːgrɔːhɑː) *n.* **1.** the policy of nonviolent resistance adopted by Mahatma Gandhi from about 1919 to oppose British rule in India. See **Gandhiism. 2.** any movement of nonviolent resistance. [via Hindi from Sanskrit, literally: insistence on truth, from *satya* truth + *agraha* fervour]

satyagrahi ('sʌtjəˌgrʌhiː) *n.* an exponent of nonviolent resistance, esp. as a form of political protest.

satyr ('sætə) *n.* **1.** *Greek myth.* one of a class of sylvan deities, represented as goatlike men who chased the nymphs. **2.** a man who has strong sexual desires. **3.** a man who has satyriasis. **4.** any of various butterflies of the genus *Satyrus* and related genera, having dark wings often marked with eyespots: family *Satyridae.* [C14: from Latin *satyrus,* from Greek *saturos*] —**satyric** (sə'tɪrɪk) *or* **sa'tyrical** *adj.* —'**satyr-ˌlike** *adj.*

satyriasis (ˌsætɪ'raɪəsɪs) *n.* a neurotic condition in men in which the symptoms are a compulsion to have sexual intercourse with as many women as possible and an inability to have lasting relationships with them. Compare **nymphomania.** [C17: via New Latin from Greek *saturiasis;* see SATYR, -IASIS]

satyrid (sə'tɪərɪd) *n.* any butterfly of the family *Satyridae,* having typically brown or dark wings with paler markings: includes the graylings, satyrs, browns, ringlets, and gatekeepers.

satyr play *n.* (in ancient Greek drama) a ribald play with a chorus of satyrs, presented at the Dionysian festival.

sauce (sɔːs) *n.* **1.** any liquid or semiliquid preparation eaten with food to enhance its flavour. **2.** anything that adds piquancy. **3.** *U.S. and Canadian.* stewed fruit. **4.** *U.S. dialect.* vegetables eaten with meat. **5.** *Informal.* impudent language or behaviour. ~*vb.* (*tr.*) **6.** to prepare (food) with sauce. **7.** to add zest to. **8.** to make agreeable or less severe. **9.** *Informal.* to be saucy to. [C14: via Old French from Latin *salsus* salted, from *salīre* to sprinkle with salt, from *sal* salt] —'**sauceless** *adj.*

sauce boat *n.* another term for **gravy boat.**

saucebox ('sɔːsˌbɒks) *n. Informal.* a saucy person.

saucepan ('sɔːspən) *n.* a metal or enamel pan with a long handle and often a lid, used for cooking food.

saucer ('sɔːsə) *n.* **1.** a small round dish on which a cup is set. **2.** any similar dish. [C14: from Old French *saussier* container for SAUCE] —'**saucerful** *n.* —'**saucerless** *adj.*

sauch *or* **saugh** (sɔːx) *n.* a sallow or willow. [C15: from Old English *salh*]

saucy ('sɔːsɪ) *adj.* **saucier, sauciest. 1.** impertinent. **2.** pert; jaunty: *a saucy hat.* —'**saucily** *adv.* —'**sauciness** *n.*

Saudi *or* **Saudi Arabian** ('saudɪ, 'sɔː-) *adj.* **1.** of or relating to Saudi Arabia, a kingdom in SW Asia, or to its people, customs, etc. ~*n.* **2.** a native or inhabitant of Saudi Arabia.

sauerbraten ('sauəˌbrɑːtᵊn; *German* 'zauərˌbraːtən) *n.* beef marinated in vinegar, sugar, and seasonings, and then braised. [German, from *sauer* SOUR + *Braten* roast]

sauerkraut ('sauəˌkraut) *n.* finely shredded and pickled cabbage. [German, from *sauer* SOUR + *Kraut* cabbage]

sauger ('sɔːgə) *n.* a small North American pikeperch, *Stizostedion canadense,* with a spotted dorsal fin: valued as a food and game fish. [C19: of unknown origin]

sauna ('sɔːnə) *n.* **1.** an invigorating bath originating in Finland in which the bather is subjected to hot steam, usually followed by a cold plunge or by being lightly beaten with birch twigs. **2.** the place in which such a bath is taken. [C20: from Finnish]

saunter ('sɔːntə) *vb.* (*intr.*) **1.** to walk in a casual manner; stroll. ~*n.* **2.** a leisurely pace or stroll. **3.** a leisurely old-time dance. [C17 (meaning: to wander aimlessly), C15 (to muse): of obscure origin] —'**saunterer** *n.*

-saur *or* **-saurus** *n. combining form.* lizard: *dinosaur.* [from New Latin *saurus*]

saurel ('sɔːrəl) *n.* a U.S. name for **horse mackerel** (sense 1). [C19: via French from Late Latin *saurus,* from Greek *sauros,* of obscure origin]

saurian ('sɔːrɪən) *adj.* **1.** of, relating to, or resembling a lizard. **2.** of, relating to, or belonging to the *Sauria,* a former suborder of reptiles (now called *Lacertilia*), which included the lizards. ~*n.* **3.** a former name for **lizard.** [C15: from New Latin *Sauria,* from Greek *sauros*]

saurischian (sɔː'rɪskɪən) *adj.* **1.** of, relating to, or belonging to the *Saurischia,* an order of late Triassic dinosaurs including the theropods and sauropods. ~*n.* **2.** any dinosaur belonging to the order *Saurischia.* [C19: from New Latin *Saurischia,* from *saurus* + ISCHIUM]

sauropod ('sɔːrəˌpɒd) *n.* any herbivorous quadrupedal saurischian dinosaur of the suborder *Sauropoda,* of Jurassic and Cretaceous times, including the brontosaurus, diplodocus, and titanosaurs. They had small heads and long necks and tails and were partly amphibious. [C19: from New Latin *sauropoda,* from Greek *sauros* lizard + *pous* foot] —**sauropodous** (sɔː'rɒpədəs) *adj.*

saury ('sɔːrɪ) *n., pl.* **-ries.** any teleost fish, such as the Atlantic *Scomberesox saurus* of the family *Scomberesocidae* of tropical and temperate seas, having an elongated body and long toothed jaws. Also called: **skipper.** [C18: perhaps from Late Latin *saurus;* see SAUREL]

sausage ('sɒsɪdʒ) *n.* **1.** finely minced meat, esp. pork or beef, mixed with fat, cereal or bread, and seasonings (**sausage meat**), and packed into a tube-shaped animal intestine or synthetic casing. **2.** an object shaped like a sausage. **3.** *Aeronautics, informal.* a captive balloon shaped like a sausage. **4. not a sausage.** nothing at all. [C15: from Old Norman French *saussiche,* from Late Latin *salsīcia,* from Latin *salsus* salted; see SAUCE] —'**sausage-ˌlike** *adj.*

sausage dog *n.* an informal name for **dachshund.**

sausage roll *n. Brit.* a roll of sausage meat in pastry.

saut (sɔːt) *n., vb., adj.* a Scot. word for **salt.**

sauté ('səuteɪ) *vb.* **-tés, -téing** *or* **-téeing, -téed. 1.** to fry (food) quickly in a little fat. ~*n.* **2.** a dish of sautéed food, esp. meat that is browned and then cooked in a sauce. ~*adj.* **3.** sautéed until lightly brown: *sauté potatoes.* [C19: from French: tossed, from *sauter* to jump, from Latin *saltāre* to dance, from *salīre* to spring]

Sauternes (səu'tɜːn) *n.* (*sometimes not cap.*) a sweet white wine made in the southern Bordeaux district of France. [C18: from *Sauternes,* the district where it is produced]

sauve qui peut *French.* (sov ki pø) *n.* a state of panic or disorder; rout. [literally: save (himself) who can]

sav (sæv) *n. Austral. and N.Z. informal.* short for **saveloy.**

savage ('sævɪdʒ) *adj.* **1.** wild; untamed: *savage beasts of the jungle.* **2.** ferocious in temper; vicious: *a savage dog.* **3.** uncivilized; crude: *savage behaviour.* **4.** (of peoples) nonliterate or primitive: *a savage tribe.* **5.** (of terrain) rugged and uncultivated. **6.** *Obsolete.* far from human habitation. ~*n.* **7.** a member of a nonliterate society, esp. one regarded as primitive. **8.** a crude or uncivilized person. **9.** a fierce or vicious person or animal. ~*vb.* (*tr.*) **10.** to criticize violently. **11.** to attack ferociously and wound: *the dog savaged the child.* [C13: from Old French *sauvage,* from Latin *silvāticus* belonging to a wood, from *silva* a wood] —'**savagedom** *n.* —'**savagely** *adv.* —'**savageness** *n.*

savagery ('sævɪdʒrɪ) *n., pl.* **-ries. 1.** an uncivilized condition. **2.** a savage act or nature. **3.** savages collectively.

savanna *or* **savannah** (sə'vænə) *n.* open grasslands, usually with scattered bushes or trees, characteristic of much of tropical Africa. Whether this is the natural climax vegetation or the result of clearing or burning by man is disputed. [C16: from Spanish *zavana,* from Taino *zabana*]

savant ('sævənt, *French* savɑ̃) *n.* a man of great learning; sage. [C18: from French, from *savoir* to know, from Latin *sapere* to be wise; see SAPIENT] —'**savante** *fem. n.*

savate (sə'væt) *n.* a form of boxing in which blows may be delivered with the feet as well as the hands. [C19: from French, literally: old worn-out shoe; related to SABOT]

save[1] (seɪv) *vb.* **1.** (*tr.*) to rescue, preserve, or guard (a person or thing) from danger or harm. **2.** to avoid the spending, waste, or loss of (money, possessions, etc.). **3.** (*tr.*) to deliver from sin; redeem. **4.** (often foll. by *up*) to set aside or reserve (money, goods, etc.) for future use. **5.** (*tr.*) to treat with care so as to avoid or lessen wear or degeneration: *use a good light to save your eyes.* **6.** (*tr.*) to prevent the necessity for; obviate the trouble of: *good work now will save future revision.* **7.** (*tr.*) *Soccer, hockey, etc.* to prevent (a goal) by stopping (a struck ball or puck). **8.** (*intr.*) *Chiefly U.S.* (of food) to admit of preservation; keep. ~*n.* **9.** *Soccer, hockey, etc.* the act of saving a goal. **10.** *Computer technol.* an instruction to write information from the memory onto a tape or disk. [C13: from Old French *salver,* via Late Latin from Latin *salvus* safe] —ˈ**savable** *or* ˈ**saveable** *adj.* —ˈ**savableness** *or* ˈ**saveableness** *n.* —ˈ**saver** *n.*

save[2] (seɪv) *Archaic or literary.* ~*prep.* **1.** (often foll. by *for*) Also: **saving.** with the exception of. ~*conj.* **2.** but; except. [C13 *sauf,* from Old French, from Latin *salvō,* from *salvus* safe]

save-all *n.* **1.** a device to prevent waste or loss. **2.** *Nautical.* **a.** a net used while loading a ship. **b.** a light sail set to catch wind spilling from another sail. **3.** *Dialect.* overalls or a pinafore. **4.** *Brit.* a dialect word for **miser.**

save as you earn *n.* (in Britain) a savings scheme operated by the government, in which monthly contributions earn tax-free interest. Abbrev.: **SAYE.**

saveloy (ˈsævɪˌlɔɪ) *n.* a smoked sausage made from salted pork, well seasoned and coloured red with saltpetre. [C19: probably via French from Italian *cervellato,* from *cervello* brain, from Latin *cerebellum,* diminutive of *cerebrum* brain]

savin *or* **savine** (ˈsævɪn) *n.* **1.** a small spreading juniper bush, *Juniperus sabina,* of Europe, N Asia, and North America. **2.** the oil derived from the shoots and leaves of this plant, formerly used in medicine to treat rheumatism, etc. **3.** another name for **red cedar** (sense 1). [C14: from Old French *savine,* from Latin *herba Sabīna* the Sabine plant]

saving (ˈseɪvɪŋ) *adj.* **1.** tending to save or preserve. **2.** redeeming or compensating (esp. in the phrase **saving grace**). **3.** thrifty or economical. **4.** *Law.* denoting or relating to an exception or reservation: *a saving clause in an agreement.* ~*n.* **5.** preservation or redemption, esp. from loss or danger. **6.** economy or avoidance of waste. **7.** reduction in cost or expenditure: *a saving of 20p.* **8.** anything saved. **9.** (*pl.*) money saved for future use. **10.** *Law.* an exception or reservation. ~*prep.* **11.** with the exception of. ~*conj.* **12.** except. —ˈ**savingly** *adv.*

savings account *n.* an account at a bank that accumulates interest.

savings and loan association *n.* a U.S. name for a **building society.**

savings bank *n.* **1.** a bank that accepts the savings of depositors and pays interest on them. **2.** a container, usually having a slot in the top, for saving coins.

savings ratio *n. Economics.* the ratio of personal savings to disposable income, esp. using the difference between national figures for disposable income and consumer spending as a measure of savings.

saviour *or U.S.* **savior** (ˈseɪvjə) *n.* a person who rescues another person or a thing from danger or harm. [C13 *saveour,* from Old French, from Church Latin *Salvātor* the Saviour; see SAVE[1]]

Saviour *or U.S.* **Savior** (ˈseɪvjə) *n. Christianity.* Jesus Christ regarded as the saviour of men from sin.

savoir-faire (ˈsævwɑːˈfɛə) *n.* the ability to do the right thing in any situation. [French, literally: a knowing how to do]

savoir-vivre (ˈsævwɑːˈviːvrə) *n.* familiarity with the customs of good society; breeding. [French, literally: a knowing how to live]

savory (ˈseɪvərɪ) *n., pl.* **-vories.** **1.** any of numerous aromatic plants of the genus *Satureja,* esp. *S. montana* (**winter savory**) and *S. hortensis* (**summer savory**), of the Mediterranean region, having narrow leaves and white, pink, or purple flowers: family *Labiatae* (labiates). **2.** the leaves of any of these plants, used as a potherb. [C14: probably from Old English *sætherie,* from Latin *saturēia,* of obscure origin]

savour *or U.S.* **savor** (ˈseɪvə) *n.* **1.** the quality in a substance that is perceived by the sense of taste or smell. **2.** a specific taste or smell: *the savour of lime.* **3.** a slight but distinctive quality or trace. **4.** the power to excite interest: *the savour of wit has been lost.* **5.** *Archaic.* reputation. ~*vb.* **6.** (*intr.;* often foll. by *of*) to possess the taste or smell (of). **7.** (*intr.;* often foll. by *of*) to have a suggestion (of). **8.** (*tr.*) to give a taste to; season. **9.** (*tr.*) to taste or smell, esp. appreciatively. **10.** (*tr.*) to relish or enjoy. [C13: from Old French *savour,* from Latin *sapor* taste, from *sapere* to taste] —ˈ**savourless** *or U.S.* ˈ**savorless** *adj.* —ˈ**savorous** *adj.*

savoury *or U.S.* **savory** (ˈseɪvərɪ) *adj.* **1.** attractive to the sense of taste or smell. **2.** salty or spicy; not sweet: *a savoury dish.* **3.** pleasant. **4.** respectable. ~*n., pl.* **-vouries.** **5.** *Chiefly Brit.* a savoury dish served as an hors d'oeuvre or dessert. [C13 *savure,* from Old French *savouré,* from *savourer* to SAVOUR] —ˈ**savourily** *or U.S.* ˈ**savorily** *adv.* —ˈ**savouriness** *or U.S.* ˈ**savoriness** *n.*

savoy (səˈvɔɪ) *n.* a cultivated variety of cabbage, *Brassica oleracea capitata,* having a compact head and wrinkled leaves. [C16: named after the *Savoy* region of SE France]

Savoyard[1] (səˈvɔɪɑːd; *French* savwajar) *n.* **1.** a native of Savoy, SE France. **2.** the dialect of French spoken in Savoy. ~*adj.* **3.** of or relating to Savoy, its inhabitants, or their dialect.

Savoyard[2] (səˈvɔɪɑːd) *n.* **1.** a person keenly interested in the operettas of Gilbert and Sullivan. **2.** a person who takes part in these operettas. [C20: from the *Savoy* Theatre, built in London in 1881 for the presentation of operettas by Gilbert and Sullivan]

savvy (ˈsævɪ) *Slang.* ~*vb.* **-vies, -vying, -vied.** **1.** to understand or get the sense of (an idea, etc.). **2. no savvy.** I don't (he doesn't, etc.) understand. ~*n.* **3.** comprehension. ~*adj.* **-vier, -viest.** **4.** *Chiefly U.S.* shrewd; well-informed. [C18: corruption of Spanish *sabe* (*usted*) (you) know, from *saber* to know, from Latin *sapere* to be wise]

saw[1] (sɔː) *n.* **1.** any of various hand tools for cutting wood, metal, etc., having a blade with teeth along one edge. **2.** any of various machines or devices for cutting by use of a toothed blade, such as a power-driven circular toothed wheel or toothed band of metal. ~*vb.* **saws, sawing, sawed; sawed** *or* **sawn.** **3.** to cut with a saw. **4.** to form by sawing. **5.** to cut as if wielding a saw: *to saw the air.* **6.** to move (an object) from side to side as if moving a saw. [Old English *sagu;* related to Old Norse *sog,* Old High German *saga,* Latin *secāre* to cut, *secūris* axe] —ˈ**sawer** *n.* —ˈ**sawˌlike** *adj.*

saw[2] (sɔː) *vb.* the past tense of **see**[1].

saw[3] (sɔː) *n.* a wise saying, maxim, or proverb. [Old English *sagu* a saying; related to SAGA]

SAW *abbrev. for* surface acoustic wave.

sawbill (ˈsɔːˌbɪl) *n.* **1.** another name for **merganser** or **motmot.** **2.** any of various hummingbirds of the genus *Ramphodon.* [C19: so called because of their serrated bills]

sawbones (ˈsɔːˌbəʊnz) *n., pl.* **bones** *or* **boneses.** *Slang.* a surgeon or doctor.

sawbuck (ˈsɔːˌbʌk) *n.* **1.** *U.S. and Canadian.* a sawhorse, esp. one having an X-shaped supporting structure. **2.** *Chiefly U.S. and Canadian slang.* a ten-dollar bill. [C19: (in the sense: sawhorse) translated from Dutch *zaagbok;* (in the sense: ten-dollar bill) from the legs of a sawbuck forming the Roman numeral X]

sawder (ˈsɔːdə) *Informal.* ~*n.* **1.** flattery; compliments (esp. in the phrase **soft sawder**). ~*vb.* (*tr.*) **2.** to flatter. [C19: metaphorical use of variant of SOLDER]

saw doctor *n. N.Z.* a sawmill specialist who sharpens and services saw blades.

sawdust (ˈsɔːˌdʌst) *n.* particles of wood formed by sawing.

sawfish (ˈsɔːˌfɪʃ) *n., pl.* **-fish** *or* **-fishes.** any sharklike ray of the family *Pristidae* of subtropical coastal waters and estuaries, having a serrated bladelike mouth.

sawfly (ˈsɔːˌflaɪ) *n., pl.* **-flies.** any of various hymenopterous insects of the family *Tenthredinidae* and related families, the females of which have a sawlike ovipositor.

sawhorse (ˈsɔːˌhɔːs) *n.* a stand for timber during sawing.

sawmill (ˈsɔːˌmɪl) *n.* **1.** an industrial establishment where timber is sawn into planks, etc. **2.** a large sawing machine.

sawn (sɔːn) *vb.* a past participle of **saw**[1].

Sawney (ˈsɔːnɪ) *n.* **1.** a derogatory word for **Scotsman.** **2.** (*also not cap.*) *Informal.* a fool. [C18: a Scots variant of *Sandy,* short for *Alexander*]

sawn-off *or esp. U.S.* **sawed-off** *adj.* **1.** (*prenominal*) (of a shotgun) having the barrel cut short, mainly to facilitate concealment of the weapon. **2.** *Informal.* (of a person) small in stature.

saw palmetto *n.* any of several dwarf prickly palms, esp. any of the genus *Sabal,* of the southeastern U.S.

saw-pit *n.* (esp. formerly) a pit above which a log is sawn into planks with a large pitsaw.

saw set *n.* a tool used for setting the teeth of a saw, consisting of a type of clamp used to bend each tooth in turn at a slight angle to the plane of the saw, alternate teeth being bent in the same direction.

sawtooth (ˈsɔːˌtuːθ) *adj.* **1.** (of a waveform) having an amplitude that varies linearly with time between two values, the interval in one direction often being much greater than the other. **2.** having or generating such a waveform.

saw-wort (ˈsɔːˌwɜːt) *n.* a perennial Old World plant, *Serratula tinctoria,* having serrated leaves that yield a yellow dye: family *Compositae* (composites).

sawyer (ˈsɔːjə) *n.* a person who saws timber for a living. [C14 *sawier,* from SAW[1] + *-ier,* variant of -ER[1]]

sax[1] (sæks) *n.* a tool resembling a small axe, used for cutting roofing slate. [Old English *seax* knife; related to Old Saxon *sahs,* Old Norse *sax*]

sax[2] (sæks) *n. Informal.* short for **saxophone.**

Sax. *abbrev. for:* **1.** Saxon. **2.** Saxony.

saxatile (ˈsæksəˌtaɪl; *as specific name* sækˈsætɪlɪ) *adj.* growing on or living among rocks. [C17: from Latin *saxitilis,* from *saxum* rock]

saxe blue (sæks) *n.* **a.** a light greyish-blue colour. **b.** (*as adj.*): *a saxe-blue dress.* [C19: from French *Saxe* Saxony, source of a dye of this colour]

saxhorn (ˈsæksˌhɔːn) *n.* a valved brass instrument used chiefly in brass and military bands, having a tube of conical bore and a brilliant tone colour. It resembles the tuba and constitutes a family of instruments related to the flugelhorn and cornet. [C19: named after Adolphe *Sax* (see SAXOPHONE), who invented it (1845)]

saxicolous (sækˈsɪkələs) *adj.* living on or among rocks: *saxicolous plants.* Also: **saxicole, saxatile** (ˈsæksəˌtaɪl). [C19: from New Latin *saxicolus,* from Latin *saxum* rock + *colere* to dwell]

saxifragaceous (ˌsæksɪfrəˈgeɪʃəs) *adj.* of, relating to, or belonging to the *Saxifragaceae,* a chiefly arctic and alpine family of plants having a basal rosette of leaves and small flowers: includes saxifrage.

saxifrage (ˈsæksɪˌfreɪdʒ) *n.* any saxifragaceous plant of the genus *Saxifraga,* having small white, yellow, purple, or pink flowers. [C15: from Late Latin *saxifraga,* literally: rock-breaker, from Latin *saxum* rock + *frangere* to break]

Saxon (ˈsæksən) *n.* **1.** a member of a West Germanic people who in Roman times spread from N Europe across NW Germany to the Rhine. Saxons raided and settled parts of S Britain in the fifth and sixth centuries A.D. In Germany they established a duchy and other dominions, which changed and shifted through the centuries, usually retaining the name Saxony. **2.** a native or inhabitant of Saxony, in Germany. **3. a.** the Low German dialect of Saxony. **b.** any of the West Germanic dialects spoken by the ancient Saxons or their descendants. ~*adj.* **4.** of, relating to, or characteristic of the ancient Saxons, the Anglo-Saxons, or their descendants. **5.** of, relating to, or characteristic of Saxony, its inhabitants, or their Low German dialect. ~See also **West Saxon, Anglo-Saxon.** [C13 (replacing Old English *Seaxe*): via Old French from Late Latin *Saxon-, Saxo,* from Greek; of Germanic origin and perhaps related to the name of a knife used by the Saxons; compare SAW[1]]

Saxon blue *n.* a dye made by dissolving indigo in a solution of sulphuric acid. [C19: named after *Saxony* in Germany, where it originated]

saxony ('sæksənɪ) *n.* **1.** a fine 3-ply yarn used for knitting and weaving. **2.** a fine woollen fabric used for coats, etc. [C19: named after *Saxony,* where it was produced]

saxophone ('sæksəˌfəʊn) *n.* a keyed wind instrument of mellow tone colour, used mainly in jazz and dance music. It is made in various sizes, has a conical bore, and a single reed. Often shortened to **sax.** [C19: named after Adolphe *Sax* (1814–94), Belgian musical-instrument maker, who invented it (1846)] —**saxophonic** (ˌsæksə'fɒnɪk) *adj.* —**saxophonist** (sæk'sɒfənɪst) *n.*

say[1] (seɪ) *vb.* **says** (sɛz), **saying, said.** (*mainly tr.*) **1.** to speak, pronounce, or utter. **2.** (*also intr.*) to express (an idea) in words; tell: *we asked his opinion but he refused to say.* **3.** (*also intr.; may take a clause as object*) to state (an opinion, fact, etc.) positively; declare; affirm. **4.** to recite: *to say grace.* **5.** (*may take a clause as object*) to report or allege: *they say we shall have rain today.* **6.** (*may take a clause as object*) to take as an assumption; suppose: *let us say that he is lying.* **7.** (*may take a clause as object*) to convey by means of artistic expression: *the artist in this painting is saying that we should look for hope.* **8.** to make a case for: *there is much to be said for either course of action.* **9.** (*usually passive*) *Irish.* to persuade or coax (someone) to do something: *If I hadn't been said by her I wouldn't be in this fix.* **10. go without saying.** to be so obvious as to need no explanation. **11. I say!** *Chiefly Brit. informal.* an exclamation of surprise. **12. not to say.** even; and indeed. **13. that is to say.** in other words; more explicitly. **14. to say nothing of.** as well as; even disregarding: *he was warmly dressed in a shirt and heavy jumper, to say nothing of a thick overcoat.* **15. to say the least.** without the slightest exaggeration; at the very least. ~*adv.* **16.** approximately: *there were, say, 20 people present.* **17.** for example: *choose a number, say, four.* ~*n.* **18.** the right or chance to speak: *let him have his say.* **19.** authority, esp. to influence a decision: *he has a lot of say in the company's policy.* **20.** a statement of opinion: *you've had your say, now let me have mine.* ~*interj.* **21.** *U.S. and Canadian informal.* an exclamation to attract attention or express surprise, etc. [Old English *secgan;* related to Old Norse *segja,* Old Saxon *seggian,* Old High German *sagēn*] —'**sayer** *n.*

say[2] (seɪ) *n. Archaic.* a type of fine woollen fabric. [C13: from Old French *saie,* from Latin *saga,* plural of *sagum* a type of woollen cloak]

Saybolt universal seconds ('seɪˌbəʊlt) *n.* (*functioning as sing.*) a U.S. measurement of viscosity similar in type to the British Redwood seconds. [named after G. M. *Saybolt* (died 1924), U.S. chemist, who proposed it]

SAYE *abbrev. for* save as you earn.

saying ('seɪɪŋ) *n.* a maxim, adage, or proverb.

say-so *n. Informal.* **1.** an arbitrary assertion. **2.** an authoritative decision. **3.** the authority to make a final decision.

sayyid, sayid ('saɪɪd), *or* **said** *n.* **1.** a Muslim claiming descent from Mohammed's grandson Husain. **2.** a Muslim honorary title. [C17: from Arabic: lord]

sazerac ('sæzəˌræk) *n. U.S.* a mixed drink of whisky, Pernod, syrup, bitters, and lemon. [C20: of uncertain origin]

Sb *the chemical symbol for* antimony. [from New Latin *stibium*]

sb. *abbrev. for* substantive.

SBA *abbrev. for* standard beam approach: a radar navigation system that gives lateral guidance to aircraft when landing.

SBS *abbrev. for* Special Boat Service.

SBU *abbrev. for* strategic business unit: a division within an organization responsible for marketing its own range of products.

sc *Printing. abbrev. for* small capitals.

Sc *the chemical symbol for* scandium.

SC *abbrev. for:* **1.** Signal Corps. **2.** South Carolina. **3.** (in Australia and New Zealand) School Certificate. **4.** (in Canada) Star of Courage.

sc. *abbrev. for:* **1.** scale. **2.** scene. **3.** science. **4.** scilicet. **5.** screw. **6.** scruple (unit of weight).

scab (skæb) *n.* **1.** the dried crusty surface of a healing skin wound or sore. **2.** a contagious disease of sheep resembling mange, caused by a mite (*Psoroptes communis*). **3.** a fungal disease of plants characterized by crusty spots on the fruits, leaves, etc. **4.** *Derogatory.* **a.** Also called: **blackleg.** a person who refuses to support a trade union's actions, esp. one who replaces a worker who is on strike. **b.** (*as modifier*): *scab labour.* **5.** a despicable person. ~*vb.* **scabs, scabbing, scabbed.** (*intr.*) **6.** to become covered with a scab. **7.** (of a road surface) to become loose so that potholes develop. **8.** to replace a striking worker. [Old English *sceabb;* related to Old Norse *skabb,* Latin *scabiēs,* Middle Low German *schabbe* scoundrel, German *schäbig* SHABBY] —'**scabˌlike** *adj.*

scabbard ('skæbəd) *n.* a holder for a bladed weapon such as a sword or bayonet; sheath. [C13 *scauberc,* from Norman French *escaubers* (pl.), of Germanic origin; related to Old High German *skār* blade and *bergan* to protect]

scabbard fish *n.* any of various marine spiny-finned fishes of the family *Trichiuridae,* esp. of the genus *Lepidopus,* having a long whiplike scaleless body and long sharp teeth: most common in warm waters.

scabble ('skæbᵊl) *vb.* (*tr.*) to shape (stone) roughly. [C17: from earlier *scapple,* from French *escapler* to shape (timber)]

scabby ('skæbɪ) *adj.* **-bier, -biest.** **1.** *Pathol.* having an area of the skin covered with scabs. **2.** *Pathol.* having scabies. **3.** *Informal.* despicable. —'**scabbily** *adv.* —'**scabbiness** *n.*

scabies ('skeɪbiːz, -bɪˌiːz) *n.* a contagious skin infection caused by the mite *Sarcoptes scaboi,* characterized by intense itching, inflammation, and the formation of vesicles and pustules. [C15: from Latin: scurf, from *scabere* to scratch; see SHAVE] —**scabietic** (ˌskeɪbɪ'ɛtɪk) *adj.*

scabious[1] ('skeɪbɪəs) *adj.* **1.** having or covered with scabs. **2.** of, relating to, or resembling scabies. [C17: from Latin *scabiōsus,* from SCABIES]

scabious[2] ('skeɪbɪəs) *n.* **1.** any plant of the genus *Scabiosa,* esp. *S. atropurpurea,* of the Mediterranean region, having blue, red, or whitish dome-shaped flower heads: family *Dipsacaceae.* **2.** any of various similar plants of the related genus *Knautia.* **3.** **devil's bit scabious.** a similar and related Eurasian marsh plant, *Succisa pratensis.* [C14: from Medieval Latin *scabiōsa herba* the scabies plant, referring to its use in treating scabies]

scablands ('skæbˌlændz) *pl. n.* a type of terrain, found for example in the NW U.S., consisting of bare rock surfaces, with little or no soil cover and scanty vegetation, that have been deeply channelled by glacial flood waters.

scabrid ('skæbrɪd) *adj.* having a rough or scaly surface. [C19: see SCABROUS] —**scabridity** (skə'brɪdɪtɪ) *n.*

scabrous ('skeɪbrəs) *adj.* **1.** roughened because of small projections; scaly. **2.** indelicate, indecent, or salacious: *scabrous humour.* **3.** difficult to deal with; knotty. [C17: from Latin *scaber* rough; related to SCABIES] —'**scabrously** *adv.* —'**scabrousness** *n.*

scad (skæd) *n., pl.* **scad** *or* **scads.** any of various carangid fishes of the genus *Trachurus,* esp. the horse mackerel. [C17: of uncertain origin; compare Swedish *skädde* flounder]

scads (skædz) *pl. n. Informal.* a large amount or number. [C19: of uncertain origin]

scaffold ('skæfəld, -fəʊld) *n.* **1.** a temporary metal or wooden framework that is used to support workmen and materials during the erection, repair, etc., of a building or other construction. **2.** a raised wooden platform on which plays are performed, tobacco, etc., is dried, or (esp. formerly) criminals are executed. ~*vb.* (*tr.*) **3.** to provide with a scaffold. **4.** to support by means of a scaffold. [C14: from Old French *eschaffaut,* from Vulgar Latin *catafalicum* (unattested); see CATAFALQUE] —'**scaffolder** *n.*

scaffolding ('skæfəldɪŋ) *n.* **1.** a scaffold or system of scaffolds. **2.** the building materials used to make scaffolds.

scag[1] *or* **skag** (skæg) *n.* a slang name for **heroin.**

scag[2] (skæg) *South Wales and southwest English dialect.* ~*n.* **1.** a tear in a garment or piece of cloth. ~*vb.* **scags, scagging, scagged.** **2.** (*tr.*) to make a tear in (cloth). [apparently related to Old Norse *skaga* to project]

scagliola (skæl'jəʊlə) *n.* imitation marble made of glued gypsum with a polished surface of coloured stone or marble dust. [C16: from Italian, diminutive of *scaglia* chip of marble, of Germanic origin; related to SHALE, SCALE[2]]

scalable ('skeɪləbᵊl) *adj.* capable of being scaled or climbed. —'**scalableness** *n.* —'**scalably** *adv.*

scalade (skə'leɪd) *or* **scalado** (skə'leɪdəʊ) *n., pl.* **-lades** *or* **-lados.** short for **escalade.** [C16: from Old Italian *scalada,* from *scala* a ladder; see SCALE[3]]

scalage ('skeɪlɪdʒ) *n.* **1.** *U.S.* a percentage deducted from the price of goods liable to shrink or leak. **2.** *Forestry, U.S. and Canadian.* the estimated amount of usable timber in a log. [C19: from SCALE[3] + -AGE]

scalar ('skeɪlə) *n.* **1.** a quantity, such as time or temperature, that has magnitude but not direction and is an even function of the coordinates. Compare **vector** (sense 1), **tensor** (sense 2), **pseudoscalar, pseudovector.** **2.** *Maths.* an element of a field associated with a vector space. ~*adj.* **3.** having magnitude but not direction. [C17 (meaning: resembling a ladder): from Latin *scālāris,* from *scāla* ladder]

scalare (skə'lɛərɪ) *n.* another name for **angelfish** (sense 2). [C19: from Latin *scālāris* of a ladder, SCALAR, referring to the runglike pattern on its body]

scalariform (skə'lærɪˌfɔːm) *adj. Biology.* resembling a ladder: *a scalariform cell.* [C19: from New Latin *scālāriformis* from Latin *scālāris* of a ladder + -FORM]

scalar multiplication *n. Maths.* an operation used in the definition of a vector space in which the product of a scalar and a vector is a vector, the operation is distributive over the addition of both scalars and vectors, and is associative with multiplication of scalars.

scalar product *n.* the product of two vectors to form a scalar, whose value is the product of the magnitudes of the vectors and the cosine of the angle between them. Written: ***A•B*** or ***AB*** Compare **vector product.** Also called: **dot product.**

scalawag ('skælə,wæg) *n.* a variant of **scallywag.**

scald[1] (skɔːld) *vb.* **1.** to burn or be burnt with or as if with hot liquid or steam. **2.** (*tr.*) to subject to the action of boiling water, esp. so as to sterilize. **3.** (*tr.*) to heat (a liquid) almost to boiling point. **4.** (*tr.*) to plunge (tomatoes, peaches, etc.) into boiling water briefly in order to skin them more easily. ~*n.* **5.** the act or result of scalding. **6.** an abnormal condition in plants, characterized by discoloration and wrinkling of the skin of the fruits, caused by exposure to excessive sunlight, gases, etc. [C13: via Old Norman French from Late Latin *excaldāre* to wash in warm water, from *calida* (*aqua*) warm (water), from *calēre* to be warm] —'**scalder** *n.*

scald[2] (skɔːld) *n.* a variant spelling of **skald.**

scald[3] (skɔːld) *Obsolete.* ~*adj. also* **scalled. 1.** scabby. ~*n.* **2.** a scab or a skin disease producing scabs. [C16: from SCALL]

scald-crow *n. Irish.* another name for **hooded crow.**

scaldfish ('skɔːld,fɪʃ, 'skɑːld-) *n., pl.* **-fish** *or* **-fishes.** a small European flatfish, *Arnoglossus laterna,* covered with large fragile scales: family *Bothidae.* [C19: from SCALD[3]]

scale[1] (skeɪl) *n.* **1.** any of the numerous plates, made of various substances resembling enamel or dentine, covering the bodies of fishes. **2. a.** any of the horny or chitinous plates covering a part or the entire body of certain reptiles and mammals. **b.** any of the numerous minute structures covering the wings of lepidoptera. **3.** a thin flat piece or flake. **4.** a thin flake of dead epidermis shed from the skin: excessive shedding may be the result of a skin disease. **5.** a specialized leaf or bract, esp. the protective covering of a bud or the dry membranous bract of a catkin. **6.** See **scale insect. 7.** a flaky black oxide of iron formed on the surface of iron or steel at high temperatures. **8.** any oxide formed on a metal during heat treatment. ~*vb.* **9.** (*tr.*) to remove the scales or coating from. **10.** to peel off or cause to peel off in flakes or scales. **11.** (*intr.*) to shed scales. **12.** to cover or become covered with scales, incrustation, etc. **13.** (*tr.*) to throw (a disc or thin flat object) edgewise through the air or along the surface of water. **14.** (*intr.*) *Austral. informal.* to ride on public transport without paying a fare. [C14: from Old French *escale,* of Germanic origin; compare Old English *scealu* SHELL] —'**scale,like** *adj.*

scale[2] (skeɪl) *n.* **1.** (*often pl.*) a machine or device for weighing. **2.** one of the pans of a balance. **3. tip the scales. a.** to exercise a decisive influence. **b.** (foll. by *at*) to amount in weight (to). ~*vb.* (*tr.*) **4.** to weigh with or as if with scales. **5.** to have a weight of. [C13: from Old Norse *skāl* bowl, related to Old High German *scāla* cup, Old English *scealu* SHELL, SCALE[1]]

scale[3] (skeɪl) *n.* **1.** a sequence of marks either at regular intervals or else representng equal steps used as a reference in making measurements. **2.** a measuring instrument having such a scale. **3. a.** the ratio between the size of something real and that of a model or representation of it: *the scale of the map was so large that we could find our house on it.* **b.** (*as modifier*): *a scale model.* **4.** a line, numerical ratio, etc., for showing this ratio. **5.** a progressive or graduated table of things, wages, etc., in order of size, value, etc.: *a wage scale for carpenters.* **6.** an established measure or standard. **7.** a relative degree or extent: *he entertained on a grand scale.* **8.** *Music.* a group of notes taken in ascending or descending order, esp. within the compass of one octave. **9.** *Maths.* the notation of a given number system: *the decimal scale.* **10.** a graded series of tests measuring mental development, etc. **11.** *Obsolete.* a ladder or staircase. ~*vb.* **12.** to climb to the top of (a height) by or as if by a ladder. **13.** (*tr.*) to make or draw (a model, plan, etc.) according to a particular ratio of proportionate reduction. **14.** (*tr.*; usually foll. by *up* or *down*) to increase or reduce proportionately in size, etc. **15.** *U.S. and Canadian.* (in forestry) to estimate the board footage of (standing timber or logs). [C15: via Italian from Latin *scāla* ladder; related to Old French *eschiele,* Spanish *escala*]

scaleboard ('skeɪl,bɔːd, 'skæbəd) *n.* **1.** a very thin piece of board, used for backing a picture, as a veneer, etc. **2.** *Printing.* a thin wooden strip used in justifying type.

scale insect *n.* any small homopterous insect of the family *Coccidae* and related families, which typically live and feed on plants and secrete a protective scale around themselves. Many species, such as the San Jose scale, are important pests.

scale leaf *n. Botany.* a modified leaf, often small and membranous, protecting buds, etc.

scale moss *n.* any of various leafy liverworts of the order *Jungermanniales,* which resemble mosses.

scalene ('skeɪliːn) *adj.* **1.** *Maths.* (of a triangle) having all sides of unequal length. **2.** *Anatomy.* of or relating to any of the scalenus muscles. [C17: from Late Latin *scalēnus* with unequal sides, from Greek *skalēnos*]

scalenus (skə'liːnəs, skeɪ-) *n., pl.* **-ni** (-naɪ). *Anatomy.* any one of the three muscles situated on each side of the neck extending from the cervical vertebrae to the first or second pair of ribs. [C18: from New Latin; see SCALENE]

scaler ('skeɪlə) *n.* **1.** a person or thing that scales. **2.** Also called: **counter, scaling circuit.** an electronic device or circuit that aggregates electric pulses and gives a single output pulse for a predetermined number of input pulses.

Scales (skeɪlz) *n.* **the.** the constellation Libra, the seventh sign of the zodiac.

scaling ladder *n.* a ladder used to climb high walls, esp. one used formerly to enter a besieged town, fortress, etc.

scall (skɔːl) *n. Pathol.* a former term for any of various diseases of the scalp characterized by itching and scab formation. [C14: from Old Norse *skalli* bald head. Compare SKULL] —**scalled** *adj.*

scallion ('skæljən) *n.* any of various onions or similar plants, such as the spring onion, that have a small bulb and long leaves and are eaten in salads. Also called: **green onion.** [C14: from Anglo-French *scalun,* from Latin *Ascalōnia* (*caepa*) Ascalonian (onion), from *Ascalo* Ascalon, a Palestinian port]

scallop ('skɒləp, 'skæl-) *n.* **1.** any of various marine bivalves of the family *Pectinidae,* having a fluted fan-shaped shell: includes free-swimming species (genus *Pecten*) and species attached to a substratum (genus *Chlamys*). See also **pecten** (sense 3). **2.** the edible adductor muscle of certain of these molluscs. **3.** either of the shell valves of any of these molluscs. **4.** a scallop shell or similarly shaped dish, in which fish, esp. shellfish, is cooked and served. **5.** one of a series of curves along an edge, esp. an edge of cloth. **6.** the shape of a scallop shell used as the badge of a pilgrim, esp. in the Middle Ages. **7.** *Chiefly Austral.* a potato cake fried in batter. ~*vb.* **8.** (*tr.*) to decorate (an edge) with scallops. **9.** to bake (food) in a scallop shell or similar dish. **10.** (*intr.*) to collect scallops. [C14: from Old French *escalope* shell, of Germanic origin; see SCALP] —'**scalloper** *n.* —'**scalloping** *n.*

scally ('skælɪ) *n., pl.* **-lies.** *Northwest English dialect.* a rascal; rogue. [C20: from SCALLYWAG]

scallywag ('skælɪ,wæg) *n.* **1.** *Informal.* a scamp; rascal. **2.** (after the U.S. Civil War) a White Southerner who supported the Republican Party and its policy of Black emancipation. Scallywags were viewed as traitors by their fellow Southerners. ~Also: **scalawag, scallawag.** [C19: (originally undersized animal) of uncertain origin]

scaloppine *or* **scaloppini** (,skælə'piːnɪ) *pl. n.* escalopes of meat, esp. veal, cooked in a rich sauce, usually of wine with seasonings. [Italian: from *scaloppa* a fillet, probably from Old French *escalope* SCALLOP]

scalp (skælp) *n.* **1.** *Anatomy.* the skin and subcutaneous tissue covering the top of the head. **2.** (among North American Indians) a part of this removed as a trophy from a slain enemy. **3.** a trophy or token signifying conquest. **4.** *Hunting, chiefly U.S.* a piece of hide cut from the head of a victim as a trophy or as proof of killing in order to collect a bounty. **5.** *Informal, chiefly U.S.* a small speculative profit taken in quick transactions. **6.** *Scottish dialect.* a projection of bare rock from vegetation. ~*vb.* (*tr.*) **7.** to cut the scalp from. **8.** *Informal, chiefly U.S.* to purchase and resell (securities) quickly so as to make several small profits. **9.** *Informal.* to buy (tickets) cheaply and resell at an inflated price. [C13: probably from Scandinavian; compare Old Norse *skalpr* sheath, Middle Dutch *schelpe,* Danish *skalp* husk] —'**scalper** *n.*

scalpel ('skælpᵊl) *n.* a surgical knife with a short thin blade. [C18: from Latin *scalpellum,* from *scalper* a knife, from *scalpere* to scrape] —**scalpellic** (skæl'pelɪk) *adj.*

scalping ('skælpɪŋ) *n.* a process in which the top portion of a metal ingot is machined away before use, thus removing the layer containing defects and impurities.

scalp lock *n.* a small tuft or plait of hair left on the shaven scalp by American Indian warriors as a challenge to enemies.

scaly ('skeɪlɪ) *adj.* **scalier, scaliest. 1.** resembling or covered in scales. **2.** peeling off in scales. —'**scaliness** *n.*

scaly anteater *n.* another name for **pangolin.**

scam (skæm) *n. Slang.* a stratagem for gain; a swindle.

scammony ('skæmənɪ) *n., pl.* **-nies. 1.** a twining Asian convolvulus plant, *Convolvulus scammonia,* having arrow-shaped leaves, white or purple flowers, and tuberous roots. **2.** a resinous juice obtained from the roots of this plant and having purgative properties. **3.** any of various similar medicinal resins or the plants that yield them. [Old English, via Latin from Greek *skammōnia,* of obscure origin] —**scammoniate** (skæ'məʊnɪɪt) *adj.*

scamp[1] (skæmp) *n.* **1.** an idle mischievous person; rascal. **2.** a mischievous child. [C18: from *scamp* (vb.) to be a highway robber, probably from Middle Dutch *schampen* to decamp, from Old French *escamper,* from *es-* EX-[1] + *-camper,* from Latin *campus* field] —'**scampish** *adj.*

scamp[2] (skæmp) *vb.* a less common word for **skimp.** —'**scamper** *n.*

scamper ('skæmpə) *vb.* (*intr.*) **1.** to run about playfully. **2.** (often foll. by *through*) to hurry quickly through (a place, task, book, etc.) ~*n.* **3.** the act of scampering. [C17: probably from *scamp* (vb.); see SCAMP[1]] —'**scamperer** *n.*

scampi ('skæmpɪ) *n.* (*usually functioning as sing.*) large prawns, usually eaten fried in breadcrumbs. [Italian: plural of *scampo* shrimp, of obscure origin]

scan (skæn) *vb.* **scans, scanning, scanned. 1.** (*tr.*) to scrutinize minutely. **2.** (*tr.*) to glance over quickly. **3.** (*tr.*) *Prosody.* to read or analyse (verse) according to the rules of metre and versification. **4.** (*intr.*) *Prosody.* to conform to the rules of metre and versification. **5.** (*tr.*) *Electronics.* to move a beam of light, electrons, etc., in a predetermined pattern over (a surface or region) to obtain information, esp. either to sense and transmit or to reproduce a television image. **6.** (*tr.*) to examine data stored on (magnetic tape, etc.), usually in order to retrieve information. **7.** to examine or search (a prescribed region) by systematically varying the direction of a radar or sonar beam. **8.** *Physics.* to examine or produce or be examined or produced by a continuous charge of some variable: *to scan a spectrum.* **9.** *Med.* to obtain an image of (a part of the body) by means of a scanner. ~*n.* **10.** the act or an instance of scanning. **11.** *Med.* **a.** the examination of a part of the body by means of a scanner: *a brain scan; ultrasound scan.* **b.** the image produced by a scanner. [C14: from Late Latin *scandere* to scan (verse), from Latin: to climb] —'**scannable** *adj.*

Scand. *or* **Scan.** *abbrev. for* Scandinavia(n).

scandal ('skændᵊl) *n.* **1.** a disgraceful action or event: *his negligence was a scandal.* **2.** censure or outrage arising from an action or event. **3.** a person whose conduct causes reproach or disgrace. **4.** malicious talk, esp. gossip about the private lives of other people. **5.** *Law.* a libellous action or statement. ~*vb.* (*tr.*) *Obsolete.* **6.** to disgrace. **7.** to scandalize. [C16: from Late Latin *scandalum* stumbling block, from Greek *skandalon* a trap] —'**scandalous** *adj.* —'**scandalously** *adv.* —'**scandalousness** *n.*

scandalize *or* **scandalise** ('skændəˌlaɪz) *vb.* (*tr.*) to shock, as by improper behaviour. —ˌ**scandali'zation** *or* ˌ**scandali'sation** *n.* —'**scandalˌizer** *or* '**scandalˌiser** *n.*

scandalmonger ('skændᵊlˌmʌŋgə) *n.* a person who spreads or enjoys scandal, gossip, etc.

Scandaroon (ˌskændə'ruːn) *n.* a large variety of fancy pigeon having a long thin body and an elongated neck and head. [from *Scandaroon* the former name of *Ishenderon* a seaport in Turkey]

scandent ('skændənt) *adj.* (of plants) having a climbing habit. [C17: from Latin *scandere* to climb]

Scandian ('skændɪən) *n.* another name for a **Scandinavian.** [C17: from Latin *Scandia* Scandinavia]

scandic ('skændɪk) *adj.* of or containing scandium.

Scandinavian (ˌskændɪ'neɪvɪən) *adj.* **1.** of, relating to, or characteristic of Scandinavia, the peninsula occupied by Norway and Sweden or (loosely) the countries of N Europe considered as a cultural unit, including Norway, Sweden, Denmark, Finland, Iceland, and the Faeroe Islands. ~*n.* **2.** a native or inhabitant of Scandinavia. **3.** Also called: **Norse.** the northern group of Germanic languages, consisting of Swedish, Danish, Norwegian, Icelandic, and Faeroese.

scandium ('skændɪəm) *n.* a rare light silvery-white metallic element occurring in minute quantities in numerous minerals. Symbol: Sc; atomic no.: 21; atomic wt.: 44.96; valency: 3; relative density: 2.99; melting pt.: 1539°C; boiling pt.: 2832°C. [C19: from New Latin, from Latin *Scandia* Scandinavia, where it was discovered]

scanner ('skænə) *n.* **1.** a person or thing that scans. **2.** a device, usually electronic, used to measure or sample the distribution of some quantity or condition in a particular system, region, or area. **3.** an aerial or similar device designed to transmit or receive signals, esp. radar signals, inside a given solid angle of space, thus allowing a particular region to be scanned. **4.** any of various devices used in medical diagnosis to obtain an image of an internal organ or part. See **CAT scanner, nuclear magnetic resonance scanner, ultrasound scanner.** **5.** *Informal.* a television outside broadcast vehicle. **6.** short for **optical scanner.**

scanning electron microscope *n.* a type of electron microscope that produces a three-dimensional image.

scansion ('skænʃən) *n.* the analysis of the metrical structure of verse. See **quantity** (sense 7), **stress** (sense 4). [C17: from Latin: climbing up, from *scandere* to climb, SCAN]

scansorial (skæn'sɔːrɪəl) *adj. Zoology.* specialized for, characterized by, or relating to climbing: *a scansorial bird.* [C19: from Latin *scānsōrius,* from *scandere* to climb]

scant (skænt) *adj.* **1.** scarcely sufficient; limited: *he paid her scant attention.* **2.** (*prenominal*) slightly short of the amount indicated; bare: *a scant ten inches.* **3.** (*postpositive;* foll. by *of*) having a short supply (of). ~*vb.* (*tr.*) **4.** to limit in size or quantity. **5.** to provide with a limited or inadequate supply of. **6.** to treat in a slighting or inadequate manner. ~*adv.* **7.** scarcely; barely. [C14: from Old Norse *skamt,* from *skammr* short; related to Old High German *scam*] —'**scantly** *adv.* —'**scantness** *n.*

scantling ('skæntlɪŋ) *n.* **1.** a piece of sawn timber, such as a rafter, that has a small cross section. **2.** the dimensions of a piece of building material or the structural parts of a ship, esp. those in cross section. **3.** a building stone, esp. one that is more than 6 feet in length. **4.** a small quantity or amount. [C16: changed (through influence of SCANT and -LING[1]) from earlier *scantillon,* a carpenter's gauge, from Old Norman French *escantillon,* ultimately from Latin *scandere* to climb; see SCAN]

scantlings ('skæntlɪŋz) *pl. n.* the structural casings of the internal gas paths in an aeroengine.

scanty ('skæntɪ) *adj.* **scantier, scantiest.** **1.** limited; barely enough; meagre. **2.** insufficient; inadequate. **3.** lacking fullness; small. —'**scantily** *adv.* —'**scantiness** *n.*

scape[1] (skeɪp) *n.* **1.** a leafless stalk in plants that arises from a rosette of leaves and bears one or more flowers. **2.** *Zoology.* a stalklike part, such as the first segment of an insect's antenna. [C17: from Latin *scāpus* stem, from (Doric) Greek *skapos;* see SHAFT] —'**scapose** *adj.*

scape[2] *or* **'scape** (skeɪp) *vb., n.* an archaic word for **escape.**

-scape *suffix forming nouns.* indicating a scene or view of something, esp. a pictorial representation: *seascape.* [abstracted from LANDSCAPE]

scapegoat ('skeɪpˌgəʊt) *n.* **1.** a person made to bear the blame for others. **2.** *Old Testament.* a goat used in the ritual of Yom Kippur (Leviticus 16); it was symbolically laden with the sins of the Israelites and sent into the wilderness to be destroyed. [C16: from ESCAPE + GOAT, coined by William Tyndale to translate Biblical Hebrew *azāzēl* (probably) goat for Azazel, mistakenly thought to mean "goat that escapes"]

scapegrace ('skeɪpˌgreɪs) *n.* an idle mischievous person. [C19: from SCAPE[2] + GRACE, alluding to a person who lacks God's grace]

scapewheel ('skeɪpˌwiːl) *n.* a less common name for **escape wheel.**

scaphoid ('skæfɔɪd) *adj. Anatomy.* an obsolete word for **navicular.** [C18: via New Latin from Greek *skaphoeidēs,* from *skaphē* boat]

scaphopod ('skæfəˌpɒd) *n.* any marine mollusc of the class *Scaphopoda,* which includes the tusk (or tooth) shells. [C20: from New Latin, from Greek *skaphē* boat + -POD]

scapolite ('skæpəˌlaɪt) *n.* any of a group of colourless, white, grey, or violet fluorescent minerals consisting of sodium or calcium aluminium silicate, carbonate, and chloride in tetragonal crystalline form. They occur mainly in impure limestones and pegmatites. Also called: **wernerite.** [C19: from German *Skapolith,* from Greek *skapos* rod + -LITE]

scapula ('skæpjʊlə) *n., pl.* **-lae** (-liː) *or* **-las.** **1.** either of two large flat triangular bones, one on each side of the back part of the shoulder in man. Nontechnical name: **shoulder blade.** **2.** the corresponding bone in most vertebrates. [C16: from Late Latin: shoulder]

scapular ('skæpjʊlə) *adj.* **1.** *Anatomy.* of or relating to the scapula. ~*n.* **2.** part of the monastic habit worn by members of many Christian, esp. Roman Catholic, religious orders, consisting of a piece of woollen cloth worn over the shoulders, and hanging down in front and behind to the ankles. **3.** two small rectangular pieces of woollen cloth joined by tapes passing over the shoulders and worn under secular clothes in token of affiliation to a religious order. **4.** any of the small feathers that are attached to the humerus of a bird and lie along the shoulder. ~Also called (for senses 2 and 3): '**scapulary.**

scar[1] (skɑː) *n.* **1.** any mark left on the skin or other tissue following the healing of a wound. **2.** a permanent change in a person's character resulting from emotional distress: *his wife's death left its scars on him.* **3.** the mark on a plant indicating the former point of attachment of a part, esp. the attachment of a leaf to a stem. **4.** a mark of damage; blemish. ~*vb.* **scars, scarring, scarred.** **5.** to mark or become marked with a scar. **6.** (*intr.*) to heal leaving a scar. [C14: via Late Latin from Greek *eskhara* scab]

scar[2] (skɑː) *n.* **1.** a bare craggy rock formation. **2.** a similar formation in a river or sea. ~Also called (Scot): **scaur.** [C14: from Old Norse *sker* low reef, SKERRY]

scarab ('skærəb) *n.* **1.** any scarabaeid beetle, esp. *Scarabaeus sacer* (**sacred scarab**), regarded by the ancient Egyptians as divine. **2.** the scarab as represented on amulets, etc., of ancient Egypt, or in hieroglyphics as a symbol of the solar deity. [C16: from Latin *scarabaeus;* probably related to Greek *karabos* horned beetle]

scarabaeid (ˌskærə'biːɪd) *or* **scarabaean** (ˌskærə'biːən) *n.* **1.** any beetle of the family *Scarabaeidae,* including the sacred scarab and other dung beetles, the chafers, goliath beetles, and rhinoceros beetles. ~*adj.* **2.** of, relating to, or belonging to the family *Scarabaeidae.* [C19: from New Latin]

scarabaeoid (ˌskærə'biːɔɪd) *adj.* **1.** Also: **scaraboid** ('skærəˌbɔɪd). of, relating to, or resembling a scarabaeid. **2.** a former word for **lamellicorn.**

scarabaeus (ˌskærə'biːəs) *n., pl.* **-baeuses** *or* **-baei** (-'biːaɪ). a less common name for **scarab.**

Scaramouch *or* **Scaramouche** ('skærəˌmaʊtʃ, -ˌmuːtʃ) *n.* a stock character who appears as a boastful coward in commedia dell'arte and farce. [C17: via French from Italian *Scaramuccia,* from *scaramuccia* a SKIRMISH]

scarce (skεəs) *adj.* **1.** rarely encountered. **2.** insufficient to meet the demand. **3. make oneself scarce.** *Informal.* to go away, esp. suddenly. ~*adv.* **4.** *Archaic or literary.* scarcely. [C13: from Old Norman French *scars,* from Vulgar Latin *excarpsus* (unattested) plucked out, from Latin *excerpere* to select; see EXCERPT] —'**scarceness** *n.*

scarcely ('skεəslɪ) *adv.* **1.** hardly at all; only just. **2.** *Often used ironically.* probably not or definitely not: *that is scarcely justification for your actions.*

▷**Usage.** See at **hardly.**

scarcement ('skɛəsmənt) *n.* a ledge in a wall. [C16: probably from obsolete sense of SCARCE to reduce + -MENT]

scarcity ('skɛəsɪtɪ) *n., pl.* **-ties.** **1.** inadequate supply; dearth; paucity. **2.** rarity or infrequent occurrence.

scare (skɛə) *vb.* **1.** to fill or be filled with fear or alarm. **2.** (*tr.*; often foll. by *away* or *off*) to drive (away) by frightening. **3.** (*tr.*) *U.S. and Canadian informal.* (foll. by *up*) to produce (a meal) quickly from what is available. *~n.* **4.** a sudden attack of fear or alarm. **5.** a period of general fear or alarm. *~adj.* **6.** causing (needless) fear or alarm: *a scare story.* [C12: from Old Norse *skirra;* related to Norwegian *skjerra,* Swedish dialect *skjarra*] —'**scarer** *n.*

scarecrow ('skɛəˌkrəʊ) *n.* **1.** an object, usually in the shape of a man, made out of sticks and old clothes to scare birds away from crops. **2.** a person or thing that appears frightening but is not actually harmful. **3.** *Informal.* **a.** an untidy-looking person. **b.** a very thin person.

scaredy-cat ('skɛədɪˌkæt) *n. Informal.* someone who is easily frightened.

scaremonger ('skɛəˌmʌŋgə) *n.* a person who delights in spreading rumours of disaster. —'**scareˌmongering** *n.*

scarf[1] (skɑːf) *n., pl.* **scarfs** *or* **scarves** (skɑːvz). **1.** a rectangular, triangular, or long narrow piece of cloth worn around the head, neck, or shoulders for warmth or decoration. *~vb.* (*tr.*) *Rare.* **2.** to wrap with or as if with a scarf. **3.** to use as or in the manner of a scarf. [C16: of uncertain origin; compare Old Norman French *escarpe,* Medieval Latin *scrippum* pilgrim's pack; see SCRIP[2]]

scarf[2] (skɑːf) *n., pl.* **scarfs.** **1.** Also called: **scarf joint, scarfed joint.** a lapped joint between two pieces of timber made by notching or grooving the ends and strapping, bolting, or gluing the two pieces together. **2.** the end of a piece of timber shaped to form such a joint. **3.** *N.Z.* a wedge-shaped cut made in a tree before felling, to determine the direction of the fall. **4.** *Whaling.* an incision made along a whale's body before stripping off the blubber. *~vb.* (*tr.*) **5.** to join (two pieces of timber) by means of a scarf. **6.** to make a scarf on (a piece of timber). **7.** to cut a scarf in (a whale). [C14: probably from Scandinavian; compare Norwegian *skarv,* Swedish *skarf,* Low German, Dutch *scherf* SCARF[1]]

scarfskin ('skɑːfˌskɪn) *n.* the outermost layer of the skin; epidermis or cuticle. [C17: from SCARF[1] (in the sense: an outer covering)]

scarificator ('skɛərɪfɪˌkeɪtə, 'skærɪ-) *n.* a surgical instrument for use in puncturing the skin or other tissue.

scarify[1] ('skɛərɪˌfaɪ, 'skærɪ-) *vb.* **-fies, -fying, -fied.** (*tr.*) **1.** *Surgery.* to make tiny punctures or superficial incisions in (the skin or other tissue), as for inoculating. **2.** *Agriculture.* **a.** to break up and loosen (soil) to a shallow depth. **b.** to scratch or abrade the outer surface of (seeds) to increase water absorption or hasten germination. **3.** to wound with harsh criticism. [C15: via Old French from Latin *scarīfāre* to scratch open, from Greek *skariphasthai* to draw, from *skariphos* a pencil] —ˌ**scarifi'cation** *n.* —'**scariˌfier** *n.*

scarify[2] ('skɛərɪˌfaɪ) *vb.* **-fies, -fying, -fied.** (*tr.*) *Informal.* to make scared; frighten. [C18: from SCARE + -IFY] —'**scariˌfyingly** *adv.*

scarious ('skɛərɪəs) *or* **scariose** ('skɛərɪˌəʊs) *adj.* (of plant parts) membranous, dry, and brownish in colour: *scarious bracts.* [C19: from New Latin *scariōsus,* of uncertain origin]

scarlatina (ˌskɑːlə'tiːnə) *n.* the technical name for **scarlet fever.** [C19: from New Latin, from Italian *scarlattina,* diminutive of *scarlatto* SCARLET] —ˌ**scarla'tinal** *adj.*

scarlet ('skɑːlɪt) *n.* **1.** a vivid red colour, sometimes with an orange tinge. **2.** cloth or clothing of this colour. *~adj.* **3.** of the colour scarlet. **4.** sinful or immoral, esp. unchaste. [C13: from Old French *escarlate* fine cloth, of unknown origin]

scarlet fever *n.* an acute communicable disease characterized by fever, strawberry-coloured tongue, and a typical rash starting on the neck and chest and spreading to the abdomen and limbs, caused by the bacterium *Streptococcus scarlatinae.* Technical name: **scarlatina.**

scarlet hat *n.* another term for **red hat.**

scarlet letter *n.* (esp. among U.S. Puritans) a scarlet letter *A* formerly worn by a person convicted of adultery.

scarlet pimpernel *n.* a primulaceous plant, *Anagallis arvensis,* of temperate regions, having small red, purple, or white star-shaped flowers that close in bad weather. Also called: **shepherd's** (*or* **poor man's**) **weatherglass.**

scarlet runner *n.* a climbing perennial bean plant, *Phaseolus multiflorus* (or *P. coccineus*), of tropical America, having scarlet flowers: widely cultivated for its long green edible pods containing edible seeds. Also called: **runner bean, string bean.**

scarlet tanager *n.* an E North American tanager, *Piranga olivacea,* the male of which has a bright red head and body with black wings and tail.

scarlet woman *n.* **1.** *New Testament.* a sinful woman described in Revelation 17, interpreted as a figure either of pagan Rome or of the Roman Catholic Church regarded as typifying vice overlaid with gaudy pageantry. **2.** any sexually promiscuous woman, esp. a prostitute.

scarp (skɑːp) *n.* **1.** a steep slope, esp. one formed by erosion or faulting; escarpment. See also **cuesta.** **2.** *Fortifications.* the side of a ditch cut nearest to and immediately below a rampart. *~vb.* **3.** (*tr.; often passive*) to wear or cut so as to form a steep slope. [C16: from Italian *scarpa*]

scarper ('skɑːpə) *Brit. slang.* *~vb.* (*intr.*) **1.** to depart in haste. *~n.* **2.** a hasty departure. [C19: probably an adaptation of Italian *scappare* to escape; perhaps influenced by folk etymology *Scapa Flow* Cockney rhyming slang for *go*]

scart (skært) *Scot.* *~vb.* **1.** to scratch or scrape. *~n.* **2.** a scratch or scrape. **3.** a stroke of a pen. **4.** a small amount; scraping. [C14: from earlier *scrat*]

scarves (skɑːvz) *n.* a plural of **scarf**[1].

scary ('skɛərɪ) *adj.* **scarier, scariest.** *Informal.* **1.** causing fear or alarm; frightening. **2.** easily roused to fear; timid.

scat[1] (skæt) *vb.* **scats, scatting, scatted.** (*intr.; usually imperative*) *Informal.* to go away in haste. [C19: perhaps from a hiss + the word *cat,* used to frighten away cats]

scat[2] (skæt) *n.* **1.** a type of jazz singing characterized by improvised vocal sounds instead of words. *~vb.* **scats, scatting, scatted.** **2.** (*intr.*) to sing jazz in this way. [C20: perhaps imitative]

scat[3] (skæt) *n.* any marine and freshwater percoid fish of the Asian family *Scatophagidae,* esp. *Scatophagus argus,* which has a beautiful coloration. [C20: shortened from *Scatophagus;* see SCATO-]

scat[4] (skæt) *n.* an animal dropping. [C20: see SCATO-]

scathe (skeɪð) *vb.* (*tr.*) **1.** *Rare.* to attack with severe criticism. **2.** *Archaic or dialect.* to injure. *~n.* **3.** *Archaic or dialect.* harm. [Old English *sceatha;* related to Old Norse *skathi,* Old Saxon *scatho*] —'**scatheless** *adj.*

scathing ('skeɪðɪŋ) *adj.* **1.** harshly critical; scornful: *a scathing remark.* **2.** damaging; painful. —'**scathingly** *adv.*

scato- *or before a vowel* **scat-** *combining form.* dung or excrement: *scatophagous.* [from Greek *skōr, skat-* dung]

scatology (skæ'tɒlədʒɪ) *n.* **1.** the scientific study of excrement, esp. in medicine for diagnostic purposes, and in palaeontology of fossilized excrement. **2.** obscenity or preoccupation with obscenity, esp. in the form of references to excrement. —**scatological** (ˌskætə'lɒdʒɪkᵊl) *or* (*less commonly*) ˌ**scato'logic** *adj.* —**sca'tologist** *n.*

scatter ('skætə) *vb.* **1.** (*tr.*) to throw about in various directions; strew. **2.** to separate and move or cause to separate and move in various directions; disperse. **3.** to deviate or cause to deviate in many directions, as in the diffuse reflection or refraction of light. *~n.* **4.** the act of scattering. **5.** a substance or a number of objects scattered about. [C13: probably a variant of SHATTER] —'**scatterable** *adj.* —'**scatterer** *n.*

scatterbrain ('skætəˌbreɪn) *n.* a person who is incapable of serious thought or concentration. —'**scatterˌbrained** *adj.*

scatter diagram *n. Statistics.* a graph that plots along two axes at right angles to each other the relationship between two variable quantities, such as height and weight.

scatter-gun *n.* a shotgun.

scattering ('skætərɪŋ) *n.* **1.** a small amount. **2.** *Physics.* the process in which particles, atoms, etc., are deflected as a result of collision.

scatter pin *n.* a small decorative pin usually worn in groups of two or three.

scatter rug *n.* a small rug used to cover a limited area.

scatty ('skætɪ) *adj.* **-tier, -tiest.** *Brit. informal.* **1.** empty-headed, frivolous, or thoughtless. **2.** distracted (esp. in **drive someone scatty**). [C20: from SCATTERBRAINED] —'**scattily** *adv.* —'**scattiness** *n.*

scaud (skɔːd) *vb., n.* a Scot. word for **scald**[1].

scaup *or* **scaup duck** (skɔːp) *n.* either of two diving ducks, *Aythya marila* (**greater scaup**) or *A. affinis* (**lesser scaup**), of Europe and America, having a black-and-white plumage in the male. Also called (U.S.): **bluebill, broadbill.** [C16: Scottish variant of SCALP]

scauper ('skɔːpə) *n.* a variant spelling of **scorper.**

scaur (skɔːr) *n.* a Scot. variant of **scar**[2].

scavenge ('skævɪndʒ) *vb.* **1.** to search for (anything usable) among discarded material. **2.** (*tr.*) to purify (a molten metal) by bubbling a suitable gas through it. The gas may be inert or may react with the impurities. **3.** to clean up filth from (streets, etc.). **4.** *Chem.* to act as a scavenger for (atoms, molecules, ions, radicals, etc.).

scavenge pump *n. Engineering.* an oil pump used in some internal-combustion engines to return oil from the crankcase to the oil tank.

scavenger ('skævɪndʒə) *n.* **1.** a person who collects things discarded by others. **2.** any animal that feeds on decaying organic matter, esp. on refuse. **3.** a substance added to a chemical reaction or mixture to counteract the effect of impurities. **4.** a person employed to clean the streets. [C16: from Anglo-Norman *scawager,* from Old Norman French *escauwage* examination, from *escauwer* to scrutinize, of Germanic origin; related to Flemish *scauwen*] —'**scavengery** *n.*

scavenger beetle *n.* any beetle of the mostly aquatic family *Hydrophilidae,* having clubbed antennae and long palps, and usually feeding on decaying vegetation.

scavenger hunt *n.* a game in which players are required to collect an assortment of miscellaneous items: usually played outdoors.

scavenge stroke *or* **scavenging stroke** *n.* (in a reciprocating engine) the stroke of a piston in a four-stroke cycle that pushes the burnt gases out as exhaust. Also called: **exhaust stroke.**

ScD *abbrev. for* Doctor of Science.

SCE (in Scotland) *abbrev. for* Scottish Certificate of Education: either of two public examinations in specific subjects taken as school-leaving qualifications or as qualifying examinations for entry into a university, college, etc. See also **higher** (sense 2), **O grade.**

scena ('ʃeɪnə) *n., pl.* **-ne** (-ˌneɪ). **1.** a scene in an opera, usually longer than a single aria. **2.** a dramatic vocal piece written in operatic style.

scenario (sɪ'nɑːrɪˌəʊ) *n., pl.* **-narios. 1.** a summary of the plot of a play, etc., including information about its characters, scenes, etc. **2.** a predicted sequence of events: *let's try another scenario, involving the demise of democracy.* [C19: via Italian from Latin *scēnārium,* from *scēna;* see SCENE] —**scenarist** ('siːnərɪst, sɪ'nɑː-) *n.*

scend *or* **send** (sɛnd) *Nautical.* ~*vb.* **scends, scending, scended** *or* **sends, sending, sent. 1.** (*intr.*) (of a vessel) to surge upwards in a heavy sea. ~*n.* **2.** the upward heaving of a vessel pitching. **3.** the forward lift given a vessel by the sea. [C17: perhaps from DESCEND or ASCEND]

scene (siːn) *n.* **1.** the place where an action or event, real or imaginary, occurs. **2.** the setting for the action of a play, novel, etc. **3.** an incident or situation, real or imaginary, esp. as described or represented. **4. a.** a subdivision of an act of a play, in which the time is continuous and the setting fixed. **b.** a single event, esp. a significant one, in a play. **5.** *Films.* a shot or series of shots that constitutes a unit of the action. **6.** the backcloths, stage setting, etc., for a play or film set; scenery. **7.** the prospect of a place, landscape, etc. **8.** a display of emotion, esp. an embarrassing one to the onlookers. **9.** *Informal.* the environment for a specific activity: *the fashion scene.* **10.** *Informal.* interest or chosen occupation: *classical music is not my scene.* **11.** *Rare.* the stage, esp. of a theatre in ancient Greece or Rome. **12. behind the scenes.** out of public view; privately. [C16: from Latin *scēna* theatrical stage, from Greek *skēnē* tent, stage]

scene dock *or* **bay** *n.* a place in a theatre where scenery is stored, usually near the stage.

scenery ('siːnərɪ) *n., pl.* **-eries. 1.** the natural features of a landscape. **2.** *Theatre.* the painted backcloths, stage structures, etc., used to represent a location in a theatre or studio. [C18: from Italian SCENARIO]

scenic ('siːnɪk, 'sɛn-) *adj.* **1.** of or relating to natural scenery. **2.** having beautiful natural scenery: *a scenic drive.* **3.** of or relating to the stage or stage scenery. **4.** (in painting) representing a scene, such as a scene of action or a historical event. —'**scenically** *adv.*

scenic railway *n.* **1.** a miniature railway used for amusement in a park, zoo, etc. **2.** a roller coaster.

scenic reserve *n. N.Z.* an area of natural beauty, set aside for public recreation.

scenography (siː'nɒgrəfɪ) *n.* **1.** the art of portraying objects or scenes in perspective. **2.** scene painting, esp. in ancient Greece. [C17: via Latin from Greek *skēnographia* a drawing in perspective, from *skēnē* SCENE] —**sce'nographer** *n.* —**scenographic** (ˌsiːnəʊ'græfɪk) *or* ˌ**sceno'graphical** *adj.* —ˌ**sceno'graphically** *adv.*

scent (sɛnt) *n.* **1.** a distinctive smell, esp. a pleasant one. **2.** a smell left in passing, by which a person or animal may be traced. **3.** a trail, clue, or guide. **4.** an instinctive ability for finding out or detecting. **5.** another word (esp. Brit.) for **perfume.** ~*vb.* **6.** (*tr.*) to recognize or be aware of by or as if by the smell. **7.** (*tr.*) to have a suspicion of; detect: *I scent foul play.* **8.** (*tr.*) to fill with odour or fragrance. **9.** (*intr.*) (of hounds, etc.) to hunt by the sense of smell. **10.** to smell (at): *the dog scented the air.* [C14: from Old French *sentir* to sense, from Latin *sentīre* to feel; see SENSE] —'**scented** *adj.* —'**scentless** *adj.*

scented orchid *n.* a slender orchid, *Gymnadenia conopsea,* with fragrant pink flowers carried in a dense spike and having a three-lobed lip; found in calcareous turf. The less common **larger scented orchid** is *G. densiflora.* Also called **fragrant orchid.**

sceptic *or archaic and U.S.* **skeptic** ('skɛptɪk) *n.* **1.** a person who habitually doubts the authenticity of accepted beliefs. **2.** a person who mistrusts people, ideas, etc., in general. **3.** a person who doubts the truth of religion, esp. Christianity. ~*adj.* **4.** of or relating to sceptics; sceptical. [C16: from Latin *scepticus,* from Greek *skeptikos* one who reflects upon, from *skeptesthai* to consider] —'**sceptical** *or archaic and U.S.* '**skeptical** *adj.* —'**sceptically** *or archaic and U.S.* '**skeptically** *adv.* —'**scepticism** *or archaic and U.S.* '**skepticism** *n.*

Sceptic *or archaic and U.S.* **Skeptic** ('skɛptɪk) *n.* **1.** a member of one of the ancient Greek schools of philosophy who believed that real knowledge of things is impossible. ~*adj.* **2.** of or relating to the Sceptics. —'**Scepticism** *or archaic and U.S.* '**Skepticism** *n.*

sceptre *or U.S.* **scepter** ('sɛptə) *n.* **1.** a ceremonial staff held by a monarch as the symbol of authority. **2.** imperial authority; sovereignty. ~*vb.* **3.** (*tr.*) to invest with authority. [C13: from Old French *sceptre,* from Latin *scēptrum,* from Greek *skeptron* staff] —'**sceptred** *or U.S.* '**sceptered** *adj.*

SCG (in Australia) *abbrev. for* Sydney Cricket Ground.

sch. *abbrev. for* school.

Schadenfreude *German.* ('ʃaːdənfrɔydə) *n.* delight in another's misfortune. [German: from *Schaden* harm + *Freude* joy]

schappe ('ʃæpə) *n.* a yarn or fabric made from waste silk. [from German]

schedule ('ʃɛdjuːl; *also, esp. U.S.* 'skɛdʒʊəl) *n.* **1.** a plan of procedure for a project, allotting the work to be done and the time for it. **2.** a list of items: *a schedule of fixed prices.* **3.** a list of times, esp. of arrivals and departures; timetable. **4.** a list of tasks to be performed, esp. within a set period. **5.** *Law.* a list or inventory, usually supplementary to a contract, will, etc. **6. on schedule.** at the expected or planned time. ~*vb.* (*tr.*) **7.** to make a schedule of or place in a schedule. **8.** to plan to occur at a certain time. [C14: earlier *cedule, sedule* via Old French from Late Latin *schedula* small piece of paper, from Latin *scheda* sheet of paper] —'**schedular** *adj.*

scheduled ('ʃɛdjuːld) *adj.* **1.** arranged or planned according to a programme, timetable, etc.: *a scheduled meeting; a change to the scheduled programmes on TV tonight.* **2.** (of an aircraft or a flight) part of a regular service, not specially chartered. **3.** *Brit.* (of a building, place of historic interest, etc.) entered on a list of places to be preserved. See also **listed building.**

scheduled castes *pl. n.* certain classes in Indian society officially granted special concessions. See **Harijan.**

scheduled territories *pl. n.* **the.** another name for **sterling area.**

scheelite ('ʃiːlaɪt) *n.* a white, brownish, or greenish mineral, usually fluorescent, consisting of calcium tungstate in tetragonal crystalline form with some tungsten often replaced by molybdenum: occurs principally in contact metamorphic rocks and quartz veins, and is an important source of tungsten and purified calcium tungstate. Formula: $CaWO_4$. [C19: from German *Scheelit,* named after K. W. *Scheele* (1742–86), Swedish chemist]

schema ('skiːmə) *n., pl.* **-mata** (-mətə). **1.** a plan, diagram, or scheme. **2.** (in Kantian philosophy) a rule or principle that enables the understanding to apply its categories and unify experience: *universal succession is the schema of causality.* **3.** *Psychol.* a mental model of aspects of the world or of the self that is structured in such a way as to facilitate the processes of cognition and perception. **4.** *Logic.* an expression using metavariables that may be replaced by object language expressions to yield a well-formed formula. Thus $A = A$ is an axiom schema for identity, representing the infinite number of axioms, $x = x$, $y = y$, $z = z$, etc. [C19: from Greek: form]

schematic (skɪ'mætɪk, skiː-) *adj.* **1.** of or relating to the nature of a diagram, plan, or schema. ~*n.* **2.** a schematic diagram, esp. of an electrical circuit. —**sche'matically** *adv.*

schematism ('skiːməˌtɪzəm) *n.* the general form, arrangement, or classification of something.

schematize *or* **schematise** ('skiːməˌtaɪz) *vb.* (*tr.*) to form into or arrange in a scheme. —ˌ**schemati'zation** *or* ˌ**schemati'sation** *n.*

scheme (skiːm) *n.* **1.** a systematic plan for a course of action. **2.** a systematic arrangement of correlated parts; system. **3.** a secret plot. **4.** a visionary or unrealizable project. **5.** a chart, diagram, or outline. **6.** an astrological diagram giving the aspects of celestial bodies at a particular time. **7.** *Chiefly Brit.* a plan formally adopted by a commercial enterprise or governmental body, as for pensions, etc. **8.** *Chiefly Scot.* an area of housing that is laid out esp. by a local authority; estate. ~*vb.* **9.** (*tr.*) to devise a system for. **10.** to form intrigues (for) in an underhand manner. [C16: from Latin *schema,* from Greek *skhēma* form] —'**schemer** *n.*

scheming ('skiːmɪŋ) *adj.* **1.** given to making plots; cunning. ~*n.* **2.** intrigues. —'**schemingly** *adv.*

scherzando (skɛə'tsændəʊ) *Music.* ~*adj., adv.* **1.** to be performed in a light-hearted manner. ~*n., pl.* **-di** (-diː) *or* **-dos. 2.** a movement, passage, etc., directed to be performed in this way. [Italian, literally: joking. See SCHERZO]

scherzo ('skɛətsəʊ) *n., pl.* **-zos** *or* **-zi** (-tsiː). a brisk lively movement, developed from the minuet, with a contrastive middle section (a trio). See **minuet** (sense 2). [Italian: joke, of Germanic origin; compare Middle High German *scherzen* to jest]

Schick test (ʃɪk) *n. Med.* a skin test to determine immunity to diphtheria: a dilute diphtheria toxin is injected into the skin; within two or three days a red inflamed area will develop if no antibodies are present. [C20: named after Bela *Schick* (1877–1967), U.S. paediatrician]

Schiff base (ʃɪf) *n.* the product of the chemical association of an aldehyde with a primary amine. [C19: named after Hugo *Schiff* (1834–1915), German chemist]

schiller ('ʃɪlə) *n.* an unusual metallic lustre in some minerals caused by internal reflection from certain inclusions such as gas cavities. [C19: from German *Schiller* iridescence, from Old High German *scilihen* to blink]

schilling ('ʃɪlɪŋ) *n.* **1.** the standard monetary unit of Austria, divided into 100 groschen. **2.** an old German coin of low denomination. [C18: from German: SHILLING]

schipperke ('ʃɪpəkɪ, 'skɪp-) *n.* a small Dutch breed of tailless dog with a foxy head, pricked ears, and usually a black coat. [C19: from Dutch, literally: little boatman (from its use as a guard dog on canal barges). See SKIPPER[1]]

schism ('sɪzəm, 'skɪz-) *n.* 1. the division of a group into opposing factions. 2. the factions so formed. 3. division within or separation from an established Church, esp. the Roman Catholic Church, not necessarily involving differences in doctrine. [C14: from Church Latin *schisma,* from Greek *skhisma* a cleft, from *skhizein* to split]

schismatic (sɪz'mætɪk, skɪz-) *or* **schismatical** *adj.* 1. of, relating to, or promoting schism. ~*n.* 2. a person who causes schism or belongs to a schismatic faction. —**schis'matically** *adv.* —**schis'maticalness** *n.*

schist (ʃɪst) *n.* any metamorphic rock that can be split into thin layers because its micaceous minerals have become aligned in thin parallel bands. [C18: from French *schiste,* from Latin *lapis schistos* stone that may be split, from Greek *skhizein* to split] —'**schistose** *adj.* —**schistosity** (ʃɪ'stɒsɪtɪ) *n.*

schistosome ('ʃɪstəˌsəʊm) *n.* any of various blood flukes of the chiefly tropical genus *Schistosoma,* which cause disease in man and domestic animals. Also called: **bilharzia.** [C19: from New Latin *Schistosoma;* see SCHIST, -SOME[3]]

schistosomiasis (ˌʃɪstəsəʊ'maɪəsɪs) *n.* a disease caused by infestation of the body with blood flukes of the genus *Schistosoma.* Also called: **bilharziasis.**

schizanthus (skɪt'sænθəs) *n.* any plant of the Chilean annual genus *Schizanthus,* some species of which are grown as pot or garden plants for their showy red, white, or yellow orchid-like flowers: family *Solanaceae.* Sometimes called: **poor man's orchid.** [New Latin, from Greek *schizein* to cut + *anthos* flower (from the deeply divided corolla)]

schizo ('skɪtsəʊ) *Informal.* ~*adj.* 1. schizophrenic. ~*n., pl.* **-os.** 2. a schizophrenic person.

schizo- *or before a vowel* **schiz-** *combining form.* indicating a cleavage, split, or division: *schizocarp; schizophrenia.* [from Greek *skhizein* to split]

schizocarp ('skɪzəˌkɑːp) *n. Botany.* a dry fruit that splits into two or more one-seeded portions at maturity. —ˌ**schizo'carpous** *or* ˌ**schizo'carpic** *adj.*

schizogenesis (ˌskɪtsəʊ'dʒɛnɪsɪs) *n.* asexual reproduction by fission of the parent organism or part. —**schizogenetic** (ˌskɪtsəʊdʒɪ'nɛtɪk) *adj.*

schizogony (skɪt'sɒgənɪ) *n.* asexual reproduction in protozoans that is characterized by multiple fission.

schizoid ('skɪtsɔɪd) *adj.* 1. *Psychol.* denoting a personality disorder characterized by extreme shyness and oversensitivity to others. 2. *Informal.* characterized by or showing conflicting or contradictory attitudes, ideas, etc. ~*n.* 3. a person who has a schizoid personality.

schizomycete (ˌskɪtsəʊmaɪ'siːt) *n.* any microscopic organism of the class *Schizomycetes,* which includes the bacteria. —**schizomycetic** (ˌskɪtsəʊmaɪ'sɛtɪk) *or* ˌ**schizomy'cetous** *adj.*

schizont ('skɪtsɒnt) *n.* a cell formed from a trophozoite during the asexual stage of the life cycle of protozoans of the class *Sporozoa,* such as the malaria parasite. [C19: from SCHIZO- + *-ont* a being, from Greek *einai* to be]

schizophrenia (ˌskɪtsəʊ'friːnɪə) *n.* 1. any of a group of psychotic disorders characterized by progressive deterioration of the personality, withdrawal from reality, hallucinations, delusions, social apathy, emotional instability, etc. See **catatonia, hebephrenia, paranoia.** 2. *Informal.* behaviour that appears to be motivated by contradictory or conflicting principles. [C20: from SCHIZO- + Greek *phrēn* mind + -IA]

schizophrenic (ˌskɪtzəʊ'frɛnɪk) *adj.* 1. exhibiting symptoms of schizophrenia. 2. *Informal.* experiencing or maintaining contradictory attitudes, emotions, etc. ~*n.* 3. a person who is schizophrenic.

schizophyceous (ˌskɪtsəʊ'fɪʃəs) *adj.* of, relating to, or belonging to the *Schizophyceae,* a group of blue-green algae that grow in salt and fresh water and often pollute drinking water. [C19: from New Latin *Schizophyceae,* from SCHIZO- + Greek *phukos* seaweed]

schizophyte ('skɪtsəʊˌfaɪt) *n.* any of various plants, such as certain fungi and bacteria, that reproduce only by multiple fission. —**schizophytic** (ˌskɪtsəʊ'fɪtɪk) *adj.*

schizopod ('skɪtsəʊˌpɒd) *n.* any of various shrimplike crustaceans of the former order *Schizopoda,* now separated into the orders *Mysidacea* (opossum shrimps) and *Euphausiacea.*

schizothymia (ˌskɪtsəʊ'θaɪmɪə) *n. Psychiatry.* the condition of being schizoid or introverted. It encompasses elements of schizophrenia but does not involve the same depth of psychological disturbance. [C20: New Latin, from SCHIZO- + *-thymia,* from Greek *thumos* spirit] —ˌ**schizo'thymic** *adj.*

schlemiel, schlemihl, *or* **shlemiel** (ʃlə'miːl) *n. U.S. slang.* a clumsy or unlucky person. [Yiddish, from German, after the hero of a novel by Chamisso (1781–1838)]

schlep (ʃlɛp) *U.S. slang.* ~*vb.* **schleps, schlepping, schlepped.** 1. to drag or lug (oneself or an object) with difficulty. ~*n.* 2. a stupid or clumsy person. 3. an arduous journey or procedure. [Yiddish, from German *schleppen*]

schlieren ('ʃlɪərən) *n.* 1. *Physics.* visible streaks produced in a transparent fluid as a result of variations in the fluid's density leading to variations in refractive index. They can be recorded by flash photography (**schlieren photography**). 2. streaks or platelike masses of mineral in a rock mass, that differ in texture or composition from the main mass. [German, plural of *Schliere* streak] —'**schlieric** *adj.*

schlock (ʃlɒk) *Chiefly U.S. slang.* ~*n.* 1. goods or produce of cheap or inferior quality; trash. ~*adj.* 2. cheap, inferior, or trashy. [Yiddish: damaged merchandise, probably from German *Schlag* a blow; related to SLAY]

schlumbergera (ʃləm'bɜːgərə) *n.* See **Christmas cactus.**

schmaltz *or* **schmalz** (ʃmælts, ʃmɔːlts) *n.* 1. excessive sentimentality, esp. in music. 2. *U.S.* animal fat used in cooking. [C20: from German (*Schmalz*) and Yiddish: melted fat, from Old High German *smalz*] —'**schmaltzy** *adj.*

Schmidt telescope *or* **camera** (ʃmɪt) *n.* a type of reflecting telescope incorporating a camera and consisting of a thin convex glass plate placed at the centre of curvature of a spherical mirror, thus correcting for spherical aberration, coma, and astigmatism. Wide areas of the sky can be photographed in one exposure. [C20: named after B.V. *Schmidt* (1879–1935), Estonian-born German inventor]

Schmitt trigger (ʃmɪt) *n. Electronics.* a bistable circuit that gives a constant output when the input voltage is above a specified value. [C20: named after O.H. *Schmitt* (born 1913), U.S. scientist]

schmo *or* **shmo** (ʃməʊ) *n., pl.* **schmoes** *or* **shmoes.** *U.S. slang.* a dull, stupid, or boring person. [from Yiddish *shmok*]

schmooze (ʃmuːz) *U.S. slang.* ~*vb.* (*intr.*) 1. to chat or gossip. ~*n.* 2. a trivial conversation; chat. [Yiddish, from *schmues* a chat, from Hebrew *shemuoth* reports]

schmuck (ʃmʌk) *n. U.S. slang.* a stupid or contemptible person; oaf. [from Yiddish *schmuck* penis, from German *Schmuck* decoration, from Middle High German *smucken* to press into]

schnapper ('ʃnæpə) *n.* a variant of **snapper** (senses 1, 2).

schnapps *or* **schnaps** (ʃnæps) *n.* 1. a Dutch spirit distilled from potatoes. 2. (in Germany) any strong spirit. [C19: from German *Schnaps,* from *schnappen* to SNAP]

schnauzer ('ʃnaʊtsə) *n.* a wire-haired breed of dog of the terrier type, originally from Germany, having a greyish coat and distinctive beard, moustache, and eyebrows. [C19: from German *Schnauze* SNOUT]

schnecken ('ʃnɛkən) *pl. n., sing.* **schnecke** ('ʃnɛkə). *Chiefly U.S.* a sweet spiral-shaped bread roll flavoured with cinnamon and nuts. [German, plural of *Schnecke* SNAIL]

schnitzel ('ʃnɪtsəl) *n.* a thin slice of meat, esp. veal. See also **Wiener schnitzel.** [German: cutlet, from *schnitzen* to carve, *schnitzeln* to whittle]

schnook (ʃnʊk) *n. U.S. slang.* a stupid or gullible person. [from Yiddish *shnok,* variant of *shmok* SCHMO]

schnorkle ('ʃnɔːkᵊl) *n., vb.* a less common variant of **snorkel.**

schnorrer ('ʃnɔːrə) *n. U.S. slang.* a person who lives off the charity of others; professional beggar. [Yiddish, from German *Schnurrer* beggar (who played an instrument), from Middle High German *snurren* to hum]

schnozzle ('ʃnɒzᵊl) *n. Chiefly U.S.* a slang word for **nose** (sense 1). [alteration of Yiddish *shnoitsl,* diminutive of *shnoits,* from German *Schnauze* SNOUT]

schola cantorum ('skəʊlə kæn'tɔːrəm) *n., pl.* **scholae cantorum** ('skəʊliː). a choir or choir school maintained by a church. [Medieval Latin: school of singers]

scholar ('skɒlə) *n.* 1. a learned person, esp. in the humanities. 2. a person, esp. a child, who studies; pupil. 3. a student of merit at an educational establishment who receives financial aid, esp. from an endowment given for such a purpose. [C14: from Old French *escoler,* via Late Latin from Latin *schola* SCHOOL] —'**scholarly** *adj.* —'**scholarliness** *n.*

scholarship ('skɒləʃɪp) *n.* 1. academic achievement; erudition; learning. 2. **a.** financial aid provided for a scholar because of academic merit. **b.** the position of a student who gains this financial aid. **c.** (*as modifier*): *a scholarship student.* 3. the qualities of a scholar.

scholar's mate *n. Chess.* a simple mate by the queen on the f7 square, achievable by white's fourth move.

scholastic (skə'læstɪk) *adj.* 1. of, relating to, or befitting schools, scholars, or education. 2. pedantic or precise. 3. (*often cap.*) characteristic of or relating to the medieval Schoolmen. ~*n.* 4. a student or pupil. 5. a person who is given to quibbling or logical subtleties; pedant. 6. (*often cap.*) a disciple or adherent of scholasticism; Schoolman. 7. **a.** a Jesuit student who is undergoing a period of probation prior to commencing his theological studies. **b.** the status and position of such a student. 8. a formalist in art. [C16: via Latin from Greek *skholastikos* devoted to learning, ultimately from *skholē* SCHOOL[1]] —**scho'lastically** *adv.*

scholasticate (skə'læstɪˌkeɪt, -kɪt) *n. R.C. Church.* the state of being a scholastic, the period during which a Jesuit student is a scholastic, or an institution where scholastics pass this period. [C19: from New Latin *scholasticātus,* from Latin *scholasticus* SCHOLASTIC]

scholasticism (skə'læstɪˌsɪzəm) *n.* 1. (*sometimes cap.*) the system of philosophy, theology, and teaching that dominated medieval western Europe and was based on the writings of the Church Fathers and (from the 12th century) Aristotle. 2. strict adherence to traditional doctrines.

scholiast ('skəʊlɪˌæst) *n.* a medieval annotator, esp. of classical texts. [C16: from Late Greek *skholiastēs,* from *skholiazein* to write a SCHOLIUM] —ˌ**scholi'astic** *adj.*

scholium ('skəʊlɪəm) *n., pl.* **-lia** (-lɪə). a commentary or annotation, esp. on a classical text. [C16: from New Latin, from Greek *skholion* exposition, from *skholē* SCHOOL[1]]

school[1] (sku:l) *n.* **1. a.** an institution or building at which children and young people usually under 19 receive education. **b.** (*as modifier*): *school bus; school day.* **c.** (*in combination*): *schoolroom; schoolwork.* **2.** any educational institution or building. **3.** a faculty, institution, or department specializing in a particular subject: *a law school.* **4.** the staff and pupils of a school. **5.** the period of instruction in a school or one session of this: *he stayed after school to do extra work.* **6.** meetings held occasionally for members of a profession, etc. **7.** a place or sphere of activity that instructs: *the school of hard knocks.* **8.** a body of people or pupils adhering to a certain set of principles, doctrines, or methods. **9.** a group of artists, writers, etc., linked by the same style, teachers, or aims: *the Venetian school of painting.* **10.** a style of life: *a gentleman of the old school.* **11.** *Informal.* a group assembled for a common purpose, esp. gambling or drinking. *~vb.* (*tr.*) **12.** to train or educate in or as in a school. **13.** to discipline or control. **14.** an archaic word for **reprimand.** [Old English *scōl,* from Latin *schola* school, from Greek *skholē* leisure spent in the pursuit of knowledge]

school[2] (sku:l) *n.* **1.** a group of porpoises or similar aquatic animals that swim together. *~vb.* **2.** (*intr.*) to form such a group. [Old English *scolu* SHOAL[2]]

school attendance officer *n.* a former name for **Educational Welfare Officer.**

school board *n.* **1.** (formerly in Britain) an elected board of ratepayers who provided local elementary schools between 1870 and 1902. **2.** (in the U.S. and Canada) a local board of education.

schoolboy ('sku:l,bɔɪ) *or* (*fem.*) **schoolgirl** *n.* a child attending school.

School Certificate *n.* (in England and Wales between 1917 and 1951 and currently in New Zealand) a certificate awarded to school pupils who pass a public examination: the equivalent of O level. Abbrev.: **SC.**

School Committee *n.* (in New Zealand) a parent group selected to support a primary school.

school crossing patrol *n.* the official name for **lollipop man** *or* **lady.**

schoolhouse ('sku:l,haʊs) *n.* **1.** a building used as a school, esp. a rural school. **2.** a house attached to a school.

schoolie ('sku:lɪ) *n. Austral. slang.* a schoolteacher.

schooling ('sku:lɪŋ) *n.* **1.** education, esp. when received at school. **2.** the process of teaching or being taught in a school. **3.** the training of an animal, esp. of a horse for dressage. **4.** an archaic word for **reprimand.**

school-leaver *n.* a pupil who is about to leave or has recently left school, esp. at the minimum school-leaving age. —'**school,leaving** *adj.*

schoolman ('sku:lmən) *n., pl.* **-men.** **1.** (*sometimes cap.*) a scholar versed in the learning of the Schoolmen. **2.** *Rare, chiefly U.S.* a professional educator or teacher.

Schoolman ('sku:lmən) *n., pl.* **-men.** (*sometimes not cap.*) a master in one of the schools or universities of the Middle Ages who was versed in scholasticism; scholastic.

schoolmarm ('sku:l,mɑ:m) *n. Informal.* **1.** a woman schoolteacher, esp. when considered to be prim, prudish, or old-fashioned. **2.** *Brit.* any woman considered to be prim, prudish, or old-fashioned. [C19: from SCHOOL + *marm,* variant of MA'AM. See MADAM] —'**school,marmish** *adj.*

schoolmaster ('sku:l,mɑ:stə) *n.* **1.** a man who teaches in or runs a school. **2.** a person or thing that acts as an instructor. **3.** a food fish, *Lutjanus apodus,* of the warm waters of the Caribbean and Atlantic: family *Lutjanidae* (snappers). *~vb.* (*intr.*) **4.** to be a schoolmaster. —'**school,mastering** *n.* —'**school,masterish** *adj.* —'**school,masterly** *adj.* —'**school,mastership** *n.*

schoolmate ('sku:l,meɪt) *or* **schoolfellow** *n.* a companion at school; fellow pupil.

school milk *n. Social welfare.* (in Britain) a third of a pint of milk, formerly provided free by the local education authority to all young pupils, now given only to children who have passed a needs or means test.

schoolmistress ('sku:l,mɪstrɪs) *n.* a woman who teaches in or runs a school. —'**school,mistressy** *adj.*

school of arts *n. Austral.* a public building in a small town, originally one used for adult education.

Schools (sku:lz) *pl. n.* **1. the.** the medieval Schoolmen collectively. **2.** (at Oxford University) **a.** the Examination Schools, the University building in which examinations are held. **b.** *Informal.* the Second Public Examination for the degree of Bachelor of Arts; finals.

school ship *n.* a ship for training young men in seamanship, for a career in the regular or merchant navy.

schoolteacher ('sku:l,ti:tʃə) *n.* a person who teaches in a school. —'**school,teaching** *n.*

school welfare officer *n.* a former name for **Educational Welfare Officer.**

school year *n.* **1.** a twelve-month period, (in Britain) usually starting in late summer and continuing for three terms until the following summer, during which pupils remain in the same class. **2.** the time during this period when the school is open.

schooner ('sku:nə) *n.* **1.** a sailing vessel with at least two masts, with all lower sails rigged fore-and-aft. **2.** *Brit.* a large glass for sherry. **3.** *U.S., Canadian, Austral., and N.Z.* a large glass for beer. [C18: origin uncertain]

schooner rig *n. Nautical.* a rig in which the mainmast is taller than the foremast.

schorl (ʃɔ:l) *n.* a black tourmaline consisting of a borosilicate of sodium, iron, and aluminium. Formula: $NaFe_3B_3Al_3(Al_3Si_6O_{27})(OH)_4$. [C18: from German *Schörl,* origin unknown] —**schor'laceous** *adj.*

schottische (ʃɒ'ti:ʃ) *n.* **1.** a 19th-century German dance resembling a slow polka. **2.** a piece of music composed for or in the manner of this dance. [C19: from German *der schottische Tanz* the Scottish dance]

Schottky defect ('ʃɒtkɪ) *n. Physics.* a crystal defect in which vacancies exist in the lattice. [C20: named after Walter *Schottky* (1886–1976), German physicist]

Schottky effect *n. Physics.* a reduction in the energy required to remove an electron from a solid surface in a vacuum when an electric field is applied to the surface.

Schottky noise *n.* another name for **shot noise.**

Schrödinger equation ('ʃrɜ:dɪŋə) *n.* an equation used in wave mechanics to describe a physical system. For a particle of mass m and potential energy V it is written $(ih/2\pi).(\partial\psi/\partial t) = (-h^2/8\pi^2 m)\nabla^2\psi + V\psi$, where $i = \sqrt{-1}$, h is the Planck constant, t the time, ∇^2 the Laplace operator, and ψ the wave function. [named after Erwin *Schrödinger* (1887–1961), Austrian physicist]

schul (ʃu:l) *n.* a variant spelling of **shul.**

schuss (ʃʊs) *Skiing.* *~n.* **1.** a straight high-speed downhill run. *~vb.* **2.** (*intr.*) to perform a schuss. [German: SHOT[1]]

schwa *or* **shwa** (ʃwɑ:) *n.* **1.** a central vowel represented in the International Phonetic Alphabet by (ə). The sound occurs in unstressed syllables in English, as in *around, mother,* and *sofa.* **2.** the symbol (ə) used to represent this sound. [C19: via German from Hebrew *shewā,* a diacritic indicating lack of a vowel sound]

Schwarzschild radius ('ʃwɔ:ts,ʃɪld; *German* 'ʃvartsʃɪlt) *n. Astronomy.* the radius of a sphere (**Schwarzschild sphere**) surrounding an object, esp. a black hole, from within which no meaningful information can escape because of gravitational forces. [C20: named after Karl *Schwarzschild* (1873–1916), U.S. astrophysicist]

sci. *abbrev. for:* **1.** science. **2.** scientific.

sciaenid (saɪ'i:nɪd) *or* **sciaenoid** *adj.* **1.** of, relating to, or belonging to the *Sciaenidae,* a family of mainly tropical and subtropical marine percoid fishes that includes the drums, grunts, and croakers. *~n.* **2.** any sciaenid fish. [C19: from Latin *sciaena* a type of fish, from Greek *skiaina*]

sciamachy (saɪ'æməkɪ), **sciomachy,** *or* **skiamachy** (skaɪ'æməkɪ) *n., pl.* **-chies.** *Rare.* a fight with an imaginary enemy. [C17: from Greek *skiamakhia* a mock fight, from *skia* a shadow + *makhesthai* to fight]

sciatic (saɪ'ætɪk) *adj.* **1.** *Anatomy.* of or relating to the hip or the hipbone. **2.** of, relating to, or afflicted with sciatica. [C16: from French *sciatique,* from Late Latin *sciaticus,* from Latin *ischiadicus* relating to pain in the hip, from Greek *iskhiadikos,* from *iskhia* hip joint]

sciatica (saɪ'ætɪkə) *n.* a form of neuralgia characterized by intense pain and tenderness along the course of the body's longest nerve (**sciatic nerve**), extending from the back of the thigh down to the calf of the leg. [C15: from Late Latin *sciatica;* see SCIATIC]

science ('saɪəns) *n.* **1.** the systematic study of the nature and behaviour of the material and physical universe, based on observation, experiment, and measurement, and the formulation of laws to describe these facts in general terms. **2.** the knowledge so obtained or the practice of obtaining it. **3.** any particular branch of this knowledge: *the pure and applied sciences.* **4.** any body of knowledge organized in a systematic manner. **5.** skill or technique. **6.** *Archaic.* knowledge. [C14: via Old French from Latin *scientia* knowledge, from *scīre* to know]

science fiction *n.* **a.** a literary genre that makes imaginative use of scientific knowledge or conjecture. **b.** (*as modifier*): *a science fiction writer.*

science park *n.* an area usually linked with a university where scientific research and commercial development are carried on in cooperation.

scienter (saɪ'ɛntə) *adv. Law.* knowingly; wilfully. [from Latin]

sciential (saɪ'ɛnʃəl) *adj.* **1.** of or relating to science. **2.** skilful or knowledgeable.

scientific (,saɪən'tɪfɪk) *adj.* **1.** (*prenominal*) of, relating to, derived from, or used in science: *scientific equipment.* **2.** (*prenominal*) occupied in science: *scientific manpower.* **3.** conforming with the principles or methods used in science: *a scientific approach.* —,**scien'tifically** *adv.*

scientific method *n.* a method of investigation in which a problem is first identified and observations, experiments, or other relevant data are then used to construct or test hypotheses that purport to solve it.

scientific socialism *n.* Marxist socialism. Compare **utopian socialism.**

scientism ('saɪən,tɪzəm) *n.* **1.** the application of, or belief in, the scientific method. **2.** the uncritical application of scientific or quasi-scientific methods to inappropriate fields of study or investigation. —,**scien'tistic** *adj.*

scientist ('saɪəntɪst) *n.* a person who studies or practises any of the sciences or who uses scientific methods.

Scientist ('saɪəntɪst) *n.* **1.** *Christian Science.* Christ as supreme spiritual healer. **2.** short for **Christian Scientist.**

Scientology (ˌsaɪən'tɒlədʒɪ) *n. Trademark.* the philosophy of the Church of Scientology, a nondenominational movement founded in the U.S. in the 1950s, which emphasizes self-knowledge as a means of realizing full spiritual potential. [C20: from Latin *scient(ia)* SCIENCE + -LOGY] —ˌ**Scien'tologist** *n.*

sci-fi ('saɪˌfaɪ) *n.* short for **science fiction.**

scilicet ('sɪlɪˌsɛt) *adv.* namely; that is: used esp. in explaining an obscure text or supplying a missing word. [Latin: shortened from *scīre licet* it is permitted to know]

scilla ('sɪlə) *n.* any liliaceous plant of the genus *Scilla,* of Old World temperate regions, having small bell-shaped flowers. See also **squill** (sense 3). [C19: via Latin from Greek *skilla;* compare SQUILL]

Scillonian (sɪ'ləʊnɪən) *adj.* **1.** of or relating to the Scilly Isles, off SW England, or to their inhabitants, customs, etc. ~*n.* **2.** a native or inhabitant of the Scilly Isles.

scimitar *or (rarely)* **simitar** ('sɪmɪtə) *n.* an oriental sword with a curved blade broadening towards the point. [C16: from Old Italian *scimitarra,* probably from Persian *shimshīr,* of obscure origin]

scincoid ('sɪŋkɔɪd) *or* **scincoidian** *adj.* **1.** of, relating to, or resembling a skink. ~*n.* **2.** any animal, esp. a lizard, resembling a skink. [C18: from New Latin *scincoidēs,* from Latin *scincus* a SKINK]

scindapsus (sɪn'dæpsəs) *n.* any plant of the tropical Asiatic climbing genus *Scindapsus,* typically stem rooting, esp. *S. aureus* and *S. pictus,* grown as greenhouse or house plants for their leathery heart-shaped variegated leaves: family *Araceae.* [New Latin, from Greek *skindapsos* an ivy-like plant]

scintigraphy (ˌsɪn'tɪgrəfɪ) *n. Med.* a diagnostic technique using a radioactive tracer and scintillation counter for producing pictures (**scintigrams**) of internal parts of the body. [C20: from SCINTI(LLATION) + -GRAPHY]

scintilla (sɪn'tɪlə) *n.* a minute amount; hint, trace, or particle. [C17: from Latin: a spark]

scintillate ('sɪntɪˌleɪt) *vb.* (*mainly intr.*) **1.** (*also tr.*) to give off (sparks); sparkle; twinkle. **2.** to be animated or brilliant. **3.** *Physics.* to give off flashes of light as a result of the impact of particles or photons. [C17: from Latin *scintillāre,* from *scintilla* a spark] —'**scintillant** *adj.* —'**scintillantly** *adv.* —'**scintilˌlating** *adj.* —'**scintilˌlatingly** *adv.*

scintillation (ˌsɪntɪ'leɪʃən) *n.* **1.** the act of scintillating. **2.** a spark or flash. **3.** the twinkling of stars, caused by rapid changes in the density of the earth's atmosphere producing uneven refraction of starlight. **4.** *Physics.* a flash of light produced when a material scintillates.

scintillation counter *n.* an instrument for detecting and measuring the intensity of high-energy radiation. It consists of a phosphor with which particles collide producing flashes of light that are detected by a photomultiplier and converted into pulses of electric current that are counted by electronic equipment.

scintillator ('sɪntɪˌleɪtə) *n. Physics.* a phosphor that produces scintillations.

scintillometer (ˌsɪntɪ'lɒmɪtə) *n. Physics.* a device for observing ionizing radiation by the scintillations it produces in a suitable material.

scintillon (sɪn'tɪlən) *n.* a luminescent body present in the cytoplasm of some dinoflagellates.

sciolism ('saɪəˌlɪzəm) *n. Rare.* the practice of opinionating on subjects of which one has only superficial knowledge. [C19: from Late Latin *sciolus* someone with a smattering of knowledge, from Latin *scīre* to know] —'**sciolist** *n.* —ˌ**scio'listic** *adj.*

sciomachy (saɪ'ɒmәkɪ) *n., pl.* **-chies.** a variant of **sciamachy.**

sciomancy ('saɪəˌmænsɪ) *n.* divination with the help of ghosts. [C17: via Latin from Greek *skia* ghost + -MANCY] —'**sciomancer** *n.* —ˌ**scio'mantic** *adj.*

scion ('saɪən) *n.* **1.** a descendant, heir, or young member of a family. **2.** a shoot or twig of a plant used to form a graft. [C14: from Old French *cion,* of Germanic origin; compare Old High German *chīnan* to sprout]

sciophyte ('saɪəˌfaɪt) *n.* any plant that grows best in the shade. [C20: via Latin from Greek *skia* shade + -PHYTE] —**sciophytic** (ˌsaɪə'fɪtɪk) *adj.*

scire facias ('saɪərɪ 'feɪʃɪˌæs) *n. Law, rare.* **1.** a judicial writ founded upon some record, such as a judgment, letters patent, etc., requiring the person against whom it is brought to show cause why the record should not be enforced or annulled. **2.** a proceeding begun by the issue of such a writ. [C15: from legal Latin, literally: cause (him) to know]

scirrhous ('sɪrəs) *adj. Pathol.* of or resembling a scirrhus; hard. —**scirrhosity** (sɪ'rɒsɪtɪ) *n.*

scirrhus ('sɪrəs) *n., pl.* **-rhi** (-raɪ) *or* **-rhuses.** *Pathol.* a firm cancerous growth composed of fibrous tissues. [C17: from New Latin, from Latin *scirros,* from Greek *skirros,* from *skiros* hard] —**scirrhoid** ('sɪrɔɪd) *adj.*

scissel ('skɪsᵊl) *n.* the waste metal left over from sheet metal after discs have been punched out of it. [C19: from French *cisaille,* from *cisailler* to clip]

scissile ('sɪsaɪl) *adj.* capable of being cut or divided. [C17: from Latin *scissilis* that can be split, from *scindere* to cut]

scission ('sɪʃən) *n.* the act or an instance of cutting, splitting, or dividing. [C15: from Late Latin *scissiō,* from *scindere* to split]

scissor ('sɪzə) *vb.* to cut (an object) with scissors.

scissors ('sɪzəz) *pl. n.* **1.** Also called: **pair of scissors.** a cutting instrument used for cloth, hair, etc., having two crossed pivoted blades that cut by a shearing action, with ring-shaped handles at one end. **2.** a wrestling hold in which a wrestler wraps his legs round his opponent's body or head, locks his feet together, and squeezes. **3.** any gymnastic or athletic feat in which the legs cross and uncross in a scissor-like movement. **4.** *Athletics.* a technique in high-jumping, now little used, in which the legs perform a scissor-like movement in clearing the bar. [C14 *sisoures,* from Old French *cisoires,* from Vulgar Latin *cīsōria* (unattested), ultimately from Latin *caedere* to cut; see CHISEL] —'**scissor-ˌlike** *adj.*

scissors kick *n.* **1.** a type of swimming kick used esp. in the sidestroke, in which one leg is moved forward and the other bent back and they are then brought together again in a scissor-like action. **2.** *Football.* a kick in which the player leaps into the air raising one leg and brings up his other leg to kick the ball.

scissure ('sɪʒə, 'sɪʃə) *n. Rare.* a longitudinal cleft. [C15: from Latin *scissūra* a rending, from Latin *scindere* to split]

sciurine ('saɪjʊrɪn, -ˌraɪn) *adj.* **1.** of, relating to, or belonging to the *Sciuridae,* a family of rodents inhabiting most parts of the world except Australia and southern South America: includes squirrels, marmots, and chipmunks. ~*n.* **2.** any sciurine animal. [C19: from Latin *sciūrus,* from Greek *skiouros* squirrel, from *skia* a shadow + *oura* a tail]

sciuroid ('saɪjʊrɔɪd, saɪ'jʊərɔɪd) *adj.* **1.** (of an animal) resembling a squirrel. **2.** (esp. of the spikes of barley) shaped like a squirrel's tail. [C19: from Latin *sciūrus* squirrel + -OID]

sclaff (sklæf) *Golf.* ~*vb.* **1.** to cause (the club) to hit (the ground) when making a stroke. ~*n.* **2.** a sclaffing stroke or shot. ~Also: **duff.** [C19: from Scottish *sclaf* to shuffle] —'**sclaffer** *n.*

sclera ('sklɪərə) *n.* the firm white fibrous membrane that forms the outer covering of the eyeball. Also called: **sclerotic.** [C19: from New Latin, from Greek *sklēros* hard]

sclere (sklɪə) *n. Zoology.* a supporting anatomical structure, esp. a sponge spicule.

sclerenchyma (sklɪə'rɛŋkɪmə) *n.* a supporting tissue in plants consisting of dead cells with very thick lignified walls. [C19: from SCLERO- + PARENCHYMA] —**sclerenchymatous** (ˌsklɪərɛŋ'kɪmətəs) *adj.*

sclerite ('sklɪəraɪt) *n. Zoology.* **1.** any of the hard chitinous plates that make up the exoskeleton of an arthropod. **2.** any calcareous or chitinous part, such as a spicule or plate. [C19: from SCLERO- + -ITE[1]] —**scleritic** (sklɪə'rɪtɪk) *adj.*

scleritis (sklɪə'raɪtɪs) *or* **sclerotitis** (ˌsklɪərəʊ'taɪtɪs) *n. Pathol.* inflammation of the sclera.

sclero- *or before a vowel* **scler-** *combining form.* **1.** indicating hardness: *sclerosis.* **2.** of or relating to the sclera: *sclerotomy.* [from Greek *sklēros* hard]

scleroderma (ˌsklɪərəʊ'dɜːmə), **sclerodermia** (ˌsklɪərəʊ'dɜːmɪə), *or* **scleriasis** (sklɪ'raɪəsɪs) *n.* a chronic progressive disease most common among women, characterized by a local or diffuse thickening and hardening of the skin. [C19: from New Latin *sclerōdermus,* from Greek, from *sklēros* hard + *derma* skin]

sclerodermatous (ˌsklɪərəʊ'dɜːmətəs) *adj.* **1.** (of animals) possessing a hard external covering of scales or plates. **2.** of or relating to scleroderma.

scleroid ('sklɪərɔɪd) *adj.* (of organisms and their parts) hard or hardened.

scleroma (sklɪə'rəʊmə) *n., pl.* **-mata** (-mətə) *or* **-mas.** *Pathol.* any small area of abnormally hard tissue, esp. in a mucous membrane. [C17: from New Latin, from Greek, from *sklēroun* to harden, from *sklēros* hard]

sclerometer (sklɪə'rɒmɪtə) *n.* an instrument that determines the hardness of a mineral or metal by means of a diamond point. —**sclerometric** (ˌsklɪərə'mɛtrɪk) *adj.*

sclerophyll ('sklɛrəʊˌfɪl) *n.* a woody plant with small leathery evergreen leaves that is the dominant plant form in certain hot dry areas, esp. the Mediterranean region. [C20: from Greek *sklēros* hard + *phullon* a leaf] —**sclerophyllous** (sklɛ'rɒfɪləs) *adj.*

scleroprotein (ˌsklɪərəʊ'prəʊtiːn) *n.* any of a group of insoluble stable proteins such as keratin, elastin, and collagen that occur in skeletal and connective tissues. Also called: **albuminoid.**

sclerosed ('sklɪərəʊst) *adj. Pathol.* hardened; sclerotic.

sclerosis (sklɪə'rəʊsɪs) *n., pl.* **-ses** (-siːz). **1.** *Pathol.* a hardening or thickening of organs, tissues, or vessels from chronic inflammation, abnormal growth of fibrous tissue, or degeneration of the myelin sheath of nerve fibres, or (esp. on the inner walls of arteries) deposition of fatty plaques. Compare **arteriosclerosis, atherosclerosis, multiple sclerosis. 2.** the hardening of a plant cell wall or tissue by the deposition of lignin. [C14: via Medieval Latin from Greek *sklērōsis* a hardening] —**scle'rosal** *adj.*

sclerotic (sklɪə'rɒtɪk) *adj.* **1.** of or relating to the sclera. **2.** of, relating to, or having sclerosis. **3.** *Botany.* characterized by the hardening and strengthening of cell walls. ~*n.* **4.** another name for **sclera.** [C16: from Medieval Latin *sclērōticus,* from Greek; see SCLEROMA]

sclerotin ('sklɛrəʊtɪn) *n.* a protein in the cuticle of insects that becomes hard and dark.

sclerotium (sklɪə'rəʊʃɪəm) *n., pl.* **-tia** (-ʃɪə). a compact mass of hyphae, that is formed by certain fungi and gives rise to new fungal growth or spore-producing structures. [C18: from New Latin, from Greek *sklēros* hard] —**scle'rotioid** *or* **scle'rotial** *adj.*

sclerotize *or* **sclerotise** ('sklɛrə,taɪz) *vb.* (*tr.; usually passive*). *Zoology.* to harden and darken (an insect's cuticle). —,**scleroti'zation** *or* ,**scleroti'sation** *n.*

sclerotomy (sklɪə'rɒtəmɪ) *n., pl.* **-mies.** surgical incision into the sclera.

sclerous ('sklɪərəs) *adj. Anatomy, pathol.* hard; bony; indurated. [C19: from Greek *sklēros* hard]

SCM (in Britain) *abbrev. for:* **1.** State Certified Midwife. **2.** Student Christian Movement.

scoff[1] (skɒf) *vb.* **1.** (*intr.;* often foll. by *at*) to speak contemptuously (about); express derision (for); mock. **2.** (*tr.*) *Obsolete.* to regard with derision. ~*n.* **3.** an expression of derision. **4.** an object of derision. [C14: probably from Scandinavian; compare Old Frisian *skof* mockery, Danish *skof, skuf* jest] —'**scoffer** *n.* —'**scoffing** *adj.* —'**scoffingly** *adv.*

scoff[2] (skɒf) *Informal, chiefly Brit.* ~*vb.* **1.** to eat (food) fast and greedily; devour. ~*n.* **2.** food or rations. [C19: variant of *scaff* food; related to Afrikaans, Dutch *schoft* quarter of the day, one of the four daily meals]

scofflaw ('skɒflɔː) *n. U.S. informal.* a person who habitually flouts or violates the law, esp. one who fails to pay debts or answer summonses.

scold (skəʊld) *vb.* **1.** to find fault with or reprimand (a person) harshly; chide. **2.** (*intr.*) to use harsh or abusive language. ~*n.* **3.** a person, esp. a woman, who constantly finds fault. [C13: from Old Norse SKALD] —'**scoldable** *adj.* —'**scolder** *n.* —'**scolding** *n.* —'**scoldingly** *adv.*

scolecite ('skɒlɪ,saɪt, 'skəʊl-) *n.* a white zeolite mineral consisting of hydrated calcium aluminium silicate in groups of radiating monoclinic crystals. Formula: $CaAl_2Si_3O_{10}.3H_2O$. [C19: *scolec-* from Greek *skōlēx* SCOLEX + -ITE[1]]

scolex ('skəʊlɛks) *n., pl.* **scoleces** (skəʊ'liːsiːz) *or* **scolices** ('skɒlɪ,siːz, 'skəʊ-). the headlike part of a tapeworm, bearing hooks and suckers by which the animal is attached to the tissues of its host. [C19: from New Latin, from Greek *skōlēx* worm]

scoliosis (,skɒlɪ'əʊsɪs) *n. Pathol.* an abnormal lateral curvature of the spine, of congenital origin or caused by trauma or disease of the vertebrae or hipbones. Compare **kyphosis, lordosis.** [C18: from New Latin, from Greek: a curving, from *skolios* bent] —**scoliotic** (,skɒlɪ'ɒtɪk) *adj.*

scollop[1] ('skɒləp) *n., vb.* a variant of **scallop.**

scollop[2] ('skɒləp) *n.* (in Ireland) a rod, pointed at both ends, used to pin down thatch. [C19: from Irish Gaelic *scolb*]

scolopendrid (,skɒlə'pɛndrɪd) *n.* any centipede of the family *Scolopendridae,* including some large and poisonous species. [C19: from New Latin *Scolopendridae,* from Latin *scolopendra,* from Greek *skolopendra* legendary sea-fish] —**scolopendrine** (,skɒlə'pɛndraɪn, -drɪn) *adj.*

scolopendrium (skɒlə'pɛndrɪəm) *n.* any of a genus of true ferns with undivided leaves, esp. hart's-tongue. [C17: from New Latin, from Greek *scolopendrion,* from a fancied resemblance of the fern and its sori to a centipede]

scombroid ('skɒmbrɔɪd) *adj.* **1.** of, relating to, or belonging to the *Scombroidea,* a suborder of marine spiny-finned fishes having a spindle-shaped body and a forked powerful tail: includes the mackerels, tunnies, bonitos, swordfish, and sailfish. ~*n.* **2.** any fish belonging to the suborder *Scombroidea.* [C19: from Greek *skombros* a mackerel; see -OID]

sconce[1] (skɒns) *n.* **1.** a bracket fixed to a wall for holding candles or lights. **2.** a flat candlestick with a handle. [C14: from Old French *esconse* hiding place, lantern, or from Late Latin *sconsa,* from *absconsa* dark lantern]

sconce[2] (skɒns) *n.* a small protective fortification, such as an earthwork. [C16: from Dutch *schans,* from Middle High German *schanze* bundle of brushwood]

sconce[3] (skɒns) (at Oxford and Cambridge Universities, esp. formerly) ~*vb.* (*tr.*) **1.** to challenge (a fellow student) on the grounds of a social misdemeanour to drink a large quantity of beer without stopping. **2.** *Obsolete.* to fine (a student) for some minor misdemeanour. ~*n.* **3.** the act of sconcing. **4.** a mug or tankard used in sconcing. [C17: of obscure origin]

sconce[4] (skɒns) *n. Archaic.* **1.** the head or skull. **2.** sense, brain, or wit. [C16: probably jocular use of SCONCE[1]]

scone *n.* **1.** (skəʊn, skɒn) a light plain doughy cake made from flour with very little fat, cooked in an oven or (esp. originally) on a griddle, usually split open and buttered. **2.** (skɒn). *Austral.* a slang word for **head** (sense 1). **3. off one's scone.** *Austral. slang.* **a.** angry. **b.** insane. [C16: Scottish, perhaps from Middle Low German *schonbrot,* Middle Dutch *schoonbrot* fine bread]

scoop (skuːp) *n.* **1.** a utensil used as a shovel or ladle, esp. a small shovel with deep sides and a short handle, used for taking up flour, corn, etc. **2.** a utensil with a long handle and round bowl used for dispensing liquids. **3.** a utensil with a round bowl and short handle, sometimes with a mechanical device to empty the bowl, for serving ice cream or mashed potato. **4.** anything that resembles a scoop in action, such as the bucket on a dredge. **5.** a spoonlike surgical instrument for scraping or extracting foreign matter, etc., from the body. **6.** the quantity taken up by a scoop. **7.** the act of scooping, dredging, etc. **8.** a hollow cavity. **9.** *Slang.* a large quick gain, as of money. **10.** a news story reported in one newspaper before all the others; an exclusive. **11.** any sensational piece of news. ~*vb.* (*mainly tr.*) **12.** (often foll. by *up*) to take up and remove (an object or substance) with or as if with a scoop. **13.** (often foll. by *out*) to hollow out with or as if with a scoop: *to scoop a hole in a hillside.* **14.** to make (a large sudden profit). **15.** to beat (rival newspapers) in uncovering a news item. **16.** *Hockey, golf, etc.* to hit (the ball) on its underside so that it rises into the air. [C14: via Middle Dutch *schōpe* from Germanic; compare Old High German *scephan* to ladle, German *schöpfen, Schaufel* SHOVEL, Dutch *schoep* vessel for baling] —'**scooper** *n.* —'**scoop,ful** *n.*

scoop neck *n.* a rounded low-cut neckline on a woman's garment.

scoosh (skuʃ) *Scot.* ~*vb.* **1.** to squirt. **2.** (*intr.*) (of liquid) to rush. ~*n.* **3.** a squirt or rush of liquid. **4.** any fizzy drink. [C19: of imitative origin]

scoot (skuːt) *vb.* **1.** to go or cause to go quickly or hastily; dart or cause to dart off or away. **2.** *Scot.* to squirt. ~*n.* **3.** the act of scooting. **4.** *Scot.* a squirt. [C19 probably of Scandinavian origin; compare SHOOT]

scooter ('skuːtə) *n.* **1.** a child's vehicle consisting of a low footboard mounted between two small wheels with a handlebar. It is propelled by pushing one foot against the ground. **2.** See **motor scooter. 3.** (in the U.S. and Canada) another term for **ice yacht.** —'**scooterist** *n.*

scop (skɒp) *n.* (in Anglo-Saxon England) a bard or minstrel. [Old English: related to Old Norse *skop, skaup,* Old High German *scof, scopf* poem]

scopa ('skəʊpə) *n., pl.* **-pae** (-,piː). a tuft of hairs on the abdomen or hind legs of bees, used for collecting pollen. [C19: from Latin, used only in pl. *scopae* twigs, brush]

scope (skəʊp) *n.* **1.** opportunity for exercising the faculties or abilities; capacity for action. **2.** range of view, perception, or grasp; outlook. **3.** the area covered by an activity, topic, etc.; range: *the scope of his thesis was vast.* **4.** *Nautical.* slack left in an anchor cable. **5.** *Logic, linguistics.* that part of an expression that is governed by a given operator: the scope of the negation in *PV–(q∧r)* is *–(q∧r).* **6.** *Informal.* short for **telescope, microscope, oscilloscope,** etc. **7.** *Archaic.* purpose or aim. [C16: from Italian *scopo* goal, from Latin *scopus,* from Greek *skopos* target; related to Greek *skopein* to watch]

-scope *n. combining form.* indicating an instrument for observing, viewing, or detecting: *microscope; stethoscope.* [from New Latin *-scopium,* from Greek *-skopion,* from *skopein* to look at] —**-scopic** *adj. combining form.*

scopolamine (skə'pɒlə,miːn, -mɪn; ,skəʊpə'læmɪn) *n.* a colourless viscous liquid alkaloid extracted from certain plants, such as henbane: used in preventing travel sickness and as an anticholinergic, sedative, and truth serum. Formula: $C_{17}H_{21}NO_4$. Also called: **hyoscine.** See also **atropine.** [C20: *scopol-* from New Latin *scopolia Japonica* Japanese belladonna (from which the alkaloid is extracted), named after G. A. *Scopoli* (1723–88), Italian naturalist, + AMINE]

scopoline ('skəʊpə,liːn, -lɪn) *n.* a soluble crystalline alkaloid obtained from the decomposition of scopolamine and used as a sedative. Formula: $C_8H_{13}NO_2$. Also called: **oscine.** [C19: from *scopol-* (as in SCOPOLAMINE) + -INE[2]]

scopula ('skɒpjʊlə) *n., pl.* **-las** *or* **-lae** (-,liː). a small tuft of dense hairs on the legs and chelicerae of some spiders. [C19: from Late Latin: a broom-twig, from *scōpa* thin twigs] —**scopulate** ('skɒpjʊ,leɪt, -lɪt) *adj.*

-scopy *n. combining form.* indicating a viewing or observation: *microscopy.* [from Greek *-skopia,* from *skopein* to look at]

scorbutic (skɔː'bjuːtɪk) *adj.* of, relating to, or having scurvy. [C17: from New Latin *scorbūticus,* from Medieval Latin *scorbūtus,* probably of Germanic origin; compare Old English *sceorf* scurf, Middle Low German *scorbuk* scurvy] —**scor'butically** *adv.*

scorch (skɔːtʃ) *vb.* **1.** to burn or become burnt, so as to affect the colour, taste, etc., or to cause or feel pain. **2.** to wither or parch or cause to wither from exposure to heat. **3.** (*intr.*) *Informal.* to be very hot: *it is scorching outside.* **4.** (*tr.*) *Informal.* to criticize harshly. **5.** (*intr.*) *Brit. slang.* to drive or ride very fast. ~*n.* **6.** a slight burn. **7.** a mark caused by the application of too great heat. **8.** *Horticulture.* a mark or series of marks on fruit, vegetables, etc., caused by pests or insecticides. [C15: probably from Old Norse *skorpna* to shrivel up] —'**scorching** *adj.*

scorched earth policy *n.* **1.** the policy in warfare of removing or destroying everything that might be useful to an invading enemy, esp. by fire. **2.** *Business.* a manoeuvre by a company expecting an unwelcome takeover bid in which apparent profitability is greatly reduced by a reversible operation, such as borrowing at an exorbitant interest rate.

scorcher ('skɔːtʃə) *n.* **1.** a person or thing that scorches. **2.** something severe or caustic. **3.** *Informal.* a very hot day. **4.** *Brit. informal.* something remarkable.

score (skɔː) *n.* **1.** an evaluative usually numerical record of a competitive game or match. **2.** the total number of points made by a side or individual in a game or match. **3.** the act of scoring, esp. a point or points. **4. the score.** *Informal.* the actual situation; the true facts: *to know the score.* **5.** *U.S. and Canadian.* the result of a test or exam. **6.** a group or set of twenty: *three score years and ten.* **7.** (*usually pl.*; foll. by *of*) a great number; lots: *I have scores of things to do.* **8.** *Music.* **a.** the written or printed form of a composition in which the instrumental or vocal parts appear on separate staves vertically arranged on large pages (**full score**) or in a condensed version, usually for piano (**short score**) or voices and piano (**vocal score**). **b.** the incidental music for a film or play. **c.** the songs, music, etc., for a stage or film musical. **9.** a mark or notch, esp. one made in keeping a tally. **10.** an account of amounts due. **11.** an amount recorded as due. **12.** a reason or account: *the book was rejected on the score of length.* **13.** a grievance. **14. a.** a line marking a division or boundary. **b.** (*as modifier*): *score line.* **15.** *Informal.* the victim of a theft or swindle. **16.** *Dancing.* notation indicating a dancer's moves. **17. over the score.** *Informal.* excessive; unfair. **18. settle** *or* **pay off a score. a.** to avenge a wrong. **b.** to repay a debt. ~*vb.* **19.** to gain (a point or points) in a game or contest. **20.** (*tr.*) to make a total score of: *to score twelve.* **21.** to keep a record of the score (of). **22.** (*tr.*) to be worth (a certain amount) in a game. **23.** (*tr.*) *U.S. and Canadian.* to evaluate (a test or exam) numerically; mark. **24.** (*tr.*) to record by making notches in. **25.** to make (cuts, lines, etc.) in or on. **26.** (*intr.*) *Slang.* to obtain something desired, esp. to purchase an illegal drug. **27.** (*intr.*) *Slang.* (of a man) to be successful in seducing a person. **28.** (*tr.*) **a.** to set or arrange (a piece of music) for specific instruments or voices. **b.** to write the music for (a film, play, etc.). **29.** to achieve (success or an advantage): *your idea really scored with the boss.* **30.** (*tr.*) *Chiefly U.S. and Canadian.* to criticize harshly; berate. **31.** to accumulate or keep a record of (a debt). [Old English *scora;* related to Old Norse *skor* notch, tally, twenty] —**'scorer** *n.*

scoreboard ('skɔːˌbɔːd) *n. Sport, etc.* a board for displaying the score of a game or match.

scorecard ('skɔːˌkɑːd) *n.* **1.** a card on which scores are recorded in various games, esp. golf. **2.** a card identifying the players in a sports match, esp. cricket or baseball.

score draw *n.* (esp. in football) a result of a match in which both sides have scored an equal number of goals.

score off *vb.* (*intr., prep.*) to gain an advantage at someone else's expense.

score out *vb.* (*tr., adv.*) to delete or cancel by marking through with a line or lines; cross out.

scoria ('skɔːrɪə) *n., pl.* **-riae** (-rɪˌiː). **1.** a rough heavy mass of solidified lava containing many cavities. **2.** refuse obtained from smelted ore; slag. [C17: from Latin: dross, from Greek *skōria*, from *skōr* excrement] —**scoriaceous** (ˌskɔːrɪ'eɪʃəs) *adj.*

scorify ('skɔːrɪˌfaɪ) *vb.* **-fies, -fying, -fied.** to remove (impurities) from metals by forming scoria. —ˌ**scorifi'cation** *n.* —'**scoriˌfier** *n.*

scoring ('skɔːrɪŋ) *n.* **1.** the act or practice of scoring. **2.** another name for **orchestration** (see **orchestrate**).

scorn (skɔːn) *n.* **1.** open contempt or disdain for a person or thing; derision. **2.** an object of contempt or derision. **3.** *Archaic.* an act or expression signifying contempt. ~*vb.* **4.** to treat with contempt or derision. **5.** (*tr.*) to reject with contempt. [C12 *schornen*, from Old French *escharnir*, of Germanic origin; compare Old High German *scerōn* to behave rowdily, obsolete Dutch *schern* mockery] —'**scorner** *n.* —'**scornful** *adj.* —'**scornfully** *adv.* —'**scornfulness** *n.*

scorpaenid (skɔː'piːnɪd) *n.* **1.** any spiny-finned marine fish of the family *Scorpaenidae*, having sharp spines on the fins and a heavy armoured head: includes the scorpion fishes, rockfishes, and redfishes. ~*adj.* **2.** of, relating to, or belonging to the family *Scorpaenidae*. [via New Latin from Latin *scorpaena* a sea-scorpion; see SCORPION]

scorpaenoid (skɔː'piːnɔɪd) *adj.* **1.** of, relating to, or belonging to the *Scorpaenoidea*, a suborder of spiny-finned fishes having bony plates covering the head: includes the sculpins, scorpion fishes, gurnards, etc. ~*n.* **2.** any fish belonging to the suborder *Scorpaenoidea*.

scorper *or* **scauper** ('skɔːpə) *n.* a kind of fine chisel with a square or curved tip used in wood engraving for clearing away large areas of the block or clearing away lines. [C19: erroneously for *scauper* scalper, from Latin *scalper* knife]

Scorpio ('skɔːpɪˌəʊ) *n.* **1.** Also called: the **Scorpion.** *Astrology.* **a.** the eighth sign of the zodiac, symbol ♏, having a fixed water classification and ruled by the planets Mars and Pluto. The sun is in this sign between about Oct. 23 and Nov. 21. **b.** a person born during a period when the sun is in this sign. **2.** *Astronomy.* another name for **Scorpius.** ~*adj.* **3.** *Astrology.* born under or characteristic of Scorpio. ~Also (for senses 1b, 3): **Scorpionic** (ˌskɔːpɪ'ɒnɪk). [Latin: SCORPION]

scorpioid ('skɔːpɪˌɔɪd) *adj.* **1.** of, relating to, or resembling scorpions or the order (*Scorpionida*) to which they belong. **2.** *Botany.* (esp. of a cymose inflorescence) having the main stem coiled during development.

scorpion ('skɔːpɪən) *n.* **1.** any arachnid of the order *Scorpionida*, of warm dry regions, having a segmented body with a long tail terminating in a venomous sting. **2. false scorpion.** any small nonvenomous arachnid of the order *Pseudoscorpionida* (or *Chelonethida*), which superficially resemble scorpions but lack the long tail. See **book scorpion. 3.** any of various other similar arachnids, such as the whip scorpion, or other arthropods, such as the water scorpion. **4.** *Old Testament.* a barbed scourge (I Kings 12:11). **5.** *History.* a war engine for hurling stones; ballista. [C13: via Old French from Latin *scorpiō*, from Greek *skorpios*, of obscure origin]

Scorpion ('skɔːpɪən) *n.* **the.** the constellation Scorpio, the eighth sign of the zodiac.

scorpion fish *n.* any of various scorpaenid fishes of the genus *Scorpaena* and related genera, of temperate and tropical seas, having venomous spines on the dorsal and anal fins.

scorpion fly *n.* any of various insects of the family *Panorpidae*, of the N hemisphere, having a scorpion-like but nonvenomous tail in the males, long antennae, and a beaklike snout: order *Mecoptera*.

scorpion grass *n.* another name for **forget-me-not.**

Scorpius ('skɔːpɪəs) *n., Latin genitive* **Scorpii** ('skɔːpɪˌaɪ). a large zodiacal constellation lying between Libra and Sagittarius and crossed by the Milky Way. It contains the first magnitude star Antares. Also called: **Scorpio.**

Scot (skɒt) *n.* **1.** a native or inhabitant of Scotland, a country in N Great Britain that is part of the United Kingdom. **2.** a member of a tribe of Celtic raiders from northern Ireland who carried out periodic attacks against the British mainland coast from the 3rd century A.D., eventually settling in N Britain during the 5th and 6th centuries.

Scot. *abbrev for:* **1.** Scotch (whisky). **2.** Scotland. **3.** Scottish.

scot and lot *n. British history.* a municipal tax paid by burgesses and others that came to be regarded as a qualification for the borough franchise in parliamentary elections (until the Reform Act of 1832). [C13 *scot* tax, from Germanic; compare Old Norse *skot;* related to Old French *escot* (French *écot*) + LOT (in the obsolete sense: tax)]

scotch[1] (skɒtʃ) *vb.* (*tr.*) **1.** to put an end to; crush: *bad weather scotched our plans.* **2.** *Archaic.* to injure so as to render harmless. **3.** *Obsolete.* to cut or score. ~*n.* **4.** *Archaic.* a gash; scratch. **5.** a line marked down, as for hopscotch. [C15: of obscure origin]

scotch[2] (skɒtʃ) *vb.* **1.** (*tr.*) to block, prop, or prevent from moving with or as if with a wedge. ~*n.* **2.** a block or wedge to prevent motion. [C17: of obscure origin]

Scotch[1] (skɒtʃ) *adj.* **1.** another word for **Scottish.** ~*n.* **2.** the Scots or their language.

▷**Usage.** In the north of England and in Scotland, *Scotch* is not used outside fixed expressions such as *Scotch whisky.* The use of *Scotch* for *Scots* or *Scottish* is otherwise felt to be incorrect, esp. when applied to persons.

Scotch[2] (skɒtʃ) *n.* **1.** Also called: **Scotch whisky.** whisky distilled esp. from fermented malted barley and made in Scotland. **2.** *Northeast English.* a type of relatively mild beer.

Scotch broth *n. Brit.* a thick soup made from mutton or beef stock, vegetables, and pearl barley.

Scotch egg *n. Brit.* a hard-boiled egg enclosed in a layer of sausage meat, covered in egg and crumbs, and fried.

Scotchman ('skɒtʃmən) *n., pl.* **-men.** (*regarded as bad usage by the Scots*) another word for **Scotsman.** —'**Scotchˌwoman** *fem. n.*

Scotch mist *n.* **1.** a heavy wet mist. **2.** drizzle. [C16: so called because it is common on Scottish hills]

Scotch pancake *n.* another name for **drop scone.**

Scotch snap *n. Music.* a rhythmical pattern consisting of a short note followed by a long one. Also called: **Scotch catch.** [C19: so named because it is characteristic of, though not exclusive to, Scottish dance music, esp. that for strathspeys]

Scotch tape *n. Trademark, chiefly U.S.* a transparent or coloured adhesive tape made of cellulose or a similar substance.

Scotch terrier *n.* another name for **Scottish terrier.**

Scotch woodcock *n.* hot toast spread with anchovies or anchovy paste and topped with creamy scrambled eggs.

scoter ('skəʊtə) *n., pl.* **-ters** *or* **-ter.** any sea duck of the genus *Melanitta*, such as *M. nigra* (**common scoter**), of northern regions. The male plumage is black with white patches around the head and eyes. [C17: origin unknown]

scot-free *adv., adj.* (*predicative*) without harm, loss, or penalty. [C16: see SCOT AND LOT]

scotia ('skəʊʃə) *n.* a deep concave moulding, esp. one used on the base of an Ionic column between the two torus mouldings. [C16: via Latin from Greek *skotia*, from *skotos* darkness (from the shadow in the cavity)]

Scotism ('skəʊtɪzəm) *n.* the doctrines of the Scottish theologian Duns Scotus (?1265–1308), esp. those holding that philosophy and theology are independent. See **haecceity.** —'**Scotist** *n., adj.* —**Sco'tistic** *adj.*

Scotland Yard *n.* the headquarters of the police force of metropolitan London, controlled directly by the British Home Office and hence having certain national responsibilities. Official name: **New Scotland Yard.**

scotoma (skɒ'təʊmə) *n., pl.* **-mas** *or* **-mata** (-mətə). **1.** *Pathol.* a blind spot; a permanent or temporary area of depressed or absent vision caused by lesions of the visual system, viewing the sun directly (**eclipse scotoma**), squinting, etc. **2.** *Psychol.* a mental blind spot; inability to understand or perceive certain matters. [C16: via Medieval Latin from Greek *skotōma* giddiness, from *skotoun* to make dark, from *skotos* darkness] —**scotomatous** (skɒ'tɒmətəs) *adj.*

scotopia (skə'təʊpɪə, skəʊ-) *n.* the ability of the eye to adjust for night vision. [New Latin, from Greek *skotos* darkness + -OPIA] —**scotopic** (skə'tɒpɪk, skəʊ-) *adj.*

Scots (skɒts) *adj.* **1.** of, relating to, or characteristic of Scotland, its people, their English dialects, or their Gaelic language. ~*n.* **2.** any of the English dialects spoken or written in Scotland. See also **Lallans.**

Scotsman ('skɒtsmən) *n., pl.* **-men.** a native or inhabitant of Scotland. —'**Scots,woman** *fem. n.*

Scots pine *or* **Scotch pine** *n.* **1.** a coniferous tree, *Pinus sylvestris,* of Europe and W and N Asia, having blue-green needle-like leaves and brown cones with a small prickle on each scale: a valuable timber tree. **2.** the wood of this tree. ~Also called: **Scots** (*or* **Scotch**) **fir.**

Scotticism ('skɒtɪ,sɪzəm) *n.* a Scottish idiom, word, etc.

Scottie *or* **Scotty** ('skɒtɪ) *n., pl.* **-ties. 1.** See **Scottish terrier. 2.** *Informal.* a Scotsman.

Scottish ('skɒtɪʃ) *adj.* **1.** of, relating to, or characteristic of Scotland, its people, their Gaelic language, or their English dialect. ~*n.* **2. the.** (*functioning as pl.*) the Scots collectively.

Scottish Blackface *n.* a common breed of hardy mountain sheep having horns and a black face, kept chiefly on the mainland of Scotland.

Scottish Certificate of Education *n.* See **SCE.**

Scottish Gaelic *n.* the Goidelic language of the Celts of Scotland, spoken in the Highlands and Western Isles.

Scottish Nationalist *n.* **1.** a member or supporter of the Scottish National Party, which advocates independence for Scotland. ~*adj.* **2.** of or relating to the aims or policies of the Scottish National Party.

Scottish terrier *n.* a small but sturdy breed of terrier, having short legs and erect ears and tail and a longish, wiry, usually black coat. Often shortened to **Scottie.** Former name: **Aberdeen terrier.**

Scottish topaz *n.* a form of yellow transparent quartz.

scoundrel ('skaʊndrəl) *n.* a worthless or villainous person. [C16: of unknown origin] —'**scoundrelly** *adj.*

scour[1] (skaʊə) *vb.* **1.** to clean or polish (a surface) by washing and rubbing, as with an abrasive cloth. **2.** to remove dirt from or have the dirt removed from. **3.** (*tr.*) to clear (a channel) by the force of water; flush. **4.** (*tr.*) to remove by or as if by rubbing. **5.** (*intr.*) (of livestock, esp. cattle) to have diarrhoea. **6.** (*tr.*) to cause (livestock) to purge their bowels. **7.** (*tr.*) to wash (wool) to remove wax, suint, and other impurities. ~*n.* **8.** the act of scouring. **9.** the place scoured, esp. by running water. **10.** something that scours, such as a cleansing agent. **11.** (*often pl.*) prolonged diarrhoea in livestock, esp. cattle. [C13: via Middle Low German *schūren,* from Old French *escurer,* from Late Latin *excūrāre* to cleanse, from *cūrāre;* see CURE] —'**scourer** *n.*

scour[2] (skaʊə) *vb.* **1.** to range over (territory), as in making a search. **2.** to move swiftly or energetically over (territory). [C14: from Old Norse *skūr*]

scourge (skɜːdʒ) *n.* **1.** a person who harasses, punishes, or causes destruction. **2.** a means of inflicting punishment or suffering. **3.** a whip used for inflicting punishment or torture. ~*vb.* (*tr.*) **4.** to whip; flog. **5.** to punish severely. [C13: from Anglo-French *escorge,* from Old French *escorgier* (unattested) to lash, from *es-* EX-[1] + Latin *corrigia* whip] —'**scourger** *n.*

scouring rush *n.* any of several horsetails, esp. *Equisetum hyemale,* that have rough-ridged stems and were formerly used for scouring and polishing.

scourings ('skaʊərɪŋz) *pl. n.* **1.** the residue left after cleaning grain. **2.** residue that remains after scouring.

scouse (skaʊs) *n. Liverpool dialect.* a stew made from left-over meat. [C19: shortened from LOBSCOUSE]

Scouse (skaʊs) *Brit. informal.* ~*n.* **1.** Also called: **Scouser.** a person who lives in or comes from Liverpool. **2.** the dialect spoken by such a person. ~*adj.* **3.** of or from Liverpool; Liverpudlian. [C20: from SCOUSE]

scout[1] (skaʊt) *n.* **1.** a person, ship, or aircraft sent out to gain information. **2.** *Military.* a person or unit despatched to reconnoitre the position of the enemy. **3.** *Sport.* a person employed by a club to seek new players. **4.** the act or an instance of scouting. **5.** (esp. at Oxford University) a college servant. Compare **gyp**[3]. **6.** (in Britain) a patrolman of a motoring organization. **7.** *Informal.* a fellow or companion. ~*vb.* **8.** to examine or observe (anything) in order to obtain information. **9.** (*tr.;* sometimes foll. by *out* or *up*) to seek. **10.** (*intr.*) to act as a scout for a sports club. **11.** (*intr.;* foll. by *about* or *around*) to go in search (for). [C14: from Old French *ascouter* to listen to, from Latin *auscultāre* to AUSCULTATE] —'**scouter** *n.*

scout[2] (skaʊt) *vb. Archaic.* to reject (a person or thing) with contempt. [C17: from Old Norse *skūta* derision]

Scout (skaʊt) *n.* (*sometimes not cap.*) a boy or (in some countries) a girl who is a member of a worldwide movement (the **Scout Association**) founded as the Boy Scouts in England in 1908 by Lord Baden-Powell with the aim of developing character and responsibility. See also **Air Scout, Girl Scout, Guide, Sea Scout, Venture Scout.**

scout car *n.* a fast lightly armoured vehicle used for reconnaissance.

Scouter ('skaʊtə) *n.* the leader of a troop of Scouts.

Scouting ('skaʊtɪŋ) *n.* **a.** the activities, programmes, principles, etc., of the Scout Association. **b.** (*as modifier*): *the international Scouting movement.*

scoutmaster ('skaʊt,mɑːstə) *n.* a former name for **Scouter.**

scow (skaʊ) *n.* **1.** an unpowered barge used for freight; lighter. **2.** (esp. in the midwestern U.S.) a sailing yacht with a flat bottom, designed to plane. [C18: via Dutch *schouw* from Low German *schalde,* related to Old Saxon *skaldan* to push (a boat) into the sea]

scowl (skaʊl) *vb.* **1.** (*intr.*) to contract the brows in a threatening or angry manner. ~*n.* **2.** a gloomy or threatening expression. [C14: probably from Scandinavian; compare Danish *skule* to look down, Old English *scūlēgede* squint-eyed] —'**scowler** *n.*

SCP *abbrev. for* single-cell protein.

SCPS (in Britain) *abbrev. for* Society of Civil and Public Servants.

SCR *abbrev. for:* **1.** (in British universities) senior common room. **2.** silicon controlled rectifier.

scr. *abbrev. for* scruple (unit of weight).

scrabble ('skræbᵊl) *vb.* **1.** (*intr.;* often foll. by *about* or *at*) to scrape (at) or grope (for), as with hands or claws. **2.** to struggle (with). **3.** (*intr.;* often foll. by *for*) to struggle to gain possession, esp. in a disorderly manner. **4.** to scribble. ~*n.* **5.** the act or an instance of scrabbling. **6.** a scribble. **7.** a disorderly struggle. [C16: from Middle Dutch *shrabbelen,* frequentative of *shrabben* to scrape] —'**scrabbler** *n.*

Scrabble ('skræbᵊl) *n. Trademark.* a board game in which words are formed by placing lettered tiles in a pattern similar to a crossword puzzle.

scrag (skræg) *n.* **1.** a thin or scrawny person or animal. **2.** the lean end of a neck of veal or mutton. **3.** *Informal.* the neck of a human being. ~*vb.* **scrags, scragging, scragged.** (*tr.*) **4.** *Informal.* to wring the neck of; throttle. [C16: perhaps variant of CRAG; related to Norwegian *skragg,* German *Kragen* collar]

scraggly ('skræglɪ) *adj.* **-glier, -gliest.** untidy or irregular.

scraggy ('skrægɪ) *adj.* **-gier, -giest. 1.** lean or scrawny. **2.** rough; unkempt. —'**scraggily** *adv.* —'**scragginess** *n.*

scram[1] (skræm) *vb.* **scrams, scramming, scrammed.** (*intr.; often imperative*) *Informal.* to go away hastily; get out. [C20: shortened from SCRAMBLE]

scram[2] (skræm) *n.* **1.** an emergency shutdown of a nuclear reactor. ~*vb.* **2.** (of a nuclear reactor) to shut down or be shut down in an emergency. [C20: perhaps from SCRAM[1]]

scramb *or* **scram** (skræm) *vb.* (*tr.*) *Brit. dialect.* to scratch with nails or claws. [from Dutch *schrammen*]

scramble ('skræmbᵊl) *vb.* **1.** (*intr.*) to climb or crawl, esp. by using the hands to aid movement. **2.** (*intr.*) to proceed hurriedly or in a disorderly fashion. **3.** (*intr.;* often foll. by *for*) to compete with others, esp. in a disordered manner: *to scramble for a prize.* **4.** (*intr.;* foll. by *through*) to deal with hurriedly and unsystematically. **5.** (*tr.*) to throw together in a haphazard manner; jumble. **6.** (*tr.*) to collect in a hurried or disorganized manner. **7.** (*tr.*) to cook (eggs that have been whisked up with milk and seasoning) in a pan containing a little melted butter. **8.** *Military.* to order (a crew or aircraft) to take off immediately or (of a crew or aircraft) to take off immediately. **9.** (*tr.*) to render (speech) unintelligible during transmission by means of an electronic scrambler. ~*n.* **10.** the act of scrambling. **11.** a climb over rocks that involves the use of the hands but not ropes, etc. **12.** a disorderly struggle, esp. to gain possession. **13.** *Military.* an immediate preparation for action, as of crew, aircraft, etc. **14.** *Brit.* a motorcycle rally in which competitors race across rough open ground. [C16: blend of SCRABBLE and RAMP]

scrambled eggs *pl. n. Slang.* gold embroidery on the peak of a high-ranking military officer's cap.

scrambler ('skræmblə) *n.* **1.** a plant that produces long weak shoots by which it grows over other plants. **2.** an electronic device that renders speech unintelligible during transmission, normal speech being restored at the receiving system.

scran (skræn) *n.* **1.** *Slang.* food; provisions. **2. bad scran to.** *Irish dialect.* bad luck to. [C18: of unknown origin]

scrannel ('skrænᵊl) *adj. Archaic.* **1.** thin. **2.** harsh. [C17: probably from Norwegian *skran* lean. Compare SCRAWNY]

scrap[1] (skræp) *n.* **1.** a small piece of something larger; fragment. **2.** an extract from something written. **3. a.** waste material or used articles, esp. metal, often collected and reprocessed. **b.** (*as modifier*): *scrap iron.* **4.** (*pl.*) pieces of discarded food. ~*vb.* **scraps, scrapping, scrapped.** (*tr.*) **5.** to make into scrap. **6.** to discard as useless. [C14: from Old Norse *skrap;* see SCRAPE]

scrap[2] (skræp) *Informal.* ~*n.* **1.** a fight or argument. ~*vb.* **scraps, scrapping, scrapped. 2.** (*intr.*) to quarrel or fight. [C17: perhaps from SCRAPE]

scrapbook ('skræp,bʊk) *n.* a book or album of blank pages in which to mount newspaper cuttings, pictures, etc.

scrape (skreɪp) *vb.* **1.** to move (a rough or sharp object) across (a surface), esp. to smooth or clean. **2.** (*tr.;* often foll. by *away* or *off*) to remove (a layer) by rubbing. **3.** to produce a harsh or grating sound by rubbing against (an instrument, surface, etc.). **4.** (*tr.*) to injure or damage by rough contact: *to scrape one's knee.* **5.** (*intr.*) to be very economical or sparing in the use (of) (esp. in the phrase **scrimp and scrape**). **6.** (*intr.*) to draw the foot backwards in making a bow. **7.** (*tr.*) to finish (a surface) by use of a scraper. **8.** (*tr.*) to make (a bearing, etc.) fit by scraping. **9. bow and scrape.** to behave with excessive humility. **10. scrape acquaintance with.** to contrive an acquaintance with. ~*n.* **11.** the act of scraping. **12.** a scraped place. **13.** a harsh or grating sound. **14.** *Informal.* an awkward or embarrassing predicament. **15.** *Informal.* a conflict or struggle. [Old English *scrapian;* related to Old Norse *skrapa,* Middle Dutch *schrapen,* Middle High German *schraffen*] —**'scrapable** *adj.* —**'scraper** *n.*

scrape in *vb.* (*intr., adv.*) to succeed in entering with difficulty or by a narrow margin: *he only just scraped into university.* Also: **scrape into.**

scraperboard ('skreɪpəˌbɔːd) *n.* **1.** thin card covered with a layer of white china clay and a black top layer of Indian ink, which can be scraped away with a special tool to leave a white line. **2.** a picture or design produced in this way.

scrape through *vb.* (*adv.*) **1.** (*intr.*) to manage or survive with difficulty. **2.** to succeed in with difficulty or by a narrow margin: *he scraped through by one mark.*

scrape together *or* **up** *vb.* (*tr., adv.*) to collect with difficulty: *to scrape together money for a new car.*

scrapheap ('skræpˌhiːp) *n.* **1.** a pile of discarded material. **2. on the scrapheap.** (of people or things) having outlived their usefulness.

scrapie ('skreɪpɪ) *n.* a usually fatal virus disease of sheep and goats affecting the central nervous system, characterized by intense itching. [C20: from SCRAPE + -IE]

scraping ('skreɪpɪŋ) *n.* **1.** the act of scraping. **2.** a sound produced by scraping. **3.** (*often pl.*) something scraped off, together, or up; a small amount.

scrappy[1] ('skræpɪ) *adj.* **-pier, -piest.** fragmentary; disjointed. —**'scrappily** *adv.* —**'scrappiness** *n.*

scrappy[2] ('skræpɪ) *adj.* **-pier, -piest.** *Informal.* pugnacious.

scratch (skrætʃ) *vb.* **1.** to mark or cut (the surface of something) with a rough or sharp instrument. **2.** (often foll. by *at, out, off,* etc.) to scrape (the surface of something), as with claws, nails, etc. **3.** to scrape (the surface of the skin) with the nails, as to relieve itching. **4.** to chafe or irritate (a surface, esp. the skin). **5.** to make or cause to make a grating sound; scrape. **6.** (*tr.;* sometimes foll. by *out*) to erase by or as if by scraping. **7.** (*tr.*) to write or draw awkwardly. **8.** (*intr.;* sometimes foll. by *along*) to earn a living, manage, etc., with difficulty. **9.** to withdraw (an entry) from a race, match, etc. **10.** (*intr.*) *Billiards, etc.* **a.** to make a shot resulting in a penalty. **b.** to make a lucky shot. **11.** (*tr.*) *U.S.* to cancel (the name of a candidate) from a party ticket in an election. **12.** (*intr.;* often foll. by *for*) *Austral. informal.* to be struggling or in difficulty, esp. in earning a living. **13. scratch the surface.** to treat (a subject) superficially. **14. you scratch my back and I will scratch yours.** if you will help me, I will help you. ~*n.* **15.** the act of scratching. **16.** a slight injury. **17.** a mark made by scratching. **18.** a slight grating sound. **19.** (in a handicap sport) **a.** a competitor or the status of a competitor who has no allowance or receives a penalty. **b.** (*as modifier*): *a scratch player.* **20.** the time, initial score, etc., of such a competitor. **21. a.** the line from which competitors start in a race. **b.** (formerly) a line drawn on the floor of a prize ring at which the contestants stood to begin or continue fighting. **22.** a withdrawn competitor in a race, etc. **23.** *Billiards, etc.* **a.** a shot that results in a penalty, as when the cue ball enters the pocket. **b.** a lucky shot. **24.** poultry food. **25. from scratch.** *Informal.* from the very beginning. **26. up to scratch.** (*usually used with a negative*) *Informal.* up to standard. ~*adj.* **27.** *Sport.* (of a team) assembled hastily. **28.** (in a handicap sport) with no allowance or penalty. **29.** *Informal.* rough or haphazard. ~See also **scratches, scratch together.** [C15: via Old French *escrater* from Germanic; compare Old High German *krazzōn* (German *kratzen*); related to Old French *gratter* to GRATE] —**'scratcher** *n.* —**'scratchy** *adj.* —**'scratchily** *adv.* —**'scratchiness** *n.*

scratches ('skrætʃɪz) *n.* (*functioning as sing.*) a disease of horses characterized by eczematous weeping lesions in the region of the fetlock. [C16: so called because it makes the pastern appear to be scratched]

scratch file *n. Computer technol.* a temporary store for use during the execution of a program.

scratchies ('skrætʃɪz) *pl. n. Austral. informal.* instant lottery tickets that reveal whether or not the holder is eligible for a prize when the surface is scratched.

scratching ('skrætʃɪŋ) *n.* a percussive effect obtained by rotating a gramophone record manually: a disc-jockey and dub technique.

scratch pad *n. Chiefly U.S.* a notebook, esp. one with detachable leaves.

scratchplate ('skrætʃˌpleɪt) *n.* a plastic or metal plate attached to the front of a guitar to protect it from pick scratches.

scratch sheet *n. U.S. and Canadian informal.* another term for a **dope sheet.**

scratch test *n. Med.* a skin test to determine allergic sensitivity to various substances by placing the allergen to be tested over an area of lightly scratched skin. A positive reaction is typically indicated by the formation of a weal.

scratch together *or* **up** *vb.* (*tr., adv.*) to assemble with difficulty: *he scratched up a team for the football match.*

scratch video *n.* the technique or practice of recycling images from films or television to make collages.

scraw (skrɑː) *n. Irish.* a sod from the surface of a peat bog or from a field. [from Irish Gaelic *scraith*]

scrawl (skrɔːl) *vb.* **1.** to write or draw (signs, words, etc.) carelessly or hastily; scribble. ~*n.* **2.** careless or scribbled writing, drawing, or marks. [C17: perhaps a blend of SPRAWL and CRAWL] —**'scrawler** *n.* —**'scrawly** *adj.*

scrawny ('skrɔːnɪ) *adj.* **scrawnier, scrawniest. 1.** very thin and bony; scraggy. **2.** meagre or stunted: *scrawny vegetation.* [C19: variant of dialect *scranny;* see SCRANNEL] —**'scrawnily** *adv.* —**'scrawniness** *n.*

screak (skriːk) *Dialect, chiefly U.S.* ~*vb.* **1.** (*intr.*) to screech or creak. ~*n.* **2.** a screech or creak. [C16: from Old Norse *skrækja.* See SCREECH, SHRIEK] —**'screaky** *adj.*

scream (skriːm) *vb.* **1.** to utter or emit (a sharp piercing cry or similar sound or sounds), esp. as of fear, pain, etc. **2.** (*intr.*) to laugh wildly. **3.** (*intr.*) to speak, shout, or behave in a wild or impassioned manner. **4.** (*tr.*) to bring (oneself) into a specified state by screaming: *she screamed herself hoarse.* **5.** (*intr.*) to be extremely conspicuous: *these orange curtains scream, you need more restful colours in a bedroom.* ~*n.* **6.** a sharp piercing cry or sound, esp. one denoting fear or pain. **7.** *Informal.* a person or thing that causes great amusement. [C13: from Germanic; compare Middle Dutch *schreem,* West Frisian *skrieme* to weep]

screamer ('skriːmə) *n.* **1.** a person or thing that screams. **2.** any goose-like aquatic bird, such as *Chauna torquata* (**crested screamer**), of the family *Anhimidae* of tropical and subtropical South America: order *Anseriformes* (ducks, geese, etc.). **3.** *Informal.* (in printing) an exclamation mark. **4.** someone or something that raises screams of laughter or astonishment. **5.** *U.S. and Canadian slang.* a sensational headline. **6.** *Austral. slang.* **a.** a person or thing that is excellent of its kind. **b.** See **two-pot screamer.**

scream therapy *n.* another name for **primal therapy.**

scree (skriː) *n.* an accumulation of weathered rock fragments at the foot of a cliff or hillside, often forming a sloping heap. Also called: **talus.** [Old English *scrīthan* to slip; related to Old Norse *skrītha* to slide, German *schreiten* to walk]

screech[1] (skriːtʃ) *n.* **1.** a shrill, harsh, or high-pitched sound or cry. ~*vb.* **2.** to utter with or produce a screech. [C16: variant of earlier *scritch,* of imitative origin] —**'screecher** *n.* —**'screechy** *adj.*

screech[2] (skriːtʃ) *n. Canadian slang.* (esp. in Newfoundland) **1.** a dark rum. **2.** any strong cheap drink. [perhaps special use of SCREECH[1]]

screech owl *n.* **1.** a small North American owl, *Otus asio,* having ear tufts and a reddish-brown or grey plumage. **2.** *Brit.* any owl that utters a screeching cry.

screed (skriːd) *n.* **1.** a long or prolonged speech or piece of writing. **2.** a strip of wood, plaster, or metal placed on a surface to act as a guide to the thickness of the cement or plaster coat to be applied. **3.** a mixture of cement, sand, and water applied to a concrete slab, etc., to give a smooth surface finish. **4.** *Scot.* a rent or tear or the sound produced by this. [C14: probably variant of Old English *scrēade* SHRED]

screen (skriːn) *n.* **1.** a light movable frame, panel, or partition serving to shelter, divide, hide, etc. **2.** anything that serves to shelter, protect, or conceal. **3.** a frame containing a mesh that is placed over a window or opening to keep out insects. **4.** a decorated partition, esp. in a church around the choir. See also **rood** (sense 1). **5.** a sieve. **6.** a system for selecting people, such as candidates for a job. **7.** the wide end of a cathode-ray tube, esp. in a television set, on which a visible image is formed. **8.** a white or silvered surface, usually fabric, placed in front of a projector to receive the enlarged image of a film or of slides. **9. the screen.** the film industry or films collectively. **10.** *Photog.* a plate of ground glass in some types of camera on which the image of a subject is focused before being photographed. **11.** *Printing.* a glass marked with fine intersecting lines, used in a camera for making half-tone reproductions. **12.** men or ships deployed around and ahead of a larger military formation to warn of attack or protect from a specific threat. **13.** *Sport, chiefly U.S. and Canadian.* a tactical ploy in which players block an opponent. **14.** *Psychoanal.* anything that prevents a person from realizing his true feelings about someone or something. **15.** *Electronics.* See **screen grid.** ~*vb.* (*tr.*) **16.** (sometimes foll. by *off*) to shelter, protect, or conceal. **17.** to sieve or sort. **18.** to test or check (an individual or group) so as to determine suitability for a task, etc. **19.** to examine for the presence of a disease, weapons, etc.: *the authorities screened five hundred cholera suspects.* **20.** to provide with a screen or screens. **21.** to project (a film) onto a screen, esp. for public viewing. **22.** *Printing.* to photograph (a picture) through a screen to render it suitable for half-tone reproduction. [C15: from Old French *escren* (French *écran*); related to Old High German *skrank,* German *Schrank* cupboard] —**'screenable** *adj.* —**'screener** *n.* —**'screenˌlike** *adj.*

screen grid *n. Electronics.* an electrode placed between the control grid and anode of a valve and having a fixed positive potential relative to the grid. It acts as an electrostatic shield preventing capacitive coupling between grid and anode, thus increasing the stability of the device. Sometimes shortened to **screen.** See also **suppressor grid.**

screenings (ˈskriːnɪŋz) *pl. n.* refuse separated by sifting.

screening test *n.* a simple test performed on a large number of people to identify those who have or are likely to develop a specified disease.

screen memory *n. Psychoanal.* a memory that is tolerable but allied to a distressing event and which is unconsciously used to hide the distressing memory.

screenplay (ˈskriːnˌpleɪ) *n.* the script for a film, including instructions for sets and camera work.

screen process *n.* a method of printing using a fine mesh of silk, nylon, etc., treated with an impermeable coating except in the areas through which ink is subsequently forced onto the paper behind. Also called: **silk-screen printing.**

screen test *n.* **1.** a filmed audition of a prospective actor or actress to test suitability. **2.** the test film so made.

screenwriter (ˈskriːnˌraɪtə) *n.* a person who writes screenplays.

screigh *or* **screich** (skriːx) *n., vb.* a Scot. word for **screech**[1].

screw (skruː) *n.* **1.** a device used for fastening materials together, consisting of a threaded and usually tapered shank that has a slotted head by which it may be rotated so as to cut its own thread as it bores through the material. **2.** Also called: **screw-bolt.** a threaded cylindrical rod that engages with a similarly threaded cylindrical hole; bolt. **3.** a thread in a cylindrical hole corresponding with that on the bolt or screw with which it is designed to engage. **4.** anything resembling a screw in shape or spiral form. **5.** a twisting movement of or resembling that of a screw. **6.** Also called: **screw-back.** *Billiards, snooker, etc.* **a.** a stroke in which the cue ball recoils or moves backward after striking the object ball, made by striking the cue ball below its centre. **b.** the motion resulting from this stroke. **7.** another name for **propeller** (sense 1). **8.** *Slang.* a prison guard. **9.** *Brit. slang.* salary, wages, or earnings. **10.** *Brit.* a small amount of salt, tobacco, etc., in a twist of paper. **11.** *Slang.* a person who is mean with money. **12.** *Slang.* an old, unsound, or worthless horse. **13.** (*often pl.*) *Slang.* force or compulsion (esp. in the phrase **put the screws on**). **14.** *Taboo slang.* sexual intercourse. **15. have a screw loose.** *Informal.* to be insane. ~*vb.* **16.** (*tr.*) to rotate (a screw or bolt) so as to drive it into or draw it out of a material. **17.** (*tr.*) to cut a screw thread in (a rod or hole) with a tap or die or on a lathe. **18.** to turn or cause to turn in the manner of a screw. **19.** (*tr.*) to attach or fasten with a screw or screws. **20.** (*tr.*) *Informal.* to take advantage of; cheat. **21.** (*tr.*; often foll. by *up*) to distort or contort: *he screwed his face into a scowl.* **22.** Also: **screw back.** to impart a screw to (a ball). **23.** (*tr.*, often foll. by *from* or *out of*) to coerce or force out of; extort. **24.** *Taboo slang.* to have sexual intercourse (with). **25.** (*tr.*) *Slang.* to burgle. **26. have one's head screwed on (the right way).** *Informal.* to be wise or sensible. ~See also **screw up.** [C15: from French *escroe,* from Medieval Latin *scrōfa* screw, from Latin: sow, presumably because the thread of the screw is like the spiral of the sow's tail] —ˈ**screwer** *n.* —ˈ**screwˌlike** *adj.*

screwball (ˈskruːˌbɔːl) *Slang, chiefly U.S. and Canadian.* ~*n.* **1.** an odd or eccentric person. ~*adj.* **2.** odd; zany; eccentric.

screw conveyor *n. Engineering.* a duct along which material is conveyed by the rotational action of a spiral vane which lies along the length of the duct. Also called: **worm conveyor.**

screwdriver (ˈskruːˌdraɪvə) *n.* **1.** a tool used for turning screws, usually having a handle of wood, plastic, etc., and a steel shank with a flattened square-cut tip that fits into a slot in the head of the screw. **2.** an alcoholic beverage consisting of orange juice and vodka.

screwed (skruːd) *adj.* **1.** fastened by a screw or screws. **2.** having spiral grooves like a screw; threaded. **3.** twisted or distorted. **4.** *Brit.* a slang word for **drunk.**

screw eye *n.* a wood screw with its shank bent into a ring.

screw jack *n.* a lifting device utilizing the mechanical advantage of a screw thread, the effort being applied through a bevel drive. Also called: **jackscrew, jack.**

screw pile *n.* a pile with a threaded tip that is screwed into the ground by a winch or capstan.

screw pine *n.* any of various pandanaceous plants of the Old World tropical genus *Pandanus,* having a spiral mass of pineapple-like leaves and heavy conelike fruits.

screw plate *n.* a steel plate with threaded holes used for making male screws.

screw propeller *n.* an early form of ship's propeller in which an Archimedes' screw is used to produce thrust by accelerating a flow of water. —ˈ**screw-proˈpelled** *adj.*

screw tap *n.* another name for **tap**[2] (sense 6).

screw thread *n.* the helical ridge on a screw formed by a die or lathe tool.

screw top *n.* **1.** a lid with a threaded rim that is turned on the corresponding thread on the neck of a bottle or container to close it securely. **2.** a bottle or container having such a lid. —ˈ**screw-ˌtop** *or* ˈ**screw-ˌtopped** *adj.*

screw up *vb.* (*tr., adv.*) **1.** to twist out of shape or distort. **2.** to summon up or call upon: *to screw up one's courage.* **3.** *Informal.* to mishandle or bungle. **4.** (*often passive*) *Informal.* to cause to become very anxious, confused, or nervous: *he is really screwed up about his exams.*

screwworm (ˈskruːˌwɜːm) *n.* **1.** the larva of a dipterous fly, *Callitroga macellaria,* that develops beneath the skin of living mammals often causing illness or death. **2. screwworm fly.** the fly producing this larva: family *Calliphoridae.*

screwy (ˈskruːɪ) *adj.* **screwier, screwiest.** *Informal.* odd, crazy, or eccentric.

scribble[1] (ˈskrɪbᵊl) *vb.* **1.** to write or draw in a hasty or illegible manner. **2.** to make meaningless or illegible marks (on). **3.** *Derogatory or facetious.* to write poetry, novels, etc. ~*n.* **4.** hasty careless writing or drawing. **5.** writing, esp. literary matter, of poor quality. **6.** meaningless or illegible marks. [C15: from Medieval Latin *scrībillāre* to write hastily, from Latin *scrībere* to write] —ˈ**scribbler** *n.* —ˈ**scribbly** *adj.*

scribble[2] (ˈskrɪbᵊl) *vb.* (*tr.*) to card (wool, etc.). [C17: probably from Low German; compare *schrubben* SCRUB[1]]

scribbly gum (ˈskribᵊlɪ) *n.* any species of the genus *Eucalyptus* with smooth white bark marked with random patterns made by wood-boring insects.

scribe (skraɪb) *n.* **1.** a person who copies documents, esp. a person who made handwritten copies before the invention of printing. **2.** a clerk or public copyist. **3.** *Old Testament.* a recognized scholar and teacher of the Jewish Law. **4.** *Judaism.* a man qualified to write certain documents in accordance with religious requirements. **5.** an author or journalist: used humorously. **6.** another name for **scriber.** ~*vb.* **7.** to score a line on (a surface) with a pointed instrument, as in metalworking. [(in the senses: writer, etc.) C14: from Latin *scrība* clerk, from *scrībere* to write; C17 (vb.): perhaps from INSCRIBE] —ˈ**scribal** *adj.*

scriber (ˈskraɪbə) *n.* a pointed steel tool used to score materials as a guide to cutting, etc. Also called: **scribe.**

scrim (skrɪm) *n.* an open-weave muslin or hessian fabric, used in upholstery, lining, building, and in the theatre to create the illusion of a solid wall or to suggest haziness, etc., according to the lighting. [C18: origin unknown]

scrimmage (ˈskrɪmɪdʒ) *n.* **1.** a rough or disorderly struggle. **2.** *American football.* the clash of opposing linemen at every down. ~*vb.* **3.** (*intr.*) to engage in a scrimmage. **4.** (*tr.*) to put (the ball) into a scrimmage. [C15: from earlier *scrimish,* variant of SKIRMISH] —ˈ**scrimmager** *n.*

scrimp (skrɪmp) *vb.* **1.** (when *intr.*, sometimes foll. by *on*) to be very economical or sparing in the use (of) (esp. in the phrase **scrimp and scrape**). **2.** (*tr.*) to treat meanly: *he is scrimping his children.* **3.** (*tr.*) to cut too small. ~*adj.* **4.** a less common word for **scant.** [C18: Scottish, origin unknown] —ˈ**scrimpy** *adj.* —ˈ**scrimpily** *adv.* —ˈ**scrimpiness** *n.*

scrimshank (ˈskrɪmˌʃæŋk) *vb.* (*intr.*) *Brit. military slang.* to shirk work. [C19: of unknown origin]

scrimshaw (ˈskrɪmˌʃɔː) *n.* **1.** the art of decorating or carving shells, ivory, etc., done by sailors as a leisure activity. **2. a.** an article made in this manner. **b.** such articles collectively. ~*vb.* **3.** to produce scrimshaw (from). [C19: origin uncertain, perhaps after a surname]

scrip[1] (skrɪp) *n.* **1.** a written certificate, list, etc. **2.** a small scrap, esp. of paper with writing on it. **3.** *Finance.* **a.** a certificate representing a claim to part of a share of stock. **b.** the shares allocated in a bonus issue. [C18: in some senses, probably from SCRIPT; otherwise, short for *subscription receipt*]

scrip[2] (skrɪp) *n. Archaic.* a small bag or wallet, as carried by pilgrims. [C14: from Old French *escreppe,* variant of *escarpe* SCARF[1]]

scrip issue *n.* another name for **bonus issue.**

scripophily (skrɪˈpɒfɪlɪ) *n.* the hobby of collecting bonds and share certificates, esp. those of historical interest. [C20: from SCRIP[1] + -O- + *-phily,* from Greek *philos* loving] —**scripophile** (ˈskrɪpəʊˌfaɪl) *n.*

script (skrɪpt) *n.* **1.** handwriting as distinguished from print, esp. cursive writing. **2.** the letters, characters, or figures used in writing by hand. **3.** any system or style of writing. **4.** written copy for the use of performers in films and plays. **5.** *Law.* **a.** an original or principal document. **b.** (esp. in England) a will or codicil or the draft for one. **6.** any of various typefaces that imitate handwriting. **7.** an answer paper in an examination. ~*vb.* **8.** (*tr.*) to write a script for. [C14: from Latin *scriptum* something written, from *scrībere* to write]

Script. *abbrev. for:* **1.** scriptural. **2.** Scripture(s).

scriptorium (skrɪpˈtɔːrɪəm) *n., pl.* **-riums** *or* **-ria** (-rɪə). a room, esp. in a monastery, set apart for the writing or copying of manuscripts. [from Medieval Latin]

scriptural (ˈskrɪptʃərəl) *adj.* **1.** (*often cap.*) of, in accordance with, or based on Scripture. **2.** of or relating to writing. —ˈ**scripturally** *adv.*

scripture (ˈskrɪptʃə) *n.* a sacred, solemn, or authoritative book or piece of writing. [C13: from Latin *scriptūra* written material, from *scrībere* to write]

Scripture (ˈskrɪptʃə) *n.* **1.** Also called: **Holy Scripture, Holy Writ, the Scriptures.** *Christianity.* the Old and New Testaments. **2.** any book or body of writings, esp. when regarded as sacred by a particular religious group.

scriptwriter (ˈskrɪptˌraɪtə) *n.* a person who prepares scripts, esp. for a film. —ˈ**scriptˌwriting** *n.*

scrivener (ˈskrɪvnə) *n. Archaic.* **1.** a person who writes out deeds, letters, etc.; copyist. **2.** a notary. [C14: from *scrivein* clerk, from Old French *escrivain,* ultimately from Latin *scrība* SCRIBE]

scrobiculate (skrəʊˈbɪkjʊlɪt, -ˌleɪt) *or* **scrobiculated** *adj. Biology.* having a surface covered with small round pits or grooves. [C19: from Latin *scrobiculus* diminutive of *scrobis* a ditch]

scrod (skrɒd) *n. U.S.* a young cod or haddock, esp. one split and prepared for cooking. [C19: perhaps from obsolete Dutch *schrood,* from Middle Dutch *schrode* SHRED (n.); the name perhaps refers to the method of preparing the fish for cooking]

scrofula (ˈskrɒfjʊlə) *n. Pathol.* (*no longer in technical use*) tuberculosis of the lymphatic glands. Also called (formerly): (the) **king's evil.** [C14: from Medieval Latin, from Late Latin *scrōfulae* swollen glands in the neck, literally: little sows (sows were thought to be particularly prone to the disease), from Latin *scrōfa* sow]

scrofulous (ˈskrɒfjʊləs) *adj.* **1.** of, relating to, resembling, or having scrofula. **2.** morally degraded. —ˈ**scrofulously** *adv.* —ˈ**scrofulousness** *n.*

scroggin (ˈskrɒgɪn) *n. N.Z. informal.* a tramper's home-made high-calorie sweetmeat.

scroll (skrəʊl) *n.* **1.** a roll of parchment, paper, etc., usually inscribed with writing. **2.** an ancient book in the form of a roll of parchment, papyrus, etc. **3. a.** a decorative carving or moulding resembling a scroll. **b.** (*as modifier*): *a scroll saw.* **c.** (*in combination*): *scrollwork.* ~*vb.* **4.** (*tr.*) to saw into scrolls. **5.** to roll up like a scroll. **6.** *Computer technol.* to move (text) from right to left or up and down on a screen in order to view text that cannot be contained within a single display image. [C15 *scrowle,* from *scrowe,* from Old French *escroe* scrap of parchment, but also influenced by ROLL]

scroll saw *n.* a saw with a narrow blade for cutting intricate ornamental curves in wood.

scrollwork (ˈskrəʊlˌwɜːk) *n.* ornamental work in scroll-like patterns, esp. when done with a scroll saw.

Scrooge (skruːdʒ) *n.* a mean or miserly person. [C19: after a character in Charles Dickens' story *A Christmas Carol* (1843)]

scroop (skruːp) *Dialect.* ~*vb.* **1.** (*intr.*) to emit a grating or creaking sound. ~*n.* **2.** such a sound. [C18: of imitative origin]

scrophulariaceous (ˌskrɒfjʊˌlɛərɪˈeɪʃəs) *adj.* of, relating to, or belonging to the *Scrophulariaceae,* a family of plants including figwort, snapdragon, foxglove, toadflax, speedwell, and mullein. [C19: from New Latin (*herba*) *scrophularia* scrofula (plant), from the use of such plants in treating scrofula]

scrotum (ˈskrəʊtəm) *n., pl.* **-ta** (-tə) *or* **-tums.** the pouch of skin containing the testes in most mammals. [C16: from Latin] —ˈ**scrotal** *adj.*

scrouge (skraʊdʒ, skruːdʒ) *vb.* (*tr.*) *Dialect.* to crowd or press. [C18: alteration of C16 *scruze* to squeeze, perhaps blend of SCREW + SQUEEZE]

scrounge (skraʊndʒ) *vb. Informal.* **1.** (when *intr.,* sometimes foll. by *around*) to search in order to acquire (something) without cost. **2.** to obtain or seek to obtain (something) by cadging or begging. [C20: variant of dialect *scrunge* to steal, of obscure origin] —ˈ**scrounger** *n.*

scrub[1] (skrʌb) *vb.* **scrubs, scrubbing, scrubbed.** **1.** to rub (a surface) hard, with or as if with a brush, soap, and water, in order to clean it. **2.** to remove (dirt), esp. by rubbing with a brush and water. **3.** (*intr.;* foll. by *up*) (of a surgeon) to wash the hands and arms thoroughly before operating. **4.** (*tr.*) to purify (a vapour or gas) by removing impurities. **5.** (*tr.*) *Informal.* to delete or cancel. **6.** (*intr.*) *Horse-racing slang.* (of jockeys) to urge a horse forwards by moving the arms and whip rhythmically forwards and backwards alongside its neck. ~*n.* **7.** the act of or an instance of scrubbing. ~See also **scrub round.** [C14: from Middle Low German *schrubben,* or Middle Dutch *schrobben*]

scrub[2] (skrʌb) *n.* **1. a.** vegetation consisting of stunted trees, bushes, and other plants growing in an arid area. **b.** (*as modifier*): *scrub vegetation.* **2.** an area of arid land covered with such vegetation. **3. a.** an animal of inferior breeding or condition. **b.** (*as modifier*): *a scrub bull.* **4.** a small or insignificant person. **5.** anything stunted or inferior. **6.** *Sport, U.S. and Canadian.* **a.** a player not in the first team. **b.** a team composed of such players. **c.** a contest between scratch or incomplete teams. **7.** **the scrub.** *Austral. informal.* a remote place, esp. one where contact with people can be avoided. ~*adj.* (*prenominal*) **8.** small, stunted, or inferior. **9.** *Sport, U.S. and Canadian.* **a.** (of a player) not in the first team. **b.** (of a team) composed of such players. **c.** (of a contest) between scratch or incomplete teams. [C16: variation of SHRUB]

scrubber[1] (ˈskrʌbə) *n.* **1.** a person or thing that scrubs. **2.** an apparatus for purifying a gas. **3.** *Derogatory Brit. and Austral. slang.* a promiscuous girl.

scrubber[2] (ˈskrʌbə) *n. Austral.* a domestic animal, esp. a bullock, that has run wild in the bush. [C19: from SCRUB[2]]

scrub bird *n.* either of two fast-running wren-like passerine birds, *Atrichornis clamosus* or *A. rufescens,* that constitute the Australian family *Atrichornithidae.*

scrubby (ˈskrʌbɪ) *adj.* **-bier, -biest.** **1.** covered with or consisting of scrub. **2.** (of trees or vegetation) stunted in growth. **3.** *Brit. informal.* messy. —ˈ**scrubbiness** *n.*

scrub fowl *or* **turkey** *n.* another name for **megapode.**

scrubland (ˈskrʌbˌlænd) *n.* an area of scrub vegetation.

scrub round *vb.* (*intr., prep.*) *Informal.* to waive; avoid or ignore: *we can scrub round the rules.*

scrub typhus *n.* an acute febrile disease characterized by severe headache, skin rash, chills, and swelling of the lymph nodes, caused by the bite of mites infected with the microorganism *Rickettsia tsutsugamushi:* occurs mainly in Asia, Australia, and the islands of the western Pacific.

scruff[1] (skrʌf) *n.* the nape of the neck (esp. in the phrase **by the scruff of the neck**). [C18: variant of *scuft,* perhaps from Old Norse *skoft* hair; related to Old High German *scuft*]

scruff[2] (skrʌf) *n.* **1.** *Informal.* an untidy scruffy person. **2.** *Informal.* a disreputable person, ruffian. **3.** another name for **scum** (sense 3).

scruffy (ˈskrʌfɪ) *adj.* **scruffier, scruffiest.** unkempt or shabby.

scrum (skrʌm) *n.* **1.** *Rugby.* the act or method of restarting play after an infringement when the two opposing packs of forwards group together with heads down and arms interlocked and push to gain ground while the scrum half throws the ball in and the hookers attempt to scoop it out to their own team. A scrum is usually called by the referee (**set scrum**) but may be formed spontaneously (**loose scrum**). **2.** *Informal.* a disorderly struggle. ~*vb.* **scrums, scrumming, scrummed.** **3.** (*intr.;* usually foll. by *down*) *Rugby.* to form a scrum. [C19: shortened from SCRUMMAGE]

scrum half *n. Rugby.* **1.** a player who puts in the ball at scrums and tries to get it away to his three-quarter backs. **2.** this position in a team.

scrummage (ˈskrʌmɪdʒ) *n., vb.* **1.** *Rugby.* another word for **scrum.** **2.** a variant of **scrimmage.** [C19: variant of SCRIMMAGE] —ˈ**scrummager** *n.*

scrump (skrʌmp) *vb. Dialect.* to steal (apples) from an orchard or garden. [dialect variant of SCRIMP]

scrumptious (ˈskrʌmpʃəs) *adj. Informal.* very pleasing; delicious. [C19: probably changed from SUMPTUOUS] —ˈ**scrumptiously** *adv.* —ˈ**scrumptiousness** *n.*

scrumpy (ˈskrʌmpɪ) *n.* a rough dry cider, brewed esp. in the West Country. [from *scrump,* variant of SCRIMP (in obsolete sense: withered), referring to the apples used]

scrunch (skrʌntʃ) *vb.* **1.** to crumple, crush, or crunch or to be crumpled, crushed, or crunched. ~*n.* **2.** the act or sound of scrunching. [C19: variant of CRUNCH]

scruple (ˈskruːpᵊl) *n.* **1.** (*often pl.*) a doubt or hesitation as to what is morally right in a certain situation. **2.** *Archaic.* a very small amount. **3.** a unit of weight equal to 20 grains (1.296 grams). **4.** an ancient Roman unit of weight equivalent to approximately one twenty-fourth of an ounce. ~*vb.* **5.** (*obsolete when tr.*) to have doubts (about), esp. from a moral compunction. [C16: from Latin *scrūpulus* a small weight, from *scrūpus* rough stone] —ˈ**scrupleless** *adj.*

scrupulous (ˈskruːpjʊləs) *adj.* **1.** characterized by careful observation of what is morally right. **2.** very careful or precise. [C15: from Latin *scrūpulōsus* punctilious] —ˈ**scrupulously** *adv.* —ˈ**scrupulousness** *n.*

scrutable (ˈskruːtəbᵊl) *adj. Rare.* open to or able to be understood by scrutiny. [C17: from Latin *scrūtārī* to inspect closely; see SCRUTINY] —ˌ**scrutaˈbility** *n.*

scrutator (skruːˈteɪtə) *n.* a person who examines or scrutinizes. [from Latin, from *scrūtārī* to search]

scrutineer (ˌskruːtɪˈnɪə) *n.* a person who examines, esp. one who scrutinizes the conduct of an election poll.

scrutinize *or* **scrutinise** (ˈskruːtɪˌnaɪz) *vb.* (*tr.*) to examine carefully or in minute detail. —ˈ**scrutiˌnizer** *or* ˈ**scrutiˌniser** *n.*

scrutiny (ˈskruːtɪnɪ) *n., pl.* **-nies.** **1.** close or minute examination. **2.** a searching look. **3. a.** (in the early Christian Church) a formal testing that catechumens had to undergo before being baptized. **b.** a similar examination of candidates for holy orders. [C15: from Late Latin *scrūtinium* an investigation, from *scrūtārī* to search (originally referring to rag-and-bone men), from *scrūta* rubbish]

scry (skraɪ) *vb.* **scries, scrying, scried.** (*intr.*) to divine, esp. by crystal gazing. [C16: from DESCRY]

scuba (ˈskjuːbə) *n.* **a.** an apparatus used in skindiving, consisting of a cylinder or cylinders containing compressed air attached to a breathing apparatus. **b.** (*as modifier*): *scuba diving.* [C20: from the initials of *self-contained underwater breathing apparatus*]

scud (skʌd) *vb.* **scuds, scudding, scudded.** **1.** (*intr.*) (esp. of clouds) to move along swiftly and smoothly. **2.** (*intr.*) *Nautical.* to run before a gale. **3.** (*tr.*) *Scot.* to hit; slap. ~*n.* **4.** the act of scudding. **5.** *Meteorol.* **a.** a formation of low fractostratus clouds driven by a strong wind beneath rain-bearing clouds. **b.** a sudden shower or gust of wind. **6.** *Scot.* a slap. [C16: probably of Scandinavian origin; related to Norwegian *skudda* to thrust, Swedish *skudda* to shake]

scudo (ˈskuːdəʊ) *n., pl.* **-di** (-diː). any of several former Italian coins. [C17: from Italian: shield, from Latin *scūtum*]

scuff (skʌf) *vb.* **1.** to scrape or drag (the feet) while walking. **2.** to rub or scratch (a surface) or (of a surface) to become rubbed or scratched. **3.** (*tr.*) *U.S.* to poke at (something) with the foot. ~*n.* **4.** the act or sound of scuffing. **5.** a rubbed place caused by scuffing. **6.** a backless slipper. [C19: probably of imitative origin]

scuffle[1] ('skʌfᵊl) *vb. (intr.)* **1.** to fight in a disorderly manner. **2.** to move by shuffling. **3.** to move in a hurried or confused manner. ~*n.* **4.** a disorderly struggle. **5.** the sound made by scuffling or shuffling. [C16: from Scandinavian; compare Swedish *skuff, skuffa* to push]

scuffle[2] ('skʌfᵊl) *n. U.S.* a type of hoe operated by pushing rather than pulling. [C18: from Dutch *schoffel* SHOVEL]

scull (skʌl) *n.* **1.** a single oar moved from side to side over the stern of a boat to propel it. **2.** one of a pair of short-handled oars, both of which are pulled by one oarsman, esp. in a racing shell. **3.** a racing shell propelled by a single oarsman pulling two oars. **4.** *(pl.)* a race between racing shells, each propelled by one oarsman pulling two oars. **5.** an act, instance, period, or distance of sculling. ~*vb.* **6.** to propel (a boat) with a scull. [C14: of unknown origin] —'**sculler** *n.*

scullery ('skʌlərɪ) *n., pl.* **-leries.** *Chiefly Brit.* a small room or part of a kitchen where washing up, vegetable preparation, etc. is done. [C15: from Anglo-Norman *squillerie,* from Old French *escuelerie,* from *escuele* a bowl, from Latin *scutella,* from *scutra* a flat tray]

scullion ('skʌljən) *n.* **1.** a mean or despicable person. **2.** *Archaic.* a servant employed to do rough household work in a kitchen. [C15: from Old French *escouillon* cleaning cloth, from *escouve* a broom, from Latin *scōpa* a broom]

sculp. *abbrev. for:* **1.** Also: **sculpt.** sculpsit. **2.** sculptor, sculptress, or sculpture.

sculpin ('skʌlpɪn) *n., pl.* **-pin** *or* **-pins.** *U.S. and Canadian.* any of various fishes of the family *Cottidae* (bullheads and sea scorpions). [C17: of unknown origin]

sculpsit ('skʌlpsɪt) he (or she) sculptured it: an inscription following the artist's name on a sculpture. [Latin]

sculpt (skʌlpt) *vb.* **1.** a variant of **sculpture** (senses 5–8). **2.** *(intr.)* to practise sculpture. ~Also: **sculp.** [C19: from French *sculpter,* from Latin *sculpere* to carve]

sculptor ('skʌlptə) *or (fem.)* **sculptress** *n.* a person who practises sculpture.

Sculptor ('skʌlptə) *n., Latin genitive* **Sculptoris** (skʌlp'tɔːrɪs). a faint constellation in the S hemisphere lying between Phoenix and Cetus.

sculpture ('skʌlptʃə) *n.* **1.** the art of making figures or designs in relief or the round by carving wood, moulding plaster, etc., or casting metals, etc. **2.** works or a work made in this way. **3.** ridges or indentations as on a shell, formed by natural processes. **4.** the gradual formation of the landscape by erosion. ~*vb.* *(mainly tr.)* **5.** *(also intr.)* to carve, cast, or fashion (stone, bronze, etc.) three-dimensionally. **6.** to portray (a person, etc.) by means of sculpture. **7.** to form in the manner of sculpture, esp. to shape (landscape) by erosion. **8.** to decorate with sculpture. ~Also (for senses 5–8): **sculpt.** [C14: from Latin *sculptūra* a carving; see SCULPT] —'**sculptural** *adj.* —'**sculpturally** *adv.*

sculpturesque (ˌskʌlptʃə'rɛsk) *adj.* resembling sculpture. —ˌ**sculptur'esquely** *adv.* —ˌ**sculptur'esqueness** *n.*

scum (skʌm) *n.* **1.** a layer of impure matter that forms on the surface of a liquid, often as the result of boiling or fermentation. **2.** the greenish film of algae and similar vegetation surface of a stagnant pond. **3.** Also called: **dross, scruff.** the skin of oxides or impurities on the surface of a molten metal. **4.** waste matter. **5.** a worthless person or group of people. ~*vb.* **scums, scumming, scummed.** **6.** *(tr.)* to remove scum from. **7.** *(intr.) Rare.* to form a layer of or become covered with scum. [C13: of Germanic origin; related to Old High German *scūm,* Middle Dutch *schūm,* Old French *escume;* see SKIM] —'**scumˌlike** *adj.* —'**scummer** *n.* —'**scummy** *adj.*

scumbag ('skʌmˌbæg) *n. Slang.* an offensive or despicable person. [C20: perhaps from earlier U.S. sense: condom, from U.S. slang *scum* semen + bag]

scumble ('skʌmbᵊl) *vb.* **1.** (in painting and drawing) to soften or blend (an outline or colour) with an upper coat of opaque colour, applied very thinly. ~*n.* **2.** the upper layer of colour applied in this way. **3.** the technique or effects of scumbling. [C18: probably from SCUM]

scuncheon ('skʌntʃən) *n.* the inner part of a door jamb or window frame. [C15: from Old French *escoinson,* from *coin* angle]

scunge (skʌndʒ) *Austral. and N.Z. slang.* ~*vb.* **1.** to borrow. ~*n.* **2.** a dirty or worthless person. **3.** a person who borrows, esp. habitually. [C20: of unknown origin]

scungy ('skʌndʒɪ) *adj.* **scungier, scungiest.** *Austral. and N.Z. informal.* miserable; sordid. [C20: of uncertain origin]

scunner ('skʌnə; *Scot.* 'skʌnər) *Dialect, chiefly Scot.* ~*vb.* **1.** *(intr.)* to feel aversion. **2.** *(tr.)* to produce a feeling of aversion in. ~*n.* **3.** a strong aversion (often in the phrase **take a scunner to**). **4.** an object of dislike; nuisance. [C14: from Scottish *skunner,* of unknown origin]

scup (skʌp) *n.* a common sparid fish, *Stenotomus chrysops,* of American coastal regions of the Atlantic. Also called: **northern porgy.** [C19: from Narraganset *mishcup,* from *mishe* big + *kuppe* close together; from the form of the scales]

scupper[1] ('skʌpə) *n.* **1.** *Nautical.* a drain or spout allowing water on the deck of a vessel to flow overboard. **2.** an opening in the side of a building for draining off water. **3.** a drain in a factory floor for running off the water from a sprinkler system. [C15 *skopper,* of uncertain origin; perhaps related to SCOOP]

scupper[2] ('skʌpə) *vb. (tr.) Brit.* **1.** *Slang.* to overwhelm, ruin, or disable. **2.** to sink (one's ship) deliberately. [C19: of unknown origin]

scuppernong ('skʌpəˌnɒŋ) *n.* **1.** a sweet American wine, slightly golden, made from a variety of muscadine grape. **2.** another name for **muscadine** (sense 2), esp. the variety from which this wine is made. [C19: named after *Scuppernong* River in North Carolina where the grape grows]

scurf (skɜːf) *n.* **1.** another name for **dandruff.** **2.** flaky or scaly matter adhering to or peeling off a surface. [Old English *scurf;* related to Old Norse *skurfōttr* scurfy, Old High German *scorf,* Danish *skurv*] —'**scurfy** *adj.*

scurrilous ('skʌrɪləs) *adj.* **1.** grossly or obscenely abusive or defamatory. **2.** characterized by gross or obscene humour. [C16: from Latin *scurrīlis* derisive, from *scurra* buffoon] —**scurrility** (skə'rɪlɪtɪ) *or* '**scurrilousness** *n.* —'**scurrilously** *adv.*

scurry ('skʌrɪ) *vb.* **-ries, -rying, -ried.** **1.** to move about or proceed hurriedly. **2.** *(intr.)* to whirl about. ~*n., pl.* **-ries.** **3.** the act or sound of scurrying. **4.** a brisk light whirling movement, as of snow. **5.** *Horse racing.* a short race or sprint. [C19: probably shortened from *hurry-scurry*]

scurvy ('skɜːvɪ) *n.* **1.** a disease caused by a lack of vitamin C, characterized by anaemia, spongy gums, bleeding beneath the skin, and (in infants) malformation of bones and teeth. ~*adj.* **-vier, -viest.** **2.** mean or despicable. [C16: see SCURF] —'**scurvily** *adv.* —'**scurviness** *n.*

scurvy grass *n.* any of various cruciferous plants of the genus *Cochlearia,* esp. *C. officinalis,* of Europe and North America, formerly used to treat scurvy.

scut (skʌt) *n.* the short tail of animals such as the deer and rabbit. [C15: probably of Scandinavian origin; compare Old Norse *skutr* end of a vessel, Icelandic *skott* tail]

scuta ('skjuːtə) *n.* the plural of **scutum.**

scutage ('skjuːtɪdʒ) *n.* (in feudal society) a payment sometimes exacted by a lord from his vassal in lieu of military service. [C15: from Medieval Latin *scūtāgium,* literally: shield dues, from Latin *scūtum* a shield]

scutate ('skjuːteɪt) *adj.* **1.** (of animals) having or covered with large bony or horny plates. **2.** *Botany.* shaped like a round shield or buckler: *a scutate leaf.* [C19: from Latin *scūtātus* armed with a shield, from *scūtum* a shield] —**scu'tation** *n.*

scutch (skʌtʃ) *vb.* **1.** *(tr.)* to separate the fibres from the woody part of (flax) by pounding. ~*n.* **2.** the tool used for this. Also called: **scutcher.** [C18: from obsolete French *escoucher,* from Vulgar Latin *excuticāre* (unattested) to beat out, from Latin EX-[1] + *quatere* to shake]

scutcheon ('skʌtʃən) *n.* **1.** a variant of **escutcheon.** **2.** any rounded or shield-shaped structure, esp. a scute. —'**scutcheonless** *adj.* —'**scutcheon-ˌlike** *adj.*

scutch grass *n.* another name for **Bermuda grass** and **couch grass.** Sometimes shortened to **scutch.** [variant of COUCH GRASS]

scute (skjuːt) *n. Zoology.* a horny or chitinous plate that makes up part of the exoskeleton in armadillos, turtles, fishes, etc. [C14 (the name of a French coin; C19 in zoological sense): from Latin *scūtum* shield]

scutellation (ˌskjuːtɪ'leɪʃən) *n. Zoology.* **1.** the way in which scales or plates are arranged in an animal. **2.** a covering of scales or scutella, as on a bird's leg. [C19: New Latin, from *scutella,* plural of SCUTELLUM + -ATION]

scutellum (skjuː'tɛləm) *n., pl.* **-la** (-lə). *Biology.* **1.** the last of three plates into which the notum of an insect's thorax is divided. **2.** one of the scales on the tarsus of a bird's leg. **3.** the cotyledon of a developing grass seed. **4.** any other small shield-shaped part or structure. [C18: from New Latin: a little shield, from Latin *scūtum* a shield] —**scu'tellar** *adj.* —**scutellate** ('skjuːtɪˌleɪt, -lɪt) *adj.*

scutiform ('skjuːtɪˌfɔːm) *adj.* (esp. of plant parts) shaped like a shield. [C17: from New Latin *scūtiformis,* from Latin *scūtum* a shield + *forma* shape]

scutter ('skʌtə) *vb., n. Brit.* an informal word for **scurry.** [C18: probably from SCUTTLE[2], with -ER[1] as in SCATTER]

scuttle[1] ('skʌtᵊl) *n.* **1.** See **coal scuttle.** **2.** *Dialect, chiefly Brit.* a shallow basket, esp. for carrying vegetables. **3.** the part of a motor-car body lying immediately behind the bonnet. [Old English *scutel* trencher, from Latin *scutella* bowl, diminutive of *scutra* platter; related to Old Norse *skutill,* Old High German *scuzzila,* perhaps to Latin *scūtum* shield]

scuttle[2] ('skʌtᵊl) *vb.* **1.** *(intr.)* to run or move about with short hasty steps. ~*n.* **2.** a hurried pace or run. [C15: perhaps from SCUD, influenced by SHUTTLE]

scuttle[3] ('skʌtᵊl) *vb.* **1.** *(tr.) Nautical.* to cause (a vessel) to sink by opening the seacocks or making holes in the bottom. **2.** *(tr.)* to give up (hopes, plans, etc.). ~*n.* **3.** *Nautical.* a small hatch or its cover. [C15 (n.): via Old French from Spanish *escotilla* a small opening, from *escote* opening in a piece of cloth, from *escotar* to cut out]

scuttlebutt ('skʌtᵊlˌbʌt) *n. Nautical.* **1.** a drinking fountain. **2.** (formerly) a cask of drinking water aboard a ship. **3.** *Chiefly U.S. slang.* rumour or gossip. [C19: from SCUTTLE[3] + BUTT[4]]

scutum ('skjuːtəm) *n., pl.* **-ta** (-tə). **1.** the middle of three plates into which the notum of an insect's thorax is divided. **2.** another word for **scute.** **3.** a large Roman shield. [Latin: shield]

Scutum (ˈskjuːtəm) *n., Latin genitive* **Scuti** (ˈskjuːtaɪ). a small faint constellation in the S hemisphere lying between Sagittarius and Aquila and crossed by the Milky Way. Also called: **Scutum Sobieskii** (sɒˈbjɛskɪ). [Latin, literally: the Shield]

scuzzy (ˈskʌzɪ) *adj.* **-zier, -ziest.** *Slang, chiefly U.S.* unkempt, dirty, or squalid. [C20: perhaps from *disgusting* or perhaps from a blend of *scum and fuzz*]

Scylla (ˈsɪlə) *n.* **between Scylla and Charybdis.** in a predicament in which avoidance of either of two dangers means exposure to the other. [after two sea monsters in Greek mythology, on opposite sides of the channel between Italy and Sicily and of equal danger to sailors]

scyphiform (ˈsaɪfɪˌfɔːm) *adj.* shaped like a cup or goblet: *a scyphiform cell.* [C19: from Greek *skuphos cup* + -FORM]

scyphistoma (saɪˈfɪstəmə) *n., pl.* **-mae** (-ˌmiː) *or* **-mas.** a sessile hydra-like individual representing the polyp stage of scyphozoans. It produces forms which become free-swimming jellyfish. [C19: from Greek *skuphos* cup + STOMA]

scyphozoan (ˌsaɪfəˈzəʊən) *n.* **1.** any marine medusoid coelenterate of the class *Scyphozoa;* a jellyfish. *~adj.* **2.** of, relating to, or belonging to the *Scyphozoa.* [C19: via New Latin from Greek *skuphos* bowl + *zōion* animal]

scyphus (ˈsaɪfəs) *n., pl.* **-phi** (-faɪ). **1.** an ancient Greek two-handled drinking cup without a footed base. **2.** *Botany.* a cuplike body formed at the end of the thallus in certain lichens. [C18: from Latin: goblet, from Greek *skuphos*]

scythe (saɪð) *n.* **1.** a manual implement for cutting grass, etc., having a long handle held with both hands and a curved sharpened blade that moves in a plane parallel to the ground. *~vb.* **2.** *(tr.)* to cut (grass, etc.) with a scythe. [Old English *sigthe;* related to Old Norse *sigthr,* Old High German *segansa*] —ˈ**scytheˌlike** *adj.*

Scythian (ˈsɪðɪən) *adj.* **1.** of or relating to Scythia, an ancient region of SE Europe, or to its inhabitants or their language. *~n.* **2.** a member of an ancient nomadic people of Scythia. **3.** the extinct language of this people, belonging to the East Iranian branch of the Indo-European family.

sd *abbrev. for:* **1.** sine die. **2.** sound. **3.** *Philosophy.* sense datum.

SD *abbrev. for:* **1.** South Dakota. **2.** Also: **sd.** *Statistics.* standard deviation. *~***3.** *international car registration for* Swaziland.

SDA *abbrev. for* Scottish Development Agency.

S. Dak. *abbrev. for* South Dakota.

SDI *abbrev. for* Strategic Defense Initiative.

SDLP *abbrev. for* Social Democratic and Labour Party.

SDP *abbrev. for* Social Democratic Party.

SDRs *abbrev. for* special drawing rights.

Se *the chemical symbol for* selenium.

SE *symbol for* southeast(ern).

sea (siː) *n.* **1. a.** (usually preceded by *the*) the mass of salt water on the earth's surface as differentiated from the land. Related adjs.: **marine, maritime. b.** (*as modifier*): *sea air.* **2.** (*cap. when part of place name*) **a.** one of the smaller areas of ocean: *the Irish Sea.* **b.** a large inland area of water: *the Caspian Sea.* **3.** turbulence or swell, esp. of considerable size: *heavy seas.* **4.** (*cap. when part of a name*) *Astronomy.* any of many huge dry plains on the surface of the moon: *Sea of Serenity.* See also **mare**². **5.** anything resembling the sea in size or apparent limitlessness. **6.** the life or career of a sailor (esp. in the phrase **follow the sea**). **7. at sea. a.** on the ocean. **b.** in a state of confusion. **8. go to sea.** to become a sailor. **9. put (out) to sea.** to embark on a sea voyage. [Old English *sǣ;* related to Old Norse *sǣr,* Old Frisian *sē,* Gothic *saiws,* Old High German *sēo*]

sea anchor *n. Nautical.* any device, such as a bucket or canvas funnel, dragged in the water to keep a vessel heading into the wind or reduce drifting.

sea anemone *n.* any of various anthozoan coelenterates, esp. of the order *Actiniaria,* having a polypoid body with oral rings of tentacles. See also **actinia.**

sea aster *n.* a composite perennial plant of salt marshes, *Aster tripolium,* having yellow and purple flowers like those of the related Michaelmas daisy.

sea bag *n.* a canvas bag, closed by a line rove through grommets at the top, used by a seaman for his belongings.

sea bass (bæs) *n.* any of various American coastal percoid fishes of the genus *Centropristes* and related genera, such as *C. striatus* (**black sea bass**), having an elongated body with a long spiny dorsal fin almost divided into two: family *Serranidae.*

Seabee (ˈsiːˌbiː) *n.* a member of the U.S. Navy's Construction Battalions established to build airstrips. [C20: from pronunciation of *CB,* for *Construction Battalion*]

sea beet *n.* a name for the wild form of *Beta vulgaris.* See **beet.**

sea bird *n.* a bird such as a gull, that lives on the sea.

sea biscuit *n.* another term for **hardtack.**

seablite (ˈsiːˌblaɪt) *n.* a prostrate annual plant of the goosefoot family, *Suaeda maritima,* of salt marshes, having fleshy alternate leaves and small green flowers. [C18: SEA + *blite,* via Latin from Greek *bliton* ORACHE]

seaboard (ˈsiːˌbɔːd) *n.* **a.** land bordering on the sea; the seashore. **b.** (*as modifier*): *seaboard towns.*

seaborne (ˈsiːˌbɔːn) *adj.* **1.** carried on or by the sea. **2.** transported by ship.

sea bream *n.* any sparid fish, esp. *Pagellus centrodontus,* of European seas, valued as a food fish.

sea breeze *n.* a wind blowing from the sea to the land, esp. during the day when the land surface is warmer.

sea buckthorn *n.* a thorny Eurasian shrub, *Hippophaë rhamnoides,* growing on sea coasts and having silvery leaves and orange fruits: family *Elaeagnaceae.*

sea butterfly *n.* another name for **pteropod.**

SEAC (ˈsiːæk) *n.* (in Britain) acronym for School Examination and Assessment Council.

sea captain *n.* the master of a ship, usually a merchant ship.

sea change *n.* a seemingly magical change, as brought about by the action of the sea. [coined by Shakespeare, in Ariel's song "Full Fathom Five" in *The Tempest*]

sea chest *n.* a usually large firm chest used by a sailor for storing personal property.

seacoast (ˈsiːˌkəʊst) *n.* land bordering on the sea; a coast.

seacock (ˈsiːˌkɒk) *n. Nautical.* a valve in the hull of a vessel below the water line for admitting sea water or for pumping out bilge water.

sea cow *n.* **1.** any sirenian mammal, such as a dugong or manatee. **2.** an archaic name for **walrus.**

sea cucumber *n.* any echinoderm of the class *Holothuroidea,* having an elongated body covered with a leathery skin and bearing a cluster of tentacles at the oral end. They usually creep on the sea bed or burrow in sand. [C17: so named because of its cucumber-like shape]

seadog (ˈsiːˌdɒg) *n.* another word for **fogbow** or **fogdog.**

sea dog *n.* an experienced or old sailor.

sea duck *n.* any of various large diving ducks, such as the eider and the scoter, that occur along coasts.

sea eagle *n.* any of various fish-eating eagles that live near the sea, esp. *Haliaetus albicilla* (**European sea eagle** or **white-tailed eagle**) having a brown plumage and white tail.

sea-ear *n.* another name for the **ormer** (sense 1).

sea elephant *n.* another name for **elephant seal.**

sea fan *n.* any of various corals of the genus *Gorgonia* and related genera, having a treelike or fan-shaped horny skeleton: order *Gorgonacea* (gorgonians).

seafarer (ˈsiːˌfɛərə) *n.* **1.** a traveller who goes by sea. **2.** a less common word for **sailor.**

seafaring (ˈsiːˌfɛərɪŋ) *adj.* (*prenominal*) **1.** travelling by sea. **2.** working as a sailor. *~n.* **3.** the act of travelling by sea. **4.** the career or work of a sailor.

sea fir *n.* another name for **hydroid** (sense 3).

seafloor spreading (ˈsiːˌflɔː) *n.* a series of processes in which new oceanic lithosphere is created at oceanic ridges, spreads away from the ridges, and returns to the earth's interior along Benioff zones. Also called: **ocean floor spreading.**

sea foam *n.* **1.** foam formed on the surface of the sea. **2.** a former name for **meerschaum** (sense 1).

seafood (ˈsiːˌfuːd) *n.* edible saltwater fish or shellfish.

sea fret *n.* a wet mist or haze coming inland from the sea.

seafront (ˈsiːˌfrʌnt) *n.* a built-up area facing the sea.

sea-girt *adj. Literary.* surrounded by the sea.

seagoing (ˈsiːˌgəʊɪŋ) *adj.* intended for or used at sea.

sea gooseberry *n.* any of various ctenophores of the genus *Pleurobrachia* and related genera, having a rounded body with longitudinal rows of cilia and hairlike tentacles.

sea green *n.* **a.** a moderate green colour, sometimes with a bluish or yellowish tinge. **b.** (*as adj.*): *a sea-green carpet.*

seagull (ˈsiːˌgʌl) *n.* **1.** a popular name for the **gull** (the bird). **2.** Also called (Austral.): **sniper.** *Austral. and N.Z.* a casual wharf labourer who is not a trade-union member.

sea hare *n.* any of various marine gastropods of the order *Aplysiomorpha* (or *Anaspidea*), esp. *Aplysia punctata,* having a soft body with an internal shell and two pairs of earlike tentacles.

sea heath *n.* a small tough perennial plant, *Frankenia laevis,* of Eurasian salt marshes, having minute leaves and pink flowers: family *Frankeniaceae.*

sea holly *n.* a European umbelliferous plant, *Eryngium maritimum,* of sandy shores, having spiny bluish-green stems and blue flowers.

sea horse *n.* **1.** any marine teleost fish of the temperate and tropical genus *Hippocampus,* having a bony-plated body, a prehensile tail, and a horselike head and swimming in an upright position: family *Syngnathidae* (pipefishes). **2.** an archaic name for the **walrus.**

sea-island cotton *n.* **1.** a cotton plant, *Gossypium barbadense,* of the Sea Islands, off the SE coast of the U.S., widely cultivated for its fine long fibres. **2.** the fibre of this plant or the material woven from it.

sea kale *n.* a European coastal cruciferous plant, *Crambe maritima,* with broad fleshy leaves and white flowers: cultivated for its edible asparagus-like shoots. Compare **kale.**

seakale beet (ˈsiːˌkeɪl) *n.* another name for **chard.**

sea king *n.* any of the greater Viking pirate chiefs who led raids on the coasts of early medieval Europe.

seal¹ (siːl) *n.* **1.** a device impressed on a piece of wax, moist clay, etc., fixed to a letter, document, etc., as a mark of authentication. **2.** a stamp, ring, etc., engraved with a device to form such an impression. **3.** a substance, esp. wax, so placed over an envelope, document, etc., that it must be broken before the object can be opened or used. **4.** any substance or device used to close or fasten tightly. **5.** a material, such as putty or cement, that is used to close an opening to prevent the passage of air, water, etc. **6.** a small amount of water contained in the trap of a drain to prevent the passage of foul smells. **7.** *Austral. and N.Z.* a road surface consolidated with bitumen, tar, etc. **8.** an agent or device for keeping something hidden or secret. **9.** anything that gives a pledge or confirmation. **10.** a decorative stamp often sold in aid of charity. **11.** *R.C. Church.* Also called: **seal of confession.** the obligation never to reveal anything said by a penitent in confession. **12. set one's seal on** (*or* **to**). **a.** to mark with one's sign or seal. **b.** to endorse. *~vb.* (*tr.*) **13.** to affix a seal to, as proof of authenticity. **14.** to stamp with or as if with a seal. **15.** to approve or authorize. **16.** (sometimes foll. by *up*) to close or secure with or as if with a seal: *to seal one's lips; seal up a letter.* **17.** (foll. by *off*) to enclose (a place) with a fence, wall, etc. **18.** to decide irrevocably. **19.** *Mormon Church.* to make (a marriage or adoption) perpetually binding. **20.** to close tightly so as to render airtight or watertight. **21.** to paint (a porous material) with a nonporous coating. **22.** *Austral. and N.Z.* to consolidate (a road surface) with bitumen, tar, etc. [C13 *seel,* from Old French, from Latin *sigillum* little figure, from *signum* a sign] —**'sealable** *adj.*

seal[2] (siːl) *n.* **1.** any pinniped mammal of the families *Otariidae* (see **eared seal**) and *Phocidae* (see **earless seal**) that are aquatic but come on shore to breed. **2.** any earless seal (family *Phocidae*), esp. the common or harbour seal or the grey seal (*Halichoerus grypus*). **3.** sealskin. *~vb.* **4.** (*intr.*) to hunt for seals. [Old English *seolh;* related to Old Norse *selr,* Old High German *selah,* Old Irish *selige* tortoise] —**'seal-ˌlike** *adj.*

sea lace *n.* a brown seaweed, *Chorda filum,* that grows on stones under sandy bottoms and produces chordlike fronds up to 8.5 metres (28 ft.) long.

sea ladder *n.* a rope ladder, set of steps, etc., by which a boat may be boarded at sea.

sea lamprey *n.* a common anadromous lamprey, *Petromyzon marinus,* a form of which occurs in the Great Lakes of N America and causes great losses of fish.

sea lane *n.* an established route for ships.

sealant ('siːlənt) *n.* **1.** any substance, such as wax, used for sealing documents, bottles, etc. **2.** any of a number of substances used for stopping leaks, waterproofing wood, etc.

sea lavender *n.* any of numerous perennial plants of the plumbaginaceous genus *Limonium,* of temperate salt marshes, having spikes of white, pink, or mauve flowers, several species of which are grown as garden plants. See also **statice.**

sea lawyer *n. Nautical slang.* a contentious seaman.

seal brown *n.* **a.** a dark brown colour often with a yellowish or greyish tinge. **b.** (*as adj.*): *a seal-brown dress.*

sealed (siːld) *vb.* **1.** the past participle of **seal**[1]. *~adj.* **2.** *Austral. and N.Z.* (of a road) having a hard surface; made-up.

sealed-beam *adj.* (esp. of a car headlight) having a lens and prefocused reflector sealed in the lamp vacuum.

sealed book *n.* another term for **closed book.**

sealed move *n. Chess.* the last move before an adjournment, which is written down by the player making it, sealed in an envelope, and kept secret from his opponent until play is resumed.

sealed orders *pl. n.* written instructions that are not to be read until a specified time.

sealed unit *n.* a hard disk that is permanently sealed to prevent damage to the read/write head. See also **Winchester disk.**

sea legs *pl. n. Informal.* **1.** the ability to maintain one's balance on board ship, esp. in rough weather. **2.** the ability to resist seasickness, esp. in rough weather.

sealer[1] ('siːlə) *n.* **1.** a person or thing that seals. **2.** (formerly in Britain and currently in the U.S.) an official who examines the accuracy of weights and measures. **3.** a coating of paint, varnish, etc., applied to a surface to prevent the absorption of subsequent coats.

sealer[2] ('siːlə) *n.* a person or ship occupied in hunting seals.

sealery ('siːlərɪ) *n., pl.* **-eries. 1.** the occupation of hunting seals. **2.** any place where seals are regularly to be found, esp. a seal rookery.

sea letter *n.* **1.** Also called: **passport.** a document issued to a merchant vessel, esp. in wartime, authorizing it to leave a port or proceed freely. **2.** (formerly) a document issued to a vessel in port, describing its cargo, crew, etc.

sea lettuce *n.* any of various green seaweeds of the genus *Ulva,* which have edible wavy translucent fronds.

sea level *n.* the level of the surface of the sea with respect to the land, taken to be the mean level between high and low tide, and used as a standard base for measuring heights and depths.

sea lily *n.* any of various sessile echinoderms, esp. of the genus *Ptilocrinus,* in which the body consists of a long stalk attached to a hard surface and bearing a central disc with delicate radiating arms: class *Crinoidea* (crinoids).

sealing wax *n.* a hard material made of shellac, turpentine, and pigment that softens when heated. It is used for sealing documents, parcels, letters, etc.

sea lion *n.* any of various large eared seals, such as *Zalophus californianus* (**Californian sea lion**), of the N Pacific, often used as a performing animal.

sea loch *n.* another name for **loch** (sense 2).

Sea Lord *n.* (in Britain) either of the two serving naval officers (**First** and **Second Sea Lords**) who sit on the admiralty board of the Ministry of Defence.

seal-point *n.* a popular variety of the Siamese cat, having a dark brown mask, paws, and tail, and a cream body.

seal ring *n.* another term for **signet ring.**

sealskin ('siːlˌskɪn) *n.* **1. a.** the skin or pelt of a fur seal, esp. when dressed with the outer hair removed and the underfur dyed dark brown. **b.** (*as modifier*): *a sealskin coat.* **2.** a garment made of this skin.

Sealyham terrier ('siːlɪəm) *n.* a short-legged wire-haired breed of terrier with a medium-length white coat. Often shortened to **Sealyham.** [named after *Sealyham,* village in S Wales, where it was bred in the 19th cent.]

seam (siːm) *n.* **1.** the line along which pieces of fabric are joined, esp. by stitching. **2.** a ridge or line made by joining two edges. **3.** a stratum of coal, ore, etc. **4. in a good seam.** *Northern English dialect.* doing well, esp. financially. **5.** a linear indentation, such as a wrinkle or scar. **6.** *Surgery.* another name for **suture** (sense 1b). **7.** *Anatomy.* another name for **raphe** (sense 3). **8.** (*modifier*) *Cricket.* of or relating to a style of bowling in which the bowler utilizes the stitched seam round the ball in order to make it swing in flight and after touching the ground: *a seam bowler.* **9. bursting at the seams.** full to overflowing. *~vb.* **10.** (*tr.*) to join or sew together by or as if by a seam. **11.** *U.S.* to make ridges in (knitting) using purl stitch. **12.** to mark or become marked with or as if with a seam or wrinkle. [Old English; related to Old Norse *saumr,* Old High German *soum*] —**'seamless** *adj.* —**'seamlessness** *n.*

seaman ('siːmən) *n., pl.* **-men. 1.** a rating trained in seamanship as opposed to electrical engineering, etc. **2.** a man who serves as a sailor. **3.** a person skilled in seamanship. —**'seaman-ˌlike** *adj.* —**'seamanly** *adj., adv.*

seamanship ('siːmənʃɪp) *n.* skill in and knowledge of the work of navigating, maintaining, and operating a vessel.

seamark ('siːˌmɑːk) *n. Nautical.* an aid to navigation, such as a conspicuous object on a shore used as a guide.

sea mat *n.* a popular name for a **bryozoan.**

seam bowler *or* **seamer** *n. Cricket.* a fast bowler who makes the ball bounce on its seam so that it will change direction. —**seam bowling** *n.*

seamer ('siːmə) *n.* **1.** a person or thing that seams. **2.** another name for **seam bowler.**

sea mew *n.* another name for **mew**[2].

sea mile *n.* an Imperial unit of length, formerly used in navigation, equal to 6000 feet or 1000 fathoms. It is equivalent to 1828.8 metres. Compare **nautical mile.**

sea milkwort *n.* a primulaceous plant, *Glaux maritima,* of estuary mud and seaside rocks of N temperate coasts, having trailing stems and small pink flowers. Also called: **saltwort, black saltwort.** Compare **milkwort.**

seamount ('siːˌmaʊnt) *n.* a submarine mountain rising more than 1000 metres above the surrounding ocean floor. Compare **guyot.**

sea mouse *n.* any of several large polychaete worms of the genus *Aphrodite* and related genera, having a broad flattened body covered dorsally with a dense mat of iridescent hairlike chaetae. [C16: so called because of its appearance]

seamstress ('sɛmstrɪs) *or* (*rarely*) **sempstress** ('sɛmpstrɪs) *n.* a woman who sews and makes clothes, esp. professionally.

seamy ('siːmɪ) *adj.* **seamier, seamiest. 1.** showing the least pleasant aspect; sordid. **2.** (esp. of the inner side of a garment) showing many seams. —**'seaminess** *n.*

Seanad Éireann ('ʃænəð 'eːrən) *n.* (in the Republic of Ireland) the upper chamber of parliament; the Senate. [from Irish, literally: senate of Ireland]

seance *or* **séance** ('seɪɑ̃ns, -ɑːns) *n.* **1.** a meeting at which spiritualists attempt to receive messages from the spirits of the dead. **2.** a meeting of a society. [C19: from French, literally: a sitting, from Old French *seoir* to sit, from Latin *sedēre*]

sea onion *n.* another name for **sea squill.**

sea otter *n.* a large marine otter, *Enhydra lutris,* of N Pacific coasts, formerly hunted for its thick dark brown fur.

sea pen *n.* any of various anthozoan coelenterates of the genus *Pennatula* and related genera, forming fleshy feather-like colonies in warm seas: order *Pennatulacea.*

sea perch *n.* **1.** any of various marine serranid fishes, such as the bass and stone bass, that have an elongated body with a very spiny dorsal fin and occur in all except polar seas. **2.** another name for **surfperch.**

sea pink *n.* another name for **thrift** (the plant).

seaplane ('siːˌpleɪn) *n.* any aircraft that lands on and takes off from water. Also called (esp. U.S.): **hydroplane.**

seaport ('siːˌpɔːt) *n.* **1.** a port or harbour accessible to seagoing vessels. **2.** a town or city located at such a place.

sea power *n.* **1.** a nation that possesses great naval strength. **2.** the naval strength of a country or nation.

sea purse *n.* a tough horny envelope containing fertilized eggs, produced by the female of certain sharks and skates. Also called: **mermaid's purse.**

sea purslane *n.* a small chenopodiaceous shrub, *Halimione portulacoides,* of salt marshes in Eurasia and parts of Africa, having oval leaves and inconspicuous flowers.

SEAQ ('siː,æk) *n.* *acronym for* Stock Exchange Automated Quotation: a computerized system that collects and displays the prices and transactions in securities.

seaquake ('siː,kweɪk) *n.* an agitation and disturbance of the sea caused by an earthquake at the sea bed.

sear[1] (sɪə) *vb.* (*tr.*) **1.** to scorch or burn the surface of. **2.** to brand with a hot iron. **3.** to cause to wither or dry up. **4.** *Rare.* to make callous or unfeeling. ~*n.* **5.** a mark caused by searing. ~*adj.* **6.** *Poetic.* dried up. [Old English *sēarian* to become withered, from *sēar* withered; related to Old High German *sōrēn*, Greek *hauos* dry, Sanskrit *sōsa* drought]

sear[2] (sɪə) *n.* the catch in the lock of a small firearm that holds the hammer or firing pin cocked. [C16: probably from Old French *serre* a clasp, from *serrer* to hold firmly, from Late Latin *serāre* to bolt, from Latin *sera* a bar]

sea ranger *n. Brit.* a senior Guide training in seamanship. U.S. equivalent: **mariner.**

sea raven *n.* a large fish, *Hemitripterus americanus*, of North American Atlantic coastal waters that inflates itself with air when caught: family *Cottidae* (bullheads and sea scorpions).

search (sɜːtʃ) *vb.* **1.** to look through (a place, records, etc.) thoroughly in order to find someone or something. **2.** (*tr.*) to examine (a person) for concealed objects by running one's hands over the clothing. **3.** to look at or examine (something) closely: *to search one's conscience.* **4.** (*tr.*; foll. by *out*) to discover by investigation. **5.** *Surgery.* **a.** to explore (a bodily cavity) during a surgical procedure. **b.** to probe (a wound). **6.** (*tr.*) *Military.* to fire all over (an area). **7.** *Computer technol.* to review (a file) to locate specific information. **8.** *Archaic.* to penetrate. **9. search me.** *Informal.* I don't know. ~*n.* **10.** the act or an instance of searching. **11.** the examination of a vessel by the right of search. **12.** *Computer technol.* **a.** a review of a file to locate specific information. **b.** (*as modifier*): *a search routine.* **13. right of search.** *International law.* the right possessed by the warships of a belligerent state in time of war to board and search merchant vessels to ascertain whether ship or cargo is liable to seizure. [C14: from Old French *cerchier*, from Late Latin *circāre* to go around, from Latin *circus* CIRCLE] —'**searchable** *adj.* —'**searcher** *n.*

searching ('sɜːtʃɪŋ) *adj.* keenly penetrating: *a searching look.* —'**searchingly** *adv.* —'**searchingness** *n.*

searchlight ('sɜːtʃ,laɪt) *n.* **1.** a device, consisting of a light source and a reflecting surface behind it, that projects a powerful beam of light in a particular direction. **2.** the beam of light produced by such a device.

search party *n.* a group of people taking part in an organized search, as for a lost, missing, or wanted person.

search warrant *n.* a written order issued by a justice of the peace authorizing a constable or other officer to enter and search premises for stolen goods, drugs, etc.

sea robin *n.* any of various American gurnards of the genus *Prionotus* and related genera, such as *P. carolinus* (**northern sea robin**).

sea room *n.* sufficient space to manoeuvre a vessel.

sea salt *n.* salt obtained by evaporation of sea water.

seascape ('siː,skeɪp) *n.* a sketch, picture, etc., of the sea.

sea scorpion *n.* any of various northern marine scorpaenoid fishes of the family *Cottidae*, esp. *Taurulus bubalis* (**long-spined sea scorpion**). They have a tapering body and a large head covered with bony plates and spines.

Sea Scout *n.* a Scout belonging to any of a number of Scout troops whose main activities are canoeing, sailing, etc., and who wear sailors' caps as part of their uniform.

sea serpent *n.* a huge legendary creature of the sea resembling a snake or dragon.

seashell ('siː,ʃɛl) *n.* the empty shell of a marine mollusc.

seashore ('siː,ʃɔː) *n.* **1.** land bordering on the sea. **2.** *Law.* the land between the marks of high and low water.

seasick ('siː,sɪk) *adj.* suffering from nausea and dizziness caused by the motion of a ship at sea. —'**sea,sickness** *n.*

seaside ('siː,saɪd) *n.* **a.** any area bordering on the sea, esp. one regarded as a resort. **b.** (*as modifier*): *a seaside hotel.*

sea slater *n.* a large (2.5 cm or 1 in.) nocturnal isopod, *Ligea oceanica*, that lives in cracks in rocks or walls around the high-water mark.

sea slug *n.* any of various shell-less marine gastropod molluscs, esp. those of the order *Nudibranchia.* See **nudibranch.**

sea snail *n.* any small spiny-finned fish of the family *Liparidae*, esp. *Liparis liparis*, of cold seas, having a soft scaleless tadpole-shaped body with the pelvic fins fused into a sucker. Also called: **snailfish.**

sea snake *n.* any venomous snake of the family *Hydrophiidae*, of tropical seas, that swims by means of a laterally compressed oarlike tail.

season ('siːzᵊn) *n.* **1.** one of the four equal periods into which the year is divided by the equinoxes and solstices, resulting from the apparent movement of the sun north and south of the equator during the course of the earth's orbit around it. These periods (spring, summer, autumn, and winter) have their characteristic weather conditions in different regions, and occur at opposite times of the year in the N and S hemispheres. **2.** a period of the year characterized by particular conditions or activities: *the rainy season.* **3.** the period during which any particular species of animal, bird, or fish is legally permitted to be caught or killed: *open season on red deer.* **4.** a period during which a particular entertainment, sport, etc., takes place: *a season at the National Theatre; the football season; the tourist season.* **5.** (esp. formerly) a period of fashionable social events in a particular place: *the London season.* **6.** any definite or indefinite period. **7.** any of the major periods into which the ecclesiastical calendar is divided, such as Lent, Advent, or Easter. **8.** (*sometimes cap.*) Christmas (esp. in the phrases **compliments of the season, Season's greetings**). **9.** a period or time that is considered proper, suitable, or natural for something. **10. in good season.** early enough. **11. in season. a.** (of game) permitted to be caught or killed. **b.** (of fresh food) readily available. **c.** Also: **in** *or* **on heat.** (of some female mammals) sexually receptive. **d.** appropriate. ~*vb.* **12.** (*tr.*) to add herbs, salt, pepper, or spice to (food). **13.** (*tr.*) to add zest to. **14.** (in the preparation of timber) to undergo or cause to undergo drying. **15.** (*tr.; usually passive*) to make or become mature or experienced: *seasoned troops.* **16.** (*tr.*) to mitigate or temper: *to season one's admiration with reticence.* [C13: from Old French *seson*, from Latin *satiō* a sowing, from *serere* to sow] —**seasoned** *adj.* —'**seasoner** *n.* —'**seasonless** *adj.*

seasonable ('siːzənəbᵊl) *adj.* **1.** suitable for the season. **2.** taking place at the appropriate time. —'**seasonableness** *n.* —'**seasonably** *adv.*

seasonal ('siːzənᵊl) *adj.* of, relating to, or occurring at a certain season or certain seasons of the year: *seasonal labour.* —'**seasonally** *adv.* —'**seasonalness** *n.*

seasonal affective disorder *n.* a state of depression sometimes experienced by people in winter, thought to be related to lack of sunlight. Abbrev.: **SAD.**

seasoning ('siːzənɪŋ) *n.* **1.** something that enhances the flavour of food, such as salt or herbs. **2.** another term (not now in technical usage) for **drying** (sense 2).

season ticket *n.* a ticket for a series of events, number of journeys, etc., within a limited time, usually obtained at a reduced rate.

sea spider *n.* a small marine arachnid, having four pairs of legs and somewhat resembling a spider, unusual in that the male carries the eggs once they are laid and cares for the offspring.

sea squill *or* **onion** *n.* a Mediterranean liliaceous plant, *Urginea maritima*, having dense spikes of small white flowers, and yielding a bulb with medicinal properties.

sea squirt *n.* any minute primitive marine animal of the class *Ascidiacea*, most of which are sedentary, having a saclike body with openings through which water enters and leaves. See also **ascidian.**

sea steps *pl. n.* projecting metal bars attached to a ship's side, used for boarding.

sea swallow *n.* a popular name for **tern**[1].

seat (siːt) *n.* **1.** a piece of furniture designed for sitting on, such as a chair or sofa. **2.** the part of a chair, bench, etc., on which one sits. **3.** a place to sit, esp. one that requires a ticket: *I have two seats for the film tonight.* **4.** another name for **buttocks** (see **buttock**). **5.** the part of a garment covering the buttocks. **6.** the part or area serving as the base of an object. **7.** the part or surface on which the base of an object rests. **8.** the place or centre in which something is located: *a seat of government.* **9.** a place of abode, esp. a country mansion that is or was originally the chief residence of a family. **10.** a membership or the right to membership in a legislative or similar body. **11.** *Chiefly Brit.* a parliamentary constituency. **12.** membership in a stock exchange. **13.** the manner in which a rider sits on a horse. **14. on seat.** *W African informal.* (of officials) in the office rather than on tour or on leave: *the agricultural advisor will be on seat tomorrow.* ~*vb.* **15.** (*tr.*) to bring to or place on a seat; cause to sit down. **16.** (*tr.*) to provide with seats. **17.** (*tr.; often passive*) to place or centre: *the ministry is seated in the capital.* **18.** (*tr.*) to set firmly in place. **19.** (*tr.*) to fix or install in a position of power. **20.** (*tr.*) to put a seat on or in (an item of furniture, garment, etc.). **21.** (*intr.*) (of garments) to sag in the area covering the buttocks: *your thin skirt has seated badly.* [Old English *gesete*; related to Old Norse *sæti*, Old High German *gasāzi*, Middle Dutch *gesaete*] —'**seatless** *adj.*

sea tangle *n.* any of various brown seaweeds, esp. any of the genus *Laminaria.*

seat belt *n.* **1.** Also called: **safety belt.** a belt or strap worn in a car to restrain forward motion in the event of a collision. **2.** a similar belt or strap worn in an aircraft at takeoff and landing and in rough weather.

-seater *n.* a settee, vehicle, cinema, etc., having a number of seats as specified: *a forty-seater coach.*

seating ('siːtɪŋ) *n.* **1.** the act of providing with a seat or seats. **2. a.** the provision of seats, as in a theatre, cinema, etc. **b.** (*as modifier*): *seating arrangements.* **3.** material used for covering or making seats.

SEATO ('siːtəʊ) *n. acronym for* Southeast Asia Treaty Organization.

sea trout *n.* **1.** a silvery marine variety of the brown trout that migrates to fresh water to spawn. Compare **brown trout. 2.** any of several marine sciaenid fishes of the genus *Cynoscion*, such as *C. nebulosus* (**spotted sea trout**) and the weakfish, of North American coastal waters.

sea urchin *n.* any echinoderm of the class *Echinoidea*, such as *Echinus esculentus* (**edible sea urchin**), typically having a globular body enclosed in a rigid spiny test and occurring in shallow marine waters.

sea wall *n.* a wall or embankment built to prevent encroachment or erosion by the sea or to serve as a breakwater. —'**sea-ˌwalled** *adj.*

seawan *or* **sewan** ('siːwən) *n.* shell beads, usually unstrung, used by certain North American Indians as money; wampum. [C18: from Narraganset *seawohn* loose]

seaward ('siːwəd) *adv.* **1.** a variant of **seawards.** ~*adj.* **2.** directed or moving towards the sea. **3.** (esp. of a wind) coming from the sea.

seawards ('siːwədz) *or* **seaward** *adv.* towards the sea.

seaware ('siːˌwɛə) *n.* any of numerous large coarse seaweeds, esp. when cast ashore and used as fertilizer. [Old English *sǣwār*, from *sǣ* SEA + *wār* seaweed]

sea wasp *n. Austral.* another name for **box jellyfish.**

seaway ('siːˌweɪ) *n.* **1.** a waterway giving access to an inland port, navigable by ocean-going ships. **2.** a vessel's progress. **3.** a rough or heavy sea. **4.** a route across the sea.

seaweed ('siːˌwiːd) *n.* **1.** any of numerous multicellular marine algae that grow on the seashore, in salt marshes, in brackish water, or submerged in the ocean. **2.** any of certain other plants that grow in or close to the sea.

seaworthy ('siːˌwɜːðɪ) *adj.* in a fit condition or ready for a sea voyage. —'**seaˌworthiness** *n.*

sea wrack *n.* any of various seaweeds found on the shore, esp. any of the larger species.

sebaceous (sɪ'beɪʃəs) *adj.* **1.** of or resembling sebum, fat, or tallow; fatty. **2.** secreting fat or a greasy lubricating substance. [C18: from Late Latin *sēbāceus*, from SEBUM]

sebaceous glands *pl. n.* the small glands in the skin that secrete sebum into hair follicles and onto most of the body surface except the soles of the feet and the palms of the hands.

sebacic acid (sɪ'bæsɪk, -'beɪ-) *n.* another name for **decanedioic acid.**

sebi- *or* **sebo-** *combining form.* fat or fatty matter: *sebiferous.* [from Latin *sēbum* tallow]

sebiferous (sɪ'bɪfərəs) *adj. Biology.* producing or carrying a fatty, oily, or waxlike substance.

seborrhoea *or esp. U.S.* **seborrhea** (ˌsɛbə'rɪə) *n.* a disease of the sebaceous glands characterized by excessive secretion of sebum and its accumulation on the skin surface. —ˌ**sebor'rhoeal,** ˌ**sebor'rhoeic** *or esp. U.S.* ˌ**sebor'rheal,** ˌ**sebor'rheic** *adj.*

sebum ('siːbəm) *n.* the oily secretion of the sebaceous glands that acts as a lubricant for the hair and skin and provides some protection against bacteria. [C19: from New Latin, from Latin: tallow]

sec[1] (sɛk) *adj.* **1.** (of wines) dry. **2.** (of champagne) of medium sweetness. [C19: from French, from Latin *siccus*]

sec[2] (sɛk) *n. Informal.* short for **second**[2]: *wait a sec.*

sec[3] (sɛk) *abbrev. for* secant.

SEC (in the U.S.) *abbrev. for* Securities and Exchange Commission.

sec. *abbrev. for:* **1.** second (of time). **2.** secondary. **3.** secretary. **4.** section. **5.** sector.

SECAM ('siːˌkæm) *n. acronym for* séquentiel couleur à mémoire: a colour-television broadcasting system adopted in France and some other countries.

secant ('siːkənt) *n.* **1.** (of an angle) a trigonometric function that in a right-angled triangle is the ratio of the length of the hypotenuse to that of the adjacent side; the reciprocal of cosine. Abbrev.: **sec. 2.** a line that intersects a curve. [C16: from Latin *secāre* to cut] —'**secantly** *adv.*

secateurs ('sɛkətəz, ˌsɛkə'tɜːz) *pl. n. Chiefly Brit.* a small pair of shears for pruning, having a pair of pivoted handles, sprung so that they are normally open, and usually a single cutting blade that closes against a flat surface. [C19: plural of French *sécateur*, from Latin *secāre* to cut]

secco ('sɛkəʊ) *n., pl.* **-cos. 1.** wall painting done on dried plaster with tempera or pigments ground in limewater. Compare **fresco. 2.** any wall painting other than true fresco. [C19: from Italian: dry, from Latin *siccus*]

secede (sɪ'siːd) *vb. (intr.;* often foll. by *from)* (of a person, section, etc.) to make a formal withdrawal of membership, as from a political alliance, church, organization, etc. [C18: from Latin *sēcēdere* to withdraw, from *sē-* apart + *cēdere* to go] —**se'ceder** *n.*

secern (sɪ'sɜːn) *vb. (tr.) Rare.* **1.** (of a gland or follicle) to secrete. **2.** to distinguish or discriminate. [C17: from Latin *sēcernere* to separate, from *sē-* apart + *cernere* to distinguish] —**se'cernment** *n.*

secession (sɪ'sɛʃən) *n.* **1.** the act of seceding. **2.** *(often cap.) Chiefly U.S.* the withdrawal in 1860–61 of 11 Southern states from the Union to form the Confederacy, precipitating the American Civil War. [C17: from Latin *sēcessiō* a withdrawing, from *sēcēdere* to SECEDE] —**se'cessional** *adj.* —**se'cessionˌism** *n.* —**se'cessionist** *n., adj.*

sech (ʃɛk, sɛtʃ, 'sɛk'eɪtʃ) *n.* hyperbolic secant; a hyperbolic function that is the reciprocal of cosh.

seclude (sɪ'kluːd) *vb. (tr.)* **1.** to remove from contact with others. **2.** to shut off or screen from view. [C15: from Latin *sēclūdere* to shut off, from *sē-* + *claudere* to imprison]

secluded (sɪ'kluːdɪd) *adj.* **1.** kept apart from the company of others: *a secluded life.* **2.** sheltered; private. —**se'cludedly** *adv.* —**se'cludedness** *n.*

seclusion (sɪ'kluːʒən) *n.* **1.** the act of secluding or the state of being secluded. **2.** a secluded place. [C17: from Medieval Latin *sēclūsiō*; see SECLUDE]

seclusive (sɪ'kluːsɪv) *adj.* **1.** tending to seclude. **2.** fond of seclusion. —**se'clusively** *adv.* —**se'clusiveness** *n.*

second[1] ('sɛkənd) *adj. (usually prenominal)* **1. a.** coming directly after the first in numbering or counting order, position, time, etc.; being the ordinal number of *two:* often written 2nd. **b.** *(as n.): the second in line.* **2.** rated, graded, or ranked between the first and third levels. **3.** alternate: *every second Thursday.* **4.** additional; extra: *a second opportunity.* **5.** resembling a person or event from an earlier period of history; unoriginal: *a second Wagner.* **6.** of lower quality; inferior: *belonging to the second class.* **7.** denoting the lowest but one forward ratio of a gearbox in a motor vehicle. **8.** *Music.* **a.** relating to or denoting a musical part, voice, or instrument lower in pitch than another part, voice, or instrument (the first): *the second tenors.* **b.** of or relating to a part, instrument, or instrumentalist regarded as subordinate to another (the first): *the second flute.* **9. at second hand.** by hearsay. ~*n.* **10.** *Brit. education.* an honours degree of the second class, usually further divided into an upper and lower designation. Full term: **second-class honours degree. 11.** the lowest but one forward ratio of a gearbox in a motor vehicle: *he changed into second on the bend.* **12.** (in boxing, duelling, etc.) an attendant who looks after a competitor. **13.** a speech seconding a motion or the person making it. **14.** *Music.* **a.** the interval between one note and another lying next above or below it in the diatonic scale. **b.** one of two notes constituting such an interval in relation to the other. See also **minor** (sense 4), **major** (sense 13), **interval** (sense 5). **15.** *(pl.)* goods of inferior quality. **16.** *(pl.) Informal.* a second helping of food. **17.** *(pl.)* the second course of a meal. ~*vb. (tr.)* **18.** to give aid or backing to. **19.** (in boxing, etc.) to act as second to (a competitor). **20.** to make a speech or otherwise express formal support for (a motion already proposed). ~*adv.* **21.** Also: **secondly.** in the second place. ~*sentence connector.* **22.** Also: **secondly.** as the second point: linking what follows with the previous statement. [C13: via Old French from Latin *secundus* coming next in order, from *sequī* to follow] —'**seconder** *n.*

second[2] ('sɛkənd) *n.* **1. a.** 1/60 of a minute of time. **b.** the basic SI unit of time: the duration of 9 192 631 770 periods of radiation corresponding to the transition between two hyperfine levels of the ground state of caesium-133. Symbol: s **2.** 1/60 of a minute of angle. Symbol: ″ **3.** a very short period of time; moment. [C14: from Old French, from Medieval Latin *pars minūta secunda* the second small part (a minute being the first small part of an hour); see SECOND[1]]

second[3] (sɪ'kɒnd) *vb. (tr.) Brit.* **1.** to transfer (an employee) temporarily to another branch, etc. **2.** *Military.* to transfer (an officer) to another post, often retiring him to a staff or non-regimental position. [C19: from French *en second* in second rank (or position)] —**se'condment** *n.*

Second Advent *n.* a less common term for the **Second Coming.**

secondary ('sɛkəndərɪ, -drɪ) *adj.* **1.** one grade or step after the first; not primary. **2.** derived from or depending on what is primary, original, or first: *a secondary source.* **3.** below the first in rank, importance, etc.; not of major importance. **4.** *(prenominal)* of or relating to the education of young people between the ages of 11 and 18: *secondary education.* **5.** (of the flight feathers of a bird's wing) growing from the ulna. **6. a.** being the part of an electric circuit, such as a transformer or induction coil, in which a current is induced by a changing current in a neighbouring coil: *a secondary coil.* **b.** (of a current) flowing in such a circuit. Compare **primary** (sense 7). **7.** (of an industry) involving the manufacture of goods from raw materials. Compare **primary** (sense 8b), **tertiary** (sense 2). **8.** *Geology.* (of minerals) formed by the alteration of pre-existing minerals. **9.** *Chem.* **a.** (of an organic compound) having a functional group attached to a carbon atom that is attached to one hydrogen atom and two other groups. **b.** (of an amine) having only two organic groups attached to a nitrogen atom; containing the group NH. **c.** (of a salt) derived from a tribasic acid by replacement of two acidic hydrogen atoms with metal atoms or electropositive groups. **10.** *Linguistics.* **a.** derived from a word that is itself a derivation from another word. Thus, *lovably* comes from *lovable* and is a secondary derivative from *love.* **b.** (of a tense in Latin, Greek, or Sanskrit) another word for **historic** (sense 3). ~*n., pl.* **-aries. 11.** a person or thing that is secondary. **12.** a subordinate, deputy, or inferior. **13.** a secondary coil, winding, inductance, or current in an electric circuit. **14.** *Ornithol.* any of the flight feathers that grow from the ulna of a bird's wing. See **primary** (sense 6). **15.** *Astronomy.* a celestial body that orbits around a specified primary body: *the moon is the secondary of the earth.* **16.** *Med.* a cancerous growth in some part of the body remote from the site of the original tumour. **17.** *American football.* **a.** (usually preceded by *the*) cornerbacks and safeties collectively. **b.** their area in the field. **18.** short for **secondary colour.** —'**secondarily** *adv.* —'**secondariness** *n.*

secondary accent *or* **stress** *n. Phonetics.* (in a system of transcribing utterances recognizing three levels of stress) the accent on a syllable of a word or breath group that is weaker than the primary accent but stronger than the lack of stress: *in the word "agriculture" the secondary accent falls on the third syllable.* Compare **primary accent.**

secondary cell *n.* an electric cell that can be recharged and can therefore be used to store electrical energy in the form of chemical energy. See also **accumulator** (sense 1). Compare **primary cell.**

secondary colour *n.* a colour formed by mixing two primary colours. Sometimes shortened to **secondary.**

secondary emission *n. Physics.* the emission of electrons (**secondary electrons**) from a solid as a result of bombardment with a beam of electrons, ions, or metastable atoms: used in electron multipliers.

secondary modern school *n. Brit.* (formerly) a secondary school offering a more technical or practical and less academic education than a grammar school.

secondary picketing *n.* the picketing by strikers of a place of work that supplies goods to or distributes goods from their employer. —**secondary picket** *n.*

secondary processes *pl. n. Psychoanal.* the logical conscious type of mental functioning, guided by external reality. Compare **primary processes.**

secondary qualities *pl. n.* (in empiricist philosophy) those properties of objects that are explained in terms of the primary properties of their parts, such as heat in terms of the motion of molecules.

secondary school *n.* a school for young people, usually between the ages of 11 and 18.

secondary sexual characteristic *n.* any of various features distinguishing individuals of different sex but not directly concerned in reproduction. Examples are the antlers of a stag and the beard of a man.

secondary stress *n.* another term for **secondary accent.**

second ballot *n.* an electoral procedure in which if no candidate emerges as a clear winner in a first ballot, candidates at the bottom of the poll are eliminated and another ballot is held among the remaining candidates.

second banana *n. Slang, chiefly U.S.* **1.** a performer in vaudeville, etc., who plays a role subordinate to another. **2.** any person in a or secondary position to another.

second-best *adj.* **1.** next to the best. **2. come off second best.** *Informal.* to be defeated in competition. ~*n.* **second best.** **3.** an inferior alternative.

second chamber *n.* the upper house of a bicameral legislative assembly.

second childhood *n.* dotage; senility (esp. in the phrases **in his, her,** etc., **second childhood**).

second class *n.* **1.** the class or grade next in value, quality, etc., to the first. ~*adj.* (**second-class** *when prenominal*). **2.** of the class or grade next to the best in quality, etc. **3.** shoddy or inferior. **4.** of or denoting the class of accommodation in a hotel or on a train, etc., lower in quality and price than first class. **5. a.** (in Britain) of or relating to letters that are handled more slowly than first-class letters. **b.** (in the U.S. and Canada) of or relating to mail that consists mainly of newspapers, etc. **6.** *Education.* See **second**[1] (sense 10). ~*adv.* **7.** by second-class mail, transport, etc.

second-class citizen *n.* a person whose rights and opportunities are treated as less important than those of other people in the same society.

Second Coming *or* (*less commonly*) **Advent** *n.* the prophesied return of Christ to earth at the Last Judgment.

second cousin *n.* the child of a first cousin of either of one's parents.

second-degree burn *n. Pathol.* See **burn**[1] (sense 21).

seconde (sɪ'kɒnd; *French* səgɔ̃d) *n.* the second of eight positions from which a parry or attack can be made in fencing. [C18: from French *seconde parade* the second parry]

second estate *n. Rare.* the nobility collectively.

second fiddle *n. Informal.* **1. a.** the second violin in a string quartet or one of the second violins in an orchestra. **b.** the musical part assigned to such an instrument. **2.** a secondary status. **3.** a person who has a secondary status.

second floor *n.* **1.** *Brit.* the storey of a building immediately above the first and two floors up from the ground. U.S. and Canadian term: **third floor.** **2.** the U.S. and Canadian term for **first floor.**

second generation *n.* **1.** offspring of parents born in a given country. ~(*modifier*) **2.** of an improved or refined stage of development in manufacture: *a second-generation robot.*

second growth *n.* natural regrowth of a forest after fire, cutting, or some other disturbance.

second-guess *vb. Informal, chiefly U.S. and Canadian.* **1.** to criticize or evaluate with hindsight. **2.** to attempt to anticipate or predict (a person or thing). —'**second-'guesser** *n.*

second hand *n.* a pointer on the face of a timepiece that indicates the seconds. Compare **hour hand, minute hand.**

second-hand *adj.* **1.** previously owned or used. **2.** not from an original source or experience. **3.** dealing in or selling goods that are not new: *a second-hand car dealer.* ~*adv.* **4.** from a source of previously owned or used goods: *he prefers to buy second-hand.* **5.** not directly: *he got the news second-hand.*

second language *n.* **1.** a language other than the mother tongue that a person or community uses for public communication, esp. in trade, higher education, and administration. **2.** a non-native language officially recognized and adopted in a multilingual country as a means of public communication.

second lieutenant *n.* an officer holding the lowest commissioned rank in the armed forces of certain nations.

secondly ('sɛkəndlɪ) *adv.* another word for **second**[1], usually used to precede the second item in a list of topics.

second man *n.* a person who assists the driver in crewing a locomotive.

second mate *n.* the next in command of a merchant vessel after the first mate. Also called: **second officer.**

second mortgage *n.* a mortgage incurred after a first mortgage and having second claim against the security.

second name *n.* another term for **surname** (sense 1).

second nature *n.* a habit, characteristic, etc., not innate but so long practised or acquired as to seem so.

secondo (sɛ'kɒndəʊ) *n., pl.* **-di** (-diː). the left-hand part in a piano duet. Compare **primo.** [Italian: SECOND[1]]

second person *n.* a grammatical category of pronouns and verbs used when referring to or describing the individual or individuals being addressed.

second-rate *adj.* **1.** not of the highest quality; mediocre. **2.** second in importance, etc. —'**second-'rater** *n.*

second reading *n.* the second presentation of a bill in a legislative assembly, as to approve its general principles (in Britain), or to discuss a committee's report on it (in the U.S.).

second sight *n.* the alleged ability to foresee the future, see actions taking place elsewhere, etc.; clairvoyance. —'**second-'sighted** *adj.* —'**second-'sightedness** *n.*

second-strike *adj.* **1.** (of a nuclear weapon) intended to be used in a counterattack in response to a nuclear attack. **2.** (of a strategy) based on the concept of surviving an initial nuclear attack with enough nuclear weaponry to retaliate.

second string *n.* **1.** *Chiefly Brit.* an alternative course of action, etc., intended to come into use should the first fail (esp. in the phrase **a second string to one's bow**). **2.** *Chiefly U.S. and Canadian.* a substitute or reserve player or team. ~*adj.* **second-string.** *Chiefly U.S. and Canadian.* **3.** *Sport.* **a.** being a substitute player. **b.** being the second-ranked player of a team in an individual sport. **4.** second-rate or inferior.

second thought *n.* (*usually pl.*) a revised opinion or idea on a matter already considered.

second wind (wɪnd) *n.* **1.** the return of the ability to breathe at a normal rate, esp. following a period of exertion. **2.** renewed ability to continue in an effort.

secrecy ('siːkrɪsɪ) *n., pl.* **-cies.** **1.** the state or quality of being secret. **2.** the state of keeping something secret. **3.** the ability or tendency to keep things secret.

secret ('siːkrɪt) *adj.* **1.** kept hidden or separate from the knowledge of others. Related adj.: **cryptic.** **2.** known only to initiates: *a secret password.* **3.** hidden from general view or use: *a secret garden.* **4.** able or tending to keep things private or to oneself. **5.** operating without the knowledge of outsiders: *a secret society.* **6.** outside the normal range of knowledge. ~*n.* **7.** something kept or to be kept hidden. **8.** something unrevealed; mystery. **9.** an underlying explanation, reason, etc., that is not apparent: *the secret of success.* **10.** a method, plan, etc., known only to initiates. **11.** *Liturgy.* a variable prayer, part of the Mass, said by the celebrant after the offertory and before the preface. **12. in the secret.** among the people who know a secret. [C14: via Old French from Latin *sēcrētus* concealed, from *sēcernere* to sift; see SECERN] —'**secretly** *adv.*

secret agent *n.* a person employed in espionage.

secretagogue (sɪ'kriːtəgɒg) *n. Med.* a substance that stimulates secretion. —**se,creta'gogic** *adj.*

secretaire (,sɛkrɪ'tɛə) *n.* an enclosed writing desk, usually having an upper cabinet section. [C19: from French *secrétaire;* see SECRETARY]

secretariat (,sɛkrɪ'tɛərɪət) *n.* **1. a.** an office responsible for the secretarial, clerical, and administrative affairs of a legislative body, executive council, or international organization. **b.** the staff of such an office. **c.** the building or rooms in which such an office is housed. **2.** a body of secretaries. **3.** a secretary's place of work; office. **4.** the position of a secretary. [C19: via French from Medieval Latin *sēcrētāriātus,* from *sēcrētārius* SECRETARY]

secretary ('sɛkrətrɪ) *n., pl.* **-taries.** **1.** a person who handles correspondence, keeps records, and does general clerical work for an individual, organization, etc. **2.** the official manager of the day-to-day business of a society or board. **3.** (in Britain) a senior civil servant who assists a government minister. **4.** (in the U.S. and New Zealand) the head of a government administrative department. **5.** (in Britain) See **secretary of state.** **6.** (in Australia) the head of a public service department. **7.** *Diplomacy.* the assistant to an ambassador or diplomatic minister of certain countries. **8.** another name for **secretaire.** [C14: from Medieval Latin *sēcrētārius,* from Latin *sēcrētum* something hidden; see SECRET] —**secretarial** (,sɛkrɪ'tɛərɪəl) *adj.* —'**secretaryship** *n.*

secretary bird *n.* a large African long-legged diurnal bird of prey, *Sagittarius serpentarius,* having a crest and tail of long

feathers and feeding chiefly on snakes: family *Sagittariidae*, order *Falconiformes* (hawks, falcons, etc.). [C18: so called because its crest resembles a group of quill pens stuck behind the ear]
secretary-general *n., pl.* **secretaries-general.** a chief administrative official, as of the United Nations.
secretary of state *n.* **1.** (in Britain) the head of any of several government departments. **2.** (in the U.S.) the head of the government department in charge of foreign affairs (**State Department**). **3.** (in certain U.S. states) an official with various duties, such as keeping records.
secrete[1] (sɪ'kriːt) *vb.* (of a cell, organ, etc.) to synthesize and release (a secretion). [C18: back formation from SECRETION] —**se'cretor** *n.*
secrete[2] (sɪ'kriːt) *vb. (tr.)* to put in a hiding place. [C18: variant of obsolete *secret* to hide away; see SECRET (n.)]
secretin (sɪ'kriːtɪn) *n.* a peptic hormone secreted by the mucosae of the duodenum and jejunum when food passes from the stomach. [C20: from SECRETION + -IN]
secretion (sɪ'kriːʃən) *n.* **1.** a substance that is released from a cell, esp. a glandular cell, and is synthesized in the cell from simple substances extracted from the blood or a similar fluid. **2.** the process involved in producing and releasing such a substance from the cell. [C17: from Medieval Latin *sēcrētiō*, from Latin: a separation; see SECERN] —**se'cretionary** *adj.*
secretive ('siːkrɪtɪv, sɪ'kriːtɪv) *adj.* **1.** inclined to secrecy; reticent. **2.** another word for **secretory.** —**'secretively** *adv.* —**'secretiveness** *n.*
secretory (sɪ'kriːtərɪ) *adj.* of, relating to, or producing a secretion: *a secretory cell; secretory function.*
secret police *n.* a police force that operates relatively secretly to check subversion or political dissent.
secret service *n.* **1.** a government agency or department that conducts intelligence or counterintelligence operations. **2.** such operations.
secret society *n.* a society or organization that conceals its rites, activities, etc., from those who are not members.
sect (sɛkt) *n.* **1.** a subdivision of a larger religious group (esp. the Christian Church as a whole) the members of which have to some extent diverged from the rest by developing deviating beliefs, practices, etc. **2.** *Often disparaging.* **a.** a schismatic religious body characterized by an attitude of exclusiveness in contrast to the more inclusive religious groups called denominations or Churches. **b.** a religious group regarded as extreme or heretical. **3.** a group of people with a common interest, doctrine, etc.; faction. [C14: from Latin *secta* faction, following, from the stem of *sequī* to follow]
sect. *abbrev. for* section.
-sect *vb. combining form.* to cut or divide, esp. into a specified number of parts: *trisect.* [from Latin *sectus* cut, from *secāre* to cut; see SAW[1]]
sectarian (sɛk'tɛərɪən) *adj.* **1.** of, belonging or relating to, or characteristic of sects or sectaries. **2.** adhering to a particular sect, faction, or doctrine. **3.** narrow-minded, esp. as a result of rigid adherence to a particular sect. ~*n.* **4.** a member of a sect or faction, esp. one who is bigoted in his adherence to its doctrines or in his intolerance towards other sects, etc. —**sec'tarian,ism** *n.*
sectarianize *or* **sectarianise** (sɛk'tɛərɪə,naɪz) *vb. (tr.)* to render sectarian.
sectary ('sɛktərɪ) *n., pl.* **-taries.** **1.** a member of a sect, esp. a person who belongs to a religious sect that is regarded as heretical or schismatic. **2.** a person excessively devoted to a particular sect. **3.** a member of a Nonconformist denomination, esp. one that is small. [C16: from Medieval Latin *sectārius*, from Latin *secta* SECT]
sectile ('sɛktaɪl) *adj.* able to be cut smoothly. [C18: from Latin *sectilis*, from *secāre* to cut] —**sectility** (sɛk'tɪlɪtɪ) *n.*
section ('sɛkʃən) *n.* **1.** a part cut off or separated from the main body of something. **2.** a part or subdivision of a piece of writing, book, etc.: *the sports section of the newspaper.* **3.** one of several component parts. **4.** a distinct part or subdivision of a country, community, etc. **5.** *U.S. and Canadian.* an area one mile square (640 acres) in a public survey, esp. in the western parts of the U.S. and Canada. **6.** *N.Z.* a plot of land for building on, esp. in a suburban area. **7.** the section of a railway track that is maintained by a single crew or is controlled by a particular signal box. **8.** the act or process of cutting or separating by cutting. **9.** a representation of a portion of a building or object exposed when cut by an imaginary vertical plane so as to show its construction and interior. **10.** *Geometry.* **a.** a plane surface formed by cutting through a solid. **b.** the shape or area of such a plane surface. ~Compare **cross section** (sense 1). **11.** *Surgery.* any procedure involving the cutting or division of an organ, structure, or part. **12.** a thin slice of biological tissue, mineral, etc., prepared for examination by microscope. **13.** a segment of an orange or other citrus fruit. **14.** a small military formation, typically comprising two or more squads or aircraft. **15.** *Austral. and N.Z.* a fare stage on a bus, tram, etc. **16.** *Music.* **a.** an extended division of a composition or movement that forms a coherent part of the structure: *the development section.* **b.** a division in an orchestra, band, etc., containing instruments belonging to the same class: *the brass section.* **17.** Also called: **signature, gathering, gather, quire.** a folded printing sheet or sheets ready for gathering and binding. ~*vb. (tr.)* **18.** to cut or divide into sections. **19.** to cut through so as to reveal a section. **20.** (in drawing, esp. mechanical drawing) to shade so as to indicate sections. **21.** *Surgery.* to cut or divide (an organ, structure, or part). **22.** *Brit., Social welfare.* to have (a mentally disturbed person) confined in a mental hospital under an appropriate section of the mental health legislation. [C16: from Latin *sectiō*, from *secāre* to cut]
sectional ('sɛkʃənᵊl) *adj.* **1.** composed of several sections. **2.** of or relating to a section. —**'sectionally** *adv.*
sectionalism ('sɛkʃənə,lɪzəm) *n.* excessive or narrow-minded concern for local or regional interests as opposed to the interests of the whole. —**'sectionalist** *n., adj.*
sectionalize *or* **sectionalise** ('sɛkʃənə,laɪz) *vb. (tr.)* **1.** to render sectional. **2.** to divide into sections, esp. geographically. —**,sectionali'zation** *or* **,sectionali'sation** *n.*
section mark *n. Printing.* a mark (§) inserted into text matter to draw attention to a footnote or to indicate a section of a book, etc. Also called: **section.**
sector ('sɛktə) *n.* **1.** a part or subdivision, esp. of a society or an economy: *the private sector.* **2.** *Geometry.* either portion of a circle included between two radii and an arc. Area: $\frac{1}{2}r^2\theta$, where r is the radius and θ is the central angle subtended by the arc (in radians). **3.** a measuring instrument consisting of two graduated arms hinged at one end. **4.** a part or subdivision of an area of military operations. **5.** *Computer technol.* the smallest addressable portion of the track on a magnetic tape, disk, or drum store. [C16: from Late Latin: sector, from Latin: a cutter, from *secāre* to cut] —**'sectoral** *adj.*
sectorial (sɛk'tɔːrɪəl) *adj.* **1.** of or relating to a sector. **2.** *Zoology.* **a.** adapted for cutting: *the sectorial teeth of carnivores.* **b.** designating a vein in the wing of an insect that links certain branches of the radius vein.
secular ('sɛkjʊlə) *adj.* **1.** of or relating to worldly as opposed to sacred things; temporal. **2.** not concerned with or related to religion. **3.** not within the control of the Church. **4.** (of an education, etc.) **a.** having no particular religious affinities. **b.** not including compulsory religious studies or services. **5.** (of clerics) not bound by religious vows to a monastic or other order. **6.** occurring or appearing once in an age or century. **7.** lasting for a long time. **8.** *Astronomy.* occurring slowly over a long period of time: *the secular perturbation of a planet's orbit.* ~*n.* **9.** a member of the secular clergy. **10.** another word for **layman.** [C13: from Old French *seculer*, from Late Latin *saeculāris* temporal, from Latin: concerning an age, from *saeculum* an age] —**'secularly** *adv.*
secularism ('sɛkjʊlə,rɪzəm) *n.* **1.** *Philosophy.* a doctrine that rejects religion, esp. in ethics. **2.** the attitude that religion should have no place in civil affairs. **3.** the state of being secular. —**'secularist** *n., adj.* —**,secular'istic** *adj.*
secularity (,sɛkjʊ'lærɪtɪ) *n., pl.* **-ties.** **1.** the state or condition of being secular. **2.** interest in or adherence to secular things. **3.** a secular concern or matter.
secularize *or* **secularise** ('sɛkjʊlə,raɪz) *vb. (tr.)* **1.** to change from religious or sacred to secular functions, etc. **2.** to dispense from allegiance to a religious order. **3.** *Law.* to transfer (property) from ecclesiastical to civil possession or use. **4.** *English legal history.* to transfer (an offender) from the jurisdiction of the ecclesiastical courts to that of the civil courts for the imposition of a more severe punishment. —**,seculari'zation** *or* **,seculari'sation** *n.* —**'secular,izer** *or* **'secular,iser** *n.*
secund (sɪ'kʌnd) *adj. Botany.* having or designating parts arranged on or turned to one side of the axis. [C18: from Latin *secundus* following, from *sequī* to follow; see SECOND[1]] —**se'cundly** *adv.*
secundine ('sɛkən,daɪn, -dɪn) *n. Botany.* the inner of two integuments surrounding the ovule of a plant. [C17: from Late Latin *secundīnae*, from Latin *secundus* following + -INE. See SECOND[1]]
secundines ('sɛkən,daɪnz, sɪ'kʌndɪnz) *pl. n. Physiol.* a technical word for **afterbirth.** [C14: from Late Latin *secundīnae*, from Latin *secundus* following; see SECOND[1]]
secure (sɪ'kjʊə) *adj.* **1.** free from danger, damage, etc. **2.** free from fear, care, etc. **3.** in safe custody. **4.** not likely to fail, become loose, etc. **5.** able to be relied on; certain: *a secure investment.* **6.** *Nautical.* stowed away or made inoperative. **7.** *Archaic.* careless or overconfident. ~*vb.* **8.** *(tr.)* to obtain or get possession of: *I will secure some good seats.* **9.** (when *intr.*, often foll. by *against*) to make or become free from danger, fear, etc. **10.** *(tr.)* to make fast or firm; fasten. **11.** (when *intr.*, often foll. by *against*) to make or become certain; guarantee: *this plan will secure your happiness.* **12.** *(tr.)* to assure (a creditor) of payment, as by giving security. **13.** *(tr.)* to make (a military position) safe from attack. **14.** *Nautical.* to make (a vessel or its contents) safe or ready by battening down hatches, stowing gear, etc. **15.** *(tr.) Nautical.* to stow or make inoperative: *to secure the radio.* [C16: from Latin *sēcūrus* free from care, from *sē-* without + *cūra* care] —**se'curable** *adj.* —**se'curely** *adv.* —**se'curement** *n.* —**se'cureness** *n.* —**se'curer** *n.*
secure tenancy *n.* (in Britain) *Social welfare.* the letting of a dwelling by a nonprivate landlord, usually a local council or housing association, under an agreement that allows security of tenure, subletting, improvements made to the property by the

tenant without consequent rent increase, and the right to buy the dwelling at a discount after three years' occupancy.

Securities and Exchange Commission *n.* a U.S. federal agency established in 1934 to supervise and regulate issues of and transactions in securities and to prosecute illegal stock manipulations. Abbrev.: **SEC.**

Securities and Investment Board *n.* a British regulatory body set up in 1986 to oversee London's financial markets, each of which has its own self-regulatory organization. Abbrev.: **SIB.**

securitization *or* **securitisation** (sɪˌkjʊərɪtaɪˈzeɪʃən) *n. Finance.* the use of such securities as eurobonds to enable investors to lend directly to borrowers with a minimum of risk but without using banks as intermediaries.

security (sɪˈkjʊərɪtɪ) *n., pl.* **-ties.** **1.** the state of being secure. **2.** assured freedom from poverty or want: *he needs the security of a permanent job.* **3.** a person or thing that secures, guarantees, etc. **4.** precautions taken to ensure against theft, espionage, etc.: *the security in the government offices was not very good.* **5.** (*often pl.*) **a.** a certificate of creditorship or property carrying the right to receive interest or dividend, such as shares or bonds. **b.** the financial asset represented by such a certificate. **6.** the specific asset that a creditor can claim title to in the event of default on an obligation. **7.** something given or pledged to secure the fulfilment of a promise or obligation. **8.** a person who undertakes to fulfil another person's obligation. **9.** the protection of data to ensure that only authorized personnel have access to computer files. **10.** *Archaic.* carelessness or overconfidence.

security blanket *n.* **1.** a policy of temporary secrecy by police or those in charge of security, in order to protect a person, place, etc., threatened with danger, from further risk. **2.** a baby's blanket, soft toy, etc., to which a baby or young child becomes very attached, using it as a comforter. **3.** *Informal.* anything used or thought of as providing reassurance.

security guard *n.* a person employed to protect buildings, people, etc., and to collect and deliver large sums of money.

security of tenure *n.* (in Britain) the right of a tenant to continue to occupy a dwelling or site unless the landlord obtains a court order for possession of the property or termination of the tenancy agreement.

security risk *n.* a person deemed to be a threat to state security in that he could be open to pressure, have subversive political beliefs, etc.

secy *or* **sec'y** *abbrev. for* secretary.

SED *abbrev. for* Scottish Education Department.

sedan (sɪˈdæn) *n.* **1.** the U.S., Canadian, and N.Z. name for a **saloon** (sense 5). **2.** short for **sedan chair.** [C17: of uncertain origin; compare Latin *sēdēs* seat]

sedan chair *n.* a closed chair for one passenger, carried on poles by two bearers. It was commonly used in the 17th and 18th centuries. Sometimes shortened to **sedan.**

sedate[1] (sɪˈdeɪt) *adj.* **1.** habitually calm and composed in manner; serene. **2.** staid, sober, or decorous. [C17: from Latin *sēdāre* to soothe; related to *sedēre* to sit] —**seˈdately** *adv.* —**seˈdateness** *n.*

sedate[2] (sɪˈdeɪt) *vb.* (*tr.*) to administer a sedative to. [C20: back formation from SEDATIVE]

sedation (sɪˈdeɪʃən) *n.* **1.** a state of calm or reduced nervous activity. **2.** the administration of a sedative.

sedative (ˈsɛdətɪv) *adj.* **1.** having a soothing or calming effect. **2.** of or relating to sedation. ~*n.* **3.** *Med.* a sedative drug or agent. [C15: from Medieval Latin *sēdātīvus*, from Latin *sēdātus* assuaged; see SEDATE[1]]

sedentary (ˈsɛdᵊntərɪ, -trɪ) *adj.* **1.** characterized by or requiring a sitting position: *sedentary work.* **2.** tending to sit about without taking much exercise. **3.** (of animals) moving about very little, usually because of attachment to a rock or other surface. **4.** (of birds) not migratory. [C16: from Latin *sedentārius*, from *sedēre* to sit] —ˈ**sedentarily** *adv.* —ˈ**sedentariness** *n.*

Seder (ˈseɪdə) *n. Judaism.* a ceremonial meal with prescribed ritual reading of the Haggadah observed in Jewish homes on the first night or first two nights of Passover. [from Hebrew *sēdher* order]

sederunt (sɪˈderʊnt, sɪˈdɛərənt) *n.* (in Scotland) **1.** a sitting of an ecclesiastical assembly, court, etc. **2.** the list of persons present. [C17: from Latin *sēdērunt* they were sitting, from *sedēre* to sit]

sedge (sɛdʒ) *n.* **1.** any grasslike cyperaceous plant of the genus *Carex*, typically growing on wet ground and having rhizomes, triangular stems, and minute flowers in spikelets. **2.** any other plant of the family *Cyperaceae.* [Old English *secg*; related to Middle High German *segge* sedge, Old English *sagu* SAW[1]] —ˈ**sedgy** *adj.*

sedge fly *n.* an angler's name for various caddis flies, notably the grey sedge, the murragh, and the cinnamon sedge.

sedge warbler *n.* a European songbird, *Acrocephalus schoenobaenus*, of reed beds and swampy areas, having a streaked brownish plumage with white eye stripes: family *Muscicapidae* (Old World flycatchers, etc.).

sedilia (sɛˈdaɪlɪə) *n.* (*functioning as sing.*) the group of three seats, each called a **sedile** (sɛˈdaɪlɪ), often recessed, on the south side of a sanctuary where the celebrant and ministers sit at certain points during High Mass. [C18: from Latin, from *sedīle* a chair, from *sedēre* to sit]

sediment (ˈsɛdɪmənt) *n.* **1.** matter that settles to the bottom of a liquid. **2.** material that has been deposited from water, ice, or wind. [C16: from Latin *sedimentum* a settling, from *sedēre* to sit] —**sedimentous** (ˌsɛdɪˈmɛntəs) *adj.*

sedimentary (ˌsɛdɪˈmɛntərɪ) *adj.* **1.** characteristic of, resembling, or containing sediment. **2.** (of rocks) formed by the accumulation and consolidation of mineral and organic fragments that have been deposited by water, ice, or wind. Compare **igneous, metamorphic.** —ˌ**sediˈmentarily** *adv.*

sedimentation (ˌsɛdɪmɛnˈteɪʃən) *n.* **1.** the process of formation of sedimentary rocks. **2.** the deposition or production of sediment. **3.** *Chem., biochem.* the process by which large molecules or macroscopic particles are concentrated in a centrifugal field in a centrifuge or ultracentrifuge.

sedimentation tank *n.* a tank into which sewage is passed to allow suspended solid matter to separate out.

sedimentology (ˌsɛdɪmɛnˈtɒlədʒɪ) *n.* the branch of geology concerned with sedimentary rocks and deposits.

sedition (sɪˈdɪʃən) *n.* **1.** speech or behaviour directed against the peace of a state. **2.** an offence that tends to undermine the authority of a state. **3.** an incitement to public disorder. **4.** *Archaic.* revolt. [C14: from Latin *sēditiō* discord, from *sēd-* apart + *itiō* a going, from *īre* to go] —**seˈditionary** *n., adj.*

seditious (sɪˈdɪʃəs) *adj.* **1.** of, like, or causing sedition. **2.** inclined to or taking part in sedition. —**seˈditiously** *adv.* —**seˈditiousness** *n.*

seduce (sɪˈdjuːs) *vb.* (*tr.*) **1.** to persuade to engage in sexual intercourse. **2.** to lead astray, as from the right action. **3.** to win over, attract, or lure. [C15: from Latin *sēdūcere* to lead apart, from *sē-* apart + *dūcere* to lead] —**seˈducible** *or* **seˈduceable** *adj.*

seducer (sɪˈdjuːsə) *or* (*fem.*) **seductress** (sɪˈdʌktrɪs) *n.* a person who entices, allures, or seduces, esp. one who entices another to engage in sexual intercourse.

seduction (sɪˈdʌkʃən) *n.* **1.** the act of seducing or the state of being seduced. **2.** a means of seduction.

seductive (sɪˈdʌktɪv) *adj.* tending to seduce or capable of seducing; enticing; alluring. —**seˈductively** *adv.* —**seˈductiveness** *n.*

sedulous (ˈsɛdjʊləs) *adj.* constant or persistent in use or attention; assiduous; diligent. [C16: from Latin *sēdulus*, of uncertain origin] —**sedulity** (sɪˈdjuːlɪtɪ) *or* ˈ**sedulousness** *n.* —ˈ**sedulously** *adv.*

sedum (ˈsiːdəm) *n.* any crassulaceous rock plant of the genus *Sedum*, having thick fleshy leaves and clusters of white, yellow, or pink flowers. See also **stonecrop, rose-root, orpine.** [C15: from Latin: houseleek]

see[1] (siː) *vb.* **sees, seeing, saw, seen.** **1.** to perceive with the eyes. **2.** (when *tr., may take a clause as object*) to perceive (an idea) mentally; understand: *I explained the problem but he could not see it.* **3.** (*tr.*) to perceive with any or all of the senses: *I hate to see you so unhappy.* **4.** (*tr.; may take a clause as object*) to be aware of in advance; foresee: *I can see what will happen if you don't help.* **5.** (when *tr., may take a clause as object*) to ascertain or find out (a fact); learn: *see who is at the door.* **6.** (when *tr., takes a clause as object;* when *intr.*, foll. by *to*) to make sure (of something) or take care (of something): *see that he gets to bed early.* **7.** (when *tr., may take a clause as object*) to consider, deliberate, or decide: *see if you can come next week.* **8.** (*tr.*) to have experience of; undergo: *he had seen much unhappiness in his life.* **9.** (*tr.*) to allow to be in a specified condition: *I cannot stand by and see a child in pain.* **10.** (*tr.*) to be characterized by: *this period of history has seen much unrest.* **11.** (*tr.*) to meet or pay a visit to: *to see one's solicitor.* **12.** (*tr.*) to receive, esp. as a guest or visitor: *the Prime Minister will see the deputation now.* **13.** (*tr.*) to frequent the company of: *she is seeing a married man.* **14.** (*tr.*) to accompany or escort: *I saw her to the door.* **15.** (*tr.*) to refer to or look up: *for further information see the appendix.* **16.** (in gambling, esp. in poker) to match (another player's bet) or match the bet of (another player) by staking an equal sum. **17. as far as I can see.** to the best of my judgment or understanding. **18. see fit.** (*takes an infinitive*) to consider proper, desirable, etc.: *I don't see fit to allow her to come here.* **19. see (someone) hanged** *or* **damned first.** *Informal.* to refuse absolutely to do what one has been asked. **20. see (someone) right.** *Brit. informal.* to ensure fair treatment of (someone): *if he has cheated you, I'll see you right.* **21. see the light (of day).** See **light**[1] (sense 23). **22. see you, see you later,** *or* **be seeing you.** an expression of farewell. **23. you see.** *Informal.* a parenthetical filler phrase used to make a pause in speaking or add slight emphasis. ~See also **see about, see into, see of, see off, see out, see over, see through.** [Old English *sēon*; related to Old Norse *sjā*, Gothic *saihwan*, Old Saxon *sehan*] —ˈ**seeable** *adj.*

see[2] (siː) *n.* the diocese of a bishop, or the place within it where his cathedral or procathedral is situated. See also **Holy See.** [C13: from Old French *sed*, from Latin *sēdēs* a seat; related to *sedēre* to sit]

see about *vb.* (*intr., prep.*) **1.** to take care of; look after: *he couldn't see about the matter because he was ill.* **2.** to investigate; enquire into: *to see about a new car.*

Seebeck (ˈsiːbɛk) *n. Philately.* **1.** any of a set of stamps issued (1890–99) in Nicaragua, Honduras, Ecuador, and El Salvador and named after Nicholas Frederick Seebeck, who provided them free to the respective governments. **2.** any of the reprints issued later for personal gain by Seebeck.

Seebeck effect ('si:bɛk; *German* 'ze:bɛk) *n.* the phenomenon in which a current is produced in a circuit containing two or more different metals when the junctions between the metals are maintained at different temperatures. Also called: **thermoelectric effect.** Compare **Peltier effect.** [C19: named after Thomas *Seebeck* (1770–1831), German physicist]

seed (si:d) *n.* **1.** *Botany.* a mature fertilized plant ovule, consisting of an embryo and its food store surrounded by a protective seed coat (testa). Related adj.: **seminal. 2.** the small hard seedlike fruit of plants such as wheat. **3.** any propagative part of a plant, such as a tuber, spore, or bulb. **4.** such parts collectively. **5.** the source, beginning, or germ of anything: *the seeds of revolt.* **6.** *Chiefly Bible.* offspring or descendants: *the seed of Abraham.* **7.** an archaic or dialect term for **sperm** or **semen. 8.** *Sport.* a seeded player. **9.** the egg cell or cells of the lobster and certain other animals. **10.** See **seed oyster. 11.** *Chem.* a small crystal added to a supersaturated solution or supercooled liquid to induce crystallization. **12. go** *or* **run to seed. a.** (of plants) to produce and shed seeds. **b.** to lose vigour, usefulness, etc. ~*vb.* **13.** to plant (seeds, grain, etc.) in (soil): *we seeded this field with oats.* **14.** (*intr.*) (of plants) to form or shed seeds. **15.** (*tr.*) to remove the seeds from (fruit, etc.). **16.** (*tr.*) *Chem.* to add a small crystal to (a supersaturated solution or supercooled liquid) in order to cause crystallization. **17.** (*tr.*) to scatter certain substances, such as silver iodide, in (clouds) in order to cause rain. **18.** (*tr.*) **a.** to arrange (the draw of a tournament) so that outstanding teams or players will not meet in the early rounds. **b.** to distribute (players or teams) in this manner. [Old English *sǣd;* related to Old Norse *sāth,* Gothic *sēths,* Old High German *sāt*] —'**seed,like** *adj.* —'**seedless** *adj.*

seedbed ('si:d,bɛd) *n.* **1.** a plot of land in which seeds or seedlings are grown before being transplanted. **2.** the place where something develops: *the seedbed of discontent.*

seedcake ('si:d,keɪk) *n.* a sweet cake flavoured with caraway seeds and lemon rind or essence.

seed capital *n. Finance.* a small amount of capital required to finance the research necessary to produce a business plan for a new company.

seed capsule *or* **seedcase** ('si:d,keɪs) *n.* the part of a fruit enclosing the seeds; pericarp.

seed coat *n.* the nontechnical name for **testa.**

seed coral *n.* small pieces of coral used in jewellery, etc.

seed corn *n.* **1.** the good quality ears or kernels of corn that are used as seed. **2.** assets or investments that are expected to provide profits in the future.

seeder ('si:də) *n.* **1.** a person or thing that seeds. **2.** a device used to remove seeds, as from fruit, etc. **3.** any of various devices for sowing grass seed or grain on the surface of the ground.

seed fern *n.* another name for **pteridosperm.**

seed leaf *n.* the nontechnical name for **cotyledon.**

seedling ('si:dlɪŋ) *n.* a plant produced from a seed, esp. a very young plant.

seed money *n.* money used for the establishment of an enterprise.

seed oyster *n.* a young oyster, esp. a cultivated oyster, ready for transplantation.

seed pearl *n.* a tiny pearl weighing less than a quarter of a grain.

seed plant *n.* the nontechnical name for **spermatophyte.**

seed pod *n.* a carpel or pistil enclosing the seeds of a plant, esp. a flowering plant.

seed potato *n.* a potato tuber used for planting.

seed vessel *n. Botany.* a dry fruit, such as a capsule.

seedy ('si:dɪ) *adj.* **seedier, seediest. 1.** shabby or unseemly in appearance: *seedy clothes.* **2.** (of a plant) at the stage of producing seeds. **3.** *Informal.* not physically fit; sickly. —'**seedily** *adv.* —'**seediness** *n.*

seeing ('si:ɪŋ) *n.* **1.** the sense or faculty of sight; vision. **2.** *Astronomy.* the condition of the atmosphere with respect to observation of stars, planets, etc.: *the bad seeing was due to turbulent air.* ~*conj.* **3.** (*subordinating;* often foll. by *that*) in light of the fact (that); inasmuch as; since.

see into *vb.* (*intr., prep.*) **1.** to examine or investigate. **2.** to discover the true nature of: *I can't see into your thoughts.*

seek (si:k) *vb.* **seeks, seeking, sought.** (*mainly tr.*) **1.** (when *intr.,* often foll. by *for* or *after*) to try to find by searching; look for: *to seek a solution.* **2.** (*also intr.*) to try to obtain or acquire: *to seek happiness.* **3.** to attempt (to do something); try: *I'm only seeking to help.* **4.** (*also intr.*) to enquire about or request (something): *to seek help.* **5.** to go or resort to: *to seek the garden for peace.* **6.** an archaic word for **explore.** [Old English *sēcan;* related to Old Norse *sōkja,* Gothic *sōkjan,* Old High German *suohhen,* Latin *sāgīre* to perceive by scent; see BESEECH] —'**seeker** *n.*

seek out *vb.* (*tr., adv.*) to search hard for a specific person or thing and find: *she sought out her friend from amongst the crowd.*

seel (si:l) *vb.* (*tr.*) **1.** to sew up the eyelids of (a hawk or falcon) so as to render it quiet and tame. **2.** *Obsolete.* to close up the eyes of, esp. by blinding. [C15 *silen,* from Old French *ciller,* from Medieval Latin *ciliāre,* from Latin *cilium* an eyelid]

seem (si:m) *vb.* (may take an infinitive) **1.** (*copula*) to appear to the mind or eye; look: *this seems nice; the car seems to be running well.* **2.** to give the impression of existing; appear to be: *there seems no need for all this nonsense.* **3.** used to diminish the force of a following infinitive to be polite, more noncommittal, etc.: *I can't seem to get through to you.* [C12: perhaps from Old Norse *soma* to beseem, from *sœmr* befitting; related to Old English *sēman* to reconcile; see SAME] —'**seemer** *n.*

seeming ('si:mɪŋ) *adj.* **1.** (*prenominal*) apparent but not actual or genuine: *seeming honesty.* ~*n.* **2.** outward or false appearance. —'**seemingly** *adv.* —'**seemingness** *n.*

seemly ('si:mlɪ) *adj.* **-lier, -liest. 1.** proper or fitting. **2.** *Obsolete.* pleasing or handsome in appearance. ~*adv.* **3.** *Archaic.* properly or decorously. [C13: from Old Norse *sœmiligr,* from *sœmr* befitting] —'**seemliness** *n.*

seen (si:n) *vb.* the past participle of **see**[1].

see of *vb.* (*tr., prep.*) to meet; be in contact with: *we haven't seen much of him since he got married.*

see off *vb.* (*tr., adv.*) **1.** to be present at the departure of (a person making a journey). **2.** *Informal.* to cause to leave or depart, esp. by force.

see out *vb.* (*tr., adv.*) **1.** to remain or endure until the end of: *we'll see the first half of the game out and then leave.* **2.** to be present at the departure of (a person from a house, room, etc.).

see over *or* **round** *vb.* (*intr., prep.*) to inspect by making a tour of: *she said she'd like to see over the house.*

seep (si:p) *vb.* **1.** (*intr.*) to pass gradually or leak through or as if through small openings; ooze. ~*n.* **2.** a small spring or place where water, oil, etc., has oozed through the ground. **3.** another word for **seepage.** [Old English *sīpian;* related to Middle High German *sīfen,* Swedish dialect *sipa*]

seepage ('si:pɪdʒ) *n.* **1.** the act or process of seeping. **2.** liquid or moisture that has seeped.

seer[1] (sɪə) *n.* **1.** a person who can supposedly see into the future; prophet. **2.** a person who professes supernatural powers. **3.** a person who sees. —'**seeress** *fem. n.*

seer[2] (sɪə) *n.* a variant spelling of **ser.**

seersucker ('sɪə,sʌkə) *n.* a light cotton, linen, or other fabric with a crinkled surface and often striped. [C18: from Hindi *śīrśakar,* from Persian *shīr o shakkar,* literally: milk and sugar]

seesaw ('si:,sɔ:) *n.* **1.** a plank balanced in the middle so that two people seated on the ends can ride up and down by pushing on the ground with their feet. **2.** the pastime of riding up and down on a seesaw. **3. a.** an up-and-down or back-and-forth movement. **b.** (*as modifier*): *a seesaw movement.* ~*vb.* **4.** (*intr.*) to move up and down or back and forth in such a manner; oscillate. [C17: reduplication of SAW[1], alluding to the movement from side to side, as in sawing]

seethe (si:ð) *vb.* **1.** (*intr.*) to boil or to foam as if boiling. **2.** (*intr.*) to be in a state of extreme agitation, esp. through anger. **3.** (*tr.*) to soak in liquid. **4.** (*tr.*) *Archaic.* to cook or extract the essence of (a food) by boiling. ~*n.* **5.** the act or state of seething. [Old English *sēothan;* related to Old Norse *sjōtha,* Old High German *siodan* to seethe] —'**seething** *adj.* —'**seethingly** *adv.*

see through *vb.* **1.** (*tr.*) to help out in time of need or trouble: *I know you're short of money, but I'll see you through.* **2.** (*tr., adv.*) to remain with until the end or completion: *let's see the job through.* **3.** (*intr., prep.*) to perceive the true nature of: *I can see through your evasion.* ~*adj.* **see-through. 4.** partly or wholly transparent or translucent, esp. (of clothes) in a titillating way: *a see-through nightie.*

sefer ('sɛfɛr, 'seɪfɛr) *n. Judaism.* **1.** in full: **sefer torah.** the scrolls of the Law. **2.** any book of Hebrew religious literature. [from Hebrew, literally: book]

segment *n.* ('sɛgmənt). **1.** *Maths.* **a.** a part of a line or curve between two points. **b.** a part of a plane or solid figure cut off by an intersecting line, plane, or planes, esp. one between a chord and an arc of a circle. **2.** one of several parts or sections into which an object is divided; portion. **3.** *Zoology.* any of the parts into which the body or appendages of an annelid or arthropod are divided. **4.** *Linguistics.* a speech sound considered in isolation. ~*vb.* (sɛg'mɛnt). **5.** to cut or divide (a whole object) into segments. [C16: from Latin *segmentum,* from *secāre* to cut] —**segmentary** ('sɛgməntərɪ, -trɪ) *adj.*

segmental (sɛg'mɛnt°l) *adj.* **1.** of, like, or having the form of a segment. **2.** divided into segments. **3.** *Linguistics.* of, relating to, or constituting an isolable speech sound. —**seg'mentally** *adv.*

segmentation (,sɛgmɛn'teɪʃən) *n.* **1.** the act or an instance of dividing into segments. **2.** *Embryol.* another name for **cleavage** (sense 4). **3.** *Zoology.* another name for **metamerism** (sense 1).

segmentation cavity *n.* another name for **blastocoel.**

segno ('sɛnjəʊ; *Italian* 'seɲɲo) *n., pl.* **-gni** (-nji:; *Italian* -ɲɲi). *Music.* a sign at the beginning or end of a section directed to be repeated. Symbol: 𝄋 or :S: [Italian: a sign, from Latin *signum*]

segregate ('sɛgrɪ,geɪt) *vb.* **1.** to set or be set apart from others or from the main group. **2.** (*tr.*) to impose segregation on (a racial or minority group). **3.** *Genetics, metallurgy.* to undergo or cause to undergo segregation. [C16: from Latin *sēgregāre,* from *sē-* apart + *grex* a flock] —**segregable** ('sɛgrɪgəb°l) *adj.* —'**segre,gative** *adj.* —'**segre,gator** *n.*

segregation (,sɛgrɪ'geɪʃən) *n.* **1.** the act of segregating or state of being segregated. **2.** *Sociol.* the practice or policy of creating separate facilities within the same society for the use of a minority group. **3.** *Genetics.* the separation at meiosis of the two members of any pair of alleles into separate gametes. See also **Mendel's laws.** **4.** *Metallurgy.* the process in which a component of an alloy or solid solution separates in small regions within the solid or on the solid's surface. —ˌ**segre'gational** *adj.*

segregationist (ˌsɛgrɪ'geɪʃənɪst) *n.* a person who favours, advocates, or practises racial segregation.

segue ('sɛgweɪ) *vb.* **segues, segueing, segued.** (*intr.*) **1.** (often foll. by *into*) to proceed from one section or piece of music to another without a break. **2.** (*imperative*) play on without pause: a musical direction. ~*n.* **3.** the practice or an instance of playing music in this way. [from Italian: follows, from *seguire* to follow, from Latin *sequī*]

seguidilla (ˌsɛgɪ'diːljə) *n.* **1.** a Spanish dance in a fast triple rhythm. **2.** a piece of music composed for or in the rhythm of this dance. **3.** *Prosody.* a stanzaic form consisting of four to seven lines and marked by a characteristic rhythm. [Spanish: a little dance, from *seguida* a dance, from *seguir* to follow, from Latin *sequī*]

seicento (*Italian* sei'tʃɛnto) *n.* the 17th century with reference to Italian art and literature. [Italian, shortened from *mille seicento* one thousand six hundred]

seiche (seɪʃ) *n.* a periodic oscillation of the surface of an enclosed or semienclosed body of water (lake, inland sea, bay, etc.) caused by such phenomena as atmospheric pressure changes, winds, tidal currents, and earthquakes. [C19: from Swiss French, first used to describe rise and fall of water in Lake Geneva; of obscure origin]

Seidlitz powder *or* **powders** ('sɛdlɪts) *n.* a laxative consisting of two powders, tartaric acid and a mixture of sodium bicarbonate and Rochelle salt. Also called: **Rochelle powder.** [C19: named after *Seidlitz,* a village in Bohemia with mineral springs having similar laxative effects]

seif dune (seɪf) *n.* (in deserts, esp. the Sahara) a long ridge of blown sand, often several miles long. [*seif,* from Arabic: sword, from the shape of the dune]

seigneur (sɛ'njɜː; *French* sɛɲœr) *n.* **1.** a feudal lord, esp. in France. **2.** (in French Canada, until 1854) the landlord of an estate that was subdivided among peasants who held their plots by a form of feudal tenure. [C16: from Old French, from Vulgar Latin *senior,* from Latin: an elderly man; see SENIOR] —**sei'gneurial** *adj.*

seigneury ('seɪnjərɪ) *n., pl.* **-gneuries.** the estate of a seigneur.

seignior ('seɪnjə) *n.* **1.** a less common name for a **seigneur. 2.** (in England) the lord of a seigniory. [C14: from Anglo-French *segnour;* see SEIGNEUR] —**seigniorial** (seɪ'njɔːrɪəl) *adj.*

seigniorage ('seɪnjərɪdʒ) *n.* **1.** something claimed by a sovereign or superior as a prerogative, right, or due. **2.** a fee payable to a government for coining bullion. **3.** the difference in value between the cost of bullion and the face value of the coin made from it.

seigniory ('seɪnjərɪ) *or* **signory** ('siːnjərɪ) *n., pl.* **-gniories** *or* **-gnories. 1.** less common names for a **seigneury. 2.** (in England) the fee or manor of a seignior; a feudal domain. **3.** the authority of a seignior or the relationship between him and his tenants. **4.** a body of lords.

seik (siːk) *adj.* a Scot. word for **sick**[1].

seine (seɪn) *n.* **1.** a large fishing net that hangs vertically in the water by means of floats at the top and weights at the bottom. ~*vb.* **2.** to catch (fish) using this net. [Old English *segne,* from Latin *sagēna,* from Greek *sagēnē;* related to Old High German *segina,* Old French *saïne*]

seise *or U.S.* **seize** (siːz) *vb.* to put into legal possession of (property, etc.). [variant of SEIZE] —'**seisable** *adj.* —'**seiser** *n.*

seisin *or U.S.* **seizin** ('siːzɪn) *n. Property law.* feudal possession of an estate in land. [C13: from Old French *seisine,* from *seisir* to SEIZE]

seism ('saɪzəm) *n.* a less common name for **earthquake.** [C19: from Greek *seismos,* from *seiein* to shake]

seismic ('saɪzmɪk) *or (less commonly)* **seismical** ('saɪzmɪk^{ə}l) *adj.* relating to or caused by earthquakes or artificially produced earth tremors. —'**seismically** *adv.*

seismic array *n.* a system of linked seismographs arranged in a regular geometric pattern to increase sensitivity to earthquake detection.

seismicity (saɪz'mɪsɪtɪ) *n.* seismic activity; the phenomenon of earthquake activity or the occurrence of artificially produced earth tremors.

seismic wave *n.* an earth vibration generated by an earthquake or explosion.

seismo- *or before a vowel* **seism-** *combining form.* earthquake: *seismology.* [from Greek *seismos*]

seismograph ('saɪzməˌgrɑːf, -ˌgræf) *n.* an instrument that registers and records the features of earthquakes. A **seismogram** is the record from such an instrument. Also called: **seis'mometer.** —**seismographic** (ˌsaɪzmə'græfɪk) *adj.* —**seismographer** (saɪz'mɒgrəfə) *n.* —**seis'mography** *n.*

seismology (saɪz'mɒlədʒɪ) *n.* the branch of geology concerned with the study of earthquakes. —**seismologic** (ˌsaɪzmə'lɒdʒɪk) *or* ˌ**seismo'logical** *adj.* —ˌ**seismo'logically** *adv.* —**seis'mologist** *n.*

seismoscope ('saɪzməˌskəʊp) *n.* an instrument that indicates the occurrence of an earthquake. Compare **seismograph.** —**seismoscopic** (ˌsaɪzmə'skɒpɪk) *adj.*

sei whale (seɪ) *n.* a rorqual, *Balaenoptera borealis,* hunted for its fine whalebone. [C20: from Norwegian *seihval,* from *sei* coalfish (see SAITHE) + *hval* whale: so called because it follows coalfish in search of food]

seize (siːz) *vb.* (*mainly tr.*) **1.** (also *intr.,* foll. by *on*) to take hold of quickly; grab: *she seized her hat and ran for the bus.* **2.** (sometimes foll. by *on* or *upon*) to grasp mentally, esp. rapidly: *she immediately seized his idea.* **3.** to take mental possession of: *alarm seized the crowd.* **4.** to take possession of rapidly and forcibly: *the thief seized the woman's purse.* **5.** to take legal possession of; take into custody. **6.** to take by force or capture: *the army seized the undefended town.* **7.** to take immediate advantage of: *to seize an opportunity.* **8.** *Nautical.* to bind (two ropes together or a piece of gear to a rope). See also **serve** (sense 19). **9.** (*intr.;* often foll. by *up*) (of mechanical parts) to become jammed, esp. because of excessive heat. **10.** (*passive;* usually foll. by *of*) to be apprised of; conversant with. **11.** the usual U.S. spelling of **seise.** [C13 *saisen,* from Old French *saisir,* from Medieval Latin *sacīre* to position, of Germanic origin; related to Gothic *satjan* to SET] —'**seizable** *adj.*

seizing ('siːzɪŋ) *n. Nautical.* a binding used for holding together two ropes, two spars, etc., esp. by lashing with a separate rope.

seizure ('siːʒə) *n.* **1.** the act or an instance of seizing or the state of being seized. **2.** *Pathol.* a sudden manifestation or recurrence of a disease, such as an epileptic convulsion.

sejant *or* **sejeant** ('siːdʒənt) *adj.* (*usually postpositive*) *Heraldry.* (of a beast) shown seated. [C16: variant of *seant,* from Old French, from *seoir* to sit, from Latin *sedēre*]

sel (sɛl) *n.* a Scot. word for **self.**

selachian (sɪ'leɪkɪən) *adj.* **1.** of, relating to, or belonging to the *Selachii* (or *Elasmobranchii*), a large subclass of cartilaginous fishes including the sharks, rays, dogfish, and skates. ~*n.* **2.** any fish belonging to the subclass *Selachii.* ~Also: **elasmobranch.** [C19: from New Latin *Selachiī,* from Greek *selakhē* a shark; related to Greek *selas* brightness]

selaginella (ˌsɛlədʒɪ'nɛlə) *n.* any club moss of the genus *Selaginella,* having stems covered in small pointed leaves and small spore-bearing cones: family *Selaginellaceae.* See also **resurrection plant.** [C19: from New Latin, diminutive of Latin *selāgō* plant similar to the savin]

selah ('siːlə) *n.* a Hebrew word of unknown meaning occurring in the Old Testament psalms, and thought to be a musical direction. [C16: from Hebrew]

seldom ('sɛldəm) *adv.* not often; rarely. [Old English *seldon;* related to Old Norse *sjāldan,* Old High German *seltan*]

select (sɪ'lɛkt) *vb.* **1.** to choose (someone or something) in preference to another or others. ~*adj. also* **selected. 2.** chosen in preference to another or others. **3.** of particular quality or excellence. **4.** limited as to membership or entry: *a select gathering.* **5.** careful in making a choice. [C16: from Latin *sēligere* to sort, from *sē-* apart + *legere* to choose] —**se'lectly** *adv.* —**se'lectness** *n.*

select committee *n.* (in Britain) a small committee composed of members of parliament, set up by either House of Parliament to investigate and report back on a specified matter of interest.

selectee (sɪˌlɛk'tiː) *n. U.S.* a person who is selected, esp. for military service.

selection (sɪ'lɛkʃən) *n.* **1.** the act or an instance of selecting or the state of being selected. **2.** a thing or number of things that have been selected. **3.** a range from which something may be selected: *this shop has a good selection of clothes.* **4.** *Biology.* the natural or artificial process by which certain organisms or characters are reproduced and perpetuated in the species in preference to others. See also **natural selection. 5.** a contestant in a race chosen as likely to win or come second or third. **6.** *Austral.* **a.** the act of free-selecting. **b.** a tract of land acquired by free-selection.

selective (sɪ'lɛktɪv) *adj.* **1.** of or characterized by selection. **2.** tending to choose carefully or characterized by careful choice. **3.** *Electronics.* occurring at, operating at, or capable of separating out a particular frequency or band of frequencies. —**se'lectively** *adv.* —**se'lectiveness** *n.*

selective attention *n. Psychol.* the process by which a person can selectively pick out one message from a mixture of messages occurring simultaneously.

selective service *n. U.S.* (formerly) compulsory military service under which men were conscripted selectively.

selective synchronization *n.* a sound-recording process that facilitates overdubs by feeding the recorded track to the performer straight from the recording head. Often shortened to **sel-sync.**

selectivity (sɪˌlɛk'tɪvɪtɪ) *n.* **1.** the state or quality of being selective. **2.** the degree to which a radio receiver or other circuit can respond to and separate the frequency of a desired signal from other frequencies by tuning. **3.** the principle that welfare services should go only to those whose need is greatest, as revealed by needs tests, means tests, etc.

selectman (sɪ'lɛktmən) *n., pl.* **-men.** any of the members of the local boards of most New England towns.

selector (sɪ'lɛktə) *n.* **1.** a person or thing that selects. **2.** a device used in automatic telephone switching that connects one circuit with any one of a number of other circuits. **3.** *Brit.* a person who chooses the members of a sports team. **4.** *Austral.* the holder of a tract of land acquired by free-selection.

selenate (ˈsɛlɪˌneɪt) *n.* any salt or ester formed by replacing one or both of the hydrogens of selenic acid with metal ions or organic groups. [C19: from SELENIUM + -ATE[1]]
selenic (sɪˈliːnɪk) *adj.* of or containing selenium, esp. in the hexavalent state.
selenic acid *n.* a colourless crystalline soluble strong dibasic acid analogous to sulphuric acid. Formula: H_2SeO_4.
selenious (sɪˈliːnɪəs) *or* **selenous** (sɪˈliːnəs) *adj.* of or containing selenium in the divalent or tetravalent state.
selenious acid *n.* a white soluble crystalline strong dibasic acid analogous to sulphurous acid. Formula: H_2SeO_3.
selenite (ˈsɛlɪˌnaɪt) *n.* a colourless glassy variety of gypsum. [C17: via Latin from Greek *selēnitēs lithos* moonstone, from *selēnē* moon; so called because it was believed to wax and wane with the moon]
selenium (sɪˈliːnɪəm) *n.* a nonmetallic element that exists in several allotropic forms. It occurs free in volcanic areas and in sulphide ores, esp. pyrite. The common form is a grey crystalline solid that is photoconductive, photovoltaic, and semiconducting: used in photocells, solar cells, and in xerography. Symbol: Se; atomic no.: 34; atomic wt.: 78.96; valency: 2, 4, or 6; relative density: 4.79 (grey); melting pt.: 217°C (grey); boiling pt.: 684.9°C (grey). [C19: from New Latin, from Greek *selēnē* moon; named by analogy to TELLURIUM (from Latin *tellus* earth)]
selenium cell *n.* a photoelectric cell containing a strip of selenium between two metal electrodes.
seleno- *or before a vowel* **selen-** *combining form.* denoting the moon: *selenology.* [from Greek *selēnē* moon]
selenodont (sɪˈliːnəˌdɒnt) *adj.* **1.** (of the teeth of certain mammals) having crescent-shaped ridges on the crowns, as in deer. *~n.* **2.** a mammal with selenodont teeth. [C19: from SELENO- (moon-shaped) + -ODONT]
selenography (ˌsiːlɪˈnɒɡrəfɪ) *n.* the branch of astronomy concerned with the description and mapping of the surface features of the moon. —**selenograph** (sɪˈliːnəʊˌɡrɑːf, -ˌɡræf) *n.* —ˌ**seleˈnographer** *or* ˌ**selleˈnographist** *n.* —**selenographic** (sɪˌliːnəʊˈɡræfɪk) *or* **seˌlenoˈgraphical** *adj.* —**seˌlenoˈgraphically** *adv.*
selenology (ˌsiːlɪˈnɒlədʒɪ) *n.* the branch of astronomy concerned with the moon, its physical characteristics, nature, origin, etc. —**selenological** (sɪˌliːnəʊˈlɒdʒɪkᵊl) *adj.* —ˌ**seleˈnologist** *n.*
selenomorphology (sɪˌliːnəʊmɔːˈfɒlədʒɪ) *n.* the study of the lunar surface and landscape.
Seleucid (sɪˈluːsɪd) *n., pl.* **-cids** *or* **-cidae** (-sɪˌdiː). **1.** a member of a royal dynasty (312–64 B.C.) that at the zenith of its power ruled over an area extending from Thrace to India. *~adj.* **2.** of, relating to, or supporting the Seleucids or their dynasty. —**Seleucidan** (sɪˈluːsɪdᵊn) *adj.*
self (sɛlf) *n., pl.* **selves** (sɛlvz). **1.** the distinct individuality or identity of a person or thing. **2.** a person's usual or typical bodily make-up or personal characteristics: *she looked her old self again.* **3. good self** (*or* **selves**). *Rare.* a polite way of referring to or addressing a person (or persons), used following *your, his, her,* or *their.* **4.** one's own welfare or interests: *he only thinks of self.* **5.** an individual's consciousness of his own identity or being. **6.** *Philosophy.* (usually preceded by *the*) that which is essential to an individual, esp. the mind or soul in Cartesian metaphysics; the ego. **7.** a bird, animal, etc., that is a single colour throughout, esp. a self-coloured pigeon. *~pron.* **8.** *Not standard.* myself, yourself, etc.: *seats for self and wife.* *~adj.* **9.** of the same colour or material: *a dress with a self belt.* See also **self-coloured. 10.** *Obsolete.* the same. [Old English *seolf;* related to Old Norse *själfr,* Gothic *silba,* Old High German *selb*]
self- *combining form.* **1.** of oneself or itself: *self-defence; self-rule.* **2.** by, to, in, due to, for, or from the self: *self-employed; self-inflicted; self-respect.* **3.** automatic or automatically: *self-propelled.*
self-abnegation *n.* the denial of one's own interests in favour of the interests of others. —ˌ**self-ˈabneˌgating** *adj.*
self-absorption *n.* **1.** preoccupation with oneself to the exclusion of others or the outside world. **2.** *Physics.* the process in which some of the radiation emitted by a material is absorbed by the material itself.
self-abuse *n.* **1.** disparagement or misuse of one's own abilities, etc. **2.** a censorious term for **masturbation.**
self-acting *adj.* not requiring an external influence or control to function; automatic. —ˌ**self-ˈaction** *n.*
self-actualization *n. Psychol.* the process of establishing oneself as a whole person, able to develop one's abilities and to understand oneself.
self-addressed *adj.* **1.** addressed for return to the sender. **2.** directed to oneself: *a self-addressed remark.*
self-advocacy *n. Social welfare.* (esp. in the U.S.) **1. a.** the practice of having mentally handicapped people speak for themselves and control their own affairs, rather than having nonhandicapped people automatically assume responsibility for them. See also **normalization. b.** (*as modifier*): *a self-advocacy group.* **2.** the act or condition of representing oneself, either generally in society or in formal proceedings, such as a court.
self-aggrandizement *n.* the act of increasing one's own power, importance, etc., esp. in an aggressive or ruthless manner. —ˌ**self-agˈgranˌdizing** *adj.*
self-annealing *adj. Metallurgy.* denoting certain metals, such as lead, tin, and zinc, that recrystallize at air temperatures and so may be cold-worked without strain-hardening.
self-annihilation *n.* the surrender of the self in mystical contemplation, union with God, etc.
self-appointed *adj.* having assumed authority without the agreement of others: *a self-appointed critic.*
self-assertion *n.* the act or an instance of putting forward one's own opinions, etc., esp. in an aggressive or conceited manner. —ˌ**self-asˈserting** *adj.* —ˌ**self-asˈsertingly** *adv.* —ˌ**self-asˈsertive** *adj.* —ˌ**self-asˈsertively** *adv.* —ˌ**self-asˈsertiveness** *n.*
self-assurance *n.* confidence in the validity, value, etc., of one's own ideas, opinions, etc.
self-assured *adj.* confident of one's own worth. —ˌ**self-asˈsuredly** *adv.* —ˌ**self-asˈsuredness** *n.*
self-catering *adj.* denoting accommodation in which the tenant or visitor provides and prepares his own food.
self-centred *adj.* totally preoccupied with one's own concerns. —ˌ**self-ˈcentredly** *adv.* —ˌ**self-ˈcentredness** *n.*
self-certification *n.* (in Britain) a formal assertion by a worker to his employer that absence from work for up to seven days was due to sickness. From 1982 this replaced a doctor's certificate for the purposes of paying sickness benefit. See also **sick note.**
self-coloured *adj.* **1.** having only a single and uniform colour: *self-coloured flowers; a self-coloured dress.* **2.** (of cloth, material, etc.) **a.** having the natural or original colour. **b.** retaining the colour of the thread before weaving.
self-command *n.* another term for **self-control.**
self-concept *n. Psychol.* the whole set of attitudes, opinions, and cognitions that a person has of himself.
self-confessed *adj.* according to one's own testimony or admission: *a self-confessed liar.*
self-confidence *n.* confidence in one's own powers, judgment, etc. —ˌ**self-ˈconfident** *adj.* —ˌ**self-ˈconfidently** *adv.*
self-conscious *adj.* **1.** unduly aware of oneself as the object of the attention of others; embarrassed. **2.** conscious of one's existence. —ˌ**self-ˈconsciously** *adv.* —ˌ**self-ˈconsciousness** *n.*
self-contained *adj.* **1.** containing within itself all parts necessary for completeness. **2.** (of a flat) having its own kitchen, bathroom, and lavatory not shared by others and usually having its own entrance. **3.** able or tending to keep one's feelings, thoughts, etc., to oneself; reserved. **4.** able to control one's feelings or emotions in the presence of others. —ˌ**self-conˈtainedly** *adv.* —ˌ**self-conˈtainedness** *n.*
self-control *n.* the ability to exercise restraint or control over one's feelings, emotions, reactions, etc. —ˌ**self-conˈtrolled** *adj.* —ˌ**self-conˈtrolling** *adj.*
self-deception *or* **self-deceit** *n.* the act or an instance of deceiving oneself, esp. as to the true nature of one's feelings or motives. —ˌ**self-deˈceptive** *adj.*
self-defence *n.* **1.** the act of defending oneself, one's actions, ideas, etc. **2.** boxing as a means of defending the person (esp. in the phrase **noble art of self-defence**). **3.** *Law.* the right to defend one's person, family, or property against attack or threat of attack by the use of no more force than is reasonable. —ˌ**self-deˈfensive** *adj.*
self-denial *n.* the denial or sacrifice of one's own desires. —ˌ**self-deˈnying** *adj.* —ˌ**self-deˈnyingly** *adv.*
self-determination *n.* **1.** the power or ability to make a decision for oneself without influence from outside. **2.** the right of a

ˌ**self-aˈbandonment** *n.*
ˌ**self-aˈbasement** *n.*
ˌ**self-abˈhorrence** *n.*
ˌ**self-abˈsorbed** *adj.*
ˌ**self-ˌaccuˈsation** *n.*
ˌ**self-acˈcusatory** *adj.*
ˌ**self-adˈhesive** *adj.*
ˌ**self-adˈjusting** *adj.*
ˌ**self-adˈministered** *adj.*
ˌ**self-ˌadmiˈration** *n.*
ˌ**self-adˈvancement** *n.*
ˌ**self-adˈvertisement** *n.*
ˌ**self-aˈligning** *adj.*
ˌ**self-aˈnalysis** *n.*
ˌ**self-apˌpreciˈation** *n.*
ˌ**self-apˈproval** *n.*
ˌ**self-asˈsessment** *n.*
ˌ**self-asˈsumed** *adj.*
ˌ**self-aˈware** *adj.*
ˌ**self-beˈtrayal** *n.*
ˌ**self-ˈcaricaˌture** *n.*
ˌ**self-ˈcensorˌship** *n.*
ˌ**self-ˈcleaning** *adj.*
ˌ**self-ˈclosing** *adj.*
ˌ**self-comˈmitment** *n.*
ˌ**self-comˈmunion** *n.*
ˌ**self-comˈplacent** *adj.*
ˌ**self-conˈceit** *n.*
ˌ**self-conˈcern** *n.*
ˌ**self-ˌcondemˈnation** *n.*
ˌ**self-conˈdemned** *adj.*
ˌ**self-conˌgratuˈlation** *n.*
ˌ**self-conˈsistency** *n.*
ˌ**self-conˈsistent** *adj.*
ˌ**self-ˈconstiˌtuted** *adj.*
ˌ**self-conˈtempt** *n.*
ˌ**self-conˈtent** *n., adj.*
ˌ**self-conˈtented** *adj.*
ˌ**self-conˈtentedly** *adv.*
ˌ**self-ˌcontraˈdicting** *adj.*
ˌ**self-ˌcontraˈdiction** *n.*
ˌ**self-ˌcontraˈdictory** *adj.*
ˌ**self-conˈvicted** *adj.*
ˌ**self-corˈrecting** *adj.*
ˌ**self-creˈated** *adj.*
ˌ**self-ˈcritical** *adj.*
ˌ**self-ˈcritiˌcism** *n.*
ˌ**self-deˈfeating** *adj.*
ˌ**self-ˌdegraˈdation** *n.*
ˌ**self-deˈlusion** *n.*
ˌ**self-deˈpendence** *n.*
ˌ**self-deˈpendent** *adj.*
ˌ**self-desˈpair** *n.*
ˌ**self-deˈstroying** *adj.*
ˌ**self-deˈstruct** *vb.*
ˌ**self-deˈstruction** *n.*

nation or people to determine its own form of government without influence from outside. —ˌ**self-deˈtermined** *adj.* —ˌ**self-deˈtermining** *adj.*

self-discipline *n.* the act of disciplining or power to discipline one's own feelings, desires, etc., esp. with the intention of improving oneself. —ˌ**self-ˈdisciplined** *adj.*

self-dissociation *n. Chem.* the splitting of the molecules of certain highly polar liquids, such as water and liquid ammonia, into ions.

self-drive *adj.* denoting or relating to a hired car that is driven by the hirer.

self-educated *adj.* **1.** educated through one's own efforts without formal instruction. **2.** educated at one's own expense, without financial aid. —ˌ**self-ˌeduˈcation** *n.*

self-effacement *n.* the act of making oneself, one's actions, etc., inconspicuous, esp. because of humility or timidity. —ˌ**self-efˈfacing** *adj.* —ˌ**self-efˈfacingly** *adv.*

self-employed *adj.* earning one's living in one's own business or through freelance work, rather than as the employee of another. —ˌ**self-emˈployment** *n.*

self-esteem *n.* **1.** respect for or a favourable opinion of oneself. **2.** an unduly high opinion of oneself; vanity.

self-evident *adj.* containing its own evidence or proof without need of further demonstration. —ˌ**self-ˈevidence** *n.* —ˌ**self-ˈevidently** *adv.*

self-examination *n.* scrutiny of one's own conduct, motives, desires, etc. —ˌ**self-exˈamining** *adj.*

self-excited *adj.* **1.** (of an electrical machine) having the current for the magnetic field system generated by the machine itself or by an auxiliary machine coupled to it. **2.** (of an oscillator) generating its own energy and depending on resonant circuits for frequency determination.

self-executing *adj.* (of a law, treaty, or clause in a deed or contract, etc.) coming into effect automatically at a specified time, no legislation or other action being needed for enforcement.

self-existent *adj. Philosophy.* existing independently of any other being or cause. —ˌ**self-exˈistence** *n.*

self-explanatory *or* (*less commonly*) **self-explaining** *adj.* understandable without explanation; self-evident.

self-expression *n.* the expression of one's own personality, feelings, etc., as in painting, poetry, or other creative activity. —ˌ**self-exˈpressive** *adj.*

self-feeder *n.* any machine or device capable of automatically supplying materials when and where they are needed, esp. one for making measured quantities of food constantly available to farm livestock.

self-fertilization *n.* fertilization in a plant or animal by the fusion of male and female gametes produced by the same individual. Compare **cross-fertilization** (sense 1). —ˌ**self-ˈfertiˌlized** *adj.* —ˌ**self-ˈfertiˌlizing** *or* ˌ**self-ˈfertile** *adj.*

self-forgetful *adj.* forgetful of one's own interests. —ˌ**self-forˈgetfully** *adv.* —ˌ**self-forˈgetfulness** *n.*

self-government *n.* **1.** the government of a country, nation, etc., by its own people. **2.** the state of being self-controlled. **3.** an archaic term for **self-control.** —ˌ**self-ˈgoverned** *adj.* —ˌ**self-ˈgoverning** *adj.*

selfheal (ˈsɛlfˌhiːl) *n.* **1.** a low-growing European herbaceous plant, *Prunella vulgaris,* with tightly clustered violet-blue flowers and reputedly having healing powers: family *Labiatae* (labiates). **2.** any of several other plants thought to have healing powers. ~Also called: **allheal, heal-all.**

self-help *n.* **1.** the act or state of providing the means to help oneself without relying on the assistance of others. **2. a.** the practice of solving one's problems by joining or forming a group designed to help those suffering from a particular problem. **b.** (*as modifier*): *a self-help group.*

selfhood (ˈsɛlfhʊd) *n.* **1.** *Philosophy.* **a.** the state of having a distinct identity. **b.** the individuality so possessed. **2.** a person's character. **3.** the quality of being egocentric.

self-identity *n.* the conscious recognition of the self as having a unique identity.

self-image *n.* one's own idea of oneself or sense of one's worth.

self-important *adj.* having or showing an unduly high opinion of one's own abilities, importance, etc. —ˌ**self-imˈportantly** *adv.* —ˌ**self-imˈportance** *n.*

self-improvement *n.* the improvement of one's status, position, education, etc., by one's own efforts.

self-induced *adj.* **1.** induced or brought on by oneself or itself. **2.** *Electronics.* produced by self-induction.

self-inductance *n.* the inherent inductance of a circuit, given by the ratio of the electromotive force produced in the circuit by self-induction to the rate of change of current producing it. It is usually expressed in henries. Symbol: *L* Also called: **coefficient of self-induction.**

self-induction *n.* the production of an electromotive force in a circuit when the magnetic flux linked with the circuit changes as a result of a change in current in the same circuit. See also **self-inductance.** Compare **mutual induction.** —ˌ**self-inˈductive** *adj.*

self-indulgent *adj.* tending to indulge one's own desires, etc. —ˌ**self-inˈdulgence** *n.* —ˌ**self-inˈdulgently** *adv.*

self-insurance *n.* the practice of insuring oneself or one's property by accumulating a reserve out of one's income or funds rather than by purchase of an insurance policy.

self-interest *n.* **1.** one's personal interest or advantage. **2.** the act or an instance of pursuing one's own interest. —ˌ**self-ˈinterested** *adj.* —ˌ**self-ˈinterestedness** *n.*

selfish (ˈsɛlfɪʃ) *adj.* **1.** chiefly concerned with one's own interest, advantage, etc., esp. to the total exclusion of the interests of others. **2.** relating to or characterized by self-interest. —ˈ**selfishly** *adv.* —ˈ**selfishness** *n.*

self-justification *n.* the act or an instance of justifying or providing excuses for one's own behaviour, etc.

self-justifying *adj.* **1.** *Printing.* (of a typesetting machine) automatically adjusting the lengths of lines of type. **2.** offering excuses for one's behaviour, often when they are not called for.

self-knowledge *n.* knowledge of one's own character, etc.

selfless (ˈsɛlflɪs) *adj.* having little concern for one's own interests. —ˈ**selflessly** *adv.* —ˈ**selflessness** *n.*

self-liquidating *adj.* **1.** (of a loan, bill of exchange, etc.) used to finance transactions whose proceeds are expected to accrue before the date of redemption or repayment. **2.** (of a business transaction, project, investment, etc.) yielding proceeds sufficient to cover the initial outlay or to finance any recurrent outlays.

self-loading *adj.* (of a firearm) utilizing some of the force of the explosion to eject the empty shell and replace it with a new one. Also: **autoloading.** See also **automatic** (sense 5), **semiautomatic** (sense 2). —ˌ**self-ˈloader** *n.*

self-love *n.* the instinct or tendency to seek one's own well-being or to further one's own interest.

self-made *adj.* **1.** having achieved wealth, status, etc., by one's own efforts. **2.** made by oneself.

self-opinionated *or* (*less commonly*) **self-opinioned** *adj.* **1.** having an unduly high regard for oneself or one's own opinions. **2.** clinging stubbornly to one's own opinions.

self-pity *n.* the act or state of pitying oneself, esp. in an exaggerated or self-indulgent manner. —ˌ**self-ˈpitying** *adj.* —ˌ**self-ˈpityingly** *adv.*

self-pollination *n.* the transfer of pollen from the anthers to the stigma of the same flower. Compare **cross-pollination.** —ˌ**self-ˈpolliˌnated** *adj.*

self-possessed *adj.* having control of one's emotions, etc. —ˌ**self-posˈsessedly** *adv.* —ˌ**self-posˈsession** *n.*

self-preservation *n.* the preservation of oneself from danger or injury, esp. as a basic instinct.

self-pronouncing *adj.* (in a phonetic transcription) of, relating to, or denoting a word that, except for additional diacritic marks of stress, may keep the letters of its ordinary orthography to represent its pronunciation.

self-propelled *adj.* (of a vehicle) provided with its own source of tractive power rather than requiring an external means of propulsion. —ˌ**self-proˈpelling** *adj.*

self-raising *adj.* (of flour) having a raising agent, such as baking powder, already added.

ˌ**self-deˈvelopment** *n.*
ˌ**self-deˈvotion** *n.*
ˌ**self-diˈrected** *adj.*
ˌ**self-disˈtrust** *n.*
ˌ**self-ˈdoubt** *n.*
ˌ**self-ˈdrive** *adj.*
ˌ**self-ˈdriven** *adj.*
ˌ**self-eˈlected** *adj.*
ˌ**self-enˈclosed** *adj.*
ˌ**self-enˈjoyment** *n.*
ˌ**self-enˈrichment** *n.*
ˌ**self-eˈvolved** *adj.*
ˌ**self-exˈertion** *n.*
ˌ**self-exˈpanding** *adj.*
ˌ**self-fiˈnanced** *adj.*
ˌ**self-fiˈnancing** *adj.*
ˌ**self-ˈflattery** *n.*
ˌ**self-ˈfocusing** *adj.*
ˌ**self-fulˈfilling** *adj.*
ˌ**self-fulˈfilment** *n.*
ˌ**self-ˈgenerˌating** *adj.*
ˌ**self-ˈgiving** *adj.*
ˌ**self-ˈhate** *n.*
ˌ**self-ˈhatred** *n.*
ˌ**self-ˈhealing** *n.*
ˌ**self-huˌmiliˈation** *n.*
ˌ**self-hypˈnosis** *n.*
ˌ**self-hypˈnotic** *adj.*
ˌ**self-ˈhypnoˌtism** *n.*
ˌ**self-ˈimage** *n.*
ˌ**self-ˌimmoˈlation** *n.*
ˌ**self-imˈposed** *adj.*
ˌ**self-inˈflicted** *adj.*
ˌ**self-inˈitiˌated** *adj.*
ˌ**self-ˈjudgment** *n.*
ˌ**self-ˈlocking** *adj.*
ˌ**self-ˈmastery** *n.*
ˌ**self-ˈmockery** *n.*
ˌ**self-ˈmotiˌvated** *adj.*
ˌ**self-ˈmoving** *adj.*
ˌ**self-ˈmurder** *n.*
ˌ**self-ˌmutiˈlation** *n.*
ˌ**self-ˈoccuˌpied** *adj.*
ˌ**self-ˈoperˌating** *adj.*
ˌ**self-oˈpinion** *n.*
ˌ**self-orˈdained** *adj.*
ˌ**self-ˈparody** *n.*
ˌ**self-perˈpetuˌating** *adj.*
ˌ**self-ˈportrait** *n.*
ˌ**self-ˈpowered** *adj.*
ˌ**self-ˈpraise** *n.*
ˌ**self-ˌprepaˈration** *n.*
ˌ**self-preˈpared** *adj.*
ˌ**self-proˈclaimed** *adj.*
ˌ**self-proˈduced** *adj.*
ˌ**self-proˈfessed** *adj.*
ˌ**self-proˈmotion** *n.*
ˌ**self-ˈpropaˌgating** *adj.*
ˌ**self-proˈpelled** *adj.*
ˌ**self-proˈpulsion** *n.*
ˌ**self-proˈtecting** *adj.*
ˌ**self-proˈtection** *n.*
ˌ**self-proˈtective** *adj.*
ˌ**self-ˈpunishment** *n.*
ˌ**self-ˈquestioning** *adj.*

self-realization *n.* the realization or fulfilment of one's own potential or abilities.
self-regard *n.* **1.** concern for one's own interest. **2.** proper esteem for oneself.
self-regarding *adj.* **1.** self-centred; egotistical. **2.** *Philosophy.* (of an action) affecting the interests of no-one other than the agent, and hence, according to Mill, immune from moral criticism.
self-regulatory organization *n.* one of five British organizations set up in 1986 under the auspices of the Securities and Investment Board to regulate the activities of London investment markets. Abbrev.: **SRO.**
self-reliance *n.* reliance on one's own abilities, decisions, etc. —ˌ**self-re'liant** *adj.* —ˌ**self-re'liantly** *adv.*
self-renunciation *n.* the renunciation of one's own rights, claims, interest, etc., esp. in favour of those of others. —ˌ**self-re'nunciatory** *adj.*
self-reproach *n.* the act of finding fault with or blaming oneself. —ˌ**self-re'proachful** *adj.* —ˌ**self-re'proachfully** *adv.*
self-respect *n.* a proper sense of one's own dignity and integrity. —ˌ**self-re'spectful** *or* ˌ**self-re'specting** *adj.*
self-restraint *n.* restraint imposed by oneself on one's own feelings, desires, etc.
self-righteous *adj.* having or showing an exaggerated awareness of one's own virtuousness or rights. —ˌ**self-'righteously** *adv.* —ˌ**self-'righteousness** *n.*
self-rule *n.* another term for **self-government** (sense 1).
self-sacrifice *n.* the sacrifice of one's own desires, interest, etc., for the sake of duty or for the well-being of others. —ˌ**self-'sacriˌficing** *adj.* —ˌ**self-'sacriˌficingly** *adv.*
selfsame ('sɛlfˌseɪm) *adj.* (*prenominal*) the very same.
self-satisfied *adj.* having or showing a complacent satisfaction with oneself, one's own actions, behaviour, etc. —ˌ**self-ˌsatis'faction** *n.*
self-sealing *adj.* (esp. of an envelope) designed to become sealed with the application of pressure only.
self-seeking *n.* **1.** the act or an instance of seeking one's own profit or interest, esp. exclusively. ~*adj.* **2.** having or showing an exclusive preoccupation with one's own profit or interest: *a self-seeking attitude.* —ˌ**self-'seeker** *n.*
self-service *adj.* **1.** of or denoting a shop, restaurant, petrol station, etc., where the customer serves himself. ~*n.* **2.** the practice of serving oneself, as in a shop, etc.
self-serving *adj.* habitually seeking one's own advantage, esp. at the expense of others.
self-sown *adj.* (of plants) growing from seed dispersed by any means other than by the agency of man or animals. Also: **self-seeded.**
self-starter *n.* **1.** an electric motor used to start an internal-combustion engine. **2.** the switch that operates this motor. **3.** a person who is strongly motivated and shows initiative, esp. at work.
self-styled *adj.* (*prenominal*) claiming to be of a specified nature, quality, profession, etc.: *a self-styled expert.*
self-sufficient *or* **self-sufficing** *adj.* **1.** able to provide for or support oneself without the help of others. **2.** *Rare.* having undue confidence in oneself, one's own abilities, etc. —ˌ**self-suf'ficiency** *n.* —ˌ**self-suf'ficiently** *adv.*
self-suggestion *n.* another term for **autosuggestion.**
self-supporting *adj.* **1.** able to support or maintain oneself without the help of others. **2.** able to stand up or hold firm without support, props, attachments, etc.
self-tapping *adj.* (of a screw) cutting its own thread when screwed into a plain hole in a metal sheet.
self-tender *n.* an offer by a company to buy back some or all of its shares from its shareholders, esp. as a protection against an unwelcome takeover bid.
self-violence *n. Euphemistic.* suicide.
self-will *n.* stubborn adherence to one's own will, desires, etc., esp. at the expense of others. —ˌ**self-'willed** *adj.*
self-winding *adj.* (of a wrist watch) having a mechanism, activated by the movements of the wearer, in which a rotating or oscillating weight rewinds the mainspring.
Seljuk (sɛl'dʒuːk) *or* **Seljukian** (sɛl'dʒuːkɪən) *n.* **1.** a member of any of the pre-Ottoman Turkish dynasties ruling over large parts of Asia in the 11th, 12th, and 13th centuries A.D. ~*adj.* **2.** of or relating to these dynasties or to their subjects. [C19: from Turkish]
selkie ('sɛlkɪ) *n. Scot.* a variant of **silkie.**
sell (sɛl) *vb.* **sells, selling, sold. 1.** to dispose of or transfer or be disposed of or transferred to a purchaser in exchange for money or other consideration; put or be on sale. **2.** to deal in (objects, property, etc.): *he sells used cars for a living.* **3.** (*tr.*) to give up or surrender for a price or reward: *to sell one's honour.* **4.** to promote or facilitate the sale of (objects, property, etc.): *publicity sells many products.* **5.** to induce or gain acceptance of: *to sell an idea.* **6.** (*intr.*) to be in demand on the market: *these dresses sell well in the spring.* **7.** (*tr.*) *Informal.* to deceive or cheat. **8.** (*tr.*; foll. by *on*) *Chiefly U.S. and Canadian.* to persuade to accept or approve (of): *to sell a buyer on a purchase.* **9. sell down the river.** *Informal.* to betray. **10. sell oneself. a.** to convince someone else of one's potential or worth. **b.** to give up one's moral or spiritual standards, etc. **11. sell short. a.** *Informal.* to disparage or belittle. **b.** *Finance.* to sell securities or goods without owning them in anticipation of buying them before delivery at a lower price. ~*n.* **12.** the act or an instance of selling. Compare **hard sell, soft sell. 13.** *Informal.* **a.** a trick, hoax, or deception. **b.** *Irish.* a great disappointment: *the service in the hotel was a sell.* ~See also **sell off, sell out, sell up.** [Old English *sellan* to lend, deliver; related to Old Norse *selja* to sell, Gothic *saljan* to offer sacrifice, Old High German *sellen* to sell, Latin *cōnsilium* advice] —'**sellable** *adj.*
sell-by date *n.* **1.** a date printed on the packaging of perishable goods, indicating the date after which the goods should not be offered for sale. **2. past one's sell-by date.** *Informal.* beyond one's prime.
seller ('sɛlə) *n.* **1.** a person who sells. **2.** an article to be sold: *this item is always a good seller.* **3.** short for **selling race.**
sellers' market *n.* a market in which demand exceeds supply and sellers can influence prices.
Sellers screw thread ('sɛləz) *n.* a thread form in a system of standard sizes proposed by Sellers in 1884 and later accepted as standard in the U.S.A., having a 60° flank angle with a flat top and foot. [named after William *Sellers* (1824–1905), U.S. engineer]
selling-plater *n.* **1.** a horse that competes, or is only good enough to compete, in a selling race. **2.** a person or thing of limited ability or value.
selling race *or* **plate** *n.* a horse race in which the winner must be offered for sale at auction.
sell off *vb.* (*tr., adv.*) to sell (remaining or unprofitable items), esp. at low prices.
Sellotape ('sɛləˌteɪp) *n.* **1.** *Trademark.* a type of transparent adhesive tape made of cellulose or a similar substance. ~*vb.* (*tr.*) **2.** to seal or stick using adhesive tape.
sell out *vb.* (*adv.*) **1.** Also (chiefly Brit.): **sell up.** to dispose of (supplies of something) completely by selling. **2.** (*tr.*) *Informal.* to betray, esp. through a secret agreement. ~*n.* **sellout. 3.** *Informal.* a performance for which all tickets are sold. **4.** a commercial success. **5.** *Informal.* a betrayal.
sell up *vb.* (*adv.*) *Chiefly Brit.* **1.** (*tr.*) to sell all (the possessions or assets) of (a bankrupt debtor) in order to discharge his debts as far as possible. **2.** (*intr.*) to sell a business.
selsyn ('sɛlsɪn) *n.* another name for **synchro.** [from SEL(F-) + SYN(CHRONOUS)]
sel-sync ('sɛlˌsɪŋk) *n.* short for **selective synchronization.**
Seltzer ('sɛltsə) *n.* **1.** a natural effervescent water with a high content of minerals. **2.** a similar synthetic water, used as a beverage. ~Also called: **Seltzer water.** [C18: changed from German *Selterser Wasser* water from (*Nieder*) *Selters,* district where mineral springs are located, near Wiesbaden, Germany]
selva ('sɛlvə) *n.* **1.** dense equatorial forest, esp. in the Amazon basin, characterized by tall broad-leaved evergreen trees, epiphytes, lianas, etc. **2.** a tract of such forest. [C19: from Spanish and Portuguese, from Latin *silva* forest]
selvage *or* **selvedge** ('sɛlvɪdʒ) *n.* **1.** the finished nonfraying edge of a length of woven fabric. **2.** a similar strip of material allowed in fabricating a metal or plastic article, used esp. for handling components during manufacture. [C15: from SELF + EDGE; related to Dutch *selfegghe,* German *Selbende*] —'**selvaged** *adj.*
selves (sɛlvz) *n.* **a.** the plural of **self. b.** (*in combination*): *ourselves, yourselves, themselves.*
sem. *abbrev. for:* **1.** semester. **2.** semicolon.
Sem. *abbrev. for:* **1.** Seminary. **2.** Semitic.
semanteme (sɪ'mæntiːm) *n.* another word for **sememe** (sense 2).
semantic (sɪ'mæntɪk) *adj.* **1.** of or relating to meaning or arising from distinctions between the meanings of different words or symbols. **2.** of or relating to semantics. **3.** *Logic.* concerned with the interpretation of a formal theory, as when truth tables are given as an account of the sentential connectives. [C19: from Greek *sēmantikos* having significance, from *sēmainein* to signify, from *sēma* a sign] —**se'mantically** *adv.*
semantics (sɪ'mæntɪks) *n.* (*functioning as sing.*) **1.** the branch of linguistics that deals with the study of meaning, changes in meaning, and the principles that govern the relationship between sentences or words and their meanings. **2.** the study of the relationships between signs and symbols and what they represent. **3.** *Logic.* **a.** the study of interpretations of a formal

ˌ**self-re'flection** *n.*
ˌ**self-'registering** *adj.*
ˌ**self-'reguˌlating** *adj.*
ˌ**self-re'peating** *adj.*
ˌ**self-re'pellent** *adj.*
ˌ**self-re'pose** *n.*
ˌ**self-re'pression** *n.*
ˌ**self-re'proof** *n.*
ˌ**self-re'sentment** *n.*
ˌ**self-re'stricted** *adj.*
ˌ**self-re'vealing** *adj.*
ˌ**self-'righting** *adj.*
ˌ**self-'schooled** *adj.*
ˌ**self-sur'render** *n.*
ˌ**self-'taught** *adj.*
ˌ**self-'torment** *n.*
ˌ**self-tor'menting** *adj.*
ˌ**self-'torture** *n.*
ˌ**self-'trained** *adj.*
ˌ**self-ˌtransfor'mation** *n.*
ˌ**self-'treatment** *n.*
ˌ**self-'trust** *n.*
ˌ**self-ˌunder'standing** *n.*
ˌ**self-ˌvindi'cation** *n.*
ˌ**self-'worship** *n.*
ˌ**self-'worth** *n.*

theory. **b.** the study of the relationship between the structure of a theory and its subject matter. **c.** (of a formal theory) the principles that determine the truth or falsehood of sentences within the theory, and the references of its terms. —**se'manticist** *n.*

semantic tableau *n. Logic.* **1.** a method of demonstrating the consistency or otherwise of a set of statements by constructing a diagrammatic representation of all the circumstances that satisfy the set of statements. **2.** the diagram so constructed.

semaphore ('sɛmə,fɔː) *n.* **1.** an apparatus for conveying information by means of visual signals, as with movable arms or railway signals, flags, etc. **2.** a system of signalling by holding a flag in each hand and moving the arms to designated positions to denote each letter of the alphabet. *~vb.* **3.** to signal (information) by means of semaphore. [C19: via French, from Greek *sēma* a signal + -PHORE] —**semaphoric** (,sɛmə'fɒrɪk) *or* **,sema'phorical** *adj.* —**,sema'phorically** *adv.*

semasiology (sɪ,meɪsɪ'ɒlədʒɪ) *n.* another name for **semantics.** [C19: from Greek *sēmasia* meaning, from *sēmainein* to signify + -LOGY] —**semasiological** (sɪ,meɪsɪə'lɒdʒɪkᵊl) *adj.* —**se,masio'logically** *adv.* —**se,masi'ologist** *n.*

sematic (sɪ'mætɪk) *adj.* (of the conspicuous coloration of certain animals) acting as a warning, esp. to potential predators. [C19: from Greek *sēma* a sign]

sematology (,sɛmə'tɒlədʒɪ) *n.* another name for **semantics.** [C19: from Greek *sēmat-, sēma* sign + -LOGY]

semblable ('sɛmbləbᵊl) *Archaic.* *~adj.* **1.** resembling or similar. **2.** apparent rather than real. *~n.* **3.** something that resembles another thing. **4.** a resemblance. [C14: from Old French, from *sembler* to seem; see SEMBLANCE] —**'semblably** *adv.*

semblance ('sɛmbləns) *n.* **1.** outward appearance, esp. without any inner substance or reality. **2.** a resemblance or copy. [C13: from Old French, from *sembler* to seem, from Latin *simulāre* to imitate, from *similis* like]

semé *or* **semée** ('sɛmeɪ; *French* səme) *adj.* (*postpositive*) (usually foll. by *of*) *Heraldry.* dotted (with): *semé of fleurs-de-lis gules.* [C16: from French, literally: sown, from *semer* to sow, from Latin *sēmināre,* from *sēmen* seed]

semei- for words beginning thus, see the more common spelling in **semi-.**

sememe ('siːmiːm) *n. Linguistics.* **1.** the meaning of a morpheme. **2.** Also called: **semanteme.** a minimum unit of meaning in terms of which it is sometimes proposed that meaning in general might be analysed. [C20 (coined in 1933 by L. Bloomfield, U.S. linguist): from Greek *sēma* a sign + -EME]

semen ('siːmɛn) *n.* **1.** the thick whitish fluid containing spermatozoa that is ejaculated from the male genital tract. **2.** another name for **sperm.** [C14: from Latin: seed]

semester (sɪ'mɛstə) *n.* **1.** *Chiefly U.S. and Canadian.* either of two divisions of the academic year, ranging from 15 to 18 weeks. **2.** (in German universities) a session of six months. [C19: via German from Latin *sēmestris* half-yearly, from *sex* six + *mensis* a month] —**se'mestral** *adj.*

semi ('sɛmɪ) *n., pl.* **semis.** *Informal.* **1.** *Brit.* short for **semidetached (house). 2.** short for **semifinal. 3.** *U.S., Canadian, Austral., and N.Z.* short for **semitrailer.**

semi- *prefix.* **1.** half: *semicircle.* Compare **demi-** (sense 1), **hemi-. 2.** partially, partly, not completely, or almost: *semiprofessional; semifinal.* **3.** occurring twice in a specified period of time: *semiannual; semiweekly.* [from Latin; compare Old English *sōm-, sām-* half, Greek *hēmi-*]

semiannual (,sɛmɪ'ænjʊəl) *adj.* **1.** occurring every half-year. **2.** lasting for half a year. —**,semi'annually** *adv.*

semiaquatic (,sɛmɪə'kwætɪk) *adj.* (of organisms, esp. plants) occurring close to the water and sometimes within it.

semiarid (,sɛmɪ'ærɪd) *adj.* characterized by scanty rainfall and scrubby vegetation, often occurring in continental interiors. —**,semia'ridity** *n.*

semiautomatic (,sɛmɪ,ɔːtə'mætɪk) *adj.* **1.** partly automatic. **2.** (of a firearm) self-loading but firing only one shot at each pull of the trigger. Compare **automatic** (sense 5a). *~n.* **3.** a semiautomatic firearm. —**,semi,auto'matically** *adv.*

Semi-Bantu *n.* **1.** a group of languages of W Africa, mainly SE Nigeria and Cameroon, that were not traditionally classed as Bantu but that show certain essential Bantu characteristics. They are now classed with Bantu in the Benue-Congo branch of the Niger-Congo family. *~adj.* **2.** relating to or belonging to this group of languages.

semibold (,sɛmɪ'bəʊld) *Printing.* *~adj.* **1.** denoting a weight of typeface between medium and bold face. **2.** denoting matter printed in this. *~n.* **3.** semibold type.

semibreve ('sɛmɪ,briːv) *n. Music.* a note, now the longest in common use, having a time value that may be divided by any power of 2 to give all other notes. Usual U.S. and Canadian name: **whole note.** See also **breve** (sense 2).

semicentennial (,sɛmɪsɛn'tɛnɪəl) *adj.* **1.** (*prenominal*) of or relating to the 50th anniversary of some event. **2.** occurring once every 50 years. *~n.* **3.** a 50th anniversary.

semicircle ('sɛmɪ,sɜːkᵊl) *n.* **1. a.** one half of a circle. **b.** half the circumference of a circle. **2.** anything having the shape or form of half a circle. —**semicircular** (,sɛmɪ'sɜːkjʊlə) *adj.* —**,semi'circularly** *adv.*

semicircular canal *n. Anatomy.* any of the three looped fluid-filled membranous tubes, at right angles to one another, that comprise the labyrinth of the ear: concerned with the sense of orientation and equilibrium.

semicolon (,sɛmɪ'kəʊlən) *n.* the punctuation mark (;) used to indicate a pause intermediate in value or length between that of a comma and that of a full stop.

semiconductor (,sɛmɪkən'dʌktə) *n.* **1.** a substance, such as germanium or silicon, that has an electrical conductivity that increases with temperature and is intermediate between that of a metal and an insulator. The behaviour may be exhibited by the pure substance (**intrinsic semiconductor**) or as a result of impurities (**extrinsic semiconductor**). **2. a.** a device, such as a transistor or integrated circuit, that depends on the properties of such a substance. **b.** (*as modifier*): *a semiconductor diode.* —**,semicon'duction** *n.*

semiconscious (,sɛmɪ'kɒnʃəs) *adj.* not fully conscious. —**,semi'consciously** *adv.* —**,semi'consciousness** *n.*

semidetached (,sɛmɪdɪ'tætʃt) *adj.* **a.** (of a building) joined to another on one side by a common wall. **b.** (*as n.*): *they live in a suburban semidetached.*

semidiurnal (,sɛmɪdaɪ'ɜːnᵊl) *adj.* **1.** of or continuing during half a day. **2.** occurring every 12 hours.

semidome ('sɛmɪ,dəʊm) *n.* a half-dome, esp. one used to cover a semicircular apse.

semielliptical (,sɛmɪɪ'lɪptɪkᵊl) *adj.* shaped like one half of an ellipse, esp. one divided along the major axis.

semifinal (,sɛmɪ'faɪnᵊl) *n.* **a.** the round before the final in a competition. **b.** (*as modifier*): *the semifinal draw.*

semifinalist (,sɛmɪ'faɪnᵊlɪst) *n.* a player or team taking part in a semifinal.

semifluid (,sɛmɪ'fluːɪd) *adj.* also (*rarely*) **semifluidic** (,sɛmɪfluː'ɪdɪk). **1.** having properties between those of a liquid and those of a solid. *~n.* **2.** a substance that has such properties because of high viscosity: *tar is a semifluid.* ~Also: **semiliquid.** —**,semiflu'idity** *n.*

semiliterate (,sɛmɪ'lɪtərɪt) *adj.* **1.** hardly able to read or write. **2.** able to read but not to write.

semilunar (,sɛmɪ'luːnə) *adj.* shaped like a crescent or half-moon.

semilunar valve *n. Anatomy.* either of two crescent-shaped valves, one in the aorta and one in the pulmonary artery, that prevent regurgitation of blood into the heart.

seminal ('sɛmɪnəl) *adj.* **1.** potentially capable of development. **2.** highly original, influential and important. **3.** rudimentary or unformed. **4.** of or relating to semen: *seminal fluid.* **5.** *Biology.* of or relating to seed. [C14: from Late Latin *sēminālis* belonging to seed, from Latin *sēmen* seed] —**,semi'nality** *n.* —**'seminally** *adv.*

seminar ('sɛmɪ,nɑː) *n.* **1.** a small group of students meeting regularly under the guidance of a tutor, professor, etc., to exchange information, discuss theories, etc. **2.** one such meeting or the place in which it is held. **3.** a higher course for postgraduates. **4.** any group or meeting for holding discussions or exchanging information. [C19: via German from Latin *sēminārium* SEMINARY]

seminarian (,sɛmɪ'nɛərɪən) *n.* a student at a seminary.

seminary ('sɛmɪnərɪ) *n., pl.* **-naries. 1.** an academy for the training of priests, rabbis, etc. **2.** *Rare.* a private secondary school, esp. for girls. **3.** *U.S.* another word for **seminar** (sense 1). **4.** a place where something is grown. [C15: from Latin *sēminārium* a nursery garden, from *sēmen* seed] —**,semi'narial** *adj.*

,semi'abstract *adj.*
,semi'active *adj.*
,semi,agri'cultural *adj.*
,semi'angular *adj.*
,semi'ani,mated *adj.*
,semiau'tonomous *adj.*
,semi'blind *adj.*
,semi'civi,lized *or* **,semi'civi,lised** *adj.*
,semi'classical *adj.*
,semi'classically *adv.*
,semi'coma *n.*
,semi'comical *adj.*
,semi'daily *adj., adv.*
,semi'darkness *n.*
,semi'deaf *adj.*
,semide'pendence *n.*
,semide'pendent *adj.*
,semidi'ameter *n.*
,semidi'rect *adj.*
,semidi'vine *adj.*
,semi,docu'mentary *adj., n., pl.* **-taries.**
,semido'mesti,cated *adj.*
,semido,mesti'cation *n.*
,semi'dry *adj.*
,semie'rect *adj.*
,semiex'posed *adj.*
,semi'fictional *adj.*
,semi'finished *adj.*
,semi'formed *adj.*
,semi'friable *adj.*
,semi'globular *adj.*
,semi'hard *adj.*
,semi-il'literate *adj.*
,semi-,inde'pendence *n.*
,semi-,inde'pendent *adj.*
,semi-in'dustrial *adj.*
,semi-in'dustrial,ized *or* **,semi-in'dustrial,ised** *adj.*
,semi-in'stinctive *adj.*
,semi-in'stinctively *adv.*
,semi-in'toxi,cated *adj.*
,semi-'invalid *n.*
,semi'legendary *adj.*
,semima'ture *adj.*
,semi'monthly *adj., adv.*
,semi'mountainous *adj.*
,semi'mystical *adj.*
,semi'mythical *adj.*

semination (ˌsɛmɪˈneɪʃən) *n. Rare.* the production, dispersal, or sowing of seed. [C16: from Late Latin *sēminātiō*, from Latin *sēmināre* to sow, from *sēmen* seed]

seminiferous (ˌsɛmɪˈnɪfərəs) *adj.* **1.** containing, conveying, or producing semen: *the seminiferous tubules of the testes.* **2.** (of plants) bearing or producing seeds. [C17: from Latin *sēmin-*, *sēmen* seed + connecting vowel + -FEROUS]

Seminole (ˈsɛmɪˌnəʊl) *n.* **1.** (*pl.* **-noles** *or* **-nole**) a member of a North American Indian people consisting of Creeks who moved into Florida in the 18th century. **2.** the language of this people, belonging to the Muskhogean family. [from Creek *simanó-li* fugitive, from American Spanish *cimarrón* runaway]

semiochemical (ˌsɛmɪəʊˈkɛmɪkəl) *n.* a chemical substance produced by an animal and used in communications, such as a pheromone. [C20: *semio-* from Greek *sēmeion* a sign + CHEMICAL]

semiology *or* **semeiology** (ˌsɛmɪˈɒlədʒɪ, ˌsiːmɪ-) *n.* another word for **semiotics.** [C17 (in the sense "sign language"): from Greek *sēmeion* sign + -LOGY] —**semiologic** (ˌsɛmɪəˈlɒdʒɪk, ˌsiːmɪ-), ˌ**semioˈlogical** *or* ˌ**semeioˈlogic,** ˌ**semeioˈlogical** *adj.* —ˌ**semiˈologist** *or* ˌ**semeiˈologist** *n.*

semiotic *or* **semeiotic** (ˌsɛmɪˈɒtɪk, ˌsiːmɪ-) *adj.* **1.** relating to signs and symbols, esp. spoken or written signs. **2.** relating to semiotics. **3.** of, relating to, or resembling the symptoms of disease; symptomatic. [C17: from Greek *sēmeiōtikos* taking note of signs, from *sēmeion* a sign]

semiotician (ˌsɛmɪəˈtɪʃən) *n.* a person who studies semiotics.

semiotics *or* **semeiotics** (ˌsɛmɪˈɒtɪks, ˌsiːmɪ-) *n.* (*functioning as sing.*) **1.** the study of signs and symbols, esp. the relations between written or spoken signs and their referents in the physical world or the world of ideas. See also **semantics, syntactics, pragmatics. 2.** the scientific study of the symptoms of disease; symptomatology. ~Also called: **semiology, semeiology.**

semipalmate (ˌsɛmɪˈpælmɪt) *or* **semipalmated** *adj.* (of the feet of some birds) having the front three toes partly webbed.

semiparasitic (ˌsɛmɪˌpærəˈsɪtɪk) *adj.* **1.** (of plants) obtaining shelter and some food from a host but undergoing photosynthesis at the same time. **2.** (of plants or animals, esp. fungi) usually parasitic but capable of living as a saprophyte. —**semiparasite** (ˌsɛmɪˈpærəsaɪt) *n.* —**semiparasitism** (ˌsɛmɪˈpærəsɪˌtɪzəm) *n.*

semipermeable (ˌsɛmɪˈpɜːmɪəbəl) *adj.* (esp. of a cell membrane) selectively permeable. —ˌ**semiˌpermeaˈbility** *n.*

semipolar bond (ˌsɛmɪˈpəʊlə) *n. Chem.* another name for **coordinate bond.**

semiporcelain (ˌsɛmɪˈpɔːslɪn) *n.* a durable porcellaneous stoneware; stone china.

semipostal (ˌsɛmɪˈpəʊstəl) *adj. Philately, chiefly U.S.* denoting stamps where all or part of the receipts from sale are given to some charitable cause.

semiprecious (ˌsɛmɪˈprɛʃəs) *adj.* (of certain stones) having less value than a precious stone.

semipro (ˈsɛmɪˌprəʊ) *adj., n., pl.* **-pros.** short for **semiprofessional.**

semiprofessional (ˌsɛmɪprəˈfɛʃənəl) *adj.* **1.** (of a person) engaged in an activity or sport part-time but for pay. **2.** (of an activity or sport) engaged in by semiprofessional people. **3.** of or relating to a person whose activities are professional in some respects: *a semiprofessional pianist.* ~*n.* **4.** a semiprofessional person. —ˌ**semiproˈfessionally** *adv.*

semiquaver (ˈsɛmɪˌkweɪvə) *n. Music.* a note having the time value of one-sixteenth of a semibreve. Usual U.S. and Canadian name: **sixteenth note.**

semirigid (ˌsɛmɪˈrɪdʒɪd) *adj.* **1.** partly but not wholly rigid. **2.** (of an airship) maintaining shape by means of a main supporting keel and internal gas pressure.

semiskilled (ˌsɛmɪˈskɪld) *adj.* partly skilled or trained but not sufficiently so to perform specialized work.

semisolid (ˌsɛmɪˈsɒlɪd) *adj.* **1. a.** having a viscosity and rigidity intermediate between that of a solid and a liquid. **b.** partly solid. ~*n.* **2.** a substance in this state.

semisolus (ˌsɛmɪˈsəʊləs) *n.* an advertisement that appears on the same page as another advertisement but not adjacent to it.

semisubmersible rig *n.* (in the oil industry) a type of drilling platform that floats supported by underwater pontoons, with much of its structure below the water line for stability in high winds: usually used only for exploratory drilling for oil or gas. Sometimes shortened to **semisubmersible.**

Semite (ˈsiːmaɪt) *or* (*less commonly*) **Shemite** *n.* **1.** a member of the group of Caucasoid peoples who speak a Semitic language, including the Jews and Arabs as well as the ancient Babylonians, Assyrians, and Phoenicians. **2.** another word for a **Jew.** [C19: from New Latin *sēmīta* descendant of Shem, eldest son of Noah]

Semitic (sɪˈmɪtɪk) *or* (*less commonly*) **Shemitic** *n.* **1.** a branch or subfamily of the Afro-Asiatic family of languages that includes Arabic, Hebrew, Aramaic, Amharic, and such ancient languages as Akkadian and Phoenician. ~*adj.* **2.** denoting, relating to, or belonging to this group of languages. **3.** denoting, belonging to, or characteristic of any of the peoples speaking a Semitic language, esp. the Jews or the Arabs. **4.** another word for **Jewish.**

Semitics (sɪˈmɪtɪks) *n.* (*functioning as sing.*) the study of Semitic languages and culture. —**Semitist** (ˈsɛmɪtɪst) *n.*

Semito-Hamitic (ˈsɛmɪtəʊhæˈmɪtɪk) *n.* **1.** a former name for the **Afro-Asiatic** family of languages. ~*adj.* **2.** denoting or belonging to this family of languages.

semitone (ˈsɛmɪˌtəʊn) *n.* an interval corresponding to a frequency difference of 100 cents as measured in the system of equal temperament, and denoting the pitch difference between certain adjacent degrees of the diatonic scale (**diatonic semitone**) or between one note and its sharpened or flattened equivalent (**chromatic semitone**); minor second. Also called (U.S. and Canadian): **half step.** Compare **whole tone.** —**semitonic** (ˌsɛmɪˈtɒnɪk) *adj.* —ˌ**semiˈtonally** *adv.*

semitrailer (ˌsɛmɪˈtreɪlə) *n.* a type of trailer or articulated lorry that has wheels only at the rear, the front end being supported by the towing vehicle.

semitropical (ˌsɛmɪˈtrɒpɪkəl) *adj.* **1.** partly tropical. **2.** another word for **subtropical.** —ˌ**semiˈtropics** *pl. n.*

semivitreous (ˌsɛmɪˈvɪtrɪəs) *adj.* **1.** partially vitreous. **2.** *Ceramics.* not wholly impervious to liquid.

semivocal (ˌsɛmɪˈvəʊkəl) *or* **semivocalic** (ˌsɛmɪvəʊˈkælɪk) *adj.* of or relating to a semivowel.

semivowel (ˈsɛmɪˌvaʊəl) *n. Phonetics.* **1.** a vowel-like sound that acts like a consonant, in that it serves the same function in a syllable carrying the same amount of prominence as a consonant relative to a true vowel, the nucleus of the syllable. In English and many other languages the chief semivowels are (w) in *well* and (j), represented as *y*, in *yell.* **2.** a frictionless continuant classified as one of the liquids; (l) or (r). ~Also called: **glide.**

semiyearly (ˌsɛmɪˈjɪəlɪ) *adj.* another word for **semiannual.**

semmit (ˈsɪmɪt, ˈsɛm-) *n. Scot.* a vest. [C15: of unknown origin]

semolina (ˌsɛməˈliːnə) *n.* the large hard grains of wheat left after flour has been bolted, used for puddings, soups, etc. [C18: from Italian *semolino*, diminutive of *semola* bran, from Latin *simila* very fine wheat flour]

semper fidelis *Latin.* (ˈsɛmpə fɪˈdeɪlɪs) always faithful.

semper paratus *Latin.* (ˈsɛmpə pəˈrɑːtəs) always prepared.

sempervivum (ˌsɛmpəˈvaɪvəm) *n.* See **houseleek.** [New Latin, from Latin *sempervivus* ever-living, from *semper* always + *vivere* to live]

sempiternal (ˌsɛmpɪˈtɜːnəl) *adj. Literary.* everlasting; eternal. [C15: from Old French *sempiternel*, from Late Latin *sempiternālis*, from Latin *sempiternus*, from *semper* always + *aeternus* ETERNAL] —ˌ**sempiˈternally** *adv.* —**sempiternity** (ˌsɛmpɪˈtɜːnɪtɪ) *n.*

semplice (ˈsɛmplɪtʃɪ) *adj., adv. Music.* to be performed in a simple manner. [Italian: simple, from Latin *simplex*]

sempre (ˈsɛmprɪ) *adv. Music.* (preceding a tempo or dynamic marking) always; consistently. It is used to indicate that a specified volume, tempo, etc., is to be sustained throughout a piece or passage. [Italian: always, from Latin *semper*]

sempstress (ˈsɛmpstrɪs) *n.* a rare word for **seamstress.**

Semtex (ˈsɛmtɛks) *n. Trademark.* a pliable plastic explosive.

sen (sɛn) *n., pl.* **sen.** a monetary unit of Indonesia, Kampuchea, and formerly of Japan (where it is still used as a unit of account), worth one hundredth of the rupiah, the riel, and the yen respectively. [C19: ultimately from Chinese *ch'ien* coin]

SEN (in Britain) *abbrev. for:* **1.** (formerly) State Enrolled Nurse. **2.** special educational needs: needs arising from any of a wide range of problems that affect a pupil's normal educational development and for which special provisions are made.

Sen. *or* **sen.** *abbrev. for:* **1.** senate. **2.** senator. **3.** senior.

sena (ˈseɪnɑː) *n.* (in India) the army: used in the names of certain paramilitary political organizations. [Hindi]

senarmontite (ˌsɛnɑːˈmɒntaɪt) *n.* a white or grey mineral consisting of antimony trioxide in cubic crystalline form. Formula: Sb_2O_3. [C19: named after Henri de *Sénarmont* (died 1862), French mineralogist]

ˌ**semiˈnormal** *adj.*
ˌ**semiˈnude** *adj.*
ˌ**semiˈnudity** *n.*
ˌ**semiofˈficial** *adj.*
ˌ**semioˈpaque** *adj.*
ˌ**semiˈorganˌized** *or* ˌ**semiˈorganˌised** *adj.*
ˌ**semiˌoriˈental** *adj.*
ˌ**semiˈpagan** *n., adj.*
ˌ**semipaˈralysis** *n.*
ˌ**semiˌparaˈlytic** *n., adj.*
ˌ**semiˈpermanent** *adj.*
ˌ**semiˈpetriˌfied** *adj.*
ˌ**semiˈplastic** *adj.*
ˌ**semipoˈlitical** *adj.*
ˌ**semiˈporous** *adj.*
ˌ**semiˈprimitive** *adj.*
ˌ**semiˈprivate** *adj.*
ˌ**semiˈpublic** *adj.*
ˌ**semiˈpurposive** *adj.*
ˌ**semireˈbellious** *adj.*
ˌ**semireˈfined** *adj.*
ˌ**semiˈresoˌlute** *adj.*
ˌ**semireˌspectaˈbility** *n.*
ˌ**semireˈspectable** *adj.*
ˌ**semireˈtired** *adj.*
ˌ**semireˈtirement** *n.*
ˌ**semiˈround** *adj.*
ˌ**semiˈrural** *adj.*
ˌ**semiˈsacred** *adj.*
ˌ**semisaˈtirical** *adj.*
ˌ**semisaˈtirically** *adv.*
ˌ**semiˈserious** *adj.*
ˌ**semiˌsocialˈistic** *adj.*
ˌ**semiˈsoft** *adj.*
ˌ**semisubˈurban** *adj.*
ˌ**semisucˈcessful** *adj.*
ˌ**semiˈsweet** *adj.*
ˌ**semitraˈditional** *adj.*
ˌ**semiˈtrained** *adj.*
ˌ**semitransˈlucent** *adj.*
ˌ**semitransˈparent** *adj.*
ˌ**semiˈtruthful** *adj.*
ˌ**semiˈurban** *adj.*
ˌ**semiˈvoluntary** *adj.*
ˌ**semiˈweekly** *adj., adv.*

senary ('siːnərɪ) *adj.* of or relating to the number six; having six parts or units. [C17: from Latin *sēnārius*, from *sēnī* six each, from *sex* SIX]

senate ('sɛnɪt) *n.* **1.** any legislative or governing body considered to resemble a Senate. **2.** the main governing body at some colleges and universities. [C13: from Latin *senātus* council of the elders, from *senex* an old man]

Senate ('sɛnɪt) *n.* (*sometimes not cap.*) **1.** the upper chamber of the legislatures of the U.S., Canada, Australia, and many other countries. **2.** the legislative council of ancient Rome. **3.** the ruling body of certain free cities in medieval and modern Europe.

senator ('sɛnətə) *n.* **1.** (*often cap.*) a member of a Senate or senate. **2.** any legislator or statesman.

senatorial (ˌsɛnə'tɔːrɪəl) *adj.* **1.** of, relating to, befitting, or characteristic of a senator. **2.** composed of senators. **3.** *Chiefly U.S.* electing or entitled to representation by a senator: *senatorial districts.* —ˌ**sena'torially** *adv.*

senatus consultum *Latin.* (sə'nɑːtəs kən'sʊltəm) *n., pl.* ***senatus consulta*** (kən'sʊltə). a decree of the Senate of ancient Rome, taking the form of advice to a magistrate.

send[1] (sɛnd) *vb.* **sends, sending, sent. 1.** (*tr.*) to cause or order (a person or thing) to be taken, directed, or transmitted to another place: *to send a letter; she sent the salesman away.* **2.** (when *intr.*, foll. by *for*; when *tr.*, *takes an infinitive*) to dispatch a request or command (for something or to do something): *he sent for a bottle of wine; he sent to his son to come home.* **3.** (*tr.*) to direct or cause to go to a place or point: *his blow sent the champion to the floor.* **4.** (*tr.*) to bring to a state or condition: *this noise will send me mad.* **5.** (*tr.*; often foll. by *forth, out,* etc.) to cause to issue; emit: *his cooking sent forth a lovely smell from the kitchen.* **6.** (*tr.*) to cause to happen or come: *misery sent by fate.* **7.** to transmit (a message) by radio, esp. in the form of pulses. **8.** (*tr.*) *Slang.* to move to excitement or rapture: *this music really sends me.* **9. send (someone) about his** *or* **her business.** to dismiss or get rid of (someone). **10. send (someone) packing.** to dismiss or get rid of (someone) peremptorily. ~*n.* **11.** another word for **swash** (sense 4). ~See also **send down, sendoff, send up.** [Old English *sendan*; related to Old Norse *senda*, Gothic *sandjan*, Old High German *senten*] —'**sendable** *adj.* —'**sender** *n.*

send[2] (sɛnd) *vb.* **sends, sending, sent,** *n.* a variant spelling of **scend.**

sendal ('sɛndᵊl) *n.* **1.** a fine silk fabric used, esp. in the Middle Ages, for ceremonial clothing, etc. **2.** a garment of such fabric. [C13: from Old French *cendal*, from Medieval Latin *cendalum*; probably related to Greek *sindōn* fine linen]

send down *vb.* (*tr., adv.*) *Brit.* **1.** to expel from a university, esp. permanently. **2.** *Informal.* to send to prison.

sendoff ('sɛndˌɒf) *n. Informal.* **1.** a demonstration of good wishes to a person about to set off on a journey, new career, etc. **2.** a start, esp. an auspicious one, to a venture. ~*vb.* **send off.** (*tr., adv.*) **3.** to cause to depart; despatch. **4.** *Soccer, rugby, etc.* (of the referee) to dismiss (a player) from the field of play for some offence. **5.** *Informal.* to give a sendoff to.

send up *vb.* (*tr., adv.*) **1.** *Slang.* to send to prison. **2.** *Brit. informal.* to make fun of, esp. by doing an imitation or parody of: *he sent up the teacher marvellously.* ~*n.* **send-up. 3.** *Brit. informal.* a parody or imitation.

Seneca ('sɛnɪkə) *n.* **1.** (*pl.* **-cas** *or* **-ca**) a member of a North American Indian people formerly living south of Lake Ontario; one of the Iroquois peoples. **2.** the language of this people, belonging to the Iroquoian family. [C19: from Dutch *Sennecaas* (plural), probably of Algonquian origin]

senecio (sɪ'niːʃɪəʊ) *n., pl.* **-cios.** See **cineraria.**

senega ('sɛnɪgə) *n.* **1.** a milkwort plant, *Polygala senega*, of the eastern U.S., with small white flowers. **2.** the root of this plant, used as an expectorant. ~Also called: **senega snakeroot, seneca snakeroot.** [C18: variant of *Seneca* (the Indian tribe)]

Senegalese (ˌsɛnɪgə'liːz) *adj.* **1.** of or relating to Senegal, a republic in W Africa, or to its people, customs, etc. ~*n.* **2.** a native or inhabitant of Senegal.

senescent (sɪ'nɛsᵊnt) *adj.* **1.** growing old. **2.** characteristic of old age. [C17: from Latin *senēscere* to grow old, from *senex* old] —**se'nescence** *n.*

seneschal ('sɛnɪʃəl) *n.* **1.** a steward of the household of a medieval prince or nobleman who took charge of domestic arrangements, etc. **2.** *Brit.* a cathedral official. [C14: from Old French, from Medieval Latin *siniscalcus*, of Germanic origin; related to Old High German *senescalh* oldest servant, from *sene-* old + *scalh* a servant]

senile ('siːnaɪl) *adj.* **1.** of, relating to, or characteristic of old age. **2.** mentally or physically weak or infirm on account of old age. **3.** (of land forms or rivers) at an advanced stage in the cycle of erosion. See **old** (sense 18). [C17: from Latin *senīlis*, from *senex* an old man] —'**senilely** *adv.* —**senility** (sɪ'nɪlɪtɪ) *n.*

senile dementia *n.* dementia starting in old age with no clear physical cause.

senior ('siːnjə) *adj.* **1.** higher in rank or length of service. **2.** older in years: *senior citizens.* **3.** of or relating to adulthood, maturity, or old age: *senior privileges.* **4.** *Education.* **a.** of, relating to, or designating more advanced or older pupils. **b.** of or relating to a secondary school. **5.** *U.S.* of, relating to, or designating students in the fourth and final year at college. ~*n.* **6.** a senior person. **7. a.** a senior pupil, student, etc. **b.** a fellow of senior rank in an English university. [C14: from Latin: older, from *senex* old]

Senior ('siːnjə) *adj. Chiefly U.S.* being the older: used to distinguish the father from the son with the same first name or names: *Charles Parker, Senior.* Abbrevs.: **Sr, Sen.**

senior aircraftman *n.* a rank in the Royal Air Force comparable to that of a private in the army, though not the lowest rank in the Royal Air Force.

senior citizen *n. Brit. and N.Z., euphemistic.* an old age pensioner.

senior common room *n.* (in British universities, colleges, etc.) a common room for the use of academic staff. Compare **junior common room.**

seniority (ˌsiːnɪ'ɒrɪtɪ) *n., pl.* **-ties. 1.** the state of being senior. **2.** precedence in rank, etc., due to senior status.

senior management *n.* another term for **top management.**

senior service *n. Brit.* the Royal Navy.

senna ('sɛnə) *n.* **1.** any of various tropical plants of the caesalpiniaceous genus *Cassia*, esp. *C. angustifolia* (**Arabian senna**) and *C. acutifolia* (**Alexandrian senna**), having typically yellow flowers and long pods. **2. senna leaf.** the dried leaflets of any of these plants, used as a cathartic and laxative. **3. senna pods.** the dried fruits of any of these plants, used as a cathartic and laxative. ~See also **bladder senna.** [C16: via New Latin from Arabic *sanā*]

sennet ('sɛnɪt) *n.* a fanfare: used as a stage direction in Elizabethan drama. [C16: probably variant of SIGNET (meaning "a sign")]

sennight *or* **se'nnight** ('sɛnaɪt) *n.* an archaic word for **week.** [Old English *seofan nihte*; see SEVEN, NIGHT]

sennit ('sɛnɪt) *n.* **1.** a flat braided cordage used on ships. **2.** plaited straw, grass, palm leaves, etc., as for making hats. [C17: of unknown origin]

señor (sɛ'njɔː; *Spanish* se'ɲor) *n., pl.* **-ñors** *or* **-ñores** (*Spanish* -'ɲores). a Spaniard or Spanish-speaking man: a title of address equivalent to *Mr* when placed before a name or *sir* when used alone. [Spanish, from Latin *senior* an older man, SENIOR]

señora (sɛ'njɔːrə; *Spanish* se'ɲora) *n., pl.* **-ras** (-rəz; *Spanish* -ras). a married Spanish or Spanish-speaking woman: a title of address equivalent to *Mrs* when placed before a name or *madam* when used alone.

señorita (ˌsɛnjɔː'riːtə; *Spanish* seɲo'rita) *n., pl.* **-tas** (-təz; *Spanish* -tas). an unmarried Spanish or Spanish-speaking woman: a title of address equivalent to *Miss* when placed before a name or *madam* or *miss* when used alone.

sensate ('sɛnseɪt) *adj.* **1.** perceived by the senses. **2.** *Obsolete.* having the power of sensation. [C16: from Late Latin *sensātus* endowed with sense, from Latin *sensus* SENSE] —'**sensately** *adv.*

sensation (sɛn'seɪʃən) *n.* **1.** the power of perceiving through the senses. **2.** a physical condition or experience resulting from the stimulation of one of the sense organs: *a sensation of warmth.* **3.** a general feeling or awareness: *a sensation of fear.* **4.** a state of widespread public excitement: *his announcement caused a sensation.* **5.** anything that causes such a state: *your speech was a sensation.* [C17: from Medieval Latin *sensātiō*, from Late Latin *sensātus* SENSATE] —**sen'sationless** *adj.*

sensational (sɛn'seɪʃənᵊl) *adj.* **1.** causing or intended to cause intense feelings, esp. of curiosity, horror, etc.: *sensational disclosures in the press.* **2.** *Informal.* extremely good: *a sensational skater.* **3.** of or relating to the faculty of sensation. **4.** *Philosophy.* of or relating to sensationalism. —**sen'sationally** *adv.*

sensationalism (sɛn'seɪʃənᵊˌlɪzəm) *n.* **1.** the use of sensational language, etc., to arouse an intense emotional response. **2.** such sensational matter itself. **3.** *Philosophy.* **a.** the doctrine that knowledge cannot go beyond the analysis of experience. **b.** *Ethics.* the doctrine that the ability to gratify the senses is the only criterion of goodness. **4.** *Psychol.* the theory that all experience and mental life may be explained in terms of sensations and remembered images. **5.** *Aesthetics.* the theory of the beauty of sensuality in the arts. ~Also called (for senses 3, 4): **sensationism.** —**sen'sationalist** *n., adj.* —**sen**ˌ**sational'istic** *adj.*

sensationalize *or* **sensationalise** (sɛn'seɪʃənəˌlaɪz) *vb.* (*tr.*) to cause (events, esp. in newspaper reports) to seem more vivid, shocking, etc., than they really are.

sense (sɛns) *n.* **1.** any of the faculties by which the mind receives information about the external world or about the state of the body. In addition to the five traditional faculties of sight, hearing, touch, taste, and smell, the term includes the means by which bodily position, temperature, pain, balance, etc., are perceived. **2.** such faculties collectively; the ability to perceive. **3.** a feeling perceived through one of the senses: *a sense of warmth.* **4.** a mental perception or awareness: *a sense of happiness.* **5.** moral discernment; understanding: *a sense of right and wrong.* **6.** (*sometimes pl.*) sound practical judgment or intelligence: *he is a man without any sense.* **7.** reason or purpose: *what is the sense of going out in the rain?* **8.** substance or gist; meaning: *what is the sense of this proverb?* **9.** specific meaning; definition: *in what sense are you using the word?* **10.** an opinion or consensus. **11.** *Maths.* one of two opposite directions measured on a directed line; the sign of the measure as contrasted with the magnitude of a vector. **12. make sense.** to be reasonable or understandable. **13.** *Logic, linguistics.* **a.** the import of an expression as contrasted with its referent. Thus *the morning star* and *the evening star* have the same reference, Venus, but different senses. **b.** the property of an expression by virtue of which its referent is determined. **c.** that which one grasps in understanding an expression. **14. take leave of one's senses.** See **leave**[2] (sense 8). ~*vb.* (*tr.*) **15.** to perceive through one or more of the senses. **16.** to apprehend or detect without or in advance of the evidence of the senses. **17.** to understand. **18.** *Computer technol.* **a.** to test or locate the position of (a part of computer hardware). **b.** to read (data). [C14: from Latin *sēnsus,* from *sentīre* to feel]

sense datum *n. Philosophy.* a sensation detached both from any information it may convey and from its putative source in the external world, such as the bare awareness of a red visual field. Sense data are held by some philosophers to be the immediate objects of experience providing certain knowledge from which knowledge of material objects is inferred. See also **representationalism** (sense 1), **apriorism.**

senseless ('sɛnslɪs) *adj.* **1.** lacking in sense; foolish: *a senseless plan.* **2.** lacking in feeling; unconscious. **3.** lacking in perception; stupid. —'**senselessly** *adv.* —'**senselessness** *n.*

sense organ *n.* a structure in animals that is specialized for receiving external or internal stimuli and transmitting them in the form of nervous impulses to the brain.

sensibilia (ˌsɛnsɪ'bɪlɪə) *n.* that which can be sensed. [Latin, neuter plural of *sensibilis* SENSIBLE]

sensibility (ˌsɛnsɪ'bɪlɪtɪ) *n., pl.* **-ties.** **1.** the ability to perceive or feel. **2.** (*often pl.*) the capacity for responding to emotion, impression, etc. **3.** (*often pl.*) the capacity for responding to aesthetic stimuli. **4.** mental responsiveness; discernment; awareness. **5.** (*usually pl.*) emotional or moral feelings: *cruelty offends most people's sensibilities.* **6.** the condition of a plant of being susceptible to external influences, esp. attack by parasites.

sensible ('sɛnsɪbᵊl) *adj.* **1.** having or showing good sense or judgment: *a sensible decision.* **2.** (of clothing) serviceable; practical: *sensible shoes.* **3.** having the capacity for sensation; sensitive. **4.** capable of being apprehended by the senses. **5.** perceptible to the mind. **6.** (sometimes foll. by *of*) having perception; aware: *sensible of your kindness.* **7.** readily perceived; considerable: *a sensible difference.* ~*n.* **8.** Also called: **sensible note.** a less common term for **leading note.** [C14: from Old French, from Late Latin *sēnsibilis,* from Latin *sentīre* to sense] —'**sensibleness** *n.* —'**sensibly** *adv.*

sensible horizon *n.* See under **horizon** (sense 2a).

sensillum (sɛn'sɪləm) *n., pl.* **-la** (-lə). a sense organ in insects, typically consisting of a receptor organ in the integument connected to sensory neurons. [New Latin, diminutive of Latin *sensus* sense (Middle Latin: sense organ)]

sensitive ('sɛnsɪtɪv) *adj.* **1.** having the power of sensation. **2.** easily irritated; delicate: *sensitive skin.* **3.** affected by external conditions or stimuli. **4.** easily offended. **5.** of or relating to the senses or the power of sensation. **6.** capable of registering small differences or changes in amounts, quality, etc.: *a sensitive instrument.* **7.** *Photog.* having a high sensitivity: *a sensitive emulsion.* **8.** connected with matters affecting national security, esp. through access to classified information. **9.** (of a stock market or prices) quickly responsive to external influences and thus fluctuating or tending to fluctuate. [C14: from Medieval Latin *sēnsitīvus,* from Latin *sentīre* to feel] —'**sensitively** *adv.* —'**sensitiveness** *n.*

sensitive plant *n.* **1.** a tropical American mimosa plant, *Mimosa pudica,* the leaflets and stems of which fold if touched. **2.** any of several similar plants, such as the caesalpiniaceous plant *Cassia nictitans* of E North America. **3.** *Informal.* a person who is easily upset.

sensitivity (ˌsɛnsɪ'tɪvɪtɪ) *n., pl.* **-ties.** **1.** the state or quality of being sensitive. **2.** *Physiol.* the state, condition, or quality of reacting or being sensitive to an external stimulus, drug, allergen, etc. **3.** *Electronics.* the magnitude or time of response of an instrument, circuit, etc., to an input signal, such as a current. **4.** *Photog.* the degree of response of an emulsion to light or other actinic radiation, esp. to light of a particular colour, expressed in terms of its speed.

sensitize *or* **sensitise** ('sɛnsɪˌtaɪz) *vb.* **1.** to make or become sensitive. **2.** (*tr.*) to render (an individual) sensitive to a drug, allergen, etc. **3.** (*tr.*) *Photog.* to make (a material) sensitive to light or to other actinic radiation, esp. to light of a particular colour, by coating it with a photographic emulsion often containing special chemicals, such as dyes. —ˌ**sensitiˈzation** *or* ˌ**sensitiˈsation** *n.* —ˈ**sensiˌtizer** *or* ˈ**sensiˌtiser** *n.*

sensitometer (ˌsɛnsɪ'tɒmɪtə) *n.* an instrument for measuring the sensitivity to light of a photographic material over a range of exposures. —ˌ**sensi'tometry** *n.*

sensor ('sɛnsə) *n.* anything, such as a photoelectric cell, that receives a signal or stimulus and responds to it. [C19: from Latin *sēnsus* perceived, from *sentīre* to observe]

sensorimotor (ˌsɛnsərɪ'məʊtə) *or* **sensomotor** (ˌsɛnsə'məʊtə) *adj.* of or relating to both the sensory and motor functions of an organism or to the nerves controlling them.

sensorium (sɛn'sɔːrɪəm) *n., pl.* **-riums** *or* **-ria** (-rɪə). **1.** the area of the brain considered responsible for receiving and integrating sensations from the outside world. **2.** *Physiol.* the entire sensory and intellectual apparatus of the body. [C17: from Late Latin, from Latin *sēnsus* felt, from *sentīre* to perceive]

sensory ('sɛnsərɪ) *or* (*less commonly*) **sensorial** (sɛn'sɔːrɪəl) *adj.* **1.** of or relating to the senses or the power of sensation. **2.** of or relating to those processes and structures within an organism that receive stimuli from the environment and convey them to the brain. [C18: from Latin *sensōrius,* from *sentīre* to feel]

sensory deprivation *n. Psychol.* an experimental situation in which all stimulation is cut off from the sensory receptors.

sensual ('sɛnsjʊəl) *adj.* **1.** of or relating to any of the senses or sense organs; bodily. **2.** strongly or unduly inclined to gratification of the senses. **3.** tending to arouse the bodily appetites, esp. the sexual appetite. **4.** of or relating to sensualism. [C15: from Late Latin *sensuālis,* from Latin *sēnsus* SENSE. Compare French *sensuel,* Italian *sensuale*] —'**sensually** *adv.* —'**sensualness** *n.*

sensualism ('sɛnsjʊəˌlɪzəm) *n.* **1.** the quality or state of being sensual. **2.** another word for **sensationalism** (senses 3a, b).

sensuality (ˌsɛnsjʊ'ælɪtɪ) *n., pl.* **-ties.** **1.** the quality or state of being sensual. **2.** excessive indulgence in sensual pleasures. —**sensualist** ('sɛnsjʊəlɪst) *n.*

sensum ('sɛnsəm) *n., pl.* **-sa** (-sə). another word for **sense datum.**

sensuous ('sɛnsjʊəs) *adj.* **1.** aesthetically pleasing to the senses. **2.** appreciative of or moved by qualities perceived by the senses. **3.** of, relating to, or derived from the senses. [C17: apparently coined by Milton to avoid the unwanted overtones of SENSUAL; not in common use until C19: from Latin *sēnsus* SENSE + -OUS] —'**sensuously** *adv.* —'**sensuousness** *n.*

sent (sɛnt) *vb.* the past tense and past participle of **send**[1] and **send**[2].

sentence ('sɛntəns) *n.* **1.** a sequence of words capable of standing alone to make an assertion, ask a question, or give a command, usually consisting of a subject and a predicate containing a finite verb. **2.** the judgment formally pronounced upon a person convicted in criminal proceedings, esp. the decision as to what punishment is to be imposed. **3.** an opinion, judgment, or decision. **4.** *Music.* another word for **period** (sense 11). **5.** any short passage of scripture employed in liturgical use: *the funeral sentences.* **6.** *Logic.* a well-formed expression, without variables. **7.** *Archaic.* a proverb, maxim, or aphorism. ~*vb.* **8.** (*tr.*) to pronounce sentence on (a convicted person) in a court of law: *the judge sentenced the murderer to life imprisonment.* [C13: via Old French from Latin *sententia* a way of thinking, from *sentīre* to feel] —**sentential** (sɛn'tɛnʃəl) *adj.* —**sen'tentially** *adv.*

sentence connector *n.* a word or phrase that introduces a clause or sentence and serves as a transition between it and a previous clause or sentence, as for example *also* in *I'm buying eggs and also I'm looking for a dessert for tonight.* It may be preceded by a coordinating conjunction such as *and* in the above example.

sentence stress *n.* the stress given to a word or words in a sentence, often conveying nuances of meaning or emphasis.

sentence substitute *n.* a word or phrase, esp. one traditionally classified as an adverb, that is used in place of a finite sentence, such as *yes, no, certainly,* and *never.*

sentential calculus *n. Logic.* the formal theory the intended interpretation of which concerns the logical relations between sentences treated only as a whole and without regard to their internal structure.

sentential function *n.* another name for **open sentence.**

sententious (sɛn'tɛnʃəs) *adj.* **1.** characterized by or full of aphorisms, terse pithy sayings, or axioms. **2.** constantly using aphorisms, etc. **3.** tending to indulge in pompous moralizing. [C15: from Latin *sententiōsus* full of meaning, from *sententia;* see SENTENCE] —**sen'tentiously** *adv.* —**sen'tentiousness** *n.*

sentience ('sɛnʃəns) *or* **sentiency** *n.* **1.** the state or quality of being sentient; awareness. **2.** sense perception not involving intelligence or mental perception; feeling.

sentient ('sɛntɪənt) *adj.* **1.** having the power of sense perception or sensation; conscious. ~*n.* **2.** *Rare.* a sentient person or thing. [C17: from Latin *sentiēns* feeling, from *sentīre* to perceive] —'**sentiently** *adv.*

sentiment ('sɛntɪmənt) *n.* **1.** susceptibility to tender, delicate, or romantic emotion: *she has too much sentiment to be successful.* **2.** (*often pl.*) a thought, opinion, or attitude. **3.** exaggerated, overindulged, or mawkish feeling or emotion. **4.** an expression of response to deep feeling, esp. in art or literature. **5.** a feeling, emotion, or awareness: *a sentiment of pity.* **6.** a mental attitude modified or determined by feeling: *there is a strong revolutionary sentiment in his country.* **7.** a feeling conveyed, or intended to be conveyed, in words. [C17: from Medieval Latin *sentīmentum,* from Latin *sentīre* to feel]

sentimental (ˌsɛntɪ'mɛntᵊl) *adj.* **1.** tending to indulge the emotions excessively. **2.** making a direct appeal to the emotions, esp. to romantic feelings. **3.** relating to or characterized by sentiment. —ˌ**senti'mentally** *adv.*

sentimentalism (ˌsɛntɪ'mɛntᵊˌlɪzəm) *n.* **1.** the state or quality of being sentimental. **2.** an act, statement, etc., that is sentimental. —ˌ**senti'mentalist** *n.*

sentimentality (ˌsɛntɪmɛn'tælɪtɪ) *n., pl.* **-ties.** **1.** the state, quality, or an instance of being sentimental. **2.** an act, statement, etc., that is sentimental.

sentimentalize *or* **sentimentalise** (ˌsɛntɪˈmɛntəˌlaɪz) *vb.* to make sentimental or behave sentimentally. —ˌ**sentiˌmentaliˈzation** *or* ˌ**sentiˌmentaliˈsation** *n.*

sentimental value *n.* the value of an article in terms of its sentimental associations for a particular person.

sentinel (ˈsɛntɪnəl) *n.* **1.** a person, such as a sentry, assigned to keep guard. **2.** *Computer technol.* a character used to indicate the beginning or end of a particular block of information. ~*vb.* **-nells, -nelling, -nelled.** (*tr.*) **3.** to guard as a sentinel. **4.** to post as a sentinel. **5.** to provide with a sentinel. [C16: from Old French *sentinelle,* from Old Italian *sentinella,* from *sentina* watchfulness, from *sentire* to notice, from Latin]

sentry (ˈsɛntrɪ) *n., pl.* **-tries. 1.** a soldier who guards or prevents unauthorized access to a place, keeps watch for danger, etc. **2.** the watch kept by a sentry. [C17: perhaps shortened from obsolete *centrinel,* C16 variant of SENTINEL]

sentry box *n.* a small shelter with an open front in which a sentry may stand to be sheltered from the weather.

Senussi *or* **Senusi** (sɛˈnuːsɪ) *n., pl.* **-sis.** a member of a zealous and aggressive Muslim sect of North Africa and Arabia, founded in 1837 by Sidi Mohammed ibn Ali al Senussi (?1787–1859). —**Seˈnussian** *or* **Seˈnusian** *adj.*

senza (ˈsɛntsɑː) *prep. Music.* without; omitting. [Italian]

sep. *abbrev. for:* **1.** sepal. **2.** separate.

Sep. *abbrev. for:* **1.** September. **2.** Septuagint.

sepal (ˈsɛpəl) *n.* any of the separate parts of the calyx of a flower. [C19: from New Latin *sepalum: sep-* from Greek *skepē* a covering + *-alum,* from New Latin *petalum* PETAL] —ˈ**sepalled** *or* **sepalous** (ˈsɛpələs) *adj.*

sepaloid (ˈsiːpəˌlɔɪd) *or* **sepaline** *adj.* (esp. of petals) resembling a sepal in structure and function.

-sepalous *adj. combining form.* having sepals of a specified type or number: *polysepalous.* —**sepaly** *n. combining form.*

separable (ˈsɛpərəbəl, ˈsɛprəbəl) *adj.* able to be separated, divided, or parted. —ˌ**separaˈbility** *or* ˈ**separableness** *n.* —ˈ**separably** *adv.*

separate *vb.* (ˈsɛpəˌreɪt). **1.** (*tr.*) to act as a barrier between: *a range of mountains separates the two countries.* **2.** to put or force or be put or forced apart. **3.** to part or be parted from a mass or group. **4.** (*tr.*) to discriminate between: *to separate the men and the boys.* **5.** to divide or be divided into component parts; sort or be sorted. **6.** to sever or be severed. **7.** (*intr.*) (of a married couple) to cease living together by mutual agreement or after obtaining a decree of judicial separation. ~*adj.* (ˈsɛprɪt, ˈsɛpərɪt). **8.** existing or considered independently: *a separate problem.* **9.** disunited or apart. **10.** set apart from the main body or mass. **11.** distinct, individual, or particular. **12.** solitary or withdrawn. **13.** (*sometimes cap.*) designating or relating to a Church or similar institution that has ceased to have associations with an original parent organization. [C15: from Latin *sēparāre,* from *sē-* apart + *parāre* to obtain] —ˈ**separately** *adv.* —ˈ**separateness** *n.*

separates (ˈsɛprɪts, ˈsɛpərɪts) *pl. n.* women's outer garments that only cover part of the body and so are worn in combination with others, usually unmatching; skirts, blouses, jackets, trousers, etc. Compare **coordinates.**

separate school *n.* (in Canada) a school for a large religious minority financed by its rates and administered by its own school board but under the authority of the provincial department of education.

separating funnel *n. Chem.* a large funnel having a tap in its output tube, used to separate immiscible liquids.

separation (ˌsɛpəˈreɪʃən) *n.* **1.** the act of separating or state of being separated. **2.** the place or line where a separation is made. **3.** a gap that separates. **4.** *Family law.* the cessation of cohabitation between a man and wife, either by mutual agreement or under a decree of a court. See **judicial separation.** Compare **divorce. 5. a.** the act of jettisoning a burnt-out stage of a multistage rocket. **b.** the instant at which such a stage is jettisoned.

separatist (ˈsɛpərətɪst, ˈsɛprə-) *or* **separationist** *n.* **a.** a person who advocates or practises secession from an organization or group. **b.** (*as modifier*): *a separatist movement.* —ˈ**separaˌtism** *n.* —ˌ**separaˈtistic** *adj.*

Separatist (ˈsɛpərətɪst, ˈsɛprə-) *n.* (*sometimes not cap.*) a person who advocates the secession of a province, esp. Quebec, from Canada. —ˈ**Separaˌtism** *n.*

separative (ˈsɛpərətɪv, ˈsɛprə-) *adj.* tending to separate or causing separation. —ˈ**separatively** *adv.* —ˈ**separativeness** *n.*

separator (ˈsɛpəˌreɪtə) *n.* **1.** a person or thing that separates. **2.** a device for separating things into constituent parts, as milk into cream, etc. —ˈ**separatory** *adj.*

separatrix (ˈsɛpəˌreɪtrɪks) *n., pl.* **separatrices** (ˌsɛpəˈreɪtrɪˌsiːz). another name for **solidus** (sense 1). [via New Latin from Late Latin, feminine of *sēparātor* one that separates]

Sephardi (sɪˈfɑːdiː) *n., pl.* **-dim** (-dɪm). *Judaism.* **1. a.** a Jew of Spanish, Portuguese, or North African descent. **b.** (loosely) any Oriental Jew. **2.** the pronunciation of Hebrew used by these Jews, and of Modern Hebrew as spoken in Israel. **3.** (*modifier*) of or pertaining to the Sephardim, esp. to their liturgy and ritual. **4.** (*modifier*) of or pertaining to the liturgy adopted by certain European, esp. Chassidic, communities who believe it to be more authentic but nonetheless differing from the genuine Oriental liturgy. ~Compare **Ashkenazi.** [C19: from Late Hebrew, from Hebrew *sepharad* a region mentioned in Obadiah 20, thought to have been Spain] —**Seˈphardic** *adj.*

sepia (ˈsiːpɪə) *n.* **1.** a dark reddish-brown pigment obtained from the inky secretion of the cuttlefish. **2.** any cuttlefish of the genus *Sepia.* **3.** a brownish tone imparted to a photograph, esp. an early one such as a calotype. It can be produced by first bleaching a print (after fixing) and then immersing it for a short time in a solution of sodium sulphide or of alkaline thiourea. **4.** a brownish-grey to dark yellowish-brown colour. **5.** a drawing or photograph in sepia. ~*adj.* **6.** of the colour sepia or done in sepia: *a sepia print.* [C16: from Latin: a cuttlefish, from Greek; related to Greek *sēpein* to make rotten]

sepiolite (ˈsiːpɪəˌlaɪt) *n.* another name for **meerschaum** (sense 1). [C19: from German *Sepiolith,* from Greek *sēpion* bone of a cuttlefish; see SEPIA, -LITE]

sepmag (ˈsɛpˌmæg) *adj.* designating a film or television programme for which the sound is recorded on separate magnetic material and run in synchronism with the picture. [C20: from SEP(ARATE) + MAG(NETIC)]

sepoy (ˈsiːpɔɪ) *n.* (formerly) an Indian soldier in the service of the British. [C18: from Portuguese *sipaio,* from Urdu *sipāhī,* from Persian: horseman, from *sipāh* army]

seppuku (sɛˈpuːkuː) *n.* another word for **hara-kiri.** [from Japanese, from Chinese *ch'ieh* to cut + *fu* bowels]

sepsis (ˈsɛpsɪs) *n.* the presence of pus-forming bacteria in the body. [C19: via New Latin from Greek *sēpsis* a rotting; related to Greek *sēpein* to cause to decay]

sept (sɛpt) *n.* **1.** *Anthropol.* a clan or group that believes itself to be descended from a common ancestor. **2.** a branch of a tribe or nation, esp. in medieval Ireland or Scotland. [C16: perhaps variant of SECT]

Sept. *abbrev. for:* **1.** September. **2.** Septuagint.

septa (ˈsɛptə) *n.* the plural of **septum.**

septal (ˈsɛptəl) *adj.* of or relating to a septum.

septarium (sɛpˈtɛərɪəm) *n., pl.* **-ia** (-ɪə). a mass of mineral substance having cracks filled with another mineral, esp. calcite. [C18: from New Latin, from Latin SEPTUM] —**sepˈtarian** *adj.*

septate (ˈsɛpteɪt) *adj.* divided by septa: *a septate plant ovary.* [C19: from New Latin *septātus* having a SEPTUM]

septavalent (ˌsɛptəˈveɪlənt) *adj. Chem.* another word for **heptavalent.** [C19: from SEPT(IVALENT) + (HEPT)AVALENT]

September (sɛpˈtɛmbə) *n.* the ninth month of the year, consisting of 30 days. [Old English, from Latin: the seventh (month) according to the calendar of ancient Rome, from *septem* seven]

Septembrist (sɛpˈtɛmbrɪst) *n. French history.* a person who took part in the September Massacre (Sept. 2–6, 1792) of royalist prisoners in Paris.

septenary (ˈsɛptɪnərɪ) *adj.* **1.** of or relating to the number seven. **2.** forming a group of seven. **3.** another word for **septennial.** ~*n., pl.* **-naries. 4.** the number seven. **5.** a group of seven things. **6.** a period of seven years. **7.** *Prosody.* a line of seven metrical feet. [C16: from Latin *septēnārius,* from *septēnī* seven each, from *septem* seven]

septennial (sɛpˈtɛnɪəl) *adj.* **1.** occurring every seven years. **2.** relating to or lasting seven years. [C17: from Latin *septennis,* from *septem* seven + *annus* a year] —**sepˈtennially** *adv.*

septennium (sɛpˈtɛnɪəm) *n., pl.* **-niums** *or* **-nia** (-nɪə). a period or cycle of seven years. [C19: from Latin, from *septem* seven + *-ennium,* from *annus* year]

septentrion (sɛpˈtɛntrɪˌɒn) *n. Archaic.* the northern regions or the north. [C14: from Latin *septentriōnēs,* literally: the seven ploughing oxen (the constellation of the Great Bear), from *septem* seven + *triōnēs* ploughing oxen] —**sepˈtentrional** *adj.*

septet *or* **septette** (sɛpˈtɛt) *n.* **1.** *Music.* a group of seven singers or instrumentalists or a piece of music composed for such a group. **2.** a group of seven people or things. [C19: from German, from Latin *septem* seven]

septi-[1] *or before a vowel* **sept-** *combining form.* seven: *septivalent.* [from Latin *septem*]

septi-[2] *combining form.* septum: *septicidal.*

septic (ˈsɛptɪk) *adj.* **1.** of, relating to, or caused by sepsis. **2.** of, relating to, or caused by putrefaction. ~*n.* **3.** *Austral. and N.Z. informal.* short for **septic tank.** [C17: from Latin *sēpticus,* from Greek *sēptikos,* from *sēptos* decayed, from *sēpein* to make rotten] —ˈ**septically** *adv.* —**septicity** (sɛpˈtɪsɪtɪ) *n.*

septicaemia *or U.S.* **septicemia** (ˌsɛptɪˈsiːmɪə) *n.* any of various diseases caused by microorganisms in the blood. Nontechnical name: **blood poisoning.** See also **bacteraemia, pyaemia.** [C19: from New Latin, from Greek *sēptik(os)* SEPTIC + -AEMIA] —ˌ**sepptiˈcaemic** *or U.S.* ˌ**septiˈcemic** *adj.*

septicidal (ˌsɛptɪˈsaɪdəl) *adj. Botany.* (of a dehiscence) characterized by splitting along the partitions of the seed capsule. [C19: from SEPTI-[2] + -CIDAL] —ˌ**septiˈcidally** *adv.*

septic tank *n.* a tank, usually below ground, for containing sewage to be decomposed by anaerobic bacteria.

septifragal (sɛpˈtɪfrəgəl) *adj.* (of a dehiscence) characterized by breaking apart from a natural line of division in the fruit. [C19: from SEPTI-[2] + *-fragal,* from Latin *frangere* to break]

septilateral (ˌsɛptɪˈlætərəl) *adj.* having seven sides.

septillion (sɛpˈtɪljən) *n., pl.* **-lions** *or* **-lion. 1.** (in Britain, France, and Germany) the number represented as one followed by 42 zeros (10^{42}). **2.** (in the U.S. and Canada) the number represented as one followed by 24 zeros (10^{24}). Brit. word: **quadrillion.** [C17: from French, from *sept* seven + *-illion,* on the model of *million*] —**sep'tillionth** *adj., n.*

septime ('sɛptiːm) *n.* the seventh of eight basic positions from which a parry or attack can be made in fencing. [C19: from Latin *septimus* seventh, from *septem* seven]

septivalent (ˌsɛptɪ'veɪlənt) *or* **septavalent** (ˌsɛptə'veɪlənt) *adj. Chem.* another word for **heptavalent.**

septuagenarian (ˌsɛptjuədʒɪ'nɛərɪən) *n.* **1.** a person who is from 70 to 79 years old. *~adj.* **2.** being between 70 and 79 years old. **3.** of or relating to a septuagenarian. [C18: from Latin *septuāgēnārius,* from *septuāgēnī* seventy each, from *septuāgintā* seventy]

Septuagesima (ˌsɛptjuə'dʒɛsɪmə) *n.* the third Sunday before Lent. [C14: from Church Latin *septuāgēsima* (*dīes*) the seventieth (day); compare QUINQUAGESIMA]

Septuagint ('sɛptjuəˌdʒɪnt) *n.* the principal Greek version of the Old Testament, including the Apocrypha, believed to have been translated by 70 or 72 scholars. [C16: from Latin *septuāgintā* seventy]

septum ('sɛptəm) *n., pl.* **-ta** (-tə). **1.** *Biology, anatomy.* a dividing partition between two tissues or cavities. **2.** a dividing partition or membrane between two cavities in a mechanical device. [C18: from Latin *saeptum* wall, from *saepīre* to enclose; related to Latin *saepēs* a fence]

septuple ('sɛptjupᵊl) *adj.* **1.** seven times as much or many; sevenfold. **2.** consisting of seven parts or members. *~vb.* **3.** (*tr.*) to multiply by seven. [C17: from Late Latin *septuplus,* from *septem* seven; compare QUADRUPLE]

septuplet (sɛp'tjuːplɪt, 'sɛptjuplɪt) *n.* **1.** *Music.* a group of seven notes played in a time value of six, eight, etc. **2.** one of seven offspring produced at one birth. **3.** a group of seven things.

septuplicate (sɛp'tjuːplɪkət) *n.* **1.** a group or set of seven things. *~adj.* **2.** having or being in seven parts; sevenfold.

sepulchral (sɪ'pʌlkrəl) *adj.* **1.** suggestive of a tomb; gloomy. **2.** of or relating to a sepulchre. —**se'pulchrally** *adv.*

sepulchre *or U.S.* **sepulcher** ('sɛpəlkə) *n.* **1.** a burial vault, tomb, or grave. **2.** Also called: **Easter sepulchre.** a separate alcove in some medieval churches in which the Eucharistic elements were kept from Good Friday until the Easter ceremonies. *~vb.* **3.** (*tr.*) to bury in a sepulchre. [C12: from Old French *sépulcre,* from Latin *sepulcrum,* from *sepelīre* to bury]

sepulture ('sɛpəltʃə) *n.* **1.** the act of placing in a sepulchre. **2.** an archaic word for **sepulchre.** [C13: via Old French from Latin *sepultūra,* from *sepultus* buried, from *sepelīre* to bury]

seq. *abbrev. for:* **1.** sequel. **2.** sequens. [Latin: the following (one)]

seqq. *abbrev. for* sequentia. [Latin: the following (ones)]

sequacious (sɪ'kweɪʃəs) *adj.* **1.** logically following in regular sequence. **2.** ready to follow any leader; pliant. [C17: from Latin *sequāx* pursuing, from *sequī* to follow] —**se'quaciously** *adv.* —**sequacity** (sɪ'kwæsɪtɪ) *n.*

sequel ('siːkwəl) *n.* **1.** anything that follows from something else; development. **2.** a consequence or result. **3.** a novel, play, etc., that continues a previously related story. [C15: from Late Latin *sequēla,* from Latin *sequī* to follow]

sequela (sɪ'kwiːlə) *n., pl.* **-lae** (-liː). (*often pl.*) *Med.* **1.** any abnormal bodily condition or disease related to or arising from a pre-existing disease. **2.** any complication of a disease. [C18: from Latin: SEQUEL]

sequence ('siːkwəns) *n.* **1.** an arrangement of two or more things in a successive order. **2.** the successive order of two or more things: *chronological sequence.* **3.** a sequentially ordered set of related things or ideas. **4.** an action or event that follows another or others. **5. a.** *Cards.* a set of three or more consecutive cards, usually of the same suit. **b.** *Bridge.* a set of two or more consecutive cards. **6.** *Music.* an arrangement of notes or chords repeated several times at different pitches. **7.** *Maths.* **a.** an ordered set of numbers or other mathematical entities in one-to-one correspondence with the integers 1 to *n.* **b.** an ordered infinite set of mathematical entities in one-to-one correspondence with the natural numbers. **8.** a section of a film constituting a single continuous uninterrupted episode. **9.** *Biochem.* the unique order of amino acids in the polypeptide chain of a protein or of nucleotides in the polynucleotide chain of DNA or RNA. **10.** *R.C. Church.* another word for **prose** (sense 4). *~vb.* (*tr.*) **11.** *Biochem.* to determine the order of the units comprising (a protein, nucleic acid, genome, etc.). [C14: from Medieval Latin *sequentia* that which follows, from Latin *sequī* to follow]

sequence of tenses *n. Grammar.* the sequence according to which the tense of a subordinate verb in a sentence is determined by the tense of the principal verb, as in *I believe he is lying, I believed he was lying,* etc.

sequencer ('siːkwənsə) *n.* **1.** an electronic device that determines the order in which a number of operations occur. **2.** an electronic device that sorts information into the required order for data processing. **3.** a unit connected to a synthesizer, which is capable of memorizing sequences of notes.

sequencing ('siːkwənsɪŋ) *n. Biochem.* the procedure of determining the order of amino acids in the polypeptide chain of a protein (**protein sequencing**) or of nucleotides in a DNA section comprising a gene (**gene sequencing**).

sequent ('siːkwənt) *adj.* **1.** following in order or succession. **2.** following as a result; consequent. *~n.* **3.** something that follows; consequence. **4.** *Logic.* a formal representation of an argument. The inference of *A* from *A* & *B* is written *A* & *B* ⊢ *A.* The sequent ⊢ *A* represents the derivation of *A* from no assumptions and thus indicates that *A* is a theorem. [C16: from Latin *sequēns,* from *sequī* to follow] —**'sequently** *adv.*

sequential (sɪ'kwɛnʃəl) *adj.* **1.** characterized by or having a regular sequence. **2.** another word for **sequent.** —**sequentiality** (sɪˌkwɛnʃɪ'ælɪtɪ) *n.* —**se'quentially** *adv.*

sequential access *n.* a method of reaching and reading data from a computer file by reading through the file from the beginning. Compare **direct access.**

sequential scanning *n.* a system of scanning a television picture along the lines in numerical sequence. Compare **interlaced scanning.**

sequester (sɪ'kwɛstə) *vb.* (*tr.*) **1.** to remove or separate. **2.** (*usually passive*) to retire into seclusion. **3.** *Law.* to take (property) temporarily out of the possession of its owner, esp. until the claims of creditors are satisfied or a court order is complied with. **4.** *International law.* to requisition or appropriate (enemy property). [C14: from Late Latin *sequestrāre* to surrender for safekeeping, from Latin *sequester* a trustee] —**se'questrable** *adj.*

sequestrant (sɪ'kwɛstrənt) *n. Chem.* any substance used to bring about sequestration, often by chelation. They are used in horticulture to counteract lime in the soil.

sequestrate (sɪ'kwɛstreɪt) *vb.* (*tr.*) **1.** *Law.* a variant of **sequester** (sense 3). **2.** *Chiefly Scots Law.* **a.** to place (the property of a bankrupt) in the hands of a trustee for the benefit of his creditors. **b.** to render (a person) bankrupt. **3.** *Archaic.* to seclude or separate. [C16: from Late Latin *sequestrāre* to SEQUESTER] —**sequestrator** ('siːkwɛsˌtreɪtə, sɪ'kwɛsˌtreɪtə) *n.*

sequestration (ˌsiːkwɛ'streɪʃən) *n.* **1.** the act of sequestering or state of being sequestered. **2.** *Law.* the sequestering of property. **3.** *Chem.* the effective removal of ions from a solution by coordination with another type of ion or molecule to form complexes that do not have the same chemical behaviour as the original ions. See also **sequestrant.**

sequestrum (sɪ'kwɛstrəm) *n., pl.* **-tra** (-trə). *Pathol.* a detached piece of necrotic bone that often migrates to a wound, abscess, etc. [C19: from New Latin, from Latin: something deposited; see SEQUESTER] —**se'questral** *adj.*

sequin ('siːkwɪn) *n.* **1.** a small piece of shiny often coloured metal foil or plastic, usually round, used to decorate garments, etc. **2.** Also called: **zecchino.** any of various gold coins formerly minted in Italy, Turkey, and Malta. [C17: via French from Italian *zecchino,* from *zecca* mint, from Arabic *sikkah* die for striking coins] —**'sequined** *adj.*

sequoia (sɪ'kwɔɪə) *n.* either of two giant Californian coniferous trees, *Sequoia sempervirens* (**redwood**) or *Sequoiadendron giganteum* (formerly *Sequoia gigantea*) (**big tree** or **giant sequoia**): family *Taxodiaceae.* [C19: New Latin, named after *Sequoya,* known also as George Guess, (?1770–1843), American Indian scholar and leader]

ser *or* **seer** (sɪə) *n.* a unit of weight used in India, usually taken as one fortieth of a maund. [from Hindi]

ser. *abbrev. for:* **1.** serial. **2.** series. **3.** sermon.

sera ('sɪərə) *n.* a plural of **serum.**

sérac ('seræk) *n.* a pinnacle of ice among crevasses on a glacier, usually on a steep slope. [C19: from Swiss French: a variety of white cheese (hence the ice that it resembles) from Medieval Latin *serācium,* from Latin *serum* whey]

seraglio (sɛ'rɑːlɪˌəu) *or* **serail** (sə'raɪ, -'raɪl, -'reɪl) *n., pl.* **-raglios** *or* **-rails.** **1.** the harem of a Muslim house or palace. **2.** a sultan's palace, esp. in the former Turkish empire. **3.** the wives and concubines of a Muslim. [C16: from Italian *serraglio* animal cage, from Medieval Latin *serrāculum* bolt, from Latin *sera* a door bar; associated also with Turkish *seray* palace]

serai (sɛ'raɪ) *n.* (in the East) a caravanserai or inn. [C17: from Turkish *saray* palace, from Persian *sarāī* palace; see CARAVANSERAI]

serape (sə'rɑːpɪ) *n.* a blanket-like shawl often of brightly coloured wool worn by men in Latin America.

seraph ('sɛrəf) *n., pl.* **-aphs** *or* **-aphim** (-əfɪm). *Theol.* a member of the highest order of angels in the celestial hierarchies, often depicted as the winged head of a child. [C17: back formation from plural *seraphim,* via Late Latin from Hebrew]

seraphic (sɪ'ræfɪk) *or* **seraphical** *adj.* **1.** of or resembling a seraph. **2.** blissfully serene; rapt. —**se'raphically** *adv.*

Serb (sɜːb) *n., adj.* another word for **Serbian.** [C19: from Serbian *Srb*]

Serb. *abbrev. for* Serbia(n).

Serbian ('sɜːbɪən) *adj.* **1.** of, relating to, or characteristic of Serbia, a republic of SE Yugoslavia, or of its people or their dialect of Serbo-Croatian. *~n.* **2.** the dialect of Serbo-Croatian spoken in Serbia. **3. a.** a native or inhabitant of Serbia. **b.** (esp. in other existing or former constituent republics of Yugoslavia) a speaker of the Serbian dialect.

Serbo-Croatian *or* **Serbo-Croat** *n.* **1.** the chief official language of Yugoslavia, belonging to the South Slavonic branch of the Indo-European family. The Serbian dialect is usually written in the Cyrillic alphabet, the Croatian in Roman. ~*adj.* **2.** of or relating to this language.

SERC *Brit. abbrev. for* Science and Engineering Research Council.

serdab ('sɜːdæb, sə'dæb) *n.* a secret chamber in an ancient Egyptian tomb. [C19 (earlier, in the sense: cellar): from Arabic: cellar, from Persian *sardāb* ice cellar, from *sard* cold + *āb* water]

sere[1] *or* **sear** (sɪə) *adj.* **1.** *Archaic.* dried up or withered. ~*vb., n.* **2.** a rare spelling of **sear**[1]. [Old English *sēar;* see SEAR[1]]

sere[2] (sɪə) *n.* the series of changes occurring in the ecological succession of a particular community. [C20: from SERIES]

serein (sə'reɪn) *n.* fine rain falling from a clear sky after sunset, esp. in the tropics. [C19: via French, from Old French *serain* dusk, from Latin *sērus* late]

serenade (ˌserɪ'neɪd) *n.* **1.** a piece of music appropriate to the evening, characteristically played outside the house of a woman. **2.** a piece of music indicative or suggestive of this. **3.** an extended composition in several movements similar to the modern suite or divertimento. ~*vb.* **4.** (*tr.*) to play a serenade for (someone). **5.** (*intr.*) to play a serenade. ~Compare **aubade.** [C17: from French *sérénade,* from Italian *serenata,* from *sereno* peaceful, from Latin *serēnus* calm; also influenced in meaning by Italian *sera* evening, from Latin *sērus* late] —ˌ**sere'nader** *n.*

serenata (ˌserɪ'nɑːtə) *n.* **1.** an 18th-century cantata, often dramatic in form. **2.** another word for **serenade.** [C18: from Italian; see SERENADE]

serendipity (ˌserən'dɪpɪtɪ) *n.* the faculty of making fortunate discoveries by accident. [C18: coined by Horace Walpole, from the Persian fairytale *The Three Princes of Serendip,* in which the heroes possess this gift] —ˌ**seren'dipitous** *adj.*

serene (sɪ'riːn) *adj.* **1.** peaceful or tranquil; calm. **2.** clear or bright: *a serene sky.* **3.** (*often cap.*) honoured: used as part of certain royal titles: *His Serene Highness.* [C16: from Latin *serēnus*] —**se'renely** *adv.* —**se'reneness** *n.*

serenity (sɪ'renɪtɪ) *n., pl.* **-ties. 1.** the state or quality of being serene. **2.** (*often cap.*) a title of honour used of certain royal personages: preceded by *his, her,* etc.

serf (sɜːf) *n.* (esp. in medieval Europe) an unfree person, esp. one bound to the land. If his lord sold the land, the serf was passed on to the new landlord. [C15: from Old French, from Latin *servus* a slave; see SERVE] —'**serfdom** *or* '**serfhood** *n.* —'**serf**ˌ**like** *adj.*

serge (sɜːdʒ) *n.* **1.** a twill-weave woollen or worsted fabric used for clothing. **2.** a similar twilled cotton, silk, or rayon fabric. [C14: from Old French *sarge,* from Vulgar Latin *sārica* (unattested), from Latin *sēricum,* from Greek *sērikon* silk, from *sērikos* silken, from *sēr* silkworm]

sergeant ('sɑːdʒənt) *n.* **1.** a noncommissioned officer in certain armies, air forces, and marine corps, usually ranking immediately above a corporal. **2. a.** (in Britain) a police officer ranking between constable and inspector. **b.** (in the U.S.) a police officer ranking below a captain. **3.** See **sergeant at arms. 4.** a court or municipal officer who has ceremonial duties. **5.** (formerly) a tenant by military service, not of knightly rank. **6.** See **serjeant at law.** ~Also: **serjeant.** [C12: from Old French *sergent,* from Latin *serviēns,* literally: serving, from *servīre* to SERVE] —**sergeancy** ('sɑːdʒənsɪ) *or* '**sergeantship** *n.*

sergeant at arms *n.* **1.** an officer of a legislative or fraternal body responsible for maintaining internal order. **2.** (formerly) an officer who served a monarch or noble, esp. as an armed attendant. ~Also called: **sergeant, serjeant at arms, serjeant.**

sergeant at law *n.* a variant spelling of **serjeant at law.**

Sergeant Baker *n.* a large brightly-coloured fish of the genus *Latropiscis,* found in temperate waters of Australia.

sergeant major *n.* **1.** a noncommissioned officer of the highest rank or having specific administrative tasks in branches of the armed forces of various countries. **2.** a large damselfish, *Abudefduf saxatilis,* having a bluish-grey body marked with black stripes.

Sergt *abbrev. for* Sergeant.

serial ('sɪərɪəl) *n.* **1.** a novel, play, etc., presented in separate instalments at regular intervals. **2.** a publication, usually regularly issued and consecutively numbered. ~*adj.* **3.** of, relating to, or resembling a series. **4.** published or presented as a serial. **5.** of or relating to such publication or presentation. **6.** *Computer technol.* of or operating on items of information, instructions, etc., in the order in which they occur. Compare **parallel** (sense 5). **7.** of, relating to, or using the techniques of serialism. **8.** *Logic, maths.* (of a relation) connected, transitive, and asymmetric, thereby imposing an order on all the members of the domain, as *less than* on the natural numbers. See also **ordering.** [C19: from New Latin *seriālis,* from Latin *seriēs* SERIES] —'**serially** *adv.*

serial correlation *n. Statistics.* another name for **autocorrelation.**

serialism ('sɪərɪəˌlɪzəm) *n.* (in 20th-century music) the use of a sequence of notes in a definite order as a thematic basis for a composition and a source from which the musical material is derived. See also **twelve-tone.**

serialize *or* **serialise** ('sɪərɪəˌlaɪz) *vb.* (*tr.*) to publish or present in the form of a serial. —ˌ**seriali'zation** *or* ˌ**seriali'sation** *n.*

serial killer *n.* a person who carries out a series of murders.

serial number *n.* any of the consecutive numbers assigned to machines, tools, books, etc.

seriate ('sɪərɪɪt) *adj.* forming a series. —'**seriately** *adv.*

seriatim (ˌsɪərɪ'ætɪm, ˌser-) *adv.* in a series; one after another in regular order. [C17: from Medieval Latin, from Latin *seriēs* SERIES]

sericeous (sɪ'rɪʃəs) *adj. Botany.* **1.** covered with a layer of small silky hairs: *a sericeous leaf.* **2.** silky. [C18: from Late Latin *sēriceus* silken, from Latin *sēricus;* see SERGE]

sericin ('serɪsɪn) *n.* a gelatinous protein found on the fibres of raw silk. [C19: from Latin *sēricum* silk + -IN]

sericulture ('serɪˌkʌltʃə) *n.* the rearing of silkworms for the production of raw silk. [C19: via French; *seri-* from Latin *sēricum* silk, from Greek *sērikos* silken, from *sēr* a silkworm] —ˌ**seri'cultural** *adj.* —ˌ**seri'culturist** *n.*

seriema (ˌserɪ'iːmə) *n.* either of two cranelike South American birds, *Cariama cristata* or *Chunga burmeisteri,* having a crest just above the bill, rounded wings, and a long tail: family *Cariamidae,* order *Gruiformes* (cranes, rails, etc.). [C19: from New Latin, from Tupi *çariama* crested]

series ('sɪəriːz, -rɪz) *n., pl.* **-ries. 1.** a group or connected succession of similar or related things, usually arranged in order. **2.** a set of radio or television programmes having the same characters and setting but different stories. **3.** a set of books having the same format, related content, etc., published by one firm. **4.** a set of stamps, coins, etc., issued at a particular time. **5.** *Maths.* the sum of a finite or infinite sequence of numbers or quantities. See also **geometric series. 6.** *Electronics.* **a.** a configuration of two or more components connected in a circuit so that the same current flows in turn through each of them (esp. in the phrase **in series**). Compare **parallel** (sense 10). **b.** (*as modifier*): *a series circuit.* **7.** *Rhetoric.* a succession of coordinate elements in a sentence. **8.** *Geology.* a stratigraphical unit that is a subdivision of a system and represents the rocks formed during an epoch. [C17: from Latin: a row, from *serere* to link]

series resonance *n.* the resonance that results when circuit elements are connected with their inductance and capacitance in series, so that the impedance of the combination falls to a minimum at the resonant frequency. Compare **parallel resonance.**

series-wound ('sɪəriːzˌwaʊnd, -rɪz-) *adj.* (of a motor or generator) having the field and armature circuits connected in series. Compare **shunt-wound.**

serif *or* (*rarely*) **seriph** ('serɪf) *n. Printing.* a small line at the extremities of a main stroke in a type character. [C19: perhaps from Dutch *schreef* dash, probably of Germanic origin, compare Old High German *screvōn* to engrave]

serigraph ('serɪˌgræf, -ˌgrɑːf) *n.* a colour print made by an adaptation of the silk-screen process. [C19: from *seri-,* from Latin *sēricum* silk + -GRAPH] —**serigraphy** (sə'rɪgrəfɪ) *n.*

serin ('serɪn) *n.* any of various small yellow-and-brown finches of the genus *Serinus,* esp. *S. serinus,* of parts of Europe. See also **canary.** [C16: from French, perhaps from Old Provençal *sirena* a bee-eater, from Latin *sīrēn,* a kind of bird, from SIREN]

serine ('seriːn, 'sɪəriːn, -rɪn) *n.* a sweet-tasting amino acid that is synthesized in the body and is involved in the synthesis of cysteine; 2-amino-3-hydroxypropanoic acid. Formula: $CH_2(OH)CH(NH_2)$-COOH. [C19: from SERICIN + -INE[2]]

seringa (sə'rɪŋgə) *n.* **1.** any of several euphorbiaceous trees of the Brazilian genus *Hevea,* that yield rubber. **2.** a deciduous simaroubaceous tree, *Kirkia acuminata,* of southern Africa with a graceful shape. [C18: from Portuguese, variant of SYRINGA]

seriocomic (ˌsɪərɪəʊ'kɒmɪk) *or* (*less commonly*) **seriocomical** *adj.* mixing serious and comic elements. —ˌ**serio'comically** *adv.*

serious ('sɪərɪəs) *adj.* **1.** grave in nature or disposition; thoughtful: *a serious person.* **2.** marked by deep feeling; in earnest; sincere: *is he serious or joking?* **3.** concerned with important matters: *a serious conversation.* **4.** requiring effort or concentration: *a serious book.* **5.** giving rise to fear or anxiety; critical: *a serious illness.* **6.** *Informal.* worthy of regard because of substantial quantity or quality: *serious money; serious wine.* [C15: from Late Latin *sēriōsus,* from Latin *sērius;* probably related to Old English *swǣr* gloomy, Gothic *swers* esteemed] —'**seriously** *adv.* —'**seriousness** *n.*

serjeant ('sɑːdʒənt) *n.* a variant spelling of **sergeant.**

serjeant at arms *n.* a variant spelling of **sergeant at arms.**

serjeant at law *n.* (formerly in England) a barrister of a special rank, to which he was raised by a writ under the Great Seal. Also called: **serjeant, sergeant at law, sergeant.**

sermon ('sɜːmən) *n.* **1. a.** an address of religious instruction or exhortation, often based on a passage from the Bible, esp. one delivered during a church service. **b.** a written version of such an address. **2.** a serious speech, esp. one administering reproof. [C12: via Old French from Latin *sermō* discourse, probably from *serere* to join together] —**sermonic** (sɜː'mɒnɪk) *or* **ser'monical** *adj.*

sermonize *or* **sermonise** ('sɜːməˌnaɪz) *vb.* to talk to or address (a person or audience) as if delivering a sermon. —'**sermon**ˌ**izer** *or* '**sermon**ˌ**iser** *n.*

sero- *combining form.* indicating a serum: *serotherapy.*

seroconvert (ˌsɪərəʊkən'vɜːt) *vb.* (*intr.*) (of an individual) to produce antibodies specific to, and in response to the presence in the blood of, a particular antigen, such as a virus or vaccine. —ˌ**serocon'version** *n.*

serology (sɪ'rɒlədʒɪ) *n.* the branch of science concerned with serums. —**serologic** (ˌsɪərə'lɒdʒɪk) *or* ˌ**sero'logical** *adj.* —**se'rologist** *n.*

seropositive (ˌsɪərəʊ'pɒzɪtɪv) *adj.* (of a person whose blood has been tested for a specific disease, such as AIDS) showing a serological reaction indicating the presence of the disease.

seropurulent (ˌsɪərəʊ'pjʊərələnt) *adj. Pathol.* composed of or containing both serum and pus.

serosa (sɪ'rəʊsə) *n.* **1.** another name for **serous membrane. 2.** one of the thin membranes surrounding the embryo in an insect's egg. [C19: from New Latin, from *serōsus* relating to SERUM]

serotherapy (ˌsɪərəʊ'θɛrəpɪ) *n.* the treatment of disease by the injection of serum containing antibodies to the disease.

serotine ('sɛrəˌtaɪn) *adj.* **1.** Also: **serotinal** (sɪ'rɒtɪnᵊl), **serotinous.** *Biology.* produced, flowering, or developing late in the season. ~*n.* **2.** either of two insectivorous bats, *Eptesicus serotinus* or *Vespertilio serotinus:* family *Vespertilionidae.* [C16: from Latin *sērōtinus* late, from *sērus* late; applied to the bat because it flies late in the evening]

serotonin (ˌsɛrə'təʊnɪn) *n.* a compound that occurs in the brain, intestines, and blood platelets and acts as a neurotransmitter, as well as inducing vasoconstriction and contraction of smooth muscle; 5-hydroxytryptamine (5HT). [from SERO- + TON(IC) + -IN]

serous ('sɪərəs) *adj.* of, resembling, producing, or containing serum. [C16: from Latin *serōsus,* from SERUM] —**serosity** (sɪ'rɒsɪtɪ) *or* '**serousness** *n.*

serous fluid *n.* a thin watery fluid found in many body cavities, esp. those lined with serous membrane.

serous membrane *n.* any of the smooth moist delicate membranes, such as the pleura or peritoneum, that line the closed cavities of the body.

serow ('sɛrəʊ) *n.* either of two antelopes, *Capricornis sumatraensis* and *C. crispus,* of mountainous regions of S and SE Asia, having a dark coat and conical backward-pointing horns. [C19: from Lepcha *să-ro* Tibetan goat]

Serpens ('sɜːpɛnz) *n., Latin genitive* **Serpentis** (sə'pɛntɪs). a faint extensive constellation situated in the N and S equatorial regions and divided into two parts, **Serpens Caput** (the head) lying between Ophiuchus and Boötes and **Serpens Cauda** (the tail) between Ophiuchus and Aquila. [Latin: SERPENT]

serpent ('sɜːpənt) *n.* **1.** a literary or dialect word for **snake. 2.** *Old Testament.* a manifestation of Satan as a guileful tempter (Genesis 3:1–5). **3.** a sly, deceitful, or unscrupulous person. **4.** an obsolete wind instrument resembling a snake in shape, the bass form of the cornett. **5.** a firework that moves about with a serpentine motion when ignited. [C14: via Old French from Latin *serpēns* a creeping thing, from *serpere* to creep; related to Greek *herpein* to crawl]

serpentine[1] ('sɜːpənˌtaɪn) *adj.* **1.** of, relating to, or resembling a serpent. **2.** twisting; winding. ~*n.* **3.** *Maths.* a curve that is symmetric about the origin of and asymptotic to the *x*-axis. [C14: from Late Latin *serpentīnus,* from *serpēns* SERPENT]

serpentine[2] ('sɜːpənˌtaɪn) *n.* **1.** a dark green or brown mineral with a greasy or silky lustre, found in igneous and metamorphic rocks. It is used as an ornamental stone; and one variety (chrysotile) is known as asbestos. Composition: hydrated magnesium silicate. Formula: $Mg_3Si_2O_5.2H_2O$. Crystal structure: monoclinic. **2.** any of a group of minerals having the general formula $(Mg,Fe)_3Si_2O_5(OH)_4$. [C15 *serpentyn,* from Medieval Latin *serpentīnum* SERPENTINE[1]; referring to the snakelike patterns of these minerals]

serpigo (sɜː'paɪgəʊ) *n. Pathol.* any progressive skin eruption, such as ringworm or herpes. [C14: from Medieval Latin, from Latin *serpere* to creep] —**serpiginous** (sɜː'pɪdʒɪnəs) *adj.*

SERPS *or* **Serps** (sɜːps) *n.* (in Britain) *acronym for* state earnings-related pension scheme.

serpulid ('sɜːpjʊlɪd) *n.* a marine polychaete worm of the family *Serpulidae,* which constructs and lives in a calcareous tube attached to stones or seaweed and has a crown of ciliated tentacles. [C19: Latin, from *serpula* a little serpent]

serra ('sɛrə) *n., pl.* **-rae** (-riː). *Zoology.* a sawlike part or organ. [C19: from Latin: saw]

serranid (sə'rænɪd, 'sɛrə-) *or* **serranoid** ('sɛrəˌnɔɪd) *n.* **1.** any of numerous mostly marine percoid fishes of the family *Serranidae:* includes the sea basses, sea perches, groupers, and jewfish. ~*adj.* **2.** of, relating to, or belonging to the family *Serranidae.* [C19: from New Latin *Serranidae,* from *serrānus* genus name from Latin *serra* sawfish]

serrate *adj.* ('sɛrɪt, -eɪt). **1.** (of leaves) having a margin of forward pointing teeth. **2.** having a notched or sawlike edge. ~*vb.* (sɛ'reɪt). **3.** (*tr.*) to make serrate. [C17: from Latin *serrātus* saw-shaped, from *serra* a saw] —**ser'rated** *adj.*

serration (sɛ'reɪʃən) *or* (*less commonly*) **serrature** ('sɛrətʃə) *n.* **1.** the state or condition of being serrated. **2.** a row of notches or toothlike projections on an edge. **3.** a single notch.

serried ('sɛrɪd) *adj.* in close or compact formation: *serried ranks of troops.* [C17: from Old French *serré* close-packed, from *serrer* to shut up; see SEAR[2]]

serriform ('sɛrɪˌfɔːm) *adj. Biology.* resembling a notched or sawlike edge. [*serri-,* from Latin *serra* saw]

serrulate ('sɛrʊˌleɪt, -lɪt) *or* **serrulated** *adj.* (esp. of leaves) minutely serrate. [C18: from New Latin *serrulātus,* from Latin *serrula* diminutive of *serra* a saw]

serrulation (ˌsɛrʊ'leɪʃən) *n.* **1.** any of the notches in a serrulate object. **2.** the condition of being serrulate.

sertularian (ˌsɜːtjʊ'lɛərɪən) *n.* any of various hydroid coelenterates of the genus *Sertularia,* forming feathery colonies of long branched stems bearing stalkless paired polyps. [C18: from New Latin *Sertulāria,* from Latin *sertula* diminutive of *serta* a garland, from *serere* to wreathe]

serum ('sɪərəm) *n., pl.* **-rums** *or* **-ra** (-rə). **1.** See **blood serum. 2.** antitoxin obtained from the blood serum of immunized animals. **3.** *Physiol., zoology.* clear watery fluid, esp. that exuded by serous membranes. **4.** a less common word for **whey.** [C17: from Latin: whey] —'**serumal** *adj.*

serum albumin *n.* a form of albumin that is the most abundant protein constituent of blood plasma. See also **albumin.**

serum globulin *n.* the blood serum component consisting of proteins with a larger molecular weight than serum albumin. See also **immunoglobulin.**

serum hepatitis *n.* another name for **hepatitis B.**

serum sickness *n.* an allergic reaction, such as vomiting, skin rash, etc., that sometimes follows injection of a foreign serum.

serv. *abbrev. for:* **1.** servant. **2.** service.

serval ('sɜːvᵊl) *n., pl.* **-vals** *or* **-val.** a slender feline mammal, *Felis serval,* of the African bush, having an orange-brown coat with black spots, large ears, and long legs. [C18: via French from Late Latin *cervālis* staglike, from Latin *cervus* a stag]

servant ('sɜːvᵊnt) *n.* **1.** a person employed to work for another, esp. one who performs household duties. **2.** See **public servant.** [C13: via Old French, from *servant* serving, from *servir* to SERVE] —'**servant-**ˌ**like** *adj.*

serve (sɜːv) *vb.* **1.** to be in the service of (a person). **2.** to render or be of service to (a person, cause, etc.); help. **3.** (in a shop) to give (customers) information about articles for sale and to hand over articles purchased. **4.** (*tr.*) to provide (guests, customers, etc.) with food, drink, etc.: *she served her guests with cocktails.* **5.** to distribute or provide (food, drink, etc.) for guests, customers, etc.: *do you serve coffee?* **6.** (*tr.*; sometimes foll. by *up*) to present (food, drink, etc.) in a specified manner: *cauliflower served with cheese sauce.* **7.** (*tr.*) to provide with a regular supply of. **8.** (*tr.*) to work actively for: *to serve the government.* **9.** (*tr.*) to pay homage to: *to serve God.* **10.** to answer the requirements of; suit: *this will serve my purpose.* **11.** (*intr.; may take an infinitive*) to have a use; function: *this wood will serve to build a fire.* **12.** to go through (a period of service, enlistment, imprisonment, etc.). **13.** (*intr.*) (of weather, conditions, etc.) to be favourable or suitable. **14.** (*tr.*) Also: **service.** (of a male animal) to copulate with (a female animal). **15.** *Tennis, squash, etc.* to put (the ball) into play. **16.** (*intr.*) *R.C. Church.* to act as server at Mass or other services. **17.** (*tr.*) to deliver (a legal document, esp. a writ or summons) to (a person). **18.** to provide (a machine, etc.) with an impulse or signal for control purposes or with a continuous supply of fuel, working material, etc. **19.** (*tr.*) *Nautical.* to bind (a rope, spar, etc.) with wire or fine cord to protect it from chafing, etc. See also **seize** (sense 8). **20. serve (a person) right.** *Informal.* to pay (a person) back, esp. for wrongful or foolish treatment or behaviour. ~*n.* **21.** *Tennis, squash, etc.* short for **service** (sense 17). [C13: from Old French *servir,* from Latin *servīre,* from *servus* a slave] —'**servable** *or* '**serveable** *adj.*

server ('sɜːvə) *n.* **1.** a person who serves. **2.** *Chiefly R.C. Church.* a person who acts as acolyte or assists the priest at Mass. **3.** something that is used in serving food and drink. **4.** the player who serves in racket games.

service[1] ('sɜːvɪs) *n.* **1.** an act of help or assistance. **2.** an organized system of labour and material aids used to supply the needs of the public: *telephone service; bus service.* **3.** the supply, installation, or maintenance of goods carried out by a dealer. **4.** the state of availability for use by the public (esp. in the phrases **into** *or* **out of service**). **5.** a periodic overhaul made on a car, machine, etc. **6.** the act or manner of serving guests, customers, etc., in a shop, hotel, restaurant, etc. **7.** a department of public employment and its employees: *civil service.* **8.** employment in or performance of work for another: *he has been in the service of our firm for ten years.* **9.** the work of a public servant. **10. a.** one of the branches of the armed forces. **b.** (*as modifier*): *service life.* **11.** the state, position, or duties of a domestic servant (esp. in the phrase **in service**). **12.** the act or manner of serving food. **13.** a complete set of dishes, cups, etc., for use at table. **14.** public worship carried out according to certain prescribed forms: *divine service.* **15.** the prescribed form according to which a specific kind of religious ceremony is to be carried out: *the burial service.* **16.** a unified collection of musical settings of the canticles and other liturgical items prescribed by the Book of Common Prayer as used in the Church of England. **17.** *Tennis, squash, etc.* **a.** the act, manner, or right of serving a ball. **b.** the game in which a particular player serves: *he has lost his service.* Often shortened to **serve. 18.** (in feudal law) the duty owed by a tenant to his lord. **19.** the serving of a writ, summons, etc., upon a person. **20.** *Nautical.* a length of tarred marline or small stuff used in serving. **21.** (of male animals) the act of mating. **22.** (*modifier*) of, relating to, or for the use of servants or employees. ~*vb.* (*tr.*) **23.** to make fit for use. **24.** to supply with assistance. **25.** to overhaul (a car, machine, etc.). **26.** (of a male animal) to mate with (a female). **27.** *Brit.* to meet interest and capital payments on (debt). ~See also **services.** [C12 *servise,* from Old French, from Latin *servitium* condition of a slave, from *servus* a slave]

service[2] ('sɜːvɪs) *n.* See **service tree.**

serviceable ('sɜːvɪsəbᵊl) *adj.* **1.** capable of or ready for service; usable. **2.** capable of giving good service; durable. **3.** *Archaic.* diligent in service. —ˌ**servicea'bility** *or* '**serviceableness** *n.* —'**serviceably** *adv.*

service area *n.* **1.** a place on a motorway providing garage services, restaurants, toilet facilities, etc. **2.** the area within which a satisfactory signal can be received from a given radio transmitter.

serviceberry ('sɜːvɪsˌbɛrɪ) *n., pl.* **-ries. 1.** Also called: **shadbush.** any of various North American rosaceous trees or shrubs of the genus *Amelanchier,* esp. *A. canadensis,* which has white flowers and edible purplish berries. **2.** the fruit of any of these plants. **3.** the fruit of the service tree. ~Also called (for senses 1, 2): **shadberry, Juneberry.**

service car *n. N.Z.* a bus operating on a long-distance route.

service ceiling *n.* the height above sea level, measured under standard conditions, at which the rate of climb of an aircraft has fallen to a specified amount. Compare **absolute ceiling.**

service charge *n.* a percentage of a bill, as at a restaurant or hotel, added to the total to pay for service.

service contract *n.* a contract between an employer and a senior employee, esp. a director, executive, etc.

service flat *n. Brit.* a flat in which domestic services are provided by the management. Also called (esp. Austral.): **serviced flat.**

service industry *n.* an industry that provides services, such as transport or entertainment, rather than goods.

service line *n.* (in certain racket games) **1.** the line at the back of the court behind which the server must stand when serving. **2.** a line indicating the boundary of a permissible service, as on the backwall of a squash court.

serviceman ('sɜːvɪsˌmæn, -mən) *n., pl.* **-men. 1.** Also called (*fem.*): '**serviceˌwoman.** a person who serves in the armed services of a country. **2.** a man employed to service and maintain equipment.

service module *n.* a section of an Apollo spacecraft housing the rocket engine, radar, fuel cells, etc., and jettisoned on re-entry into the earth's atmosphere. See also **lunar module, command module.**

service road *n. Brit.* a relatively narrow road running parallel to a main road and providing access to houses, shops, offices, factories, etc., situated along its length.

services ('sɜːvɪsɪz) *pl. n.* **1.** work performed for remuneration. **2.** (usually preceded by *the*) the armed forces. **3.** (*sometimes sing.*) *Economics.* commodities, such as banking, that are mainly intangible and usually consumed concurrently with their production. Compare **goods** (sense 2). **4.** a system of providing the public with gas, water, etc.

service station *n.* **1.** a place that supplies fuel, oil, etc., for motor vehicles and often carries out repairs, servicing, etc. **2.** a place that repairs and sometimes supplies mechanical or electrical equipment.

service tree *n.* **1.** Also called: **sorb.** a Eurasian rosaceous tree, *Sorbus domestica,* cultivated for its white flowers and brown edible apple-like fruits. **2. wild service tree.** a similar and related Eurasian tree, *Sorbus torminalis.* [*service,* from Old English *syrfe,* from Vulgar Latin *sorbea* (unattested), from Latin *sorbus* SORB]

servient tenement ('sɜːvɪənt) *n. Property Law.* the land or tenement over which an easement or other servitude is exercised. Compare **dominant tenement.**

serviette (ˌsɜːvɪ'ɛt) *n. Chiefly Brit.* a small square of cloth or paper used while eating to protect the clothes, wipe the mouth and hands, etc. [C15: from Old French, from *servir* to SERVE; formed on the model of OUBLIETTE]

servile ('sɜːvaɪl) *adj.* **1.** obsequious or fawning in attitude or behaviour; submissive. **2.** of or suitable for a slave. **3.** existing in or relating to a state of slavery. **4.** (when *postpositive,* foll. by *to*) submitting or obedient. [C14: from Latin *servīlis,* from *servus* slave] —'**servilely** *adv.* —**servility** (sɜː'vɪlɪtɪ) *or* '**servileness** *n.*

servile work *n. R.C. Church.* work of a physical nature that is forbidden on Sundays and on certain holidays.

serving ('sɜːvɪŋ) *n.* a portion or helping of food or drink.

servitor ('sɜːvɪtə) *n. Archaic.* a person who serves another. [C14: from Old French *servitour,* from Late Latin *servītor,* from Latin *servīre* to SERVE]

servitude ('sɜːvɪˌtjuːd) *n.* **1.** the state or condition of a slave; bondage. **2.** the state or condition of being subjected to or dominated by a person or thing: *servitude to drink.* **3.** *Law.* a burden attaching to an estate for the benefit of an adjoining estate or of some definite person. See also **easement. 4.** short for **penal servitude.** [C15: via Old French from Latin *servitūdō,* from *servus* a slave]

servo ('sɜːvəʊ) *adj.* **1.** (*prenominal*) of, relating to, forming part of, or activated by a servomechanism: *servo brakes.* ~*n., pl.* **-vos. 2.** *Informal.* short for **servomechanism.** [see SERVOMOTOR]

servomechanism ('sɜːvəʊˌmɛkəˌnɪzəm, ˌsɜːvəʊ'mɛk-) *n.* a mechanical or electromechanical system for control of the position or speed of an output transducer. Negative feedback is incorporated to minimize discrepancies between the output state and the input control setting. —**servomechanical** (ˌsɜːvəʊmɪ'kænɪkᵊl) *adj.*

servomotor ('sɜːvəʊˌməʊtə) *n.* any motor that supplies power to a servomechanism. [C19: from French *servo-moteur,* from Latin *servus* slave + French *moteur* MOTOR]

sesame ('sɛsəmɪ) *n.* **1.** a tropical herbaceous plant, *Sesamum indicum,* of the East Indies, cultivated, esp. in India, for its small oval seeds: family *Pedaliaceae.* **2.** the seeds of this plant, used in flavouring bread and yielding an edible oil (**benne oil** or **gingili**). ~Also called: **benne, gingili, til.** [C15: from Latin *sēsamum,* from Greek *sēsamon, sēsamē,* of Semitic origin; related to Arabic *simsim*]

sesamoid ('sɛsəˌmɔɪd) *adj. Anatomy.* **1.** of or relating to various small bones formed in tendons, such as the patella. **2.** of or relating to any of various small cartilages, esp. those of the nose. [C17: from Latin *sēsamoīdēs* like sesame (seed), from Greek]

Sesotho (sɪ'suːtʊ) *n.* the dialect of Sotho spoken by the Basotho: an official language of Lesotho. Also called: **Southern Sotho.** Former name: **Basuto.**

sesqui- *prefix.* **1.** indicating one and a half: *sesquicentennial.* **2.** (in a chemical compound) indicating a ratio of two to three: *sesquioxide.* [from Latin, contraction of SEMI- + *as* AS[2] + *-que* and]

sesquialtera (ˌsɛskwɪ'æltərə) *n. Music.* **1.** a mixture stop on an organ. **2.** another term for **hemiola.** [C16: from Latin *sesqui-* half + *alter* second, other]

sesquicarbonate (ˌsɛskwɪ'kɑːbəˌneɪt, -nɪt) *n.* a mixed salt consisting of a carbonate and a hydrogen carbonate, such as sodium sesquicarbonate, $Na_2CO_3.NaHCO_3.2H_2O$.

sesquicentennial (ˌsɛskwɪsɛn'tɛnɪəl) *adj.* **1.** of or relating to a period of 150 years. ~*n.* **2.** a period or cycle of 150 years. **3.** a 150th anniversary or its celebration. —ˌ**sesquicen'tennially** *adv.*

sesquioxide (ˌsɛskwɪ'ɒksaɪd) *n.* any of certain oxides whose molecules contain three atoms of oxygen for every two atoms of the element: *chromium sesquioxide,* Cr_2O_3.

sesquipedalian (ˌsɛskwɪpɪ'deɪlɪən) *or* (*less commonly*) **sesquipedal** (sɛs'kwɪpədᵊl) *adj.* **1.** tending to use very long words. **2.** (of words or expressions) long and ponderous; polysyllabic. ~*n.* **3.** a polysyllabic word. [C17: from Latin *sēsquipedālis* of a foot and a half (coined by Horace in *Ars Poetica*), from SESQUI- + *pedālis* of the foot, from *pēs* foot] —ˌ**sesquipe'dalianism** *n.*

sessile ('sɛsaɪl) *adj.* **1.** (of flowers or leaves) having no stalk; growing directly from the stem. **2.** (of animals such as the barnacle) permanently attached to a substratum. [C18: from Latin *sēssilis* concerning sitting, from *sedēre* to sit] —**sessility** (sɛ'sɪlɪtɪ) *n.*

sessile oak *n.* another name for the **durmast** (sense 1).

session ('sɛʃən) *n.* **1.** the meeting of a court, legislature, judicial body, etc., for the execution of its function or the transaction of business. **2.** a single continuous meeting of such a body. **3.** a series or period of such meetings. **4.** *Education.* **a.** the time during which classes are held. **b.** a school or university term or year. **5.** *Presbyterian Church.* the judicial and administrative body presiding over a local congregation and consisting of the minister and elders. **6.** a meeting of a group of musicians to record in a studio. **7.** a meeting of a group of people to pursue an activity. **8.** any period devoted to an activity. **9.** See **Court of Session.** [C14: from Latin *sessiō* a sitting, from *sedēre* to sit] —'**sessional** *adj.* —'**sessionally** *adv.*

session musician *n.* a studio musician, esp. one who works freelance.

sessions ('sɛʃənz) *pl. n.* the sittings or a sitting of justice in court. See **magistrates' court, quarter sessions.**

sesterce ('sɛstɜːs) *or* **sestertius** (sɛ'stɜːtɪəs) *n.* a silver or, later, bronze coin of ancient Rome worth a quarter of a denarius. [C16: from Latin *sēstertius* a coin worth two and a half asses, from *sēmis* half + *tertius* a third]

sestertium (sɛ'stɜːtɪəm) *n., pl.* **-tia** (-tɪə). an ancient Roman money of account equal to 1000 sesterces. [C16: from Latin, from the phrase *mille sestertium* a thousand of sesterces; see SESTERCE]

sestet (sɛ'stɛt) *n.* **1.** *Prosody.* the last six lines of a Petrarchan sonnet. **2.** *Prosody.* any six-line stanza. **3.** another word for **sextet** (sense 1). [C19: from Italian *sestetto,* from *sesto* sixth, from Latin *sextus,* from *sex* six]

sestina (sɛ'stiːnə) *n.* an elaborate verse form of Italian origin, normally unrhymed, consisting of six stanzas of six lines each and a concluding tercet. The six final words of the lines in the first stanza are repeated in a different order in each of the remaining five stanzas and also in the concluding tercet. Also called: **sextain.** [C19: from Italian, from *sesto* sixth, from Latin *sextus*]

set[1] (sɛt) *vb.* **sets, setting, set.** (*mainly tr.*) **1.** to put or place in position or into a specified state or condition: *to set a book on the table; to set someone free.* **2.** (*also intr.*; foll. by *to* or *on*) to put or be put (to); apply or be applied: *he set fire to the house; they set the dogs on the scent.* **3.** to put into order or readiness for use; prepare: *to set a trap; to set the table for dinner.* **4.** (*also intr.*) to put, form, or be formed into a jelled, firm, fixed, or rigid state: *the jelly set in three hours.* **5.** (*also intr.*) to put or be put into a position that will restore a normal state: *to set a broken bone.* **6.** to adjust (a clock or other instrument) to a position. **7.** to determine or establish: *we have set the date for our wedding.* **8.** to prescribe or allot (an undertaking, course of study, etc.): *the examiners have set "Paradise Lost".* **9.** to arrange in a particular fashion, esp. an attractive one: *she set her hair; the jeweller set the diamonds in silver.* **10.** (of clothes) to hang or fit (well or badly) when worn. **11.** Also: **set to music.** to provide music for (a poem or other text to be sung). **12.** Also: **set up.** *Printing.* to arrange or produce (type, film, etc.) from (text or copy); compose. **13.** to arrange (a stage, television studio, etc.) with scenery and props. **14.** to describe or present (a scene or the background to a literary work, story, etc.) in words: *his novel is set in Russia.* **15.** to present as a model of good or bad behaviour (esp. in the phrases **set an example, set a good example, set a bad example**). **16.** (foll. by *on* or *by*) to value (something) at a specified price or estimation of worth: *he set a high price on his services.* **17.** (foll. by *at*) to price (the value of something) at a specified sum: *he set his services at £300.* **18.** (*also intr.*) to give or be given a particular direction: *his course was set to the East.* **19.** (*also intr.*) to rig (a sail) or (of a sail) to be rigged so as to catch the wind. **20.** (*intr.*) (of the sun, moon, etc.) to disappear beneath the horizon. **21.** to leave (dough, etc.) in one place so that it may prove. **22.** to sharpen (a cutting blade) by grinding or honing the angle adjacent to the cutting edge. **23.** to displace alternate teeth of (a saw) to opposite sides of the blade in order to increase the cutting efficiency. **24.** to sink (the head of a nail) below the surface surrounding it by using a nail set. **25.** *Computer technol.* to give (a binary circuit) the value 1. **26.** (of plants) to produce (fruits, seeds, etc.) after pollination or (of fruits or seeds) to develop after pollination. **27.** to plant (seeds, seedlings, etc.). **28.** to place (a hen) on (eggs) for the purpose of incubation. **29.** (*intr.*) (of a gun dog) to turn in the direction of game, indicating its presence. **30.** *Scot. and Irish.* to let or lease: *to set a house.* **31.** *Bridge.* to defeat (one's opponents) in their attempt to make a contract. **32.** a dialect word for **sit. 33. set eyes on.** to see. ~*n.* **34.** the act of setting or the state of being set. **35.** a condition of firmness or hardness. **36.** bearing, carriage, or posture: *the set of a gun dog when pointing.* **37.** the fit or hang of a garment, esp. when worn. **38.** the scenery and other props used in and identifying the location of a stage or television production, film, etc. **39.** Also called: **set width.** *Printing.* **a.** the width of the body of a piece of type. **b.** the width of the lines of type in a page or column. **40.** *Nautical.* **a.** the cut of the sails or the arrangement of the sails, spars, rigging, etc., of a vessel. **b.** the direction from which a wind is blowing or towards which a tide or current is moving. **41.** *Psychol.* a temporary bias disposing an organism to react to a stimulus in one way rather than in others. **42.** a seedling, cutting, or similar part that is ready for planting: *onion sets.* **43.** a blacksmith's tool with a short head similar to a cold chisel set transversely onto a handle and used, when struck with a hammer, for cutting off lengths of iron bars. **44.** See **nail set. 45.** a mechanical distortion of shape or alignment. **46.** a variant spelling of **sett.** ~*adj.* **47.** fixed or established by authority or agreement: *set hours of work.* **48.** (*usually postpositive*) rigid or inflexible: *she is set in her ways.* **49.** conventional, artificial, or stereotyped, rather than spontaneous: *she made her apology in set phrases.* **50.** (*postpositive;* foll. by *on* or *upon*) resolute in intention: *he is set upon marrying.* **51.** (of a book, etc.) prescribed for students' preparation for an examination. ~See also **set about, set against, set aside, set back, set down, set forth, set in, set off, set on, set out, set to, set up, set upon.** [Old English *settan,* causative of *sittan* to SIT; related to Old Frisian *setta,* Old High German *sezzan*]

set² (set) *n.* **1.** a number of objects or people grouped or belonging together, often forming a unit or having certain features or characteristics in common: *a set of coins; John is in the top set for maths.* **2.** a group of people who associate together, esp. a clique: *he's part of the jet set.* **3.** *Maths, logic.* **a.** Also called: **class.** a collection of numbers, objects, etc., that is treated as an entity: {3, the moon} is the set the two members of which are the number 3 and the moon. **b.** (in some formulations) a class that can itself be a member of other classes. **4.** any apparatus that receives or transmits television or radio signals. **5.** *Tennis, squash, etc.* one of the units of a match, in tennis one in which one player or pair of players must win at least six games. **6. a.** the number of couples required for a formation dance. **b.** a series of figures that make up a formation dance. **7. a.** a band's or performer's concert repertoire on a given occasion: *the set included no new numbers.* **b.** a continuous performance: *the Who played two sets.* **8. make a dead set at. a.** to attack by arguing or ridiculing. **b.** (of a woman) to try to gain the attention and affections of (a man). ~*vb.* **sets, setting, set. 9.** (*intr.*) (in square dancing and country dancing) to perform a sequence of steps while facing towards another dancer: *set to your partners.* **10.** (*usually tr.*) to divide into sets: *in this school we set our older pupils for English.* [C14 (in the obsolete sense: a religious sect): from Old French *sette,* from Latin *secta* SECT; later sense development influenced by the verb SET¹]

SET (in Britain) *abbrev. for* selective employment tax: an employment payroll tax, first levied in 1966 and abolished when VAT was introduced in 1973.

seta ('siːtə) *n., pl.* **-tae** (-tiː). (in invertebrates and some plants) any bristle or bristle-like appendage. [C18: from Latin] —**setaceous** (sɪ'teɪʃəs) *adj.* —**se'taceously** *adv.* —**'setal** *adj.*

set about *vb.* (*intr., prep.*) **1.** to start or begin. **2.** to attack physically or verbally.

set against *vb.* (*tr., prep.*) **1.** to balance or compare: *to set a person's faults against his virtues.* **2.** to cause to be hostile or unfriendly to.

set aside *vb.* (*tr., adv.*) **1.** to reserve for a special purpose; put to one side. **2.** to discard, dismiss, or quash.

set-aside *n.* **a.** (in the European Community) a scheme in which a proportion of farmland is taken out of production in order to reduce surpluses or maintain or increase prices of a specific crop. **b.** (*as modifier*): *set-aside land.*

set back *vb.* (*tr., adv.*) **1.** to hinder; impede. **2.** *Informal.* to cost (a person) a specified amount. ~*n.* **setback. 3.** anything that serves to hinder or impede. **4.** a recession in the upper part of a high building, esp. one that increases the daylight at lower levels. **5.** Also called: **offset, setoff.** a steplike shelf where a wall is reduced in thickness.

set chisel *n.* another name for **cold chisel.**

set down *vb.* (*tr., adv.*) **1.** to write down or record. **2.** to judge, consider, or regard: *he set him down as an idiot.* **3.** (foll. by *to*) to ascribe; attribute: *his attitude was set down to his illness.* **4.** to reprove; rebuke. **5.** to snub; dismiss. **6.** *Brit.* to allow (passengers) to alight from a bus, taxi, etc.

se tenant *French.* (sə tənɑ̃) *adj.* **1.** denoting two postage stamps of different face values and sometimes of different designs in an unseparated pair. ~*n.* **2.** such a pair of stamps. [literally: holding together]

set forth *vb.* (*adv.*) *Formal or archaic.* **1.** (*tr.*) to state, express, or utter: *he set forth his objections.* **2.** (*intr.*) to start out on a journey: *the expedition set forth on the first of July.*

SETI ('setɪ) *n. acronym for* Search for Extraterrestrial Intelligence; a scientific programme attempting, by radio transmissions, to make contact with beings from other planets.

setiferous (sɪ'tɪfərəs) *or* **setigerous** (sɪ'tɪdʒərəs) *adj. Biology.* bearing bristles. [C19: see SETA, -FEROUS, -GEROUS]

setiform ('siːtɪˌfɔːm) *adj. Biology.* shaped like a seta.

set in *vb.* (*intr., adv.*) **1.** to become established: *the winter has set in.* **2.** (of wind) to blow or (of current) to move towards shore. ~*adj.* **set-in. 3.** (of a part) made separately and then added to a larger whole: *a set-in sleeve.*

setline ('setˌlaɪn) *n.* any of various types of fishing line that consist of a long line suspended across a stream, between buoys, etc., and having shorter hooked and baited lines attached. See **trawl** (sense 2), **trotline.**

set off *vb.* (*adv.*) **1.** (*intr.*) to embark on a journey. **2.** (*tr.*) to cause (a person) to act or do something, such as laugh or tell stories. **3.** (*tr.*) to cause to explode. **4.** (*tr.*) to act as a foil or contrast to, esp. so as to improve: *that brooch sets your dress off well.* **5.** (*tr.*) *Accounting.* to cancel a credit on (one account) against a debit on another, both of which are in the name of the same person, enterprise, etc. **6.** (*intr.*) to bring a claim by way of setoff. ~*n.* **setoff. 7.** anything that serves as a counterbalance. **8.** anything that serves to contrast with or enhance something else; foil. **9.** another name for **setback** (sense 5). **10.** a counterbalancing debt or claim offered by a debtor against a creditor. **11.** a cross claim brought by a debtor that partly offsets the creditor's claim. See also **counterclaim.**

set-off *n. Printing.* a fault in which ink is transferred from a heavily inked or undried printed sheet to the sheet next to it in a pile. Also called (esp. Brit.): **offset.**

set on *vb.* (*tr.*) **1.** (*prep.*) to cause to attack: *they set the dogs on him.* **2.** (*adv.*) to instigate or incite; urge: *he set the child on to demand food.*

setose ('siːtəʊs) *adj. Biology.* covered with setae; bristly. [C17: from Latin *saetōsus,* from *saeta* a bristle]

set out *vb.* (*adv., mainly tr.*) **1.** to present, arrange, or display: *he set the flowers out in the vase.* **2.** to give a full account of; explain exactly: *he set out the matter in full.* **3.** to plan or lay out (a garden, etc.). **4.** (*intr.*) to begin or embark on an undertaking, esp. a journey.

set piece *n.* **1.** a work of literature, music, etc., often having a conventional or prescribed theme, intended to create an impressive effect. **2.** a piece of scenery built to stand independently as part of a stage set. **3.** a display of fireworks. **4.** *Sport.* a rehearsed team manoeuvre, usually attempted in continuous games at a restart of play, esp. when the other side has been penalized for improper play.

set point *n. Tennis, etc.* a point that would enable one side to win a set.

setscrew ('setˌskruː) *n.* a screw that fits into the boss or hub of a wheel, coupling, cam, etc., and prevents motion of the part relative to the shaft on which it is mounted.

set square *n.* a thin flat piece of plastic, metal, etc., in the shape of a right-angled triangle, used in technical drawing.

sett *or* **set** (sɛt) *n.* **1.** a small rectangular paving block made of stone, such as granite, used to provide a durable road surface. Compare **cobblestone.** **2.** the burrow of a badger. **3. a.** a square in a pattern of tartan. **b.** the pattern itself. [C19: variant of SET[1] (n.)]

settee (sɛ'tiː) *n.* a seat, for two or more people, with a back and usually with arms. [C18: changed from SETTLE[2]]

setter ('sɛtə) *n.* any of various breeds of large gun dog, having silky coats and plumed tails. See **English setter, Gordon setter, Irish setter.** [C16: so called because they can be used to indicate where game is: see SET[1]]

set theory *n.* **1.** *Maths.* the branch of mathematics concerned with the properties and interrelationships of sets. **2.** *Logic.* a theory constructed within first-order logic that yields the mathematical theory of classes, esp. one that distinguishes sets from proper classes as a means of avoiding certain paradoxes.

setting ('sɛtɪŋ) *n.* **1.** the surroundings in which something is set; scene. **2.** the scenery, properties, or background, used to create the location for a stage play, film, etc. **3.** *Music.* a composition consisting of a certain text and music provided or arranged for it. **4.** the metal mounting and surround of a gem: *diamonds in an antique gold setting.* **5.** the tableware, cutlery, etc., for a single place at table. **6.** any of a series of points on a scale or dial that can be selected to control the level as of temperature, speed, etc., at which a machine functions. **7.** a clutch of eggs in a bird's nest, esp. a clutch of hen's eggs.

setting lotion *n.* a perfumed solution of gum or a synthetic resin in a solvent, used in hairdressing to make a set last longer.

setting rule *n. Printing.* a metal strip used in the hand composition of type in a stick to separate the line being set from the previous one.

settle[1] ('sɛtᵊl) *vb.* **1.** (*tr.*) to put in order; arrange in a desired state or condition: *he settled his affairs before he died.* **2.** to arrange or be arranged in a fixed or comfortable position: *he settled himself by the fire.* **3.** (*intr.*) to come to rest or a halt: *a bird settled on the hedge.* **4.** to take up or cause to take up residence: *the family settled in the country.* **5.** to establish or become established in a way of life, job, residence, etc. **6.** (*tr.*) to migrate to and form a community; colonize. **7.** to make or become quiet, calm, or stable. **8.** (*intr.*) to be cast or spread; come down: *fog settled over a wide area.* **9.** to make (a liquid) clear or (of a liquid) to become clear; clarify. **10.** to cause (sediment) to sink to the bottom, as in a liquid, or (of sediment) to sink thus. **11.** to subside or cause to subside and become firm or compact: *the dust settled.* **12.** (sometimes foll. by *up*) to pay off or account for (a bill, debt, etc.). **13.** (*tr.*) to decide, conclude, or dispose of: *to settle an argument.* **14.** (*intr.*; often foll. by *on* or *upon*) to agree or fix: *to settle upon a plan.* **15.** (*tr.*; usually foll. by *on* or *upon*) to secure (title, property, etc.) to a person, as by making a deed of settlement, will, etc.: *he settled his property on his wife.* **16.** to determine (a legal dispute, etc.) by agreement of the parties without resort to court action (esp. in the phrase **settle out of court**). ~See also **settle down, settle for, settle in, settle with.** [Old English *setlan;* related to Dutch *zetelen;* see SETTLE[2]] —'**settleable** *adj.*

settle[2] ('sɛtᵊl) *n.* a seat, for two or more people, usually made of wood with a high back and arms, and sometimes having a storage space in the boxlike seat. [Old English *setl;* related to Old Saxon, Old High German *sezzal*]

settle down *vb.* (*adv., mainly intr.*) **1.** (*also tr.*) to make or become quiet and orderly. **2.** (often foll. by *to*) to apply oneself diligently: *please settle down to work.* **3.** to adopt an orderly and routine way of life, take up a permanent post, etc., esp. after marriage.

settle for *vb.* (*intr., prep.*) to accept or agree to in spite of dispute or dissatisfaction.

settle in *vb.* (*adv.*) to become or help to become adapted to and at ease in a new home, environment, etc.

settlement ('sɛtᵊlmənt) *n.* **1.** the act or state of settling or being settled. **2.** the establishment of a new region; colonization. **3.** a place newly settled; colony. **4.** a collection of dwellings forming a community, esp. on a frontier. **5.** a community formed by members of a group, esp. of a religious sect. **6.** a public building used to provide educational and general welfare facilities for persons living in deprived areas. **7.** a subsidence of all or part of a structure. **8. a.** the payment of an outstanding account, invoice, charge, etc. **b.** (*as modifier*): settlement day. **9.** an adjustment or agreement reached in matters of finance, business, etc. **10.** *Law.* **a.** a conveyance, usually to trustees, of property to be enjoyed by several persons in succession. **b.** the deed or other instrument conveying such property. **c.** the determination of a dispute, etc., by mutual agreement without resorting to legal proceedings.

settler ('sɛtlə) *n.* a person who settles in a new country or a colony.

settler's clock *n. Austral.* (formerly) an informal name for **kookaburra.** [C19: so called because its laugh was heard at dawn and sunset]

settle with *vb.* (*prep.*) **1.** (*intr.*) to pay a debt or bill to. **2.** (*intr.*) to make an agreement with. **3.** to get one's revenge for (a wrong or injury) with (a person).

settlings ('sɛtlɪŋz) *pl. n.* any matter or substance that has settled at the bottom of a liquid; sediment; dregs.

settlor ('sɛtlə) *n. Law.* a person who settles property on someone.

set to *vb.* (*intr., adv.*) **1.** to begin working. **2.** to start fighting. ~*n.* **set-to. 3.** *Informal.* a brief disagreement or fight.

set up *vb.* (*adv., mainly tr.*) **1.** (*also intr.*) to put into a position of power, etc. **2.** (*also intr.*) to begin or enable (someone) to begin (a new venture), as by acquiring or providing means, equipment, etc. **3.** to build or construct: *to set up a shed.* **4.** to raise, cause, or produce: *to set up a wail.* **5.** to advance or propose: *to set up a theory.* **6.** to restore the health of: *the sea air will set you up again.* **7.** to establish (a record). **8.** *Informal.* to cause (a person) to be blamed, accused, etc. **9.** *Informal.* **a.** to provide (drinks, etc.) for: *set 'em up, Joe!* **b.** to pay for the drinks of: *I'll set up the next round.* **10.** *Printing.* another term for **set**[1] (sense 12). ~*n.* **setup. 11.** *Informal.* the way in which anything is organized or arranged. **12.** *Slang, chiefly U.S. and Canadian.* an event the result of which is prearranged: *it's a setup.* **13.** a prepared arrangement of materials, machines, etc., for a job or undertaking. **14.** a station at which a surveying instrument, esp. a theodolite, is set up. **15.** *Films.* the position of the camera, microphones, and performers at the beginning of a scene. ~*adj.* **set-up. 16.** physically well-built.

set upon *vb.* (*intr., prep.*) to attack: *three thugs set upon him.*

set width *n.* another name for **set**[1] (sense 39).

seven ('sɛvᵊn) *n.* **1.** the cardinal number that is the sum of six and one and is a prime number. See also **number** (sense 1). **2.** a numeral, 7, VII, etc., representing this number. **3.** the amount or quantity that is one greater than six. **4.** anything representing, represented by, or consisting of seven units, such as a playing card with seven symbols on it. **5.** Also called: **seven o'clock.** seven hours after noon or midnight. ~*determiner.* **6. a.** amounting to seven: *seven swans a-swimming.* **b.** (*as pronoun*): *you've eaten seven already.* ~Related prefixes: **hepta-, septi-.** ~See also **sevens.** [Old English *seofon;* related to Gothic *sibun,* German *sieben,* Old Norse *sjau,* Latin *septem,* Greek *hepta,* Sanskrit *saptá*]

seven deadly sins *pl. n.* a fuller name for the **deadly sins.**

sevenfold ('sɛvᵊnˌfəʊld) *adj.* **1.** equal to or having seven times as many or as much. **2.** composed of seven parts. ~*adv.* **3.** by or up to seven times as many or as much.

sevens ('sɛvᵊnz) *n.* (*functioning as sing.*) a Rugby Union match or series of matches played with seven players on each side.

seven seas *pl. n.* the oceans of the world considered as the N and S Pacific, the N and S Atlantic, and the Arctic, Antarctic, and Indian Oceans.

seven-segment display *n.* an arrangement of seven bars forming a square figure of eight, used in electronic displays of alphanumeric characters: any letter or figure can be represented by illuminating selected bars.

seventeen ('sɛvᵊn'tiːn) *n.* **1.** the cardinal number that is the sum of ten and seven and is a prime number. See also **number** (sense 1). **2.** a numeral, 17, XVII, etc., representing this number. **3.** the amount or quantity that is seven more than ten. **4.** something represented by, representing, or consisting of 17 units. ~*determiner.* **5. a.** amounting to seventeen: *seventeen attempts.* **b.** (*as pronoun*): *seventeen were sold.* [Old English *seofontīene*]

seventeenth ('sɛvᵊn'tiːnθ) *adj.* **1.** (*usually prenominal*) **a.** coming after the sixteenth in numbering or counting order, position, time, etc.; being the ordinal number of *seventeen:* often written 17th. **b.** (*as n.*): *the ship docks on the seventeenth.* ~*n.* **2. a.** one of 17 approximately equal parts of something. **b.** (*as modifier*): *a seventeenth part.* **3.** the fraction equal to one divided by 17 (1/17).

seventeen-year locust *n.* an E North American cicada, *Magicicada septendecim,* appearing in great numbers at infrequent intervals because its nymphs take 13 or 17 years to mature. Also called: **periodical cicada.**

seventh ('sɛvᵊnθ) *adj.* **1.** (*usually prenominal*) **a.** coming after the sixth and before the eighth in numbering or counting order, position, time, etc.; being the ordinal number of *seven:* often written 7th. **b.** (*as n.*): *she left on the seventh; he was the seventh to arrive.* ~*n.* **2. a.** one of seven equal or nearly equal parts of an object, quantity, measurement, etc. **b.** (*as modifier*): *a seventh part.* **3.** the fraction equal to one divided by seven (1/7). **4.** *Music.* **a.** the interval between one note and another seven notes away from it counting inclusively along the diatonic scale. **b.** one of two notes constituting such an interval in relation to the other. See also **major** (sense 13), **minor** (sense 4), **interval** (sense 5). **c.** short for **seventh chord.** ~*adv.* **5.** Also: **seventhly.** after the sixth person, position, event, etc. ~*sentence connector.* **6.** Also: **seventhly.** as the seventh point: linking what follows to the previous statements, as in a speech or argument.

seventh chord *n. Music.* a chord consisting of a triad with a seventh added above the root. See **dominant seventh chord, diminished seventh chord, major seventh chord, minor seventh chord.**

Seventh-Day Adventist *n. Protestant.* a member of that branch of the Adventists which constituted itself as a separate body after the expected Second Coming of Christ failed to be realized in 1844. They are strongly Protestant, believe that Christ's coming is imminent, and observe Saturday instead of Sunday as their Sabbath.

seventh heaven *n.* **1.** the final state of eternal bliss, esp. according to Talmudic and Muslim eschatology. **2.** a state of supreme happiness. [C19: so named from the belief that there are seven levels of heaven, the seventh and most exalted being the abode of God and the angels]

seventieth ('sɛvᵊntɪɪθ) *adj.* **1.** (*usually prenominal*) **a.** being the ordinal number of *seventy* in numbering or counting order, position, time, etc.: often written 70th. **b.** (*as n.*): *the seventieth in line.* ~*n.* **2. a.** one of 70 approximately equal parts of something. **b.** (*as modifier*): *a seventieth part.* **3.** the fraction equal to one divided by 70 (1/70).

seventy ('sɛvᵊntɪ) *n., pl.* **-ties. 1.** the cardinal number that is the product of ten and seven. See also **number** (sense 1). **2.** a numeral, 70, LXX, etc., representing this number. **3.** (*pl.*) the numbers 70–79, esp. the 70th to the 79th year of a person's life or of a particular century. **4.** the amount or quantity that is seven times as big as ten. **5.** something represented by, representing, or consisting of 70 units. ~*determiner.* **6. a.** amounting to seventy: *the seventy varieties of fabric.* **b.** (*as pronoun*): *to invite seventy to the wedding.* [Old English *seofentig*]

seven-up *n.* a card game in which the lead to each round determines the trump suit. Also called: **all fours, pitch.**

seven-year itch *n.* **1.** *Pathol.* an informal name for **scabies. 2.** *Informal.* a tendency towards infidelity, traditionally said to begin after about seven years of marriage.

sever ('sɛvə) *vb.* **1.** to put or be put apart; separate. **2.** to divide or be divided into parts. **3.** (*tr.*) to break off or dissolve (a tie, relationship, etc.). [C14 *severen,* from Old French *severer,* from Latin *sēparāre* to SEPARATE]

severable ('sɛvərəbᵊl) *adj.* **1.** able to be severed. **2.** *Law.* capable of being separated, as a clause in an agreement: *a severable contract.*

several ('sɛvrəl) *determiner.* **1. a.** more than a few; an indefinite small number: *several people objected.* **b.** (*as pronoun; functioning as pl.*): *several of them know.* ~*adj.* **2.** (*prenominal*) various; separate: *the members with their several occupations.* **3.** (*prenominal*) distinct; different: *three several times.* **4.** *Law.* capable of being dealt with separately; not shared. Compare **joint** (sense 15). [C15: via Anglo-French from Medieval Latin *sēparālis,* from Latin *sēpār,* from *sēparāre* to SEPARATE]

severally ('sɛvrəlɪ) *adv. Archaic or literary.* **1.** separately, individually, or distinctly. **2.** each in turn; respectively.

severalty ('sɛvrəltɪ) *n., pl.* **-ties. 1.** the state of being several or separate. **2.** (usually preceded by *in*) *Property law.* the tenure of property, esp. land, in a person's own right and not jointly with another or others.

severance ('sɛvərəns) *n.* **1.** the act of severing or state of being severed. **2.** a separation. **3.** *Law.* the division into separate parts of a joint estate, contract, etc.

severance pay *n.* compensation paid by an organization to an employee who leaves because, through no fault of his own, the job to which he was appointed ceases to exist, as during rationalization, and no comparable job is available to him.

severe (sɪ'vɪə) *adj.* **1.** rigorous or harsh in the treatment of others; strict: *a severe parent.* **2.** serious in appearance or manner; stern. **3.** critical or dangerous: *a severe illness.* **4.** causing misery or discomfort by its harshness: *severe weather.* **5.** strictly restrained in appearance; austere: *a severe way of dressing.* **6.** hard to endure, perform, or accomplish: *a severe test.* **7.** rigidly precise or exact. [C16: from Latin *sevērus*] —**se'verely** *adv.* —**se'vereness** *or* **severity** (sɪ'vɛrɪtɪ) *n.*

Seville orange (sə'vɪl) *n.* **1.** an orange tree, *Citrus aurantium,* of tropical and semitropical regions: grown for its bitter fruit, which is used to make marmalade. **2.** the fruit of this tree. ~Also called: **bitter orange.** [named after *Seville,* a port in SW Spain]

Sèvres (*French* sɛvrə) *n.* porcelain ware manufactured at Sèvres, near Paris, from 1756, characterized by the use of clear colours and elaborate decorative detail.

sew (səʊ) *vb.* **sews, sewing, sewed; sewn** *or* **sewed. 1.** to join or decorate (pieces of fabric, etc.) by means of a thread repeatedly passed through with a needle or similar implement. **2.** (*tr.;* often foll. by *on* or *up*) to attach, fasten, or close by sewing. **3.** (*tr.*) to make (a garment, etc.) by sewing. ~See also **sew up.** [Old English *sēowan;* related to Old Norse *sȳja,* Gothic *siujan,* Old High German *siuwen,* Latin *suere* to sew, Sanskrit *sīvjati* he sews]

sewage ('suːɪdʒ) *n.* waste matter from domestic or industrial establishments that is carried away in sewers or drains for dumping or conversion into a form that is not toxic. [C19: back formation from SEWER¹]

sewage farm *n.* a place where sewage is treated, esp. for use as manure.

sewage gas *n.* gas given off in the digestion of sewage consisting of approximately 66 per cent methane and 34 per cent carbon dioxide.

sewan ('siːwən) *n.* a variant spelling of **seawan.**

sewellel (sɪ'wɛləl) *n.* another name for **mountain beaver** (see **beaver¹** (sense 3)). [C19: probably from Chinook]

sewer¹ ('suːə) *n.* **1.** a drain or pipe, esp. one that is underground, used to carry away surface water or sewage. ~*vb.* **2.** (*tr.*) to provide with sewers. [C15: from Old French *esseveur,* from *essever* to drain, from Vulgar Latin *exaquāre* (unattested), from Latin EX-¹ +*aqua* water]

sewer² ('səʊə) *n.* a person or thing that sews.

sewer³ ('suːə) *n.* (in medieval England) a servant of high rank in charge of the serving of meals and the seating of guests. [C14: shortened from Anglo-French *asseour,* from Old French *asseoir* to cause to sit, from Latin *assidēre,* from *sedēre* to sit]

sewerage ('suːərɪdʒ) *n.* **1.** an arrangement of sewers. **2.** the removal of surface water or sewage by means of sewers. **3.** another word for **sewage.**

sewin *or* **sewen** ('sjuən) *n.* (in Wales and Ireland) another name for the **sea trout.**

sewing ('səʊɪŋ) *n.* **a.** a piece of cloth, etc., that is sewn or to be sewn. **b.** (*as modifier*): *sewing basket.*

sewing machine *n.* any machine designed to sew material. It is now usually driven by electric motor but is sometimes operated by a foot treadle or by hand.

sewn (səʊn) *vb.* a past participle of **sew.**

sew up *vb.* (*tr., adv.*) **1.** to fasten or mend completely by sewing. **2.** *U.S.* to acquire sole use or control of. **3.** *Informal.* to complete or negotiate successfully: *to sew up a deal.*

sex (sɛks) *n.* **1.** the sum of the characteristics that distinguish organisms on the basis of their reproductive function. **2.** either of the two categories, male or female, into which organisms are placed on this basis. **3.** short for **sexual intercourse. 4.** feelings or behaviour resulting from the urge to gratify the sexual instinct. **5.** sexual matters in general. ~*modifier.* **6.** of or concerning sexual matters: *sex education; sex hygiene.* **7.** based on or arising from the difference between the sexes: *sex discrimination.* ~*vb.* **8.** (*tr.*) to ascertain the sex of. [C14: from Latin *sexus;* compare *secāre* to divide]

sex- *combining form.* six: *sexcentennial.* [from Latin]

sexagenarian (ˌsɛksədʒɪ'nɛərɪən) *n.* **1.** a person from 60 to 69 years old. ~*adj.* **2.** being from 60 to 69 years old. **3.** of or relating to a sexagenarian. [C18: from Latin *sexāgēnārius,* from *sexāgēnī* sixty each, from *sexāgintā* sixty] —**sexagenary** (sɛk'sædʒɪnərɪ) *adj., n.*

Sexagesima (ˌsɛksə'dʒɛsɪmə) *n.* the second Sunday before Lent. [C16: from Latin: sixtieth, from *sexāgintā* sixty]

sexagesimal (ˌsɛksə'dʒɛsɪməl) *adj.* **1.** relating to or based on the number 60: *sexagesimal measurement of angles.* ~*n.* **2.** a fraction in which the denominator is some power of 60; a sixtieth.

sexangular (sɛks'æŋgjʊlə) *adj.* another name for **hexagonal.** —**sex'angularly** *adv.*

sex appeal *n.* the quality or power of attracting the opposite sex.

sexcentenary (ˌsɛksɛn'tiːnərɪ) *adj.* **1.** of or relating to 600 or a period of 600 years. **2.** of, relating to, or celebrating a 600th anniversary. ~*n., pl.* **-naries. 3.** a 600th anniversary or its celebration. [C18: from Latin *sexcentēnī* six hundred each]

sex change *n.* **a.** a change in a person's physical sexual characteristics to those of the opposite sex, often achieved by surgery. **b.** (*as modifier*): *a sex-change operation.*

sex chromosome *n.* either of the chromosomes determining the sex of animals. See also **X-chromosome, Y-chromosome.**

sexed (sɛkst) *adj.* **1.** (*in combination*) having a specified degree of sexuality: *undersexed.* **2.** of, relating to, or having sexual differentiation.

sexennial (sɛk'sɛnɪəl) *adj.* **1.** occurring once every six years or over a period of six years. ~*n.* **2.** a sixth anniversary. [C17: from Latin *sexennis* of six years, from *sex* six + *annus* a year] —**sex'ennially** *adv.*

sex hormone *n.* an animal hormone affecting development and growth of reproductive organs and related parts.

sexism ('sɛksɪzəm) *n.* discrimination on the basis of sex, esp. the oppression of women by men. [C20: from SEX + -ISM, on the model of RACISM] —**'sexist** *n., adj.*

sexivalent *or* **sexavalent** (ˌsɛksɪ'veɪlənt) *adj. Chem.* another word for **hexavalent.**

sexless ('sɛkslɪs) *adj.* **1.** having or showing no sexual differentiation. **2.** having no sexual desires. **3.** sexually unattractive. —**'sexlessly** *adv.* —**'sexlessness** *n.*

sex-limited *adj. Genetics.* of or designating a character or the gene producing it that appears in one sex only.

sex linkage *n. Genetics.* the condition in which a particular gene is located on a sex chromosome, esp. on the X-chromosome, so that the character controlled by the gene is associated with either of the sexes. —**'sex,linked** *adj.*

sex object *n.* a person viewed or treated as a means of obtaining sexual gratification.

sexology (sɛk'sɒlədʒɪ) *n.* the study of sexual behaviour in human beings. —**sex'ologist** *n.* —**sexological** (ˌsɛksə'lɒdʒɪkᵊl) *adj.*

sexpartite (sɛks'pɑːtaɪt) *adj.* **1.** (esp. of vaults, arches, etc.) divided into or composed of six parts. **2.** maintained by or involving six participants or groups of participants.

sexploitation (ˌsɛksplɔɪ'teɪʃən) *n.* the commercial exploitation of sex in films and other media. [C20: blend of SEX + EXPLOITATION]

sexpot ('sɛksˌpɒt) *n. Slang.* a person, esp. a young woman, considered as being sexually very attractive.

sex shop *n.* **a.** a shop selling aids purporting to increase the pleasurableness of sexual activity. **b.** a shop selling erotica and pornographic material.

sex-starved *adj.* deprived of sexual gratification.

sext (sɛkst) *n. Chiefly R.C. Church.* the fourth of the seven canonical hours of the divine office or the prayers prescribed for it:

originally the sixth hour of the day (noon). [C15: from Church Latin *sexta hōra* the sixth hour]
sextain ('sɛksteɪn) *n.* another word for **sestina.** [C17: from obsolete French *sestine* SESTINA, but also influenced by obsolete *sixain* stanza of six lines]
sextan ('sɛkstən) *adj.* (of a fever) marked by paroxysms that recur every fifth day. [C17: from Medieval Latin *sextana (febris)* (fever) of the sixth (day)]
Sextans ('sɛkstənz) *n., Latin genitive* **Sextantis** (sɛks'tæntɪs). a faint constellation lying on the celestial equator close to Leo and Hydra. [New Latin: SEXTANT]
sextant ('sɛkstənt) *n.* **1.** an optical instrument used in navigation and consisting of a telescope through which a sighting of a heavenly body is taken, with protractors for determining its angular distance above the horizon or from another heavenly body. **2.** a sixth part of a circle having an arc which subtends an angle of 60°. [C17: from Latin *sextāns* one sixth of a unit]
sextet *or* **sextette** (sɛks'tɛt) *n.* **1.** *Music.* a group of six singers or instrumentalists or a piece of music composed for such a group. **2.** a group of six people or things. [C19: variant of SESTET, with Latinization of *ses-*]
sex therapy *n.* treatment by counselling, behaviour modification, etc., for psychosexual and physical problems in sexual intercourse. —**sex therapist** *n.*
sextile ('sɛkstaɪl) *n.* **1.** *Statistics.* one of five actual or notional values of a variable dividing its distribution into six groups with equal frequencies. **2.** *Astrology, astronomy.* an aspect or position of 60° between two planets or other celestial bodies. [C16: from Latin *sextīlis* one sixth (of a circle), from *sextus* sixth]
sextillion (sɛks'tɪljən) *n., pl.* **-lions** *or* **-lion. 1.** (in Britain, France, and Germany) the number represented as one followed by 36 zeros (10^{36}). **2.** (in the U.S. and Canada) the number represented as one followed by 21 zeros (10^{21}). [C17: from French, from SEX- + *-illion*, on the model of SEPTILLION] —**sex'tillionth** *adj., n.*
sexto ('sɛkstəʊ) *n., pl.* **-tos.** *Bookbinding.* another word for **sixmo.** [C19: from Latin *sextus* sixth]
sextodecimo (ˌsɛkstəʊ'dɛsɪˌməʊ) *n., pl.* **-mos.** *Bookbinding.* another word for **sixteenmo.** [C17: from Latin *sextusdecimus* sixteenth]
sexton ('sɛkstən) *n.* **1.** a man employed to act as caretaker of a church and its contents and graveyard, and often also as bell-ringer, gravedigger, etc. **2.** another name for the **burying beetle.** [C14: from Old French *secrestein*, from Medieval Latin *sacristānus* SACRISTAN]
sextuple ('sɛkstjʊpᵊl) *n.* **1.** a quantity or number six times as great as another. ~*adj.* **2.** six times as much or many; sixfold. **3.** consisting of six parts or members. **4.** (of musical time or rhythm) having six beats per bar. [C17: Latin *sextus* sixth + *-uple*, as in QUADRUPLE]
sextuplet ('sɛkstjʊplɪt) *n.* **1.** one of six offspring born at one birth. **2.** a group of six things. **3.** *Music.* a group of six notes played in a time value of four.
sextuplicate *n.* (sɛks'tuːpləkɪt, -ˌkeɪt, -'tjuː-, -'tʌp-). **1.** a group or set of six things, esp. identical copies. ~*adj.* (sɛks'tuːpləkɪt, -ˌkeɪt, -'tjuː-, -'tʌp-). **2.** six times as many, much, or often. **3.** *Maths.* raised to the sixth power. ~*vb.* (sɛks'tuːpləˌkeɪt, -'tjuː-, -'tʌp-). **4.** to multiply or become multiplied by six. [C20: from SEXTU(PLE + DU)PLICATE]
sex-typed *adj.* characterized as appropriate for or of one sex rather than the other. —'**sex-ˌtyping** *n.*
sexual ('sɛksjʊəl) *adj.* **1.** of, relating to, or characterized by sex or sexuality. **2.** (of reproduction) characterized by the union of male and female gametes. Compare **asexual** (sense 2). [C17: from Late Latin *sexuālis*; see SEX] —'**sexually** *adv.*
sexual dimorphism *n. Biology.* differences in appearance between the males and females of a species.
sexual harassment *n.* the persistent unwelcome directing of sexual remarks, looks, etc., at a woman, esp. in the workplace.
sexual intercourse *n.* the act of sexual procreation in which the insertion of the male's erect penis into the female's vagina is followed by rhythmic thrusting usually culminating in orgasm; copulation; coitus.
sexuality (ˌsɛksjʊ'ælɪtɪ) *n.* **1.** the state or quality of being sexual. **2.** preoccupation with or involvement in sexual matters. **3.** the possession of sexual potency.
sexual reproduction *n.* reproduction involving the fusion of a male and female haploid gamete.
sexual selection *n.* an evolutionary process in animals, in which selection by females of males with certain characters, such as large antlers or bright plumage, results in the preservation of these characters in the species.
sexy ('sɛksɪ) *adj.* **sexier, sexiest.** *Informal.* **1.** provoking or intended to provoke sexual interest: *a sexy dress; a sexy book.* **2.** feeling sexual interest; aroused. **3.** interesting, exciting, or trendy: *a sexy project; a sexy new car.* —'**sexily** *adv.* —'**sexiness** *n.*
Seyfert galaxy ('saɪfət) *n.* any of a class of small spiral galaxies having a very bright nucleus and inconspicuous arms. [C20: named after Carl K. *Seyfert* (died 1960), U.S. astronomer]
sf, sf., sfz, *or* **sfz.** *Music. abbrev. for* sforzando.
SF 1. Also: **sf** *abbrev. for* science fiction. ~ **2.** *international car registration for* Finland. [from Finnish *Suomi*]
SFA *abbrev. for:* **1.** Scottish Football Association. **2.** Sweet Fanny Adams. See **fanny adams.**
sferics ('sfɛrɪks) *n.* the usual U.S. spelling of **spherics**².
SFO *abbrev. for* Superannuation Funds Office: the department of the British Inland Revenue responsible for pensions, etc.
sforzando (sfɔː'tsɑːndəʊ) *or* **sforzato** (sfɔː'tsɑːtəʊ) *Music.* ~*adj., adv.* **1.** to be played with strong initial attack. Abbrev: **sf.** ~*n.* **2.** a symbol, mark, etc., such as >, written above a note, indicating this. [C19: from Italian, from *sforzare* to force, from EX-¹ + *forzare*, from Vulgar Latin *fortiāre* (unattested) to FORCE]
sfumato (sfuː'mɑːtəʊ) *n.* (in painting) a gradual transition between areas of different colour, avoiding sharp outlines. [from Italian, from *sfumato* shaded off, from *sfumare* to shade off, from Latin EX-¹ + *fūmāre* to smoke]
sg *abbrev. for* specific gravity.
SG *abbrev. for:* **1.** (in transformational grammar) singular. **2.** solicitor general.
sgd *abbrev. for* signed.
SGHWR *abbrev. for* steam-generating heavy-water reactor.
sgian-dhu ('skiːən'duː, 'skiːn-) *n. Scot.* a dirk carried in the stocking by Highlanders. [Gaelic *sgian* knife + *dhu* black]
S. Glam *abbrev. for* South Glamorgan.
SGP *international car registration for* Singapore.
sgraffito (sgræ'fiːtəʊ) *n., pl.* **-ti** (-tɪ). **1.** a technique in mural or ceramic decoration in which the top layer of glaze, plaster, etc., is incised with a design to reveal parts of the ground. **2.** such a decoration. **3.** an object decorated in such a way. [C18: from Italian, from *sgraffire* to scratch; see GRAFFITO]
Sgt *abbrev. for* Sergeant.
Sgt Maj. *abbrev. for* Sergeant Major.
sh (*spelling pron.* ʃʃʃ) *interj.* an exclamation to request silence or quiet.
sh. *abbrev. for:* **1.** *Stock Exchange.* share. **2.** sheep. **3.** *Bookbinding.* sheet. **4.** shilling.
SHA *Navigation. abbrev. for* sidereal hour angle.
Shaban *or* **Shaaban** (ʃə'bɑːn, ʃɑː-) *n.* the eighth month of the Muslim year. [from Arabic *sha'bān*]
Shabbat (ʃɑː'bɑːt), **Shabbos,** *or* **Shabbes** ('ʃɑːbəs) *n., pl.* **Shabbatot** (ˌʃɑːbɑː'tot), **Shabbosos** (ʃɑː'bosəs), *or* **Shabbosim** (ʃɑːbosəm). *Judaism.* another word for the **Sabbath.** [from Hebrew *shabbāth*; see SABBATH]
shabby ('ʃæbɪ) *adj.* **-bier, -biest. 1.** threadbare or dilapidated in appearance. **2.** wearing worn and dirty clothes; seedy. **3.** mean, despicable, or unworthy: *shabby treatment.* **4.** dirty or squalid. [C17: from Old English *sceabb* SCAB + -Y¹] —'**shabbily** *adv.* —'**shabbiness** *n.*
shabby-genteel *adj.* preserving or aspiring to the forms and manners of gentility despite appearing shabby.
Shabuoth (ʃə'vuːəs, -əʊs; *Hebrew* ʃavuː'ɔt) *n.* a variant spelling of **Shavuot.**
Shacharis ('ʃɑxəˌras) *or* **Shaharith** (ˌʃɑxɑ'rit) *Hebrew. n. Judaism.* the morning service.
shack (ʃæk) *n.* **1.** a roughly built hut. ~*vb.* **2.** See **shack up.** [C19: perhaps from dialect *shackly* ramshackle, from dialect *shack* to shake]
shackle ('ʃækᵊl) *n.* **1.** (*often pl.*) a metal ring or fastening, usually part of a pair used to secure a person's wrists or ankles; fetter. **2.** (*often pl.*) anything that confines or restricts freedom. **3.** a rope, tether, or hobble for an animal. **4.** a U-shaped bracket, the open end of which is closed by a bolt (**shackle pin**), used for securing ropes, chains, etc. ~*vb.* (*tr.*) **5.** to confine with or as if with shackles. **6.** to fasten or connect with a shackle. [Old English *sceacel*; related to Dutch *schakel*, Old Norse *skokull* wagon pole, Latin *cingere* to surround] —'**shackler** *n.*
shacko ('ʃækəʊ) *n., pl.* **shackos** *or* **shackoes.** a variant spelling of **shako.**
shack up *vb.* (*intr., adv.*; usually foll. by *with*) *Slang.* to live or take up residence, esp. with a mistress or lover.
shad (ʃæd) *n., pl.* **shad** *or* **shads. 1.** any of various herring-like food fishes of the genus *Alosa* and related genera, such as *A. alosa* (**allis shad**) of Europe, that migrate from the sea to freshwater to spawn: family *Clupeidae* (herrings). **2.** any of various similar but unrelated fishes. [Old English *sceadd*; related to Norwegian *skadd*, German *Schade* shad, Old Irish *scatān* herring, Latin *scatēre* to well up]
shadberry ('ʃædbərɪ, -brɪ) *n., pl.* **-ries.** another name for **serviceberry** (senses 1, 2). [C19: perhaps so called because they appear when SHAD fish are in the rivers to spawn]
shadbush ('ʃæd,bʊʃ) *n.* another name for **serviceberry** (sense 1).
shadchan *Yiddish.* (*Yiddish* 'ʃatxən; *Hebrew* ʃad'xan) *n., pl.* ***shadchanim*** (ʃat'xɔnɪm) *or* ***shadchans.*** a Jewish marriage broker. [from Hebrew *shadhkhān*, from *shiddēkh* to arrange a marriage]
shaddock ('ʃædək) *n.* another name for **pomelo.** [C17: named after Captain *Shaddock*, who brought its seed from the East Indies to Jamaica in 1696]
shade (ʃeɪd) *n.* **1.** relative darkness produced by the blocking out of light. **2.** a place made relatively darker or cooler than other areas by the blocking of light, esp. sunlight. **3.** a position of relative obscurity. **4.** something used to provide a shield or protection from a direct source of light, such as a lampshade. **5.** a darker area indicated in a painting, drawing, etc., by shading. **6.** a colour that varies slightly from a standard colour due to a difference in hue, saturation, or luminosity: *a darker shade of*

green. **7.** a slight amount: *a shade of difference.* **8.** *Literary.* a ghost. **9.** an archaic word for **shadow.** **10. put in the shade.** to appear better than (another); surpass. ~*vb.* (*mainly tr.*) **11.** to screen or protect from heat, light, view, etc. **12.** to make darker or dimmer. **13.** to represent (a darker area) in (a painting, drawing, etc.), by means of hatching, using a darker colour, etc. **14.** (*also intr.*) to change or cause to change slightly. **15.** to lower (a price) slightly. [Old English *sceadu;* related to Gothic *skadus,* Old High German *skato,* Old Irish *scāth* shadow, Greek *skotos* darkness, Swedish *skäddä* fog] —'**shadeless** *adj.*

shades (ʃeɪdz) *pl. n.* **1.** gathering darkness at nightfall. **2.** a slang word for **sunglasses.** **3.** (*often cap; preceded by the*) a literary term for **Hades.** **4.** (foll. by *of*) undertones or suggestions: *shades of my father!*

shading ('ʃeɪdɪŋ) *n.* the graded areas of tone, lines, dots, etc., indicating light and dark in a painting or drawing.

shadoof *or* **shaduf** (ʃə'du:f) *n.* a mechanism for raising water, consisting of a pivoted pole with a bucket at one end and a counterweight at the other, esp. as used in Egypt and the Near East. [C19: from Egyptian Arabic]

shadow ('ʃædəʊ) *n.* **1.** a dark image or shape cast on a surface by the interception of light rays by an opaque body. **2.** an area of relative darkness. **3.** the dark portions of a picture. **4.** a hint, image, or faint semblance: *beyond a shadow of a doubt.* **5.** a remnant or vestige: *a shadow of one's past self.* **6.** a reflection. **7.** a threatening influence; blight: *a shadow over one's happiness.* **8.** a spectre. **9.** an inseparable companion. **10.** a person who trails another in secret, such as a detective. **11.** *Med.* a dark area on an x-ray film representing an opaque structure or part. **12.** (in Jungian psychology) the archetype that represents man's animal ancestors. **13.** *Archaic or rare.* protection or shelter. **14.** (*modifier*) *Brit.* designating a member or members of the main opposition party in Parliament who would hold ministerial office if their party were in power: *shadow Chancellor; shadow cabinet.* ~*vb.* (*tr.*) **15.** to cast a shadow over. **16.** to make dark or gloomy; blight. **17.** to shade from light. **18.** to follow or trail secretly. **19.** (often foll. by *forth*) to represent vaguely. **20.** *Painting, drawing, etc.* another word for **shade** (sense 13). [Old English *sceadwe,* oblique case of *sceadu* SHADE; related to Dutch *schaduw*] —'**shadower** *n.* —'**shadowless** *adj.*

shadow-box *vb.* (*intr.*) **1.** *Boxing.* to practise blows and footwork against an imaginary opponent. **2.** to act or speak unconvincingly, without saying what one means, etc.: *he's just shadow-boxing.* —'**shadow-ˌboxing** *n.*

shadowgraph ('ʃædəʊˌgrɑ:f, -ˌgræf) *n.* **1.** a silhouette made by casting a shadow, usually of the hands, on a lighted surface. **2.** another name for **radiograph.**

shadow mask *n. Television.* a perforated metal sheet mounted close to the phosphor-dotted screen in some colour television tubes. The holes are positioned so that each of the three electron beams strikes the correct phosphor dot producing the required colour mixture in the image.

shadow play *n.* a theatrical entertainment using shadows thrown by puppets or actors onto a lighted screen.

shadow price *n. Economics.* the calculated price of a good or service for which no market price exists.

shadow test *n. Med.* another name for **retinoscopy.**

shadowy ('ʃædəʊɪ) *adj.* **1.** full of shadows; dark; shady. **2.** resembling a shadow in faintness; vague. **3.** illusory or imaginary. —'**shadowiness** *n.*

shaduf (ʃə'du:f) *n.* a variant spelling of **shadoof.**

shady ('ʃeɪdɪ) *adj.* **shadier, shadiest.** **1.** full of shade; shaded. **2.** affording or casting a shade. **3.** dim, quiet, or concealed. **4.** *Informal.* dubious or questionable as to honesty or legality. —'**shadily** *adv.* —'**shadiness** *n.*

SHAEF (ʃeɪf) *n. acronym for* Supreme Headquarters Allied Expeditionary Forces.

shaft (ʃɑ:ft) *n.* **1.** the long narrow pole that forms the body of a spear, arrow, etc. **2.** something directed at a person in the manner of a missile: *shafts of sarcasm.* **3.** a ray, beam, or streak, esp. of light. **4.** a rod or pole forming the handle of a hammer, axe, golf club, etc. **5.** a revolving rod that transmits motion or power: usually used of axial rotation. Compare **rod** (sense 9). **6.** one of the two wooden poles by which an animal is harnessed to a vehicle. **7.** *Anatomy.* **a.** the middle part (diaphysis) of a long bone. **b.** the main portion of any elongated structure or part. **8.** the middle part of a column or pier, between the base and the capital. **9.** a column, obelisk, etc., esp. one that forms a monument. **10.** *Architect.* a column that supports a vaulting rib, sometimes one of a set. **11.** a vertical passageway through a building, as for a lift. **12.** a vertical passageway into a mine. **13.** *Ornithol.* the central rib of a feather. **14.** an archaic or literary word for **arrow.** **15. get the shaft.** *U.S. and Canadian slang.* to be tricked or cheated. ~*vb.* **16.** *Slang.* to have sexual intercourse with (a woman). **17.** *U.S. and Canadian slang.* to trick or cheat. [Old English *sceaft;* related to Old Norse *skapt,* German *Schaft,* Latin *scāpus* shaft, Greek *skeptron* SCEPTRE, Lettish *skeps* javelin]

shaft feather *n. Archery.* one of the two fletchings on an arrow. Compare **cock feather.**

shafting ('ʃɑ:ftɪŋ) *n.* **1.** an assembly of rotating shafts for transmitting power. **2.** the stock from which shafts are made. **3.** *Architect.* a set of shafts.

shag[1] (ʃæg) *n.* **1.** a matted tangle, esp. of hair, wool, etc. **2.** a napped fabric, usually a rough wool. **3.** shredded coarse tobacco. ~*vb.* **shags, shagging, shagged.** **4.** (*tr.*) to make shaggy. [Old English *sceacga;* related to *sceaga* SHAW, Old Norse *skegg* beard, *skagi* tip, *skōgr* forest]

shag[2] (ʃæg) *n.* **1.** another name for **cormorant,** esp. (in Britain) the **green cormorant** (*Phalacrocorax aristotelis*). **2. like a shag on a rock.** *Austral. slang.* abandoned and alone. [C16: special use of SHAG[1], with reference to its crest]

shag[3] (ʃæg) *Brit. slang.* ~*vb.* **shags, shagging, shagged.** **1.** *Taboo.* to have sexual intercourse with (a person). **2.** (*tr.; often foll. by out; usually passive*) to exhaust; tire. ~*n.* **3.** *Taboo.* an act of sexual intercourse. [C20: of unknown origin]

shagbark ('ʃægˌbɑ:k) *or* **shellbark** *n.* **1.** a North American hickory tree, *Carya ovata,* having loose rough bark and edible nuts. **2.** the wood of this tree, used for tool handles, fuel, etc. **3.** the light-coloured hard-shelled nut of this tree. [C18: so called because of the texture of its bark]

shaggy ('ʃægɪ) *adj.* **-gier, -giest.** **1.** having or covered with rough unkempt fur, hair, wool, etc.: *a shaggy dog.* **2.** rough or unkempt. **3.** (in textiles) having a nap of long rough strands. —'**shaggily** *adv.* —'**shagginess** *n.*

shaggy cap *n.* an edible saprophytic agaricaceous fungus, *Coprinus comatus,* having a white cap covered with shaggy scales.

shaggy dog story *n. Informal.* a long rambling joke ending in a deliberate anticlimax, such as a pointless punch line.

shagreen (ʃæ'gri:n) *n.* **1.** the rough skin of certain sharks and rays, used as an abrasive. **2.** a rough grainy leather made from certain animal hides. [C17: from French *chagrin,* from Turkish *çagri* rump; also associated through folk etymology with SHAG[1], GREEN]

shagroon (ʃæ'gru:n) *n. N.Z. history.* a nineteenth-century Australian settler in Canterbury. [perhaps from Irish *seachrān* wandering]

shah (ʃɑ:) *n.* a ruler of certain Middle Eastern countries, esp. (formerly) Iran. [C16: from Persian: king] —'**shahdom** *n.*

Shahaptin (ʃə'hæptɪn), **Shahaptan** (ʃə'hæptən), *or* **Shahaptian** (ʃə'hæptɪən) *n.* variants of **Sahaptin.**

Shaitan (ʃaɪ'tɑ:n) *n.* (in Muslim countries) **a.** Satan. **b.** any evil spirit. **c.** a vicious person or animal. [C17: from Arabic *shaytān,* from Hebrew *sātān;* see SATAN]

shake (ʃeɪk) *vb.* **shakes, shaking, shook, shaken** ('ʃeɪkᵊn). **1.** to move or cause to move up and down or back and forth with short quick movements; vibrate. **2.** to sway or totter or cause to sway or totter. **3.** to clasp or grasp (the hand) of (a person) in greeting, agreement, etc.: *he shook John by the hand; he shook John's hand; they shook and were friends.* **4. shake hands.** to clasp hands in greeting, agreement, etc. **5. shake on it.** *Informal.* to shake hands in agreement, reconciliation, etc. **6.** to bring or come to a specified condition by or as if by shaking: *he shook free and ran.* **7.** (*tr.*) to wave or brandish: *he shook his sword.* **8.** (*tr.;* often foll. by *up*) to rouse, stir, or agitate. **9.** (*tr.*) to shock, disturb, or upset: *he was shaken by the news of her death.* **10.** (*tr.*) to undermine or weaken: *the crisis shook his faith.* **11.** to mix (dice) by rattling in a cup or the hand before throwing. **12.** (*tr.*) *Austral. slang.* to steal. **13.** (*tr.*) *U.S. and Canadian informal.* to escape from: *can you shake that detective?* **14.** *Music.* to perform a trill on (a note). **15. shake a leg.** *Informal.* to hurry: usually used in the imperative. **16. shake in one's shoes.** to tremble with fear or apprehension. **17. shake one's head.** to indicate disagreement or disapproval by moving the head from side to side. **18. shake the dust from one's feet.** to depart gladly or with the intention not to return. ~*n.* **19.** the act or an instance of shaking. **20.** a tremor or vibration. **21. the shakes.** *Informal.* a state of uncontrollable trembling or a condition that causes it, such as a fever. **22.** *Informal.* a very short period of time; jiffy: *in half a shake.* **23.** a shingle or clapboard made from a short log by splitting it radially. **24.** a fissure or crack in timber or rock. **25.** an instance of shaking dice before casting. **26.** *Music.* another word for **trill**[1] (sense 1). **27.** a dance, popular in the 1960s, in which the body is shaken convulsively in time to the beat. **28.** an informal name for **earthquake.** **29.** short for **milk shake.** **30. no great shakes.** *Informal.* of no great merit or value; ordinary. ~See also **shake down, shake off, shake up.** [Old English *sceacan;* related to Old Norse *skaka* to shake, Old High German *untscachōn* to be driven] —'**shakable** *or* '**shakeable** *adj.*

shake down *vb.* (*adv.*) **1.** to fall or settle or cause to fall or settle by shaking. **2.** (*tr.*) *U.S. slang.* to extort money from, esp. by blackmail or threats of violence. **3.** (*tr.*) *U.S. slang.* to search thoroughly. **4.** (*tr.*) *Informal, chiefly U.S.* to submit (a vessel, etc.) to a shakedown test. **5.** (*intr.*) to go to bed, esp. to a makeshift bed. **6.** (*intr.*) (of a person, animal, etc.) to settle down. ~*n.* **shakedown.** **7.** *U.S. slang.* a swindle or act of extortion. **8.** *U.S. slang.* a thorough search. **9.** a makeshift bed, esp. of straw, blankets, etc. **10.** *Informal, chiefly U.S.* **a.** a voyage to test the performance of a ship or aircraft or to familiarize the crew with their duties. **b.** (*as modifier*): *a shakedown run.*

shake off *vb.* (*adv.*) **1.** to remove or be removed with or as if with a quick movement: *she shook off her depression.* **2.** (*tr.*) to escape from; elude: *they shook off the police.*

shake-out *n.* the process of reducing the number of people in a workforce in order to lower the costs of a company.

shaker ('ʃeɪkə) *n.* **1.** a person or thing that shakes. **2.** a container, often having a perforated top, from which something, such as a condiment, is shaken. **3.** a container in which the ingredients of alcoholic drinks are shaken together.

Shakespearean *or* **Shakespearian** (ʃeɪk'spɪərɪən) *adj.* **1.** of, relating to, or characteristic of William Shakespeare (1564–1616), English dramatist and poet, or his works. *~n.* **2.** a student of or specialist in Shakespeare's works.

Shakespeareana ('ʃeɪkˌspɪərɪ'ɑːnə, ʃeɪkˌspɪər-) *n.* (*functioning as pl.*) collected writings or items relating to Shakespeare.

Shakespearean sonnet *n.* a sonnet form developed in 16th-century England and employed by Shakespeare, having the rhyme scheme a b a b c d c d e f e f g g. Also called: **Elizabethan sonnet, English sonnet.**

shake up *vb.* (*tr., adv.*) **1.** to shake or agitate in order to mix. **2.** to reorganize drastically. **3.** to stir or rouse. **4.** to restore the shape of (a pillow, cushion, etc.). **5.** *Informal.* to disturb or shock mentally or physically. *~n.* **shake-up. 6.** *Informal.* a radical or drastic reorganization.

shaking palsy *n.* another name for **Parkinson's disease.**

shako *or* **shacko** ('ʃækəʊ) *n., pl.* **shakos, shakoes** *or* **shackos, shackoes.** a tall usually cylindrical military headdress, having a plume and often a peak, popular esp. in the 19th century. [C19: via French from Hungarian *csákó,* from Middle High German *zacke* a sharp point]

Shakta ('ʃʌktə) *n. Hinduism.* a devotee of Sakti, the wife of Siva. [from Sanskrit *śākta* concerning Sakti] —'**Shaktism** *n.* —'**Shaktist** *n.*

Shakti ('ʃʌktɪ) *n.* a variant of **Sakti.**

shaky ('ʃeɪkɪ) *adj.* **shakier, shakiest. 1.** tending to shake or tremble. **2.** liable to prove defective; unreliable. **3.** uncertain or questionable: *your arguments are very shaky.* —'**shakily** *adv.* —'**shakiness** *n.*

shale (ʃeɪl) *n.* a dark fine-grained laminated sedimentary rock formed by compression of successive layers of clay. [Old English *scealu* SHELL; compare German *Schalstein* laminated limestone; see SCALE[1], SCALE[2]] —'**shaly** *adj.*

shale oil *n.* an oil distilled from shales and used as fuel.

shall (ʃæl; *unstressed* ʃəl) *vb. past* **should.** (takes an infinitive without *to* or an implied infinitive) used as an auxiliary: **1.** (esp. with *I* or *we* as subject) to make the future tense: *we shall see you tomorrow.* Compare **will**[1] (sense 1). **2.** (with *you, he, she, it, they,* or a noun as subject) **a.** to indicate determination on the part of the speaker, as in issuing a threat: *you shall pay for this!* **b.** to indicate compulsion, now esp. in official documents: *the Tenant shall return the keys to the Landlord.* **c.** to indicate certainty or inevitability: *our day shall come.* **3.** (*with any noun or pronoun as subject, esp. in conditional clauses or clauses expressing doubt*) to indicate nonspecific futurity: *I don't think I shall ever see her again; he doubts whether he shall be in tomorrow.* [Old English *sceal;* related to Old Norse *skal,* Old High German *scal,* Dutch *zal*]

▷**Usage.** The usual rule given for the use of *shall* and *will* is that where the meaning is one of simple futurity, *shall* is used for the first person of the verb and *will* for the second and third: *I shall go tomorrow; they will be there now.* Where the meaning involves command, obligation, or determination, the positions are reversed: *it shall be done; I will definitely go.* However, *shall* has come to be largely neglected in favour of *will,* which has become the commonest form of the future in all three persons.

shalloon (ʃæ'luːn) *n.* a light twill-weave woollen fabric used chiefly for coat linings, etc. [C17: from Old French *chalon,* from the name of *Châlons-sur-Marne,* France, where it originated]

shallop ('ʃæləp) *n.* **1.** a light boat used for rowing in shallow water. **2.** (formerly) a two-masted gaff-rigged vessel. [C16: from French *chaloupe,* from Dutch *sloep* SLOOP]

shallot (ʃə'lɒt) *n.* **1.** Also called: **scallion.** an alliaceous plant, *Allium ascalonicum,* cultivated for its edible bulb. **2.** the bulb of this plant, which divides into small sections and is used in cooking for flavouring and as a vegetable. [C17: from Old French *eschalotte,* from Old French *eschaloigne,* from Latin *Ascalōnia caepa* Ascalonian onion, from *Ascalon,* a Palestinian town]

shallow ('ʃæləʊ) *adj.* **1.** having little depth. **2.** lacking intellectual or mental depth or subtlety; superficial. *~n.* **3.** (*often pl.*) a shallow place in a body of water; shoal. *~vb.* **4.** to make or become shallow. [C15: related to Old English *sceald* shallow; see SHOAL[1]] —'**shallowly** *adv.* —'**shallowness** *n.*

shalom aleichem *Hebrew.* (ʃa'lɔm a'lexɛm; *English* ʃə'lɒm ə'leɪxəm) *interj.* peace be to you: used by Jews as a greeting or farewell. Often shortened to **shalom.**

shalt (ʃælt) *vb. Archaic or dialect.* (used with the pronoun *thou* or its relative equivalent) a singular form of the present tense (indicative mood) of **shall.**

sham (ʃæm) *n.* **1.** anything that is not what it purports or appears to be. **2.** something false, fake, or fictitious that purports to be genuine. **3.** a person who pretends to be something other than he is. *~adj.* **4.** counterfeit or false; simulated. *~vb.* **shams, shamming, shammed. 5.** to falsely assume the appearance of (something); counterfeit: *to sham illness.* [C17: perhaps a Northern English dialect variant of SHAME] —'**shammer** *n.*

shaman ('ʃæmən) *n.* **1.** a priest of shamanism. **2.** a medicine man of a similar religion, esp. among certain tribes of North American Indians. [C17: from Russian *shaman,* from Tungusian *sămân,* from Pali *samana* Buddhist monk, ultimately from Sanskrit *śrama* religious exercise] —**shamanic** (ʃə'mænɪk) *adj.*

shamanism ('ʃæməˌnɪzəm) *n.* **1.** the religion of certain peoples of northern Asia, based on the belief that the world is pervaded by good and evil spirits who can be influenced or controlled only by the shamans. **2.** any similar religion involving forms of spiritualism. —'**shamanist** *n., adj.* —ˌ**shaman'istic** *adj.*

shamateur ('ʃæməˌtɜː, -ˌtjʊə, -tə, -tʃə) *n.* a sportsperson who is officially an amateur but accepts payment. [C20: from a blend of *sham* and *amateur*]

shamba ('ʃamba) *n.* (in E Africa) any field used for growing crops. [Swahili]

shamble ('ʃæmb^əl) *vb.* **1.** (*intr.*) to walk or move along in an awkward or unsteady way. *~n.* **2.** an awkward or unsteady walk. [C17: from *shamble* (adj.) ungainly, perhaps from the phrase *shamble legs* legs resembling those of a meat vendor's table; see SHAMBLES] —'**shambling** *adj., n.*

shambles ('ʃæmb^əlz) *n.* (*functioning as sing. or pl.*) **1.** a place of great disorder: *the room was a shambles after the party.* **2.** a place where animals are brought to be slaughtered. **3.** any place of slaughter or execution. **4.** *Brit. dialect.* a row of covered stalls or shops where goods, originally meat, are sold. [C14 *shamble* table used by meat vendors, from Old English *sceamel* stool, from Late Latin *scamellum* a small bench, from Latin *scamnum* stool]

shambolic (ʃæm'bɒlɪk) *adj. Informal.* completely disorganized; chaotic. [C20: irregularly formed from SHAMBLES]

shame (ʃeɪm) *n.* **1.** a painful emotion resulting from an awareness of having done something dishonourable, unworthy, degrading, etc. **2.** capacity to feel such an emotion. **3.** ignominy or disgrace. **4.** a person or thing that causes this. **5.** an occasion for regret, disappointment, etc.: *it's a shame you can't come with us.* **6. put to shame. a.** to disgrace. **b.** to surpass totally. *~vb.* (*tr.*) **7.** to cause to feel shame. **8.** to bring shame on; disgrace. **9.** (often foll. by *into*) to compel through a sense of shame: *he shamed her into making an apology.* [Old English *scamu;* related to Old Norse *skömm,* Old High German *skama*] —'**shamable** *or* '**shameable** *adj.*

shamefaced ('ʃeɪmˌfeɪst) *adj.* **1.** bashful or modest. **2.** showing a sense of shame. [C16: alteration of earlier *shamefast,* from Old English *sceamfaest;* see SHAME, FAST[1]] —**shamefacedly** (ʃeɪm'feɪsɪdlɪ, 'ʃeɪmˌfeɪstlɪ) *adv.* —**shame'facedness** *n.*

shameful ('ʃeɪmfʊl) *adj.* causing or deserving shame; scandalous. —'**shamefully** *adv.* —'**shamefulness** *n.*

shameless ('ʃeɪmlɪs) *adj.* **1.** having no sense of shame; brazen. **2.** done without shame; without decency or modesty. —'**shamelessly** *adv.* —'**shamelessness** *n.*

shammes *or* **shammash** ('ʃɑːməs; *Hebrew* ʃa'maʃ) *n., pl.* **shammosim** *or* **shammashim** (*Hebrew* ʃa'mɔsɪm). *Judaism.* **1.** an official acting as the beadle, sexton, and caretaker of a synagogue. **2.** the extra candle used on the Feast of Hanukkah to kindle the lamps or candles of the menorah. [from Hebrew *shāmmāsh,* from Aramaic *shĕmāsh* to serve]

shammy ('ʃæmɪ) *n., pl.* **-mies.** *Informal.* another word for **chamois** (sense 3). Also called: **shammy leather.** [C18: variant, influenced by the pronunciation, of CHAMOIS]

shampoo (ʃæm'puː) *n.* **1.** a liquid or cream preparation of soap or detergent to wash the hair. **2.** a similar preparation for washing carpets, etc. **3.** the process of shampooing. *~vb.* **-poos, -pooing, -pooed. 4.** (*tr.*) to wash (the hair, etc.) with such a preparation. [C18: from Hindi *chāmpo,* from *chāmpnā* to knead] —**sham'pooer** *n.*

shamrock ('ʃæmˌrɒk) *n.* a plant having leaves divided into three leaflets, variously identified as the wood sorrel, red clover, white clover, and black medick: the national emblem of Ireland. [C16: from Irish Gaelic *seamrōg,* diminutive of *seamar* clover]

shamus ('ʃɑːməs, 'ʃeɪ-) *n., pl.* **-muses.** *U.S. slang.* a police or private detective. [probably from SHAMMES, influenced by Irish *Séamas* James]

Shan (ʃɑːn) *n.* **1.** (*pl.* **Shans** *or* **Shan**) a member of a Mongoloid people living in Burma, Thailand, and SW China. **2.** the language or group of dialects spoken by the Shan, belonging to the Sino-Tibetan family and closely related to Thai.

shandrydan ('ʃændrɪˌdæn) *n.* **1.** a two-wheeled cart or chaise, esp. one with a hood. **2.** any decrepit old-fashioned conveyance. [C19: of unknown origin]

shandy ('ʃændɪ) *or U.S.* **shandygaff** ('ʃændɪˌgæf) *n., pl.* **-dies** *or* **-gaffs.** an alcoholic drink made of beer and ginger beer or lemonade. [C19: of unknown origin]

Shang (ʃæŋ) *adj.* of or relating to the pottery produced in China during the Shang dynasty (c. 18th–12th centuries B.C.).

Shangaan ('ʃaŋgɑːn) *n.* a member of any of the Tsonga-speaking Bantu peoples settled in Mozambique and NE Transvaal, esp. one who works in a gold mine.

shanghai ('ʃæŋhaɪ, ʃæŋ'haɪ) *Slang.* *~vb.* **-hais, -haiing, -haied.** (*tr.*) **1.** to kidnap (a man or seaman) for enforced service at sea, esp. on a merchant ship. **2.** to force or trick (someone) into doing something, going somewhere, etc. **3.** *Austral. and N.Z.* to shoot with a catapult. *~n.* **4.** *Austral. and N.Z.* a catapult. [C19: from the city of *Shanghai*, E China; from the forceful methods formerly used to collect crews for voyages to the Orient]

Shango ('ʃæŋgəʊ) *n.* **a.** a W African religious cult surviving in some parts of the Caribbean. **b.** (*as modifier*): *Shango ritual.* [Yoruba]

Shangri-la (ˌʃæŋgrɪ'lɑː) *n.* a remote or imaginary utopia. [C20: from the name of an imaginary valley in the Himalayas, from *Lost Horizon* (1933), a novel by James Hilton]

shank (ʃæŋk) *n.* **1.** *Anatomy.* the shin. **2.** the corresponding part of the leg in vertebrates other than man. **3.** a cut of meat from the top part of an animal's shank. **4.** the main part of a tool, between the working part and the handle. **5.** the part of a bolt between the thread and the head. **6.** the cylindrical part of a bit by which it is held in the drill. **7.** the ring or stem on the back of some buttons. **8.** the stem or long narrow part of a key, anchor, hook, spoon handle, nail, pin, etc. **9.** the band of a ring as distinguished from the setting. **10. a.** the part of a shoe connecting the wide part of the sole with the heel. **b.** the metal or leather piece used for this. **11.** *Printing.* the body of a piece of type, between the shoulder and the foot. **12.** *Engineering.* a ladle used for molten metal. **13.** *Music.* another word for **crook** (sense 6). **14.** *Rare.* the latter or remaining part of anything. ~*vb.* **15.** (*intr.*) (of fruits, roots, etc.) to show disease symptoms, esp. discoloration. **16.** (*tr.*) *Golf.* to mishit (the ball) with the foot of the shaft rather than the face of the club. [Old English *scanca;* related to Old Frisian *schanke,* Middle Low German *schenke,* Danish, Swedish *skank* leg]

shanks's pony *or U.S. and Canadian* **shanks's mare** ('ʃæŋksɪz) *n. Informal.* one's own legs as a means of transportation. [C18: from SHANK (in the sense: lower leg); probably with a pun on the surname *Shanks*]

shanny ('ʃænɪ) *n., pl.* **-nies.** a European blenny, *Blennius pholis,* of rocky coastal waters. [C19: of obscure origin]

shan't (ʃɑːnt) *contraction of* shall not.

shantung (ˌʃæn'tʌŋ) *n.* **1.** a heavy silk fabric with a knobbly surface. **2.** a cotton or rayon imitation of this. [C19: so called because it was first imported to Britain from *Shantung* province, NE China]

shanty[1] ('ʃæntɪ) *n., pl.* **-ties. 1.** a ramshackle hut; crude dwelling. **2.** *Austral. and N.Z.* a public house, esp. an unlicensed one. **3.** (formerly, in Canada) **a.** a log bunkhouse at a lumber camp. **b.** the camp itself. [C19: from Canadian French *chantier* cabin built in a lumber camp, from Old French *gantier* GANTRY]

shanty[2], **shantey** ('ʃæntɪ), **chanty,** *or U.S.* **chantey** ('ʃæntɪ, 'tʃæn-) *n., pl.* **-ties** *or* **-teys.** a song originally sung by sailors, esp. a rhythmical one forming an accompaniment to work. [C19: from French *chanter* to sing; see CHANT]

shantytown ('ʃæntɪˌtaʊn) *n.* a town or section of a town or city inhabited by very poor people living in shanties.

shape (ʃeɪp) *n.* **1.** the outward form of an object defined by outline. **2.** the figure or outline of the body of a person. **3.** a phantom. **4.** organized or definite form: *my plans are taking shape.* **5.** the form that anything assumes; guise. **6.** something used to provide or define form; pattern; mould. **7.** condition or state of efficiency: *to be in good shape.* **8. out of shape. a.** in bad physical condition. **b.** bent, twisted, or deformed. **9. take shape.** to assume a definite form. ~*vb.* **10.** (when *intr.*, often foll. by *into* or *up*) to receive or cause to receive shape or form. **11.** (*tr.*) to mould into a particular pattern or form; modify. **12.** (*tr.*) to plan, devise, or prepare: *to shape a plan of action.* **13.** an obsolete word for **appoint.** [Old English *gesceap,* literally: that which is created, from *sceppan* to create; related to *sceap* sexual organs, Old Norse *skap* destiny, Old High German *scaf* form] —'**shapable** *or* '**shapeable** *adj.* —'**shaper** *n.*

SHAPE (ʃeɪp) *n. acronym for* Supreme Headquarters Allied Powers Europe.

-shaped (ʃeɪpt) *adj. combining form.* having the shape of: *an L-shaped room; a pear-shaped figure.*

shapeless ('ʃeɪplɪs) *adj.* **1.** having no definite shape or form: *a shapeless mass; a shapeless argument.* **2.** lacking a symmetrical or aesthetically pleasing shape: *a shapeless figure.* —'**shapelessly** *adv.* —'**shapelessness** *n.*

shapely ('ʃeɪplɪ) *adj.* **-lier, -liest.** (esp. of a woman's body or legs) pleasing or attractive in shape. —'**shapeliness** *n.*

shape up *vb.* (*intr., adv.*) **1.** *Informal.* to proceed or develop satisfactorily. **2.** *Informal.* to develop a definite or proper form. ~*n.* **shapeup. 3.** *U.S. and Canadian.* (formerly) a method of hiring dockers for a day or shift by having a union hiring boss select them from a gathering of applicants.

shard (ʃɑːd) *or* **sherd** *n.* **1.** a broken piece or fragment of a brittle substance, esp. of pottery. **2.** *Zoology.* a tough sheath, scale, or shell, esp. the elytra of a beetle. [Old English *sceard;* related to Old Norse *skarth* notch, Middle High German *scharte* notch]

share[1] (ʃɛə) *n.* **1.** a part or portion of something owned, allotted to, or contributed by a person or group. **2.** (*often pl.*) any of the equal parts, usually of low par value, into which the capital stock of a company is divided: ownership of shares carries the right to receive a proportion of the company's profits. See also **ordinary shares, preference shares. 3. go shares.** *Informal.* to share (something) with another or others. ~*vb.* **4.** (*tr.*; often foll. by *out*) to divide or apportion, esp. equally. **5.** (when *intr.*, often foll. by *in*) to receive or contribute a portion of: *we can share the cost of the petrol; six people shared in the inheritance.* **6.** to join with another or others in the use of (something): *can I share your umbrella?* [Old English *scearu;* related to Old Norse *skor* amount, Old High German *scara* crowd; see SHEAR] —'**sharable** *or* '**shareable** *adj.* —'**sharer** *n.*

share[2] (ʃɛə) *n.* short for **ploughshare.** [Old English *scear;* related to Old Norse *skeri,* Old High German *scaro*]

share certificate *n.* a document issued by a company certifying ownership of one or more of its shares. U.S. equivalent: **stock certificate.**

sharecrop ('ʃɛəˌkrɒp) *vb.* **-crops, -cropping, -cropped.** *Chiefly U.S.* to cultivate (farmland) as a sharecropper.

sharecropper ('ʃɛəˌkrɒpə) *n. Chiefly U.S.* a farmer, esp. a tenant farmer, who pays over a proportion of a crop or crops as rent.

shared care *n. Social welfare.* an arrangement between a welfare agency and a family with a dependent handicapped member, whereby the agency takes the handicapped person into a home for respite care or in emergencies.

shared logic *n. Computer technol.* the sharing of a central processing unit and associated software among several terminals.

shared ownership *n.* (in Britain) a form of house purchase whereby the purchaser buys a proportion of the dwelling, usually from a local authority or housing association, and rents the rest.

shared resources *n.* (*functioning as sing.*) *Computer technol.* the sharing of peripherals among several terminals.

sharefarmer ('ʃɛəˌfɑːmə) *n. Chiefly Austral.* a farmer who shares his profits with his farm workers.

shareholder ('ʃɛəˌhəʊldə) *n.* the owner of one or more shares in a company.

share index *n.* an index showing the movement of share prices. See **Financial Times Industrial Ordinary Share Index, Financial Times Stock Exchange 100 Index.**

share-milker *n.* (in New Zealand) a person who lives on a dairy farm milking the owner's herd for an agreed share of the profits and, usually, building his own herd simultaneously.

share option *n.* a scheme giving employees an option to buy shares in the company for which they work at a favourable price or discount.

share premium *n. Brit.* the excess of the amount actually subscribed for an issue of corporate capital over its par value. Also called (esp. U.S.): **capital surplus.**

shareware ('ʃɛəˌwɛə) *n. Computer technol.* software available to all users without the need for a licence and for which a token fee is requested.

sharia *or* **sheria** (ʃə'riːə) *n.* the body of doctrines that regulate the lives of those who profess Islam. [Arabic]

sharif (ʃæ'riːf) *n.* a variant transliteration of **sherif.**

shark[1] (ʃɑːk) *n.* any of various usually ferocious selachian fishes, typically marine with a long body, two dorsal fins, rows of sharp teeth, and between five and seven gill slits on each side of the head. [C16: of uncertain origin] —'**shark,like** *adj.*

shark[2] (ʃɑːk) *n.* **1.** a person who preys on or victimizes others, esp. by swindling or extortion. ~*vb.* **2.** *Archaic.* to obtain (something) by cheating or deception. [C18: probably from German *Schurke* rogue; perhaps also influenced by SHARK[1]]

shark bell *n. Chiefly Austral.* a bell sounded to warn swimmers of the presence of sharks.

shark net *or* **mesh** *n. Chiefly Austral.* **1.** a net for catching sharks. **2.** a long piece of netting strung across a bay, inlet, etc., to exclude sharks.

shark patrol *n. Chiefly Austral.* a watch for sharks kept by an aircraft flying over beaches used by swimmers.

shark repellents *pl. n. Finance.* another name for **porcupine provisions.**

shark siren *n. Chiefly Austral.* a siren sounded to warn swimmers of the presence of sharks.

sharkskin ('ʃɑːkˌskɪn) *n.* a smooth glossy fabric of acetate rayon, used for sportswear, etc.

sharksucker ('ʃɑːkˌsʌkə) *n.* an informal name for a **remora.**

shark watcher *n. Informal.* a business consultant who assists companies in identifying and preventing unwelcome takeover bids.

sharon fruit ('ʃærən) *n.* another name for **persimmon** (sense 2).

sharp (ʃɑːp) *adj.* **1.** having a keen edge suitable for cutting. **2.** having an edge or point; not rounded or blunt. **3.** involving a sudden change, esp. in direction: *a sharp bend.* **4.** moving, acting, or reacting quickly, efficiently, etc.: *sharp reflexes.* **5.** clearly defined. **6.** mentally acute; clever; astute. **7.** sly or artful; clever in an underhand way: *sharp practice.* **8.** bitter or harsh: *sharp words.* **9.** shrill or penetrating: *a sharp cry.* **10.** having an acrid taste. **11.** keen; biting: *a sharp wind; sharp pain.* **12.** *Music.* **a.** (*immediately postpositive*) denoting a note that has been raised in pitch by one chromatic semitone: *B sharp.* **b.** (of an instrument, voice, etc.) out of tune by being or tending to be too high in pitch. Compare **flat**[1] (sense 22). **13.** *Phonetics.* a less common word for **fortis. 14.** *Informal.* **a.** stylish. **b.** too smart. **15. at the sharp end.** involved in the area of any activity where there is most difficulty, competition, danger, etc. ~*adv.* **16.** in a sharp manner. **17.** exactly: *six o'clock sharp.* **18.** *Music.* **a.** higher than a standard pitch. **b.** out of tune by being or tending to be too high in pitch: *she sings sharp.* Compare **flat**[1] (sense 28). ~*n.* **19.** *Music.* **a.** an accidental that raises the pitch of the following note by one chromatic semitone. Usual symbol: ♯ **b.** a note affected by this accidental. Compare **flat**[1] (sense 33). **20.** a thin needle with a sharp point. **21.** *Informal.* a sharper. ~*vb.* **22.** (*tr.*) *Music.* the usual U.S. and Canadian word for **sharpen.** [Old English *scearp;* related to Old Norse *skarpr,* Old High German *scarpf,* Old Irish *cerb,* Lettish *skarbs*] —'**sharply** *adv.* —'**sharpness** *n.*

sharpen ('ʃɑːpᵊn) *vb.* **1.** to make or become sharp or sharper. **2.** *Music.* to raise the pitch of (a note), esp. by one chromatic semitone. Usual U.S. and Canadian word: **sharp.** —'**sharpener** *n.*

sharper ('ʃɑːpə) *n.* a person who cheats or swindles; fraud.

sharp-eyed *adj.* **1.** having very good eyesight. **2.** observant or alert.

sharpie ('ʃɑːpɪ) *n. Austral.* a member of a teenage group having short hair and distinctive clothes. Compare **skinhead.**

sharpish ('ʃɑːpɪʃ) *adj.* **1.** fairly sharp. ~*adv.* **2.** *Informal.* promptly; quickly.

sharp-set *adj.* **1.** set to give an acute cutting angle. **2.** keenly hungry. **3.** keen or eager.

sharpshooter ('ʃɑːpˌʃuːtə) *n.* an expert marksman, esp. with a rifle. —'**sharpˌshooting** *n.*

sharp-sighted *adj.* having keen vision; sharp-eyed. —ˌ**sharp-'sightedly** *adv.* —ˌ**sharp-'sightedness** *n.*

sharp-tongued *adj.* bitter or critical in speech; sarcastic.

sharp-witted *adj.* having or showing a keen intelligence; perceptive. —ˌ**sharp-'wittedly** *adv.* —ˌ**sharp-'wittedness** *n.*

shashlik *or* **shashlick** (ʃɑːʃ'lɪk, 'ʃɑːʃlɪk) *n.* a type of kebab. [from Russian, of Turkic origin; compare *shish kebab*]

Shasta daisy ('ʃæstə) *n.* a Pyrenean plant, *Chrysanthemum maximum,* widely cultivated for its large white daisy-like flowers: family *Compositae* (composites). [named after Mount *Shasta* in California]

shastra ('ʃɑːstrə), **shaster** ('ʃɑːstə), *or* **sastra** *n.* any of the sacred writings of Hinduism. [C17: from Sanskrit *śāstra,* from *śās* to teach]

shatter ('ʃætə) *vb.* **1.** to break or be broken into many small pieces. **2.** (*tr.*) to impair or destroy: *his nerves were shattered by the torture.* **3.** (*tr.*) to dumbfound or thoroughly upset: *she was shattered by the news.* **4.** (*tr.*) *Informal.* to cause to be tired out or exhausted. **5.** an obsolete word for **scatter.** ~*n.* **6.** (*usually pl.*) *Obsolete or dialect.* a fragment. [C12: perhaps obscurely related to SCATTER] —'**shattered** *adj.* —'**shatterer** *n.* —'**shattering** *adj.* —'**shatteringly** *adv.*

shatterproof ('ʃætəˌpruːf) *adj.* designed to resist shattering.

shave (ʃeɪv) *vb.* **shaves, shaving, shaved; shaved** *or* **shaven.** (*mainly tr.*) **1.** (*also intr.*) to remove (the beard, hair, etc.) from (the face, head, or body) by scraping the skin with a razor. **2.** to cut or trim very closely. **3.** to reduce to shavings. **4.** to remove thin slices from (wood, etc.) with a sharp cutting tool; plane or pare. **5.** to touch or graze in passing. **6.** *Informal.* to reduce (a price) by a slight amount. **7.** *U.S. commerce.* to purchase (a commercial paper) at a greater rate of discount than is customary or legal. ~*n.* **8.** the act or an instance of shaving. **9.** any tool for scraping. **10.** a thin slice or shaving. **11.** an instance of barely touching something. **12. close shave.** *Informal.* a narrow escape. [Old English *sceafan;* related to Old Norse *skafa,* Gothic *skaban* to shave, Latin *scabere* to scrape] —'**shavable** *or* '**shaveable** *adj.*

shaveling ('ʃeɪvlɪŋ) *n. Archaic.* **1.** *Derogatory.* a priest or clergyman with a shaven head. **2.** a young fellow; youth.

shaven ('ʃeɪvᵊn) *adj.* **a.** closely shaved or tonsured. **b.** (*in combination*): *clean-shaven.*

shaver ('ʃeɪvə) *n.* **1.** a person or thing that shaves. **2.** Also called: **electric razor, electric shaver.** an electrically powered implement for shaving, having reciprocating or rotating blades behind a fine metal comb or pierced foil. **3.** *Informal.* a youngster, esp. a young boy. **4.** *Obsolete.* a person who makes hard or extortionate bargains.

Shavian ('ʃeɪvɪən) *adj.* **1.** of, relating to, or like George Bernard Shaw (1856–1950), Irish dramatist and critic, or his works, ideas, etc. ~*n.* **2.** an admirer of Shaw or his works. —'**Shavianism** *n.*

shaving ('ʃeɪvɪŋ) *n.* **1.** a thin paring or slice, esp. of wood, that has been shaved from something. ~*modifier.* **2.** used when shaving the face, etc.: *shaving cream.*

Shavuot *or* **Shabuoth** (ʃə'vuːəs, -əus; *Hebrew* ʃavuː'ɔt) *n.* the Hebrew name for **Pentecost** (sense 2). [from Hebrew *shābhū'ōth,* plural of *shābhūā'* week]

shaw[1] (ʃɔː) *n. Archaic or dialect.* a small wood; thicket; copse. [Old English *sceaga;* related to Old Norse *skagi* tip, *skaga* to jut out, *skōgr* forest, *skegg* beard]

shaw[2] (ʃɔː) *Scot.* ~*vb.* **1.** to show. ~*n.* **2.** a show. **3.** the part of a potato plant that is above ground.

shawl (ʃɔːl) *n.* a piece of fabric or knitted or crocheted material worn around the shoulders by women or wrapped around a baby. [C17: from Persian *shāl*]

shawl collar *n.* a collar rolled back in a continuous and tapering line along the surplice neckline of a garment.

shawlie ('ʃɔːlɪ) *n. Irish.* a disparaging term for a working-class woman who wears a shawl.

shawm (ʃɔːm) *n. Music.* a medieval form of the oboe with a conical bore and flaring bell, blown through a double reed. [C14 *shalmye,* from Old French *chalemie,* ultimately from Latin *calamus* a reed, from Greek *kalamos*]

Shawnee (ʃɔː'niː) *n.* **1.** (*pl.* **-nees** *or* **-nee**) a member of a North American Indian people formerly living along the Tennessee River. **2.** the language of this people, belonging to the Algonquian family. [C20: back formation from obsolete *Shawnese,* from Shawnee *Shaawanwaaki* people of the south, from *shaawanawa* south]

Shawwal (ʃə'wɑːl) *n.* the tenth month of the Muslim year. [from Arabic]

shay (ʃeɪ) *n.* a dialect word for **chaise.** [C18: back formation from CHAISE, mistakenly thought to be plural]

she (ʃiː) *pron.* (*subjective*) **1.** refers to a female person or animal: *she is an actress; she's a fine mare.* **2.** refers to things personified as feminine, such as cars, ships, and nations. **3.** *Austral. and N.Z.* an informal word for **it** (esp. in the phrases **she's apples, she'll be right,** etc.) ~*n.* **4. a.** a female person or animal **b.** (*in combination*): *she-cat.* [Old English *sīe,* accusative of *sēo,* feminine demonstrative pronoun]

shea ('ʃɪə) *n.* **1.** a tropical African sapotaceous tree, *Butyrospermum parkii,* with oily seeds. **2. shea butter.** the white butter-like fat obtained from the seeds of this plant and used as food, to make soaps, etc. [C18: from Bambara *si*]

sheading ('ʃiːdɪŋ) *n.* any of the six subdivisions of the Isle of Man. [variant of *shedding;* see SHED[2]]

sheaf (ʃiːf) *n., pl.* **sheaves** (ʃiːvz). **1.** a bundle of reaped but unthreshed corn tied with one or two bonds. **2.** a bundle of objects tied together. **3.** the arrows contained in a quiver. ~*vb.* **4.** (*tr.*) to bind or tie into a sheaf. [Old English *sceaf,* related to Old High German *skoub* sheaf, Old Norse *skauf* tail, Gothic *skuft* tuft of hair]

shear (ʃɪə) *vb.* **shears, shearing, sheared;** *or archaic, Austral. and N.Z. sometimes* **shore; sheared** *or* **shorn. 1.** (*tr.*) to remove (the fleece or hair) of (sheep, etc.) by cutting or clipping. **2.** to cut or cut through (something) with shears or a sharp instrument. **3.** *Engineering.* to cause (a part, member, shaft, etc.) to deform or fracture or (of a part, etc.) to deform or fracture as a result of excess torsion or transverse load. **4.** (*tr.;* often foll. by *of*) to strip or divest: *to shear someone of his power.* **5.** (when *intr.,* foll. by *through*) to move through (something) by or as if by cutting. **6.** *Scot. or dialect.* to reap (corn, etc.) with a scythe or sickle. ~*n.* **7.** the act, process, or an instance of shearing. **8.** a shearing of a sheep or flock of sheep, esp. when referred to as an indication of age: *a sheep of two shears.* **9.** a form of deformation or fracture in which parallel planes in a body or assembly slide over one another. **10.** *Physics.* the deformation of a body, part, etc., expressed as the lateral displacement between two points in parallel planes divided by the distance between the planes. **11.** either one of the blades of a pair of shears, scissors, etc. **12.** a machine that cuts sheet material by passing a knife blade through it. **13.** a device for lifting heavy loads consisting of a tackle supported by a framework held steady by guy ropes. ~See also **shears, shore**[3]. [Old English *sceran;* related to Old Norse *skera* to cut, Old Saxon, Old High German *skeran* to shear; see SHARE[2]] —'**shearer** *n.*

shearing gang *n. N.Z.* a group of itinerant workers who contract to shear, class, and bale a farmer's wool clip.

shearing shed *n. N.Z.* a farm building equipped with power machinery for sheepshearing and equipment for baling wool. Also called: **woolshed.**

shearlegs ('ʃɪəˌlɛgz) *n.* a variant spelling of **sheerlegs.**

shearling ('ʃɪəlɪŋ) *n.* **1.** a young sheep after its first shearing. **2.** the skin of such an animal.

shear pin *n.* an easily replaceable pin inserted in a machine at a critical point and designed to break and stop the machine if the stress becomes too great.

shears (ʃɪəz) *pl. n.* **1. a.** large scissors, as for cutting cloth, jointing poultry, etc. **b.** a large scissor-like and usually hand-held cutting tool with flat blades, as for cutting hedges. **2.** any of various analogous cutting or clipping implements or machines. **3.** short for **sheerlegs. 4. off the shears.** *Austral. informal.* (of a sheep) newly shorn.

shear strength *n.* the degree to which a material or bond is able to resist shear.

shearwater ('ʃɪəˌwɔːtə) *n.* any of several oceanic birds of the genera *Puffinus,* such as *P. puffinus* (**Manx shearwater**), *Procellaria,* etc., specialized for an aerial or aquatic existence: family *Procellariidae,* order *Procellariiformes* (petrels). [C17: so named because their wings seem to clip the waves when they are flying low]

sheatfish ('ʃiːtˌfɪʃ) *n., pl.* **-fish** *or* **-fishes.** another name for **European catfish** (see **silurid** (sense 1)). [C16: variant of *sheathfish;* perhaps influenced by German *Schaid* sheatfish; see SHEATH, FISH]

sheath (ʃiːθ) *n., pl.* **sheaths** (ʃiːðz). **1.** a case or covering for the blade of a knife, sword, etc. **2.** any similar close-fitting case. **3.** *Biology.* an enclosing or protective structure, such as a leaf base encasing the stem of a plant. **4.** the protective covering on an electric cable. **5.** a figure-hugging dress with a narrow tapering skirt. **6.** another name for **condom.** ~*vb.* **7.** (*tr.*) another word for **sheathe.** [Old English *scēath;* related to Old Norse *skeithir,* Old High German *sceida* a dividing; compare Old English *scādan* to divide]

sheathbill ('ʃiːθˌbɪl) *n.* either of two pigeon-like shore birds, *Chionis alba* or *C. minor,* of antarctic and subantarctic regions, constituting the family *Chionididae:* order *Charadriiformes.* They have a white plumage and a horny sheath at the base of the bill.

sheathe (ʃiːð) *vb. (tr.)* **1.** to insert (a knife, sword, etc.) into a sheath. **2.** (esp. of cats) to retract (the claws). **3.** to surface with or encase in a sheath or sheathing.

sheathing ('ʃiːðɪŋ) *n.* **1.** any material used as an outer layer, as on a ship's hull. **2.** boarding, etc., used to cover the wall studding or roof joists of a timber frame.

sheath knife *n.* a knife carried in or protected by a sheath.

sheave[1] (ʃiːv) *vb. (tr.)* to gather or bind into sheaves.

sheave[2] (ʃiːv) *n.* a wheel with a grooved rim, esp. one used as a pulley. [C14: of Germanic origin; compare Old High German *scība* disc]

sheaves (ʃiːvz) *n.* the plural of **sheaf.**

shebang (ʃɪ'bæŋ) *n. Slang, chiefly U.S. and Canadian.* **1.** a situation, matter, or affair (esp. in the phrase **the whole shebang**). **2.** a hut or shack. [C19: of uncertain origin]

Shebat (ʃɛ'vat) *n.* a variant spelling of **Shevat.**

shebeen *or* **shebean** (ʃɪ'biːn) *n.* **1.** *Irish, Scot., S. African.* a place where alcoholic drink is sold illegally. **2.** (in Ireland) alcohol, esp. home-distilled whiskey, sold without a licence. **3.** (in South Africa) a place where Black African men engage in social drinking. **4.** (in the U.S. and Ireland) weak beer. [C18: from Irish Gaelic *síbín* beer of poor quality]

Shechina *or* **Shekinah** (ʃɛ'kaɪnə; *Hebrew* ʃəxiː'na) *n. Judaism.* **1.** the radiance in which God's immanent presence in the midst of his people, esp. in the Temple, is visibly manifested. **2.** the divine presence itself as contrasted with the divine transcendence. [C17: from Hebrew *shĕkhīnāh,* from *shākhan* to dwell]

shechita ('ʃəxitɑ, 'ʃxitə) *n.* the Jewish method of killing animals for food. [from Hebrew, literally: slaughter]

shed[1] (ʃɛd) *n.* **1.** a small building or lean-to of light construction, used for storage, shelter, etc. **2.** a large roofed structure, esp. one with open sides, used for storage, repairing locomotives, sheepshearing, etc. **3.** *N.Z.* another name for **freezing works. 4. in the shed.** *N.Z.* at work. ~*vb.* **sheds, shedding, shedded.** *(tr.)* **5.** *N.Z.* to store (hay or wool) in a shed. [Old English *sced;* probably variant of *scead* shelter, SHADE] —'**shedˌlike** *adj.*

shed[2] (ʃɛd) *vb.* **sheds, shedding, shed.** *(mainly tr.)* **1.** to pour forth or cause to pour forth: *to shed tears; shed blood.* **2. shed** (*or* **throw**) **light on** *or* **upon.** to clarify or supply additional information about. **3.** to cast off or lose: *the snake shed its skin; trees shed their leaves.* **4.** (of a lorry) to drop (its load) on the road by accident. **5.** to repel: *this coat sheds water.* **6.** (*also intr.*) (in weaving) to form an opening between (the warp threads) in order to permit the passage of the shuttle. **7.** *(tr.) Dialect.* to make a parting in (the hair). ~*n.* **8.** (in weaving) the space made by shedding. **9.** short for **watershed. 10.** *Chiefly Scot.* a parting in the hair. [Old English *sceadan;* related to Gothic *skaidan,* Old High German *skeidan* to separate; see SHEATH] —'**shedable** *or* '**sheddable** *adj.*

shed[3] (ʃɛd) *vb.* **sheds, shedding, shed. 1.** *(tr.)* to separate or divide off (some farm animals) from the remainder of a group: *a good dog can shed his sheep in a matter of minutes.* ~*n.* **2.** (of a dog) the action of separating farm animals. [from SHED[2]] —'**shedding** *n.*

shed[4] (ʃɛd) *n. Physics.* a unit of nuclear cross section equal to 10^{-52} square metre. [C20: from SHED[1]; so called by comparison to BARN[2] because of its smaller size]

she'd (ʃiːd) *contraction of* she had *or* she would.

shedder ('ʃɛdə) *n.* **1.** a person or thing that sheds. **2.** an animal, such as a llama, snake, or lobster, that moults. **3.** *N.Z.* a person who milks cows in a milking shed.

shed hand *n. Chiefly Austral. and N.Z.* a worker in a sheepshearing shed.

shed out *vb. (tr., adv.) N.Z.* to separate off (sheep that have lambed) and move them to better pasture.

shed up *vb. (tr., adv.) N.Z.* to store (hay) in a shed.

sheen (ʃiːn) *n.* **1.** a gleaming or glistening brightness; lustre. **2.** *Poetic.* splendid clothing. ~*adj.* **3.** *Rare.* shining and beautiful; radiant. ~*vb.* **4.** *(intr.) Scot. and northern English dialect.* to gleam. [Old English *sciene;* related to Old Norse *skjōni* white horse, Gothic *skauns* beautiful, Old High German *scōni* bright] —'**sheeny** *adj.*

sheeny ('ʃiːnɪ) *n., pl.* **sheenies.** *Slang.* a derogatory word for a **Jew.** [C19: of unknown origin]

sheep (ʃiːp) *n., pl.* **sheep. 1.** any of various bovid mammals of the genus *Ovis* and related genera, esp. *O. aries* (**domestic sheep**), having transversely ribbed horns and a narrow face. There are many breeds of domestic sheep, raised for their wool and for meat. Related adj.: **ovine. 2. Barbary sheep.** another name for **aoudad. 3.** a meek or timid person, esp. one without initiative. **4. separate the sheep from the goats.** to pick out the members of any group who are superior in some respects. [Old English *sceap;* related to Old Frisian *skēp,* Old Saxon *scāp,* Old High German *scāf*] —'**sheepˌlike** *adj.*

sheepcote ('ʃiːpˌkəʊt) *n. Chiefly Brit.* another word for **sheepfold.**

sheep-dip *n.* **1.** any of several liquid disinfectants and insecticides in which sheep are immersed to kill vermin and germs in their fleece. **2.** a deep trough containing such a liquid.

sheepdog ('ʃiːpˌdɒg) *n.* **1.** Also called: **shepherd dog.** a dog used for herding sheep. See **Border collie. 2.** any of various breeds of dog reared originally for herding sheep. See **Old English sheepdog, Shetland sheepdog.**

sheepdog trial *n.* (*often pl.*) a competition in which sheepdogs are tested in their tasks.

sheepfold ('ʃiːpˌfəʊld) *n.* a pen or enclosure for sheep.

sheepish ('ʃiːpɪʃ) *adj.* **1.** abashed or embarrassed, esp. through looking foolish or being in the wrong. **2.** resembling a sheep in timidity or lack of initiative. —'**sheepishly** *adv.* —'**sheepishness** *n.*

sheep ked *or* **tick** *n.* a wingless dipterous fly, *Melophagus ovinus,* that is an external parasite of sheep: family *Hippoboscidae.*

sheep measles *n.* (*functioning as sing. or pl.*) a disease of sheep caused by infestation by the cysticerci of a dog tapeworm (*Taenia ovis*).

sheepo ('ʃiːpəʊ) *n., pl.* **sheepos.** *N.Z.* a person employed to bring sheep to the catching pen in a shearing shed.

sheep race *n. N.Z.* a single-file walkway for sheep at the entrance to a sheep-dip.

sheep's eyes *pl. n. Old-fashioned.* amorous or inviting glances.

sheep's fescue *n.* a temperate perennial tufted grass, *Festuca ovina,* with narrow inwardly rolled leaves. [C18: so called because it is often used for sheep pastures]

sheepshank ('ʃiːpˌʃæŋk) *n.* a knot consisting of two hitches at the ends of a bight made in a rope to shorten it temporarily.

sheepshead ('ʃiːpsˌhɛd) *n., pl.* **-head** *or* **-heads.** any of several sparid fishes with strong crushing teeth, esp. *Archosargus rhomboidalis,* of the American Atlantic, which is marked with dark bands.

sheepshearing ('ʃiːpˌʃɪərɪŋ) *n.* **1.** the act or process of shearing sheep. **2.** the season or an occasion of shearing sheep. **3.** a feast held on such an occasion. —'**sheepˌshearer** *n.*

sheepskin ('ʃiːpˌskɪn) *n.* **a.** the skin of a sheep, esp. when used for clothing, etc., or with the fleece removed and used for parchment. **b.** (*as modifier*): *a sheepskin coat.*

sheep sorrel *or* **sheep's sorrel** *n.* a polygonaceous plant, *Rumex acetosella,* of the N hemisphere, having slightly bitter-tasting leaves and small reddish flowers.

sheep station *or* **run** *n. Austral. and N.Z.* a large sheep farm. Also called: **run.**

sheep tick *n.* **1.** a tick, *Ixodes ricinus,* that is parasitic on sheep, cattle, and man and transmits the disease louping ill in sheep. **2.** another name for **sheep ked.**

sheepwalk ('ʃiːpˌwɔːk) *n. Chiefly Brit.* a tract of land for grazing sheep.

sheer[1] (ʃɪə) *adj.* **1.** perpendicular; very steep: *a sheer cliff.* **2.** (of textiles) so fine as to be transparent. **3.** (*prenominal*) absolute; unmitigated: *sheer folly.* **4.** *Obsolete.* bright or shining. ~*adv.* **5.** steeply or perpendicularly. **6.** completely or absolutely. ~*n.* **7.** any transparent fabric used for making garments. [Old English *scīr;* related to Old Norse *skīrr* bright, Gothic *skeirs* clear, Middle High German *schīr*] —'**sheerly** *adv.* —'**sheerness** *n.*

sheer[2] (ʃɪə) *vb.* (foll. by *off* or *away* (*from*)). **1.** to deviate or cause to deviate from a course. **2.** *(intr.)* to avoid an unpleasant person, thing, topic, etc. ~*n.* **3.** the upward sweep of the deck or bulwarks of a vessel. **4.** *Nautical.* the position of a vessel relative to its mooring. [C17: perhaps variant of SHEAR]

sheerlegs *or* **shearlegs** ('ʃɪəˌlɛgz) *n.* (*functioning as sing.*) a device for lifting heavy weights consisting of two or more spars lashed together at the upper ends from which a lifting tackle is suspended. Also called: **shears.** [C19: variant of *shear legs*]

sheet[1] (ʃiːt) *n.* **1.** a large rectangular piece of cotton, linen, etc., generally one of a pair used as inner bedclothes. **2. a.** a thin piece of a substance such as paper, glass, or metal, usually rectangular in form. **b.** (*as modifier*): *sheet iron.* **3.** a broad continuous surface; expanse or stretch: *a sheet of rain.* **4.** a newspaper, esp. a tabloid. **5.** a piece of printed paper to be folded into a section for a book. **6.** a page of stamps, usually of one denomination and already perforated. **7.** any thin tabular mass of rock covering a large area. ~*vb.* **8.** *(tr.)* to provide with, cover, or wrap in a sheet. **9.** *(intr.)* (of rain, snow, etc.) to fall heavily. [Old English *sciete;* related to *sceat* corner, lap, Old Norse *skaut,* Old High German *scōz* lap]

sheet[2] (ʃiːt) *n. Nautical.* a line or rope for controlling the position of a sail relative to the wind. [Old English *scēata* corner of a sail; related to Middle Low German *schōte* rope attached to a sail; see SHEET[1]]

sheet anchor *n.* **1.** *Nautical.* a large strong anchor for use in emergency. **2.** a person or thing to be relied upon in an emergency. [C17: from earlier *shute anker,* from *shoot* (obsolete) the sheet of a sail]

sheet bend *n.* a knot used esp. for joining ropes of different sizes. Also called: **becket bend, weaver's hitch.**

sheet down *vb. (intr., adv.)* (of rain) to fall heavily in sheets.

sheet-fed *adj. Printing.* involving or printing on separate sheets of paper. Compare **reel-fed.**

sheeting ('ʃiːtɪŋ) *n.* fabric from which sheets are made.

sheet lightning *n.* lightning that appears as a broad sheet, caused by the reflection of more distant lightning.
sheet metal *n.* metal in the form of a sheet, the thickness being intermediate between that of plate and that of foil.
sheet music *n.* **1.** the printed or written copy of a short composition or piece, esp. in the form of unbound leaves. **2.** music in its written or printed form.
sheet pile *n. Civil engineering.* one of a group of piles made of timber, steel, or prestressed concrete set close together to resist lateral pressure, as from earth or water. Compare **bearing pile.**
Sheffer's stroke ('ʃɛfəz) *n. Logic.* a function of two sentences, equivalent to the negation of their conjunction, and written p/q (p and q are both not true) where $p,q,$ are the arguments: p/q is false only when p,q are both true. It is possible to construct all truth functions out of this one alone. [named after H. M. *Sheffer* (born 1883), U.S. philosopher]
Sheffield Shield ('ʃɛfiːld) *n.* (in Australia) the prize of the annual interstate cricket competition. [C19: named after Lord *Sheffield,* sponsor of a visiting English side in 1891–92, who inaugurated the Sheffield Shield competition in 1892]
sheik *or* **sheikh** (ʃeɪk) *n.* **1.** (in Muslim countries) **a.** the head of an Arab tribe, village, etc. **b.** a venerable old man. **c.** a religious leader; high priest. **2.** *Informal.* an attractive man. [C16: from Arabic *shaykh* old man]
sheikdom *or* **sheikhdom** ('ʃeɪkdəm) *n.* the territory ruled by a sheik.
sheila ('ʃiːlə) *n. Austral. and N.Z.* an informal word for **girl** or **woman.** [C19: from the girl's name *Sheila*]
shekel ('ʃɛkᵊl) *n.* **1.** the standard monetary unit of Israel, divided into 100 agorot. **2.** any of several former coins and units of weight of the Near East. **3.** (*often pl.*) *Informal.* any coin or money. [C16: from Hebrew *sheqel*]
Shekinah (ʃɛ'kaınə; *Hebrew* ʃəxiː'na) *n. Judaism.* a variant spelling of **Shechina.**
shelduck ('ʃɛlˌdʌk) *or* (*masc.*) **sheldrake** ('ʃɛlˌdreɪk) *n., pl.* **-ducks, -duck** *or* **-drakes, -drake.** any of various large usually brightly coloured gooselike ducks, such as *Tadorna tadorna* (**common shelduck**), of the Old World. [C14: *shel,* probably from dialect *sheld* pied; related to Middle Dutch *schillede* variegated]
shelf (ʃɛlf) *n., pl.* **shelves** (ʃɛlvz). **1.** a thin flat plank of wood, metal, etc., fixed horizontally against a wall, etc., for the purpose of supporting objects. **2.** something resembling this in shape or function. **3.** the objects placed on a shelf, regarded collectively: *a shelf of books.* **4.** a projecting layer of ice, rock, etc., on land or in the sea. See also **continental shelf.** **5.** *Mining.* a layer of bedrock hit when sinking a shaft. **6.** *Archery.* the part of the hand on which an arrow rests when the bow is grasped. **7.** See **off the shelf.** **8. on the shelf.** put aside or abandoned: used esp. of unmarried women considered to be past the age of marriage. ~*vb.* (*tr.*) **9.** *Austral. slang.* to inform upon. [Old English *scylfe* ship's deck; related to Middle Low German *schelf* shelf, Old English *scylf* crag] —'**shelf,like** *adj.*
shelf ice *n.* a less common term for **ice shelf.**
shelf life *n.* the length of time a packaged food, chemical, etc., will last without deteriorating.
shell (ʃɛl) *n.* **1.** the protective calcareous or membranous outer layer of an egg, esp. a bird's egg. **2.** the hard outer covering of many molluscs that is secreted by the mantle. **3.** any other hard outer layer, such as the exoskeleton of many arthropods. **4.** the hard outer layer of some fruits, esp. of nuts. **5.** any hard outer case. **6.** a hollow artillery projectile filled with explosive primed to explode either during flight, on impact, or after penetration. Compare **ball**[1] (sense 7a). **7.** a small-arms cartridge comprising a hollow casing inside which is the primer, charge, and bullet. **8.** a pyrotechnic cartridge designed to explode in the air. **9.** *Rowing.* a very light narrow racing boat. **10.** the external structure of a building, esp. one that is unfinished or one that has been gutted by fire. **11.** the basic structural case of something, such as a machine, vehicle, etc. **12.** *Physics.* **a.** a class of electron orbits in an atom in which the electrons have the same principal quantum number and differences in their energy are small compared with differences in energy between shells. **b.** an analogous energy state of nucleons in certain theories (**shell models**) of the structure of the atomic nucleus. **13.** the pastry case of a pie, flan, etc. **14.** a thin slab of concrete or a skeletal framework made of wood or metal that forms a shell-like roof. **15.** *Brit.* (in some schools) a class or form. **16. come** (*or* **bring**) **out of one's shell.** to become (or help to become) less shy and reserved. ~*vb.* **17.** to divest or be divested of a shell, husk, pod, etc. **18.** to separate or be separated from an ear, husk, cob, etc. **19.** (*tr.*) to bombard with artillery shells. ~See also **shell out.** [Old English *sciell;* related to Old Norse *skel* shell, Gothic *skalja* tile, Middle Low German *schelle* shell; see SCALE[1], SHALE] —'**shell-less** *adj.* —'**shell-ˌlike** *adj.* —'**shelly** *adj.*
she'll (ʃiːl; *unstressed* ʃɪl) *contraction of* she will *or* she shall.
shellac (ʃə'læk, 'ʃɛlæk) *n.* **1.** a yellowish resin secreted by the lac insect, esp. a commercial preparation of this used in varnishes, polishes, and leather dressings. **2.** Also called: **shellac varnish.** a varnish made by dissolving shellac in ethanol or a similar solvent. **3.** a gramophone record based on shellac. ~*vb.* **-lacs, -lacking, -lacked.** (*tr.*) **4.** to coat or treat (an article) with a shellac varnish. **5.** *U.S. slang.* to defeat completely. [C18: SHELL + LAC[1], translation of French *laque en écailles,* literally: lac in scales, that is, in thin plates] —**shel'lacker** *n.*
shellacking (ʃə'lækɪŋ, 'ʃɛlækɪŋ) *n. U.S. and Canadian slang.* a complete defeat; a sound beating.
shellback ('ʃɛlˌbæk) *n.* **1.** *Informal.* a sailor who has crossed the equator. Compare **polliwog** (sense 2). **2.** an experienced or old sailor.
shellbark ('ʃɛlˌbɑːk) *n.* another name for **shagbark.** [C19: so called from the texture of its bark]
shell bean *n. U.S.* any of various bean plants that are cultivated for their edible seeds rather than for their pods.
shell company *n. Business.* **1.** a near-defunct company, esp. one with a stock-exchange listing, used as a vehicle for a thriving company. **2.** a company that has ceased to trade but retains its registration and is sold for a small sum to enable its new owners to avoid the cost and trouble of registering a new company.
shellfire ('ʃɛlˌfaɪə) *n.* the firing of artillery shells.
shellfish ('ʃɛlˌfɪʃ) *n., pl.* **-fish** *or* **-fishes.** any aquatic invertebrate having a shell or shell-like carapace, esp. such an animal used as human food. Examples are crustaceans such as crabs and lobsters and molluscs such as oysters.
shell game *n.* the U.S. name for **thimblerig.**
shell gland *n. Zoology.* a gland in certain invertebrates that secretes the components required for forming the shell of an egg.
shell jacket *n.* an army officer's waist-length mess jacket.
shell out *vb.* (*adv.*) *Informal.* to pay out or hand over (money). [C19: from SHELL (in the sense: to remove from a pod or (figuratively) a purse)]
shell program *n. Computers.* a basic low-cost computer program that provides a framework within which the user can develop the program to suit his personal requirements.
shellproof ('ʃɛlˌpruːf) *adj.* designed, intended, or able to resist shellfire.
shell shock *n.* loss of sight, memory, etc., resulting from psychological strain during prolonged engagement in warfare. Also called: **combat neurosis.** —'**shell-ˌshocked** *adj.*
shell star *n. Astronomy.* a type of star, usually of spectral type B to F, surrounded by a gaseous shell.
shell suit *n.* a lightweight tracksuit consisting of an inner cotton layer covered by a waterproof nylon layer.
Shelta ('ʃɛltə) *n.* a secret language used by some itinerant tinkers in Ireland and parts of Britain, based on systematically altered Gaelic. [C19: from earlier *sheldrū,* perhaps an arbitrary alteration of Old Irish *bēlre* speech]
shelter ('ʃɛltə) *n.* **1.** something that provides cover or protection, as from weather or danger; place of refuge. **2.** the protection afforded by such a cover; refuge. **3.** the state of being sheltered. ~*vb.* **4.** (*tr.*) to provide with or protect by a shelter. **5.** (*intr.*) to take cover, as from rain; find refuge. **6.** (*tr.*) to act as a shelter for; take under one's protection. [C16: of uncertain origin] —'**shelterer** *n.* —'**shelterless** *adj.*
shelter belt *n.* a row of trees planted to protect an area from the wind.
sheltered ('ʃɛltəd) *adj.* **1.** protected from wind or weather: *a sheltered garden.* **2.** protected from outside influences: *a sheltered upbringing.* **3.** (of buildings) specially designed to provide a safe environment for the elderly, handicapped, or disabled: *sheltered workshops for the blind.* See also **sheltered housing.**
sheltered housing *n.* accommodation designed esp. for the elderly or infirm consisting of a group of individual premises, often with some shared facilities and a caretaker. Also called: **sheltered accommodation, sheltered homes.**
shelter tent *n. U.S.* a military tent for two men.
sheltie *or* **shelty** ('ʃɛltɪ) *n., pl.* **-ties.** another name for **Shetland pony** or **Shetland sheepdog.** [C17: probably from Orkney dialect *sjalti,* from Old Norse *Hjalti* Shetlander, from *Hjaltland* Shetland]
shelve[1] (ʃɛlv) *vb.* (*tr.*) **1.** to place on a shelf. **2.** to provide with shelves. **3.** to put aside or postpone from consideration. **4.** to dismiss or cause to retire. —'**shelver** *n.*
shelve[2] (ʃɛlv) *vb.* (*intr.*) to slope away gradually; incline.
shelves (ʃɛlvz) *n.* the plural of **shelf.**
shelving ('ʃɛlvɪŋ) *n.* **1.** material for making shelves. **2.** a set of shelves; shelves collectively.
Shema (ʃə'mɑː) *n.* **1.** the central statement of Jewish belief, the sentence "Hear, O Israel: the Lord is your God; the Lord is One" (Deuteronomy 6:4). **2.** the section of the liturgy consisting of this and related biblical passages, Deuteronomy 6:4–9 and 11:13–21 and Numbers 15:37–41, recited in the morning and evening prayers and on retiring at night. [Hebrew, literally: hear]
Shemini Atseres ('ʃmini ɑ'tsɛrɛs) *or* **Shemini Atzereth** ('ʃəmini ɑ'tsɛrɛt) *n. Judaism.* the festival which follows upon Sukkoth on Tishri 22 (and 23 outside Israel), and includes Simchat Torah.
Shemite ('ʃɛmaɪt) *n.* another word for **Semite.**
Shemitic (ʃə'mɪtɪk) *n., adj.* another word for **Semitic.**
Shemona Esrei *Hebrew.* (*Hebrew* ʃəmə'na ɛs'reɪ; *Yiddish* 'ʃmonə 'ɛsreɪ) *n. Judaism.* another name for **Amidah.** [literally: eighteen (blessings)]
shemozzle (ʃɪ'mɒzᵊl) *n. Informal.* a noisy confusion or dispute; uproar. [C19: perhaps from Yiddish *shlimazl* misfortune]
shenanigan (ʃɪ'nænɪgən) *n. Informal.* **1.** (*usually pl.*) roguishness; mischief. **2.** an act of treachery; deception. [C19: of unknown origin]

shend (ʃɛnd) *vb.* **shends, shending, shent** (ʃɛnt). (*tr.*) *Archaic.* **1.** to put to shame. **2.** to chide or reproach. **3.** to injure or destroy. [Old English *gescendan,* from *scand* SHAME]

she-oak *n.* any of various Australian trees of the genus *Casuarina.* See **casuarina.** [C18 *she* (in the sense: inferior) + OAK]

Sheol (ˈʃiːəʊl, -ɒl) *n. Old Testament.* **1.** the abode of the dead. **2.** (*often not cap.*) hell. [C16: from Hebrew *shĕ'ōl*]

shepherd (ˈʃɛpəd) *n.* **1.** a person employed to tend sheep. Fem. equivalent: **shepherdess. 2.** a person, such as a clergyman, who watches over or guides a group of people. **3.** *Austral.* a miner who retains the rights to a mining claim without working it. ~*vb.* (*tr.*) **4.** to guide or watch over in the manner of a shepherd. **5.** *Austral.* to retain (a mining claim) without working it. **6.** *Australian Rules football.* to prevent opponents from tackling (a member of one's own team) by blocking their path. [from Old English *sceaphirde.* See SHEEP, HERD[2]]

shepherd dog *n.* another term for **sheepdog** (sense 1).

shepherd's needle *n.* a European umbelliferous plant, *Scandix pectenveneris,* with long needle-like fruits.

shepherd's pie *n. Chiefly Brit.* a baked dish of minced meat covered with mashed potato. Also called: **cottage pie.**

shepherd's-purse *n.* a cruciferous plant, *Capsella bursa-pastoris,* having small white flowers and flattened triangular seed pods. [C15: compare Latin *bursa pastoris,* French *bourse-de-berger,* German *Hirtentasche,* Dutch *herdentasch*]

shepherd's weatherglass *n. Brit.* another name for the **scarlet pimpernel.**

sherardize *or* **sherardise** (ˈʃɛrəˌdaɪz) *vb. Metallurgy.* to coat (iron or steel) with zinc by heating in a container with zinc dust or (of iron or steel) to be coated in this way. [C20: process named after *Sherard* Cowper-Coles (died 1936), English inventor] —ˌ**sherardiˈzation** *or* ˌ**sherardiˈsation** *n.*

Sheraton (ˈʃɛrətən) *adj.* denoting furniture made by or in the style of Thomas Sheraton (1751–1806), British furniture maker, characterized by lightness, elegance, and the extensive use of inlay.

sherbet (ˈʃɜːbət) *n.* **1.** a fruit-flavoured slightly effervescent powder, eaten as a sweet or used to make a drink: *lemon sherbet.* **2.** another word (esp. U.S. and Canadian) for **sorbet** (sense 1). **3.** *Austral. slang.* beer. **4.** a cooling Oriental drink of sweetened fruit juice. [C17: from Turkish *şerbet,* from Persian *sharbat,* from Arabic *sharbah* drink, from *shariba* to drink]

sherd (ʃɜːd) *n.* a variant of **shard.**

sheria (ʃəˈriːə) *n.* a variant spelling of **sharia.**

sherif *or* **shereef** (ʃɛˈriːf) *or* **sharif** *n., pl.* **ashraf.** *Islam.* **1.** a descendant of Mohammed through his daughter Fatima. **2.** (formerly) the governor of Mecca. **3.** an honorific title accorded to any Muslim ruler. [C16: from Arabic *sharīf* noble]

sheriff (ˈʃɛrɪf) *n.* **1.** (in the U.S.) the chief law-enforcement officer in a county: popularly elected, except in Rhode Island. **2.** (in England and Wales) the chief executive officer of the Crown in a county, having chiefly ceremonial duties. **3.** (in Scotland) a judge in any of the sheriff courts. **4.** (in Australia) an administrative officer of the Supreme Court, who enforces judgments and the execution of writs, empanels juries, etc. **5.** (in New Zealand) an officer of the High Court. [Old English *scīrgerēfa,* from *scīr* SHIRE[1] + *gerēfa* REEVE[1]] —ˈ**sheriffdom** *n.*

sheriff court *n.* (in Scotland) a court having jurisdiction to try summarily or on indictment all but the most serious crimes and to deal with most civil actions.

Sherpa (ˈʃɜːpə) *n., pl.* **-pas** *or* **-pa.** a member of a people of Mongolian origin living on the southern slopes of the Himalayas in Nepal, noted as mountaineers.

sherry (ˈʃɛrɪ) *n., pl.* **-ries.** a fortified wine, originally only from the Jerez region of southern Spain, usually drunk as an apéritif. [C16: from earlier *sherris* (assumed to be plural), from Spanish *Xeres,* now *Jerez*]

sherwani (ʃɛəˈwɑːnɪ) *n., pl.* **-nis.** a long coat closed up to the neck, worn by men in India. [Hindi]

she's (ʃiːz) *contraction of* she is *or* she has.

Shetland pony (ˈʃɛtlənd) *n.* a very small sturdy breed of pony with a long shaggy mane and tail. Also called: **sheltie.** [named after the *Shetland* Islands off the N coast of Scotland, where it originated]

Shetland sheepdog *n.* a small dog similar in appearance to a rough collie. Also called: **sheltie.**

Shetland wool *n.* a fine loosely twisted wool yarn obtained from Shetland sheep and used esp. for sweaters.

sheuch *or* **sheugh** (ʃuːx, ʃʌx) *n. Scot. dialect.* a ditch or trough. [dialect variant of SOUGH[2]]

Sheva Brachoth *or* **Sheva Brochos** *Hebrew.* (*Hebrew* ˈʃɛvɑ brɑˈxot; *Yiddish* ˈʃɛvə ˈbroxəs) *pl. n. Judaism.* **1.** the seven blessings said during the marriage service and repeated at the celebration thereafter. **2.** any of the celebratory meals held on the seven days after a wedding. [literally: seven blessings]

Shevat *or* **Shebat** (ʃɛˈvat) *n.* (in the Jewish calendar) the eleventh month of the year according to biblical reckoning and the fifth month of the civil year, usually falling within January and February. [from Hebrew]

shew (ʃəʊ) *vb.* **shews, shewing, shewed; shewn** (ʃəʊn) *or* **shewed.** an archaic spelling of **show.** —ˈ**shewer** *n.*

shewbread *or* **showbread** (ˈʃəʊˌbrɛd) *n. Old Testament.* the loaves of bread placed every Sabbath on the table beside the altar of incense in the tabernacle or temple of ancient Israel (Exodus 25:30; Leviticus 24:5–9). [on the model of German *Schaubrot,* a translation of the Greek *artoi enōpioi,* a translation of the Hebrew *lechem pānīm,* literally: bread of the presence]

SHF *or* **shf** *Radio. abbrev. for* superhigh frequency.

Shiah *or* **Shia** (ˈʃiːə) *n.* **1.** one of the two main branches of Islam, now mainly in Iran, which regards Mohammed's cousin Ali and his successors as the true imams. **2.** another name for **Shiite.** ~*adj.* **3.** designating or characteristic of this sect or its beliefs and practices. [C17: from Arabic *shī'ah* sect, from *shā'a* to follow]

shiai (ˈʃiːaɪ) *n.* a judo contest. [Japanese]

shiatsu (ˌʃiːˈætsuː) *n.* a type of massage in which pressure is applied to the same points of the body as in acupuncture. Also called: **acupressure.** [Japanese from Chinese *chī* finger + *yā* pressure]

shibboleth (ˈʃɪbəˌlɛθ) *n.* a custom, phrase, or use of language that acts as a test of belonging to, or as a stumbling block to becoming a member of, a particular social class, profession, etc. [C14: from Hebrew, literally: ear of grain; the word is used in the Old Testament by the Gileadites as a test word for the Ephraimites, who could not pronounce the sound *sh*]

shicker (ˈʃɪkə) *n. Austral. slang.* alcoholic drink; liquor. [via Yiddish from Hebrew]

shickered (ˈʃɪkəd) *adj. Austral. and N.Z. slang.* drunk; intoxicated.

shidduch *Yiddish.* (ˈʃɪdəx) *n., pl.* **shidduchim** (ʃɪˈduːxɪm). *Judaism.* **1. a.** an arranged marriage. **b.** the arrangement of a marriage. **2.** any negotiated agreement. [from Hebrew: see SHADCHAN]

shied (ʃaɪd) *vb.* the past tense and past participle of **shy**[1] and **shy**[2].

shield (ʃiːld) *n.* **1.** any protection used to intercept blows, missiles, etc., such as a tough piece of armour carried on the arm. **2.** any similar protective device. **3.** Also called: **scutcheon, escutcheon.** *Heraldry.* a pointed stylized shield used for displaying armorial bearings. **4.** anything that resembles a shield in shape, such as a prize in a sports competition. **5.** the protective outer covering of an animal, such as the shell of a turtle. **6.** *Physics.* a structure of concrete, lead, etc., placed around a nuclear reactor or other source of radiation in order to prevent the escape of radiation. **7.** a broad stable plateau of ancient Precambrian rocks forming the rigid nucleus of a particular continent. **8.** short for **dress shield. 9.** *Civil engineering.* a hollow steel cylinder that protects men driving a circular tunnel through loose, soft, or water-bearing ground. **10. the shield.** *Informal.* **a.** *Austral.* short for the **Sheffield Shield. b.** *N.Z.* short for the **Ranfurly Shield.** ~*vb.* (*tr.*) **11.** to protect, hide, or conceal (something) from danger or harm. [Old English *scield;* related to Old Norse *skjöldr,* Gothic *skildus,* Old High German *scilt* shield, Old English *sciell* SHELL] —ˈ**shielder** *n.* —ˈ**shieldˌlike** *adj.*

shield bug *n.* any shield-shaped herbivorous heteropterous insect of the superfamily *Pentamoidea,* esp. any of the family *Pentatomidae.* Also called: **stink bug.**

shield cricket *n. Austral.* the interstate cricket competition held for the Sheffield Shield.

shield fern *n.* any temperate woodland fern of the genus *Polystichum* having shield-shaped flaps covering the spore-producing bodies.

shield match *n.* **a.** *Austral.* a cricket match for the Sheffield Shield. **b.** *N.Z.* a rugby match for the Ranfurly Shield.

Shield of David *n.* another term for the **Star of David.**

shield volcano *n.* a broad volcano built up from the repeated nonexplosive eruption of basalt to form a low dome or shield, usually having a large caldera at the summit.

shieling (ˈʃiːlɪŋ) *or* **shiel** (ʃiːl) *n. Chiefly Scot.* **1.** a rough, sometimes temporary, hut or shelter used by people tending cattle on high or remote ground. **2.** pasture land for the grazing of cattle in summer. [C16: from Middle English *shale* hut, of unknown origin]

shier[1] (ˈʃaɪə) *adj.* a comparative of **shy**[1].

shier[2] *or* **shyer** (ˈʃaɪə) *n.* a horse that shies habitually.

shiest (ˈʃaɪɪst) *adj.* a superlative of **shy**[1].

shift (ʃɪft) *vb.* **1.** to move or cause to move from one place or position to another. **2.** (*tr.*) to change for another or others. **3.** to change (gear) in a motor vehicle. **4.** (*intr.*) (of a sound or set of sounds) to alter in a systematic way. **5.** (*intr.*) to provide for one's needs (esp. in the phrase **shift for oneself**). **6.** (*intr.*) to proceed by indirect or evasive methods. **7.** to remove or be removed, esp. with difficulty: *no detergent can shift these stains.* **8.** (*intr.*) *Slang.* to move quickly. **9.** *tr. Computer technol.* to move (bits held in a store location) to the left or right. ~*n.* **10.** the act or an instance of shifting. **11.** a group of workers who work for a specific period. **12.** the period of time worked by such a group. **13.** an expedient, contrivance, or artifice. **14.** the displacement of rocks, esp. layers or seams in mining, at a geological fault. **15.** an underskirt or dress with little shaping. [Old English *sciftan;* related to Old Norse *skipta* to divide, Middle Low German *schiften,* to separate] —ˈ**shifter** *n.*

shifting cultivation *n.* a land-use system, esp. in tropical Africa, in which a tract of land is cleared and the land cultivated until its fertility diminishes, when the area is abandoned until this is restored naturally.

shifting spanner *n. Austral. and N.Z.* an adjustable spanner. Also called: **shifter.**

shift key *n.* a key on a typewriter or computer keyboard used to adjust the action of the machine so that it types capital letters and certain numbers and symbols.

shiftless ('ʃɪftlɪs) *adj.* lacking in ambition or initiative. —'**shiftlessly** *adv.* —'**shiftlessness** *n.*

shiftwork ('ʃɪftˌwɜːk) *n.* a system of employment where an individual's normal hours of work are, in part, outside the period of normal day working and may follow a different pattern in consecutive periods of weeks.

shifty ('ʃɪftɪ) *adj.* **shiftier, shiftiest.** **1.** given to evasions; artful. **2.** furtive in character or appearance. **3.** full of expedients; resourceful. —'**shiftily** *adv.* —'**shiftiness** *n.*

shigella (ʃɪ'gɛlə) *n.* any rod-shaped Gram-negative bacterium of the genus *Shigella,* some species of which cause dysentery. [C20: named after K. *Shiga* (1870–1957), Japanese bacteriologist, who discovered it]

shih-tzu ('ʃiː'tsuː) *n.* a small dog of a breed derived from crossing the Pekingese and the Tibetan apso. It has a long straight dense coat and carries its tail curled over its back. [from Chinese, literally: lion]

Shiism ('ʃiːɪzəm) *n. Islam.* the beliefs and practices of Shiah.

Shiite ('ʃiːaɪt) *or* **Shiah** *Islam.* ~*n.* **1.** an adherent of Shiah. ~*adj.* **2.** of or relating to Shiah. —**Shiitic** (ʃiː'ɪtɪk) *adj.*

shikar (ʃɪ'kɑː) (in India) ~*n.* **1.** hunting, esp. big-game hunting. ~*vb.* **-kars, -karring, -karred.** **2.** to hunt (game, esp. big game). [C17: via Urdu from Persian]

shikari *or* **shikaree** (ʃɪ'kɑːrɪ) *n., pl.* **-ris** *or* **-rees.** (in India) a hunter.

shiksa ('ʃɪksə) *n. Often derogatory.* (used by Jews) **1.** a non-Jewish girl. **2.** a Jewish girl who fails to live up to traditional Jewish standards. [Yiddish *shikse,* feminine of *sheygets* non-Jewish youth, from Hebrew *sheqes* defect]

shill (ʃɪl) *n. Slang.* a confidence trickster's assistant, esp. a person who poses as an ordinary customer, gambler, etc., in order to entice others to participate. [C20: perhaps shortened from *shillaber* a circus barker, of unknown origin]

shillelagh *or* **shillala** (ʃə'leɪlə, -lɪ; *Irish* ʃɪ'leːlə) *n.* (in Ireland) a stout club or cudgel, esp. one made of oak or blackthorn. [C18: from Irish Gaelic *sail* cudgel + *éille* leash, thong]

shilling ('ʃɪlɪŋ) *n.* **1.** a former British and Australian silver or cupronickel coin worth one twentieth of a pound: not minted in Britain since 1970. Abbrev.: **s., sh.** **2.** the standard monetary unit of Kenya, Uganda, the Somali Republic, and Tanzania: divided into 100 cents. **3.** an old monetary unit of the U.S. varying in value in different states. **4.** (*in combination*) *Scot.* an indication of the strength and character of a beer, referring to the price after duty that was formerly paid per barrel: *sixty-shilling.* Usually abbreviated to: /-. [Old English *scilling;* related to Old Norse *skillingr,* Gothic *skilliggs,* Old High German *skilling*]

shilling mark *n.* another name for **solidus** (sense 1). [so named because it was used to separate shillings from pence when writing amounts less than one pound before the introduction of decimal currency in Britain. For example, *three shillings and eleven pence* was written *3/11*]

shillyshally ('ʃɪlɪˌʃælɪ) *Informal.* ~*vb.* **-lies, -lying, -lied. 1.** (*intr.*) to be indecisive, esp. over unimportant matters; hesitate. ~*adv.* **2.** in an indecisive manner. ~*adj.* **3.** indecisive or hesitant. ~*n., pl.* **-lies.** **4.** indecision or hesitation; vacillation. [C18: from *shill I shall I,* by reduplication of *shall I*] —'**shillyˌshallier** *n.*

shilpit ('ʃɪlpɪt) *adj. Scot.* puny; thin; weak-looking. [C19: of unknown origin]

shily ('ʃaɪlɪ) *adv.* a less common spelling of **shyly.**

shim (ʃɪm) *n.* **1.** a thin packing strip or washer often used with a number of similar washers or strips to adjust a clearance for gears, etc. **2.** *Physics.* a thin strip of magnetic material, such as soft iron, used to adjust a magnetic field. ~*vb.* **shims, shimming, shimmed.** **3.** *tr.* to modify a load, clearance, or magnetic field by the use of shims.

shimmer ('ʃɪmə) *vb.* **1.** (*intr.*) to shine with a glistening or tremulous light. ~*n.* **2.** a faint, glistening, or tremulous light. [Old English *scimerian;* related to Middle Low German *schēmeren* to grow dark, Old Norse *skimi* brightness] —'**shimmering** *adj.* —'**shimmeringly** *adv.* —'**shimmery** *adj.*

shimmy ('ʃɪmɪ) *n., pl.* **-mies.** **1.** an American ragtime dance with much shaking of the hips and shoulders. **2.** abnormal wobbling motion in a motor vehicle, esp. in the front wheels or steering. **3.** an informal word for **chemise.** ~*vb.* **-mies, -mying, -mied.** (*intr.*) **4.** to dance the shimmy. **5.** to vibrate or wobble. [C19: changed from CHEMISE, mistakenly assumed to be plural]

shin[1] (ʃɪn) *n.* **1.** the front part of the lower leg. **2.** the front edge of the tibia. **3.** *Chiefly Brit.* a cut of beef, the lower foreleg. ~*vb.* **shins, shinning, shinned.** **4.** (when *intr.,* often foll. by *up*) to climb (a pole, tree, etc.) by gripping with the hands or arms and the legs and hauling oneself up. **5.** (*tr.*) to kick (a person) in the shins. [Old English *scinu;* related to Old High German *scina* needle, Norwegian dialect *skina* small disc]

shin[2] (ʃɪn) *n.* the 22nd letter in the Hebrew alphabet (ש), transliterated as *sh.* [from Hebrew *shīn,* literally: tooth]

shinbone ('ʃɪnˌbəʊn) *n.* the nontechnical name for **tibia** (sense 1).

shindig ('ʃɪnˌdɪg) *n. Informal.* **1.** a noisy party, dance, etc. **2.** another word for **shindy.** [C19: variant of SHINDY]

shindy ('ʃɪndɪ) *n., pl.* **-dies.** *Informal.* **1.** a quarrel or commotion (esp. in the phrase **kick up a shindy**). **2.** another word for **shindig.** [C19: variant of SHINTY]

shine (ʃaɪn) *vb.* **shines, shining, shone.** **1.** (*intr.*) to emit light. **2.** (*intr.*) to glow or be bright with reflected light. **3.** (*tr.*) to direct the light of (a lamp, etc.): *he shone the torch in my eyes.* **4.** (*tr.; past tense and past participle* **shined**) to cause to gleam by polishing: *to shine shoes.* **5.** (*intr.*) to be conspicuously competent; excel: *she shines at tennis.* **6.** (*intr.*) to appear clearly; be conspicuous: *the truth shone out of his words.* ~*n.* **7.** the state or quality of shining; sheen; lustre. **8. come rain or (come) shine. a.** whatever the weather. **b.** regardless of circumstances. **9.** *Informal.* short for **moonshine** (whisky). **10.** *Informal.* a liking or fancy (esp. in the phrase **take a shine to**). [Old English *scīnan;* related to Old Norse *skīna,* Gothic *skeinan,* Old High German *scīnan* to shine, Greek *skia* shadow]

shiner ('ʃaɪnə) *n.* **1.** something that shines, such as a polishing device. **2.** any of numerous small North American freshwater cyprinid fishes of the genus *Notropis* and related genera, such as *N. cornutus* (**common shiner**) and *Notemigonus crysoleucas* (**golden shiner**). **3.** a popular name for the **mackerel.** **4.** *Informal.* a black eye. **5.** *N.Z. old-fashioned, informal.* a vagrant or tramp.

shingle[1] ('ʃɪŋgᵊl) *n.* **1.** a thin rectangular tile, esp. one made of wood, that is laid with others in overlapping rows to cover a roof or a wall. **2.** a woman's short-cropped hairstyle. **3.** *U.S. and Canadian.* a small signboard or nameplate fixed outside the office of a doctor, lawyer, etc. **4. a shingle short.** *Austral. informal.* unintelligent or mentally subnormal. ~*vb.* (*tr.*) **5.** to cover (a roof or a wall) with shingles. **6.** to cut (the hair) in a short-cropped style. [C12 *scingle,* from Late Latin *scindula* a split piece of wood, from Latin *scindere* to split] —'**shingler** *n.*

shingle[2] ('ʃɪŋgᵊl) *n.* **1.** coarse gravel, esp. the pebbles found on beaches. **2.** a place or area strewn with shingle. [C16: of Scandinavian origin; compare Norwegian *singl* pebbles, Frisian *singel* gravel] —'**shingly** *adj.*

shingle[3] ('ʃɪŋgᵊl) *vb.* (*tr.*) *Metallurgy.* to hammer or squeeze the slag out of (iron) after puddling in the production of wrought iron. [C17: from Old French dialect *chingler* to whip, from *chingle* belt, from Latin *cingula* girdle; see CINGULUM]

shingles ('ʃɪŋgᵊlz) *n.* (*functioning as sing.*) an acute viral disease affecting the ganglia of certain nerves, characterized by inflammation, pain, and skin eruptions along the course of the affected nerve. Technical names: **herpes zoster, zoster.** [C14: from Medieval Latin *cingulum* girdle, rendering Greek *zōnē* ZONE]

shinkin ('ʃɪŋkɪn) *n. South Wales dialect.* a worthless person. [Welsh, from the surname *Jenkin,* of Dutch origin]

shinleaf ('ʃɪnˌliːf) *n., pl.* **-leaves.** the usual U.S. name for **wintergreen** (sense 3).

shinplaster ('ʃɪnˌplɑːstə) *n. U.S., Canadian, and Austral.* a promissory note on brittle paper, issued by an individual. [C19: so called because of its resemblance to a sticking plaster]

shintaido (ʃɪn'taɪdəʊ) *n.* a form of group physical and mental exercise, developing awareness of others, interaction, etc., involving vigorous movements derived from those of the Japanese martial arts, but without aggressive intent. [C20: Japanese, from Chinese *shēn* gods + Japanese *ai* to harmonize + *do* way]

Shinto ('ʃɪntəʊ) *n.* the indigenous religion of Japan, polytheistic in character and incorporating the worship of a number of ethnic divinities, from the chief of which the emperor is believed to be descended. [C18: from Japanese: the way of the gods, from Chinese *shên* gods + *tao* way] —'**Shintoism** *n.* —'**Shintoist** *n., adj.*

shinty ('ʃɪntɪ) *or U.S. and Canadian* **shinny** ('ʃɪnɪ) *n., pl.* **-ties** *or U.S. and Canadian* **-nies.** **1.** a simple form of hockey of Scottish origin played with a ball and sticks curved at the lower end. **2.** the stick used in this game. ~*vb.* **-ties, -tying, -tied** *or U.S. and Canadian* **-nies, -nying, -nied.** (*intr.*) **3.** to play shinty. [C17: probably from the cry *shin ye* in the game]

shiny ('ʃaɪnɪ) *adj.* **shinier, shiniest.** **1.** glossy or polished; bright. **2.** (of clothes or material) worn to a smooth and glossy state, as by continual rubbing. —'**shininess** *n.*

ship (ʃɪp) *n.* **1.** a vessel propelled by engines or sails for navigating on the water, esp. a large vessel that cannot be carried aboard another, as distinguished from a boat. **2.** *Nautical.* a large sailing vessel with three or more square-rigged masts. **3.** the crew of a ship. **4.** short for **airship** or **spaceship.** **5.** *Informal.* any vehicle or conveyance. **6. when one's ship comes in** (*or* **home**). when one has become successful or wealthy. ~*vb.* **ships, shipping, shipped.** **7.** to place, transport, or travel on any conveyance, esp. aboard a ship: *ship the microscopes by aeroplane; can we ship tomorrow?* **8.** (*tr.*) *Nautical.* to take (water) over the side. **9.** to bring or go aboard a vessel: *to ship oars.* **10.** (*tr.;* often foll. by *off*) *Informal.* to send away, often in order to be rid of: *they shipped the children off to boarding school.* **11.** (*intr.*) to engage to serve aboard a ship: *I shipped aboard a Liverpool liner.* ~See also **ship out.** [Old English *scip;* related to Old Norse *skip,* Old High German *skif* ship, *scipfī* cup] —'**shippable** *adj.*

-ship *suffix forming nouns.* **1.** indicating state or condition: *fellowship.* **2.** indicating rank, office, or position: *lordship.* **3.**

indicating craft or skill: *horsemanship; workmanship; scholarship.* [Old English *-scipe;* compare SHAPE]

shipboard (ˈʃɪpˌbɔːd) *n.* **1.** (*modifier*) taking place, used, or intended for use aboard a ship: *a shipboard encounter.* **2. on shipboard.** on board a ship.

ship-broker *n.* a person who acts for a shipowner by getting cargo and passengers for his ships and also handling insurance and other matters.

shipbuilder (ˈʃɪpˌbɪldə) *n.* a person or business engaged in the building of ships. —ˈ**shipˌbuilding** *n.*

ship chandler *n.* a person or business dealing in supplies for ships. —**ship chandlery** *n.*

shipload (ˈʃɪpˌləʊd) *n.* the quantity carried by a ship.

shipmaster (ˈʃɪpˌmɑːstə) *or* **shipman** (ˈʃɪpmən) *n., pl.* **-masters** *or* **-men.** the master or captain of a ship.

shipmate (ˈʃɪpˌmeɪt) *n.* a sailor who serves on the same ship as another.

shipment (ˈʃɪpmənt) *n.* **1. a.** goods shipped together as part of the same lot: *a shipment of grain.* **b.** (*as modifier*): *a shipment schedule.* **2.** the act of shipping cargo.

ship money *n. English history.* a tax levied to finance the fitting out of warships: abolished 1640.

ship of the line *n. Nautical.* (formerly) a warship large enough to fight in the first line of battle.

ship out *vb.* (*adv.*) to depart or cause to depart by ship: *we shipped out at dawn; they shipped out the new recruits.*

shipowner (ˈʃɪpˌəʊnə) *n.* a person who owns or has shares in a ship or ships.

shipper (ˈʃɪpə) *n.* a person or company in the business of shipping freight.

shipping (ˈʃɪpɪŋ) *n.* **1. a.** the business of transporting freight, esp. by ship. **b.** (*as modifier*): *a shipping magnate; shipping office.* **2. a.** ships collectively: *there is a lot of shipping in the Channel.* **b.** the tonnage of a number of ships: *shipping for this year exceeded that of last.*

shipping agent *n.* a person or company whose business is to prepare shipping documents, arrange shipping space and insurance, and deal with customs requirements.

shipping clerk *n.* a person employed by a company to arrange, receive, record, and send shipments of goods.

shipping ton *n.* the full name for **ton**[1] (sense 5).

ship-rigged *adj.* rigged as a full-rigged ship.

ship's articles *or* **shipping articles** *pl. n.* a type of contract by which sailors agree to the conditions, payment, etc., for the ship in which they are going to work.

ship's biscuit *n.* another name for **hardtack.**

ship's boy *n.* a young man or boy employed to attend the needs of passengers or officers aboard ship.

shipshape (ˈʃɪpˌʃeɪp) *adj.* **1.** neat; orderly. *~adv.* **2.** in a neat and orderly manner.

ship's papers *pl. n.* the documents that are required by law to be carried by a ship for the purpose of ascertaining details of her ownership, nationality, destination, and cargo or to prove her neutrality.

shipway (ˈʃɪpˌweɪ) *n.* **1.** the structure on which a vessel is built, then launched. **2.** a canal used by ships.

shipworm (ˈʃɪpˌwɜːm) *n.* any wormlike marine bivalve mollusc of the genus *Teredo* and related genera and family *Teredinidae.* They bore into wooden piers, ships, etc., by means of drill-like shell valves. See also **piddock.**

shipwreck (ˈʃɪpˌrɛk) *n.* **1.** the partial or total destruction of a ship at sea. **2.** a wrecked ship or part of such a ship. **3.** ruin or destruction: *the shipwreck of all my hopes.* *~vb.* (*tr.*) **4.** to wreck or destroy (a ship). **5.** to bring to ruin or destruction. [Old English *scipwræc,* from SHIP + *wræc* something driven by the sea; see WRACK[2]]

shipwright (ˈʃɪpˌraɪt) *n.* an artisan skilled in one or more of the tasks required to build vessels.

shipyard (ˈʃɪpˌjɑːd) *n.* a place or facility for the building, maintenance, and repair of ships.

shiralee (ˌʃɪrəˈliː) *n. Austral. history, informal.* a swag; swagman's bundle. [C19: of unknown origin]

shire[1] (ʃaɪə) *n.* **1. a.** one of the British counties. **b.** (*in combination*): *Yorkshire.* **2.** (in Australia) a rural district having its own local council. **3.** See **shire horse.** **4. the Shires.** the Midland counties of England, esp. Northamptonshire and Leicestershire, famous for hunting, etc. [Old English *scīr* office; related to Old High German *scīra* business]

shire[2] (ʃaɪə) *vb.* (*tr.*) *Ulster dialect.* to refresh or rest: *let me get my head shired.* [from Old English *scīr* clear]

shire horse *n.* a large heavy breed of carthorse with long hair on the fetlocks. Often shortened to **shire.** [C19: so called because the breed was originally reared in *the Shires.* See SHIRE[1]]

shirk (ʃɜːk) *vb.* **1.** to avoid discharging (work, a duty, etc.); evade. *~n. also* **shirker.** **2.** a person who shirks. [C17: probably from German *Schurke* rogue; see SHARK[2]]

shirr (ʃɜː) *vb.* **1.** to gather (fabric) into two or more parallel rows to decorate a dress, blouse, etc., often using elastic thread. **2.** (*tr.*) to bake (eggs) out of their shells. *~n. also* **shirring.** **3.** a series of gathered rows decorating a dress, blouse, etc. [C19: of unknown origin]

shirt (ʃɜːt) *n.* **1.** a garment worn on the upper part of the body, esp. by men, usually of light material and typically having a collar and sleeves and buttoning up the front. **2.** short for **nightshirt** or **undershirt.** **3. keep your shirt on.** *Informal.* refrain from losing your temper (often used as an exhortation to another). **4. put** *or* **lose one's shirt on.** *Informal.* to bet or lose all one has on (a horse, etc.). [Old English *scyrte;* related to Old English *sceort* SHORT, Old Norse *skyrta* skirt, Middle High German *schurz* apron]

shirting (ˈʃɜːtɪŋ) *n.* fabric used in making men's shirts.

shirtsleeve (ˈʃɜːtˌsliːv) *n.* **1.** the sleeve of a shirt. **2. in one's shirtsleeves.** not wearing a jacket.

shirt-tail *n.* the part of a shirt that extends below the waist.

shirtwaister (ˈʃɜːtˌweɪstə) *or U.S. and Canadian* **shirtwaist** *n.* a woman's dress with a tailored bodice resembling a shirt.

shirty (ˈʃɜːtɪ) *adj.* **shirtier, shirtiest.** *Slang, chiefly Brit.* bad-tempered or annoyed. [C19: perhaps based on such phrases as *to get someone's shirt out* to annoy someone] —ˈ**shirtily** *adv.* —ˈ**shirtiness** *n.*

shish kebab (ˈʃiːʃ kəˈbæb) *n.* a dish consisting of small pieces of meat and vegetables threaded onto skewers and grilled. [from Turkish *şiş kebab,* from *şiş* skewer; see KEBAB]

shit (ʃɪt) *vb.* **shits, shitting; shitted** *or* **shit.** **1.** to defecate. *~n.* **2.** faeces; excrement. **3.** *Slang.* rubbish; nonsense. **4.** *Slang.* an obnoxious or worthless person. **5.** *Slang.* cannabis resin or heroin. **6. in the shit.** *Slang.* in trouble. *~interj.* **7.** *Slang.* an exclamation expressing anger, disgust, etc. ~Also (esp. dialect): **shite** (ʃaɪt). [Old English *scite* (unattested) dung, *scītan* to defecate, of Germanic origin; related to Old English *scēadan* to separate, Old Norse *skīta* to defecate, Middle Dutch *schitte* excrement] —ˈ**shitty** *adj.* —ˈ**shittily** *adv.* —ˈ**shittiness** *n.*

shithead (ˈʃɪtˌhɛd) *n. Taboo slang.* a fool; idiot: used as a term of abuse.

shittah (ˈʃɪtə) *n., pl.* **shittim** (ˈʃɪtɪm) *or* **shittahs.** a tree mentioned in the Old Testament, thought to be either of two Asian acacias, *Acacia seyal* or *A. tortilis,* having close-grained yellow-brown wood. [C17: from Hebrew *shittāh;* related to Egyptian *sout* acacia]

shittim wood (ˈʃɪtɪm) *n. Old Testament.* a kind of wood, probably acacia, from which the Ark of the Covenant and parts of the tabernacle were made. [C14: from Hebrew *shittīm,* plural of SHITTAH]

shiur (ˈʃiʊr, ʃiˈuːr) *n., pl.* **shiurim** (ʃiʊˈrim, ʃiˈuːrim) *Judaism.* a lesson, esp. one in which a passage of the Talmud is studied together by a group of people. [from Hebrew, literally: measurement]

shiv (ʃɪv) *n.* a variant spelling of **chiv.**

Shiva (ˈʃiːvə, ˈʃɪvə) *n.* a variant spelling of **Siva.** —ˈ**Shivaism** *n.* —ˈ**Shivaist** *n., adj.*

shivah (ˈʃivɑ, ˈʃivə) *n. Judaism.* **1.** the period of formal mourning lasting seven days from the funeral during which the mourner stays indoors and sits on a low stool. **2. sit shivah.** to mourn. [from Hebrew, literally: seven (days)]

shivaree (ˌʃɪvəˈriː) *n.* a variant (esp. U.S. and Canadian) of **charivari.**

shive (ʃaɪv) *n.* **1.** a flat cork or bung for wide-mouthed bottles. **2.** an archaic word for **slice.** [C13: from Middle Dutch or Middle Low German *schīve;* see SHEAVE[1]]

shiver[1] (ˈʃɪvə) *vb.* (*intr.*) **1.** to shake or tremble, as from cold or fear. **2. a.** (of a sail) to luff; flap or shake. **b.** (of a sailing vessel) to sail close enough to the wind to make the sails luff. *~n.* **3.** the act of shivering; a tremulous motion. **4. the shivers.** an attack of shivering, esp. through fear or illness. [C13 *chiveren,* perhaps variant of *chevelen* to chatter (used of teeth), from Old English *ceafl* JOWL] —ˈ**shiverer** *n.* —ˈ**shivering** *adj.*

shiver[2] (ˈʃɪvə) *vb.* **1.** to break or cause to break into fragments. *~n.* **2.** a splintered piece. [C13: of Germanic origin; compare Old High German *scivaro,* Middle Dutch *scheveren* to shiver, Old Norse *skīfa* to split]

shivery[1] (ˈʃɪvərɪ) *adj.* **1.** inclined to shiver or tremble. **2.** causing shivering, esp. through cold or fear.

shivery[2] (ˈʃɪvərɪ) *adj. Rare.* easily shattered; brittle.

shloshim (ˈʃləʃim, ˈʃlaʊʃim) *n. Judaism.* the period of thirty days' deep mourning following a death. [from Hebrew, literally: thirty (days)]

Shluh (ʃəˈluː, ʃluː) *n.* **1.** (*pl.* **Shluhs** *or* **Shluh**) a member of a Berber people inhabiting the Atlas Mountains in Morocco and Algeria. **2.** the dialect of Berber spoken by this people.

SHM *abbrev. for* simple harmonic motion.

shmatte *Yiddish.* (ˈʃmɑtə) *n.* **1.** a rag. **2.** anything shabby. **3.** (*modifier*) clothes: a jocular use: *the shmatte trade.*

shmo (ʃməʊ) *n., pl.* **shmoes.** a variant form of **schmo.**

Shoah (ˈʃɔɑː) *n.* (in secular Judaism) a Hebrew word for **holocaust** (sense 2). [literally: destruction]

shoal[1] (ʃəʊl) *n.* **1.** a stretch of shallow water. **2.** a sandbank or rocky area in a stretch of water, esp. one that is visible at low water. *~vb.* **3.** to make or become shallow. **4.** (*intr.*) *Nautical.* to sail into shallower water. *~adj. also* **shoaly.** **5.** a less common word for **shallow.** **6.** *Nautical.* (of the draught of a vessel) drawing little water. [Old English *sceald* SHALLOW] —ˈ**shoaliness** *n.*

shoal[2] (ʃəʊl) *n.* **1.** a large group of fish. **2.** a large group of people or things. *~vb.* **3.** (*intr.*) to collect together in such a group. [Old English *scolu;* related to Middle Low German, Middle Dutch *schōle* SCHOOL[2]]

shoat *or* **shote** (ʃəʊt) *n.* a piglet that has recently been weaned. [C15: related to West Flemish *schote*]

shock[1] (ʃɒk) *vb.* **1.** to experience or cause to experience extreme horror, disgust, surprise, etc.: *the atrocities shocked us; she shocks easily.* **2.** to cause a state of shock in (a person). **3.** to come or cause to come into violent contact; jar. *~n.* **4.** a sudden and violent jarring blow or impact. **5.** something that causes a sudden and violent disturbance in the emotions: *the shock of her father's death made her ill.* **6.** *Pathol.* a state of bodily collapse or near collapse caused by circulatory failure or sudden lowering of the blood pressure, as from severe bleeding, burns, fright, etc. [C16: from Old French *choc,* from *choquier* to make violent contact with, of Germanic origin; related to Middle High German *schoc*] —ˈ**shockable** *adj.* —ˌ**shockaˈbility** *n.*

shock[2] (ʃɒk) *n.* **1.** a number of sheaves set on end in a field to dry. **2.** a pile or stack of unthreshed corn. *~vb.* **3.** (*tr.*) to set up (sheaves) in shocks. [C14: probably of Germanic origin; compare Middle Low German, Middle Dutch *schok* shock of corn, group of sixty]

shock[3] (ʃɒk) *n.* **1.** a thick bushy mass, esp. of hair. *~adj.* **2.** *Rare.* bushy; shaggy. [C19: perhaps from SHOCK[2]]

shock absorber *n.* any device designed to absorb mechanical shock, esp. one fitted to a motor vehicle to damp the recoil of the road springs.

shocker (ˈʃɒkə) *n. Informal.* **1.** a person or thing that shocks or horrifies. **2.** a sensational novel, film, or play.

shockheaded (ˈʃɒkˌhɛdɪd) *adj.* having a head of bushy or tousled hair.

shock-horror *adj. Facetious.* (esp. of newspaper headlines) sensationalistic: *shock-horror stories about the British diet.* [C20: SHOCK[1] + HORROR]

shocking (ˈʃɒkɪŋ) *adj.* **1.** causing shock, horror, or disgust. **2. shocking pink.** a vivid or garish shade of pink. **3.** *Informal.* very bad or terrible: *shocking weather.* —ˈ**shockingly** *adv.* —ˈ**shockingness** *n.*

shockproof (ˈʃɒkˌpruːf) *adj.* capable of absorbing shock without damage: *a shockproof watch.*

shockstall (ˈʃɒkˌstɔːl) *n.* the loss of lift and increase of drag experienced by transonic aircraft when strong shock waves on the wings cause the airflow to separate from the wing surfaces.

shock therapy *or* **treatment** *n.* the treatment of certain psychotic conditions by injecting drugs or by passing an electric current through the brain (**electroconvulsive therapy**) to produce convulsions or coma.

shock troops *pl. n.* soldiers specially trained and equipped to carry out an assault.

shock tube *n.* an apparatus in which a gas is heated to very high temperatures by means of a shock wave, usually for spectroscopic investigation of the natures and reactions of the resulting radicals and excited molecules.

shock wave *n.* a region across which there is a rapid pressure, temperature, and density rise caused by a body moving supersonically in a gas or by a detonation. Often shortened to **shock.** See also **sonic boom, shock tube.**

shod (ʃɒd) *vb.* the past participle of **shoe.**

shoddy (ˈʃɒdɪ) *adj.* **-dier, -diest. 1.** imitating something of better quality. **2.** of poor quality; trashy. **3.** made of shoddy material. *~n., pl.* **-dies. 4.** a yarn or fabric made from wool waste or clippings. **5.** anything of inferior quality that is designed to simulate superior quality. [C19: of unknown origin] —ˈ**shoddily** *adv.* —ˈ**shoddiness** *n.*

shoe (ʃuː) *n.* **1. a.** one of a matching pair of coverings shaped to fit the foot, esp. one ending below the ankle, having an upper of leather, plastic, etc., on a sole and heel of heavier leather, rubber, or synthetic material. **b.** (*as modifier*): *shoe cleaner.* **2.** anything resembling a shoe in shape, function, position, etc., such as a horseshoe. **3.** a band of metal or wood on the bottom of the runner of a sledge. **4.** (in baccarat, etc.) a boxlike device for holding several packs of cards and allowing the cards to be dispensed singly. **5.** a base for the supports of a superstructure of a bridge, roof, etc. **6.** a metal collector attached to an electric train that slides along the third rail and picks up power for the motor. **7.** *Engineering.* a lining to protect from and withstand wear: see **brake shoe, pile shoe. 8. be in (a person's) shoes.** *Informal.* to be in (another person's) situation. *~vb.* **shoes, shoeing, shod.** (*tr.*) **9.** to furnish with shoes. **10.** to fit (a horse) with horseshoes. **11.** to furnish with a hard cover, such as a metal plate, for protection against friction or bruising. [Old English *scōh;* related to Old Norse *skōr,* Gothic *skōhs,* Old High German *scuoh*]

shoebill (ˈʃuːˌbɪl) *n.* a large wading bird, *Balaeniceps rex,* of tropical E African swamps, having a dark plumage, a large head, and a large broad bill: family *Balaenicipitidae,* order *Ciconiiformes.* [C19: so named because of the shape of its bill]

shoeblack (ˈʃuːˌblæk) *n.* (esp. formerly) a person who shines boots and shoes.

shoehorn (ˈʃuːˌhɔːn) *n.* a smooth curved implement of horn, metal, plastic, etc., inserted at the heel of a shoe to ease the foot into it.

shoelace (ˈʃuːˌleɪs) *n.* a cord or lace for fastening shoes.

shoe leather *n.* **1.** leather used to make shoes. **2. save shoe leather.** to avoid wearing out shoes, as by taking a bus rather than walking.

shoemaker (ˈʃuːˌmeɪkə) *n.* a person who makes or repairs shoes or boots. —ˈ**shoeˌmaking** *n.*

shoer (ˈʃuːə) *n. Rare.* a person who shoes horses.

shoeshine (ˈʃuːˌʃaɪn) *n.* **1.** the act or an instance of polishing a pair of shoes. **2.** the appearance or shiny surface of polished shoes.

shoestring (ˈʃuːˌstrɪŋ) *n.* **1.** another word for **shoelace. 2.** *Informal.* **a.** a very small or petty amount of money (esp. in the phrase **on a shoestring**). **b.** (*as modifier*): *a shoestring budget.*

shoetree (ˈʃuːˌtriː) *n.* a wooden or metal form inserted into a shoe or boot to stretch it or preserve its shape.

shofar *or* **shophar** (ˈʃəʊfɑː; *Hebrew* ʃɔˈfar) *n., pl.* **-fars, -phars** *or* **-froth, -phroth** (*Hebrew* -ˈfrɔt). *Judaism.* a ram's horn sounded in the synagogue daily during the month of Elul and repeatedly on Rosh Hashanah, and by the ancient Israelites as a warning, summons, etc. [from Hebrew *shōphār* ram's horn]

shogun (ˈʃəʊˌguːn) *n. Japanese history.* **1.** (from 794 A.D.) a chief military commander. **2.** (from about 1192 to 1867) any of a line of hereditary military dictators who relegated the emperors to a position of purely theoretical supremacy. [C17: from Japanese, from Chinese *chiang chün* general, from *chiang* to lead + *chün* army] —ˈ**shoˌgunal** *adj.*

shogunate (ˈʃəʊgʊnɪt, -ˌneɪt) *n. Japanese history.* the office or rule of a shogun.

shoji (ˈʃəʊʒiː, -dʒiː) *n., pl.* **-ji** *or* **-jis. 1.** a rice-paper screen in a sliding wooden frame, used in Japanese houses as a partition. **2.** any similar screen. [C19: from Japanese, from *shō* to separate, + *ji* a piece]

Shona (ˈʃɒnə) *n.* **1.** (*pl.* **-na** *or* **-nas**) a member of a Sotho people of S central Africa, living chiefly in Zimbabwe and Mozambique. **2.** the language of this people, belonging to the Bantu group of the Niger-Congo family.

shone (ʃɒn; *U.S.* ʃəʊn) *vb.* the past tense and past participle of **shine.**

shoneen (ˈʃoːniːn) *n. Irish.* an Irishman who imitates English ways. [C19: from Irish Gaelic *Seoinín,* diminutive of *Seon* John (taken as typical English name)]

shonky (ˈʃɒŋkɪ) *adj.* **-kier, -kiest.** *Austral. slang.* unreliable; deceptive; unsound. [C19: perhaps from Yiddish *shonniker* or from SH(ODDY) + (W)ONKY]

shoo (ʃuː) *interj.* **1.** go away!: used to drive away unwanted or annoying people, animals, etc. *~vb.* **shoos, shooing, shooed. 2.** (*tr.*) to drive away by or as if by crying "shoo." **3.** (*intr.*) to cry "shoo." [C15: imitative; related to Middle High German *schū,* French *shou,* Italian *scio*]

shoofly pie (ˈʃuːˌflaɪ) *n. U.S.* a dessert similar to treacle tart.

shoogle (ˈʃugᵊl) *Dialect, chiefly Scot.* *~vb.* **1.** to shake, sway, or rock back and forth. *~n.* **2.** a rocking motion; shake. [from dialectal *shog, shug;* apparently related to German *schaukeln* to shake] —ˈ**shoogly** *adj.*

shoo-in *n. U.S. and Canadian.* a person or thing that is certain to win or succeed.

shook[1] (ʃʊk) *n.* **1.** (in timber working) a set of parts ready for assembly, esp. of a barrel. **2.** a group of sheaves piled together on end; shock. [C18: of unknown origin]

shook[2] (ʃʊk) *vb.* **1.** the past tense of **shake.** *~adj.* **2. shook on.** *Austral. and N.Z. informal.* keen on; enthusiastic about.

shool (ʃuːl) *n.* a dialect word for **shovel.**

shoon (ʃuːn) *n. Dialect, chiefly Scot.* a plural of **shoe.**

shoot (ʃuːt) *vb.* **shoots, shooting, shot. 1.** (*tr.*) to hit, wound, damage, or kill with a missile discharged from a weapon. **2.** to discharge (a missile or missiles) from a weapon. **3.** to fire (a weapon) or (of a weapon) to be fired. **4.** to send out or be sent out as if from a weapon: *he shot questions at her.* **5.** (*intr.*) to move very rapidly; dart. **6.** (*tr.*) to slide or push into or out of a fastening: *to shoot a bolt.* **7.** to emit (a ray of light) or (of a ray of light) to be emitted. **8.** (*tr.*) to go or pass quickly over or through: *to shoot rapids.* **9.** (*intr.*) to hunt game with a gun for sport. **10.** (*tr.*) to pass over (an area) in hunting game. **11.** to extend or cause to extend; project. **12.** (*tr.*) to discharge down or as if down a chute. **13.** (*intr.*) (of a plant) to produce (buds, branches, etc.). **14.** (*intr.*) (of a seed) to germinate. **15.** to photograph or record (a sequence, subject, etc.). **16.** (*tr.; usually passive*) to variegate or streak, as with colour. **17.** *Soccer, hockey, etc.* to hit or propel (the ball, etc.) towards the goal. **18.** (*tr.*) *Sport, chiefly U.S. and Canadian.* to score (points, strokes, etc.): *he shot 72 on the first round.* **19.** (*tr.*) to plane (a board) to produce a straight edge. **20.** (*tr.*) *Mining.* to detonate. **21.** (*tr.*) to measure the altitude of (a celestial body). **22.** (often foll. by *up*) *Slang.* to inject (someone, esp. oneself) with (a drug, esp. heroin). **23. shoot a line.** See **line**[1] (sense 58). **24. shoot off one's mouth.** *Slang, chiefly U.S. and Canadian.* **a.** to talk indiscreetly. **b.** to boast or exaggerate. **25. shoot one's bolt.** See **bolt**[1] (sense 12). **26. shoot oneself in the foot.** *Informal.* to damage one's own cause inadvertently. *~n.* **27.** the act of shooting. **28.** the action or motion of something that is shot. **29.** the first aerial part of a plant to develop from a germinating seed. **30.** any new growth of a plant, such as a bud, young branch, etc. **31.** *Chiefly Brit.* a meeting or party organized for hunting game with guns. **32.** an area or series of coverts and woods where game can be hunted with guns. **33.** a steep descent in a stream; rapid. **34.** *Geology, mining.* a narrow workable vein of ore. **35.** *Obsolete.* the reach of a shot. **36. the whole shoot.**

Slang. everything. ~*interj.* **37.** *U.S. and Canadian.* an exclamation expressing disbelief, scepticism, etc. ~See also **shoot down, shoot out, shoot through, shoot up.** [Old English *sceōtan;* related to Old Norse *skjōta,* Old High German *skiozan* to shoot, Old Slavonic *iskydati* to throw out] —'**shooter** *n.*

shoot down *vb. (tr., adv.)* **1.** to shoot callously. **2.** to cause to fall to earth by hitting with a missile. **3.** to defeat or disprove: *he shot down her argument.*

shooting box *n.* a small country house providing accommodation for a shooting party during the shooting season. Also called: **shooting lodge.**

shooting brake *n. Brit.* another name for **estate car.**

shooting gallery *n.* **1.** an area, often enclosed, designed for target practice, shooting, etc. **2.** *Slang.* a house where heroin addicts inject themselves.

shooting iron *n. U.S. slang.* a firearm, esp. a pistol.

shooting script *n. Films.* written instructions indicating to the cameraman the order of shooting.

shooting star *n.* an informal name for **meteor.**

shooting stick *n.* a device that resembles a walking stick, having a spike at one end and a folding seat at the other.

shoot out *vb. (tr., adv.)* **1.** to fight to the finish by shooting (esp. in the phrase **shoot it out**). ~*n.* **shoot-out. 2.** a conclusive gunfight.

shoot through *vb. (intr., adv.) Chiefly Austral.* to leave; depart.

shoot up *vb. (adv.)* **1.** *(intr.)* to grow or become taller very fast. **2.** *(tr.)* to hit with a number of shots. **3.** *(tr.)* to spread terror throughout (a place) by lawless and wanton shooting. **4.** *(tr.) Slang.* to inject (someone, esp. oneself) with (a drug, esp. heroin).

shop (ʃɒp) *n.* **1.** a place, esp. a small building, for the retail sale of goods and services. **2.** an act or instance of shopping, esp. household shopping: *the weekly shop.* **3.** a place for the performance of a specified type of work; workshop. **4. all over the shop.** *Informal.* **a.** in disarray: *his papers were all over the shop.* **b.** in every direction: *I've searched for it all over the shop.* **5. shut up shop.** to close business at the end of the day or permanently. **6. talk shop.** to speak about one's work, esp. when meeting socially, sometimes with the effect of excluding those not similarly employed. ~*vb.* **shops, shopping, shopped. 7.** *(intr.;* often foll. by *for)* to visit a shop or shops in search of (goods) with the intention of buying them. **8.** *(tr.) Slang, chiefly Brit.* to inform on or betray, esp. to the police. [Old English *sceoppa* stall, booth; related to Old High German *scopf* shed, Middle Dutch *schoppe* stall]

shop around *vb. (intr., adv.) Informal.* **1.** to visit a number of shops or stores to compare goods and prices. **2.** to consider a number of possibilities before making a choice.

shop assistant *n.* a person who serves in a shop.

shop floor *n.* **1.** the part of a factory housing the machines and men directly involved in production. **2. a.** workers, esp. factory workers organized in a union. **b.** *(as modifier): shop-floor protest.*

shophar ('ʃəʊfɑː; *Hebrew* ʃɔ'far) *n., pl.* **-phars** *or* **-phroth** *(Hebrew* -'frɔt). a variant spelling of **shofar.**

shopkeeper ('ʃɒpˌkiːpə) *n.* a person who owns or manages a shop or small store. —'**shopˌkeeping** *n.*

shoplifter ('ʃɒpˌlɪftə) *n.* a person who steals goods from a shop during shopping hours. —'**shopˌlifting** *n.*

shopper ('ʃɒpə) *n.* a person who buys goods in a shop.

shopping ('ʃɒpɪŋ) *n.* **1.** a number or collection of articles purchased. **2.** the act or an instance of making purchases.

shopping bag lady *n.* another name for **bag lady.**

shopping centre *n.* **1.** a purpose-built complex of shops, restaurants, etc., for the use of pedestrians. **2.** the area of a town where most of the shops are situated.

shopping mall *n.* a large enclosed shopping centre.

shopping precinct *n.* a pedestrian area containing shops, restaurants, etc., forming a single architectural unit and usually providing car-parking facilities.

shopsoiled ('ʃɒpˌsɔɪld) *adj.* **1.** worn, faded, tarnished, etc., from being displayed in a shop or store. U.S. word: **shopworn. 2.** no longer new or fresh.

shop steward *n.* a coworker elected by trade union members to represent them in discussions and negotiations with the management.

shoptalk ('ʃɒpˌtɔːk) *n.* conversation concerning one's work, esp. when carried on outside business hours.

shopwalker ('ʃɒpˌwɔːkə) *n. Brit.* a person employed by a departmental store to supervise sales personnel, assist customers, etc. U.S. equivalent: **floorwalker.**

shopworn ('ʃɒpˌwɔːn) *adj.* the U.S. word for **shopsoiled.**

shoran ('ʃɔːræn) *n.* a short-range radar system by which an aircraft, ship, etc., can accurately determine its position by the time taken for a signal to be sent to two radar beacons at known locations and be returned. [C20: *sho(rt) ra(nge) n(avigation)*]

shore[1] (ʃɔː) *n.* **1.** the land along the edge of a sea, lake, or wide river. Related adj.: **littoral. 2. a.** land, as opposed to water (esp. in the phrase **on shore**). **b.** *(as modifier): shore duty.* **3.** *Law.* the tract of coastland lying between the ordinary marks of high and low water. **4.** *(often pl.)* a country: *his native shores.* ~*vb.* **5.** *(tr.)* to move or drag (a boat) onto a shore. [C14: probably from Middle Low German, Middle Dutch *schōre;* compare Old High German *scorra* cliff; see SHEAR]

shore[2] (ʃɔː) *n.* **1.** a prop, post, or beam used to support a wall, building, ship in dry dock, etc. ~*vb.* **2.** *(tr.;* often foll. by *up)* to prop or make safe with or as if with a shore. [C15: from Middle Dutch *schōre;* related to Old Norse *skortha* prop] —'**shoring** *n.*

shore[3] (ʃɔː) *vb. Archaic or Austral. and N.Z.* a past tense of **shear.**

shore bird *n.* any of various birds that live close to water, esp. any bird of the families *Charadriidae* or *Scolopacidae* (plovers, sandpipers, etc.). Also called (Brit.): **wader.**

shore leave *n. Naval.* **1.** permission to go ashore, esp. when granted to an officer. Compare **liberty** (sense 5). **2.** time spent ashore during leave.

shoreless ('ʃɔːlɪs) *adj.* **1.** without a shore suitable for landing. **2.** *Poetic.* boundless; vast: *the shoreless wastes.*

shoreline ('ʃɔːˌlaɪn) *n.* the edge of a body of water.

shore patrol *n. U.S.* a naval unit serving the same function as the military police.

shoreward ('ʃɔːwəd) *adj.* **1.** near or facing the shore. ~*adv. also* **shorewards. 2.** towards the shore.

shoreweed ('ʃɔːˌwiːd) *n.* a tufty aquatic perennial, *Littorella uniflora,* of the plantain family, that forms underwater mats but usually flowers only on muddy margins.

shorn (ʃɔːn) *vb.* a past participle of **shear.**

short (ʃɔːt) *adj.* **1.** of little length; not long. **2.** of little height; not tall. **3.** of limited duration. **4.** not meeting a requirement; deficient: *the number of places laid at the table was short by four.* **5.** *(postpositive;* often foll. by *of* or *on)* lacking (in) or needful (of): *I'm always short of money.* **6.** concise; succinct. **7.** lacking in the power of retentiveness: *a short memory.* **8.** abrupt to the point of rudeness: *the salesgirl was very short with him.* **9.** *Finance.* **a.** not possessing the securities or commodities that have been sold under contract and therefore obliged to make a purchase before the delivery date. **b.** of or relating to such sales, which depend on falling prices for profit. **10.** *Phonetics.* **a.** denoting a vowel of relatively brief temporal duration. **b.** classified as short, as distinguished from other vowels. Thus in English (ɪ) in *bin,* though of longer duration than (iː) in *beat,* is nevertheless regarded as a short vowel. **c.** (in popular usage) denoting the qualities of the five English vowels represented orthographically in the words *pat, pet, pit, pot, put,* and *putt.* **11.** *Prosody.* **a.** denoting a vowel that is phonetically short or a syllable containing such a vowel. In classical verse short vowels are followed by one consonant only or sometimes one consonant plus a following *l* or *r.* **b.** (of a vowel or syllable in verse that is not quantitative) not carrying emphasis or accent; unstressed. **12.** (of pastry) crumbly in texture. See also **shortcrust pastry. 13.** (of a drink of spirits) undiluted; neat. **14. get (someone) by the short hairs.** *Informal.* to have (someone) completely in one's power. **15. in short supply.** scarce. **16. short and sweet.** unexpectedly brief. **17. short for.** an abbreviation for. ~*adv.* **18.** abruptly: *to stop short.* **19.** briefly or concisely. **20.** rudely or curtly. **21.** *Finance.* without possessing the securities or commodities at the time of their contractual sale: *to sell short.* **22. caught** *or* **taken short.** having a sudden need to urinate or defecate. **23. fall short. a.** to prove inadequate. **b.** (often foll. by *of*) to fail to reach or measure up to (a standard). **24. go short.** not to have a sufficient amount, etc. **25. short of.** except: *nothing short of a miracle can save him now.* ~*n.* **26.** anything that is short. **27.** a drink of spirits as opposed to a long drink such as beer. **28.** *Phonetics, prosody.* a short vowel or syllable. **29.** *Finance.* **a.** a short contract or sale. **b.** a short seller. **30.** a short film, usually of a factual nature. **31.** See **short circuit. 32. for short.** *Informal.* as an abbreviation: *he is called Jim for short.* **33. in short. a.** as a summary. **b.** in a few words. ~*vb.* **34.** See **short circuit** (sense 2). ~See also **shorts.** [Old English *scort;* related to Old Norse *skortr* a lack, *skera* to cut, Old High German *scurz* short] —'**shortness** *n.*

short account *n.* **1.** the aggregate of short sales on an open market, esp. a stock market. **2.** the account of a stock-market speculator who sells short.

short-acting *adj.* (of a drug) quickly effective, but requiring regularly repeated doses for long-term treatment, being rapidly absorbed, distributed in the bloodstream, and excreted. Compare **intermediate-acting, long-acting.**

shortage ('ʃɔːtɪdʒ) *n.* a deficiency or lack in the amount needed, expected, or due; deficit.

short bill *n.* a bill of exchange that is payable at sight, on demand, or within less than ten days.

shortbread ('ʃɔːtˌbrɛd) *n.* a rich crumbly biscuit made from dough with a large proportion of butter. [C19: from SHORT (in the sense: crumbly)]

shortcake ('ʃɔːtˌkeɪk) *n.* **1.** a kind of shortbread made from a rich biscuit dough. **2.** a dessert made of layers of shortcake filled with fruit and cream. [C16: from SHORT (in the sense: crumbly)]

short-change *vb. (tr.)* **1.** to give less than correct change to. **2.** *Slang.* to cheat or swindle. —ˌ**short-'changer** *n.*

short circuit *n.* **1.** a faulty or accidental connection between two points of different potential in an electric circuit, bypassing the load and establishing a path of low resistance through which an excessive current can flow. It can cause damage to the components if the circuit is not protected by a fuse. ~*vb.* **short-circuit. 2.** to develop or cause to develop a short circuit. **3.** *(tr.)* to bypass (a procedure, regulation, etc.). **4.** *(tr.)* to hinder or frustrate (plans, etc.). ~Sometimes (for senses 1, 2) shortened to **short.**

shortcoming ('ʃɔːtˌkʌmɪŋ) *n.* a failing, defect, or deficiency.

short covering *n.* **1.** the purchase of securities or commodities by a short seller to meet delivery requirements. **2.** the securities or commodities purchased.

shortcrust pastry ('ʃɔːtˌkrʌst) *n.* a basic type of pastry that is made with half the quantity of fat to flour, and has a crisp but crumbly texture. Also called: **short pastry.**

short cut *n.* **1.** a route that is shorter than the usual one. **2.** a means of saving time or effort. ~*vb.* **short-cut, -cuts, -cutting, -cut. 3.** (*intr.*) to use a short cut. [C16: from CUT (in the sense: a direct route)]

short-dated *adj.* (of a gilt-edged security) having less than five years to run before redemption. Compare **medium-dated, long-dated.**

short-day *adj.* (of plants) able to flower only if exposed to short periods of daylight (less than 12 hours), each followed by a long dark period. Compare **long-day.**

short division *n.* the division of numbers, usually integers, that can be worked out mentally rather than on paper.

shorten ('ʃɔːtᵊn) *vb.* **1.** to make or become short or shorter. **2.** (*tr.*) *Nautical.* to reduce the area of (sail). **3.** (*tr.*) to make (pastry, bread, etc.) short, by adding butter or another fat. **4.** *Gambling.* to cause (the odds) to lessen or (of odds) to become less. —'**shortener** *n.*

shortening ('ʃɔːtᵊnɪŋ) *n.* butter, lard, or other fat, used in a dough, cake mixture, etc., to make the mixture short.

Shorter Catechism *n. Chiefly Presbyterian Church.* the more widely used and influential of two catechisms of religious instruction drawn up in 1647.

shortfall ('ʃɔːtˌfɔːl) *n.* **1.** failure to meet a goal or a requirement. **2.** the amount of such a failure; deficiency.

short fuse *n. Informal.* a quick temper.

shorthand ('ʃɔːtˌhænd) *n.* **a.** a system of rapid handwriting employing simple strokes and other symbols to represent words or phrases. **b.** (*as modifier*): *a shorthand typist.*

short-handed *adj.* lacking the usual or necessary number of assistants, workers, etc. —ˌ**short-'handedness** *n.*

shorthand typist *n. Brit.* a person skilled in the use of shorthand and in typing. U.S. and Canadian name: **stenographer.**

short head *n. Horse racing.* a distance shorter than the length of a horse's head.

shorthold tenancy ('ʃɔːtˌhəʊld) *n.* (in Britain) the letting of a dwelling by a nonresident private landlord for a fixed term of between one and five years at a fair rent.

shorthorn ('ʃɔːtˌhɔːn) *n.* a short-horned breed of cattle with several regional varieties. Also called: **Durham.**

short hundredweight *n.* the full name for **hundredweight** (sense 2).

shortie *or* **shorty** ('ʃɔːtɪ) *n.* **1.** *Informal.* **a.** (*pl.* **shorties**). a person or thing that is extremely short. **b.** (*as modifier*): *a shortie nightdress.* **2.** a Scot. name for **shortbread.**

short jenny *n. Billiards.* an in-off into a middle pocket. Compare **long jenny.** [from *Jenny,* pet form of *Janet*]

short leg *n. Cricket.* **a.** a fielding position on the leg side near the batsman's wicket. **b.** a fielder in this position.

short list *Chiefly Brit.* ~*n.* **1.** a list of suitable applicants for a job, post, etc., from which the successful candidate will be selected. ~*vb.* (*tr.*) **short-list. 2.** to put (someone) on a short list.

short-lived *adj.* living or lasting only for a short time.

shortly ('ʃɔːtlɪ) *adv.* **1.** in a short time; soon. **2.** in a few words; briefly. **3.** in a curt or rude manner.

short odds *pl. n.* (in betting) an almost even chance.

short order *n. Chiefly U.S. and Canadian.* **a.** food that is easily and quickly prepared. **b.** (*as modifier*): *short-order counter.*

short-range *adj.* of small or limited extent in time or distance: *a short-range forecast; a short-range gun.*

shorts (ʃɔːts) *pl. n.* **1.** trousers reaching the top of the thigh or partway to the knee, worn by both sexes for sport, relaxing in summer, etc. **2.** *Chiefly U.S. and Canadian.* men's underpants that usually reach mid-thigh. Usual Brit. word: **pants. 3.** short-dated gilt-edged securities. **4.** short-term bonds. **5.** securities or commodities that have been sold short. **6.** timber cut shorter than standard lengths. **7.** a livestock feed containing a large proportion of bran and wheat germ. **8.** items needed to make up a deficiency.

short shrift *n.* **1.** brief and unsympathetic treatment. **2.** (formerly) a brief period allowed to a condemned prisoner to make confession. **3. make short shrift of.** to dispose of quickly and unsympathetically.

short-sighted *adj.* **1.** relating to or suffering from myopia. **2.** lacking foresight: *a short-sighted plan.* —ˌ**short-'sightedly** *adv.* —ˌ**short-'sightedness** *n.*

short-spoken *adj.* tending to be abrupt in speech.

short-staffed *adj.* lacking an adequate number of staff, assistants, etc.

shortstop ('ʃɔːtˌstɒp) *n. Baseball.* **a.** the fielding position to the left of second base viewed from home plate. **b.** the player at this position.

short story *n.* a prose narrative of shorter length than the novel, esp. one that concentrates on a single theme.

short straw *n.* **draw the short straw.** be the person (as in drawing lots) to whom an unwelcome task or fate falls.

short subject *n. Chiefly U.S.* a short film, esp. one presented between screenings of a feature film.

short-tempered *adj.* easily moved to anger; irascible.

short-term *adj.* **1.** of, for, or extending over a limited period. **2.** *Finance.* extending over, maturing within, or required within a short period of time, usually twelve months: *short-term credit; short-term capital.*

short-termism *n.* the tendency to focus attention on short-term gains, often at the expense of long-term success or stability.

short-term memory *n. Psychol.* that section of the memory storage system of limited capacity (approximately seven items) that is capable of storing material for a brief period of time. Compare **long-term memory.**

short time *or* **short-time working** *n.* a system of working, usually for a temporary period, when employees are required to work and be paid for fewer than their normal hours per week due to a shortage of work.

short ton *n.* the full name for **ton**[1] (sense 2).

short-waisted *adj.* unusually short from the shoulders to the waist.

short wave *n.* **a.** a radio wave with a wavelength in the range 10–100 metres. **b.** (*as modifier*): *a short-wave broadcast.*

short-winded *adj.* **1.** tending to run out of breath, esp. after exertion. **2.** (of speech or writing) terse or abrupt.

Shoshone *or* **Shoshoni** (ʃəʊ'ʃəʊnɪ) *n.* **1.** (*pl.* **-nes, -ne** *or* **-nis, -ni**) a member of a North American Indian people of the southwestern U.S., related to the Aztecs. **2.** the language of this people, belonging to the Uto-Aztecan family.

Shoshonean *or* **Shoshonian** (ʃəʊ'ʃəʊnɪən, ˌʃəʊʃə'niːən) *n.* a subfamily of North American Indian languages belonging to the Uto-Aztecan family, spoken mainly in the southwestern U.S.

shot[1] (ʃɒt) *n.* **1.** the act or an instance of discharging a projectile. **2.** (*pl.* **shot**) a solid missile, such as an iron ball or a lead pellet, discharged from a firearm. **3. a.** small round pellets of lead collectively, as used in cartridges. **b.** metal in the form of coarse powder or small pellets. **4.** the distance that a discharged projectile travels or is capable of travelling. **5.** a person who shoots, esp. with regard to his ability: *he is a good shot.* **6.** *Informal.* an attempt; effort. **7.** *Informal.* a guess or conjecture. **8.** any act of throwing or hitting something, as in certain sports. **9.** the launching of a rocket, missile, etc., esp. to a specified destination: *a moon shot.* **10. a.** a single photograph: *I took 16 shots of the wedding.* **b.** a series of frames on cine film concerned with a single event. **c.** a length of film taken by a single camera without breaks, used with others to build up a full motion picture or television film. **11.** *Informal.* an injection, as of a vaccine or narcotic drug. **12.** *Informal.* a glass of alcoholic drink, esp. spirits. **13.** *Sport.* a heavy metal ball used in the shot put. **14.** an explosive charge used in blasting. **15.** globules of metal occurring in the body of a casting that are harder than the rest of the casting. **16.** a unit of chain length equal to 75 feet (Brit.) or 90 feet (U.S.). **17. call the shots.** *Slang.* to have control over an organization, course of action, etc. **18. have a shot at.** *Informal.* **a.** to attempt. **b.** *Austral.* to jibe at or vex. **19. like a shot.** very quickly, esp. willingly. **20. shot in the arm.** *Informal.* anything that regenerates, increases confidence or efficiency, etc.: *his arrival was a shot in the arm for the company.* **21. shot in the dark.** a wild guess. **22. that's the shot.** *Austral. informal.* that is the right thing to do. ~*vb.* **shots, shotting, shotted. 23.** (*tr.*) to weight or load with shot. [Old English *scot;* related to Old Norse *skot,* Old High German *scoz* missile; see SHOOT]

shot[2] (ʃɒt) *vb.* **1.** the past tense and past participle of **shoot.** ~*adj.* **2.** (of textiles) woven to give a changing colour effect. **3.** streaked with colour. **4.** *Slang.* exhausted. **5. get shot** *or* **shut of.** *Slang.* to get rid of.

shot-blasting *n.* the cleaning of metal, etc., by a stream of shot.

shote (ʃəʊt) *n.* a variant spelling of **shoat.**

shotgun ('ʃɒtˌgʌn) *n.* **1. a.** a shoulder firearm with unrifled bore designed for the discharge of small shot at short range and used mainly for hunting small game. **b.** (*as modifier*): *shotgun fire.* **2.** *American football.* an offensive formation in which the quarterback lines up for a snap unusually far behind the line of scrimmage. ~*adj.* **3.** *Chiefly U.S.* involving coercion or duress: *a shotgun merger.* **4.** *Chiefly U.S.* involving or relying on speculative suggestions, etc.: *a shotgun therapy.* ~*vb.* **-guns, -gunning, -gunned. 5.** (*tr.*) *U.S.* to shoot or threaten with or as if with a shotgun.

shotgun wedding *n. Informal.* a wedding into which one or both partners are coerced, usually because the woman is pregnant.

shot hole *n.* a drilled hole into which explosive is put for blasting.

shot noise *or* **effect** *n.* the inherent electronic noise arising in an electric current because of the discontinuous nature of conduction by electrons. Also called: **Schottky noise** ('ʃɒtkɪ).

shot put *n.* **1.** an athletic event in which contestants hurl or put a heavy metal ball or shot as far as possible. **2.** a single put of the shot. —'**shot-**ˌ**putter** *n.*

shott *or* **chott** (ʃɒt) *n.* **1.** a shallow temporary salt lake or marsh in the North African desert. **2.** the hollow in which it lies. [C19: via French *chott* from Arabic *shatt*]

shotten ('ʃɒtᵊn) *adj.* **1.** (of fish, esp. herring) having recently spawned. **2.** *Archaic.* worthless or undesirable. [C15: from obsolete past participle of SHOOT]

shot tower *n.* a building formerly used in the production of shot, in which molten lead was graded and dropped into water, thus cooling it and forming the shot.

should (ʃʊd) *vb.* the past tense of **shall:** used as an auxiliary verb to indicate that an action is considered by the speaker to be obligatory (*you should go*) or to form the subjunctive mood with *I* or *we* (*I should like to see you; if I should be late, go without me*). [Old English *sceold;* see SHALL]

▷**Usage.** *Should* has, as its most common meaning in modern English, the sense *ought* as in *I should go to the graduation, but I don't see how I can.* However, the older sense of the subjunctive of *shall* is often used with *I* or *we* to indicate a more polite form than *would: I should like to go, but I can't.* In much speech and writing, *should* has been replaced by *would* in contexts of this kind, but it remains in conditional subjunctives: *should* (never *would*) *I go, I should* (or *would*) *wear my black dress.*

shoulder ('ʃəʊldə) *n.* **1.** the part of the vertebrate body where the arm or a corresponding forelimb joins the trunk: the pectoral girdle and associated structures. **2.** the joint at the junction of the forelimb with the pectoral girdle. **3.** a cut of meat including the upper part of the foreleg. **4.** *Printing.* the flat surface of a piece of type from which the face rises. **5.** *Tanning.* the portion of a hide covering the shoulders and neck of the animal, usually including the cheeks. **6.** the part of a garment that covers the shoulder. **7.** anything that resembles a shoulder in shape or position. **8.** the strip of unpaved land that borders a road. **9.** *Engineering.* a substantial projection or abrupt change in shape or diameter designed to withstand thrust. **10.** *Photog.* the portion of the characteristic curve of a photographic material indicating the maximum density that can be produced on the material. **11.** *Jewellery.* the part of a ring where the shank joins the setting. **12. a shoulder to cry on.** a person one turns to for sympathy with one's troubles. **13. give (someone) the cold shoulder.** *Informal.* **a.** to treat (someone) in a cold manner; snub. **b.** to ignore or shun (someone). **14. put one's shoulder to the wheel.** *Informal.* to work very hard. **15. rub shoulders with.** See **rub** (sense 11). **16. shoulder to shoulder. a.** side by side or close together. **b.** in a corporate effort. ~*vb.* **17.** (*tr.*) to bear or carry (a burden, responsibility, etc.) as if on one's shoulders. **18.** to push (something) with or as if with the shoulder. **19.** (*tr.*) to lift or carry on the shoulders. **20. shoulder arms.** *Military.* to bring the rifle vertically close to the right side with the muzzle uppermost and held at the trigger guard. [Old English *sculdor;* related to Old High German *sculterra*]

shoulder blade *n.* the nontechnical name for **scapula.**

shoulder pad *n.* a small pad inserted to raise or give shape to the shoulder of a garment.

shoulder patch *n. Military.* an emblem worn high on the arm as an insignia. Also called: **shoulder flash.**

shoulder strap *n.* a strap over one or both of the shoulders, as to hold up a garment or to support a bag, etc.

shouldn't ('ʃʊdᵊnt) *vb. contraction of* should not.

shouldst (ʃʊdst) *or* **shouldest** ('ʃʊdɪst) *vb. Archaic or dialect.* (used with the pronoun *thou* or its relative equivalent) a form of the past tense of **shall.**

shouse (ʃaʊs) *Austral. slang.* ~*n.* **1.** a toilet; lavatory. ~*adj.* **2.** unwell or in poor spirits. [C20: shortening of *shithouse*]

shout (ʃaʊt) *n.* **1.** a loud cry, esp. to convey emotion or a command. **2.** *Informal, Brit., Austral., and N.Z.* **a.** a round, esp. of drinks. **b.** one's turn to buy a round of drinks. ~*vb.* **3.** to utter (something) in a loud cry; yell. **4.** (*intr.*) to make a loud noise. **5.** (*tr.*) *Austral. and N.Z. informal.* to treat (someone) to (something), esp. a round of drinks. [C14: probably from Old Norse *skūta* taunt; related to Old Norse *skjōta* to SHOOT] —'**shouter** *n.*

shout down *vb.* (*tr., adv.*) to drown, overwhelm, or silence by shouting or talking loudly.

shove (ʃʌv) *vb.* **1.** to give a thrust or push to (a person or thing). **2.** (*tr.*) to give a violent push to; jostle. **3.** (*intr.*) to push one's way roughly. **4.** (*tr.*) *Informal.* to put (something) somewhere, esp. hurriedly or carelessly: *shove it in the bin.* ~*n.* **5.** the act or an instance of shoving. ~See also **shove off.** [Old English *scūfan;* related to Old Norse *skūfa* to push, Gothic *afskiuban* to push away, Old High German *skioban* to shove] —'**shover** *n.*

shove-halfpenny *n. Brit.* a game in which players try to propel old halfpennies or polished discs with the hand into lined sections of a wooden or slate board.

shovel ('ʃʌvᵊl) *n.* **1.** an instrument for lifting or scooping loose material, such as earth, coal, etc., consisting of a curved blade or a scoop attached to a handle. **2.** any machine or part resembling a shovel in action. **3.** Also called: **shovelful.** the amount that can be contained in a shovel. **4.** short for **shovel hat.** ~*vb.* **-els, -elling, -elled** *or U.S.* **-els, -eling, -eled. 5.** to lift (earth, etc.) with a shovel. **6.** (*tr.*) to clear or dig (a path) with or as if with a shovel. **7.** (*tr.*) to gather, load, or unload in a hurried or careless way: *he shovelled the food into his mouth and rushed away.* [Old English *scofl;* related to Old High German *scūfla* shovel, Dutch *schoffel* hoe; see SHOVE] —'**shoveller** *or U.S.* '**shoveler** *n.*

shoveler ('ʃʌvələ) *n.* a duck, *Anas* (or *Spatula*) *clypeata,* of ponds and marshes, having a spoon-shaped bill, a blue patch on each wing, and in the male a green head, white breast, and reddish-brown body.

shovel hat *n.* a black felt hat worn by some clergymen, with a brim rolled up to resemble a shovel in shape.

shovelhead ('ʃʌvᵊlˌhɛd) *n.* a common shark, *Sphyrna tiburo,* of the Atlantic and Pacific Oceans, having a shovel-shaped head: family *Sphyrnidae* (hammerheads).

shovelnose ('ʃʌvᵊlˌnəʊz) *n.* an American freshwater sturgeon, *Scaphirhynchus platorynchus,* having a broad shovel-like snout.

shove off *vb.* (*intr., adv.; often imperative*) **1.** to move from the shore in a boat. **2.** *Informal.* to go away; depart.

show (ʃəʊ) *vb.* **shows, showing, showed; shown** *or* **showed. 1.** to make, be, or become visible or noticeable: *to show one's dislike.* **2.** (*tr.*) to present to view; exhibit: *he showed me a picture.* **3.** (*tr.*) to indicate or explain; prove: *to show that the earth moves round the sun.* **4.** (*tr.*) to exhibit or present (oneself or itself) in a specific character: *to show oneself to be trustworthy.* **5.** (*tr.;* foll. by *how* and an infinitive) to instruct by demonstration: *show me how to swim.* **6.** (*tr.*) to indicate or register: *a barometer shows changes in the weather.* **7.** (*tr.*) to grant or bestow: *to show favour to someone.* **8.** (*intr.*) to appear: *to show to advantage.* **9.** to exhibit, display, or offer (goods, etc.) for sale: *three artists were showing at the gallery.* **10.** (*tr.*) to allege, as in a legal document: *to show cause.* **11.** to present (a play, film, etc.) or (of a play, etc.) to be presented, as at a theatre or cinema. **12.** (*tr.*) to guide or escort: *please show me to my room.* **13. show in** *or* **out.** to conduct a person into or out of a room or building by opening the door for him. **14.** (*intr.*) to win a place in a horse race, etc. **15.** to give a performance of riding and handling (a horse) to display its best points. **16.** (*intr.*) *Informal.* to put in an appearance; arrive. ~*n.* **17.** a display or exhibition. **18.** a public spectacle. **19.** an ostentatious or pretentious display. **20.** a theatrical or other entertainment. **21.** a trace or indication. **22.** *Obstetrics.* a discharge of blood at the onset of labour. **23.** *U.S., Austral., and N.Z. informal.* a chance; opportunity (esp. in the phrases **give someone a show, he's got no show of winning,** etc.). **24.** a sporting event consisting of contests in which riders perform different exercises to show their skill and their horses' ability and breeding. **25.** *Slang, chiefly Brit.* a thing or affair (esp. in the phrases **good show, bad show,** etc.). **26.** *Austral. and N.Z., mining.* a slight indication of the presence of gold. **27.** a display of farm animals, with associated competitions. **28. for show.** in order to attract attention. **29. run the show.** *Informal.* to take charge of or manage an affair, business, etc. **30. steal the show.** to draw the most attention or admiration, esp. unexpectedly. **31. stop the show.** *Informal.* **a.** (of a stage act, etc.) to receive so much applause as to interrupt the performance. **b.** to be received with great enthusiasm. ~See also **show off, show up.** [Old English *scēawian;* related to Old High German *scouwōn* to look, Old Norse *örskār* careful, Greek *thuoskoos* seer]

show bill *n.* a poster advertising a play or show. Also called: **show card.**

showboat ('ʃəʊˌbəʊt) *n.* a paddle-wheel river steamer with a theatre and a repertory company.

showbread ('ʃəʊˌbrɛd) *n.* a variant spelling of **shewbread.**

show business *n.* the entertainment industry, including theatre, films, television, and radio. Informal term: **show biz.**

show card *n.* **1.** *Commerce.* a tradesman's advertisement mounted on card as a poster. **2.** another term for **show bill.**

showcase ('ʃəʊˌkeɪs) *n.* **1.** a glass case used to display objects in a museum or shop. **2.** a setting in which anything may be displayed to best advantage. ~*vb.* **3.** (*tr.*) to exhibit or display. ~*adj.* **4.** displayed or meriting display as in a showcase.

show copy *n. Films.* a positive print of a film for use at an important presentation such as a premiere.

showd (ʃaʊd) *Northeast Scot. dialect.* ~*vb.* **1.** (*intr.*) to rock or sway to and fro. **2.** (*tr.*) to rock (a baby in one's arms or in a pram). ~*n.* **3.** a rocking motion. [from Old English *scūdan* to shake]

show day *n.* (in Australia) a public holiday in a state on the date of its annual agricultural and industrial show.

showdown ('ʃəʊˌdaʊn) *n.* **1.** *Informal.* an action that brings matters to a head or acts as a conclusion or point of decision. **2.** *Poker.* the exposing of the cards in the players' hands on the table at the end of the game.

shower[1] ('ʃaʊə) *n.* **1.** a brief period of rain, hail, sleet, or snow. **2.** a sudden abundant fall or downpour, as of tears, sparks, or light. **3.** a rush; outpouring: *a shower of praise.* **4. a.** a kind of bath in which a person stands upright and is sprayed with water from a nozzle. **b.** the room, booth, etc., containing such a bath. Full name: **shower bath. 5.** *Brit. slang.* a derogatory term applied to a person or group, esp. to a group considered as being slack, untidy, etc. **6.** *U.S., Canadian, Austral., and N.Z.* a party held to honour and present gifts to a person, as to a prospective bride. **7.** a large number of particles formed by the collision of a cosmic-ray particle with a particle in the atmosphere. **8.** *N.Z.* a light fabric cover thrown over a tea table to protect the food from flies, dust, etc. ~*vb.* **9.** (*tr.*) to sprinkle or spray with or as if with a shower: *shower the powder into the milk.* **10.** (often with *it* as subject) to fall or cause to fall in the form of a shower. **11.** (*tr.*) to give (gifts, etc.) in abundance or present (a person) with (gifts, etc.): *they showered gifts on him.* **12.** (*intr.*) to take a shower. [Old English *scūr;* related to Old Norse *skūr,* Old High

German *skūr* shower, Latin *caurus* northwest wind] —'**showery** *adj.*

shower[2] ('ʃəʊə) *n.* a person or thing that shows.

showerproof ('ʃaʊəˌpruːf) *adj.* (of a garment, etc.) resistant to or partly impervious to rain. —'**showerˌproofing** *n.*

showgirl ('ʃəʊˌgɜːl) *n.* a girl who appears in variety shows, nightclub acts, etc., esp. as a singer or dancer.

showground ('ʃəʊˌgraʊnd) *n.* an open-air setting for agricultural displays, competitions, etc. Also called (Austral. and N.Z.): **showgrounds.**

show house *n.* a house on a new estate that is decorated and furnished for prospective buyers to view.

showing ('ʃəʊɪŋ) *n.* **1.** a presentation, exhibition, or display. **2.** manner of presentation; performance. **3.** evidence.

showjumping ('ʃəʊˌdʒʌmpɪŋ) *n.* the riding of horses in competitions to demonstrate skill in jumping over or between various obstacles. —'**show-ˌjumper** *n.*

showman ('ʃəʊmən) *n., pl.* **-men. 1.** a person who presents or produces a theatrical show, etc. **2.** a person skilled at presenting anything in an effective manner. —'**showmanship** *n.*

shown (ʃəʊn) *vb.* a past participle of **show.**

show off *vb. (adv.)* **1.** *(tr.)* to exhibit or display so as to invite admiration. **2.** *(intr.) Informal.* to behave in such a manner as to make an impression. ~*n.* **show-off. 3.** *Informal.* a person who makes a vain display of himself.

show of hands *n.* the raising of hands to indicate voting for or against a proposition.

showpiece ('ʃəʊˌpiːs) *n.* **1.** anything displayed or exhibited. **2.** anything prized as a very fine example of its type.

showplace ('ʃəʊˌpleɪs) *n.* a place exhibited or visited for its beauty, historic interest, etc.

showroom ('ʃəʊˌruːm, -ˌrʊm) *n.* a room in which goods, such as cars, are on display.

show stopper *n. Informal.* a stage act, etc., that receives so much applause as to interrupt the performance.

show trial *n.* a trial conducted primarily to make a particular impression on the public or on other nations, esp. one that demonstrates the power of the state over the individual.

show up *vb. (adv.)* **1.** to reveal or be revealed clearly. **2.** *(tr.)* to expose or reveal the faults or defects of by comparison. **3.** *(tr.) Informal.* to put to shame; embarrass: *he showed me up in front of my friends.* **4.** *(intr.) Informal.* to appear or arrive.

showy ('ʃəʊɪ) *adj.* **showier, showiest. 1.** gaudy, flashy, or ostentatious. **2.** making a brilliant or imposing display. —'**showily** *adv.* —'**showiness** *n.*

shpt *abbrev. for* shipment.

shr. *Stock Exchange. abbrev. for* share.

shrank (ʃræŋk) *vb.* a past tense of **shrink.**

shrapnel ('ʃræpnᵊl) *n.* **1. a.** a projectile containing a number of small pellets or bullets exploded before impact. **b.** such projectiles collectively. **2.** fragments from this or any other type of shell. [C19: named after H. *Shrapnel* (1761–1842), English army officer, who invented it]

shred (ʃrɛd) *n.* **1.** a long narrow strip or fragment torn or cut off. **2.** a very small piece or amount; scrap. ~*vb.* **shreds, shredding, shredded** *or* **shred. 3.** *(tr.)* to tear or cut into shreds. [Old English *scread;* related to Old Norse *skrjōthr* torn-up book, Old High German *scrōt* cut-off piece; see SCROLL, SHROUD, SCREED] —'**shredder** *n.*

shrew (ʃruː) *n.* **1.** Also called: **shrewmouse.** any small mouselike long-snouted mammal, such as *Sorex araneus* (**common shrew**), of the family *Soricidae:* order *Insectivora* (insectivores). See also **water shrew. 2.** a bad-tempered or mean-spirited woman. [Old English *scrēawa;* related to Old High German *scrawaz* dwarf, Icelandic *skröggr* old man, Norwegian *skrugg* dwarf]

shrewd (ʃruːd) *adj.* **1.** astute and penetrating, often with regard to business. **2.** artful and crafty: *a shrewd politician.* **3.** *Obsolete.* **a.** piercing: *a shrewd wind.* **b.** spiteful. [C14: from *shrew* (obsolete vb.) to curse, from SHREW] —'**shrewdly** *adv.* —'**shrewdness** *n.*

shrewdie ('ʃruːdɪ) *n. Austral. and N.Z. informal.* a shrewd person. [C20: from SHREWD + -IE]

shrewish ('ʃruːɪʃ) *adj.* (esp. of a woman) bad-tempered and nagging. —'**shrewishly** *adv.* —'**shrewishness** *n.*

shrew mole *n.* any of several moles, such as *Uropsilus soricipes* of E Asia or *Neurotrichus gibbsi* of E North America, having a long snout and long tail.

shrewmouse ('ʃruːˌmaʊs) *n., pl.* **-mice.** another name for **shrew,** esp. the common shrew.

shriek (ʃriːk) *n.* **1.** a shrill and piercing cry. ~*vb.* **2.** to produce or utter (words, sounds, etc.) in a shrill piercing tone. [C16: probably from Old Norse *skrækja* to SCREECH] —'**shrieker** *n.*

shrieval ('ʃriːvᵊl) *adj.* of or relating to a sheriff.

shrievalty ('ʃriːvəltɪ) *n., pl.* **-ties. 1.** the office or term of office of a sheriff. **2.** the jurisdiction of a sheriff. [C16: from SHRIEVE, on the model of *mayoralty*]

shrieve (ʃriːv) *n.* an archaic word for **sheriff.**

shrift (ʃrɪft) *n. Archaic.* the act or an instance of shriving or being shriven. See also **short shrift.** [Old English *scrift,* from Latin *scriptum* SCRIPT]

shrike (ʃraɪk) *n.* **1.** Also called: **butcherbird.** any songbird of the chiefly Old World family *Laniidae,* having a heavy hooked bill and feeding on smaller animals which they sometimes impale on thorns, barbed wire, etc. See also **bush shrike** (sense 1). **2.** any of various similar but unrelated birds, such as the cuckoo shrikes. **3. shrike thrush** *or* **tit.** another name for **thickhead** (the bird). [Old English *scrīc* thrush; related to Middle Dutch *schrīk* corncrake; see SCREECH, SHRIEK]

shrill (ʃrɪl) *adj.* **1.** sharp and high-pitched in quality. **2.** emitting a sharp high-pitched sound. ~*vb.* **3.** to utter (words, sounds, etc.) in a shrill tone. **4.** *(tr.) Rare.* to cause to produce a shrill sound. [C14: probably from Old English *scralletan;* related to German *schrill* shrill, Dutch *schrallen* to shriek] —'**shrillness** *n.* —'**shrilly** *adv.*

shrimp (ʃrɪmp) *n.* **1.** any of various chiefly marine decapod crustaceans of the genus *Crangon* and related genera, having a slender flattened body with a long tail and a single pair of pincers. **2.** any of various similar but unrelated crustaceans, such as the opossum shrimp and mantis shrimp. **3.** Also called: **freshwater shrimp.** any of various freshwater shrimplike amphipod crustaceans of the genus *Gammarus,* esp. *G. pulex.* **4.** Also called: **sand shrimp.** any of various shrimplike amphipod crustaceans of the genus *Gammarus,* esp. *G. locusta.* ~See also **opossum shrimp. 5.** *Informal.* a diminutive person, esp. a child. ~*vb.* **6.** *(intr.)* to fish for shrimps. [C14: probably of Germanic origin; compare Middle Low German *schrempen* to shrink; see SCRIMP, CRIMP] —'**shrimper** *n.*

shrine (ʃraɪn) *n.* **1.** a place of worship hallowed by association with a sacred person or object. **2.** a container for sacred relics. **3.** the tomb of a saint or other holy person. **4.** a place or site venerated for its association with a famous person or event. **5.** *R.C. Church.* a building, alcove, or shelf arranged as a setting for a statue, picture, or other representation of Christ, the Virgin Mary, or a saint. ~*vb.* **6.** short for **enshrine.** [Old English *scrīn,* from Latin *scrīnium* bookcase; related to Old Norse *skrin,* Old High German *skrīni*] —'**shrineˌlike** *adj.*

shrink (ʃrɪŋk) *vb.* **shrinks, shrinking; shrank** *or* **shrunk; shrunk** *or* **shrunken. 1.** to contract or cause to contract as from wetness, heat, cold, etc. **2.** to become or cause to become smaller in size. **3.** *(intr.;* often foll. by *from)* **a.** to recoil or withdraw: *to shrink from the sight of blood.* **b.** to feel great reluctance (at): *to shrink from killing an animal.* ~*n.* **4.** the act or an instance of shrinking. **5.** a slang word for **psychiatrist.** [Old English *scrincan;* related to Old Norse *skrokkr* torso, Old Swedish *skrunkin* wrinkled, Old Norse *hrukka* a crease, Icelandic *skrukka* wrinkled woman] —'**shrinkable** *adj.* —'**shrinker** *n.* —'**shrinking** *adj.* —'**shrinkingly** *adv.*

shrinkage ('ʃrɪŋkɪdʒ) *n.* **1.** the act or fact of shrinking. **2.** the amount by which anything decreases in size, value, weight, etc. **3.** the loss in body weight during shipment and preparation of livestock for marketing as meat. **4.** *Retail.* the loss of merchandise through shoplifting or damage.

shrink fit *n. Engineering.* a tight fit of a collar or wheel boss on a shaft obtained by expanding the collar or boss by heating to enable it to be threaded onto the shaft and then allowing it to cool, or by freezing the shaft to reduce its diameter to enable it to be threaded into the collar or boss and then allowing the shaft temperature to rise.

shrinking violet *n. Informal.* a shy person.

shrink-wrap *vb.* **-wraps, -wrapping, -wrapped.** *(tr.)* to package (a product) in a flexible plastic wrapping designed to shrink about its contours to protect and seal it.

shrive (ʃraɪv) *vb.* **shrives, shriving; shrove** *or* **shrived; shriven** ('ʃrɪvᵊn) *or* **shrived.** *Chiefly R.C. Church.* **1.** to hear the confession of (a penitent). **2.** *(tr.)* to impose a penance upon (a penitent) and grant him sacramental absolution. **3.** *(intr.)* to confess one's sins to a priest in order to obtain sacramental forgiveness. [Old English *scrīfan,* from Latin *scrībere* to write] —'**shriver** *n.*

shrivel ('ʃrɪvᵊl) *vb.* **-els, -elling, -elled** *or U.S.* **-els, -eling, -eled. 1.** to make or become shrunken and withered. **2.** to lose or cause to lose vitality. [C16: probably of Scandinavian origin; compare Swedish dialect *skryvla* wrinkle]

shroff (ʃrɒf) *n.* **1.** (in China, Japan, etc., esp. formerly) an expert employed to separate counterfeit money or base coin from the genuine. **2.** (in India) a moneychanger or banker. ~*vb.* **3.** *(tr.)* to test (money) and separate out the counterfeit and base. [C17: from Portuguese *xarrafo,* from Hindi *sarrāf* moneychanger, from Arabic]

shroud (ʃraʊd) *n.* **1.** a garment or piece of cloth used to wrap a dead body. **2.** anything that envelops like a garment: *a shroud of mist.* **3.** a protective covering for a piece of equipment. **4.** *Astronautics.* a streamlined protective covering used to protect the payload during a rocket-powered launch. **5.** *Nautical.* one of a pattern of ropes or cables used to stay a mast. **6.** any of a set of wire cables stretched between a smokestack or similar structure and the ground, to prevent side sway. **7.** Also called: **shroud line.** any of a set of lines running from the canopy of a parachute to the harness. ~*vb.* **8.** *(tr.)* to wrap in a shroud. **9.** *(tr.)* to cover, envelop, or hide. **10.** *Archaic.* to seek or give shelter. [Old English *scrūd* garment; related to Old Norse *skrūth* gear] —'**shroudless** *adj.*

shroud-laid *adj.* (of a rope) made with four strands twisted to the right, usually around a core.

shrove (ʃrəʊv) *vb.* a past tense of **shrive.**

Shrovetide (ˈʃrəʊvˌtaɪd) *n.* the Sunday, Monday, and Tuesday before Ash Wednesday, formerly a time when confessions were made in preparation for Lent.

Shrove Tuesday *n.* the last day of Shrovetide; Pancake Day.

shrub[1] (ʃrʌb) *n.* a woody perennial plant, smaller than a tree, with several major branches arising from near the base of the main stem. [Old English *scrybb;* related to Middle Low German *schrubben* coarse, uneven, Old Swedish *skrubba* to SCRUB[1]] —ˈ**shrub,like** *adj.*

shrub[2] (ʃrʌb) *n.* **1.** a mixed drink of rum, fruit juice, sugar, and spice. **2.** mixed fruit juice, sugar, and spice made commercially to be mixed with rum or other spirits. [C18: from Arabic *sharāb,* variant of *shurb* drink; see SHERBET]

shrubbery (ˈʃrʌbərɪ) *n., pl.* **-beries. 1.** a place where a number of shrubs are planted. **2.** shrubs collectively.

shrubby (ˈʃrʌbɪ) *adj.* **-bier, -biest. 1.** consisting of, planted with, or abounding in shrubs. **2.** resembling a shrub. —ˈ**shrubbiness** *n.*

shrub layer *n.* See **layer** (sense 2).

shrug (ʃrʌg) *vb.* **shrugs, shrugging, shrugged. 1.** to draw up and drop (the shoulders) abruptly in a gesture expressing indifference, contempt, ignorance, etc. ~*n.* **2.** the gesture so made. **3.** a woman's short jacket. [C14: of uncertain origin]

shrug off *vb.* (*tr., adv.*) **1.** to minimize the importance of; dismiss. **2.** to get rid of. **3.** to wriggle out of or push off (clothing).

shrunk (ʃrʌŋk) *vb.* a past participle and past tense of **shrink.**

shrunken (ˈʃrʌŋkən) *vb.* **1.** a past participle of **shrink.** ~*adj.* **2.** (*usually prenominal*) reduced in size.

shtg. *abbrev. for* shortage.

shtick (ʃtɪk) *n. Slang.* a comedian's routine; act; piece. [C20: from Yiddish *shtik* piece, from Middle High German *stücke*]

shtoom (ʃtʊm) *adj. Slang.* silent; dumb (esp. in **keep shtoom**). [from Yiddish, from German *stumm* silent]

shuck (ʃʌk) *n.* **1.** the outer covering of something, such as the husk of a grain of maize, a pea pod, or an oyster shell. ~*vb.* (*tr.*) **2.** to remove the shucks from. **3.** *Informal, chiefly U.S. and Canadian.* to throw off or remove (clothes, etc.). [C17: American dialect, of unknown origin] —ˈ**shucker** *n.*

shucks (ʃʌks) *U.S. and Canadian informal.* ~*pl. n.* **1.** something of little value (esp. in the phrase **not worth shucks**). ~*interj.* **2.** an exclamation of disappointment, annoyance, etc.

shudder (ˈʃʌdə) *vb.* **1.** (*intr.*) to shake or tremble suddenly and violently, as from horror, fear, aversion, etc. ~*n.* **2.** the act of shuddering; convulsive shiver. [C18: from Middle Low German *schōderen;* related to Old Frisian *skedda* to shake, Old High German *skutten* to shake] —ˈ**shuddering** *adj.* —ˈ**shudderingly** *adv.* —ˈ**shuddery** *adj.*

shuffle (ˈʃʌfəl) *vb.* **1.** to walk or move (the feet) with a slow dragging motion. **2.** to change the position of (something), esp. quickly or in order to deceive others. **3.** (*tr.*) to mix together in a careless manner: *he shuffled the papers nervously.* **4.** to mix up (cards in a pack) to change their order. **5.** (*intr.*) to behave in an awkward, evasive, or underhand manner; equivocate. **6.** (when *intr.*, often foll. by *into* or *out of*) to move or cause to move clumsily: *he shuffled out of the door.* **7.** (*intr.*) to dance the shuffle. ~*n.* **8.** the act or an instance of shuffling. **9.** a dance or dance step with short dragging movements of the feet. [C16: probably from Low German *schüffeln;* see SHOVE] —ˈ**shuffler** *n.*

shuffleboard (ˈʃʌfəlˌbɔːd) *n.* **1.** a game in which players push wooden or plastic discs with a long cue towards numbered scoring sections marked on a floor, esp. a ship's deck. **2.** the marked area on which this game is played.

shuffle off *vb.* (*tr., adv.*) to thrust off or put aside: *shuffle off responsibility.*

shufty *or* **shufti** (ˈʃʊftɪ, ˈʃʌftɪ) *n., pl.* **-ties.** *Brit. slang.* a look; peep. [C20: from Arabic]

shuggy (ˈʃʌgɪ) *n., pl.* **-gies.** *Northeastern English dialect.* a swing, as at a fairground. [from *shog, shug* to shake; see SHOOGLE]

shul *or* **schul** (ʃuːl) *n.* the Yiddish word for **synagogue.** [Yiddish: synagogue, from Old High German *scuola* SCHOOL[1]]

Shulchan Aruch (ʃʊlˈxɑn ɑrˈʊx, ˈʃʊlxən ˈɑʊrəx) *n.* the main codification of Jewish law derived from the Talmud, compiled by the 16th-century rabbi, Joseph Caro.

shun (ʃʌn) *vb.* **shuns, shunning, shunned.** (*tr.*) to avoid deliberately; keep away from. [Old English *scunian,* of obscure origin] —ˈ**shunnable** *adj.* —ˈ**shunner** *n.*

'shun (ʃʌn) *interj. Military.* a clipped form of **attention** (sense 7).

shunt (ʃʌnt) *vb.* **1.** to turn or cause to turn to one side; move or be moved aside. **2.** *Railways.* to transfer (rolling stock) from track to track. **3.** *Electronics.* to divert or be diverted through a shunt. **4.** (*tr.*) to evade by putting off onto someone else. **5.** (*tr.*) *Motor racing slang.* to crash (a car). ~*n.* **6.** the act or an instance of shunting. **7.** a railway point. **8.** *Electronics.* a low-resistance conductor connected in parallel across a device, circuit, or part of a circuit to provide an alternative path for a known fraction of the current. **9.** *Med.* a channel that bypasses the normal circulation of the blood: a congenital abnormality or surgically induced. **10.** *Brit. informal.* a collision which occurs when a vehicle runs into the back of the vehicle in front. [C13: perhaps from *shunen* to SHUN]

shunter (ˈʃʌntə) *n.* a small railway locomotive used for manoeuvring coaches rather than for making journeys.

shunt-wound (ˈʃʌntˌwaʊnd) *adj. Electrical engineering.* (of a motor or generator) having the field and armature circuits connected in parallel. Compare **series-wound.**

shush (ʃʊʃ) *interj.* **1.** be quiet! hush! ~*vb.* **2.** to silence or calm (someone) by or as if by saying "shush". [C20: reduplication of SH, influenced by HUSH]

shut (ʃʌt) *vb.* **shuts, shutting, shut. 1.** to move (something) so as to cover an aperture; close: *to shut a door.* **2.** to close (something) by bringing together the parts: *to shut a book.* **3.** (*tr.;* often foll. by *up*) to close or lock the doors of: *to shut up a house.* **4.** (*tr.;* foll. by *in, out,* etc.) to confine, enclose, or exclude: *to shut a child in a room.* **5.** (*tr.*) to prevent (a business, etc.) from operating. **6. shut one's eyes to.** to ignore deliberately. **7. shut the door on. a.** to refuse to think about. **b.** to render impossible. ~*adj.* **8.** closed or fastened. ~*n.* **9.** the act or time of shutting. **10.** the line along which pieces of metal are welded. **11. get shut** *or* **shot of.** *Slang.* to get rid of. ~See also **shutdown, shut-off, shutout, shut up.** [Old English *scyttan;* related to Old Frisian *sketta* to shut in, Middle Dutch *schutten* to obstruct]

shutdown (ˈʃʌtˌdaʊn) *n.* **1. a.** the closing of a factory, shop, etc. **b.** (*as modifier*): *shutdown costs.* ~*vb.* **shut down.** (*adv.*) **2.** to cease or cause to cease operation. **3.** (*tr.*) to close by lowering. **4.** (*tr.*) (of fog) to descend and envelop. **5.** (*intr.;* foll. by *on* or *upon*) *Informal.* to put a stop to; clamp down on. **6.** (*tr.*) to reduce the power level of (a nuclear reactor) to the lowest possible value.

shuteye (ˈʃʌtˌaɪ) *n.* an informal term for **sleep.**

shut-in *n.* **1.** *Chiefly U.S. and Canadian.* **a.** a person confined indoors by illness. **b.** (*as modifier*): *a shut-in patient.* **2.** *Psychiatry.* a condition in which the person is highly withdrawn and unable to express his own feelings. See also **schizoid.**

shut-off *n.* **1.** a device that shuts something off, esp. a machine control. **2.** a stoppage or cessation. ~*vb.* **shut off.** (*tr., adv.*) **3.** to stem the flow of. **4.** to block off the passage through. **5.** to isolate or separate.

shutout (ˈʃʌtˌaʊt) *n.* **1.** a less common word for a **lockout. 2.** *U.S. and Canadian, sport.* a win in which the defeated team has no score. ~*vb.* **shut out.** (*tr., adv.*) **3.** to keep out or exclude. **4.** to conceal from sight: *we planted trees to shut out the view of the road.* **5.** *U.S. and Canadian.* to prevent (an opponent) from scoring.

shut-out bid *n. Bridge.* a pre-emptive bid.

shutter (ˈʃʌtə) *n.* **1.** a hinged doorlike cover, often louvred and usually one of a pair, for closing off a window. **2. put up the shutters.** to close business at the end of the day or permanently. **3.** *Photog.* an opaque shield in a camera that, when tripped, admits light to expose the film or plate for a predetermined period, usually a fraction of a second. It is either built into the lens system or lies in the focal plane of the lens **(focal-plane shutter). 4.** *Photog.* a rotating device in a film projector that permits an image to be projected onto the screen only when the film is momentarily stationary. **5.** *Music.* one of the louvred covers over the mouths of organ pipes, operated by the swell pedal. **6.** a person or thing that shuts. ~*vb.* (*tr.*) **7.** to close with or as if with a shutter or shutters. **8.** to equip with a shutter or shutters.

shuttering (ˈʃʌtərɪŋ) *n.* another word (esp. Brit.) for **formwork.**

shutter priority *n. Photog.* an automatic exposure system in which the photographer selects the shutter speed and the camera then automatically sets the correct aperture. Compare **aperture priority.**

shuttle (ˈʃʌtəl) *n.* **1.** a bobbin-like device used in weaving for passing the weft thread between the warp threads. **2.** a small bobbin-like device used to hold the thread in a sewing machine or in tatting, knitting, etc. **3.** a bus, train, aircraft, etc., that plies between two points, esp. one that offers a frequent service over a short route. **4. a.** the movement between various countries of a diplomat in order to negotiate with rulers who refuse to meet each other. **b.** (*as modifier*): *shuttle diplomacy.* **5.** *Badminton, etc.* short for **shuttlecock.** ~*vb.* **6.** to move or cause to move by or as if by a shuttle. [Old English *scytel* bolt; related to Middle High German *schüzzel,* Swedish *skyttel.* See SHOOT, SHOT]

shuttle armature *n.* a simple H-shaped armature used in small direct-current motors.

shuttlecock (ˈʃʌtəlˌkɒk) *n.* **1.** a light cone consisting of a cork stub with feathered flights, struck to and fro in badminton and battledore. Often shortened to **shuttle. 2.** anything moved to and fro, as in an argument. ~*vb.* **3.** to move or cause to move to and fro, like a shuttlecock. [C16: from SHUTTLE + COCK[1]]

shut up *vb.* (*adv.*) **1.** (*tr.*) to prevent all access to. **2.** (*tr.*) to confine or imprison. **3.** *Informal.* to cease to talk or make a noise or cause to cease to talk or make a noise: often used in commands. **4.** (*intr.*) (of horses in a race) to cease through exhaustion from maintaining a racing pace.

shwa (ʃwɑː) *n.* a variant spelling of **schwa.**

shy[1] (ʃaɪ) *adj.* **shyer, shyest** *or* **shier, shiest. 1.** not at ease in the company of others. **2.** easily frightened; timid. **3.** (often foll. by *of*) watchful or wary. **4.** *Poker.* (of a player) without enough money to back his bet. **5.** (of plants and animals) not breeding or producing offspring freely. **6.** (foll. by *of*) *Informal, chiefly U.S. and Canadian.* short (of). **7.** (*in combination*) showing reluctance or disinclination: *workshy.* ~*vb.* **shies, shying, shied.** (*intr.*) **8.** to move suddenly, as from fear: *the horse shied at the snake in the road.* **9.** (usually foll. by *off* or *away*) to draw back; recoil. ~*n., pl.* **shies. 10.** a sudden movement, as from fear. [Old English *sceoh;* related to Old High German *sciuhen* to frighten away, Dutch *schuw* shy, Swedish *skygg*] —'**shyer** *n.* —'**shyly** *adv.* —'**shyness** *n.*

shy[2] (ʃaɪ) *vb.* **shies, shying, shied. 1.** to throw (something) with a sideways motion. ~*n., pl.* **shies. 2.** a quick throw. **3.** *Informal.* a gibe. **4.** *Informal.* an attempt; experiment. **5.** short for **cockshy.** [C18: of Germanic origin; compare Old High German *sciuhen* to make timid, Middle Dutch *schüchteren* to chase away] —'**shyer** *n.*

Shylock ('ʃaɪˌlɒk) *n.* a heartless or demanding creditor. [C19: after *Shylock,* the name of the heartless usurer in Shakespeare's *The Merchant of Venice* (1595)]

shypoo (ʃaɪ'puː) *n. Austral. informal.* **a.** liquor of poor quality. **b.** a place where this is sold. **c.** (*as modifier*): *a shypoo shanty.* [C20: of uncertain origin]

shyster ('ʃaɪstə) *n. Informal, chiefly U.S.* a person, esp. a lawyer or politician, who uses discreditable or unethical methods. [C19: probably based on *Scheuster,* name of a disreputable 19th-century New York lawyer]

si (siː) *n. Music.* a variant of **te.**

Si *the chemical symbol for* silicon.

SI **1.** *symbol for* Système International (d'Unités). See **SI unit. 2.** *N.Z. abbrev. for* South Island.

sial ('saɪəl) *n.* the silicon-rich and aluminium-rich rocks of the earth's continental upper crust, the most abundant individual rock being granite. [C20: *si(licon)* + *al(uminium)*] —**sialic** (saɪ'ælɪk) *adj.*

sialagogue *or* **sialogogue** ('saɪələˌgɒg, saɪ'æləˌgɒg) *n. Med.* any drug or agent that can stimulate the flow of saliva. [C18: from New Latin *sialagōgus,* from Greek *sialon* saliva + -AGOGUE] —**sialagogic** *or* **sialogogic** (ˌsaɪələ'gɒdʒɪk) *adj.*

sialoid ('saɪəˌlɔɪd) *adj.* resembling saliva. [from Greek *sialon* saliva + -OID]

siamang ('saɪəˌmæŋ) *n.* a large black gibbon, *Hylobates* (or *Symphalangus*) *syndactylus,* of Sumatra and the Malay Peninsula, having a large reddish-brown vocal sac beneath the chin and the second and third toes united. [C19: from Malay]

Siamese (ˌsaɪə'miːz) *n., pl.* **-mese. 1.** See **Siamese cat.** ~*adj.* **2.** characteristic of, relating to, or being a Siamese twin. ~*adj., n.* **3.** another word for **Thai.**

Siamese cat *n.* a short-haired breed of cat with a tapering tail, blue eyes, and dark ears, mask, tail, and paws. [so called because the breed is believed to have originated in *Siam* (Thailand)]

Siamese fighting fish *n.* a brightly coloured labyrinth fish, *Betta splendens,* of Thailand and Malaysia, having large sail-like fins: the males are very pugnacious.

Siamese twins *pl. n.* twin babies born joined together at some point, such as at the hips. Some have lived for many years without being surgically separated. [C19: named after a famous pair of conjoined twins, Chai and Leng (1814–74), who were born in *Siam*]

sib (sɪb) *n.* **1.** a blood relative. **2.** kinsmen collectively; kindred. **3.** any social unit that is bonded by kinship through one line of descent only. [Old English *sibb;* related to Old Norse *sifjar* relatives, Old High German *sippa* kinship, Latin *suus* one's own; see GOSSIP]

SIB (in Britain) *abbrev. for* Securities and Investments Board: a body that regulates financial dealings in the City of London.

Sib. *abbrev. for* Siberia(n).

Siberian (saɪ'bɪərɪən) *adj.* **1.** of, relating to, or characteristic of Siberia, a vast region of N Asia, chiefly in Russia, or its people, customs, climate, etc. ~*n.* **2.** a native or inhabitant of Siberia.

sibilant ('sɪbɪlənt) *adj.* **1.** *Phonetics.* relating to or denoting the consonants (s, z, ʃ, ʒ), all pronounced with a characteristic hissing sound. **2.** having a hissing sound: *the sibilant sound of wind among the leaves.* ~*n.* **3.** a sibilant consonant. [C17: from Latin *sībilāre* to hiss, of imitative origin; compare Greek *sizein* to hiss] —'**sibilance** *or* '**sibilancy** *n.* —'**sibilantly** *adv.*

sibilate ('sɪbɪˌleɪt) *vb.* to pronounce or utter (words or speech) with a hissing sound. —ˌ**sibi'lation** *n.*

sibling ('sɪblɪŋ) *n.* **1. a.** a person's brother or sister. **b.** (*as modifier*): *sibling rivalry.* **2.** any fellow member of a sib. [C19: specialized modern use of Old English *sibling* relative, from SIB; see -LING[1]]

sibship ('sɪbʃɪp) *n.* a group of children of the same parents.

sibyl ('sɪbɪl) *n.* **1.** (in ancient Greece and Rome) any of a number of women believed to be oracles or prophetesses, one of the most famous being the sibyl of Cumae, who guided Aeneas through the underworld. **2.** a witch, fortune-teller, or sorceress. [C13: ultimately from Greek *Sibulla,* of obscure origin] —**sibylline** ('sɪbɪˌlaɪn, sɪ'bɪlaɪn), **sibyllic,** *or* **sibylic** (sɪ'bɪlɪk) *adj.*

sic[1] (sɪk) *adv.* so or thus: inserted in brackets in a written or printed text to indicate that an odd or questionable reading is in fact accurate. [Latin]

sic[2] (sɪk) *vb.* **sics, sicking, sicked.** (*tr.*) **1.** to turn on or attack: used only in commands, as to a dog. **2.** to urge (a dog) to attack. [C19: dialect variant of SEEK]

sic[3] (sɪk) *determiner, adv.* a Scot. word for **such.**

Sic. *abbrev. for:* **1.** Sicilian. **2.** Sicily.

Sicanian (sɪ'keɪnɪən) *adj.* another word for **Sicilian.**

siccar ('sɪkər) *adj. Scot.* sure; certain. Also: **sicker.** [Middle English, from Latin *sēcūrus* SECURE]

siccative ('sɪkətɪv) *n.* a substance added to a liquid to promote drying: used in paints and some medicines. [C16: from Late Latin *siccātīvus,* from Latin *siccāre* to dry up, from *siccus* dry]

sice (saɪs) *n.* a variant spelling of **syce.**

sicht (sɪxt) *n., vb.* a Scot. word for **sight.**

Sicilian (sɪ'sɪlɪən) *adj.* **1.** of or relating to Sicily, an island in the Mediterranean off the tip of SW Italy, or to its people, customs, etc. ~*n.* **2.** a native or inhabitant of Sicily.

siciliano (sɪˌsɪlɪ'ɑːnəʊ, ˌsɪtʃɪ'ljɑːnəʊ) *n., pl.* **-ianos. 1.** an old dance in six-beat or twelve-beat time. **2.** music composed for or in the rhythm of this dance. [Italian; Sicilian]

sick[1] (sɪk) *adj.* **1.** inclined or likely to vomit. **2. a.** suffering from ill health. **b.** (*as collective n.;* preceded by *the*): *the sick.* **3. a.** of, relating to, or used by people who are unwell: *sick benefits.* **b.** (*in combination*): *sickbed.* **4.** deeply affected with a mental or spiritual feeling akin to physical sickness: *sick at heart.* **5.** mentally, psychologically, or spiritually disturbed. **6.** *Informal.* delighting in or catering for the macabre or sadistic; morbid: *sick humour.* **7.** (often foll. by *of*) *Informal.* Also: **sick and tired.** disgusted or weary, esp. because satiated: *I am sick of his everlasting laughter.* **8.** (often foll. by *for*) weary with longing; pining: *I am sick for my own country.* **9.** pallid or sickly. **10.** not in working order. **11.** (of land) unfit for the adequate production of certain crops. **12. look sick.** *Slang.* to be outclassed. ~*n., vb.* **13.** an informal word for **vomit.** ~See also **sick-out.** [Old English *sēoc;* related to Old Norse *skjūkr,* Gothic *siuks,* Old High German *sioh*] —'**sickish** *adj.*

sick[2] (sɪk) *vb.* a variant spelling of **sic**[2].

sickbay ('sɪkˌbeɪ) *n.* a room or area for the treatment of the sick or injured, as on board a ship.

sick building syndrome *n.* a group of symptoms, such as headaches, eye irritation, and lethargy, that may be experienced by workers in air-conditioned offices.

sicken ('sɪkən) *vb.* **1.** to make or become sick, nauseated, or disgusted. **2.** (*intr.;* often foll. by *for*) to show symptoms (of an illness).

sickener ('sɪkᵊnə) *n.* **1.** something that induces sickness or nausea. **2.** a bright red basidiomycetous fungus of either of two species of *Russula,* notably the poisonous *R. emetica.*

sickening ('sɪkənɪŋ) *adj.* **1.** causing sickness or revulsion. **2.** *Informal.* extremely annoying. —'**sickeningly** *adv.*

sick headache *n.* **1.** a headache accompanied by nausea. **2.** a nontechnical name for **migraine.**

sickie ('sɪkɪ) *n. Austral. and N.Z. informal.* a day of sick leave from work, whether for genuine sickness or not. [C20: from SICK[1] + -IE]

sickle ('sɪkᵊl) *n.* an implement for cutting grass, corn, etc., having a curved blade and a short handle. [Old English *sicol,* from Latin *sēcula;* related to *secāre* to cut]

sick leave *n.* leave of absence from work through illness.

sicklebill ('sɪkᵊlˌbɪl) *n.* any of various birds having a markedly curved bill, such as *Falculea palliata,* a Madagascan bird of the family *Vangidae, Hemignathus procerus,* a Hawaiian honey creeper, and certain hummingbirds and birds of paradise.

sickle-cell anaemia *n.* a hereditary haemolytic anaemia, occurring in Black populations, and caused by mutant haemoglobin. The red blood cells become sickle-shaped. It is characterized by fever, abdominal pain, jaundice, leg ulcers, etc.

sickle feather *n.* (*often pl.*) any of the elongated tail feathers of certain birds, esp. the domestic cock. [C17: so called because of its shape]

sickle medick *n.* a small Eurasian papilionaceous plant, *Medicago falcata,* having trifoliate leaves, yellow flowers, and sickle-shaped pods. Also called: **yellow medick.**

sick list *n.* **1.** a list of the sick, esp. in the army or navy. **2. on the sick list.** ill.

sickly ('sɪklɪ) *adj.* **-lier, -liest. 1.** disposed to frequent ailments; not healthy; weak. **2.** of, relating to, or caused by sickness. **3.** (of a smell, taste, etc.) causing revulsion or nausea. **4.** (of light or colour) faint or feeble. **5.** mawkish; insipid: *sickly affectation.* ~*adv.* **6.** in a sick or sickly manner. —'**sickliness** *n.*

sickness ('sɪknɪs) *n.* **1.** an illness or disease. **2.** nausea or queasiness. **3.** the state or an instance of being sick.

sickness benefit *n.* **1.** (in the British National Insurance scheme) a weekly payment to a person who has been off work through illness for more than three days and less than six months. **2.** (in New Zealand) a payment made by the Department of Social Welfare to a person unable to work owing to a medical condition.

sick note *n. Brit. informal.* a document given to an employer certifying that an employee's absence from work of more than four days was due to illness. If the absence is for more than seven days the note must be signed by a doctor. See also **self-certification.**

sick-out *Caribbean.* ~*n.* **1.** a form of industrial action in which all workers in a factory, etc., report sick simultaneously. ~*vb.* **sick out. 2.** (*intr., adv.*) to take part in such action.

sick pay *n.* wages paid to an employee while he is on sick leave.

sickroom ('sɪkˌruːm, -ˌrʊm) *n.* **1.** a room to which a person who is ill is confined. **2.** a room set aside, as in a school, for people who are taken ill.

sic passim *Latin.* (ˈsɪk ˈpæsɪm) a phrase used in printed works to indicate that a word, spelling, etc., occurs in the same form throughout. [literally: thus everywhere]

sic transit gloria mundi *Latin.* (ˈsɪk ˈtrænsɪt ˈglɔːrɪˌɑː ˈmʊndiː) thus passes the glory of the world.

sidalcea (sɪˈdælsɪə) *n.* any plant of the mostly perennial N American genus *Sidalcea*, related to and resembling mallow, esp. *S. malvaeflora*, grown for its spikes of lilac, pink, or red flowers: family *Malvaceae*. Also called **Greek mallow.** [New Latin, from Greek *sidē* a plant name + *alkea* a kind of mallow]

siddur *Hebrew.* (siːˈduːr; *English* ˈsɪdʊə) *n., pl.* **-durim** (-duːˈriːm) *or* **-durs.** *Judaism.* the Jewish prayer book. [literally: order]

side (saɪd) *n.* **1.** a line or surface that borders anything. **2.** *Geometry.* **a.** any line segment forming part of the perimeter of a plane geometric figure. **b.** another name for **face** (sense 13). **3.** either of two parts into which an object, surface, area, etc., can be divided, esp. by a line, median, space, etc.: *the right side and the left side.* **4.** either of the two surfaces of a flat object: *the right and wrong side of the cloth.* **5.** a surface or part of an object that extends vertically: *the side of a cliff.* **6.** either half of a human or animal body, esp. the area around the waist, as divided by the median plane: *I have a pain in my side.* **7.** the area immediately next to a person or thing: *he stood at her side.* **8.** a district, point, or direction within an area identified by reference to a central point: *the south side of the city.* **9.** the area at the edge of a room, road, etc., as distinguished from the middle. **10.** aspect or part: *look on the bright side; his cruel side.* **11.** one of two or more contesting factions, teams, etc. **12.** a page in an essay, book, etc. **13.** a position, opinion, etc., held in opposition to another in a dispute. **14.** line of descent: *he gets his brains from his mother's side.* **15.** *Informal.* a television channel. **16.** *Billiards, etc.* spin imparted to a ball by striking it off-centre with the cue. U.S. and Canadian equivalent: **English.** **17.** *Brit. slang.* insolence, arrogance, or pretentiousness: *to put on side.* **18. on one side.** set apart from the rest, as provision for emergencies, etc., or to avoid muddling. **19. on the side. a.** apart from or in addition to the main object. **b.** as a sideline. **c.** *U.S.* as a side dish. **d. bit on the side.** See **bit** (sense 11). **20. side by side. a.** close together. **b.** (foll. by *with*) beside or near to. **21. take sides.** to support one group, opinion, etc., as against another. **22. on the weak, heavy,** etc., **side.** tending to be too weak, heavy, etc. *~adj.* **23.** being on one side; lateral. **24.** from or viewed as if from one side. **25.** directed towards one side. **26.** not main; subordinate or incidental: *side door; side road.* *~vb.* **27.** (*intr.*; usually foll. by *with*) to support or associate oneself with a faction, interest, etc. **28.** (*tr.*) to provide with siding or sides. **29.** (*tr.*; often foll. by *away* or *up*) *Northern English dialect.* to tidy up or clear (dishes, a table, etc.). [Old English *sīde*; related to *sīd* wide, Old Norse *sītha* side, Old High German *sīta*]

side arms *pl. n.* weapons carried on the person, by sling, belt, or holster, such as a sword, pistol, etc.

sideband (ˈsaɪdˌbænd) *n.* the frequency band either above (**upper sideband**) or below (**lower sideband**) the carrier frequency, within which fall the spectral components produced by modulation of a carrier wave. See also **single sideband transmission.**

sideboard (ˈsaɪdˌbɔːd) *n.* a piece of furniture intended to stand at the side of a dining room, with drawers, cupboards, and shelves to hold silver, china, linen, etc.

sideboards (ˈsaɪdˌbɔːdz) *pl. n. Brit.* a man's whiskers grown down either side of the face in front of the ears. Also called: **side whiskers,** (Austral.) **sidelevers,** (esp. U.S. and Canadian) **sideburns.**

sideburns (ˈsaɪdˌbɜːnz) *pl. n.* another term (esp. U.S. and Canadian) for **sideboards.** [C19: variant of BURNSIDES]

sidecar (ˈsaɪdˌkɑː) *n.* **1.** a small car attached on one side to a motorcycle, usually for one passenger, the other side being supported by a single wheel. **2.** a cocktail containing brandy with equal parts of Cointreau and lemon juice.

side chain *n. Chem.* a group of atoms bound to an atom, usually a carbon, that forms part of a larger chain or ring in a molecule.

-sided *adj.* (*in combination*) having a side or sides as specified: *three-sided; many-sided.*

side deal *n.* a transaction between two people for their private benefit, which is subsidiary to a contract negotiated by them on behalf of the organizations they represent.

side dish *n.* a portion of food served in addition to the main dish.

side-dress *vb.* (*tr.*) to place fertilizers on or in the soil near the roots of (growing plants).

side drum *n.* a small double-headed drum carried at the side with snares that produce a rattling effect.

side effect *n.* **1.** any unwanted nontherapeutic effect caused by a drug. Compare **aftereffect** (sense 2). **2.** any secondary effect, esp. an undesirable one.

sidekick (ˈsaɪdˌkɪk) *n. Informal.* a close friend or follower who accompanies another on adventures, etc.

sidelight (ˈsaɪdˌlaɪt) *n.* **1.** light coming from the side. **2.** a side window. **3.** either of the two navigational running lights used by vessels at night, a red light on the port and a green on the starboard. **4.** *Brit.* either of two small lights on the front of a motor vehicle, used to indicate the presence of the vehicle at night rather than to assist the driver. **5.** additional or incidental information.

sideline (ˈsaɪdˌlaɪn) *n.* **1.** *Sport.* a line that marks the side boundary of a playing area. **2.** a subsidiary interest or source of income. **3.** an auxiliary business activity or line of merchandise. *~vb.* (*tr.*) *Chiefly U.S. and Canadian.* **4.** to prevent (a player) from taking part in a game. **5.** to prevent (a person) from pursuing a particular activity, operation, career, etc.

sidelines (ˈsaɪdˌlaɪnz) *pl. n.* **1.** *Sport.* the area immediately outside the playing area, where substitute players sit. **2.** the peripheral areas of any region, organization, etc.

sidelong (ˈsaɪdˌlɒŋ) *adj.* (*prenominal*) **1.** directed or inclining to one side. **2.** indirect or oblique. *~adv.* **3.** from the side; obliquely.

sideman (ˈsaɪdmən) *n., pl.* **-men.** a member of a dance band or a jazz group other than the leader.

side meat *n. U.S. informal.* salt pork or bacon. [C19: so called because it comes from the side of the pig]

sidereal (saɪˈdɪərɪəl) *adj.* **1.** of, relating to, or involving the stars. **2.** determined with reference to one or more stars: *the sidereal day.* [C17: from Latin *sīdereus*, from *sīdus* a star, a constellation] —**siˈdereally** *adv.*

sidereal day *n.* See **day** (sense 5).

sidereal hour *n.* a 24th part of a sidereal day.

sidereal month *n.* See **month** (sense 5).

sidereal period *n. Astronomy.* the period of revolution of a body about another with respect to one or more stars.

sidereal time *n.* time based upon the rotation of the earth with respect to a particular star, the **sidereal day** being the unit of measurement.

sidereal year *n.* See **year** (sense 5).

siderite (ˈsaɪdəˌraɪt) *n.* **1.** Also called: **chalybite.** a pale yellow to brownish-black mineral consisting chiefly of iron carbonate in hexagonal crystalline form. It occurs mainly in ore veins and sedimentary rocks and is an important source of iron. Formula: $FeCO_3$. **2.** a meteorite consisting principally of metallic iron. —**sideritic** (ˌsaɪdəˈrɪtɪk) *adj.*

sidero- *or before a vowel* **sider-** *combining form.* indicating iron: *siderolite.* [from Greek *sidēros*]

sideroad (ˈsaɪdˌrəʊd) *n. Canadian.* (esp. in Ontario) a road, usually north-south, going at right angles to concession roads.

siderolite (ˈsaɪdərəˌlaɪt) *n.* a meteorite consisting of a mixture of iron, nickel, and such ferromagnesian minerals as olivine and pyroxene.

siderophilin (ˌsɪdəˈrɒfəlɪn) *n.* another name for **transferrin.** [from SIDERO- + PHIL(E) + -IN]

siderosis (ˌsaɪdəˈrəʊsɪs) *n.* **1.** a lung disease caused by breathing in fine particles of iron or other metallic dust. **2.** an excessive amount of iron in the blood or tissues. —**siderotic** (ˌsɪdəˈrɒtɪk) *adj.*

siderostat (ˈsaɪdərəʊˌstæt) *n.* an astronomical instrument consisting essentially of a plane mirror rotated by a clock mechanism about two axes so that light from a celestial body, esp. the sun, is reflected along a constant direction for a long period of time. See also **heliostat.** Compare **coelostat.** [C19: from *sidero-*, from Latin *sidus* a star + -STAT, on the model of HELIOSTAT] —ˌ**sideroˈstatic** *adj.*

side-saddle *n.* **1.** a riding saddle originally designed for women riders in skirts who sit with both legs on the near side of the horse. *~adv.* **2.** on or as if on a side-saddle: *to be riding side-saddle.*

sideshow (ˈsaɪdˌʃəʊ) *n.* **1.** a small show or entertainment offered in conjunction with a larger attraction, as at a circus or fair. **2.** a subordinate event or incident.

sideslip (ˈsaɪdˌslɪp) *n.* **1.** a sideways skid, as of a motor vehicle. **2.** a sideways and downward movement towards the inside of a turn by an aircraft in a sharp bank. *~vb.* **-slips, -slipping, -slipped.** **3.** another name for **slip**[1] (sense 12).

sidesman (ˈsaɪdzmən) *n., pl.* **-men.** *Church of England.* a man elected to help the parish church warden.

side-splitting *adj.* **1.** producing great mirth. **2.** (of laughter) uproarious or very hearty.

sidestep (ˈsaɪdˌstɛp) *vb.* **-steps, -stepping, -stepped.** **1.** to step aside from or out of the way of (something). **2.** (*tr.*) to dodge or circumvent. *~n.* **side step.** **3.** a movement to one side, as in dancing, boxing, etc. —ˈ**sideˌstepper** *n.*

side street *n.* a minor or unimportant street, esp. one leading off a main thoroughfare.

sidestroke (ˈsaɪdˌstrəʊk) *n.* a type of swimming stroke in which the swimmer lies sideways in the water paddling with his arms and making a scissors kick with his legs.

sideswipe (ˈsaɪdˌswaɪp) *n.* **1.** a glancing blow or hit along or from the side. *~vb.* **2.** to strike (someone) with such a blow. —ˈ**sideˌswiper** *n.*

side tone *n.* sound diverted from a telephone microphone to the earpiece so that a speaker hears his own voice at the same level and position as that of the respondent.

sidetrack (ˈsaɪdˌtræk) *vb.* **1.** to distract or be distracted from a main subject or topic. *~n.* **2.** *U.S. and Canadian.* a railway siding. **3.** the act or an instance of sidetracking; digression.

side-valve engine *n.* a type of internal-combustion engine in which the inlet and exhaust valves are in the cylinder block at the side of the pistons. Compare **overhead-valve engine.**

sidewalk (ˈsaɪdˌwɔːk) *n.* the U.S. and Canadian word for **pavement.**

sidewall ('saɪdˌwɔːl) *n.* either of the sides of a pneumatic tyre between the tread and the rim.
sideward ('saɪdwəd) *adj.* **1.** directed or moving towards one side. ~*adv.* also **sidewards. 2.** towards one side.
sideways ('saɪdˌweɪz) *adv.* **1.** moving, facing, or inclining towards one side. **2.** from one side; obliquely. **3.** with one side forward. ~*adj.* (*prenominal*) **4.** moving or directed to or from one side. **5.** towards or from one side.
sidewheel ('saɪdˌwiːl) *n.* one of the paddle wheels of a sidewheeler.
sidewheeler ('saɪdˌwiːlə) *n.* a vessel, esp. a river boat, propelled by two large paddle wheels, one on each side. Compare **sternwheeler.**
side whiskers *pl. n.* another name for **sideboards.**
sidewinder ('saɪdˌwaɪndə) *n.* **1.** a North American rattlesnake, *Crotalus cerastes,* that moves forwards by a sideways looping motion. **2.** *Boxing, U.S.* a heavy swinging blow from the side. **3.** a U.S. air-to-air missile using infrared homing aids in seeking its target.
siding ('saɪdɪŋ) *n.* **1.** a short stretch of railway track connected to a main line, used for storing rolling stock or to enable trains on the same line to pass. **2.** a short railway line giving access to the main line for freight from a factory, mine, quarry, etc. **3.** *U.S. and Canadian.* material attached to the outside of a building to make it weatherproof.
sidle ('saɪdᵊl) *vb.* (*intr.*) **1.** to move in a furtive or stealthy manner; edge along. **2.** to move along sideways. ~*n.* **3.** a sideways movement. [C17: back formation from obsolete *sideling* sideways] —'**sidler** *n.*
SIDS *abbrev. for* sudden infant death syndrome. See **cot death.**
siècle *French.* (sjɛklə) *n.* a century, period, or era.
siege (siːdʒ) *n.* **1. a.** the offensive operations carried out to capture a fortified place by surrounding it, severing its communications and supply lines, and deploying weapons against it. **b.** (*as modifier*): *siege warfare.* **2.** a persistent attempt to gain something. **3.** a long tedious period, as of illness, etc. **4.** *Obsolete.* a seat or throne. **5. lay siege to.** to besiege. ~*vb.* **6.** (*tr.*) to besiege or assail. [C13: from Old French *sege* a seat, from Vulgar Latin *sēdicāre* (unattested) to sit down, from Latin *sedēre*]
Sieg Heil *German.* (ziːk hail) hail to victory: a Nazi salute, often accompanied by the raising of the right arm.
siemens ('siːmənz) *n., pl.* **siemens.** the derived SI unit of electrical conductance equal to 1 reciprocal ohm. Symbol: S Formerly called: **mho.** [named after Werner von *Siemens* (1816–92), German engineer]
sienna (sɪ'ɛnə) *n.* **1.** a natural earth containing ferric oxide used as a yellowish-brown pigment when untreated (**raw sienna**) or a reddish-brown pigment when roasted (**burnt sienna**). **2.** the colour of this pigment. See also **burnt sienna.** [C18: from Italian *terra di Siena* earth of Siena]
sierra (sɪ'ɛərə) *n.* a range of mountains with jagged peaks, esp. in Spain or America. [C17: from Spanish, literally: saw, from Latin *serra;* see SERRATE] —**si'erran** *adj.*
Sierra (sɪ'ɛərə) *n. Communications.* a code word for the letter *s.*
Sierra Leonean (sɪ'ɛərə lɪ'əʊnɪən) *adj.* **1.** of or relating to Sierra Leone, a republic in W Africa. ~*n.* **2.** a native or inhabitant of Sierra Leone.
siesta (sɪ'ɛstə) *n.* a rest or nap, usually taken in the early afternoon, as in hot countries. [C17: from Spanish, from Latin *sexta hōra* the sixth hour, that is, noon]
sieve (sɪv) *n.* **1.** a device for separating lumps from powdered material, straining liquids, grading particles, etc., consisting of a container with a mesh or perforated bottom through which the material is shaken or poured. **2.** *Rare.* a person who gossips and spreads secrets. **3. a memory** *or* **head like a sieve.** a very poor memory. ~*vb.* **4.** to pass or cause to pass through a sieve. **5.** (*tr.;* often foll. by *out*) to separate or remove (lumps, materials, etc.) by use of a sieve. [Old English *sife;* related to Old Norse *sef* reed with hollow stalk, Old High German *sib* sieve, Dutch *zeef*] —'**sieveˌlike** *adj.*
sievert ('siːvət) *n.* **1.** the derived SI unit of dose equivalent, equal to 1 joule per kilogram. 1 sievert is equivalent to 100 rems. Symbol: Sv **2.** (formerly) a unit of gamma radiation dose approximately equal to 8.4×10^{-2} gray. [C20: named after Rolf *Sievert* (1896–1966), Swedish physicist]
sieve tube *n. Botany.* an element of phloem tissue consisting of a longitudinal row of thin-walled elongated cells with perforations in their connecting walls through which food materials pass.
sifaka (sɪ'fɑːkə) *n.* either of two large rare arboreal lemuroid primates, *Propithecus diadema* or *P. verreauxi,* of Madagascar, having long strikingly patterned or coloured fur: family *Indriidae.* [from Malagasy]
sift (sɪft) *vb.* **1.** (*tr.*) to sieve (sand, flour, etc.) in order to remove the coarser particles. **2.** to scatter (something) over a surface through a sieve. **3.** (*tr.*) to separate with or as if with a sieve; distinguish between. **4.** (*tr.*) to examine minutely: *to sift evidence.* **5.** (*intr.*) to move as if through a sieve. [Old English *siftan;* related to Middle Low German *siften* to sift, Dutch *ziften;* see SIEVE] —'**sifter** *n.*
siftings ('sɪftɪŋz) *pl. n.* material or particles separated out by or as if by a sieve.
sig. *abbrev. for:* **1.** signature. **2.** signor. **3.** signore.
Sig. *abbrev. for:* **1.** (in prescriptions) signā. [Latin: sign] **2.** (in prescriptions) signature. **3.** signor. **4.** signore.
sigh (saɪ) *vb.* **1.** (*intr.*) to draw in and exhale audibly a deep breath as an expression of weariness, despair, relief, etc. **2.** (*intr.*) to make a sound resembling this: *trees sighing in the wind.* **3.** (*intr.;* often foll. by *for*) to yearn, long, or pine. **4.** (*tr.*) to utter or express with sighing. ~*n.* **5.** the act or sound of sighing. [Old English *sīcan,* of obscure origin] —'**sigher** *n.*
sight (saɪt) *n.* **1.** the power or faculty of seeing; perception by the eyes; vision. Related adj.: **visual. 2.** the act or an instance of seeing. **3.** the range of vision: *within sight of land.* **4.** range of mental vision; point of view; judgment: *in his sight she could do nothing wrong.* **5.** a glimpse or view (esp. in the phrases **catch sight of, lose sight of**). **6.** anything that is seen. **7.** (*often pl.*) anything worth seeing; spectacle: *the sights of London.* **8.** *Informal.* anything unpleasant or undesirable to see: *his room was a sight!* **9.** any of various devices or instruments used to assist the eye in making alignments or directional observations, esp. such a device used in aiming a gun. **10.** an observation or alignment made with such a device. **11.** an opportunity for observation. **12.** *Obsolete.* insight or skill. **13. a sight.** *Informal.* a great deal: *she's a sight too good for him.* **14. a sight for sore eyes.** a person or thing that one is pleased or relieved to see. **15. at** *or* **on sight. a.** as soon as seen. **b.** on presentation: *a bill payable at sight.* **16. know by sight.** to be familiar with the appearance of without having personal acquaintance: *I know Mr Brown by sight but we have never spoken.* **17. not by a long sight.** *Informal.* on no account; not at all. **18. out of sight.** *Slang.* **a.** extreme or very unusual. **b.** (*as interj.*) that's marvellous! **19. set one's sights on.** to have (a specified goal) in mind; aim for. **20. sight unseen.** without having seen the object at issue: *to buy a car sight unseen.* ~*vb.* **21.** (*tr.*) to see, view, or glimpse. **22.** (*tr.*) **a.** to furnish with a sight or sights. **b.** to adjust the sight of. **23.** to aim (a firearm) using the sight. [Old English *sihth;* related to Old High German *siht;* see SEE[1]] —'**sightable** *adj.*
sight bill *or* **draft** *n.* variants of **demand bill.**
sighted ('saɪtɪd) *adj.* **1.** not blind. **2.** (*in combination*) having sight of a specified kind: *short-sighted.*
sighter ('saɪtə) *n. Shooting, archery.* any of six practice shots allowed to each competitor in a tournament.
sightless ('saɪtlɪs) *adj.* **1.** blind. **2.** invisible. —'**sightlessly** *adv.* —'**sightlessness** *n.*
sightline ('saɪtˌlaɪn) *n.* an uninterrupted line of vision, as in a theatre, etc., or from a vehicle joining a road.
sightly ('saɪtlɪ) *adj.* **-lier, -liest. 1.** pleasing or attractive to see. **2.** *U.S.* providing a pleasant view. —'**sightliness** *n.*
sight-read ('saɪtˌriːd) *vb.* **-reads, -reading, -read** (-ˌrɛd). to sing or play (music in a printed or written form) without previous preparation. —'**sight-ˌreader** *n.* —'**sight-ˌreading** *n.*
sightscreen ('saɪtˌskriːn) *n. Cricket.* a large white screen placed near the boundary behind the bowler to help the batsman see the ball.
sightsee ('saɪtˌsiː) *vb.* **-sees, -seeing, -saw, -seen.** *Informal.* to visit the famous or interesting sights of (a place). —'**sightˌseeing** *n.* —'**sightˌseer** *n.*
sigil ('sɪdʒɪl) *n. Rare.* **1.** a seal or signet. **2.** a sign or image supposedly having magical power. [C17: from Latin *sigillum* a little sign, from *signum* a SIGN] —**sigillary** ('sɪdʒɪlərɪ) *adj.*
sigla ('sɪglə) *n.* the list of symbols used in a book, usually collected together as part of the preliminaries. [Latin: plural of *siglum,* diminutive of *signum* sign]
siglos ('sɪglɒs) *n., pl.* **-loi** (-lɔɪ). a silver coin of ancient Persia worth one twentieth of a daric.
sigma ('sɪgmə) *n.* **1.** the 18th letter in the Greek alphabet (Σ, σ or, when final, ς), a consonant, transliterated as *S.* **2.** *Maths.* the symbol Σ, indicating summation of the numbers or quantities indicated. [Greek, of Semitic origin; related to Hebrew SAMEKH]
sigmate ('sɪgmɪt, -meɪt) *adj.* shaped like the Greek letter sigma or the Roman *S.* —**sigmation** (sɪg'meɪʃən) *n.*
sigmoid ('sɪgmɔɪd) *adj.* also **sigmoidal. 1.** shaped like the letter S. **2.** of or relating to the sigmoid flexure of the large intestine. ~*n.* **3.** See **sigmoid flexure.** [C17: from Greek *sigmoeidēs* sigma-shaped]
sigmoid flexure *n.* **1.** the S-shaped bend in the final portion of the large intestine. **2.** *Zoology.* an S-shaped curve, as in the necks of certain birds.
sigmoidoscope (sɪg'mɔɪdəˌskəʊp) *n.* an instrument incorporating a light for the direct observation of the colon, rectum, and sigmoid flexure. —**sigmoidoscopic** (sɪgˌmɔɪdə'skɒpɪk) *adj.* —**sigmoidoscopy** (ˌsɪgmɔɪd'ɒskəpɪ) *n.*
sign (saɪn) *n.* **1.** something that indicates or acts as a token of a fact, condition, etc., that is not immediately or outwardly observable. **2.** an action or gesture intended to convey information, a command, etc. **3. a.** a board, placard, etc., displayed in public and inscribed with words or designs intended to inform, warn, etc. **b.** (*as modifier*): *a sign painter.* **4.** an arbitrary or conventional mark or device that stands for a word, phrase, etc. **5.** *Maths, logic.* **a.** any symbol indicating an operation: *a plus sign; an implication sign.* **b.** the positivity or negativity of a number, quantity, or expression: *subtraction from zero changes the sign of an expression.* **6.** an indication or vestige: *the house showed no signs of being occupied.* **7.** a portentous or significant event. **8.**

an indication, such as a scent or spoor, of the presence of an animal. **9.** *Med.* any objective evidence of the presence of a disease or disorder. Compare **symptom** (sense 1). **10.** *Astrology.* See **sign of the zodiac.** ~*vb.* **11.** to write (one's name) as a signature to (a document, etc.) in attestation, confirmation, ratification, etc. **12.** (*intr.*; often foll. by *to*) to make a sign; signal. **13.** to engage or be engaged by written agreement, as a player for a team, etc. **14.** (*tr.*) to outline in gestures a sign over, esp. the sign of the cross. **15.** (*tr.*) to indicate by or as if by a sign; betoken. **16.** (*intr.*) to use sign language. ~See also **sign away, sign in, sign off, sign on, sign out, sign up.** [C13: from Old French *signe,* from Latin *signum* a sign] —'**signable** *adj.* —'**signer** *n.*

signal ('sɪgnᵊl) *n.* **1.** any sign, gesture, token, etc., that serves to communicate information. **2.** anything that acts as an incitement to action: *the rise in prices was a signal for rebellion.* **3. a.** a variable parameter, such as a current or electromagnetic wave, by which information is conveyed through an electronic circuit, communications system, etc. **b.** the information so conveyed. **c.** (*as modifier*): *signal strength; a signal generator.* ~*adj.* **4.** distinguished or conspicuous. **5.** used to give or act as a signal. ~*vb.* **-nals, -nalling, -nalled** *or U.S.* **-nals, -naling, -naled. 6.** to communicate (a message, etc.) to (a person). [C16: from Old French *seignal,* from Medieval Latin *signāle,* from Latin *signum* SIGN] —'**signaller** *or U.S.* '**signaler** *n.*

signal box *n.* **1.** a building containing manually operated signal levers for all the railway lines in its section. **2.** a control point for a large area of a railway system, operated electrically and semiautomatically.

signal generator *n. Electrical engineering.* an apparatus used to generate a signal consisting of a known oscillating voltage, usually between 1 microvolt and 1 volt, over a range of frequencies, to test electronic equipment.

signalize *or* **signalise** ('sɪgnə,laɪz) *vb.* (*tr.*) **1.** to make noteworthy or conspicuous. **2.** to point out carefully.

signally ('sɪgnəlɪ) *adv.* conspicuously or especially.

signalman ('sɪgnᵊlmən) *n., pl.* **-men. 1.** a railway employee in charge of the signals and points within a section. **2.** a man who sends and receives signals, esp. in the navy.

signalment ('sɪgnᵊlmənt) *n. U.S.* a detailed description of a person, for identification or use in police records. [from French *signalement,* from *signaler* to distinguish]

signal-to-noise ratio *n.* the ratio of one parameter, such as power of a wanted signal to the same parameter of the noise at a specified point in an electronic circuit, etc.

signatory ('sɪgnətərɪ, -trɪ) *n., pl.* **-ries. 1.** a person who has signed a document such as a treaty or contract or an organization, state, etc., on whose behalf such a document has been signed. ~*adj.* **2.** having signed a document, treaty, etc. [C17: from Latin *signātōrius* concerning sealing, from *signāre* to mark out, seal, from *signum* a mark]

signature ('sɪgnɪtʃə) *n.* **1.** the name of a person or a mark or sign representing his name, marked by himself or by an authorized deputy. **2.** the act of signing one's name. **3.** a distinctive mark, characteristic, etc., that identifies a person or thing. **4.** *Music.* See **key signature, time signature. 5.** *U.S.* the part of a medical prescription that instructs a patient how frequently and in what amounts he should take a drug or agent. Abbrevs.: **Sig., S. 6.** *Printing.* **a.** a sheet of paper printed with several pages that upon folding will become a section or sections of a book. **b.** such a sheet so folded. **c.** a mark, esp. a letter, printed on the first page of a signature. [C16: from Old French, from Medieval Latin *signātura,* from Latin *signāre* to sign]

signature tune *n. Brit.* a melody used to introduce or identify a television or radio programme, a dance band, a performer, etc. Also called (esp. U.S. and Canadian): **theme song.**

sign away *vb.* (*tr., adv.*) to dispose of or lose by or as if by signing a document: *he signed away all his rights.*

signboard ('saɪn,bɔːd) *n.* a board carrying a sign or notice, esp. one used to advertise a product, event, etc.

signed minor *n. Maths.* another name for **cofactor.**

signed-ranks test *n. Statistics. See* **Wilcoxon test.**

signet ('sɪgnɪt) *n.* **1.** a small seal, esp. one as part of a finger ring. **2.** a seal used to stamp or authenticate documents. **3.** the impression made by such a seal. ~*vb.* **4.** (*tr.*) to stamp or authenticate with a signet. [C14: from Medieval Latin *signētum* a little seal, from Latin *signum* a SIGN]

signet ring *n.* a finger ring bearing a signet.

significance (sɪg'nɪfɪkəns) *n.* **1.** consequence or importance. **2.** something signified, expressed, or intended. **3.** the state or quality of being significant. **4.** *Statistics.* **a.** a measure of the confidence that can be placed in a result, esp. a substantive causal hypothesis, as not being merely a matter of chance. **b.** (*as modifier*): *a significance level.* Compare **confidence level.** See also **hypothesis testing.**

significance test *n. Statistics.* (in hypothesis testing) a test of whether the alternative hypothesis achieves the predetermined significance level in order to be accepted in preference to the null hypothesis.

significant (sɪg'nɪfɪkənt) *adj.* **1.** having or expressing a meaning; indicative. **2.** having a covert or implied meaning; suggestive. **3.** important, notable, or momentous. **4.** *Statistics.* of or relating to a difference between a result derived from a hypothesis and its observed value that is too large to be attributed to chance and that therefore tends to refute the hypothesis. [C16: from Latin *significāre* to SIGNIFY] —**sig'nificantly** *adv.*

significant figures *or esp. U.S.* **significant digits** *pl. n.* **1.** the figures of a number that express a magnitude to a specified degree of accuracy, rounding up or down the final figure: *3.141 59 to four significant figures is 3.142.* **2.** the number of such figures: *3.142 has four significant figures.* Compare **decimal place** (sense 2).

significant other *n. U.S. informal.* a spouse or lover.

signification (,sɪgnɪfɪ'keɪʃən) *n.* **1.** something that is signified; meaning or sense. **2.** the act of signifying.

significative (sɪg'nɪfɪkətɪv) *adj.* **1.** (of a sign, mark, etc.) symbolic. **2.** another word for **significant.** —**sig'nificatively** *adv.* —**sig'nificativeness** *n.*

signify ('sɪgnɪ,faɪ) *vb.* **-fies, -fying, -fied.** (when *tr., may take a clause as object*) **1.** (*tr.*) to indicate, show, or suggest. **2.** (*tr.*) to imply or portend: *the clouds signified the coming storm.* **3.** (*tr.*) to stand as a symbol, sign, etc. (for). **4.** (*intr.*) *Informal.* to be significant or important. [C13: from Old French *signifier,* from Latin *significāre,* from *signum* a sign, mark + *facere* to make] —'**signi,fiable** *adj.* —'**signi,fier** *n.*

sign in *vb.* (*adv.*) **1.** to sign or cause to sign a register, as at a hotel, club, etc. **2.** to make or become a member, as of a club.

sign language *n.* any system of communication by manual signs or gestures, such as one used by the deaf.

sign manual *n. Law.* a person's signature in his own hand, esp. that of a sovereign on an official document.

sign off *vb.* (*adv.*) **1.** (*intr.*) to announce the end of a radio or television programme, esp. at the end of a day. **2.** (*intr.*) *Bridge.* to make a conventional bid indicating to one's partner that one wishes the bidding to stop. **3.** (*tr.*) to withdraw or retire from (an activity). **4.** (*tr.*) (of a doctor) to declare unfit for work, because of illness.

sign of the cross *n. Chiefly R.C. Church.* a gesture in which the right hand is moved from the forehead to the breast and from the left shoulder to the right to describe the form of a cross in order to invoke the grace of Christ.

sign of the zodiac *n.* any of the 12 equal areas, 30° wide, into which the zodiac can be divided, named after the 12 zodiacal constellations. In astrology, it is thought that a person's psychological type and attitudes to life can be correlated with the sign in which the sun lay at the moment of his birth and to a lesser extent with the signs in which other planets lay at this time. Also called: **sign.** See also **planet** (sense 3), **house** (sense 9).

sign on *vb.* (*adv.*) **1.** (*tr.*) to hire or employ. **2.** (*intr.*) to commit oneself to a job, activity, etc. **3.** (*intr.*) *Brit.* to register at a labour exchange.

signor *or* **signior** ('siːnjɔː; *Italian* siɲ'ɲor) *n., pl.* **-gnors** *or* **-gnori** (*Italian* -'ɲori). an Italian man: usually used before a name as a title equivalent to *Mr.*

signora (siːn'jɔːrə; *Italian* siɲ'ɲora) *n., pl.* **-ras** *or* **-re** (*Italian* -re). a married Italian woman: a title of address equivalent to *Mrs* when placed before a name or *madam* when used alone. [Italian, feminine of SIGNORE]

signore (siːn'jɔːriː; *Italian* siɲ'ɲore) *n., pl.* **-ri** (-rɪ; *Italian* -ri). an Italian man: a title of respect equivalent to *sir* when used alone. [Italian, ultimately from Latin *senior* an elder, from *senex* an old man]

signorina (,siːnjɔː'riːnə; *Italian* siɲɲo'rina) *n., pl.* **-nas** *or* **-ne** (*Italian* -ne). an unmarried Italian woman: a title of address equivalent to *Miss* when placed before a name or *madam* or *miss* when used alone. [Italian, diminutive of SIGNORA]

signory ('siːnjərɪ) *n., pl.* **-gnories.** a variant spelling of **seigniory.**

sign out *vb.* (*adv.*) to sign (one's name) to indicate that one is leaving a place: *he signed out for the evening.*

signpost ('saɪn,pəʊst) *n.* **1.** a post bearing a sign that shows the way, as at a roadside. **2.** something that serves as a clue or indication; sign. ~*vb.* (*tr.; usually passive*) **3.** to mark with signposts. **4.** to indicate direction towards: *the camp site is signposted from the road.*

sign test *n.* a statistical test used to analyse the direction of differences of scores between the same or matched pairs of subjects under two experimental conditions.

sign up *vb.* (*adv.*) to enlist or cause to enlist, as for military service.

sika ('siːkə) *n.* a Japanese forest-dwelling deer, *Cervus nippon,* having a brown coat, spotted with white in summer, and a large white patch on the rump. [from Japanese *shika*]

sike (saɪk, sɪk) *n. Scot. and northern English dialect.* a small stream or gulley. [Old English *sīc;* related to Old Norse *sīk* ditch, Middle Low German *sīk* puddle]

Sikh (siːk) *n.* **1.** a member of an Indian religion that separated from Hinduism and was founded in the 16th century, that teaches monotheism and that has the Granth as its chief religious document, rejecting the authority of the Vedas. ~*adj.* **2.** of or relating to the Sikhs or their religious beliefs and customs. [C18: from Hindi, literally: disciple, from Sanskrit *śiksati* he studies] —'**Sikh,ism** *n.*

silage ('saɪlɪdʒ) *n.* any crop harvested while green for fodder and kept succulent by partial fermentation in a silo. Also called: **ensilage.** [C19: alteration (influenced by SILO) of ENSILAGE]

Silastic (sɪˈlæstɪk) *n. Trademark.* a flexible inert silicone rubber, used esp. in prosthetic medicine.
sild (sɪld) *n.* any of various small young herrings, esp. when prepared and canned in Norway. [Norwegian]
sile (saɪl) *vb. (intr.) Northern English dialect.* to pour with rain. [probably from Old Norse; compare Swedish and Norwegian dialect *sila* to pass through a strainer]
silence (ˈsaɪləns) *n.* **1.** the state or quality of being silent. **2.** the absence of sound or noise; stillness. **3.** refusal or failure to speak, communicate, etc., when expected: *his silence on the subject of their promotion was alarming.* **4.** a period of time without noise. **5.** oblivion or obscurity. ~*vb. (tr.)* **6.** to bring to silence. **7.** to put a stop to; extinguish: *to silence all complaint.* [C13: via Old French from Latin *silēntium,* from *silēre* to be quiet. See SILENT]
silenced (ˈsaɪlənst) *adj.* (of a clergyman) forbidden to preach or perform his clerical functions: *a silenced priest.*
silencer (ˈsaɪlənsə) *n.* **1.** any device designed to reduce noise, esp. the tubular device containing baffle plates in the exhaust system of a motor vehicle. U.S. and Canadian name: **muffler. 2.** a tubular device fitted to the muzzle of a firearm to deaden the report. **3.** a person or thing that silences.
silene (saɪˈliːnɪ) *n.* any plant of the large perennial genus *Silene,* with mostly red or pink flowers; many, esp. *S.* or *Agrostemma coeli-rosa,* are grown as garden plants: family *Carophyllaceae.* See also **campion.** [New Latin from Latin *silenus* viscaria]
silent (ˈsaɪlənt) *adj.* **1.** characterized by an absence or near absence of noise or sound: *a silent house.* **2.** tending to speak very little or not at all. **3.** unable to speak. **4.** failing to speak, communicate, etc., when expected: *the witness chose to remain silent.* **5.** not spoken or expressed: *silent assent.* **6.** not active or in operation: *a silent volcano.* **7.** (of a letter) used in the conventional orthography of a word but no longer pronounced in that word: *the "k" in "know" is silent.* **8.** denoting a film that has no accompanying soundtrack, esp. one made before 1927, when such soundtracks were developed. ~*n.* **9.** a silent film. [C16: from Latin *silēns,* from *silēre* to be quiet] —ˈ**silently** *adv.* —ˈ**silentness** *n.*
silent cop *n. Austral. informal.* a small hemispherical traffic marker at an intersection.
silent majority *n.* a presumed moderate majority of the citizens who are too passive to make their views known.
silent partner *n.* another name (esp. U.S. and Canadian) for **sleeping partner.**
silesia (saɪˈliːʃɪə) *n.* a twill-weave fabric of cotton or other fibre, used esp. for pockets, linings, etc. [C17: Latinized form of German *Schlesien* Silesia, a region of central Europe]
silex (ˈsaɪlɛks) *n.* a type of heat-resistant glass made from fused quartz. [C16: from Latin: hard stone, flint]
silhouette (ˌsɪluːˈɛt) *n.* **1.** the outline of a solid figure as cast by its shadow. **2.** an outline drawing filled in with black, often a profile portrait cut out of black paper and mounted on a light ground. ~*vb.* **3.** *(tr.)* to cause to appear in silhouette. [C18: named after Étienne de *Silhouette* (1709–67), French politician, perhaps referring to silhouettes as partial portraits, with a satirical allusion to Silhouette's brief career as controller general (1759)]
silica (ˈsɪlɪkə) *n.* **1.** the dioxide of silicon, occurring naturally as quartz, cristobalite, and tridymite. It is a refractory insoluble material used in the manufacture of glass, ceramics, and abrasives. **2.** short for **silica glass.** [C19: New Latin, from Latin: SILEX]
silica gel *n.* an amorphous form of silica capable of absorbing large quantities of water: used in drying gases and oils, as a carrier for catalysts and an anticaking agent for cosmetics.
silica glass *n.* another name for **quartz glass.**
silicate (ˈsɪlɪkɪt, -ˌkeɪt) *n.* a salt or ester of silicic acid, esp. one of a large number of usually insoluble salts with polymeric negative ions having a structure formed of tetrahedrons of SiO_4 groups linked in rings, chains, sheets, or three dimensional frameworks. Silicates constitute a large proportion of the earth's minerals and are present in cement and glass.
siliceous *or* **silicious** (sɪˈlɪʃəs) *adj.* **1.** of, relating to, or containing silica: *siliceous deposits; a siliceous clay.* **2.** (of plants) growing in or needing soil rich in silica.
silici- *or before a vowel* **silic-** *combining form.* indicating silica or silicon: *silicify.*
silicic (sɪˈlɪsɪk) *adj.* of, concerned with, or containing silicon or an acid obtained from silicon.
silicic acid *n.* a white gelatinous substance obtained by adding an acid to a solution of sodium silicate. It has an ill-defined composition and is best regarded as hydrated silica, $SiO_2.nH_2O$.
silicide (ˈsɪlɪˌsaɪd) *n.* any one of a class of binary compounds formed between silicon and certain metals.
siliciferous (ˌsɪlɪˈsɪfərəs) *adj.* containing or yielding silicon or silica.
silicify (sɪˈlɪsɪˌfaɪ) *vb.* **-fies, -fying, -fied.** to convert or be converted into silica: *silicified wood.* —**siˌlicifiˈcation** *n.*
silicium (sɪˈlɪsɪəm) *n.* a rare name for **silicon.**
silicle (ˈsɪlɪkᵊl), **silicula** (sɪˈlɪkjʊlə), *or* **silicule** (ˈsɪlɪˌkjuːl) *n. Botany.* a short broad siliqua, occurring in such cruciferous plants as honesty and shepherd's-purse. [C18: from Latin *silicula* a small pod; see SILIQUA]
silicon (ˈsɪlɪkən) *n.* **a.** a brittle metalloid element that exists in two allotropic forms; occurs principally in sand, quartz, granite, feldspar, and clay. It is usually a grey crystalline solid but is also found as a brown amorphous powder. It is used in transistors, rectifiers, solar cells, and alloys. Its compounds are widely used in glass manufacture, the building industry, and in the form of silicones. Symbol: Si; atomic no.: 14; atomic wt.: 28.09; valency: 4; relative density: 2.33; melting pt.: 1410°C; boiling pt.: 2355°C. **b.** *(modifier) (sometimes cap.)* denoting an area of a country that contains a density of high-technology industry. [C19: from SILICA, on the model of *boron, carbon*]
silicon carbide *n.* an extremely hard bluish-black insoluble crystalline substance produced by heating carbon with sand at a high temperature and used as an abrasive and refractory material. Silicon carbide whiskers have a high tensile strength and are used in composites; very pure crystals are used as semiconductors. Formula: SiC.
silicon chip *n.* another term for **chip** (sense 8).
silicon-controlled rectifier *n.* a semiconductor rectifier whose forward current between two electrodes, the anode and cathode, is initiated by means of a signal applied to a third electrode, the gate. The current subsequently becomes independent of the signal; the solid-state equivalent of the thyratron. Abbrev.: **SCR.** Also called: **thyristor.**
silicone (ˈsɪlɪˌkəʊn) *n. Chem.* **a.** any of a large class of polymeric synthetic materials that usually have resistance to temperature, water, and chemicals, and good insulating and lubricating properties, making them suitable for wide use as oils, water-repellents, resins, etc. Chemically they have alternate silicon and oxygen atoms with the silicon atoms bound to organic groups. **b.** *(as modifier): silicone rubber.* ~See also **siloxane.**
silicon rectifier *n. Electronics.* a rectifier consisting of a semiconductor diode using crystalline silicon.
silicosis (ˌsɪlɪˈkəʊsɪs) *n. Pathol.* a form of pneumoconiosis caused by breathing in tiny particles of silica, quartz, or slate, and characterized by shortness of breath and fibrotic changes in the tissues of the lungs.
siliculose (sɪˈlɪkjʊˌləʊs, -ˌləʊz) *adj.* (of certain cruciferous plants such as honesty) producing silicles. [C18: from New Latin *siliculōsus,* from *silicula* a SILICLE]
siliqua (sɪˈliːkwə, ˈsɪlɪkwə) *or* **silique** (sɪˈliːk, ˈsɪlɪk) *n., pl.* **-liquae** (-ˈliːkwiː), **-liquas,** *or* **-liques.** the long dry dehiscent fruit of cruciferous plants, such as the wallflower, consisting of two compartments separated by a central septum to which the seeds are attached. [C18: via French from Latin *siliqua* a pod] —**siliquaceous** (ˌsɪlɪˈkweɪʃəs) *adj.* —**siliquose** (ˈsɪlɪˌkwəʊs) *or* **siliquous** (ˈsɪlɪkwəs) *adj.*
silk (sɪlk) *n.* **1.** the very fine soft lustrous fibre produced by a silkworm to make its cocoon. **2. a.** thread or fabric made from this fibre. **b.** *(as modifier): a silk dress.* **3.** a garment made of this. **4.** a very fine fibre produced by a spider to build its web, nest, or cocoon. **5.** the tuft of long fine styles on an ear of maize. **6.** *Brit.* **a.** the gown worn by a Queen's (or King's) Counsel. **b.** *Informal.* a Queen's (or King's) Counsel. **c. take silk.** to become a Queen's (or King's) Counsel. ~*vb.* **7.** *(intr.) U.S. and Canadian.* (of maize) to develop long hairlike styles. [Old English *sioluc;* compare Old Norse *silki,* Greek *sērikon,* Korean *sir;* all ultimately from Chinese *ssŭ* silk] —ˈ**silkˌlike** *adj.*
silkaline *or* **silkalene** (ˌsɪlkəˈliːn) *n.* a fine smooth cotton fabric used for linings, etc. [C20: from SILK + *-aline,* from *-oline* as in CRINOLINE]
silk cotton *n.* another name for **kapok.**
silk-cotton tree *n.* any of several tropical bombacaceous trees of the genus *Ceiba,* esp. *Ceiba pentandra,* having seeds covered with silky hairs from which kapok is obtained. Also called: **kapok tree.**
silken (ˈsɪlkən) *adj.* **1.** made of silk. **2.** resembling silk in smoothness or gloss. **3.** dressed in silk. **4.** soft and delicate. **5.** *Rare.* luxurious or elegant.
silk hat *n.* a man's top hat covered with silk.
silkie (ˈsɪlkɪ) *or* **selkie** *n.* a Scot. word for a **seal** (the animal). [from earlier Scot. *selch,* Old English *seolh*]
silk-screen printing *n.* another name for **screen process.**
silkweed (ˈsɪlkˌwiːd) *n.* another name for **milkweed** (sense 1). [C19: so called because the pods contain a silklike down]
silkworm (ˈsɪlkˌwɜːm) *n.* **1.** the larva of the Chinese moth *Bombyx mori,* that feeds on the leaves of the mulberry tree: widely cultivated as a source of silk. **2.** any of various similar or related larvae. **3. silkworm moth.** the moth of any of these larvae.
silky (ˈsɪlkɪ) *adj.* **silkier, silkiest. 1.** resembling silk in texture; glossy. **2.** made of silk. **3.** (of a voice, manner, etc.) suave; smooth. **4.** *Botany.* covered with long fine soft hairs: *silky leaves.* —ˈ**silkily** *adv.* —ˈ**silkiness** *n.*
silky oak *n.* any of several trees of the Australian genus *Grevillea,* esp. *G. robusta,* having divided leaves and showy clusters of orange, red, or white flowers: cultivated in the tropics as shade trees: family *Proteaceae.*
sill (sɪl) *n.* **1.** a shelf at the bottom of a window inside a room. **2.** a horizontal piece along the outside lower member of a window, that throws water clear of the wall below. **3.** the lower horizontal member of a window or door frame. **4.** a continuous horizontal member placed on top of a foundation wall in order to carry

a timber framework. **5.** a flat usually horizontal mass of igneous rock, situated between two layers of older sedimentary rock, that was formed by an intrusion of magma. [Old English *syll;* related to Old Norse *svill* sill, Icelandic *svoli* tree trunk, Old High German *swella* sill, Latin *solum* ground]

sillabub ('sɪləˌbʌb) *n.* a variant spelling of **syllabub.**

siller ('sɪlər) *Scot.* ~*n.* **1.** silver. **2.** money. ~*adj.* **3.** silver. [a Scot. variant of SILVER]

sillimanite ('sɪlɪməˌnaɪt) *n.* a white, brown, or green fibrous mineral that consists of aluminium silicate in orthorhombic crystalline form and occurs in metamorphic rocks. Formula: Al_2SiO_5. [C19: named after Benjamin *Silliman* (1779–1864), U.S. chemist]

silly ('sɪlɪ) *adj.* **-lier, -liest. 1.** lacking in good sense; absurd. **2.** frivolous, trivial, or superficial. **3.** feeble-minded. **4.** dazed, as from a blow. **5.** *Obsolete.* homely or humble. ~*n.* **6.** (*modifier*) *Cricket.* (of a fielding position) near the batsman's wicket: *silly mid-on.* **7.** (*pl.* **-lies**) Also called: **silly-billy.** *Informal.* a foolish person. [C15 (in the sense: pitiable, hence the later senses: foolish): from Old English *sǣlig* (unattested) happy, from *sǣl* happiness; related to Gothic *sēls* good] —'**silliness** *n.*

silly season *n. Brit.* a period, usually during the hot summer months, when journalists fill space reporting on frivolous events and activities.

silo ('saɪləʊ) *n., pl.* **-los. 1.** a pit, trench, horizontal container, or tower, often cylindrical in shape, in which silage is made and stored. **2.** a strengthened underground position in which missile systems are sited for protection against attack. [C19: from Spanish, perhaps from Celtic]

siloxane (sɪ'lɒkseɪn) *n.* any of a class of compounds containing alternate silicon and oxygen atoms with the silicon atoms bound to hydrogen atoms or organic groups. Many are highly complex polymers. See also **silicone.** [C20: from SIL(ICON) + OX(YGEN) + (METH)ANE]

silt (sɪlt) *n.* **1.** a fine deposit of mud, clay, etc., esp. one in a river or lake. ~*vb.* **2.** (usually foll. by *up*) to fill or become filled with silt; choke. [C15: of Scandinavian origin; compare Norwegian, Danish *sylt* salt marsh; related to Old High German *sulza* salt marsh; see SALT] —**sil'tation** *n.* —'**silty** *adj.*

siltstone ('sɪltˌstəʊn) *n.* a variety of fine sandstone formed from consolidated silt.

Silurian (saɪ'lʊərɪən) *adj.* **1.** of, denoting, or formed in the third period of the Palaeozoic era, between the Ordovician and Devonian periods, which lasted for 40 million years, during which fishes first appeared. **2.** of or relating to the Silures, a powerful and warlike tribe of ancient Britons, living chiefly in SE Wales. ~*n.* **3. the.** the Silurian period or rock system.

silurid (saɪ'lʊərɪd) *n.* **1.** any freshwater teleost fish of the Eurasian family *Siluridae,* including catfish, such as *Silurus glanis* (**European catfish**), that have an elongated body, naked skin, and a long anal fin. ~*adj.* **2.** of, relating to, or belonging to the family *Siluridae.* [C19: from Latin *silūrus,* from Greek *silouros* a river fish]

silva ('sɪlvə) *n.* a variant spelling of **sylva.**

silvan ('sɪlvən) *adj.* a variant spelling of **sylvan.**

silver ('sɪlvə) *n.* **1. a.** a very ductile malleable brilliant greyish-white element having the highest electrical and thermal conductivity of any metal. It occurs free and in argentite and other ores: used in jewellery, tableware, coinage, electrical contacts, and in electroplating. Its compounds are used in photography. Symbol: Ag; atomic no.: 47; atomic wt.: 107.870; valency: 1 or 2; relative density: 10.5; melting pt.: 961.93°C; boiling pt.: 2212°C. **b.** (*as modifier*): *a silver coin.* Related adj.: **argent. 2.** coin made of this metal. **3.** cutlery, whether made of silver or not. **4.** any household articles made of silver. **5.** *Photog.* any of a number of silver compounds used either as photosensitive substances in emulsions or as sensitizers. **6. a.** a brilliant or light greyish-white colour. **b.** (*as adj.*): *silver hair.* **7.** short for **silver medal.** ~*adj.* **8.** well-articulated: *silver speech.* **9.** (*prenominal*) denoting the 25th in a series, esp. an annual series: *a silver wedding anniversary.* ~*vb.* **10.** (*tr.*) to coat with silver or a silvery substance: *to silver a spoon.* **11.** to become or cause to become silvery in colour. [Old English *siolfor;* related to Old Norse *silfr,* Gothic *silubr,* Old High German *silabar,* Old Slavonic *sirebro*] —'**silverer** *n.* —'**silvering** *n.*

silver age *n.* **1.** (in Greek and Roman mythology) the second of the world's major epochs, inferior to the preceding golden age and characterized by opulence and irreligion. **2.** the postclassical period of Latin literature, occupying the early part of the Roman imperial era, characterized by an overindulgence in elegance for its own sake and empty scholarly rhetoric.

silver beet *n.* a variety of beet, *Beta vulgaris cicla,* having large firm green leaves: staple cooked green vegetable in Australia and New Zealand.

silver bell *n.* any of various deciduous trees of the styracaceous genus *Halesia,* esp. *H. carolina,* of North America and China, having white bell-shaped flowers. Also called: **snowdrop tree.**

silver belly *n. N.Z.* a freshwater eel.

silver birch *n.* a betulaceous tree, *Betula pendula,* of N temperate regions of the Old World, having silvery-white peeling bark. See also **birch** (sense 1).

silver bromide *n.* a yellowish insoluble powder that darkens when exposed to light: used in making photographic emulsions. Formula: AgBr.

silver certificate *n.* (formerly) a banknote issued by the U.S. Treasury to the public and redeemable in silver.

silver chloride *n.* a white insoluble powder that darkens on exposure to light because of the production of metallic silver: used in making photographic emulsions and papers. Formula: AgCl.

silver disc *n.* (in Britain) an LP record certified to have sold 60 000 copies or a single certified to have sold 200 000 copies.

silver-eye *n. Austral. and N.Z.* another name for **white-eye.**

silver fern *n. N.Z.* **1.** another name for **ponga. 2.** a formalized spray of fern leaf, silver on a black background: the symbol of New Zealand sporting teams, esp. the All Blacks.

silver fir *n.* any of various fir trees the leaves of which have a silvery undersurface, esp. *Abies alba,* an important timber tree of central and S Europe.

silverfish ('sɪlvəˌfɪʃ) *n., pl.* **-fish** *or* **-fishes. 1.** a silver variety of the goldfish *Carassius auratus.* **2.** any of various other silvery fishes, such as the moonfish *Monodactylus argenteus.* **3.** any of various small primitive wingless insects of the genus *Lepisma,* esp. *L. saccharina,* that have long antennae and tail appendages and occur in buildings, feeding on food scraps, bookbindings, etc.: order *Thysanura* (bristletails).

silver fox *n.* **1.** an American red fox in a colour phase in which the fur is black with long silver-tipped hairs. **2.** the valuable fur or pelt of this animal.

silver frost *n.* another name for **glaze ice.**

silver-gilt *n.* silver covered with a thin film of gold.

silverhorn ('sɪlvəˌhɔːn) *n.* any of various usually darkish caddis flies of the family *Leptoceridae,* characterized by very long pale antennae. The larvae are a favourite food of trout.

silver iodide *n.* a yellow insoluble powder that darkens on exposure to light: used in photography and artificial rainmaking. Formula: AgI.

silver lining *n.* a comforting or hopeful aspect of an otherwise desperate or unhappy situation.

silver maple *n.* a North American maple tree, *Acer saccharinum,* having five-lobed leaves that are green above and silvery-white beneath.

silver medal *n.* a medal of silver awarded to a competitor who comes second in a contest or race. Compare **gold medal, bronze medal.**

silvern ('sɪlvən) *adj. Archaic or poetic.* silver.

silver nitrate *n.* a white crystalline soluble poisonous substance used in making photographic emulsions, other silver salts, and as a medical antiseptic and astringent. Formula: $AgNO_3$. See also **lunar caustic.**

silver plate *n.* **1.** a thin layer of silver deposited on a base metal. **2.** articles, esp. tableware, made of silver plate. ~*vb.* **silver-plate. 3.** (*tr.*) to coat (a metal, object, etc.) with silver, as by electroplating.

silverpoint ('sɪlvəˌpɔɪnt) *n.* a drawing technique popular esp. in the 15th and 16th centuries, using an instrument with a silver wire tip on specially prepared paper.

silver screen *n.* **the.** *Informal.* **1.** films collectively or the film industry. **2.** the screen onto which films are projected.

silver service *n.* (in restaurants) a style of serving food using a spoon and fork in one hand like a pair of tongs.

silverside ('sɪlvəˌsaɪd) *n.* **1.** *Brit. and N.Z.* a coarse cut of beef below the aitchbone and above the leg. **2.** Also called: **silversides.** any small marine or freshwater teleost fish of the family *Atherinidae,* related to the grey mullets: includes the jacksmelt.

silversmith ('sɪlvəˌsmɪθ) *n.* a craftsman who makes or repairs articles of silver. —'**silverˌsmithing** *n.*

silver standard *n.* a monetary system in which the legal unit of currency is defined with reference to silver of a specified fineness and weight and sometimes (esp. formerly) freely redeemable for it.

silvertail ('sɪlvəˌteɪl) *n. Austral. informal.* a rich and influential person.

silver thaw *n. Canadian.* **1.** a freezing rainstorm. **2.** another name for **glitter** (sense 7).

silver-tongued *adj.* persuasive; eloquent.

silverware ('sɪlvəˌwɛə) *n.* articles, esp. tableware, made of or plated with silver.

silverweed ('sɪlvəˌwiːd) *n.* **1.** a rosaceous perennial creeping plant, *Potentilla anserina,* with silvery pinnate leaves and yellow flowers. **2.** any of various convolvulaceous twining shrubs of the genus *Argyreia,* of SE Asia and Australia, having silvery leaves and showy purple flowers.

silvery ('sɪlvərɪ) *adj.* **1.** of or having the appearance of silver: *the silvery moon.* **2.** containing or covered with silver. **3.** having a clear ringing sound. —'**silveriness** *n.*

silver-Y moth *n.* a brownish noctuid moth, *Plusia gamma,* having a light Y-shaped marking on each forewing; it migrates in large flocks. Often shortened to **silver-Y.**

silviculture ('sɪlvɪˌkʌltʃə) *n.* the branch of forestry that is concerned with the cultivation of trees. [C20: *silvi-,* from Latin *silva* woodland + CULTURE] —ˌ**silvi'cultural** *adj.* —ˌ**silvi'culturist** *n.*

s'il vous plaît *French.* (sil vu plɛ) if you please; please.

sima ('saɪmə) *n.* **1.** the silicon-rich and magnesium-rich rocks of the earth's oceanic crust, the most abundant individual rock being basalt. **2.** the earth's continental lower crust, probably comprised of gabbro rather than basalt. [C20: from SI(LICA) + MA(GNESIA)] —**simatic** (saɪˈmætɪk) *adj.*

simar (sɪˈmɑː) *n.* a variant spelling of **cymar.**

simarouba *or* **simaruba** (ˌsɪməˈruːbə) *n.* **1.** any tropical American tree of the genus *Simarouba,* esp. *S. amara,* having divided leaves and fleshy fruits: family *Simaroubaceae.* **2.** the medicinal bark of any of these trees. [C18: from New Latin, from Carib *simaruba*]

simaroubaceous *or* **simarubaceous** (ˌsɪməruːˈbeɪʃəs) *adj.* of, relating to, or belonging to the *Simaroubaceae,* a mainly tropical family of trees and shrubs that includes ailanthus, seringa, and quassia.

simba (ˈsɪmbə) *n.* an E African word for **lion.** [Swahili]

Simchath Torah, Simhath Torah, *or* **Simchas Torah** (simˈxɑt tɔrˈɑː, ˈsimxɑs ˈtaʊrɔ) *n.* a Jewish festival celebrated immediately after Sukkoth on Tishri 23 (in Israel, Tishri 22) to mark the completion of the annual cycle of Torah readings and its immediate recommencement. [from Hebrew *śimḥath tōrāh,* literally: celebration of the Torah]

simian (ˈsɪmɪən) *adj.* **1.** Also (rarely): **simious** (ˈsɪmɪəs). of, relating to, or resembling a monkey or ape. ~*n.* **2.** a monkey or ape. [C17: from Latin *sīmia* an ape, probably from *sīmus* flat-nosed, from Greek *sīmos*]

similar (ˈsɪmɪlə) *adj.* **1.** showing resemblance in qualities, characteristics, or appearance; alike but not identical. **2.** *Geometry.* (of two or more figures) having corresponding angles equal and all corresponding sides in the same ratio. Compare **congruent** (sense 2). **3.** *Maths.* (of two classes) equinumerous. [C17: from Old French *similaire,* from Latin *similis*] —**similarity** (ˌsɪmɪˈlærɪtɪ) *n.* —ˈ**similarly** *adv.*

▷**Usage.** Careful writers prefer not to use *similarly* where *correspondingly* would be appropriate: *if our competitors raise their prices, we must correspondingly* (not *similarly*) *make increases in ours.*

simile (ˈsɪmɪlɪ) *n.* a figure of speech that expresses the resemblance of one thing to another of a different category, usually introduced by *as* or *like.* Compare **metaphor.** [C14: from Latin *simile* something similar, from *similis* like]

similitude (sɪˈmɪlɪˌtjuːd) *n.* **1.** likeness; similarity. **2.** a thing or sometimes a person that is like or the counterpart of another. **3.** *Archaic.* a simile, allegory, or parable. [C14: from Latin *similitūdō,* from *similis* like]

simitar (ˈsɪmɪtə) *n.* a rare spelling of **scimitar.**

simmer (ˈsɪmə) *vb.* **1.** to cook (food) gently at or just below the boiling point. **2.** (*intr.*) to be about to break out in rage or excitement. ~*n.* **3.** the act, sound, or state of simmering. [C17: perhaps of imitative origin; compare German *summen* to hum]

simmer dim (ˈsɪmər, -mə) *n. Scot.* the night-long twilight found in the Northern Isles around midsummer.

simmer down *vb.* (*adv.*) **1.** (*intr.*) *Informal.* to grow calmer or quieter, as after intense rage or excitement. **2.** (*tr.*) to reduce the volume of (a liquid) by boiling slowly.

simnel cake (ˈsɪmnᵊl) *n. Brit.* a fruit cake, often coloured with saffron and covered with a layer of marzipan, traditionally eaten in Lent or at Easter. [C13 *simenel,* from Old French, from Latin *simila* fine flour, probably of Semitic origin; related to Greek *semidalis* fine flour]

simoniac (sɪˈməʊnɪˌæk) *n.* a person who is guilty of practising simony. —**simoniacal** (ˌsaɪməˈnaɪəkᵊl) *adj.* —ˌ**simoˈniacally** *adv.*

simon-pure *adj.* real; genuine; authentic. [C19: from the phrase *the real Simon Pure,* name of a character in the play *A Bold Stroke for a Wife* (1717) by Susannah Centlivre (1669–1723) who is impersonated by another character in some scenes]

simony (ˈsaɪmənɪ) *n. Christianity.* the practice, now usually regarded as a sin, of buying or selling spiritual or Church benefits such as pardons, relics, etc., or preferments. [C13: from Old French *simonie,* from Late Latin *sīmōnia,* from the name of *Simon* Magus, a Biblical sorcerer who tried to buy miraculous powers from the apostles] —ˈ**simonist** *n.*

simoom (sɪˈmuːm) *or* **simoon** (sɪˈmuːn) *n.* a strong suffocating sand-laden wind of the deserts of Arabia and North Africa. Also called: **samiel.** [from Arabic *samūm* poisonous, from *sam* poison, from Aramaic *sammā* poison]

simp (sɪmp) *n. U.S. slang.* short for **simpleton.**

simpatico (sɪmˈpɑːtɪˌkəʊ, -ˈpæt-) *adj. Informal.* **1.** pleasant or congenial. **2.** of similar mind or temperament; compatible. [Italian: from *simpatia* SYMPATHY]

simper (ˈsɪmpə) *vb.* **1.** (*intr.*) to smile coyly, affectedly, or in a silly self-conscious way. **2.** (*tr.*) to utter (something) in a simpering manner. ~*n.* **3.** a simpering smile; smirk. [C16: probably from Dutch *simper* affected] —ˈ**simperer** *n.* —ˈ**simpering** *adj., n.* —ˈ**simperingly** *adv.*

simple (ˈsɪmpᵊl) *adj.* **1.** not involved or complicated; easy to understand or do: *a simple problem.* **2.** plain; unadorned: *a simple dress.* **3.** consisting of one element or part only; not combined or complex: *a simple mechanism.* **4.** unaffected or unpretentious: *although he became famous, he remained a simple and well-liked man.* **5.** not guileful; sincere; frank: *her simple explanation was readily accepted.* **6.** of humble condition or rank: *the peasant was of simple birth.* **7.** weak in intelligence; feeble-minded. **8.** (*prenominal*) without additions or modifications; mere: *the witness told the simple truth.* **9.** (*prenominal*) ordinary or straightforward: *a simple case of mumps.* **10.** *Chem.* (of a substance or material) consisting of only one chemical compound rather than a mixture of compounds. **11.** *Maths.* **a.** (of a fraction) containing only integers. **b.** (of an equation) containing variables to the first power only; linear. **c.** (of a root of an equation) occurring only once; not multiple. **12.** *Biology.* not divided into parts: *a simple leaf; a simple eye.* **13.** *Music.* relating to or denoting a time where the number of beats per bar may be two, three, or four. ~*n. Archaic.* **14.** a simpleton; fool. **15.** a plant, esp. a herbaceous plant, having medicinal properties. [C13: via Old French from Latin *simplex* plain] —ˈ**simpleness** *n.*

simple fraction *n.* a fraction in which the numerator and denominator are both integers expressed as a ratio rather than a decimal. Also called: **common fraction, vulgar fraction.**

simple fracture *n.* a fracture in which the broken bone does not pierce the skin. Also called: **closed fracture.** Compare **compound fracture.**

simple fruit *n.* a fruit, such as a grape or cherry, that is formed from only one ovary.

simple harmonic motion *n.* a form of periodic motion of a particle, etc., in which the acceleration is always directed towards some equilibrium point and is proportional to the displacement from this point. Abbrev.: **SHM.**

simple-hearted *adj.* free from deceit; open; frank; sincere.

simple interest *n.* interest calculated or paid on the principal alone. Compare **compound interest.**

simple machine *n.* a simple device for altering the magnitude or direction of a force. The six basic types are the lever, wheel and axle, pulley, screw, wedge, and inclined plane.

simple microscope *n.* a microscope having a single lens; magnifying glass. Compare **compound microscope.**

simple-minded *adj.* **1.** stupid; foolish; feeble-minded. **2.** **mentally defective.** **3.** unsophisticated; artless. —ˌ**simpleˈmindedly** *adv.* —ˌ**simple-ˈmindedness** *n.*

simple sentence *n.* a sentence consisting of a single main clause. Compare **compound sentence, complex sentence.**

Simple Simon *n.* a foolish man or boy; simpleton. [C20: after the name of a character in a nursery rhyme]

simple tense *n. Grammar.* a tense of verbs, in English and other languages, not involving the use of an auxiliary verb in addition to the main verb, as for example the past *He drowned* as opposed to the future *He will drown.*

simpleton (ˈsɪmpᵊltən) *n.* a foolish or ignorant person.

simplex (ˈsɪmplɛks) *adj.* **1.** permitting the transmission of signals in either direction in a radio circuit, etc., but not simultaneously. Compare **duplex** (sense 4), **diplex.** ~*n.* **2.** *Linguistics.* a simple not a compound word. **3.** *Geom.* the most elementary geometric figure in Euclidean space of a given dimension; a line in one-dimensional space or a triangle in two-dimensional space. [C16: from Latin: simple, literally: one-fold, from *sim-* one + *plex,* from *plicāre* to fold; compare DUPLEX]

simplicidentate (ˌsɪmplɪsɪˈdɛnteɪt) *adj.* **1.** of, relating to, or belonging to the *Simplicidentata,* a former suborder including all the mammals now classified as rodents: used when lagomorphs were included in the order *Rodentia.* ~*n.* **2.** any animal of this type.

simplicity (sɪmˈplɪsɪtɪ) *n.* the quality or condition of being simple.

simplify (ˈsɪmplɪˌfaɪ) *vb.* **-fies, -fying, -fied.** (*tr.*) **1.** to make less complicated, clearer, or easier. **2.** *Maths.* to reduce (an equation, fraction, etc.) to its simplest form by cancellation of common factors, regrouping of terms in the same variable, etc. [C17: via French from Medieval Latin *simplificāre,* from Latin *simplus* simple + *facere* to make] —ˌ**simplifiˈcation** *n.* —ˈ**simplificative** *adj.* —ˈ**simpliˌfier** *n.*

simplistic (sɪmˈplɪstɪk) *adj.* **1.** characterized by extreme simplicity; naive. **2.** oversimplifying complex problems; making unrealistically simple judgments or analyses. —ˈ**simplism** *n.* —**simˈplistically** *adv.*

simply (ˈsɪmplɪ) *adv.* **1.** in a simple manner. **2.** merely; only. **3.** absolutely; altogether; really: *a simply wonderful holiday.* ~*sentence modifier.* **4.** frankly; candidly.

simsim (ˈsɪmsɪm) *n.* an E African word for **sesame.** [Swahili, from Arabic]

simul (ˈsɪməl) *n.* a shortened form of **simultaneous** (sense 2).

simulacrum (ˌsɪmjʊˈleɪkrəm) *n., pl.* **-cra** (-krə). *Archaic.* **1.** any image or representation of something. **2.** a slight, unreal, or vague semblance of something; superficial likeness. [C16: from Latin: likeness, from *simulāre* to imitate, from *similis* like]

simulant (ˈsɪmjʊlənt) *adj.* **1.** simulating. **2.** (esp. of plant parts) resembling another part in structure or function.

simular (ˈsɪmjʊlə) *Archaic.* ~*n.* **1.** a person or thing that simulates or imitates; sham. ~*adj.* **2.** fake; simulated.

simulate *vb.* (ˈsɪmjʊˌleɪt). (*tr.*) **1.** to make a pretence of; feign: *to simulate anxiety.* **2.** to reproduce the conditions of (a situation, etc.), as in carrying out an experiment: *to simulate weightlessness.* **3.** to assume or have the appearance of; imitate. ~*adj.* (ˈsɪmjʊlɪt, -ˌleɪt). **4.** *Archaic.* assumed or simulated. [C17: from Latin *simulāre* to copy, from *similis* like] —ˈ**simulative** *adj.* —ˈ**simulatively** *adv.*

simulated (ˈsɪmjʊˌleɪtɪd) *adj.* **1.** (of fur, leather, pearls, etc.) being an imitation of the genuine article, usually made from cheaper material. 2. (of actions, qualities, emotions, etc.) imitated; feigned.

simulation (ˌsɪmjʊˈleɪʃən) *n.* 1. the act or an instance of simulating. 2. the assumption of a false appearance or form. 3. a representation of a problem, situation, etc., in mathematical terms, esp. using a computer. 4. *Maths, statistics, computing.* the construction of a mathematical model for some process, situation, etc., in order to estimate its characteristics or solve problems about it probabilistically in terms of the model. 5. *Psychiatry.* the conscious process of feigning illness in order to gain some particular end; malingering.

simulator (ˈsɪmjʊˌleɪtə) *n.* 1. any device or system that simulates specific conditions or the characteristics of a real process for the purposes of research or operator training: *space simulator.* 2. a person who simulates.

simulcast (ˈsɪməlˌkɑːst) *vb.* 1. (*tr.*) to broadcast (a programme, etc.) simultaneously on radio and television. ~*n.* 2. a programme, etc., so broadcast. [C20: from SIMUL(TANEOUS) + (BROAD)CAST]

simultaneous (ˌsɪməlˈteɪnɪəs; *U.S.* ˌsaɪməlˈteɪnɪəs) *adj.* 1. occurring, existing, or operating at the same time; concurrent. ~*n.* 2. *Chess.* a display in which one player plays a number of opponents at once, walking from board to board. Sometimes shortened to **simul.** [C17: formed on the model of INSTANTANEOUS from Latin *simul* at the same time, together] —ˌ**simulˈtaneously** *adv.* —ˌ**simulˈtaneousness** *or* **simultaneity** (ˌsɪməltəˈniːɪtɪ; *U.S.* ˌsaɪməltəˈniːɪtɪ) *n.*

▷**Usage.** See at **unique.**

simultaneous equations *pl. n.* a set of equations that are all satisfied by the same values of the variables, the number of variables being equal to the number of equations.

sin[1] (sɪn) *n.* 1. *Theol.* **a.** transgression of God's known will or any principle or law regarded as embodying this. **b.** the condition of estrangement from God arising from such transgression. See also **actual sin, mortal sin, original sin, venial sin.** 2. any serious offence, as against a religious or moral principle. 3. any offence against a principle or standard. 4. **live in sin.** *Informal.* (of an unmarried couple) to live together. ~*vb.* (*intr.*) **sins, sinning, sinned.** 5. *Theol.* to commit a sin. 6. (usually foll. by *against*) to commit an offence (against a person, principle, etc.). [Old English *synn;* related to Old Norse *synth,* Old High German *suntea* sin, Latin *sons* guilty] —ˈ**sinner** *n.*

sin[2] (sɪn) *prep., conj., adv.* a Scot. dialect word for **since.**

sin[3] (siːn) *n.* the 21st letter in the Hebrew alphabet (ש), transliterated as *S.*

sin[4] (saɪn) *Maths. abbrev. for* sine.

sinanthropus (sɪnˈænθrəpəs) *n.* a primitive apelike man of the genus *Sinanthropus,* now considered a subspecies of *Homo erectus.* See also **Java man, Peking man.** [C20: from New Latin, from Late Latin *Sīnae* the Chinese + *-anthropus,* from Greek *anthrōpos* man]

sinapism (ˈsɪnəˌpɪzəm) *n.* a technical name for **mustard plaster.** [C17: from Late Latin *sināpismus,* from Greek *sinapismos* application of mustard plaster, from *sinapi* mustard, of Egyptian origin]

Sinarquist (ˈsɪnɑːkɪst, -kwɪst) *n.* (in Mexico) a member of a fascist movement in the 1930s and 1940s having links with the Nazis and the Falangists: hostile towards the U.S., Communism, Jews, organized labour, etc. [C20: Mexican Spanish *sinarquista,* from Spanish *sin* without + *anarquista* anarchist] —ˈ**Sinarquism** *n.*

sin bin *n.* 1. *Slang.* (in ice hockey, etc.) an area off the field of play where a player who has committed a foul can be sent to sit for a specified period. 2. *Brit. informal.* a special unit on a separate site from a school that disruptive schoolchildren attend until they can be reintegrated into their normal classes.

since (sɪns) *prep.* 1. during or throughout the period of time after: *since May it has only rained once.* ~*conj.* (*subordinating*) 2. (sometimes preceded by *ever*) continuously from or starting from the time when: *since we last met, important things have happened.* 3. seeing that; because: *since you have no money, you can't come.* ~*adv.* 4. since that time: *he left yesterday and I haven't seen him since.* [Old English *sīththan,* literally: after that; related to Old High German *sīd* since, Latin *sērus* late]

▷**Usage.** See at **ago.**

sincere (sɪnˈsɪə) *adj.* 1. not hypocritical or deceitful; open; genuine: *a sincere person; sincere regret.* 2. *Archaic.* pure; unadulterated; unmixed. 3. *Obsolete.* sound; whole. [C16: from Latin *sincērus*] —**sinˈcerely** *adv.* —**sincerity** (sɪnˈsɛrɪtɪ) *or* **sinˈcereness** *n.*

sinciput (ˈsɪnsɪˌpʌt) *n., pl.* **sinciputs** *or* **sincipita** (sɪnˈsɪpɪtə). *Anatomy.* the forward upper part of the skull. [C16: from Latin: half a head, from SEMI- + *caput* head] —**sinˈcipital** *adj.*

Sindhi (ˈsɪndɪ) *n.* 1. (*pl.* **-dhi** *or* **-dhis**) a former inhabitant of Sind (now in SE Pakistan) when it was a province of British India. The Muslim majority now lives in Pakistan while the Hindu minority has mostly moved to India. 2. the language of this people, belonging to the Indic branch of the Indo-European family.

sine[1] (saɪn) *n.* (of an angle) **a.** a trigonometric function that in a right-angled triangle is the ratio of the length of the opposite side to that of the hypotenuse. **b.** a function that in a circle centred at the origin of a Cartesian coordinate system is the ratio of the ordinate of a point on the circumference to the radius of the circle. Abbrev.: **sin.** [C16: from Latin *sinus* a bend; in New Latin, *sinus* was mistaken as a translation of Arabic *jiba* sine (from Sanskrit *jīva,* literally: bowstring) because of confusion with Arabic *jaib* curve]

sine[2] (ˈsaɪnɪ) *prep.* (esp. in Latin phrases or legal terms) lacking; without.

sinecure (ˈsaɪnɪˌkjʊə) *n.* 1. a paid office or post involving minimal duties. 2. a Church benefice to which no spiritual or pastoral charge is attached. [C17: from Medieval Latin phrase (*beneficium*) *sine cūrā* (benefice) without cure (of souls), from Latin *sine* without + *cūra* cure, care] —ˈ**sineˌcurism** *n.* —ˈ**sineˌcurist** *n.*

sine curve *n.* a curve of the equation $y = \sin x$. Also called: **sinusoid.**

sine die *Latin.* (ˈsaɪnɪ ˈdaɪɪ) *adv., adj.* without a day fixed: *an adjournment sine die.* [literally: without a day]

sine prole *Latin.* (ˈsaɪnɪ ˈprəʊlɪ) *adj., adv. Law.* without issue (esp. in the phrase ***demisit sine prole*** (died without issue)).

sine qua non *Latin.* (ˈsaɪnɪ kweɪ ˈnɒn) *n.* an essential condition or requirement. [literally: without which not]

sinew (ˈsɪnjuː) *n.* 1. *Anatomy.* another name for **tendon.** 2. (*often pl.*) **a.** a source of strength or power. **b.** a literary word for **muscle.** [Old English *sionu;* related to Old Norse *sin,* Old Saxon *sinewa,* Old High German *senawa* sinew, Lettish *pasainis* string] —ˈ**sinewless** *adj.*

sine wave *n.* any oscillation, such as a sound wave or alternating current, whose waveform is that of a sine curve.

sinewy (ˈsɪnjʊɪ) *adj.* 1. consisting of or resembling a tendon or tendons. 2. muscular; brawny. 3. (esp. of language, style, etc.) vigorous; forceful. 4. (of meat, etc.) tough; stringy. —ˈ**sinewiness** *n.*

sinfonia (ˌsɪnfəˈnɪə) *n., pl.* **-nie** (-ˈniːeɪ). 1. another word for **symphony** (senses 2, 3). 2. (*cap. when part of a name*) a symphony orchestra. [Italian]

sinfonietta (ˌsɪnfənˈjɛtə, -fəʊn-) *n.* 1. a short or light symphony. 2. (*cap. when part of name*) a small symphony orchestra. [Italian: a little symphony, from SINFONIA]

sinful (ˈsɪnfʊl) *adj.* 1. having committed or tending to commit sin: *a sinful person.* 2. characterized by or being a sin: *a sinful act.* —ˈ**sinfully** *adv.* —ˈ**sinfulness** *n.*

sing (sɪŋ) *vb.* **sings, singing, sang, sung.** 1. to produce or articulate (sounds, words, a song, etc.) with definite and usually specific musical intonation. 2. (when *intr.,* often foll. by *to*) to perform (a song) to the accompaniment (of): *to sing to a guitar.* 3. (*intr.;* foll. by *of*) to tell a story or tale in song (about): *I sing of a maiden.* 4. (*intr.;* foll. by *to*) to address a song (to) or perform a song (for). 5. (*intr.*) to perform songs for a living, as a professional singer. 6. (*intr.*) (esp. of certain birds and insects) to utter calls or sounds reminiscent of music. 7. (when *intr.,* usually foll. by *of*) to tell (something) or give praise (to someone), esp. in verse: *the poet who sings of the Trojan dead.* 8. (*intr.*) to make a whining, ringing, or whistling sound: *the kettle is singing; the arrow sang past his ear.* 9. (*intr.*) (of the ears) to experience a continuous ringing or humming sound. 10. (*tr.*) (esp. in church services) to chant or intone (a prayer, psalm, etc.). 11. (*tr.*) to bring to a given state by singing: *to sing a child to sleep.* 12. (*intr.*) *Slang, chiefly U.S.* to confess or act as an informer. 13. (*intr.*) *Austral.* (in Aboriginal witchcraft) to bring about a person's death by incantation. The same power can sometimes be used beneficently. ~*n.* 14. *Informal.* an act or performance of singing. 15. a ringing or whizzing sound, as of bullets. ~See also **sing along, sing out.** [Old English *singan;* related to Old Norse *syngja* to sing, Gothic *siggwan,* Old High German *singan*] —ˈ**singable** *adj.* —ˈ**singing** *adj., n.*

▷**Usage.** See at **ring**[2].

sing. *abbrev. for* singular.

sing along *vb.* (*intr., adv.*) 1. to join in singing with a performer. ~*n.* **sing-along.** 2. such a singsong.

Singaporean (ˌsɪŋəˈpɔːrɪən, ˌsɪŋgə-) *adj.* 1. of or relating to Singapore, a republic in SE Asia, or to its people, customs, etc. ~*n.* 2. a native or inhabitant of Singapore.

singe (sɪndʒ) *vb.* **singes, singeing, singed.** 1. to burn or be burnt superficially; scorch: *to singe one's clothes.* 2. (*tr.*) to burn the ends of (hair, etc.). 3. (*tr.*) to expose (a carcass) to flame to remove bristles or hair. ~*n.* 4. a superficial burn. [Old English *sengan;* related to Middle High German *sengen* to singe, Dutch *sengel* spark, Norwegian *sengla* to smell of burning, Swedish *sjängla* to singe, Icelandic *sāngr*]

singer (ˈsɪŋə) *n.* 1. a person who sings, esp. one who earns a living by singing. 2. a singing bird. 3. an obsolete word for **poet.**

Singh (sɪŋ) *n.* a title assumed by a Sikh when he becomes a full member of the community. [from Hindi, from Sanskrit *sinhá* a lion]

Singhalese (ˌsɪŋəˈliːz) *n., pl.* **-leses** *or* **-lese,** *adj.* a variant spelling of **Sinhalese.**

singing telegram *n.* a greetings service in which a person is employed to present greetings by singing to the person celebrating.

single (ˈsɪŋgᵊl) *adj.* (*usually prenominal*) 1. existing alone; solitary: *upon the hill stood a single tower.* 2. distinct from other things; unique or individual. 3. composed of one part. 4. designed for one user: *a single room; a single bed.* 5. (*also* *postpositive*) unmarried. **6.** connected with the condition of being unmarried: *he led a single life.* **7.** (esp. of combat) involving two individuals; one against one. **8.** sufficient for one person or thing only: *a single portion of food.* **9.** even one: *there wasn't a single person on the beach.* **10.** (of a flower) having only one set or whorl of petals. **11.** determined; single-minded: *a single devotion to duty.* **12.** (of the eye) seeing correctly: *to consider something with a single eye.* **13.** *Rare.* honest or sincere; genuine. **14.** *Archaic.* (of ale, beer, etc.) mild in strength. ~*n.* **15.** something forming one individual unit. **16.** an unmarried person. **17.** a gramophone record with a short recording, usually of pop music, on each side: now usually 7 inches (18 centimetres) in diameter and played at 45 revolutions per minute. Compare **EP.** **18.** *Golf.* a game between two players. **19.** *Cricket.* a hit from which one run is scored. **20. a.** *Brit.* a pound note. **b.** *U.S. and Canadian.* a dollar note. **21.** See **single ticket.** ~*vb.* **22.** (*tr.*; usually foll. by *out*) to select from a group of people or things; distinguish by separation: *he singled him out for special mention.* **23.** (*tr.*) to thin out (seedlings). **24.** short for **single-foot.** ~See also **singles.** [C14: from Old French *sengle,* from Latin *singulus* individual] —ˈ**singleness** *n.*

single-acting *adj.* (of a reciprocating engine or pump) having a piston or pistons that are pressurized on one side only. Compare **double-acting** (sense 1).

single-action *n.* (*modifier*) (of a firearm) requiring the hammer to be cocked by hand before firing.

single-blind *adj.* of or relating to an experiment, esp. one to discover people's reactions to certain commodities, drugs, etc., in which the experimenters but not the subjects know the particulars of the test items during the experiment. Compare **double-blind.**

single bond *n. Chem.* a covalent bond formed between two atoms by the sharing of one pair of electrons.

single-breasted *adj.* (of a garment) having the fronts overlapping only slightly and with one row of fastenings.

single-cell protein *n.* protein that is produced by micro-organisms fermenting in liquid or gaseous petroleum fractions or other organic substances: used as a food supplement. Abbrev.: **SCP.**

single cream *n.* cream having a low fat content that does not thicken with beating.

single-cross *n. Genetics.* a hybrid of the first generation between two inbred lines.

single-cut file *n.* a file with teeth in one direction only: used for filing soft material.

single-decker *n. Brit. informal.* a bus with only one passenger deck.

single density *n. Computer technol.* a disk with the normal capacity for storage.

single-end *n. Scot. dialect.* accommodation consisting of a single room.

single-ended *adj. Electronics.* (of an amplifier) having one side of the input and one side of the output connected to earth: used for an unbalanced signal.

single entry *n.* **a.** a simple book-keeping system in which transactions are entered in one account only. Compare **double entry.** **b.** (*as modifier*): *a single-entry account.*

single file *n.* a line of persons, animals, or things ranged one behind the other, either stationary or moving.

single-foot *n.* **1.** a rapid showy gait of a horse in which each foot strikes the ground separately, as in a walk. ~*vb.* **2.** to move or cause to move at this gait.

single-handed *adj., adv.* **1.** unaided or working alone: *a single-handed crossing of the Atlantic.* **2.** having or operated by one hand or one person only. —ˌ**single-ˈhandedly** *adv.* —ˌ**single-ˈhandedness** *n.*

single-lens reflex *n.* See **reflex camera.**

single-minded *adj.* having but one aim or purpose; dedicated. —ˌ**single-ˈmindedly** *adv.* —ˌ**single-ˈmindedness** *n.*

single-parent family *n.* another term for **one-parent family.**

single-phase *adj.* (of a system, circuit, or device) having, generating, or using a single alternating voltage.

singles (ˈsɪŋgᵊlz) *pl. n. Tennis, etc.* a match played with one person on each side.

singles bar *n.* a bar or club that is a social meeting place for single people.

single-sex *adj.* (of schools, etc.) admitting members of one sex only; not coeducational.

single sideband transmission *n.* a method of transmitting radio waves in which either the upper or the lower sideband is transmitted, the carrier being either wholly or partially suppressed. This reduces the required bandwidth and improves the signal-to-noise ratio. Abbrev.: **SSB.**

single-space *vb.* (*tr.*) to type (copy) without leaving a space between the lines.

single-step *vb.* **-steps, -stepping, -stepped.** (*tr.*) *Computer technol.* to perform a single instruction on (a program), generally under the control of a debug program.

singlestick (ˈsɪŋgᵊlˌstɪk) *n.* **1.** a wooden stick used instead of a sword for fencing. **2.** fencing with such a stick. **3.** any short heavy stick.

singlet (ˈsɪŋglɪt) *n.* **1.** *Chiefly Brit.* a man's sleeveless vest. **2.** *Austral.* any vest. **3.** *Chiefly Brit.* a garment worn with shorts by athletes, boxers, etc. **4.** *N.Z.* a black woollen outer garment worn by bushmen. **5.** *Physics.* a multiplet that has only one member. **6.** *Chem.* a chemical bond consisting of one electron. [C18: from SINGLE, on the model of *doublet*]

single tax *n. U.S.* **1.** a taxation system in which a tax on one commodity, usually land, is the only source of revenue. **2.** such a tax.

single thread *n. Computer technol.* the execution of an entire task from beginning to end without interruption.

single ticket *n. Brit.* a ticket entitling a passenger to travel only to his destination, without returning. U.S. and Canadian equivalent: **one-way ticket.** Compare **return ticket.**

singleton (ˈsɪŋgᵊltən) *n.* **1.** *Bridge, etc.* an original holding of one card only in a suit. **2.** a single object, individual, etc., separated or distinguished from a pair or group. **3.** *Maths.* a set containing only one member. [C19: from SINGLE, on the model of SIMPLETON]

single-tongue *vb. Music.* to play (any nonlegato passage) on a wind instrument by obstructing and uncovering the air passage through the lips with the tongue. Compare **double-tongue, triple-tongue.** —**single tonguing** *n.*

single-track *adj.* **1.** (of a railway) having only a single pair of lines, so that trains can travel in only one direction at a time. **2.** (of a road) only wide enough for one vehicle. **3.** able to think about only one thing; one-track.

Single Transferable Vote *n.* (*modifier*) of or relating to a system of voting in which voters list the candidates in order of preference. Any candidate achieving a predetermined proportion of the votes in a constituency is elected. Votes exceeding this amount and those cast for the bottom candidate are redistributed according to the stated preferences. Redistribution continues until all the seats are filled. Abbrev.: **STV.** See **proportional representation.**

singletree (ˈsɪŋgᵊlˌtriː) *n.* a variant, esp. U.S. and Austral., of **swingletree.**

singly (ˈsɪŋglɪ) *adv.* **1.** one at a time; one by one. **2.** apart from others; separately; alone.

sing out *vb.* (*tr., adv.*) to call out in a loud voice; shout.

singsong (ˈsɪŋˌsɒŋ) *n.* **1.** an accent, metre, or intonation that is characterized by an alternately rising and falling rhythm, as in a person's voice, piece of verse, etc. **2.** *Brit.* an informal session of singing, esp. of popular or traditional songs. ~*adj.* **3.** having a regular or monotonous rising and falling rhythm: *a singsong accent.*

Singspiel *German.* (ˈzɪŋʃpiːl) *n.* a type of comic opera in German with spoken dialogue, popular during the late 18th and early 19th centuries. [literally: singing play]

singular (ˈsɪŋgjʊlə) *adj.* **1.** remarkable; exceptional; extraordinary: *a singular feat.* **2.** unusual; odd: *a singular character.* **3.** unique. **4.** denoting a word or an inflected form of a word indicating that not more than one referent is being referred to or described. **5.** *Logic.* of or referring to a specific thing or person as opposed to something general. ~*n.* **6.** *Grammar.* **a.** the singular number. **b.** a singular form of a word. [C14: from Latin *singulāris* SINGLE] —ˈ**singularly** *adv.* —ˈ**singularness** *n.*

singularity (ˌsɪŋgjʊˈlærɪtɪ) *n., pl.* **-ties.** **1.** the state, fact, or quality of being singular. **2.** something distinguishing a person or thing from others. **3.** something remarkable or unusual. **4.** *Maths.* **a.** a point at which a function is not differentiable although it is differentiable in a neighbourhood of that point. See also **pole**[2] (sense 4). **b.** another word for **discontinuity.** **5.** *Astronomy.* a hypothetical point in space at which matter is infinitely compressed to infinitesimal volume. Compare **black hole.**

singularize *or* **singularise** (ˈsɪŋgjʊləˌraɪz) *vb.* (*tr.*) **1.** to make (a word, etc.) singular. **2.** to make conspicuous. —ˌ**singulariˈzation** *or* ˌ**singulariˈsation** *n.*

singulary (ˈsɪŋgjʊlərɪ) *adj. Logic, maths.* (of an operator) monadic.

singultus (sɪŋˈgʌltəs) *n.* a technical name for **hiccup.** [C18: from Latin, literally: a sob]

sinh (ʃaɪn, sɪnʃ) *n.* hyperbolic sine; a hyperbolic function, sinh $z = \frac{1}{2}(e^z - e^{-z})$, related to sine by the expression sinh iz = i sin z, where i = $\sqrt{-1}$. [C20: from SIN(E) + H(YPERBOLIC)]

Sinhalese (ˌsɪnhəˈliːz) *or* **Singhalese** *n.* **1.** (*pl.* **-leses** *or* **-lese**) a member of a people living chiefly in Sri Lanka, where they constitute the majority of the population. **2.** the language of this people, belonging to the Indic branch of the Indo-European family: the official language of Sri Lanka. It is written in a script of Indian origin. ~*adj.* **3.** of or relating to this people or their language.

Sinicism (ˈsaɪnɪˌsɪzəm, ˈsɪn-) *n. Rare.* a Chinese custom or idiom. [C19: from Medieval Latin *Sinicus* Chinese, from Late Latin *Sīnae* the Chinese, from Greek *Sinai,* from Arabic *Sīn* China]

sinister (ˈsɪnɪstə) *adj.* **1.** threatening or suggesting evil or harm; ominous: *a sinister glance.* **2.** evil or treacherous, esp. in a mysterious way. **3.** (*usually postpositive*) *Heraldry.* of, on, or starting from the left side from the bearer's point of view and therefore on the spectator's right. **4.** *Archaic.* located on the left side. **5.** *Archaic.* (of signs, omens, etc.) unfavourable. ~Compare **dexter.** [C15: from Latin *sinister* on the left-hand side, considered by Roman augurers to be the unlucky one] —'**sinisterly** *adv.* —'**sinisterness** *n.*

sinistral ('sɪnɪstrəl) *adj.* **1.** of, relating to, or located on the left side, esp. the left side of the body. **2.** a technical term for **left-handed.** **3.** (of the shells of certain gastropod molluscs) coiling in a clockwise direction from the apex. ~Compare **dextral.** [C15 (in the obsolete sense: adverse, evil); C19 (in current senses): from Medieval Latin *sinistrālis.* See SINISTER] —'**sinistrally** *adv.*

sinistrodextral (ˌsɪnɪstrəʊ'dɛkstrəl) *adj.* going or directed from left to right: *a sinistrodextral script.* [See SINISTER, DEXTER[1]]

sinistrorse ('sɪnɪˌstrɔːs, ˌsɪnɪ'strɔːs) *adj.* (of some climbing plants) growing upwards in a spiral from right to left, or clockwise. Compare **dextrorse.** [C19: from Latin *sinistrōrsus* turned towards the left, from *sinister* on the left + *vertere* to turn] —ˌ**sinis'trorsal** *adj.* —'**sinisˌtrorsely** *adv.*

sinistrous ('sɪnɪstrəs) *adj. Archaic.* **1.** sinister or ill-omened. **2.** sinistral. —'**sinistrously** *adv.*

Sinitic (sɪ'nɪtɪk) *n.* **1.** a branch of the Sino-Tibetan family of languages, consisting of the various languages or dialects of Chinese. Compare **Tibeto-Burman.** ~*adj.* **2.** belonging or relating to this group of languages.

sink (sɪŋk) *vb.* **sinks, sinking, sank** *or* **sunk; sunk** *or* **sunken.** **1.** to descend or cause to descend, esp. beneath the surface of a liquid or soft substance. **2.** (*intr.*) to appear to move down towards or descend below the horizon. **3.** (*intr.*) to slope downwards; dip. **4.** (*intr.*; often foll. by *in* or *into*) to pass into or gradually enter a specified lower state or condition: *to sink into apathy.* **5.** to make or become lower in volume, pitch, etc. **6.** to make or become lower in value, price, etc. **7.** (*intr.*) to become weaker in health, strength, etc. **8.** to decline or cause to decline in moral value, worth, etc. **9.** (*intr.*) to seep or penetrate. **10.** (*tr.*) to suppress or conceal: *he sank his worries in drink.* **11.** (*tr.*) to dig, cut, drill, bore, or excavate (a hole, shaft, etc.). **12.** (*tr.*) to drive into the ground: *to sink a stake.* **13.** (*tr.*; usually foll. by *in* or *into*) **a.** to invest (money). **b.** to lose (money) in an unwise or unfortunate investment. **14.** (*tr.*) to pay (a debt). **15.** (*intr.*) to become hollow; cave in: *his cheeks had sunk during his illness.* **16.** (*tr.*) to hit, throw, or propel (a ball) into a hole, basket, pocket, etc.: *he sank a 15-foot putt.* **17.** (*tr.*) *Brit. informal.* to drink, esp. quickly: *he sank three pints in half an hour.* **18. sink or swim.** to take risks where the alternatives are loss and failure or security and success. ~*n.* **19.** a fixed basin, esp. in a kitchen, made of stone, earthenware, metal, etc., used for washing. **20.** See **sinkhole.** **21.** another word for **cesspool.** **22.** a place of vice or corruption. **23.** an area of ground below that of the surrounding land, where water collects. **24.** *Physics.* a device or part of a system at which energy is removed from the system: *a heat sink.* [Old English *sincan;* related to Old Norse *sökkva* to sink, Gothic *siggan,* Old High German *sincan,* Swedish *sjunka*] —'**sinkable** *adj.*

sinkage ('sɪŋkɪdʒ) *n. Rare.* the act of sinking or degree to which something sinks or has sunk.

sinker ('sɪŋkə) *n.* **1.** a weight attached to a fishing line, net, etc., to cause it to sink in water. **2.** a person who sinks shafts, etc. **3.** *U.S.* an informal word for **doughnut.** **4. hook, line, and sinker.** See **hook** (sense 19).

sinkhole ('sɪŋkˌhəʊl) *n.* **1.** Also called (esp. Brit.): **swallow hole.** a depression in the ground surface, esp. in limestone, where a surface stream disappears underground. **2.** a place into which foul matter runs.

sink in *vb.* (*intr., adv.*) to enter or penetrate the mind: *eventually the news sank in.*

sinking ('sɪŋkɪŋ) *n.* **a.** a feeling in the stomach caused by hunger or uneasiness. **b.** (*as modifier*): *a sinking feeling.*

sinking fund *n.* a fund accumulated out of a business enterprise's earnings or a government's revenue and invested to repay a long-term debt or meet a depreciation charge.

sinless ('sɪnlɪs) *adj.* free from sin or guilt; innocent; pure. —'**sinlessly** *adv.* —'**sinlessness** *n.*

Sinn Féiner (ʃɪn 'feːnə) *n.* a member or supporter of Sinn Féin, an Irish republican political movement founded about 1905.

Sino- *combining form.* Chinese: *Sino-Tibetan; Sinology.* [from French, from Late Latin *Sīnae* the Chinese, from Late Greek *Sinai,* from Arabic *Sīn* China, probably from Chinese *Ch'in*]

Sinology (saɪ'nɒlədʒɪ, sɪ-) *n.* the study of Chinese history, language, culture, etc. —**Sinological** (ˌsaɪnə'lɒdʒɪkəl, ˌsɪn-) *adj.* —**Si'nologist** *n.* —**Sinologue** ('saɪnəˌlɒg) *n.*

Sino-Tibetan ('saɪnəʊ-) *n.* **1.** a family of languages that includes most of the languages of China, as well as Tibetan, Burmese, and possibly Thai. Their most noticeable phonological characteristic is the phonemic use of tones. ~*adj.* **2.** belonging or relating to this family of languages.

sinsemilla (ˌsɪnsə'miːljə) *n.* **1.** a type of marijuana with a very high narcotic content. **2.** the plant from which it is obtained, a strain of *Cannabis sativa.* [C20: from American Spanish, literally: without seed]

sinter ('sɪntə) *n.* **1.** a whitish porous incrustation, usually consisting of silica, that is deposited from hot springs. **2.** the product of a sintering process. **3.** another name for **cinder** (sense 3). ~*vb.* **4.** (*tr.*) to form large particles, lumps, or masses from (metal powders or powdery ores) by heating or pressure or both. [C18: German: CINDER]

sinuate ('sɪnjʊɪt, -ˌeɪt) *or* **sinuated** *adj.* **1.** Also: **sinuous.** (of leaves) having a strongly waved margin. **2.** another word for **sinuous.** [C17: from Latin *sinuātus* curved; see SINUS, -ATE[1]] —'**sinuately** *adv.*

sinuosity (ˌsɪnjʊ'ɒsɪtɪ) *or* (*less commonly*) **sinuation** *n., pl.* **-osites** *or* **-ations.** **1.** the quality of being sinuous. **2.** a turn, curve, or intricacy.

sinuous ('sɪnjʊəs) *adj.* **1.** full of turns or curves; intricate. **2.** devious; not straightforward. **3.** supple; lithe. ~Also: **sinuate.** [C16: from Latin *sinuōsus* winding, from *sinus* a curve] —'**sinuously** *adv.* —'**sinuousness** *n.*

sinus ('saɪnəs) *n., pl.* **-nuses.** **1.** *Anatomy.* **a.** any bodily cavity or hollow space. **b.** a large channel for venous blood, esp. between the brain and the skull. **c.** any of the air cavities in the cranial bones. **2.** *Pathol.* a passage leading to a cavity containing pus. **3.** *Botany.* a small rounded notch between two lobes of a leaf, petal, etc. **4.** an irregularly shaped cavity. [C16: from Latin: a curve, bay]

sinusitis (ˌsaɪnə'saɪtɪs) *n.* inflammation of the membrane lining a sinus, esp. a nasal sinus.

sinusoid ('saɪnəˌsɔɪd) *n.* **1.** any of the irregular terminal blood vessels that replace capillaries in certain organs, such as the liver, heart, spleen, and pancreas. **2.** another name for **sine curve.** ~*adj.* **3.** resembling a sinus. [C19: from French *sinusoïde.* See SINUS, -OID]

sinusoidal (ˌsaɪnə'sɔɪdəl) *adj.* **1.** *Maths.* of or relating to a sine curve. **2.** *Physics.* having a magnitude that varies as a sine curve. —ˌ**sinus'oidally** *adv.*

sinusoidal projection *n.* an equal-area map projection on which all parallels are straight lines and all except the prime meridian are sine curves, often used to show tropical latitudes. Also called: **Sanson-Flamsteed projection.**

Sion ('saɪən) *n.* a variant of **Zion.**

Siouan ('suːən) *n.* a family of North American Indian languages including Sioux, probably related to Iroquoian.

Sioux (suː) *n.* **1.** (*pl.* **Sioux** (suː, suːz)) a member of a group of North American Indian peoples formerly ranging over a wide area of the Plains from Lake Michigan to the Rocky Mountains. **2.** any of the Siouan languages. [from French, shortened from *Nadowessioux,* from Chippewa *Nadoweisiw*] —'**Siouan** *adj.*

sip (sɪp) *vb.* **sips, sipping, sipped.** **1.** to drink (a liquid) by taking small mouthfuls; drink gingerly or delicately. ~*n.* **2.** a small quantity of a liquid taken into the mouth and swallowed. **3.** an act of sipping. [C14: probably from Low German *sippen*] —'**sipper** *n.*

siphon *or* **syphon** ('saɪfən) *n.* **1.** a tube placed with one end at a certain level in a vessel of liquid and the other end outside the vessel below this level, so that atmospheric pressure forces the liquid through the tube and out of the vessel. **2.** See **soda siphon.** **3.** *Zoology.* any of various tubular organs in different aquatic animals, such as molluscs and elasmobranch fishes, through which a fluid, esp. water, passes. ~*vb.* **4.** (often foll. by *off*) to pass or draw off through or as if through a siphon. [C17: from Latin *sīphō,* from Greek *siphōn* siphon] —'**siphonage** *n.* —'**siphonal** *or* **siphonic** (saɪ'fɒnɪk) *adj.*

siphon bottle *n.* another name (esp. U.S.) for **soda siphon.**

siphonophore ('saɪfənəˌfɔː, saɪ'fɒnə-) *n.* any marine colonial hydrozoan of the order *Siphonophora,* including the Portuguese man-of-war. [C19: from New Latin *siphonophora,* from Greek *siphōnophoros* tube-bearing] —**siphonophorous** (ˌsaɪfə'nɒfərəs) *adj.*

siphonostele ('saɪfənəˌstiːl) *n. Botany.* the cylinder of conducting tissue surrounding a central core of pith in certain stems. See also **stele** (sense 3). [C19: from SIPHON + STELE] —**siphonostelic** (ˌsaɪfənə'stiːlɪk) *adj.*

sipper ('sɪpə) *n. U.S. informal.* a drinking straw.

sippet ('sɪpɪt) *n.* a small piece of something, esp. a piece of toast or fried bread eaten with soup or gravy. [C16: used as diminutive of SOP; see -ET]

sir (sɜː) *n.* **1.** a polite term of address for a man. **2.** *Archaic.* a gentleman of high social status. [C13: variant of SIRE]

Sir (sɜː) *n.* **1.** a title of honour placed before the name of a knight or baronet: *Sir Walter Raleigh.* **2.** *Archaic.* a title placed before the name of a figure from ancient history.

sirdar ('sɜːdɑː) *n.* **1.** a general or military leader in Pakistan and India. **2.** (formerly) the title of the British commander in chief of the Egyptian Army. **3.** a variant spelling of **sardar.** [from Hindi *sardār,* from Persian, from *sar* head + *dār* possession]

sire (saɪə) *n.* **1.** a male parent, esp. of a horse or other domestic animal. **2.** a respectful term of address, now used only in addressing a male monarch. **3.** *Obsolete.* a man of high rank. ~*vb.* **4.** (*tr.*) (esp. of a domestic animal) to father; beget. [C13: from Old French, from Latin *senior* an elder, from *senex* an old man]

siren ('saɪərən) *n.* **1.** a device for emitting a loud wailing sound, esp. as a warning or signal, typically consisting of a rotating perforated metal drum through which air or steam is passed under pressure. **2.** (*sometimes cap.*) *Greek myth.* one of several sea nymphs whose seductive singing was believed to lure sailors to destruction on the rocks the nymphs inhabited. **3. a.** a woman considered to be dangerously alluring or seductive. **b.** (*as modifier*): *her siren charms.* **4.** any aquatic eel-like salamander of the North American family *Sirenidae,* having external gills, no hind limbs, and reduced forelimbs. [C14: from Old French *sereine,* from Latin *sīrēn,* from Greek *seirēn*]

sirenian (saɪˈriːnɪən) *adj.* **1.** of, relating to, or belonging to the *Sirenia,* an order of aquatic herbivorous placental mammals having forelimbs modified as paddles, no hind limbs, and a horizontally flattened tail: contains only the dugong and manatees. ~*n.* **2.** any animal belonging to the order *Sirenia;* a sea cow.

Sirius (ˈsɪrɪəs) *n.* the brightest star in the sky, lying in the constellation Canis Major. It is a binary star whose companion, **Sirius B,** is a very faint white dwarf. Distance: 8.7 light years. Also called: the **Dog Star, Canicula, Sothis.** [C14: via Latin from Greek *Seirios,* of obscure origin]

sirloin (ˈsɜːˌlɔɪn) *n.* a prime cut of beef from the loin, esp. the upper part. [C16 *surloyn,* from Old French *surlonge,* from *sur* above + *longe,* from *loigne* LOIN]

sirocco (sɪˈrɒkəʊ) *n., pl.* **-cos. 1.** a hot oppressive and often dusty wind usually occurring in spring, beginning in N Africa and reaching S Europe. **2.** any hot southerly wind, esp. one moving to a low pressure centre. [C17: from Italian, from Arabic *sharq* east wind]

sironize *or* **sironise** (ˈsaɪrəˌnaɪz) *vb. (tr.) Austral.* to treat (a woollen fabric) chemically to prevent it wrinkling after being washed. [C20: from (C)SIRO + *-n-* + -IZE]

siroset (ˈsaɪrəʊˌsɛt) *adj. Austral.* of or relating to the chemical treatment of woollen fabrics to give a permanent-press effect, or a garment so treated.

sirrah (ˈsɪrə) *n. Archaic.* a contemptuous term used in addressing a man or boy. [C16: probably variant of SIRE]

sirree (səˈriː) *interj. (sometimes cap.) U.S. informal.* an emphatic exclamation used with *yes* or *no.*

sir-reverence *interj. Obsolete.* an expression of apology used esp. to introduce taboo or vulgar words or phrases. [C16: short for *save your reverence*]

Sir Roger de Coverley *n.* an English country dance similar to the Virginia reel and danced to a traditional tune. [C18: alteration of *Roger of Coverley* influenced by *Sir Roger de Coverley,* a fictitious character appearing in the *Spectator* essays by Addison and Steele]

sirup (ˈsɪrəp) *n. U.S.* a less common spelling of **syrup.**

sirvente (səˈvɛnt) *n.* a verse form employed by the troubadours of Provence to satirize moral or political themes. [C19: via French from Provençal *sirventes* song of a servant (that is, of a lover serving his mistress), from *sirvent* a servant, from Latin *servīre* to SERVE]

sis (sɪs) *n. Informal.* short for **sister.**

SIS (in New Zealand) *abbrev. for* Security Intelligence Service.

sisal (ˈsaɪsᵊl) *n.* **1.** a Mexican agave plant, *Agave sisalana,* cultivated for its large fleshy leaves, which yield a stiff fibre used for making rope. **2.** the fibre of this plant. **3.** any of the fibres of certain similar or related plants. ~Also called: **sisal hemp.** [C19: from Mexican Spanish, named after *Sisal,* a port in Yucatán, Mexico]

siskin (ˈsɪskɪn) *n.* **1.** a yellow-and-black Eurasian finch, *Carduelis spinus.* **2. pine siskin.** a North American finch, *Spinus pinus,* having a streaked yellowish-brown plumage. [C16: from Middle Dutch *sīseken,* from Middle Low German *sīsek;* related to Czech *čížek,* Russian *chizh*]

sissy *or* **cissy** (ˈsɪsɪ) *n., pl.* **-sies. 1.** an effeminate, weak, or cowardly boy or man. ~*adj.* **2.** Also (informal or dialect): **ˈsissiˌfied** *or* **ˈcissiˌfied.** effeminate, weak, or cowardly.

sister (ˈsɪstə) *n.* **1.** a female person having the same parents as another person. **2.** See **half-sister, stepsister. 3.** a female person who belongs to the same group, trade union, etc., as another or others. **4.** *Informal.* a form of address to a woman or girl, used esp. by Blacks in the U.S. **5.** a senior nurse. **6.** *Chiefly R.C. Church.* a nun or a title given to a nun. **7.** a woman fellow member of a Church or religious body. **8.** *(modifier)* belonging to the same class, fleet, etc., as another or others: *a sister ship.* **9.** *(modifier) Biology.* denoting any of the cells or cell components formed by division of a parent cell or cell component: *sister nuclei.* [Old English *sweostor;* related to Old Norse *systir,* Old High German *swester,* Gothic *swistar*]

sisterhood (ˈsɪstəˌhʊd) *n.* **1.** the state of being related as a sister or sisters. **2.** a religious body or society of sisters, esp. a community, order, or congregation of nuns. **3.** the bond between women who support the Women's Movement.

sister-in-law *n., pl.* **sisters-in-law. 1.** the sister of one's husband or wife. **2.** the wife of one's brother.

sisterly (ˈsɪstəlɪ) *adj.* of, resembling, or suitable to a sister, esp. in showing kindness and affection. —**ˈsisterliness** *n.*

sistroid (ˈsɪstrɔɪd) *adj.* contained between the convex sides of two intersecting curves. Compare **cissoid** (sense 2). [C20: from SISTRUM + -OID]

sistrum (ˈsɪstrəm) *n., pl.* **-tra** (-trə). a musical instrument of ancient Egypt consisting of a metal rattle. [C14: via Latin from Greek *seistron,* from *seiein* to shake]

Sisyphean (ˌsɪsɪˈfiːən) *adj.* actually or seemingly endless and futile. [alluding to King *Sisyphus* in Greek mythology, punished in Hades by having to roll a boulder uphill eternally]

sit (sɪt) *vb.* **sits, sitting, sat.** *(mainly intr.)* **1.** *(also tr.;* when *intr.,* often foll. by *down, in,* or *on)* to adopt or rest in a posture in which the body is supported on the buttocks and thighs and the torso is more or less upright: *to sit on a chair; sit a horse.* **2.** *(tr.)* to cause to adopt such a posture. **3.** (of an animal) to adopt or rest in a posture with the hindquarters lowered to the ground. **4.** (of a bird) to perch or roost. **5.** (of a hen or other bird) to cover eggs to hatch them; brood. **6.** to be situated or located. **7.** (of the wind) to blow from the direction specified. **8.** to adopt and maintain a posture for one's portrait to be painted, etc. **9.** to occupy or be entitled to a seat in some official capacity, as a judge, elected representative, etc. **10.** (of a deliberative body) to be convened or in session. **11.** to remain inactive or unused: *his car sat in the garage for a year.* **12.** to rest or lie as specified: *the nut was sitting so awkwardly that he couldn't turn it.* **13.** (of a garment) to fit or hang as specified: *that dress sits well on you.* **14.** to weigh, rest, or lie as specified: *greatness sits easily on him.* **15.** *(tr.) Chiefly Brit.* to take (an examination): *he's sitting his bar finals.* **16.** (usually foll. by *for*) *Chiefly Brit.* to be a candidate (for a qualification): *he's sitting for a BA.* **17.** *(intr.; in combination)* to look after a specified person or thing for someone else: *granny-sit.* **18.** *(tr.)* to have seating capacity for. **19. sitting pretty.** *Informal.* well placed or established financially, socially, etc. **20. sit tight. a.** to wait patiently; bide one's time. **b.** to maintain one's position, stand, or opinion firmly. ~See also **sit back, sit down, sit-in, sit on, sit out, sit over, sit under, sit up.** [Old English *sittan;* related to Old Norse *sitja,* Gothic *sitan,* Old High German *sizzen,* Latin *sedēre* to sit, Sanskrit *sīdati* he sits]

sitar (sɪˈtɑː, ˈsɪtɑː) *n.* a stringed musical instrument, esp. of India, having a long neck, a rounded body, and movable frets. The main strings, three to seven in number, overlie other sympathetic strings, the tuning depending on the raga being performed. [from Hindi *sitār,* literally: three-stringed] —**siˈtarist** *n.*

sitatunga (ˌsɪtəˈtʊŋgə) *n.* another name for **marshbuck.**

sit back *vb. (intr., adv.)* to relax, as when action should be taken: *many people just sit back and ignore the problems of today.*

sitcom (ˈsɪtˌkɒm) *n.* an informal term for **situation comedy.**

sit down *vb. (adv.)* **1.** to adopt or cause (oneself or another) to adopt a sitting posture. **2.** *(intr.;* foll. by *under)* to suffer (insults, etc.) without protests or resistance. ~*n.* **sit-down. 3.** a form of civil disobedience in which demonstrators sit down in a public place as a protest or to draw attention to a cause. **4.** See **sit-down strike.** ~*adj.* **sit-down. 5.** (of a meal, etc.) eaten while sitting down at a table.

sit-down money *n. Austral. informal.* social security benefits.

sit-down strike *n.* a strike in which workers refuse to leave their place of employment until a settlement is reached.

site (saɪt) *n.* **1. a.** the piece of land where something was, is, or is intended to be located: *a building site; archaeological site.* **b.** *(as modifier): site office.* ~*vb.* **2.** *(tr.)* to locate, place, or install (something) in a specific place. [C14: from Latin *situs* situation, from *sinere* to be placed]

sitella (sɪˈtɛlə) *n. Austral.* any of various small generally black-and-white birds of the genus *Neositta,* having a straight sharp beak and strong claws used to run up trees in search of insects: family *Sittidae* (nuthatches). Also called: **tree-runner.** [C19: from New Latin, the diminutive of *sitta,* from Greek *sittē* nuthatch]

sitfast (ˈsɪtˌfɑːst) *n.* a sore on a horse's back caused by rubbing of the saddle. [C17: from SIT + FAST[1] (in the sense: secure, fixed)]

sith (sɪθ) *adv., conj., prep.* an archaic word for **since.** [Old English *siththa,* short for *siththan* SINCE]

sit-in *n.* **1.** a form of civil disobedience in which demonstrators occupy seats in a public place and refuse to move as a protest. **2.** another term for **sit-down strike.** ~*vb.* **sit in.** *(intr., adv.)* **3.** (often foll. by *for*) to deputize (for). **4.** (foll. by *on*) to take part (in) as a visitor or guest: *we sat in on Professor Johnson's seminar.* **5.** to organize or take part in a sit-in.

sitkamer (ˈsɪtˌkɑːmə) *n. S. African.* a sitting room; lounge. [from Afrikaans *sit* sitting + *kamer* room]

sitka spruce (ˈsɪtkə) *n.* a tall North American spruce tree, *Picea sitchensis,* having yellowish-green needle-like leaves: yields valuable timber. [C19: from *Sitka,* a town in SE Alaska]

sitology (saɪˈtɒlədʒɪ) *n.* the scientific study of food, diet, and nutrition. [C19: from Greek *sitos* food, grain + -LOGY]

sit on *vb. (intr., prep.)* **1.** to be a member of (a committee, etc.). **2.** *Informal.* to suppress. **3.** *Informal.* to check or rebuke.

sitosterol (saɪˈtɒstəˌrɒl) *n.* a white powder or waxy white solid extracted from soya beans, consisting of a mixture of isomers of the formula $C_{29}H_{50}O$ with other sterols: used in cosmetics and medicine. [C20: from Greek *sitos* food, grain + STEROL]

sit out *vb. (adv.)* **1.** *(tr.)* to endure to the end: *I sat out the play although it was terrible.* **2.** *(tr.)* to remain seated throughout (a dance, etc.). **3.** *(intr.) Chiefly Brit.* to lean backwards over the side of a light sailing boat in order to carry the centre of gravity as far to windward as possible to reduce heeling. U.S. and Canadian term: **hike out.**

sit over *vb. (intr., prep.) Cards.* to be seated in an advantageous position on the left of (the player).

sitter (ˈsɪtə) *n.* **1.** a person or animal that sits. **2.** a person who is posing for his or her portrait to be painted, carved, etc. **3.** a broody hen or other bird that is sitting on its eggs to hatch them. **4.** *(in combination)* a person who looks after a specified person or thing for someone else: *flat-sitter.* **5.** *U.S.* short for **baby-sitter. 6.** anyone, other than the medium, taking part in a seance. **7.** anything that is extremely easy, such as an easy catch in cricket.

sitting ('sɪtɪŋ) *n.* **1.** a continuous period of being seated: *I read his novel at one sitting.* **2.** such a period in a restaurant, canteen, etc., where space and other facilities are limited: *dinner will be served in two sittings.* **3.** the act or period of posing for one's portrait to be painted, carved, etc. **4.** a meeting, esp. of an official body, to conduct business. **5.** the incubation period of a bird's eggs during which the mother sits on them to keep them warm. ~*adj.* **6.** in office: *a sitting Member of Parliament.* **7.** (of a hen) brooding eggs. **8.** seated: *in a sitting position.*

sitting room *n.* a room in a private house or flat used for relaxation and entertainment of guests.

sitting target *n.* a person or thing in a defenceless or vulnerable position. Also called (informal): **sitting duck.**

sitting tenant *n.* a tenant occupying a house, flat, etc.

sitting trot *n.* a horse's trot during which the rider sits still in the saddle. Compare **rising trot.**

situate ('sɪtjʊˌeɪt) *vb.* **1.** (*tr.; often passive*) to allot a site to; place; locate. ~*adj.* **2.** (now used esp. in legal contexts) situated; located. [C16: from Late Latin *situāre* to position, from Latin *situs* a SITE]

situation (ˌsɪtjʊ'eɪʃən) *n.* **1.** physical placement, esp. with regard to the surroundings. **2. a.** state of affairs; combination of circumstances. **b.** a complex or critical state of affairs in a novel, play, etc. **3.** social or financial status, position, or circumstances. **4.** a position of employment; post. —ˌ**situ'ational** *adj.*

▷**Usage.** *Situation* is often used in contexts in which it is redundant or imprecise. Typical examples are: *the company is in a crisis situation* or *people in a job situation.* In the first example, *situation* does not add to the meaning and should be omitted. In the second example, it would be clearer and more concise to substitute a phrase such as *people at work.*

situation comedy *n.* (on television or radio) a comedy series involving the same characters in various day-to-day situations which are developed as separate stories for each episode. Also called: **sitcom.**

situla ('sɪtjʊlə) *n., pl.* **-lae** (-liː). **1.** a bucket-shaped container, usually of metal or pottery and often richly decorated: typical of the N Italian Iron Age. ~*adj.* **2.** of or relating to the type of designs usually associated with these containers. [from Latin]

sit under *vb.* (*intr., prep.*) *Cards.* to be seated on the right of (the player).

sit up *vb.* (*adv.*) **1.** to raise (oneself or another) from a recumbent to an upright or alert sitting posture. **2.** (*intr.*) to remain out of bed and awake, esp. until a late hour. **3.** (*intr.*) *Informal.* to become suddenly interested or alert: *devaluation of the dollar made the money market sit up.*

sit-up *n.* a physical exercise in which the body is brought into a sitting position from one lying on the back.

situs ('saɪtəs) *n., pl.* **-tus.** position or location, esp. the usual or right position of an organ or part of the body. [C18: from Latin: site, situation, position]

sitz bath (sɪts, zɪts) *n.* a bath in which the buttocks and hips are immersed in hot water, esp. for therapeutic effects, as after perineal or pelvic surgery. [half translation of German *Sitzbad*, from *Sitz* SEAT + *Bad* BATH]

sitzkrieg ('sɪtsˌkriːg, 'zɪts-) *n.* a period during a war in which both sides change positions very slowly or not at all. [C20: from German, from *sitzen* to sit + *Krieg* war]

sitzmark ('sɪtsˌmɑːk, 'zɪts-) *n. Skiing.* a depression in the snow where a skier has fallen. [German, literally: seat mark]

SI unit *n.* any of the units adopted for international use under the Système International d'Unités, now employed for all scientific and most technical purposes. There are seven fundamental units: the metre, kilogram, second, ampere, kelvin, candela, and mole; and two supplementary units: the radian and the steradian. All other units are derived by multiplication or division of these units without the use of numerical factors.

Siva ('siːvə, 'sɪvə) *or* **Shiva** *n. Hinduism.* the destroyer, one of the three chief divinities of the later Hindu pantheon, the other two being Brahma and Vishnu. Siva is also the god presiding over personal destinies. [from Sanskrit *Śiva*, literally: the auspicious (one)] —'**Sivaˌism** *n.* —'**Sivaist** *n.* —ˌ**Siva'istic** *adj.*

Sivan (siː'vɑːn) *n.* (in the Jewish calendar) the third month of the year according to biblical reckoning and the ninth month of the civil year, usually falling within May and June. [from Hebrew]

siwash ('saɪwɒʃ) *n.* **1.** another name for **Cowichan sweater.** ~*vb.* **2.** (*intr.*) (in the Pacific Northwest) to camp out with only natural shelter. [see SIWASH]

Siwash ('saɪwɒʃ) (*sometimes not cap.*) *Slang, derogatory.* (in the Pacific Northwest) ~*n.* **1.** a North American Indian. ~*adj.* **2.** of, characteristic of, or relating to Indians. **3.** worthless, stingy, or bad: *he's siwash.* [C19: from Chinook Jargon, from French *sauvage* SAVAGE]

six (sɪks) *n.* **1.** the cardinal number that is the sum of five and one. See also **number** (sense 1). **2.** a numeral, 6, VI, etc., representing this number. **3.** something representing, represented by, or consisting of six units, such as a playing card with six symbols on it. **4.** Also called: **six o'clock.** six hours after noon or midnight. **5.** Also called: **sixer.** *Cricket.* **a.** a stroke in which the ball crosses the boundary without bouncing. **b.** the six runs scored for such a stroke. **6.** a division of a Brownie Guide or Cub Scout pack. **7. at sixes and sevens. a.** in disagreement. **b.** in a state of confusion. **8. knock (someone) for six.** *Informal.* to upset or overwhelm (someone) completely; stun. **9. six of one and half a dozen of the other.** Also: **six and two threes.** a situation in which the alternatives are considered equivalent. ~*determiner.* **10. a.** amounting to six: *six nations.* **b.** (*as pronoun*): *set the table for six.* ~Related prefixes: **hexa-, sex-.** [Old English *siex*; related to Old Norse *sex*, Gothic *saihs*, Old High German *sehs*, Latin *sex*, Greek *hex*, Sanskrit *sastha*]

sixain ('sɪkseɪn) *n.* a stanza or poem of six lines. [from French]

six-eight time *n. Music.* a form of compound duple time in which there are six quaver beats to the bar, indicated by the time signature $^6_8$. Often shortened to **six-eight.**

sixer ('sɪksə) *n.* a leader of a Brownie Guide or Cub Scout six.

sixfold ('sɪksˌfəʊld) *adj.* **1.** equal to or having six times as many or as much. **2.** composed of six parts. ~*adv.* **3.** by or up to six times as many or as much.

six-footer *n.* a person who is at least six feet tall.

six-gun *n. U.S. informal.* another word for **six-shooter.**

sixmo ('sɪksməʊ) *n., pl.* **-mos. 1.** Also called: **sexto.** a book size resulting from folding a sheet of paper into six leaves or twelve pages, each one sixth the size of the sheet. Often written: **6mo, 6°. 2.** a book of this size.

six o'clock swill *n. Austral. and N.Z. informal.* a period of heavy drinking, esp. during the years when hotels had to close their bars at 6.00 p.m.

six-pack *n. Informal.* a package containing six units, esp. six cans of beer.

sixpence ('sɪkspəns) *n.* a small British cupronickel coin with a face value of six pennies, worth 2½ (new) pence, not minted since 1970.

sixpenny ('sɪkspənɪ) *adj.* (*prenominal*) (of a nail) two inches in length.

six-shooter *n. U.S. informal.* a revolver with six chambers. Also called: **six-gun.**

sixte (sɪkst) *n.* the sixth of eight basic positions from which a parry or attack can be made in fencing. [from French: (the) sixth (parrying position), from Latin *sextus* sixth]

sixteen ('sɪks'tiːn) *n.* **1.** the cardinal number that is the sum of ten and six. See also **number** (sense 1). **2.** a numeral, 16, XVI, etc., representing this number. **3.** *Music.* the numeral 16 used as the lower figure of a time signature to indicate that the beat is measured in semiquavers. **4.** something represented by, representing, or consisting of 16 units. ~*determiner.* **5. a.** amounting to sixteen: *sixteen tons.* **b.** (*as pronoun*): *sixteen are known to the police.*

sixteenmo ('sɪks'tiːnməʊ) *n., pl.* **-mos. 1.** Also called: **sextodecimo.** a book size resulting from folding a sheet of paper into 16 leaves or 32 pages, each one sixteenth the size of the sheet. Often written: **16mo, 16°. 2.** a book of this size.

sixteenth ('sɪks'tiːnθ) *adj.* **1.** (*usually prenominal*) **a.** coming after the fifteenth in numbering or counting order, position, time, etc.; being the ordinal number of *sixteen*: often written 16th. **b.** (*as n.*): *the sixteenth of the month.* ~*n.* **2. a.** one of 16 equal or nearly equal parts of something. **b.** (*as modifier*): *a sixteenth part.* **3.** the fraction that is equal to one divided by 16 (1/16).

sixteenth note *n.* the usual U.S. and Canadian name for **semiquaver.**

sixth (sɪksθ) *adj.* **1.** (*usually prenominal*) **a.** coming after the fifth and before the seventh in numbering or counting order, position, time, etc.; being the ordinal number of *six*: often written 6th. **b.** (*as n.*): *the sixth to go.* ~*n.* **2. a.** one of six equal or nearly equal parts of an object, quantity, measurement, etc. **b.** (*as modifier*): *a sixth part.* **3.** the fraction equal to one divided by six (1/6). **4.** *Music.* **a.** the interval between one note and another note six notes away from it counting inclusively along the diatonic scale. **b.** one of two notes constituting such an interval in relation to the other. See also **major** (sense 13), **minor** (sense 4), **interval** (sense 5). **c.** short for **sixth chord.** ~*adv.* **5.** Also: **sixthly.** after the fifth person, position, etc. ~*sentence connector.* **6.** Also: **sixthly.** as the sixth point: linking what follows to the previous statements.

sixth chord *n.* (in classical harmony) the first inversion of the triad, in which the note next above the root appears in the bass. See also **added sixth.**

sixth form *n.* (in England and Wales) the most senior class in a secondary school to which pupils, usually above the legal leaving age, may proceed to take A levels, retake GCSEs, etc. —'**sixthˌformer** *n.*

sixth-form college *n.* (in Britain) a college offering A-level and other courses to pupils over sixteen from local schools, esp. from those that do not have sixth forms.

sixth sense *n.* any supposed sense or means of perception, such as intuition or clairvoyance, other than the five senses of sight, hearing, touch, taste, and smell.

sixth year *n.* (in Scotland) the most senior class in a secondary school to which pupils, usually above the legal leaving age, may proceed to take sixth-year studies, retake or take additional Highers, etc.

sixtieth ('sɪkstɪəθ) *adj.* **1.** (*usually prenominal*) **a.** being the ordinal number of *sixty* in numbering or counting order, position, time, etc.: often written 60th. **b.** (*as n.*): *the sixtieth in a row.* ~*n.* **2. a.** one of 60 approximately equal parts of something. **b.**

(as modifier): a sixtieth part. **3.** the fraction equal to one divided by 60 (1/60).

sixty ('sɪkstɪ) *n., pl.* **-ties.** **1.** the cardinal number that is the product of ten and six. See also **number** (sense 1). **2.** a numeral, 60, LX, etc., representing sixty. **3.** something represented by, representing, or consisting of 60 units. ~*determiner.* **4. a.** amounting to sixty: *sixty soldiers.* **b.** *(as pronoun): sixty are dead.* [Old English *sixtig*]

sixty-fourmo (ˌsɪkstɪ'fɔːməʊ) *n., pl.* **-mos.** **1.** a book size resulting from folding a sheet of paper into 64 leaves or 128 pages, each one sixty-fourth the size of the sheet. Often written **64mo, 64°.** **2.** a book of this size.

sixty-fourth note *n.* the usual U.S. and Canadian name for **hemidemisemiquaver.**

sixty-four thousand dollar question *n.* a crucial question or issue. [C20: an elaboration of the earlier *sixty-four dollar question,* so called from the top prize on the U.S. radio show *Take It or Leave It* (1941–48)]

sixty-nine *n.* another term for **soixante-neuf.**

six-yard line *n. Soccer.* the line marking the limits of the goal area.

sizable *or* **sizeable** ('saɪzəbᵊl) *adj.* quite large. —'**sizableness** *or* '**sizeableness** *n.* —'**sizably** *or* '**sizeably** *adv.*

sizar ('saɪzə) *n. Brit.* (at Peterhouse, Cambridge, and Trinity College, Dublin) an undergraduate receiving a maintenance grant from the college. [C16: from earlier *sizer,* from SIZE[1] (meaning "an allowance of food, etc.")] —'**sizar,ship** *n.*

size[1] (saɪz) *n.* **1.** the dimensions, proportions, amount, or extent of something. **2.** large or great dimensions, etc. **3.** one of a series of graduated measurements, as of clothing: *she takes size 4 shoes.* **4.** *Informal.* state of affairs as summarized: *he's bankrupt, that's the size of it.* ~*vb.* **5.** to sort according to size. **6.** *(tr.)* to make or cut to a particular size or sizes. [C13: from Old French *sise,* shortened from *assise* ASSIZE] —'**sizer** *n.*

size[2] (saɪz) *n.* **1.** Also called: **sizing.** a thin gelatinous mixture, made from glue, clay, or wax, that is used as a sealer or filler on paper, cloth, or plaster surfaces. ~*vb.* **2.** *(tr.)* to treat or coat (a surface) with size. [C15: perhaps from Old French *sise;* see SIZE[1]] —'**sizy** *adj.*

sized (saɪzd) *adj.* of a specified size: *medium-sized.*

size up *vb. (adv.)* **1.** *(tr.)* to make an assessment of (a person, problem, etc.). **2.** to conform to or make so as to conform to certain specifications of dimension.

size-weight illusion *n.* a standard sense illusion that a small object is heavier than a large object of the same weight.

sizzle ('sɪzᵊl) *vb. (intr.)* **1.** to make the hissing sound characteristic of frying fat. **2.** *Informal.* to be very hot. **3.** *Informal.* to be very angry. ~*n.* **4.** a hissing sound. [C17: of imitative origin. Compare *siss* (now dialect) to hiss, West Frisian *size, siizje.* See also FIZZ and FIZZLE] —'**sizzling** *adj.*

sizzler ('sɪzlə) *n.* **1.** something that sizzles. **2.** *Informal.* a very hot day.

SJ *abbrev. for* Society of Jesus.

SJA *abbrev. for* Saint John's Ambulance (Brigade or Association).

sjambok ('ʃæmbʌk, -bɒk) (in South Africa) ~*n.* **1.** a heavy whip of rhinoceros or hippopotamus hide. ~*vb.* **-boks, -bokking, -bokked.** **2.** *(tr.)* to strike or beat with such a whip. [C19: from Afrikaans, from Malay *samboq, chamboq,* from Urdu *chābuk*]

SJC (in the U.S.) *abbrev. for* Supreme Judicial Court.

SJD *abbrev. for* Doctor of Juridical Science. [from Latin *Scientiae Juridicae Doctor*]

sk *abbrev. for* sack.

SK *abbrev. for* Saskatchewan.

ska (skɑː) *n.* a type of West Indian pop music of the 1960s, accented on the second and fourth beats of a four-beat bar.

skag (skæg) *n.* a variant spelling of **scag**[1].

skald *or* **scald** (skɔːld) *n.* (in ancient Scandinavia) a bard or minstrel. [from Old Norse, of unknown origin] —'**skaldic** *or* '**scaldic** *adj.*

skank (skæŋk) *n.* **1.** a fast dance to reggae music. ~*vb. (intr.)* **2.** to perform this dance.

skat (skæt) *n.* a three-handed card game using 32 cards, popular in German-speaking communities. [C19: from German, from Italian *scarto* played cards, from *scartare* to discard, from *s-* EX-[1] + *carta,* from Latin *charta* CARD[1]]

skate[1] (skeɪt) *n.* **1.** See **roller skate, ice skate.** **2.** the steel blade or runner of an ice skate. **3.** such a blade fitted with straps for fastening to a shoe. **4.** a current collector on an electric railway train that collects its current from a third rail. Compare **bow collector.** **5. get one's skates on.** to hurry. ~*vb. (intr.)* **6.** to glide swiftly on skates. **7.** to slide smoothly over a surface. **8. skate on thin ice.** to place oneself in a dangerous or delicate situation. [C17: via Dutch from Old French *éschasse* stilt, probably of Germanic origin]

skate[2] (skeɪt) *n., pl.* **skate** *or* **skates.** any large ray of the family *Rajidae,* of temperate and tropical seas, having flat pectoral fins continuous with the head, two dorsal fins, a short spineless tail, and a long snout. [C14: from Old Norse *skata*]

skate[3] (skeɪt) *n. U.S. slang.* a person; fellow. [from Scottish and northern English dialect *skate,* a derogatory term of uncertain origin]

skateboard ('skeɪtˌbɔːd) *n.* **1.** a plank mounted on roller-skate wheels, usually ridden while standing up. ~*vb.* **2.** *(intr.)* to ride on a skateboard. —'**skate,boarder** *n.* —'**skate,boarding** *n.*

skate over *vb. (intr., prep.)* **1.** to cross on or as if on skates. **2.** to avoid dealing with (a matter) fully.

skater ('skeɪtə) *n.* **1.** a person who skates. **2.** See **pond-skater.**

skatole ('skætəʊl) *n.* a white or brownish crystalline solid with a strong faecal odour, found in faeces, beetroot, and coal tar; B-methylindole. Formula: C_9H_9N. [C19: from Greek *skat-,* stem of *skōr* excrement + -OLE[1]]

skean (skiːn) *n.* a kind of double-edged dagger formerly used in Ireland and Scotland. [from Irish and Scottish Gaelic *scian*]

skean-dhu ('skiːən'duː, 'skiːn-) *n. Scot.* a variant of **sgian-dhu.**

skedaddle (skɪ'dædᵊl) *Informal.* ~*vb.* **1.** *(intr.)* to run off hastily. ~*n.* **2.** a hasty retreat. [C19: of unknown origin]

skeet (skiːt) *n.* a form of clay-pigeon shooting in which targets are hurled from two traps at varying speeds and angles. Also called: **skeet shooting.** [C20: changed from Old Norse *skeyti* a thrown object, from *skjōta* to shoot]

skeg (skɛg) *n. Nautical.* **1.** a reinforcing brace between the after end of a keel and the rudderpost. **2.** a support at the bottom of a rudder. **3.** a projection from the forefoot of a vessel for towing paravanes. **4.** any short keel-like projection at the stern of a boat. **5.** *Austral.* a rear fin on the underside of a surfboard. [C16: of Scandinavian origin; compare Icelandic *skegg* cutwater]

skein (skeɪn) *n.* **1.** a length of yarn, etc., wound in a long coil. **2.** something resembling this, such as a lock of hair. **3.** a flock of geese flying. Compare **gaggle** (sense 2). [C15: from Old French *escaigne,* of unknown origin]

skeleton ('skɛlɪtən) *n.* **1.** a hard framework consisting of inorganic material that supports and protects the soft parts of an animal's body and provides attachment for muscles: may be internal, as in vertebrates (see **endoskeleton**), or external, as in arthropods (see **exoskeleton**). **2.** *Informal.* a very thin emaciated person or animal. **3.** the essential framework of any structure, such as a building or leaf, that supports or determines the shape of the rest of the structure. **4.** an outline consisting of bare essentials: *the skeleton of a novel.* **5.** *(modifier)* reduced to a minimum: *a skeleton staff.* **6. skeleton in the cupboard** *or (U.S. and Canadian)* **closet.** a scandalous fact or event in the past that is kept secret. [C16: via New Latin from Greek: something desiccated, from *skellein* to dry up] —'**skeletal** *adj.* —'**skeletally** *adv.* —'**skeleton-,like** *adj.*

skeletonize *or* **skeletonise** ('skɛlɪtəˌnaɪz) *vb. (tr.)* **1.** to reduce to a minimum framework, number, or outline. **2.** to create the essential framework of.

skeleton key *n.* a key with the serrated edge filed down so that it can open numerous locks. Also called: **passkey.** [C19: so called because it has been reduced to its essential parts]

skelf (skɛlf) *n. Scot. and northern English dialect.* **1.** a splinter of wood, esp. when embedded accidentally in the skin. **2.** a thin or diminutive person. [from Scottish; see SHELF]

skellum ('skɛləm) *n. Archaic and dialect.* a rogue. [C17: via Dutch from Old High German *skelmo* devil]

skelly[1] ('skɛlɪ) *n., pl.* **-lies.** a whitefish, *Coregonus stigmaticus,* of certain lakes in the Lake District. [C18: perhaps from dialect *skell* a shell or scale, and so called because of its large scales]

skelly[2] ('skɛlɪ) *Scot. and northern English dialect.* ~*vb.* **-lies, -lying, -lied.** *(intr.)* **1.** to look sideways or squint. ~*n., pl.* **-lies.** **2.** a quick look; glance. ~*adj.* **3.** Also: **skelly-eyed.** cross-eyed. [probably from Old Norse, from *skjalgr* wry; related to Old English *sceolh* a squint]

skelp[1] (skɛlp) *Dialect.* ~*vb.* **1.** *(tr.)* to slap. ~*n.* **2.** a slap. [C15: probably of imitative origin]

skelp[2] (skɛlp) *n.* sheet or plate metal that has been curved and welded to form a tube. [C19: perhaps from Scottish Gaelic *sgealb* thin strip of wood]

sken (skɛn) *vb.* **skens, skenning, skenned.** *(intr.) Northern English dialect.* to squint or stare. [of obscure origin]

skep (skɛp) *n.* **1.** a beehive, esp. one constructed of straw. **2.** *Now chiefly dialect.* a large basket of wickerwork or straw. [Old English *sceppe,* from Old Norse *skeppa* bushel; related to Old High German *sceffil* bushel]

skeptic ('skɛptɪk) *n., adj.* an archaic, and the usual U.S., spelling of **sceptic.** —'**skeptical** *adj.* —'**skeptically** *adv.* —'**skepticalness** *n.* —'**skepticism** *n.*

skerrick ('skɛrɪk) *n. U.S., Austral., and N.Z. informal.* a small fragment or amount (esp. in the phrase **not a skerrick**). [C20: northern English dialect, probably of Scandinavian origin]

skerry ('skɛrɪ) *n., pl.* **-ries.** *Chiefly Scot.* **1.** a small rocky island. **2.** a reef. [C17: Orkney dialect, from Old Norse *sker* SCAR[2]]

sket (skɛt) *vb.* **skets, sketting, sketted.** *(tr.) South Wales dialect.* **1.** to splash (water). **2.** to splash (someone with water). [perhaps from Old Norse *skjóta* to shoot]

sketch (skɛtʃ) *n.* **1.** a rapid drawing or painting, often a study for subsequent elaboration. **2.** a brief usually descriptive and informal essay or other literary composition. **3.** a short play, often comic, forming part of a revue. **4.** a short evocative piece of instrumental music, esp. for piano. **5.** any brief outline. ~*vb.* **6.** to make a rough drawing (of). **7.** *(tr.; often foll. by out)* to make a brief description of. [C17: from Dutch *schets,* via Italian from Latin *schedius* hastily made, from Greek *skhedios* unprepared] —'**sketchable** *adj.* —'**sketcher** *n.*

sketchbook ('skɛtʃˌbʊk) *n.* **1.** a book of plain paper containing sketches or for making sketches in. **2.** a book of literary sketches.

sketchy ('skɛtʃɪ) *adj.* **sketchier, sketchiest. 1.** characteristic of a sketch; existing only in outline. **2.** superficial or slight. —'**sketchily** *adv.* —'**sketchiness** *n.*

skew (skjuː) *adj.* **1.** placed in or turning into an oblique position or course. **2.** *Machinery.* having a component that is at an angle to the main axis of an assembly or is in some other way asymmetrical: *a skew bevel gear.* **3.** *Maths.* **a.** composed of or being elements that are neither parallel nor intersecting as, for example, two lines not lying in the same plane in a three-dimensional space. **b.** (of a curve) not lying in a plane. **4.** (of a statistical distribution) not having equal probabilities above and below the mean; non-normal. **5.** distorted or biased. ~*n.* **6.** an oblique, slanting, or indirect course or position. **7.** *Psychol.* the system of relationships in a family in which one parent is extremely dominating while the other parent tends to be meekly compliant. ~*vb.* **8.** to take or cause to take an oblique course or direction. **9.** (*intr.*) to look sideways; squint. **10.** (*tr.*) to place at an angle. **11.** (*tr.*) to distort or bias. [C14: from Old Norman French *escuer* to shun, of Germanic origin; compare Middle Dutch *schuwen* to avoid]

skew arch *n.* an arch or vault, esp. one used in a bridge or tunnel, that is set at an oblique angle to the span.

skewback ('skjuːˌbæk) *n.* **1.** the sloping surface on both sides of a segmental arch that takes the thrust. **2.** one or more stones that provide such a surface. —'**skewˌbacked** *adj.*

skewbald ('skjuːˌbɔːld) *adj.* **1.** marked or spotted in white and any colour except black. ~*n.* **2.** a horse with this marking. [C17: see SKEW, PIEBALD]

skewer ('skjʊə) *n.* **1.** a long pin for holding meat in position while being cooked, etc. **2.** a similar pin having some other function. **3.** *Chess.* a tactical manoeuvre in which an attacked man is made to move and expose another man to capture. ~*vb.* **4.** (*tr.*) to drive a skewer through or fasten with a skewer. [C17: probably from dialect *skiver*]

skewness ('skjuːnɪs) *n.* **1.** the quality or condition of being skew. **2.** *Statistics.* a measure of the symmetry of a distribution around its mean, esp. the statistic $B_1 = m_3/(m_2)^{3/2}$, where m_2 and m_3 are respectively the second and third moments of the distribution around the mean. In a normal distribution, $B_1 = 0$. Compare **kurtosis.**

skew symmetry *n.* symmetry of top left with bottom right, and top right with bottom left.

skewwhiff ('skjuː'wɪf) *adj.* (*postpositive*) *Brit. informal.* not straight; askew. [C18: probably influenced by ASKEW]

ski (skiː) *n., pl.* **skis** *or* **ski. 1. a.** one of a pair of wood, metal, or plastic runners that are used for gliding over snow. Skis are commonly attached to shoes for sport, but may also be used as landing gear for aircraft, etc. **b.** (*as modifier*): *a ski boot.* **2.** a water-ski. ~*vb.* **skis, skiing; skied** *or* **ski'd. 3.** (*intr.*) to travel on skis. [C19: from Norwegian, from Old Norse *skíth* snowshoes; related to Old English *scīd* piece of split wood] —'**skiable** *adj.* —'**skier** *n.* —'**skiing** *n.*

skiamachy (skaɪ'æməkɪ) *n., pl.* **-chies.** a variant of **sciamachy.**

skiascope ('skaɪəˌskəʊp) *n. Med.* a medical instrument for examining the eye to detect errors of refraction. Also called: **retinoscope.** See also **retinoscopy.** [C19: from Greek *skia* a shadow + -SCOPE]

skiascopy (skaɪ'æskəpɪ) *n. Med.* another name for **retinoscopy.**

skibob ('skiːbɒb) *n.* a vehicle made of two short skis, the forward one having a steering handle and the rear one supporting a low seat, for gliding down snow slopes. [C20: from SKI + BOB[2]. See BOBSLEIGH] —'**skibobber** *n.* —'**skibobbing** *n.*

skid (skɪd) *vb.* **skids, skidding, skidded. 1.** to cause (a vehicle) to slide sideways or (of a vehicle) to slide sideways while in motion, esp. out of control. **2.** (*intr.*) to slide without revolving, as the wheel of a moving vehicle after sudden braking. **3.** (*tr.*) *U.S. and Canadian.* to put or haul on a skid, esp. along a special track. **4.** to cause (an aircraft) to slide sideways away from the centre of a turn when insufficiently banked or (of an aircraft) to slide in this manner. ~*n.* **5.** an instance of sliding, esp. sideways. **6.** *Chiefly U.S. and Canadian.* one of the logs forming a skidway. **7.** a support on which heavy objects may be stored and moved short distances by sliding. **8.** a shoe or drag used to apply pressure to the metal rim of a wheel to act as a brake. [C17: perhaps of Scandinavian origin; compare SKI] —'**skiddy** *adj.*

skidlid ('skɪdˌlɪd) *n.* a slang word for **crash helmet.**

skidpan ('skɪdˌpæn) *n. Chiefly Brit.* an area made slippery so that vehicle drivers can practise controlling skids.

skidproof ('skɪdˌpruːf) *adj.* (of a road surface, tyre, etc.) preventing or resistant to skidding.

skid road *n.* (in the U.S. and Canada) **1.** a track made of a set of logs laid transversely on which freshly cut timber can be hauled. **2. a.** (in the West) the part of a town frequented by loggers. **b.** another term for **skid row.**

skid row (rəʊ) *or* **skid road** *n. Slang, chiefly U.S. and Canadian.* a dilapidated section of a city inhabited by vagrants, etc.

skidway ('skɪdˌweɪ) *n. Chiefly U.S. and Canadian.* **1.** a platform on which logs ready for sawing are piled. **2.** a track made of logs for rolling objects along.

skied[1] (skaɪd) *vb.* the past tense and past participle of **sky.**

skied[2] (skiːd) *vb.* a past tense and past participle of **ski.**

skiff (skɪf) *n.* any of various small boats propelled by oars, sail, or motor. [C18: from French *esquif,* from Old Italian *schifo* a boat, of Germanic origin; related to Old High German *schif* SHIP]

skiffle[1] ('skɪfᵊl) *n.* a style of popular music of the 1950s, played chiefly on guitars and improvised percussion instruments. [C20: of unknown origin]

skiffle[2] ('skɪfᵊl) *n. Ulster dialect.* a drizzle: *a skiffle of rain.* [from Scottish *skiff,* from *skiff* to move lightly, probably changed from *skift,* from Old Norse *skipta* SHIFT]

skijoring (skiː'dʒɔːrɪŋ) *n.* a sport in which a skier is pulled over snow or ice, usually by a horse. [Norwegian *skikjöring,* literally: ski-driving] —**ski'jorer** *n.*

ski jump *n.* **1.** a high ramp overhanging a slope from which skiers compete to make the longest jump. ~*vb.* **ski-jump. 2.** (*intr.*) to perform a ski jump. —**ski jumper** *n.*

skilful *or U.S.* **skillful** ('skɪlfʊl) *adj.* **1.** possessing or displaying accomplishment or skill. **2.** involving or requiring accomplishment or skill. —'**skilfully** *or U.S.* '**skillfully** *adv.* —'**skilfulness** *or U.S.* '**skillfulness** *n.*

ski lift *n.* any of various devices for carrying skiers up a slope, such as a chair lift.

skill (skɪl) *n.* **1.** special ability in a task, sport, etc., esp. ability acquired by training. **2.** something, esp. a trade or technique, requiring special training or manual proficiency. **3.** *Obsolete.* understanding. [C12: from Old Norse *skil* distinction; related to Middle Low German *schēle,* Middle Dutch *geschil* difference] —'**skill-less** *or* '**skilless** *adj.*

skilled (skɪld) *adj.* **1.** possessing or demonstrating accomplishment, skill, or special training. **2.** (*prenominal*) involving skill or special training: *a skilled job.*

skillet ('skɪlɪt) *n.* **1.** a small frying pan. **2.** *Chiefly Brit.* a saucepan. [C15: probably from *skele* bucket, of Scandinavian origin; related to Old Norse *skjōla* bucket]

skilling ('skɪlɪŋ) *n.* a former Scandinavian coin of low denomination. [C18: from Danish and Swedish; see SHILLING]

skillion ('skɪlɪən) *n. Austral.* **a.** a part of a building having a lower, esp. sloping, roof; lean-to. **b.** (*as modifier*): *a skillion roof.* [C19: from English dialect *skilling* outhouse]

skilly ('skɪlɪ) *n. Chiefly Brit.* a thin soup or gruel. [C19: shortened from *skilligallee,* probably a fanciful formation]

Skilsaw ('skɪlˌsɔː) *n. Trademark.* a portable electric saw.

skim (skɪm) *vb.* **skims, skimming, skimmed. 1.** (*tr.*) to remove floating material from the surface of (a liquid), as with a spoon: *to skim milk.* **2.** to glide smoothly or lightly over (a surface). **3.** (*tr.*) to throw (something) in a path over a surface, so as to bounce or ricochet: *to skim stones over water.* **4.** (when *intr.*, usually foll. by *through*) to read (a book) in a superficial or cursory manner. **5.** to cover (a liquid) with a thin layer or (of liquid) to become coated in this way, as with ice, scum, etc. ~*n.* **6.** the act or process of skimming. **7.** material skimmed off a liquid, esp. off milk. **8.** the liquid left after skimming. **9.** any thin layer covering a surface. ~See also **skim off.** [C15 *skimmen,* probably from *scumen* to skim; see SCUM]

skimble-scamble ('skɪmbᵊl'skæmbᵊl) *Archaic.* ~*adj.* **1.** rambling; confused. ~*n.* **2.** meaningless discourse. [C16: whimsical formation based on dialect *scamble* to struggle]

skimmer ('skɪmə) *n.* **1.** a person or thing that skims. **2.** any of several mainly tropical coastal aquatic birds of the genus *Rhynchops,* having long narrow wings and a bill with an elongated lower mandible for skimming food from the surface of the water: family *Rynchopidae,* order *Charadriiformes.* **3.** a flat perforated spoon used for skimming fat from liquids.

skimmia ('skɪmɪə) *n.* any rutaceous shrub of the S and SE Asian genus *Skimmia,* grown for their ornamental red berries and evergreen foliage. [C18: New Latin from Japanese (*mijama-*) *shikimi,* a native name of the plant]

skim milk *n.* milk from which the cream has been removed. Also called: **skimmed milk.** Compare **whole milk.**

skimmings ('skɪmɪŋz) *pl. n.* **1.** material that is skimmed off a liquid. **2.** the froth containing concentrated ore removed during a flotation process. **3.** slag, scum, or impurities removed from molten metals.

skim off *vb.* (*tr., adv.*) to take the best part of: *the teacher skimmed off the able pupils for his class.*

skimp (skɪmp) *vb.* **1.** to be extremely sparing or supply (someone) sparingly; stint. **2.** to perform (work, etc.) carelessly, hastily, or with inadequate materials. [C17: perhaps a combination of SCANT and SCRIMP]

skimpy ('skɪmpɪ) *adj.* **skimpier, skimpiest. 1.** (of clothes, etc.) made of too little material; scanty. **2.** excessively thrifty; mean; stingy. —'**skimpily** *adv.* —'**skimpiness** *n.*

skin (skɪn) *n.* **1. a.** the tissue forming the outer covering of the vertebrate body: it consists of two layers (see **dermis, epidermis**), the outermost of which may be covered with hair, scales, feathers, etc. It is mainly protective and sensory in function. **b.** (*as modifier*): *a skin disease.* **2.** a person's complexion: *a fair skin.* **3.** any similar covering in a plant or lower animal. **4.** any coating or film, such as one that forms on the surface of a liquid. **5.** unsplit leather made from the outer covering of various mammals, reptiles, etc. Compare **hide**[2] (sense 1). **6.** the outer covering of a fur-bearing animal, dressed and finished with the hair on. **7.** a container made from animal skin. **8.** the outer covering surface of a vessel, rocket, etc. 9. a person's skin regarded as his life: *to save one's skin.* 10. (*often pl.*) *Informal.* (in jazz or pop use) a drum. 11. *Informal.* short for **skinhead.** 12. *Slang.* a cigarette paper used for rolling a cannabis cigarette. 13. *Anglo-Irish slang.* a person; sort: *he's a good old skin.* 14. **by the skin of one's teeth.** by a narrow margin; only just. 15. **get under one's skin.** *Informal.* to irritate one. 16. **jump out of one's skin.** to be very startled. 17. **no skin off one's nose.** *Informal.* not a matter that affects one adversely. 18. **thick** (*or* **thin**) **skin.** an insensitive (*or* sensitive) nature. ~*vb.* **skins, skinning, skinned.** 19. (*tr.*) to remove the outer covering from (fruit, etc.). 20. (*tr.*) to scrape a small piece of skin from (a part of oneself) in falling, etc.: *he skinned his knee.* 21. (often foll. by *over*) to cover (something) with skin or a skinlike substance or (of something) to become covered in this way. 22. (*tr.*) *Slang.* to strip of money; swindle. ~*adj.* 23. relating to or for the skin: *skin cream.* 24. *Slang, chiefly U.S.* involving or depicting nudity: *skin magazines.* [Old English *scinn,* from Old Norse *skinn*] —'**skinless** *adj.* —'**skin,like** *adj.*

skin-deep *adj.* 1. superficial; shallow. ~*adv.* 2. superficially.

skin diving *n.* the sport or activity of underwater swimming using breathing apparatus. —'**skin-,diver** *n.*

skin effect *n.* the tendency of alternating current to concentrate in the surface layer of a conductor, esp. at high frequencies, thus increasing its effective resistance.

skin flick *n. Slang.* a film containing much nudity and explicit sex for sensational purposes.

skinflint ('skɪn,flɪnt) *n.* an ungenerous or niggardly person; miser. [C18: referring to a person so avaricious that he would skin (swindle) a flint] —'**skin,flinty** *adj.*

skin food *n.* a cosmetic cream for keeping the skin in good condition.

skin friction *n.* the friction acting on a solid body when it is moving through a fluid.

skinful ('skɪn,fʊl) *n., pl.* **-fuls.** *Slang.* sufficient alcoholic drink to make one drunk (esp. in the phrase **have a skinful**).

skin game *n. Slang.* a swindling trick.

skin graft *n.* a piece of skin removed from one part of the body and surgically grafted at the site of a severe burn or similar injury.

skinhead ('skɪn,hɛd) *n. Brit.* one of a gang of White boys characterized by closely cropped hair, heavy boots, and braces.

skink (skɪŋk) *n.* any lizard of the family *Scincidae,* commonest in tropical Africa and Asia, having reduced limbs and an elongated body covered with smooth scales. [C16: from Latin *scincus* a lizard, from Greek *skinkos*]

skinned (skɪnd) *adj.* 1. stripped of the skin. 2. **a.** having a skin as specified. **b.** (*in combination*): *thick-skinned.* 3. **keep one's eyes skinned** (*or* **peeled**). to watch carefully (for).

skinner ('skɪnə) *n.* a person who prepares or deals in animal skins.

Skinner box ('skɪnə) *n.* a device for studying the learning behaviour of animals, esp. rats and pigeons, consisting of a box in which the animal can move a lever to obtain a reward, such as a food pellet, or a punishment, such as an electric shock. [C20: named after B. F. *Skinner* (1904–90), U.S. behavioural psychologist]

skinny ('skɪnɪ) *adj.* **-nier, -niest.** 1. lacking in flesh; thin. 2. consisting of or resembling skin. —'**skinniness** *n.*

skinny-dip *vb.* **-dips, -dipping, -dipped.** (*intr.*) to swim in the nude. —**skinny dipping** *n.*

skin-pop *Slang.* ~*n.* 1. the subcutaneous or intramuscular injection of a narcotic. ~*vb.* **-pops, -popping, -popped.** 2. (*intr.*) to take drugs in such a way.

skint (skɪnt) *adj.* (*usually postpositive*) *Brit. slang.* without money. [variant of *skinned,* past participle of SKIN]

skin test *n. Med.* any test to determine immunity to a disease or hypersensitivity by introducing a small amount of the test substance beneath the skin or rubbing it into a fresh scratch. See **scratch test.**

skintight ('skɪn'taɪt) *adj.* (of garments) fitting tightly over the body; clinging.

skip[1] (skɪp) *vb.* **skips, skipping, skipped.** 1. (when *intr.,* often foll. by *over, along, into,* etc.) to spring or move lightly, esp. to move by hopping from one foot to the other. 2. (*intr.*) to jump over a skipping-rope. 3. to cause (a stone, etc.) to bounce or skim over a surface or (of a stone) to move in this way. 4. to omit (intervening matter), as in passing from one part or subject to another: *he skipped a chapter of the book.* 5. (*intr.;* foll. by *through*) *Informal.* to read or deal with quickly or superficially: *he skipped through the accounts before dinner.* 6. **skip it!** *Informal.* it doesn't matter! 7. (*tr.*) *Informal.* to miss deliberately: *to skip school.* 8. (*tr.*) *Informal, chiefly U.S. and Canadian.* to leave (a place) in haste or secrecy: *to skip town.* ~*n.* 9. a skipping movement or gait. 10. the act of passing over or omitting. 11. *Music, U.S. and Canadian.* another word for **leap** (sense 10). ~See also **skip off.** [C13: probably of Scandinavian origin; related to Old Norse *skopa* to take a run, obsolete Swedish *skuppa* to skip]

skip[2] (skɪp) *n., vb.* **skips, skipping, skipped.** *Informal.* short for **skipper**[1].

skip[3] (skɪp) *n.* 1. a large open container for transporting building materials, etc. 2. a cage used as a lift in mines, etc. [C19: variant of SKEP]

skip[4] (skɪp) *n.* a college servant, esp. of Trinity College, Dublin. [C17: probably shortened from archaic *skip-kennel* a footman or lackey (from SKIP[1] + KENNEL[2])]

ski pants *pl. n.* trousers usually of stretch material and kept taut by a strap under the foot, worn for skiing or as a fashion garment.

skip distance *n.* the shortest distance between a transmitter and a receiver that will permit reception of radio waves of a specified frequency by one reflection from the ionosphere.

skipjack ('skɪp,dʒæk) *n., pl.* **-jack** *or* **-jacks.** 1. Also called: **skipjack tuna.** an important food fish, *Katsuwonus pelamis,* that has a striped abdomen and occurs in all tropical seas: family *Scombridae* (mackerels and tunas). 2. **black skipjack.** a small spotted tuna, *Euthynnus yaito,* of Indo-Pacific seas. 3. any of several other unrelated fishes, such as the alewife and bonito. 4. *Nautical.* an American sloop used for oystering and as a yacht. 5. another name for a **click beetle.** [C18: from SKIP[1] + JACK[1]]

skiplane ('skiː,pleɪn) *n.* an aircraft fitted with skis to enable it to land on and take off from snow.

skip off *vb.* (*intr., adv.*) *Brit. informal.* to leave work, school, etc., early or without authorization.

skipper[1] ('skɪpə) *n.* 1. the captain of any vessel. 2. the captain of an aircraft. 3. a manager or leader, as of a sporting team. ~*vb.* 4. to act as skipper (of). [C14: from Middle Low German, Middle Dutch *schipper* shipper]

skipper[2] ('skɪpə) *n.* 1. a person or thing that skips. 2. any small butterfly of the family *Hesperiidae,* having a hairy mothlike body and erratic darting flight. 3. another name for the **saury** (a fish).

skippet ('skɪpɪt) *n.* a small round box for preserving a document or seal. [C14: perhaps from *skeppe* SKEP]

skipping ('skɪpɪŋ) *n.* the act of jumping over a rope that is held and swung either by the person jumping or by two other people, as a game or for exercise.

skipping-rope *n. Brit.* a cord, usually having handles at each end, that is held in the hands and swung round and down so that the holder or others can jump over it.

skip-tooth saw *n.* a saw with alternate teeth absent.

skip zone *n.* a region surrounding a broadcasting station that cannot receive transmissions either directly or by reflection off the ionosphere.

skirl (skɜːl; *Scot.* skɪrl) *vb.* (*intr.*) 1. *Scot. and northern English dialect.* (esp. of bagpipes) to emit a shrill sound. 2. to play the bagpipes. ~*n.* 3. the sound of bagpipes. 4. a shrill sound. [C14: probably of Scandinavian origin; see SHRILL]

skirmish ('skɜːmɪʃ) *n.* 1. a minor short-lived military engagement. 2. any brisk clash or encounter, usually of a minor nature. ~*vb.* 3. (*intr.;* often foll. by *with*) to engage in a skirmish. [C14: from Old French *eskirmir,* of Germanic origin; related to Old High German *skirmen* to defend] —'**skirmisher** *n.*

skirr (skɜː) *vb.* 1. (*intr.;* usually foll. by *off, away,* etc.) to move, run, or fly rapidly. 2. (*tr.*) *Archaic or literary.* to move rapidly over (an area, etc.), esp. in order to find or apprehend. ~*n.* 3. a whirring or grating sound, as of the wings of birds in flight. [C16: variant of SCOUR[2]]

skirret ('skɪrɪt) *n.* an umbelliferous Old World plant, *Sium sisarum,* cultivated in parts of Europe for its edible tuberous roots. [C14 *skirwhite,* perhaps from obsolete *skir* bright (see SHEER[1]) + WHITE]

skirt (skɜːt) *n.* 1. a garment hanging from the waist, worn chiefly by women and girls. 2. the part of a dress below the waist. 3. Also called: **apron.** a frieze or circular flap, as round the base of a hovercraft. 4. the flaps on a saddle that protect a rider's legs. 5. *Brit.* a cut of beef from the flank. 6. (*often pl.*) a margin or outlying area. 7. *N.Z.* the lower part of a sheep's fleece. 8. **bit of skirt.** *Slang.* a girl or woman. ~*vb.* 9. (*tr.*) to form the edge of. 10. (*tr.*) to provide with a border. 11. (when *intr.,* foll. by *around, along,* etc.) to pass (by) or be situated (near) the outer edge of (an area, etc.). 12. (*tr.*) to avoid (a difficulty, etc.): *he skirted the issue.* 13. *Chiefly Austral. and N.Z.* to remove the trimmings or inferior wool from (a fleece). [C13: from Old Norse *skyrta* SHIRT] —'**skirted** *adj.*

skirter ('skɜːtə) *n. Austral.* a man who skirts fleeces. See **skirt** (sense 13).

skirting ('skɜːtɪŋ) *n.* 1. a border, esp. of wood or tiles, fixed round the base of an interior wall to protect it from kicks, dirt, etc. 2. material used or suitable for skirts.

skirting board *n.* a skirting made of wood. U.S. and Canadian name: **baseboard.** U.S. name: **mopboard.**

skirtings ('skɜːtɪŋz) *pl. n.* ragged edges trimmed from the fleece of a sheep.

ski run *n.* a trail, slope, or course for skiing.

ski stick *or* **pole** *n.* a stick, usually with a metal point and a disc to prevent it from sinking into the snow, used by skiers to gain momentum and maintain balance.

skit (skɪt) *n.* 1. a brief satirical theatrical sketch. 2. a short satirical piece of writing. 3. a trick or hoax. [C18: related to earlier verb *skit* to move rapidly, hence to score a satirical hit, probably of Scandinavian origin; related to Old Norse *skjóta* to shoot]

skitch (skɪtʃ) *vb.* (*tr.*) *N.Z.* (of a dog) to attack; catch.

skite[1] (skəɪt) *Scot.* ~*vb.* **1.** (*intr.*) to slide or slip, as on ice. **2.** (*tr.*) to strike with a sharp or glancing blow. ~*n.* **3.** an instance of sliding or slipping. **4.** a sharp or glancing blow. **5. on the** (*or* **a**) **skite.** *Scot., Irish.* on a drinking spree. [C18: of uncertain origin]

skite[2] (skaɪt) *Austral. and N.Z. informal.* ~*vb.* (*intr.*) **1.** to boast. ~*n.* **2.** boastful talk. **3.** a person who boasts. [C19: from Scottish and northern English dialect; see SKATE[3]]

ski touring *n.* long-distance hiking on skis over open, mountainous country; noncompetitive cross-country skiing.

ski tow *n.* a device for pulling skiers uphill, usually a motor-driven rope grasped by the skier while riding on his skis.

skitter (ˈskɪtə) *vb.* **1.** (*intr.*; often foll. by *off*) to move or run rapidly or lightly; scamper. **2.** to skim or cause to skim lightly and rapidly, as across the surface of water. **3.** (*intr.*) *Angling.* to draw a bait lightly over the surface of water. [C19: probably from dialect *skite* to dash about; related to Old Norse *skjōta* to SHOOT]

skittish (ˈskɪtɪʃ) *adj.* **1.** playful, lively, or frivolous. **2.** difficult to handle or predict. **3.** *Now rare.* coy. [C15: probably of Scandinavian origin; compare Old Norse *skjōta* to SHOOT; see -ISH] —ˈ**skittishly** *adv.* —ˈ**skittishness** *n.*

skittle (ˈskɪtᵊl) *n.* **1.** a wooden or plastic pin, typically widest just above the base. **2.** (*pl.*; *functioning as sing.*) Also called (esp. U.S.): **ninepins.** a bowling game in which players knock over as many skittles as possible by rolling a wooden ball at them. **3. beer and skittles.** (*often used with a negative*) *Informal.* an easy time; amusement. [C17: of obscure origin; perhaps related to Swedish, Danish *skyttel* shuttle]

skittle out *vb.* (*tr., adv.*) *Cricket.* to dismiss (batsmen) quickly.

skive[1] (skaɪv) *vb.* (*tr.*) to shave or remove the surface of (leather). [C19: from Old Norse *skifa*; related to English dialect *shive* a slice of bread]

skive[2] (skaɪv) *vb.* (when *intr.*, often foll. by *off*) *Brit. informal.* to evade (work or responsibility). [C20: of unknown origin]

skiver[1] (ˈskaɪvə) *n.* **1.** the tanned outer layer split from a skin. **2.** a person, tool, or machine that skives.

skiver[2] (ˈskaɪvə) *n. Brit. slang.* a person who persistently avoids work or responsibility.

skivvy[1] (ˈskɪvɪ) *n., pl.* **-vies.** **1.** *Chiefly Brit., often contemptuous.* a servant, esp. a female, who does menial work of all kinds; drudge. ~*vb.* **-vies, -vying, -vied.** **2.** (*intr.*) *Brit.* to work as a skivvy. [C20: of unknown origin]

skivvy[2] (ˈskɪvɪ) *n., pl.* **-vies.** **1.** *Slang, chiefly U.S.* a man's T-shirt or vest. **2.** (*pl.*) *Slang, chiefly U.S.* men's underwear. **3.** *Austral. and N.Z.* a garment resembling a sweater with long sleeves and a polo neck, usually made of stretch cotton or cotton and polyester and worn by either sex. [of unknown origin]

skokiaan (ˈskɔːkɪˌɑːn) *n.* (in South Africa) a potent alcoholic beverage drunk by Black Africans in shebeens. [C20: from Afrikaans, of unknown origin]

skol (skɒl) *or* **skoal** (skəʊl) *sentence substitute.* good health! (a drinking toast). [C16: from Danish *skaal* bowl, from Old Norse *skal*; see SCALE[2]]

skolly *or* **skollie** (ˈskɒlɪ) *n., pl.* **-lies.** *S. African.* a Coloured hooligan, usually one of a gang. [C20: of unknown origin]

Skt *or* **Skr.** *abbrev. for* Sanskrit.

skua (ˈskjuːə) *n.* any predatory gull-like bird of the family *Stercorariidae*, such as the **great skua** or **bonxie** (*Stercorarius skua*) or **arctic skua** (*S. parasiticus*) both of which harass terns or gulls into dropping or disgorging fish they have caught. [C17: from New Latin, from Faeroese *skūgvur*, from Old Norse *skūfr*]

skulduggery *or U.S.* **skullduggery** (skʌlˈdʌgərɪ) *n. Informal.* underhand dealing; trickery. [C19: altered from earlier Scot. *sculduddery*; of obscure origin]

skulk (skʌlk) *vb.* (*intr.*) **1.** to move stealthily so as to avoid notice. **2.** to lie in hiding; lurk. **3.** to shirk duty or evade responsibilities; malinger. ~*n.* **4.** a person who skulks. **5.** *Obsolete.* a pack of foxes or other animals that creep about stealthily. [C13: of Scandinavian origin; compare Norwegian *skulka* to lurk, Swedish *skolka*, Danish *skulke* to shirk] —ˈ**skulker** *n.*

skull (skʌl) *n.* **1.** the bony skeleton of the head of vertebrates. See **cranium.** **2.** *Often derogatory.* the head regarded as the mind or intelligence: *to have a dense skull.* **3.** a picture of a skull used to represent death or danger. [C13: of Scandinavian origin; compare Old Norse *skoltr*, Norwegian *skult*, Swedish dialect *skulle*]

skull and crossbones *n.* a picture of the human skull above two crossed thighbones, formerly on the pirate flag, now used as a warning of danger or death.

skullcap (ˈskʌlˌkæp) *n.* **1.** a rounded brimless hat fitting the crown of the head. **2.** the nontechnical name for **calvaria.** **3.** any of various perennial plants of the genus *Scutellaria*, esp. *S. galericulata*, that typically have helmet-shaped flowers: family *Labiatae* (labiates).

skunk (skʌŋk) *n., pl.* **skunk** *or* **skunks.** **1.** any of various American musteline mammals of the subfamily *Mephitinae*, esp. *Mephitis mephitis* (**striped skunk**), typically having a black and white coat and bushy tail: they eject an unpleasant-smelling fluid from the anal gland when attacked. **2.** *Informal.* a despicable person. ~*vb.* **3.** (*tr.*) *U.S. and Canadian slang.* to defeat overwhelmingly in a game. [C17: from Algonquian; compare Abnaki *segākw* skunk]

skunk cabbage *n.* **1.** a low-growing fetid aroid swamp plant, *Symplocarpus foetidus* of E North America, having broad leaves and minute flowers enclosed in a mottled greenish or purple spathe. **2.** a similar aroid plant, *Lysichitum americanum*, of the W coast of North America and N Asia. ~Also called: **skunkweed.**

sky (skaɪ) *n., pl.* **skies.** **1.** (*sometimes pl.*) the apparently dome-shaped expanse extending upwards from the horizon that is characteristically blue or grey during the day, red in the evening, and black at night. **2.** outer space, as seen from the earth. **3.** (*often pl.*) weather, as described by the appearance of the upper air: *sunny skies.* **4.** the source of divine power; heaven. **5.** *Informal.* the highest level of attainment: *the sky's the limit.* **6. to the skies.** highly; extravagantly. ~*vb.* **skies, skying, skied.** **7.** *Rowing.* to lift (the blade of an oar) too high before a stroke. **8.** (*tr.*) *Informal.* to hit (a ball) high in the air. [C13: from Old Norse *skȳ*; related to Old English *scio* cloud, Old Saxon *skio*, Old Norse *skjār* transparent skin] —ˈ**sky**ˌ**like** *adj.*

sky blue *n.* **a.** a light or pale blue colour. **b.** (*as adj.*): *a sky-blue jumper.*

sky-blue pink *n., adj.* a jocular name for a nonexistent, unknown, or unimportant colour.

skydive (ˈskaɪˌdaɪv) *vb.* **-dives, -diving, -dived** *or U.S.* **-dove; -dived.** (*intr.*) to take part in skydiving. —ˈ**sky**ˌ**diver** *n.*

skydiving (ˈskaɪˌdaɪvɪŋ) *n.* the sport of parachute jumping, in which participants perform manoeuvres before opening the parachute and attempt to land accurately.

Skye terrier (skaɪ) *n.* a short-legged long-bodied breed of terrier with long wiry hair and erect ears. [named after *Skye*, an island off the NW coast of Scotland]

sky-high *adj., adv.* **1.** at or to an unprecedented or excessive level: *prices rocketed sky-high.* ~*adv.* **2.** high into the air. **3. blow sky-high.** to destroy completely.

skyjack (ˈskaɪˌdʒæk) *vb.* (*tr.*) to commandeer (an aircraft), usually with a gun during flight, forcing the pilot to fly somewhere other than to its scheduled destination. [C20: from SKY + HIJACK] —ˈ**sky**ˌ**jacker** *n.*

skylark (ˈskaɪˌlɑːk) *n.* **1.** an Old World lark, *Alauda arvensis*, noted for singing while hovering at a great height. ~*vb.* **2.** (*intr.*) *Informal.* to romp or play jokes. —ˈ**sky**ˌ**larker** *n.*

skylight (ˈskaɪˌlaɪt) *n.* a window placed in a roof or ceiling to admit daylight. Also called: **fanlight.**

skylight filter *n. Photog.* a very slightly pink filter that absorbs ultraviolet light and reduces haze and excessive blueness.

skyline (ˈskaɪˌlaɪn) *n.* **1.** the line at which the earth and sky appear to meet; horizon. **2.** the outline of buildings, mountains, trees, etc., seen against the sky.

sky marker *n.* a parachute flare dropped to mark a target area.

sky pilot *n. Slang.* a chaplain in one of the military services.

skyrocket (ˈskaɪˌrɒkɪt) *n.* **1.** another word for **rocket**[1] (sense 1). ~*vb.* **2.** (*intr.*) *Informal.* to rise rapidly, as in price.

skysail (ˈskaɪˌseɪl) *n. Nautical.* **1.** a square sail set above the royal on a square-rigger. **2.** a triangular sail set between the trucks of a racing schooner.

skyscape (ˈskaɪˌskeɪp) *n.* a painting, drawing, photograph, etc., representing or depicting the sky.

skyscraper (ˈskaɪˌskreɪpə) *n.* a very tall multistorey building.

skyward (ˈskaɪwəd) *adj.* **1.** directed or moving towards the sky. ~*adv.* **2.** Also: **skywards.** towards the sky.

sky wave *n.* a radio wave reflected back to the earth by the ionosphere (**ionospheric wave**), permitting transmission around the curved surface of the earth. Compare **ground wave.**

skywriting (ˈskaɪˌraɪtɪŋ) *n.* **1.** the forming of words in the sky by the release of smoke or vapour from an aircraft. **2.** the words so formed. —ˈ**sky**ˌ**writer** *n.*

sl *Bibliog. abbrev. for* sine loco. [Latin: without place (of publication)]

SL *abbrev. for* Solicitor at Law.

slab (slæb) *n.* **1.** a broad flat thick piece of wood, stone, or other material. **2.** a thick slice of cake, etc. **3.** any of the outside parts of a log that are sawn off while the log is being made into planks. **4.** *Mountaineering.* a flat sheet of rock lying at an angle of between 30° and 60° from the horizontal. **5.** a printer's ink table. **6.** (*modifier*) *Austral. and N.Z.* made or constructed of coarse wooden planks: *a slab hut.* **7.** *Informal, chiefly Brit.* an operating or mortuary table. ~*vb.* **slabs, slabbing, slabbed.** (*tr.*) **8.** to cut or make into a slab or slabs. **9.** to cover or lay with slabs. **10.** to saw slabs from (a log). [C13: of unknown origin]

slabber (ˈslæbə) *vb., n.* a dialect word for **slobber.** [C16: variant of SLOBBER]

slack[1] (slæk) *adj.* **1.** not tight, tense, or taut. **2.** negligent or careless. **3.** (esp. of water, etc.) moving slowly. **4.** (of trade, etc.) not busy. **5.** *Phonetics.* another term for **lax** (sense 4). ~*adv.* **6.** in a slack manner. ~*n.* **7.** a part of a rope, etc., that is slack: *take in the slack.* **8.** a period of decreased activity. **9. a.** a patch of water without current. **b.** a slackening of a current. **10.** *Prosody.* (in sprung rhythm) the unstressed syllable or syllables. ~*vb.* **11.** to neglect (one's duty, etc.). **12.** (often foll. by *off*) to loosen; to make slack. **13.** *Chem.* a less common word for **slake** (sense 3). ~See also **slacks.** [Old English *slæc*, *sleac*;

related to Old High German *slah,* Old Norse *slākr* bad, Latin *laxus* LAX] —'**slackly** *adv.* —'**slackness** *n.*

slack[2] (slæk) *n.* small pieces of coal with a high ash content. [C15: probably from Middle Low German *slecke;* related to Dutch *slak,* German *Schlacke* dross]

slack[3] (slæk) *n. Scot. and northern English dialect.* **1.** a small valley or depression. **2.** a boggy hollow. [C14 (Scottish and northern English): from Old Norse *slakki,* of obscure origin]

slacken ('slækən) *vb.* (often foll. by *off*) **1.** to make or become looser. **2.** to make or become slower, less intense, etc.

slacker ('slækə) *n.* a person who evades work or duty; shirker.

slacks (slæks) *pl. n.* informal trousers worn by both sexes.

slack suit *n. U.S.* casual male dress consisting of slacks and a matching shirt or jacket.

slack water *n.* the period of still water around the turn of the tide, esp. at low tide.

slag (slæg) *n.* **1.** Also called: **cinder.** the fused material formed during the smelting or refining of metals by combining the flux with gangue, impurities in the metal, etc. It usually consists of a mixture of silicates with calcium, phosphorus, sulphur, etc. See also **basic slag. 2.** the mass of rough fragments of rock derived from volcanic lava; scoria. **3.** a mixture of shale, clay, coal dust, and other mineral waste produced during coal mining. **4.** *Brit. slang.* a coarse or dissipated girl or woman. ~*vb.* **slags, slagging, slagged. 5.** to convert into or become slag. **6.** (*tr.;* sometimes foll. by *off*) *Slang.* to make disparaging comments about; slander. **7.** (*intr.*) *Austral. slang.* to spit. [C16: from Middle Low German *slagge,* perhaps from *slagen* to SLAY] —'**slagging** *n.* —'**slaggy** *adj.*

slag down *vb.* (*tr., adv.*) *Prison slang.* to give a verbal lashing to.

slag heap *n.* a hillock of waste matter from coal mining, etc.

slain (sleɪn) *vb.* the past participle of **slay.**

slàinte mhath (ˌslɑːndʒə 'va) *or* **slàinte** *Scot.;* **slàinte mhaith** (ˌslɑːntə 'va) *Irish. interj.* a drinking toast; cheers. [Gaelic: good health]

slaister ('sleɪstə; *Scot.* 'sleɪstər) *Scot. and northern English dialect.* ~*vb.* **1.** (*intr.*) to make a mess. **2.** (*intr.*) to work messily, as if in mud or water. **3.** (*tr.*) to smear with mud or dirty liquid. ~*n.* **4.** a dirty or confused mess. [C18: of obscure origin]

slake (sleɪk) *vb.* **1.** (*tr.*) *Literary.* to satisfy (thirst, desire, etc.). **2.** (*tr.*) *Poetic.* to cool or refresh. **3.** Also: **slack.** to undergo or cause to undergo the process in which lime reacts with water or moist air to produce calcium hydroxide. **4.** *Archaic.* to make or become less active or intense. [Old English *slacian,* from *slæc* SLACK[1]; related to Dutch *slaken* to diminish, Icelandic *slaka*] —'**slakable** *or* '**slakeable** *adj.* —'**slaker** *n.*

slaked lime *n.* another name for **calcium hydroxide,** esp. when made by adding water to calcium oxide.

slalom ('slɑːləm) *n.* **1.** *Skiing.* a race, esp. one downhill, over a winding course marked by artificial obstacles. **2.** a similar type of obstacle race in canoes. ~*vb.* **3.** (*intr.*) to take part in a slalom. [Norwegian, from *slad* sloping + *lom* path]

slam[1] (slæm) *vb.* **slams, slamming, slammed. 1.** to cause (a door or window) to close noisily and with force or (of a door, etc.) to close in this way. **2.** (*tr.*) to throw (something) down noisily and violently. **3.** (*tr.*) *Slang.* to criticize harshly. **4.** (*intr.;* usually foll. by *into* or *out of*) *Informal.* to go (into or out of a room, etc.) in violent haste or anger. **5.** (*tr.*) to strike with violent force. **6.** (*tr.*) *Informal.* to defeat easily. ~*n.* **7.** the act or noise of slamming. **8.** *Slang.* harsh criticism or abuse. [C17: of Scandinavian origin; compare Old Norse *slamra,* Norwegian *slemma,* Swedish dialect *slämma*]

slam[2] (slæm) *n.* **1. a.** the winning of all (**grand slam**) or all but one (**little** or **small slam**) of the 13 tricks at bridge or whist. **b.** the bid to do so in bridge. **2.** an old card game. [C17: of uncertain origin]

slam-bang *adv.* **1.** another word (esp. U.S.) for **slap-bang. 2.** *U.S. informal.* carelessly; recklessly.

slam dance *vb.* to hurl oneself repeatedly into or through a crowd at a rock-music concert.

slammer ('slæmə) *n.* **the.** *Slang.* prison.

slander ('slɑːndə) *n.* **1.** *Law.* **a.** defamation in some transient form, as by spoken words, gestures, etc. **b.** a slanderous statement, etc. **2.** any false or defamatory words spoken about a person; calumny. ~*vb.* **3.** to utter or circulate slander (about). [C13: via Anglo-French from Old French *escandle,* from Late Latin *scandalum* a cause of offence; see SCANDAL] —'**slanderer** *n.* —'**slanderous** *adj.* —'**slanderously** *adv.* —'**slanderousness** *n.*

slang (slæŋ) *n.* **1. a.** vocabulary, idiom, etc., that is not appropriate to the standard form of a language or to formal contexts, may be restricted as to social status or distribution, and is characteristically more metaphorical and transitory than standard language. **b.** (*as modifier*): *a slang word.* **2.** another word for **jargon.** ~*vb.* **3.** to abuse (someone) with vituperative language; insult. [C18: of unknown origin] —'**slangy** *adj.* —'**slangily** *adv.* —'**slanginess** *n.*

slanging match *n. Brit.* a dispute in which insults and accusations are made by each party against the other.

slant (slɑːnt) *vb.* **1.** to incline or be inclined at an oblique or sloping angle. **2.** (*tr.*) to write or present (news, etc.) with a bias. **3.** (*intr.;* foll. by *towards*) (of a person's opinions) to be biased. ~*n.* **4.** an inclined or oblique line or direction; slope. **5.** a way of looking at something. **6.** a bias or opinion, as in an article. **7.** a less technical name for **solidus. 8. on a** (*or* **the**) **slant.** sloping. ~*adj.* **9.** oblique, sloping. [C17: short for ASLANT, probably of Scandinavian origin] —'**slanting** *adj.* —'**slantingly** *or* '**slantly** *adv.*

slanter ('slæntə) *n. Austral. obsolete, informal.* a variant of **slinter.**

slant rhyme *n. Prosody.* another term for **half-rhyme.**

slantwise ('slɑːntˌwaɪz) *or* **slantways** ('slɑːntˌweɪz) *adv., adj.* (*prenominal*) in a slanting or oblique direction.

slap (slæp) *n.* **1.** a sharp blow or smack, as with the open hand, something flat, etc. **2.** the sound made by or as if by such a blow. **3.** a sharp rebuke; reprimand. **4.** (**a bit of**) **slap and tickle.** *Brit. informal.* sexual play. **5. a slap in the face.** an insult or rebuff. **6. a slap on the back.** congratulation. ~*vb.* **slaps, slapping, slapped. 7.** (*tr.*) to strike (a person or thing) sharply, as with the open hand or something flat. **8.** (*tr.*) to bring down (the hand, something flat, etc.) sharply. **9.** (when *intr.,* usually foll. by *against*) to strike (something) with or as if with a slap. **10.** (*tr.*) *Informal, chiefly Brit.* to apply in large quantities, haphazardly, etc.: *she slapped butter on the bread.* **11. slap on the back.** to congratulate. ~*adv. Informal.* **12.** exactly; directly: *slap on time.* **13.** forcibly or abruptly: *to fall slap on the floor.* [C17: from Low German *slapp,* German *Schlappe,* of imitative origin] —'**slapper** *n.*

slap-bang *adv. Informal, chiefly Brit.* **1.** in a violent, sudden, or noisy manner. U.S. equivalent: **slam-bang. 2.** directly or immediately: *slap-bang in the middle.*

slapdash ('slæpˌdæʃ) *adv.* **1.** in a careless, hasty, or haphazard manner. ~*adj.* **2.** careless, hasty, or haphazard. ~*n.* **3.** slapdash activity or work. **4.** another name for **roughcast** (sense 1). [C17: from SLAP + DASH[1]]

slap down *vb.* (*tr., adv.*) *Informal.* to rebuke sharply, as for impertinence.

slaphappy ('slæpˌhæpɪ) *adj.* **-pier, -piest.** *Informal.* **1.** cheerfully irresponsible or careless. **2.** dazed or giddy from or as if from repeated blows; punch-drunk.

slapjack ('slæpˌdʒæk) *n.* **1.** a simple card game. **2.** *U.S.* another word for **pancake.** [C19: from SLAP + JACK[1]]

slapshot ('slæpˌʃɒt) *n. Ice hockey.* a fast shot impelled by a short but powerful swing of the stick.

slapstick ('slæpˌstɪk) *n.* **1. a.** comedy characterized by horseplay and physical action. **b.** (*as modifier*): *slapstick humour.* **2.** a flexible pair of paddles bound together at one end, formerly used in pantomime to strike a blow to a person with a loud clapping sound but without injury.

slap-up *adj.* (*prenominal*) *Brit. informal.* (esp. of meals) lavish; excellent; first-class.

slash (slæʃ) *vb.* (*tr.*) **1.** to cut or lay about (a person or thing) with sharp sweeping strokes, as with a sword, knife, etc. **2.** to lash with a whip. **3.** to make large gashes in: *to slash tyres.* **4.** to reduce (prices, etc.) drastically. **5.** *Chiefly U.S.* to criticize harshly. **6.** to slit (the outer fabric of a garment) so that the lining material is revealed. **7.** to clear (scrub or undergrowth) by cutting. ~*n.* **8.** a sharp, sweeping stroke, as with a sword or whip. **9.** a cut or rent made by such a stroke. **10.** a decorative slit in a garment revealing the lining material. **11.** *North American.* **a.** littered wood chips and broken branches that remain after trees have been cut down. **b.** an area so littered. **12.** another name for **solidus. 13.** *Brit. slang.* the act of urinating (esp. in the phrase **have a slash**). [C14 *slaschen,* perhaps from Old French *esclachier* to break]

slash-and-burn *adj.* denoting a short-term method of cultivation in which land is cleared by destroying and burning trees and other vegetation for temporary agricultural use.

slasher ('slæʃə) *n.* **1.** a person or thing that slashes. **2.** *Austral. and N.Z.* a wooden-handled cutting tool used for cutting scrub or undergrowth in the bush.

slasher movie *n. Slang.* a film in which victims, usually women, are slashed with knives, razors, etc.

slashing ('slæʃɪŋ) *adj.* aggressively or harshly critical (esp. in the phrase **slashing attack**). —'**slashingly** *adv.*

slash pocket *n.* a pocket in which the opening is a slit in the seam of a garment.

slat[1] (slæt) *n.* **1.** a narrow thin strip of wood or metal, as used in a Venetian blind, etc. **2.** a movable or fixed auxiliary aerofoil attached to the leading edge of an aircraft wing to increase lift, esp. during landing and takeoff. ~*vb.* **slats, slatting, slatted. 3.** (*tr.*) to provide with slats. [C14: from Old French *esclat* splinter, from *esclater* to shatter]

slat[2] (slæt) *Dialect.* ~*vb.* **slats, slatting, slatted. 1.** (*tr.*) to throw violently; fling carelessly. **2.** (*intr.*) to flap violently. ~*n.* **3.** a sudden blow. [C13: of Scandinavian origin; related to Old Norse, Icelandic *sletta* to slap]

slat[3] (slæt) *n. Irish.* a spent salmon. [C19: of uncertain origin]

slate[1] (sleɪt) *n.* **1. a.** a compact fine-grained metamorphic rock formed by the effects of heat and pressure on shale. It can be split into thin layers along natural cleavage planes and is used as a roofing and paving material. **b.** (*as modifier*): *a slate tile.* **2.** a roofing tile of slate. **3.** (formerly) a writing tablet of slate. **4.** a dark grey colour, often with a purplish or bluish tinge. **5.** *Chiefly U.S. and Canadian.* a list of candidates in an election. **6.** *Films.* **a.** the reference information written on a clapperboard. **b.**

Informal. the clapperboard itself. **7. clean slate.** a record without dishonour. **8. have a slate loose.** *Brit. and Irish informal.* to be eccentric or crazy. **9. on the slate.** *Brit. informal.* on credit. **10. wipe the slate clean.** *Informal.* to make a fresh start, esp. by forgetting past differences. ~*vb.* (*tr.*) **11.** to cover (a roof) with slates. **12.** *Chiefly U.S.* to enter (a person's name) on a list, esp. on a political slate. **13.** *U.S. and Canadian.* to choose or destine: *he was slated to go far.* ~*adj.* **14.** of the colour slate. [C14: from Old French *esclate*, from *esclat* a fragment; see SLAT[1]]

slate[2] (sleɪt) *vb.* (*tr.*) *Informal, chiefly Brit.* **1.** to criticize harshly; censure. **2.** to punish or defeat severely. [C19: probably from SLATE[1]]

slater (ˈsleɪtə) *n.* **1.** a person trained in laying roof slates. **2.** *Dialect, Austral., and N.Z.* a woodlouse. See also **sea slater.**

slatey (ˈsleɪtɪ) *adj.* **slatier, slatiest.** *Irish informal.* slightly mad; crazy.

slather (ˈslæðə) *n.* **1.** (*usually pl.*) *Informal.* a large quantity. **2. open slather.** *Austral. and N.Z. slang.* a situation in which there are no restrictions; free-for-all. ~*vb.* (*tr.*) *U.S. and Canadian slang.* **3.** to squander or waste. **4.** to spread thickly or lavishly. [C19: of unknown origin]

slating[1] (ˈsleɪtɪŋ) *n.* **1.** the act or process of laying slates. **2.** slates collectively, or material for making slates.

slating[2] (ˈsleɪtɪŋ) *n.* *Informal, chiefly Brit.* a severe reprimand or critical attack.

slattern (ˈslætən) *n.* a slovenly woman or girl; slut. [C17: probably from *slattering*, from dialect *slatter* to slop; perhaps from Scandinavian; compare Old Norse *sletta* to slap] —ˈ**slatternly** *adj.* —ˈ**slatternliness** *n.*

slaty (ˈsleɪtɪ) *adj.* **slatier, slatiest. 1.** consisting of or resembling slate. **2.** having the colour of slate. —ˈ**slatiness** *n.*

slaughter (ˈslɔːtə) *n.* **1.** the killing of animals, esp. for food. **2.** the savage killing of a person. **3.** the indiscriminate or brutal killing of large numbers of people, as in war; massacre. **4.** *Informal.* a resounding defeat. ~*vb.* (*tr.*) **5.** to kill (animals), esp. for food. **6.** to kill in a brutal manner. **7.** to kill indiscriminately or in large numbers. **8.** *Informal.* to defeat resoundingly. [Old English *sleaht*; related to Old Norse *slāttar* hammering, *slātr* butchered meat, Old High German *slahta*, Gothic *slauhts*, German *Schlacht* battle] —ˈ**slaughterer** *n.* —ˈ**slaughterous** *adj.*

slaughterhouse (ˈslɔːtəˌhaʊs) *n.* a place where animals are butchered for food; abattoir.

slaughterman (ˈslɔːtəˌmæn) *n., pl.* **-men.** a person employed to kill animals in a slaughterhouse.

Slav (slɑːv) *n.* a member of any of the peoples of E Europe or W Asia who speak a Slavonic language. [C14: from Medieval Latin *Sclāvus* a captive Slav; see SLAVE]

Slav. *abbrev. for* Slavonic *or* Slavic.

slave (sleɪv) *n.* **1.** a person legally owned by another and having no freedom of action or right to property. **2.** a person who is forced to work for another against his will. **3.** a person under the domination of another person or some habit or influence: *a slave to television.* **4.** a person who works in harsh conditions for low pay. **5. a.** a device that is controlled by or that duplicates the action of another similar device (the master device). **b.** (*as modifier*): *slave cylinder.* ~*vb.* **6.** (*intr.*: often foll. by *away*) to work like a slave. **7.** (*tr.*) an archaic word for **enslave.** [C13: via Old French from Medieval Latin *Sclāvus* a Slav, one held in bondage (from the fact that the Slavonic races were frequently conquered in the Middle Ages), from Late Greek *Sklabos* a Slav]

slave ant *n.* any of various ants, esp. *Formica fusca*, captured and forced to do the work of a colony of ants of another species (**slave-making ants**). See also **amazon ant.**

slave cylinder *n.* a small cylinder containing a piston that operates the brake shoes or pads in hydraulic brakes or the working part in any other hydraulically operated system. Compare **master cylinder.**

slave-driver *n.* **1.** (esp. formerly) a person forcing slaves to work. **2.** an employer who demands excessively hard work from his employees.

slaveholder (ˈsleɪvˌhəʊldə) *n.* a person who owns slaves. —ˈ**slaveˌholding** *n.*

slaver[1] (ˈsleɪvə) *n.* **1.** an owner of or dealer in slaves. **2.** another name for **slave ship.**

slaver[2] (ˈslævə) *vb.* (*intr.*) **1.** to dribble saliva. **2.** (often foll. by *over*) **a.** to fawn or drool (over someone). **b.** to show great desire (for); lust (after). ~*n.* **3.** saliva dribbling from the mouth. **4.** *Informal.* drivel. [C14: probably of Low Dutch origin; related to SLOBBER] —ˈ**slaverer** *n.*

slavery (ˈsleɪvərɪ) *n.* **1.** the state or condition of being a slave; a civil relationship whereby one person has absolute power over another and controls his life, liberty, and fortune. **2.** the subjection of a person to another person, esp. in being forced into work. **3.** the condition of being subject to some influence or habit. **4.** work done in harsh conditions for low pay.

slave ship *n.* a ship used to transport slaves, esp. formerly from Africa to the New World.

Slave State *n.* *U.S. history.* any of the 15 Southern states in which slavery was legal until the Civil War.

slave trade *n.* the business of trading in slaves, esp. the transportation of Black Africans to America from the 16th to 19th centuries. —ˈ**slave-ˌtrader** *n.* —ˈ**slave-ˌtrading** *n.*

slavey (ˈsleɪvɪ) *n.* *Brit. informal.* a female general servant. [C19: from SLAVE + -Y[2]]

Slavic (ˈslɑːvɪk) *n., adj.* another word (esp. U.S.) for **Slavonic.**

slavish (ˈsleɪvɪʃ) *adj.* **1.** of or befitting a slave. **2.** being or resembling a slave; servile. **3.** unoriginal; imitative. **4.** *Archaic.* ignoble. —ˈ**slavishly** *adv.* —ˈ**slavishness** *n.*

Slavism (ˈslɑːvɪzəm) *n.* anything characteristic of, peculiar to, or associated with the Slavs or the Slavonic languages.

slavocracy (sleɪˈvɒkrəsɪ) *n., pl.* **-cies.** (esp. in the U.S. before the Civil War) **1.** slaveholders as a dominant class. **2.** domination by slaveholders.

Slavonian (sləˈvəʊnɪən) *adj.* **1.** of or relating to Slavonia, a region of Croatia, or to its people, culture, etc. ~*n.* **2.** a native or inhabitant of Slavonia.

Slavonic (sləˈvɒnɪk) *or* (*esp U.S.*) **Slavic** *n.* **1.** a branch of the Indo-European family of languages, usually divided into three subbranches: **South Slavonic** (including Old Church Slavonic, Serbo-Croatian, Bulgarian, etc.), **East Slavonic** (including Ukrainian, Russian, etc.), and **West Slavonic** (including Polish, Czech, Slovak, etc.). **2.** the unrecorded ancient language from which all of these languages developed. ~*adj.* **3.** of, denoting, or relating to this group of languages. **4.** of, denoting, or relating to the people who speak these languages. [C17: from Medieval Latin *Slavonicus, Sclavonicus*, from *Slavonia*]

Slavophile (ˈslɑːvəʊfɪl, -ˌfaɪl) *or* **Slavophil** *n.* **1.** a person who admires the Slavs or their cultures. **2.** (*sometimes not cap.*) (in 19th-century Russia) a person who believed in the superiority and advocated the supremacy of the Slavs. ~*adj.* **3.** admiring the Slavs and Slavonic culture, etc. **4.** (*sometimes not cap.*) (in 19th-century Russia) of, characteristic of, or relating to the Slavophiles. —**Slavophilism** (sləˈvɒfɪˌlɪzəm, ˈslɑːvəʊfɪˌlɪzəm) *n.*

slaw (slɔː) *n.* *Chiefly U.S. and Canadian.* short for **coleslaw.** [C19: from Danish *sla*, short for *salade* SALAD]

slay (sleɪ) *vb.* **slays, slaying, slew, slain.** (*tr.*) **1.** *Archaic or literary.* to kill, esp. violently. **2.** *Slang.* to impress (someone of the opposite sex). **3.** *Obsolete.* to strike. [Old English *slēan*; related to Old Norse *slā*, Gothic, Old High German *slahan* to strike, Old Irish *slacaim* I beat] —ˈ**slayer** *n.*

SLBM *abbrev. for* submarine-launched ballistic missile.

SLCM *abbrev. for* sea-launched cruise missile: a type of cruise missile that can be launched from either a submarine or a surface ship.

sld *abbrev. for:* **1.** sailed. **2.** sealed.

SLD *abbrev. for* Social and Liberal Democrats.

sleave (sliːv) *n.* **1.** a tangled thread. **2.** a thin filament unravelled from a thicker thread. **3.** *Chiefly poetic.* anything matted or complicated. ~*vb.* **4.** to disentangle (twisted thread, etc.). [Old English *slǣfan* to divide; related to Middle Low German *slēf*, Norwegian *sleiv* big spoon]

sleaze (sliːz) *n.* *Informal.* sleaziness.

sleazy (ˈsliːzɪ) *adj.* **-zier, -ziest. 1.** sordid; disreputable: *a sleazy nightclub.* **2.** thin or flimsy, as cloth. [C17: origin uncertain] —ˈ**sleazily** *adv.* —ˈ**sleaziness** *n.*

sled dog *n.* any of various hardy thick-coated breeds of dog, such as the Eskimo dog, the husky, and the malamute, developed for hauling sledges in various parts of the highest northern latitudes.

sledge[1] (slɛdʒ) *or* (*esp. U.S. and Canadian*) **sled** (slɛd) *n.* **1.** Also called: **sleigh.** a vehicle mounted on runners, drawn by horses or dogs, for transporting people or goods, esp. over snow. **2.** a light wooden frame used, esp. by children, for sliding over snow; toboggan. **3.** *N.Z.* a farm vehicle mounted on runners, for use on rough or muddy ground. ~*vb.* **4.** to convey, travel, or go by sledge. [C17: from Middle Dutch *sleedse*; C14 *sled*, from Middle Low German, from Old Norse *slethi*, related to SLIDE] —ˈ**sledger** *n.*

sledge[2] (slɛdʒ) *n.* short for **sledgehammer.**

sledge[3] (slɛdʒ) *vb.* (*tr.*) *Austral.* to bait (an opponent, esp. a batsman in cricket) in order to upset his concentration. [of uncertain origin; perhaps from SLEDGEHAMMER]

sledgehammer (ˈslɛdʒˌhæmə) *n.* **1.** a large heavy hammer with a long handle used with both hands for heavy work such as forging iron, breaking rocks, etc. **2.** (*modifier*) resembling the action of a sledgehammer in power, ruthlessness, etc.: *a sledgehammer blow.* ~*vb.* **3.** (*tr.*) to strike (something) with or as if with a sledgehammer. [C15 *sledge*, from Old English *slecg* a large hammer; related to Old Norse *sleggja*, Middle Dutch *slegge*]

sleek (sliːk) *adj.* **1.** smooth and shiny; polished. **2.** polished in speech or behaviour; unctuous. **3.** (of an animal or bird) having a shiny healthy coat or feathers. **4.** (of a person) having a prosperous appearance. ~*vb.* (*tr.*) **5.** to make smooth and glossy, as by grooming, etc. **6.** (usually foll. by *over*) to cover (up), as by making more agreeable; gloss (over). [C16: variant of SLICK] —ˈ**sleekly** *adv.* —ˈ**sleekness** *n.* —ˈ**sleeky** *adj.*

sleekit (ˈsliːkɪt) *adj.* *Scot.* **1.** smooth, glossy. **2.** unctuous. **3.** deceitful; crafty; sly. [Scottish, from past participle of SLEEK]

sleep (sliːp) *n.* **1.** a periodic state of physiological rest during which consciousness is suspended and metabolic rate is decreased. See also **paradoxical sleep. 2.** *Botany.* the nontechnical name for **nyctitropism. 3.** a period spent sleeping. **4.** a state of quiescence or dormancy. **5.** a poetic or euphemistic word for **death. 6.** *Informal.* the dried mucoid particles often found in the corners of the eyes after sleeping. ~*vb.* **sleeps, sleeping, slept.** **7.** (*intr.*) to be in or as in the state of sleep. **8.** (*intr.*) (of plants) to show nyctitropism. **9.** (*intr.*) to be inactive or quiescent. **10.** (*tr.*) to have sleeping accommodation for (a certain number): *the boat could sleep six.* **11.** (*tr.*; foll. by *away*) to pass (time) sleeping. **12.** (*intr.*) to fail to pay attention. **13.** (*intr.*) *Poetic or euphemistic.* to be dead. **14. sleep on it.** to give (something) extended consideration, esp. overnight. ~See also **sleep around, sleep in, sleep off, sleep out, sleep with.** [Old English *slǣpan;* related to Old Frisian *slēpa,* Old Saxon *slāpan,* Old High German *slāfan,* German *schlaff* limp]

sleep around *vb.* (*intr., adv.*) *Informal.* to be sexually promiscuous.

sleeper ('sliːpə) *n.* **1.** a person, animal, or thing that sleeps. **2.** a railway sleeping car or compartment. **3.** *Brit.* one of the blocks supporting the rails on a railway track. U.S. and Canadian equivalent: **tie. 4.** a heavy timber beam, esp. one that is laid horizontally on the ground. **5.** *Chiefly Brit.* a small plain gold circle worn in a pierced ear lobe to prevent the hole from closing up. **6.** a wrestling hold in which a wrestler presses the sides of his opponent's neck, causing him to pass out. **7.** *U.S.* an unbranded calf. **8.** Also called: **sleeper goby.** any gobioid fish of the family *Eleotridae,* of brackish or fresh tropical waters, resembling the gobies but lacking a ventral sucker. **9.** *Informal.* a person or thing that achieves unexpected success after an initial period of obscurity. **10.** a spy planted in advance for future use, but not currently active.

sleep in *vb.* (*intr., adv.*) **1.** *Brit.* to sleep longer than usual. **2.** to sleep at the place of one's employment.

sleeping bag *n.* a large well-padded bag designed for sleeping in, esp. outdoors.

sleeping car *n.* a railway car fitted with compartments containing bunks for people to sleep in.

sleeping draught *n.* any drink containing a drug or agent that induces sleep.

sleeping partner *n.* a partner in a business who does not play an active role, esp. one who supplies capital.

sleeping pill *n.* a pill or tablet containing a sedative drug, such as a barbiturate, used to induce sleep.

sleeping policeman *n.* a bump built across roads, esp. in housing estates, to deter motorists from speeding.

sleeping sickness *n.* **1.** Also called: **African sleeping sickness.** an African disease caused by infection with protozoans of the genus *Trypanosoma,* characterized by fever, wasting, and sluggishness. **2.** Also called (esp. formerly): **sleepy sickness.** an epidemic viral form of encephalitis characterized by extreme drowsiness. Technical name: **encephalitis lethargica.**

sleepless ('sliːplɪs) *adj.* **1.** without sleep or rest: *a sleepless journey.* **2.** unable to sleep. **3.** always watchful or alert. **4.** *Chiefly poetic.* always active or moving: *the sleepless tides.* —'**sleeplessly** *adv.* —'**sleeplessness** *n.*

sleep movement *n.* the folding together of leaflets, petals, etc., that occurs at night in certain plants.

sleep off *vb.* (*tr., adv.*) *Informal.* to lose by sleeping: *to sleep off a hangover.*

sleep out *vb.* (*intr., adv.*) **1.** (esp. of a tramp) to sleep in the open air. **2.** to sleep away from the place of work. ~*n.* **sleep-out. 3.** *Austral. and N.Z.* an area of a veranda that has been glassed in or partitioned off so that it may be used as a bedroom.

sleepwalk ('sliːpˌwɔːk) *vb.* (*intr.*) to walk while asleep. See also **somnambulism.** —'**sleepˌwalker** *n.* —'**sleepˌwalking** *n., adj.*

sleep with *vb.* (*intr., prep.*) to have sexual intercourse and (usually) spend the night with. Also: **sleep together.**

sleepy ('sliːpɪ) *adj.* **sleepier, sleepiest. 1.** inclined to or needing sleep; drowsy. **2.** characterized by or exhibiting drowsiness, sluggishness, etc. **3.** conducive to sleep; soporific. **4.** without activity or bustle: *a sleepy town.* —'**sleepily** *adv.* —'**sleepiness** *n.*

sleepyhead ('sliːpɪˌhɛd) *n. Informal.* a sleepy or lazy person. —'**sleepyˌheaded** *adj.*

sleet (sliːt) *n.* **1.** partly melted falling snow or hail or (esp. U.S.) partly frozen rain. **2.** *Chiefly U.S.* the thin coat of ice that forms when sleet or rain freezes on cold surfaces. ~*vb.* **3.** (*intr.*) to fall as sleet. [C13: from Germanic; compare Middle Low German *slōten* hail, Middle High German *slōze,* German *Schlossen* hailstones] —'**sleety** *adj.*

sleeve (sliːv) *n.* **1.** the part of a garment covering the arm. **2.** a tubular piece that is forced or shrunk into a cylindrical bore to reduce the diameter of the bore or to line it with a different material; liner. **3.** a tube fitted externally over two cylindrical parts in order to join them; bush. **4.** a flat cardboard or plastic container to protect a gramophone record. U.S. name: **jacket. 5. (have a few tricks) up one's sleeve.** (to have options, etc.) secretly ready. **6. roll up one's sleeves.** to prepare oneself for work, a fight, etc. ~*vb.* **7.** (*tr.*) to provide with a sleeve or sleeves. [Old English *slīf, slēf;* related to Dutch *sloof* apron] —'**sleeveless** *adj.* —'**sleeveˌlike** *adj.*

sleeve board *n.* a small ironing board for pressing sleeves, fitted onto an ironing board or table.

sleeveen ('sliːviːn) *n. Irish.* a sly obsequious smooth-tongued person. [from Irish Gaelic *slíbhín*]

sleeve notes *pl. n.* the printed information on a record sleeve. U.S. equivalent: **liner notes.**

sleeve valve *n.* (in an internal-combustion engine) a valve in the form of a thin steel sleeve fitted between the cylinder and piston and having a reciprocating and rotary oscillation movement.

sleeving ('sliːvɪŋ) *n. Electronics, chiefly Brit.* tubular flexible insulation into which bare wire can be inserted. U.S. and Canadian name: **spaghetti.**

sleigh (sleɪ) *n.* **1.** another name for **sledge**[1] (sense 1). ~*vb.* **2.** (*intr.*) to travel by sleigh. [C18: from Dutch *slee,* variant of *slede* SLEDGE[1]] —'**sleigher** *n.*

sleight (slaɪt) *n. Archaic.* **1.** skill; dexterity. See also **sleight of hand. 2.** a trick or stratagem. **3.** cunning; trickery. [C14: from Old Norse *slægth,* from *slægr* SLY]

sleight of hand *n.* **1.** manual dexterity used in performing conjuring tricks. **2.** the performance of such tricks.

slender ('slɛndə) *adj.* **1.** of small width relative to length or height. **2.** (esp. of a person's figure) slim and well-formed. **3.** small or inadequate in amount, size, etc.: *slender resources.* **4.** (of hopes, etc.) having little foundation; feeble. **5.** very small: *a slender margin.* **6.** (of a sound) lacking volume. **7.** *Phonetics.* (now only in Irish phonology) relating to or denoting a close front vowel, such as *i* or *e.* [C14 *slendre,* of unknown origin] —'**slenderly** *adv.* —'**slenderness** *n.*

slenderize *or* **slenderise** ('slɛndəˌraɪz) *vb. Chiefly U.S. and Canadian.* to make or become slender.

slenter ('slɛntə) *n. Austral. obsolete, informal.* a variant of **slinter.**

slept (slɛpt) *vb.* the past tense and past participle of **sleep.**

sleuth (sluːθ) *n.* **1.** an informal word for **detective. 2.** short for **sleuthhound** (sense 1). ~*vb.* **3.** (*tr.*) to track or follow. [C19: short for *sleuthhound,* from C12 *sleuth* trail, from Old Norse *sloth;* see SLOT[2]]

sleuthhound ('sluːθˌhaʊnd) *n.* **1.** a dog trained to track people, esp. a bloodhound. **2.** an informal word for **detective.**

S level *n. Brit.* the Special level of a subject taken for the General Certificate of Education: usually taken at the same time as A levels as an additional qualification.

slew[1] (sluː) *vb.* the past tense of **slay.**

slew[2] *or* (*esp. U.S.*) **slue** (sluː) *vb.* **1.** to twist or be twisted sideways, esp. awkwardly: *he slewed around in his chair.* **2.** *Nautical.* to cause (a mast) to rotate in its step or (of a mast) to rotate in its step. ~*n.* **3.** the act of slewing. [C18: of unknown origin]

slew[3] (sluː) *n.* a variant spelling (esp. U.S.) of **slough**[1] (sense 2).

slew[4] *or* **slue** (sluː) *n. U.S. and Canadian informal.* a great number or amount; a lot. [C20: from Irish Gaelic *sluagh;* related to Old Irish *slōg* army]

slewed (sluːd) *adj.* (*postpositive*) *Brit. slang.* intoxicated; drunk. [C19: from SLEW[2]]

slew rate *n. Electronics.* the rate at which an electronic amplifier can respond to an abrupt change of input level.

slice (slaɪs) *n.* **1.** a thin flat piece cut from something having bulk: *a slice of pork.* **2.** a share or portion: *a slice of the company's revenue.* **3.** any of various utensils having a broad flat blade and resembling a spatula. **4.** (in golf, tennis, etc.) **a.** the flight of a ball that travels obliquely because it has been struck off centre. **b.** the action of hitting such a shot. **c.** the shot so hit. ~*vb.* **5.** to divide or cut (something) into parts or slices. **6.** (when *intr.,* usually foll. by *through*) to cut in a clean and effortless manner. **7.** (when *intr.,* foll. by *into* or *through*) to move or go (through something) like a knife: *the car sliced into a field.* **8.** (usually foll. by *off, from, away,* etc.) to cut or be cut (from) a larger piece. **9.** (*tr.*) to remove by use of a slicing implement. **10.** to hit (a ball) with a slice. **11.** (*tr.*) *Rowing.* to put the blade of the oar into (the water) slantwise. [C14: from Old French *esclice* a piece split off, from *esclicier* to splinter] —'**sliceable** *adj.* —'**slicer** *n.*

slice bar *n.* an iron bar used for raking out furnaces.

slicer ('slaɪsə) *n.* a machine that slices bread, etc., usually with an electrically driven band knife or circular knife.

slick (slɪk) *adj.* **1.** flattering and glib: *a slick salesman.* **2.** adroitly devised or executed: *a slick show.* **3.** *Informal, chiefly U.S. and Canadian.* shrewd; sly. **4.** *Informal.* superficially attractive: *a slick publication.* **5.** *Chiefly U.S. and Canadian.* smooth and glossy; slippery. ~*n.* **6.** a slippery area, esp. a patch of oil floating on water. **7.** a chisel or other tool used for smoothing or polishing a surface. **8.** the tyre of a racing car that has worn treads. ~*vb.* (*tr.*) **9.** *Chiefly U.S. and Canadian.* to make smooth or sleek. **10.** *U.S. and Canadian informal.* (usually foll. by *up*) to smarten or tidy (oneself). **11.** (often foll. by *up*) to make smooth or glossy. [C14: probably of Scandinavian origin; compare Icelandic, Norwegian *slikja* to be or make smooth] —'**slickly** *adv.* —'**slickness** *n.*

slickenside ('slɪkənˌsaɪd) *n.* a rock surface with a polished appearance and fine parallel scratches caused by displacement of the rock during a fault. [C18: from dialect *slicken,* variant of SLICK + SIDE]

slicker ('slɪkə) *n.* **1.** *Informal.* a sly or untrustworthy person (esp. in the phrase **city slicker**). **2.** *U.S. and Canadian.* a shiny raincoat, esp. an oilskin. **3.** a small trowel used for smoothing the surfaces of a mould. —'**slickered** *adj.*

slide (slaɪd) *vb.* **slides, sliding, slid** (slɪd); **slid** *or* **slidden** ('slɪdᵊn). **1.** to move or cause to move smoothly along a surface in continual contact with it: *doors that slide open; children sliding on the ice.* **2.** (*intr.*) to lose grip or balance: *he slid on his back.* **3.** (*intr.; usually foll. by into, out of, away from,* etc.) to pass or move gradually and unobtrusively: *she slid into the room.* **4.** (*intr.;* usually foll. by *into*) to go (into a specified condition) by degrees, unnoticeably, etc.: *he slid into loose living.* **5.** (foll. by *in, into,* etc.) to move (an object) unobtrusively or (of an object) to move in this way: *he slid the gun into his pocket.* **6.** (*intr.*) *Music.* to execute a portamento. **7. let slide.** to allow to follow a natural course, esp. one leading to deterioration: *to let things slide.* ~*n.* **8.** the act or an instance of sliding. **9.** a smooth surface, as of ice or mud, for sliding on. **10.** a construction incorporating an inclined smooth slope for sliding down in playgrounds, etc. **11.** *Rowing.* a sliding seat in a boat or its runners. **12.** a small glass plate on which specimens are mounted for microscopic study. **13.** Also called: **transparency.** a positive photograph on a transparent base, mounted in a cardboard or plastic frame or between glass plates, that can be viewed by means of a slide projector. **14.** Also called: **hair slide.** *Chiefly Brit.* an ornamental clip to hold hair in place. U.S. and Canadian name: **barrette. 15.** *Machinery.* **a.** a sliding part or member. **b.** the track, guide, or channel on or in which such a part slides. **16.** *Music.* **a.** the sliding curved tube of a trombone that is moved in or out to allow the production of different harmonic series and a wider range of notes. **b.** a portamento. **17.** *Music.* **a.** a metal or glass tube placed over a finger held against the frets of a guitar to produce a portamento. **b.** the style of guitar playing using a slide. See also **bottleneck** (sense 3). **18.** *Geology.* **a.** the downward movement of a large mass of earth, rocks, etc., caused by erosion, faulting, etc. **b.** the mass of material involved in this descent. See also **landslide.** [Old English *slīdan;* related to *slidor* slippery, *sliderian* to SLITHER, Middle High German *slīten*] —'**slidable** *adj.* —'**slider** *n.*

slide-action *adj.* (of a shoulder firearm) ejecting the empty case and reloading by means of a sliding lever.

slide fastener *n. Chiefly U.S. and Canadian.* another name for **zip** (sense 1).

slide guitar *n.* a technique of guitar playing derived from bottleneck, using a steel or glass tube on one finger across the frets.

slide over *vb.* (*intr., prep.*) **1.** to cross by or as if by sliding. **2.** to avoid dealing with (a matter) fully.

slide rest *n. Engineering.* a stack of platforms that sits on a lathe saddle and carries a tool post, and is adjustable in rotation and at right angles by a lathe operator.

slide rule *n.* a mechanical calculating device consisting of two strips, one sliding along a central groove in the other, each strip graduated in two or more logarithmic scales of numbers, trigonometric functions, etc. It employs the same principles as logarithm tables.

slide trombone *n.* See **trombone.**

slide valve *n.* **1.** a valve that slides across an aperture to expose the port or opening. **2.** (*modifier*) fitted with slide valves: *a slide-valve engine.*

sliding ('slaɪdɪŋ) *adj.* **1.** rising or falling in accordance with given specifications: *fees were charged as a sliding percentage of income.* **2.** regulated or moved by sliding.

sliding fit *n. Engineering.* a fit that enables one part to be inserted into another by sliding or pushing, rather than by hammering. Also called: **push fit.**

sliding friction *n. Engineering.* frictional resistance to relative movement of surfaces on loaded contact. Compare **rolling friction.**

sliding scale *n.* a variable scale according to which specified wages, tariffs, prices, etc., fluctuate in response to changes in some other factor, standard, or conditions.

sliding seat *n. Rowing.* a seat that slides forwards and backwards with the oarsman, lengthening his stroke.

slier ('slaɪə) *adj.* a comparative of **sly.**

sliest ('slaɪɪst) *adj.* a superlative of **sly.**

slight (slaɪt) *adj.* **1.** small in quantity or extent. **2.** of small importance; trifling. **3.** slim and delicate. **4.** lacking in strength or substance. ~*vb.* (*tr.*) **5.** to show indifference or disregard for (someone); snub. **6.** to treat as unimportant or trifling. **7.** *U.S.* to devote inadequate attention to (work, duties, etc.). ~*n.* **8.** an act or omission indicating supercilious neglect or indifference. [C13: from Old Norse *slēttr* smooth; related to Old High German *slehtr,* Gothic *slaihts,* Middle Dutch *slecht* simple] —'**slightness** *n.*

slighting ('slaɪtɪŋ) *adj.* characteristic of a slight; disparaging; disdainful: *in a slighting manner.* —'**slightingly** *adv.*

slightly ('slaɪtlɪ) *adv.* in small measure or degree.

slily ('slaɪlɪ) *adv.* a variant spelling of **slyly.**

slim (slɪm) *adj.* **slimmer, slimmest. 1.** small in width relative to height or length. **2.** small in amount or quality: *slim chances of success.* ~*vb.* **slims, slimming, slimmed. 3.** to make or become slim, esp. by diets and exercise. **4.** to reduce or decrease or cause to be reduced or decreased. [C17: from Dutch: crafty, from Middle Dutch *slimp* slanting; compare Old High German *slimbi* obliquity] —'**slimly** *adv.* —'**slimmer** *n.* —'**slimness** *n.*

Slim (slɪm) *n.* the E African name for **AIDS.** [from its wasting effects]

slime (slaɪm) *n.* **1.** soft thin runny mud or filth. **2.** any moist viscous fluid, esp. when noxious or unpleasant. **3.** a mucous substance produced by various organisms, such as fish, slugs, and fungi. ~*vb.* (*tr.*) **4.** to cover with slime. **5.** to remove slime from (fish) before canning. [Old English *slīm;* related to Old Norse *slīm,* Old High German *slīmen* to smooth, Russian *slimák* snail, Latin *līmax* snail]

slime mould *or* **fungus** *n.* another name for **myxomycete.**

slimline ('slɪmˌlaɪn) *adj.* slim; giving the appearance of or conducive to slimness.

slimming ('slɪmɪŋ) *n.* **a.** the process of or concern with becoming slim or slimmer as by losing weight. **b.** (*as modifier*): *slimming aids.*

slimsy ('slɪmzɪ) *adj.* **-sier, -siest.** *U.S. informal.* frail. [C19: from SLIM + FLIMSY]

slimy ('slaɪmɪ) *adj.* **slimier, slimiest. 1.** characterized by, covered with, containing, secreting, or resembling slime. **2.** offensive or repulsive. **3.** *Chiefly Brit.* characterized by servility. —'**slimily** *adv.* —'**sliminess** *n.*

sling[1] (slɪŋ) *n.* **1.** a simple weapon consisting of a loop of leather, etc., in which a stone is whirled and then let fly. **2.** a rope or strap by which something may be secured or lifted. **3.** a rope net swung from a crane, used for loading and unloading cargo. **4.** *Nautical.* **a.** a halyard for a yard. **b.** (*often pl.*) the part of a yard where the sling is attached. **5.** *Med.* a wide piece of cloth suspended from the neck for supporting an injured hand or arm across the front of the body. **6.** a loop or band attached to an object for carrying. **7.** *Mountaineering.* a loop of rope or tape used for support in belays, abseils, etc. **8.** the act of slinging. ~*vb.* **slings, slinging, slung. 9.** (*tr.*) to hurl with or as if with a sling. **10.** to attach a sling or slings to (a load, etc.). **11.** (*tr.*) to carry or hang loosely from or as if from a sling: *to sling washing from the line.* **12.** *Informal.* to throw. **13.** (*intr.*) *Austral. informal.* to pay a part of one's wages or profits as a bribe or tip. [C13: perhaps of Scandinavian origin; compare Old Norse *slyngva* to hurl, Old High German *slingan*] —'**slinger** *n.*

sling[2] (slɪŋ) *n.* a mixed drink with a spirit base, usually sweetened. [C19: of uncertain origin]

slingback ('slɪŋˌbæk) *n.* **a.** a shoe with a strap instead of a full covering for the heel. **b.** (*as modifier*): *slingback shoes.*

slinger ring *n.* a tubular ring around the hub of an aircraft propeller through which antifreeze solution is spread over the propeller blades by centrifugal force.

sling off *vb.* (*intr., adv.;* often foll. by *at*) *Austral. and N.Z. informal.* to laugh or jeer (at).

slingshot ('slɪŋˌʃɒt) *n.* **1.** the U.S. and Canadian name for **catapult** (sense 1). **2.** another name for **sling**[1] (sense 1).

slink (slɪŋk) *vb.* **slinks, slinking, slunk. 1.** (*intr.*) to move or act in a furtive or cringing manner from or as if from fear, guilt, etc. **2.** (*intr.*) to move in a sinuous alluring manner. **3.** (*tr.*) (of animals, esp. cows) to give birth to prematurely. ~*n.* **4. a.** an animal, esp. a calf, born prematurely. **b.** (*as modifier*): *slink veal.* [Old English *slincan;* related to Middle Low German *slinken* to shrink, Old Swedish *slinka* to creep, Danish *slunken* limp]

slinky ('slɪŋkɪ) *adj.* **slinkier, slinkiest.** *Informal.* **1.** moving in a sinuously graceful or provocative way. **2.** (of clothes) figure-hugging; clinging. **3.** characterized by furtive movements. —'**slinkily** *adv.* —'**slinkiness** *n.*

slinter ('slɪntə) *n. N.Z. informal and Austral. obsolete, informal.* a dodge, trick, or stratagem. Also (Austral. obsolete): **slanter, slenter.** [from Dutch *slenter,* perhaps via S. African *schlenter*]

sliotar ('ʃlɪtər) *n.* the ball used in hurling. [Irish Gaelic]

slip[1] (slɪp) *vb.* **slips, slipping, slipped. 1.** to move or cause to move smoothly and easily. **2.** (*tr.*) to place, insert, or convey quickly or stealthily. **3.** (*tr.*) to put on or take off easily or quickly: *to slip on a sweater.* **4.** (*intr.*) to lose balance and slide unexpectedly: *he slipped on the ice.* **5.** to let loose or be let loose. **6.** to be released from (something); escape. **7.** (*tr.*) to let go (mooring or anchor lines) over the side. **8.** (when *intr.,* often foll. by *from* or *out of*) to pass out of (the mind or memory). **9.** (*tr.*) to overlook, neglect, or miss: *to slip an opportunity.* **10.** (*intr.*) to move or pass swiftly or unperceived: *to slip quietly out of the room.* **11.** (*intr.;* sometimes foll. by *up*) to make a mistake. **12.** Also: **sideslip.** to cause (an aircraft) to slide sideways or (of an aircraft) to slide sideways. **13.** (*intr.*) to decline in health, mental ability, etc. **14.** (*intr.*) (of an intervertebral disc) to become displaced from the normal position. **15.** (*tr.*) to dislocate (a bone). **16.** (of animals) to give birth to (offspring) prematurely. **17.** (*tr.*) to pass (a stitch) from one needle to another without knitting it. **18. a.** (*tr.*) to operate (the clutch of a motor vehicle) so that it partially disengages. **b.** (*intr.*) (of the clutch of a motor vehicle) to fail to engage, esp. as a result of wear. **19. let slip. a.** to allow to escape. **b.** to say unintentionally. **20. slip one over on.** *Slang.* to hoodwink or trick. ~*n.* **21.** the act or an instance of slipping. **22.** a mistake or oversight: *a slip of the pen.* **23.** a moral lapse or failing. **24.** a woman's sleeveless undergarment, worn as a lining for and to give support to a dress. **25.** *U.S. and Canadian.* a narrow space between two piers in which vessels may dock. **26.** See **slipway. 27.** a kind of dog lead that allows for the quick release of the dog. **28.** a small block of hard steel of known thickness used for measurement, usually forming one of a set. **29.** the ratio between output speed and input speed of a transmission device when subtracted from unity, esp. of a drive belt or clutch that is not transmitting full power. **30.** *Cricket.* **a.** the position of the fielder who stands a little way behind and to the offside of the wicketkeeper. **b.** the fielder himself. **31.** the relative movement of rocks along a fault plane. **32.** a landslide, esp. one blocking a road or railway line. **33.** *Metallurgy, crystallog.* the deformation of a metallic crystal caused when one part glides over another part along a plane. **34.** the deviation of a propeller from its helical path through a fluid, expressed as the difference between its actual forward motion and its theoretical forward motion in one revolution. **35.** another name for **sideslip** (sense 1). **36. give someone the slip.** to elude or escape from someone. ~See also **slip up.** [C13: from Middle Low German or Dutch *slippen*] —'**slipless** *adj.*

slip[2] (slɪp) *n.* **1.** a narrow piece; strip. **2.** a small piece of paper: *a receipt slip.* **3.** a part of a plant that, when detached from the parent, will grow into a new plant; cutting; scion. **4.** a young slender person: *a slip of a child.* **5.** *Dialect.* a young pig. **6.** *Printing.* **a.** a long galley. **b.** a less common name for a **galley proof.** **7.** *Chiefly U.S.* a pew or similar long narrow seat. **8.** a small piece of abrasive material of tapering section used in honing. ~*vb.* **slips, slipping, slipped. 9.** (*tr.*) to detach (portions of stem, etc.) from (a plant) for propagation. [C15: probably from Middle Low German, Middle Dutch *slippe* to cut, strip]

slip[3] (slɪp) *n.* clay mixed with water to a creamy consistency, used for decorating or patching a ceramic piece. [Old English *slyppe* slime; related to Norwegian *slipa* slime on fish; see SLOP[1]]

slipcase ('slɪpˌkeɪs) *n.* a protective case for a book or set of books that is open at one end so that only the spines of the books are visible.

slipcover ('slɪpˌkʌvə) *n.* **1.** the U.S. and Canadian word for a **loose cover. 2.** *U.S. and Canadian.* a book jacket; dust cover.

slipe (slaɪp) *n. N.Z.* **a.** wool removed from the pelt of a slaughtered sheep by immersion in a chemical bath. **b.** (*as modifier*): *slipe wool.* [from English dialect]

slip flow *n. Physics.* gas flow occurring at hypersonic speeds in which molecular shearing occurs.

slip gauge *n.* a very accurately ground block of hardened steel used to measure a gap with close accuracy: used mainly in tool-making and inspection.

slipknot ('slɪpˌnɒt) *n.* **1.** Also called: **running knot.** a nooselike knot tied so that it will slip along the rope round which it is made. **2.** a knot that can be easily untied by pulling one free end.

slipnoose ('slɪpˌnuːs) *n.* a noose made with a slipknot, so that it tightens when pulled.

slip-on *adj.* **1.** (of a garment or shoe) made so as to be easily and quickly put on or off. ~*n.* **2.** a slip-on garment or shoe.

slipover ('slɪpˌəʊvə) *adj.* **1.** of or denoting a garment that can be put on easily over the head. ~*n.* **2.** such a garment, esp. a sleeveless pullover.

slippage ('slɪpɪdʒ) *n.* **1.** the act or an instance of slipping. **2.** the amount of slipping or the extent to which slipping occurs. **3. a.** an instance of not reaching a norm, target, etc. **b.** the extent of this. **4.** the power lost in a mechanical device or system as a result of slipping.

slipped disc *n. Pathol.* a herniated intervertebral disc, often resulting in pain because of pressure on the spinal nerves.

slipper ('slɪpə) *n.* **1.** a light shoe of some soft material, for wearing around the house. **2.** a woman's evening or dancing shoe. ~*vb.* **3.** (*tr.*) *Informal.* to hit or beat with a slipper. —'**slippered** *adj.* —'**slipper-ˌlike** *adj.*

slipper bath *n.* **1.** a bath in the shape of a slipper, with a covered end. **2.** (*pl.*) an establishment where members of the public pay to have a bath.

slipper satin *n.* a fine satin fabric with a mat finish.

slipperwort ('slɪpəˌwɜːt) *n.* another name for **calceolaria.** [C19: so called because of the slipper-like shape of the flower]

slippery ('slɪpərɪ, -prɪ) *adj.* **1.** causing or tending to cause objects to slip: *a slippery road.* **2.** liable to slip from the grasp, a position, etc. **3.** not to be relied upon; cunning and untrustworthy: *a slippery character.* **4.** (esp. of a situation) liable to change; unstable. [C16: probably coined by Coverdale to translate German *schlipfferig* in Luther's Bible (Psalm 35:6); related to Old English *slipor* slippery] —'**slipperily** *adv.* —'**slipperiness** *n.*

slippery dip *n. Austral. informal.* a long slide at a playground or funfair.

slippery elm *n.* **1.** a tree, *Ulmus fulva,* of E North America, having oblong serrated leaves, notched winged fruits, and a mucilaginous inner bark. **2.** the bark of this tree, used medicinally as a demulcent. ~Also called: **red elm.**

slippy ('slɪpɪ) *adj.* **-pier, -piest. 1.** *Informal or dialect.* another word for **slippery** (senses 1, 2). **2.** *Brit. informal.* alert; quick. —'**slippiness** *n.*

slip rail *n. Austral. and N.Z.* a rail in a fence that can be slipped out of place to make an opening.

slip ring *n. Electrical engineering.* a metal ring, mounted on but insulated from a rotating shaft of a motor or generator, by means of which current can be led through stationary brushes into or out of a winding on the shaft.

slip road *n. Brit.* a short road connecting a motorway, etc., to another road.

slipsheet ('slɪpˌʃiːt) *n.* **1.** a sheet of paper that is interleaved between freshly printed sheets to prevent set-off. ~*vb.* **2.** to interleave (printed sheets) with slipsheets.

slipshod ('slɪpˌʃɒd) *adj.* **1.** (of an action) negligent; careless. **2.** (of a person's appearance) slovenly; down-at-heel. [C16: from SLIP[1] + SHOD] —'**slipˌshoddiness** *or* '**slipˌshodness** *n.*

slipslop ('slɪpˌslɒp) *n.* **1.** *Archaic.* weak or unappetizing food or drink. **2.** *Informal.* maudlin or trivial talk or writing.

slip step *n.* a dance step made by moving the left foot one step sideways and closing the right foot to the left foot: used when dancing in a circle during Scottish reels and jigs.

slip stitch *n.* **1.** a sewing stitch for securing hems, etc., in which only two or three threads of the material are caught up by the needle each time, so that the stitches are nearly invisible from the right side. ~*vb.* **2.** (*tr.*) to join (two edges) using slip stitches. [C19: from SLIP[1]]

slipstream ('slɪpˌstriːm) *n.* **1.** Also called: **airstream, race. a.** the stream of air forced backwards by an aircraft propeller. **b.** a stream of air behind any moving object. ~*vb.* **2.** *Motor racing.* to follow (another car, etc.) closely in order to take advantage of the decreased wind resistance immediately behind it.

slip up *vb.* (*intr., adv.*) **1.** *Informal.* to make a blunder or mistake; err. **2.** to fall over: *he slipped up in the street.* ~*n.* **slip-up. 3.** *Informal.* a mistake, blunder, or mishap.

slipware ('slɪpˌwɛə) *n.* pottery that has been decorated with slip.

slipway ('slɪpˌweɪ) *n.* **1.** the sloping area in a shipyard, containing the ways. **2.** Also called: **marine railway.** the ways on which a vessel is launched. **3.** the ramp of a whaling factory ship. **4.** a pillowcase; pillowslip.

slit (slɪt) *vb.* **slits, slitting, slit.** (*tr.*) **1.** to make a straight long incision in; split open. **2.** to cut into strips lengthwise. **3.** to sever. ~*n.* **4.** a long narrow cut. **5.** a long narrow opening. [Old English *slītan* to slice; related to Old Norse *slíta,* Old High German *slīzen*] —'**slitter** *n.*

slither ('slɪðə) *vb.* **1.** to move or slide or cause to move or slide unsteadily, as on a slippery surface. **2.** (*intr.*) to travel with a sliding motion. ~*n.* **3.** a slithering motion. [Old English *slidrian,* from *slīdan* to SLIDE] —'**slithery** *adj.*

slit pocket *n.* a pocket on the underside of a garment, reached through a vertical opening.

slit trench *n. Military.* a narrow trench dug for the protection of a small number of people.

sliver ('slɪvə) *n.* **1.** a thin piece that is cut or broken off lengthwise; splinter. **2.** a loose strand or fibre obtained by carding. ~*vb.* **3.** to divide or be divided into splinters; split. **4.** (*tr.*) to form (wool, etc.) into slivers. [C14: from *sliven* to split] —'**sliver-ˌlike** *adj.*

slivovitz ('slɪvəvɪts, 'sliːvə-) *n.* a plum brandy from E Europe. [from Serbo-Croatian *šljivovica,* from *sljiva* plum]

Sloane Ranger (sləʊn) *n.* (in Britain) *Informal.* a young upper-class or upper-middle-class person, esp. a woman, having a home in London and in the country, characterized typically as wearing expensive informal country clothes. Also called: **Sloane.** [C20: coined by Peter York, punning on *Sloane* Square, London SW1, and *Lone Ranger,* cowboy cartoon character]

slob (slɒb) *n.* **1.** *Informal.* a slovenly, unattractive, and lazy person. **2.** *Irish.* mire. [C19: from Irish *slab* mud; compare SLAB] —'**slobbish** *adj.*

slobber ('slɒbə) *or* **slabber** *vb.* **1.** to dribble (saliva, food, etc.) from the mouth. **2.** (*intr.*) to speak or write mawkishly. **3.** (*tr.*) to smear with matter dribbling from the mouth. ~*n.* **4.** liquid or saliva spilt from the mouth. **5.** maudlin language or behaviour. [C15: from Middle Low German, Middle Dutch *slubberen;* see SLAVER[2]] —'**slobberer** *or* '**slabberer** *n.* —'**slobbery** *or* '**slabbery** *adj.*

slob ice *n. Canadian.* sludgy masses of floating ice. [see SLOB]

sloe (sləʊ) *n.* **1.** the small sour blue-black fruit of the blackthorn. **2.** another name for **blackthorn.** [Old English *slāh;* related to Old High German *slēha,* Middle Dutch *sleuuwe*]

sloe-eyed *adj.* having dark slanted or almond-shaped eyes.

sloe gin *n.* gin flavoured with sloe juice.

slog (slɒg) *vb.* **slogs, slogging, slogged. 1.** to hit with heavy blows, as in boxing. **2.** (*intr.*) to work hard; toil. **3.** (*intr.;* foll. by *down, up, along,* etc.) to move with difficulty; plod. **4.** *Cricket.* to score freely by taking large swipes at the ball. ~*n.* **5.** a tiring hike or walk. **6.** long exhausting work. **7.** a heavy blow or swipe. [C19: of unknown origin] —'**slogger** *n.*

slogan ('sləʊgən) *n.* **1.** a distinctive or topical phrase used in politics, advertising, etc. **2.** *Scottish history.* a Highland battle cry. [C16: from Gaelic *sluagh-ghairm* war cry, from *sluagh* army + *gairm* cry]

sloganeer (ˌsləʊgə'nɪə) *Chiefly U.S.* ~*n.* **1.** a person who coins or employs slogans frequently. ~*vb.* **2.** (*intr.*) to coin or employ slogans so as to sway opinion.

sloop (sluːp) *n.* a single-masted sailing vessel, rigged fore-and-aft, with the mast stepped about one third of the overall length aft of the bow. Compare **cutter** (sense 2). [C17: from Dutch *sloep;* related to French *chaloupe* launch, Old English *slūpan* to glide]

sloop of war *n.* (formerly) a small fast sailing warship mounting some 10 to 30 small calibre guns on one deck.

sloop-rigged *adj. Nautical.* rigged as a sloop, typically with a jib and a mainsail.

sloot (sluːt) *n. S. African.* a ditch for irrigation or drainage. [from Afrikaans, from Dutch *sluit, sluis* SLUICE]

slop[1] (slɒp) *vb.* **slops, slopping, slopped. 1.** (when *intr.,* often foll. by *about*) to cause (liquid) to splash or spill or (of liquid) to splash or spill. **2.** (*tr.*) to splash liquid upon. **3.** (*intr.*; foll. by *along, through*, etc.) to tramp (through) mud or slush. **4.** (*tr.*) to feed slop or swill to: *to slop the pigs*. **5.** (*tr.*) to ladle or serve, esp. clumsily. **6.** (*intr.*; foll. by *over*) *Informal, chiefly U.S. and Canadian.* to be unpleasantly effusive. ~*n.* **7.** a puddle of spilt liquid. **8.** (*pl.*) wet feed, esp. for pigs, made from kitchen waste, etc. **9.** (*pl.*) waste food or liquid refuse. **10.** (*pl.*) the beer, cider, etc., spilt from a barrel while being drawn. **11.** (*often pl.*) the residue left after spirits have been distilled. **12.** (*often pl.*) *Informal.* liquid or semiliquid food of low quality. **13.** soft mud, snow, etc. **14.** *Informal.* gushing speech or writing. [C14: probably from Old English *-sloppe* in *cūsloppe* COWSLIP; see SLIP[3]]

slop[2] (slɒp) *n.* **1.** (*pl.*) sailors' clothing and bedding issued from a ship's stores. **2.** any loose article of clothing, esp. a smock. **3.** (*pl.*) men's wide knee breeches worn in the 16th century. **4.** (*pl.*) shoddy manufactured clothing. [Old English *oferslop* surplice; related to Old Norse *slopps* gown, Middle Dutch *slop*]

slop around *vb.* (*intr.*) to move around in a casual and idle way: *he slops around the house in old slippers.* Also: **slop about.**

slop basin *n.* a bowl or basin into which the dregs from teacups are emptied at the table.

slop chest *n.* a stock of merchandise, such as clothing, tobacco, etc., maintained aboard merchant ships for sale to the crew. Compare **small stores.**

slope (sləʊp) *vb.* **1.** to lie or cause to lie at a slanting or oblique angle. **2.** (*intr.*) (esp. of natural features) to follow an inclined course: *many paths sloped down the hillside.* **3.** (*intr.*; foll. by *off, away*, etc.) to go furtively. **4.** (*tr.*) *Military.* (formerly) to hold (a rifle) in the slope position (esp. in the command **slope arms**). ~*n.* **5.** an inclined portion of ground. **6.** (*pl.*) hills or foothills. **7.** any inclined surface or line. **8.** the degree or amount of such inclination. **9.** *Maths.* **a.** (of a line) the tangent of the angle between the line and another line parallel to the *x*-axis. **b.** the first derivative of the equation of a curve at a given point. **10.** (formerly) the position adopted for British military drill when the rifle is rested on the shoulder. [C15: short for *aslope*, perhaps from the past participle of Old English *āslūpan* to slip away, from *slūpan* to slip] —**ˈsloper** *n.* —**ˈsloping** *adj.* —**ˈslopingly** *adv.* —**ˈslopingness** *n.*

slop out *vb.* (*intr., adv.*) (of prisoners) to empty chamber pots and collect water for washing.

sloppy (ˈslɒpɪ) *adj.* **-pier, -piest.** **1.** (esp. of ground conditions, etc.) wet; slushy. **2.** *Informal.* careless; untidy. **3.** *Informal.* mawkishly sentimental. **4.** (of food or drink) watery and unappetizing. **5.** splashed with slops. **6.** (of clothes) loose; baggy. —**ˈsloppily** *adv.* —**ˈsloppiness** *n.*

sloppy joe (dʒəʊ) *n. Informal.* a long baggy thin sweater.

slopwork (ˈslɒpˌwɜːk) *n.* **1.** the manufacture of cheap shoddy clothing or the clothes so produced. **2.** any work of low quality. —**ˈslopˌworker** *n.*

slosh (slɒʃ) *n.* **1.** watery mud, snow, etc. **2.** *Brit. slang.* a heavy blow. **3.** the sound of splashing liquid. ~*vb.* **4.** (*tr.*; foll. by *around, on, in*, etc.) *Informal.* to throw or pour (liquid). **5.** (when *intr.*, often foll. by *about* or *around*) *Informal.* **a.** to shake or stir (something) in a liquid. **b.** (of a person) to splash (around) in water, etc. **6.** (*tr.*) *Brit. slang.* to deal a heavy blow to. **7.** (usually foll. by *about* or *around*) *Informal.* to shake (a container of liquid) or (of liquid within a container) to be shaken. [C19: variant of SLUSH, influenced by SLOP[1]] —**ˈsloshy** *adj.*

sloshed (slɒʃt) *adj. Chiefly Brit.* a slang word for **drunk.**

slot[1] (slɒt) *n.* **1.** an elongated aperture or groove, such as one in a vending machine for inserting a coin. **2.** an air passage in an aerofoil to direct air from the lower to the upper surface, esp. the gap formed behind a slat. **3.** a vertical opening between the leech of a foresail and a mast or the luff of another sail through which air spills from one against the other to impart forward motion. **4.** *Informal.* a place in a series or scheme. ~*vb.* **slots, slotting, slotted.** **5.** (*tr.*) to furnish with a slot or slots. **6.** (usually foll. by *in* or *into*) to fit or adjust in a slot. **7.** *Informal.* to situate or be situated in a series or scheme. [C13: from Old French *esclot* the depression of the breastbone, of unknown origin] —**ˈslotter** *n.*

slot[2] (slɒt) *n.* the trail of an animal, esp. a deer. [C16: from Old French *esclot* horse's hoof-print, probably of Scandinavian origin; compare Old Norse *sloth* track; see SLEUTH]

slot aerial *or* **antenna** *n. Radio.* a transmitting aerial in which the radiating elements are open slots in a surrounding metal sheet.

sloth (sləʊθ) *n.* **1.** any of several shaggy-coated arboreal edentate mammals of the family *Bradypodidae*, esp. *Bradypus tridactylus* (**three-toed sloth** or **ai**) or *Choloepus didactylus* (**two-toed sloth** or **unau**), of Central and South America. They are slow-moving, hanging upside down by their long arms and feeding on vegetation. **2.** reluctance to work or exert oneself. [Old English *slǣwth*; from *slǣw*, variant of *slāw* SLOW]

sloth bear *n.* a bear, *Melursus ursinus*, of forests of S India and Sri Lanka, having a shaggy coat and an elongated snout specialized for feeding on termites.

slothful (ˈsləʊθfʊl) *adj.* lazy; indolent. —**ˈslothfully** *adv.* —**ˈslothfulness** *n.*

slot machine *n.* a machine, esp. one for selling small articles or for gambling, activated by placing a coin or metal disc in a slot.

slouch (slaʊtʃ) *vb.* **1.** (*intr.*) to sit or stand with a drooping bearing. **2.** (*intr.*) to walk or move with an awkward slovenly gait. **3.** (*tr.*) to cause (the shoulders) to droop. ~*n.* **4.** a drooping carriage. **5.** (*usually used in negative constructions*) *Informal.* an incompetent or slovenly person: *he's no slouch at football.* [C16: of unknown origin] —**ˈsloucher** *n.* —**ˈslouchy** *adj.* —**ˈslouchily** *adv.* —**ˈslouchiness** *n.* —**ˈslouching** *adj.* —**ˈslouchingly** *adv.*

slouch hat *n.* any soft hat with a brim that can be pulled down over the ears, esp. an Australian army hat with the left side of the brim turned up.

slough[1] (slaʊ) *n.* **1.** a hollow filled with mud; bog. **2.** (sluː) *North American.* **a.** (in the prairies) a large hole where water collects or the water in such a hole. **b.** (in the northwest) a sluggish side channel of a river. **c.** (on the Pacific coast) a marshy saltwater inlet. **3.** despair or degradation. [Old English *slōh*; related to Middle High German *sluoche* ditch, Swedish *slaga* swamp] —**ˈsloughy** *adj.*

slough[2] (slʌf) *n.* **1.** any outer covering that is shed, such as the dead outer layer of the skin of a snake, the cellular debris in a wound, etc. **2.** Also: **sluff.** *Bridge.* a discarded card. ~*vb.* **3.** (often foll. by *off*) to shed (a skin, etc.) or (of a skin, etc.) to be shed. **4.** Also: **sluff.** *Bridge.* to discard (a card or cards). [C13: of Germanic origin; compare Middle Low German *slū* husk, German *Schlauch* hose, Norwegian *slō* fleshy part of a horn] —**ˈsloughy** *adj.*

slough off (slʌf) *vb.* (*tr., adv.*) to cast off (cares, etc.).

Slovak (ˈsləʊvæk) *adj.* **1.** Also: **Sloˈvakian.** of, relating to, or characteristic of Slovakia, a region of E Czechoslovakia, or of its people or their language. ~*n.* **2.** one of the two official languages of Czechoslovakia, belonging to the West Slavonic branch of the Indo-European family. Czech and Slovak are closely related and mutually intelligible. **3.** Also: **Sloˈvakian.** a native or inhabitant of Slovakia.

sloven (ˈslʌvᵊn) *n.* a person who is habitually negligent in appearance, hygiene, or work. [C15: probably related to Flemish *sloef* dirty, Dutch *slof* negligent]

Slovene (sləʊˈviːn) *adj.* **1.** Also: **Sloˈvenian.** of, relating to, or characteristic of the republic of Slovenia (formerly part of Yugoslavia), its people, or their language. ~*n.* **2.** a South Slavonic language spoken in Slovenia, closely related to Serbo-Croatian. **3.** Also: **Sloˈvenian. a.** a native or inhabitant of Slovenia. **b.** (esp. in parts of Yugoslavia) a speaker of Slovene.

slovenly (ˈslʌvənlɪ) *adj.* **1.** frequently or habitually unclean or untidy. **2.** negligent and careless; slipshod: *slovenly manners.* ~*adv.* **3.** in a negligent or slovenly manner. —**ˈslovenliness** *n.*

slow (sləʊ) *adj.* **1.** performed or occurring during a comparatively long interval of time. **2.** lasting a comparatively long time: *a slow journey.* **3.** characterized by lack of speed: *a slow walker.* **4.** (*prenominal*) adapted to or productive of slow movement: *the slow lane of a motorway.* **5.** (of a clock, etc.) indicating a time earlier than the correct time. **6.** given to or characterized by a leisurely or lazy existence: *a slow town.* **7.** not readily responsive to stimulation; intellectually unreceptive: *a slow mind.* **8.** dull or uninteresting: *the play was very slow.* **9.** not easily aroused: *a slow temperament.* **10.** lacking promptness or immediacy: *a slow answer.* **11.** unwilling to perform an action or enter into a state: *slow to anger.* **12.** unpunctual or late: *don't be slow or you'll miss the train.* **13.** behind the times. **14.** (of trade, etc.) unproductive; slack. **15.** lacking skill or nimbleness: *slow fingers.* **16.** (of a fire) burning weakly. **17.** (of an oven) cool. **18.** *Photog.* requiring a relatively long time of exposure to produce a given density: *a slow lens.* **19.** *Sport.* (of a track, etc.) tending to reduce the speed of the ball or the competitors. **20.** *Cricket.* (of a bowler, etc.) delivering the ball slowly, usually with spin. ~*adv.* **21.** in a manner characterized by lack of speed; slowly. ~*vb.* **22.** (often foll. by *up* or *down*) to decrease or cause to decrease in speed, efficiency, etc. [Old English *slāw* sluggish; related to Old High German *slēo* dull, Old Norse *slǣr*, Dutch *sleeuw* slow] —**ˈslowly** *adv.* —**ˈslowness** *n.*

slow burn *n.* a steadily penetrating show of anger or contempt.

slowcoach (ˈsləʊˌkəʊtʃ) *n. Brit. informal.* a person who moves, acts, or works slowly. U.S. and Canadian equivalent: **slowpoke.**

slowdown (ˈsləʊˌdaʊn) *n.* **1.** the usual U.S. and Canadian word for **go-slow.** **2.** any slackening of pace.

slow handclap *n. Brit.* slow rhythmic clapping, esp. used by an audience to indicate dissatisfaction or impatience.

slow march *n. Military.* a march in slow time.

slow match *n.* a match or fuse that burns slowly without flame, esp. a wick impregnated with potassium nitrate.

slow-mo *or* **slo-mo** (ˈsləʊˌməʊ) *n., adj. Informal.* short for **slow motion.**

slow motion *n.* **1.** *Films, television, etc.* action that is made to appear slower than normal by passing the film through the taking camera at a faster rate than normal or by replaying a video tape recording more slowly. ~*adj.* **slow-motion.** **2.** of or relating to such action. **3.** moving or functioning at considerably less than usual speed.

slow neutron *n. Physics.* a neutron having a kinetic energy of less than 100 electronvolts.

slowpoke (ˈsləʊˌpəʊk) *n. Informal.* the usual U.S. and Canadian word for **slowcoach.**

slow time *n. Military.* a slow marching pace, usually 65 or 75 paces to the minute: used esp. in funeral ceremonies.

slow virus *n.* any of a class of virus-like disease-causing agents that are present in the body for a long time before becoming active or infectious and are very resistant to radiation and similar factors: believed to be the cause of BSE and scrapie.

slow-witted *adj.* slow in comprehension; unintelligent.

slowworm ('sləʊˌwɜːm) *n.* a Eurasian legless lizard, *Anguis fragilis,* with a brownish-grey snakelike body: family *Anguidae.* Also called: **blindworm.**

SLR *abbrev. for* single-lens reflex. See **reflex camera.**

slub (slʌb) *n.* **1.** a lump in yarn or fabric, often made intentionally to give a knobbly effect. **2.** a loosely twisted roll of fibre prepared for spinning. *~vb.* **slubs, slubbing, slubbed. 3.** *(tr.)* to draw out and twist (a sliver of fibre) preparatory to spinning. *~adj.* **4.** (of material) having an irregular appearance. [C18: of unknown origin]

slubberdegullion (ˌslʌbədɪ'gʌlɪən) *n. Archaic.* a slovenly or worthless person. [C17: from *slubber* (chiefly dialect variant of SLOBBER) + invented ending]

sludge (slʌdʒ) *n.* **1.** soft mud, snow, etc. **2.** any deposit or sediment. **3.** a surface layer of ice that is not frozen solid but has a slushy appearance. **4.** (in sewage disposal) the solid constituents of sewage that precipitate during treatment and are removed for subsequent purification. [C17: probably related to SLUSH] —'**sludgy** *adj.*

slue[1] (sluː) *n., vb.* a variant spelling (esp. U.S.) of **slew**[2].

slue[2] (sluː) *n.* a variant spelling of **slough**[1] (sense 2).

slue[3] (sluː) *n. U.S. informal.* a variant spelling of **slew**[4].

sluff (slʌf) *n., vb. Bridge.* a variant spelling of **slough**[2].

slug[1] (slʌg) *n.* **1.** any of various terrestrial gastropod molluscs of the genera *Limax, Arion,* etc., in which the body is elongated and the shell is absent or very much reduced. Compare **sea slug. 2.** any of various other invertebrates having a soft slimy body, esp. the larvae of certain sawflies. **3.** *Informal, chiefly U.S. and Canadian.* a slow-moving or lazy person or animal. [C15 (in the sense: a slow person or animal): probably of Scandinavian origin; compare Norwegian (dialect) *sluggje*]

slug[2] (slʌg) *n.* **1.** an fps unit of mass; the mass that will acquire an acceleration of 1 foot per second per second when acted upon by a force of 1 pound. 1 slug is approximately equal to 32.17 pounds. **2.** *Metallurgy.* a metal blank from which small forgings are worked. **3.** a bullet or pellet larger than a pellet of buckshot. **4.** *Chiefly U.S. and Canadian.* a metal token for use in slot machines, etc. **5.** *Printing.* **a.** a thick strip of type metal that is less than type-high and is used for spacing. **b.** a similar strip carrying a type-high letter, used as a temporary mark by compositors. **c.** a metal strip containing a line of characters as produced by a Linotype machine. **6.** a draught of alcoholic drink, esp. spirits. **7.** a magnetic core that is screwed into or out of an inductance coil to adjust the tuning of a radio frequency amplifier. [C17 (bullet), C19 (printing): perhaps from SLUG[1], with allusion to the shape of the animal]

slug[3] (slʌg) *vb.* **slugs, slugging, slugged. 1.** to hit very hard and solidly, as in boxing. **2.** *(intr.) U.S. and Canadian.* to plod as if through snow. **3.** *(tr.) Austral. and N.Z. informal.* to charge (someone) an exorbitant price. *~n.* **4.** an act of slugging; heavy blow. **5.** *Austral. and N.Z. informal.* an exorbitant charge or price. [C19: perhaps from SLUG[2] (bullet)]

slugabed ('slʌgəˌbɛd) *n.* a person who remains in bed through laziness. [C16: from SLUG(GARD) + ABED]

sluggard ('slʌgəd) *n.* **1.** a person who is habitually indolent. *~adj.* **2.** lazy. [C14 *slogarde;* related to SLUG[1]] —'**sluggardly** *adj.* —'**sluggardliness** *n.* —'**sluggardness** *n.*

slugger ('slʌgə) *n.* (esp. in boxing, baseball, etc.) a person who strikes hard.

sluggish ('slʌgɪʃ) *adj.* **1.** lacking energy; inactive; slow-moving. **2.** functioning at below normal rate or level. **3.** exhibiting poor response to stimulation. —'**sluggishly** *adv.* —'**sluggishness** *n.*

sluice (sluːs) *n.* **1.** Also called: **sluiceway.** a channel that carries a rapid current of water, esp. one that has a sluicegate to control the flow. **2.** the body of water controlled by a sluicegate. **3.** See **sluicegate. 4.** *Mining.* an inclined trough for washing ore, esp. one having riffles on the bottom to trap particles. **5.** an artificial channel through which logs can be floated. **6.** *Informal.* a brief wash in running water. *~vb.* **7.** *(tr.)* to draw out or drain (water, etc.) from (a pond, etc.) by means of a sluice. **8.** *(tr.)* to wash or irrigate with a stream of water. **9.** *(tr.) Mining.* to wash in a sluice. **10.** *(tr.)* to send (logs, etc.) down a sluice. **11.** *(intr.;* often foll. by *away* or *out)* (of water, etc.) to run or flow from or as if from a sluice. **12.** *(tr.)* to provide with a sluice. [C14: from Old French *escluse,* from Late Latin *exclūsa aqua* water shut out, from Latin *exclūdere* to shut out, EXCLUDE] —'**sluiceˌlike** *adj.*

sluicegate ('sluːsˌgeɪt) *n.* a valve or gate fitted to a sluice to control the rate of flow of water. Sometimes shortened to **sluice.** See also **floodgate** (sense 1).

slum (slʌm) *n.* **1.** a squalid overcrowded house, etc. **2.** *(often pl.)* a squalid section of a city, characterized by inferior living conditions and usually by overcrowding. **3.** *(modifier)* of, relating to, or characteristic of slums: *slum conditions. ~vb.* **slums, slumming, slummed.** *(intr.)* **4.** to visit slums, esp. for curiosity. **5.** Also: **slum it.** to suffer conditions below those to which one is accustomed. [C19: originally slang, of obscure origin] —'**slummer** *n.* —'**slummy** *adj.*

slumber ('slʌmbə) *vb.* **1.** *(intr.)* to sleep, esp. peacefully. **2.** *(intr.)* to be quiescent or dormant. **3.** *(tr.;* foll. by *away)* to spend (time) sleeping. *~n.* **4.** *(sometimes pl.)* sleep. **5.** a dormant or quiescent state. [Old English *slūma* sleep (n.); related to Middle High German *slummeren,* Dutch *sluimeren*] —'**slumberer** *n.* —'**slumberless** *adj.*

slumberous ('slʌmbərəs, -brəs) *adj. Chiefly poetic.* **1.** sleepy; drowsy. **2.** inducing sleep. **3.** characteristic of slumber. —'**slumberously** *adv.* —'**slumberousness** *n.*

slumber party *n. U.S. and Canadian.* a party attended by girls who dress in night clothes and pass the night eating, talking, etc.

slumgullion (slʌm'gʌljən, 'slʌmˌgʌl-) *n. U.S. and Canadian.* **1.** *Slang.* an inexpensive stew. **2.** offal, esp. the refuse from whale blubber. **3.** a reddish mud deposited in mine sluices. [C19: from *slum* in U.S. sense slime + *gullion,* perhaps variant of *cullion* testicles]

slumlord ('slʌmˌlɔːd) *n. Informal, chiefly U.S. and Canadian.* an absentee landlord of slum property, esp. one who profiteers.

slump (slʌmp) *vb. (intr.)* **1.** to sink or fall heavily and suddenly. **2.** to relax ungracefully. **3.** (of business activity, etc.) to decline suddenly; collapse. **4.** (of health, interest, etc.) to deteriorate or decline suddenly or markedly. **5.** (of soil or rock) to slip down a slope, esp. a cliff, usually with a rotational movement. *~n.* **6.** a sudden or marked decline or failure, as in progress or achievement; collapse. **7.** a decline in commercial activity, prices, etc. **8.** *Economics.* another word for **depression. 9.** the act of slumping. **10.** a slipping of earth or rock; landslide. [C17: probably of Scandinavian origin; compare Low German *slump* bog, Norwegian *slumpa* to fall]

Slump (slʌmp) *n.* **the.** another name for the **Depression.**

slumpflation (slʌmp'fleɪʃən) *n.* a situation in which economic depression is combined with increasing inflation. [C20: blend of SLUMP + INFLATION]

slump test *n. Brit.* a test to determine the relative water content of concrete, depending on the loss in height (slump) of a sample obtained from a cone-shaped mould.

slung (slʌŋ) *adj.* the past tense and past participle of **sling**[1].

slung shot *n.* a weight attached to the end of a cord and used as a weapon.

slunk (slʌŋk) *vb.* the past tense and past participle of **slink.**

slur (slɜː) *vb.* **slurs, slurring, slurred.** *(mainly tr.)* **1.** (often foll. by *over)* to treat superficially, hastily, or without due deliberation; gloss. **2.** *(also intr.)* to pronounce or utter (words, etc.) indistinctly. **3.** to speak disparagingly of or cast aspersions on. **4.** *Music.* to execute (a melodic interval of two or more notes) smoothly, as in legato performance. **5.** *(also intr.)* to blur or smear. **6.** *Archaic.* to stain or smear; sully. *~n.* **7.** an indistinct sound or utterance. **8.** a slighting remark; aspersion. **9.** a stain or disgrace, as upon one's reputation; stigma. **10.** *Music.* **a.** a performance or execution of a melodic interval of two or more notes in a part. **b.** the curved line (‿ or ⁀) indicating this. **11.** a blur or smear. [C15: probably from Middle Low German; compare Middle Low German *slūren* to drag, trail, Middle Dutch *sloren,* Dutch *sleuren*]

slurp (slɜːp) *Informal. ~vb.* **1.** to eat or drink (something) noisily. *~n.* **2.** a sound produced in this way. [C17: from Middle Dutch *slorpen* to sip; related to German *schlürfen*]

slurry ('slʌrɪ) *n., pl.* **-ries.** a suspension of solid particles in a liquid, as in a mixture of cement, clay, manure, or coal dust with water. [C15 *slory;* see SLUR]

slush (slʌʃ) *n.* **1.** any watery muddy substance, esp. melting snow. **2.** *Informal.* sloppily sentimental language. **3.** *Nautical.* waste fat from the galley of a ship. *~vb.* **4.** *(intr.;* often foll. by *along)* to make one's way through or as if through slush. **5.** *(intr.)* to make a slushing sound. [C17: related to Danish *slus* sleet, Norwegian *slusk* slops; see SLUDGE, SLOSH]

slush fund *n.* **1.** a fund for financing political or commercial corruption. **2.** *U.S. nautical.* a fund accumulated from the sale of slush from the galley.

slushy ('slʌʃɪ) *adj.* **slushier, slushiest. 1.** of, resembling, or consisting of slush. *~n., pl.* **slushies. 2.** *Austral. slang.* an unskilled kitchen assistant. —'**slushiness** *n.*

slut (slʌt) *n.* **1.** a dirty slatternly woman. **2.** an immoral woman. **3.** *Archaic.* a female dog. [C14: of unknown origin] —'**sluttish** *adj.* —'**sluttishly** *adv.* —'**sluttishness** *n.*

sly (slaɪ) *adj.* **slyer, slyest** *or* **slier, sliest. 1.** crafty; artful: *a sly dodge.* **2.** insidious; furtive: *a sly manner.* **3.** playfully mischievous; roguish: *sly humour. ~n.* **4. on the sly.** in a secretive manner. [C12: from Old Norse *slǣgr* clever, literally: able to strike, from *slā* to SLAY] —'**slyly** *or* '**slily** *adv.* —'**slyness** *n.*

slyboots ('slaɪˌbuːts) *pl. n. (functioning as sing.)* a person who is sly.

sly grog *n. Austral. and N.Z.* illicitly sold liquor.

slype (slaɪp) *n.* a covered passageway in a cathedral or church that connects the transept to the chapterhouse. [C19: probably from Middle Flemish *slijpen* to slip]

Sm *the chemical symbol for* samarium.

SM *abbrev. for* sergeant major.

s/m *abbrev. for* sadomasochism.

smack[1] (smæk) *n.* **1.** a smell or flavour that is distinctive though faint. **2.** a distinctive trace or touch: *the smack of corruption.* **3.** a small quantity, esp. a mouthful or taste. **4.** a slang word for **heroin.** *~vb. (intr.;* foll. by *of)* **5.** to have the characteristic smell or flavour (of something): *to smack of the sea.* **6.** to have an element suggestive (of something): *his speeches smacked of bigotry.* [Old English *smæc;* related to Old High German *smoc,* Icelandic *smekkr* a taste, Dutch *smaak*]

smack[2] (smæk) *vb.* **1.** (*tr.*) to strike or slap smartly, with or as if with the open hand. **2.** to strike or send forcibly or loudly or to be struck or sent forcibly or loudly. **3.** to open and close (the lips) loudly, esp. to show pleasure. **4.** (*tr.*) to kiss noisily. ~*n.* **5.** a sharp resounding slap or blow with something flat, or the sound of such a blow. **6.** a loud kiss. **7.** a sharp sound made by the lips, as in enjoyment. **8. have a smack at.** *Informal, chiefly Brit.* to attempt. **9. smack in the eye.** *Informal, chiefly Brit.* a snub or setback. ~*adv. Informal.* **10.** directly; squarely. **11.** with a smack; sharply and unexpectedly. [C16: from Middle Low German or Middle Dutch *smacken,* probably of imitative origin]

smack[3] (smæk) *n.* **1.** a sailing vessel, usually sloop-rigged, used in coasting and fishing along the British coast. **2.** a fishing vessel equipped with a well for keeping the catch alive. [C17: from Low German *smack* or Dutch *smak,* of unknown origin]

smacker (ˈsmækə) *n. Slang.* **1.** a loud kiss; smack. **2.** a pound note or dollar bill.

smacking (ˈsmækɪŋ) *adj.* brisk; lively: *a smacking breeze.*

small (smɔːl) *adj.* **1.** comparatively little; limited in size, number, importance, etc. **2.** of little importance or on a minor scale: *a small business.* **3.** lacking in moral or mental breadth or depth: *a small mind.* **4.** modest or humble: *small beginnings.* **5.** of low or inferior status, esp. socially. **6.** (of a child or animal) young; not mature. **7.** unimportant, trivial: *a small matter.* **8.** not outstanding: *a small actor.* **9.** of, relating to, or designating the ordinary modern minuscule letter used in printing and cursive writing. Compare **capital**[1] (sense 13). See also **lower case. 10.** lacking great strength or force: *a small effort.* **11.** in fine particles: *small gravel.* **12.** *Obsolete.* (of beer, etc.) of low alcoholic strength. ~*adv.* **13.** into small pieces: *cut it small.* **14.** in a small or soft manner. **15. feel small.** to be humiliated or inferior. **16. sing small.** *Rare.* to behave humbly. ~*n.* **17.** (often preceded by *the*) an object, person, or group considered to be small: *the small or the large?* **18.** a small slender part, esp. of the back. **19.** (*pl.*) *Informal, chiefly Brit.* items of personal laundry, such as underwear. [Old English *smæl;* related to Old High German *smal,* Old Norse *smali* small cattle] —ˈ**smallish** *adj.* —ˈ**smallness** *n.*

smallage (ˈsmɔːlɪdʒ) *n.* an archaic name for **wild celery.** [C13: from earlier *smalache,* from *smal* SMALL + *ache* wild celery, from Old French, from Latin *apium*]

small arms *pl. n.* portable firearms of relatively small calibre.

small beer *n.* **1.** *Informal, chiefly Brit.* people or things of no importance. **2.** *Now rare.* weak or inferior beer.

smallboy (ˈsmɔːlˌbɔɪ) *n.* the steward's assistant or deputy steward in European households in W Africa.

small calorie *n.* another name for **calorie.**

small capital *n.* a letter having the form of an upper-case letter but the same height as a lower-case letter.

small change *n.* **1.** coins, esp. those of low value. **2.** a person or thing that is not outstanding or important.

small chop *n. W African.* cocktail snacks.

small circle *n.* a circular section of a sphere that does not contain the centre of the sphere. Compare **great circle.**

small claims court *n. Brit.* a local court administered by the county court with jurisdiction to try civil actions involving small claims.

smallclothes (ˈsmɔːlˌkləʊz, -ˌkləʊðz) *pl. n.* men's close-fitting knee breeches of the 18th and 19th centuries.

small fry *pl. n.* **1.** people or things regarded as unimportant. **2.** young children. **3.** young or small fishes.

small game *n. Brit.* small animals that are hunted for sport.

small goods *pl. n. Austral. and N.Z.* meats bought from a delicatessen, such as sausages.

smallholding (ˈsmɔːlˌhəʊldɪŋ) *n.* a holding of agricultural land smaller than a small farm. —ˈ**smallˌholder** *n.*

small hours *pl. n.* **the.** the early hours of the morning, after midnight and before dawn.

small intestine *n.* the longest part of the alimentary canal, consisting of the duodenum, jejunum, and ileum, in which digestion is completed. Compare **large intestine.**

small letter *n.* a lower-case letter.

small-minded *adj.* narrow-minded; petty; intolerant; mean. —ˌ**small-ˈmindedly** *adv.* —ˌ**small-ˈmindedness** *n.*

smallmouth bass (ˈsmɔːlˌmaʊθ ˈbæs) *n.* a North American freshwater black bass, *Micropterus dolomieu,* that is a popular game fish.

small pica *n.* (formerly) a size of printer's type approximately equal to 11 point.

small potatoes *n.* (*functioning as sing. or pl.*) *U.S. and Canadian informal.* someone or something of little significance or value, esp. a small amount of money.

smallpox (ˈsmɔːlˌpɒks) *n.* an acute highly contagious viral disease characterized by high fever, severe prostration, and a pinkish rash changing in form from papules to pustules, which dry up and form scabs that are cast off, leaving pitted depressions. Technical name: **variola.** [C16: from SMALL + POX. So called to distinguish it from *the Great Pox,* an archaic name for syphilis]

small print *n.* matter in a contract, etc., printed in small type, esp. when considered to be a trap for the unwary.

small-scale *adj.* **1.** of limited size or scope. **2.** (of a map, model, etc.) giving a relatively small representation of something, usually missing out details.

small screen *n.* an informal name for **television.**

small slam *n. Bridge.* another name for **little slam.**

small stores *pl. n. Navy.* personal items, such as clothing, sold aboard ship or at a naval base. Compare **slop chest.**

small stuff *n. Nautical.* any light twine or yarn used aboard ship for serving lines, etc.

smallsword (ˈsmɔːlˌsɔːd) *n.* a light sword used in the 17th and 18th centuries: formerly a fencing weapon.

small talk *n.* light conversation for social occasions.

small-time *adj. Informal.* insignificant; minor: *a small-time criminal.* —ˈ**small-ˈtimer** *n.*

small white *n.* a small white butterfly, *Artogeia rapae,* with scanty black markings, the larvae of which feed on brassica leaves.

smalt (smɔːlt) *n.* **1.** a type of silica glass coloured deep blue with cobalt oxide. **2.** a pigment made by crushing this glass, used in colouring enamels. **3.** the blue colour of this pigment. [C16: via French from Italian SMALTO, of Germanic origin; related to SMELT[1]]

smaltite (ˈsmɔːltaɪt) *n.* a silver-white to greyish mineral consisting chiefly of cobalt arsenide with nickel in cubic crystalline form. It occurs in veins associated with silver, nickel, and copper minerals, and is an important ore of cobalt and nickel. Formula: $(Co,Ni)As_2$. [C19: from SMALT + -ITE[1]]

smalto (ˈsmɑːltəʊ) *n., pl.* **-tos** *or* **-ti** (-tiː). coloured glass, etc., used in mosaics. [C18: from Italian; see SMALT]

smaragd (ˈsmærægd) *n. Archaic.* any green gemstone, such as the emerald. [C13: via Latin from Greek *smaragdos;* see EMERALD] —**smaragdine** (sməˈrægdɪn) *adj.*

smaragdite (sməˈrægdaɪt) *n.* a green fibrous amphibole mineral.

smarm (smɑːm) *Brit. informal.* ~*vb.* **1.** (*tr.;* often foll. by *down*) to flatten (the hair, etc.) with cream or grease. **2.** (when *intr.,* foll. by *up to*) to ingratiate oneself (with). ~*n.* **3.** obsequious flattery. [C19: of unknown origin]

smarmy (ˈsmɑːmɪ) *adj.* **smarmier, smarmiest.** *Brit. informal.* obsequiously flattering or unpleasantly suave. —ˈ**smarmily** *adv.* —ˈ**smarminess** *n.*

smart (smɑːt) *adj.* **1.** astute, as in business; clever or bright. **2.** quick, witty, and often impertinent in speech: *a smart talker.* **3.** fashionable; chic: *a smart hotel.* **4.** well-kept; neat. **5.** causing a sharp stinging pain. **6.** vigorous or brisk. **7.** *Dialect.* considerable or numerous: *a smart price.* **8.** (of systems) operating as if by human intelligence by using automatic computer control. **9.** (of a projectile or bomb) containing a device that allows it to be guided to its target. ~*vb.* (*mainly intr.*) **10.** to feel, cause, or be the source of a sharp stinging physical pain or keen mental distress: *a nettle sting smarts; he smarted under their abuse.* **11.** (often foll. by *for*) to suffer a harsh penalty. ~*n.* **12.** a stinging pain or feeling. ~*adv.* **13.** in a smart manner. [Old English *smeortan;* related to Old High German *smerzan,* Latin *mordēre* to bite, Greek *smerdnos* terrible] —ˈ**smartish** *adj.* —ˈ**smartly** *adv.* —ˈ**smartness** *n.*

smart aleck (ˈælɪk) *n., pl.* **smart alecks.** *Informal.* an irritatingly oversmart person. [C19: from *Aleck, Alec,* short for *Alexander*] —ˈ**smart-ˌaleck** *or* ˈ**smart-ˌalecky** *adj.*

smartarse (ˈsmɑːtˌɑːs) *n. Derogatory slang.* **a.** a clever person, esp. one who parades his knowledge offensively. **b.** (*as modifier*): *smartarse guidebooks.* —ˈ**smartˌarsed** *adj.*

smart card *n.* a plastic card with integrated circuits used for storing and processing computer data. Also called: **laser card, intelligent card.**

smarten (ˈsmɑːtᵊn) *vb.* (usually foll. by *up*) **1.** (*intr.*) to make oneself neater. **2.** (*tr.*) to make quicker or livelier.

smart money *n.* **1. a.** money bet or invested by experienced gamblers or investors, esp. with inside information. **b.** the gamblers or investors themselves. **2.** money paid in order to extricate oneself from an unpleasant situation or agreement, esp. from military service. **3.** money paid by an employer to someone injured while working for him. **4.** *U.S. Law.* damages awarded to a plaintiff where the wrong was aggravated by fraud, malice, etc.

smarts (smɑːts) *pl. n. Slang, chiefly U.S.* know-how, intelligence, or wits: *street smarts.*

smart set *n.* (*functioning as sing. or pl.*) fashionable sophisticated people considered as a group.

smarty *or* **smartie** (ˈsmɑːtɪ) *n. Informal.* a would-be clever person.

smarty-pants (ˈsmɑːtɪˌpænts) *or* **smarty-boots** (ˈsmɑːtɪˌbuːts) *n.* (*functioning as sing.*) *Informal.* a would-be clever person.

smash (smæʃ) *vb.* **1.** to break into pieces violently and usually noisily. **2.** (when *intr.,* foll. by *against, through, into,* etc.) to throw or crash (against) vigorously, causing shattering: *he smashed the equipment; it smashed against the wall.* **3.** (*tr.*) to hit forcefully and suddenly. **4.** (*tr.*) *Tennis, etc.* to hit (the ball) fast and powerfully, esp. with an overhead stroke. **5.** (*tr.*) to defeat or wreck (persons, theories, etc.). **6.** (*tr.*) to make bankrupt. **7.** (*intr.*) to collide violently; crash. **8.** (*intr.;* often foll. by *up*) to go bankrupt. **9. smash someone's face in.** *Informal.* to beat someone severely. ~*n.* **10.** an act, instance, or sound of smashing or the state of being smashed. **11.** a violent collision, esp. of vehicles. **12.** a total failure or collapse, as of a business. **13.** *Tennis, etc.* a fast and powerful overhead stroke. **14.** *Informal.* **a.** something having popular success. **b.** (*in combination*): *smash-hit.* **15.** *Slang.* loose change; coins. ~*adv.* **16.** with a smash. [C18: probably from SM(ACK[2] + M)ASH] —**'smashable** *adj.*

smash-and-grab *adj. Informal.* of, relating to, or denoting a robbery in which a shop window is broken and the contents removed.

smashed (smæʃt) *adj. Slang.* **1.** completely intoxicated with alcohol. **2.** noticeably under the influence of a drug.

smasher ('smæʃə) *n. Informal, chiefly Brit.* a person or thing that is very attractive or outstanding.

smashing ('smæʃɪŋ) *adj. Informal, chiefly Brit.* excellent or first-rate; wonderful: *we had a smashing time.*

smash-up *Informal.* ~*n.* **1.** a bad collision, esp. of cars. ~*vb.* **smash up. 2.** (*tr., adv.*) to damage to the point of complete destruction: *they smashed the place up.*

smatch (smætʃ) *n.* a less common word for **smack**[1].

smatter ('smætə) *n.* **1.** a smattering. ~*vb.* **2.** (*intr.*) *Rare.* to prattle. **3.** (*tr.*) *Archaic.* to dabble in. [C14 (in the sense: to prattle): of uncertain origin; compare Middle High German *smetern* to gossip] —**'smatterer** *n.*

smattering ('smætərɪŋ) *n.* **1.** a slight or superficial knowledge. **2.** a small amount. —**'smatteringly** *adv.*

SMATV *abbrev. for* (originally) small master antenna television; now more commonly, satellite master antenna television: a system for relaying broadcast television signals, embodying a master receiving antenna with distribution by cable to a small group of dwellings, such as a block of flats.

smaze (smeɪz) *n. U.S.* a smoky haze, less damp than fog. [C20: from SM(OKE + H)AZE[1]]

SMD *Electronics. abbrev. for* surface-mounted device: a device such as resistor, capacitor, or integrated circuit on a printed circuit board.

SME *international car registration for* Surinam.

smear (smɪə) *vb.* (*mainly tr.*) **1.** to bedaub or cover with oil, grease, etc. **2.** to rub over or apply thickly. **3.** to rub so as to produce a smudge. **4.** to slander. **5.** *U.S. slang.* to defeat completely. **6.** (*intr.*) to be or become smeared or dirtied. ~*n.* **7.** a dirty mark or smudge. **8. a.** a slanderous attack. **b.** (*as modifier*): *smear tactics.* **9.** a preparation of blood, secretions, etc., that is smeared onto a glass slide for examination under a microscope. See also **cervical smear.** [Old English *smeoru* (n.); related to Old Norse *smjör* fat, Old High German *smero,* Greek *muron* ointment] —**'smearer** *n.* —**'smeary** *adj.* —**'smearily** *adv.* —**'smeariness** *n.*

smear test *n. Med.* another name for **Pap test.**

smectic ('smɛktɪk) *adj. Chem.* (of a substance) existing in or having a mesomorphic state in which the molecules are oriented in layers. Compare **nematic.** See also **liquid crystal.** [C17: via Latin from Greek *smēktikos,* from *smēkhein* to wash; from the soaplike consistency of a smectic substance]

smectite ('smɛktaɪt) *n.* any of a group of clay minerals of which montmorillonite and saponite are members.

smeddum ('smɛdəm) *n. Scot.* **1.** any fine powder. **2.** spirit or mettle; vigour. [Old English *smedema* fine flour]

smegma ('smɛgmə) *n. Physiol.* a whitish sebaceous secretion that accumulates beneath the prepuce. [C19: via Latin from Greek *smēgma* detergent, from *smekhein* to wash] —**smegmatic** (smɛg'mætɪk) *adj.*

smell (smɛl) *vb.* **smells, smelling, smelt** *or* **smelled. 1.** (*tr.*) to perceive the scent or odour of (a substance) by means of the olfactory nerves. **2.** (*copula*) to have a specified smell; appear to the sense of smell to be: *the beaches smell of seaweed; some tobacco smells very sweet.* **3.** (*intr.;* often foll. by *of*) to emit an odour (of): *the park smells of flowers.* **4.** (*intr.*) to emit an unpleasant odour; stink. **5.** (*tr.;* often foll. by *out*) to detect through shrewdness or instinct. **6.** (*intr.*) to have or use the sense of smell; sniff. **7.** (*intr.;* foll. by *of*) to give indications (of): *he smells of money.* **8.** (*intr.;* foll. by *around, about,* etc.) to search, investigate, or pry. **9.** (*copula*) to be or seem to be untrustworthy or corrupt. **10. smell a rat.** to detect something suspicious. ~*n.* **11.** that sense (olfaction) by which scents or odours are perceived. Related adj.: **olfactory. 12.** anything detected by the sense of smell; odour; scent. **13.** a trace or indication. **14.** the act or an instance of smelling. [C12: of uncertain origin; compare Middle Dutch *smölen* to scorch] —**'smeller** *n.* —**'smell-less** *adj.*

▷**Usage.** *Smell* in its neutral sense of emitting an odour is followed by an adjective rather than by an adverb: *this flower smells good* (rather than *well*). *Smell* in the sense of emitting an unpleasant odour is followed by an adverb: *this chemical smells unbelievably.*

smelling salts *pl. n.* a pungent preparation containing crystals of ammonium carbonate that has a stimulant action when sniffed in cases of faintness, headache, etc.

smelly ('smɛlɪ) *adj.* **smellier, smelliest.** having a strong or nasty smell. —**'smelliness** *n.*

smelt[1] (smɛlt) *vb.* (*tr.*) to extract (a metal) from (an ore) by heating. [C15: from Middle Low German, Middle Dutch *smelten;* related to Old High German *smelzan* to melt]

smelt[2] (smɛlt) *n., pl.* **smelt** *or* **smelts.** any marine or freshwater salmonoid food fish of the family *Osmeridae,* such as *Osmerus eperlanus* (**European smelt**), having a long body, greenish-grey above and silvery below, and occurring in temperate and cold northern waters. [Old English *smylt;* related to Dutch, Danish *smelt,* Norwegian *smelta,* German *Schmelz*]

smelt[3] (smɛlt) *vb.* a past tense and past participle of **smell.**

smelter ('smɛltə) *n.* **1.** a person engaged in smelting. **2.** Also called: **smeltery** ('smɛltərɪ). an industrial plant in which smelting is carried out.

smew (smju:) *n.* a merganser, *Mergus albellus,* of N Europe and Asia, having a male plumage of white with black markings. [C17: of uncertain origin]

smidgen *or* **smidgin** ('smɪdʒən) *n. Informal, chiefly U.S. and Canadian.* a very small amount or part. [C20: of obscure origin]

smilacaceous (ˌsmaɪlə'keɪʃəs) *adj.* of, relating to, or belonging to the *Smilacaceae,* a temperate and tropical family of monocotyledonous flowering plants, most of which are climbing shrubs with prickly stems: includes smilax. [C19: via New Latin from Latin SMILAX]

smilax ('smaɪlæks) *n.* **1.** any typically climbing shrub of the smilacaceous genus *Smilax,* of warm and tropical regions, having slightly lobed leaves, small greenish or yellow flowers, and berry-like fruits: includes the sarsaparilla plant and greenbrier. **2.** a fragile branched liliaceous vine, *Asparagus asparagoides,* of southern Africa: cultivated by florists for its glossy bright green foliage. [C17: via Latin from Greek: bindweed]

smile (smaɪl) *n.* **1.** a facial expression characterized by an upturning of the corners of the mouth, usually showing amusement, friendliness, etc., but sometimes scorn, etc. **2.** favour or blessing: *the smile of fortune.* **3.** an agreeable appearance. ~*vb.* **4.** (*intr.*) to wear or assume a smile. **5.** (*intr.;* foll. by *at*) **a.** to look (at) with a kindly or amused expression. **b.** to look derisively (at) instead of being annoyed. **c.** to bear (troubles, etc.) patiently. **6.** (*intr.;* foll. by *on* or *upon*) to show approval; bestow a blessing. **7.** (*tr.*) to express by means of a smile: *she smiled a welcome.* **8.** (*tr.;* often foll. by *away*) to drive away or change by smiling: *smile away one's tears.* **9. come up smiling.** to recover cheerfully from misfortune. [C13: probably of Scandinavian origin; compare Swedish *smila,* Danish *smile;* related to Middle High German *smielen*] —**'smiler** *n.* —**'smiling** *adj.* —**'smilingly** *adv.* —**'smilingness** *n.*

smir, smirr (smɪr), *or* **smur** *Scot.* ~*n.* **1.** drizzly rain. ~*vb.* **smirs** *or* **smirrs, smirring, smirred.** (*intr.*) **2.** to drizzle lightly. [C19: of uncertain origin; compare Dutch *smoor* mist]

smirch (smɜ:tʃ) *vb.* (*tr.*) **1.** to dirty; soil. ~*n.* **2.** the act of smirching or state of being smirched. **3.** a smear or stain. [C15 *smorchen,* of unknown origin] —**'smircher** *n.*

smirk (smɜ:k) *n.* **1.** a smile expressing scorn, smugness, etc., rather than pleasure. ~*vb.* **2.** (*intr.*) to give such a smile. **3.** (*tr.*) to express with such a smile. [Old English *smearcian;* related to *smer* derision, Old High German *bismer* contempt, *bismerōn* to scorn] —**'smirker** *n.* —**'smirking** *adj.* —**'smirkingly** *adv.*

smit (smɪt) *n.* **the.** *Scot. and northern English dialect.* an infection: *he's got the smit.* [Old English *smitte* a spot, and *smittian* to smear; related to Old High German *smiz,* whence Middle High German *smitz*]

smite (smaɪt) *vb.* **smites, smiting, smote; smitten** *or* **smit.** (*mainly tr.*) *Now archaic in most senses.* **1.** to strike with a heavy blow or blows. **2.** to damage with or as if with blows. **3.** to afflict or affect severely: *smitten with flu.* **4.** to afflict in order to punish. **5.** (*intr.;* foll. by *on*) to strike forcibly or abruptly: *the sun smote down on him.* [Old English *smītan;* related to Old High German *smīzan* to smear, Gothic *bismeitan,* Old Swedish *smēta* to daub] —**'smiter** *n.*

smith (smɪθ) *n.* **1. a.** a person who works in metal, esp. one who shapes metal by hammering. **b.** (*in combination*): *a silversmith.* **2.** See **blacksmith.** [Old English; related to Old Norse *smithr,* Old High German *smid,* Middle Low German *smīde* jewellery, Greek *smilē* carving knife]

smithereens (ˌsmɪðə'ri:nz) *pl. n.* little shattered pieces or fragments. [C19: from Irish Gaelic *smidirīn,* from *smiodar*]

smithery ('smɪθərɪ) *n., pl.* **-eries. 1.** the trade or craft of a blacksmith. **2.** a rare word for **smithy.**

smithsonite ('smɪθsəˌnaɪt) *n.* a white mineral consisting of zinc carbonate in hexagonal crystalline form: occurs chiefly in dry limestone regions and is a source of zinc. Formula: $ZnCO_3$. Also called (U.S.): **calamine.** [C19: named after James *Smithson* (1765–1829), British chemist and mineralogist]

smithy ('smɪðɪ) *n., pl.* **smithies.** a place in which metal, usually iron or steel, is worked by heating and hammering; forge. [Old English *smiththe;* related to Old Norse *smithja,* Old High German *smidda,* Middle Dutch *smisse*]

smitten ('smɪtᵊn) *vb.* a past participle of **smite.**

smittle ('smɪtᵊl) *adj. Scot. and northern English dialect.* infectious. [C16: see SMIT]

smock (smɒk) *n.* **1.** any loose protective garment, worn by artists, laboratory technicians, etc. **2.** a woman's loose blouse-like garment, reaching to below the waist, worn over slacks, etc. **3.** Also called: **smock frock.** a loose protective overgarment decorated with smocking, worn formerly esp. by farm workers. **4.** *Archaic.* a woman's loose undergarment, worn from the 16th to the 18th centuries. ~*vb.* **5.** to ornament (a garment) with smocking. [Old English *smocc;* related to Old High German *smocco,* Old Norse *smokkr* blouse, Middle High German *gesmuc* decoration] —'**smock,like** *adj.*

smocking ('smɒkɪŋ) *n.* ornamental needlework used to gather and stitch material in a honeycomb pattern so that the part below the gathers hangs in even folds.

smock mill *n.* a type of windmill having a revolving top.

smog (smɒg) *n.* a mixture of smoke, fog, and chemical fumes. [C20: from SM(OKE + F)OG[1]] —'**smoggy** *adj.*

smoke (sməʊk) *n.* **1.** the product of combustion, consisting of fine particles of carbon carried by hot gases and air. **2.** any cloud of fine particles suspended in a gas. **3. a.** the act of smoking tobacco or other substances, esp. in a pipe or as a cigarette or cigar. **b.** the duration of smoking such substances. **4.** *Informal.* **a.** a cigarette or cigar. **b.** a substance for smoking, such as pipe tobacco or marijuana. **5.** something with no concrete or lasting substance: *everything turned to smoke.* **6.** a thing or condition that obscures. **7.** any of various colours similar to that of smoke, esp. a dark grey with a bluish, yellowish, or greenish tinge. **8. go** *or* **end up in smoke. a.** to come to nothing. **b.** to burn up vigorously. **c.** to flare up in anger. ~*vb.* **9.** (*intr.*) to emit smoke or the like, sometimes excessively or in the wrong place. **10.** to draw in on (a burning cigarette, etc.) and exhale the smoke. **11.** (*intr.*) *Slang.* to use marijuana for smoking. **12.** (*tr.*) to bring (oneself) into a specified state by smoking. **13.** (*tr.*) to subject or expose to smoke. **14.** (*tr.*) to cure (meat, fish, cheese, etc.) by treating with smoke. **15.** (*tr.*) to fumigate or purify the air of (rooms, etc.). **16.** (*tr.*) to darken (glass, etc.) by exposure to smoke. **17.** (*intr.*) *Slang.* to move, drive, ride, etc., very fast. **18.** (*tr.*) *Obsolete.* to tease or mock. **19.** (*tr.*) *Archaic.* to suspect or detect. ~See also **smoke out.** [Old English *smoca* (n.); related to Middle Dutch *smieken* to emit smoke] —'**smokable** *or* '**smokeable** *adj.*

Smoke (sməʊk) *n.* **the.** short for **Big Smoke.**

smoke bomb *n.* a device that emits large quantities of smoke when ignited.

smoke-dried *adj.* (of fish, meat, etc.) cured in smoke.

smoked rubber *n.* a type of crude natural rubber in the form of brown sheets obtained by coagulating latex with an acid, rolling it into sheets, and drying over open wood fires. It is the main raw material for natural rubber products. Also called: **ribbed and smoked sheet.** Compare **crepe rubber.**

smokeho ('sməʊkəʊ) *n.* a variant spelling of **smoko.**

smokehouse ('sməʊk,haʊs) *n.* a building or special construction for curing meat, fish, etc., by smoking.

smokejack ('sməʊk,dʒæk) *n.* a device formerly used for turning a roasting spit, operated by the movement of ascending gases in a chimney. [C17: from SMOKE + JACK[1]]

smokeless ('sməʊklɪs) *adj.* having or producing little or no smoke: *smokeless fuel.*

smokeless powder *n.* any one of a number of explosives that burn with relatively little smoke. They consist mainly of nitrocellulose and are used as propellants.

smokeless zone *n.* an area designated by the local authority where only smokeless fuels are permitted.

smoke out *vb.* (*tr., adv.*) **1.** to subject to smoke in order to drive out of hiding. **2.** to bring into the open; expose to the public: *they smoked out the plot.*

smoker ('sməʊkə) *n.* **1.** a person who habitually smokes tobacco. **2.** Also called: **smoking compartment.** a compartment of a train where smoking is permitted. **3.** an informal social gathering, as at a club.

smoke screen *n.* **1.** *Military.* a cloud of smoke produced by artificial means to obscure movements or positions. **2.** something said or done in order to hide the truth.

smokestack ('sməʊk,stæk) *n.* a tall chimney that conveys smoke into the air. Sometimes shortened to **stack.**

smokestack industry *n. Informal.* any of the traditional British industries, esp. heavy engineering or manufacturing, as opposed to such modern industries as electronics.

smoke tree *n.* **1.** an anacardiaceous shrub, *Cotinus coggygria,* of S Europe and Asia, having clusters of yellowish feathery flowers. **2.** a related tree, *Cotinus americanus,* of the southern U.S. [C19: so named because of the similarity between its flower clusters and a cloud of smoke]

smoking jacket *n.* a man's comfortable jacket of velvet, etc., closed by a tie belt or fastenings, worn at home. [so called because it was formerly worn for smoking]

smoking room *or* (*esp. Brit.*) **smoke room** *n.* a room, esp. in a hotel or club, for those who wish to smoke.

smoko *or* **smokeho** ('sməʊkəʊ) *n., pl.* **-kos** *or* **-hos.** *Austral. and N.Z. informal.* a short break from work for tea, a cigarette, etc. [C19: from SMOKE + -O]

smoky ('sməʊkɪ) *adj.* **smokier, smokiest. 1.** emitting, containing, or resembling smoke. **2.** emitting smoke excessively or in the wrong place: *a smoky fireplace.* **3.** of or tinged with the colour smoke. **4.** having the flavour of having been cured by smoking. **5.** made dark, dirty, or hazy by smoke. —'**smokily** *adv.* —'**smokiness** *n.*

smoky quartz *n.* another name for **cairngorm.** [so named because of its colour]

smolder ('sməʊldə) *vb., n.* the U.S. spelling of **smoulder.**

smolt (sməʊlt) *n.* a young salmon at the stage when it migrates from fresh water to the sea. [C14: Scottish, of uncertain origin; perhaps related to SMELT[2]]

smooch (smu:tʃ) *Informal.* ~*vb.* (*intr.*) **1.** Also (Austral. and N.Z.): **smoodge, smooge.** (of two people) to kiss and cuddle. **2.** *Brit.* to dance very slowly and amorously with one's arms around another person, or (of two people) to dance together in such a way. ~*n.* **3.** the act of smooching. **4.** *Brit.* a piece of music played for dancing to slowly and amorously. [C20: variant of dialect *smouch,* of imitative origin]

smoodge *or* **smooge** (smu:dʒ) *vb. Austral. and N.Z.* variants of **smooch** (sense 1).

smooth (smu:ð) *adj.* **1.** resting in the same plane; without bends or irregularities. **2.** silky to the touch: *smooth velvet.* **3.** lacking roughness of surface; flat. **4.** tranquil or unruffled: *smooth temper.* **5.** lacking obstructions or difficulties. **6. a.** suave or persuasive, esp. as suggestive of insincerity. **b.** (*in combination*): *smooth-tongued.* **7.** (of the skin) free from hair. **8.** of uniform consistency: *smooth batter.* **9.** not erratic; free from jolts: *smooth driving.* **10.** not harsh or astringent: *a smooth wine.* **11.** having all projections worn away: *smooth tyres.* **12.** *Maths.* (of a curve) differential at every point. **13.** *Phonetics.* without preliminary or simultaneous aspiration. **14.** gentle to the ear; flowing. **15.** *Physics.* (of a plane, surface, etc.) regarded as being frictionless. ~*adv.* **16.** in a calm or even manner; smoothly. ~*vb.* (*mainly tr.*) **17.** (*also intr.;* often foll. by *down*) to make or become flattened or without roughness or obstructions. **18.** (often foll. by *out* or *away*) to take or rub (away) in order to make smooth: *she smoothed out the creases in her dress.* **19.** to make calm; soothe. **20.** to make easier: *smooth his path.* **21.** *Electrical engineering.* to remove alternating current ripple from the output of a direct current power supply. **22.** *Obsolete.* to make more polished or refined. ~*n.* **23.** the smooth part of something. **24.** the act of smoothing. **25.** *Tennis, etc.* the side of a racket on which the binding strings form a continuous line. Compare **rough** (sense 27). ~See also **smooth over.** [Old English *smōth;* related to Old Saxon *māthmundi* gentle-minded, *smōthi* smooth] —'**smoothable** *adj.* —'**smoother** *n.* —'**smoothly** *adv.* —'**smoothness** *n.*

smoothbore ('smu:ð,bɔ:) *n.* **1.** (*modifier*) (of a firearm) having an unrifled bore: *a smoothbore musket.* **2.** such a firearm. —'**smooth,bored** *adj.*

smooth breathing *n.* (in Greek) the sign (') placed over an initial vowel, indicating that (in ancient Greek) it was not pronounced with an *h.* Compare **rough breathing.**

smoothen ('smu:ðən) *vb.* to make or become smooth.

smooth hound *n.* any of several small sharks of the genus *Mustelus,* esp. *M. mustelus,* a species of North Atlantic coastal regions: family *Triakidae.* See also **dogfish** (sense 3). [C17: from HOUND(FISH); so called because it has no dorsal spines]

smoothie *or* **smoothy** ('smu:ðɪ) *n., pl.* **smoothies.** *Slang, usually derogatory.* a person, esp. a man, who is suave or slick, esp. in speech, dress, or manner.

smoothing circuit *n. Electrical engineering.* a circuit used to remove ripple from the output of a direct current power supply.

smoothing iron *n.* a former name for **iron** (senses 2, 3).

smooth muscle *n.* muscle that is capable of slow rhythmic involuntary contractions: occurs in the walls of the blood vessels, alimentary canal, etc. Compare **striped muscle.** [so called because there is no cross-banding on the muscle]

smooth over *vb.* (*tr.*) to ease or gloss over: *to smooth over a situation.*

smooth snake *n.* any of several slender nonvenomous colubrid snakes of the European genus *Coronella,* esp. *C. austriaca,* having very smooth scales and a reddish-brown coloration.

smooth-spoken *adj.* speaking or spoken in a gently persuasive or competent manner.

smooth-tongued *adj.* suave or persuasive in speech.

smorgasbord ('smɔ:gəs,bɔ:d, 'smɜ:-) *n.* a variety of cold or hot savoury dishes, such as pâté, smoked salmon, etc., served in Scandinavia as hors d'oeuvres or as a buffet meal. [Swedish, from *smörgås* sandwich + *bord* table]

smørrebrød (*Danish* 'smœrə,brœð) *n.* small open savoury sandwiches, served esp. in Denmark as hors d'oeuvres, etc. [Danish, from *smør* butter + *brød* bread]

smote (sməʊt) *vb.* the past tense of **smite.**

smother ('smʌðə) *vb.* **1.** to suffocate or stifle by cutting off or being cut off from the air. **2.** (*tr.*) to surround (with) or envelop (in): *he smothered her with love.* **3.** (*tr.*) to extinguish (a fire) by covering so as to cut it off from the air. **4.** to be or cause to be suppressed or stifled: *smother a giggle.* **5.** (*tr.*) to cook or serve (food) thickly covered with sauce, etc. ~*n.* **6.** anything, such as a cloud of smoke, that stifles. **7.** a profusion or turmoil. **8.** *Archaic.* a state of smouldering or a smouldering fire. [Old English *smorian* to suffocate; related to Middle Low German *smōren*] —'**smothery** *adj.*

smothered mate *n. Chess.* checkmate given by a knight when the king is prevented from moving by surrounding men.

smoulder *or U.S.* **smolder** ('sməʊldə) *vb.* (*intr.*) **1.** to burn slowly without flame, usually emitting smoke. **2.** (esp. of anger, etc.) to exist in a suppressed or half-suppressed state. **3.** to have strong repressed or half repressed feelings, esp. anger. ~*n.* **4.** dense smoke, as from a smouldering fire. **5.** a smouldering fire. [C14: from *smolder* (n.), of obscure origin]

smout *or* **smowt** (smaʊt) *n. Scot.* **1.** a variant of **smolt. 2.** a child or undersized person. [C16: a variant of SMOLT]

SMP *abbrev. for* statutory maternity pay.

smriti ('smrɪtɪ) *n.* a class of Hindu sacred literature derived from the Vedas, containing social, domestic, and religious teaching. [from Sanskrit *smrti* what is remembered, from *samarati* he remembers]

smudge (smʌdʒ) *vb.* **1.** to smear, blur, or soil or cause to do so. **2.** (*tr.*) *Chiefly U.S. and Canadian.* to fill (an area) with smoke in order to drive insects away or guard against frost. ~*n.* **3.** a smear or dirty mark. **4.** a blurred form or area: *that smudge in the distance is a quarry.* **5.** *Chiefly U.S. and Canadian.* a smoky fire for driving insects away or protecting fruit trees or plants from frost. [C15: of uncertain origin] —'**smudgeless** *adj.* —'**smudgy** *adj.* —'**smudgily** *or* '**smudgedly** *adv.* —'**smudginess** *n.*

smug (smʌg) *adj.* **smugger, smuggest. 1.** excessively self-satisfied or complacent. **2.** *Archaic.* trim or neat. [C16: of Germanic origin; compare Low German *smuck* neat] —'**smugly** *adv.* —'**smugness** *n.*

smuggle ('smʌgᵊl) *vb.* **1.** to import or export (prohibited or dutiable goods) secretly. **2.** (*tr.*; often foll. by *into* or *out of*) to bring or take secretly, as against the law or rules. **3.** (*tr.*; foll. by *away*) to conceal; hide. [C17: from Low German *smukkelen* and Dutch *smokkelen*, perhaps from Old English *smūgen* to creep; related to Old Norse *smjūga*] —'**smuggler** *n.* —'**smuggling** *n.*

smur (smʌr) *n., vb. Scot.* a variant of **smir.**

smut (smʌt) *n.* **1.** a small dark smudge or stain, esp. one caused by soot. **2.** a speck of soot or dirt. **3.** something obscene or indecent. **4. a.** any of various fungal diseases of flowering plants, esp. cereals, in which black sooty masses of spores cover the affected parts. **b.** any parasitic basidiomycetous fungus of the order *Ustilaginales* that causes such a disease. **5.** *Angling.* a minute midge or other insect relished by trout. ~*vb.* **smuts, smutting, smutted. 6.** to mark or become marked or smudged, as with soot. **7.** to affect (grain) or (of grain) to be affected with smut. **8.** (*tr.*) to remove smut from (grain). **9.** (*tr.*) to make obscene. **10.** (*intr.*) to emit soot or smut. **11.** (*intr.*) *Angling.* (of trout) to feed voraciously on smuts. [Old English *smitte*; related to Middle High German *smitze*; associated with SMUDGE, SMUTCH] —'**smutty** *adj.* —'**smuttily** *adv.* —'**smuttiness** *n.*

smutch (smʌtʃ) *vb.* **1.** (*tr.*) to smudge; mark. ~*n.* **2.** a mark; smudge. **3.** soot; dirt. [C16: probably from Middle High German *smutzen* to soil; see SMUT] —'**smutchy** *adj.*

Sn *the chemical symbol for* tin. [from New Latin *stannum*]

SN *international car registration for* Senegal.

snack (snæk) *n.* **1.** a light quick meal eaten between or in place of main meals. **2.** a sip or bite. **3.** *Rare.* a share. **4.** *Austral. informal.* a very easy task. ~*vb.* **5.** (*intr.*) to eat a snack. [C15: probably from Middle Dutch *snacken*, variant of *snappen* to SNAP]

snack bar *n.* a place where light meals or snacks can be obtained, often with a self-service system.

snackette ('snækɛt) *n.* a Caribbean name for **snack bar.**

snaffle ('snæfᵊl) *n.* **1.** Also called: **snaffle bit.** a simple jointed bit for a horse. ~*vb.* (*tr.*) **2.** *Brit. informal.* to steal or take for oneself. **3.** to equip or control with a snaffle. [C16: of uncertain origin; compare Old Frisian *snavel* mouth, Old High German *snabul* beak]

snafu (snæ'fuː) *Slang, chiefly military.* ~*n.* **1.** confusion or chaos regarded as the normal state. ~*adj.* **2.** (*postpositive*) confused or muddled up, as usual. ~*vb.* **-fues, -fuing, -fued. 3.** (*tr.*) *U.S. and Canadian.* to throw into chaos. [C20: from *s(ituation) n(ormal): a(ll) f(ucked) u(p)*]

snag (snæg) *n.* **1.** a difficulty or disadvantage: *the snag is that I have nothing suitable to wear.* **2.** a sharp protuberance, such as a tree stump. **3.** a small loop or hole in a fabric caused by a sharp object. **4.** *Engineering.* a projection that brings to a stop a sliding or rotating component. **5.** *Chiefly U.S. and Canadian.* a tree stump in a riverbed that is dangerous to navigation. **6.** (*pl.*) *Austral. slang.* sausages. ~*vb.* **snags, snagging, snagged. 7.** (*tr.*) to hinder or impede. **8.** (*tr.*) to tear or catch (fabric). **9.** (*intr.*) to develop a snag. **10.** (*intr.*) *Chiefly U.S. and Canadian.* (of a boat) to strike or be damaged by a snag. **11.** (*tr.*) *Chiefly U.S. and Canadian.* to clear (a stretch of water) of snags. **12.** (*tr.*) *U.S.* to seize (an opportunity, benefit, etc.). [C16: of Scandinavian origin; compare Old Norse *snaghyrndr* sharp-pointed, Norwegian *snage* spike, Icelandic *snagi* peg] —'**snaggy** *adj.* —'**snag,like** *adj.*

snaggletooth ('snægᵊl,tuːθ) *n., pl.* **-teeth.** a tooth that is broken or projecting. —'**snaggle,toothed** *adj.*

snail (sneɪl) *n.* **1.** any of numerous terrestrial or freshwater gastropod molluscs with a spirally coiled shell, esp. any of the family *Helicidae*, such as *Helix aspersa* (**garden snail**). **2.** any other gastropod with a spirally coiled shell, such as a whelk. **3.** a slow-moving or lazy person or animal. [Old English *snægl*; related to Old Norse *snigill*, Old High German *snecko*] —'**snail,like** *adj.*

snail cam *n. Mechanical engineering.* a cam with spiral cross section used for progressive lifting of a lever as the cam revolves.

snailfish ('sneɪl,fɪʃ) *n., pl.* **-fish** *or* **-fishes.** another name for **sea snail.**

snail's pace *n.* a very slow or sluggish speed or rate.

snake (sneɪk) *n.* **1.** any reptile of the suborder *Ophidia* (or *Serpentes*), typically having a scaly cylindrical limbless body, fused eyelids, and a jaw modified for swallowing large prey: includes venomous forms such as cobras and rattlesnakes, large nonvenomous constrictors (boas and pythons), and small harmless types such as the grass snake. **2.** Also called: **snake in the grass.** a deceitful or treacherous person. **3.** anything resembling a snake in appearance or action. **4.** (in the European Community) a former system of managing a group of currencies by allowing the exchange rate of each of them only to fluctuate within narrow limits. **5.** a tool in the form of a long flexible wire for unblocking drains. ~*vb.* **6.** (*intr.*) to glide or move like a snake. **7.** (*tr.*) *U.S.* to haul (a heavy object, esp. a log) by fastening a rope around one end of it. **8.** (*tr.*) *U.S.* (often foll. by *out*) to pull jerkily. **9.** (*tr.*) to move in or follow (a sinuous course). [Old English *snaca*; related to Old Norse *snākr* snake, Old High German *snahhan* to crawl, Norwegian *snōk* snail] —'**snake,like** *adj.*

snakebird ('sneɪk,bɜːd) *n.* another name for **darter** (the bird).

snakebite ('sneɪk,baɪt) *n.* **1.** a bite inflicted by a snake, esp. a venomous one. **2.** a drink of cider and lager.

snake charmer *n.* an entertainer, esp. in Asia, who charms or appears to charm snakes by playing music and by rhythmical body movements.

snake dance *n.* **1.** a ceremonial dance, performed by the priests of the American Hopi Indians, in which live snakes are held in the mouth. **2. a.** the swaying movements of snakes responding to a snake charmer. **b.** a Hindu dance in which performers imitate such snake movements.

snake fly *n.* any of various neuropterous insects of the family *Raphidiidae*, having an elongated thorax: order *Megaloptera.*

snake juice *n. Austral. slang.* any strong alcoholic drink, esp. when home-made. [C19: perhaps so called from its poisonous effects]

snakemouth ('sneɪk,maʊθ) *n.* a terrestrial orchid, *Pogonia ophioglossoides*, of E North America, having solitary fragrant pinkish-purple flowers. [so called because of the alleged similarity between the shape of the flower and a snake's mouth]

snakeroot ('sneɪk,ruːt) *n.* **1.** any of various North American plants, such as *Aristolochia serpentaria* (**Virginia snakeroot**) and *Eupatorium urticaefolium* (**white snakeroot**), the roots or rhizomes of which have been used as a remedy for snakebite. **2.** the rhizome or root of any such plant. **3.** another name for **bistort** (senses 1, 2). ~Also called: **snakeweed.**

snakes and ladders *n.* (*functioning as sing.*) a board game in which players move counters along a series of squares by means of dice. A ladder provides a short cut to a square nearer the finish and a snake obliges a player to return to a square nearer the start.

snake's head *n.* a European fritillary plant, *Fritillaria meleagris*, of damp meadows, having purple-and-white chequered flowers. [C19: so called because its buds are claimed to resemble a snake's head]

snakeskin ('sneɪk,skɪn) *n.* the skin of a snake, esp. when made into a leather valued for handbags, shoes, etc.

snaky ('sneɪkɪ) *adj.* **snakier, snakiest. 1.** of or like a snake; sinuous. **2.** treacherous or insidious. **3.** infested with snakes. **4.** *Austral. and N.Z. informal.* angry or bad-tempered. —'**snakily** *adv.* —'**snakiness** *n.*

snap (snæp) *vb.* **snaps, snapping, snapped. 1.** to break or cause to break suddenly, esp. with a sharp sound. **2.** to make or cause to make a sudden sharp cracking sound. **3.** (*intr.*) to give way or collapse suddenly, esp. from strain. **4.** to move, close, etc., or cause to move, close, etc., with a sudden sharp sound. **5.** to move or cause to move in a sudden or abrupt way. **6.** (*intr.*; often foll. by *at* or *up*) to seize something suddenly or quickly. **7.** (when *intr.*, often foll. by *at*) to bite at (something) bringing the jaws rapidly together. **8.** to speak (words) sharply or abruptly. **9.** (*intr.*) (of eyes) to flash or sparkle. **10.** to take a snapshot of (something). **11.** (*intr.*) *Hunting.* to fire a quick shot without taking deliberate aim. **12.** (*tr.*) *American football.* to put (the ball) into play by sending it back from the line of scrimmage to a teammate. **13. snap one's fingers at.** *Informal.* **a.** to dismiss with contempt. **b.** to defy. **14. snap out of it.** *Informal.* to recover quickly, esp. from depression, anger, or illness. ~*n.* **15.** the act of breaking suddenly or the sound produced by a sudden breakage. **16.** a sudden sharp sound, esp. of bursting, popping, or cracking. **17.** a catch, clasp, or fastener that operates with a snapping sound. **18.** a sudden grab or bite. **19.** the sudden release of something such as elastic thread. **20.** a brisk movement of the thumb against one or more fingers. **21.** a thin crisp biscuit: *ginger snaps.* **22.** *Informal.* See **snapshot. 23.** *Informal.* vigour, liveliness, or energy. **24.** *Informal.* a task or job that is easy or profitable to do. **25.** a short spell or period, esp. of cold weather. **26.** *Brit. dialect.* food, esp. a packed lunch taken to work. **27.** *Brit.* a card game in which the word *snap* is called when two cards of equal value are turned up on the separate piles dealt by each player. **28.** *American football.* the start of each play when the centre passes the ball back from the line of scrimmage to a teammate. **29.** (*modifier*) done on the spur of the moment, without consideration: *a snap decision.* **30.** (*modifier*) closed or fastened with a snap. ~*adv.* **31.** with a snap. ~*interj.* **32. a.** *Cards.* the word called while playing snap. **b.** an exclamation used to draw attention to the similarity of two things. ~See also **snap up.** [C15: from Middle Low German or Middle Dutch *snappen* to seize; related to Old Norse *snapa* to snuffle] —'**snapless** *adj.* —'**snappable** *adj.*

snapback ('snæpˌbæk) *n.* a sudden rebound or change in direction.

snap bean *n. U.S. and Canadian.* **1.** any of various bean plants that are cultivated in the U.S. for their crisp edible unripe pods. **2.** the pod of such a plant. ~See also **string bean.** [C19: so called because the pods are broken into pieces for eating]

snapdragon ('snæpˌdrægən) *n.* any of several scrophulariaceous chiefly Old World plants of the genus *Antirrhinum,* esp. *A. majus,* of the Mediterranean region, having spikes of showy white, yellow, pink, red, or purplish flowers. Also called: **antirrhinum.** [C16: so named because the flowers, which are claimed to look like a dragon's head, have a "mouth" which snaps shut if squeezed open and then released]

snap fastener *n.* another name for **press stud.**

snapper ('snæpə) *n., pl.* **-per** *or* **-pers.** **1.** any large sharp-toothed percoid food fish of the family *Lutjanidae* of warm and tropical coastal regions. See also **red snapper.** **2.** a sparid food fish, *Chrysophrys auratus,* of Australia and New Zealand, that has a pinkish body covered with blue spots. **3.** another name for the **bluefish** or the **snapping turtle.** **4.** a person or thing that snaps. **5.** *Informal.* a person who take snapshots; photographer. ~Also called (senses 1, 2): **schnapper.**

snapper up *n.* a person who snaps up bargains, etc.

snapping beetle *n.* another name for the **click beetle.**

snapping turtle *n.* any large aggressive North American river turtle of the family *Chelydridae,* esp. *Chelydra serpentina* (**common snapping turtle**), having powerful hooked jaws and a rough shell. Also called: **snapper.**

snappy ('snæpɪ) *adj.* **-pier, -piest.** **1.** Also: **snappish.** apt to speak sharply or irritably. **2.** Also: **snappish.** apt to snap or bite. **3.** crackling in sound: *a snappy fire.* **4.** brisk, sharp, or chilly: *a snappy pace; snappy weather.* **5.** smart and fashionable: *a snappy dresser.* **6. make it snappy.** *Slang.* be quick! hurry up! —'**snappily** *adv.* —'**snappiness** *n.*

snap ring *n. Mountaineering.* another name for **karabiner.**

snap roll *n.* a manoeuvre in which an aircraft makes a fast roll.

snapshot ('snæpˌʃɒt) *n.* an informal photograph taken with a simple camera. Often shortened to **snap.**

snap up *vb.* (*tr., adv.*) **1.** to avail oneself of eagerly and quickly: *she snapped up the bargains.* **2.** to interrupt abruptly.

snare[1] (snɛə) *n.* **1.** a device for trapping birds or small animals, esp. a flexible loop that is drawn tight around the prey. **2.** a surgical instrument for removing certain tumours, consisting of a wire loop that may be drawn tight around their base to sever or uproot them. **3.** anything that traps or entangles someone or something unawares. ~*vb.* (*tr.*) **4.** to catch (birds or small animals) with a snare. **5.** to catch or trap in or as if in a snare; capture by trickery. [Old English *sneare,* from Old Norse *snara;* related to Old High German *snaraha*] —'**snareless** *adj.* —'**snarer** *n.*

snare[2] (snɛə) *n. Music.* a set of gut strings wound with wire fitted against the lower drumhead of a snare drum. They produce a rattling sound when the drum is beaten. See **snare drum.** [C17: from Middle Dutch *snaer* or Middle Low German *snare* string; related to Gothic *snōrjō* basket]

snare drum *n. Music.* a cylindrical drum with two drumheads, the upper of which is struck and the lower fitted with a snare. See **snare**[2].

snarl[1] (snɑːl) *vb.* **1.** (*intr.*) (of an animal) to growl viciously, baring the teeth. **2.** to speak or express (something) viciously or angrily. ~*n.* **3.** a vicious growl, utterance, or facial expression. **4.** the act of snarling. [C16: of Germanic origin; compare Middle Low German *snarren,* Middle Dutch *snarren* to drone] —'**snarling** *adj.* —'**snarlingly** *adv.* —'**snarly** *adj.*

snarl[2] (snɑːl) *n.* **1.** a tangled mass of thread, hair, etc. **2.** a complicated or confused state or situation. **3.** a knot in wood. ~*vb.* **4.** (often foll. by *up*) to be, become, or make tangled or complicated. **5.** (*tr.;* often foll. by *up*) to confuse mentally. **6.** (*tr.*) to flute or emboss (metal) by hammering on a tool held against the under surface. [C14: of Scandinavian origin; compare Old Swedish *snarel* noose, Old Norse *snara* SNARE[1]] —'**snarler** *n.* —'**snarly** *adj.*

snarler[1] ('snɑːlə) *n.* **1.** an animal or a person that snarls. **2.** *Austral. and N.Z. informal.* a sausage.

snarler[2] ('snɑːlə) *n. Austral. slang.* a discharge. [C20: from services *no longer required*]

snarl-up *n. Informal, chiefly Brit.* a confusion, obstruction, or tangle, esp. a traffic jam.

snatch (snætʃ) *vb.* **1.** (*tr.*) to seize or grasp (something) suddenly or peremptorily: *he snatched the chocolate out of my hand.* **2.** (*intr.;* usually foll. by *at*) to seize or attempt to seize suddenly. **3.** (*tr.*) to take hurriedly: *to snatch some sleep.* **4.** (*tr.*) to remove suddenly: *she snatched her hand away.* **5.** (*tr.*) to gain, win, or rescue, esp. narrowly: *they snatched victory in the closing seconds.* **6.** (*tr.*) (in weightlifting) to lift (a weight) with a snatch. **7. snatch one's time.** *Austral. informal.* to leave a job, taking whatever pay is due. ~*n.* **8.** an act of snatching. **9.** a fragment or small incomplete part: *snatches of conversation.* **10.** a brief spell: *snatches of time off.* **11.** *Weightlifting.* a lift in which the weight is raised in one quick motion from the floor to an overhead position. **12.** *Slang, chiefly U.S.* an act of kidnapping. **13.** *Brit. slang.* a robbery: *a diamond snatch.* [C13 *snacchen;* related to Middle Dutch *snakken* to gasp, Old Norse *snaka* to sniff around] —'**snatcher** *n.*

snatch block *n. Nautical.* a block that can be opened so that a rope can be inserted from the side, without threading it through from the end. [C17: so called because the rope can be inserted quickly: figuratively, the block snatches it. See SNATCH]

snatch squad *n. Brit.* a squad of soldiers or police trained to deal with demonstrations by picking out and arresting the alleged ringleaders.

snatchy ('snætʃɪ) *adj.* **snatchier, snatchiest.** disconnected or spasmodic. —'**snatchily** *adv.*

snath (snæθ) *or* **snathe** (sneɪð) *n.* the handle of a scythe. [C16: variant of earlier *snead,* from Old English *snǣd,* of obscure origin]

snazzy ('snæzɪ) *adj.* **-zier, -ziest.** *Informal.* (esp. of clothes) stylishly and often flashily attractive. [C20: perhaps from SN(APPY + J)AZZY] —'**snazzily** *adv.* —'**snazziness** *n.*

SNCC (snɪk) *n.* (in the U.S.) *acronym for* Student Nonviolent Coordinating Committee (1960–69) and Student National Coordinating Committee (from 1969).

SNCF (in France) *abbrev. for* Société Nationale des Chemins de Fer. [French: National Society of Railways]

sneak (sniːk) *vb.* **1.** (*intr.;* often foll. by *along, off, in,* etc.) to move furtively. **2.** (*intr.*) to behave in a cowardly or underhand manner. **3.** (*tr.*) to bring, take, or put stealthily. **4.** (*intr.*) *Informal, chiefly Brit.* to tell tales (esp. in schools). **5.** (*tr.*) *Informal.* to steal. **6.** (*intr.;* foll. by *off, out, away,* etc.) *Informal.* to leave unobtrusively. ~*n.* **7.** a person who acts in an underhand or cowardly manner, esp. as an informer. **8. a.** a stealthy act or movement. **b.** (*as modifier*): *a sneak attack.* **9.** *Brit. informal.* an unobtrusive departure. [Old English *snīcan* to creep; from Old Norse *snīkja* to hanker after] —'**sneaky** *adj.* —'**sneakily** *adv.* —'**sneakiness** *n.*

sneakers ('sniːkəz) *pl. n. Chiefly U.S. and Canadian.* canvas shoes with rubber soles worn for sports or informally.

sneaking ('sniːkɪŋ) *adj.* **1.** acting in a furtive or cowardly way. **2.** secret: *a sneaking desire to marry a millionaire.* **3.** slight but nagging (esp. in the phrase **a sneaking suspicion**). —'**sneakingly** *adv.* —'**sneakingness** *n.*

sneak preview *n.* a screening of a film at an unexpected time to test audience reaction before its release.

sneak thief *n.* a person who steals paltry articles from premises, which he enters through open doors, windows, etc.

sneck[1] (snɛk) *n.* **1.** a small squared stone used in a rubble wall to fill spaces between stones of different height. **2.** *Dialect, chiefly Scot. and northern English.* the latch or catch of a door or gate. ~*vb.* **3.** *Dialect, chiefly Scot. and northern English.* to fasten (a latch). [C15 *snekk,* of uncertain origin]

sneck[2] (snɛk) *n., vb.* a Scot. word for **snick.**

sned (snɛd) *vb.* **sneds, snedding, snedded.** (*tr.*) *Scot. and northern English dialect.* to lop off or prune. [Old English *snǣdan*]

sneer (snɪə) *n.* **1.** a facial expression of scorn or contempt, typically with the upper lip curled. **2.** a scornful or contemptuous remark or utterance. ~*vb.* **3.** (*intr.*) to assume a facial expression of scorn or contempt. **4.** to say or utter (something) in a scornful or contemptuous manner. [C16: perhaps from Low Dutch; compare North Frisian *sneere* contempt] —'**sneerer** *n.* —'**sneerful** *adj.* —'**sneering** *adj., n.* —'**sneeringly** *adv.*

sneeze (sniːz) *vb.* **1.** (*intr.*) to expel air from the nose involuntarily, esp. as the result of irritation of the nasal mucous membrane. ~*n.* **2.** the act or sound of sneezing. [Old English *fnēosan* (unattested); related to Old Norse *fnȳsa,* Middle High German *fnūsen,* Greek *pneuma* breath] —'**sneezeless** *adj.* —'**sneezer** *n.* —'**sneezy** *adj.*

sneeze at *vb.* (*intr., prep.;* usually with a negative) *Informal.* to dismiss lightly: *his offer is not to be sneezed at.*

sneezewood ('sniːzˌwʊd) *n.* **1.** a tree, *Ptaeroxylon utile,* native to southern Africa: family *Ptaeroxylaceae.* **2.** the tough wood of this tree, which has a peppery smell and is used for bridges, piers, fencing posts, etc.

sneezewort ('sniːzˌwɜːt) *n.* a Eurasian plant, *Achillea ptarmica,* having daisy-like flowers and long grey-green leaves, which cause sneezing when powdered: family *Compositae* (composites). See also **yarrow.**

snell (snɛl) *adj. Scot.* biting; bitter; sharp. [Old English *snel* quick, active]

Snell's law (snɛlz) *n. Physics.* the principle that the ratio of the sine of the angle of incidence to the sine of the angle of refraction is constant when a light ray passes from one medium to another. [C17: named after Willebrord *Snell* (1591–1626), Dutch physicist]

SNG *abbrev. for* synthetic natural gas.

snib (snɪb) *Scot.* ~*n.* **1.** the bolt or fastening of a door, window, etc. ~*vb.* **snibs, snibbing, snibbed.** (*tr.*) **2.** to bolt or fasten (a door). [C19: of uncertain origin; perhaps from Low German *snibbe* beak]

snick (snɪk) *n.* **1.** a small cut; notch. **2.** a knot in thread, etc. **3.** *Cricket.* **a.** a glancing blow off the edge of the bat. **b.** the ball so hit. ~*vb. (tr.)* **4.** to cut a small corner or notch in (material, etc.). **5.** *Cricket.* to hit (the ball) with a snick. [C18: probably of Scandinavian origin; compare Old Norse *snikka* to whittle, Swedish *snicka*]

snicker ('snɪkə) *n., vb.* **1.** another word, esp. U.S. and Canadian, for **snigger.** ~*vb.* **2.** (of a horse) to whinny. [C17: probably of imitative origin]

snickersnee ('snɪkəˌsni:) *n. Archaic.* **1.** a knife for cutting or thrusting. **2.** a fight with knives. [C17 *stick or snee,* from Dutch *steken* to STICK² + *snijen* to cut]

snicket ('snɪkɪt) *n. Northern English dialect.* a passageway between walls or fences. [of obscure origin]

snide (snaɪd) *adj.* **1.** (of a remark, etc.) maliciously derogatory; supercilious. **2.** counterfeit; sham. ~*n.* **3.** *Slang.* sham jewellery. [C19: of unknown origin] —**'snidely** *adv.* —**'snideness** *n.*

sniff (snɪf) *vb.* **1.** to inhale through the nose, usually in short rapid audible inspirations, as for the purpose of identifying a scent, for clearing a congested nasal passage, or for taking a drug or intoxicating fumes. **2.** (when *intr.*, often foll. by *at*) to perceive or attempt to perceive (a smell) by inhaling through the nose. ~*n.* **3.** the act or sound of sniffing. **4.** a smell perceived by sniffing, esp. a faint scent. [C14: probably related to *snivelen* to SNIVEL] —**'sniffer** *n.* —**'sniffing** *n., adj.*

sniff at *vb. (intr., prep.)* to express contempt or dislike for.

sniffer dog *n.* a police dog trained to detect drugs or explosives by smell.

sniffle ('snɪfᵊl) *vb.* **1.** *(intr.)* to breathe audibly through the nose, as when the nasal passages are congested. ~*n.* **2.** the act, sound, or an instance of sniffling. —**'sniffler** *n.* —**'sniffly** *adj.*

sniffles ('snɪfᵊlz) *or* **snuffles** *pl. n. Informal.* **1. the.** a cold in the head. **2.** the sniffling that sometimes accompanies weeping or prolonged crying.

sniff out *vb. (tr., adv.)* to detect through shrewdness or instinct.

sniffy ('snɪfɪ) *adj.* **-fier, -fiest.** *Informal.* contemptuous or disdainful. —**'sniffily** *adv.* —**'sniffiness** *n.*

snifter ('snɪftə) *n.* **1.** a pear-shaped glass with a short stem and a bowl that narrows towards the top so that the aroma of brandy or a liqueur is retained. **2.** *Informal.* a small quantity of alcoholic drink. [C19: perhaps from dialect *snifter* to sniff, perhaps of Scandinavian origin; compare Danish *snifta* (obsolete) to sniff]

snig (snɪg) *vb. (tr.)* **snigs, snigging, snigged.** *Austral. and N.Z.* to drag (a log) along the ground by a chain fastened at one end. [from English dialect]

snigger ('snɪgə) *or U.S. and Canadian* **snicker** ('snɪkə) *n.* **1.** a sly or disrespectful laugh, esp. one partly stifled. ~*vb. (intr.)* **2.** to utter such a laugh. [C18: variant of SNICKER]

snigging chain *n. Austral. and N.Z.* a chain attached to a log when being hauled out of the bush.

sniggle ('snɪgᵊl) *vb.* **1.** *(intr.)* to fish for eels by dangling or thrusting a baited hook into cavities. **2.** *(tr.)* to catch (eels) by sniggling. ~*n.* **3.** the baited hook used for sniggling eels. [C17: from C15 *snig* young eel] —**'sniggler** *n.*

snip (snɪp) *vb.* **snips, snipping, snipped.** **1.** to cut or clip with a small quick stroke or a succession of small quick strokes, esp. with scissors or shears. ~*n.* **2.** the act of snipping. **3.** the sound of scissors or shears closing. **4.** Also called: **snipping.** a small piece of anything, esp. one that has been snipped off. **5.** a small cut made by snipping. **6.** *Chiefly Brit.* an informal word for **bargain.** **7.** *Informal.* something easily done; cinch. **8.** *U.S. and Canadian informal.* a small or insignificant person or thing, esp. an irritating or insolent one. ~*interj.* **9.** *(often reiterated)* a representation of the sound of scissors or shears closing. ~See also **snips.** [C16: from Low German, Dutch *snippen;* related to Middle High German *snipfen* to snap the fingers]

snipe (snaɪp) *n., pl.* **snipe** *or* **snipes.** **1.** any of various birds of the genus *Gallinago* (or *Capella*) and related genera, such as *G. gallinago* (**common** or **Wilson's snipe**), of marshes and river banks, having a long straight bill: family *Scolopacidae* (sandpipers, etc.), order *Charadriiformes.* **2.** any of various similar related birds, such as certain sandpipers and curlews. **3.** a shot, esp. a gunshot, fired from a place of concealment. ~*vb.* **4.** (when *intr.*, often foll. by *at*) to attack (a person or persons) with a rifle from a place of concealment. **5.** *(intr.;* often foll. by *at)* to criticize adversely a person or persons from a position of security. **6.** *(intr.)* to hunt or shoot snipe. [C14: from Old Norse *snípa;* related to Old High German *snepfa* Middle Dutch *snippe*] —**'snipeˌlike** *adj.*

snipefish ('snaɪpˌfɪʃ) *n., pl.* **-fish** *or* **-fishes.** any teleost fish of the family *Macrorhamphosidae,* of tropical and temperate seas, having a deep body, long snout, and a single long dorsal fin: order *Solenichthyes* (sea horses, etc.). Also called: **bellows fish.** [C17: so called because of the resemblance between its snout and a snipe's bill]

snipe fly *n.* any of various predatory dipterous flies of the family *Leptidae* (or *Rhagionidae*), such as *Rhagio scolopacea* of Europe, having an elongated body and long legs. [named after the snipe because its flight resembles that of the bird]

sniper ('snaɪpə) *n.* **1.** a rifleman who fires from a concealed place, esp. a military marksman who fires from cover usually at long ranges at individual enemy soldiers. **2.** *Austral.* another word for **seagull** (sense 2).

sniperscope ('snaɪpəˌskəʊp) *n.* a telescope with crosshairs mounted on a sniper's rifle.

snippet ('snɪpɪt) *n.* a small scrap or fragment. [C17: from SNIP + -ET] —**'snippetiness** *n.* —**'snippety** *adj.*

snippy ('snɪpɪ) *adj.* **-pier, -piest.** **1.** scrappy; fragmentary. **2.** *Informal.* fault-finding. **3.** *Dialect.* mean; stingy. —**'snippily** *adv.* —**'snippiness** *n.*

snips (snɪps) *pl. n.* a small pair of shears used for cutting sheet metal. Also called: **tin snips.**

snit (snɪt) *n. U.S. and Austral.* a fit of temper. [C20: of unknown origin]

snitch (snɪtʃ) *Slang.* ~*vb.* **1.** *(tr.)* to steal; take, esp. in an underhand way. **2.** *(intr.)* to act as an informer. ~*n.* **3.** an informer; telltale. **4.** the nose. [C17: of unknown origin] —**'snitcher** *n.*

snitchy ('snɪtʃɪ) *adj.* **snitchier, snitchiest.** *N.Z. informal.* bad-tempered or irritable.

snivel ('snɪvᵊl) *vb.* **-els, -elling, -elled** *or U.S.* **-els, -eling, -eled.** **1.** *(intr.)* to sniffle as a sign of distress, esp. contemptibly. **2.** to utter (something) tearfully; whine. **3.** *(intr.)* to have a runny nose. ~*n.* **4.** an instance of snivelling. [C14 *snivelen;* related to Old English *snyflung* mucus, Dutch *snuffelen* to smell out, Old Norse *snoppa* snout] —**'sniveller** *n.* —**'snivelling** *adj., n.* —**'snivelly** *adj.*

SNO *abbrev. for* Scottish National Orchestra.

snob (snɒb) *n.* **1. a.** a person who strives to associate with those of higher social status and who behaves condescendingly to others. Compare **inverted snob.** **b.** *(as modifier)*: *snob appeal.* **2.** a person having similar pretensions with regard to his tastes, etc.: *an intellectual snob.* **3.** *Austral. and N.Z. informal.* another word for **cobbler**¹ (sense 2). [C18 (in the sense: shoemaker; hence, C19: a person who flatters those of higher station, etc.): of unknown origin] —**'snobbery** *n.* —**'snobbish** *adj.* —**'snobbishly** *adv.* —**'snobbishness** *or* **'snobbism** *n.* —**'snobby** *adj.*

SNOBOL ('snəʊbɒl) *n.* String Oriented Symbolic Language: a computer-programming language for handling strings of symbols.

Sno-Cat ('snəʊˌkæt) *n. Trademark.* a type of snowmobile.

snoek (snʊk) *n.* a South African edible marine fish, *Thyrsites atun.* [Afrikaans]

snog (snɒg) *Brit. slang.* ~*vb.* **snogs, snogging, snogged.** **1.** *(intr.)* to kiss and cuddle. ~*n.* **2.** the act of kissing and cuddling. [of obscure origin]

snood (snu:d) *n.* **1.** a pouchlike hat, often of net, loosely holding a woman's hair at the back. **2.** a headband, esp. one formerly worn by young unmarried women in Scotland. ~*vb.* **3.** *(tr.)* to confine (the hair) in a snood. [Old English *snōd;* of obscure origin]

snook¹ (snu:k) *n., pl.* **snook** *or* **snooks.** **1.** any of several large game fishes of the genus *Centropomus,* esp. *C. undecimalis* of tropical American marine and fresh waters: family *Centropomidae* (robalos). **2.** *Austral.* the sea pike *Australuzza novaehollandiae.* [C17: from Dutch *snoek* pike]

snook² (snu:k) *n. Brit.* a rude gesture, made by putting one thumb to the nose with the fingers of the hand outstretched (esp. in the phrase **cock a snook**). [C19: of obscure origin]

snooker ('snu:kə) *n.* **1.** a game played on a billiard table with 15 red balls, six balls of other colours, and a white cue ball. The object is to pot the balls in a certain order. **2.** a shot in which the cue ball is left in a position such that another ball blocks the object ball. The opponent is then usually forced to play the cue ball off a cushion. ~*vb. (tr.)* **3.** to leave (an opponent) in an unfavourable position by playing a snooker. **4.** to place (someone) in a difficult situation. **5.** *(often passive)* to thwart; defeat. [C19: of unknown origin]

snoop (snu:p) *Informal.* ~*vb.* **1.** *(intr.;* often foll. by *about* or *around)* to pry into the private business of others. ~*n.* **2.** a person who pries into the business of others. **3.** an act or instance of snooping. [C19: from Dutch *snoepen* to eat furtively] —**'snoopy** *adj.*

snooper ('snu:pə) *n.* **1.** a person who snoops. **2.** *Brit. informal.* a person employed by the DSS to spy on claimants to make sure that they are not infringing the conditions of their eligibility for benefit.

snooperscope ('snu:pəˌskəʊp) *n. Military, U.S.* an instrument that enables the user to see objects in the dark by illuminating the object with infrared radiation and converting the reflected radiation to a visual image.

snoot (snu:t) *n.* **1.** *Slang.* the nose. **2.** *Photog., films, television.* a cone-shaped fitment on a studio light to control the scene area illuminated. [C20: variant of SNOUT]

snooty ('snu:tɪ) *adj.* **snootier, snootiest.** *Informal.* **1.** aloof or supercilious. **2.** snobbish or exclusive: *a snooty restaurant.* —**'snootily** *adv.* —**'snootiness** *n.*

snooze (snu:z) *Informal.* ~*vb.* **1.** *(intr.)* to take a brief light sleep. ~*n.* **2.** a nap. [C18: of unknown origin] —**'snoozer** *n.* —**'snoozy** *adj.*

snore (snɔ:) *vb.* **1.** *(intr.)* to breathe through the mouth and nose while asleep with snorting sounds caused by the soft palate vibrating. ~*n.* **2.** the act or sound of snoring. [C14: of imitative origin; related to Middle Low German, Middle Dutch *snorken;* see SNORT] —**'snorer** *n.*

snorkel ('snɔːkᵊl) *n.* **1.** a device allowing a swimmer to breathe while face down on the surface of the water, consisting of a bent tube fitting into the mouth and projecting above the surface. **2.** (on a submarine) a retractable vertical device containing air-intake and exhaust pipes for the engines and general ventilation: its use permits extended periods of submergence at periscope depth. **3.** *Military.* a similar device on a tank, enabling it to cross shallow water obstacles. **4.** a type of parka or anorak with a hood that projects beyond the face. *~vb.* **-kels, -kelling, -kelled** *or U.S.* **-kels, -keling, -keled. 5.** (*intr.*) to swim with a snorkel. [C20: from German *Schnorchel;* related to German *schnarchen* to SNORE]

snort (snɔːt) *vb.* **1.** (*intr.*) to exhale forcibly through the nostrils, making a characteristic noise. **2.** (*intr.*) (of a person) to express contempt or annoyance by such an exhalation. **3.** (*tr.*) to utter in a contemptuous or annoyed manner. **4.** (*tr.*) *Slang.* to inhale (a powdered drug) through the nostrils. *~n.* **5.** a forcible exhalation of air through the nostrils, esp. (of persons) as a noise of contempt or annoyance. **6.** *Slang.* an instance of snorting a drug. **7.** Also called: **snorter.** *Slang.* a short drink, esp. an alcoholic one. **8.** *Slang.* the snorkel on a submarine. [C14 *snorten;* probably related to *snoren* to SNORE] —'**snorting** *n., adj.* —'**snortingly** *adv.*

snorter ('snɔːtə) *n.* **1.** a person or animal that snorts. **2.** *Brit. slang.* something outstandingly impressive or difficult. **3.** *Brit. slang.* something or someone ridiculous.

snot (snɒt) *n.* (*usually considered vulgar*) **1.** nasal mucus or discharge. **2.** *Slang.* a contemptible person. [Old English *gesnot;* related to Old High German *snuzza,* Norwegian, Danish *snot,* German *schneuzen* to blow one's nose]

snotter ('snɒtər) *Scot.* *~n.* **1.** (*often pl.*) another word for **snot.** *~vb.* (*intr.*) **2.** to breathe through obstructed nostrils. **3.** to snivel or blubber.

snotty ('snɒtɪ) (*considered vulgar*) *~adj.* **-tier, -tiest. 1.** dirty with nasal discharge. **2.** *Slang.* contemptible; nasty. **3.** snobbish; conceited. *~n., pl.* **-ties. 4.** a slang word for **midshipman.** —'**snottily** *adv.* —'**snottiness** *n.*

snout (snaʊt) *n.* **1.** the part of the head of a vertebrate, esp. a mammal, consisting of the nose, jaws, and surrounding region, esp. when elongated. **2.** the corresponding part of the head of such insects as weevils. **3.** anything projecting like a snout, such as a nozzle or the lower end of a glacier. **4.** *Slang.* a person's nose. **5.** Also called: **snout moth.** a brownish noctuid moth, *Hypena proboscidalis,* that frequents nettles: named from the palps that project prominently from the head at rest. **6.** *Brit. slang.* a cigarette or tobacco. **7.** *Slang.* an informer. **8. have (got) a snout on (someone).** *Austral. slang.* to have a grudge against (someone). [C13: of Germanic origin; compare Old Norse *snyta,* Middle Low German, Middle Dutch *snūte*] —'**snouted** *adj.* —'**snoutless** *adj.* —'**snout,like** *adj.*

snout beetle *n.* another name for **weevil** (sense 1). [C19: so named because of its long proboscis]

snow (snəʊ) *n.* **1.** precipitation from clouds in the form of flakes of ice crystals formed in the upper atmosphere. **2.** a layer of snowflakes on the ground. **3.** a fall of such precipitation. **4.** anything resembling snow in whiteness, softness, etc. **5.** the random pattern of white spots on a television or radar screen, produced by noise in the receiver and occurring when the signal is weak or absent. **6.** *Slang.* cocaine. **7.** See **carbon dioxide snow.** *~vb.* **8.** (*intr.;* with *it* as subject) to be the case that snow is falling. **9.** (*tr.;* usually passive, foll. by *over, under, in,* or *up*) to cover or confine with a heavy fall of snow. **10.** (often with *it* as subject) to fall or cause to fall as or like snow. **11.** (*tr.*) *U.S. and Canadian slang.* to deceive or overwhelm with elaborate often insincere talk. See **snow job. 12. be snowed under.** to be overwhelmed, esp. with paperwork. [Old English *snāw;* related to Old Norse *snjōr,* Gothic *snaiws,* Old High German *snēo,* Greek *nipha*] —'**snowless** *adj.* —'**snow,like** *adj.*

snowball ('snəʊ,bɔːl) *n.* **1.** snow pressed into a ball for throwing, as in play. **2.** a drink made of advocaat and lemonade. **3.** *Slang.* a mixture of heroin and cocaine. **4.** a dance started by one couple who separate and choose different partners. The process continues until all present are dancing. *~vb.* **5.** (*intr.*) to increase rapidly in size, importance, etc. **6.** (*tr.*) to throw snowballs at.

snowball tree *n.* any of several caprifoliaceous shrubs of the genus *Viburnum,* esp. *V. opulus* var. *roseum,* a sterile cultivated variety with spherical clusters of white or pinkish flowers.

snowberry ('snəʊbərɪ, -brɪ) *n., pl.* **-ries. 1.** any of several caprifoliaceous shrubs of the genus *Symphoricarpos,* esp. *S. albus,* cultivated for their small pink flowers and white berries. **2.** Also called: **waxberry.** any of the berries of such a plant. **3.** any of various other white-berried plants.

snowbird ('snəʊ,bɜːd) *n.* **1.** another name for the **snow bunting. 2.** *U.S. slang.* a person addicted to cocaine, or sometimes heroin.

snow-blind *adj.* temporarily unable to see or having impaired vision because of the intense reflection of sunlight from snow. —**snow blindness** *n.*

snowblink ('snəʊ,blɪŋk) *n.* a whitish glare in the sky reflected from snow. Compare **iceblink.**

snowblower ('snəʊ,bləʊə) *n.* a snow-clearing machine that sucks in snow and blows it away to one side.

snowboard ('snəʊ,bɔːd) *n.* a shaped board, resembling a skateboard without wheels, on which a person can stand to slide across snow. [C20: on the model of SURFBOARD]

snowboarding ('snəʊ,bɔːdɪŋ) *n.* the sport of moving across snow on a snowboard.

snowbound ('snəʊ,baʊnd) *adj.* confined to one place by heavy falls or drifts of snow; snowed-in.

snow bridge *n. Mountaineering.* a mass of snow bridging a crevasse, sometimes affording a risky way across it.

snow bunting *n.* a bunting, *Plectrophenax nivalis,* of northern and arctic regions, having a white plumage with dark markings on the wings, back, and tail.

snowcap ('snəʊ,kæp) *n.* a cap of snow, as on top of a mountain. —'**snow,capped** *adj.*

snow cave *n. Mountaineering.* another name for **snow hole.**

snow devil *n. Canadian.* a whirling column of snow.

snowdrift ('snəʊ,drɪft) *n.* a bank of deep snow driven together by the wind.

snowdrop ('snəʊ,drɒp) *n.* any of several amaryllidaceous plants of the Eurasian genus *Galanthus,* esp. *G. nivalis,* having drooping white bell-shaped flowers that bloom in early spring.

snowdrop tree *n.* another name for **silver bell.**

snowfall ('snəʊ,fɔːl) *n.* **1.** a fall of snow. **2.** *Meteorol.* the amount of snow received in a specified place and time.

snow fence *n.* a portable wire-and-paling fence erected to prevent snow from drifting across a road, drive, ski run, etc.

snowfield ('snəʊ,fiːld) *n.* a large area of permanent snow.

snowflake ('snəʊ,fleɪk) *n.* **1.** one of the mass of small thin delicate arrangements of ice crystals that fall as snow. **2.** any of various European amaryllidaceous plants of the genus *Leucojum,* such as *L. vernum* (**spring snowflake**), that have white nodding bell-shaped flowers.

snow goose *n.* a North American goose, *Anser hyperboreus* (or *Chen hyperborea* or *A. caerulescens*), having a white plumage with black wing tips.

snow grass *n.* **1.** *Austral.* any of various grey-green grasses of the genus *Poa,* of SE Australian mountain regions. **2.** *N.Z.* any of various hill and high-country grasses of the genus *Danthonia.*

snow gum *n.* another name for **sallee.** [so called because it grows at high altitude]

snow hole *n. Mountaineering.* a shelter dug in deep usually drifted snow. Also called: **snow cave.**

snow-in-summer *n.* another name for **dusty miller** (sense 1). [C19: so called from the appearance of its flowers]

snow job *n. Slang, chiefly U.S. and Canadian.* an instance of deceiving or overwhelming someone with elaborate often insincere talk.

snow leopard *n.* a large feline mammal, *Panthera uncia,* of mountainous regions of central Asia, closely related to the leopard but having a long pale brown coat marked with black rosettes. Also called: **ounce.**

snow line *n.* the altitudinal or latitudinal limit of permanent snow.

snowman ('snəʊ,mæn) *n., pl.* **-men.** a figure resembling a man, made of packed snow.

snowmobile ('snəʊmə,biːl) *n.* **a.** a small open motor vehicle for travelling on snow, steered by two skis at the front and driven by a caterpillar track underneath. **b.** Also called: **bombardier.** a larger closed motor vehicle with two skis at the front and a track at each side.

snow-on-the-mountain *n.* a North American euphorbiaceous plant, *Euphorbia marginata,* having white-edged leaves and showy white bracts surrounding small flowers.

snow plant *n.* a saprophytic plant, *Sarcodes sanguinea,* of mountain pine forests of W North America, having a fleshy scaly reddish stalk, no leaves, and pendulous scarlet flowers that are often produced before the snow melts: family *Monotropaceae.*

snowplough ('snəʊ,plaʊ) *n.* **1.** an implement or vehicle for clearing away snow. **2.** *Skiing.* a technique of turning the points of the skis inwards to turn or stop.

snowshed ('snəʊ,ʃɛd) *n.* a shelter built over an exposed section of railway track to prevent its blockage by snow.

snowshoe ('snəʊ,ʃuː) *n.* **1.** a device to facilitate walking on snow, esp. a racket-shaped frame with a network of thongs stretched across it. *~vb.* **-shoes, -shoeing, -shoed. 2.** (*intr.*) to walk or go using snowshoes. —'**snow,shoer** *n.*

snowshoe hare *or* **rabbit** *n.* a N North American hare, *Lepus americanus,* having brown fur in summer, white fur in winter, and heavily furred feet.

snowstorm ('snəʊ,stɔːm) *n.* a storm with heavy snow.

snow tyre *n.* a motor vehicle tyre with deep treads and ridges to give improved grip on snow and ice.

snow-white *adj.* **1.** white as snow. **2.** pure as white snow.

snowy ('snəʊɪ) *adj.* **snowier, snowiest. 1.** covered with or abounding in snow: *snowy hills.* **2.** characterized by snow: *snowy weather.* **3.** resembling snow in whiteness, purity, etc. —'**snowily** *adv.* —'**snowiness** *n.*

snowy egret *n.* a small American egret, *Egretta thula,* having a white plumage, yellow legs, and a black bill.

snowy owl *n.* a large owl, *Nyctea scandiaca,* of tundra regions, having a white plumage flecked with brown.

SNP *abbrev. for* Scottish National Party.

Snr *or* **snr** *abbrev. for* senior.

snub (snʌb) *vb.* **snubs, snubbing, snubbed.** (*tr.*) **1.** to insult (someone) deliberately. **2.** to stop or check the motion of (a boat, horse, etc.) by taking turns of a rope or cable around a post or other fixed object. **3.** *Archaic.* to reprimand. ~*n.* **4.** a deliberately insulting act or remark. **5. a.** *Nautical.* an elastic shock absorber attached to a mooring line. **b.** (*as modifier*): *a snub rope.* ~*adj.* **6.** short and blunt. See also **snub-nosed.** [C14: from Old Norse *snubba* to scold; related to Norwegian, Swedish dialect *snubba* to cut short, Danish *snubbe*] —'**snubber** *n.* —'**snubby** *adj.*

snub-nosed *adj.* **1.** having a short turned-up nose. **2.** (of a pistol) having an extremely short barrel.

snuck (snʌk) *vb. U.S. and Canadian, not standard.* a past tense and past participle of **sneak.**

snuff[1] (snʌf) *vb.* **1.** (*tr.*) to inhale through the nose. **2.** (when *intr.*, often foll. by *at*) (esp. of an animal) to examine by sniffing. ~*n.* **3.** an act or the sound of snuffing. [C16: probably from Middle Dutch *snuffen* to snuffle, ultimately of imitative origin] —'**snuffer** *n.*

snuff[2] (snʌf) *n.* **1.** finely powdered tobacco for sniffing up the nostrils or less commonly for chewing. **2.** a small amount of this. **3.** any powdered substance, esp. one for sniffing up the nostrils. **4. up to snuff.** *Informal.* **a.** in good health or in good condition. **b.** *Chiefly Brit.* not easily deceived. ~*vb.* **5.** (*intr.*) to use or inhale snuff. [C17: from Dutch *snuf*, shortened from *snuftabale*, literally: tobacco for snuffing; see SNUFF[1]]

snuff[3] (snʌf) *vb.* (*tr.*) **1.** (often foll. by *out*) to extinguish (a light from a naked flame, esp. a candle). **2.** to cut off the charred part of (the wick of a candle, etc.). **3.** (usually foll. by *out*) *Informal.* to suppress; put an end to. **4. snuff it.** *Brit. informal.* to die. ~*n.* **5.** the burned portion of the wick of a candle. [C14 *snoffe*, of obscure origin]

snuffbox ('snʌf,bɒks) *n.* a container, often of elaborate ornamental design, for holding small quantities of snuff.

snuff-dipping *n.* the practice of absorbing nicotine by holding in one's mouth, between the cheek and the gum, a small amount of tobacco, either loose or enclosed in a sachet.

snuffer ('snʌfə) *n.* **1.** a cone-shaped implement for extinguishing candles. **2.** (*pl.*) an instrument resembling a pair of scissors for trimming the wick or extinguishing the flame of a candle. **3.** *Rare.* a person who takes snuff.

snuffle ('snʌfᵊl) *vb.* **1.** (*intr.*) to breathe noisily or with difficulty. **2.** to say or speak in a nasal tone. **3.** (*intr.*) to snivel. ~*n.* **4.** an act or the sound of snuffling. **5.** a nasal tone or voice. **6. the snuffles.** a condition characterized by snuffling. [C16: from Low German or Dutch *snuffelen*; see SNUFF[1], SNIVEL] —'**snuffler** *n.* —'**snuffly** *adj.*

snuff movie *or* **film** *n. Slang.* a pornographic film in which an unsuspecting actress or actor is murdered as the climax of the film.

snuffy ('snʌfɪ) *adj.* **snuffier, snuffiest.** **1.** of, relating to, or resembling snuff. **2.** covered with or smelling of snuff. **3.** unpleasant; disagreeable. —'**snuffiness** *n.*

snug (snʌg) *adj.* **snugger, snuggest.** **1.** comfortably warm and well-protected; cosy: *the children were snug in bed during the blizzard.* **2.** small but comfortable: *a snug cottage.* **3.** well-ordered; compact: *a snug boat.* **4.** sheltered and secure: *a snug anchorage.* **5.** fitting closely and comfortably. **6.** offering safe concealment. ~*n.* **7.** (in Britain and Ireland) one of the bars in certain pubs, offering intimate seating for only a few persons. **8.** *Engineering.* a small peg under the head of a bolt engaging with a slot in the bolted component to prevent the bolt turning when the nut is tightened. ~*vb.* **snugs, snugging, snugged.** **9.** to make or become comfortable and warm. **10.** (*tr.*) *Nautical.* to make (a vessel) ready for a storm by lashing down gear. [C16 (in the sense: prepared for storms (used of a ship)): related to Old Icelandic *snöggr* short-haired, Swedish *snygg* tidy, Low German *snögger* smart] —'**snugly** *adv.* —'**snugness** *n.*

snuggery ('snʌgərɪ) *n., pl.* **-geries.** **1.** a cosy and comfortable place or room. **2.** another name for **snug** (sense 7).

snuggle ('snʌgᵊl) *vb.* **1.** (*usually intr.*; usually foll. by *down, up,* or *together*) to nestle into or draw close to (somebody or something) for warmth or from affection. ~*n.* **2.** the act of snuggling. [C17: frequentative SNUG (vb.)]

snye (snaɪ) *n. Canadian.* a side channel of a river. [from Canadian French *chenail*, from French *chenal* CHANNEL]

so[1] (səʊ) *adv.* **1.** (foll. by an adjective or adverb and a correlative clause often introduced by *that*) to such an extent: *the river is so dirty that it smells.* **2.** (*used with a negative*; it replaces the first *as* in an equative comparison) to the same extent as: *she is not so old as you.* **3.** (intensifier): *it's so lovely; I love you so.* **4.** in the state or manner expressed or implied: *they're happy and will remain so.* **5.** (*not used with a negative*; foll. by an auxiliary verb or *do, have,* or *be* used as main verbs) also; likewise: *I can speak Spanish and so can you.* **6.** *Dialect and U.S.* indeed: used to contradict a negative statement: *You didn't tell the truth. I did so!* **7.** *Archaic.* provided that. **8. and so on** *or* **forth.** and continuing similarly. **9. just so.** See **just** (sense 19). **10. or so.** approximately: *fifty or so people came to see me.* **11. quite so.** I agree; exactly. **12. so be it.** used to express agreement or resignation. **13. so much. a.** a certain degree or amount (of). **b.** a lot (of): *it's just so much nonsense.* **14. so much for. a.** no more can or need be said about. **b.** used to express contempt for something that has failed: *so much for your bright idea.* ~*conj.* (subordinating; often foll. by *that*) **15.** in order (that): *to die so that you might live.* **16.** with the consequence (that): *he was late home, so that there was trouble.* **17. so as.** (*takes an infinitive*) in order (to): *to slim so as to lose weight.* ~*sentence connector.* **18.** in consequence; hence: *she wasn't needed, so she left.* **19.** used to introduce a sentence expressing resignation, amazement, or sarcasm: *so you're publishing a book!* **20.** thereupon; and then: *and so we ended up in France.* **21.** used to introduce a sentence or clause to add emphasis: *he's crazy, so he is.* **22. so what!** *Informal.* what importance does that have? ~*pron.* **23.** used to substitute for a clause or sentence, which may be understood: *you'll stop because I said so.* ~*adj.* **24.** (used with *is, was,* etc.) factual; true: *it can't be so.* ~*interj.* **25.** an exclamation of agreement, surprise, etc. [Old English *swā*; related to Old Norse *svā*, Old High German *sō*, Dutch *zoo*]

▷**Usage.** Careful writers of formal English consider it poor style to use *so* as a conjunction, to indicate either purpose (*he did it so he could feel happier*) or result (*he could not do it so he did not try*). In the former case *in order to* should be used instead and in the latter case *and so* or *and therefore* would be more acceptable.

so[2] (səʊ) *n. Music.* a variant spelling of **soh.**

SO (in Britain) *abbrev. for* Stationery Office.

So. *abbrev. for* south(ern).

s.o. *abbrev. for:* **1.** seller's option. **2.** shipping order.

soak (səʊk) *vb.* **1.** to make, become, or be thoroughly wet or saturated, esp. by immersion in a liquid. **2.** (when *intr.*, usually foll. by *in* or *into*) (of a liquid) to penetrate or permeate. **3.** (*tr.*; usually foll. by *in* or *up*) (of a permeable solid) to take in (a liquid) by absorption: *the earth soaks up rainwater.* **4.** (*tr.*; foll. by *out* or *out of*) to remove by immersion in a liquid: *she soaked the stains out of the dress.* **5.** (*tr.*) *Metallurgy.* to heat (a metal) prior to working. **6.** *Informal.* to drink excessively or make or become drunk. **7.** (*tr.*) *U.S. and Canadian slang.* to overcharge. **8.** (*tr.*) *Brit. slang.* to put in pawn. ~*n.* **9.** the act of immersing in a liquid or the period of immersion. **10.** the liquid in which something may be soaked, esp. a solution containing detergent. **11.** another name for **soakage** (sense 3). **12.** *Brit. informal.* a heavy rainfall. **13.** *Slang.* a person who drinks to excess. [Old English *sōcian* to cook; see SUCK] —'**soaker** *n.* —'**soaking** *n., adj.*

soakage ('səʊkɪdʒ) *n.* **1.** the process or a period in which a permeable substance is soaked in a liquid. **2.** liquid that has been soaked up or has seeped out. **3.** Also called: **soak.** *Austral.* a small pool of water or swampy patch.

soakaway ('səʊkə,weɪ) *n.* a pit filled with rubble, etc., into which rain or waste water drains.

so-and-so *n., pl.* **so-and-sos.** *Informal.* **1.** a person whose name is forgotten or ignored: *so-and-so came to see me.* **2.** *Euphemistic.* a person or thing regarded as unpleasant or difficult: *which so-and-so broke my razor?*

soap (səʊp) *n.* **1.** a cleaning or emulsifying agent made by reacting animal or vegetable fats or oils with potassium or sodium hydroxide. Soaps often contain colouring matter and perfume and act by emulsifying grease and lowering the surface tension of water, so that it more readily penetrates open materials such as textiles. See also **detergent.** **2.** any metallic salt of a fatty acid, such as palmitic or stearic acid. See also **metallic soap.** **3.** *Slang.* flattery or persuasive talk (esp. in the phrase **soft soap**). **4.** *Informal.* short for **soap opera.** **5.** *Austral. slang.* a milksop. **6.** *U.S. and Canadian slang.* money, esp. for bribery. **7. no soap.** *U.S. and Canadian slang.* not possible or successful. ~*vb.* **8.** (*tr.*) to apply soap to. **9.** (*tr.*; often foll. by *up*) *Slang.* **a.** to flatter or talk persuasively to. **b.** *U.S. and Canadian.* to bribe. [Old English *sāpe*; related to Old High German *seipfa*, Old French *savon*, Latin *sāpō*] —'**soapless** *adj.* —'**soap,like** *adj.*

soapbark ('səʊp,bɑːk) *n.* **1.** Also called: **quillai.** a W South American rosaceous tree, *Quillaja saponaria*, with undivided evergreen leaves and small white flowers. **2.** Also called: **quillai bark.** the inner bark of this tree, formerly used as soap and as a source of saponin. **3.** any of several trees or shrubs that have a bark similar to this.

soapberry ('səʊp,bɛrɪ) *n., pl.* **-ries.** **1.** any of various chiefly tropical American sapindaceous trees of the genus *Sapindus*, esp. *S. saponaria* (or *S. marginatus*), having pulpy fruit containing saponin. **2.** a related plant, *S. drummondii*, of the southwestern U.S. **3.** the fruit of any of these trees. ~Also called: **chinaberry.**

soap boiler *n.* a manufacturer of soap. —**soap boiling** *n.*

soapbox ('səʊp,bɒks) *n.* **1.** a box or crate for packing soap. **2.** a crate used as a platform for speech-making. **3.** a child's home-made racing cart consisting of a wooden box set on a wooden frame with wheels and a steerable front axle.

soap bubble *n.* **1.** a bubble formed from soapy water. **2.** something that is ephemeral but attractive.

soapolallie ('səʊpə,lælɪ) *n. Canadian.* a drink made by crushing soapberries. [from SOAP(BERRY) + *lallie* (compare *-lolly* as in LOBLOLLY)]

soap opera *n.* a serialized drama, usually dealing with domestic themes and characterized by sentimentality, broadcast on radio or television. [C20: so called because manufacturers of soap were typical sponsors]

soapstone ('səʊpˌstəʊn) *n.* a massive compact soft variety of talc, used for making tabletops, hearths, ornaments, etc. Also called: **steatite.** [C17: so called because it has a greasy feel and was sometimes used as soap]

soapsuds ('səʊpˌsʌdz) *pl. n.* foam or lather made from soap. —'**soapˌsudsy** *adj.*

soapwort ('səʊpˌwɜːt) *n.* a Eurasian caryophyllaceous plant, *Saponaria officinalis,* having rounded clusters of fragrant pink or white flowers and leaves that were formerly used as a soap substitute. Also called: **bouncing Bet.**

soapy ('səʊpɪ) *adj.* **soapier, soapiest.** **1.** containing or covered with soap: *soapy water.* **2.** resembling or characteristic of soap. **3.** *Slang.* flattering or persuasive. —'**soapily** *adv.* —'**soapiness** *n.*

soar (sɔː) *vb.* (*intr.*) **1.** to rise or fly upwards into the air. **2.** (of a bird, aircraft, etc.) to glide while maintaining altitude by the use of ascending air currents. **3.** to rise or increase in volume, size, etc.: *soaring prices.* ~*n.* **4.** the act of soaring. **5.** the altitude attained by soaring. [C14: from Old French *essorer,* from Vulgar Latin *exaurāre* (unattested) to expose to the breezes, from Latin EX-[1] + *aura* a breeze] —'**soarer** *n.*

Soay ('səʊeɪ) *n.* a breed of small horned sheep having long legs and dark brown wool that is plucked rather than shorn; found mainly on St Kilda where they were probably introduced by the Vikings. [named after *Soay,* an island in the St Kilda group, where they were first found]

sob (sɒb) *vb.* **sobs, sobbing, sobbed.** **1.** (*intr.*) to weep with convulsive gasps. **2.** (*tr.*) to utter with sobs. **3.** to cause (oneself) to be in a specified state by sobbing: *to sob oneself to sleep.* ~*n.* **4.** a convulsive gasp made in weeping. [C12: probably from Low German; compare Dutch *sabben* to suck] —'**sobber** *n.*

s.o.b. *Slang, chiefly U.S. and Canadian. abbrev. for* son of a bitch.

sobeit (səʊ'biːɪt) *conj. Archaic.* provided that. [C16: from SO + BE + IT: originally three words]

sober ('səʊbə) *adj.* **1.** not drunk. **2.** not given to excessive indulgence in drink or any other activity. **3.** sedate and rational: *a sober attitude to a problem.* **4.** (of colours) plain and dull or subdued. **5.** free from exaggeration or speculation: *he told us the sober truth.* ~*vb.* **6.** (usually foll. by *up*) to make or become less intoxicated, reckless, etc. [C14 *sobre,* from Old French, from Latin *sōbrius*] —'**sobering** *adj.* —'**soberingly** *adv.* —'**soberly** *adv.* —'**soberness** *n.*

sobersides ('səʊbəˌsaɪdz) *n.* (*functioning as sing.*) a solemn and sedate person. —'**soberˌsided** *adj.*

sobole ('səʊbəʊl) *n., pl.* **soboles** (-liːz). a creeping underground stem that produces roots and buds; a sucker. [back formation from *soboles* (originally a sing.), from Latin *soboles* a shoot, from *subolescere* to grow]

sobriety (səʊ'braɪətɪ) *n.* **1.** the state or quality of being sober. **2.** the quality of refraining from excess. **3.** the quality of being serious or sedate.

sobriquet *or* **soubriquet** ('səʊbrɪˌkeɪ) *n.* a humorous epithet, assumed name, or nickname. [C17: from French *soubriquet,* of uncertain origin]

sob sister *n.* a journalist, esp. a woman, on a newspaper or magazine who writes articles of sentimental appeal.

sob story *n.* a tale of personal distress intended to arouse sympathy, esp. one offered as an excuse or apology.

sob stuff *n.* material such as films, stories, etc., that play upon the emotions by the overuse of pathos and sentiment.

Soc. *or* **soc.** *abbrev. for:* **1.** socialist. **2.** society.

soca ('səʊkə) *n.* a mixture of soul and calypso music typical of the E Caribbean. [C20: a blend of *soul* and *calypso*]

socage ('sɒkɪdʒ) *n.* **1.** *English legal history.* the tenure of land by certain services, esp. of an agricultural nature. **2.** *English law.* the freehold tenure of land. [C14: from Anglo-French, from *soc* SOKE] —'**socager** *n.*

so-called *adj.* **a.** (*prenominal*) designated or styled by the name or word mentioned, esp. (in the speaker's opinion) incorrectly: *a so-called genius.* **b.** (also used parenthetically after a noun): *these experts, so-called, are no help.*

soccer ('sɒkə) *n.* **a.** a game in which two teams of eleven players try to kick or head a ball into their opponent's goal, only the goalkeeper on either side being allowed to touch the ball with his hands and arms except in the case of throw-ins. **b.** (*as modifier*): *a soccer player.* ~Also called: **Association Football.** [C19: from (*as*)*soc.* + *-er*]

Socceroos (ˌsɒkə'ruːz) *pl. n. Informal.* the Australian national soccer team. [from SOCCER + (KANGAR)OO]

sociable ('səʊʃəbᵊl) *adj.* **1.** friendly or companionable. **2.** (of an occasion) providing the opportunity for friendliness and conviviality. ~*n.* **3.** *Chiefly U.S.* another name for **social** (sense 9). **4.** a type of open carriage with two seats facing each other. [C16: via French from Latin *sociābilis,* from *sociāre* to unite, from *socius* an associate] —ˌ**socia'bility** *or* '**sociableness** *n.* —'**sociably** *adv.*

social ('səʊʃəl) *adj.* **1.** living or preferring to live in a community rather than alone. **2.** denoting or relating to human society or any of its subdivisions. **3.** of, relating to, or characteristic of the experience, behaviour, and interaction of persons forming groups. **4.** relating to or having the purpose of promoting companionship, communal activities, etc.: *a social club.* **5.** relating to or engaged in social services: *a social worker.* **6.** relating to or considered appropriate to a certain class of society, esp. one thought superior. **7.** (esp. of certain species of insects) living together in organized colonies: *social bees.* Compare **solitary** (sense 6). **8.** (of plant species) growing in clumps, usually over a wide area. ~*n.* **9.** an informal gathering, esp. of an organized group, to promote companionship, communal activity, etc. [C16: from Latin *sociālis* companionable, from *socius* a comrade] —'**socially** *adv.* —'**socialness** *n.*

social accounting *n.* the analysis of the economy by sectors leading to the calculation and publication of economic statistics, such as gross national product and national income. Also called: **national accounting.**

social anthropology *n.* the branch of anthropology that deals with cultural and social phenomena such as kinship systems or beliefs, esp. of nonliterate peoples.

social assistance *n.* another name for **social security.**

Social Charter *n.* a proposed declaration of the rights, minimum wages, maximum hours, etc., of workers in the European Community.

social climber *n.* a person who seeks advancement to a higher social class, esp. by obsequious behaviour. Sometimes shortened to **climber.** —**social climbing** *n.*

social contract *or* **compact** *n.* (in the theories of Locke, Hobbes, Rousseau, and others) an agreement, entered into by individuals, that results in the formation of the state or of organized society, the prime motive being the desire for protection, which entails the surrender of some or all personal liberties.

social credit *n.* payment of state grants to citizens in order to stimulate the economy, a theory proposed by British economist C. H. Douglas (1879–1952).

social democracy *n.* (*sometimes cap.*) the beliefs, principles, practices, or programme of social democrats. —**social democratic** *adj.*

social democrat *n.* **1.** any socialist who believes in the gradual transformation of capitalism into democratic socialism. **2.** (*usually cap.*) a member of a Social Democratic Party, any of several similar political parties in various countries that favours gradual reform.

social evolution *n. Sociol.* the process of social development from an early simple type of social organization to one that is complex and highly specialized.

social fund *n.* (in Britain) a social security fund from which loans or payments may be made to people in cases of extreme need.

social inquiry report *n.* (in Britain) a report on a person and his or her circumstances, which may be required by a court before sentencing and is made by a probation officer or a social worker from a local authority social services department.

social insurance *n.* government insurance providing coverage for the unemployed, the injured, the old, etc.: usually financed by contributions from employers and employees, as well as general government revenue. See also **social security, national insurance, social assistance.**

socialism ('səʊʃəˌlɪzəm) *n.* **1.** an economic theory or system in which the means of production, distribution, and exchange are owned by the community collectively, usually through the state. It is characterized by production for use rather than profit, by equality of individual wealth, by the absence of competitive economic activity, and, usually, by government determination of investment, prices, and production levels. Compare **capitalism.** **2.** any of various social or political theories or movements in which the common welfare is to be achieved through the establishment of a socialist economic system. **3.** (in Marxist theory) a transitional stage after the proletarian revolution in the development of a society from capitalism to communism: characterized by the distribution of income according to work rather than need.

socialist ('səʊʃəlɪst) *n.* **1.** a supporter or advocate of socialism or any party promoting socialism (**socialist party**). ~*adj.* **2.** of, characteristic of, implementing, or relating to socialism. **3.** (*sometimes cap.*) of, characteristic of, or relating to socialists or a socialist party.

socialistic (ˌsəʊʃə'lɪstɪk) *adj.* resembling or sympathizing with socialism. —ˌ**social'istically** *adv.*

socialist realism *n.* (in Communist countries, esp. formerly) the doctrine that art, literature, etc. should present an idealized portrayal of reality, which glorifies the achievements of the Communist Party.

socialite ('səʊʃəˌlaɪt) *n.* a person who is or seeks to be prominent in fashionable society.

sociality (ˌsəʊʃɪ'ælɪtɪ) *n., pl.* **-ties.** **1.** the tendency of groups and persons to develop social links and live in communities. **2.** the quality or state of being social.

socialization *or* **socialisation** (ˌsəʊʃəlaɪ'zeɪʃən) *n.* **1.** *Psychol.* the modification from infancy of an individual's behaviour to conform with the demands of social life. **2.** the act of socializing or the state of being socialized.

socialize *or* **socialise** ('səʊʃəˌlaɪz) *vb.* **1.** (*intr.*) to behave in a friendly or sociable manner. **2.** (*tr.*) to prepare for life in society. **3.** (*tr.*) *Chiefly U.S.* to alter or create so as to be in accordance with socialist principles, as by nationalization. —'**socialˌizable** *or* '**socialˌisable** *adj.* —'**socialˌizer** *or* '**socialˌiser** *n.*

social organization *n. Sociol.* the formation of a stable structure of relations inside a group, which provides a basis for order and patterns relationships for new members.
social psychology *n. Psychol.* the area of psychology concerned with the interaction between individuals and groups and the effect of society on behaviour.
social realism *n.* **1.** the use of realist art, literature, etc. as a medium for social or political comment. **2.** another name for **socialist realism.**
social science *n.* **1.** the study of society and of the relationship of individual members within society, including economics, history, political science, psychology, anthropology, and sociology. **2.** any of these subjects studied individually. —**social scientist** *n.*
social secretary *n.* **1.** a member of an organization who arranges its social events. **2.** a personal secretary who deals with private correspondence, etc.
social security *n.* **1.** public provision for the economic, and sometimes social, welfare of the aged, unemployed, etc., esp. through pensions and other monetary assistance. **2.** (*often cap.*) a government programme designed to provide such assistance.
social services *pl. n.* welfare activities organized by the state or a local authority and carried out by trained personnel.
social studies *n. (functioning as sing.)* the study of how people live and organize themselves in society, embracing geography, history, economics, and other subjects.
social welfare *n.* the various social services provided by a state for the benefit of its citizens.
social work *n.* any of various social services designed to alleviate the conditions of the poor and aged and to increase the welfare of children. —**social worker** *n.*
societal (səˈsaɪətᵊl) *adj.* of or relating to society, esp. human society or social relations. —**soˈcietally** *adv.*
societal marketing *n.* **1.** marketing that takes into account society's long-term welfare. **2.** the marketing of a social or charitable cause, such as an anti-apartheid campaign.
society (səˈsaɪətɪ) *n., pl.* **-ties. 1.** the totality of social relationships among organized groups of human beings or animals. **2.** a system of human organizations generating distinctive cultural patterns and institutions and usually providing protection, security, continuity, and a national identity for its members. **3.** such a system with reference to its mode of social and economic organization or its dominant class: *middle-class society.* **4.** those with whom one has companionship. **5.** an organized group of people associated for some specific purpose or on account of some common interest: *a learned society.* **6. a.** the privileged class of people in a community, esp. as considered superior or fashionable. **b.** (*as modifier*): *a society woman.* **7.** the social life and intercourse of such people: *to enter society as a debutante.* **8.** companionship; the fact or state of being together with someone else: *I enjoy her society.* **9.** *Ecology.* a small community of plants within a larger association. [C16: via Old French *societé* from Latin *societās,* from *socius* a comrade]
Society of Friends *n.* the official name for the **Quakers.**
Society of Jesus *n.* the religious order of the Jesuits, founded by Ignatius Loyola.
Socinian (səʊˈsɪnɪən) *n.* **1.** a supporter of the beliefs of Faustus Socinus (1539–1604) and his uncle Laelius Socinus (1525–62), Italian Protestant theologians and reformers, who rejected such traditional Christian doctrines as the divinity of Christ, the Trinity, and original sin, and held that those who follow Christ's virtues will be granted salvation. *~adj.* **2.** of or relating to the Socinians or their beliefs. —**Soˈcinianˌism** *n.*
socio- *combining form.* denoting social or society: *socioeconomic; sociopolitical; sociology.*
sociobiology (ˌsəʊsɪəʊbaɪˈɒlədʒɪ) *n.* the study of social behaviour in animals and humans, esp. in relation to its survival value and evolutionary origins. —**ˌsociobiˈologist** *n.*
socioeconomic (ˌsəʊsɪəʊˌiːkəˈnɒmɪk, -ˌɛkə-) *adj.* of, relating to, or involving both economic and social factors. —**ˌsocioˌecoˈnomically** *adv.*
sociol. *abbrev. for* sociology.
sociolinguistics (ˌsəʊsɪəʊlɪŋˈgwɪstɪks) *n. (functioning as sing.)* the study of language in relation to its social context. —**ˌsocioˈlinguist** *n.* —**ˌsociolinˈguistic** *adj.*
sociology (ˌsəʊsɪˈɒlədʒɪ) *n.* the study of the development, organization, functioning, and classification of human societies. —**sociological** (ˌsəʊsɪəˈlɒdʒɪkᵊl) *adj.* —**ˌsocioˈlogically** *adv.* —**ˌsociˈologist** *n.*
sociometry (ˌsəʊsɪˈɒmɪtrɪ) *n.* the study of sociological relationships, esp. of preferences, within social groups. —**sociometric** (ˌsəʊsɪəˈmɛtrɪk) *adj.* —**ˌsociˈometrist** *n.*
sociopath (ˈsəʊsɪəˌpæθ) *n. Psychiatry.* another name for **psychopath.** —**ˌsocioˈpathic** *adj.* —**sociopathy** (ˌsəʊsɪˈɒpəθɪ) *n.*
sociopolitical (ˌsəʊsɪəʊpəˈlɪtɪkᵊl) *adj.* of, relating to, or involving both political and social factors.
sock[1] (sɒk) *n.* **1.** a cloth covering for the foot, reaching to between the ankle and knee and worn inside a shoe. **2.** an insole put in a shoe, as to make it fit better. **3.** a light shoe worn by actors in ancient Greek and Roman comedy, sometimes taken to allude to comic drama in general (as in the phrase **sock and buskin**). See **buskin. 4.** another name for **windsock. 5. pull one's socks up.** *Brit. informal.* to make a determined effort, esp. in order to regain control of a situation. **6. put a sock in it.** *Brit. slang.* be quiet! *~vb.* **7.** (*tr.*) to provide with socks. **8. socked in.** *U.S. and Canadian slang.* (of an airport) closed by adverse weather conditions. [Old English *socc* a light shoe, from Latin *soccus,* from Greek *sukkhos*]
sock[2] (sɒk) *Slang.* *~vb.* **1.** (*usually tr.*) to hit with force. **2. sock it to.** to make a forceful impression on. *~n.* **3.** a forceful blow. [C17: of obscure origin]
sock away *vb. (tr.) U.S., Canadian, and N.Z. informal.* to save up.
sockdologer *or* **sockdolager** (sɒkˈdɒlədʒə) *n. Slang, chiefly U.S.* **1.** a decisive blow or remark. **2.** an outstanding person or thing. [C19: of uncertain origin; perhaps from SOCK[2] + DOXOLOGY (in the sense: the closing act of a church service) + -ER]
socket (ˈsɒkɪt) *n.* **1.** a device into which an electric plug can be inserted in order to make a connection in a circuit. **2.** *Chiefly Brit.* such a device mounted on a wall and connected to the electricity supply. Informal Brit. names: **point, plug.** U.S. and Canadian name: **outlet. 3.** a part with an opening or hollow into which some other part, such as a pipe, probe, etc., can be fitted. **4.** a spanner head having a recess suitable to be fitted over the head of a bolt. **5.** *Anatomy.* **a.** a bony hollow into which a part or structure fits: *a tooth socket; an eye socket.* **b.** the receptacle of a ball-and-socket joint. *~vb.* **6.** (*tr.*) to furnish with or place into a socket. [C13: from Anglo-Norman *soket* a little ploughshare, from *soc,* of Celtic origin; compare Cornish *soch* ploughshare]
socket wrench *n.* a wrench having a handle onto which socketed heads of various sizes can be fitted.
sockeye (ˈsɒkˌaɪ) *n.* a Pacific salmon, *Oncorhynchus nerka,* having red flesh and valued as a food fish. Also called: **red salmon.** [by folk etymology from Salishan *sukkegh*]
socle (ˈsəʊkᵊl) *n.* another name for **plinth** (sense 1). [C18: via French from Italian *zoccolo,* from Latin *socculus* a little shoe, from *soccus* a SOCK[1]]
socman (ˈsɒkmən, ˈsəʊk-) *or* **sokeman** (ˈsəʊkmən) *n., pl.* **-men.** *English history.* a tenant holding land by socage. [C16: from Anglo-Latin *socmannus;* see SOKE]
Socratic (sɒˈkrætɪk) *adj.* **1.** of or relating to the Athenian philosopher Socrates (?470–399 B.C.), his methods, philosophy, etc. *~n.* **2.** a person who follows the teachings of Socrates. —**Soˈcratically** *adv.* —**Soˈcratiˌcism** *n.* —**Socratist** (ˈsɒkrətɪst) *n.*
Socratic irony *n. Philosophy.* a means by which the pretended ignorance of a skilful questioner leads the person answering to expose his own ignorance.
Socratic method *n. Philosophy.* the method of instruction by question and answer used by Socrates in order to elicit from his pupils truths he considered to be implicitly known by all rational beings. Compare **maieutic.**
Socred (ˈsəʊkrɛd) *Canadian.* *~n.* **1.** a supporter or member of a Social Credit movement or party. *~adj.* **2.** of or relating to Social Credit.
sod[1] (sɒd) *n.* **1.** a piece of grass-covered surface soil held together by the roots of the grass; turf. **2.** *Poetic.* the ground. *~vb.* **sods, sodding, sodded. 3.** (*tr.*) to cover with sods. [C15: from Low German; compare Middle Low German, Middle Dutch *sode;* related to Old Frisian *sātha*]
sod[2] (sɒd) *Slang, chiefly Brit.* *~n.* **1.** a person considered to be obnoxious. **2.** a jocular word for a person. *~interj.* **3.** a strong exclamation of annoyance. See also **sod off.** [C19: shortened from SODOMITE] —**ˈsodding** *adj.*
soda (ˈsəʊdə) *n.* **1.** any of a number of simple inorganic compounds of sodium, such as sodium carbonate (**washing soda**), sodium bicarbonate (**baking soda**), and sodium hydroxide (**caustic soda**). **2.** See **soda water. 3.** *U.S. and Canadian.* a fizzy drink. **4.** the top card of the pack in faro. **5. a soda.** *Austral. slang.* something easily done; a pushover. [C16: from Medieval Latin, from *sodanum* barilla, a plant that was burned to obtain a type of sodium carbonate, perhaps of Arabic origin]
soda ash *n.* the anhydrous commercial form of sodium carbonate.
soda biscuit *n.* a biscuit leavened with sodium bicarbonate.
soda bread *n.* a type of bread leavened with sodium bicarbonate combined with milk and cream of tartar.
soda fountain *n. U.S. and Canadian.* **1.** a counter that serves drinks, snacks, etc. **2.** an apparatus dispensing soda water.
soda jerk *n. U.S. slang.* a person who serves at a soda fountain.
soda lake *n.* a salt lake that has a high content of sodium salts, esp. chlorides and sulphates.
soda lime *n.* a solid mixture of sodium and calcium hydroxides used to absorb carbon dioxide and to dry gases.
sodalite (ˈsəʊdəˌlaɪt) *n.* a blue, grey, yellow, or colourless mineral consisting of sodium aluminium silicate and sodium chloride in cubic crystalline form. It occurs in basic igneous rocks. Formula: $Na_4Al_3Si_3O_{12}Cl$. [C19: from SODA + -LITE]
sodality (səʊˈdælɪtɪ) *n., pl.* **-ties. 1.** *R.C. Church.* a religious or charitable society. **2.** fraternity; fellowship. [C16: from Latin *sodālitās* fellowship, from *sodālis* a comrade]
sodamide (ˈsəʊdəˌmaɪd) *n.* a white crystalline compound used as a dehydrating agent, as a chemical reagent, and in making sodium cyanide. Formula: $NaNH_2$. Also called: **sodium amide.** [C19: from SOD(IUM) + AMIDE]
soda nitre *n.* another name for **Chile saltpetre.**
soda pop *n. U.S. informal.* a fizzy drink.

soda siphon *n.* a sealed bottle containing and dispensing soda water. The water is forced up a tube reaching to the bottom of the bottle by the pressure of gas above the water. Also called (esp. U.S.): **siphon bottle.**

soda water *n.* an effervescent beverage made by charging water with carbon dioxide under pressure. Sometimes shortened to **soda.**

sodden (ˈsɒdᵊn) *adj.* **1.** completely saturated. **2. a.** dulled, esp. by excessive drinking. **b.** (*in combination*): *a drink-sodden mind.* **3.** heavy or doughy, as bread is when improperly cooked. **4.** *Archaic.* cooked by boiling. ~*vb.* **5.** to make or become sodden. [C13 *soden,* past participle of SEETHE] —ˈ**soddenly** *adv.* —ˈ**soddenness** *n.*

sodger (ˈsodʒər) *n., vb.* a dialect variant of **soldier.**

sodium (ˈsəʊdɪəm) *n.* **a.** a very reactive soft silvery-white element of the alkali metal group occurring principally in common salt, Chile saltpetre, and cryolite. Sodium and potassium ions maintain the essential electrolytic balance in living cells. It is used in the production of chemicals, in metallurgy, and, alloyed with potassium, as a cooling medium in nuclear reactors. Symbol: Na; atomic no.: 11; atomic wt.: 22.99; valency: 1; relative density: 0.97; melting pt.: 97.81°C; boiling pt.: 892°C. **b.** (*as modifier*): *sodium light.* [C19: New Latin, from SODA + -IUM]

sodium amytal *n.* another name for **Amytal.**

sodium benzoate *n.* a white crystalline soluble compound used as an antibacterial and antifungal agent in preserving food **(E211)**, as an antiseptic, and in making dyes and pharmaceuticals. Formula: $Na(C_6H_5COO)$. Also called: **benzoate of soda.**

sodium bicarbonate *n.* a white crystalline soluble compound usually obtained by the Solvay process and used in effervescent drinks, baking powders, fire extinguishers, and in medicine as an antacid; sodium hydrogen carbonate. Formula: $NaHCO_3$. Also called: **bicarbonate of soda, baking soda.**

sodium carbonate *n.* a colourless or white odourless soluble crystalline compound existing in several hydrated forms and used in the manufacture of glass, ceramics, soap, and paper and as an industrial and domestic cleansing agent. It is made by the Solvay process and commonly obtained as the decahydrate (**washing soda** or **sal soda**) or a white anhydrous powder (**soda ash**). Formula: Na_2CO_3.

sodium chlorate *n.* a colourless crystalline soluble compound used as a bleaching agent, weak antiseptic, and weedkiller. Formula: $NaClO_3$.

sodium chloride *n.* common table salt; a soluble colourless crystalline compound occurring naturally as halite and in sea water: widely used as a seasoning and preservative for food and in the manufacture of chemicals, glass, and soap. Formula: NaCl. Also called: **salt.**

sodium cyanide *n.* a white odourless crystalline soluble poisonous compound with an odour of hydrogen cyanide when damp. It is used for extracting gold and silver from their ores and for case-hardening steel. Formula: NaCN.

sodium dichromate *n.* a soluble crystalline solid compound, usually obtained as red or orange crystals and used as an oxidizing agent, corrosion inhibitor, and mordant. Formula $Na_2Cr_2O_7$. Also called (not in technical usage): **sodium bichromate.**

sodium fluoroacetate (ˌflʊərəʊˈæsɪˌteɪt) *n.* a white crystalline odourless poisonous compound, used as a rodenticide. Formula: $Na(CH_2FCOO)$.

sodium glutamate (ˈgluːtəˌmeɪt) *n.* another name for **monosodium glutamate.**

sodium hydroxide *n.* a white deliquescent strongly alkaline solid used in the manufacture of rayon, paper, aluminium, soap, and sodium compounds. Formula: NaOH. Also called: **caustic soda.** See also **lye.**

sodium hyposulphite *n.* another name (not in technical usage) for **sodium thiosulphate.**

sodium lamp *n.* another name for **sodium-vapour lamp.**

sodium nitrate *n.* a white crystalline soluble solid compound occurring naturally as Chile saltpetre and caliche and used in matches, explosives, and rocket propellants, as a fertilizer, and as a curing salt for preserving food such as bacon, ham, and cheese **(E251)**. Formula: $NaNO_3$.

Sodium Pentothal *n. Trademark.* another name for **thiopentone sodium.**

sodium perborate *n.* a white odourless crystalline compound used as an antiseptic and deodorant. It is sodium metaborate with both water and hydrogen peroxide of crystallization. Formula: $NaBO_2.H_2O_2.3H_2O$.

sodium peroxide *n.* a yellowish-white odourless soluble powder formed when sodium reacts with an excess of oxygen: used as an oxidizing agent in chemical preparations, a bleaching agent, an antiseptic, and in removing carbon dioxide from air in submarines, etc. Formula: Na_2O_2.

sodium phosphate *n.* any sodium salt of any phosphoric acid, esp. one of three salts of orthophosphoric acid having formulas NaH_2PO_4 (**monosodium dihydrogen orthophosphate**), Na_2HPO_4 (**disodium monohydrogen orthophosphate**), and Na_3PO_4 (**trisodium orthophosphate**).

sodium propionate *n.* a transparent crystalline soluble substance used as a medical fungicide and to prevent the growth of moulds, esp. to retard spoilage in packed foods. Formula: $Na(C_2H_5COO)$.

sodium silicate *n.* **1.** Also called: **soluble glass.** a substance having the general formula, $Na_2O.xSiO_2$, where x varies between 3 and 5, existing as an amorphous powder or present in a usually viscous aqueous solution. See **water glass. 2.** any sodium salt of orthosilicic acid or metasilicic acid.

sodium sulphate *n.* a solid white substance that occurs naturally as thenardite and is usually used as the white anhydrous compound (**salt cake**) or the white crystalline decahydrate (**Glauber's salt**) in making glass, detergents, and pulp. Formula: Na_2SO_4.

sodium thiosulphate *n.* a white soluble substance used, in the pentahydrate form, in photography as a fixer to dissolve unchanged silver halides and also to remove excess chlorine from chlorinated water. Formula: $Na_2S_2O_3$. Also called (not in technical usage): **sodium hyposulphite, hypo.**

sodium-vapour lamp *n.* a type of electric lamp consisting of a glass tube containing neon and sodium vapour at low pressure through which an electric current is passed to give an orange light. They are used in street lighting.

sod off *vb.* (*intr., adv.; usually imperative*) *Taboo slang, chiefly Brit.* to go away; depart.

Sodom (ˈsɒdəm) *n.* a place notorious for depravity. [named after the biblical city destroyed by God for its wickedness and depravity (Genesis 19:24)]

sodomite (ˈsɒdəˌmaɪt) *n.* a person who practises sodomy.

sodomy (ˈsɒdəmɪ) *n.* anal intercourse committed by a man with another man or a woman. Compare **buggery.** [C13: via Old French *sodomie* from Latin (Vulgate) *Sodoma* Sodom]

Sod's law (sɒdz) *n. Informal.* a humorous or facetious precept stating that if something can go wrong or turn out inconveniently it will. Also called: **Murphy's Law.**

soever (səʊˈevə) *adv.* in any way at all: used to emphasize or make less precise a word or phrase, usually in combination with *what, where, when, how,* etc., or else separated by intervening words. Compare **whatsoever.**

sofa (ˈsəʊfə) *n.* an upholstered seat with back and arms for two or more people. [C17 (in the sense: dais upholstered as a seat): from Arabic *suffah*]

sofa bed *n.* a sofa that can be converted into a bed.

sofar (ˈsəʊfɑː) *n.* a system for determining a position at sea, esp. that of survivors of a disaster, by exploding a charge underwater at that point. The times taken for the shock waves to travel through the water to three widely separated shore stations are used to calculate their position. [C20: from *so(und) f(ixing) a(nd) r(anging)*]

soffit (ˈsɒfɪt) *n.* **1.** the underside of a part of a building or a structural component, such as an arch, beam, stair, etc. **2.** the upper inner surface of a drain or sewer. Compare **invert** (sense 5a). [C17: via French from Italian *soffitto,* from Latin *suffixus* something fixed underneath, from *suffigere,* from *sub-* under + *figere* to fasten]

S. of Sol. *Bible. abbrev. for* Song of Solomon.

soft (sɒft) *adj.* **1.** easy to dent, work, or cut without shattering; malleable. **2.** not hard; giving little or no resistance to pressure or weight. **3.** fine, light, smooth, or fluffy to the touch. **4.** gentle; tranquil. **5.** (of music, sounds, etc.) low and pleasing. **6.** (of light, colour, etc.) not excessively bright or harsh. **7.** (of a breeze, climate, etc.) temperate, mild, or pleasant. **8.** *Dialect.* drizzly or rainy: *a soft day; the weather has turned soft.* **9.** slightly blurred; not sharply outlined: *soft focus.* **10.** (of a diet) consisting of easily digestible foods. **11.** kind or lenient, often excessively so. **12.** easy to influence or impose upon. **13.** prepared to compromise; not doctrinaire: *the soft left.* **14.** *Informal.* feeble or silly; simple (often in the phrase **soft in the head**). **15.** unable to endure hardship, esp. through too much pampering. **16.** physically out of condition; flabby: *soft muscles.* **17.** loving; tender: *soft words.* **18.** *Informal.* requiring little exertion; easy: *a soft job.* **19.** *Chem.* (of water) relatively free of mineral salts and therefore easily able to make soap lather. **20.** (of a drug such as cannabis) nonaddictive or only mildly addictive. Compare **hard** (sense 19). **21.** *Phonetics.* **a.** an older word for **lenis. b.** (not in technical usage) denoting the consonants *c* and *g* in English when they are pronounced as palatal or alveolar fricatives or affricates (s, dʒ, ʃ, ð, tʃ) before *e* and *i,* rather than as velar stops (k, g). **c.** (in the Slavonic languages) palatalized before a front vowel or a special character (**soft sign**) written as **ь 22. a.** unprotected against attack: *a soft target.* **b.** *Military.* unarmoured, esp. as applied to a truck by comparison with a tank. **23.** *Finance, chiefly U.S.* (of prices, a market, etc.) unstable and tending to decline. **24.** (of a currency) in relatively little demand, esp. because of a weak balance of payments situation. **25.** (of radiation, such as x-rays and ultraviolet radiation) having low energy and not capable of deep penetration of materials. **26.** *Physics.* (of valves or tubes) only partially evacuated. **27. soft on** *or* **about. a.** gentle, sympathetic, or lenient towards. **b.** feeling affection or infatuation for. ~*adv.* **28.** in a soft manner: *to speak soft.* ~*n.* **29.** a soft object, part, or piece. **30.** *Informal.* See **softy.** ~*interj. Archaic.* **31.** quiet! **32.** wait! [Old English *sōfte;* related to Old Saxon *sāfti,* Old High German *semfti* gentle] —ˈ**softly** *adv.*

softa ('sɒftə) *n.* a Muslim student of divinity and jurisprudence, esp. in Turkey. [C17: from Turkish, from Persian *sōkhtah* aflame (with love of learning)]

softball ('sɒft,bɔːl) *n.* **1.** a variation of baseball using a larger softer ball, pitched underhand. **2.** the ball used. **3.** *Cookery.* the stage in the boiling of a sugar syrup at which it may be rubbed into balls after dipping in cold water.

soft-boiled *adj.* **1.** (of an egg) boiled for a short time so that the yolk is still soft. **2.** *Informal.* softhearted.

soft-centred *adj.* (of a chocolate or boiled sweet) having a centre consisting of cream, jelly, etc.

soft chancre *n. Pathol.* a venereal ulcer caused by an infection that is not syphilitic. Also called: **chancroid.**

soft clam *n.* another name for the **soft-shell clam.**

soft coal *n.* another name for **bituminous coal.**

soft commodities *pl. n.* nonmetal commodities such as cocoa, sugar, and grains, bought and sold on a futures market. Also called: **softs.**

soft-core *adj.* (of pornography) suggestive and titillating through not being totally explicit or detailed.

soft-cover *adj.* a less common word for **paperback.**

soft drink *n.* a nonalcoholic drink, usually cold.

soften ('sɒfᵊn) *vb.* **1.** to make or become soft or softer. **2.** to make or become gentler. **3.** (*intr.*) *Commerce.* **a.** (of demand, a market, etc.) to weaken. **b.** (of a price) to fall.

softener ('sɒfᵊnə) *n.* **1.** a substance added to another substance to increase its softness, pliability, or plasticity. **2.** a substance, such as a zeolite, for softening water.

softening of the brain *n.* an abnormal softening of the tissues of the cerebrum characterized by various degrees of mental impairment.

soften up *vb.* (*adv.*) **1.** to make or become soft. **2.** (*tr.*) to weaken (an enemy's defences) by shelling, bombing, etc. **3.** (*tr.*) to weaken the resistance of (a person) by persuasive talk, advances, etc.

soft-finned *adj.* (of certain teleost fishes) having fins that are supported by flexible cartilaginous rays. See also **malacopterygian.** Compare **spiny-finned.**

soft-focus lens *n. Photog.* a lens designed to produce an image that is uniformly very slightly out of focus: typically used for portrait work.

soft fruit *n. Brit.* any of various types of small edible stoneless fruit, such as strawberries, raspberries, and currants, borne mainly on low-growing plants or bushes.

soft furnishings *pl. n. Brit.* curtains, hangings, rugs, etc.

soft goods *pl. n.* textile fabrics and related merchandise.

soft-headed *adj. Informal.* feeble-minded; stupid; simple. —,**soft-'headedness** *n.*

softhearted (,sɒft'hɑːtɪd) *adj.* easily moved to pity. —,**soft'heartedly** *adv.* —,**soft'heartedness** *n.*

soft hyphen *n.* a hyphen, used in word processing to divide a word, which prints only when it appears at the end of a line. Also called: **optional hyphen.**

soft iron *n.* **a.** iron that has a low carbon content and is easily magnetized and demagnetized with a small hysteresis loss. **b.** (*as modifier*): *a soft-iron core.*

soft landing *n.* **1.** a landing by a spacecraft on the moon or a planet at a sufficiently low velocity for the equipment or occupants to remain unharmed. **2.** a painless resolution of a problem, esp. an economic problem. ~Compare **hard landing.**

soft line *n.* a moderate flexible attitude or policy. —,**soft'liner** *n.*

soft loan *n.* a loan on which interest is not charged, such as a loan made to an undeveloped country.

softly-softly *adj.* gradual, cautious, and discreet.

softness ('sɒftnɪs) *n.* **1.** the quality or an instance of being soft. **2.** *Metallurgy.* the tendency of a metal to distort easily. Compare **brittleness** (sense 2), **toughness** (sense 2).

soft option *n.* in a number of choices, the one considered to be easy or the easiest to do, involving the least difficulty or exertion.

soft palate *n.* the posterior fleshy portion of the roof of the mouth. It forms a movable muscular flap that seals off the nasopharynx during swallowing and speech.

soft paste *n.* **a.** artificial porcelain made from clay, bone ash, etc. **b.** (*as modifier*): *softpaste porcelain.* [C19: from PASTE (in the sense: the mixture from which porcelain is made); so called because of its consistency]

soft-pedal *vb.* **-als, -alling, -alled** *or U.S.* **-als, -aling, -aled.** (*tr.*) **1.** to mute the tone of (a piano) by depressing the soft pedal. **2.** *Informal.* to make (something, esp. something unpleasant) less obvious by deliberately failing to emphasize or allude to it. ~*n.* **soft pedal. 3.** a foot-operated lever on a piano, the left one of two, that either moves the whole action closer to the strings so that the hammers strike with less force or causes fewer of the strings to sound. Compare **sustaining pedal.** See **piano**[1].

soft porn *n. Informal.* soft-core pornography.

soft rot *n.* any of various bacterial or fungal plant diseases characterized by watery disintegration of fruits, roots, etc.

softs (sɒfts) *pl. n.* another name for **soft commodities.**

soft sell *n.* a method of selling based on indirect suggestion or inducement. Compare **hard sell.**

soft-shell clam *n.* any of several marine clams of the genus *Mya,* esp. *M. arenaria,* an edible species of coastal regions of the U.S. and Europe, having a thin brittle shell. Sometimes shortened to **soft-shell.** Compare **quahog.**

soft-shell crab *n.* a crab, esp. of the edible species *Cancer pagurus,* that has recently moulted and has not yet formed its new shell. Compare **hard-shell crab.**

soft-shelled turtle *n.* any freshwater turtle of the family *Trionychidae,* having a flattened soft shell consisting of bony plates covered by a leathery skin.

soft-shoe *n.* (*modifier*) relating to a type of tap dancing performed wearing soft-soled shoes: *the soft-shoe shuffle.*

soft shoulder *or* **verge** *n.* a soft edge along the side of a road that is unsuitable for vehicles to drive on.

soft soap *n.* **1.** *Med.* another name for **green soap. 2.** *Informal.* flattering, persuasive, or cajoling talk. ~*vb.* **soft-soap. 3.** *Informal.* to use such talk on (a person).

soft-spoken *adj.* **1.** speaking or said with a soft gentle voice. **2.** able to persuade or impress by glibness of tongue.

soft spot *n.* a sentimental fondness (esp. in the phrase **have a soft spot for**).

soft tissue *n.* the soft parts of the human body as distinct from bone and cartilage.

soft top *n.* a convertible car with a roof made of fabric rather than metal.

soft touch *n. Informal.* a person easily persuaded or imposed on, esp. to lend money.

software ('sɒft,wɛə) *n.* **1.** *Computer technol.* the programs that can be used with a particular computer system. Compare **hardware** (sense 2). **2.** video cassettes and discs for use with a particular video system.

software house *n.* a commercial organization that specializes in the production of computer software packages.

soft wheat *n.* a type of wheat with soft kernels and a high starch content.

softwood ('sɒft,wʊd) *n.* **1.** the open-grained wood of any of numerous coniferous trees, such as pine and cedar, as distinguished from that of a dicotyledonous tree. **2.** any tree yielding this wood. ~Compare **hardwood.**

softy *or* **softie** ('sɒftɪ) *n., pl.* **softies.** *Informal.* a person who is sentimental, weakly foolish, or lacking in physical endurance.

SOGAT ('səʊgæt) *n.* (in Britain) *acronym for* Society of Graphical and Allied Trades.

Sogdian ('sɒgdɪən) *n.* **1.** a member of the people who lived in Sogdiana, a region of ancient central Asia. **2.** the language of this people, now almost extinct, belonging to the East Iranian branch of the Indo-European family. ~*adj.* **3.** of or relating to Sogdiana, its people, or their language.

soggy ('sɒgɪ) *adj.* **-gier, -giest. 1.** soaked with liquid. **2.** (of bread, pastry, etc.) moist and heavy. **3.** *Informal.* lacking in spirit or positiveness. [C18: probably from dialect *sog* marsh, of obscure origin] —'**soggily** *adv.* —'**sogginess** *n.*

soh *or* **so** (səʊ) *n. Music.* (in tonic sol-fa) the name used for the fifth note or dominant of any scale. [C13: see GAMUT]

soho (səʊ'həʊ) *interj.* **1.** *Hunting.* an exclamation announcing the sighting of a hare. **2.** an exclamation announcing the discovery of something unexpected. [an Anglo-French hunting call, probably of exclamatory origin]

soi-disant *French.* (swadizɑ̃) *adj.* so-called; self-styled. [literally: calling oneself]

soigné *or* (*fem.*) **soignée** ('swɑːnjeɪ; *French* swaɲe) *adj.* well-groomed; elegant. [French, from *soigner* to take good care of, of Germanic origin; compare Old Saxon *sunnea* care]

soil[1] (sɔɪl) *n.* **1.** the top layer of the land surface of the earth that is composed of disintegrated rock particles, humus, water, and air. See **zonal soil, azonal soil, intrazonal soil, horizon** (senses 4, 5). **2.** a type of this material having specific characteristics: *loamy soil.* **3.** land, country, or region: *one's native soil.* **4. the soil.** life and work on a farm; land: *he belonged to the soil, as his forefathers had.* **5.** any place or thing encouraging growth or development. [C14: from Anglo-Norman, from Latin *solium* a seat, but confused with Latin *solum* the ground]

soil[2] (sɔɪl) *vb.* **1.** to make or become dirty or stained. **2.** (*tr.*) to pollute with sin or disgrace; sully; defile: *he soiled the family honour by his cowardice.* ~*n.* **3.** the state or result of soiling. **4.** refuse, manure, or excrement. [C13: from Old French *soillier* to defile, from *soil* pigsty, probably from Latin *sūs* a swine]

soil[3] (sɔɪl) *vb.* (*tr.*) to feed (livestock) freshly cut green fodder either to fatten or purge them. [C17: perhaps from obsolete vb. (C16) *soil* to manure, from SOIL[2] (n.)]

soilage ('sɔɪlɪdʒ) *n.* green fodder, esp. when freshly cut and fed to livestock in a confined area.

soil bank *n.* (in the U.S.) a federal programme by which farmers are paid to divert land to soil-enriching crops.

soil conservation *n.* the preservation of soil against deterioration or erosion, and the maintenance of the fertilizing elements for crop production.

soil creep *n.* the gradual downhill movement, under the force of gravity, of soil and loose rock material on a slope.

soil mechanics *n.* (*functioning as sing.*) the study of the physical properties of soil, esp. those properties that affect its ability to bear weight, such as water content, density, strength, etc.

soil pipe *n.* a pipe that conveys sewage or waste water from a toilet, etc., to a soil drain or sewer.

soilure ('sɔɪljə) *n. Archaic.* **1.** the act of soiling or the state of being soiled. **2.** a stain or blot. [C13: from Old French *soilleure,* from *soillier* to SOIL[2]]

soiree ('swɑːreɪ) *n.* an evening party or other gathering given usually at a private house, esp. where guests are invited to listen to, play, or dance to music. [C19: from French, from Old French *soir* evening, from Latin *sērum* a late time, from *sērus* late]

soixante-neuf French. (swasɑ̃tnœf) *n.* a sexual activity in which two people simultaneously stimulate each other's genitalia with their mouths. Also called: **sixty-nine.** [literally: sixty-nine, from the position adopted by the participants]

sojourn ('sɒdʒɜːn, 'sʌdʒ-) *n.* **1.** a temporary stay. *~vb.* **2.** (*intr.*) to stay or reside temporarily. [C13: from Old French *sojorner,* from Vulgar Latin *subdiurnāre* (unattested) to spend a day, from Latin *sub-* during + Late Latin *diurnum* day] —'**sojourner** *n.*

soke (səʊk) *n. English legal history.* **1.** the right to hold a local court. **2.** the territory under the jurisdiction of a particular court. [C14: from Medieval Latin *sōca,* from Old English *sōcn* a seeking; see SEEK]

sokeman ('səʊkmən) *n., pl.* **-men.** (in the Danelaw) a freeman enjoying extensive rights, esp. over his land.

n. Music. another name for **soh.** [C14: see GAMUT]

sol[2] (səʊl) *n.* a former French copper or silver coin, usually worth 12 deniers. [C16: from Old French, from Late Latin: SOLIDUS]

sol[3] (sɒl) *n.* a colloid that has a continuous liquid phase, esp. one in which a solid is suspended in a liquid. [C20: shortened from HYDROSOL]

Sol (sɒl) *n.* a poetic word for the **sun.** [from Latin *sōl* sun]

sol. *abbrev. for:* **1.** soluble. **2.** solution.

Sol. *abbrev. for:* **1.** Also: **Solr** solicitor. **2.** *Bible.* Solomon.

sola Latin. ('səʊlə) *adj.* the feminine form of **solus.**

solace ('sɒlɪs) *n.* **1.** comfort in misery, disappointment, etc. **2.** something that gives comfort or consolation. *~vb.* (*tr.*) **3.** to give comfort or cheer to (a person) in time of sorrow, distress, etc. **4.** to alleviate (sorrow, misery, etc.). [C13: from Old French *solas,* from Latin *sōlātium* comfort, from *sōlārī* to console] —'**solacer** *n.*

solan *or* **solan goose** ('səʊlən) *n.* an archaic name for the **gannet.** [C15 *soland,* of Scandinavian origin; compare Old Norse *sūla* gannet, *ōnd* duck]

solanaceous (ˌsɒlə'neɪʃəs) *adj.* of, relating to, or belonging to the *Solanaceae,* a family of plants having typically tubular flowers with reflexed petals, protruding anthers, and often poisonous or narcotic properties: includes the potato, tobacco, henbane, mandrake, and several nightshades. [C19: from New Latin *Sōlānāceae,* from Latin *sōlānum* nightshade]

solander (sə'lændə) *n.* a box for botanical specimens, maps, colour plates, etc., made in the form of a book, the front cover being the lid. [C18: named after D. D. *Solander* (1736–82), Swedish botanist]

solanum (səʊ'leɪnəm) *n.* any tree, shrub, or herbaceous plant of the mainly tropical solanaceous genus *Solanum:* includes the potato, aubergine, and certain nightshades. [C16: from Latin: nightshade]

solar ('səʊlə) *adj.* **1.** of or relating to the sun: *solar eclipse.* **2.** operating by or utilizing the energy of the sun: *solar cell.* **3.** *Astronomy.* determined from the motion of the earth relative to the sun: *solar year.* **4.** *Astrology.* subject to the influence of the sun. [C15: from Latin *sōlāris,* from *sōl* the sun]

solar apex *n.* another name for **apex** (sense 4).

solar cell *n.* a photovoltaic cell that produces electricity from the sun's rays, used esp. in spacecraft.

solar constant *n.* the rate at which the sun's energy is received per unit area on the earth's surface when the sun is at its mean distance from the earth and atmospheric absorption has been corrected for. Its value is 1388 watts per square metre.

solar day *n.* See under **day** (sense 6).

solar eclipse *n.* See under **eclipse** (sense 1).

solar energy *n.* energy obtained from solar power.

solar flare *n.* a brief powerful eruption of intense high-energy radiation from the sun's surface, associated with sunspots and causing radio and magnetic disturbances on earth. Sometimes shortened to **flare.** See also **solar wind.**

solar furnace *n.* a furnace utilizing the sun as a heat source, sunlight being concentrated at the focus of a system of concave mirrors.

solar heating *n.* heat radiation from the sun collected by heat-absorbing panels through which water is circulated: used for domestic hot water, central heating, and heating swimming pools.

solarimeter (ˌsəʊlə'rɪmɪtə) *n.* any of various instruments for measuring solar radiation, as by use of a bolometer or thermopile. Also called: **pyranometer.**

solarism ('səʊləˌrɪzəm) *n.* the explanation of myths in terms of the movements and influence of the sun. —'**solarist** *n.*

solarium (səʊ'lɛərɪəm) *n., pl.* **-laria** (-'lɛərɪə) *or* **-lariums. 1.** a room built largely of glass to afford exposure to the sun. **2.** a bed equipped with ultraviolet lights used for acquiring an artificial suntan. **3.** an establishment offering such facilities. [C19: from Latin: a terrace, from *sōl* sun]

solarize *or* **solarise** ('səʊləˌraɪz) *vb.* (*tr.*) **1.** to treat by exposure to the sun's rays. **2.** *Photog.* to reverse some of the tones of (a negative or print) and introduce pronounced outlines of highlights, by exposing it briefly to light after developing and washing, and then redeveloping. **3.** to expose (a patient) to the therapeutic effects of solar or ultraviolet light. —ˌ**solari'zation** *or* ˌ**solari'sation** *n.*

solar month *n.* See under **month** (sense 4).

solar myth *n.* a myth explaining or allegorizing the origin or movement of the sun.

solar panel *n.* a panel exposed to radiation of heat from the sun, used to heat water or, when mounted with solar cells, to produce electricity direct, esp. for powering instruments in satellites.

solar plexus *n.* **1.** *Anatomy.* the network of sympathetic nerves situated behind the stomach that supply the abdominal organs. **2.** (*not in technical usage*) the part of the stomach beneath the diaphragm; pit of the stomach. [C18: referring to resemblance between the radial network of nerves and ganglia and the rays of the sun]

solar power *n.* heat radiation from the sun converted to electrical power by specially designed steam boilers and turbogenerators.

solar system *n.* the system containing the sun and the bodies held in its gravitational field, including the planets (Mercury, Venus, Earth, Mars, Jupiter, Saturn, Uranus, Neptune, Pluto), the asteroids, and comets.

solar wind (wɪnd) *n.* the stream of charged particles, such as protons, emitted by the sun at high velocities, its intensity increasing during periods of solar activity. It affects terrestial magnetism, some of the particles being trapped by the magnetic lines of force, and causes auroral displays. See also **Van Allen belt, magnetosphere.**

solar year *n.* See under **year** (sense 4).

solation (səʊ'leɪʃən) *n. Chem.* the liquefaction of a gel.

solatium (səʊ'leɪʃɪəm) *n., pl.* **-tia** (-ʃɪə). *Law, chiefly U.S.* compensation awarded to a party for injury to the feelings as distinct from physical suffering and pecuniary loss. [C19: from Latin: see SOLACE]

sold (səʊld) *vb.* **1.** the past tense and past participle of **sell.** *~adj.* **2. sold on.** *Slang.* uncritically attached to or enthusiastic about.

soldan ('sɒldən, 'sɒl-) *n.* an archaic word for **sultan.** [C13: via Old French from Arabic: SULTAN]

solder ('sɒldə; *U.S.* 'sɒdər) *n.* **1.** an alloy for joining two metal surfaces by melting the alloy so that it forms a thin layer between the surfaces. **Soft solders** are alloys of lead and tin; **brazing solders** are alloys of copper and zinc. **2.** something that joins things together firmly; a bond. *~vb.* **3.** to join or mend or be joined or mended with or as if with solder. [C14: via Old French from Latin *solidāre* to strengthen, from *solidus* SOLID] —'**solderable** *adj.* —'**solderer** *n.*

soldering iron *n.* a hand tool consisting of a handle fixed to an iron or copper tip that is heated, electrically or in a flame, and used to melt and apply solder.

soldier ('səʊldʒə) *n.* **1. a.** a person who serves or has served in an army. **b.** Also called: **common soldier.** a noncommissioned member of an army as opposed to a commissioned officer. **2.** a person who works diligently for a cause. **3.** *Zoology.* **a.** an individual in a colony of social insects, esp. ants, that has powerful jaws adapted for defending the colony, crushing large food particles, etc. **b.** (*as modifier*): *soldier ant.* *~vb.* (*intr.*) **4.** to serve as a soldier. **5.** *Obsolete slang.* to malinger or shirk. [C13: from Old French *soudier,* from *soude* (army) pay, from Late Latin *solidus* a gold coin, from Latin: firm]

soldier beetle *n.* a yellowish-red cantharid beetle, *Rhagonycha fulva,* having a somewhat elongated body.

soldierly ('səʊldʒəlɪ) *adj.* of or befitting a good soldier. —'**soldierliness** *n.*

soldier of fortune *n.* a man who seeks money or adventure as a soldier; mercenary.

soldier on *vb.* (*intr., adv.*) to persist in one's efforts in spite of difficulties, pressure, etc.

soldier orchid *n.* a European orchid, *Orchis militaris,* having pale purple flowers with a four-lobed lower lip. Also called: **military orchid.** [from an imagined resemblance to a soldier]

soldier settlement *n. Austral.* the allocation of Crown land for farming to ex-servicemen. —**soldier settler** *n.*

soldiery ('səʊldʒərɪ) *n., pl.* **-dieries. 1.** soldiers collectively. **2.** a group of soldiers. **3.** the profession of being a soldier.

soldo ('sɒldəʊ; *Italian* 'soldo) *n., pl.* **-di** (-diː; *Italian* -di). a former Italian copper coin worth one twentieth of a lira. [C16: from Italian, from Late Latin *solidum* a gold coin; see SOLDIER]

sole[1] (səʊl) *adj.* **1.** (*prenominal*) being the only one; only. **2.** (*prenominal*) of or relating to one individual or group and no other: *sole rights on a patent.* **3.** *Law.* having no wife or husband. See also **feme sole. 4.** an archaic word for **solitary.** [C14: from Old French *soule,* from Latin *sōlus* alone] —'**soleness** *n.*

sole[2] (səʊl) *n.* **1.** the underside of the foot. **2.** the underside of a shoe. **3. a.** the bottom of a furrow. **b.** the bottom of a plough. **4.** the underside of a golf-club head. **5.** the bottom of an oven, furnace, etc. *~vb.* (*tr.*) **6.** to provide (a shoe) with a sole. **7.** *Golf.* to rest (the club) on the ground, as when preparing to make a stroke. [C14: via Old French from Latin *solea* sandal; probably related to *solum* the ground] —'**soleless** *adj.*

sole[3] (səʊl) *n., pl.* **sole** *or* **soles. 1.** any tongue-shaped flatfish of the family *Soleidae,* esp. *Solea solea* (**European sole**): common in warm seas and valued as food fishes. **2.** any of certain other similar fishes. [C14: via Old French from Vulgar Latin *sola* (unattested), from Latin *solea* a sandal (from the fish's shape)]

solecism (ˈsɒlɪˌsɪzəm) *n.* **1. a.** the nonstandard use of a grammatical construction. **b.** any mistake, incongruity, or absurdity. **2.** a violation of good manners. [C16: from Latin *soloecismus,* from Greek *soloikismos,* from *soloikos* speaking incorrectly, from *Soloi* an Athenian colony of Cilicia where the inhabitants spoke a corrupt form of Greek] —ˈ**solecist** *n.* —ˌ**soleˈcistic** *or* ˌ**soleˈcistical** *adj.* —ˌ**soleˈcistically** *adv.*

solely (ˈsəʊllɪ) *adv.* **1.** only; completely; entirely. **2.** without another or others; singly; alone. **3.** for one thing only.

solemn (ˈsɒləm) *adj.* **1.** characterized or marked by seriousness or sincerity: *a solemn vow.* **2.** characterized by pomp, ceremony, or formality. **3.** serious, glum, or pompous. **4.** inspiring awe: *a solemn occasion.* **5.** performed with religious ceremony. **6.** gloomy or sombre: *solemn colours.* [C14: from Old French *solempne,* from Latin *sōllemnis* appointed, perhaps from *sollus* whole] —ˈ**solemnly** *adv.* —ˈ**solemnness** *or* ˈ**solemness** *n.*

solemnify (səˈlɛmnɪˌfaɪ) *vb.* **-fies, -fying, -fied.** (*tr.*) to make serious or grave. —**soˌlemnifiˈcation** *n.*

solemnity (səˈlɛmnɪtɪ) *n., pl.* **-ties. 1.** the state or quality of being solemn. **2.** (*often pl.*) solemn ceremony, observance, celebration, etc. **3.** *Law.* a formality necessary to validate a deed, act, contract, etc.

solemnize *or* **solemnise** (ˈsɒləmˌnaɪz) *vb.* (*tr.*) **1.** to celebrate or observe with rites or formal ceremonies, as a religious occasion. **2.** to celebrate or perform the ceremony of (marriage). **3.** to make solemn or serious. **4.** to perform or hold (ceremonies, etc.) in due manner. —ˌ**solemniˈzation** *or* ˌ**solemniˈsation** *n.* —ˈ**solemˌnizer** *or* ˈ**solemˌniser** *n.*

Solemn League and Covenant *n.* See **Covenant.**

solenette (ˈsəʊləˌnɛt, ˈsəʊlˌnɛt) *n.* a small European sole, *Buglossidium luteum,* up to 13 cm (5 in.) in length; not caught commercially. [SOLE[3] + -ETTE]

solenodon (səˈlɛnədən) *n.* either of two rare shrewlike nocturnal mammals of the West Indies, *Atopogale cubana* **(Cuban solenodon)** or *Solenodon paradoxus* **(Haitian solenodon),** having a long hairless tail and an elongated snout: family *Solenodontidae,* order *Insectivora* (insectivores). [C19: from New Latin, from Latin *sōlēn* sea mussel, razor-shell (from Greek: pipe) + Greek *odōn* tooth]

solenoid (ˈsəʊlɪˌnɔɪd) *n.* **1.** a coil of wire, usually cylindrical, in which a magnetic field is set up by passing a current through it. **2.** a coil of wire, partially surrounding an iron core, that is made to move inside the coil by the magnetic field set up by a current: used to convert electrical to mechanical energy, as in the operation of a switch. **3.** such a device used as a relay, as in a motor vehicle for connecting the battery directly to the starter motor when activated by the ignition switch. [C19: from French *solénoïde,* from Greek *sōlēn* a pipe, tube] —ˌ**soleˈnoidal** *adj.* —ˌ**soleˈnoidally** *adv.*

sole parent *n. Austral.* the usual name for **solo parent.**

sol-fa (ˈsɒlˈfɑː) *n.* **1.** short for **tonic sol-fa.** ~*vb.* **-fas, -faing, -faed. 2.** *U.S.* to use tonic sol-fa syllables in singing (a tune). [C16: see GAMUT]

solfatara (ˌsɒlfəˈtɑːrə) *n.* a volcanic vent emitting only sulphurous gases and water vapour or sometimes hot mud. [C18: from Italian: a sulphurous volcano near Naples, from *solfo* SULPHUR] —ˌ**solfaˈtaric** *adj.*

solfeggio (sɒlˈfɛdʒɪəʊ) *or* **solfège** (sɒlˈfɛʒ) *n., pl.* **-feggi** (-ˈfɛdʒiː), **-feggios,** *or* **-fèges.** *Music.* **1.** a voice exercise in which runs, scales, etc., are sung to the same syllable or syllables. **2.** solmization, esp. the French or Italian system, in which the names correspond to the notes of the scale of C major. [C18: from Italian *solfeggiare* to use the syllables sol-fa; see GAMUT]

solferino (ˌsɒlfəˈriːnəʊ) *n.* **a.** a moderate purplish-red colour. **b.** (*as adj.*): *a solferino suit.* [C19: from a dye discovered in 1859, the year a battle was fought at *Solferino,* a town in Italy]

soli (ˈsəʊlɪ) *adj., adv. Music.* (of a piece or passage) to be performed by or with soloists. Compare **tutti.** [plural of SOLO]

solicit (səˈlɪsɪt) *vb.* **-its, -iting, -ited. 1.** (when *intr.,* foll. by *for*) to make a request, application, or entreaty to (a person for business, support, etc.). **2.** to accost (a person) with an offer of sexual relations in return for money. **3.** to provoke or incite (a person) to do something wrong or illegal. [C15: from Old French *solliciter* to disturb, from Latin *sollicitāre* to harass, from *sollicitus* agitated, from *sollus* whole + *citus,* from *ciēre* to excite] —**soˌliciˈtation** *n.*

solicitor (səˈlɪsɪtə) *n.* **1.** (in Britain) a lawyer who advises clients on matters of law, draws up legal documents, prepares cases for barristers, etc., and who may plead in certain courts. Compare **barrister. 2.** (in the U.S.) an officer responsible for the legal affairs of a town, city, etc. **3.** a person who solicits. —**soˈlicitorship** *n.*

Solicitor General *n., pl.* **Solicitors General. 1.** (in Britain) the law officer of the Crown ranking next to the Attorney General (in Scotland to the Lord Advocate) and acting as his assistant. **2.** (in New Zealand) the government's chief lawyer: head of the Crown Law Office and prosecutor for the Crown.

solicitous (səˈlɪsɪtəs) *adj.* **1.** showing consideration, concern, attention, etc. **2.** keenly anxious or willing; eager. [C16: from Latin *sollicitus* anxious; see SOLICIT] —**soˈlicitously** *adv.* —**soˈlicitousness** *n.*

solicitude (səˈlɪsɪˌtjuːd) *n.* **1.** the state or quality of being solicitous. **2.** (*often pl.*) something that causes anxiety or concern. **3.** anxiety or concern.

solid (ˈsɒlɪd) *adj.* **1.** of, concerned with, or being a substance in a physical state in which it resists changes in size and shape. Compare **liquid** (sense 1), **gas** (sense 1). **2.** consisting of matter all through. **3.** of the same substance all through: *solid rock.* **4.** sound; proved or provable: *solid facts.* **5.** reliable or sensible; upstanding: *a solid citizen.* **6.** firm, strong, compact, or substantial: *a solid table; solid ground.* **7.** (of a meal or food) substantial. **8.** (*often postpositive*) without interruption or respite; continuous: *solid bombardment.* **9.** financially sound or solvent: *a solid institution.* **10.** strongly linked or consolidated: *a solid relationship.* **11.** *Geometry.* having or relating to three dimensions: *a solid figure; solid geometry.* **12.** (of a word composed of two or more other words or elements) written or printed as a single word without a hyphen. **13.** *Printing.* with no space or leads between lines of type. **14. solid for.** unanimously in favour of. **15.** (of a writer, work, performance, etc.) adequate; sensible. **16.** of or having a single uniform colour or tone. **17.** *N.Z. informal.* excessive; unreasonably expensive. ~*n.* **18.** *Geometry.* **a.** a closed surface in three-dimensional space. **b.** such a surface together with the volume enclosed by it. **19.** a solid substance, such as wood, iron, or diamond. [C14: from Old French *solide,* from Latin *solidus* firm; related to Latin *sollus* whole] —**solidity** (səˈlɪdɪtɪ) *n.* —ˈ**solidly** *adv.* —ˈ**solidness** *n.*

solidago (ˌsɒlɪˈdeɪgəʊ) *n., pl.* **-gos.** any plant of the chiefly American genus *Solidago,* which includes the goldenrods: family *Compositae* (composites). [C18: via New Latin from Medieval Latin *soldago* a plant reputed to have healing properties, from *soldāre* to strengthen, from Latin *solidāre,* from *solidus* SOLID]

solid angle *n.* a geometric surface consisting of lines originating from a common point (the vertex) and passing through a closed curve or polygon: measured in steradians.

solidarity (ˌsɒlɪˈdærɪtɪ) *n., pl.* **-ties.** unity of interests, sympathies, etc., as among members of the same class.

solidary (ˈsɒlɪdərɪ, -drɪ) *adj.* marked by unity of interests, responsibilities, etc. [C19: from French *solidaire,* from *solide* SOLID]

solid fuel *n.* **1.** a domestic or industrial fuel, such as coal or coke, that is a solid rather than an oil or gas. **2.** Also called: **solid propellant.** a rocket fuel that is a solid rather than a liquid or a gas.

solid geometry *n.* the branch of geometry concerned with the properties of three-dimensional geometric figures.

solidify (səˈlɪdɪˌfaɪ) *vb.* **-fies, -fying, -fied. 1.** to make or become solid or hard. **2.** to make or become strong, united, determined, etc. —**soˈlidiˌfiable** *adj.* —**soˌlidifiˈcation** *n.* —**soˈlidiˌfier** *n.*

solid injection *n.* injection of fuel directly into the cylinder of an internal-combustion engine without the assistance of an air blast to atomize the fuel. Also called (in a petrol engine): **direct injection.** Compare **blast injection.**

solid solution *n. Chem.* a crystalline material in which two or more elements or compounds share a common lattice.

solid-state *n.* **1.** (*modifier*) (of an electronic device) activated by a semiconductor component in which current flow is through solid material rather than in a vacuum. **2.** (*modifier*) of, concerned with, characteristic of, or consisting of solid matter.

solid-state physics *n.* (*functioning as sing.*) the branch of physics concerned with experimental and theoretical investigations of the properties of solids, such as superconductivity, photoconductivity, and ferromagnetism.

solidus (ˈsɒlɪdəs) *n., pl.* **-di** (-ˌdaɪ). **1.** Also called: **diagonal, separatrix, shilling mark, slash, stroke, virgule.** a short oblique stroke used in text to separate items of information, such as days, months, and years in dates (*18/7/80*), alternative words (*and/or*), numerator from denominator in fractions (*55/103*), etc. **2.** a gold coin of the Byzantine empire. [C14: from Late Latin *solidus* (*nummus*) a gold coin (from *solidus* solid); in Medieval Latin, *solidus* referred to a shilling and was indicated by a long *s,* which ultimately became the virgule]

solifidian (ˌsɒlɪˈfɪdɪən) *n. Christianity.* a person who maintains that man is justified by faith alone. [C16: from New Latin *sōlifidius,* from Latin *sōlus* sole + *fides* faith] —ˌ**soliˈfidianˌism** *n.*

solifluction *or* **solifluxion** (ˈsɒlɪˌflʌkʃən, ˈsəʊlɪ-) *n.* slow downhill movement of soil, saturated with meltwater, over a permanently frozen subsoil in tundra regions. [C20: from Latin *solum* soil + *fluctio* act of flowing]

soliloquize *or* **soliloquise** (səˈlɪləˌkwaɪz) *vb.* (*intr.*) to utter a soliloquy. —**soliloquist** (səˈlɪləkwɪst) *or* **soˈliloˌquizer, soˈliloˌquiser** *n.*

soliloquy (səˈlɪləkwɪ) *n., pl.* **-quies. 1.** the act of speaking alone or to oneself, esp. as a theatrical device. **2.** a speech in a play that is spoken in soliloquy: *Hamlet's first soliloquy.* [C17: via Late Latin *sōliloquium,* from Latin *sōlus* sole + *loquī* to speak]

solipsism (ˈsɒlɪpˌsɪzəm) *n. Philosophy.* the extreme form of scepticism which denies the possibility of any knowledge other than of one's own existence. [C19: from Latin *sōlus* alone + *ipse* self] —ˈ**solipsist** *n., adj.* —ˌ**solipˈsistic** *adj.*

solitaire (ˈsɒlɪˌtɛə, ˌsɒlɪˈtɛə) *n.* **1.** Also called: **pegboard.** a game played by one person, esp. one involving moving and taking pegs in a pegboard or marbles on an indented circular board with the object of being left with only one. **2.** the U.S. name for **patience** (the card game). **3.** a gem, esp. a diamond, set alone in a ring. **4.** any of several extinct birds of the genus *Pezophaps*, related to the dodo. **5.** any of several dull grey North American songbirds of the genus *Myadestes*: subfamily *Turdinae* (thrushes). [C18: from Old French: SOLITARY]

solitary ('sɒlɪtərɪ, -trɪ) *adj.* **1.** following or enjoying a life of solitude: *a solitary disposition.* **2.** experienced or performed alone: *a solitary walk.* **3.** (of a place) unfrequented. **4.** (*prenominal*) single; sole: *a solitary speck in the sky.* **5.** having few companions; lonely. **6.** (of animals) not living in organized colonies or large groups: *solitary bees; a solitary elephant.* Compare **social** (sense 7), **gregarious** (sense 2). **7.** (of flowers) growing singly. ~*n., pl.* **-taries. 8.** a person who lives in seclusion; hermit; recluse. **9.** *Informal.* short for **solitary confinement.** [C14: from Latin *sōlitārius*, from *sōlus* SOLE[1]] —'**solitarily** *adv.* —'**solitariness** *n.*

solitary confinement *n.* isolation imposed on a prisoner, as by confinement in a special cell.

solitude ('sɒlɪˌtjuːd) *n.* **1.** the state of being solitary or secluded. **2.** *Poetic.* a solitary place. [C14: from Latin *sōlitūdō*, from *sōlus* alone, SOLE[1]] —ˌ**soli'tudinous** *adj.*

solleret (ˌsɒlə'rɛt) *n.* a protective covering for the foot consisting of riveted plates of armour. [C19: from French, diminutive of Old French *soller* shoe, from Late Latin *subtēl* arch beneath the foot, from SUB- + *tālus* ankle]

sollicker ('sɒlɪkə) *n. Austral. slang.* something very large. [C19: from English dialect]

solmization *or* **solmisation** (ˌsɒlmɪ'zeɪʃən) *n. Music.* a system of naming the notes of a scale by syllables instead of letters derived from the 11th-century hexachord system of Guido d'Arezzo, which assigns the names *ut* (or *do*), *re, mi, fa, sol, la, si* (or *ti*) to the degrees of the major scale of C (**fixed system**) or (excluding the syllables *ut* and *si*) to the major scale in any key (**movable system**). See also **tonic sol-fa.** [C18: from French *solmisation*, from *solmiser* to use the sol-fa syllables, from SOL[1] + MI]

solo ('səʊləʊ) *n., pl.* **-los. 1.** (*pl.* **-los** *or* **-li** (-liː)) a musical composition for one performer with or without accompaniment. **2.** any of various card games in which each person plays on his own instead of in partnership with another, such as solo whist. **3.** a flight in which an aircraft pilot is unaccompanied. **4. a.** any performance, mountain climb, or other undertaking carried out by an individual without assistance from others. **b.** (*as modifier*): *a solo attempt.* ~*adj.* **5.** *Music.* unaccompanied: *a sonata for cello solo.* ~*adv.* **6.** by oneself; alone: *to fly solo.* ~*vb.* **7.** to undertake a venture alone, esp. to operate an aircraft alone or climb alone. [C17: via Italian from Latin *sōlus* alone, SOLE[1]]

soloist ('səʊləʊɪst) *n.* a person who performs a solo.

Solo man *n.* a type of early man, *Homo soloensis*, of late Pleistocene times, having a skull resembling that of Neanderthal man but with a smaller cranial capacity. [C20: after *Solo*, site in central Java where remains were found]

Solomon Islands Pidgin ('sɒləmən) *n.* the variety of Neo-Melanesian spoken in the Solomon Islands, an archipelago in the SW Pacific, and in neighbouring islands.

Solomon's seal *n.* **1.** another name for **Star of David. 2.** any of several liliaceous plants of the genus *Polygonatum* of N temperate regions, having greenish or yellow paired flowers, long narrow waxy leaves, and a thick underground stem with prominent leaf scars. [C16: translation of Medieval Latin *sigillum Solomonis*, perhaps referring to the resemblance of the leaf scars to seals]

solo mother *n. N.Z.* a mother with a dependent child or dependent children and no husband.

solonchak (ˌsɒlən'tʃæk) *n.* a type of intrazonal soil of arid regions with a greyish surface crust: contains large quantities of soluble salts. [Russian, literally: salt marsh]

solonetz *or* **solonets** (ˌsɒlə'nɛts) *n.* a type of intrazonal soil with a high saline content characterized by leaching. [Russian *solonets* salt not obtained through decoction]

so long *sentence substitute. Informal.* farewell; goodbye.

solo parent *n. N.Z.* a person who has a dependent child or dependent children and who is widowed, divorced, or unmarried. Also called (Austral.): **sole parent.**

solo stop *n.* any of various organ stops designed to imitate a solo performance on a particular musical instrument.

solo whist *n.* a version of whist for four players acting independently, each of whom may bid to win or lose a fixed number of tricks before play starts, trumps having usually been decided by cutting.

solstice ('sɒlstɪs) *n.* **1.** either the shortest day of the year (**winter solstice**) or the longest day of the year (**summer solstice**). **2.** either of the two points on the ecliptic at which the sun is overhead at the tropic of Cancer or Capricorn at the summer and winter solstices. [C13: via Old French from Latin *sōlstitium*, literally: the (apparent) standing still of the sun, from *sōl* sun + *sistere* to stand still] —**solstitial** (sɒl'stɪʃəl) *adj.*

solubility (ˌsɒljʊ'bɪlɪtɪ) *n., pl.* **-ties. 1.** the ability of a substance to dissolve; the quality of being soluble. **2.** a measure of this ability for a particular substance in a particular solvent, equal to the quantity of substance dissolving in a fixed quantity of solvent to form a saturated solution under specified temperature and pressure. It is expressed in grams per cubic decametre, grams per hundred grams of solvent, moles per mole, etc.

solubilize *or* **solubilise** ('sɒljʊbɪˌlaɪz) *vb.* to make or become soluble, as in the addition of detergents to fats to make them dissolve in water.

soluble ('sɒljʊbᵊl) *adj.* **1.** (of a substance) capable of being dissolved, esp. easily dissolved in some solvent, usually water. **2.** capable of being solved or answered. [C14: from Late Latin *solūbilis*, from Latin *solvere* to dissolve] —'**solubleness** *n.* —'**solubly** *adv.*

soluble glass *n.* another name for **sodium silicate** (sense 1).

soluble RNA *n.* another name for **transfer RNA.**

solum ('səʊləm) *n., pl.* **-lums** *or* **-la** (-lə). the upper layers of the soil profile, affected by climate and vegetation. [C19: New Latin from Latin: the ground]

solus ('səʊləs) *adj.* **1.** alone; separate. **2.** of or denoting the position of an advertising poster or press advertisement that is separated from competing advertisements: *a solus position.* **3.** of or denoting a retail outlet, such as a petrol station, that sells the products of one company exclusively: *a solus site.* **4.** (*fem.* **sola**) alone; by oneself (formerly used in stage directions). [C17: from Latin *sōlus* alone]

solute (sɒ'ljuːt) *n.* **1.** the component of a solution that changes its state in forming the solution or the component that is not present in excess; the substance that is dissolved in another substance. Compare **solvent.** ~*adj.* **2.** *Botany.* loose or unattached; free. [C16: from Latin *solūtus* free, unfettered, from *solvere* to release]

solution (sə'luːʃən) *n.* **1.** a homogeneous mixture of two or more substances in which the molecules or atoms of the substances are completely dispersed. The constituents can be solids, liquids, or gases. **2.** the act or process of forming a solution. **3.** the state of being dissolved (esp. in the phrase **in solution**). **4.** a mixture of two or more substances in which one or more components are present as small particles with colloidal dimension; colloid: *a colloidal solution.* **5.** a specific answer to or way of answering a problem. **6.** the act or process of solving a problem. **7.** *Maths.* **a.** the unique set of values that yield a true statement when substituted for the variables in an equation. **b.** a member of a set of assignments of values to variables under which a given statement is satisfied; a member of a solution set. **8.** the stage of a disease, following a crisis, resulting in its termination. **9.** *Law.* the payment, discharge, or satisfaction of a claim, debt, etc. [C14: from Latin *solūtiō* an unloosing, from *solūtus*; see SOLUTE]

solution set *n.* another name for **truth set.**

Solutrean (sə'luːtrɪən) *adj.* of or relating to an Upper Palaeolithic culture of Europe that was characterized by leaf-shaped flint blades. [C19: named after *Solutré*, village in central France where traces of this culture were originally found]

solvable ('sɒlvəbᵊl) *adj.* another word for **soluble.** —ˌ**solva'bility** *or* '**solvableness** *n.*

solvate ('sɒlveɪt) *vb. Chem.* to undergo, cause to undergo, or partake in solvation. [C20: from SOLVENT]

solvation (sɒl'veɪʃən) *n.* the process in which there is some chemical association between the molecules of a solute and those of the solvent. An example is an aqueous solution of copper sulphate which contains complex ions of the type $[Cu(H_2O)_4]^{2+}$.

Solvay process ('sɒlveɪ) *n.* an industrial process for manufacturing sodium carbonate. Carbon dioxide is passed into a solution of sodium chloride saturated with ammonia. Sodium bicarbonate is precipitated and heated to form the carbonate. [C19: named after Ernest *Solvay* (1838–1922), Belgian chemist who invented it]

solve (sɒlv) *vb.* (*tr.*) **1.** to find the explanation for or solution to (a mystery, problem, etc.). **2.** *Maths.* **a.** to work out the answer to (a mathematical problem). **b.** to obtain the roots of (an equation). [C15: from Latin *solvere* to loosen, release, free from debt] —'**solver** *n.*

solvency ('sɒlvənsɪ) *n.* ability to pay all debts.

solvent ('sɒlvənt) *adj.* **1.** capable of meeting financial obligations. **2.** (of a substance, esp. a liquid) capable of dissolving another substance. ~*n.* **3.** a liquid capable of dissolving another substance: *water is a solvent for salt.* **4.** the component of a solution that does not change its state in forming the solution or the component that is present in excess. Compare **solute. 5.** something that solves. [C17: from Latin *solvēns* releasing, from *solvere* to free, SOLVE] —'**solvently** *adv.*

solvent abuse *n.* the deliberate inhaling of intoxicating fumes given off by certain solvents such as toluene. See also **glue-sniffing.**

solvolysis (sɒl'vɒlɪsɪs) *n.* a chemical reaction occurring between a dissolved substance and its solvent. See also **hydrolysis.** [from SOLV(ENT) + -LYSIS]

Som. *abbrev. for* Somerset.

soma[1] ('səʊmə) *n., pl.* **-mata** (-mətə) *or* **-mas.** the body of an organism, esp. an animal, as distinct from the germ cells. [C19: via New Latin from Greek *sōma* the body]

soma[2] ('səʊmə) *n.* an intoxicating plant juice drink used in Vedic rituals. [from Sanskrit]

somaesthesia, *U.S.* **somesthesia** (ˌsɒmɪs'θiːzɪə), *or* **somaesthesis,** *U.S.* **somesthesis** (ˌsɒmɪs'θiːsɪs) *n.* sensory perception of bodily feelings like touch, pain, position of the limbs, etc. [C20:

from Greek *sōma* body + AESTHESIA] —**somaesthetic** *or U.S.* **somesthetic** (ˌsɒmɪsˈθɛtɪk) *adj.*

Somali (səʊˈmɑːlɪ) *n.* **1.** (*pl.* **-lis** *or* **-li**) a member of a tall dark-skinned people inhabiting Somalia, a republic in NE Africa. **2.** the language of this people, belonging to the Cushitic subfamily of the Afro-Asiatic family of languages. ~*adj.* **3.** Also: **Soˈmalian.** of, relating to, or characteristic of Somalia, the Somalis, or their language.

somatic (səʊˈmætɪk) *adj.* **1.** of or relating to the soma: *somatic cells.* **2.** of or relating to an animal body or body wall as distinct from the viscera, limbs, and head. **3.** of or relating to the human body as distinct from the mind: *a somatic disease.* [C18: from Greek *sōmatikos* concerning the body, from *sōma* the body] —**soˈmatically** *adv.*

somatic cell *n.* any of the cells of a plant or animal except the reproductive cells. Compare **germ cell.**

somatic nervous system *n. Physiol.* the section of the nervous system responsible for sensation and control of the skeletal muscles. Compare **autonomic nervous system.**

somato- *or before a vowel* **somat-** *combining form.* body: *somatoplasm.* [from Greek *sōma, sōmat-* body]

somatogenic (səˌmætəʊˈdʒɛnɪk) *adj. Med.* originating in the cells of the body: of organic, rather than mental, origin: *a somatogenic disorder.*

somatology (ˌsəʊməˈtɒlədʒɪ) *n.* **1.** the branch of biology concerned with the structure and function of the body. **2.** the branch of anthropology dealing with the physical characteristics of man. —**somatologic** (ˌsəʊmətəˈlɒdʒɪk) *or* ˌ**somatoˈlogical** *adj.* —ˌ**somatoˈlogically** *adv.* —ˌ**somaˈtologist** *n.*

somatomedin (ˌsəʊmətəˈmiːdɪn) *n.* a protein hormone that promotes tissue growth under the influence of growth hormone. [C20: from SOMATO- + Latin *medius* middle + -IN]

somatoplasm (ˈsəʊmətəˌplæzəm) *n. Biology.* **a.** the protoplasm of a somatic cell. **b.** the somatic cells collectively. Compare **germ plasm** (sense 1). —ˌ**somatoˈplastic** *adj.*

somatopleure (ˈsəʊmətəˌplʊə, -ˌplɜː) *n.* a mass of tissue in embryo vertebrates that is formed by fusion of the ectoderm with the outer layer of mesoderm: develops into the amnion, chorion, and part of the body wall. [C19: from New Latin *somatopleura,* from SOMATO- + Greek *pleura* a side] —ˌ**somatoˈpleural** *or* ˌ**somatoˈpleuric** *adj.*

somatostatin (ˌsəʊmətəˈstætɪn) *n.* a peptide hormone that prevents the release of growth hormone from the pituitary gland. [C20: from SOMATO- + -STAT + -IN]

somatotonia (ˌsəʊmətəʊˈtəʊnɪə) *n.* a personality type characterized by assertiveness and energy: said to be correlated with a mesomorph body type. Compare **cerebrotonia, viscerotonia.**

somatotrophin (ˌsəʊmətəʊˈtrəʊfɪn) *or* **somatotropin** (ˌsəʊmətəʊˈtrəʊpɪn) *n.* other names for **growth hormone.** —ˌ**somatoˈtrophic** *or* ˌ**somatoˈtropic** *adj.*

somatotype (ˈsəʊmətəˌtaɪp) *n.* a type or classification of physique or body build. See **endomorph, mesomorph, ectomorph.**

sombre *or U.S.* **somber** (ˈsɒmbə) *adj.* **1.** dismal; melancholy: *a sombre mood.* **2.** dim, gloomy, or shadowy. **3.** (of colour, clothes, etc.) sober, dull, or dark. [C18: from French, from Vulgar Latin *subumbrāre* (unattested) to shade, from Latin *sub* beneath + *umbra* shade] —ˈ**sombrely** *or U.S.* ˈ**somberly** *adv.* —ˈ**sombreness** *or U.S.* ˈ**somberness** *n.* —**sombrous** (ˈsɒmbrəs) *adj.*

sombrero (sɒmˈbrɛərəʊ) *n., pl.* **-ros.** a felt or straw hat with a wide brim, as worn by men in Mexico. [C16: from Spanish, from *sombrero de sol* shade from the sun]

some (sʌm; *unstressed* səm) *determiner.* **1. a.** (a) certain unknown or unspecified: *some lunatic drove into my car; some people never learn.* **b.** (*as pronoun; functioning as sing. or pl.*): *some can teach and others can't.* **2. a.** an unknown or unspecified quantity or amount of: *there's some rice on the table; he owns some horses.* **b.** (*as pronoun; functioning as sing. or pl.*): *we'll buy some.* **3. a.** a considerable number or amount of: *he lived some years afterwards.* **b.** a little: *show him some respect.* **4.** (*usually stressed*) *Informal.* an impressive or remarkable: *that was some game!* **5.** a certain amount (more) (in the phrases **some more** and (informal) **and then some**). **6.** about; approximately: *he owes me some thirty pounds.* ~*adv.* **7.** *U.S., not standard.* to a certain degree or extent: *I guess I like him some.* [Old English *sum;* related to Old Norse *sumr,* Gothic *sums,* Old High German *sum* some, Sanskrit *samá* any, Greek *hamē* somehow]

-some[1] *suffix forming adjectives.* characterized by; tending to: *awesome; tiresome.* [Old English *-sum;* related to Gothic *-sama,* German *-sam*]

-some[2] *suffix forming nouns.* indicating a group of a specified number of members: *threesome.* [Old English *sum,* special use of SOME (determiner)]

-some[3] (-səʊm) *n. combining form.* a body: *chromosome.* [from Greek *sōma* body]

somebody (ˈsʌmbədɪ) *pron.* **1.** some person; someone. ~*n., pl.* **-bodies.** **2.** a person of greater importance than others: *he is somebody in this town.*

▷**Usage.** See at **everyone.**

someday (ˈsʌmˌdeɪ) *adv.* at some unspecified time in the (distant) future.

somehow (ˈsʌmˌhaʊ) *adv.* **1.** in some unspecified way. **2.** Also: **somehow or other.** by any means that are necessary.

someone (ˈsʌmˌwʌn, -wən) *pron.* some person; somebody.

▷**Usage.** See at **everyone.**

someplace (ˈsʌmˌpleɪs) *adv. U.S. and Canadian informal.* in, at, or to some unspecified place or region.

somersault *or* **summersault** (ˈsʌməˌsɔːlt) *n.* **1. a.** a forward roll in which the head is placed on the ground and the trunk and legs are turned over it. **b.** a similar roll in a backward direction. **2.** an acrobatic feat in which either of these rolls are performed in midair, as in diving or gymnastics. **3.** a complete reversal of opinion, policy, etc. ~*vb.* **4.** (*intr.*) to perform a somersault. [C16: from Old French *soubresault,* probably from Old Provençal *sobresaut,* from *sobre* over (from Latin *super*) + *saut* a jump, leap (from Latin *saltus*)]

something (ˈsʌmθɪŋ) *pron.* **1.** an unspecified or unknown thing; some thing: *he knows something you don't; take something warm with you.* **2. something or other.** one unspecified thing or an alternative thing. **3.** an unspecified or unknown amount; bit: *something less than a hundred.* **4.** an impressive or important person, thing, or event: *isn't that something?* ~*adv.* **5.** to some degree; a little; somewhat: *to look something like me.* **6.** (*foll. by an adj.*) *Informal.* (intensifier): *it hurts something awful.*

sometime (ˈsʌmˌtaɪm) *adv.* **1.** at some unspecified point of time. ~*adj.* **2.** (*prenominal*) having been at one time; former: *the sometime President.* **3.** (*prenominal*) *Archaic or U.S.* occasional; infrequent.

sometimes (ˈsʌmˌtaɪmz) *adv.* **1.** now and then; from time to time; occasionally. **2.** *Obsolete.* formerly; sometime.

someway (ˈsʌmˌweɪ) *adv.* in some unspecified manner.

somewhat (ˈsʌmˌwɒt) *adv.* (*not used with a negative*) rather; a bit: *she found it somewhat less easy than he.*

somewhere (ˈsʌmˌwɛə) *adv.* **1.** in, to, or at some unknown or unspecified place or point: *somewhere in England; somewhere between 3 and 4 o'clock.* **2. get somewhere.** *Informal.* to make progress.

somewise (ˈsʌmˌwaɪz) *adv.* in some way or to some degree; somehow (archaic, except in the phrase **in somewise**). [C15: from SOME + -WISE]

somite (ˈsəʊmaɪt) *n.* **1.** *Embryol.* any of a series of dorsal paired segments of mesoderm occurring along the notochord in vertebrate embryos. It develops into muscle and bone in the adult animal. **2.** *Zoology.* another name for **metamere.** [C19: from Greek *sōma* a body] —**somital** (ˈsəʊmɪtᵊl) *or* **somitic** (səʊˈmɪtɪk) *adj.*

sommelier (ˈsʌməlˌjeɪ) *n.* a wine steward in a restaurant or hotel. [French: butler, via Old French from Old Provençal *saumalier* pack-animal driver, from Late Latin *sagma* a packsaddle, from Greek]

somnambulate (sɒmˈnæmbjʊˌleɪt) *vb.* (*intr.*) to walk while asleep. [C19: from Latin *somnus* sleep + *ambulāre* to walk] —**somˈnambulance** *n.* —**somˈnambulant** *adj., n.* —**somˌnambuˈlation** *n.* —**somˈnambuˌlator** *n.*

somnambulism (sɒmˈnæmbjʊˌlɪzəm) *n.* a condition characterized by walking while asleep or in a hypnotic trance. Also called: **noctambulism.** —**somˈnambulist** *n.* —**somˌnambuˈlistic** *adj.*

somni- *or before a vowel* **somn-** *combining form.* sleep: *somniferous.* [from Latin *somnus*]

somniferous (sɒmˈnɪfərəs) *or* **somnific** *adj. Rare.* tending to induce sleep. [C17: from Latin *somnifer* (from *somnus* sleep + *ferre* to do) + -OUS] —**somˈniferously** *adv.*

somniloquy (sɒmˈnɪləkwɪ) *n., pl.* **-quies.** *Rare.* the act of talking in one's sleep. [C19: from Latin *somnus* sleep + *loqui* to speak; compare SOLILOQUY] —**somˈniloquist** *n.* —**somˈniloquous** *adj.*

somnolent (ˈsɒmnələnt) *adj.* **1.** drowsy; sleepy. **2.** causing drowsiness. [C15: from Latin *somnus* sleep] —ˈ**somnolence** *or* ˈ**somnolency** *n.* —ˈ**somnolently** *adv.*

son (sʌn) *n.* **1.** a male offspring; a boy or man in relation to his parents. **2.** a male descendant. **3.** (*often cap.*) a familiar term of address for a boy or man. **4.** a male from a certain country, place, etc., or one closely connected with a certain environment: *a son of the circus.* ~Related adj.: **filial.** [Old English *sunu;* related to Old Norse *sunr,* Gothic *sunus,* Old High German *sunu,* Lithuanian *sūnus,* Sanskrit *sūnu*] —ˈ**sonless** *adj.* —ˈ**sonˌlike** *adj.*

Son (sʌn) *n. Christianity.* the second person of the Trinity, Jesus Christ.

sonant (ˈsəʊnənt) *adj.* **1.** *Phonetics.* denoting a voiced sound capable of forming a syllable or syllable nucleus. **2.** inherently possessing, exhibiting, or producing a sound. **3.** *Rare.* resonant; sounding. ~*n.* **4.** *Phonetics.* a voiced sound belonging to the class of frictionless continuants or nasals (l, r, m, n, ŋ) considered from the point of view of being a vowel and, in this capacity, able to form a syllable or syllable nucleus. [C19: from Latin *sonāns* sounding, from *sonāre* to make a noise, resound] —ˈ**sonance** *n.* —**sonantal** (səʊˈnæntᵊl) *or* **soˈnantic** *adj.*

sonar (ˈsəʊnɑː) *n.* a communication and position-finding device used in underwater navigation and target detection using echolocation. [C20: from *so(und) na(vigation and) r(anging)*]

sonata (səˈnɑːtə) *n.* **1.** an instrumental composition, usually in three or more movements, for piano alone (**piano sonata**) or for any other instrument with or without piano accompaniment (**violin sonata, cello sonata,** etc.). See also **sonata form,**

symphony (sense 1), **concerto** (sense 1). **2.** a one-movement keyboard composition of the baroque period. [C17: from Italian, from *sonare* to sound, from Latin]

sonata form *n.* a musical structure consisting of an expanded ternary form whose three sections (exposition, development, and recapitulation), followed by a coda, are characteristic of the first movement in a sonata, symphony, string quartet, concerto, etc.

sonatina (ˌsɒnəˈtiːnə) *n.* a short sonata. [C19: from Italian]

sondage (sɒnˈdɑːʒ) *n., pl.* **-dages** (-ˈdɑːʒɪz, -ˈdɑːʒ). *Archaeology.* a deep trial trench for inspecting stratigraphy. [C20: from French: a sounding, from *sonder* to sound]

sonde (sɒnd) *n.* a rocket, balloon, or probe used for observing in the upper atmosphere. [C20: from French: plummet, plumb line; see SOUND[3]]

sone (səʊn) *n.* a unit of loudness equal to 40 phons. [C20: from Latin *sonus* a sound]

son et lumière (ˈsɒn eɪ ˈluːmɪˌɛə; *French* sɔ̃n e lymjɛr) *n.* an entertainment staged at night at a famous building, historical site, etc., whereby the history of the location is presented by means of lighting effects, sound effects, and narration. [French, literally: sound and light]

song (sɒŋ) *n.* **1. a.** a piece of music, usually employing a verbal text, composed for the voice, esp. one intended for performance by a soloist. **b.** the whole repertory of such pieces. **c.** (*as modifier*): *a song book.* **2.** poetical composition; poetry. **3.** the characteristic tuneful call or sound made by certain birds or insects. **4.** the act or process of singing: *they raised their voices in song.* **5. for a song.** at a bargain price. **6. on song.** *Brit. informal.* performing at peak efficiency or ability. [Old English *sang;* related to Gothic *saggws,* Old High German *sang;* see SING] —ˈ**song**ˌ**like** *adj.*

song and dance *n. Informal.* **1.** *Brit.* a fuss, esp. one that is unnecessary. **2.** *U.S. and Canadian.* a long or elaborate story or explanation, esp. one that is evasive.

songbird (ˈsɒŋˌbɜːd) *n.* **1.** any passerine bird of the suborder *Oscines,* having highly developed vocal organs and, in most, a musical call. **2.** any bird having a musical call.

song cycle *n.* any of several groups of songs written by composers during and after the Romantic period, each series employing texts, usually by one poet, relating a story or grouped around a central motif.

song form *n.* another name for **ternary form.**

songful (ˈsɒŋfʊl) *adj.* tuneful; melodious. —ˈ**songfully** *adv.* —ˈ**songfulness** *n.*

Songhai (sɒŋˈgaɪ) *n.* **1.** (*pl.* **-ghai** *or* **-ghais**) a member of a Nilotic people of W Africa, living chiefly in Mali and Niger in the central Niger valley. **2.** the language or group of dialects spoken by this people, now generally regarded as forming a branch of the Nilo-Saharan family.

songkok (ˈsɒŋkɒ) *n.* (in Malaysia and Indonesia) a kind of oval brimless hat, resembling a skull. [from Malay]

songololo (ˌsɒŋgəˈləʊləʊ) *n., pl.* **-los.** *S. African.* a millipede, *Jurus terrestris,* having a hard shiny dark brown segmented exoskeleton. [Nguni]

song sparrow *n.* a common North American finch, *Melospiza melodia,* having brown-and-white plumage and a melodious song.

songster (ˈsɒŋstə) *n.* **1.** a singer or poet. **2.** a singing bird; songbird. —ˈ**songstress** *fem. n.*

song thrush *n.* a common Old World thrush, *Turdus philomelos,* that has a brown back and spotted breast and is noted for its song.

songwriter (ˈsɒŋˌraɪtə) *n.* a person who composes the words or music for songs in a popular idiom.

sonic (ˈsɒnɪk) *adj.* **1.** of, involving, or producing sound. **2.** having a speed about equal to that of sound in air: 332 metres per second (743 miles per hour). [C20: from Latin *sonus* sound]

sonic barrier *n.* another name for **sound barrier.**

sonic boom *n.* a loud explosive sound caused by the shock wave of an aircraft, etc., travelling at supersonic speed.

sonic depth finder *n.* an instrument for detecting the depth of water or of a submerged object by means of sound waves; Fathometer. See also **sonar.**

sonics (ˈsɒnɪks) *n.* (*functioning as sing.*) *Physics.* the study of mechanical vibrations in matter.

soniferous (sɒˈnɪfərəs) *adj.* carrying or producing sound.

son-in-law *n., pl.* **sons-in-law.** the husband of one's daughter.

sonnet (ˈsɒnɪt) *Prosody.* ~*n.* **1.** a verse form of Italian origin consisting of 14 lines in iambic pentameter with rhymes arranged according to a fixed scheme, usually divided either into octave and sestet or, in the English form, into three quatrains and a couplet. ~*vb.* **2.** (*intr.*) to compose sonnets. **3.** (*tr.*) to celebrate in a sonnet. [C16: via Italian from Old Provençal *sonet* a little poem, from *son* song, from Latin *sonus* a sound]

sonneteer (ˌsɒnɪˈtɪə) *n.* a writer of sonnets.

sonny (ˈsʌnɪ) *n., pl.* **-nies.** *Often patronizing.* a familiar term of address to a boy or man. [C19: from SON + -Y[2]]

sonobuoy (ˈsəʊnəˌbɔɪ) *n.* a buoy equipped to detect underwater noises and transmit them by radio. [from SONIC + BUOY]

son of a bitch *n., pl.* **sons of bitches.** *Slang, chiefly U.S. and Canadian.* **1.** a worthless or contemptible person: used as an insult. **2.** a humorous or affectionate term for a person, esp. a man: *a lucky son of a bitch.*

son of a gun *n., pl.* **sons of guns.** *Slang, chiefly U.S. and Canadian.* a rogue or rascal: used as a jocular form of address.

son of God *n. Bible.* **1.** an angelic being. **2.** a Christian believer.

Son of Man *n. Bible.* a title of Jesus Christ.

sonogram (ˈsəʊnəˌgræm) *n. Physics.* a three-dimensional representation of a sound signal, using coordinates of frequency, time, and intensity.

sonorant (ˈsɒnərənt) *n. Phonetics.* **1.** one of the frictionless continuants or nasals (l, r, m, n, ŋ) having consonantal or vocalic functions depending on its situation within the syllable. **2.** either of the two consonants represented in English orthography by *w* or *y* and regarded as either consonantal or vocalic articulations of the vowels (iː) and (uː). [from Latin *sonor* a noise + -ANT]

sonorous (səˈnɔːrəs, ˈsɒnərəs) *adj.* **1.** producing or capable of producing sound. **2.** (of language, sound, etc.) deep or resonant. **3.** (esp. of speech) high-flown; grandiloquent. [C17: from Latin *sonōrus* loud, from *sonor* a noise] —**sonority** (səˈnɒrɪtɪ) *n.* —**so**ˈ**norously** *adv.* —**so**ˈ**norousness** *n.*

sonsy *or* **sonsie** (ˈsɒnsɪ) *adj.* **-sier, -siest.** *Scot., Irish, and English dialect.* **1.** plump; buxom; comely. **2.** cheerful; good-natured. **3.** lucky. [C16: from Gaelic *sonas* good fortune]

sook[1] (sʊk) *n.* **1.** *Southwest English dialect.* a baby. **2.** *Derogatory.* a coward. **3.** *N.Z. informal.* a calf. [perhaps from Old English *sūcan* to suck, influenced by Welsh *swci swead* tame]

sook[2] *or* **souk** (suːk) *Scot.* ~*vb.* **1.** to suck. ~*n.* **2.** the act or an instance of sucking. **3.** a sycophant; toady. [Old English *sūcan*]

sool (suːl) *vb.* (*tr.*) to incite (a dog) to attack. [C17: from English dialect *sowl* (esp. of a dog) to pull or seize roughly]

soon (suːn) *adv.* **1.** in or after a short time; in a little while; before long: *the doctor will soon be here.* **2. as soon as.** at the very moment that: *she burst into tears as soon as she saw him.* **3. as soon...as.** used to indicate that the second alternative mentioned is not preferable to the first: *I'd just as soon go by train as drive.* [Old English *sōna;* related to Old High German *sāno,* Gothic *suns*]

sooner (ˈsuːnə) *adv.* **1.** the comparative of **soon:** *he came sooner than I thought.* **2.** rather; in preference: *I'd sooner die than give up.* **3. no sooner...than.** immediately after or when: *no sooner had he got home than the rain stopped; no sooner said than done.* **4. sooner or later.** eventually; inevitably.

soot (sʊt) *n.* **1.** finely divided carbon deposited from flames during the incomplete combustion of organic substances such as coal. ~*vb.* **2.** (*tr.*) to cover with soot. [Old English *sōt;* related to Old Norse, Middle Low German *sōt,* Lithuanian *sódis,* Old Slavonic *sažda,* Old Irish *sūide*]

sooth (suːθ) *Archaic or poetic.* ~*n.* **1.** truth or reality (esp. in the phrase **in sooth**). ~*adj.* **2.** true or real. **3.** smooth. [Old English *sōth;* related to Old Norse *sathr* true, Old High German *sand,* Gothic *sunja* truth, Latin *sōns* guilty, *sonticus* critical] —ˈ**soothly** *adv.*

soothe (suːð) *vb.* **1.** (*tr.*) to make calm or tranquil. **2.** (*tr.*) to relieve or assuage (pain, longing, etc.). **3.** (*intr.*) to bring tranquillity or relief. [C16 (in the sense: to mollify): from Old English *sōthian* to prove; related to Old Norse *sanna* to assert; see SOOTH] —ˈ**soother** *n.* —ˈ**soothing** *adj.* —ˈ**soothingly** *adv.* —ˈ**soothingness** *n.*

soothfast (ˈsuːθˌfɑːst) *adj. Archaic.* **1.** truthful. **2.** loyal; true. [from Old English *sōthfæst;* see SOOTH, FAST[1]]

soothsay (ˈsuːθˌseɪ) *vb.* **-says, -saying, -said.** (*intr.*) to predict the future. —ˈ**sooth**ˌ**saying** *n.*

soothsayer (ˈsuːθˌseɪə) *n.* a seer or prophet.

sooty (ˈsʊtɪ) *adj.* **sootier, sootiest.** **1.** covered with soot. **2.** resembling or consisting of soot. —ˈ**sootily** *adv.* —ˈ**sootiness** *n.*

sooty mould *n.* **1.** a fungal plant disease characterized by a blackish growth covering the surface of leaves, fruits, etc. **2.** any of various fungi, such as species of *Meliola* or *Capnodium,* that cause this disease.

sop (sɒp) *n.* **1.** (*often pl.*) food soaked in a liquid before being eaten. **2.** a concession, bribe, etc., given to placate or mollify: *a sop to one's feelings.* **3.** *Informal.* a stupid or weak person. ~*vb.* **sops, sopping, sopped.** **4.** (*tr.*) to dip or soak (food) in liquid. **5.** (when *intr.,* often foll. by *in*) to soak or be soaked. ~See also **sop up.** [Old English *sopp;* related to Old Norse *soppa* SOUP, Old High German *sopfa* milk with bread; see SUP[2]]

SOP *abbrev. for* standard operating procedure.

sop. *abbrev. for* soprano.

sophism (ˈsɒfɪzəm) *n.* an instance of sophistry. Compare **paralogism.** [C14: from Latin *sophisma,* from Greek: ingenious trick, from *sophizesthai* to use clever deceit, from *sophos* wise, clever]

sophist (ˈsɒfɪst) *n.* **1.** (*often cap.*) one of the pre-Socratic philosophers who were itinerant professional teachers of oratory and argument and who were prepared to enter into debate on any matter however specious. **2.** a person who uses clever or quibbling arguments that are fundamentally unsound. [C16: from Latin *sophista,* from Greek *sophistēs* a wise man, from *sophizesthai* to act craftily]

sophister (ˈsɒfɪstə) *n.* **1.** (esp. formerly) a second-year undergraduate at certain British universities. **2.** *Rare.* another word for **sophist.**

sophistic (sə'fɪstɪk) *or* **sophistical** *adj.* **1.** of or relating to sophists or sophistry. **2.** consisting of sophisms or sophistry; specious. —**so'phistically** *adv.*

sophisticate *vb.* (sə'fɪstɪˌkeɪt). **1.** (*tr.*) to make (someone) less natural or innocent, as by education. **2.** to pervert or corrupt (an argument, etc.) by sophistry. **3.** (*tr.*) to make more complex or refined. **4.** *Rare.* to falsify (a text, etc.) by alterations. ~*n.* (sə'fɪstɪˌkeɪt, -kɪt). **5.** a sophisticated person. [C14: from Medieval Latin *sophisticāre,* from Latin *sophisticus* sophistic] —**soˌphisti'cation** *n.* —**so'phistiˌcator** *n.*

sophisticated (sə'fɪstɪˌkeɪtɪd) *adj.* **1.** having refined or cultured tastes and habits. **2.** appealing to sophisticates: *a sophisticated restaurant.* **3.** unduly refined or cultured. **4.** pretentiously or superficially wise. **5.** (of machines, methods, etc.) complex and refined. —**so'phistiˌcatedly** *adv.*

sophistry ('sɒfɪstrɪ) *n., pl.* **-ries. 1. a.** a method of argument that is seemingly plausible though actually invalid and misleading. **b.** the art of using such arguments. **2.** subtle but unsound or fallacious reasoning. **3.** an instance of this; sophism.

Sophoclean (ˌsɒfə'kliːən) *adj.* of or relating to the Greek dramatist Sophocles (?496–406 B.C.) or to his works or dramatic style.

sophomore ('sɒfəˌmɔː) *n. Chiefly U.S. and Canadian.* a second-year student at a secondary (high) school or college. [C17: perhaps from earlier *sophumer,* from *sophum,* variant of SOPHISM + -ER[1]]

Sophy *or* **Sophi** ('səʊfɪ) *n., pl.* **-phies.** (formerly) a title of the Persian monarchs. [C16: from Latin *sophī* wise men, from Greek *sophos* wise]

-sophy *n. combining form.* indicating knowledge or an intellectual system: *philosophy; theosophy.* [from Greek *-sophia,* from *sophia* wisdom, from *sophos* wise] —**-sophic** *or* **-sophical** *adj. combining form.*

sopor ('səʊpə) *n.* an abnormally deep sleep; stupor. [C17: from Latin: a deep sleep, death; related to *somnus* sleep]

soporific (ˌsɒpə'rɪfɪk) *adj. also (archaic)* **soporiferous. 1.** inducing sleep. **2.** drowsy; sleepy. ~*n.* **3.** a drug or other agent that induces sleep. —ˌ**sopo'rifically** *adv.*

sopping ('sɒpɪŋ) *adj.* completely soaked; wet through. Also: **sopping wet.**

soppy ('sɒpɪ) *adj.* **-pier, -piest. 1.** wet or soggy. **2.** *Brit. informal.* silly or sentimental. **3. soppy on.** *Brit. informal.* foolishly charmed or affected by. —'**soppily** *adv.* —'**soppiness** *n.*

sopranino (ˌsɒprə'niːnəʊ) *n., pl.* **-nos. a.** the instrument with the highest possible pitch in a family of instruments. **b.** (*as modifier*): *a sopranino recorder.* [Italian, diminutive of SOPRANO]

soprano (sə'prɑːnəʊ) *n., pl.* **-pranos** *or* **-prani** (-'prɑːniː). **1.** the highest adult female voice, having a range approximately from middle C to the A a thirteenth above it. **2.** the voice of a young boy before puberty. **3.** a singer with such a voice. **4.** the highest part of a piece of harmony. **5. a.** the highest or second highest instrument in a family of instruments. **b.** (*as modifier*): *a soprano saxophone.* ~See also **treble.** [C18: from Italian, from *sopra* above, from Latin *suprā*]

soprano clef *n.* the clef that establishes middle C as being on the bottom line of the staff. See also **C clef.**

sop up *vb. (tr., adv.)* to mop or take up (spilt water, etc.) with or as if with a sponge.

sora ('sɔːrə) *n.* a North American rail, *Porzana carolina,* with a greyish-brown plumage and yellow bill. [C18: of unknown origin]

sorb (sɔːb) *n.* **1.** another name for **service tree** (sense 1). **2.** any of various related trees, esp. the mountain ash. **3.** Also called: **sorb apple.** the fruit of any of these trees. [C16: from Latin *sorbus* the sorb, service tree] —'**sorbic** *adj.*

Sorb (sɔːb) *n.* a member of a Slavonic people living chiefly in the rural areas of E Germany and SW Poland (Lusatia). Also called: **Wend, Lusatian.**

sorbefacient (ˌsɔːbɪ'feɪʃənt) *adj.* **1.** inducing absorption. ~*n.* **2.** a sorbefacient drug. [C19: from Latin *sorbē(re)* to absorb + -FACIENT]

sorbet ('sɔːbeɪ, -bɪt) *n.* **1.** a water ice made from fruit juice, egg whites, milk, etc. **2.** a U.S. word for **sherbet** (sense 1). [C16: from French, from Old Italian *sorbetto,* from Turkish *şerbet,* from Arabic *sharbah* a drink]

Sorbian ('sɔːbɪən) *n.* **1.** a West Slavonic language spoken in the rural areas of E Germany and SW Poland; modern Wendish. ~*adj.* **2.** of or relating to the Sorbs or their language.

sorbic acid *n.* a white crystalline unsaturated carboxylic acid found in berries of the mountain ash and used to inhibit the growth of moulds and as an additive for certain synthetic coatings, as of cheese (**E200**); 2,4-hexadienoic acid. It exists as *cis-* and *trans-* isomers, the latter being the one usually obtained. Formula: $CH_3CH{:}CHCH{:}CHCOOH$. [C19: from SORB (the tree), from its discovery in the berries of the mountain ash]

sorbitol ('sɔːbɪˌtɒl) *n.* a white water-soluble crystalline alcohol with a sweet taste, found in certain fruits and berries and manufactured by the catalytic hydrogenation of sucrose: used as a sweetener (**E420**) and in the manufacture of ascorbic acid and synthetic resins. Formula: $C_6H_8(OH)_6$. [C19: from SORB + -ITOL]

sorbo rubber ('sɔːbəʊ) *n. Brit.* a spongy form of rubber. [C20: from ABSORB]

sorbose ('sɔːbəʊs) *n. Biochem.* a sweet-tasting hexose sugar derived from the berries of the mountain ash by bacterial action: used in the synthesis of ascorbic acid. Formula: $CH_2OH(CHOH)_3COCH_2OH$. [C19: from SORB + -OSE[2]]

sorcerer ('sɔːsərə) *or (fem.)* **sorceress** ('sɔːsərɪs) *n.* a person who seeks to control and use magic powers; a wizard or magician. [C16: from Old French *sorcier,* from Vulgar Latin *sortiārius* (unattested) caster of lots, from Latin *sors* lot]

sorcery ('sɔːsərɪ) *n., pl.* **-ceries.** the art, practices, or spells of magic, esp. black magic, by which it is sought to harness occult forces or evil spirits in order to produce preternatural effects in the world. [C13: from Old French *sorcerie,* from *sorcier* SORCERER] —'**sorcerous** *adj.*

sordes ('sɔːdiːz) *pl. n. Med.* dark incrustations on the lips and teeth of patients with prolonged fever. [C18: from Latin *sordēs* filth]

sordid ('sɔːdɪd) *adj.* **1.** dirty, foul, or squalid. **2.** degraded; vile; base: *a sordid affair.* **3.** selfish and grasping: *sordid avarice.* [C16: from Latin *sordidus,* from *sordēre* to be dirty] —'**sordidly** *adv.* —'**sordidness** *n.*

sordino (sɔː'diːnəʊ) *n., pl.* **-ni** (-niː). **1.** a mute for a stringed or brass musical instrument. **2.** any of the dampers that arrest the vibrations of piano strings. **3. con sordino** *or* **sordini.** a musical direction to play with a mute. **4. senza sordino** *or* **sordini.** a musical direction to remove or play without the mute or (on the piano) with the sustaining pedal pressed down. ~See also **sourdine.** [Italian: from *sordo* deaf, from Latin *surdus*]

sore (sɔː) *adj.* **1.** (esp. of a wound, injury, etc.) painfully sensitive; tender. **2.** causing annoyance: *a sore point.* **3.** resentful; irked: *he was sore that nobody believed him.* **4.** urgent; pressing: *in sore need.* **5.** (*postpositive*) grieved; distressed. **6.** causing grief or sorrow. ~*n.* **7.** a painful or sensitive wound, injury, etc. **8.** any cause of distress or vexation. ~*adv.* **9.** *Archaic.* direly; sorely (now only in such phrases as **sore pressed, sore afraid**). [Old English *sār;* related to Old Norse *sārr,* Old High German *sēr,* Gothic *sair* sore, Latin *saevus* angry] —'**soreness** *n.*

soredium (sɔː'riːdɪəm) *n.* an organ of vegetative reproduction in lichens consisting of a cluster of algal cells enclosed in fungal hyphae: dispersed by wind, insects, or other means. [C19: New Latin, from Greek *sōros* a heap]

sorehead ('sɔːˌhɛd) *n. Informal, chiefly U.S. and Canadian.* a peevish or disgruntled person. —ˌ**sore'headedly** *adv.* —ˌ**sore'headedness** *n.*

sorely ('sɔːlɪ) *adv.* **1.** painfully or grievously: *sorely wounded.* **2.** pressingly or greatly: *to be sorely taxed.*

sorghum ('sɔːgəm) *n.* any grass of the Old World genus *Sorghum,* having solid stems, large flower heads, and glossy seeds: cultivated for grain, hay, and as a source of syrup. See also **kaffir corn, durra.** [C16: from New Latin, from Italian *sorgo,* probably from Vulgar Latin *Syricum grānum* (unattested) Syrian grain]

sorgo *or* **sorgho** ('sɔːgəʊ) *n., pl.* **-gos** *or* **-ghos.** any of several varieties of sorghum that have watery sweet juice and are grown for fodder, silage, or syrup. [Italian]

sori ('sɔːraɪ) *n.* the plural of **sorus.**

soricine ('sɒrɪˌsaɪn) *adj.* of, relating to, or resembling the shrews or the family (*Soricidae*) to which they belong. [C18: from Latin *sōricīnus,* from *sōrex* a shrew]

sorites (sɒ'raɪtiːz) *n. Logic.* **a.** a polysyllogism in which the premises are arranged so that intermediate conclusions are omitted, being understood, and only the final conclusion is stated. **b.** a paradox of the form: *these few grains of sand do not constitute a heap, and the addition of a single grain never makes what is not yet a heap into a heap; so no matter how many single grains one adds it never becomes a heap.* [C16: via Latin from Greek *sōreitēs,* literally: heaped, from *sōros* a heap] —**soritical** (sɒ'rɪtɪkᵊl) *or* **so'ritic** *adj.*

sorn (sɔːn) *vb.* (*intr.,* often foll. by *on* or *upon*) *Scot.* to obtain food, lodging, etc., from another person by presuming on his generosity. [C16: from earlier *sorren* a feudal obligation requiring vassals to offer free hospitality to their lord and his men, from obsolete Irish *sorthan* free quarters]

Soroptimist (sə'rɒptɪmɪst) *n.* a member of an organization of clubs (Soroptimist International) for professional and executive businesswomen. [C20: from Latin *soror* sister + OPTIMIST]

sororate ('sɒrəˌreɪt) *n.* the custom in some societies of a widower marrying his deceased wife's younger sister. [C20: from Latin *soror* a sister]

sororicide (sə'rɒrɪˌsaɪd) *n.* **1.** the act of killing one's own sister. **2.** a person who kills his or her sister. [C17: from Latin *sorōricīda* one who murders his sister, from *soror* sister + *caedere* to slay] —**soˌrori'cidal** *adj.*

sorority (sə'rɒrɪtɪ) *n., pl.* **-ties.** *Chiefly U.S.* a social club or society for university women. [C16: from Medieval Latin *sorōritās,* from Latin *soror* sister]

sorosis (sə'rəʊsɪs) *n., pl.* **-ses** (-siːz). a fleshy multiple fruit, such as that of the pineapple and mulberry, formed from flowers that are crowded together on a fleshy stem. [C19: from New Latin, from Greek *sōros* a heap]

sorption ('sɔːpʃən) *n.* the process in which one substance takes up or holds another; adsorption or absorption. [C20: back formation from ABSORPTION, ADSORPTION]

sorrel[1] ('sɒrəl) *n.* **1. a.** a light brown to brownish-orange colour. **b.** (*as adj.*): *a sorrel carpet.* **2.** a horse of this colour. [C15: from

Old French *sorel,* from *sor* a reddish brown, of Germanic origin; related to Middle Dutch *soor* desiccated]

sorrel[2] ('sɒrəl) *n.* **1.** any of several polygonaceous plants of the genus *Rumex,* esp. *R. acetosa,* of Eurasia and North America, having acid-tasting leaves used in salads and sauces. See also **dock**[4], **sheep sorrel. 2.** short for **wood sorrel.** [C14: from Old French *surele,* from *sur* sour, of Germanic origin; related to Old High German *sūr* SOUR]

sorrel tree *n.* a deciduous ericaceous tree, *Oxydendrum arboreum,* of E North America, having deeply fissured bark, sour-tasting leaves, and small white flowers. Also called: **sourwood.** [C17: so called because the bitter flavour of the leaves is reminiscent of sorrel]

sorrow ('sɒrəʊ) *n.* **1.** the characteristic feeling of sadness, grief, or regret associated with loss, bereavement, sympathy for another's suffering, for an injury done, etc. **2.** a particular cause or source of regret, grief, etc. **3.** Also called: **sorrowing.** the outward expression of grief or sadness. ~*vb.* **4.** (*intr.*) to mourn or grieve. [Old English *sorg;* related to Old Norse *sorg,* Gothic *saurga,* Old High German *sworga*] —'**sorrower** *n.* —'**sorrowful** *adj.* —'**sorrowfully** *adv.* —'**sorrowfulness** *n.*

sorry ('sɒrɪ) *adj.* **-rier, -riest. 1.** (*usually postpositive;* often foll. by *for*) feeling or expressing pity, sympathy, remorse, grief, or regret: *I feel sorry for him.* **2.** pitiful, wretched, or deplorable: *a sorry sight.* **3.** poor; paltry: *a sorry excuse.* **4.** affected by sorrow; sad. **5.** causing sorrow or sadness. ~*interj.* **6.** an exclamation expressing apology, used esp. at the time of the misdemeanour, offence, etc. [Old English *sārig;* related to Old High German *sērag;* see SORE] —'**sorrily** *adv.* —'**sorriness** *n.*

sort (sɔːt) *n.* **1.** a class, group, kind, etc., as distinguished by some common quality or characteristic. **2.** *Informal.* type of character, nature, etc.: *he's a good sort.* **3.** a more or less definable or adequate example: *it's a sort of review.* **4.** (*often pl.*) *Printing.* any of the individual characters making up a fount of type. **5.** *Archaic.* manner; way: *in this sort we struggled home.* **6. after a sort.** to some extent. **7. of sorts** *or* **of a sort. a.** of an inferior kind. **b.** of an indefinite kind. **8. out of sorts.** not in normal good health, temper, etc. **9. sort of.** in some way or other; as it were; rather. ~*vb.* **10.** (*tr.*) to arrange according to class, type, etc. **11.** (*tr.*) to put (something) into working order. **12.** (*tr.*) to arrange (computer information) by machine in an order convenient to the computer user. **13.** (*tr.;* foll. by *with*) *Scot.* to supply (with). **14.** (*intr.;* foll. by *with, together,* etc.) *Archaic or dialect.* to associate, as on friendly terms. **15.** (*intr.*) *Archaic.* to agree; accord. [C14: from Old French, from Medieval Latin *sors* kind, from Latin: fate] —'**sortable** *adj.* —'**sortably** *adv.* —'**sorter** *n.*

▷**Usage.** See at **kind**[2].

sortal ('sɔːtəl) *n. Logic, linguistics.* **1.** a concept grasp of which includes knowledge of criteria of individuation and reidentification, such as *dog* or *concerto,* but not *flesh* or *music.* **2.** a count noun representing such a concept.

sortie ('sɔːtɪ) *n.* **1. a.** (of troops, etc.) the act of emerging from a contained or besieged position. **b.** the troops doing this. **2.** an operational flight made by one aircraft. ~*vb.* **-ties, -tieing, -tied. 3.** (*intr.*) to make a sortie. [C17: from French: a going out, from *sortir* to go out]

sortilege ('sɔːtɪlɪdʒ) *n.* **1.** the act or practice of divination by drawing lots. **2.** magic or sorcery. [C14: via Old French from Medieval Latin *sortilegium,* from Latin *sortilegus* a soothsayer, from *sors* fate + *legere* to select]

sortition (sɔː'tɪʃən) *n.* the act of casting lots. [C16: from Latin *sortitio,* from *sortiri* to cast lots]

sort out *vb.* (*tr., adv.*) **1.** to find a solution to (a problem, etc.), esp. to make clear or tidy: *it took a long time to sort out the mess.* **2.** to take or separate, as from a larger group: *he sorted out the most likely ones.* **3.** to organize into an orderly and disciplined group. **4.** *Informal.* to beat or punish.

sorus ('sɔːrəs) *n., pl.* **-ri** (-raɪ). **1.** a cluster of sporangia on the undersurface of certain fern leaves. **2.** any of various similar spore-producing structures in some lichens and fungi. [C19: via New Latin from Greek *sōros* a heap]

SOS *n.* **1.** an internationally recognized distress signal in which the letters SOS are repeatedly spelt out, as by radio-telegraphy: used esp. by ships and aircraft. **2.** a message broadcast in an emergency for people otherwise unobtainable. **3.** *Informal.* a call for help. [C20: letters chosen as the simplest to transmit and receive in Morse code; by folk etymology taken to be abbrev. for *save our souls*]

sosatie (sə'sɑːtɪ) *n. S. African.* a skewer of curried meat pieces. [Afrikaans]

so-so *Informal.* ~*adj.* **1.** (*postpositive*) neither good nor bad. ~*adv.* **2.** in an average or indifferent manner.

sostenuto (ˌsɒstə'nuːtəʊ) *adj., adv. Music.* (preceded by a tempo marking) to be performed in a smooth sustained manner. [C18: from Italian, from *sostenere* to sustain, from Latin *sustinēre* to uphold]

sostenuto pedal *n.* another word for **sustaining pedal.**

sot[1] (sɒt) *n.* **1.** a habitual or chronic drunkard. **2.** a person stupefied by or as if by drink. [Old English, from Medieval Latin *sottus;* compare French *sot* a fool] —'**sottish** *adj.*

sot[2] (sɒt) *adv. Scot.* indeed: used to contradict a negative statement: *I am not!—You are sot!* [a variant of SO[1], altered to rhyme with *not*]

soteriology (sɒˌtɪərɪ'ɒlədʒɪ) *n. Theol.* the doctrine of salvation. [C19: from Greek *sōtēria* deliverance (from *sōtēr* a saviour) + -LOGY] —**soteriologic** (sɒˌtɪərɪə'lɒdʒɪk) *or* **soˌterio'logical** *adj.*

Sothic ('səʊθɪk, 'sɒθ-) *adj.* relating to the star Sirius or to the rising of this star. [C19: from Greek *Sōthis,* from Egyptian, name of Sirius]

Sothic year *n.* the fixed year of the ancient Egyptians, 365 days 6 hours long, beginning with the appearance of the star Sirius on the eastern horizon at dawn, which heralded the yearly flooding of the Nile. A **Sothic cycle** contained 1460 such years.

Sothis ('səʊθɪs) *n.* another name for **Sirius.** [Greek; see SOTHIC]

Sotho ('suːtʊ, 'səʊtəʊ) *n.* **1.** (*pl.* **-tho** *or* **-thos**) a member of a large grouping of Negroid peoples of southern Africa, living chiefly in Botswana, South Africa, and Lesotho. **2.** the group of mutually intelligible languages of this people, including Lesotho, Tswana, and Pedi. It belongs to the Bantu group of the Niger-Congo family. **3.** (*pl.* **-tho** *or* **-thos**) *S. African.* a member of the Basotho people; a Mosotho. **4.** *S. African.* the dialect of Sotho spoken by the Basotho; Sesotho. It is an official language of Lesotho along with English. ~Former name (for senses 3, 4): **Basuto.**

sotto voce ('sɒtəʊ 'vəʊtʃɪ) *adv.* in an undertone. [C18: from Italian: under (one's) voice]

sou (suː) *n.* **1.** a former French coin of low denomination. **2.** a very small amount of money: *I haven't a sou to my name.* [C19: from French, from Old French *sol,* from Latin: SOLIDUS]

soubise (suː'biːz) *n.* a purée of onions mixed into a thick white sauce and served over eggs, fish, etc. Also called: **soubise sauce.** [C18: named after Charles de Rohan *Soubise* (1715–87), marshal of France]

soubrette (suː'brɛt) *n.* **1.** a minor female role in comedy, often that of a pert lady's maid. **2.** any pert or flirtatious girl. [C18: from French: maidservant, from Provençal *soubreto,* from *soubret* conceited, from *soubra* to exceed, from Latin *superāre* to surmount, from *super* above] —**sou'brettish** *adj.*

soubriquet ('səʊbrɪˌkeɪ) *n.* a variant spelling of **sobriquet.**

souchong ('suː'ʃɒŋ, -'tʃɒŋ) *n.* a black tea with large leaves. [C18: from Chinese *hsiao-chung* small kind]

souffle ('suːfᵊl) *n. Med.* a blowing sound or murmur heard in auscultation. [C19: from French, from *souffler* to blow]

soufflé ('suːfleɪ) *n.* **1.** a very light fluffy dish made with egg yolks and stiffly beaten egg whites combined with cheese, fish, etc. **2.** a similar sweet or savoury cold dish, set with gelatin. ~*adj., also* **souffléed. 3.** made light and puffy, as by beating and cooking. [C19: from French, from *souffler* to blow, from Latin *sufflāre*]

sough[1] (saʊ) *vb.* **1.** (*intr.*) (esp. of the wind) to make a characteristic sighing sound. ~*n.* **2.** a soft continuous murmuring sound. [Old English *swōgan* to resound; related to Gothic *gaswogjan* to groan, Lithuanian *svageti* to sound, Latin *vāgīre* to lament]

sough[2] (sʌf) *n. Northern English dialect.* a sewer or drain or an outlet channel. [of obscure origin]

sought (sɔːt) *vb.* the past tense and past participle of **seek.**

sought-after *adj.* in demand; wanted.

souk[1] *or* **suq** (suːk) *n.* (in Muslim countries, esp. North Africa and the Middle East) an open-air marketplace. [C20: from Arabic *sūq*]

souk[2] (suːk) *vb., n. Scot.* a variant spelling of **sook**[2].

soukous ('suːkʊs) *n.* a style of African popular music that originated in Zaïre, characterized by syncopated rhythms and intricate contrasting guitar melodies. [C20: perhaps from French *secouer* to shake]

soul (səʊl) *n.* **1.** the spirit or immaterial part of man, the seat of human personality, intellect, will, and emotions, regarded as an entity that survives the body after death. **2.** *Christianity.* the spiritual part of a person, capable of redemption from the power of sin through divine grace. **3.** the essential part or fundamental nature of anything. **4.** a person's feelings or moral nature as distinct from other faculties. **5. a.** Also called: **soul music.** a type of Black music resulting from the addition of jazz, gospel, and pop elements to the urban blues style. **b.** (*as modifier*): *a soul singer.* **6.** (*modifier*) of or relating to Black Americans and their culture: *soul brother; soul food.* **7.** nobility of spirit or temperament: *a man of great soul and courage.* **8.** an inspiring spirit or leading figure, as of a cause or movement. **9. the life and soul.** See **life** (sense 27). **10.** a person regarded as typifying some characteristic or quality: *the soul of discretion.* **11.** a person; individual: *an honest soul.* **12. upon my soul!** an exclamation of surprise. [Old English *sāwol;* related to Old Frisian *sēle,* Old Saxon *sēola,* Old High German *sēula* soul] —'**soul-ˌlike** *adj.*

Soul (səʊl) *n. Christian Science.* another word for **God.**

soul-destroying *adj.* (of an occupation, situation, etc.) unremittingly monotonous.

soul food *n. Informal.* food, such as chitterlings or yams, traditionally eaten by southern U.S. Negroes.

soulful ('səʊlfʊl) *adj. Sometimes ironic.* expressing profound thoughts or feelings: *soulful music.* —'**soulfully** *adv.* —'**soulfulness** *n.*

soulless ('səʊllɪs) *adj.* **1.** lacking any humanizing qualities or influences; dead; mechanical: *soulless work.* **2.** (of a person) lacking in sensitivity or nobility. 3. heartless; cruel. —'**soullessly** *adv.* —'**soullessness** *n.*

soul mate *n.* a person for whom one has a deep affinity, esp. a lover, wife, husband, etc.

soul-searching *n.* **1.** deep or critical examination of one's motives, actions, beliefs, etc. ~*adj.* **2.** displaying the characteristics of deep or painful self-analysis.

sou marqué ('suː mɑː'keɪ; *French* su marke) *n., pl.* **sous marqués** ('su mɑː'keɪz; *French* su marke). a French copper coin of the 18th century. [French, literally: a marked sou]

sound[1] (saʊnd) *n.* **1. a.** a periodic disturbance in the pressure or density of a fluid or in the elastic strain of a solid, produced by a vibrating object. It has a velocity in air at sea level at 0°C of 332 metres per second (743 miles per hour) and travels as longitudinal waves. **b.** (*as modifier*): *a sound wave.* **2.** (*modifier*) of or relating to radio as distinguished from television: *sound broadcasting; sound radio.* **3.** the sensation produced by such a periodic disturbance in the organs of hearing. **4.** anything that can be heard. **5.** a particular instance, quality, or type of sound: *the sound of running water.* **6.** volume or quality of sound: *a radio with poor sound.* **7.** the area or distance over which something can be heard: *to be born within the sound of Big Ben.* **8.** the impression or implication of something: *I don't like the sound of that.* **9.** *Phonetics.* the auditory effect produced by a specific articulation or set of related articulations. **10.** (*often pl.*) *Slang.* music, esp. rock, jazz, or pop. **11.** *Rare.* report, news, or information, as about a person, event, etc. ~*vb.* **12.** to cause (something, such as an instrument) to make a sound or (of an instrument, etc.) to emit a sound. **13.** to announce or be announced by a sound: *to sound the alarm.* **14.** (*intr.*) (of a sound) to be heard. **15.** (*intr.*) to resonate with a certain quality or intensity: *to sound loud.* **16.** (*copula*) to give the impression of being as specified when read, heard, etc.: *to sound reasonable.* **17.** (*tr.*) to pronounce distinctly or audibly: *to sound one's consonants.* **18.** (*intr.*; usually foll. by *in*) *Law.* to have the essential quality or nature (of): *an action sounding in damages.* ~See also **sound off.** [C13: from Old French *soner* to make a sound, from Latin *sonāre,* from *sonus* a sound] —'**soundable** *adj.*

sound[2] (saʊnd) *adj.* **1.** free from damage, injury, decay, etc. **2.** firm; solid; substantial: *a sound basis.* **3.** financially safe or stable: *a sound investment.* **4.** showing good judgment or reasoning; sensible; wise: *sound advice.* **5.** valid, logical, or justifiable: *a sound argument.* **6.** holding approved beliefs; ethically correct; upright; honest. **7.** (of sleep) deep; peaceful; unbroken. **8.** thorough; complete: *a sound examination.* **9.** *Law.* (of a title, etc.) free from defect; legally valid. **10.** constituting a valid and justifiable application of correct principles; orthodox: *sound theology.* **11.** *Logic.* **a.** (of a deductive argument) valid. **b.** (of an inductive argument) according with whatever principles ensure the high probability of the truth of the conclusion given the truth of the premises. **c.** another word for **consistent** (sense 4b). ~*adv.* **12.** soundly; deeply: now archaic except when applied to sleep. [Old English *sund;* related to Old Saxon *gisund,* Old High German *gisunt*] —'**soundly** *adv.* —'**soundness** *n.*

sound[3] (saʊnd) *vb.* **1.** to measure the depth of (a well, the sea, etc.) by lowering a plumb line, by sonar, etc. **2.** to seek to discover (someone's views, etc.), as by questioning. **3.** (*intr.*) (of a whale, etc.) to dive downwards swiftly and deeply. **4.** *Med.* **a.** to probe or explore (a bodily cavity or passage) by means of a sound. **b.** to examine (a patient) by means of percussion and auscultation. ~*n.* **5.** *Med.* an instrument for insertion into a bodily cavity or passage to dilate strictures, dislodge foreign material, etc. ~See also **sound out.** [C14: from Old French *sonder,* from *sonde* sounding line, probably of Germanic origin; related to Old English *sundgyrd* sounding pole, Old Norse *sund* strait, SOUND[4]; see SWIM]

sound[4] (saʊnd) *n.* **1.** a relatively narrow channel between two larger areas of sea or between an island and the mainland. **2.** an inlet or deep bay of the sea. **3.** the air bladder of a fish. [Old English *sund* swimming, narrow sea; related to Middle Low German *sunt* strait; see SOUND[3]]

sound barrier *n.* (*not in technical usage*) a hypothetical barrier to flight at or above the speed of sound, when a sudden large increase in drag occurs. Also called: **sonic barrier, transonic barrier.**

sound bite *n.* a short pithy sentence or phrase extracted from a longer speech for use on radio or television.

sound bow (bəʊ) *n.* the thick part of a bell against which the hammer strikes.

soundbox ('saʊndˌbɒks) *n.* the resonating chamber of the hollow body of a violin, guitar, etc.

sound check *n.* an on-the-spot rehearsal by a band before a gig to enable the sound engineer to set up the mixer.

sound effect *n.* any sound artificially produced, reproduced from a recording, etc., to create a theatrical effect, such as the bringing together of two halves of a hollow coconut shell to simulate a horse's gallop; used in plays, films, etc.

sounder[1] ('saʊndə) *n.* an electromagnetic device formerly used in telegraphy to convert electric signals sent over wires into audible sounds.

sounder[2] ('saʊndə) *n.* a person or device that measures the depth of water, etc.

sound head *n.* the part of a film projector that reproduces the sound in a film.

sound hole *n.* any of variously shaped apertures in the sounding board of certain stringed instruments, such as the *'f'* shaped holes of a violin.

sounding[1] ('saʊndɪŋ) *adj.* **1.** resounding; resonant. **2.** having an imposing sound and little content; pompous: *sounding phrases.* —'**soundingly** *adv.*

sounding[2] ('saʊndɪŋ) *n.* **1.** (*sometimes pl.*) the act or process of measuring depth of water or examining the bottom of a river, lake, etc., as with a sounding line. **2.** an observation or measurement of atmospheric conditions, as made using a radiosonde or rocketsonde. **3.** (*often pl.*) measurements taken by sounding. **4.** (*pl.*) a place where a sounding line will reach the bottom, esp. less than 100 fathoms in depth. **5. on** (*or* **off**) **soundings.** in waters less than (or more than) 100 fathoms in depth.

sounding board *n.* **1.** Also called: **soundboard.** a thin wooden board in a piano or comprising the upper surface of a resonating chamber in a violin, cello, etc., serving to amplify the vibrations produced by the strings passing across it. See also **belly** (sense 6). **2.** Also called: **soundboard.** a thin screen suspended over a pulpit, stage, etc., to reflect sound towards an audience. **3.** a person, group, experiment, etc., used to test a new idea, policy, etc., for acceptance or applicability.

sounding lead (lɛd) *n.* a lead weight, usually conical and having a depression in the base for a dab of grease so that, when dropped to the bottom on a sounding line, a sample of sand, gravel, etc., can be retrieved.

sounding line *n.* a line marked off to indicate its length and having a sounding lead at one end. It is dropped over the side of a vessel to determine the depth of the water.

soundless[1] ('saʊndlɪs) *adj.* extremely still or silent. —'**soundlessly** *adv.* —'**soundlessness** *n.*

soundless[2] ('saʊndlɪs) *adj. Chiefly poetic.* extremely deep.

sound mixer *n. Films, radio, etc.* **1.** the person who mixes various sound sources into a composite programme. **2.** a piece of equipment designed for mixing sound.

sound off *vb.* (*intr., adv.*) **1.** to proclaim loudly, as in venting one's opinions, grievances, etc. **2.** to speak angrily.

sound out *vb.* (*tr., adv.*) to question (someone) in order to discover (opinions, facts, etc.).

soundpost ('saʊndˌpəʊst) *n. Music.* a small post, usually of pine, on guitars, violins, etc., that joins the front surface to the back, helps to support the bridge, and allows the whole body of the instrument to vibrate.

soundproof ('saʊndˌpruːf) *adj.* **1.** not penetrable by sound. ~*vb.* **2.** (*tr.*) to render soundproof.

sound ranging *n.* the determination of the location of a source of sound waves by measuring the time lapse between their transmission and their reception at microphones situated at three or more known positions.

sound shift *n.* a gradual alteration or series of alterations in the pronunciation of a set of sounds, esp. of vowels. See also **Great Vowel Shift.**

sound spectrograph *n.* an electronic instrument that produces a record (**sound spectrogram**) of the way in which the frequencies and intensities of the components of a sound, such as a spoken word, vary with time.

sound system *n.* **1.** any system of sounds, as in the speech of a language. **2.** integrated equipment for producing amplified sound, as in a hi-fi or a mobile disco, or as a public-address system on stage.

soundtrack ('saʊndˌtræk) *n.* **1.** the recorded sound accompaniment to a film. Compare **commentary** (sense 2). **2.** a narrow strip along the side of a spool of film, which carries the sound accompaniment.

sound truck *n.* the U.S. and Canadian name for a **loudspeaker van.**

sound wave *n.* a wave that propagates sound.

soup (suːp) *n.* **1.** a liquid food made by boiling or simmering meat, fish, vegetables, etc., usually served hot at the beginning of a meal. **2.** *Informal.* a photographic developer. **3.** *Informal.* anything resembling soup in appearance or consistency, esp. thick fog. See also **peasouper.** **4.** a slang name for **nitroglycerin.** **5. in the soup.** *Informal.* in trouble or difficulties. [C17: from Old French *soupe,* from Late Latin *suppa,* of Germanic origin; compare Middle High German *suppe,* Old Norse *soppa* soup]

soupçon *French.* (supsɔ̃) *n.* a slight amount; dash. [C18: from French, ultimately from Latin *suspicio* SUSPICION]

soupfin *or* **soupfin shark** ('suːpˌfɪn) *n.* a Pacific requiem shark, *Galeorhinus zyopterus,* valued for its fins, which are used to make soup.

soup kitchen *n.* **1.** a place or mobile stall where food and drink, esp. soup, is served to destitute people. **2.** *Military.* a mobile kitchen.

soup plate *n.* a deep plate with a wide rim, used esp. for drinking soup.

soup up *vb.* (*tr., adv.*) *Slang.* to modify (a car or motorcycle engine) in order to increase its power. Also: **hot up** *or* (esp. U.S. and Canadian) **hop up.**

soupy ('suːpɪ) *adj.* **soupier, soupiest.** **1.** having the appearance or consistency of soup. **2.** *Informal, chiefly U.S. and Canadian.* emotional or sentimental.

sour ('saʊə) *adj.* **1.** having or denoting a sharp biting taste like that of lemon juice or vinegar. Compare **bitter** (sense 1). **2.** made acid or bad, as in the case of milk or alcohol, by the action of microorganisms. **3.** having a rancid or unwholesome smell. **4.** (of a person's temperament) sullen, morose, or disagreeable. **5.** (esp. of the weather or climate) harsh and unpleasant. **6.** disagreeable; distasteful: *a sour experience.* **7.** (of land, etc.) lacking in fertility, esp. due to excessive acidity. **8.** (of oil, gas, or petrol) containing a relatively large amount of sulphur compounds. **9. go** *or* **turn sour.** to become unfavourable or inharmonious: *his marriage went sour.* ~*n.* **10.** something sour. **11.** *Chiefly U.S.* any of several iced drinks usually made with spirits, lemon juice, and ice: *a whiskey sour.* **12.** an acid used in laundering and bleaching clothes or in curing animal skins. ~*vb.* **13.** to make or become sour. [Old English *sūr;* related to Old Norse *sūrr,* Lithuanian *suras* salty, Old Slavonic *syrŭ* wet, raw, *surovu* green, raw, Sanskrit *surā* brandy] —'**sourish** *adj.* —'**sourly** *adv.* —'**sourness** *n.*

source (sɔːs) *n.* **1.** the point or place from which something originates. **2. a.** a spring that forms the starting point of a stream; headspring. **b.** the area where the headwaters of a river rise: *the source of the Nile.* **3.** a person, group, etc., that creates, issues, or originates something: *the source of a complaint.* **4. a.** any person, book, organization, etc., from which information, evidence, etc., is obtained. **b.** (*as modifier*): *source material.* **5.** anything, such as a story or work of art, that provides a model or inspiration for a later work. **6.** *Electronics.* the electrode region in a field-effect transistor from which majority carriers flow into the interelectrode conductivity channel. **7. at source.** at the point of origin. ~*vb.* **8.** (*tr.*) to establish an originator or source of (a product, piece of information, etc.). [C14: from Old French *sors,* from *sourdre* to spring forth, from Latin *surgere* to rise]

source document *n.* a document that has been or will be transcribed to a word processor or to the memory bank of a computer.

source program *n.* an original computer program written by a programmer that is converted into the equivalent object program, written in machine language, by the compiler or assembler.

sour cherry *n.* **1.** a Eurasian rosaceous tree, *Prunus cerasus,* with white flowers: cultivated for its tart red fruits. **2.** the fruit of this tree. Compare **sweet cherry.** See also **morello, amarelle.**

sour cream *n.* cream soured by lactic acid bacteria, used in making salads, dips, etc. Also called: **soured cream.**

sourdine (sʊə'diːn) *n. Music.* **1.** a soft stop on an organ or harmonium. **2.** another word for **sordino.** [C17 (meaning: a muted trumpet): from French: a mute, from Italian; see SORDINO]

sourdough ('saʊəˌdəʊ) *adj.* **1.** *Dialect.* (of bread) made with fermented dough used as a leaven. ~*n.* **2.** (in Western U.S., Canada, and Alaska) an old-time prospector or pioneer.

sour gourd *n.* **1.** a large bombacaceous tree, *Adansonia gregorii,* of N Australia, having gourdlike fruit. **2.** the acid-tasting fruit of this tree, which has a woody rind and large seeds. **3.** the fruit of the baobab tree.

sour grapes *n.* (*functioning as sing.*) the attitude of affecting to despise something because one cannot or does not have it oneself. [from a fable by Aesop]

sour gum *n.* a cornaceous tree, *Nyssa sylvatica,* of the eastern U.S., having glossy leaves, soft wood, and sour purplish fruits. Also called: **black gum, pepperidge.** See also **tupelo.** Compare **sweet gum.**

sour mash *n. U.S.* **1.** a grain mash for use in distilling certain whiskeys, consisting of a mixture of new and old mash. **2.** any whiskey distilled from such a mash.

sourpuss ('saʊəˌpʊs) *n. Informal.* a person whose facial expression or nature is habitually gloomy or sullen. [C20: from SOUR + PUSS[2]]

soursop ('saʊəˌsɒp) *n.* **1.** a small West Indian tree, *Annona muricata,* having large spiny fruit: family *Annonaceae.* **2.** the fruit of this tree, which has a tart edible pulp. Compare **sweetsop.** [C19: so called because of the flavour and consistency of the pulp]

sourwood ('saʊəˌwʊd) *n.* another name for **sorrel tree.**

sousaphone ('suːzəˌfəʊn) *n. Music.* a large tuba that encircles the player's body and has a bell facing forwards. [C20: named after J. P. *Sousa* (1854–1932), U.S. bandmaster and composer] —'**sousaˌphonist** *n.*

souse[1] (saʊs) *vb.* **1.** to plunge (something, oneself, etc.) into water or other liquid. **2.** to drench or be drenched. **3.** (*tr.*) to pour or dash (liquid) over (a person or thing). **4.** to steep or cook (food) in a marinade. **5.** (*tr.*) *Slang.* to make drunk. ~*n.* **6.** the liquid or brine used in pickling. **7.** the act or process of sousing. **8.** *Slang.* a habitual drunkard. [C14: from Old French *sous,* of Germanic origin; related to Old High German *sulza* brine]

souse[2] (saʊs) *Falconry.* (of hawks or falcons) ~*vb.* (*intr.*) **1.** (often foll. by *on* or *upon*) to swoop suddenly downwards (on a prey). ~*n.* **2.** a sudden downward swoop. [C16: perhaps a variant of obsolete vb. sense of SOURCE]

souslik ('suːslɪk) *n.* a variant spelling of **suslik.**

sou-sou *or* **susu** ('suːsuː) *n. Caribbean.* an arrangement made among friends whereby each person makes regular contributions to a fund, the money being drawn out periodically by each individual in turn. [probably of W African origin, influenced by French *sou* small coin, via Creole]

soutache (suː'tæʃ) *n.* a narrow braid used as a decorative trimming. [C19: from French, from Hungarian *sujtas*]

soutane (suː'tæn) *n. R.C. Church.* a priest's cassock. [C19: from French, from Old Italian *sottana,* from Medieval Latin *subtanus* (adj.) (worn) beneath, from Latin *subtus* below]

souter *or* **soutar** ('suːtər) *n. Scot. and northern English.* a shoemaker or cobbler. [Old English *sūtere,* from Latin *sutor,* from *suere* to sew]

souterrain ('suːtəˌreɪn) *n. Archaeol.* an underground chamber or passage. [C18: from French]

south (saʊθ) *n.* **1.** one of the four cardinal points of the compass, at 180° from north and 90° clockwise from east and anticlockwise from west. **2.** the direction along a meridian towards the South Pole. **3. the south.** (*often cap.*) any area lying in or towards the south. Related adjs.: **meridional, austral.** **4.** (*usually cap.*) *Cards.* the player or position at the table corresponding to south on the compass. ~*adj.* **5.** situated in, moving towards, or facing the south. **6.** (esp. of the wind) from the south. ~*adv.* **7.** in, to, or towards the south. **8.** *Archaic.* (of the wind) from the south. ~Symbol: **S** [Old English *sūth;* related to Old Norse *suthr* southward, Old High German *sundan* from the south]

South (saʊθ) *n.* **the. 1.** the southern part of a country, esp. the southern area of England or the southern states of the U.S. **2.** the countries of the world that are not economically and technically advanced. ~*adj.* **3. a.** of or denoting the southern part of a specified country, area, etc. **b.** (*cap. as part of a name*): *the South Pacific.*

South African *adj.* **1.** of or relating to the Republic of South Africa, its inhabitants, or any of their languages. ~*n.* **2.** a native or inhabitant of the Republic of South Africa.

South African Dutch *n.* (not used in South Africa) another name for **Afrikaans.**

South American *adj.* **1.** of or relating to the continent of South America, or to its peoples, climate, vegetation, etc. ~*n.* **2.** a native or inhabitant of South America.

South American trypanosomiasis *n. Pathol.* another name for **Chagas' disease.**

southbound ('saʊθˌbaʊnd) *adj.* going or leading towards the south.

south by east *n.* **1.** one point on the compass east of south; 168° 45′ clockwise from north. ~*adj., adv.* **2.** in, from, or towards this direction.

south by west *n.* **1.** one point on the compass west of south; 191° 15′ clockwise from north. ~*adj., adv.* **2.** in, from, or towards this direction.

Southdown ('saʊθˌdaʊn) *n.* an English breed of sheep with short wool and a greyish-brown face and legs. [C18: so called because it was originally bred on the *South Downs,* S England]

southeast (ˌsaʊθ'iːst; *Nautical* ˌsaʊ'iːst) *n.* **1.** the point of the compass or the direction midway between south and east, 135° clockwise from north. ~*adj. also* **southeastern.** **2.** (*sometimes cap.*) of or denoting the southeastern part of a specified country, area, etc. **3.** situated in, proceeding towards, or facing the southeast. **4.** (esp. of the wind) from the southeast. ~*adv.* **5.** in, to, towards, or (esp. of the wind) from the southeast. ~Symbol: **SE** —ˌ**south'easternmost** *adj.*

southeast by east *n.* **1.** one point on the compass north of southeast; 123° 45′ clockwise from north. ~*adj., adv.* **2.** in, from, or towards this direction.

southeast by south *n.* **1.** one point on the compass south of southeast; 146° 15′ clockwise from north. ~*adj., adv.* **2.** in, from, or towards this direction.

southeaster (ˌsaʊθ'iːstə; *Nautical* ˌsaʊ'iːstə) *n.* a strong wind or storm from the southeast.

southeasterly (ˌsaʊθ'iːstəlɪ; *Nautical* ˌsaʊ'iːstəlɪ) *adj., adv.* **1.** in, towards, or (esp. of a wind) from the southeast. ~*n., pl.* **-lies.** **2.** a strong wind or storm from the southeast.

southeastward (ˌsaʊθ'iːstwəd; *Nautical* ˌsaʊ'iːstwəd) *adj.* **1.** towards or (esp. of a wind) from the southeast. ~*n.* **2.** a direction towards or area in the southeast. ~*adv.* **3.** a variant of **southeastwards.**

southeastwards (ˌsaʊθ'iːstwədz; *Nautical* ˌsaʊ'iːstwədz) *or* **southeastward** *adv.* to the southeast.

souther ('saʊðə) *n.* a strong wind or storm from the south.

southerly ('sʌðəlɪ) *adj.* **1.** of, relating to, or situated in the south. ~*adv., adj.* **2.** towards or in the direction of the south. **3.** from the south: *a southerly wind.* ~*n., pl.* **-lies.** **4.** a wind from the south. —'**southerliness** *n.*

southerly buster *n.* (*sometimes caps.*) a sudden violent cold wind on the SE coast of Australia causing a rapid drop in temperature. Sometimes shortened to **southerly.**

southern ('sʌðən) *adj.* **1.** situated in or towards the south. **2.** (of a wind, etc.) coming from the south. **3.** native to, inhabiting, or growing in the south. **4.** (*sometimes cap.*) of, relating to, or characteristic of the south or South. **5.** (*sometimes cap.*) *Astronomy.* south of the celestial equator.

Southern British English *n.* the dialect of spoken English regarded as standard in England and considered as having high social status in comparison with other British English dialects. Historically, it is derived from the S East Midland dialect of Middle English. Abbrev.: **SBE.** See also **Received Pronunciation.**

Southern Cross *n.* **1.** a small conspicuous constellation in the S hemisphere lying in the Milky Way near Centaurus. The four brightest stars form a cross the longer arm of which points to the south celestial pole. Formal names: **Crux, Crux Australis. 2.** *Austral.* the flag flown at the Eureka Stockade.

Southerner (ˈsʌðənə) *n.* (*sometimes not cap.*) a native or inhabitant of the south of any specified region, esp. the South of England or the Southern states of the U.S.

southern hemisphere *n.* (*often caps.*) **1.** that half of the earth lying south of the equator. **2.** *Astronomy.* that half of the celestial sphere lying south of the celestial equator. ~Abbrev.: **S hemisphere.**

southern lights *pl. n.* another name for **aurora australis.**

southernly (ˈsʌðənlɪ) *adj., adv.* a less common word for **southerly.**

southernmost (ˈsʌðənˌməʊst) *adj.* situated or occurring farthest south.

Southern Sotho *n.* another name for **Sesotho.**

southernwood (ˈsʌðənˌwʊd) *n.* an aromatic shrubby wormwood, *Artemisia abrotanum,* of S Europe, having finely dissected leaves and small drooping heads of yellowish flowers. Also called: **old man, lad's love.** [Old English. See SOUTHERN, WOOD]

southing (ˈsaʊðɪŋ) *n.* **1.** *Navigation.* movement, deviation, or distance covered in a southerly direction. **2.** *Astronomy.* a south or negative declination.

southpaw (ˈsaʊθˌpɔː) *Informal.* ~*n.* **1.** a boxer who leads with his right hand and off his right foot as opposed to the orthodox style of leading with the left. **2.** any left-handed person. ~*adj.* **3.** of or relating to a southpaw. [C20: from PAW (in the sense: hand): originally a term applied to a left-handed baseball player: perhaps so called because baseball pitchers traditionally face west, so that a left-handed pitcher would throw with the hand on the south side of his body]

South Pole *n.* **1.** the southernmost point on the earth's axis, at the latitude of 90°S. **2.** *Astronomy.* the point of intersection, in the constellation Octans, of the earth's extended axis and the southern half of the celestial sphere. **3.** (*usually not caps.*) the south-seeking pole of a freely suspended magnet.

Southron (ˈsʌðrən) *n.* **1.** *Chiefly Scot.* a Southerner, esp. an Englishman. **2.** *Scot.* the English language as spoken in England. **3.** *Dialect, chiefly southern U.S.* an inhabitant of the South, esp. at the time of the Civil War. ~*adj.* **4.** *Chiefly Scot.* of or relating to the South or to England. [C15: Scottish variant of SOUTHERN]

South Sea Bubble *n. Brit. history.* the financial crash that occurred in 1720 after the **South Sea Company** had taken over the national debt in return for a monopoly of trade with the South Seas, causing feverish speculation in their stocks. [so named because the rapid expansion and sudden collapse of investment resembled the blowing up and bursting of a bubble]

south-southeast *n.* **1.** the point on the compass or the direction midway between southeast and south; 157° 30′ clockwise from north. ~*adj., adv.* **2.** in, from, or towards this direction. ~Symbol: **SSE**

south-southwest *n.* **1.** the point on the compass or the direction midway between south and southwest; 202° 30′ clockwise from north. ~*adj., adv.* **2.** in, from, or towards this direction. ~Symbol: **SSW**

southward (ˈsaʊθwəd; *Nautical* ˈsʌðəd) *adj.* **1.** situated, directed, or moving towards the south. ~*n.* **2.** the southward part, direction, etc.; the south. ~*adv.* **3.** a variant of **southwards.** —ˈ**southwardly** *adj., adv.*

southwards (ˈsaʊθwədz; *Nautical* ˈsʌðədz) *or* **southward** *adv.* towards the south.

southwest (ˌsaʊθˈwɛst; *Nautical* ˌsaʊˈwɛst) *n.* **1.** the point of the compass or the direction midway between west and south, 225° clockwise from north. ~*adj. also* **southwestern. 2.** (*sometimes cap.*) of or denoting the southwestern part of a specified country, area, etc.: *southwest Italy.* **3.** situated in or towards the southwest. **4.** (esp. of the wind) from the southwest. ~*adv.* **5.** in, to, towards, or (esp. of the wind) from the southwest. ~Symbol: **SW** —ˌ**south**ˈ**westernmost** *adj.*

southwest by south *n.* **1.** one point on the compass south of southwest; 213° 45′ clockwise from north. ~*adj., adv.* **2.** in, from, or towards this direction.

southwest by west *n.* **1.** one point on the compass north of southwest, 236° 15′ clockwise from north. ~*adj., adv.* **2.** in, from, or towards this direction.

southwester (ˌsaʊθˈwɛstə; *Nautical* ˌsaʊˈwɛstə) *n.* a strong wind or storm from the southwest.

southwesterly (ˌsaʊθˈwɛstəlɪ; *Nautical* ˌsaʊˈwɛstəlɪ) *adj., adv.* **1.** in, towards, or (esp. of a wind) from the southwest. ~*n., pl.* **-lies. 2.** a wind or storm from the southwest.

southwestward (ˌsaʊθˈwɛstwəd; *Nautical* ˌsaʊˈwɛstwəd) *adj.* **1.** from or towards the southwest. ~*adv.* **2.** a variant of **southwestwards.** ~*n.* **3.** a direction towards or area in the southwest. —ˌ**south**ˈ**westwardly** *adj., adv.*

southwestwards (ˌsaʊθˈwɛstwədz; *Nautical* ˌsaʊˈwɛstwədz) *or* **southwestward** *adv.* to the southwest.

souvenir (ˌsuːvəˈnɪə, ˈsuːvəˌnɪə) *n.* **1.** an object that recalls a certain place, occasion, or person; memento. **2.** *Rare.* a thing recalled. ~*vb.* (*tr.*) **3.** *Austral. and N.Z., euphemistic.* to steal or keep (something, esp. a small article) for one's own use; purloin. [C18: from French, from (*se*) *souvenir* to remember, from Latin *subvenīre* to come to mind, from *sub-* up to + *venīre* to come]

souvlakia (suːˈvlækɪə) *n.* a Greek dish of kebabs, esp. made with lamb. [C20: from Modern Greek]

sou'wester (saʊˈwɛstə) *n.* a waterproof hat having a very broad rim behind, worn esp. by seamen. [C19: a contraction of SOUTHWESTER]

sovereign (ˈsɒvrɪn) *n.* **1.** a person exercising supreme authority, esp. a monarch. **2.** a former British gold coin worth one pound sterling. ~*adj.* **3.** supreme in rank or authority: *a sovereign lord.* **4.** excellent or outstanding: *a sovereign remedy.* **5.** of, relating to, or characteristic of a sovereign. **6.** independent of outside authority: *a sovereign state.* [C13: from Old French *soverain,* from Vulgar Latin *superānus* (unattested), from Latin *super* above; also influenced by REIGN] —ˈ**sovereignly** *adv.*

sovereigntist (ˈsɒvrəntɪst) *n.* (in Canada) a supporter of sovereignty association.

sovereignty (ˈsɒvrəntɪ) *n., pl.* **-ties. 1.** supreme and unrestricted power, as of a state. **2.** the position, dominion, or authority of a sovereign. **3.** an independent state.

sovereignty association *n.* (in Canada) a proposed arrangement by which Quebec would become independent but would maintain a formal association with Canada.

soviet (ˈsəʊvɪət, ˈsɒv-) *n.* **1.** (in the former Soviet Union) an elected government council at the local, regional, and national levels, culminating in the Supreme Soviet. **2.** (in prerevolutionary Russia) a local revolutionary council. ~*adj.* **3.** of or relating to a soviet. [C20: from Russian *sovyet* council, from Old Russian *sŭvětŭ*]

Soviet (ˈsəʊvɪət, ˈsɒv-) *adj.* of, characteristic of, or relating to the former Soviet Union, its people, or its government.

sovietism (ˈsəʊvɪɪˌtɪzəm, ˈsɒv-) *n.* (*sometimes cap.*) **1.** the principle or practice of government through soviets, esp. as practised in the former Soviet Union. **2.** any characteristic deemed representative of Soviet ideology. —ˈ**sovietist** *n., adj.* —ˌ**soviet**ˈ**istic** *adj.*

sovietize *or* **sovietise** (ˈsəʊvɪɪˌtaɪz, ˈsɒv-) *vb.* (*tr.*) (*often cap.*) **1.** to bring (a country, person, etc.) under Soviet control or influence. **2.** to cause (a country) to conform to the Soviet model in its social, political, and economic structure. —ˌ**sovieti**ˈ**zation** *or* ˌ**sovieti**ˈ**sation** *n.*

Sovietologist (ˌsəʊvɪəˈtɒlədʒɪst, ˌsɒv-) *n.* a person who studies the political policies and developments of the former Soviet government.

Soviets (ˈsəʊvɪəts, ˈsɒv-) *n.* (formerly) the people or government of the Soviet Union.

sovkhoz (sɒfˈkɒz; *Russian* safˈxɔs) *n., pl.* **sovkhozy** (sɒfˈkɒzɪ; *Russian* safˈxɔzi). (in the former Soviet Union) a large mechanized farm owned by the state. [C20: Russian, from *sovetskoe khozyaistvo* soviet economy]

sovran (ˈsɒvrən) *n., adj.* a literary word for **sovereign.** —ˈ**sovranly** *adv.* —ˈ**sovranty** *n.*

sow[1] (səʊ) *vb.* **sows, sowing, sowed; sown** *or* **sowed. 1.** to scatter or place (seed, a crop, etc.) in or on (a piece of ground, field, etc.) so that it may grow: *to sow wheat; to sow a strip of land.* **2.** (*tr.*) to implant or introduce: *to sow a doubt in someone's mind.* [Old English *sāwan;* related to Old Norse *sá,* Old High German *sāen,* Old Slavonic *seja,* Latin *serere* to sow] —ˈ**sowable** *adj.* —ˈ**sower** *n.*

sow[2] (saʊ) *n.* **1.** a female adult pig. **2.** the female of certain other animals, such as the mink. **3.** *Metallurgy.* **a.** the channels for leading molten metal to the moulds in casting pig iron. **b.** iron that has solidified in these channels. [Old English *sugu;* related to Old Norse *sýr,* Old High German *sū,* Latin *sūs,* Norwegian *sugga,* Dutch *zeug:* see SWINE]

sowback (ˈsaʊˌbæk) *n.* another name for **hogback** (sense 1).

sowbread (ˈsaʊˌbrɛd) *n.* a S European primulaceous plant, *Cyclamen hederifolium,* with heart-shaped leaves and pink nodding flowers. See also **cyclamen** (sense 1). [C16: from SOW[2] + BREAD, based on Medieval Latin *panis porcinus;* the tuberous roots are eaten by swine]

sow bug (saʊ) *n. U.S. and Canadian.* any of various woodlice, esp. any of the genera *Oniscus* and *Porcellio.* [C18: from its resemblance to a pig in shape]

sowens (ˈsəʊənz, ˈsuː-) *n. Scot.* a pudding made from oatmeal husks steeped and boiled. [C16: from Scottish Gaelic *sūghan,* from *sūgh* sap; related to Old High German *sūgan* to SUCK]

sown (səʊn) *vb.* a past participle of **sow**[1].

sow thistle (saʊ) *n.* any of various plants of the Old World genus *Sonchus,* esp. *S. oleraceus,* having milky juice, prickly leaves, and heads of yellow flowers: family *Compositae* (composites). Also called: **milk thistle,** (N.Z.) **puha,** (N.Z.) **rauriki.** [C13: from *sugethistel,* perhaps variant of Old English *thugethistel, thuthistel* thowthistle, a dialect name of the sow thistle. See SOW[2], THISTLE]

soya bean (ˈsɔɪə) *or U.S. and Canadian* **soybean** (ˈsɔɪˌbiːn) *n.* **1.** an Asian bean plant, *Glycine max* (or *G. soja*), cultivated for its nutritious seeds, for forage, and to improve the soil. **2.** the seed of this plant, used as food, forage, and as the source of an oil.

[C17 *soya,* via Dutch *soya* from Japanese *shōyu,* from Chinese *chiang yu,* from *chiang* paste + *yu* sauce]

soy sauce (sɔɪ) *n.* a salty dark brown sauce made from fermented soya beans, used esp. in Chinese cookery. Also called: **soya sauce.**

sozzled ('sɒzəld) *adj.* an informal word for **drunk.** [C19: perhaps from obsolete *sozzle* stupor; related to SOUSE[1]]

sp *abbrev. for* without issue. [from Latin *sine prole*]

SP *abbrev. for* starting price.

sp. *abbrev. for:* **1.** special. **2.** (*pl.* **spp.**) species. **3.** specific. **4.** specimen. **5.** spelling.

Sp. *abbrev. for:* **1.** Spain. **2.** Spaniard. **3.** Spanish.

spa (spɑː) *n.* a mineral spring or a place or resort where such a spring is found. [C17: named after *Spa,* a town in E Belgium noted for medicinal mineral springs]

SpA *abbrev. for* Società per Azioni. [Italian: limited company]

space (speɪs) *n.* **1.** the unlimited three-dimensional expanse in which all material objects are located. Related adj.: **spatial. 2.** an interval of distance or time between two points, objects, or events. **3.** a blank portion or area. **4. a.** unoccupied area or room: *there is no space for a table.* **b.** (*in combination*): *space-saving.* Related adj.: **spacious. 5. a.** the region beyond the earth's atmosphere containing the other planets of the solar system, stars, galaxies, etc.; universe. **b.** (*as modifier*): *a space probe; space navigation.* **6. a.** the region beyond the earth's atmosphere occurring between the celestial bodies of the universe. The density is normally negligible although cosmic rays, meteorites, gas clouds, etc., can occur. It can be divided into **cislunar space** (between the earth and moon), **interplanetary space, interstellar space,** and **intergalactic space. b.** (*as modifier*): *a space station; a space simulator.* **7.** a seat or place, as on a train, aircraft, etc. **8.** *Printing.* a piece of metal, less than type-high, used to separate letters or words. **9.** *Music.* any of the gaps between the lines that make up the staff. **10.** *Maths.* a collection of unspecified points having properties that obey a specified set of axioms: *Euclidean space.* **11.** Also called: **spacing.** *Telegraphy.* the period of time that separates complete letters, digits, and other characters in Morse code. ~*vb.* (*tr.*) **12.** to place or arrange at intervals or with spaces between. **13.** to divide into or by spaces: *to space one's time evenly.* **14.** *Printing.* to separate (letters, words, or lines) by the insertion of spaces. [C13: from Old French *espace,* from Latin *spatium*] —'**spacer** *n.*

space age *n.* **1.** the period in which the exploration of space has become possible. ~*adj.* **space-age. 2.** (*usually prenominal*) futuristic or ultramodern, esp. when suggestive of space technology.

spaceband ('speɪsˌbænd) *n. Printing.* a device on a linecaster for evening up the spaces between words.

space-bar *n.* a horizontal bar on a typewriter that is depressed in order to leave a space between words, letters, etc.

space blanket *n.* a plastic insulating body wrapping coated on one or both sides with aluminium foil which reflects back most of the body heat lost by radiation: carried by climbers, mountaineers, etc., for use in cases of exposure or exhaustion. [C20: material originally developed as part of the U.S. space programme]

space cadet *n. U.S. slang.* a person who is or appears to be habitually intoxicated through taking drugs.

space capsule *n.* a vehicle, sometimes carrying men or animals, designed to obtain scientific information from space, planets, etc., and be recovered on returning to earth.

space character *n. Computer technol.* a keyed space in text or data.

spacecraft ('speɪsˌkrɑːft) *n.* a manned or unmanned vehicle designed to orbit the earth or travel to celestial objects for the purpose of research, exploration, etc.

spaced out *adj. Slang.* intoxicated through or as if through taking a drug. Often shortened to **spaced.**

space heater *n.* a heater used to warm the air in an enclosed area, such as a room or office.

Space Invaders *n. Trademark.* a video game, found in pubs, amusement arcades, etc., the object of which is to obliterate a series of symbols moving down a television screen, representing invaders from outer space, by operating levers or buttons on a console below.

spacelab ('speɪsˌlæb) *n.* a laboratory in space where scientific experiments are performed, esp. one developed by the European Space Agency and carried on a space shuttle.

space lattice *n. Crystallog.* the more formal name for **lattice** (sense 4).

spaceless ('speɪslɪs) *adj. Chiefly literary.* **1.** having no limits in space; infinite or boundless. **2.** occupying no space.

spaceman ('speɪsˌmæn) *or (fem.)* **spacewoman** *n., pl.* **-men** *or (fem.)* **-women.** a person who travels in outer space, esp. one trained to participate in a space flight.

space medicine *n.* the branch of medicine concerned with the effects on man of flight outside the earth's atmosphere. Compare **aviation medicine.**

space opera *n.* a science fiction drama, such as a film or television programme, esp. one dealing with interplanetary flight.

space platform *n.* another name for **space station.**

spaceport ('speɪsˌpɔːt) *n.* a base equipped to launch, maintain, and test spacecraft.

space probe *n.* a vehicle, such as a satellite, equipped to obtain scientific information, normally transmitted back to earth by radio, about the atmosphere, surface, and temperature of a planet, conditions in space, etc.

spaceship ('speɪsˌʃɪp) *n.* a manned spacecraft.

space shuttle *n.* a vehicle, such as a two-stage rocket and aircraft, designed to be used for at least 100 space flights, carrying men and materials to space stations in orbit around the earth or to bases on the moon, etc.

space station *n.* any large manned artificial satellite designed to orbit the earth during a long period of time thus providing a base for scientific and medical research in space and a construction site, launching pad, and docking arrangements for spacecraft. Also called: **space platform, space laboratory.**

spacesuit ('speɪsˌsuːt, -ˌsjuːt) *n.* any of various types of sealed and pressurized suits worn by astronauts or cosmonauts that provide an artificial atmosphere, acceptable temperature, radiocommunication link, and protection from radiation for work outside a spacecraft.

space-time *or* **space-time continuum** *n. Physics.* the four-dimensional continuum having three spatial coordinates and one time coordinate that together completely specify the location of a particle or an event.

spacewalk ('speɪsˌwɔːk) *n.* **1.** the act or an instance of floating and manoeuvring in space, outside but attached by a lifeline to a spacecraft. Technical name: **extravehicular activity.** ~*vb.* **2.** (*intr.*) to float and manoeuvre in space while outside but attached to a spacecraft.

space writer *n.* a writer paid by the area of his copy.

spacey ('speɪsɪ) *adj.* **spacier, spaciest.** *Slang.* vague and dreamy, as if under the influence of drugs. [C20: SPACE + -EY]

spacial ('speɪʃəl) *adj.* a variant spelling of **spatial.**

spacing ('speɪsɪŋ) *n.* **1.** the arrangement of letters, words, etc., on a page in order to achieve legibility or aesthetic appeal. **2.** the arrangement of objects in a space.

spacious ('speɪʃəs) *adj.* having a large capacity or area. [C14: from Latin *spātiosus,* from *spatium* SPACE] —'**spaciously** *adv.* —'**spaciousness** *n.*

spade[1] (speɪd) *n.* **1.** a tool for digging, typically consisting of a flat rectangular steel blade attached to a long wooden handle. **2. a.** an object or part resembling a spade in shape. **b.** (*as modifier*): *a spade beard.* **3.** a heavy metallic projection attached to the trail of a gun carriage that embeds itself into the ground and so reduces recoil. **4.** a type of oar blade that is comparatively broad and short. Compare **spoon** (sense 6). **5.** a cutting tool for stripping the blubber from a whale or skin from a carcass. **6. call a spade a spade.** to speak plainly and frankly. ~*vb.* **7.** (*tr.*) to use a spade on. [Old English *spadu;* related to Old Norse *spathi,* Old High German *spato,* Greek *spathē* blade] —'**spader** *n.*

spade[2] (speɪd) *n.* **1. a.** the black symbol on a playing card resembling a heart-shaped leaf with a stem. **b.** a card with one or more of these symbols or (*when pl.*) the suit of cards so marked, usually the highest ranking of the four. **2.** a derogatory word for a Negro. **3. in spades.** *Informal.* in an extreme or emphatic way. [C16: from Italian *spada* sword, used as an emblem on playing cards, from Latin *spatha,* from Greek *spathē* blade, broadsword]

spadefish ('speɪdˌfɪʃ) *n., pl.* **-fish** *or* **-fishes.** any spiny-finned food fish of the family *Ephippidae,* esp. *Chaetodipterus faber* of American Atlantic coastal waters, having a deeply compressed body.

spade foot *n.* a spadelike projection at the end of a chair leg.

spade guinea *n. Brit. history.* a guinea decorated with a spade-shaped shield, coined during the reign of George III.

spadework ('speɪdˌwɜːk) *n.* dull or routine preparatory work.

spadiceous (speɪ'dɪʃəs) *adj.* **1.** *Botany.* producing or resembling a spadix. **2.** of a bright brown colour. [C17: from New Latin *spādīceus,* from Latin *spādix* palm branch; see SPADIX]

spadille (spə'dɪl) *n. Cards.* (in ombre and quadrille) the ace of spades. [C18: from French, from Spanish *espadilla,* diminutive of *espada* sword; see SPADE[2]]

spadix ('speɪdɪks) *n., pl.* **spadices** (speɪ'daɪsiːz). a racemose inflorescence having many small sessile flowers borne on a fleshy stem, the whole being enclosed in a spathe: occurs in aroid plants. [C18: from Latin: pulled-off branch of a palm, with its fruit, from Greek: torn-off frond; related to Greek *span* to pull off]

spae (speɪ) *vb. Scot.* to foretell (the future). [C14: from Old Norse]

spaewife ('speˌwaɪf) *n., pl.* **-wives.** *Scot.* a woman who can supposedly foretell the future.

spag[1] (spæg) *vb.* **spags, spagging, spagged.** (*tr.*) *South Wales dialect.* (of a cat) to scratch (a person) with the claws. [of uncertain origin]

spag[2] (spæg) *n. Austral. slang offensive.* an Italian. [from SPAGHETTI]

spaghetti (spə'gɛtɪ) *n.* pasta in the form of long strings. [C19: from Italian: little cords, from *spago* a cord]

spaghetti junction *n.* an interchange, usually between motorways, in which there are a large number of underpasses and overpasses and intersecting roads used by a large volume of high-speed traffic. [C20: from the nickname of the Gravelly Hill Interchange, Birmingham, where the M6, A38M, A38, and A5127 intersect]

spaghetti western *n.* a cowboy film about the American West made, esp. by an Italian director, in Europe.

spagyric (spəˈdʒɪrɪk) *or* **spagyrical** *adj. Rare.* of or relating to alchemy. [C16: from New Latin *spagiricus,* probably coined by Paracelsus, of obscure origin] —**spaˈgyrically** *adv.*

spahi *or* **spahee** (ˈspɑːhiː, ˈspɑːiː) *n., pl.* **-his** *or* **-hees. 1.** (formerly) an irregular cavalryman in the Turkish armed forces. **2.** a member of a body of native Algerian cavalrymen in the French armed forces: disbanded after 1962. [C16: from Old French, from Turkish *sipahi,* from Persian *sipāhī* soldier; see SEPOY]

spake (speɪk) *vb. Archaic or dialect.* a past tense of **speak.**

spall (spɔːl) *n.* **1.** a splinter or chip of ore, rock, or stone. ~*vb.* **2.** to split or cause to split into such fragments. [C15: of unknown origin]

spallation (spəˈleɪʃən) *n. Physics.* a type of nuclear reaction in which a photon or particle hits a nucleus and causes it to emit other particles or photons. [C20: from SPALL + -ATION]

spalpeen (ˈspælpiːn) *n. Irish.* **1.** an itinerant seasonal labourer. **2.** a rascal or layabout. [C18: from Irish Gaelic *spailpīn* itinerant labourer]

Spam (spæm) *n. Trademark.* a kind of tinned luncheon meat, made largely from pork.

span[1] (spæn) *n.* **1.** the interval, space, or distance between two points, such as the ends of a bridge or arch. **2.** the complete duration or extent: *the span of his life.* **3.** *Psychol.* the amount of material that can be processed in a single mental act: *apprehension span; span of attention.* **4.** short for **wingspan. 5.** a unit of length based on the width of an expanded hand, usually taken as nine inches. ~*vb.* **spans, spanning, spanned.** (*tr.*) **6.** to stretch or extend across, over, or around. **7.** to provide with something that extends across or around: *to span a river with a bridge.* **8.** to measure or cover, esp. with the extended hand. [Old English *spann;* related to Old Norse *sponn,* Old High German *spanna*]

span[2] (spæn) *n.* a team of horses or oxen, esp. two matched animals. [C16 (in the sense: yoke): from Middle Dutch: something stretched, from *spannen* to stretch; see SPAN[1]]

span[3] (spæn) *vb. Archaic or dialect.* a past tense of **spin.**

Span. *abbrev. for* Spanish.

spancel (ˈspænsᵊl) *n.* **1.** a length of rope for hobbling an animal, esp. a horse or cow. ~*vb.* **-cels, -celling, -celled** *or U.S.* **-cels, -celing, -celed. 2.** (*tr.*) to hobble (an animal) with a loose rope. [C17: from Low German *spansel,* from *spannen* to stretch; see SPAN[2]]

spandex (ˈspændɛks) *n.* a type of synthetic stretch fabric made from polyurethane fibre. [C20: coined from an anagram of *expands*]

spandrel *or* **spandril** (ˈspændrəl) *n. Architect.* **1.** an approximately triangular surface bounded by the outer curve of an arch and the adjacent wall. **2.** the surface area between two adjacent arches and the horizontal cornice above them. [C15 *spaundrell,* from Anglo-French *spaundre* spandrel, from Old French *spandre* to spread, EXPAND]

spang (spæŋ) *adv. U.S. and Canadian informal.* exactly, firmly, or straight: *spang on target.* [C19: of unknown origin]

spangle (ˈspæŋgᵊl) *n.* **1.** a small thin piece of metal or other shiny material used as a decoration, esp. on clothes; sequin. **2.** any glittering or shiny spot or object. ~*vb.* **3.** (*intr.*) to glitter or shine with or like spangles. **4.** (*tr.*) to decorate or cover with spangles. [C15: diminutive of *spange,* perhaps from Middle Dutch: clasp; compare Old Norse *spöng*] —ˈ**spangly** *adj.*

Spaniard (ˈspænjəd) *n.* **1.** a native or inhabitant of Spain, a kingdom of SW Europe. **2.** *N.Z.* short for **wild Spaniard.**

spaniel (ˈspænjəl) *n.* **1.** any of several breeds of gundog with long drooping ears, a silky coat, and the tail usually docked. See **clumber spaniel, cocker spaniel, field spaniel, springer spaniel, Sussex spaniel, water spaniel. 2.** either of two toy breeds of spaniel: see **King Charles spaniel. 3.** an obsequiously devoted person. [C14: from Old French *espaigneul* Spanish (dog), from Old Provençal *espanhol,* ultimately from Latin *Hispāniolus* Spanish]

Spanish (ˈspænɪʃ) *n.* **1.** the official language of Spain, Mexico, and most countries of South and Central America except Brazil: also spoken in Africa, the Far East, and elsewhere. It is the native language of approximately 200 million people throughout the world. Spanish is an Indo-European language belonging to the Romance group. **2. the Spanish.** (*functioning as pl.*) Spaniards collectively. ~*adj.* **3.** of or relating to the Spanish language or its speakers. **4.** of or relating to Spain or Spaniards.

Spanish-American *adj.* **1.** of or relating to any of the Spanish-speaking countries of the Americas (Spanish America) or to the peoples of these countries. ~*n.* **2.** a native or inhabitant of Spanish America. **3.** a Spanish-speaking person in the U.S.

Spanish bayonet *n.* any of several American liliaceous plants of the genus *Yucca,* esp. *Y. aloifolia,* that have a tall woody stem, stiff pointed leaves, and large clusters of white flowers: cultivated for ornament. See also **Adam's-needle.**

Spanish cedar *n.* a tall meliaceous tree, *Cedrela odorata,* of tropical America, the East Indies, and Australia, having smooth bark, pinnate leaves, yellow flowers, and light-coloured aromatic wood.

Spanish customs *or* **practices** *pl. n. Informal.* irregular practices among a group of workers to gain increased financial allowances, reduced working hours, etc. Also called: **old Spanish customs** *or* **practices.**

Spanish fly *n.* **1.** a European blister beetle, *Lytta vesicatoria* (family *Meloidae*), the dried bodies of which yield the pharmaceutical product cantharides. **2.** another name for **cantharides.**

Spanish guitar *n.* the classic form of the guitar; a six-stringed instrument with a waisted body and a central sound hole.

Spanish Inquisition *n.* the institution that guarded the orthodoxy of Catholicism in Spain, chiefly by the persecution of heretics, Jews, etc., esp. from the 15th to 17th centuries. See also **Inquisition.**

Spanish mackerel *n.* **1.** Also called: **kingfish.** any scombroid food fish of the genus *Scomberomorus,* esp. *S. maculatus,* of American coastal regions of the Atlantic: family *Scombridae* (mackerels, tunnies, etc.). **2.** a mackerel, *Scomber colias,* of European and E North American coasts that is similar to the common Atlantic mackerel.

Spanish moss *n.* **1.** an epiphytic bromeliaceous plant, *Tillandsia usneoides,* growing in tropical and subtropical regions as long bluish-grey strands suspended from the branches of trees. **2.** a tropical lichen, *Usnea longissima,* growing as long trailing green threads from the branches of trees. ~Also called: **long moss.**

Spanish omelette *n.* an omelette made by adding green peppers, onions, tomato, etc., to the eggs.

Spanish onion *n.* any of several varieties of large mild-flavoured onions.

Spanish paprika *n.* a mild seasoning made from a variety of red pepper grown in Spain.

Spanish rice *n.* rice cooked with tomatoes, onions, green peppers, etc., and often flavoured with saffron.

Spanish topaz *n.* an orange-brown form of quartz, used as a gemstone.

Spanish windlass *n.* a stick used as a device for twisting and tightening a rope or cable.

spank[1] (spæŋk) *vb.* **1.** (*tr.*) to slap or smack with the open hand, esp. on the buttocks. ~*n.* **2.** a slap or series of slaps with the flat of the hand. [C18: probably of imitative origin]

spank[2] (spæŋk) *vb.* (*intr.*) to go at a quick and lively pace. [C19: back formation from SPANKING[2]]

spanker (ˈspæŋkə) *n.* **1.** *Nautical.* a fore-and-aft sail or a mast that is aftermost in a sailing vessel. **2.** *Informal.* a person or animal that moves at a quick smart pace. **3.** *Informal.* something outstandingly fine or large.

spanking[1] (ˈspæŋkɪŋ) *n.* a series of spanks, esp. on the buttocks, usually as a punishment for children.

spanking[2] (ˈspæŋkɪŋ) *adj.* (*prenominal*) **1.** *Informal.* outstandingly fine, smart, large, etc. **2.** quick and energetic; lively. **3.** (esp. of a breeze) fresh and brisk. [C17: of uncertain origin. Compare Danish *spanke* to strut]

spanner (ˈspænə) *n.* **1.** a steel hand tool with a handle carrying jaws or a hole of particular shape designed to grip a nut or bolt head. **2. spanner in the works.** *Brit. informal.* a source of impediment or annoyance (esp. in the phrase **throw a spanner in the works**). [C17: from German, from *spannen* to stretch, SPAN[1]]

span-new *adj. Archaic or dialect.* absolutely new. [C14: from Old Norse *spānnýr,* from *spānn* chip + *nýr* NEW]

span of apprehension *n. Psychol.* the maximum number of objects that can be correctly assessed after a brief presentation.

span roof *n.* a roof consisting of two equal sloping sides.

span saw *n. Building trades.* another name for **frame saw.**

spanspek (ˈspɑnˌspɛk) *n. S. African.* a sweet rough-skinned melon; a cantaloupe: family *Cucurbitaceae.*

spansule (ˈspænsjuːl) *n.* a time-release capsule of a drug.

spar[1] (spɑː) *n.* **1. a.** any piece of nautical gear resembling a pole and used as a mast, boom, gaff, etc. **b.** (*as modifier*): *a spar buoy.* **2.** a principal supporting structural member of an aerofoil that runs from tip to tip or root to tip. [C13: from Old Norse *sperra* beam; related to Old High German *sparro,* Old French *esparre*]

spar[2] (spɑː) *vb.* **spars, sparring, sparred.** (*intr.*) **1.** *Boxing, martial arts.* to fight using light blows, as in training. **2.** to dispute or argue. **3.** (of gamecocks) to fight with the feet or spurs. ~*n.* **4.** an unaggressive fight. **5.** an argument or wrangle. [Old English, perhaps from SPUR]

spar[3] (spɑː) *n.* any of various minerals, such as feldspar or calcite, that are light-coloured, microcrystalline, transparent to translucent, and easily cleavable. [C16: from Middle Low German *spar;* related to Old English *spærstān;* see FELDSPAR]

sparable (ˈspærəbᵊl) *n.* a small nail with no head, used for fixing the soles and heels of shoes. [C17: changed from *sparrow-bill,* referring to the nail's shape]

sparaxis (spəˈræksɪs) *n.* any plant of the cormous S African genus *Sparaxis,* esp. *S. grandiflora* and *S. tricolor,* grown for their dainty spikes of star-shaped purple, red, or orange flowers: family *Iridaceae.* [New Latin, from Greek *sparassein* to tear (from the appearance of the spathes)]

spar buoy *n. Nautical.* a buoy resembling a vertical log.

spare (spɛə) *vb.* **1.** (*tr.*) to refrain from killing, punishing, harming, or injuring. **2.** (*tr.*) to release or relieve, as from pain, suffering, etc. **3.** (*tr.*) to refrain from using: *spare the rod, spoil the child.* **4.** (*tr.*) to be able to afford or give: *I can't spare the time.* **5.** (*usually passive*) (esp. of Providence) to allow to survive: *I'll* *see you again next year if we are spared.* **6.** (*intr.*) *Now rare.* to act or live frugally. **7.** (*intr.*) *Rare.* to show mercy. **8. not spare oneself.** to exert oneself to the full. **9. to spare.** more than is required: *two minutes to spare.* ~*adj.* **10.** (*often immediately postpositive*) in excess of what is needed; additional: *are there any seats spare?* **11.** able to be used when needed: *a spare part.* **12.** (of a person) thin and lean. **13.** scanty or meagre. **14.** (*postpositive*) *Brit. slang.* upset, angry, or distracted (esp. in the phrase **go spare**). ~*n.* **15.** a duplicate kept as a replacement in case of damage or loss. **16.** a spare tyre. **17.** *Tenpin bowling.* **a.** the act of knocking down all the pins with the two bowls of a single frame. **b.** the score thus made. Compare **strike** (sense 39). [Old English *sparian* to refrain from injuring; related to Old Norse *spara,* Old High German *sparōn*] —ˈ**sparely** *adv.* —ˈ**spareness** *n.* —ˈ**sparer** *n.*

spare part *n.* a duplicate or replacement component for a machine or other equipment.

spare-part surgery *n.* surgical replacement of defective or damaged organs by transplant or insertion of artificial devices.

sparerib (ˌspɛəˈrɪb) *n.* a cut of pork ribs with most of the meat trimmed off.

spare tyre *n.* **1.** an additional tyre, usually mounted on a wheel, carried by a motor vehicle in case of puncture. **2.** *Brit. slang, jocular.* a deposit of fat just above the waist.

sparge (spɑːdʒ) *vb. Rare.* to sprinkle or scatter (something). [C16: from Latin *spargere* to sprinkle] —ˈ**sparger** *n.*

sparid (ˈspærɪd) *or* **sparoid** *n.* **1.** any marine percoid fish of the chiefly tropical and subtropical family *Sparidae,* having a deep compressed body and well-developed teeth: includes the sea breams and porgies. ~*adj.* **2.** of, relating to, or belonging to the family *Sparidae.* [C20: from New Latin *Sparidae,* from Latin *sparus* a sea bream, from Greek *sparos*]

sparing (ˈspɛərɪŋ) *adj.* **1.** (sometimes foll. by *of*) economical or frugal (with). **2.** scanty; meagre. **3.** merciful or lenient. —ˈ**sparingly** *adv.* —ˈ**sparingness** *n.*

spark[1] (spɑːk) *n.* **1.** a fiery particle thrown out or left by burning material or caused by the friction of two hard surfaces. **2. a.** a momentary flash of light accompanied by a sharp crackling noise, produced by a sudden electrical discharge through the air or some other insulating medium between two points. **b.** the electrical discharge itself. **c.** (*as modifier*): *a spark gap.* **3.** anything that serves to animate, kindle, or excite. **4.** a trace or hint: *she doesn't show a spark of interest.* **5.** vivacity, enthusiasm, or humour. **6.** a small piece of diamond, as used in the cutting of glass. ~*vb.* **7.** (*intr.*) to give off sparks. **8.** (*intr.*) (of the sparking plug or ignition system of an internal-combustion engine) to produce a spark. **9.** (*tr.*; often foll. by *off*) to kindle, excite, or animate. ~See also **spark off, sparks.** [Old English *spearca;* related to Middle Low German *sparke,* Middle Dutch *spranke,* Lettish *spirgsti* cinders, Latin *spargere* to strew]

spark[2] (spɑːk) *Rare* (*except for sense 2*). ~*n.* **1.** a fashionable or gallant young man. **2. bright spark.** *Brit., usually ironic.* a person who appears clever or witty: *some bright spark left the papers next to the open window.* ~*vb.* **3.** to woo (a person). [C16 (in the sense: beautiful or witty woman): perhaps of Scandinavian origin; compare Old Norse *sparkr* vivacious] —ˈ**sparkish** *adj.*

spark chamber *n. Physics.* a device for detecting ionizing radiation, consisting of two oppositely charged metal plates in a chamber containing inert gas, so that a particle passing through the chamber ionizes the gas and causes a spark to jump between the electrodes.

spark coil *n.* an induction coil used to produce spark discharges.

spark erosion *n. Engineering.* a method of machining using a shaped electrode which erodes the workpiece by an electric spark discharge between itself and the workpiece.

spark gap *n.* the space between two electrodes across which a spark can jump. Sometimes shortened to **gap.**

sparking plug *n.* a device screwed into the cylinder head of an internal-combustion engine to ignite the explosive mixture by means of an electric spark which jumps across a gap between a point earthed to the body of the plug and the tip of a central insulated rod. Also called: **spark plug.**

sparkle (ˈspɑːkᵊl) *vb.* **1.** to issue or reflect or cause to issue or reflect bright points of light. **2.** (*intr.*) (of wine, mineral water, etc.) to effervesce. **3.** (*intr.*) to be vivacious or witty. ~*n.* **4.** a point of light, spark, or gleam. **5.** vivacity or wit. [C12 *sparklen,* frequentative of *sparken* to SPARK[1]]

sparkler (ˈspɑːklə) *n.* **1.** a type of firework that throws out showers of sparks. **2.** *Informal.* a sparkling gem.

sparkling wine *n.* a wine made effervescent by carbon dioxide gas, introduced artificially or produced naturally by secondary fermentation.

spark off *vb.* (*tr., adv.*) to bring into being or action; activate or initiate: *to spark off an argument.*

spark plug *n.* another name for **sparking plug.**

sparks (spɑːks) *n.* (*functioning as sing.*) *Informal.* **1.** an electrician. **2.** a radio officer, esp. on a ship.

spark transmitter *n.* an early type of radio transmitter in which power is generated by discharging a capacitor through an inductor in series with a spark gap.

sparky (ˈspɑːkɪ) *adj.* **sparkier, sparkiest.** lively; vivacious; spirited.

sparling (ˈspɑːlɪŋ) *n., pl.* **-lings** *or* **-ling.** **1.** another name for the **European smelt** (see **smelt** (the fish)). **2.** a young herring. [C14 *sperlynge,* from Old French *esperling,* from Middle Dutch *spierlinc,* from *spier* young shoot]

sparoid (ˈspærɔɪd) *adj., n.* another word for **sparid.** [C19: from New Latin *Sparoīdēs;* see SPARID]

sparring partner (ˈspɑːrɪŋ) *n.* **1.** a person who practises with a boxer during training. **2.** a person with whom one has friendly arguments.

sparrow (ˈspærəʊ) *n.* **1.** any weaverbird of the genus *Passer* and related genera, esp. the house sparrow, having a brown or grey plumage and feeding on seeds or insects. **2.** *U.S. and Canadian.* any of various North American finches, such as the chipping sparrow (*Spizella passerina*), that have a dullish streaked plumage. ~See also **hedge sparrow, tree sparrow, song sparrow.** [Old English *spearwa;* related to Old Norse *spörr,* Old High German *sparo*] —ˈ**sparrow-ˌlike** *adj.*

sparrowgrass (ˈspærəʊˌgrɑːs) *n.* a dialect or popular name for **asparagus.** [C17: variant of ASPARAGUS, associated by folk etymology with SPARROW and GRASS]

sparrowhawk (ˈspærəʊˌhɔːk) *n.* any of several small hawks, esp. *Accipiter nisus,* of Eurasia and N Africa that prey on smaller birds.

sparrow hawk *n.* a very small North American falcon, *Falco sparverius,* that is closely related to the kestrels.

sparry (ˈspɑːrɪ) *adj. Geology.* containing, relating to, or resembling spar: *sparry coal.*

sparse (spɑːs) *adj.* scattered or scanty; not dense. [C18: from Latin *sparsus,* from *spargere* to scatter] —ˈ**sparsely** *adv.* —ˈ**sparseness** *or* ˈ**sparsity** *n.*

Spartacist (ˈspɑːtəsɪst) *n.* a member of a group of German radical socialists formed in 1916 and in 1919 becoming the German Communist Party. [C20: from the pen name *Spartacus* adopted by its leader, Karl Liebknecht (1871–1919)]

Spartan (ˈspɑːtᵊn) *adj.* **1.** of or relating to Sparta, an ancient Greek city state, or to its citizens, who were known for their militaristic and austere lifestyle. **2.** (*sometimes not cap.*) very strict or austere: *a Spartan upbringing.* **3.** (*sometimes not cap.*) possessing courage and resolve. ~*n.* **4.** a citizen of Sparta. **5.** (*sometimes not cap.*) a disciplined or brave person. —ˈ**Spartanism** *n.*

sparteine (ˈspɑːtɪˌiːn, -ɪn) *n.* a viscous oily alkaloid extracted from the broom plant and lupin seeds. It has been used in medicine to treat heart arrhythmias. [C19: from New Latin *Spartium,* from Greek *spartos* broom]

spasm (ˈspæzəm) *n.* **1.** an involuntary muscular contraction, esp. one resulting in cramp or convulsion. **2.** a sudden burst of activity, emotion, etc. [C14: from Latin *spasmus,* from Greek *spasmos* a cramp, from *span* to tear]

spasmodic (spæzˈmɒdɪk) *or* (*rarely*) **spasmodical** *adj.* **1.** taking place in sudden brief spells. **2.** of or characterized by spasms. [C17: New Latin, from Greek *spasmos* SPASM] —**spasˈmodically** *adv.*

spastic (ˈspæstɪk) *n.* **1.** a person who is affected by spasms or convulsions, esp. one who has cerebral palsy. **2.** *Derogatory slang.* a clumsy, incapable, or incompetent person. ~*adj.* **3.** affected by or resembling spasms. **4.** *Offensive slang.* clumsy, incapable or incompetent. [C18: from Latin *spasticus,* from Greek *spastikos,* from *spasmos* SPASM] —ˈ**spastically** *adv.*

spat[1] (spæt) *n.* **1.** *Now rare.* a slap or smack. **2.** a slight quarrel. ~*vb.* **spats, spatting, spatted.** **3.** *Now rare.* to slap (someone). **4.** (*intr.*) *U.S., Canadian, and* (*rarely*) *N.Z.* to have a slight quarrel. [C19: probably imitative of the sound of quarrelling]

spat[2] (spæt) *vb.* a past tense and past participle of **spit**[1].

spat[3] (spæt) *n.* another name for **gaiter** (sense 2). [C19: short for SPATTERDASH]

spat[4] (spæt) *n.* **1.** a larval oyster or similar bivalve mollusc, esp. when it settles to the sea bottom and starts to develop a shell. **2.** such oysters or other molluscs collectively. [C17: from Anglo-Norman *spat;* perhaps related to SPIT[1]]

spatchcock (ˈspætʃˌkɒk) *n.* **1.** a chicken or game bird split down the back and grilled. Compare **spitchcock.** ~*vb.* (*tr.*) **2.** to interpolate (words, a story, etc.) into a sentence, narrative, etc., esp. inappropriately. [C18: perhaps variant of *spitchcock* eel when prepared and cooked]

spate (speɪt) *n.* **1.** a fast flow, rush, or outpouring: *a spate of words.* **2.** *Chiefly Brit.* a sudden flood: *the rivers were in spate.* **3.** *Chiefly Brit.* a sudden heavy downpour. [C15 (Northern and Scottish): of unknown origin]

spathe (speɪð) *n.* a large bract, often coloured, that encloses the inflorescence of any of several members of the lily family. [C18: from Latin *spatha,* from Greek *spathē* a blade] —**spathaceous** (spəˈθeɪʃəs) *adj.* —**spathed** *adj.*

spathic (ˈspæθɪk) *or* **spathose** (ˈspæθəʊs) *adj.* (of minerals) resembling spar, esp. in having good cleavage. [C18: from German *spat, spath* SPAR[3]; related to Old High German *spān* chip; see SPOON]

spathulate (ˈspæθjʊlɪt) *adj.* another word for **spatulate** (sense 2).

spatial *or* **spacial** (ˈspeɪʃəl) *adj.* **1.** of or relating to space. **2.** existing or happening in space. —**spatiality** (ˌspeɪʃɪˈælɪtɪ) *n.* —ˈ**spatially** *adv.*

spatial frequency *n. Television.* the measure of fine detail in an optical image in terms of cycles per millimetre.

spatiotemporal (ˌspeɪʃɪəʊˈtɛmpərəl, -ˈtɛmprəl) *adj.* **1.** of or existing in both space and time. **2.** of or concerned with space-time. [C20: from Latin *spatium* space + *temporālis,* from *tempus* time] —ˌ**spatioˈtemporally** *adv.*

spatter (ˈspætə) *vb.* **1.** to scatter or splash (a substance, esp. a liquid) or (of a substance) to splash (something) in scattered drops: *to spatter mud on the car; mud spattered in her face.* **2.** (*tr.*) to sprinkle, cover, or spot (with a liquid). **3.** (*tr.*) to slander or defame. **4.** (*intr.*) to shower or rain down: *bullets spattered around them.* ~*n.* **5.** the sound of something spattering. **6.** something spattered, such as a spot or splash. **7.** the act or an instance of spattering. [C16: of imitative origin; related to Low German, Dutch *spatten* to spout, Frisian *spatteren* to splash]

spatterdash (ˈspætəˌdæʃ) *n.* **1.** *U.S.* another name for **roughcast.** **2.** (*pl.*) long leather leggings worn in the 18th century, as to protect from mud when riding. [C17: see SPATTER, DASH[1]]

spatula (ˈspætjʊlə) *n.* a utensil with a broad flat, often flexible blade, used for lifting, spreading, or stirring foods, etc. [C16: from Latin: a broad piece, from *spatha* a flat wooden implement; see SPATHE] —ˈ**spatular** *adj.*

spatulate (ˈspætjʊlɪt) *adj.* **1.** shaped like a spatula. **2.** Also: **spathulate.** *Botany.* having a narrow base and a broad rounded apex: *a spatulate leaf.*

spavin (ˈspævɪn) *n. Vet. science.* enlargement of the hock of a horse by a bony growth (**bony spavin**) or distension of the ligament (**bog spavin**), usually caused by inflammation or injury, and often resulting in lameness. [C15: from Old French *espavin,* of unknown origin]

spavined (ˈspævɪnd) *adj.* **1.** *Vet. science.* affected with spavin; lame. **2.** decrepit or worn out.

spawn (spɔːn) *n.* **1.** the mass of eggs deposited by fish, amphibians, or molluscs. **2.** *Often derogatory.* offspring, product, or yield. **3.** *Botany.* the nontechnical name for **mycelium.** ~*vb.* **4.** (of fish, amphibians, etc.) to produce or deposit (eggs). **5.** *Often derogatory.* (of people) to produce (offspring). **6.** (*tr.*) to produce or engender. [C14: from Anglo-Norman *espaundre,* from Old French *spandre* to spread out, EXPAND] —ˈ**spawner** *n.*

spay (speɪ) *vb.* (*tr.*) to remove the ovaries from (a female animal). [C15: from Old French *espeer* to cut with the sword, from *espee* sword, from Latin *spatha*]

SPCK (in Britain) *abbrev. for* Society for Promoting Christian Knowledge.

SPD *abbrev. for* Sozialdemokratische Partei Deutschlands. [German: Social Democratic Party of Germany]

speak (spiːk) *vb.* **speaks, speaking, spoke, spoken. 1.** to make (verbal utterances); utter (words). **2.** to communicate or express (something) in or as if in words: *I speak the truth.* **3.** (*intr.*) to deliver a speech, discourse, etc. **4.** (*tr.*) to know how to talk in (a language or dialect): *he does not speak German.* **5.** (*intr.*) to make a characteristic sound: *the clock spoke.* **6.** (*intr.*) (of dogs, esp. hounds used in hunting) to give tongue; bark. **7.** (*tr.*) *Nautical.* to hail and converse or communicate with (another vessel) at sea. **8.** (*intr.*) (of a musical instrument) to produce a sound. **9.** (*intr.*; foll. by *for*) to be a representative or advocate (of): *he speaks for all the members.* **10. on speaking terms.** on good terms; friendly. **11. so to speak.** in a manner of speaking; as it were. **12. speak one's mind.** to express one's opinions frankly and plainly. **13. to speak of.** of a significant or worthwhile nature: *we have had no support to speak of.* ~See also **speak for, speak out, speak to, speak up.** [Old English *specan;* related to Old High German *spehhan,* Middle High German *spechten* to gossip, Middle Dutch *speken;* see SPEECH] —ˈ**speakable** *adj.*

-speak *suffix forming nouns. Informal.* the language or jargon of a specific group, organization, or field: *computerspeak.* [C20: formed on the pattern of NEWSPEAK]

speakeasy (ˈspiːkˌiːzɪ) *n., pl.* **-easies.** *U.S.* a place where alcoholic drink was sold illicitly during Prohibition. [C19: from SPEAK + EASY (in the sense: gently, quietly)]

speaker (ˈspiːkə) *n.* **1.** a person who speaks, esp. at a formal occasion. **2.** See **loudspeaker.** —ˈ**speakership** *n.*

Speaker (ˈspiːkə) *n.* the presiding officer in any of numerous legislative bodies, including the House of Commons in Britain and Canada and the House of Representatives in the U.S., Australia, and New Zealand.

speak for *vb.* (*intr., prep.*) **1.** to speak as a representative of (other people). **2. speak for itself.** to be so evident that no further comment is necessary. **3. speak for yourself.** *Informal.* (used as an imperative) do not presume that other people agree with you.

speaking (ˈspiːkɪŋ) *adj.* **1.** (*prenominal*) eloquent, impressive, or striking. **2. a.** able to speak. **b.** (*in combination*) able to speak a particular language: *French-speaking.*

speaking clock *n. Brit.* a telephone service that gives a precise verbal statement of the correct time.

speaking in tongues *n.* another term for **gift of tongues.**

speaking trumpet *n.* a trumpet-shaped instrument used to carry the voice a great distance or held to the ear by a deaf person to aid his hearing.

speaking tube *n.* a tube or pipe for conveying a person's voice from one room, area, or building to another.

speak out *vb.* (*intr., adv.*) **1.** to state one's beliefs, objections, etc., bravely and firmly. **2.** to speak more loudly and clearly.

speak to *vb.* (*intr., prep.*) **1.** to address (a person). **2.** to reprimand: *your father will speak to you later.* **3.** *Formal.* to give evidence of or comments on (a subject): *who will speak to this item?*

speak up *vb.* (*intr., adv.*) **1.** to speak more loudly. **2.** to state one's beliefs, objections, etc., bravely and firmly.

spear[1] (spɪə) *n.* **1.** a weapon consisting of a long shaft with a sharp pointed end of metal, stone, or wood that may be thrown or thrust. **2.** a similar implement used to catch fish. **3.** another name for **spearman.** ~*vb.* **4.** to pierce (something) with or as if with a spear. [Old English *spere;* related to Old Norse *spjör* spears, Greek *sparos* gilthead] —ˈ**spearer** *n.*

spear[2] (spɪə) *n.* a shoot, slender stalk or blade, as of grass, asparagus, or broccoli. [C16: probably variant of SPIRE[1], influenced by SPEAR[1]]

spearfish (ˈspɪəˌfɪʃ) *n., pl.* **-fish** *or* **-fishes.** another name for **marlin.** [so named because of its long pointed jaw]

spear grass *n. N.Z.* another name for **wild Spaniard.**

spear gun *n.* a device for shooting spears underwater.

spearhead (ˈspɪəˌhɛd) *n.* **1.** the pointed head of a spear. **2.** the leading force in a military attack. **3.** any person or thing that leads or initiates an attack, a campaign, etc. ~*vb.* **4.** (*tr.*) to lead or initiate (an attack, a campaign, etc.).

spearman (ˈspɪəmən) *n., pl.* **-men.** a soldier armed with a spear.

Spearman's rank-order coefficient (ˈspɪəmənz) *n.* a statistic measuring the extent to which two sets of discrete data place the distinct items in the same order, given by $r_S = 1 - 6\Sigma d^2/n(n^2 - 1)$, where Σd^2 is the sum of the squares of the differences of ranks between the two orderings and n is the number of items in each. Also called: **Spearman's rank-order correlation coefficient.** [named after Charles E. *Spearman* (1863–1945), British mathematician and statistician]

spearmint (ˈspɪəmɪnt) *n.* a purple-flowered mint plant, *Mentha spicata,* of S and central Europe, cultivated for its leaves, which yield an oil used for flavouring. [C16: so called because of its long narrow leaves]

spear side *n.* the male side or branch of a family. Compare **distaff side.**

spearwort (ˈspɪəˌwɜːt) *n.* any of several Eurasian ranunculaceous plants of the genus *Ranunculus,* such as *R. flammula* (**lesser spearwort**) and *R. lingua* (**great spearwort**), which grow in wet places and have long narrow leaves and yellow flowers. See also **buttercup.**

spec (spɛk) *Informal.* ~*n.* **1. on spec.** as a speculation or gamble: *all the tickets were sold so I went to the theatre on spec.* ~*adj.* **2.** (*prenominal*) *Austral. and N.Z.* speculative: *a spec developer.* [C19: short for SPECULATION or SPECULATIVE]

spec. *abbrev. for:* **1.** special. **2.** specification. **3.** speculation.

special (ˈspɛʃəl) *adj.* **1.** distinguished, set apart from, or excelling others of its kind. **2.** (*prenominal*) designed or reserved for a particular purpose: *a special tool for working leather.* **3.** not usual or commonplace. **4.** (*prenominal*) particular or primary: *his special interest was music.* **5.** denoting or relating to the education of physically or mentally handicapped children: *a special school.* ~*n.* **6.** a special person or thing, such as an extra edition of a newspaper or a train reserved for a particular purpose. **7.** a dish or meal given prominence, esp. at a low price, in a café, etc. **8.** *Austral. slang.* a convict given special treatment on account of his education, social class, etc. **9.** short for **special constable. 10.** *Austral., N.Z., U.S. and Canadian informal.* an item in a store that is advertised at a reduced price; a loss leader. ~*vb.* **-cials, -cialling, -cialled.** (*tr.*) **11.** *N.Z. informal.* to advertise and sell (an item) at a reduced price: *we are specialling butter this week.* [C13: from Old French *especial,* from Latin *speciālis* individual, special, from *speciēs* appearance, SPECIES] —ˈ**specially** *adv.* —ˈ**specialness** *n.*

▷**Usage.** See at **especial.**

special assessment *n.* (in the U.S.) a special charge levied on property owners by a county or municipality to help pay the costs of a civic improvement that increases the value of their property.

Special Branch *n.* (in Britain) the department of the police force that is concerned with political security.

special case *n. Law.* an agreed written statement of facts submitted by litigants to a court for a decision on a point of law.

special clearing *n. Banking.* (in Britain) the clearing of a cheque through a bank in less than the usual three days, for an additional charge.

special constable *n.* a person recruited for temporary or occasional police duties, esp. in time of emergency.

special delivery *n.* the delivery of a piece of mail outside the time of a scheduled delivery.

special drawing rights *pl. n.* (*sometimes caps.*) the reserve assets of the International Monetary Fund on which member nations may draw in proportion to their contribution to the Fund. Abbrev.: **SDRs.**

special effects *pl. n. Films.* techniques used in the production of scenes that cannot be achieved by normal techniques.

specialism (ˈspɛʃəˌlɪzəm) *n.* the act or process of specializing in something, or the thing itself.

specialist (ˈspɛʃəlɪst) *n.* **1. a.** a person who specializes in or devotes himself to a particular area of activity, field of research, etc. **b.** (*as modifier*): *specialist knowledge.* **2.** an enlisted rank in the U.S. Army denoting technical qualifications that entitle the holder to a noncommissioned officer's pay. **3.** *Ecology.* an organism that has special nutritional requirements and lives in a restricted habitat that provides these. Compare **generalist.** —ˌ**special'istic** *adj.*

speciality (ˌspɛʃɪ'ælɪtɪ) *or chiefly U.S. and Canadian* **specialty** *n., pl.* **-ties.** **1.** a special interest or skill. **2. a.** a service or product specialized in, as at a restaurant: *roast beef was a speciality of the house.* **b.** (*as modifier*): *a speciality dish.* **3.** a special or distinguishing feature or characteristic.

specialize *or* **specialise** ('spɛʃəˌlaɪz) *vb.* **1.** (*intr.*) to train in or devote oneself to a particular area of study, occupation, or activity. **2.** (*usually passive*) to cause (organisms or their parts) to develop in a way most suited to a particular environment or way of life or (of organisms, etc.) to develop in this way. **3.** (*tr.*) to modify or make suitable for a special use or purpose. **4.** (*tr.*) to mention specifically; specify. **5.** (*tr.*) to endorse (a commercial paper) to a specific payee. —ˌ**speciali'zation** *or* ˌ**speciali'sation** *n.*

special jury *n.* (formerly) a jury whose members were drawn from some profession or rank of society as well as possessing the usual qualifications for jury service.

special licence *n. Brit.* a licence permitting a marriage to take place by dispensing with the usual legal conditions.

special pleading *n. Law.* **1.** a pleading that alleges new facts that offset those put forward by the other side rather than directly admitting or denying those facts. **2.** a pleading that emphasizes the favourable aspects of a case while omitting the unfavourable.

special privilege *n.* a legally endorsed privilege granted exclusively to some individual or group.

special school *n. Brit.* a school for children who are unable to benefit from ordinary schooling because they are educationally subnormal, physically or mentally handicapped, etc.

special sort *n. Printing.* a character, such as an accented letter, that is not a usual member of any fount. Also called: **peculiar, arbitrary.**

special team *n. American football.* any of several predetermined permutations of the players within a team that play in situations, such as kick offs and attempts at field goals, where the standard offensive and defensive formations are not appropriate.

special theory of relativity *n.* the theory proposed in 1905 by Einstein, which assumes that the laws of physics are equally valid in all nonaccelerated frames of reference and that the speed of electromagnetic radiation in free space has the same value for all inertial observers. It leads to the idea of a space-time continuum and the equivalence of mass and energy. In combination with quantum mechanics it forms the basis of the theory of elementary particles. Also called: **special relativity.** See also **general theory of relativity, Einstein's law** (sense 1).

specialty ('spɛʃəltɪ) *n., pl.* **-ties.** **1.** *Law.* a formal contract or obligation expressed in a deed. **2.** another word, chiefly U.S. and Canadian, for **speciality.**

speciate ('spiːsɪˌeɪt) *vb.* to form or develop into a new biological species. [C20: back formation from SPECIATION]

speciation (ˌspiːʃɪ'eɪʃən) *n.* the evolutionary development of a biological species, as by geographical isolation of a group of individuals from the main stock. [C20: from SPECIES + -ATION]

specie ('spiːʃiː) *n.* **1.** coin money, as distinguished from bullion or paper money. **2. in specie. a.** (of money) in coin. **b.** in kind. **c.** *Law.* in the actual form specified. [C16: from the Latin phrase *in speciē* in kind]

specie point *n.* another name for **gold point.**

species ('spiːʃiːz; *Latin* 'spiːʃɪˌiːz) *n., pl.* **-cies.** **1.** *Biology.* **a.** any of the taxonomic groups into which a genus is divided, the members of which are capable of interbreeding: often containing subspecies, varieties, or races. A species is designated in italics by the genus name followed by the specific name, for example *Felis domesticus* (the domestic cat). Abbrev.: **sp. b.** the animals of such a group. **c.** any group of related animals or plants not necessarily of this taxonomic rank. **2.** (*modifier*) denoting a plant that is a natural member of a species rather than a hybrid or cultivar: *a species clematis.* **3.** *Logic.* a group of objects or individuals, all sharing at least one common attribute, that forms a subdivision of a genus. **4.** a kind, sort, or variety: *a species of treachery.* **5.** *Chiefly R.C. Church.* the outward form of the bread and wine in the Eucharist. **6.** *Obsolete.* an outward appearance or form. **7.** *Obsolete.* specie. [C16: from Latin: appearance, from *specere* to look]

speciesism ('spiːʃiːzˌɪzəm) *n.* a belief by humans that all other species of animals are inferior and may therefore be used for human benefit without regard to the suffering inflicted. [C20: from SPECIES + -ISM]

specif. *abbrev. for* specifically.

specifiable ('spɛsɪˌfaɪəbᵊl) *adj.* able to be specified.

specific (spɪ'sɪfɪk) *adj.* **1.** explicit, particular, or definite: *please be more specific.* **2.** relating to a specified or particular thing: *a specific treatment for arthritis.* **3.** of or relating to a biological species: *specific differences.* **4.** (of a disease) caused by a particular pathogenic agent. **5.** *Physics.* **a.** characteristic of a property of a particular substance, esp. in relation to the same property of a standard reference substance: *specific gravity.* **b.** characteristic of a property of a particular substance per unit mass, length, area, volume, etc.: *specific heat.* **c.** (of an extensive physical quantity) divided by mass: *specific heat capacity; specific volume.* **6.** Also (rare): **specifical.** *International trade.* denoting a tariff levied at a fixed sum per unit of weight, quantity, volume, etc., irrespective of value. ~*n.* **7.** (*sometimes pl.*) a designated quality, thing, etc. **8.** *Med.* any drug used to treat a particular disease. [C17: from Medieval Latin *specificus,* from Latin SPECIES] —**spe'cifically** *adv.* —**specificity** (ˌspɛsɪ'fɪsɪtɪ) *n.*

specification (ˌspɛsɪfɪ'keɪʃən) *n.* **1.** the act or an instance of specifying. **2.** (in patent law) a written statement accompanying an application for a patent that describes the nature of an invention. **3.** a detailed description of the criteria for the constituents, construction, appearance, performance, etc., of a material, apparatus, etc., or of the standard of workmanship required in its manufacture. **4.** an item, detail, etc., specified.

specific charge *n. Physics.* the charge-to-mass ratio of an elementary particle.

specific gravity *n.* the ratio of the density of a substance to that of water. See **relative density.**

specific heat capacity *n.* the heat required to raise unit mass of a substance by unit temperature interval under specified conditions, such as constant pressure: usually measured in joules per kelvin per kilogram. Symbol: c_p (for constant pressure). Also called: **specific heat.**

specific humidity *n.* the mass of water vapour in a sample of moist air divided by the mass of the sample.

specific impulse *n.* the ratio of the thrust produced by a rocket engine to the rate of fuel consumption: it has units of time and is the length of time that unit weight of propellant would last if used to produce one unit of thrust continuously.

specific performance *n. Law.* a remedy awarded by a court where damages are an insufficient remedy.

specific resistance *n.* the former name for **resistivity.**

specific viscosity *n. Physics.* a measure of the resistance to flow of a fluid, expressed as the ratio of the absolute viscosity of the fluid to that of a reference fluid (usually water in the case of liquids).

specific volume *n. Physics.* the volume of matter per unit mass; the reciprocal of the density. Symbol: v

specify ('spɛsɪˌfaɪ) *vb.* **-fies, -fying, -fied.** (*tr.; may take a clause as object*) **1.** to refer to or state specifically. **2.** to state as a condition. **3.** to state or include in the specification of. [C13: from Medieval Latin *specificāre* to describe] —**specificative** ('spɛsɪfɪˌkeɪtɪv) *adj.* —'**speciˌfier** *n.*

specimen ('spɛsɪmɪn) *n.* **1. a.** an individual, object, or part regarded as typical of the group or class to which it belongs. **b.** (*as modifier*): *a specimen signature; a specimen page.* **2.** *Med.* a sample of tissue, blood, urine, etc., taken for diagnostic examination or evaluation. **3.** the whole or a part of an organism, plant, rock, etc., collected and preserved as an example of its class, species, etc. **4.** *Informal, often derogatory.* a person. [C17: from Latin: mark, evidence, proof, from *specere* to look at]

speciosity (ˌspiːʃɪ'ɒsɪtɪ) *n., pl.* **-ties.** **1.** a thing or person that is deceptively attractive or plausible. **2.** the state of being specious. **3.** *Obsolete.* the state of being beautiful.

specious ('spiːʃəs) *adj.* **1.** apparently correct or true, but actually wrong or false. **2.** deceptively attractive in appearance. [C14 (originally: fair): from Latin *speciōsus* plausible, from *speciēs* outward appearance, from *specere* to look at] —'**speciously** *adv.* —'**speciousness** *n.*

speck (spɛk) *n.* **1.** a very small mark or spot. **2.** a small or tiny piece of something. ~*vb.* **3.** (*tr.*) to mark with specks or spots. [Old English *specca;* related to Middle Dutch *spekelen* to sprinkle]

speckle ('spɛkᵊl) *n.* **1.** a small or slight mark usually of a contrasting colour, as on the skin, a bird's plumage, or eggs. ~*vb.* **2.** (*tr.*) to mark with or as if with speckles. [C15: from Middle Dutch *spekkel;* see SPECK] —'**speckled** *adj.*

speckled trout *n.* another name for **brook trout.**

speckled wood *n.* a common woodland brown satyrid butterfly, *Pararge aegeria,* marked with pale orange or yellowish-white spots.

speckle interferometry *n. Astronomy.* a technique to increase the resolution of photographs taken by telescopes that are impaired by atmospheric turbulence, in which the information from a number of exposures of very short duration are combined.

specs (spɛks) *pl. n. Informal.* **1.** short for **spectacles. 2.** short for **specifications.**

spectacle ('spɛktəkᵊl) *n.* **1.** a public display or performance, esp. a showy or ceremonial one. **2.** a thing or person seen, esp. an unusual or ridiculous one: *he makes a spectacle of himself.* **3.** a strange or interesting object or phenomenon. ~See also **spectacles.** [C14: via Old French from Latin *spectaculum* a show, from *spectāre* to watch, from *specere* to look at]

spectacled ('spɛktəkᵊld) *adj.* **1.** wearing glasses. **2.** (of an animal) having markings around the eyes resembling a pair of glasses.

spectacles ('spɛktəkᵊlz) *pl. n.* **1.** a pair of glasses for correcting defective vision. Often (informal) shortened to **specs. 2. pair of spectacles.** *Cricket.* a score of 0 in each innings of a match.

spectacular (spɛk'tækjʊlə) *adj.* **1.** of or resembling a spectacle; impressive, grand, or dramatic. **2.** unusually marked or great: *a spectacular increase in spending.* ~*n.* **3.** a lavishly produced performance. —**spec'tacularly** *adv.*

spectate (spɛk'teɪt) *vb.* (*intr.*) to be a spectator; watch. [C20: back formation from SPECTATOR]
spectator (spɛk'teɪtə) *n.* a person viewing anything; onlooker; observer. [C16: from Latin, from *spectāre* to watch; see SPECTACLE]
spectator sport *n.* a sport that attracts people as spectators rather than as participants.
spectra ('spɛktrə) *n.* the plural of **spectrum.**
spectral ('spɛktrəl) *adj.* **1.** of or like a spectre. **2.** of or relating to a spectrum: *spectral colours.* **3.** *Physics.* (of a physical quantity) relating to a single wavelength of radiation: *spectral luminous efficiency.* —**spectrality** (spɛk'trælɪtɪ) *or* '**spectralness** *n.* —'**spectrally** *adv.*
spectral luminous efficiency *n.* a measure of the efficiency of radiation of a given wavelength in producing a visual sensation. It is equal to the ratio of the radiant flux at a standard wavelength to that at the given wavelength when the standard wavelength is chosen so that the maximum value of this ratio is unity. Symbol: $V(\lambda)$ (for photopic vision) or $V'(\lambda)$ (for scotopic vision).
spectral type *or* **class** *n.* any of various groups into which stars are classified according to characteristic spectral lines and bands. The most important classification (**Harvard classification**) has a series of classes W, O, B, A, F, G, K, M, R, N, S, the series also being a scale of diminishing surface temperature.
spectre *or U.S.* **specter** ('spɛktə) *n.* **1.** a ghost; phantom; apparition. **2.** a mental image of something unpleasant or menacing: *the spectre of redundancy.* [C17: from Latin *spectrum,* from *specere* to look at]
spectrin ('spɛktrɪn) *n.* any one of a class of fibrous proteins found in the membranes of red blood cells, the brain, the intestine, etc. [C20: from SPECTR(E) + -IN, referring to the ghosts (isolated cell membranes) of red blood cells, the source of the first known member of the class]
spectro- *combining form.* indicating a spectrum: *spectrogram.*
spectrobolometer (ˌspɛktrəʊbəʊ'lɒmɪtə) *n.* a combined spectroscope and bolometer for determining the wavelength distribution of radiant energy emitted by a source. —**spectrobolometric** (ˌspɛktrəˌbəʊlə'mɛtrɪk) *adj.*
spectrofluorimeter (ˌspɛktrəʊflʊə'rɪmɪtə) *or* **spectrofluorometer** *n.* an instrument for recording fluorescence emission and absorption spectra.
spectrograph ('spɛktrəʊˌgrɑːf, -ˌgræf) *n.* a spectroscope or spectrometer that produces a photographic record (**spectrogram**) of a spectrum. See also **sound spectrograph.** —ˌ**spectro'graphic** *adj.* —ˌ**spectro'graphically** *adv.* —**spec'trography** *n.*
spectroheliograph (ˌspɛktrəʊ'hiːlɪəˌgrɑːf, -ˌgræf) *n.* an instrument used to photograph the sun in light of a particular wavelength, usually that of calcium or hydrogen, to show the distribution of the element over the surface and in the atmosphere. The photograph obtained is a **spectroheliogram.** [C19: from SPECTRO- + HELIO- + -GRAPH] —ˌ**spectroˌhelio'graphic** *adj.*
spectrohelioscope (ˌspɛktrəʊ'hiːlɪəʊˌskəʊp) *n.* an instrument, similar to the spectroheliograph, used for observing solar radiation at one particular wavelength. —**spectrohelioscopic** (ˌspɛktrəʊˌhiːlɪəʊ'skɒpɪk) *adj.*
spectrometer (spɛk'trɒmɪtə) *n.* any instrument for producing a spectrum, esp. one in which wavelength, energy, intensity, etc., can be measured. See also **mass spectrometer.** —**spectrometric** (ˌspɛktrəʊ'mɛtrɪk) *adj.* —**spec'trometry** *n.*
spectrophotometer (ˌspɛktrəʊfəʊ'tɒmɪtə) *n.* an instrument for producing or recording a spectrum and measuring the photometric intensity of each wavelength present, esp. such an instrument used for infrared, visible, and ultraviolet radiation. See also **spectrometer.** [C19: from SPECTRO- + PHOTO- + -METER] —**spectrophotometric** (ˌspɛktrəʊˌfəʊtə'mɛtrɪk) *adj.* —ˌ**spectropho'tometry** *n.*
spectroscope ('spɛktrəˌskəʊp) *n.* any of a number of instruments for dispersing electromagnetic radiation and thus forming or recording a spectrum. See also **spectrometer.** [C19: from SPECTRO- + -SCOPE; from French, or on the model of German *Spektroskop*] —**spectroscopic** (ˌspɛktrə'skɒpɪk) *or* ˌ**spectro'scopical** *adj.* —ˌ**spectro'scopically** *adv.*
spectroscopic analysis *n.* the use of spectroscopy in determining the chemical or physical constitution of substances.
spectroscopy (spɛk'trɒskəpɪ) *n.* the science and practice of using spectrometers and spectroscopes and of analysing spectra, the methods employed depending on the radiation being examined. The techniques are widely used in chemical analysis and in studies of the properties of atoms, molecules, ions, etc. —**spec'troscopist** *n.*
spectrum ('spɛktrəm) *n., pl* **-tra** (-trə). **1.** the distribution of colours produced when white light is dispersed by a prism or diffraction grating. There is a continuous change in wavelength from red, the longest wavelength, to violet, the shortest. Seven colours are usually distinguished: violet, indigo, blue, green, yellow, orange, and red. **2.** the whole range of electromagnetic radiation with respect to its wavelength or frequency. **3.** any particular distribution of electromagnetic radiation often showing lines or bands characteristic of the substance emitting the radiation or absorbing it. See also **absorption spectrum, emission spectrum.** **4.** any similar distribution or record of the energies, velocities, masses, etc., of atoms, ions, electrons, etc.: *a mass spectrum.* **5.** any range or scale, as of capabilities, emotions, or moods. **6.** another name for an **afterimage.** [C17: from Latin: appearance, image, from *spectāre* to observe, from *specere* to look at]
spectrum analyser *n.* an instrument that splits an input waveform into its frequency components, which are then displayed.
spectrum analysis *n.* the analysis of a spectrum to determine the properties of its source, such as the analysis of the emission spectrum of a substance to determine the electron distribution in its molecules.
specular ('spɛkjʊlə) *adj.* **1.** of, relating to, or having the properties of a mirror: *specular reflection.* **2.** of or relating to a speculum. [C16: from Latin *speculāris,* from *speculum* a mirror, from *specere* to look at] —'**specularly** *adv.*
speculate ('spɛkjʊˌleɪt) *vb.* **1.** (when *tr., takes a clause as object*) to conjecture without knowing the complete facts. **2.** (*intr.*) to buy or sell securities, property, etc., in the hope of deriving capital gains. **3.** (*intr.*) to risk loss for the possibility of considerable gain. **4.** (*intr.*) *N.Z. rugby.* to make an emergency forward kick of the ball without taking any particular aim. [C16: from Latin *speculārī* to spy out, from *specula* a watchtower, from *specere* to look at]
speculation (ˌspɛkjʊ'leɪʃən) *n.* **1.** the act or an instance of speculating. **2.** a supposition, theory, or opinion arrived at through speculating. **3.** investment involving high risk but also the possibility of high profits.
speculative ('spɛkjʊlətɪv) *adj.* relating to or characterized by speculation, esp. financial speculation. —'**speculatively** *adv.* —'**speculativeness** *n.*
speculator ('spɛkjʊˌleɪtə) *n.* **1.** a person who speculates. **2.** *N.Z. rugby.* an undirected kick of the ball.
speculum ('spɛkjʊləm) *n., pl.* **-la** (-lə) *or* **-lums.** **1.** a mirror, esp. one made of polished metal for use in a telescope, etc. **2.** *Med.* an instrument for dilating a bodily cavity or passage to permit examination of its interior. **3.** a patch of distinctive colour on the wing of a bird, esp. in certain ducks. [C16: from Latin: mirror, from *specere* to look at]
speculum metal *n.* a white hard brittle corrosion-resistant alloy of copper (55–70 per cent) and tin with smaller amounts of other metals. It takes a high polish and is used for mirrors, lamp reflectors, ornamental ware, etc.
sped (spɛd) *vb.* a past tense and past participle of **speed.**
speech (spiːtʃ) *n.* **1. a.** the act or faculty of speaking, esp. as possessed by persons: *to have speech with somebody.* **b.** (*as modifier*): *speech therapy.* **2.** that which is spoken; utterance. **3.** a talk or address delivered to an audience. **4.** a person's characteristic manner of speaking. **5.** a national or regional language or dialect. **6.** *Linguistics.* another word for **parole** (sense 5). [Old English *spēc;* related to *specan* to SPEAK]
speech act *n. Philosophy.* **1.** an utterance that constitutes some act in addition to the mere act of uttering. **2.** an act or type of act capable of being so performed. ~See also **performative.**
speech community *n.* a community consisting of all the speakers of a particular language or dialect.
speech day *n. Brit.* (in schools) an annual day on which prizes are presented, speeches are made by guest speakers, etc.
speech from the throne *n.* (in Britain and the dominions of the Commonwealth) the speech at the opening of each session of Parliament in which the Government outlines its legislative programme. It is read by the sovereign or his or her representative. Also called (esp. Brit.): **Queen's** (*or* **King's**) **speech.**
speechify ('spiːtʃɪˌfaɪ) *vb.* **-fies, -fying, -fied.** (*intr.*) **1.** to make a speech or speeches. **2.** to talk pompously and boringly. —ˌ**speechifi'cation** *n.* —'**speechiˌfier** *n.*
speechless ('spiːtʃlɪs) *adj.* **1.** not able to speak. **2.** temporarily deprived of speech. **3.** not expressed or able to be expressed in words: *speechless fear.* —'**speechlessly** *adv.* —'**speechlessness** *n.*
speech-reading *n.* another name for **lip-reading.**
speech recognition *n.* the understanding of continuous speech by a computer.
speech therapy *n.* treatment to improve the speech of children who have difficulty in learning to speak, for example because of partial deafness or brain damage, or to help restore the power of speech to adults who have lost it or partly lost it through accident or illness. —**speech therapist** *n.*
speed (spiːd) *n.* **1.** the act or quality of acting or moving fast; rapidity. **2.** the rate at which something moves, is done, or acts. **3.** *Physics.* **a.** a scalar measure of the rate of movement of a body expressed either as the distance travelled divided by the time taken (**average speed**) or the rate of change of position with respect to time at a particular point (**instantaneous speed**). It is measured in metres per second, miles per hour, etc. **b.** another word for **velocity** (sense 2). **4.** a rate of rotation, usually expressed in revolutions per unit time. **5. a.** a gear ratio in a motor vehicle, bicycle, etc. **b.** (*in combination*): *a three-speed gear.* **6.** *Photog.* a numerical expression of the sensitivity to light of a particular type of film, paper, or plate. See also **ASA/BS, DIN.** **7.** *Photog.* a measure of the ability of a lens to pass light from an object to the image position, determined by the aperture and also the transmitting power of the lens. It increases as the f-number is decreased and vice versa. **8.** a slang word for **amphetamine.** **9.** *Archaic.* prosperity or success. **10.**

at speed. quickly. ~*vb.* **speeds, speeding; sped** *or* **speeded.** **11.** to move or go or cause to move or go quickly. **12.** (*intr.*) to drive (a motor vehicle) at a high speed, esp. above legal limits. **13.** (*tr.*) to help further the success or completion of. **14.** (*intr.*) *Slang.* to take or be under the influence of amphetamines. **15.** (*intr.*) to operate or run at a high speed. **16.** *Archaic.* **a.** (*intr.*) to prosper or succeed. **b.** (*tr.*) to wish success to. ~See also **speed up.** [Old English *spēd* (originally in the sense: success); related to *spōwan* to succeed, Latin *spēs* hope, Old Slavonic *spěti* to be lucky] —'**speeder** *n.*

speedball ('spiːdˌbɔːl) *n.* **1.** *Slang.* a mixture of heroin with amphetamine or cocaine. **2.** *Austral.* a meat rissole with laxative properties, eaten esp. by shearers.

speedboat ('spiːdˌbəʊt) *n.* a high-speed motorboat having either an inboard or outboard motor.

speed chess *n.* a form of chess in which each player's game is limited to a total stipulated time, usually half an hour; the first player to exceed the time limit loses.

speedfreak ('spiːdˌfriːk) *n. Slang.* an amphetamine addict.

speed limit *n.* the maximum permitted speed at which a vehicle may travel on certain roads.

speedo ('spiːdəʊ) *n., pl.* **speedos.** an informal name for **speedometer** or (Austral.) **odometer.**

speedometer (spɪ'dɒmɪtə) *n.* a device fitted to a vehicle to measure and display the speed of travel. See also **mileometer.**

speedster ('spiːdstə) *n.* a fast car, esp. a sports model.

speed trap *n.* a section of road on which the police check the speed of vehicles, often using radar.

speed up *vb.* (*adv.*) **1.** to increase or cause to increase in speed or rate; accelerate. ~*n.* **speed-up. 2.** an instance of this; acceleration.

speedway ('spiːdˌweɪ) *n.* **1. a.** the sport of racing on light powerful motorcycles round cinder tracks. **b.** (*as modifier*): *a speedway track.* **2.** the track or stadium where such races are held. **3.** *U.S. and Canadian.* **a.** a racetrack for cars. **b.** a road on which fast driving is allowed.

speedwell ('spiːdˌwɛl) *n.* any of various temperate scrophulariaceous plants of the genus *Veronica,* such as *V. officinalis* (**common speedwell**) and *V. chamaedrys* (**germander speedwell**), having small blue or pinkish white flowers. [C16: from SPEED + WELL[1]]

Speedwriting ('spiːdˌraɪtɪŋ) *n. Trademark.* a form of shorthand in which alphabetic combinations are used to represent groups of sounds or short common words.

speedy ('spiːdɪ) *adj.* **speedier, speediest. 1.** characterized by speed of motion. **2.** done or decided without delay; quick. —'**speedily** *adv.* —'**speediness** *n.*

speel (spiːl) *n. Manchester dialect.* a splinter of wood. [probably from Old Norse; compare Norwegian *spela, spila,* Swedish *spjela, spjele* SPILL[2]]

speir *or* **speer** (spiːr) *vb. Scot.* to ask; inquire. [Old English *spyrian* to seek after, search for]

speiss (spaɪs) *n.* the arsenides and antimonides that form when ores containing arsenic or antimony are smelted. [C18: from German *Speise* food]

spek (spek) *n. S. African.* bacon, fat, or fatty pork used for larding venison or other game. [Afrikaans]

spelaean *or* **spelean** (spɪ'liːən) *adj.* of, found in, or inhabiting caves: *spelaean animals.* [C19: via New Latin, from Latin *spēlaeum* a cave, from Greek *spēlaion*]

speleology *or* **spelaeology** (ˌspiːlɪ'ɒlədʒɪ) *n.* **1.** the scientific study of caves, esp. in respect of their geological formation, flora and fauna, etc. **2.** the sport or pastime of exploring caves. [C19: from Latin *spēlaeum* cave] —**speleological** *or* **spelaeological** (ˌspiːlɪə'lɒdʒɪkᵊl) *adj.* —ˌ**spele'ologist** *or* ˌ**spelae'ologist** *n.*

spelk (spɛlk) *n. Scot. and northern English dialect.* a splinter of wood. [from Old English *spelc, spilc* surgical splint; related to Old Norse *spelkur* splints]

spell[1] (spɛl) *vb.* **spells, spelling; spelt** *or* **spelled. 1.** to write or name in correct order the letters that comprise the conventionally accepted form of (a word or part of a word). **2.** (*tr.*) (of letters) to go to make up the conventionally established form of (a word) when arranged correctly: *d-o-g spells dog.* **3.** (*tr.*) to indicate or signify: *such actions spell disaster for our cause.* ~See also **spell out.** [C13: from Old French *espeller,* of Germanic origin; related to Old Norse *spialla* to talk, Middle High German *spellen*] —'**spellable** *adj.*

spell[2] (spɛl) *n.* **1.** a verbal formula considered as having magical force. **2.** any influence that can control the mind or character; fascination. **3.** a state induced by or as if by the pronouncing of a spell; trance: *to break the spell.* **4. under a spell.** held in or as if in a spell. ~*vb.* **5.** (*tr.*) *Rare.* to place under a spell. [Old English *spell* speech; related to Old Norse *spjall* tale, Gothic *spill,* Old High German *spel*]

spell[3] (spɛl) *n.* **1.** an indeterminate, usually short, period of time: *a spell of cold weather.* **2.** a period or tour of duty after which one person or group relieves another. **3.** *Scot., Austral., and N.Z.* a period or interval of rest. ~*vb.* **4.** (*tr.*) to take over from (a person) for an interval of time; relieve temporarily. **5. spell a paddock.** *N.Z.* to give a field a rest period by letting it lie fallow. [Old English *spelian* to take the place of, of obscure origin]

spellbind ('spɛlˌbaɪnd) *vb.* **-binds, -binding, -bound.** (*tr.*) to cause to be spellbound; entrance or enthral.

spellbinder ('spɛlˌbaɪndə) *n.* **1.** a person capable of holding others spellbound, esp. a political speaker. **2.** a novel, play, etc., that holds one enthralled.

spellbound ('spɛlˌbaʊnd) *adj.* having one's attention held as though one is bound by a spell: *a spellbound audience.*

speller ('spɛlə) *n.* **1.** a person who spells words in the manner specified: *a bad speller.* **2.** a book designed to teach or improve spelling.

spellican ('spɛlɪkən) *n.* a variant spelling of **spillikin.**

spelling ('spɛlɪŋ) *n.* **1.** the act or process of writing words by using the letters conventionally accepted for their formation; orthography. **2.** the art or study of orthography. **3.** the actual way in which a word is spelt. **4.** the ability of a person to spell: *John's spelling is good.*

spelling bee *n.* a contest in which players are required to spell words according to orthographic conventions. [C19: from BEE[2]]

spelling pronunciation *n.* a pronunciation of a word that is influenced by the word's orthography and often comes about as the modification of an earlier or original rendering, such as the pronunciation of the British name *Mainwaring,* usually ('mænərɪŋ), as ('meɪnˌwɛərɪŋ).

spell out *vb.* (*tr., adv.*) **1.** to make clear, distinct, or explicit; clarify in detail: *let me spell out the implications.* **2.** to read laboriously or with difficulty, working out each word letter by letter. **3.** to discern by study; puzzle out.

spelt[1] (spɛlt) *vb.* a past tense and past participle of **spell**[1].

spelt[2] (spɛlt) *n.* a species of wheat, *Triticum spelta,* that was formerly much cultivated and was used to develop present-day cultivated wheats. [Old English; related to Old Saxon *spelta,* Old High German *spelza*]

spelter ('spɛltə) *n.* impure zinc, usually containing about 3 per cent of lead and other impurities. [C17: probably from Middle Dutch *speauter,* of obscure origin; compare Old French *peautre* pewter, Italian *peltro* PEWTER]

spelunker (spɪ'lʌŋkə) *n.* a person whose hobby is the exploration and study of caves. [C20: from Latin *spēlunca,* from Greek *spēlunx* a cave] —**spe'lunking** *n.*

spence (spɛns) *n. Dialect.* **a.** a larder or pantry. **b.** any monetary allowance. **c.** a parlour, esp. in a cottage. [C14: from Old French *despense,* from Latin *dispendere* to distribute; see DISPENSE]

spencer[1] ('spɛnsə) *n.* **1.** a short fitted coat or jacket. **2.** a woman's knitted vest. [C18: named after Earl *Spencer* (1758–1834)]

spencer[2] ('spɛnsə) *n. Nautical.* a large loose-footed gaffsail on a square-rigger or barque. [C19: perhaps after the surname *Spencer*]

spend (spɛnd) *vb.* **spends, spending, spent. 1.** to pay out (money, wealth, etc.). **2.** (*tr.*) to concentrate (time, effort, thought, etc.) upon an object, activity, etc. **3.** (*tr.*) to pass (time) in a specific way, activity, place, etc. **4.** (*tr.*) to use up completely: *the hurricane spent its force.* **5.** (*tr.*) to give up (one's blood, life, etc.) in a cause. **6.** (*intr.*) *Obsolete.* to be used up or exhausted. **7. spend a penny.** *Brit. informal.* to urinate. ~*n.* **8.** an amount of money spent, esp. regularly, or allocated to be spent. ~See also **spends.** [Old English *spendan,* from Latin *expendere;* influenced also by Old French *despendre* to spend, from Latin *dispendere;* see EXPEND, DISPENSE] —'**spendable** *adj.*

spender ('spɛndə) *n.* a person who spends money in a manner specified: *a big spender.*

spending money *n.* an allowance for small personal expenses; pocket money.

spends (spɛndz) *pl. n. Lancashire dialect.* a child's pocket money.

spendthrift ('spɛndˌθrɪft) *n.* **1.** a person who spends money in an extravagant manner. ~*adj.* **2.** (*usually prenominal*) of or like a spendthrift: *spendthrift economies.* [C17: from SPEND + THRIFT]

Spenserian (spɛn'sɪərɪən) *adj.* **1.** relating to, in the style of, or characteristic of the English poet Edmund Spenser (?1552–99) or his poetry. ~*n.* **2.** a student or imitator of Edmund Spenser.

Spenserian sonnet *n. Prosody.* a sonnet form used by the poet Spenser having the rhyme scheme a b a b b c b c c d c d e e.

Spenserian stanza *n. Prosody.* the stanza form used by the poet Spenser in his poem *The Faerie Queene,* consisting of eight lines in iambic pentameter and a concluding Alexandrine, rhyming a b a b b c b c c.

spent (spɛnt) *vb.* **1.** the past tense and past participle of **spend.** ~*adj.* **2.** used up or exhausted; consumed. **3.** (of a fish) exhausted by spawning.

spent gnat *n.* an angler's name for the spinner of various mayflies, esp. *Ephemeris danica* and *E. vulgata,* particularly when lying spent on the water surface after mating and egg-laying.

speos ('spiːɒs) *n.* (esp. in ancient Egypt) a temple or tomb cut into a rock face. [C19: Greek, literally: a cave, grotto]

sperm[1] (spɜːm) *n.* **1.** another name for **semen. 2.** a male reproductive cell; male gamete. [C14: from Late Latin *sperma,* from Greek; related to Greek *speirein* to sow]

sperm[2] (spɜːm) *n.* short for **sperm whale, spermaceti,** or **sperm oil.**

-sperm *n. combining form.* (in botany) a seed: *gymnosperm.* —**-spermous** *or* **-spermal** *adj. combining form.*

spermaceti (ˌspɜːmə'sɛtɪ, -'siːtɪ) *n.* a white waxy substance obtained from oil from the head of the sperm whale: used in cosmetics, candles, ointments, etc. [C15: from Medieval Latin *sperma cētī* whale's sperm, from *sperma* SPERM[1] + Latin *cētus* whale, from Greek *kētos*]

spermary ('spɜːmərɪ) *n., pl.* **-maries.** any organ in which spermatozoa are produced, esp. a testis.

spermatheca (ˌspɜːmə'θiːkə) *n.* a sac or cavity within the body of many female invertebrates, esp. insects, used for storing spermatozoa before fertilization takes place. [C19: see SPERM[1], THECA] —ˌ**sperma'thecal** *adj.*

spermatic (spɜː'mætɪk), **spermic** ('spɜːmɪk), *or* **spermous** ('spɜːməs) *adj.* **1.** of or relating to spermatozoa: *spermatic fluid.* **2.** of or relating to the testis: *the spermatic artery.* **3.** of or relating to a spermary. [C16: from Late Latin *spermaticus,* from Greek *spermatikos* concerning seed, from *sperma* seed, SPERM[1]] —**sper'matically** *adv.*

spermatic cord *n.* a cord in many male mammals that passes from each testis to the abdominal cavity and contains the spermatic artery and vein, vas deferens, and lymphatics.

spermatic fluid *n.* another name for **semen.**

spermatid ('spɜːmətɪd) *n. Zoology.* any of four immature male gametes that are formed from a spermatocyte, each of which develops into a spermatozoon.

spermatium (spɜː'meɪtɪəm) *n., pl.* **-tia** (-tɪə). a nonmotile male reproductive cell in red algae and some fungi. [C19: New Latin, from Greek *spermation* a little seed; see SPERM[1]]

spermato-, spermo- *or before a vowel* **spermat-, sperm-** *combining form.* **1.** indicating sperm: *spermatogenesis.* **2.** indicating seed: *spermatophyte.* [from Greek *sperma, spermat-,* seed; see SPERM[1]]

spermatocide ('spɜːmətəʊˌsaɪd) *n.* a less common word for **spermicide.** —ˌ**spermato'cidal** *adj.*

spermatocyte ('spɜːmətəʊˌsaɪt) *n.* **1.** *Zoology.* an immature male germ cell, developed from a spermatogonium, that gives rise, by meiosis, to four spermatids. **2.** *Botany.* a male germ cell that develops into an antherozoid.

spermatogenesis (ˌspɜːmətəʊ'dʒɛnɪsɪs) *n.* the formation and maturation of spermatozoa in the testis. See also **spermatocyte** (sense 1). —**spermatogenetic** (ˌspɜːmətəʊdʒə'nɛtɪk) *adj.*

spermatogonium (ˌspɜːmətə'gəʊnɪəm) *n., pl.* **-nia** (-nɪə). *Zoology.* an immature male germ cell that divides to form many spermatocytes. [C19: from SPERMATO- + -GONIUM] —ˌ**spermato'gonial** *adj.*

spermatophore ('spɜːmətəʊˌfɔː) *n.* a capsule of spermatozoa extruded by some molluscs, crustaceans, annelids, and amphibians. —**spermatophoral** (ˌspɜːmə'tɒfərəl) *adj.*

spermatophyte ('spɜːmətəʊˌfaɪt) *or* **spermophyte** *n.* any plant of the major division *Spermatophyta,* which includes all seed-bearing plants: divided into the *Angiospermae* (see **angiosperm**) and the *Gymnospermae* (see **gymnosperm**). Former name: **phanerogam.** —**spermatophytic** (ˌspɜːmətəʊ'fɪtɪk) *adj.*

spermatorrhoea *or esp. U.S.* **spermatorrhea** (ˌspɜːmətəʊ'rɪə) *n.* involuntary emission of semen.

spermatozoid (ˌspɜːmətəʊ'zəʊɪd) *n. Botany.* another name for **antherozoid.**

spermatozoon (ˌspɜːmətəʊ'zəʊɒn) *n., pl.* **-zoa** (-'zəʊə). any of the male reproductive cells released in the semen during ejaculation, consisting of a flattened egg-shaped head, a long neck, and a whiplike tail by which it moves to fertilize the female ovum. Also called: **sperm, zoosperm.** —ˌ**spermato'zoal,** ˌ**spermato'zoan,** *or* ˌ**spermato'zoic** *adj.*

sperm bank *n.* a place in which semen is stored until it is required for artificial insemination.

spermic ('spɜːmɪk) *adj.* another word for **spermatic.**

spermicide ('spɜːmɪˌsaɪd) *n.* any drug or other agent that kills spermatozoa. —ˌ**spermi'cidal** *adj.*

spermine ('spɜːmiːn, -mɪn) *n.* a white or colourless basic water-soluble amine that is found in semen, sputum, and animal tissues; diaminopropyltetramethylenediamine. Formula: $C_{10}H_{26}N_4$.

spermiogenesis (ˌspɜːmɪəʊ'dʒɛnɪsɪs) *n.* the stage in spermatogenesis in which spermatozoa are formed from spermatids. —**spermiogenetic** (ˌspɜːmɪəʊdʒə'nɛtɪk) *adj.*

spermogonium (ˌspɜːmə'gəʊnɪəm) *n., pl.* **-nia** (-nɪə). a reproductive body in some fungi and lichens, in which spermatia are formed.

sperm oil *n.* an oil obtained from the head of the sperm whale, used as a lubricant.

spermophile ('spɜːməʊˌfaɪl) *n.* any of various North American ground squirrels of the genera *Citellus, Spermophilopsis,* etc., regarded as pests in many regions. [C19: from SPERMO- + -PHILE, on the model of New Latin *spermophilus* a seed-lover]

spermophyte ('spɜːməʊˌfaɪt) *n.* a variant spelling of **spermatophyte.**

spermous ('spɜːməs) *adj.* **1.** of or relating to the sperm whale or its products. **2.** another word for **spermatic.**

sperm whale *n.* a large toothed whale, *Physeter catodon,* having a square-shaped head and hunted for sperm oil, spermaceti, and ambergris: family *Physeteridae.* Also called: **cachalot.** [C19: short for SPERMACETI *whale*]

sperrylite ('spɛrɪˌlaɪt) *n.* a white metallic mineral consisting of platinum arsenide in cubic crystalline form. Formula: $PtAs_2$. [C19: named after F. L. *Sperry,* Canadian chemist]

spessartite ('spɛsəˌtaɪt) *n.* a brownish red garnet that consists of manganese aluminium silicate and is used as a gemstone. Formula: $Mn_3Al_2(SiO_4)_3$. [C19: named after *Spessart,* mountain range in Germany]

speug (spjʌg) *n. Scot.* a sparrow. [of unknown origin]

spew (spjuː) *vb.* **1.** to eject (the contents of the stomach) involuntarily through the mouth; vomit. **2.** to spit (spittle, phlegm, etc.) out of the mouth. **3.** (usually foll. by *out*) to send or be sent out in a stream: *flames spewed out.* ~*n.* **4.** something ejected from the mouth. ~Also (archaic): **spue.** [Old English *spīwan;* related to Old Norse *spȳja,* Gothic *speiwan,* Old High German *spīwan,* Latin *spuere,* Lithuanian *spiauti*] —'**spewer** *n.*

sp. gr. *abbrev. for* specific gravity.

sphagnum ('sfægnəm) *n.* any moss of the genus *Sphagnum,* of temperate bogs, having leaves capable of holding much water: layers of these mosses decay to form peat. Also called: **peat moss, bog moss.** [C18: from New Latin, from Greek *sphagnos* a variety of moss] —'**sphagnous** *adj.*

sphairee (sfaɪ'riː) *n. Austral.* a game resembling tennis played with wooden bats and a perforated plastic ball, devised by F. A. Beck in 1961. [from Greek *sphaira* a ball]

sphalerite ('sfæləˌraɪt, 'sfeɪlə-) *n.* a yellow to brownish-black mineral consisting of zinc sulphide in cubic crystalline form with varying amounts of iron, manganese, cadmium, gallium, and indium: the chief source of zinc. Formula: ZnS. Also called: **zinc blende.** [C19: from Greek *sphaleros* deceitful, from *sphallein* to cause to stumble]

sphene (sfiːn) *n.* a brown, yellow, green, or grey lustrous mineral consisting of calcium titanium silicate in monoclinic crystalline form. It occurs in metamorphic and acid igneous rocks and is used as a gemstone. Formula: $CaTiSiO_5$. Also called: **titanite.** [C19: from French *sphène,* from Greek *sphēn* a wedge, alluding to its crystals]

sphenic ('sfiːnɪk) *adj.* having the shape of a wedge. [from Greek *sphēn* a wedge]

spheno- *or before a vowel* **sphen-** *combining form.* having the shape of a wedge: *sphenogram.* [from Greek *sphēn* wedge]

sphenodon ('sfiːnəˌdɒn) *n.* the technical name for the **tuatara.** [C19: from Greek *sphēn* a wedge + *odōn* a tooth]

sphenogram ('sfiːnəˌgræm) *n.* a character used in cuneiform script.

sphenoid ('sfiːnɔɪd) *adj. also* **sphenoidal. 1.** wedge-shaped. **2.** of or relating to the sphenoid bone. ~*n.* **3.** See **sphenoid bone.**

sphenoid bone *n.* the large butterfly-shaped compound bone at the base of the skull, containing a protective depression for the pituitary gland.

spheral ('sfɪərəl) *adj.* **1.** of or shaped like a sphere; spherical. **2.** perfectly rounded; symmetrical.

sphere (sfɪə) *n.* **1.** *Maths.* **a.** a three-dimensional closed surface such that every point on the surface is equidistant from a given point, the centre. **b.** the solid figure bounded by this surface or the space enclosed by it. Equation: $(x-a)^2 + (y-b)^2 + (z-c)^2 = r^2$, where r is the radius and (a, b, c) are the coordinates of the centre; surface area: $4\pi r^2$; volume: $4\pi r^3/3$. **2.** any object having approximately this shape; globe. **3.** the night sky considered as a vaulted roof; firmament. **4.** any heavenly object such as a planet, natural satellite, or star. **5.** (in the Ptolemaic or Copernican systems of astronomy) one of a series of revolving hollow globes, arranged concentrically, on whose transparent surfaces the sun (or in the Copernican system the earth), the moon, the planets, and fixed stars were thought to be set, revolving around the earth (or in the Copernican system the sun). **6.** particular field of activity; environment: *that's out of my sphere.* **7.** a social class or stratum of society. ~*vb.* (*tr.*) *Chiefly poetic.* **8.** to surround or encircle. **9.** to place aloft or in the heavens. [C14: from Late Latin *sphēra,* from Latin *sphaera* globe, from Greek *sphaira*]

-sphere *n. combining form.* **1.** having the shape or form of a sphere: *bathysphere.* **2.** indicating a spherelike enveloping mass: *atmosphere.* —**-spheric** *adj. combining form.*

sphere of influence *n.* a region of the world in which one state is dominant.

spherical ('sfɛrɪkᵊl) *or* **spheric** *adj.* **1.** shaped like a sphere. **2.** of or relating to a sphere: *spherical geometry.* **3.** *Geom.* formed on the surface of or inside a sphere: *a spherical triangle.* **4. a.** of or relating to heavenly bodies. **b.** of or relating to the spheres of the Ptolemaic or the Copernican system. —'**spherically** *adv.* —'**sphericalness** *n.*

spherical aberration *n. Physics.* a defect of optical systems that arises when light striking a mirror or lens near its edge is focused at different points on the axis to the light striking near the centre. The effect occurs when the mirror or lens has spherical surfaces. See also **aberration** (sense 4).

spherical angle *n.* an angle formed at the intersection of two great circles of a sphere.

spherical coordinates *pl. n.* three coordinates that define the location of a point in three-dimensional space in terms of its radius vector, r, the angle, θ, which this vector makes with one axis, and the angle, ϕ, which the plane of this vector makes with a mutually perpendicular axis. Usually written (r, θ, ϕ).

spherical geometry *n.* the branch of geometry concerned with the properties of figures formed on the surface of a sphere.

spherical polygon *n.* a closed geometric figure formed on the surface of a sphere that is bounded by three or more arcs of great circles.

spherical triangle *n.* a closed geometric figure formed on the surface of a sphere that is bounded by arcs of three great circles.

spherical trigonometry *n.* the branch of trigonometry concerned with the measurement of the angles and sides of spherical triangles.

sphericity (sfɪˈrɪsɪtɪ) *n.* the state or form of being spherical.

spherics^1 (ˈsfɛrɪks) *n.* (*functioning as sing.*) the geometry and trigonometry of figures on the surface of a sphere.

spherics^2 *or U.S.* **sferics** (ˈsfɛrɪks, ˈsfɪər-) *n.* (*functioning as sing.*) short for **atmospherics.**

spheroid (ˈsfɪərɔɪd) *n. Maths.* another name for **ellipsoid of revolution.**

spheroidal (sfɪəˈrɔɪdəl) *adj.* **1.** shaped like an ellipsoid of revolution; approximately spherical. **2.** of or relating to an ellipsoid of revolution. —**spheˈroidally** *or* **spheˈroidically** *adv.*

spheroidicity (ˌsfɪərɔɪˈdɪsɪtɪ) *n.* the state or form of being spheroidal.

spherometer (sfɪəˈrɒmɪtə) *n.* an instrument for measuring the curvature of a surface.

spherule (ˈsfɛruːl) *n.* a very small sphere or globule. [C17: from Late Latin *sphaerula* a little SPHERE] —**ˈspherular** *adj.*

spherulite (ˈsfɛrʊˌlaɪt) *n.* any of several spherical masses of radiating needle-like crystals of one or more minerals occurring in rocks such as obsidian. —**spherulitic** (ˌsfɛrʊˈlɪtɪk) *adj.*

sphery (ˈsfɪərɪ) *adj. Poetic.* **1.** resembling a sphere. **2.** resembling a celestial body or bodies; starlike.

sphincter (ˈsfɪŋktə) *n. Anatomy.* a ring of muscle surrounding the opening of a hollow organ or body and contracting to close it. [C16: from Late Latin, from Greek *sphinktēr,* from *sphingein* to grip tightly] —**ˈsphincteral** *adj.*

sphingomyelin (ˌsfɪŋgəʊˈmaɪəlɪn) *n. Biochem.* any of a group of phospholipids, derived from sphingosine, that occur in biological membranes, being especially abundant in the brain. [from *sphingo-,* from Greek *sphingein* to bind + MYELIN]

sphingosine (ˈsfɪŋgəsɪn, -ˌsiːn) *n. Biochem.* a long-chain compound occurring in sphingomyelins and cerebrosides, and from which it can be released by hydrolysis. Formula: $CH_3(CH_2)_{12}$-$CH{:}CHCH(OH)CH(NH_2)CH_2OH$. [from *sphingos-,* from Greek *sphingein* to hold fast + -INE^2]

sphinx (sfɪŋks) *n., pl.* **sphinxes** *or* **sphinges** (ˈsfɪndʒiːz). **1.** any of a number of huge stone statues built by the ancient Egyptians, having the body of a lion and the head of a man. **2.** an inscrutable person.

sphinxlike (ˈsfɪŋksˌlaɪk) *adj.* like the Sphinx; enigmatic or inscrutable.

sphinx moth *n. U.S. and Canadian.* another name for the **hawk moth.**

sphragistics (sfrəˈdʒɪstɪks) *n.* (*functioning as sing.*) the study of seals and signet rings. [C19: from Greek *sphragistikos,* from *sphragizein* to seal, from *sphragis* a seal] —**sphraˈgistic** *adj.*

sp. ht *abbrev. for* specific heat.

sphygmic (ˈsfɪgmɪk) *adj. Physiol.* of or relating to the pulse.

sphygmo- *or before a vowel* **sphygm-** *combining form.* indicating the pulse: *sphygmometer.* [from Greek *sphugmos* pulsation, from *sphuzein* to throb]

sphygmograph (ˈsfɪgməʊˌgrɑːf, -ˌgræf) *n. Med.* an instrument for making a recording (**sphygmogram**) of variations in blood pressure and pulse. —**sphygmographic** (ˌsfɪgməʊˈgræfɪk) *adj.* —**sphygmography** (sfɪgˈmɒgrəfɪ) *n.*

sphygmoid (ˈsfɪgmɔɪd) *adj. Physiol.* resembling the pulse.

sphygmomanometer (ˌsfɪgməʊməˈnɒmɪtə) *n. Med.* an instrument for measuring arterial blood pressure. [C19: from SPHYGMO- + MANOMETER, on the model of French *sphygmomanomètre*]

spic, spick, *or* **spik** (spɪk) *n. U.S. slang.* a derogatory word for a person from a Spanish-speaking country in South or Central America or a Spanish-speaking community in the U.S. [C20: perhaps alluding to a foreigner's mispronunciation of *speak*]

spica (ˈspaɪkə) *n., pl.* **-cae** (-siː) *or* **-cas.** **1.** *Med.* a spiral bandage formed by a series of overlapping figure-of-eight turns. **2.** *Botany.* another word for **spike^2** (sense 1). [C15: from Latin: ear of corn]

Spica (ˈspiːkə) *n.* the brightest star in the constellation Virgo. Distance: 120 light years.

spicate (ˈspaɪkeɪt) *adj. Botany.* having, arranged in, or relating to spikes: *a spicate inflorescence.* [C17: from Latin *spīcātus* having spikes, from *spīca* a point]

spiccato (spɪˈkɑːtəʊ) *Music.* ~*n.* **1.** a style of playing a bowed stringed instrument in which the bow bounces lightly off the strings. ~*adj., adv.* **2.** to be played in this manner. [Italian: detached, from *spiccare* to make distinct]

spice (spaɪs) *n.* **1. a.** any of a variety of aromatic vegetable substances, such as ginger, cinnamon, nutmeg, used as flavourings. **b.** these substances collectively. **2.** something that represents or introduces zest, charm, or gusto. **3.** *Rare.* a small amount. **4.** *Yorkshire dialect.* confectionery. ~*vb.* (*tr.*) **5.** to prepare or flavour (food) with spices. **6.** to introduce charm or zest into. [C13: from Old French *espice,* from Late Latin *speciēs* (pl.) spices, from Latin *speciēs* (sing.) kind; also associated with Late Latin *spīcea* (unattested) fragrant herb, from Latin *spīceus* having spikes of foliage; see SPICA] —**ˈspicer** *n.*

spiceberry (ˈspaɪsbərɪ, -brɪ) *n., pl.* **-ries.** **1.** a myrtaceous tree, *Eugenia rhombea,* of the Caribbean and Florida, with orange or black edible fruits. **2.** the fruit of this tree. **3.** any of various other aromatic plants or shrubs having spicy edible berries, such as wintergreen.

spicebush (ˈspaɪsˌbʊʃ) *n.* a North American lauraceous shrub, *Lindera benzoin,* having yellow flowers and aromatic leaves and bark.

spicery (ˈspaɪsərɪ) *n., pl.* **-eries.** **1.** spices collectively. **2.** the piquant or fragrant quality associated with spices. **3.** *Obsolete.* a place to store spices.

spick-and-span *or* **spic-and-span** (ˈspɪkənˈspæn) *adj.* **1.** extremely neat and clean. **2.** new and fresh. [C17: shortened from *spick-and-span-new,* from obsolete *spick* spike, nail + SPAN-NEW]

spicule (ˈspɪkjuːl) *n.* **1.** Also called: **spiculum.** a small slender pointed structure or crystal, esp. any of the calcareous or siliceous elements of the skeleton of sponges, corals, etc. **2.** *Astronomy.* a spiked ejection of hot gas occurring over 5000 kilometres above the sun's surface (in its atmosphere) and having a diameter of about 1100 kilometres. [C18: from Latin: SPICULUM] —**spiculate** (ˈspɪkjʊˌleɪt, -lɪt) *adj.*

spiculum (ˈspɪkjʊləm) *n., pl.* **-la** (-lə). another word for **spicule** (sense 1). [C18: from Latin: small sharp point, from SPICA]

spicy (ˈspaɪsɪ) *adj.* **spicier, spiciest.** **1.** seasoned with or containing spice. **2.** highly flavoured; pungent. **3.** *Informal.* suggestive of scandal or sensation. **4.** producing or yielding spices. —**ˈspicily** *adv.* —**ˈspiciness** *n.*

spider (ˈspaɪdə) *n.* **1.** any predatory silk-producing arachnid of the order *Araneae,* having four pairs of legs and a rounded unsegmented body consisting of abdomen and cephalothorax. See also **wolf spider, trap-door spider, tarantula, black widow.** **2.** any of various similar or related arachnids. **3.** a hub fitted with radiating spokes or arms that serve to transmit power or support a load. **4.** *Agriculture.* an instrument used with a cultivator to pulverize soil. **5.** any implement or tool having the shape of a spider. **6.** *Nautical.* a metal frame fitted at the base of a mast to which halyards are tied when not in use. **7.** any part of a machine having a number of radiating spokes, tines, or arms. **8.** Also called: **octopus.** *Brit.* a cluster of elastic straps fastened at a central point and used to hold a load on a car rack, motorcycle, etc. **9.** *Snooker, etc.* a rest having long legs, used to raise the cue above the level of the height of the ball. **10.** *Angling.* an artificial fly tied with a hackle and no wings, perhaps originally thought to imitate a spider. **11.** *Austral. informal.* another name for **ice-cream soda.** **12.** short for **spider phaeton.** [Old English *spīthra;* related to Danish *spinder,* German *Spinne;* see SPIN]

spider crab *n.* any of various crabs of the genera *Macropodia, Libinia,* etc., having a small triangular body and very long legs.

spider hole *n. Military.* a small hole in the ground in which a sniper hides.

spider-hunting wasp *n.* any solitary wasp of the superfamily *Pompiloidea,* having a slender elongated body: the fast-running female hunts spiders as a food store for her larvae.

spiderman (ˈspaɪdəˌmæn) *n., pl.* **-men.** *Informal.* **1.** *Chiefly Brit.* a person who erects the steel structure of a building. **2.** another name for a **steeplejack.**

spider mite *n.* any of various plant-feeding mites of the family *Tetranychidae,* esp. *Panonychus ulmi* (**red spider mite**), which is a serious orchard pest.

spider monkey *n.* **1.** any of several arboreal New World monkeys of the genus *Ateles,* of Central and South America, having very long legs, a long prehensile tail, and a small head. **2.** **woolly spider monkey.** a rare related monkey, *Brachyteles arachnoides,* of SE Brazil. [C18: so called because its long limbs resemble the legs of a spider]

spider orchid *n.* any of several European orchids of the genus *Ophrys,* esp. *O. sphegodes,* having a flower with yellow, green, or pink sepals and a broad brown velvety lip.

spider phaeton *n.* (formerly) a light horse-drawn carriage with a high body and large slender wheels. Sometimes shortened to **spider.**

spider plant *n.* a name for various house plants, esp. for *Chlorophytum elatum:* see **chlorophytum.**

spiderwort (ˈspaɪdəˌwɜːt) *n.* **1.** any of various plants of the American genus *Tradescantia,* esp. *T. virginiana,* having blue, purplish, or pink flowers and widely grown as house plants: family *Commelinaceae.* See also **tradescantia.** **2.** any of various similar or related plants. [C17: so called because of the spidery shape of its stamens]

spidery (ˈspaɪdərɪ) *adj.* thin and angular like a spider's legs: *spidery handwriting.*

spiegeleisen (ˈspiːgəlˌaɪzən) *n.* a type of pig iron that is rich in manganese and carbon. [C19: German, from *Spiegel* mirror + *Eisen* IRON]

spiel (ʃpiːl) *n.* **1.** a glib plausible style of talk, associated esp. with salesmen. ~*vb.* **2.** (*intr.*) to deliver a prepared spiel. **3.** (*tr.;* usually foll. by *off*) to recite (a prepared oration). [C19: from German *Spiel* play] —**ˈspieler** *n.*

spier (ˈspaɪə) *n. Archaic.* a person who spies or scouts.

spif (spɪf) *n. Informal, chiefly Brit.* a postage stamp perforated with the initials of a firm to avoid theft by employees. Former name: **perfin.** [C20: from *s*(*tamp*) *p*(*erforated with*) *i*(*nitials of*) *f*(*irm*)]

spiffing (ˈspɪfɪŋ) *adj. Brit. slang, old-fashioned.* excellent; splendid. [C19: probably from dialect *spiff* spruce, smartly dressed]

spiffy (ˈspɪfɪ) *adj.* **-fier, -fiest.** *U.S. and Canadian slang.* smart; stylish. [C19: from dialect *spiff*] —ˈ**spiffily** *adv.* —ˈ**spiffiness** *n.*

spiflicate *or* **spifflicate** (ˈspɪflɪˌkeɪt) *vb.* (*tr.*) *Brit. school slang.* to destroy; annihilate. [C18: a humorous coinage]

spignel (ˈspɪgnəl) *n.* a European umbelliferous plant, *Meum athamanticum,* of mountain regions, having white flowers and finely divided aromatic leaves. Also called: **baldmoney, meu.** [C16: of uncertain origin]

spigot (ˈspɪgət) *n.* **1.** a stopper for the vent hole of a cask. **2.** a tap, usually of wood, fitted to a cask. **3.** a U.S. name for **tap**[2] (sense 1). **4.** a short cylindrical projection on one component designed to fit into a hole on another, esp. the male part of a joint (**spigot and socket joint**) between two pipes. [C14: probably from Old Provençal *espiga* a head of grain, from Latin *spīca* a point]

spik (spɪk) *n.* a variant spelling of **spic.**

spike[1] (spaɪk) *n.* **1.** a sharp point. **2.** any sharp-pointed object, esp. one made of metal. **3.** a long metal nail. **4.** *Physics.* **a.** a transient variation in voltage or current in an electric circuit. **b.** a graphical recording of this, such as one of the peaks on an electroencephalogram. **5.** (*pl.*) shoes with metal projections on the sole and heel for greater traction, as used by athletes. **6.** the straight unbranched antler of a young deer. **7.** *Brit. slang.* another word for **dosshouse.** ~*vb.* (*tr.*) **8.** to secure or supply with or as with spikes. **9.** to render ineffective or block the intentions of; thwart. **10.** to impale on a spike. **11.** to add alcohol to (a drink). **12.** *Journalism.* to reject (a news story). **13.** *Volleyball.* to hit (a ball) sharply downwards with an overarm motion from the front of one's own court into the opposing court. **14.** (formerly) to render (a cannon) ineffective by blocking its vent with a spike. **15. spike (someone's) guns.** to thwart (someone's) purpose. [C13 *spyk;* related to Old English *spīcing* nail, Old Norse *spīk* splinter, Middle Low German *spīker* spike, Norwegian *spīk* SPOKE[2], Latin *spīca* sharp point; see SPIKE[2]]

spike[2] (spaɪk) *n. Botany.* **1.** an inflorescence consisting of a raceme of sessile flowers, as in the gladiolus. **2.** an ear of wheat, barley, etc. [C14: from Latin *spīca* ear of corn]

spike heel *n.* a very high heel on a woman's shoe, tapering to a very narrow tip. Often shortened to: **spike.** Also called (esp. Brit.): **stiletto, stiletto heel.**

spike lavender *n.* a Mediterranean lavender plant, *Lavandula latifolia,* having pale purple flowers and yielding an oil used in paints. [C17: from dialect *spick* lavender, via Old French and Old Provençal from Latin *spīca* SPIKE[2]]

spikelet (ˈspaɪklɪt) *n. Botany.* a small spike, esp. the inflorescence characteristic of most grasses and sedges.

spikenard (ˈspaɪknɑːd, ˈspaɪkəˌnɑːd) *n.* **1.** an aromatic Indian valerianaceous plant, *Nardostachys jatamans,* having rose-purple flowers. **2.** an aromatic ointment obtained from this plant. **3.** any of various similar or related plants. **4.** a North American araliaceous plant, *Aralia racemosa,* having small green flowers and an aromatic root. ~Also called (for senses 1, 2): **nard.** [C14: from Medieval Latin *spīca nardī;* see SPIKE[2], NARD]

spike-rush *n.* any perennial plant of the temperate cyperaceous genus *Eleocharis,* occurring esp. by ponds, and having underground stems, narrow leaves, and small flowers.

spiky (ˈspaɪkɪ) *adj.* **spikier, spikiest. 1.** resembling a spike. **2.** having a spike or spikes. **3.** *Brit. informal.* ill-tempered. —ˈ**spikily** *adv.* —ˈ**spikiness** *n.*

spile (spaɪl) *n.* **1.** a heavy timber stake or pile. **2.** *U.S. and Canadian.* a spout for tapping sap from the sugar maple tree. **3.** a plug or spigot. ~*vb.* (*tr.*) **4.** to provide or support with a spile. **5.** *U.S.* to tap (a tree) with a spile. [C16: probably from Middle Dutch *spile* peg; related to Icelandic *spila* skewer, Latin *spīna* thorn]

spill[1] (spɪl) *vb.* **spills, spilling; spilt** *or* **spilled.** (*mainly tr.*) **1.** (when *intr.*, usually foll. by *from, out of,* etc.) to fall or cause to fall from or as from a container, esp. unintentionally. **2.** to disgorge (contents, occupants, etc.) or (of contents, occupants, etc.) to be disgorged: *the car spilt its passengers onto the road; the crowd spilt out of the theatre.* **3.** to shed (blood). **4.** Also: **spill the beans.** *Informal.* to disclose something confidential. **5.** *Nautical.* to let (wind) escape from a sail or (of the wind) to escape from a sail. ~*n.* **6.** *Informal.* a fall or tumble. **7.** short for **spillway. 8.** a spilling of liquid, etc., or the amount spilt. **9.** *Austral.* the declaring of several political jobs vacant when one higher up becomes so: *the Prime Minister's resignation could mean a Cabinet spill.* [Old English *spillan* to destroy; related to *spildan,* Old High German *spaltan* to split; see SPOIL] —ˈ**spiller** *n.*

spill[2] (spɪl) *n.* **1.** a splinter of wood or strip of twisted paper with which pipes, fires, etc., are lit. **2.** a small peg or rod made of metal. [C13: of Germanic origin; compare Old High German *spilla,* Middle Dutch *spile* stake]

spillage (ˈspɪlɪdʒ) *n.* **1.** an instance or the process of spilling. **2.** something spilt or the amount spilt.

spillikin, spilikin (ˈspɪlɪkɪn), *or* **spellican** (ˈspelɪkən) *n.* a thin strip of wood, cardboard, or plastic, esp. one used in spillikins.

spillikins (ˈspɪlɪkɪnz) *n.* (*functioning as sing.*) *Brit.* a game in which players try to pick each spillikin from a heap without moving any of the others. Also called: **jackstraws.** [C18: from SPILL[2] + diminutive ending. See -KIN]

spill over *vb.* **1.** (*intr., adv.*) to overflow or be forced out of an area, container, etc. ~*n.* **spillover. 2.** *Chiefly U.S. and Canadian.* the act of spilling over. **3.** *Chiefly U.S. and Canadian.* the excess part of something. **4.** *Economics.* any indirect effect of public expenditure.

spillway (ˈspɪlˌweɪ) *n.* a channel that carries away surplus water, as from a dam. Also called: **wasteweir, spill.**

spilt (spɪlt) *vb.* a past tense and past participle of **spill**[1].

spin (spɪn) *vb.* **spins, spinning, spun. 1.** to rotate or cause to rotate rapidly, as on an axis. **2. a.** to draw out and twist (natural fibres, as of silk or cotton) into a long continuous thread. **b.** to make such a thread or filament from (synthetic resins, etc.), usually by forcing through a nozzle. **3.** (of spiders, silkworms, etc.) to form (webs, cocoons, etc.) from a silky fibre exuded from the body. **4.** (*tr.*) to shape (metal) into a rounded form on a lathe. **5.** (*tr.*) *Informal.* to tell (a tale, story, etc.) by drawing it out at great length (esp. in the phrase **spin a yarn**). **6.** to bowl, pitch, hit, or kick (a ball) so that it rotates in the air and changes direction or speed on bouncing, or (of a ball) to be projected in this way. **7.** (*intr.*) (of wheels) to revolve rapidly without causing propulsion. **8.** to cause (an aircraft) to dive in a spiral descent or (of an aircraft) to dive in a spiral descent. **9.** (*intr.;* foll. by *along*) to drive or travel swiftly. **10.** (*tr.*) Also: **spin-dry.** to rotate (clothes) in a washing machine in order to extract surplus water. **11.** (*intr.*) to reel or grow dizzy, as from turning around: *my head is spinning.* **12.** (*intr.*) to fish by drawing a revolving lure through the water. ~*n.* **13.** a swift rotating motion; instance of spinning. **14.** *Physics.* **a.** the intrinsic angular momentum of an elementary particle or atomic nucleus, as distinguished from any angular momentum resulting from its motion. **b.** a quantum number determining values of this angular momentum in units of the Dirac constant, having integral or half-integral values. Symbol: *S* or *s* **15.** a condition of loss of control of an aircraft or an intentional flight manoeuvre in which the aircraft performs a continuous spiral descent because the angle of maximum lift is less than the angle of incidence. **16.** a spinning motion imparted to a ball, etc. **17.** (in skating) any of various movements involving spinning rapidly on the spot. **18.** *Informal.* a short or fast drive, ride, etc., esp. in a car, for pleasure. **19. flat spin.** *Informal, chiefly Brit.* a state of agitation or confusion. **20.** *Austral. and N.Z. informal.* a period of time or an experience; chance or luck; fortune: *a bad spin.* **21.** *Commerce, informal.* a sudden downward trend in prices, values, etc. ~See also **spin out.** [Old English *spinnan;* related to Old Norse *spinna,* Old High German *spinnan* to spin, Lithuanian *pinu* to braid]

spina bifida (ˈspaɪnə ˈbɪfɪdə) *n.* a congenital condition in which the meninges of the spinal cord protrude through a gap in the backbone, sometimes causing enlargement of the skull (due to accumulation of cerebrospinal fluid) and paralysis. [New Latin; see SPINE, BIFID]

spinach (ˈspɪnɪdʒ, -ɪtʃ) *n.* **1.** a chenopodiaceous annual plant, *Spinacia oleracea,* cultivated for its dark green edible leaves. **2.** the leaves of this plant, eaten as a vegetable. [C16: from Old French *espinache,* from Old Spanish *espinaca,* from Arabic *isfānākh,* from Persian]

spinal (ˈspaɪnᵊl) *adj.* **1.** of or relating to the spine or the spinal cord. **2.** denoting a laboratory animal in which the spinal cord has been severed: *a spinal rat.* ~*n.* **3.** short for **spinal anaesthesia.** —ˈ**spinally** *adv.*

spinal anaesthesia *n.* **1.** *Surgery.* anaesthesia of the lower half of the body produced by injecting an anaesthetic beneath the arachnoid membrane surrounding the spinal cord. See also **epidural** (sense 2). **2.** *Pathol.* loss of sensation in some part of the body as the result of injury of the spinal cord.

spinal canal *n.* the natural passage through the centre of the spinal column that contains the spinal cord.

spinal column *n.* a series of contiguous or interconnecting bony or cartilaginous segments that surround and protect the spinal cord. Also called: **spine, vertebral column.** Nontechnical name: **backbone.**

spinal cord *n.* the thick cord of nerve tissue within the spinal canal, which in man gives rise to 31 pairs of spinal nerves, and together with the brain forms the central nervous system.

spin bowler *n. Cricket.* a bowler who specializes in bowling balls with a spinning motion.

spindle (ˈspɪndᵊl) *n.* **1.** a rod or stick that has a notch in the top, used to draw out natural fibres for spinning into thread, and a long narrow body around which the thread is wound when spun. **2.** one of the thin rods or pins bearing bobbins upon which spun thread is wound in a spinning wheel or machine. **3.** any of various parts in the form of a rod, esp. a rotating rod that acts as an axle, mandrel, or arbor. **4.** a piece of wood that has been turned, such as a baluster or table leg. **5.** a small square metal shaft that passes through the lock of a door and to which the door knobs or handles are fixed. **6.** a measure of length of yarn equal to 18 hanks (15 120 yards) for cotton or 14 400 yards for linen. **7.** *Biology.* a spindle-shaped structure formed from microtubules during mitosis or meiosis which draws the duplicated chromosomes apart as the cell divides. **8.** a less common name for a **hydrometer. 9.** a tall pole with a marker at the top, fixed to an underwater obstruction as an aid to navigation. **10.** a device consisting of a sharp upright spike on a pedestal on which bills, order forms, etc., are impaled. ~*vb.* **11.** (*tr.*) to form into a spindle or equip with spindles. **12.** (*intr.*) *Rare.* (of a plant, stem, shoot, etc.) to grow rapidly and become elongated and thin. [Old English *spinel;* related to *spinnan* to SPIN, Old Saxon *spinnila* spindle, Old High German *spinnala*]

spindle-legged *or* **spindle-shanked** *adj.* having long thin legs.

spindlelegs ('spɪndᵊl,lɛgz) *or* **spindleshanks** *pl. n.* **1.** long thin legs. **2.** (*functioning as sing.*) a person who has long thin legs.

spindle tree *n.* any of various shrubs or trees of the genus *Euonymus,* esp. *E. europaeus,* of Europe and W Asia, typically having red fruits and yielding a hard wood formerly used in making spindles: family *Celastraceae.*

spindling ('spɪndlɪŋ) *adj.* **1.** long and slender, esp. disproportionately so. **2.** (of stalks, shoots, etc.) becoming long and slender. ~*n.* **3.** a spindling person or thing.

spindly ('spɪndlɪ) *adj.* **-dlier, -dliest.** tall, slender, and frail; attenuated.

spin doctor *n. Informal.* a person who provides a favourable slant to an item of news, potentially unpopular policy, etc., esp. on behalf of a political personality or party. [C20: from the spin given to a ball in various sports to make it go in the desired direction]

spindrift ('spɪn,drɪft) *n.* **1.** spray blown up from the surface of the sea. **2.** powdery snow blown off a mountain. ~Also called: **spoondrift.** [C17: of Scottish origin, possibly from a variant of obsolete *spoon* to scud + DRIFT]

spin-dry *vb.* **-dries, -drying, -dried.** (*tr.*) to dry (clothes, linen, etc.) in a spin-dryer.

spin-dryer *n.* a device that extracts water from clothes, linen, etc., by spinning them in a perforated drum.

spine (spaɪn) *n.* **1.** the spinal column. **2.** the sharply pointed tip or outgrowth of a leaf, stem, etc. **3.** *Zoology.* a hard pointed process or structure, such as the ray of a fin, the quill of a porcupine, or the ridge on a bone. **4.** the back of a book, record sleeve, etc. **5.** a ridge, esp. of a hill. **6.** strength of endurance, will, etc. **7.** anything resembling the spinal column in function or importance; main support or feature. [C14: from Old French *espine* spine, from Latin *spīna* thorn, backbone] —**spined** *adj.*

spine-bashing *n. Austral. informal.* loafing or resting. —'**spine-,basher** *n.*

spine-chiller *n.* a book, film, etc., that arouses terror. —'**spine-,chilling** *adj.*

spinel (spɪ'nɛl) *n.* any of a group of hard glassy minerals of variable colour consisting of oxides of aluminium, magnesium, iron, zinc, or manganese and occurring in the form of octahedral crystals: used as gemstones. Formula: $MgAl_2O_4$. [C16: from French *spinelle,* from Italian *spinella,* diminutive of *spina* a thorn, from Latin; so called from the shape of the crystals]

spineless ('spaɪnlɪs) *adj.* **1.** lacking a backbone; invertebrate. **2.** having no spiny processes: *spineless stems.* **3.** lacking strength of character, resolution, or courage. —'**spinelessly** *adv.* —'**spinelessness** *n.*

spinescent (spaɪ'nɛsᵊnt) *adj. Biology.* **1.** having or resembling a spine or spines. **2.** becoming spiny. [C18: from Late Latin *spīnēscere* to become thorny, from Latin *spīna* a thorn] —**spi'nescence** *n.*

spinet (spɪ'nɛt, 'spɪnɪt) *n.* a small type of harpsichord having one manual. [C17: from Italian *spinetta,* perhaps from Giovanni *Spinetti,* 16th-century Italian maker of musical instruments and its supposed inventor]

spine-tingling *adj.* causing a sensation of fear.

spiniferous (spaɪ'nɪfərəs) *or* **spinigerous** (spaɪ'nɪdʒərəs) *adj.* (esp. of plants) bearing spines or thorns. [C17: from Late Latin *spīnifer* having spines, from Latin *spīna* a thorn, spine + *ferre* to bear]

spinifex ('spɪnɪ,fɛks) *n.* **1.** any Australian grass of the genus *Spinifex,* having pointed leaves and spiny seed heads: often planted to bind loose sand. **2.** Also called: **porcupine grass.** *Austral.* any of various coarse spiny-leaved inland grasses of the genus *Triodia.* [C19: from New Latin, from Latin *spīna* a thorn + *-fex* maker, from *facere* to make]

spinnaker ('spɪnəkə; *Nautical* 'spæŋkə) *n.* a large light triangular racing sail set from the foremast of a yacht when running or on a broad reach. [C19: probably from SPIN + (MO)NIKER, but traditionally derived from *Sphinx,* the yacht that first adopted this type of sail]

spinner ('spɪnə) *n.* **1.** a person or thing that spins. **2.** *Cricket.* **a.** a ball that is bowled with a spinning motion. **b.** a bowler who specializes in bowling such balls. **3.** a streamlined fairing that fits over and revolves with the hub of an aircraft propeller. **4.** a fishing lure with a fin or wing that revolves when drawn through the water. **5.** an angler's name for the mature adult form (imago) of various flies, especially the mayflies. Compare **dun**[2] (sense 3).

spinneret ('spɪnə,rɛt) *n.* **1.** any of several organs in spiders and certain insects through which silk threads are exuded. **2.** a finely perforated dispenser through which a viscous liquid is extruded in the production of synthetic fibres. [C18: from SPINNER + -ET]

spinney ('spɪnɪ) *n. Chiefly Brit.* a small wood or copse. [C16: from Old French *espinei,* from *espine* thorn, from Latin *spīna*]

spinning ('spɪnɪŋ) *n.* **1. a.** the act or process of spinning. **b.** (*as modifier*): *spinning yarn.* **2.** the act or technique of casting and drawing a revolving lure through the water so as to imitate the movement of a live fish, etc.

spinning jenny *n.* an early type of spinning frame with several spindles, invented by James Hargreaves in 1764. [C18: see JENNY; the reason for the adoption of the woman's name is unclear]

spinning mule *n. Textiles.* See **mule**[1] (sense 3).

spinning top *n.* another name for **top**[2] (the toy).

spinning wheel *n.* a wheel-like machine for spinning at home, having one hand- or foot-operated spindle.

spinode ('spaɪnəʊd) *n. Maths.* another name for **cusp** (sense 4). [C19: from Latin *spīna* spine + NODE]

spin-off *n.* any product or development derived incidentally from the application of existing knowledge or enterprise.

spinose ('spaɪnəʊs, spaɪ'nəʊs) *adj.* (esp. of plants) bearing many spines. [C17: from Latin *spīnōsus* prickly, from *spīna* a thorn] —'**spinosely** *adv.* —**spinosity** (spaɪ'nɒsɪtɪ) *n.*

spinous ('spaɪnəs) *adj. Biology.* **1.** resembling a spine or thorn: *the spinous process of a bone.* **2.** having spines or spiny projections. **3.** another word for **spinose.**

spin out *vb.* (*tr., adv.*) **1.** to extend or protract (a story, etc.) by including superfluous detail; prolong. **2.** to spend or pass (time). **3.** to contrive to cause (money, etc.) to last as long as possible. ~*n.* **spinout. 4.** a spinning skid in a car that causes it to run off the road.

Spinozism (spɪ'nəʊzɪzəm) *n.* the philosophical system of Baruch Spinoza (1632–77), Dutch philosopher, esp. the concept of God as the unique reality possessing an infinite number of attributes of which we can know at least thought and extension. —**Spi'nozist** *n.*

spin stabilization *n.* a technique by which a bullet, rocket, etc., is made to spin around its longitudinal axis to assist it in maintaining a steady flight path.

spinster ('spɪnstə) *n.* **1.** an unmarried woman regarded as being beyond the age of marriage. **2.** *Law.* (in legal documents) a woman who has never married. Compare **feme sole. 3.** (formerly) a woman who spins thread for her living. [C14 (in the sense: a person, esp. a woman, whose occupation is spinning; C17: a woman still unmarried): from SPIN + -STER] —'**spinster,hood** *n.* —'**spinsterish** *adj.*

spinthariscope (spɪn'θærɪ,skəʊp) *n.* a device for observing ionizing radiation, consisting of a tube with a magnifying lens at one end and a phosphorescent screen at the other. A particle hitting the screen produces a scintillation. [C20: from Greek *spintharis* a little spark + -SCOPE]

spinule ('spaɪnju:l) *n. Biology.* a very small spine, thorn, or prickle. [C18: from Late Latin *spīnula*] —**spinulose** ('spaɪnjʊ,ləʊs) *adj.*

spiny ('spaɪnɪ) *adj.* **spinier, spiniest. 1.** (of animals) having or covered with quills or spines. **2.** (of plants) covered with spines; thorny. **3.** troublesome to handle; puzzling. **4.** shaped like a spine. —'**spininess** *n.*

spiny anteater *n.* another name for **echidna.**

spiny-finned *adj.* (of certain fishes) having fins that are supported by stiff bony spines. See also **acanthopterygian.** Compare **soft-finned.**

spiny lobster *n.* any of various large edible marine decapod crustaceans of the genus *Palinurus* and related genera, having a very tough spiny carapace. Also called: **rock lobster, crawfish, langouste.**

spiracle ('spaɪərəkᵊl, 'spaɪrə-) *n.* **1.** any of several paired apertures in the cuticle of an insect, by which air enters and leaves the trachea. **2.** a small paired rudimentary gill slit just behind the head in skates, rays, and related fishes. **3.** any similar respiratory aperture, such as the blowhole in whales. **4.** *Geology.* a small vent in a lava flow, formed by escaping gases. [C14 (originally: breath): from Latin *spīrāculum* vent, from *spīrāre* to breathe] —**spiracular** (spɪ'rækjʊlə) *adj.* —**spi'raculate** *adj.*

spiraea *or esp. U.S.* **spirea** (spaɪ'rɪə) *n.* any rosaceous plant of the genus *Spiraea,* having sprays of small white or pink flowers. See also **meadowsweet** (sense 2), **hardhack.** [C17: via Latin from Greek *speiraia,* from *speira* SPIRE[2]]

spiral ('spaɪərəl) *n.* **1.** *Geometry.* one of several plane curves formed by a point winding about a fixed point at an ever-increasing distance from it. Polar equation of **Archimedes spiral:** $r = a\theta$; of **logarithmic spiral:** $\log r = a\theta$; of **hyperbolic spiral:** $r\theta = a$, (where a is a constant). **2.** another name for **helix** (sense 1). **3.** something that pursues a winding, usually upward, course or that displays a twisting form or shape. **4.** a flight manoeuvre in which an aircraft descends describing a helix of comparatively large radius with the angle of attack within the normal flight range. Compare **spin** (sense 15). **5.** *Economics.* a continuous upward or downward movement in economic activity or prices, caused by interaction between prices, wages, demand, and production. ~*adj.* **6.** having the shape of a spiral. ~*vb.* **-rals, -ralling, -ralled** *or U.S.* **-rals, -raling, -raled. 7.** to assume or cause to assume a spiral course or shape. **8.** (*intr.*) to increase or decrease with steady acceleration: *wages and prices continue to spiral.* [C16: via French from Medieval Latin *spīrālis,* from Latin *spīra* a coil; see SPIRE[2]] —'**spirally** *adv.*

spiral galaxy *n.* a galaxy consisting of an ellipsoidal nucleus of old stars from opposite sides of which arms, containing younger stars, spiral outwards around the nucleus. In a **barred spiral** the arms originate at the ends of a bar-shaped nucleus.

spiral of Archimedes *n. Maths.* a spiral having the equation $r = a\theta$, where a is a constant. It is the locus of a point moving to or from the origin at a constant speed along a line rotating around that origin at a constant speed.

spiral staircase *n.* a staircase constructed around a central axis.

spirant ('spaɪrənt) *adj.* **1.** *Phonetics.* another word for **fricative.** ~*n.* **2.** a fricative consonant. [C19: from Latin *spīrāns* breathing, from *spīrāre* to breathe]

spire[1] (spaɪə) *n.* **1.** Also called: **steeple.** a tall structure that tapers upwards to a point, esp. one on a tower or roof or one that forms the upper part of a steeple. **2.** a slender tapering shoot or stem, such as a blade of grass. **3.** the apical part of any tapering formation; summit. ~*vb.* **4.** (*intr.*) to assume the shape of a spire; point up. **5.** (*tr.*) to furnish with a spire or spires. [Old English *spīr* blade; related to Old Norse *spīra* stalk, Middle Low German *spīr* shoot, Latin *spīna* thorn] —**'spiry** *adj.*

spire[2] (spaɪə) *n.* **1.** any of the coils or turns in a spiral structure. **2.** the apical part of a spiral shell. [C16: from Latin *spīra* a coil, from Greek *speira*] —**spiriferous** (spaɪə'rɪfərəs) *adj.*

spirelet ('spaɪəlɪt) *n.* another name for **flèche** (sense 1).

spireme ('spaɪriːm) *n. Cytology.* the tangled mass of chromatin threads into which the nucleus of a cell is resolved at the start of mitosis. [C19: from Greek *speirēma* a coil, from *speira* a coil, SPIRE[2]]

spirillum (spaɪ'rɪləm) *n., pl.* **-la** (-lə). **1.** any bacterium having a curved or spirally twisted rodlike body. Compare **coccus** (sense 1), **bacillus** (sense 1). **2.** any bacterium of the genus *Spirillum,* such as *S. minus,* which causes ratbite fever. [C19: from New Latin, literally: a little coil, from *spīra* a coil] —**spi'rillar** *adj.*

spirit[1] ('spɪrɪt) *n.* **1.** the force or principle of life that animates the body of living things. **2.** temperament or disposition: *truculent in spirit.* **3.** liveliness; mettle: *they set to it with spirit.* **4.** the fundamental, emotional, and activating principle of a person; will: *the experience broke his spirit.* **5.** a sense of loyalty or dedication: *team spirit.* **6.** the prevailing element; feeling: *a spirit of joy pervaded the atmosphere.* **7.** state of mind or mood; attitude: *he did it in the wrong spirit.* **8.** (*pl.*) an emotional state, esp. with regard to exaltation or dejection: *in high spirits.* **9.** a person characterized by some activity, quality, or disposition: *a leading spirit of the movement.* **10.** the deeper more significant meaning as opposed to a pedantic interpretation: *the spirit of the law.* **11.** that which constitutes a person's intangible being as contrasted with his physical presence: *I shall be with you in spirit.* **12. a.** an incorporeal being, esp. the soul of a dead person. **b.** (*as modifier*): *spirit world.* ~*vb.* (*tr.*) **13.** (usually foll. by *away* or *off*) to carry off mysteriously or secretly. **14.** (often foll. by *up*) to impart animation or determination to. [C13: from Old French *esperit,* from Latin *spīritus* breath, spirit; related to *spīrāre* to breathe]

spirit[2] ('spɪrɪt) *n.* **1.** (*often pl.*) any distilled alcoholic liquor such as brandy, rum, whisky, or gin. **2.** *Chem.* **a.** an aqueous solution of ethanol, esp. one obtained by distillation. **b.** the active principle or essence of a substance, extracted as a liquid, esp. by distillation. **3.** *Pharmacol.* **a.** a solution of a volatile substance, esp. a volatile oil, in alcohol. **b.** (*as modifier*): *a spirit burner.* **4.** *Alchemy.* any of the four substances sulphur, mercury, sal ammoniac, or arsenic. [C14: special use of SPIRIT[1], name applied to alchemical substances (as in sense 4), hence extended to distilled liquids]

Spirit ('spɪrɪt) *n.* **the. 1. a.** another name for the **Holy Ghost. b.** God, esp. when regarded as transcending material limitations. **2.** the influence of God or divine things upon the soul. **3.** *Christian Science.* God or divine substance.

spirited ('spɪrɪtɪd) *adj.* **1.** displaying animation, vigour, or liveliness. **2.** (*in combination*) characterized by mood, temper, or disposition as specified: *high-spirited; public-spirited.* —**'spiritedly** *adv.* —**'spiritedness** *n.*

spirit gum *n.* a glue made from gum dissolved in ether used to stick a false beard, etc., onto the face.

spiritism ('spɪrɪˌtɪzəm) *n.* a less common word for **spiritualism.** —**'spiritist** *n.* —ˌ**spirit'istic** *adj.*

spirit lamp *n.* a lamp that burns methylated or other spirits instead of oil.

spiritless ('spɪrɪtlɪs) *adj.* lacking courage or liveliness; melancholic. —**'spiritlessly** *adv.* —**'spiritlessness** *n.*

spirit level *n.* a device for setting horizontal surfaces, consisting of an accurate block of material in which a sealed slightly curved tube partially filled with liquid is set so that the air bubble rests between two marks on the tube when the block is horizontal.

spiritoso (ˌspɪrɪ'təʊsəʊ) *adj., adv. Music.* (often preceded by a tempo marking) to be played in a spirited or animated manner: *allegro spiritoso.* [Italian, from *spirito* spirit, from Latin *spīritus* breath; see SPIRIT[1]]

spiritous ('spɪrɪtəs) *adj.* **1.** a variant spelling of **spirituous. 2.** *Archaic.* high-spirited. **3.** *Archaic.* ethereal; pure.

spirits of ammonia *n.* (*functioning as sing. or pl.*) another name for **sal volatile** (sense 2).

spirits of hartshorn *n.* (*functioning as sing. or pl.*) another name for **aqueous ammonia.** See **ammonium hydroxide.**

spirits of salt *n.* (*functioning as sing. or pl.*) a solution of hydrochloric acid in water.

spirits of turpentine *n.* (*functioning as sing. or pl.*) another name for **turpentine** (sense 3).

spirits of wine *n.* (*functioning as sing. or pl.*) another name for **alcohol** (sense 1).

spiritual ('spɪrɪtjʊəl) *adj.* **1.** relating to the spirit or soul and not to physical nature or matter; intangible. **2.** of, relating to, or characteristic of sacred things, the Church, religion, etc. **3.** standing in a relationship based on communication between the souls or minds of the persons involved: *a spiritual father.* **4.** having a mind or emotions of a high and delicately refined quality. ~*n.* **5.** See **Negro spiritual. 6.** (*often pl.*) the sphere of religious, spiritual, or ecclesiastical matters, or such matters in themselves. **7. the.** the realm of spirits. —**'spiritually** *adv.* —**'spiritualness** *n.*

spiritual bouquet *n. R.C. Church.* a collection of private devotional acts and prayers chosen and performed by one person for the benefit of another.

spiritual incest *n. R.C. Church.* **1.** marriage or a sexual relationship between persons related by spiritual affinity or with a person under a solemn vow of chastity. **2.** the holding of two benefices by the same priest or bishop.

spiritualism ('spɪrɪtjʊəˌlɪzəm) *n.* **1.** the belief that the disembodied spirits of the dead, surviving in another world, can communicate with the living in this world, esp. through mediums. **2.** the doctrines and practices associated with this belief. **3.** *Philosophy.* the belief that because reality is to some extent immaterial it is therefore spiritual. **4.** any doctrine (in philosophy, religion, etc.) that prefers the spiritual to the material. **5.** the condition or quality of being spiritual. —**'spiritualist** *n.* —ˌ**spiritua'listic** *adj.*

spirituality (ˌspɪrɪtjʊ'ælɪtɪ) *n., pl.* **-ties. 1.** the state or quality of being dedicated to God, religion, or spiritual things or values, esp. as contrasted with material or temporal ones. **2.** the condition or quality of being spiritual. **3.** a distinctive approach to religion or prayer: *the spirituality of the desert Fathers.* **4.** (*often pl.*) Church property or revenue or a Church benefice.

spiritualize or **spiritualise** ('spɪrɪtjʊəˌlaɪz) *vb.* (*tr.*) to make spiritual or infuse with spiritual content. —ˌ**spirituali'zation** *or* ˌ**spirituali'sation** *n.* —**'spiritualˌizer** *or* **'spiritualˌiser** *n.*

spiritualty ('spɪrɪtjʊəltɪ) *n., pl.* **-ties.** *Archaic.* **1.** the clergy collectively. **2.** another word for **spirituality.**

spirituel (ˌspɪrɪtjʊ'ɛl) *adj.* having a refined and lively mind or wit. Also (fem.): **spirituelle** (ˌspɪrɪtjʊ'ɛl). [C17: from French]

spirituous ('spɪrɪtjʊəs) *adj.* **1.** characterized by or containing alcohol. **2.** (of a drink) being a spirit. —**spirituosity** (ˌspɪrɪtjʊ'ɒsɪtɪ) *or* **'spirituousness** *n.*

spiritus asper ('spɪrɪtəs 'æspə) *n.* another term for **rough breathing.** [Latin: rough breath]

spiritus lenis *n.* another term for **smooth breathing.** [Latin: gentle breath]

spirit varnish *n.* a varnish consisting of a gum or resin, such as shellac or copal, dissolved in alcohol.

spirketting ('spɜːkɪtɪŋ) *n. Nautical.* **1.** deck planking near the bulwarks. **2.** the interior lining between ports and the overhead interior surface of the cabin. [C18: from obsolete *spirket* space between floor timbers in a ship]

spiro-[1] *combining form.* indicating breath or respiration: *spirograph.* [from Latin *spīrāre* to breathe]

spiro-[2] *combining form.* spiral; coil: *spirochaete.* [from Latin *spīra,* from Greek *speira* a coil]

spirochaete *or U.S.* **spirochete** ('spaɪrəʊˌkiːt) *n.* any of a group of spirally coiled rodlike bacteria that includes the causative agent of syphilis. See **treponema.** [C19: from New Latin *spīrochaeta;* see SPIRO-[2], CHAETA]

spirochaetosis *or U.S.* **spirochetosis** (ˌspaɪrəʊkɪ'təʊsɪs) *n.* any disease caused by a spirochaete.

spirograph ('spaɪrəˌgrɑːf, -ˌgræf) *n. Med.* an instrument for recording the movements of breathing. —ˌ**spiro'graphic** *adj.*

spirogyra (ˌspaɪrə'dʒaɪərə) *n.* any green freshwater multicellular alga of the genus *Spirogyra,* consisting of minute filaments containing spirally coiled chloroplasts. [C20: from New Latin, from SPIRO-[2] + Greek *guros* a circle]

spiroid ('spaɪrɔɪd) *adj.* resembling a spiral or displaying a spiral form. [C19: from New Latin *spīroīdēs,* from Greek *speiroeidēs,* from *speira* a coil]

spirometer (spaɪ'rɒmɪtə) *n.* an instrument for measuring the air capacity of the lungs. Compare **pneumatometer.** —**spirometric** (ˌspaɪrə'mɛtrɪk) *adj.* —**spi'rometry** *n.*

spironolactone (ˌspaɪrənəʊ'læktəʊn) *n.* a diuretic that increases water loss from the kidneys and is much used to treat oedema in heart and kidney failure. [C20: from SPIRO-[2] + linking syllable *-no-* + LACTONE]

spirt (spɜːt) *n.* a variant spelling of **spurt.**

spirula ('spaɪrʊlə) *n.* a tropical cephalopod mollusc, *Spirula peronii,* having prominent eyes, short arms, and a small flattened spirally coiled internal shell: order *Decapoda* (cuttlefish and squids). [C19: via New Latin from Late Latin: a small twisted cake, from Latin *spīra* a coil]

spiry ('spaɪərɪ) *adj. Poetic.* of spiral form; helical.

spit[1] (spɪt) *vb.* **spits, spitting, spat** *or* **spit. 1.** (*intr.*) to expel saliva from the mouth; expectorate. **2.** (*intr.*) *Informal.* to show disdain or hatred by spitting. **3.** (of a fire, hot fat, etc.) to eject (fragments of coal, sparks, etc.) violently and with an explosive sound; splutter. **4.** (*intr.*) to rain very lightly. **5.** (*tr.*; often foll. by *out*) to eject or discharge (something) from the mouth: *he spat the food out; to spit blood.* **6.** (*tr.*; often foll. by *out*) to utter (short sharp words or syllables), esp. in a violent manner. **7. spit chips.** Also (N.Z.): **spit tacks.** *Austral. slang.* to be very angry. **8. spit it out!** *Brit. informal.* a command given to someone that he should speak forthwith. ~*n.* **9.** another name for **spittle. 10.** a light or brief fall of rain, snow, etc. **11.** the act or an instance of spitting. **12.** *Informal, chiefly Brit.* another word for **spitting image.** [Old English *spittan;* related to *spǣtan* to spit, German dialect *spitzen*] —**'spitter** *n.*

spit[2] (spɪt) *n.* **1.** a pointed rod on which meat is skewered and roasted before or over an open fire. **2.** Also called: **rotisserie, rotating spit.** a similar device rotated by electricity or clockwork, fitted onto a cooker. **3.** an elongated often hooked strip of sand or shingle projecting from the shore, deposited by longshore drift, and usually above water. ~*vb.* **spits, spitting, spitted. 4.** (*tr.*) to impale on or transfix with or as if with a spit. [Old English *spitu;* related to Old High German *spiz* spit, Norwegian *spit* tip]

spit[3] (spɪt) *n.* the depth of earth cut by a spade; a spade's depth. [C16: from Middle Dutch and Middle Low German *spit*]

spital ('spɪtᵊl) *n. Obsolete.* **1.** a hospital, esp. for the needy sick. **2.** a highway shelter. [C13 *spitel,* changed from Medieval Latin *hospitāle* HOSPITAL]

spit and polish *n. Informal.* punctilious attention to neatness, discipline, etc., esp. in the armed forces.

spitchcock ('spɪtʃˌkɒk) *n.* an eel split and grilled or fried. Compare **spatchcock.** [C16: of unknown origin; see SPATCHCOCK]

spit curl *n.* the U.S. and Canadian name for **kiss curl.** [perhaps so called because it is sometimes plastered down with spittle]

spite (spaɪt) *n.* **1.** maliciousness involving the desire to harm another; venomous ill will. **2.** an instance of such malice; grudge. **3.** *Archaic.* something that induces vexation. **4. in spite of.** (*prep.*) in defiance of; regardless of; notwithstanding. ~*vb.* (*tr.*) **5.** to annoy in order to vent spite. **6.** *Archaic.* to offend. [C13: variant of DESPITE]

spiteful ('spaɪtfʊl) *adj.* full of or motivated by spite; vindictive. —**'spitefully** *adv.* —**'spitefulness** *n.*

spitfire ('spɪtˌfaɪə) *n.* a person given to outbursts of spiteful temper and anger, esp. a woman or girl.

spitsticker ('spɪtˌstɪkə) *n.* a wood-engraving tool with a fine prow-shaped point for cutting curved lines.

spitting distance *n.* a short space or distance.

spitting image *n. Informal.* a person who bears a strong physical resemblance to another, esp. to a relative. Also called: **spit, spit and image.** [C19: modification of *spit and image,* from SPIT[1] (as in the phrase *the very spit of,* the exact likeness of (someone))]

spitting snake *n.* another name for the **ringhals.**

spittle ('spɪtᵊl) *n.* **1.** the fluid secreted in the mouth; saliva or spit. **2.** Also called: **cuckoo spit, frog spit.** the frothy substance secreted on plants by the larvae of certain froghoppers. [Old English *spǣtl* saliva; see SPIT[1]]

spittle insect *or* **spittlebug** ('spɪtᵊlˌbʌg) *n.* other names for the **froghopper.**

spittoon (spɪ'tuːn) *n.* a receptacle for spit, usually in a public place. [C19: from SPIT[1] + *-oon:* see SALOON, BALLOON, etc.]

spitz (spɪts) *n.* any of various breeds of dog characterized by very dense hair, a stocky build, a pointed muzzle, erect ears, and a tightly curled tail. [C19: from German, from *spitz* pointed]

spiv (spɪv) *n. Brit. slang.* a man or boy who makes a living by underhand dealings or swindling; black marketeer. [C20: back formation from dialect *spiving* smart; compare SPIFFY, SPIFFING] —**'spivvy** *adj.*

splake (spleɪk) *n.* a type of hybrid trout bred by Canadian zoologists. [from *sp(eckled)* + *lake (trout)*]

splanchnic ('splæŋknɪk) *adj.* of or relating to the viscera; visceral: *a splanchnic nerve.* [C17: from New Latin *splanchnicus,* from Greek *splankhnikos* concerning the entrails, from *splankhna* the entrails]

splash (splæʃ) *vb.* **1.** to scatter (liquid) about in blobs; spatter. **2.** to descend or cause to descend upon in scattered blobs: *he splashed his jacket; rain splashed against the window.* **3.** to make (one's way) by or as if by splashing: *he splashed through the puddle.* **4.** (*tr.*) to print (a story or photograph) prominently in a newspaper. ~*n.* **5.** an instance or sound of splashing. **6.** an amount splashed. **7.** a mark or patch created by or as if by splashing: *a splash of colour.* **8.** *Informal.* an extravagant display, usually for effect (esp. in the phrase **make a splash**). **9.** a small amount of soda water, water, etc., added to an alcoholic drink. [C18: alteration of PLASH[1]]

splashback ('splæʃˌbæk) *n.* a sheet of glass, plastic, etc., attached to a wall above a basin to protect the wall against splashing.

splashboard ('splæʃˌbɔːd) *n.* **1.** a guard on a vehicle to protect people from splashing water, mud, etc. **2.** *Nautical.* another word for **washboard** (sense 4).

splashdown ('splæʃˌdaʊn) *n.* **1.** the controlled landing of a spacecraft on water at the end of a space flight. **2.** the time scheduled for this event. ~*vb.* **splash down. 3.** (*intr., adv.*) (of a spacecraft) to make a splashdown.

splasher ('splæʃə) *n.* anything used for protection against splashes.

splash out *vb.* (*adv.;* often foll. by *on*) *Informal, chiefly Brit.* to spend (money) freely or extravagantly (on something).

splashy ('splæʃɪ) *adj.* **splashier, splashiest. 1.** having irregular marks. **2.** *Informal.* done to attract attention or make a sensation; showy. **3.** making a splash or splashes. —**'splashily** *adv.* —**'splashiness** *n.*

splat[1] (splæt) *n.* a wet slapping sound. [C19: of imitative origin]

splat[2] (splæt) *n.* a wide flat piece of wood, esp. one that is the upright central part of a chair back. [C19: perhaps related to Old English *splātan* to SPLIT]

splatter ('splætə) *vb.* **1.** to splash with small blobs; spatter. ~*n.* **2.** a splash of liquid, mud, etc.

splay (spleɪ) *adj.* **1.** spread out; broad and flat. **2.** turned outwards in an awkward manner. ~*vb.* **3.** to spread out; turn out or expand. **4.** (*tr.*) *Vet. science.* to dislocate (a bone). ~*n.* **5.** a surface of a wall that forms an oblique angle to the main flat surfaces, esp. at a doorway or window opening. **6.** enlargement. [C14: short for DISPLAY]

Splayd (spleɪd) *n. Austral. trademark.* an implement combining the functions of knife, fork, and spoon. [from SP(OON) + (BL)ADE]

splayfoot ('spleɪˌfʊt) *n., pl.* **-feet. 1.** *Pathol.* another word for **flatfoot** (sense 1). **2.** a foot of which the toes are spread out, as in certain breeds of dog used in hunting waterfowl. —**'splay-ˌfooted** *adj.* —**'splayˌfootedly** *adv.*

spleen (spliːn) *n.* **1.** a spongy highly vascular organ situated near the stomach in man. It forms lymphocytes, produces antibodies, aids in destroying worn-out red blood cells, and filters bacteria and foreign particles from the blood. **2.** the corresponding organ in other animals. **3.** spitefulness or ill humour; peevishness: *to vent one's spleen.* **4.** *Archaic.* the organ in the human body considered to be the seat of the emotions. **5.** *Archaic.* another word for **melancholy. 6.** *Obsolete.* whim; mood. [C13: from Old French *esplen,* from Latin *splēn,* from Greek; related to Latin *lien* spleen] —**'spleenish** *or* **'spleeny** *adj.*

spleenful ('spliːnfʊl) *adj.* affected by spleen; bad-tempered or irritable. —**'spleenfully** *adv.*

spleenwort ('spliːnˌwɜːt) *n.* any of various ferns of the genus *Asplenium,* esp. *A. trichomanes,* that often grows on walls, having linear or oblong sori on the undersurface of the fronds. See also **asplenium.**

splendent ('splɛndənt) *adj. Archaic.* **1.** shining brightly; lustrous: *a splendent sun.* **2.** famous; illustrious. [C15: from Latin *splendēns* brilliant, from *splendēre* to shine]

splendid ('splɛndɪd) *adj.* **1.** brilliant or fine, esp. in appearance. **2.** characterized by magnificence; imposing. **3.** glorious or illustrious: *a splendid reputation.* **4.** brightly gleaming; radiant: *her splendid face; splendid colours.* **5.** very good or satisfactory: *a splendid time.* [C17: from Latin *splendidus,* from *splendēre* to shine] —**'splendidly** *adv.* —**'splendidness** *n.*

splendiferous (splɛn'dɪfərəs) *adj. Facetious.* grand; splendid: *a really splendiferous meal.* [C15: from Medieval Latin *splendiferus,* from Latin *splendor* radiance + *ferre* to bring] —**splen'diferously** *adv.* —**splen'diferousness** *n.*

splendour *or U.S.* **splendor** ('splɛndə) *n.* **1.** the state or quality of being splendid. **2. sun in splendour.** *Heraldry.* a representation of the sun with rays and a human face. —**'splendorous** *or* **splendrous** ('splɛndrəs) *adj.*

splenectomy (splɪ'nɛktəmɪ) *n., pl.* **-mies.** surgical removal of the spleen.

splenetic (splɪ'nɛtɪk) *adj.* **1.** of or relating to the spleen. **2.** spiteful or irritable; peevish. **3.** *Obsolete.* full of melancholy. ~*n.* **4.** a spiteful or irritable person. [C16: from Late Latin *splēnēticus,* from Latin *splēn* SPLEEN] —**sple'netically** *adv.*

splenic ('splɛnɪk, 'spliː-) *adj.* **1.** of, relating to, or in the spleen. **2.** having a disease or disorder of the spleen.

splenitis (splɪ'naɪtɪs) *n.* inflammation of the spleen.

splenius ('spliːnɪəs) *n., pl.* **-nii** (-nɪˌaɪ). *Anatomy.* either of two flat muscles situated at the back of the neck that rotate, flex, and extend the head and neck. [C18: via New Latin from Greek *splēnion* a plaster] —**'splenial** *adj.*

splenomegaly (ˌspliːnəʊ'mɛgəlɪ) *n. Pathol.* abnormal enlargement of the spleen. [C20: from Greek *splēno-,* from *splēn* SPLEEN + *megalo-,* from *megas* large + -Y[3]]

splice (splaɪs) *vb.* (*tr.*) **1.** to join (two ropes) by intertwining the strands. **2.** to join up the trimmed ends of (two pieces of wire, film, magnetic tape, etc.) with solder or an adhesive material. **3.** to join (timbers) by overlapping and binding or bolting the ends together. **4.** (*passive*) *Informal.* to enter into marriage: *the couple got spliced last Saturday.* **5. splice the mainbrace.** *Nautical.* to issue and partake of an extra allocation of alcoholic spirits. ~*n.* **6.** a join made by splicing. **7.** the place where such a join occurs. **8.** the wedge-shaped end of a cricket-bat handle or similar instrument that fits into the blade. [C16: probably from Middle Dutch *splissen;* related to German *spleissen,* Swedish *splitsa;* see SPLIT] —**'splicer** *n.*

spliff (splɪf) *n. Caribbean slang.* a cannabis cigarette.

spline (splaɪn) *n.* **1.** any one of a series of narrow keys (**external splines**) formed longitudinally around the circumference of a shaft that fit into corresponding grooves (**internal splines**) in a mating part: used to prevent movement between two parts, esp.

in transmitting torque. **2.** a long narrow strip of wood, metal, etc.; slat. **3.** a thin narrow strip made of wood, metal, or plastic fitted into a groove in the edge of a board, tile, etc., to connect it to another. *~vb.* **4.** (*tr.*) to provide (a shaft, part, etc.) with splines. [C18: East Anglian dialect; perhaps related to Old English *splin* spindle; see SPLINT]

splint (splɪnt) *n.* **1.** a rigid support for restricting movement of an injured part, esp. a broken bone. **2.** a thin sliver of wood, esp. one that is used to light cigars, a fire, etc. **3.** a thin strip of wood woven with others to form a chair seat, basket, etc. **4.** *Vet. science.* a bony enlargement of the cannon bone of a horse. **5.** one of the overlapping metal plates used in armour after about 1330. **6.** another word for **splinter.** *~vb.* **7.** to apply a splint to (a broken arm, etc.). [C13: from Middle Low German *splinte;* related to Middle Dutch *splinte* splint, Old High German *spaltan* to split] —'**splint,like** *adj.*

splint bone *n.* one of the rudimentary metacarpal or metatarsal bones in horses and similar animals, occurring on each side of the cannon bone.

splinter ('splɪntə) *n.* **1.** a very small sharp piece of wood, glass, metal, etc., characteristically long and thin, broken off from a whole. **2.** a metal fragment, from the container of a shell, bomb, etc., thrown out during an explosion. *~vb.* **3.** to reduce or be reduced to sharp fragments; shatter. **4.** to break or be broken off in small sharp fragments. [C14: from Middle Dutch *splinter;* see SPLINT] —'**splintery** *adj.*

splinter group *n.* a number of members of an organization, political party, etc., who split from the main body and form an independent association of their own, usually as the result of dissension.

split (splɪt) *vb.* **splits, splitting, split.** **1.** to break or cause to break, esp. forcibly, by cleaving into separate pieces, often into two roughly equal pieces: *to split a brick.* **2.** to separate or be separated from a whole: *he split a piece of wood from the block.* **3.** to separate or be separated into factions, usually through discord. **4.** (often foll. by *up*) to separate or cause to separate through a disagreement. **5.** (when *tr.*, often foll. by *up*) to divide or be divided among two or more persons: *split up the pie among the three of us.* **6.** *Slang.* to depart; leave: *let's split; we split the scene.* **7.** (*tr.*) to separate (something) into its components by interposing something else: *to split a word with hyphens.* **8.** (*intr.;* usually foll. by *on*) *Slang.* to betray the trust, plans, etc. (of); inform: *he split on me to the cops.* **9.** (*tr.*) *U.S. politics.* to mark (a ballot, etc.) so as to vote for the candidates of more than one party: *he split the ticket.* **10.** (*tr.*) to separate (an animal hide or skin) into layers. **11. split hairs.** to make a fine but needless distinction. **12. split one's sides.** to laugh very heartily. **13. split the difference. a.** to settle a dispute by effecting a compromise in which both sides give way to the same extent. **b.** to divide a remainder equally. *~n.* **14.** the act or process of splitting. **15.** a gap or rift caused or a piece removed by the process of splitting. **16.** a breach or schism in a group or the faction resulting from such a breach. **17.** a dessert of sliced fruit and ice cream, covered with whipped cream, nuts, etc.: *banana split.* **18.** See **Devonshire split.** **19. a.** a separated layer of an animal hide or skin other than the outer layer. **b.** leather made from such a layer. **20.** *Tenpin bowling.* a formation of the pins after the first bowl in which there is a large gap between two pins or groups of pins. **21.** *Informal.* an arrangement or process of dividing up loot or money. *~adj.* **22.** having been split; divided: *split logs.* **23.** having a split or splits: *hair with split ends.* ~See also **splits, split up.** [C16: from Middle Dutch *splitten* to cleave; related to Middle High German *splīzen;* see SPLICE] —'**splitter** *n.*

split brain *n.* a brain in which the tracts connecting the two halves of the cerebral cortex have been surgically split or are missing from birth.

split cane *n. Angling.* bamboo split into strips of triangular section, tapered, and glued to form a stiff but flexible hexagonal rod: used, esp. formerly, for making fishing rods.

split decision *n. Boxing.* the award of a fight on a majority verdict of the judges as opposed to a unanimous decision.

split infinitive *n.* (in English grammar) an infinitive used with another word between *to* (the infinitive marker) and the verb itself, as in *I want to really finish it this time.*

▷**Usage.** The traditional rule against placing an adverb between *to* and its verb is gradually disappearing. Although it is true that a split infinitive may result in a clumsy sentence (*he decided to firmly and definitively deal with the problem*), this is not enough to justify the absolute condemnation that this practice has attracted. Indeed, very often the most natural position of the adverb is between *to* and the verb (*he decided to really try next time*) and to change it would result in an artificial and awkward construction (*he really decided to try next time*). The current view is therefore that the split infinitive is not a grammatical error. Nevertheless, many writers prefer to avoid splitting infinitives in formal written English, since readers with a more traditional point of view are likely to interpret this type of construction as incorrect.

split keyboarding *n. Computer technol.* the act or practice of editing data from one terminal on another terminal.

split-level *adj.* (of a house, room, etc.) having the floor level of one part about half a storey above or below the floor level of an adjoining part.

split-new *adj. Scot.* brand-new.

split pea *n.* a pea dried and split and used in soups, pease pudding, or as a vegetable.

split personality *n.* **1.** the tendency to change rapidly in mood or temperament. **2.** a nontechnical term for **multiple personality.**

split pin *n.* a metal pin made by bending double a wire, often of hemispherical section, so that it can be passed through a hole in a nut, shaft, etc., to secure another part by bending back the ends of the wire.

split ring *n.* a steel ring having two helical turns, often used as a key ring.

splits (splɪts) *n.* (*functioning as sing.*) (in gymnastics, etc.) the act of sinking to the floor to achieve a sitting position in which both legs are straight, pointing in opposite directions, and at right angles to the body.

split-screen technique *n.* a cinematic device by which two or more complete images are projected simultaneously onto separate parts of the screen. Also called: **split screen.**

split second *n.* **1.** an infinitely small period of time; instant. *~adj.* **split-second.** (*prenominal*) **2.** made or arrived at in an infinitely short time: *a split-second decision.* **3.** depending upon minute precision: *split-second timing.*

split shift *n.* a work period divided into two parts that are separated by an interval longer than a normal rest period.

split ticket *n.* See **split** (sense 9). See also **straight ticket.**

split tin *n. Brit.* a long loaf of bread split on top, giving a greater crust area.

splitting ('splɪtɪŋ) *adj.* **1.** (of a headache) intolerably painful; acute. **2.** (of the head) assailed by an overpowering unbearable pain. *~n.* **3.** *Psychoanal.* the Freudian defence mechanism in which an object or idea (or, alternatively, the ego) is separated into two or more parts in order to remove its threatening meaning.

split up *vb.* (*adv.*) **1.** (*tr.*) to separate out into parts; divide. **2.** (*intr.*) to become separated or parted through disagreement: *they split up after years of marriage.* **3.** to break down or be capable of being broken down into constituent parts: *I have split up the question into three parts.* *~n.* **split-up.** **4.** the act or an instance of separating.

split wings *pl. n. Angling.* **a.** wings (of an artificial fly) that are dressed cocked up and separated into a V shape. **b.** (*as modifier*): *a split-wing pattern.*

splodge (splɒdʒ) *n.* **1.** a large irregular spot or blot. *~vb.* **2.** (*tr.*) to mark (something) with such a blot or blots. [C19: alteration of earlier SPLOTCH] —'**splodgy** *adj.*

splore (splɔːr) *n. Scot.* a revel; binge; escapade. [C18: of obscure origin]

splotch (splɒtʃ) *n., vb.* the usual U.S. word for **splodge.** [C17: perhaps a blend of SPOT + BLOTCH] —'**splotchy** *adj.*

splurge (splɜːdʒ) *n.* **1.** an ostentatious display, esp. of wealth. **2.** a bout of unrestrained extravagance. *~vb.* **3.** (often foll. by *on*) to spend (money) unrestrainedly or extravagantly. [C19: of uncertain origin]

splutter ('splʌtə) *vb.* **1.** to spit out (saliva, food particles, etc.) from the mouth in an explosive manner, as through choking or laughing. **2.** to utter (words) with spitting sounds, as through rage or choking. **3.** to eject or be ejected in an explosive manner: *sparks spluttered from the fire.* **4.** (*tr.*) to bespatter (a person) with tiny particles explosively ejected: *he spluttered the boy next to him with ink.* *~n.* **5.** the process or noise of spluttering. **6.** spluttering incoherent speech, esp. in argument. **7.** anything ejected through spluttering. [C17: variant of SPUTTER, influenced by SPLASH] —'**splutterer** *n.*

spode (spəʊd) *n.* (*often cap.*) china or porcelain manufactured by Josiah Spode, British potter (1754–1827), or his company.

spodumene ('spɒdjʊˌmiːn) *n.* a greyish-white, green, or lilac pyroxene mineral consisting of lithium aluminium silicate in monoclinic crystalline form. It is an important ore of lithium and is used in the manufacture of glass and ceramics and as a gemstone. Formula: $LiAlSi_2O_6$. [C19: from French *spodumène,* from German *Spodumen,* from Greek *spodoumenos,* from *spodousthai* to be burnt to ashes, from *spodos* wood ash]

spoil (spɔɪl) *vb.* **spoils, spoiling, spoilt** *or* **spoiled.** **1.** (*tr.*) to cause damage to (something), in regard to its value, beauty, usefulness, etc. **2.** (*tr.*) to weaken the character of (a child) by complying unrestrainedly with its desires. **3.** (*intr.*) (of perishable substances) to become unfit for consumption or use: *the fruit must be eaten before it spoils.* **4.** (*intr.*) *Sport.* to disrupt the play or style of an opponent, as to prevent him from settling into a rhythm. **5.** *Archaic.* to strip (a person or place) of (property or goods) by force or violence. **6. be spoiling for.** to have an aggressive desire for (a fight, etc). *~n.* **7.** waste material thrown up by an excavation. **8.** any treasure accumulated by a person: *this gold ring was part of the spoil.* **9.** *Obsolete.* **a.** the act of plundering. **b.** a strategically placed building, city, etc., captured as plunder. ~See also **spoils.** [C13: from Old French *espoillier,* from Latin *spoliāre* to strip, from *spolium* booty]

spoilage ('spɔɪlɪdʒ) *n.* **1.** the act or an instance of spoiling or the state or condition of being spoilt. **2.** an amount of material that has been wasted by being spoilt: *the spoilage of corn was considerable.*

spoiled priest *n. Irish.* a person who was a student for the priesthood but who has withdrawn or been dismissed.

spoiler ('spɔɪlə) *n.* **1.** plunderer or robber. **2.** a person or thing that causes spoilage or corruption. **3.** a device fitted to an aircraft wing to increase drag and reduce lift. It is usually extended into the airflow to assist descent and banking. Compare **air brake** (sense 2). **4.** a similar device fitted to a car. **5.** *Sport.* a competitor who adopts spoiling tactics, as in boxing. **6.** a magazine, newspaper, etc. produced specifically to coincide with the production of a rival magazine, newspaper, etc. in order to divert public interest and reduce its sales.

spoilfive ('spɔɪl,faɪv) *n.* a card game for two or more players with five cards each.

spoils (spɔɪlz) *pl. n.* **1.** (*sometimes sing.*) valuables seized by violence, esp. in war. **2.** *Chiefly U.S.* the rewards and benefits of public office regarded as plunder for the winning party or candidate. See also **spoils system.**

spoilsman ('spɔɪlzmən) *n., pl.* **-men.** *U.S. politics.* a person who shares in the spoils of office or advocates the spoils system.

spoilsport ('spɔɪl,spɔːt) *n. Informal.* a person who spoils the pleasure of other people by his actions or attitudes.

spoils system *n. Chiefly U.S.* the practice of filling appointive public offices with friends and supporters of the ruling political party. Compare **merit system.**

spoilt (spɔɪlt) *vb.* a past tense and past participle of **spoil.**

spoke[1] (spəʊk) *vb.* **1.** the past tense of **speak.** **2.** *Archaic or dialect.* a past participle of **speak.**

spoke[2] (spəʊk) *n.* **1.** a radial member of a wheel, joining the hub to the rim. **2.** a radial projection from the rim of a wheel, as in a ship's wheel. **3.** a rung of a ladder. **4. put a spoke in someone's wheel.** *Brit.* to thwart someone's plans. ~*vb.* **5.** (*tr.*) to equip with or as if with spokes. [Old English *spāca*]

spoken ('spəʊkən) *vb.* **1.** the past participle of **speak.** ~*adj.* **2.** uttered through the medium of speech. Compare **written.** **3.** (*in combination*) having speech as specified: *soft-spoken.* **4. spoken for.** engaged, reserved, or allocated.

spokeshave ('spəʊk,ʃeɪv) *n.* a small plane with two handles, one on each side of its blade, used for shaping or smoothing cylindrical wooden surfaces, such as spokes.

spokesman ('spəʊksmən), **spokesperson** ('spəʊks,pɜːsᵊn), *or* (*fem.*) **spokeswoman** ('spəʊks,wʊmən) *n., pl.* **-men, -persons** *or* **-people,** *or* **-women.** a person authorized to speak on behalf of another person, group of people, or organization.

spoliate ('spəʊlɪ,eɪt) *vb.* a less common word for **despoil.**

spoliation (,spəʊlɪ'eɪʃən) *n.* **1.** the act or an instance of despoiling or plundering. **2.** the authorized seizure or plundering of neutral vessels on the seas by a belligerent state in time of war. **3.** *Law.* the material alteration of a document so as to render it invalid. **4.** *English ecclesiastical law.* the taking of the fruits of a benefice by a person not entitled to them. [C14: from Latin *spoliātiō,* from *spoliāre* to SPOIL] —'**spoliatory** *adj.*

spondaic (spɒn'deɪɪk) *adj. Prosody.* of, relating to, or consisting of spondees.

spondee ('spɒndiː) *n. Prosody.* a metrical foot consisting of two long syllables (– –). [C14: from Old French *spondée,* from Latin *spondēus,* from Greek *spondeios,* from *spondē* a ritual libation; from the use of spondee in the music that characteristically accompanied such ceremonies]

spondulix *or* **spondulicks** (spɒn'djuːlɪks) *n. Slang.* money. [C19: of obscure origin]

spondylitis (,spɒndɪ'laɪtɪs) *n.* inflammation of the vertebrae. [C19: from New Latin, from Greek *spondulos* vertebra; see -ITIS]

sponge (spʌndʒ) *n.* **1.** any multicellular typically marine animal of the phylum *Porifera,* usually occurring in complex sessile colonies in which the porous body is supported by a fibrous, calcareous, or siliceous skeletal framework. **2.** a piece of the light porous highly absorbent elastic skeleton of certain sponges, used in bathing, cleaning, etc. See also **spongin.** **3.** any of a number of light porous elastic materials resembling a sponge. **4.** another word for **sponger** (sense 1). **5.** *Informal.* a person who indulges in heavy drinking. **6.** leavened dough, esp. before kneading. **7.** See **sponge cake.** **8.** Also called: **sponge pudding.** *Brit.* a light steamed or baked pudding, spongy in texture, made with various flavourings or fruit. **9.** porous metal produced by electrolysis or by reducing a metal compound without fusion or sintering and capable of absorbing large quantities of gas: *platinum sponge.* **10.** a rub with a sponge. **11. throw in** (*or* **up**) **the sponge** (*or* **towel**). See **throw in** (sense 4). ~*vb.* **12.** (*tr.;* often foll. by *off* or *down*) to clean (something) by wiping or rubbing with a damp or wet sponge. **13.** (*tr.;* usually foll. by *off, away, out,* etc.) to remove (marks, etc.) by rubbing with a damp or wet sponge or cloth. **14.** (when *tr.,* often foll. by *up*) to absorb (liquids, esp. when spilt) in the manner of a sponge. **15.** (*tr.;* often foll. by *off*) to get (something) from (someone) by presuming on his generosity: *to sponge a meal off someone.* **16.** (*intr.;* often foll. by *off* or *on*) to obtain one's subsistence, welfare, etc., unjustifiably (from): *he sponges off his friends.* **17.** (*intr.*) to go collecting sponges. ~See also **sponge down.** [Old English, from Latin *spongia,* from Greek] —'**sponge,like** *adj.*

sponge bag *n.* a small bag made of plastic, etc., that holds toilet articles, used esp. when travelling.

sponge bath *n.* a washing of the body with a wet sponge or cloth, but without immersion in water.

sponge cake *n.* a light porous cake, made of eggs, sugar, flour, and flavourings traditionally without any fat.

sponge cloth *n.* any of various porous fabrics, usually made in a loose honeycomb weave.

sponge down *vb.* (*tr., adv.*) **1.** to wipe clean with a damp sponge or cloth. ~*n.* **sponge-down.** **2.** the act or instance of sponging down.

sponger ('spʌndʒə) *n.* **1.** *Informal.* a person who lives off other people by continually taking advantage of their generosity; parasite or scrounger. **2.** a person or ship employed in collecting sponges.

spongiform ('spʌndʒɪ,fɔːm) *adj.* **1.** resembling a sponge in appearance, esp. in having many holes. **2.** denoting diseases characterized by this appearance of affected tissues.

spongin ('spʌndʒɪn) *n.* a fibrous horny protein that forms the skeletal framework of the bath sponge and related sponges. [C19: from German, from Latin *spongia* SPONGE + -IN]

spongioblast ('spʌndʒɪəʊ,blɑːst) *n.* any of numerous columnar epithelial cells in the brain and spinal cord that develop into neuroglia. [C20: from Greek *spongia* SPONGE + -BLAST] —**spongioblastic** (,spʌndʒɪəʊ'blæstɪk) *adj.*

spongy ('spʌndʒɪ) *adj.* **-gier, -giest.** **1.** of or resembling a sponge, esp. in texture, porosity, elasticity, or compressibility: *spongy bread; spongy bone.* **2.** of or like a sponge in respect of its capacity to absorb fluid and yield it when compressed. —'**spongily** *adv.* —'**sponginess** *n.*

sponsion ('spɒnʃən) *n.* **1.** the act or process of becoming surety; sponsorship. **2.** (*often pl.*) *International law.* an unauthorized agreement made by a public officer, esp. an admiral or general in time of war, requiring ratification by the government of the state concerned. **3.** any act or promise, esp. one made on behalf of someone else. [C17: from Latin *sponsiō,* from *spondēre* to pledge]

sponson ('spɒnsən) *n.* **1.** *Naval.* an outboard support for a gun enabling it to fire fore and aft. **2.** a semicircular gun turret on the side of a tank. **3.** a float or flotation chamber along the gunwale of a canoe. **4.** a structural projection from the side of a paddle steamer for supporting a paddle wheel. **5.** a structural unit attached to a helicopter fuselage by fixed struts, housing the main landing gear and inflatable flotation bags. [C19: perhaps from EXPANSION]

sponsor ('spɒnsə) *n.* **1.** a person or group that provides funds for an activity, esp.: **a.** a commercial organization that pays all or part of the cost of putting on a concert, sporting event, etc. **b.** a person who donates money to a charity when the person requesting the donation has performed a specified activity as part of an organized fund-raising effort. **2.** *Chiefly U.S. and Canadian.* a person or business firm that pays the costs of a radio or television programme in return for advertising time. **3.** a legislator who presents and supports a bill, motion, etc. **4.** Also called: **godparent. a.** an authorized witness who makes the required promises on behalf of a person to be baptized and thereafter assumes responsibility for his Christian upbringing. **b.** a person who presents a candidate for confirmation. **5.** *Chiefly U.S.* a person who undertakes responsibility for the actions, statements, obligations, etc., of another, as during a period of apprenticeship; guarantor. ~*vb.* **6.** (*tr.*) to act as a sponsor for. [C17: from Latin, from *spondēre* to promise solemnly] —**sponsorial** (spɒn'sɔːrɪəl) *adj.* —'**sponsor,ship** *n.*

sponsored ('spɒnsəd) *adj.* denoting an activity organized to raise money for a charity in which sponsors agree to donate money on completion of the activity, or a specified period or amount of it, by participants: *a sponsored walk.*

spontaneity (,spɒntə'niːɪtɪ, -'neɪ-) *n., pl.* **-ties.** **1.** the state or quality of being spontaneous. **2.** (*often pl.*) the exhibiting of actions, impulses, or behaviour that are stimulated by internal processes.

spontaneous (spɒn'teɪnɪəs) *adj.* **1.** occurring, produced, or performed through natural processes without external influence: *spontaneous movement.* **2.** arising from an unforced personal impulse; voluntary; unpremeditated: *a spontaneous comment.* **3.** (of plants) growing naturally; indigenous. [C17: from Late Latin *spontāneus,* from Latin *sponte* voluntarily] —**spon'taneously** *adv.* —**spon'taneousness** *n.*

spontaneous combustion *n.* the ignition of a substance or body as a result of internal oxidation processes, without the application of an external source of heat, occurring in finely powdered ores, coal, straw, etc.

spontaneous generation *n.* another name for **abiogenesis.**

spontaneous recovery *n. Psychol.* the reappearance of a response after its extinction has been followed by a period of rest.

spontoon (spɒn'tuːn) *n.* a form of halberd carried by some junior infantry officers in the 18th and 19th centuries. [C18: from French *esponton,* from Italian *spuntone,* from *punto* POINT]

spoof (spuːf) *Informal.* ~*n.* **1.** a mildly satirical mockery or parody; lampoon: *a spoof on party politics.* **2.** a good-humoured deception or trick; prank. ~*vb.* **3.** to indulge in a spoof of (a person or thing). [C19: coined by A. Roberts (1852–1933), British comedian, to designate a game of his own invention] —'**spoofer** *n.*

spook (spuːk) *Informal.* ~*n.* **1.** a ghost or a person suggestive of this. **2.** *U.S. and Canadian.* a spy. ~*vb.* (*tr.*) *U.S. and Canadian.* **3.** to frighten: *to spook horses; to spook a person.* **4.** (of a ghost) to haunt. [C19: Dutch *spook,* from Middle Low German *spōk* ghost] —**'spookish** *adj.*

spooky ('spuːkɪ) *adj.* **spookier, spookiest.** *Informal.* **1.** ghostly or eerie: *a spooky house.* **2.** resembling or appropriate to a ghost. **3.** *U.S.* easily frightened; highly strung. —**'spookily** *adv.* —**'spookiness** *n.*

spool (spuːl) *n.* **1.** a device around which magnetic tape, film, cotton, etc., can be automatically wound, with plates at top and bottom to prevent it from slipping off. **2.** anything round which other materials, esp. thread, are wound. ~*vb.* **3.** (sometimes foll. by *up*) to wind or be wound onto a spool or reel. [C14: of Germanic origin; compare Old High German *spuolo,* Middle Dutch *spoele*]

spoon (spuːn) *n.* **1.** a metal, wooden, or plastic utensil having a shallow concave part, usually elliptical in shape, attached to a handle, used in eating or serving food, stirring, etc. **2.** Also called: **spoonbait.** an angling lure for spinning or trolling, consisting of a bright piece of metal which swivels on a trace to which are attached a hook or hooks. **3.** a golf club: a No. 3 wood with a shorter shaft and shallower face than a brassie, giving more lift. **4. be born with a silver spoon in one's mouth.** to inherit wealth or social standing. **5. wooden spoon.** *Brit.* another name for **booby prize.** **6.** *Rowing.* a type of oar blade that is curved at the edges and tip to gain a firm grip on the water. Compare **spade**[1] (sense 4). ~*vb.* **7.** (*tr.*) to scoop up or transfer (food, liquid, etc.) from one container to another with or as if with a spoon. **8.** (*intr.*) *Slang, old-fashioned.* to kiss and cuddle. **9.** to hollow out (a cavity or spoon-shaped bowl) (in something). **10.** *Sport.* to hit (a ball) with a weak lifting motion, as in golf, cricket, etc. [Old English *spōn* splinter; related to Old Norse *spōnn* spoon, chip, Old High German *spān*]

spoonbill ('spuːnˌbɪl) *n.* any of several wading birds of warm regions, such as *Platalea leucorodia* (**common spoonbill**) and *Ajaia ajaja* (**roseate spoonbill**), having a long horizontally flattened bill: family *Threskiornithidae,* order *Ciconiiformes.*

spoondrift ('spuːnˌdrɪft) *n.* a less common spelling of **spindrift.**

spoonerism ('spuːnəˌrɪzəm) *n.* the transposition of the initial consonants or consonant clusters of a pair of words, often resulting in an amusing ambiguity of meaning, such as *hush my brat* for *brush my hat.* [C20: named after W. A. *Spooner* (1844–1930), British clergyman renowned for slips of this kind]

spoon-feed *vb.* **-feeds, -feeding, -fed.** (*tr.*) **1.** to feed with a spoon. **2.** to overindulge or spoil. **3.** to provide (a person) with ready-made opinions, judgments, etc., depriving him of original thought or action.

spoonful ('spuːnˌfʊl) *n., pl.* **-fuls.** **1.** the amount that a spoon is able to hold. **2.** a small quantity.

spoony *or* **spooney** ('spuːnɪ) *Slang, rare, old-fashioned.* ~*adj.* **spoonier, spooniest.** **1.** foolishly or stupidly amorous. ~*n., pl.* **spoonies.** **2.** a fool or silly person, esp. one in love.

spoor (spʊə, spɔː) *n.* **1.** the trail of an animal or person, esp. as discernible to the human eye. ~*vb.* **2.** to track (an animal) by following its trail. [C19: from Afrikaans, from Middle Dutch *spor;* related to Old English *spor* track, Old High German *spor;* see SPUR] —**'spoorer** *n.*

sporadic (spəˈrædɪk) *adj.* **1.** occurring at irregular points in time; intermittent: *sporadic firing.* **2.** scattered; isolated: *a sporadic disease.* [C17: from Medieval Latin *sporadicus,* from Greek *sporadikos,* from *sporas* scattered; related to Greek *speirein* to sow; see SPORE] —**spo'radically** *adv.* —**spo'radicalness** *n.*

sporangium (spəˈrændʒɪəm) *n., pl.* **-gia** (-dʒɪə). any organ, esp. in fungi, in which asexual spores are produced. [C19: from New Latin, from SPORO- + Greek *angeion* receptacle] —**spo'rangial** *adj.*

spore (spɔː) *n.* **1.** a reproductive body, produced by some protozoans and many plants, that develops into a new individual. A **sexual spore** is formed after the fusion of gametes and an **asexual spore** is the result of asexual reproduction. **2.** a germ cell, seed, dormant bacterium, or similar body. ~*vb.* **3.** (*intr.*) to produce, carry, or release spores. [C19: from New Latin *spora,* from Greek: a sowing; related to Greek *speirein* to sow]

spore case *n.* the nontechnical name for **sporangium.**

spore print *n. Botany.* the pattern produced by placing the cap of a mushroom on a piece of paper and allowing the spores to fall.

sporo- *or before a vowel* **spor-** *combining form.* (in botany) spore: *sporophyte.* [from New Latin *spora*]

sporocarp ('spɔːrəʊˌkɑːp, 'spɒ-) *n.* **1.** a specialized leaf branch in certain aquatic ferns that encloses the sori. **2.** the spore-producing structure in certain algae, lichens, and fungi.

sporocyst ('spɔːrəʊˌsɪst, 'spɒ-) *n.* **1.** a thick-walled rounded structure produced by protozoans of the class *Sporozoa,* in which sporozoites are formed. **2.** the saclike larva of a trematode worm that produces redia larvae by asexual reproduction. **3.** any similar structure containing spores.

sporocyte ('spɔːrəʊˌsaɪt, 'spɒ-) *n.* a diploid cell that divides by meiosis to produce four haploid spores.

sporogenesis (ˌspɔːrəʊˈdʒɛnɪsɪs, ˌspɒ-) *n.* the process of spore formation in plants and animals. —**sporogenous** (spɔːˈrɒdʒɪnəs, spɒ-) *adj.*

sporogonium (ˌspɔːrəʊˈgəʊnɪəm, ˌspɒ-) *n., pl.* **-nia** (-nɪə). a structure in mosses and liverworts consisting of a spore-bearing capsule on a short stalk that arises from the parent plant (the sporophyte). —ˌ**sporo'gonial** *adj.*

sporogony (spɔːˈrɒgənɪ, -ˈrɒdʒ-, spɒ-) *n.* the process in sporozoans by which sporozoites are formed from an encysted zygote by multiple fission.

sporophore ('spɔːrəʊˌfɔː, 'spɒ-) *n.* an organ in fungi that produces or carries spores, esp. the massive spore-bearing body of mushrooms, etc.

sporophyll *or* **sporophyl** ('spɔːrəʊfɪl, 'spɒ-) *n.* a leaf in mosses, ferns, and related plants that bears the sporangia. See also **megasporophyll, microsporophyll.**

sporophyte ('spɔːrəʊˌfaɪt, 'spɒ-) *n.* the diploid form of plants that have alternation of generations. It develops from a zygote and produces asexual spores. Compare **gametophyte.** —**sporophytic** (ˌspɔːrəˈfɪtɪk, ˌspɒ-) *adj.*

-sporous *adj. combining form.* (in botany) having a specified type or number of spores: *homosporous.*

sporozoan (ˌspɔːrəˈzəʊən, ˌspɒ-) *n.* **1.** any parasitic protozoan of the class *Sporozoa,* characterized by a complex life cycle, part of which is passed in the cells of the host, and the production of asexual spores: includes the malaria parasite. See **plasmodium** (sense 2). ~*adj.* **2.** of, relating to, or belonging to the *Sporozoa.*

sporozoite (ˌspɔːrəˈzəʊaɪt, ˌspɒ-) *n.* any of numerous small mobile usually infective individuals produced in sporozoans by sporogony.

sporran ('spɒrən) *n.* a large pouch, usually of fur, worn hanging from a belt in front of the kilt in men's Scottish Highland dress. [C19: from Scottish Gaelic *sporan* purse; compare Irish Gaelic *sparān* purse, Late Latin *bursa* bag]

sport (spɔːt) *n.* **1.** an individual or group activity pursued for exercise or pleasure, often involving the testing of physical capabilities and taking the form of a competitive game such as football, tennis, etc. **2.** such activities considered collectively. **3.** any particular pastime indulged in for pleasure. **4.** the pleasure derived from a pastime, esp. hunting, shooting, or fishing: *we had good sport today.* **5.** playful or good-humoured joking: *to say a thing in sport.* **6.** derisive mockery or the object of such mockery: *to make sport of someone.* **7.** someone or something that is controlled by external influences: *the sport of fate.* **8.** *Informal.* (sometimes qualified by *good, bad,* etc.) a person who reacts cheerfully in the face of adversity, esp. a good loser. **9.** *Informal.* a person noted for being scrupulously fair and abiding by the rules of a game. **10.** *Informal.* a person who leads a merry existence, esp. a gambler: *he's a bit of a sport.* **11.** *Austral. and N.Z. informal.* a form of address used esp. between males. **12.** *Biology.* **a.** an animal or plant that differs conspicuously in one or more aspects from other organisms of the same species, usually because of a mutation. **b.** an anomalous characteristic of such an organism. ~*vb.* **13.** (*tr.*) *Informal.* to wear or display in an ostentatious or proud manner: *she was sporting a new hat.* **14.** (*intr.*) to skip about or frolic happily. **15.** to amuse (oneself), esp. in outdoor physical recreation. **16.** (*intr.;* often foll. by *with*) to dally or trifle (with). **17.** (*tr.;* often foll. by *away*) *Rare.* to squander (time or money): *sporting one's life away.* **18.** (*intr.;* often foll. by *with*) *Archaic.* to make fun (of). **19.** (*intr.*) Biology. to produce or undergo a mutation. ~See also **sports.** [C15 *sporten,* variant of *disporten* to DISPORT] —**'sporter** *n.* —**'sportful** *adj.* —**'sportfully** *adv.* —**'sportfulness** *n.*

sporting ('spɔːtɪŋ) *adj.* **1.** (*prenominal*) of, relating to, or used or engaged in a sport or sports: *several sporting interests.* **2.** relating or conforming to sportsmanship; fair. **3.** of, relating to, or characterized by an interest in gambling. **4.** willing to take a risk. —**'sportingly** *adv.*

sporting house *n.* **1.** *U.S., rare.* a euphemistic word for **brothel.** **2.** *Archaic.* a tavern or inn frequented by gamblers or other sportsmen.

sportive ('spɔːtɪv) *adj.* **1.** playful or joyous. **2.** done in jest rather than seriously. **3.** of, relating to, or interested in sports. **4.** *Obsolete.* wanton or amorous: *a sportive wench.* —**'sportively** *adv.* —**'sportiveness** *n.*

sports (spɔːts) *n.* **1.** (*modifier*) relating to, concerned with, or used in sports: *sports equipment.* **2.** Also called: **sports day.** *Brit.* a meeting held at a school or college for competitions in various athletic events.

sports car *n.* a production car designed for speed, high acceleration, and manoeuvrability, having a low body and usually adequate seating for only two persons.

sportscast ('spɔːtsˌkɑːst) *n.* a radio or television broadcast consisting of sports news. —**'sportsˌcaster** *n.*

sports coat *n. U.S., Austral., and N.Z.* another name for **sports jacket.**

sports jacket *n.* a man's informal jacket, made esp. of tweed: worn with trousers of different material. Also called (U.S., Austral., and N.Z.): **sports coat.**

sportsman ('spɔːtsmən) *n., pl.* **-men.** **1.** a man who takes part in sports, esp. of the outdoor type. **2.** a person who exhibits qualities highly regarded in sport, such as fairness, generosity, observance of the rules, and good humour when losing. —**'sportsman-ˌlike** *or* **'sportsmanly** *adj.* —**'sportsmanˌship** *n.*

sports medicine *n.* the branch of medicine concerned with injuries sustained through sport.

sportsperson ('spɔːtsˌpɜːsən) *n.* a person who takes part in sports, esp. of the outdoor type.

sports shirt *n.* a man's informal shirt, sometimes of knitted wool or cotton, which may be worn outside the trousers.

sportswear ('spɔːtsˌwɛə) *n.* clothes worn for sport or outdoor leisure wear.

sportswoman ('spɔːtsˌwʊmən) *n., pl.* **-women.** a woman who takes part in sports, esp. of the outdoor type.

sporty ('spɔːtɪ) *adj.* **sportier, sportiest. 1.** (of a person) fond of sport or outdoor activities. **2.** (of clothes) having the appearance of sportswear. **3.** (of a car) having the performance or appearance of a sports car. —**'sportily** *adv.* —**'sportiness** *n.*

sporulate ('spɒrjʊˌleɪt) *vb.* (*intr.*) to produce spores, esp. by multiple fission. —ˌ**sporu'lation** *n.*

sporule ('spɒruːl) *n.* a spore, esp. a very small spore. [C19: from New Latin *sporula* a little SPORE]

spot (spɒt) *n.* **1.** a small mark on a surface, such as a circular patch or stain, differing in colour or texture from its surroundings. **2.** a geographical area that is restricted in extent: *a beauty spot.* **3.** a location: *this is the exact spot on which he died.* **4.** a blemish of the skin, esp. a pimple or one occurring through some disease. **5.** a blemish on the character of a person; moral flaw. **6.** *Informal.* a place of entertainment: *we hit all the night spots.* **7.** *Informal, chiefly Brit.* a small quantity or amount: *a spot of lunch.* **8.** *Informal.* an awkward situation: *that puts me in a bit of a spot.* **9.** a short period between regular television or radio programmes that is used for advertising. **10.** a position or length of time in a show assigned to a specific performer. **11.** short for **spotlight. 12.** (in billiards) **a.** Also called: **spot ball.** the white ball that is distinguished from the plain by a mark or spot. **b.** the player using this ball. **13.** *Billiards, snooker, etc.* one of several small black dots on a table that mark where a ball is to be placed. **14.** (*modifier*) **a.** denoting or relating to goods, currencies, or securities available for immediate delivery and payment: *spot goods.* See also **spot market, spot price. b.** involving immediate cash payment: *spot sales.* **15. change one's spots.** (*used mainly in negative constructions*) to reform one's character. **16. high spot.** an outstanding event: *the high spot of the holiday was the visit to the winery.* **17. knock spots off.** to outstrip or outdo with ease. **18. on the spot. a.** immediately. **b.** at the place in question. **c.** in the best possible position to deal with a situation. **d.** in an awkward predicament. **e.** without moving from the place of one's location, etc. **f.** (*as modifier*): *our on-the-spot reporter.* **19. soft spot.** a special sympathetic affection or weakness for a person or thing. **20. tight spot.** a serious, difficult, or dangerous situation. **21. weak spot. a.** some aspect of a character or situation that is susceptible to criticism. **b.** a flaw in a person's knowledge: *classics is my weak spot.* ~*vb.* **spots, spotting, spotted. 22.** (*tr.*) to observe or perceive suddenly, esp. under difficult circumstances; discern. **23.** to put stains or spots upon (something). **24.** (*intr.*) (of some fabrics) to be susceptible to spotting by or as if by water: *silk spots easily.* **25.** (*tr.*) to place here and there: *they spotted observers along the border.* **26.** to look out for and note (trains, talent, etc.). **27.** (*intr.*) to rain slightly; spit. **28.** (*tr.*) *Billiards.* to place (a ball) on one of the spots. **29.** *Military.* to adjust fire in order to correct deviations from (the target) by observation. **30.** (*tr.*) *U.S. informal.* to yield (an advantage or concession) to (one's opponent): *to spot someone a piece in chess.* [C12 (in the sense: moral blemish): of German origin; compare Middle Dutch *spotte,* Old Norse *spotti*] —**'spottable** *adj.*

spot check *n.* **1.** a quick random examination. **2.** a check made without prior warning. ~*vb.* **spot-check. 3.** (*tr.*) to perform a spot check on.

spot height *n.* a mark on a map indicating the height of a hill, mountain, etc.

spotless ('spɒtlɪs) *adj.* **1.** free from stains; immaculate. **2.** free from moral impurity; unsullied: *a spotless character.* —**'spotlessly** *adv.* —**'spotlessness** *n.*

spotlight ('spɒtˌlaɪt) *n.* **1.** a powerful light focused so as to illuminate a small area, usually mounted so that it can be directed at will. **2. the.** the focus of attention. ~*vb.* **-lights, -lighting, -lit** *or* **-lighted.** (*tr.*) **3.** to direct a spotlight on. **4.** to focus attention on.

spot market *n. Commerce.* a market in which commodities, currencies, or securities are traded for immediate delivery. Compare **forward market.**

spot-on *adj. Brit. informal.* absolutely correct; very accurate.

spot price *n.* the price of goods, currencies, or securities that are offered for immediate delivery and payment.

spotted ('spɒtɪd) *adj.* **1.** characterized by spots or marks, esp. in having a pattern of spots. **2.** stained or blemished; soiled or bespattered.

spotted crake *n.* a Eurasian rail, *Porzana porzana,* of swamps and marshes, having a buff speckled plumage and dark brown wings.

spotted dick *n. Brit.* a steamed or boiled suet pudding containing dried fruit. [C19: perhaps from the man's name *Dick* (short for *Richard*), or from dialect *dick* pudding. The dried fruit gives it a speckled appearance]

spotted dog *n.* **1.** an informal name for a **Dalmatian. 2.** another name for **spotted dick.**

spotted fever *n.* any of various severe febrile diseases characterized by small irregular spots on the skin, as in Rocky Mountain spotted fever or tick fever.

spotted flycatcher *n.* a European woodland songbird, *Muscicapa striata,* with a greyish-brown streaked plumage: family *Muscicapidae* (Old World flycatchers).

spotted gum *n.* **1.** an Australian eucalyptus tree, *Eucalyptus maculata.* **2.** the wood of this tree, used for shipbuilding, sleepers, etc.

spotted orchid *n.* **1.** any of various common Eurasian orchids, esp. the **heath** and **common spotted orchids** (*Dactylorchis maculata* and *D. fuchsii*). The flowers are variable but usually have dark blotches. **2.** a tall orchid, *Dipodium punctatum,* with white pink-spotted flowers, found in Australia.

spotted sandpiper *n.* a North American sandpiper, *Actitis macularia,* having a spotted breast in its breeding plumage. Also called (U.S.): **peetweet.**

spotter ('spɒtə) *n.* **1. a.** a person or thing that watches or observes. **b.** (*as modifier*): *a spotter plane.* **2.** a person who makes a hobby of watching for and noting numbers or types of trains, buses, etc.: *a train spotter.* **3.** *Military.* a person who orders or advises adjustment of fire on a target by observations. **4.** a person, esp. one engaged in civil defence, who watches for enemy aircraft. **5.** *U.S. informal.* an employee assigned to spy on his colleagues in order to check on their honesty. **6.** *Films.* **a.** a person who checks against irregularities and inconsistencies. **b.** a person who searches for new material, performers, etc.

spottie ('spɒtɪ) *n. N.Z.* a young deer of up to three months of age.

spotty ('spɒtɪ) *adj.* **-tier, -tiest. 1.** abounding in or characterized by spots or marks, esp. on the skin: *a spotty face.* **2.** not consistent or uniform; irregular or uneven, often in quality. —**'spottily** *adv.* —**'spottiness** *n.*

spot-weld *vb.* **1.** (*tr.*) to join (two pieces of metal, esp. in the form of wire or sheet) by one or more small circular welds by means of heat, usually electrically generated, and pressure. ~*n.* **2.** a weld so formed. —**'spot-ˌwelder** *n.*

spousal ('spaʊzᵊl) *n.* **1.** (*often pl.*) **a.** the marriage ceremony. **b.** a wedding. ~*adj.* **2.** of or relating to marriage. —**'spousally** *adv.*

spouse *n.* (spaʊs, spaʊz). **1.** a person's partner in marriage. Related adj.: **spousal.** ~*vb.* (spaʊz, spaʊs). **2.** (*tr.*) *Obsolete.* to marry. [C12: from Old French *spus* (masculine), *spuse* (feminine), from Latin *sponsus, sponsa* betrothed man or woman, from *spondēre* to promise solemnly]

spout (spaʊt) *vb.* **1.** to discharge (a liquid) in a continuous jet or in spurts, esp. through a narrow gap or under pressure, or (of a liquid) to gush thus. **2.** (of a whale, etc.) to discharge air through the blowhole, so that it forms a spray at the surface of the water. **3.** *Informal.* to utter (a stream of words) on a subject, often at length. ~*n.* **4.** a tube, pipe, chute, etc., allowing the passage or pouring of liquids, grain, etc. **5.** a continuous stream or jet of liquid. **6.** short for **waterspout. 7. up the spout.** *Slang.* **a.** ruined or lost: *any hope of rescue is right up the spout.* **b.** pregnant. [C14: perhaps from Middle Dutch *spouten,* from Old Norse *spyta* to spit] —**'spouter** *n.*

spouting ('spaʊtɪŋ) *n. N.Z.* **a.** a rainwater downpipe on the exterior of a building. **b.** such pipes collectively.

spp. *abbrev. for* species (plural).

SPQR *abbrev. for* Senatus Populusque Romanus. [Latin: the Senate and People of Rome].

SPR *abbrev. for* Society for Psychical Research.

sprag (spræg) *n.* **1.** a chock or steel bar used to prevent a vehicle from running backwards on an incline. **2.** a support or post used in mining. **3.** *N.Z. mining.* a steel bar inserted into the wheels of a box to act as a brake. [C19: of uncertain origin]

sprain (spreɪn) *vb.* **1.** (*tr.*) to injure (a joint) by a sudden twisting or wrenching of its ligaments. ~*n.* **2.** the resulting injury to such a joint, characterized by swelling and temporary disability. [C17: of uncertain origin]

spraint (spreɪnt) *n.* (*often pl.*) a piece of otter's dung. [C15 *sprayntes* (pl.), from Medieval French *espraintes* otter's dung, from *espreindre* to press out: compare EXPRESS]

sprang (spræŋ) *vb.* the past tense of **spring.**

sprat (spræt) *n.* **1.** a small marine food fish, *Clupea sprattus,* of the NE Atlantic Ocean and North Sea: family *Clupeidae* (herrings). See also **brisling. 2.** any of various small or young herrings. [C16: variant of Old English *sprott;* related to Middle Low German *sprott,* Norwegian *sprot* small rod]

sprawl (sprɔːl) *vb.* **1.** (*intr.*) to sit or lie in an ungainly manner with one's limbs spread out. **2.** to fall down or knock down with the limbs spread out in an ungainly way. **3.** to spread out or cause to spread out in a straggling fashion: *his handwriting sprawled all over the paper.* ~*n.* **4.** the act or an instance of sprawling. **5.** a sprawling posture or arrangement of items. **6. a.** the urban area formed by the expansion of a town or city into surrounding countryside: *the urban sprawl.* **b.** the process by which this has happened. [Old English *spreawlian;* related to Old English *spryttan* to sprout, SPURT, Greek *speirein* to scatter] —**'sprawler** *n.* —**'sprawly** *adj.*

spray[1] (spreɪ) *n.* **1.** fine particles of a liquid. **2. a.** a liquid, such as perfume, paint, etc., designed to be discharged from an aerosol or atomizer: *hair spray.* **b.** the aerosol or atomizer itself. **3.** a quantity of small objects flying through the air: *a spray of bullets.* ~*vb.* **4.** to scatter (liquid) in the form of fine particles. **5.** to discharge (a liquid) from an aerosol or atomizer. **6.** (*tr.*) to treat or bombard with a spray: *to spray the lawn.* [C17: from Middle Dutch *sprāien;* related to Middle High German *spræjen*] —'**sprayer** *n.*

spray[2] (spreɪ) *n.* **1.** a single slender shoot, twig, or branch that bears buds, leaves, flowers, or berries, either growing on or detached from a plant. **2.** a small decorative bouquet or corsage of flowers and foliage. **3.** a piece of jewellery designed to resemble a spray of flowers, leaves, etc. [C13: of Germanic origin; compare Old English *sprǣc* young shoot, Old Norse *sprek* brittle wood, Old High German *sprahhula* splinter]

spray gun *n.* a device that sprays a fluid in a finely divided form by atomizing the fluid in an air jet.

spread (sprɛd) *vb.* **spreads, spreading, spread. 1.** to extend or unfold or be extended or unfolded to the fullest width: *she spread the map on the table.* **2.** to extend or cause to extend over a larger expanse of space or time: *the milk spread all over the floor; the political unrest spread over several years.* **3.** to apply or be applied in a coating: *butter does not spread very well when cold.* **4.** to distribute or be distributed over an area or region. **5.** to display or be displayed in its fullest extent: *the landscape spread before us.* **6.** (*tr.*) to prepare (a table) for a meal. **7.** (*tr.*) to lay out (a meal) on a table. **8.** to send or be sent out in all directions; disseminate or be disseminated: *someone has been spreading rumours; the disease spread quickly.* **9.** (of rails, wires, etc.) to force or be forced apart. **10.** to increase the breadth of (a part), esp. to flatten the head of a rivet by pressing, hammering, or forging. **11.** (*tr.*) *Agriculture.* **a.** to lay out (hay) in a relatively thin layer to dry. **b.** to scatter (seed, manure, etc.) over a relatively wide area. **12.** (*tr.;* often foll. by *around*) *Informal.* to make (oneself) agreeable to a large number of people, often of the opposite sex. **13.** *Phonetics.* to narrow and lengthen the aperture of (the lips) as for the articulation of a front vowel, such as (iː) in English *see* (siː). ~*n.* **14.** the act or process of spreading; diffusion, dispersion, expansion, etc.: *the spread of the Christian religion.* **15.** *Informal.* the wingspan of an aircraft. **16.** an extent of space or time; stretch: *a spread of 50 years.* **17.** *Informal, chiefly U.S. and Canadian.* a ranch or relatively large tract of land. **18.** the limit of something fully extended: *the spread of a bird's wings.* **19.** a covering for a table or bed. **20.** *Informal.* a large meal or feast, esp. when it is laid out on a table. **21.** a food which can be spread on bread, etc.: *salmon spread.* **22.** two facing pages in a book or other publication. **23.** a widening of the hips and waist: *middle-age spread.* **24.** *Stock Exchange.* **a.** the difference between the bid and offer prices quoted by a market maker. **b.** the excess of the price at which stock is offered for public sale over the price paid for the same stock by an underwriter. **c.** *Chiefly U.S.* a double option. Compare **straddle** (sense 9). **25.** *Jewellery.* the apparent size of a gemstone when viewed from above expressed in carats: *a diamond with a spread of four carats.* ~*adj.* **26.** extended or stretched out, esp. to the fullest extent. **27.** (of a gem) shallow and flat. **28.** *Phonetics.* **a.** (of the lips) forming a long narrow aperture. **b.** (of speech sounds) articulated with spread lips: (iː) *in English "feel" is a spread vowel.* [Old English *sprǣdan;* related to Old High German *spreiten* to spread, Old Lithuanian *sprainas* stiff] —ˌ**spreadaˈbility** *n.* —'**spreadable** *adj.*

spread eagle *n.* **1.** the representation of an eagle with outstretched wings, used as an emblem of the U.S. **2.** an acrobatic skating figure.

spread-eagle *adj. also* **spread-eagled. 1.** lying or standing with arms and legs outstretched. ~*vb.* **2.** to assume or cause to assume the shape of a spread eagle. **3.** (*intr.*) *Skating.* to execute a spread eagle.

spreader ('sprɛdə) *n.* **1.** a machine or device used for scattering bulk materials, esp. manure or fertilizer, over a relatively wide area. **2.** a device for keeping apart or spacing parallel objects, such as electric wires.

spread sampling *n.* the selection of a corpus for statistical analysis by selecting a number of short passages at random throughout the work and considering their aggregation. Compare **block sampling.**

spreadsheet ('sprɛdˌʃiːt) *n.* a computer program that allows easy entry and manipulation of figures, equations, and text, used esp. for financial planning and budgeting.

spreathed (spriːðd) *adj. Southwestern English and south Wales dialect.* sore; chapped. [from *spreathe* to make sore: of obscure origin]

sprechgesang (*German* 'ʃprɛçgəzaŋ) *n. Music.* a type of vocalization between singing and recitation in which the voice sings the beginning of each note and then falls rapidly from the notated pitch. It was originated by Arnold Schoenberg, who used it in *Pierrot Lunaire* (1912). [C20: from German, literally: speaking-song]

sprechstimme (*German* 'ʃprɛçʃtɪmə) *n. Music.* a vocal part employing sprechgesang. [C20: from German: speaking voice]

spree (spriː) *n.* **1.** a session of considerable overindulgence, esp. in drinking, squandering money, etc. **2.** a romp. [C19: perhaps changed from Scottish *spreath* plundered cattle, ultimately from Latin *praeda* booty]

sprekelia (sprə'kiːlɪə) *n.* a bulbous plant, *Sprekelia formosissima,* from Mexico and Guatemala, related to hippeastrum and grown for its striking crimson or white pendent flowers, in the form of a cross: family *Amaryllidaceae.* [named after J. H. von *Sprekelsen* (died 1764), German botanist]

sprig (sprɪg) *n.* **1.** a shoot, twig, or sprout of a tree, shrub, etc.; spray. **2.** an ornamental device resembling a spray of leaves or flowers. **3.** Also called: **dowel pin.** a small wire nail without a head. **4.** *Informal, rare.* a youth. **5.** *Informal, rare.* a person considered as the descendant of an established family, social class, etc. **6.** *N.Z.* another name for **stud**[1] (sense 7). ~*vb.* **sprigs, sprigging, sprigged.** (*tr.*) **7.** to fasten or secure with sprigs. **8.** to ornament (fabric, wallpaper, etc.) with a design of sprigs. **9.** to make sprays from (twigs and branches). [C15: probably of Germanic origin; compare Low German *sprick,* Swedish *sprygg*] —'**sprigger** *n.* —'**spriggy** *adj.*

sprightly ('spraɪtlɪ) *adj.* **-lier, -liest. 1.** full of vitality; lively and gay. ~*adv.* **2.** *Obsolete.* in a gay or lively manner. [C16: from *spright,* variant of SPRITE + -LY[1]] —'**sprightliness** *n.*

spring (sprɪŋ) *vb.* **springs, springing, sprang** *or* **sprung; sprung. 1.** to move or cause to move suddenly upwards or forwards in a single motion. **2.** to release or be released from a forced position by elastic force: *the bolt sprang back.* **3.** (*tr.*) to leap or jump over. **4.** (*intr.*) to come, issue, or arise suddenly. **5.** (*intr.*) (of a part of a mechanism, etc.) to jump out of place. **6.** to make (wood, etc.) warped or split or (of wood, etc.) to become warped or split. **7.** to happen or cause to happen unexpectedly: *to spring a surprise; the boat sprung a leak.* **8.** (*intr.*) to develop or originate: *the idea sprang from a chance meeting.* **9.** (*intr.;* usually foll. by *from*) to be descended: *he sprang from peasant stock.* **10.** (*intr.;* often foll. by *up*) to come into being or appear suddenly: *factories springing up.* **11.** (*tr.*) (of a gun dog) to rouse (game) from cover. **12.** (*intr.*) (of game or quarry) to start or rise suddenly from cover. **13.** (*intr.*) to appear to have a strong upward movement: *the beam springs away from the pillar.* **14.** to explode (a mine) or (of a mine) to explode. **15.** (*tr.*) to provide with a spring or springs. **16.** (*tr.*) *Informal.* to arrange the escape of (someone) from prison. **17.** (*intr.*) *Archaic or poetic.* (of daylight or dawn) to begin to appear. ~*n.* **18.** the act or an instance of springing. **19.** a leap, jump, or bound. **20. a.** the quality of resilience; elasticity. **b.** (*as modifier*): *spring steel.* **21.** the act or an instance of moving rapidly back from a position of tension. **22. a.** a natural outflow of ground water, as forming the source of a stream. **b.** (*as modifier*): *spring water.* **23. a.** a device, such as a coil or strip of steel, that stores potential energy when it is compressed, stretched, or bent and releases it when the restraining force is removed. **b.** (*as modifier*): *a spring mattress.* **24.** a structural defect such as a warp or bend. **25. a.** (*sometimes cap.*) the season of the year between winter and summer, astronomically from the March equinox to the June solstice in the N hemisphere and from the September equinox to the December solstice in the S hemisphere. **b.** (*as modifier*): *spring showers.* Related adj.: **vernal. 26.** the earliest or freshest time of something. **27.** a source or origin. **28.** one of a set of strips of rubber, steel, etc., running down the inside of the handle of a cricket bat, hockey stick, etc. **29.** Also called: **spring line.** *Nautical.* a mooring line, usually one of a pair that cross amidships. **30.** a flock of teal. **31.** *Architect.* another name for **springing.** [Old English *springan;* related to Old Norse *springa,* Old High German *springan,* Sanskrit *sprhayati* he desires, Old Slavonic *pragu* grasshopper] —'**springless** *adj.* —'**springˌlike** *adj.*

spring balance *or esp. U.S.* **spring scale** *n.* a device in which an object to be weighed is attached to the end of a helical spring, the extension of which indicates the weight of the object on a calibrated scale.

spring beauty *n.* a pale green annual plant (*Claytonia perfoliata*) of the purslane family, originally North American, having small white flowers above fused leaves that encircle the stem.

springboard ('sprɪŋˌbɔːd) *n.* **1.** a flexible board, usually projecting low over the water, used for diving. **2.** a similar board used for gaining height or momentum in gymnastics. **3.** *Austral. and N.Z.* a board inserted into the trunk of a tree at some height above the ground on which a lumberjack stands to chop down the tree. **4.** anything that serves as a point of departure or initiation.

springbok *or* (*less commonly*) **springbuck** ('sprɪŋˌbʌk) *n., pl.* **-bok, -boks** *or* **-buck, -bucks.** an antelope, *Antidorcas marsupialis,* of semidesert regions of southern Africa, which moves in leaps exposing a patch of white erectile hairs on the rump that are usually covered by a fold of skin. [C18: from Afrikaans, from Dutch *springen* to SPRING + *bok* goat, BUCK[1]]

Springbok ('sprɪŋˌbʌk, -ˌbɒk) *n.* an amateur athlete who has represented South Africa in international competitions.

spring chicken *n.* **1.** Also called: **springer.** *Chiefly U.S. and Canadian.* a young chicken, tender for cooking, esp. one from two to ten months old. **2.** *Informal.* (*usually used with a negative*) a young, inexperienced, or unsophisticated person.

spring-clean *vb.* **1.** to clean (a house) thoroughly: traditionally at the end of the winter. ~*n.* **2.** an instance of spring-cleaning. —ˌ**spring-'cleaning** *n.*

springe (sprɪndʒ) *n.* **1.** a snare set to catch small wild animals or birds and consisting of a loop attached to a bent twig or branch under tension. ~*vb.* **2.** (*intr.*) to set such a snare. **3.** (*tr.*) to catch (small wild animals or birds) with such a snare. [C13: related to Old English *springan* to SPRING]

springer ('sprɪŋə) *n.* **1.** short for **springer spaniel. 2.** Also called: **springing cow.** a cow about to give birth. **3.** a person or thing that springs. **4.** *Architect.* **a.** the first and lowest stone of an arch. **b.** the impost of an arch.

springer spaniel *n.* either of two breeds of large quick-moving spaniels bred to spring game, having a slightly domed head and ears of medium length. The **English springer spaniel** is the larger and can be of various colours; the **Welsh springer spaniel** is always a rich red and white.

spring fever *n.* the feeling of restlessness experienced by many people at the onset of spring.

Springfield rifle ('sprɪŋˌfiːld) *n.* a magazine-fed bolt-action breech-loading .30 calibre rifle formerly used by the U.S. Army. [from *Springfield,* Massachusetts, formerly the site of the U.S. arsenal and armoury]

springhaas ('sprɪŋˌhɑːs) *n., pl.* **-haas** *or* **-hase** (-ˌhɑːzə). a S and E African nocturnal rodent, *Pedetes capensis,* resembling a small kangaroo: family *Pedetidae.* [from Afrikaans: spring hare]

springhalt ('sprɪŋˌhɔːlt) *n. Vet. science.* another name for **stringhalt.** [C17: probably an alteration, influenced by SPRING, of STRINGHALT]

springhead ('sprɪŋˌhɛd) *n.* the source of a stream; spring.

springhouse ('sprɪŋˌhaʊs) *n.* a storehouse built over a spring for keeping dairy products and meat cool and fresh.

springing ('sprɪŋɪŋ) *n.* the level where an arch or vault rises from a support. Also called: **spring, springing line, springing point.**

springlet ('sprɪŋlɪt) *n.* a small spring; brooklet or rill.

spring lock *n.* a type of lock having a spring-loaded bolt, a key being required only to unlock it.

spring mattress *n.* a mattress containing an arrangement of spiral springs.

spring onion *n.* an immature form of the onion (*Allium cepa*), widely cultivated for its tiny bulb and long green leaves which are eaten in salads, etc. Also called: **green onion, scallion.**

spring roll *n.* a Chinese dish consisting of a savoury mixture of vegetables and meat rolled up in a thin pancake and fried.

springtail ('sprɪŋˌteɪl) *n.* any primitive wingless insect of the order *Collembola,* having a forked springing organ with which it projects itself forward.

spring tide *n.* **1.** either of the two tides that occur at or just after new moon and full moon when the tide-generating force of the sun acts in the same direction as that of the moon, reinforcing it and causing the greatest rise and fall in tidal level. The highest spring tides (**equinoctial springs**) occur at the equinoxes. Compare **neap tide. 2.** any great rush or flood.

springtime ('sprɪŋˌtaɪm) *n.* **1.** Also called: **springtide** ('sprɪŋˌtaɪd). the season of spring. **2.** the earliest, usually the most attractive, period of the existence of something.

springwood ('sprɪŋˌwʊd) *n.* the wood that is produced by a plant in the spring and early summer and consists of large thin-walled xylem cells. Compare **summerwood.**

springy ('sprɪŋɪ) *adj.* **springier, springiest. 1.** possessing or characterized by resilience or bounce. **2.** (of a place) having many wells or springs of water. —'**springily** *adv.* —'**springiness** *n.*

sprinkle ('sprɪŋkᵊl) *vb.* **1.** to scatter (liquid, powder, etc.) in tiny particles or droplets over (something). **2.** (*tr.*) to distribute over (something): *the field was sprinkled with flowers.* **3.** (*intr.*) to drizzle slightly. ~*n.* **4.** the act or an instance of sprinkling or a quantity that is sprinkled. **5.** a slight drizzle. [C14: probably from Middle Dutch *sprenkelen;* related to Old English *spearca* SPARK[1]]

sprinkler ('sprɪŋklə) *n.* **1.** a device perforated with small holes that is attached to a garden hose or watering can and used to spray plants, lawns, etc., with water. **2.** a person or thing that sprinkles. **3.** See **sprinkler system.**

sprinkler system *n.* a fire-extinguishing system that releases water from overhead pipes through nozzles opened automatically by a rise in temperature.

sprinkling ('sprɪŋklɪŋ) *n.* a small quantity or amount: *a sprinkling of commonsense.*

sprint (sprɪnt) *n.* **1.** *Athletics.* a short race run at top speed, such as the 100 metres. **2.** a fast finishing speed at the end of a longer race, as in running or cycling, etc. **3.** any quick run. ~*vb.* (*intr.*) **4.** to go at top speed, as in running, cycling, etc. [C16: from Scandinavian; related to Old English *gesprintan* to emit, Old Norse *spretta* to jump up, Old High German *sprinzan* to jump up, Swedish *sprata* to kick] —'**sprinter** *n.*

sprit (sprɪt) *n. Nautical.* a light spar pivoted at the mast and crossing a fore-and-aft quadrilateral sail diagonally to the peak. [Old English *spreot;* related to Old High German *spriuzen* to support, Dutch *spriet* sprit, Norwegian *sprÿta*]

sprite (spraɪt) *n.* **1.** (in folklore) a nimble elflike creature, esp. one associated with water. **2.** a small dainty person. [C13: from Old French *esprit,* from Latin *spīritus* SPIRIT[1]]

spritsail ('sprɪtˌseɪl; *Nautical* 'sprɪtsəl) *n. Nautical.* **1.** a rectangular sail mounted on a sprit in some 19th century small vessels. **2.** (in medieval rigging) a square sail mounted on a yard on the bowsprit.

spritzer ('sprɪtsə) *n.* a drink, usually white wine, with soda water added. [from German *spritzen* to splash]

spritzig ('sprɪtsɪg; *German* 'ʃprɪtsɪç) *adj.* (of wine) sparkling. [German, from *spritzen* to splash]

sprocket ('sprɒkɪt) *n.* **1.** Also called: **sprocket wheel.** a relatively thin wheel having teeth projecting radially from the rim, esp. one that drives or is driven by a chain. **2.** an individual tooth on such a wheel. **3.** a cylindrical wheel with teeth on one or both rims for pulling film through a camera or projector. **4.** a small wedge-shaped piece of wood used to extend a roof over the eaves. [C16: of unknown origin]

sprog (sprɒg) *n. Slang.* **1.** a child; baby. **2.** (esp. in RAF) a recruit.

sprout (spraʊt) *vb.* **1.** (of a plant, seed, etc.) to produce (new leaves, shoots, etc.). **2.** (*intr.;* often foll. by *up*) to begin to grow or develop: *new office blocks are sprouting up all over the city.* ~*n.* **3.** a newly grown shoot or bud. **4.** something that grows like a sprout. **5.** See **Brussels sprout.** [Old English *sprūtan;* related to Middle High German *sprūzen* to sprout, Lettish *sprausties* to jostle]

spruce[1] (spruːs) *n.* **1.** any coniferous tree of the N temperate genus *Picea,* cultivated for timber and for ornament: family *Pinaceae.* They grow in a pyramidal shape and have needle-like leaves and light-coloured wood. See also **Norway spruce, blue spruce, white spruce, black spruce. 2.** the wood of any of these trees. [C17: short for *Spruce fir,* from C14 *Spruce* Prussia, changed from *Pruce,* via Old French from Latin *Prussia*]

spruce[2] (spruːs) *adj.* neat, smart, and trim. [C16: perhaps from *Spruce leather* a fashionable leather imported from Prussia; see SPRUCE[1]] —'**sprucely** *adv.* —'**spruceness** *n.*

spruce beer *n.* an alcoholic drink made of fermented molasses flavoured with spruce twigs and cones.

spruce pine *n.* **1.** a large pine tree, *Pinus glabra,* of the southeastern U.S. **2.** any of several similar plants, such as certain pines, hemlocks, and spruces.

spruce up *vb.* (*adv.*) to make (oneself, a person, or thing) smart and neat.

sprue[1] (spruː) *n.* **1.** a vertical channel in a mould through which plastic or molten metal is introduced or out of which it flows when the mould is filled. **2.** plastic or metal that solidifies in a sprue. [C19: of unknown origin]

sprue[2] (spruː) *n.* a chronic disease, esp. of tropical climates, characterized by flatulence, diarrhoea, frothy foul-smelling stools, and emaciation. [C19: from Dutch *spruw;* related to Middle Low German *sprūwe* tumour]

sprue[3] (spruː) *n. London dialect.* an inferior type of asparagus. [C19: of unknown origin]

spruik ('spruːɪk) *vb.* (*intr.*) *Austral. slang.* to speak in public (used esp. of a showman or salesman). [C20: of unknown origin] —'**spruiker** *n.*

spruit (spreɪt) *n. S. African.* a small tributary stream or watercourse. [Afrikaans]

sprung (sprʌŋ) *vb.* the past participle and a past tense of **spring.**

sprung rhythm *n. Prosody.* a type of poetic rhythm characterized by metrical feet of irregular composition, each having one strongly stressed syllable, often the first, and an indefinite number of unstressed syllables.

spry (spraɪ) *adj.* **spryer, spryest** *or* **sprier, spriest.** active and brisk; nimble. [C18: perhaps of Scandinavian origin; compare Swedish dialect *spragg* SPRIG] —'**spryly** *adv.* —'**spryness** *n.*

spt *abbrev. for* seaport.

SPUC (spʌk) *n. acronym for* Society for the Protection of the Unborn Child.

spud (spʌd) *n.* **1.** an informal word for **potato** (sense 1). **2.** a narrow-bladed spade for cutting roots, digging up weeds, etc. **3.** Also called: **spudder.** a tool, resembling a chisel, for removing bark from trees. ~*vb.* **spuds, spudding, spudded. 4.** (*tr.*) to remove (bark) or eradicate (weeds) with a spud. **5.** (*intr.*) to drill the first foot of an oil-well. [C15 *spudde* short knife, of unknown origin; applied later to a digging tool, and hence to a potato]

spud-bashing *n. Brit. slang, chiefly military.* the task of peeling potatoes, given as a punishment.

spue (spjuː) *vb.* **spues, spuing, spued.** an archaic spelling of **spew.** —'**spuer** *n.*

spuggy ('spʊgɪ) *or* **spug** (spʊg) *n., pl.* **spuggies** *or* **spugs.** *Northeast English dialect.* a house sparrow. Compare **speug.** [variant of Scottish *sprug,* of obscure origin]

spume (spjuːm) *n.* **1.** foam or surf, esp. on the sea; froth. ~*vb.* **2.** (*intr.*) to foam or froth. [C14: from Old French *espume,* from Latin *spūma;* related to *spuere* to SPEW] —'**spumous** *or* '**spumy** *adj.*

spumescent (spjuːˈmɛsᵊnt) *adj.* producing or resembling foam or froth. —**spu'mescence** *n.*

spumone *or* **spumoni** (spuːˈməʊnɪ; *Italian* spuˈmoːne) *n., pl.* **-ni** (-nɪ). a creamy Italian ice cream, made in sections of different colouring, usually containing candied fruit and nuts. [Italian, from *spuma* foam, SPUME]

spun (spʌn) *vb.* **1.** the past tense and past participle of **spin.** ~*adj.* **2.** formed or manufactured by spinning: *spun gold; spun glass.*

spunk (spʌŋk) *n.* **1.** *Informal.* courage or spirit. **2.** *Taboo, Brit.* a slang word for **semen. 3.** touchwood or tinder, esp. originally made from various spongy types of fungus. **4.** *Austral. informal.*

a person, esp. male, who is attractive to the opposite sex. [C16 (in the sense: a spark): from Scottish Gaelic *spong* tinder, sponge, from Latin *spongia* sponge] —ˈ**spunky** *adj.* —ˈ**spunkily** *adv.*

spun silk *n.* yarn or fabric made from silk waste.

spun sugar *n. U.S.* another term for **candyfloss.**

spun yarn *n. Nautical.* small stuff made from rope yarns twisted together.

spur (spɜː) *n.* **1.** a pointed device or sharp spiked wheel fixed to the heel of a rider's boot to enable him to urge his horse on. **2.** anything serving to urge or encourage: *the increase in salary was a spur to their production.* **3.** a sharp horny projection from the leg just above the claws in male birds, such as the domestic cock. **4.** a pointed process in any of various animals; calcar. **5.** a tubular extension at the base of the corolla in flowers such as larkspur. **6.** a short or stunted branch of a tree. **7.** a ridge projecting laterally from a mountain or mountain range. **8.** a wooden prop or a masonry reinforcing pier. **9.** another name for **groyne. 10.** Also called: **spur track.** a railway branch line or siding. **11.** a short side road leading off a main road: *a motorway spur.* **12.** a sharp cutting instrument attached to the leg of a gamecock. **13. on the spur of the moment.** on impulse. **14. win one's spurs. a.** *History.* to earn knighthood. **b.** to prove one's ability; gain distinction. ~*vb.* **spurs, spurring, spurred. 15.** (*tr.*) to goad or urge with or as if with spurs. **16.** (*intr.*) to go or ride quickly; press on. **17.** (*tr.*) to injure or strike with a spur. **18.** (*tr.*) to provide with a spur or spurs. [Old English *spura;* related to Old Norse *spori,* Old High German *sporo*]

spurge (spɜːdʒ) *n.* any of various euphorbiaceous plants of the genus *Euphorbia* that have milky sap and small flowers typically surrounded by conspicuous bracts. Some species have purgative properties. [C14: from Old French *espurge,* from *espurgier* to purge, from Latin *expurgāre* to cleanse, from EX-[1] + *purgāre* to PURGE]

spur gear *or* **wheel** *n.* a gear having involuted teeth either straight or helically cut on a cylindrical surface. Two such gears are used to transmit power between parallel shafts.

spurge laurel *n.* See **laurel** (sense 4).

spurious (ˈspjʊərɪəs) *adj.* **1.** not genuine or real. **2.** (of a plant part or organ) having the appearance of another part but differing from it in origin, development, or function; false: *a spurious fruit.* **3.** (of radiation) produced at an undesired frequency by a transmitter, causing interference, etc. **4.** *Rare.* illegitimate. [C17: from Latin *spurius* of illegitimate birth] —ˈ**spuriously** *adv.* —ˈ**spuriousness** *n.*

spurn (spɜːn) *vb.* **1.** to reject (a person or thing) with contempt. **2.** (when *intr.*, often foll. by *against*) *Archaic.* to kick (at). ~*n.* **3.** an instance of spurning. **4.** *Archaic.* a kick or thrust. [Old English *spurnan;* related to Old Norse *sporna,* Old High German *spurnan,* Latin *spernere* to despise, Lithuanian *spiriu* to kick] —ˈ**spurner** *n.*

spurrier (ˈspʌrɪə) *n.* a maker of spurs.

spurry *or* **spurrey** (ˈspʌrɪ) *n., pl.* **-ries.** any of several low-growing caryophyllaceous plants of the European genus *Spergula,* esp. *S. arvensis,* having whorled leaves and small white flowers. [C16: from Dutch *spurrie,* perhaps from Medieval Latin *spergula;* related to German *Spergel*]

spurt *or* **spirt** (spɜːt) *vb.* **1.** to gush or cause to gush forth in a sudden stream or jet. **2.** to make a sudden effort. ~*n.* **3.** a sudden forceful stream or jet. **4.** a short burst of activity, speed, or energy. [C16: perhaps related to Middle High German *sprützen* to squirt]

sputter (ˈspʌtə) *vb.* **1.** another word for **splutter** (senses 1-3). **2.** *Physics.* **a.** to undergo or cause to undergo a process in which atoms of a solid are removed from its surface by the impact of high-energy ions, as in a discharge tube. **b.** to coat (a film of a metal) onto (a solid surface) by using this process. ~*n.* **3.** the process or noise of sputtering. **4.** incoherent stammering speech. **5.** something that is ejected while sputtering. [C16: from Dutch *sputteren,* of imitative origin] —ˈ**sputterer** *n.*

sputum (ˈspjuːtəm) *n., pl.* **-ta** (-tə). **1.** a mass of salivary matter ejected from the mouth. **2.** saliva ejected from the mouth mixed with mucus or pus exuded from the respiratory passages, as in bronchitis or bronchiectasis. [C17: from Latin: spittle, from *spuere* to spit out]

spy (spaɪ) *n., pl.* **spies. 1.** a person employed by a state or institution to obtain secret information from rival countries, organizations, companies, etc. **2.** a person who keeps secret watch on others. **3.** *Obsolete.* a close view. **4. spy in the cab.** an informal name for **tachograph.** ~*vb.* **spies, spying, spied. 5.** (*intr.;* usually foll. by *on*) to keep a secret or furtive watch (on). **6.** (*intr.*) to engage in espionage. **7.** (*tr.*) to catch sight of; descry. [C13 *spien,* from Old French *espier,* of Germanic origin; related to Old High German *spehōn,* Middle Dutch *spien*]

spyglass (ˈspaɪˌglɑːs) *n.* a small telescope.

spyhole (ˈspaɪˌhəʊl) *n.* a small hole in a door, etc. through which one may watch secretly; peephole.

spy out *vb.* (*tr., adv.*) **1.** to discover by careful observation: *to spy out a route.* **2.** to make a close scrutiny of: *to spy out the land.*

Spy Wednesday *n.* (in Ireland) the Wednesday before Easter, named for Judas' becoming a spy for the Sanhedrin.

sq. *abbrev. for:* **1.** sequence. **2.** square. **3.** (*pl.* **sqq.**) the following one. [from Latin *sequens*]

Sq. *abbrev. for:* **1.** Squadron. **2.** (in place names) Square.

sqn *abbrev. for* squadron.

Sqn Ldr *abbrev. for* squadron leader.

sqq. *abbrev. for* the following ones. [from Latin *sequentia*]

squab (skwɒb) *n., pl.* **squabs** *or* **squab. 1.** a young unfledged bird, esp. a pigeon. **2.** a short fat person. **3. a.** a well-stuffed bolster or cushion. **b.** a sofa. ~*adj.* **4.** (of birds) recently hatched and still unfledged. **5.** short and fat. [C17: probably of Germanic origin; compare Swedish dialect *sqvabb* flabby skin, *sqvabba* fat woman, German *Quabbe* soft mass, Norwegian *kvabb* mud] —ˈ**squabby** *adj.*

squabble (ˈskwɒbᵊl) *vb.* **1.** (*intr.*) to quarrel over a small matter. **2.** (*tr.*) *Printing.* to disarrange (composed type). ~*n.* **3.** a petty quarrel. **4.** a printing fault in which a letter or letters are misplaced into an adjacent line. [C17: probably of Scandinavian origin; related to Swedish dialect *sqvabbel* to quarrel] —ˈ**squabbler** *n.*

squacco (ˈskwækəʊ) *n., pl.* **-cos.** a S European heron, *Ardeola ralloides,* with a short thick neck and a buff-coloured plumage with white wings. [C17: Italian dialect]

squad (skwɒd) *n.* **1.** the smallest military formation, typically comprising a dozen soldiers, used esp. as a drill formation. **2.** any small group of people engaged in a common pursuit. **3.** *Sport.* a number of players from which a team is to be selected. [C17: from Old French *esquade,* from Old Spanish *escuadra,* from *escuadrar* to SQUARE, from the square formations used]

squaddie *or* **squaddy** (ˈskwɒdɪ) *n., pl.* **-dies.** *Brit. slang.* a private soldier. Compare **swaddy.** [C20: from SQUAD]

squadron (ˈskwɒdrən) *n.* **1. a.** a subdivision of a naval fleet detached for a particular task. **b.** a number of naval units usually of similar type and consisting of two or more divisions. **2.** a cavalry unit comprising two or more troops, headquarters, and supporting arms. **3.** the basic tactical and administrative air force unit comprising two or more flights. ~Abbrev.: **sqn.** [C16: from Italian *squadrone* soldiers drawn up in square formation, from *squadro* SQUARE]

squadron leader *n.* an officer holding commissioned rank, between flight lieutenant and wing commander in the air forces of Britain and certain other countries.

squalene (ˈskweɪˌliːn) *n. Biochem.* a terpene first found in the liver of sharks but also present in the livers of most higher animals: an important precursor of cholesterol. [C20: from New Latin *squalus* genus name of the shark]

squalid (ˈskwɒlɪd) *adj.* **1.** dirty and repulsive, esp. as a result of neglect or poverty. **2.** sordid. [C16: from Latin *squālidus,* from *squālēre* to be stiff with dirt] —**squalidity** (skwɒˈlɪdɪtɪ) *or* ˈ**squalidness** *n.* —ˈ**squalidly** *adv.*

squall[1] (skwɔːl) *n.* **1.** a sudden strong wind or brief turbulent storm. **2.** any sudden commotion or show of temper. ~*vb.* **3.** (*intr.*) to blow in a squall. [C18: perhaps a special use of SQUALL[2]] —ˈ**squallish** *adj.* —ˈ**squally** *adj.*

squall[2] (skwɔːl) *vb.* **1.** (*intr.*) to cry noisily; yell. ~*n.* **2.** a shrill or noisy yell or howl. [C17: probably of Scandinavian origin; compare Icelandic *skvala* to shout; see SQUEAL] —ˈ**squaller** *n.*

squall line *n.* a narrow zone along a cold front along which squalls occur. See also **line squall.**

squalor (ˈskwɒlə) *n.* the condition or quality of being squalid; disgusting dirt and filth. [C17: from Latin]

squama (ˈskweɪmə) *n., pl.* **-mae** (-miː). *Biology.* a scale or scale-like structure. [C18: from Latin] —**squamate** (ˈskweɪmeɪt) *adj.*

squamation (skweɪˈmeɪʃən) *n.* **1.** the condition of having or forming scales or squamae. **2.** the arrangement of scales in fishes or reptiles.

squamiform (ˈskweɪmɪˌfɔːm) *adj. Biology.* resembling a scale: *squamiform cells.*

squamosal (skwəˈməʊsᵊl) *n.* **1.** a thin platelike paired bone in the skull of vertebrates: in mammals it forms part of the temporal bone. ~*adj.* **2.** of or relating to this bone. **3.** a less common word for **squamous.**

squamous (ˈskweɪməs) *or* **squamose** (ˈskweɪməʊs) *adj. Biology.* **1.** (of epithelium) consisting of a single layer of flat platelike cells. **2.** covered with, formed of, or resembling scales. [C16: from Latin *squāmōsus,* from *squāma* a scale] —ˈ**squamously** *or* ˈ**squamosely** *adv.* —ˈ**squamousness** *or* ˈ**squamoseness** *n.*

squamulose (ˈskwæmjʊˌləʊs, -ˌləʊz, ˈskweɪ-) *adj.* (esp. of plants or their parts) covered with minute scales. [C19: from Latin *squāmula* diminutive of *squāma* a scale]

squander (ˈskwɒndə) *vb.* (*tr.*) **1.** to spend wastefully or extravagantly; dissipate. **2.** an obsolete word for **scatter.** ~*n.* **3.** *Rare.* extravagance or dissipation. [C16: of unknown origin] —ˈ**squanderer** *n.*

square (skwɛə) *n.* **1.** a plane geometric figure having four equal sides and four right angles. Compare **rectangle, rhombus. 2.** any object, part, or arrangement having this or a similar shape: *a square of carpet; a square on a chess board.* **3.** (*cap. when part of name*) an open area in a town, sometimes including the surrounding buildings, which may form a square. **4.** *Maths.* the product of two equal factors; the second power: *9 is the square of 3, written* 3^2. **5.** an instrument having two strips of wood, metal, etc., set in the shape of a T or L, used for constructing or testing right angles. **6.** a body of soldiers drawn up in the form of a square. **7.** *Rowing.* the position of the blade of an oar perpendicular to the surface of the water just before and during a stroke. **8.** *Informal.* a person who is old-fashioned in views, customs, appearance, etc. **9.** *Astrology.* an aspect of about 90° between two planets, etc. Compare **conjunction** (sense 5), **opposition** (sense 9), **trine** (sense 1). **10.** *Obsolete.* a standard, pattern, or rule. **11. back to square one.** indicating a return to the starting-point of an investigation, experiment, etc., because of failure, lack of progress, etc. **12. on the square. a.** at right angles. **b.** on equal terms. **c.** *Informal.* honestly and openly. **d.** *Slang.* a phrase identifying someone as a Freemason: *he is on the square.* **13. out of square. a.** not at right angles or not having a right angle. **b.** not in order or agreement. ~*adj.* **14.** being a square in shape. **15.** having or forming one or more right angles or being at right angles to something. **16.** square or rectangular in section: *a square bar.* **17. a.** (*prenominal*) denoting a measure of area of any shape: *a circle of four square feet.* **b.** (*immediately postpositive*) denoting a square having a specified length on each side: *a board four feet square contains 16 square feet.* **18.** fair and honest (esp. in the phrase **a square deal**). **19.** straight, even, or level: *a square surface.* **20.** *Cricket.* at right angles to the wicket: *square leg.* **21.** *Soccer, hockey, etc.* in a straight line across the pitch: *a square pass.* **22.** *Nautical.* (of the sails of a square-rigger) set at right angles to the keel. **23.** *Informal.* old-fashioned in views, customs, appearance, etc. **24.** stocky or sturdy: *square shoulders.* **25.** (*postpositive*) having no remaining debts or accounts to be settled. **26.** (of a horse's gait) sound, steady, or regular. **27.** (*prenominal*) unequivocal or straightforward: *a square contradiction.* **28.** (*postpositive*) neat and tidy. **29.** *Maths.* (of a matrix) having the same number of rows and columns. **30. all square.** on equal terms; even in score. **31. square peg (in a round hole).** *Informal.* a person or thing that is a misfit, such as an employee in a job for which he is unsuited. ~*vb.* (*mainly tr.*) **32.** to make into a square or similar shape. **33.** *Maths.* to raise (a number or quantity) to the second power. **34.** to test or adjust for deviation with respect to a right angle, plane surface, etc. **35.** (sometimes foll. by *off*) to divide into squares. **36.** to position so as to be rectangular, straight, or level: *square the shoulders.* **37.** (sometimes foll. by *up*) to settle (debts, accounts, etc.). **38.** to level (the score) in a game, etc. **39.** (*also intr.*; often foll. by *with*) to agree or cause to agree: *your ideas don't square with mine.* **40.** *Rowing.* to turn (an oar) perpendicular to the surface of the water just before commencing a stroke. **41.** (in canoeing) to turn (a paddle) perpendicular to the direction of the canoe at the commencement of a stroke. Compare **feather** (sense 16). **42.** to arrange (something), esp. by a corrupt method or come to an arrangement with (someone), as by bribery. **43. square the circle.** to attempt the impossible (in reference to the insoluble problem of constructing a square having exactly the same area as a given circle). ~*adv.* **44.** in order to be square. **45.** at right angles. **46.** *Soccer, hockey, etc.* in a straight line across the pitch: *pass the ball square.* **47.** *Informal.* squarely. ~See also **square away, square off, square up.** [C13: from Old French *esquare,* from Vulgar Latin *exquadra* (unattested), from Latin EX-[1] + *quadrāre* to make square; see QUADRANT] —'**squareness** *n.* —'**squarer** *n.* —'**squarish** *adj.*

square away *vb.* (*adv.*) **1.** to set the sails of (a square-rigger) at right angles to the keel. **2.** (*tr.*) *U.S. and Canadian.* to make neat and tidy.

square-bashing *n. Brit. military slang.* drill on a barrack square.

square bracket *n.* **1.** either of a pair of characters [ ], used to enclose a section of writing or printing to separate it from the main text. **2.** Also called: **bracket.** either of these characters used as a sign of aggregation in mathematical or logical expressions indicating that the expression contained in the brackets is to be evaluated first and treated as a unit in the evaluation of the whole.

square dance *n.* **1.** *Chiefly U.S. and Canadian.* any of various formation dances, such as a quadrille, in which the couples form squares. ~*vb.* **square-dance.** **2.** (*intr.*) to perform such a dance. —'**square-ˌdancer** *n.*

square knot *n.* another name for **reef knot.**

square leg *n. Cricket.* **1.** a fielding position on the on side approximately at right angles to the batsman. **2.** a person who fields in this position.

squarely ('skwɛəlɪ) *adv.* **1.** in a direct way; straight: *he hit me squarely on the nose.* **2.** in an honest, frank, and just manner. **3.** at right angles.

square matrix *n. Maths.* a matrix in which the number of rows is equal to the number of columns.

square meal *n.* a substantial meal consisting of enough food to satisfy.

square measure *n.* a unit or system of units for measuring areas.

square number *n.* an integer, such as 1, 4, 9, or 16, that is the square of an integer.

square off *vb.* (*intr., adv.*) to assume a posture of offence or defence, as in boxing.

square of opposition *n.* See **opposition** (sense 10b).

square piano *n. Music.* an obsolete form of piano, horizontally strung and with an oblong frame.

square-rigged *adj. Nautical.* rigged with square sails.

square-rigger *n. Nautical.* a square-rigged ship.

square root *n.* a number or quantity that when multiplied by itself gives a given number or quantity: *2 is the square root of 4, usually written* $\sqrt{}4$, $\sqrt{4}$, $4^{1/2}$.

square sail *n. Nautical.* a rectangular or square sail set on a horizontal yard rigged more or less athwartships.

square shooter *n. Informal, chiefly U.S.* an honest or frank person. —**square shooting** *n.*

square tin *n. Brit.* a medium-sized loaf having a crusty top, baked in a tin with a square base.

square up *vb.* (*adv.*) **1.** to pay or settle (bills, debts, etc.). **2.** *Informal.* to arrange or be arranged satisfactorily. **3.** (*intr.*; foll. by *to*) to prepare to be confronted (with), esp. courageously. **4.** (*tr.*; foll. by *to*) to adopt a position of readiness to fight (an opponent). **5.** (*tr.*) to transfer (a drawing) by aid of a network of squares.

square wave *n.* an oscillation, for example in voltage pulse, that alternates between two fixed values with a negligible transition time between the two, giving a rectangular waveform.

Squarial ('skwɛərɪəl) *n. Trademark.* (formerly) a flat-plate square aerial used for receiving British Satellite Broadcasting TV transmissions.

squarrose ('skwærəʊz, 'skwɒ-) *adj.* **1.** *Biology.* having a rough surface, caused by the presence of projecting hairs, scales, etc. **2.** *Botany.* having or relating to overlapping parts that are pointed or recurved: *squarrose bracts.* [C18: from Latin *squarrōsus* scabby]

squash[1] (skwɒʃ) *vb.* **1.** to press or squeeze or be pressed or squeezed in or down so as to crush, distort, or pulp. **2.** (*tr.*) to suppress or overcome. **3.** (*tr.*) to humiliate or crush (a person), esp. with a disconcerting retort. **4.** (*intr.*) to make a sucking, splashing, or squelching sound. **5.** (often foll. by *in* or *into*) to enter or insert in a confined space. ~*n.* **6.** *Brit.* a still drink made from fruit juice or fruit syrup diluted with water. **7.** a crush, esp. of people in a confined space. **8.** something that is squashed. **9.** the act or sound of squashing or the state of being squashed. **10.** Also called: **squash rackets, squash racquets.** a game for two or four players played in an enclosed court with a small rubber ball and light long-handled rackets. The ball may be hit against any of the walls but must hit the facing wall at a point above a horizontal line. See also **rackets.** **11.** Also called: **squash tennis.** a similar game played with larger rackets and a larger pneumatic ball. [C16: from Old French *esquasser,* from Vulgar Latin *exquassāre* (unattested), from Latin EX-[1] + *quassāre* to shatter] —'**squasher** *n.*

squash[2] (skwɒʃ) *n., pl.* **squashes** *or* **squash.** *U.S. and Canadian.* **1.** any of various marrow-like cucurbitaceous plants of the genus *Cucurbita,* esp. *C. pepo* and *C. moschata,* the fruits of which have a hard rind surrounding edible flesh. **2.** the fruit of any of these plants, eaten as a vegetable. [C17: from Narraganset *askutasquash,* literally: green vegetable eaten green]

squash bug *n.* any of various heteropterous insects of the family *Coreidae,* esp. a North American species, *Anasa tristis,* which is a pest of squash, pumpkin, and related plants.

squash ladder *n.* a list showing the relative order of merit of a set of squash players determined by the winning player in each match taking the higher of the two players' positions.

squashy ('skwɒʃɪ) *adj.* **squashier, squashiest.** **1.** easily squashed; pulpy: *a squashy peach.* **2.** soft and wet; marshy: *squashy ground.* **3.** having a squashed appearance: *a squashy face.* —'**squashily** *adv.* —'**squashiness** *n.*

squat (skwɒt) *vb.* **squats, squatting, squatted.** (*intr.*) **1.** to rest in a crouching position with the knees bent and the weight on the feet. **2.** to crouch down, esp. in order to hide. **3.** *Law.* to occupy land or property to which the occupant has no legal title. ~*adj.* **4.** Also: **squatty** ('skwɒtɪ). short and broad: *a squat chair.* ~*n.* **5.** a squatting position. **6.** a house occupied by squatters. [C13: from Old French *esquater,* from *es-* EX-[1] + *catir* to press together, from Vulgar Latin *coactīre* (unattested), from Latin *cōgere* to compress, from CO- + *agere* to drive] —'**squatly** *adv.* —'**squatness** *n.*

squatter ('skwɒtə) *n.* **1.** (in Britain) a person who occupies property or land to which he has no legal title. **2.** (in Australia) **a.** a person who occupies a tract of land, esp. pastoral land, as tenant of the Crown. **b.** a farmer of sheep or cattle on a large scale. **3.** (in New Zealand) a 19th-century settler who took up large acreage on a Crown lease.

squatter sovereignty *n.* a contemptuous term for **popular sovereignty,** used by its critics.

squat thrust *n.* an exercise in which the hands are kept on the floor with the arms held straight while the legs are straightened out behind and quickly drawn in towards the body again.

squattocracy (skwɒ'tɒkrəsɪ) *n. Chiefly Austral.* squatters collectively, regarded as rich and influential. See **squatter** (sense 2b). [C19: from SQUATTER + -CRACY]

squaw (skwɔː) *n.* **1.** *Offensive.* a North American Indian woman. **2.** *Slang, usually facetious.* a woman or wife. [C17: of Algonquian origin; compare Natick *squa* female creature]

squawk (skwɔːk) *n.* **1.** a loud raucous cry; screech. **2.** *Informal.* a loud complaint or protest. ~*vb.* **3.** to utter a squawk or with a squawk. **4.** (*intr.*) *Informal.* to complain loudly. [C19: of imitative origin] —'**squawker** *n.*

squaw man *n. Derogatory.* a White or other non-Indian married to a North American Indian woman.

squeak (skwiːk) *n.* **1.** a short shrill cry or high-pitched sound. **2.** *Informal.* an escape (esp. in the phrases **narrow squeak, near squeak**). ~*vb.* **3.** to make or cause to make a squeak. **4.** (*intr.*;

usually foll. by *through* or *by*) to pass with only a narrow margin: *to squeak through an examination.* **5.** (*intr.*) *Informal.* to confess information about oneself or another. **6.** (*tr.*) to utter with a squeak. [C17: probably of Scandinavian origin; compare Swedish *skväka* to croak] —'**squeaker** *n.* —'**squeaky** *adj.* —'**squeakily** *adv.* —'**squeakiness** *n.*

squeaky-clean *adj.* **1.** (of hair) washed so clean that wet strands squeak when rubbed. **2.** completely clean.

squeal (skwiːl) *n.* **1.** a high shrill yelp, as of pain. **2.** a screaming sound, as of tyres when a car brakes suddenly. ~*vb.* **3.** to utter a squeal or with a squeal. **4.** (*intr.*) *Slang.* to confess information about another. **5.** (*intr.*) *Informal, chiefly Brit.* to complain or protest loudly. [C13 *squelen,* of imitative origin] —'**squealer** *n.*

squeamish ('skwiːmɪʃ) *adj.* **1.** easily sickened or nauseated, as by the sight of blood. **2.** easily shocked; fastidious or prudish. **3.** easily frightened: *squeamish about spiders.* [C15: from Anglo-French *escoymous,* of unknown origin] —'**squeamishly** *adv.* —'**squeamishness** *n.*

squeegee ('skwiːdʒiː) *or* (*less commonly*) **squilgee** *n.* **1.** an implement with a rubber blade used for wiping away surplus water from a surface, such as a windowpane. **2.** any of various similar devices used in photography for pressing the water out of wet prints or negatives or for squeezing prints onto a glazing surface. ~*vb.* **-gees, -geeing, -geed. 3.** to remove (water or other liquid) from (something) by use of a squeegee. **4.** (*tr.*) to press down (a photographic print, etc.) with a squeegee. [C19: probably of imitative origin, influenced by SQUEEZE]

squeeze (skwiːz) *vb.* (*mainly tr.*) **1.** to grip or press firmly, esp. so as to crush or distort; compress. **2.** to crush or press (something) so as to extract (a liquid): *to squeeze the juice from an orange; to squeeze an orange.* **3.** to apply gentle pressure to, as in affection or reassurance: *he squeezed her hand.* **4.** to push or force in a confined space: *to squeeze six lettuces into one box; to squeeze through a crowd.* **5.** to hug closely. **6.** to oppress with exacting demands, such as excessive taxes. **7.** to exert pressure on (someone) in order to extort (something): *to squeeze money out of a victim by blackmail.* **8.** (*intr.*) to yield under pressure. **9.** to make an impression of (a coin, etc.) in a soft substance. **10.** *Bridge, whist.* to lead a card that forces (opponents) to discard potentially winning cards. ~*n.* **11.** the act or an instance of squeezing or of being squeezed. **12.** a hug or handclasp. **13.** a crush of people in a confined space. **14.** *Chiefly Brit.* a condition of restricted credit imposed by a government to counteract price inflation. **15.** an impression, esp. of a coin, etc., made in a soft substance. **16.** an amount extracted by squeezing: *add a squeeze of lemon juice.* **17.** *Commerce.* any action taken by a trader or traders on a market that forces buyers to make purchases and prices to rise. **18.** *Informal.* pressure brought to bear in order to extort something (esp. in the phrase **put the squeeze on**). **19.** Also called: **squeeze play.** *Bridge, whist.* a manoeuvre that forces opponents to discard potentially winning cards. [C16: from Middle English *queysen* to press, from Old English *cwȳsan*] —'**squeezable** *adj.* —'**squeezer** *n.*

squeeze-box *n.* an informal name for **concertina, accordion.**

squelch (skwɛltʃ) *vb.* **1.** (*intr.*) to walk laboriously through soft wet material or with wet shoes, making a sucking noise. **2.** (*intr.*) to make such a noise. **3.** (*tr.*) to crush completely; squash. **4.** (*tr.*) *Informal.* to silence, as by a crushing retort. ~*n.* **5.** a squelching sound. **6.** something that has been squelched. **7.** *Electronics.* a circuit that cuts off the audio-frequency amplifier of a radio receiver in the absence of an input signal, in order to suppress background noise. **8.** *Informal.* a crushing remark. [C17: of imitative origin] —'**squelcher** *n.* —'**squelching** *adj.* —'**squelchy** *adj.*

squeteague (skwɪ'tiːg) *n., pl.* **-teague** *or* **-teagues.** any of various sciaenid food fishes of the genus *Cynoscion,* esp. *C. regalis,* of the North American coast of the Atlantic Ocean. [C19: from Narraganset *pesukwiteag,* literally: they give glue; so called because glue is made from them]

squib (skwɪb) *n.* **1.** a firework, usually having a tube filled with gunpowder, that burns with a hissing noise and culminates in a small explosion. **2.** a firework that does not explode because of a fault; dud. **3.** a short witty attack; lampoon. **4.** an electric device for firing a rocket engine. **5.** *Obsolete.* an insignificant person. **6.** *Austral. and N.Z. slang.* a coward. **7. damp squib.** something intended but failing to impress. ~*vb.* **squibs, squibbing, squibbed. 8.** (*intr.*) to sound, move, or explode like a squib. **9.** (*intr.*) to let off or shoot a squib. **10.** to write a squib against (someone). **11.** (*intr.*) to move in a quick irregular fashion. **12.** (*intr.*) *Austral. slang.* to behave in a cowardly fashion. [C16: probably imitative of a quick light explosion]

squid (skwɪd) *n., pl.* **squid** *or* **squids. 1.** any of various fast-moving pelagic cephalopod molluscs of the genera *Loligo, Ommastrephes,* etc., of most seas, having a torpedo-shaped body ranging from about 10 centimetres to 16.5 metres long and a pair of triangular tail fins: order *Decapoda* (decapods). See also **cuttlefish.** ~*vb.* **squids, squidding, squidded. 2.** (*intr.*) (of a parachute) to assume an elongated squidlike shape owing to excess air pressure. [C17: of unknown origin]

squidgy ('skwɪdʒɪ) *adj.* **squidgier, squidgiest.** soft, moist, and squashy. [of imitative origin]

squiffy ('skwɪfɪ) *adj.* **-fier, -fiest.** *Brit. informal.* slightly drunk. Also: **squiffed.** [C19: of unknown origin]

squiggle ('skwɪgᵊl) *n.* **1.** a mark or movement in the form of a wavy line; curlicue. **2.** an illegible scrawl. ~*vb.* **3.** (*intr.*) to wriggle. **4.** (*intr.*) to form or draw squiggles. **5.** (*tr.*) to make into squiggles. [C19: perhaps a blend of SQUIRM + WIGGLE] —'**squiggler** *n.* —'**squiggly** *adj.*

squilgee ('skwɪldʒiː) *n.* a variant of **squeegee.** [C19: perhaps from SQUEEGEE, influenced by SQUELCH]

squill (skwɪl) *n.* **1.** See **sea squill. 2.** the bulb of the sea squill, which is sliced, dried, and used medicinally, as an expectorant. **3.** any Old World liliaceous plant of the genus *Scilla,* such as *S. verna* (**spring squill**) of Europe, having small blue or purple flowers. [C14: from Latin *squilla* sea onion, from Greek *skilla,* of obscure origin]

squilla ('skwɪlə) *n., pl.* **-las** *or* **-lae** (-liː). any mantis shrimp of the genus *Squilla.* [C16: from Latin *squilla* shrimp, of obscure origin]

squinch (skwɪntʃ) *n.* a small arch, corbelling, etc., across an internal corner of a tower, used to support a superstructure such as a spire. Also called: **squinch arch.** [C15: from obsolete *scunch,* from Middle English *sconcheon,* from Old French *escoinson,* from *es-* EX-[1] + *coin* corner]

squint (skwɪnt) *vb.* **1.** (*usually intr.*) to cross or partly close (the eyes). **2.** (*intr.*) to have a squint. **3.** (*intr.*) to look or glance sideways or askance. ~*n.* **4.** the nontechnical name for **strabismus. 5.** the act or an instance of squinting; glimpse. **6.** Also called: **hagioscope.** a narrow oblique opening in a wall or pillar of a church to permit a view of the main altar from a side aisle or transept. **7.** *Informal.* a quick look; glance. ~*adj.* **8.** having a squint. **9.** *Informal.* crooked; askew. [C14: short for ASQUINT] —'**squinter** *n.* —'**squinty** *adj.*

squint-eyed *adj.* **1.** having a squint. **2.** looking sidelong.

squire (skwaɪə) *n.* **1.** a country gentleman in England, esp. the main landowner in a rural community. **2.** *Feudal history.* a young man of noble birth, who attended upon a knight. **3.** *Rare.* a man who courts or escorts a woman. **4.** *Informal, chiefly Brit.* a term of address used by one man to another, esp., unless ironic, to a member of a higher social class. **5.** *Austral.* an immature snapper (see **snapper** (sense 2)). ~*vb.* **6.** (*tr.*) (of a man) to escort (a woman). [C13: from Old French *esquier;* see ESQUIRE]

squirearchy *or* **squirarchy** ('skwaɪəˌrɑːkɪ) *n., pl.* **-chies. 1.** government by squires. **2.** squires collectively, esp. as a political or social force. [C19: from SQUIRE + -ARCHY, on the model of HIERARCHY, MONARCHY, etc.] —**squire'archal, squir'archal** *or* **squire'archical, squir'archical** *adj.*

squireen (skwaɪ'riːn) *or* **squireling** ('skwaɪəlɪŋ) *n. Rare.* a petty squire. [C19: from SQUIRE + *-een,* Anglo-Irish diminutive suffix, from Irish Gaelic *-ín*]

squirm (skwɜːm) *vb.* (*intr.*) **1.** to move with a wriggling motion; writhe. **2.** to feel deep mental discomfort, guilt, embarrassment, etc. ~*n.* **3.** a squirming movement. [C17: of imitative origin (perhaps influenced by WORM)] —'**squirmer** *n.* —'**squirming** *adj.* —'**squirmingly** *adv.* —'**squirmy** *adj.*

squirrel ('skwɪrəl; *U.S.* 'skwɜːrəl, 'skwʌr-) *n., pl.* **-rels** *or* **-rel. 1.** any arboreal sciurine rodent of the genus *Sciurus,* such as *S. vulgaris* (**red squirrel**) or *S. carolinensis* (**grey squirrel**), having a bushy tail and feeding on nuts, seeds, etc. **2.** any other rodent of the family *Sciuridae,* such as a ground squirrel or a marmot. **3.** the fur of such an animal. **4.** *Informal.* a person who hoards things. ~*vb.* **-rels, -relling, -relled** *or* (esp. U.S.) **-rels, -reling, -reled. 5.** (*tr.;* usually foll. by *away*) *Informal.* to store for future use; hoard. [C14: from Old French *esquireul,* from Late Latin *sciūrus,* from Greek *skiouros,* from *skia* shadow + *oura* tail] —'**squirrel-ˌlike** *adj.*

squirrel cage *n.* **1.** a cage consisting of a cylindrical framework that is made to rotate by a small animal running inside the framework. **2.** a repetitive purposeless task, way of life, etc. **3.** Also called: **squirrel-cage motor.** *Electrical engineering.* the rotor of an induction motor with a cylindrical winding having copper bars around the periphery parallel to the axis. **4.** an electric fan with many long narrow blades arranged in parallel so as to form a cylinder about an axis around which they spin.

squirrel corn *n.* a North American plant, *Dicentra canadensis,* having yellow flowers and tubers resembling grains of corn: family *Fumariaceae.* Also called: **colicweed.**

squirrelfish ('skwɪrəlˌfɪʃ) *n., pl.* **-fish** *or* **-fishes.** any tropical marine brightly coloured teleost fish of the family *Holocentridae.* [C18: so called because it can make a squirrel-like noise]

squirrel monkey *n.* **1.** a small New World monkey, *Saimiri sciureus,* of N South American forests, having a yellowish-green coat and orange feet and limbs. **2. red-backed squirrel monkey.** a related species, *Saimiri oerstedi,* of Central America, having a reddish coat and dark brown limbs. [C18: so called because it is small and tree-dwelling]

squirrel-tail grass *n.* an annual grass, *Hordeum marinum,* of salt marsh margins of Europe, having bushy awns.

squirt (skwɜːt) *vb.* **1.** to force (a liquid) or (of a liquid) to be forced out of a narrow opening. **2.** (*tr.*) to cover or spatter with liquid so ejected. ~*n.* **3.** a jet or amount of liquid so ejected. **4.** the act or an instance of squirting. **5.** an instrument used for squirting. **6.** *Informal.* **a.** a person regarded as insignificant or contemptible. **b.** a short person. [C15: of imitative origin] —'**squirter** *n.*

squirt gun *n. U.S. and Canadian.* another name for **water pistol.**

squirting cucumber *n.* a hairy cucurbitaceous plant, *Ecballium elaterium,* of the Mediterranean region, having a fruit that discharges its seeds explosively when ripe.

squish (skwɪʃ) *vb.* **1.** (*tr.*) to crush, esp. so as to make a soft splashing noise. **2.** (*intr.*) (of mud, etc.) to make a splashing noise: *the ground squishes as you tread.* ~*n.* **3.** a soft squashing sound: *the ripe peach fell with a squish.* [C17: of imitative origin] —'**squishy** *adj.*

squit (skwɪt) *n. Brit. slang.* **1.** an insignificant person. **2.** nonsense; rubbish. [C19: dialectal variant of SQUIRT]

squiz (skwɪz) *n., pl.* **squizzes.** *Austral. and N.Z. slang.* a look or glance, esp. an inquisitive one. [C20: perhaps a blend of SQUINT and QUIZ]

sr *symbol for* steradian.

Sr *abbrev. for:* **1.** (after a name) senior. **2.** Señor. **3.** Sir. **4.** Sister (religious). **5.** *the chemical symbol for* strontium.

Sra *abbrev. for* Señora.

SRCN (in Britain) *abbrev. for* State Registered Children's Nurse.

S-R connection *n. Psychol.* stimulus-response connection; the basic unit of learning according to behaviourist learning theory. See also **reflex arc.**

Sri (ʃriː) *n. Hinduism.* **1.** the consort of Vishnu. **2.** a title of honour used when addressing a distinguished Hindu. [literally: majesty, holiness]

Sri Lankan (ˌsriː 'læŋkən) *adj.* **1.** of or relating to Sri Lanka, an island republic in S Asia, or to its people, customs, etc. ~*n.* **2.** a native or inhabitant of Sri Lanka.

SRN (formerly in Britain) *abbrev. for* State Registered Nurse.

SRO *abbrev. for:* **1.** standing room only. **2.** *Brit.* Statutory Rules and Orders. **3.** self-regulatory organization.

Srta *abbrev. for* Señorita.

SS *abbrev. for:* **1.** (in Nazi Germany) Schutzstaffel. [German: protection squad] **2.** steamship. **3.** Sunday school.

ss. *abbrev. for* sections.

SS. *abbrev. for* Saints.

SSB *abbrev. for* single sideband (transmission).

SSC *abbrev. for:* **1.** (in India) Secondary School Certificate. **2.** (in Scotland) solicitor to the Supreme Court.

SSD (in Britain) *abbrev. for* Social Services Department.

SSE *symbol for* south-southeast.

SSHA *abbrev. for* Scottish Special Housing Association.

SSM *abbrev. for* surface-to-surface missile.

SSN *abbrev. for* severely subnormal; used of a person of very limited intelligence who needs special schooling.

SSP (in Britain) *abbrev. for* statutory sick pay.

ssp (*pl.* **sspp.**) *Biology. abbrev. for* subspecies.

SSR (formerly) *abbrev. for* Soviet Socialist Republic.

SSRC *abbrev. for* Social Science Research Council.

SSSI (in Britain) *abbrev. for* site of special scientific interest: an area identified by the Nature Conservancy Council as having flora, fauna, or geological features of special interest.

SST *abbrev. for* supersonic transport.

SSTA *abbrev. for* Scottish Secondary Teachers' Association.

SSW *symbol for* south-southwest.

st *abbrev. for* short ton.

St *abbrev. for* Saint (all entries that are usually preceded by *St* are in this dictionary listed alphabetically under **Saint**).

st. *abbrev. for:* **1.** stanza. **2.** statute. **3.** *Cricket.* stumped by.

St. *abbrev. for:* **1.** statute. **2.** Strait. **3.** Street.

-st *suffix.* a variant of **-est**[2].

Sta (in the names of places or churches) *abbrev. for* Saint (female). [Italian *Santa*]

sta. *abbrev. for:* **1.** station. **2.** stationary.

stab (stæb) *vb.* **stabs, stabbing, stabbed. 1.** (*tr.*) to pierce or injure with a sharp pointed instrument. **2.** (*tr.*) (of a sharp pointed instrument) to pierce or wound: *the knife stabbed her hand.* **3.** (when *intr.*, often foll. by *at*) to make a thrust (at); jab: *he stabbed at the doorway.* **4.** (*tr.*) to inflict with a sharp pain. **5.** **stab in the back. a.** (*vb.*) to do damage to the reputation of (a person, esp. a friend) in a surreptitious way. **b.** (*n.*) a treacherous action or remark that causes the downfall of or injury to a person. ~*n.* **6.** the act or an instance of stabbing. **7.** an injury or rift made by stabbing. **8.** a sudden sensation, esp. an unpleasant one: *a stab of pity.* **9.** *Informal.* an attempt (esp. in the phrase **make a stab at**). [C14: from *stabbe* stab wound; probably related to Middle English *stob* stick] —'**stabber** *n.*

Stabat Mater ('stɑːbæt 'mɑːtə) *n.* **1.** *R.C. Church.* a Latin hymn, probably of the 13th century, commemorating the sorrows of the Virgin Mary at the crucifixion and used in the Mass and various other services. **2.** a musical setting of this hymn. [from the opening words, literally: the mother was standing]

stabile ('steɪbaɪl) *n.* **1.** *Arts.* a stationary abstract construction, usually of wire, metal, wood, etc. Compare **mobile** (sense 6a). ~*adj.* **2.** fixed; stable. **3.** resistant to chemical change. [C18: from Latin *stabilis*]

stability (stə'bɪlɪtɪ) *n., pl.* **-ties. 1.** the quality of being stable. **2.** the ability of an aircraft to resume its original flight path after inadvertent displacement. **3.** *Meteorol.* **a.** the condition of an air mass characterized by no upward movement. **b.** the degree of susceptibility of an air mass to disturbance by convection currents. **4.** *Ecology.* the ability of an ecosystem to resist change. **5.** *Electrical engineering.* the ability of an electrical circuit to cope with changes in the operational conditions. **6.** a vow taken by every Benedictine monk attaching him perpetually to the monastery where he is professed.

stabilize *or* **stabilise** ('steɪbɪˌlaɪz) *vb.* **1.** to make or become stable or more stable. **2.** to keep or be kept stable. **3.** to put or keep (an aircraft, vessel, etc.) in equilibrium by one or more special devices, or (of an aircraft, vessel, etc.) to become stable. —ˌ**stabili'zation** *or* ˌ**stabili'sation** *n.*

stabilizer *or* **stabiliser** ('steɪbɪˌlaɪzə) *n.* **1.** any device for stabilizing an aircraft. See also **horizontal stabilizer, vertical stabilizer. 2.** a substance added to something to maintain it in a stable or unchanging state, such as an additive to food to preserve its texture during distribution and storage. **3.** *Nautical.* **a.** a system of one or more pairs of fins projecting from the hull of a ship and controllable to counteract roll. **b.** See **gyrostabilizer. 4.** either of a pair of brackets supporting a small wheel that can be fitted to the back wheel of a bicycle to help an inexperienced cyclist to maintain balance. **5.** an electronic device for producing a direct current supply of constant voltage. **6.** *Economics.* a measure, such as progressive taxation, interest-rate control, or unemployment benefit, used to restrict swings in prices, employment, production, etc., in a free economy. **7.** a person or thing that stabilizes.

stab kick *n. Australian Rules football.* a rapid kick of the ball from one player to another member of his team. Also called: **stab pass.**

stable[1] ('steɪbᵊl) *n.* **1.** a building, usually consisting of stalls, for the lodging of horses or other livestock. **2.** the animals lodged in such a building, collectively. **3. a.** the racehorses belonging to a particular establishment or owner. **b.** the establishment itself. **c.** (*as modifier*): *stable companion.* **4.** *Informal.* a source of training, such as a school, theatre, etc.: *the two athletes were out of the same stable.* **5.** a number of people considered as a source of a particular talent: *a stable of writers.* **6.** (*modifier*) of, relating to, or suitable for a stable: *stable manners.* ~*vb.* **7.** to put, keep, or be kept in a stable. [C13: from Old French *estable* cowshed, from Latin *stabulum* shed, from *stāre* to stand]

stable[2] ('steɪbᵊl) *adj.* **1.** steady in position or balance; firm. **2.** lasting or permanent: *a stable relationship.* **3.** steadfast or firm of purpose. **4.** (of an elementary particle, atomic nucleus, etc.) not undergoing decay; not radioactive: *a stable nuclide.* **5.** (of a chemical compound) not readily partaking in a chemical change. **6.** (of electronic equipment) with no tendency to self-oscillation. [C13: from Old French *estable,* from Latin *stabilis* steady, from *stāre* to stand] —'**stableness** *n.* —'**stably** *adv.*

stableboy ('steɪbᵊlˌbɔɪ) *or* **stableman** ('steɪbᵊlˌmæn, -mən) *n., pl.* **-boys** *or* **-men.** a boy or man who works in a stable.

stable door *n.* a door with an upper and lower leaf that may be opened separately. U.S. and Canadian equivalent: **Dutch door.**

stable fly *n.* a blood-sucking muscid fly, *Stomoxys calcitrans,* that attacks man and domestic animals.

stable lad *n.* a person who looks after the horses in a racing stable.

stabling ('steɪblɪŋ) *n.* stable buildings or accommodation.

stablish ('stæblɪʃ) *vb.* an archaic variant of **establish.**

stacc. *Music. abbrev. for* staccato.

staccato (stə'kɑːtəʊ) *adj.* **1.** *Music.* (of notes) short, clipped, and separate. **2.** characterized by short abrupt sounds, as in speech: *a staccato command.* ~*adv.* **3.** (esp. used as a musical direction) in a staccato manner. [C18: from Italian, from *staccare* to detach, shortened from *distaccare*]

stachys ('steɪkɪs) *n.* any plant of the genus *Stachys,* esp. *S. lanata* (lamb's ears) and *S. officinalis* (betony). [New Latin, from Greek *stachys* ear of corn, used as a plant name]

stack (stæk) *n.* **1.** an ordered pile or heap. **2.** a large orderly pile of hay, straw, etc., for storage in the open air. **3.** (*often pl.*) *Library science.* compactly spaced bookshelves, used to house collections of books in an area usually prohibited to library users. **4.** a number of aircraft circling an airport at different altitudes, awaiting their signal to land. **5.** a large amount: *a stack of work.* **6.** *Military.* a pile of rifles or muskets in the shape of a cone. **7.** *Brit.* a measure of coal or wood equal to 108 cubic feet. **8.** See **chimney stack, smokestack. 9.** a vertical pipe, such as the funnel of a ship or the soil pipe attached to the side of a building. **10.** a high column of rock, esp. one isolated from the mainland by the erosive action of the sea. **11.** an area in a computer memory for temporary storage. ~*vb.* (*tr.*) **12.** to place in a stack; pile: *to stack bricks on a lorry.* **13.** to load or fill up with piles of something: *to stack a lorry with bricks.* **14.** to control (a number of aircraft waiting to land at an airport) so that each flies at a different altitude. **15. stack the cards.** to prearrange the order of a pack of cards secretly so that the deal will benefit someone. [C13: from Old Norse *stakkr* haystack, of Germanic origin; related to Russian *stog*] —'**stackable** *adj.* —'**stacker** *n.*

stacked (stækt) *adj. Slang.* a variant of **well-stacked.**

stacking ('stækɪŋ) *n.* the arrangement of aircraft traffic in busy flight lanes, esp. while waiting to land at an airport, with a minimum vertical separation for safety of 1000 feet below 29 000 feet and 2000 feet above 29 000 feet.

stacking truck *n.* another name for **pallet truck.**

stacte ('stækti:) *n. Old Testament.* one of several sweet-smelling spices used in incense (Exodus 30:34). [C14: via Latin from Greek *staktē* oil of myrrh, from *staktos* distilling a drop at a time, from *stazein* to flow, drip]

staddle ('stædᵊl) *n.* **1.** a support or prop, esp. a low flat-topped stone structure for supporting hay or corn stacks about two feet above ground level. **2.** a supporting frame for such a stack. **3.** the lower part of a hay or corn stack. [Old English *stathol* base; related to Old Norse *stothull* cow pen, Old High German *stadal* barn]

staddlestone ('stædᵊl,stəʊn) *n.* (formerly) one of several supports for a hayrick, consisting of a truncated conical stone surmounted by a flat circular stone.

stadholder *or* **stadtholder** ('stæd,həʊldə) *n.* **1.** the chief magistrate of the former Dutch republic or of any of its provinces (from about 1580 to 1802). **2.** a viceroy or governor of a province. [C16: partial translation of Dutch *stad houder,* from *stad* city (see STEAD) + *houder* holder] —'**stad,holder,ate, 'stad,holdership** *or* '**stadt,holder,ate, 'stadt,holdership** *n.*

stadia[1] ('steɪdɪə) *n.* **1. a.** tacheometry that makes use of a telescopic surveying instrument and a graduated staff calibrated to correspond with the distance from the observer. **b.** (*as modifier*): *stadia surveying.* **2.** the two parallel cross hairs or **stadia hairs** in the eyepiece of the instrument used. **3.** the staff used. [C19: probably from STADIA[2]]

stadia[2] ('steɪdɪə) *n.* a plural of **stadium.**

stadiometer (,steɪdɪ'ɒmɪtə) *n.* an instrument that measures the length of curves, dashes, etc., by running a toothed wheel along them. [C19: from *stadio-,* from STADIUM + -METER]

stadium ('steɪdɪəm) *n., pl.* **-diums** *or* **-dia** (-dɪə). **1.** a sports arena with tiered seats for spectators. **2.** (in ancient Greece) a course for races, usually located between two hills providing natural slopes for tiers of seats. **3.** an ancient Greek measure of length equivalent to about 607 feet or 184 metres. **4.** (in many arthropods) the interval between two consecutive moultings. **5.** a particular period or stage in the development of a disease. [C16: via Latin from Greek *stadion,* changed from *spadion* a racecourse, from *spān* to pull; also influenced by Greek *stadios* steady]

staff[1] (stɑ:f) *n., pl.* **staffs** *for senses 1, 3, 4;* **staffs** *or* **staves** (steɪvz) *for senses 5–9.* **1.** a group of people employed by a company, individual, etc., for executive, clerical, sales work, etc. **2.** (*modifier*) attached to or provided for the staff of an establishment: *a staff doctor.* **3.** the body of teachers or lecturers of an educational institution, as distinct from the students. **4.** the officers appointed to assist a commander, service, or central headquarters organization in establishing policy, plans, etc. **5.** a stick with some special use, such as a walking stick or an emblem of authority. **6.** something that sustains or supports: *bread is the staff of life.* **7.** a pole on which a flag is hung. **8.** *Chiefly Brit.* a graduated rod used in surveying, esp. for sighting to with a levelling instrument. Usual U.S. name: **rod. 9.** Also called: **stave.** *Music.* **a.** the system of horizontal lines grouped into sets of five (four in the case of plainsong) upon which music is written. The spaces between them are also used, being employed in conjunction with a clef in order to give a graphic indication of pitch. **b.** any set of five lines in this system together with its clef: *the treble staff.* ~*vb.* **10.** (*tr.*) to provide with a staff. [Old English *stæf;* related to Old Frisian *stef,* Old Saxon *staf,* German *Stab,* Old Norse *stafr,* Gothic *Stafs;* see STAVE]

staff[2] (stɑ:f) *n. U.S.* a mixture of plaster and hair used to cover the external surface of temporary structures and for decoration. [C19: of unknown origin]

staff association *n.* an association of employees that performs some of the functions of a trade union, such as representing its members in discussions with the management, and may also have other social and professional purposes.

staff college *n.* a training centre for executive military personnel.

staff corporal *n.* a noncommissioned rank in the British Army above that of staff sergeant and below that of warrant officer.

staffer ('stɑ:fə) *n. Informal.* a member of staff, esp., in journalism, of editorial staff.

staffman ('stɑ:f,mæn) *n., pl.* **-men.** *Brit.* a person who holds the levelling staff when a survey is being made.

staff nurse *n.* a qualified nurse ranking immediately below a sister.

staff of Aesculapius (,i:skjʊ'leɪpɪəs) *n.* an emblem consisting of a staff with a serpent entwined around it, used by the Royal Medical Corps and the American Medical Association. Compare **caduceus** (sense 2).

staff officer *n.* a commissioned officer serving on the staff of a commander, service, or central headquarters.

Staffordshire bull terrier ('stæfəd,ʃɪə, -ʃə) *n.* a breed of smooth-coated terrier with a stocky frame and generally a pied or brindled coat. See also **bull terrier.**

Staffs (stæfs) *abbrev. for* Staffordshire.

staff sergeant *n. Military.* **1.** *Brit.* a noncommissioned officer holding a rank between sergeant and warrant officer and employed on administrative duties. **2.** *U.S.* a noncommissioned officer who ranks: **a.** (in the Army) above sergeant and below sergeant first class. **b.** (in the Air Force) above airman first class and below technical sergeant. **c.** (in the Marine Corps) above sergeant and below gunnery sergeant.

stag (stæg) *n.* **1.** the adult male of a deer, esp. a red deer. **2.** a man unaccompanied by a woman at a social gathering. **3.** *Stock Exchange. Brit.* **a.** a speculator who applies for shares in a new issue in anticipation of a rise in price when trading commences in order to make a quick profit on resale. **b.** (*as modifier*): *stag operations.* **4.** (*modifier*) (of a social gathering) attended by men only. **5.** (*modifier*) pornographic in content: *a stag show.* ~*adv.* **6.** without a female escort. ~*vb.* (*tr.*) **7.** *Stock Exchange.* to apply for (shares in a new issue) with the intention of selling them for a quick profit when trading commences. [Old English *stagga* (unattested); related to Old Norse *steggr* male bird]

stag beetle *n.* any lamellicorn beetle of the family *Lucanidae,* the males of which have large branched mandibles.

stage (steɪdʒ) *n.* **1.** a distinct step or period of development, growth, or progress: *a child at the toddling stage.* **2.** a raised area or platform. **3.** the platform in a theatre where actors perform. **4. the.** the theatre as a profession. **5.** any scene regarded as a setting for an event or action. **6.** a portion of a journey or a stopping place after such a portion. **7.** short for **stagecoach. 8.** *Brit.* a division of a bus route for which there is a fixed fare. **9.** one of the separate propulsion units of a rocket that can be jettisoned when it has burnt out. See also **multistage** (sense 1). **10.** any of the various distinct periods of growth or development in the life of an organism, esp. an insect: *a larval stage; pupal stage.* **11.** the organism itself at such a period of growth. **12.** a small stratigraphical unit; a subdivision of a rock series or system. **13.** the platform on a microscope on which the specimen is mounted for examination. **14.** *Electronics.* a part of a complex circuit, esp. one of a number of transistors with the associated elements required to amplify a signal in an amplifier. **15.** a university subject studied for one academic year: *Stage II French.* **16. by** *or* **in easy stages.** not hurriedly: *he learnt French by easy stages.* ~*vb.* **17.** (*tr.*) to perform (a play), esp. on a stage: *we are going to stage "Hamlet".* **18.** (*tr.*) to set the action of (a play) in a particular time or place. **19.** (*tr.*) to plan, organize, and carry out (an event). **20.** (*intr.*) *Obsolete.* to travel by stagecoach. [C13: from Old French *estage* position, from Vulgar Latin *staticum* (unattested), from Latin *stāre* to stand]

stagecoach ('steɪdʒ,kəʊtʃ) *n.* a large four-wheeled horse-drawn vehicle formerly used to carry passengers, mail, etc., on a regular route between towns and cities.

stagecraft ('steɪdʒ,krɑ:ft) *n.* skill in or the art of writing or staging plays.

stage direction *n. Theatre.* an instruction to an actor or director, written into the script of a play.

stage door *n.* a door at a theatre leading backstage.

stage effect *n.* a special effect created on the stage by lighting, sound, etc.

stage fright *n.* nervousness or panic that may beset a person about to appear in front of an audience.

stagehand ('steɪdʒ,hænd) *n.* a person who sets the stage, moves props, etc., in a theatrical production.

stage left *n.* the part of the stage to the left of a performer facing the audience.

stage-manage *vb.* **1.** to work as stage manager for (a play, etc.). **2.** (*tr.*) to arrange, present, or supervise from behind the scenes: *to stage-manage a campaign.*

stage manager *n.* a person who supervises the stage arrangements of a theatrical production.

stager ('steɪdʒə) *n.* **1.** a person of experience; veteran (esp. in the phrase **old stager**). **2.** an archaic word for **actor.**

stage right *n.* the part of the stage to the right of a performer facing the audience.

stage-struck *adj.* infatuated with the glamour of theatrical life, esp. with the desire to act.

stage whisper *n.* **1.** a loud whisper from one actor to another onstage intended to be heard by the audience. **2.** any loud whisper that is intended to be overheard.

stagey ('steɪdʒɪ) *adj.* **stagier, stagiest.** a variant spelling (in the U.S.) of **stagy.** —'**stagily** *adv.* —'**staginess** *n.*

stagflation (stæg'fleɪʃən) *n.* a situation in which inflation is combined with stagnant or falling output and employment. [C20: blend of STAGNATION + INFLATION]

staggard ('stægəd) *n.* a male red deer in the fourth year of life. [C15: see STAG, -ARD]

stagger ('stægə) *vb.* **1.** (*usually intr.*) to walk or cause to walk unsteadily as if about to fall. **2.** (*tr.*) to astound or overwhelm, as with shock: *I am staggered by his ruthlessness.* **3.** (*tr.*) to place or arrange in alternating or overlapping positions or time periods to prevent confusion or congestion: *a staggered junction; to stagger holidays.* **4.** (*intr.*) to falter or hesitate: *his courage staggered in the face of the battle.* **5.** (*tr.*) to set (the wings of a biplane) so that the leading edge of one extends beyond that of the other. ~*n.* **6.** the act or an instance of staggering. **7.** a staggered arrangement on a biplane, etc. ~See also **staggers.** [C13 dialect *stacker,* from Old Norse *staka* to push] —'**staggerer** *n.* —'**staggering** *adj.* —'**staggeringly** *adv.*

staggerbush ('stægə,bʊʃ) *n.* an ericaceous deciduous shrub, *Lyonia mariana,* of E North America, having white or pinkish flowers: it is poisonous to livestock. [C19: so named because it was believed to cause STAGGERS in sheep]

staggered directorships *pl. n. Business.* a defence against unwelcome takeover bids in which a company resolves that its directors should serve staggered terms of office and that no director can be removed from office without just cause, thus preventing a bidder from controlling the board for some years.

staggered hours *pl. n.* a system of working in which the employees of an organization do not all arrive and leave at the same time, but have large periods of overlap.

staggers (ˈstæɡəz) *n.* (*functioning as sing. or pl.*) **1.** a form of vertigo associated with decompression sickness. **2.** Also called: **blind staggers.** a disease of horses and some other domestic animals characterized by a swaying unsteady gait, caused by infection or lesions of the central nervous system.

staghound (ˈstæɡˌhaʊnd) *n.* a breed of hound similar in appearance to the foxhound but larger.

staging (ˈsteɪdʒɪŋ) *n.* any temporary structure used in the process of building, esp. the horizontal platforms supported by scaffolding. [C14: from STAGE + -ING[1]]

staging area *n.* a general locality used as a checkpoint or regrouping area for military formations in transit.

staging post *n.* a place where a journey is usually broken, esp. a stopover on a flight.

Stagirite (ˈstædʒɪˌraɪt) *n.* an inhabitant or native of Stagira, an ancient city in Macedonia and the birthplace of Aristotle.

stagnant (ˈstæɡnənt) *adj.* **1.** (of water, etc.) standing still; without flow or current. **2.** brackish and foul from standing still. **3.** stale, sluggish, or dull from inaction. **4.** not growing or developing; static. [C17: from Latin *stagnāns,* from *stagnāre* to be stagnant, from *stagnum* a pool] —ˈ**stagnancy** *or* ˈ**stagnance** *n.* —ˈ**stagnantly** *adv.*

stagnate (stæɡˈneɪt, ˈstæɡˌneɪt) *vb.* (*intr.*) to be or become stagnant. —**stagˈnation** *n.*

stag night *or* **party** *n.* a party for men only, esp. one held for a man before he is married. Compare **hen night, hen party.**

stag's horn *or* **staghorn** (ˈstæɡˌhɔːn) *n.* **1.** the antlers of a stag used as a material for carved implements. **2.** a creeping variety of club moss, *Lycopodium clavatum,* growing on moors and mountains, having silvery hair points on its leaves.

stagy *or U.S.* **stagey** (ˈsteɪdʒɪ) *adj.* **stagier, stagiest.** excessively theatrical or dramatic. —ˈ**stagily** *adv.* —ˈ**staginess** *n.*

staid (steɪd) *adj.* **1.** of a settled, sedate, and steady character. **2.** *Now rare.* permanent. [C16: obsolete past participle of STAY[1]] —ˈ**staidly** *adv.* —ˈ**staidness** *n.*

stain (steɪn) *vb.* (*mainly tr.*) **1.** to mark or discolour with patches of something that dirties: *the dress was stained with coffee.* **2.** to dye with a penetrating dyestuff or pigment. **3.** to bring disgrace or shame on: *to stain someone's honour.* **4.** to colour (specimens) for microscopic study by treatment with a dye or similar reagent. **5.** (*intr.*) to produce indelible marks or discoloration: *does ink stain?* ~*n.* **6.** a spot, mark, or discoloration. **7.** a moral taint; blemish or slur. **8.** a dye or similar reagent, used to colour specimens for microscopic study. **9.** a solution or liquid used to penetrate the surface of a material, esp. wood, and impart a rich colour without covering up the surface or grain. **10.** any dye that is made into a solution and used to colour textiles and hides. [C14 *steynen* (vb.), shortened from *disteynen* to remove colour from, from Old French *desteindre* to discolour, from *des-* DIS-[1] + *teindre,* from Latin *tingere* to TINGE] —ˈ**stainable** *adj.* —ˌ**stainaˈbility** *n.* —ˈ**stainer** *n.*

stained glass *n.* **a.** glass that has been coloured in any of various ways, as by fusing with a film of metallic oxide or burning pigment into the surface, used esp. for church windows. **b.** (*as modifier*): *a stained-glass window.*

stainless (ˈsteɪnlɪs) *adj.* **1.** resistant to discoloration, esp. discoloration resulting from corrosion; rust-resistant: *stainless steel.* **2.** having no blemish: *a stainless reputation.* ~*n.* **3.** stainless steel. —ˈ**stainlessly** *adv.*

stainless steel *n.* **a.** a type of steel resistant to corrosion as a result of the presence of large amounts of chromium (12–15 per cent). The carbon content depends on the application, being 0.2–0.4 per cent for steel used in cutlery, etc., and about 1 per cent for use in scalpels and razor blades. **b.** (*as modifier*): *stainless-steel cutlery.*

stair (stɛə) *n.* **1.** one of a flight of stairs. **2.** a series of steps: *a narrow stair.* ~See also **stairs.** [Old English *stæger;* related to *stīg* narrow path, *stīgan* to ascend, descend, Old Norse *steigurligr* upright, Middle Dutch *steiger* ladder]

staircase (ˈstɛəˌkeɪs) *n.* a flight of stairs, its supporting framework, and, usually, a handrail or banisters.

stairhead (ˈstɛəˌhɛd) *n.* the top of a flight of stairs.

stair rod *n.* any of a series of rods placed in the angles between the steps of a carpeted staircase, used to hold the carpet in position.

stairs (stɛəz) *pl. n.* **1.** a flight of steps leading from one storey or level to another, esp. indoors. **2. below stairs.** *Brit.* in the servants' quarters; in domestic service.

stairway (ˈstɛəˌweɪ) *n.* a means of access consisting of stairs; staircase or flight of steps.

stairwell (ˈstɛəˌwɛl) *n.* a vertical shaft or opening that contains a staircase.

stake[1] (steɪk) *n.* **1.** a stick or metal bar driven into the ground as a marker, part of a fence, support for a plant, etc. **2.** one of a number of vertical posts that fit into sockets around a flat truck or railway wagon to hold the load in place. **3.** a method or the practice of executing a person by binding him to a stake in the centre of a pile of wood that is then set on fire. **4.** *Mormon Church.* an administrative district consisting of a group of wards under the jurisdiction of a president. **5. pull up stakes.** to leave one's home or temporary resting place and move on. ~*vb.* (*tr.*) **6.** to tie, fasten, or tether with or to a stake. **7.** (often foll. by *out* or *off*) to fence or surround with stakes. **8.** (often foll. by *out*) to lay (a claim) to land, rights, etc. **9.** to support with a stake. [Old English *staca* pin; related to Old Frisian *staka,* Old High German *stehho,* Old Norse *stjaki;* see STICK]

stake[2] (steɪk) *n.* **1.** the money or valuables that a player must hazard in order to buy into a gambling game or make a bet. **2.** an interest, often financial, held in something: *a stake in the company's future.* **3.** (*often pl.*) the money that a player has available for gambling. **4.** (*often pl.*) a prize in a race, etc., esp. one made up of contributions from contestants or owners. **5.** (*pl.*) *Horse racing.* a race in which all owners of competing horses contribute to the prize money. **6.** *U.S. and Canadian informal.* short for **grubstake** (sense 1). **7. at stake.** at risk: *two lives are at stake.* ~*vb.* (*tr.*) **8.** to hazard (money, etc.) on a result. **9.** to invest in or support by supplying with money, etc.: *to stake a business enterprise.* [C16: of uncertain origin]

stakeout (ˈsteɪkaʊt) *Slang, chiefly U.S. and Canadian.* ~*n.* **1.** a police surveillance of an area, house, or criminal suspect. **2.** an area or house kept under such surveillance. ~*vb.* **stake out. 3.** (*tr., adv.*) to keep under surveillance.

Stakhanovism (stæˈkænəˌvɪzəm) *n.* (in the former Soviet Union) a system designed to raise production by offering incentives to efficient workers. [C20: named after A. G. *Stakhanov* (1906–77), Soviet coal miner, the worker first awarded benefits under the system in 1935] —**Staˈkhanovˌite** *n.*

stalactite (ˈstælәkˌtaɪt) *n.* a cylindrical mass of calcium carbonate hanging from the roof of a limestone cave: formed by precipitation from continually dripping water. Compare **stalagmite.** [C17: from New Latin *stalactites,* from Greek *stalaktos* dripping, from *stalassein* to drip] —**stalactiform** (stəˈlæktɪˌfɔːm) *adj.* —**stalactitic** (ˌstæləkˈtɪtɪk) *or* ˌ**stalacˈtitical** *adj.*

stalag (ˈstælæɡ; *German* ˈʃtalak) *n.* a German prisoner-of-war camp in World War II, esp. for noncommissioned officers and other ranks. [short for *Stammlager* base camp, from *Stamm* base (related to STEM[1]) + *Lager* camp]

stalagmite (ˈstæləɡˌmaɪt) *n.* a cylindrical mass of calcium carbonate projecting upwards from the floor of a limestone cave: formed by precipitation from continually dripping water. Compare **stalactite.** [C17: from New Latin *stalagmites,* from Greek *stalagmos* dripping; related to Greek *stalassein* to drip; compare STALACTITE] —**stalagmitic** (ˌstæləɡˈmɪtɪk) *or* ˌ**stalagˈmitical** *adj.*

stale[1] (steɪl) *adj.* **1.** (esp. of food) hard, musty, or dry from being kept too long. **2.** (of beer, etc.) flat and tasteless from being kept open too long. **3.** (of air) stagnant; foul. **4.** uninteresting from overuse; hackneyed: *stale clichés.* **5.** no longer new: *stale news.* **6.** lacking in energy or ideas through overwork or lack of variety. **7.** *Banking* (of a cheque) not negotiable by a bank as a result of not having been presented within six months of being written. **8.** *Law.* (of a claim, etc.) having lost its effectiveness or force, as by failure to act or by the lapse of time. ~*vb.* **9.** to make or become stale. [C13 (originally applied to liquor in the sense: well matured): probably via Norman French from Old French *estale* (unattested) motionless, of Frankish origin; related to STALL[1], INSTALL] —ˈ**stalely** *adv.* —ˈ**staleness** *n.*

stale[2] (steɪl) *vb.* **1.** (*intr.*) (of livestock) to urinate. ~*n.* **2.** the urine of horses or cattle. [C15: perhaps from Old French *estaler* to stand in one position; see STALL[1]; compare Middle Low German *stallen* to urinate, Greek *stalassein* to drip]

stale bull *n. Business.* a dealer or speculator who holds unsold commodities after a rise in market prices but who cannot trade because there are no buyers at the new levels and because his financial commitments prevent him from making further purchases.

stalemate (ˈsteɪlˌmeɪt) *n.* **1.** a chess position in which any of a player's possible moves would place his king in check: in this position the game ends in a draw. **2.** a situation in which two opposing forces find that further action is impossible or futile; deadlock. ~*vb.* **3.** (*tr.*) to subject to a stalemate. [C18: from obsolete *stale,* from Old French *estal* STALL[1] + MATE[2]]

Stalinism (ˈstɑːlɪˌnɪzəm) *n.* the theory and form of government associated with Soviet leader Joseph Stalin (1879–1953): a variant of Marxism-Leninism characterized by totalitarianism, rigid bureaucracy, and loyalty to the Soviet state. —ˈ**Stalinist** *n., adj.*

stalk[1] (stɔːk) *n.* **1.** the main stem of a herbaceous plant. **2.** any of various subsidiary plant stems, such as a leafstalk (petiole) or flower stalk (peduncle). **3.** a slender supporting structure in animals such as crinoids and certain protozoans, coelenterates, and barnacles. **4.** any long slender supporting shaft or column. [C14: probably a diminutive formed from Old English *stalu* upright piece of wood; related to Old Frisian *staal* handle] —**stalked** *adj.* —ˈ**stalkless** *adj.* —ˈ**stalkˌlike** *adj.*

stalk[2] (stɔːk) *vb.* **1.** to follow or approach (game, prey, etc.) stealthily and quietly. **2.** to spread over (a place) in a menacing or grim manner: *fever stalked the camp.* **3.** (*intr.*) to walk in a haughty, stiff, or threatening way: *he stalked out in disgust.* **4.**

to search or draw (a piece of land) for prey. ~*n.* **5.** the act of stalking. **6.** a stiff or threatening stride. [Old English *bestealcian* to walk stealthily; related to Middle Low German *stolkeren,* Danish *stalke*] —'**stalker** *n.*

stalking-horse *n.* **1.** a horse or an imitation one used by a hunter to hide behind while stalking his quarry. **2.** something serving as a means of concealing plans; pretext. **3.** *Chiefly U.S.* a candidate put forward by one group to divide the opposition or mask the candidacy of another person for whom the stalking-horse would then withdraw.

stalky ('stɔːkɪ) *adj.* **stalkier, stalkiest. 1.** like a stalk; slender and tall. **2.** having or abounding in stalks. —'**stalkily** *adv.* —'**stalkiness** *n.*

stall[1] (stɔːl) *n.* **1. a.** a compartment in a stable or shed for confining or feeding a single animal. **b.** another name for **stable**[1] (sense 1). **2.** a small often temporary stand or booth for the display and sale of goods. **3.** (in a church) **a.** one of a row of seats, usually divided from the others by armrests or a small screen, for the use of the choir or clergy. **b.** a pen. **4.** an instance of an engine stalling. **5.** a condition of an aircraft in flight in which a reduction in speed or an increase in the aircraft's angle of attack causes a sudden loss of lift resulting in a downward plunge. **6.** any small room or compartment. **7.** *Brit.* **a.** a seat in a theatre or cinema that resembles a chair, usually fixed to the floor. **b.** (*pl.*) the area of seats on the ground floor of a theatre or cinema nearest to the stage or screen. **8.** a tubelike covering for a finger, as in a glove. **9.** (*pl.*) short for **starting stalls.** ~*vb.* **10.** to cause (a motor vehicle or its engine) to stop, usually by incorrect use of the clutch or incorrect adjustment of the fuel mixture, or (of an engine or motor vehicle) to stop, usually for these reasons. **11.** to cause (an aircraft) to go into a stall or (of an aircraft) to go into a stall. **12.** to stick or cause to stick fast, as in mud or snow. **13.** (*tr.*) to confine (an animal) in a stall. [Old English *steall* a place for standing; related to Old High German *stall,* and *stellen* to set]

stall[2] (stɔːl) *vb.* **1.** to employ delaying tactics towards (someone); be evasive. **2.** (*intr.*) *Sport, chiefly U.S.* to play or fight below one's best in order to deceive. ~*n.* **3.** an evasive move; pretext. [C16: from Anglo-French *estale* bird used as a decoy, influenced by STALL[1]]

stall-feed *vb.* **-feeds, -feeding, -fed.** (*tr.*) to keep and feed (an animal) in a stall, esp. as an intensive method of fattening it for slaughter.

stallholder ('stɔːlˌhəʊldə) *n.* a person who sells goods at a market stall.

stalling angle *n.* the angle between the chord line of an aerofoil and the undisturbed relative airflow at which stalling occurs. Also called: **stall angle, critical angle.**

stallion ('stæljən) *n.* an uncastrated male horse, esp. one used for breeding. [C14: *staloun,* from Old French *estalon,* of Germanic origin; related to Old High German *stal* STALL[1]]

stalwart ('stɔːlwət) *adj.* **1.** strong and sturdy; robust. **2.** solid, dependable, and courageous: *stalwart citizens.* **3.** resolute and firm. ~*n.* **4.** a stalwart person, esp. a supporter. [Old English *stǣlwirthe* serviceable, from *stǣl,* shortened from *stathol* support + *wierthe* WORTH[1]] —'**stalwartly** *adv.* —'**stalwartness** *n.*

stamen ('steɪmɛn) *n., pl.* **stamens** *or* **stamina** ('stæmɪnə). the male reproductive organ of a flower, consisting of a stalk (filament) bearing an anther in which pollen is produced. [C17: from Latin: the warp in an upright loom, from *stāre* to stand] —**staminal** ('stæmɪnəl) *adj.* —**staminiferous** (ˌstæmɪ'nɪfərəs) *adj.*

stamina[1] ('stæmɪnə) *n.* enduring energy, strength, and resilience. [C19: identical with STAMINA[2], from Latin *stāmen* thread, hence the threads of life spun out by the Fates, hence energy, etc.] —'**staminal** *adj.*

stamina[2] ('stæmɪnə) *n.* a plural of **stamen.**

staminate ('stæmɪnɪt, -ˌneɪt) *adj.* (of plants) having stamens, esp. having stamens but no carpels; male. [C19: from Latin *stāminātus* consisting of threads. See STAMEN, -ATE[1]]

staminode ('stæmɪˌnəʊd) *or* **staminodium** (ˌstæmɪ'nəʊdɪəm) *n., pl.* **-nodes** *or* **-nodia** (-'nəʊdɪə). a vestigial stamen that produces no pollen. [C19: from STAMEN + -ODE[1]]

staminody ('stæmɪˌnəʊdɪ) *n.* the development of any of various plant organs, such as petals or sepals, into stamens.

stammel ('stæməl) *n.* **1.** a coarse woollen cloth in former use for undergarments, etc., and usually dyed red. **2.** the bright red colour of this cloth. [C16: from Old French *estamin,* from Latin *stāmineus* made of threads, from *stāmen* a thread; see STAMEN]

stammer ('stæmə) *vb.* **1.** to speak or say (something) in a hesitant way, esp. as a result of a speech disorder or through fear, stress, etc. ~*n.* **2.** a speech disorder characterized by involuntary repetitions and hesitations. [Old English *stamerian;* related to Old Saxon *stamarōn,* Old High German *stamm*] —'**stammerer** *n.* —'**stammering** *n., adj.* —'**stammeringly** *adv.*

stamp (stæmp) *vb.* **1.** (when *intr.,* often foll. by *on*) to bring (the foot) down heavily (on the ground, etc.). **2.** (*intr.*) to walk with heavy or noisy footsteps. **3.** (*intr.;* foll. by *on*) to repress, extinguish, or eradicate: *he stamped on any criticism.* **4.** (*tr.*) to impress or mark (a particular device or sign) on (something). **5.** to mark (something) with an official impress, seal, or device: *to stamp a passport.* **6.** (*tr.*) to fix or impress permanently: *the date was stamped on her memory.* **7.** (*tr.*) to affix a postage stamp to. **8.** (*tr.*) to distinguish or reveal: *that behaviour stamps him as a cheat.* **9.** to pound or crush (ores, etc.). ~*n.* **10.** the act or an instance of stamping. **11. a.** See **postage stamp. b.** a mark applied to postage stamps for cancellation purposes. **12.** a similar piece of gummed paper used for commercial or trading purposes. **13.** a block, die, etc., used for imprinting a design or device. **14.** a design, device, or mark that has been stamped. **15.** a characteristic feature or trait; hallmark: *the story had the stamp of authenticity.* **16.** a piece of gummed paper or other mark applied to official documents to indicate payment of a fee, validity, ownership, etc. **17.** *Brit. informal.* a national insurance contribution, formerly recorded by means of a stamp on an official card. **18.** type or class: *we want to employ men of his stamp.* **19.** an instrument or machine for crushing or pounding ores, etc., or the pestle in such a device. ~See also **stamp out.** [Old English *stampe;* related to Old High German *stampfōn* to stamp, Old Norse *stappa*] —'**stamper** *n.*

stamp collecting *n.* another name for **philately.** —**stamp collector** *n.*

stamp duty *or* **tax** *n.* a tax on legal documents, publications, etc., the payment of which is certified by the attaching or impressing of official stamps.

stampede (stæm'piːd) *n.* **1.** an impulsive headlong rush of startled cattle or horses. **2.** headlong rush of a crowd: *a stampede of shoppers.* **3.** any sudden large-scale movement or other action, such as a rush of people to support a candidate. ~*vb.* **4.** to run away or cause to run away in a stampede. [C19: from American Spanish *estampida,* from Spanish: a din, from *estampar* to stamp, of Germanic origin; see STAMP] —**stam'peder** *n.*

stamping ground *n.* a habitual or favourite meeting or gathering place.

stamp mill *n. Metallurgy.* a machine for crushing ore.

stamp out *vb.* (*tr., adv.*) **1.** to put out or extinguish by stamping: *to stamp out a fire.* **2.** to crush or suppress by force: *to stamp out a rebellion.*

stance (stæns, stɑːns) *n.* **1.** the manner and position in which a person or animal stands. **2.** *Sport.* the posture assumed when about to play the ball, as in golf, cricket, etc. **3.** general emotional or intellectual attitude: *a leftist stance.* **4.** *Scot.* a place where buses or taxis wait. **5.** *Mountaineering.* a place at the top of a pitch where a climber can stand and belay. [C16: via French from Italian *stanza* place for standing, from Latin *stāns,* from *stāre* to stand]

stanch (stɑːntʃ) *or* **staunch** (stɔːntʃ) *vb.* **1.** to stem the flow of (a liquid, esp. blood) or (of a liquid) to stop flowing. **2.** to prevent the flow of a liquid, esp. blood, from (a hole, wound, etc.). **3.** an archaic word for **assuage.** ~*n.* **4.** a primitive form of lock in which boats are carried over shallow parts of a river in a rush of water released by the lock. [C14: from Old French *estanchier,* from Vulgar Latin *stanticāre* (unattested) to cause to stand, from Latin *stāre* to stand, halt] —'**stanchable** *or* '**staunchable** *adj.* —'**stancher** *or* '**stauncher** *n.*

stanchion ('stɑːnʃən) *n.* **1.** any vertical pole, beam, rod, etc., used as a support. ~*vb.* **2.** (*tr.*) to provide or support with a stanchion or stanchions. [C14: from Old French *estanchon,* from *estance,* from Vulgar Latin *stantia* (unattested) a standing, from Latin *stāre* to stand]

stand (stænd) *vb.* **stands, standing, stood.** (*mainly intr.*) **1.** (*also tr.*) to be or cause to be in an erect or upright position. **2.** to rise to, assume, or maintain an upright position. **3.** (*copula*) to have a specified height when standing: *to stand six feet.* **4.** to be situated or located: *the house stands in the square.* **5.** to be or exist in a specified state or condition: *to stand in awe of someone.* **6.** to adopt or remain in a resolute position or attitude. **7.** (*may take an infinitive*) to be in a specified position: *I stand to lose money in this venture; he stands high in the president's favour.* **8.** to remain in force or continue in effect: *whatever the difficulties, my orders stand.* **9.** to come to a stop or halt, esp. temporarily. **10.** (of water, etc.) to collect and remain without flowing. **11.** (often foll. by *at*) (of a score, account, etc.) to indicate the specified position of the parties involved: *the score stands at 20 to 1.* **12.** (*also tr.;* when *intr.,* foll. by *for*) to tolerate or bear: *I won't stand for your nonsense any longer; I can't stand spiders.* **13.** (*tr.*) to resist; survive: *to stand the test of time.* **14.** (*tr.*) to submit to: *to stand trial.* **15.** (often foll. by *for*) *Chiefly Brit.* to be or become a candidate: *will he stand for Parliament?* **16.** to navigate in a specified direction: *we were standing for Madeira when the storm broke.* **17.** (of a gun dog) to point at game. **18.** to halt, esp. to give action, repel attack, or disrupt an enemy advance when retreating. **19.** (of a male domestic animal, esp. a stallion) to be available as a stud. **20.** (*also tr.*) *Printing.* to keep (type that has been set) or (of such type) to be kept, for possible use in future printings. **21.** (*tr.*) *Informal.* to bear the cost of; pay for: *to stand someone a drink.* **22. stand a chance.** to have a hope or likelihood of winning, succeeding, etc. **23. stand fast.** to maintain one's position firmly. **24. stand one's ground.** to maintain a stance or position in the face of opposition. **25. stand still. a.** to remain motionless. **b.** (foll. by *for*) *U.S.* to tolerate: *I won't stand still for your threats.* **26. stand to (someone).** *Irish informal.* to be useful to (someone): *your knowledge of English will stand to you.* ~*n.* **27.** the act or an instance of standing. **28.** an opinion, esp. a resolutely held one: *he took a stand on capital* *punishment.* **29.** a halt or standstill. **30.** a place where a person or thing stands. **31.** *Austral. and N.Z.* **a.** a position on the floor of a shearing shed allocated to one shearer. **b.** the shearing equipment belonging to such a position. **32.** a structure, usually of wood, on which people can sit or stand. **33.** a frame or rack on which such articles as coats and hats may be hung. **34.** a small table or piece of furniture where articles may be placed or stored: *a music stand.* **35.** a supporting framework, esp. for a tool or instrument. **36.** a stall, booth, or counter from which goods may be sold. **37.** an exhibition area in a trade fair. **38.** a halt to give action, etc., esp. one taken during a retreat and having some duration or some success. **39.** *Cricket.* an extended period at the wicket by two batsmen. **40.** a growth of plants in a particular area, esp. trees in a forest or a crop in a field. **41.** a stop made by a touring theatrical company, pop group, etc., to give a performance (esp. in the phrase **one-night stand**). **42.** *S. African.* a plot or site earmarked for the erection of a building. **43.** (of a gun dog) the act of pointing at game. **44.** a complete set, esp. of arms or armour for one man. **45. stand of colours.** *Military.* the flags of a regiment. ~See also **stand by, stand down, stand for, stand in, standoff, stand on, stand out, stand over, stand pat, stand to, stand up.** [Old English *standan;* related to Old Norse *standa,* Old High German *stantan,* Latin *stāre* to stand; see STEAD] —'**stander** *n.*

stand-alone *adj. Computer technol.* (of a device or system) capable of operating independently of any other device or system.

standard ('stændəd) *n.* **1.** an accepted or approved example of something against which others are judged or measured. **2.** (*often pl.*) a principle of propriety, honesty, and integrity: *she has no standards.* **3.** a level of excellence or quality: *a low standard of living.* **4.** any distinctive flag, device, etc., as of a nation, sovereign, or special cause. **5. a.** any of a variety of naval or military flags. **b.** the colours of a cavalry regiment. **6.** a flag or emblem formerly used to show the central or rallying point of an army in battle. **7.** a large tapering flag ending in two points, originally borne by a sovereign or high-ranking noble. **8.** the commodity or commodities in which is stated the value of a basic monetary unit: *the gold standard.* **9.** an authorized model of a unit of measure or weight. **10.** a unit of board measure equal to 1980 board feet. **11.** (in coinage) the prescribed proportion by weight of precious metal and base metal that each coin must contain. **12.** an upright pole or beam, esp. one used as a support. **13. a.** a piece of furniture consisting of an upright pole or beam on a base or support. **b.** (*as modifier*): *a standard lamp.* **14. a.** a plant, esp. a fruit tree, that is trained so that it has an upright stem free of branches. **b.** (*as modifier*): *a standard cherry.* **15.** the largest petal of a papilionaceous flower, such as a sweetpea. **16.** (in New Zealand and, formerly, in England and Wales) a class or level of attainment in an elementary school. ~*adj.* **17.** of the usual, regularized, medium, or accepted kind: *a standard size.* **18.** of recognized authority, competence, or excellence: *the standard work on Greece.* **19.** denoting or characterized by idiom, vocabulary, etc., that is regarded as correct and acceptable by educated native speakers. Compare **nonstandard, informal.** **20.** *Brit.* (formerly) (of eggs) of a size that is smaller than *large* and larger than *medium.* [C12: from Old French *estandart* gathering place, flag to mark such a place, probably of Germanic origin; compare Old High German *stantan* to stand, Old High German *ort* place]

standard amenities *pl. n.* (in Britain) *Social welfare.* the sanitary facilities recommended for all dwellings by the housing law: a fixed bath or shower, wash-hand basin, and sink, all supplied with hot and cold water, and a flush toilet.

standard assessment tasks *pl. n. Brit. Education.* externally devised assessments in core subjects which complement those carried out by teachers. Abbrev.: **SATS** ('sæts).

standard-bearer *n.* **1.** an officer or man who carries a standard. **2.** a leader of a cause or party.

standard-bred *n.* a U.S. and Canadian breed of trotting and pacing horse, used esp. for harness-racing. [C19: so called because they are bred to attain a prescribed standard of speed]

standard candle *n.* another name for **candela:** not in scientific usage because of possible confusion with the former **international candle.**

standard cell *n.* a voltaic cell producing a constant and accurately known electromotive force that can be used to calibrate voltage-measuring instruments.

standard cost *n. Accounting.* the predetermined budgeted cost of a regular manufacturing process against which actual costs are compared.

standard deviation *n. Statistics.* a measure of dispersion obtained by extracting the square root of the mean of the squared deviations of the observed values from their mean in a frequency distribution.

standard error *n. Statistics.* the estimated standard deviation of a parameter, the value of which is not known exactly.

standard function *n. Computer technol.* a subprogram provided by a translator that carries out a task, for example the computation of a mathematical function, such as sine, square root, etc.

standard gauge *n.* **1.** a railway track with a distance of 4 ft. 8½ in. (1.435 m) between the lines; used on most railways. See also **narrow gauge, broad gauge.** ~*adj.* **standard-gauge** *or* **standard-gauged. 2.** of, relating to, or denoting a railway with a standard gauge.

Standard Grade *n.* (in Scotland) a type of examination designed to test skills and the application of knowledge, replacing O grade.

standard housing benefit *n.* (in Britain) *Social welfare.* a rebate of a proportion of a person's eligible housing costs paid by a local authority and calculated on the basis of level of income and family size.

standardize *or* **standardise** ('stændəˌdaɪz) *vb.* **1.** to make or become standard. **2.** (*tr.*) to test by or compare with a standard. —ˌ**standardi'zation** *or* ˌ**standardi'sation** *n.* —'**standardˌizer** *or* '**standardˌiser** *n.*

standard model *n. Physics.* a theory of fundamental interactions in which the electromagnetic, weak, and strong interactions are described in terms of the exchange of virtual particles.

standard normal distribution *n. Statistics.* a normal distribution with mean zero and variance 1, with probability density function $[\exp(-\frac{1}{2}x^2)]/\sqrt{2\pi}$.

standard of living *n.* a level of subsistence or material welfare of a community, class, or person.

standard scratch score. *n. Golf.* the number of strokes a scratch player would need to go round a particular course, based on the length of each hole to the green and allowing 35 putts for the round.

standard time *n.* the official local time of a region or country determined by the distance from Greenwich of a line of longitude passing through the area.

stand by *vb.* **1.** (*intr., adv.*) to be available and ready to act if needed or called upon. **2.** (*intr., adv.*) to be present as an onlooker or without taking any action: *he stood by at the accident.* **3.** (*intr., prep.*) to be faithful to: *to stand by one's principles.* **4.** (*tr., adv.*) *English law.* (of the Crown) to challenge (a juror) without needing to show cause. ~*n.* **stand-by. 5. a.** a person or thing that is ready for use or can be relied on in an emergency. **b.** (*as modifier*): *stand-by provisions.* **6. on stand-by.** in a state of readiness for action or use. ~*adj.* **7.** (of an airline passenger, fare, or seat) not booked in advance but awaiting or subject to availability.

stand down *vb.* (*adv.*) **1.** (*intr.*) to resign or withdraw, esp. in favour of another. **2.** (*intr.*) to leave the witness box in a court of law after giving evidence. **3.** *Chiefly Brit.* to go or be taken off duty.

standee (stæn'diː) *n.* a person who stands, esp. when there are no vacant seats.

standfast ('stændˌfɑːst) *n. Rare.* a fixed position. [C19: from STAND + FAST[1] (in the sense: firm, secure)]

stand for *vb.* (*intr., prep.*) **1.** to represent or mean. **2.** *Chiefly Brit.* to be or become a candidate for. **3.** to support or recommend. **4.** *Informal.* to tolerate or bear: *he won't stand for any disobedience.*

stand in *vb.* **1.** (*intr., adv.;* usually foll. by *for*) to act as a substitute. **2. stand (someone) in good stead.** to be of benefit or advantage to (someone). ~*n.* **stand-in. 3. a.** a person or thing that serves as a substitute. **b.** (*as modifier*): *a stand-in teacher.* **4.** a person who substitutes for an actor during intervals of waiting or in dangerous stunts.

standing ('stændɪŋ) *n.* **1.** social or financial position, status, or reputation: *a man of some standing.* **2.** length of existence, experience, etc. **3.** (*modifier*) used to stand in or on: *standing room.* ~*adj.* **4.** *Athletics.* **a.** (of the start of a race) begun from a standing position without the use of starting blocks. **b.** (of a jump, leap, etc.) performed from a stationary position without a run-up. **5.** (*prenominal*) permanent, fixed, or lasting. **6.** (*prenominal*) still or stagnant: *a standing pond.* **7.** *Printing.* (of type) set and stored for future use. Compare **dead** (sense 17).

standing army *n.* a permanent army of paid soldiers maintained by a nation.

standing chop *n. N.Z.* (in an axemen's competition) a chop with the log standing upright. Compare **underhand chop.**

standing committee *n.* a permanent committee appointed to deal with a specified subject.

standing order *n.* **1.** Also called: **banker's order.** an instruction to a bank by a depositor to pay a stated sum at regular intervals. Compare **direct debit. 2.** a rule or order governing the procedure, conduct, etc., of a legislative body. **3.** *Military.* one of a number of orders which have or are likely to have long-term validity.

standing rigging *n.* the stays, shrouds, and other more or less fixed, though adjustable, wires and ropes that support the masts of a sailing vessel. Compare **running rigging.**

standing wave *n. Physics.* the periodic disturbance in a medium resulting from the combination of two waves of equal frequency and intensity travelling in opposite directions. There are generally two kinds of displacement, and the maximum value of the amplitude of one of these occurs at the same points as the minimum value of the amplitude of the other. Thus in the case of electromagnetic radiation the amplitude of the oscillations of the electric field has its greatest value at the points where the magnetic oscillation is zero, and vice versa. Also called: **stationary wave.** Compare **node, antinode.**

standish ('stændɪʃ) *n.* a stand, usually of metal, for pens, ink bottles, etc. [C15: of unknown origin]

standoff (ˈstænd,ɒf) *n.* **1.** *U.S. and Canadian.* the act or an instance of standing off or apart. **2.** a deadlock or stalemate. **3.** any situation or disposition of forces that counterbalances or neutralizes. **4.** *Rugby.* short for **stand-off half.** ~*vb.* **stand off** (*adv.*) **5.** (*intr.*) to navigate a vessel so as to avoid the shore, an obstruction, etc. **6.** (*tr.*) to keep or cause to keep at a distance. **7.** (*intr.*) to reach a deadlock or stalemate. **8.** (*tr.*) to dismiss (workers), esp. temporarily.

stand-off half *n. Rugby.* **1.** a player who acts as a link between his scrum half and three-quarter backs and who marks the opposing scrum half. **2.** this position in a team. ~Also called: **fly half.**

standoffish (,stændˈɒfɪʃ) *adj.* reserved, haughty, or aloof. —,**standˈoffishly** *adv.* —,**standˈoffishness** *n.*

standoff missile *n.* a missile capable of striking a distant target after launch by an aircraft outside the range of missile defences.

stand oil *n.* a thick drying oil made by heating linseed, tung, or soya to over 300°C: used in oil enamel paints.

stand on *vb.* (*intr.*) **1.** (*adv.*) to continue to navigate a vessel on the same heading. **2.** (*prep.*) to insist on: *to stand on ceremony.* **3. stand on one's own (two) feet.** *Informal.* to be independent or self-reliant.

stand out *vb.* (*intr., adv.*) **1.** to be distinctive or conspicuous. **2.** to refuse to agree, consent, or comply: *they stood out for a better price.* **3.** to protrude or project. **4.** to navigate a vessel away from a port, harbour, anchorage, etc. ~*n.* **standout. 5.** *U.S. and Canadian informal.* a person or thing that is distinctive or outstanding. **6.** a person who refuses to agree or consent.

stand over *vb.* **1.** (*intr., prep.*) to watch closely; keep tight control over. **2.** (*adv.*) to postpone or be postponed. **3.** (*intr., prep.*) *Austral. and N.Z. informal.* to threaten or intimidate (a person). ~*n.* **standover. 4.** *Austral. and N.Z. informal.* a threatening or intimidating act.

standover man (ˈstænd,əʊvə) *n. Austral. informal.* a person who extorts money by intimidation.

stand pat *vb.* (*intr.*) **1.** *Poker.* to refuse the right to change any of one's cards; keep one's hand unchanged. **2.** to resist change or remain unchanged. —**standˈpatter** *n.*

standpipe (ˈstænd,paɪp) *n.* **1.** a vertical pipe, open at the upper end, attached to a pipeline or tank serving to limit the pressure head to that of the height of the pipe. **2.** a temporary freshwater outlet installed in a street during a period when household water supplies are cut off.

standpoint (ˈstænd,pɔɪnt) *n.* a physical or mental position from which things are viewed.

standstill (ˈstænd,stɪl) *n.* a complete cessation of movement; stop; halt: *the car came to a standstill.*

standstill agreement *n.* an agreement that preserves the status quo, esp. one between two countries when one country cannot pay its debts to the other that a certain fixed extension of time will be given to repay the debts.

stand to *vb.* **1.** (*adv.*) *Military.* to assume positions or cause to assume positions to resist a possible attack. **2. stand to reason.** to conform with the dictates of reason: *it stands to reason that pigs can't fly.*

stand up *vb.* (*adv.*) **1.** (*intr.*) to rise to the feet. **2.** (*intr.*) to resist or withstand wear, criticism, etc. **3.** (*tr.*) *Informal.* to fail to keep an appointment with, esp. intentionally. **4. stand up for. a.** to support, side with, or defend. **b.** *U.S.* to serve as best man for (the groom) at a wedding. **5. stand up to. a.** to confront or resist courageously. **b.** to withstand or endure (wear, criticism, etc.). ~*adj.* **stand-up.** (*prenominal*) **6.** having or being in an erect position: *a stand-up collar.* **7.** done, performed, taken, etc., while standing: *a stand-up meal.* **8.** (of a comedian) performing solo, while standing before an audience. **9.** *Informal.* (of a boxer) having an aggressive style without much leg movement: *a stand-up fighter.*

stane (stein) *n.* a Scot. word for **stone.**

Stanford-Binet test (ˈstænfədbɪˈneɪ) *n. Psychol.* a revision, esp. for U.S. use, of the Binet-Simon scale designed to measure mental ability by comparing the performance of an individual with the average performance for his age group. See also **Binet-Simon scale, intelligence test.** [C20: named after *Stanford University,* California, and Alfred *Binet* (1857–1911), French psychologist]

stang[1] (stæŋ) *vb. Archaic or dialect.* a past tense of **sting.**

stang[2] (stæŋ) *Scot. and northern English dialect.* ~*vb.* **1.** to throb or cause to throb with pain. ~*n.* **2.** a throbbing pain. [C18: ultimately from Old Norse *stanga* to prick, goad. Compare Old Norse *stinga* to STING]

stanhope (ˈstænəp) *n.* a light one-seater carriage with two or four wheels. [C18: named after Fitzroy *Stanhope* (1787–1864), British clergyman for whom it was first built]

stank[1] (stæŋk) *vb.* a past tense of **stink.**

stank[2] (stæŋk) *n.* **1.** a small cofferdam, esp. one of timber made watertight with clay. **2.** *Scot. and northern English dialect.* a pond or pool. ~*vb.* **3.** (*tr.*) to make (a stream, cofferdam, etc.) watertight, esp. with clay. [C13: from Old French *estanc,* probably from *estancher* to stanch]

stank[3] (stæŋk) *n. Dialect.* **1.** a drain, as in a roadway. **2.** a draining board adjacent to a sink unit. [special use of STANK[2] (in the sense: pool, pond)]

stann- *combining form.* denoting tin: *stannite.* [from Late Latin *stannum* tin]

stannary (ˈstænərɪ) *n., pl.* **-ries.** a place or region where tin is mined or worked. [C15: from Medieval Latin *stannāria,* from Late Latin: STANNUM, tin]

stannic (ˈstænɪk) *adj.* of or containing tin, esp. in the tetravalent state. [C18: from Late Latin *stannum* tin]

stannic sulphide *n.* an insoluble solid compound of tin usually existing as golden crystals or as a yellowish-brown powder: used as a pigment. Formula: SnS_2. See also **mosaic gold.**

stanniferous (stəˈnɪfərəs) *adj.* containing tin; tin-bearing. [C18: from Late Latin *stannum* tin + -FEROUS]

stannite (ˈstænaɪt) *n.* a grey metallic mineral that consists of a sulphide of tin, copper, and iron and is a source of tin. Formula: Cu_2FeSnS_4. [C19: from STANNUM + -ITE[1]]

stannous (ˈstænəs) *adj.* of or containing tin, esp. in the divalent state.

stannum (ˈstænəm) *n.* an obsolete name for **tin** (the metal). [C18: from Late Latin: tin, from Latin: alloy of silver and lead, perhaps of Celtic origin; compare Welsh *ystaen* tin]

stanza (ˈstænzə) *n.* **1.** *Prosody.* a fixed number of verse lines arranged in a definite metrical pattern, forming a unit of a poem. **2.** *U.S. and Austral.* a half or a quarter in a football match. [C16: from Italian: halting place, from Vulgar Latin *stantia* (unattested) station, from Latin *stāre* to stand] —**ˈstanzaed** *adj.* —**stanzaic** (stænˈzeɪɪk) *adj.*

stapelia (stəˈpiːlɪə) *n.* any fleshy cactus-like leafless African plant of the asclepiadaceous genus *Stapelia,* having thick four-angled stems and large typically fetid mottled flowers. [C18: from New Latin, named after J. B. van *Stapel,* (died 1636), Dutch botanist]

stapes (ˈsteɪpiːz) *n., pl.* **stapes** *or* **stapedes** (stæˈpiːdiːz). the stirrup-shaped bone that is the innermost of three small bones in the middle ear of mammals. Nontechnical name: **stirrup bone.** Compare **incus, malleus.** [C17: via New Latin from Medieval Latin, perhaps a variant of *staffa, stapeda* stirrup, influenced in form by Latin *stāre* to stand + *pēs* a foot] —**stapedial** (stæˈpiːdɪəl) *adj.*

staphylo- *combining form.* **1.** uvula: *staphyloplasty.* **2.** resembling a bunch of grapes: *staphylococcus.* [from Greek *staphulē* bunch of grapes, uvula]

staphylococcus (,stæfɪləʊˈkɒkəs) *n., pl.* **-cocci** (-ˈkɒksaɪ). any spherical Gram-positive bacterium of the genus *Staphylococcus,* typically occurring in clusters and including many pathogenic species, causing boils, infection in wounds, and septicaemia: family *Micrococcaceae.* Often shortened to **staph.** [C19: from STAPHYLO- (in the sense: like a bunch of grapes) + COCCUS; so called because of their shape] —**staphylococcal** (,stæfɪləʊˈkɒkəl) *or* **staphylococcic** (,stæfɪləʊˈkɒksɪk) *adj.*

staphyloplasty (ˈstæfɪləʊ,plæstɪ) *n.* plastic surgery or surgical repair involving the soft palate or the uvula. [C19: from STAPHYLO- + -PLASTY] —,**staphyloˈplastic** *adj.*

staphylorrhaphy (,stæfɪˈlɒrəfɪ) *n.* repair of a cleft palate by means of staphyloplasty and suturing. [C19: from STAPHYLO- (in the sense: uvula) + Greek *raphē* a sewing or suture] —**staphylorrhaphic** (,stæfɪlɒˈræfɪk) *adj.*

staple[1] (ˈsteɪpəl) *n.* **1.** a short length of thin wire bent into a square U-shape, used to fasten papers, cloth, etc. **2.** a short length of stiff wire formed into a U-shape with pointed ends, used for holding a hasp to a post, securing electric cables, etc. ~*vb.* **3.** (*tr.*) to secure (papers, wire, etc.) with a staple or staples. [Old English *stapol* prop, of Germanic origin; related to Middle Dutch *stapel* step, Old High German *staffal*]

staple[2] (ˈsteɪpəl) *adj.* **1.** of prime importance; principal: *staple foods.* **2.** (of a commodity) forming a predominant element in the product, consumption, or trade of a specified nation, region, etc. ~*n.* **3.** a staple commodity. **4.** a main constituent; integral part. **5.** *Chiefly U.S. and Canadian.* a principal raw material produced or grown in a region. **6.** the fibre of wool, cotton, etc., graded as to length and degree of fineness. **7.** (in medieval Europe) a town specially appointed to be the exclusive market for one or more major exports of the land. ~*vb.* **8.** (*tr.*) to arrange or sort (wool, cotton, etc.) according to length and fineness. [C15: from Middle Dutch *stapel* warehouse; see STAPLE[1]]

staple gun *n.* a mechanism that fixes staples to a surface.

stapler (ˈsteɪplə) *n.* a machine that inserts staples into sheets of paper, etc., to hold them together.

star (stɑː) *n.* **1.** any of a vast number of celestial objects that are visible in the clear night sky as points of light. **2. a.** a hot gaseous mass, such as the sun, that radiates energy, esp. as heat and light, usually derived from thermonuclear reactions in the interior, and in some cases as radio waves and x-rays. The surface temperature can range from about 1500 to 100 000°C. See also **Hertzsprung-Russell diagram, giant star, white dwarf, neutron star, black hole. b.** (*as modifier*): *a star catalogue.* Related adjs.: **astral, sidereal, stellar. 3.** *Astrology.* **a.** a celestial body, esp. a planet, supposed to influence events, personalities, etc. **b.** (*pl.*) another name for **horoscope** (sense 1). **4.** an emblem shaped like a conventionalized star, usually with five or more points, often used as a symbol of rank, an award, etc. **5.** a small white blaze on the forehead of an animal, esp. a horse. **6.** Also called: **star facet.** any of the eight triangular facets cut in the crown of a brilliant. **7. a.** a distinguished or glamorous celebrity, often from the entertainment world. **b.** (*as modifier*): *star quality.* **8.** another word for **asterisk. 9.** *Prison slang.* a convict serving his first prison sentence. **10. see stars.** to see or seem to see bright moving pinpoints of light, as from a blow on the head, increased blood pressure, etc. ~*vb.* **stars, starring, starred.** **11.** (*tr.*) to mark or decorate with a star or stars. **12.** to feature or be featured as a star: *"Greed" starred Erich von Stroheim; Olivier starred in "Hamlet".* [Old English *steorra;* related to Old Frisian *stēra,* Old Norse *stjarna,* German *Stern,* Latin *stella*] —'**starless** *adj.* —'**star,like** *adj.*

star-apple *n.* **1.** a West Indian sapotaceous tree, *Chrysophyllum cainito,* with smooth-skinned edible greenish-purple fruit. **2.** the fruit of this tree which, when cut across, reveals a star-shaped arrangement of seeds.

starboard ('stɑːbəd, -ˌbɔːd) *n.* **1.** the right side of an aeroplane or vessel when facing the nose or bow. Compare **port**[2]. ~*adj.* **2.** relating to or on the starboard. ~*vb.* **3.** to turn or be turned towards the starboard. [Old English *stēorbord,* literally: steering side, from *stēor* steering paddle + *bord* side; see STEER[1], BOARD; from the fact that boats were formerly steered by a paddle held over the right-hand side]

starch (stɑːtʃ) *n.* **1.** a polysaccharide composed of glucose units that occurs widely in plant tissues in the form of storage granules, consisting of amylose and amylopectin. **2.** Also called: **amylum.** a starch obtained from potatoes and some grain: it is fine white powder that forms a translucent viscous solution on boiling with water and is used to stiffen fabric and in many industrial processes. **3.** any food containing a large amount of starch, such as rice and potatoes. **4.** stiff or pompous formality of manner or conduct. ~*vb.* **5.** (*tr.*) to stiffen with or soak in starch. ~*adj.* **6.** (of a person) formal; stiff. [Old English *stercan* (unattested except by the past participle *sterced*) to stiffen; related to Old Saxon *sterkian,* Old High German *sterken* to strengthen, Dutch *sterken;* see STARK] —'**starcher** *n.* —'**starch,like** *adj.*

Star Chamber *n.* **1.** *English history.* the Privy Council sitting as a court of equity, esp. powerful under the Tudor monarchs; abolished 1641. **2.** (*sometimes not caps.*) any arbitrary tribunal dispensing summary justice. **3.** (*sometimes not caps.*) (in Britain, in a Conservative government) a group of senior ministers who make the final decision on the public spending of each government department.

starch-reduced *adj.* (of food, esp. bread) having the starch content reduced, as in proprietary slimming products.

starchy ('stɑːtʃɪ) *adj.* **starchier, starchiest.** **1.** of, relating to, or containing starch: *starchy foods.* **2.** extremely formal, stiff, or conventional: *a starchy manner.* **3.** stiffened with starch. —'**starchily** *adv.* —'**starchiness** *n.*

star connection *n.* a connection used in a polyphase electrical device or system of devices in which the windings each have one end connected to a common junction, the **star point,** and the other end to a separate terminal. See also **Y connection.** Compare **delta connection.**

star-crossed *adj.* dogged by ill luck; destined to misfortune. [C16: from CROSS (in the sense: thwart): so called because of the astrological belief that the stars affect people's destinies]

stardom ('stɑːdəm) *n.* **1.** the fame and prestige of being a star in films, sport, etc. **2.** the world of celebrities.

stardust ('stɑːˌdʌst) *n.* **1.** a large number of distant stars appearing to the observer as a cloud of dust. **2.** a dreamy romantic or sentimental quality or feeling.

stare[1] (stɛə) *vb.* **1.** (*intr.*) (often foll. by *at*) to look or gaze fixedly, often with hostility or rudeness. **2.** (*intr.*) (of an animal's fur, bird's feathers, etc.) to stand on end because of fear, ill health, etc. **3.** (*intr.*) to stand out as obvious; glare. **4. stare one in the face.** to be glaringly obvious or imminent. ~*n.* **5.** the act or an instance of staring. [Old English *starian;* related to Old Norse *stara,* Old High German *starēn* to stare, Greek *stereos* stiff, Latin *consternāre* to confuse] —'**starer** *n.*

stare[2] (stɛə) *n. Dialect.* a starling. [Old English *stær*]

stare out *or* **down** *vb.* (*tr., adv.*) to look at (a person or animal) fixedly until his gaze is turned away.

starfish ('stɑːˌfɪʃ) *n., pl.* **-fish** *or* **-fishes.** any echinoderm of the class *Asteroidea,* such as *Asterias rubens,* typically having a flattened body covered with a flexible test and five arms radiating from a central disc.

starflower ('stɑːˌflaʊə) *n.* any of several plants with starlike flowers, esp. the star-of-Bethlehem.

star fruit *n.* another name for **carambola.**

stargaze ('stɑːˌgeɪz) *vb.* (*intr.*) **1.** to observe the stars. **2.** to daydream. —'**star,gazer** *n.* —'**star,gazing** *n., adj.*

star grass *n.* any of various temperate and tropical plants of the amaryllidaceous genus *Hypoxis,* having long grasslike leaves and yellow star-shaped flowers.

stark (stɑːk) *adj.* **1.** (*usually prenominal*) devoid of any elaboration; blunt: *the stark facts.* **2.** grim; desolate: *a stark landscape.* **3.** (*usually prenominal*) utter; absolute: *stark folly.* **4.** *Archaic.* severe; violent. **5.** *Archaic or poetic.* rigid, as in death (esp. in the phrases **stiff and stark, stark dead**). **6.** short for **stark-naked.** ~*adv.* **7.** completely: *stark mad.* **8.** *Rare.* starkly. [Old English *stearc* stiff; related to Old Norse *sterkr,* Gothic *gastaurknan* to stiffen] —'**starkly** *adv.* —'**starkness** *n.*

stark-naked *adj.* completely naked. Informal word (*postpositive*): **starkers** ('stɑːkəz). [C13 *stert naket,* literally: tail naked; *stert,* from Old English *steort* tail; related to Old Norse *stertr* tail + NAKED]

starlet ('stɑːlɪt) *n.* **1.** a young and inexperienced actress who is projected as a potential star. **2.** a small star.

starlight ('stɑːˌlaɪt) *n.* **1.** the light emanating from the stars. ~*adj. also* **starlighted. 2.** of or like starlight. **3.** Also: **starlit** ('stɑːˌlɪt). illuminated by starlight.

starling[1] ('stɑːlɪŋ) *n.* any gregarious passerine songbird of the Old World family *Sturnidae,* esp. *Sturnus vulgaris,* which has a blackish plumage and a short tail. [Old English *stærlinc,* from *stær* starling (related to Icelandic *stari*) + *-line* -LING[1]]

starling[2] ('stɑːlɪŋ) *n.* an arrangement of piles that surround a pier of a bridge to protect it from debris, etc. [C17: probably changed from *staddling,* from STADDLE]

star-nosed mole *n.* an E North American amphibious mole, *Condylura cristata,* having a ring of pink fleshy tentacles around the nose.

star-of-Bethlehem ('bɛθlɪˌhɛm, -lɪəm) *n.* **1.** Also called: **star-flower.** a Eurasian liliaceous plant, *Ornithogalum umbellatum,* naturalized in the eastern U.S., having narrow leaves and starlike white flowers. **2.** any of several similar and related plants.

Star of Bethlehem *n.* the star that is supposed to have appeared above Bethlehem at the birth of Christ.

Star of Courage *n.* a Canadian award for bravery.

Star of David ('deɪvɪd) *n.* an emblem symbolizing Judaism and consisting of a six-pointed star formed by superimposing one inverted equilateral triangle upon another of equal size. Also called: **Magen David.**

starred (stɑːd) *adj.* **a.** having luck or fortune as specified. **b.** (*in combination*): *ill-starred.*

star ruby *n.* a ruby that resembles a starlike figure in reflected light because of its crystalline structure.

starry ('stɑːrɪ) *adj.* **-rier, -riest.** **1.** filled, covered with, or illuminated by stars. **2.** of, like, or relating to a star or stars. —'**starrily** *adv.* —'**starriness** *n.*

starry-eyed *adj.* given to naive wishes, judgments, etc.; full of unsophisticated optimism; gullible.

Stars and Bars *n.* (*functioning as sing.*) **the.** the flag of the Confederate States of America.

Stars and Stripes *n.* (*functioning as sing.*) **the.** the national flag of the United States of America, consisting of 50 white stars representing the present states on a blue field and seven red and six white horizontal stripes representing the original states. Also called: the **Star-Spangled Banner.**

star sapphire *n.* a sapphire showing a starlike figure in reflected light because of its crystalline structure.

star shell *n.* an artillery shell containing a flare or other illuminant: often containing a parachute to prolong the descent of the illuminating material.

star-spangled *adj.* marked or decorated with stars.

Star-Spangled Banner *n.* **the.** **1.** the national anthem of the United States of America. **2.** another term for the **Stars and Stripes.**

star stream *n.* one of two main streams of stars that, because of the rotation of the Milky Way, appear to move in opposite directions, one towards Orion, the other towards Ara.

star-studded *adj.* featuring a large proportion of well-known actors or other performers: *a star-studded cast.*

star system *n.* **1.** *Astronomy.* a group of celestial bodies that are associated as a result of natural laws. **2.** the practice of casting one or two famous actors or actresses in a film, play, etc., so that their popularity ensures its success. **3.** a design for laying cables for cable television in which each house is fed by an individual cable from a local central distribution point.

start (stɑːt) *vb.* **1.** to begin or cause to begin (something or to do something); come or cause to come into being, operation, etc.: *he started a quarrel; they started to work.* **2.** (when *intr.,* sometimes foll. by *on*) to make or cause to make a beginning of (a process, series of actions, etc.): *they started on the project.* **3.** (sometimes foll. by *up*) to set or be set in motion: *he started up the machine.* **4.** (*intr.*) to make a sudden involuntary movement of one's body, from or as if from fright; jump. **5.** (*intr.;* sometimes foll. by *up, away,* etc.) to spring or jump suddenly from a position or place. **6.** to establish or be established; set up: *to start a business.* **7.** (*tr.*) to support (someone) in the first part of a venture, career, etc. **8.** to work or cause to work loose. **9.** to enter or be entered in a race. **10.** (*intr.*) to flow violently from a source: *wine started from a hole in the cask.* **11.** (*tr.*) to rouse (game) from a hiding place, lair, etc. **12.** (*intr.*) (esp. of eyes) to bulge; pop. **13.** an archaic word for **startle.** **14.** (*intr.*) *Brit. informal.* to commence quarrelling or causing a disturbance. **15. to start with.** in the first place. ~*n.* **16.** the first or first part of a series of actions or operations, a journey, etc. **17.** the place or time of starting, as of a race or performance. **18.** a signal to proceed, as in a race. **19.** a lead or advantage, either in time or distance and usually of specified extent, in a competitive activity: *he had an hour's start on me.* **20.** a slight involuntary movement of the body, as through fright, surprise, etc.: *she gave a start as I entered.* **21.** an opportunity to enter a career, undertake a project, etc. **22.** *Informal.* a surprising incident. **23.** a part that has come loose or been disengaged. **24. by fits and starts.** spasmodically; without concerted effort. **25. for a start.** in the first place. ~See also **start in, start off, start on, start out, start up.** [Old English *styrtan;* related to Old Norse *sterta* to crease, Old High German *sturzen* to rush]

START (stɑːt) *n. acronym for* Strategic Arms Reduction Talks.

starter ('stɑːtə) *n.* **1.** Also called: **self-starter.** a device for starting an internal-combustion engine, usually consisting of a powerful electric motor that engages with the flywheel. **2.** *U.S.* a person who organizes the timely departure of buses, trains, etc. **3.** a person who supervises and signals the start of a race. **4.** a competitor who starts in a race or contest. **5.** *Austral. and N.Z. informal.* an acceptable or practicable proposition, plan, idea, etc. **6.** *Austral. and N.Z. informal.* a person who is willing to engage in a particular activity. **7.** a culture of bacteria used to start fermentation, as in making cheese or yoghurt. **8.** *Chiefly Brit.* the first course of a meal. **9.** (*modifier*) designed to be used by a novice: *a starter kit.* **10. for starters.** *Slang.* in the first place. **11. under starter's orders. a.** (of horses in a race) awaiting the start signal. **b.** (of a person) eager or ready to begin.

starter home *n.* a compact flat or house marketed by price and size specifications to suit the requirements of first-time home buyers.

star thistle *n.* any of several plants of the genus *Centaurea,* esp. *C. calcitrapa,* of Eurasia, which has spiny purplish flower heads: family *Compositae* (composites). See also **centaury** (sense 2). [C16: so called because it has a thistle-shaped flower surrounded by radiating spines]

start in *vb.* (*adv.*) to undertake (something or doing something); commence or begin.

starting block *n.* one of a pair of adjustable devices with pads or blocks against which a sprinter braces his feet in crouch starts.

starting gate *n.* **1.** a movable barrier so placed on the starting line of a racecourse that the raising of it releases all the contestants simultaneously. **2.** the U.S. name for **starting stalls.**

starting grid *n. Motor racing.* a marked section of the track at the start where the cars line up according to their times in practice, the fastest occupying the front position.

starting price *n.* (esp. in horse racing) the latest odds offered by bookmakers at the start of a race.

starting stalls *pl. n. Brit.* a line of stalls in which horses are enclosed at the start of a race and from which they are released by the simultaneous springing open of retaining barriers at the front of each stall.

startle ('stɑːtᵊl) *vb.* to be or cause to be surprised or frightened, esp. so as to start involuntarily. [Old English *steartlian* to stumble; related to Middle High German *starzen,* to strut, Norwegian *sterta* to strain oneself] —'**startler** *n.* —'**startling** *adj.* —'**startlingly** *adv.*

startle colour *n. Zoology.* a bright region of an animal's coloration, normally hidden from view and often part of a design resembling birds' eyes, etc., exposed when the animal is disturbed by a predator.

start off *vb.* (*adv.*) **1.** (*intr.*) to set out on a journey. **2.** to be or make the first step in an activity; initiate: *he started the show off with a lively song.* **3.** (*tr.*) to cause (a person) to act or do something, such as to laugh, to tell stories, etc.

start on *vb.* (*intr., prep.*) *Brit. informal.* to pick a quarrel with (someone).

start out *vb.* (*intr., adv.*) **1.** to set out on a journey. **2.** to take the first steps, as in life, one's career, etc.: *he started out as a salesman.* **3.** to take the first actions in an activity in a particular way or specified aim: *they started out wanting a house, but eventually bought a flat.*

start up *vb.* (*adv.*) **1.** to come or cause to come into being for the first time; originate. **2.** (*intr.*) to spring or jump suddenly from a position or place. **3.** to set in or go into motion, activity, etc.: *he started up the engine; the orchestra started up.* ~*adj.* **start-up. 4.** of or relating to input, usually financial, made to establish a new project or business: *a start-up mortgage.*

starvation (stɑː'veɪʃən) *n.* **a.** the act or an instance of starving or state of being starved. **b.** (*as modifier*): *a starvation diet; starvation wages.*

starve (stɑːv) *vb.* **1.** to die or cause to die from lack of food. **2.** to deprive (a person or animal) or (of a person, etc.) to be deprived of food. **3.** (*intr.*) *Informal.* to be very hungry. **4.** (foll. by *of* or *for*) to deprive or be deprived (of something necessary), esp. so as to cause suffering or malfunctioning: *the engine was starved of fuel.* **5.** (*tr.*; foll. by *into*) to bring (to) a specified condition by starving: *to starve someone into submission.* **6.** *Archaic or Brit. dialect.* to be or cause to be extremely cold. [Old English *steorfan* to die; related to Old Frisian *sterva* to die, Old High German *sterban* to die] —'**starver** *n.*

starveling ('stɑːvlɪŋ) *Archaic.* ~*n.* **1. a.** a starving or poorly fed person, animal, etc. **b.** (*as modifier*): *a starveling child.* ~*adj.* **2.** insufficient; meagre; scant. [C16: from STARVE + -LING[1]]

Star Wars *n.* (*functioning as sing.*) **1.** (in the U.S.) a proposed system of artificial satellites armed with lasers to destroy enemy missiles in space. Formal name: **Strategic Defense Initiative.** Abbrev.: **SDI. 2.** (modifier) (*sometimes not caps.*) of, relating to, or denoting this system: *Star Wars defence; star wars policy.* [C20: popularly named after the science fiction film *Star Wars* (1977) by George Lucas]

starwort ('stɑːˌwɜːt) *n.* **1.** any of several plants with star-shaped flowers, esp. the stitchwort. **2. water starwort.** any of several aquatic plants of the genus *Callitriche,* having a star-shaped rosette of floating leaves: family *Callitrichaceae.*

stash (stæʃ) ~*vb.* **1.** (*tr.*; often foll. by *away*) *Informal.* to put or store (money, valuables, etc.) in a secret place, as for safekeeping. ~*n.* **2.** *Informal, chiefly U.S. and Canadian.* a secret store or the place where this is hidden. **3.** *Slang.* drugs kept for personal consumption. [C20: origin unknown]

stashie ('stæʃɪ) *n. Scot.* a variant of **stushie.**

stasis ('steɪsɪs) *n.* **1.** *Pathol.* a stagnation in the normal flow of bodily fluids, such as the blood or urine. **2.** *Literature.* a state or condition in which there is no action or progress; static situation: *dramatic stasis.* [C18: via New Latin from Greek: a standing, from *histanai* to cause to stand; related to Latin *stāre* to stand]

stat. *abbrev. for:* **1.** (in prescriptions) immediately. [from Latin *statim*] **2.** stationary. **3.** statue. **4.** statutary. **5.** statute.

-stat *n. combining form.* indicating a device that causes something to remain stationary or constant: *thermostat.* [from Greek *-statēs,* from *histanai* to cause to stand]

statant ('steɪtᵊnt) *adj. Heraldry.* (of an animal) in profile with all four feet on the ground. [C15: from Latin, apparently from irregularly formed present participle of *stāre* to stand]

state (steɪt) *n.* **1.** the condition of a person, thing, etc., with regard to main attributes. **2.** the structure, form, or constitution of something: *a solid state.* **3.** any mode of existence. **4.** position in life or society; estate. **5.** ceremonious style, as befitting wealth or dignity: *to live in state.* **6.** a sovereign political power or community. **7.** the territory occupied by such a community. **8.** the sphere of power in such a community: *affairs of state.* **9.** (*often cap.*) one of a number of areas or communities having their own governments and forming a federation under a sovereign government, as in the U.S. **10.** (*often cap.*) the body politic of a particular sovereign power, esp. as contrasted with a rival authority such as the Church. **11.** *Obsolete.* a class or order; estate. **12.** *Informal.* a nervous, upset, or excited condition (esp. in the phrase **in a state**). **13. lie in state.** (of a body) to be placed on public view before burial. **14. state of affairs.** a situation; present circumstances or condition. ~*modifier.* **15.** controlled or financed by a state: *state university.* **16.** of, relating to, or concerning the State: *State trial.* **17.** involving ceremony or concerned with a ceremonious occasion: *state visit.* ~*vb.* (*tr.*; *may take a clause as object*) **18.** to articulate in words; utter. **19.** to declare formally or publicly: *to state one's innocence.* **20.** to resolve. [C13: from Old French *estat,* from Latin *status* a standing, from *stāre* to stand] —'**statable** *or* '**stateable** *adj.* —'**statehood** *n.*

state bank *n.* (in the U.S.) a commercial bank incorporated under a State charter and not required to be a member of the Federal Reserve System. Compare **national bank.**

state capitalism *n.* a form of capitalism in which the state owns or controls most of the means of production and other capital: often very similar to state socialism.

statecraft ('steɪtˌkrɑːft) *n.* the art of conducting public affairs; statesmanship.

stated ('steɪtɪd) *adj.* **1.** (esp. of a sum) determined by agreement; fixed. **2.** explicitly formulated or narrated: *a stated argument.* **3.** *Rare.* (of an official, etc.) appointed.

stated case *n.* another term for **case stated.**

State Department *n.* the U.S. government department in charge of foreign affairs.

state function *n. Physics.* a thermodynamic quantity that has definite values for given states of a system, such as entropy, enthalpy, free energy, etc.

state house *n. N.Z.* a house built by the government for renting.

stateless ('steɪtlɪs) *adj.* **1.** without nationality: *stateless persons.* **2.** without a state or states. **3.** *Chiefly Brit.* without ceremonial dignity. —'**statelessness** *n.*

stately ('steɪtlɪ) *adj.* **-lier, -liest. 1.** characterized by a graceful, dignified, and imposing appearance or manner. ~*adv.* **2.** in a stately manner. —'**stateliness** *n.*

stately home *n. Brit.* a large mansion, esp. one open to the public.

statement ('steɪtmənt) *n.* **1.** the act of stating. **2.** something that is stated, esp. a formal prepared announcement or reply. **3.** *Law.* a declaration of matters of fact, esp. in a pleading. **4.** an account containing a summary of bills or invoices and displaying the total amount due. **5.** an account prepared by a bank for each of its clients, usually at regular intervals, to show all credits and debits since the last account and the balance at the end of the period. **6.** *Music.* the presentation of a musical theme or idea, such as the subject of a fugue or sonata. **7.** a computer instruction written in a source language, such as FORTRAN, which is converted into one or more machine code instructions by a compiler. **8.** *Logic.* the content of a sentence that affirms or denies something and may be true or false; what is thereby affirmed or denied abstracted from the act of uttering it. Thus *I am warm* said by me and *you are warm* said to me make the same statement. Compare **proposition** (sense 2b). **9.** *Brit. education.* a legally binding account of the provisions that will be made to meet the needs of a pupil with special educational needs.

statement of attainment *n. Brit. education.* a programme of specific objectives that pupils should achieve within their own levels of attainment in a particular subject.

statement of claim *n. Law.* (in England) the first pleading made by the plaintiff in a High Court action showing the facts upon which he relies in support of his claim and the relief asked for.

state of the art *n.* **1.** the level of knowledge and development achieved in a technique, science, etc., esp. at present. ~*adj.* (*prenominal*) **state-of-the-art. 2.** the most recent and therefore considered the best; up-to-the-minute: *a state-of-the-art amplifier.*

state of war *n.* **1.** a period of armed conflict between states, regardless of whether or not war has been officially declared. **2.** a legal condition begun by a declaration of war and ended formally, during which the rules of international law applicable to warfare may be invoked.

state prayers *pl. n. Church of England.* prayers for the Sovereign, the royal family, the clergy, and Parliament said at matins and evensong.

State prison *n.* (in the U.S.) a prison where persons convicted of serious crimes are confined.

stater ('steɪtə) *n.* any of various usually silver coins of ancient Greece. [C14: via Late Latin from Greek *statēr* a standard of weight, from *histanai* to stand]

stateroom ('steɪtˌruːm, -ˌrʊm) *n.* **1.** a private cabin or room on a ship, train, etc. **2.** *Chiefly Brit.* a large room in a palace or other building for use on state occasions.

state school *n.* any school maintained by the state, in which education is free.

state services *pl. n. Church of England.* services appointed to commemorate days of national celebration or deliverance such as the accession of a sovereign.

state's evidence *n.* (in the U.S.) **1.** the evidence for the prosecution given on behalf of a state in a criminal prosecution. **2.** evidence given for the state by an accomplice against his former associates in crime (esp. in the phrase **turn state's evidence**). Brit. equivalent: **queen's** (or **king's**) **evidence.**

stateside ('steɪtˌsaɪd) *adj., adv. U.S.* of, in, to, or towards the U.S.

statesman ('steɪtsmən) *n., pl.* **-men. 1.** a political leader whose wisdom, integrity, etc., win great respect. **2.** a person active and influential in the formulation of high government policy, such as a cabinet member. **3.** a politician. —'**statesman-ˌlike** *or* '**statesmanly** *adj.* —'**statesmanship** *n.* —'**statesˌwoman** *fem. n.*

state socialism *n.* a variant of socialism in which the power of the state is employed for the purpose of creating an egalitarian society by means of public control of major industries, banks, etc., coupled with economic planning and a social security system. —**state socialist** *n.*

states' rights *pl. n.* (*often caps.*) (in the U.S.) **1.** the rights and powers generally conceded to the states, or all those powers claimed for the states under some interpretations of the Constitution. **2.** a doctrine advocating the severe curtailment of Federal powers by such an interpretation of the Constitution. —**states' righter** *n.*

state trooper *n. U.S.* a state policeman.

static ('stætɪk) *adj. also* **statical. 1.** not active or moving; stationary. **2.** (of a weight, force, or pressure) acting but causing no movement. **3.** of or concerned with forces that do not produce movement. Compare **dynamic** (sense 1). **4.** relating to or causing stationary electric charges; electrostatic. **5.** of or relating to interference in the reception of radio or television transmissions. **6.** of or concerned with statics. **7.** *Sociol.* characteristic of or relating to a society that has reached a state of equilibrium so that no changes are taking place. **8.** *Computer technol.* (of a memory) not needing its contents refreshed periodically. Compare **dynamic** (sense 5). ~*n.* **9.** random hissing or crackling or a speckled picture caused by the interference of electrical disturbances in the reception of radio or television transmissions. **10.** electric sparks or crackling produced by friction. ~See also **statics.** [C16: from New Latin *staticus,* from Greek *statikos* causing to stand, from *histanai* to stand, put on the scales] —'**statically** *adv.*

statice ('stætɪsɪ) *n.* a plant name formerly held to include both *Armeria* (see **thrift**) and *Limonium* (see **sea lavender**). The gardener's statice comprises various species of the latter, esp. those whose flowers can be dried and kept: family *Plumbaginaceae.* [Latin: thrift, from Greek *statikē,* from *statikos* astringent (from a medicinal use of thrift)]

static line *n.* a line attaching the pack of a parachute to an aircraft, so that the parachute is opened when it has fallen clear of the aircraft.

statics ('stætɪks) *n.* (*functioning as sing.*) the branch of mechanics concerned with the forces that produce a state of equilibrium in a system of bodies. Compare **dynamics** (sense 1).

static tube *n.* an open-ended tube used to measure the static pressure at a point in a moving fluid and positioned in such a way that it is unaffected by the fluid's motion.

station ('steɪʃən) *n.* **1.** the place or position at which a thing or person stands or is supposed to stand. **2. a.** a place along a route or line at which a bus, train, etc., stops for fuel or to pick up or let off passengers or goods, esp. one with ancillary buildings and services: *railway station.* **b.** (*as modifier*): *a station buffet.* **3. a.** the headquarters or local offices of an official organization such as the police or fire services. **b.** (*as modifier*): *a station sergeant.* See **police station, fire station. 4.** a building, depot, etc., with special equipment for some particular purpose: *power station; petrol station; television station.* **5.** *Military.* a place of duty: *an action station.* **6.** *Navy.* **a.** a location to which a ship or fleet is assigned for duty. **b.** an assigned location for a member of a ship's crew. **7.** a radio or television channel. **8.** a position or standing, as in a particular society or organization. **9.** the type of one's occupation; calling. **10.** (in British India) a place where the British district officials or garrison officers resided. **11.** *Biology.* the type of habitat occupied by a particular animal or plant. **12.** *Austral. and N.Z.* a large sheep or cattle farm. **13.** *Surveying.* a point at which a reading is made or which is used as a point of reference. **14.** (*sometimes cap.*) *R.C. Church.* **a.** one of the stations of the Cross. **b.** any of the churches (**station churches**) in Rome that have been used from ancient times as points of assembly for religious processions and ceremonies on particular days (**station days**). **15.** (*pl.*) (in rural Ireland) mass, preceded by confessions, held annually in a parishioner's dwelling and attended by other parishioners. ~*vb.* **16.** (*tr.*) to place in or assign to a station. [C14: via Old French from Latin *statiō* a standing still, from *stāre* to stand]

stationary ('steɪʃənərɪ) *adj.* **1.** not moving; standing still. **2.** not able to be moved. **3.** showing no change: *the doctors said his condition was stationary.* **4.** tending to remain in one place. [C15: from Latin *statiōnārius,* from *statiō* STATION] —'**stationarily** *adv.* —'**stationariness** *n.*

stationary engine *n.* an engine that remains in a fixed position, esp. one in a building that drives generators or other machinery. —**stationary engineer** *n.*

stationary orbit *n. Astronautics.* a synchronous orbit lying in or approximately in the plane of the equator.

stationary point *n.* **1.** a point on a curve at which the tangent is either horizontal or vertical, such as a maximum, a minimum, or a point of inflection. **2.** *Astronomy.* a point in the apparent path of a planet when it reverses direction.

stationary wave *n.* another name for **standing wave.**

stationer ('steɪʃənə) *n.* **1.** a person who sells stationery or a shop where stationery is sold. **2.** *Obsolete.* a publisher or bookseller. [C14: from Medieval Latin *stationarius* a person having a regular station, hence a shopkeeper (esp. a bookseller) as distinguished from an itinerant tradesman; see STATION]

stationery ('steɪʃənərɪ) *n.* any writing materials, such as paper, envelopes, pens, ink, rulers, etc.

station house *n. Chiefly U.S.* a house that is situated by or serves as a station, esp. as a police or fire station.

stationmaster ('steɪʃənˌmɑːstə) *or* **station manager** *n.* the senior official in charge of a railway station.

stations of the Cross *pl. n. R.C. Church.* **1.** a series of 14 crosses, often accompanied by 14 pictures or carvings, arranged in order around the walls of a church, to commemorate 14 supposed stages in Christ's journey to Calvary. **2.** a devotion consisting of 14 prayers relating to each of these stages.

station wagon *n.* a U.S., Canadian, Austral., and N.Z. name for **estate car.**

statism ('steɪtɪzəm) *n.* the theory or practice of concentrating economic and political power in the state, resulting in a weak position for the individual or community with respect to the government.

statist ('steɪtɪst) *n.* **1.** an advocate of statism. **2.** a less common name for a **statistician. 3.** *Archaic.* a politician or statesman. ~*adj.* **4.** of, characteristic of, advocating, or relating to statism.

statistic (stə'tɪstɪk) *n.* any function of a number of random variables, usually identically distributed, that may be used to estimate a population parameter. See also **sampling statistic, estimator** (sense 2), **parameter** (sense 3). —**sta'tistical** *adj.* —**sta'tistically** *adv.*

statistical dependence *n.* (of two random variables) not independent. X and Y are **positively dependent** if the conditional probability, $P(X|Y)$, of X given Y is greater than the probability, $P(X)$, of X, or equivalently if $P(X\&Y) > P(X).P(Y)$. They are **negatively dependent** if the inequalities are reversed.

statistical inference *n.* the theory, methods, and practice of forming judgments about the parameters of a population, usually on the basis of random sampling. Also called: **inferential statistics.** Compare **hypothesis testing.**

statistical mechanics *n.* (*functioning as sing.*) the study of the properties of physical systems as predicted by the statistical behaviour of their constituent particles.

statistical tables *pl. n.* tables showing the values of the cumulative distribution functions, probability functions, or probability density functions of certain common distributions for different values of their parameters, and used esp. to determine whether or not a particular statistical result exceeds the required significance level. See **hypothesis testing.**

statistician (ˌstætɪ'stɪʃən) *n.* **1.** a person who specializes in or is skilled at statistics. **2.** a person who compiles statistics.

statistics (stə'tɪstɪks) *n.* **1.** (*functioning as pl.*) quantitative data on any subject, esp. data comparing the distribution of some quantity for different subclasses of the population: *statistics for earnings by different age groups.* **2.** (*functioning as sing.*) **a.** the classification and interpretation of such data in accordance with probability theory and the application of methods such as hypothesis testing to them. **b.** the mathematical study of the theoretical nature of such distributions and tests. See also **descriptive statistics, statistical inference.** [C18 (originally "science dealing with facts of a state"): via German *Statistik,* from New Latin *statisticus* concerning state affairs, from Latin *status* STATE]

stative ('steɪtɪv) *Grammar.* ~*adj.* **1.** denoting a verb describing a state rather than an activity, act, or event, such as *know* and *want* as opposed to *leave* and *throw.* Compare **nonstative.** ~*n.* **2.** a stative verb. [C19: from New Latin *statīvus,* from Latin *stāre* to stand]

stato- *combining form.* static; standing; fixed: *statolith.* [from Greek *statos* standing, set]

statoblast ('stætəʊˌblɑːst) *n. Zoology.* an encapsulated bud produced asexually by certain bryozoans that can survive adverse conditions and that gives rise to a new colony.

statocyst ('stætəʊsɪst) *n.* an organ of balance in some invertebrates, such as crustaceans, that consists of a sensory vesicle containing small granules (see **statolith**).

statolatry (steɪ'tɒlətrɪ) *n. Rare.* the act or practice of idolizing the state. [C19: from STATE + -LATRY]

statolith ('stætəʊlɪθ) *n.* **1.** Also called: **otolith.** any of the granules of calcium carbonate occurring in a statocyst: movement of statoliths, caused by a change in position of the animal, stimulates hair cells, which convey the information to the brain by nerve fibres. **2.** any of various movable inclusions, such as starch grains, that occur in plant cells and are thought to function in geotropic responses. —ˌ**stato'lithic** *adj.*

stator ('steɪtə) *n.* **1.** the stationary part of a rotary machine or device, esp. of a motor or generator. **2.** a system of nonrotating radially arranged parts within a rotating assembly, esp. the fixed blades of an axial flow compressor in a gas turbine. ~Compare **rotor** (sense 1). [C20: from Latin: one who stands (by), from *stāre* to stand]

statoscope ('stætəˌskəʊp) *n.* a very sensitive form of aneroid barometer used to detect and measure small variations in atmospheric pressure, such as one used in an aircraft to indicate small changes in altitude.

statuary ('stætjʊərɪ) *n.* **1.** statues collectively. **2.** the art of making statues. ~*adj.* **3.** of, relating to, or suitable for statues. [C16: from Latin *statuārius*]

statue ('stætjuː) *n.* a wooden, stone, metal, plaster, or other kind of sculpture of a human or animal figure, usually life-size or larger. [C14: via Old French from Latin *statua,* from *statuere* to set up; compare STATUTE]

statued ('stætjuːd) *adj.* decorated with or portrayed in a statue or statues.

statuesque (ˌstætjʊ'ɛsk) *adj.* like a statue, esp. in possessing great formal beauty or dignity. [C19: from STATUE + -ESQUE, on the model of PICTURESQUE] —ˌ**statu'esquely** *adv.* —ˌ**statu'esqueness** *n.*

statuette (ˌstætjʊ'ɛt) *n.* a small statue.

stature ('stætʃə) *n.* **1.** the height of something, esp. a person or animal when standing. **2.** the degree of development of a person: *the stature of a champion.* **3.** intellectual or moral greatness: *a man of stature.* [C13: via Old French from Latin *statūra,* from *stāre* to stand]

status ('steɪtəs) *n., pl.* **-tuses.** **1.** a social or professional position, condition, or standing to which varying degrees of responsibility, privilege, and esteem are attached. **2.** the relative position or standing of a person or thing. **3.** a high position or standing; prestige: *he has acquired a new status since he has been in that job.* **4.** the legal standing or condition of a person. **5.** a state of affairs. [C17: from Latin: posture, from *stāre* to stand]

status quo (kwəʊ) *n.* (usually preceded by *the*) the existing state of affairs. [literally: the state in which]

status symbol *n.* a possession which is regarded as proof of the owner's social position, wealth, prestige, etc.

statutable ('stætjʊtəbᵊl) *adj.* a variant of **statutory** (senses 2, 3). —'**statutably** *adv.*

statute ('stætjuːt) *n.* **1. a.** an enactment of a legislative body expressed in a formal document. **b.** this document. **2.** a permanent rule made by a body or institution for the government of its internal affairs. [C13: from Old French *estatut,* from Late Latin *statūtum,* from Latin *statuere* to set up, decree, ultimately from *stāre* to stand]

statute book *n. Chiefly Brit.* a register of enactments passed by the legislative body of a state, usually made up of a series of volumes that form a complete official record: *not on the statute book.*

statute law *n.* **1.** a law enacted by a legislative body. **2.** a particular example of this. ~Compare **common law, equity.**

statute mile *n.* a legal or formal name for **mile** (sense 1).

statute of limitations *n.* a legislative enactment prescribing the period of time within which proceedings must be instituted to enforce a right or bring an action at law. See also **laches.**

statutory ('stætjʊtərɪ, -trɪ) *adj.* **1.** of, relating to, or having the nature of a statute. **2.** prescribed or authorized by statute. **3.** (of an offence) **a.** recognized by statute. **b.** subject to a punishment or penalty prescribed by statute. —'**statutorily** *adv.*

statutory declaration *n. Law.* a declaration made under statutory authority before a justice of the peace or commissioner for oaths which may in certain cases be substituted for a statement on oath.

statutory order *n.* a statute that applies further legislation to an existing act.

statutory rape *n.* (in the U.S.) the criminal offence of having sexual intercourse with a girl who has not reached the age of consent.

staun (stɔːn) *vb., n.* a Scot. word for **stand.**

staunch[1] (stɔːntʃ) *adj.* **1.** loyal, firm, and dependable: *a staunch supporter.* **2.** solid or substantial in construction. **3.** *Rare.* (of a ship, etc.) watertight; seaworthy. [C15: (originally): watertight): from Old French *estanche,* from *estanchier* to STANCH] —'**staunchly** *adv.* —'**staunchness** *n.*

staunch[2] (stɔːntʃ) *vb., n.* a variant spelling of **stanch.**

staurolite ('stɔːrəˌlaɪt) *n.* a brown glassy mineral consisting of iron aluminium silicate in the form of prismatic crystals: used as a gemstone. Formula: $FeAl_4Si_2O_{10}(OH)_2$. [C19: from Greek *stauros* a cross + -LITE] —**staurolitic** (ˌstɔːrə'lɪtɪk) *adj.*

stauroscope ('stɔːrəˌskəʊp) *n.* an optical instrument for studying the crystal structure of minerals under polarized light. [C19: from Greek *stauros* a cross + -SCOPE] —**stauroscopic** (ˌstɔːrə'skɒpɪk) *adj.* —ˌ**stauro'scopically** *adv.*

stave (steɪv) *n.* **1.** any one of a number of long strips of wood joined together to form a barrel, bucket, boat hull, etc. **2.** any of various bars, slats, or rods, usually of wood, such as a rung of a ladder or a crosspiece bracing the legs of a chair. **3.** any stick, staff, etc. **4.** a stanza or verse of a poem. **5.** *Music.* **a.** *Brit.* an individual group of five lines and four spaces used in staff notation. **b.** another word for **staff**[1] (sense 9). ~*vb.* **staves, staving, staved** *or* **stove.** **6.** (often foll. by *in*) to break or crush (the staves of a boat, barrel, etc.) or (of the staves of a boat) to be broken or crushed. **7.** (*tr.*; usually foll. by *in*) to burst or force (a hole in something). **8.** (*tr.*) to provide (a ladder, chair, etc.) with a stave or staves. **9.** (*tr.*) *Scot.* to sprain (a finger, toe, etc.). [C14: back formation from *staves,* plural of STAFF[1]]

stave off *vb.* (*tr., adv.*) to avert or hold off (something undesirable or harmful), esp. temporarily: *to stave off hunger.*

staves (steɪvz) *n.* a plural of **staff**[1] or **stave.**

stavesacre ('steɪvzˌeɪkə) *n.* **1.** a Eurasian ranunculaceous plant, *Delphinium staphisagria,* having purple flowers and poisonous seeds. **2.** the seeds of this plant, which have strong emetic and cathartic properties. [C14 *staphisagre,* from Latin *staphis agria,* from Greek, from *staphis* raisin + *agria* wild]

stay[1] (steɪ) *vb.* **1.** (*intr.*) to continue or remain in a certain place, position, etc.: *to stay outside.* **2.** (*copula*) to continue to be; remain: *to stay awake.* **3.** (*intr.*; often foll. by *at*) to reside temporarily, esp. as a guest: *to stay at a hotel.* **4.** (*tr.*) to remain for a specified period: *to stay the weekend.* **5.** (*intr.*) *Scot. and S. African.* to reside permanently or habitually; live. **6.** *Archaic.* to stop or cause to stop. **7.** (*intr.*) to wait, pause, or tarry. **8.** (*tr.*) to delay or hinder. **9.** (*tr.*) **a.** to discontinue or suspend (a judicial proceeding). **b.** to hold in abeyance or restrain from enforcing (an order, decree, etc.). **10.** to endure (something testing or difficult, such as a race): *a horse that stays the course.* **11.** (*intr.*; usually foll. by *with*) to keep pace (with a competitor in a race, etc.). **12.** (*intr.*) *Poker.* to raise one's stakes enough to stay in a round. **13.** (*tr.*) to hold back or restrain: *to stay one's anger.* **14.** (*tr.*) to satisfy or appease (an appetite, etc.) temporarily. **15.** (*tr.*) *Archaic.* to quell or suppress. **16.** (*intr.*) *Archaic.* to stand firm. **17. stay put.** See **put** (sense 18). ~*n.* **18.** the act of staying or sojourning in a place or the period during which one stays. **19.** the act of stopping or restraining or state of being stopped, etc. **20.** the suspension of a judicial proceeding, etc.: *stay of execution.* ~See also **stay out.** [C15 *staien,* from Anglo-French *estaier* to stay, from Old French *ester* to stay, from Latin *stāre* to stand]

stay[2] (steɪ) *n.* **1.** anything that supports or steadies, such as a prop or buttress. **2.** a thin strip of metal, plastic, bone, etc., used to stiffen corsets, etc. ~*vb.* (*tr.*) *Archaic.* **3.** (often foll. by *up*) to prop or hold. **4.** (often foll. by *up*) to comfort or sustain. **5.** (foll. by *on* or *upon*) to cause to rely or depend. ~See also **stays** (sense 1). [C16: from Old French *estaye,* of Germanic origin; compare STAY[3]]

stay[3] (steɪ) *n.* a rope, cable, or chain, usually one of a set, used for bracing uprights, such as masts, funnels, flagpoles, chimneys, etc.; guy. ~See also **stays** (senses 2, 3). [Old English *stæg;* related to Old Norse *stag,* Middle Low German *stach,* Norwegian *stagle* wooden post]

stay-at-home *adj.* **1.** (of a person) enjoying a quiet, settled, and unadventurous use of leisure. ~*n.* **2.** a stay-at-home person.

stayer ('steɪə) *n.* **1.** a person or thing that stays. **2.** *Informal.* **a.** a persistent or tenacious person. **b.** *Horse racing.* a persistent horse.

staying power *n.* endurance; stamina.

Stayman ('steɪmən) *n.* (in contract bridge) a conventional response in clubs to a partner's opening no-trump bid, as a request for the partner to show any four-card major. [C20: named after Samuel M. *Stayman* (born 1909), U.S. bridge expert]

stay out *vb.* (*adv.*) **1.** (*intr.*) to remain away from home: *the cat stayed out all night.* **2.** (*tr.*) to remain beyond the end of: *to stay out a welcome.* **3.** (*tr.*) to remain throughout: *to stay the night out.*

stays (steɪz) *pl. n.* **1.** *Now rare.* corsets with bones in them. **2.** a position of a sailing vessel relative to the wind so that the sails are luffing or aback. Compare **irons** (sense 2). **3. miss stays.** Also: **refuse stays.** (of a sailing vessel) to fail to come about.

staysail ('steɪˌseɪl; *Nautical* 'steɪsᵊl) *n.* an auxiliary sail, often triangular, set to catch the wind, as between the masts of a yawl (**mizzen staysail**), aft of a spinnaker (**spinnaker staysail**), etc.

stay stitching *n.* a line of stitches made in the seam allowance to prevent the edges from stretching.

stbd *abbrev. for* starboard.
STC (in India) *abbrev. for* State Trading Corporation.
std *abbrev. for* standard.
STD *abbrev. for:* **1.** subscriber trunk dialling. **2.** *N.Z.* subscriber toll dialling. **3.** sexually transmitted disease. **4.** Doctor of Sacred Theology.
STD code *n. Brit.* a code of two or more digits, other than those comprising a subscriber's local telephone number, that determines the routing of a call. [C20: *s(ubscriber) t(runk) d(ialling)*]
Ste *abbrev. for* Saint (female). [French *Sainte*]
stead (stɛd) *n.* **1.** (preceded by *in*) *Rare.* the place, function, or position that should be taken by another: *to come in someone's stead.* **2. stand (someone) in good stead.** to be useful or of good service to (someone). *~vb.* **3.** (*tr.*) *Archaic.* to help or benefit. [Old English *stede;* related to Old Norse *stathr* place, Old High German *stat* place, Latin *statiō* a standing, *statim* immediately]
steadfast *or* **stedfast** (ˈstɛdfəst, -ˌfɑːst) *adj.* **1.** (esp. of a person's gaze) fixed in intensity or direction; steady. **2.** unwavering or determined in purpose, loyalty, etc.: *steadfast resolve.* —ˈ**steadfastly** *or* ˈ**stedfastly** *adv.* —ˈ**steadfastness** *or* ˈ**stedfastness** *n.*
steading (ˈstɛdɪŋ) *n. Brit.* **1.** a farmstead. **2.** the outbuildings of a farm. [C15: from STEAD + -ING[1]]
steady (ˈstɛdɪ) *adj.* **steadier, steadiest.** **1.** not able to be moved or disturbed easily; stable. **2.** free from fluctuation: *the level stayed steady.* **3.** not easily excited; imperturbable. **4.** staid; sober. **5.** regular; habitual: *a steady drinker.* **6.** continuous: *a steady flow.* **7.** *Nautical.* (of a vessel) keeping upright, as in heavy seas. *~vb.* **steadies, steadying, steadied.** **8.** to make or become steady. *~adv.* **9.** in a steady manner. **10. go steady.** *Informal.* to date one person regularly. *~n., pl.* **steadies.** **11.** *Informal.* one's regular boyfriend or girlfriend. *~interj.* **12.** *Nautical.* an order to the helmsman to stay on a steady course. **13.** a warning to keep calm, be careful, etc. **14.** *Brit.* a command to get set to start, as in a race: *ready, steady, go!* [C16: from STEAD + -Y[1]; related to Old High German *stātīg,* Middle Dutch *stēdig*] —ˈ**steadier** *n.* —ˈ**steadily** *adv.* —ˈ**steadiness** *n.*
steady state *n. Physics.* the condition of a system when some or all of the quantities describing it are independent of time but not necessarily in thermodynamic or chemical equilibrium. See also **equilibrium** (sense 6).
steady-state theory *n.* a cosmological theory postulating that the universe exists throughout time in a steady state such that the average density of matter does not vary with distance or time. Matter is continuously created in the space left by the receding stars and galaxies of the expanding universe. Compare **big-bang theory.**
steak (steɪk) *n.* **1.** See **beefsteak.** **2.** any of various cuts of beef of varying quality, used for braising, stewing, etc. **3.** a thick slice of pork, veal, etc., or of a large fish, esp. cod or salmon. **4.** minced meat prepared in the same way as steak: *hamburger steak.* [C15: from Old Norse *steik* roast; related to *steikja* to roast on a spit; see STICK[1]]
steakhouse (ˈsteɪkˌhaʊs) *n.* a restaurant that has steaks as its speciality.
steak tartare *or* **tartar** *n.* raw minced steak, mixed with onion, seasonings, and raw egg. Also called: **tartare steak, tartar steak.**
steal (stiːl) *vb.* **steals, stealing, stole, stolen.** **1.** to take (something) from someone, etc. without permission or unlawfully, esp. in a secret manner. **2.** (*tr.*) to obtain surreptitiously. **3.** (*tr.*) to appropriate (ideas, etc.) without acknowledgment, as in plagiarism. **4.** to move or convey stealthily: *they stole along the corridor.* **5.** (*intr.*) to pass unnoticed: *the hours stole by.* **6.** (*tr.*) to win or gain by strategy or luck, as in various sports: *to steal a few yards.* **7. steal a march on.** to obtain an advantage over, esp. by a secret or underhand measure. **8. steal someone's thunder.** to detract from the attention due to another by forestalling him. **9. steal the show.** to be looked upon as the most interesting, popular, etc., esp. unexpectedly. *~n. Informal.* **10.** the act of stealing. **11.** something stolen or acquired easily or at little cost. [Old English *stelan;* related to Old Frisian, Old Norse *stela,* Gothic *stilan,* German *stehlen*] —ˈ**stealer** *n.*
stealth (stɛlθ) *n.* **1.** the act or characteristic of moving with extreme care and quietness, esp. so as to avoid detection: *the stealth of a cat.* **2.** cunning or underhand procedure or dealing. **3.** *Archaic.* the act of stealing. [C13 *stelthe;* see STEAL, -TH[1]] —ˈ**stealthful** *adj.*
Stealth (stɛlθ) *n.* (*modifier*) denoting or referring to technology that aims to reduce the radar, thermal, and acoustic recognizability of aircraft and missiles: *Stealth bomber.*
stealthy (ˈstɛlθɪ) *adj.* **stealthier, stealthiest.** characterized by great caution, secrecy, etc.; furtive. —ˈ**stealthily** *adv.* —ˈ**stealthiness** *n.*
steam (stiːm) *n.* **1.** the gas or vapour into which water is changed when boiled. **2.** the mist formed when such gas or vapour condenses in the atmosphere. **3.** any vaporous exhalation. **4.** *Informal.* power, energy, or speed. **5. get up steam. a.** (of a ship, etc.) to work up a sufficient head of steam in a boiler to drive an engine. **b.** *Informal.* to go quickly. **6. let off steam.** *Informal.* to release pent-up energy or emotions. **7. under one's own steam.** without the assistance of others. **8.** *Austral. slang.* cheap wine. **9.** (*modifier*) driven, operated, heated, powered, etc., by steam: *a steam radiator.* **10.** (*modifier*) treated by steam: *steam ironed; steam cleaning.* **11.** (*modifier*) *Humorous.* old-fashioned; outmoded: *steam radio.* *~vb.* **12.** to emit or be emitted as steam. **13.** (*intr.*) to generate steam, as a boiler, etc. **14.** (*intr.*) to move or travel by steam power, as a ship, etc. **15.** (*intr.*) *Informal.* to proceed quickly and sometimes forcefully. **16.** to cook or be cooked in steam. **17.** (*tr.*) to treat with steam or apply steam to, as in cleaning, pressing clothes, etc. ~See also **steam up.** [Old English; related to Dutch *stoom* steam, perhaps to Old High German *stioban* to raise dust, Gothic *stubjus* dust]
steam bath *n.* **1.** a room or enclosure that can be filled with steam in which people bathe to induce sweating and refresh or cleanse themselves. **2.** an act of taking such a bath. **3.** an enclosure through which steam can be passed continuously, used in laboratories for sterilizing equipment, maintaining a constant temperature, etc.
steamboat (ˈstiːmˌbəʊt) *n.* a boat powered by a steam engine.
steam-boiler *n.* a vessel in which water is boiled to generate steam. An industrial boiler usually consists of a system of parallel tubes through which water passes, suspended above a furnace.
steam-chest *n.* a chamber that encloses the slide valve of a steam engine and forms a manifold for the steam supply to the valve.
steam coal *n.* coal suitable for use in producing steam, as in a steam-boiler.
steam-engine *n.* an engine that uses the thermal energy of steam to produce mechanical work, esp. one in which steam from a boiler is expanded in a cylinder to drive a reciprocating piston.
steamer (ˈstiːmə) *n.* **1.** a boat or ship driven by steam engines. **2.** Also called: **steam box.** an apparatus for steaming wooden beams and planks to make them pliable for shipbuilding. **3.** a vessel used to cook food by steam. **4.** *Austral. slang.* a clash of sporting teams characterized by rough play.
steam-generating heavy-water reactor *n.* a nuclear reactor using heavy water as the moderator, light water (H_2O) as the coolant, and uranium oxide cased in zirconium alloy as the fuel. Abbrev.: **SGHWR.**
steamie (ˈstiːmɪ) *n. Scot. urban dialect.* a public wash house.
steaming (ˈstiːmɪŋ) *adj.* **1.** very hot. **2.** *Informal.* angry. **3.** *Slang.* drunk. *~n.* **4.** *Informal.* robbery, esp. of passengers in a railway carriage or bus, by a large gang of armed youths.
steam iron *n.* an electric iron that emits steam from channels in the iron face to facilitate the pressing and ironing of clothes, etc., the steam being produced from water contained within the iron.
steam jacket *n. Engineering.* a jacket containing steam that surrounds and heats a cylinder.
steam organ *n.* a type of organ powered by steam, once common at fairgrounds, in which the pipes are sounded either by a keyboard or in a sequence determined by a moving punched card. U.S. name: **calliope.**
steam point *n.* the temperature at which the maximum vapour pressure of water is equal to one atmosphere (1.01325×10^5 N/m^2). It has the value of 100° on the Celsius scale. Compare **ice point.**
steam reforming *n. Chem.* a process in which methane from natural gas is heated, with steam, usually with a catalyst, to produce a mixture of carbon monoxide and hydrogen used in organic synthesis and as a fuel.
steamroller (ˈstiːmˌrəʊlə) *n.* **1. a.** a steam-powered vehicle with heavy rollers at the front and rear used for compressing road surfaces during road-making. **b.** another word for **roadroller.** **2. a.** an overpowering force or a person with such force that overcomes all opposition. **b.** (*as modifier*): *steamroller tactics.* *~vb.* **3.** (*tr.*) to crush (opposition, etc.) by overpowering force.
steam room *n.* a room that can be filled with steam for use as a steam bath.
steamship (ˈstiːmˌʃɪp) *n.* a ship powered by one or more steam engines.
steam-shovel *n.* a steam-driven mechanical excavator, esp. one having a large bucket or grab on a beam slung from a revolving jib.
steamtight (ˈstiːmˌtaɪt) *adj.* (of joints, cylinders, etc.) being sealed in such a way that steam cannot leak out. —ˈ**steamˌtightness** *n.*
steam trap *n.* a device in a steam pipe that collects and discharges condensed water.
steam turbine *n.* a turbine driven by steam.
steam up *vb.* (*adv.*) **1.** to cover (windows, etc.) or (of windows, etc.) to become covered with a film of condensed steam. **2.** (*tr.; usually passive*) *Slang.* to excite or make angry: *he's all steamed up about the delay.*
steam whistle *n.* a type of whistle sounded by a blast of steam, as used formerly in factories, on locomotives, etc.
steamy (ˈstiːmɪ) *adj.* **steamier, steamiest.** **1.** of, resembling, full of, or covered with steam. **2.** *Informal.* lustful or erotic: *steamy nightlife.* —ˈ**steamily** *adv.* —ˈ**steaminess** *n.*
steapsin (stɪˈæpsɪn) *n. Biochem.* a pancreatic lipase. [C19: from Greek *stear* fat + PEPSIN]
stearate (ˈstɪəˌreɪt) *n.* any salt or ester of stearic acid.
stearic (stɪˈærɪk) *adj.* **1.** of or relating to suet or fat. **2.** of, consisting of, containing, or derived from stearic acid. [C19: from French *stéarique,* from Greek *stear* fat, tallow]

stearic acid *n.* a colourless odourless insoluble waxy carboxylic acid used for making candles and suppositories; octadecanoic acid. Formula: $CH_3(CH_2)_{16}COOH$. See also **stearin** (sense 2).

stearin *or* **stearine** ('stɪərɪn) *n.* **1.** Also called: **tristearin.** a colourless crystalline ester of glycerol and stearic acid, present in fats and used in soap and candles; glycerol tristearate; glycerol trioctadecanoate. Formula: $(C_{17}H_{35}COO)_3C_3H_5$. **2.** another name for **stearic acid,** esp. a commercial grade containing other fatty acids. **3.** fat in its solid form. [C19: from French *stéarine,* from Greek *stear* fat, tallow + -IN]

stearoptene (ˌstɪə'rɒptiːn) *n.* the part of an essential oil that separates out as a solid on cooling or standing. [C19: from New Latin *stearoptenum,* from Greek *stear* fat + *-ptenum,* from *ptēnos* winged (volatile)]

steatite ('stɪəˌtaɪt) *n.* another name for **soapstone.** [C18: from Latin *steatītēs,* from Greek *stear* fat + -ITE[1]] —**steatitic** (ˌstɪə'tɪtɪk) *adj.*

steato- *combining form.* denoting fat. [from Greek *stear, steat-* fat, tallow]

steatolysis (ˌstɪə'tɒlɪsɪs) *n. Physiol.* **1.** the digestive process whereby fats are emulsified and then hydrolysed to fatty acids and glycerin. **2.** the breaking down of fat.

steatopygia (ˌstɪətəʊ'pɪdʒɪə, -'paɪ-) *or* **steatopyga** (ˌstɪətəʊ'paɪgə) *n.* excessive fatness of the buttocks. [C19: from New Latin, from STEATO- + Greek *pugē* the buttocks] —**steatopygic** (ˌstɪətəʊ'pɪdʒɪk) *or* **steatopygous** (ˌstɪə'tɒpɪgəs) *adj.*

steatorrhoea *or esp. U.S.* **steatorrhea** (ˌstɪətə'rɪə) *n. Pathol.* **1.** a condition in which the stools are abnormally fatty. **2.** another word for **seborrhoea.**

stedfast ('stɛdfəst, -ˌfɑːst) *adj.* a less common spelling of **steadfast.**

steed (stiːd) *n. Archaic or literary.* a horse, esp. one that is spirited or swift. [Old English *stēda* stallion; related to German *Stute* female horse; see STUD[2]]

steel (stiːl) *n.* **1. a.** any of various alloys based on iron containing carbon (usually 0.1–1.7 per cent) and often small quantities of other elements such as phosphorus, sulphur, manganese, chromium, and nickel. Steels exhibit a variety of properties, such as strength, machinability, malleability, etc., depending on their composition and the way they have been treated. **b.** (*as modifier*): *steel girders.* See also **stainless steel. 2.** something that is made of steel. **3.** a steel stiffener in a corset, etc. **4.** a ridged steel rod with a handle used for sharpening knives. **5.** the quality of hardness, esp. with regard to a person's character or attitudes. **6.** *Stock Exchange.* the quotation for steel shares. See also **steels. 7.** (*modifier*) resembling steel: *steel determination.* ~*vb.* (*tr.*) **8.** to fit, plate, edge, or point with steel. **9.** to make hard and unfeeling: *he steeled his heart against her sorrow; he steeled himself for the blow.* [Old English *stēli;* related to Old High German *stehli,* Middle Dutch *stael*] —'**steely** *adj.* —'**steeliness** *n.*

steel band *n. Music.* a type of instrumental band, popular in the Caribbean Islands, consisting mainly of tuned percussion instruments made chiefly from the heads of oil drums, hammered or embossed to obtain different notes.

steel blue *n.* **a.** a dark bluish-grey colour. **b.** (*as adj.*): *steel-blue eyes.*

steel-die printing *n.* any form of intaglio printing, such as engraving.

steel engraving *n.* **a.** a method or art of engraving (letters, etc.) on a steel plate. **b.** a print made from such a plate.

steel grey *n.* **a.** a dark grey colour, usually slightly purple. **b.** (*as adj.*): *a steel-grey suit.*

steel guitar *n.* See **Hawaiian guitar, pedal steel guitar.**

steelhead ('stiːlˌhɛd) *n., pl.* **-heads** *or* **-head.** a silvery North Pacific variety of the rainbow trout (*Salmo gairdneri*).

steels (stiːlz) *pl. n. Stock Exchange.* shares and bonds of steel companies.

steel wool *n.* a tangled or woven mass of fine steel fibres, used for cleaning or polishing.

steelwork ('stiːlˌwɜːk) *n.* a frame, foundation, building, or article made of steel: *the steelwork of a skyscraper.* —'**steelˌworking** *n.*

steelworks ('stiːlˌwɜːks) *n.* (*functioning as sing. or pl.*) a plant in which steel is made from iron ore and rolled or forged into blooms, billets, bars, or sheets. —'**steelˌworker** *n.*

steelyard ('stiːlˌjɑːd) *n.* a portable balance consisting of a pivoted bar with two unequal arms. The load is suspended from the shorter one and the bar is returned to the horizontal by adding weights to the longer one. [C17: from STEEL + YARD[1] (in the archaic sense: a rod or pole)]

steenbok ('stiːnˌbɒk) *n., pl.* **-boks** *or* **-bok.** a small antelope, *Raphicerus campestris,* of central and southern Africa, having a reddish-brown coat and straight smooth horns. Also called: **steinbok.** [C18: from Afrikaans, from Dutch *steen* stone + *bok* BUCK[1]; Compare STEINBOCK]

steep[1] (stiːp) *adj.* **1. a.** having or being a slope or gradient approaching the perpendicular. **b.** (*as n.*): *the steep.* **2.** *Informal.* (of a fee, price, demand, etc.) unduly high; unreasonable (esp. in the phrase **that's a bit steep**). **3.** *Informal.* excessively demanding or ambitious: *a steep task.* **4.** *Brit. informal.* (of a statement) extreme or far-fetched. **5.** *Obsolete.* elevated. [Old English *steap;* related to Old Frisian *stāp,* Old High German *stouf* cliff, Old Norse *staup*] —'**steeply** *adv.* —'**steepness** *n.*

steep[2] (stiːp) *vb.* **1.** to soak or be soaked in a liquid in order to soften, cleanse, extract an element, etc. **2.** (*tr.; usually passive*) to saturate; imbue: *steeped in ideology.* ~*n.* **3.** an instance or the process of steeping or the condition of being steeped. **4.** a liquid or solution used for the purpose of steeping something. [Old English *stēpan;* related to *steap* vessel, cup, Old High German *stouf,* Old Norse *staup,* Middle Dutch *stōp*] —'**steeper** *n.*

steepen ('stiːpᵊn) *vb.* to become or cause to become steep or steeper.

steeple ('stiːpᵊl) *n.* **1.** a tall ornamental tower that forms the superstructure of a church, temple, etc. **2.** such a tower with the spire above it. **3.** any spire or pointed structure. [Old English *stēpel;* see STEEP[1]] —'**steepled** *adj.*

steeplebush ('stiːpᵊlˌbʊʃ) *n.* another name for **hardhack.** [C19: so called because of the shape of its flower clusters]

steeplechase ('stiːpᵊlˌtʃeɪs) *n.* **1.** a horse race over a course equipped with obstacles to be jumped, esp. artificial hedges, ditches, water jumps, etc. **2.** a track race, usually of 3000 metres, in which the runners have to leap hurdles, a water jump, etc. **3.** *Archaic.* **a.** a horse race across a stretch of open countryside including obstacles to be jumped. **b.** a rare word for **point-to-point.** ~*vb.* **4.** (*intr.*) to take part in a steeplechase. [C19: so called because it originally took place cross-country, with a church tower serving as a landmark to guide the riders] —'**steepleˌchaser** *n.* —'**steepleˌchasing** *n.*

steeplejack ('stiːpᵊlˌdʒæk) *n.* a person trained and skilled in the construction and repair of steeples, chimneys, etc. [C19: from STEEPLE + JACK[1] (in the sense: a man or fellow)]

steer[1] (stɪə) *vb.* **1.** to direct the course of (a vehicle or vessel) with a steering wheel, rudder, etc. **2.** (*tr.*) to guide with tuition: *his teachers steered him through his exams.* **3.** (*tr.*) to direct the movements or course of (a person, conversation, etc.). **4.** to pursue (a specified course). **5.** (*intr.*) (of a vessel, vehicle, etc.) to admit of being guided in a specified fashion: *this boat does not steer properly.* **6. steer clear of.** to keep away from; shun. ~*n.* **7.** *Chiefly U.S.* information; guidance (esp. in the phrase **a bum steer**). [Old English *stieran;* related to Old Frisian *stiūra,* Old Norse *stȳra,* German *stevern;* see STARBOARD, STERN[2]] —'**steerable** *adj.* —'**steerer** *n.*

steer[2] (stɪə) *n.* a castrated male ox or bull; bullock. [Old English *stēor;* related to Old Norse *stjōrr,* Gothic *stiur,* Old High German *stior,* Middle Dutch *stēr*]

steerage ('stɪərɪdʒ) *n.* **1.** the cheapest accommodation on a passenger ship, originally the compartments containing the steering apparatus. **2.** an instance or the practice of steering and the effect of this on a vessel or vehicle.

steerageway ('stɪərɪdʒˌweɪ) *n. Nautical.* enough forward movement to allow a vessel to be steered.

steering column *n.* (in a motor vehicle) the shaft on which a steering wheel is mounted and by which it is connected with the steering gear.

steering committee *n.* a committee set up to prepare and arrange topics to be discussed, the order of business, etc., for a legislative assembly or other body.

steering gear *n.* any mechanism used for steering a vehicle, ship, aircraft, etc.

steering wheel *n.* a wheel turned by the driver of a motor vehicle, ship, etc., when he wishes to change direction. It is connected to the front wheels, rudder, etc.

steersman ('stɪəzmən) *n., pl.* **-men.** the helmsman of a vessel.

steeve[1] (stiːv) *n.* **1.** a spar having a pulley block at one end, used for stowing cargo on a ship. ~*vb.* **2.** (*tr.*) to stow (cargo) securely in the hold of a ship. [C15 *steven,* probably from Spanish *estibar* to pack tightly, from Latin *stīpāre* to cram full]

steeve[2] (stiːv) *Nautical.* ~*vb.* **1.** to incline (a bowsprit or other spar) upwards or (of a bowsprit) to incline upwards at an angle from the horizontal. ~*n.* **2.** such an angle. [C17: of uncertain origin]

Stefan's law ('stɛfənz) *n.* the principle that the energy radiated per second by unit area of a black body at thermodynamic temperature T is directly proportional to T^4. The constant of proportionality is the **Stefan constant,** equal to 5.6697×10^{-8} $Wm^{-2} K^{-4}$. Also called: **Stefan-Boltzmann law.** [C19: named after Josef *Stefan* (1835–93), Austrian physicist]

stegodon ('stɛgəˌdɒn) *or* **stegodont** ('stɛgəˌdɒnt) *n.* any proboscidean mammal of the genus *Stegodon,* of Pliocene to Pleistocene times, similar to the mastodons. [C19: New Latin (literally: ridge-toothed), from Greek *stegos* roof, from *stegein* to cover + *odōn* tooth]

stegomyia (ˌstɛgə'maɪə) *n.* a former name for **aedes.** [C19: from Greek *stegos* roof + *-myia,* from *muia* a fly]

stegosaur ('stɛgəˌsɔː) *or* **stegosaurus** (ˌstɛgə'sɔːrəs) *n.* any quadrupedal herbivorous ornithischian dinosaur of the suborder *Stegosauria,* esp. any of the genus *Stegosaurus,* of Jurassic and early Cretaceous times, having an armour of bony plates. [C19: from Greek *stegos* roof + -SAUR]

stein (staɪn) *n.* **1.** an earthenware beer mug, esp. of a German design. **2.** the quantity contained in such a mug. [German, literally: STONE]

steinbock ('staɪnˌbɒk) *n.* another name for **ibex.** [C17: from German *Steinbock;* compare STEENBOK]

steinbok ('staɪnˌbɒk) *n., pl.* **-boks** *or* **-bok.** a variant spelling of **steenbok.**

stele ('stiːlɪ, stiːl) *n., pl.* **stelae** ('stiːliː) *or* **steles** ('stiːlɪz, stiːlz). **1.** an upright stone slab or column decorated with figures or inscriptions, common in prehistoric times. **2.** a prepared vertical surface that has a commemorative inscription or design, esp. one on the face of a building. **3.** the conducting tissue of the stems and roots of plants, which is in the form of a cylinder, principally containing xylem, phloem, and pericycle. See also **protostele, siphonostele.** ~Also called (for senses 1, 2): **stela** ('stiːlə). [C19: from Greek *stēlē*; related to Greek *histanai* to stand, Latin *stāre*] —**stelar** ('stiːlə) *adj.*

stellar ('stɛlə) *adj.* **1.** of, relating to, involving, or resembling a star or stars. **2.** of or relating to star entertainers. [C17: from Late Latin *stellāris*, from Latin *stella* star]

stellarator ('stɛləˌreɪtə) *n. Physics.* an apparatus used in research into thermonuclear reactions, consisting of a toroidal vessel designed so that a plasma may be contained within it by a magnetic field. [C20: from STELLAR + (GENER)ATOR]

stellar evolution *n. Astronomy.* the sequence of changes that occurs in a star as it ages.

stellate ('stɛlɪt, -eɪt) *or* **stellated** *adj.* resembling a star in shape; radiating from the centre: *a stellate arrangement of petals.* [C16: from Latin *stellātus* starry, from *stellāre* to stud with stars, from *stella* a star] —'**stellately** *adv.*

stelliferous (stɛ'lɪfərəs) *adj.* full of stars. [C16: from Latin *stellifer* star-bearing, from *stella* star; see -FEROUS]

stelliform ('stɛlɪˌfɔːm) *adj.* star-shaped. [C18: from New Latin *stelliformis*, from Latin *stella* star + *forma* shape]

stellify ('stɛlɪˌfaɪ) *vb.* **-fies, -fying, -fied.** to change or be changed into a star. [C14: from Latin *stella* a star]

Stellite ('stɛlaɪt) *n. Trademark.* any of various alloys containing cobalt, chromium, carbon, tungsten, and molybdenum: characteristically very hard and wear resistant, they are used as castings or hard surface-coatings.

stellular ('stɛljʊlə) *adj.* **1.** displaying or abounding in small stars: *a stellular pattern.* **2.** resembling a little star or little stars. [C18: from Late Latin *stellula*, diminutive of Latin *stella* star] —'**stellularly** *adv.*

stem[1] (stɛm) *n.* **1.** the main axis of a plant, which bears the leaves, axillary buds, and flowers and contains a hollow cylinder of vascular tissue. **2.** any similar subsidiary structure in such plants that bears a flower, fruit, or leaf. **3.** a corresponding structure in algae and fungi. **4.** any long slender part, such as the hollow part of a tobacco pipe that lies between the bit and the bowl, or the support between the base and the bowl of a wineglass, goblet, etc. **5.** a banana stalk with several bunches attached. **6.** the main line of descent or branch of a family. **7.** a round pin in some locks on which a socket in the end of a key fits and about which it rotates. **8.** any shank or cylindrical pin or rod, such as the pin that carries the winding knob on a watch. **9.** *Linguistics.* the form of a word that remains after removal of all inflectional affixes; the root of a word, esp. as occurring together with a thematic element. Compare **root**[1] (sense 9). **10.** the main, usually vertical, stroke of a letter or of a musical note such as a minim. **11.** *Electronics.* the tubular glass section projecting from the base of a light bulb or electronic valve, on which the filament or electrodes are mounted. **12. a.** the main upright timber or structure at the bow of a vessel. **b.** the very forward end of a vessel (esp. in the phrase **from stem to stern**). ~*vb.* **stems, stemming, stemmed. 13.** (*intr.*; usually foll. by *from*) to be derived; originate. **14.** (*tr.*) to make headway against (a tide, wind, etc.). **15.** (*tr.*) to remove or disengage the stem or stems from. **16.** (*tr.*) to supply (something) with a stem or stems. [Old English *stemn*; related to Old Norse *stafn* stem of a ship, German *Stamm* tribe, Gothic *stōma* basis, Latin *stāmen* thread] —'**stemˌlike** *adj.* —'**stemmer** *n.*

stem[2] (stɛm) *vb.* **stems, stemming, stemmed. 1.** (*tr.*) to restrain or stop (the flow of something) by or as if by damming up. **2.** (*tr.*) to pack tightly or stop up. **3.** *Skiing.* to manoeuvre (a ski or skis), as in performing a stem. ~*n.* **4.** *Skiing.* a technique in which the heel of one ski or both skis is forced outwards from the direction of movement in order to slow down or turn. [C15 *stemmen*, from Old Norse *stemma*; related to Old Norse *stamr* blocked, stammering, German *stemmen* to prop; see STAMMER] —'**stemmer** *n.*

stem-and-leaf diagram *n. Statistics.* a histogram in which the data points falling within each class interval are listed in order.

stem cell *n. Histology.* an undifferentiated cell that gives rise to specialized cells, such as blood cells.

stem ginger *n.* the choice pieces of the underground stem of the ginger plant, which are crystallized or preserved in syrup and eaten as a sweetmeat.

stemhead ('stɛmˌhɛd) *n. Nautical.* the head of the stem of a vessel.

stemma ('stɛmə) *n.* a family tree; pedigree. [C19: via Latin from Greek *stemma* garland, wreath, from *stephein* to crown, wreathe]

stemmed (stɛmd) *adj.* **1. a.** having a stem. **b.** (*in combination*): *a thin-stemmed plant; a long-stemmed glass.* **2.** having had the stem or stems removed.

stemson ('stɛmsən) *n. Nautical.* a curved timber scarfed into or bolted to the stem and keelson at the bow of a wooden vessel. Compare **sternson.** [C18: from STEM[1] + (KEEL)SON]

stem turn *n. Skiing.* a turn in which the heel of one ski is stemmed and the other ski is brought parallel. Also called: **stem.**

stemware ('stɛmˌwɛə) *n.* a collective term for glasses, goblets, etc., with stems.

stem-winder *n.* a watch wound by an expanded crown on the bar projecting outside the case, as opposed to one wound by a separate key. Also called: **stem-winding watch.**

stench (stɛntʃ) *n.* a strong and extremely offensive odour; stink. [Old English *stenc*; related to Old Saxon, Old High German *stank*; see STINK]

stench trap *n.* a trap in a sewer that by means of a water seal prevents the upward passage of foul-smelling gases. Also called: **stink trap.**

stencil ('stɛnsᵊl) *n.* **1.** a device for applying a design, characters, etc., to a surface, consisting of a thin sheet of plastic, metal, cardboard, etc. in which the design or characters have been cut so that ink or paint can be applied through the incisions onto the surface. **2.** a decoration, design, or characters produced in this way. ~*vb.* **-cils, -cilling, -cilled** *or U.S.* **-cils, -ciling, -ciled.** (*tr.*) **3.** to mark (a surface) with a stencil. **4.** to produce (characters or a design) with a stencil. [C14 *stanselen* to decorate with bright colours, from Old French *estenceler*, from *estencele* a spark, from Latin *scintilla*] —'**stenciller** *n.*

stengah ('stɛŋgə) *n.* another name for **stinger** (sense 2). [from Malay *sa tengah* one half]

Sten gun (stɛn) *n.* a light 9 mm sub-machine-gun formerly used in the British Army and Commonwealth forces. [C20: from *s* and *t* (initials of Shepherd and Turpin, the inventors) + *-en*, as in BREN GUN]

steno ('stɛnəʊ) *n., pl.* **stenos.** *U.S. and Canadian informal.* short for **stenographer.**

steno- *or before a vowel* **sten-** *combining form.* indicating narrowness or contraction: *stenography; stenosis.* [from Greek *stenos* narrow]

stenograph ('stɛnəˌgræf, -ˌgrɑːf) *n.* **1.** any of various keyboard machines for writing in shorthand. **2.** any character used in shorthand. ~*vb.* **3.** (*tr.*) to record (speeches, minutes, letters, etc.) in shorthand.

stenographer (stə'nɒgrəfə) *n.* the U.S. and Canadian name for **shorthand typist.**

stenography (stə'nɒgrəfɪ) *n.* **1.** the act or process of writing in shorthand by hand or machine. **2.** matter written in shorthand. —**stenographic** (ˌstɛnə'græfɪk) *or* ˌ**steno'graphical** *adj.* —ˌ**steno'graphically** *adv.*

stenohaline (ˌstɛnəʊ'heɪliːn, -laɪn) *adj.* (of certain aquatic animals) able to exist only within a narrow range of salinity. Compare **euryhaline.** [C20: from STENO- + *haline*, from Greek *hals* salt + -INE[1]]

stenopetalous (ˌstɛnəʊ'pɛtᵊləs) *adj.* (of flowers) having narrow petals.

stenophagous (stə'nɒfəgəs) *adj.* (of animals) feeding on a single type or limited variety of food. [C17: from STENO- + *-phagous* (via Latin from Greek *phagos* eating)]

stenophyllous (ˌstɛnəʊ'fɪləs) *adj.* (of plants) having narrow leaves.

stenosis (stɪ'nəʊsɪs) *n., pl.* **-ses** (-siːz). *Pathol.* an abnormal narrowing of a bodily canal or passage. [C19: via New Latin from Greek *stenōsis*, from *stenoun* to constrict, from *stenos* narrow] —**stenotic** (stɪ'nɒtɪk) *adj.*

stenothermal (ˌstɛnə'θɜːməl) *adj.* (of animals or plants) able to exist only within a narrow range of temperature. Compare **eurythermal.**

stenotopic (ˌstɛnəʊ'tɒpɪk) *adj. Ecology.* (of a species, group, etc.) able to tolerate only a narrow range of environmental changes. Also (sometimes (influenced by -TROPIC)): **stenotropic.** Compare **eurytopic.** [from STENO- + *top* from Greek *topos* place + -IC]

Stenotype ('stɛnəˌtaɪp) *n.* **1.** *Trademark.* a machine with a keyboard for recording speeches, etc., in a phonetic shorthand. **2.** any machine resembling this. **3.** the phonetic symbol typed in one stroke of such a machine.

stenotypy ('stɛnəˌtaɪpɪ) *n.* a form of shorthand in which alphabetic combinations are used to represent groups of sounds or short common words. [C19: from STENO- + TYPE + -Y[3], on the model of STENOGRAPHY] —**stenotypic** (ˌstɛnə'tɪpɪk) *adj.* —'**stenoˌtypist** *n.*

stentor ('stɛntɔː) *n.* **1.** a person with an unusually loud voice. **2.** any trumpet-shaped protozoan of the genus *Stentor*, having a ciliated spiral feeding funnel at the wider end: class *Ciliata* (ciliates). [C19: after *Stentor* in Greek mythology, a herald with a powerful voice]

stentorian (stɛn'tɔːrɪən) *adj.* (of the voice, etc.) uncommonly loud: *stentorian tones.*

step (stɛp) *n.* **1.** the act of motion brought about by raising the foot and setting it down again in coordination with the transference of the weight of the body. **2.** the distance or space covered by such a motion. **3.** the sound made by such a movement. **4.** the impression made by such movement of the foot; footprint. **5.** the manner of walking or moving the feet; gait: *he received his prize with a proud step.* **6.** a sequence of foot movements that make up a particular dance or part of a dance: *I have mastered the steps of the waltz.* **7.** any of several paces or rhythmic movements in marching, dancing, etc.: *the goose step.* **8.** (*pl.*) a course followed by a person in walking or as walking: *they followed in their leader's steps.* **9.** one of a sequence of separate consecutive stages in the progression towards some goal: *another step towards socialism.* **10.** a rank or grade in a series or scale: *he was always a step behind.* **11.** an object or device that offers support for the foot when ascending or descending. **12.** (*pl.*) a flight of stairs, esp. out of doors. **13.** (*pl.*) another name for **stepladder. 14.** a very short easily walked distance: *it is only a step to my place.* **15.** *Music.* a melodic interval of a second. See **whole tone, half-step. 16.** an offset or change in the level of a surface similar to the step of a stair. **17.** a strong block or frame bolted onto the keel of a vessel and fitted to receive the base of a mast. **18.** a ledge cut in mining or quarrying excavations. **19. break step.** to cease to march in step. **20. keep step.** to remain walking, marching, dancing, etc., in unison or in a specified rhythm. **21. in step. a.** marching, dancing, etc., in conformity with a specified pace or moving in unison with others. **b.** *Informal.* in agreement or harmony. **22. out of step. a.** not moving in conformity with a specified pace or in accordance with others. **b.** *Informal.* not in agreement; out of harmony. **23. step by step.** with care and deliberation; gradually. **24. take steps.** to undertake measures (to do something) with a view to the attainment of some end. **25. watch one's step. a.** *Informal.* to conduct oneself with caution and good behaviour. **b.** to walk or move carefully. ~*vb.* **steps, stepping, stepped. 26.** (*intr.*) to move by raising the foot and then setting it down in a different position, transferring the weight of the body to this foot and repeating the process with the other foot. **27.** (*intr.;* often foll. by *in, out,* etc.) to move or go on foot, esp. for a short distance: *step this way, ladies.* **28.** (*intr.*) *Informal, chiefly U.S.* to move, often in an attractive graceful manner, as in dancing: *he can really step around.* **29.** (*intr.;* usually foll. by *on* or *upon*) to place or press the foot; tread: *to step on the accelerator.* **30.** (*intr.;* usually foll. by *into*) to enter (into a situation) apparently with ease: *she stepped into a life of luxury.* **31.** (*tr.*) to walk or take (a number of paces, etc.): *to step ten paces.* **32.** (*tr.*) to perform the steps of: *they step the tango well.* **33.** (*tr.*) to set or place (the foot). **34.** (*tr.;* usually foll. by *off* or *out*) to measure (some distance of ground) by stepping. **35.** (*tr.*) to arrange in or supply with a series of steps so as to avoid coincidence or symmetry. **36.** (*tr.*) to raise (a mast) and fit it into its step. ~See also **step down, step in, step on, step out, step up.** [Old English *stepe, stæpe;* related to Old Frisian *stap, stepe,* Old High German *stapfo* (German *Stapfe* footprint), Old Norse *stapi* high rock] —**'step,like** *adj.*

STEP (stɛp) *n. acronym for* Special Temporary Employment Programme.

step- *combining form.* indicating relationship through the previous marriage of a spouse or parent rather than by blood: *stepson; stepfather.* [Old English *stēop-;* compare *āstȳpan* to bereave]

stepbrother ('stɛp,brʌðə) *n.* a son of one's stepmother or stepfather by a union with someone other than one's father or mother respectively.

stepchild ('stɛp,tʃaɪld) *n., pl.* **-children.** a stepson or stepdaughter.

stepdame ('stɛp,deɪm) *n.* an archaic word for **stepmother.** [C14: from STEP- + DAME (in the archaic sense: mother; see DAM[2])]

step dance *n.* a dance in which a display of steps is more important than gesture or posture, esp. a solo dance.

stepdaughter ('stɛp,dɔːtə) *n.* a daughter of one's husband or wife by a former union.

step down *vb.* (*adv.*) **1.** (*tr.*) to reduce gradually. **2.** (*intr.*) *Informal.* to resign or abdicate (from a position). **3.** (*intr.*) *Informal.* to assume an inferior or less senior position. ~*adj.* **step-down.** (*prenominal*) **4.** (of a transformer) reducing a high voltage applied to the primary winding to a lower voltage on the secondary winding. Compare **step-up** (sense 3). **5.** decreasing or falling by stages. ~*n.* **step-down. 6.** *Informal.* a decrease in quantity or size.

stepfather ('stɛp,fɑːðə) *n.* a man who has married one's mother after the death or divorce of one's father.

step function *n.* an electrical waveform that rises or falls instantly from one level to another.

stephanotis (,stɛfə'nəʊtɪs) *n.* any climbing asclepiadaceous shrub of the genus *Stephanotis,* esp. *S. floribunda,* of Madagascar and Malaya: cultivated for their fragrant white waxy flowers. [C19: via New Latin from Greek: fit for a crown, from *stephanos* a crown]

step in *vb.* **1.** (*intr., adv.*) *Informal.* to intervene or involve oneself, esp. dramatically or at a senior level. ~*adj.* **step-in. 2.** (*prenominal*) (of garments, etc.) put on by being stepped into; without fastenings. **3.** (of a ski binding) engaging automatically when the boot is positioned on the ski. ~*n.* **step-in. 4.** (*often pl.*) a step-in garment, esp. underwear.

stepladder ('stɛp,lædə) *n.* a folding portable ladder that is made of broad flat steps fixed to a supporting frame hinged at the top to another supporting frame.

stepmother ('stɛp,mʌðə) *n.* a woman who has married one's father after the death or divorce of one's mother.

step on *vb.* (*intr., prep.*) **1.** to place or press the foot on. **2.** *Informal.* to behave harshly or contemptuously towards. **3.** *Drugs slang.* to adulterate. **4. step on it.** *Informal.* to go more quickly, hurry up.

step out *vb.* (*intr., adv.*) **1.** to go outside or leave a room, building, etc., esp. briefly. **2.** to begin to walk more quickly and take longer strides. **3.** *U.S. and Canadian informal.* to withdraw from involvement; bow out.

step-parent ('stɛp,pɛərənt) *n.* a stepfather or stepmother. —**'step-,parenting** *n.*

steppe (stɛp) *n.* (*often pl.*) an extensive grassy plain usually without trees. Compare **prairie, pampas.** [C17: from Old Russian *step* lowland]

stepper ('stɛpə) *n.* a person who or animal that steps, esp. a horse or a dancer.

steppes (stɛps) *pl. n.* (*sometimes cap.*) **the.** the huge grasslands of Eurasia.

stepping stone *n.* **1.** one of a series of stones acting as footrests for crossing streams, marshes, etc. **2.** a circumstance that assists progress towards some goal.

stepsister ('stɛp,sɪstə) *n.* a daughter of one's stepmother or stepfather by a union with someone other than one's father or mother respectively.

stepson ('stɛp,sʌn) *n.* a son of one's husband or wife by a former union.

step up *vb.* (*adv.*) *Informal.* **1.** (*tr.*) to increase or raise by stages; accelerate. **2.** (*intr.*) to make progress or effect an advancement; be promoted. ~*adj.* **step-up.** (*prenominal*) **3.** (of a transformer) increasing a low voltage applied to the primary winding to a higher voltage on the secondary winding. Compare **step-down** (sense 4). **4.** *Informal.* involving a rise by stages. ~*n.* **step-up. 5.** *Informal.* an increment in quantity, size, etc.

stepwise ('stɛp,waɪz) *adj.* **1.** arranged in the manner of or resembling steps. **2.** *Music, U.S.* proceeding by melodic intervals of a second. ~*adv.* **3.** with the form or appearance of steps; step by step. **4.** *Music, U.S.* in a stepwise motion.

ster. *abbrev. for* sterling.

-ster *suffix forming nouns.* **1.** indicating a person who is engaged in a certain activity: *prankster; songster.* Compare **-stress. 2.** indicating a person associated with or being something specified: *mobster; youngster.* [Old English *-estre*]

steradian (stə'reɪdɪən) *n.* an SI unit of solid angle; the angle that, having its vertex in the centre of a sphere, cuts off an area of the surface of the sphere equal to the square of the length of the radius. Symbol: sr [C19: from STEREO- + RADIAN]

stercoraceous (,stɜːkə'reɪʃəs) *adj.* of, relating to, or consisting of dung or excrement. [C18: from Latin *stercus* dung + -ACEOUS]

stercoricolous (,stɜːkə'rɪkələs) *adj.* (of organisms) living in dung. [C19: from Latin *stercus* dung + *colere* to live]

sterculiaceous (stɜː,kjuːlɪ'eɪʃəs) *adj.* of, relating to, or belonging to the *Sterculiaceae,* a chiefly tropical family of plants that includes cacao and cola. [C18: via New Latin from Latin *Sterculius* god of manuring, from *stercus* dung, alluding to the odour of some species]

stere (stɪə) *n.* a unit used to measure volumes of stacked timber equal to one cubic metre (35.315 cubic feet). [C18: from French *stère,* from Greek *stereos* solid]

stereo ('stɛrɪəʊ, 'stɪər-) *adj.* **1.** short for **stereophonic** or **stereoscopic.** ~*n., pl.* **stereos. 2.** stereophonic sound: *to broadcast in stereo.* **3.** a stereophonic record player, tape recorder, etc. **4.** *Photog.* **a.** stereoscopic photography. **b.** a stereoscopic photograph. **5.** *Printing.* short for **stereotype.** [C20: shortened form]

stereo- *or sometimes before a vowel* **stere-** *combining form.* indicating three-dimensional quality or solidity: *stereoscope.* [from Greek *stereos* solid]

stereobate ('stɛrɪəʊ,beɪt, 'stɪər-) *n.* **1.** another name for **stylobate. 2.** a foundation of a building in the form of a platform of masonry. [C19: via Latin, from Greek *stereobatēs* from *stereos* solid + *-batēs* base, from *bainein* to walk]

stereochemistry (,stɛrɪəʊ'kɛmɪstrɪ, ,stɪər-) *n.* the study of the spatial arrangement of atoms in molecules and the effect of spatial arrangement on chemical properties.

stereochrome ('stɛrɪəʊ,krəʊm, 'stɪər-) *n.* **1.** a picture made by stereochromy. ~*vb.* **2.** (*tr.*) to produce (a picture) by the process of stereochromy.

stereochromy ('stɛrɪə,krəʊmɪ, 'stɪər-) *n.* a method of wall painting in which water glass is used either as a painting medium or as a final fixative coat. [C19: via German *Stereochromie,* from STEREO- + Greek *khrōma* colour]

stereognosis (,stɛrɪɒg'nəʊsɪs, ,stɪər-) *n.* the perception of depth or three-dimensionality through any of the senses. [C20: STEREO- + GNOSIS]

stereogram ('stɛrɪə,græm, 'stɪər-) *n.* **1.** *Brit.* a stereo radiogram. **2.** another name for **stereograph.**

stereograph ('stɛrɪə,græf, -,grɑːf, 'stɪər-) *n.* two almost identical pictures, or one special picture, that when viewed through special glasses or a stereoscope form a single three-dimensional image. Also called: **stereogram.**

stereography (,stɛrɪ'ɒgrəfɪ, ,stɪər-) *n.* **1.** the study and construction of geometrical solids. **2.** the art of drawing a solid figure on a flat surface. —**stereographic** (,stɛrɪə'græfɪk, ,stɪər-) *or* **,stereo'graphical** *adj.* —**,stereo'graphically** *adv.*

stereoisomer (,stɛrɪəʊ'aɪsəmə, ,stɪər-) *n. Chem.* one of the isomers of a compound that exhibits stereoisomerism.

stereoisomerism (ˌstɛrɪəʊaɪˈsɒməˌrɪzəm, ˌstɪər-) *n. Chem.* isomerism caused by differences in the spatial arrangement of atoms in molecules. —**stereoisometric** (ˌstɛrɪəʊˌaɪsəˈmɛtrɪk, ˌstɪər-) *adj.*

stereome (ˈstɛrɪˌəʊm) *n. Botany.* the tissue of a plant that provides mechanical support.

stereometry (ˌstɛrɪˈɒmɪtrɪ, ˌstɪər-) *n.* the measurement of volume. —**stereometric** (ˌstɛrɪəʊˈmɛtrɪk, ˌstɪər-) *or* ˌ**stereoˈmetrical** *adj.*

stereophonic (ˌstɛrɪəˈfɒnɪk, ˌstɪər-) *adj.* (of a system for recording, reproducing, or broadcasting sound) using two or more separate microphones to feed two or more loudspeakers through separate channels in order to give a spatial effect to the sound. Often shortened to **stereo.** Compare **monophonic, quadraphonics.** —ˌ**stereoˈphonically** *adv.* —**stereophony** (ˌstɛrɪˈɒfənɪ, ˌstɪər-) *n.*

stereopsis (ˌstɛrɪˈɒpsɪs, ˌstɪər-) *n.* stereoscopic vision. [from STEREO- + Greek *opsis* vision]

stereopticon (ˌstɛrɪˈɒptɪk^{ə}n, ˌstɪər-) *n.* a type of projector with two complete units arranged so that one picture dissolves as the next is forming. [C19: from STEREO- + Greek *optikon,* neuter form of *optikos* OPTIC]

stereoscope (ˈstɛrɪəˌskəʊp, ˈstɪər-) *n.* an optical instrument for viewing two-dimensional pictures and giving them an illusion of depth and relief. It has a binocular eyepiece through which two slightly different pictures of the same object are viewed, one with each eye.

stereoscopic (ˌstɛrɪəˈskɒpɪk, ˌstɪər-) *adj.* **1.** of, concerned with, or relating to seeing space three-dimensionally as a result of binocular disparity: *stereoscopic vision.* **2.** of, relating to, or formed by a stereoscope. —ˌ**stereoˈscopically** *adv.*

stereoscopy (ˌstɛrɪˈɒskəpɪ, ˌstɪər-) *n.* **1.** the viewing or appearance of objects in or as if in three dimensions. **2.** the study and use of the stereoscope. —ˌ**stereˈoscopist** *n.*

stereospecific (ˌstɛrɪəʊspɪˈsɪfɪk, ˌstɪər-) *adj. Chem.* relating to or having fixed position in space, as in the spatial arrangements of atoms in certain polymers.

stereospecific catalyst *n. Chem.* a catalyst for stereospecific chemical reactions. See also **Ziegler catalyst.**

stereospecific polymer *n.* an organic polymer in which the steric arrangements of groups on assymetric carbon atoms occur in a regular sequence. Many natural and synthetic rubbers are stereospecific polymers.

stereotactic (ˌstɛrɪəˈtæktɪk, ˌstɪər-) *adj.* **1.** of or relating to stereotaxis. **2.** *Med.* of or relating to precise localization of a tissue, esp. in the brain: *stereotactic surgery.* —ˌ**stereoˈtactically** *adv.*

stereotaxis (ˌstɛrɪəˈtæksɪs, ˌstɪər-) *n.* the movement of an organism in response to the stimulus of contact with a solid object. [C20: from STEREO- + -TAXIS]

stereotomy (ˌstɛrɪˈɒtəmɪ, ˌstɪər-) *n.* the art of cutting three-dimensional solids into particular shapes. [C18: from French *stéréotomie.* See STEREO-, -TOMY]

stereotropism (ˌstɛrɪˈɒtrəˌpɪzəm, ˌstɪər-) *n.* another name for **thigmotropism.** —**stereotropic** (ˌstɛrɪəˈtrɒpɪk, ˌstɪər-) *adj.*

stereotype (ˈstɛrɪəˌtaɪp, ˈstɪər-) *n.* **1. a.** a method of producing cast-metal printing plates from a mould made from a forme of type matter in papier-mâché or some other material. **b.** the plate so made. **2.** another word for **stereotypy. 3.** an idea, trait, convention, etc., that has grown stale through fixed usage. **4.** *Sociol.* a standardized image or conception shared by all members of a social group. ~*vb.* (*tr.*) **5. a.** to make a stereotype of. **b.** to print from a stereotype. **6.** to impart a fixed usage or convention to. —ˈ**stereoˌtyper** *or* ˈ**stereoˌtypist** *n.* —**stereotypic** (ˌstɛrɪəˈtɪpɪk, ˌstɪər-) *or* ˌ**stereoˈtypical** *adj.*

stereotyped (ˈstɛrɪəˌtaɪpt, ˈstɪər-) *adj.* **1.** lacking originality or individuality; conventional; trite. **2.** reproduced from or on a stereotype printing plate.

stereotypy (ˈstɛrɪəˌtaɪpɪ, ˈstɪər-) *n.* **1.** the act or process of making stereotype printing plates. **2.** a tendency to think or act in rigid, repetitive, and often meaningless patterns.

stereovision (ˈstɛrɪəʊˌvɪʒən, ˈstɪər-) *n.* the perception or exhibition of three-dimensional objects in three dimensions.

steric (ˈstɛrɪk, ˈstɪər-) *or* **sterical** *adj. Chem.* of, concerned with, or caused by the spatial arrangement of atoms in a molecule. [C19: from STEREO- + -IC] —ˈ**sterically** *adv.*

sterigma (stəˈrɪgmə) *n. Botany.* a minute stalk bearing a spore or chain of spores in certain fungi. [C19: New Latin from Greek *stērigma* support, from *stērizein* to sustain]

sterilant (ˈstɛrɪlənt) *n.* any substance or agent used in sterilization.

sterile (ˈstɛraɪl) *adj.* **1.** unable to produce offspring; infertile. **2.** free from living, esp. pathogenic, microorganisms; aseptic. **3.** (of plants or their parts) not producing or bearing seeds, fruit, spores, stamens, or pistils. **4.** lacking inspiration or vitality; fruitless. **5.** *Economics, U.S.* (of gold) not being used to support credit creation or an increased money supply. [C16: from Latin *sterilis*] —ˈ**sterilely** *adv.* —**sterility** (stɛˈrɪlɪtɪ) *n.*

sterilization *or* **sterilisation** (ˌstɛrɪlaɪˈzeɪʃən) *n.* **1.** the act or procedure of sterilizing or making sterile. **2.** the state of being sterile; sterilized condition.

sterilize *or* **sterilise** (ˈstɛrɪˌlaɪz) *vb.* (*tr.*) to render sterile; make infertile or barren. —ˈ**steriˌlizable** *or* ˈ**steriˌlisable** *adj.* —ˈ**steriˌlizer** *or* ˈ**steriˌliser** *n.*

sterlet (ˈstɜːlɪt) *n.* a small sturgeon, *Acipenser ruthenus,* of seas and rivers in N Asia and E Europe: used as a food fish and a source of caviar. [C16: from Russian *sterlyad,* of Germanic origin; compare Old High German *sturio* sturgeon]

sterling (ˈstɜːlɪŋ) *n.* **1. a.** British money: *pound sterling.* **b.** (*as modifier*): *sterling reserves.* **2.** the official standard of fineness of British coins: for gold 0.91666 and for silver 0.925. **3. a.** short for **sterling silver. b.** (*as modifier*): *a sterling bracelet.* **4.** an article or articles manufactured from sterling silver. **5.** a former British silver penny. ~*adj.* **6.** (*prenominal*) genuine and reliable; first-class: *sterling quality.* [C13: probably from Old English *steorra* STAR + -LING[1]; referring to a small star on early Norman pennies; related to Old French *esterlin*]

sterling area *n.* a group of countries that use sterling as a medium of international payments and sometimes informally as a currency against which to peg their own currencies. For these purposes they deposit sterling balances and hold gold and dollar reserves in the Bank of England. Also called: **sterling bloc, scheduled territories.**

sterling silver *n.* **1.** an alloy containing not less than 92.5 per cent of silver, the remainder usually being copper. **2.** sterling-silver articles collectively.

stern[1] (stɜːn) *adj.* **1.** showing uncompromising or inflexible resolve; firm, strict, or authoritarian. **2.** lacking leniency or clemency; harsh or severe. **3.** relentless; unyielding: *the stern demands of parenthood.* **4.** having an austere or forbidding appearance or nature. [Old English *styrne;* related to Old High German *stornēn* to alarm, Latin *sternāx* stubborn, Greek *stereos* hard] —ˈ**sternly** *adv.* —ˈ**sternness** *n.*

stern[2] (stɜːn) *n.* **1.** the rear or after part of a vessel, opposite the bow or stem. **2.** the rear part of any object. **3.** the tail of certain breeds of dog, such as the foxhound or beagle. ~*adj.* **4.** relating to or located at the stern. [C13: from Old Norse *stjōrn* steering; see STEER[1]]

stern-chaser *n.* a gun mounted at the stern of a vessel for firing aft at a pursuing vessel.

sternforemost (ˈstɜːnˈfɔːməʊst) *adv. Nautical.* backwards.

sternmost (ˈstɜːnˌməʊst) *adj. Nautical.* **1.** farthest to the stern; aftmost. **2.** nearest the stern.

sternpost (ˈstɜːnˌpəʊst) *n. Nautical.* the main upright timber or structure at the stern of a vessel.

stern sheets *pl. n. Nautical.* the part of an open boat near the stern.

sternson (ˈstɜːns^{ə}n) *n. Nautical.* a timber scarfed into or bolted to the sternpost and keelson at the stern of a wooden vessel. Compare **stemson.** [C19: from STERN[2] + *-son,* on the model of KEELSON]

sternum (ˈstɜːnəm) *n., pl.* **-na** (-nə) *or* **-nums. 1.** (in man) a long flat vertical bone, situated in front of the thorax, to which are attached the collarbone and the first seven pairs of ribs. Nontechnical name: **breastbone. 2.** the corresponding part in many other vertebrates. **3.** a cuticular plate covering the ventral surface of a body segment of an arthropod. Compare **tergum.** [C17: via New Latin from Greek *sternon* breastbone] —ˈ**sternal** *adj.*

sternutation (ˌstɜːnjʊˈteɪʃən) *n.* a sneeze or the act of sneezing. [C16: from Late Latin *sternūtāre* to sneeze, from *sternuere* to sputter (of a light)]

sternutator (ˈstɜːnjʊˌteɪtə) *n.* a substance that causes sneezing, coughing, and tears; used in chemical warfare.

sternutatory (stɜːˈnjuːtətərɪ, -trɪ) *adj.* *also* **sternutative. 1.** causing or having the effect of sneezing. ~*n., pl.* **-tories. 2.** an agent or substance that causes sneezing.

sternwards (ˈstɜːnwədz) *or* **sternward** *adv. Nautical.* towards the stern; astern.

sternway (ˈstɜːnˌweɪ) *n. Nautical.* movement of a vessel sternforemost.

stern-wheeler *n.* a vessel, esp. a riverboat, propelled by a large paddle wheel at the stern. Compare **sidewheeler.**

steroid (ˈstɪərɔɪd, ˈstɛr-) *n. Biochem.* any of a large group of fat-soluble organic compounds containing a characteristic chemical ring system. The majority, including the sterols, many hormones, and the D vitamins, have important physiological action. [C20: from STEROL + -OID] —**steˈroidal** *adj.*

sterol (ˈstɛrɒl) *n. Biochem.* any of a group of natural steroid alcohols, such as cholesterol and ergosterol, that are waxy insoluble substances. [C20: shortened from CHOLESTEROL, ERGOSTEROL, etc.]

stertor (ˈstɜːtə) *n.* laborious or noisy breathing caused by obstructed air passages. [C17: from New Latin, from Latin *stertere* to snore]

stertorous (ˈstɜːtərəs) *adj.* **1.** marked or accompanied by heavy snoring. **2.** breathing in this way. —ˈ**stertorously** *adv.* —ˈ**stertorousness** *n.*

stet (stɛt) *n.* **1.** a word or mark indicating that certain deleted typeset or written matter is to be retained. Compare **dele.** ~*vb.* **stets, stetting, stetted. 2.** (*tr.*) to mark (matter to be retained) with a stet. [Latin, literally: let it stand]

stethoscope (ˈstɛθəˌskəʊp) *n. Med.* an instrument for listening to the sounds made within the body, typically consisting of a hollow disc that transmits the sound through hollow tubes to earpieces. [C19: from French, from Greek *stēthos* breast + -SCOPE]

—**stethoscopic** (ˌstɛθəˈskɒpɪk) *adj.* —**stethoscopy** (stɛˈθɒskəpɪ) *n.*

stetson (ˈstɛtsᵊn) *n.* a man's felt slouch hat with a broad brim and high crown. [C20: named after John *Stetson* (1830–1906), American hatmaker who designed it]

stevedore (ˈstiːvɪˌdɔː) *n.* **1.** a person employed to load or unload ships. ~*vb.* **2.** to load or unload (a ship, ship's cargo, etc.). [C18: from Spanish *estibador* a packer, from *estibar* to load (a ship), from Latin *stīpāre* to pack full]

stevedore's knot *n.* a knot forming a lump in a line, used by stevedores to secure ropes passing through holes.

Stevengraph (ˈstiːvᵊnˌgrɑːf) *or* **Stevensgraph** *n.* a picture, usually small, woven in silk. [named after Thomas *Stevens* (1828–88), British weaver]

stew[1] (stjuː) *n.* **1. a.** a dish of meat, fish, or other food, cooked by stewing. **b.** (*as modifier*): *stew pot.* **2.** *Informal.* a difficult or worrying situation or a troubled state (esp. in the phrase **in a stew**). **3.** a heterogeneous mixture: *a stew of people of every race.* **4.** (*usually pl.*) *Archaic.* a brothel. **5.** *Obsolete.* a public room for hot steam baths. ~*vb.* **6.** to cook or cause to cook by long slow simmering. **7.** (*intr.*) *Informal.* to be troubled or agitated. **8.** (*intr.*) *Informal.* to be oppressed with heat or crowding. **9.** to cause (tea) to become bitter or (of tea) to become bitter through infusing for too long. **10. stew in one's own juice.** to suffer unaided the consequences of one's actions. [C14 *stuen* to take a very hot bath, from Old French *estuver,* from Vulgar Latin *extūfāre* (unattested), from EX-[1] + (unattested) *tūfus* vapour, from Greek *tuphos*]

stew[2] (stjuː) *n. Brit.* **1.** a fishpond or fishtank. **2.** an artificial oyster bed. [C14: from Old French *estui,* from *estoier* to shut up, confine, ultimately from Latin *studium* STUDY]

steward (ˈstjʊəd) *n.* **1.** a person who administers the property, house, finances, etc., of another. **2.** a person who manages the eating arrangements, staff, or service at a club, hotel, etc. **3.** a waiter on a ship or aircraft. **4.** a mess attendant in a naval mess afloat or ashore. **5.** a person who helps to supervise some event or proceedings in an official capacity. **6.** short for **shop steward.** ~*vb.* **7.** to act or serve as a steward (of something). [Old English *stigweard,* from *stig* hall (see STY[1]) + *weard* WARD] —ˈ**stewardˌship** *n.*

stewardess (ˈstjʊədɪs, ˌstjʊəˈdɛs) *n.* a woman who performs a steward's job on an aircraft or ship.

stewed (stjuːd) *adj.* **1.** (of meat, fruit, etc.) cooked by stewing. **2.** *Brit.* (of tea) having a bitter taste through having been left to infuse for too long. **3.** a slang word for **drunk** (sense 1).

St. Ex. *abbrev. for* stock exchange.

stg *abbrev. for* sterling.

stge *abbrev. for* storage.

Sth *abbrev. for* South.

sthenic (ˈsθɛnɪk) *adj.* abounding in energy or bodily strength; active or strong. [C18: from New Latin *sthenicus,* from Greek *sthenos* force, on the model of *asthenic*]

stibine (ˈstɪbaɪn) *n.* **1.** a colourless slightly soluble poisonous gas with an offensive odour: made by the action of hydrochloric acid on an alloy of antimony and zinc. Formula: SbH_3. **2.** any one of a class of stibine derivatives in which one or more hydrogen atoms have been replaced by organic groups. [C19: from Latin STIBIUM + -INE[2]]

stibium (ˈstɪbɪəm) *n.* an obsolete name for **antimony.** [C14: from Latin: antimony (used as a cosmetic in ancient Rome), via Greek from Egyptian *stm*] —ˈ**stibial** *adj.*

stibnite (ˈstɪbnaɪt) *n.* a soft greyish mineral consisting of antimony sulphide in orthorhombic crystalline form. It occurs in quartz veins and is the chief ore of antimony. Formula: Sb_2S_3. [C19: from obsolete *stibine* stibnite + -ITE[1]]

stich (stɪk) *n.* a line of poetry; verse. [C18: from Greek *stikhos* row, verse; related to *steikhein* to walk] —ˈ**stichic** *adj.* —ˈ**stichically** *adv.*

stichometry (stɪˈkɒmɪtrɪ) *n. Prosody.* the practice of writing out a prose text in lines that correspond to the sense units and indicate the phrasal rhythms. [C18: from Late Greek *stikhometria.* See STICH, -METRY] —**stichometric** (ˌstɪkəʊˈmɛtrɪk) *or* ˌ**stichoˈmetrical** *adj.*

stichomythia (ˌstɪkəʊˈmɪθɪə) *or* **stichomythy** (stɪˈkɒmɪθɪ) *n.* a form of dialogue originating in Greek drama in which single lines are uttered by alternate speakers. [C19: from Greek *stikhomuthein* to speak alternate lines, from *stikhos* line + *muthos* speech; see MYTH] —ˌ**stichoˈmythic** *adj.*

-stichous *adj. combining form.* having a certain number of rows: *distichous.* [from Late Latin *-stichus,* from Greek *-stikhos,* from *stikhos* line, row; see STICH]

stick[1] (stɪk) *n.* **1.** a small thin branch of a tree. **2. a.** any long thin piece of wood. **b.** such a piece of wood having a characteristic shape for a special purpose: *a walking stick; a hockey stick.* **c.** a baton, wand, staff, or rod. **3.** an object or piece shaped like a stick: *a stick of celery; a stick of dynamite.* **4.** See **control stick.** **5.** *Informal.* the lever used to change gear in a motor vehicle. **6.** *Nautical.* a mast or yard. **7.** *Printing.* See **composing stick.** **8. a.** a group of bombs arranged to fall at intervals across a target. **b.** a number of paratroops jumping in sequence. **9.** *Slang.* **a.** verbal abuse, criticism: *I got some stick for that blunder.* **b.** physical power, force (esp. in the phrase **give it some stick**). **10.** (*usually pl.*) a piece of furniture: *these few sticks are all I have.* **11.** (*pl.*) *Informal.* a rural area considered remote or backward (esp. in the phrase **in the sticks**). **12.** (*pl.*) *W and NW Canadian informal.* the wooded interior part of the country. **13.** (*pl.*) *Hockey.* a declaration made by the umpire if a player's stick is above the shoulders. **14.** (*pl.*) *Austral.* goal posts. **15.** *U.S. obsolete.* a cannabis cigarette. **16.** a means of coercion. **17.** *Informal.* a dull boring person. **18.** (usually preceded by *old*) *Informal.* a familiar name for a person: *not a bad old stick.* **19. in a cleft stick.** in a difficult position. **20. wrong end of the stick.** a complete misunderstanding of a situation, explanation, etc. ~*vb.* **sticks, sticking, sticked.** **21.** to support (a plant) with sticks; stake. **22.** *Printing.* to set (type) in a composing stick. [Old English *sticca;* related to Old Norse *stikka,* Old High German *stecca*]

stick[2] (stɪk) *vb.* **sticks, sticking, stuck.** **1.** (*tr.*) to pierce or stab with or as if with something pointed. **2.** to thrust or push (a sharp or pointed object) or (of a sharp or pointed object) to be pushed into or through another object. **3.** (*tr.*) to fasten in position by pushing or forcing a point into something: *to stick a peg in a hole.* **4.** (*tr.*) to fasten in position by or as if by pins, nails, etc.: *to stick a picture on the wall.* **5.** (*tr.*) to transfix or impale on a pointed object. **6.** (*tr.*) to cover with objects piercing or set in the surface. **7.** (when *intr.*, foll. by *out, up, through,* etc.) to put forward or be put forward; protrude or cause to protrude: *to stick one's head out of the window.* **8.** (*tr.*) *Informal.* to place or put in a specified position: *stick your coat on this chair.* **9.** to fasten or be fastened by or as if by an adhesive substance: *stick the pages together; they won't stick.* **10.** (*tr.*) *Informal.* to cause to become sticky. **11.** (when *tr., usually passive*) to come or cause to come to a standstill: *we were stuck for hours in a traffic jam; the wheels stuck.* **12.** (*intr.*) to remain for a long time: *the memory sticks in my mind.* **13.** (*tr.*) *Slang, chiefly Brit.* to tolerate; abide: *I can't stick that man.* **14.** (*intr.*) to be reluctant. **15.** (*tr.; usually passive*) *Informal.* to cause to be at a loss; baffle, puzzle, or confuse: *I was totally stuck for an answer.* **16.** (*tr.*) *Slang.* to force or impose something unpleasant on: *they stuck me with the bill for lunch.* **17.** (*tr.*) to kill by piercing or stabbing. **18. stick in one's throat** (*or* **craw**). *Informal.* to be difficult, or against one's conscience, for one to accept, utter, or believe. **19. stick one's nose into.** See **nose** (sense 17). **20. stick to the ribs.** *Informal.* (of food) to be hearty and satisfying. ~*n.* **21.** the state or condition of adhering. **22.** *Informal.* a substance causing adhesion. **23.** *Obsolete.* something that causes delay or stoppage. ~See also **stick around, stick at, stick by, stick down, stick out, stick to, stick together, stick-up, stick with, stuck.** [Old English *stician;* related to Old High German *stehhan* to sting, Old Norse *steikja* to roast on a spit]

stick around *or* **about** *vb.* (*intr., adv.*) *Informal.* to remain in a place, esp. awaiting something.

stick at *vb.* (*intr., prep.*) **1.** to continue constantly at: *to stick at one's work.* **2. stick at nothing.** to be prepared to do anything; be unscrupulous or ruthless.

stick by *vb.* (*intr., prep.*) to remain faithful to; adhere to.

stick down *vb.* (*tr., adv.*) *Informal.* to write: *stick your name down here.*

sticker (ˈstɪkə) *n.* **1.** an adhesive label, poster, or paper. **2.** a person or thing that sticks. **3.** a persevering or industrious person. **4.** something prickly, such as a thorn, that clings to one's clothing, etc. **5.** *Informal.* something that perplexes. **6.** *Informal.* a knife used for stabbing or piercing.

stick float *n. Angling.* a float attached at the top and bottom to the line.

stickful (ˈstɪkˌfʊl) *n., pl.* **-fuls.** *Printing.* the amount of type required to fill a composing stick.

sticking plaster *n.* a thin cloth with an adhesive substance on one side, used for covering slight or superficial wounds. Usual U.S. term: **adhesive tape.**

stick insect *n.* any of various mostly tropical insects of the family *Phasmidae* that have an elongated cylindrical body and long legs and resemble twigs: order *Phasmida.* Also called (U.S. and Canadian): **walking stick.** See also **leaf insect.**

stick-in-the-mud *n. Informal.* a staid or predictably conservative person who lacks initiative or imagination.

stickle (ˈstɪkᵊl) *vb.* (*intr.*) **1.** to dispute stubbornly, esp. about minor points. **2.** to refuse to agree or concur, esp. by making petty stipulations. [C16 *stightle* (in the sense: to arbitrate): frequentative of Old English *stihtan* to arrange; related to Old Norse *stētta* to support]

stickleback (ˈstɪkᵊlˌbæk) *n.* any small teleost fish of the family *Gasterosteidae,* such as *Gasterosteus aculeatus* (**three-spined stickleback**) of rivers and coastal regions and *G. pungitius* (**ten-spined stickleback**) confined to rivers. They have a series of spines along the back and occur in cold and temperate northern regions. [C15: from Old English *stickel* prick, sting + BACK[1]]

stickler (ˈstɪklə) *n.* **1.** (usually foll. by *for*) a person who makes insistent demands: *a stickler for accuracy.* **2.** a problem or puzzle: *the investigation proved to be a stickler.*

stick out *vb.* (*adv.*) **1.** to project or cause to project. **2.** (*tr.*) *Informal.* to endure (something disagreeable) (esp. in the phrase **stick it out**). **3. stick out a mile** *or* **like a sore thumb.** *Informal.* to be extremely obvious. **4. stick out for** (*intr.*) to insist on (a demand), refusing to yield until it is met: *the unions stuck out for a ten per cent wage rise.*

stick pin *n.* the U.S. name for **tiepin.**

stickseed ('stɪkˌsiːd) *n.* any of various Eurasian and North American plants of the boraginaceous genus *Lappula,* having red-and-blue flowers and small prickly fruits. Also called: **beggar's-lice.** [C19: from STICK[2]; so called because its seeds have adhesive hooks on them]

stick shift *n. U.S. and Canadian.* **1. a.** a manually operated transmission system in a motor vehicle. **b.** a motor vehicle having manual transmission. **2.** a gear lever.

sticktight ('stɪkˌtaɪt) *n.* any of various plants, esp. the bur marigold, that have barbed clinging fruits.

stick to *vb. (prep., mainly intr.)* **1.** *(also tr.)* to adhere or cause to adhere to. **2.** to continue constantly at. **3.** to remain faithful to. **4.** not to move or digress from: *the speaker stuck closely to his subject.* **5. stick to someone's fingers.** *Informal.* to be stolen by someone.

stick together *vb. (intr., adv.) Informal.* to remain loyal or friendly to one another.

stick-up *n.* **1.** *Slang, chiefly U.S.* a robbery at gunpoint; hold-up. ~*vb.* **stick up.** *(adv.)* **2.** *(tr.) Slang, chiefly U.S.* to rob, esp. at gunpoint. **3.** *(intr.;* foll. by *for) Informal.* to support or defend: *stick up for oneself.*

stickweed ('stɪkˌwiːd) *n.* any of several plants that have clinging fruits or seeds, esp. the ragweed.

stick with *vb. (intr., prep.) Informal.* to persevere with; remain faithful to.

sticky ('stɪkɪ) *adj.* **stickier, stickiest. 1.** covered or daubed with an adhesive or viscous substance: *sticky fingers.* **2.** having the property of sticking to a surface. **3.** (of weather or atmosphere) warm and humid; muggy. **4.** (of prices) tending not to fall in deflationary conditions. **5.** *Informal.* difficult, awkward, or painful: *a sticky business.* **6.** *U.S. informal.* sentimental. ~*vb.* **stickies, stickying, stickied. 7.** *(tr.) Informal.* to make sticky. ~*n., pl.* **stickies.** *Austral. informal.* **8.** short for **stickybeak. 9.** an inquisitive look or stare (esp. in the phrase **have a sticky at**). —'**stickily** *adv.* —'**stickiness** *n.*

stickybeak ('stɪkɪˌbiːk) *Austral. and N.Z. informal.* ~*n.* **1.** an inquisitive person. ~*vb.* **2.** *(intr.)* to pry. [from STICKY + BEAK[1] (in the slang sense: a human nose)]

sticky end *n. Informal.* an unpleasant finish or death (esp. in the phrase **come to** *or* **meet a sticky end**).

sticky-fingered *adj. Informal.* given to thieving.

sticky wicket *n.* **1.** a cricket pitch that is rapidly being dried by the sun after rain and is particularly conducive to spin. **2.** *Informal.* a difficult or awkward situation (esp. in the phrase **on a sticky wicket**).

sticky willie *n.* another name for **cleavers.**

stiction ('stɪkʃən) *n.* the frictional force to be overcome to set one object in motion when it is in contact with another. [C20: blend of STATIC + FRICTION]

stiff (stɪf) *adj.* **1.** not easily bent; rigid; inflexible. **2.** not working or moving easily or smoothly: *a stiff handle.* **3.** difficult to accept in its severity or harshness: *a stiff punishment.* **4.** moving with pain or difficulty; not supple: *a stiff neck.* **5.** difficult; arduous: *a stiff climb.* **6.** unrelaxed or awkward; formal. **7.** firmer than liquid in consistency; thick or viscous. **8.** powerful; strong: *a stiff breeze; a stiff drink.* **9.** excessively high: *a stiff price.* **10.** *Nautical.* (of a sailing vessel) relatively resistant to heeling or rolling. Compare **tender**[1] (sense 11). **11.** lacking grace or attractiveness. **12.** stubborn or stubbornly maintained: *a stiff fight.* **13.** *Obsolete.* tightly stretched; taut. **14.** *Dialect, chiefly Scot. and northern English.* sturdy and stocky. **15.** *Slang, chiefly Austral.* unlucky. **16.** *Slang.* intoxicated. **17. stiff upper lip.** See **lip** (sense 9). **18. stiff with.** *Informal.* amply provided with. ~*n.* **19.** *Slang.* a corpse. **20.** *Slang.* anything thought to be a loser or a failure; flop. ~*adv.* **21.** completely or utterly: *bored stiff; frozen stiff.* ~*vb.* **22.** *(intr.) Slang.* to fail: *the film stiffed.* **23.** *(tr.) Slang, chiefly U.S.* to cheat or swindle. [Old English *stīf;* related to Old Norse *stīfla* to dam up, Middle Low German *stīf* stiff, Latin *stīpēs* wooden post, *stīpāre* to press] —'**stiffish** *adj.* —'**stiffly** *adv.* —'**stiffness** *n.*

stiffen ('stɪfᵊn) *vb.* **1.** to make or become stiff or stiffer. **2.** *(intr.)* to become suddenly tense or unyielding. —'**stiffener** *n.*

stiff-necked *adj.* haughtily stubborn or obstinate.

stifle[1] ('staɪfᵊl) *vb.* **1.** *(tr.)* to smother or suppress: *stifle a cough.* **2.** to feel or cause to feel discomfort and difficulty in breathing. **3.** to prevent or be prevented from breathing so as to cause death. **4.** *(tr.)* to crush or stamp out. [C14: variant of *stuflen,* probably from Old French *estouffer* to smother] —'**stifler** *n.*

stifle[2] ('staɪfᵊl) *n.* the joint in the hind leg of a horse, dog, etc., between the femur and tibia. [C14: of unknown origin]

stifling ('staɪflɪŋ) *adj.* oppressively hot or stuffy: *a stifling atmosphere.* —'**stiflingly** *adv.*

stigma ('stɪgmə) *n., pl.* **stigmas** *or* **stigmata** ('stɪgmətə, stɪg'mɑːtə). **1.** a distinguishing mark of social disgrace: *the stigma of having been in prison.* **2.** a small scar or mark such as a birthmark. **3.** *Pathol.* **a.** any mark on the skin, such as one characteristic of a specific disease. **b.** any sign of a mental deficiency or emotional upset. **4.** *Botany.* the terminal part of the ovary, at the end of the style, where deposited pollen enters the gynoecium. **5.** *Zoology.* **a.** a pigmented eyespot in some protozoans and other invertebrates. **b.** the spiracle of an insect. **6.** *Archaic.* a mark branded on the skin. **7.** *(pl.) Christianity.* marks resembling the wounds of the crucified Christ, believed to appear on the bodies of certain individuals. [C16: via Latin from Greek: brand, from *stizein* to tattoo]

stigmasterol (stɪg'mæstəˌrɒl) *n. Biochem.* a sterol obtained from Calabar beans and soya beans and used in the manufacture of progesterone. Formula: $C_{29}H_{47}OH$. [C20: from New Latin *(physo)stigma* genus name of the Calabar bean + STEROL; see PHYSOSTIGMINE]

stigmatic (stɪg'mætɪk) *adj.* **1.** relating to or having a stigma or stigmata. **2.** another word for **anastigmatic.** ~*n. also* **stigmatist** ('stɪgmətɪst). **3.** *Chiefly R.C. Church.* a person marked with the stigmata.

stigmatism ('stɪgməˌtɪzəm) *n.* **1.** *Physics.* the state or condition of being anastigmatic. **2.** *Pathol.* the condition resulting from or characterized by stigmata.

stigmatize *or* **stigmatise** ('stɪgməˌtaɪz) *vb. (tr.)* **1.** to mark out or describe (as something bad). **2.** to mark with a stigma or stigmata. —ˌ**stigmati'zation** *or* ˌ**stigmati'sation** *n.* —'**stigmaˌtizer** *or* '**stigmaˌtiser** *n.*

stilb (stɪlb) *n. Physics.* a unit of luminance equal to 1 candela per square centimetre. Symbol: sb [C20: from Greek *stilbē* lamp]

stilbene ('stɪlbiːn) *n.* a colourless or slightly yellow crystalline water-insoluble unsaturated hydrocarbon used in the manufacture of dyes; *trans-1,2-*diphenylethene. Formula: $C_6H_5CH{:}CHC_6H_5$. [C19: from Greek *stilbos* glittering + -ENE]

stilbite ('stɪlbaɪt) *n.* a white or yellow zeolite mineral consisting of hydrated calcium sodium aluminium silicate, often in the form of sheaves of monoclinic crystals. Formula: $(Na_2Ca)Al_2Si_6O_{16}.6H_2O$. [C19: from Greek *stilbos* glittering (from *stilbein* to shine) + -ITE[1]]

stilboestrol *or U.S.* **stilbestrol** (stɪl'biːstrəl) *n.* a synthetic hormone having derivatives with oestrogenic properties. Formula: $OHC_6H_4CH{:}CHC_6H_4OH$. Also called: **diethylstilboestrol.** [C20: from STILBENE + OESTRUS + -OL[1]]

stile[1] (staɪl) *n.* **1.** a set of steps or rungs in a wall or fence to allow people, but not animals, to pass over. **2.** short for **turnstile.** [Old English *stigel;* related to *stīgan* to climb, Old High German *stigilla;* see STAIR]

stile[2] (staɪl) *n.* a vertical framing member in a door, window frame, or piece of panelling. Compare **rail**[1] (sense 3). [C17: probably from Dutch *stijl* pillar, ultimately from Latin *stilus* writing instrument; see STYLE]

stiletto (stɪ'lɛtəʊ) *n., pl.* **-tos. 1.** a small dagger with a slender tapered blade. **2.** a sharply pointed tool used to make holes in leather, cloth, etc. **3.** Also called: **spike heel, stiletto heel.** a very high heel on a woman's shoe, tapering to a very narrow tip. ~*vb.* **-toes, -toeing, -toed. 4.** *(tr.)* to stab with a stiletto. [C17: from Italian, from *stilo* a dagger, from Latin *stilus* a stake, pen; see STYLUS]

still[1] (stɪl) *adj.* **1.** *(usually predicative)* motionless; stationary. **2.** undisturbed or tranquil; silent and calm. **3.** not sparkling or effervescent: *a still wine.* **4.** gentle or quiet; subdued. **5.** *Obsolete.* (of a child) dead at birth. ~*adv.* **6.** continuing now or in the future as in the past: *do you still love me?* **7.** up to this or that time; yet: *I still don't know your name.* **8.** (often used with a comparative) even or yet: *still more insults.* **9.** quiet or without movement: *sit still.* **10.** *Poetic and dialect.* always. ~*n.* **11.** *Poetic.* silence or tranquillity: *the still of the night.* **12. a.** a still photograph, esp. of a scene from a motion-picture film. **b.** *(as modifier): a still camera.* ~*vb.* **13.** to make or become still, quiet, or calm. **14.** *(tr.)* to allay or relieve: *her fears were stilled.* ~*sentence connector.* **15.** even then; nevertheless: *the child has some new toys and still cries.* [Old English *stille;* related to Old Saxon, Old High German *stilli,* Dutch *stollen* to curdle, Sanskrit *sthānús* immobile] —'**stillness** *n.*

still[2] (stɪl) *n.* **1.** an apparatus for carrying out distillation, consisting of a vessel in which a mixture is heated, a condenser to turn the vapour back to liquid, and a receiver to hold the distilled liquid, used esp. in the manufacture of spirits. **2.** a place where spirits are made; distillery. [C16: from Old French *stiller* to drip, from Latin *stillāre,* from *stilla* a drip; see DISTIL]

stillage ('stɪlɪdʒ) *n.* **1.** a frame or stand for keeping things off the ground, such as casks in a brewery. **2.** a container in which goods, machinery, etc., are transported. [C16: probably from Dutch *stillagie* frame, scaffold, from *stellen* to stand; see -AGE]

stillbirth ('stɪlˌbɜːθ) *n.* **1.** birth of a dead fetus or baby. **2.** a stillborn fetus or baby.

stillborn ('stɪlˌbɔːn) *adj.* **1.** (of a fetus) dead at birth. **2.** (of an idea, plan, etc.) fruitless; abortive; unsuccessful. ~*n.* **3.** a stillborn fetus or baby.

still frame *n.* continuous display of a single frame of a film or of a single picture from a television signal.

still hunt *n.* **1.** the hunting of game by stalking or ambushing. ~*vb.* **still-hunt. 2.** to hunt (quarry) in this way.

stillicide ('stɪlɪˌsaɪd) *n. Law.* a right or duty relating to the drainage of water from the eaves of a roof onto adjacent land. [C17: from Latin *stillicidium,* from *stilla* drop + *-cidium,* from *cadere* to fall]

stilliform ('stɪlɪˌfɔːm) *adj. Rare.* having the shape of a drop or globule. [C20: from Latin *stilla* a drop + -FORM]

still life *n., pl.* **still lifes. 1. a.** a painting or drawing of inanimate objects, such as fruit, flowers, etc. **b.** *(as modifier): a still-life painting.* **2.** the genre of such paintings.

still room *n. Brit.* **1.** a room in which distilling is carried out. **2.** a pantry or storeroom, as in a large house.
Stillson wrench ('stɪlsᵊn) *n. Trademark.* a large wrench having adjustable jaws that tighten as the pressure on the handle is increased.
stilly *adv.* ('stɪllɪ). **1.** *Archaic or literary.* quietly or calmly. *~adj.* ('stɪlɪ). **2.** *Poetic.* still, quiet, or calm.
stilt (stɪlt) *n.* **1.** either of a pair of two long poles with footrests on which a person stands and walks, as used by circus clowns. **2.** a long post or column that is used with others to support a building above ground level. **3.** any of several shore birds of the genera *Himantopus* and *Cladorhynchus,* similar to the avocets but having a straight bill. *~vb.* **4.** (*tr.*) to raise or place on or as if on stilts. [C14 (in the sense: crutch, handle of a plough): related to Low German *stilte* pole, Norwegian *stilta*]
stilted ('stɪltɪd) *adj.* **1.** (of speech, writing, etc.) formal, pompous, or bombastic. **2.** not flowing continuously or naturally: *stilted conversation.* **3.** *Architect.* (of an arch) having vertical piers between the impost and the springing. —'**stiltedly** *adv.* —'**stiltedness** *n.*
Stilton ('stɪltən) *n. Trademark.* either of two rich cheeses made from whole milk, blue-veined (**blue Stilton**) or white (**white Stilton**), both very strong in flavour. [C18: named after *Stilton,* Cambridgeshire, where it was originally sold]
stim (stɪm) *n. Irish.* (*used with a negative*) a very small amount: *I couldn't see a stim; she hasn't a stim of sense.* [of uncertain origin]
stimulant ('stɪmjʊlənt) *n.* **1.** a drug or similar substance that increases physiological activity, esp. of a particular organ. **2.** any stimulating agent or thing. *~adj.* **3.** increasing physiological activity; stimulating. [C18: from Latin *stimulāns* goading, from *stimulāre* to urge on; see STIMULUS]
stimulate ('stɪmjʊˌleɪt) *vb.* **1.** (*tr.*) to arouse or quicken the activity or senses of. **2.** (*tr.*) *Physiol.* to excite (a nerve, organ, etc.) with a stimulus. **3.** (*intr.*) to act as a stimulant or stimulus. [C16: from Latin *stimulāre;* see STIMULANT] —'**stimulable** *adj.* —'**stimuˌlating** *adj.* —'**stimuˌlatingly** *adv.* —ˌ**stimu'lation** *n.* —'**stimulative** *adj., n.* —'**stimuˌlator** *or* '**stimuˌlater** *n.*
stimulus ('stɪmjʊləs) *n., pl.* **-li** (-ˌlaɪ, -ˌliː). **1.** something that stimulates or acts as an incentive. **2.** any drug, agent, electrical impulse, or other factor able to cause a response in an organism. **3.** an object or event that is apprehended by the senses. **4.** *Med.* another word for a **stimulant.** [C17: from Latin: a cattle goad]
sting (stɪŋ) *vb.* **stings, stinging, stung. 1.** (of certain animals and plants) to inflict a wound on (an organism) by the injection of poison. **2.** to feel or cause to feel a sharp mental or physical pain. **3.** (*tr.*) to goad or incite (esp. in the phrase **sting into action**). **4.** (*tr.*) *Informal.* to cheat, esp. by overcharging. *~n.* **5.** a skin wound caused by the poison injected by certain insects or plants. **6.** pain caused by or as if by the sting of a plant or animal. **7.** a mental pain or pang: *a sting of conscience.* **8.** a sharp pointed organ, such as the ovipositor of a wasp, by which poison can be injected into the prey. **9.** the ability to sting: *a sharp sting in his criticism.* **10.** something as painful or swift of action as a sting: *the sting of death.* **11.** a sharp stimulus or incitement. **12.** *Botany.* another name for **stinging hair. 13.** *Slang.* a deceptive ruse. [Old English *stingan;* related to Old Norse *stinga* to pierce, Gothic *usstangan* to pluck out, Greek *stakhus* ear of corn] —'**stinging** *adj.* —'**stingingly** *adv.* —'**stingingness** *n.*
stingaree ('stɪŋəˌriː, ˌstɪŋə'riː) *n. U.S., Canadian, and Austral.* a popular name for the **stingray.** [C19: variant of STINGRAY]
stinger ('stɪŋə) *n.* **1.** a person, plant, animal, etc., that stings or hurts. **2.** Also called: **stengah.** a whisky and soda with crushed ice.
stinging hair *n.* a multicellular hair in plants, such as the stinging nettle, that injects an irritant fluid when in contact with an animal.
stinging nettle *n.* See **nettle** (sense 1).
stingo ('stɪŋgəʊ) *n.* a strong English beer, originally made in Yorkshire. [C17: from STING + -O; so called because of its sharp taste]
stingray ('stɪŋˌreɪ) *n.* any ray of the family *Dasyatidae,* having a whiplike tail bearing a serrated venomous spine capable of inflicting painful weals on man.
stingy[1] ('stɪndʒɪ) *adj.* **-gier, -giest. 1.** unwilling to spend or give. **2.** insufficient or scanty. [C17 (perhaps in the sense: ill-tempered): perhaps from *stinge,* dialect variant of STING] —'**stingily** *adv.* —'**stinginess** *n.*
stingy[2] ('stɪŋɪ) *adj.* **stingier, stingiest. 1.** *Informal.* stinging or capable of stinging. *~n., pl.* **stingies. 2.** *South Wales dialect.* a stinging nettle: *I put my hand on a stingy.*
stink (stɪŋk) *n.* **1.** a strong foul smell; stench. **2.** *Slang.* a great deal of trouble (esp. in the phrase **to make** *or* **raise a stink**). **3. like stink.** intensely; furiously. *~vb.* **stinks, stinking, stank** *or* **stunk; stunk.** (*mainly intr.*) **4.** to emit a foul smell. **5.** *Slang.* to be thoroughly bad or abhorrent: *this town stinks.* **6.** *Informal.* to have a very bad reputation: *his name stinks.* **7.** to be of poor quality. **8.** (foll. by *of* or *with*) *Slang.* to have or appear to have an excessive amount (of money). **9.** (*tr.;* usually foll. by *up*) *Informal.* to cause to stink. *~*See also **stink out.** [Old English *stincan;* related to Old Saxon *stinkan,* German *stinken,* Old Norse *stökkva* to burst; see STENCH]
stink ball *n.* another name for **stinkpot** (sense 4).
stink bomb *n.* a small glass globe, used by practical jokers: it releases a liquid with an offensive smell when broken.
stinker ('stɪŋkə) *n.* **1.** a person or thing that stinks. **2.** *Slang.* a difficult or very unpleasant person or thing. **3.** *Slang.* something of very poor quality. **4.** *Informal.* any of several fulmars or related birds that feed on carrion.
stinkhorn ('stɪŋkˌhɔːn) *n.* any of various basidiomycetous saprophytic fungi of the genus *Phallus,* such as *P. impudicus,* having an offensive odour.
stinking ('stɪŋkɪŋ) *adj.* **1.** having a foul smell. **2.** *Informal.* unpleasant or disgusting. **3.** (*postpositive*) *Slang.* very drunk. **4. cry stinking fish.** to decry or defame something, esp. one's own products. *~adv.* **5.** *Informal.* (intensifier, expressing contempt for the person referred to): *stinking rich.* —'**stinkingly** *adv.* —'**stinkingness** *n.*
stinking badger *n.* another name for **teledu.**
stinking iris *n.* an iris plant, *Iris foetidissima,* of W Europe and N Africa, having purplish flowers and a strong unpleasant smell when bruised. Also called: **gladdon.**
stinking smut *n.* a smut that affects wheat and is caused by the fungus *Tilletia caries.* Also called: **bunt.**
stinko ('stɪŋkəʊ) *adj.* (*postpositive*) a slang word for **drunk.**
stink out *vb.* (*tr., adv.*) **1.** to drive out or away by a foul smell. **2.** *Brit.* to cause to stink: *the smell of orange peel stinks out the room.*
stinkpot ('stɪŋkˌpɒt) *n.* **1.** *Slang.* a person or thing that stinks. **2.** *Slang.* a person considered to be unpleasant. **3.** another name for **musk turtle. 4.** Also called: **stink ball.** *Military.* (formerly) a container filled with material that gives off noxious or suffocating vapours.
stinkstone ('stɪŋkˌstəʊn) *n.* any of various rocks producing a fetid odour when struck, esp. certain limestones.
stink trap *n.* another name for **stench trap.**
stinkweed ('stɪŋkˌwiːd) *n.* **1.** Also called: **wall mustard.** a cruciferous plant, *Diplotaxis muralis,* naturalized in Britain and S and central Europe, having pale yellow flowers, cylindrical seed pods, and a disagreeable smell when bruised. **2.** any of various other ill-smelling plants, such as mayweed.
stinkwood ('stɪŋkˌwʊd) *n.* **1.** any of various trees having offensive-smelling wood, esp. *Ocotea bullata,* a southern African lauraceous tree yielding a hard wood used for furniture. **2.** the heavy durable wood of any of these trees.
stint[1] (stɪnt) *vb.* **1.** to be frugal or miserly towards (someone) with (something). **2.** *Archaic.* to stop or check (something). *~n.* **3.** an allotted or fixed amount of work. **4.** a limitation or check. **5.** *Obsolete.* a pause or stoppage. [Old English *styntan* to blunt; related to Old Norse *stytta* to cut short; see STUNT[1]] —'**stinter** *n.*
stint[2] (stɪnt) *n.* any of various small sandpipers of the chiefly northern genus *Calidris* (or *Erolia*), such as *C. minuta* (**little stint**). [Old English; related to Middle High German *stinz* small salmon, Swedish dialect *stinta* teenager; see STUNT[1]]
stipe (staɪp) *n.* **1.** a stalk in plants that bears reproductive structures, esp. the stalk bearing the cap of a mushroom. **2.** the stalk that bears the leaflets of a fern or the thallus of a seaweed. **3.** *Zoology.* any stalklike part; stipes. [C18: via French from Latin *stīpes* tree trunk; related to Latin *stīpāre* to pack closely; see STIFF]
stipel ('staɪpᵊl) *n.* a small paired leaflike structure at the base of certain leaflets; secondary stipule. [C19: via New Latin from Latin *stipula,* diminutive of *stīpes* a log] —**stipellate** (staɪ'pɛlɪt, -eɪt) *adj.*
stipend ('staɪpɛnd) *n.* a fixed or regular amount of money paid as a salary or allowance, as to a clergyman. [C15: from Old French *stipende,* from Latin *stīpendium* tax, from *stips* a contribution + *pendere* to pay out]
stipendiary (staɪ'pɛndɪərɪ) *adj.* **1.** receiving or working for regular pay: *a stipendiary magistrate.* **2.** paid for by a stipend. *~n., pl.* **-aries. 3.** a person who receives regular payment. [C16: from Latin *stīpendiārius* concerning tribute, from *stīpendium* STIPEND]
stipes ('staɪpiːz) *n., pl.* **stipites** ('stɪpɪˌtiːz). *Zoology.* **1.** the second maxillary segment in insects and crustaceans. **2.** the eyestalk of a crab or similar crustacean. **3.** any similar stemlike structure. [C18: from Latin; see STIPE] —**stipiform** ('staɪpɪˌfɔːm) *or* **stipitiform** ('stɪpɪtɪˌfɔːm) *adj.*
stipitate ('stɪpɪˌteɪt) *adj. Botany.* possessing or borne on the end of a stipe. [C18: from New Latin *stīpitātus* having a stalk, from Latin *stīpes;* see STIPE]
stipple ('stɪpᵊl) *vb.* (*tr.*) **1.** to draw, engrave, or paint using dots or flecks. **2.** to apply paint, powder, etc., to (something) with many light dabs. **3.** to give (wet paint, cement, etc.) a granular effect. *~n. also* **stippling. 4.** the technique of stippling or a picture produced by or using stippling. [C18: from Dutch *stippelen,* from *stippen* to prick, from *stip* point] —'**stippler** *n.*
stipulate[1] ('stɪpjʊˌleɪt) *vb.* **1.** (*tr.; may take a clause as object*) to specify, often as a condition of an agreement. **2.** (*intr.;* foll. by *for*) to insist (on) as a term of an agreement. **3.** *Roman law.* to make (an oral contract) in the form of question and answer necessary to render it legally valid. **4.** (*tr.; may take a clause as object*) to guarantee or promise. [C17: from Latin *stipulārī,* probably from Old Latin *stipulus* firm, but perhaps from *stipula* a stalk, from the convention of breaking a straw to ratify a prom-

ise] —**stipulable** (ˈstɪpjʊləbᵊl) *adj.* —ˌ**stipuˈlation** *n.* —ˈ**stipuˌlator** *n.* —**stipulatory** (ˈstɪpjʊlətərɪ, -trɪ) *adj.*

stipulate[2] (ˈstɪpjʊlɪt, -ˌleɪt) *adj.* (of a plant) having stipules.

stipule (ˈstɪpjuːl) *n.* a small paired usually leaflike outgrowth occurring at the base of a leaf or its stalk. [C18: from Latin; see STIPE, STIPES] —**stipular** (ˈstɪpjʊlə) *adj.*

stir[1] (stɜː) *vb.* **stirs, stirring, stirred.** **1.** to move an implement such as a spoon around in (a liquid) so as to mix up the constituents: *she stirred the porridge.* **2.** to change or cause to change position; disturb or be disturbed: *he stirred in his sleep.* **3.** (*intr.*; often foll. by *from*) to venture or depart (from one's usual or preferred place): *he won't stir from the fireside.* **4.** (*intr.*) to be active after a rest; be up and about. **5.** (*tr.*) to excite or stimulate, esp. emotionally. **6.** to move (oneself) briskly or vigorously; exert (oneself). **7.** (*tr.*) to rouse or awaken: *to stir someone from sleep; to stir memories.* **8.** *Informal.* (when *tr.*, foll. by *up*) to cause or incite others to cause (trouble, arguments, etc.). **9. stir one's stumps.** *Informal.* to move or become active. ~*n.* **10.** the act or an instance of stirring or the state of being stirred. **11.** a strong reaction, esp. of excitement: *his publication caused a stir.* **12.** a slight movement. **13.** *N.Z. informal.* a noisy party. ~See also **stir up.** [Old English *styrian;* related to Middle High German *stürn* to poke, stir, Norwegian *styrja* to cause a commotion; see STORM, STURGEON] —ˈ**stirrable** *adj.*

stir[2] (stɜː) *n.* a slang word for **prison:** *in stir.* [C19: perhaps from Romany *stariben* prison]

Stir. *abbrev. for* Stirlingshire.

stirabout (ˈstɜːrəˌbaʊt) *n.* **1.** a kind of porridge orginally made in Ireland. **2.** a bustling person.

stir-crazy *adj. Slang, chiefly U.S. and Canadian.* mentally disturbed as a result of being in prison or otherwise confined.

stir-fry (ˈstɜːˈfraɪ) *vb.* **-fries, -frying, -fried.** to cook (small pieces of meat, vegetables, etc.) rapidly by stirring them in a wok or frying pan over a high heat: used esp. for Chinese food.

stirk (stɜːk) *n.* **1.** a heifer of 6 to 12 months old. **2.** a yearling heifer or bullock. [Old English *stierc;* related to Middle Low German *sterke,* Old High German *stero* ram, Latin *sterilis* sterile, Greek steira; see STEER]

Stirling engine (ˈstɜːlɪŋ) *n.* an external-combustion engine that uses air or an inert gas as the working fluid operating on a highly efficient thermodynamic cycle (the **Stirling cycle**). [named after Robert *Stirling* (1790–1878), British engineer who invented it]

Stirling's formula *n.* a formula giving the approximate value of the factorial of a large number *n*, as $n! \approx (n/e)^n\sqrt{2\pi n}$. [named after James *Stirling* (1692–1770), Scottish mathematician]

stirps (stɜːps) *n., pl.* **stirpes** (ˈstɜːpiːz). **1.** *Genealogy.* a line of descendants from an ancestor; stock or strain. **2.** *Botany.* a race or variety, esp. one in which the characters are maintained by cultivation. [C17: from Latin: root, family origin]

stirrer (ˈstɜːrə) *n.* **1.** a person or thing that stirs. **2.** *Informal.* a person who deliberately causes trouble. **3.** *Austral. and N.Z. informal.* a political activist or agitator.

stirring (ˈstɜːrɪŋ) *adj.* **1.** exciting the emotions; stimulating. **2.** active, lively, or busy. —ˈ**stirringly** *adv.*

stirrup (ˈstɪrəp) *n.* **1.** Also called: **stirrup iron.** either of two metal loops on a riding saddle, with a flat footpiece through which a rider puts his foot for support. They are attached to the saddle by **stirrup leathers. 2.** a U-shaped support or clamp made of metal, wood, leather, etc. **3.** *Nautical.* one of a set of ropes fastened to a yard at one end and having a thimble at the other through which a footrope is rove for support. **4.** the usual U.S. name for **étrier.** [Old English *stigrāp,* from *stīg* path, step (related to Old High German *stīgan* to move up) + *rāp* ROPE; related to Old Norse *stigreip,* Old High German *stegareif*]

stirrup bone *n.* the nontechnical name for **stapes.** [C17: so called because of its stirrup-like shape]

stirrup cup *n.* a cup containing an alcoholic drink offered to a horseman ready to ride away.

stirrup pump *n.* a hand-operated reciprocating pump, the base of the cylinder of which is placed in a bucket of water: used in fighting fires.

stir up *vb.* (*tr., adv.*) to set in motion; instigate: *he stirred up trouble.*

stishie (ˈstɪʃɪ) *n. Scot.* a variant of **stushie.**

stitch (stɪtʃ) *n.* **1.** a link made by drawing a thread through material by means of a needle. **2.** a loop of yarn formed around an implement used in knitting, crocheting, etc. **3.** a particular method of stitching or shape of stitch. **4.** a sharp spasmodic pain in the side resulting from running or exercising. **5.** (*usually used with a negative*) *Informal.* the least fragment of clothing: *he wasn't wearing a stitch.* **6.** *Agriculture.* the ridge between two furrows. **7. in stitches.** *Informal.* laughing uncontrollably. **8. drop a stitch.** to allow a loop of wool to fall off a knitting needle accidentally while knitting. ~*vb.* **9.** (*tr.*) to sew, fasten, etc., with stitches. **10.** (*intr.*) to be engaged in sewing. **11.** (*tr.*) to bind together (the leaves of a book, pamphlet, etc.) with wire staples or thread. ~*n., vb.* **12.** an informal word for **suture** (senses 1b, 6). [Old English *stice* sting; related to Old Frisian *steke,* Old High German *stih,* Gothic *stiks,* Old Norse *tikta* sharp] —ˈ**stitcher** *n.*

stitchery (ˈstɪtʃərɪ) *n.* needlework, esp. modern embroidery.

stitch wheel *n.* a notched wheel used by a harness maker to mark out the spacing for stitching.

stitchwort (ˈstɪtʃˌwɜːt) *n.* any of several low-growing N temperate herbaceous plants of the caryophyllaceous genus *Stellaria,* having small white star-shaped flowers. [C13: so named because it was once thought to be a remedy for stitches in the side]

stithy (ˈstɪðɪ) *n., pl.* **stithies. 1.** *Archaic or dialect.* a forge or anvil. ~*vb.* **stithies, stithying, stithied. 2.** (*tr.*) *Obsolete.* to forge on an anvil. [C13: from Old Norse *stedhi*]

stiver (ˈstaɪvə) *n.* **1.** a former Dutch coin worth one twentieth of a guilder. **2.** a small amount, esp. of money. [C16: from Dutch *stuiver;* related to Middle Low German *stüver,* Danish *styver*]

stk *abbrev. for* stock.

stoa (ˈstəʊə) *n., pl.* **stoae** (ˈstəʊiː) *or* **stoas.** a covered walk that has a colonnade on one or both sides, esp. as used in ancient Greece. [C17: from Greek]

stoat (stəʊt) *n.* a small Eurasian musteline mammal, *Mustela erminea,* closely related to the weasels, having a brown coat and a black-tipped tail: in the northern parts of its range it has a white winter coat and is then known as an ermine. [C15: of unknown origin]

stob (stɒb) *n. Scot., Northern English, and U.S. dialect.* a post or stump. [C14: variant of STUB]

stochastic (stɒˈkæstɪk) *adj.* **1.** *Statistics.* **a.** (of a random variable) having a probability distribution, usually with finite variance. **b.** (of a process) involving a random variable the successive values of which are not independent. **c.** (of a matrix) square with non-negative elements that add to unity in each row. **2.** *Rare.* involving conjecture. [C17: from Greek *stokhastikos* capable of guessing, from *stokhazesthai* to aim at, conjecture, from *stokhos* a target] —**stoˈchastically** *adv.*

stock (stɒk) *n.* **1. a.** (*sometimes pl.*) the total goods or raw material kept on the premises of a shop or business. **b.** (*as modifier*): *a stock clerk; stock book.* **2.** a supply of something stored for future use: *he keeps a good stock of whisky.* **3.** *Finance.* **a.** the capital raised by a company through the issue and subscription of shares entitling their holders to dividends, partial ownership, and usually voting rights. **b.** the proportion of such capital held by an individual shareholder. **c.** the shares of a specified company or industry. **d.** (formerly) the part of an account or tally given to a creditor. **e.** the debt represented by this. **4.** standing or status. **5. a.** farm animals, such as cattle and sheep, bred and kept for their meat, skins, etc. **b.** (*as modifier*): *stock farming.* **6.** the trunk or main stem of a tree or other plant. **7.** *Horticulture.* **a.** a rooted plant into which a scion is inserted during grafting. **b.** a plant or stem from which cuttings are taken. See also **rootstock. 8.** the original type from which a particular race, family, group, etc., is derived. **9.** a race, breed, or variety of animals or plants. **10.** (*often pl.*) a small pen in which a single animal can be confined. **11.** a line of descent. **12.** any of the major subdivisions of the human species; race or ethnic group. **13.** the part of a rifle, sub-machine-gun, etc., into which the barrel and firing mechanism is set: held by the firer against the shoulder. **14.** the handle of something, such as a whip or fishing rod. **15.** the main body of a tool, such as the block of a plane. **16.** short for **diestock, gunstock,** or **rolling stock. 17.** (formerly) the part of a plough to which the irons and handles were attached. **18.** the main upright part of a supporting structure. **19.** a liquid or broth in which meat, fish, bones, or vegetables have been simmered for a long time. **20.** film material before exposure and processing. **21.** *Metallurgy.* **a.** a portion of metal cut from a bar upon which a specific process, such as forging, is to be carried out. **b.** the material that is smelted in a blast furnace. **22.** Also called: **gillyflower.** any of several cruciferous plants of the genus *Matthiola,* such as *M. incana* and *M. bicornis* (**evening** or **night-scented stock**), of the Mediterranean region: cultivated for their brightly coloured flowers. **23. Virginian stock.** a similar and related North American plant, *Malcomia maritima.* **24.** a long usually white neckcloth wrapped around the neck, worn in the 18th century and as part of modern riding dress. **25.** *Cards.* a pile of cards left after the deal in certain games, from which players draw. **26. a.** the repertoire of plays available to a repertory company. **b.** (*as modifier*): *a stock play.* **27.** (on some types of anchors) a crosspiece at the top of the shank under the ring. **28.** the centre of a wheel. **29.** an exposed mass of igneous rock that is the uppermost part of an underlying batholith. **30.** a log or block of wood. **31.** See **laughing stock. 32.** an archaic word for **stocking. 33. in stock. a.** stored on the premises or available for sale or use. **b.** supplied with goods of a specified kind. **34. out of stock. a.** not immediately available for sale or use. **b.** not having goods of a specified kind immediately available. **35. take stock. a.** to make an inventory. **b.** to make a general appraisal, esp. of prospects, resources, etc. **36. take stock in.** to attach importance to. **37. lock, stock, and barrel.** See **lock**[1] (sense 7). ~*adj.* **38.** staple, standard: *stock sizes in clothes.* **39.** (*prenominal*) being a cliché; hackneyed: *a stock phrase.* ~*vb.* **40.** (*tr.*) to keep (goods) for sale. **41.** (*intr.*; usually foll. by *up* or *up on*) to obtain a store of (something) for future use or sale: *to stock up on beer.* **42.** (*tr.*) to supply with live animals, fish, etc.: *to stock a farm.* **43.** (*intr.*) (of a plant) to put forth new shoots. **44.** (*tr.*) *Obsolete.* to punish by putting in the stocks. ~See also **stocks.** [Old English *stocc* trunk (of a tree), stem, stick (the various senses developed from these meanings, as trunk of a tree, hence line of descent; structures made of timber; a store of timber or other goods for future use, hence an aggregate of goods, animals, etc.); related to Old Saxon, Old High German *stock* stick, stump] —'**stocker** *n.*

stockade (stɒ'keɪd) *n.* **1.** an enclosure or barrier of stakes and timbers. **2.** *U.S.* a military prison or detention area. ~*vb.* **3.** (*tr.*) to surround with a stockade. [C17: from Spanish *estacada*, from *estaca* a stake, post, of Germanic origin; see STAKE[1]]

stock and station agent *n. Austral. and N.Z.* a firm dealing in and financing farm activities.

stockbreeder ('stɒkˌbriːdə) *n.* a person who breeds or rears livestock as an occupation. —'**stockˌbreeding** *n.*

stockbroker ('stɒkˌbrəʊkə) *n.* a person who buys and sells securities on a commission basis for customers. Often shortened to **broker.** —**stockbrokerage** ('stɒkˌbrəʊkərɪdʒ) *or* '**stockˌbroking** *n.*

stockbroker belt *n. Brit. informal.* the area outside a city, esp. London, in which rich commuters live. Compare **exurbia.**

stock car *n.* **1. a.** a car, usually a production saloon, strengthened and modified for a form of racing in which the cars often collide. **b.** (*as modifier*): *stock-car racing.* **2.** the U.S. and Canadian term for **cattle truck.**

stock certificate *n.* the U.S. equivalent of **share certificate.**

stock company *n.* **1.** *U.S.* a business enterprise the capital of which is divided into transferable shares. **2.** a U.S. term for **repertory company.**

stock dove *n.* a European dove, *Columba oenas*, smaller than the wood pigeon and having a uniformly grey plumage. [C14: so called because it lives in tree trunks. See STOCK]

stock exchange *n.* (*often caps.*) **1.** Also called: **stock market. a.** a highly organized market facilitating the purchase and sale of securities and operated by professional stockbrokers and market makers according to fixed rules. **b.** a place where securities are regularly traded. **c.** (*as modifier*): *a stock-exchange operator; stock-exchange prices.* **2.** the prices or trading activity of a stock exchange: *the stock exchange fell heavily today.*

stock farm *n.* a farm on which livestock is bred. —**stock farmer** *n.* —**stock farming** *n.*

stockfish ('stɒkˌfɪʃ) *n., pl.* **-fish** *or* **-fishes.** fish, such as cod or haddock, cured by splitting and drying in the air. [C13: of uncertain origin. Perhaps from STOCK (in the sense: stem, tree trunk) because it was dried on wooden racks. Compare Middle Dutch *stocvisch*]

stockholder ('stɒkˌhəʊldə) *n.* **1.** an owner of corporate capital stock. **2.** *Austral.* a person who keeps livestock. —'**stockˌholding** *n.*

stockhorse ('stɒkˌhɔːs) *n. Austral.* a horse trained in the handling of stock.

stockinet (ˌstɒkɪ'nɛt) *n.* a machine-knitted elastic fabric used, esp. formerly, for stockings, undergarments, etc. [C19: perhaps changed from earlier *stocking-net*]

stocking ('stɒkɪŋ) *n.* **1.** one of a pair of close-fitting garments made of knitted yarn to cover the foot and part or all of the leg. **2.** something resembling this in position, function, appearance, etc. **3. in (one's) stocking** *or* **stockinged feet.** wearing stockings or socks but no shoes. [C16: from dialect *stock* stocking + -ING[1]] —'**stockinged** *adj.*

stocking cap *n.* a conical knitted cap, often with a tassel.

stockinger ('stɒkɪŋə) *n.* a person who knits on a stocking frame.

stocking filler *n. Brit.* a present, esp. a toy, of a size suitable for inclusion in a child's Christmas stocking.

stocking frame *n.* a type of knitting machine. Also called: **stocking loom, stocking machine.**

stocking mask *n.* a nylon stocking worn over the face by a criminal to disguise the features.

stocking stitch *n.* a pattern of stitches in knitting consisting of alternate rows of plain and purl stitch. [C19: so named because of its use in hosiery]

stock in trade *n.* **1.** goods in stock necessary for carrying on a business. **2.** anything constantly used by someone as a part of his profession, occupation, or trade: *friendliness is the salesman's stock in trade.*

stockish ('stɒkɪʃ) *adj.* stupid or dull. —'**stockishly** *adv.* —'**stockishness** *n.*

stockist ('stɒkɪst) *n. Commerce, Brit.* a dealer who undertakes to maintain stocks of a specified product at or above a certain minimum in return for favourable buying terms granted by the manufacturer of the product.

stockjobber ('stɒkˌdʒɒbə) *n.* **1.** *Brit.* (formerly) a wholesale dealer on a stock exchange who sold securities to brokers without transacting directly with the public. Often shortened to **jobber.** See also **market maker. 2.** *U.S., disparaging.* a stockbroker, esp. one dealing in worthless securities. —'**stockˌjobbery** *or* '**stockˌjobbing** *n.*

stock lock *n.* a lock that is enclosed in a wooden case.

stockman ('stɒkmən, -ˌmæn) *n., pl.* **-men. 1. a.** a man engaged in the rearing or care of farm livestock, esp. cattle. **b.** an owner of cattle or other livestock. **2.** *U.S. and Canadian.* a man employed in a warehouse or stockroom.

stock market *n.* **1.** another name for **stock exchange** (sense 1). **2.** the usual U.S. name for **stock exchange** (sense 2).

stockpile ('stɒkˌpaɪl) *vb.* **1.** to acquire and store a large quantity of (something). ~*n.* **2.** a large store or supply accumulated for future use. —'**stockˌpiler** *n.*

stockpot ('stɒkˌpɒt) *n. Chiefly Brit.* a pot in which stock for soup, etc., is made or kept.

stockroom ('stɒkˌruːm, -ˌrʊm) *n.* a room in which a stock of goods is kept, as in a shop or factory.

stockroute ('stɒkˌruːt) *n. Austral. and N.Z.* a route designated for droving sheep or cattle.

stocks (stɒks) *pl. n.* **1.** *History.* an instrument of punishment consisting of a heavy wooden frame with holes in which the feet, hands, or head of an offender were locked. **2.** a frame in which an animal is held while receiving veterinary attention or while being shod. **3.** a frame used to support a boat while under construction. **4.** *Nautical.* a vertical post or shaft at the forward edge of a rudder, extended upwards for attachment to the steering controls. **5. on the stocks.** in preparation or under construction. **6. stocks and stones.** inanimate objects.

stock saddle *n. Chiefly U.S.* a cowboy's saddle, esp. an ornamental one.

stock-still *adv.* absolutely still; motionless.

stocktaking ('stɒkˌteɪkɪŋ) *n.* **1.** the examination, counting, and valuing of goods on hand in a shop or business. **2.** a reassessment of one's current situation, progress, prospects, etc.

stock unit *n. N.Z.* **a.** the tax basis for evaluating farmers' stock. Cattle, sheep, and deer are each given differing stock-unit values, the basic measure being the ewe equivalent. **b.** (*as modifier*): *stock-unit values.*

stock watering *n. Business.* the creation of more new shares in a company than is justified by its assets.

stock whip *n.* a whip with a long lash and a short handle, as used to herd cattle.

stocky ('stɒkɪ) *adj.* **stockier, stockiest.** (usually of a person) thickset; sturdy. —'**stockily** *adv.* —'**stockiness** *n.*

stockyard ('stɒkˌjɑːd) *n.* a large yard with pens or covered buildings where farm animals are assembled, sold, etc.

stodge (stɒdʒ) *Informal.* ~*n.* **1.** heavy filling starchy food. **2.** *Dialect, chiefly southern English.* baked or steamed pudding. **3.** a dull person or subject. ~*vb.* **4.** to stuff (oneself or another) with food. [C17: perhaps a blend of STUFF + PODGE]

stodgy ('stɒdʒɪ) *adj.* **stodgier, stodgiest. 1.** (of food) heavy or uninteresting. **2.** excessively formal and conventional. [C19: from STODGE] —'**stodgily** *adv.* —'**stodginess** *n.*

stogy *or* **stogey** ('stəʊgɪ) *n., pl.* **-gies.** *U.S.* any long cylindrical inexpensive cigar. [C19: from *stoga*, short for *Conestoga*, a town in Pennsylvania]

stoic ('stəʊɪk) *n.* **1.** a person who maintains stoical qualities. ~*adj.* **2.** a variant of **stoical.**

Stoic ('stəʊɪk) *n.* **1.** a member of the ancient Greek school of philosophy founded by Zeno of Citium (?336–?264 B.C.), holding that virtue and happiness can be attained only by submission to destiny and the natural law. ~*adj.* **2.** of or relating to the doctrines of the Stoics. [C16: via Latin from Greek *stōikos*, from *stoa* the porch in Athens where Zeno taught]

stoical ('stəʊɪkəl) *adj.* characterized by impassivity or resignation. —'**stoically** *adv.* —'**stoicalness** *n.*

stoichiology, stoicheiology, *or* **stoechiology** (ˌstɔɪkɪ'ɒlədʒɪ) *n.* the branch of biology concerned with the study of the cellular components of animal tissues. [C19: from Greek *stoikheion* element + -LOGY] —**stoichiological, stoicheiological,** *or* **stoechiological** (ˌstɔɪkɪə'lɒdʒɪkəl) *adj.*

stoichiometric, stoicheiometric, *or* **stoechiometric** (ˌstɔɪkɪə'mɛtrɪk) *adj. Chem.* **1.** concerned with, involving, or having the exact proportions for a particular chemical reaction: *a stoichiometric mixture.* **2.** (of a compound) having its component elements present in the exact proportions indicated by its formula. **3.** of or concerned with stoichiometry. [C19: see STOICHIOMETRY]

stoichiometry, stoicheiometry, *or* **stoechiometry** (ˌstɔɪkɪ'ɒmɪtrɪ) *n.* the branch of chemistry concerned with the proportions in which elements are combined in compounds and the quantitative relationships between reactants and products in chemical reactions. [C19: from Greek *stoikheion* element + -METRY]

stoicism ('stəʊɪˌsɪzəm) *n.* **1.** indifference to pleasure and pain. **2.** (*cap.*) the philosophy of the Stoics.

stoke (stəʊk) *vb.* **1.** to feed, stir, and tend (a fire, furnace, etc.). **2.** (*tr.*) to tend the furnace of; act as a stoker for. ~See also **stoke up.** [C17: back formation from STOKER]

stokehold ('stəʊkˌhəʊld) *n. Nautical.* **1.** a coal bunker for a ship's furnace. **2.** the hold for a ship's boilers; fire room.

stokehole ('stəʊkˌhəʊl) *n.* **1.** another word for **stokehold. 2.** a hole in a furnace through which it is stoked.

stoker ('stəʊkə) *n.* a person employed to tend a furnace, as on a steamship. [C17: from Dutch, from *stoken* to STOKE]

stokes (stəʊks) *or* **stoke** *n.* the cgs unit of kinematic viscosity, equal to the viscosity of a fluid in poise divided by its density in grams per cubic centimetre. 1 stokes is equivalent to 10^{-4} square metre per second. Symbol: St [C20: named after Sir George *Stokes* (1819–1903), British physicist]

stoke up *vb.* (*adv.*) **1.** to feed and tend (a fire, etc.) with fuel. **2.** (*intr.*) to fill oneself with food.

STOL (stɒl) *n.* **1.** a system in which an aircraft can take off and land in a short distance. **2.** an aircraft using this system. Compare **VTOL.** [C20: *s(hort) t(ake) o(ff and) l(anding)*]
stole[1] (stəʊl) *vb.* the past tense of **steal.**
stole[2] (stəʊl) *n.* **1.** a long scarf or shawl, worn by women. **2.** a long narrow scarf worn by various officiating clergymen. [Old English *stole,* from Latin *stola,* Greek *stolē* clothing; related to *stellein* to array]
stolen ('stəʊlən) *vb.* the past participle of **steal.**
stolid ('stɒlɪd) *adj.* showing little or no emotion or interest. [C17: from Latin *stolidus* dull; compare Latin *stultus* stupid; see STILL[1]] —**stolidity** (stɒ'lɪdɪtɪ) *or* '**stolidness** *n.* —'**stolidly** *adv.*
stollen ('stəʊlən; *German* 'ʃtɔlən) *n.* a rich sweet bread containing nuts, raisins, etc. [German, from *Stollen* wooden post, prop; so called from its shape; see STALL[1]]
stolon ('stəʊlən) *n.* **1.** another name for **runner** (sense 13). **2.** a branching structure in lower animals, esp. the anchoring rootlike part of colonial organisms, such as hydroids, on which the polyps are borne. [C17: from Latin *stolō* shoot] —**stoloniferous** (ˌstəʊlə'nɪfərəs) *adj.*
stoma ('stəʊmə) *n., pl.* **stomata** ('stəʊmətə, 'stɒm-, stəʊ'mɑːtə). **1.** *Botany.* an epidermal pore, present in large numbers in plant leaves, that controls the passage of gases into and out of a plant. **2.** *Zoology, anatomy.* a mouth or mouthlike part. **3.** *Surgery.* an artificial opening made in a tubular organ, esp. the colon or ileum. See **colostomy, ileostomy.** [C17: via New Latin from Greek: mouth]
stomach ('stʌmək) *n.* **1.** (in vertebrates) the enlarged muscular saclike part of the alimentary canal in which food is stored until it has been partially digested and rendered into chyme. Related adj.: **gastric. 2.** the corresponding digestive organ in invertebrates. **3.** the abdominal region. **4.** desire, appetite, or inclination: *I have no stomach for arguments.* **5.** an archaic word for **temper. 6.** an obsolete word for **pride.** ~*vb.* (*tr.; used mainly in negative constructions*) **7.** to tolerate; bear: *I can't stomach his bragging.* **8.** to eat or digest: *he cannot stomach oysters.* [C14: from Old French *stomaque,* from Latin *stomachus* (believed to be the seat of the emotions), from Greek *stomakhos,* from *stoma* mouth]
stomachache ('stʌməkˌeɪk) *n.* pain in the stomach or abdominal region, as from acute indigestion. Technical name: **gastralgia.** Also called: **stomach upset, upset stomach.**
stomacher ('stʌməkə) *n.* a decorative V-shaped panel of stiff material worn over the chest and stomach by men and women in the 16th century, later only by women.
stomachic (stə'mækɪk) *adj.* *also* **stomachical. 1.** stimulating gastric activity. **2.** of or relating to the stomach. ~*n.* **3.** a stomachic medicine.
stomach pump *n. Med.* a suction device for removing stomach contents by a tube inserted through the mouth.
stomach worm *n.* any of various nematode worms that are parasitic in the stomach of mammals, esp. *Haemonchus contortus,* which infests sheep: family *Trichostrongylidae.*
stomachy ('stʌməkɪ) *adj.* **1.** having a large belly; paunchy. **2.** *Dialect.* easily angered; irritable.
stomack ('stʌmək) *n.* **have a stomack.** *E African informal.* to be pregnant.
stomata ('stəʊmətə, 'stɒm-, stəʊ'mɑːtə) *n.* the plural of **stoma.**
stomatal ('stəʊmətᵊl, 'stɒm-) *or* **stomatous** ('stɒmətəs, 'stəʊ-) *adj.* of, relating to, or possessing stomata or a stoma.
stomatic (stəʊ'mætɪk) *adj.* of or relating to a mouth or mouthlike part.
stomatitis (ˌstəʊmə'taɪtɪs, ˌstɒm-) *n.* inflammation of the mouth. —**stomatitic** (ˌstəʊmə'tɪtɪk, ˌstɒm-) *adj.*
stomato- *or before a vowel* **stomat-** *combining form.* indicating the mouth or a mouthlike part: *stomatology.* [from Greek *stoma, stomat-*]
stomatology (ˌstəʊmə'tɒlədʒɪ) *n.* the branch of medicine or dentistry concerned with the structures, functions, and diseases of the mouth. —**stomatological** (ˌstəʊmətə'lɒdʒɪkᵊl) *adj.*
stomatoplasty ('stɒmətəˌplæstɪ, 'stəʊ-) *n.* plastic surgery or surgical repair involving the mouth.
stomatopod ('stɒmətəˌpɒd, 'stəʊ-) *n.* any marine crustacean of the order *Stomatopoda,* having abdominal gills: subclass *Malacostraca.* The group includes the mantis shrimp. [C19: via New Latin from Greek *stoma* mouth + *-podos, pous* foot]
-stome *n. combining form.* indicating a mouth or opening resembling a mouth: *peristome.* [from Greek *stoma* mouth, and *stomion* little mouth]
stomodaeum *or* **stomodeum** (ˌstəʊmə'diːəm, ˌstɒm-) *n., pl.* **daea** *or* **dea** (-'diːə). the oral cavity of a vertebrate embryo, which is formed from an invagination of the ectoderm and develops into the part of the alimentary canal between the mouth and stomach. [C19: from New Latin, from Greek *stoma* mouth + *hodaios* on the way, from *hodos* way] —ˌ**stomo'daeal** *or* ˌ**stomo'deal** *adj.*
-stomous *adj. combining form.* having a specified type of mouth: *monostomous.*
stomp (stɒmp) *vb.* (*intr.*) **1.** *Informal.* to tread or stamp heavily. ~*n.* **2.** a rhythmical stamping jazz dance. [variant of STAMP] —'**stomper** *n.*
-stomy *n. combining form.* indicating a surgical operation performed to make an artificial opening into or for a specified part: *cytostomy.* [from Greek *-stomia,* from *stoma* mouth]
stone (stəʊn) *n.* **1.** the hard compact nonmetallic material of which rocks are made. **2.** a small lump of rock; pebble. **3.** *Jewellery.* short for **gemstone. 4. a.** a piece of rock designed or shaped for some particular purpose. **b.** (*in combination*): *gravestone; millstone.* **5. a.** something that resembles a stone. **b.** (*in combination*): *hailstone.* **6.** the woody central part of such fruits as the peach and plum, that contains the seed; endocarp. **7.** any similar hard part of a fruit, such as the stony seed of a date. **8.** (*pl.* **stone**) *Brit.* a unit of weight, used esp. to express human body weight, equal to 14 pounds or 6.350 kilograms. **9.** Also called: **granite.** the rounded heavy mass of granite or iron used in the game of curling. **10.** *Pathol.* a nontechnical name for **calculus. 11.** *Printing.* a table with a very flat iron or stone surface upon which pages are composed into formes; imposition table. **12.** *Rare.* (in certain games) a piece or man. **13.** (*usually pl.*) a rare word for **testicle. 14. a.** any of various dull grey colours. **b.** (*as adj.*): *stone paint.* **15.** (*modifier*) relating to or made of stone: *a stone house.* **16.** (*modifier*) made of stoneware: *a stone jar.* **17. cast a stone (at).** cast aspersions (upon). **18. heart of stone.** an obdurate or unemotional nature. **19. leave no stone unturned.** to do everything possible to achieve an end. ~*adv.* **20.** (*in combination*) completely: *stone-cold; stone-deaf.* ~*vb.* (*tr.*) **21.** to throw stones at, esp. to kill. **22.** to remove the stones from. **23.** to furnish or provide with stones. **24. stone the crows.** *Brit. and Austral. slang.* an expression of surprise, dismay, etc. [Old English *stān;* related to Old Saxon *stēn,* German *Stein,* Old Norse *steinn,* Gothic *stains,* Greek *stion* pebble] —'**stonable** *or* '**stoneable** *adj.* —'**stoneless** *adj.* —'**stonelessness** *n.* —'**stoneˌlike** *adj.* —'**stoner** *n.*
Stone Age *n.* **1.** a period in human culture identified by the use of stone implements and usually divided into the Palaeolithic, Mesolithic, and Neolithic stages. ~*modifier.* **Stone-Age. 2.** (*sometimes not caps.*) of or relating to this period: *stone-age man.*
stone axe *n.* **1.** a primitive axe made of chipped stone. **2.** a blunt axe used for cutting stone.
stone bass (bæs) *n.* a large sea perch, *Polyprion americanus,* of the Atlantic and Mediterranean. Also called: **wreckfish.**
stone-blind *adj.* completely blind. Compare **sand-blind.**
stoneboat ('stəʊnˌbəʊt) *n. U.S. and Canadian.* a type of sleigh used for moving rocks from fields, for hauling milk cans, etc.
stone boiling *n.* a primitive method of boiling liquid with heated stones.
stone bramble *n.* a herbaceous Eurasian rosaceous plant, *Rubus saxatilis,* of stony places, having white flowers and berrylike scarlet fruits (drupelets). See also **bramble** (sense 1). [C18: so called because it grows in stony places]
stonecast ('stəʊnˌkɑːst) *n.* a less common name for **stone's throw.**
stonechat ('stəʊnˌtʃæt) *n.* an Old World songbird, *Saxicola torquata,* having a black plumage with a reddish-brown breast: subfamily *Turdinae* (thrushes). [C18: so called from its cry, which sounds like clattering pebbles]
stone-cold *adj.* **1.** completely cold. ~*adv.* **2.** (intensifier): *stone-cold sober.*
stonecrop ('stəʊnˌkrɒp) *n.* **1.** any of various N temperate crassulaceous plants of the genus *Sedum,* having fleshy leaves and typically red, yellow, or white flowers. **2.** any of various similar or related plants. [Old English: so named because it grows on rocks and walls]
stone curlew *n.* any of several brownish shore birds of the family *Burhinidae,* esp. *Burhinus oedicnemus,* having a large head and eyes: order *Charadriiformes.* Also called: **thick-knee.** [C17: so called because it is found in stony habitats and resembles a curlew]
stonecutter ('stəʊnˌkʌtə) *n.* **1.** a person who is skilled in cutting and carving stone. **2.** a machine used to dress stone. —'**stoneˌcutting** *n.*
stoned (stəʊnd) *adj. Slang.* under the influence of drugs or alcohol.
stone-dead *adj.* completely lifeless.
stone-deaf *adj.* completely deaf.
stonefish ('stəʊnˌfɪʃ) *n., pl.* **-fish** *or* **-fishes.** a venomous tropical marine scorpaenid fish, *Synanceja verrucosa,* that resembles a piece of rock on the seabed.
stonefly ('stəʊnˌflaɪ) *n., pl.* **-flies.** any insect of the order *Plecoptera,* in which the larvae are aquatic, living beneath stones, and the adults have long antennae and two pairs of large wings and occur near water. [C15: so called because its larvae live under stones in rivers]
stone fruit *n.* the nontechnical name for **drupe.**
stoneground ('stəʊnˌgraʊnd) *adj.* (of flour) ground with millstones.
stone-lily *n.* the fossil of any of several species of sea lily or other crinoid.
stone marten *n.* **1.** a marten, *Martes foina,* of Eurasian woods and forests, having a brown coat with a pale underfur. **2.** the highly valued fur of this animal.
stonemason ('stəʊnˌmeɪsᵊn) *n.* a person who is skilled in preparing stone for building. —'**stoneˌmasonry** *n.*
stone parsley *n.* a roadside umbelliferous plant, *Sison amomum,* of W Europe and the Mediterranean region, having clusters of small white flowers and aromatic seeds.

stone pine *n.* a Mediterranean pine tree, *Pinus pinea,* having a short bole and radiating branches forming an umbrella shape. Also called: **umbrella pine.**
stone pit *n.* a less common name for **quarry.**
stone roller *n.* a small silvery freshwater cyprinid fish, *Campostoma anomalum,* of the eastern U.S., having a narrow black stripe on the dorsal and anal fins. [C19: so called because it pushes stones about in building its nest]
stone saw *n.* an untoothed iron saw used to cut stone.
stone shoot *n. Mountaineering.* a long steeply sloping line of loose boulder-strewn scree.
stone's throw *n.* a short distance. Also called: **stonecast.**
stonewall (ˌstəʊnˈwɔːl) *vb.* **1.** (*intr.*) *Cricket.* (of a batsman) to play defensively. **2.** to obstruct or hinder (parliamentary business). —ˌ**stoneˈwaller** *n.*
stoneware (ˈstəʊnˌwɛə) *n.* **1.** a hard opaque pottery, fired at a very high temperature. ~*adj.* **2.** made of stoneware.
stonewashed (ˈstəʊnˌwɒʃt) *adj.* (of new clothes or fabric, esp. denim jeans) given a worn faded look by being subjected to the abrasive action of many small pieces of pumice.
stonework (ˈstəʊnˌwɜːk) *n.* **1.** any structure or part of a building made of stone. **2.** the process of dressing or setting stones. —ˈ**stoneˌworker** *n.*
stonewort (ˈstəʊnˌwɜːt) *n.* any of various green algae of the genus *Chara,* which grow in brackish or fresh water and have jointed fronds encrusted with lime.
stonk (stɒŋk) *vb.* (*tr.*) **1.** to bombard (soldiers, buildings, etc.) with artillery. ~*n.* **2.** a concentrated bombardment by artillery. [C20: from *st(andard) (linear) (c)onc(entration)*]
stonkered (ˈstɒŋkəd) *adj. Slang.* completely exhausted or beaten; whacked. [C20: from *stonker* to beat, of unknown origin]
stony *or* **stoney** (ˈstəʊnɪ) *adj.* **stonier, stoniest. 1.** of or resembling stone. **2.** abounding in stone or stones. **3.** unfeeling, heartless, or obdurate. **4.** short for **stony-broke.** —ˈ**stonily** *adv.* —ˈ**stoniness** *n.*
stony-broke *adj. Brit. slang.* completely without money; penniless. U.S. and Canadian term: **stone-broke.**
stony coral *n.* any coral of the order *Madreporaria,* having a calcareous skeleton, aggregations of which form reefs and islands.
stony-hearted *adj.* unfeeling; hardhearted. —ˌ**stonyˈheartedness** *n.*
stony meteorite *n.* a meteorite composed mainly of silicates.
stood (stʊd) *vb.* the past tense and past participle of **stand.**
stooge (stuːdʒ) *n.* **1.** an actor who feeds lines to a comedian or acts as his foil or butt. **2.** *Slang.* someone who is taken advantage of by another. ~*vb.* (*intr.*) **3.** *Slang.* to act as a stooge. **4.** (foll. by *about* or *around*) *Slang.* (esp. in the RAF) to fly or move about aimlessly. [C20: of unknown origin]
stook (stuːk) *n.* **1.** a number of sheaves set upright in a field to dry with their heads together. ~*vb.* **2.** (*tr.*) to set up (sheaves) in stooks. [C15: variant of *stouk,* of Germanic origin; compare Middle Low German *stūke,* Old High German *stūhha* sleeve] —ˈ**stooker** *n.*
stookie (ˈstʊkɪ) *n. Scot.* **1.** stucco. **2.** plaster; plaster of Paris. **3.** a statue: *he stood there like a stookie.*
stool (stuːl) *n.* **1.** a simple seat or footrest consisting of a small flat piece of wood, etc., resting on three or four legs, a pedestal, etc. **2.** a rootstock or base of a plant from which shoots, etc., are produced. **3.** a cluster of shoots growing from such a base. **4.** *Chiefly U.S.* a decoy used in hunting. **5.** waste matter evacuated from the bowels. **6.** a lavatory seat. **7.** (in W Africa, esp. Ghana) a chief's throne. **8. fall between two stools.** to fail through vacillation between two alternatives. ~*vb.* (*intr.*) **9.** (of a plant) to send up shoots from the base of the stem, rootstock, etc. **10.** to lure wildfowl with a decoy. [Old English *stōl;* related to Old Norse *stōll,* Gothic *stōls,* Old High German *stuol* chair, Greek *stulos* pillar]
stool ball *n.* a game resembling cricket, still played by girls and women in Sussex, England.
stool pigeon *n.* **1.** a living or dummy pigeon used to decoy others. **2.** an informer for the police; nark. **3.** *U.S. slang.* a person acting as a decoy.
stoop[1] (stuːp) *vb.* (*mainly intr.*) **1.** (*also tr.*) to bend (the body or the top half of the body) forward and downward. **2.** to carry oneself with head and shoulders habitually bent forward. **3.** (often foll. by *to*) to abase or degrade oneself. **4.** (often foll. by *to*) to condescend; deign. **5.** (of a bird of prey) to swoop down. **6.** *Archaic.* to give in. ~*n.* **7.** the act, position, or characteristic of stooping. **8.** a lowering from a position of dignity or superiority. **9.** a downward swoop, esp. of a bird of prey. [Old English *stūpan;* related to Middle Dutch *stupen* to bow, Old Norse *stūpa,* Norwegian *stupa* to fall; see STEEP[1]] —ˈ**stooper** *n.* —ˈ**stooping** *adj.* —ˈ**stoopingly** *adv.*
stoop[2] (stuːp) *n. U.S. and Canadian.* a small platform with steps up to it at the entrance to a building. [C18: from Dutch *stoep,* of Germanic origin; compare Old High German *stuofa* stair, Old English *stōpel* footprint; see STEP]
stoop[3] (stuːp) *n. Archaic or northern Brit. dialect.* a pillar or post. [C15: variant of dialect *stulpe,* probably from Old Norse *stolpe;* see STELE]
stoop[4] (stuːp) *n.* a less common spelling of **stoup.**
stoor (stuːr) *n. Scot.* a variant of **stour.**
stop (stɒp) *vb.* **stops, stopping, stopped. 1.** to cease from doing or being (something); discontinue: *stop talking.* **2.** to cause (something moving) to halt or (of something moving) to come to a halt: *to stop a car; the car stopped.* **3.** (*tr.*) to prevent the continuance or completion of: *to stop a show.* **4.** (*tr.;* often foll. by *from*) to prevent or restrain: *to stop George from fighting.* **5.** (*tr.*) to keep back: *to stop supplies to the navy.* **6.** (*tr.*) to intercept or hinder in transit: *to stop a letter.* **7.** (*tr.;* often foll. by *up*) to block or plug, esp. so as to close: *to stop up a pipe.* **8.** (*tr.;* often foll. by *up*) to fill a hole or opening in: *to stop up a wall.* **9.** (*tr.*) to staunch or stem: *to stop a wound.* **10.** (*tr.*) to instruct a bank not to honour (a cheque). **11.** (*tr.*) to deduct (money) from pay. **12.** (*tr.*) *Brit.* to provide with punctuation. **13.** (*tr.*) *Boxing.* to beat (an opponent) either by a knockout or a technical knockout. **14.** (*tr.*) *Informal.* to receive (a blow, hit, etc.). **15.** (*intr.*) to stay or rest: *we stopped at the Robinsons' for three nights.* **16.** (*tr.*) *Rare.* to defeat, beat, or kill. **17.** (*tr.*) *Music.* **a.** to alter the vibrating length of (a string on a violin, guitar, etc.) by pressing down on it at some point with the finger. **b.** to alter the vibrating length of an air column in a wind instrument by closing (a finger hole, etc.). **c.** to produce (a note) in this manner. **18.** (*tr.*) to place a hand inside (the bell of a French horn) to alter the tone colour and pitch or play (a note) on a French horn in such a manner. **19.** *Bridge.* to have a protecting card or winner in (a suit in which one's opponents are strong). **20. stop at nothing.** to be prepared to do anything; be unscrupulous or ruthless. ~*n.* **21.** an arrest of movement or progress. **22.** the act of stopping or the state of being stopped. **23.** a place where something halts or pauses: *a bus stop.* **24.** a stay in or as if in the course of a journey. **25.** the act or an instance of blocking or obstructing. **26.** a plug or stopper. **27.** a block, screw, or other device or object that prevents, limits, or terminates the motion of a mechanism or moving part. **28.** *Brit.* a punctuation mark, esp. a full stop. **29.** Also called: **stop thrust.** *Fencing.* a counterthrust made without a parry in the hope that one's blade will touch before one's opponent's blade. **30.** short for **stop payment** or **stop order. 31.** *Music.* **a.** the act of stopping the string, finger hole, etc., of an instrument. **b.** a set of organ pipes or harpsichord strings that may be allowed to sound as a group by muffling or silencing all other such sets. **c.** a knob, lever, or handle on an organ, etc., that is operated to allow sets of pipes to sound. **d.** an analogous device on a harpsichord or other instrument with variable registers, such as an electrophonic instrument. **32. pull out all the stops. a.** to play at full volume. **b.** to spare no effort. **33.** *Austral.* a stud on a football boot. **34.** the angle between the forehead and muzzle of a dog or cat, regarded as a point in breeding. **35.** *Nautical.* a short length of line or small stuff used as a tie, esp. for a furled sail. **36.** Also called: **stop consonant.** *Phonetics.* any of a class of consonants articulated by first making a complete closure at some point of the vocal tract and then releasing it abruptly with audible plosion. Stops include the labials (p, b), the alveolars or dentals (t, d), the velars (k, g). Compare **continuant. 37.** Also called: **f-stop.** *Photog.* **a.** a setting of the aperture of a camera lens, calibrated to the corresponding f-number. **b.** another name for **diaphragm** (sense 4). **38.** a block or carving used to complete the end of a moulding. **39.** Also called: **stopper.** *Bridge.* a protecting card or winner in a suit in which one's opponents are strong. ~See also **stop down, stop off, stop out, stopover, stops.** [C14: from Old English *stoppian* (unattested), as in *forstoppian* to plug the ear, ultimately from Late Latin *stuppāre* to stop with a tow, from Latin *stuppa* tow, from Greek *stuppē*] —ˈ**stoppable** *adj.*
stopbank (ˈstɒpˌbæŋk) *n. N.Z.* an embankment to prevent flooding.
stop bath *n.* a weakly acidic solution used in photographic processing to stop the action of a developer on a film, plate, or paper before the material is immersed in fixer.
stop chorus *n. Jazz.* a solo during which the rhythm section plays only the first beat of each phrase of music.
stopcock (ˈstɒpˌkɒk) *n.* a valve used to control or stop the flow of a fluid in a pipe.
stop down *vb.* (*adv.*) to reduce the size of the aperture of (a camera lens).
stope (stəʊp) *n.* **1.** a steplike excavation made in a mine to extract ore. ~*vb.* **2.** to mine (ore, etc.) by cutting stopes. [C18: probably from Low German *stope;* see STOOP[2]]
stopgap (ˈstɒpˌgæp) *n.* **a.** a temporary substitute for something else. **b.** (*as modifier*): *a stopgap programme.*
stop-go *adj. Brit.* (of economic policy) characterized by deliberate alternate expansion and contraction of aggregate demand in an effort to curb inflation and eliminate balance of payments deficits, and yet maintain full employment.
stoping (ˈstəʊpɪŋ) *n. Geology.* the process by which country rock is broken up and engulfed by the upward movement of magma. Also called: **magmatic stoping.** See also **stope.**
stoplight (ˈstɒpˌlaɪt) *n.* **1.** a red light on a traffic signal indicating that vehicles or pedestrians coming towards it should stop. **2.** another word for **brake light.**
stop-loss *adj. Business.* of or relating to an order to a broker in a commodity or security market to close an open position at a specified price in order to limit any loss.
stop off, stop in, *or esp. U.S.* **stop by** *vb.* **1.** (*intr., adv.;* often foll. by *at*) to halt and call somewhere, as on a visit or errand, esp. en

route to another place. ~*n.* **stopoff.** **2. a.** a break in a journey. **b.** (*as modifier*): *stopoff point.*
stop order *n. Stock Exchange.* an instruction to a broker to sell one or more shares when the price offered for them falls below a stipulated level. Also called: **stop-loss order.**
stop out *vb.* (*tr., adv.*) to cover (part of the area) of a piece of cloth, printing plate, etc., to prevent it from being dyed, etched, etc.
stopover ('stɒpˌəʊvə) *n.* **1.** a stopping place on a journey. ~*vb.* **stop over. 2.** (*intr., adv.*) to make a stopover.
stoppage ('stɒpɪdʒ) *n.* **1.** the act of stopping or the state of being stopped. **2.** something that stops or blocks. **3.** a deduction of money, as from pay. **4.** an organized cessation of work, as during a strike.
stoppage time *n. Soccer, rugby, etc.* another name for **injury time.**
stop payment *n.* an instruction to a bank by the drawer of a cheque to refuse payment on it.
stopped (stɒpt) *adj.* (of a pipe or tube, esp. an organ pipe) closed at one end and thus sounding an octave lower than an open pipe of the same length.
stopper ('stɒpə) *n.* **1.** Also called: **stopple** ('stɒpᵊl). a plug or bung for closing a bottle, pipe, duct, etc. **2.** a person or thing that stops or puts an end to something. **3.** *Bridge.* another name for **stop** (sense 39). ~*vb.* **4.** (*tr.*) Also: **stopple.** to close or fit with a stopper.
stopping ('stɒpɪŋ) *n.* **1.** *Brit. informal.* a dental filling. **2.** a solid barrier in a mine tunnel to seal off harmful gases, fire, fresh air from used air, etc. ~*adj.* **3.** *Chiefly Brit.* making many stops in a journey: *a stopping train.*
stopping power *n. Physics.* a measure of the effect a substance has on the kinetic energy of a particle passing through it.
stop press *n. Brit.* **1.** news items inserted into a newspaper after the printing has been started. **2.** the space regularly left blank for this.
stops (stɒps) *n.* (*functioning as sing.*) any one of several card games in which players must play their cards in certain sequences.
stop thrust *n. Fencing.* another name for **stop** (sense 29).
stop time *n. Jazz.* a passage where the beat stops temporarily.
stopwatch ('stɒpˌwɒtʃ) *n.* a type of watch used for timing events, such as sporting events, accurately, having a device for stopping the hand or hands instantly.
storage ('stɔːrɪdʒ) *n.* **1.** the act of storing or the state of being stored. **2.** space or area reserved for storing. **3.** a charge made for storing. **4.** *Computer technol.* **a.** the act or process of storing information in a computer memory or on a magnetic tape, disk, etc. **b.** (*as modifier*): *a storage device; storage capacity.*
storage battery *n.* another name (esp. U.S.) for **accumulator** (sense 1).
storage capacity *n.* the maximum number of bits, bytes, words, or items that can be held in a memory system such as that of a computer or of the brain.
storage device *n.* a piece of computer equipment, such as a magnetic tape, disk, drum, etc., in or on which data and instructions can be stored, usually in binary form.
storage heater *n.* an electric device capable of accumulating and radiating heat generated by off-peak electricity.
storage tube *n. Electronics.* an electron tube in which information is stored as charges for a predetermined time.
storax ('stɔːræks) *n.* **1.** any of numerous styracaceous trees or shrubs of the genus *Styrax*, of tropical and subtropical regions, having drooping showy white flowers. **2.** a vanilla-scented solid resin obtained from one of these trees, *Styrax officinalis* of the Mediterranean region and SW Asia, formerly used as incense and in perfumery and medicine. **3.** a liquid aromatic balsam obtained from liquidambar trees, esp. *Liquidambar orientalis* of SW Asia, and used in perfumery and medicine. [C14: via Late Latin from Greek, variant of STYRAX]
store (stɔː) *vb.* **1.** (*tr.*) to keep, set aside, or accumulate for future use. **2.** (*tr.*) to place in a warehouse, depository, etc., for safekeeping. **3.** (*tr.*) to supply, provide, or stock. **4.** (*intr.*) to be put into storage. **5.** *Computer technol.* to enter or retain (information) in a storage device. ~*n.* **6. a.** an establishment for the retail sale of goods and services. **b.** (*in combination*): *storefront.* **7. a.** a large supply or stock kept for future use. **b.** (*as modifier*): *store ship.* **8.** short for **department store. 9. a.** a storage place such as a warehouse or depository. **b.** (*in combination*): *storeman.* **10.** the state of being stored (esp. in the phrase **in store**). **11.** a large amount or quantity. **12.** *Computer technol., chiefly Brit.* another name for **memory** (sense 7). **13.** Also called: **store pig.** a pig that has not yet been weaned and weighs less than 40 kg. **14. a.** an animal bought lean to be fattened up for market. **b.** (*as modifier*): *store cattle.* **15. in store.** forthcoming or imminent. **16. lay, put,** *or* **set store by.** to value or reckon as important. ~See also **stores.** [C13: from Old French *estor*, from *estorer* to restore, from Latin *instaurāre* to refresh; related to Greek *stauros* stake] —'**storable** *adj.*
store and forward *vb.* to store (information) in a computer for later forward transmission through a telecommunication network.
store card *n.* another name for **charge card.**
storehouse ('stɔːˌhaʊs) *n.* a place where things are stored.
storekeeper ('stɔːˌkiːpə) *n.* a manager, owner, or keeper of a store. —'**storeˌkeeping** *n.*
store of value *n. Economics.* the function of money that enables goods and services to be paid for a considerable time after they have been acquired.
storeroom ('stɔːˌruːm, -ˌrʊm) *n.* **1.** a room in which things are stored. **2.** room for storing.
stores (stɔːz) *pl. n.* **1.** a supply or stock of something, esp. essentials, for a specific purpose: *the ship's stores.* **2.** specifically, munitions slung externally on a military aircraft airframe.
storey *or U.S.* **story** ('stɔːrɪ) *n., pl.* **-reys** *or* **-ries. 1.** a floor or level of a building. **2.** a set of rooms on one level. [C14: from Anglo-Latin *historia*, picture, from Latin: narrative, probably arising from the pictures on medieval windows]
storeyed *or U.S.* **storied** ('stɔːrɪd) *adj.* **a.** having a storey or storeys. **b.** (*in combination*): *a two-storeyed house.*
storey house *n.* (in W Africa) a house having more than one storey.
storiated ('stɔːrɪˌeɪtɪd) *adj.* another word for **historiated** or **storied** (sense 2).
storied ('stɔːrɪd) *adj.* **1.** recorded in history or in a story; fabled. **2.** decorated with narrative scenes or pictures.
stork (stɔːk) *n.* **1.** any large wading bird of the family *Ciconiidae*, chiefly of warm regions of the Old World, having very long legs and a long stout pointed bill, and typically having a white-and-black plumage: order *Ciconiiformes.* **2.** (*sometimes cap.*) a variety of domestic fancy pigeon resembling the fairy swallow. [Old English *storc*; related to Old High German *storah*, Old Norse *storkr*, Old English *stearc* stiff; from the stiff appearance of its legs; see STARK]
storksbill ('stɔːksˌbɪl) *n.* any of various geraniaceous plants of the genus *Erodium*, esp. *E. cicutarium* (**common storksbill**), having pink or reddish-purple flowers and fruits with a beaklike process.
storm (stɔːm) *n.* **1. a.** a violent weather condition of strong winds, rain, hail, thunder, lightning, blowing sand, snow, etc. **b.** (*as modifier*): *storm signal; storm sail.* **c.** (*in combination*): *stormproof.* **2.** *Meteorol.* a violent gale of force 10 on the Beaufort scale reaching speeds of 55 to 63 mph. **3.** a strong or violent reaction: *a storm of protest.* **4.** a direct assault on a stronghold. **5.** a heavy discharge or rain, as of bullets or missiles. **6.** short for **storm window** (sense 1). **7. storm in a teacup.** *Brit.* a violent fuss or disturbance over a trivial matter. U.S. equivalent: **tempest in a teapot. 8. take by storm. a.** to capture or overrun by a violent assault. **b.** to overwhelm and enthral. ~*vb.* **9.** to attack or capture (something) suddenly and violently. **10.** (*intr.*) to be vociferously angry. **11.** (*intr.*) to move or rush violently or angrily. **12.** (*intr.*; with *it* as subject) to rain, hail, or snow hard and be very windy, often with thunder or lightning. [Old English, related to Old Norse *stormr*, German *Sturm*; see STIR[1]] —'**stormˌlike** *adj.*
storm belt *n.* an area of the earth's surface in which storms are frequent.
stormbound ('stɔːmˌbaʊnd) *adj.* detained or harassed by storms.
storm centre *n.* **1.** the centre of a cyclonic storm, etc., where pressure is lowest. **2.** the centre of any disturbance or trouble.
storm cloud *n.* **1.** a heavy dark cloud presaging rain or a storm. **2.** a herald of disturbance, anger, or violence: *the storm clouds of war.*
storm-cock *n.* another name for **missel thrush.** [C18: so called because it was believed to give forewarning of bad weather]
storm collar *n.* a high collar on a coat.
storm cone *n. Brit.* a canvas cone hoisted as a warning of high winds.
storm door *n.* an extra outer door for protection in bad weather.
storm glass *n.* a sealed tube containing a solution supposed to change in appearance according to the weather.
storm lantern *n.* another name for **hurricane lamp.**
storm petrel *n.* any small petrel, such as the northern *Hydrobates pelagicus*, of the family *Hydrobatidae*, typically having a dark plumage with paler underparts. Also called: **Mother Carey's chicken, stormy petrel.** [C19: so named because it was thought to be a harbinger of rough weather]
stormproof ('stɔːmˌpruːf) *adj.* withstanding or giving protection against storms.
storm trooper *n.* **1.** a member of the Nazi SA. **2.** a member of a force of shock troops.
storm warning *n.* **1.** a pattern of lights, flags, etc., displayed at certain ports as a warning to shipping of an approaching storm. **2.** an announcement on radio or television of an approaching storm. **3.** any warning of approaching danger or trouble.
storm window *n.* **1.** an additional window fitted to the outside of an ordinary window to provide insulation against wind, cold, rain, etc. **2.** a type of dormer window.
stormy ('stɔːmɪ) *adj.* **stormier, stormiest. 1.** characterized by storms. **2.** subject to, involving, or characterized by violent disturbance or emotional outburst. —'**stormily** *adv.* —'**storminess** *n.*
stormy petrel *n.* **1.** another name for **storm petrel. 2.** a person who brings or portends trouble.
story[1] ('stɔːrɪ) *n., pl.* **-ries. 1.** a narration of a chain of events told or written in prose or verse. **2.** Also called: **short story.** a piece of fiction, briefer and usually less detailed than a novel. **3.** Also

called: **story line.** the plot of a book, film, etc. **4.** an event that could be the subject of a narrative. **5.** a report or statement on a matter or event. **6.** the event or material for such a report. **7.** *Informal.* a lie, fib, or untruth. **8. cut** (*or* **make**) **a long story short.** to leave out details in a narration. **9. quite another story now.** things or circumstances have changed. **10.** *Informal.* **the same old story.** the familiar or regular course of events. **11. the story goes.** it is commonly said or believed. *~vb.* **-ries, -rying, -ried.** (*tr.*) **12.** to decorate (a pot, wall, etc.) with scenes from history or legends. **13.** *Archaic.* to tell the story of. [C13: from Anglo-French *estorie,* from Latin *historia;* see HISTORY]

story[2] (ˈstɔːrɪ) *n., pl.* **-ries.** another spelling (esp. U.S.) of **storey.**

storyboard (ˈstɔːrɪˌbɔːd) *n.* (in films, television, advertising, etc.) a series of sketches or photographs showing the sequence of shots or images planned for a film.

storybook (ˈstɔːrɪˌbʊk) *n.* **1.** a book containing stories, esp. for children. *~adj.* **2.** unreal or fantastic: *a storybook world.*

story line *n.* the plot of a book, film, play, etc.

storyteller (ˈstɔːrɪˌtɛlə) *n.* **1.** a person who tells stories. **2.** *Informal.* a liar. —ˈ**storyˌtelling** *n., adj.*

stoss (stɒs; *German* ʃtoːs) *adj.* (of the side of a hill, crag, etc.) facing the onward flow of a glacier or the direction in which a former glacier flowed. [German, from *stossen* to thrust]

stot[1] (stɒt) *n. Dialect.* **1.** a bullock. **2.** a castrated male ox. [Old English]

stot[2] (stɒt, stot) *vb.* **stots, stotting, stotted.** *Scot. and northern English dialect.* **1.** to bounce or cause to bounce. **2.** (*intr.*) Also: **stotter.** to stagger. [of obscure origin]

stotinka (stɒˈtɪŋkə) *n., pl.* **-ki** (-kɪ). a Bulgarian monetary unit worth one hundredth of a lev. [from Bulgarian; related to *suto* hundred]

stotious (ˈstəʊʃəs) *adj. Now chiefly Irish, dialect.* drunk; inebriated. [of obscure origin; perhaps from STOT[2]]

stotter (ˈstɒtə; *Scot.* ˈstotər) *Scot. dialect, chiefly Glasgow.* *~vb.* (*intr.*) **1.** to stagger. *~n.* **2.** anything outstanding, esp. a good-looking person. [from STOT[2]]

stound (staʊnd) *n. Obsolete or Brit. dialect.* **1.** a short while; instant. **2.** a pang or pain. [Old English *stund;* related to Old High German *stunta* period of time, hour]

stoup *or* **stoop** (stuːp) *n.* **1.** a small basin for holy water. **2.** *Scot. and northern English dialect.* Also: **stowp.** a bucket or drinking vessel. [C14 (in the sense: bucket): of Scandinavian origin; compare Old Norse *staup* beaker, Old English *stēap* flagon; see STEEP[1]]

stour (staʊə) *or Scot.* **stoor** (stuːr) *n. Archaic or Scot. and northern English dialect.* **1.** turmoil or conflict. **2.** dust; a cloud of dust. [C14: from Old French *estour* armed combat, of Germanic origin; related to Old High German *sturm* STORM]

stoush (staʊʃ) *Austral. and N.Z. slang.* *~vb.* **1.** (*tr.*) to hit or punch. *~n.* **2.** fighting, violence, or a fight. [C19: of uncertain origin]

stout (staʊt) *adj.* **1.** solidly built or corpulent. **2.** (*prenominal*) resolute or valiant: *stout fellow.* **3.** strong, substantial, and robust. **4. a stout heart.** courage; resolution. *~n.* **5.** strong porter highly flavoured with malt. [C14: from Old French *estout* bold, of Germanic origin; related to Middle High German *stolz* proud, Middle Dutch *stolt* brave] —ˈ**stoutish** *adj.* —ˈ**stoutly** *adv.* —ˈ**stoutness** *n.*

stouthearted (ˌstaʊtˈhɑːtɪd) *adj.* valiant; brave. —ˌ**stoutˈheartedly** *adv.* —ˌ**stoutˈheartedness** *n.*

stove[1] (stəʊv) *n.* **1.** another word for **cooker** (sense 1). **2.** any heating apparatus, such as a kiln. *~vb.* (*tr.*) **3.** to process (ceramics, metalwork, etc.) by heating in a stove. **4.** *Scot.* to stew (meat, vegetables, etc.). [Old English *stofa* bathroom; related to Old High German *stuba* steam room, Greek *tuphos* smoke]

stove[2] (stəʊv) *vb.* a past tense and past participle of **stave.**

stove enamel *n.* a type of enamel made heatproof by treatment in a stove.

stovepipe (ˈstəʊvˌpaɪp) *n.* **1.** a pipe that serves as a flue to a stove. **2.** Also called: **stovepipe hat.** a man's tall silk hat.

stovepipes (ˈstəʊvˌpaɪps) *pl. n. Informal.* tight trousers with narrow legs.

stover (ˈstəʊvə) *n.* **1.** *Chiefly Brit.* fodder. **2.** *U.S.* cornstalks used as fodder. [C14: shortened from ESTOVER]

stovies (ˈstovɪz, ˈstəʊ-) *pl. n. Scot.* potatoes stewed with onions. [from STOVE[1]]

stow (stəʊ) *vb.* (*tr.*) **1.** (often foll. by *away*) to pack or store. **2.** to fill by packing. **3.** *Nautical.* to pack or put away (cargo, sails and other gear, etc.). **4.** to have enough room for. **5.** (*usually imperative*) *Brit. slang.* to cease from: *stow your noise! stow it!* [Old English *stōwian* to keep, hold back, from *stōw* a place; related to Old High German *stouwen* to accuse, Gothic *stōjan* to judge, Old Slavonic *staviti* to place]

stowage (ˈstəʊɪdʒ) *n.* **1.** space, room, or a charge for stowing goods. **2.** the act or an instance of stowing or the state of being stowed. **3.** something that is stowed.

stowaway (ˈstəʊəˌweɪ) *n.* **1.** a person who hides aboard a vehicle, ship, or aircraft in order to gain free passage. *~vb.* **stow away.** **2.** (*intr., adv.*) to travel in such a way.

stowp (staʊp) *n. Scot.* a variant of **stoup** (sense 2).

STP *abbrev. for:* **1.** *Trademark.* scientifically treated petroleum: an oil substitute promising renewed power for an internal-combustion engine. **2.** Also: **NTP.** standard temperature and pressure: standard conditions of 0°C temperature and 101.325 kPa (760 mmHg) pressure. **3.** Professor of Sacred Theology. [from Latin: *Sanctae Theologiae Professor*] *~n.* **4.** a synthetic hallucinogenic drug related to mescaline. [from humorous reference to the extra power resulting from scientifically treated petroleum]

str *abbrev. for* steamer.

str. *abbrev. for:* **1.** straight. **2.** *Music.* **a.** strings. **b.** stringed. **3.** strait. **4.** street. **5.** stroke oar.

strabismus (strəˈbɪzməs) *n.* abnormal alignment of one or both eyes, characterized by a turning inwards or outwards from the nose thus preventing parallel vision: caused by paralysis of an eye muscle, etc. Also called: **squint.** [C17: via New Latin from Greek *strabismos,* from *strabizein* to squint, from *strabos* cross-eyed] —**straˈbismal, straˈbismic,** *or* **straˈbismical** *adj.*

strabotomy (strəˈbɒtəmɪ) *n., pl.* **-mies.** a former method of treating strabismus by surgical division of one or more muscles of the eye. [C19: from French *strabotomie,* from Greek *strabos* squinting + -TOMY]

straddle (ˈstrædᵊl) *vb.* **1.** (*tr.*) to have one leg, part, or support on each side of. **2.** (*tr.*) *U.S. and Canadian informal.* to be in favour of both sides of (something). **3.** (*intr.*) to stand, walk, or sit with the legs apart. **4.** (*tr.*) to spread (the legs) apart. **5.** *Gunnery.* to fire a number of shots slightly beyond and slightly short of (a target) to determine the correct range. **6.** (*intr.*) (in poker, of the second player after the dealer) to double the ante before looking at one's cards. *~n.* **7.** the act or position of straddling. **8.** a noncommittal attitude or stand. **9.** *Business.* a contract or option permitting its purchaser to either sell or buy securities or commodities within a specified period of time at specified prices. It is a combination of a put and a call option. Compare **spread** (sense 24c). **10.** *Athletics.* a high-jumping technique in which the body is parallel with the bar and the legs straddle it at the highest point of the jump. **11.** (in poker) the stake put up after the ante in poker by the second player after the dealer. **12.** *Irish.* a wooden frame placed on a horse's back to which panniers are attached. [C16: frequentative formed from obsolete *strad-* (Old English *strode*), past stem of STRIDE] —ˈ**straddler** *n.*

Stradivarius (ˌstrædɪˈvɛərɪəs) *n.* any of a number of violins manufactured by Antonio Stradivari (?1644–1737), Italian maker of stringed instruments, or his family. Often shortened to (informal) **Strad.**

strafe (streɪf, strɑːf) *vb.* (*tr.*) **1.** to machine-gun (troops, etc.) from the air. **2.** *Slang.* to punish harshly. *~n.* **3.** an act or instance of strafing. [C20: from German *strafen* to punish] —ˈ**strafer** *n.*

straggle (ˈstrægᵊl) *vb.* (*intr.*) **1.** to go, come, or spread in a rambling or irregular way; stray. **2.** to linger behind or wander from a main line or part. [C14: of uncertain origin; perhaps related to STRAKE and STRETCH] —ˈ**straggler** *n.* —ˈ**straggling** *adj.* —ˈ**stragglingly** *adv.* —ˈ**straggly** *adj.*

straight (streɪt) *adj.* **1.** not curved or crooked; continuing in the same direction without deviating. **2.** straightforward, outright, or candid: *a straight rejection.* **3.** even, level, or upright in shape or position. **4.** in keeping with the facts; accurate. **5.** honest, respectable, or reliable. **6.** accurate or logical: *straight reasoning.* **7.** continuous; uninterrupted. **8.** (esp. of an alcoholic drink) undiluted; neat. **9.** not crisp, kinked, or curly: *straight hair.* **10.** correctly arranged; orderly. **11.** (of a play, acting style, etc.) straightforward or serious. **12.** *Journalism.* (of a story, article, etc.) giving the facts without unnecessary embellishment. **13.** *U.S.* sold at a fixed unit price irrespective of the quantity sold. **14.** *Boxing.* (of a blow) delivered with an unbent arm: *a straight left.* **15.** (of the cylinders of an internal-combustion engine) in line, rather than in a V-formation or in some other arrangement: *a straight eight.* **16.** a slang word for **heterosexual.** **17.** *Informal.* no longer owing or being owed something: *if you buy the next round we'll be straight.* **18.** *Slang.* conventional in views, customs, appearance, etc. **19.** *Slang.* not using narcotics; not addicted. *~adv.* **20.** in a straight line or direct course. **21.** immediately; at once: *he came straight back.* **22.** in an even, level, or upright position. **23.** without cheating, lying, or unreliability: *tell it to me straight.* **24.** continuously; uninterruptedly. **25.** *U.S.* without discount regardless of the quantity sold. **26.** (often foll. by *out*) frankly; candidly: *he told me straight out.* **27. go straight.** *Informal.* to reform after having been dishonest or a criminal. *~n.* **28.** the state of being straight. **29.** a straight line, form, part, or position. **30.** *Brit.* a straight part of a racetrack. U.S. name: **straightaway.** **31.** *Poker.* **a.** five cards that are in sequence irrespective of suit. **b.** a hand containing such a sequence. **c.** (*as modifier*): *a straight flush.* **32.** *Slang.* a conventional person. **33.** *Slang.* a heterosexual. **34.** *Slang.* a cigarette containing only tobacco, without marijuana, etc. [C14: from the past participle of Old English *streccan* to STRETCH] —ˈ**straightly** *adv.* —ˈ**straightness** *n.*

straight and narrow *n. Informal.* the proper, honest, and moral path of behaviour. [perhaps an alteration of *strait and narrow,* an allusion to Matthew 7:14: "strait is the gate, and narrow is the way, which leadeth unto life"]

straight angle *n.* an angle of 180°.

straight-arm *adj.* **1.** *Rugby.* (of a tackle) performed with the arm fully extended. *~vb.* **2.** (*tr.*) to ward off (an opponent) with the arm outstretched.

straight arm lift *n.* a wrestling attack, in which a wrestler twists his opponent's arm against the joint and lifts him by it, often using his shoulder as a fulcrum.

straightaway (ˌstreɪtəˈweɪ) *adv. also* **straight away.** 1. at once. ~*n.* 2. the U.S. word for **straight** (sense 30).

straight bat *n.* 1. *Cricket.* a bat held vertically. 2. *Brit. informal.* honest or honourable behaviour.

straight chain *n.* **a.** an open chain of atoms in a molecule with no attached side chains. **b.** (*as modifier*): *a straight-chain hydrocarbon.* ~Compare **branched chain.**

straight chair *n.* a straight-backed side chair.

straightedge (ˈstreɪtˌɛdʒ) *n.* a stiff strip of wood or metal with one edge straight and true, used for ruling and testing straight lines. —ˈ**straightˌedged** *adj.*

straighten (ˈstreɪtᵊn) *vb.* (sometimes foll. by *up* or *out*) 1. to make or become straight. 2. (*tr.*) to make neat or tidy: *straighten your desk.* —ˈ**straightener** *n.*

straighten out *vb.* (*adv.*) 1. to make or become less complicated or confused: *the situation will straighten out.* 2. *U.S. and Canadian.* to reform or become reformed.

straighten up *vb.* (*adv.*) 1. to become or cause to become erect. 2. *Chiefly U.S.* to reform or become reformed.

straight face *n.* a serious facial expression, esp. one that conceals the impulse to laugh. —ˈ**straight-ˈfaced** *adj.*

straight fight *n.* a contest between two candidates only.

straight flush *n.* (in poker) five consecutive cards of the same suit.

straightforward (ˌstreɪtˈfɔːwəd) *adj.* 1. (of a person) honest, frank, or simple. 2. *Chiefly Brit.* (of a task, etc.) simple; easy. ~*adv., adj.* 3. in a straight course. —ˌ**straightˈforwardly** *adv.* —ˌ**straightˈforwardness** *n.*

straightjacket (ˈstreɪtˌdʒækɪt) *n.* a less common spelling of **straitjacket.**

straight joint *n.* a vertical joint in brickwork that is directly above a vertical joint in the course below.

straight-laced *adj.* a variant spelling of **strait-laced.**

straight-line *n.* (*modifier*) 1. (of a machine) having components that are arranged in a row or that move in a straight line when in operation. 2. of or relating to a method of depreciation whereby equal charges are made against gross profit for each year of an asset's expected life.

straight man *n.* a subsidiary actor who acts as stooge to a comedian.

straight off *adv. Informal.* without deliberation or hesitation: *tell me the answer straight off.*

straight-out *adj. U.S. informal.* 1. complete; thoroughgoing. 2. frank or honest.

straight razor *n.* another name for **cutthroat** (sense 2).

straight ticket *n. U.S.* a ballot for all the candidates of one and only one political party. Compare **split ticket.**

straight up *sentence substitute. Brit. slang.* honestly; truly; exactly.

straightway (ˈstreɪtˌweɪ) *adv. Archaic.* at once.

strain[1] (streɪn) *vb.* 1. to draw or be drawn taut; stretch tight. 2. to exert, tax, or use (resources) to the utmost extent. 3. to injure or damage or be injured or damaged by overexertion: *he strained himself.* 4. to deform or be deformed as a result of a stress. 5. (*intr.*) to make intense or violent efforts; strive. 6. to subject or be subjected to mental tension or stress. 7. to pour or pass (a substance) or (of a substance) to be poured or passed through a sieve, filter, or strainer. 8. (*tr.*) to draw off or remove (one part of a substance or mixture from another) by or as if by filtering. 9. (*tr.*) to clasp tightly; hug. 10. (*tr.*) *Obsolete.* to force or constrain. 11. (*intr.*; foll. by *at*) **a.** to push, pull, or work with violent exertion (upon). **b.** to strive (for). **c.** to balk or scruple (from). ~*n.* 12. the act or an instance of straining. 13. the damage resulting from excessive exertion. 14. an intense physical or mental effort. 15. *Music.* (*often pl.*) a theme, melody, or tune. 16. a great demand on the emotions, resources, etc. 17. a feeling of tension and tiredness resulting from overwork, worry, etc.; stress. 18. a particular style or recurring theme in speech or writing. 19. *Physics.* the change in dimension of a body under load expressed as the ratio of the total deflection or change in dimension to the original unloaded dimension. It may be a ratio of lengths, areas, or volumes. [C13: from Old French *estreindre* to press together, from Latin *stringere* to bind tightly]

strain[2] (streɪn) *n.* 1. the main body of descendants from one ancestor. 2. a group of organisms within a species or variety, distinguished by one or more minor characteristics. 3. a variety of bacterium or fungus, esp. one used for a culture. 4. a streak; trace. 5. *Archaic.* a kind, type, or sort. [Old English *strēon*; related to Old High German *gistriuni* gain, Latin *struere* to CONSTRUCT]

strained (streɪnd) *adj.* 1. (of an action, performance, etc.) not natural or spontaneous. 2. (of an atmosphere, relationship, etc.) not relaxed; tense.

strainer (ˈstreɪnə) *n.* 1. a sieve used for straining sauces, vegetables, tea, etc. 2. a gauze or simple filter used to strain liquids. 3. *Austral. and N.Z.* a self-locking device or a tool for tightening fencing wire. 4. *Austral. and N.Z.* the main post in a wire fence, often diagonally braced.

strain gauge *n.* a device for measuring strain in a machine or other structure, usually consisting of a metal filament that is attached to it and receives the same strain. The strain can be measured by the change in the electrical properties of the filament.

strain hardening *n.* a process in which a metal is permanently deformed in order to increase its resistance to further deformation.

straining piece *or* **beam** *n.* a horizontal tie beam that connects the top of two queen posts of a roof truss.

strait (streɪt) *n.* 1. (*often pl.*) **a.** a narrow channel of the sea linking two larger areas of sea. **b.** (*cap. as part of a name*): *the Strait of Gibraltar.* 2. (*often pl.*) a position of acute difficulty (often in the phrase **in dire** *or* **desperate straits**). 3. *Archaic.* a narrow place or passage. ~*adj. Archaic.* 4. (of spaces, etc.) affording little room. 5. (of circumstances, etc.) limiting or difficult. 6. severe, strict, or scrupulous. [C13: from Old French *estreit* narrow, from Latin *strictus* constricted, from *stringere* to bind tightly] —ˈ**straitly** *adv.* —ˈ**straitness** *n.*

straiten (ˈstreɪtᵊn) *vb.* 1. (*tr.*; *usually passive*) to embarrass or distress, esp. financially. 2. (*tr.*) to limit, confine, or restrict. 3. *Archaic.* to make or become narrow.

straitjacket (ˈstreɪtˌdʒækɪt) *n.* 1. Also called: **straightjacket** a jacket made of strong canvas material with long sleeves for binding the arms of violent prisoners or mental patients. 2. a severe restriction or limitation. ~*vb.* 3. (*tr.*) to confine in or as if in a straitjacket.

strait-laced *or* **straight-laced** *adj.* prudish or puritanical.

strake (streɪk) *n.* 1. **a.** a curved metal plate forming part of the metal rim on a wooden wheel. **b.** any metal plate let into a rubber tyre. 2. Also called: **streak.** *Nautical.* one of a continuous range of planks or plates forming the side of a vessel. 3. a profiled piece of wood carried on an arm that rotates round a fixed post: used to sweep the internal shape of a mould, as for a bell or a ship's propeller blade, in sand or loam. [C14: related to Old English *streccan* to STRETCH]

stramash (strəˈmæʃ) *Scot.* ~*n.* 1. an uproar; tumult; brawl. ~*vb.* (*tr.*) 2. to destroy; smash. [C18: perhaps expanded from SMASH]

stramonium (strəˈməʊnɪəm) *n.* 1. a preparation of the dried leaves and flowers of the thorn apple, containing hyoscyamine and used as a drug to treat nervous disorders. 2. another name for **thorn apple** (sense 1). [C17: from New Latin, of uncertain origin]

strand[1] (strænd) *vb.* 1. to leave or drive (ships, fish, etc.) aground or ashore or (of ships, fish, etc.) to be left or driven ashore. 2. (*tr.*; *usually passive*) to leave helpless, as without transport or money, etc. ~*n. Chiefly poetic.* 3. a shore or beach. 4. a foreign country. [Old English; related to Old Norse *strönd* side, Middle High German *strant* beach, Latin *sternere* to spread]

strand[2] (strænd) *n.* 1. a set of or one of the individual fibres or threads of string, wire, etc., that form a rope, cable, etc. 2. a single length of string, hair, wool, wire, etc. 3. a string of pearls or beads. 4. a constituent element in a complex whole: *one strand of her argument.* ~*vb.* 5. (*tr.*) to form (a rope, cable, etc.) by winding strands together. [C15: of uncertain origin]

Strandloper (ˈstrantˌluəpə) *n.* a member of an extinct tribe of Hottentots or Bushmen who lived on sea food gathered on the beaches of southern Africa. [C19: from Afrikaans *strand* beach + *loper* walker]

strandwolf (ˈstrændˌwʊlf; *Afrikaans* ˈstrantˌvɔlf) *n., pl.* **-wolves.** a species of hyena (*Hyaena brunnea*) that scavenges on shores of southern Africa. Also called: **brown hyena.** [C19: Afrikaans, from Dutch *strand* beach + Afrikaans *wolf* hyena]

strange (streɪndʒ) *adj.* 1. odd, unusual, or extraordinary in appearance, effect, manner, etc.; peculiar. 2. not known, seen, or experienced before; unfamiliar: *a strange land.* 3. not easily explained: *a strange phenomenon.* 4. (usually foll. by *to*) inexperienced (in) or unaccustomed (to): *strange to a task.* 5. not of one's own kind, locality, etc.; alien; foreign. 6. shy; distant; reserved. 7. **strange to say.** it is unusual or surprising that. 8. *Physics.* **a.** denoting a particular flavour of quark. **b.** denoting or relating to a hypothetical form of matter composed of such quarks: *strange matter; a strange star.* ~*adv.* 9. *Not standard.* in a strange manner. [C13: from Old French *estrange,* from Latin *extrāneus* foreign; see EXTRANEOUS] —ˈ**strangely** *adv.*

strange attractor *n. Maths.* a pattern existing in abstract mathematical space, representing the path traced by a point that expresses the essential parameters of a chaotic system.

strangeness (ˈstreɪndʒnɪs) *n.* 1. the state or quality of being strange. 2. *Physics.* a property of certain elementary particles, characterized by a quantum number (**strangeness number**) conserved in strong but not in weak interactions. This number is equivalent to the hypercharge minus the baryon number.

stranger (ˈstreɪndʒə) *n.* 1. any person whom one does not know. 2. a person who is new to a particular locality, from another region, town, etc. 3. a guest or visitor. 4. (foll. by *to*) a person who is unfamiliar (with) or new (to) something: *he is no stranger to computers.* 5. *Law.* a person who is neither party nor privy to a transaction. 6. **little stranger.** *Jocular.* a new-born child.

stranger's gallery *n.* another name for **public gallery.**

strangle (ˈstræŋgᵊl) *vb.* 1. (*tr.*) to kill by compressing the windpipe; throttle. 2. (*tr.*) to prevent or inhibit the growth or development of: *to strangle originality.* 3. (*tr.*) to suppress (an utterance) by or as if by swallowing suddenly: *to strangle a cry.*

~See also **strangles.** [C13: via Old French, ultimately from Greek *strangalē* a halter] —'**strangler** *n.*

stranglehold ('stræŋgᵊl,həʊld) *n.* **1.** a wrestling hold in which a wrestler's arms are pressed against his opponent's windpipe. See also **Japanese stranglehold.** **2.** complete power or control over a person or situation.

strangles ('stræŋgᵊlz) *n.* (*functioning as sing.*) an acute bacterial disease of horses caused by infection with *Streptococcus equi,* characterized by inflammation of the mucous membranes of the respiratory tract. Also called: **equine distemper.** [C18: from STRANGLE]

strangulate ('stræŋgjʊ,leɪt) *vb.* (*tr.*) **1.** to constrict (a hollow organ, vessel, etc.) so as to stop the natural flow of air, blood, etc., through it. **2.** another word for **strangle.** [C18: from Latin *strangulāt-,* past participle stem of *strangulāre* to STRANGLE] —,**strangu'lation** *n.*

strangury ('stræŋgjʊrɪ) *n. Pathol.* painful excretion of urine, drop by drop, caused by muscular spasms of the urinary tract. [C14: from Latin *strangūria,* from Greek, from *stranx* a drop squeezed out + *ouron* urine]

strap (stræp) *n.* **1.** a long strip of leather or similar material, for binding trunks, baggage, or other objects. **2.** a strip of leather or similar material used for carrying, lifting, or holding. **3.** a loop of leather, rubber, etc., suspended from the roof in a bus or train for standing passengers to hold on to. **4.** a razor strop. **5.** *Business.* a triple option on a security or commodity consisting of one put option and two call options at the same price and for the same period. Compare **strip** (sense 2). **6.** *Irish, derogatory slang.* a shameless or promiscuous woman. **7. the strap.** a beating with a strap as a punishment. **8.** short for **shoulder strap.** ~*vb.* **straps, strapping, strapped.** (*tr.*) **9.** to tie or bind with a strap. **10.** to beat with a strap. **11.** to sharpen with a strap or strop. [C16: variant of STROP]

straphanger ('stræp,hæŋə) *n. Informal.* a passenger in a bus, train, etc., who has to travel standing, esp. by holding on to a strap. —'**strap,hanging** *n.*

strap hinge *n.* a hinge with a long leaf or flap attached to the face of a door, gate, etc.

strapless ('stræplɪs) *adj.* (of a woman's formal dress, brassiere, etc.) without straps over the shoulders.

strapline ('stræp,laɪn) *n.* a subheading in a newspaper or magazine article or in any advertisement.

strap-oil *n. Slang.* a beating.

strappado (strə'peɪdəʊ, -'pɑː-) *n., pl.* **-does.** a system of torture in which a victim was hoisted by a rope tied to his wrists and then allowed to drop until his fall was suddenly checked by the rope. [C16: from French *strapade,* from Italian *strappare* to tug sharply, probably of Germanic origin; related to German (dialect) *strapfen* to make taut]

strapped (stræpt) *adj.* (*postpositive;* often foll. by *for*) *Slang.* badly in need (of money, manpower, etc.); short of.

strapper ('stræpə) *n. Informal.* a strapping person.

strapping ('stræpɪŋ) *adj.* (*prenominal*) tall and sturdy. [C17: from STRAP (in the archaic sense: to work vigorously)]

strap work *n. Architect.* decorative work resembling interlacing straps.

strass (stræs) *n. Jewellery.* another word for **paste**[1] (sense 6). [C19: German, named after J. *Strasser,* 18th-century German jeweller who invented it]

strata ('strɑːtə) *n.* a plural of **stratum.**

▷**Usage.** In careful usage, *strata* is the standard plural of *stratum* and is not treated as a singular noun.

stratagem ('strætɪdʒəm) *n.* a plan or trick, esp. one to deceive an enemy. [C15: ultimately from Greek *stratēgos* a general, from *stratos* an army + *agein* to lead]

strata title *n. Austral.* a system of registered ownership of space in multistorey buildings, to be equivalent to the ownership of the land of a single-storey building. N.Z. equivalent: **stratum title.**

strategic (strə'tiːdʒɪk) *or* **strategical** *adj.* **1.** of, relating to, or characteristic of strategy. **2.** important to a strategy or to strategy in general. **3.** (of weapons, attacks, etc.) directed against an enemy's homeland rather than used on a battlefield: *a strategic missile: strategic bombing.* —**stra'tegically** *adv.*

strategics (strə'tiːdʒɪks) *n.* (*functioning as sing.*) strategy, esp. in a military sense.

strategist ('strætɪdʒɪst) *n.* a specialist or expert in strategy.

strategy ('strætɪdʒɪ) *n., pl.* **-gies.** **1.** the art or science of the planning and conduct of a war; generalship. **2.** a particular long-term plan for success, esp. in business or politics. Compare **tactics** (sense 2). **3.** a plan or stratagem. [C17: from French *stratégie,* from Greek *stratēgia* function of a general; see STRATAGEM]

strath (stræθ) *n. Scot.* a broad flat river valley. [C16: from Scot. and Irish Gaelic *srath,* Welsh *ystrad*]

strathspey (,stræθ'speɪ) *n.* **1.** a Scottish dance with gliding steps, slower than a reel. **2.** a piece of music in four-four time composed for this dance.

strati- *combining form.* indicating stratum or strata: *stratiform; stratigraphy.*

straticulate (strə'tɪkjʊlɪt, -,leɪt) *adj.* (of a rock formation) composed of very thin even strata. [C19: from New Latin *strāticulum* (unattested), diminutive of Latin *strātum* something strewn; see STRATUS] —**stra,ticu'lation** *n.*

stratification (,strætɪfɪ'keɪʃən) *n.* **1.** the arrangement of sedimentary rocks in distinct layers (strata), each layer representing the sediment deposited over a specific period. **2.** the act of stratifying or state of being stratified. [C17 (in the obsolete sense: the act of depositing in layers) and C18 (in the current senses): from New Latin *strātificātiōnem,* from *stratificāre* to STRATIFY] —,**stratifi'cational** *adj.*

stratificational grammar *n. Linguistics.* a theory of grammar analysing language in terms of several structural strata or layers with different syntactic rules.

stratified sample *n. Statistics.* a sample that is not drawn at random from the whole population, but separately from a number of disjoint strata of the population in order to ensure a more representative sample. See also **frame** (sense 13).

stratiform ('strætɪ,fɔːm) *adj.* **1.** (of rocks) occurring as or arranged in strata. **2.** *Meteorol.* resembling a stratus cloud.

stratify ('strætɪ,faɪ) *vb.* **-fies, -fying, -fied.** **1.** to form or be formed in layers or strata. **2.** (*tr.*) to preserve or render fertile (seeds) by storing between layers of sand or earth. **3.** *Sociol.* to divide (a society) into horizontal status groups or (of a society) to develop such groups. [C17: from French *stratifier,* from New Latin *stratificāre,* from Latin STRATUM]

stratigraphy (strə'tɪgrəfɪ) *n.* **1.** the study of the composition, relative positions, etc., of rock strata in order to determine their geological history. Abbrev.: **stratig.** **2.** *Archaeol.* a vertical section through the earth showing the relative positions of the human artefacts and therefore the chronology of successive levels of occupation. —**stratigrapher** (strə'tɪgrəfə) *or* **stratigraphist** (strə'tɪgrəfɪst) *n.* —**stratigraphic** (,strætɪ'græfɪk) *or* ,**strati'graphical** *adj.*

strato- *combining form.* **1.** denoting stratus: *stratocumulus.* **2.** denoting the stratosphere: *stratopause.*

stratocracy (strə'tɒkrəsɪ) *n., pl.* **-cies.** military rule. [C17: from Greek *stratos* an army + -CRACY] —**stratocrat** ('strætə,kræt) *n.* —**stratocratic** (,strætə'krætɪk) *adj.*

stratocumulus (,strætəʊ'kjuːmjʊləs, ,streɪtəʊ-) *n., pl.* **-li** (-,laɪ). *Meteorol.* a uniform stretch of cloud containing dark grey globular masses.

stratopause ('strætə,pɔːz) *n. Meteorol.* the transitional zone of maximum temperature between the stratosphere and the mesosphere.

stratosphere ('strætə,sfɪə) *n.* the atmospheric layer that lies between the troposphere and the mesosphere, in which temperature generally increases with height. —**stratospheric** (,strætə'sfɛrɪk) *or* ,**strato'spherical** *adj.*

stratum ('strɑːtəm) *n., pl.* **-ta** (-tə) *or* **-tums.** **1.** (*usually pl.*) any of the distinct layers into which sedimentary rocks are divided. **2.** *Biology.* a single layer of tissue or cells. **3.** a layer of any material, esp. one of several parallel layers. **4.** a layer of ocean or atmosphere either naturally or arbitrarily demarcated. **5.** a level of a social hierarchy that is distinguished according to such criteria as educational achievement or caste status. [C16: via New Latin from Latin: something strewn, from *sternere* to scatter] —'**stratal** *adj.*

stratum title *n.* the N.Z. name for **strata title.**

stratus ('streɪtəs) *n., pl.* **-ti** (-taɪ). a grey layer cloud. Compare **cirrus** (sense 1), **cumulus.** [C19: via New Latin from Latin: strewn, from *sternere* to extend]

stravaig (strə'veɪg) *vb.* (*intr.*) *Scot. and northern English dialect.* to wander aimlessly. [C19: perhaps a variant of obsolete *extravage,* from Medieval Latin *extrāvagārī,* from *vagārī* to wander]

straw[1] (strɔː) *n.* **1. a.** stalks of threshed grain, esp. of wheat, rye, oats, or barley, used in plaiting hats, baskets, etc., or as fodder. **b.** (*as modifier*): *a straw hat.* **2.** a single dry or ripened stalk, esp. of a grass. **3.** a long thin hollow paper or plastic tube or stem of a plant, used for sucking up liquids into the mouth. **4.** (*usually used with a negative*) anything of little value or importance: *I wouldn't give a straw for our chances.* **5.** a measure or remedy that one turns to in desperation (esp. in the phrases **clutch** *or* **grasp at a straw** *or* **straws**). **6. a.** a pale yellow colour. **b.** (*as adj.*): *straw hair.* **7. the last straw.** a small incident, setback, etc. that, coming after others, proves intolerable. **8. straw in the wind.** a hint or indication. ~*adj.* **9.** *Chiefly U.S.* having little value or substance. ~See also **man of straw.** [Old English *streaw;* related to Old Norse *strā,* Old Frisian *strē,* Old High German *strō;* see STREW] —'**straw,like** *adj.* —'**strawy** *adj.*

straw[2] (strɔː) *vb. Archaic.* another word for **strew.**

strawberry ('strɔːbərɪ, -brɪ) *n., pl.* **-ries.** **1. a.** any of various low-growing rosaceous plants of the genus *Fragaria,* such as *F. vesca* (**wild strawberry**) and *F. ananassa* (**garden strawberry**), which have white flowers and red edible fruits and spread by runners. **b.** (*as modifier*): *a strawberry patch.* **2. a.** the fruit of any of these plants, consisting of a sweet fleshy receptacle bearing small seedlike parts (the true fruits). **b.** (*as modifier*): *strawberry ice cream.* **3. barren strawberry.** a related Eurasian plant, *Potentilla sterilis,* that does not produce edible fruit. **4. a.** a purplish-red colour. **b.** (*as adj.*): *strawberry shoes.* [Old English *streawberige;* perhaps from the strawlike appearance of the runners]

strawberry blonde *adj.* **1.** (of hair) reddish blonde. ~*n.* **2.** a woman with such hair.

strawberry bush *n.* **1.** an E North American shrub or small tree, *Euonymus americanus,* having pendulous capsules that split when ripe to reveal scarlet seeds: family *Celastraceae.* **2.** any of various similar or related plants.

strawberry mark *n.* a soft vascular red birthmark. Technical name: **haemangioma simplex.** Also called: **strawberry.**

strawberry tomato *n.* **1.** a tropical solanaceous annual plant, *Physalis peruviana,* having bell-shaped whitish-yellow flowers and small edible round yellow berries. **2.** a similar and related plant, *Physalis pubescens.* **3.** the fruit of either of these plants, eaten fresh or made into preserves and pickles. ~Also called: **Cape gooseberry.**

strawberry tree *n.* a S European evergreen tree, *Arbutus unedo,* having white or pink flowers and red strawberry-like berries. See also **arbutus.**

strawboard (ˈstrɔːˌbɔːd) *n.* a board made of compressed straw and adhesive, used esp. in book covers.

strawflower (ˈstrɔːˌflauə) *n.* an Australian plant, *Helichrysum bracteatum,* in which the coloured bracts retain their colour when the plant is dried: family *Compositae* (composites). See also **immortelle.**

straw man *n. Chiefly U.S.* **1.** a figure of a man made from straw. **2.** another term for **man of straw.**

straw poll *or* (*chiefly U.S., Canadian, and N.Z.*) **vote** *n.* an unofficial poll or vote taken to determine the opinion of a group or the public on some issue.

straw wine *n.* any of several wines made from grapes dried on straw mats to increase their sugar strength.

strawworm (ˈstrɔːˌwɜːm) *n.* another name for a **caddis worm.**

stray (streɪ) *vb.* (*intr.*) **1.** to wander away, as from the correct path or from a given area. **2.** to wander haphazardly. **3.** to digress from the point, lose concentration, etc. **4.** to deviate from certain moral standards. ~*n.* **5. a.** a domestic animal, fowl, etc., that has wandered away from its place of keeping and is lost. **b.** (*as modifier*): *stray dogs.* **6.** a lost or homeless person, esp. a child: *waifs and strays.* **7.** an isolated or random occurrence, specimen, etc., that is out of place or outside the usual pattern. ~*adj.* **8.** scattered, random, or haphazard: *a stray bullet grazed his thigh.* [C14: from Old French *estraier,* from Vulgar Latin *estragāre* (unattested), from Latin *extrā-* outside + *vagārī* to roam; see ASTRAY, EXTRAVAGANT, STRAVAIG] —**ˈstrayer** *n.*

strays (streɪz) *pl. n.* **1.** Also called: **stray capacitance.** *Electronics.* undesired capacitance in equipment, occurring between the wiring, between the wiring and the chassis, or between components and the chassis. **2.** *Telecomm.* another word for **static** (sense 9).

streak[1] (striːk) *n.* **1.** a long thin mark, stripe, or trace of some contrasting colour. **2. a.** (of lightning) a sudden flash. **b.** (*as modifier*): *streak lightning.* **3.** an element or trace, as of some quality or characteristic. **4.** a strip, vein, or layer: *fatty streaks.* **5.** a short stretch or run, esp. of good or bad luck. **6.** *Mineralogy.* the powdery mark made by a mineral when rubbed on a hard or rough surface: its colour is an important distinguishing characteristic. **7.** *Bacteriol.* the inoculation of a culture medium by drawing a wire contaminated with the microorganisms across the surface of the medium. **8.** *Informal.* an act or the practice of running naked through a public place. ~*vb.* **9.** (*tr.*) to mark or daub with a streak or streaks. **10.** (*intr.*) to form streaks or become streaked. **11.** (*intr.*) to move rapidly in a straight line. **12.** (*intr.*) *Informal.* to run naked through a crowd of people in a public place in order to shock or amuse them. [Old English *strica,* related to Old Frisian *strike,* Old High German *strih,* Norwegian, Swedish *strika*] —**streaked** *adj.* —**ˈstreaker** *n.* —**ˈstreakˌlike** *adj.*

streak[2] (striːk) *n.* a variant spelling of **strake** (sense 2).

streaking (ˈstriːkɪŋ) *n.* **1.** an act or instance of running naked through a public place. **2.** *Television.* light or dark streaks to the right of a bright object in a television picture, caused by distortion in the transmission chain.

streaky (ˈstriːkɪ) *adj.* **streakier, streakiest. 1.** marked with streaks. **2.** occurring in streaks. **3.** (of bacon) having alternate layers of meat and fat. **4.** of varying or uneven quality. —**ˈstreakily** *adv.* —**ˈstreakiness** *n.*

stream (striːm) *n.* **1.** a small river; brook. **2.** any steady flow of water or other fluid. **3.** something that resembles a stream in moving continuously in a line or particular direction. **4.** a rapid or unbroken flow of speech, etc.: *a stream of abuse.* **5.** *Brit.* any of several parallel classes of schoolchildren, or divisions of children within a class, grouped together because of similar ability. **6. go** (*or* **drift**) **with the stream.** to conform to the accepted standards. **7. off stream.** (of an industrial plant, manufacturing process, etc.) shut down or not in production. **8. on stream.** (of an industrial plant, manufacturing process, etc.) in or about to go into operation or production. ~*vb.* **9.** to emit or be emitted in a continuous flow: *his nose streamed blood.* **10.** (*intr.*) to move in unbroken succession, as a crowd of people, vehicles, etc. **11.** (*intr.*) to float freely or with a waving motion: *bunting streamed in the wind.* **12.** (*tr.*) to unfurl (a flag, etc.). **13.** (*intr.*) to move causing a trail of light, condensed gas, etc., as a jet aircraft. **14.** (when *intr.,* often foll. by *for*) *Mining.* to wash (earth, gravel, etc.) in running water in prospecting (for gold, etc.), to expose the particles of ore or metal. **15.** *Brit. education.* to group or divide (children) in streams. [Old English; related to Old Frisian *strām,* Old Norse *straumr,* Old High German *stroum,* Greek *rheuma*] —**ˈstreamlet** *n.* —**ˈstreamˌlike** *adj.*

streamer (ˈstriːmə) *n.* **1.** a long narrow flag or part of a flag. **2.** a long narrow coiled ribbon of coloured paper that becomes unrolled when tossed. **3.** a stream of light, esp. one appearing in some forms of the aurora. **4.** *Journalism.* a large heavy headline printed across the width of a page of a newspaper. **5.** *Computers.* an electromechanical device that enables a hard disk to copy data byte by byte onto magnetic tape for security or storage.

streamline (ˈstriːmˌlaɪn) *n.* **1.** a contour on a body that offers the minimum resistance to a gas or liquid flowing around it. **2.** a line in a fluid such that the tangent at any point indicates the direction of the velocity of a particle of the fluid at that point. ~*vb.* (*tr.*) **3.** to make streamlined.

streamlined (ˈstriːmˌlaɪnd) *adj.* **1.** offering or designed to offer the minimum resistance to the flow of a gas or liquid. **2.** made more efficient, esp. by simplifying.

streamline flow *n.* flow of a fluid in which its velocity at any point is constant or varies in a regular manner. Also called: **viscous flow.** Compare **turbulent flow.** See also **laminar flow.**

stream of consciousness *n.* **1.** *Psychol.* the continuous flow of ideas, thoughts, and feelings forming the content of an individual's consciousness. **2. a.** a literary technique that reveals the flow of thoughts and feelings of characters through long passages of soliloquy. **b.** (*as modifier*): *a stream-of-consciousness novel.*

streamy (ˈstriːmɪ) *adj.* **streamier, streamiest.** *Chiefly poetic.* **1.** (of an area, land, etc.) having many streams. **2.** flowing or streaming. —**ˈstreaminess** *n.*

streel (striːl) *n. Irish.* a slovenly woman. [from Irish Gaelic *straoill*]

street (striːt) *n.* **1. a.** (*cap. when part of a name*) a public road that is usually lined with buildings, esp. in a town: *Oxford Street.* **b.** (*as modifier*): *a street directory.* **2.** the buildings lining a street. **3.** the part of the road between the pavements, used by vehicles. **4.** the people living, working, etc., in a particular street. **5.** (*modifier*) of or relating to the urban counterculture: *street style; street drug.* **6. man in the street.** an ordinary or average citizen. **7. on the streets. a.** earning a living as a prostitute. **b.** homeless. **8. (right) up one's street.** *Informal.* (just) what one knows or likes best. **9. streets ahead of.** *Informal.* superior to, more advanced than, etc. **10. streets apart.** *Informal.* markedly different. ~*vb.* (*tr.*) **11.** *Austral.* to outdistance. [Old English *strǣt,* from Latin *via strāta* paved way (*strāta,* from *strātus,* past participle of *sternere* to stretch out); compare Old Frisian *strēte,* Old High German *strāza;* see STRATUS]

street Arab *n. Offensive.* a homeless child, esp. one who survives by begging and stealing; urchin.

streetcar (ˈstriːtˌkɑː) *n.* the usual U.S. and Canadian name for **tram**[1] (sense 1).

street credibility *n.* a convincing command or display of the style, fashions, knowledge, etc., associated with urban counterculture. Sometimes shortened to **street cred.** —ˌ**street-ˈcredible** *adj.*

street cry *n.* (*often pl.*) the cry of a street hawker.

street door *n.* the door of a house that opens onto the street.

street furniture *n.* pieces of equipment, such as streetlights and pillar boxes, placed in the street for the benefit of the public.

streetlight (ˈstriːtˌlaɪt) *or* **streetlamp** *n.* a light, esp. one carried on a lamppost, that illuminates a road, etc.

street piano *n.* another name for **barrel organ.**

street theatre *n.* dramatic entertainments performed esp. in shopping precincts.

street value *n.* the monetary worth of a commodity, usually an illicit commodity such as a drug, considered as the price it would fetch when sold to the ultimate user.

streetwalker (ˈstriːtˌwɔːkə) *n.* a prostitute who solicits on the streets. —**ˈstreetˌwalking** *n., adj.*

streetwise (ˈstriːtˌwaɪz) *adj.* attuned to and adept at surviving in an urban, poor and often criminal environment. Also: **street-smart.** —**street wisdom** *n.*

strelitzia (strɛˈlɪtsɪə) *n.* any southern African perennial herbaceous plant of the musaceous genus *Strelitzia,* cultivated for its showy flowers: includes the bird-of-paradise flower. [C18: named after Charlotte of Mecklenburg-*Strelitz* (1744–1818), queen of Great Britain and Ireland]

strength (strɛŋθ) *n.* **1.** the state or quality of being physically or mentally strong. **2.** the ability to withstand or exert great force, stress, or pressure. **3.** something that is regarded as being beneficial or a source of power: *their chief strength is technology.* **4.** potency, as of a drink, drug, etc. **5.** power to convince; cogency: *the strength of an argument.* **6.** degree of intensity or concentration of colour, light, sound, flavour, etc. **7.** the full or part of the full complement as specified: *at full strength; below strength.* **8.** *Finance.* firmness of or a rising tendency in prices, esp. security prices. **9.** *Archaic or poetic.* a stronghold or fortress. **10.** *Austral. and N.Z. informal.* the general idea, the main purpose: *to get the strength of something.* **11. from strength to strength.** with ever-increasing success. **12. in strength.** in large numbers. **13. on the strength of.** on the basis of or relying upon. [Old English *strengthu;* related to Old High German *strengida;* see STRONG]

strengthen (ˈstrɛŋθən) *vb.* to make or become stronger. —ˈ**strengthener** *n.*

strenuous (ˈstrɛnjʊəs) *adj.* **1.** requiring or involving the use of great energy or effort. **2.** characterized by great activity, effort, or endeavour. [C16: from Latin *strēnuus* brisk, vigorous] —**strenuosity** (ˌstrɛnjʊˈɒsɪtɪ) *or* ˈ**strenuousness** *n.* —ˈ**strenuously** *adv.*

strep (strɛp) *n. Informal.* short for **streptococcus.**

strepitoso (ˈstrɛpɪˈtəʊsəʊ) *adj., adv. Music.* (to be performed) boisterously. [Italian, literally; noisily].

strepitous (ˈstrɛpɪtəs) *or* **strepitant** *adj. Rare.* noisy; boisterous. [C17: from Latin *strepitus* a din]

strepto- *combining form.* **1.** indicating a shape resembling a twisted chain: *streptococcus.* **2.** indicating streptococcus: *streptolysin.* [from Greek *streptos* twisted, from *strephein* to twist]

streptocarpus (ˌstrɛptəˈkɑːpəs) *n.* any plant of the typically stemless subtropical perennial genus *Streptocarpus,* some species of which are grown as greenhouse plants for their tubular flowers in a range of bright colours: family *Gesneriaceae.* [New Latin, from Greek *streptos* twisted + *karpos* fruit (from the shape of the capsule)]

streptococcus (ˌstrɛptəʊˈkɒkəs) *n., pl.* **-cocci** (-ˈkɒksaɪ). any Gram-positive spherical bacterium of the genus *Streptococcus,* typically occurring in chains and including many pathogenic species, such as *S. pyogenes,* which causes scarlet fever, sore throat, etc.: family *Lactobacillaceae.* Often shortened to **strep.** —**streptococcal** (ˌstrɛptəʊˈkɒkəl) *or (less commonly)* **streptococcic** (ˌstrɛptəʊˈkɒksɪk) *adj.*

streptokinase (ˌstrɛptəʊˈkaɪneɪs) *n.* an enzyme produced by streptococci that causes the fibrin of certain animal species to undergo lysis.

streptomycin (ˌstrɛptəʊˈmaɪsɪn) *n.* an antibiotic obtained from the bacterium *Streptomyces griseus:* used in the treatment of tuberculosis and Gram-negative bacterial infections. Formula: $C_{21}H_{39}N_7O_{12}$. [from *Streptomyces,* genus name of bacteria (from STREPTO- + Greek *mukēs* fungus + -IN)]

streptothricin (ˌstrɛptəʊˈθraɪsɪn) *n.* an antibiotic active against bacteria and some fungi, produced by the bacterium *Streptomyces lavendulae.* [*from Streptothrix,* genus name of bacteria (from STREPTO- + Greek *thrix* hair + -IN)]

stress (strɛs) *n.* **1.** special emphasis or significance attached to something. **2.** mental, emotional, or physical strain or tension. **3.** emphasis placed upon a syllable by pronouncing it more loudly than those that surround it. **4.** such emphasis as part of a regular rhythmic beat in music or poetry. **5.** a syllable so emphasized. **6.** *Physics.* **a.** force or a system of forces producing deformation or strain. **b.** the force acting per unit area. ~*vb.* (*tr.*) **7.** to give emphasis or prominence to. **8.** to pronounce (a word or syllable) more loudly than those that surround it. **9.** to subject to stress or strain. [C14: *stresse,* shortened from DISTRESS] —ˈ**stressful** *adj.* —ˈ**stressfully** *adv.* —ˈ**stressfulness** *n.*

-stress *suffix forming nouns.* indicating a woman who performs or is engaged in a certain activity: *songstress; seamstress.* Compare **-ster** (sense 1). [from -ST(E)R + -ESS]

stressor (ˈstrɛsə) *n.* an event, experience, etc., that causes stress.

stretch (strɛtʃ) *vb.* **1.** to draw out or extend or be drawn out or extended in length, area, etc. **2.** to extend or be extended to an undue degree, esp. so as to distort or lengthen permanently. **3.** to extend (the limbs, body, etc.). **4.** (*tr.*) to reach or suspend (a rope, etc.) from one place to another. **5.** (*tr.*) to draw tight; tighten. **6.** (often foll. by *out, forward,* etc.) to reach or hold (out); extend. **7.** (*intr.;* usually foll. by *over*) to extend in time: *the course stretched over three months.* **8.** (*intr.;* foll. by *for, over,* etc.) (of a region, etc.) to extend in length or area. **9.** (*intr.*) (esp. of a garment) to be capable of expanding, as to a larger size: *socks that will stretch.* **10.** (*tr.*) to put a great strain upon or extend to the limit. **11.** to injure (a muscle, tendon, ligament, etc.) by means of a strain or sprain. **12.** (*tr.;* often foll. by *out*) to make do with (limited resources): *to stretch one's budget.* **13.** (*tr.*) *Informal.* to expand or elaborate (a story, etc.) beyond what is credible or acceptable: *that's stretching it a bit.* **14.** (*tr.; often passive*) to extend, as to the limit of one's abilities or talents. **15.** *Archaic or slang.* to hang or be hanged by the neck. **16. stretch a point. a.** to make a concession or exception not usually made. **b.** to exaggerate. **17. stretch one's legs.** to take a walk, esp. after a period of inactivity. ~*n.* **18.** the act of stretching or state of being stretched. **19.** a large or continuous expanse or distance: *a stretch of water.* **20.** extent in time, length, area, etc. **21. a.** capacity for being stretched, as in some garments. **b.** (*as modifier*): *stretch pants.* **22.** *Horse racing.* the section or sections of a racecourse that are straight, esp. the final straight section leading to the finishing line. **23.** *Slang.* a term of imprisonment. **24. at a stretch.** *Chiefly Brit.* **a.** with some difficulty; by making a special effort. **b.** if really necessary or in extreme circumstances. [Old English *streccan;* related to Old Frisian *strekka,* Old High German *strecken;* see STRAIGHT, STRAKE] —ˈ**stretchable** *adj.* —ˌ**stretchaˈbility** *n.*

stretcher (ˈstrɛtʃə) *n.* **1.** a device for transporting the ill, wounded, or dead, consisting of a frame covered by canvas or other material. **2.** a strengthening often decorative member joining the legs of a chair, table, etc. **3.** the wooden frame on which canvas is stretched and fixed for oil painting. **4.** a tie beam or brace used in a structural framework. **5.** a brick or stone laid horizontally with its length parallel to the length of a wall. Compare **header** (sense 4). **6.** *Rowing.* a fixed board across a boat on which an oarsman braces his feet. **7.** *Austral. and N.Z.* a camp bed. **8.** *Slang.* an exaggeration or lie. ~*vb.* (*tr.*) **9.** to transport (a sick or injured person) on a stretcher.

stretcher-bearer *n.* a person who helps to carry a stretcher, esp. in wartime.

stretch limo *n. Informal.* a limousine that has been lengthened to provide extra seating accommodation and more legroom. In full: **stretch limousine.**

stretchmarks (ˈstrɛtʃˌmɑːks) *pl. n.* marks that remain visible on the abdomen after its distension in pregnancy.

stretchy (ˈstrɛtʃɪ) *adj.* **stretchier, stretchiest.** characterized by elasticity. —ˈ**stretchiness** *n.*

stretto (ˈstrɛtəʊ) *n., pl.* **-tos** *or* **-ti** (-tiː). **1.** (in a fugue) the close overlapping of two parts or voices, the second one entering before the first has completed its statement of the subject. **2.** Also called: **stretta** (ˈstrɛtə). a concluding passage in a composition, played at a faster speed than the earlier material. [C17: from Italian, from Latin *strictus* tightly bound; see STRICT]

streusel (ˈstruːsəl, ˈstrɔɪ-; *German* ˈʃtrɔyzəl) *n. Chiefly U.S.* a crumbly topping for rich pastries. [German, from *streuen* to STREW]

strew (struː) *vb.* **strews, strewing, strewed; strewn** *or* **strewed.** to spread or scatter or be spread or scattered, as over a surface or area. [Old English *streowian;* related to Old Norse *strā,* Old High German *streuwen,* Latin *struere* to spread] —ˈ**strewer** *n.*

strewth (struːθ) *interj.* an expression of surprise or dismay. [C19: alteration of *God's truth*]

stria (ˈstraɪə) *n., pl.* **striae** (ˈstraɪiː). (*often pl.*) **1.** Also called: **striation.** *Geology.* any of the parallel scratches or grooves on the surface of a rock over which a glacier has flowed or on the surface of a crystal. **2.** *Biology, anatomy.* a narrow band of colour or a ridge, groove, or similar linear mark, usually occurring in a parallel series. **3.** *Architect.* a narrow channel, such as a flute on the shaft of a column. [C16: from Latin: a groove]

striate *adj.* (ˈstraɪɪt), *also* **striated. 1.** marked with striae; striped. ~*vb.* (ˈstraɪeɪt). **2.** (*tr.*) to mark with striae. [C17: from Latin *striāre* to make grooves, from STRIA]

striation (straɪˈeɪʃən) *n.* **1.** an arrangement or pattern of striae. **2.** the condition of being striate. **3.** another word for **stria** (sense 1).

strick (strɪk) *n. Textiles.* any bast fibres preparatory to being made into slivers. [C15 *stric,* perhaps of Low German origin; compare Middle Dutch *stric,* Middle Low German *strik* rope]

stricken (ˈstrɪkən) *adj.* **1.** laid low, as by disease or sickness. **2.** deeply affected, as by grief, love, etc. **3.** *Archaic.* wounded or injured. **4. stricken in years.** made feeble by age. [C14: past participle of STRIKE] —ˈ**strickenly** *adv.*

strickle (ˈstrɪkəl) *n.* **1.** Also called: **strike.** a board used for sweeping off excess material in a container. **2.** a template used for shaping a mould. **3.** a bar of abrasive material for sharpening a scythe. ~*vb.* **4.** (*tr.*) to level, form, or sharpen with a strickle. [Old English *stricel;* related to Latin *strigilis* scraper, German *Striegel;* see STRIKE]

strict (strɪkt) *adj.* **1.** adhering closely to specified rules, ordinances, etc.: *a strict faith.* **2.** complied with or enforced stringently; rigorous: *a strict code of conduct.* **3.** severely correct in attention to rules of conduct or morality: *a strict teacher.* **4.** (of a punishment, etc.) harsh; severe. **5.** (*prenominal*) complete; absolute: *in strict secrecy.* **6.** *Logic, maths.* (of a relation) **a.** applying more narrowly than some other relation often given the same name, as *strict inclusion,* which holds only between pairs of sets that are distinct, while *simple inclusion* permits the case in which they are identical. See also **proper** (sense 9), **ordering. b.** distinguished from a relation of the same name that is not the subject of formal study. **7.** *Botany, rare.* very straight, narrow, and upright: *strict panicles.* [C16: from Latin *strictus,* from *stringere* to draw tight] —ˈ**strictly** *adv.* —ˈ**strictness** *n.*

striction (ˈstrɪkʃən) *n. Rare.* the act of constricting. [C19: from Late Latin *strictiō;* see STRICT]

stricture (ˈstrɪktʃə) *n.* **1.** a severe criticism; censure. **2.** *Pathol.* an abnormal constriction of a tubular organ, structure, or part. **3.** *Obsolete.* severity. [C14: from Latin *strictūra* contraction; see STRICT] —ˈ**strictured** *adj.*

stride (straɪd) *n.* **1.** a long step or pace. **2.** the space measured by such a step. **3.** a striding gait. **4.** an act of forward movement by an animal, completed when the legs have returned to their initial relative positions. **5.** progress or development (esp. in the phrase **make rapid strides**). **6.** a regular pace or rate of progress: *to get into one's stride; to be put off one's stride.* **7.** *Rowing.* the distance covered between strokes. **8.** Also called: **stride piano.** *Jazz.* a piano style characterized by single bass notes on the first and third beats and chords on the second and fourth. **9.** (*pl.*) *Informal, chiefly Austral.* men's trousers. **10. take (something) in one's stride.** to do (something) without difficulty or effort. ~*vb.* **strides, striding, strode, stridden. 11.** (*intr.*) to walk with long regular or measured paces, as in haste, etc. **12.** (*tr.*) to cover or traverse by striding: *he strode thirty miles.* **13.** (often foll. by *over, across,* etc.) to cross (over a space, obstacle, etc.) with a stride. **14.** (*intr.*) *Rowing.* to achieve the desired rhythm in a racing shell. **15.** *Archaic or poetic.* to straddle or bestride. [Old English *strīdan;* related to Old High German *strītan* to quarrel; see STRADDLE] —'**strider** *n.*

strident ('straɪdᵊnt) *adj.* **1.** (of a shout, voice, etc.) having or making a loud or harsh sound. **2.** urgent, clamorous, or vociferous: *strident demands.* [C17: from Latin *strīdēns,* from *strīdēre* to make a grating sound] —'**stridence** *or* '**stridency** *n.* —'**stridently** *adv.*

stridor ('straɪdɔː) *n.* **1.** *Pathol.* a high-pitched whistling sound made during respiration, caused by obstruction of the air passages. **2.** *Chiefly literary.* a harsh or shrill sound. [C17: from Latin; see STRIDENT]

stridulate ('strɪdjʊˌleɪt) *vb.* (*intr.*) (of insects such as the cricket) to produce sounds by rubbing one part of the body against another. [C19: back formation from *stridulation,* from Latin *strīdulus* creaking, hissing, from *strīdēre* to make a harsh noise] —ˌ**stridu'lation** *n.* —'**striduˌlator** *n.* —**stridulatory** ('strɪdjʊˌleɪtərɪ) *adj.*

stridulous ('strɪdjʊləs) *or* **stridulant** *adj.* **1.** making a harsh, shrill, or grating noise. **2.** *Pathol.* of, relating to, or characterized by stridor. [C17: from Latin *strīdulus,* from *strīdēre* to make a harsh noise. See STRIDENT] —'**stridulously** *or* '**stridulantly** *adv.* —'**stridulousness** *or* '**stridulance** *n.*

strife (straɪf) *n.* **1.** angry or violent struggle; conflict. **2.** rivalry or contention, esp. of a bitter kind. **3.** *Austral. and N.Z.* trouble or discord of any kind: *to get into strife.* **4.** *Archaic.* striving. [C13: from Old French *estrif,* probably from *estriver* to STRIVE]

strigiform ('strɪdʒɪˌfɔːm) *adj.* of, relating to, or belonging to the *Strigiformes,* an order of birds comprising the owls. [via New Latin from Latin *strix* a screech owl]

strigil ('strɪdʒɪl) *n.* **1.** a curved blade used by the ancient Romans and Greeks to scrape the body after bathing. **2.** *Architect.* a decorative fluting, esp. one in the shape of the letter *S* as used in Roman architecture. [C16: from Latin *strigilis,* from *stringere* to graze]

strigose ('straɪgəʊs) *adj.* **1.** *Botany.* bearing stiff hairs or bristles: *strigose leaves.* **2.** *Zoology.* marked with fine closely set grooves or ridges. [C18: via New Latin *strigōsus,* from *striga* a bristle, from Latin: grain cut down]

strike (straɪk) *vb.* **strikes, striking, struck.** **1.** to deliver (a blow or stroke) to (a person). **2.** to come or cause to come into sudden or violent contact (with). **3.** (*tr.*) to make an attack on. **4.** to produce (fire, sparks, etc.) or (of fire, sparks, etc.) to be produced by ignition. **5.** to cause (a match) to light by friction or (of a match) to be lighted. **6.** to press (the key of a piano, organ, etc.) or to sound (a specific note) in this or a similar way. **7.** to indicate (a specific time) by the sound of a hammer striking a bell or by any other percussive sound. **8.** (of a venomous snake) to cause injury by biting. **9.** (*tr.*) to affect or cause to affect deeply, suddenly, or radically, as if by dealing a blow: *her appearance struck him as strange; I was struck on his art.* **10.** (*past participle* **struck** *or* **stricken**) (*tr.; passive;* usually foll. by *with*) to render incapable or nearly so: *she was stricken with grief.* **11.** (*tr.*) to enter the mind of: *it struck me that he had become very quiet.* **12.** (*past participle* **struck** *or* **stricken**) to render: *I was struck dumb.* **13.** (*tr.*) to be perceived by; catch: *the glint of metal struck his eye.* **14.** to arrive at or come upon (something), esp. suddenly or unexpectedly: *to strike the path for home; to strike upon a solution.* **15.** (*intr.;* sometimes foll. by *out*) to set (out) or proceed, esp. upon a new course: *to strike for the coast.* **16.** (*tr.; usually passive*) to afflict with a disease, esp. unexpectedly: *he was struck with polio when he was six.* **17.** (*tr.*) to discover or come upon a source of (ore, petroleum, etc.). **18.** (*tr.*) (of a plant) to produce or send down (a root or roots). **19.** (*tr.*) to take apart or pack up; break (esp. in the phrase **strike camp**). **20.** (*tr.*) to take down or dismantle (a stage set, formwork, etc.). **21.** (*tr.*) *Nautical.* **a.** to lower or remove (a specified piece of gear). **b.** to haul down or dip (a flag, sail, etc.) in salute or in surrender. **c.** to lower (cargo, etc.) into the hold of a ship. **22.** to attack (an objective) with the intention of causing damage to, seizing, or destroying it. **23.** to impale the hook in the mouth of (a fish) by suddenly tightening or jerking the line after the bait or fly has been taken. **24.** (*tr.*) to form or impress (a coin, metal, etc.) by or as if by stamping. **25.** to level (a surface) by use of a flat board. **26.** (*tr.*) to assume or take up (an attitude, posture, etc.). **27.** (*intr.*) (of workers in a factory, etc.) to cease work collectively as a protest against working conditions, low pay, etc. **28.** (*tr.*) to reach by agreement: *to strike a bargain.* **29.** (*tr.*) to form (a jury, esp. a special jury) by cancelling certain names among those nominated for jury service until only the requisite number remains. See also **special jury.** **30.** (*tr.*) *Rowing.* to make (a certain number of strokes) per minute: *Oxford were striking 38.* **31.** to make a stroke or kick in swimming. **32.** (*tr.*) (in Malaysia) to win (a lottery or raffle). **33. strike home. a.** to deliver an effective blow. **b.** to achieve the intended effect. **34. strike it rich.** *Informal.* **a.** to discover an extensive deposit of a mineral, petroleum, etc. **b.** to have an unexpected financial success. ~*n.* **35.** an act or instance of striking. **36.** a cessation of work by workers in a factory, industry, etc., as a protest against working conditions or low pay: *the workers are on strike again.* **37.** a military attack, esp. an air attack on a surface target: *air strike.* **38.** *Baseball.* a pitched ball judged good but missed or not swung at, three of which cause a batter to be out. **39.** Also called: **ten-strike.** *Tenpin bowling.* **a.** the act or an instance of knocking down all the pins with the first bowl of a single frame. **b.** the score thus made. Compare **spare** (sense 17). **40.** a sound made by striking. **41.** the mechanism that makes a clock strike. **42.** the discovery of a source of ore, petroleum, etc. **43.** the horizontal direction of a fault, rock stratum, etc., which is perpendicular to the direction of the dip. **44.** *Angling.* the act or an instance of striking. **45.** the number of coins or medals made at one time. **46.** another name for **strickle** (sense 1). **47.** *Informal.* an unexpected or complete success, esp. one that brings financial gain. **48. take strike.** *Cricket.* (of a batsman) to prepare to play a ball delivered by the bowler. ~See also **strike down, strike off, strike out, strike through, strike up.** [Old English *strīcan;* related to Old Frisian *strīka* to stroke, Old High German *strīhhan* to smooth, Latin *stria* furrow] —'**strikeless** *adj.*

strikebound ('straɪkˌbaʊnd) *adj.* (of a factory, etc.) closed or made inoperative by a strike.

strikebreaker ('straɪkˌbreɪkə) *n.* a person who tries to make a strike ineffectual by working or by taking the place of those on strike. —'**strikeˌbreaking** *n., adj.*

strike down *vb.* (*tr., adv.*) to cause to die, esp. suddenly: *he was struck down in his prime.*

strike fault *n.* a fault that runs parallel to the strike of the affected rocks.

strike note *or esp. U.S.* **strike tone** *n.* the note produced by a bell when struck, defining its musical pitch.

strike off *vb.* (*tr.*) **1.** to remove or erase from (a list, record, etc.) by or as if by a stroke of the pen. **2.** (*adv.*) to cut off or separate by or as if by a blow: *she was struck off from the inheritance.* **3.** (*adv.*) *Printing.* **a.** to take (a proof) from a relief forme by beating paper with a brush against the inked forme. **b.** to print: *they will strike off 3000 copies.* ~*n.* **strike-off.** **4.** *Printing.* a proof obtained in this manner.

strike out *vb.* (*adv.*) **1.** (*tr.*) to remove or erase. **2.** (*intr.*) to start out or begin: *to strike out on one's own.* **3.** *Baseball.* to put out or be put out on strikes. **4.** (*intr.*) *U.S. and Canadian informal.* to fail utterly.

strike pay *n.* money paid to strikers from the funds of a trade union.

striker ('straɪkə) *n.* **1.** a person who is on strike. **2.** the hammer in a timepiece that rings a bell or alarm. **3.** any part in a mechanical device that strikes something, such as the firing pin of a gun. **4.** *Soccer, informal.* an attacking player, esp. one who generally positions himself near his opponent's goal in the hope of scoring. **5.** *Cricket.* the batsman who is about to play a ball. **6. a.** a person who harpoons whales or fish. **b.** the harpoon itself.

strike-slip fault *n.* a geological fault on which the movement is along the strike of the fault.

strike through *vb.* (*tr.*) to draw (a line) through (something) to delete it.

strike up *vb.* (*adv.*) **1.** (of a band, orchestra, etc.) to begin to play or sing. **2.** (*tr.*) to bring about; cause to begin: *to strike up a friendship.* **3.** (*tr.*) to emboss (patterns, etc.) on (metal).

striking ('straɪkɪŋ) *adj.* **1.** attracting attention; fine; impressive: *a striking beauty.* **2.** conspicuous; noticeable: *a striking difference.* —'**strikingly** *adv.* —'**strikingness** *n.*

striking circle *n. Hockey.* the semicircular area in front of each goal, which an attacking player must have entered before scoring a goal.

Strine (straɪn) *n.* a humorous transliteration of Australian pronunciation, as in *Gloria Soame* for *glorious home.* [C20: a jocular rendering, coined by Alastair Morrison, of the Australian pronunciation of *Australian*]

string (strɪŋ) *n.* **1.** a thin length of cord, twine, fibre, or similar material used for tying, hanging, binding, etc. **2.** a group of objects threaded on a single strand: *a string of beads.* **3.** a series or succession of things, events, acts, utterances, etc.: *a string of oaths.* **4.** a number, chain, or group of similar things, animals, etc., owned by or associated with one person or body: *a string of girlfriends.* **5.** a tough fibre or cord in a plant: *the string of an orange; the string of a bean.* **6.** *Music.* a tightly stretched wire, cord, etc., found on stringed instruments, such as the violin, guitar, and piano. **7.** short for **bowstring.** **8.** *Architect.* short for **string course** or **stringer** (sense 1). **9.** *Maths, linguistics.* a sequence of symbols or words. **10.** *Linguistics.* a linear sequence, such as a sentence as it is spoken. **11.** *Physics.* a one-dimensional entity postulated to be a fundamental component of matter in some theories of particle physics. See also **cosmic string.** **12.** *Billiards.* another word for **lag**[1] (sense 6). **13.** a group of characters that can be treated as a unit by a computer program. **14.** (*pl.;* usually preceded by *the*) **a.** violins, violas, cellos, and double basses collectively. **b.** the section of a symphony orchestra constituted by such instruments. **15.** (*pl.*) complications or conditions (esp. in the phrase **no strings attached**). **16.** (*modifier*) composed of stringlike strands woven in a large mesh: *a string bag; string vest.* **17. first (second, etc.) string.** a person or thing regarded as a primary (secondary, etc.) source of strength. **18. keep on a string.** to have control or a hold over (a person), esp. emotionally. **19. pull strings.** *Informal.* to exert personal influence, esp. secretly or unofficially. **20. pull the strings.** to have real or ultimate control of something. ~*vb.* **strings, stringing, strung** (strʌŋ). **21.** (*tr.*) to provide with a string or strings. **22.** (*tr.*) to suspend or stretch from one point to another. 23. (*tr.*) to thread on a string. 24. (*tr.*) to form or extend in a line or series. 25. (foll. by *out*) to space or spread out at intervals. 26. (*tr.*; usually foll. by *up*) *Informal.* to kill (a person) by hanging. 27. (*tr.*) to remove the stringy parts from (vegetables, esp. beans). 28. (*intr.*) (esp. of viscous liquids) to become stringy or ropy. 29. (*tr.*; often foll. by *up*) to cause to be tense or nervous. 30. *Billiards.* another word for **lag**[1] (sense 3). [Old English *streng*; related to Old High German *strang*, Old Norse *strengr*; see STRONG] —'**string,like** *adj.*

string along *vb.* (*adv.*) *Informal.* 1. (*intr.*; often foll. by *with*) to agree or appear to be in agreement (with). 2. (*tr.*) Also: **string on.** to deceive, fool, or hoax, esp. in order to gain time.

string band *n.* 1. a band consisting of stringed instruments. 2. an informal name for **string orchestra.**

string bass (beɪs) *n.* another name for **double bass.**

string bean *n.* 1. any of several bean plants, such as the scarlet runner, cultivated for their edible unripe pods. See also **green bean, wax bean.** 2. *Informal.* a tall thin person.

stringboard ('strɪŋ,bɔːd) *n.* a skirting that covers the ends of the steps in a staircase. Also called: **stringer.**

string course *n.* another name for **cordon** (sense 4).

stringed (strɪŋd) *adj.* (of musical instruments) having or provided with strings.

stringed instrument *n.* any musical instrument in which sound is produced by the vibration of a string across a soundboard or soundbox. Also called: **chordophone.**

stringendo (strɪn'dʒendəʊ) *adj., adv. Music.* to be performed with increasing speed. [Italian, from *stringere* to compress, from Latin: to draw tight; see STRINGENT]

stringent ('strɪndʒənt) *adj.* 1. requiring strict attention to rules, procedure, detail, etc. 2. *Finance.* characterized by or causing a shortage of credit, loan capital, etc. 3. *Rare.* convincing; forcible. [C17: from Latin *stringere* to bind] —'**stringency** *n.* —'**stringently** *adv.*

stringer ('strɪŋə) *n.* 1. *Architect.* a. a long horizontal beam that is used for structural purposes. b. another name for **stringboard.** 2. *Nautical.* a longitudinal structural brace for strengthening the hull of a vessel. 3. a journalist retained by a newspaper or news service on a part-time basis to cover a particular town or area.

stringhalt ('strɪŋ,hɔːlt) *n. Vet. science.* a sudden spasmodic lifting of the hind leg of a horse, resulting from abnormal contraction of the flexor muscles of the hock. Also called: **springhalt.** [C16: probably STRING + HALT[2]]

string line *n. Billiards.* another name for **baulk line** (sense 1).

string orchestra *n.* an orchestra consisting only of violins, violas, cellos, and double basses.

stringpiece ('strɪŋ,piːs) *n.* a long horizontal timber beam used to strengthen or support a framework.

string quartet *n. Music.* 1. an instrumental ensemble consisting of two violins, one viola, and one cello. 2. a piece of music written for such a group, usually having the form and commonest features of a sonata.

string tie *n.* a very narrow tie, usually tied in a bow.

string variable *n. Computer programming.* data on which arithmetical operations will not be performed.

stringy ('strɪŋɪ) *adj.* **stringier, stringiest.** 1. made of strings or resembling strings. 2. (of meat, etc.) fibrous. 3. (of a person's build) wiry; sinewy. 4. (of liquids) forming in strings. —'**stringily** *adv.* —'**stringiness** *n.*

stringy-bark *n. Austral.* any of several eucalyptus trees having a fibrous bark.

strip[1] (strɪp) *vb.* **strips, stripping, stripped.** 1. to take or pull (the covering, clothes, etc.) off (oneself, another person, or thing): *to strip a wall; to strip a bed.* 2. (*intr.*) a. to remove all one's clothes. b. to perform a striptease. 3. (*tr.*) to denude or empty completely. 4. (*tr.*) to deprive: *he was stripped of his pride.* 5. (*tr.*) to rob or plunder. 6. (*tr.*) to remove (paint, varnish, etc.) from (a surface, furniture, etc.) by sanding, with a solvent, etc.: *stripped pine.* 7. (*tr.*) Also: **pluck.** to pull out the old coat of hair from (dogs of certain long- and wire-haired breeds). 8. a. to remove the leaves from the stalks of (tobacco, etc.). b. to separate the two sides of a leaf from the stem of (tobacco, etc.). 9. (*tr.*) *Agriculture.* to draw the last milk from each of the teats of (a cow). 10. to dismantle (an engine, mechanism, etc.). 11. to tear off or break (the thread) from (a screw, bolt, etc.) or (the teeth) from (a gear). 12. (often foll. by *down*) to remove the accessories from (a motor vehicle): *his car was stripped down.* 13. to remove (the most volatile constituent) from (a mixture of liquids) by boiling, evaporation, or distillation. 14. *Printing.* (usually foll. by *in*) to combine (pieces of film or paper) to form a composite sheet from which a plate can be made. 15. (*tr.*) (in freight transport) to unpack (a container). See also **stuffing and stripping.** ~*n.* 16. the act or an instance of undressing or of performing a striptease. ~See also **strip out.** [Old English *bestriepan* to plunder; related to Old High German *stroufen* to plunder, strip]

strip[2] (strɪp) *n.* 1. a relatively long, flat, narrow piece of something. 2. short for **airstrip.** 3. *Philately.* a horizontal or vertical row of three or more unseparated postage stamps. 4. the clothes worn by the members of a team, esp. a football team. 5. *Business.* a triple option on a security or commodity consisting of one call option and two put options at the same price and for the same period. Compare **strap** (sense 5). 6. *N.Z.* short for **dosing strip.** 7. **tear (someone) off a strip.** *Informal.* to rebuke (someone) angrily. ~*vb.* **strips, stripping, stripped.** 8. to cut or divide into strips. [C15: from Middle Dutch *strīpe* STRIPE[1]]

strip cartoon *n.* another term for **comic strip.**

strip club *n.* a small club in which striptease performances take place.

strip cropping *n.* a method of growing crops in strips or bands arranged to serve as barriers against erosion.

stripe[1] (straɪp) *n.* 1. a relatively long band of distinctive colour or texture that differs from the surrounding material or background. 2. a fabric having such bands. 3. a strip, band, or chevron of fabric worn on a military uniform, etc., esp. one that indicates rank. 4. *Chiefly U.S. and Canadian.* kind; sort; type: *a man of a certain stripe.* ~*vb.* 5. (*tr.*) to mark with a stripe or stripes. [C17: probably from Middle Dutch *strīpe*; related to Middle High German *strīfe*, of obscure origin]

stripe[2] (straɪp) *n.* a stroke from a whip, rod, cane, etc. [C15: perhaps from Middle Low German *strippe*; related to STRIPE[1]]

striped (straɪpt) *adj.* marked or decorated with stripes.

striped muscle *or* **striated muscle** *n.* a type of contractile tissue that is marked by transverse striations; it is concerned with moving skeletal parts to which it is usually attached. Compare **smooth muscle.**

striper ('straɪpə) *n. Military slang.* an officer who has a stripe or stripes on his uniform, esp. in the navy: *a two-striper* (lieutenant).

strip lighting *n.* electric lighting by means of long glass tubes that are fluorescent lamps or that contain long filaments.

stripling ('strɪplɪŋ) *n.* a lad. [C13: from STRIP[2] + -LING[1]]

strip mill *n.* a mill in which steel slabs are rolled into strips.

strip mining *n.* another term (esp. U.S.) for **opencast mining.**

strip out *vb.* (*tr., adv.*) to remove the working parts of (a machine).

stripped-down *adj.* reduced to the bare essentials; spare.

stripper ('strɪpə) *n.* 1. a striptease artist. 2. a person or thing that strips. 3. a device or substance for removing paint, varnish, etc.

strip poker *n.* a card game in which a player's losses are paid by removing an article of clothing.

strip-searching *n.* the practice by police or customs officials of stripping a prisoner or suspect naked to search him or her for contraband, narcotics, etc. —'**strip-,search** *n., vb.*

striptease ('strɪp,tiːz) *n.* a. a form of erotic entertainment in which a person gradually undresses to music. b. (*as modifier*): *a striptease club.* [from STRIP[1] + TEASE] —'**strip,teaser** *n.*

stripy ('straɪpɪ) *adj.* **stripier, stripiest.** marked by or with stripes; striped.

strive (straɪv) *vb.* **strives, striving, strove, striven** ('strɪvᵊn). 1. (*may take a clause as object or an infinitive*) to make a great and tenacious effort: *to strive to get promotion.* 2. (*intr.*) to fight; contend. [C13: from Old French *estriver*, of Germanic origin; related to Middle High German *streben* to strive, Old Norse *strītha* to fight] —'**striver** *n.*

strobe (strəʊb) *n.* 1. short for **strobe lighting** or **stroboscope.** ~*vb.* 2. to give the appearance of arrested or slow motion by using intermittent illumination.

strobe lighting *n.* 1. a high-intensity flashing beam of light produced by rapid electrical discharges in a tube or by a perforated disc rotating in front of an intense light source: used in discotheques, etc. 2. the use of or the apparatus for producing such light. Sometimes shortened to **strobe.**

strobe tuner *n.* an electronic instrument tuner that uses stroboscopic light.

strobic ('strəʊbɪk) *adj.* spinning or appearing to spin. [C19: from Greek *strobos* act of spinning]

strobila ('strəʊbɪlə) *n., pl.* **-bilae** (-bɪliː). 1. the body of a tapeworm, consisting of a string of similar segments (proglottides). 2. a less common name for **scyphistoma.** [C19: from New Latin, from Greek *strobilē* plug of lint twisted into a cone shape, from *strobilos* a fir cone]

strobilaceous (,strəʊbɪ'leɪʃəs) *adj. Botany.* relating to or resembling a cone or cones.

strobilation (,strəʊbɪ'leɪʃən) *n.* asexual reproduction by division into segments, as in tapeworms and jellyfishes.

strobilus ('strəʊbɪləs) *or* **strobile** ('strəʊbaɪl) *n., pl.* **-biluses, -bili** (-bɪlaɪ), *or* **-biles.** *Botany.* the technical name for **cone** (sense 3). [C18: via Late Latin from Greek *strobilos* a fir cone; see STROBILA]

stroboscope ('strəʊbə,skəʊp) *n.* 1. an instrument producing a flashing light, the frequency of which can be synchronized with some multiple of the frequency of rotation, vibration, or operation of an object, etc., making it appear stationary. It is used to determine speeds of rotation or vibration, or to adjust objects or parts. Sometimes shortened to **strobe.** 2. a similar device synchronized with the opening of the shutter of a camera so that a series of still photographs can be taken of a moving object. [C19: from *strobo-*, from Greek *strobos* a twisting, whirling + -SCOPE] —**stroboscopic** (,strəʊbə'skɒpɪk) *or* ,**strobo'scopical** *adj.* —,**strobo'scopically** *adv.*

strode (strəʊd) *vb.* the past tense of **stride.**

stroganoff ('strɒgə,nɒf) *n.* short for **beef stroganoff.**

stroke (strəʊk) *n.* 1. the act or an instance of striking; a blow, knock, or hit. 2. a sudden action, movement, or occurrence: *a stroke of luck.* 3. a brilliant or inspired act or feat: *a stroke of* *genius*. **4.** *Pathol.* apoplexy; rupture of a blood vessel in the brain resulting in loss of consciousness, often followed by paralysis, or embolism or thrombosis affecting a cerebral vessel. **5. a.** the striking of a clock. **b.** the hour registered by the striking of a clock: *on the stroke of three.* **6.** a mark, flourish, or line made by a writing implement. **7.** another name for **solidus**, used esp. when dictating or reading aloud. **8.** a light touch or caress, as with the fingers. **9.** a pulsation, esp. of the heart. **10.** a single complete movement or one of a series of complete movements. **11.** *Sport.* the act or manner of striking the ball with a racket, club, bat, etc. **12.** any one of the repeated movements used by a swimmer to propel himself through the water. **13.** a manner of swimming, esp. one of several named styles such as the crawl or butterfly. **14. a.** any one of a series of linear movements of a reciprocating part, such as a piston. **b.** the distance travelled by such a part from one end of its movement to the other. **15.** a single pull on an oar or oars in rowing. **16.** manner or style of rowing. **17.** the oarsman who sits nearest the stern of a shell, facing the cox, and sets the rate of striking for the rest of the crew. **18.** *U.S. informal.* a compliment or comment that enhances a persons self-esteem. **19.** (*modifier*) *Slang, chiefly U.S.* pornographic; masturbatory: *stroke magazines.* **20. a stroke (of work).** (*usually used with a negative*) a small amount of work. **21. off one's stroke.** performing or working less well than usual. **22. on the stroke.** punctually. ~*vb.* **23.** (*tr.*) to touch, brush, or caress lightly or gently. **24.** (*tr.*) to mark a line or a stroke on or through. **25.** to act as the stroke of (a racing shell). **26.** (*tr.*) *Sport.* to strike (a ball) with a smooth swinging blow. **27.** (*tr.*) *U.S. and Canadian informal.* to handle or influence (someone) with care, using persuasion, flattery, etc. [Old English *strācian;* related to Middle Low German *strēken;* see STRIKE]

stroke play *n. Golf.* **a.** scoring by counting the number of strokes taken. **b.** (*as modifier*): *a strokeplay tournament.* ~Also called: **medal play.** Compare **match play.**

stroll (strəʊl) *vb.* **1.** to walk about in a leisurely manner. **2.** (*intr.*) to wander from place to place. ~*n.* **3.** a leisurely walk. [C17: probably from dialect German *strollen,* of obscure origin; compare German *Strolch* tramp]

stroller ('strəʊlə) *n.* the usual U.S., Canadian, and Austral. word for **pushchair.**

stroma ('strəʊmə) *n., pl.* **-mata** (-mətə). *Biology.* **1.** the dense colourless framework of a chloroplast and certain cells. **2.** the fibrous connective tissue forming the matrix of the mammalian ovary and testis. **3.** a dense mass of hyphae that is produced by certain fungi and gives rise to spore-producing bodies. [C19: via New Latin from Late Latin: a mattress, from Greek; related to Latin *sternere* to strew] —**stromatic** (strəʊ'mætɪk) *or* '**stromatous** *adj.*

stromatolite (strəʊ'mætəˌlaɪt) *n.* a rocky mass consisting of layers of calcareous material formed by the prolific growth of blue-green algae: such structures date back to Precambrian times. [C20: from Greek, from *strōma* covering + -LITE] —**stromatolitic** (strəʊˌmætə'lɪtɪk) *adj.*

Strombolian (strɒm'bəʊlɪən) *adj.* relating to or denoting a type of volcanic eruption characterized by repeated small explosions caused by gas escaping through lava. [named after *Stromboli,* an island off the N coast of Sicily famous for its active volcano]

strong (strɒŋ) *adj.* **stronger** ('strɒŋgə), **strongest** ('strɒŋgɪst). **1.** involving or possessing physical or mental strength. **2.** solid or robust in construction; not easily broken or injured. **3.** having a resolute will or morally firm and incorruptible character. **4.** intense in quality; not faint or feeble: *a strong voice; a strong smell.* **5.** easily defensible; incontestable or formidable. **6.** concentrated; not weak or diluted. **7. a.** (*postpositive*) containing or having a specified number: *a navy 40 000 strong.* **b.** (*in combination*): *a 40 000-strong navy.* **8.** having an unpleasantly powerful taste or smell. **9.** having an extreme or drastic effect: *strong discipline.* **10.** emphatic or immoderate: *strong language.* **11.** convincing, effective, or cogent. **12.** (of a colour) having a high degree of saturation or purity; being less saturated than a vivid colour but more so than a moderate colour; produced by a concentrated quantity of colouring agent. **13.** *Grammar.* **a.** denoting or belonging to a class of verbs, in certain languages including the Germanic languages, whose conjugation shows vowel gradation, as *sing, sang, sung.* **b.** belonging to any part-of-speech class, in any of various languages, whose inflections follow the less regular of two possible patterns. Compare **weak** (sense 10). **14.** (of a wind, current, etc.) moving fast. **15.** (of a syllable) accented or stressed. **16.** (of an industry, market, currency, securities, etc.) firm in price or characterized by firm or increasing prices. **17.** (of certain acids and bases) producing high concentrations of hydrogen or hydroxide ions in aqueous solution. **18.** *Irish.* prosperous; well-to-do (esp. in the phrase **a strong farmer**). **19. have a strong stomach.** not to be prone to nausea. ~*adv.* **20.** *Informal.* in a strong way; effectively: *going strong.* **21. come on strong.** to make a forceful or exaggerated impression. [Old English *strang;* related to Old Norse *strangr,* Middle High German *strange,* Lettish *strans* courageous] —'**strongish** *adj.* —'**strongly** *adv.* —'**strongness** *n.*

strong-arm *Informal.* ~*n.* **1.** (*modifier*) relating to or involving physical force or violence: *strong-arm tactics.* ~*vb.* **2.** (*tr.*) to show violence towards.

strongbox ('strɒŋˌbɒks) *n.* a specially designed box or safe in which valuables are locked for safety.

strong breeze *n. Meteorol.* a considerable wind of force six on the Beaufort scale, reaching speeds of 25–31 mph.

strong drink *n.* alcoholic drink.

strong-eye dog *n. N.Z.* a dog trained to control sheep by its gaze.

strong gale *n. Meteorol.* a strong wind of force nine on the Beaufort scale, reaching speeds of 47–54 mph: capable of causing minor structural damage to buildings.

stronghold ('strɒŋˌhəʊld) *n.* **1.** a defensible place; fortress. **2.** a major centre or area of predominance. [C15: from STRONG + HOLD[1] (in the archaic sense: a fortified place)]

strong interaction *or* **force** *n. Physics.* an interaction between elementary particles responsible for the forces between nucleons in the nucleus. It operates at distances less than about 10^{-15} metres, and is about a hundred times more powerful than the electromagnetic interaction. Also called: **strong nuclear interaction** *or* **force.** See **interaction** (sense 2).

strongman ('strɒŋˌmæn) *n., pl.* **-men. 1.** a performer, esp. one in a circus, who performs feats of strength. **2.** any person regarded as a source of power, capability, initiative, etc.

strong meat *n.* anything arousing fear, anger, repulsion, etc., except among a tolerant or receptive minority: *some scenes in the film were strong meat.*

strong-minded *adj.* having strength of mind; firm, resolute, and determined. —ˌ**strong-'mindedly** *adv.* —ˌ**strong'mindedness** *n.*

strong point *n.* something at which one excels; forte: *tactfulness was never his strong point.*

strongpoint ('strɒŋˌpɔɪnt) *n. Military.* **1.** a location that is by its site and nature easily defended. **2.** a spot in a defensive position that is heavily defended.

strongroom ('strɒŋˌruːm, -ˌrʊm) *n.* a specially designed room in which valuables are locked for safety.

strong waters *pl. n.* an archaic name for alcoholic drink.

strong-willed *adj.* having strength of will.

strongyle ('strɒndʒɪl) *or* **strongyl** ('strɒndʒəl) *n.* any parasitic nematode worm of the family *Strongylidae,* chiefly occurring in the intestines of horses. [C19: via New Latin *Strongylus,* from Greek *strongulos* round]

strongyloidiasis (ˌstrɒndʒɪlɔɪ'daɪəsɪs) *or* **strongyloidosis** (-'dəʊsɪs) *n.* an intestinal disease caused by infection with the nematode worm *Strongyloides stercoralis.*

strontia ('strɒntɪə) *n.* another name for **strontium monoxide.** [C19: changed from STRONTIAN]

strontian ('strɒntɪən) *n.* **1.** another name for **strontianite. 2.** another name for **strontium** or **strontium monoxide.** [C18: named after a parish in the Scottish Highlands, where it was discovered]

strontianite ('strɒntɪəˌnaɪt) *n.* a white, lightly coloured, or colourless mineral consisting of strontium carbonate in orthorhombic crystalline form: it is a source of strontium compounds. Formula: $SrCO_3$.

strontium ('strɒntɪəm) *n.* a soft silvery-white element of the alkaline earth group of metals, occurring chiefly in celestite and strontianite. Its compounds burn with a crimson flame and are used in fireworks. The radioisotope **strontium-90,** with a half-life of 28.1 years, is used in nuclear power sources and is a hazardous nuclear fall-out product. Symbol: Sr; atomic no.: 38; atomic wt.: 87.62; valency: 2; relative density: 2.54; melting pt.: 769°C; boiling pt.: 1384°C. [C19: from New Latin, from STRONTIAN]

strontium monoxide *n.* a white insoluble solid substance used in making strontium salts and purifying sugar. Formula: SrO. Also called: **strontium oxide, strontia.**

strontium unit *n.* a unit expressing the concentration of strontium-90 in an organic medium, such as soil, milk, bone, etc., relative to the concentration of calcium in the same medium. Abbrev.: **SU.**

strop (strɒp) *n.* **1.** a leather strap or an abrasive strip for sharpening razors. **2.** a rope or metal band around a block or deadeye for support. ~*vb.* **strops, stropping, stropped. 3.** (*tr.*) to sharpen (a razor, etc.) on a strop. [C14 (in nautical use: a strip of rope): via Middle Low German or Middle Dutch *strop,* ultimately from Latin *stroppus,* from Greek *strophos* cord; see STROPHE]

strophanthin (strəʊ'fænθɪn) *n.* a toxic glycoside or mixture of glycosides obtained from the ripe seeds of certain species of strophanthus: used as a cardiac stimulant.

strophanthus (strəʊ'fænθəs) *n.* **1.** any small tree or shrub of the apocynaceous genus *Strophanthus,* of tropical Africa and Asia, having strap-shaped twisted petals. The seeds of certain species yield the drug strophanthin. **2.** the seeds of any of these plants. [C19: New Latin, from Greek *strophos* twisted cord + *anthos* flower]

strophe ('strəʊfɪ) *n. Prosody.* **1.** (in ancient Greek drama) **a.** the first of two movements made by a chorus during the performance of a choral ode. **b.** the first part of a choral ode sung during this movement. **2.** (in classical verse) the first division of the threefold structure of a Pindaric ode. **3.** the first of two metrical systems used alternately within a poem. ~See **antistrophe, epode.** [C17: from Greek: a verse, literally: a turning, from *strephein* to twist]

strophic ('strɒfɪk, 'strəʊ-) *or* (*less commonly*) **strophical** *adj.* **1.** of, relating to, or employing a strophe or strophes. **2.** (of a song) having identical or related music in each verse. Compare **through-composed. 3.** *Botany.* denoting the twisting growth of a plant organ in response to a directional stimulus.

stroppy ('strɒpɪ) *adj.* **-pier, -piest.** *Brit. informal.* angry or awkward. [C20: changed and shortened from OBSTREPEROUS] —'**stroppily** *adv.* —'**stroppiness** *n.*

stroud (straʊd) *n.* a coarse woollen fabric. [C17: perhaps named after *Stroud,* textile centre in Gloucestershire]

strove (strəʊv) *vb.* the past tense of **strive.**

strow (strəʊ) *vb.* **strows, strowing, strowed; strown** *or* **strowed.** an archaic variant of **strew.**

stroy (strɔɪ) *vb.* an archaic variant of **destroy.** —'**stroyer** *n.*

struck (strʌk) *vb.* **1.** the past tense and past participle of **strike.** ~*adj.* **2.** *Chiefly U.S. and Canadian.* (of an industry, factory, etc.) shut down or otherwise affected by a labour strike.

struck measure *n.* a measure of grain, etc., in which the contents are made level with the top of the container rather than being heaped.

structural ('strʌktʃərəl) *adj.* **1.** of, relating to, or having structure or a structure. **2.** of, relating to, or forming part of the structure of a building. **3.** of or relating to the structure of rocks and other features of the earth's crust. **4.** of or relating to the structure of organisms; morphological. **5.** *Chem.* of, concerned with, caused by, or involving the arrangement of atoms in molecules. —'**structurally** *adv.*

structural formula *n.* a chemical formula showing the composition and structure of a molecule. The atoms are represented by symbols and the structure is indicated by showing the relative positions of the atoms in space and the bonds between them: *H–C≡C–H is the structural formula of acetylene.* See also **empirical formula, molecular formula.**

structuralism ('strʌktʃərəˌlɪzəm) *n.* **1.** an approach to anthropology and other social sciences and to literature that interprets and analyses its material in terms of oppositions, contrasts, and hierarchical structures, esp. as they might reflect universal mental characteristics or organizing principles. Compare **functionalism. 2.** an approach to linguistics that analyses and describes the structure of language, as distinguished from its comparative and historical aspects. —'**structuralist** *n., adj.*

structural linguistics *n.* (*functioning as sing.*) a descriptive approach to a synchronic or diachronic analysis of language on the basis of its structure as reflected by irreducible units of phonological, morphological, and semantic features.

structural psychology *n.* (formerly) a school of psychology using introspection to analyse experience into basic units.

structural steel *n.* a strong mild steel used in construction work.

structural unemployment *n. Economics.* unemployment resulting from changes in the structure of an industry as a result of changes in either technology or taste.

structure ('strʌktʃə) *n.* **1.** a complex construction or entity. **2.** the arrangement and interrelationship of parts in a construction, such as a building. **3.** the manner of construction or organization: *the structure of society.* **4.** *Biology.* morphology; form. **5.** *Chem.* the arrangement of atoms in a molecule of a chemical compound: *the structure of benzene.* **6.** *Geology.* the way in which a mineral, rock, rock mass or stratum, etc., is made up of its component parts. **7.** *Now rare.* the act of constructing. ~*vb.* **8.** (*tr.*) to impart a structure to. [C15: from Latin *structūra,* from *struere* to build]

structured ('strʌktʃəd) *adj.* **1.** having a distinct physical shape or form, often provided by an internal structure. **2.** planned in broad outline; organized: *structured play for preschoolers.* **3.** having a definite predetermined pattern; rigid: *structured hierarchy.*

structured interview *n. Marketing.* an interview in which the respondent answers only "yes", "no", or "don't know".

strudel ('struːdᵊl; *German* 'ʃtruːdəl) *n.* a thin sheet of filled dough rolled up and baked: *apple strudel.* [German, from Middle High German *strodel* eddy, whirlpool, so called from the way the pastry is rolled]

struggle ('strʌgᵊl) *vb.* **1.** (*intr.;* usually foll. by *for* or *against; may take an infinitive*) to exert strength, energy, and force; work or strive: *to struggle to obtain freedom.* **2.** (*intr.*) to move about strenuously so as to escape from something confining. **3.** (*intr.*) to contend, battle, or fight. **4.** (*intr.*) to go or progress with difficulty. ~*n.* **5.** a laboured or strenuous exertion or effort. **6.** a fight or battle. **7.** the act of struggling. [C14: of obscure origin] —'**struggler** *n.* —'**struggling** *adj.* —'**strugglingly** *adv.*

struggle for existence *n.* (*not in technical usage*) competition between organisms of a population, esp. as a factor in the evolution of plants and animals. See also **natural selection.**

strum (strʌm) *vb.* **strums, strumming, strummed. 1.** to sound (the strings of a guitar, banjo, etc.) with a downward or upward sweep of the thumb or of a plectrum. **2.** to play (chords, a tune, etc.) in this way. [C18: probably of imitative origin; see THRUM[1]] —'**strummer** *n.*

struma ('struːmə) *n., pl.* **-mae** (-miː). **1.** *Pathol.* an abnormal enlargement of the thyroid gland; goitre. **2.** *Botany.* a swelling, esp. one at the base of a moss capsule. **3.** another word for **scrofula.** [C16: from Latin: a scrofulous tumour, from *struere* to heap up] —**strumatic** (struː'mætɪk), **strumous** ('struːməs), *or* **strumose** ('struːməʊs) *adj.*

strumpet ('strʌmpɪt) *n. Archaic.* a prostitute or promiscuous woman. [C14: of unknown origin]

strung (strʌŋ) *vb.* **1.** a past tense and past participle of **string.** ~*adj.* **2. a.** (of a piano, etc.) provided with strings, esp. of a specified kind or in a specified manner. **b.** (*in combination*): *gut-strung.* **3. highly strung.** very nervous or volatile in character. Usual U.S. and Canadian phrase: **high-strung.**

strung out *adj. Slang.* **1.** addicted to a drug. **2.** (of a drug addict) suffering or distressed because of the lack of a drug.

strung up *adj.* (*postpositive*) *Informal.* tense or nervous.

strut (strʌt) *vb.* **struts, strutting, strutted. 1.** (*intr.*) to walk in a pompous manner; swagger. **2.** (*tr.*) to support or provide with struts. ~*n.* **3.** a structural member used mainly in compression, esp. as part of a framework. **4.** an affected, proud, or stiff walk. [C14 *strouten* (in the sense: swell, stand out; C16: to walk stiffly), from Old English *strūtian* to stand stiffly; related to Low German *strutt* stiff] —'**strutter** *n.* —'**strutting** *adj.* —'**struttingly** *adv.*

struthious ('struːθɪəs) *adj.* **1.** (of birds) related to or resembling the ostrich. **2.** of, relating to, or designating all flightless (ratite) birds. [C18: from Late Latin *strūthiō,* from Greek *strouthiōn,* from *strouthos* an ostrich]

strychnic ('strɪknɪk) *adj.* of, relating to, or derived from strychnine.

strychnine ('strɪkniːn) *n.* a white crystalline very poisonous alkaloid, obtained from the plant nux vomica: used in small quantities as a stimulant of the central nervous system and the appetite. Formula: $C_{21}H_{22}O_2N_2$. [C19: via French from New Latin *Strychnos,* from Greek *strukhnos* nightshade]

strychninism ('strɪknɪˌnɪzəm) *n. Pathol.* poisoning caused by the excessive or prolonged use of strychnine.

Stuart ('stjʊət) *adj.* of or relating to the royal house that ruled in Scotland from 1371 to 1714 and in England from 1603 to 1714.

stub (stʌb) *n.* **1.** a short piece remaining after something has been cut, removed, etc.: *a cigar stub.* **2.** the residual piece or section of a receipt, ticket, cheque, etc. **3.** the usual U.S. and Canadian word for **counterfoil. 4.** any short projection or blunted end. **5.** the stump of a tree or plant. ~*vb.* **stubs, stubbing, stubbed.** (*tr.*) **6.** to strike (one's toe, foot, etc.) painfully against a hard surface. **7.** (usually foll. by *out*) to put (out a cigarette or cigar) by pressing the end against a surface. **8.** to clear (land) of stubs. **9.** to dig up (the roots) of (a tree or bush). [Old English *stubb;* related to Old Norse *stubbi,* Middle Dutch *stubbe,* Greek *stupos* stem, stump]

stub axle *n.* a short axle that carries one of the front steered wheels of a motor vehicle and is capable of limited angular movement about a kingpin.

Stubbies ('stʌbɪz) *pl. n. Austral. trademark.* a type of shorts.

stubble ('stʌbᵊl) *n.* **1. a.** the stubs of stalks left in a field where a crop has been cut and harvested. **b.** (*as modifier*): *a stubble field.* **2.** any bristly growth or surface. [C13: from Old French *estuble,* from Latin *stupula,* variant of *stipula* stalk, stem, stubble] —**stubbled** *or* '**stubbly** *adj.*

stubble-jumper *n. Canadian slang.* a prairie grain farmer.

stubborn ('stʌbᵊn) *adj.* **1.** refusing to comply, agree, or give in; obstinate. **2.** difficult to handle, treat, or overcome. **3.** persistent and dogged: *a stubborn crusade.* [C14 *stoborne,* of obscure origin] —'**stubbornly** *adv.* —'**stubbornness** *n.*

stubby ('stʌbɪ) *adj.* **-bier, -biest. 1.** short and broad; stumpy or thickset. **2.** bristling and stiff. ~*n.* **3.** *Austral. slang.* a small bottle of beer. —'**stubbily** *adv.* —'**stubbiness** *n.*

stub nail *n.* **1.** a short thick nail. **2.** a worn nail in a horseshoe.

STUC *abbrev. for* Scottish Trades Union Congress.

stucco ('stʌkəʊ) *n., pl.* **-coes** *or* **-cos. 1.** a weather-resistant mixture of dehydrated lime, powdered marble, and glue, used in decorative mouldings on buildings. **2.** any of various types of cement or plaster used for coating outside walls. **3.** Also called: **stuccowork.** decorative work moulded in stucco. ~*vb.* **-coes** *or* **-cos, -coing, -coed. 4.** (*tr.*) to apply stucco to. [C16: from Italian, of Germanic origin; compare Old High German *stukki* a fragment, crust, Old English *stycce*] —'**stuccoer** *n.*

stuck (stʌk) *vb.* **1.** the past tense and past participle of **stick**[2]. ~*adj.* **2.** *Informal.* baffled or nonplussed. **3.** (foll. by *on*) *Slang.* keen (on) or infatuated (with). **4. get stuck in** *or* **into.** *Informal.* **a.** to perform (a task) with determination. **b.** to attack (a person) verbally or physically.

stuck-up *adj. Informal.* conceited, arrogant, or snobbish. —'**stuck-'upness** *n.*

stud[1] (stʌd) *n.* **1.** a large-headed nail or other projection protruding from a surface, usually as decoration. **2.** a type of fastener consisting of two discs at either end of a short shank, used to fasten shirtfronts, collars, etc. **3.** *Building.* a vertical member made of timber, steel, etc., that is used with others to construct the framework of a wall. **4.** a headless bolt that is threaded at both ends, the centre portion being unthreaded. **5.** any short projection on a machine, such as the metal cylinder that forms a journal for the gears on a screw-cutting lathe. **6.** the crossbar in the centre of a link of a heavy chain. **7.** one of a number of rounded projections on the sole of a boot or shoe to give better grip, as on a football boot. ~*vb.* **studs, studding, studded.** (*tr.*) **8.** to provide, ornament, or make with studs. **9.** to dot or cover (with): *the park was studded with daisies.* **10.** *Building.* to provide or support (a wall, partition, etc.) with studs. [Old English *studu;* related to Old Norse *stoth* post, Middle High German *stud* post]

stud[2] (stʌd) *n.* **1.** a group of pedigree animals, esp. horses, kept for breeding purposes. **2.** any male animal kept principally for breeding purposes, esp. a stallion. **3.** a farm or stable where a stud is kept. **4.** the state or condition of being kept for breeding purposes: *at stud; put to stud.* **5.** (*modifier*) of or relating to such animals or the place where they are kept: *a stud farm; a stud horse.* **6.** *Slang.* a virile or sexually active man. **7.** short for **stud poker.** [Old English *stōd;* related to Old Norse *stōth,* Old High German *stuot*]

studbook ('stʌdˌbʊk) *n.* a written record of the pedigree of a purebred stock, esp. of racehorses.

studding ('stʌdɪŋ) *n.* **1.** building studs collectively, esp. as used to form a wall or partition. See also **stud**[1] (sense 3). **2.** material that is used to form studs or serve as studs.

studdingsail ('stʌdɪŋˌseɪl; *Nautical* 'stʌnsᵊl) *n. Nautical.* a light auxiliary sail set outboard on spars on either side of a square sail. Also called: **stunsail, stuns'l.** [C16: *studding,* perhaps from Middle Low German, Middle Dutch *stōtinge,* from *stōten* to thrust; related to German *stossen*]

student ('stjuːdᵊnt) *n.* **1. a.** a person following a course of study, as in a school, college, university, etc. **b.** (*as modifier*): *student teacher.* **2.** a person who makes a thorough study of a subject. **3.** *Rare.* a person who likes to study. [C15: from Latin *studēns* diligent, from *studēre* to be zealous; see STUDY]

student adviser *n.* another word for **counsellor** (sense 6).

studentship ('stjuːdᵊntʃɪp) *n.* **1.** the role or position of a student. **2.** another word for **scholarship** (sense 3).

Student's t *n.* a statistic often used to test the hypothesis that a random sample of normally distributed observations has a given mean, μ; given by $t = (\bar{x}-\mu)\sqrt{n}/s$ where $\bar{x}$ is the mean of the sample, *s* is its standard deviation, and *n* is the size of the sample. [after *Student,* the pen name of W. S. Gosset (1876–1937), British statistician and research scientist]

student teacher *n.* a person who is teaching in a school for a limited period under supervision as part of a course to qualify as a teacher.

studhorse ('stʌdˌhɔːs) *n.* another word for **stallion.**

studied ('stʌdɪd) *adj.* **1.** carefully practised, designed, or premeditated: *a studied reply.* **2.** an archaic word for **learned.** —'**studiedly** *adv.* —'**studiedness** *n.*

studio ('stjuːdɪˌəʊ) *n., pl.* **-dios. 1.** a room in which an artist, photographer, or musician works. **2.** a room used to record television or radio programmes, make films, etc. **3.** (*pl.*) the premises of a radio, television, or film company. [C19: from Italian, literally: study, from Latin *studium* diligence]

studio couch *n.* an upholstered couch, usually backless, convertible into a double bed.

studio flat *n.* a flat with one main room.

studious ('stjuːdɪəs) *adj.* **1.** given to study. **2.** of a serious, thoughtful, and hard-working character. **3.** showing deliberation, care, or precision. [C14: from Latin *studiōsus* devoted to, from *studium* assiduity] —'**studiously** *adv.* —'**studiousness** *n.*

stud poker *n.* a variety of poker in which the first card is dealt face down before each player and the next four are dealt face up (**five-card stud**) or in which the first two cards and the last card are dealt face down and the intervening four cards are dealt face up (**seven-card stud**), with bets made after each round. Often shortened to **stud.** [C19: from STUD[2] + POKER[2]]

stud welding *n.* the semiautomatic welding of a stud or similar piece of metal to a flat part, usually by means of an accurately timed electric arc.

studwork ('stʌdˌwɜːk) *n.* **1.** work decorated with studs. **2.** the supporting framework of a wall or partition.

study ('stʌdɪ) *vb.* **studies, studying, studied. 1.** to apply the mind to the learning or understanding of (a subject), esp. by reading: *to study languages; to study all night.* **2.** (*tr.*) to investigate or examine, as by observation, research, etc.: *to study the effects of heat on metal.* **3.** (*tr.*) to look at minutely; scrutinize. **4.** (*tr.*) to give much careful or critical thought to. **5.** to take a course in (a subject), as at a college. **6.** (*tr.*) to try to memorize: *to study a part for a play.* **7.** (*intr.*) to meditate or contemplate; reflect. ~*n., pl.* **studies. 8. a.** the act or process of studying **b.** (*as modifier*): *study group.* **9.** a room used for studying, reading, writing, etc. **10.** (*often pl.*) work relating to a particular discipline: *environmental studies.* **11.** an investigation and analysis of a subject, situation, etc.: *a study of transport provision in rural districts.* **12.** a product of studying, such as a written paper or book. **13.** a drawing, sculpture, etc., executed for practice or in preparation for another work. **14.** a musical composition intended to develop one aspect of performing technique: *a study in spiccato bowing.* **15. in a brown study.** in a reverie or daydream. [C13: from Old French *estudie,* from Latin *studium* zeal, inclination, from *studēre* to be diligent]

stuff (stʌf) *vb.* (*mainly tr.*) **1.** to pack or fill completely; cram. **2.** (*intr.*) to eat large quantities. **3.** to force, shove, or squeeze: *to stuff money into a pocket.* **4.** to fill (food such as poultry or tomatoes) with a stuffing. **5.** to fill (an animal's skin) with material so as to restore the shape of the live animal. **6.** *Taboo slang.* to have sexual intercourse with (a woman). **7.** *Tanning.* to treat (an animal skin or hide) with grease. **8.** *U.S. and Canadian.* to fill (a ballot box) with a large number of fraudulent votes. **9.** (in marine transport) to pack (a container). See also **stuffing and stripping.** ~*n.* **10.** the raw material or fabric of something. **11.** woollen cloth or fabric. **12.** any general or unspecified substance or accumulation of objects. **13.** stupid or worthless actions, speech, ideas, etc. **14.** subject matter, skill, etc.: *he knows his stuff.* **15.** a slang word for **money. 16.** *Slang.* a drug, esp. cannabis. **17.** *Informal.* **do one's stuff.** to do what is expected of one. **18. that's the stuff.** that is what is needed. **19.** *Brit. slang.* a girl or woman considered sexually (esp. in the phrase **bit of stuff**). [C14: from Old French *estoffe,* from *estoffer* to furnish, provide, of Germanic origin; related to Middle High German *stopfen* to cram full] —'**stuffer** *n.*

stuffed (stʌft) *adj.* **1.** filled with something, esp. (of poultry and other food) filled with stuffing. **2.** (foll. by *up*) (of the nasal passages) blocked with mucus. **3. get stuffed!** *Brit. taboo slang.* an exclamation of contemptuous anger or annoyance, esp. against another person.

stuffed shirt *n. Informal.* a pompous or formal person.

stuff gown *n. Brit.* a woollen gown worn by a barrister who has not taken silk.

stuffing ('stʌfɪŋ) *n.* **1.** the material with which something is stuffed. **2.** a mixture of chopped and seasoned ingredients with which poultry, meat, etc., is stuffed before cooking. **3. knock the stuffing out of (someone).** to defeat (someone) utterly.

stuffing and stripping *n.* (in marine transport) the packing and unpacking of containers.

stuffing box *n.* a small chamber in which an annular packing is compressed around a reciprocating or rotating rod or shaft to form a seal. Also called: **packing box.**

stuffing nut *n.* a large nut that is tightened to compress the packing in a stuffing box.

stuffy ('stʌfɪ) *adj.* **stuffier, stuffiest. 1.** lacking fresh air. **2.** excessively dull, staid, or conventional. **3.** (of the nasal passages) blocked with mucus. —'**stuffily** *adv.* —'**stuffiness** *n.*

stull (stʌl) *n. Mining.* a timber prop or platform in a stope. [C18: perhaps from German *Stollen,* from Old High German *stollo*]

stultify ('stʌltɪˌfaɪ) *vb.* **-fies, -fying, -fied.** (*tr.*) **1.** to make useless, futile, or ineffectual, esp. by routine. **2.** to cause to appear absurd or inconsistent. **3.** to prove (someone) to be of unsound mind and thus not legally responsible. [C18: from Latin *stultus* stupid + *facere* to make] —ˌ**stultifi'cation** *n.* —'**stultiˌfier** *n.*

stum (stʌm) (in wine-making) ~*n.* **1.** a less common word for **must**[2]. **2.** partly fermented wine added to fermented wine as a preservative. ~*vb.* **stums, stumming, stummed. 3.** to preserve (wine) by adding stum. [C17: from Dutch *stom* dumb; related to German *stumm*]

stumble ('stʌmbᵊl) *vb.* (*intr.*) **1.** to trip or fall while walking or running. **2.** to walk in an awkward, unsteady, or unsure way. **3.** to make mistakes or hesitate in speech or actions. **4.** (foll. by *across* or *upon*) to come (across) by accident. **5.** to commit a grave mistake or sin. ~*n.* **6.** a false step, trip, or blunder. **7.** the act of stumbling. [C14: related to Norwegian *stumla,* Danish dialect *stumle;* see STAMMER] —'**stumbler** *n.* —'**stumbling** *adj.* —'**stumblingly** *adv.*

stumbling block *n.* any impediment or obstacle.

stumer ('stjuːmə) *n.* **1.** *Slang.* a forgery or cheat. **2.** *Irish dialect.* a poor bargain. **3.** *Scot.* a stupid person. **4. come a stumer.** *Austral. slang.* to crash financially. [of unknown origin]

stump (stʌmp) *n.* **1.** the base part of a tree trunk left standing after the tree has been felled or has fallen. **2.** the part of something, such as a tooth, limb, or blade, that remains after a larger part has been removed. **3.** *Informal, facetious.* **a.** (*often pl.*) a leg. **b. stir one's stumps.** to move or become active. **4.** *Cricket.* any of three upright wooden sticks that, with two bails laid across them, form a wicket (the **stumps**). **5.** Also called: **tortillon.** a short sharply-pointed stick of cork or rolled paper or leather, used in drawing and shading. **6.** a heavy tread or the sound of heavy footsteps. **7.** a platform used by an orator when addressing a meeting. **8. on the stump.** *Chiefly U.S. and Canadian.* engaged in campaigning, esp. by political speech-making. **9.** (*often pl.*) *Austral.* a pile used to support a house. ~*vb.* **10.** (*tr.*) to stop, confuse, or puzzle. **11.** (*intr.*) to plod or trudge heavily. **12.** (*tr.*) *Cricket.* (of a fielder, esp. a wicketkeeper) to dismiss (a batsman) by breaking his wicket with the ball or with the ball in the hand while he is out of his crease. **13.** *Chiefly U.S. and Canadian.* to campaign or canvass (an area), esp. by political speech-making. **14.** (*tr.*) to reduce to a stump; lop. **15.** (*tr.*) to clear (land) of stumps. [C14: from Middle Low German *stump;* related to Dutch *stomp,* German *Stumpf;* see STAMP] —'**stumper** *n.*

stumpage ('stʌmpɪdʒ) *n.* **1.** *U.S. and Canadian.* standing timber or its value. **2.** *U.S. and Canadian.* the right to fell timber on another person's land. **3.** *Canadian.* a tax or royalty payable on each tree felled, esp. on crown land.

stump-jump plough *n. Austral.* a plough designed for use on land not cleared of stumps.

stump ranch *or* **farm** *n. Canadian informal.* (in British Columbia) an undeveloped ranch in the bush where animals graze among the stumps of felled trees.

stump up *vb.* (*adv.*) *Brit. informal.* to give (the money required).

stumpwork ('stʌmpˌwɜːk) *n.* a type of embroidery of the 15th to 17th centuries featuring raised or embossed figures, padded with cotton wool or hair.

stumpy ('stʌmpɪ) *adj.* **stumpier, stumpiest.** **1.** short and thick-set like a stump; stubby. **2.** abounding in or full of stumps. —'**stumpiness** *n.*

stun (stʌn) *vb.* **stuns, stunning, stunned.** (*tr.*) **1.** to render unconscious, as by a heavy blow or fall. **2.** to shock or overwhelm. **3.** to surprise or astound. ~*n.* **4.** the state or effect of being stunned. [C13 *stunen,* from Old French *estoner* to daze, stupefy, from Vulgar Latin *extonāre* (unattested), from Latin EX-[1] + *tonāre* to thunder]

stung (stʌŋ) *vb.* **1.** the past tense and past participle of **sting.** ~*adj.* **2.** *Austral. slang.* drunk; intoxicated.

stun gun *n.* a device designed to immobilize an animal or person temporarily without inflicting serious injury.

stunk (stʌŋk) *vb.* a past tense and past participle of **stink.**

stunner ('stʌnə) *n. Informal.* a person or thing of great beauty, quality, size, etc.

stunning ('stʌnɪŋ) *adj. Informal.* very attractive, impressive, astonishing, etc. —'**stunningly** *adv.*

stunsail *or* **stuns'l** ('stʌnsᵊl) *n.* another word for **studdingsail.**

stunt[1] (stʌnt) *vb.* **1.** (*tr.*) to prevent or impede (the growth or development) of (a plant, animal, etc.). ~*n.* **2.** the act or an instance of stunting. **3.** a person, animal, or plant that has been stunted. [C17 (as vb.: to check the growth of): perhaps from C15 *stont* of short duration, from Old English *stunt* simple, foolish; sense probably influenced by Old Norse *stuttr* short in stature, dwarfed] —'**stunted** *adj.* —'**stuntedness** *n.*

stunt[2] (stʌnt) *n.* **1. a.** a feat of daring or skill. **b.** (*as modifier*): *a stunt man; stunt flying.* **2.** anything spectacular or unusual done for attention. ~*vb.* **3.** (*intr.*) to perform a stunt or stunts. [C19: U.S. student slang, of unknown origin]

stupa ('stuːpə) *n.* a domed edifice housing Buddhist or Jain relics. Also called: **tope.** [C19: from Sanskrit: dome]

stupe[1] (stjuːp) *n. Med.* a hot damp cloth, usually sprinkled with an irritant, applied to the body to relieve pain by counterirritation. [C14: from Latin *stuppa* flax, from Greek *stuppē*]

stupe[2] (stjuːp) *n. U.S. slang.* a stupid person; clot.

stupefacient (ˌstjuːpɪ'feɪʃɪənt) *n.* **1.** a drug that causes stupor. ~*adj.* **2.** of, relating to, or designating this type of drug. [C17: from Latin *stupefacere* to make senseless, from *stupēre* to be stunned + *facere* to make]

stupefaction (ˌstjuːpɪ'fækʃən) *n.* **1.** astonishment. **2.** the act of stupefying or the state of being stupefied.

stupefy ('stjuːpɪˌfaɪ) *vb.* **-fies, -fying, -fied.** (*tr.*) **1.** to render insensitive or lethargic. **2.** to confuse or astound. [C16: from Old French *stupefier,* from Latin *stupefacere;* see STUPEFACIENT] —'**stupeˌfier** *n.* —'**stupeˌfying** *adj.* —'**stupeˌfyingly** *adv.*

stupendous (stjuː'pɛndəs) *adj.* astounding, wonderful, huge, etc. [C17: from Latin *stupēre* to be amazed] —**stu'pendously** *adv.* —**stu'pendousness** *n.*

stupid ('stjuːpɪd) *adj.* **1.** lacking in common sense, perception, or normal intelligence. **2.** (*usually postpositive*) stunned, dazed, or stupefied: *stupid from lack of sleep.* **3.** having dull mental responses; slow-witted. **4.** trivial, silly, or frivolous. ~*n.* **5.** *Informal.* a stupid person. [C16: from French *stupide,* from Latin *stupidus* silly, from *stupēre* to be amazed] —'**stupidly** *adv.* —'**stupidness** *n.*

stupidity (stjuː'pɪdɪtɪ) *n., pl.* **-ties.** **1.** the quality or state of being stupid. **2.** a stupid act, remark, etc.

stupor ('stjuːpə) *n.* **1.** a state of unconsciousness. **2.** mental dullness; torpor. [C17: from Latin, from *stupēre* to be aghast] —'**stuporous** *adj.*

sturdy[1] ('stɜːdɪ) *adj.* **-dier, -diest.** **1.** healthy, strong, and vigorous. **2.** strongly built; stalwart. [C13 (in the sense: rash, harsh): from Old French *estordi* dazed, from *estordir* to stun, perhaps ultimately related to Latin *turdus* a thrush (taken as representing drunkenness)] —'**sturdily** *adv.* —'**sturdiness** *n.*

sturdy[2] ('stɜːdɪ) *n. Vet. science.* another name for **staggers** (sense 2). [C17: from STURDY[1] (in the obsolete sense: giddy)] —'**sturdied** *adj.*

sturgeon ('stɜːdʒən) *n.* any primitive bony fish of the family *Acipenseridae,* of temperate waters of the N hemisphere, having an elongated snout and rows of spines along the body: valued as a source of caviar and isinglass. [C13: from Old French *estourgeon,* of Germanic origin; related to Old English *styria,* Old High German *sturio*]

Sturmer ('stɜːmə) *n.* a variety of eating apple having a pale green skin and crisp sweet flesh. [C19: named after *Sturmer,* Suffolk]

stushie ('stʊʃɪ), **stishie,** *or* **stashie** *n. Scot.* **1.** a commotion, rumpus, or row. **2.** a state of excitement or anxiety; a tizzy. ~Also called: **stooshie, stoushie.** [C19: perhaps shortened from *ecstasy*]

stutter ('stʌtə) *vb.* **1.** to speak (a word, phrase, etc.) with recurring repetition of consonants, esp. initial ones. **2.** to make (an abrupt sound) repeatedly: *the gun stuttered.* ~*n.* **3.** the act or habit of stuttering. **4.** a stuttering sound. [C16: related to Middle Low German *stötern,* Old High German *stōzan* to push against, Latin *tundere* to beat] —'**stutterer** *n.* —'**stuttering** *n., adj.* —'**stutteringly** *adv.*

STV *abbrev. for* **1.** Scottish Television. **2.** single transferable vote.

sty[1] (staɪ) *n., pl.* **sties.** **1.** a pen in which pigs are housed and fed. **2.** any filthy or corrupt place. ~*vb.* **sties, stying, stied.** **3.** to enclose or be enclosed in a sty. [Old English *stig;* related to Old Norse *stīa* pen, fold, Old High German *stīga,* Middle Dutch *stije*]

sty[2] *or* **stye** (staɪ) *n., pl.* **sties** *or* **styes.** inflammation of a sebaceous gland of the eyelid, usually caused by bacteria. [C15 *styanye* (mistakenly taken as *sty on eye*), from Old English *stīgend* rising, hence swelling, sty + *ye* eye]

Stygian ('stɪdʒɪən) *adj. Chiefly literary.* **a.** dark, gloomy, or hellish. **b.** completely inviolable, as a vow sworn by the river Styx. [C16: from Latin *Stygius,* from Greek *Stugios,* from *Stux* Styx (a river in Hades); related to *stugein* to hate]

style (staɪl) *n.* **1.** a form of appearance, design, or production; type or make: *a new style of house.* **2.** the way in which something is done: *good or bad style.* **3.** the manner in which something is expressed or performed, considered as separate from its intrinsic content, meaning, etc. **4.** a distinctive, formal, or characteristic manner of expression in words, music, painting, etc. **5.** elegance or refinement of manners, dress, etc. **6.** prevailing fashion in dress, looks, etc. **7.** a fashionable or ostentatious mode of existence: *to live in style.* **8.** the particular mode of orthography, punctuation, design, etc., followed in a book, journal, etc., or in a printing or publishing house. **9.** *Chiefly Brit.* the distinguishing title or form of address of a person or firm. **10.** *Botany.* the long slender extension of the ovary, bearing the stigma. **11.** *Zoology.* a slender pointed structure, such as the piercing mouthparts of certain insects. **12.** a method of expressing or calculating dates. See **Old Style, New Style.** **13.** another word for **stylus** (sense 1). **14.** the arm of a sundial. ~*vb.* (*mainly tr.*) **15.** to design, shape, or tailor: *to style hair.* **16.** to adapt or make suitable (for). **17.** to make consistent or correct according to a printing or publishing style. **18.** to name or call; designate: *to style a man a fool.* **19.** (*intr.*) to decorate objects using a style or stylus. [C13: from Latin *stylus, stilus* writing implement, hence characteristics of the writing, style] —'**stylar** *adj.* —'**styler** *n.*

stylebook ('staɪlˌbʊk) *n.* a book containing rules and examples of punctuation, typography, etc., for the use of writers, editors, and printers.

stylet ('staɪlɪt) *n.* **1.** *Surgery.* **a.** a wire for insertion into a flexible cannula or catheter to maintain its rigidity or patency during passage. **b.** a slender probe. **2.** *Zoology.* any small pointed bristle-like part. [C17: from French *stilet,* from Old Italian STILETTO; influenced in spelling by Latin *stylus* STYLE]

styliform ('staɪlɪˌfɔːm) *adj. Zoology.* shaped like a stylus or bristle: *a styliform antenna.* [C16: from New Latin *stiliformis,* from Latin STYLUS]

styling mousse *n. Hairdressing.* a light foamy substance applied to the hair before styling in order to retain the shape of the style.

stylish ('staɪlɪʃ) *adj.* having style; smart; fashionable. —'**stylishly** *adv.* —'**stylishness** *n.*

stylist ('staɪlɪst) *n.* **1.** a person who performs, writes, or acts with attention to style. **2.** a designer of clothes, décor, etc. **3.** a hairdresser who styles hair. **4.** a designer whose job is to coordinate the style of products, advertising material, etc.

stylistic (staɪ'lɪstɪk) *adj.* of or relating to style, esp. artistic or literary style. —**sty'listically** *adv.*

stylistics (staɪ'lɪstɪks) *n.* (*functioning as sing. or pl.*) a branch of linguistics concerned with the study of characteristic choices in use of language, esp. literary language, as regards sound, form, or vocabulary, made by different individuals or social groups in different situations of use.

stylite ('staɪlaɪt) *n. Christianity.* one of a class of recluses who in ancient times lived on the top of high pillars. [C17: from Late Greek *stulitēs,* from Greek *stulos* a pillar] —**stylitic** (staɪ'lɪtɪk) *adj.*

stylize *or* **stylise** ('staɪlaɪz) *vb.* (*tr.*) to give a conventional or established stylistic form to. —ˌ**styli'zation** *or* ˌ**styli'sation** *n.* —'**stylizer** *or* '**styliser** *n.*

stylo- *or before a vowel* **styl-** *combining form.* **1.** (in biology) a style: *stylopodium.* **2.** indicating a column or point: *stylobate; stylograph.* [from Greek *stulos* column]

stylobate ('staɪləˌbeɪt) *n.* a continuous horizontal course of masonry that supports a colonnade. [C17: from Latin *stylobatēs,* from Greek *stulos* pillar + *-batēs,* from *bainein* to tread, walk]

stylograph ('staɪləˌgræf, -ˌgrɑːf) *n.* a fountain pen having a fine hollow tube as the writing point instead of a nib. [C19: from STYL(US) + -GRAPH]

stylographic (ˌstaɪlə'græfɪk) *or* **stylographical** *adj.* of or relating to a stylograph or stylography. —ˌ**stylo'graphically** *adv.*

stylography (staɪ'lɒgrəfɪ) *n.* the art or method of writing, drawing, or engraving with a stylus or style.

styloid ('staɪlɔɪd) *adj.* **1.** resembling a stylus. **2.** *Anatomy.* of or relating to a projecting process of the temporal bone. [C18: from New Latin *styloides,* from Greek *stuloeidēs* like a STYLUS; influenced also by Greek *stulos* pillar]

stylolite ('staɪləˌlaɪt) *n.* any of the small striated columnar structures within the strata of some limestones. [C19: from Greek *stulos* pillar + -LITE] —**stylolitic** (ˌstaɪlə'lɪtɪk) *adj.*

stylophone ('staɪləˌfəʊn) *n.* a type of battery-powered electronic instrument played with a steel-tipped penlike stylus. [C20: from STYL(US) + -PHONE]

stylopize *or* **stylopise** ('staɪlə,paɪz) *vb.* (*tr.*) (of a stylops) to parasitize (a host): *the bee was stylopized.*

stylopodium (,staɪlə'pəʊdɪəm) *n., pl.* **-dia** (-dɪə). *Botany.* a swelling at the base of the style in umbelliferous plants. [C19: New Latin, from Greek *stulos* pillar + -PODIUM]

stylops ('staɪlɒps) *n., pl.* **-lopes** (-lə,pi:z). any insect of the order *Strepsiptera,* including the genus *Stylops,* living as a parasite in other insects, esp. bees and wasps: the females remain in the body of the host but the males move between hosts. [C19: New Latin, from Greek, from *stulos* a pillar + *ōps* an eye, from the fact that the male insect has stalked compound eyes]

stylostixis (,staɪləʊ'stɪksɪs) *n. Med.* another name for **acupuncture.** [C20: New Latin, from Greek *stulos* style (pointed instrument) + *stixis* mark, spot]

stylus ('staɪləs) *n., pl.* **-li** (-laɪ) *or* **-luses. 1.** Also called: **style.** a pointed instrument for engraving, drawing, or writing. **2.** a tool used in ancient times for writing on wax tablets, which was pointed at one end and blunt at the other for erasing mistakes. **3.** a device attached to the cartridge in the pick-up arm of a record player that rests in the groove in the record, transmitting the vibrations to the sensing device in the cartridge. It consists of or is tipped with a hard material, such as diamond or sapphire. [C18: from Latin, variant of *stilus* writing implement; see STYLE] —'**stylar** *adj.*

stymie *or* **stymy** ('staɪmɪ) *vb.* **-mies, -mieing, -mied** *or* **-mies, -mying, -mied.** (*tr.; often passive*) **1.** to hinder or thwart. **2.** *Golf.* to impede with a stymie. ~*n., pl.* **-mies. 3.** *Golf.* (formerly) a situation on the green in which an opponent's ball is blocking the line between the hole and the ball about to be played: an obstructing ball may now be lifted and replaced by a marker. **4.** a situation of obstruction. [C19: of uncertain origin]

stypsis ('stɪpsɪs) *n.* the action, application, or use of a styptic. [C19: via New Latin from Late Latin: astringency, from Greek *stupsis,* from *stuphein* to contract]

styptic ('stɪptɪk) *adj.* **1.** contracting the blood vessels or tissues. ~*n.* **2.** a styptic drug. [C14: via Late Latin, from Greek *stuptikos* capable of contracting; see STYPSIS] —**stypticity** (stɪp'tɪsɪtɪ) *n.*

styptic pencil *n.* a styptic agent in the form of a small stick, for application to razor nicks, etc.

styracaceous (,staɪrə'keɪʃəs) *adj.* of, relating to, or belonging to the *Styracaceae,* a family of Asian and American trees and shrubs having leathery leaves: includes storax and silver bell. [C19: *styrac-,* from STYRAX]

styrax ('staɪræks) *n.* any tropical or subtropical tree of the genus *Styrax,* which includes the storaxes. [C16: via Latin from Greek *sturax*]

styrene ('staɪri:n) *n.* a colourless oily volatile flammable water-insoluble liquid made from ethylene and benzene. It is an unsaturated compound and readily polymerizes: used in making synthetic plastics and rubbers. Formula: $C_6H_5CH{:}CH_2$. See also **polystyrene.** [C20: from STYR(AX) + -ENE]

SU *abbrev. for* strontium unit.

suable ('sju:əbᵊl) *adj.* liable to be sued in a court. [C17: from SUE + -ABLE] —,**sua'bility** *n.*

suasion ('sweɪʒən) *n.* a rare word for **persuasion.** [C14: from Latin *suāsiō,* from *suādēre* to PERSUADE] —'**suasive** *adj.*

suave (swɑ:v) *adj.* (esp. of a man) displaying smoothness and sophistication in manner or attitude; urbane. [C16: from Latin *suāvis* sweet] —'**suavely** *adv.* —**suavity** ('swɑ:vɪtɪ) *or* '**suaveness** *n.*

sub (sʌb) *n.* **1.** short for several words beginning with *sub-,* such as **subaltern, subeditor, submarine, subordinate, subscription, substandard, substitute,** and **substratum** (in photography). **2.** *Brit. informal.* an advance payment of wages or salary. Formal term: **subsistence allowance.** ~*vb.* **subs, subbing, subbed. 3.** (*intr.*) to serve as a substitute. **4.** (*intr.*) *Informal.* to act as a substitute (for). **5.** *Brit. informal.* to grant or receive (an advance payment of wages or salary). **6.** (*tr.*) *Informal.* short for **subedit. 7.** (*tr.*) *Photog.* to apply a substratum to (a film or plate base).

sub. *abbrev. for:* **1.** subeditor. **2.** subito (in music). **3.** subscription. **4.** substitute. **5.** suburb(an). **6.** subway.

sub- *prefix.* **1.** situated under or beneath: *subterranean.* **2.** secondary in rank; subordinate: *subeditor.* **3.** falling short of; less than or imperfectly: *subarctic; subhuman.* **4.** forming a subdivision or subordinate part of a whole: *subcommittee.* **5.** (in chemistry) **a.** indicating that a compound contains a relatively small proportion of a specified element: *suboxide.* **b.** indicating that a salt is basic salt: *subacetate.* [from Latin *sub*]

subacetate (sʌb'æsɪ,teɪt) *n.* any one of certain crystalline basic acetates containing hydroxide ions in addition to acetate ions. For example, the subacetate of aluminium is probably $Al_3(OH)_2(CH_3COO)$.

subacid (sʌb'æsɪd) *adj.* (esp. of some fruits) moderately acid or sour. —**subacidity** (,sʌbə'sɪdɪtɪ) *or* **sub'acidness** *n.* —**sub'acidly** *adv.*

subacute (,sʌbə'kju:t) *adj.* intermediate between acute and chronic.

subadar *or* **subahdar** ('su:bə,dɑ:) *n.* (formerly) the chief native officer of a company of Indian soldiers in the British service. Also called: **subah.** [C17: via Urdu from Persian, from *sūba* province + *-dār* holding]

subah ('su:bɑ:) *n.* (in India) **1.** a province in the Mogul empire. **2.** another word for **subadar.** [C18: via Urdu and Persian from Arabic *sūba* province]

subalpine (sʌb'ælpaɪn) *adj.* **1.** situated in or relating to the regions at the foot of mountains. **2.** (of plants) growing below the treeline in mountainous regions.

subaltern ('sʌbᵊltən) *n.* **1.** a commissioned officer below the rank of captain in certain armies, esp. the British. **2.** a person of inferior rank or position. **3.** *Logic.* **a.** the relation of one proposition to another when the first is implied by the second, esp. the relation of a particular to a universal proposition. **b.** (*as modifier*): *a subaltern relation.* ~*adj.* **4.** of inferior position or rank. [C16: from Late Latin *subalternus,* from Latin SUB- + *alternus* alternate, from *alter* the other]

subalternate (sʌb'ɔ:ltənɪt) *adj.* **1.** (of leaves) having an arrangement intermediate between alternate and opposite. **2.** following in turn. **3.** of lesser quality or status. —**subalternation** (sʌb,ɔ:ltə'neɪʃən) *n.*

subantarctic (,sʌbænt'ɑ:ktɪk) *adj.* of or relating to latitudes immediately north of the Antarctic Circle.

subapostolic (,sʌbæpə'stɒlɪk) *adj. Christianity.* of or relating to the era after that of the Apostles.

subaqua (,sʌb'ækwə) *adj.* of or relating to underwater sport: *subaqua swimming; a subaqua club.* [from SUB- + Latin *aqua* water]

subaquatic (,sʌbə'kwætɪk, -'kwɒt-) *adj.* **1.** living or growing partly in water and partly on land. **2.** of or relating to conditions, existence, or activities under water.

subaqueous (sʌb'eɪkwɪəs, -'ækwɪ-) *adj.* occurring, appearing, formed, or used under water.

subarctic (sʌb'ɑ:ktɪk) *adj.* of or relating to latitudes immediately south of the Arctic Circle.

subarid (sʌb'ærɪd) *adj.* receiving slightly more rainfall than arid regions; moderately dry.

subassembly (,sʌbə'sɛmblɪ) *n., pl.* **-blies.** a number of machine components integrated into a unit forming part of a larger assembly.

subastral (sʌb'æstrəl) *adj.* a rare word for **terrestrial.**

subatomic (,sʌbə'tɒmɪk) *adj.* **1.** of, relating to or being a particle making up an atom or a process occurring within atoms: *the electron is a subatomic particle.* **2.** having dimensions smaller than atomic dimensions.

subaudition (,sʌbɔ:'dɪʃən) *n.* **1.** something that is not directly stated but implied. **2.** the ability or act of understanding that which is only implied. [C18: from Late Latin *subaudīre,* from SUB- + Latin *audīre* to hear]

subauricular (,sʌbɔ:'rɪkjulə) *adj. Anatomy.* situated below the auricle of the ear.

subaxillary (,sʌb'æksɪlərɪ) *adj.* **1.** situated or growing beneath the axil of a plant: *subaxillary bracts.* **2.** situated beneath the armpit.

subbase ('sʌb,beɪs) *n.* the lowest part of a pedestal, base, or skirting. Compare **surbase.**

subbasement ('sʌb,beɪsmənt) *n.* an underground storey of a building beneath the main basement.

subbass *or* **subbase** ('sʌb,beɪs) *n.* another name for **bourdon.**

subcalibre *or U.S.* **subcaliber** (sʌb'kælɪbə) *adj.* **1.** (of a projectile) having a calibre less than that of the firearm from which it is discharged and therefore either fitted with a disc or fired through a tube inserted into the barrel. **2.** of, relating to, or firing subcalibre projectiles.

subcarrier ('sʌb,kærɪə) *n.* a subsidiary carrier wave that is modulated with information and applied as modulation to a main carrier wave that is already modulated with other information.

subcartilaginous (sʌb,kɑ:tɪ'lædʒɪnəs) *adj.* **1.** composed partly of cartilage: *a subcartilaginous skeleton.* **2.** situated beneath a cartilage or a cartilaginous structure.

subcelestial (,sʌbsɪ'lɛstɪəl) *adj.* **1.** beneath the heavens; terrestrial. ~*n.* **2.** a subcelestial object.

subception (səb'sɛpʃən) *n. Psychol.* another word for **subliminal perception.**

subchloride (sʌb'klɔ:raɪd) *n.* a chloride of an element that contains less chlorine than its common chloride.

subclass ('sʌb,klɑ:s) *n.* **1.** a principal subdivision of a class. **2.** *Biology.* a taxonomic group that is a subdivision of a class. **3.**

sub'abbot *n.*
,subab'dominal *adj.*
,subad'ministrative *adj.*
,subad'minis,trator *n.*
sub'agent *n.*
,subal'liance *n.*
'sub,area *n.*
'sub,article *n.*
,subas,soci'ation *n.*
,subat'torney *n.*
sub'average *adj.*
'sub,branch *n.*
'sub,breed *n.*
'sub,bureau *n., pl.* **-reaus** *or* **-reaux.**
sub'category *n., pl.* **-ries.**
'sub,cell *n.*
'sub,cellar *n.*
'sub,chapter *n.*
'sub,chief *n.*
'sub,clan *n.*

Maths. another name for **subset** (sense 1). ~*vb.* **4.** (*tr.*) to assign to a subclass.

subclavian (sʌbˈkleɪvɪən) *adj. Anatomy.* (of an artery, vein, area, etc.) situated below the clavicle. [C17: from New Latin *subclāvius,* from Latin SUB- + *clavis* key]

subclimax (sʌbˈklaɪmæks) *n. Ecology.* a community in which development has been arrested before climax has been attained. —**subclimactic** (ˌsʌbklaɪˈmæktɪk) *adj.*

subclinical (sʌbˈklɪnɪkᵊl) *adj. Med.* of or relating to the stage in the course of a disease before the symptoms are first noted. —**subˈclinically** *adv.*

subconscious (sʌbˈkɒnʃəs) *adj.* **1.** acting or existing without one's awareness: *subconscious motive.* ~*n.* **2.** *Psychoanal.* that part of the mind which is on the fringe of consciousness and contains material of which it is possible to become aware by redirecting attention. Compare **preconscious** (sense 2), **unconscious** (sense 5). —**subˈconsciously** *adv.* —**subˈconsciousness** *n.*

subcontinent (sʌbˈkɒntɪnənt) *n.* a large land mass that is a distinct part of a continent, such as India is of Asia. —**subcontinental** (ˌsʌbkɒntɪˈnɛntᵊl) *adj.*

subcontract *n.* (sʌbˈkɒntrækt). **1.** a subordinate contract under which the supply of materials, services, or labour is let out to someone other than a party to the main contract. ~*vb.* (ˌsʌbkənˈtrækt). **2.** (*intr.*; often foll. by *for*) to enter into or make a subcontract. **3.** (*tr.*) to let out (work) on a subcontract.

subcontractor (ˌsʌbkənˈtræktə) *n.* a person, company, etc., that enters into a subcontract, esp. a firm that undertakes to complete part of another's contract.

subcontrary (sʌbˈkɒntrərɪ) *Logic.* ~*adj.* **1.** (of a pair of propositions) related such that they cannot both be false at once, although they may be true together. Compare **contrary** (sense 5), **contradictory** (sense 3). ~*n., pl.* **-ries. 2.** a statement that cannot be false when a given statement is false.

subcortex (sʌbˈkɔːtɛks) *n., pl.* **-tices** (-tɪˌsiːz). *Anatomy.* the matter of the brain situated beneath the cerebral cortex. —**subcortical** (sʌbˈkɔːtɪkᵊl) *adj.*

subcritical (sʌbˈkrɪtɪkᵊl) *adj. Physics.* (of a nuclear reaction, power station, etc.) having or involving a chain reaction that is not self-sustaining; not yet critical.

subculture *n.* (ˈsʌbˌkʌltʃə). **1.** a subdivision of a national culture or an enclave within it with a distinct integrated network of behaviour, beliefs, and attitudes. **2.** a culture of microorganisms derived from another culture. ~*vb.* (sʌbˈkʌltʃə). **3.** (*tr.*) to inoculate (bacteria from one culture medium) onto another medium. —**subˈcultural** *adj.*

subcutaneous (ˌsʌbkjuːˈteɪnɪəs) *adj. Med.* situated, used, or introduced beneath the skin: *a subcutaneous injection.* [C17: from Late Latin *subcutāneus,* from SUB- + Latin *cutis* skin + -EOUS] —ˌ**subcuˈtaneously** *adv.*

subdeacon (ˌsʌbˈdiːkən) *n. Chiefly R.C. Church.* **1.** a cleric who assists at High Mass. **2.** (formerly) a person ordained to the lowest of the major orders. —**subdeaconate** (sʌbˈdiːkənɪt) *n.*

subdelirium (ˌsʌbdəˈlɪrɪəm) *n., pl.* **-liriums** *or* **-liria** (-ˈlɪrɪə). mild or intermittent delirium.

subdiaconate (ˌsʌbdaɪˈækənɪt, -ˌneɪt) *n.* the rank or office of a subdeacon. [C18: from Medieval Latin *subdiaconus* subdeacon + -ATE[2]; see DEACON] —ˌ**subdiˈaconal** *adj.*

subdivide (ˌsʌbdɪˈvaɪd, ˈsʌbdɪˌvaɪd) *vb.* **1.** to divide (something) resulting from an earlier division. **2.** (*tr.*) *U.S. and Canadian.* to divide (land) into lots for sale. —ˌ**subdiˈvider** *n.*

subdivision (ˈsʌbdɪˌvɪʒən) *n.* **1.** the process, instance, or state of being divided again following upon an earlier division. **2.** a portion that is the result of subdividing. **3.** *U.S. and Canadian.* a tract of land for building resulting from subdividing land. **4.** *Canadian.* a housing development built on such a tract. —ˌ**subdiˈvisional** *adj.*

subdominant (sʌbˈdɒmɪnənt) *Music.* ~*n.* **1.** the fourth degree of a major or minor scale. **2.** a key or chord based on this. ~*adj.* **3.** of or relating to the subdominant.

subduct (səbˈdʌkt) *vb.* (*tr.*) **1.** *Physiol.* to draw or turn (the eye, etc.) downwards. **2.** *Rare.* to take away; deduct. [C17: from Latin *subdūcere,* from SUB- + *dūcere* to lead, bring]

subduction (səbˈdʌkʃən) *n.* **1.** the act of subducting, esp. of turning the eye downwards. **2.** *Geology.* the process of one tectonic plate sliding under another, resulting in tensions in the earth's crust, with earthquakes and volcanic eruptions.

subduction zone *n. Geology.* another name for **Benioff zone.**

subdue (səbˈdjuː) *vb.* **-dues, -duing, -dued.** (*tr.*) **1.** to establish ascendancy over by force. **2.** to overcome and bring under control, as by intimidation or persuasion. **3.** to hold in check or repress (feelings, emotions, etc.). **4.** to render less intense or less conspicuous. [C14 *sobdue,* from Old French *soduire* to mislead, from Latin *subdūcere* to remove; English sense influenced by Latin *subdere* to subject] —**subˈduable** *adj.* —**subˈduably** *adv.* —**subˈdual** *n.*

subdued (səbˈdjuːd) *adj.* **1.** cowed, passive, or shy. **2.** gentle or quiet: *a subdued whisper.* **3.** (of colours, etc.) not harsh or bright: *subdued lighting.* —**subˈduedly** *adv.* —**subˈduedness** *n.*

subdural (sʌbˈdjʊərəl) *adj. Anatomy.* between the dura mater and the arachnoid: *subdural haematoma.*

subedit (sʌbˈɛdɪt) *vb.* to edit and correct (written or printed material).

subeditor (sʌbˈɛdɪtə) *n.* a person who checks and edits copy, esp. on a newspaper.

subequatorial (sʌbˌɛkwəˈtɔːrɪəl) *adj.* situated in or characteristic of regions immediately north or south of equatorial regions.

suberic acid (sjuːˈbɛrɪk) *n.* another name for **octanedioic acid.** [C18: from French *subérique,* from Latin *sūber* cork (from which the acid is obtained)]

suberin (ˈsjuːbərɪn) *n.* a fatty or waxy substance that is present in the walls of cork cells, making them impermeable to water and resistant to decay. [C19: from Latin *sūber* cork + -IN]

suberize *or* **suberise** (ˈsjuːbəˌraɪz) *vb.* (*tr.*) *Botany.* to impregnate (cell walls) with suberin during the formation of corky tissue. —ˌ**suberiˈzation** *or* ˌ**suberiˈsation** *n.*

suberose (ˈsjuːbəˌrəʊs), **subereous** (sjuːˈbɛrɪəs), *or* **suberic** (sjuːˈbɛrɪk) *adj. Botany.* relating to, resembling, or consisting of cork; corky.

subfamily (ˈsʌbˌfæmɪlɪ) *n., pl.* **-lies. 1.** *Biology.* a taxonomic group that is a subdivision of a family. **2.** any analogous subdivision, as of a family of languages.

subfloor (ˈsʌbˌflɔː) *n.* a rough floor that forms a base for a finished floor.

subfusc (ˈsʌbfʌsk) *adj.* **1.** devoid of brightness or appeal; drab, dull, or dark. ~*n.* **2.** (at Oxford University) formal academic dress. [C18: from Latin *subfuscus* dusky, from *fuscus* dark]

subgenus (sʌbˈdʒiːnəs, -ˈdʒɛn-; ˈsʌbˌdʒiːnəs, -ˌdʒɛn-) *n., pl.* **-genera** (-ˈdʒɛnərə) *or* **-genuses.** *Biology.* a taxonomic group that is a subdivision of a genus but of higher rank than a species. —**subgeneric** (ˌsʌbdʒəˈnɛrɪk) *adj.*

subglacial (sʌbˈgleɪsɪəl) *adj.* formed or occurring at the bottom of a glacier. —**subˈglacially** *adv.*

subgrade (ˈsʌbˌgreɪd) *n.* the ground beneath a roadway or pavement.

subgroup (ˈsʌbˌgruːp) *n.* **1.** a distinct and often subordinate division of a group. **2.** a mathematical group whose members are members of another group, both groups being subject to the same rule of combination.

subharmonic (ˌsʌbhɑːˈmɒnɪk) *n.* an integral submultiple of a frequency.

subheading (ˈsʌbˌhɛdɪŋ) *or* **subhead** *n.* **1.** the heading or title of a subdivision or subsection of a printed work. **2.** a division subordinate to a main heading or title.

subhuman (sʌbˈhjuːmən) *adj.* **1.** of, relating to, or designating animals that are below man (*Homo sapiens*) in evolutionary development. **2.** less than human.

subimago (ˌsʌbɪˈmeɪgəʊ) *n., pl.* **-imagoes** *or* **-imagines** (-ɪˈmædʒəˌniːz). the first winged stage of the mayfly, with dull opaque wings, known to anglers as a **dun,** before it metamorphoses into the shiny gauzy imago or **spinner.**

subindex (sʌbˈɪndɛks) *n., pl.* **-dices** (-dɪˌsiːz) *or* **-dexes. 1.** another word for **subscript** (sense 2). **2.** *U.S.* an index to a subcategory.

subinfeudate (ˌsʌbɪnˈfjuːdeɪt) *vb.* to grant (lands) by subinfeudation.

subinfeudation (ˌsʌbɪnfjʊˈdeɪʃən) *n.* **1.** (in feudal society) the granting of land by a vassal to another man who became his vassal. **2.** the tenure or relationship so established.

subinfeudatory (ˌsʌbɪnˈfjuːdətərɪ, -trɪ) (in feudal society) ~*n., pl.* **-ries. 1.** a man who held his fief by a subinfeudation. ~*adj.* **2.** of or relating to subinfeudation.

subirrigate (sʌbˈɪrɪˌgeɪt) *vb.* to irrigate (land) by means of an underground system of pipe lines or by natural moisture in the subsoil. —ˌ**subirriˈgation** *n.*

subitize *or* **subitise** (ˈsʌbɪˌtaɪz) *vb. Psychol.* to perceive the number of (a group of items) at a glance and without counting: *the maximum number of items that can be subitized is about five.* [C20: from Latin *subitus* sudden + -IZE]

subito (ˈsuːbɪˌtəʊ) *adv. Music.* (preceding or following a dynamic marking, etc.) suddenly; immediately. Abbrev.: **sub.** [C18: via

ˌ**subˌclassifiˈcation** *n.*
subˈclassiˌfy *vb.*, -ˌ**fies,** -ˌ**fying,** -ˌ**fied.**
ˈ**subˌclause** *n.*
ˈ**subˌclerk** *n.*
subˈclimate *n.*
ˌ**subcomˈmander** *n.*
ˈ**subcomˌmission** *n.*
ˌ**subcomˈmissioner** *n.*
ˈ**subcomˌmittee** *n.*
ˌ**subconstelˈlation** *n.*
subˈcouncil *n.*
subˈcranial *adj.*
ˌ**subcuˈrator** *n.*
ˌ**subdefiˈnition** *n.*
ˌ**subdeˈpartment** *n.*
ˌ**subdepartˈmental** *adj.*
ˈ**subˌdepot** *n.*
subˈdiaˌlect *n.*
ˌ**subdiˈrector** *n.*
ˌ**subdisˈtinction** *n.*
ˈ**subˌdistrict** *n.*
subˈdorsal *adj.*
subˈecho *n., pl.* **-oes.**
subˈelement *n.*
ˌ**subeleˈmental** *adj.*
subˈentry *n., pl.* **-tries.**
subˈepoch *n.*
subˈfertile *adj.*
ˌ**subferˈtility** *n.*
ˈ**subˌfile** *n.*
subˈforeman *n., pl.* **-men.**
subˈfraction *n.*
subˈfractional *adj.*
subˈfreezing *adj.*
ˈ**subˌfunction** *n.*
subˈgenital *adj.*
subˈglottal *adj.*
ˈ**subˌitem** *n.*

Italian from Latin: suddenly, from *subitus* sudden, from *subīre* to approach, from SUB- (indicating stealth) + *īre* to go]
subj. *abbrev. for:* **1.** subject. **2.** subjective(ly). **3.** subjunctive.
subjacent (sʌb'dʒeɪsᵊnt) *adj.* **1.** forming a foundation; underlying. **2.** lower than though not directly below: *tall peaks and their subjacent valley.* [C16: from Latin *subjacēre* to lie close, adjoin, be under, from SUB- + *jacēre* to lie] —**sub'jacency** *n.* —**sub'jacently** *adv.*
subject *n.* ('sʌbdʒɪkt). **1. a.** the predominant theme or topic, as of a book, discussion, etc. **b.** (*in combination*): *subject-heading.* **2.** any branch of learning considered as a course of study. **3.** *Grammar, logic.* a word, phrase, or formal expression about which something is predicated or stated in a sentence; for example, *the cat* in the sentence *The cat catches mice.* **4.** a person or thing that undergoes experiment, analysis, treatment, etc. **5.** a person who lives under the rule of a monarch, government, etc. **6.** an object, figure, scene, etc., as selected by an artist or photographer for representation. **7.** *Philosophy.* **a.** that which thinks or feels as opposed to the object of thinking and feeling; the self or the mind. **b.** a substance as opposed to its attributes. **8.** Also called: **theme.** *Music.* a melodic or thematic phrase used as the principal motif of a fugue, the basis from which the musical material is derived in a sonata-form movement, or the recurrent figure in a rondo. **9.** *Logic.* **a.** the term of a categorial statement of which something is predicated. **b.** the reference or denotation of the subject term of a statement. The subject of *John is tall* is not the name *John,* but John himself. **10.** an originating motive. **11. change the subject.** to select a new topic of conversation. ~*adj.* ('sʌbdʒɪkt). (*usually postpositive* and foll. by *to*) **12.** being under the power or sovereignty of a ruler, government, etc.: *subject peoples.* **13.** showing a tendency (towards): *a child subject to indiscipline.* **14.** exposed or vulnerable: *subject to ribaldry.* **15.** conditional upon: *the results are subject to correction.* ~*adv.* **16. subject to.** (*prep.*) under the condition that: *we accept, subject to her agreement.* ~*vb.* (səb'dʒɛkt). (*tr.*) **17.** (foll. by *to*) to cause to undergo the application (of): *they subjected him to torture.* **18.** (*often passive;* foll. by *to*) to expose or render vulnerable or liable (to some experience): *he was subjected to great danger.* **19.** (foll. by *to*) to bring under the control or authority (of): *to subject a soldier to discipline.* **20.** *Now rare.* to subdue or subjugate. **21.** *Rare.* to present for consideration; submit. **22.** *Obsolete.* to place below. ~Abbrev.: **subj.** [C14: from Latin *subjectus* brought under, from *subicere* to place under, from SUB- + *jacere* to throw] —**sub'jectable** *adj.* —**sub,jecta'bility** *n.* —**'subjectless** *adj.* —**'subject-,like** *adj.*
subject catalogue *n. Library science.* a catalogue with entries arranged by subject in a classified sequence.
subjectify (səb'dʒɛktɪ,faɪ) *vb.* **-fies, -fying, -fied.** (*tr.*) to make subjective or interpret subjectively. —**sub,jectifi'cation** *n.*
subjection (səb'dʒɛkʃən) *n.* the act or process of subjecting or the state of being subjected.
subjective (səb'dʒɛktɪv) *adj.* **1.** belonging to, proceeding from, or relating to the mind of the thinking subject and not the nature of the object being considered. **2.** of, relating to, or emanating from a person's emotions, prejudices, etc.: *subjective views.* **3.** relating to the inherent nature of a person or thing; essential. **4.** existing only as perceived and not as a thing in itself. **5.** *Med.* (of a symptom, condition, etc.) experienced only by the patient and incapable of being recognized or studied by anyone else. **6.** *Grammar.* denoting a case of nouns and pronouns, esp. in languages having only two cases, that identifies the subject of a finite verb and (in formal use in English) is selected for predicate complements, as in *It is I.* See also **nominative** (sense 1). ~*n.* **7.** *Grammar.* **a.** the subjective case. **b.** a subjective word or speech element. ~Abbrev.: **subj.** Compare **objective.** —**sub'jectively** *adv.* —**,subjec'tivity** *or* **sub'jectiveness** *n.*
subjective idealism *n. Philosophy.* the theory that all experience is of ideas in the mind.
subjective intension *n. Logic.* the associations that an expression has for an individual; the intension he believes it to have.
subjectivism (səb'dʒɛktɪ,vɪzəm) *n.* **1.** the meta-ethical doctrine that there are no absolute moral values but that these are variable in the same way as taste is. **2.** any similar philosophical theory, for example, about truth or perception. **3.** any theological theory that attaches primary importance to religious experience. **4.** the quality or condition of being subjective. —**sub'jectivist** *n.* —**sub,jecti'vistic** *adj.* —**sub,jecti'vistically** *adv.*
subject matter *n.* the substance or main theme of a book, discussion, debate, etc.
subject-raising *n. Transformational grammar.* a rule that moves the subject of a complement clause into the clause in which it is embedded, as in the derivation of *He is likely to be late* from *It is likely that he will be late.*
subjoin (sʌb'dʒɔɪn) *vb.* (*tr.*) to add or attach at the end of something spoken, written, etc. [C16: from French *subjoindre,* from Latin *subjungere* to add to, from *sub-* in addition + *jungere* to JOIN] —**sub'joinder** *n.* —**subjunction** (sʌb'dʒʌŋkʃən) *n.*
sub judice ('dʒuːdɪsɪ) *adj.* (*usually postpositive*) before a court of law or a judge; under judicial consideration. [Latin]
subjugate ('sʌbdʒʊ,geɪt) *vb.* (*tr.*) **1.** to bring into subjection. **2.** to make subservient or submissive. [C15: from Late Latin *subjugāre* to subdue, from Latin SUB- + *jugum* yoke] —**subjugable** ('sʌbdʒəgəbᵊl) *adj.* —**,subju'gation** *n.* —**'subju,gator** *n.*
subjunctive (səb'dʒʌŋktɪv) *adj.* **1.** *Grammar.* denoting a mood of verbs used when the content of the clause is being doubted, supposed, feared true, etc., rather than being asserted. The rules for its use and the range of meanings it may possess vary considerably from language to language. In the following sentence, *were* is in the subjunctive: *I'd think very seriously about that if I were you.* Compare **indicative.** ~*n.* **2.** *Grammar.* **a.** the subjunctive mood. **b.** a verb in this mood. ~Abbrev.: **subj.** [C16: via Late Latin *subjunctīvus,* from Latin *subjungere* to SUBJOIN] —**sub'junctively** *adv.*
subkingdom (sʌb'kɪŋdəm) *n. Biology.* a taxonomic group that is a subdivision of a kingdom.
sublapsarianism (,sʌblæp'sɛərɪə,nɪzəm) *n.* another word for **infralapsarianism.** [C17 *sublapsarian,* via New Latin, from Latin SUB- + *lāpsus* a fall] —**,sublap'sarian** *n., adj.*
sublease *n.* ('sʌb,liːs). **1.** a lease of property made by a person who is himself a lessee or tenant of that property. ~*vb.* (sʌb'liːs). **2.** to grant a sublease of (property); sublet. **3.** (*tr.*) to take, obtain, or hold by sublease. —**sublessee** (,sʌblɛ'siː) *n.* —**sublessor** (,sʌblɛ'sɔː) *n.*
sublet *vb.* (sʌb'lɛt), **-lets, -letting, -let. 1.** to grant a sublease of (property). **2.** to let out (work, etc.) under a subcontract. ~*n.* ('sʌb,lɛt). **3.** *Informal, chiefly U.S.* a sublease.
sublieutenant (,sʌblə'tɛnənt) *n.* the most junior commissioned officer in the Royal Navy and certain other navies. —**,sublieu'tenancy** *n.*
sublimate ('sʌblɪ,meɪt) *vb.* **1.** *Psychol.* to direct the energy of (a primitive impulse, esp. a sexual one) into activities that are considered to be socially more acceptable. **2.** (*tr.*) to make purer; refine. ~*n.* **3.** *Chem.* the material obtained when a substance is sublimed. ~*adj.* **4.** exalted or purified. [C16: from Latin *sublīmāre* to elevate, from *sublīmis* lofty; see SUBLIME] —**sublimable** ('sʌbləməbᵊl) *adj.*
sublimation (,sʌblɪ'meɪʃən) *n.* **1.** (in Freudian psychology) the diversion of psychic energy derived from sexual impulses into nonsexual activity, esp. of a creative nature. **2.** the process or an instance of sublimating. **3.** something sublimated. **4.** *Chem.* the process or instance or subliming.
sublime (sə'blaɪm) *adj.* **1.** of high moral, aesthetic, intellectual, or spiritual value; noble; exalted. **2.** inspiring deep veneration, awe, or uplifting emotion because of its beauty, nobility, grandeur, or immensity. **3.** unparalleled; supreme: *a sublime compliment.* **4.** *Poetic.* of proud bearing or aspect. **5.** *Archaic.* raised up. ~*n.* **the sublime. 6.** something that is sublime. **7.** the ultimate degree or perfect example: *the sublime of folly.* ~*vb.* **8.** (*tr.*) to make higher or purer. **9.** to change or cause to change directly from a solid to a vapour or gas without first melting: *to sublime iodine; many mercury salts sublime when heated.* **10.** to undergo or cause to undergo this process followed by a reverse change directly from a vapour to a solid: *to sublime iodine onto glass.* [C14: from Latin *sublīmis* lofty, perhaps from *sub-* up to + *līmen* lintel] —**sub'limely** *adv.* —**sublimity** (sə'blɪmɪtɪ) *n.*
subliminal (sʌb'lɪmɪnᵊl) *adj.* **1.** resulting from processes of which the individual is not aware. **2.** (of stimuli) less than the minimum intensity or duration required to elicit a response. [C19: from Latin SUB- below + *līmen* threshold] —**sub'liminally** *adv.*
subliminal advertising *n.* a form of advertising on film or television that employs subliminal images to influence the viewer unconsciously.
subliminal perception *n. Psychol.* perception of or reaction to a stimulus that occurs without awareness or consciousness. Also called: **subception.**
sublingual (sʌb'lɪŋgwəl) *adj. Anatomy.* situated beneath the tongue.
sublittoral (sʌb'lɪtərəl) *adj.* **1.** (of marine organisms) growing, living, or situated close to the seashore: *a sublittoral plant.* **2.** of or relating to the zone between the seashore and the edge of the continental shelf.
sublunary (sʌb'luːnərɪ) *adj.* **1.** situated between the moon and the earth. **2.** of or relating to the earth or world. [C16: via Late Latin, from Latin SUB- + *lūna* moon]
subluxate (sʌb'lʌkseɪt) *vb.* (*tr.*) *Pathol.* to partially dislocate. —**,sublux'ation** *n.*
sub-machine-gun *n.* a portable automatic or semiautomatic light gun with a short barrel, firing pistol ammunition: designed to be fired from the hip or shoulder.
submarginal (sʌb'mɑːdʒɪnᵊl) *adj.* **1.** below the minimum requirements. **2.** situated close to the margin of an organ or part. **3.** (of land) infertile and unprofitable for cultivation. —**sub'marginally** *adv.*
submarine ('sʌbmə,riːn, ,sʌbmə'riːn) *n.* **1.** a vessel, esp. one designed for warfare, capable of operating for protracted periods below the surface of the sea. Often shortened to **sub. 2.** (*modifier*) **a.** of or relating to a submarine: *a submarine captain.* **b.**

sub'manager *n.*

occurring or situated below the surface of the sea: *a submarine cable.*
submariner (sʌbˈmærɪnə) *n.* a crewman in a submarine.
submaxillary (ˌsʌbmækˈsɪlərɪ) *adj.* of, relating to, or situated close to the lower jaw.
submaxillary gland *n.* (in mammals) either of a pair of salivary glands situated on each side behind the lower jaw.
submediant (sʌbˈmiːdɪənt) *Music.* ~*n.* **1.** the sixth degree of a major or minor scale. **2.** a key or chord based on this. ~*adj.* **3.** of or relating to the submediant. ~Also (U.S. and Canadian): **superdominant.**
submental (sʌbˈmentᵊl) *adj. Anatomy.* situated beneath the chin. [from SUB- + Latin *mentum* chin]
submerge (səbˈmɜːdʒ) *or* **submerse** (səbˈmɜːs) *vb.* **1.** to plunge, sink, or dive or cause to plunge, sink, or dive below the surface of water, etc. **2.** (*tr.*) to cover with water or some other liquid. **3.** (*tr.*) to hide; suppress. **4.** (*tr.*) to overwhelm, as with work, difficulties, etc. [C17: from Latin *submergere,* from SUB- + *mergere* to immerse] —**subˈmergence** *or* **submersion** (səbˈmɜːʃᵊn) *n.*
submerged (səbˈmɜːdʒd) *or* **submersed** (səbˈmɜːst) *adj.* **1.** (of plants or plant parts) growing beneath the surface of the water. **2.** hidden; obscured. **3.** overwhelmed or overburdened.
submerged arc welding *n.* a type of heavy electric-arc welding using mechanically fed bare wire with the arc submerged in powdered flux to keep out oxygen.
submersible (səbˈmɜːsəbᵊl) *or* **submergible** (səbˈmɜːdʒɪbᵊl) *adj.* **1.** able to be submerged. **2.** capable of operating under water, etc. ~*n.* **3.** a vessel designed to operate under water for short periods. **4.** a submarine taking one or more men that is designed and equipped to carry out work in deep water below the levels at which divers can work. —**subˌmersiˈbility** *or* **subˌmergiˈbility** *n.*
submicroscopic (ˌsʌbmaɪkrəˈskɒpɪk) *adj.* too small to be seen through an optical microscope. —ˌ**submicroˈscopically** *adv.*
subminiature (sʌbˈmɪnɪətʃə) *adj.* smaller than miniature.
subminiature camera *n.* a pocket-sized camera, usually using 16 millimetre film with a very fine grain so that negatives can produce considerably enlarged prints.
subminiaturize *or* **subminiaturise** (sʌbˈmɪnɪətʃəˌraɪz) *vb.* (*tr.*) to make subminiature, as in the manufacture of electronic equipment, etc. —**subˌminiaturiˈzation** *or* **subˌminiaturiˈsation** *n.*
submiss (səbˈmɪs) *adj. Archaic or poetic.* **1.** docile; submissive. **2.** soft in tone. [C16: from Latin *submissus* lowered, gentle, from *submittere* to reduce, from SUB- + *mittere* to send]
submission (səbˈmɪʃən) *n.* **1.** an act or instance of submitting. **2.** something submitted; a proposal, argument, etc. **3.** the quality or condition of being submissive to another. **4.** the act of referring a document, etc., for the consideration of someone else. **5.** *Law.* **a.** an agreement by the parties to a dispute to refer the matter to arbitration. **b.** the instrument referring a disputed matter to arbitration. **6.** (in wrestling) the act of causing such pain to one's opponent that he submits. Compare **fall** (sense 48). **7.** *Archaic.* a confession of error.
submissive (səbˈmɪsɪv) *adj.* of, tending towards, or indicating submission, humility, or servility. —**subˈmissively** *adv.* —**subˈmissiveness** *n.*
submit (səbˈmɪt) *vb.* **-mits, -mitting, -mitted.** **1.** (often foll. by *to*) to yield (oneself), as to the will of another person, a superior force, etc. **2.** (foll. by *to*) to subject or be voluntarily subjected (to analysis, treatment, etc.). **3.** (*tr.;* often foll. by *to*) to refer (something to someone) for judgment or consideration: *to submit a claim.* **4.** (*tr.; may take a clause as object*) to state, contend, or propose deferentially. **5.** (*intr.;* often foll. by *to*) to defer or accede (to the decision, opinion, etc., of another). [C14: from Latin *submittere* to place under, from SUB- + *mittere* to send] —**subˈmittable** *or* **subˈmissible** *adj.* —**subˈmittal** *n.* —**subˈmitter** *n.*
submontane (sʌbˈmɒnteɪn) *adj.* **1.** situated on or characteristic of the lower slopes of a mountain. **2.** beneath a mountain or mountain range. [C19: from Latin SUB- + *mōns* mountain] —**subˈmontanely** *adv.*
submucosa (ˌsʌbmjuːˈkəʊsə) *n., pl.* **-cosae** (-ˈkəʊsiː). *Anatomy.* the connective tissue beneath a mucous membrane.
submultiple (sʌbˈmʌltɪpᵊl) *n.* **1.** a number that can be divided into another number an integral number of times without a remainder: *three is a submultiple of nine.* ~*adj.* **2.** being a submultiple of a quantity or number.
subnormal (sʌbˈnɔːməl) *adj.* **1.** less than the normal. **2.** having a low intelligence, esp. having an IQ of less than 70. ~*n.* **3.** a subnormal person. —**subnormality** (ˌsʌbnɔːˈmælɪtɪ) *n.* —**subˈnormally** *adv.*
subnuclear (sʌbˈnjuːklɪə) *adj.* **1.** of or relating to particles within the nucleus of an atom. **2.** of a lesser level of organization than the nucleus of an atom.
suboceanic (sʌbˌəʊʃɪˈænɪk) *adj.* formed or situated beneath the ocean or ocean floor.
suborbital (sʌbˈɔːbɪtᵊl) *adj.* **1.** (of a rocket, missile, etc.) having a flight path that is less than one complete orbit of the earth or other celestial body. **2.** *Anatomy.* situated beneath the orbit of the eye.
suborder (ˈsʌbˌɔːdə) *n. Biology.* a taxonomic group that is a subdivision of an order. —**subˈordinal** *adj.*
subordinary (sʌbˈɔːdɪnərɪ, -dɪnrɪ) *n., pl.* **-naries.** any of several heraldic bearings of secondary importance to the ordinary, such as the lozenge, the orle, and the fret.
subordinate *adj.* (səˈbɔːdɪnɪt). **1.** of lesser order or importance. **2.** under the authority or control of another: *a subordinate functionary.* ~*n.* (səˈbɔːdɪnɪt). **3.** a person or thing that is subordinate. ~*vb.* (səˈbɔːdɪˌneɪt). (*tr.;* usually foll. by *to*) **4.** to put in a lower rank or position (than). **5.** to make subservient: *to subordinate mind to heart.* [C15: from Medieval Latin *subordināre,* from Latin SUB- + *ordō* rank] —**subˈordinately** *adv.* —**subˌordiˈnation** *or* **subˈordinateness** *n.* —**subˈordinative** *adj.*
subordinate clause *n. Grammar.* a clause with an adjectival, adverbial, or nominal function, rather than one that functions as a separate sentence in its own right. Compare **coordinate clause, main clause.**
subordinating conjunction *n.* a conjunction that introduces subordinate clauses, such as *if, because, although,* and *until.* Compare **coordinating conjunction.**
subordinationism (səˌbɔːdɪˈneɪʃəˌnɪzəm) *n.* either of two interpretations of the doctrine of the Trinity, often regarded as heretical, according to which the Son is subordinate to the Father or the Holy Ghost is subordinate to both. —**subˌordiˈnationist** *n.*
suborn (səˈbɔːn) *vb.* (*tr.*) **1.** to bribe, incite, or instigate (a person) to commit a wrongful act. **2.** *Criminal law.* to induce (a witness) to commit perjury. [C16: from Latin *subornāre,* from *sub-* secretly + *ornāre* to furnish] —**subornation** (ˌsʌbɔːˈneɪʃən) *n.* —**subornative** (sʌˈbɔːnətɪv) *adj.* —**subˈorner** *n.*
suboxide (sʌbˈɒksaɪd) *n.* an oxide of an element containing less oxygen than the common oxide formed by the element: *carbon suboxide,* C_3O_2.
subphylum (sʌbˈfaɪləm) *n., pl.* **-la** (-lə). *Biology.* a taxonomic group that is a subdivision of a phylum. —**subˈphylar** *adj.*
subplot (ˈsʌbˌplɒt) *n.* a subordinate or auxiliary plot in a novel, play, film, etc.
subpoena (səbˈpiːnə) *n.* **1.** a writ issued by a court of justice requiring a person to appear before the court at a specified time. ~*vb.* **-nas, -naing, -naed.** **2.** (*tr.*) to serve with a subpoena. [C15: from Latin: under penalty]
subpopulation (ˌsʌbpɒpjʊˈleɪʃən) *n. Statistics.* a subgroup of a statistical population.
sub-post office *n.* (in Britain) a post office run by a **sub-postmaster** or **sub-postmistress** as a self-employed agent for the Post Office.
subprincipal (sʌbˈprɪnsɪpᵊl) *n.* a vice-principal in a college, etc.
subregion (sʌbˈriːdʒən) *n.* a subdivision of a region, esp. a zoogeographical or ecological region. —**subˈregional** *adj.*
subreption (səbˈrɛpʃən) *n.* **1.** *Now rare.* the concealment of facts in order to obtain a benefit, esp. an ecclesiastical benefit or, in Scots Law, a grant from the Crown. Compare **obreption.** **2.** any deceitful misrepresentation or concealment of facts. [C17: from Latin *subreptiō* theft, from *subripere,* from *sub-* secretly + *rapere* to seize] —**subreptitious** (ˌsʌbrɛpˈtɪʃəs) *adj.*
subrogate (ˈsʌbrəˌgeɪt) *vb.* (*tr.*) *Law.* to put (one person or thing) in the place of another in respect of a right or claim. [C16: from Latin *subrogāre,* from *sub-* in place of + *rogāre* to ask]
subrogation (ˌsʌbrəˈgeɪʃən) *n. Law.* the substitution of one person or thing for another, esp. the placing of a surety who has paid the debt in the place of the creditor, entitling him to payment from the original debtor.
sub rosa (ˈrəʊzə) *adv.* in secret. [Latin, literally: under the rose; from the rose that, in ancient times, was hung over the council table, as a token of secrecy]
subroutine (ˈsʌbruːˌtiːn) *n.* a section of a computer program that is stored once but can be used when required at different points in the program, thus saving space. Also called: **procedure.**
subscapular (sʌbˈskæpjʊlə) *adj.* **1.** (of a muscle or artery) situated beneath the scapula. ~*n.* **2.** any subscapular muscle or artery.
subscribe (səbˈskraɪb) *vb.* **1.** (usually foll. by *to*) to pay or promise to pay (a sum of money) as a contribution (to a fund or charity, for a magazine, etc.), esp. at regular intervals. **2.** to inscribe or sign (one's name, etc.) at the end of a contract, will, or other document. **3.** (*intr.;* foll. by *to*) to give support or approval: *to subscribe to the theory of transubstantiation.* [C15: from Latin *subscrībere* to write underneath, from SUB- + *scrībere* to write] —**subˈscriber** *n.*

subˈmember *n.*
ˌsubmoˈlecular *adj.*
subˈoffice *n.*
subˈofficer *n.*
ˌsubofˈficial *n.*
subˈoral *adj.*
subˈparaˌgraph *n.*
ˈsubˌpart *n.*
ˌsubparˈtition *n.*
subˈpattern *n.*
subˈpolar *adj.*
subˈprovince *n.*
ˈsubˌrace *n.*
ˈsubˌrule *n.*
ˈsubˌsale *n.*
ˌsubsatuˈration *n.*
subˈschedule *n.*

subscriber trunk dialling *n. Brit.* a service by which telephone subscribers can obtain trunk calls by dialling direct without the aid of an operator. Abbrev.: **STD.** U.S. and Canadian equivalent: **direct distance dialing.**
subscript ('sʌbskrɪpt) *adj.* **1.** *Printing.* (of a character) written or printed below the base line. Compare **superscript.** ~*n.* **2.** Also called: **subindex.** a subscript character.
subscription (səb'skrɪpʃən) *n.* **1.** a payment or promise of payment for consecutive issues of a magazine, newspaper, book, etc., over a specified period of time. **2. a.** the advance purchase of tickets for a series of concerts, operas, etc. **b.** (*as modifier*): *a subscription concert.* **3.** an amount of money paid or promised, as to a charity, or the fund raised in this way. **4.** an offer to buy shares or bonds issued by a company. **5.** the act of signing one's name to a document, etc. **6.** a signature or other appendage attached to the bottom of a document, etc. **7.** agreement, consent, or acceptance expressed by or as if by signing one's name. **8.** a signed document, statement, etc. **9.** *Chiefly Brit.* the membership dues or fees paid to a society or club. **10.** acceptance of a fixed body of articles of faith, doctrines, or principles laid down as universally binding upon all the members of a Church. **11.** *Med.* that part of a written prescription directing the pharmacist how to mix and prepare the ingredients: rarely seen today as modern drugs are mostly prepackaged by the manufacturers. **12.** an advance order for a new product. **13. a.** the sale of books, etc., prior to printing. **b.** (*as modifier*): *a subscription edition.* **14.** *Archaic.* allegiance; submission. Abbrev.: **sub.** —**sub'scriptive** *adj.*
subscription library *n.* a commercial lending library.
subscription television *n.* another name for **pay television.**
subsellium (sʌb'sɛlɪəm) *n.* a rare word for **misericord** (sense 1). [C19: from Latin, from SUB- + *sella* seat]
subsequence ('sʌbsɪkwəns; *for sense 3* ˌsʌb'siːkwəns) *n.* **1.** the fact or state of being subsequent. **2.** a subsequent incident or occurrence. **3.** *Maths.* a sequence derived from a given sequence by selecting certain of its terms and retaining their order. Thus, $\langle a_2, a_3 \rangle$ is a subsequence of $\langle a_1, a_2, a_3 \rangle$, while $\langle a_3, a_2 \rangle$ is not.
subsequent ('sʌbsɪkwənt) *adj.* occurring after; succeeding. [C15: from Latin *subsequēns* following on, from *subsequī*, from *sub-* near + *sequī* to follow] —**'subsequently** *adv.* —**'subsequentness** *n.*
subsere ('sʌbˌsɪə) *n.* a secondary sere arising when the progress of a sere towards its climax has been interrupted. [C20: SUB- + SERE[2]]
subserve (səb'sɜːv) *vb.* (*tr.*) **1.** to be helpful or useful to. **2.** *Obsolete.* to be subordinate to. [C17: from Latin *subservīre* to be subject to, from SUB- + *servīre* to serve]
subservient (səb'sɜːvɪənt) *adj.* **1.** obsequious in behaviour or attitude. **2.** serving as a means to an end. **3.** a less common word for **subordinate** (sense 2). [C17: from Latin *subserviēns* complying with, from *subservīre* to SUBSERVE] —**sub'serviently** *adv.* —**sub'servience** *or* **sub'serviency** *n.*
subset ('sʌbˌsɛt) *n.* **1.** *Maths.* **a.** a set the members of which are all members of some given class: *A is a subset of B* is usually written $A \subseteq B$. **b. proper subset.** one that is strictly contained within a larger class and excludes some of its members. Symbol: $A \subset B$. **2.** a set within a larger set.
subshrub ('sʌbˌʃrʌb) *n.* a small bushy plant that is woody except for the tips of the branches. —**'subˌshrubby** *adj.*
subside (səb'saɪd) *vb.* (*intr.*) **1.** to become less loud, excited, violent, etc.; abate. **2.** to sink or fall to a lower level. **3.** (of the surface of the earth, etc.) to cave in; collapse. **4.** (of sediment, etc.) to sink or descend to the bottom; settle. [C17: from Latin *subsīdere* to settle down, from *sub-* down + *sīdere* to settle] —**sub'sider** *n.*
subsidence (səb'saɪdᵊns, 'sʌbsɪdᵊns) *n.* **1.** the act or process of subsiding or the condition of having subsided. **2.** *Geology.* the gradual sinking of landforms to a lower level as a result of earth movements, mining operations, etc.
subsidiaries (səb'sɪdɪərɪz) *pl. n. Printing, Brit.* a less common name for **back matter.**
subsidiary (səb'sɪdɪərɪ) *adj.* **1.** serving to aid or supplement; auxiliary. **2.** of lesser importance; subordinate in function. ~*n., pl.* **-aries. 3.** a person who or thing that is subsidiary. **4.** short for **subsidiary company.** [C16: from Latin *subsidiārius* supporting, from *subsidium* SUBSIDY] —**sub'sidiarily** *adv.* —**sub'sidiariness** *n.*
subsidiary coin *n.* a coin of denomination smaller than that of the standard monetary unit.
subsidiary company *n.* a company with at least half of its capital stock owned by another company.
subsidize *or* **subsidise** ('sʌbsɪˌdaɪz) *vb.* (*tr.*) **1.** to aid or support with a subsidy. **2.** to obtain the aid of by means of a subsidy. —ˌ**subsi'dizable** *or* ˌ**subsi'disable** *adj.* —ˌ**subsidi'zation** *or* ˌ**subsidi'sation** *n.* —**'subsiˌdizer** *or* **'subsiˌdiser** *n.*
subsidy ('sʌbsɪdɪ) *n., pl.* **-dies. 1.** a financial aid supplied by a government, as to industry, for reasons of public welfare, the balance of payments, etc. **2.** *English history.* a financial grant made originally for special purposes by Parliament to the Crown. **3.** any monetary aid, grant, or contribution. [C14: from Anglo-Norman *subsidie*, from Latin *subsidium* assistance, from *subsidēre* to remain, from *sub-* down + *sedēre* to sit]
subsist (səb'sɪst) *vb.* (*mainly intr.*) **1.** (often foll. by *on*) to be sustained; manage to live: *to subsist on milk.* **2.** to continue in existence. **3.** (foll. by *in*) to lie or reside by virtue (of); consist. **4.** *Philosophy.* **a.** to exist as a concept or relation rather than a fact. **b.** to be conceivable. **5.** (*tr.*) *Obsolete.* to provide with support. [C16: from Latin *subsistere* to stand firm, from *sub-* up + *sistere* to make a stand] —**sub'sistent** *adj.* —**sub'sister** *n.*
subsistence (səb'sɪstəns) *n.* **1.** the means by which one maintains life. **2.** the act or condition of subsisting. **3.** a thing that has real existence. **4.** the state of being inherent. **5.** *Philosophy.* an inferior mode of being ascribed to the references of general terms which do not in fact exist. See also **nonbeing.**
subsistence allowance *n. Chiefly Brit.* **1.** an advance paid to an employee before his first regular payday. **2.** a payment to an employee made in order to reimburse expenses, as while on assignments.
subsistence farming *n.* a type of farming in which most of the produce (**subsistence crop**) is consumed by the farmer and his family, leaving little or nothing to be marketed.
subsistence level *n.* a standard of living barely adequate to support life.
subsistence wage *n.* the lowest wage upon which a worker and his family can survive.
subsocial (sʌb'səʊʃəl) *adj.* lacking a complex or definite social structure. —**sub'socially** *adv.*
subsoil ('sʌbˌsɔɪl) *n.* **1. a.** Also called: **undersoil.** the layer of soil beneath the surface soil and overlying the bedrock. **b.** (*as modifier*): *a subsoil plough.* ~*vb.* **2.** (*tr.*) to plough (land) to a depth below the normal ploughing level and so break up the subsoil. —**'subˌsoiler** *n.*
subsolar (sʌb'səʊlə) *adj.* **1.** (of a point on the earth's surface) located directly below the sun. **2.** situated between the tropics; equatorial.
subsong ('sʌbˌsɒŋ) *n.* a subdued form of birdsong modified from the full territorial song and used by some birds esp. in courtship.
subsonic (sʌb'sɒnɪk) *adj.* being, having, or travelling at a velocity below that of sound: *a subsonic aircraft.*
subspecies ('sʌbˌspiːʃiːz) *n., pl.* **-cies.** *Biology.* a taxonomic group that is a subdivision of a species: usually occurs because of isolation within a species. Abbrev.: **ssp.** —**subspecific** (ˌsʌbspɪ'sɪfɪk) *adj.* —ˌ**subspe'cifically** *adv.*
subst. *abbrev. for:* **1.** substantive. **2.** substitute.
substage ('sʌbˌsteɪdʒ) *n.* the part of a microscope below the stage, usually consisting of an adjustable assembly holding a condenser lens for illuminating the specimen.
substance ('sʌbstəns) *n.* **1.** the tangible basic matter of which a thing consists. **2.** a specific type of matter, esp. a homogeneous material with definite or fairly definite chemical composition. **3.** the essence, meaning, etc., of a discourse, thought, or written article. **4.** solid or meaningful quality: *an education of substance.* **5.** material density or body: *a vacuum has no substance.* **6.** material possessions or wealth: *a man of substance.* **7.** *Philosophy.* **a.** the supposed immaterial substratum that can receive modifications and in which attributes and accidents inhere. **b.** a thing considered as a continuing whole that survives the changeability of its properties. **8.** *Christian Science.* that which is eternal. **9. in substance.** with regard to the salient points. [C13: via Old French from Latin *substantia*, from *substāre*, from SUB- + *stāre* to stand] —**'substanceless** *adj.*
substandard (sʌb'stændəd) *adj.* **1.** below an established or required standard. **2.** another word for **nonstandard.**
substantial (səb'stænʃəl) *adj.* **1.** of a considerable size or value: *substantial funds.* **2.** worthwhile; important; of telling effect: *a substantial reform.* **3.** having wealth or importance: *a substantial member of the community.* **4.** (of food or a meal) sufficient and nourishing. **5.** solid or strong in construction, quality, or character: *a substantial door.* **6.** real; actual; true: *such evidence cannot be considered substantial.* **7.** of or relating to the basic or fundamental substance or aspects of a thing. **8.** *Philosophy.* of or relating to substance rather than to attributes, accidents, or modifications. ~*n.* **9.** (*often pl.*) *Rare.* an essential or important element. —**substantiality** (səbˌstænʃɪ'ælɪtɪ) *or* **sub'stantialness** *n.* —**sub'stantially** *adv.*
substantialism (səb'stænʃəˌlɪzəm) *n. Philosophy.* **1.** the doctrine that a substantial reality underlies phenomena. **2.** the doctrine that matter is a real substance. —**sub'stantialist** *n.*
substantialize *or* **substantialise** (səb'stænʃəˌlaɪz) *vb.* to make or become substantial or actual.
substantiate (səb'stænʃɪˌeɪt) *vb.* (*tr.*) **1.** to establish as valid or genuine. **2.** to give form or real existence to. [C17: from New Latin *substantiāre*, from Latin *substantia* SUBSTANCE] —**sub**ˌ**stanti'ation** *n.* —**sub'stantiative** *adj.* —**sub'stantiˌator** *n.*
substantive ('sʌbstəntɪv) *n.* **1.** *Grammar.* a noun or pronoun used in place of a noun. ~*adj.* **2.** of, relating to, containing, or being the essential element of a thing. **3.** having independent function, resources, or existence. **4.** of substantial quantity. **5.** solid in foundation or basis. **6.** *Grammar.* denoting, relating to, or standing in place of a noun. **7.** (səb'stæntɪv). relating to the

'**sub**ˌ**sect** *n.* '**sub**ˌ**section** *n.* **sub'segment** *n.* **sub'series** *n., pl.* **-ries.**

essential legal principles administered by the courts, as opposed to practice and procedure. Compare **adjective** (sense 3). **8.** (səb'stæntɪv). (of a dye or colour) staining the material directly without use of a mordant. ~Abbrevs.: **s., sb., subst.** [C15: from Late Latin *substantīvus,* from Latin *substāre* to stand beneath; see SUBSTANCE] —**substantival** (ˌsʌbstən'taɪvᵊl) *adj.* —ˌ**substan'tivally** *adv.* —'**substantively** *adv.* —'**substantiveness** *n.*

substantive agreements *pl. n.* collective agreements that regulate jobs, pay, and conditions.

substantive rank (səb'stæntɪv) *n.* a permanent rank in the armed services obtained by length of service, selection, etc.

substantivize *or* **substantivise** ('sʌbstəntɪˌvaɪz) *vb.* (*tr.*) to make (a word other than a noun) play the grammatical role of a noun in a sentence. —ˌ**substantivi'zation** *or* ˌ**substantivi'sation** *n.*

substation ('sʌbˌsteɪʃən) *n.* **1.** a subsidiary station. **2.** an installation at which electrical energy is received from one or more power stations for conversion from alternating to direct current, stepping down the voltage, or switching before distribution by a low-tension network.

substituent (sʌb'stɪtjʊənt) *n.* **1.** *Chem.* an atom or group that replaces another atom or group in a molecule or can be regarded as replacing an atom in a parent compound. ~*adj.* **2.** substituted or substitutable. [C19: from Latin *substituere* to SUBSTITUTE]

substitute ('sʌbstɪˌtjuːt) *vb.* **1.** (often foll. by *for*) to serve or cause to serve in place of another person or thing. **2.** *Chem.* to replace (an atom or group in a molecule) with (another atom or group). **3.** *Logic, maths.* to replace (one expression) by (another) in the context of a third, as replacing $x + y$ for x in $3x = k$ gives $3x + 3y = k$. ~*n.* **4. a.** a person or thing that serves in place of another, such as a player in a game who takes the place of an injured colleague. **b.** (*as modifier*): *a substitute goalkeeper.* Often shortened to **sub.** **5.** *Grammar.* another name for **pro-form.** **6.** *Nautical.* another word for **repeater** (sense 5). **7.** (formerly) a person paid to replace another due for military service. [C16: from Latin *substituere,* from *sub-* in place of + *statuere* to set up] —ˌ**substi'tutable** *adj.* —ˌ**substiˌtuta'bility** *n.*

substitution (ˌsʌbstɪ'tjuːʃən) *n.* **1.** the act of substituting or state of being substituted. **2.** something or someone substituted. **3.** *Maths.* the replacement of a term of an equation by another that is known to have the same value in order to simplify the equation. **4.** *Maths, logic.* **a.** the uniform replacement of one expression by another. **b. substitution instance.** an expression so derived from another.

substitutive ('sʌbstɪˌtjuːtɪv) *adj.* **1.** acting or able to act as a substitute. **2.** of, relating to, or involving substitution. —'**substiˌtutively** *adv.*

substitutivity (ˌsʌbstɪtjuː'tɪvɪtɪ) *n. Logic, philosophy.* the principle that expressions with the same reference can be substituted for one another without affecting the truth-value of any context in which they occur. See also **transparent context, opaque context.**

substrate ('sʌbstreɪt) *n.* **1.** *Biochem.* the substance upon which an enzyme acts. **2.** another word for **substratum.** **3.** *Electronics.* the semiconductor base on which other material is deposited, esp. in the construction of integrated circuits.

substratum (sʌb'strɑːtəm, -'streɪ-) *n., pl.* **-strata** (-'strɑːtə, -'streɪtə). **1.** any layer or stratum lying underneath another. **2.** a basis or foundation; groundwork. **3.** the nonliving material on which an animal or plant grows or lives. **4.** *Geology.* **a.** the solid rock underlying soils, gravels, etc.; bedrock. **b.** the layer of soil beneath the surface layer; subsoil. **5.** *Sociol.* any of several subdivisions or grades within a stratum. **6.** *Photog.* a binding layer by which an emulsion is made to adhere to a glass or film base. Sometimes shortened to **sub.** **7.** *Philosophy.* substance considered as that in which attributes and accidents inhere. **8.** *Linguistics.* the language of an indigenous population when replaced by the language of a conquering or colonizing population, esp. as it influences the form of the dominant language or of any mixed languages arising from their contact. Compare **superstratum.** [C17: from New Latin, from Latin *substrātus* strewn beneath, from *substernere* to spread under, from SUB- + *sternere* to spread] —**sub'strative** *or* **sub'stratal** *adj.*

substructure ('sʌbˌstrʌktʃə) *n.* **1.** a structure, pattern, etc., that forms the basis of anything. **2.** a structure forming a foundation or framework for a building or other construction. —**sub'structural** *adj.*

subsume (səb'sjuːm) *vb.* (*tr.*) **1.** to incorporate (an idea, proposition, case, etc.) under a comprehensive or inclusive classification or heading. **2.** to consider (an instance of something) as part of a general rule or principle. [C16: from New Latin *subsumere,* from Latin SUB- + *sumere* to take] —**sub'sumable** *adj.*

subsumption (səb'sʌmpʃən) *n.* the act of subsuming or the state of being subsumed. —**sub'sumptive** *adj.*

subtangent (sʌb'tændʒənt) *n. Geometry.* a segment of the x-axis lying between the x-coordinate of the point at which a tangent is drawn to a curve and the intercept of the tangent with the axis; the projection of the tangent on the axis.

subteen (ˌsʌb'tiːn) *n. U.S. and Canadian informal.* a young person who has not yet become a teenager.

subtemperate (sʌb'tɛmpərɪt) *adj.* of or relating to the colder temperate regions.

subtenant (sʌb'tɛnənt) *n.* a person who rents or leases property from a tenant. —**sub'tenancy** *n.*

subtend (səb'tɛnd) *vb.* (*tr.*) **1.** *Geometry.* to be opposite to and delimit (an angle or side). **2.** (of a bract, stem, etc.) to have (a bud or similar part) growing in its axil. **3.** to mark off. **4.** to underlie; be inherent in. [C16: from Latin *subtendere* to extend beneath, from SUB- + *tendere* to stretch out]

subterfuge ('sʌbtəˌfjuːdʒ) *n.* a stratagem employed to conceal something, evade an argument, etc. [C16: from Late Latin *subterfugium,* from Latin *subterfugere* to escape by stealth, from *subter* secretly + *fugere* to flee]

subterminal (sʌb'tɜːmɪnᵊl) *adj.* almost at an end.

subternatural (ˌsʌbtə'nætʃərəl, -'nætʃrəl) *adj. Rare.* falling below what is accepted as natural; less than natural. [C19: from Latin *subter-* below + NATURAL]

subterranean (ˌsʌbtə'reɪnɪən) *adj.* **1.** Also: **subterraneous, subterrestrial.** situated, living, or operating below the surface of the earth. **2.** existing or operating in concealment. [C17: from Latin *subterrāneus,* from SUB- + *terra* earth] —ˌ**subter'raneanly** *or* ˌ**subter'raneously** *adv.*

subtile ('sʌtᵊl) *adj.* a rare spelling of **subtle.** —'**subtilely** *adv.* —**subtility** (sʌb'tɪlɪtɪ) *or* '**subtileness** *n.* —'**subtilty** *n.*

subtilize *or* **subtilise** ('sʌtɪˌlaɪz) *vb.* **1.** (*tr.*) to bring to a purer state; refine. **2.** to debate subtly. **3.** (*tr.*) to make (the mind, etc.) keener. —ˌ**subtili'zation** *or* ˌ**subtili'sation** *n.* —'**subtilˌizer** *or* '**subtilˌiser** *n.*

subtitle ('sʌbˌtaɪtᵊl) *n.* **1.** an additional subordinate title given to a literary or other work. **2.** (*often pl.*) Also called: **caption.** *Films.* **a.** a written translation superimposed on a film that has foreign dialogue. **b.** explanatory text on a silent film. ~*vb.* **3.** (*tr.; usually passive*) to provide a subtitle for. —**subtitular** (sʌb'tɪtjʊlə, -'tɪtʃə-) *adj.*

subtle ('sʌtᵊl) *adj.* **1.** not immediately obvious or comprehensible. **2.** difficult to detect or analyse, often through being delicate or highly refined: *a subtle scent.* **3.** showing or making or capable of showing or making fine distinctions of meaning. **4.** marked by or requiring mental acuteness or ingenuity; discriminating. **5.** delicate or faint: *a subtle shade.* **6.** cunning or wily: *a subtle rogue.* **7.** operating or executed in secret: *a subtle intrigue.* [C14: from Old French *soutil,* from Latin *subtīlis* finely woven] —'**subtleness** *n.* —'**subtly** *adv.*

subtlety ('sʌtᵊltɪ) *n., pl.* **-ties.** **1.** the state or quality of being subtle; delicacy. **2.** a fine distinction or the ability to make such a distinction. **3.** something subtle.

subtonic (sʌb'tɒnɪk) *n. Music.* the seventh degree of a major or minor scale. Also called: **leading note.**

subtopia (sʌb'təʊpɪə) *n. Brit.* suburban development that encroaches on rural areas yet appears to offer the attractions of country life to suburban dwellers. [C20: blend of SUBURB + UTOPIA] —**sub'topian** *adj.*

subtorrid (sʌb'tɒrɪd) *adj.* a less common word for **subtropical.**

subtotal (sʌb'təʊtᵊl, 'sʌbˌtəʊtᵊl) *n.* **1.** the total made up by a column of figures, etc., forming part of the total made up by a larger column or group. ~*vb.* **-tals, -talling, -talled** *or U.S.* **-tals, -taling, -taled.** **2.** to establish or work out a subtotal for (a column, group, etc.).

subtract (səb'trækt) *vb.* **1.** to calculate the difference between (two numbers or quantities) by subtraction. **2.** to remove (a part of a thing, quantity, etc.) from the whole. [C16: from Latin *subtractus* withdrawn, from *subtrahere* to draw away from beneath, from SUB- + *trahere* to draw] —**sub'tracter** *n.*

subtraction (səb'trækʃən) *n.* **1.** the act or process of subtracting. **2.** a mathematical operation in which the difference between two numbers or quantities is calculated. Usually indicated by the symbol (–).

subtractive (səb'træktɪv) *adj.* **1.** able or tending to remove or subtract. **2.** indicating or requiring subtraction; having a minus sign: $-x$ *is a subtractive quantity.*

subtractive process *n.* a photographic process in which all but the desired colours are removed by passing the illuminating light through subtractive filters. Compare **additive process.**

subtrahend ('sʌbtrəˌhɛnd) *n.* the number to be subtracted from another number (the **minuend**). [C17: from Latin *subtrahendus,* from *subtrahere* to SUBTRACT]

subtreasury (sʌb'trɛʒərɪ) *n. pl.* **-uries.** *U.S.* a branch treasury. —**sub'treasurer** *n.* —**sub'treasurership** *n.*

subtropics (sʌb'trɒpɪks) *pl. n.* the region lying between the tropics and temperate lands. —**sub'tropical** *adj.*

subtype ('sʌbˌtaɪp) *n.* a secondary or subordinate type or genre, esp. a specific one considered as falling under a general classification. —**subtypical** (sʌb'tɪpɪkᵊl) *adj.*

subulate ('suːbjʊlɪt, -ˌleɪt) *adj.* (esp. of plant parts) tapering to a point; awl-shaped. [C18: from New Latin *subulatus* like an awl, from Latin *sūbula* awl]

sub'surface *adj.* '**subˌsystem** *n.* '**subˌtopic** *n.* '**subˌtribe** *n.*

suburb ('sʌbɜːb) *n.* a residential district situated on the outskirts of a city or town. [C14: from Latin *suburbium,* from *sub-* close to + *urbs* a city] —'**suburbed** *adj.*
suburban (sə'bɜːbᵊn) *adj.* **1.** of, relating to, situated in, or inhabiting a suburb or the suburbs. **2.** characteristic of or typifying a suburb or the suburbs. **3.** *Mildly derogatory.* narrow or unadventurous in outlook. ~*n.* **4.** another word for **suburbanite.**
suburbanite (sə'bɜːbəˌnaɪt) *n.* a person who lives in a suburb.
suburbanize *or* **suburbanise** (sʌ'bɜːbəˌnaɪz) *vb.* (*tr.*) to make suburban.
suburbia (sə'bɜːbɪə) *n.* **1.** suburbs or the people living in them considered as an identifiable community or class in society. **2.** the life, customs, etc., of suburbanites.
suburbicarian (səˌbɜːbɪ'kɛərɪən) *adj. R.C. Church.* situated near the city of Rome: used esp. of the dioceses surrounding Rome. [C17: from Late Latin *suburbicārius,* from *suburbium* SUBURB]
subvene (səb'viːn) *vb.* (*intr.*) *Rare.* to happen in such a way as to be of assistance, esp. in preventing something. [C18: from Latin *subvenīre,* from *venīre* to come]
subvention (səb'venʃən) *n.* **1.** a grant, aid, or subsidy, as from a government to an educational institution. **2.** the act or process of providing aid or help of any sort. **3.** *Sport.* a fee paid indirectly to a supposedly amateur athlete for appearing at a meeting. [C15: from Late Latin *subventiō* assistance, from Latin *subvenīre* to SUBVENE] —**sub'ventionary** *adj.*
subversion (səb'vɜːʃən) *n.* **1.** the act or an instance of subverting or overthrowing a legally constituted government, institution, etc. **2.** the state of being subverted; destruction or ruin. **3.** something that brings about an overthrow. [C14: from Late Latin *subversiō* destruction, from Latin *subvertere* to SUBVERT]
subversive (səb'vɜːsɪv) *adj.* **1.** liable to subvert or overthrow a government, legally constituted institution, etc. ~*n.* **2.** a person engaged in subversive activities, etc. —**sub'versively** *adv.* —**sub'versiveness** *n.*
subvert (səb'vɜːt) *vb.* (*tr.*) **1.** to bring about the complete downfall or ruin of (something existing or established by a system of law, etc.). **2.** to undermine the moral principles of (a person, etc.); corrupt. [C14: from Latin *subvertere* to overturn, from *sub-* from below + *vertere* to turn] —**sub'verter** *n.*
subviral (sʌb'vaɪrəl) *adj.* of, caused by, or denoting a part of the structure of a virus.
subway ('sʌbˌweɪ) *n.* **1.** *Brit.* an underground passage or tunnel enabling pedestrians to cross a road, railway, etc. **2.** an underground passage or tunnel for traffic, electric power supplies, etc. **3.** *Chiefly U.S. and Canadian.* an underground railway.
subzero (sʌb'zɪərəʊ) *adj.* (esp. of temperature) lower or less than zero.
succah (su'kɑ, 'sukɔ, 'sukə) *n. Judaism.* a variant spelling of **sukkah.**
succedaneum (ˌsʌksɪ'deɪnɪəm) *n., pl.* **-nea** (-nɪə). something that is used as a substitute, esp. any medical drug or agent that may be taken or prescribed in place of another. [C17: from Latin *succēdāneus* following after, from *succēdere* to SUCCEED] —ˌ**succe'daneous** *adj.*
succeed (sək'siːd) *vb.* **1.** (*intr.*) to accomplish an aim, esp. in the manner desired: *he succeeded in winning.* **2.** (*intr.*) to happen in the manner desired: *the plan succeeded.* **3.** (*intr.*) to acquit oneself satisfactorily or do well, as in a specified field: *to succeed in publishing.* **4.** (when *intr.,* often foll. by *to*) to come next in order (after someone or something). **5.** (when *intr.,* often foll. by *to*) to take over an office, post, etc. (from a person): *he succeeded to the vice presidency.* **6.** (*intr.;* usually foll. by *to*) to come into possession (of property, etc.); inherit. **7.** (*intr.*) to have a result according to a specified manner: *the plan succeeded badly.* **8.** (*intr.*) to devolve upon: *the estate succeeded to his son.* [C15: from Latin *succēdere* to follow after, from *sub-* after + *cēdere* to go] —**suc'ceedable** *adj.* —**suc'ceeder** *n.* —**suc'ceeding** *adj.* —**suc'ceedingly** *adv.*
succentor (sək'sentə) *n.* the deputy of the precentor of a cathedral that has retained its statutes from pre-Reformation days. [C17: from Late Latin: one who accompanies singing, from *succinere* to accompany, from Latin *canere* to sing] —**suc'centorship** *n.*
succès de scandale *French.* (syksɛ də skɑ̃dal) *n., pl.* ***succès de scandale.*** success of a play, book, etc., because of notoriety or its scandalous character. [literally: success of scandal]
succès d'estime *French.* (syksɛ dɛstim) *n., pl.* ***succès d'estime.*** success, as of a book, play, etc., based on the appreciation of the critics rather than popular acclaim. [literally: success of esteem]
succès fou *French.* (syksɛ fu) *n., pl.* ***succès fous*** (syksɛ fu). a fantastic success. [literally: mad success]
success (sək'sɛs) *n.* **1.** the favourable outcome of something attempted. **2.** the attainment of wealth, fame, etc. **3.** an action, performance, etc., that is characterized by success. **4.** a person or thing that is successful. **5.** *Obsolete.* any outcome. [C16: from Latin *successus* an outcome, from *succēdere* to SUCCEED] —**suc'cessless** *adj.*

'**subˌunit** *n.*

successful (sək'sɛsfʊl) *adj.* **1.** having succeeded in one's endeavours. **2.** marked by a favourable outcome. **3.** having obtained fame, wealth, etc. —**suc'cessfully** *adv.* —**suc'cessfulness** *n.*
succession (sək'sɛʃən) *n.* **1.** the act or an instance of one person or thing following another. **2.** a number of people or things following one another in order. **3.** the act, process, or right by which one person succeeds to the office, etc., of another. **4.** the order that determines how one person or thing follows another. **5.** a line of descent to a title, etc. **6.** *Ecology.* the sum of the changes in the composition of a community that occur during its development towards a stable climax community. **7. in succession.** in a manner such that one thing is followed uninterruptedly by another. [C14: from Latin *successio,* from *succēdere* to SUCCEED] —**suc'cessional** *adj.* —**suc'cessionally** *adv.*
succession state *n.* any of a number of usually new states that are established in or expand over the territory formerly ruled by one large state: *Czechoslovakia is a succession state of the Austro-Hungarian monarchy.*
successive (sək'sɛsɪv) *adj.* **1.** following another without interruption. **2.** of or involving succession: *a successive process.* —**suc'cessively** *adv.* —**suc'cessiveness** *n.*
successor (sək'sɛsə) *n.* **1.** a person or thing that follows, esp. a person who succeeds another in an office. **2.** *Logic.* the element related to a given element by a serial ordering, esp. the natural number next larger to a given one. The successor of n is $n + 1$, usually written Sn or n'. —**suc'cessoral** *adj.*
succinate ('sʌksɪˌneɪt) *n.* any salt or ester of succinic acid. [C18: from SUCCIN(IC) + -ATE[2]]
succinct (sək'sɪŋkt) *adj.* **1.** marked by brevity and clarity; concise. **2.** compressed into a small area. **3.** *Archaic.* **a.** encircled by or as if by a girdle. **b.** drawn up tightly; closely fitting. [C15: from Latin *succinctus* girt about, from *succingere* to gird from below, from *sub-* from below + *cingere* to gird] —**suc'cinctly** *adv.* —**suc'cinctness** *n.*
succinic (sʌk'sɪnɪk) *adj.* **1.** of, relating to, or obtained from amber. **2.** of, consisting of, containing, or derived from succinic acid. [C18: from French *succinique,* from Latin *succinum* amber]
succinic acid *n.* a colourless odourless water-soluble dicarboxylic acid found in plant and animal tissues: used in making lacquers, dyes, perfumes, etc.; 1,4-butanedioic acid. Formula: $HOOCCH_2{:}CH_2COOH$.
succise (sək'saɪz) *adj. Botany.* ending abruptly, as if cut off: *succise leaves.* [from Latin *succisus* cut below]
succory ('sʌkərɪ) *n., pl.* **-cories.** another name for **chicory.** [C16: variant of *cicoree* CHICORY; related to Middle Low German *suckerie,* Dutch *suikerei*]
succotash ('sʌkəˌtæʃ) *n. U.S. and Canadian.* a mixture of cooked sweet corn kernels and lima beans, served as a vegetable. [C18: from Narraganset *msiquatash,* literally: broken pieces]
Succoth ('sʊkəʊt, -kəʊθ; *Hebrew* suː'kɔt) *n.* a variant spelling of **Sukkoth.**
succour *or U.S.* **succor** ('sʌkə) *n.* **1.** help or assistance, esp. in time of difficulty. **2.** a person or thing that provides help. ~*vb.* **3.** (*tr.*) to give aid to. [C13: from Old French *sucurir,* from Latin *succurrere* to hurry to help, from *sub-* under + *currere* to run] —'**succourable** *or U.S.* '**succorable** *adj.* —'**succourer** *or U.S.* '**succorer** *n.* —'**succourless** *or U.S.* '**succorless** *adj.*
succubus ('sʌkjʊbəs) *n., pl.* **-bi** (-ˌbaɪ). **1.** Also called: **succuba.** a female demon fabled to have sexual intercourse with sleeping men. Compare **incubus.** **2.** any evil demon. [C16: from Medieval Latin, from Late Latin *succuba* harlot, from Latin *succubāre* to lie beneath, from SUB- + *cubāre* to lie]
succulent ('sʌkjʊlənt) *adj.* **1.** abundant in juices; juicy. **2.** (of plants) having thick fleshy leaves or stems. **3.** *Informal.* stimulating interest, desire, etc. ~*n.* **4.** a plant that is able to exist in arid conditions by using water stored in its fleshy tissues. [C17: from Latin *succulentus,* from *sūcus* juice] —'**succulence** *or* '**succulency** *n.* —'**succulently** *adv.*
succumb (sə'kʌm) *vb.* (*intr.;* often foll. by *to*) **1.** to give way in face of the overwhelming force (of) or desire (for). **2.** to be fatally overwhelmed (by disease, old age, etc.); die (of). [C15: from Latin *succumbere* to be overcome, from SUB- + *-cumbere* from *cubāre* to lie down] —**suc'cumber** *n.*
succursal (sʌ'kɜːsᵊl) *adj.* **1.** (esp. of a religious establishment) subsidiary. ~*n.* **2.** a subsidiary establishment. [C19: from French, from Medieval Latin *succursus,* from Latin *succurrere* to SUCCOUR]
succuss (sʌ'kʌs) *vb.* **1.** *Med.* to shake (a patient) to detect the sound of fluid in the thoracic or another bodily cavity. **2.** *Rare.* to shake, esp. with sudden force. [C17: from Latin *succussus* flung aloft, from *succutere* to toss up, from *sub-* from below + *quatere* to shake] —**succussion** (sʌ'kʌʃən) *n.* —**suc'cussive** *adj.*
such (sʌtʃ) (often foll. by a corresponding subordinate clause introduced by *that* or *as*) ~*determiner.* **1. a.** of the sort specified or understood: *such books shouldn't be sold here.* **b.** (*as pronoun*): *such is life; robbers, rapists, and such.* **2.** so great; so much: *such a help; I've never seen such weeping.* **3. a. as such.** in the capacity previously specified or understood: *a judge as such hasn't so much power.* **b.** in itself or themselves: *intelli-*

'**subvaˌriety** *n., pl.* **-ties.**

gence as such can't guarantee success. **4. such and such.** specific, but not known or named: *at such and such a time.* **5. such as. a.** for example: *animals, such as elephants and tigers.* **b.** of a similar kind as; like: *people such as your friend John make me angry.* **c.** of the (usually small) amount, etc.: *the food, such as there was, was excellent.* **6. such that.** so that: used to express purpose or result: *power such that it was effortless.* ~*adv.* **7.** (intensifier): *such nice people; such a nice person that I gave him a present.* [Old English *swilc;* related to Old Frisian *sālik,* Old Norse *slīkr,* Gothic *swaleiks,* Old High German *sulih*]

suchlike ('sʌtʃˌlaɪk) *adj.* **1.** (*prenominal*) of such a kind; similar: *John, Ken, and other suchlike idiots.* ~*n.* **2.** such or similar persons or things: *hyenas, jackals, and suchlike.*

suck (sʌk) *vb.* **1.** to draw (a liquid or other substance) into the mouth by creating a partial vacuum in the mouth. **2.** to draw in (fluid, etc.) by or as if by a similar action: *plants suck moisture from the soil.* **3.** to drink milk from (a mother's breast); suckle. **4.** (*tr.*) to extract fluid content from (a solid food): *to suck a lemon.* **5.** (*tr.*) to take into the mouth and moisten, dissolve, or roll around with the tongue: *to suck one's thumb.* **6.** (*tr.*; often foll. by *down, in,* etc.) to draw by using irresistible force: *the whirlpool sucked him down.* **7.** (*intr.*) (of a pump) to draw in air because of a low supply level or leaking valves, pipes, etc. **8.** (*tr.*) to assimilate or acquire (knowledge, comfort, etc.). ~*n.* **9.** the act or an instance of sucking. **10.** something that is sucked, esp. milk from the mother's breast. **11. give suck to.** to give (a baby or young animal) milk from the breast or udder. **12.** an attracting or sucking force: *the suck of the whirlpool was very strong.* **13.** a sound caused by sucking. ~See also **suck in, suck off, sucks, suck up to.** [Old English *sūcan;* related to Old Norse *súga,* Middle Dutch *sūgen,* Latin *sūgere* to suck, exhaust; see SOAK] —'**suckless** *adj.*

sucker ('sʌkə) *n.* **1.** a person or thing that sucks. **2.** *Slang.* a person who is easily deceived or swindled. **3.** *Slang.* a person who cannot resist the attractions of a particular type of person or thing: *he's a sucker for blondes.* **4.** a young animal that is not yet weaned, esp. a suckling pig. **5.** *Zoology.* an organ that is specialized for sucking or adhering. **6.** a cup-shaped device, generally made of rubber, that may be attached to articles allowing them to adhere to a surface by suction. **7.** *Botany.* **a.** a strong shoot that arises in a mature plant from a root, rhizome, or the base of the main stem. **b.** a short branch of a parasitic plant that absorbs nutrients from the host. **8.** a pipe or tube through which a fluid is drawn by suction. **9.** any small mainly North American cyprinoid fish of the family *Catostomidae,* having toothless jaws and a large sucking mouth. **10.** any of certain fishes that have sucking discs, esp. the clingfish or sea snail. **11.** a piston in a suction pump or the valve in such a piston. ~*vb.* **12.** (*tr.*) to strip off the suckers from (a plant). **13.** (*intr.*) (of a plant) to produce suckers.

suckerfish ('sʌkəˌfɪʃ) *or* **suckfish** *n., pl.* **-fish** *or* **-fishes.** other names for **remora.** [C18: so called because of the suction disc on its head]

suck in *vb.* (*adv.*) **1.** (*tr.*) to attract by using an inexorable force, inducement, etc.: *the current sucked him in.* **2.** to draw in (one's breath) sharply. **3.** (*tr.*) *Slang.* to deceive or defraud.

sucking ('sʌkɪŋ) *adj.* **1.** not yet weaned: *sucking pig.* **2.** not yet fledged: *sucking dove.*

sucking louse *n.* any insect of the order *Anoplura.* See **louse** (sense 1). [so named because it has a mouth adapted for sucking the body fluids of its host]

suckle ('sʌkᵊl) *vb.* **1.** to give (a baby or young animal) milk from the breast or (of a baby, etc.) to suck milk from the breast. **2.** (*tr.*) to bring up; nurture. [C15: probably back formation from SUCKLING] —'**suckler** *n.*

suckling ('sʌklɪŋ) *n.* **1.** an infant or young animal that is still taking milk from the mother. **2.** a very young child. [C15: see SUCK, -LING[1]; related to Middle Dutch *sūgeling,* Middle High German *sögelinc*]

suck off *vb.* (*tr., adv.*) *Taboo slang.* to perform the act of fellatio or cunnilingus on.

sucks (sʌks) *interj. Slang.* **1.** an expression of disappointment. **2.** an exclamation of defiance or derision (esp. in the phrase **yah boo sucks to you**).

suck up to *vb.* (*intr., adv.* + *prep.*) *Informal.* to flatter for one's own profit; toady.

sucrase ('sjuːkreɪz) *n.* another name for **invertase.** [C19: from French *sucre* sugar + -ASE]

sucre (*Spanish* 'sukre) *n.* the standard monetary unit of Ecuador, divided into 100 centavos. [C19: after Antonio José de *Sucre* (1795–1830), Venezuelan-born liberator and statesman]

sucrose ('sjuːkrəʊz, -krəʊs) *n.* the technical name for **sugar** (sense 1). [C19: from French *sucre* sugar + -OSE[2]]

suction ('sʌkʃən) *n.* **1.** the act or process of sucking. **2.** the force or condition produced by a pressure difference, as the force holding a suction cap onto a surface. **3.** the act or process of producing such a force or condition. [C17: from Late Latin *suctiō* a sucking, from Latin *sūgere* to suck] —'**suctional** *adj.*

suction pump *n.* a pump for raising water or a similar fluid by suction. It usually consists of a cylinder containing a piston fitted with a flap valve.

suction stop *n. Phonetics.* another word for **click** (sense 3).

suction valve *n.* a nonreturn valve in a pump suction to prevent the pump draining or depriming when not in service. Also called: **foot valve.**

suctorial (sʌk'tɔːrɪəl) *adj.* **1.** specialized for sucking or adhering: *the suctorial mouthparts of certain insects.* **2.** relating to or possessing suckers or suction. [C19: from New Latin *suctōrius,* from Latin *sūgere* to suck]

Sudanese (ˌsuːdᵊ'niːz) *adj.* **1.** of or relating to Sudan, a republic in NE Africa, or to its people, customs, etc. ~*n.* **2.** a native or inhabitant of Sudan.

Sudanic (suː'dænɪk) *n.* **1.** a group of languages spoken in scattered areas of the Sudan, most of which are now generally assigned to the Chari-Nile branch of the Nilo-Saharan family. ~*adj.* **2.** relating to or belonging to this group of languages. **3.** of or relating to the Sudan.

sudarium (sjʊ'dɛərɪəm) *n., pl.* **-daria** (-'dɛərɪə). another word for **sudatorium** or **veronica**[2]. [C17: from Latin, from *sūdāre* to sweat]

sudatorium (ˌsjuːdə'tɔːrɪəm) *or* **sudatory** *n., pl.* **-toria** (-'tɔːrɪə) *or* **-tories.** a room, esp. in a Roman bathhouse, where sweating is induced by heat. [C18: from Latin, from *sūdāre* to sweat]

sudatory ('sjuːdətərɪ, -trɪ) *adj.* **1.** relating to or producing sweating; sudorific. ~*n., pl.* **-ries. 2.** *Med.* a sudatory agent. **3.** another word for **sudatorium.**

sudd (sʌd) *n.* floating masses of reeds and weeds that occur on the White Nile and obstruct navigation. [C19: from Arabic, literally: obstruction]

sudden ('sʌdᵊn) *adj.* **1.** occurring or performed quickly and without warning. **2.** marked by haste; abrupt. **3.** *Rare.* rash; precipitate. ~*n.* **4.** *Archaic.* an abrupt occurrence or the occasion of such an occurrence (in the phrase **on a sudden**). **5. all of a sudden.** without warning; unexpectedly. ~*adv.* **6.** *Chiefly poetic.* without warning; suddenly. [C13: via French from Late Latin *subitāneus,* from Latin *subitus* unexpected, from *subīre* to happen unexpectedly, from *sub-* secretly + *īre* to go] —'**suddenly** *adv.* —'**suddenness** *n.*

sudden death *n.* **1.** (in sports, etc.) an extra game or contest to decide the winner of a tied competition. **2.** an unexpected or quick death.

sudden infant death syndrome *n.* a technical term for **cot death.** Abbrev.: **SIDS.**

sudor ('sjuːdɔː) *n.* a technical name for **sweat.** [Latin] —**sudoral** ('sjuːdərəl) *adj.*

sudoriferous (ˌsjuːdə'rɪfərəs) *adj.* producing or conveying sweat. Also: **sudoriparous** (ˌsjuːdə'rɪpərəs). [C16: via New Latin from SUDOR + Latin *ferre* to bear] —ˌ**sudor'iferousness** *n.*

sudorific (ˌsjuːdə'rɪfɪk) *adj.* **1.** producing or causing sweating; sudatory. ~*n.* **2.** a sudorific agent. [C17: from New Latin *sūdōrificus,* from SUDOR + Latin *facere* to make]

Sudra ('sjuːdrə) *n.* the lowest of the four main Hindu castes, the workers. [C17: from Sanskrit]

suds (sʌdz) *pl. n.* **1.** the bubbles on the surface of water in which soap, detergents, etc., have been dissolved; lather. **2.** soapy water. **3.** *Slang, chiefly U.S. and Canadian.* beer or the bubbles floating on it. [C16: probably from Middle Dutch *sudse* marsh; related to Middle Low German *sudde* swamp; see SEETHE] —'**sudsy** *adj.*

sue (sjuː, suː) *vb.* **sues, suing, sued. 1.** to institute legal proceedings (against). **2.** to make suppliant requests of (someone for something). **3.** *Archaic.* to pay court (to). [C13: via Anglo-Norman from Old French *sivre,* from Latin *sequī* to follow] —'**suer** *n.*

suede (sweɪd) *n.* **a.** a leather finished with a fine velvet-like nap, usually on the flesh side of the skin or hide, produced by abrasive action. **b.** (*as modifier*): *a suede coat.* [C19: from French *gants de Suède,* literally: gloves from Sweden]

suet ('suːɪt, 'sjuːɪt) *n.* a hard waxy fat around the kidneys and loins in sheep, cattle, etc., used in cooking and making tallow. [C14: from Old French *seu,* from Latin *sēbum*] —'**suety** *adj.*

suet pudding *n. Brit.* any of a variety of sweet or savoury puddings made with suet and steamed or boiled.

suf. *abbrev. for* suffix.

suff. *abbrev. for:* **1.** sufficient. **2.** suffix.

Suff. *abbrev. for:* **1.** Suffolk. **2.** Suffragan.

suffer ('sʌfə) *vb.* **1.** to undergo or be subjected to (pain, punishment, etc.). **2.** (*tr.*) to undergo or experience (anything): *to suffer a change of management.* **3.** (*intr.*) to be set at a disadvantage: *this author suffers in translation.* **4.** to be prepared to endure (pain, death, etc.): *he suffers for the cause of freedom.* **5.** (*tr.*) *Archaic.* to permit (someone to do something): *suffer the little children to come unto me.* **6. suffer from. a.** to be ill with, esp. recurrently. **b.** to be given to: *he suffers from a tendency to exaggerate.* [C13: from Old French *soffrir,* from Latin *sufferre,* from SUB- + *ferre* to bear] —'**sufferer** *n.*

sufferable ('sʌfərəbᵊl, 'sʌfrə-) *adj.* able to be tolerated or suffered; endurable. —'**sufferably** *adv.*

sufferance ('sʌfərəns, 'sʌfrəns) *n.* **1.** tolerance arising from failure to prohibit; tacit permission. **2.** capacity to endure pain, injury, etc. **3.** the state or condition of suffering. **4.** *Archaic.* patient endurance. **5. on sufferance.** with reluctance. [C13: via Old French from Late Latin *sufferentia* endurance, from Latin *sufferre* to SUFFER]

suffering (ˈsʌfərɪŋ, ˈsʌfrɪŋ) *n.* **1.** the pain, misery, or loss experienced by a person who suffers. **2.** the state or an instance of enduring pain, etc. —**ˈsufferingly** *adv.*
suffice (səˈfaɪs) *vb.* **1.** to be adequate or satisfactory for (something). **2. suffice it to say that.** (*takes a clause as object*) let us say no more than that; I shall just say that. [C14: from Old French *suffire,* from Latin *sufficere* from *sub-* below + *facere* to make] —**sufˈficer** *n.*
sufficiency (səˈfɪʃənsɪ) *n., pl.* **-cies. 1.** the quality or condition of being sufficient. **2.** an adequate amount or quantity, as of income. **3.** *Archaic.* efficiency.
sufficient (səˈfɪʃənt) *adj.* **1.** enough to meet a need or purpose; adequate. **2.** *Logic.* (of a condition) assuring the truth of a statement; requiring but not necessarily required by some other state of affairs. Compare **necessary** (sense 3e). **3.** *Archaic.* competent; capable. ~*n.* **4.** a sufficient quantity. [C14: from Latin *sufficiens* supplying the needs of, from *sufficere* to SUFFICE] —**sufˈficiently** *adv.*
sufficient reason *n. Philosophy.* **1.** the principle that nothing happens by pure chance, but that an explanation must always be available. **2.** the view that such an explanation is a reason for God to have chosen one alternative rather than another.
suffix *n.* (ˈsʌfɪks). **1.** *Grammar.* an affix that follows the stem to which it is attached, as for example *-s* and *-ness* in *dogs* and *softness.* Compare **prefix** (sense 1). **2.** anything that is added at the end of something else. ~*vb.* (ˈsʌfɪks, səˈfɪks). **3.** (*tr.*) *Grammar.* to add (a morpheme) as a suffix to the end of a word. [C18: from New Latin *suffixum,* from Latin *suffixus* fastened below, from *suffīgere,* from SUB- + *fīgere* to fasten] —**suffixal** (ˈsʌfɪksəl) *adj.* —**suffixion** (sʌˈfɪkʃən) *n.*
sufflate (sʌˈfleɪt) *vb.* an archaic word for **inflate.** [C17: from Latin *sufflāre* from SUB- + *flāre* blow] —**sufˈflation** *n.*
suffocate (ˈsʌfəˌkeɪt) *vb.* **1.** to kill or be killed by the deprivation of oxygen, as by obstruction of the air passage or inhalation of noxious gases. **2.** to block the air passages or have the air passages blocked. **3.** to feel or cause to feel discomfort from heat and lack of air. [C16: from Latin *suffōcāre,* from SUB- + *faucēs* throat] —**ˈsuffoˌcating** *adj.* —**ˈsuffoˌcatingly** *adv.* —**ˌsuffoˈcation** *n.* —**ˈsuffoˌcative** *adj.*
Suffolk (ˈsʌfək) *n.* a black-faced breed of sheep originating in Suffolk, SE England.
Suffolk punch *n.* a breed of draught horse with a chestnut coat and short legs. [C18: from dialect *punch* squat, short and thick]
Suffr. *abbrev. for* Suffragan.
suffragan (ˈsʌfrəgən) *adj.* **1. a.** (of any bishop of a diocese) subordinate to and assisting his superior archbishop or metropolitan. **b.** (of any assistant bishop) having the duty of assisting the bishop of the diocese to which he is appointed but having no ordinary jurisdiction in that diocese. ~*n.* **2.** a suffragan bishop. [C14: from Medieval Latin *suffragāneus,* from *suffrāgium* assistance, from Latin: SUFFRAGE] —**ˈsuffraganship** *n.*
suffrage (ˈsʌfrɪdʒ) *n.* **1.** the right to vote, esp. in public elections; franchise. **2.** the exercise of such a right; casting a vote. **3.** a supporting vote. **4.** a prayer, esp. a short intercessory prayer. [C14: from Latin *suffrāgium*]
suffragette (ˌsʌfrəˈdʒɛt) *n.* a female advocate of the extension of the franchise to women, esp. a militant one, as in Britain at the beginning of the 20th century. [C20: from SUFFRAG(E) + -ETTE] —**ˌsuffraˈgettism** *n.*
suffragist (ˈsʌfrədʒɪst) *n.* an advocate of the extension of the franchise, esp. to women. —**ˈsuffragism** *n.*
suffruticose (səˈfruːtɪˌkəʊz) *adj.* (of a plant) having a permanent woody base and herbaceous branches. [C18: from New Latin *suffruticōsus,* from Latin SUB- + *frutex* a shrub]
suffumigate (səˈfjuːmɪˌgeɪt) *vb.* (*tr.*) to fumigate from or as if from beneath. [C16: from Latin *suffūmigāre,* from SUB- + *fūmigāre* to FUMIGATE] —**sufˌfumiˈgation** *n.*
suffuse (səˈfjuːz) *vb.* (*tr.; usually passive*) to spread or flood through or over (something): *the evening sky was suffused with red.* [C16: from Latin *suffūsus* overspread with, from *suffundere,* from SUB- + *fundere* to pour] —**suffusion** (səˈfjuːʒən) *n.* —**sufˈfusive** *adj.*
Sufi (ˈsuːfɪ) *n., pl.* **-fis.** an adherent of any of various Muslim mystical orders or teachings, which emphasize the direct personal experience of God. [C17: from Arabic *ṣūfīy,* literally: (man) of wool, from *ṣūf* wool; probably from the ascetic's woollen garments] —**ˈSufic** *adj.* —**ˈSufism** *n.*
sug (sʌg) *vb.* **sugging, sugged.** (*intr.*) to use the pretence of conducting a survey in order to try to sell something to a person. [C20: from *s*elling *u*nder the *g*uise (of market research)] —**ˈsugging** *n.*
súgán (ˈsuːgɑːn) *n. Irish.* **1.** a straw rope. **2. súgán chair.** a chair with a seat made from woven súgáns. [Irish Gaelic]
sugar (ˈʃʊgə) *n.* **1.** Also called: **sucrose, saccharose.** a white crystalline sweet carbohydrate, a disaccharide, found in many plants and extracted from sugar cane and sugar beet: it is used esp. as a sweetening agent in food and drinks. Formula: $C_{12}H_{22}O_{11}$. Related adj.: **saccharine. 2.** any of a class of simple water-soluble carbohydrates, such as sucrose, lactose, and fructose. **3.** *Informal, chiefly U.S. and Canadian.* a term of affection, esp. for one's sweetheart. **4.** *Rare.* a slang word for **money. 5.** a slang name for **LSD.** ~*vb.* **6.** (*tr.*) to add sugar to; make sweet. **7.** (*tr.*) to cover or sprinkle with sugar. **8.** (*intr.*) to produce sugar. **9. sugar the pill** *or* **medicine.** to make something unpleasant more agreeable by adding something pleasant: *the government stopped wage increases but sugared the pill by reducing taxes.* [C13 *suker,* from Old French *çucre,* from Medieval Latin *zuccārum,* from Italian *zucchero,* from Arabic *sukkar,* from Persian *shakar,* from Sanskrit *śarkarā*] —**ˈsugarless** *adj.* —**ˈsugar-ˌlike** *adj.*
sugarallie (ˈʃʊgərˈælɪ) *n. Scot.* liquorice. [C19: from earlier *sugar alicreesh*]
sugar apple *n.* another name for **sweetsop.**
sugar bag *n. Austral. and N.Z.* a small hessian bag occasionally still used, esp. in rural areas, as a rough-and-ready measure for dry goods.
sugar beet *n.* a variety of the plant *Beta vulgaris* that is cultivated for its white roots from which sugar is obtained. Compare **sugar cane.**
sugar bird *n.* a South African nectar-eating bird, *Promerops cafer,* with a long curved bill and long tail: family *Meliphagidae* (honey-eaters).
sugar bush *n.* an anacardiaceous evergreen shrub, *Rhus ovata,* of S California and Arizona, having pale oval leaves, spikes of yellow-tinged red flowers, and deep red fruits.
sugar candy *n.* **1.** Also called: **rock candy.** large crystals of sugar formed by suspending strings in a strong sugar solution that hardens on the strings, used chiefly for sweetening coffee. **2.** *Chiefly U.S.* confectionery; sweets.
sugar cane *n.* a coarse perennial grass, *Saccharum officinarum,* of Old World tropical regions, having tall stout canes that yield sugar: cultivated chiefly in the West Indies and the southern U.S. Compare **sugar beet.**
sugar-coat *vb.* (*tr.*) **1.** to coat or cover with sugar. **2.** to cause to appear more attractive; make agreeable.
sugar corn *n.* another name for **sweet corn** (sense 1).
sugar daddy *n. Slang.* a rich usually middle-aged or old man who bestows expensive gifts on a young person in return for companionship or sexual favours.
sugar diabetes *n.* an informal name for **diabetes mellitus** (see **diabetes**).
sugared (ˈʃʊgəd) *adj.* made sweeter or more appealing with or as with sugar.
sugar glider *n.* a common Australian phalanger, *Petaurus breviceps,* that glides from tree to tree feeding on insects and nectar.
sugar gum *n. Austral.* a small eucalyptus tree, *Eucalyptus cladocalyx,* having smooth bark and barrel-shaped fruits and grown for timber and ornament. It has sweet-tasting leaves which are often eaten by livestock.
sugar loaf *n.* **1.** a large conical mass of hard refined sugar. See also **loaf sugar. 2.** something resembling this in shape.
sugar maple *n.* a North American maple tree, *Acer saccharum,* that is grown as a source of sugar, which is extracted from the sap, and for its hard wood.
sugar of lead (lɛd) *n.* another name for **lead acetate.**
sugar of milk *n.* another name for **lactose.**
sugar pea *n.* another name for **mangetout.**
sugar pine *n.* a pine tree, *Pinus lambertiana,* of California and Oregon, having spreading pendulous branches, light brown cones, and sugary resin.
sugarplum (ˈʃʊgəˌplʌm) *n.* a crystallized plum.
sugar soap *n.* an alkaline compound used for cleaning or stripping paint.
sugary (ˈʃʊgərɪ) *adj.* **1.** of, like, or containing sugar. **2.** containing too much sugar; excessively sweet. **3.** deceptively pleasant; insincere. —**ˈsugariness** *n.*
suggest (səˈdʒɛst, *U.S.* səgˈdʒɛst) *vb.* (*tr.; may take a clause as object*) **1.** to put forward (a plan, idea, etc.) for consideration: *I suggest Smith for the post; a plan suggested itself.* **2.** to evoke (a person, thing, etc.) in the mind of someone by the association of ideas: *that painting suggests home to me.* **3.** to give an indirect or vague hint of: *his face always suggests his peace of mind.* [C16: from Latin *suggerere* to bring up, from SUB- + *gerere* to bring] —**sugˈgester** *n.*
suggestibility (səˌdʒɛstɪˈbɪlɪtɪ) *n. Psychol.* a state, esp. under hypnosis, in which a person will accept the suggestions of another person and act accordingly.
suggestible (səˈdʒɛstɪbᵊl) *adj.* **1.** easily influenced by ideas provided by other persons. **2.** characteristic of something that can be suggested. —**sugˈgestibleness** *n.* —**sugˈgestibly** *adv.*
suggestion (səˈdʒɛstʃən) *n.* **1.** something that is suggested. **2.** a hint or indication: *a suggestion of the odour of violets.* **3.** *Psychol.* the process whereby the mere presentation of an idea to a receptive individual leads to the acceptance of that idea. See also **autosuggestion.**
suggestive (səˈdʒɛstɪv) *adj.* **1.** (*postpositive;* foll. by *of*) conveying a hint (of something): *this painting is suggestive of a hot summer day.* **2.** tending to suggest something improper or indecent. **3.** able or liable to suggest an idea, plan, etc. —**sugˈgestively** *adv.* —**sugˈgestiveness** *n.*
suicidal (ˌsuːɪˈsaɪdᵊl, ˌsjuː-) *adj.* **1.** involving, indicating, or tending towards suicide. **2.** liable to result in suicide: *a suicidal attempt.* **3.** liable to destroy one's own interests or prospects; dangerously rash. —**ˌsuiˈcidally** *adv.*

suicide (ˈsuːɪˌsaɪd, ˈsjuː-) *n.* **1.** the act or an instance of killing oneself intentionally. **2.** the self-inflicted ruin of one's own prospects or interests: *a merger would be financial suicide.* **3.** a person who kills himself intentionally. **4.** (*modifier*) reckless; extremely dangerous: *a suicide mission.* **5.** (*modifier*) (of an action) undertaken or (of a person) undertaking an action in the knowledge that it will result in the death of the person performing it in order that maximum damage may be inflicted on an enemy: *a suicide attack; suicide bomber.* [C17: from New Latin *suīcīdium,* from Latin *suī* of oneself + *-cīdium,* from *caedere* to kill]

sui generis (ˌsuːaɪ ˈdʒɛnərɪs) *adj.* unique. [Latin, literally: of its own kind]

sui juris (ˈsuːaɪ ˈdʒʊərɪs) *adj.* (*usually postpositive*) *Law.* of full age and not under disability; legally competent to manage one's own affairs; independent. [C17: from Latin, literally: of one's own right]

suint (ˈsuːɪnt, swɪnt) *n.* a water-soluble substance found in the fleece of sheep, consisting of peptides, organic acids, metal ions, and inorganic cations and formed from dried perspiration. [C18: from French *suer* to sweat, from Latin *sūdāre*]

suit (suːt, sjuːt) *n.* **1.** any set of clothes of the same or similar material designed to be worn together, now usually (for men) a jacket with matching trousers or (for women) a jacket with matching or contrasting skirt or trousers. **2.** (*in combination*) any outfit worn for a specific purpose: *a spacesuit.* **3.** any set of items, such as the full complement of sails of a vessel or parts of personal armour. **4.** any of the four sets of 13 cards in a pack of playing cards, being spades, hearts, diamonds, and clubs. The cards in each suit are two to ten, jack, queen, and king in the usual order of ascending value, with ace counting as either the highest or lowest according to the game. **5.** a civil proceeding; lawsuit. **6.** the act or process of suing in a court of law. **7.** a petition or appeal made to a person of superior rank or status or the act of making such a petition. **8.** a man's courting of a woman. **9. follow suit. a.** to play a card of the same suit as the card played immediately before it. **b.** to act in the same way as someone else. **10. strong** *or* **strongest suit.** something that one excels in. *~vb.* **11.** to make or be fit or appropriate for: *that dress suits you.* **12.** to meet the requirements or standards (of). **13.** to be agreeable or acceptable to (someone). **14.** (*tr.*) *Archaic.* to supply with clothing. **15. suit oneself.** to pursue one's own intentions without reference to others. [C13: from Old French *sieute* set of things, from *sivre* to follow; compare SUE] —ˈ**suitˌlike** *adj.*

suitable (ˈsuːtəbᵊl, ˈsjuːt-) *adj.* appropriate; proper; fit. —ˌ**suitaˈbility** *or* ˈ**suitableness** *n.* —ˈ**suitably** *adv.*

suitcase (ˈsuːtˌkeɪs, ˈsjuːt-) *n.* a portable rectangular travelling case, usually stiffened, for carrying clothing, etc.

suite (swiːt) *n.* **1.** a series of items intended to be used together; set. **2.** a number of connected rooms in a hotel forming one living unit: *the presidential suite.* **3.** a matching set of furniture, esp. of two armchairs and a settee. **4.** a number of attendants or followers. **5.** *Music.* **a.** an instrumental composition consisting of several movements in the same key based on or derived from dance rhythms, esp. in the baroque period. **b.** an instrumental composition in several movements less closely connected than a sonata. **c.** a piece of music containing movements based on or extracted from music already used in an opera, ballet, play, etc. [C17: from French, from Old French *sieute;* see SUIT]

suiting (ˈsuːtɪŋ, ˈsjuːt-) *n.* a fabric used for suits.

suitor (ˈsuːtə, ˈsjuːt-) *n.* **1.** a man who courts a woman; wooer. **2.** *Law.* a person who brings a suit in a court of law; plaintiff. **3.** *Rare.* a person who makes a request or appeal for anything. [C13: from Anglo-Norman *suter,* from Latin *secūtor* follower, from *sequī* to follow]

sukiyaki (ˌsuːkɪˈjɑːkɪ) *n.* a Japanese dish consisting of very thinly sliced beef or other meat, vegetables, and seasonings cooked together quickly, usually at the table. [from Japanese]

sukkah *or* **succah** (suˈkɑ, ˈsukɔ, ˈsukə) *n.* a temporary structure with a roof of branches in which orthodox Jews eat and, if possible, sleep during the festival of Sukkoth. Also called: **tabernacle.** [from Hebrew, literally: tabernacle]

Sukkoth *or* **Succoth** (ˈsʊkəʊt, -kəʊθ; *Hebrew* suːˈkɔt) *n.* an eight-day Jewish harvest festival beginning on Tishri 15, which commemorates the period when the Israelites lived in the wilderness. Also called: **Feast of Tabernacles.** [from Hebrew, literally: tabernacles]

sulcate (ˈsʌlkeɪt) *adj. Biology.* marked with longitudinal parallel grooves: *sulcate stems.* [C18: via Latin *sulcātus* from *sulcāre* to plough, from *sulcus* a furrow] —**sulˈcation** *n.*

sulcus (ˈsʌlkəs) *n., pl.* **-ci** (-saɪ). **1.** a linear groove, furrow, or slight depression. **2.** any of the narrow grooves on the surface of the brain that mark the cerebral convolutions. Compare **fissure.** [C17: from Latin]

sulf- *combining form.* a U.S. variant of **sulph-.**

sulfamethazine (ˌsʌlfəˈmɛθəˌziːn) *n.* U.S. name for **sulphadimidine.**

sulfur (ˈsʌlfə) *n.* the U.S. preferred spelling of **sulphur.**

sulk (sʌlk) *vb.* **1.** (*intr.*) to be silent and resentful because of a wrong done to one, esp. in order to gain sympathy; brood sullenly: *the child sulked in a corner after being slapped.* *~n.* **2.** (*often pl.*) a state or mood of feeling resentful or sullen: *he's in a sulk because he lost the game; he's got the sulks.* **3.** Also: **sulker.** a person who sulks. [C18: perhaps a back formation from SULKY[1]]

sulky[1] (ˈsʌlkɪ) *adj.* **sulkier, sulkiest. 1.** sullen, withdrawn, or moody, through or as if through resentment. **2.** dull or dismal: *sulky weather.* [C18: perhaps from obsolete *sulke* sluggish, probably related to Old English *āseolcan* to be lazy] —ˈ**sulkily** *adv.* —ˈ**sulkiness** *n.*

sulky[2] (ˈsʌlkɪ) *n., pl.* **sulkies.** a light two-wheeled vehicle for one person, usually drawn by one horse. [C18: from SULKY[1], because it can carry only one person]

sullage (ˈsʌlɪdʒ) *n.* **1.** filth or waste, esp. sewage. **2.** sediment deposited by running water. [C16: perhaps from French *souiller* to sully; compare Old English *sol* mud]

sullen (ˈsʌlən) *adj.* **1.** unwilling to talk or be sociable; sulky; morose. **2.** sombre; gloomy: *a sullen day.* **3.** *Literary.* sluggish; slow: *a sullen stream.* **4.** *Obsolete.* threatening. *~n.* **5.** (*pl.*) *Archaic.* a sullen mood. [C16: perhaps from Anglo-French *solain* (unattested), ultimately related to Latin *sōlus* alone] —ˈ**sullenly** *adv.* —ˈ**sullenness** *n.*

sully (ˈsʌlɪ) *vb.* **-lies, -lying, -lied. 1.** to stain or tarnish (a reputation, etc.) or (of a reputation) to become stained or tarnished. *~n., pl.* **-lies. 2.** a stain. **3.** the act of sullying. [C16: probably from French *souiller* to soil] —ˈ**sulliable** *adj.*

sulph- *or U.S.* **sulf-** *combining form.* containing sulphur: *sulphate; sulphonic acid.*

sulphadiazine (ˌsʌlfəˈdaɪəˌziːn) *n.* an important sulpha drug used chiefly in combination with an antibiotic. Formula: $C_{10}H_{10}N_4O_2S$.

sulphadimidine (ˌsʌlfəˈdaɪmɪˌdiːn) *n.* a sulpha drug used in human and veterinary medicine. There is concern that residues of the drug in pork products may cause cancer, but this has not yet been proved. U.S. name: **sulfamethazine.**

sulpha drug (ˈsʌlfə) *n.* any of a group of sulphonamide compounds that inhibit the activity of bacteria and are used in medicine to treat bacterial infections.

sulphanilamide (ˌsʌlfəˈnɪləˌmaɪd) *n.* a white odourless crystalline compound formerly used in medicine in the treatment of bacterial infections. Formula: $NH_2C_6H_4SO_2NH_2$. See also **sulpha drug.**

sulphate (ˈsʌlfeɪt) *n.* **1.** any salt or ester of sulphuric acid, such as sodium sulphate, Na_2SO_4, sodium hydrogen sulphate, or diethyl sulphate, $(C_2H_5)_2SO_4$. *~vb.* **2.** (*tr.*) to treat with a sulphate or convert into a sulphate. **3.** to undergo or cause to undergo the formation of a layer of lead sulphate on the plates of an accumulator. [C18: from New Latin *sulfātum;* see SULPHUR] —**sulˈphation** *n.*

sulphate-resisting cement *n.* a type of cement that resists normal concentrations of sulphates: used in concrete for flues and underwater work.

sulphathiazole (ˌsʌlfəˈθaɪəˌzəʊl) *n.* a sulpha drug used in veterinary medicine and formerly in clinical medicine. Formula: $C_9H_9N_3O_2S_2$.

sulphide (ˈsʌlfaɪd) *n.* **1.** a compound of sulphur with a more electropositive element. **2.** another name for **thio-ether.**

sulphinyl (ˈsʌlfənɪl) *n.* (*modifier*) another term (no longer in technical usage) for **thionyl.** [C20: from SULF- + -IN + -YL]

sulphisoxazole (ˌsʌlfɪˈsɒksəˌzəʊl) *n.* a sulpha drug used in the treatment of meningitis and certain diseases of the eye, such as trachoma. Formula: $C_{11}H_{13}N_3O_3S$.

sulphite (ˈsʌlfaɪt) *n.* any salt or ester of sulphurous acid, containing the ions SO_3^{2-} or HSO_3^- (**hydrogen sulphite**) or the groups SO_3 or HSO_3. The salts are usually soluble crystalline compounds. —**sulphitic** (sʌlˈfɪtɪk) *adj.*

sulphonamide (sʌlˈfɒnəˌmaɪd) *n.* any of a class of organic compounds that are amides of sulphonic acids containing the group $-SO_2NH_2$ or a group derived from this. An important class of sulphonamides are the sulpha drugs.

sulphonate (ˈsʌlfəˌneɪt) *Chem.* *~n.* **1.** a salt or ester of any sulphonic acid containing the ion RSO_2O^- or the group RSO_2O-, R being an organic group. *~vb.* **2.** (*tr.*) to introduce a sulphonic acid group, SO_2OH, into (a molecule).

sulphone (ˈsʌlfəʊn) *n.* any of a class of organic compounds containing the divalent group SO_2 linked to two other organic groups. Certain sulphones are used in the treatment of leprosy and tuberculosis.

sulphonic acid (sʌlˈfɒnɪk) *n.* any of a large group of strong organic acids that contain the group $-SO_2OH$ and are used in the manufacture of dyes and drugs.

sulphonium compound *or* **salt** (sʌlˈfəʊnɪəm) *n.* any one of a class of salts derived by the addition of a proton to the sulphur atom of a thiol or thio-ether thus producing a positive ion (**sulphonium ion**).

sulphonmethane (ˌsʌlfɒnˈmiːθeɪn) *n.* a colourless crystalline compound used medicinally as a hypnotic. Formula: $C_7H_{16}O_4S_2$.

sulphonyl (ˈsʌlfənɪl) *n.* (*modifier*) another term for **sulphuryl.**

sulphur *or U.S.* **sulfur** (ˈsʌlfə) *n.* **a.** an allotropic nonmetallic element, occurring free in volcanic regions and in combined state in gypsum, pyrite, and galena. The stable yellow rhombic form converts on heating to monoclinic needles. It is used in the production of sulphuric acid, in the vulcanization of rubber, and in fungicides. Symbol: S; atomic no.: 16; atomic wt.: 32.064; valency: 2, 4, or 6; relative density: 2.07 (rhombic), 1.96 (monoclinic); melting pt.: 112.8°C (rhombic), 119.0°C (monoclinic); boiling pt.: 444.6°C. **b.** (*as modifier*): *sulphur springs.* [C14 *soufre,* from Old French, from Latin *sulfur*] —**sulphuric** *or U.S.* **sulfuric** (sʌlˈfjʊərɪk) *adj.*

sulphurate (ˈsʌlfjʊˌreɪt) *vb.* (*tr.*) to combine or treat with sulphur or a sulphur compound. —ˌ**sulphuˈration** *n.*

sulphur-bottom *n.* another name for **blue whale.**

sulphur dioxide *n.* a colourless soluble pungent gas produced by burning sulphur. It is both an oxidizing and a reducing agent and is used in the manufacture of sulphuric acid, the preservation of a wide range of foodstuffs (**E220**), bleaching, and disinfecting. Formula: SO_2. Systematic name: **sulphur(IV) oxide.**

sulphureous (sʌlˈfjʊərɪəs) *adj.* **1.** another word for **sulphurous** (sense 1). **2.** of the yellow colour of sulphur. —**sulˈphureously** *adv.* —**sulˈphureousness** *n.*

sulphuret (ˈsʌlfjʊˌrɛt) *vb.* **-rets, -retting, -retted** *or U.S.* **-rets, -reting, -reted.** (*tr.*) to treat or combine with sulphur.

sulphuretted hydrogen *n.* another name for **hydrogen sulphide.**

sulphuric acid *n.* a colourless dense oily corrosive liquid produced by the reaction of sulphur trioxide with water and used in accumulators and in the manufacture of fertilizers, dyes, and explosives. Formula: H_2SO_4. Systematic name: **sulphuric(VI) acid.**

sulphurize *or* **sulphurise** (ˈsʌlfjʊˌraɪz) *vb.* (*tr.*) to combine or treat with sulphur or a sulphur compound. —ˌ**sulphuriˈzation** *or* ˌ**sulfuriˈsation** *n.*

sulphurous (ˈsʌlfərəs) *adj.* **1.** Also: **sulphureous.** of, relating to, or resembling sulphur: *a sulphurous colour.* **2.** of or containing sulphur with an oxidation state of 4: *sulphurous acid.* **3.** of or relating to hellfire. **4.** hot-tempered. —ˈ**sulphurously** *adv.* —ˈ**sulphurousness** *n.*

sulphurous acid *n.* an unstable acid produced when sulphur dioxide dissolves in water: used as a preservative for food and a bleaching agent. Formula: H_2SO_3. Systematic name: **sulphuric(IV) acid.**

sulphur trioxide *n.* a white corrosive substance existing in three crystalline forms of which the stable (*alpha-*) form is usually obtained as silky needles. It is produced by the oxidation of sulphur dioxide, and is used in the sulphonation of organic compounds. Formula: SO_3. Systematic name: **sulphur(VI) oxide.**

sulphur tuft *n.* a poisonous basidiomycetous fungus, *Hypholoma fasciculare,* having a sulphurous yellow cap and found in clumps on and around broad-leaved trees.

sulphuryl (ˈsʌlfjʊrɪl, -fərɪl) *n.* (*modifier*) of, consisting of, or containing the divalent group, $=SO_2$: *sulphuryl chloride.* Also: **sulphonyl** (ˈsʌlfəˌnɪl).

sultan (ˈsʌltən) *n.* **1.** the sovereign of a Muslim country, esp. of the former Ottoman Empire. **2.** an arbitrary ruler; despot. **3.** a small domestic fowl with a white crest and heavily feathered legs and feet: originated in Turkey. [C16: from Medieval Latin *sultānus,* from Arabic *sultān* rule, from Aramaic *salita* to rule] —**sultanic** (sʌlˈtænɪk) *adj.* —ˈ**sultan-ˌlike** *adj.* —ˈ**sultanship** *n.*

sultana (sʌlˈtɑːnə) *n.* **1. a.** the dried fruit of a small white seedless grape, originally produced in SW Asia: used in cakes, curries, etc.; seedless raisin. **b.** the grape itself. **2.** Also called: **sultaness.** a wife, concubine, or female relative of a sultan. **3.** a mistress; concubine. [C16: from Italian, feminine of *sultano* SULTAN]

sultanate (ˈsʌltəˌneɪt) *n.* **1.** the territory or a country ruled by a sultan. **2.** the office, rank, or jurisdiction of a sultan.

sultry (ˈsʌltrɪ) *adj.* **-trier, -triest. 1.** (of weather or climate) oppressively hot and humid. **2.** characterized by or emitting oppressive heat. **3.** displaying or suggesting passion; sensual: *sultry eyes.* [C16: from obsolete *sulter* to SWELTER + -Y[1]] —ˈ**sultrily** *adv.* —ˈ**sultriness** *n.*

sum (sʌm) *n.* **1. a.** the result of the addition of numbers, quantities, objects, etc. **b.** the cardinality of the union of disjoint sets whose cardinalities are the given numbers. **2.** one or more columns or rows of numbers to be added, subtracted, multiplied, or divided. **3.** *Maths.* the limit of a series of sums of the first *n* terms of a converging infinite series as *n* tends to infinity. **4.** (*pl.*) another name for **number work. 5.** a quantity, esp. of money: *he borrows enormous sums.* **6.** the essence or gist of a matter (esp. in the phrases **in sum, in sum and substance**). **7.** a less common word for **summary. 8.** *Archaic.* the summit or maximum. **9.** (*modifier*) complete or final (esp. in the phrase **sum total**). ~*vb.* **sums, summing, summed. 10.** (often foll. by *up*) to add or form a total of (something). **11.** (*tr.*) to calculate the sum of (the terms in a sequence). ~See also **sum up.** [C13 *summe,* from Old French, from Latin *summa* the top, sum, from *summus* highest, from *superus* in a higher position; see SUPER]

sumach *or U.S.* **sumac** (ˈsuːmæk, ˈʃuː-) *n.* **1.** any temperate or subtropical shrub or small tree of the anacardiaceous genus *Rhus,* having compound leaves, clusters of green flowers, and red hairy fruits. See also **poison sumach. 2.** a preparation of powdered leaves of certain species of *Rhus,* esp. *R. coriaria,* used in dyeing and tanning. **3.** the wood of any of these plants. [C14: via Old French from Arabic *summāq*]

Sumatran (sʊˈmɑːtrᵊn) *adj.* **1.** of or relating to Sumatra, an island in W Indonesia, or to its people, culture, etc. ~*n.* **2.** a native or inhabitant of Sumatra.

Sumerian (suːˈmɪərɪən, -ˈmɛər-) *n.* **1.** a member of a people who established a civilization in Sumer, the S region of Babylonia in SW Asia, during the 4th millennium B.C. **2.** the extinct language of this people, of no known relationship to any other language. ~*adj.* **3.** of or relating to ancient Sumer, its inhabitants, or their language or civilization.

summa (ˈsʊmɑː) *n., pl.* **-mae** (-miː). **1.** *Medieval Christianity theol.* a compendium of theology, philosophy, or canon law, or sometimes of all three together. The **Summa Theologica** of St Thomas Aquinas, written between 1265 and 1274, was the most famous of all such compendia. **2.** *Rare.* a comprehensive work or survey. [C15: from Latin: SUM]

summa cum laude (ˈsʊmɑː kʊm ˈlaʊdeɪ) *adv., adj. Chiefly U.S.* with the utmost praise: the highest of three designations for above-average achievement in examinations. In Britain it is sometimes used to designate a first-class honours degree. [from Latin]

summand (ˈsʌmænd, sʌˈmænd) *n.* a number or quantity forming part of a sum. [C19: from Medieval Latin *summandus,* from Latin *summa* SUM]

summarize *or* **summarise** (ˈsʌməˌraɪz) *vb.* (*tr.*) to make or be a summary of; express concisely. —ˈ**summaˌrizable** *or* ˈ**summaˌrisable** *adj.* —ˌ**summariˈzation** *or* ˌ**summariˈsation** *n.* —ˈ**summaˌrizer,** ˈ**summaˌriser,** *or* ˈ**summarist** *n.*

summary (ˈsʌmərɪ) *n., pl.* **-maries. 1.** a brief account giving the main points of something. ~*adj.* (*usually prenominal*). **2.** performed arbitrarily and quickly, without formality: *a summary execution.* **3.** (of legal proceedings) short and free from the complexities and delays of a full trial. **4. summary jurisdiction.** the right a court has to adjudicate immediately upon some matter arising during its proceedings. **5.** giving the gist or essence. [C15: from Latin *summārium,* from *summa* SUM] —ˈ**summarily** *adv.* —ˈ**summariness** *n.*

summary offence *n.* an offence that is triable in a magistrates' court.

summation (sʌˈmeɪʃən) *n.* **1.** the act or process of determining a sum; addition. **2.** the result of such an act or process. **3.** a summary. **4.** *U.S. law.* the concluding statements made by opposing counsel in a case before a court. [C18: from Medieval Latin *summātiō,* from *summāre* to total, from Latin *summa* SUM] —**sumˈmational** *adj.* —ˈ**summative** *adj.*

summative assessment (ˈsʌmətɪv) *n. Brit. educ.* general assessment of a pupil's achievements over a range of subjects by means of a combined appraisal of formative assessments.

summer[1] (ˈsʌmə) *n.* **1.** (*sometimes cap.*) **a.** the warmest season of the year, between spring and autumn, astronomically from the June solstice to the September equinox in the N hemisphere and at the opposite time of year in the S hemisphere. **b.** (*as modifier*): *summer flowers; a summer dress.* Related adj.: **aestival. 2.** the period of hot weather associated with the summer. **3.** a time of blossoming, greatest happiness, etc. **4.** *Chiefly poetic.* a year represented by this season: *a child of nine summers.* ~*vb.* **5.** (*intr.*) to spend the summer (at a place). **6.** (*tr.*) to keep or feed (farm animals) during the summer: *they summered their cattle on the mountain slopes.* [Old English *sumor;* related to Old Frisian *sumur,* Old Norse *sumar,* Old High German *sumar,* Sanskrit *samā* season] —ˈ**summerless** *adj.* —ˈ**summer-ˌlike** *adj.* —ˈ**summerly** *adj., adv.* —ˈ**summery** *adj.* —ˈ**summeriness** *n.*

summer[2] (ˈsʌmə) *n.* **1.** Also called: **summer tree.** a large horizontal beam or girder, esp. one that supports floor joists. **2.** another name for **lintel. 3.** a stone on the top of a column, pier, or wall that supports an arch or lintel. [C14: from Anglo-Norman *somer,* from Old French *somier* beam, packhorse, from Late Latin *sagmārius* (*equus*) pack(horse), from *sagma* a packsaddle, from Greek]

summer cypress *n.* another name for **kochia.**

summerhouse (ˈsʌməˌhaʊs) *n.* a small building in a garden or park, used for shade or recreation in the summer.

summer pudding *n. Brit.* a pudding made by filling a bread-lined basin with a purée of fruit, leaving it to soak, and then turning it out.

summersault (ˈsʌməˌsɔːlt) *n., vb.* a variant spelling of **somersault.**

summer school *n.* a school, academic course, etc., held during the summer.

summer solstice *n.* **1.** the time at which the sun is at its northernmost point in the sky (southernmost point in the S hemisphere), appearing at noon at its highest altitude above the horizon. It occurs about June 21 (December 22 in the S hemisphere). **2.** *Astronomy.* the point on the celestial sphere, opposite the **winter solstice,** at which the ecliptic is furthest north from the celestial equator. Right ascension: 6 hours; declination: 23.5°.

summertime (ˈsʌməˌtaɪm) *n.* the period or season of summer.

summer time *n. Brit.* any daylight-saving time, esp. British Summer Time.

summerweight (ˈsʌməˌweɪt) *adj.* (of clothes) suitable in weight for wear in the summer; relatively light.

summerwood (ˈsʌməˌwʊd) *n.* the wood that is produced by a plant near the end of the growing season: consists of small thick-walled xylem cells. Compare **springwood.**

summing-up *n.* **1.** a review or summary of the main points of an argument, speech, etc. **2.** a direction regarding the law and a summary of the evidence, given by a judge in his address to the jury before they retire to consider their verdict.

summit ('sʌmɪt) *n.* **1.** the highest point or part, esp. of a mountain or line of communication; top. **2.** the highest possible degree or state; peak or climax: *the summit of ambition.* **3.** the highest level, importance, or rank: *a meeting at the summit.* **4. a.** a meeting of chiefs of governments or other high officials. **b.** (*as modifier*): *a summit conference.* [C15: from Old French *somet,* diminutive of *som,* from Latin *summum;* see SUM] —'**summital** *adj.* —'**summitless** *adj.*

summitry ('sʌmɪtrɪ) *n. Chiefly U.S.* the practice of conducting international negotiations by summit conferences.

summon ('sʌmən) *vb.* (*tr.*) **1.** to order to come; send for, esp. to attend court, by issuing a summons. **2.** to order or instruct (to do something) or call (to something): *the bell summoned them to their work.* **3.** to call upon to meet or convene. **4.** (often foll. by *up*) to muster or gather (one's strength, courage, etc.). **5.** *Archaic.* to call upon to surrender. [C13: from Latin *summonēre* to give a discreet reminder, from *monēre* to advise] —'**summonable** *adj.*

summons ('sʌmənz) *n., pl.* **-monses. 1.** a call, signal, or order to do something, esp. to appear in person or attend at a specified place or time. **2. a.** an official order requiring a person to attend court, either to answer a charge or to give evidence. **b.** the writ making such an order. Compare **warrant. 3.** a call or command given to the members of an assembly to convene a meeting. ~*vb.* **4.** to take out a summons against (a person). [C13: from Old French *somonse,* from *somondre* to SUMMON]

summum bonum *Latin.* ('sʊmʊm 'bɒnʊm) *n.* the principle of goodness in which all moral values are included or from which they are derived; highest or supreme good.

sumo ('suːməʊ) *n.* the national style of wrestling of Japan, the object of which is to force one's opponent to touch the ground with any part of his body except the soles of his feet or to step out of the ring. [from Japanese *sumō*]

sump (sʌmp) *n.* **1.** a receptacle, such as the lower part of the crankcase of an internal-combustion engine, into which liquids, esp. lubricants, can drain to form a reservoir. **2.** another name for **cesspool. 3.** *Mining.* **a.** a depression at the bottom of a shaft where water collects before it is pumped away. **b.** the front portion of a shaft or tunnel, ahead of the main bore. **4.** *Brit. dialect.* a muddy pool or swamp. [C17: from Middle Dutch *somp* marsh; see SWAMP]

sumph (sʌmf) *n. Scot.* a stupid person; simpleton. [C18: of uncertain origin]

sumpter ('sʌmptə) *n. Archaic.* a packhorse, mule, or other beast of burden. [C14: from Old French *sometier* driver of a baggage horse, from Vulgar Latin *sagmatārius* (unattested), from Late Latin *sagma* packsaddle]

sumptuary ('sʌmptjʊərɪ) *adj.* relating to or controlling expenditure or extravagance. [C17: from Latin *sumptuārius* concerning expense, from *sumptus* expense, from *sūmere* to spend]

sumptuary law *n.* (formerly) a law imposing restraint on luxury, esp. by limiting personal expenditure or by regulating personal conduct in religious and moral spheres.

sumptuous ('sʌmptjʊəs) *adj.* **1.** expensive or extravagant: *sumptuous costumes.* **2.** magnificent; splendid: *a sumptuous scene.* [C16: from Old French *somptueux,* from Latin *sumptuōsus* costly, from *sumptus;* see SUMPTUARY] —'**sumptuously** *adv.* —'**sumptuousness** *or* **sumptuosity** (ˌsʌmptjʊ'ɒsɪtɪ) *n.*

sum up *vb.* (*adv.*) **1.** to summarize (feelings, the main points of an argument, etc.): *the judge began to sum up.* **2.** (*tr.*) to form a quick opinion of: *I summed him up in five minutes.*

sun (sʌn) *n.* **1.** the star that is the source of heat and light for the planets in the solar system. It is a gaseous body having a highly compressed core, in which energy is generated by thermonuclear reactions (at about 20 million °C), surrounded by a less dense convective zone serving to transport the energy to the surface (the **photosphere**). The atmospheric layers (the **chromosphere** and **corona**) are normally invisible except during a total eclipse. Mass and diameter: 333 000 and 109 times that of earth respectively; mean distance from earth: 149.6 million km (1 astronomical unit). Related adj.: **solar. 2.** any star around which a planetary system revolves. **3.** the sun as it appears at a particular time or place: *the winter sun.* **4.** the radiant energy, esp. heat and light, received from the sun; sunshine. **5.** a person or thing considered as a source of radiant warmth, glory, etc. **6.** a pictorial representation of the sun, often depicted with a human face. **7.** *Poetic.* a year or a day. **8.** *Poetic.* a climate. **9.** *Archaic.* sunrise or sunset (esp. in the phrase **from sun to sun**). **10. catch the sun.** to become slightly sunburnt. **11. place in the sun.** a prominent or favourable position. **12. take** *or* **shoot the sun.** *Nautical.* to measure the altitude of the sun in order to determine latitude. **13. touch of the sun.** slight sunstroke. **14. under** *or* **beneath the sun.** on earth; at all: *nobody under the sun eats more than you do.* ~*vb.* **suns, sunning, sunned. 15.** to expose (oneself) to the sunshine. **16.** (*tr.*) to expose to the sunshine in order to warm, tan, etc. [Old English *sunne;* related to Old High German *sunna,* Old Frisian *senne,* Gothic *sunno*] —'**sunˌlike** *adj.*

Sun. *abbrev. for* Sunday.

sunbake ('sʌnˌbeɪk) *Austral. informal.* ~*vb.* (*intr.*) **1.** to sunbathe, esp. in order to become tanned. ~*n.* **2.** a period of sunbaking.

sunbaked ('sʌnˌbeɪkt) *adj.* **1.** (esp. of roads, etc.) dried or cracked by the sun's heat. **2.** baked hard by the heat of the sun: *sunbaked bricks.*

sun bath *n.* the exposure of the body to the rays of the sun or a sun lamp, esp. in order to get a suntan.

sunbathe ('sʌnˌbeɪð) *vb.* (*intr.*) to bask in the sunshine, esp. in order to get a suntan. —'**sunˌbather** *n.*

sunbeam ('sʌnˌbiːm) *n.* **1.** a beam, ray, or stream of sunlight. **2.** *Austral. slang.* a piece of crockery or cutlery laid for a meal but remaining unused. —'**sunˌbeamed** *or* '**sunˌbeamy** *adj.*

sun bear *n.* a small bear, *Helarctos malayanus,* of tropical forests in S and SE Asia, having a black coat and a yellowish snout and feeding mostly on honey and insects. Also called: **honey bear.**

sunbird ('sʌnˌbɜːd) *n.* any small songbird of the family *Nectariniidae,* of tropical regions of the Old World, esp. Africa, having a long slender curved bill and a bright plumage in the males.

sun bittern *n.* a cranelike bird, *Eurypyga helias,* of tropical American forests, having a greyish plumage with orange and brown wings: family *Eurypygidae,* order *Gruiformes* (cranes, rails, etc.).

sun blind *n. Chiefly Brit.* a blind, such as a Venetian blind, that shades a room from the sun's glare.

sun block *n.* a chemical, usually in the form of a cream, applied to exposed skin to block out all or almost all of the ultraviolet rays of the sun.

sunbonnet ('sʌnˌbɒnɪt) *n.* a hat that shades the face and neck from the sun, esp. one of cotton with a projecting brim now worn esp. by babies. —'**sunˌbonneted** *adj.*

sunbow ('sʌnˌbəʊ) *n.* a bow of prismatic colours similar to a rainbow, produced when sunlight shines through spray.

sunburn ('sʌnˌbɜːn) *n.* **1.** inflammation of the skin caused by overexposure to the sun. Technical name: **erythema solare. 2.** another word for **suntan.** —'**sunˌburnt** *or* '**sunˌburned** *adj.*

sunburst ('sʌnˌbɜːst) *n.* **1.** a burst of sunshine, as through a break in the clouds. **2.** a pattern or design resembling that of the sun. **3.** a jewelled brooch with this pattern.

sunburst pleats *pl. n.* the U.S. term for **sunray pleats.**

sun-cured *adj.* cured or preserved by exposure to the sun.

sundae ('sʌndɪ, -deɪ) *n.* ice cream topped with a sweet sauce, nuts, whipped cream, etc. [C20: of uncertain origin]

sun dance *n.* a North American Indian ceremony associated with the sun, performed at the summer solstice.

Sunday ('sʌndɪ) *n.* the first day of the week and the Christian day of worship. [Old English *sunnandæg,* translation of Latin *diēs sōlis* day of the sun, translation of Greek *hēmera hēliou;* related to Old Norse *sunnu dagr,* German *Sonntag*]

Sunday best *n.* one's best clothes, esp. regarded as those most suitable for churchgoing.

Sunday painter *n.* a person who paints pictures as a hobby.

Sunday punch *n. Informal, chiefly U.S.* **1.** *Boxing.* a heavy blow intended to knock out one's opponent. **2.** any manoeuvre or action intended to crush an opponent.

Sunday school *n.* **1. a.** a school for the religious instruction of children on Sundays, usually held in a church and formerly also providing secular education. **b.** (*as modifier*): *a Sunday-school outing.* **2.** the members of such a school.

sun deck *n.* **1.** an upper open deck on a passenger ship. **2.** *Austral. and N.Z.* a balcony or deck attached to a house, used for sunbathing.

sunder ('sʌndə) *Archaic or literary.* ~*vb.* **1.** to break or cause to break apart or in pieces. ~*n.* **2. in sunder.** into pieces; apart. [Old English *sundrian;* related to Old Norse *sundr* asunder, Gothic *sundrō* apart, Old High German *suntar,* Latin *sine* without] —'**sunderable** *adj.* —'**sunderance** *n.* —'**sunderer** *n.*

sundew ('sʌnˌdjuː) *n.* any of several bog plants of the genus *Drosera,* having leaves covered with sticky hairs that trap and digest insects: family *Droseraceae.* [C16: translation of Latin *ros solis*]

sundial ('sʌnˌdaɪəl) *n.* a device indicating the time during the hours of sunlight by means of a stationary arm (the **gnomon**) that casts a shadow onto a plate or surface marked in hours at right angles to the gnomon.

sun disc *n.* a disc symbolizing the sun, esp. one flanked by two serpents and the extended wings of a vulture, used as a religious figure in ancient Egypt.

sundog ('sʌnˌdɒg) *n.* **1.** another word for **parhelion. 2.** a small rainbow or halo near the horizon.

sundown ('sʌnˌdaʊn) *n.* another name for **sunset.**

sundowner ('sʌnˌdaʊnə) *n.* **1.** *Austral. and N.Z. obsolete slang.* a tramp, esp. one who seeks food and lodging at sundown when it is too late to work. **2.** *Nautical.* a strict ship's officer. **3.** *Informal, chiefly Brit.* an alcoholic drink taken at sunset. **4.** *N.Z. slang.* a lazy sheepdog.

sundress ('sʌnˌdrɛs) *n.* a dress for hot weather that exposes the shoulders, arms, and back, esp. one with straps over the shoulders.

sun-dried *adj.* dried or preserved by exposure to the sun.

sundry ('sʌndrɪ) *determiner.* **1.** several or various; miscellaneous. ~*pron.* **2. all and sundry.** all the various people, individually and collectively. ~*n., pl.* **-dries. 3.** (*pl.*) miscellaneous unspecified items. **4.** the Austral. name for **extra** (sense 6).

[Old English *syndrig* separate; related to Old High German *suntarīg;* see SUNDER, -Y[1]]

sundry shop *n.* (in Malaysia) a shop, similar to a delicatessen, that sells predominantly Chinese foodstuffs.

sunfast ('sʌnˌfɑːst) *adj. Chiefly U.S. and Canadian.* not fading in sunlight.

sunfish ('sʌnˌfɪʃ) *n., pl.* **-fish** *or* **-fishes. 1.** any large plectognath fish of the family *Molidae,* of temperate and tropical seas, esp. *Mola mola,* which has a large rounded compressed body, long pointed dorsal and anal fins, and a fringelike tail fin. **2.** any of various small predatory North American freshwater percoid fishes of the family *Centrarchidae,* typically having a compressed brightly coloured body.

sunflower ('sʌnˌflaʊə) *n.* **1.** any of several American plants of the genus *Helianthus,* esp. *H. annuus,* having very tall thick stems, large flower heads with yellow rays, and seeds used as food, esp. for poultry: family *Compositae* (composites). See also **Jerusalem artichoke. 2. sunflower seed oil.** the oil extracted from sunflower seeds, used as a salad oil, in the manufacture of margarine, etc.

sung (sʌŋ) *vb.* **1.** the past participle of **sing.** *~adj.* **2.** produced by singing: *a sung syllable.*

▷**Usage.** See at **ring**[2].

Sung *or* **Song** (sʊŋ) *adj.* of or relating to an imperial dynasty of China (960–1279 A.D.), notable for its art, literature, and philosophy: *Sung pottery.*

sunglass ('sʌnˌglɑːs) *n.* a convex lens used to focus the sun's rays and thus produce heat or ignition; burning glass.

sunglasses ('sʌnˌglɑːsɪz) *pl. n.* glasses with darkened or polarizing lenses that protect the eyes from the sun's glare.

sunglow ('sʌnˌgləʊ) *n.* a pinkish glow often seen in the sky before sunrise or after sunset. It is caused by scattering or diffraction of sunlight by particles in the atmosphere.

sun-god *n.* **1.** the sun considered as a personal deity. **2.** a deity associated with the sun or controlling its movements.

sungrebe ('sʌnˌgriːb) *n.* another name for **finfoot.**

sunhat ('sʌnˌhæt) *n.* a hat that shades the face and neck from the sun.

sunk (sʌŋk) *vb.* **1.** a past tense and past participle of **sink.** *~adj.* **2.** *Informal.* with all hopes dashed; ruined: *if the police come while we're opening the safe, we'll be sunk.* *~n.* **3.** *Scot. dialect.* a cellar or basement.

sunken ('sʌŋkən) *vb.* **1.** a past participle of **sink.** *~adj.* **2.** unhealthily hollow: *sunken cheeks.* **3.** situated at a lower level than the surrounding or usual one. **4.** situated under water; submerged. **5.** depressed; low: *sunken spirits.*

sunk fence *n.* a ditch, one side of which is made into a retaining wall so as to enclose an area of land while remaining hidden in the total landscape. Also called: **ha-ha.**

sun lamp *n.* **1.** a lamp that generates ultraviolet rays, used for obtaining an artificial suntan, for muscular therapy, etc. **2.** a lamp used in film studios, etc., to give an intense beam of light by means of parabolic mirrors.

sunless ('sʌnlɪs) *adj.* **1.** without sun or sunshine. **2.** gloomy; depressing. —'**sunlessly** *adv.* —'**sunlessness** *n.*

sunlight ('sʌnlaɪt) *n.* **1.** the light emanating from the sun. **2.** an area or the time characterized by sunshine. —'**sunlit** *adj.*

sun lounge *or U.S.* **sun parlor** *n.* a room with large windows positioned to receive as much sunlight as possible.

sunn (sʌn) *n.* **1.** a leguminous plant, *Crotalaria juncea,* of the East Indies, having yellow flowers. **2.** the hemplike fibre obtained from the inner bark of this plant, used in making rope, sacking, etc. [C18: from Hindi *san,* from Sanskrit *śāṇá* hempen]

Sunna ('sʌnə) *n.* the body of traditional Islamic law accepted by most orthodox Muslims as based on the words and acts of Mohammed. [C18: from Arabic *sunnah* rule]

Sunni ('sʌnɪ) *n.* **1.** one of the two main branches of orthodox Islam (the other being the Shiah), consisting of those who acknowledge the authority of the Sunna. **2.** (*pl.* **-ni**) a less common word for **Sunnite.**

Sunnite ('sʌnaɪt) *n. Islam.* an adherent of the Sunni.

sunny ('sʌnɪ) *adj.* **-nier, -niest. 1.** full of or exposed to sunlight. **2.** radiating good humour. **3.** of or resembling the sun. —'**sunnily** *adv.* —'**sunniness** *n.*

sunny side *n.* **1.** the cheerful aspect or point of view: *look on the sunny side of things.* **2. on the sunny side of.** *Informal.* younger than (a specified age).

sunny-side up *adj.* (of eggs) fried on one side only.

sunray pleats ('sʌnˌreɪ) *pl. n. Brit.* bias-cut knife pleats that are narrower at the top than at the bottom, producing a flared effect, used esp. for skirts. U.S. term: **sunburst pleats.**

sunrise ('sʌnˌraɪz) *n.* **1.** the daily appearance of the sun above the horizon. **2.** the atmospheric phenomena accompanying this appearance. **3.** Also called (esp. U.S.): **sunup.** the time at which the sun rises at a particular locality. **4.** (*modifier*) of or relating to sunrise industry: *sunrise technology; sunrise sector.*

sunrise industry *n.* any of the high-technology industries, such as electronics, that hold promise of future development.

sunroof ('sʌnˌruːf) *or* **sunshine roof** *n.* a panel, often translucent, that may be opened in the roof of a car.

sunset ('sʌnˌsɛt) *n.* **1.** the daily disappearance of the sun below the horizon. **2.** the atmospheric phenomena accompanying this disappearance. **3.** Also called: **sundown.** the time at which the sun sets at a particular locality. **4.** the final stage or closing period, as of a person's life.

sunshade ('sʌnˌʃeɪd) *n.* a device, esp. a parasol or awning, serving to shade from the sun.

sunshine ('sʌnˌʃaɪn) *n.* **1.** the light received directly from the sun. **2.** the warmth from the sun. **3.** a sunny area. **4.** a light-hearted or ironic term of address. —'**sunˌshiny** *adj.*

sunspot ('sʌnˌspɒt) *n.* any of the dark cool patches, with a diameter of up to several thousand kilometres, that appear on the surface of the sun and last about a week. They occur in approximately 11-year cycles and possess a strong magnetic field. —'**sunˌspotted** *adj.*

sunstar ('sʌnˌstɑː) *n.* any starfish of the genus *Solaster,* having up to 13 arms radiating from a central disc.

sunstone ('sʌnˌstəʊn) *n.* another name for **aventurine** (sense 2). [C17: so called because it contains red and gold flecks which reflect the light]

sunstroke ('sʌnˌstrəʊk) *n.* heatstroke caused by prolonged exposure to intensely hot sunlight.

sunsuit ('sʌnˌsuːt, -ˌsjuːt) *n.* a child's outfit consisting of a brief top and shorts or a short skirt.

suntan ('sʌnˌtæn) *n.* **a.** a brownish colouring of the skin caused by the formation of the pigment melanin within the skin on exposure to the ultraviolet rays of the sun or a sunlamp. Often shortened to **tan. b.** (*as modifier*): *suntan oil.* —'**sunˌtanned** *adj.*

suntrap ('sʌnˌtræp) *n.* a very sunny sheltered place.

sunup ('sʌnˌʌp) *n.* another name (esp. U.S.) for **sunrise** (sense 3).

sunward ('sʌnwəd) *adj.* **1.** directed or moving towards the sun. *~adv.* **2.** a variant of **sunwards.**

sunwards ('sʌnwədz) *or* **sunward** *adv.* towards the sun.

sunwise ('sʌnˌwaɪz) *adv.* moving in the same direction as the sun; clockwise.

suo jure ('suːəʊ 'dʒʊərɪ) *adv. Chiefly law.* in one's own right. [Latin]

suo loco ('suːəʊ 'lɒkəʊ) *adv. Chiefly law.* in a person or thing's own or rightful place. [Latin]

sup[1] (sʌp) *vb.* **sups, supping, supped. 1.** (*intr.*) *Archaic.* to have supper. **2.** (*tr.*) *Obsolete.* to provide with supper. [C13: from Old French *soper;* see SUP[2]]

sup[2] (sʌp) *vb.* **sups, supping, supped. 1.** to partake of (liquid) by swallowing a little at a time. **2.** *Scot. and northern English dialect.* to drink. *~n.* **3.** a sip. [Old English *sūpan;* related to Old High German *sūfan,* German *saufen;* see also SUP[1]]

sup. *abbrev. for:* **1.** above. [from Latin *supra*] **2.** superior. **3.** *Grammar.* superlative. **4.** supine (noun). **5.** supplement. **6.** supplementary. **7.** supply.

sup. ben. *Informal. abbrev. for* supplementary benefit.

super ('suːpə) *adj.* **1.** *Informal.* outstanding; exceptionally fine. *~n.* **2.** petrol with a high octane rating. **3.** *Informal.* a superintendent or supervisor. **4.** *Austral. and N.Z. informal.* superannuation benefits. **5.** *Austral. and N.Z. informal.* superphosphate. *~interj.* **6.** *Brit. informal.* an enthusiastic expression of approval or assent. [from Latin: above]

super. *abbrev. for:* **1.** superfine. **2.** superior. **3.** supernumerary.

super- *prefix.* **1.** placed above or over: *superscript.* **2.** of greater size, extent, quality, etc.: *supermarket.* **3.** surpassing others; outstanding: *superstar.* **4.** beyond a standard or norm; exceeding or exceedingly: *supersonic.* **5.** indicating that a chemical compound contains a specified element in a higher proportion than usual: *superoxide.* [from Latin *super* above]

superable ('suːpərəbᵊl, -prəbᵊl) *adj.* able to be surmounted or overcome. [C17: from Latin *superābilis,* from *superāre* to overcome] —ˌ**superaˈbility** *or* '**superableness** *n.* —'**superably** *adv.*

superabound (ˌsuːpərəˈbaʊnd) *vb.* **1.** (*intr.*) to abound abnormally; be in surplus. **2.** *Rare.* to be more abundant than (something else). —**superabundance** (ˌsuːpərəˈbʌndəns) *n.* —ˌ**superaˈbundant** *adj.*

superadd (ˌsuːpərˈæd) *vb.* (*tr.*) to add (something) to something that has already been added; add as extra. —ˌ**superadˈdition** *n.* —ˌ**superadˈditional** *adj.*

superaerodynamics (ˌsuːpəˌɛərəʊdaɪˈnæmɪks) *n.* (*functioning as sing.*) the study of aerodynamics at very high altitudes, where the air density is very low.

superaltar ('suːpərˌɔːltə) *n. Christianity.* a consecrated portable stone slab for use on an unconsecrated altar.

superannuate (ˌsuːpərˈænjʊˌeɪt) *vb.* (*tr.*) **1.** to pension off. **2.** to discard as obsolete or old-fashioned.

superannuated (ˌsuːpərˈænjʊˌeɪtɪd) *adj.* **1.** discharged, esp. with a pension, owing to age or illness. **2.** too old to serve usefully. **3.** obsolete. [C17: from Medieval Latin *superannātus* aged more than one year, from Latin SUPER- + *annus* a year]

ˌ**superacˈcommodating** *adj.*
ˌ**superacˈcomplished** *adj.*
ˌ**superˈactive** *adj.*
ˌ**superamˈbitious** *adj.*

superannuation (ˌsuːpərˌænjʊˈeɪʃən) *n.* **1. a.** the amount deducted regularly from employees' incomes in a contributory pension scheme. **b.** the pension finally paid to such employees. **2.** the act or process of superannuating or the condition of being superannuated.

superb (sʊˈpɜːb, sjʊ-) *adj.* **1.** surpassingly good; excellent: *a superb actor.* **2.** majestic or imposing: *a superb mansion.* **3.** magnificently rich; luxurious: *the jubilee was celebrated with a superb banquet.* [C16: from Old French *superbe,* from Latin *superbus* distinguished, from *super* above] —**suˈperbly** *adv.* —**suˈperbness** *n.*

superbazaar *or* **superbazar** (ˈsuːpəbəˈzɑː) *n.* (in India) a large department store or supermarket, esp. one set up as a cooperative store by the government.

Super Bowl *n. American football.* the main championship game of the sport, held annually in January between the champions of the American Football Conference and the National Football Conference.

supercalender (ˌsuːpəˈkæləndə) *n.* **1.** a calender with a number of rollers that gives a high gloss to paper. ~*vb.* **2.** (*tr.*) to produce a glossy finish on (paper) by pressing in a supercalender. —ˌ**superˈcalendered** *adj.*

supercargo (ˌsuːpəˈkɑːgəʊ) *n., pl.* **-goes.** an officer on a merchant ship who supervises commercial matters and is in charge of the cargo. [C17: changed from Spanish *sobrecargo,* from *sobre* over (from Latin SUPER) + *cargo* CARGO]

supercharge (ˈsuːpəˌtʃɑːdʒ) *vb.* (*tr.*) **1.** to increase the intake pressure of (an internal-combustion engine) with a supercharger; boost. **2.** to charge (the atmosphere, a remark, etc.) with an excess amount of (tension, emotion, etc.). **3.** to apply pressure to (a fluid); pressurize.

supercharger (ˈsuːpəˌtʃɑːdʒə) *n.* a device, usually a fan or compressor, that increases the mass of air drawn into an internal-combustion engine by raising the intake pressure. Also called: **blower, booster.**

superciliary (ˌsuːpəˈsɪlɪərɪ) *adj.* relating to or situated over the eyebrow or a corresponding region in lower animals. [C18: from New Latin *superciliaris,* from Latin *supercilium,* from SUPER- + *cilium* eyelid]

supercilious (ˌsuːpəˈsɪlɪəs) *adj.* displaying arrogant pride, scorn, or indifference. [C16: from Latin *superciliōsus,* from *supercilium* eyebrow; see SUPERCILIARY] —ˌ**superˈciliously***adv.* —ˌ**superˈciliousness** *n.*

superclass (ˈsuːpəˌklɑːs) *n.* a taxonomic group that is a subdivision of a subphylum.

supercolumnar (ˌsuːpəkəˈlʌmnə) *adj. Architect.* **1.** having one colonnade above another. **2.** placed above a colonnade or a column. —ˌ**supercolˌumniˈation** *n.*

supercomputer (ˌsuːpəkəmˈpjuːtə) *n.* a powerful computer that can process large quantities of data of a similar type very quickly.

superconductivity (ˌsuːpəˌkɒndʌkˈtɪvɪtɪ) *n. Physics.* the property of certain substances that have no electrical resistance. In metals it occurs at very low temperatures, but higher temperature superconductivity occurs in some ceramic materials. —**superconduction** (ˌsuːpəkənˈdʌkʃən) *n.* —ˌ**superconˈductive** *or* ˌ**superconˈducting** *adj.* —ˌ**superconˈductor** *n.*

supercontinent (ˈsuːpəˌkɒntɪnənt) *n.* a great landmass thought to have existed in the geological past and to have split into smaller landmasses, which drifted and formed the present continents.

supercool (ˌsuːpəˈkuːl) *vb. Chem.* to cool or be cooled without freezing or crystallization to a temperature below that at which freezing or crystallization should occur. Supercooled liquids are not in equilibrium.

superdense theory (ˌsuːpəˈdɛns) *n. Astronomy.* another name for the **big-bang theory.**

superdominant (ˌsuːpəˈdɒmɪnənt) *n. U.S. and Canadian.* another word for **submediant.**

super-duper (ˈsuːpəˈduːpə) *adj. Informal.* extremely pleasing, impressive, etc.: often used as an exclamation.

superego (ˌsuːpərˈiːgəʊ, -ˈɛgəʊ) *n., pl.* **-gos.** *Psychoanal.* that part of the unconscious mind that acts as a conscience for the ego, developing mainly from the relationship between a child and his parents. See also **id, ego.**

superelastic (ˌsuːpərɪˈlæstɪk) *adj. Physics.* (of collisions) involving an overall increase in translational kinetic energy.

superelevation (ˌsuːpərˌɛlɪˈveɪʃən) *n.* **1.** another name for **bank**[2] (sense 7). **2.** the difference between the heights of the sides of a road or railway track on a bend.

supereminent (ˌsuːpərˈɛmɪnənt) *adj.* of distinction, dignity, or rank superior to that of others; pre-eminent. —ˌ**superˈeminence** *n.* —ˌ**superˈeminently** *adv.*

supererogate (ˌsuːpərˈɛrəˌgeɪt) *vb.* (*intr.*) *Obsolete.* to do or perform more than is required. [C16: from Late Latin *superērogāre* to spend over and above, from Latin SUPER- + *ērogāre* to pay out] —ˌ**superˈeroˌgator** *n.*

supererogation (ˌsuːpərˌɛrəˈgeɪʃən) *n.* **1.** the performance of work in excess of that required or expected. **2.** *R.C. Church.* supererogatory prayers, devotions, etc.

supererogatory (ˌsuːpərɛˈrɒgətərɪ, -trɪ) *adj.* **1.** performed to an extent exceeding that required or expected. **2.** exceeding what is needed; superfluous. **3.** *R.C. Church.* of, characterizing, or relating to prayers, good works, etc., performed over and above those prescribed as obligatory. [C16: from Medieval Latin *superērogātōrius;* see SUPEREROGATE] —ˌ**supereˈrogatorily** *adv.*

superette (ˌsuːpəˈrɛt) *n. N.Z. informal.* a small store or dairy laid out along the lines of a supermarket.

superfamily (ˈsuːpəˌfæmɪlɪ) *n., pl.* **-lies. 1.** *Biology.* a taxonomic group that is a subdivision of a suborder. **2.** any analogous group, such as a group of related languages.

superfecundation (ˌsuːpəˌfiːkənˈdeɪʃən) *n. Physiol.* the fertilization of two or more ova, produced during the same menstrual cycle, by sperm ejaculated during two or more acts of sexual intercourse.

superfemale (ˈsuːpəˌfiːmeɪl) *n.* a former name for **metafemale.**

superfetation (ˌsuːpəfiːˈteɪʃən) *n. Physiol.* the presence in the uterus of two fetuses developing from ova fertilized at different times. [C17 *superfetate,* from Latin *superfētāre* to fertilize when already pregnant, from SUPER- + *fētāre* to impregnate, from *fētus* offspring] —**superfetate** (ˌsuːpəˈfiːteɪt) *adj.*

superficial (ˌsuːpəˈfɪʃəl) *adj.* **1.** of, relating to, being near, or forming the surface: *superficial bruising.* **2.** displaying a lack of thoroughness or care: *a superficial inspection.* **3.** only outwardly apparent rather than genuine or actual: *the similarity was merely superficial.* **4.** of little substance or significance; trivial: *superficial differences.* **5.** lacking originality or profundity: *the film's plot was quite superficial.* **6.** (of measurements) involving only the surface area. [C14: from Late Latin *superficiālis* of the surface, from Latin SUPERFICIES] —**superficiality** (ˌsuːpəˌfɪʃɪˈælɪtɪ) *or* (*less commonly*) ˌ**superˈficialness** *n.* —ˌ**superˈficially** *adv.*

superficies (ˌsuːpəˈfɪʃiːz) *n., pl.* **-cies.** *Rare.* **1.** a surface or outer face. **2.** the outward form of a thing. [C16: from Latin: upper side, from SUPER- + *faciēs* face]

superfine (ˌsuːpəˈfaɪn) *adj.* **1.** of exceptional fineness or quality. **2.** excessively refined. —ˌ**superˈfineness** *n.*

superfix (ˈsuːpəˌfɪks) *n. Linguistics.* a suprasegmental feature distinguishing the meaning or grammatical function of one word or phrase from that of another, as stress does for example between the noun *conduct* and the verb *conduct.* [from SUPER- + *-fix,* on the model of PREFIX, SUFFIX]

superfluid (ˌsuːpəˈfluːɪd) *n.* **1.** *Physics.* a fluid in a state characterized by a very low viscosity, high thermal conductivity, high capillarity, etc. The only known example is that of liquid helium at temperatures close to absolute zero. ~*adj.* **2.** being or relating to a superfluid.

superfluidity (ˌsuːpəfluːˈɪdɪtɪ) *n. Physics.* the state of being or property of becoming a superfluid.

superfluity (ˌsuːpəˈfluːɪtɪ) *n.* **1.** the condition of being superfluous. **2.** a quantity or thing that is in excess of what is needed. **3.** a thing that is not needed. [C14: from Old French *superfluité,* via Late Latin from Latin *superfluus* SUPERFLUOUS]

superfluous (sʊˈpɜːflʊəs) *adj.* **1.** exceeding what is sufficient or required. **2.** not necessary or relevant; uncalled-for. **3.** *Obsolete.* extravagant in expenditure or oversupplied with possessions. [C15: from Latin *superfluus* overflowing, from SUPER- + *fluere* to flow] —**suˈperfluously** *adv.* —**suˈperfluousness** *n.*

superfuse (ˌsuːpəˈfjuːz) *vb. Obsolete.* to pour or be poured so as to cover something. [C17: from Latin *superfūsus* poured over, from *superfundere,* from SUPER- + *fundere* to pour] —ˌ**superˈfusion** *n.*

supergiant (ˈsuːpəˌdʒaɪənt) *n.* any of a class of extremely bright stars, such as Betelgeuse, which have expanded to a diameter hundreds or thousands of times greater than that of the sun and have an extremely low mean density. Compare **giant star, white dwarf.**

superglacial (ˌsuːpəˈgleɪsɪəl) *adj.* on or originating from the surface of a glacier.

superglue (ˈsuːpəˌgluː) *n.* any of various impact adhesives that quickly make an exceptionally strong bond.

supergrass (ˈsuːpəˌgrɑːs) *n.* an informer whose information implicates a large number of people in terrorist activities or other major crimes.

supergravity (ˌsuːpəˈgrævɪtɪ) *n. Physics.* any of various theories in which supersymmetry is applied to the theory of gravitation.

supergroup (ˈsuːpəˌgruːp) *n.* a rock band whose members are individually famous from previous groups.

ˌ**superˈbold** *adj.*
ˌ**supercoˈlossal** *adj.*
ˌ**superˈcomplex** *adj.*
ˌ**superˈconfident** *adj.*
ˌ**superconˈformity** *n.*
ˌ**superconˈgested** *adj.*
ˌ**superconˈservative** *adj.*
ˌ**superˈcriminal** *n., adj.*
ˌ**superˈcritical** *adj.*
ˌ**superˈcurious** *adj.*
ˌ**superˈcynical** *adj.*
ˌ**superˈdeficit** *n.*
ˌ**superdeˈvotion** *n.*
ˌ**superˈdifficult** *adj.*
ˌ**superdiˈplomacy** *n.*
ˌ**superˈdose** *n.*
ˌ**superefˈfective** *adj.*
ˌ**superefˈficient** *adj.*
ˌ**superexˈcited** *adj.*
ˌ**superexˈpressive** *adj.*
ˌ**superˈfinite** *adj.*
ˌ**superˈgenerous** *adj.*

superheat (ˌsuːpəˈhiːt) *vb. (tr.)* **1.** to heat (a vapour, esp. steam) to a temperature above its saturation point for a given pressure. **2.** to heat (a liquid) to a temperature above its boiling point without boiling occurring. **3.** to heat excessively; overheat. —ˌ**super'heater** *n.*

superheavy (ˌsuːpəˈhɛvɪ) *n. Physics.* denoting or relating to elements of high atomic number (above 109) postulated to exist with special stability as a consequence of the shell model of the nucleus.

superhero (ˈsuːpəˌhɪərəʊ) *n., pl.* **-roes.** any of various comic-strip characters with superhuman abilities or magical powers, wearing a distinctive costume, and fighting against evil.

superhet (ˈsuːpəˌhɛt) *n.* See **superheterodyne receiver.**

superheterodyne receiver (ˌsuːpəˈhɛtərəˌdaɪn) *n.* a radio receiver that combines two radio-frequency signals by heterodyne action, to produce a signal above the audible frequency limit. This signal is amplified and demodulated to give the desired audio-frequency signal. Sometimes shortened to **superhet.** [C20: from SUPER(SONIC) + HETERODYNE]

superhigh frequency (ˈsuːpəˌhaɪ) *n.* a radio-frequency band or radio frequency lying between 30 000 and 3000 megahertz. Abbrev.: **SHF.**

superhighway (ˈsuːpəˌhaɪweɪ) *n. Chiefly U.S.* a fast dual-carriage-way road.

superhuman (ˌsuːpəˈhjuːmən) *adj.* **1.** having powers above and beyond those of mankind. **2.** exceeding normal human ability or experience. —ˌ**superhu'manity** *or* ˌ**super'humanness** *n.* —ˌ**super'humanly** *adv.*

superhumeral (ˌsuːpəˈhjuːmərəl) *n.* an ecclesiastical vestment worn over the shoulders. [C17: from Late Latin *superhumerāle;* see SUPER-, HUMERAL]

superimpose (ˌsuːpərɪmˈpəʊz) *vb. (tr.)* **1.** to set or place on or over something else. **2.** (usually foll. by *on* or *upon*) to add (to). —ˌ**superˌimpo'sition** *n.*

superincumbent (ˌsuːpərɪnˈkʌmbənt) *adj.* **1.** lying or being on top of something else. **2.** situated or suspended above; overhanging. —ˌ**superin'cumbence** *or* ˌ**superin'cumbency** *n.* —ˌ**superin'cumbently** *adv.*

superinduce (ˌsuːpərɪnˈdjuːs) *vb. (tr.)* to introduce as an additional feature, factor, etc. —ˌ**superin'ducement** *n.* —**superinduction** (ˌsuːpərɪnˈdʌkʃən) *n.*

superintend (ˌsuːpərɪnˈtɛnd, ˌsuːprɪn-) *vb.* to undertake the direction or supervision (of); manage. [C17: from Church Latin *superintendere,* from Latin SUPER- + *intendere* to give attention to] —ˌ**superin'tendence** *n.*

superintendency (ˌsuːpərɪnˈtɛndənsɪ, ˌsuːprɪn-) *n., pl.* **-cies. 1.** the office or jurisdiction of a superintendent. **2.** a district under the jurisdiction of a superintendent.

superintendent (ˌsuːpərɪnˈtɛndənt, ˌsuːprɪn-) *n.* **1.** a person who directs and manages an organization, office, etc. **2.** (in Britain) a senior police officer higher in rank than an inspector but lower than a chief superintendent. **3.** (in the U.S.) the head of a police department. **4.** *Chiefly U.S. and Canadian.* a caretaker, esp. of a block of apartments. ~*adj.* **5.** of or relating to supervision; superintending. [C16: from Church Latin *superintendens* overseeing]

superior (suːˈpɪərɪə) *adj.* **1.** greater in quality, quantity, etc. **2.** of high or extraordinary worth, merit, etc. **3.** higher in rank or status: *a superior tribunal.* **4.** displaying a conscious sense of being above or better than others; supercilious. **5.** (*often postpositive;* foll. by *to*) not susceptible (to) or influenced (by). **6.** placed higher up; situated further from the base. **7.** *Astronomy.* **a.** (of a planet) having an orbit further from the sun than the orbit of the earth. **b.** (of a conjunction) occurring when the sun lies between the earth and an inferior planet. **8.** (of a plant ovary) situated above the calyx and other floral parts. **9.** *Anatomy.* (of one part in relation to another) situated above or higher. **10.** *Printing.* (of a character) written or printed above the line; superscript. ~*n.* **11.** a person or thing of greater rank or quality. **12.** *Printing.* a character set in a superior position. **13.** (*often cap.*) the head of a community in a religious order. [C14: from Latin, from *superus* placed above, from *super* above] —**su'perioress** *fem. n.* —**superiority** (suːˌpɪərɪˈɒrɪtɪ) *n.* —**su'periorly** *adv.*

superior court *n.* **1.** (in England) a higher court not subject to control by any other court except by way of appeal. See also **Supreme Court of Judicature. 2.** *U.S.* (in several states) a court of general jurisdiction ranking above the inferior courts and below courts of last resort.

superiority complex *n. Informal.* an inflated estimate of one's own merit, usually manifested in arrogance.

superior planet *n.* any of the six planets (Mars, Jupiter, Saturn, Uranus, Neptune, and Pluto) whose orbit lies outside that of the earth.

superjacent (ˌsuːpəˈdʒeɪsᵊnt) *adj.* lying immediately above or upon. [C17: from Late Latin *superjacēre,* from Latin SUPER- + *jacēre* to lie]

superl. *abbrev. for* superlative.

superlative (suːˈpɜːlətɪv) *adj.* **1.** of outstanding quality, degree, etc.; supreme. **2.** *Grammar.* denoting the form of an adjective or adverb that expresses the highest or a very high degree of quality. In English the superlative degree is usually marked by the suffix *-est* or the word *most,* as in *loudest* or *most loudly.* Compare **positive** (sense 10), **comparative** (sense 3). **3.** (of language or style) excessive; exaggerated. ~*n.* **4.** a thing that excels all others or is of the highest quality. **5.** *Grammar.* the superlative form of an adjective. **6.** the highest degree; peak. [C14: from Old French *superlatif,* via Late Latin from Latin *superlātus* extravagant, from *superferre* to carry beyond, from SUPER- + *ferre* to bear] —**su'perlatively** *adv.* —**su'perlativeness** *n.*

superload (ˈsuːpəˌləʊd) *n.* another name for **live load.**

superluminal (ˌsuːpəˈluːmɪnəl) *adj. Physics.* of or relating to a speed or velocity exceeding the speed of light.

superlunar (ˌsuːpəˈluːnə) *adj.* situated beyond the moon; celestial. —ˌ**super'lunary** *adj.*

supermale (ˈsuːpəˌmeɪl) *n.* a former name for **metamale.**

superman (ˈsuːpəˌmæn) *n., pl.* **-men. 1.** (in the philosophy of Nietzsche) an ideal man who through personal integrity and creative ability would rise above good and evil and who represents the goal of human evolution. **2.** any man of apparently superhuman powers.

supermarket (ˈsuːpəˌmɑːkɪt) *n.* a large self-service store retailing food and household supplies.

supermembrane (ˌsuːpəˈmɛmbreɪn) *n. Physics.* a type of membrane postulated in certain theories of elementary particles that involve supersymmetry.

supermundane (ˌsuːpəˈmʌndeɪn) *adj.* of or relating to what is elevated above earthly things.

supernal (suːˈpɜːnᵊl, sjuː-) *adj. Literary.* **1.** of or from the world of the divine; celestial. **2.** of or emanating from above or from the sky. [C15: from Medieval Latin *supernālis,* from Latin *supernus* that is on high, from *super* above] —**su'pernally** *adv.*

supernatant (ˌsuːpəˈneɪtᵊnt) *adj.* **1.** floating on the surface or over something. **2.** *Chem.* (of a liquid) lying above a sediment or settled precipitate. [C17: from Latin *supernatāre* to float, from SUPER- + *natāre* to swim] —ˌ**superna'tation** *n.*

supernational (ˌsuːpəˈnæʃnᵊl) *adj.* a less common word for **supranational.** —ˌ**super'nationalism** *n.* —ˌ**super'nationalist** *n.* —ˌ**super'nationally** *adv.*

supernatural (ˌsuːpəˈnætʃrəl, -ˈnætʃərəl) *adj.* **1.** of or relating to things that cannot be explained according to natural laws. **2.** characteristic of or caused by or as if by a god; miraculous. **3.** of, involving, or ascribed to occult beings. **4.** exceeding the ordinary; abnormal. ~*n.* **5. the.** supernatural forces, occurrences, and beings collectively or their realm. —ˌ**super'naturally** *adv.* —ˌ**super'naturalness** *n.*

supernaturalism (ˌsuːpəˈnætʃrəlɪzəm, -ˈnætʃərə-)) *n.* **1.** the quality or condition of being supernatural. **2.** a supernatural agency, the effects of which are felt to be apparent in this world. **3.** belief in supernatural forces or agencies as producing effects in this world. —ˌ**super'naturalist** *n., adj.* —ˌ**superˌnatural'istic** *adj.*

supernormal (ˌsuːpəˈnɔːməl) *adj.* greatly exceeding the normal. —**supernormality** (ˌsuːpənɔːˈmælɪtɪ) *n.* —ˌ**super'normally** *adv.*

supernova (ˌsuːpəˈnəʊvə) *n., pl.* **-vae** (-viː) *or* **-vas.** a star that explodes catastrophically owing to instabilities following the exhaustion of its nuclear fuel, becoming for a few days up to one hundred million times brighter than the sun. The expanding shell of debris (the **supernova remnant**) creates a nebula that radiates radio waves, x-rays, and light, for hundreds or thousands of years. Compare **nova.**

supernumerary (ˌsuːpəˈnjuːmərərɪ, -ˈnjuːmrərɪ) *adj.* **1.** exceeding a regular or proper number; extra. **2.** functioning as a substitute or assistant with regard to a regular body or staff. ~*n., pl.* **-aries. 3.** a person or thing that exceeds the normal, required, or regular number. **4.** a person who functions as a substitute or assistant. **5.** an actor who has no lines, esp. a nonprofessional one. [C17: from Late Latin *supernumerārius,* from Latin SUPER- + *numerus* number]

superorder (ˈsuːpərˌɔːdə) *n. Biology.* a taxonomic group that is a subdivision of a subclass.

superordinate *adj.* (ˌsuːpərˈɔːdɪnɪt). **1.** of higher status or condition. ~*n.* (ˌsuːpərˈɔːdɪnɪt). **2.** a person or thing that is superordinate. **3.** a word the meaning of which includes the meaning of another word or words: *"red" is a superordinate of "scarlet", "vermilion", and "crimson".* Compare **hyponym, synonym, antonym.** ~*vb.* (ˌsuːpərˈɔːdɪˌneɪt). **4.** *(tr.) Rare.* to make superordinate.

superorganic (ˌsuːpərɔːˈgænɪk) *adj. Sociol.* (no longer widely used) relating to those aspects of a culture that are conceived as being superior to the individual members of the society. —ˌ**superor'ganicism** *n.* —ˌ**superor'ganicist** *n.*

ˌ**super'ignorant** *adj.*
ˌ**superim'portant** *adj.*
ˌ**superin'difference** *n.*
ˌ**superin'sist** *vb.*
ˌ**superˌintel'lectual** *adj.*
ˌ**superin'telligent** *adj.*
ˌ**super'logical** *adj.*
ˌ**super'lucky** *adj.*
ˌ**superlux'urious** *adj.*
ˌ**super'negligent** *adj.*
ˌ**superˌobli'gation** *n.*
ˌ**superof'ficious** *adj.*
ˌ**super'optimist** *n.*

superoxide (ˌsuːpərˈɒksaɪd) *n.* any of certain metal oxides that contain the O_2^- ion: *potassium superoxide, KO_2.*
superphosphate (ˌsuːpəˈfɒsfeɪt) *n.* **1.** a mixture of the diacid calcium salt of orthophosphoric acid $Ca(H_2PO_4)_2$ with calcium sulphate and small quantities of other phosphates: used as a fertilizer. **2.** a salt of phosphoric acid formed by incompletely replacing its acidic hydrogen atoms; acid phosphate; hydrogen phosphate.
superphysical (ˌsuːpəˈfɪzɪkᵊl) *adj.* not explained by the known physical laws and phenomena; supernatural.
superplastic (ˌsuːpəˈplæstɪk) *adj.* **1.** (of a metal, alloy, etc.) very easily moulded at high temperatures without fracturing. *~n.* **2.** such a metal, alloy, etc. —ˌ**superplasˈticity** *n.*
superpose (ˌsuːpəˈpəʊz) *vb.* (*tr.*) **1.** *Geometry.* to transpose (the coordinates of one geometric figure) to coincide with those of another. **2.** a rare word for **superimpose** (sense 1). [C19: from French *superposer*, from Latin *superpōnere*, from SUPER- + *pōnere* to place] —ˌ**superˈposable** *adj.*
superposition (ˌsuːpəpəˈzɪʃən) *n.* **1.** the act of superposing or state of being superposed. **2.** *Geology.* the principle that in any sequence of sedimentary rocks which has not been disturbed, the oldest strata lie at the bottom and the youngest at the top.
superpower (ˈsuːpəˌpaʊə) *n.* **1.** an extremely powerful state, such as the U.S. **2.** extremely high power, esp. electrical or mechanical. —ˈ**superˌpowered** *adj.*
superrealism (ˌsuːpəˈrɪəˌlɪzəm) *n.* another name for **surrealism.** —ˌ**superˈrealist** *n., adj.*
supersaturated (ˌsuːpəˈsætʃəˌreɪtɪd) *adj.* **1.** (of a solution) containing more solute than a saturated solution and therefore not in equilibrium. **2.** (of a vapour) containing more material than a saturated vapour and therefore not in equilibrium. —ˌ**superˌsatuˈration** *n.*
superscribe (ˌsuːpəˈskraɪb) *vb.* (*tr.*) to write (an inscription, name, etc.) above, on top of, or outside. [C16: from Latin *superscrībere*, from SUPER- + *scrībere* to write]
superscript (ˈsuːpəˌskrɪpt) *adj.* **1.** *Printing.* (of a character) written or printed above the line; superior. Compare **subscript.** *~n.* **2.** a superscript or superior character. **3.** *Obsolete.* a superscription on a document, letter, etc. [C16: from Latin *superscriptus;* see SUPERSCRIBE]
superscription (ˌsuːpəˈskrɪpʃən) *n.* **1.** the act of superscribing. **2.** a superscribed title, address, etc. **3.** the symbol (℞) at the head of a medical prescription, which stands for the Latin word *recipe* (take).
supersede (ˌsuːpəˈsiːd) *vb.* (*tr.*) **1.** to take the place of (something old-fashioned or less appropriate); supplant. **2.** to replace in function, office, etc.; succeed. **3.** to discard or set aside or cause to be set aside as obsolete or inferior. [C15: via Old French from Latin *supersedēre* to sit above, from SUPER- + *sedēre* to sit] —ˌ**superˈsedable** *adj.* —ˌ**superˈsedence** *n.* —ˌ**superˈseder** *n.* —**supersedure** (ˌsuːpəˈsiːdʒə) *n.* —**supersession** (ˌsuːpəˈsɛʃən) *n.*
supersensible (ˌsuːpəˈsɛnsɪbᵊl) *or* **supersensory** (ˌsuːpəˈsɛnsərɪ) *adj.* imperceptible to or beyond reach of the senses. —ˌ**superˈsensibly** *adv.*
supersex (ˈsuːpəˌsɛks) *n. Genetics.* a sterile organism in which the ratio between the sex chromosomes is disturbed. See **metafemale, metamale.**
supersonic (ˌsuːpəˈsɒnɪk) *adj.* being, having, or capable of reaching a velocity in excess of the velocity of sound: *supersonic aircraft.* —ˌ**superˈsonically** *adv.*
supersonics (ˌsuːpəˈsɒnɪks) *n.* (*functioning as sing.*) **1.** the study of supersonic motion. **2.** a less common name for **ultrasonics.**
superstar (ˈsuːpəˌstɑː) *n.* a popular singer, film star, etc., who is idolized by fans and elevated to a position of importance in the entertainment industry.
superstition (ˌsuːpəˈstɪʃən) *n.* **1.** irrational belief usually founded on ignorance or fear and characterized by obsessive reverence for omens, charms, etc. **2.** a notion, act or ritual that derives from such belief. **3.** any irrational belief, esp. with regard to the unknown. [C15: from Latin *superstitiō* dread of the supernatural, from *superstāre* to stand still by something (as in amazement)]
superstitious (ˌsuːpəˈstɪʃəs) *adj.* **1.** disposed to believe in superstition. **2.** of or relating to superstition. —ˌ**superˈstitiously** *adv.* —ˌ**superˈstitiousness** *n.*
superstore (ˈsuːpəˌstɔː) *n.* a very large supermarket, often selling household goods, clothes, etc., as well as food.
superstratum (ˌsuːpəˈstrɑːtəm, -ˈstreɪ-) *n., pl.* **-ta** (-tə) *or* **-tums.** **1.** *Geology.* a layer or stratum overlying another layer or similar structure. **2.** *Linguistics.* the language of a conquering or colonizing population as it supplants that of an indigenous population, as for example French and English in the West Indies. Compare **substratum** (sense 8).
superstring (ˈsuːpəˌstrɪŋ) *n. Physics.* a type of string (sense 11) postulated in certain theories of elementary particles that involve supersymmetry.
superstruct (ˌsuːpəˈstrʌkt) *vb.* (*tr.*) to erect upon a foundation or on top of another building or part.
superstructure (ˈsuːpəˌstrʌktʃə) *n.* **1.** the part of a building above its foundation. **2.** any structure or concept erected on something else. **3.** *Nautical.* any structure above the main deck of a ship with sides flush with the sides of the hull. **4.** the part of a bridge supported by the piers and abutments. **5.** (in Marxist theory) an edifice of interdependent agencies of the state, including legal and political institutions and ideologies, each possessing some autonomy but remaining products of the dominant mode of economic production. —ˈ**superˌstructural** *adj.*
supersymmetry (ˌsuːpəˈsɪmɪtrɪ) *n. Physics.* a symmetry of elementary particles having a higher order than that in the standard model, postulated to encompass the behaviour of both bosons and fermions.
supertanker (ˈsuːpəˌtæŋkə) *n.* a large fast tanker of more than 275 000 tons capacity.
supertax (ˈsuːpəˌtæks) *n.* a tax levied in addition to the basic or normal tax, esp. a graduated surtax on incomes above a certain level.
supertonic (ˌsuːpəˈtɒnɪk) *n. Music.* **1.** the second degree of a major or minor scale. **2.** a key or chord based on this.
supervene (ˌsuːpəˈviːn) *vb.* (*intr.*) **1.** to follow closely; ensue. **2.** to occur as an unexpected or extraneous development. [C17: from Latin *supervenīre* to come upon, from SUPER- + *venīre* to come] —ˌ**superˈvenience** *or* **supervention** (ˌsuːpəˈvɛnʃən) *n.*
supervenient (ˌsuːpəˈviːnɪənt) *adj.* **1.** supervening. **2.** *Philosophy.* (of a property) inseparable from the other properties of something. Two objects may be identical except that one is red and the other not, but they cannot be identical except that one is beautiful and the other not; beauty is thus a supervenient property.
supervise (ˈsuːpəˌvaɪz) *vb.* (*tr.*) **1.** to direct or oversee the performance or operation of. **2.** to watch over so as to maintain order, etc. [C16: from Medieval Latin *supervidēre*, from Latin SUPER- + *vidēre* to see] —**supervision** (ˌsuːpəˈvɪʒən) *n.*
supervision order *n.* (in Britain) *Social welfare.* an order by a juvenile court requiring a named probation officer or local-authority social worker to advise, assist, and befriend a child or young person who is the subject of care proceedings, over a period of up to three years.
supervisor (ˈsuːpəˌvaɪzə) *n.* **1.** a person who manages or supervises. **2.** a foreman or forewoman. **3.** (in some British universities) a tutor supervising the work, esp. research work, of a student. **4.** (in some U.S. schools) an administrator running a department of teachers. **5.** (in some U.S. states) the elected chief official of a township or other subdivision of a county. **6.** *Obsolete.* a spectator. —ˈ**superˌvisorship** *n.*
supervisory (ˈsuːpəˌvaɪzərɪ) *adj.* of, involving, or limited to supervision: *a supervisory capacity.*
supervisory board *n.* a board of management of which non-managerial workers are members, having supervisory powers over some aspects of management decision-making.
superwoman (ˈsuːpəˌwʊmən) *n., pl.* **-women.** a woman who fulfils her many roles with apparently superhuman efficiency.
supinate (ˈsuːpɪˌneɪt, ˈsjuː-) *vb.* to turn (the hand and forearm) so that the palm faces up or forwards. [C19: from Latin *supīnāre* to lay on the back, from *supīnus* SUPINE] —ˌ**supiˈnation** *n.*
supinator (ˈsuːpɪˌneɪtə, ˈsjuː-) *n. Anatomy.* the muscle of the forearm that can produce the motion of supination.
supine *adj.* (suːˈpaɪn, sjuː-; ˈsuːpaɪn, ˈsjuː-). **1.** lying or resting on the back with the face, palm, etc., upwards. **2.** displaying no interest or animation; lethargic. *~n.* (ˈsuːpaɪn, ˈsjuː-). **3.** *Grammar.* a noun form derived from a verb in Latin, often used to express purpose with verbs of motion. Abbrev.: **sup.** [C15: from Latin *supīnus* related to *sub* under, up; (in grammatical sense) from Latin *verbum supīnum* supine word (the reason for this use is unknown)] —**suˈpinely** *adv.* —**suˈpineness** *n.*
suplex (ˈsuːplɛks) *n.* a wrestling hold in which a wrestler grasps his opponent round the waist from behind and carries him backwards. [C20: of uncertain origin]
supp. *or* **suppl.** *abbrev. for* supplement(ary).
supper (ˈsʌpə) *n.* **1.** an evening meal, esp. a light one. **2.** an evening social event featuring a supper. **3. sing for one's supper.** to obtain something by performing a service. *~vb.* **4.** (*tr.*) *Rare.* to give supper to. **5.** (*intr.*) *Rare.* to eat supper. [C13: from Old French *soper;* see SUP[1]] —ˈ**supperless** *adj.*
supper club *n. U.S. and Canadian.* a small expensive nightclub.

ˌ**superpoˈlite** *adj.*
ˌ**superˈpolymer** *n.*
ˌ**superpreˈcise** *adj.*
ˌ**superpreˈpared** *adj.*
ˌ**superˈpure** *adj.*
ˌ**superreˈfine** *vb.*
ˌ**superreˈliance** *n.*
ˌ**superreˈspectable** *adj.*
ˌ**superreˈstriction** *n.*
ˌ**superˈrich** *adj.*
ˌ**superˈrighteous** *adj.*
ˌ**superˈsacred** *adj.*
ˌ**supersarˈcastic** *adj.*
ˌ**superˈsecret** *adj.*
ˌ**superˈsensitive** *adj.*
ˌ**superseˈvere** *adj.*
ˌ**supersimˈplicity** *n.*
ˌ**supersoˈphisticate** *n.*
ˌ**supersoˈphistiˌcated** *adj.*
ˌ**superˈspecialˌize** *or* ˌ**superˈspecialˌise** *vb.*
ˌ**superˈstrict** *adj.*
ˌ**superˈstylish** *adj.*
ˌ**supersufˈficiency** *n.*
ˌ**superˈsweet** *adj.*
ˌ**superˈtension** *n.*
ˌ**superˈthorough** *adj.*
ˌ**superˈvigilant** *adj.*
ˌ**superˈvirulent** *adj.*

supplant (sə'plɑːnt) *vb.* (*tr.*) to take the place of, often by trickery or force: *he easily supplanted his rival.* [C13: via Old French from Latin *supplantāre* to trip up, from *sub-* from below + *planta* sole of the foot] —**supplantation** (ˌsʌplɑːn'teɪʃən) *n.* —**sup'planter** *n.*

supple ('sʌpᵊl) *adj.* **1.** bending easily without damage. **2.** capable of or showing easy or graceful movement; lithe. **3.** mentally flexible; responding readily. **4.** disposed to agree, sometimes to the point of servility. ~*vb.* **5.** *Rare.* to make or become supple. [C13: from Old French *souple,* from Latin *supplex* bowed] —'**suppleness** *n.*

supplejack ('sʌpᵊlˌdʒæk) *n.* **1.** a North American twining rhamnaceous woody vine, *Berchemia scandens,* that has greenish-white flowers and purple fruits. **2.** a bush plant of New Zealand, *Rhipogonum scandens,* having tough climbing vines. **3.** a tropical American woody sapindaceous vine, *Paullinia curassavica,* having strong supple wood. **4.** any of various other vines with strong supple stems. **5.** *U.S.* a walking stick made from the wood of *Paullinia curassavica.* [C18: from SUPPLE + JACK[1]]

supplement *n.* ('sʌplɪmənt). **1.** an addition designed to complete, make up for a deficiency, etc. **2.** a section appended to a publication to supply further information, correct errors, etc. **3.** a magazine or section inserted into a newspaper or periodical, such as one with colour photographs issued every week. **4.** *Geometry.* **a.** either of a pair of angles whose sum is 180°. **b.** an arc of a circle that when added to another arc forms a semicircle. ~Abbrevs.: **sup., supp.** ~*vb.* ('sʌplɪˌmɛnt). **5.** (*tr.*) to provide a supplement to, esp. in order to remedy a deficiency. [C14: from Latin *supplēmentum,* from *supplēre* to SUPPLY] —ˌ**supplemen'tation** *n.* —'**suppleˌmenter** *n.*

supplementary (ˌsʌplɪ'mɛntərɪ, -trɪ) *adj.* **1.** Also (*less commonly*): **supplemental** (ˌsʌplɪ'mɛntᵊl). forming or acting as a supplement. ~*n., pl.* **-ries. 2.** a person or thing that is a supplement. —ˌ**supple'mentarily** *or* (*less commonly*) ˌ**supple'mentally** *adv.*

supplementary angle *n.* either of two angles whose sum is 180°. Compare **complementary angle.**

supplementary benefit *n.* (in Britain) a weekly allowance formerly paid to various groups of people by the state to bring their incomes up to minimum levels established by law: replaced by income support in 1988.

suppletion (sə'pliːʃən) *n.* the use of an unrelated word to complete the otherwise defective paradigm of a given word, as for example the use of *went* for the past tense of *go.* [C14: from Medieval Latin *supplētiō* a completing, from Latin *supplēre* to SUPPLY[1]] —**sup'pletive** *n., adj.*

suppletory ('sʌplɪtərɪ, -trɪ) *adj. Archaic.* remedying deficiencies; supplementary. —'**suppletorily** *adv.*

suppliant ('sʌplɪənt) *adj.* **1.** expressing entreaty or supplication. ~*n., adj.* **2.** another word for **supplicant.** [C15: from French *supplier* to beseech, from Latin *supplicāre* to kneel in entreaty; see SUPPLE] —'**suppliantly** *adv.* —'**suppliance** *n.*

supplicant ('sʌplɪkənt) *or* **suppliant** *n.* **1.** a person who supplicates. ~*adj.* **2.** entreating humbly; supplicating. [C16: from Latin *supplicāns* beseeching; see SUPPLE]

supplicate ('sʌplɪˌkeɪt) *vb.* **1.** to make a humble request to (someone); plead. **2.** (*tr.*) to ask for or seek humbly. [C15: from Latin *supplicāre* to beg on one's knees; see SUPPLE] —'**suppliˌcatory** *adj.*

supplication (ˌsʌplɪ'keɪʃən) *n.* **1.** the act of supplicating. **2.** a humble entreaty or petition; prayer.

supply[1] (sə'plaɪ) *vb.* **-plies, -plying, -plied. 1.** (*tr.;* often foll. by *with*) to furnish with something that is required: *to supply the community with good government.* **2.** (*tr.;* often foll. by *to* or *for*) to make available or provide (something that is desired or lacking): *to supply books to the library.* **3.** (*tr.*) to provide for adequately; make good; satisfy: *who will supply their needs?* **4.** to serve as a substitute, usually temporary, in (another's position, etc.): *there are no clergymen to supply the pulpit.* **5.** (*tr.*) *Brit.* to fill (a vacancy, position, etc.). ~*n., pl.* **-plies. 6. a.** the act of providing or something that is provided. **b.** (*as modifier*): *a supply dump.* **7.** (*often pl.*) an amount available for use; stock. **8.** (*pl.*) food, equipment, etc., needed for a campaign or trip. **9.** *Economics.* **a.** willingness and ability to offer goods and services for sale. **b.** the amount of a commodity that producers are willing and able to offer for sale at a specified price. Compare **demand** (sense 9). **10.** *Military.* **a.** the management and disposal of food and equipment. **b.** (*as modifier*): *supply routes.* **11.** (*often pl.*) a grant of money voted by a legislature for government expenses, esp. those not covered by other revenues. **12.** (in Parliament and similar legislatures) the money voted annually for the expenses of the civil service and armed forces. **13. a.** a person who acts as a temporary substitute. **b.** (*as modifier*): *a supply vicar.* **14.** a source of electrical energy, gas, etc. **15.** *Obsolete.* aid or assistance. [C14: from Old French *souppleier,* from Latin *supplēre* to complete, from *sub-* up + *plēre* to fill] —**sup'pliable** *adj.* —**sup'plier** *n.*

supply[2] ('sʌplɪ) *or* **supplely** ('sʌpᵊlɪ) *adv.* in a supple manner.

supply-side economics *n.* (*functioning as sing.*) a school of economic thought that emphasizes the importance to a strong economy of policies that remove impediments to supply.

supply teacher *n.* a teacher employed to replace other teachers when they are absent.

support (sə'pɔːt) *vb.* (*tr.*) **1.** to carry the weight of. **2.** to bear or withstand (pressure, weight, etc.). **3.** to provide the necessities of life for (a family, person, etc.). **4.** to tend to establish (a theory, statement, etc.) by providing new facts; substantiate. **5.** to speak in favour of (a motion). **6.** to give aid or courage to. **7.** to give approval to (a cause, principle, etc.); subscribe to: *to support a political candidature.* **8.** to endure with forbearance: *I will no longer support bad behaviour.* **9.** to give strength to; maintain: *to support a business.* **10.** (*tr.*) (in a concert) to perform earlier than (the main attraction). **11.** *Films, theatre.* **a.** to play a subordinate role to. **b.** to accompany (the feature) in a film programme. **12.** to act or perform (a role or character). ~*n.* **13.** the act of supporting or the condition of being supported. **14.** a thing that bears the weight or part of the weight of a construction. **15.** a person who or thing that furnishes aid. **16.** the means of maintenance of a family, person, etc. **17.** a band or entertainer not topping the bill. **18.** (often preceded by *the*) an actor or group of actors playing subordinate roles. **19.** *Med.* an appliance worn to ease the strain on an injured bodily structure or part. **20.** the solid material on which a painting is executed, such as canvas. **21.** See **athletic support.** [C14: from Old French *supporter,* from Latin *supportāre* to bring, from *sub-* up + *portāre* to carry] —**sup'portless** *adj.*

supportable (sə'pɔːtəbᵊl) *adj.* able to be supported or endured; bearable. —**supˌporta'bility** *or* **sup'portableness** *n.* —**sup'portably** *adv.*

support area *n. Military.* an area containing concentrations of personnel and materiel ready to support a force in the field.

supporter (sə'pɔːtə) *n.* **1.** a person who or thing that acts as a support. **2.** a person who backs a sports team, politician, etc. **3.** a garment or device worn to ease the strain on or restrict the movement of a bodily structure or part. **4.** *Heraldry.* a figure or beast in a coat of arms depicted as holding up the shield.

supporting (sə'pɔːtɪŋ) *adj.* **1.** (of a role) being a fairly important but not leading part, esp. in a play or film. **2.** (of an actor or actress) playing a supporting role.

supportive (sə'pɔːtɪv) *adj.* providing support, esp. moral or emotional support. —**sup'portively** *adv.* —**sup'portiveness** *n.*

supportive therapy *n.* **1.** *Med.* any treatment, such as the intravenous administration of certain fluids, designed to reinforce or sustain the physiological well-being of a patient. **2.** *Psychol.* a form of therapy for mental disturbances employing guidance and encouragement to develop the patient's own resources.

suppose (sə'pəʊz) *vb.* (*tr.; may take a clause as object*) **1.** to presume (something) to be true without certain knowledge: *I suppose he meant to kill her.* **2.** to consider as a possible suggestion for the sake of discussion, elucidation, etc.; postulate: *suppose that he wins the election.* **3.** (of theories, propositions, etc.) to imply the inference or assumption (of): *your policy supposes full employment.* [C14: from Old French *supposer,* from Medieval Latin *suppōnere,* from Latin: to substitute, from SUB- + *pōnere* to put] —**sup'posable** *adj.* —**sup'poser** *n.*

supposed (sə'pəʊzd, -'pəʊzɪd) *adj.* **1.** (*prenominal*) presumed to be true without certain knowledge: *his supposed date of birth.* **2.** (*prenominal*) believed to be true on slight grounds; highly doubtful: *the supposed existence of ghosts.* **3.** (sə'pəʊzd). (*postpositive;* foll. by *to*) expected or obliged (to): *I'm supposed to be there at nine.* **4.** (*postpositive; used in negative;* foll. by *to*) expected or obliged not (to): *you're not supposed to walk on the grass.* —**supposedly** (sə'pəʊzɪdlɪ) *adv.*

supposition (ˌsʌpə'zɪʃən) *n.* **1.** the act of supposing. **2.** a fact, theory, etc., that is supposed. —ˌ**suppo'sitional** *adj.* —ˌ**suppo'sitionally** *adv.* —ˌ**suppo'sitionless** *adj.*

suppositious (ˌsʌpə'zɪʃəs) *adj.* deduced from supposition; hypothetical. —ˌ**suppo'sitiously** *adv.* —ˌ**suppo'sitiousness** *n.*

supposititious (səˌpɒzɪ'tɪʃəs) *adj.* substituted with intent to mislead or deceive. —**supˌposi'titiously** *adv.* —**supˌposi'titiousness** *n.*

suppositive (sə'pɒzɪtɪv) *adj.* **1.** of, involving, or arising out of supposition. **2.** *Grammar.* denoting a conjunction introducing a clause expressing a supposition, as for example *if, supposing,* or *provided that.* ~*n.* **3.** *Grammar.* a suppositive conjunction. —**sup'positively** *adv.*

suppository (sə'pɒzɪtərɪ, -trɪ) *n., pl.* **-ries.** *Med.* an encapsulated or solid medication for insertion into the vagina, rectum, or urethra, where it melts and releases the active substance. [C14: from Medieval Latin *suppositōrium,* from Latin *suppositus* placed beneath, from *suppōnere;* see SUPPOSE]

suppress (sə'prɛs) *vb.* (*tr.*) **1.** to put an end to; prohibit. **2.** to hold in check; restrain: *I was obliged to suppress a smile.* **3.** to withhold from circulation or publication: *to suppress seditious pamphlets.* **4.** to stop the activities of; crush: *to suppress a rebellion.* **5.** *Electronics.* **a.** to reduce or eliminate (unwanted oscillations) in a circuit. **b.** to eliminate (a particular frequency or group of frequencies) in a signal. **6.** *Psychiatry.* **a.** to resist consciously (an idea or a desire entering one's mind). **b.** to exercise self-control by preventing the expression of (certain desires). Compare **repress** (sense 3). [C14: from Latin *suppressus* held down, from *supprimere* to restrain, from *sub-*

down + *premere* to press] —**sup'pressible** *adj.* —**sup'pressor** *or* **sup'presser** *n.*

suppressed carrier modulation *n. Radio.* an amplitude-modulated wave in which only the sidebands are transmitted, the carrier being removed.

suppression (sə'prɛʃən) *n.* **1.** the act or process of suppressing or the condition of being suppressed. **2.** *Psychiatry.* the conscious avoidance of unpleasant thoughts. Compare **repression.** **3.** *Electronics.* the act or process of suppressing a frequency, oscillation, etc. **4.** *Biology.* the failure of an organ or part to develop. **5.** *Med.* the cessation of any physiological process.

suppressive (sə'prɛsɪv) *adj.* **1.** tending or acting to suppress; involving suppression. **2.** *Psychiatry.* tending to prevent the expression of certain of one's desires or to resist the emergence of mental symptoms.

suppressor grid *n.* an electrode placed between the screen grid and anode of a valve. Its negative potential, relative to both screen and anode, prevents secondary electrons from the anode reaching the screen.

suppurate ('sʌpjʊˌreɪt) *vb.* (*intr.*) *Pathol.* (of a wound, sore, etc.) to discharge pus; fester. [C16: from Latin *suppūrāre,* from SUB- + *pūs* PUS]

suppuration (ˌsʌpjʊ'reɪʃən) *n.* **1.** the discharging of pus from a wound, sore, etc. **2.** the discharge itself.

suppurative ('sʌpjʊrətɪv) *adj.* **1.** causing suppuration. ~*n.* **2.** any suppurative drug.

supr. *abbrev. for* supreme.

supra ('suːprə) *adv.* above, esp. referring to earlier parts of a book etc. [C15: from Latin; related to SUPER-]

supra- *prefix.* over, above, beyond, or greater than: *supranational; supramolecular.* [from Latin *suprā* above]

supraglottal (ˌsuːprə'glɒtᵊl, ˌsjuː-) *adj. Anatomy.* situated above the glottis: *supraglottal obstruction.*

supralapsarian (ˌsuːprəlæp'sɛərɪən, ˌsjuː-) *n. Christian theol., chiefly Calvinist.* a person who believes that God decreed the election or nonelection of individuals to salvation even before the Fall. Compare **infralapsarian.** [C17: from New Latin *suprālapsārius,* from Latin SUPRA- + *lapsus* a fall] —ˌ**supralap'sarianism** *n.*

supraliminal (ˌsuːprə'lɪmɪnᵊl, ˌsjuː-) *adj.* of or relating to any stimulus that is above the threshold of sensory awareness. Compare **subliminal.** —ˌ**supra'liminally** *adv.*

supramaxillary (ˌsuːprəmæk'sɪlərɪ) *adj.* of or relating to the upper jaw.

supramolecular (ˌsuːprəmə'lɛkjʊlə, ˌsjuː-) *adj.* **1.** more complex than a molecule. **2.** consisting of more than one molecule.

supranational (ˌsuːprə'næʃnᵊl, ˌsjuː-) *adj.* involving or relating to more than one nation. —ˌ**supra'nationalism** *n.* —ˌ**supra'nationally** *adv.*

supraorbital (ˌsuːprə'ɔːbɪtᵊl, ˌsjuː-) *adj. Anatomy.* situated above the orbit.

suprarenal (ˌsuːprə'riːnᵊl, ˌsjuː-) *adj. Anatomy.* situated above a kidney. [C19: from New Latin *suprārēnālis.* See SUPRA-, RENAL]

suprarenal gland *n.* another name for **adrenal gland.**

suprasegmental (ˌsuːprəsɛg'mɛntᵊl, ˌsjuː-) *adj. Linguistics.* denoting those features of a sound or sequence of sounds that accompany rather than form part of the consecutive segments of a word or sentence, as for example stress and pitch in English. —ˌ**supraseg'mentally** *adv.*

supremacist (sʊ'prɛməsɪst, sjʊ-) *n.* **1.** a person who promotes or advocates the supremacy of any particular group. ~*adj.* **2.** characterized by belief in the supremacy of any particular group. —**su'prematism** *n.*

supremacy (sʊ'prɛməsɪ, sjʊ-) *n.* **1.** supreme power; authority. **2.** the quality or condition of being supreme.

Suprematism (sʊ'prɛməˌtɪzəm, sjʊ-) *n.* a form of pure cubist art, launched in Russia in 1913, and based on the principle that paintings should be composed only of rectangles, circles, triangles, or crosses. [C20: from *suprematist* a supporter of this theory, from French *suprémacie* SUPREMACY] —**Su'prematist** *n., adj.*

supreme (sʊ'priːm, sjʊ-) *adj.* **1.** of highest status or power: *a supreme tribunal.* **2.** (*usually prenominal*) of highest quality, importance, etc.: *supreme endeavour.* **3.** greatest in degree; extreme: *supreme folly.* **4.** (*prenominal*) final or last, esp. being last in one's life or progress; ultimate: *the supreme judgment.* [C16: from Latin *suprēmus* highest, from *superus* that is above, from *super* above] —**su'premely** *adv.* —**su'premeness** *n.*

suprême (sʊ'priːm, -'prɛm, sjʊ-) *n.* **1.** Also called: **suprême sauce.** a rich velouté sauce made with a base of veal or chicken stock, with cream or egg yolks added. **2.** the best or most delicate part of meat, esp. the breast and wing of chicken, cooked in suprême sauce. [French: SUPREME]

Supreme Being *n.* the most exalted being; God.

supreme commander *n.* the military officer in overall command of all forces in one theatre of operations.

Supreme Court *n.* (in the U.S.) **1.** the highest Federal court, possessing final appellate jurisdiction and exercising supervisory jurisdiction over the lower courts. **2.** (in many states) the highest state court.

Supreme Court of Judicature *n.* (in England) a court formed in 1873 by the amalgamation of several superior courts into two divisions, the High Court of Justice and the Court of Appeal.

supreme sacrifice *n.* **the.** the sacrifice of one's life.

supremo (sʊ'priːməʊ, sjʊ-) *n., pl.* **-mos.** *Brit. informal.* a person in overall authority. [C20: from SUPREME]

Supt *or* **supt** *abbrev. for* superintendent.

suq (suːk) *n.* a variant spelling of **souk**[1].

sur-[1] *prefix.* over; above; beyond: *surcharge; surrealism.* Compare **super-.** [from Old French, from Latin SUPER-]

sur-[2] *prefix.* a variant of **sub-** before *r: surrogate.*

sura ('sʊərə) *n.* any of the 114 chapters of the Koran. [C17: from Arabic *sūrah* section]

surah ('sʊərə) *n.* a twill-weave fabric of silk or rayon, used for dresses, blouses, etc. [C19: from the French pronunciation of *Surat,* W India]

sural ('sjʊərəl) *adj. Anatomy.* of or relating to the calf of the leg. [C17: via New Latin from Latin *sūra* calf]

surat (sjʊ'ræt) *n.* (formerly) a cotton fabric from the Surat area of W India.

surbase ('sɜːˌbeɪs) *n.* the uppermost part, such as a moulding, of a pedestal, base, or skirting. Compare **subbase.** —**sur'basement** *n.*

surbased ('sɜːˌbeɪst) *adj. Architect.* **1.** having a surbase. **2.** (of an arch) having a rise of less than half the span. [C18: from French *surbaisser* to depress, from *sur-* (intensive) + *baisser* to lower, from *bas* low; see BASE[1]]

surcease (sɜː'siːs) *Archaic.* ~*n.* **1.** cessation or intermission. ~*vb.* **2.** to desist from (some action). **3.** to cease or cause to cease. [C16: from earlier *sursesen,* from Old French *surseoir,* from Latin *supersedēre;* see SUPERSEDE]

surcharge *n.* ('sɜːˌtʃɑːdʒ). **1.** a charge in addition to the usual payment, tax, etc. **2.** an excessive sum charged, esp. when unlawful. **3.** an extra and usually excessive burden or supply. **4.** *Law.* the act or an instance of surcharging. **5.** an overprint that alters the face value of a postage stamp. ~*vb.* (sɜː'tʃɑːdʒ, 'sɜːˌtʃɑːdʒ). (*tr.*) **6.** to charge an additional sum, tax, etc. **7.** to overcharge (a person) for something. **8.** to put an extra physical burden upon; overload. **9.** to fill to excess; overwhelm. **10.** *Law.* to insert credits that have been omitted in (an account). **11.** to overprint a surcharge on (a stamp). —**sur'charger** *n.*

surcingle ('sɜːˌsɪŋgᵊl) *n.* **1.** a girth for a horse which goes around the body, used esp. with a racing saddle. **2.** the belt worn with a cassock. ~*vb.* **3.** to put a surcingle on or over (a horse). [C14: from Old French *surcengle,* from *sur-* over + *cengle* a belt, from Latin *cingulum*]

surcoat ('sɜːˌkəʊt) *n.* **1.** a tunic, often embroidered with heraldic arms, worn by a knight over his armour during the Middle Ages. **2.** an outer coat or other garment.

surculose ('sɜːkjʊˌləʊs) *adj.* (of a plant) bearing suckers. [C19: from Latin *surculōsus* woody, from *surculus* twig, from *sūrus* a branch]

surd (sɜːd) *n.* **1.** *Maths.* an expression containing one or more irrational roots of numbers, such as $2\sqrt{3} + 3\sqrt{2} + 6$. **2.** *Phonetics.* a voiceless consonant, such as (t). ~*adj.* **3.** of or relating to a surd. [C16: from Latin *surdus* muffled]

sure (ʃʊə, ʃɔː) *adj.* **1.** (sometimes foll. by *of*) free from hesitancy or uncertainty (with regard to a belief, conviction, etc.): *we are sure of the accuracy of the data; I am sure that he is lying.* **2.** (foll. by *of*) having no doubt, as of the occurrence of a future state or event: *sure of success.* **3.** always effective; unfailing: *a sure remedy.* **4.** reliable in indication or accuracy: *a sure criterion.* **5.** (of persons) worthy of trust or confidence: *a sure friend.* **6.** not open to doubt: *sure proof.* **7.** admitting of no vacillation or doubt: *he is very sure in his beliefs.* **8.** bound to be or occur; inevitable: *victory is sure.* **9.** (*postpositive*) bound inevitably (to be or do something); certain: *she is sure to be there tonight.* **10.** physically secure or dependable: *a sure footing.* **11.** *Obsolete.* free from exposure to harm or danger. **12. be sure.** (*usually imperative or dependent imperative; takes a clause as object or an infinitive,* sometimes with *to* replaced by *and*) to be careful or certain: *be sure and shut the door; I told him to be sure to shut the door.* **13. for sure.** without a doubt; surely. **14. make sure. a.** (*takes a clause as object*) to make certain; ensure. **b.** (foll. by *of*) to establish or confirm power or possession (over). **15. sure enough.** *Informal.* as might have been confidently expected; definitely: often used as a sentence substitute. **16. to be sure. a.** without doubt; certainly. **b.** it has to be acknowledged; admittedly. ~*adv.* **17.** (*sentence modifier*) *U.S. and Canadian informal.* without question; certainly. **18.** (*sentence substitute*) *U.S. and Canadian informal.* willingly; yes. [C14: from Old French *seur,* from Latin *sēcūrus* SECURE] —**'sureness** *n.*

sure-fire *adj.* (*usually prenominal*) *Informal.* certain to succeed or meet expectations; assured.

sure-footed *adj.* **1.** unlikely to fall, slip, or stumble. **2.** not likely to err or fail, as in judgment. —ˌ**sure-'footedly** *adv.* —ˌ**sure-'footedness** *n.*

surely ('ʃʊəlɪ, 'ʃɔː-) *adv.* **1.** without doubt; assuredly: *things could surely not have been worse.* **2.** without fail; inexorably (esp. in the phrase **slowly but surely**). **3.** (*sentence modifier*) am I not right in thinking that?; I am sure that: *surely you don't mean it?* **4.** *Rare.* in a sure manner. **5.** *Archaic.* safely; securely. **6.**

(*sentence substitute*) *Chiefly U.S. and Canadian.* willingly; of course; yes.

sure thing *Informal.* **1.** (*sentence substitute*) *Chiefly U.S.* all right! yes indeed! used to express enthusiastic assent. ~*n.* **2.** something guaranteed to be successful.

surety (ˈʃʊətɪ, ˈʃʊərɪtɪ) *n., pl.* **-ties.** **1.** a person who assumes legal responsibility for the fulfilment of another's debt or obligation and himself becomes liable if the other defaults. **2.** security given against loss or damage or as a guarantee that an obligation will be met. **3.** *Obsolete.* the quality or condition of being sure. **4.** *Obsolete.* a means of assurance or safety. **5. stand surety.** to act as a surety. [C14: from Old French *seurte,* from Latin *sēcūritās* SECURITY] —ˈ**surety,ship** *n.*

surf (sɜːf) *n.* **1.** waves breaking on the shore or on a reef. **2.** foam caused by the breaking of waves. ~*vb.* **3.** (*intr.*) to take part in surfing. [C17: probably variant of SOUGH[1]] —ˈ**surfable** *adj.* —ˈ**surf,like** *adj.* —ˈ**surfy** *adj.*

surface (ˈsɜːfɪs) *n.* **1. a.** the exterior face of an object or one such face. **b.** (*as modifier*): *surface gloss.* **2. a.** the area or size of such a face. **b.** (*as modifier*): *surface measurements.* **3.** material resembling such a face, with length and width but without depth. **4. a.** the superficial appearance as opposed to the real nature. **b.** (*as modifier*): *a surface resemblance.* **5.** *Geom.* **a.** the complete boundary of a solid figure. **b.** a continuous two-dimensional configuration. **6. a.** the uppermost level of the land or sea. **b.** (*as modifier*): *surface transportation.* **7. come to the surface.** to emerge; become apparent. **8. on the surface.** to all appearances. ~*vb.* **9.** to rise or cause to rise to or as if to the surface (of water, etc.). **10.** (*tr.*) to treat the surface of, as by polishing, smoothing, etc. **11.** (*tr.*) to furnish with a surface. **12.** (*intr.*) *Mining.* **a.** to work at or near the ground surface. **b.** to wash surface ore deposits. **13.** (*intr.*) to become apparent; emerge. **14.** (*intr.*) *Informal.* **a.** to wake up. **b.** to get up. [C17: from French, from *sur* on + *face* FACE, probably on the model of Latin SUPERFICIES] —ˈ**surfaceless** *adj.* —ˈ**surfacer** *n.*

surface acoustic wave *n.* an acoustic wave generated on the surface of a piezoelectric substrate: used as a filter in electronic circuits.

surface-active *adj.* (of a substance, esp. a detergent) capable of lowering the surface tension of a liquid, usually water. See also **surfactant.**

surface condenser *n.* a steam condenser usually associated with a steam turbine in which the steam is condensed on the surface of tubes through which water is passed. Compare **jet condenser.**

surface friction drag *n.* the part of the drag on a body moving through a fluid that is dependent on the nature of the surface of the body. Also called: **skin friction.**

surface mail *n.* mail transported by land or sea. Compare **air mail.**

surface noise *n.* noise produced by the friction of the needle or stylus of a record player with the rotating record, caused by a static charge, dust, or irregularities on the surface of a record.

surface plate *n.* another name for **faceplate** (sense 2).

surface structure *n. Generative grammar.* a representation of a string of words or morphemes as they occur in a sentence, together with labels and brackets that represent syntactic structure. Compare **deep structure.**

surface tension *n.* **1.** a property of liquids caused by intermolecular forces near the surface leading to the apparent presence of a surface film and to capillarity, etc. **2.** a measure of this property expressed as the force acting normal to one side of a line of unit length on the surface: measured in newtons per metre. Symbol: T, γ, or σ

surface-to-air *adj.* of or relating to a missile launched from the surface of the earth against airborne targets.

surface-to-surface *adj.* of or relating to a missile launched from the surface of the earth against surface targets.

surfactant (sɜːˈfæktənt) *n.* **1.** Also called: **surface-active agent.** a substance, such as a detergent, that can reduce the surface tension of a liquid and thus allow it to foam or penetrate solids; a wetting agent. ~*adj.* **2.** having the properties of a surfactant. [C20: *surf(ace)-act(ive) a(ge)nt*]

surfbird (ˈsɜːf,bɜːd) *n.* an American shore bird, *Aphriza virgata,* having a spotted plumage, with a black and white tail: family *Scolopacidae* (sandpipers, etc.), order *Charadriiformes.*

surfboard (ˈsɜːf,bɔːd) *n.* **1.** a long narrow board used in surfing. **2.** a wrestling hold in which a wrestler sits on the floor and locks his feet round his opponent's ankles, seizes the arms or head, and bends his opponent's body backwards, placing his knees against his opponent's back.

surfboat (ˈsɜːf,bəʊt) *n.* a boat with a high bow and stern and flotation chambers, equipped for use in rough surf.

surfcasting (ˈsɜːf,kɑːstɪŋ) *n.* fishing from the shore by casting into the surf. —ˈ**surf,caster** *n.*

surfeit (ˈsɜːfɪt) *n.* **1.** (usually foll. by *of*) an excessive or immoderate amount. **2.** overindulgence, esp. in eating or drinking. **3.** disgust, nausea, etc., caused by such overindulgence. ~*vb.* **4.** (*tr.*) to supply or feed excessively; satiate. **5.** (*intr.*) *Archaic.* to eat, drink, or be supplied to excess. **6.** (*intr.*) *Obsolete.* to feel uncomfortable as a consequence of overindulgence. [C13: from French *sourfait,* from *sourfaire* to overdo, from SUR-[1] + *faire,* from Latin *facere* to do] —ˈ**surfeiter** *n.*

surfie (ˈsɜːfɪ) *n. Austral. and N.Z. slang.* a young man whose main interest is in surfing, esp. when considered as a cult figure.

surfing (ˈsɜːfɪŋ) *n.* the sport of riding towards shore on the crest of a wave by standing or lying on a surfboard. —ˈ**surfer** *or* ˈ**surf,rider** *n.*

surf mat *n. Austral. informal.* a small inflatable rubber mattress used to ride on waves.

surf music *n.* a U.S. West Coast style of pop music of the early 1960s, characterized by high harmony vocals and strong trebly guitar riffs.

surfperch (ˈsɜːf,pɜːtʃ) *n.* any viviparous marine percoid fish of the family *Embiotocidae,* of North American Pacific coastal waters. Also called: **sea perch.**

surf scoter *or* **duck** *n.* a North American scoter, *Melanitta perspicillata,* having white patches on the head.

surg. *abbrev. for:* **1.** surgeon. **2.** surgery. **3.** surgical.

surge (sɜːdʒ) *n.* **1.** a strong rush or sweep; sudden increase: *a surge of anger.* **2.** the rolling swell of the sea, esp. after the passage of a large wave. **3.** a heavy rolling motion or sound: *the surge of the trumpets.* **4.** an undulating rolling surface, as of hills. **5.** a billowing cloud or volume. **6.** *Nautical.* a temporary release or slackening of a rope or cable. **7.** a large momentary increase in the voltage or current in an electric circuit. **8.** an instability or unevenness in the power output of an engine. **9.** *Astronomy.* a short-lived disturbance, occurring during the eruption of a solar flare. ~*vb.* **10.** (*intr.*) (of waves, the sea, etc.) to rise or roll with a heavy swelling motion. **11.** (*intr.*) to move like a heavy sea. **12.** *Nautical.* to slacken or temporarily release (a rope or cable) from a capstan or (of a rope, etc.) to be slackened or released and slip back. **13.** (*intr.*) (of an electric current or voltage) to undergo a large momentary increase. **14.** (*tr.*) *Rare.* to cause to move in or as if in a wave or waves. [C15: from Latin *surgere* to rise, from *sub-* up + *regere* to lead] —ˈ**surgeless** *adj.* —ˈ**surger** *n.*

surgeon (ˈsɜːdʒən) *n.* **1.** a medical practioner who specializes in surgery. **2.** a medical officer in the Royal Navy. [C14: from Anglo-Norman *surgien,* from Old French *cirurgien;* see SURGERY]

surgeoncy (ˈsɜːdʒənsɪ) *n., pl.* **-cies.** *Chiefly Brit.* the office, duties, or position of a surgeon, esp. in the army or navy.

surgeonfish (ˈsɜːdʒən,fɪʃ) *n., pl.* **-fish** *or* **-fishes.** any tropical marine spiny-finned fish of the family *Acanthuridae,* having a compressed brightly coloured body with one or more knifelike spines at the base of the tail.

surgeon general *n., pl.* **surgeons general.** **1.** (in the British, U.S., and certain other armies and navies) the senior officer of the medical service. **2.** the head of the public health service in the U.S.

surgeon's knot *n.* a knot used by surgeons in tying ligatures, etc.

surgery (ˈsɜːdʒərɪ) *n., pl.* **-geries.** **1.** the branch of medicine concerned with treating disease, injuries, etc., by means of manual or operative procedures, esp. by incision into the body. **2.** the performance of such procedures by a surgeon. **3.** *Brit.* a place where a doctor, dentist, etc., can be consulted. **4.** *Brit.* an occasion when an MP, lawyer, etc., is available for consultation. **5.** *U.S. and Canadian.* an operating theatre where surgical operations are performed. [C14: via Old French from Latin *chirurgia,* from Greek *kheirurgia,* from *kheir* hand + *ergon* work]

surge tank *n. Engineering.* a tank used to absorb surges in flow.

surgical (ˈsɜːdʒɪkəl) *adj.* of, relating to, involving, or used in surgery. —ˈ**surgically** *adv.*

surgical boot *n.* a specially designed boot or shoe that compensates for deformities of the foot or leg.

surgical spirit *n.* methylated spirit containing small amounts of oil of wintergreen and castor oil: used medically for sterilizing.

suricate (ˈsjʊərɪ,keɪt) *n.* another name for **slender-tailed meerkat** (see **meerkat**). [C18: from French *surikate,* probably from a native South African word]

Surinam toad (,sʊərɪˈnæm) *n.* another name for **pipa.**

surjection (sɜːˈdʒɛkʃən) *n.* a mathematical function or mapping for which every element of the image space is a value for some members of the domain. See also **injection** (sense 5), **bijection.** [C20: from SUR-[1] + *-jection,* on the model of PROJECTION] —**sur**ˈ**jective** *adj.*

surly (ˈsɜːlɪ) *adj.* **-lier, -liest.** **1.** sullenly ill-tempered or rude. **2.** (of an animal) ill-tempered or refractory. **3.** dismal. **4.** *Obsolete.* arrogant. [C16: from obsolete *sirly* haughty; see SIR] —ˈ**surlily** *adv.* —ˈ**surliness** *n.*

surmise *vb.* (sɜːˈmaɪz). **1.** (when *tr., may take a clause as object*) to infer (something) from incomplete or uncertain evidence. ~*n.* (sɜːˈmaɪz, ˈsɜːmaɪz). **2.** an idea inferred from inconclusive evidence. [C15: from Old French, from *surmettre* to accuse, from Latin *supermittere* to throw over, from SUPER- + *mittere* to send] —**sur**ˈ**misable** *adj.* —**sur**ˈ**miser** *n.*

surmount (sɜːˈmaʊnt) *vb.* (*tr.*) **1.** to prevail over; overcome: *to surmount tremendous difficulties.* **2.** to ascend and cross to the opposite side of. **3.** to lie on top of or rise above. **4.** to put something on top of or above. **5.** *Obsolete.* to surpass or exceed. [C14: from Old French *surmonter,* from SUR-[1] + *monter* to MOUNT[1]] —**sur**ˈ**mountable** *adj.* —**sur**ˈ**mountableness** *n.* —**sur**ˈ**mounter** *n.*

surmullet (sɜːˈmʌlɪt) *n.* a U.S. name for the **red mullet.** [C17: from French *sormulet,* from *sor* brown + MULLET]

surname (ˈsɜːˌneɪm) *n.* 1. Also called: **last name, second name.** a family name as opposed to a Christian name. 2. (formerly) a descriptive epithet attached to a person's name to denote a personal characteristic, profession, etc.; nickname. ~*vb.* 3. (*tr.*) to furnish with or call by a surname. [C14: via Anglo-French from Old French *surnom.* See SUR-[1], NAME] —ˈ**surˌnamer** *n.*

surpass (sɜːˈpɑːs) *vb.* (*tr.*) 1. to be greater than in degree, extent, etc. 2. to be superior to in achievement or excellence. 3. to overstep the limit or range of: *the theory surpasses my comprehension.* [C16: from French *surpasser,* from SUR-[1] + *passer* to PASS] —**surˈpassable** *adj.*

surpassing (sɜːˈpɑːsɪŋ) *adj.* 1. exceptional; extraordinary. ~*adv.* 2. *Obsolete or poetic.* (intensifier): *surpassing fair.* —**surˈpassingly** *adv.*

surplice (ˈsɜːplɪs) *n.* a loose wide-sleeved liturgical vestment of linen, reaching to the knees, worn over the cassock by clergymen, choristers, and acolytes. [C13: via Anglo-French from Old French *sourpelis,* from Medieval Latin *superpellīcium,* from SUPER- + *pellīcium* coat made of skins, from Latin *pellis* a skin] —ˈ**surpliced** *adj.*

surplus (ˈsɜːpləs) *n., pl.* **-pluses.** 1. a quantity or amount in excess of what is required. 2. *Accounting.* **a.** an excess of total assets over total liabilities. **b.** an excess of actual net assets over the nominal value of capital stock. **c.** an excess of revenues over expenditures during a certain period of time. 3. *Economics.* **a.** an excess of government revenues over expenditures during a certain financial year. **b.** an excess of receipts over payments on the balance of payments. ~*adj.* 4. being in excess; extra. [C14: from Old French, from Medieval Latin *superplūs,* from Latin SUPER- + *plūs* more]

surplusage (ˈsɜːpləsɪdʒ) *n.* 1. *Law.* (in pleading, etc.) irrelevant matter, such as a superfluous allegation. 2. an excess of words. 3. a less common word for **surplus.**

surprint (ˈsɜːˌprɪnt) *vb.* 1. (*tr.*) to print (additional matter) over something already printed; overprint. ~*n.* 2. marks, printed matter, etc., that have been surprinted.

surprise (səˈpraɪz) *vb.* (*tr.*) 1. to cause to feel amazement or wonder. 2. to encounter or discover unexpectedly or suddenly. 3. to capture or assault suddenly and without warning. 4. to present with something unexpected, such as a gift. 5. (foll. by *into*) to provoke (someone) to unintended action by a trick, etc.: *to surprise a person into an indiscretion.* 6. (often foll. by *from*) to elicit by unexpected behaviour or by a trick: *to surprise information from a prisoner.* ~*n.* 7. the act or an instance of surprising; the act of taking unawares. 8. a sudden or unexpected event, gift, etc. 9. the feeling or condition of being surprised; astonishment. 10. (*modifier*) causing, characterized by, or relying upon surprise: *a surprise move.* 11. **take by surprise. a.** to come upon suddenly and without warning. **b.** to capture unexpectedly or catch unprepared. **c.** to astonish; amaze. [C15: from Old French, from *surprendre* to overtake, from SUR-[1] + *prendre* from Latin *prehendere* to grasp; see PREHENSILE] —**surˈprisal** *n.* —**surˈprised** *adj.* —**surprisedly** (səˈpraɪzɪdlɪ) *adv.* —**surˈpriser** *n.*

surprising (səˈpraɪzɪŋ) *adj.* causing surprise; unexpected or amazing. —**surˈprisingly** *adv.* —**surˈprisingness** *n.*

surra (ˈsʊərə) *n.* a tropical febrile disease of cattle, horses, camels, and dogs, characterized by severe emaciation: caused by the protozoan *Trypanosoma evansi* and transmitted by fleas. [from Marathi]

surreal (səˈrɪəl) *adj.* 1. suggestive of surrealism; dreamlike. ~*n.* 2. **the.** the atmosphere or qualities evoked by surrealism.

surrealism (səˈrɪəˌlɪzəm) *n.* (*sometimes cap.*) a movement in art and literature in the 1920s, which developed esp. from dada, characterized by the evocative juxtaposition of incongruous images in order to include unconscious and dream elements. [C20: from French *surréalisme,* from SUR-[1] + *réalisme* REALISM] —**surˈrealist** *n., adj.* —**surˌrealˈistic** *adj.* —**surˌrealˈistically** *adv.*

surrebuttal (ˌsɜːrɪˈbʌtᵊl) *n. Law.* (in pleading) the giving of evidence in support of a surrebutter.

surrebutter (ˌsɜːrɪˈbʌtə) *n. Law.* (in pleading) the plaintiff's reply to the defendant's rebutter.

surrejoinder (ˌsɜːrɪˈdʒɔɪndə) *n. Law.* (in pleading) the plaintiff's reply to the defendant's rejoinder.

surrender (səˈrɛndə) *vb.* 1. (*tr.*) to relinquish to the control or possession of another under duress or on demand: *to surrender a city.* 2. (*tr.*) to relinquish or forego (an office, position, etc.), esp. as a voluntary concession to another: *he surrendered his place to a lady.* 3. to give (oneself) up physically, as or as if to an enemy. 4. to allow (oneself) to yield, as to a temptation, influence, etc. 5. (*tr.*) to give up (hope, etc.) 6. (*tr.*) *Law.* to give up or restore (an estate), esp. to give up a lease before expiration of the term. 7. (*tr.*) *Obsolete.* to return or render (thanks, etc.). 8. **surrender to bail.** to present oneself at court at the appointed time after having been on bail. ~*n.* 9. the act or instance of surrendering. 10. *Insurance.* the voluntary discontinuation of a life policy by its holder in return for a consideration (the **surrender value**). 11. *Law.* **a.** the yielding up or restoring of an estate, esp. the giving up of a lease before its term has expired. **b.** the giving up to the appropriate authority of a fugitive from justice. **c.** the act of surrendering or being surrendered to bail. **d.** the deed by which a legal surrender is effected. [C15: from Old French *surrendre* to yield, from SUR-[1] + *rendre* to RENDER] —**surˈrenderer** *n.*

surreptitious (ˌsʌrəpˈtɪʃəs) *adj.* 1. done, acquired, etc., in secret or by improper means. 2. operating by stealth. 3. characterized by fraud or misrepresentation of the truth. [C15: from Latin *surreptīcius* furtive, from *surripere* to steal, from *sub-* secretly + *rapere* to snatch] —ˌ**surrepˈtitiously** *adv.* —ˌ**surrepˈtitiousness** *n.*

surrey (ˈsʌrɪ) *n.* a light four-wheeled horse-drawn carriage having two or four seats. [C19: shortened from *Surrey cart,* after Surrey, SE England, where it was originally made]

surrogate *n.* (ˈsʌrəgɪt). 1. a person or thing acting as a substitute. 2. *Chiefly Brit.* a deputy, such as a clergyman appointed to deputize for a bishop in granting marriage licences. 3. *Psychiatry.* a person who is a substitute for someone else, esp. in childhood when different persons, such as a brother or teacher, can act as substitutes for the parents. 4. (in some U.S. states) a judge with jurisdiction over the probate of wills, etc. 5. (*modifier*) of, relating to, or acting as a surrogate: *a surrogate pleasure.* ~*vb.* (ˈsʌrəˌgeɪt). (*tr.*) 6. to put in another's position as a deputy, substitute, etc. 7. to appoint as a successor to oneself. [C17: from Latin *surrogāre* to substitute; see SUBROGATE] —ˈ**surrogateship** *n.* —ˌ**surroˈgation** *n.*

surrogate motherhood *or* **surrogacy** (ˈsʌrəgəsɪ) *n.* the role of a woman who bears a child on behalf of a couple unable to have a child, either by artificial insemination from the man or implantation of an embryo from the woman. —**surrogate mother** *n.*

surround (səˈraʊnd) *vb.* (*tr.*) 1. to encircle or enclose or cause to be encircled or enclosed. 2. to deploy forces on all sides of (a place or military formation), so preventing access or retreat. 3. to exist around: *I dislike the people who surround her.* ~*n.* 4. *Chiefly Brit.* a border, esp. the area of uncovered floor between the walls of a room and the carpet or around an opening or panel. 5. *Chiefly U.S.* **a.** a method of capturing wild beasts by encircling the area in which they are believed to be. **b.** the area so encircled. [C15 *surrounden* to overflow, from Old French *suronder,* from Late Latin *superundāre,* from Latin SUPER- + *undāre* to abound, from *unda* a wave] —**surˈrounding** *adj.*

surroundings (səˈraʊndɪŋz) *pl. n.* the conditions, scenery, etc., around a person, place, or thing; environment.

surround sound *n.* a system of sound recording and reproduction that uses three or more independent recording channels and loudspeakers in order to give the impression that the listener is surrounded by the sound sources. Compare **quadraphonics.** See also **ambisonics.**

sursum corda (ˈsɜːsəm ˈkɔːdə) *n.* 1. *R.C. Church.* a Latin versicle meaning *Lift up your hearts,* said by the priest at Mass. 2. a cry of exhortation, hope, etc. [C16: Latin, literally: up hearts]

surtax (ˈsɜːˌtæks) *n.* 1. a tax, usually highly progressive, levied on the amount by which a person's income exceeds a specific level. 2. an additional tax on something that has already been taxed. ~*vb.* 3. (*tr.*) to assess for liability to surtax; charge with an extra tax.

surtitles (ˈsɜːˌtaɪtᵊlz) *pl. n.* brief translations of the text of an opera that is being sung in a foreign language, projected above the stage.

surtout (ˈsɜːtuː; *French* syrtu) *n.* a man's overcoat resembling a frock coat, popular in the late 19th century. [C17: from French, from *sur* over + *tout* all]

surv. *abbrev. for:* 1. Also: **survey.** surveying. 2. surveyor.

surveillance (sɜːˈveɪləns) *n.* close observation or supervision maintained over a person, group, etc., esp. one in custody or under suspicion. [C19: from French, from *surveiller* to watch over, from SUR-[1] + *veiller* to keep watch (from Latin *vigilāre;* see VIGIL)] —**surˈveillant** *adj., n.*

survey *vb.* (sɜːˈveɪ, ˈsɜːveɪ). 1. (*tr.*) to view or consider in a comprehensive or general way: *to survey the situation.* 2. (*tr.*) to examine carefully, as or as if to appraise value: *to survey oneself in a mirror.* 3. to plot a detailed map of (an area of land) by measuring or calculating distances and height. 4. *Brit.* to inspect a building to determine its condition and value. 5. to examine a vessel thoroughly in order to determine its seaworthiness. 6. (*tr.*) to run a statistical survey on (incomes, opinions, etc.). ~*n.* (ˈsɜːveɪ). 7. a comprehensive or general view: *a survey of English literature.* 8. a critical, detailed, and formal inspection: *a survey of the nation's hospitals.* 9. *Brit.* an inspection of a building to determine its condition and value. 10. a report incorporating the results of such an inspection. 11. **a.** a body of surveyors. **b.** an area surveyed. 12. *Statistics.* a random sample. [C15: from French *surveoir,* from SUR-[1] + *veoir* to see, from Latin *vidēre*] —**surˈveyable** *adj.*

surveying (sɜːˈveɪɪŋ) *n.* 1. the study or practice of measuring altitudes, angles, and distances on the land surface so that they can be accurately plotted on a map. 2. the setting out on the ground of the positions of proposed construction or engineering works.

surveyor (sɜːˈveɪə) *n.* 1. a person whose occupation is to survey land or buildings. See also **quantity surveyor.** 2. *Chiefly Brit.* a person concerned with the official inspection of something for purposes of measurement and valuation. 3. a person who carries out surveys, esp. of ships (**marine surveyor**) to determine

seaworthiness, etc. **4.** a customs official. **5.** *Archaic.* a supervisor. —**sur'veyor,ship** *n.*
surveyor's chain *n.* a measuring chain 22 yards in length; Gunter's chain. See **chain** (sense 7).
surveyor's level *n.* another term for **level** (sense 19).
surveyor's measure *n.* the system of measurement based on the chain (66 feet) as a unit.
survival (sə'vaɪvᵊl) *n.* **1.** a person or thing that survives, such as a custom. **2. a.** the act or fact of surviving or condition of having survived. **b.** (*as modifier*): *survival kit.*
survival bag *n.* a large plastic bag carried by climbers for use in an emergency as protection against exposure.
survivalist (sə'vaɪvəlɪst) *n. U.S.* **a.** a person who believes in ensuring his personal survival of a catastrophic event by arming himself and often by living in the wild. **b.** (*as modifier*): *survivalist weapons.* —**sur'vival,ism** *n.*
survival of the fittest *n.* a popular term for **natural selection.**
survive (sə'vaɪv) *vb.* **1.** (*tr.*) to live after the death of (another): *he survived his wife by 12 years.* **2.** to continue in existence or use after (a passage of time, an adversity, etc.). **3.** *Informal.* to endure (something): *I don't know how I survive such an awful job.* [C15: from Old French *sourvivre,* from Latin *supervīvere,* from SUPER- + *vīvere* to live] —**sur'vivable** *adj.* —**sur,viva'bility** *n.*
survivor (sə'vaɪvə) *n.* **1.** a person or thing that survives. **2.** *Property law.* one of two or more specified persons having joint interests in property who lives longer than the other or others and thereby becomes entitled to the whole property. —**sur'vivor,ship** *n.*
sus (sʌs) *Brit. slang.* ~*n.* **1.** suspicion. **2.** a suspect. ~*adj.* **3.** suspicious. ~*vb.* **4.** a variant spelling of **suss** (sense 2). ~See also **sus laws.** [C20: shortened from SUSPICION]
susceptance (sə'sɛptəns) *n. Physics.* the imaginary component of the admittance. [C19: from SUSCEPT(IBILITY) + -ANCE]
susceptibility (sə,sɛptə'bɪlɪtɪ) *n., pl.* **-ties. 1.** the quality or condition of being susceptible. **2.** the ability or tendency to be impressed by emotional feelings; sensitivity. **3.** (*pl.*) emotional sensibilities; feelings. **4.** *Physics.* **a.** Also called: **electric susceptibility.** (of a dielectric) the amount by which the relative permittivity differs from unity. Symbol: Χ **b.** Also called: **magnetic susceptibility.** (of a magnetic medium) the amount by which the relative permeability differs from unity. Symbol: Κ
susceptible (sə'sɛptəbᵊl) *adj.* **1.** (*postpositive;* foll. by *of* or *to*) yielding readily (to); capable (of): *hypotheses susceptible of refutation; susceptible to control.* **2.** (*postpositive;* foll. by *to*) liable to be afflicted (by): *susceptible to colds.* **3.** easily impressed emotionally. [C17: from Late Latin *susceptibilis,* from Latin *suscipere* to take up, from SUB- + *capere* to take] —**sus'ceptibleness** *n.* —**sus'ceptibly** *adv.*
susceptive (sə'sɛptɪv) *adj.* **1.** another word for **receptive. 2.** a variant of **susceptible.** —**susceptivity** (,sʌsɛp'tɪvɪtɪ) *or* **sus'ceptiveness** *n.*
sushi ('suːʃɪ) *n.* a Japanese dish consisting of small cakes of cold rice with a topping esp. of raw fish. [from Japanese]
Susian ('suːzɪən) *n., adj.* another word for **Elamite.** [C16: from *Susiana,* a province of the ancient Persian Empire with its capital at *Susa*]
sus laws *or* **suss laws** *pl. n. Brit. slang* laws authorizing the arrest and punishment of suspected persons frequenting, or loitering in, public places with criminal intent. In England, the sus law formed part of the Vagrancy Act of 1824, repealed in 1981.
suslik ('sʌslɪk) *or* **souslik** *n.* a central Eurasian ground squirrel, *Citellus citellus,* of dry open areas, having large eyes and small ears. [from Russian]
suspect *vb.* (sə'spɛkt). **1.** (*tr.*) to believe guilty of a specified offence without proof. **2.** (*tr.*) to think false, questionable, etc.: *she suspected his sincerity.* **3.** (*tr.; may take a clause as object*) to surmise to be the case; think probable: *to suspect fraud.* **4.** (*intr.*) to have suspicion. ~*n.* ('sʌspɛkt). **5.** a person who is under suspicion. ~*adj.* ('sʌspɛkt). **6.** causing or open to suspicion. [C14: from Latin *suspicere* to mistrust, from SUB- + *specere* to look] —**sus'pecter** *n.* —**'suspectless** *adj.*
suspend (sə'spɛnd) *vb.* **1.** (*tr.*) to hang from above so as to permit free movement. **2.** (*tr.; passive*) to cause to remain floating or hanging: *a cloud of smoke was suspended over the town.* **3.** (*tr.*) to render inoperative or cause to cease, esp. temporarily: *to suspend interest payments.* **4.** (*tr.*) to hold in abeyance; postpone action on: *to suspend a decision.* **5.** (*tr.*) to debar temporarily from privilege, office, etc., as a punishment. **6.** (*tr.*) *Chem.* to cause (particles) to be held in suspension in a fluid. **7.** (*tr.*) *Music.* to continue (a note) until the next chord is sounded, with which it usually forms a dissonance. See **suspension** (sense 11). **8.** (*intr.*) to cease payment, as from incapacity to meet financial obligations. **9.** (*tr.*) *Obsolete.* to put or keep in a state of anxiety or wonder. **10.** (*intr.*) *Rare.* to come to a stop, esp. temporarily. **11.** (*intr.*) *Obsolete.* to be attached from above. [C13: from Latin *suspendere* from SUB- + *pendere* to hang] —**sus'pendible** *or* **sus'pensible** *adj.* —**sus,pendi'bility** *n.*
suspended animation *n.* a temporary cessation of the vital functions, as by freezing an organism.
suspended sentence *n.* a sentence of imprisonment that is not served by an offender unless he commits a further offence during its currency. Compare **deferred sentence.**
suspender (sə'spɛndə) *n.* **1.** (*often pl.*) *Brit.* **a.** an elastic strap attached to a belt or corset having a fastener at the end, for holding up women's stockings. **b.** a similar fastener attached to a garter worn by men in order to support socks. U.S. and Canadian equivalent: **garter. 2.** (*pl.*) the U.S. and Canadian name for **braces. 3.** a person or thing that suspends, such as one of the vertical cables in a suspension bridge.
suspender belt *n.* a belt with suspenders hanging from it to hold up women's stockings. U.S. and Canadian name: **garter belt.**
suspense (sə'spɛns) *n.* **1.** the condition of being insecure or uncertain: *the matter of the succession remained in suspense for many years.* **2.** mental uncertainty; anxiety: *their father's illness kept them in a state of suspense.* **3.** excitement felt at the approach of the climax: *a play of terrifying suspense.* **4.** the condition of being suspended. [C15: from Medieval Latin *suspensum* delay, from Latin *suspendere* to hang up; see SUSPEND] —**sus'penseful** *adj.*
suspense account *n. Book-keeping.* an account in which entries are made until determination of their proper disposition.
suspension (sə'spɛnʃən) *n.* **1.** an interruption or temporary revocation: *the suspension of a law.* **2.** a temporary debarment, as from position, privilege, etc. **3.** a deferment, esp. of a decision, judgment, etc. **4.** *Law.* **a.** a postponement of execution of a sentence or the deferring of a judgment, etc. **b.** a temporary extinguishment of a right or title. **5.** cessation of payment of business debts, esp. as a result of insolvency. **6.** the act of suspending or the state of being suspended. **7.** a system of springs, shock absorbers, etc., that supports the body of a wheeled or tracked vehicle and insulates it and its occupants from shocks transmitted by the wheels. See also **hydraulic suspension. 8.** a device or structure, usually a wire or spring, that serves to suspend or support something, such as the pendulum of a clock. **9.** *Chem.* a dispersion of fine solid or liquid particles in a fluid, the particles being supported by buoyancy. See also **colloid. 10.** the process by which eroded particles of rock are transported in a river. **11.** *Music.* one or more notes of a chord that are prolonged until a subsequent chord is sounded, usually to form a dissonance.
suspension bridge *n.* a bridge that has a deck suspended by cables or rods from other cables or chains that hang between two towers and are anchored at both ends.
suspension point *n. Chiefly U.S.* one of a group of dots, usually three, used in written material to indicate the omission of a word or words. Compare **ellipsis** (sense 2).
suspensive (sə'spɛnsɪv) *adj.* **1.** having the power of deferment; effecting suspension. **2.** causing, characterized by, or relating to suspense. **3.** inclined to defer judgment; undecided. **4.** *Rare.* characterized by physical suspension. —**sus'pensively** *adv.* —**sus'pensiveness** *n.*
suspensoid (sə'spɛnsɔɪd) *n. Chem.* a system consisting of a suspension of solid particles in a liquid.
suspensor (sə'spɛnsə) *n.* **1.** another name for **suspensory** (sense 1). **2.** *Botany.* (in a seed) a row of cells attached to the embryo plant, by means of which it is pushed into the endosperm.
suspensory (sə'spɛnsərɪ) *n., pl.* **-ries. 1.** Also called: **suspensor.** *Anatomy.* a ligament or muscle that holds a structure or part in position. **2.** *Med.* a bandage, sling, etc., for supporting a dependent part. **3.** another name (esp. U.S.) for **athletic support.** ~*adj.* **4.** suspending or supporting. **5.** *Anatomy.* (of a ligament or muscle) supporting or holding a structure or part in position.
suspicion (sə'spɪʃən) *n.* **1.** the act or an instance of suspecting; belief without sure proof, esp. that something is wrong. **2.** the feeling of mistrust of a person who suspects. **3.** the state of being suspected: *to be shielded from suspicion.* **4.** a slight trace. **5. above suspicion.** in such a position that no guilt may be thought or implied, esp. through having an unblemished reputation. **6. on suspicion.** as a suspect. **7. under suspicion.** regarded with distrust. [C14: from Old French *sospeçon,* from Latin *suspīciō* distrust, from *suspicere* to mistrust; see SUSPECT] —**sus'picional** *adj.* —**sus'picionless** *adj.*
suspicious (sə'spɪʃəs) *adj.* **1.** exciting or liable to excite suspicion; questionable. **2.** disposed to suspect something wrong. **3.** indicative or expressive of suspicion. —**sus'piciously** *adv.* —**sus'piciousness** *n.*
suspire (sə'spaɪə) *vb. Archaic or poetic.* **1.** to sigh or utter with a sigh; yearn. **2.** (*intr.*) to breathe; respire. [C15: from Latin *suspīrāre* to take a deep breath, from SUB- + *spīrāre* to breathe] —**suspiration** (,sʌspɪ'reɪʃən) *n.*
suss (sʌs) *vb.* (*tr.*) *Slang.* **1.** (often foll. by *out*) to attempt to work out (a situation, person's character, etc.), esp. using one's intuition. **2.** Also: **sus.** to become aware of; suspect (esp. in the phrase **suss it**). ~*n.* **3.** sharpness of mind; social astuteness. ~See also **sus laws.** [C20: shortened from SUSPECT]
Sussex ('sʌsɪks) *n.* **1.** a breed of red beef cattle originally from Sussex, SE England. **2.** a heavy and long-established breed of domestic fowl used principally as a table bird.
Sussex spaniel *n.* a short-legged breed of spaniel with a golden-liver coloured coat. [so named because it was bred in Sussex, in the late 18th century]
susso ('sʌsəʊ) *n., pl.* **-sos.** *Austral. slang.* **a.** money paid by the government to an unemployed person. **b.** an unemployed person receiving such money. [C20: from SUSTENANCE]

sustain (sə'steɪn) *vb.* (*tr.*) **1.** to hold up under; withstand: *to sustain great provocation.* **2.** to undergo (an injury, loss, etc.); suffer: *to sustain a broken arm.* **3.** to maintain or prolong: *to sustain a discussion.* **4.** to support physically from below. **5.** to provide for or give support to, esp. by supplying necessities: *to sustain one's family; to sustain a charity.* **6.** to keep up the vitality or courage of. **7.** to uphold or affirm the justice or validity of: *to sustain a decision.* **8.** to establish the truth of; confirm. ~*n.* **9.** *Music.* the prolongation of a note, by playing technique or electronics. [C13: via Old French from Latin *sustinēre* to hold up, from SUB- + *tenēre* to hold] —**sus'tained** *adj.* —**sustainedly** (sə'steɪnɪdlɪ) *adv.* —**sus'taining** *adj.* —**sus'tainingly** *adv.* —**sus'tainment** *n.*

sustainable (sə'steɪnəbᵊl) *adj.* **1.** capable of being sustained. **2.** (of economic development, energy sources, etc.) capable of being maintained at a steady level without exhausting natural resources or causing severe ecological damage: *sustainable development.*

sustainer (sə'steɪnə) *n.* a rocket engine that maintains the velocity of a space vehicle after the booster has been jettisoned.

sustaining pedal *n. Music.* a foot-operated lever on a piano, usually the right one of two, that keeps the dampers raised from the strings when keys are released, allowing them to continue to vibrate. Compare **soft pedal.**

sustaining program *n. U.S. and Canadian.* a television or radio programme promoted by the broadcasting network or station itself and not by a commercial sponsor.

sustenance ('sʌstənəns) *n.* **1.** means of sustaining health or life; nourishment. **2.** means of maintenance; livelihood. **3.** Also: **sustention** (sə'stɛnʃən). the act or process of sustaining or the quality of being sustained. [C13: from Old French *sostenance,* from *sustenir* to SUSTAIN]

sustentacular (ˌsʌstɛn'tækjʊlə) *adj. Anatomy.* (of fibres, cells, etc.) supporting or forming a support. [C19: from Latin *sustentāculum* a stay, from *sustentāre* to support, from *sustinēre* to SUSTAIN]

sustentation (ˌsʌstɛn'teɪʃən) *n.* a less common word for **sustenance.** [C14: from Latin *sustentātio,* from *sustentāre,* frequentative of *sustinēre* to SUSTAIN]

sustentation fund *n.* a fund, esp. in the Church of Scotland, to augment the support of ministers.

susu ('suːsuː) *n.* a variant form of **sou-sou.**

Susu ('suːsuː) *n.* **1.** (*pl.* **-su** *or* **-sus**) a member of a Negroid people of W Africa, living chiefly in Guinea, the Sudan, and Sierra Leone. **2.** the language of this people, belonging to the Mande branch of the Niger-Congo family.

susurrate ('sjuːsəˌreɪt) *vb.* (*intr.*) *Literary.* to make a soft rustling sound; whisper; murmur. [C17: from Latin *susurrāre* to whisper] —**susurrant** (sjuː'sʌrənt) *adj.* —ˌ**susur'ration** *or* **'susurrus** *n.*

Suth. *abbrev. for* Sutherland.

sutler ('sʌtlə) *n.* (formerly) a merchant who accompanied an army in order to sell provisions to the soldiers. [C16: from obsolete Dutch *soeteler,* from Middle Low German *suteler,* from Middle High German *sudelen* to do dirty work; related to SOOT, SEETHE] —**'sutlerˌship** *n.*

sutra ('suːtrə) *n.* **1.** *Hinduism.* Sanskrit sayings or collections of sayings on Vedic doctrine dating from about 200 A.D. onwards. **2.** (*modifier*) *Hinduism.* **a.** of or relating to the last of the Vedic literary periods, from about 500 to 100 B.C.: *the sutra period.* **b.** of or relating to the sutras or compilations of sutras of about 200 A.D. onwards. **3.** *Buddhism.* collections of dialogues and discourses of classic Mahayana Buddhism dating from the 2nd to the 6th centuries A.D. [C19: from Sanskrit: list of rules]

suttee (sʌ'tiː, 'sʌtiː) *n.* **1.** the former Hindu custom whereby a widow burnt herself to death on her husband's funeral pyre. **2.** a Hindu widow who immolated herself in this way. [C18: from Sanskrit *satī* virtuous woman, from *sat* good] —**sut'teeism** *n.*

suture ('suːtʃə) *n.* **1.** *Surgery.* **a.** catgut, silk thread, or wire used to stitch together two bodily surfaces. **b.** the surgical seam formed after joining two surfaces. **2.** *Anatomy.* a type of immovable joint, esp. between the bones of the skull (**cranial suture**). **3.** a seam or joining, as in sewing. **4.** *Zoology.* a line of junction in a mollusc shell, esp. the line between adjacent chambers of a nautiloid shell. **5.** *Botany.* a line marking the point of dehiscence in a seed pod or capsule. ~*vb.* **6.** (*tr.*) *Surgery.* to join (the edges of a wound, etc.) by means of sutures. [C16: from Latin *sūtūra,* from *suere* to SEW] —**'sutural** *adj.* —**'suturally** *adv.*

suzerain ('suːzəˌreɪn) *n.* **1. a.** a state or sovereign exercising some degree of dominion over a dependent state, usually controlling its foreign affairs. **b.** (*as modifier*): *a suzerain power.* **2. a.** a feudal overlord. **b.** (*as modifier*): *suzerain lord.* [C19: from French, from *sus* above (from Latin *sursum* turned upwards, from *sub-* up + *vertere* to turn) + *-erain,* as in *souverain* SOVEREIGN]

suzerainty ('suːzərəntɪ) *n., pl.* **-ties.** **1.** the position, power, or dignity of a suzerain. **2.** the relationship between suzerain and subject.

sv *abbrev. for:* **1.** sailing vessel. **2.** side valve. **3.** sub verbo *or* voce. [Latin: under the word *or* voice]

SV *abbrev. for:* **1.** Sancta Virgo. [Latin: Holy Virgin] **2.** Sanctitas Vestra. [Latin: Your Holiness]

svelte (svɛlt, sfɛlt) *adj.* **1.** attractively or gracefully slim; slender. **2.** urbane or sophisticated. [C19: from French, from Italian *svelto,* from *svellere* to pull out, from Latin *ēvellere,* from EX-[1] + *vellere* to pull]

Svengali (svɛn'gɑːlɪ) *n.* a person who controls another's mind, usually with sinister intentions. [after a character in British writer George Du Maurier's novel *Trilby* (1894)]

SW **1.** *symbol for* southwest(ern). **2.** *abbrev. for* short wave.

Sw. *abbrev. for:* **1.** Sweden. **2.** Swedish.

swab (swɒb) *n.* **1.** *Med.* **a.** a small piece of cotton, gauze, etc., for use in applying medication, cleansing a wound, or obtaining a specimen of a secretion, etc. **b.** the specimen so obtained. **2.** a mop for cleaning floors, decks, etc. **3.** a brush used to clean a firearm's bore. **4.** *Slang.* an uncouth or worthless fellow. ~*vb.* **swabs, swabbing, swabbed.** **5.** (*tr.*) to clean or medicate with or as if with a swab. **6.** (*tr.;* foll. by *up*) to take up with a swab. [C16: probably from Middle Dutch *swabbe* mop; related to Norwegian *svabba* to splash, Dutch *zwabberen* to mop, German *schwappen* to slop over]

swabber ('swɒbə) *n.* **1.** a person who uses a swab. **2.** a device designed for swabbing. **3.** *Slang.* an uncouth fellow.

swacked (swækt) *adj. Slang.* in a state of intoxication, stupor, or euphoria induced by drugs or alcohol. [C20: perhaps from Scottish *swack* a heavy blow, of imitative origin]

swaddle ('swɒdᵊl) *vb.* (*tr.*) **1.** to wind a bandage round. **2.** to wrap (a baby) in swaddling clothes. **3.** to restrain as if by wrapping with bandages; smother. ~*n.* **4.** *Chiefly U.S.* swaddling clothes. [C15: from Old English *swæthel* swaddling clothes; related to *swathian* to SWATHE]

swaddling clothes *pl. n.* **1.** long strips of linen or other cloth formerly wrapped round a newly born baby. **2.** restrictions or supervision imposed on the immature.

swaddy *or* **swaddie** ('swɒdɪ) *n., pl.* **-dies.** *Brit. slang.* a private soldier. Compare **squaddie.** [C19: from dialect *swad* a country bumpkin]

Swadeshi (swə'deɪʃɪ) *adj.* **1.** (in present-day India) produced within the country; not imported. ~*n.* **2.** (in British India) the encouragement of domestic production and boycott of foreign goods as part of the campaign for independence. [C20: from Bengali *svadesī,* from Sanskrit *svadeśin,* from *sva* one's own + *deśa* country]

swag (swæg) *n.* **1.** *Slang.* property obtained by theft or other illicit means. **2.** *Slang.* goods; valuables. **3.** an ornamental festoon of fruit, flowers, or drapery or a representation of this. **4.** a swaying movement; lurch. **5.** *Midland England dialect.* a depression filled with water, resulting from mining subsidence. **6.** *Austral. and N.Z. informal.* a swagman's pack containing personal belongings. **7.** **go on the swag.** *Austral. and N.Z. informal.* to become a tramp. **8.** **swags of.** *Austral. and N.Z. informal.* lots of. ~*vb.* **swags, swagging, swagged.** **9.** *Chiefly Brit.* to lurch or sag or cause to lurch or sag. **10.** (*tr.*) to adorn or arrange with swags. **11.** (*intr.*) *Austral. informal.* to tramp about carrying a pack of personal belongings. [C17: perhaps of Scandinavian origin; compare Norwegian *svagga* to SWAY]

swage (sweɪdʒ) *n.* **1.** a shaped tool or die used in forming cold metal by hammering, pressing, etc. **2.** a decorative moulding. ~*vb.* **3.** (*tr.*) to form (metal) with a swage. [C19: from French *souage,* of unknown origin] —**'swager** *n.*

swage block *n.* an iron block cut with holes, recesses, and grooves to assist in the cold-working of metal.

swagger[1] ('swægə) *vb.* **1.** (*intr.*) to walk or behave in an arrogant manner. **2.** (*intr.;* often foll. by *about*) to brag loudly. **3.** (*tr.*) *Rare.* to force, influence, etc., by blustering. ~*n.* **4.** arrogant gait, conduct, or manner. ~*adj.* **5.** *Brit. informal, rare.* elegantly fashionable. [C16: probably from SWAG] —**'swaggerer** *n.* —**'swaggering** *adj.* —**'swaggeringly** *adv.*

swagger[2] ('swægə) *or* **swaggie** ('swægɪ) *n.* other names for **swagman.**

swagger stick *or esp. Brit.* **swagger cane** *n.* a short cane or stick carried on occasion mainly by army officers.

swaggie ('swægɪ) *n. Austral. and N.Z. slang.* short for **swagman.**

swagman ('swægˌmæn, -mən) *n., pl.* **-men.** *Austral. and N.Z. informal.* a labourer who carries his personal possessions in a pack or swag while travelling about in search of work; vagrant worker. Also called: **swagger, swaggie.**

Swahili (swɑː'hiːlɪ) *n.* **1.** a language of E Africa that is an official language of Kenya and Tanzania and is widely used as a lingua franca throughout E and central Africa. It is a member of the Bantu group of the Niger-Congo family, originally spoken in Zanzibar, and has a large number of loan words taken from Arabic and other languages. **2.** (*pl.* **-lis** *or* **-li**) a member of a people speaking this language, living chiefly in Zanzibar. ~*adj.* **3.** of or relating to the Swahilis or their language. [C19: from Arabic *sawāhil* coasts] —**Swa'hilian** *adj.*

swain (sweɪn) *n. Archaic or poetic.* **1.** a male lover or admirer. **2.** a country youth. [Old English *swān* swineherd; related to Old High German *swein,* Old Norse *sveinn* boy; see SWINE] —**'swainish** *adj.*

swale (sweɪl) *n. Chiefly U.S.* **a.** a moist depression in a tract of land, usually with rank vegetation. **b.** (*as modifier*): *swell and swale topography.* [C16: probably of Scandinavian origin; compare Old Norse *svala* to chill]

Swaledale (ˈsweɪlˌdeɪl) *n.* a breed of small hardy sheep kept esp. in northern England for its coarse wool which is used for making tweeds and carpets. [from *Swaledale,* Yorkshire]

SWALK (swɔːlk) *acronym for* sealed with a loving kiss: sometimes written on the back of envelopes.

swallow[1] (ˈswɒləʊ) *vb.* (*mainly tr.*) **1.** to pass (food, drink, etc.) through the mouth to the stomach by means of the muscular action of the oesophagus. **2.** (often foll. by *up*) to engulf or destroy as if by ingestion: *Nazi Germany swallowed up several small countries.* **3.** *Informal.* to believe gullibly: *he will never swallow such an excuse.* **4.** to refrain from uttering or manifesting: *to swallow one's disappointment.* **5.** to endure without retaliation. **6.** to enunciate (words, etc.) indistinctly; mutter. **7.** (often foll. by *down*) to eat or drink reluctantly. **8.** (*intr.*) to perform or simulate the act of swallowing, as in gulping. **9.** **swallow one's words.** to retract a statement, argument, etc., often in humiliating circumstances. ~*n.* **10.** the act of swallowing. **11.** the amount swallowed at any single time; mouthful. **12.** Also called: **crown, throat.** *Nautical.* the opening between the shell and the groove of the sheave of a block, through which the rope is passed. **13.** *Rare.* another word for **throat** or **gullet.** **14.** *Rare.* a capacity for swallowing; appetite. [Old English *swelgan;* related to Old Norse *svelga,* Old High German *swelgan* to swallow, Swedish *svalg* gullet] —ˈ**swallowable** *adj.* —ˈ**swallower** *n.*

swallow[2] (ˈswɒləʊ) *n.* **1.** any passerine songbird of the family *Hirundinidae,* esp. *Hirundo rustica* (**common** or **barn swallow**), having long pointed wings, a forked tail, short legs, and a rapid flight. **2.** See **fairy swallow.** [Old English *swealwe;* related to Old Frisian *swale,* Old Norse *svala,* Old High German *swalwa*] —ˈ**swallow-ˌlike** *adj.*

swallow dive *n.* a type of dive in which the diver arches back while in the air, keeping his legs straight and together and his arms outstretched, finally entering the water headfirst. U.S. and Canadian equivalent: **swan dive.**

swallow hole *n. Chiefly Brit.* another word for **sinkhole** (sense 1).

swallowtail (ˈswɒləʊˌteɪl) *n.* **1.** any of various butterflies of the genus *Papilio* and related genera, esp. *P. machaon* of Europe, having a tail-like extension of each hind wing: family *Papilionidae.* **2.** the forked tail of a swallow or similar bird. **3.** short for **swallow-tailed coat.**

swallow-tailed *adj.* **1.** (of a bird) having a deeply forked tail. **2.** having a part resembling a swallow's tail.

swallow-tailed coat *n.* another name for **tail coat.**

swallowwort (ˈswɒləʊˌwɜːt) *n.* **1.** any of several Eurasian vines of the genus *Cynanchum,* esp. *C. nigrum,* having small brownish-purple flowers: family *Asclepiadaceae.* **2.** a related European herbaceous plant, *Vincetoxicum officinale* (or *Cynanchum vincetoxicum*), having an emetic root. **3.** another name for **greater celandine.** [C16: so called because the shape of its pod is reminiscent of a flying swallow]

swam (swæm) *vb.* the past tense of **swim.**

swami (ˈswɑːmɪ) *n., pl.* **-mies** *or* **-mis.** (in India) a title of respect for a Hindu saint or religious teacher. [C18: from Hindi *svāmī,* from Sanskrit *svāmin* master, from *sva* one's own]

swamp (swɒmp) *n.* **1. a.** permanently waterlogged ground that is usually overgrown and sometimes partly forested. Compare **marsh. b.** (*as modifier*): *swamp fever.* ~*vb.* **2.** to drench or submerge or be drenched or submerged. **3.** *Nautical.* to cause (a boat) to sink or fill with water or (of a boat) to sink or fill with water. **4.** to overburden or overwhelm or be overburdened or overwhelmed, as by excess work or great numbers: *we have been swamped with applications.* **5.** to sink or stick or cause to sink or stick in or as if in a swamp. **6.** (*tr.*) to render helpless. [C17: probably from Middle Dutch *somp;* compare Middle High German *sumpf,* Old Norse *svöppr* sponge, Greek *somphos* spongy] —ˈ**swampish** *adj.* —ˈ**swampless** *adj.* —ˈ**swampy** *adj.*

swamp boat *n.* a shallow-draught boat powered by an æroplane engine mounted on a raised structure for use in swamps. Also called: **airboat.**

swamp buggy *n.* (esp. in the U.S. and Canada) a light aerofoil conveyance for use in regions with swamps, lakes, etc.

swamp cypress *n.* a North American deciduous coniferous tree, *Taxodium distichum,* that grows in swamps and sends up aerial roots from its base. Also called: **bald cypress.**

swamper (ˈswɒmpə) *n.* **1.** *U.S.* **a.** a person who lives or works in a swampy region, esp. in the southern U.S. **b.** a person who clears a swamp of trees and undergrowth or who clears a path in a forest for transporting logs. **2.** *Austral.* **a.** a bullock driver's assistant. **b.** a person getting a lift in return for a small service.

swamp fever *n.* **1.** Also called: **equine infectious anaemia.** a viral disease of horses characterized by recurring fever, staggering gait, and general debility. **2.** *U.S.* another name for **malaria.**

swampland (ˈswɒmpˌlænd) *n.* a permanently waterlogged area; marshland.

swan (swɒn) *n.* **1.** any large aquatic bird of the genera *Cygnus* and *Coscoroba,* having a long neck and usually a white plumage: family *Anatidae,* order *Anseriformes.* **2.** *Rare, literary.* **a.** a poet. **b.** (*cap. when part of a title or epithet*): *the Swan of Avon* (Shakespeare). ~*vb.* **swans, swanning, swanned. 3.** (*intr.;* usually foll. by *around* or *about*) *Informal.* to wander idly. [Old English; related to Old Norse *svanr,* Middle Low German *swōn*] —ˈ**swanˌlike** *adj.*

swan dive *n.* the U.S. and Canadian name for **swallow dive.**

swanherd (ˈswɒnˌhɜːd) *n.* a person who herds swans.

swank (swæŋk) *Informal.* ~*vb.* **1.** (*intr.*) to show off or swagger. ~*n.* **2.** Also called: **swankpot.** *Brit.* a swaggering or conceited person. **3.** *Chiefly U.S.* elegance or style, esp. of a showy kind. **4.** swagger; ostentation. ~*adj.* **5.** another word (esp. U.S.) for **swanky.** [C19: perhaps from Middle High German *swanken* to sway; see SWAG]

swanky (ˈswæŋkɪ) *adj.* **swankier, swankiest.** *Informal.* **1.** expensive and showy; stylish: *a swanky hotel.* **2.** boastful or conceited. —ˈ**swankily** *adv.* —ˈ**swankiness** *n.*

swan maiden *n.* any of a group of maidens in folklore who by magic are transformed into swans.

Swanndri (ˈswɒnˌdraɪ) *n., pl.* **-dris.** *N.Z. trademark.* an all-weather heavy woollen shirt. Also called: **swannie** (ˈswɒnɪ).

swan neck *n.* a tube, rail, etc., curved like a swan's neck.

swannery (ˈswɒnərɪ) *n., pl.* **-neries.** a place where swans are kept and bred.

swan's-down *n.* **1.** the fine soft down feathers of a swan, used to trim powder puffs, clothes, etc. **2.** a thick soft fabric of wool with silk, cotton, or rayon, used for infants' clothing, etc. **3.** a cotton fabric with a heavy nap.

swanskin (ˈswɒnˌskɪn) *n.* **1.** the skin of a swan with the feathers attached. **2.** a fine twill-weave flannel fabric.

swan song *n.* **1.** the last act, appearance, publication, or utterance of a person before retirement or death. **2.** the song that a dying swan is said to sing.

swan-upping *n. Brit.* **1.** the practice or action of marking nicks in swans' beaks as a sign of ownership. **2.** the annual swan-upping of royal cygnets on the River Thames. [C16: from UP (in the archaic sense: to catch and mark a swan)]

swap *or* **swop** (swɒp) *vb.* **swaps, swapping, swapped** *or* **swops, swopping, swopped. 1.** to trade or exchange (something or someone) for another. ~*n.* **2.** an exchange. **3.** something that is exchanged. **4.** *Finance.* Also called: **swap option, swaption.** a contract in which the parties to it exchange liabilities on outstanding debts, often exchanging fixed interest-rate for floating-rate debts (**debt swap**), either as a means of debt management or in trading (**swap trading**). [C14 (in the sense: to shake hands on a bargain, strike): probably of imitative origin] —ˈ**swapper** *or* ˈ**swopper** *n.*

SWAPO *or* **Swapo** (ˈswɑːpəʊ) *n. acronym for* South-West Africa People's Organization.

swap shop *n.* a place or occasion at which articles no longer wanted may be exchanged for other articles.

swaption (ˈswɒpʃən) *n.* another name for **swap** (sense 4).

swaraj (swəˈrɑːdʒ) *n.* (in British India) self-government; independence. [C20: from Sanskrit *svarāj,* from *sva* self + *rājya* rule] —**swaˈrajism** *n.* —**swaˈrajist** *n., adj.*

sward (swɔːd) *n.* **1.** turf or grass or a stretch of turf or grass. ~*vb.* **2.** to cover or become covered with grass. [Old English *sweard* skin; related to Old Frisian *swarde* scalp, Middle High German *swart* hide]

swarf (swɔːf, swɑːf) *n.* material removed by cutting or grinding tools in the machining of metals, stone, etc. [C16: of Scandinavian origin; related to Old Norse *svarf* metallic dust]

swarm[1] (swɔːm) *n.* **1.** a group of social insects, esp. bees led by a queen, that has left the parent hive in order to start a new colony. **2.** a large mass of small animals, esp. insects. **3.** a throng or mass, esp. when moving or in turmoil. ~*vb.* **4.** (*intr.*) (of small animals, esp. bees) to move in or form a swarm. **5.** (*intr.*) to congregate, move about or proceed in large numbers. **6.** (when *intr.,* often foll. by *with*) to overrun or be overrun (with): *the house swarmed with rats.* **7.** (*tr.*) to cause to swarm. [Old English *swearm;* related to Old Norse *svarmr* uproar, Old High German *swaram* swarm]

swarm[2] (swɔːm) *vb.* (when *intr.,* usually foll. by *up*) to climb (a ladder, etc.) by gripping with the hands and feet: *the boys swarmed up the rigging.* [C16: of unknown origin]

swarm cell *or* **spore** *n.* another name for **zoospore.**

swart (swɔːt) *or* **swarth** (swɔːθ) *adj. Archaic or dialect.* swarthy. [Old English *sweart;* related to Old Frisian *swart,* Old Norse *svartr,* Old High German *swarz* black, Latin *sordēs* dirt; see SORDID] —ˈ**swartness** *or* ˈ**swarthness** *n.*

swarthy (ˈswɔːðɪ) *adj.* **swarthier, swarthiest.** dark-hued or dark-complexioned. [C16: from obsolete *swarty,* from SWART + -Y[1]] —ˈ**swarthily** *adv.* —ˈ**swarthiness** *n.*

swash (swɒʃ) *vb.* **1.** (*intr.*) (esp. of water or things in water) to wash or move with noisy splashing. **2.** (*tr.*) to dash (a liquid, esp. water) against or upon. **3.** (*intr.*) *Archaic.* to swagger or bluster. ~*n.* **4.** Also called: **send.** the dashing movement or sound of water, such as that of waves on a beach. Compare **backwash. 5.** any other swashing movement or sound. **6.** a sandbar washed by the waves. **7.** Also called: **swash channel.** a channel of moving water cutting through or running behind a sandbank. **8.** *Archaic.* **a.** swagger or bluster. **b.** a swashbuckler. [C16: probably of imitative origin]

swashbuckler (ˈswɒʃˌbʌklə) *n.* a swaggering or flamboyant adventurer. [C16: from SWASH (in the archaic sense: to make the noise of a sword striking a shield) + BUCKLER]

swashbuckling (ˈswɒʃˌbʌklɪŋ) *adj.* (*usually prenominal*) **1.** of or characteristic of a swashbuckler, esp. in being swaggering or flamboyant. **2.** (esp. of films in period costume) full of adventure and excitement.

swash letter *n. Printing.* a decorative letter, esp. an ornamental italic capital. [C17 *swash* (n., in the sense: the decorative flourish of an ornamental letter) from *aswash* aslant]

swash plate *n. Engineering.* a collar or face plate on a shaft that is inclined at an oblique angle to the axis of rotation and either imparts reciprocating motion to push rods parallel to the shaft axis as in a **swash plate pump** or, conversely, converts reciprocating motion to rotation as in a **swash plate motor.** Also called: **wobble plate.** [from *swash* (obsolete n.) an oblique figure or ornament, from *aswash:* see SWASH LETTER]

swastika (ˈswɒstɪkə) *n.* **1.** a primitive religious symbol or ornament in the shape of a Greek cross, usually having the ends of the arms bent at right angles in either a clockwise or anticlockwise direction. **2.** this symbol with clockwise arms, officially adopted in 1935 as the emblem of Nazi Germany. [C19: from Sanskrit *svastika,* from *svasti* prosperity; from the belief that it brings good luck]

swat[1] (swɒt) *vb.* **swats, swatting, swatted.** (*tr.*) **1.** to strike or hit sharply: *to swat a fly.* ~*n.* **2.** another word (esp. Brit.) for **swatter** (sense 1). **3.** a sharp or violent blow. ~Also: **swot.** [C17: northern English dialect and U.S. variant of SQUAT]

swat[2] (swɒt) *vb.* **swats, swatting, swatted.** *n.* a variant of **swot**[1].

swatch (swɒtʃ) *n.* **1.** a sample of cloth. **2.** a number of such samples, usually fastened together in book form. [C16: Scottish and northern English, of uncertain origin]

swath (swɔːθ) *or* **swathe** (sweɪð) *n., pl.* **swaths** (swɔːðz) *or* **swathes. 1.** the width of one sweep of a scythe or of the blade of a mowing machine. **2.** the strip cut by either of these in one course. **3.** the quantity of cut grass, hay, or similar crop left in one course of such mowing. **4.** a long narrow strip or belt. [Old English *swæth;* related to Old Norse *svath* smooth patch]

swathe (sweɪð) *vb.* (*tr.*) **1.** to bandage (a wound, limb, etc.), esp. completely. **2.** to wrap a band, garment, etc., around, esp. so as to cover completely; swaddle. **3.** to envelop. ~*n.* **4.** a bandage or wrapping. **5.** a variant spelling of **swath.** [Old English *swathian;* related to *swæthel* swaddling clothes, Old High German *swedil,* Dutch *zwadel;* see SWADDLE] —ˈ**swathable** *or* ˈ**swatheable** *adj.*

swats (swæts) *pl. n. Scot. and northern English dialect.* newly brewed ale or beer. [Old English *swātan* (plural) beer]

swatter (ˈswɒtə) *n.* **1.** a device for killing insects, esp. a meshed flat attached to a handle. **2.** a person who swats.

sway (sweɪ) *vb.* **1.** (*usually intr.*) to swing or cause to swing to and fro: *the door swayed in the wind.* **2.** (*usually intr.*) to lean or incline or cause to lean or incline to one side or in different directions in turn. **3.** (*usually intr.*) to vacillate or cause to vacillate between two or more opinions. **4.** to be influenced or swerve or influence or cause to swerve to or from a purpose or opinion. **5.** (*tr.*) *Nautical.* to hoist (a yard, mast, or other spar). **6.** *Archaic or poetic.* to rule or wield power (over). **7.** (*tr.*) *Archaic.* to wield (a weapon). ~*n.* **8.** control; power. **9.** a swinging or leaning movement. **10.** *Archaic.* dominion; governing authority. **11. hold sway.** to be master; reign. [C16: probably from Old Norse *sveigja* to bend; related to Dutch *zwaaien,* Low German *swājen*] —ˈ**swayable** *adj.* —ˈ**swayer** *n.* —ˈ**swayful** *adj.*

sway-back *n. Vet. science.* an abnormal sagging or concavity of the spine in horses. —ˈ**sway-ˌbacked** *adj.*

Swazi (ˈswɑːzɪ) *n.* **1.** (*pl.* **-zis** *or* **-zi**) a member of a racially mixed people of southern Africa living chiefly in the kingdom of Swaziland, who first formed into a strong political group in the late 19th century. **2.** the language of this people: an official language of Swaziland along with English. It belongs to the Niger-Congo family and is closely related to Xhosa and Zulu.

swear (swɛə) *vb.* **swears, swearing, swore, sworn. 1.** to declare or affirm (a statement) as true, esp. by invoking a deity, etc., as witness. **2.** (foll. by *by*) **a.** to invoke (a deity, etc.) by name as a witness or guarantee to an oath. **b.** to trust implicitly; have complete confidence (in). **3.** (*intr.;* often foll. by *at*) to curse, blaspheme, or use swearwords. **4.** (when *tr., may take a clause as object or an infinitive*) to promise solemnly on oath; vow. **5.** (*tr.*) to assert or affirm with great emphasis or earnestness. **6.** (*intr.*) to give evidence or make any statement or solemn declaration on oath. **7.** to take an oath in order to add force or solemnity to (a statement or declaration). ~*n.* **8.** a period of swearing. [Old English *swerian;* related to Old Norse *sverja,* Gothic *swaran,* Old Frisian *swera,* German *schwören*] —ˈ**swearer** *n.*

swear in *vb.* (*tr., adv.*) to administer an oath to (a person) on his assuming office, entering the witness box to give evidence, etc.

swear off *vb.* (*intr., prep.*) to promise to abstain from something: *to swear off drink.*

swear out *vb.* (*tr., adv.*) *U.S.* to secure the issue of (a warrant for an arrest) by making a charge under oath.

swearword (ˈswɛəˌwɜːd) *n.* a socially taboo word or phrase of a profane, obscene, or insulting character.

sweat (swɛt) *n.* **1.** the secretion from the sweat glands, esp. when profuse and visible, as during strenuous activity, from excessive heat, etc.; perspiration. **2.** the act or process of secreting this fluid. **3.** the act of inducing the exudation of moisture. **4.** drops of moisture given forth or gathered on the surface of something. **5.** *Informal.* a state or condition of worry or eagerness (esp. in the phrase **in a sweat**). **6.** *Slang.* drudgery or hard labour: *mowing lawns is a real sweat!* **7.** *Chiefly U.S.* an exercise gallop given to a horse, esp. on the day of a race. **8.** *Slang, chiefly Brit.* a soldier, esp. one who is old and experienced. **9. no sweat!** (*interj.*) *Slang.* an expression suggesting that something can be done without problems or difficulty. ~*vb.* **sweats, sweating; sweat** *or* **sweated. 10.** to secrete (sweat) through the pores of the skin, esp. profusely; perspire. **11.** (*tr.*) to make wet or stain with perspiration. **12.** to give forth or cause to give forth (moisture) in droplets: *a sweating cheese; the maple sweats sap.* **13.** (*intr.*) to collect and condense moisture on an outer surface: *a glass of beer sweating in the sun.* **14.** (*intr.*) (of a liquid) to pass through a porous surface in droplets. **15.** (of tobacco leaves, cut and dried hay, etc.) to exude moisture and, sometimes, begin to ferment or to cause (tobacco leaves, etc.) to exude moisture. **16.** (*tr.*) to heat (food, esp. vegetables) slowly in butter in a tightly closed saucepan. **17.** (*tr.*) to join (pieces of metal) by pressing together and heating. **18.** (*tr.*) to heat (solder) until it melts. **19.** (*tr.*) to heat (a partially fused metal) to extract an easily fusible constituent. **20.** to shake together (coins, esp. gold coins) so as to remove particles for illegal use. **21.** *Informal.* to suffer anxiety, impatience, or distress. **22.** *Informal.* to overwork or be overworked. **23.** (*tr.*) *Informal.* to employ at very low wages and under bad conditions. **24.** (*tr.*) *Informal.* to extort, esp. by torture: *to sweat information out of a captive.* **25.** (*intr.*) *Informal.* to suffer punishment: *you'll sweat for this!* **26. sweat blood.** *Informal.* **a.** to work very hard. **b.** to be filled with anxiety or impatience. ~See also **sweat off, sweat out.** [Old English *swǣtan* to sweat, from *swāt* sweat; related to Old Saxon *swēt,* Old Norse *sveiti,* Old High German *sweiz,* Latin *sūdor,* Sanskrit *svedas*] —ˈ**sweatless** *adj.*

sweatband (ˈswɛtˌbænd) *n.* **1.** a band of material set in a hat or cap to protect it from sweat. **2.** a piece of cloth tied around the forehead to keep sweat out of the eyes or around the wrist to keep the hands dry, as in sports.

sweatbox (ˈswɛtˌbɒks) *n.* **1.** a device for causing tobacco leaves, fruit, or hides to sweat. **2.** a very small pen or cubicle where a pig is fattened intensively. **3.** *Informal, chiefly U.S.* a narrow room or cell for a prisoner. **4.** *Informal.* any place where a person sweats on account of confinement, heat, etc.

sweated (ˈswɛtɪd) *adj.* **1.** made by exploited labour: *sweated goods.* **2.** (of workers, etc.) forced to work in poor conditions for low pay.

sweater (ˈswɛtə) *n.* **1. a.** a garment made of knitted or crocheted material covering the upper part of the body, esp. a heavy one worn for warmth. **b.** (*as modifier*): *a sweater dress.* **2.** a person or thing that sweats. **3.** an employer who overworks and underpays his employees.

sweater girl *n. Slang, now rare.* a young woman or girl with large breasts who wears tight sweaters.

sweat gland *n.* any of the coiled tubular subcutaneous glands that secrete sweat by means of a duct that opens on to the surface of the skin.

sweating sickness *n.* **1.** the nontechnical name for **miliary fever. 2.** an acute infectious febrile disease that was widespread in Europe during the late 15th century, characterized by profuse sweating. **3.** a disease of cattle, esp. calves, prevalent in southern Africa and transmitted by ticks.

sweat off *or* **away** *vb.* (*tr., adv.*) *Informal.* to get rid of (weight) by strenuous exercise or sweating.

sweat out *vb.* (*tr., adv.*) **1.** to cure or lessen the effects of (a cold, respiratory infection, etc.) by sweating. **2.** *Informal.* to endure (hardships) for a time (often in the phrase **sweat it out**). **3. sweat one's guts out.** *Informal.* to work extremely hard.

sweats (swɛts) *pl. n.* sweatshirts and sweat-suit trousers: *jeans and sweats.*

sweatshirt (ˈswɛtˌʃɜːt) *n.* a long-sleeved knitted cotton sweater worn by athletes, etc.

sweatshop (ˈswɛtˌʃɒp) *n.* a workshop where employees work long hours under bad conditions for low wages.

sweat suit *n.* a suit worn by athletes for training comprising knitted cotton trousers fitting closely at the ankle and a light cotton sweater.

sweaty (ˈswɛtɪ) *adj.* **sweatier, sweatiest. 1.** covered with perspiration; sweating. **2.** smelling of or like sweat. **3.** causing sweat. —ˈ**sweatily** *adv.* —ˈ**sweatiness** *n.*

swede (swiːd) *n.* **1.** a Eurasian cruciferous plant, *Brassica napobrassica,* cultivated for its bulbous edible root, which is used as a vegetable and as cattle fodder. **2.** the root of this plant. ~Also called: **Swedish turnip.** U.S. and Canadian name: **rutabaga.** [C19: so called after being introduced into Scotland from Sweden in the 18th century]

Swede (swiːd) *n.* a native, citizen, or inhabitant of Sweden, a kingdom in NW Europe.

Swedenborgianism (ˌswiːdᵊnˈbɔːdʒɪəˌnɪzəm, -gɪ-) *or* **Swedenborgism** (ˈswiːdᵊnˌbɔːdʒɪzəm, -gɪz-) *n.* the system of philosophical and religious doctrines of Emanuel Swedenborg (1688–1772), Swedish scientist and theologian, emphasizing the spiritual structure of the universe, the possibility of direct contact with spirits, and the divinity of Christ. —ˌ**Swedenˈborgian** *n., adj.*

Swedish (ˈswiːdɪʃ) *adj.* **1.** of, relating to, or characteristic of Sweden, a kingdom in NW Europe, its people, or their language. ~*n.* **2.** the official language of Sweden, belonging to the North Germanic branch of the Indo-European family: one of the two official languages of Finland. **3. the Swedish.** (*functioning as pl.*) the people of Sweden collectively.

Swedish massage *n.* massage combined with a system (**Swedish movements** or **gymnastics**) of passive and active exercising of muscles and joints.

Swedish mile *n.* a unit of length used in Sweden, equal to 10 kilometres.

sweeny (ˈswiːnɪ) *n. Vet. science.* a wasting of the shoulder muscles of a horse, esp. as the result of a nerve injury. [C19: probably from German dialect *Schweine* emaciation, atrophy]

sweep (swiːp) *vb.* **sweeps, sweeping, swept. 1.** to clean or clear (a space, chimney, etc.) with a brush, broom, etc. **2.** (often foll. by *up*) to remove or collect (dirt, rubbish, etc.) with a brush, broom, etc. **3.** to move in a smooth or continuous manner, esp. quickly or forcibly: *cars swept along the road.* **4.** to move in a proud or dignified fashion: *she swept past.* **5.** to spread or pass rapidly across, through, or along (a region, area, etc.): *the news swept through the town.* **6.** (*tr.*) to direct (the gaze, line of fire, etc.) over; survey. **7.** (*tr.*; foll. by *away* or *off*) to overwhelm emotionally: *she was swept away by his charm.* **8.** (*tr.*) to brush or lightly touch (a surface, etc.): *the dress swept along the ground.* **9.** (*tr.*; often foll. by *away*) to convey, clear, or abolish, esp. with strong or continuous movements: *the sea swept the sandcastle away; secondary modern schools were swept away.* **10.** (*intr.*) to extend gracefully or majestically, esp. in a wide circle: *the plains sweep down to the sea.* **11.** to search (a body of water) for mines, etc., by dragging. **12.** to search (a room, area, etc.) electronically to detect spying devices. **13.** (*tr.*) to win overwhelmingly, esp. in an election: *Labour swept the country.* **14.** *Cricket.* to play (a ball) with a sweep. **15.** (*tr.*) to propel (a boat) with sweeps. **16. sweep the board. a.** (in gambling) to win all the cards or money. **b.** to win every event or prize in a contest. **17. sweep (something) under the carpet.** to conceal (something, esp. a problem) in the hope that it will be overlooked by others. ~*n.* **18.** the act or an instance of sweeping; removal by or as if by a brush or broom. **19.** a swift or steady movement, esp. in an arc: *with a sweep of his arms.* **20.** the distance, arc, etc., through which something, such as a pendulum, moves. **21.** a wide expanse or scope: *the sweep of the plains.* **22.** any curving line or contour. **23.** *Cards.* **a.** the winning of every trick in a hand of whist. **b.** the taking, by pairing, of all exposed cards in cassino. **24.** short for **sweepstake. 25.** *Cricket.* a shot in which the ball is hit more or less square on the leg side from a half-kneeling position with the bat held nearly horizontal. **26. a.** a long oar used on an open boat. **b.** *Austral.* a person steering a surf boat with such an oar. **27.** any of the sails of a windmill. **28.** *Electronics.* a steady horizontal or circular movement of an electron beam across or around the fluorescent screen of a cathode-ray tube. **29.** *Agriculture.* **a.** a rakelike attachment for the front of a motor vehicle for pushing hay into piles. **b.** a triangular blade on a cultivator used to cut through roots below the surface of the soil. **30.** a curving driveway. **31.** *Chiefly Brit.* See **chimney sweep. 32.** another name for **swipe** (sense 4). **33. clean sweep. a.** an overwhelming victory or success. **b.** a complete change; purge: *to make a clean sweep.* [C13 *swepen;* related to Old English *swāpan,* Old Norse *sveipa;* see SWIPE, SWOOP] —ˈ**sweepy** *adj.*

sweepback (ˈswiːpˌbæk) *n.* the rearward inclination of a component or surface, such as an aircraft wing, fin, etc.

sweeper (ˈswiːpə) *n.* **1.** a person employed to sweep, such as a roadsweeper. **2.** any device for sweeping: *a carpet sweeper.* **3.** *Informal, soccer.* a player who supports the main defenders, as by intercepting loose balls, etc.

sweep hand *n. Horology.* a long hand that registers seconds or fractions of seconds on the perimeter of the dial.

sweeping (ˈswiːpɪŋ) *adj.* **1.** comprehensive and wide-ranging: *sweeping reforms.* **2.** indiscriminate or without reservations: *sweeping statements.* **3.** decisive or overwhelming: *a sweeping victory.* **4.** taking in a wide area: *a sweeping glance.* **5.** driving steadily onwards, esp. over a large area: *a sweeping attack.* —ˈ**sweepingly** *adv.* —ˈ**sweepingness** *n.*

sweepings (ˈswiːpɪŋz) *pl. n.* debris, litter, or refuse.

sweepo (ˈswiːpəʊ) *n., pl.* **sweepos.** another name for **broomie.**

sweep-saw *n.* a saw with a thin blade that can be used for cutting curved shapes.

sweepstake (ˈswiːpˌsteɪk) *or esp. U.S.* **sweepstakes** *n.* **1. a.** a lottery in which the stakes of the participants constitute the prize. **b.** the prize itself. **2.** any event involving a lottery, esp. a horse race in which the prize is the competitors' stakes. ~Often shortened to **sweep.** [C15: originally referring to someone who *sweeps* or takes all the stakes in a game]

sweer (swiːr) *vb. Scot.* a variant spelling of **sweir**[1] and **sweir**[2].

sweet (swiːt) *adj.* **1.** having or denoting a pleasant taste like that of sugar. **2.** agreeable to the senses or the mind: *sweet music.* **3.** having pleasant manners; gentle: *a sweet child.* **4.** (of wine, etc.) having a relatively high sugar content; not dry. **5.** (of foods) not decaying or rancid: *sweet milk.* **6.** not salty: *sweet water.* **7.** free from unpleasant odours: *sweet air.* **8.** containing no corrosive substances: *sweet soil.* **9.** (of petrol) containing no sulphur compounds. **10.** sentimental or unrealistic. **11.** *Jazz.* performed with a regular beat, with the emphasis on clearly outlined melody and little improvisation. **12.** *Austral. slang.* satisfactory or in order; all right. **13.** *Archaic.* respected; dear (used in polite forms of address): *sweet sir.* **14.** smooth and precise; perfectly executed: *a sweet shot.* **15. sweet on.** fond of or infatuated with. **16. at one's own sweet will.** as it suits oneself alone. **17. keep (someone) sweet.** to ingratiate oneself in order to ensure cooperation. ~*adv.* **18.** *Informal.* in a sweet manner. ~*n.* **19.** a sweet taste or smell; sweetness in general. **20.** (*often pl.*) *Brit.* any of numerous kinds of confectionery consisting wholly or partly of sugar, esp. of sugar boiled and crystallized (**boiled sweets**). **21.** *Brit.* a pudding, fruit, or any sweet dish served as a dessert. **22.** dear; sweetheart (used as a form of address). **23.** anything that is sweet. **24.** (*often pl.*) a pleasurable experience, state, etc.: *the sweets of success.* **25.** *U.S.* See **sweet potato.** [Old English *swēte;* related to Old Saxon *swōti,* Old High German *suozi,* Old Norse *sœtr,* Latin *suādus* persuasive, *suāvis* sweet, Greek *hēdus,* Sanskrit *svādu;* see PERSUADE, SUAVE] —ˈ**sweetish** *adj.* —ˈ**sweetly** *adv.* —ˈ**sweetness** *n.*

sweet alyssum *n.* a Mediterranean cruciferous plant, *Lobularia maritima,* having clusters of small fragrant white or violet flowers: widely grown in gardens. See also **alyssum.**

sweet-and-sour *adj.* (of food) cooked in a sauce made from sugar and vinegar and other ingredients.

sweet basil *n.* See **basil** (sense 1).

sweet bay *n.* **1.** a small tree, *Magnolia virginiana,* of SE North America, having large fragrant white flowers: family *Magnoliaceae* (magnolias). Sometimes shortened to **bay. 2.** another name for **bay**[4] (sense 2).

sweetbread (ˈswiːtˌbrɛd) *n.* the pancreas (**stomach sweetbread**) or the thymus gland (**neck** or **throat sweetbread**) of an animal, used for food. [C16: SWEET + BREAD, perhaps from Old English *brǣd* meat; related to Old Saxon *brādo* ham, Old High German *brāt,* Old Norse *brāth*]

sweetbrier (ˈswiːtˌbraɪə) *n.* a Eurasian rose, *Rosa rubiginosa,* having a tall bristly stem, fragrant leaves, and single pink flowers. Also called: **eglantine.**

sweet cherry *n.* **1.** either of two types of cherry tree that are cultivated for their red edible sweet fruit, the gean having tender-fleshed fruit, the bigarreau having firm-fleshed fruit. **2.** the fruit of any of these trees. See also **heart cherry.** ~Also called: **dessert cherry.** Compare **sour cherry.**

sweet chestnut *n.* See **chestnut** (sense 1).

sweet cicely *n.* **1.** Also called: **myrrh.** an aromatic umbelliferous European plant, *Myrrhis odorata,* having compound leaves and clusters of small white flowers. **2.** the leaves of this plant, formerly used in cookery for their flavour of aniseed. **3.** any of various plants of the umbelliferous genus *Osmorhiza,* of Asia and America, having aromatic roots and clusters of small white flowers.

sweet cider *n.* **1.** *Brit.* cider having a high sugar content. **2.** *U.S. and Canadian.* unfermented apple juice. Compare **hard cider.**

sweet clover *n.* another name for **melilot.**

sweet corn *n.* **1.** Also called: **sugar corn, green corn.** a variety of maize, *Zea mays saccharata,* whose kernels are rich in sugar and eaten as a vegetable when young. **2.** the unripe ears of maize, esp. the sweet kernels removed from the cob, cooked as a vegetable.

sweeten (ˈswiːtᵊn) *vb.* (*mainly tr.*) **1.** (*also intr.*) to make or become sweet or sweeter. **2.** to mollify or soften (a person). **3.** to make more agreeable. **4.** (*also intr.*) *Chem.* to free or be freed from unpleasant odours, acidic or corrosive substances, or the like. **5.** *Finance, chiefly U.S.* to raise the value of (loan collateral) by adding more securities. **6.** *Informal, poker.* to enlarge (the pot) by adding chips.

sweetener (ˈswiːtᵊnə) *n.* **1.** a sweetening agent, esp. one that does not contain sugar. **2.** a slang word for **bribe.**

sweetening (ˈswiːtᵊnɪŋ) *n.* something that sweetens.

sweet fern *n.* a North American shrub, *Comptonia* (or *Myrica*) *asplenifolia,* having scented fernlike leaves and heads of brownish flowers: family *Myricaceae.*

sweet flag *n.* an aroid marsh plant, *Acorus calamus,* having swordlike leaves, small greenish flowers, and aromatic roots. Also called: **calamus.** [C18: see FLAG[2]]

sweet gale *n.* a shrub, *Myrica gale,* of northern swamp regions, having yellow catkin-like flowers and aromatic leaves: family *Myricaceae.* Also called: **bog myrtle.** Often shortened to **gale.** [C17: see GALE[2]]

sweet gum *n.* **1.** a North American liquidambar tree, *Liquidambar styraciflua,* having prickly spherical fruit clusters and fragrant sap: the wood (called **satin walnut**) is used to make furniture. Compare **sour gum. 2.** the sap of this tree. ~Also called: **red gum.**

sweetheart (ˈswiːtˌhɑːt) *n.* **1.** a person loved by another. **2.** *Informal.* a lovable, generous, or obliging person. **3.** a term of endearment for a beloved or lovable person. ~*adj.* **4.** of or relating to a garment with a sweetheart neckline: *sweetheart cardigan.*

sweetheart agreement *n.* **1.** an industrial agreement made at a local level between an employer and employees, often with clauses advantageous to the employer, such as no strikes, but without the recognition of the national union representing the employees. **2.** *Austral.* an industrial agreement negotiated directly between employers and employees, without resort to arbitration.

sweetheart neckline *n.* a neckline on a woman's dress that is low at the front and shaped like the top of a heart.

sweetie[1] (ˈswiːtɪ) *n. Informal.* **1.** sweetheart; darling: used as a term of endearment. **2.** *Brit.* another word for **sweet** (sense 20). **3.** *Chiefly Brit.* an endearing person.

sweetie[2] (ˈswiːtɪ) *n.* a large seedless variety of grapefruit which has a green to yellow rind and juicy sweet pulp.

sweetiewife (ˈswiːtɪˌwaɪf) *n., pl.* **-wives.** *Scot. dialect.* **1.** a garrulous person. **2.** (formerly) a woman selling sweets.

sweeting (ˈswiːtɪŋ) *n.* **1.** a variety of sweet apple. **2.** an archaic word for **sweetheart.**

sweetman (ˈswiːtˌmæn) *n., pl.* **-men.** (in the Caribbean) a man kept by a woman.

sweet marjoram *n.* another name for **marjoram** (sense 1).

sweet marten *n.* a name for the pine marten, referring to the fact that its scent glands produce a less offensive scent marker than that of the polecat (the foul marten or foumart).

sweetmeal (ˈswiːtˌmiːl) *adj.* (of biscuits) sweet and wholemeal.

sweetmeat (ˈswiːtˌmiːt) *n.* a sweetened delicacy, such as a preserve, sweet, or, formerly, a cake or pastry.

sweetness and light *n.* an apparently affable reasonableness. [C19: adopted by Matthew Arnold from Swift's *Battle of the Books* (1704)]

sweet oil *n.* another name for **olive oil.**

sweet pea *n.* a climbing papilionaceous plant, *Lathyrus odoratus,* of S Europe, widely cultivated for its butterfly-shaped fragrant flowers of delicate pastel colours.

sweet pepper *n.* **1.** a pepper plant, *Capsicum frutescens grossum,* with large bell-shaped fruits that are eaten unripe (**green pepper**) or ripe (**red pepper**). **2.** the fruit of this plant.

sweet potato *n.* **1.** a convolvulaceous twining plant, *Ipomoea batatas,* of tropical America, cultivated in the tropics for its edible fleshy yellow root. **2.** the root of this plant. ~Also called (N.Z.): **kumera.**

sweet shop *n. Chiefly Brit.* a shop solely or largely selling sweets, esp. boiled sweets.

sweetsop (ˈswiːtˌsɒp) *n.* **1.** a small West Indian tree, *Annona squamosa,* having yellowish-green fruit: family *Annonaceae.* **2.** the fruit of this tree, which has a sweet edible pulp. ~Also called: **sugar apple, custard apple.** Compare **soursop.** [C19: so called because of the flavour and consistency of its pulp]

sweet-talk *Informal.* ~*vb.* **1.** to coax, flatter, or cajole (someone). ~*n.* **sweet talk. 2.** cajolery; coaxing.

sweet tooth *n.* a strong liking for sweet foods.

sweet william *n.* a widely cultivated Eurasian caryophyllaceous plant, *Dianthus barbatus,* with flat clusters of white, pink, red, or purple flowers.

sweet woodruff *n.* a Eurasian and North African rubiaceous plant, *Galium odoratum* (or *Asperula odorata*), having whorls of leaves and clusters of fragrant white flowers.

sweir[1] (swiːr) *vb., n.* a Scot. word for **swear.**

sweir[2] (swiːr) *adj. Scot.* **1.** lazy. **2.** loath; disinclined. [Old English]

swell (swɛl) *vb.* **swells, swelling, swelled; swollen** *or* **swelled. 1.** to grow or cause to grow in size, esp. as a result of internal pressure. Compare **contract** (senses 1,3). **2.** to expand or cause to expand at a particular point or above the surrounding level; protrude. **3.** to grow or cause to grow in size, amount, intensity, or degree: *the party is swelling with new recruits.* **4.** to puff or be puffed up with pride or another emotion. **5.** (*intr.*) (of seas or lakes) to rise in waves. **6.** (*intr.*) to well up or overflow. **7.** (*tr.*) to make (a musical phrase) increase gradually in volume and then diminish. ~*n.* **8. a.** the undulating movement of the surface of the open sea. **b.** a succession of waves or a single large wave. **9.** a swelling or being swollen; expansion. **10.** an increase in quantity or degree; inflation. **11.** a bulge; protuberance. **12.** a gentle hill. **13.** *Informal.* a person very fashionably dressed. **14.** *Informal.* a man of high social or political standing. **15.** *Music.* a crescendo followed by an immediate diminuendo. **16.** Also called: **swell organ.** *Music.* **a.** a set of pipes on an organ housed in a box (**swell box**) fitted with a shutter operated by a pedal, which can be opened or closed to control the volume. **b.** the manual on an organ controlling this. Compare **choir** (sense 4), **great** (sense 21). ~*adj.* **17.** *Informal.* stylish or grand. **18.** *Slang.* excellent; first-class. [Old English *swellan;* related to Old Norse *svella,* Old Frisian *swella,* German *schwellen*]

swelled head *or* **swollen head** *Informal.* ~*n.* **1.** an inflated view of one's own worth, often caused by sudden success. ~*adj.* **swelled-headed, swell-headed,** *or* **swollen-headed. 2.** conceited.

swellfish (ˈswɛlˌfɪʃ) *n., pl.* **-fish** *or* **-fishes.** a popular name for **puffer** (sense 2).

swelling (ˈswɛlɪŋ) *n.* **1.** the act of expansion or inflation. **2.** the state of being or becoming swollen. **3.** a swollen or inflated part or area. **4.** an abnormal enlargement of a bodily structure or part, esp. as the result of injury. Related adj.: **tumescent.**

swelter (ˈswɛltə) *vb.* **1.** (*intr.*) to suffer under oppressive heat, esp. to perspire and feel faint. **2.** (*tr.*) *Archaic.* to exude (venom). **3.** (*tr.*) *Rare.* to cause to suffer under oppressive heat. ~*n.* **4.** a sweltering condition (esp. in the phrase **in a swelter**). **5.** oppressive humid heat. [C15 *swelten,* from Old English *sweltan* to die; related to Old Norse *svelta* to starve, Old High German *swelzan* to burn with passion; see SULTRY]

sweltering (ˈswɛltərɪŋ) *adj.* oppressively hot and humid: *a sweltering day.* —ˈ**swelteringly** *adv.*

swept (swɛpt) *vb.* the past tense of **sweep.**

sweptback (ˈswɛptˌbæk) *adj.* (of an aircraft wing) having leading edge and trailing edges inclined backwards towards the rear of the fuselage.

swept volume *n.* another term for **volumetric displacement.**

sweptwing (ˈswɛptˌwɪŋ) *adj.* (of an aircraft, winged missile, etc.) having wings swept (usually) backwards.

swerve (swɜːv) *vb.* **1.** to turn or cause to turn aside, usually sharply or suddenly, from a course. ~*n.* **2.** the act, instance, or degree of swerving. [Old English *sweorfan* to scour; related to Old High German *swerban* to wipe off, Gothic *afswairban* to wipe off, Old Norse *sverfa* to file] —ˈ**swervable** *adj.* —ˈ**swerver** *n.*

sweven (ˈswɛvᵊn) *n. Archaic.* a vision or dream. [Old English *swefn;* related to Old Norse *svefn* dream, sleep, Lithuanian *sāpnas,* Old Slavonic *sunu,* Latin *somnus*]

SWG Standard Wire Gauge; a notation for the diameters of metal rods or thickness of metal sheet ranging from 16 mm to 0.02 mm or from 0.5 inch to 0.001 inch.

swift (swɪft) *adj.* **1.** moving or able to move quickly; fast. **2.** occurring or performed quickly or suddenly; instant: *a swift response.* **3.** (*postpositive;* foll. by *to*) prompt to act or respond: *swift to take revenge.* ~*adv.* **4. a.** swiftly or quickly. **b.** (*in combination*): *swift-moving.* ~*n.* **5.** any bird of the families *Apodidae* and *Hemiprocnidae,* such as *Apus apus* (**common swift**) of the Old World: order *Apodiformes.* They have long narrow wings and spend most of the time on the wing. **6.** (*sometimes cap.*) a variety of domestic fancy pigeon originating in Egypt and Syria and having an appearance somewhat similar to a swift. **7.** short for **swift moth. 8.** any of certain North American lizards of the genera *Sceloporus* and *Uta* that can run very rapidly: family *Iguanidae* (iguanas). **9.** the main cylinder in a carding machine. **10.** an expanding circular frame used to hold skeins of silk, wool, etc. [Old English, from *swīfan* to turn; related to Old Norse *svifa* to rove, Old Frisian *swīvia* to waver, Old High German *sweib* a reversal; see SWIVEL] —ˈ**swiftly** *adv.* —ˈ**swiftness** *n.*

swifter (ˈswɪftə) *n. Nautical.* a line run around the ends of capstan bars to prevent their falling out of their sockets. [C17: related to the nautical term *swift* to fasten with tight-drawn ropes; probably Scandinavian in origin: compare Old Norse *svipta* to reef]

swift fox *n.* a small fox, *Vulpes velox,* of the plains of W North America. Also called: **kit fox.**

swiftie *or* **swifty** (ˈswɪftɪ) *n. Slang, chiefly Austral.* a trick, ruse, or deception.

swiftlet (ˈswɪftlɪt) *n.* any of various small swifts of the Asian genus *Collocalia* that often live in caves and use echolocation: the nests, which are made of hardened saliva, are used in oriental cookery to make birds' nest soup.

swift moth *n.* any of five species of fast-flying moths of the family *Hepialidae,* regarded as primitive in development, having forewings and hind wings similar in size and shape: the best known is the **ghost swift,** *Hepialus humili.* Often shortened to **swift.**

swig (swɪg) *Informal.* ~*n.* **1.** a large swallow or deep drink, esp. from a bottle. ~*vb.* **swigs, swigging, swigged. 2.** to drink (some liquid) deeply, esp. from a bottle. [C16: of unknown origin] —ˈ**swigger** *n.*

swill (swɪl) *vb.* **1.** to drink large quantities of (liquid, esp. alcoholic drink); guzzle. **2.** (*tr.;* often foll. by *out*) *Chiefly Brit.* to drench or rinse in large amounts of water. **3.** (*tr.*) to feed swill to (pigs, etc.). ~*n.* **4.** wet feed, esp. for pigs, consisting of kitchen waste, skim milk, etc. **5.** garbage or refuse, esp. from a kitchen. **6.** a deep draught of drink, esp. beer. **7.** any liquid mess. **8.** the act of swilling. [Old English *swilian* to wash out] —ˈ**swiller** *n.*

swim (swɪm) *vb.* **swims, swimming, swam, swum. 1.** (*intr.*) to move along in water, etc., by means of movements of the body or parts of the body, esp. the arms and legs, or (in the case of fish) tail and fins. **2.** (*tr.*) to cover (a distance or stretch of water) in this way. **3.** (*tr.*) to compete in (a race) in this way. **4.** (*intr.*) to be supported by and on a liquid; float. **5.** (*tr.*) to use (a particular stroke) in swimming. **6.** (*intr.*) to move smoothly, usually through air or over a surface. **7.** (*intr.*) to reel or seem to reel: *my head swam; the room swam around me.* **8.** (*intr.;* often foll. by *in* or *with*) to be covered or flooded with water or other liquid. **9.** (*intr.;* often foll. by *in*) to be liberally supplied (with): *he's swimming in money.* **10.** (*tr.*) to cause to float or swim. **11.** (*tr.*) to provide (something) with water deep enough to float in. **12. swim with** (*or* **against**) **the stream** *or* **tide.** to conform to (or resist) prevailing opinion. ~*n.* **13.** the act, an instance, or period of swimming. **14.** any graceful gliding motion. **15.** a condition of dizziness; swoon. **16.** a pool in a river good for fishing. **17. in the swim.** *Informal.* fashionable or active in social or political activities. [Old English *swimman;* related to Old Norse *svima,* German *schwimmen,* Gothic *swumsl* pond, Norwegian *svamla* to paddle] —ˈ**swimmable** *adj.* —ˈ**swimmer** *n.* —ˈ**swimming** *n., adj.*

swim bladder *n. Ichthyol.* another name for **air bladder** (sense 1).

swimfeeder ('swɪmˌfiːdə) *n. Angling.* a device containing bait, attached to the line to ensure the gradual baiting of the swim from under the surface.

swimmeret ('swɪməˌrɛt) *n.* any of the small paired appendages on the abdomen of crustaceans, used chiefly in locomotion and reproduction. Also called: **pleopod.** [C19: from SWIM + -ER[1] + -ET]

swimming bath *n.* (*often pl.*) an indoor swimming pool.

swimming costume *or* **bathing costume** *n. Chiefly Brit.* any apparel worn for swimming or sunbathing, such as a woman's one-piece garment covering most of the torso but not the limbs.

swimmingly ('swɪmɪŋlɪ) *adv.* successfully, effortlessly, or well (esp. in the phrase **go swimmingly**).

swimming pool *n.* an artificial pool for swimming.

swimsuit ('swɪmˌsuːt, -ˌsjuːt) *n.* a woman's one-piece swimming garment that leaves the arms and legs bare.

swindle ('swɪndᵊl) *vb.* **1.** to cheat (someone) of money, etc.; defraud. **2.** (*tr.*) to obtain (money, etc.) by fraud. *~n.* **3.** a fraudulent scheme or transaction. [C18: back formation from German *Schwindler,* from *schwindeln,* from Old High German *swintilōn,* frequentative of *swintan* to disappear] —'**swindler** *n.*

swindle sheet *n.* a slang term for **expense account.**

swine (swaɪn) *n.* **1.** (*pl.* **swines**) a coarse or contemptible person. **2.** (*pl.* **swine**) another name for a **pig.** [Old English *swīn;* related to Old Norse *svīn,* Gothic *swein,* Latin *suīnus* relating to swine] —'**swineˌlike** *adj.* —'**swinish** *adj.* —'**swinishly** *adv.* —'**swinishness** *n.*

swine fever *n.* an infectious viral disease of pigs, characterized by fever, refusal to eat, weight loss, and diarrhoea. U.S. term: **hog cholera.**

swineherd ('swaɪnˌhɜːd) *n.* a person who looks after pigs.

swinepox ('swaɪnˌpɒks) *n.* **1.** Also called: **variola porcina** (pɔː'saɪnə). an acute infectious viral disease of pigs characterized by skin eruptions. **2.** a form of chickenpox in which the skin eruptions are not pitted.

swine's cress *n.* another name for **wart cress.**

swine vesicular disease *n.* a viral disease of swine characterized by vesicular lesions on the feet, legs, snout, and tongue.

swing (swɪŋ) *vb.* **swings, swinging, swung. 1.** to move or cause to move rhythmically to and fro, as a free-hanging object; sway. **2.** (*intr.*) to move, walk, etc., with a relaxed and swaying motion. **3.** to pivot or cause to pivot, as on a hinge. **4.** to move or cause to move in a curve: *the car swung around the bend.* **5.** to move or cause to move by suspending or being suspended. **6.** to hang or be hung so as to be able to turn freely. **7.** (*intr.*) *Slang.* to be hanged: *he'll swing for it.* **8.** to alter or cause to alter habits, a course, etc. **9.** (*tr.*) *Informal.* to influence or manipulate successfully: *I hope he can swing the deal.* **10.** (*tr.;* foll. by *up*) to raise or hoist, esp. in a sweeping motion. **11.** (*intr.;* often foll. by *at*) to hit out or strike (at), esp. with a sweeping motion. **12.** (*tr.*) to wave (a weapon, etc.) in a sweeping motion; flourish. **13.** to arrange or play (music) with the rhythmically flexible and compulsive quality associated with jazz. **14.** (*intr.*) (of popular music, esp. jazz, or of the musicians who play it) to have this quality. **15.** *Slang.* to be lively and modern. **16.** (*intr.*) *Slang.* to swap sexual partners in a group, esp. habitually. **17.** (*intr.*) *Cricket.* to bowl (a ball) with swing or (of a ball) to move with a swing. **18.** to turn (a ship or aircraft) in order to test compass error. **19. swing both ways.** *Slang.* to enjoy sexual partners of both sexes. **20. swing the lead.** *Informal.* to malinger or make up excuses. *~n.* **21.** the act or manner of swinging or the distance covered while swinging: *a wide swing.* **22.** a sweeping stroke or blow. **23.** *Boxing.* a wide punch from the side similar to but longer than a hook. **24.** *Cricket.* the lateral movement of a bowled ball through the air. **25.** any free-swaying motion. **26.** any curving movement; sweep. **27.** something that swings or is swung, esp. a suspended seat on which a person may sit and swing back and forth. **28. a.** a kind of popular dance music influenced by jazz, usually played by big bands and originating in the 1930s. **b.** (*as modifier*): *swing music.* **29.** *Prosody.* a steady distinct rhythm or cadence in prose or verse. **30.** *Informal.* the normal round or pace: *get into the swing of things.* **31. a.** a fluctuation, as in some business activity, voting pattern etc. **b.** (*as modifier*) able to bring about a swing in a voting pattern: *swing party.* **32.** *U.S. informal.* free scope; freedom of activity. **33.** *Chiefly U.S.* a circular tour. **34.** *Canadian.* a tour of a particular area or region. **35. go with a swing.** to go well; be successful. **36. in full swing.** at the height of activity. [Old English *swingan;* related to Old Frisian *swinga,* Old High German *swingan*]

swingboat ('swɪŋˌbəʊt) *n.* a piece of fairground equipment consisting of a boat-shaped carriage for swinging in.

swing bridge *n.* **1.** Also called: **pivot bridge, turn bridge.** a low bridge that can be rotated about a vertical axis, esp. to permit the passage of ships. Compare **drawbridge. 2.** *N.Z.* a pedestrian bridge over a river, suspended by heavy wire cables.

swing door *or* **swinging door** *n.* a door pivoted or hung on double-sided hinges so that it can open either way.

swinge (swɪndʒ) *vb.* **swinges, swingeing** *or* **swinging, swinged.** (*tr.*) *Archaic.* to beat, flog, or punish. [Old English *swengan;* related to Old Frisian *swenga* to drench, Gothic *afswaggwjan* to cause to sway; see SWING]

swingeing ('swɪndʒɪŋ) *adj. Chiefly Brit.* punishing; severe.

swinger ('swɪŋə) *n. Slang.* a person regarded as being modern and lively. —'**swinging** *adj.* —'**swingingly** *adv.*

swinging voter *n.* an Austral. and N.Z. informal term for **floating voter.**

swingle ('swɪŋgᵊl) *n.* **1.** a flat-bladed wooden instrument used for beating and scraping flax or hemp to remove coarse matter from it. *~vb.* (*tr.*) **2.** to use a swingle on. [Old English *swingel* stroke; related to Middle High German *swüngel,* Middle Dutch *swinghel*]

swingletree ('swɪŋgᵊlˌtriː) *n.* a crossbar in a horse's harness to which the ends of the traces are attached. Also called: **whippletree,** (esp. U.S.) **whiffletree.** [C15: from SWINGLE + TREE (in the sense: a post or bar)]

swingometer (swɪŋ'ɒmɪtə) *n.* a device used in television broadcasting during a general election to indicate the swing of votes from one political party to another.

swing shift *n. U.S. and Canadian informal.* **1.** the evening work shift, usually from the middle of the afternoon until midnight. **2.** the employees working such a shift. —**swing shifter** *n.*

swing-wing *adj.* **1.** of or relating to a variable-geometry aircraft. *~n.* **2. a.** such an aircraft. **b.** either of the two wings of such an aircraft.

swingy ('swɪŋɪ) *adj.* **swingier, swingiest.** (of a garment, esp. a skirt) styled so that it swings as the wearer moves.

swink (swɪŋk) *Archaic or Brit. dialect.* *~vb.* **1.** (*intr.*) to toil or drudge. *~n.* **2.** toil or drudgery. [Old English *swinc,* from *swincan*] —'**swinker** *n.*

swipe (swaɪp) *vb.* **1.** (when *intr.*, usually foll. by *at*) *Informal.* to hit hard with a sweeping blow. **2.** (*tr.*) *Slang.* to steal. *~n.* **3.** *Informal.* a hard blow. **4.** Also called: **sweep.** a type of lever for raising and lowering a weight, such as a bucket in a well. [C19: perhaps related to SWEEP]

swipes (swaɪps) *pl. n. Brit. slang.* beer, esp. when poor or weak. [C18: probably related to SWEEP]

swipple *or* **swiple** ('swɪpᵊl) *n.* the part of a flail that strikes the grain. [C15 *swipyl,* variant of *swepyl,* from *swep(en)* to SWEEP + *-yl,* suffix denoting an instrument]

swirl (swɜːl) *vb.* **1.** to turn or cause to turn in a twisting spinning fashion. **2.** (*intr.*) to be dizzy; swim: *my head was swirling.* *~n.* **3.** a whirling or spinning motion, esp. in water. **4.** a whorl; curl. **5.** the act of swirling or stirring. **6.** dizzy confusion or disorder. [C15: probably from Dutch *zwirrelen;* related to Norwegian *svirla,* German *schwirren*] —'**swirling** *adj.* —'**swirlingly** *adv.* —'**swirly** *adj.*

swish (swɪʃ) *vb.* **1.** to move with or make or cause to move with or make a whistling or hissing sound. **2.** (*intr.*) (esp. of fabrics) to rustle. **3.** (*tr.*) *Slang, now rare.* to whip; flog. **4.** (*tr.;* foll. by *off*) to cut with a swishing blow. *~n.* **5.** a hissing or rustling sound or movement. **6.** a rod for flogging or a blow from such a rod. **7.** *U.S. slang.* an effeminate male homosexual. **8.** a W African building material composed of mortar and mud or laterite, or more recently of cement and earth. *~adj.* **9.** *Informal, chiefly Brit.* fashionable; smart. **10.** *U.S. slang.* effeminate and homosexual. [C18: of imitative origin] —'**swisher** *n.* —'**swishing** *adj.* —'**swishingly** *adv.* —'**swishy** *adj.*

Swiss (swɪs) *adj.* **1.** of, relating to, or characteristic of Switzerland, a federal republic in W central Europe, or of its inhabitants or their dialects of German, French, and Italian. *~n.* **2.** a native, inhabitant, or citizen of Switzerland.

Swiss chard *n.* another name for **chard.**

Swiss cheese *n.* a hard white or pale yellow cheese with holes, such as Gruyère or Emmenthal.

Swiss cheese plant *n.* See **monstera.**

swiss muslin *n.* a fine muslin dress fabric, usually having a raised or woven pattern of dolls or figures. [C19: so called because it was formerly imported from Switzerland]

swiss roll *n.* a sponge cake spread with jam, cream, or some other filling, and rolled up.

Swiss tournament *n. Chess.* a tournament system in which players are paired in each round according to the scores they then have, playing a new opponent each time. More players can take part than in an all-play-all tournament of the same duration. [named from such a tournament in Zürich, Switzerland, in 1895]

switch (swɪtʃ) *n.* **1.** a mechanical, electrical, or electronic device for opening or closing a circuit or for diverting a current from one part of a circuit to another. **2.** a swift and usually sudden shift or change. **3.** an exchange or swap. **4.** a flexible rod or twig, used esp. for punishment. **5.** the sharp movement or blow of such an instrument. **6.** a tress of false hair used to give added length or bulk to a woman's own hairstyle. **7.** the tassel-like tip of the tail of cattle and certain other animals. **8.** any of various card games in which the suit is changed during play. **9.** *U.S. and Canadian.* a railway siding. **10.** *U.S. and Canadian.* a railway point. **11.** *Austral. informal.* See **switchboard.** *~vb.* **12.** to shift, change, turn aside, or change the direction of (something). **13.** to exchange (places); replace (something by something else): *the battalions switched fronts.* **14.** *Chiefly U.S. and Canadian.* to transfer (rolling stock) from one railway track to another. **15.** (*tr.*) to cause (an electric current) to start or stop flowing or to change its path by operating a switch. **16.** to swing or cause to swing, esp. back and forth. **17.** (*tr.*) to lash or whip with or as if with a switch. ~See also **switch off, switch on.** [C16: perhaps from Middle Dutch *swijch* branch, twig] —'**switcher** *n.* —'**switch,like** *adj.*

switchback ('swɪtʃ,bæk) *n.* **1.** a steep mountain road, railway, or track with hairpin bends or a hairpin bend on such a road, etc. **2.** another word (esp. Brit.) for **big dipper.**

switchblade *or* **switchblade knife** ('swɪtʃ,bleɪd) *n.* another name (esp. U.S. and Canadian) for **flick knife.**

switchboard ('swɪtʃ,bɔːd) *n.* **1.** an installation in a telephone exchange, office, hotel, etc., at which the interconnection of telephone lines is manually controlled. **2.** a similar installation of switches, terminals, etc., by which certain electrical equipment is operated.

switched-star *adj.* denoting or relating to a cable television system in which only one or two programme channels are fed to each subscriber, who can select other channels by remote control of a central switching point: *a switched-star network.* Compare **tree-and-branch.**

switcheroo (,swɪtʃə'ruː) *n. U.S. slang.* a surprising or unexpected change or variation. [C20: from SWITCH]

switchgear ('swɪtʃ,gɪə) *n. Electrical engineering.* any of several devices used for opening and closing electric circuits, esp. those that pass high currents.

switchgirl ('swɪtʃ,gɜːl) *n. Informal, chiefly Austral.* a woman who operates a telephone switchboard.

switch-hitter *n. U.S. and Canadian.* **1.** *Baseball.* a batsman who can hit either right- or left-handed. **2.** *Slang.* a bisexual person.

switchman ('swɪtʃmən) *n., pl.* **-men.** the U.S. and Canadian name for **pointsman.**

switch off *vb. (adv.)* **1.** to cause (a device) to stop operating by or as if by moving a switch, knob, or lever; turn off. **2.** *Informal.* to cease to interest or be interested; make or become bored, alienated, etc.

switch on *vb. (adv.)* **1.** to cause (a device) to operate by or as if by moving a switch, knob, or lever; turn on. **2.** *(tr.) Informal.* to produce (charm, tears, etc.) suddenly or automatically. **3.** *(tr.) Informal.* (now slightly dated) to make up-to-date, esp. regarding outlook, dress, etc. **4.** *(tr.) Slang.* to arouse emotionally or sexually. **5.** *(intr.) Slang.* to take or become intoxicated by drugs. **6.** *(tr.) Slang.* to introduce (someone) to drugs.

switch selling *n.* a system of selling, now illegal in Britain, whereby potential customers are attracted by a special offer on some goods but the salesman's real aim is to sell other more expensive goods instead.

switch yard *n. U.S. and Canadian.* an area in a railway system where rolling stock is shunted, as in forming trains.

swither ('swɪðər) *Scot.* ~*vb. (intr.)* **1.** to hesitate; vacillate; be perplexed. ~*n.* **2.** hesitation; perplexity; agitation. [C16: of unknown origin]

Switz. *or* **Swit.** *abbrev. for* Switzerland.

Switzer ('swɪtsə) *n.* **1.** a less common word for **Swiss. 2.** a member of the Swiss Guard, the bodyguard of the pope or (formerly) the Swiss mercenary bodyguard of the French kings. [C16: from Middle High German, from *Swīz* Switzerland]

swive (swaɪv) *vb. Archaic.* to have sexual intercourse with (a person). [Old English *swīfan* to revolve, SWIVEL]

swivel ('swɪvᵊl) *n.* **1.** a coupling device which allows an attached object to turn freely. **2.** such a device made of two parts which turn independently, such as a compound link of a chain. **3. a.** a pivot on which is mounted a gun that may be swung from side to side in a horizontal plane. **b.** Also called: **swivel gun.** the gun itself. ~*vb.* **-els, -elling, -elled** *or U.S.* **-els, -eling, -eled. 4.** to turn or swing on or as if on a pivot. **5.** *(tr.)* to provide with, secure by, or support with a swivel. [C14: from Old English *swīfan* to turn; see SWIFT] —'**swivel-,like** *adj.*

swivel chair *n.* a chair, the seat of which is joined to the legs by a swivel and which thus may be spun round.

swivel pin *n.* another name for **kingpin** (sense 3).

swiz *or* **swizz** (swɪz) *n. Brit. informal.* a swindle or disappointment; swizzle.

swizzle ('swɪzᵊl) *n.* **1.** *U.S.* an unshaken cocktail. **2.** a Caribbean drink of milk and rum. **3.** *Brit. informal.* a swiz. ~*vb.* **4.** *(tr.)* to stir a swizzle stick in (a drink). **5.** *Brit. informal.* to swindle; cheat. [C19: of unknown origin]

swizzle stick *n.* a small rod used to agitate an effervescent drink to facilitate the escape of carbon dioxide.

swob (swɒb) *n., vb.,* **swobs, swobbing, swobbed.** a less common word for **swab.**

swollen ('swəʊlən) *vb.* **1.** a past participle of **swell.** ~*adj.* **2.** tumid or enlarged by or as if by swelling. **3.** turgid or bombastic. —'**swollenly** *adv.* —'**swollenness** *n.*

swollen head *n.* another term for **swelled head.**

swollen-headed *adj. Informal.* conceited.

swoon (swuːn) *vb. (intr.)* **1.** a literary word for **faint. 2.** to become ecstatic. ~*n.* **3.** an instance of fainting. ~Also (archaic or dialect): **swound.** [Old English *geswōgen* insensible, past participle of *swōgan* (unattested except in compounds) to suffocate] —'**swooning** *adj.* —'**swooningly** *adv.*

swoop (swuːp) *vb.* **1.** *(intr.; usually foll. by down, on, or upon)* to sweep or pounce suddenly. **2.** *(tr.; often foll. by up, away, or off)* to seize or scoop suddenly. ~*n.* **3.** the act of swooping. **4.** a swift descent. [Old English *swāpan* to sweep; related to Old High German *sweifan* to swing around, Old Norse *sveipa* to throw]

swoosh (swʊʃ) *vb.* **1.** to make or cause to make a rustling or swirling sound, esp. when moving or pouring out. ~*n.* **2.** a swirling or rustling sound or movement. [C20: of imitative origin (probably influenced by SWISH and SWOOP)]

swop (swɒp) *n., vb.,* **swops, swopping, swopped.** a variant spelling of **swap.**

sword (sɔːd) *n.* **1.** a thrusting, striking, or cutting weapon with a long blade having one or two cutting edges, a hilt, and usually a crosspiece or guard. **2.** such a weapon worn on ceremonial occasions as a symbol of authority. **3.** something resembling a sword, such as the snout of a swordfish. **4. cross swords.** to argue or fight. **5. the sword. a.** violence or power, esp. military power. **b.** death; destruction: *to put to the sword.* [Old English *sweord;* related to Old Saxon *swerd,* Old Norse *sverth,* Old High German *swert*] —'**swordless** *adj.* —'**sword,like** *adj.*

sword bayonet *n.* a bayonet with a swordlike blade and hilt, capable of use as a sword.

swordbearer ('sɔːd,bɛərə) *n.* an official who carries a ceremonial sword.

sword belt *n.* a belt with a sling or strap for a sword.

swordbill ('sɔːd,bɪl) *n.* a South American hummingbird, *Ensifera ensifera,* having a bill as long as its body.

sword cane *n.* another name for **swordstick.**

swordcraft ('sɔːd,krɑːft) *n.* the art of using a sword.

sword dance *n.* a dance in which the performers dance nimbly over swords on the ground or brandish them in the air. —**sword dancer** *n.* —**sword dancing** *n.*

sword fern *n.* any of numerous ferns having sword-shaped fronds.

swordfish ('sɔːd,fɪʃ) *n., pl.* **-fish** *or* **-fishes.** a large scombroid fish, *Xiphias gladius,* with a very long upper jaw: valued as a food and game fish: family *Xiphiidae.*

sword grass *n.* any of various grasses and other plants having sword-shaped sharp leaves.

sword knot *n.* a loop on the hilt of a sword by which it was attached to the wrist, now purely decorative.

sword lily *n.* another name for **gladiolus** (sense 1). [C18: so called because of its sword-shaped leaves]

Sword of Damocles *n.* a closely impending disaster. [after a sycophant forced by Dionysius, tyrant of ancient Syracuse, to sit under a sword suspended by a hair]

swordplay ('sɔːd,pleɪ) *n.* **1.** the action or art of fighting with a sword. **2.** verbal sparring. —'**sword,player** *n.*

swordsman ('sɔːdzmən) *n., pl.* **-men.** one who uses or is skilled in the use of a sword. —'**swordsman,ship** *n.*

swordstick ('sɔːd,stɪk) *n.* a hollow walking stick containing a short sword or dagger.

sword-swallower *n.* a performer who simulates the swallowing of swords.

swordtail ('sɔːd,teɪl) *n.* any of several small freshwater cyprinodont fishes of the genus *Xiphophorus,* esp. *X. helleri,* of Central America, having a long swordlike tail.

swore (swɔː) *vb.* the past tense of **swear.**

sworn (swɔːn) *vb.* **1.** the past participle of **swear.** ~*adj.* **2.** bound, pledged, or made inveterate, by or as if by an oath: *a sworn statement; he was sworn to God.*

swot[1] (swɒt) *Brit. informal.* ~*vb.* **swots, swotting, swotted. 1.** (often foll. by *up*) to study (a subject) intensively, as for an examination; cram. ~*n.* **2.** Also called: **swotter** ('swɒtə). a person who works or studies hard. **3.** hard work or grind. ~Also: **swat.** [C19: dialect variant of SWEAT (n.)]

swot[2] (swɒt) *vb.* **swots, swotting, swotted,** *n.* a variant of **swat**[1].

SWOT *abbrev. for* strengths, weaknesses, opportunities, and threats: an analysis of a product made before it is marketed.

swound (swaʊnd) *n., vb.* an archaic or dialect word for **swoon.**

swounds *or* **'swounds** (zwaʊndz, zaʊndz) *interj. Archaic.* less common spellings of **zounds.**

swum (swʌm) *vb.* the past participle of **swim.**

swung (swʌŋ) *vb.* the past tense and past participle of **swing.**

swung dash *n.* a mark, ~, traditionally used in text to indicate the omission of a word or part of a word.

swy (swaɪ) *n. Austral.* another name for **two-up.** [C20: from German *zwei* two]

SY *international car registration for* Seychelles.

sybarite ('sɪbə,raɪt) *n.* **1.** *(sometimes cap.)* a devotee of luxury and the sensual vices. ~*adj.* **2.** luxurious; sensuous. [C16: from Latin *Sybarīta,* from Greek *Subaritēs* inhabitant of Sybaris, an ancient Greek colony in S Italy notorious for its luxurious living] —**sybaritic** (,sɪbə'rɪtɪk) *or (less commonly)* **,syba'ritical** *adj.* —**,syba'ritically** *adv.* —'**sybaritism** *n.*

sybo, syboe, *or* **sybow** ('saɪbɪ, 'saɪ-, -bo) *n., pl.* **syboes, sybows.** *Scot.* a spring onion. [C16: from *cibol,* from French *ciboule,* from Latin *cepulla* onion bed, from *cepa* onion]

sycamine ('sɪkə,maɪn) *n.* a mulberry tree mentioned in the Bible, thought to be the black mulberry, *Morus nigra.* [C16: from Latin *sȳcamīnus,* from Greek *sukaminon,* from Hebrew *shiqmāh*]

sycamore ('sɪkə,mɔː) *n.* **1.** a Eurasian maple tree, *Acer pseudoplatanus,* naturalized in Britain and North America, having five-lobed leaves, yellow flowers, and two-winged fruits. **2.** *U.S. and Canadian.* an American plane tree, *Platanus occidentalis.* See **plane tree. 3.** a moraceous tree, *Ficus sycomorus,* of N Africa and W Asia, having an edible figlike fruit.

[C14: from Old French *sicamor,* from Latin *sȳcomorus,* from Greek *sukomoros,* from *sukon* fig + *moron* mulberry]

syce, sice, *or* **saice** (saɪs) *n.* **1.** (formerly, in India) a servant employed to look after horses, drive carriages, etc. **2.** (in Malaysia) a driver or chauffeur. [C17: from Urdu *sā'is,* from Arabic, from *sāsa* to administer]

sycee *or* **sycee silver** (saɪ'siː) *n.* silver ingots formerly used as a medium of exchange in China. [C18: from Chinese *saì sz* fine silk; so called because the silver can be made into threads as fine as silk]

syconium (saɪ'kəʊnɪəm) *n., pl.* **-nia** (-nɪə). *Botany.* the fleshy fruit of the fig, consisting of a greatly enlarged receptacle. [C19: from New Latin, from Greek *sukon* fig]

sycophant ('sɪkəfənt) *n.* a person who uses flattery to win favour from individuals wielding influence; toady. [C16: from Latin *sȳcophanta,* from Greek *sukophantēs,* literally: the person showing a fig, apparently referring to the fig sign used in making an accusation, from *sukon* fig + *phainein* to show; sense probably developed from "accuser" to "informer, flatterer"] —**'sycophancy** *n.* —**sycophantic** (ˌsɪkə'fæntɪk) *adj.* —ˌ**syco'phantically** *adv.*

sycosis (saɪ'kəʊsɪs) *n.* chronic inflammation of the hair follicles, esp. those of the beard, caused by a staphylococcal infection. [C16: via New Latin from Greek *sukōsis,* from *sukon* fig]

Sydenham's chorea ('sɪdᵊnəmz) *n.* a form of chorea affecting children, often associated with rheumatic fever. Nontechnical name: **Saint Vitus's dance.** [named after T. *Sydenham* (1624–89), English physician]

Sydneysider ('sɪdnɪˌsaɪdə) *n. Chiefly Austral.* a resident of Sydney, SE Australia.

Sydney silky ('sɪdnɪ) *n.* a small silky-coated breed of terrier, originally from Australia.

syenite ('saɪəˌnaɪt) *n.* a light-coloured coarse-grained plutonic igneous rock consisting of feldspars with hornblende or biotite. [C18: from French *syénite,* from Latin *syēnītēs lapis* stone from *Syene* (Aswan), SE Egypt, where it was originally quarried] —**syenitic** (ˌsaɪə'nɪtɪk) *adj.*

SYHA *abbrev. for* Scottish Youth Hostels Association.

syl. *or* **syll.** *abbrev. for:* **1.** syllable. **2.** syllabus.

syllabary ('sɪləbərɪ) *n., pl.* **-baries.** **1.** a table or list of syllables. **2.** a set of symbols used in certain writing systems, such as one used for Japanese, in which each symbol represents a spoken syllable. [C16: from New Latin *syllabārium,* from Latin *syllaba* SYLLABLE]

syllabi ('sɪləˌbaɪ) *n.* a plural of **syllabus.**

syllabic (sɪ'læbɪk) *adj.* **1.** of or relating to syllables or the division of a word into syllables. **2.** denoting a kind of verse line based on a specific number of syllables rather than being regulated by stresses or quantities. **3.** (of a consonant) constituting a syllable. **4.** (of plainsong and similar chanting) having each syllable sung to a different note. *~n.* **5.** a syllabic consonant. —**syl'labically** *adv.*

syllabify (sɪ'læbɪˌfaɪ) *or* **syllabicate** *vb.* **-fies, -fying, -fied** *or* **-cates, -cating, -cated.** (*tr.*) to divide (a word) into its constituent syllables. —**sylˌlabifi'cation** *or* **sylˌlabi'cation** *n.*

syllabism ('sɪləˌbɪzəm) *n.* use of a writing system consisting of characters for syllables rather than for individual sounds or whole words. Also called: **syllabography.**

syllable ('sɪləbᵊl) *n.* **1.** a combination or set of one or more units of sound in a language that must consist of a sonorous element (a sonant or vowel) and may or may not contain less sonorous elements (consonants or semivowels) flanking it on either or both sides: for example "paper" has two syllables. See also **open** (sense 34b), **closed** (sense 6a). **2.** (in the writing systems of certain languages, esp. ancient ones) a symbol or set of symbols standing for a syllable. **3.** the least mention in speech or print: *don't breathe a syllable of it.* **4. in words of one syllable.** simply; bluntly. *~vb.* **5.** to pronounce syllables of (a text); articulate. **6.** (*tr.*) to write down in syllables. [C14: via Old French from Latin *syllaba,* from Greek *sullabē,* from *sullambanein* to collect together, from *sul-* SYN- + *lambanein* to take]

syllabogram (sɪ'læbəʊˌgræm) *n.* a written symbol representing a single syllable.

syllabography (ˌsɪlə'bɒgrəfɪ) *n.* another word for **syllabism.** Compare **logography, phonography.**

syllabub *or* **sillabub** ('sɪləˌbʌb) *n.* **1.** a spiced drink made of milk with rum, port, brandy, or wine, often hot. **2.** *Brit.* a cold dessert made from milk or cream beaten with sugar, wine, and lemon juice. [C16: of unknown origin]

syllabus ('sɪləbəs) *n., pl.* **-buses** *or* **-bi** (-ˌbaɪ). **1.** an outline of a course of studies, text, etc. **2.** *Brit.* **a.** the subjects studied for a particular course. **b.** a list of these subjects. [C17: from Late Latin, erroneously from Latin *sittybus* parchment strip giving title and author, from Greek *sittuba*]

syllepsis (sɪ'lɛpsɪs) *n., pl.* **-ses** (-siːz). **1.** (in grammar or rhetoric) the use of a single sentence construction in which a verb, adjective, etc. is made to cover two syntactical functions, as the verb form *have* in *she and they have promised to come.* **2.** another word for **zeugma.** [C16: from Late Latin, from Greek *sullēpsis,* from *sul-* SYN- + *lēpsis* a taking, from *lambanein* to take] —**syl'leptic** *adj.* —**syl'leptically** *adv.*

syllogism ('sɪləˌdʒɪzəm) *n.* **1.** a deductive inference consisting of two premises and a conclusion, all of which are categorial propositions. The subject of the conclusion is the **minor term** and its predicate the **major term;** the **middle term** occurs in both premises but not the conclusion. There are 256 such arguments but only 24 are valid. *Some men are mortal; some men are angelic; so some mortals are angelic* is invalid, while *some temples are in ruins; all ruins are fascinating; so some temples are fascinating* is valid. Here *fascinating, in ruins,* and *temples* are respectively major, middle, and minor terms. **2.** a deductive inference of certain other forms with two premises, such as the **hypothetical syllogism,** *if P then Q; if Q then R; so if P then R.* **3.** a piece of deductive reasoning from the general to the particular. **4.** a subtle or deceptive piece of reasoning. [C14: via Latin from Greek *sullogismos,* from *sullogizesthai* to reckon together, from *sul-* SYN- + *logizesthai* to calculate, from *logos* a discourse]

syllogistic (ˌsɪlə'dʒɪstɪk) *adj. also* **syllogistical.** **1.** of, relating to or consisting of syllogisms. *~n.* (*often pl.*) **2.** the branch of logic concerned with syllogisms. **3.** reasoning by means of syllogisms. —ˌ**syllo'gistically** *adv.*

syllogize *or* **syllogise** ('sɪləˌdʒaɪz) *vb.* to reason or infer by using syllogisms. [C15: via Old French from Late Latin *syllogizāre,* from Greek *sullogizesthai;* see SYLLOGISM] —ˌ**syllogi'zation** *or* ˌ**syllogi'sation** *n.* —**'sylloˌgizer** *or* **'sylloˌgiser** *n.*

sylph (sɪlf) *n.* **1.** a slender graceful girl or young woman. **2.** any of a class of imaginary beings assumed to inhabit the air. [C17: from New Latin *sylphus,* probably coined from Latin *silva* wood + Greek *numphē* NYMPH] —**'sylphˌlike** *or* (*less commonly*) **'sylphic, 'sylphish,** *or* **'sylphy** *adj.*

sylva *or* **silva** ('sɪlvə) *n., pl.* **-vas** *or* **-vae** (-viː). the trees growing in a particular region. [C17: Latin *silva* a wood]

sylvan *or* **silvan** ('sɪlvən) *Chiefly poetic.* *~adj.* **1.** of, characteristic of, or consisting of woods or forests. **2.** living or located in woods or forests. **3.** idyllically rural or rustic. *~n.* **4.** an inhabitant of the woods, esp. a spirit. [C16: from Latin *silvānus,* from *silva* forest]

sylvanite ('sɪlvəˌnaɪt) *n.* a silver-white mineral consisting of a telluride of gold and silver in the form of elongated striated crystals: a source of gold in Australia and North America. Formula: $(Au,Ag)Te_2$. [C18: from *(Tran)sylvan(ia)* + -ITE[1], with reference to the region in Romania where it was first found]

sylvatic (sɪl'vætɪk) *adj.* growing, living, or occurring in a wood or beneath a tree. Also: **sylvestral** (sɪl'vɛstrəl).

sylviculture ('sɪlvɪˌkʌltʃə) *n.* a variant spelling of **silviculture.**

sylvite ('sɪlvaɪt) *or* **sylvine** ('sɪlviːn) *n.* a soluble colourless, white, or coloured mineral consisting of potassium chloride in cubic crystalline form with sodium impurities: it occurs chiefly in sedimentary beds and is an important ore of potassium. Formula: KCl. [C19: *sylvite,* alteration of *sylvine,* from New Latin *sal digestiva Sylvii* digestive salt of Sylvius, after Franciscus *Sylvius* (died 1672), German anatomist. See -ITE[1], -INE[2]]

sym. *abbrev. for:* **1.** symbol. **2.** *Chem.* symmetrical. **3.** symphony. **4.** symptom.

sym- *prefix.* a variant of **syn-** before *b, p,* and *m.*

symbiont ('sɪmbɪˌɒnt) *n.* an organism living in a state of symbiosis. [C19: from Greek *sumbioun* to live together, from *bioun* to live] —ˌ**symbi'ontic** *adj.* —ˌ**symbi'ontically** *adv.*

symbiosis (ˌsɪmbɪ'əʊsɪs) *n.* **1.** a close association of two animal or plant species that are dependent on one another. **2.** a similar relationship between interdependent persons or groups. [C19: via New Latin from Greek: a living together; see SYMBIONT] —ˌ**symbi'otic** *or* (*less commonly*) ˌ**symbi'otical** *adj.*

symbol ('sɪmbᵊl) *n.* **1.** something that represents or stands for something else, usually by convention or association, esp. a material object used to represent something abstract. **2.** an object, person, idea, etc., used in a literary work, film, etc., to stand for or suggest something else with which it is associated either explicitly or in some more subtle way. **3.** a letter, figure, or sign used in mathematics, science, music, etc. to represent a quantity, phenomenon, operation, function, etc. **4.** *Psychoanal.* the end product, in the form of an object or act, of a conflict in the unconscious between repression processes and the actions and thoughts being repressed: *the symbols of dreams.* **5.** *Psychol.* any mental process that represents some feature of external reality. *~vb.* **-bols, -bolling, -bolled** *or U.S.* **-bols, -boling, -boled.** **6.** (*tr.*) another word for **symbolize.** [C15: from Church Latin *symbolum,* from Greek *sumbolon* sign, from *sumballein* to throw together, from SYN- + *ballein* to throw]

symbolic (sɪm'bɒlɪk) *or* **symbolical** *adj.* **1.** of or relating to a symbol or symbols. **2.** serving as a symbol. **3.** characterized by the use of symbols or symbolism. —**sym'bolically** *adv.* —**sym'bolicalness** *n.*

symbolical books *pl. n. Christianity.* the books containing the creeds, beliefs, or doctrine of religious groups that have emerged since the Reformation.

symbolic logic *n.* another term for **formal logic.**

symbolism ('sɪmbəˌlɪzəm) *n.* **1.** the representation of something in symbolic form or the attribution of symbolic meaning or character to something. **2.** a system of symbols or symbolic representation. **3.** a symbolic significance or quality. **4.** (*often cap.*) a late 19th-century movement in art that sought to express mystical or abstract ideas through the symbolic use of images. See also **synthetism.** **5.** *Theol.* any symbolist interpretation of the Eucharist.

symbolist ('sɪmbəlɪst) *n.* **1.** a person who uses or can interpret symbols, esp. as a means to revealing aspects of truth and reality. **2.** an artist or writer who practises symbolism in his work. **3.** (*usually cap.*) a writer associated with the symbolist movement in French and Belgian poetry in the late 19th century, which sought to use words and imagery to suggest states of mind. **4.** (*often cap.*) an artist associated with the movement of symbolism. **5.** *Christian theol.* a person who rejects any interpretation of the Eucharist that suggests that Christ is really present in it, and who maintains that the bread and wine are only symbols of his body and blood. *~adj.* **6.** of, relating to, or characterizing symbolism or symbolists. —ˌ**symbol'istic** *adj.* —ˌ**symbol'istically** *adv.*

symbolize *or* **symbolise** ('sɪmbəˌlaɪz) *vb.* **1.** (*tr.*) to serve as or be a symbol of. **2.** (*tr.*; usually foll. by *by*) to represent by a symbol or symbols. **3.** (*intr.*) to use symbols. **4.** (*tr.*) to treat or regard as symbolic or figurative. —ˌ**symboli'zation** *or* ˌ**symboli'sation** *n.*

symbology (sɪm'bɒlədʒɪ) *n.* the use, study, or interpretation of symbols. —**symbological** (ˌsɪmbə'lɒdʒɪkᵊl) *adj.* —**sym'bologist** *n.*

symbol retailer *n.* any member of a voluntary group of independent retailers, often using a common name or symbol, formed to obtain better prices from wholesalers or manufacturers in competition with supermarket chains. Also called: **voluntary retailer.**

symmetallism *or U.S.* **symmetalism** (sɪ'mɛtəˌlɪzəm) *n.* **1.** the use of an alloy of two or more metals in fixed relative value as the standard of value and currency. **2.** the economic policies and doctrine supporting a symmetallic standard. [C19: from SYM- + *-metallism,* on the model of BIMETALLISM]

symmetric (sɪ'mɛtrɪk) *adj.* **1.** *Logic, maths.* (of a relation) holding between a pair of arguments *x* and *y* when and only when it holds between *y* and *x*, as ... *is a sibling of* ... but not ... *is a brother of* .... Compare **asymmetric** (sense 5), **antisymmetric, nonsymmetric. 2.** another word for **symmetrical** (sense 5).

symmetrical (sɪ'mɛtrɪkᵊl) *adj.* **1.** possessing or displaying symmetry. Compare **asymmetric. 2.** *Maths.* **a.** (of two points) capable of being joined by a line that is bisected by a given point or bisected perpendicularly by a given line or plane: *the points* (*x, y*) *and* (*–x, –y*) *are symmetrical about the origin.* **b.** (of a configuration) having pairs of points that are symmetrical about a given point, line, or plane: *a circle is symmetrical about a diameter.* **c.** (of an equation or function of two or more variables) remaining unchanged in form after an interchange of two variables: *x + y = z is a symmetrical equation.* **3.** *Chem.* (of a compound) having a molecular structure in which substituents are symmetrical about the molecule. **4.** *Botany.* another word for **actinomorphic. 5.** Also: **symmetric.** (of a disease, infection, etc.) affecting both sides of the body or corresponding parts, such as both legs. —**sym'metrically** *adv.* —**sym'metricalness** *n.*

symmetric matrix *n. Maths.* a square matrix that is equal to its transpose, being symmetrical about its main diagonal. A **skew symmetric matrix** is equal to the negation of its transpose. Compare **orthogonal matrix.**

symmetrize *or* **symmetrise** ('sɪmɪˌtraɪz) *vb.* (*tr.*) to render symmetrical or perfectly balanced. —ˌ**symmetri'zation** *or* ˌ**symmetri'sation** *n.*

symmetry ('sɪmɪtrɪ) *n., pl.* **-tries. 1.** similarity, correspondence, or balance among systems or parts of a system. **2.** *Maths.* an exact correspondence in position or form about a given point, line, or plane. See **symmetrical** (sense 2). **3.** beauty or harmony of form based on a proportionate arrangement of parts. **4.** *Physics.* the independence of a property with respect to direction; isotropy. [C16: from Latin *symmetria,* from Greek *summetria* proportion, from SYN- + *metron* measure]

sympathectomy (ˌsɪmpə'θɛktəmɪ) *n., pl.* **-mies.** the surgical excision or chemical destruction (**chemical sympathectomy**) of one or more parts of the sympathetic nervous system. [C20: from SYMPATHETIC + -ECTOMY]

sympathetic (ˌsɪmpə'θɛtɪk) *adj.* **1.** characterized by, feeling, or showing sympathy; understanding. **2.** in accord with the subject's personality or mood; congenial: *a sympathetic atmosphere.* **3.** (when *postpositive,* often foll. by *to* or *towards*) showing agreement (with) or favour (towards): *sympathetic to the proposals.* **4.** *Anatomy, physiol.* of or relating to the division of the autonomic nervous system that acts in opposition to the parasympathetic system accelerating the heartbeat, dilating the bronchi, inhibiting the smooth muscles of the digestive tract, etc. Compare **parasympathetic. 5.** relating to vibrations occurring as a result of similar vibrations in a neighbouring body: *sympathetic strings on a sitar.* —ˌ**sympa'thetically** *adv.*

sympathetic ink *n.* another term for **invisible ink.**

sympathetic magic *n.* a type of magic in which it is sought to produce a large-scale effect, often at a distance, by performing some small-scale ceremony resembling it, such as the pouring of water on an altar to induce rainfall.

sympathin ('sɪmpəθɪn) *n.* a substance released at certain sympathetic nerve endings: thought to be identical with adrenaline. [C20: from SYMPATH(ETIC) + -IN]

sympathize *or* **sympathise** ('sɪmpəˌθaɪz) *vb.* (*intr.*; often foll. by *with*) **1.** to feel or express compassion or sympathy (for); commiserate: *he sympathized with my troubles.* **2.** to share or understand the sentiments or ideas (of); be in sympathy (with). —'**sympaˌthizer** *or* '**sympaˌthiser** *n.*

sympatholytic (ˌsɪmpəθəʊ'lɪtɪk) *Med.* *~adj.* **1. a.** inhibiting or antagonistic to nerve impulses of the sympathetic nervous system. **b.** of or relating to such inhibition. *~n.* **2.** a sympatholytic drug. Compare **sympathomimetic.** [C20: from SYMPATH(ETIC) + -LYTIC]

sympathomimetic (ˌsɪmpəθəʊmɪ'mɛtɪk) *Med.* *~adj.* **1.** causing a physiological effect similar to that produced by stimulation of the sympathetic nervous system. *~n.* **2.** a sympathomimetic drug. Compare **sympatholytic.** [C20: from SYMPATH(ETIC) + MIMETIC]

sympathy ('sɪmpəθɪ) *n., pl.* **-thies. 1.** the sharing of another's emotions, esp. of sorrow or anguish; pity; compassion. **2.** an affinity or harmony, usually of feelings or interests, between persons or things: *to be in sympathy with someone.* **3.** mutual affection or understanding arising from such a relationship; congeniality. **4.** the condition of a physical system or body when its behaviour is similar or corresponds to that of a different system that influences it, such as the vibration of sympathetic strings. **5.** (*sometimes pl.*) a feeling of loyalty, support, or accord, as for an idea, cause, etc. **6.** *Physiol.* the mutual relationship between two organs or parts whereby a change in one has an effect on the other. [C16: from Latin *sympathīa,* from Greek *sumpatheia,* from *sumpathēs,* from SYN- + *pathos* suffering]

sympathy strike *n.* a strike organized in support of another section of workers or a cause and not because of direct grievances. Also called: **sympathetic strike.**

sympatric (sɪm'pætrɪk) *adj.* (of biological speciation or species) taking place or existing in the same or overlapping geographical areas. Compare **allopatric.** [C20: from SYN- + *-patric,* from Greek *patra* native land, from *patēr* father] —**sym'patrically** *adv.*

sympetalous (sɪm'pɛtələs) *adj. Botany.* another word for **gamopetalous.**

symphile ('sɪmfaɪl) *n.* an insect or other organism that lives in the nests of social insects, esp. ants and termites, and is fed and reared by the inmates. Compare **synoekete.** [C20: from Greek *sumphilein* to love mutually; see SYN-, -PHILE]

symphonic poem *n. Music.* an extended orchestral composition, originated by Liszt, based on nonmusical material, such as a work of literature or folk tale. Also called: **tone poem.**

symphonious (sɪm'fəʊnɪəs) *adj. Literary.* harmonious or concordant. —**sym'phoniously** *adv.*

symphonist ('sɪmfənɪst) *n.* a person who composes symphonies.

symphony ('sɪmfənɪ) *n., pl.* **-nies. 1.** an extended large-scale orchestral composition, usually with several movements, at least one of which is in sonata form. The classical form of the symphony was fixed by Haydn and Mozart, but the innovations of subsequent composers have freed it entirely from classical constraints. It continues to be a vehicle for serious, large-scale orchestral music. **2.** a piece of instrumental music in up to three very short movements, used as an overture to or interlude in a baroque opera. **3.** any purely orchestral movement in a vocal work, such as a cantata or oratorio. **4.** short for **symphony orchestra. 5.** (in musical theory, esp. of classical Greece) **a.** another word for **consonance** (sense 3). Compare **diaphony** (sense 2). **b.** the interval of unison. **6.** anything distinguished by a harmonious composition: *the picture was a symphony of green.* **7.** *Archaic.* harmony in general; concord. [C13: from Old French *symphonie,* from Latin *symphōnia* concord, concert, from Greek *sumphōnia,* from SYN- + *phōnē* sound] —**symphonic** (sɪm'fɒnɪk) *adj.* —**sym'phonically** *adv.*

symphony orchestra *n. Music.* an orchestra capable of performing symphonies, esp. the large orchestra comprising strings, brass, woodwind, harp and percussion.

symphysis ('sɪmfɪsɪs) *n., pl.* **-ses** (-ˌsiːz). **1.** *Anatomy, botany.* a growing together of parts or structures, such as two bony surfaces joined by an intermediate layer of fibrous cartilage. **2.** a line marking this growing together. **3.** *Pathol.* an abnormal adhesion of two or more parts or structures. [C16: via New Latin from Greek *sumphusis,* from *sumphuein,* from SYN- + *phuein* to grow] —**symphysial** *or* **symphyseal** (sɪm'fɪzɪəl) *adj.* —**symphystic** (sɪm'fɪstɪk) *or* **sym'phytic** *adj.*

symplast ('sɪmplæst) *n. Botany.* the continuous system of protoplasts, linked by plasmodesmata and bounded by the cell wall. —**sym'plastic** *adj.*

sympodium (sɪm'pəʊdɪəm) *n., pl.* **-dia** (-dɪə). the main axis of growth in the grapevine and similar plants: a number of lateral branches that arise from just behind the apex of the main stem, which ceases to grow. Compare **monopodium.** [C19: from New Latin, from SYN- + Greek *podion* a little foot, from *pous* foot] —**sym'podial** *adj.* —**sym'podially** *adv.*

symposiac (sɪm'pəʊzɪˌæk) *adj.* **1.** of, suitable for, or occurring at a symposium. *~n.* **2.** an archaic word for **symposium.** [C17: from Latin *symposiacus;* see SYMPOSIUM]

symposiarch (sɪm'pəʊzɪˌɑːk) *n.* **1.** the president of a symposium, esp. in classical Greece. **2.** a rare word for **toastmaster.** [C17: from Greek; see SYMPOSIUM, -ARCH]

symposiast (sɪm'pəʊzɪˌæst) *n.* a person who takes part in a symposium.

symposium (sɪm'pəʊzɪəm) *n., pl.* **-siums** *or* **-sia** (-zɪə). **1.** a conference or meeting for the discussion of some subject, esp. an academic topic or social problem. **2.** a collection of scholarly contributions, usually published together, on a given subject. **3.** (in classical Greece) a drinking party with intellectual conversation, music, etc. [C16: via Latin from Greek *sumposion,* from *sumpinein* to drink together, from *sum-* SYN- + *pinein* to drink]

symptom ('sɪmptəm) *n.* **1.** *Med.* any sensation or change in bodily function experienced by a patient that is associated with a particular disease. Compare **sign** (sense 9). **2.** any phenomenon or circumstance accompanying something and regarded as evidence of its existence; indication. [C16: from Late Latin *symptōma,* from Greek *sumptōma* chance, from *sumpiptein* to occur, from SYN- + *piptein* to fall] —**'symptomless** *adj.*

symptomatic (ˌsɪmptə'mætɪk) *adj.* **1.** (often foll. by *of*) being a symptom; indicative: *symptomatic of insanity.* **2.** of or relating to a symptom or symptoms. **3.** according to symptoms: *a symptomatic analysis of a case.* —ˌ**sympto'matically** *adv.*

symptomatology (ˌsɪmptəmə'tɒlədʒɪ) *n.* the branch of medicine concerned with the study and classification of the symptoms of disease.

syn (saɪn, sɪn) *adv., prep., conj.* a variant of **syne,** a Scot. word for **since.**

syn. *abbrev. for* synonym(ous).

syn- *prefix.* **1.** with or together: *synecology.* **2.** fusion: *syngamy.* [from Greek *sun* together, with]

synaeresis (sɪ'nɪərɪsɪs) *n.* a variant spelling of **syneresis.**

synaesthesia *or U.S.* **synesthesia** (ˌsɪniːs'θiːzɪə) *n.* **1.** *Physiol.* a sensation experienced in a part of the body other than the part stimulated. **2.** *Psychol.* the subjective sensation of a sense other than the one being stimulated. For example, a sound may evoke sensations of colour. [from New Latin, from SYN- + *-esthesia,* from Greek *aisthēsis* sensation] —**synaesthetic** *or U.S.* **synesthetic** (ˌsɪnɪs'θɛtɪk) *adj.*

synagogue ('sɪnəˌgɒg) *n.* **1. a.** a building for Jewish religious services and usually also for religious instruction. **b.** (*as modifier*): *synagogue services.* **2.** a congregation of Jews who assemble for worship or religious study. **3.** the religion of Judaism as organized in such congregations. [C12: from Old French *sinagogue,* from Late Latin *synagōga,* from Greek *sunagōgē* a gathering, from *sunagein* to bring together, from SYN- + *agein* to lead] —**synagogical** (ˌsɪnə'gɒdʒɪkᵊl) *or* **synagogal** ('sɪnəˌgɒgᵊl) *adj.*

synalepha *or* **synaloepha** (ˌsɪnə'liːfə) *n. Linguistics.* vowel elision, esp. as it arises when one word ends in a vowel and the following word begins with one. [C16: from Late Latin *synaloepha,* from Greek *sunaliphē,* from SYN- + *aleiphein* to melt, smear]

synapse ('saɪnæps) *n.* the point at which a nerve impulse is relayed from the terminal portion of an axon to the dendrites of an adjacent neuron.

synapsis (sɪ'næpsɪs) *n., pl.* **-ses** (-siːz). **1.** *Cytology.* the association in pairs of homologous chromosomes at the start of meiosis. **2.** another word for **synapse.** [C19: from New Latin, from Greek *sunapsis* junction, from *sunaptein* to join together, from SYN- + *haptein* to connect] —**synaptic** (sɪ'næptɪk) *or* **syn'aptical** *adj.* —**syn'aptically** *adv.*

synarchy ('sɪnəkɪ) *n., pl.* **-chies.** joint rule. [C18: from Greek *sunarchia,* from *sunarchein* to rule jointly]

synarthrosis (ˌsɪnɑː'θrəʊsɪs) *n., pl.* **-ses** (-siːz). *Anatomy.* any of various joints which lack a synovial cavity and are virtually immovable; a fixed joint. [via New Latin from Greek *sunarthrōsis,* from *sunarthrousthai* to be connected by joints, from *sun-* SYN- + *arthron* a joint] —ˌ**synar'throdial** *adj.* —ˌ**synar'throdially** *adv.*

sync *or* **synch** (sɪŋk) *Films, television, computers, etc.* ~*vb.* **1.** an informal word for **synchronize.** ~*n.* **2.** an informal word for **synchronization** (esp. in the phrases **in** *or* **out of sync**).

syncarp ('sɪnkɑːp) *n. Botany.* a fleshy multiple fruit, formed from two or more carpels of one flower or the aggregated fruits of several flowers. [C19: from New Latin *syncarpium,* from SYN- + Greek *karpos* fruit]

syncarpous (sɪn'kɑːpəs) *adj.* **1.** (of the ovaries of certain flowering plants) consisting of united carpels. Compare **apocarpous. 2.** of or relating to a syncarp. —**syncarpy** ('sɪnkɑːpɪ) *n.*

syncategorematic (sɪnˌkætəˌgɒːrə'mætɪk) *adj. Philosophy.* applying to expressions that are not in any of Aristotle's categories, but form meaningful expressions together with them, such as conjunctions and adverbs.

synchro ('sɪŋkrəʊ) *n., pl.* **-chros. 1.** any of a number of electrical devices in which the angular position of a rotating part is transformed into a voltage, or vice versa. Also called: **selsyn. 2.** short for **synchronized swimming.**

synchro- *combining form.* indicating synchronization: *synchroflash.*

synchrocyclotron (ˌsɪŋkrəʊ'saɪkləˌtrɒn) *n.* a type of cyclotron in which the frequency of the electric field is modulated to allow for relativistic effects at high velocities and thus produce higher energies.

synchroflash ('sɪŋkrəʊˌflæʃ) *n.* a mechanism in a camera that enables the shutter to be fully open while the light from a flashbulb or electronic flash is at its brightest.

synchromesh ('sɪŋkrəʊˌmɛʃ) *adj.* **1.** (of a gearbox, etc.) having a system of clutches that synchronizes the speeds of the driving and driven members before engagement to avoid shock in gear changing and to reduce noise and wear. ~*n.* **2.** a gear system having these features. [C20: shortened from *synchronized mesh*]

synchronic (sɪn'krɒnɪk) *adj.* **1.** concerned with the events or phenomena at a particular period without considering historical antecedents: *synchronic linguistics.* Compare **diachronic. 2.** synchronous. —**syn'chronically** *adv.*

synchronicity (ˌsɪnkrə'nɪsɪtɪ) *n.* an apparently meaningful coincidence in time of two or more similar or identical events that are causally unrelated. [C20: coined by Carl Jung from SYNCHRONIC + -ITY]

synchronism ('sɪŋkrəˌnɪzəm) *n.* **1.** the quality or condition of being synchronous. **2.** a chronological usually tabular list of historical persons and events, arranged to show parallel or synchronous occurrence. **3.** the representation in a work of art of one or more incidents that occurred at separate times. [C16: from Greek *sunkhronismos;* see SYNCHRONOUS, -ISM] —ˌ**synchro'nistic** *adj.* —ˌ**synchro'nistically** *adv.*

synchronize *or* **synchronise** ('sɪŋkrəˌnaɪz) *vb.* **1.** (when *intr.,* usually foll. by *with*) to occur or recur or cause to occur or recur at the same time or in unison. **2.** to indicate or cause to indicate the same time: *synchronize your watches.* **3.** (*tr.*) *Films.* to establish (the picture and soundtrack records) in their correct relative position. **4.** (*tr.*) to designate (events) as simultaneous. —ˌ**synchroni'zation** *or* ˌ**synchroni'sation** *n.* —**'synchroˌnizer** *or* **'synchroˌniser** *n.*

synchronized swimming *n.* the art or sport of one or more swimmers moving in patterns in the water in time to music. Sometimes shortened to **synchro** *or* **synchro swimming.**

synchronous ('sɪŋkrənəs) *adj.* **1.** occurring at the same time; contemporaneous. **2.** *Physics.* (of periodic phenomena, such as voltages) having the same frequency and phase. **3.** occurring or recurring exactly together and at the same rate: *the synchronous flapping of a bird's wings.* [C17: from Late Latin *synchronus,* from Greek *sunkhronos,* from SYN- + *khronos* time] —**'synchronously** *adv.* —**'synchronousness** *n.*

synchronous converter *n.* a synchronous machine that converts alternating current to direct current, or vice versa.

synchronous machine *n.* an electrical machine, whose rotating speed is proportional to the frequency of the alternating-current supply and independent of the load.

synchronous motor *n.* an alternating-current motor that runs at a speed that is equal to or is a multiple of the frequency of the supply.

synchronous orbit *n. Astronautics.* an earth orbit in which a satellite makes one complete revolution in the period taken for the earth to rotate about its axis.

synchroscope ('sɪŋkrəˌskəʊp) *or* **synchronoscope** (sɪŋ'krɒnəˌskəʊp) *n.* an instrument used to indicate whether two periodic quantities or motions are synchronous.

synchrotron ('sɪŋkrəˌtrɒn) *n.* a type of particle accelerator similar to a betatron but having an electric field of fixed frequency as well as a changing magnetic field. It is capable of producing very high energies in the GeV range. [C20: from SYNCHRO- + (ELEC)TRON]

synchrotron radiation *n.* electromagnetic radiation emitted in narrow beams tangential to the orbit of very high energy charged particles, such as electrons, spiralling along the lines of force in a strong magnetic field. It occurs in synchrotron accelerators and in supernova remnants such as the Crab Nebula.

synclastic (sɪŋ'klæstɪk) *adj. Maths.* (of a surface) having a curvature at a given point and in a particular direction that is of the same sign as the curvature at that point in perpendicular direction. Compare **anticlastic.** [C19: from SYN- (alike) + Greek *klastos* bent, from *klan* to bend]

syncline ('sɪŋklaɪn) *n.* a downward fold of stratified rock in which the strata slope towards a vertical axis. Compare **anticline.** [C19: from SYN- + Greek *klīnein* to lean] —**syn'clinal** *adj.*

synclinorium (ˌsɪŋklɪ'nɔːrɪəm) *n., pl.* **-ria** (-rɪə). a vast elongated syncline with its strata further folded into anticlines and synclines. [C19: New Latin, from SYNCLINE + *-orium,* suffix indicating a place]

Syncom ('sɪnˌkɒm) *n.* a communications satellite in stationary orbit. [C20: from *syn(chronous) com(munication)*]

syncopate ('sɪŋkəˌpeɪt) *vb.* (*tr.*) **1.** *Music.* to modify or treat (a beat, rhythm, note, etc.) by syncopation. **2.** to shorten (a word) by omitting sounds or letters from the middle. [C17: from Medieval Latin *syncopāre* to omit a letter or syllable, from Late Latin *syncopa* SYNCOPE] —**'syncoˌpator** *n.*

syncopation (ˌsɪŋkə'peɪʃən) *n.* **1.** *Music.* **a.** the displacement of the usual rhythmical accent away from a strong beat onto a weak beat. **b.** a note, beat, rhythm, etc., produced by syncopation. **2.** another word for **syncope** (sense 2).

syncope ('sɪŋkəpɪ) *n.* **1.** *Pathol.* a technical word for a **faint. 2.** the omission of one or more sounds or letters from the middle of a word. [C16: from Late Latin *syncopa,* from Greek *sunkopē* a cutting off, from SYN- + *koptein* to cut] —**syncopic** (sɪŋ'kɒpɪk) *or* **'syncopal** *adj.*

syncretism ('sɪŋkrɪˌtɪzəm) *n.* **1.** the tendency to syncretize. **2.** the historical tendency of languages to reduce their use of inflection, as in the development of Old English with all its case endings into Modern English. [C17: from New Latin *syncrētismus,* from Greek *sunkrētismos* alliance of Cretans, from *sunkrētizein* to join forces (in the manner of the Cretan towns), from SYN- + *Krēs* a Cretan] —**syncretic** (sɪŋ'krɛtɪk) *or* ˌ**syncre'tistic** *adj.* —**'syncretist** *n.*

syncretize *or* **syncretise** ('sɪŋkrɪˌtaɪz) *vb.* to combine or attempt to combine the characteristic teachings, beliefs, or practices of (differing systems of religion or philosophy). —ˌ**syncreti'zation** *or* ˌ**syncreti'sation** *n.*

syncrisis ('sɪŋkrɪsɪs) *n. Rare.* a rhetorical device by which opposites are compared. [via Late Latin from Greek *sunkrisis* comparison, from SYN- + *krinein* to assess]

syncytium (sɪn'sɪtɪəm) *n., pl.* **-cytia** (-'sɪtɪə). *Zoology.* a mass of cytoplasm containing many nuclei and enclosed in a cell membrane. [C19: New Latin; see SYN-, CYTO-, -IUM] —**syn'cytial** *adj.*

synd (sʌnd) *vb., n. Scot.* a variant of **syne**[2].

synd. *abbrev. for* syndicate.

syndactyl (sɪn'dæktɪl) *adj.* **1.** (of certain animals) having two or more digits growing fused together. ~*n.* **2.** an animal with this arrangement of digits. —**syn'dactylism** *n.*

syndesis (sɪn'diːsɪs) *n. Grammar.* **1.** the use of syndetic constructions. **2.** another name for **polysyndeton** (sense 2). [C20: from Greek, from *sundein* to bind together, from SYN- + *dein* to bind]

syndesmosis (ˌsɪndɛs'məʊsɪs) *n., pl.* **-ses** (-siːz). *Anatomy.* a type of joint in which the articulating bones are held together by a ligament of connective tissue. [New Latin, from Greek *sundein* to bind together; see SYNDESIS] —**syndesmotic** (ˌsɪndɛs'mɒtɪk) *adj.*

syndetic (sɪn'dɛtɪk) *adj.* denoting a grammatical construction in which two clauses are connected by a conjunction. Compare **asyndetic** (sense 2). [C17: from Greek *sundetikos,* from *sundetos* bound together; see SYNDESIS] —**syn'detically** *adv.*

syndeton (sɪn'diːtᵊn) *n. Grammar.* a syndetic construction. Compare **asyndeton** (sense 2). [C20: from Greek *sundeton* a bond, from *sundein* to bind together; see SYNDESIS]

syndic ('sɪndɪk) *n.* **1.** *Brit.* a business agent of some universities or other bodies. **2.** (in several countries) a government administrator or magistrate with varying powers. [C17: via Old French from Late Latin *syndicus,* from Greek *sundikos* defendant's advocate, from SYN- + *dikē* justice] —'**syndic**ˌ**ship** *n.* —'**syndical** *adj.*

syndicalism ('sɪndɪkəˌlɪzəm) *n.* **1.** a revolutionary movement and theory advocating the seizure of the means of production and distribution by syndicates of workers through direct action, esp. a general strike. **2.** an economic system resulting from such action. —'**syndical** *adj.* —'**syndicalist** *adj., n.* —ˌ**syndical'istic** *adj.*

syndicate *n.* ('sɪndɪkɪt). **1.** an association of business enterprises or individuals organized to undertake a joint project requiring considerable capital. **2.** a news agency that sells articles, photographs, etc., to a number of newspapers for simultaneous publication. **3.** any association formed to carry out an enterprise or enterprises of common interest to its members. **4.** a board of syndics or the office of syndic. **5.** (in Italy under the Fascists) a local organization of employers or employees. ~*vb.* ('sɪndɪˌkeɪt). **6.** (*tr.*) to sell (articles, photographs, etc.) to several newspapers for simultaneous publication. **7.** (*tr.*) *U.S.* to sell (a programme or programmes) to several local commercial television or radio stations. **8.** to form a syndicate of (people). [C17: from Old French *syndicat* office of a SYNDIC] —ˌ**syndi'cation** *n.*

syndicated research *n. Marketing.* a large-scale marketing research project undertaken without being commissioned and subsequently offered to interested parties.

syndiotactic (ˌsɪndɪəʊ'tæktɪk) *adj. Chem.* (of a stereospecific polymer) having alternating stereochemical configurations of the groups on successive carbon atoms in the chain. Compare **isotactic.** [C20: from *syndyo,* from Greek *sunduo* two together + -TACTIC]

syndrome ('sɪndrəʊm) *n.* **1.** *Med.* any combination of signs and symptoms that are indicative of a particular disease or disorder. **2.** a symptom, characteristic, or set of symptoms or characteristics indicating the existence of a condition, problem, etc. [C16: via New Latin from Greek *sundromē,* literally: a running together, from SYN- + *dramein* to run] —**syndromic** (sɪn'drɒmɪk) *adj.*

syne[1] *or* **syn** (sʌɪn) *adv., prep., conj.* a Scot. word for **since.** [C14: probably related to Old English *sīth* since]

syne[2] (sʌɪn) *or* **synd** *Scot.* ~*vb.* (*tr.*) **1.** to rinse; wash out. ~*n.* **2.** a rinse. [C14: of uncertain origin]

synecdoche (sɪn'ɛkdəkɪ) *n.* a figure of speech in which a part is substituted for a whole or a whole for a part, as in *50 head of cattle* for *50 cows,* or *the army* for *a soldier.* [C14: via Latin from Greek *sunekdokhē,* from SYN- + *ekdokhē* interpretation, from *dekhesthai* to accept] —**synecdochic** (ˌsɪnɛk'dɒkɪk) *or* ˌ**synec'dochical** *adj.* —ˌ**synec'dochically** *adv.*

synecious (sɪ'niːʃəs) *adj.* a variant spelling of **synoecious.**

synecology (ˌsɪnɪ'kɒlədʒɪ) *n.* the ecological study of communities of plants and animals. Compare **autecology.** —**synecologic** (sɪnˌɛkə'lɒdʒɪk) *or* **syn**ˌ**eco'logical** *adj.* —**syn**ˌ**eco'logically** *adv.*

synectics (sɪ'nɛktɪks) *n.* (*functioning as sing.*) a method of identifying and solving problems that depends on creative thinking, the use of analogy, and informal conversation among a small group of individuals with diverse experience and expertise. [C20: from SYN- + ECTO- + -ICS, in the sense: working together from outside]

syneresis *or* **synaeresis** (sɪ'nɪərɪsɪs) *n.* **1.** *Chem.* the process in which a gel contracts on standing and exudes liquid, as in the separation of whey in cheese-making. **2.** the contraction of two vowels into a diphthong. **3.** another word for **synizesis.** [C16: via Late Latin from Greek *sunairesis* a shortening, from *sunairein* to draw together, from SYN- + *hairein* to take]

synergetic (ˌsɪnə'dʒɛtɪk) *or* **synergistic** (ˌsɪnə'dʒɪstɪk) *adj.* acting together. [C17: from Greek *sunergētikos,* from SYN- + *-ergētikos,* from *ergon* work; see ENERGY] —ˌ**syner'getically** *or* ˌ**syner'gistically** *adv.*

synergism ('sɪnəˌdʒɪzəm, sɪ'nɜː-) *n.* **1.** Also called: **synergy.** the working together of two or more drugs, muscles, etc., to produce an effect greater than the sum of their individual effects. **2.** another name for **synergy** (sense 1). **3.** *Christian theol.* the doctrine or belief that the human will cooperates with the Holy Spirit and with divine grace, esp. in the act of conversion or regeneration. [C18: from New Latin *synergismus,* from Greek *sunergos,* from SYN- + *ergon* work]

synergist ('sɪnədʒɪst, sɪ'nɜː-) *n.* **1.** a drug, muscle, etc., that increases the action of another. **2.** *Christian theol.* an upholder of synergism. ~*adj.* **3.** of or relating to synergism.

synergy ('sɪnədʒɪ) *n., pl.* **-gies. 1.** Also called: **synergism.** the potential ability of individual organizations or groups to be more successful or productive as a result of a merger. **2.** another name for **synergism** (sense 1). [C19: from New Latin *synergia,* from Greek *sunergos;* see SYNERGISM] —**synergic** (sɪ'nɜːdʒɪk) *adj.*

synesis ('sɪnɪsɪs) *n.* a grammatical construction in which the inflection or form of a word is conditioned by the meaning rather than the syntax, as for example the plural form *have* with the singular noun **group** in the sentence *the group have already assembled.* [via New Latin from Greek *sunesis* union, from *sunienai* to bring together, from SYN- + *hienai* to send]

synesthesia (ˌsɪniːs'θiːzɪə) *n.* the usual U.S. spelling of **synaesthesia.** —**synesthetic** (ˌsɪniːs'θɛtɪk) *adj.*

syngamy ('sɪŋgəmɪ) *or* **syngenesis** (sɪn'dʒɛnɪsɪs) *n.* other names for **sexual reproduction.** —**syngamic** (sɪŋ'gæmɪk) *or* **syngamous** ('sɪŋgəməs) *adj.*

synizesis (ˌsɪnɪ'ziːsɪs) *n.* **1.** *Phonetics.* the contraction of two vowels originally belonging to separate syllables into a single syllable, without diphthongization. Compare **syneresis. 2.** *Cytology.* the contraction of chromatin towards one side of the nucleus during the prophase of meiosis. [C19: via Late Latin from Greek *sunizēsis* a collapse, from *sunizanein* to sink down, from SYN- + *hizein* to sit]

synkaryon (sɪn'kærɪˌɒn) *n. Biology.* the nucleus of a fertilized egg. [C20: New Latin, from SYN- + Greek *karuon* a nut] —**syn**ˌ**kary'onic** *adj.*

synod ('sɪnəd, 'sɪnɒd) *n.* **1.** a local or special ecclesiastical council, esp. of a diocese, formally convened to discuss ecclesiastical affairs. **2.** *Rare.* any council, esp. for discussion. [C14: from Late Latin *synodus,* from Greek *sunodos,* from SYN- + *hodos* a way] —'**synodal** *or* (*less commonly*) **syn'odical** *adj.*

synodic (sɪ'nɒdɪk) *adj.* relating to or involving a conjunction or two successive conjunctions of the same star, planet, or satellite: *the synodic month.*

synodic month *n.* See **month** (sense 6).

synoecious, synecious (sɪ'niːʃəs), *or* **synoicous** (sɪ'nɔɪkəs) *adj.* (of plants) having male and female organs on the same flower or corresponding structure. [C19: SYN- + *-oecious,* from Greek *oikion* diminutive of *oikos* house]

synoekete (sɪ'niːkiːt) *or* **synoecete** (sɪ'niːsiːt) *n.* an insect that lives in the nests of social insects, esp. ants, without receiving any attentions from the inmates. Compare **symphile.** [C20: from Greek *sunoiketēs* house-fellow, from *sunoikia* community]

synonym ('sɪnənɪm) *n.* **1.** a word that means the same or nearly the same as another word, such as *bucket* and *pail.* **2.** a word or phrase used as another name for something, such as *Hellene* for a *Greek.* **3.** *Biology.* a taxonomic name that has been superseded or rejected. [C16: via Late Latin from Greek *sunōnumon,* from SYN- + *onoma* name] —ˌ**syno'nymic** *or* ˌ**syno'nymical** *adj.* —ˌ**syno'nymity** *n.*

synonymize *or* **synonymise** (sɪ'nɒnɪˌmaɪz) *vb.* (*tr.*) to analyse the synonyms of or provide with synonyms.

synonymous (sɪ'nɒnɪməs) *adj.* **1.** (often foll. by *with*) being a synonym (of). **2.** (*postpositive;* foll. by *with*) closely associated (with) or suggestive (of): *his name was synonymous with greed.* —**syn'onymously** *adv.* —**syn'onymousness** *n.*

synonymy (sɪ'nɒnɪmɪ) *n., pl.* **-mies. 1.** the study of synonyms. **2.** the character of being synonymous; equivalence. **3.** a list or collection of synonyms, esp. one in which their meanings are discriminated. **4.** *Biology.* a collection of the synonyms of a species or group.

synop. *abbrev. for* synopsis.

synopsis (sɪ'nɒpsɪs) *n., pl.* **-ses** (-siːz). a condensation or brief review of a subject; summary. [C17: via Late Latin from Greek *sunopsis,* from SYN- + *opsis* view]

synopsize *or* **synopsise** (sɪ'nɒpsaɪz) *vb.* (*tr.*) **1.** *U.S.* variants of **epitomize. 2.** *U.S. and Canadian.* to make a synopsis of.

synoptic (sɪ'nɒptɪk) *adj.* **1.** of or relating to a synopsis. **2.** (*often cap.*) *Bible.* **a.** (of the Gospels of Matthew, Mark, and Luke) presenting the narrative of Christ's life, ministry, etc. from a point of view held in common by all three, and with close similarities in content, order, etc. **b.** of, relating to, or characterizing these three Gospels. **3.** *Meteorol.* showing or concerned with the distribution of meteorological conditions over a wide area at a given time: *a synoptic chart.* **4.** *Rare.* viewing any phenomenon from the same standpoint. ~*n.* **5.** (*often cap.*) *Bible.* **a.** any of the three synoptic Gospels. **b.** any of the authors of these three Gospels. [C18: from Greek *sunoptikos,* from SYNOPSIS] —**syn'optically** *adv.* —**syn'optist** *n.*

synovia (saɪ'nəʊvɪə, sɪ-) *n.* a transparent viscid lubricating fluid, secreted by the membrane lining joints, tendon sheaths, etc. [C17: from New Latin, probably from SYN- + Latin *ōvum* egg] —**syn'ovial** *adj.* —**syn'ovially** *adv.*

synovitis (ˌsaɪnəʊ'vaɪtɪs, ˌsɪn-) *n.* inflammation of the membrane surrounding a joint. —**synovitic** (ˌsaɪnəʊ'vɪtɪk, ˌsɪn-) *adj.*

synroc ('sɪnˌrɒk) *n.* a titanium-ceramic substance that can incorporate nuclear waste in its crystals. [from *syn(thetic)* + *roc(k)*]

synsepalous (sɪn'sɛpələs) *adj.* another word for **gamosepalous.**

syntactic (sɪn'tæktɪk) *adj.* **1.** Also: **syntactical.** relating to or determined by syntax. **2.** *Logic, linguistics.* describable wholly with respect to the grammatical structure of an expression or the rules of well-formedness of a formal system. —**syn'tactically** *adv.*

syntactics (sɪn'tæktɪks) *n.* (*functioning as sing.*) the branch of semiotics that deals with the formal properties of symbol systems; proof theory.

syntagma (sɪn'tægmə) *or* **syntagm** ('sɪnˌtæm) *n., pl.* **-tagmata** (-'tægmətə) *or* **-tagms.** **1.** a syntactic unit or a word or phrase forming a syntactic unit. **2.** a systematic collection of statements or propositions. [C17: from Late Latin, from Greek, from *suntassein* to put in order; see SYNTAX]

syntagmatic (ˌsɪntæg'mætɪk) *adj.* **1.** of or denoting a syntagma. **2.** Also: **syntagmic** (sɪn'tægmɪk). *Linguistics.* denoting or concerning the relationship between a word and other members of a syntactic unit containing it.

syntax ('sɪntæks) *n.* **1.** the branch of linguistics that deals with the grammatical arrangement of words and morphemes in the sentences of a language or of languages in general. **2.** the totality of facts about the grammatical arrangement of words in a language. **3.** a systematic statement of the rules governing the grammatical arrangement of words and morphemes in a language. **4.** *Logic.* a systematic statement of the rules governing the properly formed formulas of a logical system. **5.** any orderly arrangement or system. [C17: from Late Latin *syntaxis,* from Greek *suntaxis,* from *suntassein* to put in order, from SYN- + *tassein* to arrange]

synth (sɪnθ) *n.* short for **synthesizer.**

synthesis ('sɪnθɪsɪs) *n., pl.* **-ses** (-ˌsiːz). **1.** the process of combining objects or ideas into a complex whole. Compare **analysis.** **2.** the combination or whole produced by such a process. **3.** the process of producing a compound by a chemical reaction or series of reactions, usually from simpler or commonly available starting materials. **4.** *Linguistics.* the use of inflections rather than word order and function words to express the syntactic relations in a language. Compare **analysis** (sense 5). **5.** *Philosophy, archaic.* synthetic reasoning. **6.** *Philosophy.* **a.** (in the writings of Kant) the unification of one concept with another not contained in it. Compare **analysis** (sense 7). **b.** the final stage in the Hegelian dialectic, that resolves the contradiction between thesis and antithesis. [C17: via Latin from Greek *sunthesis,* from *suntithenai* to put together, from SYN- + *tithenai* to place] —**'synthesist** *n.*

synthesis gas *n. Chem.* **1.** a mixture of carbon dioxide, carbon monoxide, and hydrogen formerly made by using water gas and reacting it with steam to enrich the proportion of hydrogen for use in the synthesis of ammonia. **2.** a similar mixture of gases made by steam reforming natural gas, used for synthesizing organic chemicals and as a fuel.

synthesize ('sɪnθɪˌsaɪz), **synthetize** *or* **synthesise, synthetise** *vb.* **1.** to combine or cause to combine into a whole. **2.** (*tr.*) to produce by synthesis. —ˌ**synthesi'zation,** ˌ**syntheti'zation** *or* ˌ**synthesi'sation,** ˌ**syntheti'sation** *n.*

synthesizer ('sɪnθɪˌsaɪzə) *n.* **1.** an electrophonic instrument, usually operated by means of a keyboard and pedals, in which sounds are produced by voltage-controlled oscillators, filters, and amplifiers, with an envelope generator module that controls attack, decay, sustain, and release. **2.** a person or thing that synthesizes.

synthetic (sɪn'θɛtɪk) *adj. also* **synthetical.** **1.** (of a substance or material) made artificially by chemical reaction. **2.** not genuine; insincere: *synthetic compassion.* **3.** denoting languages, such as Latin, whose morphology is characterized by synthesis. Compare **polysynthetic, agglutinative** (sense 2), **analytic** (sense 3). **4.** *Philosophy.* **a.** (of a proposition) having a truth-value that is not determined solely by virtue of the meanings of the words, as in *all men are arrogant.* **b.** contingent. Compare **a posteriori, empirical.** ~*n.* **5.** a synthetic substance or material. [C17: from New Latin *syntheticus,* from Greek *sunthetikos* expert in putting together, from *suntithenai* to put together; see SYNTHESIS] —**syn'thetically** *adv.*

synthetic resin *n.* See **resin** (sense 2).

synthetic rubber *n.* any of various synthetic materials, similar to natural rubber, made by polymerizing unsaturated hydrocarbons, such as isoprene and butadiene.

synthetism ('sɪnθɪˌtɪzəm) *n.* (*often cap.*) the symbolism of Gauguin and the Nabis, who reacted against the impressionists and realists by seeking to produce brightly coloured abstractions of their inner experience. [C19: from Greek *sunthetos* composite; see SYNTHETIC] —**'synthetist** *n.*

syntonic (sɪn'tɒnɪk) *adj. Psychol.* emotionally in harmony with one's environment. [C20: from Greek *suntonos* in harmony with; see SYN-, TONE] —**syn'tonically** *adv.*

sypher ('saɪfə) *vb.* (*tr.*) to lap (a chamfered edge of one plank over that of another) in order to form a flush surface. [C19: variant of CIPHER] —**'syphering** *n.*

syphilis ('sɪfɪlɪs) *n.* a venereal disease caused by infection with the microorganism *Treponema pallidum:* characterized by an ulcerating chancre, usually on the genitals and progressing through the lymphatic system to nearly all tissues of the body, producing serious clinical manifestations. [C18: from New Latin *Syphilis* (*sive Morbus Gallicus*) "Syphilis (or the French disease)", title of a poem (1530) by G. Fracastoro, Italian physician and poet, in which a shepherd *Syphilus* is portrayed as the first victim of the disease] —**syphilitic** (ˌsɪfɪ'lɪtɪk) *adj.* —ˌ**syphi'litically** *adv.* —**'syphiˌloid** *adj.*

syphilology (ˌsɪfɪ'lɒlədʒɪ) *n.* the branch of medicine concerned with the study and treatment of syphilis. —ˌ**syphi'lologist** *n.*

syphiloma (ˌsɪfɪ'ləʊmə) *n., pl.* **-mas** *or* **-mata** (-mətə). *Pathol.* a tumour or gumma caused by infection with syphilis. [C19: from SYPHILIS + *-oma,* as in *sarcoma*]

syphon ('saɪfᵊn) *n.* a variant spelling of **siphon.**

SYR *international car registration for* Syria.

Syr. *abbrev. for:* **1.** Syria. **2.** Syriac. **3.** Syrian.

Syriac ('sɪrɪˌæk) *n.* a dialect of Aramaic spoken in Syria until about the 13th century A.D. and still in use as a liturgical language of certain Eastern churches.

Syrian ('sɪrɪən) *adj.* **1.** of, relating to, or characteristic of Syria, a republic in W Asia, or of its people or their dialect of Arabic. **2.** *Eastern Church.* of or relating to Christians who belong to churches with Syriac liturgies. ~*n.* **3.** a native or inhabitant of Syria. **4.** *Eastern Church.* a Syrian Christian.

syringa (sɪ'rɪŋgə) *n.* another name for **mock orange** and **lilac** (sense 1). [C17: from New Latin, from Greek *surinx* tube, alluding to the use of its hollow stems for pipes]

syringe ('sɪrɪndʒ, sɪ'rɪndʒ) *n.* **1.** *Med.* an instrument, such as a hypodermic syringe or a rubber ball with a slender nozzle, for use in withdrawing or injecting fluids, cleaning wounds, etc. **2.** any similar device for injecting, spraying, or extracting liquids by means of pressure or suction. ~*vb.* **3.** (*tr.*) to cleanse, inject, or spray with a syringe. [C15: from Late Latin, from Latin: SYRINX]

syringomyelia (səˌrɪŋgəʊmaɪ'iːlɪə) *n.* a chronic progressive disease of the spinal cord in which cavities form in the grey matter: characterized by loss of the sense of pain and temperature. [C19: *syringo-,* from Greek: SYRINX + *-myelia* from Greek *muelos* marrow] —**syringomyelic** (səˌrɪŋgəʊmaɪ'ɛlɪk) *adj.*

syrinx ('sɪrɪŋks) *n., pl.* **syringes** (sɪ'rɪndʒiːz) *or* **syrinxes.** **1.** the vocal organ of a bird, which is situated in the lower part of the trachea. **2.** (in classical Greek music) a panpipe or set of panpipes. **3.** *Anatomy.* another name for the **Eustachian tube.** [C17: via Latin from Greek *surinx* pipe] —**syringeal** (sɪ'rɪndʒɪəl) *adj.*

Syro- ('saɪrəʊ-) *combining form.* **1.** indicating Syrian and: *Syro-Lebanese.* **2.** indicating Syriac and: *Syro-Aramaic.* [from Greek *Suro-,* from *Suros* a Syrian]

syrphid ('sɜːfɪd) *n.* any dipterous fly of the family *Syrphidae,* typically having a coloration mimicking that of certain bees and wasps: includes the hover flies. [C19: from Greek *surphos* gnat]

syrup ('sɪrəp) *n.* **1.** a solution of sugar dissolved in water and often flavoured with fruit juice: used for sweetening fruit, etc. **2.** any of various thick sweet liquids prepared for cooking or table use from molasses, sugars, etc. **3.** *Informal.* cloying sentimentality. **4.** a liquid medicine containing a sugar solution for flavouring or preservation. ~*vb.* (*tr.*) **5.** to bring to the consistency of syrup. **6.** to cover, fill, or sweeten with syrup. ~Also: **sirup.** [C15: from Medieval Latin *syrupus,* from Arabic *sharāb* a drink, from *shariba* to drink] —**'syrup-ˌlike** *adj.* —**'syrupy** *adj.*

syssarcosis (ˌsɪsɑː'kəʊsɪs) *n., pl.* **-ses** (-siːz). *Anatomy.* the union or articulation of bones by muscle. [C17: from New Latin, from Greek *sussarkōsis,* from *sussarkousthai,* from *sus-* SYN- + *sarkoun* to become fleshy, from *sarx* flesh] —**syssarcotic** (ˌsɪsɑː'kɒtɪk) *adj.*

syst. *abbrev. for* system.

systaltic (sɪ'stæltɪk) *adj.* (esp. of the action of the heart) of, relating to, or characterized by alternate contractions and dilations; pulsating. [C17: from Late Latin *systalticus,* from Greek *sustaltikos,* from *sustellein* to contract, from SYN- + *stellein* to place]

system ('sɪstəm) *n.* **1.** a group or combination of interrelated, interdependent, or interacting elements forming a collective entity; a methodical or coordinated assemblage of parts, facts, concepts, etc.: *a system of currency; the Copernican system.* **2.** any scheme of classification or arrangement: *a chronological system.* **3.** a network of communications, transportation, or distribution. **4.** a method or complex of methods: *he has a perfect system at roulette.* **5.** orderliness; an ordered manner. **6.** **the system.** (*often cap.*) society seen as an environment exploiting, restricting, and repressing individuals. **7.** an organism considered as a functioning entity. **8.** any of various bodily parts or structures that are anatomically or physiologically related: *the digestive system.* **9.** one's physiological or psychological constitution: *get it out of your system.* **10.** any assembly of electronic, electrical, or mechanical components with interdependent functions, usually forming a self-contained unit: *a brake system.* **11.** a group of celestial bodies that are associated as a result of natural laws, esp. gravitational attraction: *the solar system.* **12.** *Chem.* a sample of matter in which there are one or more substances in one or more phases. See also **phase rule. 13.** a point of view or doctrine used to interpret a branch of knowledge. **14.** *Mineralogy.* one of a group of divisions into which crystals may be placed on the basis of the lengths and inclinations of their axes. **15.** *Geology.* a stratigraphical unit for the rock strata formed during a period of geological time. It can be subdivided into series. [C17: from French *système,* from Late Latin *systēma,* from Greek *sustēma,* from SYN- + *histanai* to cause to stand] —**'systemless** *adj.*

systematic (ˌsɪstɪ'mætɪk) *adj.* **1.** characterized by the use of order and planning; methodical: *a systematic administrator.* **2.** comprising or resembling a system: *systematic theology.* **3.** Also: **systematical** (sɪstə'mætɪkᵊl). *Biology.* of or relating to the taxonomic classification of organisms. —ˌ**system'atically** *adv.*

systematic desensitization *n. Psychol.* a treatment of phobias in which the patient while relaxed is exposed, often only in imagination, to progressively more frightening aspects of the phobia.

systematics (ˌsɪstɪ'mætɪks) *n.* (*functioning as sing.*) the study of systems and the principles of classification and nomenclature.

systematism ('sɪstɪməˌtɪzəm) *n.* **1.** the practice of classifying or systematizing. **2.** adherence to a system. **3.** a systematic classification; systematized arrangement.

systematist ('sɪstɪmətɪst) *n.* **1.** a person who constructs systems. **2.** an adherent of a system. **3.** a taxonomist.

systematize ('sɪstɪməˌtaɪz), **systemize** *or* **systematise, systemise** *vb.* (*tr.*) to arrange in a system. —ˌ**systemati'zation,** ˌ**systemati'sation** *or* ˌ**systemi'zation,** ˌ**systemi'sation** *n.* —**'systemaˌtizer, 'systemaˌtiser** *or* **'systemˌizer, 'systemˌiser** *n.*

systematology (ˌsɪstɪmə'tɒlədʒɪ) *n.* the study of the nature and formation of systems.

system building *n.* a method of building in which prefabricated components are used to speed the construction of buildings. —ˌ**system 'built** *adj.*

Système International d'Unités (*French* sistɛm ɛ̃tɛrnasjɔnal dynite) *n.* the International System of units. See **SI unit.**

systemic (sɪ'stɛmɪk, -'stiː-) *adj.* **1.** another word for **systematic** (senses 1, 2). **2.** *Physiol.* (of a poison, disease, etc.) affecting the entire body. **3.** (of a pesticide, fungicide, etc.) spreading through all the parts of a plant and making it toxic to pests or parasites without destroying it. ~*n.* **4.** a systemic pesticide, fungicide, etc. —**sys'temically** *adv.*

systemic grammar *n.* a grammar in which description is founded on the relationships among the various units at different ranks of a language, and in which language is viewed as a system of meaning-creating choices. Compare **transformational grammar, case grammar.**

systems analysis *n.* the analysis of the requirements of a task and the expression of those requirements in a form that permits the assembly of computer hardware and software to perform the task. —**systems analyst** *n.*

systems disk *n.* a disk used to store computer programs, esp. the basic operating programs of a computer.

systems diskette *n.* a small flexible disk used to store computer programs, esp. the basic operating programs of a microprocessor.

systems engineering *n.* the branch of engineering, based on systems analysis and information theory, concerned with the design of integrated systems.

systems theory *n.* an approach to industrial relations which likens the enterprise to an organism with interdependent parts, each with its own specific function and interrelated responsibilities.

systole ('sɪstəlɪ) *n.* contraction of the heart, during which blood is pumped into the aorta and the arteries that lead to the lungs. Compare **diastole.** [C16: via Late Latin from Greek *sustolē,* from *sustellein* to contract; see SYSTALTIC] —**systolic** (sɪ'stɒlɪk) *adj.*

syver *or* **siver** ('saɪvər) *n. Scot.* **1.** a street drain or the grating over it. **2.** a street gutter. [C17: of uncertain origin]

syzygy ('sɪzɪdʒɪ) *n., pl.* **-gies. 1.** either of the two positions (conjunction or opposition) of a celestial body when sun, earth, and the body lie in a straight line: *the moon is at syzygy when full.* **2.** (in classical prosody) a metrical unit of two feet. **3.** *Rare.* any pair, usually of opposites. **4.** *Zoology.* the aggregation in a mass of certain protozoans, esp. when occurring before sexual reproduction. [C17: from Late Latin *syzygia,* from Greek *suzugia,* from *suzugos* yoked together, from SYN- + *zugon* a yoke] —**syzygial** (sɪ'zɪdʒɪəl), **syzygetic** (ˌsɪzɪ'dʒɛtɪk), *or* **syzygal** ('sɪzɪgᵊl) *adj.* —ˌ**syzy'getically** *adv.*

t *or* **T** (tiː) *n., pl.* **t's, T's,** *or* **Ts. 1.** the 20th letter and 16th consonant of the modern English alphabet. **2.** a speech sound represented by this letter, usually a voiceless alveolar stop, as in *tame.* **3. a.** something shaped like a T. **b.** (*in combination*): *a T-junction.* **4. to a T.** in every detail; perfectly: *the work suited her to a T.*

t *symbol for:* **1.** tonne(s). **2.** troy (weight). **3.** *Statistics.* distribution. **4.** *Statistics.* See **Student's t.**

T *symbol for:* **1.** absolute temperature. **2.** tera-. **3.** *Chem.* tritium. **4.** tesla. **5.** surface tension. ~**6.** *international car registration for* Thailand.

t. *abbrev. for:* **1.** *Commerce.* tare. **2.** teaspoon(ful). **3.** temperature. **4.** *Music.* tempo. **5.** tempore. [Latin: in the time of] **6.** tenor. **7.** *Grammar.* tense. **8.** ton(s). **9.** transitive.

T. *abbrev. for:* **1.** tablespoon(ful). **2.** territory. **3.** time. **4.** Tuesday. **5.** Also: **Th.** Thursday.

't *contraction of* it.

T- *abbrev. for* trainer (aircraft): *T-37.*

ta (tɑː) *interj. Brit. informal.* thank you. [C18: imitative of baby talk]

Ta *the chemical symbol for* tantalum.

TA (in Britain) *abbrev. for* Territorial Army (now superseded by **TAVR).**

TAA *abbrev. for* Trans-Australia Airlines.

Taal (tɑːl) *n.* **the.** another name for **Afrikaans.** [Dutch: speech; see TALE]

taata ('tata) *n. E African.* a child's word for **father.**

tab[1] (tæb) *n.* **1.** a small flap of material, esp. one on a garment for decoration or for fastening to a button. **2.** any similar flap, such as a piece of paper attached to a file for identification. **3.** a small auxiliary aerofoil on the trailing edge of a rudder, aileron, or elevator, etc., to assist in the control of the aircraft in flight. See also **trim tab. 4.** *Brit. military.* the insignia on the collar of a staff officer. **5.** *Chiefly U.S. and Canadian.* a bill, esp. one for a meal or drinks. **6.** *Scot. and northern English dialect.* a cigarette. **7. keep tabs on.** *Informal.* to keep a watchful eye on. ~*vb.* **tabs, tabbing, tabbed. 8.** (*tr.*) to supply (files, clothing, etc.) with a tab or tabs. [C17: of unknown origin]

tab[2] (tæb) *n.* short for **tabulator** or **tablet.**

TAB *abbrev. for:* **1.** typhoid-paratyphoid A and B (vaccine). **2.** *Austral. and N.Z.* Totalizator Agency Board.

tab. *abbrev. for* table (list or chart).

tabanid ('tæbənɪd) *n.* any stout-bodied fly of the dipterous family *Tabanidae,* the females of which have mouthparts specialized for sucking blood: includes the horseflies. [C19: from Latin *tabānus* horsefly]

tabard ('tæbəd) *n.* a sleeveless or short-sleeved jacket, esp. one worn by a herald, bearing a coat of arms, or by a knight over his armour. [C13: from Old French *tabart,* of uncertain origin]

tabaret ('tæbərɪt) *n.* a hard-wearing fabric of silk or similar cloth with stripes of satin or moire, used esp. for upholstery. [C19: perhaps from TABBY[1]]

Tabasco (tə'bæskəʊ) *n. Trademark.* a very hot red sauce made from matured capsicums.

tabby[1] ('tæbɪ) *n.* a fabric with a watered pattern, esp. silk or taffeta. [C17: from Old French *tabis* silk cloth, from Arabic *al-'attabiya,* literally: the quarter of (Prince) 'Attab, the part of Baghdad, Iraq, where the fabric was first made]

tabby[2] ('tæbɪ) *adj.* **1.** (esp. of cats) brindled with dark stripes or wavy markings on a lighter background. **2.** having a wavy or striped pattern, particularly in colours of grey and brown. ~*n., pl.* **-bies. 3.** a tabby cat. **4.** any female domestic cat. **5.** *Brit. informal.* a gossiping old woman. **6.** *Austral. slang.* any girl or woman. [C17: from *Tabby,* pet form of the girl's name *Tabitha,* probably influenced by TABBY[1]]

tabernacle ('tæbəˌnækᵊl) *n.* **1.** (*often cap.*) *Old Testament.* **a.** the portable sanctuary in the form of a tent in which the ancient Israelites carried the Ark of the Covenant (Exodus 27–27). **b.** the Jewish Temple regarded as the shrine of the divine presence. **2.** *Judaism.* an English word for **sukkah. 3.** any place of worship that is not called a church. **4.** a small ornamented cupboard or box used for the reserved sacrament of the Eucharist. **5.** the human body regarded as the temporary dwelling of the soul. **6.** *Chiefly R.C. Church.* a canopied niche or recess forming the shrine of an icon. **7.** *Nautical.* a strong framework for holding the foot of a mast stepped on deck, allowing it to be swung down horizontally to pass under low bridges, etc. [C13: from Latin *tabernāculum* a tent, from *taberna* a hut; see TAVERN] —ˌ**taber'nacular** *adj.*

Tabernacles ('tæbəˌnækᵊlz) *pl. n. Judaism.* an English name for **Sukkoth.**

tabes ('teɪbiːz) *n., pl.* **tabes. 1.** a wasting of a bodily organ or part. **2.** short for **tabes dorsalis.** [C17: from Latin: a wasting away] —**tabetic** (tə'bɛtɪk) *adj.*

tabescent (tə'bɛsᵊnt) *adj.* **1.** progressively emaciating; wasting away. **2.** of, relating to, or having tabes. [C19: from Latin *tābēscere,* from TABES] —**ta'bescence** *n.*

tabes dorsalis (dɔː'sɑːlɪs) *n.* a form of late syphilis that attacks the spinal cord causing degeneration of the nerve fibres, pains in the legs, paralysis of the leg muscles, acute abdominal pain, etc. Also called: **locomotor ataxia.** [New Latin, literally: tabes of the back; see TABES, DORSAL]

tabla ('tʌblə, 'tɑːblɑː) *n.* a musical instrument of India consisting of a pair of drums whose pitches can be varied. [Hindu, from Arabic *tabla* drum]

tablature ('tæblətʃə) *n.* **1.** *Music.* any of a number of forms of musical notation, esp. for playing the lute, consisting of letters and signs indicating rhythm and fingering. **2.** an engraved or painted tablet or other flat surface. [C16: from French, ultimately from Latin *tabulātum* wooden floor, from *tabula* a plank]

table ('teɪbᵊl) *n.* **1.** a flat horizontal slab or board supported by one or more legs, on which objects may be placed. **2. a.** such a slab or board on which food is served: *we were six at table.* **b.** (*as modifier*): *table linen.* **c.** (*in combination*): *a tablecloth.* **3.** food as served in a particular household or restaurant: *a good table.* **4.** such a piece of furniture specially designed for any of various purposes: *a backgammon table; bird table.* **5. a.** a company of persons assembled for a meal, game, etc. **b.** (*as modifier*): *table talk.* **6.** any flat or level area, such as a plateau. **7.** a rectangular panel set below or above the face of a wall. **8.** *Architect.* another name for **cordon** (sense 4). **9.** an upper horizontal facet of a cut gem. **10.** *Music.* the sounding board of a violin, guitar, or similar stringed instrument. **11. a.** an arrangement of words, numbers, or signs, usually in parallel columns, to display data or relations: *a table of contents.* **b.** See **multiplication table. 12.** a tablet on which laws were inscribed by the ancient Romans, the Hebrews, etc. **13.** *Palmistry.* an area of the palm's surface bounded by four lines. **14.** *Printing.* a slab of smooth metal on which ink is rolled to its proper consistency. **15. a.** either of the two bony plates that form the inner and outer parts of the flat bones of the cranium. **b.** any thin flat plate, esp. of bone. **16. turn the tables on (someone).** to cause a complete reversal of circumstances, esp. to defeat or get the better of (someone) who was previously in a stronger position. ~*vb.* (*tr.*) **17.** to place on a table. **18.** *Brit.* to submit (a bill, etc.) for consideration by a legislative body. **19.** *U.S.* to suspend discussion of (a bill, etc.) indefinitely or for some time. **20.** to enter in or form into a list; tabulate. [C12: via Old French from Latin *tabula* a writing tablet] —'**tableful** *n.* —'**tableless** *adj.*

tableau ('tæbləʊ) *n., pl.* **-leaux** (-ləʊ, -ləʊz) *or* **-leaus. 1.** See ***tableau vivant.* 2.** a pause during or at the end of a scene on stage when all the performers briefly freeze in position. **3.** any dramatic group or scene. **4.** *Logic.* short for **semantic tableau.** [C17: from French, from Old French *tablel* a picture, diminutive of TABLE]

tableau vivant *French.* (tablo vivɑ̃) *n., pl.* ***tableaux vivants*** (tablo vivɑ̃). a representation of a scene, painting, sculpture, etc., by a person or group posed silent and motionless. [C19: literally: living picture]

tablecloth ('teɪbᵊlˌklɒθ) *n.* a cloth for covering the top of a table, esp. during meals.

table d'hôte ('tɑːbᵊl 'dəʊt; *French* tablə dot) *adj.* **1.** (of a meal) consisting of a set number of courses with limited choice of dishes offered at a fixed price. Compare **à la carte, prix fixe.** ~*n., pl.* **tables d'hôte** ('tɑːbᵊlz 'dəʊt; *French* tablə dot). **2.** a table d'hôte meal or menu. [C17: from French, literally: the host's table]

tableland ('teɪbᵊlˌlænd) *n.* flat elevated land; a plateau.

table licence *n.* a licence authorizing the sale of alcoholic drinks with meals only.

table money *n.* an allowance for official entertaining of visitors, clients, etc., esp. in the army.

table napkin *n.* See **napkin** (sense 1).

table-rapping *n.* the sounds of knocking or tapping made without any apparent physical agency while a group of people sit round a table, and attributed by spiritualists to the spirit of a dead person using this as a means of communication with the living.

table salt *n.* salt that is used at table rather than for cooking.

tablespoon ('teɪbᵊlˌspuːn) *n.* **1.** a spoon, larger than a dessert-spoon, used for serving food, etc. **2.** Also called: **tablespoonful.** the amount contained in such a spoon. **3.** a unit of capacity used in cooking, medicine, etc., equal to half a fluid ounce or three teaspoons.

tablet ('tæblɪt) *n.* **1.** a pill made of a compressed powdered medicinal substance. **2.** a flattish cake of some substance, such as soap. **3.** *Scot.* a sweet made of butter, sugar, and condensed milk, usually shaped in a flat oblong block. **4.** a slab of stone, wood, etc., esp. one formerly used for inscriptions. **5. a.** a thinner rigid sheet, as of bark, ivory, etc., used for similar purposes. **b.** (*often pl.*) a set or pair of these fastened together, as in a book. **6.** a pad of writing paper. **7.** *N.Z.* a token giving right of way to the driver of a train on a single line section. [C14: from Old French *tablete* a little table, from Latin *tabula* a board]

table talk *n.* informal conversation on a range of topics, as that at table during and after a meal.

table tennis *n.* a miniature form of tennis played on a table with small bats and a light hollow ball.

table-turning *n.* **1.** the movement of a table attributed by spiritualists to the power of spirits working through a group of persons placing their hands or fingers on the table top. **2.** *Often derogatory.* spiritualism in general.

tableware ('teɪbəl,wɛə) *n.* articles such as dishes, plates, knives, forks, etc., used at meals.

table wine *n.* a wine considered suitable for drinking with a meal.

tabloid ('tæblɔɪd) *n.* **1.** a newspaper with pages about 30 cm (12 inches) by 40 cm (16 inches), usually characterized by an emphasis on photographs and a concise and often sensational style. **2.** (*modifier*) designed to appeal to a mass audience or readership; sensationalist: *the tabloid press; tabloid television.* [C20: from earlier *Tabloid,* a trademark for a medicine in tablet form]

taboo *or* **tabu** (tə'buː) *adj.* **1.** forbidden or disapproved of; placed under a social prohibition or ban: *taboo words.* **2.** (in Polynesia and other islands of the South Pacific) marked off as simultaneously sacred and forbidden. ~*n., pl.* **-boos** *or* **-bus. 3.** any prohibition resulting from social or other conventions. **4.** ritual restriction or prohibition, esp. of something that is considered holy or unclean. ~*vb.* **5.** (*tr.*) to place under a taboo. [C18: from Tongan *tabu*]

tabor *or* **tabour** ('teɪbə) *n. Music.* a small drum used esp. in the Middle Ages, struck with one hand while the other held a three-holed pipe. See **pipe**[1] (sense 7). [C13: from Old French *tabour,* perhaps from Persian *tabīr*] —**'taborer** *or* **'tabourer** *n.*

taboret *or* **tabouret** ('tæbərɪt) *n.* **1.** a low stool, originally in the shape of a drum. **2.** a frame, usually round, for stretching out cloth while it is being embroidered. **3.** Also called: **taborin, tabourin** ('tæbərɪn). a small tabor. [C17: from French *tabouret,* diminutive of TABOR]

tabular ('tæbjʊlə) *adj.* **1.** arranged in systematic or table form. **2.** calculated from or by means of a table. **3.** like a table in form; flat. [C17: from Latin *tabulāris* concerning boards, from *tabula* a board] —**'tabularly** *adv.*

tabula rasa ('tæbjʊlə 'rɑːsə) *n., pl.* **tabulae rasae** ('tæbjʊliː 'rɑːsiː). **1.** *Philosophy.* the mind in its uninformed original state. **2.** an opportunity for a fresh start; clean slate. [Latin: a scraped tablet (one from which the writing has been erased)]

tabulate *vb.* ('tæbjʊ,leɪt). (*tr.*) **1.** Also: **tabularize** ('tæbjʊlə,raɪz). to set out, arrange, or write in tabular form. **2.** to form or cut with a flat surface. ~*adj.* ('tæbjʊlɪt, -,leɪt). **3.** having a flat surface. **4.** (of certain corals) having transverse skeletal plates. [C18: from Latin *tabula* a board] —**'tabulable** *adj.* —**,tabu'lation** *n.*

tabulator ('tæbjʊ,leɪtə) *n.* **1.** a device for setting the automatic stops that locate the column margins on a typewriter. **2.** *Computer technol.* a machine that reads data from one medium, such as punched cards, producing lists, tabulations, or totals, usually on a continuous sheet of paper. **3.** any machine that tabulates data.

tabun (tɑː'buːn) *n.* an organic compound used in chemical warfare as a lethal nerve gas. Formula: $C_2H_5OP(O)(CN)N(CH_3)_2$. [C20: from German, of uncertain origin]

tacamahac ('tækəmə,hæk) *or* **tacmahack** *n.* **1.** any of several strong-smelling resinous gums obtained from certain trees, used in making ointments, incense, etc. **2.** any tree yielding this resin, esp. the balsam poplar. [C16: from Spanish *tacamahaca,* from Nahuatl *tecomahca* aromatic resin]

Tacan ('tækən) *n.* an electronic ultrahigh-frequency navigation system for aircraft which gives a continuous indication of bearing and distance from a transmitting station. [C20: *tac(tical) a(ir) n(avigation)*]

tace (tæs, teɪs) *n.* a less common word for **tasset.**

tacet ('teɪsɛt, 'tæs-) *vb.* (*intr.*) (on a musical score) a direction indicating that a particular instrument or singer does not take part in a movement or part of a movement. [C18: from Latin: it is silent, from *tacēre* to be quiet]

tache[1] (tæʃ, tɑːʃ) *n. Archaic.* a buckle, clasp, or hook. [C17: from Old French, of Germanic origin; compare TACK[1]]

tache[2] (tæʃ) *n. Informal.* short for **moustache.**

tacheo- *combining form.* a variant of **tachy-.**

tacheometer (,tækɪ'ɒmɪtə) *or* **tachymeter** *n. Surveying.* a type of theodolite designed for the rapid measurement of distances, elevations, and directions.

tacheometry (,tækɪ'ɒmɪtrɪ) *or* **tachymetry** *n. Surveying.* the measurement of distance, etc., using a tacheometer. —**tacheometric** (,tækɪə'mɛtrɪk), **,tacheo'metrical** *or* **,tachy'metric, ,tachy'metrical** *adj.* —**,tacheo'metrically** *or* **,tachy'metrically** *adv.*

tachina fly ('tækɪnə) *n.* any bristly fly of the dipterous family *Tachinidae,* the larvae of which live parasitically in caterpillars, beetles, hymenopterans, and other insects. [C19: via New Latin *Tachina,* from Greek *takhinos* swift, from *takhos* fleetness]

tachisme ('tɑːʃɪzəm; *French* taʃism) *n.* a type of action painting evolved in France in which haphazard dabs and blots of colour are treated as a means of instinctive or unconscious expression. [C20: French, from *tache* stain]

tachistoscope (tə'kɪstə,skəʊp) *n.* an instrument, used mainly in experiments on perception and memory, for displaying visual images for very brief intervals, usually a fraction of a second. [C20: from Greek *takhistos* swiftest (see TACHY-) + -SCOPE] —**tachistoscopic** (tə,kɪstə'skɒpɪk) *adj.* —**ta,chisto'scopically** *adv.*

tacho- *combining form.* speed: *tachograph; tachometer.* [from Greek *takhos*]

tachograph ('tækə,grɑːf, -,græf) *n.* a tachometer that produces a graphical record (**tachogram**) of its readings, esp. a device for recording the speed of and distance covered by a heavy goods vehicle. Often shortened to **tacho.**

tachometer (tæ'kɒmɪtə) *n.* any device for measuring speed, esp. the rate of revolution of a shaft. Tachometers (rev counters) are often fitted to cars to indicate the number of revolutions per minute of the engine. —**tachometric** (,tækə'mɛtrɪk) *or* **,tacho'metrical** *adj.* —**,tacho'metrically** *adv.* —**ta'chometry** *n.*

tachy- *or* **tacheo-** *combining form.* swift or accelerated: *tachycardia; tachygraphy; tachylyte; tachyon; tachyphylaxis.* [from Greek *takhus* swift]

tachycardia (,tækɪ'kɑːdɪə) *n. Pathol.* abnormally rapid beating of the heart, esp. over 100 beats per minute. Compare **bradycardia.** —**tachycardiac** (,tækɪ'kɑːdɪ,æk) *adj.*

tachygraphy (tæ'kɪgrəfɪ) *n.* shorthand, esp. as used in ancient Rome or Greece. —**ta'chygrapher** *or* **ta'chygraphist** *n.* —**tachygraphic** (,tækɪ'græfɪk) *adj.* —**,tachy'graphically** *adv.*

tachylyte *or* **tachylite** ('tækɪ,laɪt) *n.* a black glassy basalt often found on the edges of intrusions of basalt. [C19: from German *tachylit,* from TACHY- + Greek *lutos* soluble, melting, from *luein* to release; so called because it fuses easily when heated. The form *tachylite* is influenced by -LITE stone] —**tachylytic** (,tækɪ'lɪtɪk) *or* **,tachy'litic** *adj.*

tachymeter (tæ'kɪmɪtə) *n.* another name for **tacheometer.**

tachymetry (tæ'kɪmɪtrɪ) *n.* another name for **tacheometry.**

tachyon ('tækɪ,ɒn) *n. Physics.* a hypothetical elementary particle capable of travelling faster than the velocity of light. [C20: from TACHY- + -ON]

tachyphylaxis (,tækɪfɪ'læksɪs) *n.* very rapid development of tolerance or immunity to the effects of a drug. [New Latin, from TACHY- + *phylaxis* on the model of *prophylaxis.* See PROPHYLACTIC]

tachypnoea *or U.S.* **tachypnea** (,tækɪp'nɪə) *n. Pathol.* abnormally rapid breathing.

tacit ('tæsɪt) *adj.* **1.** implied or inferred without direct expression; understood: *a tacit agreement.* **2.** created or having effect by operation of law, rather than by being directly expressed. [C17: from Latin *tacitus,* past participle of *tacēre* to be silent] —**'tacitly** *adv.* —**'tacitness** *n.*

taciturn ('tæsɪ,tɜːn) *adj.* habitually silent, reserved, or uncommunicative; not inclined to conversation. [C18: from Latin *taciturnus,* from *tacitus* silent, from *tacēre* to be silent] —**,taci'turnity** *n.* —**'taci,turnly** *adv.*

tack[1] (tæk) *n.* **1.** a short sharp-pointed nail, usually with a flat and comparatively large head. **2.** *Brit.* a long loose temporary stitch used in dressmaking, etc. **3.** See **tailor's-tack. 4.** a temporary fastening. **5.** stickiness, as of newly applied paint, varnish, etc. **6.** *Nautical.* the heading of a vessel sailing to windward, stated in terms of the side of the sail against which the wind is pressing. **7.** *Nautical.* **a.** a course sailed by a sailing vessel with the wind blowing from forward of the beam. **b.** one such course or a zigzag pattern of such courses. **8.** *Nautical.* **a.** a sheet for controlling the weather clew of a course. **b.** the weather clew itself. **9.** *Nautical.* the forward lower clew of a fore-and-aft sail. **10.** a course of action differing from some previous course: *he went off on a fresh tack.* **11. on the wrong tack.** under a false impression. ~*vb.* **12.** (*tr.*) to secure by a tack or series of tacks. **13.** *Brit.* to sew (something) with long loose temporary stitches. **14.** (*tr.*) to attach or append: *tack this letter onto the other papers.* **15.** *Nautical.* to change the heading of (a sailing vessel) to the opposite tack. **16.** *Nautical.* to steer (a sailing vessel) on alternate tacks. **17.** (*intr.*) *Nautical.* (of a sailing vessel) to proceed on a different tack or to alternate tacks. **18.** (*intr.*) to follow a zigzag route; keep changing one's course of action. [C14 *tak* fastening, nail; related to Middle Low German *tacke* pointed instrument] —**'tacker** *n.* —**'tackless** *adj.*

tack[2] (tæk) *n. Informal.* food, esp. when regarded as inferior or distasteful. See also **hardtack.** [C19: of unknown origin]

tack[3] (tæk) *n.* **a.** riding harness for horses, such as saddles, bridles, etc. **b.** (*as modifier*): *the tack room.* [C20: shortened from TACKLE]

tack[4] (tæk) *n. Scot.* **1.** a lease. **2.** an area of land held on a lease. [C15: from *tak* a Scots word for *take*]

tacket ('tækɪt) *n. Scot. and northern English dialect.* a nail, esp. a hobnail. [C14: from TACK[1]]

tack hammer *n.* a light hammer for driving tacks.

tackies ('tækız) *pl. n., sing.* **tacky.** *S. African informal.* tennis shoes or plimsolls. [C20: probably from TACKY[1], with reference to their nonslip rubber soles]

tackle ('tæk^əl; *Nautical often* 'teık^əl) *n.* **1.** any mechanical system for lifting or pulling, esp. an arrangement of ropes and pulleys designed to lift heavy weights. **2.** the equipment required for a particular occupation, etc.: *fishing tackle.* **3.** *Nautical.* the halyards and other running rigging aboard a vessel. **4.** *Sport.* a physical challenge to an opponent, as to prevent his progress with the ball. **5.** *American football.* a defensive player. ~*vb.* **6.** (*tr.*) to undertake (a task, problem, etc.). **7.** (*tr.*) to confront (a person, esp. an opponent) with a difficult proposition. **8.** *Sport.* (esp. in football games) to challenge (an opponent) with a tackle. [C13: related to Middle Low German *takel* ship's rigging, Middle Dutch *taken* to TAKE] —'**tackler** *n.*

tack rag *n. Building trades.* a cotton cloth impregnated with an oil, used to remove dust from a surface prior to painting.

tacksman ('tæksmən) *n., pl.* **-men.** *Scot.* a leaseholder, esp. a tenant in the Highlands who sublets. [C16: from TACK[4]]

tack welding *n. Engineering.* short intermittent welds made to hold components in place before full welding is begun.

tacky[1] *or* **tackey** ('tækı) *adj.* **tackier, tackiest.** slightly sticky or adhesive: *the varnish was still tacky.* [C18: from TACK[1] (in the sense: stickiness)] —'**tackily** *adv.* —'**tackiness** *n.*

tacky[2] ('tækı) *adj.* **tackier, tackiest.** *Informal.* **1.** shabby or shoddy. **2.** ostentatious and vulgar. **3.** *U.S.* (of a person) dowdy; seedy. [C19: from dialect *tacky* an inferior horse, of unknown origin] —'**tackiness** *n.*

tacmahack ('tækmə,hæk) *n.* a variant of **tacamahac.**

tacnode ('tæk,nəʊd) *n.* another name for **osculation** (sense 1). [C19: from Latin *tactus* touch (from *tangere* to touch) + NODE]

taco ('tɑːkəʊ) *n., pl.* **-cos.** *Mexican cookery.* a tortilla folded into a roll with a filling and usually fried. [from Mexican Spanish, from Spanish: literally, a snack, a bite to eat]

taconite ('tækə,naıt) *n.* a fine-grained sedimentary rock containing magnetite, haematite, and silica, which occurs in the Lake Superior region of North America: a low-grade iron ore. [C20: named after the *Taconic* Mountains in New England]

tact (tækt) *n.* **1.** a sense of what is fitting and considerate in dealing with others, so as to avoid giving offence or to win good will; discretion. **2.** skill or judgment in handling difficult or delicate situations; diplomacy. **3.** *Archaic.* the sense of touch. [C17: from Latin *tactus* a touching, from *tangere* to touch] —'**tactful** *adj.* —'**tactfully** *adv.* —'**tactfulness** *n.* —'**tactless** *adj.* —'**tactlessly** *adv.* —'**tactlessness** *n.*

tactic ('tæktık) *n.* a piece of tactics; tactical move. See also **tactics.**

-tactic *adj. combining form.* having a specified kind of pattern or arrangement or having an orientation determined by a specified force: *syndiotactic; phototactic.* [from Greek *taktikos* relating to order or arrangement; see TACTICS]

tactical ('tæktık^əl) *adj.* **1.** of, relating to, or employing tactics: *a tactical error.* **2.** (of weapons, attacks, etc.) used in or supporting limited military operations: *a tactical missile; tactical bombing.* **3.** skilful, adroit, or diplomatic: *a tactical manoeuvre.* —'**tactically** *adv.*

tactical voting *n.* (in an election) the practice of casting one's vote not for the party of one's choice but for the second strongest contender in order to defeat the likeliest winner.

tactics ('tæktıks) *pl. n.* **1.** (*functioning as sing.*) *Military.* the art and science of the detailed direction and control of movement or manoeuvre of forces in battle to achieve an aim or task. **2.** the manoeuvres used or plans followed to achieve a particular short-term aim. [C17: from New Latin *tactica,* from Greek *ta taktika* the matters of arrangement, neuter plural of *taktikos* concerning arrangement or order, from *taktos* arranged (for battle), from *tassein* to arrange] —**tac'tician** *n.*

tactile ('tæktaıl) *adj.* **1.** of, relating to, affecting, or having a sense of touch: *a tactile organ; tactile stimuli.* **2.** *Now rare.* capable of being touched; tangible. [C17: from Latin *tactilis,* from *tangere* to touch] —**tactility** (tæk'tılıtı) *n.*

taction ('tækʃən) *n. Obsolete.* the act of touching; contact. [C17: from Latin *tactiō* a touching, from *tangere* to touch]

tactual ('tæktjʊəl) *adj.* **1.** caused by touch; causing a tactile sensation. **2.** of or relating to the tactile sense or the organs of touch. [C17: from Latin *tactus* a touching; see TACT] —'**tactually** *adv.*

tad (tæd) *n. Informal, chiefly U.S. and Canadian.* **1.** a small boy; lad. **2.** a small bit or piece. **3. a tad.** a little; rather: *she may be a tad short but she got a top modelling job.* [C20: short for TADPOLE]

tadpole ('tæd,pəʊl) *n.* the aquatic larva of frogs, toads, etc., which develops from a limbless tailed form with external gills into a form with internal gills, limbs, and a reduced tail. [C15 *taddepol,* from *tadde* TOAD + *pol* head, POLL]

Tadzhik, Tadjik, *or* **Tajik** ('tɑːdʒık, tɑː'dʒiːk) *n., pl.* **-dzhik, -djik,** *or* **-jik.** a member of a Persian-speaking Muslim people inhabiting the former Soviet republic of Tadzhikistan and parts of Sinkiang in W China.

Tadzhiki (tɑː'dʒıkiː, -'dʒiː-) *n.* **1.** the language of the Tadzhiks, belonging to the West Iranian subbranch of the Indo-European family. ~*adj.* **2.** of or relating to the Tadzhiks or their language.

tae[1] (te) *prep., adv.* a Scot. word for **to.**

tae[2] (te) *adv.* a Scot. word for **too.**

tae[3] (te) *n.* a Scot. word for **toe.**

taedium vitae ('tiːdıəm 'viːtaı, 'vaıtiː) *n.* the feeling that life is boring and dull. [Latin, literally: weariness of life]

tae kwon do ('taı 'kwɒn 'dəʊ, 'teı) *n.* a Korean martial art that resembles karate. [C20: Korean *tae* kick + *kwon* fist + *do* way, method]

tael (teıl) *n.* **1.** a unit of weight, used in the Far East, having various values between one to two and a half ounces. **2.** (formerly) a Chinese monetary unit equivalent in value to a tael weight of standard silver. [C16: from Portuguese, from Malay *tahil* weight, perhaps from Hindi *tolā* weight of a new rupee, from Sanskrit *tulā* weight]

ta'en (teın) *vb.* a poetic contraction of **taken.**

taenia *or U.S.* **tenia** ('tiːnıə) *n., pl.* **-niae** (-nı,iː). **1.** (in ancient Greece) a narrow fillet or headband for the hair. **2.** *Architect.* the fillet between the architrave and frieze of a Doric entablature. **3.** *Anatomy.* any bandlike structure or part. **4.** any tapeworm of the genus *Taenia,* such as *T. soleum,* a parasite of man that uses the pig as its intermediate host. [C16: via Latin from Greek *tainia* narrow strip; related to Greek *teinein* to stretch]

taeniacide *or U.S.* **teniacide** ('tiːnıə,saıd) *n.* a substance, esp. a drug, that kills tapeworms.

taeniafuge *or U.S.* **teniafuge** ('tiːnıə,fjuːdʒ) *n.* a substance, esp. a drug, that expels tapeworms from the body of their host.

taeniasis *or U.S.* **teniasis** (tiː'naıəsıs) *n. Pathol.* infestation with tapeworms of the genus *Taenia.*

TAFE ('tæfı) *n.* (in Australia) *acronym for* Technical and Further Education.

taffeta ('tæfıtə) *n.* **1. a.** a thin crisp lustrous plain-weave fabric of silk, rayon, etc., used esp. for women's clothes. **b.** (*as modifier*): *a taffeta petticoat.* **2.** any of various similar fabrics. [C14: from Medieval Latin *taffata,* from Persian *tāftah* spun, from *tāftan* to spin]

taffrail ('tæf,reıl) *n. Nautical.* **1.** a rail at the stern or above the transom of a vessel. **2.** the upper part of the transom of a vessel, esp. a sailing vessel, often ornately decorated. [C19: changed (through influence of RAIL[1]) from earlier *tafferel,* from Dutch *taffereel* panel (hence applied to the part of a vessel decorated with carved panels), variant of *tafeleel* (unattested), from *tafel* TABLE]

taffy ('tæfı) *n., pl.* **-fies.** **1.** *U.S. and Canadian.* a chewy sweet made of brown sugar or molasses and butter, boiled and then pulled so that it becomes glossy. **2.** *Chiefly U.S. and Canadian.* a less common term for **toffee.** [C19: perhaps from TAFIA]

Taffy ('tæfı) *n., pl.* **-fies.** a slang word or nickname for a Welshman. [C17: from the supposed Welsh pronunciation of *Davy* (from *David,* Welsh *Dafydd*), a common Welsh Christian name]

tafia *or* **taffia** ('tæfıə) *n.* a type of rum, esp. from Guyana or the West Indies. [C18: from French, from West Indian Creole, probably from RATAFIA]

tag[1] (tæg) *n.* **1.** a piece or strip of paper, plastic, leather, etc., for attaching to something by one end as a mark or label: *a price tag.* **2.** an electronic device worn, usually on the wrist or ankle, by an offender serving a noncustodial sentence, which monitors the offender's whereabouts by means of a link to a central computer through the telephone system. Also called: **electronic tag.** **3.** a small piece of material hanging from or loosely attached to a part or piece. **4.** a point of metal or other hard substance at the end of a cord, lace, etc., to prevent it from fraying and to facilitate threading. **5.** an epithet or verbal appendage, the refrain of a song, the moral of a fable, etc. **6.** a brief quotation, esp. one in a foreign language: *his speech was interlarded with Horatian tags.* **7.** *Grammar.* **a.** Also called: **tag question.** a clause added on to another clause to invite the hearer's agreement or conversational cooperation. Tags are usually in the form of a question with a pronoun as subject, the antecedent of which is the subject of the main clause; as *isn't it* in *the bread is on the table, isn't it?* **b.** a linguistic item added on to a sentence but not forming part of it, as *John* in *are you there, John?* **8.** an ornamental flourish as at the end of a signature. **9.** the contrastingly coloured tip to an animal's tail. **10.** a matted lock of wool or hair. **11.** *Angling.* a strand of tinsel, wire, etc., tied to the body of an artificial fly. ~*vb.* **tags, tagging, tagged.** (*mainly tr.*) **12.** to mark with a tag. **13.** to monitor the whereabouts of (an offender) by means of an electronic tag. **14.** to add or append as a tag. **15.** to supply (prose or blank verse) with rhymes. **16.** (*intr.; usually foll. by on or along*) to trail (behind): *many small boys tagged on behind the procession.* **17.** to name or call (someone something): *they tagged him Lanky.* **18.** to cut the tags of wool or hair from (an animal). [C15: of uncertain origin; related to Swedish *tagg* point, perhaps also to TACK[1]]

tag[2] (tæg) *n.* **1.** Also called: **tig.** a children's game in which one player chases the others in an attempt to catch one of them who will then become the chaser. **2.** the act of tagging one's partner in tag wrestling. **3.** (*modifier*) denoting or relating to a wrestling contest between two teams of two wrestlers, in which only one from each team may be in the ring at one time. The contestant outside the ring may change places with his team-mate inside the ring after touching his hand. ~*vb.* **tags, tagging, tagged.** (*tr.*)

4. to catch (another child) in the game of tag. 5. (in tag wrestling) to touch the hand of (one's partner). [C18: perhaps from TAG¹]

Tagalog (tə'gɑːlɒg) *n.* 1. (*pl.* **-logs** *or* **-log**) a member of a people of the Philippines, living chiefly in the region around the capital, Manila. 2. the language of this people, belonging to the Malayo-Polynesian family: the official language of the Philippines. ~*adj.* 3. of or relating to this people or their language.

tag end *n.* 1. *Chiefly U.S. and Canadian.* the last part of something: *the tag end of the day.* 2. a loose end of cloth, thread, etc.

tagetes (tæ'dʒiːtiːz) *n.* See **marigold** (sense 1).

taggers ('tægəz) *pl. n.* very thin iron or steel sheet coated with tin. [C19: perhaps so called because it was used to make tags for laces]

tagliatelle (ˌtæljə'tɛlɪ) *n.* a form of pasta made in narrow strips. [Italian, from *tagliare* to cut]

tagma ('tægmə) *n., pl.* **-mata** (-mətə). *Zoology.* a distinct region of the body of an arthropod, such as the head, thorax, or abdomen of an insect. [C19: from Greek: something arranged, from *tassein* to put in order]

tagmeme ('tægmiːm) *n. Linguistics.* a class of speech elements all of which may fulfil the same grammatical role in a sentence; the minimum unit of analysis in tagmemics. [C20: from Greek *tagma* order, from *tassein* to put in order + -EME] —**tag'memic** *adj.*

tagmemics (tæg'miːmɪks) *pl. n.* (*functioning as sing.*) *Linguistics.* a type of grammatical analysis based on the concept of function in sentence slots and the determination of classes of words that can fill each slot.

taguan ('tægˌwæn) *n.* a large nocturnal flying squirrel, *Petaurista petaurista,* of high forests in the East Indies that uses its long tail as a rudder. [C19: its Filipino name]

tahini (tə'hiːnɪ) *or* **tahina** (tə'hiːnə) *n.* a paste made from sesame seeds originating in the Middle East, often used as an ingredient of hummus and other dips. [from Arabic]

Tahitian (tə'hiːtɪən, tə'hiːʃɪən) *adj.* 1. of or relating to Tahiti, a French Polynesian island in the S Pacific, or its people. ~*n.* 2. a native or inhabitant of Tahiti.

Tahltan ('tæltən) *n.* 1. a member of a North American Indian people inhabiting NW British Columbia, Canada. 2. the language of this people, belonging to the Athapascan group of the Na-Dene phylum.

tahr *or* **thar** (tɑː) *n.* any of several goatlike bovid mammals of the genus *Hemitragus,* such as *H. jemlahicus* (**Himalayan tahr**), of mountainous regions of S and SW Asia, having a shaggy coat and curved horns. [from Nepali *thār*]

tahsil (tə'siːl) *n.* an administrative division of a zila in certain states in India. [Urdu, from Arabic: collection]

tahsildar (tə'siːldɑː) *n.* the officer in charge of the collection of revenues, etc., in a tahsil. [C18: via Hindi from Persian, from TAHSIL + Persian *-dār* having]

Tai (taɪ) *adj., n.* a variant spelling of **Thai.**

taiaha ('taɪəˌhɑː) *n. N.Z.* a carved weapon in the form of a staff, now used in Maori ceremonial oratory. [Maori]

t'ai chi ch'uan ('taɪ dʒiː 'tʃwɑːn) *n.* a Chinese system of callisthenics characterized by coordinated and rhythmic movements. Often shortened to **t'ai chi** ('taɪ 'dʒiː). [Chinese, literally: great art of boxing]

taig (teɪg) *n. Ulster dialect, often derogatory.* a Roman Catholic. [variant of the Irish name *Tadhg,* originally signifying any Irishman]

taiga ('taɪgə) *n.* the coniferous forests extending across much of subarctic North America and Eurasia, bordered by tundra to the north and steppe to the south. [from Russian, of Turkic origin; compare Turkish *dağ* mountain]

taihoa ('taɪhəʊə) *interj. N.Z.* hold on! no hurry!

tail¹ (teɪl) *n.* 1. the region of the vertebrate body that is posterior to or above the anus and contains an elongation of the vertebral column, esp. forming a flexible movable appendage. Related adj.: **caudal.** 2. anything resembling such an appendage in form or position; the bottom, lowest, or rear part: *the tail of a shirt.* 3. the last part or parts: *the tail of the storm.* 4. the rear part of an aircraft including the fin, tail plane, and control surfaces; empennage. 5. *Astronomy.* the luminous stream of gas and dust particles, up to 200 million kilometres long, driven from the head of a comet, when close to the sun, under the effect of the solar wind. 6. the rear portion of a bomb, rocket, missile, etc., usually fitted with guiding or stabilizing vanes. 7. a line of people or things. 8. a long braid or tress of hair: *a ponytail; a pigtail.* 9. *Angling.* Also called: **'tailˌfly.** the lowest fly on a wet-fly cast. 10. a final short line in a stanza. 11. *Informal.* a person employed to follow and spy upon another or others. 12. an informal word for **buttocks.** 13. *Taboo slang.* **a.** the female genitals. **b.** a woman considered sexually (esp. in the phrases **piece of tail, bit of tail**). 14. *Printing.* **a.** the margin at the foot of a page. **b.** the bottom edge of a book. 15. the lower end of a pool or part of a stream. 16. *Informal.* the course or track of a fleeing person or animal: *the police are on my tail.* 17. (*modifier*) coming from or situated in the rear: *a tail wind.* 18. **turn tail.** to run away; escape. 19. **with one's tail between one's legs.** in a state of utter defeat or confusion. ~*vb.* 20. to form or cause to form the tail. 21. to remove the tail of (an animal); dock. 22. (*tr.*) to remove the stalk of: *to top and tail the gooseberries.* 23. (*tr.*) to connect (objects, ideas, etc.) together by or as if by the tail. 24. (*tr.*) *Informal.* to follow stealthily. 25. (*tr.*) *Austral.* to tend (cattle) on foot. 26. (*intr.*) (of a vessel) to assume a specified position, as when at a mooring. 27. to build the end of (a brick, joist, etc.) into a wall or (of a brick, etc.) to have one end built into a wall. ~See also **tail off, tail out, tails.** [Old English *tægel;* related to Old Norse *tagl* horse's tail, Gothic *tagl* hair, Old High German *zagal* tail] —**'tailless** *adj.* —**'taillessly** *adv.* —**'taillessness** *n.* —**'tail-ˌlike** *adj.*

tail² (teɪl) *Property law.* ~*n.* 1. the limitation of an estate or interest to a person and the heirs of his body. See also **entail.** ~*adj.* 2. (*immediately postpositive*) (of an estate or interest) limited in this way. [C15: from Old French *taille* a division; see TAILOR, TALLY] —**'tailless** *adj.*

tailback ('teɪlˌbæk) *n.* a queue of traffic stretching back from an obstruction.

tailboard ('teɪlˌbɔːd) *n.* a board at the rear of a lorry, wagon, etc., that can be removed or let down on a hinge.

tail coat *n.* 1. Also called: **tails.** a man's black coat having a horizontal cut over the hips and a tapering tail with a vertical slit up to the waist: worn as part of full evening dress. 2. Also called: **swallow-tailed coat.** another name for **morning coat.**

tail covert *n.* any of the covert feathers of a bird covering the bases of the tail feathers.

tail end *n.* the last, endmost, or final part.

tail fan *n.* the fanned structure at the hind end of a lobster or related crustacean, formed from the telson and uropods.

tailgate ('teɪlˌgeɪt) *n.* 1. another name for **tailboard.** ~*vb.* 2. to drive very close behind (a vehicle).

tail gate *n.* a gate that is used to control the flow of water at the lower end of a lock. Compare **head gate.**

tail-heavy *adj.* (of an aircraft) having too much weight at the rear because of overloading or poor design.

tailing ('teɪlɪŋ) *n.* the part of a beam, rafter, projecting brick or stone, etc., embedded in a wall.

tailings ('teɪlɪŋz) *pl. n.* waste left over after certain processes, such as from an ore-crushing plant or in milling grain.

taille (taɪ; *French* tɑj) *n., pl.* **tailles** (taɪ, taɪz; *French* tɑj). (in France before 1789) a tax levied by a king or overlord on his subjects. [C17: from French, from Old French *taillier* to shape; see TAILOR]

taillight ('teɪlˌlaɪt) *or* **taillamp** *n.* the U.S. and Canadian names for **rear light.**

tail off *or* **away** *vb.* (*adv., usually intr.*) to decrease or cause to decrease in quantity, degree, etc., esp. gradually: *his interest in collecting stamps tailed off over the years.*

tailor ('teɪlə) *n.* 1. a person who makes, repairs, or alters outer garments, esp. menswear. Related adj.: **sartorial.** 2. a voracious and active marine food fish, *Pomatomus saltator,* of Australia with scissor-like teeth. ~*vb.* 3. to cut or style (material, clothes, etc.) to satisfy certain requirements. 4. (*tr.*) to adapt so as to make suitable for something specific: *he tailored his speech to suit a younger audience.* 5. (*intr.*) to follow the occupation of a tailor. [C13: from Anglo-Norman *taillour,* from Old French *taillier* to cut, from Latin *tālea* a cutting; related to Greek *talis* girl of marriageable age]

tailorbird ('teɪləˌbɜːd) *n.* any of several tropical Asian warblers of the genus *Orthotomus,* which build nests by sewing together large leaves using plant fibres.

tailor-made *adj.* 1. made by a tailor to fit exactly: *a tailor-made suit.* 2. perfectly meeting a particular purpose: *a girl tailor-made for him.* ~*n.* 3. a tailor-made garment. 4. *Slang.* a cigarette made in a factory rather than rolled by hand.

tailor's chalk *n.* pipeclay used by tailors and dressmakers to mark seams, darts, etc., on material.

tailor's-tack *n.* one of a series of loose looped stitches used to transfer markings for seams, darts, etc., from a paper pattern to material.

tail out *vb.* (*tr., adv.*) to guide (timber) as it emerges from a power saw.

tailpiece ('teɪlˌpiːs) *n.* 1. an extension or appendage that lengthens or completes something. 2. *Printing.* a decorative design at the foot of a page or end of a chapter. 3. *Music.* a piece of wood to which the strings of a violin, etc., are attached at their lower end. It is suspended between the taut strings and the bottom of the violin by a piece of gut or metal. 4. Also called: **tail beam.** *Architect.* a short beam or rafter that has one end embedded in a wall.

tailpipe ('teɪlˌpaɪp) *n.* a pipe from which the exhaust gases from an internal-combustion engine are discharged, esp. the terminal pipe of the exhaust system of a motor vehicle.

tailplane ('teɪlˌpleɪn) *n.* a small horizontal wing at the tail of an aircraft to provide longitudinal stability. Also called (esp. U.S.): **horizontal stabilizer.**

tailrace ('teɪlˌreɪs) *n.* 1. a channel that carries water away from a water wheel, turbine, etc. Compare **headrace.** 2. *Mining.* the channel for removing tailings in water.

tail rotor *n.* a small propeller fitted to the rear of a helicopter to counteract the torque reaction of the main rotor and thus prevent the body of the helicopter from rotating in an opposite direction.

tails (teɪlz) *pl. n.* 1. an informal name for **tail coat.** ~*interj., adv.* 2. with the reverse side of a coin uppermost: used as a call before tossing a coin. Compare **heads.**

tailskid (ˈteɪlˌskɪd) *n.* **1.** a runner under the tail of an aircraft. **2.** a rear-wheel skid of a motor vehicle.

tailspin (ˈteɪlˌspɪn) *n.* **1.** *Aeronautics.* another name for **spin** (sense 15). **2.** *Informal.* a state of confusion or panic.

tailstock (ˈteɪlˌstɒk) *n.* a casting that slides on the bed of a lathe in alignment with the headstock and is locked in position to support the free end of a workpiece.

tail wheel *n.* a wheel fitted to the rear of a vehicle, esp. the landing wheel under the tail of an aircraft.

tailwind (ˈteɪlˌwɪnd) *n.* a wind blowing in the same direction as the course of an aircraft or ship. Compare **headwind.**

tain (teɪn) *n.* tinfoil used in backing mirrors. [from French, from *étain* tin, from Old French *estain,* from Latin *stagnum* alloy of silver and lead; see STANNUM]

Taino (ˈtaɪnəʊ) *n.* **1.** (*pl.* **-nos** *or* **-no**) a member of an extinct American Indian people of the Greater Antilles and the Bahamas in the West Indies. **2.** the language of this people, belonging to the Arawakan family.

taint (teɪnt) *vb.* **1.** to affect or be affected by pollution or contamination: *oil has tainted the water.* **2.** to tarnish (someone's reputation, etc.). ~*n.* **3.** a defect or flaw: *a taint on someone's reputation.* **4.** a trace of contamination or infection. [C14: (influenced by *attaint* infected, from ATTAIN) from Old French *teindre* to dye, from Latin *tingere* to dye] —ˈ**taintless** *adj.*

taipan (ˈtaɪˌpæn) *n.* a large highly venomous elapid snake, *Oxyuranus scutellatus,* of NE Australia. [C20: from a native Australian language]

Taiping (ˈtaɪˈpɪŋ) *n. History.* a person who supported or took part in the movement of religious mysticism and agrarian unrest in China between 1850 and 1864 (Taiping rebellion), which weakened the Manchu dynasty but was eventually suppressed with foreign aid. [C19: from Chinese, from *t'ai* great + *p'ing* peace]

Taisho (taɪˈʃəʊ) *n.* the period of Japanese history and artistic style associated with the reign of Emperor Yoshihito (1912–26).

Taiwanese (ˌtaɪwɑːˈniːz) *adj.* **1.** of or relating to the island of Taiwan, principal territory of Nationalist China, or its people or culture. ~*n.* **2.** a native or inhabitant of Taiwan.

taj (tɑːdʒ) *n.* a tall conical cap worn as a mark of distinction by Muslims. [via Arabic from Persian: crown, crest]

Tajik (ˈtɑːdʒɪk, tɑːˈdʒiːk) *n., pl.* **-jik.** a variant spelling of **Tadzhik.**

taka (ˈtɑːkɑː) *n.* the standard monetary unit of Bangladesh. [from Bengali]

takahe (ˈtɑːkəˌhiː) *n* a very rare flightless New Zealand rail, *Notornis mantelli.* [from Maori, of imitative origin]

take (teɪk) *vb.* **takes, taking, took, taken.** (*mainly tr.*) **1.** (*also intr.*) to gain possession of (something) by force or effort. **2.** to appropriate or steal: *to take other people's belongings.* **3.** to receive or accept into a relationship with oneself: *to take a wife.* **4.** to pay for or buy. **5.** to rent or lease: *to take a flat in town.* **6.** to receive or obtain by regular payment: *we take a newspaper every day.* **7.** to obtain by competing for; win: *to take first prize.* **8.** to obtain or derive from a source: *he took his good manners from his older brother.* **9.** to assume the obligations of: *to take office.* **10.** to endure, esp. with fortitude: *to take punishment.* **11.** to adopt as a symbol of duty, obligation, etc.: *to take the veil.* **12.** to receive or react to in a specified way: *she took the news very well.* **13.** to adopt as one's own: *to take someone's part in a quarrel.* **14.** to receive and make use of: *to take advice.* **15.** to receive into the body, as by eating, inhaling, etc.: *to take a breath.* **16.** to eat, drink, etc., esp. habitually: *to take sugar in one's tea.* **17.** to have or be engaged in for one's benefit or use: *to take a rest.* **18.** to work at or study: *to take economics at college.* **19.** to make, do, or perform (an action): *to take a leap.* **20.** to make use of: *to take an opportunity.* **21.** to put into effect; adopt: *to take measures.* **22.** (*also intr.*) to make a photograph of or admit of being photographed. **23.** to act or perform: *she takes the part of the Queen.* **24.** to write down or copy: *to take notes.* **25.** to experience or feel: *to take pride in one's appearance; to take offence.* **26.** to consider, believe, or regard: *I take him to be honest.* **27.** to consider or accept as valid: *I take your point.* **28.** to hold or maintain in the mind: *his father took a dim view of his career.* **29.** to deal or contend with: *the tennis champion took her opponent's best strokes without difficulty.* **30.** to use as a particular case: *take hotels for example.* **31.** (*intr.*; often foll. by *from*) to diminish or detract: *the actor's bad performance took from the effect of the play.* **32.** to confront successfully: *the horse took the jump at the third attempt.* **33.** (*intr.*) to have or produce the intended effect; succeed: *her vaccination took; the glue is taking well.* **34.** (*intr.*) (of seeds, plants, etc.) to start growing successfully. **35.** to aim or direct: *he took a swipe at his opponent.* **36.** to deal a blow to in a specified place. **37.** *Archaic.* to have sexual intercourse with. **38.** to carry off or remove from a place. **39.** to carry along or have in one's possession: *don't forget to take your umbrella.* **40.** to convey or transport: *the train will take us out of the city.* **41.** to use as a means of transport: *I shall take the bus.* **42.** to conduct or lead: *this road takes you to the station.* **43.** to escort or accompany: *may I take you out tonight?* **44.** to bring or deliver to a state, position, etc.: *his ability took him to the forefront in his field.* **45.** to go to look for; seek: *to take cover.* **46.** to ascertain or determine by measuring, computing, etc.: *to take a pulse; take a reading from a dial.* **47.** (*intr.*) (of a mechanism) to catch or engage (a part). **48.** to put an end to; destroy: *she took her own life.* **49.** to come upon unexpectedly; discover. **50.** to contract: *he took a chill.* **51.** to affect or attack: *the fever took him one night.* **52.** (*copula*) to become suddenly or be rendered (ill): *he took sick; he was taken sick.* **53.** (*also intr.*) to absorb or become absorbed by something: *to take a polish.* **54.** (*usually passive*) to charm or captivate: *she was very taken with the puppy.* **55.** (*intr.*) to be or become popular; win favour. **56.** to require or need: *this job will take a lot of attention; that task will take all your time.* **57.** to subtract or deduct: *to take six from ten leaves four.* **58.** to hold or contain: *the suitcase won't take all your clothes.* **59.** to quote or copy: *he has taken several paragraphs from the book for his essay.* **60.** to proceed to occupy: *to take a seat.* **61.** (often foll. by *to*) to use or employ: *to take steps to ascertain the answer.* **62.** to win or capture (a trick, counter, piece, etc.). **63.** (*also intr.*) to catch as prey or catch prey. **64.** *Slang.* to cheat, deceive, or victimize. **65. take amiss.** to be annoyed or offended by. **66. take at one's word.** See **word** (sense 17). **67. take care.** to pay attention; be heedful. **68. take care of.** to assume responsibility for; look after. **69. take chances** *or* **a chance.** to behave in a risky manner. **70. take five** (*or* **ten**). *Informal, chiefly U.S. and Canadian.* to take a break of five (or ten) minutes. **71. take heart.** to become encouraged. **72. take it. a.** to assume; believe: *I take it you'll be back later.* **b.** *Informal.* to stand up to or endure criticism, abuse, harsh treatment, etc. **73. take one's time.** to use as much time as is needed; not rush. **74. take place.** to happen or occur. **75. take (someone's) name in vain. a.** to use a name, esp. of God, disrespectfully or irreverently. **b.** *Jocular.* to say (someone's) name. **76. take (something) upon oneself.** to assume the right to do or responsibility for (something). ~*n.* **77.** the act of taking. **78.** the number of quarry killed or captured on one occasion. **79.** *Informal, chiefly U.S.* the amount of anything taken, esp. money. **80.** *Films, music.* **a.** one of a series of recordings from which the best will be selected for release. **b.** the process of taking one such recording. **c.** a scene or part of a scene photographed without interruption. **81.** *Informal.* **a.** any objective indication of a successful vaccination, such as a local skin reaction. **b.** a successful skin graft. **82.** *Printing.* a part of an article, story, etc., given to a compositor or keyboard operator for setting in type. **83.** *Informal.* a try or attempt. ~See also **take aback, take after, take apart, take away, take back, take down, take for, take in, take off, take on, take out, take over, take to, take up.** [Old English *tacan,* from Old Norse *taka;* related to Gothic *tekan* to touch] —ˈ**takable** *or* ˈ**takeable** *adj.*

take aback *vb.* (*tr., adv.*) to astonish or disconcert.

take after *vb.* (*intr., prep.*) **1.** to resemble in appearance, character, behaviour, etc. **2.** to follow as an example.

take apart *vb.* (*tr., adv.*) **1.** to separate (something) into component parts. **2.** to criticize or punish severely: *the reviewers took the new play apart.*

take away *vb.* (*tr., adv.*) **1.** to deduct; subtract: *take away four from nine to leave five.* ~*prep.* **2.** minus: *nine take away four is five.* ~*adj.* **takeaway.** *Brit., Austral., and N.Z.* **3.** sold for consumption away from the premises on which it is prepared: *a takeaway meal.* **4.** preparing and selling food for consumption away from the premises: *a takeaway Indian restaurant.* ~*n.* **takeaway.** *Brit. and N.Z.* **5.** a shop or restaurant that sells such food: *let's go to the Chinese takeaway.* **6.** a meal bought at such a shop or restaurant: *we'll have a Chinese takeaway tonight to save cooking.* ~Scot. word (for senses 3–6) **carry-out.** U.S. and Canadian word (for senses 3–6) **takeout.**

take back *vb.* (*adv., mainly tr.*) **1.** to retract or withdraw (something said, written, promised, etc.). **2.** to regain possession of. **3.** to return for exchange: *to take back a substandard garment.* **4.** to accept (someone) back (into one's home, affections, etc.). **5.** to remind one of the past; cause one to reminisce: *that tune really takes me back.* **6.** (*also intr.*) *Printing.* to move (copy) to the previous line.

take down *vb.* (*tr., adv.*) **1.** to record in writing. **2.** to dismantle or tear down: *to take down an old shed.* **3.** to lower or reduce in power, arrogance, etc. (esp. in the phrase **to take down a peg).** ~*adj.* **take-down.** **4.** made or intended to be disassembled.

take for *vb.* (*tr., prep.*) *Informal.* to consider or suppose to be, esp. mistakenly: *the fake coins were taken for genuine; who do you take me for?*

take-home pay *n.* the remainder of one's pay after all income tax and other compulsory deductions have been made.

take in *vb.* (*tr., adv.*) **1.** to comprehend or understand. **2.** to include or comprise: *his thesis takes in that point.* **3.** to receive into one's house in exchange for payment: *to take in washing; take in lodgers.* **4.** to make (an article of clothing, etc.) smaller by altering seams. **5.** to include: *the tour takes in the islands as well as the mainland.* **6.** *Informal.* to cheat or deceive. **7.** *U.S.* to go to; visit: *let's take in a movie tonight.* ~*n.* **take-in.** **8.** *Informal.* the act or an instance of cheating or deceiving.

taken (ˈteɪkən) *vb.* **1.** the past participle of **take.** ~*adj.* **2.** (*postpositive*; foll. by *with*) enthusiastically impressed (by); infatuated (with).

take off *vb.* (*adv.*) **1.** (*tr.*) to remove or discard (a garment). **2.** (*intr.*) (of an aircraft) to become airborne. **3.** *Informal.* to set out or cause to set out on a journey: *they took off for Spain.* **4.** (*tr.*) (of a disease) to prove fatal to; kill. **5.** (*tr.*) *Informal.* to mimic or imitate, esp. in an amusing or satirical manner. **6.** (*intr.*) *Informal.* to become successful or popular, esp. suddenly. ~*n.* **take-off. 7.** the act or process of making an aircraft airborne. **8.** the stage of a country's economic development when rapid and sustained economic growth is first achieved. **9.** *Informal.* an act of mimicry; imitation.

take on *vb.* (*adv., mainly tr.*) **1.** to employ or hire: *to take on new workmen.* **2.** to assume or acquire: *his voice took on a plaintive note.* **3.** to agree to do; undertake: *I'll take on that job for you.* **4.** to compete against, oppose, or fight: *I will take him on at tennis; I'll take him on any time.* **5.** (*intr.*) *Informal.* to exhibit great emotion, esp. grief.

take out *vb.* (*tr., adv.*) **1.** to extract or remove. **2.** to obtain or secure (a licence, patent, etc.) from an authority. **3.** to go out with; escort: *George is taking Susan out next week.* **4.** *Bridge.* to bid a different suit from (one's partner) in order to rescue him from a difficult contract. **5.** *Slang.* to kill or destroy. **6.** *Austral. informal.* to win, esp. in sport: *he took out the tennis championship.* **7. take it** *or* **a lot out of.** *Informal.* to sap the energy or vitality of. **8. take out on.** *Informal.* to vent (anger, frustration, etc.) on (esp. an innocent person). **9. take someone out of himself.** *Informal.* to make someone forget his anxieties, problems, etc. ~*adj.* **takeout. 10.** *Bridge.* of or designating a conventional informatory bid, asking one's partner to bid another suit. ~*adj., n.* **11.** an informal word (chiefly U.S. and Canadian) for **takeaway** (senses 3–6).

take over *vb.* (*adv.*) **1.** to assume the control or management of. **2.** *Printing.* to move (copy) to the next line. ~*n.* **takeover. 3. a.** the act of seizing or assuming power, control, etc. **b.** (*as modifier*): *takeover bid.* **4.** *Sport.* another word for **changeover** (sense 3).

taker ('teɪkə) *n.* a person who takes something, esp. a bet, wager, or offer of purchase.

take to *vb.* (*intr., prep.*) **1.** to make for; flee to: *to take to the hills.* **2.** to form a liking for, esp. after a short acquaintance: *I took to him straightaway.* **3.** to have recourse to: *to take to the bottle.* **4. take to heart.** to regard seriously.

take up *vb.* (*adv., mainly tr.*) **1.** to adopt the study, practice, or activity of: *to take up gardening.* **2.** *Austral. and N.Z.* to occupy and break in (uncultivated land): *he took up some hundreds of acres in the back country.* **3.** to shorten (a garment or part of a garment): *she took all her skirts up three inches.* **4.** to pay off (a note, mortgage, etc.). **5.** to agree to or accept (an invitation, etc.). **6.** to pursue further or resume (something): *he took up French where he left off.* **7.** to absorb (a liquid). **8.** to adopt as a protégé; act as a patron to. **9.** to occupy or fill (space or time). **10.** to interrupt, esp. in order to contradict or criticize. **11. take up on. a.** to argue or dispute with (someone): *can I take you up on two points in your talk?* **b.** to accept what is offered by (someone): *let me take you up on your invitation.* **12. take up with. a.** to discuss with (someone); refer to: *to take up a fault with the manufacturers.* **b.** (*intr.*) to begin to keep company or associate with. ~*n.* **take-up. 13. a.** the claiming or acceptance of something, esp. a state benefit, that is due or available. **b.** (*as modifier*): *take-up rate.* **14.** *Machinery.* the distance through which a part must move to absorb the free play in a system. **15.** (*modifier*) denoting the part of a mechanism on which film, tape, or wire is wound up: *a take-up spool on a tape recorder.*

takin ('tɑːkiːn) *n.* a massive bovid mammal, *Budorcas taxicolor,* of mountainous regions of S Asia, having a shaggy coat, short legs, and horns that point backwards and upwards. [C19: from Mishmi]

taking ('teɪkɪŋ) *adj.* **1.** charming, fascinating, or intriguing. **2.** *Informal.* infectious; catching. ~*n.* **3.** something taken. **4.** (*pl.*) receipts; earnings. —'**takingly** *adv.* —'**takingness** *n.*

Talaing (tɑː'laɪŋ) *n.* another name for **Mon.**

talapoin ('tæləˌpɔɪn) *n.* **1.** the smallest of the guenon monkeys, *Cercopithecus talapoin,* of swampy central W African forests, having olive-green fur and slightly webbed digits. **2. a.** (in Burma and Thailand) a Buddhist monk. **b.** a title of respect used in addressing such a monk. [C16: from French, literally: Buddhist monk, from Portuguese *talapão,* from Mon *tala pōi* our lord; originally jocular, from the appearance of the monkey]

talbot ('tɔːlbət) *n.* (formerly) an ancient breed of large hound, usually white or light-coloured, having pendulous ears and strong powers of scent. [C16: supposed to have been brought to England by the *Talbot* family]

talc (tælk) *n. also* **talcum. 1.** See **talcum powder. 2.** a white, grey, brown, or pale green mineral, found in metamorphic rocks. It is used in the manufacture of talcum powder and electrical insulators. Composition: hydrated magnesium silicate. Formula: $Mg_3Si_4O_{10}(OH)_2$. Crystal structure: monoclinic. ~*vb.* **talcs, talcking, talcked** *or* **talcs, talcing, talced. 3.** (*tr.*) to apply talc to. [C16: from Medieval Latin *talcum,* from Arabic *talq* mica, from Persian *talk*] —'**talcose** *or* '**talcous** *adj.*

talcum powder ('tælkəm) *n.* a powder made of purified talc, usually scented, used for perfuming the body and for absorbing excess moisture. Often shortened to **talc.**

tale (teɪl) *n.* **1.** a report, narrative, or story. **2.** one of a group of short stories connected by an overall narrative framework. **3. a.** a malicious or meddlesome rumour or piece of gossip: *to bear tales against someone.* **b.** (*in combination*): *talebearer; taleteller.* **4.** a fictitious or false statement. **5. tell tales. a.** to tell fanciful lies. **b.** to report malicious stories, trivial complaints, etc., esp. to someone in authority. **6. tell a tale.** to reveal something important. **7. tell its own tale.** to be self-evident. **8.** *Archaic.* **a.** a number; amount. **b.** computation or enumeration. **9.** an obsolete word for **talk.** [Old English *talu* list; related to Old Frisian *tele* talk, Old Saxon, Old Norse *tala* talk, number, Old High German *zala* number]

talent ('tælənt) *n.* **1.** innate ability, aptitude, or faculty, esp. when unspecified; above average ability: *a talent for cooking; a child with talent.* **2.** a person or persons possessing such ability. **3.** any of various ancient units of weight and money. **4.** *Informal.* members of the opposite sex collectively, esp. those living in a particular place: *the local talent.* **5.** an obsolete word for **inclination.** [Old English *talente,* from Latin *talenta,* pl. of *talentum* sum of money, from Greek *talanton* unit of money or weight; in Medieval Latin the sense was extended to ability through the influence of the parable of the talents (Matthew 25:14–30)] —'**talented** *adj.*

talent scout *n.* a person whose occupation is the search for talented artists, sportsmen, performers, etc., for engagements as professionals.

taler ('tɑːlə) *n., pl.* **-ler** *or* **-lers.** a variant spelling of **thaler.**

tales ('teɪliːz) *n. Law.* **1.** (*functioning as pl.*) a group of persons summoned from among those present in court or from bystanders to fill vacancies on a jury panel. **2.** (*functioning as sing.*) the writ summoning such jurors. [C15: from Medieval Latin phrase *tālēs dē circumstantibus* such men from among the bystanders, from Latin *tālis* such] —'**talesman** *n.*

taligrade ('tælɪˌgreɪd) *adj.* (of mammals) walking on the outer side of the foot. [C20: from New Latin, from Latin *tālus* ankle, heel + -GRADE]

talion ('tælɪən) *n.* the system or legal principle of making the punishment correspond to the crime; retaliation. [C15: via Old French from Latin *tāliō,* from *tālis* such]

taliped ('tælɪˌpɛd) *adj.* **1.** *Pathol.* having a club foot. ~*n.* **2.** a club-footed person. [C19: see TALIPES]

talipes ('tælɪˌpiːz) *n.* **1.** a congenital deformity of the foot by which it is twisted in any of various positions. **2.** a technical name for **club foot.** [C19: New Latin, from Latin *tālus* ankle + *pēs* foot]

talipot *or* **talipot palm** ('tælɪˌpɒt) *n.* a palm tree, *Corypha umbraculifera,* of the East Indies, having large leaves that are used for fans, thatching houses, etc. [C17: from Bengali: palm leaf, from Sanskrit *tālī* fan palm + *pattra* leaf]

talisman ('tælɪzmən) *n., pl.* **-mans. 1.** a stone or other small object, usually inscribed or carved, believed to protect the wearer from evil influences. **2.** anything thought to have magical or protective powers. [C17: via French or Spanish from Arabic *tilsam,* from Medieval Greek *telesma* ritual, from Greek: consecration, from *telein* to perform a rite, complete, from *telos* end, result] —**talismanic** (ˌtælɪz'mænɪk) *adj.*

talk (tɔːk) *vb.* **1.** (*intr.;* often foll. by *to* or *with*) to express one's thoughts, feelings, or desires by means of words (to); speak (to). **2.** (*intr.*) to communicate or exchange thoughts by other means: *lovers talk with their eyes.* **3.** (*intr.;* usually foll. by *about*) to exchange ideas, pleasantries, or opinions (about): *to talk about the weather.* **4.** (*intr.*) to articulate words; verbalize: *his baby can talk.* **5.** (*tr.*) to give voice to; utter: *to talk rubbish.* **6.** (*tr.*) to hold a conversation about; discuss: *to talk business.* **7.** (*intr.*) to reveal information: *the prisoner talked after torture.* **8.** (*tr.*) to know how to communicate in (a language or idiom): *he talks English.* **9.** (*intr.*) to spread rumours or gossip: *we don't want the neighbours to talk.* **10.** (*intr.*) to make sounds suggestive of talking. **11.** (*intr.*) to be effective or persuasive: *money talks.* **12. now you're talking.** *Informal.* at last you're saying something agreeable. **13. talk big.** to boast or brag. **14. talk shop.** to speak about one's work, esp. when meeting socially, sometimes with the effect of excluding those not similarly employed. **15. you can talk.** *Informal.* you don't have to worry about doing a particular thing yourself. **16. you can** *or* **can't talk.** *Informal.* you yourself are guilty of offending in the very matter you are upholding or decrying. ~*n.* **17.** a speech or lecture: *a talk on ancient Rome.* **18.** an exchange of ideas or thoughts: *a business talk with a colleague.* **19.** idle chatter, gossip, or rumour: *there has been a lot of talk about you two.* **20.** a subject of conversation; theme: *our talk was of war.* **21.** (*often pl.*) a conference, discussion, or negotiation: *talks about a settlement.* **22.** a specific manner of speaking: *children's talk.* ~See also **talk about, talk at, talk back, talk down, talk into, talk out, talk round, talk up.** [C13 *talkien* to talk; related to Old English *talu* TALE, Frisian *talken* to talk] —'**talkable** *adj.* —ˌ**talka'bility** *n.* —'**talker** *n.*

talk about *vb.* (*intr., prep.*) **1.** to discuss. **2.** used informally and often ironically to add emphasis to a statement: *all his plays have such ridiculous plots—talk about good drama!* **3. know what one is talking about.** to have thorough or specialized knowledge.

talk at *vb.* (*intr., prep.*) to speak to (a person) in a way that indicates a response is not really wanted: *I wish he'd talk to me rather than at me.*

talkative ('tɔːkətɪv) *adj.* given to talking a great deal. —'**talkatively** *adv.* —'**talkativeness** *n.*

talk back *vb.* (*intr., adv.*) **1.** to answer boldly or impudently. **2.** *N.Z.* to conduct a telephone dialogue for immediate transmission over the air. ~*n.* **talkback. 3.** *Television, radio.* a system of telephone links enabling spoken directions to be given during the production of a programme. **4.** *N.Z.* **a.** a broadcast telephone dialogue. **b.** (*as modifier*): *a talkback show.*

talkbox (ˈtɔːkˌbɒks) *n.* another name for **voice box** (sense 2).

talk down *vb.* (*adv.*) **1.** (*intr.*; often foll. by *to*) to behave (towards) in a superior or haughty manner. **2.** (*tr.*) to override (a person or argument) by continuous or loud talking. **3.** (*tr.*) to give instructions to (an aircraft) by radio to enable it to land.

talkie (ˈtɔːkɪ) *n. Informal.* an early film with a soundtrack. Full name: **talking picture.**

talking book *n.* a tape recording or gramophone record of a book, designed to be used by the blind.

talking head *n.* (on television) a person, such as a newscaster, who is shown only from the shoulders up, and speaks without the use of any illustrative material.

talking-to *n. Informal.* a session of criticism, as of the work or attitude of a subordinate by a person in authority.

talk into *vb.* (*tr., prep.*) to persuade to by talking: *I talked him into buying the house.*

talk out *vb.* (*adv.*) **1.** (*tr.*) to resolve or eliminate by talking: *they talked out their differences.* **2.** (*tr.*) *Brit.* to block (a bill, etc.) in a legislative body by lengthy discussion. **3. talk out of.** to dissuade from by talking: *she was talked out of marriage.*

talk round *vb.* **1.** (*tr., adv.*) Also: **talk over.** to persuade to one's opinion: *I talked him round to buying a car.* **2.** (*intr., prep.*) to discuss the arguments relating to (a subject), esp. without coming to a conclusion: *to talk round the problem of the human condition.* **3.** (*intr., prep.*) to discuss (a subject) vaguely without considering basic facts: *they talked round the idea of moving house quite forgetting they hadn't enough money.*

talk show *n.* another name for **chat show.**

talk up *vb.* (*tr., adv.*) to speak of or discuss favourably in order to arouse interest or support.

talky (ˈtɔːkɪ) *adj.* **talkier, talkiest.** *U.S. and Canadian.* containing too much dialogue or inconsequential talk: *a talky novel.*

tall (tɔːl) *adj.* **1.** of more than average height. **2. a.** (*postpositive*) having a specified height: *a woman five feet tall.* **b.** (*in combination*): *a twenty-foot-tall partition.* **3.** *Informal.* exaggerated or incredible: *a tall story.* **4.** *Informal.* difficult to accomplish: *a tall order.* **5.** an archaic word for **excellent.** [C14 (in the sense: big, comely, valiant); related to Old English *getæl* prompt, Old High German *gizal* quick, Gothic *untals* foolish] —ˈ**tallness** *n.*

tallage (ˈtælɪdʒ) *English history.* ~*n.* **1. a.** a tax levied by the Norman and early Angevin kings on their Crown lands and royal towns. **b.** a toll levied by a lord upon his tenants or by a feudal lord upon his vassals. ~*vb.* **2.** (*tr.*) to levy a tax (upon); impose a tax (upon). [C13: from Old French *taillage,* from *taillier* to cut; see TAILOR]

tallboy (ˈtɔːlˌbɔɪ) *n.* **1.** a high chest of drawers made in two sections and placed one on top of the other; chest-on-chest. **2.** a fitting on the top of a chimney to prevent downdraughts. [C18: from TALL + BOY]

tallis (ˈtɑlis) *or* **tallith** (tɑˈlit) *n. Judaism.* a fringed shawl worn by Jewish men during morning prayers. [from Hebrew, literally: a cover]

tallith (ˈtælɪθ; *Hebrew* taˈliːt) *n., pl.* **tallaisim** (tæˈleɪsɪm), **tallithes,** *or* **talitoth** (*Hebrew* -liːˈtɔt). **1.** a white shawl with fringed corners worn over the head and shoulders by Jewish males during religious services. **2.** a smaller form of this worn under the outer garment during waking hours by some Jewish males. [C17: from Hebrew *tallīt*]

tall oil *n.* any of various oily liquid mixtures obtained by acidifying the liquor resulting from the treatment of wood pulp with sodium hydroxide: it contains chiefly rosin acids and fatty acids and is used in making soaps and lubricants. [C20: partial translation of German *Tallöl,* from Swedish *tallolja,* from *tall* pine + *olja* OIL]

tallow (ˈtæləʊ) *n.* **1.** a fatty substance consisting of a mixture of glycerides, including stearic, palmitic, and oleic acids and extracted chiefly from the suet of sheep and cattle: used for making soap, candles, food, etc. ~*vb.* **2.** (*tr.*) to cover or smear with tallow. [Old English *tælg,* a dye; related to Middle Low German *talch* tallow, Dutch *talk,* Icelandic *tólg*] —ˈ**tallowy** *adj.*

tallow wood *n. Austral.* a tall eucalyptus tree, *Eucalyptus microcorys,* of coastal regions, having soft fibrous bark and conical fruits and yielding a greasy timber.

tall poppy *n. Austral. informal.* a person who has a high salary or is otherwise prominent. [perhaps from the decapitation by Tarquin, king of Rome, of the tallest poppies in his garden, to indicate the fate of the most prominent citizens of Gabii]

tall poppy syndrome *n. Austral. informal.* a tendency to disparage any person who has achieved great prominence or wealth.

tall ship *n.* any square-rigged sailing ship.

tally (ˈtælɪ) *vb.* **-lies, -lying, -lied. 1.** (*intr.*) to correspond one with the other: *the two stories don't tally.* **2.** (*tr.*) to supply with an identifying tag. **3.** (*intr.*) to keep score. **4.** (*tr.*) *Obsolete.* to record or mark. ~*n., pl.* **-lies. 5.** any record of debit, credit, the score in a game, etc. **6.** a ticket, label, or mark, used as a means of identification, classification, etc. **7.** a counterpart or duplicate of something, such as the counterfoil of a cheque. **8.** a stick used (esp. formerly) as a record of the amount of a debt according to the notches cut in it. **9.** a notch or mark cut in or made on such a stick. **10.** a mark or number of marks used to represent a certain number in counting. **11.** *Austral. and N.Z.* the total number of sheep shorn by one shearer in a specified period of time. [C15: from Medieval Latin *tālea,* from Latin: a stick; related to Latin *tālus* heel] —ˈ**tallier** *n.*

tally clerk *n.* a person, esp. on a wharf or dock or in an airport, who checks the count of goods being loaded or unloaded.

tally-ho (ˌtælɪˈhəʊ) *interj.* **1.** the cry of a participant at a hunt to encourage the hounds when the quarry is sighted. ~*n., pl.* **-hos. 2.** an instance of crying tally-ho. **3.** another name for a **four-in-hand** (sense 1). ~*vb.* **-hos, -hoing, -hoed** *or* **-ho'd. 4.** (*intr.*) to make the cry of tally-ho. [C18: perhaps from French *taïaut* cry used in hunting]

tallyman (ˈtælɪmən) *n., pl.* **-men. 1.** a scorekeeper or recorder. **2.** *Dialect.* a travelling salesman for a firm specializing in hire-purchase. —ˈ**tally,woman** *fem. n.*

Talmud (ˈtælmʊd) *n. Judaism.* **1.** the primary source of Jewish religious law, consisting of the Mishnah and the Gemara. **2.** either of two recensions of this compilation, the Palestinian Talmud of about 375 A.D., or the longer and more important Babylonian Talmud of about 500 A.D. [C16: from Hebrew *talmūdh,* literally: instruction, from *lāmadh* to learn] —**Talˈmudic** *or* **Talˈmudical** *adj.* —ˈ**Talmudism** *n.*

Talmudist (ˈtælmʊdɪst) *n.* **1.** a scholar specializing in the study of the Talmud. **2.** any of the writers of or contributors to the Talmud.

talon (ˈtælən) *n.* **1.** a sharply hooked claw, esp. of a bird of prey. **2.** anything resembling a bird's claw. **3.** the part of a lock that the key presses on when it is turned. **4.** *Piquet, etc.* the pile of cards left after the deal. **5.** *Architect.* another name for **ogee. 6.** *Stock Exchange.* a printed slip attached to some bearer bonds to enable the holder to apply for a new sheet of coupons. [C14: from Old French: heel, from Latin *tālus* heel] —ˈ**taloned** *adj.*

taluk (ˈtɑːlʊk, tɑːˈlʊk), **taluka,** *or* **talooka** (tɑːˈluːkə) *n.* (in India) **1.** a subdivision of a district; a group of several villages organized for revenue purposes. **2.** a hereditary estate. [C18: from Urdu *ta' alluk* estate, ultimately from Arabic]

talus[1] (ˈteɪləs) *n., pl.* **-li** (-laɪ). the bone of the ankle that articulates with the leg bones to form the ankle joint. Nontechnical name: **anklebone.** [C18: from Latin: ankle]

talus[2] (ˈteɪləs) *n., pl.* **-luses. 1.** *Geology.* another name for **scree. 2.** *Fortifications.* the sloping side of a wall. [C17: from French, from Latin *talūtium* slope, perhaps of Iberian origin]

talweg (ˈtɑːlvɛg) *n.* a variant spelling of **thalweg.**

tam (tæm) *n.* short for **tam-o'-shanter.**

tamale (təˈmɑːlɪ) *n.* a Mexican dish made of minced meat mixed with crushed maize and seasonings, wrapped in maize husks and steamed. [C19: erroneously for *tamal,* from Mexican Spanish, from Nahuatl *tamalli*]

tamandua (ˌtæmənˈdʊə) *or* **tamandu** (ˈtæmənˌduː) *n.* a small toothless arboreal edentate mammal, *Tamandua tetradactyla,* of Central and South America, having a prehensile tail and tubular mouth specialized for feeding on termites: family *Myrmecophagidae.* Also called: **lesser anteater.** [C17: via Portuguese from Tupi: ant trapper, from *taixi* ant + *mondê* to catch]

tamarack (ˈtæməˌræk) *n.* **1.** any of several North American larches, esp. *Larix laricina,* which has reddish-brown bark, bluish-green needle-like leaves, and shiny oval cones. **2.** the wood of any of these trees. [C19: from Algonquian]

tamarau *or* **tamarao** (ˈtæməˌraʊ) *n.* a small rare member of the cattle tribe, *Anoa mindorensis,* of lowland areas of Mindora in the Philippines. Compare **anoa.** [from Tagalog *tamaráw*]

tamari (təˈmɒːrɪ) *n.* a Japanese variety of soy sauce. [Japanese]

tamarillo (ˌtæməˈrɪləʊ) *n., pl.* **-los.** another name for **tree tomato.**

tamarin (ˈtæmərɪn) *n.* any of numerous small monkeys of the genera *Saguinus* (or *Leontocebus*) and *Leontideus,* of South and Central American forests; similar to the marmosets: family *Callithricidae.* [C18: via French from Galibi]

tamarind (ˈtæmərɪnd) *n.* **1.** a caesalpiniaceous tropical evergreen tree, *Tamarindus indica,* having pale yellow red-streaked flowers and brown pulpy pods, each surrounded by a brittle shell. **2.** the acid fruit of this tree, used as a food and to make beverages and medicines. **3.** the wood of this tree. [C16: from Medieval Latin *tamarindus,* ultimately from Arabic *tamr hindī* Indian date, from *tamr* date + *hindī* Indian, from *Hind* India]

tamarisk (ˈtæmərɪsk) *n.* any of various ornamental trees and shrubs of the genus *Tamarix,* of the Mediterranean region and S and SE Asia, having scalelike leaves, slender branches, and feathery clusters of pink or whitish flowers: family *Tamaricaceae.* [C15: from Late Latin *tamariscus,* from Latin *tamarix*]

tamasha (təˈmɑːʃə) *n.* (in India) a show; entertainment. [C17: via Urdu from Arabic: a stroll, saunter]

tambac (ˈtæmbæk) *n.* a variant spelling of **tombac.**

tambour (ˈtæmbʊə) *n.* **1.** *Real Tennis.* the sloping buttress on one side of the receiver's end of the court. **2.** a small round embroidery frame, consisting of two concentric hoops over which the fabric is stretched while being worked. **3.** embroidered work done on such a frame. **4.** a sliding door on desks, cabinets, etc., made of thin strips of wood glued side by side onto a canvas backing. **5.** *Architect.* a wall that is circular in plan, esp. one that supports a dome or one that is surrounded by a colonnade. **6.** a drum. ~*vb.* **7.** to embroider (fabric or a design) on a tambour. [C15: from French, from *tabour* TABOR]

tamboura (tæm'bʊərə) *n.* an instrument with a long neck, four strings, and no frets, used in Indian music to provide a drone. [from Persian *tanbūr*, from Arabic *tunbūr*]

tambourin ('tæmbʊrɪn) *n.* **1.** an 18th-century Provençal folk dance. **2.** a piece of music composed for or in the rhythm of this dance. **3.** a small drum. [C18: from French: a little drum, from TAMBOUR]

tambourine (ˌtæmbə'riːn) *n. Music.* a percussion instrument consisting of a single drumhead of skin stretched over a circular wooden frame hung with pairs of metal discs that jingle when it is struck or shaken. [C16: from Middle Flemish *tamborijn* a little drum, from Old French: TAMBOURIN] —ˌ**tambou'rinist** *n.*

tame (teɪm) *adj.* **1.** changed by man from a naturally wild state into a tractable, domesticated, or cultivated condition. **2.** (of animals) not fearful of human contact. **3.** lacking in spirit or initiative; meek or submissive: *a tame personality.* **4.** flat, insipid, or uninspiring: *a tame ending to a book.* **5.** slow-moving: *a tame current.* ~*vb.* (*tr.*) **6.** to make tame; domesticate. **7.** to break the spirit of, subdue, or curb. **8.** to tone down, soften, or mitigate. [Old English *tam*; related to Old Norse *tamr*, Old High German *zam*] —'**tamable** *or* '**tameable** *adj.* —ˌ**tama'bility,** ˌ**tamea'bility** *or* '**tamableness,** '**tameableness** *n.* —'**tameless** *adj.* —'**tamely** *adv.* —'**tameness** *n.* —'**tamer** *n.*

Tamil ('tæmɪl) *n.* **1.** (*pl.* **-ils** *or* **-il**) a member of a mixed Dravidian and Caucasoid people of S India and Sri Lanka. **2.** the language of this people: the state language of Tamil Nadu, also spoken in Sri Lanka and elsewhere, belonging to the Dravidian family of languages. ~*adj.* **3.** of or relating to this people or their language.

tamis ('tæmɪ, -ɪs) *n., pl.* **-ises** (-ɪz, -ɪsɪz). a less common word for **tammy**[3] (sense 1).

tammar ('tæmə) *n.* a small scrub wallaby, *Macropus eugenii*, of Australia, having a thick dark-coloured coat. [C19: from a native Australian language]

Tammuz ('tæmuːz, -ʊz) *n.* (in the Jewish calendar) the fourth month of the year according to biblical reckoning and the tenth month of the civil year, usually falling within June and July. [from Hebrew]

tammy[1] ('tæmɪ) *n., pl.* **-mies.** a glazed woollen or mixed fabric, used for linings, undergarments, etc. [C17: of unknown origin]

tammy[2] ('tæmɪ) *n., pl.* **-mies.** another word for **tam-o'-shanter.**

tammy[3] ('tæmɪ) *n., pl.* **-mies.** **1.** Also called: **tammy cloth, tamis.** (esp. formerly) a rough-textured woollen cloth used for straining sauces, soups, etc. ~*vb.* **-mies, -mying, -mied.** **2.** (*tr.*) (esp. formerly) to strain (sauce, soup, etc.) through a tammy. [C18: changed (through influence of TAMMY[1]) from French *tamis*, perhaps of Celtic origin; compare Breton *tamouez* strainer]

tam-o'-shanter (ˌtæmə'ʃæntə) *n.* a Scottish brimless wool cap with a bobble in the centre, usually worn pulled down at one side. Also called: **tam, tammy.** [C19: named after the hero of Robert Burns' poem *Tam o' Shanter* (1790)]

tamp[1] (tæmp) *vb.* (*tr.*) **1.** to force or pack down firmly by repeated blows. **2.** to pack sand, earth, etc. into (a drill hole) over an explosive. [C17: probably a back formation from *tampin* (obsolete variant of TAMPION), which was taken as being a present participle *tamping*]

tamp[2] (tæmp) *vb. South Wales dialect.* **1.** (*tr.*) to bounce (a ball). **2.** (*intr.*; usually foll. by *down*) to pour with rain. [probably special use of TAMP[1]]

tamper[1] ('tæmpə) *vb.* (*intr.*) **1.** (usually foll. by *with*) to interfere or meddle. **2.** to use corrupt practices such as bribery or blackmail. **3.** (usually foll. by *with*) to attempt to influence or corrupt, esp. by bribery: *to tamper with the jury.* [C16: alteration of TEMPER (vb.)] —'**tamperer** *n.*

tamper[2] ('tæmpə) *n.* **1.** a person or thing that tamps, esp. an instrument for packing down tobacco in a pipe. **2.** a casing around the core of a nuclear weapon to increase its efficiency by reflecting neutrons and delaying the expansion.

tamping *or* **tamping mad** ('tæmpɪŋ) *adj.* (*postpositive*) *South Wales dialect.* very angry. [see TAMP[1]]

tampion ('tæmpɪən) *or* **tompion** *n.* a plug placed in a gun's muzzle when the gun is not in use to keep out moisture and dust. [C15: from French: TAMPON]

tampon ('tæmpɒn) *n.* **1.** a plug of lint, cotton wool, cotton, etc., inserted into an open wound or body cavity to stop the flow of blood, absorb secretions, etc., esp. one inserted into the vagina to absorb menstrual blood. ~*vb.* **2.** (*tr.*) to plug (a wound, etc.) with a tampon. [C19: via French from Old French *tapon* a little plug, from *tape* a plug, of Germanic origin] —'**tamponage** *n.*

tam-tam *n.* another name for **gong** (sense 1). [from Hindi: see TOM-TOM]

tamworth ('tæmwəθ) *n.* (*often cap.*) any of a hardy breed of long-bodied reddish pigs. [named after *Tamworth* in Staffordshire, where it was developed]

tan[1] (tæn) *n.* **1.** the brown colour produced by the skin after intensive exposure to ultraviolet rays, esp. those of the sun. **2.** a light or moderate yellowish-brown colour. **3.** short for **tanbark.** ~*vb.* **tans, tanning, tanned.** **4.** to go brown or cause to go brown after exposure to ultraviolet rays: *she tans easily.* **5.** to convert (a skin or hide) into leather by treating it with a tanning agent, such as vegetable tannins, chromium salts, fish oils, or formaldehyde. **6.** (*tr.*) *Slang.* to beat or flog. ~*adj.* **tanner, tannest.** **7.** of the colour tan: *tan gloves.* **8.** used in or relating to tanning. [Old English *tannian* (unattested as infinitive, attested as *getanned*, past participle), from Medieval Latin *tannāre*, from *tannum* tanbark, perhaps of Celtic origin; compare Irish *tana* thin] —'**tannable** *adj.* —'**tannish** *adj.*

tan[2] (tæn) *abbrev. for* tangent (sense 2).

tana ('tɑːnə) *n.* **1.** a small Madagascan lemur, *Phaner furcifer.* **2.** a large tree shrew, *Tupaia tana*, of Sumatra and Borneo. [C19: from Malay *tūpai tana* ground squirrel]

Tanach *Hebrew.* (ta'nax) *n.* the Hebrew Bible as used by Jews, divided into the Torah, Prophets, and Hagiographa. [from Hebrew, acronym formed from *torāh* (the Pentateuch), *nebi'im* (the prophets), and *ketūbim* (the Hagiographa)]

tanager ('tænədʒə) *n.* any American songbird of the family *Thraupidae*, having a short thick bill and a brilliantly coloured male plumage. [C19: from New Latin *tanagra*, based on Tupi *tangara*]

Tanagra ('tænəgrə) *n.* any of the terracotta figurines first discovered in the ancient Greek Boeotian town of Tanagra.

tanbark ('tænˌbɑːk) *n.* the bark of certain trees, esp. the oak and hemlock, used as a source of tannin. Often shortened to **tan.**

T & E *abbrev. for* tired and emotional, a euphemism for slightly drunk.

tandem ('tændəm) *n.* **1.** a bicycle with two sets of pedals and two saddles, arranged one behind the other for two riders. **2.** a two-wheeled carriage drawn by two horses harnessed one behind the other. **3.** a team of two horses so harnessed. **4.** any arrangement of two things in which one is placed behind the other. **5.** **in tandem.** together or in conjunction. ~*adj.* **6.** *Brit.* used as, used in, or routed through an intermediate automatic telephone exchange: *a tandem exchange.* ~*adv.* **7.** one behind the other: *to ride tandem.* [C18: whimsical use of Latin *tandem* at length, to indicate a vehicle of elongated appearance]

tandem roller *n.* a type of road roller in which the front and back wheels consist of rollers of about the same diameter.

T & G *abbrev. for* Transport and General Workers' Union.

tandoori (tæn'dʊərɪ) *n.* **a.** an Indian method of cooking meat or vegetables on a spit in a clay oven. **b.** (*as modifier*): *tandoori chicken.* [from Urdu, from *tandoor* an oven]

tang (tæŋ) *n.* **1.** a strong taste or flavour: *the tang of the sea.* **2.** a pungent or characteristic smell: *the tang of peat fires.* **3.** a trace, touch, or hint of something: *a tang of cloves in the apple pie.* **4.** the pointed end of a tool, such as a chisel, file, knife, etc., which is fitted into a handle, shaft, or stock. [C14: from Old Norse *tangi* point; related to Danish *tange* point, spit]

Tang (tæŋ) *adj.* of, relating to, or characteristic of the imperial dynasty of China from 618 to 907 A.D.

tanga ('tæŋgə) *n.* a type of very brief bikini.

tangelo ('tændʒəˌləʊ) *n., pl.* **-los.** **1.** a hybrid produced by crossing a tangerine tree with a grapefruit tree. **2.** the fruit of this hybrid, having orange acid-tasting flesh. [C20: from TANG(ERINE) + (POM)ELO]

tangent ('tændʒənt) *n.* **1.** a geometric line, curve, plane, or curved surface that touches another curve or surface at one point but does not intersect it. **2.** (of an angle) a trigonometric function that in a right-angled triangle is the ratio of the length of the opposite side to that of the adjacent side; the ratio of sine to cosine. Abbrev.: **tan.** **3.** the straight part on a survey line between curves. **4.** *Music.* a part of the action of a clavichord consisting of a small piece of metal that strikes the string and curtails its vibrations almost immediately. **5.** **on** *or* **at a tangent.** on a completely different or divergent course, esp. of thought: *to go off at a tangent.* ~*adj.* **6.** **a.** of or involving a tangent. **b.** touching at a single point. **7.** touching. **8.** almost irrelevant. [C16: from Latin phrase *līnea tangēns* the touching line, from *tangere* to touch] —'**tangency** *n.*

tangent galvanometer *n.* a type of galvanometer having a vertical coil of wire with a horizontal magnetic needle at its centre. The current to be measured is passed through the coil and produces a proportional magnetic field which deflects the needle.

tangential (tæn'dʒɛnʃəl) *adj.* **1.** of, being, relating to, or in the direction of a tangent. **2.** Also: **transverse.** *Astronomy.* (of velocity) in a direction perpendicular to the line of sight of a celestial object. Compare **radial** (sense 6). **3.** of superficial relevance only; digressive. —**tanˌgenti'ality** *n.* —**tan'gentially** *or* **tan'gentally** *adv.*

tangerine (ˌtændʒə'riːn) *n.* **1.** an Asian citrus tree, *Citrus reticulata*, cultivated for its small edible orange-like fruits. **2.** the fruit of this tree, having a loose rind and sweet spicy flesh. **3.** **a.** a reddish-orange colour. **b.** (*as adj.*): *a tangerine door.* [C19: from *Tangier*]

Tangerine (ˌtændʒə'riːn) *n.* **1.** a native or inhabitant of Tangier, a port in N Morocco. ~*adj.* **2.** of or relating to Tangier.

tangi ('tʌŋiː) *n., pl.* **-gis.** *N.Z.* **1.** a Maori funeral ceremony. **2.** *Informal.* a lamentation. [Maori]

tangible ('tændʒəbᵊl) *adj.* **1.** capable of being touched or felt; having real substance: *a tangible object.* **2.** capable of being clearly grasped by the mind; substantial rather than imaginary: *tangible evidence.* **3.** having a physical existence; corporeal: *tangible assets.* ~*n.* **4.** (*often pl.*) a tangible thing or asset. [C16:

from Late Latin *tangibilis,* from Latin *tangere* to touch] —ˌ**tangi'bility** *or* '**tangibleness** *n.* —'**tangibly** *adv.*

tangle[1] ('tæŋgᵊl) *n.* **1.** a confused or complicated mass of hairs, lines, fibres, etc., knotted or coiled together. **2.** a complicated problem, condition, or situation. ~*vb.* **3.** to become or cause to become twisted together in a confused mass. **4.** (*intr.;* often foll. by *with*) to come into conflict; contend: *to tangle with the police.* **5.** (*tr.*) to involve in matters which hinder or confuse: *to tangle someone in a shady deal.* **6.** (*tr.*) to ensnare or trap, as in a net. [C14 *tangilen,* variant of *tagilen,* probably of Scandinavian origin; related to Swedish dialect *taggla* to entangle] —'**tanglement** *n.* —'**tangler** *n.* —'**tangly** *adj.*

tangle[2] *or* **tangle weed** ('tæŋgᵊl) *n.* alternative names (esp. Scot.) for **oarweed.** [C16: of Scandinavian origin: compare Danish *tang* seaweed]

tango ('tæŋgəʊ) *n., pl.* **-gos. 1.** a Latin American dance in duple time, characterized by long gliding steps and sudden pauses. **2.** a piece of music composed for or in the rhythm of this dance. ~*vb.* **-goes, -going, -goed. 3.** (*intr.*) to perform this dance. [C20: from American Spanish, probably of Niger-Congo origin; compare Ibibio *tamgu* to dance] —'**tangoist** *n.*

Tango ('tæŋgəʊ) *n. Communications.* a code word for the letter *t.*

tangram ('tæŋgræm) *n.* a Chinese puzzle in which a square, cut into a parallelogram, a square, and five triangles, is formed into figures. [C19: perhaps from Chinese *t'ang* Chinese + -GRAM]

tangy ('tæŋɪ) *adj.* **tangier, tangiest.** having a pungent, fresh, or briny flavour or aroma: *a tangy sea breeze.*

tanh (θæn, tænʃ) *n.* hyperbolic tangent; a hyperbolic function that is the ratio of sinh to cosh. [C20: from TAN(GENT) + H(YPERBOLIC)]

tanist ('tænɪst) *n. History.* the heir apparent of a Celtic chieftain chosen by election during the chief's lifetime: usually the worthiest of his kin. [C16: from Irish Gaelic *tánaiste,* literally: the second person] —'**tanistry** *n.*

taniwha ('tʌniːfɑː, 'tænəwɑː) *n. N.Z.* a legendary Maori monster. [Maori]

tank (tæŋk) *n.* **1.** a large container or reservoir for the storage of liquids or gases: *tanks for storing oil.* **2. a.** an armoured combat vehicle moving on tracks and armed with guns, etc. **b.** (*as modifier*): *a tank commander; a tank brigade.* **3.** *Brit. or U.S. dialect.* a reservoir, lake, or pond. **4.** *Photog.* **a.** a light-tight container inside which a film can be processed in daylight, the solutions and rinsing waters being poured in and out without light entering. **b.** any large dish or container used for processing a number of strips or sheets of film. **5.** *Slang, chiefly U.S.* **a.** a jail. **b.** a jail cell. **6.** Also called: **tankful.** the quantity contained in a tank. **7.** *Austral.* a dam formed by excavation. ~*vb.* **8.** (*tr.*) to put or keep in a tank. **9.** (*intr.*) to move like a tank, esp. heavily and rapidly. **10.** *Slang.* to defeat heavily. ~See also **tank up.** [C17: from Gujarati *tānkh* artificial lake, but influenced also by Portuguese *tanque,* from *estanque* pond, from *estancar* to dam up, from Vulgar Latin *stanticāre* (unattested) to block, STANCH] —'**tankless** *adj.* —'**tank,like** *adj.*

tanka ('tɑːŋkə) *n., pl.* **-kas** *or* **-ka.** a Japanese verse form consisting of five lines, the first and third having five syllables, the others seven. [C19: from Japanese, from *tan* short + *ka* verse]

tankage ('tæŋkɪdʒ) *n.* **1.** the capacity or contents of a tank or tanks. **2.** the act of storing in a tank or tanks, or a fee charged for such storage. **3.** *Agriculture.* **a.** fertilizer consisting of the dried and ground residues of animal carcasses. **b.** a protein supplement feed for livestock.

tankard ('tæŋkəd) *n.* **a.** a large one-handled drinking vessel, commonly made of silver, pewter, or glass, sometimes fitted with a hinged lid. **b.** the quantity contained in a tankard. [C14: related to Middle Dutch *tankaert,* French *tanquart*]

tank engine *or* **locomotive** *n.* a steam locomotive that carries its water supply in tanks mounted around its boiler.

tanker ('tæŋkə) *n.* a ship, lorry, or aeroplane designed to carry liquid in bulk, such as oil.

tank farming *n.* another name for **hydroponics.** —**tank farmer** *n.*

tank top *n.* a sleeveless upper garment with wide shoulder straps and a low neck, usually worn over a shirt, blouse, or jumper. [C20: named after *tank suits,* one-piece bathing costumes of the 1920s worn in tanks or swimming pools]

tank trap *n.* any obstacle, such as a number of concrete stumps set in the ground, designed to stop a military tank.

tank up *vb.* (*adv.*) *Chiefly Brit.* **1.** to fill the tank of (a vehicle) with petrol. **2.** *Slang.* to imbibe or cause to imbibe a large quantity of alcoholic drink.

tank wagon *or esp. U.S. and Canadian* **tank car** *n.* a form of railway wagon carrying a tank for the transport of liquids.

tannage ('tænɪdʒ) *n.* **1.** the act or process of tanning. **2.** a skin or hide that has been tanned.

tannate ('tæneɪt) *n.* any salt or ester of tannic acid.

tanner[1] ('tænə) *n.* a person who tans skins and hides.

tanner[2] ('tænə) *n. Brit.* (formerly) an informal word for **sixpence.** [C19: of unknown origin]

tannery ('tænərɪ) *n., pl.* **-neries.** a place or building where skins and hides are tanned.

tannic ('tænɪk) *adj.* of, relating to, containing, or produced from tan, tannin, or tannic acid.

tannin ('tænɪn) *n.* any of a class of yellowish or brownish solid compounds found in many plants and used as tanning agents, mordants, medical astringents, etc. Tannins are derivatives of gallic acid with the approximate formula $C_{76}H_{52}O_{46}$. Also called: **tannic acid.** [C19: from French *tanin,* from TAN[1]]

Tannoy ('tænɔɪ) *n. Trademark.* a sound-amplifying apparatus used as a public-address system esp. in a large building, such as a university.

tansy ('tænzɪ) *n., pl.* **-sies. 1.** any of numerous plants of the genus *Tanacetum,* esp. *T. vulgare,* having yellow flowers in flat-topped clusters and formerly used in medicine and for seasoning: family *Compositae* (composites). **2.** any of various similar plants. [C15: from Old French *tanesie,* from Medieval Latin *athanasia* tansy (with reference to its alleged power to prolong life), from Greek: immortality]

tantalate ('tæntəˌleɪt) *n.* any of various salts of tantalic acid formed when the pentoxide of tantalum dissolves in an alkali.

tantalic (tæn'tælɪk) *adj.* of or containing tantalum, esp. in the pentavalent state.

tantalic acid *n.* a white gelatinous substance produced by hydrolysis of tantalic halides. It dissolves in strong bases to give tantalates.

tantalite ('tæntəˌlaɪt) *n.* a heavy brownish mineral consisting of a tantalum oxide of iron and manganese in orthorhombic crystalline form: it occurs in coarse granite, often with columbite, and is an ore of tantalum. Formula: $(Fe,Mn)(Ta,Nb)_2O_6$. [C19: from TANTALUM + -ITE[1]]

tantalize *or* **tantalise** ('tæntəˌlaɪz) *vb.* (*tr.*) to tease or make frustrated, as by tormenting with the sight of something greatly desired but inaccessible. [C16: from the punishment of *Tantalus,* legendary Greek king condemned to stand in water that receded when he tried to drink] —ˌ**tantali'zation** *or* ˌ**tantali'sation** *n.* —'**tantaˌlizer** *or* '**tantaˌliser** *n.* —'**tantaˌlizing** *or* '**tantaˌlising** *adj.* —'**tantaˌlizingly** *or* '**tantaˌlisingly** *adv.*

tantalous ('tæntələs) *adj.* of or containing tantalum in the trivalent state. [C19: from TANTAL(UM) + -OUS]

tantalum ('tæntələm) *n.* a hard greyish-white metallic element that occurs with niobium in tantalite and columbite: used in electrolytic components and in alloys to increase hardness and chemical resistance, esp. in surgical instruments. Symbol: Ta; atomic no.: 73; atomic wt.: 180.95; valency: 2, 3, 4, or 5; relative density: 16.65; melting pt.: 2996°C; boiling pt.: 5425°C. [C19: named after *Tantalus,* with reference to the metal's incapacity to absorb acids; see TANTALIZE]

tantalus ('tæntələs) *n. Brit.* a case in which bottles may be locked with their contents tantalizingly visible.

tantamount ('tæntəˌmaʊnt) *adj.* (*postpositive;* foll. by *to*) as good (as); equivalent in effect (to): *his statement was tantamount to an admission of guilt.* [C17: basically from Anglo-French *tant amunter* to amount to as much, from *tant* so much + *amunter* to AMOUNT]

tantara ('tæntərə, tæn'tɑːrə) *n.* a fanfare or blast, as on a trumpet or horn. [C16: from Latin *taratantara,* imitative of the sound of the tuba]

tantivy (tæn'tɪvɪ) *adv.* **1.** at full speed; rapidly. ~*n., pl.* **-tivies,** *interj.* **2.** a hunting cry, esp. at full gallop. [C17: perhaps imitative of galloping hooves]

tant mieux *French.* (tɑ̃ mjø) so much the better.

tanto ('tæntəʊ; *Italian* 'tanto) *adv.* too much; excessively: *allegro ma non tanto.* See **non troppo.** [C19: from Italian, from Latin *tantum* so much]

tant pis *French.* (tɑ̃ pi) so much the worse.

Tantra ('tæntrə, 'tʌn-) *n. Hinduism, Buddhism.* the sacred books of Tantrism, written between the 7th and 17th centuries A.D., mainly in the form of a dialogue between the god Siva and his wife. [C18: from Sanskrit: warp, hence underlying principle, from *tanoti* he weaves]

Tantrism ('tæntrɪzəm) *n.* **1.** a movement within Hinduism combining magical and mystical elements and with sacred writings of its own. **2.** a similar movement within Buddhism. [C18: from Sanskrit *tantra,* literally: warp, hence, doctrine] —'**Tantric** *adj.* —'**Tantrist** *n.*

tantrum ('tæntrəm) *n.* (*often pl.*) a childish fit of rage; outburst of bad temper. [C18: of unknown origin]

Tanzanian (ˌtænzə'nɪən) *adj.* **1.** of or relating to Tanzania, a republic in E Africa, or to its people or culture. ~*n.* **2.** a native or inhabitant of Tanzania.

Tao (taʊ) *n.* (in the philosophy of Taoism) **1.** that in virtue of which all things happen or exist. **2.** the rational basis of human conduct. **3.** the course of life and its relation to eternal truth. [Chinese, literally: path, way]

Taoiseach ('tiːʃæx) *n.* the prime minister of the Republic of Ireland. [from Irish Gaelic, literally: leader]

Taoism ('taʊɪzəm) *n.* a popular Chinese system of religion and philosophy based on the teachings of the Chinese philosopher Lao Zi (?604–?531 B.C.), which advocates a simple honest life and noninterference with the course of natural events. —'**Taoist** *n., adj.* —**Tao'istic** *adj.*

taonga (tɑ'ɔŋgə) *n. N.Z.* anything highly prized. [Maori]

tap[1] (tæp) *vb.* **taps, tapping, tapped. 1.** to strike (something) lightly and usually repeatedly: *to tap the table; to tap on the table.* **2.** (*tr.*) to produce by striking in this way: *to tap a rhythm.* **3.** (*tr.*) to strike lightly with (something): *to tap one's finger on the desk.*

4. (*intr.*) to walk with a tapping sound: *she tapped across the floor.* 5. (*tr.*) to attach metal or leather reinforcing pieces to (the toe or heel of a shoe). ~*n.* 6. a light blow or knock, or the sound made by it. 7. the metal piece attached to the toe or heel of a shoe used for tap-dancing. 8. short for **tap-dancing.** 9. *Phonetics.* the contact made between the tip of the tongue and the alveolar ridge as the tongue is flicked upwards in the execution of a flap or vibrates rapidly in the execution of a trill or roll. ~See also **taps.** [C13 *tappen,* probably from Old French *taper,* of Germanic origin; related to Middle Low German *tappen* to pluck, Swedish dialect *täpa* to tap] —'**tappable** *adj.*

tap[2] (tæp) *n.* 1. a valve by which a fluid flow from a pipe can be controlled by opening and closing an orifice. U.S. name: **faucet.** 2. a stopper to plug a cask or barrel and enable the contents to be drawn out in a controlled flow. 3. a particular quality of alcoholic drink, esp. when contained in casks: *an excellent tap.* 4. *Brit.* short for **taproom.** 5. the surgical withdrawal of fluid from a bodily cavity: *a spinal tap.* 6. Also called: **screw tap.** a tool for cutting female screw threads, consisting of a threaded steel cylinder with longitudinal grooves forming cutting edges. Compare **die**[2] (sense 2). 7. *Electronics, chiefly U.S. and Canadian.* a connection made at some point between the end terminals of an inductor, resistor, or some other component. Usual Brit. name: **tapping.** 8. *Stock Exchange.* **a.** an issue of a government security released slowly onto the market when its market price reaches a predetermined level. **b.** (*as modifier*): *tap stock; tap issue.* 9. a concealed listening or recording device connected to a telephone or telegraph wire for the purpose of obtaining information secretly. 10. **on tap. a.** *Informal.* ready for immediate use. **b.** (of drinks) on draught. ~*vb.* **taps, tapping, tapped.** (*tr.*) 11. to furnish with a tap. 12. to draw off with or as if with a tap. 13. to cut into (a tree) and draw off sap from it. 14. *Brit. informal.* to ask or beg (someone) for money: *he tapped me for a fiver.* 15. **a.** to connect a tap to (a telephone or telegraph wire). **b.** to listen in secret to (a telephone message, etc.) by means of a tap. 16. to make a connection to (a pipe, drain, etc.). 17. to cut a female screw thread in (an object or material) by use of a tap. 18. to withdraw (fluid) from (a bodily cavity). [Old English *tæppa;* related to Old Norse *tappi* tap, Old High German *zapfo*] —'**tappable** *adj.* —'**tapper** *n.*

tap[3] (tæp) *n., vb.* a Scot. word for **top**[1].

tapa ('tɑːpə) *n.* 1. the inner bark of the paper mulberry. 2. a paper-like cloth made from this in the Pacific islands. [C19: from Marquesan and Tahitian]

tapadera (ˌtæpə'dɛərə) *n.* the leather covering for the stirrup on an American saddle. [via American Spanish from Spanish: cover, from *tapar* to cover, of Germanic origin; compare TAMPON, TAP[2]]

tap dance *n.* 1. a step dance in which the performer wears shoes equipped with taps that make a rhythmic sound on the stage as he dances. ~*vb.* **tap-dance.** (*intr.*) 2. to perform a tap dance. —'**tap-ˌdancer** *n.* —'**tap-ˌdancing** *n.*

tape (teɪp) *n.* 1. a long thin strip, made of cotton, linen, etc., used for binding, fastening, etc. 2. any long narrow strip of cellulose, paper, metal, etc., having similar uses. 3. a string stretched across the track at the end of a race course. 4. *Military slang, chiefly Brit.* another word for **stripe**[1] (sense 3). 5. See **magnetic tape, ticker tape, paper tape, tape recording.** ~*vb.* (*mainly tr.*) 6. to furnish with tapes. 7. to bind, measure, secure, or wrap with tape. 8. (*usually passive*) *Brit. informal.* to take stock of (a person or situation); sum up: *he's got the job taped.* 9. (*also intr.*) Also: **tape-record.** to record (speech, music, etc.). [Old English *tæppe;* related to Old Frisian *tapia* to pull, Middle Dutch *tapen* to tear] —'**tapeˌlike** *adj.* —'**taper** *n.*

tape deck *n.* the platform supporting the spools, cassettes, or cartridges of a tape recorder, incorporating the motor or motors that drive them and the playback, recording, and erasing heads. Sometimes shortened to **deck.**

tape echo *n.* a means of delaying the repeat of a sound by adjusting the time lapse between the recording and playback heads of a tape recorder. Also called: **tape slap.**

tape grass *n.* any of several submerged freshwater plants of the genus *Vallisneria,* esp. *V. spiralis,* of warm temperate regions, having ribbon-like leaves: family *Hydrocharitaceae.*

tape machine *n. Stock Exchange.* a telegraphic receiving device that records current stock quotations electronically or on ticker tape. U.S. equivalent: **ticker.**

tape measure *n.* a tape or length of metal marked off in inches, centimetres, etc., used principally for measuring and fitting garments. Also called (esp. U.S.): '**tapeˌline.**

taper ('teɪpə) *vb.* 1. to become or cause to become narrower towards one end: *the spire tapers to a point.* 2. (often foll. by *off*) to become or cause to become smaller or less significant. ~*n.* 3. a thin candle. 4. a thin wooden or waxed strip for transferring a flame; spill. 5. a narrowing. 6. *Engineering.* (in conical parts) the amount of variation in the diameter per unit of length. 7. any feeble source of light. [Old English *tapor,* probably from Latin *papȳrus* PAPYRUS (from its use as a wick)] —'**taperer** *n.* —'**tapering** *adj.* —'**taperingly** *adv.*

tape-record *vb.* to make a tape recording (of).

tape recorder *n.* an electrical device used for recording sounds on magnetic tape and usually also for reproducing them, consisting of a tape deck and one or more amplifiers and loudspeakers.

tape recording *n.* 1. the act or process of recording on magnetic tape. 2. the magnetized tape used in making such a recording. 3. the speech, music, etc., so recorded.

tapered roller bearing *n. Engineering.* a rolling bearing that uses tapered rollers running in coned races and is able to accept axial thrust as well as providing shaft location. Compare **thrust bearing.**

taper pin *n.* a short round metal rod having a small amount of taper so that when driven into a hole it tightens on the taper so that it can act as a stop or wedge.

tape slap *n.* another term for **tape echo.**

tapestry ('tæpɪstrɪ) *n., pl.* **-tries.** 1. a heavy ornamental fabric, often in the form of a picture, used for wall hangings, furnishings, etc., and made by weaving coloured threads into a fixed warp. 2. another word for **needlepoint.** [C15: from Old French *tapisserie* carpeting, from Old French *tapiz* carpet; see TAPIS] —'**tapestried** *adj.* —'**tapestry-ˌlike** *adj.*

tapestry moth *n.* one of the larger tineid moths, *Trichophaga tapetzella,* the larvae of which devour animal fibres. It is brown, with white-tipped forewings, and prefers damp environments.

tape transport *n.* the motorized mechanism that moves tape evenly across the recording and playback heads of a tape recorder or cassette player.

tapetum (tə'piːtəm) *n., pl.* **-ta** (-tə). 1. a layer of nutritive cells in the sporangia of ferns and anthers of flowering plants that surrounds developing spore cells. 2. **a.** a membranous reflecting layer of cells in the choroid of the eye of nocturnal vertebrates. **b.** a similar structure in the eyes of certain nocturnal insects. 3. *Anatomy.* a covering layer of cells. [C18: from New Latin, from Medieval Latin: covering, from Latin *tapēte* carpet, from Greek *tapēs* carpet] —**ta'petal** *adj.*

tapeworm ('teɪpˌwɜːm) *n.* any parasitic ribbon-like flatworm of the class *Cestoda,* having a body divided into many egg-producing segments and lacking a mouth and gut. The adults inhabit the intestines of vertebrates. See also **echinococcus, taenia.**

taphephobia (ˌtæfɪ'fəʊbɪə) *n. Med.* a pathological fear of being buried alive. [from Greek *taphos* grave + -PHOBIA] —ˌ**taphe'phobic** *adj.*

taphole ('tæpˌhəʊl) *n.* a hole in a furnace for running off molten metal or slag.

taphonomy (tə'fɒnəmɪ) *n.* the study of the processes affecting an organism after death that result in its fossilization. [C20: from Greek *taphos* grave + -NOMY] —**taphonomic** (ˌtæfə'nɒmɪk) *or* ˌ**tapho'nomical** *adj.*

taphouse ('tæpˌhaʊs) *n. Now rare.* an inn or bar.

taphrogenesis (ˌtæfrəʊ'dʒɛnɪsɪs) *n. Geology.* vertical movement of the earth's crust, resulting in major faults. [C20: from German *tafrogenese,* from Greek *taphros* pit + -GENESIS]

tapioca (ˌtæpɪ'əʊkə) *n.* a beadlike starch obtained from cassava root, used in cooking as a thickening agent, esp. in puddings. [C18: via Portuguese from Tupi *tipioca* pressed-out juice, from *tipi* residue + *ok* to squeeze out]

tapir ('teɪpə) *n., pl.* **-pirs** *or* **-pir.** any perissodactyl mammal of the genus *Tapirus,* such as *T. indicus* (**Malayan tapir**), of South and Central America and SE Asia, having an elongated snout, three-toed hind legs, and four-toed forelegs: family *Tapiridae.* [C18: from Tupi *tapiira*]

tapis ('tæpiː, 'tæpɪ; *French* tapi) *n., pl.* **tapis.** 1. tapestry or carpeting, esp. as formerly used to cover a table in a council chamber. 2. **on the tapis.** currently under consideration or discussion. [C17: from French, from Old French *tapiz,* from Greek *tapētion* rug, from *tapēs* carpet]

tappet ('tæpɪt) *n.* a mechanical part that reciprocates to receive or transmit intermittent motion, esp. the part of an internal-combustion engine that transmits motion from the camshaft to the push rods or valves. [C18: from TAP[1] + -ET]

tappit-hen ('tæpɪt'hɛn) *n. Scot.* 1. a hen with a crest. 2. a pewter tankard, usually with a distinctive knob on the lid. [C18: from Scottish *tappit* topped, crested + HEN]

taproom ('tæpˌruːm, -ˌrʊm) *n.* a bar, as in a hotel or pub.

taproot ('tæpˌruːt) *n.* the large single root of plants such as the dandelion, which grows vertically downwards and bears smaller lateral roots. [C17: from TAP[2] + ROOT[1]] —'**tapˌrooted** *adj.*

taps (tæps) *n.* (*functioning as sing.*) 1. *Chiefly U.S.* **a.** (in army camps, etc.) a signal given on a bugle, drum, etc., indicating that lights are to be put out. **b.** any similar signal, as at a military funeral. 2. (in the Guide movement) a closing song sung at an evening camp fire or at the end of a meeting. [C19: from TAP[1]]

tapsalteerie ('tæpsəl'tiːrɪ) *adj., adv., n. Scot.* topsy-turvy. [C17: of uncertain origin]

tapster ('tæpstə) *n.* 1. *Rare.* a barman. 2. (in W Africa) a man who taps palm trees to collect and sell palm wine. [Old English *tæppestre,* feminine of *tæppere,* from *tappian* to TAP[2]] —'**tapstress** *fem. n.*

tapu ('tɑːpuː) *adj. N.Z.* sacred; forbidden.

tap water *n.* water drawn off through taps from pipes in a house, as distinguished from distilled water, mineral water, etc.

tar[1] (tɑː) *n.* 1. any of various dark viscid substances obtained by the destructive distillation of organic matter such as coal, wood, or peat. 2. another name for **coal tar.** ~*vb.* **tars, tarring, tarred.** (*tr.*) 3. to coat with tar. 4. **tar and feather.** to punish by smearing tar and feathers over (someone). 5. **tarred with the same brush.** having the same faults. [Old English *teoru;*

related to Old Frisian *tera,* Old Norse *tjara,* Middle Low German *tere* tar, Gothic *triu* tree] —'**tarry** *adj.* —'**tarriness** *n.*

tar[2] (tɑː) *n.* an informal word for **seaman.** [C17: short for TARPAULIN]

taradiddle ('tærəˌdɪdᵊl) *n.* another spelling of **tarradiddle.**

tarakihi ('tærəˌkiːhiː) *or* **terakihi** *n., pl.* **-kihis.** a common edible sea fish of New Zealand waters.

taramasalata (ˌtærəməsə'lɑːtə) *n.* a creamy pale pink pâté, made from the roe of grey mullet or smoked cod and served as an hors d'oeuvre. [C20: from Modern Greek, from *tarama* cod's roe]

Taranaki gate (ˌtærə'nækiː) *n. N.Z.* a rough-and-ready gate in a fence made from wire and battens. [first used on dairy farms in *Taranaki,* province of N.Z.]

tarantass (ˌtɑːrən'tæs) *n.* a large horse-drawn four-wheeled Russian carriage without springs. [C19: from Russian *tarantas,* from Kazan Tatar *taryntas*]

tarantella (ˌtærən'tɛlə) *n.* **1.** a peasant dance from S Italy. **2.** a piece of music composed for or in the rhythm of this dance, in fast six-eight time. [C18: from Italian, from *Taranto,* a port in SE Italy; associated with TARANTISM]

tarantism ('tærənˌtɪzəm) *n.* a nervous disorder marked by uncontrollable bodily movement, widespread in S Italy during the 15th to 17th centuries: popularly thought to be caused by the bite of a tarantula. [C17: from New Latin *tarantismus,* from *Taranto*; see TARANTULA]

tarantula (tə'ræntjʊlə) *n., pl.* **-las** *or* **-lae** (-ˌliː). **1.** any of various large hairy mostly tropical spiders of the American family *Theraphosidae.* **2.** a large hairy spider, *Lycosa tarentula* of S Europe, the bite of which was formerly thought to cause tarantism. [C16: from Medieval Latin, from Old Italian *tarantola,* from *Taranto*]

Tararua biscuit ('tɑːrɑːˌruːə) *n. N.Z. informal.* a tramper's home-made biscuit with a high calorie content.

taraxacum (tə'ræksəkəm) *n.* **1.** any perennial plant of the genus *Taraxacum,* such as the dandelion, having dense heads of small yellow flowers and seeds with a feathery attachment: family *Compositae* (composites). **2.** the dried root of the dandelion, used as a laxative, diuretic, and tonic. [C18: from Medieval Latin, from Arabic *tarakhshaqūn* wild chicory, perhaps of Persian origin]

tarboosh, tarbush, *or* **tarbouche** (tɑː'buːʃ) *n.* a felt or cloth brimless cap resembling the fez, usually red and often with a silk tassel, worn alone or as part of a turban by Muslim men. [C18: from Arabic *tarbūsh*]

tar boy *n. Austral. and N.Z. informal.* a boy who applies tar to the skin of sheep cut during shearing.

Tardenoisian (ˌtɑːdə'nɔɪzɪən) *adj.* of or referring to a Mesolithic culture characterized by small flint instruments. [C20: after *Tardenois,* France, where implements were found]

tardigrade ('tɑːdɪˌgreɪd) *n.* **1.** any minute aquatic segmented eight-legged invertebrate of the phylum *Tardigrada,* related to the arthropods, occurring in soil, ditches, etc. Popular name: **water bear.** ~*adj.* **2.** of, relating to, or belonging to the *Tardigrada.* [C17: via Latin *tardigradus,* from *tardus* sluggish + *gradī* to walk]

tardy ('tɑːdɪ) *adj.* **-dier, -diest. 1.** occurring later than expected: *tardy retribution.* **2.** slow in progress, growth, etc.: *a tardy reader.* [C15: from Old French *tardif,* from Latin *tardus* slow] —'**tardily** *adv.* —'**tardiness** *n.*

tare[1] (tɛə) *n.* **1.** any of various vetch plants, such as *Vicia hirsuta* (**hairy tare**) of Eurasia and N Africa. **2.** the seed of any of these plants. **3.** *Bible.* a troublesome weed, thought to be the darnel. [C14: of unknown origin]

tare[2] (tɛə) *n.* **1.** the weight of the wrapping or container in which goods are packed. **2.** a deduction from gross weight to compensate for this. **3.** the weight of a vehicle unladen with cargo, passengers, etc. **4.** an empty container used as a counterbalance in determining net weight. ~*vb.* **5.** (*tr.*) to weigh (a package, etc.) in order to calculate the amount of tare. [C15: from Old French: waste, from Medieval Latin *tara,* from Arabic *tarhah* something discarded, from *taraha* to reject]

targe (tɑːdʒ) *n.* an archaic word for **shield.** [C13: from Old French, of Germanic origin; related to Old High German *zarga* rim, frame, Old Norse *targa* shield]

target ('tɑːgɪt) *n.* **1. a.** an object or area at which an archer or marksman aims, usually a round flat surface marked with concentric rings. **b.** (*as modifier*): *target practice.* **2. a.** any point or area aimed at; the object of an attack or a takeover bid. **b.** (*as modifier*): *target area; target company.* **3.** a fixed goal or objective: *the target for the appeal is £10 000.* **4.** a person or thing at which an action or remark is directed or the object of a person's feelings: *a target for the teacher's sarcasm.* **5.** a joint of lamb consisting of the breast and neck. **6.** *Surveying.* a marker on which sights are taken, such as the sliding marker on a levelling staff. **7.** (formerly) a small round shield. **8.** *Physics, electronics.* **a.** a substance, object, or system subjected to bombardment by electrons or other particles, or to irradiation. **b.** an electrode in a television camera tube whose surface, on which image information is stored, is scanned by the electron beam. **9.** *Electronics.* an object detected by the reflection of a radar or sonar signal, etc. **10. on target.** on the correct course to meet a target or objective. ~*vb.* **-gets, -geting, -geted.** (*tr.*) **11.** to make a target of. **12.** to direct or aim: *to target benefits at those most in need.* [C14: from Old French *targette* a little shield, from Old French TARGE] —'**targetless** *adj.*

target language *n.* **1.** the language into which a text, document, etc., is translated. **2.** a language that is being or is to be learnt.

target man *n. Soccer.* an attacking player to whom high crosses and centres are played, esp. a tall forward.

Targum ('tɑːgəm; *Hebrew* tar'gum) *n.* an Aramaic translation, usually in the form of an expanded paraphrase, of various books or sections of the Old Testament. [C16: from Aramaic: interpretation] —**Targumic** (tɑː'guːmɪk) *or* **Tar'gumical** *adj.* —'**Targumist** *n.*

tariff ('tærɪf) *n.* **1. a.** a tax levied by a government on imports or occasionally exports for purposes of protection, support of the balance of payments, or the raising of revenue. **b.** a system or list of such taxes. **2.** any schedule of prices, fees, fares, etc. **3.** *Chiefly Brit.* **a.** a method of charging for the supply of services, esp. public services, such as gas and electricity: *block tariff.* **b.** a schedule of such charges. **4.** *Chiefly Brit.* a bill of fare with prices listed; menu. ~*vb.* (*tr.*) **5.** to set a tariff on. **6.** to set a price on according to a schedule of tariffs. [C16: from Italian *tariffa,* from Arabic *ta'rīfa* to inform] —'**tariffless** *adj.*

tariff office *n. Insurance.* a company whose premiums are based on a tariff agreed with other insurance companies.

tarlatan ('tɑːlətən) *n.* an open-weave cotton fabric, used for stiffening garments. [C18: from French *tarlatane,* variant of *tarnatane* type of muslin, perhaps of Indian origin]

Tarmac ('tɑːmæk) *n.* **1.** *Trademark.* (*often not cap.*) a paving material that consists of crushed stone rolled and bound with a mixture of tar and bitumen, esp. as used for a road, airport runway, etc. Full name: **Tarmacadam** (ˌtɑːmə'kædəm). See also **macadam.** ~*vb.* **-macs, -macking, -macked.** (*tr.*) **2.** (*usually not cap.*) to apply Tarmac to.

tarn (tɑːn) *n.* a small mountain lake or pool. [C14: of Scandinavian origin; related to Old Norse *tjörn* pool]

tarnal ('tɑːnᵊl) *U.S. dialect.* ~*adj.* **1.** (*prenominal*) damned. ~*adv.* **2.** (intensifier): *tarnal lucky!* [C18: aphetic dialect pronunciation of ETERNAL] —'**tarnally** *adv.*

tarnation (tɑː'neɪʃən) *n.* a euphemism for **damnation.**

tarnish ('tɑːnɪʃ) *vb.* **1.** to lose or cause to lose the shine, esp. by exposure to air or moisture resulting in surface oxidation; discolour: *silver tarnishes quickly.* **2.** to stain or become stained; taint or spoil: *a fraud that tarnished his reputation.* ~*n.* **3.** a tarnished condition, surface, or film. [C16: from Old French *ternir* to make dull, from *terne* lustreless of Germanic origin; related to Old High German *tarnen* to conceal, Old English *dierne* hidden] —'**tarnishable** *adj.* —'**tarnisher** *n.*

taro ('tɑːrəʊ) *n., pl.* **-ros. 1.** an Asian aroid plant, *Colocasia esculenta,* cultivated in the tropics for its large edible rootstock. **2.** the rootstock of this plant. ~Also called: **elephant's-ear, dasheen, eddo, Chinese eddo.** [C18: from Tahitian and Maori]

tarot ('tærəʊ) *n.* **1.** one of a special pack of cards, now used mainly for fortune-telling, consisting of 78 cards (4 suits of 14 cards each (the minor arcana), and 22 other cards (the major arcana)). **2.** a card in a tarot pack with distinctive symbolic design, such as the Wheel of Fortune. ~*adj.* **3.** relating to tarot cards. [C16: from French, from Old Italian *tarocco,* of unknown origin]

tarp (tɑːp) *n. Austral.* an informal word for **tarpaulin.**

tarpan ('tɑːpæn) *n.* a European wild horse, *Equus caballus gomelini,* common in prehistoric times but now extinct. [from Kirghiz Tatar]

tarpaulin (tɑː'pɔːlɪn) *n.* **1.** a heavy hard-wearing waterproof fabric made of canvas or similar material coated with tar, wax, or paint, for outdoor use as a protective covering against moisture. **2.** a sheet of this fabric. **3.** a hat of or covered with this fabric, esp. a sailor's hat. **4.** a rare word for **seaman.** [C17: probably from TAR[1] + PALL[1] + -ING[1]]

tarpon ('tɑːpən) *n., pl.* **-pons** *or* **-pon. 1.** a large silvery clupeoid game fish, *Tarpon atlanticus,* of warm Atlantic waters, having a compressed body covered with large scales: family *Elopidae.* **2.** any similar related fish. [C17: perhaps from Dutch *tarpoen,* of unknown origin]

tarradiddle ('tærəˌdɪdᵊl) *n.* **1.** a trifling lie. **2.** nonsense; twaddle. [of unknown origin]

tarragon ('tærəgən) *n.* **1.** an aromatic perennial plant, *Artemisia dracunculus,* of the Old World, having whitish flowers and small toothed leaves, which are used as seasoning: family *Compositae* (composites). **2.** the leaves of this plant. ~Also called: **estragon.** [C16: from Old French *targon,* from Medieval Latin *tarcon,* from Arabic *tarkhūn,* perhaps from Greek *drakontion* adderwort]

tarriance ('tærɪəns) *n.* an archaic word for **delay.**

tarry ('tærɪ) *vb.* **-ries, -rying, -ried. 1.** (*intr.*) to delay in coming or going; linger. **2.** (*intr.*) to remain temporarily or briefly. **3.** (*intr.*) to wait or stay. **4.** (*tr.*) *Archaic or poetic.* to await. ~*n., pl.* **-ries. 5.** *Rare.* a stay. [C14 *tarien,* of uncertain origin] —'**tarrier** *n.*

tarsal ('tɑːsᵊl) *adj.* **1.** of, relating to, or constituting the tarsus or tarsi. ~*n.* **2.** a tarsal bone.

tar sand *n.* a sandstone in which hydrocarbons have been trapped; the lighter compounds evaporate, leaving a residue of asphalt in the rock pores.

tarseal ('tɑːˌsiːl) *n. N.Z.* **1.** the bitumen surface of a road. **2. the.** the main highway.

tarsia ('tɑːsɪə) *n.* another term for **intarsia.** [C17: from Italian, from Arabic *tarsi'*; see INTARSIA]

tarsier ('tɑːsɪə) *n.* any of several nocturnal arboreal prosimian primates of the genus *Tarsius,* of Indonesia and the Philippines, having huge eyes, long hind legs, and digits ending in pads to facilitate climbing: family *Tarsiidae.* [C18: from French, from *tarse* the flat of the foot; see TARSUS]

tarsometatarsus (ˌtɑːsəʊˌmɛtə'tɑːsəs) *n., pl.* **-si** (-saɪ). a bone in the lower part of a bird's leg consisting of the metatarsal bones and some of the tarsal bones fused together. [C19: *tarso-* from TARSUS + METATARSUS] —ˌ**tarsoˌmeta'tarsal** *adj.*

tarsus ('tɑːsəs) *n., pl.* **-si** (-saɪ). **1.** the bones of the ankle and heel, collectively. **2. a.** the corresponding part in other mammals and in amphibians and reptiles. **b.** another name for **tarsometatarsus.** **3.** the dense connective tissue supporting the free edge of each eyelid. **4.** the part of an insect's leg that lies distal to the tibia. [C17: from New Latin, from Greek *tarsos* flat surface, instep]

tart[1] (tɑːt) *n.* a pastry case often having no top crust, with a sweet filling of fruit, jam, custard, etc. [C14: from Old French *tarte,* of uncertain origin; compare Medieval Latin *tarte*]

tart[2] (tɑːt) *adj.* **1.** (of a flavour, food, etc.) sour, acid, or astringent. **2.** cutting, sharp, or caustic: *a tart remark.* [Old English *teart* rough; related to Dutch *tarten* to defy, Middle High German *traz* defiance] —'**tartish** *adj.* —'**tartishly** *adv.* —'**tartly** *adv.* —'**tartness** *n.*

tart[3] (tɑːt) *n. Informal.* a promiscuous woman, esp. a prostitute: often a term of abuse. See also **tart up.** [C19: shortened from SWEETHEART] —'**tarty** *adj.*

tartan[1] ('tɑːtᵊn) *n.* **1. a.** a design of straight lines, crossing at right angles to give a chequered appearance, esp. the distinctive design or designs associated with each Scottish clan: *the Buchanan tartan.* **b.** (*as modifier*): *a tartan kilt.* **2.** a woollen fabric or garment with this design. **3. the tartan.** Highland dress. [C16: perhaps from Old French *tertaine* linsey-woolsey, from Old Spanish *tiritaña* a fine silk fabric, from *tiritar* to rustle] —'**tartaned** *adj.*

tartan[2] ('tɑːtᵊn) *n.* a single-masted vessel used in the Mediterranean, usually with a lateen sail. [C17: from French, perhaps from Provençal *tartana* falcon, buzzard, since a ship was frequently given the name of a bird]

tartanry ('tɑːtᵊnrɪ) *n. Derogatory.* the excessive use of tartan and other Scottish imagery to produce a distorted sentimental view of Scotland and its history. [C20: TARTAN[1] + -RY]

tartar[1] ('tɑːtə) *n.* **1.** *Dentistry.* a hard crusty deposit on the teeth, consisting of food, cellular debris, and mineral salts. **2.** Also called: **argol.** a brownish-red substance consisting mainly of potassium hydrogen tartrate, present in grape juice and deposited during the fermentation of wine. [C14: from Medieval Latin *tartarum,* from Medieval Greek *tartaron*]

tartar[2] ('tɑːtə) *n.* (*sometimes cap.*) a fearsome or formidable person. [C16: special use of TARTAR]

Tartar ('tɑːtə) *n., adj.* a variant spelling of **Tatar.** —**Tartarian** (tɑː'tɛərɪən) *or* **Tartaric** (tɑː'tærɪk) *adj.*

tartare *or* **tartar sauce** *n.* a mayonnaise sauce mixed with hard-boiled egg yolks, chopped herbs, capers, and gherkins. [from French *sauce tartare,* from TARTAR]

Tartarean (tɑː'tɛərɪən, -'tɑːrɪ-) *adj. Literary.* of or relating to Tartarus, a place of punishment in Hades; infernal.

tartar emetic *n.* another name for **antimony potassium tartrate.**

tartaric (tɑː'tærɪk) *adj.* of, concerned with, containing, or derived from tartar or tartaric acid. Systematic name: **2,3-dihydroxybutanedioic acid.**

tartaric acid *n.* a colourless or white odourless crystalline water-soluble dicarboxylic acid existing in four stereoisomeric forms, the commonest being the dextrorotatory (*d*-) compound which is found in many fruits: used as a food additive (**E334**) in soft drinks, confectionery, and baking powders and in tanning and photography. Formula: HOOCCH(OH)CH(OH)COOH.

tartarize *or* **tartarise** ('tɑːtəˌraɪz) *vb.* (*tr.*) to impregnate or treat with tartar or tartar emetic. —ˌ**tartari'zation** *or* ˌ**tartari'sation** *n.*

tartarous ('tɑːtərəs) *adj.* consisting of, containing, or resembling tartar.

tartar steak *n.* a variant term for **steak tartare.**

tartlet ('tɑːtlɪt) *n. Brit.* an individual pastry case with a filling of fruit or other sweet or savoury mixture.

tartrate ('tɑːtreɪt) *n.* any salt or ester of tartaric acid.

tartrated ('tɑːtreɪtɪd) *adj.* being in the form of a tartrate.

tartrazine ('tɑːtrəˌziːn, -zɪn) *n.* an azo dye that produces a yellow colour: widely used as a food additive (**E102**) in convenience foods, soft drinks, sweets, etc., and in drugs, and also to dye textiles.

Tartuffe *or* **Tartufe** (tɑː'tʊf, -'tuːf) *n.* a person who hypocritically pretends to be deeply pious. [from the character in the comedy *Tartuffe* (1664) by French dramatist Molière (1622–73)] —**Tar'tuffian** *or* **Tar'tufian** *adj.*

tart up *vb.* (*tr., adv.*) *Brit. informal.* **1.** to dress and make (oneself) up in a provocative or promiscuous way. **2.** *Informal.* to decorate or improve the appearance of: *to tart up a bar.*

tarwhine ('tɑːˌwaɪn) *n.* a bream, *Rhabdosargus sarba,* of E Australia, silver in colour with gold streaks. [from a native Australian language]

Tarzan ('tɑːzən) *n.* (*sometimes not cap.*) *Informal, often ironical.* a man with great physical strength, agility, and virility. [C20: after the hero of a series of stories by Edgar Rice Burroughs (1875–1950), U.S. novelist]

Tas. *abbrev. for* Tasmania.

Tashi Lama ('tɑːʃɪ 'lɑːmə) *n.* another name for the **Panchen Lama.** [from *Tashi* (*Lumpo*), name of Tibetan monastery over which this Lama presides]

tasimeter (tə'sɪmɪtə) *n.* a device for measuring small temperature changes. It depends on the changes of pressure resulting from expanding or contracting solids. [C19 *tasi-,* from Greek *tasis* tension + -METER] —**tasimetric** (ˌtæsɪ'mɛtrɪk) *adj.* —**ta'simetry** *n.*

task (tɑːsk) *n.* **1.** a specific piece of work required to be done as a duty or chore. **2.** an unpleasant or difficult job or duty. **3.** any piece of work. **4. take to task.** to criticize or reprove. ~*vb.* (*tr.*) **5.** to assign a task to. **6.** to subject to severe strain; tax. [C13: from Old French *tasche,* from Medieval Latin *tasca,* from *taxa* tax, from Latin *taxāre* to TAX] —'**tasker** *n.* —'**taskless** *adj.*

task force *n.* **1.** a temporary grouping of military units formed to undertake a specific mission. **2.** any semipermanent organization set up to carry out a continuing task.

taskmaster ('tɑːskˌmɑːstə) *n.* a person, discipline, etc., that enforces work, esp. hard or continuous work: *his teacher is a hard taskmaster.* —'**taskˌmistress** *fem. n.*

taskwork ('tɑːskˌwɜːk) *n.* **1.** hard or unpleasant work. **2.** a rare word for **piecework.**

Tasmanian (tæz'meɪnɪən) *adj.* **1.** of or relating to the Australian island state of Tasmania, south of the mainland, or its people. ~*n.* **2.** a native or inhabitant of Tasmania.

Tasmanian devil *n.* a small ferocious carnivorous marsupial, *Sarcophilus harrisi,* of Tasmania, having black fur with pale markings, strong jaws, and short legs: family *Dasyuridae.* Also called: **ursine dasyure.**

Tasmanian wolf *or* **tiger** *n.* other names for **thylacine.**

tass (tæs) *or* **tassie** ('tæsɪ) *n. Scot. and northern English dialect.* **1.** a cup, goblet, or glass. **2.** the contents of such a vessel. [C15: from Old French *tasse* cup, from Arabic *tassah* basin, from Persian *tast*]

tassel ('tæsᵊl) *n.* **1.** a tuft of loose threads secured by a knot or ornamental knob, used to decorate soft furnishings, clothes, etc. **2.** anything resembling this tuft, esp. the tuft of stamens at the tip of a maize inflorescence. ~*vb.* **-sels, -selling, -selled** *or U.S.* **-sels, -seling, -seled.** **3.** (*tr.*) to adorn with a tassel or tassels. **4.** (*intr.*) (of maize) to produce stamens in a tuft. **5.** (*tr.*) to remove the tassels from. [C13: from Old French, from Vulgar Latin *tassellus* (unattested), changed from Latin *taxillus* a small die, from *tālus* gaming die] —'**tasselly** *adj.*

tasset ('tæsɪt), **tasse** (tæs), *or* (*less commonly*) **tace** *n.* a piece of armour consisting of one or more plates fastened on to the bottom of a cuirass to protect the thigh. [C19: from French *tassette* small pouch, from Old French *tasse* purse]

Tassie *or* **Tassy** ('tæzɪ) *n., pl.* **-sies.** *Austral. informal.* a native or inhabitant of Tasmania.

taste (teɪst) *n.* **1.** the sense by which the qualities and flavour of a substance are distinguished by the taste buds. **2.** the sensation experienced by means of the taste buds. **3.** the act of tasting. **4.** a small amount eaten, drunk, or tried on the tongue. **5.** a brief experience of something: *a taste of the whip.* **6.** a preference or liking for something; inclination: *to have a taste for danger.* **7.** the ability to make discerning judgments about aesthetic, artistic, and intellectual matters; discrimination: *to have taste.* **8.** judgment of aesthetic or social matters according to a generally accepted standard: *bad taste.* **9.** discretion; delicacy: *that remark lacks taste.* **10.** *Obsolete.* the act of testing. ~*vb.* **11.** to distinguish the taste of (a substance) by means of the taste buds. **12.** (*usually tr.*) to take a small amount of (a food, liquid, etc.) into the mouth, esp. in order to test the quality: *to taste the wine.* **13.** (often foll. by *of*) to have a specific flavour or taste: *the tea tastes of soap; this apple tastes sour.* **14.** (when *intr.,* usually foll. by *of*) to have an experience of (something): *to taste success.* **15.** (*tr.*) an archaic word for **enjoy.** **16.** (*tr.*) *Obsolete.* to test by touching. [C13: from Old French *taster,* ultimately from Latin *taxāre* to appraise] —'**tastable** *adj.*

taste bud *n.* any of the elevated oval-shaped sensory end organs on the surface of the tongue, by means of which the sensation of taste is experienced.

tasteful ('teɪstfʊl) *adj.* **1.** indicating good taste: *a tasteful design.* **2.** a rare word for **tasty.** —'**tastefully** *adv.* —'**tastefulness** *n.*

tasteless ('teɪstlɪs) *adj.* **1.** lacking in flavour; insipid. **2.** lacking social or aesthetic taste. **3.** *Rare.* unable to taste. —'**tastelessly** *adv.* —'**tastelessness** *n.*

taster ('teɪstə) *n.* **1.** a person who samples food or drink for quality. **2.** any device used in tasting or sampling. **3.** a person employed, esp. formerly, to taste food and drink prepared for a king, etc., to test for poison.

tasty ('teɪstɪ) *adj.* **tastier, tastiest.** **1.** having a pleasant flavour. **2.** *Brit. informal.* attractive: used chiefly by men when talking of women. —'**tastily** *adv.* —'**tastiness** *n.*

tat[1] (tæt) *vb.* **tats, tatting, tatted.** to make (something) by tatting. [C19: of unknown origin]

tat[2] (tæt) *n.* **1.** tatty articles or a tatty condition. **2.** tasteless articles. **3.** a tangled mass. [C20: back formation from TATTY]

tat[3] (tæt) *n.* See **tit for tat.**

ta-ta (tæ'tɑː) *sentence substitute. Brit. informal.* goodbye; farewell. [C19: of unknown origin]

tatami (tə'tɑːmɪ, tæ'tæmɪ) *n., pl.* **-mi** *or* **-mis.** a thick rectangular mat of woven straw, used as a standard to measure a Japanese room. [Japanese]

Tatar *or* **Tartar** ('tɑːtə) *n.* **1. a.** a member of a Mongoloid people who established a vast and powerful state in central Asia from the 13th century until conquered by Russia in 1552. **b.** a descendant of this people, now scattered throughout the former Soviet Union but living chiefly in Russia, around the middle Volga. **2.** any of the languages spoken by the present-day Tatars, belonging to various branches of the Turkic family of languages, esp. Kazan Tatar. *~adj.* **3.** of, relating to, or characteristic of the Tatars. [C14: from Old French *Tartare,* from Medieval Latin *Tartarus* (associated with Latin *Tartarus* the underworld), from Persian *Tātār*] —**Tatarian** (tɑː'tɛərɪən), **Tar'tarian** *or* **Tataric** (tɑː'tærɪk), **Tar'taric** *adj.*

tater ('teɪtə) *n.* a dialect word for **potato.**

tatouay ('tætʊˌeɪ, ˌtɑːtʊ'aɪ) *n.* a large armadillo, *Cabassous tatouay,* of South America. [C16: from Spanish *tatuay,* from Guarani *tatu ai,* from *tatu* armadillo + *ai* worthless (because inedible)]

tatter ('tætə) *vb.* **1.** to make or become ragged or worn to shreds. *~n.* **2.** a torn or ragged piece, esp. of material. **3. in tatters. a.** torn to pieces; in shreds. **b.** destroyed or ruined. [C14: of Scandinavian origin; compare Icelandic *töturr* rag, Old English *tættec,* Old High German *zæter* rag]

tatterdemalion (ˌtætədɪ'meɪljən, -'mæl-) *n. Rare.* **a.** a person dressed in ragged clothes. **b.** (*as modifier*): *a tatterdemalion dress.* [C17: from TATTER + *-demalion,* of uncertain origin]

tattersall ('tætəˌsɔːl) *n.* **a.** a fabric, sometimes brightly coloured, having stripes or bars in a checked or squared pattern. **b.** (*as modifier*): *a tattersall coat.* [C19: after *Tattersall's,* a London horse market where the horse blankets originally had this pattern]

tattie *or* **tatty** ('tætɪ) *n., pl.* **-ties.** a Scot. or dialect word for **potato.**

tattie-bogle (ˌtætɪ'bogᵊl) *n. Scot.* a scarecrow. [TATTIE + BOGLE]

tattie-peelin ('tætɪ'piːlɪn) *adj. Central Scot. dialect* (esp. of speech) highfalutin, affected, or pretentious. [from *potato-peeling;* sense development obscure]

tatting ('tætɪŋ) *n.* **1.** an intricate type of lace made by looping a thread of cotton or linen by means of a hand shuttle. **2.** the act or work of producing this. [C19: of unknown origin]

tattle ('tætᵊl) *vb.* **1.** (*intr.*) to gossip about another's personal matters or secrets. **2.** (*tr.*) to reveal by gossiping: *to tattle a person's secrets.* **3.** (*intr.*) to talk idly; chat. *~n.* **4.** the act or an instance of tattling. **5.** a scandalmonger or gossip. [C15 (in the sense: to stammer, hesitate): from Middle Dutch *tatelen* to prate, of imitative origin]

tattler ('tætlə) *n.* **1.** a person who tattles; gossip. **2.** any of several sandpipers of the genus *Heteroscelus,* such as *H. incanus* (**Polynesian tattler**), of Pacific coastal regions.

tattletale ('tætᵊlˌteɪl) *Chiefly U.S. and Canadian.* *~n.* **1.** a scandalmonger or gossip. *~adj.* **2.** another word for **telltale** (sense 1).

tattoo[1] (tæ'tuː) *n., pl.* **-toos.** **1.** (formerly) a signal by drum or bugle ordering the military to return to their quarters. **2.** a military display or pageant, usually at night. **3.** any similar beating on a drum, etc. [C17: from Dutch *taptoe,* from the command *tap toe!* turn off the taps! from *tap* tap of a barrel + *toe* to shut]

tattoo[2] (tæ'tuː) *vb.* **-toos, -tooing, -tooed.** **1.** to make (pictures or designs) on (the skin) by pricking and staining with indelible colours. *~n., pl.* **-toos.** **2.** a design made by this process. **3.** the practice of tattooing. [C18: from Tahitian *tatau*] —**tat'tooer** *or* **tat'tooist** *n.*

tatty ('tætɪ) *adj.* **-tier, -tiest.** *Chiefly Brit.* worn out, shabby, tawdry, or unkempt. [C16: of Scottish origin, probably related to Old English *tættec* a tatter] —**'tattily** *adv.* —**'tattiness** *n.*

tau (tɔː, taʊ) *n.* the 19th letter in the Greek alphabet (Τ or τ), a consonant, transliterated as *t.* [C13: via Latin from Greek, of Semitic origin; see TAV]

tau cross *n.* a cross shaped like the Greek letter tau. Also called: **Saint Anthony's cross.**

taught (tɔːt) *vb.* the past tense and past participle of **teach.**

tau neutrino *n. Physics.* a type of neutrino associated with the decay of tau particles.

taunt[1] (tɔːnt) *vb.* (*tr.*) **1.** to provoke or deride with mockery, contempt, or criticism. **2.** to tease; tantalize. *~n.* **3.** a jeering remark. **4.** *Archaic.* the object of mockery. [C16: from French phrase *tant pour tant* like for like, rejoinder] —**'taunter** *n.* —**'taunting** *adj.* —**'tauntingly** *adv.*

taunt[2] (tɔːnt) *adj. Nautical.* (of the mast or masts of a sailing vessel) unusually tall. [C15: of uncertain origin]

tauon ('taʊɒn) *or* **tau particle** *n. Physics.* a negatively charged elementary particle of high mass classed as a lepton, with an associated antiparticle and neutrino. [C20: from Greek letter TAU + -ON]

taupe (təʊp) *n.* **a.** a brownish-grey colour. **b.** (*as adj.*): *a taupe coat.* [C20: from French, literally: mole, from Latin *talpa*]

taurine[1] ('tɔːraɪn) *adj.* of, relating to, or resembling a bull. [C17: from Latin *taurīnus,* from *taurus* a bull]

taurine[2] ('tɔːriːn, -rɪn) *n.* a derivative of the amino acid, cysteine, obtained from the bile of animals; 2-aminoethanesulphonic acid. Formula: $NH_2CH_2CH_2SO_3H$. [C19: from TAURO- (as in *taurocholic* acid, so called because discovered in ox bile) + -INE[2]]

tauro- *or before a vowel* **taur-** *combining form.* denoting a bull: *tauromachy.* [from Latin *taurus* bull, Greek *tauros*]

tauromachy (tɔː'rɒməkɪ) *n.* the art or act of bullfighting. [C19: Greek *tauromakhia,* from TAURO- + *makhē* fight] —**tauromachian** (ˌtɔːrə'meɪkɪən) *adj.*

Taurus ('tɔːrəs) *n., Latin genitive* **Tauri** ('tɔːraɪ). **1.** *Astronomy.* a zodiacal constellation in the N hemisphere lying close to Orion and between Aries and Gemini. It contains the star Aldebaran, the star clusters Hyades and Pleiades, and the Crab Nebula. **2.** *Astrology.* **a.** Also called: the **Bull.** the second sign of the zodiac, symbol ♉, having a fixed earth classification and ruled by the planet Venus. The sun is in this sign between about April 20 and May 20. **b.** a person born when the sun is in this sign. *~adj.* **3.** born under or characteristic of Taurus. *~*Also (for senses 2b, 3): **Taurean** ('tɔːrɪən, tɔː'rɪən). [C14: from Latin: bull]

taut (tɔːt) *adj.* **1.** tightly stretched; tense. **2.** showing nervous strain; stressed. **3.** *Chiefly nautical.* in good order; neat. [C14 *tought;* probably related to Old English *togian* to TOW[1]] —**'tautly** *adv.* —**'tautness** *n.*

tauten ('tɔːtᵊn) *vb.* to make or become taut or tense.

tauto- *or before a vowel* **taut-** *combining form.* identical or same: *tautology; tautonym.* [from Greek *tauto,* from *to auto*]

tautog (tɔː'tɒg) *n.* a large dark-coloured wrasse, *Tautoga onitis,* of the North American coast of the Atlantic Ocean: used as a food fish. Also called: **blackfish.** [C17: from Narraganset *tautauog,* plural of *tautau* sheepshead]

tautologize *or* **tautologise** (tɔː'tɒləˌdʒaɪz) *vb.* (*intr.*) to express oneself tautologically. —**tau'tologist** *n.*

tautology (tɔː'tɒlədʒɪ) *n., pl.* **-gies.** **1.** the use of words that merely repeat elements of the meaning already conveyed, as in the sentence *Will these supplies be adequate enough?* in place of *Will these supplies be adequate?* **2.** *Logic.* a statement that is always true, esp. a truth-functional expression that takes the value true for all combinations of values of its components, as in *either the sun is out or the sun is not out.* Compare **inconsistency** (sense 3), **contingency** (sense 4). [C16: from Late Latin *tautologia,* from Greek, from *tautologos*] —**tautological** (ˌtɔːtᵊ'lɒdʒɪkᵊl), ˌ**tauto'logic,** *or* **tau'tologous** *adj.* —ˌ**tauto'logically** *or* **tau'tologously** *adv.*

tautomer ('tɔːtəmə) *n.* either of the two forms of a chemical compound that exhibits tautomerism.

tautomerism (tɔː'tɒməˌrɪzəm) *n.* the ability of certain chemical compounds to exist as a mixture of two interconvertible isomers in equilibrium. See also **keto-enol tautomerism.** [C19: from TAUTO- + ISOMERISM] —**tautomeric** (ˌtɔːtə'mɛrɪk) *adj.*

tautonym ('tɔːtənɪm) *n. Biology.* a taxonomic name in which the generic and specific components are the same, as in *Rattus rattus* (black rat). [C20: from Greek *tautonymos.* See TAUTO-, -ONYM] —ˌ**tauto'nymic** *or* **tautonymous** (tɔː'tɒnɪməs) *adj.* —**tau'tonymy** *n.*

tav *or* **taw** (tɑːv, tɑːf; *Hebrew* tav, taf) *n.* the 23rd and last letter in the Hebrew alphabet (ת), transliterated as *t* or when final *th.* [from Hebrew: cross, mark]

Tavel (tɑː'vɛl) *n.* a fine rosé wine produced in the Rhône valley near the small town of Tavel in S France.

tavern ('tævən) *n.* **1.** a less common word for **pub.** **2.** *U.S., Canadian, and N.Z.* a place licensed for the sale and consumption of alcoholic drink. [C13: from Old French *taverne,* from Latin *taberna* hut]

taverna (tə'vɜːnə) *n.* **1.** (in Greece) a guesthouse that has its own bar. **2.** a Greek restaurant. [C20: Modern Greek, from Latin *taberna*]

taverner ('tævənə) *n.* **1.** *Archaic.* a keeper of a tavern. **2.** *Obsolete.* a constant frequenter of taverns.

TAVR *abbrev. for* Territorial and Army Volunteer Reserve.

taw[1] (tɔː) *n.* **1.** the line from which the players shoot in marbles. **2. back to taws.** *Austral. informal.* back to the beginning. **3.** a large marble used for shooting. **4.** a game of marbles. [C18: of unknown origin]

taw[2] (tɔː) *vb.* (*tr.*) **1.** to convert (skins) into white leather by treatment with mineral salts, such as alum and salt, rather than by normal tanning processes. **2.** *Archaic or dialect.* to flog; beat. [Old English *tawian;* compare Old High German *zouwen* to prepare, Gothic *taujan* to make] —**'tawer** *n.*

tawa ('tɑːwə) *n.* a tall timber tree, *Beilschmiedia tawa,* of New Zealand, having edible purple berries. [Maori]

tawai ('tɑːˌwaɪ) *or* **tawhai** ('tɑːˌhwaɪ) *n.* any of various species of beech of the genus *Nothofagus* of New Zealand, originally called "birches" by the settlers. [Maori]

tawdry ('tɔːdrɪ) *adj.* **-drier, -driest.** cheap, showy, and of poor quality: *tawdry jewellery.* [C16 *tawdry lace,* shortened and altered from *Seynt Audries lace,* finery sold at the fair of St *Audrey* (Etheldrida), 7th-century queen of Northumbria and patron saint of Ely, Cambridgeshire] —**'tawdrily** *adv.* —**'tawdriness** *n.*

tawny *or* **tawney** ('tɔːnɪ) *n.* **a.** a light brown to brownish-orange colour. **b.** (*as adj.*): *tawny port.* [C14: from Old French *tané,* from *taner* to TAN[1]] —'**tawniness** *n.*
tawny owl *n.* a European owl, *Strix aluco,* having a reddish-brown or grey plumage, black eyes, and a round head. Also called: **brown owl, wood owl.**
Tawny Owl *n.* a name (no longer in official use) for an assistant Brownie Guider.
tawny pipit *n.* a small sandy-brown European bird of the wagtail family; an irregular migrant to some parts of Britain.
tawse *or* **taws** (tɔːz) *Chiefly Scot.* ~*n.* **1.** a leather strap having one end cut into thongs, formerly used as an instrument of punishment by a schoolteacher. ~*vb.* **2.** to punish (someone) with or as if with a tawse; whip. [C16: probably plural of obsolete *taw* strip of leather; see TAW[2]]
tax (tæks) *n.* **1.** a compulsory financial contribution imposed by a government to raise revenue, levied on the income or property of persons or organizations, on the production costs or sales prices of goods and services, etc. **2.** a heavy demand on something; strain: *a tax on our resources.* ~*vb.* (*tr.*) **3.** to levy a tax on (persons, companies, etc., or their incomes, etc.). **4.** to make heavy demands on; strain: *to tax one's intellect.* **5.** to accuse, charge, or blame: *he was taxed with the crime.* **6.** to determine (the amount legally chargeable or allowable to a party to a legal action), as by examining the solicitor's bill of costs: *to tax costs.* [C13: from Old French *taxer,* from Latin *taxāre* to appraise, from *tangere* to touch] —'**taxer** *n.* —'**taxless** *adj.*
taxable ('tæksəbᵊl) *adj.* **1.** capable of being taxed; able to bear tax. **2.** subject to tax. ~*n.* **3.** (*often pl.*) *U.S.* a person, income, property, etc., that is subject to tax. —ˌ**taxa'bility** *or* '**taxableness** *n.* —'**taxably** *adv.*
taxaceous (tæk'seɪʃəs) *adj.* of, relating to, or belonging to the *Taxaceae,* a family of coniferous trees that includes the yews. [C19: from New Latin *taxāceus,* from Latin *taxus* a yew]
taxation (tæk'seɪʃən) *n.* **1.** the act or principle of levying taxes or the condition of being taxed. **2. a.** an amount assessed as tax. **b.** a tax rate. **3.** revenue from taxes. —**tax'ational** *adj.*
tax avoidance *n.* reduction or minimization of tax liability by lawful methods. Compare **tax evasion.**
tax-deductible *adj.* (of an expense, loss, etc.) legally deductible from income or wealth before tax assessment.
tax disc *n.* a paper disc displayed on the windscreen of a motor vehicle showing that the tax due on it has been paid.
taxeme ('tæksiːm) *n. Linguistics.* any element of speech that may differentiate one utterance from another with a different meaning, such as the occurrence of a particular phoneme, the presence of a certain intonation, or a distinctive word order. [C20: from Greek *taxis* order, arrangement + -EME] —**tax'emic** *adj.*
tax evasion *n.* reduction or minimization of tax liability by illegal methods. Compare **tax avoidance.**
tax-exempt *adj. U.S.* **1.** (of an income or property) exempt from taxation. **2.** (of an asset) earning income that is not subject to taxation.
tax exile *n.* a person having a high income who chooses to live abroad so as to avoid paying high taxes.
tax haven *n.* a country or state having a lower rate of taxation than elsewhere.
tax holiday *n.* a period during which tax concessions are made for some reason; examples include an export incentive or an incentive to start a new business given by some governments, in which a company is excused all or part of its tax liability.
taxi ('tæksɪ) *n., pl.* **taxis** *or* **taxies. 1.** Also called: **cab, taxicab.** a car, usually fitted with a taximeter, that may be hired to carry passengers to any specified destination. ~*vb.* **taxies, taxiing** *or* **taxying, taxied. 2.** to cause (an aircraft) to move along the ground under its own power, esp. before takeoff and after landing, or (of an aircraft) to move along the ground in this way. **3.** (*intr.*) to travel in a taxi. [C20: shortened from *taximeter cab*]
taxi dancing *n.* a system, as in a dance hall or hotel, whereby a person pays to get a partner (**taxi dancer**) for a dance, payment being required for each individual dance during an evening.
taxidermy ('tæksɪˌdɜːmɪ) *n.* the art or process of preparing, stuffing, and mounting animal skins so that they have a lifelike appearance. [C19: from Greek *taxis* arrangement + *-dermy,* from Greek *derma* skin] —ˌ**taxi'dermal** *or* ˌ**taxi'dermic** *adj.* —'**taxiˌdermist** *n.*
taximeter ('tæksɪˌmiːtə) *n.* a meter fitted to a taxi to register the fare, based on the length of the journey. [C19: from French *taximètre;* see TAX, -METER]
taxing ('tæksɪŋ) *adj.* demanding, onerous, and wearing. —'**taxingly** *adv.*
taxiplane ('tæksɪˌpleɪn) *n. U.S.* an aircraft that is available for hire.
taxi rank *n.* a place where taxis wait to be hired.
taxis ('tæksɪs) *n.* **1.** the movement of a cell or organism in a particular direction in response to an external stimulus. **2.** *Surgery.* the repositioning of a displaced organ or part by manual manipulation only. [C18: via New Latin from Greek: arrangement, from *tassein* to place in order]
-taxis *or* **-taxy** *n. combining form.* **1.** indicating movement towards or away from a specified stimulus: *thermotaxis.* **2.** order or arrangement: *phyllotaxis.* [from New Latin, from Greek *taxis* order] —**-tactic** *or* **-taxic** *adj. combining form.*
taxi truck *n. Austral.* a truck with a driver that can be hired.
taxiway ('tæksɪˌweɪ) *n.* a marked path along which aircraft taxi to or from a runway, parking area, etc. Also called: **taxi strip, peritrack.**
tax loss *n.* a loss sustained by a company that can be set against future profits for tax purposes.
taxon ('tæksɒn) *n., pl.* **taxa** ('tæksə). *Biology.* any taxonomic group or rank. [C20: back formation from TAXONOMY]
taxonomy (tæk'sɒnəmɪ) *n.* **1. a.** the branch of biology concerned with the classification of organisms into groups based on similarities of structure, origin, etc. **b.** the practice of arranging organisms in this way. **2.** the science or practice of classification. [C19: from French *taxonomie,* from Greek *taxis* order + -NOMY] —**taxonomic** (ˌtæksə'nɒmɪk) *or* ˌ**taxo'nomical** *adj.* —ˌ**taxo'nomically** *adv.* —**tax'onomist** *or* **tax'onomer** *n.*
taxpayer ('tæksˌpeɪə) *n.* a person or organization that pays taxes or is liable to taxation. —'**taxˌpaying** *adj.*
tax rate *n.* the percentage of income, wealth, etc., assessed as payable in taxation.
tax return *n.* a declaration of personal income made annually to the tax authorities and used as a basis for assessing an individual's liability for taxation.
tax shelter *n. Commerce.* a form into which business or financial activities may be organized to minimize taxation.
-taxy *n. combining form.* a variant of **-taxis.**
tay (teɪ) *n.* an Irish dialect word for **tea.**
tayberry ('teɪbərɪ) *n., pl.* **-ries. 1.** a hybrid shrub produced by crossing a blackberry, raspberry, and loganberry. **2.** the large sweet red fruit of this plant. [C20: so named because first grown at Blairgowrie on *Tayside,* Scotland]
Taylor's series ('teɪləz) *n. Maths.* an infinite sum giving the value of a function f(*z*) in the neighbourhood of a point *a* in terms of the derivatives of the function evaluated at *a.* Under certain conditions, the series has the form $f(z) = f(a) + [f'(a)(z-a)]/1! + [f''(a)(z-a)^2]/2! + \ldots$ See also **Maclaurin's series.** [C18: named after Brook *Taylor* (1685–1731), English mathematician]
tayra ('taɪrə) *n.* a large arboreal musteline mammal, *Eira barbara,* of Central and South America, having a dark brown body and paler head. [C19: from Tupi *taira*]
Tay-Sachs disease (ˌteɪ'sæks) *n.* an inherited disorder, caused by a faulty recessive gene, in which lipids accumulate in the brain, leading to mental retardation and blindness. It occurs mostly in Ashkenazi Jews. [C20: named after W. *Tay* (1843–1927), British physician, and B. *Sachs* (1858–1944), U.S. neurologist]
tazza ('tætsə) *n.* a wine cup with a shallow bowl and a circular foot. [C19: from Italian, probably from Arabic *tassah* bowl]
tb *abbrev. for:* **1.** trial balance. **2.** Also: **TB.** tuberculosis.
Tb *the chemical symbol for* terbium.
TB *abbrev. for:* **1.** torpedo boat. **2.** Also: **tb.** tuberculosis.
T-bar *n.* **1.** a T-shaped wrench for use with a socket. **2.** a metal bar having a T-shaped cross section. **3.** a T-shaped bar on a ski tow which skiers hold on to while being pulled up slopes. **4.** (*modifier*) another term for **T-strap.**
T-bone steak *n.* a large choice steak cut from the sirloin of beef, containing a T-shaped bone.
tbs. *or* **tbsp.** *abbrev. for* tablespoon(ful).
TBT *abbrev. for* tri-*n*-butyl tin: a biocide used in marine paints to prevent fouling.
Tc *the chemical symbol for* technetium.
TC (on cars, etc.) *abbrev. for* twin carburettors.
TCA cycle *abbrev. for* tricarboxylic acid cycle: another name for **Krebs cycle.**
T-cell *n.* another name for **T-lymphocyte.**
Tchebychev's inequality (ˌtʃɛbɪ'ʃɒfs) *n.* See **Chebyshev's inequality.**
TCP *n. Trademark.* a mild disinfectant used for cleansing minor wounds, gargling, etc. [abbrev. for *t(ri)c(hloro)p(henylmethyliodisalicyl)*]
TD *abbrev. for:* **1.** (in Ireland) Teachta Dála. [Irish Gaelic: member of the Dáil]. **2.** technical drawing. **3.** (in Britain) Territorial Decoration. **4.** Also: **td.** touchdown.
t.d.c. *abbrev. for* top dead-centre.
t distribution *n.* See **Student's t.**
tdm *abbrev. for* time-division multiplex. See **multiplex** (sense 1).
te *or* **ti** (tiː) *n. Music.* (in tonic sol-fa) the syllable used for the seventh note or subtonic of any scale. [see GAMUT]
Te *the chemical symbol for* tellurium.
tea (tiː) *n.* **1.** an evergreen shrub or small tree, *Camellia sinensis,* of tropical and subtropical Asia, having toothed leathery leaves and white fragrant flowers: family *Theaceae.* **2. a.** the dried shredded leaves of this shrub, used to make a beverage by infusion in boiling water. **b.** such a beverage, served hot or iced. **c.** (*as modifier*): *tea caddy; tea urn.* **3. a.** any of various plants that are similar to *Camellia sinensis* or are used to make a tealike beverage. **b.** any such beverage. **4.** *Chiefly Brit.* **a.** Also called: **afternoon tea.** a light meal eaten in mid-afternoon, usually consisting of tea and cakes, biscuits, or sandwiches. **b.** (*as modifier*): *a tea party.* **c.** Also called: **high tea.** afternoon tea that also includes a light cooked dish. **5.** *Brit., Austral., and N.Z.* the main evening meal. **6.** *U.S. and Canadian dated slang.* marijuana. **7. tea and sympathy.** *Informal.* a caring attitude, esp. to

someone in trouble. [C17: from Chinese (Amoy) *t'e,* from Ancient Chinese *d'a*]
tea bag *n.* a small bag of paper or cloth containing tea leaves, infused in boiling water to make tea.
tea ball *n. Chiefly U.S.* a perforated metal ball filled with tea leaves and put in boiling water to make tea.
teaberry ('tiːbərɪ, -brɪ) *n., pl.* **-ries. 1.** the berry of the wintergreen (*Gaultheria procumbens*). **2.** another name for **wintergreen** (sense 1). [C19: so called because its dried leaves have been used as a substitute for tea]
tea biscuit *n. Brit.* any of various semisweet biscuits.
teabread ('tiːˌbrɛd) *n.* **1.** a loaf-shaped cake that contains dried fruit which has been steeped in cold tea before baking: served sliced and buttered. **2.** any of a variety of loaf-shaped, usually light, cakes: *banana teabread.*
tea break *n. Brit.* a short rest period during working hours during which tea, coffee, etc. is drunk.
teacake ('tiːˌkeɪk) *n. Brit.* a flat cake made from a yeast dough with raisins in it, usually eaten toasted and buttered.
teacart ('tiːˌkɑːt) *n.* a U.S. and Canadian word for **tea trolley.**
teach (tiːtʃ) *vb.* **teaches, teaching, taught. 1.** (*tr.; may take a clause as object or an infinitive;* often foll. by *how*) to help to learn; tell or show (how): *to teach someone to paint; to teach someone how to paint.* **2.** to give instruction or lessons in (a subject) to (a person or animal): *to teach French; to teach children; she teaches.* **3.** (*tr.; may take a clause as object or an infinitive*) to cause to learn or understand: *experience taught him that he could not be a journalist.* **4.** Also: **teach (someone) a lesson.** *Informal.* to cause (someone) to suffer the unpleasant consequences of some action or behaviour. [Old English *tǣcan;* related to *tācen* TOKEN, Old Frisian *tēken,* Old Saxon *tēkan,* Old High German *zeihhan,* Old Norse *teikn* sign] —'**teachable** *adj.*
teacher ('tiːtʃə) *n.* **1.** a person whose occupation is teaching others, esp. children. **2.** a personified concept that teaches: *nature is a good teacher.* —'**teacherless** *adj.*
teachers' centre *n.* (in Britain) a place that provides a central store of educational aids, such as films and display material, and also in-service training, and is available for use to all the teachers within a particular area.
teach-in *n.* an informal conference, esp. on a topical subject, usually held at a university or college and involving a panel of visiting speakers, lecturers, students, etc.
teaching ('tiːtʃɪŋ) *n.* **1.** the art or profession of a teacher. **2.** (*sometimes pl.*) something taught; precept. **3.** (*modifier*) denoting a person or institution that teaches: *a teaching hospital.* **4.** (*modifier*) used in teaching: *teaching aids.*
teaching aid *n.* any device, object, or machine used by a teacher to clarify or enliven a subject.
teaching fellow *n.* a postgraduate student who is given tuition, accommodation, expenses, etc., in return for some teaching duties. —**teaching fellowship** *n.*
teaching hospital *n.* a hospital that is affiliated to a medical school and provides the students with teaching and supervised practical experience.
teaching machine *n.* a machine that presents information and questions to the user, registers the answers, and indicates whether these are correct or acceptable.
teaching practice *n.* a temporary period of teaching in a school undertaken under supervision by a person who is training to become a teacher.
tea cloth *n.* another name for **tea towel.**
tea cosy *n.* a covering for a teapot to keep the contents hot, often having holes for the handle and spout.
teacup ('tiːˌkʌp) *n.* **1.** a cup out of which tea may be drunk, larger than a coffee cup. **2.** Also called: **teacupful.** the amount a teacup will hold, about four fluid ounces.
tea dance *n.* a dance held in the afternoon at which tea is served.
tea garden *n.* **1.** an open-air restaurant that serves tea and light refreshments. **2.** a tea plantation.
tea gown *n.* (formerly) a long loose decorative dress worn esp. when entertaining guests to afternoon tea.
teahouse ('tiːˌhaʊs) *n.* a restaurant, esp. in Japan or China, where tea and light refreshments are served.
teak (tiːk) *n.* **1.** a large verbenaceous tree, *Tectona grandis,* of the East Indies, having white flowers and yielding a valuable wood. **2.** the hard resinous yellowish-brown wood of this tree, used for furniture making, etc. **3.** any of various similar trees or their wood. **4.** a brown or yellowish-brown colour. [C17: from Portuguese *teca,* from Malayalam *tēkka*]
teakettle ('tiːˌkɛtᵊl) *n.* a kettle for boiling water to make tea.
teal (tiːl) *n., pl.* **teals** *or* **teal. 1.** any of various small ducks, such as the Eurasian *Anas crecca* **(common teal)** that are related to the mallard and frequent ponds, lakes, and marshes. **2.** a greenish-blue colour. [C14: related to Middle Low German *tēlink,* Middle Dutch *tēling*]
tea lady *n.* a woman employed in a factory, office, etc. to make tea during a tea break.
tea leaf *n.* **1.** the dried leaf of the tea shrub, used to make tea. **2.** (*usually pl.*) shredded parts of these leaves, esp. after infusion. **3.** *Brit. and Austral. slang.* a thief. [sense 3 rhyming slang]
team (tiːm) *n.* (*sometimes functioning as pl.*) **1.** a group of people organized to work together. **2.** a group of players forming one of the sides in a sporting contest. **3.** two or more animals working together to pull a vehicle or agricultural implement. **4.** such animals and the vehicle: *the coachman riding his team.* **5.** *Dialect.* a flock, herd, or brood. **6.** *Obsolete.* ancestry. ~*vb.* **7.** (when *intr.,* often foll. by *up*) to make or cause to make a team: *he teamed George with Robert.* **8.** (*tr.*) *U.S. and Canadian.* to drag or transport in or by a team. **9.** (*intr.*) *U.S. and Canadian.* to drive a team. [Old English *team* offspring; related to Old Frisian *tām* bridle, Old Norse *taumr* chain yoking animals together, Old High German *zoum* bridle]
tea-maker *n.* a spoon with a perforated cover used to infuse tea in a cup of boiling water. Also called (esp. Brit.): **infuser, tea egg.**
team-mate *n.* a fellow member of a team.
team spirit *n.* willingness to cooperate as part of a team.
teamster ('tiːmstə) *n.* **1.** a driver of a team of horses used for haulage. **2.** *U.S. and Canadian.* the driver of a lorry.
team teaching *n.* a system whereby two or more teachers pool their skills, knowledge, etc., to teach combined classes.
teamwork ('tiːmˌwɜːk) *n.* **1.** the cooperative work done by a team. **2.** the ability to work efficiently as a team.
tea party *n.* a social gathering in the afternoon at which tea is served.
teapot ('tiːˌpɒt) *n.* a container with a lid, spout, and handle, in which tea is made and from which it is served.
teapoy ('tiːpɔɪ) *n.* **1.** a small table or stand with a tripod base. **2.** a tea caddy on such a table or stand. [C19: from Hindi *tipāī,* from Sanskrit *tri* three + *pāda* foot; compare Persian *sīpœ* three-legged stand]
tear[1] (tɪə) *n.* **1.** a drop of the secretion of the lacrimal glands. See **tears. 2.** something shaped like a falling drop: *a tear of amber.* ~Also called: **teardrop.** [Old English *tēar,* related to Old Frisian, Old Norse *tār,* Old High German *zahar,* Greek *dakri*] —'**tearless** *adj.*
tear[2] (tɛə) *vb.* **tears, tearing, tore, torn. 1.** to cause (material, paper, etc.) to come apart or (of material, etc.) to come apart; rip. **2.** (*tr.*) to make (a hole or split) in (something): *to tear a hole in a dress.* **3.** (*intr.;* often foll. by *along*) to hurry or rush: *to tear along the street.* **4.** (*tr.;* usually foll. by *away* or *from*) to remove or take by force. **5.** (when *intr.,* often foll. by *at*) to cause pain, distress, or anguish (to): *it tore at my heartstrings to see the starving child.* **6. tear one's hair.** *Informal.* to be angry, frustrated, very worried, etc. ~*n.* **7.** a hole, cut, or split. **8.** the act of tearing. **9.** a great hurry; rush. ~See also **tear away, tear down, tear into, tear off, torn.** [Old English *teran;* related to Old Saxon *terian,* Gothic *gatairan* to destroy, Old High German *zeran* to destroy] —'**tearable** *adj.* —'**tearer** *n.*
tear away (tɛə) *vb.* **1.** (*tr., adv.*) to persuade (oneself or someone else) to leave: *I couldn't tear myself away from the television.* ~*n.* **tearaway. 2.** *Brit.* **a.** a reckless impetuous unruly person. **b.** (*as modifier*): *a tearaway young man.*
tear down (tɛə) *vb.* (*tr., adv.*) to destroy or demolish: *to tear a wall down; to tear down an argument.*
tear duct (tɪə) *n.* the nontechnical name for **lacrimal duct.**
tearful ('tɪəful) *adj.* **1.** about to cry. **2.** accompanying or indicative of weeping: *a tearful expression.* **3.** tending to produce tears; sad. —'**tearfully** *adv.* —'**tearfulness** *n.*
tear gas (tɪə) *n.* any one of a number of gases or vapours that make the eyes smart and water, causing temporary blindness; usually dispersed from grenades and used in warfare and to control riots. Also called: **lacrimator.**
tearing ('tɛərɪŋ) *adj.* violent or furious (esp. in the phrase **tearing hurry** *or* **rush**).
tear into (tɛə) *vb.* (*intr., prep.*) *Informal.* to attack vigorously and damagingly.
tear-jerker ('tɪəˌdʒɜːkə) *n. Informal.* an excessively sentimental film, play, book, etc.
tear off (tɛə) *vb.* **1.** (*tr.*) to separate by tearing. **2.** (*intr., adv.*) to rush away; hurry. **3.** (*tr., adv.*) to produce in a hurry; do quickly and carelessly: *to tear off a letter.* **4. tear (someone) off a strip.** *Brit. informal.* to reprimand or rebuke (someone) forcibly. ~*adj.* **tear-off. 5.** (of paper, etc.) produced in a roll or block and marked with perforations so that one section at a time can be torn off.
tearoom ('tiːˌruːm, -ˌrʊm) *n.* another name for **teashop.**
tea rose *n.* **1.** any of several varieties of hybrid rose that are derived from *Rosa odorata* and have pink or yellow flowers with a scent resembling that of tea. **2. a.** a yellowish-pink colour. **b.** (*as adj.*): *tea-rose walls.*
tears (tɪəz) *pl. n.* **1.** the clear salty solution secreted by the lacrimal glands that lubricates and cleanses the surface of the eyeball and inner surface of the eyelids. **2.** a state of intense frustration (esp. in the phrase **bored to tears**). **3. in tears.** weeping. **4. without tears.** presented so as to be easily assimilated: *reading without tears.*
tear sheet (tɛə) *n.* a page in a newspaper or periodical that is cut or perforated so that it can be easily torn out.
tease (tiːz) *vb.* **1.** to annoy (someone) by deliberately offering something with the intention of delaying or withdrawing the offer. **2.** to arouse sexual desire in (someone) with no intention of satisfying it. **3.** to vex (someone) maliciously or playfully, esp. by ridicule. **4.** (*tr.*) to separate the fibres of; comb; card. **5.** (*tr.*) to raise the nap of (a fabric) with a teasel. **6.** another word (esp. U.S. and Canadian) for **backcomb. 7.** (*tr.*) to loosen or pull

apart (biological tissues, etc.) by delicate agitation or prodding with an instrument. ~*n.* **8.** a person or thing that teases. **9.** the act of teasing. [Old English *tǣsan;* related to Old High German *zeisan* to pick] —'**teasing** *adj.* —'**teasingly** *adv.*

teasel, teazel, *or* **teazle** ('ti:zəl) *n.* **1.** any of various stout biennial plants of the genus *Dipsacus,* of Eurasia and N Africa, having prickly leaves and prickly heads of yellow or purple flowers: family *Dipsacaceae.* See also **fuller's teasel. 2. a.** the prickly dried flower head of the fuller's teasel, used for teasing. **b.** any manufactured implement used for the same purpose. ~*vb.* **-sels, -selling, -selled** *or U.S.* **-sels, -seling, -seled. 3.** (*tr.*) to tease (a fabric). [Old English *tǣsel;* related to Old High German *zeisala* teasel, Norwegian *tīsl* undergrowth, *tīsla* to tear to bits; see TEASE] —'**teaseller** *n.*

teaser ('ti:zə) *n.* **1.** a person who teases. **2.** a preliminary advertisement in a campaign that attracts attention by making people curious to know what product is being advertised. **3.** a difficult question.

tea service *or* **set** *n.* the china or pottery articles used in serving tea, including a teapot, cups, saucers, etc.

teashop ('ti:ˌʃɒp) *n. Brit.* a restaurant where tea and light refreshments are served. Also called: **tearoom.**

teaspoon ('ti:ˌspu:n) *n.* **1.** a small spoon used for stirring tea, eating certain desserts, etc. **2.** Also called: **teaspoonful** ('ti:ˌspu:nfʊl). the amount contained in such a spoon. **3.** a unit of capacity used in cooking, medicine, etc., equal to about one fluid dram.

teat (ti:t) *n.* **1. a.** the nipple of a mammary gland. **b.** (in cows, etc.) any of the projections from the udder through which milk is discharged. See **nipple. 2.** something resembling a teat in shape or function, such as the rubber mouthpiece of a feeding bottle. [C13: from Old French *tete,* of Germanic origin; compare Old English *titt,* Middle High German *zitze*]

tea towel *or* **cloth** *n.* a towel for drying dishes and kitchen utensils. U.S. name: **dishtowel.**

tea tree *n.* any of various myrtaceous trees of the genus *Leptospermum,* of Australia and New Zealand, the leaves of which were formerly used to make tea.

tea trolley *n. Brit.* a trolley from which tea is served.

tea wagon *n.* a U.S. and Canadian name for **tea trolley.**

Tebet (te'vet) *n.* a variant spelling of **Tevet.**

TEC ('tɛk) *n. acronym for* Training and Enterprise Council.

tech (tɛk) *n. Informal.* short for **technical college.**

tech. *abbrev. for:* **1.** technical. **2.** technology.

technetium (tɛk'ni:ʃɪəm) *n.* a silvery-grey metallic element, artificially produced by bombardment of molybdenum by deuterons: used to inhibit corrosion in steel. The radioisotope **technetium-99m,** with a half-life of six hours, is used in radiotherapy. Symbol: Tc; atomic no.: 43; half-life of most stable isotope, ^{97}Tc: 2.6 × 10^6 years; valency: 2, 4, 5, 6, or 7; relative density: 11.5 (approx.); melting pt.: 2200°C (approx.); boiling pt.: 5030°C. [C20: New Latin, from Greek *tekhnētos* manmade, from *tekhnasthai* to devise artificially, from *tekhnē* skill]

technic *n.* **1.** (tɛk'ni:k). another word for **technique. 2.** ('tɛknɪk). another word for **technics.** [C17: from Latin *technicus,* from Greek *tekhnikos,* from *tekhnē* art, skill]

technical ('tɛknɪkᵊl) *adj.* **1.** of, relating to, or specializing in industrial, practical, or mechanical arts and applied sciences: *a technical institute.* **2.** skilled in practical and mechanical arts rather than theoretical or abstract thinking. **3.** relating to or characteristic of a particular field of activity: *the technical jargon of linguistics.* **4.** existing by virtue of a strict application of the rules or a strict interpretation of the wording: *a technical loophole in the law; a technical victory.* **5.** of, derived from, or showing technique: *technical brilliance.* **6.** (of a financial market) having prices determined by internal speculative or manipulative factors rather than by general or economic conditions: *a technical rally.* —'**technically** *adv.* —'**technicalness** *n.*

technical college *n. Brit.* an institution for further education that provides courses in technology, art, secretarial skills, agriculture, etc. Sometimes shortened to (informal) **tech.**

technical drawing *n.* the study and practice, esp. as a subject taught in school, of the basic techniques of draughtsmanship, as employed in mechanical drawing, architecture, etc. Abbrev.: **TD.**

technical institute *n. N.Z.* a higher-education institution. Sometimes shortened to (informal): **tech.**

technicality (ˌtɛknɪ'kælɪtɪ) *n., pl.* **-ties. 1.** a petty formal point arising from a strict interpretation of rules, etc.: *the case was dismissed on a technicality.* **2.** the state or quality of being technical. **3.** technical methods and vocabulary.

technical knockout *n. Boxing.* a judgment of a knockout given when a boxer is in the referee's opinion too badly beaten to continue without risk of serious injury.

technical sergeant *n.* a noncommissioned officer in the U.S. Marine Corps or Air Force ranking immediately subordinate to a master sergeant.

technician (tɛk'nɪʃən) *n.* **1.** a person skilled in mechanical or industrial techniques or in a particular technical field. **2.** a person employed in a laboratory, technical college, or scientific establishment to do mechanical and practical work. **3.** a person having specific artistic or mechanical skill, esp. if lacking original flair or genius.

Technicolor ('tɛknɪˌkʌlə) *n. Trademark.* the process of producing colour film by means of superimposing synchronized films of the same scene, each of which has a different colour filter, to obtain the desired mix of colour.

technicolour ('tɛknɪˌkʌlə) *or* **technicoloured** ('tɛknɪˌkʌləd) *adj.* brightly, showily, or garishly coloured; vividly noticeable.

technics ('tɛknɪks) *n. (functioning as sing.)* the study or theory of industry and industrial arts; technology.

technique *or* **technic** (tɛk'ni:k) *n.* **1.** a practical method, skill, or art applied to a particular task. **2.** proficiency in a practical or mechanical skill. **3.** special facility; knack: *he had the technique of turning everything to his advantage.* [C19: from French, from *technique* (adj.) TECHNIC]

techno- *combining form.* **1.** craft or art: *technology; technography.* **2.** technological or technical: *technocracy.* **3.** relating to or using technology: *technophobia.* [from Greek *tekhnē* skill]

technocracy (tɛk'nɒkrəsɪ) *n., pl.* **-cies. 1.** a theory or system of society according to which government is controlled by scientists, engineers, and other experts. **2.** a body of such experts. **3.** a state considered to be governed or organized according to these principles. —**technocrat** ('tɛknəˌkræt) *n.* —ˌ**techno'cratic** *adj.*

technography (tɛk'nɒgrəfɪ) *n.* the study and description of the historical development of the arts and sciences in the context of their ethnic and geographical background.

technol. *abbrev. for:* **1.** technological. **2.** technology.

technology (tɛk'nɒlədʒɪ) *n., pl.* **-gies. 1.** the application of practical or mechanical sciences to industry or commerce. **2.** the methods, theory, and practices governing such application: *a highly developed technology.* **3.** the total knowledge and skills available to any human society for industry, art, science, etc. [C17: from Greek *tekhnologia* systematic treatment, from *tekhnē* art, skill] —**technological** (ˌtɛknə'lɒdʒɪkᵊl) *adj.* —ˌ**techno'logically** *adv.* —**tech'nologist** *n.*

technology agreement *n.* a framework designed by trade unions for negotiating changes in employment caused by the introduction of new technology.

technophobia (ˌtɛknəʊ'fəʊbɪə) *n.* **1.** fear of the effects of technological developments on society or the environment. **2.** fear of using technological devices, such as computers.

technostructure ('tɛknəʊˌstrʌktʃə) *n.* the people who control the technology of a society, such as professional administrators, experts in business management, etc.

techy ('tɛtʃɪ) *adj.* **techier, techiest.** a variant spelling of **tetchy.** —'**techily** *adv.* —'**techiness** *n.*

tectibranch ('tɛktɪˌbræŋk) *n.* a mollusc of the suborder *Tectibranchia* (or *Tectibranchiata*) (order: *Opisthobranchia*), which includes the sea slugs and sea hares. [C19: New Latin, from *tectus* covered, from *tegere* to cover + *branchia:* see -BRANCH]

tectonic (tɛk'tɒnɪk) *adj.* **1.** denoting or relating to construction or building. **2.** *Geology.* **a.** (of landforms, rock masses, etc.) resulting from distortion of the earth's crust due to forces within it. **b.** (of processes, movements, etc.) occurring within the earth's crust and causing structural deformation. [C17: from Late Latin *tectonicus,* from Greek *tektonikos* belonging to carpentry, from *tektōn* a builder] —**tec'tonically** *adv.*

tectonics (tɛk'tɒnɪks) *n. (functioning as sing.)* **1.** the art and science of construction or building. **2.** the study of the processes by which the earth's surface has attained its present structure. See also **plate tectonics.**

tectorial membrane (tɛk'tɔ:rɪəl) *n.* the membrane in the inner ear that covers the organ of Corti. [C19: *tectorial,* from Latin *tectōrium* a covering, from *tegere* to cover]

tectrix ('tɛktrɪks) *n., pl.* **tectrices** ('tɛktrɪˌsi:z, tɛk'traɪsi:z). (*usually pl.*) *Ornithol.* another name for **covert** (sense 7). [C19: New Latin, from Latin *tector* plasterer, from *tegere* to cover] —**tectricial** (tɛk'trɪʃəl) *adj.*

ted[1] (tɛd) *vb.* **teds, tedding, tedded.** to shake out and loosen (hay), so as to dry it. [C15: from Old Norse *tethja;* related to *tad* dung, Old High German *zetten* to spread]

ted[2] (tɛd) *n. Informal.* short for **teddy boy.**

tedder ('tɛdə) *n.* **1.** a machine equipped with a series of small rotating forks for tedding hay. **2.** a person who teds.

teddy ('tɛdɪ) *n., pl.* **-dies.** a woman's one-piece undergarment, incorporating a chemise top and panties.

teddy bear *n.* a stuffed toy bear made from soft or fluffy material. Often shortened to **teddy.** [C20: from *Teddy,* from *Theodore,* after Theodore Roosevelt (1858–1919), U.S. president, who was well known as a hunter of bears]

teddy boy *n.* **1.** (in Britain, esp. in the mid-1950s) one of a cult of youths who wore mock Edwardian fashions, such as tight narrow trousers, pointed shoes, and long sideboards. Often shortened to **ted. 2.** any tough or delinquent youth. [C20: from *Teddy,* from *Edward,* referring to the Edwardian dress]

teddy girl *n.* a girl companion to a teddy boy.

Te Deum (ˌti: 'di:əm) *n.* **1.** an ancient Latin hymn in rhythmic prose, sung or recited at matins in the Roman Catholic Church and in English translation at morning prayer in the Church of England and used by both Churches as an expression of thanksgiving on special occasions. **2.** a musical setting of this hymn. **3.** a service of thanksgiving in which the recital of this hymn forms a central part. [from the Latin canticle beginning *Tē Deum laudāmus,* literally: Thee, God, we praise]

tedious (ˈtiːdɪəs) *adj.* **1.** causing fatigue or tedium; monotonous. **2.** *Obsolete.* progressing very slowly. —**ˈtediously** *adv.* —**ˈtediousness** *n.*

tedium (ˈtiːdɪəm) *n.* the state of being bored or the quality of being boring; monotony. [C17: from Latin *taedium,* from *taedēre* to weary]

tee[1] (tiː) *n.* **1.** a pipe fitting in the form of a letter T, used to join three pipes. **2.** a metal section with a cross section in the form of a letter T, such as a rolled-steel joist. **3.** any part or component shaped like a T.

tee[2] (tiː) *Golf.* ~*n.* **1.** Also called: **teeing ground.** an area, often slightly elevated, from which the first stroke of a hole is made. **2.** a support for a golf ball, usually a small wooden or plastic peg, used when teeing off or in long grass, etc. ~*vb.* **tees, teeing, teed. 3.** (when *intr.*, often foll. by *up*) to position (the ball) ready for striking, on or as if on a tee. ~See also **tee off.** [C17 *teaz,* of unknown origin]

tee[3] (tiː) *n.* a mark used as a target in certain games such as curling and quoits. [C18: perhaps from T-shaped marks, which may have originally been used in curling]

tee-hee *or* **te-hee** (ˈtiːˈhiː) *interj.* **1.** an exclamation of laughter, esp. when mocking. ~*n.* **2.** a chuckle. ~*vb.* **-hees, -heeing, -heed. 3.** (*intr.*) to snigger or laugh, esp. derisively. [C14: of imitative origin]

tee-joint *n.* a variant spelling of **T-joint.**

teem[1] (tiːm) *vb.* **1.** (*intr.;* usually foll. by *with*) to be prolific or abundant (in); abound (in). **2.** *Obsolete.* to bring forth (young). [Old English *tēman* to produce offspring; related to West Saxon *tīeman;* see TEAM]

teem[2] (tiːm) *vb.* **1.** (*intr.;* often foll. by *down* or *with rain*) to pour in torrents: *it's teeming down.* **2.** (*tr.*) to pour or empty out. [C15 *temen* to empty, from Old Norse *tœma;* related to Old English *tōm,* Old High German *zuomīg* empty] —**ˈteemer** *n.*

teen[1] (tiːn) *adj. Informal.* another word for **teenage.**

teen[2] (tiːn) *n. Obsolete.* affliction or woe. [Old English *tēona;* related to Old Saxon *tiono,* Old Frisian *tiona* injury]

-teen *n. combining form.* ten: added to modified forms of the numbers 3 to 9 to form the numbers 13 to 19. [Old English *-tēne, -tȳne*] —**-teenth** *adj. combining form.*

teenage (ˈtiːnˌeɪdʒ) *adj. also* **teenaged. 1.** (*prenominal*) of or relating to the time in a person's life between the ages of 13 and 19 inclusive. ~*n.* **2.** this period of time.

teenager (ˈtiːnˌeɪdʒə) *n.* a person between the ages of 13 and 19 inclusive.

teens (tiːnz) *pl. n.* **1.** the years of a person's life between the ages of 13 and 19 inclusive. **2.** all the numbers that end in *-teen.*

teeny (ˈtiːnɪ) *adj.* **-nier, -niest.** extremely small; tiny. Also: **teeny-weeny** (ˈtiːnɪˈwiːnɪ) *or* **teensy-weensy** (ˈtiːnzɪˈwiːnzɪ). [C19: variant of TINY]

teenybopper (ˈtiːnɪˌbɒpə) *n. Slang.* a young teenager, usually a girl, who avidly follows fashions in clothes and pop music. [C20: *teeny,* from TEENAGE + *-bopper* see BOP[1]]

tee off *vb.* (*adv.*) **1.** *Golf.* to strike (the ball) from a tee, as when starting a hole. **2.** *Informal.* to begin; start.

teepee (ˈtiːpiː) *n.* a variant spelling of **tepee.**

tee-piece *n.* a variant spelling of **T-piece.**

tee-plate *n.* a variant spelling of **T-plate.**

tee shirt *n.* a variant of **T-shirt.**

tee-square *n.* a variant spelling of **T-square.**

teeter (ˈtiːtə) *vb.* **1.** to move or cause to move unsteadily; wobble. ~*n., vb.* **2.** another word for **seesaw.** [C19: from Middle English *titeren,* related to Old Norse *titra* to tremble, Old High German *zittarōn* to shiver]

teeth (tiːθ) *n.* **1.** the plural of **tooth. 2.** the most violent part: *the teeth of the gale.* **3.** the power to produce a desired effect: *that law has no teeth.* **4. by the skin of one's teeth.** See **skin** (sense 11). **5. get one's teeth into.** to become engrossed in. **6. in the teeth of.** in direct opposition to; against: *in the teeth of violent criticism he went ahead with his plan.* **7. to the teeth.** to the greatest possible degree: *armed to the teeth.* **8. show one's teeth.** to threaten, esp. in a defensive manner.

teethe (tiːð) *vb.* (*intr.*) to cut one's baby (deciduous) teeth.

teething ring *n.* a plastic, hard rubber, or bone ring on which babies may bite while teething.

teething troubles *pl. n.* the difficulties or problems that arise during the initial stages of a project, enterprise, etc.

teetotal (tiːˈtəʊtᵊl) *adj.* **1.** of, relating to, or practising abstinence from alcoholic drink. **2.** *Dialect.* complete. [C19: allegedly coined in 1833 by Richard Turner, English advocate of total abstinence from alcoholic liquors; probably from TOTAL, with emphatic reduplication] —**teeˈtotaller** *n.* —**teeˈtotally** *adv.* —**teeˈtotalism** *n.*

teetotum (tiːˈtəʊtəm) *n. Archaic.* **1.** a spinning top bearing letters of the alphabet on its four sides. **2.** such a top used as a die in gambling games. [C18: from *T totum,* from *T* initial inscribed on one of the faces + *totum* the name of the toy, from Latin *tōtum* the whole]

tef *or* **teff** (tɛf) *n.* an annual grass, *Eragrostis abyssinica,* of NE Africa, grown for its grain. [C18: from Amharic *ṭēf*]

tefillah *or* **tephillah** (təˈfiːlə) *n., pl.* **-lin** (-lɪn). *Judaism.* another name for **phylactery** (sense 1). [from Hebrew]

TEFL *abbrev. for* Teaching (of) English as a Foreign Language.

Teflon (ˈtɛflɒn) *n.* a trademark for **polytetrafluoroethylene.**

teg (tɛg) *n.* **1.** a two-year-old sheep. **2.** the fleece of a two-year-old sheep. [C16: of unknown origin]

tegmen (ˈtɛgmən) *n., pl.* **-mina** (-mɪnə). **1.** either of the leathery forewings of the cockroach and related insects. **2.** the delicate inner covering of a seed. **3.** any similar covering or layer. [C19: from Latin: a cover, variant of *tegimen,* from *tegere* to cover] —**ˈtegminal** *adj.*

tegular (ˈtɛgjʊlə) *adj.* **1.** of, relating to, or resembling a tile or tiles. **2.** *Biology.* overlapping like a series of tiles: *tegular scales.* [C18: from Latin *tēgula* a tile, from *tegere* to cover] —**ˈtegularly** *adv.*

tegument (ˈtɛgjʊmənt) *n.* a less common word for **integument.** [C15: from Latin *tegumentum* a covering, from *tegere* to cover] —**tegumental** (ˌtɛgjʊˈmɛntᵊl) *or* ˌ**teguˈmentary** *adj.*

te-hee (ˈtiːˈhiː) *interj., n., vb.* a variant spelling of **tee-hee.**

te igitur *Latin.* (teɪ ˈɪgɪˌtʊə; *English* teɪ ˈɪdʒɪˌtʊə) *n. R.C. Church.* the first prayer of the canon of the Mass, which begins *Te igitur clementissime Pater* (*Thee, therefore, most merciful Father*).

teind (tiːnd) *n., vb.* a Scot. and northern English word for **tithe.**

tektite (ˈtɛktaɪt) *n.* a small dark glassy object found in several areas around the world, thought to be a product of meteorite impact. See also **moldavite.** [C20: from Greek *tēktos* molten]

tel. *abbrev. for:* **1.** telegram. **2.** telegraph(ic). **3.** telephone.

tel- *combining form.* a variant of **tele-** and **telo-** before a vowel.

tela (ˈtiːlə) *n., pl.* **-lae** (-liː). *Anatomy.* any delicate tissue or weblike structure. [from New Latin, from Latin: a web]

telaesthesia *or U.S.* **telesthesia** (ˌtɛlɪsˈθiːzɪə) *n.* the alleged perception of events that are beyond the normal range of perceptual processes. Compare **telegnosis, clairvoyance.** —**telaesthetic** *or U.S.* **telesthetic** (ˌtɛlɪsˈθɛtɪk) *adj.*

telamon (ˈtɛləmən) *n., pl.* **telamones** (ˌtɛləˈməʊniːz) *or* **-mons.** a column in the form of a male figure, used to support an entablature. Also called: **atlas.** Compare **caryatid.** [C18: via Latin from Greek, from *tlēnai* to bear]

telangiectasis (tɪˌlændʒɪˈɛktəsɪs) *or* **telangiectasia** (tɪˌlændʒɪɛkˈteɪzɪə) *n., pl.* **-ses** (-ˌsiːz). *Pathol.* an abnormal dilation of the capillaries or terminal arteries producing blotched red spots, esp. on the face or thighs. [C19: New Latin, from Greek *telos* end + *angeion* vessel + *ektasis* dilation] —**telangiectatic** (tɪˌlændʒɪɛkˈtætɪk) *adj.*

Telautograph (tɛlˈɔːtəˌgræf, -ˌgrɑːf) *n. Trademark.* a telegraphic device for reproducing handwriting, drawings, etc., the movements of an electromagnetically controlled pen at one end being transmitted along a line to a similar pen at the receiving end. —**telˌautoˈgraphic** *adj.* —**telautography** (ˌtɛlɔːˈtɒgrəfɪ) *n.*

tele- *or before a vowel* **tel-** *combining form.* **1.** at or over a distance; distant: *telescope; telegony; telekinesis; telemeter.* **2.** television: *telecast.* **3.** by means of or via telephone or television. [from Greek *tele* far]

telecast (ˈtɛlɪˌkɑːst) *vb.* **-casts, -casting, -cast** *or* **-casted. 1.** to broadcast (a programme) by television. ~*n.* **2.** a television broadcast. —**ˈteleˌcaster** *n.*

telecine (ˈtɛlɪˌsɪnɪ) *n.* apparatus for producing a television signal from cinematograph film.

telecom (ˈtɛlɪˌkɒm) *or* **telecoms** (ˈtɛlɪˌkɒmz) *n.* (*functioning as sing.*) short for **telecommunications.**

telecommunication (ˌtɛlɪkəˌmjuːnɪˈkeɪʃən) *n.* the telegraphic or telephonic communication of audio or video information over a distance by means of radio waves, optical signals, etc., or along a transmission line.

telecommunications (ˌtɛlɪkəˌmjuːnɪˈkeɪʃənz) *n.* (*functioning as sing.*) the science and technology of communications by telephony, radio, television, etc.

telecommuting (ˌtɛlɪkəˈmjuːtɪŋ) *n.* the use of home computers, telephones, etc., to enable a person to work from home while maintaining contact with colleagues, customers, or a central office. Also called: **teleworking.** —ˌ**telecomˈmuter** *n.*

teledu (ˈtɛlɪˌduː) *n.* a badger, *Mydaus javanensis,* of SE Asia and Indonesia, having dark brown hair with a white stripe along the back and producing a fetid secretion from the anal glands when attacked. [C19: from Malay]

téléférique (teɪleɪferˈiːk) *n.* a variant spelling of **téléphérique.**

teleg. *abbrev. for:* **1.** telegram. **2.** telegraph(ic). **3.** telegraphy.

telega (tɛˈleɪgə) *n.* a rough four-wheeled cart used in Russia. [C16: from Russian]

telegenic (ˌtɛlɪˈdʒɛnɪk) *adj.* having or showing a pleasant television image. [C20: from TELE(VISION) + (PHOTO)GENIC] —ˌ**teleˈgenically** *adv.*

telegnosis (ˌtɛləˈnəʊsɪs, ˌtɛləg-) *n.* knowledge about distant events alleged to have been obtained without the use of any normal sensory mechanism. Compare **clairvoyance.** [C20: from TELE- + *-gnosis,* from Greek *gnōsis* knowledge] —**telegnostic** (ˌtɛləˈnɒstɪk, ˌtɛləg-) *adj.*

telegony (tɪˈlɛgənɪ) *n. Genetics.* the supposed influence of a previous sire on offspring borne by a female to other sires. [C19: from TELE- + -GONY. Compare Greek *tēlegonos* "born far from one's homeland"] —**telegonic** (ˌtɛlɪˈgɒnɪk) *or* **teˈlegonous** *adj.*

telegram (ˈtɛlɪˌgræm) *n.* a communication transmitted by telegraph. See also **cable** (sense 5), **Telemessage.** —**telegrammatic** (ˌtɛlɪgrəˈmætɪk) *or* ˌ**teleˈgrammic** *adj.*

telegraph ('tɛlɪˌgræf, -ˌgrɑːf) *n.* **1. a.** a device, system, or process by which information can be transmitted over a distance, esp. using radio signals or coded electrical signals sent along a transmission line connected to a transmitting and a receiving instrument. **b.** (*as modifier*): *telegraph pole.* **2.** a message transmitted by such a device, system, or process; telegram. *~vb.* **3.** to send a telegram to (a person or place); wire. **4.** (*tr.*) to transmit or send by telegraph. **5.** (*tr.*) *Boxing, informal.* to prepare to deliver (a punch) so obviously that one's opponent has ample time to avoid it. **6.** (*tr.*) to give advance notice of (anything), esp. unintentionally. **7.** (*tr.*) *Canadian informal.* to cast (votes) illegally by impersonating registered voters. —**telegrapher** (tɪ'lɛgrəfə) *or* **te'legraphist** *n.*

telegraphic (ˌtɛlɪ'græfɪk) *adj.* **1.** used in or transmitted by telegraphy. **2.** of or relating to a telegraph. **3.** having a concise style; clipped: *telegraphic speech.* —ˌ**tele'graphically** *adv.*

telegraph plant *n.* a small tropical Asian leguminous shrub, *Desmodium gyrans,* having small leaflets that turn in various directions during the day and droop at night.

telegraphy (tɪ'lɛgrəfɪ) *n.* **1.** a system of telecommunications involving any process providing reproduction at a distance of written, printed, or pictorial matter. See also **facsimile** (sense 2). **2.** the skill or process of operating a telegraph.

Telegu ('tɛləˌguː) *n., adj.* a variant spelling of **Telugu.**

telekinesis (ˌtɛlɪkɪ'niːsɪs, -kaɪ-) *n.* **1.** the movement of a body caused by thought or willpower without the application of a physical force. **2.** the ability to cause such movement. —**telekinetic** (ˌtɛlɪkɪ'nɛtɪk, -kaɪ-) *adj.*

telemark ('tɛlɪˌmɑːk) *n.* **1.** *Skiing.* a turn in which one ski is placed far forward of the other and turned gradually inwards. **2.** a step in ballroom dancing involving a heel pivot. [C20: named after *Telemark,* county in Norway]

telemarketing ('tɛlɪˌmɑːkɪtɪŋ) *n.* another name for **telesales.** [C20: short for TELE(PHONE) MARKETING] —'**teleˌmarketer** *n.*

Telemessage ('tɛlɪˌmɛsɪdʒ) *n. Trademark.* a message sent by telephone or telex and delivered in printed form; in Britain, it has replaced the telegram.

telemeter (tɪ'lɛmɪtə) *n.* **1.** any device for recording or measuring a distant event and transmitting the data to a receiver or observer. **2.** any device or apparatus used to measure a distance without directly comparing it with a measuring rod, etc., esp. one that depends on the measurement of angles. *~vb.* **3.** (*tr.*) to obtain and transmit (data) from a distant source, esp. from a spacecraft. —**telemetric** (ˌtɛlɪ'mɛtrɪk) *or* ˌ**tele'metrical** *adj.* —ˌ**tele'metrically** *adv.*

telemetry (tɪ'lɛmɪtrɪ) *n.* **1.** the use of radio waves, telephone lines, etc., to transmit the readings of measuring instruments to a device on which the readings can be indicated or recorded. See also **radiotelemetry.** **2.** the measurement of linear distance using a tellurometer.

telencephalon (ˌtɛlɛn'sɛfəˌlɒn) *n.* the cerebrum together with related parts of the hypothalamus and the third ventricle. —**telencephalic** (ˌtɛlɛnsɪ'fælɪk) *adj.*

teleological argument *n. Philosophy.* the argument purporting to prove the existence of God from empirical facts, the premise being that the universe shows evidence of order and hence design. Also called: **argument from design.** Compare **ontological argument, cosmological argument.**

teleology (ˌtɛlɪ'ɒlədʒɪ, ˌtiːlɪ-) *n.* **1.** *Philosophy.* **a.** the doctrine that there is evidence of purpose or design in the universe, and esp. that this provides proof of the existence of a Designer. **b.** the belief that certain phenomena are best explained in terms of purpose rather than cause. **c.** the systematic study of such phenomena. ~See also **final cause.** **2.** *Biology.* the belief that natural phenomena have a predetermined purpose and are not determined by mechanical laws. [C18: from New Latin *teleologia,* from Greek *telos* end + -LOGY] —**teleological** (ˌtɛlɪə'lɒdʒɪkᵊl, ˌtiːlɪ-) *or* ˌ**teleo'logic** *adj.* —ˌ**teleo'logically** *adv.* —ˌ**tele'ologism** *n.* —ˌ**tele'ologist** *n.*

teleost ('tɛlɪˌɒst, 'tiːlɪ-) *n.* **1.** any bony fish of the subclass *Teleostei,* having rayed fins and a swim bladder: the group contains most of the bony fishes, including the herrings, carps, eels, cod, perches, etc. *~adj.* **2.** of, relating to, or belonging to the *Teleostei.* [C19: from New Latin *teleosteī* (pl.) creatures having complete skeletons, from Greek *teleos* complete + *osteon* bone]

telepath ('tɛlɪˌpæθ) *n.* **1.** a person who is telepathic. *~vb.* (*intr.*) **2.** to practise telepathy.

telepathize *or* **telepathise** (tɪ'lɛpəˌθaɪz) *vb.* (*intr.*) to practise telepathy.

telepathy (tɪ'lɛpəθɪ) *n. Psychol.* the communication between people of thoughts, feelings, desires, etc., involving mechanisms that cannot be understood in terms of known scientific laws. Also called: **thought transference.** Compare **telegnosis, clairvoyance.** [C19: from TELE- + Greek *patheia* feeling, perception: see -PATHY] —**telepathic** (ˌtɛlɪ'pæθɪk) *adj.* —ˌ**tele'pathically** *adv.* —**te'lepathist** *n.*

téléphérique *or* **téléférique** (teɪleɪfeɪ'riːk) *n.* **1.** a mountain cable car. **2.** a cableway. [C20: from French]

telephone ('tɛlɪˌfəʊn) *n.* **1. a.** Also called: **telephone set.** an electrical device for transmitting speech, consisting of a microphone and receiver mounted on a handset. **b.** (*as modifier*): *a telephone receiver.* **2. a.** a worldwide system of communications using telephones. The microphone in one telephone converts sound waves into electrical oscillations that are transmitted along a telephone wire or by radio to one or more distant sets, the receivers of which reconvert the incoming signal into the original sound. **b.** (*as modifier*): *a telephone exchange; a telephone call.* **3.** See **telephone box.** *~vb.* **4.** to call or talk to (a person) by telephone. **5.** to transmit (a recorded message, radio or television programme, or other information) by telephone, using special transmitting and receiving equipment. ~Often shortened to **phone.** —'**teleˌphoner** *n.* —**telephonic** (ˌtɛlɪ'fɒnɪk) *adj.* —ˌ**tele'phonically** *adv.*

telephone answering machine *n.* the full name for **answering machine.**

telephone box *n.* a soundproof enclosure from which a paid telephone call can be made. Also called: **telephone kiosk, telephone booth.**

telephone directory *n.* a book listing the names, addresses, and telephone numbers of subscribers in a particular area.

telephone number *n.* a set of figures identifying the telephone of a particular subscriber, and used in making connections to that telephone.

telephone selling *n.* another name for **telesales.**

telephonist (tɪ'lɛfənɪst) *n. Brit.* a person who operates a telephone switchboard. Also called (esp. U.S.): **telephone operator.**

telephony (tɪ'lɛfənɪ) *n.* a system of telecommunications for the transmission of speech or other sounds.

telephotography (ˌtɛlɪfə'tɒgrəfɪ) *n.* the process or technique of photographing distant objects using a telephoto lens. —**telephotographic** (ˌtɛlɪˌfəʊtə'græfɪk) *adj.*

telephoto lens ('tɛlɪˌfəʊtəʊ) *n.* a compound camera lens in which the focal length is greater than that of a simple lens of the same dimensions and thus produces a magnified image of a distant object. See also **zoom lens.**

teleport ('tɛlɪˌpɔːt) *vb.* (*tr.*) to move by means of telekinesis. [C20: from TELE- + PORT[5]]

teleprinter ('tɛlɪˌprɪntə) *n.* **1.** a telegraph apparatus consisting of a keyboard transmitter, which converts a typed message into coded pulses for transmission along a wire or cable, and a printing receiver, which converts incoming signals and prints out the message. U.S. name: **teletypewriter.** See also **telex, radioteletype.** **2.** a network of such devices, widely used for communicating information, etc. **3.** a similar device used for direct input/output of data into a computer at a distant location.

teleprocessing (ˌtɛlɪ'prəʊsɛsɪŋ) *n.* the use of remote computer terminals connected to a central computer to process data.

Teleprompter ('tɛlɪˌprɒmptə) *n. Trademark.* the U.S. and Canadian name for **Autocue.**

Teleran ('tɛləˌræn) *n. Trademark.* an electronic navigational aid in which the image of a ground-based radar system is televised to aircraft in flight so that a pilot can see the position of his aircraft in relation to others. [C20: from *Tele(vision) R(adar) A(ir) N(avigation)*]

telerecording (ˌtɛlɪrɪ'kɔːdɪŋ) *n.* the recording of television signals on tape or, more usually, on film.

telesales ('tɛlɪˌseɪlz) *n.* (*functioning as sing.*) the selling or attempted selling of a particular commodity or service by a salesman who makes his initial approach by telephone. Also called: **telemarketing, telephone selling.**

telescience ('tɛlɪˌsaɪəns) *n. Astronautics.* the investigation of remotely controlled scientific experiments.

telescope ('tɛlɪˌskəʊp) *n.* **1.** an optical instrument for making distant objects appear closer by use of a combination of lenses (**refracting telescope**) or lenses and curved mirrors (**reflecting telescope**). See also **terrestrial telescope, astronomical telescope, Cassegrainian telescope, Galilean telescope, Newtonian telescope.** **2.** any instrument, such as a radio telescope, for collecting, focusing, and detecting electromagnetic radiation from space. *~vb.* **3.** to crush together or be crushed together, as in a collision: *the front of the car was telescoped by the impact.* **4.** to fit together like a set of cylinders that slide into one another, thus allowing extension and shortening. **5.** to make or become smaller or shorter: *the novel was telescoped into a short play.* [C17: from Italian *telescopio* or New Latin *telescopium,* literally: far-seeing instrument; see TELE-, -SCOPE]

telescopic (ˌtɛlɪ'skɒpɪk) *adj.* **1.** of or relating to a telescope. **2.** seen through or obtained by means of a telescope. **3.** visible only with the aid of a telescope. **4.** able to see far. **5.** having or consisting of parts that telescope: *a telescopic umbrella.* —ˌ**tele'scopically** *adv.*

telescopic sight *n.* a telescope mounted on a rifle, etc., used for sighting.

Telescopium (ˌtɛlɪ'skəʊpɪəm) *n., Latin genitive* **Telescopii** (ˌtɛlɪ'skəʊpɪˌaɪ). an inconspicuous constellation in the S hemisphere, close to Sagittarius and Ara. [New Latin; see TELESCOPE]

telescopy (tɪ'lɛskəpɪ) *n.* the branch of astronomy concerned with the use and design of telescopes.

telesis ('tɛlɪsɪs) *n.* the purposeful use of natural and social processes to obtain specific social goals. [C19: from Greek: event, from *telein* to fulfil, from *telos* end]

telesoftware (ˌtɛlɪ'sɒftwɛə) *n.* the transmission of computer programs on a teletext system.

telespectroscope (ˌtɛlɪˈspɛktrəˌskəʊp) *n.* a combination of a telescope and a spectroscope, used for spectroscopic analysis of radiation from stars and other celestial bodies.
telestereoscope (ˌtɛlɪˈstɪərɪəˌskəʊp, -ˈstɛrɪə-) *n.* an optical instrument for obtaining stereoscopic images of distant objects.
telesthesia (ˌtɛlɪsˈθiːzɪə) *n.* the usual U.S. spelling of **telaesthesia.** —**telesthetic** (ˌtɛlɪsˈθɛtɪk) *adj.*
telestich (tɪˈlɛstɪk, ˈtɛlɪˌstɪk) *n.* a short poem in which the last letters of each successive line form a word. [C17: from Greek *telos* end + STICH]
teletex (ˈtɛlɪˌtɛks) *n.* an international means of communicating text between a variety of terminals.
Teletext (ˈtɛlɪˌtɛkst) *n.* *Trademark.* a form of Videotex in which information is broadcast by a television station and received on an adapted television set. **Ceefax** is provided by the BBC and **Oracle** by ITV.
telethon (ˈtɛləˌθɒn) *n.* a lengthy television programme to raise charity funds, etc. [C20: from TELE- + MARATHON]
Teletype (ˈtɛlɪˌtaɪp) *n.* **1.** *Trademark.* a type of teleprinter. **2.** (*sometimes not cap.*) a network of such devices, used for communicating messages, information, etc. ~*vb.* **3.** (*sometimes not cap.*) to transmit (a message) by Teletype.
Teletypesetter (ˌtɛlɪˈtaɪpˌsɛtə, ˈtɛlɪˌtaɪp-) *n.* *Trademark, printing.* a keyboard device whose output can either be punched tape, which can be used directly to operate a line-casting machine, or be transmitted by cable or wire to operate such a machine indirectly. —ˌ**teleˈtypeˌsetting** *n.*
teletypewriter (ˌtɛlɪˈtaɪpˌraɪtə, ˈtɛlɪˌtaɪp-) *n.* a U.S. name for **teleprinter.**
teleutospore (tɪˈluːtəˌspɔː) *n.* another name for **teliospore.** [C19: from Greek *teleutē,* from *telos* end + SPORE] —**teˌleutoˈsporic** *adj.*
televangelist (ˌtɛlɪˈvændʒəlɪst) *n.* *U.S.* an evangelical preacher who appears regularly on television, preaching the gospel and appealing for donations from viewers. [C20: from TELE(VISION + E)VANGELIST]
televise (ˈtɛlɪˌvaɪz) *vb.* **1.** to put (a programme) on television. **2.** (*tr.*) to transmit (a programme, signal, etc.) by television.
television (ˈtɛlɪˌvɪʒən) *n.* **1.** the system or process of producing on a distant screen a series of transient visible images, usually with an accompanying sound signal. Electrical signals, converted from optical images by a camera tube, are transmitted by UHF or VHF radio waves or by cable and reconverted into optical images by means of a television tube inside a television set. **2.** Also called: **television set.** a device designed to receive and convert incoming electrical signals into a series of visible images on a screen together with accompanying sound. **3.** the content, etc., of television programmes. **4.** the occupation or profession concerned with any aspect of the broadcasting of television programmes: *he's in television.* **5.** (*modifier*) of, relating to, or used in the transmission or reception of video and audio UHF or VHF radio signals: *a television transmitter.* ~Abbrev.: **TV** [C20: from TELE- + VISION] —ˌ**teleˈvisional** *adj.* —ˌ**teleˈvisionally** *adv.* —ˌ**teleˈvisionary** *adj.*
television tube *n.* a cathode-ray tube designed for the reproduction of television pictures. Sometimes shortened to **tube.** Also called: **picture tube.**
televisual (ˌtɛlɪˈvɪʒʊəl, -zjʊ-) *adj.* relating to, shown on, or suitable for production on television. —ˌ**teleˈvisually** *adv.*
teleworking (ˌtɛlɪˈwɜːkɪŋ) *n.* another name for **telecommuting.**
telewriter (ˈtɛlɪˌraɪtə) *n.* a telegraphic device for reproducing handwriting by converting the manually controlled movements of a pen into signals that, after transmission, control the movements of a similar pen.
telex (ˈtɛlɛks) *n.* **1.** an international telegraph service in which teleprinters are rented out to subscribers for the purpose of direct communication. **2.** a teleprinter used in such a service. **3.** a message transmitted or received by telex. ~*vb.* **4.** to transmit (a message) to (a person, office, etc.) by telex. [C20: from *tel(eprinter) ex(change)*]
telfer (ˈtɛlfə) *n.* a variant spelling of **telpher.**
telferage (ˈtɛlfərɪdʒ) *n.* a variant spelling of **telpherage.**
telic (ˈtɛlɪk) *adj.* **1.** directed or moving towards some goal; purposeful. **2.** (of a clause or phrase) expressing purpose. [C19: from Greek *telikos* final, from *telos* end]
Telidon (ˈtɛlɪˌdɒn) *n.* *Trademark.* a Canadian interactive Viewdata service.
teliospore (ˈtiːlɪəˌspɔː) *n.* any of the dark noninfective spores that are produced in each telium of the rust fungi and remain dormant during the winter. Also called: **teleutospore.** [C20: from TELIUM + SPORE]
telium (ˈtiːlɪəm, ˈtɛl-) *n., pl.* **telia** (ˈtiːlɪə, ˈtɛlɪə). the spore-producing body of some rust fungi in which the teliospores are formed. [C20: New Latin, from Greek *teleion,* from *teleios* complete, from *telos* end] —ˈ**telial** *adj.*
tell[1] (tɛl) *vb.* **tells, telling, told. 1.** (when *tr., may take a clause as object*) to let know or notify: *he told me that he would go.* **2.** (*tr.*) to order or instruct (someone to do something): *I told her to send the letter airmail.* **3.** (when *intr.*, usually foll. by *of*) to give an account or narration (of something): *she told me her troubles.* **4.** (*tr.*) to communicate by words; utter: *to tell the truth.* **5.** (*tr.*) to make known; disclose: *to tell fortunes.* **6.** (*intr.;* often foll. by *of*) to serve as an indication: *her blush told of her embarrassment.* **7.** (*tr.;* used with *can,* etc.; *may take a clause as object*) to comprehend, discover, or discern: *I can tell what is wrong.* **8.** (*tr.;* used with *can,* etc.) to distinguish or discriminate: *he couldn't tell chalk from cheese.* **9.** (*intr.*) to have or produce an impact, effect, or strain: *every step told on his bruised feet.* **10.** (*intr.;* sometimes foll. by *on*) *Informal.* to reveal secrets or gossip (about): *don't tell! she told on him.* **11.** (*tr.*) to assure: *I tell you, I've had enough!* **12.** (*tr.*) to count (votes). **13.** (*intr.*) *Dialect.* to talk or chatter. **14. tell it like it is.** *Informal, chiefly U.S.* to tell the truth no matter how unpleasant it is. **15. tell the time.** to read the time from a clock. **16. you're telling me.** *Slang.* I know that very well. ~See also **tell apart, tell off.** [Old English *tellan;* related to Old Saxon *tellian,* Old High German *zellen* to tell, count, Old Norse *telja*] —ˈ**tellable** *adj.*
tell[2] (tɛl) *n.* a large mound resulting from the accumulation of rubbish on a long-settled site, esp. one with mudbrick buildings, particularly in the Middle East. [C19: from Arabic *tall*]
tell apart *vb.* (*tr., adv.*) to distinguish between; discern: *can you tell the twins apart?*
teller (ˈtɛlə) *n.* **1.** another name for **cashier**[1] (sense 2). **2.** a person appointed to count votes in a legislative body, assembly, etc. **3.** a person who tells; narrator. —ˈ**tellerˌship** *n.*
tellin (ˈtɛlɪn) *n.* any of various slim marine bivalve molluscs of the genus *Tellina* (or *Macoma*) that live in intertidal sand, esp. the smooth oval delicately tinted *T. tenuis.* [from New Latin *tellina,* from Greek *tellinē* a shellfish]
telling (ˈtɛlɪŋ) *adj.* **1.** having a marked effect or impact: *a telling blow.* **2.** revealing: *a telling smile.* —ˈ**tellingly** *adv.*
tell off *vb.* (*tr., adv.*) **1.** *Informal.* to reprimand; scold: *they told me off for stealing apples.* **2.** to count and dismiss: *he told off four more soldiers.*
telltale (ˈtɛlˌteɪl) *n.* **1.** a person who tells tales about others. **2. a.** an outward indication of something concealed. **b.** (*as modifier*): *a telltale paw mark.* **3.** any of various indicators or recording devices used to monitor a process, machine, etc. **4.** *Nautical.* **a.** another word for **dogvane. b.** one of a pair of light vanes mounted on the main shrouds of a sailing boat to indicate the apparent direction of the wind.
tellurate (ˈtɛljʊˌreɪt) *n.* any salt or ester of telluric acid.
tellurian (tɛˈlʊərɪən) *adj.* **1.** of or relating to the earth. ~*n.* **2.** (esp. in science fiction) an inhabitant of the earth. [C19: from Latin *tellūs* the earth]
telluric[1] (tɛˈlʊərɪk) *adj.* **1.** of, relating to, or originating on or in the earth or soil; terrestrial. **2.** *Astronomy.* (of spectral lines or bands) observed in the spectra of celestial objects and caused by absorption of oxygen, water vapour, and carbon dioxide in the earth's atmosphere. [C19: from Latin *tellūs* the earth]
telluric[2] (tɛˈlʊərɪk) *adj.* of or containing tellurium, esp. in a high valence state. [C20: from TELLUR(IUM) + -IC]
telluric acid *n.* a white crystalline dibasic acid produced by the oxidation of tellurium by hydrogen peroxide. Formula: H_6TeO_6.
telluride (ˈtɛljʊˌraɪd) *n.* any compound of tellurium, esp. one formed between tellurium and a more electropositive element or group.
tellurion *or* **tellurian** (tɛˈlʊərɪən) *n.* an instrument that shows how day and night and the seasons result from the tilt of the earth, its rotation on its axis, and its revolution around the sun. [C19: from Latin *tellūs* the earth]
tellurite (ˈtɛljʊˌraɪt) *n.* any salt or ester of tellurous acid.
tellurium (tɛˈlʊərɪəm) *n.* a brittle silvery-white nonmetallic element occurring both uncombined and in combination with metals: used in alloys of lead and copper and as a semiconductor. Symbol: Te; atomic no.: 52; atomic wt.: 127.60; valency: 2, 4, or 6; relative density: 6.24; melting pt.: 449.5°C; boiling pt.: 989.8°C. [C19: New Latin, from Latin *tellūs* the earth, formed by analogy with URANIUM]
tellurize *or* **tellurise** (ˈtɛljʊˌraɪz) *vb.* (*tr.*) to mix or combine with tellurium.
tellurometer (ˌtɛljʊˈrɒmɪtə) *n.* *Surveying.* an electronic instrument for measuring distances of up to about 30 miles that consists of two units, one at each end of the distance to be measured, between which radio waves are transmitted. [C20: from Latin *tellūs* the earth + -METER]
tellurous (ˈtɛljʊrəs, tɛˈlʊərəs) *adj.* of or containing tellurium, esp. in a low valence state.
telly (ˈtɛlɪ) *n., pl.* **-lies.** *Informal, chiefly Brit.* short for **television.**
telo- *or before a vowel* **tel-** *combining form.* **1.** complete; final; perfect: *telophase.* **2.** end; at the end: *telencephalon.* [from Greek *telos* end]
telocentric (ˌtɛləˈsɛntrɪk) *adj.* *Genetics.* (of a chromosome) having the centromere at or close to the end.
telomerization *or* **telomerisation** (tɛˌlɒməraɪˈzeɪʃən) *n.* *Chem.* polymerization in the presence of a chain transfer agent to yield a series of products of low molecular weight. [C20: from TELO- + -MER]
telophase (ˈtɛləˌfeɪz) *n.* **1.** the final stage of mitosis, during which the chromosomes at each end of the cell are dispersed into nuclear material and a nuclear membrane forms around the two new nuclei. See also **prophase, metaphase, anaphase. 2.** the corresponding stage of the first division of meiosis. —ˌ**teloˈphasic** *adj.*
telpher *or* **telfer** (ˈtɛlfə) *n.* **1.** a load-carrying car in a telpherage. **2. a.** another word for **telpherage. b.** (*as modifier*): *a telpher*

line; a telpher system. ~*vb.* **3.** (*tr.*) to transport (a load) by means of a telpherage. [C19: changed from *telephore,* from TELE- + -PHORE] —**'telpheric** *or* **'telferic** *adj.*

telpherage *or* **telferage** ('tɛlfərɪdʒ) *n.* an overhead transport system in which an electrically driven truck runs along a single rail or cable, the load being suspended in a separate car beneath. Also called: **telpher line, telpher.**

telson ('tɛlsən) *n.* the last segment or an appendage on the last segment of the body of crustaceans and arachnids. [C19: from Greek: a boundary; probably related to *telos* end] —**telsonic** (tɛl'sɒnɪk) *adj.*

Telstar ('tɛl,stɑː) *n.* either of two low-altitude active communications satellites launched in 1962 and 1963 by the U.S. and used in the transmission of television programmes, telephone messages, etc.

Telugu *or* **Telegu** ('tɛlə,guː) *n.* **1.** a language of SE India, belonging to the Dravidian family of languages: the state language of Andhra Pradesh. **2.** (*pl.* **-gus** *or* **-gu**) a member of the people who speak this language. ~*adj.* **3.** of or relating to this people or their language.

temblor ('tɛmblə, -blɔː) *n., pl.* **temblors** *or* **temblores** (tɛm'blɔːreɪz). *Chiefly U.S.* an earthquake or earth tremor. [C19: American Spanish, from Spanish *temblar* to shake, tremble]

temerity (tɪ'mɛrɪtɪ) *n.* rashness or boldness. [C15: from Latin *temeritās* accident, from *temere* at random] —**temerarious** (,tɛmə'rɛərɪəs) *adj.*

Temne ('tɛmnɪ, 'tɪm-) *n.* **1.** (*pl.* **-nes** *or* **-ne**) a member of a Negroid people of N Sierra Leone. **2.** the language of this people, closely related to Bantu.

temp (tɛmp) *Informal.* ~*n.* **1.** a person, esp. a typist or other office worker, employed on a temporary basis. ~*vb.* (*intr.*) **2.** to work as a temp.

temp. *abbrev. for:* **1.** temperate. **2.** temperature. **3.** temporary. **4.** tempore. [Latin: in the time of]

temper ('tɛmpə) *n.* **1.** a frame of mind; mood or humour: *a good temper.* **2.** a sudden outburst of anger; tantrum. **3.** a tendency to exhibit uncontrolled anger; irritability. **4.** a mental condition of moderation and calm (esp. in the phrases **keep one's temper, lose one's temper, out of temper**). **5.** the degree of hardness, elasticity, or a similar property of a metal or metal object. **6.** *Archaic.* a middle course between two extremes. ~*vb.* (*tr.*) **7.** to make more temperate, acceptable, or suitable by adding something else; moderate: *he tempered his criticism with kindly sympathy.* **8.** to strengthen or toughen (a metal or metal article) by heat treatment, as by heating and quenching. **9.** *Music.* **a.** to adjust the frequency differences between the notes of a scale on (a keyboard instrument) in order to allow modulation into other keys. **b.** to make such an adjustment to the pitches of notes in (a scale). **10.** a rare word for **adapt. 11.** an archaic word for **mix.** [Old English *temprian* to mingle, (influenced by Old French *temprer*), from Latin *temperāre* to mix, probably from *tempus* time] —**'temperable** *adj.* —**,tempera'bility** *n.* —**'temperer** *n.*

tempera ('tɛmpərə) *n.* **1.** a painting medium for powdered pigments, consisting usually of egg yolk and water. **2. a.** any emulsion used as a painting medium, with casein, glue, wax, etc., as a base. **b.** the paint made from mixing this with pigment. **3.** the technique of painting with tempera. [C19: from Italian phrase *pingere a tempera* painting in tempera, from *temperare* to mingle; see TEMPER]

temperament ('tɛmpərəmənt, -prəmənt) *n.* **1.** an individual's character, disposition, and tendencies as revealed in his reactions. **2.** excitability, moodiness, or anger, esp. when displayed openly: *an actress with temperament.* **3.** the characteristic way an individual behaves, esp. towards other people. See also **character, personality. 4. a.** an adjustment made to the frequency differences between notes on a keyboard instrument to allow modulation to other keys. **b.** any of several systems of such adjustment, such as **just temperament,** a system theoretically impossible on keyboard instruments (see **just intonation**), **mean-tone temperament,** a system giving an approximation to natural tuning, and **equal temperament,** the system commonly used in keyboard instruments, giving a scale based on an octave divided into twelve exactly equal semitones. **5.** *Obsolete.* the characteristic way an individual behaves, viewed as the result of the influence of the four humours (blood, phlegm, yellow bile, and black bile). **6.** *Archaic.* compromise or adjustment. **7.** an obsolete word for **temperature.** [C15: from Latin *temperāmentum* a mixing in proportion, from *temperāre* to TEMPER]

temperamental (,tɛmpərə'mɛntᵊl, -prə'mɛntᵊl) *adj.* **1.** easily upset or irritated; excitable; volatile. **2.** of, relating to, or caused by temperament. **3.** *Informal.* working erratically and inconsistently; unreliable: *a temperamental sewing machine.* —**,tempera'mentally** *adv.*

temperance ('tɛmpərəns) *n.* **1.** restraint or moderation, esp. in yielding to one's appetites or desires. **2.** abstinence from alcoholic drink. [C14: from Latin *temperantia,* from *temperāre* to regulate]

temperate ('tɛmpərɪt, 'tɛmprɪt) *adj.* **1.** having a climate intermediate between tropical and polar; moderate or mild in temperature. **2.** mild in quality or character; exhibiting temperance. [C14: from Latin *temperātus*] —**'temperately** *adv.* —**'temperateness** *n.*

Temperate Zone *n.* those parts of the earth's surface lying between the Arctic Circle and the tropic of Cancer and between the Antarctic Circle and the tropic of Capricorn.

temperature ('tɛmprɪtʃə) *n.* **1.** the degree of hotness of a body, substance, or medium; a physical property related to the average kinetic energy of the atoms or molecules of a substance. **2.** a measure of this degree of hotness, indicated on a scale that has one or more fixed reference points. **3.** *Informal.* a body temperature in excess of the normal. **4.** *Archaic.* **a.** compromise. **b.** temperament. **c.** temperance. [C16 (originally: a mingling): from Latin *temperātūra* proportion, from *temperāre* to TEMPER]

temperature gradient *n.* the rate of change in temperature in a given direction, esp. in altitude.

temperature-humidity index *n.* an index of the effect on human comfort of temperature and humidity levels, 65 being the highest comfortable level.

temperature inversion *n. Meteorol.* an abnormal increase in temperature with height in the troposphere.

tempered ('tɛmpəd) *adj.* **1.** *Music.* **a.** (of a scale) having the frequency differences between notes adjusted in accordance with the system of equal temperament. See **temperament. b.** (of an interval) expanded or contracted from the state of being pure. **2.** (*in combination*) having a temper or temperament as specified: *ill-tempered.*

tempest ('tɛmpɪst) *n.* **1.** *Chiefly literary.* a violent wind or storm. **2.** a violent commotion, uproar, or disturbance. ~*vb.* **3.** (*tr.*) *Poetic.* to agitate or disturb violently. [C13: from Old French *tempeste,* from Latin *tempestās* storm, from *tempus* time]

tempestuous (tɛm'pɛstjʊəs) *adj.* **1.** of or relating to a tempest. **2.** violent or stormy: *a tempestuous love affair.* —**tem'pestuously** *adv.* —**tem'pestuousness** *n.*

tempi ('tɛmpiː) *n.* (in musical senses) the plural of **tempo.**

Templar ('tɛmplə) *n.* **1.** a member of a military religious order (**Knights of the Temple of Solomon**) founded by Crusaders in Jerusalem around 1118 to defend the Holy Sepulchre and Christian pilgrims; suppressed in 1312. **2.** (*sometimes not cap.*) *Brit.* a lawyer, esp. a barrister, who lives or has chambers in the Inner or Middle Temple, two of the chief law societies in London. [C13: from Medieval Latin *templārius* of the temple, from Latin *templum* TEMPLE[1]; first applied to the knightly order because their house was near the site of the Temple of Solomon]

template *or* **templet** ('tɛmplɪt) *n.* **1.** a gauge or pattern, cut out in wood or metal, used in woodwork, etc., to help shape something accurately. **2.** a pattern cut out in card or plastic, used in various crafts to reproduce shapes. **3.** a short beam, made of metal, wood, or stone, that is used to spread a load, as over a doorway. **4.** *Biochem.* the molecular structure of a compound that serves as a pattern for the production of the molecular structure of another specific compound in a reaction. [C17 *templet* (later spelling influenced by PLATE), probably from French, diminutive of TEMPLE[3]]

temple[1] ('tɛmpᵊl) *n.* **1.** a building or place dedicated to the worship of a deity or deities. **2.** a Mormon church. **3.** *U.S.* another name for a **synagogue. 4.** any Christian church, esp. a large or imposing one. **5.** any place or object regarded as a shrine where God makes himself present, esp. the body of a person who has been sanctified or saved by grace. **6.** a building regarded as the focus of an activity, interest, or practice: *a temple of the arts.* [Old English *tempel,* from Latin *templum;* probably related to Latin *tempus* TIME, Greek *temenos* sacred enclosure, literally: a place cut off, from *temnein* to cut] —**'templed** *adj.* —**'temple,like** *adj.*

temple[2] ('tɛmpᵊl) *n.* the region on each side of the head in front of the ear and above the cheek bone. [C14: from Old French *temple,* from Latin *tempora* the temples, from *tempus* temple of the head]

temple[3] ('tɛmpᵊl) *n.* the part of a loom that keeps the cloth being woven stretched to the correct width. [C15: from French, from Latin *templum* a small timber]

tempo ('tɛmpəʊ) *n., pl.* **-pos** *or* **-pi** (-piː). **1.** the speed at which a piece or passage of music is meant to be played, usually indicated by a musical direction (**tempo marking**) or metronome marking. **2.** rate or pace. [C18: from Italian, from Latin *tempus* time]

tempolabile (,tɛmpəʊ'leɪbaɪl) *adj. Chem.* changing irregularly with time.

temporal[1] ('tɛmpərəl, 'tɛmprəl) *adj.* **1.** of or relating to time. **2.** of or relating to secular as opposed to spiritual or religious affairs: *the lords spiritual and temporal.* **3.** lasting for a relatively short time. **4.** *Grammar.* of or relating to tense or the linguistic expression of time in general: *a temporal adverb.* [C14: from Latin *temporālis,* from *tempus* time] —**'temporally** *adv.* —**'temporalness** *n.*

temporal[2] ('tɛmpərəl, 'tɛmprəl) *adj. Anatomy.* of, relating to, or near the temple or temples. [C16: from Late Latin *temporālis* belonging to the temples; see TEMPLE[2]]

temporal bone *n.* either of two compound bones forming part of the sides and base of the skull: they surround the organs of hearing.

temporality (,tɛmpə'rælɪtɪ) *n., pl.* **-ties. 1.** the state or quality of being temporal. **2.** something temporal. **3.** (*often pl.*) a secular possession or revenue belonging to a Church, a group within the Church, or the clergy.

temporal lobe *n.* the laterally protruding portion of each cerebral hemisphere, situated below the parietal lobe and associated with sound perception and interpretation: it is thought to be the centre for memory recall.

temporary ('tɛmpərərɪ, 'tɛmprərɪ) *adj.* **1.** not permanent; provisional: *temporary accommodation.* **2.** lasting only a short time; transitory: *temporary relief from pain.* ~*n., pl.* **-raries. 3.** a person, esp. a secretary or other office worker, employed on a temporary basis. Often shortened to **temp.** [C16: from Latin *temporārius,* from *tempus* time] —'**temporarily** *adv.* —'**temporariness** *n.*

temporary hardness *n. Chem.* hardness of water due to the presence of magnesium and calcium hydrogencarbonates, which can be precipitated as carbonates by boiling.

temporize *or* **temporise** ('tɛmpəˌraɪz) *vb. (intr.)* **1.** to delay, act evasively, or protract a discussion, negotiation, etc., esp. in order to gain time or effect a compromise. **2.** to adapt oneself to the circumstances or occasion, as by temporary or apparent agreement. [C16: from French *temporiser,* from Medieval Latin *temporizāre,* from Latin *tempus* time] —ˌ**tempori'zation** *or* ˌ**tempori'sation** *n.* —'**tempoˌrizer** *or* '**tempoˌriser** *n.*

tempt (tɛmpt) *vb. (tr.)* **1.** to attempt to persuade or entice to do something, esp. something morally wrong or unwise. **2.** to allure, invite, or attract. **3.** to give rise to a desire in (someone) to do something; dispose: *their unfriendliness tempted me to leave the party.* **4.** to risk provoking (esp. in the phrase **tempt fate**). [C13: from Old French *tempter,* from Latin *temptāre* to test] —'**temptable** *adj.* —'**tempter** *n.*

temptation (tɛmp'teɪʃən) *n.* **1.** the act of tempting or the state of being tempted. **2.** a person or thing that tempts.

Tempter ('tɛmptə) *n.* **the.** Satan regarded as trying to lead men into sin.

tempting ('tɛmptɪŋ) *adj.* attractive or inviting: *a tempting meal.* —'**temptingly** *adv.* —'**temptingness** *n.*

temptress ('tɛmptrɪs) *n.* a woman who sets out to allure or seduce a man or men; seductress.

tempura ('tɛmpərə) *n.* a Japanese dish of seafood or vegetables dipped in batter and deep-fried, often at the table. [from Japanese: fried food]

tempus fugit *Latin.* ('tɛmpəs 'fjuːdʒɪt, -gɪt) time flies.

ten (tɛn) *n.* **1.** the cardinal number that is the sum of nine and one. It is the base of the decimal number system and the base of the common logarithm. See also **number** (sense 1). **2.** a numeral, 10, X, etc., representing this number. **3.** something representing, represented by, or consisting of ten units, such as a playing card with ten symbols on it. **4.** Also called: **ten o'clock.** ten hours after noon or midnight. ~*determiner.* **5. a.** amounting to ten: *ten tigers.* **b.** *(as pronoun): to sell only ten.* ~Related adj.: **decimal.** Related prefixes: **deca-, deci-.** [Old English *tēn;* related to Old Saxon *tehan,* Old High German *zehan,* Gothic *taihun,* Latin *decem,* Greek *deka,* Sanskrit *dasa*]

ten. *Music. abbrev. for:* **1.** tenor. **2.** tenuto.

ten- *combining form.* a variant of **teno-** before a vowel.

tenable ('tɛnəbᵊl) *adj.* able to be upheld, believed, maintained, or defended. [C16: from Old French, from *tenir* to hold, from Latin *tenēre*] —ˌ**tena'bility** *or* '**tenableness** *n.* —'**tenably** *adv.*

tenace ('tɛneɪs) *n. Bridge, whist.* a holding of two nonconsecutive high cards of a suit, such as the ace and queen. [C17: from French, from Spanish *tenaza* forceps, ultimately from Latin *tenāx* holding fast, from *tenēre* to hold]

tenacious (tɪ'neɪʃəs) *adj.* **1.** holding or grasping firmly; forceful: *a tenacious grip.* **2.** retentive: *a tenacious memory.* **3.** stubborn or persistent: *a tenacious character.* **4.** holding together firmly; tough or cohesive: *tenacious cement.* **5.** tending to stick or adhere: *tenacious mud.* [C16: from Latin *tenāx,* from *tenēre* to hold] —**te'naciously** *adv.* —**te'naciousness** *or* **tenacity** (tɪ'næsɪtɪ) *n.*

ten-acre block *n. N.Z.* a block of subdivided farming land, usually within commuting distance of a city, that provides a semi-rural way of life.

tenaculum (tɪ'nækjʊləm) *n., pl.* **-la** (-lə). a surgical or dissecting instrument for grasping and holding parts, consisting of a slender hook mounted in a handle. [C17: from Late Latin, from Latin *tenēre* to hold]

tenaille (tɛ'neɪl) *n. Fortifications.* a low outwork in the main ditch between two bastions. [C16: from French, literally: tongs, from Late Latin *tenācula,* pl. of TENACULUM]

tena koe (tə'nɑː 'kwɔɪ) *interj. N.Z.* a Maori greeting to one person.

tenancy ('tɛnənsɪ) *n., pl.* **-cies. 1.** the temporary possession or holding by a tenant of lands or property owned by another. **2.** the period of holding or occupying such property. **3.** the period of holding office, a position, etc. **4.** property held or occupied by a tenant.

tenant ('tɛnənt) *n.* **1.** a person who holds, occupies, or possesses land or property by any kind of right or title, esp. from a landlord under a lease. **2.** a person who has the use of a house, flat, etc., subject to the payment of rent. **3.** any holder or occupant. ~*vb.* **4.** *(tr.)* to hold (land or property) as a tenant. **5.** *(intr.;* foll. by *in) Rare.* to dwell. [C14: from Old French, literally: (one who is) holding, from *tenir* to hold, from Latin *tenēre*] —'**tenantable** *adj.* —'**tenantless** *adj.* —'**tenant-ˌlike** *adj.*

tenant farmer *n.* a person who farms land rented from another, the rent usually taking the form of part of the crops grown or livestock reared.

tenant-in-chief *n.* (in feudal society) a tenant who held some or all of his lands directly from the king.

tenantry ('tɛnəntrɪ) *n.* **1.** tenants collectively, esp. those with the same landlord. **2.** the status or condition of being a tenant.

tenants association *n.* an organization of tenants, usually with a written constitution and charitable status, whose aim is to improve the housing conditions, amenities, community life, and contractual positions of its members. See also **community association, residents association.**

tenants' charter *n.* (in Britain) a package of legal rights to which tenants of local authorities, new towns, and housing associations are entitled, including security of tenure, and the rights to buy the dwelling cheaply, to take in lodgers, and to sublet.

tench (tɛntʃ) *n.* a European freshwater cyprinid game fish, *Tinca tinca,* having a thickset dark greenish body with a barbel at each side of the mouth. [C14: from Old French *tenche,* from Late Latin *tinca*]

tend[1] (tɛnd) *vb.* (when *intr.,* usually foll. by *to* or *towards*) **1.** (when *tr., takes an infinitive*) to have a general disposition (to do something); be inclined: *children tend to prefer sweets to meat.* **2.** *(intr.)* to have or be an influence (towards a specific result); be conducive: *the party atmosphere tends to hilarity.* **3.** *(intr.)* to go or move (in a particular direction): *to tend to the south.* [C14: from Old French *tendre,* from Latin *tendere* to stretch]

tend[2] (tɛnd) *vb.* **1.** *(tr.)* to care for: *to tend wounded soldiers.* **2.** (when *intr.,* often foll. by *on* or *to*) to attend (to): *to tend on someone's wishes.* **3.** *(tr.)* to handle or control: *to tend a fire.* **4.** *(intr.;* often foll. by *to) Informal, chiefly U.S. and Canadian.* to pay attention. [C14: variant of ATTEND]

tendance ('tɛndəns) *n.* **1.** *Rare.* care and attention; ministration. **2.** *Obsolete.* attendants collectively.

tendency ('tɛndənsɪ) *n., pl.* **-cies. 1.** (often foll. by *to*) an inclination, predisposition, propensity, or leaning: *she has a tendency to be frivolous; a tendency to frivolity.* **2.** the general course, purport, or drift of something, esp. a written work. [C17: from Medieval Latin *tendentia,* from Latin *tendere* to TEND[1]]

tendentious *or* **tendencious** (tɛn'dɛnʃəs) *adj.* having or showing an intentional tendency or bias, esp. a controversial one. [C20: from TENDENCY] —**ten'dentiously, ten'denciously** *or* **ten'dentially, ten'dencially** *adv.* —**ten'dentiousness** *or* **ten'denciousness** *n.*

tender[1] ('tɛndə) *adj.* **1.** easily broken, cut, or crushed; soft; not tough: *a tender steak.* **2.** easily damaged; vulnerable or sensitive: *a tender youth; at a tender age.* **3.** having or expressing warm and affectionate feelings: *a tender smile.* **4.** kind, merciful, or sympathetic: *a tender heart.* **5.** arousing warm feelings; touching: *a tender memory.* **6.** gentle and delicate: *a tender breeze.* **7.** requiring care in handling; ticklish: *a tender question.* **8.** painful or sore: *a tender wound.* **9.** sensitive to moral or spiritual feelings: *a tender conscience.* **10.** *(postpositive;* foll. by *of)* careful or protective: *tender of one's emotions.* **11.** (of a sailing vessel) easily keeled over by a wind; crank. Compare **stiff** (sense 10). ~*vb.* **12.** *(tr.) Rare.* **a.** to make tender. **b.** to treat tenderly. [C13: from Old French *tendre,* from Latin *tener* delicate] —'**tenderly** *adv.* —'**tenderness** *n.*

tender[2] ('tɛndə) *vb.* **1.** *(tr.)* to give, present, or offer: *to tender one's resignation; tender a bid.* **2.** *(intr.;* foll. by *for)* to make a formal offer or estimate for (a job or contract). **3.** *(tr.) Law.* to offer (money or goods) in settlement of a debt or claim. ~*n.* **4.** the act or an instance of tendering; offer. **5.** *Commerce.* a formal offer to supply specified goods or services at a stated cost or rate. **6.** something, esp. money, used as an official medium of payment: *legal tender.* [C16: from Anglo-French *tendre,* from Latin *tendere* to extend; see TEND[1]] —'**tenderable** *adj.* —'**tenderer** *n.*

tender[3] ('tɛndə) *n.* **1.** a small boat, such as a dinghy, towed or carried by a yacht or ship. **2.** a vehicle drawn behind a steam locomotive to carry the fuel and water. **3.** an ancillary vehicle used to carry supplies, spare parts, etc., for a mobile operation, such as an outside broadcast. **4.** a person who tends. [C15: variant of *attender*]

tenderfoot ('tɛndəˌfʊt) *n., pl.* **-foots** *or* **-feet. 1.** a newcomer, esp. to the mines or ranches of the southwestern U.S. **2.** (formerly) a beginner in the Scouts or Guides.

tenderhearted (ˌtɛndə'hɑːtɪd) *adj.* having a compassionate, kindly, or sensitive disposition. —ˌ**tender'heartedly** *adv.* —ˌ**tender'heartedness** *n.*

tenderize *or* **tenderise** ('tɛndəˌraɪz) *vb. (tr.)* to make (meat) tender by pounding it to break down the fibres, by steeping it in a marinade, or by treating it with a tenderizer. —ˌ**tenderi'zation** *or* ˌ**tenderi'sation** *n.*

tenderizer *or* **tenderiser** ('tɛndəˌraɪzə) *n.* a substance, such as the plant enzyme papain, rubbed onto meat to soften the fibres and make it more tender.

tenderloin ('tɛndəˌlɔɪn) *n.* **1.** a tender cut of pork or other meat from between the sirloin and ribs. **2.** *U.S.* a district of a city that is particularly noted for vice and corruption. [sense 2 from *Tenderloin,* former district of New York City, regarded as an easy source of bribes for a corrupt policeman]

tendinous ('tɛndɪnəs) *adj.* of, relating to, possessing, or resembling tendons; sinewy. [C17: from New Latin *tendinōsus,* from Medieval Latin *tendō* TENDON]

tendon (ˈtɛndən) *n.* a cord or band of white inelastic collagenous tissue that attaches a muscle to a bone or some other part; sinew. [C16: from Medieval Latin *tendō,* from Latin *tendere* to stretch; related to Greek *tenōn* sinew]

tendril (ˈtɛndrɪl) *n.* **1.** a specialized threadlike leaf or stem that attaches climbing plants to a support by twining or adhering. **2.** something resembling a tendril, such as a wisp of hair. [C16: perhaps from Old French *tendron* tendril (confused with Old French *tendron* bud), from Medieval Latin *tendō* TENDON] —ˈ**tendrillar** *or* ˈ**tendrilous** *adj.*

Tenebrae (ˈtɛnəˌbreɪ) *n.* (*functioning as sing. or pl.*) *R.C. Church.* (formerly) the matins and lauds for Thursday, Friday, and Saturday of Holy Week, usually sung in the evenings or at night. [C17: from Latin: darkness]

tenebrism (ˈtɛnəˌbrɪzəm) *n.* (*sometimes cap.*) a school, style, or method of painting, adopted chiefly by 17th-century Spanish and Neapolitan painters, characterized by large areas of dark colours, usually relieved with a shaft of light. —ˈ**tenebrist** *n., adj.*

tenebrous (ˈtɛnəbrəs) *or* **tenebrious** (təˈnɛbrɪəs) *adj.* gloomy, shadowy, or dark. [C15: from Latin *tenebrōsus* from *tenebrae* darkness] —**tenebrosity** (ˌtɛnəˈbrɒsɪtɪ), ˈ**tenebrousness,** *or* **teˈnebriousness** *n.*

tenement (ˈtɛnəmənt) *n.* **1.** Also called: **tenement building.** (now esp. in Scotland) a large building divided into separate flats. **2.** a dwelling place or residence, esp. one intended for rent. **3.** *Chiefly Brit.* a room or flat for rent. **4.** *Property law.* any form of permanent property, such as land, dwellings, offices, etc. [C14: from Medieval Latin *tenementum,* from Latin *tenēre* to hold] —**tenemental** (ˌtɛnəˈmɛntᵊl) *or* ˌ**teneˈmentary** *adj.* —ˈ**teneˌmented** *adj.*

tenesmus (tɪˈnɛzməs, -ˈnɛs-) *n. Pathol.* an ineffective painful straining to empty the bowels or bladder. [C16: from Medieval Latin, from Latin *tēnesmos,* from Greek *teinesmos,* from *teinein* to strain] —**teˈnesmic** *adj.*

tenet (ˈtɛnɪt, ˈtiːnɪt) *n.* a belief, opinion, or dogma. [C17: from Latin, literally: he (it) holds, from *tenēre* to hold]

tenfold (ˈtɛnˌfəʊld) *adj.* **1.** equal to or having 10 times as many or as much: *a tenfold increase in population.* **2.** composed of 10 parts. ~*adv.* **3.** by or up to 10 times as many or as much: *the population increased tenfold.*

ten-gallon hat *n.* (in the U.S. and Canada) a cowboy's broad-brimmed felt hat with a very high crown. [C20: so called because of its large size]

tenia (ˈtiːnɪə) *n., pl.* **-niae** (-nɪˌiː). the U.S. spelling of **taenia.**

teniacide (ˈtiːnɪəˌsaɪd) *n.* the U.S. spelling of **taeniacide.**

teniafuge (ˈtiːnɪəˌfjuːdʒ) *n.* the U.S. spelling of **taeniafuge.**

teniasis (tiːˈnaɪəsɪs) *n.* the U.S. spelling of **taeniasis.**

Tenn. *abbrev. for* Tennessee.

tenner (ˈtɛnə) *n. Informal.* **1.** *Brit.* **a.** a ten-pound note. **b.** the sum of ten pounds. **2.** *U.S.* a ten-dollar bill.

Tennessee Walking Horse (ˌtɛnɪˈsiː) *n.* an American breed of horse, developed in the state of Tennessee, marked by its stamina and trained to move at a fast running walk. Often shortened to **Walking Horse.**

tennis (ˈtɛnɪs) *n.* **a.** a racket game played between two players or pairs of players who hit a ball to and fro over a net on a rectangular court of grass, asphalt, clay, etc. See also **lawn tennis, real tennis, court tennis, table tennis. b.** (*as modifier*): *tennis court; tennis racket.* [C14: probably from Anglo-French *tenetz* hold (imperative), from Old French *tenir* to hold, from Latin *tenēre*]

tennis ball *n.* a hollow rubber ball covered with felt, used in tennis.

tennis elbow *n.* a painful inflammation of the elbow caused by exertion in playing tennis and similar games.

tennis shoe *n.* a rubber-soled canvas shoe tied with laces.

tenno (ˈtɛnəʊ) *n., pl.* **-no** *or* **-nos.** the formal title of the Japanese emperor, esp. when regarded as a divine religious leader. [from Japanese *tennō*]

Tennysonian (ˌtɛnɪˈsəʊnɪən) *adj.* of, relating to, or in the style of the British poet Alfred, Lord Tennyson (1809–92).

teno- *or before a vowel* **ten-** *combining form.* tendon: *tenosynovitis.* [from Greek *tenōn*]

tenon (ˈtɛnən) *n.* **1.** the projecting end of a piece of wood formed to fit into a corresponding mortise in another piece. ~*vb. (tr.)* **2.** to form a tenon on (a piece of wood). **3.** to join with a tenon and mortise. [C15: from Old French, from *tenir* to hold, from Latin *tenēre*] —ˈ**tenoner** *n.*

tenon saw *n.* a small fine-toothed saw with a strong back, used esp. for cutting tenons.

tenor (ˈtɛnə) *n.* **1.** *Music.* **a.** the male voice intermediate between alto and baritone, having a range approximately from the B a ninth below middle C to the G a fifth above it. **b.** a singer with such a voice. **c.** a saxophone, horn, recorder, etc., intermediate in compass and size between the alto and baritone or bass. **d.** (*as modifier*): *a tenor sax.* **2.** general drift of thought; purpose: *to follow the tenor of an argument.* **3. a.** (in early polyphonic music) the part singing the melody or the cantus firmus. **b.** (in four-part harmony) the second lowest part lying directly above the bass. **4.** *Change-ringing.* **a.** the heaviest and lowest-pitched bell in a ring. **b.** (*as modifier*): *a tenor bell.* **5.** a settled course of progress. **6.** *Archaic.* general tendency. **7.** *Finance.* the time required for a bill of exchange or promissory note to become due for payment. **8.** *Law.* **a.** the exact words of a deed, etc., as distinct from their effect. **b.** an exact copy or transcript. [C13 (originally: general meaning or sense): from Old French *tenour,* from Latin *tenor* a continuous holding to a course, from *tenēre* to hold; musical sense via Italian *tenore,* referring to the voice part that was continuous, that is, to which the melody was assigned] —ˈ**tenorless** *adj.*

tenor clef *n.* the clef that establishes middle C as being on the fourth line of the staff, used for the writing of music for the bassoon, cello, or tenor trombone. See also **C clef.**

tenorite (ˈtɛnəˌraɪt) *n.* a black mineral found in copper deposits and consisting of copper oxide in the form of either metallic scales or earthy masses. Formula: CuO. [C19: named after G. *Tenore* (died 1861), Italian botanist]

tenorrhaphy (tɪˈnɒrəfɪ) *n., pl.* **-phies.** *Surgery.* the union of torn or divided tendons by means of sutures. [C19: from TENO- + Greek *raphē* a sewing or suture]

tenosynovitis (ˈtɛnəʊˌsaɪnəʊˈvaɪtɪs) *n.* painful swelling and inflammation of tendons, usually of the wrist, often the result of repetitive movements such as typing.

tenotomy (təˈnɒtəmɪ) *n., pl.* **-mies.** surgical division of a tendon. —**teˈnotomist** *n.*

tenpenny (ˈtɛnpənɪ) *adj.* (*prenominal*) *U.S. and Canadian.* (of a nail) three inches in length.

tenpin (ˈtɛnˌpɪn) *n.* one of the pins used in tenpin bowling. See also **tenpins.**

tenpin bowling *n.* a bowling game in which heavy bowls are rolled down a long lane to knock over the ten target pins at the other end. Also called (esp. U.S. and Canadian): **tenpins.**

tenpins (ˈtɛnˌpɪnz) *n.* (*functioning as sing.*) the U.S. and Canadian name for **tenpin bowling.**

tenrec (ˈtɛnrɛk) *n.* any small mammal, such as *Tenrec ecaudatus* (**tailless tenrec**), of the Madagascan family *Tenrecidae,* resembling hedgehogs or shrews: order *Insectivora* (insectivores). [C18: via French from Malagasy *tràndraka*]

tense[1] (tɛns) *adj.* **1.** stretched or stressed tightly; taut or rigid. **2.** under mental or emotional strain. **3.** producing mental or emotional strain: *a tense day.* **4.** (of a speech sound) pronounced with considerable muscular effort and having relatively precise accuracy of articulation and considerable duration: *in English the vowel* (iː) *in "beam" is tense.* Compare **lax** (sense 4). ~*vb.* **5.** (often foll. by *up*) to make or become tense. [C17: from Latin *tensus* taut, from *tendere* to stretch] —ˈ**tensely** *adv.* —ˈ**tenseness** *n.*

tense[2] (tɛns) *n. Grammar.* a category of the verb or verbal inflections, such as present, past, and future, that expresses the temporal relations between what is reported in a sentence and the time of its utterance. [C14: from Old French *tens* time, from Latin *tempus*] —ˈ**tenseless** *adj.*

tense logic *n. Logic.* the study of the logical properties of tense operators, and of the logical relations between sentences having tense, by means of consideration of appropriate formal systems.

tensible (ˈtɛnsəbᵊl) *adj.* capable of being stretched; tensile. —ˌ**tensiˈbility** *or* ˈ**tensibleness** *n.* —ˈ**tensibly** *adv.*

tensile (ˈtɛnsaɪl) *adj.* **1.** of or relating to tension. **2.** sufficiently ductile to be stretched or drawn out. **3.** *Rare.* (of musical instruments) producing sounds through the vibration of stretched strings. [C17: from New Latin *tensilis,* from Latin *tendere* to stretch] —ˈ**tensilely** *adv.* —**tensility** (tɛnˈsɪlɪtɪ) *or* ˈ**tensileness** *n.*

tensile strength *n.* a measure of the ability of a material to withstand a longitudinal stress, expressed as the greatest stress that the material can stand without breaking.

tensimeter (tɛnˈsɪmɪtə) *n.* a device that measures differences in vapour pressures. It is used to determine transition points by observing changes of vapour pressure with temperature. [C20: from TENSI(ON) + -METER]

tensiometer (ˌtɛnsɪˈɒmɪtə) *n.* **1.** an instrument for measuring the tensile strength of a wire, beam, etc. **2.** an instrument used to compare the vapour pressures of two liquids, usually consisting of two sealed bulbs containing the liquids, each being connected to one limb of a manometer. **3.** an instrument for measuring the surface tension of a liquid, usually consisting of a sensitive balance for measuring the force needed to pull a wire ring from the surface of the liquid. **4.** an instrument for measuring the moisture content of soil.

tension (ˈtɛnʃən) *n.* **1.** the act of stretching or the state or degree of being stretched. **2.** mental or emotional strain; stress. **3.** a situation or condition of hostility, suspense, or uneasiness. **4.** *Physics.* a force that tends to produce an elongation of a body or structure. **5.** *Physics.* **a.** voltage, electromotive force, or potential difference. **b.** (*in combination*): *high-tension; low-tension.* **6.** a device for regulating the tension in a part, string, thread, etc., as in a sewing machine. **7.** *Knitting.* the degree of tightness or looseness with which a person knits. [C16: from Latin *tensiō,* from *tendere* to strain] —ˈ**tensional** *adj.* —ˈ**tensionless** *adj.*

tensity (ˈtɛnsɪtɪ) *n.* a rare word for **tension** (senses 1–3).

tensive (ˈtɛnsɪv) *adj.* of or causing tension or strain.

tensor (ˈtɛnsə, -sɔː) *n.* **1.** *Anatomy.* any muscle that can cause a part to become firm or tense. **2.** *Maths.* a set of components, functions of the coordinates of any point in space, that transform linearly between coordinate systems. For three dimensional space there are 3^r components, where r is the rank. A tensor of zero rank is a scalar, of rank one, a vector. [C18: from New Latin, literally: a stretcher] —**tensorial** (tɛnˈsɔːrɪəl) *adj.*

ten-strike *n. Tenpin bowling.* another word for **strike** (sense 39).

tent[1] (tɛnt) *n.* **1. a.** a portable shelter of canvas, plastic, or other waterproof material supported on poles and fastened to the ground by pegs and ropes. **b.** (*as modifier*): *tent peg.* **2.** something resembling this in function or shape. ~*vb.* **3.** (*intr.*) to camp in a tent. **4.** (*tr.*) to cover with or as if with a tent or tents. **5.** (*tr.*) to provide with a tent as shelter. [C13: from Old French *tente*, from Latin *tentōrium* something stretched out, from *tendere* to stretch] —ˈ**tented** *adj.* —ˈ**tentless** *adj.* —ˈ**tent,like** *adj.*

tent[2] (tɛnt) *Med.* ~*n.* **1.** a plug of soft material for insertion into a bodily canal, etc., to dilate it or maintain its patency. ~*vb.* **2.** (*tr.*) to insert such a plug into (a bodily canal, etc.). [C14 (in the sense: a probe): from Old French *tente* (n.), ultimately from Latin *temptāre* to try; see TEMPT]

tent[3] (tɛnt) *n. Obsolete.* a red table wine from Alicante, Spain. [C16: from Spanish *tinto* dark-coloured; see TINT]

tent[4] (tɛnt) *Scot.* ~*n.* **1.** heed; attention. ~*vb.* (*tr.*) **2.** to pay attention to; take notice of. **3.** to attend to. [C14: from *attent* ATTEND and INTENT] —ˈ**tenter** *n.*

tentacle (ˈtɛntəkᵊl) *n.* **1.** any of various elongated flexible organs that occur near the mouth in many invertebrates and are used for feeding, grasping, etc. **2.** any of the hairs on the leaf of an insectivorous plant that are used to capture prey. **3.** something resembling a tentacle, esp. in its ability to grasp. [C18: from New Latin *tentāculum*, from Latin *tentāre*, variant of *temptāre* to feel] —ˈ**tentacled** *adj.* —ˈ**tentacle-,like** *or* **tentaculoid** (tɛnˈtækjʊ,lɔɪd) *adj.* —**tentacular** (tɛnˈtækjʊlə) *adj.*

tentage (ˈtɛntɪdʒ) *n.* **1.** tents collectively. **2.** a supply of tents or tenting equipment.

tentation (tɛnˈteɪʃən) *n.* a method of achieving the correct adjustment of a mechanical device by a series of trials. [C14: from Latin *tentātiō*, variant of *temptātiō* TEMPTATION]

tentative (ˈtɛntətɪv) *adj.* **1.** provisional or experimental; conjectural. **2.** hesitant, uncertain, or cautious. [C16: from Medieval Latin *tentātīvus*, from Latin *tentāre* to test] —ˈ**tentatively** *adv.* —ˈ**tentativeness** *n.*

tent caterpillar *n.* the larva of various moths of the family *Lasiocampidae*, esp. *Malacosoma americana* of North America, which build communal webs in trees.

tent dress *n.* a very full tent-shaped dress, having no darts, waistline, etc.

tenter (ˈtɛntə) *n.* **1.** a frame on which cloth is stretched during the manufacturing process in order that it may retain its shape while drying. **2.** a person who stretches cloth on a tenter. ~*vb.* **3.** (*tr.*) to stretch (cloth) on a tenter. [C14: from Medieval Latin *tentōrium*, from Latin *tentus* stretched, from *tendere* to stretch]

tenterhook (ˈtɛntə,hʊk) *n.* **1.** one of a series of hooks or bent nails used to hold cloth stretched on a tenter. **2. on tenterhooks.** in a state of tension or suspense.

tenth (tɛnθ) *adj.* **1.** (*usually prenominal*) **a.** coming after the ninth in numbering or counting order, position, time, etc.; being the ordinal number of *ten:* often written 10th. **b.** (*as n.*): *see you on the tenth; tenth in line.* ~*n.* **2. a.** one of 10 approximately equal parts of something. **b.** (*as modifier*): *a tenth part.* **3.** one of 10 equal divisions of a particular measurement, etc. Related prefix: **deci-**: *decibel.* **4.** the fraction equal to one divided by ten (1/10). **5.** *Music.* **a.** an interval of one octave plus a third. **b.** one of two notes constituting such an interval in relation to the other. ~*adv.* **6.** Also: **tenthly.** after the ninth person, position, event, etc. ~*sentence connector.* **7.** Also: **tenthly.** as the 10th point: linking what follows with the previous statements, as in a speech or argument. [C12 *tenthe*, from Old English *tēotha*; see TEN, -TH[2]]

tent stitch *n.* another term for **petit point** (sense 1). [C17: of uncertain origin]

tenuis (ˈtɛnjʊɪs) *n., pl.* **tenues** (ˈtɛnjʊ,iːz). (in the grammar of classical Greek) any of the voiceless stops as represented by kappa, pi, or tau (k, p, t). [C17: from Latin: thin]

tenuous (ˈtɛnjʊəs) *adj.* **1.** insignificant or flimsy: *a tenuous argument.* **2.** slim, fine, or delicate: *a tenuous thread.* **3.** diluted or rarefied in consistency or density: *a tenuous fluid.* [C16: from Latin *tenuis*] —**tenuity** (tɛˈnjuːɪtɪ) *or* ˈ**tenuousness** *n.* —ˈ**tenuously** *adv.*

tenure (ˈtɛnjʊə, ˈtɛnjə) *n.* **1.** the possession or holding of an office or position. **2.** the length of time an office, position, etc., lasts; term. **3.** *U.S. and Canadian.* the improved security status of a person after having been in the employ of the same company or institution for a specified period. **4.** *Property law.* **a.** the holding or occupying of property, esp. realty, in return for services rendered, etc. **b.** the duration of such holding or occupation. [C15: from Old French, from Medieval Latin *tenitūra*, ultimately from Latin *tenēre* to hold] —**tenˈurial** *adj.* —**tenˈurially** *adv.*

tenuto (tɪˈnjuːtəʊ) *adj., adv. Music.* (of a note) to be held for or beyond its full time value. Symbol: ˉ (written above a note). [from Italian, literally: held, from *tenere* to hold, from Latin *tenēre*]

teocalli (,tiːəʊˈkælɪ) *n., pl.* **-lis.** any of various truncated pyramids built by the Aztecs as bases for their temples. [C17: from Nahuatl, from *teotl* god + *calli* house]

teosinte (,tiːəʊˈsɪntɪ) *n.* a tall Central American annual grass, *Euchlaena mexicana*, resembling maize and grown for forage in the southern U.S. [C19: from Nahuatl *teocentli*, from *teotl* god + *centli* dry ear of corn]

tepal (ˈtiːpᵊl, ˈtɛpᵊl) *n.* any of the subdivisions of a perianth that is not clearly differentiated into calyx and corolla. [C20: from French *tépale* changed (on analogy with *sépale* sepal) from *pétale* PETAL]

tepee *or* **teepee** (ˈtiːpiː) *n.* a cone-shaped tent of animal skins used by certain North American Indians. [C19: from Siouan *tīpī*, from *ti* to dwell + *pi* used for]

tepefy (ˈtɛpɪ,faɪ) *vb.* **-fies, -fying, -fied.** to make or become tepid. [C17: from Latin *tepēre*] —**tepefaction** (,tɛpɪˈfækʃən) *n.*

tephra (ˈtɛfrə) *n. Chiefly U.S.* solid matter ejected during a volcanic eruption. [C20: Greek, literally: ashes]

tephrite (ˈtɛfraɪt) *n.* a variety of basalt containing augite, nepheline, or leucite. [C17: from Greek *tephros*, from *tephra* ashes; see -ITE[1]] —**tephritic** (tɪˈfrɪtɪk) *adj.*

tepid (ˈtɛpɪd) *adj.* **1.** slightly warm; lukewarm. **2.** relatively unenthusiastic or apathetic: *the play had a tepid reception.* [C14: from Latin *tepidus*, from *tepēre* to be lukewarm] —**teˈpidity** *or* ˈ**tepidness** *n.* —ˈ**tepidly** *adv.*

tequila (tɪˈkiːlə) *n.* **1.** a spirit that is distilled in Mexico from an agave plant and forms the basis of many mixed drinks. **2.** the plant, *Agave tequilana*, from which this drink is made. [C19: from Mexican Spanish, from *Tequila*, district in Mexico]

ter. *abbrev. for:* **1.** terrace. **2.** territory.

ter- *combining form.* three, third, or three times: *tercentenary.* [from Latin *ter* thrice; related to *trēs* THREE]

tera- *prefix.* denoting 10^{12}: *terameter.* Symbol: T [from Greek *teras* monster]

teraglin (təˈræglən) *n.* an edible marine fish, *Zeluco atelodus*, of Australia which has fine scales and is blue in colour. [from a native Australian language]

Terai (təˈraɪ) *n.* (*sometimes not cap.*) a felt hat with a wide brim worn in subtropical regions. [from *Terai*, a belt of marshy land at the foot of the Himalayas in India]

terakihi (,tɛrəˈkiːhiː) *n., pl.* **-kihis.** See **tarakihi.**

teraph (ˈtɛrəf) *n., pl.* **-aphim** (-əfɪm). *Old Testament.* any of various small household gods or images venerated by ancient Semitic peoples. (Genesis 31:19–21; I Samuel 19:13–16). [C14: from Hebrew, of uncertain origin]

terat- *or* **terato-** *combining form.* indicating a monster or something abnormal: *teratism; teratoid.* [from Greek *terat-*, *teras* monster, prodigy]

teratism (ˈtɛrə,tɪzəm) *n.* a malformed animal or human, esp. in the fetal stage; monster.

teratogen (ˈtɛrətədʒən, tɪˈrætə-) *n.* any substance, organism, or process that causes malformations in a fetus. Teratogens include certain drugs (such as thalidomide), infections (such as German measles), and ionizing radiation. —,**teratoˈgenic** *adj.*

teratoid (ˈtɛrə,tɔɪd) *adj. Biology.* resembling a monster.

teratology (,tɛrəˈtɒlədʒɪ) *n.* **1.** the branch of biology that is concerned with the structure, development, etc., of monsters. **2.** a collection of tales about mythical or fantastic creatures, monsters, etc. —**teratologic** (,tɛrətəˈlɒdʒɪk) *or* ,**teratoˈlogical** *adj.* —,**teraˈtologist** *n.*

teratoma (,tɛrəˈtəʊmə) *n., pl.* **-mata** (-mətə) *or* **-mas.** a tumour or group of tumours composed of tissue foreign to the site of growth.

teratophobia (,tɛrətəʊˈfəʊbɪə) *n. Psychiatry.* fear of giving birth to a monster.

terbia (ˈtɜːbɪə) *n.* another name (not in technical usage) for **terbium oxide.**

terbium (ˈtɜːbɪəm) *n.* a soft malleable silvery-grey element of the lanthanide series of metals, occurring in gadolinite and monazite and used in lasers and for doping solid-state devices. Symbol: Tb; atomic no.: 65; atomic wt.: 158.925; valency: 3 or 4; relative density: 8.234; melting pt.: 1360°C; boiling pt.: 3041°C. [C19: from New Latin, named after *Ytterby*, Sweden, village where it was discovered] —ˈ**terbic** *adj.*

terbium metal *n. Chem.* any of a group of related lanthanides, including terbium, europium, and gadolinium.

terbium oxide *n.* an amorphous white insoluble powder. Formula: Tb_2O_3. Also called: **terbia.**

terce (tɜːs) *or* **tierce** *n. Chiefly R.C. Church.* the third of the seven canonical hours of the divine office, originally fixed at the third hour of the day, about 9 a.m. [a variant of TIERCE]

tercel (ˈtɜːsᵊl) *or* **tiercel** *n.* a male falcon or hawk, esp. as used in falconry. [C14: from Old French, from Vulgar Latin *tertiolus* (unattested), from Latin *tertius* third, referring to the tradition that only one egg in three hatched a male chick]

tercentenary (,tɜːsɛnˈtiːnərɪ) *or* **tercentennial** *adj.* **1.** of or relating to a period of 300 years. **2.** of or relating to a 300th anniversary or its celebration. ~*n., pl.* **-tenaries** *or* **-tennials.** **3.** an anniversary of 300 years or its celebration. ~Also: **tricentennial.**

tercet (ˈtɜːsɪt, tɜːˈsɛt) *n.* a group of three lines of verse that rhyme together or are connected by rhyme with adjacent groups of three lines. [C16: from French, from Italian *terzetto*, diminutive of *terzo* third, from Latin *tertius*]

terebene (ˈtɛrə,biːn) *n.* a mixture of hydrocarbons prepared from oil of turpentine and sulphuric acid, used to make paints and varnishes and medicinally as an expectorant and antiseptic. [C19: from TEREB(INTH) + -ENE]

terebic acid (tɛˈrɛbɪk) *n.* a white crystalline carboxylic acid produced by the action of nitric acid on turpentine. Formula: $C_7H_{10}O_4$. [C19: from TEREB(INTH) + -IC]
terebinth (ˈtɛrɪbɪnθ) *n.* a small anacardiaceous tree, *Pistacia terebinthus,* of the Mediterranean region, having winged leafstalks and clusters of small flowers, and yielding a turpentine. [C14: from Latin *terebinthus,* from Greek *terebinthos* turpentine tree]
terebinthine (ˌtɛrɪˈbɪnθaɪn) *adj.* **1.** of or relating to terebinth or related plants. **2.** of, consisting of, or resembling turpentine.
terebrate (ˈtɛrɪˌbreɪt) *adj.* (of animals, esp. insects) having a boring or penetrating organ, such as a sting. [C20: from Latin *terebra* borer + -ATE[1]]
teredo (tɛˈriːdəʊ) *n., pl.* **-dos** *or* **-dines** (-dɪˌniːz). any marine bivalve mollusc of the genus *Teredo.* See **shipworm.** [C17: via Latin from Greek *terēdōn* wood-boring worm; related to Greek *tetrainein* to pierce]
terephthalic acid (ˌtɛrɛfˈθælɪk) *n.* a white crystalline water-insoluble carboxylic acid used in making polyester resins such as Terylene; 1,4-benzenedicarboxylic acid. Formula: $C_6H_4(COOH)_2$. [C20: from TEREBENE + PHTHALIC ACID]
terete (ˈtɛriːt) *adj.* (esp. of plant parts) cylindrical and tapering. [C17: from Latin *teres* smooth, from *terere* to rub]
tergiversate (ˈtɜːdʒɪvəˌseɪt) *vb. (intr.)* **1.** to change sides or loyalties; apostatize. **2.** to be evasive or ambiguous; equivocate. [C17: from Latin *tergiversārī* to turn one's back, from *tergum* back + *vertere* to turn] —ˌ**tergiverˈsation** *n.* —ˈ**tergiverˌsator** *or* **tergiversant** (ˈtɜːdʒɪˌvɜːsᵊnt) *n.* —ˌ**tergiˈversatory** *adj.*
tergum (ˈtɜːgəm) *n., pl.* **-ga** (-gə). a cuticular plate covering the dorsal surface of a body segment of an arthropod. Compare **sternum** (sense 3). [C19: from Latin: the back] —ˈ**tergal** *adj.*
teriyaki (ˌtɛrɪˈjækɪ) *adj.* **1.** *Japanese cookery.* marinated in soy sauce and rice wine and grilled, usually over charcoal. ~*n.* **2.** a dish of meat prepared in this way. [from Japanese, from *teri* shine, gloss + *yaki* to broil]
term (tɜːm) *n.* **1.** a name, expression, or word used for some particular thing, esp. in a specialized field of knowledge: *a medical term.* **2.** any word or expression. **3.** a limited period of time: *his second term of office; a prison term.* **4.** any of the divisions of the academic year during which a school, college, etc., is in session. **5.** a point in time determined for an event or for the end of a period. **6.** Also called: **full term.** the period at which childbirth is imminent. **7.** *Law.* **a.** an estate or interest in land limited to run for a specified period: *a term of years.* **b.** the duration of an estate, etc. **c.** (formerly) a period of time during which sessions of courts of law were held. **d.** time allowed to a debtor to settle. **8.** *Maths.* either of the expressions the ratio of which is a fraction or proportion, any of the separate elements of a sequence, or any of the individual addends of a polynomial or series. **9.** *Logic.* **a.** the word or phrase that forms either the subject or predicate of a proposition. **b.** a name or variable, as opposed to a predicate. **c.** one of the relata of a relation. **d.** any of the three subjects or predicates occurring in a syllogism. **10.** Also called: **terminal, terminus, terminal figure.** *Architect.* a sculptured post, esp. one in the form of an armless bust or an animal on the top of a square pillar. **11.** *Australian Rules football.* the usual word for **quarter** (sense 10). **12.** *Archaic.* a boundary or limit. ~*vb.* **13.** *(tr.)* to designate; call: *he was termed a thief.* ~See also **terms.** [C13: from Old French *terme,* from Latin *terminus* end] —ˈ**termly** *adv.*
term. *abbrev. for:* **1.** terminal. **2.** termination.
termagant (ˈtɜːməgənt) *n.* **a.** a shrewish woman; scold. **b.** (*as modifier*): *a termagant woman.* [C13: from earlier *Tervagaunt,* from Old French *Tervagan,* from Italian *Trivigante;* after an arrogant character in medieval mystery plays who was supposed to be a Muslim deity] —ˈ**termagancy** *n.* —ˈ**termagantly** *adv.*
termer (ˈtɜːmə) *n.* a variant spelling of **termor.**
-termer *n. (in combination)* a person serving a specified length of time in prison: *a short-termer.*
terminable (ˈtɜːmɪnəbᵊl, ˈtɜːmnəbᵊl) *adj.* **1.** able to be terminated. **2.** terminating after a specific period or event: *a terminable annuity.* —ˌ**terminaˈbility** *or* ˈ**terminableness** *n.* —ˈ**terminably** *adv.*
terminal (ˈtɜːmɪnᵊl) *adj.* **1.** of, being, or situated at an end, terminus, or boundary: *a terminal station; terminal buds.* **2.** of, relating to, or occurring after or in a term: *terminal leave; terminal examinations.* **3.** (of a disease) terminating in death: *terminal cancer.* **4.** *Informal.* extreme: *terminal boredom.* **5.** of or relating to the storage or delivery of freight at a warehouse: *a terminal service.* ~*n.* **6.** a terminating point, part, or place. **7. a.** a point at which current enters or leaves an electrical device, such as a battery or a circuit. **b.** a conductor by which current enters or leaves at such a point. **8.** *Computer technol.* a device having input/output links with a computer but situated at a distance from the computer. **9.** *Architect.* **a.** an ornamental carving at the end of a structure. **b.** another name for **term** (sense 10). **10. a.** a point or station usually at the end of the line of a railway, serving as an important access point for passengers or freight. **b.** a less common name for **terminus.** **11.** a purpose-built reception and departure structure at the terminus of a bus, sea, or air transport route. **12.** a site where raw material is unloaded, stored, in some cases reprocessed, and reloaded for further transportation, esp. an onshore installation designed to receive offshore oil or gas from tankers or a pipeline. **13.** *Physiol.* **a.** the smallest arteriole before its division into capillaries. **b.** either of two veins that collect blood from the thalamus and surrounding structures and empty it into the internal cerebral vein. **c.** the portion of a bronchiole just before it subdivides into the air sacs of the lungs. [C15: from Latin *terminālis,* from *terminus* end] —ˈ**terminally** *adv.*
terminal market *n.* a commodity market in a trading centre rather than at a producing centre.
terminal platform *n.* (in the oil industry) an offshore platform from which oil or gas is pumped ashore through a pipeline.
terminal velocity *n.* **1.** the constant maximum velocity reached by a body falling under gravity through a fluid, esp. the atmosphere. **2.** the velocity of a missile or projectile when it reaches its target. **3.** the maximum velocity attained by a rocket, missile, or shell flying in a parabolic flight path. **4.** the maximum velocity that an aircraft can attain, as determined by its total drag.
terminate (ˈtɜːmɪˌneɪt) *vb.* **1.** (when *intr.,* often foll. by *in* or *with*) to form, be, or put an end (to); conclude: *to terminate a pregnancy; their relationship terminated amicably.* **2.** *(tr.)* to connect (suitable circuitry) to the end of an electrical transmission line to absorb the energy and avoid reflections. **3.** *(intr.) Maths.* (of a decimal expansion) to have only a finite number of digits. [C16: from Latin *terminātus* limited, from *termināre* to set boundaries, from *terminus* end] —ˈ**terminative** *adj.* —ˈ**terminatory** *adj.*
termination (ˌtɜːmɪˈneɪʃən) *n.* **1.** the act of terminating or the state of being terminated. **2.** something that terminates. **3.** a final result. —ˌ**termiˈnational** *adj.*
terminator (ˈtɜːmɪˌneɪtə) *n.* the line dividing the illuminated and dark part of the moon or planet.
terminology (ˌtɜːmɪˈnɒlədʒɪ) *n., pl.* **-gies.** **1.** the body of specialized words relating to a particular subject. **2.** the study of terms. [C19: from Medieval Latin *terminus* term, from Latin: end] —**terminological** (ˌtɜːmɪnəˈlɒdʒɪkᵊl) *adj.* —ˌ**terminoˈlogically** *adv.* —ˌ**termiˈnologist** *n.*
term insurance *n.* life assurance, usually low in cost and offering no cash value, that provides for the payment of a specified sum of money only if the insured dies within a stipulated period of time.
terminus (ˈtɜːmɪnəs) *n., pl.* **-ni** (-naɪ) *or* **-nuses.** **1.** the last or final part or point. **2.** either end of a railway, bus route, etc., or a station or town at such a point. **3.** a goal aimed for. **4.** a boundary or boundary marker. **5.** *Architect.* another name for **term** (sense 10). [C16: from Latin: end; related to Greek *termōn* boundary]
terminus ad quem *Latin.* (ˈtɜːmɪˌnʊs æd ˈkwɛm) *n.* the aim or terminal point. [literally: the end to which]
terminus a quo *Latin.* (ˈtɜːmɪˌnʊs ɑː ˈkwəʊ) *n.* the starting point; beginning. [literally: the end from which]
termitarium (ˌtɜːmɪˈtɛərɪəm) *n., pl.* **-ia** (-ɪə). the nest of a termite colony. [C20: from TERMITE + -ARIUM]
termite (ˈtɜːmaɪt) *n.* any whitish ant-like social insect of the order *Isoptera,* of warm and tropical regions. Some species feed on wood, causing damage to furniture, buildings, trees, etc. Also called: **white ant.** [C18: from New Latin *termitēs* white ants, pl. of *termes,* from Latin: a woodworm; related to Greek *tetrainein* to bore through] —**termitic** (tɜːˈmɪtɪk) *adj.*
termless (ˈtɜːmlɪs) *adj.* **1.** without limit or boundary. **2.** unconditional. **3.** an archaic word for **indescribable.**
termor *or* **termer** (ˈtɜːmə) *n. Property law.* a person who holds an estate for a term of years or until he dies. [C14: from Anglo-French *termer,* from *terme* TERM]
terms (tɜːmz) *pl. n.* **1.** (usually specified prenominally) the actual language or mode of presentation used: *he described the project in loose terms.* **2.** conditions of an agreement: *you work here on our terms.* **3.** a sum of money paid for a service or credit; charges. **4.** (usually preceded by *on*) mutual relationship or standing: *they are on affectionate terms.* **5. bring to terms.** to cause to agree or submit. **6. in terms of.** as expressed by; regarding: *in terms of money he was no better off.* **7. come to terms.** to reach acceptance or agreement: *to come to terms with one's failings.*
terms of trade *pl. n. Economics, Brit.* the ratio of export prices to import prices. It measures a nation's trading position, which improves when export prices rise faster or fall slower than import prices.
tern[1] (tɜːn) *n.* any aquatic bird of the subfamily *Sterninae,* having a forked tail, long narrow wings, a pointed bill, and a typically black-and-white plumage: family *Laridae* (gulls, etc.), order *Charadriiformes.* [C18: from Old Norse *therna;* related to Norwegian *terna,* Swedish *tärna*]
tern[2] (tɜːn) *n.* **1.** a three-masted schooner. **2.** *Rare.* a group of three. [C14: from Old French *terne,* from Italian *terno,* from Latin *ternī* three each; related to Latin *ter* thrice, *trēs* three]
ternary (ˈtɜːnərɪ) *adj.* **1.** consisting of three or groups of three. **2.** *Maths.* **a.** (of a number system) to the base three. **b.** involving or containing three variables. **3.** (of an alloy, mixture, or chemical compound) having three different components or composed of three different elements. ~*n., pl.* **-ries.** **4.** a group of three. [C14: from Latin *ternārius,* from *ternī* three each]
ternary form *n.* a musical structure consisting of two contrasting sections followed by a repetition of the first; the form *aba.* Also called: **song form.**

ternate ('tɜːnɪt, -neɪt) *adj.* **1.** (esp. of a leaf) consisting of three leaflets or other parts. **2.** (esp. of plants) having groups of three members. [C18: from New Latin *ternātus,* from Medieval Latin *ternāre* to increase threefold] —'**ternately** *adv.*

terne (tɜːn) *n.* **1.** Also called: **terne metal.** an alloy of lead containing tin (10–20 per cent) and antimony (1.5–2 per cent). **2.** Also called: **terne plate.** steel plate coated with this alloy. [C16: perhaps from French *terne* dull, from Old French *ternir* to TARNISH]

ternion ('tɜːnɪən) *n.* **1.** *Rare.* a group of three. **2.** *Printing.* a gathering of three sheets of paper folded once, making six leaves or 12 pages. [C16: from Latin *terniō* triad, from *ternī* three each; related to *ter* thrice]

terotechnology (ˌtɪərəʊtɛk'nɒlədʒɪ, ˌtɛr-) *n.* a branch of technology that utilizes management, financial, and engineering expertise in the installation and efficient operation and maintenance of equipment and machinery. [C20: from Greek *tērein* to care for + TECHNOLOGY]

terpene ('tɜːpiːn) *n.* any one of a class of unsaturated hydrocarbons, such as limonene, pinene, and the carotenes, that are found in the essential oils of many plants, esp. conifers. Their molecules contain isoprene units and have the general formula $(C_5H_8)_n$. [C19: *terp-* from obsolete *terpentine* TURPENTINE + -ENE] —**ter'penic** *adj.*

terpineol (tɜː'pɪnɪˌɒl) *n.* a terpene alcohol with an odour of lilac, existing in three isomeric forms that occur in several essential oils. A mixture of the isomers is used as a solvent and in flavourings and perfumes. Formula: $C_{10}H_{17}OH$. [C20: from TERPENE + -INE[2] + -OL[1]]

Terpsichorean (ˌtɜːpsɪkə'rɪən, -'kɔːrɪən) *Often used facetiously.* ~*adj. also* **Terpsichoreal. 1.** of or relating to dancing or the art of dancing. ~*n.* **2.** a dancer. [from *Terpsichore,* the Muse of the dance, via Latin from Greek, from *terpsikhoros* delighting in the dance, from *terpein* to delight + *khoros* dance; see CHORUS]

terr. *abbrev. for:* **1.** terrace. **2.** territory.

terra ('tɛrə) *n.* (in legal contexts) earth or land. [from Latin]

terra alba ('ælbə) *n.* **1.** a white finely powdered form of gypsum, used to make paints, paper, etc. **2.** any of various other white earthy substances, such as kaolin, pipeclay, and magnesia. [from Latin, literally: white earth]

terrace ('tɛrəs) *n.* **1.** a horizontal flat area of ground, often one of a series in a slope. **2. a.** a row of houses, usually identical and having common dividing walls, or the street onto which they face. **b.** (*cap. when part of a street name*): *Grosvenor Terrace.* **3.** a paved area alongside a building, serving partly as a garden. **4.** a balcony or patio. **5.** the flat roof of a house built in a Spanish or Oriental style. **6.** a flat area bounded by a short steep slope formed by the down-cutting of a river or by erosion. **7.** (*usually pl.*) **a.** unroofed tiers around a football pitch on which the spectators stand. **b.** the spectators themselves. ~*vb.* (*tr.*) **8.** to make into or provide with a terrace or terraces. [C16: from Old French *terrasse,* from Old Provençal *terrassa* pile of earth, from *terra* earth, from Latin] —'**terraceless** *adj.*

terraced house *n. Brit.* a house that is part of a terrace. U.S. and Canadian names: **row house, town house.** —**terraced housing** *n.*

terracing ('tɛrəsɪŋ) *n.* **1.** a series of terraces, esp. one dividing a slope into a steplike system of flat narrow fields. **2.** the act of making a terrace or terraces. **3.** another name for **terrace** (sense 7a).

terracotta (ˌtɛrə'kɒtə) *n.* **1.** a hard unglazed brownish-red earthenware, or the clay from which it is made. **2.** something made of terracotta, such as a sculpture. **3.** a strong reddish-brown to brownish-orange colour. ~*adj.* **4.** made of terracotta: *a terracotta urn.* **5.** of the colour terracotta: *a terracotta carpet.* [C18: from Italian, literally: baked earth]

terra firma ('fɜːmə) *n.* the solid earth; firm ground. [C17: from Latin]

terrain (tə'reɪn, 'tɛreɪn) *n.* **1.** ground or a piece of ground, esp. with reference to its physical character or military potential: *radio reception can be difficult in mountainous terrain; a rocky terrain.* **2.** a variant spelling of **terrane.** [C18: from French, ultimately from Latin *terrēnum* ground, from *terra* earth]

terra incognita *Latin.* ('tɛrə ɪn'kɒgnɪtə) *n.* an unexplored or unknown land, region, or area for study.

Terramycin (ˌtɛrə'maɪsɪn) *n. Trademark.* a broad-spectrum antibiotic used in treating various infections.

terrane *or* **terrain** ('tɛreɪn) *n.* a series of rock formations, esp. one having a prevalent type of rock. [C19: see TERRAIN]

terrapin ('tɛrəpɪn) *n.* any of various web-footed chelonian reptiles that live on land and in fresh water and feed on small aquatic animals: family *Emydidae.* Also called: **water tortoise.** [C17: of Algonquian origin; compare Delaware *torope* turtle]

terrarium (tɛ'rɛərɪəm) *n., pl.* **-rariums** *or* **-raria** (-'rɛərɪə). **1.** an enclosure for keeping small land animals. **2.** a glass container, often a globe, in which plants are grown. [C19: New Latin, from Latin *terra* earth]

terra sigillata ('tɛrə ˌsɪdʒɪ'lɑːtə) *n.* **1.** a reddish-brown clayey earth found on the Aegean island of Lemnos: formerly used as an astringent and in the making of earthenware pottery. **2.** any similar earth resembling this. **3.** earthenware pottery made from this or a similar earth, esp. Samian ware. [from Latin: sealed earth]

terrazzo (tɛ'rætsəʊ) *n.* a floor or wall finish made by setting marble or other stone chips into a layer of mortar and polishing the surface. [C20: from Italian: TERRACE]

terrene (tɛ'riːn) *adj.* **1.** of or relating to the earth; worldly; mundane. **2.** *Rare.* of earth; earthy. ~*n.* **3.** a land. **4.** a rare word for **earth.** [C14: from Anglo-Norman, from Latin *terrēnus,* from *terra* earth] —**ter'renely** *adv.*

terreplein ('tɛəˌpleɪn) *n.* **1.** the top of a rampart where guns are placed behind the parapet. **2.** an embankment with a level top surface. [C16: from French, from Medieval Latin phrase *terrā plēnus* filled with earth]

terrestrial (tə'rɛstrɪəl) *adj.* **1.** of or relating to the earth. **2.** of or belonging to the land as opposed to the sea or air. **3.** (of animals and plants) living or growing on the land. **4.** earthly, worldly, or mundane. **5.** (of television signals) sent over the earth's surface from a transmitter on land, rather than by satellite. ~*n.* **6.** an inhabitant of the earth. [C15: from Latin *terrestris,* from *terra* earth] —**ter'restrially** *adv.* —**ter'restrialness** *n.*

terrestrial guidance *n.* a method of missile or rocket guidance in which the flight path is controlled by reference to the strength and direction of the earth's gravitational or magnetic field. Compare **inertial guidance.**

terrestrial telescope *n.* a telescope for use on earth rather than for making astronomical observations. Such telescopes contain an additional lens or prism system to produce an erect image. Compare **astronomical telescope.**

terret ('tɛrɪt) *n.* **1.** either of the two metal rings on a harness saddle through which the reins are passed. **2.** the ring on a dog's collar for attaching the lead. [C15: variant of *toret,* from Old French, diminutive of *tor* loop; see TOUR]

terre-verte ('tɛəˌvɜːt) *n.* **1.** a greyish-green pigment used in paints, consisting of powdered glauconite. ~*adj.* **2.** of a greyish-green colour. [C17: from French, literally: green earth]

terrible ('tɛrəbᵊl) *adj.* **1.** very serious or extreme: *a terrible cough.* **2.** *Informal.* of poor quality; unpleasant or bad: *a terrible meal; a terrible play.* **3.** causing terror. **4.** causing awe: *the terrible nature of God.* [C15: from Latin *terribilis,* from *terrēre* to terrify] —'**terribleness** *n.*

terribly ('tɛrəblɪ) *adv.* **1.** in a terrible manner. **2.** (intensifier): *you're terribly kind.*

terricolous (tɛ'rɪkələs) *adj.* living on or in the soil. [C19: from Latin *terricola,* from *terra* earth + *colere* to inhabit]

terrier[1] ('tɛrɪə) *n.* any of several usually small, active, and short-bodied breeds of dog, originally trained to hunt animals living underground. [C15: from Old French *chien terrier* earth dog, from Medieval Latin *terrārius* belonging to the earth, from Latin *terra* earth]

terrier[2] ('tɛrɪə) *n. English legal history.* a register or survey of land. [C15: from Old French, from Medieval Latin *terrārius* of the land, from Latin *terra* land]

Terrier ('tɛrɪə) *n. Informal.* a member of the British Army's Territorial and Volunteer Reserve.

terrific (tə'rɪfɪk) *adj.* **1.** very great or intense: *a terrific noise.* **2.** *Informal.* very good; excellent: *a terrific singer.* **3.** very frightening. [C17: from Latin *terrificus,* from *terrēre* to frighten; see -FIC] —**ter'rifically** *adv.*

terrify ('tɛrɪˌfaɪ) *vb.* **-fies, -fying, -fied.** (*tr.*) to inspire fear or dread in; frighten greatly. [C16: from Latin *terrificāre,* from *terrēre* to alarm + *facere* to cause] —'**terriˌfier** *n.* —'**terriˌfying** *adj.* —'**terriˌfyingly** *adv.*

terrigenous (tɛ'rɪdʒɪnəs) *adj.* **1.** of or produced by the earth. **2.** (of geological deposits) formed in the sea from material derived from the land by erosion. [C17: from Latin *terrigenus,* from *terra* earth + *gignere* to beget]

terrine (tɛ'riːn) *n.* **1.** an oval earthenware cooking dish with a tightly fitting lid used for pâtés, etc. **2.** the food cooked or served in such a dish, esp. pâté. **3.** another word for **tureen.** [C18: earlier form of TUREEN]

territorial (ˌtɛrɪ'tɔːrɪəl) *adj.* **1.** of or relating to a territory or territories. **2.** restricted to or owned by a particular territory: *the Indian territorial waters.* **3.** local or regional. **4.** pertaining to a territorial army, providing a reserve of trained men for use in emergency. —ˌ**terri'torially** *adv.*

Territorial (ˌtɛrɪ'tɔːrɪəl) *n.* a member of a territorial army, esp. the British Army's Territorial and Volunteer Reserve.

territorial court *n.* a court in a U.S. territory with both local and federal jurisdiction.

territorialism (ˌtɛrɪ'tɔːrɪəlɪzəm) *n.* **1.** a social system under which the predominant force in the state is the landed class. **2.** a former Protestant theory that the civil government has the right to determine the religious beliefs of the subjects of a state. —ˌ**terri'torialist** *n.*

territoriality (ˌtɛrɪˌtɔːrɪ'ælɪtɪ) *n.* **1.** the state or rank of being a territory. **2.** the behaviour shown by an animal when establishing and defending its territory.

territorialize *or* **territorialise** (ˌtɛrɪ'tɔːrɪəˌlaɪz) *vb.* (*tr.*) **1.** to make a territory of. **2.** to place on a territorial basis: *the militia was territorialized.* **3.** to enlarge (a country) by acquiring more territory. **4.** to make territorial. —ˌ**terriˌtoriali'zation** *or* ˌ**terriˌtoriali'sation** *n.*

territorial waters *pl. n.* the waters over which a nation exercises jurisdiction and control.

Territorian (ˌtɛrɪˈtɔːrɪən) *n. Austral.* an inhabitant of the Northern Territory in N central Australia.

territory (ˈtɛrɪtərɪ, -trɪ) *n., pl.* **-ries.** **1.** any tract of land; district. **2.** the geographical domain under the jurisdiction of a political unit, esp. of a sovereign state. **3.** the district for which an agent, etc., is responsible: *a salesman's territory.* **4.** an area inhabited and defended by an individual animal or a breeding pair of animals. **5.** an area of knowledge: *science isn't my territory.* **6.** (in football, hockey, etc.) the area defended by a team. **7.** (*often cap.*) a region of a country, esp. of a federal state, that enjoys less autonomy and a lower status than most constituent parts of the state. **8.** (*often cap.*) a protectorate or other dependency of a country. [C15: from Latin *territōrium* land surrounding a town, from *terra* land]

terror (ˈtɛrə) *n.* **1.** great fear, panic, or dread. **2.** a person or thing that inspires great dread. **3.** *Informal.* a troublesome person or thing, esp. a child. **4.** terrorism. [C14: from Old French *terreur,* from Latin *terror,* from *terrēre* to frighten; related to Greek *trein* to run away in terror] —ˈ**terrorful** *adj.* —ˈ**terrorless** *adj.*

terrorism (ˈtɛrəˌrɪzəm) *n.* **1.** systematic use of violence and intimidation to achieve some goal. **2.** the act of terrorizing. **3.** the state of being terrorized.

terrorist (ˈtɛrərɪst) *n.* **a.** a person who employs terror or terrorism, esp. as a political weapon. **b.** (*as modifier*): *terrorist tactics.* —ˌ**terrorˈistic** *adj.*

terrorize *or* **terrorise** (ˈtɛrəˌraɪz) *vb.* (*tr.*) **1.** to coerce or control by violence, fear, threats, etc. **2.** to inspire with dread; terrify. —ˌ**terroriˈzation** *or* ˌ**terroriˈsation** *n.* —ˈ**terrorˌizer** *or* ˈ**terrorˌiser** *n.*

terror-stricken *or* **terror-struck** *adj.* in a state of terror.

terry (ˈtɛrɪ) *n., pl.* **-ries.** **1.** an uncut loop in the pile of towelling or a similar fabric. **2. a.** a fabric with such a pile on both sides. **b.** (*as modifier*): *a terry towel.* [C18: perhaps variant of TERRET]

terse (tɜːs) *adj.* **1.** neatly brief and concise. **2.** curt; abrupt. [C17: from Latin *tersus* precise, from *tergēre* to polish] —ˈ**tersely** *adv.* —ˈ**terseness** *n.*

tertial (ˈtɜːʃəl) *adj., n.* another word for **tertiary** (senses 5, 6). [C19: from Latin *tertius* third, from *ter* thrice, from *trēs* three]

tertian (ˈtɜːʃən) *adj.* **1.** (of a fever or the symptoms of a disease, esp. malaria) occurring every other day. ~*n.* **2.** a tertian fever or symptoms. [C14: from Latin *febris tertiāna* fever occurring every third day, reckoned inclusively, from *tertius* third]

tertiary (ˈtɜːʃərɪ) *adj.* **1.** third in degree, order, etc. **2.** (of an industry) involving services as opposed to extraction or manufacture, such as transport, finance, etc. Compare **primary** (sense 8b), **secondary** (sense 7). **3.** *R.C. Church.* of or relating to a Third Order. **4.** *Chem.* **a.** (of an organic compound) having a functional group attached to a carbon atom that is attached to three other groups. **b.** (of an amine) having three organic groups attached to a nitrogen atom. **c.** (of a salt) derived from a tribasic acid by replacement of all its acidic hydrogen atoms with metal atoms or electropositive groups. **5.** Also: **tertial.** *Ornithol., rare.* of, relating to, or designating any of the small flight feathers attached to the part of the humerus nearest to the body. ~*n., pl.* **-tiaries.** **6.** Also called: **tertial.** *Ornithol., rare.* any of the tertiary feathers. **7.** *R.C. Church.* a member of a Third Order. [C16: from Latin *tertiārius* containing one third, from *tertius* third]

Tertiary (ˈtɜːʃərɪ) *adj.* **1.** of, denoting, or formed in the first period of the Cenozoic era, which lasted for 69 million years, during which mammals became dominant. ~*n.* **2. the.** the Tertiary period or rock system, divided into Palaeocene, Eocene, Oligocene, Miocene, and Pliocene epochs or series.

tertiary bursary *n. N.Z.* a noncompetitive award granted to all pupils who have passed a university entrance examination.

tertiary college *n. Brit.* a college system incorporating the secondary school sixth form and vocational courses.

tertiary colour *n.* a colour formed by mixing two secondary colours.

tertium quid (ˈtɜːtɪəm ˈkwɪd) *n.* an unknown or indefinite thing related in some way to two known or definite things, but distinct from both: *there is either right or wrong, with no tertium quid.* [C18: from Late Latin, rendering Greek *triton ti* some third thing]

tervalent (tɜːˈveɪlənt) *adj. Chem.* another word for **trivalent.** —**terˈvalency** *n.*

Terylene (ˈtɛrɪˌliːn) *n. Trademark.* a synthetic polyester fibre or fabric based on terephthalic acid, characterized by lightness and crease resistance and used for clothing, sheets, ropes, sails, etc. U.S. name (trademark): **Dacron.**

terza rima (ˈtɛətsə ˈriːmə) *n., pl.* **terze rime** (ˈtɛətseɪ ˈriːmeɪ). a verse form of Italian origin consisting of a series of tercets in which the middle line of one tercet rhymes with the first and third lines of the next. [C19: from Italian, literally: third rhyme]

terzetto (tɜːˈtsɛtəʊ) *n., pl.* **-tos** *or* **-ti** (-tɪ). *Music.* a trio, esp. a vocal one. [C18: Italian: trio; see TERCET]

TES *abbrev. for* Times Educational Supplement.

TESL *abbrev. for* Teaching (of) English as a Second Language.

tesla (ˈtɛslə) *n.* the derived SI unit of magnetic flux density equal to a flux of 1 weber in an area of 1 square metre. Symbol: T [C20: named after Nikola *Tesla* (1857–1943), U.S. electrical engineer and inventor]

tesla coil *n.* a step-up transformer with an air core, used for producing high voltages at high frequencies. The secondary circuit is tuned to resonate with the primary winding. [C20: named after Nikola *Tesla*]

TESSA (ˈtɛsə) *n.* (in Britain) *acronym for* Tax Exempt Special Savings Account; a savings scheme introduced in 1991 enabling interest on up to £1800 p.a. to be paid tax free if the capital remains intact for five years.

tessellate (ˈtɛsɪˌleɪt) *vb.* **1.** (*tr.*) to construct, pave, or inlay with a mosaic of small tiles. **2.** (*intr.*) (of identical shapes) to fit together exactly: *triangles will tessellate but octagons will not.* [C18: from Latin *tessellātus* checked, from *tessella* small stone cube, from TESSERA]

tessellation (ˌtɛsɪˈleɪʃən) *n.* **1.** the act of tessellating. **2.** the form or a specimen of tessellated work.

tessera (ˈtɛsərə) *n., pl.* **-serae** (-səˌriː). **1.** a small square tile of stone, glass, etc., used in mosaics. **2.** a die, tally, etc., used in classical times, made of bone or wood. [C17: from Latin, from Ionic Greek *tesseres* four] —ˈ**tesseral** *adj.*

tessitura (ˌtɛsɪˈtʊərə) *n. Music.* **1.** the general pitch level of a piece of vocal music: *an uncomfortably high tessitura.* **2.** the compass or range of a voice. [Italian: texture, from Latin *textura;* see TEXTURE]

test[1] (tɛst) *vb.* **1.** to ascertain (the worth, capability, or endurance) of (a person or thing) by subjection to certain examinations; try. **2.** (often foll. by *for*) to carry out an examination on (a substance, material, or system) by applying some chemical or physical procedure designed to indicate the presence of a substance or the possession of a property: *to test food for arsenic; to test for magnetization.* **3.** (*intr.*) to achieve a specified result in a test: *a quarter of the patients at the clinic tested positive for the AIDS virus.* **4. test the water.** to make an exploratory or initial approach; sound out. ~*n.* **5.** a method, practice, or examination designed to test a person or thing. **6.** a series of questions or problems designed to test a specific skill or knowledge: *an intelligence test.* **7.** a standard of judgment; criterion. **8. a.** a chemical reaction or physical procedure for testing a substance, material, etc. **b.** a chemical reagent used in such a procedure: *litmus is a test for acids.* **c.** the result of the procedure or the evidence gained from it: *the test for alcohol was positive.* **9.** *Sport.* See **test match.** **10.** *Archaic.* a declaration or confirmation of truth, loyalty, etc.; oath. **11.** (*modifier*) performed as a test: *test drive; test flight.* [C14 (in the sense: vessel used in treating metals): from Latin *testum* earthen vessel] —ˈ**testable** *adj.* —ˌ**testaˈbility** *n.* —ˈ**testing** *adj.*

test[2] (tɛst) *n.* **1.** the hard or tough outer covering of certain invertebrates and tunicates. **2.** a variant of **testa.** [C19: from Latin *testa* shell]

testa (ˈtɛstə) *n., pl.* **-tae** (-tiː). a hard protective outer layer of the seeds of flowering plants; seed coat. [C18: from Latin: shell; see TEST[2]]

testaceous (tɛˈsteɪʃəs) *adj. Biology.* **1.** of, relating to, or possessing a test or testa. **2.** of the reddish-brown colour of terra cotta. [C17: from Latin *testāceus,* from TESTA]

testament (ˈtɛstəmənt) *n.* **1.** *Law.* a will setting out the disposition of personal property (esp. in the phrase **last will and testament**). **2.** a proof, attestation, or tribute: *his success was a testament to his skills.* **3. a.** a covenant instituted between God and man, esp. the covenant of Moses or that instituted by Christ. **b.** a copy of either the Old or the New Testament, or of the complete Bible. [C14: from Latin: a will, from *testārī* to bear witness, from *testis* a witness] —ˌ**testaˈmental** *adj.*

Testament (ˈtɛstəmənt) *n.* **1.** either of the two main parts of the Bible; the Old Testament or the New Testament. **2.** the New Testament as distinct from the Old.

testamentary (ˌtɛstəˈmɛntərɪ) *adj.* **1.** of or relating to a will or testament. **2.** derived from, bequeathed, or appointed by a will. **3.** contained or set forth in a will.

testate (ˈtɛsteɪt, ˈtɛstɪt) *adj.* **1.** having left a legally valid will at death. ~*n.* **2.** a person who dies testate. ~Compare **intestate.** [C15: from Latin *testārī* to make a will; see TESTAMENT] —**testacy** (ˈtɛstəsɪ) *n.*

testator (tɛˈsteɪtə) *or* (*fem.*) **testatrix** (tɛˈsteɪtrɪks) *n.* a person who makes a will, esp. one who dies testate. [C15: from Anglo-French *testatour,* from Late Latin *testātor,* from Latin *testārī* to make a will; see TESTAMENT]

test ban *n.* an agreement among nations to forgo tests of some or all types of nuclear weapons.

test-bed *n. Engineering.* an area equipped with instruments, etc., used for testing machinery, engines, etc., under working conditions.

test card *or* **pattern** *n.* a complex pattern used to test the characteristics of a television transmission system.

test case *n.* a legal action that serves as a precedent in deciding similar succeeding cases.

test-drive *vb.* (*tr.*) **-drives, -driving, -drove, -driven.** to drive (a car or other motor vehicle) for a limited period in order to assess its capabilities and limitations.

tester[1] (ˈtɛstə) *n.* a person or thing that tests or is used for testing.

tester[2] (ˈtɛstə) *n.* (in furniture) a canopy, esp. the canopy over a four-poster bed. [C14: from Medieval Latin *testerium,* from Late Latin *testa* a skull, from Latin: shell]

tester[3] (ˈtɛstə) *n.* another name for **teston** (sense 2).

testes ('tɛstiːz) *n.* the plural of **testis.**

testicle ('tɛstɪkᵊl) *n.* either of the two male reproductive glands, in most mammals enclosed within the scrotum, that produce spermatozoa and the hormone testosterone. Also called: **testis.** [C15: from Latin *testiculus,* diminutive of *testis* testicle] —**testicular** (tɛ'stɪkjʊlə) *adj.*

testiculate (tɛ'stɪkjʊlɪt) *adj. Botany.* having an oval shape: *the testiculate tubers of certain orchids.* [C18: from Late Latin *testiculātus;* see TESTICLE]

testify ('tɛstɪˌfaɪ) *vb.* **-fies, -fying, -fied. 1.** (when *tr., may take a clause as object*) to state (something) formally as a declaration of fact: *I testify that I know nothing about him.* **2.** *Law.* to declare or give (evidence) under oath, esp. in court. **3.** (when *intr.,* often foll. by *to*) to be evidence (of); serve as witness (to): *the money testified to his good faith.* **4.** (*tr.*) to declare or acknowledge openly. [C14: from Latin *testificārī,* from *testis* witness] —ˌ**testifi'cation** *n.* —'**testiˌfier** *n.*

testimonial (ˌtɛstɪ'məʊnɪəl) *n.* **1. a.** a recommendation of the character, ability, etc., of a person or of the quality of a consumer product or service, esp. by a person whose opinion is valued. **b.** (*as modifier*): *testimonial advertising.* **2.** a formal statement of truth or fact. **3.** a tribute given for services or achievements. ~*adj.* **4.** of or relating to a testimony or testimonial.

testimony ('tɛstɪmənɪ) *n., pl.* **-nies. 1.** a declaration of truth or fact. **2.** *Law.* evidence given by a witness, esp. orally in court under oath or affirmation. **3.** evidence testifying to something: *her success was a testimony to her good luck.* **4.** *Old Testament.* **a.** the Ten Commandments, as inscribed on the two stone tables. **b.** the Ark of the Covenant as the receptacle of these (Exodus 25:16; 16:34). [C15: from Latin *testimōnium,* from *testis* witness]

testing station *n. N.Z.* an establishment licensed to issue warrants of fitness for motor vehicles.

testis ('tɛstɪs) *n., pl.* **-tes** (-tiːz). another word for **testicle.** [C17: from Latin, literally: witness (to masculinity)]

test marketing *n.* the use of a representative segment of a total market for experimental purposes, as to test a new product about to be launched or a price change.

test match *n.* (in various sports, esp. cricket) any of a series of international matches.

teston ('tɛstən) *or* **testoon** (tɛ'stuːn) *n.* **1.** a French silver coin of the 16th century. **2.** Also called: **tester.** an English silver coin of the 16th century, originally worth one shilling, bearing the head of Henry VIII. [C16: from Italian *testone,* from *testa* head, from Late Latin: skull, from Latin: shell]

testosterone (tɛ'stɒstəˌrəʊn) *n.* a potent steroid hormone secreted mainly by the testes. It can be extracted from the testes of animals or synthesized and used to treat androgen deficiency or promote anabolis. Formula: $C_{19}H_{28}O_2$. [C20: from TESTIS + STEROL + -ONE]

test paper *n.* **1.** *Chem.* paper impregnated with an indicator for use in chemical tests. See also **litmus. 2.** *Brit. education.* **a.** the question sheet of a test. **b.** the paper completed by a test candidate.

test pilot *n.* a pilot who flies aircraft of new design to test their performance in the air.

test tube *n.* **1.** a cylindrical round-bottomed glass tube open at one end: used in scientific experiments. **2.** (*modifier*) made synthetically in, or as if in, a test tube: *a test-tube product.*

test-tube baby *n.* **1.** a fetus that has developed from an ovum fertilized in an artificial womb. **2.** a baby conceived by artificial insemination.

testudinal (tɛ'stjuːdɪnᵊl) *or* **testudinary** *adj.* of, relating to, or resembling a tortoise or turtle or the shell of either of these animals. [C19: from Latin TESTUDO]

testudo (tɛ'stjuːdəʊ) *n., pl.* **-dines** (-dɪˌniːz). a form of shelter used by the ancient Roman Army for protection against attack from above, consisting either of a mobile arched structure or of overlapping shields held by the soldiers over their heads. [C17: from Latin: a tortoise, from *testa* a shell]

testy ('tɛstɪ) *adj.* **-tier, -tiest.** irritable or touchy. [C14: from Anglo-Norman *testif* headstrong, from Old French *teste* head, from Late Latin *testa* skull, from Latin: shell] —'**testily** *adv.* —'**testiness** *n.*

tetanic (tə'tænɪk) *adj.* **1.** of, relating to, or producing tetanus or the spasms of tetanus. ~*n.* **2.** a tetanic drug or agent. —**te'tanically** *adv.*

tetanize *or* **tetanise** ('tɛtəˌnaɪz) *vb.* (*tr.*) to induce tetanus in (a muscle); affect (a muscle) with tetanic spasms. —ˌ**tetani'zation** *or* ˌ**tetani'sation** *n.*

tetanus ('tɛtənəs) *n.* **1.** Also called: **lockjaw.** an acute infectious disease in which sustained muscular spasm, contraction, and convulsion are caused by the release of exotoxins from the bacterium, *Clostridium tetani:* infection usually occurs through a contaminated wound. **2.** *Physiol.* any tense contraction of a muscle, esp. when produced by electric shocks. [C16: via Latin from Greek *tetanos,* from *tetanos* taut, from *teinein* to stretch] —'**tetanal** *adj.* —'**tetaˌnoid** *adj.*

tetany ('tɛtənɪ) *n. Pathol.* an abnormal increase in the excitability of nerves and muscles resulting in spasms of the arms and legs, caused by a deficiency of parathyroid secretion. [C19: from French *tétanie.* See TETANUS]

tetartohedral (tɪˌtɑːtəʊ'hiːdrəl) *adj.* (of a crystal) having one quarter of the number of faces necessary for the full symmetry of its crystal system. [C19: from Greek *tetartos* one fourth + -HEDRAL] —**teˌtarto'hedrally** *adv.* —**teˌtarto'hedralism** *or* **teˌtarto'hedrism** *n.*

tetchy ('tɛtʃɪ) *adj.* **tetchier, tetchiest.** being or inclined to be cross, irritable, or touchy. [C16: probably from obsolete *tetch* defect, from Old French *tache* spot, of Germanic origin] —'**tetchily** *adv.* —'**tetchiness** *n.*

tête-à-tête (ˌteɪtə'teɪt) *n., pl.* **-têtes** *or* **-tête. 1. a.** a private conversation between two people. **b.** (*as modifier*): *a tête-à-tête conversation.* **2.** a small sofa for two people, esp. one that is S-shaped in plan so that the sitters are almost face to face. ~*adv.* **3.** intimately; in private. [C17: from French, literally: head to head]

tête-bêche (tɛt'bɛʃ) *adj. Philately.* (of an unseparated pair of stamps) printed so that one is inverted in relation to the other. [C19: from French, from *tête* head + *bêche,* from obsolete *béchevet* double-headed (originally of a bed)]

teth (tɛs; *Hebrew* tɛt) *n.* the ninth letter of the Hebrew alphabet (ט) transliterated as *t* and pronounced more or less like English *t* with pharyngeal articulation.

tether ('tɛðə) *n.* **1.** a restricting rope, chain, etc., by which an animal is tied to a particular spot. **2.** the range of one's endurance, etc. **3. at the end of one's tether.** distressed or exasperated to the limit of one's endurance. ~*vb.* (*tr.*) **4.** to tie or limit with or as if with a tether. [C14: from Old Norse *tjothr;* related to Middle Dutch *tūder* tether, Old High German *zeotar* pole of a wagon]

tetra ('tɛtrə) *n., pl.* **-ra** *or* **-ras.** any of various brightly coloured tropical freshwater fishes of the genus *Hemigrammus* and related genera: family *Characidae* (characins). [C20: short for New Latin *tetragonopterus* (former genus name), from TETRAGON + -O- + *-pterous,* from Greek *pteron* wing]

tetra- *or before a vowel* **tetr-** *combining form.* four: *tetrameter.* [from Greek]

tetrabasic (ˌtɛtrə'beɪsɪk) *adj.* (of an acid) containing four replaceable hydrogen atoms. —**tetrabasicity** (ˌtɛtrəbeɪ'sɪsɪtɪ) *n.*

tetrabrach ('tɛtrəˌbræk) *n.* (in classical prosody) a word or metrical foot composed of four short syllables (⏑⏑⏑⏑). [C19: from Greek *tetrabrakhus,* from TETRA- + *brakhus* short]

tetrabranchiate *adj.* (ˌtɛtrə'bræŋkɪɪt, -ˌeɪt). **1.** of, relating to, or belonging to the *Tetrabranchiata,* a former order of cephalopod molluscs having four gills and including the pearly nautilus. ~*n.* (ˌtɛtrə'bræŋkɪˌeɪt). **2.** any mollusc belonging to the *Tetrabranchiata.*

tetrachloride (ˌtɛtrə'klɔːraɪd) *n.* any compound that contains four chlorine atoms per molecule: *carbon tetrachloride,* CCl_4.

tetrachloromethane ('tɛtrəklɔːrəʊˌmiːθeɪn) *n.* the systematic name for **carbon tetrachloride.**

tetrachord ('tɛtrəˌkɔːd) *n.* (in musical theory, esp. of classical Greece) any of several groups of four notes in descending order, in which the first and last notes form a perfect fourth. [C17: from Greek *tetrakhordos* four-stringed, from TETRA- + *khordē* a string] —ˌ**tetra'chordal** *adj.*

tetracid (tɛ'træsɪd) *adj.* (of a base) capable of reacting with four molecules of a monobasic acid.

tetracyclic (ˌtɛtrə'saɪklɪk) *adj. Chem.* (of a compound) containing four rings in its molecular structure.

tetracycline (ˌtɛtrə'saɪklaɪn, -klɪn) *n.* an antibiotic synthesized from chlortetracycline or derived from the bacterium *Streptomyces viridifaciens:* used in treating rickettsial infections and various bacterial and viral infections. Formula: $C_{22}H_{24}N_2O_8$. [C20: from TETRA- + CYCL(IC) + -INE[2]]

tetrad ('tɛtræd) *n.* **1.** a group or series of four. **2.** the number four. **3.** *Botany.* a group of four cells formed by meiosis from one diploid cell. **4.** *Genetics.* a four-stranded structure, formed during the pachytene stage of meiosis, consisting of paired homologous chromosomes that have each divided into two chromatids. **5.** *Chem.* an element, atom, group, or ion with a valency of four. **6.** *Ecology.* a square of 2 × 2 km used in distribution mapping. [C17: from Greek *tetras,* from *tettares* four]

tetradactyl (ˌtɛtrə'dæktɪl) *n.* **1.** a four-toed animal. ~*adj. also* ˌ**tetra'dactylous. 2.** having four toes or fingers. [C19: from Greek *tetradaktulos,* from TETRA- + *dactulos* finger]

tetradymite (tɛ'trædɪˌmaɪt) *n.* a grey metallic mineral consisting of a telluride and sulphide of bismuth. Formula: Bi_2Te_2S. [C19: from Late Greek *tetradumos* fourfold, from Greek TETRA- + *didumos* double]

tetradynamous (ˌtɛtrə'daɪnəməs, -'dɪn-) *adj.* (of plants) having six stamens, two of which are shorter than the others. [C19: from TETRA- + Greek *dunamis* power]

tetraethyl lead (ˌtɛtrə'iːθaɪl lɛd) *n.* a colourless oily insoluble liquid used in petrol to prevent knocking. Formula: $Pb(C_2H_5)_4$. Systematic name: **lead tetraethyl.**

tetrafluoroethene ('tɛtrəˌflʊərəʊ'ɛθiːn) *n. Chem.* a dense colourless gas that is polymerized to make polytetrafluorethene (PTFE). Formula: $F_2C{:}CF_2$. Also called: **tetrafluoroethylene.** [C20: from TETRA- + FLUORO- + ETHENE]

tetragon ('tɛtrəˌgɒn) *n.* a less common name for **quadrilateral** (sense 2). [C17: from Greek *tetragōnon;* see TETRA-, -GON]

tetragonal (tɛ'trægənᵊl) *adj.* **1.** Also: **dimetric.** *Crystallog.* relating or belonging to the crystal system characterized by three mutually perpendicular axes of which only two are equal. **2.** of, relating to, or shaped like a quadrilateral. —**te'tragonally** *adv.* —**te'tragonalness** *n.*

tetragram ('tɛtrəˌgræm) *n.* any word of four letters.

Tetragrammaton (ˌtɛtrə'græmətᵊn) *n. Bible.* the Hebrew name for God revealed to Moses on Mount Sinai (Exodus 3), consisting of the four consonants Y H V H (or Y H W H) and regarded by Jews as too sacred to be pronounced. It is usually transliterated as *Jehovah* or *Yahweh.* Sometimes shortened to **Tetragram.** [C14: from Greek, from *tetragrammatos* having four letters, from TETRA- + *gramma* letter]

tetrahedrite (ˌtɛtrə'hiːdraɪt) *n.* a grey metallic mineral consisting of a sulphide of copper, iron, and antimony, often in the form of tetrahedral crystals: it is a source of copper. Formula: $(Cu,Fe)_{12}Sb_4S_{13}$.

tetrahedron (ˌtɛtrə'hiːdrən) *n., pl.* **-drons** *or* **-dra** (-drə). **1.** a solid figure having four plane faces. A **regular tetrahedron** has faces that are equilateral triangles. See also **polyhedron. 2.** any object shaped like a tetrahedron. [C16: from New Latin, from Late Greek *tetraedron;* see TETRA-, -HEDRON] —ˌ**tetra'hedral** *adj.* —ˌ**tetra'hedrally** *adv.*

tetralogy (tɛ'trælədʒɪ) *n., pl.* **-gies. 1.** a series of four related works, as in drama or opera. **2.** (in ancient Greece) a group of four dramas, the first three tragic and the last satiric. [C17: from Greek *tetralogia;* see TETRA-, -LOGY]

tetramerous (tɛ'træmərəs) *adj.* **1.** (esp. of animals or plants) having or consisting of four parts. **2.** (of certain flowers) having parts arranged in whorls of four members. [C19: from New Latin *tetramerus,* from Greek *tetramerēs*] —**te'tramerism** *n.*

tetrameter (tɛ'træmɪtə) *n. Prosody.* **1.** a line of verse consisting of four metrical feet. **2.** a verse composed of such lines. **3.** (in classical prosody) a line of verse composed of four dipodies.

tetramethyldiarsine (ˌtɛtrəˌmiːθaɪldaɪ'ɑːsiːn) *n.* an oily slightly water-soluble poisonous liquid with garlic-like odour. Its derivatives are used as accelerators for rubber. Also called (not in technical usage): **cacodyl, dicacodyl.**

tetraplegia (ˌtɛtrə'pliːdʒɪə) *n.* another name for **quadriplegia.** [from TETRA- + Greek *plegē* a blow, from *plēssein* to strike] —ˌ**tetra'plegic** *adj.*

tetraploid ('tɛtrəˌplɔɪd) *Genetics.* ~*adj.* **1.** having four times the haploid number of chromosomes in the nucleus. ~*n.* **2.** a tetraploid organism, nucleus, or cell.

tetrapod ('tɛtrəˌpɒd) *n.* **1.** any vertebrate that has four limbs. **2.** Also called: **caltrop.** a device consisting of four arms radiating from a central point, each at 120° to the others, so that regardless of its position on a surface, three arms form a supporting tripod and the fourth is vertical. **3.** *Engineering.* a very large cast concrete structure of a similar shape piled in large numbers round breakwaters and sea defence systems to dissipate the energy of the waves.

tetrapody (tɛ'træpədɪ) *n., pl.* **-dies.** *Prosody.* a metrical unit consisting of four feet. —**tetrapodic** (ˌtɛtrə'pɒdɪk) *adj.*

tetrapterous (tɛ'træptərəs) *adj.* **1.** (of certain insects) having four wings. **2.** *Biology.* having four winglike extensions or parts. [C19: from New Latin *tetrapterus,* from Greek *tetrapteros,* from TETRA- + *pteron* wing]

tetrarch ('tɛtrɑːk) *n.* **1.** the ruler of one fourth of a country. **2.** a subordinate ruler, esp. of Syria under the Roman Empire. **3.** the commander of one of the smaller subdivisions of a Macedonian phalanx. **4.** any of four joint rulers. [C14: from Greek *tetrarkhēs;* see TETRA-, -ARCH] —**tetrarchate** (tɛ'trɑːˌkeɪt, -kɪt) *n.* —**te'trarchic** *or* **te'trarchical** *adj.* —**'tetrarchy** *n.*

tetraspore ('tɛtrəˌspɔː) *n.* any of the asexual spores that are produced in groups of four in the sporangium (**tetrasporangium**) of any of the red algae. —**tetrasporic** (ˌtɛtrə'spɒrɪk) *or* **tetrasporous** (ˌtɛtrə'spɔːrəs, tɪ'træspərəs) *adj.*

tetrastich ('tɛtrəˌstɪk) *n.* a poem, stanza, or strophe that consists of four lines. [C16: via Latin from Greek *tetrastikhon,* from TETRA- + *stikhos* row] —**tetrastichic** (ˌtɛtrə'stɪkɪk) *or* **tetrastichal** (tɛ'træstɪkᵊl) *adj.*

tetrastichous (tɛ'træstɪkəs) *adj.* (of flowers or leaves on a stalk) arranged in four vertical rows.

tetrasyllable (ˌtɛtrə'sɪləbᵊl) *n.* a word of four syllables. —**tetrasyllabic** (ˌtɛtrəsɪ'læbɪk) *or* ˌ**tetrasyl'labical** *adj.*

tetratomic (ˌtɛtrə'tɒmɪk) *adj.* composed of four atoms or having four atoms per molecule: *phosgene has tetratomic molecules.*

tetravalent (ˌtɛtrə'veɪlənt) *adj. Chem.* **1.** having a valency of four. **2.** Also: **quadrivalent.** having four valencies. —ˌ**tetra'valency** *n.*

tetrode ('tɛtrəʊd) *n.* **1.** an electronic valve having four electrodes, namely a cathode, control grid, screen grid, and anode. **2.** (*modifier*) (of a transistor) having two terminals on the base or gate to improve the performance at high frequencies.

tetroxide (tɛ'trɒksaɪd) *or* **tetroxid** (tɛ'trɒksɪd) *n.* any oxide that contains four oxygen atoms per molecule: *osmium tetroxide,* OsO_4.

tetryl ('tɛtrɪl) *n.* a yellow crystalline explosive solid used in detonators; trinitrophenylmethylnitramine. Formula: $(NO_2)_3C_6H_2N(NO_2)CH_3$. Also called: **nitramine.**

tetter ('tɛtə) *n.* **1.** a blister or pimple. **2.** *Informal.* any of various skin eruptions, such as eczema. [Old English *teter;* related to Old High German *zitaroh,* Sanskrit *dadru,* Late Latin *derbita*]

teuchter ('tjuːxtər) *n. Scot.* (*sometimes cap.*) **a.** a derogatory word used by Lowlanders for a Highlander. **b.** (*as modifier*): *teuchter music.* [C20: of uncertain origin]

Teucrian ('tjuːkrɪən) *n., adj.* another word for **Trojan.** [from *Teucer,* founder of Troy in Greek mythology]

Teut. *abbrev. for* Teuton(ic).

Teuton ('tjuːtən) *n.* **1.** a member of an ancient Germanic people from the Jutland peninsula of N Europe who migrated to S Gaul in the 2nd century B.C.: annihilated by a Roman army in 102 B.C. **2.** a member of any people speaking a Germanic language, esp. a German. ~*adj.* **3.** Teutonic. [C18: from Latin *Teutonī* the Teutons, of Germanic origin]

Teutonic (tjuː'tɒnɪk) *adj.* **1.** characteristic of or relating to the German people: *Teutonic thoroughness.* **2.** of or relating to the ancient Teutons. **3.** (not used in linguistics) of or relating to the Germanic languages. ~*n.* **4.** an obsolete name for **Germanic.** —**Teu'tonically** *adv.*

Teutonism ('tjuːtəˌnɪzəm) *n.* **1.** a German idiom, custom, or characteristic. **2.** German society or civilization.

Teutonize *or* **Teutonise** ('tjuːtəˌnaɪz) *vb.* to make or become German or Germanic; Germanize. —ˌ**Teutoni'zation** *or* ˌ**Teutoni'sation** *n.*

Tevet *or* **Tebet** (te'vet) *n.* (in the Jewish calendar) the tenth month of the year according to biblical reckoning and the fourth month of the civil year, usually falling within December and January. [from Hebrew]

Tex. *abbrev. for:* **1.** Texan. **2.** Texas.

Texan ('tɛksən) *adj.* **1.** of, relating to, or characteristic of Texas, a state of the southwestern U.S., or its people. ~*n.* **2.** a native or inhabitant of Texas.

Texas fever ('tɛksəs) *n.* an infectious disease of cattle caused by the protozoan *Babesia bigemina* and transmitted by the bite of a tick.

Texel ('tɛksᵊl) *n.* a breed of sheep originating from the Netherlands having a heavy white fleece: kept for the production of lean lambs. [C20: named after *Texel,* one of the West Frisian Islands off the Netherlands]

Tex-Mex ('tɛksˌmɛks) *adj.* of, relating to, or denoting the Texan version of something Mexican, such as music, food, or language.

text (tɛkst) *n.* **1.** the main body of a printed or written work as distinct from commentary, notes, illustrations, etc. **2.** the words of something printed or written. **3.** (*often pl.*) a book prescribed as part of a course of study. **4.** *Computer technol.* the words printed, written, or displayed on a visual display unit. **5.** the original exact wording of a work, esp. the Bible, as distinct from a revision or translation. **6.** a short passage of the Bible used as a starting point for a sermon or adduced as proof of a doctrine. **7.** the topic or subject of a discussion or work. **8.** *Printing.* any one of several styles of letters or types. **9.** short for **textbook.** [C14: from Medieval Latin *textus* version, from Latin *textus* texture, from *texere* to compose] —**'textless** *adj.*

textbook ('tɛkstˌbʊk) *n.* **a.** a book used as a standard source of information on a particular subject. **b.** (*as modifier*): *a textbook example.* —**'textˌbookish** *adj.*

textile ('tɛkstaɪl) *n.* **1.** any fabric or cloth, esp. woven. **2.** raw material suitable to be made into cloth; fibre or yarn. ~*adj.* **3.** of or relating to fabrics or the making of fabrics. [C17: from Latin *textilis* woven, from *texere* to weave]

text processing *n.* the handling of alphabetic characters by a computer.

textual ('tɛkstjʊəl) *adj.* **1.** of or relating to a text or texts. **2.** based on or conforming to a text. —**'textually** *adv.*

textual criticism *n.* **1.** the scholarly study of manuscripts, esp. of the Bible, in an effort to establish the original text. **2.** literary criticism emphasizing a close analysis of the text. —**textual critic** *n.*

textualism ('tɛkstjʊəˌlɪzəm) *n.* **1.** doctrinaire adherence to a text, esp. of the Bible. **2.** textual criticism, esp. of the Bible. —**'textualist** *n., adj.*

textuary ('tɛkstjʊərɪ) *adj.* **1.** of, relating to, or contained in a text. ~*n., pl.* **-aries. 2.** a textual critic.

texture ('tɛkstʃə) *n.* **1.** the surface of a material, esp. as perceived by the sense of touch: *a wall with a rough texture.* **2.** the structure, appearance, and feel of a woven fabric. **3.** the general structure and disposition of the constituent parts of something: *the texture of a cake.* **4.** the distinctive character or quality of something: *the texture of life in America.* **5.** the nature of a surface other than smooth: *woollen cloth has plenty of texture.* **6.** *Art.* the representation of the nature of a surface: *the painter caught the grainy texture of the sand.* **7. a.** music considered as the interrelationship between the horizontally presented aspects of melody and rhythm and the vertically represented aspect of harmony: *a contrapuntal texture.* **b.** the nature and quality of the instrumentation of a passage, piece, etc. ~*vb.* **8.** (*tr.*) to give a distinctive usually rough or grainy texture to. [C15: from Latin *textūra* web, from *texere* to weave] —**'textural** *adj.* —**'texturally** *adv.* —**'textureless** *adj.*

tg *Biology. abbrev. for* type genus.

TG **1.** *abbrev. for* transformational grammar. ~**2.** *international car registration for* Togo.

TGAT ('tiːgæt) *n.* (in Britain) *Education. acronym for* Task Group on Assessment and Testing.

T-group *n. Psychol.* a group that meets for educational or therapeutic purposes to study its own communication. [C20: from *(Sensitivity) T(raining) Group*]
TGWU (in Britain) *abbrev. for* Transport and General Workers' Union.
Th *the chemical symbol for* thorium.
Th. *abbrev. for* Thursday.
-th[1] *suffix forming nouns.* **1.** *(from verbs)* indicating an action or its consequence: *growth.* **2.** *(from adjectives)* indicating a quality: *width.* [from Old English *-thu, -tho*]
-th[2] *or* **-eth** *suffix.* forming ordinal numbers: *fourth; thousandth.* [from Old English *-(o)tha, -(o)the*]
Thai (taɪ) *adj.* **1.** of, relating to, or characteristic of Thailand, a kingdom in SE Asia, its people, or their language. ~*n.* **2.** *(pl.* **Thais** *or* **Thai)** a native or inhabitant of Thailand. **3.** the language of Thailand, sometimes classified as belonging to the Sino-Tibetan family. ~Also called: **Siamese.**
thalamencephalon (ˌθæləmɛnˈsɛfəˌlɒn) *n., pl.* **-lons** *or* **-la** (-lə). *Anatomy.* **1.** the part of the diencephalon of the brain that includes the thalamus, pineal gland, and adjacent structures. **2.** another name for **diencephalon.** —**thalamencephalic** (ˌθæləˌmɛnsəˈfælɪk) *adj.*
thalamus (ˈθæləməs) *n., pl.* **-mi** (-ˌmaɪ). **1.** either of the two contiguous egg-shaped masses of grey matter at the base of the brain. **2.** both of these masses considered as a functional unit. **3.** the receptacle or torus of a flower. [C18: from Latin, Greek *thalamos* inner room; probably related to Greek *tholos* vault] —**thalamic** (θəˈlæmɪk) *adj.* —**thaˈlamically** *adv.*
thalassaemia *or U.S.* **thalassemia** (ˌθæləˈsiːmɪə) *n.* a hereditary disease, common in many parts of the world, resulting from defects in the synthesis of the red blood pigment haemoglobin. Also called: **Cooley's anaemia** (ˈkuːlɪz). [New Latin, from Greek *thalassa* sea + -AEMIA, from it being esp. prevalent round the eastern Mediterranean Sea]
thalassic (θəˈlæsɪk) *adj.* **1.** of or relating to the sea. **2.** of or relating to small or inland seas, as opposed to open waters. **3.** inhabiting or growing in the sea; marine: *thalassic fauna.* [C19: from French *thalassique,* from Greek *thalassa* sea]
thalassocracy (ˌθæləˈsɒkrəsɪ) *or* **thalattocracy** *n.* the government of a nation having dominion over large expanses of the seas. [C19: from Attic Greek *thalassocratia,* from *thalassa* sea + -CRACY]
thalassotherapy (ˌθæləsəʊˈθɛrəpɪ) *n.* therapeutic bathing in sea water. [C20: from Greek *thalassa* sea + THERAPY]
thaler *or* **taler** (ˈtɑːlə) *n., pl.* **-ler** *or* **-lers.** a former German, Austrian, or Swiss silver coin. [from German; see DOLLAR]
thalidomide (θəˈlɪdəˌmaɪd) *n.* **a.** a synthetic drug formerly used as a sedative and hypnotic but withdrawn from the market when found to cause abnormalities in developing fetuses. Formula: $C_{13}H_{10}N_2O_4$. **b.** *(as modifier): a thalidomide baby.* [C20: from THALLIC + *-id-* (from IMIDE) + IMIDE]
thallic (ˈθælɪk) *adj.* of or containing thallium, esp. in the trivalent state.
thallium (ˈθælɪəm) *n.* a soft malleable highly toxic white metallic element used as a rodent and insect poison and in low-melting glass. Its compounds are used as infrared detectors and in photoelectric cells. Symbol: Tl; atomic no.: 81; atomic wt.: 204.37; valency: 1 or 3; relative density: 11.85; melting pt.: 303.5° C; boiling pt.: 1457° C. [C19: from New Latin, from Greek *thallos* a green shoot; referring to the green line in its spectrum]
thallophyte (ˈθæləˌfaɪt) *n.* any plant of the group (or former division) *Thallophyta,* lacking true stems, leaves, and roots: includes the algae, fungi, lichens, and bacteria, all now regarded as separate divisions. [C19: from New Latin *thallophyta,* from Greek *thallos* a young shoot + *phuton* a plant] —**thallophytic** (ˌθæləˈfɪtɪk) *adj.*
thallous (ˈθæləs) *adj.* of or containing thallium, esp. in the monovalent state.
thallus (ˈθæləs) *n., pl.* **thalli** (ˈθælaɪ) *or* **thalluses.** the undifferentiated plant body of algae, fungi, and lichens. [C19: from Latin, from Greek *thallos* green shoot, from *thallein* to bloom] —**ˈthalloid** *adj.*
thalweg *or* **talweg** (ˈtɑːlvɛg) *n. Geography, rare.* **1.** the longitudinal outline of a riverbed from source to mouth. **2.** the line of steepest descent from any point on the land surface. [C19: from German, from *Thal* valley + *Weg* way, path]
Thammuz (ˈtæmuːz, -uz) *n.* a variant spelling of **Tammuz.**
than (ðæn; *unstressed* ðən) *conj. (coordinating), prep.* **1.** used to introduce the second element of a comparison, the first element of which expresses difference: *shorter than you; couldn't do otherwise than love him; he swims faster than I run.* **2.** used after adverbs such as *rather* or *sooner* to introduce a rejected alternative in an expression of preference: *rather than be imprisoned, I shall die.* **3. other than.** besides; in addition to. [Old English *thanne;* related to Old Saxon, Old High German *thanna;* see THEN]
▷**Usage.** In sentences such as *he does it far better than I, than* is usually regarded in careful usage as a conjunction governing an unexpressed verb: *he does it far better than I (do it).* The case of any pronoun therefore depends on whether it is the subject or the object of that unexpressed verb: *she likes him more than I (like him); she likes him more than (she likes) me.* However, in informal usage *than* is often treated as a preposition and any pronoun is therefore used in its objective form, so that *she likes him more than me* is ambiguous.
thanatology (ˌθænəˈtɒlədʒɪ) *n.* the scientific study of death and the phenomena and practices relating to it. [C19: from Greek *thanatos* death + -LOGY]
thanatopsis (ˌθænəˈtɒpsɪs) *n.* a meditation on death, as in a poem. [C19: from Greek *thanatos* death + *opsis* a view]
Thanatos (ˈθænəˌtɒs) *n.* (in Freudian theory) a universal death instinct. Compare **Eros.** —**Thanatotic** (ˌθænəˈtɒtɪk) *adj.*
thane *or (less commonly)* **thegn** (θeɪn) *n.* **1.** (in Anglo-Saxon England) a member of an aristocratic class, ranking below an ealdorman, whose status was hereditary and who held land from the king or from another nobleman in return for certain services. **2.** (in medieval Scotland) **a.** a person of rank, often the chief of a clan, holding land from the king. **b.** a lesser noble who was a Crown official holding authority over an area of land. [Old English *thegn;* related to Old Saxon, Old High German *thegan* thane] —**thanage** (ˈθeɪnɪdʒ) *n.*
thank (θæŋk) *vb. (tr.)* **1.** to convey feelings of gratitude to. **2.** to hold responsible; *he has his creditors to thank for his bankruptcy.* **3.** used in exclamations of relief: *thank goodness; thank God.* **4. I'll thank you to.** used ironically to intensify a command, request, etc.: *I'll thank you to mind your own business.* [Old English *thancian;* related to Old Frisian *thankia,* Old Norse *thakka,* Old Saxon, Old High German *thancōn*]
thankful (ˈθæŋkfʊl) *adj.* grateful and appreciative. —**ˈthankfully** *adv.* —**ˈthankfulness** *n.*
thankless (ˈθæŋklɪs) *adj.* **1.** receiving no thanks or appreciation: *a thankless job.* **2.** ungrateful: *a thankless pupil.* —**ˈthanklessly** *adv.* —**ˈthanklessness** *n.*
thanks (θæŋks) *pl. n.* **1.** an expression of appreciation or gratitude or an acknowledgment of services or favours given. **2. thanks to.** because of: *thanks to him we lost the match.* ~*interj.* **3.** *Informal.* an exclamation expressing acknowledgment, gratitude, or appreciation.
thanksgiving (ˈθæŋksˌgɪvɪŋ; *U.S.* θæŋksˈgɪvɪŋ) *n.* **1.** the act of giving thanks. **2. a.** an expression of thanks to God. **b.** a public act of religious observance or a celebration in acknowledgment of divine favours.
Thanksgiving Day *n.* an annual day of holiday celebrated in thanksgiving to God on the fourth Thursday of November in the United States, and on the second Monday of October in Canada. Often shortened to **Thanksgiving.**
thank you *interj., n.* a conventional expression of gratitude.
thar (tɑː) *n.* a variant spelling of **tahr.**
that (ðæt; *unstressed* ðət) *determiner. (used before a singular n.)* **1. a.** used preceding a noun that has been mentioned at some time or is understood: *that idea of yours.* **b.** *(as pronoun): don't eat that; that's what I mean.* **2. a.** used preceding a noun that denotes something more remote or removed: *that dress is cheaper than this one; that building over there is for sale.* **b.** *(as pronoun): that is John and this is his wife; give me that.* Compare **this. 3.** used to refer to something that is familiar: *that old chap from across the street.* **4. and (all) that.** *Informal.* everything connected with the subject mentioned: *he knows a lot about building and that.* **5. at that.** *(completive-intensive)* additionally, all things considered, or nevertheless: *he's a pleasant fellow at that; I might decide to go at that.* **6. like that. a.** with ease; effortlessly: *he gave me the answer just like that.* **b.** of such a nature, character, etc.: *he paid for all our tickets—he's like that.* **7. that is. a.** to be precise. **b.** in other words. **c.** for example. **8. that's more like it.** that is better, an improvement, etc. **9. that's that.** there is no more to be done, discussed, etc. **10. with** *(or* **at) that.** thereupon; having said or done that. ~*conj. (subordinating)* **11.** used to introduce a noun clause: *I believe that you'll come.* **12.** Also: **so that, in order that.** used to introduce a clause of purpose: *they fought that others might have peace.* **13.** used to introduce a clause of result: *he laughed so hard that he cried.* **14.** used to introduce a clause after an understood sentence expressing desire, indignation, or amazement: *oh, that I had never lived!* ~*adv.* **15.** used with adjectives or adverbs to reinforce the specification of a precise degree already mentioned: *go just that fast and you should be safe.* **16.** Also: **all that.** *(usually used with a negative) Informal.* (intensifier): *he wasn't that upset at the news.* **17.** *Dialect.* (intensifier): *the cat was that weak after the fight.* ~*pron.* **18.** used to introduce a restrictive relative clause: *the book that we want.* **19.** used to introduce a clause with the verb *to be* to emphasize the extent to which the preceding noun is applicable: *genius that she is, she outwitted the computer.* [Old English *thæt;* related to Old Frisian *thet,* Old Norse, Old Saxon *that,* Old High German *daz,* Greek *to,* Latin *istud,* Sanskrit *tad*]
▷**Usage.** Precise stylists maintain a distinction between *that* and *which: that* is used as a relative pronoun in restrictive clauses and *which* in nonrestrictive clauses. In *the book that is on the table is mine,* the clause *that is on the table* is used to distinguish one particular book (the one on the table) from another or others (which may be anywhere, but not on the table). In *the book, which is on the table, is mine,* the *which* clause is merely descriptive or incidental. The more formal the level of language, the more important it is to preserve the distinction between the two relative pronouns; but in informal or colloquial usage, the words are often used interchangeably.

thatch (θætʃ) *n.* **1. a.** Also called: **thatching.** a roofing material that consists of straw, reed, etc. **b.** a roof made of such a material. **2.** anything resembling this, such as the hair of the head. **3.** Also called: **thatch palm.** any of various palms with leaves suitable for thatching. *~vb.* **4.** to cover (a roof) with thatch. [Old English *theccan* to cover; related to *thæc* roof, Old Saxon *thekkian* to thatch, Old High German *decchen,* Old Norse *thekja*] —**'thatcher** *n.* —**'thatchless** *adj.* —**'thatchy** *adj.*

Thatcherism ('θætʃəˌrɪzəm) *n.* the policies of monetarism, privatization, and self-help promoted by Margaret Thatcher (born 1925), British stateswoman. —**Thatcherite** ('θætʃəˌraɪt) *n., adj.*

thaumato- *or before a vowel* **thaumat-** *combining form.* miracle; marvel: *thaumaturge.* [from Greek *thauma, thaumat-* a marvel]

thaumatology (ˌθɔːmə'tɒlədʒɪ) *n.* the study of or a treatise on miracles.

thaumatrope ('θɔːməˌtrəʊp) *n.* a toy in which partial pictures on the two sides of a card appear to merge when the card is twirled rapidly. [C19: from THAUMATO- + -TROPE] —**thaumatropical** (ˌθɔːmə'trɒpɪkᵊl) *adj.*

thaumaturge ('θɔːməˌtɜːdʒ) *n. Rare.* a performer of miracles; magician. [C18: from Medieval Latin *thaumaturgus,* from Greek *thaumatourgos* miracle-working, from THAUMATO- + *-ourgos* working, from *ergon* work] —**'thaumaˌturgy** *n.* —**ˌthauma'turgic** *adj.*

thaw (θɔː) *vb.* **1.** to melt or cause to melt from a solid frozen state: *the snow thawed.* **2.** to become or cause to become unfrozen; defrost. **3.** (*intr.*) to be the case that the ice or snow is melting: *it's thawing fast.* **4.** (*intr.*) to become more sociable, relaxed, or friendly. *~n.* **5.** the act or process of thawing. **6.** a spell of relatively warm weather, causing snow or ice to melt. **7.** an increase in relaxation or friendliness. [Old English *thawian;* related to Old High German *douwen* to thaw, Old Norse *theyja* to thaw, Latin *tabēre* to waste away] —**'thawer** *n.* —**'thawless** *adj.*

ThB *abbrev. for* Bachelor of Theology.

THC *abbrev. for:* **1.** tetrahydrocannabinol: the main active principle in cannabis. **2.** (in New Zealand) Tourist Hotel Corporation.

ThD *abbrev. for* Doctor of Theology.

the[1] (*stressed or emphatic* ðiː; *unstressed before a consonant* ðə; *unstressed before a vowel* ðɪ) *determiner.* (*article*) **1.** used preceding a noun that has been previously specified: *the pain should disappear soon; the man then opened the door.* Compare: **a**[1]. **2.** used with a qualifying word or phrase to indicate a particular person, object, etc., as distinct from others: *ask the man standing outside; give me the blue one.* Compare **a**[1]. **3.** used preceding certain nouns associated with one's culture, society, or community: *to go to the doctor; listen to the news; watch the television.* **4.** used preceding present participles and adjectives when they function as nouns: *the singing is awful; the dead salute you.* **5.** used preceding titles and certain uniquely specific or proper nouns, such as place names: *the United States; the Honourable Edward Brown; the Chairman; the moon.* **6.** used preceding a qualifying adjective or noun in certain names or titles: *William the Conqueror; Edward the First.* **7.** used preceding a noun to make it refer to its class generically: *the white seal is hunted for its fur; this is good for the throat; to play the piano.* **8.** used instead of *my, your, her,* etc., with parts of the body: *take me by the hand.* **9.** (usually stressed) the best, only, or most remarkable: *Harry's is the club in this town.* **10.** used with proper nouns when qualified: *written by the young Hardy.* **11.** another word for **per**, esp. with nouns or noun phrases of cost: *fifty pence the pound.* **12.** *Often facetious or derogatory.* my; our: *the wife goes out on Thursdays.* **13.** used preceding a unit of time in phrases or titles indicating an outstanding person, event, etc.: *match of the day; housewife of the year.* [Middle English, from Old English *thē,* a demonstrative adjective that later superseded *sē* (masculine singular) and *sēo, sio* (feminine singular); related to Old Frisian *thi,* thin, Old High German *der, diu*]

the[2] (ðə, ðɪ) *adv.* **1.** (often foll. by *for*) used before comparative adjectives or adverbs for emphasis: *she looks the happier for her trip.* **2.** used correlatively before each of two comparative adjectives or adverbs to indicate equality: *the sooner you come, the better; the more I see you, the more I love you.* [Old English *thī, thȳ,* instrumental case of THE[1] and THAT; related to Old Norse *thī,* Gothic *thei*]

the- *combining form.* a variant of **theo-** before a vowel.

theaceous (θiː'eɪʃəs) *adj.* of, relating to, or belonging to the *Theaceae,* a family of evergreen trees and shrubs of tropical and warm regions: includes the tea plant.

theanthropism (θiː'ænθrəˌpɪzəm) *n.* **1.** the ascription of human traits or characteristics to a god or gods. **2.** *Christian theol.* the doctrine of the hypostatic union of the divine and human natures in the single person of Christ. [C19: from Ecclesiastical Greek *theanthrōpos* (from *theos* god + *anthrōpos* man) + -ISM] —**ˌthean'thropic** *adj.* —**the'anthropist** *n.*

thearchy ('θiːɑːkɪ) *n., pl.* **-chies.** rule or government by God or gods; theocracy. [C17: from Church Greek *thearkhia;* see THEO-, -ARCHY] —**the'archic** *adj.*

theatre *or U.S.* **theater** ('θɪətə) *n.* **1. a.** a building designed for the performance of plays, operas, etc. **b.** (*as modifier*): *a theatre ticket.* **c.** (*in combination*): *a theatregoer.* **2.** a large room or hall, usually with a raised platform and tiered seats for an audience, used for lectures, film shows, etc. **3.** Also called: **operating theatre.** a room in a hospital or other medical centre equipped for surgical operations. **4.** plays regarded collectively as a form of art. **5. the theatre.** the world of actors, theatrical companies, etc.: *the glamour of the theatre.* **6.** a setting for dramatic or important events. **7.** writing that is suitable for dramatic presentation: *a good piece of theatre.* **8.** *U.S., Austral., N.Z.* the usual word for **cinema** (sense 1). **9.** a major area of military activity: *the theatre of operations.* **10.** a circular or semicircular open-air building with tiers of seats. [C14: from Latin *theātrum,* from Greek *theatron* place for viewing, from *theasthai* to look at; related to Greek *thauma* miracle]

theatre-in-the-round *n., pl.* **theatres-in-the-round. 1.** a theatre with seats arranged around a central acting area. **2.** drama written or designed for performance in such a theatre. ~Also called: **arena theatre.**

theatre of cruelty *n.* a type of theatre that seeks to communicate to its audience a sense of pain, suffering, and evil, using gesture, movement, sound, and symbolism rather than language.

theatre of the absurd *n.* drama in which normal conventions and dramatic structure are ignored or modified in order to present life as irrational or meaningless.

theatrical (θɪ'ætrɪkᵊl) *adj.* **1.** of or relating to the theatre or dramatic performances. **2.** exaggerated and affected in manner or behaviour; histrionic. —**theˌatri'cality** *or* **the'atricalness** *n.* —**the'atrically** *adv.*

theatricals (θɪ'ætrɪkᵊlz) *pl. n.* dramatic performances and entertainments, esp. as given by amateurs.

theatrics (θɪ'ætrɪks) *n.* (*functioning as sing.*) **1.** the art of staging plays. **2.** exaggerated mannerisms or displays of emotions.

thebaine ('θiːbəˌiːn, θɪ'beɪiːn, -aɪn) *n.* a poisonous white crystalline alkaloid, extracted from opium and used in medicine. Formula: $C_{19}H_{21}NO_3$. Also called: **paramorphine.** [C19: from New Latin *thebaia* opium of Thebes in ancient Egypt (with reference to Egypt as a chief source of opium) + -INE[2]]

Theban ('θiːbən) *adj.* **1.** of or relating to Thebes, ancient Egyptian city on the river Nile. **2.** of or relating to Thebes, ancient Greek city of Boeotia. *~n.* **3.** a native or inhabitant of either of these cities.

theca ('θiːkə) *n., pl.* **-cae** (-siː). **1.** *Botany.* an enclosing organ, cell, or spore case, esp. the capsule of a moss. **2.** *Zoology.* a hard outer covering, such as the cup-shaped container of a coral polyp. [C17: from Latin *thēca,* from Greek *thēkē* case; related to Greek *tithenai* to place] —**'thecal** *or* **'thecate** *adj.*

thecodont ('θiːkəˌdɒnt) *adj.* **1.** (of mammals and certain reptiles) having teeth that grow in sockets. **2.** of or relating to teeth of this type. *~n.* **3.** any extinct reptile of the order *Thecodontia,* of Triassic times, having teeth set in sockets: they gave rise to the dinosaurs, crocodiles, pterodactyls, and birds. [C20: New Latin *Thecondontia,* from Greek *thēkē* case + -ODONT]

thé dansant *French.* (te dɑ̃sɑ̃) *n., pl.* ***thés dansant*** (te dɑ̃sɑ̃). a dance held while afternoon tea is served, popular in the 1920s and 1930s. [literally: dancing tea]

thee (ðiː) *pron.* **1.** the objective form of **thou**[1]. **2.** (*subjective*) *Rare.* refers to the person addressed: used mainly by members of the Society of Friends. [Old English *thē;* see THOU[1]]

theft (θɛft) *n.* **1.** *Criminal law.* the dishonest taking of property belonging to another person with the intention of depriving the owner permanently of its possession. **2.** *Rare.* something stolen. [Old English *thēofth;* related to Old Norse *thȳfth,* Old Frisian *thiūvethe,* Middle Dutch *düfte;* see THIEF] —**'theftless** *adj.*

thegn (θeɪn) *n.* a variant spelling of **thane.**

theine ('θiːiːn, -ɪn) *n.* another name for **caffeine,** esp. when present in tea. [C19: from New Latin *thea* tea + -INE[2]]

their (ðɛə) *determiner.* **1.** of, belonging to, or associated in some way with them: *their finest hour; their own clothes; she tried to combat their mocking her.* **2.** belonging to or associated in some way with people in general not including the speaker or people addressed: *in many countries they wash their clothes in the river.* **3.** belonging to or associated in some way with an indefinite antecedent such as *one, whoever,* or *anybody: everyone should bring their own lunch.* [C12: from Old Norse *theira* (genitive plural); see THEY, THEM]

▷**Usage.** The use of *their* as in sense 3 is sometimes regarded as unacceptable in formal contexts, though it has existed in the language for at least five centuries, and is common in informal contexts.

theirs (ðɛəz) *pron.* **1.** something or someone belonging to or associated in some way with them: *theirs is difficult.* **2.** *Not standard.* something or someone belonging to or associated in some way with an indefinite antecedent such as *one, whoever,* or *anybody: everyone thinks theirs is best.* **3. of theirs.** belonging to or associated with them.

theism ('θiːɪzəm) *n.* **1.** the form of the belief in one God as the transcendent creator and ruler of the universe that does not necessarily entail further belief in divine revelation. Compare **deism.** **2.** the belief in the existence of a God or gods. Compare **atheism.** [C17: from Greek *theos* god + -ISM] —**'theist** *n., adj.* —**the'istic** *or* **the'istical** *adj.* —**the'istically** *adv.*

them (ðɛm; *unstressed* ðəm) *pron.* **1.** (*objective*) refers to things or people other than the speaker or people addressed: *I'll kill them; what happened to them?* **2.** *Chiefly U.S.* a dialect word for

themselves when used as an indirect object: *they got them a new vice president.* ~*determiner.* **3.** a nonstandard word for **those:** *three of them oranges.* [Old English *thǣm,* influenced by Old Norse *theim;* related to Old Frisian *thām,* Old Saxon, Old High German *thēm,* Old Norse *theimr,* Gothic *thaim*]

▷**Usage.** See at **me.**

thematic (θɪˈmætɪk) *adj.* **1.** of, relating to, or consisting of a theme or themes. **2.** *Linguistics.* denoting a word that is the theme of a sentence. **3.** *Grammar.* **a.** denoting a vowel or other sound or sequence of sounds that occurs between the root of a word and any inflectional or derivational suffixes. **b.** of or relating to the stem or root of a word. ~*n.* **4.** *Grammar.* a thematic vowel: *"-o-" is a thematic in the combining form "psycho-".* —**theˈmatically** *adv.*

thematic apperception test *n. Psychol.* a projective test in which drawings of interacting people are shown and the person being tested is asked to make up a story about them.

thematization *or* **thematisation** (ˌθiːmətaɪˈzeɪʃən) *n. Linguistics.* the mental act or process of selecting particular topics as themes in discourse or words as themes in sentences.

theme (θiːm) *n.* **1.** an idea or topic expanded in a discourse, discussion, etc. **2.** (in literature, music, art, etc.) a unifying idea, image, or motif, repeated or developed throughout a work. **3.** *Music.* a group of notes forming a recognizable melodic unit, often used as the basis of the musical material in a composition. **4.** a short essay, esp. one set as an exercise for a student. **5.** *Linguistics.* the first major constituent of a sentence, usually but not necessarily the subject. In the sentence *history I do like,* "history" is the theme of the sentence, even though it is the object of the verb. **6.** *Grammar.* another word for **root**[1] (sense 9) or **stem**[1] (sense 9). **7.** (in the Byzantine Empire) a territorial unit consisting of several provinces under a military commander. **8.** (*modifier*) planned or designed round one unifying subject, image, etc.: *a theme holiday.* ~*vb.* (*tr.*) **9.** to design, decorate, arrange, etc., in accordance with a theme. [C13: from Latin *thema,* from Greek: deposit, from *tithenai* to lay down] —ˈ**themeless** *adj.*

theme park *n.* an area planned as a leisure attraction, in which all the displays, buildings, activities, etc., are based on or relate to one particular subject.

theme song *n.* **1.** a melody used, esp. in a film score, to set a mood, introduce a character, etc. **2.** another term for **signature tune.**

themselves (ðəmˈsɛlvz) *pron.* **1. a.** the reflexive form of *they* or *them.* **b.** (intensifier): *the team themselves voted on it.* **2.** (*preceded by a copula*) their normal or usual selves: *they don't seem themselves any more.* **3.** Also: **themself.** *Not standard.* a reflexive form of an indefinite antecedent such as *one, whoever,* or *anybody: everyone has to look after themselves.*

▷**Usage.** See at **myself.**

then (ðɛn) *adv.* **1.** at that time; over that period of time. **2.** (*sentence modifier*) in that case; that being so: *then why don't you ask her? if he comes, then you'll have to leave; go on then, take it.* **3. then and there.** a variant of **there and then:** see **there** (sense 6). ~*sentence connector.* **4.** after that; with that: *then John left the room and didn't return.* ~*n.* **5.** that time: *before then; from then on.* ~*adj.* **6.** (*prenominal*) existing, functioning, etc., at that time: *the then prime minister.* [Old English *thenne;* related to Old Saxon, Old High German *thanna;* see THAN]

thenar (ˈθiːnɑː) *Anatomy.* ~*n.* **1.** the palm of the hand. **2.** the fleshy area of the palm at the base of the thumb. ~*adj.* **3.** of or relating to the palm or the region at the base of the thumb. [C17: via New Latin from Greek; related to Old High German *tenar* palm of the hand]

thenardite (θɪˈnɑːdaɪt, tɪ-) *n.* a whitish vitreous mineral that consists of anhydrous sodium sulphate and occurs in saline residues. Formula: Na_2SO_4. [C19: named after Baron L. J. *Thénard* (1777–1857), French chemist; see -ITE[1]]

Thénard's blue (ˈteɪnɑːz, -nɑːdz) *n.* another name for **cobalt blue.** [C19: named after Baron L. J. *Thénard;* see THENARDITE]

thence (ðɛns) *adv.* **1.** from that place. **2.** Also: **thenceforth** (ˈðɛnsˈfɔːθ). from that time or event; thereafter. **3.** therefore. [C13: *thannes,* from *thanne,* from Old English *thanon;* related to Gothic *thanana,* Old Norse *thanan*]

thenceforward (ˈðɛnsˈfɔːwəd) *or* **thenceforwards** *adv.* from that time or place on; thence.

theo- *or before a vowel* **the-** *combining form.* indicating God or gods: *theology.* [from Greek *theos* god]

theobromine (ˌθiːəʊˈbrəʊmiːn, -mɪn) *n.* a white crystalline slightly water-soluble alkaloid that occurs in many plants, such as tea and cacao: used to treat coronary heart disease and headaches. Formula: $C_7H_8N_4O_2$. See also **xanthine** (sense 2). [C18: from New Latin *theobroma* genus of trees, literally: food of the gods, from THEO- + Greek *brōma* food + -INE[2]]

theocentric (ˌθɪəˈsɛntrɪk) *adj. Theol.* having God as the focal point of attention. —ˌ**theocenˈtricity** *n.* —ˌ**theoˈcentrism** *or* **theocentricism** (ˌθiːəʊˈsɛntrɪˌsɪzəm) *n.*

theocracy (θɪˈɒkrəsɪ) *n., pl.* **-cies.** **1.** government by a deity or by a priesthood. **2.** a community or political unit under such government. —ˈ**theoˌcrat** *n.* —ˌ**theoˈcratic** *or* ˌ**theoˈcratical** *adj.* —ˌ**theoˈcratically** *adv.*

theocrasy (θɪˈɒkrəsɪ) *n.* **1.** a mingling into one of deities or divine attributes previously regarded as distinct. **2.** the union of the soul with God in mysticism. [C19: from Greek *theokrasia,* from THEO- + *-krasia* from *krasis* a blending]

theodicy (θɪˈɒdɪsɪ) *n., pl.* **-cies.** the branch of theology concerned with defending the attributes of God against objections resulting from physical and moral evil. [C18: coined by the German philosopher Gottfried Leibnitz (1646–1716) in French as *théodicée,* from THEO- + Greek *dikē* justice] —**theˌodiˈcean** *adj.*

theodolite (θɪˈɒdəˌlaɪt) *n.* a surveying instrument for measuring horizontal and vertical angles, consisting of a small tripod-mounted telescope that is free to move in both the horizontal and vertical planes. Also called (in the U.S. and Canada): **transit.** [C16: from New Latin *theodolitus,* of uncertain origin] —**theodolitic** (θɪˌɒdəˈlɪtɪk) *adj.*

theogony (θɪˈɒgənɪ) *n., pl.* **-nies.** **1.** the origin and descent of the gods. **2.** an account of this, often recited in epic poetry. [C17: from Greek *theogonia;* see THEO-, -GONY] —**theogonic** (ˌθɪəˈgɒnɪk) *adj.* —**theˈogonist** *n.*

theol. *abbrev. for:* **1.** theologian. **2.** theological. **3.** theology.

theologian (ˌθɪəˈləʊdʒɪən) *n.* a person versed in or engaged in the study of theology, esp. Christian theology.

theological (ˌθɪəˈlɒdʒɪkᵊl) *adj.* **1.** of, relating to, or based on theology. **2.** based on God's revelation to man of his nature, his designs, and his will. —ˌ**theoˈlogically** *adv.*

theological virtues *pl. n.* (esp. among the scholastics) those virtues that are infused into man by a special grace of God, specifically faith, hope, and charity. Compare **natural virtues.**

theologize *or* **theologise** (θɪˈɒləˌdʒaɪz) *vb.* **1.** (*intr.*) to speculate upon theological subjects, engage in theological study or discussion, or formulate theological arguments. **2.** (*tr.*) to render theological or treat from a theological point of view. —**theˌologiˈzation** *or* **theˌologiˈsation** *n.* —**theˈoloˌgizer** *or* **theˈoloˌgiser** *n.*

theology (θɪˈɒlədʒɪ) *n., pl.* **-gies.** **1.** the systematic study of the existence and nature of the divine and its relationship to and influence upon other beings. **2.** the systematic study of Christian revelation concerning God's nature and purpose, esp. through the teaching of the Church. **3.** a specific system, form, or branch of this study, esp. for those preparing for the ministry or priesthood. [C14: from Late Latin *theologia,* from Latin; see THEO-, -LOGY] —**theˈologist** *n.*

theomachy (θɪˈɒməkɪ) *n., pl.* **-chies.** a battle among the gods or against them. [C16: from Greek *theomakhia,* from THEO- + *makhē* battle]

theomancy (ˈθiːəʊmænsɪ) *n.* divination or prophecy by an oracle or by people directly inspired by a god. [C17: from THEO- + -MANCY]

theomania (ˌθɪəˈmeɪnɪə) *n.* religious madness, esp. when it takes the form of believing oneself to be a god. —ˌ**theoˈmaniˌac** *n.*

theomorphic (ˌθɪəˈmɔːfɪk) *adj.* of or relating to the conception or representation of man as having the form of God or a deity. [C19: from Greek *theomorphos,* from THEO- + *morphē* form] —ˌ**theoˈmorphism** *n.*

theonomy (θɪˈɒnəmɪ) *n.* the state of being governed by God.

theopathy (θɪˈɒpəθɪ) *n.* religious emotion engendered by the contemplation of or meditation upon God. [C18: from THEO- + *-pathy,* from SYMPATHY] —**theopathetic** (ˌθɪəpəˈθɛtɪk) *or* **theopathic** (ˌθɪəˈpæθɪk) *adj.*

theophagy (θɪˈɒfədʒɪ) *n., pl.* **-gies.** the sacramental eating of a god.

theophany (θɪˈɒfənɪ) *n., pl.* **-nies.** *Theol.* a manifestation of a deity to man in a form that, though visible, is not necessarily material. [C17: from Late Latin *theophania,* from Late Greek *theophaneia,* from THEO- + *phainein* to show] —**theophanic** (θɪəˈfænɪk) *or* **theˈophanous** *adj.*

theophobia (ˌθɪəˈfəʊbɪə) *n.* morbid fear or hatred of God. —ˌ**theoˈphobiˌac** *n.*

theophylline (ˌθɪəˈfɪliːn, -ɪn; θɪˈɒfɪlɪn) *n.* a white crystalline slightly water-soluble alkaloid that is an isomer of theobromine: it occurs in plants such as tea and is used to treat heart disease and headaches. Formula: $C_7H_8N_4O_2$. See also **xanthine** (sense 2). [C19: from THEO(BROMINE) + PHYLLO- + -INE[2]]

theorbo (θɪˈɔːbəʊ) *n., pl.* **-bos.** *Music.* an obsolete form of the lute, having two necks, one above the other, the second neck carrying a set of unstopped sympathetic bass strings. [C17: from Italian *teorba,* probably from Venetian, variant of *tuorba* travelling bag, ultimately from Turkish *torba* bag] —**theˈorbist** *n.*

theorem (ˈθɪərəm) *n. Maths, logic.* a statement or formula that can be deduced from the axioms of a formal system by means of its rules of inference. [C16: from Late Latin *theōrēma,* from Greek: something to be viewed, from *theōrein* to view] —**theorematic** (ˌθɪərəˈmætɪk) *or* **theoremic** (ˌθɪəˈrɛmɪk) *adj.* —ˌ**theoreˈmatically** *adv.*

theoretic (ˌθɪəˈrɛtɪk) *adj.* **1.** another word for **theoretical.** ~*n.* **2.** another word for **theoretics.**

theoretical (ˌθɪəˈrɛtɪkᵊl) *or* **theoretic** *adj.* **1.** of or based on theory. **2.** lacking practical application or actual existence; hypothetical. **3.** using or dealing in theory; impractical. —ˌ**theoˈretically** *adv.*

theoretician (ˌθɪərɪˈtɪʃən) *n.* a student or user of the theory rather than the practical aspects of a subject.

theoretics (ˌθɪəˈrɛtɪks) *n.* (*functioning as sing. or pl.*) the theory of a particular subject. Also called (less commonly): **theoretic.**

theorize *or* **theorise** (ˈθɪəˌraɪz) *vb.* (*intr.*) to produce or use theories; speculate. —ˈ**theorist** *n.* —ˌ**theoriˈzation** *or* ˌ**theoriˈsation** *n.* —ˈ**theoˌrizer** *or* ˈ**theoˌriser** *n.*

theory (ˈθɪərɪ) *n., pl.* **-ries. 1.** a system of rules, procedures, and assumptions used to produce a result. **2.** abstract knowledge or reasoning. **3.** a speculative or conjectural view or idea: *I have a theory about that.* **4.** an ideal or hypothetical situation (esp. in the phrase **in theory**). **5.** a set of hypotheses related by logical or mathematical arguments to explain and predict a wide variety of connected phenomena in general terms: *the theory of relativity.* **6.** a nontechnical name for **hypothesis** (sense 1). [C16: from Late Latin *theōria,* from Greek: a sight, from *theōrein* to gaze upon]

theory-laden *adj.* (of an expression) capable of being understood only within the context of a specific theory, as for example *superego,* which requires the apparatus of Freudian theory in explanation.

theory of games *n.* another name for **game theory.**

theos. *abbrev. for:* **1.** theosophical. **2.** theosophy.

theosophy (θɪˈɒsəfɪ) *n.* **1.** any of various religious or philosophical systems claiming to be based on or to express an intuitive insight into the divine nature. **2.** the system of beliefs of the Theosophical Society founded in 1875, claiming to be derived from the sacred writings of Brahmanism and Buddhism, but denying the existence of any personal God. [C17: from Medieval Latin *theosophia,* from Late Greek; see THEO-, -SOPHY] —**theosophical** (ˌθɪəˈsɒfɪkᵊl) *or* ˌ**theoˈsophic** *adj.* —ˌ**theoˈsophically** *adv.* —**theˈosophism** *n.* —**theˈosophist** *n.*

therap. *or* **therapeut.** *abbrev. for:* **1.** therapeutic. **2.** therapeutics.

therapeutic (ˌθɛrəˈpjuːtɪk) *adj.* **1.** of or relating to the treatment of disease; curative. **2.** serving or performed to maintain health: *therapeutic abortion.* [C17: from New Latin *therapeuticus,* from Greek *therapeutikos,* from *therapeuein* to minister to, from *theraps* an attendant] —ˌ**theraˈpeutically** *adv.*

therapeutics (ˌθɛrəˈpjuːtɪks) *n.* (*functioning as sing.*) the branch of medicine concerned with the treatment of disease.

therapist (ˈθɛrəpɪst) *n.* a person skilled in a particular type of therapy: *a physical therapist.*

therapsid (θəˈræpsɪd) *n.* any extinct reptile of the order *Therapsida,* of Permian to Triassic times: considered to be the ancestors of mammals. [C20: from New Latin *Therapsida,* from Greek *theraps* attendant]

therapy (ˈθɛrəpɪ) *n., pl.* **-pies. a.** the treatment of physical, mental, or social disorders or disease. **b.** (*in combination*): *physiotherapy; electrotherapy.* [C19: from New Latin *therapia,* from Greek *therapeia* attendance; see THERAPEUTIC]

Theravada (ˌθɛrəˈvɑːdə) *n.* the southern school of Buddhism, the name preferred by Hinayana Buddhists for their doctrines. [from Pali: doctrine of the elders]

there (ðɛə) *adv.* **1.** in, at, or to that place, point, case, or respect: *we never go there; I'm afraid I disagree with you there.* ~*pron.* **2.** used as a grammatical subject with some verbs, esp. *be,* when the true subject is an indefinite or mass noun phrase following the verb as complement: *there is a girl in that office; there doesn't seem to be any water left.* ~*adj.* **3.** (*postpositive*) who or which is in that place or position: *that boy there did it.* **4. all there.** (*predicative*) having his wits about him; of normal intelligence. **5. so there.** an exclamation that usually follows a declaration of refusal or defiance: *you can't have any more, so there!* **6. there and then.** on the spot; immediately; instantly. **7. there it is.** that is the state of affairs. **8. there you are. a.** an expression used when handing a person something requested or desired. **b.** an exclamation of triumph: *there you are, I knew that would happen!* ~*n.* **9.** that place: *near there; from there.* ~*interj.* **10.** an expression of sympathy, as in consoling a child. [Old English *thǣr;* related to Old Frisian *thēr,* Old Saxon, Old High German *thār,* Old Norse, Gothic *thar*]

▷**Usage.** Careful writers and speakers ensure that the verb agrees with the number of the subject in such constructions as *there is a man waiting* and *there are several people waiting.* However, where the subject is compound even careful speakers frequently use the singular as in *there is a pen and a book on the table.*

thereabouts (ˈðɛərəˌbaʊts) *or U.S.* **thereabout** *adv.* near that place, time, amount, etc.: *fifty or thereabouts.*

thereafter (ˌðɛərˈɑːftə) *adv.* from that time on or after that time: *thereafter, he ceased to pay attention.*

thereat (ˌðɛərˈæt) *adv. Rare.* **1.** at that point or time. **2.** for that reason.

thereby (ˌðɛəˈbaɪ, ˈðɛəˌbaɪ) *adv.* **1.** by that means; because of that. **2.** *Archaic.* by or near that place; thereabouts.

therefor (ˌðɛəˈfɔː) *adv. Archaic or law.* for this, that, or it: *he will be richer therefor.*

therefore (ˈðɛəˌfɔː) *sentence connector.* **1.** thus; hence: used to mark an inference on the speaker's part: *those people have their umbrellas up; therefore, it must be raining.* **2.** consequently; as a result: *they heard the warning on the radio and therefore took another route.*

therefrom (ˌðɛəˈfrɒm) *adv. Archaic.* from that or there: *the roads that lead therefrom.*

therein (ˌðɛərˈɪn) *adv. Formal or law.* in or into that place, thing, etc.

thereinafter (ˌðɛərɪnˈɑːftə) *adv. Formal or law.* from this point on in that document, statement, etc.

thereinto (ˌðɛərˈɪntuː) *adv. Formal or law.* into that place, circumstance, etc.

thereof (ˌðɛərˈɒv) *adv. Formal or law.* **1.** of or concerning that or it. **2.** from or because of that.

thereon (ˌðɛərˈɒn) *adv.* an archaic word for **thereupon.**

thereto (ˌðɛəˈtuː) *adv.* **1.** *Formal or law.* to that or it: *the form attached thereto.* **2.** *Obsolete.* in addition to that.

theretofore (ˌðɛətʊˈfɔː) *adv. Formal or law.* before that time; previous to that.

thereunder (ˌðɛərˈʌndə) *adv. Formal or law.* **1.** (in documents, etc.) below that or it; subsequently in that; thereafter. **2.** under the terms or authority of that.

thereupon (ˌðɛərəˈpɒn) *adv.* **1.** immediately after that; at that point: *thereupon, the whole class applauded.* **2.** *Formal or law.* upon that thing, point, subject, etc.

therewith (ˌðɛəˈwɪθ, -ˈwɪð) *or* **therewithal** *adv.* **1.** *Formal or law.* with or in addition to that. **2.** a less common word for **thereupon** (sense 1). **3.** *Archaic.* by means of or on account of that.

therianthropic (ˌθɪərɪənˈθrɒpɪk) *adj.* **1.** (of certain mythical creatures or deities) having a partly animal, partly human form. **2.** of or relating to such creatures or deities. [C19: from Greek *thērion* wild animal + *anthrōpos* man] —**therianthropism** (ˌθɪərɪˈænθrəˌpɪzəm) *n.*

theriomorphic (ˌθɪərɪəʊˈmɔːfɪk) *or* **theriomorphous** *adj.* (esp. of a deity) possessing or depicted in the form of a beast. [C19: from Greek *thēriomorphos,* from *thērion* wild animal + *morphē* shape] —ˈ**therioˌmorph** *n.*

therm (θɜːm) *n. Brit.* a unit of heat equal to 100 000 British thermal units. One therm is equal to $1.055\,056 \times 10^{8}$ joules. [C19: from Greek *thermē* heat]

thermae (ˈθɜːmiː) *pl. n.* public baths or hot springs, esp. in ancient Greece or Rome. [C17: from Latin, from Greek *thermai,* pl. of *thermē* heat]

thermaesthesia *or U.S.* **thermesthesia** (ˌθɜːmɪsˈθiːzɪə) *n.* sensitivity to various degrees of heat and cold. [C19: from New Latin, from THERM- + Greek *aisthēsis* feeling]

thermal (ˈθɜːməl) *adj.* **1.** Also: **thermic** (ˈθɜːmɪk). of, relating to, caused by, or generating heat or increased temperature. **2.** hot or warm: *thermal baths; thermal spring.* **3.** (of garments or fabrics) specially designed so as to have exceptional heat-retaining properties. ~*n.* **4.** *Meteorol.* a column of rising air caused by local unequal heating of the land surface, and used by gliders and birds to gain height. **5.** (*pl.*) thermal garments, esp. underclothes. —ˈ**thermally** *adv.*

thermal barrier *n.* an obstacle to flight at very high speeds as a result of the heating effect of air friction. Also called: **heat barrier.**

thermal conductivity *n.* a measure of the ability of a substance to conduct heat, determined by the rate of heat flow normally through an area in the substance divided by the area and by minus the component of the temperature gradient in the direction of flow: measured in watts per metre per kelvin. Symbol: λ or *k.* Sometimes shortened to **conductivity.**

thermal efficiency *n.* the ratio of the work done by a heat engine to the energy supplied to it. Compare **efficiency.**

thermal equator *n.* an imaginary line round the earth running through the point on each meridian with the highest average temperature. It lies mainly to the north because of the larger landmasses and therefore greater summer heating.

thermalize *or* **thermalise** (ˈθɜːməˌlaɪz) *vb. Physics.* to undergo or cause to undergo a process in which neutrons lose energy in a moderator and become thermal neutrons. —ˌ**thermaliˈzation** *or* ˌ**thermaliˈsation** *n.*

thermal neutrons *pl. n.* slow neutrons that are approximately in thermal equilibrium with a moderator. They have a distribution of speeds similar to that of the molecules of a gas at the temperature of the moderator. Data concerning nuclear interactions are often given for standard thermal neutrons of speed 2200 metres per second, which is approximately the most probable speed at normal laboratory temperatures.

thermal noise *n.* electrical noise caused by thermal agitation of conducting electrons.

thermal printer *n. Computer technol.* another name for **electrothermal printer.**

thermal reactor *n.* a nuclear reactor in which most of the fission is caused by thermal neutrons.

thermal shock *n.* a fluctuation in temperature causing stress in a material. It often results in fracture, esp. in brittle materials such as ceramics.

thermette (θɜːˈmɛt) *n. N.Z.* a device, used outdoors, for boiling water rapidly.

Thermidor *French.* (tɛrmidɔr) *n.* the month of heat: the eleventh month of the French revolutionary calendar, extending from July 20 to Aug. 18. Also called: **Fervidor.** [C19: from French, from Greek *thermē* heat + *dōron* gift]

thermion (ˈθɜːmɪən) *n. Physics.* an electron or ion emitted by a body at high temperature.

thermionic (ˌθɜːmɪˈɒnɪk) *adj.* of, relating to, or operated by electrons emitted from materials at high temperatures: *a thermionic valve.*

thermionic current *n.* an electric current produced between two electrodes as a result of electrons emitted by thermionic emission.

thermionic emission *n.* the emission of electrons from very hot solids or liquids: used for producing electrons in valves, electron microscopes, x-ray tubes, etc.

thermionics (ˌθɜːmɪˈɒnɪks) *n.* (*functioning as sing.*) the branch of electronics concerned with the emission of electrons by hot bodies and with devices based on this effect, esp. the study and design of thermionic valves.

thermionic valve *or esp. U.S. and Canadian* **tube** *n.* an electronic valve in which electrons are emitted from a heated rather than a cold cathode.

thermistor (θɜːˈmɪstə) *n.* a semiconductor device having a resistance that decreases rapidly with an increase in temperature. It is used for temperature measurement, to compensate for temperature variations in a circuit, etc. [C20: from THERMO- + (RES)ISTOR]

Thermit (ˈθɜːmɪt) *or* **Thermite** (ˈθɜːmaɪt) *n. Trademark.* a mixture of aluminium powder and a metal oxide, such as iron oxide, which when ignited reacts with the evolution of heat to yield aluminium oxide and molten metal: used for welding and in some types of incendiary bombs.

thermite process *n.* another name for **aluminothermy.**

thermo- *or before a vowel* **therm-** *combining form.* related to, caused by, or measuring heat: *thermodynamics; thermophile.* [from Greek *thermos* hot, *thermē* heat]

thermobarograph (ˌθɜːməʊˈbærəˌgrɑːf, -ˌgræf) *n.* a device that simultaneously records the temperature and pressure of the atmosphere.

thermobarometer (ˌθɜːməʊbəˈrɒmɪtə) *n.* an apparatus that provides an accurate measurement of pressure by observation of the change in the boiling point of a fluid.

thermochemistry (ˌθɜːməʊˈkɛmɪstrɪ) *n.* the branch of chemistry concerned with the study and measurement of the heat evolved or absorbed during chemical reactions. —ˌ**thermoˈchemical** *adj.* —ˌ**thermoˈchemically** *adv.* —ˌ**thermoˈchemist** *n.*

thermocline (ˈθɜːməʊˌklaɪn) *n.* a temperature gradient in a thermally stratified body of water, such as a lake.

thermocouple (ˈθɜːməʊˌkʌpᵊl) *n.* **1.** a device for measuring temperature consisting of a pair of wires of different metals or semiconductors joined at both ends. One junction is at the temperature to be measured, the second at a fixed temperature. The electromotive force generated depends upon the temperature difference. **2.** a similar device with only one junction between two dissimilar metals or semiconductors. [C19: from THERMO- + COUPLE]

thermodynamic (ˌθɜːməʊdaɪˈnæmɪk) *or* **thermodynamical** *adj.* **1.** of or concerned with thermodynamics. **2.** determined by or obeying the laws of thermodynamics. —ˌ**thermodyˈnamically** *adv.*

thermodynamic equilibrium *n.* the condition of a system in which the quantities that specify its properties, such as pressure, temperature, etc., all remain unchanged. Sometimes shortened to **equilibrium.**

thermodynamics (ˌθɜːməʊdaɪˈnæmɪks) *n.* (*functioning as sing.*) the branch of physical science concerned with the interrelationship and interconversion of different forms of energy and the behaviour of systems in terms of certain basic quantities, such as pressure, temperature, etc. See also **law of thermodynamics.**

thermodynamic temperature *n.* temperature defined in terms of the laws of thermodynamics and not in terms of the properties of any real material. It is usually expressed on the Kelvin scale. Also called: **absolute temperature.**

thermoelectric (ˌθɜːməʊɪˈlɛktrɪk) *or* **thermoelectrical** *adj.* **1.** of, relating to, used in, or operated by the generation of an electromotive force by the Seebeck effect or the Thomson effect: *a thermoelectric thermometer.* **2.** of, relating to, used in, or operated by the production or absorption of heat by the Peltier effect: *a thermoelectric cooler.* —ˌ**thermoeˈlectrically** *adv.*

thermoelectric effect *n.* another name for the **Seebeck effect** or **Peltier effect.**

thermoelectricity (ˌθɜːməʊɪlɛkˈtrɪsɪtɪ) *n.* **1.** electricity generated by a thermocouple. **2.** the study of the relationship between heat and electrical energy. See also **Seebeck effect, Peltier effect.**

thermoelectron (ˌθɜːməʊɪˈlɛktrɒn) *n.* an electron emitted at high temperature, such as one produced in a thermionic valve.

thermogenesis (ˌθɜːməʊˈdʒɛnɪsɪs) *n.* the production of heat by metabolic processes. —**thermogenous** (θɜːˈmɒdʒɪnəs) *or* **thermogenetic** (ˌθɜːməʊdʒɪˈnɛtɪk) *adj.*

thermogram (ˈθɜːməʊˌgræm) *n.* **1.** *Med.* a picture produced by thermography, using photographic film sensitive to infrared radiation. **2.** the record produced by a thermograph.

thermograph (ˈθɜːməʊˌgrɑːf, -ˌgræf) *n.* a type of thermometer that produces a continuous record of a fluctuating temperature.

thermography (θɜːˈmɒgrəfɪ) *n.* **1.** any writing, printing, or recording process involving the use of heat. **2.** *Med.* the measurement and recording of heat produced by a part of the body: used in the diagnosis of tumours, esp. of the breast (**mammothermography**), which have an increased blood supply and therefore generate more heat than normal tissue. See also **thermogram.** —**therˈmographer** *n.* —**thermographic** (ˌθɜːməʊˈgræfɪk) *adj.*

thermojunction (ˌθɜːməʊˈdʒʌŋkʃən) *n.* a point of electrical contact between two dissimilar metals across which a voltage appears, the magnitude of which depends on the temperature of the contact and the nature of the metals. See also **Seebeck effect.**

thermolabile (ˌθɜːməʊˈleɪbɪl) *adj.* (of certain biochemical and chemical compounds) easily decomposed or subject to a loss of characteristic properties by the action of heat: *a thermolabile enzyme.* Compare **thermostable** (sense 1). [C20: from THERMO- + LABILE]

thermoluminescence (ˌθɜːməʊˌluːmɪˈnɛsəns) *n.* phosphorescence of certain materials or objects as a result of heating. It is caused by pre-irradiation of the material inducing defects which are removed by the heat, the energy released appearing as light: used in archaeological dating. —ˌ**thermoˌlumiˈnescent** *adj.*

thermolysis (θɜːˈmɒlɪsɪs) *n.* **1.** *Physiol.* loss of heat from the body. **2.** the dissociation of a substance as a result of heating. —**thermolytic** (ˌθɜːməʊˈlɪtɪk) *adj.*

thermomagnetic (ˌθɜːməʊmægˈnɛtɪk) *adj.* of or concerned with the relationship between heat and magnetism, esp. the change in temperature of a body when it is magnetized or demagnetized. Former term: **pyromagnetic.**

thermometer (θəˈmɒmɪtə) *n.* an instrument used to measure temperature, esp. one in which a thin column of liquid, such as mercury, expands and contracts within a graduated sealed tube. See also **clinical thermometer, gas thermometer, resistance thermometer, thermocouple, pyrometer.**

thermometry (θəˈmɒmɪtrɪ) *n.* the branch of physics concerned with the measurement of temperature and the design and use of thermometers and pyrometers. —**thermometric** (ˌθɜːməˈmɛtrɪk) *or* ˌ**thermoˈmetrical** *adj.* —ˌ**thermoˈmetrically** *adv.*

thermomotor (ˌθɜːməʊˈməʊtə) *n.* an engine that produces force from the expansion of a heated fluid.

thermonasty (ˈθɜːməʊˌnæstɪ) *n. Botany.* a nastic movement in response to a temperature change, as occurs in the opening of certain flowers.

thermonuclear (ˌθɜːməʊˈnjuːklɪə) *adj.* **1.** involving nuclear fusion: *a thermonuclear reaction; thermonuclear energy.* **2.** involving thermonuclear weapons: *a thermonuclear war.*

thermonuclear bomb *n.* another name for **fusion bomb.**

thermonuclear reaction *n.* a nuclear fusion reaction occurring at a very high temperature: responsible for the energy produced in the sun, nuclear weapons, and fusion reactors. See **nuclear fusion, hydrogen bomb.**

thermoperiodism (ˌθɜːməʊˈpɪərɪədɪzəm) *or* **thermoperiodicity** (ˌθɜːməʊˌpɪərɪəˈdɪsɪtɪ) *n. Botany.* the response of a plant to cycles of temperature fluctuation. —ˌ**thermoˌperiˈodic** *adj.*

thermophile (ˈθɜːməʊˌfaɪl) *or* **thermophil** (ˈθɜːməʊˌfɪl) *n.* **1.** an organism, esp. a bacterium or plant, that thrives under warm conditions. ~*adj.* **2.** thriving under warm conditions. —ˌ**thermoˈphilic** *or* **thermophilous** (θɜːˈmɒfɪləs) *adj.*

thermophyllous (ˌθɜːməʊˈfɪləs) *adj.* (of plants) having leaves only in the warmer part of the year; deciduous.

thermopile (ˈθɜːməʊˌpaɪl) *n.* an instrument for detecting and measuring heat radiation or for generating a thermoelectric current. It consists of a number of thermocouple junctions, usually joined together in series. [C19: from THERMO- + PILE (in the sense: voltaic pile)]

thermoplastic (ˌθɜːməʊˈplæstɪk) *adj.* **1.** (of a material, esp. a synthetic plastic or resin) becoming soft when heated and rehardening on cooling without appreciable change of properties. Compare **thermosetting.** ~*n.* **2.** a synthetic plastic or resin, such as polystyrene, with these properties. —**thermoplasticity** (ˌθɜːməʊplæˈstɪsɪtɪ) *n.*

Thermos *or* **Thermos flask** (ˈθɜːməs) *n. Trademark.* a type of stoppered vacuum flask used to preserve the temperature of its contents. See also **Dewar flask.**

thermoscope (ˈθɜːməˌskəʊp) *n.* a device that indicates a change in temperature, esp. one that does not measure the actual temperature. —**thermoscopic** (ˌθɜːməˈskɒpɪk) *or* ˌ**thermoˈscopical** *adj.* —ˌ**thermoˈscopically** *adv.*

thermosetting (ˌθɜːməʊˈsɛtɪŋ) *adj.* (of a material, esp. a synthetic plastic or resin) hardening permanently after one application of heat and pressure. Thermosetting plastics, such as phenol-formaldehyde, cannot be remoulded. Compare **thermoplastic.**

thermosiphon (ˌθɜːməʊˈsaɪfən) *n.* a system in which a coolant is circulated by convection caused by a difference in density between the hot and cold portions of the liquid.

thermosphere (ˈθɜːməˌsfɪə) *n.* an atmospheric layer lying between the mesosphere and the exosphere, reaching an altitude of about 400 kilometres where the temperature is over 1000° C.

thermostable (ˌθɜːməʊˈsteɪbᵊl) *adj.* **1.** (of certain chemical and biochemical compounds) capable of withstanding moderate heat without loss of characteristic properties: *a thermostable plastic.* Compare **thermolabile.** **2.** not affected by high temperatures. —**thermostability** (ˌθɜːməʊstəˈbɪlɪtɪ) *n.*

thermostat (ˈθɜːməˌstæt) *n.* **1.** a device that maintains a system at a constant temperature. It often consists of a bimetallic strip that bends as it expands and contracts with temperature, thus breaking and making contact with an electrical power supply. **2.** a similar device that actuates equipment, such as a sprinkler,

when a certain temperature is reached. —ˌ**thermo'static** *adj.* —ˌ**thermo'statically** *adv.*
thermostatics (ˌθɜːməˈstætɪks) *n.* (*functioning as sing.*) the branch of science concerned with thermal equilibrium.
thermotaxis (ˌθɜːməʊˈtæksɪs) *n.* the directional movement of an organism in response to the stimulus of a source of heat. —ˌ**thermo'taxic** *adj.*
thermotensile (ˌθɜːməʊˈtɛnsaɪl) *adj.* of or relating to tensile strength in so far as it is affected by temperature.
thermotherapy (ˌθɜːməʊˈθɛrəpɪ) *n. Med.* treatment of a bodily structure or part by the application of heat.
thermotolerant (ˌθɜːməʊˈtɒlərənt) *adj.* (of plants) able to tolerate, but not thriving in, high temperatures.
thermotropism (ˌθɜːməʊˈtrəʊpɪzəm) *n.* the directional growth of a plant in response to the stimulus of heat. —ˌ**thermo'tropic** *adj.*
-thermy *n. combining form.* indicating heat: *diathermy.* [from New Latin *-thermia,* from Greek *thermē*] —**-thermic** *or* **-thermal** *adj. combining form.*
theroid (ˈθɪərɔɪd) *adj.* of, relating to, or resembling a beast. [C19: from Greek *thēroeidēs,* from *thēr* wild animal; see -OID]
therophyte (ˈθɪərəˌfaɪt) *n.* a plant that overwinters as a seed. [from Greek *theros* summer + -PHYTE]
theropod (ˈθɪərəpɒd) *n.* any bipedal carnivorous saurischian dinosaur of the suborder *Theropoda,* having strong hind legs and grasping hands. They lived in Triassic to Cretaceous times and included tyrannosaurs and megalosaurs. [C19: from New Latin *theropoda,* from Greek *thēr* beast + *pous* foot] —**theropodan** (θɪˈrɒpədᵊn) *n., adj.*
thersitical (θəˈsɪtɪkᵊl) *adj. Rare.* abusive and loud. [C17: from *Thersites,* evil-tongued fighter on the Greek side in the Trojan War]
thesaurus (θɪˈsɔːrəs) *n., pl.* **-ri** (-raɪ) *or* **-ruses.** **1.** a book containing systematized lists of synonyms and related words. **2.** a dictionary of selected words or topics. **3.** *Rare.* a treasury. [C18: from Latin, Greek: TREASURE]
these (ðiːz) *determiner.* **a.** the form of **this** used before a plural noun: *these men.* **b.** (*as pronoun*): *I don't much care for these.*
thesis (ˈθiːsɪs) *n., pl.* **-ses** (-siːz). **1.** a dissertation resulting from original research, esp. when submitted by a candidate for a degree or diploma. **2.** a doctrine maintained or promoted in argument. **3.** a subject for a discussion or essay. **4.** an unproved statement, esp. one put forward as a premise in an argument. **5.** *Music.* the downbeat of a bar, as indicated in conducting. **6.** (in classical prosody) the syllable or part of a metrical foot not receiving the ictus. Compare **arsis.** **7.** *Philosophy.* the first stage in the Hegelian dialectic, that is challenged by the antithesis. [C16: via Late Latin from Greek: a placing, from *tithenai* to place]
Thespian (ˈθɛspɪən) *adj.* **1.** of or relating to Thespis, 6th-century B.C. Greek poet, regarded as the founder of tragic drama. **2.** of or relating to drama and the theatre; dramatic. ~*n.* **3.** *Often facetious.* an actor or actress.
Thess. *Bible. abbrev. for* Thessalonians.
theta (ˈθiːtə) *n.* **1.** the eighth letter of the Greek alphabet (Θ, θ), a consonant, transliterated as *th.* **2.** the lower-case form of this letter used in phonetic transcription to represent the voiceless dental fricative *th* as in *thick, both.* Compare **edh.** [C17: from Greek, of Semitic origin; compare Hebrew *tēth*]
thetic (ˈθɛtɪk) *adj.* **1.** (in classical prosody) of, bearing, or relating to a metrical stress. **2.** positive and arbitrary; prescriptive. [C17: from Greek *thetikos,* from *thetos* laid down, from *tithenai* to place] —ˈ**thetically** *adv.*
theurgy (ˈθiːˌɜːdʒɪ) *n., pl.* **-gies.** **1. a.** the intervention of a divine or supernatural agency in the affairs of man. **b.** the working of miracles by such intervention. **2.** beneficent magic as taught and performed by Egyptian Neoplatonists and others. [C16: from Late Latin *theūrgia,* from Late Greek *theourgia* the practice of magic, from *theo-* THEO- + *-urgia,* from *ergon* work] —**the'urgic** *or* **the'urgical** *adj.* —**the'urgically** *adv.* —ˈ**theurgist** *n.*
thew (θjuː) *n.* **1.** muscle, esp. if strong or well-developed. **2.** (*pl.*) muscular strength. [Old English *thēaw;* related to Old Saxon, Old High German *thau* discipline, Latin *tuērī* to observe, *tūtus* secure] —ˈ**thewy** *adj.* —ˈ**thewless** *adj.*
they (ðeɪ) *pron.* (*subjective*) **1.** refers to people or things other than the speaker or people addressed: *they fight among themselves.* **2.** refers to unspecified people or people in general not including the speaker or people addressed: *in Australia they have Christmas in the summer.* **3.** *Not standard.* refers to an indefinite antecedent such as *one, whoever,* or *anybody: if anyone objects, they can go.* **4.** an archaic word for **those:** *blessed are they that mourn.* [C12: *thei* from Old Norse *their,* masculine nominative plural, equivalent to Old English *thā*]
they'd (ðeɪd) *contraction of* they would *or* they had.
they'll (ðeɪl) *contraction of* they will *or* they shall.
they're (ðɛə, ˈðeɪə) *contraction of* they are.
they've (ðeɪv) *contraction of* they have.
THI *abbrev. for* temperature-humidity index.
thi- *combining form.* a variant of **thio-.**
thiamine (ˈθaɪəˌmiːn, -mɪn) *or* **thiamin** (ˈθaɪəmɪn) *n. Biochem.* a soluble white crystalline vitamin that occurs in the outer coat of rice and other grains. It forms part of the vitamin B complex and is essential for carbohydrate metabolism: deficiency leads to nervous disorders and to the disease beriberi. Formula: $C_{12}H_{17}ON_4SCl.H_2O$. Also called: **vitamin B_1, aneurin.** [C20: THIO- + (VIT)AMIN]
thiazine (ˈθaɪəˌziːn, -ˌzaɪn) *n.* any of a group of organic compounds containing a ring system composed of four carbon atoms, a sulphur atom, and a nitrogen atom.
thiazole (ˈθaɪəˌzəʊl) *or* **thiazol** (ˈθaɪəˌzɒl) *n.* **1.** a colourless liquid with a pungent smell that contains a ring system composed of three carbon atoms, a sulphur atom, and a nitrogen atom. It is used in dyes and fungicides. Formula: C_3H_3NS. **2.** any of a group of compounds derived from this substance that are used in dyes.
thick (θɪk) *adj.* **1.** of relatively great extent from one surface to the other; fat, broad, or deep: *a thick slice of bread.* **2. a.** (*postpositive*) of specific fatness: *ten centimetres thick.* **b.** (*in combination*): *a six-inch-thick wall.* **3.** having a relatively dense consistency; not transparent: *thick soup.* **4.** abundantly covered or filled: *a piano thick with dust.* **5.** impenetrable; dense: *a thick fog.* **6.** stupid, slow, or insensitive: *a thick person.* **7.** throaty or badly articulated: *a voice thick with emotion.* **8.** (of accents, etc.) pronounced. **9.** *Informal.* very friendly (esp. in the phrase **thick as thieves**). **10. a bit thick.** *Brit.* unfair or excessive. **11. a thick ear.** *Informal.* a blow on the ear delivered as punishment, in anger, etc. ~*adv.* **12.** in order to produce something thick: *to slice bread thick.* **13.** profusely; in quick succession (esp. in the phrase **thick and fast**). **14. lay it on thick.** *Informal.* **a.** to exaggerate a story, statement, etc. **b.** to flatter excessively. ~*n.* **15.** a thick piece or part. **16. the thick.** the most intense or active part. **17. through thick and thin.** in good times and bad. [Old English *thicce;* related to Old Saxon, Old High German *thikki,* Old Norse *thykkr*] —ˈ**thickish** *adj.* —ˈ**thickly** *adv.*
thicken (ˈθɪkən) *vb.* **1.** to make or become thick or thicker: *thicken the soup by adding flour.* **2.** (*intr.*) to become more involved: *the plot thickened.* —ˈ**thickener** *n.*
thickening (ˈθɪkənɪŋ) *n.* **1.** something added to a liquid to thicken it. **2.** a thickened part or piece.
thicket (ˈθɪkɪt) *n.* a dense growth of small trees, shrubs, and similar plants. [Old English *thiccet;* see THICK]
thickhead (ˈθɪkˌhɛd) *n.* **1.** a stupid or ignorant person; fool. **2.** Also called: **whistler.** any of various Australian and SE Asian songbirds of the family *Muscicapidae* (flycatchers, etc.). —ˌ**thick'headed** *adj.* —ˌ**thick'headedness** *n.*
thickie *or* **thicky** (ˈθɪkɪ) *n., pl.* **-ies.** *Brit. slang.* a slow-witted unintelligent person.
thick-knee *n.* another name for **stone curlew.** [C19: so called because it has thick knee joints]
thickleaf (ˈθɪkˌliːf) *n., pl.* **-leaves.** any of various succulent plants of the crassulaceous genus *Crassula,* having sessile or short-stalked fleshy leaves.
thickness (ˈθɪknɪs) *n.* **1.** the state or quality of being thick. **2.** the dimension through an object, as opposed to length or width. **3.** a layer of something. **4.** a thick part.
thickset (ˌθɪkˈsɛt) *adj.* **1.** stocky in build; sturdy. **2.** densely planted or placed. ~*n.* **3.** a rare word for **thicket.**
thick-skinned *adj.* insensitive to criticism or hints; not easily upset or affected.
thick-witted *or* **thick-skulled** *adj.* stupid, dull, or slow to learn. —ˌ**thick-'wittedly** *adv.* —ˌ**thick-'wittedness** *n.*
thief (θiːf) *n., pl.* **thieves** (θiːvz). **1.** a person who steals something from another. **2.** *Criminal law.* a person who commits theft. [Old English *thēof;* related to Old Frisian *thiāf,* Old Saxon *thiof,* Old High German *diob,* Old Norse *thjōfr,* Gothic *thiufs*] —ˈ**thievish** *adj.* —ˈ**thievishly** *adv.* —ˈ**thievishness** *n.*
thieve (θiːv) *vb.* to steal (someone's possessions). [Old English *thēofian,* from *thēof* THIEF] —ˈ**thievery** *n.* —ˈ**thieving** *adj.*
thigh (θaɪ) *n.* **1.** the part of the leg between the hip and the knee in man. **2.** the corresponding part in other vertebrates and insects. ~Related adj.: **femoral.** [Old English *thēh;* related to Old Frisian *thiāch,* Old High German *dioh* thigh, Old Norse *thjō* buttock, Old Slavonic *tyku* fat]
thighbone (ˈθaɪˌbəʊn) *n.* a nontechnical name for the **femur.**
thigmotaxis (ˌθɪgməˈtæksɪs) *n.* another name for **stereotaxis.** [C19: from Greek *thigma* touch + -TAXIS] —ˌ**thigmo'tactic** *adj.* —ˌ**thigmo'tactically** *adv.*
thigmotropism (ˌθɪgməʊˈtrəʊpɪzəm) *n.* the directional growth of a plant, in response to the stimulus of direct contact. Also called: **haptotropism, stereotropism.** [C19: from Greek *thigma* touch + -TROPISM] —ˌ**thigmo'tropic** *adj.*
thill (θɪl) *n. Archaic.* another word for **shaft** (sense 6). [C14: perhaps related to Old English *thille* board, planking, Old High German *dilla* plank, Old Norse *thili*]
thimble (ˈθɪmbᵊl) *n.* **1.** a cap of metal, plastic, etc., used to protect the end of the finger when sewing. **2.** any small metal cap resembling this. **3.** *Nautical.* a loop of metal having a groove at its outer edge for a rope or cable, for lining the inside of an eye. **4.** short for **thimbleful.** [Old English *thȳmel* thumbstall, from *thūma* THUMB]
thimbleful (ˈθɪmbᵊlˌfʊl) *n.* a very small amount, esp. of a liquid.
thimblerig (ˈθɪmbᵊlˌrɪg) *n.* **1.** a game in which the operator rapidly moves about three inverted thimbles, often with sleight of hand, one of which conceals a token, the other player betting on which thimble the token is under. ~*vb.* **-rigs, -rigging,**

-rigged. (*tr.*) **2.** to cheat or swindle, as in this game. [C19: from THIMBLE + *rig* (in obsolete sense: a trick, scheme)] —'**thimble,rigger** *n.*

thimbleweed ('θɪmbᵊl,wi:d) *n. U.S.* any of various plants having a thimble-shaped fruit, esp. an American anemone, *Anemone virginiana*, and a rudbeckia, *Rudbeckia laciniata*.

thimblewit ('θɪmbᵊl,wɪt) *n. Chiefly U.S.* a silly or dimwitted person; dunce. —'**thimble,witted** *adj.*

thimerosal (θaɪ'mɛrə,sæl) *n.* a creamy white crystalline compound of mercury, used in solution as an antiseptic. Formula: $C_9H_9HgNaO_2S$. [C20: from THIO- + MER(CURY) + SAL(ICYLATE)]

thin (θɪn) *adj.* **thinner, thinnest. 1.** of relatively small extent from one side or surface to the other; fine or narrow. **2.** slim or lean. **3.** sparsely placed; meagre: *thin hair.* **4.** of relatively low density or viscosity: *a thin liquid.* **5.** weak; poor; insufficient: *a thin disguise.* **6.** (of a photographic negative) having low density, usually insufficient to produce a satisfactory positive. **7.** *Mountaineering.* a climb or pitch on which the holds are few and small. **8. thin on the ground.** few in number; scarce. ~*adv.* **9.** in order to produce something thin: *to cut bread thin.* ~*vb.* **thins, thinning, thinned. 10.** to make or become thin or sparse. [Old English *thynne;* related to Old Frisian *thenne,* Old Saxon, Old High German *thunni,* Old Norse *thunnr,* Latin *tenuis* thin, Greek *teinein* to stretch] —'**thinly** *adv.* —'**thinness** *n.*

thine (ðaɪn) *determiner. Archaic.* **a.** (*preceding a vowel*) of, belonging to, or associated in some way with you (thou): *thine eyes.* **b.** (*as pronoun*): *thine is the greatest burden.* ~Compare **thy.** [Old English *thīn;* related to Old High German *dīn,* Gothic *theina*]

thin-film *adj.* (of an electronic component, device, or circuit) composed of one or more extremely thin layers of metal, semiconductor, etc., deposited on a ceramic or glass substrate: *thin-film capacitor.*

thing[1] (θɪŋ) *n.* **1.** an object, fact, affair, circumstance, or concept considered as being a separate entity. **2.** any inanimate object. **3.** an object or entity that cannot or need not be precisely named. **4.** *Informal.* a person or animal regarded as the object of pity, contempt, etc.: *you poor thing.* **5.** an event or act. **6.** a thought or statement. **7.** *Law.* any object or right that may be the subject of property (as distinguished from a person). **8.** a device, means, or instrument. **9.** (*often pl.*) a possession, article of clothing, etc. **10.** *Informal.* a mental attitude, preoccupation or obsession (esp. in the phrase **have a thing about**). **11.** an activity or mode of behaviour satisfying to one's personality (esp. in the phrase **do one's (own) thing**). **12. the thing.** the latest fashion. **13. be on to a good thing.** to be in a profitable situation or position. **14. make a thing of.** to make a fuss about; exaggerate the importance of. [Old English *thing* assembly; related to Old Norse *thing* assembly, Old High German *ding* assembly]

thing[2] (θɪŋ, tɪŋ) *n.* (*often cap.*) a law court or public assembly in the Scandinavian countries. Also: **ting**[2]. [C19: from Old Norse *thing* assembly (the same word as THING[1])]

thing-in-itself *n.* (in Kantian philosophy) an element of the noumenal rather than the phenomenal world, of which the senses give no knowledge but whose bare existence can be inferred from the nature of experience.

thingumabob *or* **thingamabob** ('θɪŋəmə,bɒb) *n. Informal.* a person or thing the name of which is unknown, temporarily forgotten, or deliberately overlooked. Also: **thingumajig, thingamajig** ('θɪŋəmə,dʒɪg), *or* **thingummy** ('θɪŋəmɪ). [C18: from THING[1], with humorous suffix]

think (θɪŋk) *vb.* **thinks, thinking, thought. 1.** (*tr.; may take a clause as object*) to consider, judge, or believe: *he thinks my ideas impractical.* **2.** (*intr.;* often foll. by *about*) to exercise the mind as in order to make a decision; ponder. **3.** (*intr.*) to be capable of conscious thought: *man is the only animal that thinks.* **4.** to remember; recollect: *I can't think what his name is.* **5.** (*intr.;* foll. by *of*) to make the mental choice (of): *think of a number.* **6.** (*may take a clause as object or an infinitive*) **a.** to expect; suppose: *I didn't think to see you here.* **b.** to be considerate or aware enough (to do something): *he did not think to thank them.* **7.** (*intr.;* foll. by *of*) to consider; regard: *she thinks of herself as a poet.* **8.** (*intr.*) to focus the attention on being: *think thin; think big.* **9.** (*tr.*) to bring into or out of a specified condition by thinking: *to think away one's fears.* **10. I don't think.** *Slang.* a phrase added to an ironical statement: *you're the paragon of virtue, I don't think.* **11. think again.** to reconsider one's decision, opinion, etc. **12. think better of. a.** to change one's mind about (a course of action, decision, etc.). **b.** to have a more favourable opinion of (a person). **13. think much of.** (*usually negative*) to have a high opinion of. **14. think nothing of. a.** to regard as routine, easy, or natural. **b.** to have no compunction or hesitation about. **c.** to have a very low opinion of. **15. think twice.** to consider carefully before deciding (about something). ~*n.* **16.** *Informal.* a careful, open-minded assessment: *let's have a fresh think about this problem.* **17.** (*modifier*) *Informal.* characterized by or involving thinkers, thinking, or thought: *a think session.* **18. you've (he's, she's, etc.) got another think coming.** *Slang.* you (etc.) are mistaken and will soon have to alter your opinion. ~See also **think out, think over, think up.** [Old English *thencan;* related to Old Frisian *thenza,* Old Saxon *thenkian,* Old High German *denken,* Old Norse *thekkja,* Gothic *thagkjan*] —'**thinker** *n.*

thinkable ('θɪŋkəbᵊl) *adj.* able to be conceived or considered; possible; feasible.

thinking ('θɪŋkɪŋ) *n.* **1.** opinion or judgment. **2.** the process of thought. ~*adj.* **3.** (*prenominal*) using or capable of using intelligent thought: *thinking people.* **4. put on one's thinking cap.** to ponder a matter or problem.

think out *or* **through** *vb.* (*tr., adv.*) to consider carefully and rationally in order to reach a conclusion.

think over *vb.* (*tr., adv.*) to ponder or consider: *to think over a problem.*

think-tank *n. Informal.* a group of specialists organized by a business enterprise, governmental body, etc., and commissioned to undertake intensive study and research into specified problems.

think up *vb.* (*tr., adv.*) to invent or devise: *to think up a plan.*

thinner ('θɪnə) *n.* (*often pl., functioning as sing.*) a solvent, such as turpentine, added to paint or varnish to dilute it, reduce its opacity or viscosity, or increase its penetration into the ground.

thin-skinned *adj.* sensitive to criticism or hints; easily upset or affected.

thio- *or before a vowel* **thi-** *combining form.* indicating that a chemical compound contains sulphur, esp. denoting that a compound is derived from a specified compound by the replacement of an oxygen atom with a sulphur atom: *thiol; thiosulphate.* [from Greek *theion* sulphur]

thioalcohol (,θaɪəʊ'ælkə,hɒl) *n.* another name for a **thiol.**

thiocarbamide (,θaɪəʊ'kɑ:bə,maɪd) *n.* another name for **thiourea.**

thiocyanate (,θaɪəʊ'saɪə,neɪt) *n.* any salt or ester of thiocyanic acid.

thiocyanic acid (,θaɪəʊsaɪ'ænɪk) *n.* an unstable acid known in the form of thiocyanate salts. Formula: HSCN.

thio-ether (,θaɪəʊ'i:θə) *n.* any of a class of organic compounds in which a sulphur atom is bound to two hydrocarbon groups.

thiofuran (,θaɪəʊ'fjʊəræn) *n.* another name for **thiophen.** [C20: from THIO- + FURAN]

thiol ('θaɪɒl) *n.* any of a class of sulphur-containing organic compounds with the formula RSH, where R is an organic group. Also called (not in technical usage): **mercaptan.**

thionate ('θaɪə,neɪt) *n.* any salt or ester of thionic acid.

thionic (θaɪ'ɒnɪk) *adj.* of, relating to, or containing sulphur.

thionine ('θaɪəʊ,ni:n, -,naɪn) *or* **thionin** ('θaɪənɪn) *n.* **1.** a crystalline derivative of thiazine used as a violet dye to stain microscope specimens. **2.** any of a class of related dyes. [C19: by shortening, from *ergothioneine,* a crystalline betaine found in ergot and blood]

thionyl ('θaɪənɪl) *n.* (*modifier*) of, consisting of, or containing the divalent group SO: *a thionyl group or radical; thionyl chloride.* Also: **sulphinyl.** [C19 *thion-,* from Greek *theion* sulphur + -YL]

thiopentone sodium (,θaɪəʊ'pɛntəʊn) *or* **thiopental sodium** (,θaɪəʊ'pɛntæl) *n.* a barbiturate drug used in medicine as an intravenous general anaesthetic. Formula: $C_{11}H_{17}NaN_2O_2S$. Also called: **Sodium Pentothal.** See also **truth drug.**

thiophen ('θaɪəʊ,fɛn) *or* **thiophene** ('θaɪəʊ,fi:n) *n.* a colourless liquid heterocyclic compound found in the benzene fraction of coal tar and manufactured from butane and sulphur. It has an odour resembling that of benzene and is used as a solvent and in the manufacture of dyes, pharmaceuticals, and resins. Formula: C_4H_4S. Also called: **thiofuran.**

thiosinamine (,θaɪəʊ'sɪnə,mi:n, -sɪ'næmɪn) *n.* a white crystalline bitter-tasting compound with a slight garlic-like odour, occurring in mustard oil and used in organic synthesis; 1-allyl-2-thiourea. Formula: CH_2:$CHCH_2NHCSNH_2$. [C19: from THIO- + *sin-* (from Latin *sināpis* mustard) + AMINE]

thiosulphate (,θaɪəʊ'sʌlfeɪt) *n.* any salt of thiosulphuric acid.

thiosulphuric acid (,θaɪəʊsʌl'fjʊərɪk) *n.* an unstable acid known only in solutions and in the form of its salts. Formula: $H_2S_2O_3$.

thiouracil (,θaɪəʊ'jʊərəsɪl) *n.* a white crystalline water-insoluble substance with an intensely bitter taste, used in medicine to treat hyperthyroidism; 2-thio-4-oxypyrimidine. Formula: $C_4H_4N_2OS$. [from THIO- + *uracil* (URO-[1] + AC(ETIC) + *-il* -ILE)]

thiourea (,θaɪəʊ'jʊərɪə) *n.* a white water-soluble crystalline substance with a bitter taste that forms addition compounds with metal ions and is used in photographic fixing, rubber vulcanization, and the manufacture of synthetic resins. Formula: H_2NCSNH_2.

third (θɜ:d) *adj.* (*usually prenominal*) **1. a.** coming after the second and preceding the fourth in numbering or counting order, position, time, etc.; being the ordinal number of *three:* often written 3rd. **b.** (*as n.*): *he arrives on the third; the third got a prize.* **2.** rated, graded, or ranked below the second level. **3.** denoting the third from lowest forward ratio of a gearbox in a motor vehicle. ~*n.* **4. a.** one of three equal or nearly equal parts of an object, quantity, etc. **b.** (*as modifier*): *a third part.* **5.** the fraction equal to one divided by three (1/3). **6.** the forward ratio above second of a gearbox in a motor vehicle. In some vehicles it is the top gear. **7. a.** the interval between one note and another three notes away from it counting inclusively along the diatonic scale. **b.** one of two notes constituting such an interval in relation to the other. See also **interval** (sense 5), **major** (sense 13a), **minor** (sense 4d). **8.** *Brit.* an honours degree of the third and usually the lowest class. Full term: **third class honours degree. 9.** (*pl.*) goods of a standard lower than that of seconds. *~adv.* **10.** Also: **thirdly.** in the third place. *~sentence connector.* **11.** Also: **thirdly.** as the third point: linking what follows with the previous statements as in a speech or argument. [Old English *thirda,* variant of *thridda;* related to Old Frisian *thredda,* Old Saxon *thriddio,* Old High German *drittio,* Old Norse *thrithi,* Latin *tertius*] —'**thirdly** *adv.*

Third Age *n.* **the.** old age, esp. when viewed as an opportunity for travel, further education, etc.

third class *n.* **1.** the class or grade next in value, quality, etc., to the second. *~adj.* (**third-class** *when prenominal*). **2.** of the class or grade next in value, quality, etc., to the second. **3.** of or denoting the class of accommodation in a hotel, on a ship, etc., next in quality and price to the second: usually the cheapest. **4.** (in the U.S. and Canada) of or relating to a class of mail consisting largely of unsealed printed matter. **5.** *Brit.* See **third** (sense 8). *~adv.* **6.** by third-class mail, transport, etc.

third degree *n. Informal.* torture or bullying, esp. used to extort confessions or information.

third-degree burn *n. Pathol.* See **burn**[1] (sense 21).

third dimension *n.* the additional dimension by which a solid object may be distinguished from a two-dimensional drawing or picture of it or from any planar object.

third estate *n.* the third order or class in a country or society divided into estates, esp. for representation in a parliament; the commons, townsmen, or middle class.

third eyelid *n.* another name for **nictitating membrane.**

third house *n. U.S.* a political lobby for a special interest.

third-line forcing *n.* the deprecated practice of forcing a buyer to purchase a supply of a product that he does not want as a condition of supplying him with the product he does want.

third man *n. Cricket.* **a.** a fielding position on the off side near the boundary behind the batsman's wicket. **b.** a fielder in this position.

third man argument *n.* (in Aristotelian philosophy) the argument against the existence of Platonic Forms that since the Form of Man is itself a perfect man, a further form (the "third" man) would be required to explain this, and so ad infinitum.

Third Market *n.* a market established by the London Stock Exchange in 1987 to trade in shares in companies required to provide less detailed information than that required by the main market or the unlisted securities market.

Third Order *n. R.C. Church.* a religious society of laymen affiliated to one of the religious orders and following a mitigated form of religious rule.

third party *n.* **1.** a person who is involved by chance or only incidentally in a legal proceeding, agreement, or other transaction, esp. one against whom a defendant claims indemnity. *~adj.* **2.** *Insurance.* providing protection against liability caused by accidental injury or death of other persons or damage to their property.

third person *n.* a grammatical category of pronouns and verbs used when referring to objects or individuals other than the speaker or his addressee or addressees.

third rail *n.* an extra rail from which an electric train picks up current by means of a sliding collector to feed power to its motors.

third-rate *adj.* not of high quality; mediocre or inferior.

third reading *n.* (in a legislative assembly) **1.** *Brit.* the process of discussing the committee's report on a bill. **2.** *U.S.* the final consideration of a bill.

Third Reich *n.* See **Reich** (sense 4).

thirdstream ('θɜːdˌstriːm) *adj.* **1.** (of music) combining jazz and classical elements. *~n.* **2.** such music.

Third World *n.* the countries of Africa, Asia, and Latin America collectively, esp. when viewed as underdeveloped and as neutral in the former East-West alignment.

thirl[1] (θɜːl) *vb. (tr.) Dialect.* **a.** to bore or drill. **b.** to thrill. [Old English *thyrelian,* from *thyrel* hole; see NOSTRIL]

thirl[2] (θɪrl, θɜːl) *vb. (tr.) Chiefly Scot.* to enslave; bind. [C16: variant of earlier *thrill* THRALL]

thirlage ('θɜːlɪdʒ) *n. Scots Law.* (formerly) **1.** an obligation imposed upon tenants of certain lands requiring them to have their grain ground at a specified mill. **2.** the fee paid for grinding the grain. [C16: variant of earlier *thrillage,* from *thrill,* Scottish variant of THRALL]

thirst (θɜːst) *n.* **1.** a craving to drink, accompanied by a feeling of dryness in the mouth and throat. **2.** an eager longing, craving, or yearning: *a thirst for knowledge.* *~vb. (intr.)* **3.** to feel a thirst: *to thirst for a drink; to thirst after righteousness.* [Old English *thyrstan,* from *thurst* thirst; related to Old Norse *thyrsta* to thirst, Old High German *dursten* to thirst, Latin *torrēre* to parch] —'**thirster** *n.*

thirsty ('θɜːstɪ) *adj.* **thirstier, thirstiest. 1.** feeling a desire to drink. **2.** dry; arid: *the thirsty soil.* **3.** (foll. by *for*) feeling an eager desire: *thirsty for information.* **4.** causing thirst: *thirsty work.* —'**thirstily** *adv.* —'**thirstiness** *n.*

thirteen ('θɜː'tiːn) *n.* **1.** the cardinal number that is the sum of ten and three and is a prime number. See also **number** (sense 1). **2.** a numeral, 13, XIII, etc., representing this number. **3.** the amount or quantity that is three more than ten; baker's dozen. **4.** something represented by, representing, or consisting of 13 units. *~determiner.* **5. a.** amounting to thirteen: *thirteen buses.* **b.** (*as pronoun*): *thirteen of them fell.* [Old English *threotēne;* see THREE, -TEEN]

thirteenth ('θɜː'tiːnθ) *adj.* **1.** (*usually prenominal*) **a.** coming after the twelfth in numbering or counting order, position, time, etc.; being the ordinal number of *thirteen:* often written 13th. **b.** (*as n.*): *Friday the thirteenth.* *~n.* **2. a.** one of 13 equal or nearly equal parts of something. **b.** (*as modifier*): *a thirteenth part.* **3.** the fraction equal to one divided by 13 (1/13). **4.** *Music.* **a.** an interval of one octave plus a sixth. See also **interval** (sense 5). **b.** short for **thirteenth chord.**

thirteenth chord *n.* a chord much used in jazz and pop, consisting of a major or minor triad upon which are superimposed the seventh, ninth, eleventh, and thirteenth above the root. Often shortened to **thirteenth.**

thirtieth ('θɜːtɪɪθ) *adj.* **1.** (*usually prenominal*) **a.** being the ordinal number of *thirty* in counting order, position, time, etc.: often written 30th. **b.** (*as n.*): *the thirtieth of the month.* *~n.* **2. a.** one of 30 approximately equal parts of something. **b.** (*as modifier*): *a thirtieth part.* **3.** the fraction equal to one divided by 30 (1/30).

thirty ('θɜːtɪ) *n., pl.* **-ties. 1.** the cardinal number that is the product of ten and three. See also **number** (sense 1). **2.** a numeral, 30, XXX, etc., representing this number. **3.** (*pl.*) the numbers 30-39, esp. the 30th to the 39th year of a person's life or of a century. **4.** the amount or quantity that is three times as big as ten. **5.** something representing, represented by, or consisting of 30 units. *~determiner.* **6. a.** amounting to thirty: *thirty trees.* **b.** (*as pronoun*): *thirty are broken.* [Old English *thrītig;* see THREE, -TY[1]]

Thirty-nine Articles *pl. n.* a set of formulas defining the doctrinal position of the Church of England, drawn up in the 16th century, to which the clergy are required to give general consent.

thirty-second note *n.* the usual U.S. and Canadian name for **demisemiquaver.**

thirty-three *n.* a former name for **LP**[1]. [C20: so called because it is played at thirty-three and a third revolutions per minute]

thirty-twomo (ˌθɜːtɪ'tuːməʊ) *n., pl.* **-mos.** a book size resulting from folding a sheet of paper into 32 leaves or 64 pages. Often written: **32mo, 32°.**

this (ðɪs) *determiner.* (*used before a singular n.*) **1. a.** used preceding a noun referring to something or someone that is closer: distinct from **that:** *this dress is cheaper than that one; look at this picture.* **b.** (*as pronoun*): *this is Mary and that is her boyfriend; take this.* **2. a.** used preceding a noun that has just been mentioned or is understood: *this plan of yours won't work.* **b.** (*as pronoun*): *I first saw this on Sunday.* **3. a.** used to refer to something about to be said, read, etc.: *consider this argument.* **b.** (*as pronoun*): *listen to this.* **4. a.** the present or immediate: *this time you'll know better.* **b.** (*as pronoun*): *before this, I was mistaken.* **5.** *Informal.* an emphatic form of **a**[1] or **the**[1]: used esp. on relating a story: *I saw this big brown bear.* **6. this and that.** various unspecified and trivial actions, matters, objects, etc. **7. this here.** *U.S., not standard.* an emphatic form of **this** (senses 1–3). **8. with** (*or* **at**) **this.** after this; thereupon. *~adv.* **9.** used with adjectives and adverbs to specify a precise degree that is about to be mentioned: *go just this fast and you'll be safe.* [Old English *thēs, thēos, this* (masculine, feminine, neuter singular); related to Old Saxon *thit,* Old High German *diz,* Old Norse *thessi*]

thistle ('θɪsᵊl) *n.* **1.** any of numerous plants of the genus *Cirsium,* having prickly-edged leaves, pink, purple, yellow, or white dense flower heads, and feathery hairs on the seeds: family *Compositae* (composites). **2.** any of various similar or related plants, such as the star thistle. **3.** a thistle, or a representation of one, as the national emblem of Scotland. [Old English *thīstel,* related to Old Saxon, Old High German *thīstil,* Old Norse *thīstill*] —'**thistly** *adj.*

Thistle ('θɪsᵊl) *n.* **the. 1.** See **Order of the Thistle. 2.** (*sometimes not cap.*) **a.** the emblem of this Order. **b.** membership of this Order.

thistledown ('θɪsᵊlˌdaʊn) *n.* **1.** the mass of feathery plumed seeds produced by a thistle. **2.** anything resembling this.

thither ('ðɪðə) *or* **thitherward** *adv. Obsolete or formal.* to or towards that place; in that direction. [Old English *thider,* variant of *thæder,* influenced by *hider* HITHER; related to Old Norse *thathra* there]

thitherto (ˌðɪðə'tuː, 'ðɪðəˌtuː) *adv. Obsolete or formal.* until that time.

thixotropic (ˌθɪksə'trɒpɪk) *adj.* (of fluids and gels) having a reduced viscosity when stress is applied, as when stirred: *thixotropic paints.* [C20: from Greek *thixis* the act of touching + -TROPIC] —**thixotropy** (θɪk'sɒtrəpɪ) *n.*

tho *or* **tho'** (ðəʊ) *conj., adv. U.S. or poetic.* a variant spelling of **though.**

thole[1] (θəʊl) *or* **tholepin** ('θəʊlˌpɪn) *n.* a wooden pin or one of a pair, set upright in the gunwales of a rowing boat to serve as a fulcrum in rowing. [Old English *tholl,* related to Middle Low German *dolle,* Norwegian *toll,* Icelandic *thollr*]

thole[2] (θəʊl) *vb.* **1.** (*tr.*) *Scot. and northern English dialect.* to put up with; bear. **2.** an archaic word for **suffer.** [Old English *tholian;* related to Old Saxon, Old High German *tholōn,* Old Norse *thola* to endure: compare Latin *tollere* to bear up]

tholos ('θəʊlɒs) *n., pl.* **-loi** (-lɔɪ). a dry-stone beehive-shaped tomb associated with the Mycenaean culture of Greece in the 16th to the 12th century B.C. [C17: from Greek]

Thomism ('təʊmɪzəm) *n.* the comprehensive system of philosophy and theology developed by the Italian scholar Saint Thomas Aquinas in the 13th century and since taught and maintained by his followers, esp. in the Dominican order. —'**Thomist** *n., adj.* —**Tho'mistic** *or* **Tho'mistical** *adj.*

Thompson sub-machine-gun ('tɒmpsən, 'tɒmsən) *n. Trademark.* a .45 calibre sub-machine-gun. Also called: **Tommy gun.** [C20: after John T. *Thompson* (1860–1940), U.S. Army Officer, its coinventor]

Thomson effect ('tɒmsən) *n. Physics.* the phenomenon in which a temperature gradient along a metallic (or semiconductor) wire or strip causes an electric potential gradient to form along its length. [named after Sir William *Thomson*, later Lord Kelvin (1824–1907), British physicist who discovered it]

thon (ðɒn) *determiner.* a Scot. word for **yon.** [C19: of uncertain origin]

-thon *suffix forming nouns.* indicating a large-scale event or operation of a specified kind: *telethon.* [C20: on the pattern of MARATHON]

thonder ('ðɒndər) *adv., determiner.* a Scot. word for **yonder.** [C19: of uncertain origin]

thong (θɒŋ) *n.* **1.** a thin strip of leather or other material, such as one used for lashing things together. **2.** a whip or whiplash, esp. one made of leather. **3.** *U.S., Canadian, Austral., and N.Z.* the usual name for **flip-flop** (sense 5). [Old English *thwang;* related to Old High German *dwang* reins, Old Norse *thvengr* strap]

thoracentesis (ˌθɔːrəsɛn'tiːsɪs) *or* **thoracocentesis** (ˌθɔːrəkəʊsɛn'tiːsɪs) *n. Med.* the surgical puncture of the pleural cavity using a hollow needle, in order to withdraw fluid, drain blood, etc. Also called: **pleurocentesis.**

thoracic (θɔː'ræsɪk) *adj.* of, near, or relating to the thorax.

thoracic duct *n.* the major duct of the lymphatic system, beginning below the diaphragm and ascending in front of the spinal column to the base of the neck.

thoraco- *or before a vowel* **thorac-** *combining form.* thorax: *thoracotomy.*

thoracoplasty ('θɔːrəkəʊˌplæstɪ) *n., pl.* **-ties.** **1.** plastic surgery of the thorax. **2.** surgical removal of several ribs or a part of them to permit the collapse of a diseased lung, used in cases of pulmonary tuberculosis and bronchiectasis.

thoracoscope ('θɔːrəkəʊˌskəʊp) *n. Med.* an instrument used for examining the pleural cavity.

thoracotomy (ˌθɔːrə'kɒtəmɪ) *n., pl.* **-mies.** surgical incision into the chest wall.

thorax ('θɔːræks) *n., pl.* **thoraxes** *or* **thoraces** ('θɔːrəˌsiːz, θɔː'reɪsiːz). **1.** the part of the human body enclosed by the ribs. **2.** the corresponding part in other vertebrates. **3.** the part of an insect's body between the head and abdomen, which bears the wings and legs. [C16: via Latin from Greek *thōrax* breastplate, chest]

thoria ('θɔːrɪə) *n.* another name for **thorium dioxide.** [C19: THORIUM + *-a*, on the model of *magnesia*]

thorianite ('θɔːrɪəˌnaɪt) *n.* a rare black mineral consisting of thorium and uranium oxides. Formula: $ThO_2.U_3O_8$.

thorite ('θɔːraɪt) *n.* an orange-yellow, brownish, or black radioactive mineral consisting of thorium silicate in tetragonal crystalline form. It occurs in coarse granite and is a source of thorium. Formula: $ThSiO_4$.

thorium ('θɔːrɪəm) *n.* a soft ductile silvery-white metallic element. It is radioactive and occurs in thorite and monazite: used in gas mantles, magnesium alloys, electronic equipment, and as a nuclear power source. Symbol: Th; atomic no.: 90; atomic wt.: 232.04; half-life of most stable isotope, ^{232}Th: 1.41×10^{10} years; valency: 4; relative density: 11.72; melting pt.: 1750°C; boiling pt.: 3800°C (approx.). [C19: New Latin, from *Thor*, Norse god of thunder, + -IUM] —'**thoric** *adj.*

thorium dioxide *n.* a heavy insoluble white powder used in incandescent mantles. Formula: ThO_2. Also called: **thoria.**

thorium series *n.* a radioactive series that starts with thorium–232 and ends with lead–208.

thorn (θɔːn) *n.* **1.** a sharp pointed woody extension of a stem or leaf. Compare **prickle** (sense 1). **2. a.** any of various trees or shrubs having thorns, esp. the hawthorn. **b.** the wood of any of these plants. **3.** short for **thorn moth.** **4.** a Germanic character of runic origin (þ) used in Old and Modern Icelandic to represent the voiceless dental fricative sound of *th,* as in *thin, bath.* Its use in phonetics for the same purpose is now obsolete. See **theta.** **5.** this same character as used in Old and Middle English as an alternative to *edh,* but indistinguishable from it in function or sound. Compare **edh.** **6.** *Zoology.* any of various sharp spiny parts. **7.** a source of irritation (esp. in the phrases **a thorn in one's side** *or* **flesh**). [Old English; related to Old High German *dorn,* Old Norse *thorn*] —'**thornless** *adj.*

thorn apple *n.* **1.** a poisonous solanaceous plant, *Datura stramonium,* of the N hemisphere, having white funnel-shaped flowers and spiny capsule fruits. U.S. name: **jimson weed.** See also **stramonium.** **2.** any other plant of the genus *Datura.* **3.** the fruit of certain types of hawthorn.

thornback ('θɔːnˌbæk) *n.* **1.** a European ray, *Raja clavata,* having a row of spines along the back and tail. **2.** a similar fish, *Platyrhinoidis triseriata,* of the Pacific Ocean.

thornbill ('θɔːnˌbɪl) *n.* **1.** any of various South American hummingbirds of the genera *Chalcostigma, Ramphomicron,* etc., having a thornlike bill. **2.** Also called: **thornbill warbler.** any of various Australasian wrens of the genus *Acanthiza* and related genera: family *Muscicapidae.* **3.** any of various other birds with thornlike bills.

thorn moth *n.* any of various woodland geometrid moths, typified by the **large thorn** (*Ennomos autumnaria*), having wings set somewhat at an angle and held up when at rest. Often shortened to **thorn.**

thorny ('θɔːnɪ) *adj.* **thornier, thorniest.** **1.** bearing or covered with thorns. **2.** difficult or unpleasant: *a thorny problem.* **3.** sharp. —'**thornily** *adv.* —'**thorniness** *n.*

thoron ('θɔːrɒn) *n.* a radioisotope of radon that is a decay product of thorium. Symbol: Tn or ^{220}Rn; atomic no.: 86; half-life: 54.5s. [C20: from THORIUM + -ON]

thorough ('θʌrə) *adj.* **1.** carried out completely and carefully: *a thorough search.* **2.** (*prenominal*) utter: *a thorough bore.* **3.** painstakingly careful: *our accountant is thorough.* [Old English *thurh;* related to Old Frisian *thruch,* Old Saxon *thuru,* Old High German *duruh;* see THROUGH] —'**thoroughly** *adv.* —'**thoroughness** *n.*

thorough bass (beɪs) *n.* **a.** Also called: **basso continuo, continuo.** (esp. during the baroque period) a bass part underlying a piece of concerted music. It is played on a keyboard instrument, usually supported by a cello, viola da gamba, etc. See also **figured bass.** **b.** (*as adj.*): *a thorough-bass part; thorough-bass technique.*

thorough brace *n. Chiefly U.S.* either of two strong leather straps upon which the body of certain types of carriage is supported. —'**thorough-ˌbraced** *adj.*

thoroughbred ('θʌrəˌbrɛd) *adj.* **1.** purebred. ~*n.* **2.** a pedigree animal; purebred. **3.** a person regarded as being of good breeding.

Thoroughbred ('θʌrəˌbrɛd) *n.* a British breed of horse the ancestry of which can be traced to English mares and Arab sires; most often used as a racehorse.

thoroughfare ('θʌrəˌfɛə) *n.* **1.** a road from one place to another, esp. a main road. **2.** way through, access, or passage: *no thoroughfare.*

thoroughgoing ('θʌrəˌgəʊɪŋ) *adj.* **1.** extremely thorough. **2.** (*usually prenominal*) absolute; complete: *thoroughgoing incompetence.* —'**thoroughˌgoingly** *adv.* —'**thoroughˌgoingness** *n.*

thoroughpaced ('θʌrəˌpeɪst) *adj.* **1.** (of a horse) showing performing ability in all paces. **2.** thoroughgoing.

thoroughpin ('θʌrəˌpɪn) *n.* an inflammation and swelling on both sides of the hock joint of a horse affecting the sheath of the deep flexor tendon. [C18: so called because it makes the leg look as if it has a pin stuck through it]

thorp *or* **thorpe** (θɔːp) *n. Obsolete except in place names.* a small village. [Old English; related to Old Norse *thorp* village, Old High German *dorf,* Gothic *thaurp*]

those (ðəʊz) *determiner.* the form of **that** used before a plural noun. [Old English *thās,* plural of THIS]

thou[1] (ðaʊ) *pron.* (*subjective*) **1.** *Archaic or Brit. dialect.* refers to the person addressed: used mainly in familiar address or to a younger person or inferior. **2.** (*usually cap.*) refers to God when addressed in prayer, etc. [Old English *thū;* related to Old Saxon *thū,* Old High German *du,* Old Norse *thū,* Latin *tū,* Doric Greek *tu*]

thou[2] (θaʊ) *n., pl.* **thous** *or* **thou.** **1.** one thousandth of an inch. 1 thou is equal to 0.0254 millimetre. **2.** *Informal.* short for **thousand.**

though (ðəʊ) *conj.* (*subordinating*) **1.** (sometimes preceded by *even*) despite the fact that: *though he tries hard, he always fails; poor though she is, her life is happy.* **2. as though.** as if: *he looked as though he'd seen a ghost.* ~*adv.* **3.** nevertheless; however: *he can't dance; he sings well, though.* [Old English *theah;* related to Old Frisian *thāch,* Old Saxon, Old High German *thōh* Old Norse *thō*]

thought (θɔːt) *vb.* **1.** the past tense and past participle of **think.** ~*n.* **2.** the act or process of thinking; deliberation, meditation, or reflection. **3.** a concept, opinion, or idea. **4.** philosophical or intellectual ideas typical of a particular time or place: *German thought in the 19th century.* **5.** application of mental attention; consideration: *he gave the matter some thought.* **6.** purpose or intention: *I have no thought of giving up.* **7.** expectation: *no thought of reward.* **8.** a small amount; trifle: *you could be a thought more enthusiastic.* **9.** kindness or regard: *he has no thought for his widowed mother.* [Old English *thōht;* related to Old Frisian *thochta,* Old Saxon, Old High German *githācht*]

thought disorder *n. Psychiatry.* a cognitive disorder in which the patient's thoughts or conversations are characterized by irrationality or sudden changes of subject.

thoughtful ('θɔːtfʊl) *adj.* **1.** considerate in the treatment of other people. **2.** showing careful thought. **3.** pensive; reflective. —'**thoughtfully** *adv.* —'**thoughtfulness** *n.*

thoughtless ('θɔːtlɪs) *adj.* **1.** inconsiderate: *a thoughtless remark.* **2.** having or showing lack of thought: *a thoughtless essay.* **3.** unable to think; not having the power of thought. —'**thoughtlessly** *adv.* —'**thoughtlessness** *n.*

thought-out *adj.* conceived and developed by careful thought: *a well thought-out scheme.*

thought transference *n. Psychol.* another name for **telepathy.**

thousand ('θaʊzənd) *n.* **1.** the cardinal number that is the product of 10 and 100. See also **number** (sense 1). **2.** a numeral, 1000, 10^3, M, etc., representing this number. **3.** (*often pl.*) a very large but unspecified number, amount, or quantity: *they are thousands of miles away.* **4.** (*pl.*) the numbers 2000–9999: *the price of the picture was in the thousands.* **5.** the amount or quantity that is one hundred times greater than ten. **6.** something represented by, representing, or consisting of 1000 units. **7.** *Maths.* the position containing a digit representing that number followed by three zeros: *in 4760, 4 is in the thousand's place.* ~*determiner.* **8. a.** amounting to a thousand: *a thousand ships.* **b.** (*as pronoun*): *a thousand is hardly enough.* **9.** amounting to 1000 times a particular scientific unit. Related prefix: **kilo-.** ~Related adj.: **millenary.** [Old English *thūsend;* related to Old Saxon *thūsind,* Old High German *thūsunt,* Old Norse *thūsund*]

Thousand Island dressing *n.* a salad dressing made from mayonnaise with ketchup, chopped gherkins, etc. [probably from the *Thousand Islands* group in the upper St Lawrence River bordering the U.S. and Canada]

thousandth ('θaʊzənθ) *adj.* **1.** (*usually prenominal*) **a.** being the ordinal number of 1000 in numbering or counting order, position, time, etc. **b.** (*as n.*): *the thousandth in succession.* ~*n.* **2. a.** one of 1000 approximately equal parts of something. **b.** (*as modifier*): *a thousandth part.* **3.** one of 1000 equal divisions of a particular scientific quantity. Related prefix: **milli-:** *millivolt.* **4.** the fraction equal to one divided by 1000 (1/1000).

Thracian ('θreɪʃɪən) *n.* **1.** a member of an ancient Indo-European people who lived in Thrace, in the SE corner of the Balkan Peninsula. **2.** the ancient language spoken by this people, belonging to the Thraco-Phrygian branch of the Indo-European family: extinct by the early Middle Ages. ~*adj.* **3.** of or relating to Thrace, its inhabitants, or the extinct Thracian language.

Thraco-Phrygian (ˌθreɪkəʊ'frɪdʒɪən) *n.* **1.** a branch of the Indo-European family of languages, all members of which are extinct except for Armenian. ~*adj.* **2.** relating to or belonging to this group of languages. [from *Thraco-,* from Greek *Thraikē* Thrace; see PHRYGIAN]

thrall (θrɔːl) *n.* **1.** Also called: **thraldom** or (U.S.) **thralldom** ('θrɔːldəm). the state or condition of being in the power of another person. **2.** a person who is in such a state. **3.** a person totally subject to some need, desire, appetite, etc. ~*vb.* **4.** (*tr.*) to enslave or dominate. [Old English *thrǣl* slave, from Old Norse *thrǣll*]

thrang (θræŋ) *Scot.* ~*n.* **1.** a throng; crowd. ~*vb.* **2.** to throng; crowd. ~*adj.* **3.** crowded; busy. **4.** engaged or occupied; busy. [Scot. variant of THRONG]

thrapple ('θræpᵊl) *Scot.* ~*n.* **1.** the throat or windpipe. ~*vb.* **2.** to throttle; strangle. [C18: a variant of earlier *thropple,* of uncertain origin]

thrash (θræʃ) *vb.* **1.** (*tr.*) to beat soundly, as with a whip or stick. **2.** (*tr.*) to defeat totally; overwhelm. **3.** (*intr.*) to beat or plunge about in a wild manner. **4.** (*intr.*) to move the legs up and down in the water, as in certain swimming strokes. **5.** to sail (a boat) against the wind or tide or (of a boat) to sail in this way. **6.** another word for **thresh.** ~*n.* **7.** the act of thrashing; blow; beating. **8.** *Informal.* a party or similar social gathering. [Old English *threscan;* related to Old High German *dreskan,* Old Norse *thriskja*]

thrasher[1] ('θræʃə) *n.* another name for **thresher** (the shark).

thrasher[2] ('θræʃə) *n.* any of various brown thrushlike American songbirds of the genus *Toxostoma* and related genera, having a long downward-curving bill and long tail: family *Mimidae* (mockingbirds). [C19: perhaps from English dialect *thresher, thrusher* a thrush]

thrashing ('θræʃɪŋ) *n.* a physical assault; flogging.

thrash metal *n.* a type of very fast, very loud rock music that combines elements of heavy metal and punk rock. Often shortened to **thrash.**

thrash out *vb.* (*tr., adv.*) to discuss fully or vehemently, esp. in order to come to a solution or agreement.

thrasonical (θrə'sɒnɪkᵊl) *adj. Rare.* bragging; boastful. [C16: from Latin *Thrasō* name of boastful soldier in *Eunuchus,* a play by the Roman dramatist Terence (?190–159 B.C.), from Greek *Thrasōn,* from *thrasus* forceful] —**thra'sonically** *adv.*

thrave (θreɪv) *n. Scot. and northern English dialect.* twenty-four sheaves of corn. [Old English *threfe,* of Scandinavian origin]

thrawn (θrɔːn) *adj. Scot. and northern English dialect.* **1.** crooked or twisted. **2.** stubborn; perverse. [Northern English dialect, variant of THROWN, from Old English *thrāwan* to twist about, THROW]

thread (θrɛd) *n.* **1.** a fine strand, filament or fibre of some material. **2.** a fine cord of twisted filaments, esp. of cotton, used in sewing, weaving, etc. **3.** any of the filaments of which a spider's web is made. **4.** any fine line, stream, mark, or piece: *from the air, the path was a thread of white.* **5.** a helical groove in a cylindrical hole (**female thread**), formed by a tap or lathe tool, or a helical ridge on a cylindrical bar, rod, shank, etc. (**male thread**), formed by a die or lathe tool. **6.** a very thin seam of coal or vein of ore. **7.** something acting as the continuous link or theme of a whole: *the thread of the story.* **8.** the course of an individual's life believed in Greek mythology to be spun, measured, and cut by the Fates. ~*vb.* **9.** (*tr.*) to pass (thread, film, magnetic tape, etc.) through (something): *to thread a needle; to thread cotton through a needle.* **10.** (*tr.*) to string on a thread: *she threaded the beads.* **11.** to make (one's way) through or over (something). **12.** (*tr.*) to produce a screw thread by cutting, rolling, tapping, or grinding. **13.** (*tr.*) to pervade: *hysteria threaded his account.* **14.** (*intr.*) (of boiling syrup) to form a fine thread when poured from a spoon. [Old English *thrǣd;* related to Old Frisian *thrēd,* Old High German *drāt,* Old Norse *thrāthr* thread] —'**threader** *n.* —'**threadless** *adj.* —'**thread,like** *adj.*

threadbare ('θrɛdˌbɛə) *adj.* **1.** (of cloth, clothing, etc.) having the nap worn off so that the threads are exposed; worn out. **2.** meagre or poor: *a threadbare existence.* **3.** hackneyed: *a threadbare argument.* **4.** wearing threadbare clothes; shabby. —'**thread,bareness** *n.*

threadfin ('θrɛdˌfɪn) *n., pl.* **-fin** *or* **-fins.** any spiny-finned tropical marine fish of the family *Polynemidae,* having pectoral fins consisting partly of long threadlike rays.

thread mark *n.* a mark put into paper money to prevent counterfeiting, consisting of a pattern of silk fibres.

thread rolling *n. Engineering.* the production of a screw thread by a rolling swaging process using hardened profiled rollers. Rolled threads have greater strength than threads machined by a cutting tool.

threadworm ('θrɛdˌwɜːm) *n.* any of various nematodes, esp. the pinworm.

thready ('θrɛdɪ) *adj.* **threadier, threadiest. 1.** of, relating to, or resembling a thread or threads. **2.** *Med.* (of the pulse) barely perceptible; weak; fine. **3.** sounding thin, weak, or reedy: *a thready tenor.* —'**threadiness** *n.*

threap *or* **threep** (θriːp) *vb.* (*tr.*) *Scot. and northern English dialect.* **1.** to scold. **2.** to contradict. [Old English *thrēapian* to blame; related to Old Frisian *thrūwa,* Old High German *threwen,* Old Norse *threa*] —'**threaper** *or* '**threeper** *n.*

threat (θrɛt) *n.* **1.** a declaration of the intention to inflict harm, pain, or misery. **2.** an indication of imminent harm, danger, or pain. **3.** a person or thing that is regarded as dangerous or likely to inflict pain or misery. ~*vb.* **4.** an archaic word for **threaten.** [Old English; related to Old Norse *thraut,* Middle Low German *drōt*]

threaten ('θrɛtᵊn) *vb.* **1.** (*tr.*) to be a threat to. **2.** to be a menacing indication of (something); portend: *dark clouds threatened rain.* **3.** (when *tr., may take a clause as object*) to express a threat to (a person or people). —'**threatener** *n.* —'**threatening** *adj.* —'**threateningly** *adv.*

three (θriː) *n.* **1.** the cardinal number that is the sum of two and one and is a prime number. See also **number** (sense 1). **2.** a numeral, 3, III, (iii), representing this number. **3.** the amount or quantity that is one greater than two. **4.** something representing, represented by, or consisting of three units such as a playing card with three symbols on it. **5.** Also called: **three o'clock.** three hours after noon or midnight. ~*determiner.* **6. a.** amounting to three: *three ships.* **b.** (*as pronoun*): *three were killed.* ~Related adjs.: **ternary, tertiary, treble, triple.** Related prefixes: **tri-, ter-.** [Old English *thrēo;* related to Old Norse *thrīr,* Old High German *drī,* Latin *trēs,* Greek *treis*]

three-card trick *n.* a game in which players bet on which of three inverted playing cards is the queen.

three-colour *adj.* of, relating to, or comprising a colour print or a photomechanical process in which a picture is reproduced by superimposing three prints from half-tone plates in inks corresponding to the three primary colours.

three-D *or* **3-D** *n.* a three-dimensional effect.

three-day event *n.* See **eventing.**

three-day measles *n. Pathol.* an informal name for **rubella.**

three-decker *n.* **1. a.** anything having three levels or layers. **b.** (*as modifier*): *a three-decker sandwich.* **2.** a warship with guns on three decks.

three-dimensional, three-D, *or* **3-D** *adj.* **1.** of, having, or relating to three dimensions: *three-dimensional space.* **2.** (of a film, transparency, etc.) simulating the effect of depth by presenting slightly different views of a scene to each eye. **3.** having volume. **4.** lifelike or real.

threefold ('θriːˌfəʊld) *adj.* **1.** equal to or having three times as many or as much; triple: *a threefold decrease.* **2.** composed of three parts: *a threefold purpose.* ~*adv.* **3.** by or up to three times as many or as much.

three-four time *n. Music.* a form of simple triple time in which there are three crotchet beats to the bar, indicated by the time signature $\frac{3}{4}$. Often shortened to **three-four.** Also called (esp. U.S. and Canadian): **three-quarter time.**

three-gaited *adj. Chiefly U.S.* (of a horse) having the three usual paces, the walk, trot, and canter.

three-legged race *n.* a race in which pairs of competitors run with their adjacent legs tied together.

three-line whip *n.* See **whip** (sense 20c).

three-mile limit *n. International law.* the range of a nation's territorial waters, extending to three nautical miles from shore.

threep (θriːp) *vb.* a variant spelling of **threap.**

threepenny bit *or* **thrupenny bit** ('θrʌpnɪ, -ənɪ, 'θrɛp-) *n.* a twelve-sided British coin of nickel-brass, valued at three old pence, obsolete since 1971.

three-phase *adj.* (of an electrical system, circuit, or device) having, generating, or using three alternating voltages of the same frequency, displaced in phase by 120°.
three-piece *adj.* **1.** having three pieces, esp. (of a suit, suite, etc.) consisting of three matching parts. ~*n.* **2.** a three-piece suite, suit, etc.
three-ply *adj.* **1.** having three layers or thicknesses. **2. a.** (of knitting wool, etc.) three-stranded. **b.** (*as n.*): *the sweater was knitted in three-ply.*
three-point landing *n.* **1.** an aircraft landing in which the two main wheels and the nose or tail wheel all touch the ground simultaneously. **2.** a successful conclusion.
three-point turn *n.* a turn reversing the direction of motion of a motor vehicle using forward and reverse gears alternately, and completed after only three movements.
three-quarter *adj.* **1.** being three quarters of something: *a three-quarter turn.* **2.** being of three quarters the normal length: *a three-quarter coat.* ~*n.* **3.** *Rugby.* **a.** any of the four players between the full back and the forwards. **b.** this position. **c.** (*as modifier*): *three-quarter play.*
three-quarter binding *n.* a bookbinding style in which the spine and much of the sides are in a different material from the rest of the covers.
three-ring circus *n. U.S. and Canadian.* **1.** a circus with three rings in which separate performances are carried on simultaneously. **2.** a situation of confusion, characterized by a bewildering variety of events or activities.
three Rs *pl. n.* **the.** the three skills regarded as the fundamentals of education; reading, writing, and arithmetic. [from the humorous spelling *reading, 'riting,* and *'rithmetic*]
threescore ('θriːˈskɔː) *determiner.* an archaic word for **sixty.**
threesome ('θriːsəm) *n.* **1.** a group of three. **2.** *Golf.* a match in which a single player playing his own ball competes against two others playing alternate strokes on the same ball. **3.** any game, etc., for three people. **4.** (*modifier*) performed by three: *a threesome game.*
three-square *adj.* having a cross section that is an equilateral triangle: *a three-square file.*
three-way *adj.* **1.** providing connections to three routes from a central point. **2.** involving three things or people.
three-wheeler *n.* a light car that has three wheels.
thremmatology (ˌθrɛməˈtɒlədʒɪ) *n.* the science of breeding domesticated animals and plants. [C19: from Greek *thremma* nursling + -LOGY]
threnody ('θrɛnədɪ, 'θriː-) *or* **threnode** ('θriːnəʊd, 'θrɛn-) *n., pl.* **threnodies** *or* **threnodes.** an ode, song, or speech of lamentation, esp. for the dead. [C17: from Greek *thrēnōidia,* from *thrēnos* dirge + *ōidē* song] —**threnodial** (θrɪˈnəʊdɪəl) *or* **threnodic** (θrɪˈnɒdɪk) *adj.* —**threnodist** ('θrɛnədɪst, 'θriː-) *n.*
threonine ('θriːəˌniːn, -nɪn) *n.* an essential amino acid that occurs in certain proteins. [C20: *threon-,* probably from Greek *eruthron,* from *eruthros* red (see ERYTHRO-) + -INE[2]]
thresh (θrɛʃ) *vb.* **1.** to beat or rub stalks of ripe corn or a similar crop either with a hand implement or a machine to separate the grain from the husks and straw. **2.** (*tr.*) to beat or strike. **3.** (*intr.*; often foll. by *about*) to toss and turn; thrash. ~*n.* **4.** the act of threshing. [Old English *threscan;* related to Gothic *thriskan,* Old Norse *thriskja;* see THRASH]
thresher ('θrɛʃə) *n.* **1.** a person who threshes. **2.** short for **threshing machine. 3.** Also called: **thrasher, thresher shark.** any of various large sharks of the genus *Alopias,* esp. *A. vulpinus,* occurring in tropical and temperate seas: family *Alopiidae.* They have a very long whiplike tail with which they are thought to round up the small fish on which they feed.
threshing machine *n.* a machine for threshing crops.
threshold ('θrɛʃəʊld, 'θrɛʃˌhəʊld) *n.* **1.** Also called: **doorsill.** a sill, esp. one made of stone or hardwood, placed at a doorway. **2.** any doorway or entrance. **3.** the starting point of an experience, event, or venture: *on the threshold of manhood.* **4.** *Psychol.* the strength at which a stimulus is just perceived: *the threshold of consciousness.* Compare **absolute threshold, difference threshold. 5. a.** a level or point at which something would happen, would cease to happen, or would take effect, become true, etc. **b.** (*as modifier*): *threshold price; threshold effect.* **6. a.** the minimum intensity or value of a signal, etc., that will produce a response or specified effect: *a frequency threshold.* **b.** (*as modifier*): *a threshold current.* **7.** (*modifier*) designating or relating to a pay agreement, clause, etc., that raises wages to compensate for increases in the cost of living. ~Related adj.: **liminal.** [Old English *therscold;* related to Old Norse *threskoldr,* Old High German *driscubli,* Old Swedish *thriskuldi*]
threshold agreement *n.* an agreement between an employer and employees or their union to increase wages by a specified sum if inflation exceeds a specified level in a specified time.
thresh out *vb.* another term for **thrash out.**
threw (θruː) *vb.* the past tense of **throw.**
thrice (θraɪs) *adv.* **1.** three times. **2.** in threefold degree. **3.** *Archaic.* greatly. [Old English *thrīwa, thrīga;* see THREE]
thrift (θrɪft) *n.* **1.** wisdom and caution in the management of money. **2.** Also called: **sea pink.** any of numerous perennial plumbaginaceous low-growing plants of the genus *Armeria,* esp. *A. maritima,* of Europe, W Asia, and North America, having narrow leaves and round heads of pink or white flowers. **3.** *Rare.* vigorous thriving or growth, as of a plant. **4.** an obsolete word for **prosperity.** [C13: from Old Norse: success; see THRIVE] —**'thriftless** *adj.* —**'thriftlessly** *adv.* —**'thriftlessness** *n.*
thrifty ('θrɪftɪ) *adj.* **thriftier, thriftiest. 1.** showing thrift; economical or frugal. **2.** *Rare.* thriving or prospering. —**'thriftily** *adv.* —**'thriftiness** *n.*
thrill (θrɪl) *n.* **1.** a sudden sensation of excitement and pleasure: *seeing his book for sale gave him a thrill.* **2.** a situation producing such a sensation: *it was a thrill to see Rome for the first time.* **3.** a trembling sensation caused by fear or emotional shock. **4.** *Pathol.* an abnormal slight tremor associated with a heart or vascular murmur, felt on palpation. ~*vb.* **5.** to feel or cause to feel a thrill. **6.** to tremble or cause to tremble; vibrate or quiver. [Old English *thȳrlian* to pierce, from *thyrel* hole; see NOSTRIL, THROUGH]
thriller ('θrɪlə) *n.* **1.** a book, film, play, etc., depicting crime, mystery, or espionage in an atmosphere of excitement and suspense. **2.** a person or thing that thrills.
thrilling ('θrɪlɪŋ) *adj.* **1.** very exciting or stimulating. **2.** vibrating or trembling. —**'thrillingly** *adv.*
thrips (θrɪps) *n., pl.* **thrips.** any of various small slender-bodied insects of the order *Thysanoptera,* typically having piercing mouthparts and narrow feathery wings and feeding on plant sap. Some species are serious plant pests. [C18: via New Latin from Greek: woodworm]
thrive (θraɪv) *vb.* **thrives, thriving; thrived** *or* **throve; thrived** *or* **thriven** ('θrɪvᵊn). (*intr.*) **1.** to grow strongly and vigorously. **2.** to do well; prosper. [C13: from Old Norse *thrīfask* to grasp for oneself, reflexive of *thrīfa* to grasp, of obscure origin] —**'thriver** *n.* —**'thriving** *adj.* —**'thrivingly** *adv.*
thro' *or* **thro** (θruː) *prep., adv. Informal or poetic.* variant spellings of **through.**
throat (θrəʊt) *n.* **1. a.** that part of the alimentary and respiratory tracts extending from the back of the mouth (nasopharynx) to just below the larynx. **b.** the front part of the neck. **2.** something resembling a throat, esp. in shape or function: *the throat of a chimney.* **3.** *Botany.* the gaping part of a tubular corolla or perianth. **4.** *Informal.* a sore throat. **5. cut one's (own) throat.** to bring about one's own ruin. **6. have by the throat.** to have compete control over (a person or thing). **7. jump down someone's throat.** See **jump** (sense 24). **8. ram** *or* **force (something) down someone's throat.** to insist that someone listen to or accept (something): *he rammed his own opinions down my throat.* **9. stick in one's throat** (*or* **craw**). *Informal.* to be difficult, or against one's conscience, for one to accept, utter, or believe. ~Related adjs.: **guttural, laryngeal.** [Old English *throtu;* related to Old High German *drozza* throat, Old Norse *throti* swelling]
throatlash ('θrəʊtˌlæʃ) *or* **throatlatch** *n.* the strap that holds a bridle in place, fastening under the horse's jaw.
throat microphone *n.* a type of microphone that is held against the throat to pick up voice vibrations. Also called: **throat mike.**
throaty ('θrəʊtɪ) *adj.* **throatier, throatiest. 1.** indicating a sore throat; hoarse: *a throaty cough.* **2.** of, relating to, or produced in or by the throat. **3.** deep, husky, or guttural. —**'throatily** *adv.* —**'throatiness** *n.*
throb (θrɒb) *vb.* **throbs, throbbing, throbbed.** (*intr.*) **1.** to pulsate or beat repeatedly, esp. with increased force: *to throb with pain.* **2.** (of engines, drums, etc.) to have a strong rhythmic vibration or beat. ~*n.* **3.** the act or an instance of throbbing, esp. a rapid pulsation as of the heart: *a throb of pleasure.* [C14: perhaps of imitative origin] —**'throbbing** *adj.* —**'throbbingly** *adv.*
throe (θrəʊ) *n. Rare.* a pang or pain. [Old English *thrāwu* threat; related to Old High German *drawa* threat, Old Norse *thrā* desire, *thrauka* to endure]
throes (θrəʊz) *pl. n.* **1.** a condition of violent pangs, pain, or convulsions: *death throes.* **2. in the throes of.** struggling with great effort with: *a country in the throes of revolution.*
thrombin ('θrɒmbɪn) *n. Biochem.* an enzyme that acts on fibrinogen in blood causing it to clot.
thrombo- *or sometimes before a vowel* **thromb-** *combining form.* indicating a blood clot: *thromboembolism.* [from Greek *thrombos* lump, clot]
thrombocyte ('θrɒmbəˌsaɪt) *n.* another name for **platelet.** —**thrombocytic** (ˌθrɒmbəˈsɪtɪk) *adj.*
thrombocytopenia (ˌθrɒmbəʊˌsaɪtəʊˈpiːnɪə) *n. Pathol.* an abnormal decrease in the number of platelets in the blood. [C20: from German *thrombocytopenie* from THROMBOCYTE + Greek *penia* poverty]
thromboembolism (ˌθrɒmbəʊˈɛmbəˌlɪzəm) *n. Pathol.* the obstruction of a blood vessel by a thrombus that has become detached from its original site.
thrombogen ('θrɒmbəˌdʒɛn) *n.* a protein present in blood that is essential for the formation of thrombin.
thrombokinase (ˌθrɒmbəʊˈkaɪneɪs) *n.* another name for **thromboplastin.**
thrombophlebitis (ˌθrɒmbəʊflɪˈbaɪtɪs) *n.* inflammation of a vein associated with the formation of a thrombus.
thromboplastic (ˌθrɒmbəʊˈplæstɪk) *adj.* causing or enhancing the formation of a blood clot.
thromboplastin (ˌθrɒmbəʊˈplæstɪn) *n.* any of a group of substances that are liberated from damaged blood platelets and other

tissues and convert prothrombin to thrombin. Also called: **thrombokinase.**

thrombose ('θrɒmbəʊz) *vb.* to become or affect with a thrombus. [C19: back formation from THROMBOSIS]

thrombosis (θrɒm'bəʊsɪs) *n., pl.* **-ses** (siːz). **1.** the formation or presence of a thrombus. **2.** *Informal.* short for **coronary thrombosis.** [C18: from New Latin, from Greek: curdling, from *thrombousthai* to clot, from *thrombos* THROMBUS] —**thrombotic** (θrɒm'bɒtɪk) *adj.*

thrombus ('θrɒmbəs) *n., pl.* **-bi** (-baɪ). a clot of coagulated blood that forms within a blood vessel or inside the heart and remains at the site of its formation, often impeding the flow of blood. Compare **embolus.** [C17: from New Latin, from Greek *thrombos* lump, of obscure origin]

throne (θrəʊn) *n.* **1.** the ceremonial seat occupied by a monarch, bishop, etc. on occasions of state. **2.** the power, duties, or rank ascribed to a royal person. **3.** a person holding royal rank. **4.** (*pl.; often cap.*) the third of the nine orders into which the angels are traditionally divided in medieval angelology. ~*vb.* **5.** to place or be placed on a throne. [C13: from Old French *trone,* from Latin *thronus,* from Greek *thronos* throne] —'**throneless** *adj.*

throng (θrɒŋ) *n.* **1.** a great number of people or things crowded together. ~*vb.* **2.** to gather in or fill (a place) in large numbers; crowd. **3.** (*tr.*) to hem in (a person); jostle. ~*adj.* **4.** *Yorkshire dialect.* (*postpositive*) busy. [Old English *gethrang;* related to Old Norse *throug,* Old High German *drangōd*]

throstle ('θrɒsᵊl) *n.* **1.** a poetic name for **thrush**[1], esp. the song thrush. **2.** a spinning machine for wool or cotton in which the fibres are twisted and wound continuously. [Old English; related to Old Saxon *throsla,* Old Norse *thröstr,* Middle High German *drostel*]

throttle ('θrɒtᵊl) *n.* **1.** Also called: **throttle valve.** any device that controls the quantity of fuel or fuel and air mixture entering an engine. **2.** an informal or dialect word for **throat.** ~*vb.* (*tr.*) **3.** to kill or injure by squeezing the throat. **4.** to suppress: *to throttle the press.* **5.** to control or restrict (a flow of fluid) by means of a throttle valve. [C14: *throtelen,* from *throte* THROAT] —'**throttler** *n.*

through (θruː) *prep.* **1.** going in or starting at one side and coming out or stopping at the other side of: *a path through the wood.* **2.** occupying or visiting several points scattered around in (an area). **3.** as a result of; by means of: *the thieves were captured through his vigilance.* **4.** *Chiefly U.S.* up to and including: *Monday through Friday.* **5.** during: *through the night.* **6.** at the end of; having (esp. successfully) completed. **7. through with.** having finished with (esp. when dissatisfied with). ~*adj.* **8.** (*postpositive*) having successfully completed some specified activity. **9.** (on a telephone line) connected. **10.** (*postpositive*) no longer able to function successfully in some specified capacity: *as a journalist, you're through.* **11.** (*prenominal*) (of a route, journey, etc.) continuous or unbroken: *a through train.* ~*adv.* **12.** through some specified thing, place, or period of time. **13. through and through.** thoroughly; completely. ~Also: **thro'** *or* **thro** (informal or poetic), **thru** (chiefly U.S.). [Old English *thurh;* related to Old Frisian *thruch,* Old Saxon *thuru,* Old High German *duruh*]

through bridge *n. Civil engineering.* a bridge in which the track is carried by the lower horizontal members.

through-composed *adj. Music.* of or relating to a song in stanzaic form, in which different music is provided for each stanza. Compare **strophic** (sense 2).

throughly ('θruːlɪ) *adv. Archaic.* thoroughly; completely.

through-other *adj. Scot.* **1.** untidy or dishevelled. **2.** mixed up; in disorder. [a literal translation of Irish Gaelic *trí n-a chéile* through each other, hence, mixed up with each other]

throughout (θruː'aʊt) *prep.* **1.** right through; through the whole of (a place or a period of time): *throughout the day.* ~*adv.* **2.** throughout some specified period or area.

throughput ('θruːˌpʊt) *n.* the quantity of raw material processed in a given period, esp. by a computer.

throughway ('θruːˌweɪ) *n. U.S.* a thoroughfare, esp. a motorway.

throve (θrəʊv) *vb.* a past tense of **thrive.**

throw (θrəʊ) *vb.* **throws, throwing, threw, thrown.** (*mainly tr.*) **1.** (*also intr.*) to project or cast (something) through the air, esp. with a rapid motion of the arm and wrist. **2.** (foll. by *in, on, onto,* etc.) to put or move suddenly, carelessly, or violently: *she threw her clothes onto the bed.* **3.** to bring to or cause to be in a specified state or condition, esp. suddenly or unexpectedly: *the news threw the family into a panic.* **4.** to direct or cast (a shadow, light, etc.). **5.** to project (the voice) so as to make it appear to come from other than its source. **6.** to give or hold (a party). **7.** to cause to fall or be upset; dislodge: *the horse soon threw his rider.* **8. a.** to tip (dice) out onto a flat surface. **b.** to obtain (a specified number) in this way. **9.** to shape on a potter's wheel. **10.** to move (a switch or lever) to engage or disengage a mechanism. **11.** to be subjected to (a fit). **12.** to turn (wood, etc.) on a lathe. **13.** *Informal.* to baffle or astonish; confuse: *the last question on the test paper threw me.* **14.** *Boxing.* to deliver (a punch). **15.** *Wrestling.* to hurl (an opponent) to the ground. **16.** *Informal.* to lose (a contest, fight, etc.) deliberately, esp. in boxing. **17. a.** to play (a card). **b.** to discard (a card). **18.** (of a female animal, esp. a cow) to give birth to (young). **19.** to twist or spin (filaments) into thread. **20. throw cold water on (something).** *Informal.* to be unenthusiastic about or discourage (something). **21. throw oneself at.** to strive actively to attract the attention or affection of. **22. throw oneself into.** to involve oneself enthusiastically in. **23. throw oneself on.** to rely entirely upon: *he threw himself on the mercy of the police.* ~*n.* **24.** the act or an instance of throwing. **25.** the distance or extent over which anything may be thrown: *a stone's throw.* **26.** *Informal.* a chance, venture, or try. **27.** an act or result of throwing dice. **28. a.** the eccentricity of a cam. **b.** the radial distance between the central axis of a crankshaft and the axis of a crankpin forming part of the shaft. **29.** *U.S. and Canadian.* a decorative light blanket or cover, as thrown over a chair. **30.** a sheet of fabric used for draping over an easel or unfinished painting, etc., to keep the dust off. **31.** *Geology.* the vertical displacement of rock strata at a fault. **32.** *Physics.* the deflection of a measuring instrument as a result of a sudden fluctuation. ~See also **throw about, throwaway, throwback, throw in, throw off, throw out, throw over, throw together, throw up.** [Old English *thrāwan* to turn, torment; related to Old High German *drāen* to twist, Latin *terere* to rub] —'**thrower** *n.*

throw about *vb.* (*tr., adv.*) **1.** to spend (one's money) in a reckless and flaunting manner. **2. throw one's weight about.** *Informal.* to act in an authoritarian or aggressive manner.

throwaway ('θrəʊəˌweɪ) *adj.* (*prenominal*) **1.** said or done incidentally, esp. for rhetorical effect; casual: *a throwaway remark.* **2. a.** anything designed to be discarded after use rather than reused, refilled, etc.; disposable. **b.** (*as modifier*): *a throwaway carton.* ~*n.* **3.** *Chiefly U.S. and Canadian.* a handbill or advertisement distributed in a public place. ~*vb.* **throw away.** (*tr., adv.*) **4.** to get rid of; discard. **5.** to fail to make good use of; waste: *to throw away all one's money on horses.*

throwback ('θrəʊˌbæk) *n.* **1. a.** a person, animal, or plant that has the characteristics of an earlier or more primitive type. **b.** a reversion to such an organism. ~*vb.* **throw back.** (*adv.*) **2.** (*intr.*) to revert to an earlier or more primitive type. **3.** (*tr.;* foll. by *on*) to force to depend (on): *the crisis threw her back on her faith in God.*

throw in *vb.* (*tr., adv.*) **1.** to add (something extra) at no additional cost. **2.** to contribute or interpose (a remark, argument, etc.), esp. in a discussion. **3. throw in one's hand. a.** (in cards) to concede defeat by putting one's cards down. **b.** to give in and accept defeat; discontinue a venture. **4. throw in the towel** (*or* **sponge**). **a.** (in boxing) to concede defeat by the throwing of a towel (or sponge) into the ring by a second. **b.** to give in and accept defeat; discontinue a venture. ~*n.* **throw-in. 5.** *Soccer.* the method of putting the ball into play after it has gone into touch by throwing it two-handed from behind the head to a teammate, both feet being kept on the ground.

throwing stick *n.* a primitive device for hurling a spear with greater leverage, consisting of a rod with a groove in it and a hook or projection at the back end to hold the weapon until its release.

thrown (θrəʊn) *vb.* the past participle of **throw.**

throw off *vb.* (*mainly tr., adv.*) **1.** to free oneself of; discard. **2.** to produce or utter in a casual manner: *to throw off a witty remark.* **3.** to escape from or elude: *the fox rapidly threw off his pursuers.* **4.** to confuse or disconcert: *the interruption threw the young pianist off.* **5.** (*intr.*, often foll. by *at*) *Austral. and N.Z. informal.* to deride or ridicule.

throw out *vb.* (*tr., adv.*) **1.** to discard or reject. **2.** to expel or dismiss, esp. forcibly. **3.** to construct (something projecting or prominent, such as a wing of a building). **4.** to put forward or offer: *the chairman threw out a new proposal.* **5.** to utter in a casual or indirect manner: *to throw out a hint.* **6.** to confuse or disconcert: *the noise threw his concentration out.* **7.** to give off or emit. **8.** *Cricket.* (of a fielder) to put (the batsman) out by throwing the ball to hit the wicket. **9.** *Baseball.* to make a throw to a teammate who in turn puts out (a base runner).

throw over *vb.* (*tr., adv.*) to forsake or abandon; jilt.

throwster ('θrəʊstə) *n.* a person who twists silk or other fibres into yarn. [C15 *throwestre,* from THROW + -STER]

throw together *vb.* (*tr., adv.*) **1.** to assemble hurriedly. **2.** to cause to become casually acquainted.

throw up *vb.* (*adv., mainly tr.*) **1.** to give up; abandon, relinquish. **2.** to build or construct hastily. **3.** to reveal; produce: *every generation throws up its own leaders.* **4.** (*also intr.*) *Informal.* to vomit.

throw weight *n.* the maximum weight of supplementary mechanisms that can be lifted by the boost stages of a particular missile.

thru (θruː) *prep., adv., adj. Chiefly U.S.* a variant spelling of **through.**

thrum[1] (θrʌm) *vb.* **thrums, thrumming, thrummed. 1.** to strum rhythmically but without expression on (a musical instrument). **2.** (*intr.*) to drum incessantly: *rain thrummed on the roof.* **3.** to repeat (something) monotonously. ~*n.* **4.** a repetitive strumming or recitation. [C16: of imitative origin] —'**thrummer** *n.*

thrum[2] (θrʌm) *Textiles.* ~*n.* **1. a.** any of the unwoven ends of warp thread remaining on the loom when the web has been removed. **b.** such ends of thread collectively. **2.** a fringe or tassel of short unwoven threads. ~*vb.* **thrums, thrumming,**

thrummed. 3. (*tr.*) to trim with thrums. [C14: from Old English; related to Old High German *drum* remnant, Dutch *dreum*]
thrum-eyed *adj.* (of flowers, esp. primulas) having the stigma on a short style below the anthers, which lie in the mouth of the corolla on big stamens. Compare **pin-eyed.** [C19: from THRUM², because of the ring of anthers visible at the neck of the corolla]
thrupenny bit ('θrʌpnɪ, -ənɪ, 'θrɛp-) *n.* a variant spelling of **threepenny bit.**
thrush¹ (θrʌʃ) *n.* any songbird of the subfamily *Turdinae,* esp. those having a brown plumage with a spotted breast, such as the mistle thrush and song thrush: family *Muscicapidae.* Compare **water thrush.** [Old English *thrȳsce;* related to Old High German *drōsca;* see THROSTLE, THROAT]
thrush² (θrʌʃ) *n.* **1. a.** a fungal disease of the mouth, esp. of infants, and the vagina, characterized by the formation of whitish spots and caused by infection with the fungus *Candida albicans.* **b.** another word for **sprue**². **2.** a softening of the frog of a horse's hoof characterized by inflammation and a thick foul discharge. [C17: related to Old Danish *törsk,* Danish *troske*]
thrust (θrʌst) *vb.* **thrusts, thrusting, thrust. 1.** (*tr.*) to push (someone or something) with force or sudden strength: *she thrust him away; she thrust it into the fire.* **2.** (*tr.*) to force or impose upon (someone) or into (some condition or situation): *they thrust extra responsibilities upon her; she was thrust into the limelight.* **3.** (*tr.;* foll. by *through*) to pierce; stab. **4.** (*intr.;* usually foll. by *through* or *into*) to force a passage or entrance. **5.** (*intr.*) to push forwards, upwards, or outwards. **6.** (*intr.;* foll. by *at*) to make a stab or lunge at (a person or thing). ~*n.* **7.** a forceful drive, push, stab, or lunge. **8.** a force, esp. one that produces motion. **9. a.** a propulsive force produced by the fluid pressure or the change of momentum of the fluid in a jet engine, rocket engine, etc. **b.** a similar force produced by a propeller. **10.** a pressure that is exerted continuously by one part of an object, structure, etc., against another. **11.** *Geology.* **a.** the compressive force in the earth's crust that produces recumbent folds. **b.** See **thrust fault. 12.** *Civil engineering.* a force exerted in a downwards and outwards direction, as by an arch or a rafter. **13.** force, impetus, or drive: *a man with thrust and energy.* **14.** the essential or most forceful part: *the thrust of the argument.* [C12: from Old Norse *thrysta;* related to Latin *trūdere;* see INTRUDE]
thrust bearing *n. Engineering* a low-friction bearing on a rotating shaft that resists axial thrust in the shaft. Usually it consists of a collar which bears against a ring of well lubricated stationary and sometimes tilting pads. Compare **tapered roller bearing.**
thruster ('θrʌstə) *n.* **1.** a person or thing that thrusts. **2.** Also called: **vernier rocket.** a small rocket engine, esp. one used to correct the altitude or course of a spacecraft. **3.** an auxiliary propeller on a ship, capable of acting athwartships.
thrust fault *n.* a fault in which the rocks on the lower side of an inclined fault plane have been displaced downwards, usually by compression; a reverse fault.
thud (θʌd) *n.* **1.** a dull heavy sound: *the book fell to the ground with a thud.* **2.** a blow or fall that causes such a sound. ~*vb.* **thuds, thudding, thudded. 3.** to make or cause to make such a sound. [Old English *thyddan* to strike; related to *thoddettan* to beat, perhaps of imitative origin]
thug (θʌg) *n.* **1.** a tough and violent man, esp. a criminal. **2.** (*sometimes cap.*) (formerly) a member of an organization of robbers and assassins in India who typically strangled their victims. [C19: from Hindi *thag* thief, from Sanskrit *sthaga* scoundrel, from *sthagati* to conceal] —'**thuggery** *n.* —'**thuggish** *adj.*
thuggee (θʌ'giː) *n. History.* the methods and practices of the thugs of India. [C19: from Hindi *thagī;* see THUG]
thuja *or* **thuya** ('θuːjə) *n.* any of various coniferous trees of the genus *Thuja,* of North America and East Asia, having scalelike leaves, small cones, and an aromatic wood: family *Pinaceae.* See also **arbor vitae.** [C18: from New Latin, from Medieval Latin *thuia,* ultimately from Greek *thua* name of an African tree]
thulium ('θjuːlɪəm) *n.* a malleable ductile silvery-grey element occurring principally in monazite. The radioisotope **thulium-170** is used as an electron source in portable x-ray units. Symbol: Tm; atomic no.: 69; atomic wt.: 168.93; valency: 2 or 3; relative density: 9.31; melting pt.: 1545°C; boiling pt.: 1727°C. [C19: New Latin, from *Thule,* northernmost or faraway unknown region, + -IUM]
thumb (θʌm) *n.* **1.** the first and usually shortest and thickest of the digits of the hand, composed of two short bones. Technical name: **pollex. 2.** the corresponding digit in other vertebrates. **3.** the part of a glove shaped to fit the thumb. **4.** *Architect.* another name for **ovolo. 5. all thumbs.** clumsy. **6. thumbs down.** an indication of refusal, disapproval, or negation: *he gave the thumbs down on our proposal.* **7. thumbs up.** an indication of encouragement, approval, or acceptance. **8. under someone's thumb.** at someone's mercy or command. ~*vb.* **9.** (*tr.*) to touch, mark, or move with the thumb. **10.** to attempt to obtain (a lift or ride) by signalling with the thumb. **11.** (when *intr.,* often foll. by *through*) to flip the pages of (a book, magazine, etc.) perfunctorily in order to glance at the contents. **12. thumb one's nose at.** to deride or mock, esp. by placing the thumb on the nose with fingers extended. [Old English *thūma;* related to Old Saxon *thūma,* Old High German *thūmo,* Old Norse *thumall* thumb of a glove, Latin *tumēre* to swell] —'**thumbless** *adj.* —'**thumb,like** *adj.*
thumb index *n.* **1.** a series of indentations cut into the fore edge of a book to facilitate quick reference. ~*vb.* **thumb-index. 2.** (*tr.*) to furnish with a thumb index.
thumb knot *n.* another name for **overhand knot.**
thumbnail ('θʌm,neɪl) *n.* **1.** the nail of the thumb. **2.** (*modifier*) concise and brief: *a thumbnail sketch.*
thumbnut ('θʌm,nʌt) *n.* a nut with projections enabling it to be turned by the thumb and forefinger; wing nut.
thumb piano *n.* another name for **mbira.**
thumbprint ('θʌm,prɪnt) *n.* an impression of the upper part of the thumb, used esp. for identification purposes. See **fingerprint.**
thumbscrew ('θʌm,skruː) *n.* **1.** an instrument of torture that pinches or crushes the thumbs. **2.** a screw with projections on its head enabling it to be turned by the thumb and forefinger.
thumbstall ('θʌm,stɔːl) *n.* a protective sheathlike cover for the thumb.
thumbtack ('θʌm,tæk) *n.* the U.S. and Canadian name for **drawing pin.**
thump (θʌmp) *n.* **1.** the sound of a heavy solid body hitting or pounding a comparatively soft surface. **2.** a heavy blow with the hand: *he gave me a thump on the back.* ~*vb.* **3.** (*tr.*) to strike or beat heavily; pound. **4.** (*intr.*) to throb, beat, or pound violently: *his heart thumped with excitement.* [C16: related to Icelandic, Swedish dialect *dumpa* to thump; see THUD, BUMP] —'**thumper** *n.*
thumping ('θʌmpɪŋ) *adj.* (*prenominal*) *Slang.* huge or excessive: *a thumping loss.* —'**thumpingly** *adv.*
thunbergia (θʊn'bɜːdʒɪə) *n.* any plant of the typically climbing tropical genus *Thunbergia* such as black-eyed Susan: family *Acanthaceae.* [named after K. P. *Thunberg* (1743–1822), Swedish traveller and botanist]
thunder ('θʌndə) *n.* **1.** a loud cracking or deep rumbling noise caused by the rapid expansion of atmospheric gases which are suddenly heated by lightning. **2.** any loud booming sound. **3.** *Rare.* a violent threat or denunciation. **4. steal someone's thunder.** to detract from the attention due to another by forestalling him. ~*vb.* **5.** to make (a loud sound) or utter (words) in a manner suggesting thunder. **6.** (*intr.;* with *it* as subject) to be the case that thunder is being heard. **7.** (*intr.*) to move fast and heavily: *the bus thundered downhill.* **8.** (*intr.*) to utter vehement threats or denunciation; rail. [Old English *thunor;* related to Old Saxon *thunar,* Old High German *donar,* Old Norse *thōrr;* see THURSDAY] —'**thunderer** *n.* —'**thundery** *adj.*
thunderbird ('θʌndə,bɜːd) *n.* a legendary bird that produces thunder, lightning, and rain according to the folk belief of several North American Indian peoples.
thunderbolt ('θʌndə,bəʊlt) *n.* **1.** a flash of lightning accompanying thunder. **2.** the imagined agency of destruction produced by a flash of lightning. **3.** (in mythology) the destructive weapon wielded by several gods, esp. the Greek god Zeus. **4.** something very startling.
thunderbox ('θʌndə,bɒks) *n. Slang.* **1.** a portable boxlike lavatory seat that can be placed over a hole in the ground. **2.** any portable lavatory.
thunderclap ('θʌndə,klæp) *n.* **1.** a loud outburst of thunder. **2.** something as violent or unexpected as a clap of thunder.
thundercloud ('θʌndə,klaʊd) *n.* **1.** a towering electrically charged cumulonimbus cloud associated with thunderstorms. **2.** anything that is threatening.
thunderhead ('θʌndə,hɛd) *n. Chiefly U.S. and Canadian.* the anvil-shaped top of a cumulonimbus cloud.
thundering ('θʌndərɪŋ) *adj.* (*prenominal*) *Slang.* very great or excessive: *a thundering idiot.* —'**thunderingly** *adv.*
thunderous ('θʌndərəs) *adj.* **1.** resembling thunder, esp. in loudness: *thunderous clapping.* **2.** threatening and extremely angry: *she gave him a thunderous look.* —'**thunderously** *adv.*
thunder sheet *n.* a large sheet of metal that can be shaken to produce a noise resembling thunder as a sound effect for a theatrical production.
thundershower ('θʌndə,ʃaʊə) *n.* a heavy shower during a thunderstorm.
thunderstone ('θʌndə,stəʊn) *n.* **1.** a long tapering stone, fossil, or similar object, formerly thought to be a thunderbolt. **2.** an archaic word for **thunderbolt.**
thunderstorm ('θʌndə,stɔːm) *n.* a storm caused by strong rising air currents and characterized by thunder and lightning and usually heavy rain or hail.
thunderstruck ('θʌndə,strʌk) *or* **thunderstricken** ('θʌndə,strɪkən) *adj.* **1.** completely taken aback; amazed or shocked. **2.** *Rare.* struck by lightning.
thurible ('θjʊərɪbᵊl) *n.* another word for **censer.** [C15: from Latin *tūribulum* censer, from *tūs* incense]
thurifer ('θjʊərɪfə) *n.* a person appointed to carry the censer at religious ceremonies. [C19: from Latin, from *tūs* incense + *ferre* to carry]
Thurs. *abbrev. for* Thursday.
Thursday ('θɜːzdɪ) *n.* the fifth day of the week; fourth day of the working week. [Old English *Thursdæg,* literally: Thor's day, Thor being the Norse god of thunder; related to Old High German *Donares tag;* see THUNDER, DAY]
thus (ðʌs) *adv.* **1.** in this manner: *do it thus.* **2.** to such a degree: *thus far and no further.* ~ *sentence connector.* **3.** therefore: *We*

have failed. Thus we have to take the consequences. [Old English; related to Old Frisian, Old Saxon *thus*]
thuya ('θuːjə) *n.* a variant spelling of **thuja.**
thwack (θwæk) *vb.* **1.** to beat, hit, or flog, esp. with something flat. *~n.* **2. a.** a blow with something flat. **b.** the sound made by it. *~interj.* **3.** an exclamation imitative of this sound. [C16: of imitative origin] —'**thwacker** *n.*
thwaite (θweɪt) *n. Obsolete except in place names.* a piece of land cleared from forest or reclaimed from wasteland. [from Old Norse *thveit* paddock]
thwart (θwɔːt) *vb.* **1.** to oppose successfully or prevent; frustrate: *they thwarted the plan.* **2.** *Obsolete.* to be or move across. *~n.* **3.** *Nautical.* **a.** a seat lying across a boat and occupied by an oarsman. **b.** a crosspiece that spreads the gunwales of a boat. *~adj.* **4.** passing or being situated across. **5.** *Archaic.* perverse or stubborn. *~prep., adv.* **6.** *Obsolete.* across. [C13: from Old Norse *thvert,* from *thverr* transverse; related to Old English *thweorh* crooked, Old High German *twerh* transverse] —'**thwartedly** *adv.* —'**thwarter** *n.*
thy (ðaɪ) *determiner. (usually preceding a consonant) Archaic or Brit. dialect.* belonging to or associated in some way with you (thou): *thy goodness and mercy.* Compare **thine.** [C12: variant of THINE]
thylacine ('θaɪləˌsaɪn) *n.* an extinct or very rare doglike carnivorous marsupial, *Thylacinus cynocephalus,* of Tasmania, having greyish-brown fur with dark vertical stripes on the back: family *Dasyuridae.* Also called: **Tasmanian wolf.** [C19: from New Latin *thȳlacīnus,* from Greek *thulakos* pouch, sack]
thyme (taɪm) *n.* any of various small shrubs of the temperate genus *Thymus,* having a strong mintlike odour, small leaves, and white, pink, or red flowers: family *Labiatae* (labiates). [C14: from Old French *thym,* from Latin *thymum,* from Greek *thumon,* from *thuein* to make a burnt offering] —'**thymy** *adj.*
thymectomy (θaɪ'mɛktəmɪ) *n. pl.* **-mies.** surgical removal of the thymus.
thymelaeaceous (ˌθɪmɪlɪ'eɪʃəs) *adj.* of, relating to, or belonging to the *Thymelaeaceae,* a family of trees and shrubs having tough acrid bark and simple leaves: includes spurge laurel, leatherwood, and mezereon. [C19: via New Latin, from Greek *thumelaia,* from *thumon* THYME + *elaia* olive]
-thymia *n. combining form.* indicating a certain emotional condition, mood, or state of mind: *cyclothymia.* [New Latin, from Greek *thumos* temper]
thymic ('θaɪmɪk) *adj.* of or relating to the thymus.
thymidine ('θaɪmɪˌdiːn) *n.* the crystalline nucleoside of thymine, found in DNA. Formula: $C_{10}H_{14}N_2O_5$. [C20: from THYM(INE) + -IDE + -INE[2]]
thymidylic acid (ˌθaɪmɪ'dɪlɪk) *n.* a nucleotide consisting of thymine, deoxyribose, and a phosphate group. It is a constituent of DNA. Also called: **thymidine monophosphate.**
thymine ('θaɪmiːn) *n.* a white crystalline pyrimidine base found in DNA. Formula: $C_5H_6N_2O_2$. [C19: from THYMIC + -INE[2]]
thymocyte ('θaɪməsaɪt) *n.* a lymphocyte found in the thymus.
thymol ('θaɪmɒl) *n.* a white crystalline substance with an aromatic odour, obtained from the oil of thyme and used as a fungicide, antiseptic, and anthelmintic and in perfumery and embalming; 2-isopropylphenol. Formula: $(CH_3)_2CHC_6H_3(CH_3)$-OH. [C19: from THYME + -OL[2]]
thymus ('θaɪməs) *n., pl.* **-muses** *or* **-mi** (-maɪ). a glandular organ of vertebrates, consisting in man of two lobes situated below the thyroid. In early life it produces lymphocytes and is thought to influence certain immunological responses. It atrophies with age and is almost nonexistent in the adult. [C17: from New Latin, from Greek *thumos* sweetbread]
thyratron ('θaɪrəˌtrɒn) *n.* an electronic relay consisting of a gas-filled tube, usually a triode, in which a signal applied to the control grid initiates a transient anode current but subsequently loses control over it. See also **silicon controlled rectifier.** [C20: originally a trademark, from Greek *thura* door, valve + -TRON]
thyristor (θaɪ'rɪstə) *n.* another name for **silicon controlled rectifier.** [C20: from THYR(ATRON) + (TRANS)ISTOR]
thyro- *or before a vowel* **thyr-** *combining form.* thyroid: *thyrotoxicosis; thyrotropin.*
thyrocalcitonin (ˌθaɪrəʊˌkælsɪ'təʊnɪn) *n.* another name for **calcitonin.** [C20: from THYRO- + CALCITONIN]
thyroid ('θaɪrɔɪd) *adj.* **1.** of or relating to the thyroid gland. **2.** of or relating to the largest cartilage of the larynx. *~n.* **3.** see **thyroid gland. 4.** the powdered preparation made from the thyroid gland of certain animals, used to treat hypothyroidism. [C18: from New Latin *thyroidēs,* from Greek *thureoeidēs,* from *thureos* oblong (literally: door-shaped) shield, from *thura* door]
thyroidectomy (ˌθaɪrɔɪ'dɛktəmɪ) *n., pl.* **-mies.** surgical removal of all or part of the thyroid gland.
thyroid gland *n.* an endocrine gland of vertebrates, consisting in man of two lobes near the base of the neck. It secretes hormones that control metabolism and body growth.
thyroiditis (ˌθaɪrɔɪ'daɪtɪs) *n.* inflammation of the thyroid gland.
thyroid-stimulating hormone *n.* another name for **thyrotropin.** Abbrev.: **TSH.**
thyrotoxicosis (ˌθaɪrəʊˌtɒksɪ'kəʊsɪs) *n.* another name for **hyperthyroidism.**
thyrotropin (ˌθaɪrəʊ'trəʊpɪn) *or* **thyrotrophin** *n.* a glycoprotein hormone secreted by the anterior lobe of the pituitary gland: it stimulates activity of the thyroid gland. Also called: **thyroid-stimulating hormone.** [C20: from THYRO- + -TROPE + -IN]
thyroxine (θaɪ'rɒksiːn, -sɪn) *or* **thyroxin** (θaɪ'rɒksɪn) *n.* the principal hormone produced by the thyroid gland: it increases the metabolic rate of tissues and also controls growth, as in amphibian metamorphosis. It can be synthesized or extracted from the thyroid glands of animals and used to treat hypothyroidism. Chemical name: tetra-iodothyronine; formula: $C_{15}H_{11}I_4NO_4$. [C19: from THYRO- + OXY-[2] + -INE[2]]
thyrse (θɜːs) *or* **thyrsus** ('θɜːsəs) *n., pl.* **thyrses** *or* **thyrsi** ('θɜːsaɪ). *Botany.* a type of inflorescence, occurring in the lilac and grape, in which the main branch is racemose and the lateral branches cymose. [C17: from French: THYRSUS] —'**thyrsoid** *adj.*
thyrsus ('θɜːsəs) *n., pl.* **-si** (-saɪ). **1.** *Greek myth.* a staff, usually one tipped with a pine cone, borne by Dionysus (Bacchus), the god of wine, and his followers. **2.** a variant spelling of **thyrse.** [C18: from Latin, from Greek *thursos* stalk]
thysanuran (ˌθɪsə'njuərən) *n.* **1.** any primitive wingless insect of the order *Thysanura,* which comprises the bristletails. *~adj.* **2.** of, relating to, or belonging to the order *Thysanura.* [C19: from New Latin, from Greek *thusanos* fringe + *oura* tail] —ˌ**thysa'nurous** *adj.*
thyself (ðaɪ'sɛlf) *pron. Archaic.* **a.** the reflexive form of *thou* or *thee.* **b.** (intensifier): *thou, thyself, wouldst know.*
ti[1] (tiː) *n. Music.* a variant spelling of **te.**
ti[2] (tiː) *n., pl.* **tis. 1.** a woody palmlike agave plant, *Cordyline terminalis,* of the East Indies, having, white, mauve, or reddish flowers. The sword-shaped leaves are used for garments, fodder, thatch, etc., and the root for food and liquor. **2.** a similar and related plant, *Cordyline australis,* of New Zealand. [of Polynesian origin]
Ti *the chemical symbol for* titanium.
Tia Maria ('tɪə mə'rɪə) *n. Trademark.* a coffee-flavoured liqueur from the West Indies.
tiara (tɪ'ɑːrə) *n.* **1.** a woman's semicircular jewelled headdress for formal occasions. **2.** a high headdress worn by Persian kings in ancient times. **3.** *R.C. Church.* **a.** a headdress worn by the pope, consisting of a beehive-shaped diadem surrounded by three coronets. **b.** the office or rank of pope. [C16: via Latin from Greek, of Oriental origin] —**ti'araed** *adj.*
Tibetan (tɪ'bɛtᵊn) *adj.* **1.** of, relating to, or characteristic of Tibet, a region in the Himalayas, its people, or their language. *~n.* **2.** a native or inhabitant of Tibet. **3.** the language of Tibet, belonging to the Sino-Tibetan family.
Tibetan terrier *n.* a breed of dog with a long dense shaggy coat: it resembles a small Old English sheepdog.
Tibeto-Burman (tɪ'bɛtəʊ'bɜːmən) *n.* **1.** a branch of the Sino-Tibetan family of languages, sometimes regarded as a family in its own right. Compare **Sinitic.** *~adj.* **2.** belonging or relating to this group of languages.
tibia ('tɪbɪə) *n., pl.* **tibiae** ('tɪbɪˌiː) *or* **tibias. 1.** Also called: **shinbone.** the inner and thicker of the two bones of the human leg between the knee and ankle. Compare **fibula. 2.** the corresponding bone in other vertebrates. **3.** the fourth segment of an insect's leg, lying between the femur and the tarsus. [C16: from Latin: leg, pipe] —'**tibial** *adj.*
tibiotarsus (ˌtɪbɪəʊ'tɑːsəs) *n.* the bone in the leg of a bird formed by fusion of the tibia and some of the tarsal bones. [C19: from *tibio-* (combining form of TIBIA) + TARSUS]
tic (tɪk) *n. Pathol.* **1.** spasmodic twitching of a particular group of muscles. **2.** See **tic douloureux.** [C19: from French, of uncertain origin; compare Italian *ticche*]
tical (tɪ'kɑːl, -'kɔːl; 'tiːkᵊl) *n., pl.* **-cals** *or* **-cal. 1.** the former standard monetary unit of Thailand, replaced by the baht in 1928. **2.** a unit of weight, formerly used in Thailand, equal to about half an ounce or 14 grams. [C17: via Siamese and Portuguese from Malay *tikal* monetary unit]
tic douloureux ('tɪk ˌduːlə'ruː) *n.* a condition of momentary stabbing pain along the trigeminal nerve. Also called: **trigeminal neuralgia.** [C19: from French, literally: painful tic]
tichy ('tɪtʃɪ) *adj.* **tichier, tichiest.** a variant spelling of **titchy.**
tick[1] (tɪk) *n.* **1.** a recurrent metallic tapping or clicking sound, such as that made by a clock or watch. **2.** *Brit. informal.* a moment or instant. **3.** a mark (✓) or dash used to check off or indicate the correctness of something. *~vb.* **4.** to produce a recurrent tapping sound or indicate by such a sound: *the clock ticked the minutes away.* **5.** (when *tr.,* often foll. by *off*) to mark or check (something, such as a list) with a tick. **6. what makes someone tick.** *Informal.* the basic drive or motivation of a person. ~See also **tick off, tick over.** [C13: from Low German *tikk* touch; related to Old High German *zekōn* to pluck, Norwegian *tikke* to touch]
tick[2] (tɪk) *n.* **1.** any of various small parasitic arachnids of the families *Ixodidae* (**hard ticks**) and *Argasidae,* (**soft ticks**), typically living on the skin of warm-blooded animals and feeding on the blood and tissues of their hosts: order *Acarina* (mites and ticks). See also **sheep tick** (sense 1). **2.** any of certain other arachnids of the order *Acarina.* **3.** any of certain insects of the dipterous family *Hippoboscidae* that are ectoparasitic on horses, cattle, sheep, etc., esp. the sheep ked. [Old English *ticca;* related to Middle High German *zeche* tick, Middle Irish *dega* stag beetle]

tick^{3} (tɪk) *n.* **1.** the strong covering of a pillow, mattress, etc. **2.** *Informal.* short for **ticking.** [C15: probably from Middle Dutch *tīke;* related to Old High German *ziecha* pillow cover, Latin *tēca* case, Greek *thēkē*]

tick^{4} (tɪk) *n. Brit. informal.* account or credit (esp. in the phrase **on tick**). [C17: shortened from TICKET]

tick-bird *n.* another name for **oxpecker.** [C19: so called because it eats insects off animals' backs]

tick-borne typhus *n.* another name for **Rocky Mountain spotted fever.**

ticker ('tɪkə) *n.* **1.** *Slang.* **a.** the heart. **b.** a watch. **2.** a person or thing that ticks. **3.** *Stock Exchange.* the U.S. word for **tape machine.**

ticker tape *n.* **1.** *Stock Exchange.* a continuous paper ribbon on which a tape machine automatically prints current stock quotations. **2. ticker-tape reception** (*or* **parade**). (mainly in New York) the showering of the motorcade of a distinguished politician, visiting head of state, etc., with ticker tape as a sign of welcome.

ticket ('tɪkɪt) *n.* **1. a.** a piece of paper, cardboard, etc., showing that the holder is entitled to certain rights, such as travel on a train or bus, entry to a place of public entertainment, etc. **b.** (*modifier*) concerned with or relating to the issue, sale, or checking of tickets: *a ticket office; ticket collector.* **2.** a piece of card, cloth, etc., attached to an article showing information such as its price, size, or washing instructions. **3.** a summons served for a parking offence or violation of traffic regulations. **4.** *Informal.* the certificate of competence issued to a ship's captain or an aircraft pilot. **5.** *Chiefly U.S. and N.Z.* the group of candidates nominated by one party in an election; slate. **6.** *Chiefly U.S.* the declared policy of a political party at an election. **7.** *Brit. informal.* a certificate of discharge from the armed forces. **8.** *Informal.* the right or appropriate thing: *that's the ticket.* **9. have (got) tickets on oneself.** *Austral. informal.* to be conceited. ~*vb.* **-ets, -eting, -eted.** (*tr.*) **10.** to issue or attach a ticket or tickets to. **11.** *Informal.* to earmark for a particular purpose. [C17: from Old French *etiquet,* from *estiquier* to stick on, from Middle Dutch *steken* to STICK^{2}]

ticket day *n.* (on the London Stock Exchange) the day on which selling brokers receive from buying brokers the names of investors who have made purchases during the previous account. Also called: **name day.** Compare **account day.**

ticket of leave *n.* (formerly in Britain) a permit allowing a convict (**ticket-of-leave man**) to leave prison, after serving only part of his sentence, with certain restrictions placed on him.

ticket tout *n.* See **tout** (sense 6).

tickety-boo (ˌtɪkɪtɪ'buː) *adj. Brit. old-fashioned informal.* as it should be; correct; satisfactory. [C20: of obscure origin]

tickey ('tɪkɪ) *n.* a South African threepenny piece, which was replaced by the five-cent coin in 1961. [of uncertain origin]

tick fever *n.* **1.** any acute infectious febrile disease caused by the bite of an infected tick. **2.** another name for **Rocky Mountain spotted fever.**

ticking ('tɪkɪŋ) *n.* a strong cotton fabric, often striped, used esp. for mattress and pillow covers. [C17: from TICK^{3}]

tickle ('tɪkᵊl) *vb.* **1.** to touch, stroke, or poke (a person, part of the body, etc.) so as to produce pleasure, laughter, or a twitching sensation. **2.** (*tr.*) to excite pleasurably; gratify. **3.** (*tr.*) to delight or entertain (often in the phrase **tickle one's fancy**). **4.** (*intr.*) to itch or tingle. **5.** (*tr.*) to catch (a fish, esp. a trout) by grasping it with the hands and gently moving the fingers into its gills. **6. tickle pink** *or* **to death.** *Informal.* to please greatly: *he was tickled pink to be elected president.* ~*n.* **7.** a sensation of light stroking or itching. **8.** the act of tickling. [C14: related to Old English *tinclian,* Old High German *kizziton,* Old Norse *kitla,* Latin *titillāre* to TITILLATE] —'**tickly** *adj.*

tickler ('tɪklə) *n.* **1.** *Informal, chiefly Brit.* a difficult or delicate problem. **2.** Also called: **tickler file.** *U.S.* a memorandum book or file. **3.** *Accounting, U.S.* a single-entry business journal. **4.** a person or thing that tickles.

tickler coil *n.* a small inductance coil connected in series in the anode circuit of a valve and magnetically coupled to a coil in the grid circuit to provide feedback.

ticklish ('tɪklɪʃ) *adj.* **1.** susceptible and sensitive to being tickled. **2.** delicate or difficult: *a ticklish situation.* **3.** easily upset or offended. —'**ticklishly** *adv.* —'**ticklishness** *n.*

tick off *vb.* (*tr., adv.*) **1.** to mark with a tick. **2.** *Informal, chiefly Brit.* to scold; reprimand.

tick over *vb.* (*intr., adv.*) **1.** Also: **idle.** *Brit.* (of an engine) to run at low speed with the throttle control closed and the transmission disengaged. **2.** to run smoothly without any major changes: *keep the firm ticking over until I get back.* ~*n.* **tick-over. 3.** *Brit.* **a.** the speed of an engine when it is ticking over. **b.** (*as modifier*): *tick-over speed.*

ticktack ('tɪkˌtæk) *n.* **1.** *Brit.* a system of sign language, mainly using the hands, by which bookmakers transmit their odds to each other at racecourses. **2.** *U.S.* a ticking sound, as made by a clock. [from TICK^{1}]

tick-tack-toe (ˌtɪktæk'təʊ) *or* **tick-tack-too** (ˌtɪktæk'tuː) *n.* the usual U.S. and Canadian term for **noughts and crosses.** [C19: from TICKTACK (meaning: an obsolete variety of backgammon)]

ticktock ('tɪkˌtɒk) *n.* **1.** a ticking sound as made by a clock. ~*vb.* **2.** (*intr.*) to make a ticking sound.

tick trefoil *n.* any of various tropical and subtropical leguminous plants of the genus *Desmodium,* having trifoliate leaves, clusters of small purplish or white flowers, and sticky jointed seed pods, which separate into segments that cling to animals. Also called: **beggar-ticks.**

t.i.d. (in prescriptions) *abbrev. for* ter in die. [Latin: three times a day]

tidal ('taɪdᵊl) *adj.* **1.** relating to, characterized by, or affected by tides: *a tidal estuary.* **2.** dependent on the state of the tide: *a tidal ferry.* **3.** (of a glacier) reaching the sea and discharging floes or icebergs. —'**tidally** *adv.*

tidal basin *n.* a basin for vessels that is filled at high tide.

tidal energy *n.* energy obtained by harnessing tidal power.

tidal power *n.* the use of the rise and fall of tides involving very large volumes of water at low heads to generate electric power.

tidal volume *n.* **1.** the volume of water associated with a rising tide. **2.** *Physiol.* the amount of air passing into and out of the lungs during normal breathing.

tidal wave *n.* **1.** a name (not accepted in technical usage) for **tsunami. 2.** an unusually large incoming wave, often caused by high winds and spring tides. **3.** a forceful and widespread movement in public opinion, action, etc.

tidbit ('tɪdˌbɪt) *n.* the usual U.S. spelling of **titbit.**

tiddler ('tɪdlə) *n. Brit. informal.* **1.** a very small fish or aquatic creature, esp. a stickleback, minnow, or tadpole. **2.** a small child, esp. one undersized for its age. [C19: from dialectal *tittlebat,* childish variant of STICKLEBACK, influenced by TIDDLY^{1}]

tiddly^{1} ('tɪdlɪ) *adj.* **-dlier, -dliest.** *Brit.* small; tiny. [C19: childish variant of LITTLE]

tiddly^{2} ('tɪdlɪ) *adj.* **-dlier, -dliest.** *Slang, chiefly Brit.* slightly drunk. [C19 (meaning: a drink): of unknown origin]

tiddlywink ('tɪdlɪˌwɪŋk) *n.* any of the discs used in the game of tiddlywinks.

tiddlywinks ('tɪdlɪˌwɪŋks) *n.* (*functioning as sing.*) a game in which players try to flick discs of plastic into a cup by pressing them sharply on the side with other larger discs. [C19: probably from TIDDLY^{1} + dialect *wink,* variant of WINCH^{1}]

tide^{1} (taɪd) *n.* **1.** the cyclic rise and fall of sea level caused by the gravitational pull of the sun and moon. There are usually two high tides and two low tides in each lunar day. See also **tide-generating force, neap tide, spring tide. 2.** the current, ebb, or flow of water at a specified place resulting from these changes in level: *the tide is coming in.* **3.** See **ebb** (sense 3) and **flood** (sense 3). **4.** a widespread tendency or movement: *the tide of resentment against the government.* **5.** a critical point in time; turning point: *the tide of his fortunes.* **6.** *Northern English dialect.* a fair or holiday. **7.** *Archaic except in combination.* a season or time: *Christmastide.* **8.** *Rare.* any body of mobile water, such as a stream. **9.** *Archaic.* a favourable opportunity. ~*vb.* **10.** to carry or be carried with or as if with the tide. **11.** (*intr.*) to ebb and flow like the tide. [Old English *tīd* time; related to Old High German *zīt,* Old Norse *tīthr* time] —'**tideless** *adj.* —'**tideˌlike** *adj.*

tide^{2} (taɪd) *vb.* (*intr.*) *Archaic.* to happen. [Old English *tīdan;* related to Old Frisian *tīdia* to proceed to, Middle Low German *tīden* to hurry, Old Norse *tītha* to desire]

tide-gauge *n.* a gauge used to measure extremes or the present level of tidal movement.

tide-generating force *n.* the difference between the force of gravity exerted by the moon or the sun on a particle of water in the ocean and that exerted on an equal mass of matter at the centre of the earth. The lunar tide-generating forces are about 2.2 times greater than are the solar ones. See also **neap tide, spring tide, tide.**

tideland ('taɪdˌlænd) *n. U.S.* land between high-water and low-water marks.

tidemark ('taɪdˌmɑːk) *n.* **1.** a mark left by the highest or lowest point of a tide. **2.** a marker indicating the highest or lowest point reached by a tide. **3.** *Chiefly Brit.* a mark showing a level reached by a liquid: *a tidemark on the bath.* **4.** *Informal, chiefly Brit.* a dirty mark on the skin, indicating the extent to which someone has washed.

tide over *vb.* (*tr.*) to help to get through (a period of difficulty, distress, etc.): *the money tided him over until he got a job.*

tide race *n.* a fast-running tidal current.

tide-rip *n.* another word for **riptide** (sense 1).

tide table *n.* a table showing the height of the tide at different times of day over a period at a particular place.

tidewaiter ('taɪdˌweɪtə) *n.* (formerly) a customs officer who boarded and inspected incoming ships.

tidewater ('taɪdˌwɔːtə) *n.* **1.** water that advances and recedes with the tide. **2.** water that covers land that is dry at low tide. **3.** *U.S.* **a.** coastal land drained by tidal streams. **b.** (*as modifier*): *tidewater regions.*

tideway ('taɪdˌweɪ) *n.* a strong tidal current or its channel, esp. the tidal part of a river.

tidings ('taɪdɪŋz) *pl. n.* information or news. [Old English *tīdung;* related to Middle Low German *tīdinge* information, Old Norse *tidhendi* events; see TIDE^{2}]

tidy ('taɪdɪ) *adj.* **-dier, -diest. 1.** characterized by or indicating neatness and order. **2.** *Informal.* considerable: *a tidy sum of money.* ~*vb.* **-dies, -dying, -died. 3.** (when *intr.,* usually foll.

by *up*) to put (things) in order; neaten. ~*n., pl.* **-dies. 4. a.** a small container in which odds and ends are kept. **b. sink tidy.** a container with holes in the bottom, kept in the sink to retain rubbish that might clog the plug hole. **5.** *Chiefly U.S. and Canadian.* an ornamental protective covering for the back or arms of a chair. [C13 (in the sense: timely, seasonable, excellent): from TIDE[1] + -Y[1]; related to Dutch *tijdig* timely] —'**tidily** *adv.* —'**tidiness** *n.*

tie (taɪ) *vb.* **ties, tying, tied. 1.** (when *tr.*, often foll. by *up*) to fasten or be fastened with string, thread, etc. **2.** to make (a knot or bow) in (something): *to tie a knot; tie a ribbon.* **3.** (*tr.*) to restrict or secure. **4.** to equal the score of a competitor or fellow candidate. **5.** (*tr.*) *Informal.* to unite in marriage. **6.** *Music.* **a.** to execute (two successive notes of the same pitch) as though they formed one note of composite time value. **b.** to connect (two printed notes) with a tie. **7. fit to be tied.** *Slang.* very angry or upset. ~*n.* **8.** a bond, link, or fastening. **9.** a restriction or restraint. **10.** a string, wire, ribbon, etc., with which something is tied. **11.** a long narrow piece of material worn, esp. by men, under the collar of a shirt, tied in a knot close to the throat with the ends hanging down the front. U.S. name: **necktie. 12. a.** an equality in score, attainment, etc., in a contest. **b.** the match or competition in which such a result is attained. **13.** a structural member such as a tie beam or tie rod. **14.** *Sport, Brit.* a match or game in an eliminating competition: *a cup tie.* **15.** (*usually pl.*) a shoe fastened by means of laces. **16.** the U.S. and Canadian name for **sleeper** (on a railway track). **17.** *Music.* a slur connecting two notes of the same pitch indicating that the sound is to be prolonged for their joint time value. **18.** *Surveying.* one of two measurements running from two points on a survey line to a point of detail to fix its position. **19.** *Lacemaking.* another name for **bride**[2]. ~See also **tie in, tie up.** [Old English *tīgan* to tie; related to Old Norse *teygja* to draw, stretch out, Old English *tēon* to pull; see TUG, TOW[1], TIGHT]

tieback ('taɪˌbæk) *n.* **a.** a length of cord, ribbon, or other fabric used for tying a curtain to one side. **b.** a curtain having such a device.

tie beam *n.* a horizontal beam that serves to prevent two other structural members from separating, esp. one that connects two corresponding rafters in a roof or roof truss.

tie-break *or* **tiebreaker** ('taɪˌbreɪkə) *n.* **1.** *Tennis.* a method of deciding quickly the result of a set drawn at six-all, usually involving the playing of one deciding game for the best of twelve points in which each player serves alternately. **2.** any contest or game played to decide a winner when contestants have tied scores.

tie clasp *n.* a clip, often ornamental, which holds a tie in place against a shirt. Also called: **tie clip.**

tied (taɪd) *adj. Brit.* **1.** (of a public house, retail shop, etc.) obliged to sell only the beer, products, etc. of a particular producer: *a tied house; tied outlet.* **2.** (of a house or cottage) rented out to the tenant for as long as he is employed by the owner. **3.** (of a loan) made by one nation to another on condition that the money is spent on goods or services provided by the lending nation.

tie-dyeing *n.* a method of dyeing textiles to produce patterns by tying sections of the cloth together so that they will not absorb the dye. Also called: **tie-and-dye.** —'**tie-ˌdyed** *adj.*

tie in *vb.* (*adv.*) **1.** to come or bring into a certain relationship; coordinate. ~*n.* **tie-in. 2.** a link, relationship, or coordination. **3.** publicity material, a book, tape, etc., linked to a film or broadcast programme or series. **4.** *U.S.* **a.** a sale or advertisement offering products of which a purchaser must buy one or more in addition to his purchase. **b.** an item sold or advertised in this way, esp. the extra item. **c.** (*as modifier*): *a tie-in sale.*

tie line *n.* a telephone line between two private branch exchanges or private exchanges that may or may not pass through a main exchange.

tiemannite ('tiːməˌnaɪt) *n.* a grey mineral consisting of mercury selenide. Formula: HgSe. [C19: named after J. C. W. F. *Tiemann* (1848–99), German scientist]

tiepin ('taɪˌpɪn) *n.* an ornamental pin of various shapes used to pin the two ends of a tie to a shirt.

tier[1] (tɪə) *n.* **1.** one of a set of rows placed one above and behind the other, such as theatre seats. **2. a.** a layer or level. **b.** (*in combination*): *a three-tier cake.* **3.** a rank, order, or row. ~*vb.* **4.** to be or arrange in tiers. [C16: from Old French *tire* rank, of Germanic origin; compare Old English *tīr* embellishment]

tier[2] ('taɪə) *n.* a person or thing that ties.

tierce (tɪəs) *n.* **1.** a variant of **terce. 2.** the third of eight basic positions from which a parry or attack can be made in fencing. **3.** (tɜːs). *Piquet, etc.* a sequence of three cards in the same suit. **4.** an obsolete measure of capacity equal to 42 wine gallons. **5.** in Western Australia, a betting system in which the punter selects the first three place winners in any order. [C15: from Old French, feminine of *tiers* third, from Latin *tertius*]

tierce de Picardie (*French* tjɛrs də pikardi) *n.* another term for **Picardy third.**

tiercel ('tɪəsᵊl) *n.* a variant of **tercel.**

tie rod *n.* any rod or bar designed to prevent the separation of two parts, as in a vehicle.

tie up *vb.* (*adv.*) **1.** (*tr.*) to attach or bind securely with or as if with string, rope, etc. **2.** to moor (a vessel). **3.** (*tr.; often passive*) to engage the attentions of: *he's tied up at the moment and can't see you.* **4.** (*tr.; often passive*) to conclude (the organization of something): *the plans for the trip were tied up well in advance.* **5.** to come or bring to a complete standstill. **6.** (*tr.*) to invest or commit (funds, etc.) and so make unavailable for other uses. **7.** (*tr.*) to subject (property) to conditions that prevent sale, alienation, or other action. ~*n.* **tie-up. 8.** a link or connection. **9.** *Chiefly U.S. and Canadian.* a standstill. **10.** *Chiefly U.S. and Canadian.* an informal term for **traffic jam.**

tiff[1] (tɪf) *n.* **1.** a petty quarrel. **2.** a fit of ill humour. ~*vb.* **3.** (*intr.*) to have or be in a tiff. [C18: of unknown origin]

tiff[2] (tɪf) *n. Archaic.* a small draught of alcoholic drink; dram. [C18: see TIFFIN]

tiffany ('tɪfənɪ) *n., pl.* **-nies.** a sheer fine gauzy fabric. [C17: (in the sense: a fine dress worn on Twelfth Night): from Old French *tifanie,* from ecclesiastical Latin *theophania* Epiphany; see THEOPHANY]

Tiffany glass ('tɪfənɪ) *n.* another term for **Favrile glass.** [named after Louis C. *Tiffany* (1848–1933), U.S. glass-maker and craftsman who created it]

tiffin ('tɪfɪn) *n.* (in India) a light meal, esp. one taken at midday. [C18: probably from obsolete *tiffing,* from *tiff* to sip]

tig (tɪg) *n., vb.* **tigs, tigging, tigged.** another name for **tag**[2] (senses 1, 4).

tiger ('taɪgə) *n.* **1.** a large feline mammal, *Panthera tigris,* of forests in most of Asia, having a tawny yellow coat with black stripes. **2.** (*not in technical use*) any of various other animals, such as the jaguar, leopard, and thylacine. **3.** a dynamic, forceful, or cruel person. **4.** *Archaic.* a servant in livery, esp. a page or groom. **5.** short for **tiger moth. 6. get off the tiger** (*or* **the tiger's back**). *Informal.* to extricate oneself from a difficult or embarrassing situation. **7. have a tiger by the tail.** *Informal.* to find oneself in a situation that has turned out to be much more difficult to control than one had expected. [C13: from Old French *tigre,* from Latin *tigris,* from Greek, of Iranian origin] —'**tigerish** *or* '**tigrish** *adj.* —'**tigerishly** *adv.* —'**tigerishness** *n.* —'**tiger-like** *adj.*

Tiger ('taɪgə) *n.* See **TIGR.**

Tiger balm *n. Trademark.* (in Malaysia) a mentholated ointment widely used as a panacea.

tiger beetle *n.* any active predatory beetle of the family *Cicindelidae,* chiefly of warm dry regions, having powerful mandibles and long legs. [C19: so called because it has patterned, sometimes striped, wing covers]

tiger cat *n.* **1.** a medium-sized feline mammal, *Felis tigrina,* of Central and South America, having a dark-striped coat. **2.** any similar feline with tiger-like markings, such as the margay.

tiger lily *n.* **1.** a lily plant, *Lilium tigrinum,* of China and Japan, cultivated for its flowers, which have black-spotted orange reflexed petals. **2.** any of various similar lilies.

tiger moth *n.* any of a group of arctiid moths, mostly boldly marked, often in black, orange, and yellow, of the genera *Arctia Parasemia, Euplagia,* etc., producing woolly bear larvae and typified by the **garden tiger** (*Arctia caja*). Often shortened to **tiger.**

tiger's-eye ('taɪgəzˌaɪ) *or* **tigereye** ('taɪgərˌaɪ) *n.* **1.** a golden brown silicified variety of crocidolite, used as an ornamental stone. **2.** a glaze resembling this, used on pottery.

tiger shark *n.* **1.** a voracious omnivorous requiem shark, *Galeocerdo cuvieri,* chiefly of tropical waters, having a striped or spotted body. **2.** any of certain other spotted sharks, such as *Stegostoma tigrinum,* of the Indian Ocean.

tiger snake *n.* a highly venomous brown-and-yellow elapid snake, *Notechis scutatus,* of Australia and Tasmania.

tight (taɪt) *adj.* **1.** stretched or drawn so as not to be loose; taut: *a tight cord.* **2.** fitting or covering in a close manner: *a tight dress.* **3.** held, made, fixed, or closed firmly and securely: *a tight knot.* **4. a.** of close and compact construction or organization, esp. so as to be impervious to water, air, etc. **b.** (*in combination*): *watertight; airtight.* **5.** unyielding or stringent: *to keep a tight hold on resources.* **6.** cramped or constricted: *a tight fit.* **7.** mean or miserly. **8.** difficult and problematic: *a tight situation.* **9.** hardly profitable: *a tight bargain.* **10.** *Economics.* **a.** (of a commodity) difficult to obtain; in excess demand. **b.** (of funds, money, etc.) difficult and expensive to borrow because of high demand or restrictive monetary policy. **c.** (of markets) characterized by excess demand or scarcity with prices tending to rise. Compare **easy** (sense 8). **11.** (of a match or game) very close or even. **12.** (of a team or group, esp. of a pop group) playing well together, in a disciplined coordinated way. **13.** *Informal.* drunk. **14.** *Informal.* (of a person) showing tension. **15.** *Archaic or dialect.* neat. ~*adv.* **16.** in a close, firm, or secure way: *pull it tight.* **17. sit tight. a.** to wait patiently; bide one's time. **b.** to maintain one's position, stand, or opinion firmly. **18. sleep tight.** to sleep soundly. [C14: probably variant of *thight,* from Old Norse *thēttr* close; related to Middle High German *dīhte* thick] —'**tightly** *adv.* —'**tightness** *n.*

tighten ('taɪtᵊn) *vb.* **1.** to make or become tight or tighter. **2. tighten one's belt.** to economize. —'**tightener** *n.*

tightfisted (ˌtaɪt'fɪstɪd) *adj.* mean; miserly.

tight head *n. Rugby.* the prop on the hooker's right in the front row of a scrum. Compare **loose head.**

tightknit (ˌtaɪt'nɪt) *adj.* **1.** closely integrated: *a tightknit community.* **2.** organized carefully and concisely.

tight-lipped *adj.* **1.** reticent, secretive, or taciturn. **2.** with the lips pressed tightly together, as through anger.
tightrope ('taɪt,rəʊp) *n.* a rope or cable stretched taut above the ground on which acrobats walk or perform balancing feats.
tightrope walker *n.* an acrobat who performs on a tightrope. —**tightrope walking** *n.*
tights (taɪts) *pl. n.* **1.** Also called (U.S., Canadian, Austral., and N.Z.): **pantihose.** a one-piece clinging garment covering the body from the waist to the feet, worn by women in place of stockings and also by acrobats, dancers, etc. **2.** a similar garment formerly worn by men, as in the 16th century with a doublet.
tightwad ('taɪt,wɒd) *n. U.S. and Canadian slang.* a stingy person; miser.
tiglic acid ('tɪglɪk) *n.* a syrupy liquid or crystalline colourless unsaturated carboxylic acid, with the *trans*-configuration, found in croton oil and used in perfumery; *trans*-2-methyl-2-butenoic acid. Formula: $CH_3CH{:}C(CH_3)COOH$. [C19 *tiglic,* from New Latin phrase *Croton tiglium* (name of the croton plant), of uncertain origin]
tigon ('taɪgən) *or* **tiglon** ('tɪglɒn) *n.* the hybrid offspring of a male tiger and a female lion.
TIGR *abbrev. for* Treasury Investment Growth Receipts: a bond denominated in dollars and linked to U.S. treasury bonds, the yield on which is taxed in the UK as income when it is cashed or redeemed. Also called: **Tiger.**
Tigrean (tɪ'greɪən) *adj.* **1.** of or relating to Tigré, a province in N Ethiopia. ~*n.* **2.** a native or inhabitant of Tigré.
Tigré ('tiːgreɪ) *n.* a language of NE Ethiopia, belonging to the SE Semitic subfamily of the Afro-Asiatic family.
tigress ('taɪgrɪs) *n.* **1.** a female tiger. **2.** a fierce, cruel, or wildly passionate woman.
tigridia (taɪ'grɪdɪə) *n.* any plant of the bulbous genus *Tigridia,* native to subtropical and tropical America, esp. *T. pavonia,* the tiger flower or peacock tiger flower, grown for its large strikingly marked red, white, or yellow concave flowers: family *Iridaceae.* [New Latin, from Greek *tigris, tigridis* tiger]
Tigrinya (tɪ'griːnjə) *n.* a language of N Ethiopia, belonging to the SE Semitic subfamily of the Afro-Asiatic family.
TIG welding (tɪg) *n.* tungsten-electrode inert gas welding: a method of welding in which the arc is maintained by a tungsten electrode and shielded from the access of air by an inert gas. Compare **MIG welding.**
tike (taɪk) *n.* a variant spelling of **tyke.**
tiki ('tiːkɪ) *n.* an amulet or figurine in the form of a carved representation of an ancestor, worn in some Maori cultures. [from Maori]
tikka ('tiːkə) *adj.* (*immediately postpositive*) *Indian cookery.* (of meat, esp. chicken or lamb) marinated in spices then dry-roasted, usually in a clay oven.
tikoloshe (,tɪkɒ'lɒʃ, -'lɒʃɪ) *n.* a vari nt of **tokoloshe.**
til (tɪl, tiːl) *n.* another name for **sesame,** esp. a variety grown in India. [C19: from Hindi, from Sanskrit *tila* sesame]
tilak ('tɪlək) *n., pl.* **-ak** *or* **-aks.** a coloured spot or mark worn by Hindus, esp. on the forehead, often indicating membership of a religious sect, caste, etc., or (in the case of a woman) marital status. [from Sanskrit *tilaka*]
tilapia (tɪ'læpɪə, -'leɪ-) *n.* any mouthbrooding cichlid fish of the African freshwater genus *Tilapia:* used as food fishes. [C18: from New Latin]
tilbury ('tɪlbərɪ, -brɪ) *n., pl.* **-buries.** a light two-wheeled horse-drawn open carriage, seating two people. [C19: probably named after the inventor]
tilde ('tɪldə) *n.* the diacritical mark (~) placed over a letter to indicate a palatal nasal consonant, as in Spanish *señor.* This symbol is also used in the International Phonetic Alphabet to represent any nasalized vowel. [C19: from Spanish, from Latin *titulus* title, superscription]
tile (taɪl) *n.* **1.** a flat thin slab of fired clay, rubber, linoleum, etc., usually square or rectangular and sometimes ornamental, used with others to cover a roof, floor, wall, etc. **2.** a short pipe made of earthenware, concrete, or plastic, used with others to form a drain. **3.** tiles collectively. **4.** a rectangular block used as a playing piece in mahjong and other games. **5.** *Brit. old-fashioned slang.* a hat. **6. on the tiles.** *Informal.* on a spree, esp. of drinking or debauchery. ~*vb.* **7.** (*tr.*) to cover with tiles. [Old English *tīgele,* from Latin *tēgula;* related to German *Ziegel*] —'**tiler** *n.*
tilefish ('taɪl,fɪʃ) *n., pl.* **-fish** *or* **-fishes.** a large brightly coloured deep-sea percoid food fish, *Lopholatilus chamaeleonticeps,* of warm and tropical seas, esp. the North American coast of the Atlantic: family *Branchiostegidae.* [C19: from New Latin *-tilus,* ending of genus name *Lopholatilus;* perhaps also from a resemblance between its colours and patterning and ornamental tiles]
tiliaceous (,tɪlɪ'eɪʃəs) *adj.* of, relating to, or belonging to the *Tiliaceae,* a family of flowering plants, mostly trees and shrubs of warm and tropical regions: includes linden and jute. [C19: from Late Latin *tiliāceus,* from Latin *tilia* linden]
tiling ('taɪlɪŋ) *n.* **1.** tiles collectively. **2.** something made of or surfaced with tiles.
till[1] (tɪl) *conj., prep.* **1.** short for **until.** Also (not standard): **'til.** **2.** *Scot.* to; towards. **3.** *Dialect.* in order that: *come here till I tell you.* [Old English *til;* related to Old Norse *til* to, Old High German *zil* goal, aim]
▷**Usage.** *Till* is a variant of *until* that is acceptable at all levels of language. *Until* is, however, often preferred at the beginning of a sentence in formal writing: *until his behaviour improves, he cannot become a member.*
till[2] (tɪl) *vb.* (*tr.*) **1.** to cultivate and work (land) for the raising of crops. **2.** another word for **plough.** [Old English *tilian* to try, obtain; related to Old Frisian *tilia* to obtain, Old Saxon *tilōn* to obtain, Old High German *zilōn* to hasten towards] —'**tillable** *adj.* —'**tiller** *n.*
till[3] (tɪl) *n.* a box, case, or drawer into which the money taken from customers is put, now usually part of a cash register. [C15 *tylle,* of obscure origin]
till[4] (tɪl) *n.* an unstratified glacial deposit consisting of rock fragments of various sizes. The most common is boulder clay. [C17: of unknown origin]
tillage ('tɪlɪdʒ) *n.* **1.** the act, process, or art of tilling. **2.** tilled land.
tillandsia (tɪ'lændzɪə) *n.* any bromeliaceous epiphytic plant of the genus *Tillandsia,* such as Spanish moss, of tropical and subtropical America. [C18: New Latin, named after Elias *Tillands* (died 1693), Finno-Swedish botanist]
tiller[1] ('tɪlə) *n. Nautical.* a handle fixed to the top of a rudderpost to serve as a lever in steering it. [C14: from Anglo-French *teiler* beam of a loom, from Medieval Latin *tēlārium,* from Latin *tēla* web] —'**tillerless** *adj.*
tiller[2] ('tɪlə) *n.* **1.** a shoot that arises from the base of the stem in grasses. **2.** a less common name for **sapling.** ~*vb.* **3.** (*intr.*) (of a plant) to produce tillers. [Old English *telgor* twig; related to Icelandic *tjalga* branch]
tillicum ('tɪlɪkəm) *n. North American informal.* (in the Pacific Northwest) a friend. [from Chinook Jargon, from Chinook *tlxam* kin, esp. as distinguished from chiefs]
tilt[1] (tɪlt) *vb.* **1.** to incline or cause to incline at an angle. **2.** (*usually intr.*) to attack or overthrow (a person or people) in a tilt or joust. **3.** (when *intr.,* often foll. by *at*) to aim or thrust: *to tilt a lance.* **4.** (*tr.*) to work or forge with a tilt hammer. ~*n.* **5.** a slope or angle: *at a tilt.* **6.** the act of tilting. **7.** (esp. in medieval Europe) **a.** a jousting contest. **b.** a thrust with a lance or pole delivered during a tournament. **8.** any dispute, contest, or similar encounter. **9.** See **tilt hammer.** **10. (at) full tilt.** at full speed or force. [Old English *tealtian;* related to Dutch *touteren* to totter, Norwegian *tylta* to tiptoe, *tylten* unsteady] —'**tilter** *n.*
tilt[2] (tɪlt) *n.* **1.** an awning or canopy, usually of canvas, for a boat, booth, etc. ~*vb.* **2.** (*tr.*) to cover or provide with a tilt. [Old English *teld;* related to Old High German *zelt* tent, Old Norse *tjald* tent]
tilth (tɪlθ) *n.* **1.** the act or process of tilling land. **2.** the condition of soil or land that has been tilled, esp. with respect to suitability for promoting plant growth. [Old English *tilthe;* see TILL[2]]
tilt hammer *n.* a drop hammer consisting of a heavy head moving at the end of a pivoted arm; used in forging.
tiltyard ('tɪlt,jɑːd) *n.* (formerly) an enclosed area for tilting.
Tim. *Bible. abbrev. for* Timothy.
timbal *or* **tymbal** ('tɪmbᵊl) *n. Music.* a type of kettledrum. [C17: from French *timbale,* from Old French *tamballe,* (associated also with *cymbale* cymbal), from Old Spanish *atabal,* from Arabic *at-tabl* the drum]
timbale (tæm'bɑːl; *French* tɛ̃bal) *n.* **1.** a mixture of meat, fish, etc., in a rich sauce, cooked in a mould lined with potato or pastry. **2.** a plain straight-sided mould in which such a dish is prepared. [C19: from French: kettledrum]
timber ('tɪmbə) *n.* **1. a.** wood, esp. when regarded as a construction material. **b.** (*as modifier*): *a timber cottage.* Usual U.S. and Canadian word: **lumber.** **2. a.** trees collectively. **b.** *Chiefly U.S.* woodland. **3.** a piece of wood used in a structure. **4.** *Nautical.* a frame in a wooden vessel. **5.** potential material, for a post, rank, etc.: *he is managerial timber.* ~*vb.* **6.** (*tr.*) to provide with timbers. ~*interj.* **7.** a lumberjack's shouted warning when a tree is about to fall. [Old English; related to Old High German *zimbar* wood, Old Norse *timbr* timber, Latin *domus* house]
timbered ('tɪmbəd) *adj.* **1.** made of or containing timber or timbers. **2.** covered with trees; wooded.
timberhead ('tɪmbə,hɛd) *n. Nautical.* a timber, the top of which rises above deck level and is used as a bollard.
timber hitch *n.* a knot used for tying a rope round a spar, log, etc., for haulage.
timbering ('tɪmbərɪŋ) *n.* **1.** timbers collectively. **2.** work made of timber.
timberland ('tɪmbə,lænd) *n. U.S.* land covered with trees grown for their timber.
timber line *n.* the altitudinal or latitudinal limit of normal tree growth. See also **tree line.**
timberman ('tɪmbəmən) *n., pl.* **-men.** any of various longicorn beetles that have destructive wood-eating larvae. Also called: **timberman beetle.**
timber wolf *n.* a variety of the wolf, *Canis lupus,* having a grey brindled coat and occurring in forested northern regions, esp. of North America. Also called: **grey wolf.**
timberwork ('tɪmbə,wɜːk) *n.* a structure made of timber.
timberyard ('tɪmbə,jɑːd) *n. Brit.* an establishment where timber and sometimes other building materials are stored or sold. U.S. and Canadian word: **lumberyard.**

timbre ('tɪmbə, 'tæmbə; *French* tɛ̃brə) *n.* **1.** *Phonetics.* the distinctive tone quality differentiating one vowel or sonant from another. **2.** *Music.* tone colour or quality of sound, esp. a specific type of tone colour. [C19: from French: note of a bell, from Old French: drum, from Medieval Greek *timbanon,* from Greek *tumpanon* drum]

timbrel ('tɪmbrəl) *n. Chiefly biblical.* another word for **tambourine.** [C16: from Old French; see TIMBRE]

Timbuktu (ˌtɪmbʌk'tuː) *n.* any distant or outlandish place: *from here to Timbuktu.* [after a town in central Mali, W Africa]

time (taɪm) *n.* **1. a.** the continuous passage of existence in which events pass from a state of potentiality in the future, through the present, to a state of finality in the past. **b.** (*as modifier*): *time travel.* Related adj.: **temporal. 2.** *Physics.* a quantity measuring duration, usually with reference to a periodic process such as the rotation of the earth or the vibration of electromagnetic radiation emitted from certain atoms (see **caesium clock, second**[2] (sense 1)). In classical mechanics, time is absolute in the sense that the time of an event is independent of the observer. According to the theory of relativity it depends on the observer's frame of reference. Time is considered as a fourth coordinate required, along with three spatial coordinates, to specify an event. See **space-time continuum. 3.** a specific point on this continuum expressed in terms of hours and minutes: *the time is four o'clock.* **4.** a system of reckoning for expressing time: *Greenwich mean time.* **5. a.** a definite and measurable portion of this continuum. **b.** (*as modifier*): *time limit.* **6. a.** an accepted period such as a day, season, etc. **b.** (*in combination*): *springtime.* **7.** an unspecified interval; a while: *I was there for a time.* **8.** (*often pl.*) a period or point marked by specific attributes or events: *the Victorian times; time for breakfast.* **9.** a sufficient interval or period: *have you got time to help me?* **10.** an instance or occasion: *I called you three times.* **11.** an occasion or period of specified quality: *have a good time; a miserable time.* **12.** the duration of human existence. **13.** the heyday of human life: *in her time she was a great star.* **14.** a suitable period or moment: *it's time I told you.* **15.** the expected interval in which something is done: *the flying time from New York to London was seven hours.* **16.** a particularly important moment, esp. childbirth or death: *her time had come.* **17.** (*pl.*) indicating a degree or amount calculated by multiplication with the number specified: *ten times three is thirty; he earns four times as much as me.* **18.** (*often pl.*) the fashions, thought, etc., of the present age (esp. in the phrases **ahead of one's time, behind the times**). **19.** *Brit.* (in bars, pubs, etc.) short for **closing time. 20.** *Informal.* a term in jail (esp. in the phrase **do time**). **21. a.** a customary or full period of work. **b.** the rate of pay for this period. **22.** Also (esp. U.S.): **metre. a.** the system of combining beats or pulses in music into successive groupings by which the rhythm of the music is established. **b.** a specific system having a specific number of beats in each grouping or bar: *duple time.* **23.** *Music.* short for **time value. 24.** *Prosody.* a unit of duration used in the measurement of poetic metre; mora. **25. against time.** in an effort to complete something in a limited period. **26. ahead of time.** before the deadline. **27. all in good time.** in due course. **28. all the time.** continuously. **29. at one time. a.** once; formerly. **b.** simultaneously. **30. at the same time. a.** simultaneously. **b.** nevertheless; however. **31. at times.** sometimes. **32. beat time.** (of a conductor, etc.) to indicate the tempo or pulse of a piece of music by waving a baton or a hand, tapping out the beats, etc. **33. before one's time.** prematurely. **34. for the time being.** for the moment; temporarily. **35. from time to time.** at intervals; occasionally. **36. gain time.** See **gain**[1] (sense 9). **37. have no time for.** to have no patience with; not tolerate. **38. in good time. a.** early. **b.** quickly. **39. in no time.** very quickly; almost instantaneously. **40. in one's own time. a.** outside paid working hours. **b.** at one's own rate. **41. in time. a.** early or at the appointed time. **b.** eventually. **c.** *Music.* at a correct metrical or rhythmical pulse. **42. keep time.** to observe correctly the accent or rhythmical pulse of a piece of music in relation to tempo. **43. lose time.** (of a timepiece) to operate too slowly. **44. lose no time.** to do something without delay. **45. make time. a.** to find an opportunity. **b.** (often foll. by *with*) *U.S. informal.* to succeed in seducing. **46. mark time.** See **mark** (sense 35). **47. in the nick of time.** at the last possible moment; at the critical moment. **48. on time. a.** at the expected or scheduled time. **b.** *U.S.* payable in instalments. **49. pass the time of day.** to exchange casual greetings (with an acquaintance). **50. time about.** *Scot.* alternately; turn and turn about. **51. time and again.** frequently. **52. time off.** a period when one is absent from work for a holiday, through sickness, etc. **53. time on.** the Austral. equivalent of **extra time. 54. time out of mind.** from time immemorial. **55. time of one's life.** a memorably enjoyable time. **56.** (*modifier*) operating automatically at or for a set time, for security or convenience: *time lock; time switch.* ~*vb.* (*tr.*) **57.** to ascertain or calculate the duration or speed of. **58.** to set a time for. **59.** to adjust to keep accurate time. **60.** to pick a suitable time for. **61.** *Sport.* to control the execution or speed of (an action, esp. a shot or stroke) so that it has its full effect at the right moment. ~*interj.* **62.** the word called out by a publican signalling that it is closing time. [Old English *tīma;* related to Old English *tīd* time, Old Norse *tīmi,* Alemannic *zīme;* see TIDE[1]]

time and a half *n.* the rate of pay equalling one and a half times the normal rate, often offered for overtime work.

time and motion study *n.* the analysis of industrial or work procedures to determine the most efficient methods of operation. Also: **time and motion, time study, motion study.**

time bomb *n.* a bomb containing a timing mechanism that determines the time at which it will detonate.

time capsule *n.* a container holding articles, documents, etc., representative of the current age, buried in the earth or in the foundations of a new building for discovery in the future.

timecard ('taɪmˌkɑːd) *n.* a card used with a time clock.

time charter *n.* the hire of a ship or aircraft for a specified period. Compare **voyage charter.**

time clock *n.* a clock which records, by punching or stamping cards inserted into it, the time of arrival or departure of people, such as employees in a factory.

time code *n.* (on video or audio tape) a separate track on which time references are continually recorded in digital form as an aid to editing.

time constant *n. Electronics.* the time required for the current or voltage in a circuit to rise or fall exponentially through approximately 63 per cent of its amplitude.

time-consuming *adj.* taking up or involving a great deal of time.

time deposit *n.* a bank deposit from which withdrawals may be made only after advance notice or at a specified future date. Compare **demand deposit.**

time dilation *or* **dilatation** *n.* the principle predicted by relativity that time intervals between events in a system have larger values measured by an observer moving with respect to the system than those measured by an observer at rest with respect to it.

time-division multiplex *n.* See **multiplex** (sense 1).

time exposure *n.* **1.** an exposure of a photographic film for a relatively long period, usually a few seconds. **2.** a photograph produced by such an exposure.

time-honoured *adj.* having been observed for a long time and sanctioned by custom.

time immemorial *n.* **1.** the distant past beyond memory or record. **2.** *Law.* time beyond legal memory, fixed by English statute as before the reign of Richard I (1189).

timekeeper ('taɪmˌkiːpə) *n.* **1.** a person or thing that keeps or records time. **2.** an employee who maintains a record of the hours worked by the other employees. **3.** a device for indicating time; timepiece. **4.** an employee with respect to his record of punctuality: *a good timekeeper.* —'**timeˌkeeping** *n.*

time-lag *n.* an interval between two connected events.

time-lapse photography *n.* the technique of recording a very slow process, such as the withering of a flower, by taking a large number of photographs on a strip of film at regular intervals. The film is then projected at normal speed.

timeless ('taɪmlɪs) *adj.* **1.** unaffected or unchanged by time; ageless. **2.** eternal. **3.** an archaic word for **untimely.** —'**timelessly** *adv.* —'**timelessness** *n.*

time loan *n.* a loan repayable before or at a specified future date. Compare **call loan.**

timely ('taɪmlɪ) *adj.* **-lier, -liest,** *adv.* **1.** at the right or an opportune or appropriate time. **2.** an archaic word for **early.** —'**timeliness** *n.*

time machine *n.* (in science fiction) a machine in which people or objects can be transported into the past or the future.

timeous ('taɪməs) *adj. Scot.* in good time; sufficiently early: *a timeous warning.* [C15: Scottish; see TIME, -OUS] —'**timeously** *adv.*

time-out *n. Chiefly U.S. and Canadian.* **1.** *Sport.* an interruption in play during which players rest, discuss tactics, or make substitutions. **2.** a break taken during working hours.

timepiece ('taɪmˌpiːs) *n.* **1.** any of various devices, such as a clock, watch, or chronometer, which measure and indicate time. **2.** a device which indicates the time but does not strike or otherwise audibly mark the hours.

timer ('taɪmə) *n.* **1.** a device for measuring, recording, or indicating time. **2.** a switch or regulator that causes a mechanism to operate at a specific time or at predetermined intervals. **3.** a person or thing that times.

timesaving ('taɪmˌseɪvɪŋ) *adj.* shortening the length of time required for an operation, activity, etc. —'**timeˌsaver** *n.*

timescale ('taɪmˌskeɪl) *n.* the span of time within which certain events occur or are scheduled to occur considered in relation to any broader period of time.

time series *n. Statistics.* a series of values of a variable taken in successive periods of time.

time-served *adj.* (of a craftsman or tradesman) having completed an apprenticeship; fully trained and competent: *a time-served mechanic.*

timeserver ('taɪmˌsɜːvə) *n.* a person who compromises and changes his opinions, way of life, etc., to suit the current fashions. —'**timeˌserving** *adj., n.*

time-share *adj.* denoting, relating to, or forming part of time sharing of property: *time-share villas.*

time sharing *n.* **1. a.** a system of part ownership of a property, such as a flat or villa, for use as a holiday home, whereby each participant buys the right to use the property for the same fixed period annually. **b.** (*as modifier*): *a time-sharing system.* **2. a.** a system by which users at different terminals of a computer can, because of its high speed, apparently communicate with it at the same time. Compare **batch processing. b.** (*as modifier*): *a time-sharing computer.*

time sheet *n.* a card on which are recorded the hours spent working by an employee or employees.

time signal *n.* an announcement of the correct time, esp. on radio or television.

time signature *n. Music.* a sign usually consisting of two figures, one above the other, the upper figure representing the number of beats per bar and the lower one the time value of each beat. This sign is placed after the key signature at the outset of a piece or section of a piece.

time study *n.* short for **time and motion study.**

time switch *n.* an electric switch that can be set to operate an appliance, such as a light or an oven, at a particular time.

timetable ('taɪm,teɪbᵊl) *n.* **1.** a list or table of events arranged according to the time when they take place; schedule. ~*vb.* **2.** (*tr.*) to include in or arrange according to a timetable. **3.** (*intr.*) to draw up a timetable.

time trial *n.* (esp. in cycling) a race in which the competitors compete against the clock over a specified course. —'**time-,trialling** *n.*

time value *n. Music.* the duration of a given printed note relative to other notes in a composition or section and considered in relation to the basic tempo. Often shortened to **time.** Also called: **note value, time.**

time warp *n.* **1.** any distortion of space-time. **2.** a hypothetical distortion of time in which people and events from one age can be imagined to exist in another age. **3.** *Informal.* an illusion in which time appears to stand still: *he is living in a time warp.*

timework ('taɪm,wɜːk) *n.* work paid for by the length of time taken, esp. by the hour or the day. Compare **piecework.** —'**time,worker** *n.*

timeworn ('taɪm,wɔːn) *adj.* **1.** showing the adverse effects of overlong use or of old age. **2.** hackneyed; trite.

time zone *n.* a region throughout which the same standard time is used. There are 24 time zones in the world, demarcated approximately by meridians at 15° intervals, an hour apart. See also **zonetime.**

timid ('tɪmɪd) *adj.* **1.** easily frightened or upset, esp. by human contact; shy. **2.** indicating shyness or fear. [C16: from Latin *timidus,* from *timēre* to fear] —**ti'midity** *or* '**timidness** *n.* —'**timidly** *adv.*

timing ('taɪmɪŋ) *n.* the process or art of regulating actions or remarks in relation to others to produce the best effect, as in music, the theatre, sport, etc.

timing gear *n.* (in an internal-combustion engine) the drive between the crankshaft and the camshaft, usually giving a ratio of 2:1.

timocracy (taɪ'mɒkrəsɪ) *n., pl.* **-cies. 1.** a political unit or system in which possession of property serves as the first requirement for participation in government. **2.** a political unit or system in which love of honour is deemed the guiding principle of government. [C16: from Old French *tymocracie,* ultimately from Greek *timokratia,* from *timē* worth, honour, price + -CRACY] —**timocratic** (,taɪmə'krætɪk) *adj. or* ,**timo'cratical** *adj.*

timorous ('tɪmərəs) *adj.* **1.** fearful or timid. **2.** indicating fear or timidity. [C15: from Old French *temoros,* from Medieval Latin *timōrōsus,* from Latin *timor* fear, from *timēre* to be afraid] —'**timorously** *adv.* —'**timorousness** *n.*

timothy grass *or* **timothy** ('tɪməθɪ) *n.* a perennial grass, *Phleum pratense,* of temperate regions, having erect stiff stems and cylindrical flower spikes: grown for hay and pasture. [C18: apparently named after a *Timothy Hanson,* who brought it to colonial Carolina in the present-day U.S.]

timpani *or* **tympani** ('tɪmpənɪ) *pl. n.* (*sometimes functioning as sing.*) a set of kettledrums, two or more in number. Often shortened to **timps** (informal). [from Italian, pl. of *timpano* kettledrum, from Latin: TYMPANUM] —'**timpanist** *or* '**tympanist** *n.*

tin (tɪn) *n.* **1.** a metallic element, occurring in cassiterite, that has several allotropes; the ordinary malleable silvery-white metal slowly changes below 13.2°C to a grey powder. It is used extensively in alloys, esp. bronze and pewter, and as a noncorroding coating for steel. Symbol: Sn; atomic no.: 50; atomic wt.: 118.69; valency: 2 or 4; relative density: 5.75 (grey), 7.31 (white); melting pt.: 231.89°C; boiling pt.: 2270°C. **2.** Also called (esp. U.S. and Canadian): **can.** an airtight sealed container of thin sheet metal, usually iron, coated with tin, used for preserving and storing food or drink. **3.** any container made of metallic tin. **4. fill her tins.** *N.Z.* to complete a home baking of cakes, biscuits, etc. **5.** Also called: **tinful.** the contents of a tin or the amount a tin will hold. **6.** *Brit., Austral., and N.Z.* corrugated or galvanized iron: *a tin roof.* **7.** any metal regarded as cheap or flimsy. **8.** *Brit.* a loaf of bread with a rectangular shape, baked in a tin. **9.** *Slang.* money. ~*vb.* **tins, tinning, tinned.** (*tr.*) **10.** to put (food, etc.) into a tin or tins; preserve in a tin. **11.** to plate or coat with tin. **12.** to prepare (a metal) for soldering or brazing by applying a thin layer of solder to the surface. ~Related adjs.: **stannic, stannous.** [Old English; related to Old Norse *tin,* Old High German *zin*] —'**tin,like** *adj.*

tinamou ('tɪnə,muː) *n.* any bird of the order *Tinamiformes* of Central and South America, having small wings, a heavy body, and an inconspicuous plumage. [C18: via French from Carib (Galibi) *tinamu*]

tincal ('tɪŋkᵊl) *n.* another name for **borax** (sense 1). [C17: from Malay *tingkal,* from Sanskrit *tankana*]

tin can *n.* a metal food container, esp. when empty.

tinct (tɪŋkt) *n., vb.* **1.** an obsolete word for **tint.** ~*adj.* **2.** *Poetic.* tinted or coloured. [C15: from Latin *tinctus,* from *tingere* to colour]

tinct. *abbrev. for* tincture.

tinctorial (tɪŋk'tɔːrɪəl) *adj.* **1.** of or relating to colouring, staining, or dyeing. **2.** imbuing with colour. [C17: from Latin *tinctōrius,* from *tingere* to tinge] —**tinc'torially** *adv.*

tincture ('tɪŋktʃə) *n.* **1.** *Pharmacol.* a medicinal extract in a solution of alcohol. **2.** a tint, colour, or tinge. **3.** a slight flavour, aroma, or trace. **4.** any one of the colours or either of the metals used on heraldic arms. **5.** *Obsolete.* a dye or pigment. ~*vb.* **6.** (*tr.*) to give a tint or colour to. [C14: from Latin *tinctūra* a dyeing, from *tingere* to dye]

tinder ('tɪndə) *n.* **1.** dry wood or other easily combustible material used for lighting a fire. **2.** anything inflammatory or dangerous: *his speech was tinder to the demonstrators' unrest.* [Old English *tynder;* related to Old Norse *tundr,* Old High German *zuntara*] —'**tindery** *adj.*

tinderbox ('tɪndə,bɒks) *n.* **1.** a box used formerly for holding tinder, esp. one fitted with a flint and steel. **2.** a person or thing that is particularly touchy or explosive.

tine (taɪn) *n.* **1.** a slender prong, esp. of a fork. **2.** any of the sharp terminal branches of a deer's antler. [Old English *tind;* related to Old Norse *tindr,* Old High German *zint*] —**tined** *adj.*

tinea ('tɪnɪə) *n.* any fungal skin disease, esp. ringworm. [C17: from Latin: worm] —'**tineal** *adj.*

tineid ('tɪnɪɪd) *n.* **1.** any moth of the family *Tineidae,* which includes the clothes moths. ~*adj.* **2.** of, relating to, or belonging to the family *Tineidae.* [C19: from New Latin *Tineidae,* from Latin: TINEA]

tinfoil ('tɪn,fɔɪl) *n.* **1.** thin foil made of tin or an alloy of tin and lead. **2.** thin foil made of aluminium; used for wrapping foodstuffs.

ting[1] (tɪŋ) *n.* **1.** a high metallic sound such as that made by a small bell. ~*vb.* **2.** to make or cause to make such a sound. [C15: of imitative origin]

ting[2] (tɪŋ) *n.* (*often cap.*) a variant spelling of **thing**[2].

ting-a-ling ('tɪŋə'lɪŋ) *n.* the sound of a small bell.

tinge (tɪndʒ) *n.* **1.** a slight tint or colouring: *her hair had a tinge of grey.* **2.** any slight addition. ~*vb.* **tinges, tingeing** *or* **tinging, tinged.** (*tr.*) **3.** to colour or tint faintly. **4.** to impart a slight trace to: *her thoughts were tinged with nostalgia.* [C15: from Latin *tingere* to colour]

tingle ('tɪŋgᵊl) *vb.* **1.** (*usually intr.*) to feel or cause to feel a prickling, itching, or stinging sensation of the flesh, as from a cold plunge or electric shock. ~*n.* **2.** a sensation of tingling. **3.** *Rare.* a tinkle. [C14: perhaps a variant of TINKLE] —'**tingler** *n.* —'**tingling** *adj.* —'**tinglingly** *adv.* —'**tingly** *adj.*

tin god *n.* **1.** a self-important dictatorial person. **2.** a person erroneously regarded as holy or venerable.

tin hat *n. Informal.* a steel helmet worn by military personnel for protection against small metal fragments.

tinhorn ('tɪn,hɔːn) *U.S. slang.* ~*n.* **1.** a cheap pretentious person, esp. a gambler with extravagant claims. ~*adj.* **2.** cheap and showy.

tinker ('tɪŋkə) *n.* **1.** (esp. formerly) a travelling mender of pots and pans. **2.** a clumsy worker. **3.** the act of tinkering. **4.** *Scot. and Irish.* another name for a **Gypsy. 5.** *Brit. informal.* a mischievous child. **6.** any of several small mackerels that occur off the North American coast of the Atlantic. ~*vb.* **7.** (*intr.;* foll. by *with*) to play, fiddle, or meddle (with machinery, etc.), esp. while undertaking repairs. **8.** to mend (pots and pans) as a tinker. [C13 *tinkere,* perhaps from *tink* tinkle, of imitative origin] —'**tinkerer** *n.*

tinker's damn *or* **cuss** *n. Slang.* the slightest heed (esp. in the phrase **not give a tinker's damn** *or* **cuss).**

tinkle ('tɪŋkᵊl) *vb.* **1.** to ring or cause to ring with a series of high tinny sounds, like a small bell. **2.** (*tr.*) to announce or summon by such a ringing. **3.** (*intr.*) *Brit. informal.* to urinate. ~*n.* **4.** a high clear ringing sound. **5.** the act of tinkling. **6.** *Brit. informal.* a telephone call. [C14: of imitative origin] —'**tinkling** *adj., n.* —'**tinkly** *adj.*

tin lizzie ('lɪzɪ) *n. Informal.* an old or decrepit car; jalopy. [originally a nickname for the Model T Ford car]

tinned (tɪnd) *adj.* **1.** plated, coated, or treated with tin. **2.** *Chiefly Brit.* preserved or stored in airtight tins: *tinned soup.* **3.** coated with a layer of solder.

tinned dog *n. Slang, chiefly Austral.* tinned meat.

tinner ('tɪnə) *n.* **1.** a tin miner. **2.** a worker in tin; tinsmith. **3.** a person or organization that puts food, etc., into tins; canner.

tinnitus (tɪ'naɪtəs) *n. Pathol.* a ringing, hissing, or booming sensation in one or both ears, caused by infection of the middle or inner ear, a side effect of certain drugs, etc. [C19: from Latin, from *tinnīre* to ring]

tinny ('tɪnɪ) *adj.* **-nier, -niest. 1.** of, relating to, or resembling tin. **2.** cheap, badly made, or shoddy. **3.** (of a sound) high, thin, and

metallic. 4. (of food or drink) flavoured with metal, as from a container. 5. *Austral. informal.* lucky. ~*n., pl.* **-nies.** 6. *Austral. slang.* a can of beer. —'**tinnily** *adv.* —'**tinniness** *n.*
tin-opener *n.* a small tool for opening tins.
Tin Pan Alley *n.* 1. a district in a city concerned with the production of popular music, originally a small district in New York. 2. *Derogatory.* the strictly commercial side of show business and pop music.
tin plate *n.* 1. thin steel sheet coated with a layer of tin that protects the steel from corrosion. ~*vb.* **tin-plate.** 2. (*tr.*) to coat (a metal or object) with a layer of tin, usually either by electroplating or by dipping in a bath of molten tin. —'**tin-ˌplater** *n.*
tinpot ('tɪnˌpɒt) *adj.* (*prenominal*) *Brit. informal.* 1. inferior, cheap, or worthless. 2. paltry; unimportant.
tinsel ('tɪnsəl) *n.* 1. a decoration consisting of a piece of string with thin strips of metal foil attached along its length. 2. a yarn or fabric interwoven with strands of glittering thread. 3. anything cheap, showy, and gaudy. ~*vb.* **-sels, -selling, -selled** *or U.S.* **-sels, -seling, -seled.** (*tr.*) 4. to decorate with or as if with tinsel: *snow tinsels the trees.* 5. to give a gaudy appearance to. ~*adj.* 6. made of or decorated with tinsel. 7. showily but cheaply attractive; gaudy. [C16: from Old French *estincele* a spark, from Latin *scintilla;* compare STENCIL] —'**tinsel-ˌlike** *adj.* —'**tinselly** *adj.*
tinsmith ('tɪnˌsmɪθ) *n.* a person who works with tin or tin plate.
tin soldier *n.* 1. a miniature toy soldier, usually made of lead. 2. a person who enjoys playing at being a soldier.
tinstone ('tɪnˌstəʊn) *n.* another name for **cassiterite.**
tint (tɪnt) *n.* 1. a shade of a colour, esp. a pale one. 2. a colour that is softened or desaturated by the addition of white. 3. a tinge. 4. a semipermanent dye for the hair. 5. a trace or hint: *a tint of jealousy in his voice.* 6. *Engraving.* uniform shading, produced esp. by hatching. 7. *Printing.* a panel of colour serving as a background to letters or other matter. ~*vb.* 8. (*tr.*) to colour or tinge. 9. (*tr.*) to change or influence slightly: *his answer was tinted by his prior knowledge.* 10. (*intr.*) to acquire a tint. [C18: from earlier TINCT] —'**tinter** *n.*
tintinnabulation (ˌtɪntɪˌnæbjʊ'leɪʃən) *n.* the act or an instance of the ringing or pealing of bells. —ˌ**tintin'nabular,** ˌ**tintin'nabulary,** *or* ˌ**tintin'nabulous** *adj.*
tintinnabulum (ˌtɪntɪ'næbjʊləm) *n., pl.* **-la** (-lə). a small high-pitched bell. [C16: from Latin, from *tintinnāre* to tinkle, from *tinnīre* to ring; see TINNITUS]
tintometer (tɪn'tɒmɪtə) *n.* another name for **colorimeter** (sense 1).
tint tool *n.* a kind of burin used in wood engraving for carving lines of even thickness, as in hatching.
tintype ('tɪnˌtaɪp) *n.* another name for **ferrotype** (senses 1, 2).
tinware ('tɪnˌwɛə) *n.* objects made of tin plate.
tin whistle *n.* another name for **penny whistle.**
tinwork ('tɪnˌwɜːk) *n.* objects made of tin.
tinworks ('tɪnˌwɜːks) *n.* (*functioning as sing. or pl.*) a place where tin is mined, smelted, or rolled.
tiny ('taɪnɪ) *adj.* **tinier, tiniest.** very small; minute. [C16 *tine,* of uncertain origin] —'**tinily** *adv.* —'**tininess** *n.*
-tion *suffix forming nouns.* indicating state, condition, action, process, or result: *election; prohibition.* Compare **-ation, -ion.** [from Old French, from Latin *-tiō, -tiōn-*]
tip[1] (tɪp) *n.* 1. the extreme end of something, esp. a narrow or pointed end. 2. the top or summit. 3. a small piece forming an extremity or end: *a metal tip on a cane.* ~*vb.* **tips, tipping, tipped.** (*tr.*) 4. to adorn or mark the tip of. 5. to cause to form a tip. [C15: from Old Norse *typpa;* related to Middle Low German, Middle Dutch *tip*] —'**tipless** *adj.*
tip[2] (tɪp) *vb.* **tips, tipping, tipped.** 1. to tilt or cause to tilt. 2. (usually foll. by *over* or *up*) to tilt or cause to tilt, so as to overturn or fall. 3. *Brit.* to dump (rubbish, etc.). 4. **tip one's hat.** to take off, raise, or touch one's hat in salutation. ~*n.* 5. the act of tipping or the state of being tipped. 6. *Brit.* a dump for refuse, etc. [C14: of uncertain origin; related to TOP[1], TOPPLE] —'**tippable** *adj.*
tip[3] (tɪp) *n.* 1. a payment given for services in excess of the standard charge; gratuity. 2. a helpful hint, warning, or other piece of information. 3. a piece of inside information, esp. in betting or investing. ~*vb.* **tips, tipping, tipped.** 4. to give a tip to (a person). [C18: perhaps from TIP[4]]
tip[4] (tɪp) *vb.* **tips, tipping, tipped.** (*tr.*) 1. to hit or strike lightly. 2. to hit (a ball) indirectly so that it glances off the bat in cricket. ~*n.* 3. a light blow. 4. a glancing hit in cricket. [C13: perhaps from Low German *tippen*]
tip and run *n.* 1. a form of cricket in which the batsman must run if his bat touches the ball. ~*adj.* **tip-and-run.** 2. (*prenominal*) characterized by a rapid departure immediately after striking: *a tip-and-run raid.*
tipcat ('tɪpˌkæt) *n.* a game in which a short sharp-ended piece of wood (the cat) is tipped in the air with a stick.
tipi ('tiːpɪ) *n., pl.* **-pis.** a variant spelling of **tepee.**
tip-off *n.* 1. a warning or hint, esp. given confidentially and based on inside information. 2. *Basketball.* the act or an instance of putting the ball in play by a jump ball. ~*vb.* **tip off.** 3. (*tr., adv.*) to give a hint or warning to.
tipper ('tɪpə) *n.* 1. a person who gives or leaves a tip: *he is a generous tipper.* 2. short for **tipper truck.**
tipper truck *or* **lorry** *n.* a truck or lorry the rear platform of which can be pneumatically raised at the front end to enable the load to be discharged by gravity. Also called: **tip truck.**
tippet ('tɪpɪt) *n.* 1. a woman's fur cape for the shoulders, often consisting of the whole fur of a fox, marten, etc. 2. the long stole of Anglican clergy worn during a service. 3. a long streamer-like part to a sleeve, hood, etc., esp. in the 16th century. 4. the ruff of a bird. 5. a tippet feather or something similar used in dressing some artificial angling flies. [C14: perhaps from TIP[1]]
tipple[1] ('tɪpᵊl) *vb.* 1. to make a habit of taking (alcoholic drink), esp. in small quantities. ~*n.* 2. alcoholic drink. [C15: back formation from obsolete *tippler* tapster, of unknown origin] —'**tippler** *n.*
tipple[2] ('tɪpᵊl) *n.* 1. a device for overturning ore trucks, mine cars, etc., so that they discharge their load. 2. a place at which such trucks are tipped and unloaded. ~*vb.* 3. *Northern English dialect.* to fall or cause to fall. [C19: from *tipple* to overturn, from TIP[2]]
tippler ('tɪplə) *n.* (*sometimes cap.*) 1. a variety of domestic pigeon bred mainly for flying. Also called: **high-flying tippler.** 2. a domestic fancy pigeon of a smaller rounder type kept mainly for exhibition. Usual name: **show tippler.** [C19: from TIPPLE[2] + -ER[1]]
tipstaff ('tɪpˌstɑːf) *n.* 1. a court official having miscellaneous duties, mostly concerned with the maintenance of order in court. 2. a metal-tipped staff formerly used as a symbol of office. [C16 *tipped staff;* see TIP[1], STAFF[1]]
tipster ('tɪpstə) *n.* a person who sells tips on horse racing, the stock market, etc.
tipsy ('tɪpsɪ) *adj.* **-sier, -siest.** 1. slightly drunk. 2. slightly tilted or tipped; askew. [C16: from TIP[2]] —'**tipsily** *adv.* —'**tipsiness** *n.*
tipsy cake *n. Brit.* a kind of trifle made from a sponge cake soaked with white wine or sherry and decorated with almonds and crystallized fruit.
tip-tilted *adj.* (of a nose) slightly turned up.
tiptoe ('tɪpˌtəʊ) *vb.* **-toes, -toeing, -toed.** (*intr.*) 1. to walk with the heels off the ground and the weight supported by the ball of the foot and the toes. 2. to walk silently or stealthily. ~*n.* 3. **on tiptoe. a.** on the tips of the toes or on the ball of the foot and the toes. **b.** eagerly anticipating something. **c.** stealthily or silently. ~*adv.* 4. on tiptoe. ~*adj.* 5. walking or standing on tiptoe. 6. stealthy or silent.
tiptop (ˌtɪp'tɒp) *adj., adv.* 1. at the highest point of health, excellence, etc. 2. at the topmost point. ~*n.* 3. the best in quality. 4. the topmost point.
tip truck *n.* another name for **tipper truck.**
tip-up *adj.* (*prenominal*) able to be turned upwards around a hinge or pivot: *a tip-up seat.*
TIR (on continental lorries) *abbrev. for* Transports Internationaux Routiers. [French: International Road Transport]
tirade (taɪ'reɪd) *n.* 1. a long angry speech or denunciation. 2. *Prosody, rare.* a speech or passage dealing with a single theme. [C19: from French, literally: a pulling, from Italian *tirata,* from *tirare* to pull, of uncertain origin]
tire[1] ('taɪə) *vb.* 1. (*tr.*) to reduce the energy of, esp. by exertion; weary. 2. (*tr.; often passive*) to reduce the tolerance of; bore or irritate: *I'm tired of the children's chatter.* 3. (*intr.*) to become wearied or bored; flag. [Old English *tēorian,* of unknown origin] —'**tiring** *adj.*
tire[2] ('taɪə) *n., vb.* the U.S. spelling of **tyre.**
tire[3] ('taɪə) *vb., n.* an archaic word for **attire.**
tired ('taɪəd) *adj.* 1. weary; fatigued. 2. (foll. by *of*) **a.** having lost interest in; bored: *I'm tired of playing cards.* **b.** having lost patience with; exasperated by: *I'm tired of his eternal excuses.* 3. hackneyed; stale: *the same tired old jokes.* 4. **tired and emotional.** a euphemism for slightly drunk. Sometimes shortened to **T & E.** —'**tiredly** *adv.* —'**tiredness** *n.*
tireless ('taɪəlɪs) *adj.* unable to be tired; indefatigable. —'**tirelessly** *adv.* —'**tirelessness** *n.*
tiresome ('taɪəsəm) *adj.* boring and irritating; irksome. —'**tiresomely** *adv.* —'**tiresomeness** *n.*
tirewoman ('taɪəˌwʊmən) *n., pl.* **-women.** an obsolete term for **lady's maid.** [C17: see TIRE[3]]
tiring room *n. Archaic.* a dressing room in a theatre.
tiro ('taɪrəʊ) *n., pl.* **-ros.** a variant spelling of **tyro.**
Tirolese (ˌtɪrə'liːz) *or* **Tirolean** (ˌtɪrə'lɪən) *adj., n.* variants of **Tyrolese.**
'tis (tɪz) *Poetic or dialect. contraction of* it is.
tisane (tɪ'zæn) *n.* an infusion of dried or fresh leaves or flowers, as camomile. [C19: from French, from Latin *ptisana* barley water; see PTISAN]
Tishah b'Av (ti'ʃa bə'av) *n. Judaism.* the ninth day of the month of Av observed as a fast day in memory of the destruction of the First and Second Temples in ancient Jerusalem.
Tishri (tɪʃ'riː) *n.* (in the Jewish calendar) the seventh month of the year according to biblical reckoning and the first month of the civil year, usually falling within September and October. [from Hebrew]
tissue ('tɪsjuː, 'tɪʃuː) *n.* 1. a part of an organism consisting of a large number of cells having a similar structure and function:

connective tissue; nerve tissue. **2.** a thin piece of soft absorbent paper, usually of two or more layers, used as a disposable handkerchief, towel, etc. **3.** See **tissue paper. 4.** an interwoven series: *a tissue of lies.* **5.** a woven cloth, esp. of a light gauzy nature, originally interwoven with threads of gold or silver. *~vb. (tr.)* **6.** *Rare.* to weave into tissue. **7.** to decorate or clothe with tissue or tissue paper. [C14: from Old French *tissu* woven cloth, from *tistre* to weave, from Latin *texere*]

tissue culture *n.* **1.** the growth of small pieces of animal or plant tissue in a sterile controlled medium. **2.** the tissue produced as a result of this process.

tissue paper *n.* very thin soft delicate paper used to wrap breakable goods, as decoration, etc.

tissue type *n.* the inherited chemical characteristics of the bodily tissue of an individual that are recognized and, when grafted, are accepted or rejected by the immune system of another individual. The tissue type is determined by the histocompatibility antigens.

tit[1] (tɪt) *n.* **1.** any of numerous small active Old World songbirds of the family *Paridae* (titmice), esp. those of the genus *Parus* (bluetit, great tit, etc.). They have a short bill and feed on insects and seeds. **2.** any of various similar small birds. **3.** *Archaic or dialect.* a worthless or worn-out horse; nag. [C16: perhaps of imitative origin, applied to small animate or inanimate objects; compare Icelandic *tittr* pin]

tit[2] (tɪt) *n.* **1.** *Slang.* a female breast. **2.** a teat or nipple. **3.** *Derogatory.* a girl or young woman. **4.** *Taboo slang.* a despicable or unpleasant person: often used as a term of address. [Old English *titt;* related to Middle Low German *title,* Norwegian *titta*]

Tit. *Bible. abbrev. for* Titus.

titan (ˈtaɪtᵊn) *n.* a person of great strength or size. [C17: from *Titan,* a primordial Greek god]

titanate (ˈtaɪtəˌneɪt) *n.* any salt or ester of titanic acid.

Titanesque (ˌtaɪtəˈnɛsk) *adj.* resembling a Titan; gigantic.

titania (taɪˈteɪnɪə) *n.* another name for **titanium dioxide.**

titanic[1] (taɪˈtænɪk) *adj.* of or containing titanium, esp. in the tetravalent state.

titanic[2] (taɪˈtænɪk) *adj.* possessing or requiring colossal strength: *a titanic battle.* —**tiˈtanically** *adv.*

titanic acid *n.* any of various white substances regarded as hydrated forms of titanium dioxide, typical formulas being H_4TiO_4 and H_2TiO_3.

titanic oxide *n.* another name for **titanium dioxide.**

titaniferous (ˌtaɪtəˈnɪfərəs) *adj.* of or containing titanium; bearing titanium: *a titaniferous ore.*

Titanism (ˈtaɪtəˌnɪzəm) *n.* a spirit of defiance of and rebellion against authority, social convention, etc.

titanite (ˈtaɪtəˌnaɪt) *n.* another name for **sphene.** [C19: from German *Titanit,* so named because it contained TITANIUM]

titanium (taɪˈteɪnɪəm) *n.* a strong malleable white metallic element, which is very corrosion-resistant and occurs in rutile and ilmenite. It is used in the manufacture of strong lightweight alloys, esp. aircraft parts. Symbol: Ti; atomic no.: 22; atomic wt.: 47.90; valency: 2, 3, or 4; relative density: 4.54; melting pt.: 1675°C; boiling pt.: 3620°C. [C18: New Latin; see TITAN, -IUM]

titanium dioxide *n.* a white insoluble powder occurring naturally as rutile and used chiefly as a pigment of high covering power and durability. Formula: TiO_2. Also called: **titanium oxide, titanic oxide, titania.**

titanosaur (taɪˈtænəˌsɔː) *n.* any of various herbivorous quadrupedal dinosaurs of the family *Titanosauridae,* of Jurassic and Cretaceous times: suborder *Sauropoda* (sauropods). [C19: from New Latin *Tītānosaurus,* from Greek *Titan;* see TITAN + -SAUR]

titanothere (taɪˈtænəˌθɪə) *n.* any of various very large horse-like perissodactyl mammals of the genera *Menodus, Brontotherium,* etc., that lived in Eocene and Oligocene times in North America. See also **chalicothere.** [C19: from New Latin *Tītānotherium* giant animal, from Greek *Titan* + *thēr* wild beast]

titanous (taɪˈtænəs) *adj.* of or containing titanium, esp. in the trivalent state.

titarakura (ˈtiːtɑːrəˌkuːrə) *n. N.Z.* another name for **bully**[2].

titbit (ˈtɪtˌbɪt) *or esp. U.S.* **tidbit** *n.* **1.** a tasty small piece of food; dainty. **2.** a pleasing scrap of anything, such as scandal. [C17: perhaps from dialect *tid* tender, of obscure origin]

titchy *or* **tichy** (ˈtɪtʃɪ) *adj.* **titchier, titchiest.** *Brit. slang.* very small; tiny. [C20: from *tich* or *titch* a small person, from *Little Tich,* the stage name of Harry Relph (1867–1928), English actor noted for his small stature]

titer (ˈtaɪtə, ˈtiː-) *n.* the usual U.S. spelling of **titre.**

titfer (ˈtɪtfə) *n. Brit. slang.* a hat. [from rhyming slang *tit for tat* hat]

tit for tat *n.* an equivalent given in return or retaliation; blow for blow. [C16: from earlier *tip for tap*]

tithable (ˈtaɪðəbᵊl) *adj.* **1.** (until 1936) liable to pay tithes. **2.** (of property, etc.) subject to the payment of tithes.

tithe (taɪð) *n.* **1.** *(often pl.) Christianity.* a tenth part of agricultural or other produce, personal income, or profits, contributed either voluntarily or as a tax for the support of the church or clergy or for charitable purposes. **2.** any levy, esp. of one tenth. **3.** a tenth or very small part of anything. *~vb.* **4.** *(tr.)* **a.** to exact or demand a tithe or tithes from (an individual or group). **b.** to levy a tithe upon (a crop or amount of produce, etc.). **5.** *(intr.)* to pay a tithe or tithes. [Old English *teogoth;* related to Old Frisian *tegotha,* Old Saxon *tegotho,* Old High German *zehando,* Old Norse *tīundi,* Gothic *taihunda*] —**ˈtither** *n.*

tithe barn *n.* a large barn where, formerly, the agricultural tithe of a parish was stored.

tithing (ˈtaɪðɪŋ) *n. English history.* **1. a.** a tithe; tenth. **b.** the exacting or paying of tithes. **2.** a company of ten householders in the system of frankpledge. **3.** a rural division, originally regarded as a tenth of a hundred.

titi[1] (ˈtiːtiː) *n., pl.* **-tis.** any of several small omnivorous New World monkeys of the genus *Callicebus,* of South America, having long beautifully coloured fur and a long nonprehensile tail. [via Spanish from Aymaran, literally: little cat]

titi[2] (ˈtiːtiː) *n., pl.* **-tis.** any of various evergreen shrubs or small trees of the family *Cyrillaceae* of the southern U.S., esp. the leatherwood and *Cliftonia monophyllia,* which has white or pinkish fragrant flowers. [C19: of American Indian origin]

Titian (ˈtɪʃən) *adj. (sometimes not cap.)* reddish-gold, like the hair colour used in many of the works of the Italian painter Titian (?1490–1576). Also called: **Titian red.**

titillate (ˈtɪtɪˌleɪt) *vb. (tr.)* **1.** to arouse, tease, interest, or excite pleasurably and often superficially. **2.** to cause a tickling or tingling sensation in, esp. by touching. [C17: from Latin *tītillāre*] —**ˈtitilˌlating** *adj.* —**ˈtitilˌlatingly** *adv.* —**ˌtitilˈlation** *n.* —**ˈtitilˌlative** *adj.*

titivate *or* **tittivate** (ˈtɪtɪˌveɪt) *vb.* **1.** to smarten up (oneself or another), as by making up, doing the hair, etc. **2.** *(tr.)* to smarten up (a thing): *to titivate a restaurant.* **3.** *(tr.) Rare.* another word for **titillate.** [C19: earlier *tidivate,* perhaps based on TIDY and CULTIVATE] —**ˌtitiˈvation** *or* **ˌtittiˈvation** *n.* —**ˈtitiˌvator** *or* **ˈtittiˌvator** *n.*

titlark (ˈtɪtˌlɑːk) *n.* another name for **pipit,** esp. the meadow pipit (*Anthus pratensis*). [C17: from TIT[1] + LARK[1]]

title (ˈtaɪtᵊl) *n.* **1.** the distinctive name of a work of art, musical or literary composition, etc. **2.** a descriptive name, caption, or heading of a section of a book, speech, etc. **3.** See **title page. 4.** a name or epithet signifying rank, office, or function. **5.** a formal designation, such as *Mr, Mrs,* or *Miss.* **6.** an appellation designating nobility. **7.** *Films.* **a.** short for **subtitle** (sense 2). **b.** written material giving credits in a film or television programme. **8.** *Sport.* a championship. **9.** *Property law.* **a.** the legal right to possession of property, esp. real property. **b.** the basis of such right. **c.** the documentary evidence of such right: *title deeds.* **10.** *Law.* **a.** the heading or a division of a statute, book of law, etc. **b.** the heading of a suit or action at law. **11. a.** any customary or established right. **b.** a claim based on such a right. **12.** a definite spiritual charge or office in the church, without appointment to which a candidate for holy orders cannot lawfully be ordained. **13.** *R.C. Church.* a titular church. *~vb.* **14.** *(tr.)* to give a title to. [C13: from Old French, from Latin *titulus*]

titled (ˈtaɪtᵊld) *adj.* having a title: *the titled classes.*

title deed *n.* a deed or document evidencing a person's legal right or title to property, esp. real property.

titleholder (ˈtaɪtᵊlˌhəʊldə) *n.* a person who holds a title, esp. a sporting championship. —**ˈtitleˌholding** *adj.*

title page *n.* the page in a book that bears the title, author's name, publisher's imprint, date of publication, etc.

title role *n.* the role of the character after whom a play, etc., is named.

titman (ˈtɪtmən) *n., pl.* **-men.** (of pigs) the runt of a litter. [*tit-* (as in TITMOUSE) + MAN]

titmouse (ˈtɪtˌmaʊs) *n., pl.* **-mice.** *(usually pl.)* any small active songbird of the family *Paridae,* esp. those of the genus *Parus* (see **tit**[1]). [C14 *titemous,* from *tite* (see TIT[1]) + MOUSE]

Titoism (ˈtiːtəʊˌɪzəm) *n.* **1.** the variant of Communism practised by the Yugoslav statesman Tito (1892–1980), characterized by independence from the Soviet bloc and neutrality in East-West controversies, a considerable amount of decentralization, and a large degree of worker control of industries. **2.** any variant of Communism resembling Titoism. —**ˈTitoist** *n., adj.*

titrant (ˈtaɪtrənt) *n.* the solution in a titration that is added from a burette to a measured quantity of another solution.

titrate (ˈtaɪtreɪt) *vb. (tr.)* to measure the volume or concentration of (a solution) by titration. [C19: from French *titrer;* see TITRE] —**tiˈtratable** *adj.*

titration (taɪˈtreɪʃən) *n.* an operation, used in volumetric analysis, in which a measured amount of one solution is added to a known quantity of another solution until the reaction between the two is complete. If the concentration of one solution is known, that of the other can be calculated.

titre *or U.S.* **titer** (ˈtaɪtə, ˈtiː-) *n.* **1. a.** the concentration of a solution as determined by titration. **b.** the minimum quantity of a solution required to complete a reaction in a titration. **2.** the quantity of antibody present in an organism. [C19: from French *titre* proportion of gold or silver in an alloy, from Old French *title* TITLE]

titter (ˈtɪtə) *vb.* **1.** *(intr.)* to snigger, esp. derisively or in a suppressed way. **2.** *(tr.)* to express by tittering. *~n.* **3.** a suppressed laugh, chuckle, or snigger. [C17: of imitative origin] —**ˈtitterer** *n.* —**ˈtittering** *adj.* —**ˈtitteringly** *adv.*

tittivate (ˈtɪtɪˌveɪt) *vb.* a less common spelling of **titivate.**

tittle (ˈtɪtᵊl) *n.* **1.** a small mark in printing or writing, esp. a diacritic. **2.** a jot; particle. [C14: from Medieval Latin *titulus* label, from Latin: TITLE]

tittle-tattle *n.* **1.** idle chat or gossip. ~*vb.* **2.** (*intr.*) to chatter or gossip. —ˈ**tittle-ˌtattler** *n.*

tittup (ˈtɪtəp) *vb.* **-tups, -tupping, -tupped** *or U.S.* **-tups, -tuping, -tuped. 1.** (*intr.*) to prance or frolic. ~*n.* **2.** a caper. **3.** the sound made by high-heeled shoes. [C18 (in the sense: a horse's gallop): probably imitative]

titubation (ˌtɪtjuˈbeɪʃən) *n. Pathol.* **1.** a disordered gait characterized by stumbling or staggering, often caused by a lesion of the cerebellum. **2.** Also called: **lingual titubation.** stuttering or stammering. [C17: from Latin *titubātiō,* from *titubāre* to reel]

titular (ˈtɪtjʊlə) *or* **titulary** (ˈtɪtjʊlərɪ) *adj.* **1.** of, relating to, or of the nature of a title. **2.** in name only. **3.** bearing a title. **4.** giving a title. **5.** *R.C. Church.* designating any of certain churches in Rome to whom cardinals or bishops are attached as their nominal incumbents. ~*n., pl.* **-lars** *or* **-laries. 6.** the bearer of a title. **7.** the bearer of a nominal office. [C18: from French *titulaire,* from Latin *titulus* TITLE] —ˈ**titularly** *adv.*

Tiv (tɪv) *n.* **1.** (*pl.* **Tivs** *or* **Tiv**) a member of a Negroid people of W Africa, living chiefly in the savanna of the Benue area of S Nigeria and noted by anthropologists for having no chiefs. **2.** the language of this people, belonging to the Benue-Congo branch of the Niger-Congo family.

tizzy (ˈtɪzɪ) *n., pl.* **-zies.** *Informal.* a state of confusion, anxiety, or excitement. Also called: **tizz, tiz-woz** (ˈtɪzˌwɒz). [C19: of unknown origin]

T-joint *n.* a right-angled joint, esp. one in wood, making the shape of the letter T.

T-junction *n.* a road junction in which one road joins another at right angles but does not cross it.

TKO *Boxing. abbrev. for* technical knockout.

Tl *the chemical symbol for* thallium.

TLC *Informal. abbrev. for* tender loving care.

Tlingit (ˈtlɪŋgɪt) *n.* **1.** (*pl.* **-gits** *or* **-git**) a member of a seafaring group of North American Indian peoples inhabiting S Alaska and N British Columbia. **2.** the language of these peoples, belonging to the Na-Dene phylum.

TLS *abbrev. for* Times Literary Supplement.

T-lymphocyte *n.* a type of lymphocyte that matures in the thymus gland and has an important role in the immune response. There are several subclasses: **killer T-cells** are responsible for killing cells that are infected by a virus; **helper T-cells** induce other cells (**B-lymphocytes**) to produce antibodies. Also called: **T-cell.**

Tm *the chemical symbol for* thulium.

TM *abbrev. for* transcendental meditation.

T-man *n., pl.* **-men.** *U.S.* a law-enforcement agent of the U.S. Treasury.

tmesis (təˈmiːsɪs, ˈmiːsɪs) *n.* interpolation of a word or group of words between the parts of a compound word. [C16: via Latin from Greek, literally: a cutting, from *temnein* to cut]

TN 1. *abbrev. for* Tennessee. ~ **2.** *international car registration for* Tunisia.

tng *abbrev. for* training.

TNT *n.* 2,4,6-trinitrotoluene; a yellow solid: used chiefly as a high explosive and is also an intermediate in the manufacture of dyestuffs. Formula: $CH_3C_6H_2(NO_2)_3$.

T-number *or* **T number** *n. Photog.* a function of the f-number of a camera lens that takes into account the amount of light actually transmitted by the lens. [from *T(otal Light Transmission) Number*]

to (tuː; *unstressed before vowels* tʊ; *unstressed before consonants* tə) *prep.* **1.** used to indicate the destination of the subject or object of an action: *he climbed to the top.* **2.** used to mark the indirect object of a verb in a sentence: *telling stories to children.* **3.** used to mark the infinitive of a verb: *he wanted to go.* **4.** as far as; until: *working from Monday to Friday.* **5.** used to indicate equality: *16 ounces to the pound.* **6.** against; upon; onto: *put your ear to the wall.* **7.** before the hour of: *five to four.* **8.** accompanied by: *dancing to loud music.* **9.** as compared with, as against: *the score was eight to three.* **10.** used to indicate a resulting condition: *he tore her dress to shreds; they starved to death.* **11.** a dialect word for **at:** *he's to town; where's it to.* ~*adv.* **12.** towards a fixed position, esp. (of a door) closed. [Old English *tō;* related to Old Frisian, Old Saxon *to,* Old High German *zuo,* Latin *do-* as in *dōnec* until]

▷**Usage.** In formal usage, *to* is always used with an infinitive and never omitted as in *come see the show.* The use of *and* instead of *to* (*try and come*) is very common in informal speech but is avoided by careful writers.

toad (təʊd) *n.* **1.** any anuran amphibian of the class *Bufonidae,* such as *Bufo bufo* (**common toad**) of Europe. They are similar to frogs but are more terrestrial, having a drier warty skin. **2.** any of various similar amphibians of different families. **3.** a loathsome person. [Old English *tādige,* of unknown origin; see TADPOLE] —ˈ**toadish** *or* ˈ**toadˌlike** *adj.*

toadeater (ˈtəʊdˌiːtə) *n.* a rare word for **toady** (sense 1). [C17: originally a mountebank's assistant who would pretend to eat toads (believed to be poisonous), hence a servile flatterer, toady]

toadfish (ˈtəʊdˌfɪʃ) *n., pl.* **-fish** *or* **-fishes.** any spiny-finned bottom-dwelling marine fish of the family *Batrachoididae,* of tropical and temperate seas, having a flattened tapering body and a wide mouth.

toadflax (ˈtəʊdˌflæks) *n.* any of various scrophulariaceous plants of the genus *Linaria,* esp. *L. vulgaris,* having narrow leaves and spurred two-lipped yellow-orange flowers. Also called: **butter-and-eggs.**

toad-in-the-hole *n. Brit. and Austral.* a dish made of sausages baked in a batter.

toad spit *or* **spittle** *n.* another name for **cuckoo spit.**

toadstone (ˈtəʊdˌstəʊn) *n.* an amygdaloidal basalt occurring in the limestone regions of Derbyshire. [C18: perhaps from a supposed resemblance to a toad's spotted skin]

toadstool (ˈtəʊdˌstuːl) *n.* (*not in technical use*) any basidiomycetous fungus with a capped spore-producing body that is poisonous. Compare **mushroom** (sense 1a). [C14: from TOAD + STOOL]

toady (ˈtəʊdɪ) *n., pl.* **toadies. 1.** a person who flatters and ingratiates himself in a servile way; sycophant. **2.** *Austral.* an informal name for **toadfish.** ~*vb.* **toadies, toadying, toadied. 3.** to fawn on and flatter (someone). [C19: shortened from TOAD-EATER] —ˈ**toadyish** *adj.* —ˈ**toadyism** *n.*

to and fro *adj.,* **to-and-fro** *adv.* **1.** back and forth. **2.** here and there. —ˈ**toing and** ˈ**froing** *n.*

toast[1] (təʊst) *n.* **1.** sliced bread browned by exposure to heat, usually under a grill, over a fire, or in a toaster. ~*vb.* **2.** (*tr.*) to brown under a grill or over a fire: *to toast cheese.* **3.** to warm or be warmed in a similar manner: *to toast one's hands by the fire.* [C14: from Old French *toster,* from Latin *tōstus* parched, baked from *torrēre* to dry with heat; see THIRST, TORRID] —ˈ**toasty** *adj.*

toast[2] (təʊst) *n.* **1.** a tribute or proposal of health, success, etc., given to a person or thing by a company of people and marked by raising glasses and drinking together. **2.** a person or thing honoured by such a tribute or proposal. **3.** (esp. formerly) an attractive woman to whom such tributes are frequently made: *she was the toast of the town.* ~*vb.* **4.** to propose or drink a toast to (a person or thing). **5.** (*intr.*) to add vocal effects to a prerecorded track: a disc-jockey technique. See also **rap**[1] (sense 6). [C17 (in the sense: a lady to whom the company is asked to drink): from TOAST[1], from the idea that the name of the lady would flavour the drink like a piece of spiced toast] —ˈ**toaster** *n.*

toaster (ˈtəʊstə) *n.* a device for toasting bread, usually electric, and often equipped with an automatic timer.

toastmaster (ˈtəʊstˌmɑːstə) *n.* a person who introduces after-dinner speakers, proposes or announces toasts, etc., at public or formal dinners. —ˈ**toastˌmistress** *fem. n.*

toast rack *n.* a small stand consisting of a usually oblong base with a number of open-sided partitions between which pieces of toast may be stood upright.

toasty *or* **toastie** (ˈtəʊstɪ) *n., pl.* **toasties.** a toasted sandwich.

Tob. *Bible. abbrev. for* Tobit.

tobacco (təˈbækəʊ) *n., pl.* **-cos** *or* **-coes. 1.** any of numerous solanaceous plants of the genus *Nicotiana,* having mildly narcotic properties, tapering hairy leaves, and tubular or funnel-shaped fragrant flowers. The species *N. tabacum* is cultivated as the chief source of commercial tobacco. **2.** the leaves of certain of these plants dried and prepared for snuff, chewing, or smoking. [C16: from Spanish *tabaco,* perhaps from Taino: leaves rolled for smoking, assumed by the Spaniards to be the name of the plant] —**toˈbaccoless** *adj.*

tobacco mosaic virus *n.* the virus that causes mosaic disease in tobacco and related plants: its discovery in 1892 provided the first evidence of the existence of viruses. Abbrev.: **TMV.**

tobacconist (təˈbækənɪst) *n. Chiefly Brit.* a person or shop that sells tobacco, cigarettes, pipes, etc.

-to-be *adj.* (*in combination*) about to be; future: *a mother-to-be; the bride-to-be.*

toboggan (təˈbɒgən) *n.* **1.** a light wooden frame on runners used for sliding over snow and ice. **2.** a long narrow sledge made of a thin board curved upwards and backwards at the front. ~*vb.* **-gans, -ganing, -ganed.** (*intr.*) **3.** to ride on a toboggan. [C19: from Canadian French, from Algonquian; related to Abnaki *udābāgan*] —**toˈbogganer** *or* **toˈbogganist** *n.*

toby (ˈtəʊbɪ) *n., pl.* **-bies.** *N.Z.* a water stopcock at the boundary of a street and house section.

toby jug (ˈtəʊbɪ) *n.* a beer mug or jug typically in the form of a stout seated man wearing a three-cornered hat and smoking a pipe. Also called: **toby.** [C19: from the familiar form of the Christian name *Tobias*]

toccata (təˈkɑːtə) *n.* a rapid keyboard composition for organ, harpsichord, etc., dating from the baroque period, usually in a rhythmically free style. [C18: from Italian, literally: touched, from *toccare* to play (an instrument), TOUCH]

Tocharian *or* **Tokharian** (tɒˈkɑːrɪən) *n.* **1.** a member of an Asian people with a complex material culture, sometimes thought to be of European origin, who lived in the Tarim Basin in present-day NW China until overcome by the Uighurs around 800 A.D. **2.** the language of this people, known from records in a N Indian script of the 7th and 8th centuries A.D. It belongs to the Indo-European family, is regarded as forming an independent branch, and shows closer affinities with the W or European group than with the E or Indo-Iranian group. The language is recorded in two dialects, known as **Tocharian A** and **Tocharian B.** [C20: ultimately from Greek *Tokharoi,* name of uncertain origin]

tocher (ˈtɒxər) *Scot.* ~*n.* **1.** a dowry. ~*vb.* (*tr.*) **2.** to give a dowry to. [C15: from Irish Gaelic *tochar;* Scot. Gaelic *tochradh*]

tocology *or* **tokology** (tɒˈkɒlədʒɪ) *n.* the branch of medicine concerned with childbirth; obstetrics. [C19: from Greek *tokos* childbirth, from *tiktein* to bear]

tocopherol (tɒˈkɒfəˌrɒl) *n. Biochem.* any of a group of fat-soluble alcohols that occur in wheat-germ oil, watercress, lettuce, egg yolk, etc. They are thought to be necessary for healthy human reproduction. Also called: **vitamin E.** [C20: from *toco-*, from Greek *tokos* offspring (see TOCOLOGY) + *-pher-*, from *pherein* to bear + -OL[1]]

tocsin (ˈtɒksɪn) *n.* **1.** an alarm or warning signal, esp. one sounded on a bell. **2.** an alarm bell. [C16: from French, from Old French *toquassen,* from Old Provençal *tocasenh,* from *tocar* to TOUCH + *senh* bell, from Latin *signum*]

tod[1] (tɒd) *n. Brit.* a unit of weight, used for wool, etc., usually equal to 28 pounds. [C15: probably related to Frisian *todde* rag, Old High German *zotta* tuft of hair]

tod[2] (tɒd) *n.* **on one's tod.** *Brit. slang.* on one's own. [C19: rhyming slang *Tod Sloan/alone,* after *Tod* Sloan, a jockey]

tod[3] (tɒd) *n.* a Scot. and northern English dialect word for a **fox.** [C12: of unknown origin]

today (təˈdeɪ) *n.* **1.** this day, as distinct from yesterday or tomorrow. **2.** the present age: *children of today.* ~*adv.* **3.** during or on this day. **4.** nowadays. [Old English *tō dæge,* literally: on this day, from TO + *dæge,* dative of *dæg* DAY]

toddle (ˈtɒdəl) *vb.* (*intr.*) **1.** to walk with short unsteady steps, as a child does when learning to walk. **2.** (foll. by *off*) *Jocular.* to depart. **3.** (foll. by *round, over,* etc.) *Jocular.* to stroll; amble. ~*n.* **4.** the act or an instance of toddling. [C16 (Scottish and northern English): of obscure origin]

toddler (ˈtɒdlə) *n.* **1.** a young child, usually one between the ages of one and two and a half. **2.** (*modifier*) designed or suitable for a toddler: *toddler suits.*

toddy (ˈtɒdɪ) *n., pl.* **-dies.** **1.** a drink made from spirits, esp. whisky, with hot water, sugar, and usually lemon juice. **2. a.** the sap of various palm trees (**toddy** or **wine palms**), used as a beverage. **b.** the liquor prepared from this sap. **3.** (in Malaysia) a milky-white sour alcoholic drink made from fermented coconut milk, drunk chiefly by Indians. [C17: from Hindi *tārī* juice of the palmyra palm, from *tār* palmyra palm, from Sanskrit *tāra,* probably of Dravidian origin]

to-do (təˈduː) *n., pl.* **-dos.** a commotion, fuss, or quarrel.

tody (ˈtəʊdɪ) *n., pl.* **-dies.** any small bird of the family *Todidae* of the West Indies, having a red-and-green plumage and long straight bill: order *Coraciiformes* (kingfishers, etc.). [C18: from French *todier,* from Latin *todus* small bird]

toe (təʊ) *n.* **1.** any one of the digits of the foot. **2.** the corresponding part in other vertebrates. **3.** the part of a shoe, sock, etc., covering the toes. **4.** anything resembling a toe in shape or position. **5.** the front part of the head of a golf club, hockey stick, etc. **6.** the lower bearing of a vertical shaft assembly. **7.** the tip of a cam follower that engages the cam profile. **8. dip one's toe** (*or* **toes**) **in.** *Informal.* to begin doing or try something new or unfamiliar. **9. on one's toes.** alert. **10. tread on someone's toes.** to offend or insult a person, esp. by trespassing on his field of responsibility. **11. turn up one's toes.** *Informal.* to die. **12.** *Austral. slang.* speed: *a player with plenty of toe.* ~*vb.* **toes, toeing, toed.** **13.** (*tr.*) to touch, kick, or mark with the toe. **14.** (*tr.*) *Golf.* to strike (the ball) with the toe of the club. **15.** (*tr.*) to drive (a nail, spike, etc.) obliquely. **16.** (*intr.*) to walk with the toes pointing in a specified direction: *to toe inwards.* **17. toe the line.** to conform to expected standards, attitudes, etc. [Old English *tā;* related to Old Frisian *tāne,* Old Norse *tā,* Old High German *zēha,* Latin *digitus* finger] —ˈ**toe**ˌ**like** *adj.*

toea (ˈtəʊɑː) *n.* a monetary unit of Papua New Guinea; one-hundredth of a kina. [from a Papuan language]

toe and heel *n.* a technique used by racing drivers while changing gear on sharp bends, in which the brake is operated by the toe (or heel) of the right foot while the heel (or toe) simultaneously operates the accelerator.

toecap (ˈtəʊˌkæp) *n.* a reinforced covering for the toe of a boot or shoe.

toe crack *n. Vet. science.* a sand crack occurring on the forepart of the hind foot of a horse.

toed (təʊd) *adj.* **1.** having a part resembling a toe. **2.** (of a vertical or oblique member of a timber frame) fixed by nails driven in at the foot. **3.** (*in combination*) having a toe or toes as specified: *five-toed; thick-toed.*

toe dance *n.* **1.** a dance performed on tiptoe. ~*vb.* **toe-dance.** **2.** (*intr.*) *Ballet.* to dance on pointes. —**toe dancer** *n.*

toehold (ˈtəʊˌhəʊld) *n.* **1.** a small foothold to facilitate climbing. **2.** any means of gaining access, support, etc.: *the socialist party gained a toehold in the local elections.* **3.** a wrestling hold in which the opponent's toe is held and his leg twisted against the joints.

toe-in *n.* a slight forward convergence given to the wheels of motor vehicles to improve steering and equalize tyre wear.

toenail (ˈtəʊˌneɪl) *n.* **1.** a thin horny translucent plate covering part of the dorsal surface of the end joint of each toe. **2.** *Carpentry.* a nail driven obliquely, as in joining one beam at right angles to another. **3.** *Printers' slang.* a parenthesis. ~*vb.* **4.** (*tr.*) *Carpentry.* to join (beams) by driving nails obliquely.

toerag (ˈtəʊˌræg) *n. Brit. slang.* a contemptible or despicable person. [C20: originally, a beggar, tramp: from the pieces of rag they wrapped round their feet]

toetoe (ˈtɔɪtɔɪ, ˈtəʊiːˌtəʊiː, ˌtəʊiːˈtəʊiː) *n.* See **toitoi**[1].

toey (ˈtəʊɪ) *adj. Austral. slang.* **1.** (of a person) nervous or anxious. **2.** *Rare.* (of a horse) eager to race.

toff (tɒf) *n. Brit. slang.* a rich, well-dressed, or upper-class person, esp. a man. [C19: perhaps variant of TUFT, nickname for a titled student at Oxford University, wearing a cap with a gold tassel]

toffee *or* **toffy** (ˈtɒfɪ) *n., pl.* **-fees** *or* **-fies.** **1.** a sweet made from sugar or treacle boiled with butter, nuts, etc. **2. for toffee.** (preceded by *can't*) *Informal.* to be incompetent at a specified activity: *he can't sing for toffee.* [C19: variant of earlier TAFFY]

toffee-apple *n.* an apple fixed on a stick and coated with a thin layer of toffee.

toffee-nosed *adj. Slang, chiefly Brit.* pretentious or supercilious; used esp. of snobbish people. [C20: perhaps coined as a pun on *toffy* stylish, grand: see TOFF]

toft (tɒft) *n. Brit. history.* **1.** a homestead. **2.** an entire holding, consisting of a homestead and the attached arable land. [Old English, from Old Norse *topt*]

tofu (ˈtəʊˌfuː) *n.* unfermented soya-bean curd, a food with a soft cheeselike consistency made from soya-bean milk. [from Japanese]

tog[1] (tɒg) *Informal.* ~*vb.* **togs, togging, togged.** **1.** (often foll. by *up* or *out*) to dress oneself, esp. in smart clothes. ~*n.* **2.** See **togs.** [C18: probably short for obsolete cant *togemans* coat, from Latin *toga* TOGA + *-mans,* of uncertain origin]

tog[2] (tɒg) *n.* **a.** a unit of thermal resistance used to measure the power of insulation of a fabric, garment, quilt, etc. The tog-value of an article is equal to ten times the temperature difference between its two faces, in degrees Celsius, when the flow of heat across it is equal to one watt per m^2. **b.** (*as modifier*): *tog-rating.* [C20: arbitrary coinage from TOG[1] (n.)]

toga (ˈtəʊgə) *n.* **1.** a garment worn by citizens of ancient Rome, consisting of a piece of cloth draped around the body. **2.** the official vestment of certain offices. [C16: from Latin, related to *tegere* to cover] —**togaed** (ˈtəʊgəd) *adj.*

toga praetexta (priːˈtɛkstə) *n.* (in ancient Rome) a toga with a broad purple border worn by certain magistrates and priests and by boys until they assumed the toga virilis. [Latin, literally: bordered toga]

toga virilis (vɪˈraɪlɪs) *n.* (in ancient Rome) the toga assumed by a youth at the age of 14 as a symbol of manhood and citizenship. [Latin, literally: manly (i.e., man's) toga]

together (təˈgɛðə) *adv.* **1.** with cooperation and interchange between constituent elements, members, etc.: *we worked together.* **2.** in or into contact or union with each other: *to stick papers together.* **3.** in or into one place or assembly; with each other: *the people are gathered together.* **4.** at the same time: *we left school together.* **5.** considered collectively or jointly: *all our wages put together couldn't buy that car.* **6.** continuously: *working for eight hours together.* **7.** closely, cohesively, or compactly united or held: *water will hold the dough together.* **8.** mutually or reciprocally: *to multiply seven and eight together.* **9.** *Informal.* organized: *to get things together.* **10. together with.** in addition to. ~*adj.* **11.** *Slang.* self-possessed, competent, and well-organized; mentally and emotionally stable: *she's a very together lady.* [Old English *tōgædre;* related to Old Frisian *togadera,* Middle High German *gater;* see GATHER]

▷**Usage.** See at **plus.**

togetherness (təˈgɛðənɪs) *n.* a feeling of closeness or affection from being united with other people.

toggery (ˈtɒgərɪ) *n. Informal.* clothes; togs.

toggle (ˈtɒgəl) *n.* **1.** a wooden peg or metal rod fixed crosswise through an eye at the end of a rope, chain, or cable, for fastening temporarily by insertion through an eye in another rope, chain, etc. **2.** a wooden or plastic bar-shaped button inserted through a loop for fastening. **3.** a pin inserted into a nautical knot to keep it secure. **4.** *Machinery.* a toggle joint or a device having such a joint. ~*vb.* **5.** (*tr.*) to supply or fasten with a toggle or toggles. [C18: of unknown origin] —ˈ**toggler** *n.*

toggle iron *n.* a whaling harpoon with a pivoting barb near its head to prevent a harpooned whale pulling free. Also called: **toggle harpoon.**

toggle joint *n.* a device consisting of two arms pivoted at a common joint and at their outer ends and used to apply pressure by straightening the angle between the two arms.

toggle switch *n.* **1.** an electric switch having a projecting lever that is manipulated in a particular way to open or close a circuit. **2.** a computer device that is used to turn a feature on or off.

Togolese (ˌtəʊgəˈliːz) *adj.* **1.** of or relating to Togo, a republic in W Africa, or its people. ~*n.* **2.** a native or inhabitant of Togo.

togs (tɒgz) *pl. n. Informal.* **1.** clothes. **2.** *Austral., N.Z., and Irish.* a swimming costume. [from TOG[1]]

toheroa (ˌtəʊəˈrəʊə) *n.* **1.** a bivalve mollusc, *Amphidesma* (or *Semele*) *ventricosum,* of New Zealand. **2.** a greenish soup made of this. [from Maori]

tohunga (ˈtɒhʊŋə, tɒˈhʊŋə) *n. N.Z.* a Maori priest, the repository of traditional lore.

toil[1] (tɔɪl) *n.* **1.** hard or exhausting work. **2.** an obsolete word for **strife.** ~*vb.* **3.** (*intr.*) to labour. **4.** (*intr.*) to progress with slow painful movements: *to toil up a hill.* **5.** (*tr.*) *Archaic.* to achieve by toil. [C13: from Anglo-French *toiler* to struggle, from Old French *toeillier* to confuse, from Latin *tudiculāre* to stir, from *tudicula* machine for bruising olives, from *tudes* a hammer, from *tundere* to beat] —'**toiler** *n.*

toil[2] (tɔɪl) *n.* **1.** (*often pl.*) a net or snare: *the toils of fortune had ensnared him.* **2.** *Archaic.* a trap for wild beasts. [C16: from Old French *toile,* from Latin *tēla* loom]

toile (twɑːl) *n.* **1.** a transparent linen or cotton fabric. **2.** a garment of exclusive design made up in cheap cloth so that alterations and experiments can be made. [C19: from French, from Latin *tēla* a loom]

toilet ('tɔɪlɪt) *n.* **1.** another word for **lavatory. 2.** the act of dressing and preparing oneself: *to make one's toilet.* **3.** a dressing table or the articles used when making one's toilet. **4.** *Rare.* costume. **5.** the cleansing of a wound, etc., after an operation or childbirth. [C16: from French *toilette* dress, from TOILE]

toilet paper *or* **tissue** *n.* thin absorbent paper, often wound in a roll round a cardboard cylinder (**toilet roll**), used for cleaning oneself after defecation or urination.

toiletry ('tɔɪlɪtrɪ) *n., pl.* **-ries.** an object or cosmetic used in making up, dressing, etc.

toilet set *n.* a matching set consisting of a hairbrush, comb, mirror, and clothes brush.

toilet soap *n.* a mild soap, often coloured and scented, used for washing oneself.

toilette (twɑː'lɛt; *French* twalɛt) *n. Usually literary or affected.* another word for **toilet** (sense 2). [C16: from French; see TOILET]

toilet training *n.* the process of teaching young children to control the timing of bladder and bowel movements and to use the lavatory.

toilet water *n.* a form of liquid perfume lighter than cologne. Compare **cologne.** Also called: **eau de toilette.**

toilsome ('tɔɪlsəm) *or* **toilful** *adj.* laborious. —'**toilsomely** *adv.* —'**toilsomeness** *n.*

toitoi[1] ('tɔɪtɔɪ) *or* **toetoe** *n., pl.* **-tois** *or* **-toes.** any of various tall grasses of the genus *Cortaderia* of New Zealand, with feathery fronds. [Maori]

toitoi[2] ('tɔɪtɔɪ) *n. N.Z.* another name for **bully**[2].

tokamak ('tɒkəˌmæk) *n. Physics.* a toroidal reactor used in thermonuclear experiments, in which strong axial magnetic fields keep the plasma from contacting the external walls. [C20: from Russian *to(roidál'naya) kám(era s) ak(siál'nym magnitnym pólem),* toroidal chamber with magnetic field]

tokay ('təʊkeɪ) *n.* a small gecko, *Gekko gecko,* of S and SE Asia, having a retractile claw at the tip of each digit. [from Malay *toke,* of imitative origin]

Tokay (təʊ'keɪ) *n.* **1.** a fine sweet wine made near Tokaj, Hungary. **2.** a variety of large sweet grape used to make this wine. **3.** a similar wine made elsewhere.

toke (təʊk) *Slang.* ~*n.* **1.** a draw on a cigarette, pipe, etc. ~*vb.* (*intr.*) **2.** to take a draw on a cigarette, pipe, etc.

token ('təʊkən) *n.* **1.** an indication, warning, or sign of something. **2.** a symbol or visible representation of something. **3.** something that indicates authority, proof, or authenticity. **4.** a metal or plastic disc, such as a substitute for currency for use in slot machines. **5.** a memento. **6.** a gift voucher that can be used as payment for goods of a specified value. **7.** (*modifier*) as a matter of form only; nominal: *a token increase in salary.* **8.** *Linguistics.* a symbol regarded as an individual concrete mark, not as a class of identical symbols. Compare **type** (sense 11). **9.** *Philosophy.* an individual instance: if the same sentence has different truth-values on different occasions of utterance the truth-value may be said to attach to the sentence-token. Compare **type** (sense 13). **10. by the same token.** moreover and for the same or a similar reason. ~*vb.* **11.** (*tr.*) to act or serve as a warning or symbol of; betoken. [Old English *tācen;* related to Old Frisian *tēken,* Old Saxon *tēkan,* Old High German *zeihhan,* Old Norse *teikn;* see TEACH]

token economy *n.* a type of psychotherapy in which the inmates of an institution are rewarded for good behaviour with tokens that can be exchanged for privileges.

tokenism ('təʊkəˌnɪzəm) *n.* the practice of making only a token effort or doing no more than the minimum, esp. in order to comply with a law. —ˌ**token'istic** *adj.*

token money *n.* coins of the regular issue having greater face value than the value of their metal content.

token payment *n.* a small payment made in acknowledgment of the existence of debt.

token strike *n.* a brief strike intended to convey strength of feeling on a disputed issue.

token vote *n.* a Parliamentary vote of money in which the amount quoted to aid discussion is not intended to be binding.

Tokharian (tɒ'kɑːrɪən) *n.* a variant spelling of **Tocharian.**

tokology (tɒ'kɒlədʒɪ) *n.* a variant spelling of **tocology.**

tokoloshe (ˌtɒkɒ'lɒʃ, -'lɒʃɪ) *n.* (in Bantu folklore) a malevolent mythical manlike animal of short stature. Also called: **tikoloshe.** [from Xhosa *uthikoloshe*]

tola ('təʊlə) *n.* a unit of weight, used in India, equal to 180 ser or 180 grains. [C17: from Hindi *tolā,* from Sanskrit *tulā* scale, from *tul* to weigh]

tolan ('təʊlæn) *or* **tolane** ('təʊleɪn) *n.* a white crystalline derivative of acetylene; diphenylacetylene; diphenylethyne. Formula: $C_6H_5C{:}CC_6H_5$. [C19: from TOL(UENE) + *-an* (see -ANE)]

tolbooth ('təʊlˌbuːθ, -ˌbuːð, 'tɒl-) *n.* a variant spelling of **tollbooth.**

tolbutamide (tɒl'bjuːtəˌmaɪd) *n.* a synthetic crystalline compound administered orally in the treatment of diabetes to lower blood glucose levels. Formula: $C_{12}H_{18}N_2O_3S$. [C20: from TOL(UYL) + BUT(YRIC ACID) + AMIDE]

told (təʊld) *vb.* **1.** the past tense and past participle of **tell**[1]. ~*adj.* **2.** See **all told.**

tole (təʊl) *n.* enamelled or lacquered metal ware, usually gilded, popular in the 18th century. [from French *tôle* sheet metal, from French (dialect): table, from Latin *tabula* table]

Toledo (tɒ'leɪdəʊ) *n.* a fine-tapered sword or sword blade. [after *Toledo,* a city in central Spain famous for steel and swords]

tolerable ('tɒlərəbᵊl) *adj.* **1.** able to be tolerated; endurable. **2.** permissible. **3.** *Informal.* fairly good. —'**tolerableness** *or* ˌ**tolera'bility** *n.* —'**tolerably** *adv.*

tolerance ('tɒlərəns) *n.* **1.** the state or quality of being tolerant. **2.** capacity to endure something, esp. pain or hardship. **3.** the permitted variation in some measurement or other characteristic of an object or workpiece. **4.** *Physiol.* the capacity of an organism to endure the effects of a poison or other substance, esp. after it has been taken over a prolonged period.

tolerant ('tɒlərənt) *adj.* **1.** able to tolerate the beliefs, actions, opinions, etc., of others. **2.** permissive. **3.** able to withstand extremes, as of heat and cold. **4.** *Med.* (of a patient) exhibiting tolerance to a drug. —'**tolerantly** *adv.*

tolerate ('tɒləˌreɪt) *vb.* (*tr.*) **1.** to treat with indulgence, liberality, or forbearance. **2.** to permit. **3.** to be able to bear; put up with. **4.** *Med.* to have tolerance for (a drug, poison, etc.). [C16: from Latin *tolerāre* sustain; related to THOLE[2]] —'**tolerative** *adj.* —'**tolerˌator** *n.*

toleration (ˌtɒlə'reɪʃən) *n.* **1.** the act or practice of tolerating. **2.** freedom to hold religious opinions that differ from the established or prescribed religion of a country. —ˌ**toler'ationism** *n.* —ˌ**toler'ationist** *n.*

tolidine ('tɒlɪˌdiːn) *n.* any of several isomeric compounds, esp. the *ortho-* isomer, which is a white or reddish crystalline substance used in the manufacture of dyes and resins. Formula: $(C_6H_3NH_2CH_3)_2$. [C19: from TOL(UENE) + -ID[3] + -INE[2]]

toll[1] (təʊl) *vb.* **1.** to ring or cause to ring slowly and recurrently. **2.** (*tr.*) to summon, warn, or announce by tolling. **3.** *U.S. and Canadian.* to decoy (game, esp. ducks). ~*n.* **4.** the act or sound of tolling. [C15: perhaps related to Old English *-tyllan,* as in *fortyllan* to attract]

toll[2] (təʊl, tɒl) *n.* **1. a.** an amount of money levied, esp. for the use of certain roads, bridges, etc., to cover the cost of maintenance. **b.** (*as modifier*): *toll road; toll bridge.* **2.** loss or damage incurred through an accident, disaster, etc.: *the war took its toll of the inhabitants.* **3.** Also called: '**tollage.** (formerly) the right to levy a toll. **4.** Also called: **toll charge.** *N.Z.* a charge for a telephone call beyond a free-dialling area. [Old English *toln;* related to Old Frisian *tolene,* Old High German *zol* toll, from Late Latin *telōnium* customs house, from Greek *telónion,* ultimately from *telos* tax]

tollbooth *or* **tolbooth** ('təʊlˌbuːθ, -ˌbuːð, 'tɒl-) *n.* **1.** a booth or kiosk at which a toll is collected. **2.** *Chiefly Scot., archaic.* **a.** a town hall or guildhall. **b.** a town jail. Often, a building fulfilling both these functions.

toll call *n.* **1.** *Brit. obsolete.* a short-distance trunk call. **2.** *U.S.* a long-distance telephone call at a rate higher than that for a local call. **3.** *N.Z.* a telephone call beyond a free-dialling area for which a charge is made.

tollgate ('təʊlˌgeɪt, 'tɒl-) *n.* a gate across a toll road or bridge at which travellers must stop and pay.

tollhouse ('təʊlˌhaʊs, 'tɒl-) *n.* a small house at a tollgate occupied by a toll collector.

tolly *or* **tollie** ('tɒlɪ) *n., pl.* **-lies.** *S. African.* a castrated calf. [C19: from Xhosa *ithole* calf on which the horns have begun to appear]

Toltec ('tɒltɛk) *n., pl.* **-tecs** *or* **-tec.** **1.** a member of a Central American Indian people who dominated the valley of Mexico from their capital Tula from about 950 to 1160 A.D., when the valley was overrun by the Aztecs. ~*adj. also* **Toltecan. 2.** of or relating to this people. [C19: from Spanish *tolteca,* of American Indian origin]

tolu (tɒ'luː) *n.* an aromatic balsam obtained from a South American tree, *Myroxylon balsamum.* See **balsam** (sense 1). [C17: after *Santiago de Tolu,* Colombia, from which it was exported]

toluate ('tɒljʊˌeɪt) *n.* any salt or ester of any of the three isomeric forms of toluic acid. [C19: from TOLU(IC ACID) + -ATE[1]]

toluene ('tɒljʊˌiːn) *n.* a colourless volatile flammable liquid with an odour resembling that of benzene, obtained from petroleum and coal tar and used as a solvent and in the manufacture of many organic chemicals. Formula: $C_6H_5CH_3$. [C19: from TOLU + -ENE, since it was previously obtained from tolu]

toluic acid (tɒ'luːɪk) *n.* a white crystalline derivative of toluene existing in three isomeric forms; methylbenzoic acid. The *ortho-* and *para-* isomers are used in synthetic resins and the *meta-* isomer is used as an insect repellent. Formula: $C_6H_4CH_3COOH$. [C19: from TOLU(ENE) + -IC]

toluidine (tɒ'ljuːɪˌdiːn) *n.* an amine derived from toluene existing in three isomeric forms; aminotoluene. The *ortho-* and *meta-* isomers are liquids and the *para-* isomer is a crystalline solid.

All three are used in making dyes. Formula: $C_6H_4CH_3NH_2$. [C19: from TOLU(ENE) + -IDE + -INE[2]]
toluol ('tɒljʊˌɒl) *n.* another name for **toluene.**
toluyl ('tɒljʊɪl) *n.* (*modifier*) of, consisting of, or containing any of three isomeric groups $CH_3C_6H_4CO$-, derived from a toluic acid by removal of the hydroxyl group: *toluyl group or radical.* [C19: from TOLU(ENE) + -YL]
tolyl ('tɒlɪl) *n.* **1.** (*modifier*) of, consisting of, or containing any of three isomeric groups, $CH_3C_6H_4$-, derived from toluene: *tolyl group or radical.* **2.** (*modifier*) another word for **benzyl.** Also called: **α-tolyl.** [C19: from TOLU (see TOLUENE) + -YL]
tom[1] (tɒm) *n.* **a.** the male of various animals, esp. the cat. **b.** (*as modifier*): *a tom turkey.* **c.** (*in combination*): *a tomcat.* [C16: special use of the shortened form of *Thomas,* applied to any male, often implying a common or ordinary type of person, etc.]
tom[2] (tɒm) *n. Austral. and N.Z.* a temporary supporting post. [from a specialized use of TOM[1]]
tomahawk ('tɒməˌhɔːk) *n.* **1.** a fighting axe, with a stone or later an iron head, used by the North American Indians. **2.** *Chiefly Austral.* the usual word for **hatchet.** ~*vb.* (*tr.*) **3.** *Austral. slang.* to shear (a sheep) roughly or so as to cut the skin. [C17: from Virginia Algonquian *tamahaac*]
tomalley ('tɒmælɪ) *n.* fat from a lobster, called "liver", and eaten as a delicacy. [C17: of Caribbean origin; compare Galibi *tumali* sauce of crab or lobster liver]
toman (tə'mɑːn) *n.* a gold coin formerly issued in Persia. [C16: from Persian, of Mongolian origin]
Tom and Jerry *n. U.S.* a hot mixed drink containing rum, brandy, egg, nutmeg, and sometimes milk.
tomato (tə'mɑːtəʊ) *n., pl.* **-toes. 1.** a solanaceous plant, *Lycopersicon* (or *Lycopersicum*) *esculentum,* of South America, widely cultivated for its red fleshy many-seeded edible fruits. **2.** the fruit of this plant, which has slightly acid-tasting flesh and is eaten in salads, as a vegetable, etc. **3.** *U.S. and Canadian slang.* a girl or woman. [C17 *tomate,* from Spanish, from Nahuatl *tomatl*]
tomb (tuːm) *n.* **1.** a place, esp. a vault beneath the ground, for the burial of a corpse. **2.** a stone or other monument to the dead. **3. the tomb.** a poetic term for **death. 4.** anything serving as a burial place: *the sea was his tomb.* ~*vb.* **5.** (*tr.*) *Rare.* to place in a tomb; entomb. [C13: from Old French *tombe,* from Late Latin *tumba* burial mound, from Greek *tumbos;* related to Latin *tumēre* to swell, Middle Irish *tomm* hill] —'**tombˌlike** *adj.*
tombac ('tɒmbæk) *or* **tambac** ('tæmbæk) *n.* any of various brittle alloys containing copper and zinc and sometimes tin and arsenic: used for making cheap jewellery, etc. [C17: from French, from Dutch *tombak,* from Malay *tambâga* copper, apparently from Sanskrit *tāmraka,* from *tāmra* dark coppery red]
tombola (tɒm'bəʊlə) *n. Brit.* a type of lottery, esp. at a fête, in which tickets are drawn from a revolving drum. [C19: from Italian, from *tombolare* to somersault; see TUMBLE]
tombolo ('tɒmbəˌləʊ) *n., pl.* **-los.** a narrow sand or shingle bar linking a small island with another island or the mainland. [C20: from Italian, from Latin *tumulus* mound; see TUMULUS]
tomboy ('tɒmˌbɔɪ) *n.* a girl who acts or dresses in a boyish way, liking rough outdoor activities. —'**tomˌboyish** *adj.* —'**tomˌboyishly** *adv.* —'**tomˌboyishness** *n.*
tombstone ('tuːmˌstəʊn) *n.* another word for **gravestone.**
Tom Collins ('kɒlɪnz) *n.* a long drink consisting of gin, lime or lemon juice, sugar or syrup, and soda water.
Tom, Dick, and (or) Harry *n.* an ordinary, undistinguished, or common person (esp. in the phrases **every Tom, Dick, and Harry; any Tom, Dick, or Harry**).
tome (təʊm) *n.* **1.** a large weighty book. **2.** one of the several volumes of a work. [C16: from French, from Latin *tomus* section of larger work, from Greek *tomos* a slice, from *temnein* to cut; related to Latin *tondēre* to shear]
-tome *n. combining form.* indicating an instrument for cutting: *osteotome.* [from Greek *tomē* a cutting, *tomos* a slice, from *temnein* to cut]
tomentum (tə'mɛntəm) *n., pl.* **-ta** (-tə). **1.** a feltlike covering of downy hairs on leaves and other plant parts. **2.** a network of minute blood vessels occurring in the human brain between the pia mater and cerebral cortex. [C17: New Latin, from Latin: stuffing for cushions; related to Latin *tumēre* to swell] —**tomentose** (tə'mɛntəʊs) *adj.*
tomfool (ˌtɒm'fuːl) *n.* **a.** a fool. **b.** (*as modifier*): *tomfool ideas.* [C14: from TOM[1] + FOOL[1]] —ˌ**tom'foolish** *adj.* —ˌ**tom'foolishness** *n.*
tomfoolery (ˌtɒm'fuːlərɪ) *n., pl.* **-eries. 1.** foolish behaviour. **2.** utter nonsense; rubbish.
tommy ('tɒmɪ) *n., pl.* **-mies.** (*often cap.*) *Brit. informal.* a private in the British Army. Also called: **Tommy Atkins** ('ætkɪnz). [C19: originally *Thomas Atkins,* a name representing a typical private in specimen forms; compare TOM[1]]
tommy bar *n.* a short bar used as a lever to provide torque for tightening a box spanner or key.
Tommy gun *n.* an informal name for **Thompson sub-machine-gun.**
tommyrot ('tɒmɪˌrɒt) *n.* utter nonsense; tomfoolery.
tomography (tə'mɒgrəfɪ) *n.* any of a number of techniques used to obtain an x-ray photograph of a selected plane section of the human body or some other solid object. [C20: from Greek *tomē* a cutting + -GRAPHY]
tomorrow (tə'mɒrəʊ) *n.* **1.** the day after today. **2.** the future. ~*adv.* **3.** on the day after today. **4.** at some time in the future. [Old English *tō morgenne,* from TO (at, on) + *morgenne,* dative of *morgen* MORNING; see MORROW]
tompion ('tɒmpɪən) *n.* a variant of **tampion.**
Tom Thumb *n.* a dwarf; midget. [after *Tom Thumb,* the tiny hero of several English folk tales]
tomtit ('tɒmˌtɪt) *n. Brit.* any of various tits, esp. the bluetit.
tom-tom *n.* **1.** a drum associated either with the American Indians or with Eastern cultures, usually beaten with the hands as a signalling instrument. **2.** a standard cylindrical drum, normally with one drumhead. **3.** a monotonous drumming or beating sound. [C17: from Hindi *tamtam,* of imitative origin]
-tomy *n. combining form.* indicating a surgical cutting of a specified part or tissue: *lobotomy.* [from Greek *-tomia;* see -TOME]
ton[1] (tʌn) *n.* **1.** Also called: **long ton.** *Brit.* a unit of weight equal to 2240 pounds or 1016.046 909 kilograms. **2.** Also called: **short ton, net ton.** *U.S.* a unit of weight equal to 2000 pounds or 907.184 kilograms. **3.** Also called: **metric ton, tonne.** a unit of weight equal to 1000 kilograms. **4.** Also called: **freight ton.** a unit of volume or weight used for charging or measuring freight in shipping. It depends on the type of material being shipped but is often taken as 40 cubic feet, 1 cubic metre, or 1000 kilograms: *freight is charged at £40 per ton of 1 cubic metre.* **5.** Also called: **measurement ton, shipping ton.** a unit of volume used in shipping freight, equal to 40 cubic feet, irrespective of the commodity shipped. **6.** Also called: **displacement ton.** a unit used for measuring the displacement of a ship, equal to 35 cubic feet of sea water or 2240 pounds. **7.** Also called: **register ton.** a unit of internal capacity of ships equal to 100 cubic feet. ~*adv.* **8. tons.** (intensifier): *the new flat is tons better than the old one.* [C14: variant of TUN]
ton[2] *French.* (tɔ̃) *n.* style, fashion, or distinction. [C18: from French, from Latin *tonus* TONE]
ton[3] (tʌn) *n. Slang, chiefly Brit.* a score or achievement of a hundred, esp. a hundred miles per hour, as on a motorcycle. [C20: special use of TON[1] applied to quantities of one hundred]
tonal ('təʊnᵊl) *adj.* **1.** of or relating to tone. **2.** of, relating to, or utilizing the diatonic system; having an established key. Compare **atonal. 3. a.** (of an answer in a fugue) not having the same melodic intervals as the subject, so as to remain in the original key. **b.** denoting a fugue as having such an answer. Compare **real**[1] (sense 10). —'**tonally** *adv.*
tonality (təʊ'nælɪtɪ) *n., pl.* **-ties. 1.** *Music.* **a.** the actual or implied presence of a musical key in a composition. **b.** the system of major and minor keys prevalent in Western music since the decline of modes. Compare **atonality. 2.** the overall scheme of colours and tones in a painting.
to-name *n. Scot.* a nickname used to distinguish one person from others of the same name.
tondo ('tɒndəʊ) *n., pl.* **-di** (-diː). a circular easel painting or relief carving. [C19: from Italian: a circle, shortened from *rotondo* round]
tone (təʊn) *n.* **1.** sound with reference to quality, pitch, or volume. **2.** short for **tone colour. 3.** *U.S. and Canadian.* another word for **note** (sense 10). **4.** (in acoustic analysis) a sound resulting from periodic or regular vibrations, composed either of a simple sinusoidal waveform (**pure tone**) or of several such waveforms superimposed upon one main one (**compound tone**). **5.** an interval of a major second; whole tone. **6.** Also called: **Gregorian tone.** any of several plainsong melodies or other chants used in the singing of psalms. **7.** *Linguistics.* any of the pitch levels or pitch contours at which a syllable may be pronounced, such as high tone, falling tone, etc. **8.** the quality or character of a sound: *a nervous tone of voice.* **9.** general aspect, quality, or style: *I didn't like the tone of his speech.* **10.** high quality or style: *to lower the tone of a place.* **11.** the quality of a given colour, as modified by mixture with white or black; shade; tint: *a tone of red.* **12.** *Physiol.* **a.** the normal tension of a muscle at rest. **b.** the natural firmness of the tissues and normal functioning of bodily organs in health. **13.** the overall effect of the colour values and gradations of light and dark in a picture. **14.** *Photog.* a colour or shade of colour, including black or grey, of a particular area on a negative or positive that can be distinguished from surrounding lighter or darker areas. ~*vb.* **15.** (*intr.; often foll. by with*) to be of a matching or similar tone (to): *the curtains tone with the carpet.* **16.** (*tr.*) to give a tone to or correct the tone of. **17.** (*tr.*) *Photog.* to soften or change the colour of the tones of (a photographic image) by chemical means. **18.** an archaic word for **intone.** ~See also **tone down, tone up.** [C14: from Latin *tonus,* from Greek *tonos* tension, tone, from *teinein* to stretch]
tone arm *n.* another name for **pick-up** (sense 1).
tone cluster *n. Music.* a group of adjacent notes played simultaneously, either in an orchestral score or, on the piano, by depressing a whole set of adjacent keys.
tone colour *n.* the quality of a musical sound that is conditioned or distinguished by the upper partials or overtones present in it. Often shortened to **tone.** See also **timbre** (sense 2).

tone control *n.* a device in a radio, etc., by which the relative intensities of high and low frequencies may be varied.

tone-deaf *adj.* unable to distinguish subtle differences in musical pitch. —**tone deafness** *n.*

tone down *vb.* (*adv.*) to moderate or become moderated in tone: *to tone down an argument; to tone down a bright colour.*

tone language *n.* a language, such as Chinese or certain African languages, in which differences in tone may make differences in meaning.

toneless ('təʊnlɪs) *adj.* **1.** having no tone. **2.** lacking colour or vitality. —'**tonelessly** *adv.* —'**tonelessness** *n.*

toneme ('təʊniːm) *n. Linguistics.* a phoneme that is distinguished from another phoneme only by its tone. [C20: from TONE + -EME] —**to'nemic** *adj.*

tone poem *n.* another term for **symphonic poem.**

toner ('təʊnə) *n.* **1.** a person or thing that tones or produces tones, esp. a concentrated pure organic pigment. **2.** a cosmetic preparation that is applied to produce a required effect, such as one that softens or alters hair colour or one that reduces the oiliness of the skin. **3.** *Photog.* a chemical solution that softens or alters the colour of the tones of a photographic image.

tone row *or* **series** *n. Music.* a group of notes having a characteristic pattern or order that forms the basis of the musical material in a serial composition, esp. one consisting of the twelve notes of the chromatic scale. Also called: **note row.** See also **serialism, twelve-tone.**

tonetic (təʊ'nɛtɪk) *adj.* (of a language) distinguishing words semantically by distinction of tone as well as by other sounds. See **tone language.** [C20: from TONE + *-etic,* as in PHONETIC] —**to'netically** *adv.*

tone up *vb.* (*adv.*) to make or become more vigorous, healthy, etc.: *exercise tones up the muscles.*

tong[1] (tɒŋ) *vb.* (*tr.*) **1.** to gather or seize with tongs. **2.** to curl or style (hair) with curling tongs.

tong[2] (tɒŋ) *n.* (formerly) a Chinese secret society or association, esp. one popularly assumed to engage in criminal activities. [C20: from Chinese (Cantonese) *t'ong* meeting place]

tonga ('tɒŋgə) *n.* a light two-wheeled vehicle used in rural areas of India. [C19: from Hindi *tāngā*]

Tonga ('tɒŋgə, 'tɒŋə) *n.* **1.** (*pl.* **-gas** *or* **-ga**) a member of a Negroid people of S central Africa, living chiefly in Zambia and Zimbabwe. **2.** the language of this people, belonging to the Bantu group of the Niger-Congo family.

Tongan ('tɒŋən) *adj.* **1.** of or relating to the kingdom of Tonga in the SW Pacific, its inhabitants, or their language. ~*n.* **2.** a member of the people that inhabits Tonga. **3.** the language of this people, belonging to the Polynesian family.

tongs (tɒŋz) *pl. n.* a tool for grasping or lifting, consisting of a hinged, sprung, or pivoted pair of arms or levers, joined at one end. Also called: **pair of tongs.** [plural of Old English *tange;* related to Old Saxon *tanga,* Old High German *zanga,* Old Norse *tong*]

tongue (tʌŋ) *n.* **1.** a movable mass of muscular tissue attached to the floor of the mouth in most vertebrates. It is the organ of taste and aids the mastication and swallowing of food. In man it plays an important part in the articulation of speech sounds. Related adj.: **lingual.** **2.** an analogous organ in invertebrates. **3.** the tongue of certain animals used as food. **4.** a language, dialect, or idiom: *the English tongue.* **5.** the ability to speak: *to lose one's tongue.* **6.** a manner of speaking: *a glib tongue.* **7.** utterance or voice (esp. in the phrase **give tongue**). **8.** (*pl.*) See **gift of tongues.** **9.** *Archaic.* a people or tribe, esp. one having its own language. **10.** anything which resembles a tongue in shape or function: *a tongue of flame; a tongue of the sea.* **11.** a promontory or spit of land. **12.** a flap of leather on a shoe, either for decoration or under the laces or buckles to protect the instep. **13.** *Music.* the reed of an oboe or similar instrument. **14.** the clapper of a bell. **15.** the harnessing pole of a horse-drawn vehicle. **16.** a long and narrow projection on a machine part that serves as a guide for assembly or as a securing device. **17.** a projecting strip along an edge of a board that is made to fit a corresponding groove in the edge of another board. **18. hold one's tongue.** to keep quiet. **19. on the tip of one's tongue.** about to come to mind: *her name was on the tip of his tongue.* **20. with (one's) tongue in (one's) cheek.** Also: **tongue in cheek.** with insincere or ironical intent. ~*vb.* **tongues, tonguing, tongued.** **21.** to articulate (notes played on a wind instrument) by the process of tonguing. **22.** (*tr.*) to lick, feel, or touch with the tongue. **23.** (*tr.*) *Carpentry.* to provide (a board) with a tongue. **24.** (*intr.*) (of a piece of land) to project into a body of water. **25.** (*tr.*) *Obsolete.* to reproach; scold. [Old English *tunge;* related to Old Saxon, Old Norse *tunga,* Old High German *zunga,* Latin *lingua*] —'**tongueless** *adj.* —'**tongue,like** *adj.*

tongue-and-groove joint *n.* a joint made between two boards by means of a tongue along the edge of one board that fits into a groove along the edge of the other board.

tongued (tʌŋd) *adj.* **1. a.** having a tongue or tongues. **b.** (*in combination*): *long-tongued.* **2.** (*in combination*) having a manner of speech as specified: *sharp-tongued.*

tongue-lash *vb.* (*tr.*) to reprimand severely; scold. —'**tongue,lashing** *n., adj.*

tongue-tie *n.* a congenital condition in which the tongue has restricted mobility as the result of an abnormally short frenulum.

tongue-tied *adj.* **1.** speechless, esp. with embarrassment or shyness. **2.** having a condition of tongue-tie.

tongue twister *n.* a sentence or phrase that is difficult to articulate clearly and quickly, such as *Peter Piper picked a peck of pickled pepper.*

tonguing ('tʌŋɪŋ) *n.* a technique of articulating notes on a wind instrument. See **single-tongue, double-tongue, triple-tongue.**

tonic ('tɒnɪk) *n.* **1.** a medicinal preparation that improves and strengthens the functioning of the body or increases the feeling of wellbeing. **2.** anything that enlivens or strengthens: *his speech was a tonic to the audience.* **3.** Also called: **tonic water.** a mineral water, usually carbonated and containing quinine and often mixed with gin or other alcoholic drinks. **4.** *Music.* **a.** the first degree of a major or minor scale and the tonal centre of a piece composed in a particular key. **b.** a key or chord based on this. **5.** a stressed syllable in a word. ~*adj.* **6.** serving to enliven and invigorate: *a tonic wine.* **7.** of or relating to a tone or tones. **8.** *Music.* of or relating to the first degree of a major or minor scale. **9.** of or denoting the general effect of colour and light and shade in a picture. **10.** *Physiol.* of, relating to, characterized by, or affecting normal muscular or bodily tone: *a tonic spasm.* **11.** of or relating to stress or the main stress in a word. **12.** denoting a tone language. [C17: from New Latin *tonicus,* from Greek *tonikos* concerning tone, from *tonos* TONE] —'**tonically** *adv.*

tonic accent *n.* **1.** emphasis imparted to a note by virtue of its having a higher pitch, rather than greater stress or long duration relative to other notes. **2.** another term for **pitch accent.**

tonicity (təʊ'nɪsɪtɪ) *n.* **1.** the state, condition, or quality of being tonic. **2.** *Physiol.* another name for **tonus.**

tonic sol-fa *n.* a method of teaching music, esp. singing, used mainly in Britain, by which the syllables of a movable system of solmization are used as names for the notes of the major scale in any key. In this system *sol* is usually replaced by *so* as the name of the fifth degree. See **solmization.**

tonight (tə'naɪt) *n.* **1.** the night or evening of this present day. ~*adv.* **2.** in or during the night or evening of this day. **3.** *Obsolete or western Brit. dialect.* last night. [Old English *tōniht,* from TO (at) + NIGHT]

tonk (tɒŋk) *n. Austral. slang.* an effete or effeminate man. [C20: origin unknown]

tonka bean ('tɒŋkə) *n.* **1.** a tall leguminous tree, *Coumarouna odorata,* of tropical America, having fragrant black almond-shaped seeds. **2.** the seeds of this tree, used in the manufacture of perfumes, snuff, etc. [C18: probably from Tupi *tonka*]

tonnage *or* **tunnage** ('tʌnɪdʒ) *n.* **1.** the capacity of a merchant ship expressed in tons, for which purpose a ton is considered as 40 cubic feet of freight or 100 cubic feet of bulk cargo, unless such an amount would weigh more than 2000 pounds in which case the actual weight is used. **2.** the weight of the cargo of a merchant ship. **3.** the total amount of shipping of a port or nation, estimated by the capacity of its ships. **4.** a duty on ships based either on their capacity or their register tonnage. [C15: from Old French, from *tonne* barrel]

tonne (tʌn) *n.* a unit of mass equal to 1000 kg or 2204.6 pounds. Also called (not in technical use): **metric ton.** [from French]

tonneau ('tɒnəʊ) *n., pl.* **-neaus** *or* **-neaux** (-nəʊ, -nəʊz). **1.** Also called: **tonneau cover. a.** a detachable cover to protect the rear part of an open car when it is not carrying passengers. **b.** a similar cover that fits over all the passenger seats, but not the driver's, in an open vehicle. **2.** *Rare.* the part of an open car in which the rear passengers sit. [C20: from French: special type of vehicle body, from Old French *tonnel* cask, from *tonne* tun]

tonometer (təʊ'nɒmɪtə) *n.* **1.** an instrument for measuring the pitch of a sound, esp. one consisting of a set of tuning forks. **2.** any of various types of instrument for measuring pressure or tension, such as the blood pressure, vapour pressure, etc. [C18: from Greek *tonos* TONE + -METER] —**tonometric** (ˌtɒnə'mɛtrɪk, ˌtəʊ-) *adj.* —**to'nometry** *n.*

tonoplast ('təʊnəˌplæst) *n. Botany.* the membrane enclosing a vacuole in a plant cell. [C20: from Greek *tonos* tone + -PLAST]

tonsil ('tɒnsəl) *n.* **1.** Also called: **palatine tonsil.** either of two small masses of lymphatic tissue situated one on each side of the back of the mouth. **2.** *Anatomy.* any small rounded mass of tissue, esp. lymphatic tissue. [C17: from Latin *tōnsillae* (pl.) tonsils, of uncertain origin] —'**tonsillar** *or* '**tonsillary** *adj.*

tonsillectomy (ˌtɒnsɪ'lɛktəmɪ) *n., pl.* **-mies.** surgical removal of the palatine tonsils.

tonsillitis (ˌtɒnsɪ'laɪtɪs) *n.* inflammation of the palatine tonsils, causing enlargement, occasionally to the extent that they nearly touch one another. —**tonsillitic** (ˌtɒnsɪ'lɪtɪk) *adj.*

tonsillotomy (ˌtɒnsɪ'lɒtəmɪ) *n., pl.* **-mies.** surgical incision into one or both of the palatine tonsils, usually followed by removal (tonsillectomy).

tonsorial (tɒn'sɔːrɪəl) *adj. Often facetious.* of or relating to barbering or hairdressing. [C19: from Latin *tōnsōrius* concerning shaving, from *tondēre* to shave]

tonsure ('tɒnʃə) *n.* **1.** (in certain religions and monastic orders) **a.** the shaving of the head or the crown of the head only. **b.** the part of the head left bare by shaving. **c.** the state of being shaven thus. *~vb.* **2.** *(tr.)* to shave the head of. [C14: from Latin *tōnsūra* a clipping, from *tondēre* to shave] —ˈ**tonsured** *adj.*

tontine (ˈtɒntiːn, tɒnˈtiːn) *n.* **1. a.** an annuity scheme by which several subscribers accumulate and invest a common fund out of which they receive an annuity that increases as subscribers die until the last survivor takes the whole. **b.** the subscribers to such a scheme collectively. **c.** the share of each subscriber. **d.** the common fund accumulated. **e.** *(as modifier): a tontine fund.* **2.** a system of mutual life assurance by which benefits are received by those participants who survive and maintain their policies throughout a stipulated period (the **tontine period**). [C18: from French, named after Lorenzo *Tonti,* Neapolitan banker who devised the scheme]

ton-up *Brit. informal.* *~adj.* *(prenominal)* **1.** (esp. of a motorcycle) capable of speeds of a hundred miles per hour or more. **2.** liking to travel at such speeds: *a ton-up boy.* *~n.* **3.** a person who habitually rides at such speeds.

tonus (ˈtəʊnəs) *n. Physiol.* the normal tension of a muscle at rest; tone. [C19: from Latin, from Greek *tonos* TONE]

tony (ˈtəʊnɪ) *adj.* **tonier, toniest.** *U.S. and Canadian informal.* stylish or distinctive; classy. [C20: from TONE]

Tony (ˈtəʊnɪ) *n., pl.* **Tonies** *or* **Tonys.** any of several medallions awarded annually in the United States by a professional school for the performing arts for outstanding achievement in the theatre. [from *Tony,* the nickname of Antoinette Perry (died 1946), U.S. actress and producer]

too (tuː) *adv.* **1.** as well; in addition; also: *can I come too?* **2.** in or to an excessive degree; more than a fitting or desirable amount: *I have too many things to do.* **3.** extremely: *you're too kind.* **4.** *U.S. and Canadian informal.* indeed: used to reinforce a command: *you will too do it!* **5. too right!** *Brit., Austral., and N.Z.* certainly; indeed. [Old English *tō;* related to Old Frisian, Old Saxon *to,* Old High German *zou;* see TO]

▷**Usage.** See at **very.**

toodle-oo (ˌtuːdᵊlˈluː) *or* **toodle-pip** *sentence substitute. Brit. informal, rare.* goodbye. [C20: perhaps imitative of the horn of a car]

took (tʊk) *vb.* the past tense of **take.**

tool (tuːl) *n.* **1. a.** an implement, such as a hammer, saw, or spade, that is used by hand. **b.** a power-driven instrument; machine tool. **c.** *(in combination): a toolkit.* **2.** the cutting part of such an instrument. **3. a.** any of the instruments used by a bookbinder to impress a design on a book cover. **b.** a design so impressed. **4.** anything used as a means of performing an operation or achieving an end: *he used his boss's absence as a tool for gaining influence.* **5.** a person used to perform dishonourable or unpleasant tasks for another. **6.** a necessary medium for or adjunct to one's profession: *numbers are the tools of the mathematician's trade.* **7.** *Taboo slang.* another word for **penis.** **8.** *Brit.* an underworld slang word for **gun.** *~vb.* **9.** to work, cut, shape, or form (something) with a tool or tools. **10.** *(tr.)* to decorate (a book cover) with a bookbinder's tool. **11.** *(tr.;* often foll. by *up)* to furnish with tools. **12.** (when *intr.,* often foll. by *along)* to drive (a vehicle) or (of a vehicle) to be driven, esp. in a leisurely or casual style. [Old English *tōl;* related to Old Norse *tōl* weapon, Old English *tawian* to prepare; see TAW^{2}] —ˈ**tooler** *n.* —ˈ**tool-less** *adj.*

tooled up *adj. Slang.* equipped with a weapon, esp. a gun.

tooling (ˈtuːlɪŋ) *n.* **1.** any decorative work done with a tool, esp. a design stamped onto a book cover, piece of leatherwork, etc. **2.** the selection, provision, and setting up of tools, esp. for a machining operation.

tool-maker (ˈtuːlˌmeɪkə) *n.* a person who specializes in the production or reconditioning of precision tools, cutters, etc. —ˈ**tool-ˌmaking** *n.*

tool post *n.* the rigid holding device which holds the cutting tool on a lathe and some other machine tools.

tool pusher *n.* a foreman who supervises drilling operations on an oil rig.

toolroom (ˈtuːlruːm, -rʊm) *n.* a room, as in a machine shop, where tools are made or stored.

tool shed *n.* a small shed in the garden or yard of a house used for storing tools, esp. those for gardening.

tool steel *n.* any of various steels whose hardness and ability to retain a cutting edge make them suitable for use in tools for cutting wood and metal.

toon (tuːn) *n.* **1.** a large meliaceous tree, *Cedrela toona,* of the East Indies and Australia, having clusters of flowers from which a dye is obtained. **2.** the close-grained red wood of this tree, used for furniture, carvings, etc. [from Hindi *tūn,* from Sanskrit *tunna*]

toorie *or* **tourie** (ˈtʊrɪ) *n. Scot.* **1.** a tassel or bobble on a bonnet. **2.** Also: **toorie bonnet.** a bonnet with a toorie. [C19: from Scot. *toor* tower]

toot^{1} (tuːt) *vb.* **1.** to give or cause to give (a short blast, hoot, or whistle): *to toot a horn; to toot a blast; the train tooted.* *~n.* **2.** the sound made by or as if by a horn, whistle, etc. **3.** *Slang.* any drug for snorting, esp. cocaine. **4.** *U.S. and Canadian slang.* a drinking spree. **5.** *Austral. slang.* a lavatory. [C16: from Middle Low German *tuten,* of imitative origin] —ˈ**tooter** *n.*

toot^{2} (tuːt) *n. N.Z.* an informal name for **tutu^{2}.**

tooth (tuːθ) *n., pl.* **teeth** (tiːθ). **1.** any of various bonelike structures set in the jaws of most vertebrates and modified, according to the species, for biting, tearing, or chewing. Related adj.: **dental.** **2.** any of various similar structures in invertebrates, occurring in the mouth or alimentary canal. **3.** anything resembling a tooth in shape, prominence, or function: *the tooth of a comb.* **4.** any of the various small indentations occurring on the margin of a leaf, petal, etc. **5.** any one of a number of uniform projections on a gear, sprocket, rack, etc., by which drive is transmitted. **6.** taste or appetite (esp. in the phrase **sweet tooth**). **7. long in the tooth.** old or ageing: used originally of horses, because their gums recede with age. **8. tooth and nail.** with ferocity and force: *we fought tooth and nail.* *~vb.* (tuːð, tuːθ). **9.** *(tr.)* to provide with a tooth or teeth. **10.** *(intr.)* (of two gearwheels) to engage. [Old English *tōth;* related to Old Saxon *tand,* Old High German *zand,* Old Norse *tonn,* Gothic *tunthus,* Latin *dens*] —ˈ**toothless** *adj.* —ˈ**toothˌlike** *adj.*

toothache (ˈtuːθˌeɪk) *n.* a pain in or about a tooth. Technical name: **odontalgia.**

toothache tree *n.* another name for **prickly ash.**

toothbrush (ˈtuːθˌbrʌʃ) *n.* a small brush, usually with a long handle, for cleaning the teeth.

toothed (tuːθt) *adj.* **a.** having a tooth or teeth. **b.** *(in combination): sabre-toothed; six-toothed.*

toothed whale *n.* any whale belonging to the cetacean suborder *Odontoceti,* having a single blowhole and numerous simple teeth and feeding on fish, smaller mammals, molluscs, etc.: includes dolphins and porpoises. Compare **whalebone whale.**

toothpaste (ˈtuːθˌpeɪst) *n.* a paste used for cleaning the teeth, applied with a toothbrush.

toothpick (ˈtuːθˌpɪk) *n.* **1.** a small sharp sliver of wood, plastic, etc., used for extracting pieces of food from between the teeth. **2.** a slang word for **bowie knife.**

tooth powder *n.* a powder used for cleaning the teeth, applied with a toothbrush.

tooth shell *n.* another name for the **tusk shell.**

toothsome (ˈtuːθsəm) *adj.* **1.** of delicious or appetizing appearance, flavour, or smell. **2.** attractive; alluring. —ˈ**toothsomely** *adv.* —ˈ**toothsomeness** *n.*

toothwort (ˈtuːθˌwɜːt) *n.* **1.** an orobanchaceous European plant, *Lathraea squamaria,* having scaly cream or pink stems and pinkish flowers and a rhizome covered with toothlike scales. **2.** any cruciferous North American or Eurasian plant of the genus *Dentaria,* having creeping rhizomes covered with toothlike projections. See also **crinkleroot.**

toothy (ˈtuːθɪ) *adj.* **toothier, toothiest.** having or showing numerous, large, or projecting teeth: *a toothy grin.* —ˈ**toothily** *adv.* —ˈ**toothiness** *n.*

tootle^{1} (ˈtuːtᵊl) *vb.* **1.** to toot or hoot softly or repeatedly: *the flute tootled quietly.* *~n.* **2.** a soft hoot or series of hoots. [C19: from TOOT^{1}] —ˈ**tootler** *n.*

tootle^{2} (ˈtuːtᵊl) *Brit. informal.* *~vb.* **1.** *(intr.)* to go, esp. by car. *~n.* **2.** a drive, esp. a short pleasure trip. [C19: from TOOTLE^{1}, imitative of the horn of a car]

toots (tʊts) *or* **tootsy** *n., pl.* **tootses** *or* **tootsies.** *Informal, chiefly U.S.* darling; sweetheart. [C20: perhaps related to earlier dialect *toot* worthless person, of obscure origin]

tootsy, tootsie (ˈtʊtsɪ), *or* **tootsy-wootsy** (ˈtʊtsɪˈwʊtsɪ) *n., pl.* **-sies.** a child's word for **foot.**

top^{1} (tɒp) *n.* **1.** the highest or uppermost part of anything: *the top of a hill.* **2.** the most important or successful position: *to be at the top of the class; the top of the table.* **3.** the part of a plant that is above ground: *carrot tops.* **4.** a thing that forms or covers the uppermost part of anything, esp. a lid or cap: *put the top on the saucepan.* **5.** the highest degree or point: *at the top of his career.* **6.** the most important person: *he's the top of this organization.* **7.** the best or finest part of anything: *we've got the top of this year's graduates.* **8.** the loudest or highest pitch (esp. in the phrase **top of one's voice**). **9.** short for **top gear.** **10.** *Cards.* the highest card of a suit in a player's hand. **11.** *Sport.* **a.** a stroke that hits the ball above its centre. **b.** short for **topspin.** **12.** a platform around the head of a lower mast of a sailing vessel, the edges of which serve to extend the topmast shrouds. **13.** *Chem.* the part of a volatile liquid mixture that distils first. **14.** a garment, esp. for a woman, that extends from the shoulders to the waist or hips. **15. a.** the high-frequency content of an audio signal. **b.** *(as modifier): this amplifier has a good top response.* **16. blow one's top.** *Informal.* to lose one's temper. **17. on top of. a.** in addition to: *on top of his accident, he caught pneumonia.* **b.** *Informal.* in complete control of (a difficult situation, job, etc.). **18. off the top of one's head.** with no previous preparation; extempore. **19. over the top. a.** over the parapet or leading edge of a trench. **b.** over the limit; excessive(ly); lacking restraint or a sense of proportion. **20. the top of the morning.** a morning greeting regarded as characteristic of Irishmen. *~adj.* **21.** of, relating to, serving as, or situated on the top: *the top book in a pile.* *~vb.* **tops, topping, topped.** *(mainly tr.)* **22.** to form a top on (something): *to top a cake with whipped cream.* **23.** to remove the top of or from: *to top carrots.* **24.** to reach or pass the top of: *we topped the mountain.* **25.** to be at the top of: *he tops the team.* **26.** to exceed or surpass. **27.** *Slang.* to kill, esp. by hanging. **28.** *(also intr.) Sport.* **a.** to hit (a ball) above the centre. **b.** to make (a stroke) by hitting the ball in this way. **29.** *Chem.* to distil off (the most volatile part) from a liquid mixture. **30.** to add other colorants to (a dye) in order to modify the shade produced. ~See also **top off, top out, tops, top up.** [Old English *topp;* related to Old High German *zopf* plait, Old Norse *toppr* tuft]

top[2] (tɒp) *n.* **1.** a toy that is spun on its pointed base by a flick of the fingers, by pushing a handle at the top up and down, etc. **2.** anything that spins or whirls around. **3. sleep like a top.** to sleep very soundly. [Old English, of unknown origin]

top- *combining form.* a variant of **topo-** before a vowel.

topagnosia (ˌtɒpæg'nəʊzɪə) *or* **topagnosis** (ˌtɒpæg'nəʊsɪs) *n.* a symptom of disease of or damage to the brain in which a person cannot identify a part of the body that has been touched.

topalgia (tɒ'pældʒɪə) *n.* pain restricted to a particular spot: a neurotic or hysterical symptom.

toparch ('tɒpɑːk) *n.* the ruler of a small state or realm. [C17: from Greek *toparchēs,* from *topos* a place + -ARCH] —'**toparchy** *n.*

topaz ('təʊpæz) *n.* **1.** a white or colourless mineral often tinted by impurities, found in cavities in igneous rocks and in quartz veins. It is used as a gemstone. Composition: hydrated aluminium silicate. Formula: $Al_2SiO_4(F,OH)_2$. Crystal structure: orthorhombic. **2. oriental topaz.** a yellowish-brown variety of sapphire. **3. false topaz.** another name for **citrine. 4. a.** a yellowish-brown colour, as in some varieties of topaz. **b.** (*as adj.*): *topaz eyes.* **5.** either of two South American hummingbirds, *Topaza pyra* and *T. pella.* [C13: from Old French *topaze,* from Latin *topazus,* from Greek *topazos*]

topazolite (təʊ'pæzəˌlaɪt) *n.* a yellowish-green variety of andradite garnet. [C19: from TOPAZ + -LITE; so called because it is the same colour as some topaz]

top banana *n. Slang, chiefly U.S.* **1.** the leading comedian in vaudeville, burlesque, etc. **2.** the leader; boss.

top boot *n.* a high boot, often with a decorative or contrasting upper section.

top brass *n.* (*functioning as pl.*) *Informal.* the most important or high-ranking officials or leaders, as in politics, industry, etc. See also **brass** (sense 5).

topcoat ('tɒpˌkəʊt) *n.* an outdoor coat worn over a suit, etc.

top dead-centre *n. Engineering.* the position of the crank of a reciprocating engine or pump when the piston is at the top of its stroke. Abbrev.: **t.d.c.**

top dog *n. Informal.* the leader or chief of a group.

top-down *adj.* controlled, directed, or organized from the top.

top drawer *n.* people of the highest standing, esp. socially (esp. in the phrase **out of the top drawer**).

top-dress *vb.* (*tr.*) to spread manure or fertilizer on the surface of (land) without working it into the soil.

top dressing *n.* **1.** a surface application of manure or fertilizer to land. **2.** a thin layer of loose gravel that covers the top of a road surface.

tope[1] (təʊp) *vb.* to consume (alcoholic drink) as a regular habit, usually in large quantities. [C17: from French *toper* to keep an agreement, from Spanish *topar* to take a bet; probably because a wager was generally followed by a drink] —'**toper** *n.*

tope[2] (təʊp) *n.* **1.** a small grey requiem shark, *Galeorhinus galeus,* of European coastal waters. **2.** any of various other small sharks. [C17: of uncertain origin; compare Norfolk dialect *toper* dogfish]

tope[3] (təʊp) *n.* another name for a **stupa.** [C19: from Hindi *tōp;* compare Sanskrit *stūpa* STUPA]

topee *or* **topi** ('təʊpiː, -pɪ) *n., pl.* **-pees** *or* **-pis.** another name for **pith helmet.** [C19: from Hindi *topī* hat]

top end *n.* (in vertical engines) another name for **little end** (sense 1).

top-flight *adj.* of superior or excellent quality; outstanding.

topfull ('tɒpˌfʊl) *adj. Rare.* full to the top.

topgallant (ˌtɒp'gælənt; *Nautical* tə'gælənt) *n.* **1.** Also called: **topgallant mast.** a mast on a square-rigger above a topmast or an extension of a topmast. **2.** Also called: **topgallant sail.** a sail set on a yard of a topgallant mast. **3.** (*modifier*) of or relating to a topgallant. [C16: from TOP[1] + GALLANT]

top gear *n.* the highest gear in a motor vehicle, often shortened to **top.**

top hat *n.* a man's hat with a tall cylindrical crown and narrow brim, often made of silk, now worn for some formal occasions. Also called: **high hat.**

top-hat scheme *n. Informal.* a pension scheme for the senior executives of an organization.

top-heavy *adj.* **1.** unstable or unbalanced through being overloaded at the top. **2.** *Finance.* (of an enterprise or its capital structure) characterized by or containing too much debt capital in relation to revenue or profit so that too little is left over for dividend distributions; overcapitalized. **3.** (of a business enterprise) having too many executives. —ˌ**top-'heavily** *adv.* —ˌ**top'heaviness** *n.*

top-hole *interj., adj. Brit. informal.* excellent; splendid.

tophus ('təʊfəs) *n., pl.* **-phi** (-faɪ). *Pathol.* a deposit of sodium urate in the helix of the ear or surrounding a joint: a diagnostic of advanced or chronic gout. Also called: **chalkstone.** [C16: from Latin, variant of *tōfus* TUFA, TUFF] —**tophaceous** (təʊ'feɪʃəs) *adj.*

topi *n., pl.* **-pis. 1.** ('təʊpɪ). an antelope, *Damaliscus korrigum,* of grasslands and semideserts of Africa, having angular curved horns and an elongated muzzle. **2.** ('təʊpiː, -pɪ). another name for **pith helmet.** [C19: from Hindi: hat]

topiary ('təʊpɪərɪ) *adj.* **1.** of, relating to, or characterized by the trimming or training of trees or bushes into artificial decorative animal, geometric, or other shapes. ~*n.* **2.** (*pl.* **-aries**) **a.** topiary work. **b.** a topiary garden. **3.** the art of topiary. [C16: from French *topiaire,* from Latin *topia* decorative garden work, from Greek *topion* little place, from *topos* place] —**topiarian** (ˌtəʊpɪ'ɛərɪən) *adj.* —'**topiarist** *n.*

topic ('tɒpɪk) *n.* **1.** a subject or theme of a speech, essay, book, etc. **2.** a subject of conversation; item of discussion. **3.** (in rhetoric, logic, etc.) a category or class of arguments or ideas which may be drawn on to furnish proofs. [C16: from Latin *topica* translating Greek *ta topika,* literally: matters relating to commonplaces, title of an Aristotelian treatise, from *topoi,* pl. of *topos* place, commonplace]

topical ('tɒpɪkᵊl) *adj.* **1.** of, relating to, or constituting current affairs. **2.** relating to a particular place; local. **3.** of or relating to a topic or topics. **4.** (of a drug, ointment, etc.) for application to the body surface; local. —**topicality** (ˌtɒpɪ'kælɪtɪ) *n.* —'**topically** *adv.*

topic sentence *n.* a sentence in a paragraph that expresses the main idea or point of the whole paragraph.

topknot ('tɒpˌnɒt) *n.* **1.** a crest, tuft, decorative bow, chignon, etc., on the top of the head. **2.** any of several European flatfishes of the genus *Zeugopterus* and related genera, esp. *Z. punctatus,* which has an oval dark brown body marked with darker blotches: family *Bothidae* (turbot, etc.).

topless ('tɒplɪs) *adj.* **1.** having no top. **2. a.** denoting a costume which has no covering for the breasts. **b.** wearing such a costume. **3.** *Archaic.* immeasurably high. —'**toplessness** *n.*

top-level *n.* (*modifier*) of, involving, or by those on the highest level of influence or authority: *top-level talks.*

toplofty ('tɒpˌlɒftɪ) *adj. Informal.* haughty or pretentious. —'**topˌloftily** *adv.* —'**topˌloftiness** *n.*

top management *or* **senior management** *n.* the most senior staff of an organization or business, including the heads of various divisions or departments led by the chief executive. Compare **middle management.**

topmast ('tɒpˌmɑːst; *Nautical* 'tɒpməst) *n.* the mast next above a lower mast on a sailing vessel.

topminnow ('tɒpˌmɪnəʊ) *n., pl.* **-now** *or* **-nows.** any of various small American freshwater cyprinodont fishes that are either viviparous (genera *Heterandria, Gambusia,* etc.) or egg-laying (genus *Fundulus*). [from TOP[1] + MINNOW; so called because they are small and swim near the surface of the water]

topmost ('tɒpˌməʊst) *adj.* highest; at or nearest the top.

topnotch ('tɒp'nɒtʃ) *adj. Informal.* excellent; superb. —'**top'notcher** *n.*

topo ('tɒpəʊ) *n. Mountaineering.* a picture of a mountain with details of climbing routes superimposed on it. [C20: shortened from *topographical picture*]

topo- *or before a vowel* **top-** *combining form.* indicating place or region: *topography; topology; toponym; topotype.* [from Greek *topos* a place, commonplace]

topochemistry ('tɒpəˌkɛmɪstrɪ) *n. Chem.* the study of reactions that only occur at specific regions in a system.

top off *vb.* (*tr., adv.*) to finish or complete, esp. with some decisive action: *he topped off the affair by committing suicide.*

topog. *abbrev. for:* **1.** topographical. **2.** topography.

topography (tə'pɒgrəfɪ) *n., pl.* **-phies. 1.** the study or detailed description of the surface features of a region. **2.** the detailed mapping of the configuration of a region. **3.** the land forms or surface configuration of a region. **4.** the surveying of a region's surface features. **5.** the study or description of the configuration of any object. —**to'pographer** *n.* —**topographic** (ˌtɒpə'græfɪk) *or* ˌ**topo'graphical** *adj.* —ˌ**topo'graphically** *adv.*

topological group *n. Maths.* a group, such as the set of all real numbers, that constitutes a topological space and in which multiplication and inversion are continuous.

topological space *n. Maths.* a set *S* with an associated family of subsets τ that is closed under set union and finite intersection. *S* and the empty set are members of τ.

topology (tə'pɒlədʒɪ) *n.* **1.** the branch of mathematics concerned with generalization of the concepts of continuity, limit, etc. **2.** a branch of geometry describing the properties of a figure that are unaffected by continuous distortion, such as stretching or knotting. Former name: **analysis situs. 3.** *Maths.* a family of subsets of a given set *S,* such that *S* is a topological space. **4.** the arrangement and interlinking of computers in a computer network. **5.** the study of the topography of a given place, esp. as far as it reflects its history. **6.** the anatomy of any specific bodily area, structure, or part. —**topologic** (ˌtɒpə'lɒdʒɪk) *or* ˌ**topo'logical** *adj.* —ˌ**topo'logically** *adv.* —**to'pologist** *n.*

toponym ('tɒpənɪm) *n.* **1.** the name of a place. **2.** any name derived from a place name.

toponymy (tə'pɒnɪmɪ) *n.* **1.** the study of place names. **2.** *Rare.* the anatomical nomenclature of bodily regions, as distinguished from that of specific organs or structures. —**toponymic** (ˌtɒpə'nɪmɪk) *or* ˌ**topo'nymical** *adj.*

topos ('tɒpɒs) *n., pl.* **-oi** (-ɔɪ). a basic theme or concept, esp. a stock topic in rhetoric. [C20: Greek, literally: place]

topotype ('tɒpə,taɪp) *n.* a specimen plant or animal taken from an area regarded as the typical habitat.

top out *vb. (adv.)* to place the highest stone on (a building) or perform a ceremony on this occasion.

topper ('tɒpə) *n.* **1.** an informal name for **top hat.** **2.** a person or thing that tops. **3.** *Informal.* a remark that caps the one before. **4.** *Informal.* a good chap.

topping ('tɒpɪŋ) *n.* **1.** something that tops something else, esp. a sauce or garnish for food. **2.** *Angling.* part of a brightly coloured feather, usually from a golden pheasant crest, used to top some artificial flies. *~adj.* **3.** high or superior in rank, degree, etc. **4.** *Brit. slang.* excellent; splendid.

topping lift *n. Nautical.* a line or cable for raising the end of a boom that is away from the mast.

topple ('tɒpᵊl) *vb.* **1.** to tip over or cause to tip over, esp. from a height. **2.** *(intr.)* to lean precariously or totter. **3.** *(tr.)* to overthrow; oust. [C16: frequentative of TOP[1] (vb.)]

tops (tɒps) *Slang.* *~n.* **1. the tops.** a person or thing of top quality. *~adj.* **2.** *(postpositive)* excellent; superb.

TOPS (tɒps) *n.* (in Britain) *acronym for* Training Opportunities Scheme.

topsail ('tɒp,seɪl; *Nautical* 'tɒpsᵊl) *n.* a square sail carried on a yard set on a topmast.

top-secret *adj.* containing information whose disclosure would cause exceedingly grave damage to the nation and therefore classified as needing the highest level of secrecy and security.

top-shell *n.* any marine gastropod mollusc of the mainly tropical Old World family *Trochidae,* having a typically brightly coloured top-shaped or conical shell.

topside ('tɒp,saɪd) *n.* **1.** the uppermost side of anything. **2.** *Brit. and N.Z.* a lean cut of beef from the thigh containing no bone. **3.** *(often pl.)* **a.** the part of a ship's sides above the waterline. **b.** the parts of a ship above decks.

topsoil ('tɒp,sɔɪl) *n.* **1.** the surface layer of soil. *~vb.* **2.** *(tr.)* to spread topsoil on (land). **3.** *(tr.)* to remove the topsoil from (land).

topspin ('tɒp,spɪn) *n. Tennis, etc.* spin imparted to make a ball bounce or travel exceptionally far, high, or quickly, as by hitting it with a sharp forward and upward stroke. Compare **backspin.**

topsy-turvy ('tɒpsɪ'tɜːvɪ) *adj.* **1.** upside down. **2.** in a state of confusion. *~adv.* **3.** in a topsy-turvy manner. *~n.* **4.** a topsy-turvy state. [C16: probably from *tops,* plural of TOP[1] + obsolete *tervy* to turn upside down; perhaps related to Old English *tearflian* to roll over]

top up *vb. (tr., adv.) Brit.* **1.** to raise the level of (a liquid, powder, etc.) in (a container), usually bringing it to the brim of the container: *top up the sugar in those bowls.* **2. a.** to increase the benefits from (an insurance scheme), esp. to increase a pension when a salary rise enables higher premiums to be paid. **b.** to add money to (a loan, bank account, etc.) in order to keep it at a constant or acceptable level. *~n.* **top-up. 3. a.** an amount added to something in order to raise it to or maintain it at a desired level. **b.** *(as modifier): a top-up loan; a top-up policy.*

toque (təʊk) *n.* **1.** a woman's small round brimless hat, popular esp. in Edwardian times. **2.** a hat with a small brim and a pouched crown, popular in the 16th century. **3.** *Canadian.* a close-fitting knitted hat often with a tassel or pompon. **4.** a chef's tall white hat. [C16: from French, from Old Spanish *toca* headdress, probably from Basque *tauka* hat]

tor (tɔː) *n.* **1.** a high hill, esp. a bare rocky one. **2.** *Chiefly southwestern Brit.* a prominent rock or heap of rocks, esp. on a hill. [Old English *torr,* probably of Celtic origin; compare Scottish Gaelic *torr* pile, Welsh *twr*]

Torah ('tɔːrə; *Hebrew* tɔ'ra) *n.* **1. a.** the Pentateuch. **b.** the scroll on which this is written, used in synagogue services. **2.** the whole body of traditional Jewish teaching, including the Oral Law. **3.** *(modifier)* promoting or according with traditional Jewish Law. [C16: from Hebrew: precept, from *yārāh* to instruct]

torbernite ('tɔːbə,naɪt) *n.* a green secondary mineral consisting of hydrated copper uranium phosphate in the form of square platelike crystals. Formula: $Cu(UO_2)(PO_4)_2.12H_2O$. [C19: named after *Torbern* O. Bergman (1735–84), Swedish chemist; see -ITE[1]]

torc (tɔːk) *n.* another spelling of **torque** (sense 1).

torch (tɔːtʃ) *n.* **1.** a small portable electric lamp powered by one or more dry batteries. U.S. and Canadian word: **flashlight. 2.** a wooden or tow shaft dipped in wax or tallow and set alight. **3.** anything regarded as a source of enlightenment, guidance, etc.: *the torch of evangelism.* **4.** any apparatus that burns with a hot flame for welding, brazing, or soldering. **5. carry a torch for.** to be in love with, esp. unrequitedly. **6. put to the torch.** to set fire to; burn down: *the looted monastery was put to the torch.* [C13: from Old French *torche* handful of twisted straw, from Vulgar Latin *torca* (unattested), from Latin *torquēre* to twist] —**'torch,like** *adj.*

torchbearer ('tɔːtʃ,bɛərə) *n.* **1.** a person or thing that carries a torch. **2.** a person who leads or inspires.

torchère (tɔː'ʃɛə) *n.* a tall narrow stand for holding a candelabrum. [C20: from French, from *torche* TORCH]

torchier *or* **torchiere** ('tɔːtʃɪə) *n.* a standing lamp with a bowl for casting light upwards and so giving all-round indirect illumination. [C20: from TORCHÈRE]

torchon lace ('tɔːʃən; *French* tɔrʃɔ̃) *n.* a coarse linen or cotton lace with a simple openwork pattern. [C19 *torchon,* from French: a cleaning cloth, from *torcher* to wipe, from Old French *torche* bundle of straw; see TORCH]

torch song *n.* a sentimental or romantic popular song, usually sung by a woman. [C20: from the phrase *to carry a torch for (someone)*] —**torch singer** *n.*

torchwood ('tɔːtʃ,wʊd) *n.* **1.** any of various rutaceous trees or shrubs of the genus *Amyris,* esp. *A. balsamifera,* of Florida and the West Indies, having hard resinous wood used for torches. **2.** any of various similar trees the wood of which is used for torches. **3.** the wood of any of these trees.

tore[1] (tɔː) *vb.* the past tense of **tear[2].**

tore[2] (tɔː) *n. Architect.* another name for **torus** (sense 1). [C17: from French, from Latin: TORUS]

toreador ('tɒrɪə,dɔː) *n.* a bullfighter. [C17: from Spanish, from *torear* to take part in bullfighting, from *toro* a bull, from Latin *taurus;* compare STEER[2]]

toreador pants *pl. n.* tight-fitting women's trousers reaching to midcalf or above the ankle.

torero (tɒ'rɛərəʊ) *n., pl.* **-ros.** a bullfighter, esp. one who fights on foot. [C18: from Spanish, from Late Latin *taurārius,* from Latin *taurus* a bull]

toreutics (tə'ruːtɪks) *n. (functioning as sing. or pl.)* the art of making detailed ornamental reliefs, esp. in metal, by embossing and chasing. [C19: from Greek *toreutikos* concerning work in relief, from *toreuein* to bore through, from *toreus* tool for boring] —**to'reutic** *adj.*

tori ('tɔːraɪ) *n.* the plural of **torus.**

toric ('tɒrɪk) *adj.* of, relating to, or having the form of a torus.

toric lens *n.* a lens used to correct astigmatism, having one of its surfaces shaped like part of a torus so that its focal lengths are different in different meridians.

torii ('tɔːrɪ,iː) *n., pl.* **-rii.** a gateway, esp. one at the entrance to a Japanese Shinto temple. [C19: from Japanese, literally: a perch for birds]

torment *vb.* (tɔː'mɛnt). *(tr.)* **1.** to afflict with great pain, suffering, or anguish; torture. **2.** to tease or pester in an annoying way: *stop tormenting the dog.* *~n.* ('tɔːmɛnt). **3.** physical or mental pain. **4.** a source of pain, worry, annoyance, etc. **5.** *Archaic.* an instrument of torture. **6.** *Archaic.* the infliction of torture. [C13: from Old French, from Latin *tormentum,* from *torquēre*] —**tor'mented** *adj.* —**tor'mentedly** *adv.* —**tor'menting** *adj.* —**tor'mentingly** *adv.*

tormentil ('tɔːməntɪl) *n.* a rosaceous downy perennial plant, *Potentilla erecta,* of Europe and W Asia, having serrated leaves, four-petalled yellow flowers, and an astringent root used in medicine, tanning, and dyeing. Also called: **bloodroot.** [C15: from Old French *tormentille,* from Medieval Latin *tormentilla,* from Latin *tormentum* agony; referring to its use in relieving pain; see TORMENT]

tormentor *or* **tormenter** (tɔː'mɛntə) *n.* **1.** a person or thing that torments. **2.** a curtain or movable piece of stage scenery at either side of the proscenium arch, used to mask lights or exits and entrances. **3.** *Films.* a panel of sound-insulating material placed outside the field of the camera to control the acoustics on the sound stage.

torn (tɔːn) *vb.* **1.** the past participle of **tear[2]. 2. that's torn it.** *Brit. slang.* an unexpected event or circumstance has upset one's plans. *~adj.* **3.** split or cut. **4.** divided or undecided, as in preference: *he was torn between staying and leaving.*

tornado (tɔː'neɪdəʊ) *n., pl.* **-does** *or* **-dos. 1.** Also called: **cyclone** or (U.S. and Canadian informal) **twister.** a violent storm with winds whirling around a small area of extremely low pressure, usually characterized by a dark funnel-shaped cloud causing damage along its path. **2.** a small but violent squall or whirlwind, such as those occurring on the West African coast. **3.** any violently active or destructive person or thing. [C16: probably alteration of Spanish *tronada* thunderstorm (from *tronar* to thunder, from Latin *tonāre*), through influence of *tornar* to turn, from Latin *tornāre* to turn in a lathe] —**tornadic** (tɔː'nædɪk) *adj.* —**tor'nado-,like** *adj.*

toroid ('tɔːrɔɪd) *n.* **1.** *Geometry.* a surface generated by rotating a closed plane curve about a coplanar line that does not intersect the curve. **2.** the solid enclosed by such a surface. See also **torus.** —**to'roidal** *adj.*

torose ('tɔːrəʊz, tɔː'rəʊz) *or* **torous** ('tɔːrəs) *adj. Biology.* (of a cylindrical part) having irregular swellings; knotted. [C18: from Latin *torōsus* muscular, from *torus* a swelling] —**torosity** (tɔː'rɒsɪtɪ) *n.*

torpedo (tɔː'piːdəʊ) *n., pl.* **-does. 1.** a cylindrical self-propelled weapon carrying explosives that is launched from aircraft, ships, or submarines and follows an underwater path to hit its target. **2.** *Obsolete.* a submarine mine. **3.** *U.S. and Canadian.* a firework containing gravel and a percussion cap that explodes when dashed against a hard surface. **4.** *U.S. and Canadian.* a detonator placed on a railway line as a danger signal. **5.** any of various electric rays of the genus *Torpedo.* *~vb.* **-does, -doing, -doed.** *(tr.)* **6.** to attack or hit (a ship, etc.) with one or a number of torpedoes. **7.** to render ineffective; destroy or wreck: *to torpedo the administration's plan.* [C16: from Latin: crampfish (whose electric discharges can cause numbness), from *torpēre* to be inactive; see TORPID] —**tor'pedo-,like** *adj.*

torpedo boat *n.* (formerly) a small high-speed warship designed to carry out torpedo attacks in coastal waters.

torpedo-boat destroyer *n.* (formerly) a large powerful high-speed torpedo boat designed to destroy enemy torpedo boats: a forerunner of the modern destroyer, from which the name is derived.

torpedo tube *n.* the tube from which a torpedo is discharged from submarines or surface ships.

torpid ('tɔːpɪd) *adj.* **1.** apathetic, sluggish, or lethargic. **2.** (of a hibernating animal) dormant; having greatly reduced metabolic activity. **3.** unable to move or feel. [C17: from Latin *torpidus*, from *torpēre* to be numb, motionless] —**tor'pidity** *n.* —**'torpidly** *adv.*

torpor ('tɔːpə) *n.* a state of torpidity. [C17: from Latin: inactivity, from *torpēre* to be motionless] —ˌ**torpor'ific** *adj.*

torque (tɔːk) *n.* **1.** Also: **torc.** a necklace or armband made of twisted metal, worn esp. by the ancient Britons and Gauls. **2.** any force or system of forces that causes or tends to cause rotation. **3.** the ability of a shaft to cause rotation. [C19: from Latin *torquēs* necklace, and *torquēre* to twist]

torque converter *n.* a hydraulic device for the smooth transmission of power in which an engine-driven impeller transmits its momentum to a fluid held in a sealed container, which in turn drives a rotor. Also called: **hydraulic coupling.**

torque meter *n. Engineering.* a device designed to determine the torque or torsion in a shaft, usually by measuring the twist in a calibrated length of shafting. Also called: **torsion meter.**

torques ('tɔːkwiːz) *n.* a distinctive band of hair, feathers, skin, or colour around the neck of an animal; a collar. [C17: from Latin: necklace, from *torquēre* to twist] —**torquate** ('tɔːkwɪt, -kweɪt) *adj.*

torque spanner *n.* a spanner having a torque-limiting mechanism which can be set to a predetermined value.

torque wrench *n.* a type of wrench with a gauge attached to indicate the torque applied to the workpiece.

torr (tɔː) *n., pl.* **torr.** a unit of pressure equal to one millimetre of mercury (133.322 newtons per square metre). [C20: named after Evangelista *Torricelli* (1608–47), Italian physicist and mathematician]

torrefy ('tɒrɪˌfaɪ) *vb.* **-fies, -fying, -fied.** (*tr.*) to dry (drugs, ores, etc.) by subjection to intense heat; roast. [C17: from French *torréfier*, from Latin *torrefacere*, from *torrēre* to parch + *facere* to make] —**torrefaction** (ˌtɒrɪ'fækʃən) *n.*

Torrens title *n. Austral.* legal title to land based on record of registration rather than on title deeds. [from Sir Robert Richard *Torrens* (1814–84), who introduced the system as premier of South Australia in 1857]

torrent ('tɒrənt) *n.* **1.** a fast, voluminous, or violent stream of water or other liquid. **2.** an overwhelming flow of thoughts, words, sound, etc. ~*adj.* **3.** *Rare.* like or relating to a torrent. [C17: from French, from Latin *torrēns* (n.), from *torrēns* (adj.) burning, from *torrēre* to burn]

torrential (tɒ'rɛnʃəl, tə-) *adj.* **1.** of or relating to a torrent. **2.** pouring or flowing fast, violently, or heavily: *torrential rain.* **3.** abundant, overwhelming, or irrepressible: *torrential abuse.* —**tor'rentially** *adv.*

Torricellian tube (ˌtɒrɪ'sɛlɪən) *n.* a vertical glass tube partly evacuated and partly filled with mercury, the height of which is used as a measure of atmospheric pressure. [C17: named after its inventor, E. *Torricelli*; see TORR]

Torricellian vacuum *n.* the vacuum at the top of a Torricellian tube.

torrid ('tɒrɪd) *adj.* **1.** so hot and dry as to parch or scorch. **2.** arid or parched. **3.** highly charged emotionally: *a torrid love scene.* [C16: from Latin *torridus*, from *torrēre* to scorch] —**tor'ridity** *or* **'torridness** *n.* —**'torridly** *adv.*

Torrid Zone *n. Rare.* that part of the earth's surface lying between the tropics of Cancer and Capricorn.

torsade (tɔː'seɪd) *n.* an ornamental twist or twisted cord, as on hats. [C19: from French, from obsolete *tors* twisted, from Late Latin *torsus*, from Latin *torquēre* to twist]

torsi ('tɔːsɪ) *n. Rare.* a plural of **torso.**

torsibility (ˌtɔːsə'bɪlɪtɪ) *n.* **1.** the ability to be twisted. **2.** the degree of resistance to or the capacity of recovering from being twisted.

torsion ('tɔːʃən) *n.* **1. a.** the twisting of a part by application of equal and opposite torques. **b.** the condition of twist and shear stress produced by a torque on a part or component. **2.** the act of twisting or the state of being twisted. [C15: from Old French, from medical Latin *torsiō* griping pains, from Latin *torquēre* to twist, torture] —**'torsional** *adj.* —**'torsionally** *adv.*

torsion balance *n.* an instrument used to measure small forces, esp. electric or magnetic forces, by the torsion they produce in a thin wire, thread, or rod.

torsion bar *n.* a metal bar acting as a torsional spring, esp. as used in the suspensions of some motor vehicles.

torsion meter *n.* another name for **torque meter.**

torsk (tɔːsk) *n., pl.* **torsks** *or* **torsk.** a gadoid food fish, *Brosmius brosme*, of northern coastal waters, having a single long dorsal fin. Usual U.S. and Canadian name: **cusk.** [C17: of Scandinavian origin; related to Old Norse *thorskr* codfish, Danish *torsk*]

torso ('tɔːsəʊ) *n., pl.* **-sos** *or* **-si** (-sɪ). **1.** the trunk of the human body. **2.** a statue of a nude human trunk, esp. without the head or limbs. **3.** something regarded as incomplete or truncated. [C18: from Italian: stalk, stump, from Latin: THYRSUS]

tort (tɔːt) *n. Law.* a civil wrong or injury arising out of an act or failure to act, independently of any contract, for which an action for damages may be brought. [C14: from Old French, from Medieval Latin *tortum*, literally: something twisted, from Latin *torquēre* to twist]

torte (tɔːt; *German* 'tɔrtə) *n.* a rich cake, originating in Austria, usually decorated or filled with cream, fruit, nuts, and jam. [C16: ultimately perhaps from Late Latin *tōrta* a round loaf, of uncertain origin]

tortellini (ˌtɔːtə'liːnɪ) *n.* pasta cut into small rounds, folded about a filling, and boiled. [from Italian, diminutive of *tortelli* a type of pie, ultimately from Late Latin *tōrta* a round loaf or cake; see TORTE]

tort-feasor ('tɔːt'fiːzə) *n. Law.* a person guilty of tort. [C17: from Old French, literally: wrongdoer, from TORT + *faiseur*, from *faire* to do]

torticollis (ˌtɔːtɪ'kɒlɪs) *n. Pathol.* an abnormal position of the head, usually with the neck bent to one side, caused congenitally by contracture of muscles, muscular spasm, etc. [C19: New Latin, from Latin *tortus* twisted (from *torquēre* to twist) + *collum* neck] —ˌ**torti'collar** *adj.*

tortile ('tɔːtaɪl) *adj. Rare.* twisted or coiled. [C17: from Latin *tortilis* winding, from *tortus* twisted, from *torquēre* to twist] —**tortility** (tɔː'tɪlɪtɪ) *n.*

tortilla (tɔː'tiːə) *n. Mexican cookery.* a kind of thin pancake made from corn meal and cooked on a hot griddle until dry. [C17: from Spanish: a little cake, from *torta* a round cake, from Late Latin; see TORTE]

tortillon (ˌtɔːtiː'ɒn, -'əʊn; *French* tɔrtijɔ̃) *n.* another word for **stump** (sense 5). [from French: something twisted, from Old French *tortiller* to twist]

tortious ('tɔːʃəs) *adj. Law.* having the nature of or involving a tort; wrongful. [C14: from Anglo-French *torcious*, from *torcion*, literally: a twisting, from Late Latin *tortiō* torment, from Latin *torquēre* to twist; influenced in meaning by TORT] —**'tortiously** *adv.*

tortoise ('tɔːtəs) *n.* **1.** any herbivorous terrestrial chelonian reptile of the family *Testudinidae*, of most warm regions, having a heavy dome-shaped shell and clawed limbs. **2. water tortoise.** another name for **terrapin.** **3.** a slow-moving person. **4.** another word for **testudo.** ~See also **giant tortoise.** [C15: probably from Old French *tortue* (influenced by Latin *tortus* twisted), from Medieval Latin *tortūca*, from Late Latin *tartarūcha* coming from Tartarus, from Greek *tartaroukhos;* referring to the belief that the tortoise originated in the underworld]

tortoise beetle *n.* a metallic-coloured leaf beetle of the genus *Cassida*, in which the elytra and terga cover the body like a shell.

tortoiseshell ('tɔːtəsˌʃɛl) *n.* **1.** a horny translucent yellow-and-brown mottled substance obtained from the outer layer of the shell of the hawksbill turtle: used for making ornaments, jewellery, etc. **2.** a similar synthetic substance, esp. plastic or celluloid, now more widely used than the natural product. **3.** a breed of domestic cat, usually female, having black, cream, and brownish markings. **4.** any of several nymphalid butterflies of the genus *Nymphalis*, and related genera, having orange-brown wings with black markings. **5. tortoiseshell turtle.** another name for **hawksbill turtle.** **6. a.** a yellowish-brown mottled colour. **b.** (*as adj.*): *a tortoiseshell décor.* **7.** (*modifier*) made of tortoiseshell: *a tortoiseshell comb.*

tortoni (tɔː'təʊnɪ) *n.* a rich ice cream often flavoured with sherry. [from Italian: probably from the name of a 19th-century Italian caterer in Paris]

tortricid ('tɔːtrɪsɪd) *n.* **1.** any small moth of the chiefly temperate family *Tortricidae*, the larvae of which live concealed in leaves, which they roll or tie together, and are pests of fruit and forest trees: includes the codling moth. ~*adj.* **2.** of, relating to, or belonging to the family *Tortricidae.* [C19: from New Latin *Tortrīcidae*, from *tortrix*, feminine of *tortor*, literally: twister, referring to the leaf-rolling of the larvae, from *torquēre* to twist]

tortuosity (ˌtɔːtjʊ'ɒsɪtɪ) *n., pl.* **-ties.** **1.** the state or quality of being tortuous. **2.** a twist, turn, or coil.

tortuous ('tɔːtjʊəs) *adj.* **1.** twisted or winding: *a tortuous road.* **2.** devious or cunning: *a tortuous mind.* **3.** intricate. —**'tortuously** *adv.* —**'tortuousness** *n.*

torture ('tɔːtʃə) *vb.* (*tr.*) **1.** to cause extreme physical pain to, esp. in order to extract information, break resistance, etc.: *to torture prisoners.* **2.** to give mental anguish to. **3.** to twist into a grotesque form. ~*n.* **4.** physical or mental anguish. **5.** the practice of torturing a person. **6.** a cause of mental agony or worry. [C16: from Late Latin *tortūra* a twisting, from *torquēre* to twist] —**'tortured** *adj.* —**'torturedly** *adv.* —**'torturer** *n.* —**'torturesome** *or* **'torturous** *adj.* —**'torturing** *adj.* —**'torturingly** *adv.* —**'torturously** *adv.*

torus ('tɔːrəs) *n., pl.* **-ri** (-raɪ). **1.** Also called: **tore.** a large convex moulding approximately semicircular in cross section, esp. one used on the base of a classical column. **2.** *Geom.* a ring-shaped surface generated by rotating a circle about a coplanar line that does not intersect the circle. Area: $4\pi^2 Rr$; volume: $2\pi^2 Rr^2$, where r is the radius of the circle and R is the distance from the line to the centre of the circle. **3.** *Botany.* another name for receptacle (sense 2). 4. *Anatomy.* a ridge, fold, or similar linear elevation. [C16: from Latin: a swelling, of obscure origin]

Tory ('tɔːrɪ) *n., pl.* **-ries.** 1. a member of the Conservative Party in Great Britain or Canada. 2. a member of the English political party that opposed the exclusion of James, Duke of York from the royal succession (1679–80). Tory remained the label for subsequent major conservative interests. 3. an American supporter of the British cause; loyalist. Compare **Whig.** 4. (*sometimes not cap.*) an ultraconservative or reactionary. 5. (in the 17th century) an Irish Roman Catholic, esp. an outlaw who preyed upon English settlers. ~*adj.* 6. of, characteristic of, or relating to Tories. 7. (*sometimes not cap.*) ultraconservative or reactionary. [C17: from Irish *tōraidhe* outlaw, from Middle Irish *tōir* pursuit] —'**Toryish** *adj.* —'**Toryism** *n.*

tosh (tɒʃ) *n. Slang, chiefly Brit.* nonsense; rubbish. [C19: of unknown origin]

toss (tɒs) *vb.* 1. (*tr.*) to throw lightly or with a flourish, esp. with the palm of the hand upwards. 2. to fling or be flung about, esp. constantly or regularly in an agitated or violent way: *a ship tosses in a storm.* 3. to discuss or put forward for discussion in an informal way. 4. (*tr.*) (of an animal such as a horse) to throw (its rider). 5. (*tr.*) (of an animal) to butt with the head or the horns and throw into the air: *the bull tossed the matador.* 6. (*tr.*) to shake, agitate, or disturb. 7. to toss up a coin with (someone) in order to decide or allot something: *I'll toss you for it; let's toss for it.* 8. (*intr.*) to move away angrily or impatiently: *she tossed out of the room.* ~*n.* 9. an abrupt movement. 10. a rolling or pitching motion. 11. the act or an instance of tossing. 12. the act of tossing up a coin. See **toss-up.** 13. **argue the toss.** to wrangle or dispute at length. 14. a fall from a horse or other animal. [C16: of Scandinavian origin; related to Norwegian, Swedish *tossa* to strew]

tosser ('tɒsə) *n. Brit. slang.* a stupid or despicable person. [C20: probably from TOSS OFF (to masturbate)]

toss off *vb.* (*adv.*) 1. (*tr.*) to perform, write, consume, etc., quickly and easily: *he tossed off a letter to Jim.* 2. (*tr.*) to drink quickly at one draught. 3. (*intr.*) *Brit. taboo.* to masturbate.

tosspot ('tɒsˌpɒt) *n. Archaic or literary.* a habitual drinker.

toss up *vb.* (*adv.*) 1. to spin (a coin) in the air in order to decide between alternatives by guessing which side will fall uppermost. 2. (*tr.*) to prepare (food) quickly. ~*n.* **toss-up.** 3. an instance of tossing up a coin. 4. *Informal.* an even chance or risk; gamble.

tot[1] (tɒt) *n.* 1. a young child; toddler. 2. *Chiefly Brit.* a small amount of anything. 3. a small measure of spirits. [C18: perhaps short for *totterer;* see TOTTER]

tot[2] (tɒt) *vb.* **tots, totting, totted.** (usually foll. by *up*) *Chiefly Brit.* to total; add. [C17: shortened from TOTAL or from Latin *totum* all]

total ('təʊtᵊl) *n.* 1. the whole, esp. regarded as the complete sum of a number of parts. ~*adj.* 2. complete; absolute: *the evening was a total failure; a total eclipse.* 3. (*prenominal*) being or related to a total: *the total number of passengers.* ~*vb.* **-tals, -talling, -talled** *or U.S.* **-tals, -taling, -taled.** 4. (when *intr.*, sometimes foll. by *to*) to amount: *to total six pounds.* 5. (*tr.*) to add up: *to total a list of prices.* 6. (*tr.*) *Slang.* to kill or destroy. [C14: from Old French, from Medieval Latin *tōtālis,* from Latin *tōtus* all] —'**totally** *adv.*

total allergy syndrome *n.* a condition in which a person suffers from a large number of symptoms that are claimed to be caused by allergies to various substances used or encountered in modern life.

total depravity *n. Chiefly Calvinist theol.* the doctrine that man's nature is totally corrupt as a result of the Fall.

total eclipse *n.* an eclipse as seen from a particular area of the earth's surface where the eclipsed body is completely hidden. Compare **annular eclipse, partial eclipse.**

total football *n.* an attacking style of play, popularized by the Dutch national team of the 1970s, in which there are no fixed positions and every outfield player can join in the attack.

total heat *n.* another term for **enthalpy.**

total internal reflection *n. Physics.* the complete reflection of a light ray at the boundary of two media, when the ray is in the medium with greater refractive index.

totalitarian (təʊˌtælɪ'tɛərɪən) *adj.* of, denoting, relating to, or characteristic of a dictatorial one-party state that regulates every realm of life. [from TOTALITY + -ARIAN] —**toˌtali'tarianism** *n.*

totality (təʊ'tælɪtɪ) *n., pl.* **-ties.** 1. the whole amount. 2. the state of being total. 3. the state or period of an eclipse when light from the eclipsed body is totally obscured.

totalizator ('təʊtᵊlaɪˌzeɪtə), **totalizer** *or* **totalisator, totaliser** *n.* 1. a system of betting on horse races in which the aggregate stake, less an administration charge and tax, is paid out to winners in proportion to their stake. 2. the machine that records bets in this system and works out odds, pays out winnings, etc. 3. an apparatus for registering totals, as of a particular function or measurement. ~U.S. and Canadian term (for senses 1, 2): **pari-mutuel.**

totalize *or* **totalise** ('təʊtᵊˌlaɪz) *vb.* to combine or make into a total. —ˌ**totali'zation** *or* ˌ**totali'sation** *n.*

totalizer *or* **totaliser** ('təʊtᵊˌlaɪzə) *n.* 1. a variant of **totalizator.** 2. *Chiefly U.S.* an adding machine.

total recall *n. Psychol.* the faculty or an instance of complete and clear recall of every detail of something.

total serialism *or* **serialization** *n.* (in some music after 1945) the use of serial techniques applied to such elements as rhythm, dynamics, and tone colour.

totaquine ('təʊtəˌkwiːn, -kwɪn) *n.* a mixture of quinine and other alkaloids derived from cinchona bark, used as a substitute for quinine in treating malaria. [C20: from New Latin *tōtaquīna,* from TOTA(L) + Spanish *quina* cinchona bark; see QUININE]

totara ('təʊtərə) *n.* a tall coniferous forest tree, *Podocarpus totara,* of New Zealand, having a hard durable wood. [Maori]

tote[1] (təʊt) *Informal.* ~*vb.* 1. (*tr.*) to carry, convey, or drag. ~*n.* 2. the act of or an instance of toting. 3. something toted. [C17: of obscure origin] —'**toter** *n.*

tote[2] (təʊt) *n.* (usually preceded by *the*) *Informal.* short for **totalizator** (senses 1, 2).

tote bag *n.* a large roomy handbag or shopping bag.

totem ('təʊtəm) *n.* 1. (in some societies, esp. among North American Indians) an object, species of animal or plant, or natural phenomenon symbolizing a clan, family, etc., often having ritual associations. 2. a representation of such an object. [C18: from Ojibwa *nintōtēm* mark of my family] —**totemic** (təʊ'tɛmɪk) *adj.* —**to'temically** *adv.*

totemism ('təʊtəˌmɪzəm) *n.* 1. the belief in kinship of groups or individuals having a common totem. 2. the rituals, taboos, and other practices associated with such a belief. —'**totemist** *n.* —ˌ**totem'istic** *adj.*

totem pole *n.* a pole carved or painted with totemic figures set up by certain North American Indians, esp. those of the NW Pacific coast, within a village as a tribal symbol or, sometimes, in memory of a dead person.

tother *or* **t'other** ('tʌðə) *adj., n. Archaic or dialect.* the other. [C13 *the tother,* by mistaken division from *thet other* (*thet,* from Old English *thæt,* neuter of THE[1])]

totipalmate (ˌtəʊtɪ'pælmɪt, -ˌmeɪt) *adj.* (of certain birds) having all four toes webbed. [C19: from Latin *tōtus* entire + *palmate,* from Latin *palmātus* shaped like a hand, from *palma* PALM[1]] —ˌ**totipal'mation** *n.*

totipotent (təʊ'tɪpətənt) *adj.* (of an animal cell) capable of differentiation and so forming a new individual, tissue, organ, etc. [C20: from Latin *tōtus* entire + POTENT] —**to'tipotency** *n.*

totter ('tɒtə) *vb.* (*intr.*) 1. to walk or move in an unsteady manner, as from old age. 2. to sway or shake as if about to fall. 3. to be failing, unstable, or precarious. ~*n.* 4. the act or an instance of tottering. [C12: perhaps from Old English *tealtrian* to waver, and Middle Dutch *touteren* to stagger] —'**totterer** *n.* —'**tottering** *adj.* —'**totteringly** *adv.* —'**tottery** *adj.*

tottie *or* **totty** ('tɒtɪ) *adj. Chiefly Scot.* very small; tiny. [from TOT[1]]

totting ('tɒtɪŋ) *n. Brit.* the practice of searching through rubbish for usable or saleable items. [C19: of unknown origin]

toucan ('tuːkən) *n.* any tropical American arboreal fruit-eating bird of the family *Ramphastidae,* having a large brightly coloured bill with serrated edges and a bright plumage. [C16: from French, from Portuguese *tucano,* from Tupi *tucana,* probably imitative of its cry]

touch (tʌtʃ) *n.* 1. the sense by which the texture and other qualities of objects can be experienced when they come in contact with a part of the body surface, esp. the tips of the fingers. Related adj.: **tactile.** 2. the quality of an object as perceived by this sense; feel; feeling. 3. the act or an instance of something coming into contact with the body. 4. a gentle push, tap, or caress. 5. a small amount; hint: *a touch of sarcasm.* 6. a noticeable effect; influence: *the house needed a woman's touch.* 7. any slight stroke or mark: *with a touch of his brush he captured the scene.* 8. characteristic manner or style: *the artist had a distinctive touch.* 9. a detail of some work, esp. a literary or artistic work: *she added a few finishing touches to the book.* 10. a slight attack, as of a disease: *a touch of bronchitis.* 11. a specific ability or facility: *the champion appeared to have lost his touch.* 12. the state of being aware of a situation or in contact with someone: *to get in touch with someone.* 13. the state of being in physical contact. 14. a trial or test (esp. in the phrase **put to the touch**). 15. *Rugby, soccer, etc.* the area outside the touchlines, beyond which the ball is out of play (esp. in the phrase **in touch**). 16. *Archaic.* **a.** an official stamp on metal indicating standard purity. **b.** the die stamp used to apply this mark. Now usually called: **hallmark.** 17. a scoring hit in competitive fencing. 18. an estimate of the amount of gold in an alloy as obtained by use of a touchstone. 19. the technique of fingering a keyboard instrument. 20. the quality of the action of a keyboard instrument with regard to the relative ease with which the keys may be depressed: *this piano has a nice touch.* 21. *Bell-ringing.* any series of changes where the permutations are fewer in number than for a peal. 22. *Slang.* **a.** the act of asking for money as a loan or gift, often by devious means. **b.** the money received in this way. **c.** a person asked for money in this way: *he was an easy touch.* ~*vb.* 23. (*tr.*) to cause or permit a part of the body to come into contact with. 24. (*tr.*) to tap, feel, or strike, esp. with the hand: *don't touch the cake!* 25. to come or cause (something) to come into contact with (something else): *their hands touched briefly; he touched the match to the fuse.* 26. (*intr.*) to be in contact. 27. (*tr.; usually used with a negative*) to take hold of (a person or thing), esp. in violence: *don't touch the baby!* **28.** to be adjacent to (each other): *the two properties touch.* **29.** (*tr.*) to move or disturb by handling: *someone's touched my desk.* **30.** (*tr.*) to have an effect on: *the war scarcely touched our town.* **31.** (*tr.*) to produce an emotional response in: *his sad story touched her.* **32.** (*tr.*) to affect; concern. **33.** (*tr.; usually used with a negative*) to partake of, eat, or drink. **34.** (*tr.; usually used with a negative*) to handle or deal with: *I wouldn't touch that business.* **35.** (when *intr.*, often foll. by *on*) to allude (to) briefly or in passing: *the speech touched on several subjects.* **36.** (*tr.*) to tinge or tint slightly: *brown hair touched with gold.* **37.** (*tr.*) to spoil or injure slightly: *blackfly touched the flowers.* **38.** (*tr.*) to mark, as with a brush or pen. **39.** (*tr.*) to compare to in quality or attainment; equal or match: *there's no-one to touch him.* **40.** (*tr.*) to reach or attain: *he touched the high point in his career.* **41.** (*intr.*) to dock or stop briefly: *the ship touches at Tenerife.* **42.** (*tr.*) *Slang.* to ask for a loan or gift of money from. **43.** *Rare.* **a.** to finger (the keys or strings of an instrument). **b.** to play (a tune, piece of music, etc.) in this way. **44.** (*tr.*) *Archaic.* to apply a stamp to (metal) indicating standard purity. ~See also **touch-down, touch off, touch up.** [C13: from Old French *tochier,* from Vulgar Latin *toccāre* (unattested) to strike, ring (a bell), probably imitative of a tapping sound] —'**touchable** *adj.* —'**touchableness** *n.* —'**toucher** *n.* —'**touchless** *adj.*

touch and go *adj.* (**touch-and-go** *when prenominal*) risky or critical: *a touch-and-go situation.*

touchback ('tʌtʃˌbæk) *n. American football.* a play in which the ball is put down by a player behind his own goal line when the ball has been put across the goal line by an opponent. Compare **safety** (sense 4b.).

touchdown ('tʌtʃˌdaʊn) *n.* **1.** the moment at which a landing aircraft or spacecraft comes into contact with the landing surface. **2.** *Rugby.* the act of placing or touching the ball on the ground behind the goal line, as in scoring a try. **3.** *American football.* a scoring play worth six points, achieved by being in possession of the ball in the opposing team's end zone. Abbrev.: **TD.** See also **field goal.** ~*vb.* **touch down.** (*intr., adv.*) **4.** (of a space vehicle, aircraft, etc.) to land. **5.** *Rugby.* to place the ball behind the goal line, as when scoring a try.

touché (tuːˈʃeɪ) *interj.* **1.** an acknowledgment that a scoring hit has been made in a fencing competition. **2.** an acknowledgment of the striking home of a remark or the capping of a witticism. [from French, literally: touched]

touched (tʌtʃt) *adj.* (*postpositive*) **1.** moved to sympathy or emotion; affected. **2.** showing slight insanity.

touch football *n.* an informal version of football chiefly characterized by players being touched rather than tackled.

touchhole ('tʌtʃˌhəʊl) *n.* a hole in the breech of early cannon and firearms through which the charge was ignited.

touching ('tʌtʃɪŋ) *adj.* **1.** evoking or eliciting tender feelings: *your sympathy is touching.* ~*prep.* **2.** on the subject of; relating to. —'**touchingly** *adv.* —'**touchingness** *n.*

touch-in goal *n. Rugby.* the area at each end of a pitch between the goal line and the dead-ball line.

touch judge *n.* one of the two linesmen in rugby.

touchline ('tʌtʃˌlaɪn) *n.* either of the lines marking the side of the playing area in certain games, such as rugby.

touchmark ('tʌtʃˌmɑːk) *n.* a maker's mark stamped on pewter objects.

touch-me-not *n.* any of several balsaminaceous plants of the genus *Impatiens,* esp. *I. noli-me-tangere,* having yellow spurred flowers and seed pods that burst open at a touch when ripe. Also called: **noli-me-tangere.**

touch off *vb.* (*tr., adv.*) **1.** to cause to explode, as by touching with a match. **2.** to cause (a disturbance, violence, etc.) to begin: *the marchers' action touched off riots.*

touchpaper ('tʌtʃˌpeɪpə) *n.* paper soaked in saltpetre and used for firing gunpowder.

touchstone ('tʌtʃˌstəʊn) *n.* **1.** a criterion or standard by which judgment is made. **2.** a hard dark siliceous stone, such as basalt or jasper, that is used to test the quality of gold and silver from the colour of the streak they produce on it.

touch system *n.* a typing system in which the fingers are trained to find the correct keys, permitting the typist to read and type copy without looking at the keyboard.

touch-type *vb.* (*intr.*) to type without having to look at the keys of the typewriter. —'**touch-ˌtypist** *n.*

touch up *vb.* (*tr., adv.*) **1.** to put extra or finishing touches to. **2.** to enhance, renovate, or falsify by putting extra touches to: *to touch up a photograph.* **3.** to stimulate or rouse as by a tap or light blow. **4.** *Brit. slang.* to touch or caress (someone), esp. to arouse sexual feelings. ~*n.* **touch-up.** **5.** a renovation or retouching, as of a painting.

touchwood ('tʌtʃˌwʊd) *n.* something, esp. dry wood or fungus material such as amadou, used as tinder. [C16: TOUCH (in the sense: to kindle) + WOOD]

touchy ('tʌtʃɪ) *adj.* **touchier, touchiest.** **1.** easily upset or irritated; oversensitive. **2.** extremely risky. **3.** easily ignited. —'**touchily** *adv.* —'**touchiness** *n.*

tough (tʌf) *adj.* **1.** strong or resilient; durable: *a tough material.* **2.** not tender: *he could not eat the tough steak.* **3.** having a great capacity for endurance; hardy and fit: *a tough mountaineer.* **4.** rough or pugnacious: *a tough gangster.* **5.** resolute or intractable: *a tough employer.* **6.** difficult or troublesome to do or deal with: *a tough problem.* **7.** *Informal.* unfortunate or unlucky: *it's tough on him.* ~*n.* **8.** a rough, vicious, or pugnacious person. ~*adv.* **9.** *Informal.* violently, aggressively, or intractably: *to treat someone tough.* ~*vb.* (*tr.*) **10.** *Slang.* to stand firm, hold out against (a difficulty or difficult situation) (esp. in **tough it out**). [Old English *tōh;* related to Old High German *zāhi* tough, Old Norse *tā* trodden ground in front of a house] —'**toughish** *adj.* —'**toughly** *adv.*

toughen ('tʌfən) *vb.* to make or become tough or tougher.

tough love *n.* the practice of taking a stern attitude towards a relative or friend suffering from an addiction, etc., to help the addict overcome the problem.

tough-minded *adj.* practical, unsentimental, or intractable. —ˌ**tough-'mindedly** *adv.* —ˌ**tough-'mindedness** *n.*

toughness ('tʌfnɪs) *n.* **1.** the quality or an instance of being tough. **2.** *Metallurgy.* the ability of a metal to withstand repeated twisting and bending, measured by the energy in kilojoules needed to break it. Compare **brittleness** (sense 2), **softness** (sense 2).

toun (tuːn) *n. Scot.* **1.** a town. **2.** a farmstead.

toupee ('tuːpeɪ) *n.* **1.** a wig or hairpiece worn, esp. by men, to cover a bald or balding place. **2.** (formerly) a prominent lock on a periwig, esp. in the 18th century. [C18: apparently from French *toupet* forelock, from Old French *toup* top, of Germanic origin; see TOP[1]]

tour (tʊə) *n.* **1.** an extended journey, usually taken for pleasure, visiting places of interest along the route. **2.** *Military.* a period of service, esp. in one place of duty. **3.** a short trip, as for inspection. **4.** a trip made by a theatre company, orchestra, etc., to perform in several different places: *a concert tour.* **5.** an overseas trip made by a cricket or rugby team, etc., to play in several places. ~*vb.* **6.** to make a tour of (a place). [C14: from Old French: a turn, from Latin *tornus* a lathe, from Greek *tornos;* compare TURN]

touraco *or* **turaco** ('tʊərəˌkəʊ) *n., pl.* **-cos.** any brightly coloured crested arboreal African bird of the family *Musophagidae:* order *Cuculiformes* (cuckoos, etc.). [C18: of West African origin]

tourbillion (tʊəˈbɪljən) *n.* a rare word for **whirlwind.** [C15: from French *tourbillon,* ultimately from Latin *turbō* something that spins, from *turbāre* to confuse]

tour de force *French.* (tur də fɔrs; *English* ˈtʊə də ˈfɔːs) *n., pl.* ***tours de force*** (tur; *English* ˈtʊə). a masterly or brilliant stroke, creation, effect, or accomplishment. [literally: feat of skill or strength]

tourer ('tʊərə) *n.* a large open car with a folding top, usually seating a driver and four passengers. Also called (esp. U.S.): **touring car.**

Tourette syndrome (tʊəˈrɛt) *n.* a brain disorder characterized by involuntary outbursts of swearing, spitting, barking, etc., and sudden involuntary movements. Also called: **Gilles de la Tourette syndrome, Tourette's syndrome, Tourette's.** [C20: named after Georges Gilles de la *Tourette* 1857–1904, French neurologist]

tourie ('tʊrɪ) *n. Scot.* a variant spelling of **toorie.**

tourism ('tʊərɪzəm) *n.* tourist travel and the services connected with it, esp. when regarded as an industry.

tourist ('tʊərɪst) *n.* **1. a.** a person who travels for pleasure, usually sightseeing and staying in hotels. **b.** (*as modifier*): *tourist attractions.* **2.** a person on an excursion or sightseeing tour. **3.** a person travelling abroad as a member of a sports team that is playing a series of usually international matches. **4.** Also called: **tourist class.** the lowest class of accommodation on a passenger ship. ~*adj.* **5.** of or relating to tourist accommodation. —**tour'istic** *adj.*

touristy ('tʊərɪstɪ) *adj. Informal, often derogatory.* abounding in or designed for tourists.

tourmaline ('tʊəməˌliːn) *n.* any of a group of hard glassy minerals of variable colour consisting of complex borosilicates of aluminium with quantities of lithium, sodium, potassium, iron, and magnesium in hexagonal crystalline form: used in optical and electrical equipment and in jewellery. [C18: from German *Turmalin,* from Sinhalese *toramalli* carnelian] —**tourmalinic** (ˌtʊəməˈlɪnɪk) *adj.*

tournament ('tʊənəmənt, 'tɔː-, 'tɜː-) *n.* **1.** a sporting competition in which contestants play a series of games to determine an overall winner. **2.** a meeting for athletic or other sporting contestants: *an archery tournament.* **3.** *Medieval history* **a.** (originally) a martial sport or contest in which mounted combatants fought for a prize. **b.** (later) a meeting for knightly sports and exercises. [C13: from Old French *torneiement,* from *torneier* to fight on horseback, literally: to turn, from the constant wheeling round of the combatants; see TOURNEY]

tournedos ('tʊənəˌdəʊ) *n., pl.* **-dos** (-ˌdəʊz). a thick round steak of beef cut from the fillet or undercut of sirloin. [from French, from *tourner* to TURN + *dos* back]

tourney ('tʊənɪ, 'tɔː-) *Medieval history.* ~*n.* **1.** a knightly tournament. ~*vb.* **2.** (*intr.*) to engage in a tourney. [C13: from Old French *torneier,* from Vulgar Latin *tornidiāre* (unattested) to turn constantly, from Latin *tornāre* to TURN (in a lathe); see TOURNAMENT] —'**tourneyer** *n.*

tourniquet ('tʊənɪˌkeɪ, 'tɔː-) *n. Med.* any instrument or device for temporarily constricting an artery of the arm or leg to control bleeding. [C17: from French: device that operates by turning, from *tourner* to TURN]

tour operator *n.* a person or company that provides package holidays.

tousle ('tauz^{ə}l) *vb.* *(tr.)* **1.** to tangle, ruffle, or disarrange. **2.** to treat roughly. *~n.* **3.** a disorderly, tangled, or rumpled state. **4.** a dishevelled or disordered mass, esp. of hair. [C15: from Low German *tūsen* to shake; related to Old High German *zirzūsōn* to tear to pieces]

tous-les-mois (ˌtuːleɪ'mwɑː) *n.* **1.** a large widely cultivated plant, *Canna edulis,* of the West Indies and South America, having purplish stems and leaves, bright red flowers and edible tubers: family *Cannaceae.* **2.** the tuber of this plant, used as a source of starch. [C19: from French, literally: all the months, probably an attempt to give phonetic reproduction of *tolomane,* from native West Indian name]

tout (taʊt) *vb.* **1.** to solicit (business, customers, etc.) or hawk (merchandise), esp. in a brazen way. **2.** *(intr.)* **a.** to spy on racehorses being trained in order to obtain information for betting purposes. **b.** to sell, or attempt to sell, such information or to take bets, esp. in public places. **3.** *(tr.) Informal.* to recommend flatteringly or excessively. *~n.* **4. a.** a person who spies on racehorses so as to obtain betting information to sell. **b.** a person who sells information obtained by such spying. **5.** a person who solicits business in a brazen way. **6.** Also called: **ticket tout.** a person who sells tickets unofficially for a heavily booked sporting event, concert, etc., at greatly inflated prices. **7.** *Northern Ireland.* a police informer. [C14 (in the sense: to peer, look out): related to Old English *tȳtan* to peep out] —'**touter** *n.*

tout à fait *French.* (tut a fɛ) *adv.* completely; absolutely.

tout court *French.* (tu kur) *adv.* simply; briefly.

tout de suite *French.* (tud sɥit) *adv.* at once; immediately.

tout ensemble *French.* (tut ɑ̃sɑ̃blə) *adv.* **1.** everything considered; all in all. *~n.* **2.** the total impression or effect.

tout le monde *French.* (tu lə mɔ̃d) *n.* all the world; everyone.

touzle ('tauz^{ə}l) *vb., n.* a rare spelling of **tousle.**

tovarisch, tovarich, *or* **tovarish** (tə'vɑːrɪʃ; *Russian* ta'varjɪʃtʃ) *n.* comrade: a term of address. [from Russian]

tow[1] (təʊ) *vb.* **1.** *(tr.)* to pull or drag (a vehicle, boat, etc.), esp. by means of a rope or cable. *~n.* **2.** the act or an instance of towing. **3.** the state of being towed (esp. in the phrases **in tow, under tow, on tow**). **4.** something towed. **5.** something used for towing. **6. in tow.** in one's charge or under one's influence. **7.** *Informal.* (in motor racing, etc.) the act of taking advantage of the slipstream of another car (esp. in the phrase **get a tow**). **8.** short for **ski tow.** [Old English *togian;* related to Old Frisian *togia,* Old Norse *toga,* Old High German *zogōn*] —'**towable** *adj.*

tow[2] (təʊ) *n.* **1.** the fibres of hemp, flax, jute, etc., in the scutched state. **2.** synthetic fibres preparatory to spinning. **3.** the coarser fibres discarded after combing. [Old English *tōw;* related to Old Saxon *tou,* Old Norse *tō* tuft of wool, Dutch *touwen* to spin] —'**towy** *adj.*

towage ('təʊɪdʒ) *n.* **1.** a charge made for towing. **2.** the act of towing or the state of being towed.

toward *adj.* ('təʊəd). **1.** *Now rare.* in progress; afoot. **2.** *Obsolete.* about to happen; imminent. **3.** *Obsolete.* promising or favourable. *~prep.* (tə'wɔːd, tɔːd). **4.** a variant of **towards.** [Old English *tōweard;* see TO, -WARD]

towardly ('təʊədlɪ) *adj. Archaic.* **1.** compliant. **2.** propitious or suitable. —'**towardliness** *or* '**towardness** *n.*

towards (tə'wɔːdz, tɔːdz) *prep.* **1.** in the direction or vicinity of: *towards London.* **2.** with regard to: *her feelings towards me.* **3.** as a contribution or help to: *money towards a new car.* **4.** just before: *towards one o'clock.* **5.** *Irish.* in comparison with: *it's no work towards having to do it by hand.* ~Also: **toward.**

towbar ('təʊˌbɑː) *n.* a rigid metal bar or frame used for towing vehicles. Compare **towrope, towline.**

towboat ('təʊˌbəʊt) *n.* another word for **tug** (the boat).

tow-coloured *adj.* pale yellow; flaxen.

towel ('tauəl) *n.* **1.** a square or rectangular piece of absorbent cloth or paper used for drying the body. **2.** a similar piece of cloth used for drying plates, cutlery, etc. **3. throw in the towel.** See **throw in** (sense 4). *~vb.* **-els, -elling, -elled** *or U.S.* **-els, -eling, -eled. 4.** *(tr.)* to dry or wipe with a towel. **5.** *(tr.;* often foll. by *up) Austral. slang.* to assault or beat (a person). [C13: from Old French *toaille,* of Germanic origin; related to Old High German *dwahal* bath, Old Saxon *twahila* towel, Gothic *thwahan* to wash]

towelling ('tauəlɪŋ) *n.* an absorbent fabric, esp. with a nap, used for making towels, bathrobes, etc.

towel rail *n.* a rail or frame in a bathroom, etc., for hanging towels on.

tower ('tauə) *n.* **1.** a tall, usually square or circular structure, sometimes part of a larger building and usually built for a specific purpose: *a church tower; a control tower.* **2.** a place of defence or retreat. **3.** a mobile structure used in medieval warfare to attack a castle, etc. **4. tower of strength.** a person who gives support, comfort, etc. *~vb.* **5.** *(intr.)* to be or rise like a tower; loom. [C12: from Old French *tur,* from Latin *turris,* from Greek]

tower crane *n.* a rotatable cantilever jib on top of a steelwork tower used on building sites where the operator needs to command a good view of the site.

towered ('tauəd) *adj.* **a.** having a tower or towers. **b.** *(in combination): four-towered; high-towered.*

towering ('tauərɪŋ) *adj.* **1.** very tall; lofty. **2.** outstanding, as in importance or stature. **3.** *(prenominal)* very intense: *a towering rage.* —'**toweringly** *adv.*

tow-haired (ˌtəʊ'hɛəd) *adj.* having blond and sometimes tousled hair.

towhead ('təʊˌhɛd) *n. Often disparaging.* **1.** a person with blond or yellowish hair. **2.** a head of such hair. [from TOW[2] (flax)] —ˌ**tow'headed** *adj.*

towhee ('tauhɪ, 'təʊ-) *n.* any of various North American brownish-coloured sparrows of the genera *Pipilo* and *Chlorura.* [C18: imitative of its note]

towing path *n.* another name for **towpath.**

towkay (tau'keɪ) *n.* sir; master: used as a form of address. [of Chinese origin]

towline ('təʊˌlaɪn) *n.* another name for **towrope.**

town (taun) *n.* **1. a.** a densely populated urban area, typically smaller than a city and larger than a village, having some local powers of government and a fixed boundary. **b.** *(as modifier): town life.* **2.** a city, borough, or other urban area. **3.** (in the U.S.) a territorial unit of local government that is smaller than a county; township. **4.** the nearest town or commercial district. **5.** London or the chief city of an area. **6.** the inhabitants of a town. **7.** the permanent residents of a university town as opposed to the university staff and students. Compare **gown** (sense 3). **8. go to town. a.** to make a supreme or unrestricted effort; go all out. **b.** *Austral. and N.Z. informal.* to lose one's temper. **9. on the town.** seeking out entertainments and amusements. [Old English *tūn* village; related to Old Saxon, Old Norse *tūn,* Old High German *zūn* fence, Old Irish *dūn*] —'**townish** *adj.* —'**townless** *adj.*

town clerk *n.* **1.** (in Britain until 1974) the secretary and chief administrative officer of a town or city. **2.** (in the U.S.) the official who keeps the records of a town.

town crier *n.* (formerly) a person employed by a town to make public announcements in the streets.

townee (tau'niː) *or U.S.* **townie** *or* **towny** ('taunɪ) *n.* **1.** *Informal, often disparaging.* a permanent resident in a town, esp. as distinct from country dwellers or students. **2.** *Midlands dialect.* a slick and flashy male city dweller.

town gas *n.* coal gas manufactured for domestic and industrial use.

town hall *n.* the chief building in which municipal business is transacted, often with a hall for public meetings.

townhall clock ('taunˌhɔːl) *n. Brit.* another name for **moschatel.**

town house *n.* **1.** a terraced house in an urban area, esp. a fashionable one, often having the main living room on the first floor with an integral garage on the ground floor. **2.** a person's town residence as distinct from his country residence. **3.** another name (now chiefly *Scot.*) for **town hall. 4.** a U.S. and Canadian name for **terraced house.**

townland ('taunlænd) *n. Irish.* a division of land of various sizes.

town meeting *n. U.S.* **1.** an assembly of the inhabitants of a town. **2.** (esp. in New England) an assembly of the qualified voters of a town. Such a meeting may exercise all the powers of local government.

town milk *n. N.Z.* milk treated by pasteurization for direct consumption, as opposed to dairy factory milk for the production of butter, cheese, etc.

town planning *n.* the comprehensive planning of the physical and social development of a town, including the construction of facilities. U.S. term: **city planning.** —**town planner** *n.*

townscape ('taunskeɪp) *n.* a view of an urban scene.

township ('taunʃɪp) *n.* **1.** a small town. **2.** (in the Scottish Highlands and islands) a small crofting community. **3.** (in the U.S. and Canada) a territorial area, esp. a subdivision of a county: often organized as a unit of local government. **4.** (in South Africa) a planned urban settlement of Black Africans or Coloureds. Compare **location** (sense 4). **5.** *English history.* **a.** any of the local districts of a large parish, each division containing a village or small town. **b.** the particular manor or parish itself as a territorial division. **c.** the inhabitants of a township collectively.

townsman ('taunzmən) *n., pl.* **-men. 1.** an inhabitant of a town. **2.** a person from the same town as oneself. —'**towns,woman** *fem. n.*

townspeople ('taunzˌpiːp^{ə}l) *or* **townsfolk** *n.* the inhabitants of a town; citizens.

towpath ('təʊˌpɑːθ) *n.* a path beside a canal or river, used by people or animals towing boats. Also called: **towing path.**

towrope ('təʊˌrəʊp) *n.* a rope or cable used for towing a vehicle or vessel. Also called: **towline.**

tow truck *n.* a U.S. and Canadian name for **breakdown van.**

tox. *or* **toxicol.** *abbrev. for* toxicology.

tox-, toxic- *or before a consonant* **toxo-, toxico-** *combining form.* indicating poison: *toxalbumin.* [from Latin *toxicum*]

toxaemia *or U.S.* **toxemia** (tɒk'siːmɪə) *n.* **1.** a condition characterized by the presence of bacterial toxins in the blood. **2.** the condition in pregnancy of pre-eclampsia or eclampsia. [C19: from TOX- + -AEMIA] —**tox'aemic** *or U.S.* **tox'emic** *adj.*

toxalbumin (ˌtɒksælˈbjuːmɪn) *n. Biochem.* any of a group of toxic albumins that occur in certain plants, such as toadstools, and in snake venom.
toxaphene (ˈtɒksəˌfiːn) *n.* an amber waxy solid with a pleasant pine odour, consisting of chlorinated terpenes, esp. chlorinated camphene: used as an insecticide.
toxic (ˈtɒksɪk) *adj.* **1.** of, relating to, or caused by a toxin or poison; poisonous. **2.** harmful or deadly. [C17: from medical Latin *toxicus*, from Latin *toxicum* poison, from Greek *toxikon (pharmakon)* (poison) used on arrows, from *toxon* arrow] —ˈ**toxically** *adv.*
toxicant (ˈtɒksɪkənt) *n.* **1.** a toxic substance; poison. **2.** a rare word for **intoxicant.** ~*adj.* **3.** poisonous; toxic. [C19: from Medieval Latin *toxicāre* to poison; see TOXIC]
toxicity (tɒkˈsɪsɪtɪ) *n.* **1.** the degree of strength of a poison. **2.** the state or quality of being poisonous.
toxicogenic (ˌtɒksɪkəʊˈdʒenɪk) *adj.* **1.** producing toxic substances or effects. **2.** caused or produced by a toxin.
toxicology (ˌtɒksɪˈkɒlədʒɪ) *n.* the branch of science concerned with poisons, their nature, effects, and antidotes. —**toxicological** (ˌtɒksɪkəˈlɒdʒɪkᵊl) *or* ˌ**toxicoˈlogic** *adj.* —ˌ**toxicoˈlogically** *adv.* —ˌ**toxiˈcologist** *n.*
toxicosis (ˌtɒksɪˈkəʊsɪs) *n.* any disease or condition caused by poisoning. [C19: from New Latin, from TOXIC + -OSIS]
toxic shock syndrome *n.* a potentially fatal condition in women, characterized by fever, stomachache, a painful rash, and a drop in blood pressure, that is caused by staphylococcal blood poisoning, most commonly from a retained tampon during menstruation.
toxin (ˈtɒksɪn) *n.* **1.** any of various poisonous substances produced by microorganisms that stimulate the production of neutralizing substances (antitoxins) in the body. See also **endotoxin, exotoxin. 2.** any other poisonous substance of plant or animal origin.
toxin-antitoxin *n.* a mixture of a specific toxin and antitoxin. The diphtheria toxin-antitoxin was formerly used in the U.S. for active immunization.
toxocariasis (ˌtɒksəkəˈraɪəsɪs) *n.* the infection of humans with the larvae of a genus of roundworms, *Toxocara*, of dogs and cats. It can cause swelling of the liver and, sometimes, damage to the eyes.
toxoid (ˈtɒksɔɪd) *n.* a toxin that has been treated to reduce its toxicity and is used in immunization to stimulate production of antitoxins.
toxophilite (tɒkˈsɒfɪˌlaɪt) *Formal.* ~*n.* **1.** an archer. ~*adj.* **2.** of or relating to archery. [C18: from *Toxophilus*, the title of a book (1545) by the English writer and scholar Roger Ascham, designed to mean: a lover of the bow, from Greek *toxon* bow + *philos* loving] —**toxˈophily** *n.*
toxoplasmosis (ˌtɒksəʊplæzˈməʊsɪs) *n.* a protozoal disease that is characterized by jaundice, enlarged liver and spleen, and convulsions, caused by infection with *Toxoplasma gondii.* —ˌ**toxoˈplasmic** *adj.*
toy (tɔɪ) *n.* **1.** an object designed to be played with. **2. a.** something that is a nonfunctioning replica of something else, esp. a miniature one. **b.** (*as modifier*): *a toy guitar.* **3.** any small thing of little value; trifle. **4. a.** something small or miniature, esp. a miniature variety of a breed of dog. **b.** (*as modifier*): *a toy poodle.* ~*vb.* **5.** (*intr.*; usually foll. by *with*) to play, fiddle, or flirt. [C16 (in the sense: amorous dalliance): of uncertain origin] —ˈ**toyer** *n.* —ˈ**toyless** *adj.* —ˈ**toyˌlike** *adj.*
toy boy *n.* the much younger male lover of an older woman.
TPI *abbrev. for* tax and price index: a measure of the increase in taxable income needed to compensate for an increase in retail prices.
T-piece *n.* a strut or part shaped like a T.
T-plate *n.* a metal plate shaped like a T used to strengthen or effect a right-angled joint between two beams, etc.
TPN *n. Biochem.* triphosphopyridine nucleotide; a former name for **NADP.**
Tpr *abbrev. for* Trooper.
tr *abbrev. for* treasurer.
TR *international car registration for* Turkey.
tr. *abbrev. for:* **1.** transitive. **2.** translated. **3.** translator. **4.** *Music.* trill. **5.** trustee.
trabeated (ˈtreɪbɪˌeɪtɪd) *or* **trabeate** (ˈtreɪbɪɪt, -ˌeɪt) *adj. Architect.* constructed with horizontal beams as opposed to arches. Compare **arcuate.** [C19: back formation from *trabeation*, from Latin *trabs* a beam] —ˌ**trabeˈation** *n.*
trabecula (trəˈbekjʊlə) *n., pl.* **-lae** (-ˌliː). *Anatomy, botany.* **1.** any of various rod-shaped structures that support other organs. **2.** any of various rod-shaped cells or structures that bridge a cavity, as within the capsule of a moss. [C19: via New Latin from Latin: a little beam, from *trabs* a beam] —**traˈbecular** *or* **traˈbeculate** *adj.*
tracasserie (trəˈkæsərɪ) *n.* a turmoil; annoyance. [from French, from *tracasser* to fuss about]
trace[1] (treɪs) *n.* **1.** a mark or other sign that something has been in a place; vestige. **2.** a tiny or scarcely detectable amount or characteristic. **3.** a footprint or other indication of the passage of an animal or person. **4.** any line drawn by a recording instrument or a record consisting of a number of such lines. **5.** something drawn, such as a tracing. **6.** *Chiefly U.S.* a beaten track or path. **7.** the postulated alteration in the cells of the nervous system that occurs as the result of any experience or learning. See also **memory trace, engram. 8.** *Geom.* the intersection of a surface with a coordinate plane. **9.** *Maths.* the sum of the diagonal entries of a square matrix. **10.** *Linguistics.* a symbol inserted in the constituent structure of a sentence to mark the position from which a constituent has been moved in a generative process. **11.** *Meteorol.* an amount of precipitation that is too small to be measured. **12.** *Archaic.* a way taken; route. ~*vb.* **13.** (*tr.*) to follow, discover, or ascertain the course or development of (something): *to trace the history of China.* **14.** (*tr.*) to track down and find, as by following a trail. **15.** to copy (a design, map, etc.) by drawing over the lines visible through a superimposed sheet of transparent paper or other material. **16.** (*tr.*; often foll. by *out*) **a.** to draw or delineate a plan or diagram of: *she spent hours tracing the models one at a time.* **b.** to outline or sketch (an idea, policy, etc.): *he traced out his scheme for the robbery.* **17.** (*tr.*) to decorate with tracery. **18.** (*tr.*) to imprint (a design) on cloth, etc. **19.** (usually foll. by *back*) to follow or be followed to source; date back: *his ancestors trace back to the 16th century.* **20.** *Archaic.* to make one's way over, through, or along (something). [C13: from French *tracier*, from Vulgar Latin *tractiāre* (unattested) to drag, from Latin *tractus*, from *trahere* to drag] —ˈ**traceable** *adj.* —ˌ**traceaˈbility** *or* ˈ**traceableness** *n.* —ˈ**traceably** *adv.* —ˈ**traceless** *adj.* —ˈ**tracelessly** *adv.*
trace[2] (treɪs) *n.* **1.** either of the two side straps that connect a horse's harness to the whiffletree. **2.** *Angling.* a length of nylon or, formerly, gut attaching a hook or fly to a line. **3. kick over the traces.** to escape or defy control. [C14 *trais*, from Old French *trait*, ultimately from Latin *trahere* to drag]
trace element *n.* any of various chemical elements, such as iron, manganese, zinc, copper, and iodine, that occur in very small amounts in organisms and are essential for many physiological and biochemical processes.
trace fossil *n.* the fossilized remains of a track, trail, footprint, burrow, etc., of an organism.
tracer (ˈtreɪsə) *n.* **1.** a person or thing that traces. **2. a.** a projectile that can be observed when in flight by the burning of chemical substances in its base. **b.** ammunition consisting of such projectiles. **c.** (*as modifier*): *tracer fire.* **3.** *Med.* any radioactive isotope introduced into the body to study metabolic processes, absorption, etc., by following its progress through the body with a gamma camera or other detector. **4.** an investigation to trace missing cargo, mail, etc.
tracer bullet *n.* a round of small arms ammunition containing a tracer.
tracery (ˈtreɪsərɪ) *n., pl.* **-eries. 1.** a pattern of interlacing ribs, esp. as used in the upper part of a Gothic window, etc. **2.** any fine pattern resembling this. —ˈ**traceried** *adj.*
trachea (trəˈkiːə) *n., pl.* **-cheae** (-ˈkiːiː). **1.** *Anatomy, zoology.* the membranous tube with cartilaginous rings that conveys inhaled air from the larynx to the bronchi. Nontechnical name: **windpipe. 2.** any of the tubes in insects and related animals that convey air from the spiracles to the tissues. **3.** *Botany.* another name for **vessel** (sense 5). [C16: from Medieval Latin, from Greek *trakheia*, shortened from (*artēria*) *trakheia* rough (artery), from *trakhus* rough] —**traˈcheal** *or* **traˈcheate** *adj.*
tracheid (ˈtreɪkɪɪd) *or* **tracheide** *n. Botany.* an element of xylem tissue consisting of an elongated lignified cell with tapering ends. [C19: from TRACHEA (in the sense: a vessel in a plant) + -ID[2]] —**tracheidal** (trəˈkiːɪdᵊl, ˌtreɪkɪˈaɪdᵊl) *adj.*
tracheitis (ˌtreɪkɪˈaɪtɪs) *n.* inflammation of the trachea.
tracheo- *or before a vowel* **trache-** *combining form.* denoting the trachea: *tracheotomy.*
tracheophyte (ˈtreɪkɪəʊˌfaɪt) *n.* any plant that has a conducting system of xylem and phloem elements; a vascular plant.
tracheostomy (ˌtrækɪˈɒstəmɪ) *n., pl.* **-mies.** the surgical formation of a temporary or permanent opening into the trachea following tracheotomy.
tracheotomy (ˌtrækɪˈɒtəmɪ) *n., pl.* **-mies.** surgical incision into the trachea, usually performed when the upper air passage has been blocked.
trachoma (trəˈkəʊmə) *n.* a chronic contagious disease of the eye characterized by inflammation of the conjunctiva and cornea and the formation of scar tissue, caused by infection with the virus-like bacterium *Chlamydia trachomatis.* [C17: from New Latin, from Greek *trakhōma* roughness, from *trakhus* rough] —**trachomatous** (trəˈkɒmətəs, -ˈkəʊ-) *adj.*
trachyte (ˈtreɪkaɪt, ˈtræ-) *n.* a light-coloured fine-grained volcanic rock of rough texture consisting of feldspars with small amounts of pyroxene or amphibole. [C19: from French, from Greek *trakhutēs*, from *trakhus* rough] —**trachytoid** (ˈtrækɪˌtɔɪd, ˈtreɪ-) *adj.*
trachytic (trəˈkɪtɪk) *adj.* (of the texture of certain igneous rocks) characterized by a parallel arrangement of crystals, which mark the flow of the lava when still molten.
tracing (ˈtreɪsɪŋ) *n.* **1.** a copy made by tracing. **2.** the act of making a trace. **3.** a record made by an instrument.
tracing paper *n.* strong transparent paper used for tracing.
track (træk) *n.* **1.** the mark or trail left by something that has passed by: *the track of an animal.* **2.** any road or path affording passage, esp. a rough one. **3.** a rail or pair of parallel rails on which a vehicle, such as a locomotive, runs, esp. the rails together

with the sleepers, ballast, etc., on a railway. **4.** a course of action, thought, etc.: *don't start on that track again!* **5.** a line of motion or travel, such as flight. **6.** an endless jointed metal band driven by the wheels of a vehicle such as a tank or tractor to enable it to move across rough or muddy ground. **7.** *Physics.* the path of a particle of ionizing radiation as observed in a cloud chamber, bubble chamber, or photographic emulsion. **8. a.** a course for running or racing. **b.** (*as modifier*): *track events.* **9.** *U.S. and Canadian.* **a.** sports performed on a track. **b.** track and field events as a whole. **10.** a path on a magnetic recording medium, esp. magnetic tape, on which information, such as music or speech, from a single input channel is recorded. **11.** Also called: **band.** any of a number of separate sections in the recording on either side of a gramophone record. **12.** the distance between the points of contact with the ground of a pair of wheels, such as the front wheels of a motor vehicle or the paired wheels of an aircraft undercarriage. **13.** a hypothetical trace made on the surface of the earth by a point directly below an aircraft in flight. **14. keep** (*or* **lose**) **track of.** to follow (or fail to follow) the passage, course, or progress of. **15. off the beaten track.** See **beaten** (sense 4). **16. off the track.** away from what is correct or true. **17. on the track of.** on the scent or trail of; pursuing. **18. the right** (*or* **wrong**) **track.** pursuing the correct (or incorrect) line of investigation, inquiry, etc. ~*vb.* **19.** to follow the trail of (a person, animal, etc.). **20.** to follow the flight path of (a satellite, spacecraft, etc.) by picking up radio or radar signals transmitted or reflected by it. **21.** *U.S. railways.* **a.** to provide with a track. **b.** to run on a track of (a certain width). **22.** (of a camera or camera operator) to follow (a moving object) in any direction while operating. **23.** to move (a camera) towards the scene (**track in**) or away from the scene (**track out**). **24.** to follow a track through (a place): *to track the jungles.* **25.** (*intr.*) (of the pick-up, stylus, etc., of a record player) to follow the groove of a record: *the pick-up tracks badly.* ~See also **tracks.** [C15: from Old French *trac,* probably of Germanic origin; related to Middle Dutch *tracken* to pull, Middle Low German *trecken;* compare Norwegian *trakke* to trample] —**'trackable** *adj.* —**'tracker** *n.*

track down *vb.* (*tr., adv.*) to find by tracking or pursuing.

tracker dog *n.* a dog specially trained to hunt fugitives or to search for missing people.

track event *n.* a competition in athletics, such as relay running or sprinting, that takes place on a running track.

tracking ('trækɪŋ) *n.* **1.** the act or process of following something or someone. **2.** *Electrical engineering.* a leakage of electric current between two insulated points caused by dirt, carbon particles, moisture, etc.

tracking radar *n.* a radar system emitting a narrow beam which oscillates about the target, thus compensating for abrupt changes of direction.

tracking shot *n.* a camera shot in which the cameraman follows a specific person or event in the action.

tracking station *n.* a station that can use a radio or radar beam to determine and follow the path of an object, esp. a spacecraft or satellite, in space or in the atmosphere.

tracklaying ('træk,leɪɪŋ) *adj.* (of a vehicle) having an endless jointed metal band around the wheels.

trackless ('træklɪs) *adj.* **1.** having or leaving no trace or trail: *a trackless jungle.* **2.** (of a vehicle) using or having no tracks. —**'tracklessly** *adv.* —**'tracklessness** *n.*

trackman ('trækmən) *n., pl.* **-men.** the U.S. and Canadian name for **platelayer.**

track meet *n. U.S. and Canadian.* an athletics meeting.

track record *n. Informal.* the past record of the accomplishments and failures of a person, business, etc.

track rod *n.* the rod connecting the two front wheels of a motor vehicle ensuring that they turn at the same angle.

tracks (træks) *pl. n.* **1.** (*sometimes sing.*) marks, such as footprints, tyre impressions, etc., left by someone or something that has passed. **2. in one's tracks.** on the very spot where one is standing (esp. in the phrase **stop in one's tracks**). **3. make tracks.** to leave or depart. **4. make tracks for.** to go or head towards. **5. born on the wrong side of the tracks.** *U.S.* in the unfashionable or poor district or stratum of a community.

track shoe *n.* either of a pair of light running shoes fitted with steel spikes for better grip. Also called: **spike.**

tracksuit ('træk,su:t, -,sju:t) *n.* a warm suit worn by athletes, etc., usually over the clothes, esp. during training.

tract[1] (trækt) *n.* **1.** an extended area, as of land. **2.** *Anatomy.* a system of organs, glands, or other tissues that has a particular function: *the digestive tract.* **3.** a bundle of nerve fibres having the same function, origin, and termination: *the optic tract.* **4.** *Archaic.* an extended period of time. [C15: from Latin *tractus* a stretching out, from *trahere* to drag]

tract[2] (trækt) *n.* a treatise or pamphlet, esp. a religious or moralistic one. [C15: from Latin *tractātus* TRACTATE]

tract[3] (trækt) *n. R.C. Church.* an anthem in some Masses. [C14: from Medieval Latin *tractus cantus* extended song; see TRACT[1]]

tractable ('træktəbᵊl) *adj.* **1.** easily controlled or persuaded. **2.** readily worked; malleable. [C16: from Latin *tractābilis,* from *tractāre* to manage, from *trahere* to draw] —,**tracta'bility** *or* **'tractableness** *n.* —**'tractably** *adv.*

Tractarianism (træk'tɛərɪə,nɪzəm) *n.* another name for the **Oxford Movement.** —**Trac'tarian** *n., adj.*

tractate ('trækteɪt) *n.* **1.** a short tract; treatise. **2.** *Judaism.* one of the volumes of the Talmud. [C15: from Latin *tractātus,* from *tractāre* to handle; see TRACTABLE]

tractile ('træktaɪl) *adj.* capable of being drawn out; ductile. [C17: from Latin *trahere* to drag] —**tractility** (træk'tɪlɪtɪ) *n.*

traction ('trækʃən) *n.* **1.** the act of drawing or pulling, esp. by motive power. **2.** the state of being drawn or pulled. **3.** *Med.* the application of a steady pull on a part during healing of a fractured or dislocated bone, using a system of weights and pulleys or splints. **4.** the adhesive friction between a wheel and a surface, as between a driving wheel of a motor vehicle and the road. [C17: from Medieval Latin *tractiō,* from Latin *tractus* dragged; see TRACTILE] —**'tractional** *adj.* —**tractive** ('træktɪv) *adj.*

traction engine *n.* a steam-powered locomotive used, esp. formerly, for drawing heavy loads along roads or over rough ground. It usually has two large rear wheels and a rope drum for haulage purposes.

traction load *n. Geology.* the solid material that is carried along the bed of a river.

tractive force *n.* the force measured in the drawbar of a locomotive or tractor.

tractor ('træktə) *n.* **1.** a motor vehicle used to pull heavy loads, esp. farm machinery such as a plough or harvester. It usually has two large rear wheels with deeply treaded tyres. **2.** a short motor vehicle with a powerful engine and a driver's cab, used to pull a trailer, as in an articulated lorry. **3.** an aircraft with its propeller or propellers mounted in front of the engine. [C18: from Late Latin: one who pulls, from *trahere* to drag]

tractorfeed ('træktə,fi:d) *n. Computer technol.* the automatic movement of a continuous roll of edge-perforated paper through the platen of the printer.

trad (træd) *n.* **1.** *Chiefly Brit.* traditional jazz, as revived in the 1950s. ~*adj.* **2.** short for **traditional.**

trade (treɪd) *n.* **1.** the act or an instance of buying and selling goods and services either on the domestic (wholesale and retail) markets or on the international (import, export, and entrepôt) markets. **2.** a personal occupation, esp. a craft requiring skill. **3.** the people and practices of an industry, craft, or business. **4.** exchange of one thing for something else. **5.** the regular clientele of a firm or industry. **6.** amount of custom or commercial dealings; business. **7.** a specified market or business: *the tailoring trade.* **8.** an occupation in commerce, as opposed to a profession. **9.** commercial customers, as opposed to the general public: *trade only; trade advertising.* **10.** *Homosexual slang.* a sexual partner or sexual partners collectively. **11.** *Archaic.* a custom or habit. ~*vb.* **12.** (*tr.*) to buy and sell (commercial merchandise). **13.** to exchange (one thing) for another. **14.** (*intr.*) to engage in trade. **15.** (*intr.*) to deal or do business (with): *we trade with them regularly.* ~*adj.* **16.** intended for or available only to people in industry or business: *trade prices.* ~See also **trade-in, trade on.** [C14 (in the sense: track, hence, a regular business): related to Old Saxon *trada,* Old High German *trata* track; see TREAD] —**'tradable** *or* **'tradeable** *adj.* —**'tradeless** *adj.*

trade agreement *n.* a commercial treaty between two or more nations.

trade association *n.* an association of organizations in the same trade formed to further their collective interests, esp. in negotiating with governments, trade unions, etc.

trade bill *n.* a bill of exchange drawn on and accepted (**trade acceptance**) by a trader in payment for goods.

trade book *or* **edition** *n.* an ordinary edition of a book sold in the normal way in shops, as opposed to a de luxe or mail-order edition.

trade cycle *n.* the recurrent fluctuation between boom and depression in the economic activity of a capitalist country. Also called (esp. U.S. and Canadian): **business cycle.**

trade discount *n.* a sum or percentage deducted from the list price of a commodity allowed by a manufacturer, distributor, or wholesaler to a retailer or by one enterprise to another in the same trade.

traded option *n. Stock Exchange.* an option that can itself be bought and sold on a stock exchange. Compare **traditional option.**

trade down *vb.* (*intr., adv.*) to sell a large or relatively expensive house, car, etc., and replace it with a smaller or less expensive one.

trade gap *n.* the amount by which the value of a country's visible imports exceeds that of visible exports; an unfavourable balance of trade.

trade-in *n.* **1. a.** a used article given in part payment for the purchase of a new article. **b.** a transaction involving such part payment. **c.** the valuation put on the article traded in. **d.** (*as modifier*): *a trade-in dealer.* ~*vb.* **trade in. 2.** (*tr., adv.*) to give (a used article) as part payment for the purchase of a new article.

trade journal *n.* a periodical containing new developments, discussions, etc., concerning a trade or profession.

trade-last *n. U.S. informal.* a compliment that one has heard about someone, which one offers to tell to that person in exchange for a compliment heard about oneself.

trademark (ˈtreɪdˌmɑːk) *n.* **1.** the name or other symbol used to identify the goods produced by a particular manufacturer or distributed by a particular dealer and to distinguish them from products associated with competing manufacturers or dealers. A trademark that has been officially registered and is therefore legally protected is known as a **Registered Trademark. 2.** any distinctive sign or mark of the presence of a person or animal. ~*vb.* (*tr.*) **3.** to label with a trademark. **4.** to register as a trademark.

trade name *n.* **1.** the name used by a trade to refer to a commodity, service, etc. **2.** the name under which a commercial enterprise operates in business.

trade-off *n.* an exchange, esp. as a compromise.

trade on *vb.* (*intr., prep.*) to exploit or take advantage of: *he traded on her endless patience.*

trade plate *n.* a numberplate attached temporarily to a vehicle by a dealer, etc., before the vehicle has been registered.

trader (ˈtreɪdə) *n.* **1.** a person who engages in trade; dealer; merchant. **2.** a vessel regularly employed in foreign or coastal trade. **3.** *Stock Exchange, U.S.* a member who operates mainly on his own account rather than for customers' accounts. —ˈ**traderˌship** *n.*

trade reference *n.* a reference in which one trader gives his opinion as to the credit worthiness of another trader in the same trade, esp. to a supplier.

tradescantia (ˌtrædɛsˈkænʃɪə) *n.* any plant of the American genus *Tradescantia,* widely cultivated for their striped variegated leaves: family *Commelinaceae.* See also **wandering Jew, spiderwort.** [C18: New Latin, named after John *Tradescant* (1608–62), English naturalist and gardener]

trade school *n.* a school or teaching unit organized by an industry or large company to provide trade training, apprentice education, and similar courses.

trade secret *n.* a secret formula, technique, process, etc., known and used to advantage by only one manufacturer.

tradesman (ˈtreɪdzmən) *n., pl.* **-men. 1.** a man engaged in trade, esp. a retail dealer. **2.** a skilled worker. —ˈ**tradesˌwoman** *fem. n.*

tradespeople (ˈtreɪdzˌpiːpᵊl) *or* **tradesfolk** (ˈtreɪdzˌfəʊk) *pl. n. Chiefly Brit.* people engaged in trade, esp. shopkeepers.

trade union *or* **trades union** *n.* an association of employees formed to improve their incomes and working conditions by collective bargaining with the employer or employer organizations. —**trade unionism** *or* **trades unionism** *n.* —**trade unionist** *or* **trades unionist** *n.*

trade up *vb.* (*intr., adv.*) to sell a small or relatively inexpensive house, car, etc., and replace it with a larger or more expensive one.

trade wind (wɪnd) *n.* a wind blowing obliquely towards the equator either from the northeast in the N hemisphere or the southeast in the S hemisphere, approximately between latitudes 30° N and S, forming part of the planetary wind system. [C17: from *to blow trade* to blow steadily in one direction, from TRADE in the obsolete sense: a track]

trading estate *n. Chiefly Brit.* a large area in which a number of commercial or industrial firms are situated. Also called: **industrial estate.**

trading post *n.* **1.** a general store established by a trader in an unsettled or thinly populated region. **2.** *Stock Exchange.* a booth or location on an exchange floor at which a particular security is traded.

trading stamp *n.* (esp. formerly) a stamp of stated value given by some retail organizations to customers, according to the value of their purchases and redeemable for articles offered on a premium list.

tradition (trəˈdɪʃən) *n.* **1.** the handing down from generation to generation of the same customs, beliefs, etc., esp. by word of mouth. **2.** the body of customs, thought, practices, etc., belonging to a particular country, people, family, or institution over a relatively long period. **3.** a specific custom or practice of long standing. **4.** *Christianity.* a doctrine or body of doctrines regarded as having been established by Christ or the apostles though not contained in Scripture. **5.** (*often cap.*) *Judaism.* a body of laws regarded as having been handed down from Moses orally and only committed to writing in the 2nd century A.D. **6.** the beliefs and customs of Islam supplementing the Koran, esp. as embodied in the Sunna. **7.** *Law, chiefly Roman and Scots.* the act of formally transferring ownership of movable property; delivery. [C14: from Latin *trāditiō* a handing down, surrender, from *trādere* to give up, transmit, from TRANS- + *dāre* to give] —**traˈditionless** *adj.* —**traˈditionist** *n.*

traditional (trəˈdɪʃənᵊl) *adj.* **1.** of, relating to, or being a tradition. **2.** of or relating to the style of New Orleans jazz, characterized by collective improvisation by a front line of trumpet, trombone, and clarinet accompanied by various rhythm instruments. —**traditionality** (trəˌdɪʃəˈnælɪtɪ) *n.* —**traˈditionally** *adv.*

traditionalism (trəˈdɪʃənᵊˌlɪzəm) *n.* **1.** the doctrine that all knowledge originates in divine revelation and is perpetuated by tradition. **2.** adherence to tradition, esp. in religion. —**traˈditionalist** *n., adj.* —**traˌditionalˈistic** *adj.*

traditional option *n. Stock Exchange.* an option that once purchased cannot be resold. Compare **traded option.**

traditional policy *n.* a life assurance policy in which the policyholder's premiums are paid into a general fund and his investment benefits are calculated according to actuarial formulae. Compare **unit-linked policy.**

traditor (ˈtrædɪtə) *n., pl.* **traditores** (ˌtrædɪˈtɔːriːz) *or* **traditors.** *Early Church.* a Christian who betrayed his fellow Christians at the time of the Roman persecutions. [C15: from Latin: traitor, from *trādere* to hand over]

traduce (trəˈdjuːs) *vb.* (*tr.*) to speak badly or maliciously of. [C16: from Latin *trādūcere* to lead over, transmit, disgrace, from TRANS- + *dūcere* to lead] —**traˈducement** *n.* —**traˈducer** *n.* —**traˈducible** *adj.*

traducianism (trəˈdjuːʃəˌnɪzəm) *n.* the theory that the soul is transmitted to a child in the act of generation or concomitantly with its body. Compare **creationism.** [C18: from Church Latin *trādūciānus,* from *trādux* transmission; see TRADUCE] —**traˈducianist** *or* **traˈducian** *n., adj.* —**traˌducianˈistic** *adj.*

traffic (ˈtræfɪk) *n.* **1. a.** the vehicles coming and going in a street, town, etc. **b.** (*as modifier*): *traffic lights.* **2.** the movement of vehicles, people, etc., in a particular place or for a particular purpose: *sea traffic.* **3. a.** the business of commercial transportation by land, sea, or air. **b.** the freight, passengers, etc., transported. **4.** (usually foll. by *with*) dealings or business: *have no traffic with that man.* **5.** trade, esp. of an illicit or improper kind: *drug traffic.* **6.** the aggregate volume of messages transmitted through a communications system in a given period. **7.** *Chiefly U.S.* the number of customers patronizing a commercial establishment in a given time period. ~*vb.* **-fics, -ficking, -ficked.** (*intr.*) **8.** (often foll. by *in*) to carry on trade or business, esp. of an illicit kind. **9.** (usually foll. by *with*) to have dealings. [C16: from Old French *trafique,* from Old Italian *traffico,* from *trafficare* to engage in trade] —ˈ**trafficker** *n.* —ˈ**trafficless** *adj.*

trafficator (ˈtræfɪˌkeɪtə) *n.* (formerly) an illuminated arm on a motor vehicle that was raised to indicate a left or right turn. Compare **indicator** (sense 4).

traffic circle *n.* the U.S. and Canadian name for **roundabout** (sense 2).

traffic cop *n.* **1.** *Brit. informal.* a policeman who supervises road traffic. **2.** *N.Z. informal.* a traffic officer.

traffic court *n. Law.* a magistrates' court dealing with traffic offences.

traffic engineering *n.* a discipline which includes the design of highways and pedestrian ways, the study and application of traffic statistics, and the environmental aspects of the transportation of goods and people.

traffic island *n.* a raised area in the middle of a road, designed as a guide for traffic flow and to provide a stopping place for pedestrians crossing.

traffic jam *n.* a number of vehicles so obstructed that they can scarcely move. —ˈ**traffic-ˌjammed** *adj.*

traffic light *or* **signal** *n.* one of a set of coloured lights placed at crossroads, junctions, etc., to control the flow of traffic. A red light indicates that traffic must stop and a green light that it may go: usually an amber warning light is added between the red and the green.

traffic officer *n. N.Z.* an officer appointed by the Ministry of Transport or a local authority to control road traffic.

traffic pattern *n.* a pattern of permitted lanes in the air around an airport to which an aircraft is restricted.

traffic warden *n. Brit.* a person who is appointed to supervise road traffic and report traffic offences.

tragacanth (ˈtrægəˌkænθ) *n.* **1.** any of various spiny leguminous plants of the genus *Astragalus,* esp. *A. gummifer,* of Asia, having clusters of white, yellow, or purple flowers, and yielding a substance that is made into a gum. **2.** the gum obtained from any of these plants, used in the manufacture of pills and lozenges and in calico printing. [C16: from French *tragacante,* from Latin *tragacantha* goat's thorn, from Greek *tragakantha,* from *tragos* goat + *akantha* thorn]

tragedian (trəˈdʒiːdɪən) *or* (*fem.*) **tragedienne** (trəˌdʒiːdɪˈɛn) *n.* **1.** an actor who specializes in tragic roles. **2.** a writer of tragedy.

tragedy (ˈtrædʒɪdɪ) *n., pl.* **-dies. 1.** (esp. in classical and Renaissance drama) a play in which the protagonist, usually a man of importance and outstanding personal qualities, falls to disaster through the combination of a personal failing and circumstances with which he cannot deal. **2.** (in later drama) a play in which the protagonist is overcome by a combination of social and psychological circumstances. **3.** any dramatic or literary composition dealing with serious or sombre themes and ending with disaster. **4.** (in medieval literature) a literary work in which a great person falls from prosperity to disaster, often through no fault of his own. **5.** the branch of drama dealing with such themes. **6.** the unfortunate aspect of something. **7.** a shocking or sad event; disaster. ~Compare **comedy.** [C14: from Old French *tragédie,* from Latin *tragoedia,* from Greek *tragōidia,* from *tragos* goat + *ōidē* song; perhaps a reference to the goat-satyrs of Peloponnesian plays]

tragic (ˈtrædʒɪk) *or* (*less commonly*) **tragical** *adj.* **1.** of, relating to, or characteristic of tragedy. **2.** mournful or pitiable: *a tragic face.* —ˈ**tragically** *adv.*

tragic flaw *n.* a failing of character in the hero of a tragedy that brings about his downfall.

tragic irony *n.* the use of dramatic irony in a tragedy (originally, in Greek tragedy), so that the audience is aware that a character's words or actions will bring about a tragic or fatal result, while the character himself is not.

tragicomedy (ˌtrædʒɪˈkɒmɪdɪ) *n., pl.* **-dies.** **1. a.** a drama in which aspects of both tragedy and comedy are found. **b.** the dramatic genre of works of this kind. **2.** an event or incident having both comic and tragic aspects. [C16: from French, ultimately from Late Latin *tragicōmoedia;* see TRAGEDY, COMEDY] —ˌ**tragiˈcomic** *or* ˌ**tragiˈcomical** *adj.* —ˌ**tragiˈcomically** *adv.*

tragopan (ˈtræɡəˌpæn) *n.* any pheasant of the genus *Tragopan,* of S and SE Asia, having a brilliant plumage and brightly coloured fleshy processes on the head. [C19: via Latin from Greek, from *tragos* goat + *Pan,* goatlike Greek god]

tragus (ˈtreɪɡəs) *n., pl.* **-gi** (-dʒaɪ). **1.** the cartilaginous fleshy projection that partially covers the entrance to the external ear. **2.** any of the hairs that grow just inside this entrance. [C17: from Late Latin, from Greek *tragos* hairy projection of the ear, literally: goat] —ˈ**tragal** *adj.*

trail (treɪl) *vb.* **1.** to drag or stream, or permit to drag or stream along a surface, esp. the ground: *her skirt trailed; she trailed her skipping rope.* **2.** to make (a track or path) through (a place): *to trail a way; to trail a jungle.* **3.** to chase, follow, or hunt (an animal or person) by following marks or tracks. **4.** (when *intr.,* often foll. by *behind*) to lag or linger behind (a person or thing). **5.** (*intr.*) (esp. of plants) to extend, hang, or droop over or along a surface. **6.** (*intr.*) to be falling behind in a race or competition: *the favourite is trailing at the last fence.* **7.** (*tr.*) to tow (a boat, caravan, etc.) behind a motor vehicle. **8.** (*tr.*) to carry (a rifle) at the full length of the right arm in a horizontal position, with the muzzle to the fore. **9.** (*intr.*) to move wearily or slowly: *we trailed through the city.* **10.** (*tr.*) (on television or radio) to advertise (a future programme) with short extracts. **11. trail one's coat.** to invite a quarrel by deliberately provocative behaviour. ~*n.* **12.** a print, mark, or marks made by a person, animal, or object. **13.** the act or an instance of trailing. **14.** the scent left by a moving person or animal that is followed by a hunting animal. **15.** a path, track, or road, esp. one roughly blazed. **16.** something that trails behind or trails in loops or strands. **17.** the part of a towed gun carriage and limber that connects the two when in movement and rests on the ground as a partial support when unlimbered. **18.** *Engineering.* the distance between the point of contact of a steerable wheel and a line drawn from the swivel pin axis to the ground. [C14: from Old French *trailler* to draw, tow, from Vulgar Latin *tragulāre* (unattested), from Latin *trāgula* dragnet, from *trahere* to drag; compare Middle Dutch *traghelen* to drag] —ˈ**trailing** *adj.* —ˈ**trailingly** *adv.* —ˈ**trail-less** *adj.*

trail away *or* **off** *vb.* (*intr., adv.*) to become fainter, quieter, or weaker: *his voice trailed off.*

trail bike *n.* a motorcycle adapted for riding on rough tracks.

trailblazer (ˈtreɪlˌbleɪzə) *n.* **1.** a leader or pioneer in a particular field. **2.** a person who blazes a trail. —ˈ**trailˌblazing** *adj., n.*

trailer (ˈtreɪlə) *n.* **1.** a road vehicle, usually two-wheeled, towed by a motor vehicle: used for transporting boats, etc. **2.** the part of an articulated lorry that is drawn by the cab. **3.** a series of short extracts from a film, used to advertise it in a cinema or on television. **4.** a person or thing that trails. **5.** the U.S. and Canadian name for **caravan** (sense 1).

trailing arbutus *n.* a creeping evergreen ericaceous plant, *Epigaea repens,* of E North America, having clusters of fragrant pink or white flowers. Also called: **mayflower.**

trailing edge *n.* **1.** the rear edge of a propeller blade or aerofoil. Compare **leading edge. 2.** *Physics.* the edge of a pulse signal as its amplitude falls.

trailing vortex drag *n.* drag arising from vortices that occur behind a body moving through a gas or liquid. Often shortened to **vortex drag.** Former name: **induced drag.**

trail mix *n.* a mixture of nuts, dried fruits, and seeds, eaten as a snack, esp. originally by hikers.

trail rope *n.* **1.** another name for **dragrope** (sense 2). **2.** a long rope formerly used for various military purposes, esp. to allow a vehicle, horses, or men to pull a gun carriage.

train (treɪn) *vb.* **1.** (*tr.*) to guide or teach (to do something), as by subjecting to various exercises or experiences: *to train a man to fight.* **2.** (*tr.*) to control or guide towards a specific goal: *to train a plant up a wall.* **3.** (*intr.*) to do exercises and prepare for a specific purpose: *the athlete trained for the Olympics.* **4.** (*tr.*) to improve or curb by subjecting to discipline: *to train the mind.* **5.** (*tr.*) to focus or bring to bear (on something): *to train a telescope on the moon.* ~*n.* **6. a.** a line of coaches or wagons coupled together and drawn by a railway locomotive. **b.** (*as modifier*): *a train ferry.* **7.** a sequence or series, as of events, objects, etc.: *a train of disasters.* **8.** a procession of people, vehicles, etc., travelling together, such as one carrying supplies of ammunition or equipment in support of a military operation. **9.** a series of interacting parts through which motion is transmitted: *a train of gears.* **10.** a fuse or line of gunpowder to an explosive charge, etc. **11.** something drawn along, such as the long back section of a dress that trails along the floor behind the wearer. **12.** a retinue or suite. **13.** proper order or course. [C14: from Old French *trahiner,* from Vulgar Latin *tragīnāre* (unattested) to draw; related to Latin *trahere* to drag] —ˈ**trainable** *adj.* —ˈ**trainless** *adj.*

trainband (ˈtreɪnˌbænd) *n.* a company of English militia from the 16th to the 18th century. [C17: altered from *trained band*]

trainbearer (ˈtreɪnˌbɛərə) *n.* an attendant in a procession who holds up the train of a dignitary's robe.

trainee (treɪˈniː) *n.* **a.** a person undergoing training. **b.** (*as modifier*): *a trainee journalist.*

trainer (ˈtreɪnə) *n.* **1.** a person who trains athletes in a sport. **2.** a piece of equipment employed in training, such as a simulated aircraft cockpit. **3.** *Horse racing.* a person who schools racehorses and prepares them for racing. **4.** (*pl.*) an informal name for **training shoes.**

training (ˈtreɪnɪŋ) *n.* **1. a.** the process of bringing a person, etc., to an agreed standard of proficiency, etc., by practice and instruction: *training for the priesthood; physical training.* **b.** (*as modifier*): *training college.* **2. in training. a.** undergoing physical training. **b.** physically fit. **3. out of training.** physically unfit.

training shoes *pl. n.* **1.** running shoes for sports training, esp. in contrast to studded or spiked shoes worn for the sport itself. **2.** shoes in the style of those used for sports training. ~Also called: **trainers.**

train oil *n.* oil obtained from the blubber of various marine animals, esp. the whale: used in the manufacture of margarine and soap, in dressing leather, and as a lubricant. [C16: from earlier *train* or *trane,* from Middle Low German *trān* or Middle Dutch *traen* tear, exudation]

train spotter *n.* a person who collects the numbers of railway locomotives.

traipse *or* **trapes** (treɪps) *Informal.* ~*vb.* **1.** (*intr.*) to walk heavily or tiredly. ~*n.* **2.** a long or tiring walk; trudge. [C16: of unknown origin]

trait (treɪt, treɪ) *n.* **1.** a characteristic feature or quality distinguishing a particular person or thing. **2.** *Rare.* a touch or stroke. [C16: from French, from Old French: a pulling, from Latin *tractus,* from *trahere* to drag]

traitor (ˈtreɪtə) *n.* a person who is guilty of treason or treachery, in betraying friends, country, a cause or trust, etc. [C13: from Old French *traitour,* from Latin *trāditor* TRADITOR] —ˈ**traitorous** *adj.* —ˈ**traitorously** *adv.* —ˈ**traitorˌship** *n.* —ˈ**traitress** *fem. n.*

traject (trəˈdʒɛkt) *vb.* (*tr.*) *Archaic.* to transport or transmit. [C17: from Latin *trājectus* cast over, from *trāicere* to throw across, from TRANS- + *iacere* to throw] —**traˈjection** *n.*

trajectory (trəˈdʒɛktərɪ, -trɪ) *n., pl.* **-ries. 1.** the path described by an object moving in air or space under the influence of such forces as thrust, wind resistance, and gravity, esp. the curved path of a projectile. **2.** *Geometry.* a curve that cuts a family of curves or surfaces at a constant angle. —**trajectile** (trəˈdʒɛktaɪl) *adj.*

tra-la *or* **tra-la-la** a set of nonsensical syllables used in humming music, esp. for a melody or refrain.

tram[1] (træm) *n.* **1.** Also called: **tramcar.** an electrically driven public transport vehicle that runs on rails let into the surface of the road, power usually being taken from an overhead wire. U.S. and Canadian names: **streetcar, trolley car. 2.** a small vehicle on rails for carrying loads in a mine; tub. [C16 (in the sense: shaft of a cart): probably from Low German *traam* beam; compare Old Norse *thrömr,* Middle Dutch *traem* beam, tooth of a rake] —ˈ**tramless** *adj.*

tram[2] (træm) *n.* **1.** *Machinery.* a fine adjustment that ensures correct function or alignment. ~*vb.* **trams, tramming, trammed. 2.** (*tr.*) to adjust (a mechanism) to a fine degree of accuracy. [C19: short for TRAMMEL]

tram[3] (træm) *n.* (in weaving) a weft yarn of two or more twisted strands of silk. [C17: from French *trame,* from Latin *trāma;* related to Latin *trāns* across, *trāmes* footpath]

tramline (ˈtræmˌlaɪn) *n.* **1.** (*often pl.*) Also called: **tramway.** the tracks on which a tram runs. **2.** the route taken by a tram. **3.** (*often pl.*) the outer markings along the sides of a tennis or badminton court. **4.** (*pl.*) a set of guiding principles.

trammel (ˈtræməl) *n.* **1.** (*often pl.*) a hindrance to free action or movement. **2.** Also called: **trammel net.** a fishing net in three sections, the two outer nets having a large mesh and the middle one a fine mesh. **3.** *Rare.* a fowling net. **4.** *U.S.* a fetter or shackle, esp. one used in teaching a horse to amble. **5.** a device for drawing ellipses consisting of a flat sheet of metal, plastic, or wood having a cruciform slot in which run two pegs attached to a beam. The free end of the beam describes an ellipse. **6.** (*sometimes pl.*) another name for **beam compass. 7.** Also called: **tram.** a gauge for setting up machines correctly. **8.** a device set in a fireplace to support cooking pots. ~*vb.* **-els, -elling, -elled** *or U.S.* **-els, -eling, -eled.** (*tr.*) **9.** to hinder or restrain. **10.** to catch or ensnare. **11.** to produce an accurate setting of (a machine adjustment), as with a trammel. [C14: from Old French *tramail* three-mesh net, from Late Latin *trēmaculum,* from Latin *trēs* three + *macula* hole, mesh in a net] —ˈ**trammeller** *or U.S.* ˈ**trammeler** *n.*

trammie (ˈtræmɪ) *n. Austral. informal.* the conductor or driver of a tram.

tramontane (trəˈmɒnteɪn) *adj. also* **transmontane. 1.** being or coming from the far side of the mountains, esp. from the other side of the Alps as seen from Italy. **2.** foreign or barbarous. **3.** (of a wind) blowing down from the mountains. ~*n.* **4.** an inhabitant of a tramontane country. **5.** Also called: **tramontana.** a cold dry wind blowing south or southwest from the mountains in Italy and the W Mediterranean. **6.** *Rare.* a foreigner or barbarian. [C16: from Italian *tramontano,* from Latin *trānsmontānus,* from TRANS- + *montānus,* from *mōns* mountain]

tramp (træmp) *vb.* **1.** (*intr.*) to walk long and far; hike. **2.** to walk heavily or firmly across or through (a place); march or trudge. **3.** (*intr.*) to wander about as a vagabond or tramp. **4.** (*tr.*) to make (a journey) or traverse (a place) on foot, esp. laboriously or wearily: *to tramp the streets in search of work.* **5.** (*tr.*) to tread or trample. **6.** (*intr.*) *N.Z.* to walk for sport or recreation, esp. in the bush. ~*n.* **7.** a person who travels about on foot, usually with no permanent home, living by begging or doing casual work. **8.** a long hard walk; hike. **9.** a heavy or rhythmic step or tread. **10.** the sound of heavy treading. **11.** Also called: **tramp steamer.** a merchant ship that does not run between ports on a regular schedule but carries cargo wherever the shippers desire. **12.** *Slang, chiefly U.S. and Canadian.* a prostitute or promiscuous girl or woman. **13.** an iron plate on the sole of a boot. [C14: probably from Middle Low German *trampen;* compare Gothic *ana-trimpan* to press heavily upon, German *trampen* to hitchhike] —**'tramper** *n.* —**'tramping** *n.* —**'trampish** *adj.*

tramping club *n. N.Z.* an organization of bush walkers.

tramping hut *n. N.Z.* a hut in the bush for the use of trampers.

trample ('træmpᵊl) *vb.* (when *intr.,* usually foll. by *on, upon,* or *over*) **1.** to stamp or walk roughly (on): *to trample the flowers.* **2.** to encroach (upon) so as to violate or hurt: *to trample on someone's feelings.* ~*n.* **3.** the action or sound of trampling. [C14: frequentative of TRAMP; compare Middle High German *trampeln*] —**'trampler** *n.*

trampoline ('træmpəlɪn, -ˌliːn) *n.* **1.** a tough canvas sheet suspended by springs or elasticated cords from a frame, used by acrobats, gymnasts, etc. ~*vb.* **2.** (*intr.*) to exercise on a trampoline. [C18: via Spanish from Italian *trampolino,* from *trampoli* stilts, of Germanic origin; compare TRAMPLE] —**'trampoliner** *or* **'trampolinist** *n.*

tramway ('træmˌweɪ) *n.* **1.** another name for **tramline** (sense 1). **2.** *Brit.* **a.** a public transportation system using trams. **b.** the company owning or running such a system. **3.** Also called (esp. U.S.): **tramroad.** a small or temporary railway for moving freight along tracks, as in a quarry.

trance (trɑːns) *n.* **1.** a hypnotic state resembling sleep. **2.** any mental state in which a person is unaware or apparently unaware of the environment, characterized by loss of voluntary movement, rigidity, and lack of sensitivity to external stimuli. **3.** a dazed or stunned state. **4.** a state of ecstasy or mystic absorption so intense as to cause a temporary loss of consciousness at the earthly level. **5.** *Spiritualism.* a state in which a medium, having temporarily lost consciousness, can supposedly be controlled by an intelligence from without as a means of communication with the dead. ~*vb.* **6.** (*tr.*) to put into or as into a trance. [C14: from Old French *transe,* from *transir* to faint, pass away, from Latin *trānsīre* to go over, from TRANS- + *īre* to go] —**'trance,like** *adj.*

tranche (trɑːnʃ) *n.* a portion or instalment of a usually large sum of money, such as a loan borrowed by a government. [from French, literally: a slice]

trannie *or* **tranny** ('trænɪ) *n., pl.* **-nies.** *Informal, chiefly Brit.* a transistor radio.

tranquil ('træŋkwɪl) *adj.* calm, peaceful or quiet. [C17: from Latin *tranquillus*] —**'tranquilly** *adv.* —**'tranquilness** *n.*

tranquillity *or U.S. (sometimes)* **tranquility** (træŋ'kwɪlɪtɪ) *n.* a state of calm or quietude.

tranquillize, tranquillise, *or U.S.* **tranquilize** ('træŋkwɪˌlaɪz) *vb.* to make or become calm or calmer. —ˌ**tranquilli'zation,** ˌ**tranquilli'sation,** *or U.S.* ˌ**tranquili'zation** *n.*

tranquillizer, tranquilliser, *or U.S.* **tranquilizer** ('træŋkwɪˌlaɪzə) *n.* **1.** a drug that calms a person without affecting clarity of consciousness. **2.** anything that tranquillizes.

trans. *abbrev. for:* **1.** transaction. **2.** transferred. **3.** transitive. **4.** translated. **5.** translator. **6.** transport(ation). **7.** transparent. **8.** transpose. **9.** transverse.

trans- *or sometimes before* s- **tran-** *prefix.* **1.** across, beyond, crossing, on the other side: *transoceanic; trans-Siberian; transatlantic.* **2.** changing thoroughly: *transliterate.* **3.** transcending: *transubstantiation.* **4.** transversely: *transect.* **5.** (*often in italics*) indicating that a chemical compound has a molecular structure in which two identical groups or atoms are on opposite sides of a double bond: *trans*-butadiene. Compare **cis-** (sense 2). [from Latin *trāns* across, through, beyond]

transact (træn'zækt) *vb.* to do, conduct, or negotiate (business, a deal, etc.). [C16: from Latin *trānsactus,* from *trānsigere,* literally: to drive through, from TRANS- + *agere* to drive] —**trans'actor** *n.*

transactinide (ˌtræns'æktɪˌnaɪd) *n.* any artificially produced element with an atomic number greater than 103. [C20: from TRANS- + ACTINIDE]

transaction (træn'zækʃən) *n.* **1.** something that is transacted, esp. a business deal or negotiation. **2.** the act of transacting or the state of being transacted. **3.** (*pl.*) the published records of the proceedings of a society, conference, etc. **4.** (in business computing) the act of obtaining and paying for an item or service. **5.** (in general computing) the transmission and processing of an item of data. —**trans'actional** *adj.* —**trans'actionally** *adv.*

transactional analysis *n. Psychol.* a form of psychotherapy that attributes neuroses to lack of balance in the personality between the conflicting ego-states of child, adult, and parent.

transalpine (trænz'ælpaɪn) *adj.* (*prenominal*) **1.** situated in or relating to places beyond the mountains of the Alps, esp. from Italy. **2.** passing over the Alps. ~*n.* **3.** a transalpine person.

transaminase (trænz'æmɪˌneɪz, -ˌneɪs) *n. Biochem.* an enzyme that catalyses the transfer of an amino group from one molecule, esp. an amino acid, to another, esp. a keto acid, in the process of **transamination.**

transatlantic (ˌtrænzət'læntɪk) *adj.* **1.** on or from the other side of the Atlantic Ocean. **2.** crossing the Atlantic.

transcalent (træns'keɪlənt) *adj. Rare.* permitting the passage of heat. [C19: TRANS- + *-calent,* from Latin *calēre* to be hot] —**trans'calency** *n.*

Transcaucasian (ˌtrænskɔː'keɪzjən) *adj.* **1.** of, relating to, coming from, or situated in Transcaucasia, a region in the SW of the former Soviet Union. ~*n.* **2.** a native or inhabitant of Transcaucasia.

transceiver (træn'siːvə) *n.* a combined radio transmitter and receiver. [C20: from TRANS(MITTER) + (RE)CEIVER]

transcend (træn'sɛnd) *vb.* **1.** to go above or beyond (a limit, expectation, etc.), as in degree or excellence. **2.** (*tr.*) to be superior to. **3.** *Philosophy, theol.* (esp. of the Deity) to exist beyond (the material world). [C14: from Latin *trānscendere* to climb over, from TRANS- + *scandere* to climb] —**trans'cendingly** *adv.*

transcendent (træn'sɛndənt) *adj.* **1.** exceeding or surpassing in degree or excellence. **2. a.** (in Kantian philosophy) beyond or before experience; a priori. **b.** (of a concept) falling outside a given set of categories. **c.** beyond consciousness or direct apprehension. **3.** *Theol.* (of God) having continuous existence outside the created world. **4.** free from the limitations inherent in matter. ~*n.* **5.** *Philosophy.* a transcendent thing. —**tran'scendence** *n.* —**tran'scendency** *n.* —**tran'scendently** *adv.* —**tran'scendentness** *n.*

transcendental (ˌtrænsɛn'dɛntᵊl) *adj.* **1.** transcendent, superior, or surpassing. **2.** (in Kantian philosophy) **a.** (of a judgment or logical deduction) being both synthetic and a priori. **b.** of or relating to knowledge of the presuppositions of thought. **3.** *Philosophy.* beyond our experience of phenomena, although not beyond potential knowledge. **4.** *Theol.* surpassing the natural plane of reality or knowledge; supernatural or mystical. —ˌ**transcenden'tality** *n.* —ˌ**transcen'dentally** *adv.*

transcendental argument *n. Philosophy.* an argument designed to make explicit the conditions under which a certain kind of knowledge is possible, esp. those of Kant.

transcendental function *n. Maths.* a function that is not capable of expression in terms of a finite number of arithmetical operations, such as sin x.

transcendental idealism *n. Philosophy.* the Kantian doctrine that reality consists not of appearances, but of some other order of being whose existence can be inferred from the nature of human reason.

transcendentalism (ˌtrænsɛn'dɛntəˌlɪzəm) *n.* **1. a.** any system of philosophy holding that the key to knowledge of the nature of reality lies in the critical examination of the processes of reason on which depends the nature of experience. **b.** any system of philosophy that emphasizes intuition as a means to knowledge or the importance of the search for the divine. **2.** vague philosophical speculation. **3.** the state of being transcendental. **4.** something, such as thought or language, that is transcendental. —ˌ**transcen'dentalist** *n., adj.*

transcendental meditation *n.* a technique, based on Hindu traditions, for relaxing and refreshing the mind and body through the silent repetition of a mantra.

transcendental number *n. Maths.* a number or quantity that is real but nonalgebraic, that is, one that is not a root of any polynomial with rational coefficients such as π or e.

transcontinental (ˌtrænzkɒntɪ'nɛntᵊl) *adj.* **1.** crossing a continent. **2.** on or from the far side of a continent. —ˌ**transconti'nentally** *adv.*

transcribe (træn'skraɪb) *vb.* (*tr.*) **1.** to write, type, or print out fully from speech, notes, etc. **2.** to make a phonetic transcription of. **3.** to transliterate or translate. **4.** to make an electrical recording of (a programme or speech) for a later broadcast. **5.** *Music.* to rewrite (a piece of music) for an instrument or medium other than that originally intended; arrange. **6.** *Computer technol.* **a.** to transfer (information) from one storage device, such as punched cards, to another, such as magnetic tape. **b.** to transfer (information) from a computer to an external storage device. **7.** (*usually passive*) *Biochem.* to convert the genetic information in (a strand of DNA) into a strand of RNA, esp. messenger RNA. See also **genetic code, translate** (sense 6). [C16: from Latin *transcrībere,* from TRANS- + *scrībere* to write] —**tran'scribable** *adj.* —**tran'scriber** *n.*

transcript ('trænskrɪpt) *n.* **1.** a written, typed, or printed copy or manuscript made by transcribing. **2.** *Education, chiefly U.S. and Canadian.* an official record of a student's school progress and achievements. **3.** any reproduction or copy. [C13: from Latin *transcriptum,* from *transcrībere* to TRANSCRIBE]

transcriptase (træn'skrɪpteɪz) *n.* See **reverse transcriptase.**

transcription (træn'skrɪpʃən) *n.* **1.** the act or an instance of transcribing or the state of being transcribed. **2.** something transcribed. **3.** a representation in writing of the actual pronunciation of a speech sound, word, or piece of continuous text, using not a conventional orthography but a symbol or set of symbols specially designated as standing for corresponding phonetic values. —**tran'scriptional** *or* **tran'scriptive** *adj.* —**tran'scriptionally** *or* **tran'scriptively** *adv.*

transculturation (ˌtrænzkʌltʃʊ'reɪʃən) *n.* the introduction of foreign elements into an established culture.

transcurrent (trænz'kʌrənt) *adj.* running across; transverse.

transducer (trænz'djuːsə) *n.* any device, such as a microphone or electric motor, that converts one form of energy into another. [C20: from Latin *transducere* to lead across, from TRANS- + *ducere* to lead]

transduction (trænz'dʌkʃən) *n. Genetics.* the transfer by a bacteriophage of genetic material from one bacterium to another. [C17: from Latin *transductiō*, variant of *trāductiō* a leading along, from *trādūcere* to lead over; see TRADUCE]

transect *vb.* (*tr.*) (træn'sɛkt) **1.** to cut or divide crossways. ~*n.* ('trænsɛkt). **2.** a sample strip of land used to monitor plant distribution, animal populations, etc., within a given area. [C17: from Latin TRANS- + *secāre* to cut] —**tran'section** *n.*

transept ('trænsɛpt) *n.* either of the two wings of a cruciform church at right angles to the nave. [C16: from Anglo-Latin *transeptum*, from Latin TRANS- + *saeptum* enclosure] —**tran'septal** *adj.*

transeunt ('trænsɪənt) *or* **transient** *adj. Philosophy.* (of a mental act) causing effects outside the mind. Compare **immanent** (sense 2). [C17: from Latin *transiēns* going over, from *transīre* to pass over; see TRANCE]

transf. *abbrev. for* transferred.

transfect (træns'fɛkt) *vb.* (*tr.*) to bring about transfection in. [from TRANS- + (IN)FECT]

transfection (træns'fɛkʃən) *n.* the transfer into another cell of genetic material isolated from a cell or virus.

transfer *vb.* (træns'fɜː), **-fers, -ferring, -ferred. 1.** to change or go or cause to change or go from one thing, person, or point to another: *they transferred from the Park Hotel to the Imperial; she transferred her affections to her dog.* **2.** to change (buses, trains, etc.). **3.** *Law.* to make over (property, etc.) to another; convey. **4.** to displace (a drawing, design, etc.) from one surface to another. **5.** (of a football player, esp. a professional) to change clubs or (of a club, manager, etc.) to sell or release (a player) to another club. **6.** to leave one school, college, etc., and enrol at another. **7.** to change (the meaning of a word, etc.), esp. by metaphorical extension. ~*n.* ('trænsfɜː). **8.** the act, process, or system of transferring, or the state of being transferred. **9. a.** a person or thing that transfers or is transferred. **b.** (*as modifier*): *a transfer student.* **10.** a design or drawing that is transferred from one surface to another, as by ironing a printed design onto cloth. **11.** *Law.* the passing of title to property or other right from one person to another by act of the parties or by operation of law; conveyance. **12.** *Finance.* **a.** the act of transferring the title of ownership to shares or registered bonds in the books of the issuing enterprise. **b.** (*as modifier*): *transfer deed; transfer form.* **13.** any document or form effecting or regulating a transfer. **14.** *Chiefly U.S. and Canadian.* a ticket that allows a passenger to change routes. [C14: from Latin *transferre*, from TRANS- + *ferre* to carry] —**trans'ferable** *or* **trans'ferrable** *adj.* —ˌ**transfera'bility** *n.*

transferable vote *n.* a vote that is transferred to a second candidate indicated by the voter if the first is eliminated from the ballot.

transferase ('trænsfəˌreɪs) *n.* any enzyme that catalyses the transfer of a chemical group from one substance to another.

transfer characteristic *n. Electronics.* the relationship between output and input of an electronic or electromechanical system, esp. as depicted graphically.

transferee (ˌtrænsfə'riː) *n.* **1.** *Property law.* a person to whom property is transferred. **2.** a person who is transferred.

transference ('trænsfərəns, -frəns) *n.* **1.** the act or an instance of transferring or the state of being transferred. **2.** *Psychoanal.* the redirection of attitudes and emotions towards a substitute, such as towards the analyst during therapy. —**transferential** (ˌtrænsfə'rɛnʃəl) *adj.*

transfer fee *n.* a sum of money paid by one football club to another for a transferred player.

transfer list *n.* a list of football players available for transfer.

transferor *or* **transferrer** (træns'fɜːrə) *n. Property law.* a person who makes a transfer, as of property.

transfer payment *n.* (*usually pl.*) money received by an individual or family from the state or other body, often a pension or unemployment benefit. It is not reckoned when calculating the national income as it is money transferred rather than paid for merchandise or a service rendered.

transferrin (træns'fɜːrɪn) *n. Biochem.* any of a group of blood glycoproteins that transport iron. Also called: **beta globulin, siderophilin.** [C20: from TRANS- + FERRO- + -IN]

transfer RNA *n. Biochem.* any of several soluble forms of RNA of low molecular weight, each of which transports a specific amino acid to a ribosome during protein synthesis. Sometimes shortened to **t-RNA.** Also called: **soluble RNA.** See also **messenger RNA, genetic code.**

transfiguration (ˌtrænsfɪgjʊ'reɪʃən) *n.* the act or an instance of transfiguring or the state of being transfigured.

Transfiguration (ˌtrænsfɪgjʊ'reɪʃən) *n.* **1.** *New Testament.* the change in the appearance of Christ that took place before three disciples (Matthew 17:1–9). **2.** the Church festival held in commemoration of this on Aug. 6.

transfigure (træns'fɪgə) *vb.* (*usually tr.*) **1.** to change or cause to change in appearance. **2.** to become or cause to become more exalted. [C13: from Latin *transfigūrāre*, from TRANS- + *figūra* appearance] —**trans'figurement** *n.*

transfinite (træns'faɪnaɪt) *adj.* extending beyond the finite.

transfinite number *n.* a cardinal or ordinal number used in the comparison of infinite sets for which several types of infinity can be classified: *the set of integers and the set of real numbers have different transfinite numbers.*

transfix (træns'fɪks) *vb.* **-fixes, -fixing, -fixed** *or* **-fixt.** (*tr.*) **1.** to render motionless, esp. with horror or shock. **2.** to impale or fix with a sharp weapon or other device. **3.** *Med.* to cut through (a limb or other organ), as in amputation. [C16: from Latin *transfīgere* to pierce through, from TRANS- + *fīgere* to thrust in] —**transfixion** (træns'fɪkʃən) *n.*

transform *vb.* (træns'fɔːm). **1.** to alter or be altered radically in form, function, etc. **2.** (*tr.*) to convert (one form of energy) to another form. **3.** (*tr.*) *Maths.* to change the form of (an equation, expression, etc.) by a mathematical transformation. **4.** (*tr.*) to increase or decrease (an alternating current or voltage) using a transformer. ~*n.* ('trænsˌfɔːm). **5.** *Maths.* the result of a mathematical transformation, esp. (of a matrix or an element of a group) another related to the given one by $B=X^{-1}AX$ for some appropriate X. [C14: from Latin *transformāre*, from TRANS- + *formāre* to FORM] —**trans'formable** *adj.* —**trans'formative** *adj.*

transformation (ˌtrænsfə'meɪʃən) *n.* **1.** a change or alteration, esp. a radical one. **2.** the act of transforming or the state of being transformed. **3.** *Maths.* **a.** a change in position or direction of the reference axes in a coordinate system without an alteration in their relative angle. **b.** an equivalent change in an expression or equation resulting from the substitution of one set of variables by another. **4.** *Physics.* a change in an atomic nucleus to a different nuclide as the result of the emission of either an alpha-particle or a beta-particle. Compare **transition** (sense 5). **5.** *Linguistics.* another word for **transformational rule. 6.** an apparently miraculous change in the appearance of a stage set. —ˌ**transfor'mational** *adj.*

transformational grammar *n.* a grammatical description of a language making essential use of transformational rules. Such grammars are usually but not necessarily generative grammars. Compare **systemic grammar, case grammar.**

transformational rule *n.* **1.** *Generative grammar.* a rule that converts one phrase marker into another. Taken together, these rules, which form the **transformational component** of the grammar, convert the deep structures of sentences into their surface structures. **2.** (*pl.*) *Logic.* a rule that specifies in purely syntactic terms a method by which theorems may be derived from the axioms of a formal system.

transformer (træns'fɔːmə) *n.* **1.** a device that transfers an alternating current from one circuit to one or more other circuits, usually with an increase (**step-up transformer**) or decrease (**step-down transformer**) of voltage. The input current is fed to a primary winding, the output being taken from a secondary winding or windings inductively linked to the primary. **2.** a person or thing that transforms.

transformism (træns'fɔːmɪzəm) *n.* a less common word for **evolution,** esp. the theory of evolution. —**trans'formist** *n.*

transfuse (træns'fjuːz) *vb.* (*tr.*) **1.** to permeate or infuse: *a blush transfused her face.* **2. a.** to inject (blood, etc.) into a blood vessel. **b.** to give a transfusion to (a patient). **3.** *Rare.* to transfer from one vessel to another, esp. by pouring. [C15: from Latin *transfundere* to pour out, from TRANS- + *fundere* to pour] —**trans'fuser** *n.* —**trans'fusible** *or* **trans'fusable** *adj.* —**trans'fusive** *adj.*

transfusion (træns'fjuːʒən) *n.* **1.** the act or an instance of transfusing. **2.** the injection of blood, blood plasma, etc., into the blood vessels of a patient.

transgenic (trænz'dʒɛnɪk) *adj.* (of an animal or plant) containing genetic material artificially transferred from another species.

transgress (trænz'grɛs) *vb.* **1.** to break (a law, etc.). **2.** to go beyond or overstep (a limit). [C16: from Latin *transgredī*, from TRANS- + *gradī* to step] —**trans'gressive** *adj.* —**trans'gressively** *adv.* —**trans'gressor** *n.*

transgression (trænz'grɛʃən) *n.* **1.** a breach of a law, etc.; sin or crime. **2.** the act or an instance of transgressing.

tranship (træn'ʃɪp) *vb.* **-ships, -shipping, -shipped.** a variant spelling of **transship.** —**tran'shipment** *n.*

transhumance (træns'hjuːməns) *n.* the seasonal migration of livestock to suitable grazing grounds. [C20: from French, from *transhumer* to change one's pastures, from Spanish *trashumar*, from Latin TRANS- + *humus* ground] —**trans'humant** *adj.*

transient ('trænzɪənt) *adj.* **1.** for a short time only; temporary or transitory. **2.** *Philosophy.* a variant of **transeunt.** ~*n.* **3.** a transient person or thing. **4.** *Physics.* a brief change in the state of a system, such as a sudden short-lived oscillation in the current flowing through a circuit. [C17: from Latin *transiēns* going over, from *transīre* to pass over, from TRANS- + *īre* to go] —**'transiently** *adv.* —**'transience** *or* **'transiency** *n.*

transilient (træn'sɪlɪənt) *adj.* passing quickly from one thing to another. [C19: from Latin *transilīre* to jump over, from TRANS- + *salīre* to leap] —**tran'silience** *n.*

transilluminate (ˌtrænzɪ'luːmɪˌneɪt) *vb.* (*tr.*) *Med.* to pass a light through the wall of (a bodily cavity, membrane, etc.) in order to detect fluid, lesions, etc. —**ˌtransilˌlumi'nation** *n.* —**ˌtransil'lumiˌnator** *n.*

transistor (træn'zɪstə) *n.* **1.** a semiconductor device, having three or more terminals attached to electrode regions, in which current flowing between two electrodes is controlled by a voltage or current applied to one or more specified electrodes. The device is capable of amplification, etc., and has replaced the valve in most circuits since it is much smaller, more robust, and works at a much lower voltage. See also **junction transistor, field-effect transistor.** **2.** *Informal.* a transistor radio. [C20: originally a trademark, from TRANSFER + RESISTOR, referring to the transfer of electric signals across a resistor]

transistorize *or* **transistorise** (træn'zɪstəˌraɪz) *vb.* **1.** to convert (a system, device, industry, etc.) to the use or manufacture of or operation by transistors and other solid-state components. **2.** to equip (a device or circuit) with transistors and other solid-state components.

transit ('trænsɪt, 'trænz-) *n.* **1. a.** the passage or conveyance of goods or people. **b.** (*as modifier*): *a transit visa.* **2.** a change or transition. **3.** a route. **4.** *Astronomy.* **a.** the passage of a celestial body or satellite across the face of a relatively larger body as seen from the earth. **b.** the apparent passage of a celestial body across the meridian, caused by the earth's diurnal rotation. **5.** *Astrology.* the passage of a planet across some special point on the zodiac. **6. in transit.** while being conveyed; during passage. ~*vb.* **7.** to make a transit through or over (something). **8.** *Astronomy.* to make a transit across (a celestial body or the meridian). **9.** to cause (the telescope of a surveying instrument) to turn over or (of such a telescope) to be turned over in a vertical plane so that it points in the opposite direction. [C15: from Latin *transitus* a going over, from *transīre* to pass over; see TRANSIENT] —**'transitable** *adj.*

transit camp *n.* a camp in which refugees, soldiers, etc., live temporarily before moving to another destination.

transit instrument *n.* an astronomical instrument, mounted on an E-W axis, in which the reticle of a telescope is always in the plane of the meridian. It is used to time the transit of a star, etc., across the meridian.

transition (træn'zɪʃən) *n.* **1.** change or passage from one state or stage to another. **2.** the period of time during which something changes from one state or stage to another. **3.** *Music.* **a.** a movement from one key to another; modulation. **b.** a linking passage between two divisions in a composition; bridge. **4.** Also called: **transitional.** a style of architecture that was used in western Europe in the late 11th and early 12th century, characterized by late Romanesque forms combined with early Gothic details. **5.** *Physics.* a change in the configuration of an atomic nucleus, involving either a change in energy level resulting from the emission of a gamma-ray photon or a transformation to another element or isotope. **6.** a sentence, passage, etc., that connects a topic to one that follows or that links sections of a written work. [C16: from Latin *transitio;* see TRANSIENT] —**tran'sitional** *or* (*rarely*) **tran'sitionary** *adj.* —**tran'sitionally** *adv.*

transition element *or* **metal** *n. Chem.* any element belonging to one of three series of elements with atomic numbers between 21 and 30, 39 and 48, and 57 and 80. They have an incomplete penultimate electron shell and tend to exhibit more than one valency and to form complexes.

transition point *n.* **1.** the point in a stream of fluid flow at which laminar flow changes to turbulent flow. **2.** See **transition temperature.**

transition temperature *n.* the temperature at which a sudden change of physical properties occurs, such as a change of phase, crystalline structure, or conductivity.

transitive ('trænsɪtɪv) *adj.* **1.** *Grammar.* **a.** denoting an occurrence of a verb when it requires a direct object or denoting a verb that customarily requires a direct object. **b.** (*as n.*): *these verbs are transitives.* **2.** *Grammar.* denoting an adjective, such as *fond,* or a noun, such as *husband,* that requires a noun phrase and cannot be used without some implicit or explicit reference to such a noun phrase. **3.** *Logic, maths.* having the property that if one object bears a relationship to a second object that also bears the same relationship to a third object, then the first object bears this relationship to the third object: *mathematical equality is transitive, since if* $x = y$ *and* $y = z$ *then* $x = z$. ~Compare **intransitive.** [C16: from Late Latin *transitīvus,* from Latin *transitus* a going over; see TRANSIENT] —**'transitively** *adv.* —**ˌtransi'tivity** *or* **'transitiveness** *n.*

transitory ('trænsɪtərɪ, -trɪ) *adj.* of short duration; transient or ephemeral. [C14: from Church Latin *transitōrius* passing, from Latin *transitus* a crossing over; see TRANSIENT] —**'transitorily** *adv.* —**'transitoriness** *n.*

transitory action *n. Law.* an action that can be brought in any country regardless of where it originated.

transit theodolite *n.* a theodolite the telescope of which can be rotated completely about its horizontal axis.

transl. *abbrev. for:* **1.** translated. **2.** translator.

translate (træns'leɪt, trænz-) *vb.* **1.** to express or be capable of being expressed in another language or dialect: *he translated Shakespeare into Afrikaans; his books translate well.* **2.** (*intr.*) to act as translator. **3.** (*tr.*) to express or explain in simple or less technical language. **4.** (*tr.*) to interpret or infer the significance of (gestures, symbols, etc.). **5.** (*tr.*) to transform or convert: *to translate hope into reality.* **6.** (*tr.; usually passive*) *Biochem.* to transform the molecular structure of (messenger RNA) into a polypeptide chain by means of the information stored in the genetic code. See also **transcribe** (sense 7). **7.** to move or carry from one place or position to another. **8.** (*tr.*) **a.** to transfer (a cleric) from one ecclesiastical office to another. **b.** to transfer (a see) from one place to another. **9.** (*tr.*) *R.C. Church.* to transfer (the body or the relics of a saint) from one resting place to another. **10.** (*tr.*) *Theol.* to transfer (a person) from one place or plane of existence to another, as from earth to heaven. **11.** *Maths, physics.* to move (a figure or body) laterally, without rotation, dilation, or angular displacement. **12.** (*intr.*) (of an aircraft, missile, etc.) to fly or move from one position to another. **13.** (*tr.*) *Archaic.* to bring to a state of spiritual or emotional ecstasy. [C13: from Latin *translātus* transferred, carried over, from *transferre* to TRANSFER] —**trans'latable** *adj.* —**ˌtranslata'bility** *n.*

translation (træns'leɪʃən, trænz-) *n.* **1.** something that is or has been translated, esp. a written text. **2.** the act of translating or the state of being translated. **3.** *Maths.* a transformation in which the origin of a coordinate system is moved to another position so that each axis retains the same direction or, equivalently, a figure or curve is moved so that it retains the same orientation to the axes. —**trans'lational** *adj.*

translator (træns'leɪtə, trænz-) *n.* **1.** a person or machine that translates speech or writing. **2.** *Radio.* a relay transmitter that retransmits a signal on a carrier frequency different from that on which it was received. **3.** *Computer technol.* a computer program that converts a program from one language to another. —**ˌtransla'torial** *adj.*

transliterate (trænz'lɪtəˌreɪt) *vb.* (*tr.*) to transcribe (a word, etc., in one alphabet) into corresponding letters of another alphabet: *the Greek word* λογοσ *can be transliterated as "logos".* [C19: TRANS- + *-literate,* from Latin *līttera* LETTER] —**ˌtransliter'ation** *n.* —**trans'literˌator** *n.*

translocate (ˌtrænzləʊ'keɪt) *vb.* (*tr.*) to move; displace.

translocation (ˌtrænzləʊ'keɪʃən) *n.* **1.** *Genetics.* the transfer of one part of a chromosome to another part of the same or a different chromosome, resulting in rearrangement of the genes. **2.** *Botany.* the transport of minerals, sugars, etc., in solution within a plant. **3.** a movement from one position or place to another.

translucent (trænz'luːsᵊnt) *adj.* allowing light to pass through partially or diffusely; semitransparent. [C16: from Latin *translūcēre* to shine through, from TRANS- + *lūcēre* to shine] —**trans'lucence** *or* **trans'lucency** *n.* —**trans'lucently** *adv.*

translunar (trænz'luːnə) *or* **translunary** (trænz'luːnərɪ) *adj.* **1.** lying beyond the moon. Compare **cislunar.** **2.** unworldly or ethereal.

transmarine (ˌtrænzmə'riːn) *adj.* a less common word for **overseas.** [C16: from Latin *transmarīnus,* from TRANS- + *marīnus,* from *mare* sea]

transmigrant (trænz'maɪgrənt, 'trænzmɪgrənt) *n.* **1.** an emigrant on the way to the country of immigration. ~*adj.* **2.** passing through from one place or stage to another.

transmigrate (ˌtrænzmaɪ'greɪt) *vb.* (*intr.*) **1.** to move from one place, state, or stage to another. **2.** (of souls) to pass from one body into another at death. —**ˌtransmi'gration** *n.* —**ˌtransmi'grational** *adj.* —**trans'migrative** *adj.* —**ˌtransmi'grator** *n.* —**trans'migratory** *adj.*

transmissible spongiform encephalopathy *n.* the full name for **TSE.**

transmission (trænz'mɪʃən) *n.* **1.** the act or process of transmitting. **2.** something that is transmitted. **3.** the extent to which a body or medium transmits light, sound, or some other form of energy. **4.** the transference of motive force or power. **5.** a system of shafts, gears, torque converters, etc., that transmits power, esp. the arrangement of such parts that transmits the power of the engine to the driving wheels of a motor vehicle. **6.** the act or process of sending a message, picture, or other information from one location to one or more other locations by means of radio waves, electrical signals, light signals, etc. **7.** a radio or television broadcast. [C17: from Latin *transmissiō* a sending across; see TRANSMIT] —**trans'missible** *adj.* —**transˌmissi'bility** *n.* —**trans'missive** *adj.* —**trans'missively** *adv.* —**trans'missiveness** *n.*

transmission density *n. Physics.* a measure of the extent to which a substance transmits light or other electromagnetic radiation, equal to the logarithm to base ten of the reciprocal of the transmittance. Symbol: τ Also called: **absorbance.** Former name: **optical density.**

transmission line *n.* a coaxial cable, waveguide, or other system of conductors that transfers electrical signals from one location to another. Sometimes shortened to **line.**

transmissivity (ˌtrænzmɪˈsɪvɪtɪ) *n. Physics.* a measure of the ability of a material to transmit radiation, equal to the internal transmittance of the material under conditions in which the path of the radiation has unit length.

transmit (trænzˈmɪt) *vb.* **-mits, -mitting, -mitted. 1.** (*tr.*) to pass or cause to go from one place or person to another; transfer. **2.** (*tr.*) to pass on or impart (a disease, infection, etc.). **3.** (*tr.*) to hand down to posterity. **4.** (*tr.; usually passive*) to pass (an inheritable characteristic) from parent to offspring. **5.** to allow the passage of (particles, energy, etc.): *radio waves are transmitted through the atmosphere.* **6. a.** to send out (signals) by means of radio waves or along a transmission line. **b.** to broadcast (a radio or television programme). **7.** (*tr.*) to transfer (a force, motion, power, etc.) from one part of a mechanical system to another. [C14: from Latin *transmittere* to send across, from TRANS- + *mittere* to send] —**transˈmittable** *or* **transˈmittible** *adj.* —**transˈmittal** *n.*

transmittance (trænzˈmɪtᵊns) *n.* **1.** the act of transmitting. **2.** Also called: **transmission factor.** *Physics.* a measure of the ability of anything to transmit radiation, equal to the ratio of the transmitted flux to the incident flux; the reciprocal of the opacity. For a plate of material the ratio of the flux leaving the entry surface to that reaching the exit surface is the **internal transmittance.** Symbol: τ Compare **reflectance, absorptance.**

transmittancy (trænzˈmɪtᵊnsɪ) *n. Physics.* a measure of the extent to which a solution transmits radiation. It is equal to the ratio of the transmittance of the solution to the transmittance of a pure solvent of the same dimensions.

transmitter (trænzˈmɪtə) *n.* **1.** a person or thing that transmits. **2.** the equipment used for generating and amplifying a radio-frequency carrier, modulating the carrier with information, and feeding it to an aerial for transmission. **3.** the microphone in a telephone that converts sound waves into audio-frequency electrical signals. **4.** a device that converts mechanical movements into coded electrical signals transmitted along a telegraph circuit. **5.** *Physiol.* a substance released by nerve endings that transmits impulses across synapses.

transmittivity (ˌtrænzmɪˈtɪvɪtɪ) *n. Physics.* the transmittance of unit thickness of a substance, neglecting any scattering effects.

transmogrify (trænzˈmɒgrɪˌfaɪ) *vb.* **-fies, -fying, -fied.** (*tr.*) *Jocular.* to change or transform into a different shape, esp. a grotesque or bizarre one. [C17: of unknown origin] —**transˌmogrifiˈcation** *n.*

transmontane (ˌtrænzmɒnˈteɪn) *adj., n.* another word for **tramontane.**

transmundane (trænzˈmʌndeɪn) *adj.* beyond this world or worldly considerations.

transmutation (ˌtrænzmjuːˈteɪʃən) *n.* **1.** the act or an instance of transmuting. **2.** the change of one chemical element into another by a nuclear reaction. **3.** the attempted conversion, by alchemists, of base metals into gold or silver. —ˌ**transmuˈtational** *or* **transˈmutative** *adj.* —ˌ**transmuˈtationist** *n., adj.*

transmute (trænzˈmjuːt) *vb.* (*tr.*) **1.** to change the form, character, or substance of. **2.** to alter (an element, metal, etc.) by alchemy. [C15: via Old French from Latin *transmūtāre* to shift, from TRANS- + *mūtāre* to change] —**transˌmutaˈbility** *n.* —**transˈmutable** *adj.* —**transˈmutably** *adv.* —**transˈmuter** *n.*

transnational (trænzˈnæʃənᵊl) *adj.* extending beyond the boundaries, interests, etc., of a single nation.

Trans-New Guinea phylum *n.* the largest grouping of the non-Austronesian languages of Papua and New Guinea and the surrounding regions N of Australia. Older term: **New Guinea Macrophylum.**

transoceanic (ˈtrænzˌəʊʃɪˈænɪk) *adj.* **1.** on or from the other side of an ocean. **2.** crossing an ocean.

transom (ˈtrænsəm) *n.* **1.** Also called: **traverse.** a horizontal member across a window. Compare **mullion. 2.** a horizontal member that separates a door from a window over it. **3.** the usual U.S. name for **fanlight. 4.** *Nautical.* **a.** a surface forming the stern of a vessel, either vertical or canted either forwards (**reverse transom**) or aft at the upper side. **b.** any of several transverse beams used for strengthening the stern of a vessel. [C14: earlier *traversayn,* from Old French *traversin,* from TRAVERSE] —ˈ**transomed** *adj.*

transonic (trænˈsɒnɪk) *adj.* of or relating to conditions when travelling at or near the speed of sound.

transonic barrier *n.* another name for **sound barrier.**

transp. *abbrev. for* transport(ation).

transpacific (ˌtrænzpəˈsɪfɪk) *adj.* **1.** crossing the Pacific Ocean. **2.** on or from the other side of the Pacific.

transpadane (ˈtrænzpəˌdeɪn, trænsˈpeɪdeɪn) *adj.* (*prenominal*) on or from the far (or north) side of the River Po, as viewed from Rome. Compare **cispadane.** [C17: from Latin *Transpadānus,* from TRANS- + *Padus* the River Po]

transparency (trænsˈpærənsɪ, -ˈpɛər-) *n., pl.* **-cies. 1.** Also called: **transparence.** the state of being transparent. **2.** Also called: **slide.** a positive photograph on a transparent base, usually mounted in a frame or between glass plates. It can be viewed by means of a slide projector.

transparent (trænsˈpærənt, -ˈpɛər-) *adj.* **1.** permitting the uninterrupted passage of light; clear: *a window is transparent.* **2.** easy to see through, understand, or recognize; obvious. **3.** (of a substance or object) permitting the free passage of electromagnetic radiation: *a substance that is transparent to x-rays.* **4.** candid, open, or frank. [C15: from Medieval Latin *transpārēre* to show through, from Latin TRANS- + *pārēre* to appear] —**transˈparently** *adv.* —**transˈparentness** *n.*

transparent context *n. Philosophy, logic.* an expression in which any term may be replaced by another with the same reference without changing its truth-value. Compare **opaque context.**

transpicuous (trænˈspɪkjʊəs) *adj.* a less common word for **transparent.** [C17: from Medieval Latin *transpicuus,* from Latin *transpicere* to look through, from TRANS- + *specere* to look] —**tranˈspicuously** *adv.*

transpierce (trænsˈpɪəs) *vb.* (*tr.*) to pierce through.

transpire (trænˈspaɪə) *vb.* **1.** (*intr.*) to come to light; be known. **2.** (*intr.*) *Informal.* to happen or occur. **3.** *Physiol.* to give off or exhale (water or vapour) through the skin, a mucous membrane, etc. **4.** (of plants) to lose (water in the form of water vapour), esp. through the stomata of the leaves. [C16: from Medieval Latin *transpīrāre,* from Latin TRANS- + *spīrāre* to breathe] —**tranˈspirable** *adj.* —**transpiration** (ˌtrænspəˈreɪʃən) *n.* —**tranˈspiratory** *adj.*

▷**Usage.** It is often maintained that *transpire* should not be used to mean happen or occur, as in *the event transpired late in the evening,* and that the word is properly used to mean become known, as in *it transpired later that the thief had been caught.* The word is, however, widely used in the former sense, esp. in spoken English.

transplant *vb.* (trænsˈplɑːnt). **1.** (*tr.*) to remove or transfer (esp. a plant) from one place to another. **2.** (*intr.*) to be capable of being transplanted. **3.** *Surgery.* to transfer (an organ or tissue) from one part of the body to another or from one person or animal to another during a grafting or transplant operation. ~*n.* (ˈtrænsˌplɑːnt). **4.** *Surgery.* **a.** the procedure involved in such a transfer. **b.** the organ or tissue transplanted. —**transˈplantable** *adj.* —ˌ**transplanˈtation** *n.* —**transˈplanter** *n.*

transpolar (trænzˈpəʊlə) *adj.* crossing a polar region.

transponder *or* **transpondor** (trænˈspɒndə) *n.* **1.** a type of radio or radar transmitter-receiver that transmits signals automatically when it receives predetermined signals. **2.** the receiver and transmitter in a communications or broadcast satellite, relaying received signals back to earth. [C20: from TRANSMITTER + RESPONDER]

transpontine (trænzˈpɒntaɪn) *adj.* **1.** on or from the far side of a bridge. **2.** *Archaic.* on or from the south side of the River Thames in London. [C19: TRANS- + *-pontine,* from Latin *pōns* bridge]

transport *vb.* (trænsˈpɔːt). (*tr.*) **1.** to carry or cause to go from one place to another, esp. over some distance. **2.** to deport or exile to a penal colony. **3.** (*usually passive*) to have a strong emotional effect on. ~*n.* (ˈtrænsˌpɔːt). **4. a.** the business or system of transporting goods or people. **b.** (*as modifier*): *a modernized transport system.* **5.** *Brit.* freight vehicles generally. **6. a.** a vehicle used to transport goods or people, esp. lorries or ships used to convey troops. **b.** (*as modifier*): *a transport plane.* **7.** the act of transporting or the state of being transported. **8.** ecstasy, rapture, or any powerful emotion. **9.** a convict sentenced to be transported. [C14: from Latin *transportāre,* from TRANS- + *portāre* to carry] —**transˈportable** *adj.* —ˌ**transportaˈbility** *n.* —**transˈporter** *n.* —**transˈportive** *adj.*

transportation (ˌtrænspɔːˈteɪʃən) *n.* **1.** a means or system of transporting. **2.** the act of transporting or the state of being transported. **3.** (esp. formerly) deportation to a penal colony. **4.** *Chiefly U.S.* a ticket or fare.

transport café *n. Brit.* an inexpensive eating place on a main route, used mainly by long-distance lorry drivers.

transporter bridge *n.* a bridge consisting of a movable platform suspended from cables, for transporting vehicles, etc., across a body of water.

transpose (trænsˈpəʊz) *vb.* **1.** (*tr.*) to alter the positions of; interchange, as words in a sentence; put into a different order. **2.** *Music.* **a.** to play (notes, music, etc.) in a different key from that originally intended. **b.** to move (a note or series of notes) upwards or downwards in pitch. **3.** (*tr.*) *Maths.* to move (a term) from one side of an equation to the other with a corresponding reversal in sign. ~*n.* **4.** *Maths.* the matrix resulting from interchanging the rows and columns of a given matrix. [C14: from Old French *transposer,* from Latin *transpōnere* to remove, from TRANS- + *pōnere* to place] —**transˈposable** *adj.* —**transˌposaˈbility** *n.* —**transˈposal** *n.* —**transˈposer** *n.*

transposing instrument *n.* a musical instrument, esp. a horn or clarinet, pitched in a key other than C major, but whose music is written down as if its basic scale were C major. A piece of music in the key of F intended to be played on a horn pitched in F is therefore written down a fourth lower than an ordinary part in that key and has the same key signature as a part written in C.

transposition (ˌtrænspəˈzɪʃən) *n.* **1.** the act of transposing or the state of being transposed. **2.** something transposed. —ˌ**transpoˈsitional** *or* **transpositive** (trænsˈpɒzɪtɪv) *adj.*

transposon (trænsˈpəʊzɒn) *n. Genetics.* a fragment of bacterial nucleic acid that can move from one site in a chromosome to another site in the same or a different chromosome and thus alter the genetic constitution of the bacterium. [C20: TRANS-POS(E) + -ON]

transputer (trænz'pju:tə) *n. Computer technol.* a type of fast, powerful microchip that is the equivalent of a 32-bit microprocessor with its own RAM facility. [C20: from TRANS(ISTOR) + (COM)PUTER]

transsexual (trænz'sɛksjʊəl) *n.* **1.** a person who permanently acts the part of and is completely identified with the opposite sex. **2.** a person who has undergone medical and surgical procedures to alter external sexual characteristics to those of the opposite sex.

transsexualism (trænz'sɛksjʊə,lɪzəm) *n.* an abnormally strong desire to change sex.

transship (træns'ʃɪp) *or* **tranship** *vb.* **-ships, -shipping, -shipped.** to transfer or be transferred from one vessel or vehicle to another. —**trans'shipment** *or* **tran'shipment** *n.*

transubstantiate (,trænsəb'stænʃɪ,eɪt) *vb.* **1.** (*intr.*) *R.C. theol.* (of the Eucharistic bread and wine) to undergo transubstantiation. **2.** (*tr.*) to change (one substance) into another; transmute. [C16: from Medieval Latin *transsubstantiāre,* from Latin TRANS- + *substantia* SUBSTANCE] —,**transub'stantial** *adj.* —,**transub'stantially** *adv.*

transubstantiation (,trænsəb,stænʃɪ'eɪʃən) *n.* **1.** (esp. in Roman Catholic theology) **a.** the doctrine that the whole substance of the bread and wine changes into the substance of the body and blood of Christ when consecrated in the Eucharist. **b.** the mystical process by which this is believed to take place during consecration. Compare **consubstantiation. 2.** a substantial change; transmutation. —,**transub,stanti'ationalist** *n.*

transudate ('trænsʊ,deɪt) *n.* **1.** *Physiol.* any fluid that passes through a membrane, esp. through the wall of a capillary. **2.** anything that has been transuded.

transude (træn'sju:d) *vb.* (of a fluid) to ooze or pass through interstices, pores, or small holes. [C17: from New Latin *transūdāre,* from Latin TRANS- + *sūdāre* to sweat] —**transudation** (,trænsjʊ'deɪʃən) *n.* —**tran'sudatory** *adj.*

transuranic (,trænzjʊ'rænɪk), **transuranian** (,trænzjʊ'reɪnɪən), *or* **transuranium** *adj.* **1.** (of an element) having an atomic number greater than that of uranium. **2.** of, relating to, or having the behaviour of transuranic elements. [C20: from TRANS- + *uranic,* from URANIUM]

transvalue (trænz'vælju:) *vb.* **-ues, -uing, -ued.** (*tr.*) to evaluate by a principle that varies from the accepted standards. —**trans,valu'ation** *n.* —**trans'valuer** *n.*

transversal (trænz'vɜ:səl) *n.* **1.** *Geometry.* a line intersecting two or more other lines. ~*adj.* **2.** a less common word for **transverse.** —**trans'versally** *adv.*

transverse (trænz'vɜ:s) *adj.* **1.** crossing from side to side; athwart; crossways. **2.** *Geometry.* denoting the axis that passes through the foci of a hyperbola. **3.** (of a flute, etc.) held almost at right angles to the player's mouth, so that the breath passes over a hole in the side to create a vibrating air column within the tube of the instrument. **4.** *Astronomy.* another word for **tangential** (sense 2). ~*n.* **5.** a transverse piece or object. [C16: from Latin *transversus,* from *transvertere* to turn across, from TRANS- + *vertere* to turn] —**trans'versely** *adv.* —**trans'verseness** *n.*

transverse colon *n. Anatomy.* the part of the large intestine passing transversely in front of the liver and stomach.

transverse flute *n.* the normal orchestral flute, as opposed to the recorder (or **fipple flute**).

transverse process *n. Anatomy.* either of the projections that arise from either side of a vertebra and provide articulation for the ribs.

transverse wave *n.* a wave, such as an electromagnetic wave, that is propagated in a direction perpendicular to the direction of displacement of the transmitting field or medium. Compare **longitudinal wave.**

transverter (trænz'vɜ:tə) *n.* a piece of equipment attached to a radio transceiver to enable it to transmit and receive on additional frequencies.

transvestite (trænz'vɛstaɪt) *n.* a person who seeks sexual pleasure from wearing clothes that are normally associated with the opposite sex. [C19: from German *Transvestit,* from TRANS- + Latin *vestītus* clothed, from *vestīre* to clothe] —**trans'vestism** *or* **trans'vestitism** *n.*

trap[1] (træp) *n.* **1.** a mechanical device or enclosed place or pit in which something, esp. an animal, is caught or penned. **2.** any device or plan for tricking a person or thing into being caught unawares. **3.** anything resembling a trap or prison. **4.** a fitting for a pipe in the form of a U-shaped or S-shaped bend that contains standing water to prevent the passage of gases. **5.** any similar device. **6.** a device that hurls clay pigeons into the air to be fired at by trapshooters. **7.** *Greyhound racing.* any one of a line of boxlike stalls in which greyhounds are enclosed before the start of a race. **8.** See **trap door. 9.** a light two-wheeled carriage. **10.** a slang word for **mouth. 11.** *Golf.* an obstacle or hazard, esp. a bunker. **12.** (*pl.*) *Jazz slang.* percussion instruments. **13.** (*usually pl.*) *Austral. slang.* a policeman. ~*vb.* **traps, trapping, trapped. 14.** (*tr.*) to catch, take, or pen in a trap; entrap. **15.** (*tr.*) to ensnare by trickery; trick. **16.** (*tr.*) to provide (a pipe) with a trap. **17.** to set traps in (a place), esp. for animals. [Old English *træppe;* related to Middle Low German *trappe,* Medieval Latin *trappa*] —'**trap,like** *adj.*

trap[2] (træp) *n.* **1.** an obsolete word for **trappings** (sense 2). ~*vb.* **traps, trapping, trapped. 2.** (*tr.*; often foll. by *out*) to dress or adorn. ~See also **traps.** [C11: probably from Old French *drap* cloth]

trap[3] (træp) *or* **traprock** *n.* **1.** any fine-grained often columnar dark igneous rock, esp. basalt. **2.** any rock in which oil or gas has accumulated. [C18: from Swedish *trappa* stair (from its steplike formation); see TRAP[1]]

trap[4] (træp) *n. Scot. dialect.* a ladder or flight of steps. [C18: probably of Low German origin; compare Dutch *trap* flight of steps]

trapan (trə'pæn) *vb.* **-pans, -panning, -panned,** *n.* a variant spelling of **trepan**[2]. —**tra'panner** *n.*

trap door *n.* **1.** a door or flap flush with and covering an opening, esp. in a ceiling. **2.** the opening so covered.

trap-door spider *n.* any of various spiders of the family *Ctenizidae* that construct a silk-lined hole in the ground closed by a hinged door of earth and silk.

trapes (treɪps) *vb., n.* a less common spelling of **traipse.**

trapeze (trə'pi:z) *n.* **1.** a free-swinging bar attached to two ropes, used by circus acrobats, etc. **2.** a sling like a bosun's chair at one end of a line attached to the masthead of a light racing sailing boat, used in sitting out. [C19: from French *trapèze,* from New Latin; see TRAPEZIUM]

trapeziform (trə'pi:zɪ,fɔ:m) *adj. Rare.* shaped like a trapezium: *a trapeziform part.*

trapezium (trə'pi:zɪəm) *n., pl.* **-ziums** *or* **-zia** (-zɪə). **1.** *Chiefly Brit.* a quadrilateral having two parallel sides of unequal length. Usual U.S. and Canadian name: **trapezoid. 2.** *Now chiefly U.S. and Canadian.* a quadrilateral having neither pair of sides parallel. **3.** a small bone of the wrist near the base of the thumb. [C16: via Late Latin from Greek *trapezion,* from *trapeza* table] —**tra'pezial** *adj.*

trapezius (trə'pi:zɪəs) *n., pl.* **-uses.** either of two flat triangular muscles, one covering each side of the back and shoulders, that rotate the shoulder blades. [C18: from New Latin *trapezius* (*musculus*) trapezium-shaped (muscle)]

trapezohedron (trə,pi:zəʊ'hi:drən) *n., pl.* **-drons** *or* **-dra** (-drə). *Crystallog.* a crystal form in which all the crystal's faces are trapeziums. [C19: from *trapezo-* combining form of TRAPEZIUM + -HEDRON, on the model of TETRAHEDRON] —**tra,pezo'hedral** *adj.*

trapezoid ('træpɪ,zɔɪd) *n.* **1.** a quadrilateral having neither pair of sides parallel. **2.** the usual U.S. and Canadian name for **trapezium. 3.** a small bone of the wrist near the base of the index finger. [C18: from New Latin *trapezoidēs,* from Late Greek *trapezoeidēs* trapezium-shaped, from *trapeza* table]

trappean ('træpɪən, trə'pɪən) *adj. Rare.* of, relating to, or consisting of igneous rock, esp. a basalt. [C19: from TRAP[3]]

trapper ('træpə) *n.* a person who traps animals, esp. for their furs or skins.

trappings ('træpɪŋz) *pl. n.* **1.** the accessories and adornments that characterize or symbolize a condition, office, etc.: *the visible trappings of success.* **2.** ceremonial harness for a horse or other animal, including bridles, saddles, etc. [C16: from TRAP[2]]

Trappist ('træpɪst) *n.* **a.** a member of a branch of the Cistercian order of Christian monks, the Reformed Cistercians of the Strict Observance, which originated at La Trappe in France in 1664. They are noted for their rule of silence. **b.** (*as modifier*): *a Trappist monk.*

traprock ('træp,rɒk) *n.* another name for **trap**[3].

traps (træps) *pl. n.* belongings; luggage. [C19: probably shortened from TRAPPINGS]

trapshooting ('træp,ʃu:tɪŋ) *n.* the sport of shooting at clay pigeons thrown up by a trap. —'**trap,shooter** *n.*

trapunto (trə'pʊntəʊ) *n., pl.* **-tos.** a type of quilting that is only partly padded, in a design. [Italian, from *trapungere* to embroider, from *pungere* to prick (from Latin)]

trash[1] (træʃ) *n.* **1.** foolish ideas or talk; nonsense. **2.** *Chiefly U.S. and Canadian.* useless or unwanted matter or objects. **3.** a literary or artistic production of poor quality. **4.** *Chiefly U.S. and Canadian.* a poor or worthless person or a group of such people. **5.** bits that are broken or lopped off, esp. the trimmings from trees or plants. **6.** the dry remains of sugar cane after the juice has been extracted. **7. poor White trash.** (used derogatorily) the poor White people living in the depressed areas of the southern U.S. ~*vb.* **8.** to remove the outer leaves and branches from (growing plants, esp. sugar cane). **9.** *Slang.* to attack or destroy (someone or something) wilfully or maliciously. [C16: of obscure origin; perhaps related to Norwegian *trask*] —'**trashery** *n.*

trash[2] (træʃ) *Archaic.* ~*vb.* **1.** (*tr.*) to restrain with or as if with a lead. ~*n.* **2.** a lead for a dog. [C17: perhaps from obsolete French *tracier* to track, TRACE[1]]

trash can *n.* a U.S. name for **dustbin.** Also called: **ash can, garbage can.**

trash farming *n. U.S.* cultivation by leaving stubble, etc., on the surface of the soil to serve as a mulch.

trashy ('træʃɪ) *adj.* **trashier, trashiest.** cheap, worthless, or badly made. —'**trashily** *adv.* —'**trashiness** *n.*

trass (træs) *n.* a variety of the volcanic rock tuff, used to make a hydraulic cement. [from Dutch *tras, tarasse,* from Italian *terrazza* worthless earth; see TERRACE]

trattoria (ˌtrætəˈrɪə) *n.* an Italian restaurant. [C19: from Italian, from *trattore* innkeeper, from French *traiteur,* from Old French *tretier* to TREAT]

trauma (ˈtrɔːmə) *n., pl.* **-mata** (-mətə) *or* **-mas.** **1.** *Psychol.* a powerful shock that may have long-lasting effects. **2.** *Pathol.* any bodily injury or wound. [C18: from Greek: a wound] —**traumatic** (trɔːˈmætɪk) *adj.* —**trauˈmatically** *adv.*

traumatism (ˈtrɔːməˌtɪzəm) *n.* **1.** any abnormal bodily condition caused by injury, wound, or shock. **2.** (not in technical usage) another name for **trauma** (sense 2).

traumatize *or* **traumatise** (ˈtrɔːməˌtaɪz) *vb.* **1.** (*tr.*) to wound or injure (the body). **2.** to subject or be subjected to mental trauma. —ˌ**traumatiˈzation** *or* ˌ**traumatiˈsation** *n.*

travail (ˈtræveɪl) *Literary.* ~*n.* **1.** painful or excessive labour or exertion. **2.** the pangs of childbirth; labour. ~*vb.* **3.** (*intr.*) to suffer or labour painfully, esp. in childbirth. [C13: from Old French *travaillier,* from Vulgar Latin *tripaliāre* (unattested) to torture, from Late Latin *trepālium* instrument of torture, from Latin *tripālis* having three stakes, from *trēs* three + *pālus* stake]

trave (treɪv) *n.* **1.** a stout wooden cage in which difficult horses are shod. **2.** another name for **crossbeam.** **3.** a bay formed by crossbeams. [C15: from Old French *trave* beam, from Latin *trabs*]

travel (ˈtrævᵊl) *vb.* **-els, -elling, -elled** *or U.S.* **-els, -eling, -eled.** (*mainly intr.*) **1.** to go, move, or journey from one place to another: *he travels to improve his mind; she travelled across France.* **2.** (*tr.*) to go, move, or journey through or across (an area, region, etc.): *he travelled the country.* **3.** to go, move, or cover a specified or unspecified distance. **4.** to go from place to place as a salesman: *to travel in textiles.* **5.** (esp. of perishable goods) to withstand a journey. **6.** (of light, sound, etc.) to be transmitted or move: *the sound travelled for miles.* **7.** to progress or advance. **8.** *Basketball.* to take an excessive number of steps while holding the ball. **9.** (of part of a mechanism) to move in a fixed predetermined path. **10.** *Informal.* to move rapidly: *that car certainly travels.* **11.** (often foll. by *with*) *Informal.* to be in the company (of); associate. ~*n.* **12. a.** the act of travelling. **b.** (*as modifier*): *a travel brochure.* Related adj.: **itinerant.** **13.** (*usually pl.*) a tour or journey. **14.** the distance moved by a mechanical part, such as the stroke of a piston. **15.** movement or passage. [C14 *travaillen* to make a journey, from Old French *travaillier* to TRAVAIL]

travel agency *or* **bureau** *n.* an agency that arranges and negotiates flights, holidays, etc., for travellers. —**travel agent** *n.*

travelator (ˈtrævəˌleɪtə) *n.* a variant spelling of **travolator.**

travelled *or U.S.* **traveled** (ˈtrævəld) *adj.* having experienced or undergone much travelling: *a travelled urbane epicure.*

traveller *or U.S.* **traveler** (ˈtrævələ, ˈtrævlə) *n.* **1.** a person who travels, esp. habitually. **2.** See **travelling salesman.** **3.** (*sometimes cap.*) a member of the travelling people. **4.** a part of a mechanism that moves in a fixed course. **5.** *Nautical.* **a.** a thimble fitted to slide freely on a rope, spar, or rod. **b.** the fixed rod on which such a thimble slides. **6.** *Austral.* a swagman.

traveller's cheque *n.* a cheque in any of various denominations sold for use abroad by a bank, etc., to the bearer, who signs it on purchase and can cash it by signing it again.

traveller's joy *n.* a ranunculaceous Old World climbing plant, *Clematis vitalba,* having white flowers and heads of feathery plumed fruits. Also called: **old man's beard.**

travelling people *or* **folk** *pl. n.* (*sometimes caps.*) *Brit.* Gypsies or other itinerant people: a term used esp. by such people of themselves.

travelling salesman *n.* a salesman who travels within an assigned territory in order to sell merchandise or to solicit orders for the commercial enterprise he represents by direct personal contact with customers and potential customers. Also called: **commercial traveller, traveller.**

travelling wave *n.* **a.** a wave carrying energy away from its source. **b.** (*as modifier*): *a travelling-wave aerial.*

travelling-wave tube *n.* an electronic tube in which an electron beam interacts with a high-frequency magnetic field so that energy is transferred from the beam to the field.

travelogue *or U.S.* (*sometimes*) **travelog** (ˈtrævᵊlɒg) *n.* a film, lecture, or brochure on travels and travelling. [C20: from TRAVEL + -LOGUE]

travel-sick *adj.* nauseated from riding in a moving vehicle. —**ˈtravel-ˌsickness** *n.*

traverse (ˈtrævɜːs, trəˈvɜːs) *vb.* **1.** to pass or go over or back and forth over (something); cross. **2.** (*tr.*) to go against; oppose; obstruct. **3.** to move or cause to move sideways or crosswise. **4.** (*tr.*) to extend or reach across. **5.** to turn (an artillery gun) laterally on its pivot or mount or (of an artillery gun) to turn laterally. **6.** (*tr.*) to look over or examine carefully. **7.** (*tr.*) *Law.* to deny (an allegation of fact), as in pleading. **8.** (*intr.*) *Fencing.* to slide one's blade towards an opponent's hilt while applying pressure against his blade. **9.** *Mountaineering.* to move across (a face) horizontally. **10.** (*tr.*) *Nautical.* to brace (a yard) fore and aft. ~*n.* **11.** something being or lying across, such as a transom. **12.** a gallery or loft inside a building that crosses it. **13.** *Maths.* another name for **transversal** (sense 1). **14.** an obstruction or hindrance. **15.** *Fortifications.* a protective bank or other barrier across a trench or rampart. **16.** a railing, screen, or curtain. **17.** the act or an instance of traversing or crossing. **18.** a path or road across. **19.** *Nautical.* the zigzag course of a vessel tacking frequently. **20.** *Law.* the formal denial of a fact alleged in the opposite party's pleading. **21.** *Surveying.* a survey consisting of a series of straight lines, the length of each and the angle between them being measured. **22.** *Mountaineering.* a horizontal move across a face. ~*adj.* **23.** being or lying across; transverse. ~*adv.* **24.** an archaic word for **across.** [C14: from Old French *traverser,* from Late Latin *trānsversāre,* from Latin *trānsversus* TRANSVERSE] —**ˈtraversable** *adj.* —**traˈversal** *n.* —**ˈtraverser** *n.*

travertine *or* **travertin** (ˈtrævətɪn) *n.* a porous rock consisting of calcium carbonate, used for building. Also called: **calc-sinter.** [C18: from Italian *travertino* (influenced by *tra-* TRANS-), from Latin *lapis Tīburtīnus* Tiburtine stone, from *Tībur*s the district around Tibur (now Tivoli in central Italy)]

travesty (ˈtrævɪstɪ) *n., pl.* **-ties.** **1.** a farcical or grotesque imitation; mockery; parody. ~*vb.* **-ties, -tying, -tied.** (*tr.*) **2.** to make or be a travesty of. [C17: from French *travesti* disguised, from *travestir* to disguise, from Italian *travestire,* from *tra-* TRANS- + *vestire* to clothe]

travois (trəˈvɔɪ) *n., pl.* **-vois** (-ˈvɔɪz). a sled formerly used by the Plains Indians of North America, consisting of two poles joined by a frame and dragged by an animal. [from Canadian French, from French *travail* TRAVE]

travolator *or* **travelator** (ˈtrævəˌleɪtə) *n.* a moving pavement for transporting pedestrians, as in a shopping precinct or an airport. [C20: coined on the model of ESCALATOR]

trawl (trɔːl) *n. Sea fishing.* **1.** Also called: **trawl net.** a large net, usually in the shape of a sock or bag, drawn at deep levels behind special boats (trawlers). **2.** Also called: **trawl line.** a long line to which numerous shorter hooked lines are attached, suspended between buoys. See also **setline, trotline.** **3.** the act of trawling. ~*vb.* **4.** *Sea fishing.* to catch or try to catch (fish) with a trawl net or trawl line. **5.** *Sea fishing.* (*tr.*) to drag (a trawl net) or suspend (a trawl line). **6.** (*intr.*; foll. by *for*) to seek or gather (something, such as information, or someone, such as a likely appointee) from a wide variety of sources. ~*n., vb.* **7.** *Angling.* another word for **troll**[1]. [C17: from Middle Dutch *traghelen* to drag, from Latin *trāgula* dragnet; see TRAIL]

trawler (ˈtrɔːlə) *n.* **1.** a vessel used for trawling. **2.** a person who trawls.

tray (treɪ) *n.* **1.** a thin flat board or plate of metal, plastic, etc., usually with a raised edge, on which things can be carried. **2.** a shallow receptacle for papers, etc., sometimes forming a drawer in a cabinet or box. [Old English *trieg;* related to Old Swedish *trö* corn measure, Old Norse *treyja* carrier, Greek *driti* tub, German *Trog* TROUGH]

traymobile (ˈtreɪməˌbiːl) *n. Austral.* an informal word for **trolley.**

treacherous (ˈtrɛtʃərəs) *adj.* **1.** betraying or likely to betray faith or confidence. **2.** unstable, unreliable, or dangerous: *treacherous weather; treacherous ground.* —**ˈtreacherously** *adv.* —**ˈtreacherousness** *n.*

treachery (ˈtrɛtʃərɪ) *n., pl.* **-eries.** **1.** the act or an instance of wilful betrayal. **2.** the disposition to betray. [C13: from Old French *trecherie,* from *trechier* to cheat; compare TRICK]

treacle (ˈtriːkᵊl) *n.* **1.** Also called: **black treacle.** *Brit.* a dark viscous syrup obtained during the refining of sugar. **2.** *Brit.* another name for **golden syrup.** **3.** anything sweet and cloying. **4.** *Obsolete.* any of various preparations used as an antidote to poisoning. [C14: from Old French *triacle,* from Latin *thēriaca* antidote to poison] —**ˈtreacly** *adj.* —**ˈtreacliness** *n.*

treacle mustard *n.* a N temperate cruciferous annual plant, *Erysimum cheiranthoides,* having small yellow flowers. It is a common weed in cultivated ground. [C16: so called because of its alleged medicinal properties. See TREACLE]

tread (trɛd) *vb.* **treads, treading, trod, trodden** *or* **trod.** **1.** to walk or trample in, on, over, or across (something). **2.** (when *intr.,* foll. by *on*) to crush or squash by or as if by treading: *to tread grapes; to tread on a spider.* **3.** (*intr.*; sometimes foll. by *on*) to subdue or repress, as by doing injury (to): *to tread on one's inferiors.* **4.** (*tr.*) to do by walking or dancing: *to tread a measure.* **5.** (*tr.*) (of a male bird) to copulate with (a female bird). **6. tread lightly.** to proceed with delicacy or tact. **7. tread on (someone's) toes.** to offend or insult (someone), esp. by infringing on his sphere of action, etc. **8. tread water.** to stay afloat in an upright position by moving the legs in a walking motion. ~*n.* **9.** a manner or style of walking, dancing, etc.: *a light tread.* **10.** the act of treading. **11.** the top surface of a step in a staircase. **12.** the outer part of a tyre or wheel that makes contact with the road, esp. the grooved surface of a pneumatic tyre. **13.** the part of a rail that wheels touch. **14.** the part of a shoe that is generally in contact with the ground. **15.** a rare word for **footprint.** [Old English *tredan;* related to Old Norse *trotha,* Old High German *tretan,* Swedish *träda*] —**ˈtreader** *n.*

treadle (ˈtrɛdᵊl) *n.* **1. a.** a rocking lever operated by the foot to drive a machine. **b.** (*as modifier*): *a treadle sewing machine.* ~*vb.* **2.** to work (a machine) with a treadle. [Old English *tredel,* from *trēde* something firm, from *tredan* to TREAD] —**ˈtreadler** *n.*

treadmill ('trɛd,mɪl) *n.* **1.** Also called: **treadwheel.** (formerly) an apparatus used to produce rotation, in which the weight of men or animals climbing steps on or around the periphery of a cylinder or wheel caused it to turn. **2.** a dreary round or routine. **3.** an exercise machine that consists of a continuous moving belt on which to walk or jog.

treas. *abbrev. for:* **1.** treasurer. **2.** treasury.

treason ('triːzᵊn) *n.* **1.** violation or betrayal of the allegiance that a person owes his sovereign or his country, esp. by attempting to overthrow the government; high treason. **2.** any treachery or betrayal. [C13: from Old French *traïson,* from Latin *trāditiō* a handing over; see TRADITION, TRADITOR] —'**treasonable** *or* '**treasonous** *adj.* —'**treasonableness** *n.* —'**treasonably** *adv.*

treasure ('trɛʒə) *n.* **1.** wealth and riches, usually hoarded, esp. in the form of money, precious metals, or gems. **2.** a thing or person that is highly prized or valued. ~*vb.* (*tr.*) **3.** to prize highly as valuable, rare, or costly. **4.** to store up and save; hoard. [C12: from Old French *tresor,* from Latin *thēsaurus* anything hoarded, from Greek *thēsauros*] —'**treasurable** *adj.* —'**treasureless** *adj.*

treasure flower *n.* another name for **gazania.**

treasure hunt *n.* a game in which players act upon successive clues and are eventually directed to a prize.

treasurer ('trɛʒərə) *n.* a person appointed to look after the funds of a society, company, city, or other governing body. —'**treasurership** *n.*

treasure-trove *n.* **1.** *Law.* any articles, such as coins, bullion, etc., found hidden in the earth or elsewhere and of unknown ownership. Such articles become the property of the Crown. **2.** anything similarly discovered that is of value. [C16: from Anglo-French *tresor trové* treasure found, from Old French *tresor* TREASURE + *trover* to find]

treasury ('trɛʒərɪ) *n., pl.* **-uries. 1.** a storage place for treasure. **2.** the revenues or funds of a government, private organization, or individual. **3.** a place where funds are kept and disbursed. **4.** Also: **treasure house.** a collection or source of valuable items: *a treasury of information.* [C13: from Old French *tresorie,* from *tresor* TREASURE]

Treasury ('trɛʒərɪ) *n.* (in various countries) the government department in charge of finance. In Britain the Treasury is also responsible for economic strategy.

Treasury bill *n.* a short-term noninterest-bearing obligation issued by the Treasury, payable to bearer and maturing usually in three months, within which it is tradable on a discount basis on the open market.

treasury bond *n.* a long-term interest-bearing bond issued by the U.S. Treasury.

treasury certificate *n.* a short-term obligation issued by the U.S. Treasury, maturing in 12 months with interest payable by coupon redemption.

treasury note *n.* a note issued by a government treasury and generally receivable as legal tender for any debt, esp.: **a.** a medium-term interest-bearing obligation issued by the U.S. Treasury, maturing in from one to five years. **b.** Also called: **currency note.** a note issued by the British Treasury in 1914 to the value of £1 or ten shillings: amalgamated with banknotes in 1928.

treasury tag *n.* a short piece of cord having metal ends one of which can be slotted inside the other: used for holding papers together or fastening them into a file.

treat (triːt) *n.* **1.** a celebration, entertainment, gift, or feast given for or to someone and paid for by another. **2.** any delightful surprise or specially pleasant occasion. **3.** the act of treating. ~*vb.* **4.** (*tr.*) to deal with or regard in a certain manner: *she treats school as a joke.* **5.** (*tr.*) to apply treatment to: *to treat a patient for malaria.* **6.** (*tr.*) to subject to a process or to the application of a substance: *to treat photographic film with developer.* **7.** (often foll. by *to*) to provide (someone) (with) as a treat: *he treated the children to a trip to the zoo.* **8.** (*intr.;* usually foll. by *of*) *Formal.* to deal (with), as in writing or speaking. **9.** (*intr.*) *Formal.* to discuss settlement; negotiate. [C13: from Old French *tretier,* from Latin *tractāre* to manage, from *trahere* to drag] —'**treatable** *adj.* —'**treater** *n.*

treatise ('triːtɪz) *n.* **1.** a formal work on a subject, esp. one that deals systematically with its principles and conclusions. **2.** an obsolete word for **narrative.** [C14: from Anglo-French *tretiz,* from Old French *tretier* to TREAT]

treatment ('triːtmənt) *n.* **1.** the application of medicines, surgery, psychotherapy, etc., to a patient or to a disease or symptom. **2.** the manner of handling or dealing with a person or thing, as in a literary or artistic work. **3.** the act, practice, or manner of treating. **4.** *Films.* an expansion of a script into sequence form, indicating camera angles, dialogue, etc. **5. the treatment.** *Slang.* the usual manner of dealing with a particular type of person (esp. in the phrase **give someone the (full) treatment**).

treaty ('triːtɪ) *n., pl.* **-ties. 1. a.** a formal agreement or contract between two or more states, such as an alliance or trade arrangement. **b.** the document in which such a contract is written. **2.** any international agreement. **3.** any pact or agreement. **4.** an agreement between two parties concerning the purchase of property at a price privately agreed between them. **5.** *Archaic.* negotiation towards an agreement. **6.** (in Canada) **a.** any of the formal agreements between Indian bands and the federal government by which the Indians surrender their land rights in return for various forms of aid. **b.** (*as modifier*): *treaty Indians; treaty money.* **7.** an obsolete word for **entreaty.** [C14: from Old French *traité,* from Medieval Latin *tractātus* treaty, from Latin: discussion, from *tractāre* to manage; see TREAT] —'**treatyless** *adj.*

treaty port *n.* (in China, Japan, and Korea during the last half of the 19th and first half of the 20th century) a city, esp. a port, in which foreigners, esp. Westerners, were allowed by treaty to conduct trade.

treble ('trɛbᵊl) *adj.* **1.** threefold; triple. **2.** of, relating to, or denoting a soprano voice or part or a high-pitched instrument. ~*n.* **3.** treble the amount, size, etc. **4.** a soprano voice or part or a high-pitched instrument. **5.** the highest register of a musical instrument. **6. a.** the high-frequency response of an audio amplifier, esp. in a record player or tape recorder. **b.** a control knob on such an instrument by means of which the high-frequency gain can be increased or decreased. **7.** *Change-ringing.* the lightest and highest bell in a ring. **8. a.** the narrow inner ring on a dartboard. **b.** a hit on this ring. ~*vb.* **9.** to make or become three times as much. [C14: from Old French, from Latin *triplus* threefold, TRIPLE] —'**trebleness** *n.* —'**trebly** *adv., adj.*

treble chance *n.* a method of betting in football pools in which the chances of winning are related to the number of draws and the number of home and away wins forecast by the competitor.

treble clef *n. Music.* the clef that establishes G a fifth above middle C as being on the second line of the staff. Symbol: 𝄞

trebuchet ('trɛbjʊ,ʃɛt) *or* **trebucket** ('triːbʌkɪt) *n.* a large medieval siege engine for hurling missiles consisting of a sling on a pivoted wooden arm set in motion by the fall of a weight. [C13: from Old French, from *trebuchier* to stumble, from *tre-* TRANS- + *-buchier,* from *buc* trunk of the body, of Germanic origin; compare Old High German *būh* belly, Old English *buc*]

trecento (treɪ'tʃɛntəʊ) *n.* the 14th century, esp. with reference to Italian art and literature. [C19: shortened from Italian *mille trecento* one thousand three hundred] —**tre'centist** *n.*

tree (triː) *n.* **1.** any large woody perennial plant with a distinct trunk giving rise to branches or leaves at some distance from the ground. Related adj.: **arboreal. 2.** any plant that resembles this but has a trunk not made of wood, such as a palm tree. **3.** a wooden post, bar, etc. **4.** See **family tree, shoetree, saddletree. 5.** *Chem.* a treelike crystal growth; dendrite. **6. a.** a branching diagrammatic representation of something, such as the grammatical structure of a sentence. **b.** (*as modifier*): *a tree diagram.* **7.** an archaic word for **gallows. 8.** *Archaic.* the cross on which Christ was crucified. **9. at the top of the tree.** in the highest position of a profession, etc. **10. up a tree.** *U.S. and Canadian informal.* in a difficult situation; trapped or stumped. ~*vb.* **trees, treeing, treed.** (*tr.*) **11.** to drive or force up a tree. **12.** *U.S. and Canadian informal.* to force into a difficult situation. **13.** to shape or stretch (a shoe) on a shoetree. [Old English *treo;* related to Old Frisian, Old Norse *trē,* Old Saxon *trio,* Gothic *triu,* Greek *doru* wood, *drus* tree] —'**treeless** *adj.* —'**treelessness** *n.* —'**tree,like** *adj.*

tree-and-branch *adj.* denoting a cable television system in which all available programme channels are fed to each subscriber. Compare **switched-star.**

tree creeper *n.* any small songbird of the family *Certhiidae* of the N hemisphere, having a brown-and-white plumage and slender downward-curving bill. They creep up trees to feed on insects.

tree farm *n.* an area of forest in which the growth of the trees is managed on a commercial basis.

tree fern *n.* any of numerous large tropical ferns, mainly of the family *Cyatheaceae,* having a trunklike stem bearing fronds at the top.

tree frog *n.* **1.** any arboreal frog of the family *Hylidae,* chiefly of SE Asia, Australia, and America. They are strong jumpers and have long toes ending in adhesive discs, which assist in climbing. **2.** any of various other arboreal frogs of different families.

tree heath *n.* another name for **briar**[1] (sense 1).

treehopper ('triː,hɒpə) *n.* any homopterous insect of the family *Membracidae,* which live among trees and other plants and typically have a large hoodlike thoracic process curving backwards over the body.

tree kangaroo *n.* any of several arboreal kangaroos of the genus *Dendrolagus,* of New Guinea and N Australia, having hind and forelegs of a similar length and a long tail.

tree layer *n.* See **layer** (sense 2).

tree line *n.* the zone, at high altitudes or high latitudes, beyond which no trees grow. Trees growing between the timber line and the tree line are typically stunted.

tree mallow *n.* a malvaceous treelike plant, *Lavatera arborea,* of rocky coastal areas of Europe and N Africa, having a woody stem, rounded leaves, and red-purple flowers.

treen ('triːən) *adj.* **1.** made of wood; wooden. ~*n.* **2.** another name for **treenware. 3.** the art of making treenware. [Old English *trēowen,* from *trēow* TREE]

treenail, trenail ('triːneɪl, 'trɛnᵊl), *or* **trunnel** ('trʌnᵊl) *n.* a dowel used for pinning planks or timbers together.

treenware ('triːən,wɛə) *n.* dishes and other household utensils made of wood, as by pioneers in North America. [from TREEN + WARE[1]]
tree of heaven *n.* another name for **ailanthus.**
tree of knowledge of good and evil *n. Old Testament.* the tree in the Garden of Eden bearing the forbidden fruit that Adam and Eve ate, thus incurring loss of primal innocence (Genesis 2:9; 3:2–7).
tree of life *n.* **1.** *Old Testament.* a tree in the Garden of Eden, the fruit of which had the power of conferring eternal life (Genesis 2:9; 3:22). **2.** *New Testament.* a tree in the heavenly Jerusalem, for the healing of the nations (Revelation 22:2).
tree ring *n.* another name for **annual ring.**
tree runner *n. Austral.* another name for **sitella.**
tree shrew *n.* any of numerous small arboreal prosimian primates of the family *Tupaiidae,* of SE Asia, having large eyes and resembling squirrels.
tree snake *n.* any of various slender arboreal colubrid snakes of the genera *Chlorophis* (**green tree snakes**), *Chrysopelea* (**golden tree snakes**), etc.
tree sparrow *n.* **1.** a small European weaverbird, *Passer montanus,* similar to the house sparrow but having a brown head. **2.** a small North American finch, *Spizella arborea,* having a reddish-brown head, grey underparts, and brown striped back and wings.
tree surgery *n.* the treatment of damaged trees by filling cavities, applying braces, etc. —**tree surgeon** *n.*
tree toad *n.* a less common name for **tree frog.**
tree tomato *n.* **1.** an arborescent shrub, *Cyphomandra betacea* or *C. crassifolia,* native to South America but widely cultivated, esp. commercially in New Zealand, bearing red egg-shaped edible fruit: family *Solanaceae.* **2.** the fruit of this plant. ~Also called: **tamarillo.**
tref, treif (treɪf), *or* **treifa** ('treɪfə) *adj. Judaism.* ritually unfit to be eaten; not kosher. [Yiddish, from Hebrew *terēphāh,* literally: torn (i.e., animal meat torn by beasts), from *tāraf* to tear]
trefoil ('trɛfɔɪl) *n.* **1.** any of numerous leguminous plants of the temperate genus *Trifolium,* having leaves divided into three leaflets and dense heads of small white, yellow, red, or purple flowers. **2.** any of various related plants having leaves divided into three leaflets, such as bird's-foot trefoil. **3.** a flower or leaf having three lobes. **4.** *Architect.* an ornament in the form of three arcs arranged in a circle. [C14: from Anglo-French *trifoil,* from Latin *trifolium* three-leaved herb, from TRI- + *folium* leaf] —'**trefoiled** *adj.*
trehala (trɪ'hɑːlə) *n.* an edible sugary substance obtained from the pupal cocoon of an Asian weevil, *Larinus maculatus.* [C19: from Turkish *tīgāla,* from Persian *tīghāl*]
trehalose ('triːhə,ləʊs, -,ləʊz) *n.* a white crystalline disaccharide that occurs in yeast and certain fungi. Formula: $C_{12}H_{22}O_{11}$. [C19: from TREHALA]
treillage ('treɪlɪdʒ) *n.* latticework; trellis. [C17: from French, from Old French *treille* bower, from Latin *trichila;* see -AGE]
trek (trɛk) *n.* **1.** a long and often difficult journey. **2.** *S. African.* a journey or stage of a journey, esp. a migration by ox wagon. ~*vb.* **treks, trekking, trekked. 3.** (*intr.*) to make a trek. **4.** (*tr.*) *S. African.* (of an ox, etc.) to draw (a load). [C19: from Afrikaans, from Middle Dutch *trekken* to travel; related to Old Frisian *trekka*] —'**trekker** *n.*
trellis ('trɛlɪs) *n.* **1.** a structure or pattern of latticework, esp. one used to support climbing plants. **2.** an arch made of latticework. ~*vb.* (*tr.*) **3.** to interweave (strips of wood, etc.) to make a trellis. **4.** to provide or support with a trellis. [C14: from Old French *treliz* fabric of open texture, from Late Latin *trilīcius* woven with three threads, from Latin TRI- + *līcium* thread] —'**trellis-,like** *adj.*
trelliswork ('trɛlɪs,wɜːk) *n.* **a.** work or patterns of trellis; latticework. **b.** (*as modifier*): *a trelliswork fence.*
trematode ('trɛmə,təʊd, 'triː-) *n.* any parasitic flatworm of the class *Trematoda,* which includes the flukes. [C19: from New Latin *Trematoda,* from Greek *trēmatōdēs* full of holes, from *trēma* a hole]
tremble ('trɛmbᵊl) *vb.* (*intr.*) **1.** to vibrate with short slight movements; quiver. **2.** to shake involuntarily, as with cold or fear; shiver. **3.** to experience fear or anxiety. ~*n.* **4.** the act or an instance of trembling. [C14: from Old French *trembler,* from Medieval Latin *tremulāre,* from Latin *tremulus* quivering, from *tremere* to quake] —'**trembling** *adj.* —'**tremblingly** *adv.* —'**trembly** *adj.*
trembler ('trɛmblə) *n. Electrical engineering.* a device that vibrates to make or break an electrical circuit.
trembles ('trɛmbᵊlz) *n.* (*functioning as sing.*) **1.** Also called: **milk sickness.** a disease of cattle and sheep characterized by muscular incoordination and tremor, caused by ingestion of white snakeroot or rayless goldenrod. **2.** a nontechnical name for **Parkinson's disease.**
trembling poplar *n.* another name for **aspen.**
tremendous (trɪ'mɛndəs) *adj.* **1.** vast; huge. **2.** *Informal.* very exciting or unusual. **3.** *Informal.* (intensifier): *a tremendous help.* **4.** *Archaic.* terrible or dreadful. [C17: from Latin *tremendus* terrible, literally: that is to be trembled at, from *tremere* to quake] —**tre'mendously** *adv.* —**tre'mendousness** *n.*
tremie ('trɛmɪ) *n. Civil engineering.* a large metal hopper and pipe used to distribute freshly mixed concrete over an underwater site. [C20: from French, from Italian *tramoggia,* from Latin *trimodia* a three-peck measure]
tremolite ('trɛmə,laɪt) *n.* a white or pale green mineral of the amphibole group consisting of calcium magnesium silicate and used as a form of asbestos. Formula: $Ca_2(Mg,Fe)_5Si_8O_{22}(OH)_2$. [C18: from *Tremola,* name of Swiss valley where it was found + -ITE[1]]
tremolo ('trɛmə,ləʊ) *n., pl.* **-los.** *Music.* **1. a.** (in playing the violin, cello, etc.) the rapid repetition of a single note produced by a quick back-and-forth movement of the bow. **b.** the rapid reiteration of two notes usually a third or greater interval apart (**fingered tremolo**). Compare **trill**[1] (sense 1). **2.** (in singing) a fluctuation in pitch. Compare **vibrato. 3.** a vocal ornament of late renaissance music consisting of the increasingly rapid reiteration of a single note. **4.** another word for **tremulant.** [C19: from Italian: quavering, from Medieval Latin *tremulāre* to TREMBLE]
tremolo arm *n.* a metal lever attached to the bridge of an electric guitar, used to vary the pitch of a played note.
tremor ('trɛmə) *n.* **1.** an involuntary shudder or vibration, as from illness, fear, shock, etc. **2.** any trembling or quivering movement. **3.** a vibrating or trembling effect, as of sound or light. **4.** Also called: **earth tremor.** a minor earthquake. ~*vb.* (*intr.*) **5.** to tremble. [C14: from Latin: a shaking, from *tremere* to tremble, quake] —'**tremorless** *adj.* —'**tremorous** *adj.*
tremulant ('trɛmjʊlənt) *n. Music.* **a.** a device on an organ by which the wind stream is made to fluctuate in intensity producing a tremolo effect. **b.** a device on an electrophonic instrument designed to produce a similar effect. [C19: from Medieval Latin *tremulāre* to TREMBLE]
tremulous ('trɛmjʊləs) *adj.* **1.** vibrating slightly; quavering; trembling: *a tremulous voice.* **2.** showing or characterized by fear, anxiety, excitement, etc. [C17: from Latin *tremulus* quivering, from *tremere* to shake] —'**tremulously** *adv.* —'**tremulousness** *n.*
trenail ('triːneɪl, 'trɛnᵊl) *n.* a variant spelling of **treenail.**
trench (trɛntʃ) *n.* **1.** a deep ditch or furrow. **2.** a ditch dug as a fortification, having a parapet of the excavated earth. ~*vb.* **3.** to make a trench in (a place). **4.** (*tr.*) to fortify with a trench or trenches. **5.** to slash or be slashed. **6.** (*intr.;* foll. by *on* or *upon*) to encroach or verge. ~See also **trenches.** [C14: from Old French *trenche* something cut, from *trenchier* to cut, from Latin *truncāre* to cut off]
trenchant ('trɛntʃənt) *adj.* **1.** keen or incisive: *trenchant criticism.* **2.** vigorous and effective: *a trenchant foreign policy.* **3.** distinctly defined: *a trenchant outline.* **4.** *Archaic or poetic.* sharp: *a trenchant sword.* [C14: from Old French *trenchant* cutting, from *trenchier* to cut; see TRENCH] —'**trenchancy** *n.* —'**trenchantly** *adv.*
trench coat *n.* a belted double-breasted waterproof coat of gaberdine, etc., resembling a military officer's coat.
trencher[1] ('trɛntʃə) *n.* **1.** (esp. formerly) a wooden board on which food was served or cut. **2.** Also called: **trencher cap.** another name for **mortarboard** (sense 1). [C14 *trenchour* knife, plate for carving on, from Old French *trencheoir,* from *trenchier* to cut; see TRENCH]
trencher[2] ('trɛntʃə) *n.* a person or thing that digs trenches.
trencherman ('trɛntʃəmən) *n., pl.* **-men. 1.** a person who enjoys food; hearty eater. **2.** *Archaic.* a person who sponges on others; parasite. [C16: from TRENCHER[1] + MAN]
trenches ('trɛntʃɪz) *pl. n.* a system of excavations used for the protection of troops, esp. those (**the Trenches**) used at the front line in World War I.
trench fever *n.* an acute infectious disease characterized by fever and muscular aches and pains, caused by the microorganism *Rickettsia quintana* and transmitted by the bite of a body louse.
trench foot *n.* a form of frostbite affecting the feet of persons standing for long periods in cold water.
trench knife *n.* a double-edged steel knife for close combat. [C20: so called because such knives were carried by patrols in the Trenches during World War I]
trench mortar *n.* a portable mortar used in trench warfare to shoot projectiles at a high trajectory over a short range.
trench mouth *n.* a bacterial ulcerative disease characterized by inflammation of the tonsils, gums, etc. [C20: so called because it was prevalent in soldiers in the Trenches during World War I]
trench warfare *n.* a type of warfare in which opposing armies face each other in entrenched positions.
trend (trɛnd) *n.* **1.** general tendency or direction. **2.** fashion; mode. ~*vb.* **3.** (*intr.*) to take a certain trend. [Old English *trendan* to turn; related to Middle Low German *trenden*]
trendsetter ('trɛnd,sɛtə) *n.* a person or thing that creates, or may create, a new fashion. —'**trend,setting** *adj.*
trendy ('trɛndɪ) *Brit. informal, often derogatory.* ~*adj.* **trendier, trendiest. 1.** consciously fashionable. ~*n., pl.* **trendies. 2.** a trendy person. —'**trendily** *adv.* —'**trendiness** *n.*
trente et quarante (*French* trɑ̃t e karɑ̃t) *n.* another name for **rouge et noir.** [C17: French, literally: thirty and forty; referring to the rule that forty is the maximum number that may be dealt and the winning colour is the one closest to thirty-one]

trepan[1] (trɪˈpæn) *n.* **1.** *Surgery.* an instrument resembling a carpenter's brace and bit formerly used to remove circular sections of bone from (esp. the skull). Compare **trephine. 2.** a tool for cutting out circular blanks or for making grooves around a fixed centre. **3. a.** the operation of cutting a hole with such a tool. **b.** the hole so produced. *~vb.* **-pans, -panning, -panned.** (*tr.*) **4.** to cut (a hole or groove) with a trepan. **5.** *Surgery.* another word for **trephine.** [C14: from Medieval Latin *trepanum* rotary saw, from Greek *trupanon* auger, from *trupan* to bore, from *trupa* a hole] —**trepanation** (ˌtrɛpəˈneɪʃən) *n.* —**treˈpanner** *n.*

trepan[2] (trɪˈpæn) *or* **trapan** (trəˈpæn) *Archaic.* *~vb.* **-pans, -panning, -panned.** (*tr.*) **1.** to entice, ensnare, or entrap. **2.** to swindle or cheat. *~n.* **3.** a person or thing that traps. [C17: of uncertain origin]

trepang (trɪˈpæŋ) *n.* any of various large sea cucumbers of tropical Oriental seas, the dried body walls of which are used as food by the Chinese. Also called: **bêche-de-mer.** [C18: from Malay *tĕripang*]

trephine (trɪˈfiːn) *n.* **1.** a surgical sawlike instrument for removing circular sections of bone, esp. from the skull. *~vb.* **2.** (*tr.*) to remove a circular section of bone from (esp. the skull). ~Also called: **trepan.** [C17: from French *tréphine*, from obsolete English *trefine* TREPAN[1], allegedly from Latin *trēs fīnēs* literally: three ends; influenced also by English *trepane* TREPAN[1]] —**trephination** (ˌtrɛfɪˈneɪʃən) *n.*

trepidation (ˌtrɛpɪˈdeɪʃən) *n.* **1.** a state of fear or anxiety. **2.** a condition of quaking or palpitation, esp. one caused by anxiety. [C17: from Latin *trepidātiō*, from *trepidāre* to be in a state of alarm; compare INTREPID]

treponema (ˌtrɛpəˈniːmə) *or* **treponeme** (ˈtrɛpəniːm) *n., pl.* **-nemas, -nemata** (-ˈniːmətə), *or* **-nemes.** any anaerobic spirochaete bacterium of the genus *Treponema*, such as *T. pallidum* which causes syphilis. [C19: from New Latin, from Greek *trepein* to turn + *nēma* thread] —**treponematous** (ˌtrɛpəˈnɛmətəs) *adj.*

trespass (ˈtrɛspəs) *vb.* (*intr.*) **1.** (often foll. by *on* or *upon*) to go or intrude (on the property, privacy, or preserves of another) with no right or permission. **2.** *Law.* to commit trespass, esp. to enter wrongfully upon land belonging to another. **3.** *Archaic.* (often foll. by *against*) to sin or transgress. *~n.* **4.** *Law.* **a.** any unlawful act committed with force or violence, actual or implied, which causes injury to another person, his property, or his rights. **b.** a wrongful entry upon another's land. **c.** an action to recover damages for such injury or wrongful entry. **5.** an intrusion on another's privacy or preserves. **6.** a sin or offence. [C13: from Old French *trespas* a passage, from *trespasser* to pass through, from *tres-* TRANS- + *passer*, ultimately from Latin *passus* a PACE[1]] —ˈ**trespasser** *n.*

tress (trɛs) *n.* **1.** (*often pl.*) a lock of hair, esp. a long lock of woman's hair. **2.** a plait or braid of hair. *~vb.* (*tr.*) **3.** to arrange in tresses. [C13: from Old French *trece*, of uncertain origin] —ˈ**tressy** *adj.*

tressed (trɛst) *adj.* (*in combination*) having a tress or tresses as specified: *gold-tressed; long-tressed.*

tressure (ˈtrɛʃə, ˈtrɛsjʊə) *n. Heraldry.* a narrow inner border on a shield, usually decorated with fleurs-de-lis. [C14: from Old French *tressour*, from *trecier* to plait, from *trece* TRESS] —ˈ**tressured** *adj.*

trestle (ˈtrɛsᵊl) *n.* **1.** a framework in the form of a horizontal member supported at each end by a pair of splayed legs, used to carry scaffold boards, a table top, etc. **2. a.** a braced structural tower-like framework of timber, metal, or reinforced concrete that is used to support a bridge or ropeway. **b.** a bridge constructed of such frameworks. [C14: from Old French *trestel*, ultimately from Latin *trānstrum* TRANSOM]

trestletree (ˈtrɛsᵊlˌtriː) *n. Nautical.* either of a pair of fore-and-aft timbers fixed horizontally on opposite sides of a lower masthead to support an upper mast.

trestlework (ˈtrɛsᵊlˌwɜːk) *n.* an arrangement of trestles, esp. one that supports or makes a bridge.

tret (trɛt) *n. Commerce.* (formerly) an allowance according to weight granted to purchasers for waste due to transportation. It was calculated after deduction for tare. [C15: from Old French *trait* pull, tilt of the scale; see TRAIT]

trevally (trɪˈvælɪ) *n., pl.* **-lies.** *Austral. and N.Z.* any of various marine food and game fishes of the genus *Caranx*: family *Carangidae*. [C19: probably alteration of *cavally*; see CAVALLA]

trews (truːz) *pl. n. Chiefly Brit.* close-fitting trousers, esp. of tartan cloth and worn by certain Scottish soldiers. [C16: from Scottish Gaelic *triubhas*, from Old French *trebus*; see TROUSERS]

trey (treɪ) *n.* any card or dice throw with three spots. [C14: from Old French *treis* three, from Latin *trēs*]

TRH *abbrev. for* Their Royal Highnesses.

tri- *prefix.* **1.** three or thrice: *triaxial; trigon; trisect.* **2.** occurring every three: *trimonthly.* [from Latin *trēs*, Greek *treis*]

triable (ˈtraɪəbᵊl) *adj.* **1. a.** liable to be tried judicially. **b.** subject to examination or determination by a court of law. **2.** *Rare.* able to be tested. —ˈ**triableness** *n.*

triacid (traɪˈæsɪd) *adj.* (of a base) capable of reacting with three molecules of a monobasic acid.

triad (ˈtraɪæd) *n.* **1.** a group of three; trio. **2.** *Chem.* an atom, element, group, or ion that has a valency of three. **3.** *Music.* a three-note chord consisting of a note and the third and fifth above it. **4.** an aphoristic literary form used in medieval Welsh and Irish literature. **5.** the U.S. strategic nuclear force, consisting of intercontinental ballistic missiles, submarine-launched ballistic missiles, and bombers. [C16: from Late Latin *trias*, from Greek; related to Greek *treis* three] —**triˈadic** *adj.* —ˈ**triadism** *n.*

Triad (ˈtraɪæd) *n.* any of several Chinese secret societies, esp. one involved in criminal activities, such as drug trafficking.

triage (ˈtraɪɪdʒ) *n.* **1.** the principle or practice of sorting casualties in battle or disaster into categories of priority for treatment. **2.** the principle or practice of allocating limited resources, as of food or foreign aid, on a basis of expediency rather than according to moral principles or the needs of the recipients. [C18 (in the sense: sorting (goods) according to quality): from French; see TRY, -AGE]

trial[1] (ˈtraɪəl, traɪl) *n.* **1. a.** the act or an instance of trying or proving; test or experiment. **b.** (*as modifier*): *a trial run.* **2.** *Law.* **a.** the judicial examination of the issues in a civil or criminal cause by a competent tribunal and the determination of these issues in accordance with the law of the land. **b.** the determination of an accused person's guilt or innocence after hearing evidence for the prosecution and for the accused and the judicial examination of the issues involved. **c.** (*as modifier*): *trial proceedings.* **3.** an effort or attempt to do something: *we had three trials at the climb.* **4.** trouble or grief. **5.** an annoying or frustrating person or thing. **6.** (*often pl.*) a competition for individuals: *sheepdog trials.* **7.** *Ceramics.* a piece of sample material used for testing the heat of a kiln and its effects. **8. on trial. a.** undergoing trial, esp. before a court of law. **b.** being tested, as before a commitment to purchase. [C16: from Anglo-French, from *trier* to TRY]

trial[2] (ˈtraɪəl) *n. Grammar.* **1.** a grammatical number occurring in some languages for words in contexts where exactly three of their referents are described or referred to. **2.** (*modifier*) relating to or inflected for this number. [C19: from TRI- + -AL[1]]

trial and error *n.* a method of discovery, solving problems, etc., based on practical experiment and experience rather than on theory: *he learnt to cook by trial and error.*

trial balance *n. Book-keeping.* a statement of all the debit and credit balances in the ledger of a double-entry system, drawn up to test their equality.

trial balloon *n.* a tentative action or statement designed to test public opinion on a controversial matter. Compare **ballon d'essai.**

trial by battle *or* **trial by combat** *n. History.* a method of trying an accused person or of settling a dispute by a personal fight between the two parties involved or, in some circumstances, their permitted champions, in the presence of a judge. It was introduced to England after the Norman Conquest and abolished in 1819.

trial court *n. Law.* the first court before which the facts of a case are decided.

trial run *n.* **1.** a test drive in a vehicle to assess its performance. **2.** a test or rehearsal of something new or untried to assess its effectiveness.

triangle (ˈtraɪˌæŋgᵊl) *n.* **1.** *Geometry.* a three-sided polygon that can be classified by angle, as in an acute triangle, or by side, as in an equilateral triangle. Sum of interior angles: 180°; area: ½ base × height. **2.** any object shaped like a triangle. **3.** any situation involving three parties or points of view. See also **eternal triangle. 4.** *Music.* a percussion instrument consisting of a sonorous metal bar bent into a triangular shape, beaten with a metal stick. **5.** a group of three. [C14: from Latin *triangulum* (n.), from *triangulus* (adj.), from TRI- + *angulus* corner] —ˈ**triˌangled** *adj.*

triangle of forces *n. Physics.* a triangle whose sides represent the magnitudes and directions of three forces in equilibrium whose resultant is zero and which are therefore in equilibrium.

triangular (traɪˈæŋgjʊlə) *adj.* **1.** Also: **trigonal.** of, shaped like, or relating to a triangle; having three corners or sides. **2.** of or involving three participants, pieces, or units. **3.** *Maths.* having a base shaped like a triangle. —**triangularity** (traɪˌæŋgjʊˈlærɪtɪ) *n.* —**triˈangularly** *adv.*

triangulate *vb.* (traɪˈæŋgjʊˌleɪt). (*tr.*) **1. a.** to survey by the method of triangulation. **b.** to calculate trigonometrically. **2.** to divide into triangles. **3.** to make triangular. *~adj.* (traɪˈæŋgjʊlɪt, -ˌleɪt). **4.** marked with or composed of triangles. —**triˈangulately** *adv.*

triangulation (traɪˌæŋgjʊˈleɪʃən) *n.* **1.** a method of surveying in which an area is divided into triangles, one side (the base line) and all angles of which are measured and the lengths of the other lines calculated trigonometrically. **2.** the network of triangles so formed. **3.** the fixing of an unknown point, as in navigation, by making it one vertex of a triangle, the other two being known. **4.** *Chess.* a key manoeuvre in the endgame in which the king moves thrice in a triangular path to leave the opposing king with the move and at a disadvantage.

triangulation station *n.* a point used in triangulation as a basis for making maps. Triangulation stations are marked in a number of ways, such as by a tapering stone pillar on a hilltop. Also called (informal): **trig point,** (Austral. and N.Z.) **trig.**

Triangulum (traɪˈæŋgjʊləm) *n., Latin genitive* **Trianguli** (traɪˈæŋgjʊˌlaɪ). a small triangular constellation in the N hemisphere, close to Perseus and Aries.

Triangulum Australe (ɒˈstreɪlɪ) *n., Latin genitive* **Trianguli Australis** (ɒˈstreɪlɪs). a small bright triangular constellation in the S hemisphere, lying between Ara and the Southern Cross, that contains an open star cluster. [New Latin: southern triangle]

triarchy (ˈtraɪɑːkɪ) *n., pl.* **-chies.** 1. government by three people; a triumvirate. 2. a country ruled by three people. 3. an association of three territories each governed by its own ruler. 4. any of the three such territories.

Triassic (traɪˈæsɪk) *adj.* 1. of, denoting, or formed in the first period of the Mesozoic era that lasted for 45 million years and during which reptiles flourished. ~*n.* 2. **the.** Also called: **Trias.** the Triassic period or rock system. [C19: from Latin *trias* triad, with reference to the three subdivisions]

triathlon (traɪˈæθlɒn) *n.* an athletic contest in which each athlete competes in three different events, swimming, cycling, and horse riding. [C20: from TRI- + Greek *athlon* contest] —ˌ**triˈathlete** *n.*

triatomic (ˌtraɪəˈtɒmɪk) *adj. Chem.* having three atoms in the molecule. —ˌ**triaˈtomically** *adv.*

triaxial (traɪˈæksɪəl) *adj.* having three axes.

triazine (ˈtraɪəˌziːn, -zɪn; traɪˈæziːn, -zɪn) *or* **triazin** (ˈtraɪəzɪn, traɪˈæzɪn) *n.* 1. any of three azines that contain three nitrogen atoms in their molecules. Formula: $C_3H_3N_3$. 2. any substituted derivative of any of these compounds.

triazole (ˈtraɪəˌzɒl, -ˌzəʊl; traɪˈæzɒl, -zəʊl) *n.* 1. any of four heterocyclic compounds having a five-membered ring with the formula $C_2H_3N_3$. 2. any substituted derivative of any of these compounds. [C19: from TRI- + AZOLE] —**triazolic** (ˌtraɪəˈzɒlɪk) *adj.*

tribade (ˈtrɪbəd) *n.* a lesbian, esp. one who practises tribadism. [C17: from Latin *tribas,* from Greek *tribein* to rub] —**tribadic** (trɪˈbædɪk) *adj.*

tribadism (ˈtrɪbəˌdɪzəm) *n.* a lesbian practice in which one partner lies on top of the other and simulates the male role in heterosexual intercourse.

tribalism (ˈtraɪbəˌlɪzəm) *n.* 1. the state of existing as a separate tribe or tribes. 2. the customs and beliefs of a tribal society. 3. loyalty to a tribe or tribal values. —ˈ**tribalist** *n., adj.* —ˌ**tribalˈistic** *adj.*

tribasic (traɪˈbeɪsɪk) *adj.* 1. (of an acid) containing three replaceable hydrogen atoms in the molecule. 2. (of a molecule) containing three monovalent basic atoms or groups in the molecule.

tribe (traɪb) *n.* 1. a social division of a people, esp. of a preliterate people, defined in terms of common descent, territory, culture, etc. 2. an ethnic or ancestral division of ancient cultures, esp. of one of the following: **a.** any of the three divisions of the ancient Romans, the Latins, Sabines, and Etruscans. **b.** one of the later political divisions of the Roman people. **c.** any of the 12 divisions of ancient Israel, each of which was named after and believed to be descended from one of the 12 patriarchs. **d.** a phyle of ancient Greece. 3. *Informal, often jocular.* **a.** a large number of persons, animals, etc. **b.** a specific class or group of persons. **c.** a family, esp. a large one. 4. *Biology.* a taxonomic group that is a subdivision of a subfamily. 5. *Stockbreeding.* a strain of animals descended from a common female ancestor through the female line. [C13: from Latin *tribus;* probably related to Latin *trēs* three] —ˈ**tribal** *adj.* —ˈ**tribally** *adv.* —ˈ**tribeless** *adj.*

tribesman (ˈtraɪbzmən) *n., pl.* **-men.** a member of a tribe.

triblet (ˈtrɪblɪt) *n.* a spindle or mandrel used in making rings, tubes, etc. [C17: from French *triboulet,* of unknown origin]

tribo- *combining form.* indicating friction: *triboelectricity.* [from Greek *tribein* to rub]

triboelectricity (ˌtraɪbəʊɪlɛkˈtrɪsɪtɪ, -ˌiːlɛk-) *n.* electricity generated by friction. Also called: **frictional electricity.** —ˌ**triboeˈlectric** *adj.*

tribology (traɪˈbɒlədʒɪ) *n.* the study of friction, lubrication, and wear between moving surfaces.

triboluminescence (ˌtraɪbəʊˌluːmɪˈnɛsəns) *n.* luminescence produced by friction, such as the emission of light when certain crystals are crushed. —ˌ**triboˌlumiˈnescent** *adj.*

tribrach[1] (ˈtraɪbræk, ˈtrɪb-) *n. Prosody.* a metrical foot of three short syllables (˘˘˘). [C16: from Latin *tribrachys,* from Greek *tribrakhus,* from TRI- + *brakhus* short] —**triˈbrachic** *or* **triˈbrachial** *adj.*

tribrach[2] (ˈtrɪbræk) *n. Archaeol.* a three-armed object, esp. a flint implement. [C19: from TRI- + Greek *brakhiōn* arm]

tribromoethanol (traɪˌbrəʊməʊˈɛθəˌnɒl) *n.* a soluble white crystalline compound with a slight aromatic odour, used as a general anaesthetic; 2,2,2-tribromoethanol. Formula: CBr_3CH_2OH.

tribulation (ˌtrɪbjʊˈleɪʃən) *n.* 1. a cause of distress. 2. a state of suffering or distress. [C13: from Old French, from Church Latin *trībulātiō,* from Latin *trībulāre* to afflict, from *trībulum* a threshing board, from *terere* to rub]

tribunal (traɪˈbjuːnᵊl, trɪ-) *n.* 1. a court of justice or any place where justice is administered. 2. (in England) a special court, convened by the government to inquire into a specific matter. 3. a raised platform containing the seat of a judge or magistrate, originally that in a Roman basilica. [C16: from Latin *tribūnus* TRIBUNE[1]]

tribunate (ˈtrɪbjʊnɪt) *or* **tribuneship** *n.* the office or rank of a tribune.

tribune[1] (ˈtrɪbjuːn) *n.* 1. (in ancient Rome) **a.** an officer elected by the plebs to protect their interests. Originally there were two of these officers but finally there were ten. **b.** a senior military officer. 2. a person or institution that upholds public rights; champion. [C14: from Latin *tribunus,* probably from *tribus* TRIBE] —ˈ**tribunary** *adj.*

tribune[2] (ˈtrɪbjuːn) *n.* 1. **a.** the apse of a Christian basilica that contains the bishop's throne. **b.** the throne itself. 2. a gallery or raised area in a church. 3. *Rare.* a raised platform from which a speaker may address an audience; dais. [C17: via French from Italian *tribuna,* from Medieval Latin *tribūna,* variant of Latin *tribūnal* TRIBUNAL]

tributary (ˈtrɪbjʊtərɪ, -trɪ) *n., pl.* **-taries.** 1. a stream, river, or glacier that feeds another larger one. 2. a person, nation, or people that pays tribute. ~*adj.* 3. (of a stream, etc.) feeding a larger stream. 4. given or owed as a tribute. 5. paying tribute. —ˈ**tributarily** *adv.*

tribute (ˈtrɪbjuːt) *n.* 1. a gift or statement made in acknowledgment, gratitude, or admiration. 2. **a.** a payment by one ruler or state to another, usually as an acknowledgment of submission. **b.** any tax levied for such a payment. 3. (in feudal society) homage or a payment rendered by a vassal to his lord. 4. the obligation to pay tribute. [C14: from Latin *tribūtum,* from *tribuere* to grant (originally: to distribute among the tribes), from *tribus* TRIBE]

tricarboxylic acid cycle (traɪˌkɑːbɒkˈsɪlɪk) *n. Biochem.* another name for **Krebs cycle.** Abbrev.: **TCA cycle.**

trice[1] (traɪs) *n.* moment; instant (esp. in the phrase **in a trice**). [C15 (in the phrase *at* or *in a trice,* in the sense: at one tug): apparent substantive use of TRICE[2]]

trice[2] (traɪs) *vb. (tr.;* often foll. by *up) Nautical.* to haul up or secure. [C15: from Middle Dutch *trīsen,* from *trīse* pulley]

tricentenary (ˌtraɪsɛnˈtiːnərɪ) *or* **tricentennial** (ˌtraɪsɛnˈtɛnɪəl) *adj.* 1. of or relating to a period of 300 years. 2. of or relating to a 300th anniversary or its celebration. ~*n.* 3. an anniversary of 300 years or its celebration. ~Also: **tercentenary, tercentennial.**

triceps (ˈtraɪsɛps) *n., pl.* **-cepses** (-sɛpsɪz) *or* **-ceps.** any muscle having three heads, esp. the one (*triceps brachii*) that extends the forearm. [C16: from Latin, from TRI- + *caput* head]

triceratops (traɪˈsɛrəˌtɒps) *n.* any rhinoceros-like herbivorous dinosaur of the ornithischian genus *Triceratops,* of Cretaceous times, having a heavily armoured neck and three horns on the skull. [C19: from New Latin, from TRI- + Greek *kerat-, keras* horn + *ōps* eye]

trich- *combining form.* a variant of **tricho-** before a vowel.

trichiasis (trɪˈkaɪəsɪs) *n. Pathol.* 1. an abnormal position of the eyelashes that causes irritation when they rub against the eyeball. 2. the presence of hairlike filaments in the urine. [C17: via Late Latin from Greek *trikhiasis,* from *thrix* a hair + -IASIS]

trichina (trɪˈkaɪnə) *n., pl.* **-nae** (-niː). a parasitic nematode worm, *Trichinella spiralis,* occurring in the intestines of pigs, rats, and man and producing larvae that form cysts in skeletal muscle. [C19: from New Latin, from Greek *trikhinos* relating to hair, from *thrix* a hair]

trichinize *or* **trichinise** (ˈtrɪkɪˌnaɪz) *vb. (tr.)* to infest (an organism) with trichinae. —ˌ**trichiniˈzation** *or* ˌ**trichiniˈsation** *n.*

trichinosis (ˌtrɪkɪˈnəʊsɪs) *n.* a disease characterized by nausea, fever, diarrhoea, and swelling of the muscles, caused by ingestion of pork infected with trichina larvae. Also called: **trichiniasis** (ˌtrɪkɪˈnaɪəsɪs). [C19: from New Latin TRICHINA]

trichinous (ˈtrɪkɪnəs) *adj.* 1. of, relating to, or having trichinosis. 2. infested with trichinae.

trichite (ˈtrɪkaɪt) *n.* 1. any of various needle-shaped crystals that occur in some glassy volcanic rocks. 2. *Botany.* any of numerous long slender crystals assumed to be present in a starch grain. —**trichitic** (trɪˈkɪtɪk) *adj.*

trichloride (traɪˈklɔːraɪd) *n.* any compound that contains three chlorine atoms per molecule.

trichloroacetic acid (traɪˌklɔːrəʊəˈsiːtɪk, -ˈsɛtɪk) *n.* a corrosive deliquescent crystalline acid with a characteristic odour, used as a veterinary astringent and antiseptic. Formula: CCl_3COOH.

trichloroethane (traɪˌklɔːrəʊˈiːθeɪn) *n.* a volatile nonflammable colourless liquid with low toxicity used for cleaning electrical apparatus and as a solvent; 1,2,3-trichloroethane. Formula: CH_3CCl_3. Also called: **methyl chloroform.**

trichloroethylene (traɪˌklɔːrəʊˈɛθɪˌliːn) *or* **trichlorethylene** *n.* a volatile nonflammable mobile colourless liquid with an odour resembling that of chloroform. It is a good solvent for certain organic materials and is also an inhalation anaesthetic. Formula $CHCl{:}CCl_2$.

trichlorophenoxyacetic acid (traɪˈklɔːrəʊfəˌnɒksɪəˈsiːtɪk) *n.* an insoluble crystalline solid; 2,4,5-trichlorophenoxyacetic acid. It is a plant hormone and is used as a weedkiller. Formula: $C_8H_5Cl_3O_3$. Also called: **2,4,5-T.**

tricho- *or before a vowel* **trich-** *combining form.* indicating hair or a part resembling hair: *trichocyst.* [from Greek *thrix* (genitive *thrikhos*) hair]

trichocyst (ˈtrɪkəˌsɪst) *n.* any of various cavities on the surface of some ciliate protozoans, each containing a sensory thread that can be ejected. —ˌ**trichoˈcystic** *adj.*

trichogyne ('trɪkəˌdʒaɪn, -dʒɪn) *n.* a hairlike projection of the female reproductive organs of certain algae, fungi, and lichens, which receives the male gametes before fertilization takes place. [C19: from TRICHO- + Greek *gunē* woman] —ˌ**tricho'gynial** *or* ˌ**tricho'gynic** *adj.*

trichoid ('trɪkɔɪd) *adj. Zoology.* resembling a hair; hairlike.

trichology (trɪ'kɒlədʒɪ) *n.* the branch of medicine concerned with the hair and its diseases. —**trichological** (ˌtrɪkə'lɒdʒɪkᵊl) *adj.* —**tri'chologist** *n.*

trichome ('traɪkəʊm, 'trɪk-) *n.* **1.** any hairlike outgrowth from the surface of a plant. **2.** any of the threadlike structures that make up the filaments of blue-green algae. [C19: from Greek *trikhōma,* from *trikhoun* to cover with hair, from *thrix* a hair] —**trichomic** (trɪ'kɒmɪk) *adj.*

trichomonad (ˌtrɪkəʊ'mɒnæd) *n.* any parasitic protozoan of the genus *Trichomonas,* occurring in the digestive and reproductive systems of man and animals: class *Mastigophora* (or *Flagellata*). —**trichomonadal** (ˌtrɪkəʊ'mɒnədəl) *or* **trichomonal** (ˌtrɪkə'mɒnᵊl, -'məʊ-; trɪ'kɒmənᵊl) *adj.*

trichomoniasis (ˌtrɪkəʊmə'naɪəsɪs) *n.* **1.** inflammation of the vagina characterized by a frothy discharge, caused by infection with parasitic protozoa (*Trichomonas vaginalis*). **2.** any infection caused by parasitic protozoa of the genus *Trichomonas.* [C19: New Latin; see TRICHOMONAD, -IASIS]

trichopteran (traɪ'kɒptərən) *n.* **1.** any insect of the order *Trichoptera,* which comprises the caddis flies. ~*adj.* **2.** Also: **trichopterous** (trɪ'kɒptərəs). of, relating to, or belonging to the order *Trichoptera.* [C19: from New Latin *Trichoptera,* literally: having hairy wings, from Greek *thrix* a hair + *pteron* wing]

trichosis (trɪ'kəʊsɪs) *n.* any abnormal condition or disease of the hair. [C19: via New Latin from Greek *trikhōsis* growth of hair]

trichotomy (traɪ'kɒtəmɪ) *n., pl.* **-mies. 1.** division into three categories. **2.** *Theol.* the division of man into body, spirit, and soul. [C17: probably from New Latin *trichotomia,* from Greek *trikhotomein* to divide into three, from *trikha* triple + *temnein* to cut] —**trichotomic** (ˌtrɪkə'tɒmɪk) *or* **tri'chotomous** *adj.* —**tri'chotomously** *adv.*

trichroism ('traɪkrəʊˌɪzəm) *n.* a property of biaxial crystals as a result of which they show a perceptible difference in colour when viewed along three different axes. See **pleochroism.** [C19: from Greek *trikhroos* three-coloured, from TRI- + *khrōma* colour] —**tri'chroic** *adj.*

trichromat ('traɪkrəʊˌmæt) *n.* any person with normal colour vision, who can therefore see the three primary colours.

trichromatic (ˌtraɪkrəʊ'mætɪk) *or* **trichromic** (traɪ'krəʊmɪk) *adj.* **1.** *Photog., printing.* involving the combination of three primary colours in the production of any colour. **2.** of, relating to, or having normal colour vision. **3.** having or involving three colours.

trichromatism (traɪ'krəʊməˌtɪzəm) *n.* **1.** the use or combination of three primary colours for colour reproduction in photography, printing, television, etc. **2.** *Rare.* the state of being trichromatic.

trichuriasis (ˌtrɪkjʊə'raɪəsɪs) *n.* infection of the large intestine with the whipworm *Trichuris trichiura,* resulting in anaemia, weakness, etc.

trick (trɪk) *n.* **1.** a deceitful, cunning, or underhand action or plan. **2. a.** a mischievous, malicious, or humorous action or plan; joke: *the boys are up to their tricks again.* **b.** (*as modifier*): *a trick spider.* **3.** an illusory or magical feat or device. **4.** a simple feat learned by an animal or person. **5.** an adroit or ingenious device; knack: *a trick of the trade.* **6.** a behavioural trait, habit, or mannerism. **7.** a turn or round of duty or work. **8.** *Cards.* **a.** a batch of cards containing one from each player, usually played in turn and won by the player or side that plays the card with the highest value. **b.** a card that can potentially win a trick. **9. can't take a trick.** *Austral. slang.* to be consistently unsuccessful or unlucky. **10. do the trick.** *Informal.* to produce the right or desired result. **11. how's tricks?** *Slang.* how are you? **12. turn a trick.** *Slang.* (of a prostitute) to gain a customer. ~*vb.* **13.** to defraud, deceive, or cheat (someone), esp. by means of a trick. [C15: from Old Northern French *trique,* from *trikier* to deceive, from Old French *trichier,* ultimately from Latin *trīcārī* to play tricks] —'**tricker** *n.* —'**trickless** *adj.*

trick cyclist *n.* a slang term for **psychiatrist.**

trickery ('trɪkərɪ) *n., pl.* **-eries.** the practice or an instance of using tricks: *he obtained the money by trickery.*

trickle ('trɪkᵊl) *vb.* **1.** to run or cause to run in thin or slow streams: *she trickled the sand through her fingers.* **2.** (*intr.*) to move, go, or pass gradually: *the crowd trickled away.* ~*n.* **3.** a thin, irregular, or slow flow of something. **4.** the act of trickling. [C14: perhaps of imitative origin] —'**trickling** *adj.* —'**tricklingly** *adv.* —'**trickly** *adj.*

trickle charger *n.* a small mains-operated battery charger, esp. one that delivers less than 5 amperes and is used by car owners.

trick or treat *n. Chiefly U.S. and Canadian.* the cry by children at Hallowe'en when they call at houses, indicating that they want a present or money otherwise they will play a trick on the householder.

trick out *or* **up** *vb.* (*tr., adv.*) to dress up; deck out: *tricked out in frilly dresses.*

trickster ('trɪkstə) *n.* a person who deceives or plays tricks.

tricksy ('trɪksɪ) *adj.* **-sier, -siest. 1.** playing tricks habitually; mischievous. **2.** crafty or difficult to deal with. **3.** *Archaic.* well-dressed; spruce; smart. —'**tricksiness** *n.*

ticktrack ('trɪkˌtræk) *n.* a variant spelling of **trictrac.**

tricky ('trɪkɪ) *adj.* **trickier, trickiest. 1.** involving snags or difficulties: *a tricky job.* **2.** needing careful and tactful handling: *a tricky situation.* **3.** characterized by tricks; sly; wily: *a tricky dealer.* —'**trickily** *adv.* —'**trickiness** *n.*

triclinic (traɪ'klɪnɪk) *adj.* relating to or belonging to the crystal system characterized by three unequal axes, no pair of which are perpendicular. Also: **anorthic.**

triclinium (traɪ'klɪnɪəm) *n., pl.* **-ia** (-ɪə). (in ancient Rome) **1.** an arrangement of three couches around a table for reclining upon while dining. **2.** a dining room, esp. one containing such an arrangement of couches. [C17: from Latin, from Greek *triklinion,* from TRI- + *klinē* a couch]

tricolour *or U.S.* **tricolor** ('trɪkələ, 'traɪˌkʌlə) *adj. also* **tricoloured** *or U.S.* **tricolored** ('traɪˌkʌləd). **1.** having or involving three colours. ~*n.* **2.** (*often cap.*) the French national flag, having three equal vertical stripes in blue, white, and red. **3.** any flag, badge, ribbon, etc., with three colours.

tricorn ('traɪˌkɔːn) *n. also* **tricorne. 1.** a cocked hat with opposing brims turned back and caught in three places. **2.** an imaginary animal having three horns. ~*adj. also* **tricornered. 3.** having three horns or corners. [C18: from Latin *tricornis,* from TRI- + *cornu* HORN]

tricostate (traɪ'kɒsteɪt) *adj. Biology.* having three ribs or riblike parts: *tricostate leaves.* [C19: from TRI- + COSTATE]

tricot ('trɪkəʊ, 'triː-) *n.* **1.** a thin rayon or nylon fabric knitted or resembling knitting, used for dresses, etc. **2.** a type of ribbed dress fabric. [C19: from French, from *tricoter* to knit, of unknown origin]

tricotine (ˌtrɪkə'tiːn, ˌtriː-) *n.* a twill-weave woollen fabric resembling gaberdine. [C20: from French; see TRICOT]

tricrotic (traɪ'krɒtɪk) *adj. Physiol.* (of the pulse) having a tracing characterized by three elevations with each beat. [C19: from Greek *trikrotos* having three beats, from TRI- + *krotos* a beat] —**tricrotism** ('traɪkrəˌtɪzəm, 'trɪk-) *n.*

trictrac *or* **ticktrack** ('trɪkˌtræk) *n.* a game similar to backgammon. [C17: from French, imitative]

tricuspid (traɪ'kʌspɪd) *Anatomy.* ~*adj. also* **tricuspidal. 1. a.** having three points, cusps, or segments: *a tricuspid tooth; a tricuspid valve.* **b.** of or relating to such a tooth or valve. ~*n.* **2.** a tooth having three cusps.

tricycle ('traɪsɪkᵊl) *n.* **1.** a three-wheeled cycle, esp. one driven by pedals. **2.** a three-wheeler for invalids. ~*vb.* **3.** (*intr.*) to ride a tricycle. —'**tricyclist** *n.*

tricyclic (traɪ'saɪklɪk) *adj.* **1.** (of a chemical compound) containing three rings in the molecular structure. ~*n.* **2.** an antidepressant drug having a tricyclic molecular structure.

tridactyl (traɪ'dæktᵊl) *or* **tridactylous** *adj.* having three digits on one hand or foot.

trident ('traɪdᵊnt) *n.* **1.** a three-pronged spear, originally from the East. **2.** a three-pronged instrument, weapon, or symbol. ~*adj.* **3.** having three prongs. [C16: from Latin *tridēns* three-pronged, from TRI- + *dēns* tooth]

tridentate (traɪ'dɛnteɪt) *or* **tridental** *adj. Anatomy, botany.* having three prongs, teeth, or points.

Tridentine (traɪ'dɛntaɪn) *adj.* **1.** *History.* **a.** of or relating to the Council of Trent (1545–63), held by the Roman Catholic Church at Trento, N Italy. **b.** in accord with Tridentine doctrine. ~*n.* **2.** an orthodox Roman Catholic. [C16: from Medieval Latin *Tridentīnus,* from *Tridentum* Trent]

tridimensional (ˌtraɪdɪ'mɛnʃənᵊl, -daɪ-) *adj.* a less common word for **three-dimensional.** —ˌ**tridiˌmension'ality** *n.* —ˌ**tridi'mensionally** *adv.*

triduum ('trɪdjʊəm, 'traɪ-) *n. R.C. Church.* a period of three days for prayer before a feast. [C19: Latin, perhaps from *triduum spatium* a space of three days]

triecious (traɪ'iːʃəs) *adj.* a variant spelling of **trioecious.**

tried (traɪd) *vb.* the past tense and past participle of **try.**

triella (traɪ'ɛlə) *n. Austral.* three nominated horse races in which the punter bets on selecting the three winners.

triene ('traɪˌiːn) *n.* a chemical compound containing three double bonds.

triennial (traɪ'ɛnɪəl) *adj.* **1.** relating to, lasting for, or occurring every three years. ~*n.* **2.** a third anniversary. **3.** a triennial period, thing, or occurrence. [C17: from Latin TRIENNIUM] —**tri'ennially** *adv.*

triennium (traɪ'ɛnɪəm) *n., pl.* **-niums** *or* **-nia** (-nɪə). a period or cycle of three years. [C19: from Latin, from TRI- + *annus* a year]

trier ('traɪə) *n.* a person or thing that tries.

trierarch ('traɪəˌrɑːk) *n. Greek history.* **1.** a citizen responsible for fitting out a state trireme, esp. in Athens. **2.** the captain of a trireme. [C17: from Latin, from Greek *triērarkhos,* from *triērēs* equipped with three banks of oars + *arkhein* to command]

trierarchy ('traɪəˌrɑːkɪ) *n., pl.* **-chies.** *Greek history.* **1.** the responsibility for fitting out a state trireme, esp. in Athens. **2.** the office of a trierarch. **3.** trierarchs collectively.

trifacial (traɪ'feɪʃəl) *adj.* another word for **trigeminal.**

trifecta (traɪ'fɛktə) *n. Austral.* a form of betting in which the punter selects the first three place-winners in a horse race in the correct order. [from TRI- + (*per*)*fecta,* a U.S. system of betting]

triffid ('trɪfɪd) *n.* any of a species of fictional plants that supposedly grew to a gigantic size, were capable of moving about, and could kill humans. [from the science fiction novel *The Day of the Triffids* (1951) by the British writer John Wyndham]

trifid ('traɪfɪd) *adj.* divided or split into three parts or lobes. [C18: from Latin *trifidus* from TRI- + *findere* to split]

trifle ('traɪfᵊl) *n.* **1.** a thing of little or no value or significance. **2.** a small amount; bit: *a trifle more enthusiasm.* **3.** *Brit.* a cold dessert made with sponge cake spread with jam or fruit, soaked in wine or sherry, covered with a custard sauce and cream, and decorated. **4.** a type of pewter of medium hardness. **5.** articles made from this pewter. ~*vb.* **6.** (*intr.*; usually foll. by *with*) to deal (with) as if worthless; dally: *to trifle with a person's affections.* **7.** to waste (time) frivolously. [C13: from Old French *trufle* mockery, from *trufler* to cheat] —'**trifler** *n.*

trifling ('traɪflɪŋ) *adj.* **1.** insignificant or petty. **2.** frivolous or idle. —'**triflingly** *adv.* —'**triflingness** *n.*

trifocal *adj.* (traɪ'fəʊkᵊl). **1.** having three focuses. **2.** having three focal lengths. ~*n.* (traɪ'fəʊkᵊl, 'traɪˌfəʊkᵊl). **3.** (*pl.*) glasses that have trifocal lenses.

trifold ('traɪˌfəʊld) *adj.* a less common word for **triple.**

trifoliate (traɪ'fəʊlɪɪt, -ˌeɪt) *or* **trifoliated** *adj.* having three leaves, leaflike parts, or (of a compound leaf) leaflets.

trifolium (traɪ'fəʊlɪəm) *n.* any leguminous plant of the temperate genus *Trifolium,* having leaves divided into three leaflets and dense heads of small white, yellow, red, or purple flowers: includes the clovers and trefoils. [C17: from Latin, from TRI- + *folium* leaf]

triforium (traɪ'fɔːrɪəm) *n., pl.* **-ria** (-rɪə). an arcade above the arches of the nave, choir, or transept of a church. [C18: from Anglo-Latin, apparently from Latin TRI- + *foris* a doorway; referring to the fact that each bay characteristically had three openings] —**tri'forial** *adj.*

trifurcate ('traɪfɜːkɪt, -ˌkeɪt) *or* **trifurcated** *adj.* having three branches or forks. [from Latin *trifurcus,* from TRI- + *furca* a fork] —ˌ**trifur'cation** *n.*

trig[1] (trɪg) *Archaic or dialect.* ~*adj.* **1.** neat or spruce. ~*vb.* **trigs, trigging, trigged.** **2.** to make or become trim or spruce. [C12 (originally: trusty): of Scandinavian origin; related to Old Norse *tryggr* true] —'**trigly** *adv.* —'**trigness** *n.*

trig[2] (trɪg) *Chiefly dialect.* ~*n.* **1.** a wedge or prop. ~*vb.* **trigs, trigging, trigged.** (*tr.*) **2.** to block or stop. **3.** to prop or support. [C16: probably of Scandinavian origin; compare Old Norse *tryggja* to make secure; see TRIG[1]]

trig. *abbrev. for:* **1.** trigonometry. **2.** trigonometrical.

trigeminal (traɪ'dʒɛmɪnᵊl) *adj. Anatomy.* of or relating to the trigeminal nerve. [C19: from Latin *trigeminus* triplet, from TRI- + *geminus* twin]

trigeminal nerve *n.* either one of the fifth pair of cranial nerves, which supply the muscles of the mandible and maxilla. Their ophthalmic branches supply the area around the orbit of the eye, the nasal cavity, and the forehead.

trigeminal neuralgia *n. Pathol.* another name for **tic douloureux.**

trigger ('trɪgə) *n.* **1.** a small projecting lever that activates the firing mechanism of a firearm. **2.** *Machinery.* a device that releases a spring-loaded mechanism or a similar arrangement. **3.** any event that sets a course of action in motion. ~*vb.* (*tr.*) **4.** (usually foll. by *off*) to give rise (to); set off. **5.** to fire or set in motion by or as by pulling a trigger. [C17 *tricker,* from Dutch *trekker,* from *trekken* to pull; see TREK] —'**triggered** *adj.* —'**triggerless** *adj.*

triggerfish ('trɪgəˌfɪʃ) *n., pl.* **-fish** *or* **-fishes.** any plectognath fish of the family *Balistidae,* of tropical and temperate seas. They have a compressed body with erectile spines in the first dorsal fin.

trigger-happy *adj. Informal.* **1.** tending to resort to the use of firearms or violence irresponsibly. **2.** tending to act rashly or without due consideration.

trigger plant *n. Austral.* any of several small grasslike plants of the genus *Stylidium,* having sensitive stamens that are erected when disturbed: family *Stylidiaceae.*

triglyceride (traɪ'glɪsəˌraɪd) *n.* any ester of glycerol and one or more carboxylic acids, in which each glycerol molecule has combined with three carboxylic acid molecules. Most natural fats and oils are triglycerides.

triglyph ('traɪˌglɪf) *n. Architect.* a stone block in a Doric frieze, having three vertical channels. [C16: via Latin from Greek *trigluphos* three-grooved, from *tri-* TRI- + *gluphē* carving. See GLYPH] —**tri'glyphic** *adj.*

trigon ('traɪgɒn) *n.* **1.** (in classical Greece or Rome) a triangular harp or lyre. **2.** an archaic word for **triangle.** [C17: via Latin from Greek *trigōnon* triangle. See TRI-, -GON]

trigonal ('trɪgənᵊl) *adj.* **1.** another word for **triangular** (sense 1). **2.** Also: **rhombohedral.** relating or belonging to the crystal system characterized by three equal axes that are equally inclined and not perpendicular to each other.

trigonometric function *n.* **1.** Also called: **circular function.** any of a group of functions of an angle expressed as a ratio of two of the sides of a right-angled triangle containing the angle. The group includes sine, cosine, tangent, secant, cosecant, and cotangent. **2.** any function containing only sines, cosines, etc., and constants.

trigonometry (ˌtrɪgə'nɒmɪtrɪ) *n.* the branch of mathematics concerned with the properties of trigonometric functions and their application to the determination of the angles and sides of triangles. Used in surveying, navigation, etc. Abbrev.: **trig.** [C17: from New Latin *trigōnometria,* from Greek *trigōnon* triangle] —**trigonometric** (ˌtrɪgənə'mɛtrɪk) *or* ˌ**trigono'metrical** *adj.* —ˌ**trigono'metrically** *adv.*

trigonous ('trɪgənəs) *adj.* (of stems, seeds, and similar parts) having a triangular cross section.

trig point *n.* an informal name for **triangulation station.** Also called (Austral. and N.Z.): **trig.**

trigraph ('traɪˌgrɑːf, -ˌgræf) *n.* a combination of three letters used to represent a single speech sound or phoneme, such as *eau* in French *beau.* —**trigraphic** (traɪ'græfɪk) *adj.*

trihalomethane (traɪˌheɪləʊ'miːθeɪn) *n.* a type of chemical compound in which three of the hydrogen atoms in a methane molecule have been replaced by halogen atoms, esp. by chlorine in drinking water. Trihalomethanes are thought to be carcinogenic.

trihedral (traɪ'hiːdrəl) *adj.* **1.** having or formed by three plane faces meeting at a point. ~*n.* **2.** a figure formed by the intersection of three lines in different planes. [C18: from TRI- + Greek *hedra* base, seat + -AL[1]]

trihedron (traɪ'hiːdrən) *n., pl.* **-drons** *or* **-dra** (-drə). a figure determined by the intersection of three planes.

trihydrate (traɪ'haɪdreɪt) *n. Chem.* a substance that contains three molecules of water. —**tri'hydrated** *adj.*

trihydric (traɪ'haɪdrɪk) *or* **trihydroxy** (ˌtraɪhaɪ'drɒksɪ) *adj.* (of an alcohol or similar compound) containing three hydroxyl groups.

triiodomethane (ˌtraɪaɪˌəʊdəʊ'miːθeɪn) *n.* another name for **iodoform.**

triiodothyronine (ˌtraɪaɪˌəʊdəʊ'θaɪrəˌniːn) *n.* an amino acid hormone that contains iodine and is secreted by the thyroid gland with thyroxine, to which it has a similar action. Formula: $C_{15}H_{12}I_3NO_4$. [C20: from TRI- + IODO- + THYRO- + -INE[2]]

trike (traɪk) *n.* **1.** short for **tricycle.** **2.** short for **trichloroethylene.**

trilateral (traɪ'lætərəl) *adj.* having three sides. —**tri'laterally** *adv.*

trilateration (ˌtraɪlætə'reɪʃən) *n.* a method of surveying in which a whole area is divided into triangles, the sides of which are measured, usually by electromagnetic distance measuring for geodetic control or by chain survey for a detailed survey.

trilby ('trɪlbɪ) *n., pl.* **-bies.** **1.** *Chiefly Brit.* a man's soft felt hat with an indented crown. **2.** (*pl.*) *Slang.* feet. [C19: named after *Trilby,* the heroine of a dramatized novel (1893) of that title by the British writer George Du Maurier (1834–96)]

trilemma (traɪ'lɛmə) *n.* **1.** a quandary posed by three alternative courses of action. **2.** an argument one of the premises of which is the disjunction of three statements from each of which the same conclusion is derived. [C17: formed on the model of DILEMMA, from TRI- + Greek *lēmma* assumption]

trilinear (traɪ'lɪnɪə) *adj.* consisting of, bounded by, or relating to three lines.

trilingual (traɪ'lɪŋgwəl) *adj.* **1.** able to speak three languages fluently. **2.** expressed or written in three languages. —**tri'lingualism** *n.* —**tri'lingually** *adv.*

triliteral (traɪ'lɪtərəl) *adj.* **1.** having three letters. **2.** (of a word root in Semitic languages) consisting of three consonants. ~*n.* **3.** a word root of three consonants.

trilithon (traɪ'lɪθɒn, 'traɪlɪˌθɒn) *or* **trilith** ('traɪlɪθ) *n.* a structure consisting of two upright stones with a third placed across the top, such as those of the prehistoric monument Stonehenge in S England. [C18: from Greek; see TRI-, -LITH] —**trilithic** (traɪ'lɪθɪk) *adj.*

trill[1] (trɪl) *n.* **1.** *Music.* a melodic ornament consisting of a rapid alternation between a principal note and the note a whole tone or semitone above it. Usual symbol: *tr.* or *tr.*~~~ (written above a note). **2.** a shrill warbling sound, esp. as made by some birds. **3.** *Phonetics.* **a.** the articulation of an (r) sound produced by holding the tip of the tongue close to the alveolar ridge, allowing the tongue to make a succession of taps against the ridge. **b.** the production of a similar effect using the uvula against the back of the tongue. ~*vb.* **4.** to sound, sing, or play (a trill or with a trill). **5.** (*tr.*) to pronounce (an (r) sound) by the production of a trill. [C17: from Italian *trillo,* from *trillare,* apparently from Middle Dutch *trillen* to vibrate]

trill[2] (trɪl) *vb., n.* an archaic or poetic word for **trickle.** [C14: probably of Scandinavian origin; related to Norwegian *trilla* to roll; see TRILL[1]]

trillion ('trɪljən) *n.* **1.** (in Britain, France, and Germany) the number represented as one followed by eighteen zeros (10^{18}); a million million million. U.S. and Canadian word: **quintillion.** **2.** (in the U.S. and Canada) the number represented as one followed by twelve zeros (10^{12}); a million million. Brit. word: **billion.** **3.** (*often pl.*) an exceptionally large but unspecified number. ~*determiner.* **4.** (preceded by *a* or a numeral) **a.** amounting to a trillion: *a trillion stars.* **b.** (*as pronoun*): *there are three trillion.* [C17: from French, on the model of *million*] —'**trillionth** *n., adj.*

trillium ('trɪljəm) *n.* any herbaceous plant of the genus *Trillium,* of Asia and North America, having a whorl of three leaves at the top of the stem with a single central white, pink, or purple three-petalled flower: family *Trilliaceae*. [C18: from New Latin, modification by Linnaeus of Swedish *trilling* triplet]

trilobate (traɪˈləʊbeɪt, ˈtraɪləˌbeɪt) *adj.* (esp. of a leaf) consisting of or having three lobes or parts.

trilobite (ˈtraɪləˌbaɪt) *n.* any extinct marine arthropod of the group *Trilobita*, abundant in Palaeozoic times, having a segmented exoskeleton divided into three parts. [C19: from New Latin *Trilobītēs*, from Greek *trilobos* having three lobes; see TRI-, LOBE] —**trilobitic** (ˌtraɪləˈbɪtɪk) *adj.*

trilocular (traɪˈlɒkjʊlə) *adj.* (esp. of a plant ovary or anther) having or consisting of three chambers or cavities. [C18: from TRI- + Latin *loculus* compartment (from *locus* place) + -AR]

trilogy (ˈtrɪlədʒɪ) *n., pl.* **-gies.** **1.** a series of three related works, esp. in literature, etc. **2.** (in ancient Greece) a series of three tragedies performed together at the Dionysian festivals. [C19: from Greek *trilogia*; see TRI-, -LOGY]

trim (trɪm) *adj.* **trimmer, trimmest. 1.** neat and spruce in appearance. **2.** slim; slender. **3.** in good condition. ~*vb.* **trims, trimming, trimmed.** (*mainly tr.*) **4.** to put in good order, esp. by cutting or pruning. **5.** to shape and finish (timber). **6.** to adorn or decorate. **7.** (sometimes foll. by *off* or *away*) to cut so as to remove: *to trim off a branch.* **8.** to cut down to the desired size or shape: *to trim material to a pattern.* **9.** *Dialect.* to decorate: *to trim a Christmas tree.* **10.** *Nautical.* **a.** (*also intr.*) to adjust the balance of (a vessel) or (of a vessel) to maintain an even balance, by distribution of ballast, cargo, etc. **b.** (*also intr.*) to adjust (a vessel's sails) to take advantage of the wind. **c.** to stow (cargo). **11.** to balance (an aircraft) before flight by adjusting the position of the load or in flight by the use of trim tabs, fuel transfer, etc. **12.** (*also intr.*) to modify (one's opinions, etc.) to suit opposing factions or for expediency. **13.** *Informal.* to thrash or beat. **14.** *Informal.* to rebuke. **15.** *Obsolete.* to furnish or equip. ~*n.* **16.** a decoration or adornment. **17.** the upholstery and decorative facings, as on the door panels, of a car's interior. **18.** proper order or fitness; good shape: *in trim.* **19.** a haircut that neatens but does not alter the existing hairstyle. **20.** *Nautical.* **a.** the general set and appearance of a vessel. **b.** the difference between the draught of a vessel at the bow and at the stern. **c.** the fitness of a vessel. **d.** the position of a vessel's sails relative to the wind. **e.** the relative buoyancy of a submarine. **21.** dress or equipment. **22.** *U.S.* window-dressing. **23.** the attitude of an aircraft in flight when the pilot allows the main control surfaces to take up their own positions. **24.** *Films.* a section of shot cut out during editing. **25.** material that is trimmed off. **26.** decorative mouldings, such as architraves, picture rails, etc. [Old English *trymman* to strengthen; related to *trum* strong, Old Irish *druma* tree, Russian *drom* thicket] —ˈ**trimly** *adv.* —ˈ**trimness** *n.*

trimaran (ˈtraɪməˌræn) *n.* a vessel, usually of shallow draught, with two hulls flanking the main hull. [C20: from TRI- + (CATA)MARAN]

trimer (ˈtraɪmə) *n.* a polymer or a molecule of a polymer consisting of three identical monomers. —**trimeric** (traɪˈmɛrɪk) *adj.*

trimerous (ˈtrɪmərəs) *adj.* **1.** (of plants) having parts arranged in groups of three. **2.** consisting of or having three parts.

trimester (traɪˈmɛstə) *n.* **1.** a period of three months. **2.** (in some U.S. and Canadian universities or schools) any of the three academic sessions. [C19: from French *trimestre*, from Latin *trimēstris* of three months, from TRI- + *mēnsis* month] —**triˈmestral** *or* **triˈmestrial** *adj.*

trimeter (ˈtrɪmɪtə) *Prosody.* ~*n.* **1.** a verse line consisting of three metrical feet. ~*adj.* **2.** designating such a line.

trimethadione (ˌtraɪmɛθəˈdaɪəʊn) *n.* a crystalline compound with a bitter taste and camphor-like odour, used in the treatment of epilepsy. Formula: $C_6H_9NO_3$. [from TRI- + METH(YL) + DI-[1] + -ONE]

trimetric (traɪˈmɛtrɪk) *or* **trimetrical** *adj.* **1.** *Prosody.* of, relating to, or consisting of a trimeter or trimeters. **2.** *Crystallog.* another word for **orthorhombic.**

trimetric projection *n.* a geometric projection, used in mechanical drawing, in which the three axes are at arbitrary angles, often using different linear scales.

trimetrogon (traɪˈmɛtrəˌgɒn) *n.* **a.** a method of aerial photography for rapid topographic mapping, in which one vertical and two oblique photographs are taken simultaneously. **b.** (*as modifier*): *trimetrogon photography.* [from TRI- + *metro-*, from Greek *metron* measure + -GON]

trimmer (ˈtrɪmə) *n.* **1.** Also called: **trimmer joist.** a beam in a floor or roof structure attached to truncated joists in order to leave an opening for a staircase, chimney, etc. **2.** a machine for trimming timber. **3.** Also called: **trimming capacitor.** *Electronics.* a variable capacitor of small capacitance used for making fine adjustments, etc. **4.** a person who alters his opinions on the grounds of expediency. **5.** a person who fits out motor vehicles.

trimming (ˈtrɪmɪŋ) *n.* **1.** an extra piece used to decorate or complete. **2.** (*pl.*) usual or traditional accompaniments: *roast turkey with all the trimmings.* **3.** (*pl.*) parts that are cut off. **4.** (*pl.*) *Dialect.* ornaments; decorations: *Christmas trimmings.* **5.** *Informal.* a reproof, beating, or defeat.

trimolecular (ˌtraɪməˈlɛkjʊlə) *adj. Chem.* of, concerned with, formed from, or involving three molecules.

trimonoecious (ˌtraɪməˈniːʃəs) *adj.* (of a plant) having separate male, female, and hermaphrodite flowers on the same plant.

trimonthly (traɪˈmʌnθlɪ) *adj., adv.* every three months.

trimorph (ˈtraɪmɔːf) *n.* **1.** a substance, esp. a mineral, that exists in three distinct forms. **2.** any of the forms in which such a structure exists.

trimorphism (traɪˈmɔːfɪzəm) *n.* **1.** *Biology.* the property exhibited by certain species of having or occurring in three different forms. **2.** the property of certain minerals of existing in three crystalline forms. [C19: from Greek *trimorphos* (from TRI- + *morphē* form) + -ISM] —**triˈmorphic** *or* **triˈmorphous** *adj.*

trim size *n.* the size of a book or a page of a book after all excess material has been trimmed off.

trim tab *n.* a small control surface attached to the trailing edge of a main control surface to enable the pilot to trim an aircraft.

Trimurti (trɪˈmʊətɪ) *n.* the triad of the three chief gods of later Hinduism, consisting of Brahma the Creator, Vishnu the Sustainer, and Siva the Destroyer. [from Sanskrit, from *tri* three + *mūrti* form]

trinary (ˈtraɪnərɪ) *adj.* **1.** made up of three parts; ternary. **2.** going in threes. [C15: from Late Latin *trīnārius* of three sorts, from Latin *trīnī* three each, from *trēs* three]

trine (traɪn) *n.* **1.** *Astrology.* an aspect of 120° between two planets, an orb of 8° being allowed. Compare **conjunction** (sense 5), **opposition** (sense 9), **square** (sense 9). **2.** anything comprising three parts. ~*adj.* **3.** of or relating to a trine. **4.** threefold; triple. [C14: from Old French *trin*, from Latin *trīnus* triple, from *trēs* three] —ˈ**trinal** *adj.*

Trinidadian (ˌtrɪnɪˈdædɪən) *adj.* **1.** of or relating to Trinidad, an island in the West Indies, or its people. ~*n.* **2.** a native or inhabitant of Trinidad.

Trinil man (ˈtriːnɪl) *n.* another name for **Java man.** [C20: named after the village in Java where remains were found]

Trinitarian (ˌtrɪnɪˈtɛərɪən) *n.* **1.** a person who believes in the doctrine of the Trinity. **2.** a member of the Holy Trinity. See **Trinity** (sense 3). ~*adj.* **3.** of or relating to the doctrine of the Trinity or those who uphold it. **4.** of or relating to the Holy Trinity. —ˌ**Triniˈtarianˌism** *n.*

trinitrobenzene (traɪˌnaɪtrəʊˈbɛnziːn, -bɛnˈziːn) *n.* any of three explosive crystalline isomeric compounds with the formula $C_6H_3(NO_2)_3$. They are less sensitive to impact than TNT but more powerful in their explosive force.

trinitrocresol (traɪˌnaɪtrəʊˈkriːsɒl) *n.* a yellow crystalline highly explosive compound. Formula: $CH_3C_6H(OH)(NO_2)_3$.

trinitroglycerin (traɪˌnaɪtrəʊˈglɪsərɪn) *n.* the full name for **nitroglycerin.**

trinitrophenol (traɪˌnaɪtrəʊˈfiːnɒl) *n.* another name for **picric acid.**

trinitrotoluene (traɪˌnaɪtrəʊˈtɒljʊˌiːn) *or* **trinitrotoluol** (traɪˌnaɪtrəʊˈtɒljʊˌɒl) *n.* the full name for **TNT.**

trinity (ˈtrɪnɪtɪ) *n., pl.* **-ties.** **1.** a group of three. **2.** the state of being threefold. [C13: from Old French *trinite*, from Late Latin *trīnitās*, from Latin *trīnus* triple]

Trinity (ˈtrɪnɪtɪ) *n.* **1.** Also called: **Holy Trinity, Blessed Trinity.** *Christian theol.* the union of three persons, the Father, Son, and Holy Ghost, in one Godhead. **2.** See **Trinity Sunday.** **3.** **Holy Trinity.** a religious order founded in 1198.

Trinity Sunday *n.* the Sunday after Whit Sunday.

Trinity term *n.* the summer term at the Inns of Court and some educational establishments.

trinket (ˈtrɪŋkɪt) *n.* **1.** a small or worthless ornament or piece of jewellery. **2.** a trivial object; trifle. [C16: perhaps from earlier *trenket* little knife, via Old Northern French, from Latin *truncāre* to lop] —ˈ**trinketry** *n.*

trinocular (traɪˈnɒkjʊlə) *adj.* of or relating to a binocular microscope having a lens for photographic recording while direct visual observation is taking place. [C20: from TRI- + (BI)NOCULAR]

trinomial (traɪˈnəʊmɪəl) *adj.* **1.** *Maths.* consisting of or relating to three terms. **2.** *Biology.* denoting or relating to the three-part name of an organism that incorporates its genus, species, and subspecies. ~*n.* **3.** *Maths.* a polynomial consisting of three terms, such as $ax^2 + bx + c$. **4.** *Biology.* the third word in the trinomial name of an organism, which distinguishes between subspecies. [C18: TRI- + *-nomial* on the model of *binomial*] —**triˈnomially** *adv.*

trio (ˈtriːəʊ) *n., pl.* **trios.** **1.** a group of three people or things. **2.** *Music.* **a.** a group of three singers or instrumentalists or a piece of music composed for such a group. **b.** a subordinate section in a scherzo, minuet, etc., that is contrastive in style and often in a related key. **3.** *Piquet.* three cards of the same rank. [C18: from Italian, ultimately from Latin *trēs* three; compare DUO]

triode (ˈtraɪəʊd) *n.* **1.** an electronic valve having three electrodes, a cathode, an anode, and a grid, the potential of the grid controlling the flow of electrons between the cathode and anode. It has been replaced by the transistor. **2.** any electronic device, such as a thyratron, having three electrodes. [C20: TRI- + ELECTRODE]

trioecious *or* **triecious** (traɪˈiːʃəs) *adj.* (of a plant species) having male, female, and hermaphrodite flowers in three different plants. [C18: from New Latin *trioecia*, from Greek TRI- + *oikos* house]

triol ('traɪɒl) *n.* any of a class of alcohols that have three hydroxyl groups per molecule. Also called: **trihydric alcohol.** [from TRI- + -OL[1]]

triolein (traɪ'əʊlɪɪn) *n.* a naturally occurring glyceride of oleic acid, found in fats and oils. Formula: $(C_{17}H_{33}COO)_3C_3H_5$. Also called: **olein.**

triolet ('triːəʊˌlɛt) *n.* a verse form of eight lines, having the first line repeated as the fourth and seventh and the second line as the eighth, rhyming a b a a a b a b. [C17: from French: a little TRIO]

triose ('traɪəʊz, -əʊs) *n.* a simple monosaccharide produced by the oxidation of glycerol. Formula: $CH_2OHCHOHCHO$.

trio sonata *n.* **1.** a type of baroque composition in several movements scored for two upper parts and a bass part. **2.** a similar type of composition played on a keyboard instrument, esp. an organ.

trioxide (traɪ'ɒksaɪd) *n.* any oxide that contains three oxygen atoms per molecule: *sulphur trioxide,* SO_3.

trip (trɪp) *n.* **1.** an outward and return journey, often for a specific purpose. **2.** any tour, journey, or voyage. **3.** a false step; stumble. **4.** any slip or blunder. **5.** a light step or tread. **6.** a manoeuvre or device to cause someone to trip. **7.** Also called: **tripper. a.** any catch on a mechanism that acts as a switch. **b.** (*as modifier*): *trip button.* **8.** *Informal.* a hallucinogenic drug experience. **9.** *Informal.* any stimulating, profound, etc., experience. ~*vb.* **trips, tripping, tripped. 10.** (often foll. by *up*, or when *intr.*, by *on* or *over*) to stumble or cause to stumble. **11.** to make or cause to make a mistake or blunder. **12.** (*tr.;* often foll. by *up*) to trap or catch in a mistake. **13.** (*intr.*) to go on a short tour or journey. **14.** (*intr.*) to move or tread lightly. **15.** (*intr.*) *Informal.* to experience the effects of LSD or any other hallucinogenic drug. **16.** (*tr.*) **a.** to activate (a mechanical trip). **b. trip a switch.** to switch electric power off by moving the switch armature to disconnect the supply. ~See also **trip out.** [C14: from Old French *triper* to tread, of Germanic origin; related to Low German *trippen* to stamp, Middle Dutch *trippen* to walk trippingly, *trepelen* to trample] —'**trippingly** *adv.*

tripalmitin (traɪ'pælmɪtɪn) *n.* another name for **palmitin.**

tripartite (traɪ'pɑːtaɪt) *adj.* **1.** divided into or composed of three parts. **2.** involving three participants. **3.** (esp. of leaves) consisting of three parts formed by divisions extending almost to the base. —**tri'partitely** *adv.*

tripartition (ˌtraɪpɑː'tɪʃən) *n.* division into or among three.

tripe (traɪp) *n.* **1.** the stomach lining of an ox, cow, or other ruminant, prepared for cooking. **2.** *Informal.* something silly; rubbish. **3.** (*pl.*) *Archaic, informal.* intestines; belly. [C13: from Old French, of unknown origin]

tripersonal (traɪ'pɜːsənᵊl) *adj. Christian theol.* (of God) existing as the Trinity. Compare **unipersonal.** —ˌ**triperson'ality** *n.*

triphammer ('trɪpˌhæmə) *n.* a power hammer that is raised or tilted by a cam and allowed to fall under gravity.

triphenylmethane (traɪˌfiːnaɪl'miːθeɪn, -ˌfɛn-) *n.* a colourless crystalline solid used for the preparation of many dyes. Formula: $(C_6H_5)_3CH$.

triphibious (traɪ'fɪbɪəs) *adj.* (esp. of military operations) occurring on land, at sea, and in the air. [C20: from TRI- + (AM)PHIBIOUS]

triphthong ('trɪfθɒŋ, 'trɪp-) *n.* **1.** a composite vowel sound during the articulation of which the vocal organs move from one position through a second, ending in a third. **2.** a trigraph representing a composite vowel sound such as this. [C16: via New Latin from Medieval Greek *triphthongos,* from TRI- + *phthongos* sound; compare DIPHTHONG] —**triph'thongal** *adj.*

triphylite ('trɪfɪˌlaɪt) *n.* a bluish-grey rare mineral that consists of lithium iron phosphate in orthorhombic crystalline form and occurs in pegmatites. Formula: $LiFePO_4$. [C19: from TRI- + *phyl-,* from Greek *phulon* family + -ITE[1], referring to its three bases]

tripinnate (traɪ'pɪnɪt, -eɪt) *adj.* (of a leaf) having pinnate leaflets that are bipinnately arranged. —**tri'pinnately** *adv.*

Tripitaka (ˌtrɪpɪ'tɑːkə) *n. Buddhism.* the three collections of books making up the Buddhist canon of scriptures. [from Pali *tri* three + *pitaka* basket]

tripl. *abbrev. for* triplicate.

triplane ('traɪˌpleɪn) *n.* an aeroplane having three wings arranged one above the other.

triple ('trɪpᵊl) *adj.* **1.** consisting of three parts; threefold. **2.** (of musical time or rhythm) having three beats in each bar. **3.** three times as great or as much. ~*n.* **4.** a threefold amount. **5.** a group of three. ~*vb.* **6.** to increase or become increased threefold; treble. [C16: from Latin *triplus*] —'**triply** *adv.*

triple A *n. Military.* anti-aircraft artillery.

triple bond *n.* a type of chemical bond consisting of three distinct covalent bonds linking two atoms in a molecule.

triple expansion engine *n.* (formerly) a steam engine in which the steam is expanded in three stages in cylinders of increasing diameter to accommodate the increasing volume of the steam.

triple jump *n.* an athletic event in which the competitor has to perform successively a hop, a step, and a jump in continuous movement. Also called: **hop, step, and jump.**

triple-nerved *adj.* (of a leaf) having three main veins.

triple point *n. Chem.* the temperature and pressure at which the three phases of a substance are in equilibrium. The triple point of water, 273.16 K at a pressure of 611.2 Pa, is the basis of the definition of the kelvin.

triplet ('trɪplɪt) *n.* **1.** a group or set of three similar things. **2.** one of three offspring born at one birth. **3.** *Music.* a group of three notes played in a time value of two, four, etc. **4.** *Chem.* a state of a molecule or free radical in which there are two unpaired electrons. [C17: from TRIPLE, on the model of *doublet*]

tripletail ('trɪpᵊlˌteɪl) *n., pl.* **-tail** *or* **-tails.** any percoid fish of the family *Lobotidae,* esp. *Lobotes surinamensis,* of brackish waters of SE Asia, having tail-like dorsal and anal fins.

triple time *n.* musical time with three beats in each bar.

triple-tongue *vb. Music.* to play (very quick staccato passages of notes grouped in threes) on a wind instrument by a combination of single- and double-tonguing. Compare **single-tongue, double-tongue.** —**triple tonguing** *n.*

triplex ('trɪplɛks) *adj.* a less common word for **triple.** [C17: from Latin: threefold, from TRI- + *-plex* -FOLD]

Triplex ('trɪplɛks) *n. Brit. trademark.* a laminated safety glass, as used in car windows.

triplicate *adj.* ('trɪplɪkɪt). **1.** triple. ~*vb.* ('trɪplɪˌkeɪt). **2.** to multiply or be multiplied by three. ~*n.* ('trɪplɪkɪt). **3. a.** a group of three things. **b.** one of such a group. **4. in triplicate.** written out three times. [C15: from Latin *triplicāre* to triple, from TRIPLEX] —ˌ**tripli'cation** *n.*

triplicity (trɪ'plɪsɪtɪ) *n., pl.* **-ties. 1.** a group of three things. **2.** the state of being three. **3.** *Astrology.* any of four groups, earth, air, fire, and water, each consisting of three signs of the zodiac that are thought to have something in common in their nature. [C14: from Late Latin *triplicitās,* from Latin *triplex* threefold; see TRIPLEX]

triploblastic (ˌtrɪpləʊ'blæstɪk) *adj.* (of all multicellular animals except coelenterates) having a body developed from all three germ layers. Compare **diploblastic.** [C19: from *triplo-* threefold (from Greek *triploos*) + -BLAST]

triploid ('trɪplɔɪd) *adj.* **1.** having or relating to three times the haploid number of chromosomes: *a triploid organism.* ~*n.* **2.** a triploid organism. [C19: from Greek *tripl(oos)* triple + (HAPL)OID]

tripod ('traɪpɒd) *n.* **1.** an adjustable and usually collapsible three-legged stand to which a camera, etc., can be attached to hold it steady. **2.** a stand or table having three legs. [C17: via Latin from Greek *tripod-, tripous* three-footed, from TRI- + *pous* foot] —**tripodal** ('trɪpədᵊl) *adj.*

tripody ('trɪpədɪ) *n., pl.* **-dies.** *Prosody.* a metrical unit consisting of three feet.

tripoli ('trɪpəlɪ) *n.* a lightweight porous siliceous rock derived by weathering and used in a powdered form as a polish, filter, etc. [C17: named after *Tripoli,* port in Libya or in Lebanon]

tripos ('traɪpɒs) *n. Brit.* the final honours degree examinations in all subjects at Cambridge University. [C16: from Latin *tripūs,* influenced by Greek noun ending *-os*]

trip out *vb.* (*adv.*) (of an electrical circuit) to disconnect or be disconnected or (of a machine) to stop or be stopped by means of a trip switch or trip button.

tripper ('trɪpə) *n.* **1.** a person who goes on a trip. **2.** *Chiefly Brit.* a tourist; excursionist. **3.** another word for **trip** (sense 7). **4. a.** any device that generates a signal causing a trip to operate. **b.** the signal so generated.

trippet ('trɪpɪt) *n.* any mechanism that strikes or is struck at regular intervals, as by a cam. [C15 (in the sense: a piece of wood used in a game): from *trippen* to TRIP]

trip switch *n.* an electric switch arranged to interrupt a circuit suddenly and disconnect power from a running machine so that the machine is stopped.

triptane ('trɪpteɪn) *n.* a colourless highly flammable liquid alkane hydrocarbon, isomeric with heptane, used in aviation fuel; 2,2,3-trimethylbutane. Formula: $CH_3C(CH_3)_2CH(CH_3)CH_3$. [C20: shortened and altered from *trimethylbutane;* see TRI-, METHYL, BUTANE]

tripterous ('trɪptərəs) *adj.* (of fruits, seeds, etc.) having three winglike extensions or parts. [C19: from TRI- + Greek *-pteros,* from *pteron* wing]

triptych ('trɪptɪk) *n.* **1.** a set of three pictures or panels, usually hinged so that the two wing panels fold over the larger central one: often used as an altarpiece. **2.** a set of three hinged writing tablets. [C18: from Greek *triptukhos,* from TRI- + *ptux* plate; compare DIPTYCH]

triptyque (trɪp'tiːk) *n.* a customs permit for the temporary importation of a motor vehicle. [from French: TRIPTYCH (referring to its three sections)]

tripwire ('trɪpˌwaɪə) *n.* a wire that activates a trap, mine, etc., when tripped over.

triquetrous (traɪ'kwiːtrəs, -'kwɛ-) *adj.* triangular, esp. in cross section: *a triquetrous stem.* [C17: from Latin *triquetrus* having three corners]

triradiate (traɪ'reɪdɪɪt, -ˌeɪt) *adj. Biology.* having or consisting of three rays or radiating branches. —**tri'radiately** *adv.*

trireme ('traɪriːm) *n.* a galley, developed by the ancient Greeks as a warship, with three banks of oars on each side. [C17: from Latin *trirēmis,* from TRI- + *rēmus* oar]

trisaccharide (traɪ'sækəˌraɪd) *n.* an oligosaccharide whose molecules have three linked monosaccharide molecules.

trisect (traɪˈsɛkt) *vb.* (*tr.*) to divide into three parts, esp. three equal parts. [C17: TRI- + *-sect* from Latin *secāre* to cut] —**trisection** (traɪˈsɛkʃən) *n.* —**triˈsector** *n.*

triserial (traɪˈsɪərɪəl) *adj.* arranged in three rows or series.

trishaw (ˈtraɪˌʃɔː) *n.* another name for **rickshaw** (sense 2). [C20: from TRI- + RICKSHAW]

triskaidekaphobia (ˌtrɪskaɪˌdɛkəˈfəʊbɪə) *n.* an abnormal fear of the number thirteen. [C20: from Greek *triskaideka* thirteen + -PHOBIA] —ˌ**triskaiˌdekaˈphobic** *adj., n.*

triskelion (trɪˈskɛlɪˌɒn, -ən) *or* **triskele** (ˈtrɪskiːl) *n., pl.* **triskelia** (trɪˈskɛlɪə) *or* **triskeles.** a symbol consisting of three bent limbs or lines radiating from a centre. [C19: from Greek *triskelēs* three-legged, from TRI- + *skelos* leg]

trismus (ˈtrɪzməs) *n. Pathol.* the state or condition of being unable to open the mouth because of sustained contractions of the jaw muscles, caused by a form of tetanus. Nontechnical name: **lockjaw.** [C17: from New Latin, from Greek *trismos* a grinding] —ˈ**trismic** *adj.*

trisoctahedron (trɪsˌɒktəˈhiːdrən) *n., pl.* **-drons** *or* **-dra** (-drə). a solid figure having 24 identical triangular faces, groups of three faces being formed on an underlying octahedron. [C19: from Greek *tris* three times + OCTAHEDRON] —**trisˌoctaˈhedral** *adj.*

trisomy (ˈtraɪsəʊmɪ) *n.* the condition of having one chromosome of the set represented three times in an otherwise diploid organism, cell, etc. Trisomy of chromosome 21 results in Down's syndrome. [C20: from TRI- + (CHROMO)SOM(E) + -Y[3]] —**trisomic** (traɪˈsəʊmɪk) *adj.*

tristate (ˈtraɪˌsteɪt) *adj.* (of a digital logic device) having high, low, and floating output states.

triste (triːst) *or* **tristful** (ˈtrɪstfʊl) *adj.* archaic words for **sad.** [from French] —ˈ**tristfully** *adv.* —ˈ**tristfulness** *n.*

tristearin (traɪˈstɪərɪn) *n.* another name for **stearin.**

tristich (ˈtrɪstɪk) *n. Prosody.* a poem, stanza, or strophe that consists of three lines. [C19: from Greek, from TRI- + *stikhos* STICH, on the model of DISTICH] —**trisˈtichic** *adj.*

tristichous (ˈtrɪstɪkəs) *adj.* arranged in three rows, esp. (of plants) having three vertical rows of leaves.

tristimulus values (traɪˈstɪmjʊləs) *pl. n.* three values that together are used to describe a colour and are the amounts of three reference colours that can be mixed to give the same visual sensation as the colour considered. Symbol: X, Y, Z. See also **chromaticity coordinates.**

trisulphide (traɪˈsʌlfaɪd) *n.* any sulphide containing three sulphur atoms per molecule.

trisyllable (traɪˈsɪləbᵊl) *n.* a word of three syllables. —**trisyllabic** (ˌtraɪsɪˈlæbɪk) *adj.* —ˌ**trisylˈlabically** *adv.*

tritanopia (ˌtraɪtəˈnəʊpɪə, ˌtrɪt-) *n.* a form of colour blindness in which there is a tendency to confuse blues and greens and in which sensitivity to blue is reduced. [C19/20: from New Latin, from Greek *tritos* third + New Latin *anopia* blindness; signifying that only two thirds of the spectrum can be distinguished] —**tritanopic** (ˌtraɪtəˈnɒpɪk, ˌtrɪt-) *adj.*

trite (traɪt) *adj.* **1.** hackneyed; dull: *a trite comment.* **2.** *Archaic.* frayed or worn out. [C16: from Latin *trītus* worn down, from *terere* to rub] —ˈ**tritely** *adv.* —ˈ**triteness** *n.*

tritheism (ˈtraɪθɪˌɪzəm) *n. Theol.* belief in three gods, esp. in the Trinity as consisting of three distinct gods. —ˈ**tritheist** *n., adj.* —ˌ**tritheˈistic** *or* ˌ**tritheˈistical** *adj.*

tritiate (ˈtrɪtɪˌeɪt) *vb.* (*tr.*) to replace normal hydrogen atoms in (a compound) by those of tritium. [C20: from TRITI(UM) + -ATE[1]] —ˌ**tritiˈation** *n.*

triticale (ˌtrɪtɪˈkɑːlɪ) *n.* a fertile hybrid cereal, a cross between wheat (*Triticum*) and rye (*Secale*), produced by polyploidy. [C20: from *Tritic(um)* + (*Sec*)*ale*]

triticum (ˈtrɪtɪkəm) *n.* any annual cereal grass of the genus *Triticum,* which includes the wheats. [C19: Latin, literally: wheat, probably from *tritum,* supine of *terere* to grind]

tritium (ˈtrɪtɪəm) *n.* a radioactive isotope of hydrogen, occurring in trace amounts in natural hydrogen and produced in a nuclear reactor. Tritiated compounds are used as tracers. Symbol: T or ^{3}H; half-life: 12.5 years. [C20: New Latin, from Greek *tritos* third]

triton[1] (ˈtraɪtᵊn) *n.* any of various chiefly tropical marine gastropod molluscs of the genera *Triton, Cymatium,* etc., having large beautifully-coloured spiral shells. [C16: via Latin from Greek *tritōn*]

triton[2] (ˈtraɪtɒn) *n. Physics.* a nucleus of an atom of tritium, containing two neutrons and one proton. [C20: from TRIT(IUM) + -ON]

tritone (ˈtraɪˌtəʊn) *n.* a musical interval consisting of three whole tones; augmented fourth.

tritonia (traɪˈtəʊnɪə) *n.* any plant of the perennial cormous S. African genus *Tritonia,* with typically scarlet or orange flowers. The gardener's montbretia is a cross between *Tritonia* and the related *Crocosmia:* family *Iridaceae.* [New Latin, from Greek *tritōn*]

triturate (ˈtrɪtjʊˌreɪt) *vb.* **1.** (*tr.*) to grind or rub into a fine powder or pulp; masticate. ~*n.* **2.** the powder or pulp resulting from this grinding. [C17: from Late Latin *trītūrāre* to thresh, from Latin *trītūra* a threshing, from *terere* to grind] —ˈ**triturable** *adj.* —ˈ**trituˌrator** *n.*

trituration (ˌtrɪtjʊˈreɪʃən) *n.* **1.** the act of triturating or the state of being triturated. **2.** *Pharmacol.* a mixture of one or more finely ground powdered drugs.

triumph (ˈtraɪəmf) *n.* **1.** the feeling of exultation and happiness derived from a victory or major achievement. **2.** the act or condition of being victorious; victory. **3.** (in ancient Rome) a ritual procession to the Capitoline Hill held in honour of a victorious general. **4.** *Obsolete.* a public display or celebration. **5.** *Cards.* an obsolete word for **trump.** ~*vb.* (*intr.*) **6.** (often foll. by *over*) to win a victory or control: *to triumph over one's weaknesses.* **7.** to rejoice over a victory. **8.** to celebrate a Roman triumph. [C14: from Old French *triumphe,* from Latin *triumphus,* from Old Latin *triumpus;* probably related to Greek *thriambos* Bacchic hymn] —ˈ**triumpher** *n.*

triumphal (traɪˈʌmfəl) *adj.* **1.** celebrating a triumph: *a triumphal procession.* **2.** resembling triumph. —**triˈumphalˌism** *n.*

triumphal arch *n.* an arch built to commemorate a victory.

triumphant (traɪˈʌmfənt) *adj.* **1.** experiencing or displaying triumph. **2.** exultant through triumph. **3.** *Obsolete.* **a.** magnificent. **b.** triumphal. —**triˈumphantly** *adv.*

triumvir (traɪˈʌmvə) *n., pl.* **-virs** *or* **-viri** (-vɪˌriː). (esp. in ancient Rome) a member of a triumvirate. [C16: from Latin: one of three administrators, from *trium virōrum* of three men, from *trēs* three + *vir* man] —**triˈumviral** *adj.*

triumvirate (traɪˈʌmvɪrɪt) *n.* **1.** (in ancient Rome) a board of three officials jointly responsible for some task. **2.** joint rule by three men. **3.** any group of three men associated in some way. **4.** the office of a triumvir.

triune (ˈtraɪjuːn) *adj.* **1.** constituting three in one, esp. the three persons in one God of the Trinity. ~*n.* **2.** a group of three. **3.** (*often cap.*) another word for **Trinity.** [C17: TRI- + *-une,* from Latin *ūnus* one] —**triˈunity** *n.*

Triunitarian (traɪˌjuːnɪˈtɛərɪən) *n., adj.* a less common word for **Trinitarian.**

trivalent (traɪˈveɪlənt, ˈtrɪvələnt) *adj. Chem.* **1.** having a valency of three. **2.** having three valencies. ~Also: **tervalent.** —**triˈvalency** *n.*

trivet (ˈtrɪvɪt) *n.* **1.** a stand, usually three-legged and metal, on which cooking vessels are placed over a fire. **2.** a short metal stand on which hot dishes are placed on a table. **3. as right as a trivet.** in perfect health. [Old English *trefet* (influenced by Old English *thrifēte* having three feet), from Latin *tripēs* having three feet]

trivia (ˈtrɪvɪə) *n.* (*functioning as sing. or pl.*) petty details or considerations; trifles; trivialities. [from New Latin, plural of Latin *trivium* junction of three roads; for meaning, see TRIVIAL]

trivial (ˈtrɪvɪəl) *adj.* **1.** of little importance; petty or frivolous: *trivial complaints.* **2.** ordinary or commonplace; trite: *trivial conversation.* **3.** *Maths.* (of the solutions of a set of homogeneous equations) having zero values for all the variables. **4.** *Biology.* denoting the specific name of an organism in binomial nomenclature. **5.** *Biology, chemistry.* denoting the popular name of an organism or substance, as opposed to the scientific one. **6.** of or relating to the trivium. [C15: from Latin *triviālis* belonging to the public streets, common, from *trivium* crossroads, junction of three roads, from TRI- + *via* road] —ˈ**trivially** *adv.* —ˈ**trivialness** *n.*

triviality (ˌtrɪvɪˈælɪtɪ) *n., pl.* **-ties.** **1.** the state or quality of being trivial. **2.** something, such as a remark, that is trivial. ~Also called: **trivialism** (ˈtrɪvɪəˌlɪzəm).

trivialize *or* **trivialise** (ˈtrɪvɪəˌlaɪz) *vb.* (*tr.*) to cause to seem trivial or more trivial; minimize: *he trivialized his injuries.* —ˌ**trivialiˈzation** *or* ˌ**trivialiˈsation** *n.*

trivium (ˈtrɪvɪəm) *n., pl.* **-ia** (-ɪə). (in medieval learning) the lower division of the seven liberal arts, consisting of grammar, rhetoric, and logic. Compare **quadrivium.** [C19: from Medieval Latin, from Latin: crossroads; see TRIVIAL]

triweekly (traɪˈwiːklɪ) *adj., adv.* **1.** every three weeks. **2.** three times a week. ~*n., pl.* **-lies.** **3.** a triweekly publication.

-trix *suffix forming nouns.* indicating a feminine agent, corresponding to nouns ending in *-tor: executrix.* [from Latin]

t-RNA *abbrev. for* **transfer RNA.**

troat (trəʊt) *vb.* (*intr.*) (of a rutting buck) to call or bellow. [C17: probably related to Old French *trout, trut,* a cry used by hunters to urge on the dogs]

trocar (ˈtrəʊkɑː) *n.* a surgical instrument for removing fluid from bodily cavities, consisting of a puncturing device situated inside a tube. [C18: from French *trocart* literally: with three sides, from *trois* three + *carre* side]

trochaic (trəʊˈkeɪɪk) *Prosody.* ~*adj.* **1.** of, relating to, or consisting of trochees. ~*n.* **2.** another word for **trochee.** **3.** a verse composed of trochees. —**troˈchaically** *adv.*

trochal (ˈtrəʊkᵊl) *adj. Zoology.* shaped like a wheel: *the trochal disc of a rotifer.* [C19: from Greek *trokhos* wheel]

trochanter (trəʊˈkæntə) *n.* **1.** any of several processes on the upper part of the vertebrate femur, to which muscles are attached. **2.** the third segment of an insect's leg. [C17: via French from Greek *trokhantēr,* from *trekhein* to run]

troche (trəʊʃ) *n. Med.* another name for **lozenge** (sense 1). [C16: from French *trochisque,* from Late Latin *trochiscus,* from Greek *trokhiskos* little wheel, from *trokhos* wheel]

trochee (ˈtrəʊkiː) *n. Prosody.* a metrical foot of two syllables, the first long and the second short (-˘). Compare **iamb.** [C16: via Latin from Greek *trokhaios pous,* literally: a running foot, from *trekhein* to run]

trochelminth (ˈtrɒkəlˌmɪnθ) *n.* any invertebrate of the former taxonomic group *Trochelminthes*, which included the rotifers and gastrotrichs, now classed as separate phyla. [C19: from New Latin *trochelminthes*, from Greek *trokhos* wheel, from *trekhein* to run + HELMINTH]

trochilus (ˈtrɒkɪləs) *n., pl.* **-li** (-ˌlaɪ). **1.** another name for **hummingbird. 2.** any of several Old World warblers, esp. *Phylloscopus trochilus* (willow warbler). [C16: via Latin from Greek *trokhilos* name of a small Egyptian bird said by ancient writers to pick the teeth of crocodiles, from *trekhein* to run]

trochlea (ˈtrɒklɪə) *n., pl.* **-leae** (-lɪˌiː). any bony or cartilaginous part with a grooved surface over which a bone, tendon, etc., may slide or articulate. [C17: from Latin, from Greek *trokhileia* a sheaf of pulleys; related to *trokhos* wheel, *trekhein* to run]

trochlear (ˈtrɒklɪə) *adj.* **1.** of or relating to a trochlea or trochlear nerve. **2.** *Botany.* shaped like a pulley. ~*n.* **3.** See **trochlear nerve.**

trochlear nerve *n.* either one of the fourth pair of cranial nerves, which supply the superior oblique muscle of the eye.

trochoid (ˈtrəʊkɔɪd) *n.* **1.** the curve described by a fixed point on the radius or extended radius of a circle as the circle rolls along a straight line. ~*adj. also* **trochoidal. 2.** rotating or capable of rotating about a central axis. **3.** *Anatomy.* (of a structure or part) resembling or functioning as a pivot or pulley. [C18: from Greek *trokhoeidēs* circular, from *trokhos* wheel] —**troˈchoidally** *adv.*

trochophore (ˈtrɒkəˌfɔː) *or* **trochosphere** (ˈtrɒkəsˌfɪə) *n.* the ciliated planktonic larva of many invertebrates, including polychaete worms, molluscs, and rotifers. [C19: from Greek *trokhos* wheel + -PHORE]

trod (trɒd) *vb.* the past tense and a past participle of **tread.**

trodden (ˈtrɒdᵊn) *vb.* a past participle of **tread.**

trode (trəʊd) *vb. Archaic.* a past tense of **tread.**

trog (trɒg) *vb.* **trogs, trogging, trogged.** (*intr.*; often foll. by *along*) *Brit. informal.* to walk, esp. aimlessly or heavily; stroll. [C20: perhaps a blend of TRUDGE and SLOG]

troglodyte (ˈtrɒgləˌdaɪt) *n.* **1.** a cave dweller, esp. one of the prehistoric peoples thought to have lived in caves. **2.** *Informal.* a person who lives alone and appears eccentric. [C16: via Latin from Greek *trōglodutēs* one who enters caves, from *trōglē* hole + *duein* to enter] —**troglodytic** (ˌtrɒgləˈdɪtɪk) *or* **ˌtrogloˈdytical** *adj.*

trogon (ˈtrəʊgɒn) *n.* any bird of the order *Trogoniformes* of tropical and subtropical regions of America, Africa, and Asia. They have a brilliant plumage, short hooked bill, and long tail. See also **quetzal.** [C18: from New Latin, from Greek *trōgōn*, from *trōgein* to gnaw]

troika (ˈtrɔɪkə) *n.* **1.** a Russian vehicle drawn by three horses abreast. **2.** three horses harnessed abreast. **3.** a triumvirate. [C19: from Russian, from *troe* three]

troilism (ˈtrɔɪlɪzəm) *n.* sexual activity involving three people. [C20: perhaps from French *trois* three (compare MÉNAGE À TROIS) + *-l-*, as in DUALISM] —ˈ**troilist** *adj.*

Trojan (ˈtrəʊdʒən) *n.* **1.** a native or inhabitant of ancient Troy in NW Asia Minor (the Asian part of present-day Turkey). **2.** a person who is hard-working and determined. ~*adj.* **3.** of or relating to ancient Troy or its inhabitants.

Trojan Horse *n.* **1.** a trap intended to undermine an enemy. **2.** *Computer technol.* a bug inserted into a program or system designed to be activated after a certain time or a certain number of operations. [after the huge wooden horse in Greek mythology inside which Greek attackers entered Troy]

troll[1] (trəʊl) *vb.* **1.** *Angling.* **a.** to draw (a baited line, etc.) through the water, often from a boat. **b.** to fish (a stretch of water) by trolling. **c.** to fish (for) by trolling. **2.** to roll or cause to roll. **3.** *Archaic.* to sing (a refrain, chorus, etc.) or (of a refrain, etc.) to be sung in a loud hearty voice. **4.** (*intr.*) *Brit. informal.* to walk or stroll. **5.** (*intr.*) *Homosexual slang.* to stroll around looking for sexual partners; cruise. ~*n.* **6.** the act or an instance of trolling. **7.** *Angling.* a bait or lure used in trolling, such as a spinner. [C14: from Old French *troller* to run about; related to Middle High German *trollen* to run with short steps] —ˈ**troller** *n.*

troll[2] (trəʊl) *n.* (in Scandinavian folklore) one of a class of supernatural creatures that dwell in caves or mountains and are depicted either as dwarfs or as giants. [C19: from Old Norse: demon; related to Danish *trold*]

trolley (ˈtrɒlɪ) *n.* **1.** *Brit.* a small table on casters used for conveying food, drink, etc. **2.** *Brit.* a wheeled cart or stand pushed by hand and used for moving heavy items, such as shopping in a supermarket or luggage at a railway station. **3.** *Brit.* (in a hospital) a bed mounted on casters and used for moving patients who are unconscious, immobilized, etc. **4.** *Brit.* See **trolley-bus. 5.** *U.S. and Canadian.* See **trolley car. 6.** a device that collects the current from an overhead wire (**trolley wire**), third rail, etc., to drive the motor of an electric vehicle. **7.** a pulley or truck that travels along an overhead wire in order to support a suspended load. **8.** *Chiefly Brit.* a low truck running on rails, used in factories, mines, etc., and on railways. **9.** a truck, cage, or basket suspended from an overhead track or cable for carrying loads in a mine, quarry, etc. **10. off one's trolley.** *Slang.* **a.** mentally confused or disorganized. **b.** insane. [C19: probably from TROLL[1]]

trolleybus (ˈtrɒlɪˌbʌs) *n.* an electrically driven public-transport vehicle that does not run on rails but takes its power from an overhead wire through a trolley.

trolley car *n.* a U.S. and Canadian name for **tram**[1] (sense 1).

trollius (ˈtrɒlɪəs) *n.* See **globeflower.** [New Latin, from German *Trollblume* globeflower]

trollop (ˈtrɒləp) *n.* **1.** a promiscuous woman, esp. a prostitute. **2.** an untidy woman; slattern. [C17: perhaps from German dialect *Trolle* prostitute; perhaps related to TRULL] —ˈ**trollopy** *adj.*

tromba marina (ˈtrɒmbə məˈriːnə) *n.* an obsolete viol with a long thin body and a single string. It resembled the natural trumpet in its range of notes (limited to harmonics) and its tone. [from Italian, literally: marine trumpet]

trombidiasis (ˌtrɒmbɪˈdaɪəsɪs) *n. Pathol.* infestation with mites of the family *Trombiculidae*. [C20: New Latin, from *Trombid(ium)* genus name + -IASIS]

trombone (trɒmˈbəʊn) *n.* **1.** a brass instrument, a low-pitched counterpart of the trumpet, consisting of a tube the effective length of which is varied by means of a U-shaped slide. The usual forms of this instrument are the **tenor trombone** (range: about two and a half octaves upwards from E) and the **bass trombone** (pitched a fourth lower). **2.** a person who plays this instrument in an orchestra. [C18: from Italian, from *tromba* a trumpet, from Old High German *trumba*] —**tromˈbonist** *n.*

trommel (ˈtrɒməl) *n.* a revolving cylindrical sieve used to screen crushed ore. [C19: from German: a drum]

trompe (trɒmp) *n.* an apparatus for supplying the blast of air in a forge, consisting of a thin column down which water falls, drawing in air through side openings. [C19: from French, literally: trumpet]

trompe l'oeil (*French* trɔ̃p lœj) *n., pl.* **trompe l'oeils** (trɔ̃p lœj). **1.** a painting or decoration giving a convincing illusion of reality. **2.** an effect of this kind. [from French, literally: deception of the eye]

tron (trɒn) *n.* **1.** a public weighing machine. **2.** the place where a tron is set up; marketplace. [C15: from Old French *trone*, from Latin *trutina*, from Greek *trutanē* balance, set of scales]

-tron *suffix forming nouns.* **1.** indicating a vacuum tube: *magnetron*. **2.** indicating an instrument for accelerating atomic or subatomic particles: *synchrotron*. [from Greek, suffix indicating instrument]

trona (ˈtrəʊnə) *n.* a greyish mineral that consists of hydrated sodium carbonate and occurs in salt deposits. Formula: $Na_2CO_3NaHCO_3.2H_2O$. [C18: from Swedish, probably from Arabic *natrūn* NATRON]

tronc (trɒŋk) *n.* a pool into which waiters, waitresses, hotel workers, etc., pay their tips and into which some managements pay service charges for later distribution to staff by a **tronc master**, according to agreed percentages. [C20: from French: collecting box]

troop (truːp) *n.* **1.** a large group or assembly; flock: *a troop of children*. **2.** a subdivision of a cavalry squadron or artillery battery of about platoon size. **3.** (*pl.*) armed forces; soldiers. **4.** a large group of Scouts comprising several patrols. **5.** an archaic spelling of **troupe.** ~*vb.* **6.** (*intr.*) to gather, move, or march in or as if in a crowd. **7.** (*tr.*) *Military, chiefly Brit.* to parade (the colour or flag) ceremonially: *trooping the colour*. **8.** (*tr.*) *Brit. military slang.* (formerly) to report (a serviceman) for a breach of discipline. **9.** (*intr.*) an archaic word for **consort** (sense 1). [C16: from French *troupe*, from *troupeau* flock, of Germanic origin]

troop carrier *n.* a vehicle, aircraft, or ship designed for the carriage of troops.

trooper (ˈtruːpə) *n.* **1.** a soldier in a cavalry regiment. **2.** *U.S. and Austral.* a mounted policeman. **3.** *U.S.* a state policeman. **4.** a cavalry horse. **5.** *Informal, chiefly Brit.* a troopship.

troopship (ˈtruːpˌʃɪp) *n.* a ship, usually a converted merchant ship, used to transport military personnel.

troostite (ˈtruːstaɪt) *n.* a reddish or greyish mineral that is a variety of willemite in which some of the zinc is replaced by manganese. [C19: named after Gerard *Troost* (died 1850), U.S. geologist]

trop. *abbrev. for* tropic(al).

tropaeolin (trəʊˈpiːəlɪn) *n.* any of certain yellow and orange azo dyes of complex structure. [C19: see TROPAEOLUM, -IN]

tropaeolum (trəʊˈpiːələm) *n., pl.* **-lums** *or* **-la** (-lə). any garden plant of the genus *Tropaeolum*, esp. the nasturtium. [C18: from New Latin, from Latin *tropaeum* TROPHY; referring to the shield-shaped leaves and helmet-shaped flowers]

trope (trəʊp) *n.* **1.** *Rhetoric.* a word or expression used in a figurative sense. **2.** an interpolation of words or music into the plainsong settings of the Roman Catholic liturgy. [C16: from Latin *tropus* figurative use of a word, from Greek *tropos* style, turn; related to *trepein* to turn]

-trope *n. combining form.* indicating a turning towards, development in the direction of, or affinity to: *heliotrope*. [from Greek *tropos* a turn]

trophallaxis (ˌtrɒfəˈlæksɪs) *n.* the exchange of regurgitated food that occurs between adults and larvae in colonies of social insects. [C19/20: from New Latin, from TROPHO- + Greek *allaxis* exchange, from *allassein* to change, from *allos* other] —ˌ**trophalˈlactic** *adj.*

trophic ('trɒfɪk) *adj.* of or relating to nutrition: *the trophic levels of a food chain.* [C19: from Greek *trophikos,* from *trophē* food, from *trephein* to feed] —'**trophically** *adv.*

tropho- *or before a vowel* **troph-** *combining form.* indicating nourishment or nutrition: *trophozoite.* [from Greek *trophē* food, from *trephein* to feed]

trophoblast ('trɒfəˌblæst) *n.* a membrane that encloses the embryo of placental mammals, becoming attached to the uterus wall and absorbing nourishment from the uterine fluids. [C19: from TROPHO- + -BLAST] —ˌ**tropho'blastic** *adj.*

trophoplasm ('trɒfəˌplæzəm) *n. Biology.* the cytoplasm that is involved in the nutritive processes of a cell.

trophozoite (ˌtrɒfə'zəʊaɪt) *n.* the form of a protozoan of the class *Sporozoa* in the feeding stage. In the malaria parasite this stage occurs in the human red blood cell. Compare **merozoite.**

trophy ('trəʊfɪ) *n., pl.* **-phies. 1.** an object such as a silver or gold cup that is symbolic of victory in a contest, esp. a sporting contest; prize. **2.** a memento of success, esp. one taken in war or hunting. **3.** (in ancient Greece and Rome) **a.** a memorial to a victory, usually consisting of captured arms raised on the battlefield or in a public place. **b.** a representation of such a memorial. **4.** an ornamental carving that represents a group of weapons, etc. [C16: from French *trophée,* from Latin *tropaeum,* from Greek *tropaion,* from *tropē* a turning, defeat of the enemy; related to Greek *trepein* to turn]

-trophy *n. combining form.* indicating a certain type of nourishment or growth: *dystrophy.* [from Greek *-trophia,* from *trophē* nourishment] —**-trophic** *adj. combining form.*

tropic ('trɒpɪk) *n.* **1.** (*sometimes cap.*) either of the parallel lines of latitude at about 23½°N (**tropic of Cancer**) and 23½°S (**tropic of Capricorn**) of the equator. **2. the tropics.** (*often cap.*) that part of the earth's surface between the tropics of Cancer and Capricorn; the Torrid Zone. **3.** *Astronomy.* either of the two parallel circles on the celestial sphere having the same latitudes and names as the corresponding lines on the earth. ~*adj.* **4.** a less common word for **tropical.** [C14: from Late Latin *tropicus* belonging to a turn, from Greek *tropikos,* from *tropos* a turn; from the ancient belief that the sun turned back at the solstices]

-tropic *adj. combining form.* turning or developing in response to a certain stimulus: *heliotropic.* [from Greek *tropos* a turn; see TROPE]

tropical ('trɒpɪkᵊl) *adj.* **1.** situated in, used in, characteristic of, or relating to the tropics. **2.** (of weather) very hot, esp. when humid. **3.** *Rhetoric.* of or relating to a trope. —ˌ**tropi'cality** *n.* —'**tropically** *adv.*

tropicalize *or* **tropicalise** ('trɒpɪkᵊˌlaɪz) *vb.* (*tr.*) to adapt to tropical use, temperatures, etc. —ˌ**tropicali'zation** *or* ˌ**tropicali'sation** *n.*

tropical year *n.* another name for **solar year.** See **year** (sense 4).

tropicbird ('trɒpɪkˌbɜːd) *n.* any aquatic bird of the tropical family *Phaethontidae,* having long slender tail feathers and a white plumage with black markings: order *Pelecaniformes* (pelicans, cormorants, etc.). [C17: so called because it is found in the tropical regions]

tropine ('trəʊpiːn, -pɪn) *n.* a white crystalline poisonous hygroscopic alkaloid obtained by heating atropine or hyoscyamine with barium hydroxide. Formula: $C_8H_{15}NO$. [C19: shortened from ATROPINE]

tropism ('trəʊpɪzəm) *n.* the response of an organism, esp. a plant, to an external stimulus by growth in a direction determined by the stimulus. [from Greek *tropos* a turn] —ˌ**tropis'matic** *adj.* —**tropistic** (trəʊ'pɪstɪk) *adj.*

-tropism *or* **-tropy** *n. combining form.* indicating a tendency to turn or develop in response to a certain stimulus: *phototropism.* [from Greek *tropos* a turn]

tropo- *combining form.* indicating change or a turning: *tropophyte.* [from Greek *tropos* a turn]

tropology (trɒ'pɒlədʒɪ) *n., pl.* **-gies. 1.** *Rhetoric.* the use of figurative language in speech or writing. **2.** *Christian theol.* the educing of moral or figurative meanings from the Scriptures. **3.** a treatise on tropes or figures of speech. [C16: via Late Latin from Greek *tropalogia;* see TROPE, -LOGY] —ˌ**tropo'logic** *or* ˌ**tropo'logical** *adj.*

tropopause ('trɒpəˌpɔːz) *n. Meteorol.* the plane of discontinuity between the troposphere and the stratosphere, characterized by a sharp change in the lapse rate and varying in altitude from about 18 kilometres (11 miles) above the equator to 6 km (4 miles) at the Poles.

tropophilous (trɒ'pɒfɪləs) *adj.* (of plants) able to adapt to seasonal changes in temperature, rainfall, etc.

tropophyte ('trɒpəˌfaɪt) *n.* a plant that is able to adapt to seasonal changes in temperature, rainfall, etc. —**tropophytic** (ˌtrɒpə'fɪtɪk) *adj.*

troposphere ('trɒpəˌsfɪə) *n.* the lowest atmospheric layer, about 18 kilometres (11 miles) thick at the equator to about 6 km (4 miles) at the Poles, in which air temperature decreases normally with height at about 6.5°C per km. Most meteorological phenomena occur in this layer. —ˌ**tropo'spheric** *adj.*

-tropous *adj. combining form.* indicating a turning away: *anatropous.* [from Greek *-tropos* concerning a turn]

troppo[1] ('trɒpəʊ) *adv. Music.* too much; excessively. See **non troppo.** [Italian]

troppo[2] ('trɒpəʊ) *adj. Austral. slang.* mentally affected by a tropical climate.

trot (trɒt) *vb.* **trots, trotting, trotted. 1.** to move or cause to move at a trot. **2.** *Angling.* to fish (a fast-moving stream or river) by using a float and weighted line that carries the baited hook just above the bottom. ~*n.* **3.** a gait of a horse or other quadruped, faster than a walk, in which diagonally opposite legs come down together. See also **jog trot, rising trot, sitting trot. 4.** a steady brisk pace. **5.** (in harness racing) a race for horses that have been trained to trot fast. **6.** *Angling.* **a.** one of the short lines attached to a trotline. **b.** the trotline. **7.** *Austral. and N.Z. informal.* a run of luck: *a good trot.* **8.** *Chiefly Brit.* a small child; tot. **9.** *U.S. slang.* a student's crib. **10. on the trot.** *Informal.* **a.** one after the other: *to read two books on the trot.* **b.** busy, esp. on one's feet. **11. the trots.** *Informal.* **a.** diarrhoea. **b.** *N.Z.* trotting races. [C13: from Old French *trot,* from *troter* to trot, of Germanic origin; related to Middle High German *trotten* to run]

Trot (trɒt) *n. Informal.* a follower of the Russian communist Trotsky; Trotskyite.

troth (trəʊθ) *n. Archaic.* **1.** a pledge or oath of fidelity, esp. a betrothal. **2.** truth (esp. in the phrase **in troth**). **3.** loyalty; fidelity. [Old English *trēowth;* related to Old High German *gitriuwida* loyalty; see TRUTH]

trothplight ('trəʊθˌplaɪt) *Archaic.* ~*n.* **1.** a betrothal. ~*vb.* **2.** (*tr.*) to betroth. ~*adj.* **3.** betrothed; engaged. [C14: from TROTH + PLIGHT[2]]

trotline ('trɒtˌlaɪn) *n. Angling.* a long line suspended across a stream, river, etc., to which shorter hooked and baited lines are attached. Compare **trawl** (sense 2). See also **setline.**

trot out *vb.* (*tr., adv.*) *Informal.* to bring forward, as for approbation or admiration, esp. repeatedly: *he trots out the same excuses every time.*

Trotskyism ('trɒtskɪˌɪzəm) *n.* the theory of communism proposed by the Russian revolutionary Leon Trotsky (1879–1940), in which he called for immediate worldwide revolution by the proletariat. —'**Trotskyite** *or* '**Trotskyist** *n., adj.*

trotter ('trɒtə) *n.* **1.** a person or animal that trots, esp. a horse that is specially trained to trot fast. **2.** (*usually pl.*) the foot of certain animals, esp. of pigs.

trotting race *n.* the N.Z. term for **harness race.**

trotyl ('trəʊtɪl, -tiːl) *n.* another name for **TNT.** [C20: from (TRINI)TROT(OLUENE) + -YL]

troubadour ('truːbəˌdʊə) *n.* **1.** any of a class of lyric poets who flourished principally in Provence, SE France, and in N Italy from the 11th to the 13th centuries, writing chiefly on courtly love in complex metric form. **2.** a singer. [C18: from French, from Old Provençal *trobador,* from *trobar* to write verses, perhaps ultimately from Latin *tropus* TROPE]

trouble ('trʌbᵊl) *n.* **1.** a state or condition of mental distress or anxiety. **2.** a state or condition of disorder or unrest: *industrial trouble.* **3.** a condition of disease, pain, or malfunctioning: *she has liver trouble.* **4.** a cause of distress, disturbance, or pain; problem: *what is the trouble?* **5.** effort or exertion taken to do something: *he took a lot of trouble over this design.* **6.** liability to suffer punishment or misfortune (esp. in the phrase **be in trouble**): *he's in trouble with the police.* **7.** a personal quality that is regarded as a weakness, handicap, or cause of annoyance: *his trouble is that he's too soft.* **8.** (*pl.*) **a.** political unrest or public disturbances. **b. the Troubles.** political violence in Ireland during the 1920s or in Northern Ireland since the late 1960s. **9.** the condition of an unmarried girl who becomes pregnant (esp. in the phrase **in trouble**). ~*vb.* **10.** (*tr.*) to cause trouble to; upset, pain, or worry. **11.** (*intr.;* usually with a negative and foll. by *about*) to put oneself to inconvenience; be concerned: *don't trouble about me.* **12.** (*intr.;* usually with a negative) to take pains; exert oneself: *please don't trouble to write everything down.* **13.** (*tr.*) to cause inconvenience or discomfort to: *does this noise trouble you?* **14.** (*tr.; usually passive*) to agitate or make rough: *the seas were troubled.* **15.** (*tr.*) *Caribbean.* to interfere with: *he wouldn't like anyone to trouble his new bicycle.* [C13: from Old French *troubler,* from Vulgar Latin *turbulāre* (unattested), from Late Latin *turbidāre,* from *turbidus* confused, from *turba* commotion] —'**troubled** *adj.* —'**troubler** *n.*

troublemaker ('trʌbᵊlˌmeɪkə) *n.* a person who makes trouble, esp. between people. —'**troubleˌmaking** *adj., n.*

troubleshooter ('trʌbᵊlˌʃuːtə) *n.* a person who locates the cause of trouble and removes or treats it. —'**troubleˌshooting** *n., adj.*

troublesome ('trʌbᵊlsəm) *adj.* **1.** causing a great deal of trouble; worrying, upsetting, or annoying. **2.** characterized by violence; turbulent. **3.** *Archaic.* agitated or disturbed. —'**troublesomely** *adv.* —'**troublesomeness** *n.*

trouble spot *n.* a place of recurring trouble, esp. of political unrest.

troublous ('trʌbləs) *adj. Archaic or literary.* unsettled; agitated. —'**troublously** *adv.* —'**troublousness** *n.*

trou-de-loup (ˌtruːdᵊ'luː) *n., pl.* **trous-de-loup** (ˌtruːdᵊ'luː). *Military.* any of a series of conical-shaped pits with a stake fixed in the centre, formerly used as protection against enemy cavalry. [C18: from French, literally: wolf's hole]

trough (trɒf) *n.* **1.** a narrow open container, esp. one in which food or water for animals is put. **2.** a narrow channel, gutter, or gulley. **3.** a narrow depression either in the land surface, ocean bed, or between two successive waves. **4.** *Meteorol.* an elongated area of low pressure, esp. an extension of a depression. Compare **ridge** (sense 6). **5.** a single or temporary low point; depression. **6.** *Physics.* the portion of a wave, such as a light wave, in which the amplitude lies below its average value. **7.** *Economics.* the lowest point or most depressed stage of the trade cycle. [Old English *trōh;* related to Old Saxon, Old Norse *trog* trough, Dutch *trügge* ladle] —ˈ**trough,like** *adj.*

trounce (traʊns) *vb.* (*tr.*) to beat or defeat utterly; thrash. [C16: of unknown origin]

troupe (truːp) *n.* **1.** a company of actors or other performers, esp. one that travels. ~*vb.* **2.** (*intr.*) (esp. of actors) to move or travel in a group. [C19: from French; see TROOP]

trouper (ˈtruːpə) *n.* **1.** a member of a troupe. **2.** an experienced or dependable worker or associate.

troupial (ˈtruːpɪəl) *n.* any of various American orioles of the genus *Icterus,* esp. *I. icterus,* a bright orange-and-black South American bird. [C19: from French *troupiale,* from *troupe* flock; referring to its gregarious habits]

trouse (traʊz) *pl. n. Brit.* close-fitting breeches worn in Ireland. [from Irish and Scot. Gaelic *triubhas:* compare TREWS]

trouser (ˈtraʊzə) *n.* (*modifier*) of or relating to trousers: *trouser buttons.*

trousers (ˈtraʊzəz) *pl. n.* **1.** a garment shaped to cover the body from the waist to the ankles or knees with separate tube-shaped sections for both legs. **2. wear the trousers.** *Brit. informal.* to have control, esp. in a marriage. U.S. equivalent: **wear the pants.** [C17: from earlier *trouse,* a variant of TREWS, influenced by DRAWERS] —ˈ**trousered** *adj.* —ˈ**trouserless** *adj.*

trouser suit *n. Chiefly Brit.* a woman's suit of a jacket or top and trousers. Also called (esp. U.S. and Canadian): **pant suit.**

trousseau (ˈtruːsəʊ) *n., pl.* **-seaux** *or* **-seaus** (-səʊz). the clothes, linen, etc., collected by a bride for her marriage. [C19: from Old French, literally: a little bundle, from *trusse* a bundle; see TRUSS]

trout (traʊt) *n., pl.* **trout** *or* **trouts. 1.** any of various game fishes, esp. *Salmo trutta* and related species, mostly of fresh water in northern regions: family *Salmonidae* (salmon). They resemble salmon but are smaller and spotted. **2.** any of various similar or related fishes, such as a sea trout. **3.** *Brit. informal.* a person, esp. an unattractive woman. [Old English *trūht,* from Late Latin *tructa,* from Greek *tröktēs* sharp-toothed fish]

trouvère (truːˈvɛə; *French* truvɛr) *or* **trouveur** (*French* truvœr) *n.* any of a group of poets of N France during the 12th and 13th centuries who composed chiefly narrative works. [C19: from French, from Old French *troveor,* from *trover* to compose; related to TROUBADOUR]

trove (trəʊv) *n.* See **treasure-trove.**

trover (ˈtrəʊvə) *n. Law.* (formerly) the act of wrongfully assuming proprietary rights over personal goods or property belonging to another. [C16: from Old French, from *trover* to find; see TROUVÈRE, TROUBADOUR]

trow (trəʊ) *vb. Archaic.* to think, believe, or trust. [Old English *treow;* related to Old Frisian *triūwe,* Old Saxon *treuwa,* Old High German *triuwa;* see TROTH, TRUE]

trowel (ˈtraʊəl) *n.* **1.** any of various small hand tools having a flat metal blade attached to a handle, used for scooping or spreading plaster or similar materials. **2.** a similar tool with a curved blade used by gardeners for lifting plants, etc. ~*vb.* **-els, -elling, -elled** *or U.S.* **-els, -eling, -eled. 3.** (*tr.*) to use a trowel on (plaster, soil, etc.). [C14: from Old French *truele,* from Latin *trulla* a scoop, from *trua* a stirring spoon] —ˈ**troweller** *or U.S.* ˈ**troweler** *n.*

troy weight *or* **troy** (trɔɪ) *n.* a system of weights used for precious metals and gemstones, based on the grain, which is identical to the avoirdupois grain. 24 grains = 1 pennyweight; 20 pennyweights = 1 (troy) ounce; 12 ounces = 1 (troy) pound. [C14: named after the city of *Troyes,* France, where it was first used]

truant (ˈtruːənt) *n.* **1.** a person who is absent without leave, esp. from school. ~*adj.* **2.** being or relating to a truant. ~*vb.* **3.** (*intr.*) to play truant. [C13: from Old French: vagabond, probably of Celtic origin; compare Welsh *truan* miserable, Old Irish *trōg* wretched] —ˈ**truancy** *n.*

truce (truːs) *n.* **1.** an agreement to stop fighting, esp. temporarily. **2.** temporary cessation of something unpleasant. [C13: from the plural of Old English *treow* TROW; see TRUE, TRUST]

truck[1] (trʌk) *n.* **1.** *Brit.* a vehicle for carrying freight on a railway; wagon. **2.** another name (esp. U.S., Canadian, and Austral.) for **lorry** (sense 1). **3.** a frame carrying two or more pairs of wheels and usually springs and brakes, attached under an end of a railway coach, etc. **4.** *Nautical.* **a.** a disc-shaped block fixed to the head of a mast having sheave holes for receiving signal halyards. **b.** the head of a mast itself. **5.** any wheeled vehicle used to move goods. ~*vb.* **6.** to convey (goods) in a truck. **7.** (*intr.*) *Chiefly U.S. and Canadian.* to drive a truck. [C17: perhaps shortened from TRUCKLE[2]]

truck[2] (trʌk) *n.* **1.** commercial goods. **2.** dealings (esp. in the phrase **have no truck with**). **3.** commercial exchange. **4.** *Archaic.* payment of wages in kind. **5.** miscellaneous articles. **6.** *Informal.* rubbish. **7.** *U.S. and Canadian.* vegetables grown for market. ~*vb.* **8.** *Archaic.* to exchange (goods); barter. **9.** (*intr.*) to traffic or negotiate. [C13: from Old French *troquer* (unattested) to barter, equivalent to Medieval Latin *trocare,* of unknown origin]

truckage (ˈtrʌkɪdʒ) *n. U.S.* **1.** conveyance of cargo by truck. **2.** the charge for this.

trucker[1] (ˈtrʌkə) *n. Chiefly U.S. and Canadian.* **1.** a lorry driver. **2.** a person who arranges for the transport of goods by lorry.

trucker[2] (ˈtrʌkə) *n. U.S. and Canadian.* **1.** a market gardener. **2.** another word for **hawker**[1].

truck farm *n. U.S. and Canadian.* a market garden. —**truck farmer** *n.* —**truck farming** *n.*

truckie (ˈtrʌkɪ) *n. Austral. informal.* a truck driver.

trucking[1] (ˈtrʌkɪŋ) *n. Chiefly U.S. and Canadian.* the transportation of goods by lorry.

trucking[2] (ˈtrʌkɪŋ) *n.* **1.** the usual U.S. and Canadian term for **market gardening. 2.** commercial exchange; barter.

truckle[1] (ˈtrʌkᵊl) *vb.* (*intr.;* usually foll. by *to*) to yield weakly; give in. [C17: from obsolete *truckle* to sleep in a truckle bed; see TRUCKLE[2]] —ˈ**truckler** *n.*

truckle[2] (ˈtrʌkᵊl) *n.* **1.** a small wheel; caster. **2.** a small barrel-shaped cheese. ~*vb.* **3.** (*intr.*) to roll on truckles. **4.** (*tr.*) to push (a piece of furniture) along on truckles. [C15 *trokel,* from Anglo-Norman *trocle,* from Latin *trochlea* sheaf of a pulley; see TROCHLEA]

truckle bed *n.* a low bed on wheels, stored under a larger bed, used esp. formerly by a servant.

truckload (ˈtrʌkˌləʊd) *n.* the amount carried by a truck.

truck system *n.* a system during the early years of the Industrial Revolution of forcing workers to accept payment of wages in kind, usually to the employer's advantage. [C19: from TRUCK[2]]

truculent (ˈtrʌkjʊlənt) *adj.* **1.** defiantly aggressive, sullen, or obstreperous. **2.** *Archaic.* savage, fierce, or harsh. [C16: from Latin *truculentus,* from *trux* fierce] —ˈ**truculence** *or* ˈ**truculency** *n.* —ˈ**truculently** *adv.*

trudge (trʌdʒ) *vb.* **1.** (*intr.*) to walk or plod heavily or wearily. **2.** (*tr.*) to pass through or over by trudging. ~*n.* **3.** a long tiring walk. [C16: of obscure origin] —ˈ**trudger** *n.*

trudgen (ˈtrʌdʒən) *n.* a type of swimming stroke that uses over-arm action, as in the crawl, and a scissors kick. [C19: named after John *Trudgen,* English swimmer, who introduced it]

true (truː) *adj.* **truer, truest. 1.** not false, fictional, or illusory; factual or factually accurate; conforming with reality. **2.** (*prenominal*) being of real or natural origin; genuine; not synthetic: *true leather.* **3. a.** unswervingly faithful and loyal to friends, a cause, etc.: *a true follower.* **b.** (*as collective n.;* preceded by *the*): *the loyal and the true.* **4.** faithful to a particular concept of truth, esp. of religious truth: *a true believer.* **5.** conforming to a required standard, law, or pattern: *a true aim; a true fit.* **6.** exactly in tune: *a true note.* **7.** (of a compass bearing) according to the earth's geographical rather than magnetic poles: *true north.* **8.** *Biology.* conforming to the typical structure of a designated type: *sphagnum moss is a true moss, Spanish moss is not.* **9.** *Physics.* not apparent or relative; taking into account all complicating factors: *the true expansion of a liquid takes into account the expansion of the container.* Compare **apparent** (sense 3). **10. not true.** *Informal.* unbelievable; remarkable: *she's got so much money it's not true.* **11. true to life.** exactly comparable with reality. ~*n.* **12.** correct alignment (esp. in the phrases **in true, out of true**). ~*adv.* **13.** truthfully; rightly. **14.** precisely or unswervingly: *he shot true.* **15.** *Biology.* without variation from the ancestral type: *to breed true.* ~*vb.* **trues, truing, trued. 16.** (*tr.*) to adjust so as to make true. [Old English *triewe;* related to Old Frisian *triūwe,* Old Saxon, Old High German *triuwi* loyal, Old Norse *tryggr;* see TROW, TRUST] —ˈ**trueness** *n.*

true bill *n. Criminal law.* (formerly in Britain; now only U.S.) the endorsement made on a bill of indictment by a grand jury certifying it to be supported by sufficient evidence to warrant committing the accused to trial.

true-blue *adj.* **1.** unwaveringly or staunchly loyal, esp. to a person, a cause, etc. ~*n.* **true blue. 2.** *Chiefly Brit.* a staunch royalist or Conservative.

true-born *adj.* being such by birth: *a true-born Japanese.*

true level *n.* a hypothetical surface that is perpendicular at every point to the plumb line, such as the mean sea level or geoid: *a still liquid surface is at true level.*

true-life *adj.* directly comparable to reality: *a true-life romance.*

truelove (ˈtruːˌlʌv) *n.* **1.** someone truly loved; sweetheart. **2.** another name for **herb Paris.**

truelove knot *or* **true-lovers' knot** *n.* a complicated bowknot that is hard to untie, symbolizing ties of love.

true north *n.* the direction from any point along a meridian towards the North Pole. Also called: **geographic north.** Compare **magnetic north.**

true rib *n.* any of the upper seven pairs of ribs in man.

true time *n.* the time shown by a sundial; solar time. When the sun is at the highest point in its daily path, the true time is exactly noon. Compare **mean time.**

truffle (ˈtrʌfᵊl) *n.* **1.** Also called: **earthnut.** any of various edible saprophytic ascomycetous subterranean fungi of the European genus *Tuber.* They have a tuberous appearance and are regarded as a delicacy. **2.** Also called: **rum truffle.** *Chiefly Brit.* a sweet resembling this fungus in shape, flavoured with chocolate or rum. [C16: from French *truffe,* from Old Provençal *trufa,* ultimately from Latin *tūber*]

trug (trʌg) *n. Brit.* a long shallow basket made of curved strips of wood and used for carrying flowers, fruit, etc. [C16: perhaps dialect variant of TROUGH]

trugo ('truːgəʊ) *n. Austral.* a game similar to croquet, originally improvised in the state of Victoria from the rubber discs used as buffers on railway carriages. [from *true go,* when the wheel is hit between the goal posts]

truism ('truːɪzəm) *n.* an obvious truth; platitude. [C18: from TRUE + -ISM] —**tru'istic** *adj.*

trull (trʌl) *n. Archaic.* a prostitute; harlot. [C16: from German *Trulle;* see TROLLOP]

truly ('truːlɪ) *adv.* **1.** in a true, just, or faithful manner. **2.** (intensifier): *a truly great man.* **3.** indeed; really. ~See also **yours truly.**

trumeau (truː'məʊ) *n., pl.* **-meaux** (-məʊz). *Architect.* a section of a wall or pillar between two openings. [from French]

trump[1] (trʌmp) *n.* **1.** Also called: **trump card. a.** any card from the suit chosen as trumps. **b.** this suit itself; trumps. **2.** Also called: **trump card.** a decisive or advantageous move, resource, action, etc. **3.** *Informal.* a fine or reliable person. ~*vb.* **4.** to play a trump card on (a suit, or a particular card of a suit, that is not trumps). **5.** (*tr.*) to outdo or surpass. ~See also **trumps, trump up.** [C16: variant of TRIUMPH] —**'trumpless** *adj.*

trump[2] (trʌmp) *Archaic or literary.* ~*n.* **1.** a trumpet or the sound produced by one. **2. the last trump.** the final trumpet call that according to the belief of some will awaken and raise the dead on the Day of Judgment. ~*vb.* **3.** (*intr.*) to produce a sound upon or as if upon the trumpet. **4.** (*tr.*) to proclaim or announce with or as if with a fanfare. [C13: from Old French *trompe,* from Old High German *trumpa* trumpet; compare TROMBONE]

trumpery ('trʌmpərɪ) *n., pl.* **-eries. 1.** foolish talk or actions. **2.** a useless or worthless article; trinket. ~*adj.* **3.** useless or worthless. [C15: from Old French *tromperie* deceit, from *tromper* to cheat]

trumpet ('trʌmpɪt) *n.* **1.** a valved brass instrument of brilliant tone consisting of a narrow tube of cylindrical bore ending in a flared bell, normally pitched in B flat. Range: two and a half octaves upwards from F sharp on the fourth line of the bass staff. **2.** any instrument consisting of a valveless tube ending in a bell, esp. a straight instrument used for fanfares, signals, etc. **3.** a person who plays a trumpet in an orchestra. **4.** a loud sound such as that of a trumpet, esp. when made by an animal: *the trumpet of the elephants.* **5.** an eight-foot reed stop on an organ. **6.** something resembling a trumpet in shape, esp. in having a flared bell. **7.** short for **ear trumpet. 8. blow one's own trumpet.** to boast about oneself; brag. ~*vb.* **-pets, -peting, -peted. 9.** to proclaim or sound loudly. [C13: from Old French *trompette* a little TRUMP[2]] —**'trumpet-,like** *adj.*

trumpeter ('trʌmpɪtə) *n.* **1.** a person who plays the trumpet, esp. one whose duty it is to play fanfares, signals, etc. **2.** any of three birds of the genus *Psophia* of the forests of South America, having a rounded body, long legs, and a glossy blackish plumage: family *Psophiidae,* order *Gruiformes* (cranes, rails, etc.). **3.** (*sometimes cap.*) a breed of domestic fancy pigeon with a long ruff.

trumpeter swan *n.* a large swan, *Cygnus buccinator,* of W North America, having a white plumage and black bill.

trumpet flower *n.* **1.** any of various plants having trumpet-shaped flowers. **2.** the flower of any of these plants.

trumpet honeysuckle *n.* a North American honeysuckle shrub, *Lonicera sempervirens,* having orange, scarlet, or yellow trumpet-shaped flowers.

trumpetweed ('trʌmpɪt,wiːd) *n. U.S.* any of various eupatorium plants, esp. joe-pye weed. [C19: so called because it has a hollow stem which children sometimes use as imitation trumpets]

trumps (trʌmps) *pl. n.* **1.** (*sometimes sing.*) *Cards.* any one of the four suits, decided by cutting or bidding, that outranks all the other suits for the duration of a deal or game. **2. turn up trumps.** (of a person) to bring about a happy or successful conclusion (to an event, problem, etc.), esp. unexpectedly.

trump up *vb.* (*tr., adv.*) to concoct or invent (a charge, accusation, etc.) so as to deceive or implicate someone.

truncate *vb.* (trʌŋ'keɪt, 'trʌŋkeɪt). **1.** (*tr.*) to shorten by cutting off a part, end, or top. ~*adj.* ('trʌŋkeɪt). **2.** cut short; truncated. **3.** *Biology.* having a blunt end, as though cut off at the tip: *a truncate leaf.* [C15: from Latin *truncāre* to lop] —**'truncately** *adv.* —**trun'cation** *n.*

truncated (trʌŋ'keɪtɪd) *adj.* **1.** *Maths.* (of a cone, pyramid, prism, etc.) having an apex or end removed by a plane intersection that is usually nonparallel to the base. **2.** (of a crystal) having edges or corners cut off. **3.** shortened by or as if by cutting off; truncate.

truncheon ('trʌntʃən) *n.* **1.** *Chiefly Brit.* a short thick club or cudgel carried by a policeman. **2.** a baton of office: *a marshal's truncheon.* **3.** *Archaic.* a short club or cudgel. **4.** the shaft of a spear. ~*vb.* **5.** (*tr.*) to beat with a truncheon. [C16: from Old French *tronchon* stump, from Latin *truncus* trunk; see TRUNCATE]

trundle ('trʌndᵊl) *vb.* **1.** to move heavily on or as if on wheels: *the bus trundled by.* **2.** (*tr.*) *Archaic.* to rotate or spin. ~*n.* **3.** the act or an instance of trundling. **4.** a small wheel or roller. **5. a.** the pinion of a lantern. **b.** any of the bars in a lantern pinion. **6.** a small truck with low wheels. [Old English *tryndel;* related to Middle High German *trendel* disc]

trundle bed *n.* a less common word for **truckle bed.**

trundler ('trʌndlə) *n. N.Z.* **1.** a golf bag or shopping trolley. **2.** a child's pushchair.

trunk (trʌŋk) *n.* **1.** the main stem of a tree, usually thick and upright, covered with bark and having branches at some distance from the ground. **2.** a large strong case or box used to contain clothes and other personal effects when travelling and for storage. **3.** *Anatomy.* the body excluding the head, neck, and limbs; torso. **4.** the elongated prehensile nasal part of an elephant; proboscis. **5.** the U.S. and Canadian name for **boot**[1] (sense 2). **6.** *Anatomy.* the main stem of a nerve, blood vessel, etc. **7.** *Nautical.* a watertight boxlike cover within a vessel with its top above the waterline, such as one used to enclose a centreboard. **8.** an enclosed duct or passageway for ventilation, etc. **9.** (*modifier*) of or relating to a main road, railway, etc., in a network: *a trunk line.* ~See also **trunks.** [C15: from Old French *tronc,* from Latin *truncus,* from *truncus* (adj.) lopped] —**'trunk,ful** *n.* —**'trunkless** *adj.*

trunk cabin *n. Nautical.* a long relatively low cabin above the deck of a yacht.

trunk call *n. Chiefly Brit.* a long-distance telephone call.

trunk curl *n.* another name for **sit-up.**

trunkfish ('trʌŋk,fɪʃ) *n., pl.* **-fish** *or* **-fishes.** any tropical plectognath fish of the family *Ostraciidae,* having the body encased in bony plates with openings for the fins, eyes, mouth, etc. Also called: **boxfish, cowfish.**

trunk hose *n.* a man's puffed-out breeches reaching to the thighs and worn with tights in the 16th century. [C17: of uncertain origin; perhaps from the obsolete *trunk* to truncate]

trunking ('trʌŋkɪŋ) *n.* **1.** *Telecomm.* the cables that take a common route through an exchange building linking ranks of selectors. **2.** plastic housing used to conceal wires, etc.; casing. **3.** the delivery of goods over long distances, esp. by road vehicles to local distribution centres, from which deliveries and collections are made.

trunk line *n.* **1.** a direct link between two telephone exchanges or switchboards that are a considerable distance apart. **2.** the main route or routes on a railway.

trunk road *n. Brit.* a main road, esp. one that is suitable for heavy vehicles.

trunks (trʌŋks) *pl. n.* **1.** Also called: **swimming trunks.** a man's garment worn for swimming, either fairly loose and extending from the waist to the thigh or briefer and close-fitting. **2.** shorts worn for some sports. **3.** *Chiefly Brit.* men's underpants with legs that reach midthigh.

trunnel ('trʌnᵊl) *n.* a variant spelling of **treenail.**

trunnion ('trʌnjən) *n.* **1.** one of a pair of coaxial projections attached to opposite sides of a container, cannon, etc., to provide a support about which it can turn in a vertical. **2.** the structure supporting such a projection. [C17: from Old French *trognon* trunk] —**'trunnioned** *adj.*

truss (trʌs) *vb.* (*tr.*) **1.** (sometimes foll. by *up*) to tie, bind, or bundle: *to truss up a prisoner.* **2.** to fasten or bind the wings and legs of (a fowl) before cooking to keep them in place. **3.** to support or stiffen (a roof, bridge, etc.) with structural members. **4.** *Informal.* to confine (the body or a part of it) in tight clothes. **5.** *Falconry.* (of falcons) to hold (the quarry) in the stoop without letting go. **6.** *Med.* to supply or support with a truss. ~*n.* **7.** a structural framework of wood or metal, esp. one arranged in triangles, used to support a roof, bridge, etc. **8.** *Med.* a device for holding a hernia in place, typically consisting of a pad held in position by a belt. **9.** *Horticulture.* a cluster of flowers or fruit growing at the end of a single stalk. **10.** *Nautical.* a metal fitting fixed to a yard at its centre for holding it to a mast while allowing movement. **11.** *Architect.* another name for **corbel. 12.** a bundle or pack. **13.** *Chiefly Brit.* a bundle of hay or straw, esp. one having a fixed weight of 36, 56, or 60 pounds. [C13: from Old French *trousse,* from *trousser,* apparently from Vulgar Latin *torciāre* (unattested), from *torca* (unattested) a bundle, TORCH] —**'trusser** *n.*

truss bridge *n.* a bridge that is constructed of trusses.

trussing ('trʌsɪŋ) *n. Engineering.* **1.** a system of trusses, esp. for strengthening or reinforcing a structure. **2.** the parts or members that form a truss.

trust (trʌst) *n.* **1.** reliance on and confidence in the truth, worth, reliability, etc., of a person or thing; faith. Related adj.: **fiducial. 2.** a group of commercial enterprises combined to monopolize and control the market for any commodity: illegal in the U.S. **3.** the obligation of someone in a responsible position: *a position of trust.* **4.** custody, charge, or care: *a child placed in my trust.* **5.** a person or thing in which confidence or faith is placed. **6.** commercial credit. **7. a.** an arrangement whereby a person to whom the legal title to property is conveyed (the trustee) holds such property for the benefit of those entitled to the beneficial interest. **b.** property that is the subject of such an arrangement. **c.** the confidence put in the trustee. Related adj.: **fiduciary. 8.** See **trust company, trust account** (sense 2). **9.** (*modifier*) of or relating to a trust or trusts: *trust property.* ~*vb.* **10.** (*tr.; may take a clause as object*) to expect, hope, or suppose: *I trust that you are well.* **11.** (when *tr., may take an infinitive;* when *intr.,* often foll. by *in* or *to*) to place confidence in (someone to do something);

have faith (in); rely (upon): *I trust him to tell her.* 12. (*tr.*) to consign for care: *the child was trusted to my care.* 13. (*tr.*) to allow (someone to do something) with confidence in his or her good sense or honesty: *I trust my daughter to go.* 14. (*tr.*) to extend business credit to. [C13: from Old Norse *traust;* related to Old High German *Trost* solace] —'**trustable** *adj.* —ˌ**trustaˈbility** *n.* —'**truster** *n.*

trust account *n.* 1. Also called: **trustee account.** a savings account deposited in the name of a trustee who controls it during his lifetime, after which the balance is payable to a prenominated beneficiary. 2. property under the control of a trustee or trustees.

trustbuster ('trʌstˌbʌstə) *n. U.S. informal.* a person who seeks the dissolution of corporate trusts, esp. a federal official who prosecutes trusts under the antitrust laws. —'**trustˌbusting** *n.*

trust company *n.* a commercial bank or other enterprise organized to perform trustee functions. Also called: **trust corporation.**

trust deed *n.* a document that transfers the legal title to property to a trustee.

trustee (trʌ'stiː) *n.* 1. a person to whom the legal title to property is entrusted to hold or use for another's benefit. 2. a member of a board that manages the affairs and administers the funds of an institution or organization.

trustee in bankruptcy *n.* a person entrusted with the administration of a bankrupt's affairs and with realizing his assets for the benefit of the creditors.

trustee investment *n. Stock Exchange.* an investment in which trustees are authorized to invest money belonging to a trust fund.

trusteeship (trʌ'stiːʃɪp) *n.* 1. the office or function of a trustee. 2. a. the administration or government of a territory by a foreign country under the supervision of the **Trusteeship Council** of the United Nations. b. (*often cap.*) any such dependent territory; trust territory.

trustful ('trʌstfʊl) *or* **trusting** *adj.* characterized by a tendency or readiness to trust others. —'**trustfully** *or* '**trustingly** *adv.* —'**trustfulness** *or* '**trustingness** *n.*

trust fund *n.* money, securities, etc., held in trust.

trust hotel *or* **tavern** *n. N.Z.* a licensed hotel or a bar owned by a publicly elected committee as trustees, the profits of which go to public amenities.

trustless ('trʌstlɪs) *adj. Archaic or literary.* 1. untrustworthy; deceitful. 2. distrusting; suspicious; wary. —'**trustlessly** *adv.* —'**trustlessness** *n.*

trust territory *n.* (*sometimes cap.*) another name for a **trusteeship** (sense 2).

trustworthy ('trʌstˌwɜːðɪ) *adj.* worthy of being trusted; honest, reliable, or dependable. —'**trustˌworthily** *adv.* —'**trustˌworthiness** *n.*

trusty ('trʌstɪ) *adj.* **trustier, trustiest.** 1. faithful or reliable. 2. *Archaic.* trusting. ~*n., pl.* **trusties.** 3. someone who is trusted, esp. a convict to whom special privileges are granted. —'**trustily** *adv.* —'**trustiness** *n.*

truth (truːθ) *n.* 1. the quality of being true, genuine, actual, or factual: *the truth of his statement was attested.* 2. something that is true as opposed to false: *you did not tell me the truth.* 3. a proven or verified principle or statement; fact: *the truths of astronomy.* 4. (*usually pl.*) a system of concepts purporting to represent some aspect of the world: *the truths of ancient religions.* 5. fidelity to a required standard or law. 6. faithful reproduction or portrayal: *the truth of a portrait.* 7. an obvious fact; truism; platitude. 8. honesty, reliability, or veracity: *the truth of her nature.* 9. accuracy, as in the setting, adjustment, or position of something, such as a mechanical instrument. 10. the state or quality of being faithful; allegiance. ~Related adjs.: **veritable, veracious.** [Old English *triewth;* related to Old High German *gitriuwida* fidelity, Old Norse *tryggr* true] —'**truthless** *adj.*

truth-condition *n. Logic, philosophy.* 1. the circumstances under which a statement is true. 2. a statement of these circumstances: sometimes identified with the meaning of the statement.

truth drug *or* **serum** *n. Informal.* any of various drugs supposed to have the property of making people tell the truth, as by relaxing them.

truthful ('truːθfʊl) *adj.* 1. telling or expressing the truth; honest or candid. 2. realistic: *a truthful portrayal of the king.* —'**truthfully** *adv.* —'**truthfulness** *n.*

truth-function *n. Logic.* 1. a function that determines the truth-value of a complex sentence solely in terms of the truth-values of the component sentences without reference to their meaning. 2. a complex sentence whose truth-value is so determined, such as a negation or conjunction.

truth set *n.* 1. *Logic, maths.* Also called: **solution set.** the set of values that satisfy an open sentence, equation, inequality, etc., having no unique solution. 2. *Logic.* the set of possible worlds in which a statement is true.

truth table *n.* 1. a table, used in logic, indicating the truth-value of a compound statement for every truth-value of its component propositions. 2. a similar table, used in transistor technology, to indicate the value of the output signal of a logic circuit for every value of input signal.

truth-value *n. Logic.* a. either of the values, true or false, that may be taken by a statement. b. by analogy, any of the values that a semantic theory may accord to a statement.

truth-value gap *n. Logic.* the possibility in certain semantic systems of a statement being neither true nor false while also not being determinately of any third truth-value, as *all my children are asleep* uttered by a childless person.

try (traɪ) *vb.* **tries, trying, tried.** 1. (when *tr., may take an infinitive,* sometimes with *to* replaced by *and*) to make an effort or attempt: *he tried to climb a cliff.* 2. (*tr.;* often foll. by *out*) to sample, test, or give experimental use to (something) in order to determine its quality, worth, etc.: *try her cheese flan.* 3. (*tr.*) to put strain or stress on: *he tries my patience.* 4. (*tr.; often passive*) to give pain, affliction, or vexation to: *I have been sorely tried by those children.* 5. a. to examine and determine the issues involved in (a cause) in a court of law. b. to hear evidence in order to determine the guilt or innocence of (an accused). c. to sit as judge at the trial of (an issue or person). 6. (*tr.*) to melt (fat, lard, etc.) in order to separate out impurities. 7. (*tr.;* usually foll. by *out*) *Obsolete.* to extract (a material) from an ore, mixture, etc., usually by heat; refine. ~*n., pl.* **tries.** 8. an experiment or trial. 9. an attempt or effort. 10. *Rugby.* the act of an attacking player touching the ball down behind the opposing team's goal line, scoring four or, in Rugby League, three points. 11. Also called: **try for a point.** *American football.* an attempt made after a touchdown to score an extra point by kicking a goal or, for two extra points, by running the ball or completing a pass across the opponents' goal line. [C13: from Old French *trier* to sort, sift, of uncertain origin]

trying ('traɪɪŋ) *adj.* upsetting, difficult, or annoying: *a trying day at the office.* —'**tryingly** *adv.* —'**tryingness** *n.*

trying plane *n.* a plane with a long body for planing the edges of long boards.

tryma ('traɪmə) *n., pl.* **-mata** (-mətə). *Botany.* a drupe produced by the walnut and similar plants, in which the endocarp is a hard shell and the epicarp is dehiscent. [C19: from New Latin, from Greek *truma* a hole (referring to the hollow drupe), from *truein* to wear away]

try on *vb.* (*tr., adv.*) 1. to put on (an article of clothing) to find out whether it fits or is suitable. 2. **try it on.** *Informal.* to attempt to deceive or fool someone. ~*n.* **try-on.** 3. *Brit. informal.* an action or statement made to test out a person's gullibility, tolerance, etc.

try out *vb.* (*adv.*) 1. (*tr.*) to test or put to experimental use: *I'm going to try the new car out.* 2. (when *intr.,* usually foll. by *for*) *U.S. and Canadian.* (of an athlete, actor, etc.) to undergo a test or to submit (an athlete, actor, etc.) to a test to determine suitability for a place in a team, an acting role, etc. ~*n.* **tryout.** 3. *Chiefly U.S. and Canadian.* a trial or test, as of an athlete or actor.

trypan blue ('trɪpən, 'trɪpæn, trɪ'pæn) *n.* a dye obtained from tolidine that is absorbed by the macrophages of the reticuloendothelial system and is therefore used for staining cells in biological research. [so called because it is *trypanocidal:* see TRYPANOSOME, -CIDE]

trypanosome ('trɪpənəˌsəʊm) *n.* any parasitic protozoan of the genus *Trypanosoma,* which lives in the blood of vertebrates, is transmitted by certain insects, and causes sleeping sickness and certain other diseases: class *Mastigophora* (or *Flagellata*). [C19: from New Latin *Trypanosoma,* from Greek *trupanon* borer + *sōma* body] —ˌ**trypano'somal** *or* **trypanosomic** (ˌtrɪpənə'sɒmɪk) *adj.*

trypanosomiasis (ˌtrɪpənəsə'maɪəsɪs) *n.* any infection of an animal or human with a trypanosome. See also **sleeping sickness, Chagas' disease.**

tryparsamide (trɪ'pɑːsəmɪd) *n.* a synthetic crystalline compound of arsenic used in the treatment of trypanosomal and other protozoan infections. Formula: $C_8H_{10}AsN_2O_4Na.\frac{1}{2}H_2O$. [C20: from a trademark]

trypsin ('trɪpsɪn) *n.* an enzyme occurring in pancreatic juice: it catalyses the hydrolysis of proteins to peptides and is secreted from the pancreas in the form of trypsinogen. See also **chymotrypsin.** [C19 *tryp-,* from Greek *tripsis* a rubbing, from *tribein* to rub + -IN; referring to the fact that it was originally produced by rubbing the pancreas with glycerin] —**tryptic** ('trɪptɪk) *adj.*

trypsinogen (trɪp'sɪnədʒən) *n.* the inactive precursor of trypsin that is converted to trypsin by the enzyme enterokinase.

tryptophan ('trɪptəˌfæn) *n.* an essential amino acid; a component of proteins necessary for growth. [C20: from TRYPT(IC) + -O- + *-phan,* variant of -PHANE]

trysail ('traɪˌseɪl; *Nautical* 'traɪsᵊl) *n.* a small fore-and-aft sail, triangular or square, set on the mainmast of a sailing vessel in foul weather to help keep her head to the wind. Also called: **storm trysail.**

try square *n.* a device for testing or laying out right angles, consisting of a grooved metal ruler along which a movable frame runs, one edge of the frame always being perpendicular to the ruler.

tryst (trɪst, traɪst) *Archaic or literary.* ~*n.* 1. an appointment to meet, esp. secretly. 2. the place of such a meeting or the meeting itself. ~*vb.* 3. (*intr.*) to meet at or arrange a tryst. [C14: from Old French *triste* lookout post, apparently of Scandinavian origin; compare Old Norse *traust* trust] —'**tryster** *n.*

tsade ('tsɑːdiː, 'sɑː-; *Hebrew* 'tsadi) *n.* a variant spelling of **sadhe.**

tsar *or* **czar** (zɑː) *n.* **1.** (until 1917) the emperor of Russia. **2.** a tyrant; autocrat. **3.** *Informal.* a person in authority; leader. **4.** (formerly) any of several S Slavonic rulers, such as any of the princes of Serbia in the 14th century. ~Also (less commonly) **tzar.** [from Russian *tsar,* via Gothic *kaisar* from Latin *Caesar,* Roman emperor] —**'tsardom** *or* **'czardom** *n.*

tsarevitch *or* **czarevitch** ('zɑːrəvɪtʃ) *n.* a son of a Russian tsar, esp. the eldest son. [from Russian *tsarevich,* from TSAR + *-evich,* masculine patronymic suffix]

tsarevna *or* **czarevna** (zɑː'rɛvnə) *n.* **1.** a daughter of a Russian tsar. **2.** the wife of a Russian tsarevitch. [from Russian, from TSAR + *-evna,* feminine patronymic suffix]

tsarina, czarina (zɑː'riːnə) *or* **tsaritsa, czaritza** (zɑː'rɪtsə) *n.* the wife of a Russian tsar; Russian empress. [from Russian, from TSAR + *-ina,* feminine suffix]

tsarism *or* **czarism** ('zɑːrɪzəm) *n.* **1.** a system of government by a tsar, esp. in Russia until 1917. **2.** absolute rule; dictatorship. —**'tsarist** *or* **'czarist** *n., adj.*

TSB *abbrev. for* Trustee Savings Bank.

TSE *abbrev. for* transmissible spongiform encephalopathy: any of a group of degenerative brain diseases, including BSE in cattle, that can be transmitted from one individual or species to another.

tsetse fly *or* **tzetze fly** ('tsɛtsɪ) *n.* any of various bloodsucking African dipterous flies of the genus *Glossina,* which transmit the pathogens of various diseases: family *Muscidae.* [C19: via Afrikaans from Tswana]

TSH *abbrev. for* thyroid-stimulating hormone; another name for **thyrotropin.**

Tshiluba (tʃɪ'luːbə) *n.* the language of the Luba people, used as a trade language in Zaïre. See **Luba.**

T-shirt *or* **tee shirt** *n.* a lightweight simple garment for the upper body, usually short-sleeved. [so called because of its shape]

tsitsith ('tsɪtsɪs, tsiː'tsiːt) *n.* (*functioning as sing. or pl.*) *Judaism.* the tassels or fringes of thread attached to the four corners of the tallith. [from Hebrew *sīsīth*]

Tsonga ('tsɒŋgə) *n.* **1.** (*pl.* **-ga** *or* **-gas**) a member of a Negroid people of S Mozambique, Swaziland, and South Africa. **2.** the language of this people, belonging to the Bantu group of the Niger-Congo family.

tsotsi ('tsɒtsɪ, 'tsɔː-) *n., pl.* **-tsis.** *S. African informal.* a violent usually young criminal who operates mainly in Black African townships and lives by his wits. [C20: of unknown origin; probably from a Bantu language]

tsp. *abbrev. for* teaspoon.

T-square *n.* a T-shaped ruler used in mechanical drawing, consisting of a short crosspiece, which slides along the edge of the drawing board, and a long horizontal piece: used for drawing horizontal lines and to support set squares when drawing vertical and inclined lines.

T-stop *n.* a setting of the lens aperture on a camera calibrated photometrically and assigned a T-number.

T-strap *n.* (*modifier*) denoting a type of woman's shoe fastened with a T-shaped strap having one part passing across the ankle and the other attached to it in the middle and lying along the length of the foot. Also called: **T-bar.**

tsunami (tsʊ'næmɪ) *n., pl.* **-mis** *or* **-mi.** a large, often destructive, sea wave produced by a submarine earthquake, subsidence, or volcanic eruption. Sometimes incorrectly called a tidal wave. [from Japanese, from *tsu* port + *nami* wave]

tsutsugamushi disease (ˌtsʊtsʊgə'mʊʃɪ) *n.* **1.** one of the five major groups of acute infectious rickettsial diseases affecting man, common in Asia and including scrub typhus. It is caused by the microorganism *Rickettsia tsutsugamushi,* transmitted by the bite of mites. **2.** another name for **scrub typhus.** [from Japanese, from *tsutsuga* disease + *mushi* insect]

Tswana ('tswɑːnə) *n.* **1.** (*pl.* **-na** *or* **-nas**) a member of a mixed Negroid and Bushman people of the Sotho group of southern Africa, living chiefly in Botswana. **2.** the language of this people, belonging to the Bantu group of the Niger-Congo family: the principal language of Botswana.

TT *abbrev. for:* **1.** teetotal. **2.** teetotaller. **3.** telegraphic transfer: a method of sending money abroad by cabled transfer between banks. **4.** Tourist Trophy (annual motorcycle races held in the Isle of Man). **5.** tuberculin-tested. ~**6.** *international car registration for* Trinidad and Tobago.

TTL *abbrev. for:* **1.** transistor transistor logic: a method of constructing electronic logic circuits. **2.** through-the-lens: denoting a system of light metering in cameras.

TU *abbrev. for* trade union.

Tu. *abbrev. for* Tuesday.

tuan[1] ('tuːɑːn) *n.* (in Malay-speaking countries) sir; lord: a form of address used as a mark of respect. [Malay]

tuan[2] ('tuːən, 'tjuː-) *n.* a flying phalanger, *Phascogale tapoatafa,* of Australia. It is about the size of a rat, bluish grey in colour, brush-tailed, arboreal, and nocturnal. Also called: **wambenger, brush-tailed phascogale.** [C19: from a native Australian language]

Tuareg ('twɑːrɛg) *n.* **1.** (*pl.* **-reg** *or* **-regs**) a member of a nomadic Berber people of the Sahara desert, N Africa. **2.** the dialect of Berber spoken by this people.

tuart ('tuːɑːt) *n.* a eucalyptus tree, *Eucalyptus gomphocephala,* of Australia, yielding a very durable light-coloured timber. [from a native Australian language]

tuatara (ˌtuːə'tɑːrə) *n.* a greenish-grey lizard-like rhynchocephalian reptile, *Sphenodon punctatus,* occurring only on certain small islands near New Zealand: it is the sole surviving member of a group common in Mesozoic times. [C19: from Maori, from *tua* back + *tara* spine]

tub (tʌb) *n.* **1.** a low wide open container, typically round, originally one made of wood and used esp. for washing: now made of wood, plastic, metal, etc., and used in a variety of domestic and industrial situations. **2.** a small plastic or cardboard container of similar shape for ice cream, margarine, etc. **3.** Also called: **bathtub.** another word (esp. U.S. and Canadian) for **bath**[1] (sense 1). **4.** Also called: **tubful.** the amount a tub will hold. **5.** a clumsy slow boat or ship. **6.** *Informal.* (in rowing) a heavy wide boat used for training novice oarsmen. **7. a.** Also called: **tram, hutch.** a small vehicle on rails for carrying loads in a mine. **b.** a container for lifting coal or ore up a mine shaft; skip. ~*vb.* **tubs, tubbing, tubbed. 8.** *Brit. informal.* to wash (oneself or another) in a tub. **9.** (*tr.*) to keep or put in a tub. [C14: from Middle Dutch *tubbe*] —**'tubbable** *adj.* —**'tubber** *n.*

tuba ('tjuːbə) *n., pl.* **-bas** *or* **-bae** (-biː). **1.** a valved brass instrument of bass pitch, in which the bell points upwards and the mouthpiece projects at right angles. The tube is of conical bore and the mouthpiece cup-shaped. **2.** any other bass brass instrument such as the euphonium, helicon, etc. **3.** a powerful reed stop on an organ. **4.** a form of trumpet of ancient Rome. [Latin]

tubal ('tjuːbəl) *adj.* **1.** of or relating to a tube. **2.** of, relating to, or developing in a Fallopian tube: *a tubal pregnancy.*

tubate ('tjuːbeɪt) *adj.* a less common word for **tubular.**

tubby ('tʌbɪ) *adj.* **-bier, -biest. 1.** plump. **2.** shaped like a tub. **3.** *Rare.* having little resonance. —**'tubbiness** *n.*

tube (tjuːb) *n.* **1.** a long hollow and typically cylindrical object, used for the passage of fluids or as a container. **2.** a collapsible cylindrical container of soft metal or plastic closed with a cap, used to hold viscous liquids or pastes. **3.** *Anatomy.* **a.** short for **Eustachian tube** or **Fallopian tube. b.** any hollow cylindrical structure. **4.** *Botany.* **a.** the lower part of a gamopetalous corolla or gamosepalous calyx, below the lobes. **b.** any other hollow structure in a plant. **5.** (*sometimes cap.*) *Brit.* **a. the tube.** Also called: **the underground.** an underground railway system, esp. that in London. U.S. and Canadian equivalent: **subway. b.** the tunnels through which the railway runs. **c.** the train itself. **6.** *Electronics.* **a.** another name for **valve** (sense 3). **b.** See **electron tube, cathode-ray tube, television tube. 7.** (preceded by *the*) *Slang.* a television set. **8.** *Austral. slang.* a bottle or can of beer. **9.** *Surfing.* the cylindrical passage formed when a wave breaks and the crest tips forward. **10.** an archaic word for **telescope.** ~*vb.* (*tr.*) **11.** to fit or supply with a tube or tubes. **12.** to carry or convey in a tube. **13.** to shape like a tube. [C17: from Latin *tubus*] —**'tubeless** *adj.*

tube fly *n. Angling.* an artificial fly with the body tied on a hollow tube that can slide up the leader when a fish takes.

tube foot *n.* any of numerous tubular outgrowths of the body wall of most echinoderms that are used as organs of locomotion and respiration and to aid ingestion of food.

tubeless tyre *n.* a pneumatic tyre in which the outer casing makes an airtight seal with the rim of the wheel so that an inner tube is unnecessary.

tuber ('tjuːbə) *n.* **1.** a fleshy underground stem (as in the potato) or root (as in the dahlia) that is an organ of vegetative reproduction and food storage. **2.** *Anatomy.* a raised area; swelling. [C17: from Latin *tūber* hump]

tubercle ('tjuːbəkəl) *n.* **1.** any small rounded nodule or elevation, esp. on the skin, on a bone, or on a plant. **2.** any small rounded pathological lesion of the tissues, esp. one characteristic of tuberculosis. [C16: from Latin *tūberculum* a little swelling, diminutive of TUBER]

tubercle bacillus *n.* a rodlike Gram-positive bacterium, *Mycobacterium tuberculosis,* that causes tuberculosis: family *Mycobacteriaceae.*

tubercular (tjʊ'bɜːkjʊlə) *adj.* **1.** of, relating to, or symptomatic of tuberculosis. **2.** of or relating to a tubercle or tubercles. **3.** characterized by the presence of tubercles. ~*n.* **4.** a person with tuberculosis. —**tu'bercularly** *adv.*

tuberculate (tjʊ'bɜːkjʊlɪt) *adj.* covered with tubercles. —**tu'berculately** *adv.* —**tuˌbercu'lation** *n.*

tuberculin (tjʊ'bɜːkjʊlɪn) *n.* a sterile liquid prepared from cultures of attenuated tubercle bacillus and used in the diagnosis of tuberculosis.

tuberculin-tested *adj.* (of milk) produced by cows that have been certified as free of tuberculosis.

tuberculosis (tjʊˌbɜːkjʊ'ləʊsɪs) *n.* a communicable disease caused by infection with the tubercle bacillus, most frequently affecting the lungs (**pulmonary tuberculosis**). Also called: **consumption, phthisis.** Abbrev.: **TB.** [C19: from New Latin; see TUBERCLE, -OSIS]

tuberculous (tjʊ'bɜːkjʊləs) *adj.* of or relating to tuberculosis or tubercles; tubercular. —**tu'berculously** *adv.*

tuberose *n.* ('tjuːbəˌrəʊz) **1.** a perennial Mexican agave plant, *Polianthes tuberosa,* having a tuberous root and spikes of white fragrant lily-like flowers. ~*adj.* ('tjuːbəˌrəʊs). **2.** a variant of

tuberous. [C17: from Latin *tūberōsus* full of lumps; referring to its root]
tuberosity (ˌtjuːbəˈrɒsɪtɪ) *n., pl.* **-ties.** any protuberance on a bone, esp. for the attachment of a muscle or ligament.
tuberous (ˈtjuːbərəs) *or* **tuberose** (ˈtjuːbəˌrəʊs) *adj.* **1.** (of plants or their parts) forming, bearing, or resembling a tuber or tubers: *a tuberous root.* **2.** *Anatomy.* of, relating to, or having warty protuberances or tubers. [C17: from Latin *tūberōsus* full of knobs; see TUBER]
tube worm *n.* any of various polychaete worms that construct and live in a tube made of sand, lime, etc.
tubicolous (tjuːˈbɪkələs) *adj.* (of certain invertebrate animals) living in a self-constructed tube.
tubifex (ˈtjuːbɪˌfɛks) *n., pl.* **-fex** *or* **-fexes.** any small reddish freshwater oligochaete worm of the genus *Tubifex;* it characteristically lives in a tube in sand and is used as food for aquarium fish. [C19: from New Latin, from Latin *tubus* tube + *facere* to make, do]
tubing (ˈtjuːbɪŋ) *n.* **1.** tubes collectively. **2.** a length of tube. **3.** a system of tubes. **4.** fabric in the form of a tube, used for pillowcases and some cushions; piping.
tub-thumper *n.* a noisy, violent, or ranting public speaker. —**ˈtub-ˌthumping** *adj., n.*
tubular (ˈtjuːbjʊlə) *adj.* **1.** Also: **tubiform** (ˈtjuːbɪˌfɔːm). having the form of a tube or tubes. **2.** of or relating to a tube or tubing. —**ˌtubuˈlarity** *n.* —**ˈtubularly** *adv.*
tubular bells *pl. n. Music.* an orchestral percussion instrument of 18 chromatically tuned metal tubes suspended vertically and struck near the top.
tubulate *vb.* (ˈtjuːbjʊˌleɪt). (*tr.*) **1.** to form or shape into a tube. **2.** to fit or furnish with a tube. ~*adj.* (ˈtjuːbjʊlɪt, -ˌleɪt). **3.** a less common word for **tubular.** [C18: from Latin *tubulātus,* from *tubulus* a little pipe, from *tubus* pipe] —**ˌtubuˈlation** *n.* —**ˈtubuˌlator** *n.*
tubule (ˈtjuːbjuːl) *n.* any small tubular structure, esp. one in an animal, as in the kidney, testis, etc. [C17: from Latin *tubulus* a little TUBE]
tubuliflorous (ˌtjuːbjʊlɪˈflɔːrəs) *adj.* (of plants) having flowers or florets with tubular corollas. [C19: from TUBULE + -FLOROUS]
tubulous (ˈtjuːbjʊləs) *adj.* **1.** tube-shaped; tubular. **2.** characterized by or consisting of small tubes. [C17: from New Latin *tubulōsus*] —**ˈtubulously** *adv.*
TUC (in Britain) *abbrev. for* Trades Union Congress.
Tucana (tuːˈkɑːnə) *n., Latin genitive* **Tucanae** (tuːˈkɑːniː). a faint extensive constellation in the S hemisphere close to Hydrus and Eridanus, containing most of the Small Magellanic Cloud. [probably from Tupi: toucan]
tuchun (tuːˈtʃuːn) *n.* (formerly) a Chinese military governor or warlord. [from Chinese, from *tu* to superintend + *chün* troops]
tuck[1] (tʌk) *vb.* **1.** (*tr.*) to push or fold into a small confined space or concealed place or between two surfaces: *to tuck a letter into an envelope.* **2.** (*tr.*) to thrust the loose ends or sides of (something) into a confining space, so as to make neat and secure: *to tuck the sheets under the mattress.* **3.** to make a tuck or tucks in (a garment). **4.** (*usually tr.*) to draw together, contract, or pucker. ~*n.* **5.** a tucked object or part. **6.** a pleat or fold in a part of a garment, usually stitched down so as to make it a better fit or as decoration. **7.** the part of a vessel where the after ends of the planking or plating meet at the sternpost. **8.** *Brit.* **a.** an informal or schoolchild's word for **food,** esp. cakes and sweets. **b.** (*as modifier*): *a tuck box.* **9.** a position of the body in certain dives in which the legs are bent with the knees drawn up against the chest and tightly clasped. ~See also **tuck away, tuck in.** [C14: from Old English *tūcian* to torment; related to Middle Dutch *tucken* to tug, Old High German *zucchen* to twitch]
tuck[2] (tʌk) *n. Archaic.* a rapier. [C16: from French *estoc* sword, from Old French: tree trunk, sword, of Germanic origin]
tuck[3] (tʌk) *Dialect.* ~*n.* **1.** a touch, blow, or stroke. ~*vb.* **2.** (*tr.*) to touch or strike. **3.** (*intr.*) to throb or bump. [C16: from Middle English *tukken* to beat a drum, from Old Northern French *toquer* to TOUCH; compare TUCKET]
tuck away *vb.* (*tr., adv.*) *Informal.* **1.** to eat (a large amount of food). **2.** to store, esp. in a place difficult to find.
tucker[1] (ˈtʌkə) *n.* **1.** a person or thing that tucks. **2.** a detachable yoke of lace, linen, etc., often white, worn over the breast, as of a low-cut dress. **3.** an attachment on a sewing machine used for making tucks at regular intervals. **4.** *Austral. and N.Z.* an informal word for **food.**
tucker[2] (ˈtʌkə) *vb.* (*tr.; often passive;* usually foll. by *out*) *Informal, chiefly U.S. and Canadian.* to weary or tire completely.
tucker-bag *or* **tuckerbox** (ˈtʌkəˌbɒks) *n. Austral. informal.* a bag used for carrying food.
tucket (ˈtʌkɪt) *n. Archaic.* a flourish on a trumpet. [C16: from Old Northern French *toquer* to sound (on a drum)]
tuck in *vb.* (*adv.*) **1.** (*tr.*) Also: **tuck into.** to put to bed and make snug. **2.** (*tr.*) to thrust the loose ends or sides of (something) into a confining space: *tuck the blankets in.* **3.** (*intr.*) Also: **tuck into.** *Informal.* to eat, esp. heartily. ~*n.* **tuck-in.** **4.** *Brit. informal.* a meal, esp. a large one.
tuck shop *n. Chiefly Brit.* a shop, esp. one in or near a school, where food such as cakes and sweets are sold.
tucotuco (ˌtuːkəʊˈtuːkəʊ) *or* **tucutucu** (ˌtuːkuːˈtuːkuː) *n.* any of various colonial burrowing South American hystricomorph rodents of the genus *Ctenomys,* having long-clawed feet and a stocky body: family *Ctenomyidae.* [C19: of South American Indian origin]
-tude *suffix forming nouns.* indicating state or condition: *plenitude.* [from Latin *-tūdō*]
Tudor (ˈtjuːdə) *adj.* **1.** of or relating to an English royal house descended from a Welsh squire, Owen Tudor (died 1461), and ruling from 1485 to 1603: *a Tudor monarch.* **2.** denoting a style of architecture of the late perpendicular period and characterized by half-timbered houses.
Tues. *abbrev. for* Tuesday.
Tuesday (ˈtjuːzdɪ) *n.* the third day of the week; second day of the working week. [Old English *tīwesdæg,* literally: day of Tiw (Tiu), Anglo-Saxon god of war, representing Latin *diēs Martis* day of Mars, Roman god of war; compare Old Norse *týsdagr,* Old High German *zīostag;* see DAY]
tufa (ˈtjuːfə) *n.* a soft porous rock consisting of calcium carbonate deposited from springs rich in lime. Also called: **calc-tufa.** [C18: from Italian *tufo,* from Late Latin *tōfus*] —**tufaceous** (tjuːˈfeɪʃəs) *adj.*
tuff (tʌf) *n.* a rock formed by the fusing together on the ground of small rock fragments (less than 2 mm across) ejected from a volcano. [C16: from Old French *tuf,* from Italian *tufo;* see TUFA] —**tuffaceous** (tʌˈfeɪʃəs) *adj.*
tuffet (ˈtʌfɪt) *n.* a small mound or low seat. [C16: alteration of TUFT]
tuft (tʌft) *n.* **1.** a bunch of feathers, grass, hair, etc., held together at the base. **2.** a cluster of threads drawn tightly through upholstery, a mattress, a quilt, etc., to secure and strengthen the padding. **3.** a small clump of trees or bushes. **4.** (formerly) a gold tassel on the cap worn by titled undergraduates at English universities. **5.** a person entitled to wear such a tassel. ~*vb.* **6.** (*tr.*) to provide or decorate with a tuft or tufts. **7.** to form or be formed into tufts. **8.** to secure and strengthen (a mattress, quilt, etc.) with tufts. [C14: perhaps from Old French *tufe,* of Germanic origin; compare TOP[1]] —**ˈtufter** *n.* —**ˈtufty** *adj.*
tufted (ˈtʌftɪd) *adj.* **1.** having a tuft or tufts. **2.** (of plants or plant parts) having or consisting of one or more groups of short branches all arising at the same level.
tufted duck *n.* a European lake-dwelling duck, *Aythya fuligula,* the male of which has a black plumage with white underparts and a long black drooping crest.
tug (tʌg) *vb.* **tugs, tugging, tugged.** **1.** (when *intr.,* sometimes foll. by *at*) to pull or drag with sharp or powerful movements: *the boy tugged at the door handle.* **2.** (*tr.*) to tow (a vessel) by means of a tug. **3.** (*intr.*) to work; toil. ~*n.* **4.** a strong pull or jerk: *he gave the rope a tug.* **5.** Also called: **tugboat.** a boat with a powerful engine, used for towing barges, ships, etc. **6.** a hard struggle or fight. **7.** a less common word for **trace**[2] (sense 1). [C13: related to Old English *tēon* to TOW[1]] —**ˈtugger** *n.*
tug of love *n.* a conflict over custody of a child between divorced parents or between natural parents and foster or adoptive parents.
tug of war *n.* **1.** a contest in which two people or teams pull opposite ends of a rope in an attempt to drag the opposition over a central line. **2.** any hard struggle, esp. between two equally matched factions.
tugrik *or* **tughrik** (ˈtuːˌgriːk) *n.* the standard monetary unit of Mongolia, divided into 100 mongos. [from Mongolian]
tui (ˈtuːɪ) *n., pl.* **tuis.** a New Zealand honeyeater, *Prosthemadera novaeseelandiae,* having a glossy bluish-green plumage with white feathers at the throat: it mimics human speech and the songs of other birds. [from Maori]
tuition (tjuːˈɪʃən) *n.* **1.** instruction, esp. that received in a small group or individually. **2.** the payment for instruction, esp. in colleges or universities. [C15: from Old French *tuicion,* from Latin *tuitiō* a guarding, from *tuērī* to watch over] —**tuˈitional** *adj.*
tuktu *or* **tuktoo** (ˈtʌkˌtuː) *n.* (in Canada) another name for **caribou.** [from Eskimo]
tularaemia *or U.S.* **tularemia** (ˌtuːləˈriːmɪə) *n.* an acute infectious bacterial disease of rodents, transmitted to man by infected ticks or flies or by handling contaminated flesh. It is characterized by fever, chills, and inflammation of the lymph glands. Also called: **rabbit fever.** [C19/20: from New Latin, from *Tulare,* county in California where it was first observed; see -AEMIA] —**ˌtulaˈraemic** *or* **ˌtulaˈremic** *adj.*
tulip (ˈtjuːlɪp) *n.* **1.** any spring-blooming liliaceous plant of the temperate Eurasian genus *Tulipa,* having tapering bulbs, long broad pointed leaves, and single showy bell-shaped flowers. **2.** the flower or bulb of any of these plants. [C17: from New Latin *tulipa,* from Turkish *tülbend* turban, which the opened bloom was thought to resemble] —**ˈtulip-ˌlike** *adj.*
tulip tree *n.* **1.** Also called: **tulip poplar, yellow poplar.** a North American magnoliaceous forest tree, *Liriodendron tulipifera,* having tulip-shaped greenish-yellow flowers and long conelike fruits. **2.** any of various other trees with tulip-shaped flowers, such as the magnolia.
tulipwood (ˈtjuːlɪpˌwʊd) *n.* **1.** Also called: **white poplar, yellow poplar.** the light soft wood of the tulip tree, used in making furniture and veneer. **2.** any of several woods having stripes or streaks of colour, esp. that of *Dalbergia variabilis,* a tree of tropical South America.

tulle (tjuːl) *n.* a fine net fabric of silk, rayon, etc., used for evening dresses, as a trimming for hats, etc. [C19: from French, from *Tulle*, city in S central France, where it was first manufactured]

tum[1] (tʊm) *or* **tyum** (tjʊm) *adj. Scot. and northeast English dialect.* empty. [from Old English *tōm;* related to Old Norse *tōmr*]

tum[2] (tʌm) *n.* an informal or childish word for **stomach.**

tumatakuru (ˈtuːˌmɑːtəˈkʊruː) *n. N.Z.* another name for **matagouri.** [Maori]

tumble (ˈtʌmbᵊl) *vb.* **1.** to fall or cause to fall, esp. awkwardly, precipitately, or violently. **2.** (*intr.;* usually foll. by *about*) to roll or twist, esp. in playing: *the kittens tumbled about on the floor.* **3.** (*intr.*) to perform leaps, somersaults, etc. **4.** to go or move in a heedless or hasty way. **5.** (*tr.*) to polish (gemstones) in a tumbler. **6.** (*tr.*) to disturb, rumple, or toss around: *to tumble the bedclothes.* ~*n.* **7.** the act or an instance of tumbling. **8.** a fall or toss. **9.** an acrobatic feat, esp. a somersault. **10.** a state of confusion. **11.** a confused heap or pile: *a tumble of clothes.* [Old English *tumbian*, from Old French *tomber;* related to Old High German *tūmōn* to turn]

tumbledown (ˈtʌmbᵊlˌdaʊn) *adj.* falling to pieces; dilapidated; crumbling.

tumble-dry *vb.* **-dries, -drying, -dried.** (*tr.*) to dry (laundry) in a tumble dryer.

tumble dryer *n.* a machine that dries wet laundry by rotating it in warmed air inside a metal drum. Also called: **tumbler dryer, tumbler.**

tumblehome (ˈtʌmbᵊlˌhəʊm) *n.* the inward curvature of the upper parts of the sides of a vessel at or near the stern.

tumbler (ˈtʌmblə) *n.* **1. a.** a flat-bottomed drinking glass with no handle or stem. Originally, a tumbler had a round or pointed base and so could not stand upright. **b.** Also called: **tumblerful.** the contents or quantity such a glass holds. **2.** a person, esp. a professional entertainer, who performs somersaults and other acrobatic feats. **3.** another name for **tumble dryer. 4.** Also called: **tumbling box.** a pivoted box or drum rotated so that the contents (usually inferior gemstones) tumble about and become smooth and polished. **5.** the part of a lock that retains or releases the bolt and is moved by the action of a key. **6.** a lever in a gunlock that receives the action of the mainspring when the trigger is pressed and thus forces the hammer forwards. **7. a.** a part that moves a gear in a train of gears into and out of engagement. **b.** a single cog or cam that transmits motion to the part with which it engages. **8.** a toy, often a doll, that is so weighted that it rocks when touched. **9.** (*often cap.*) a breed of domestic pigeon kept for exhibition or flying. The performing varieties execute backward somersaults in flight.

tumbler gear *n.* a train of gears in which the gear-selection mechanism is operated by tumblers.

tumbler switch *n.* a switch that is turned over to connect or disconnect an electric current.

tumble to *vb.* (*intr., prep.*) *Informal.* to understand; become aware of: *she tumbled to his plan quickly.*

tumbleweed (ˈtʌmbᵊlˌwiːd) *n.* any densely branched plant that breaks off near the ground on withering and is rolled about by the wind, esp. one of several amaranths of the western U.S. and Australia.

tumbrel *or* **tumbril** (ˈtʌmbrəl) *n.* **1.** a farm cart for carrying dung, esp. one that tilts backwards to deposit its load. A cart of this type was used to take condemned prisoners to the guillotine during the French Revolution (1789–99). **2.** (formerly) a covered cart that accompanied artillery in order to carry ammunition, tools, etc. **3.** an obsolete word for a **ducking stool.** [C14 *tumberell* ducking stool, from Medieval Latin *tumbrellum*, from Old French *tumberel* dump cart, from *tomber* to tumble, of Germanic origin]

tumefacient (ˌtjuːmɪˈfeɪʃɪənt) *adj.* producing or capable of producing swelling: *a tumefacient drug.* [C16: from Latin *tumefacere* to cause to swell, from *tumēre* to swell + *facere* to cause]

tumefaction (ˌtjuːmɪˈfækʃən) *n.* **1.** the act or process of swelling. **2.** a puffy or swollen structure or part.

tumefy (ˈtjuːmɪˌfaɪ) *vb.* **-fies, -fying, -fied.** to make or become tumid; swell or puff up. [C16: from French *tuméfier*, from Latin *tumefacere;* see TUMEFACIENT]

tumescent (tjuːˈmɛsənt) *adj.* swollen or becoming swollen. [C19: from Latin *tumescere* to begin to swell, from *tumēre*] —**tuˈmescence** *n.*

tumid (ˈtjuːmɪd) *adj.* **1.** (of an organ or part) enlarged or swollen. **2.** bulging or protuberant. **3.** pompous or fulsome in style: *tumid prose.* [C16: from Latin *tumidus*, from *tumēre* to swell] —**tuˈmidity** *or* ˈ**tumidness** *n.* —ˈ**tumidly** *adv.*

tummy (ˈtʌmɪ) *n., pl.* **-mies.** an informal or childish word for **stomach.**

tummy tuck *n. Informal.* the surgical removal of abdominal fat and skin for cosmetic purposes.

tumour *or U.S.* **tumor** (ˈtjuːmə) *n.* **1.** *Pathol.* **a.** any abnormal swelling. **b.** a mass of tissue formed by a new growth of cells, normally independent of the surrounding structures. **2.** *Obsolete.* pompous style or language. [C16: from Latin, from *tumēre* to swell] —ˈ**tumorous** *or* ˈ**tumoral** *adj.*

tump (tʌmp) *n. Western English dialect.* a small mound or clump. [C16: of unknown origin]

tumpline (ˈtʌmpˌlaɪn) *n.* (in the U.S. and Canada, esp. formerly) a leather or cloth band strung across the forehead or chest and attached to a pack or load in order to support it. Also called: **tump.** [C19: from *tump*, of Algonquian origin + LINE[1]; compare Abnaki *mădŭmbi* pack strap]

tumular (ˈtjuːmjʊlə) *adj.* of, relating to, or like a mound.

tumulose (ˈtjuːmjʊləʊs) *or* **tumulous** (ˈtjuːmjʊləs) *adj.* **1.** abounding in small hills or mounds. **2.** being or resembling a mound. [C18: from Latin *tumulōsus*, from *tumulus* a hillock] —**tumulosity** (ˌtjuːmjʊˈlɒsɪtɪ) *n.*

tumult (ˈtjuːmʌlt) *n.* **1.** a loud confused noise, as of a crowd; commotion. **2.** violent agitation or disturbance. **3.** great emotional or mental agitation. [C15: from Latin *tumultus*, from *tumēre* to swell up]

tumultuous (tjuːˈmʌltjʊəs) *adj.* **1.** uproarious, riotous, or turbulent: *a tumultuous welcome.* **2.** greatly agitated, confused, or disturbed: *a tumultuous dream.* **3.** making a loud or unruly disturbance: *tumultuous insurgents.* —**tuˈmultuously** *adv.* —**tuˈmultuousness** *n.*

tumulus (ˈtjuːmjʊləs) *n., pl.* **-li** (-ˌlaɪ). *Archaeol.* (no longer in technical usage) another word for **barrow**[2]. [C17: from Latin: a hillock, from *tumēre* to swell up]

tun (tʌn) *n.* **1.** a large beer cask. **2.** a measure of capacity, usually equal to 252 wine gallons. **3.** a cask used during the manufacture of beer: *a mash tun.* ~*vb.* **tuns, tunning, tunned. 4.** (*tr.*) to put into or keep in tuns. [Old English *tunne;* related to Old High German, Old Norse *tunna*, Medieval Latin *tunna*]

tuna[1] (ˈtjuːnə) *n., pl.* **-na** *or* **-nas.** another name for **tunny** (sense 1). [C20: from American Spanish, from Spanish *atún*, from Arabic *tūn*, from Latin *thunnus* tunny, from Greek]

tuna[2] (ˈtjuːnə) *n.* **1.** any of various tropical American prickly pear cacti, esp. *Opuntia tuna*, that are cultivated for their sweet edible fruits. **2.** the fruit of any of these cacti. [C16: via Spanish from Taino]

tunable *or* **tuneable** (ˈtjuːnəbᵊl) *adj.* **1.** able to be tuned. **2.** *Archaic or poetic.* melodious or tuneful.

tundra (ˈtʌndrə) *n.* **a.** a vast treeless zone lying between the ice cap and the timber line of North America and Eurasia and having a permanently frozen subsoil. **b.** (*as modifier*): *tundra vegetation.* [C19: from Russian, from Lapp *tundar* hill; related to Finnish *tunturi* treeless hill]

tune (tjuːn) *n.* **1.** a melody, esp. one for which harmony is not essential. **2.** the most important part in a musical texture: *the cello has the tune at that point.* **3.** the condition of producing accurately pitched notes, intervals, etc. (esp. in the phrases **in tune, out of tune**): *he can't sing in tune.* **4.** accurate correspondence of pitch and intonation between instruments (esp. in the phrases **in tune, out of tune**): *the violin is not in tune with the piano.* **5.** the correct adjustment of a radio, television, or some other electronic circuit with respect to the required frequency (esp. in the phrases **in tune, out of tune**). **6.** a frame of mind; disposition or mood. **7.** *Obsolete.* a musical sound; note. **8. call the tune.** to be in control of the proceedings. **9. change one's tune** *or* **sing another** (*or* **a different**) **tune.** to alter one's attitude or tone of speech. **10. to the tune of.** *Informal.* to the amount or extent of: *costs to the tune of a hundred pounds.* ~*vb.* **11.** to adjust (a musical instrument or a changeable part of one) to a certain pitch. **12.** to adjust (a note, etc.) so as to bring it into harmony or concord. **13.** (*tr.*) to adapt or adjust (oneself); attune: *to tune oneself to a slower life.* **14.** (*tr.;* often foll. by *up*) to make fine adjustments to (an engine, machine, etc.) to obtain optimum performance. **15.** *Electronics.* to adjust (one or more circuits) for resonance at a desired frequency. **16.** *Obsolete.* to utter (something) musically or in the form of a melody; sing. ~See also **tune in, tune up.** [C14: variant of TONE]

tuneful (ˈtjuːnfʊl) *adj.* **1.** having a pleasant or catchy tune; melodious. **2.** producing a melody or music: *a tuneful blackbird.* —ˈ**tunefully** *adv.* —ˈ**tunefulness** *n.*

tune in *vb.* (*adv.;* often foll. by *to*) **1.** to adjust (a radio or television) to receive (a station or programme). **2.** *Slang.* to make or become more aware, knowledgeable, etc. (about).

tuneless (ˈtjuːnlɪs) *adj.* **1.** having no melody or tune. **2.** *Chiefly poetic.* not producing or able to produce music; silent. —ˈ**tunelessly** *adv.* —ˈ**tunelessness** *n.*

tuner (ˈtjuːnə) *n.* **1.** a person who tunes instruments, esp. pianos. **2.** the part of a radio or television receiver for selecting only those signals having a particular frequency.

tunesmith (ˈtjuːnˌsmɪθ) *n. Informal, chiefly U.S.* a composer of light or popular music and songs.

tune up *vb.* (*adv.*) **1.** to adjust (a musical instrument) to a particular pitch, esp. a standard one. **2.** (esp. of an orchestra or other instrumental ensemble) to tune (instruments) to a common pitch. **3.** (*tr.*) to adjust (an engine) in (a car, etc.) to improve performance. ~*n.* **tune-up. 4.** adjustments made to an engine to improve its performance.

tung oil (tʌŋ) *n.* a fast-drying oil obtained from the seeds of a central Asian euphorbiaceous tree, *Aleurites fordii*, used in paints, varnishes, etc., as a drying agent and to give a water-resistant finish. Also called: **Chinese wood oil.** [partial translation of Chinese *yu t'ung* tung tree oil, from *yu* oil + *t'ung* tung tree]

tungstate (ˈtʌŋsteɪt) *n.* a salt of tungstic acid. [C20: from TUNGST(EN) + -ATE[1]]

tungsten (ˈtʌŋstən) *n.* a hard malleable ductile greyish-white element. It occurs principally in wolframite and scheelite and is used in lamp filaments, electrical contact points, x-ray targets, and, alloyed with steel, in high-speed cutting tools. Symbol: W; atomic no.: 74; atomic wt.: 183.85; valency: 2–6; relative density: 19.3; melting pt.: 3410°C; boiling pt.: 5927°C. Also called: **wolfram.** [C18: from Swedish *tung* heavy + *sten* STONE]

tungsten carbide *n.* a fine very hard crystalline grey powder produced by heating tungsten and carbon to a very high temperature: used in the manufacture of drill bits, dies, etc. Symbol: WC; melting pt.: 2870°C.

tungsten lamp *n.* a lamp in which light is produced by a tungsten filament heated to incandescence by an electric current. The glass bulb enclosing the filament contains a low pressure of inert gas, usually argon. Sometimes small amounts of a halogen, such as iodine, are added to improve the intensity (**tungsten-halogen lamp**).

tungsten steel *n.* any of various hard steels containing tungsten (1–20 per cent) and traces of carbon. They are resistant to wear at high temperatures and are used in tools.

tungstic (ˈtʌŋstɪk) *adj.* of or containing tungsten, esp. in a high valence state. [C18: from TUNGST(EN) + -IC]

tungstic acid *n.* any of various oxyacids of tungsten obtained by neutralizing alkaline solutions of tungstates. They are often polymeric substances, typical examples being H_2WO_4 (**orthotungstic acid**), $H_2W_4O_{13}$ (**metatungstic acid**), and $H_{10}W_{12}O_{14}$ (**paratungstic acid**).

tungstite (ˈtʌŋstaɪt) *n.* a yellow earthy rare secondary mineral that consists of tungsten oxide and occurs with tungsten ores. Formula: WO_3. [C20: from TUNGST(EN) + -ITE[1]]

tungstous (ˈtʌŋstəs) *adj.* of or containing tungsten in a low valence state.

Tungus (ˈtʊŋgʊs) *n.* **1.** (*pl.* **-guses** *or* **-gus**) a member of a formerly nomadic Mongoloid people of E Siberia. **2.** Also called: **Evenki.** the language of this people, belonging to the Tungusic branch of the Altaic family.

Tungusic (tʊŋˈgʊsɪk) *n.* **1.** a branch or subfamily of the Altaic family of languages, including Tungus and Manchu. ~*adj. also* **Tungusian. 2.** of or relating to these languages or their speakers.

tunic (ˈtjuːnɪk) *n.* **1.** any of various hip-length or knee-length garments, such as the loose sleeveless garb worn in ancient Greece or Rome, the jacket of some soldiers, or a woman's hip-length garment, worn with a skirt or trousers. **2.** Also called: **tunica.** *Anatomy, botany, zoology.* a covering, lining, or enveloping membrane of an organ or part. **3.** *Chiefly R.C. Church.* another word for **tunicle.** [Old English *tunice* (unattested except in the accusative case), from Latin *tunica*]

tunicate (ˈtjuːnɪkɪt, -ˌkeɪt) *n.* **1.** any minute primitive marine chordate animal of the subphylum *Tunicata* (or *Urochordata, Urochorda*). The adults have a saclike unsegmented body enclosed in a cellulose-like outer covering (tunic) and only the larval forms have a notochord: includes the sea squirts. See also **ascidian.** ~*adj. also* **tunicated. 2.** of, relating to, or belonging to the subphylum *Tunicata.* **3.** (esp. of a bulb) having or consisting of concentric layers of tissue. [C18: from Latin *tunicātus* clad in a TUNIC]

tunicle (ˈtjuːnɪkᵊl) *n. Chiefly R.C. Church.* the liturgical vestment worn by the subdeacon and bishops at High Mass and other religious ceremonies. [C14: from Latin *tunicula* a little TUNIC]

tuning (ˈtjuːnɪŋ) *n. Music.* **1.** a set of pitches to which the open strings of a guitar, violin, etc., are tuned: *the normal tuning on a violin is G, D, A, E.* **2.** the accurate pitching of notes and intervals by a choir, orchestra, etc.; intonation.

tuning fork *n.* a two-pronged metal fork that when struck produces a pure note of constant specified pitch. It is used to tune musical instruments and in acoustics.

tuning key *n.* a small square-sectioned tube, open at one end and forming a keylike handle at the other, that may be placed over a wrest pin on a piano, etc., and turned to alter the tension and pitch of a string.

Tunisian (tjuːˈnɪzɪən, -ˈnɪsɪən) *adj.* **1.** of or relating to Tunisia, a republic in N Africa, or its people or culture. ~*n.* **2.** a native or inhabitant of Tunisia.

tunnage (ˈtʌnɪdʒ) *n.* a variant spelling of **tonnage.**

tunnel (ˈtʌnᵊl) *n.* **1.** an underground passageway, esp. one for trains or cars that passes under a mountain, river, or a congested urban area. **2.** any passage or channel through or under something. **3.** a dialect word for **funnel. 4.** *Obsolete.* the flue of a chimney. ~*vb.* **-nels, -nelling, -nelled** *or U.S.* **-nels, -neling, -neled. 5.** (*tr.*) to make or force (a way) through or under (something): *to tunnel a hole in the wall; to tunnel the cliff.* **6.** (*intr.;* foll. by *through, under,* etc.) to make or force a way (through or under something): *he tunnelled through the bracken.* [C15: from Old French *tonel* cask, from *tonne* tun, from Medieval Latin *tonna* barrel, of Celtic origin] —ˈ**tunneller** *or U.S.* ˈ**tunneler** *n.*

tunnel diode *n.* an extremely stable semiconductor diode, having a very narrow highly doped p-n junction, in which electrons travel across the junction by means of the tunnel effect. Also called: **Esaki diode.**

tunnel disease *n.* another name (esp. formerly) for **decompression sickness.** [so called because it used to be common among people who were digging tunnels]

tunnel effect *n. Physics.* the phenomenon in which an object, usually an elementary particle, tunnels through a potential barrier even though it does not have sufficient energy to surmount the barrier. It is explained by wave mechanics and is the cause of alpha decay, field emission, and certain conduction processes in semiconductors.

tunnel vault *n.* another name for **barrel vault.**

tunnel vision *n.* **1.** a condition in which peripheral vision is greatly restricted. **2.** narrowness of viewpoint resulting from concentration on a single idea, opinion, etc., to the exclusion of others.

tunny (ˈtʌnɪ) *n., pl.* **-nies** *or* **-ny. 1.** Also called: **tuna.** any of various large marine spiny-finned fishes of the genus *Thunnus,* esp. *T. thynnus,* chiefly of warm waters: family *Scombridae.* They have a spindle-shaped body and widely forked tail, and are important food fishes. **2.** any of various similar and related fishes. [C16: from Old French *thon,* from Old Provençal *ton,* from Latin *thunnus,* from Greek]

tup (tʌp) *n.* **1.** *Chiefly Brit.* an uncastrated male sheep; ram. **2.** the head of a pile-driver or steam hammer. ~*vb.* **tups, tupping, tupped.** (*tr.*) **3.** to cause (a ram) to mate with a ewe, or (of a ram) to mate with (a ewe). **4.** *Lancashire dialect.* to butt (someone), as in a fight. [C14: of unknown origin]

Tupamaro (ˌtuːpəˈmɑːrəʊ) *n., pl.* **-ros.** any of a group of Marxist urban guerrillas in Uruguay. [C20: after *Tupac Amaru,* 18th-century Peruvian Indian who led a rebellion against the Spaniards]

tupelo (ˈtjuːpɪˌləʊ) *n., pl.* **-los. 1.** any of several cornaceous trees of the genus *Nyssa,* esp. *N. aquatica,* a large tree of deep swamps and rivers of the southern U.S. **2.** the light strong wood of any of these trees. [C18: from Creek *ito opilwa,* from *ito* tree + *opilwa* swamp]

Tupi (tuːˈpiː) *n.* **1.** (*pl.* **-pis** *or* **-pi**) a member of a South American Indian people of Brazil and Paraguay. **2.** the language of this people, belonging to the Tupi-Guarani family. —**Tuˈpian** *adj.*

Tupi-Guarani *n.* a family of South American Indian languages spoken in Brazil, Paraguay, and certain adjacent regions: possibly distantly related to Quechua. —ˈ**Tupi**ˌ**Guaraˈnian** *adj.*

tupik *or* **tupek** (ˈtuːpək) *n. Canadian.* (esp. in the Arctic) a tent of animal skins, a traditional type of Inuit summer dwelling. [from Eskimo *tupiq*]

-tuple *n. and adj. combining form.* indicating a set of the number specified.

tuppence (ˈtʌpəns) *n. Brit.* a variant spelling of **twopence.**

tuppenny (ˈtʌpənɪ) *adj.* a variant spelling of **twopenny.**

tuque (tuːk) *n.* (in Canada) a knitted cap with a long tapering end. [C19: from Canadian French, from French: TOQUE]

tu quoque *Latin.* (tjuː ˈkwəʊkwɪ) *interj.* you likewise: a retort made by a person accused of a crime implying that the accuser is also guilty of the same crime.

turaco (ˈtʊərəˌkəʊ) *n., pl.* **-cos.** a variant spelling of **touraco.**

Turanian (tjʊˈreɪnɪən) *n.* **1.** a member of any of the peoples inhabiting ancient Turkestan in central Asia, or their descendants. **2.** another name for **Ural-Altaic.** ~*adj.* **3.** of or relating to the Ural-Altaic languages or any of the peoples who speak them. **4.** of or relating to Turkestan or its people.

turban (ˈtɜːbᵊn) *n.* **1.** a man's headdress, worn esp. by Muslims, Hindus, and Sikhs, made by swathing a length of linen, silk, etc., around the head or around a caplike base. **2.** a woman's brimless hat resembling this. **3.** any headdress resembling this. [C16: from Turkish *tülbend,* from Persian *dulband*] —ˈ**turbaned** *adj.* —ˈ**turban-**ˌ**like** *adj.*

turbary (ˈtɜːbərɪ) *n., pl.* **-ries. 1.** land where peat or turf is cut or has been cut. **2.** Also called: **common of turbary.** (in England) the legal right to cut peat for fuel on a common. [C14: from Old French *turbarie,* from Medieval Latin *turbāria,* from *turba* peat, TURF]

turbellarian (ˌtɜːbɪˈlɛərɪən) *n.* **1.** any typically aquatic free-living flatworm of the class *Turbellaria,* having a ciliated epidermis and a simple life cycle: includes the planarians. ~*adj.* **2.** of, relating to, or belonging to the class *Turbellaria.* [C19: from New Latin *Turbellāria,* from Latin *turbellae* (pl.) bustle, from *turba* brawl, referring to the swirling motion created in the water]

turbid (ˈtɜːbɪd) *adj.* **1.** muddy or opaque, as a liquid clouded with a suspension of particles. **2.** dense, thick, or cloudy: *turbid fog.* **3.** in turmoil or confusion. [C17: from Latin *turbidus,* from *turbāre* to agitate, from *turba* crowd] —**turˈbidity** *or* ˈ**turbidness** *n.* —ˈ**turbidly** *adv.*

turbidimeter (ˌtɜːbɪˈdɪmɪtə) *n.* a device that measures the turbidity of a liquid.

turbidite (ˈtɜːbɪˌdaɪt) *n.* a sediment deposited by a turbidity current. [C20: from TURBID + -ITE[1]]

turbidity current *n.* a swirling mass of water and suspended material stirred up by a tsunami, a storm, a river in flood, etc.

turbinate (ˈtɜːbɪnɪt, -ˌneɪt) *or* **turbinal** (ˈtɜːbɪnᵊl) *adj. also* **turbinated. 1.** *Anatomy.* of or relating to any of the thin scroll-shaped bones situated on the walls of the nasal passages. **2.** shaped like a spiral or scroll. **3.** (esp. of the shells of certain molluscs) shaped like an inverted cone. ~*n.* **4.** Also called: **nasal concha.** a turbinate bone. **5.** a turbinate shell. [C17: from Latin *turbō* spinning top] —ˌ**turbiˈnation** *n.*

turbine (ˈtɜːbɪn, -baɪn) *n.* any of various types of machine in which the kinetic energy of a moving fluid is converted into mechanical energy by causing a bladed rotor to rotate. The moving fluid may be water, steam, air, or combustion products of a fuel. See also **reaction turbine, impulse turbine, gas turbine.** [C19: from French, from Latin *turbō* whirlwind, from *turbāre* to throw into confusion]
turbine blade *n.* any of a number of bladelike vanes assembled around the periphery of a turbine rotor to guide the steam or gas flow.
turbit (ˈtɜːbɪt) *n.* a crested breed of domestic pigeon. [C17: from Latin *turbō* top, with reference to the bird's shape; compare TURBOT]
turbo- *combining form.* of, relating to, or driven by a turbine: *turbofan.*
turbocar (ˈtɜːbəʊˌkɑː) *n.* a car driven by a gas turbine.
turbocharger (ˈtɜːbəʊˌtʃɑːdʒə) *n.* a centrifugal compressor driven by an exhaust-gas turbine.
turbo-electric (ˌtɜːbəʊɪˈlɛktrɪk) *adj.* of, relating to, or using an electric generator driven by a turbine: *turbo-electric propulsion.*
turbofan (ˌtɜːbəʊˈfæn) *n.* **1.** Also called: **high bypass ratio engine.** a type of bypass engine in which a large fan driven by a turbine and housed in a short duct forces air rearwards around the exhaust gases in order to increase the propulsive thrust. **2.** an aircraft driven by one or more turbofans. **3.** the ducted fan in such an engine. ~Also called (for senses 1, 2): **fanjet.**
turbogenerator (ˌtɜːbəʊˈdʒɛnəˌreɪtə) *n.* a large electrical generator driven by a steam turbine.
turbojet (ˌtɜːbəʊˈdʒɛt) *n.* **1.** short for **turbojet engine. 2.** an aircraft powered by one or more turbojet engines.
turbojet engine *n.* a gas turbine in which the exhaust gases provide the propulsive thrust to drive an aircraft.
turboprop (ˌtɜːbəʊˈprɒp) *n.* **1.** a gas turbine for driving an aircraft propeller. **2.** an aircraft powered by turboprops.
turbosupercharger (ˌtɜːbəʊˈsuːpəˌtʃɑːdʒə) *n.* a supercharging device for an internal-combustion engine, consisting of a turbine driven by the exhaust gases.
turbot (ˈtɜːbət) *n., pl.* **-bot** *or* **-bots. 1.** a European flatfish, *Scophthalmus maximus,* having a pale brown speckled scaleless body covered with tubercles: family *Bothidae.* It is highly valued as a food fish. **2.** any of various similar or related fishes. [C13: from Old French *tourbot,* from Medieval Latin *turbō,* from Latin: top, from a fancied similarity in shape; see TURBIT, TURBINE]
turbulence (ˈtɜːbjʊləns) *or (rarely)* **turbulency** *n.* **1.** a state or condition of confusion, movement, or agitation; disorder. **2.** *Meteorol.* instability in the atmosphere causing considerable gusty air currents and cumulonimbus clouds. **3.** turbulent flow in a liquid or gas.
turbulent (ˈtɜːbjʊlənt) *adj.* **1.** being in a state of turbulence. **2.** wild or insubordinate; unruly. [C16: from Latin *turbulentus,* from *turba* confusion] —ˈ**turbulently** *adv.*
turbulent flow *n.* flow of a fluid in which its velocity at any point varies rapidly in an irregular manner. Compare **laminar flow.** See also **streamline flow.**
Turco (ˈtɜːkəʊ) *n., pl.* **-cos.** (formerly) an Algerian serving in the light infantry of the French army. [C19: via French from Italian: a Turk]
Turco- *or* **Turko-** *combining form.* indicating Turkey or Turkish: *Turco-Greek.*
turd (tɜːd) *n. Taboo.* **1.** a lump of dung; piece of excrement. **2.** *Slang.* an unpleasant or contemptible person or thing. [Old English *tord;* related to Old Norse *tordy fill* dung beetle, Dutch *tort* dung]
turdine (ˈtɜːdaɪn, -dɪn) *adj.* of, relating to, or characteristic of thrushes. [C19: from Latin *turdus* thrush]
tureen (təˈriːn) *n.* a large deep usually rounded dish with a cover, used for serving soups, stews, etc. [C18: from French *terrine* earthenware vessel, from *terrin* made of earthenware, from Vulgar Latin *terrīnus* (unattested) earthen, from Latin *terra* earth]
turf (tɜːf) *n., pl.* **turfs** *or* **turves** (tɜːvz). **1.** the surface layer of fields and pastures, consisting of earth containing a dense growth of grasses with their roots; sod. **2.** a piece cut from this layer, used to form lawns, verges, etc. **3. the turf. a.** a track, usually of grass or dirt, where horse races are run. **b.** horse racing as a sport or industry. **4.** *U.S. slang.* the territory claimed by a juvenile gang as its own. **5.** *Chiefly U.S. informal.* an area of knowledge or influence: *he's on home turf when it comes to music.* **6.** another term for **peat.** ~*vb.* **7.** *(tr.)* to cover with pieces of turf. [Old English; related to Old Norse *torfa,* Old High German *zurba,* Sanskrit *darbha* tuft of grass]
turf accountant *n. Brit.* a formal name for a **bookmaker.**
turfman (ˈtɜːfmən) *n., pl.* **-men.** *Chiefly U.S.* a person devoted to horse racing. Also called: **turfite** (ˈtɜːfaɪt).
turf out *vb. (tr., adv.) Brit. informal.* to throw out or dismiss; eject: *we were turfed out of the club.*
turfy (ˈtɜːfɪ) *adj.* **turfier, turfiest. 1.** of, covered with, or resembling turf. **2.** relating to or characteristic of horse racing or persons connected with it. —ˈ**turfiness** *n.*
turgent (ˈtɜːdʒənt) *adj.* an obsolete word for **turgid.** [C15: from Latin *turgēre* to swell] —ˈ**turgently** *adv.*
turgescent (tɜːˈdʒɛsᵊnt) *adj.* becoming or being swollen; inflated; tumid. —**tur**ˈ**gescence** *or* **tur**ˈ**gescency** *n.*
turgid (ˈtɜːdʒɪd) *adj.* **1.** swollen and distended; congested. **2.** (of style or language) pompous and high-flown; bombastic. [C17: from Latin *turgidus,* from *turgēre* to swell] —**tur**ˈ**gidity** *or* ˈ**turgidness** *n.* —ˈ**turgidly** *adv.*
turgite (ˈtɜːdʒaɪt) *n.* a red or black mineral consisting of hydrated ferric oxide. Formula: $Fe_2O_3.nH_2O$.
turgor (ˈtɜːgə) *n.* **1.** the normal rigid state of a cell, caused by pressure of the cell contents against the cell wall or membrane. **2.** *Rare.* turgidity. [C19: from Late Latin: a swelling, from Latin *turgēre* to swell]
Turing machine (ˈtjʊərɪŋ) *n.* a hypothetical universal computing machine able to modify its original instructions by reading, erasing, or writing a new symbol on a moving tape of fixed length that acts as its program. The concept was instrumental in the early development of computer systems. [C20: named after Alan *Turing* (1912–54), British mathematician who proposed it]
Turing test *n.* a proposed test of a computer's ability to think, requiring that the covert substitution of the computer for one of the participants in a teletype dialogue should be undetectable by the remaining human participant.
turion (ˈtʊərɪən) *n.* a perennating bud produced by many aquatic plants: it detaches from the parent plant and remains dormant until the following spring. [C17: from French *turion,* from Latin *turio*]
Turk (tɜːk) *n.* **1.** a native, inhabitant, or citizen of Turkey, a country in W Asia and SE Europe. **2.** a native speaker of any Turkic language. **3.** *Obsolete, derogatory.* a violent, brutal, or domineering person.
Turk. *abbrev. for:* **1.** Turkey. **2.** Turkish.
turkey (ˈtɜːkɪ) *n., pl.* **-keys** *or* **-key. 1.** a large gallinaceous bird, *Meleagris gallopavo,* of North America, having a bare wattled head and neck and a brownish iridescent plumage. The male is brighter and has a fan-shaped tail. A domestic variety is widely bred for its flesh. **2.** the flesh of the turkey used as food. **3.** a similar and related bird, *Agriocharis ocellata* (**ocellated turkey**), of Central and N South America. **4.** *Slang, chiefly U.S. and Canadian.* **a.** a dramatic production that fails; flop. **b.** a thing or person that fails; dud. **5.** *Slang, chiefly U.S. and Canadian.* a stupid, incompetent, or unappealing person. **6.** *Slang.* (in tenpin bowling) three strikes in a row. **7.** See **cold turkey. 8. talk turkey.** *Informal, chiefly U.S. and Canadian.* to discuss frankly and practically. [C16: shortened from *Turkey cock (hen),* used at first to designate the African guinea fowl (apparently because the bird was brought through Turkish territory), later applied by mistake to the American bird]
turkey brown *n.* an angler's name for a species of mayfly, *Paraleptophlebia submarginata.*
turkey buzzard *or* **vulture** *n.* a New World vulture, *Cathartes aura,* having a dark plumage and naked red head.
Turkey carpet *n.* a wool carpet made in one piece and having a deep velvety pile and rich glowing colours.
turkey cock *n.* **1.** a male turkey. **2.** an arrogant person.
turkey nest *n. Austral.* a small earth dam adjacent to, and higher than, a larger earth dam, to feed water by gravity to a cattle trough, etc.
Turkey oak *n.* an oak tree, *Quercus cerris,* of W and S Europe, with deeply lobed hairy leaves. [C18: so called because its acorns are often eaten by turkeys]
Turkey red *n.* **1. a.** a moderate or bright red colour. **b.** *(as adj.): a Turkey-red fabric.* **2.** a cotton fabric of a bright red colour.
turkey trot *n.* an early ragtime one-step, popular in the period of World War I.
Turki (ˈtɜːkɪ) *adj.* **1.** of or relating to the Turkic languages, esp. those spoken in central Asia. **2.** of or relating to speakers of these languages. ~*n.* **3.** these languages collectively; Turkic, esp. Eastern Turkic.
Turkic (ˈtɜːkɪk) *n.* a branch or subfamily of the Altaic family of languages, including Turkish, Turkmen, Kirghiz, Tatar, etc., members of which are found from Turkey to NE China, esp. in central Asia.
Turkish (ˈtɜːkɪʃ) *adj.* **1.** of, relating to, or characteristic of Turkey, a country in W Asia and SE Europe, or to its people or their language. ~*n.* **2.** the official language of Turkey, belonging to the Turkic branch of the Altaic family. See also **Osmanli.** —ˈ**Turkishness** *n.*
Turkish bath *n.* **1.** a type of bath in which the bather sweats freely in a steam room, is then washed, often massaged, and has a cold plunge or shower. **2.** *(sometimes pl.)* an establishment where such a bath is obtainable.
Turkish coffee *n.* very strong black coffee made with finely ground coffee beans.
Turkish delight *n.* a jelly-like sweet flavoured with flower essences, usually cut into cubes and covered in icing sugar.
Turkish tobacco *n.* a fragrant dark tobacco cultivated in E Europe, esp. Turkey and Greece.
Turkish towel *n.* a rough loose-piled towel; terry towel.
Turkism (ˈtɜːkɪzəm) *n. Rare.* **1.** the culture, beliefs, and customs of the Turks. **2.** a Turkish word, fashion, etc.
Turkmen (ˈtɜːkmɛn) *n.* the language of the Turkomans, belonging to the Turkic branch of the Altaic family.
Turko- *combining form.* a variant spelling of **Turco-.**

Turkoman ('tɜːkəmən) *or* **Turkman** *n.* **1.** (*pl.* **-mans** *or* **-men**) a member of a formerly nomadic people of central Asia, now living chiefly in the former Soviet republic of Turkmenistan and in NE Iran. **2.** the Turkmen language. ~*adj.* **3.** of or relating to this people or their language. [C16: from Medieval Latin *Turcomannus,* from Persian *turkumān* resembling a Turk, from *turk* Turk + *māndan* to be like]

Turk's-cap lily *n.* any of several cultivated lilies, such as *Lilium martagon* and *L. superbum,* that have brightly coloured flowers with reflexed petals. See also **martagon.** [C17: so called because of a fancied resemblance between the shape of its flowers and a turban]

Turk's-head *n.* an ornamental turban-like knot made by weaving small cord around a larger rope.

turmeric ('tɜːmərɪk) *n.* **1.** a tropical Asian zingiberaceous plant, *Curcuma longa,* having yellow flowers and an aromatic underground stem. **2.** the powdered stem of this plant, used as a condiment and as a yellow dye. **3.** any of several other plants with similar roots. [C16: from Old French *terre merite,* from Medieval Latin *terra merita,* literally: meritorious earth, name applied for obscure reasons to curcuma]

turmeric paper *n. Chem.* paper impregnated with turmeric used as a test for alkalis, which turn it brown, and for boric acid, which turns it reddish brown.

turmoil ('tɜːmɔɪl) *n.* **1.** violent or confused movement; agitation; tumult. ~*vb.* **2.** *Archaic.* to make or become turbulent. [C16: perhaps from TURN + MOIL]

turn (tɜːn) *vb.* **1.** to move or cause to move around an axis: *a wheel turning; to turn a knob.* **2.** (sometimes foll. by *round*) to change or cause to change positions by moving through an arc of a circle: *he turned the chair to face the light.* **3.** to change or cause to change in course, direction, etc.: *he turned left at the main road.* **4.** (of soldiers, ships, etc.) to alter the direction of advance by changing direction simultaneously or (of a commander) to cause the direction of advance to be altered simultaneously. **5.** to go or pass to the other side of (a corner, etc.). **6.** to assume or cause to assume a rounded, curved, or folded form: *the road turns here.* **7.** to reverse or cause to reverse position. **8.** (*tr.*) to pass round (an enemy or enemy position) so as to attack it from the flank or rear: *the Germans turned the Maginot line.* **9.** (*tr.*) to perform or do by a rotating movement: *to turn a somersault.* **10.** (*tr.*) to shape or cut a thread in (a workpiece, esp. one of metal, wood, or plastic) by rotating it on a lathe against a fixed cutting tool. **11.** (when *intr.,* foll. by *into* or *to*) to change or convert or be changed or converted: *the alchemists tried to turn base metals into gold.* **12.** (foll. by *into*) to change or cause to change in nature, character, etc.: *the frog turned into a prince.* **13.** (*copula*) to change so as to become: *he turned nasty when he heard the price.* **14.** to cause (foliage, etc.) to change colour or (of foliage, etc.) to change colour: *frost turned the trees a vivid orange.* **15.** to cause (milk, etc.) to become rancid or sour or (of milk, etc.) to become rancid or sour. **16.** to change or cause to change in subject, trend, etc.: *the conversation turned to fishing.* **17.** to direct or apply or be directed or applied: *he turned his attention to the problem.* **18.** (*intr.;* usually foll. by *to*) to appeal or apply (to) for help, advice, etc.: *she was very frightened and didn't know where to turn.* **19.** to reach, pass, or progress beyond in age, time, etc.: *she has just turned twenty.* **20.** (*tr.*) to cause or allow to go: *to turn an animal loose.* **21.** to affect or be affected with nausea: *the sight of the dead body turned his stomach.* **22.** to affect or be affected with giddiness: *my head is turning.* **23.** (*tr.*) to affect the mental or emotional stability of (esp. in the phrase **turn (someone's) head**). **24.** (*tr.*) to release from a container: *she turned the fruit into a basin.* **25.** (*tr.*) to render into another language. **26.** (usually foll. by *against* or *from*) to transfer or reverse or cause to transfer or reverse (one's loyalties, affections, etc.). **27.** (*tr.*) to cause (an enemy agent) to become a double agent working for one's own side: *the bureau turned some of the spies it had caught.* **28.** (*tr.*) to bring (soil) from lower layers to the surface. **29.** to blunt (an edge) or (of an edge) to become blunted. **30.** (*tr.*) to give a graceful form to: *to turn a compliment.* **31.** (*tr.*) to reverse (a cuff, collar, etc.) in order to hide the outer worn side. **32.** (*intr.*) *U.S.* to be merchandised as specified: *shirts are turning well this week.* **33.** *Cricket.* to spin (the ball) or (of the ball) to spin. **34. turn one's hand to.** to undertake (something, esp. something practical). **35. turn tail.** to run away; flee. **36. turn the tables (on someone).** See **table** (sense 16). **37. turn the tide.** to reverse the general course of events. ~*n.* **38.** an act or instance of turning or the state of being turned or the material turned: *a turn of a rope around a bollard.* **39.** a movement of complete or partial rotation. **40.** a change or reversal of direction or position. **41.** direction or drift: *his thoughts took a new turn.* **42.** a deviation or departure from a course or tendency. **43.** the place, point, or time at which a deviation or change occurs. **44.** another word for **turning** (sense 1). **45.** the right or opportunity to do something in an agreed order or succession: *we'll take turns to play; now it's George's turn; you must not play out of turn.* **46.** a change in nature, condition, etc.: *his illness took a turn for the worse.* **47.** a period of action, work, etc. **48.** a short walk, ride, or excursion: *to take a turn in the park.* **49.** natural inclination: *he is of a speculative turn of mind; she has a turn for needlework.* **50.** distinctive form or style: *a neat turn of phrase.* **51.** requirement, need, or advantage: *to serve someone's turn.* **52.** a deed performed that helps or hinders someone: *to do an old lady a good turn.* **53.** a twist, bend, or distortion in shape. **54.** *Music.* a melodic ornament that makes a turn around a note, beginning with the note above, in a variety of sequences. **55.** *Theatre, chiefly Brit.* a short theatrical act, esp. in music hall, cabaret, etc. **56.** *Stock Exchange.* **a.** *Brit.* the difference between a market maker's bid and offer prices, representing the market maker's profit. **b.** a transaction including both a purchase and a sale. **57.** a military manoeuvre in which men or ships alter their direction of advance together. **58.** *Austral. slang.* a party. **59.** *Informal.* a shock or surprise: *the bad news gave her quite a turn.* **60. at every turn.** on all sides or occasions. **61. by turns.** one after another; alternately. **62. on the turn.** *Informal.* **a.** at the point of change. **b.** about to go rancid. **63. out of turn. a.** not in the correct or agreed order of succession. **b.** improperly, inappropriately, or inopportunely. **64. turn and turn about.** one after another; alternately. **65. to a turn.** to the proper amount; perfectly: *cooked to a turn.* ~See also **turn against, turn away, turn down, turn in, turn off, turn on, turn out, turn over, turn to, turn up.** [Old English *tyrnian,* from Old French *torner,* from Latin *tornāre* to turn in a lathe, from *tornus* lathe, from Greek *tornos* dividers] —'**turnable** *adj.*

turnabout ('tɜːnə,baʊt) *n.* **1.** the act of turning so as to face a different direction. **2.** a change or reversal of opinion, attitude, etc. ~Also called: **turnround.**

turn against *vb.* (*prep.*) to change or cause to change one's attitude so as to become hostile or to retaliate.

turnaround ('tɜːnə,raʊnd) *n.* another word (esp. U.S. and Canadian) for **turnround.**

turnaround time *n. Computer technol.* the total time taken between the submission of a program for execution and the return of the complete output to the customer.

turn away *vb.* (*adv.*) **1.** to move or cause to move in a different direction so as not to face something. **2.** (*tr.*) to refuse admittance or assistance to: *dozens of people were turned away from the hostel.*

turn bridge *n.* another name for **swing bridge.**

turnbuckle ('tɜːn,bʌkəl) *n.* an open mechanical sleeve usually having a swivel at one end and a thread at the other to enable a threaded wire or rope to be tightened. [C19: from TURN + BUCKLE]

turncoat ('tɜːn,kəʊt) *n.* a person who deserts one cause or party for the opposite faction; renegade.

turncock ('tɜːn,kɒk) *n.* an official employed to turn on the water for the mains supply.

turn down *vb.* (*tr., adv.*) **1.** to reduce (the volume or brightness) of (something): *please turn the radio down.* **2.** to reject or refuse. **3.** to fold down (a collar, sheets on a bed, etc.). ~*adj.* **turndown.** **4.** (*prenominal*) capable of being or designed to be folded or doubled down.

turned comma *n. Printing.* a single inverted comma (‘), esp. as used in Britain as a quotation mark.

turned period *n. Printing.* an inverted full stop (·), used chiefly as a decimal point.

turner ('tɜːnə) *n.* **1.** a person or thing that turns, esp. a person who operates a lathe. **2.** *U.S.* a member of a society of gymnasts.

turnery ('tɜːnərɪ) *n., pl.* **-eries.** **1.** objects made on a lathe. **2.** Also called: **turning.** the process or skill of turning objects on a lathe. **3.** the workshop of a lathe operator.

turn in *vb.* (*adv.*) *Informal.* **1.** (*intr.*) to go to bed for the night. **2.** (*tr.*) to hand in; deliver: *to turn in an essay.* **3.** to give up or conclude (something): *we turned in the game when it began to rain.* **4.** (*tr.*) to record (a score, etc.). **5. turn in on oneself.** to withdraw or cause to withdraw from contact with others and become preoccupied with one's own problems.

turning ('tɜːnɪŋ) *n.* **1.** Also called: **turn.** a road, river, or path that turns off the main way: *the fourth turning on the right.* **2.** the point where such a way turns off. **3.** a bend in a straight course. **4.** an object made on a lathe. **5.** another name for **turnery** (sense 2). **6.** (*pl.*) the waste produced in turning on a lathe.

turning circle *n.* the smallest circle in which a vehicle can turn.

turning point *n.* **1.** a moment when the course of events is changed: *the turning point of his career.* **2.** a point at which there is a change in direction or motion. **3.** *Maths.* a stationary point at which the first derivative of a function changes sign, so that typically its graph does not cross a horizontal tangent. **4.** *Surveying.* a point to which a foresight and a backsight are taken in levelling; change point.

turnip ('tɜːnɪp) *n.* **1.** a widely cultivated cruciferous plant, *Brassica rapa,* of the Mediterranean region, with a large yellow or white edible root. **2.** the root of this plant, which is eaten as a vegetable. **3.** any of several similar or related plants. **4. turnip cabbage.** another name for **kohlrabi.** ~Also called (for senses 1, 2): **navew.** [C16: from earlier *turnepe,* perhaps from TURN (indicating its rounded shape) + *nepe,* from Latin *nāpus* turnip; see NEEP]

turnip moth *n.* a common noctuid moth, *Agrotis segetum,* drab grey-brown in colour, the larvae of which feed on root crops and brassica stems.

turnkey ('tɜːn,kiː) *n.* **1.** *Archaic.* a keeper of the keys, esp. in a prison; warder or jailer. ~*adj.* **2.** denoting a project, as in civil engineering, in which a single contractor has responsibility for the complete job from the start to the time of installation or occupancy.

turnkey project *n. Engineering.* a complete project usually including many major units of plant completed under one overall contract, such as a chemical works or power station complex. [C20: from use of *turnkey* in the construction industry to describe the day a job will be completed and the owner able to turn the key in the door]

turnkey system *n.* a computer or computer system supplied to a customer in such a complete form that it can be put to immediate use.

turn off *vb.* **1.** (*intr.*) to leave (a road, pathway, etc.). **2.** (*intr.*) (of a road, pathway, etc.) to deviate from (another road, etc.). **3.** (*tr., adv.*) to cause (something) to cease operating by turning a knob, pushing a button, etc.: *to turn off the radio.* **4.** (*tr.*) *Informal.* to cause (a person, etc.) to feel dislike or distaste for (something): *this music turns me off.* **5.** (*tr., adv.*) *Brit. informal.* to dismiss from employment. *~n.* **turn-off. 6.** a road or other way branching off from the main thoroughfare. **7.** *Informal.* a person or thing that elicits dislike or distaste.

turn on *vb.* **1.** (*tr., adv.*) to cause (something) to operate by turning a knob, etc.: *to turn on the light.* **2.** (*intr., prep.*) to depend or hinge on: *the success of the party turns on you.* **3.** (*prep.*) to change or cause to change one's attitude so as to become hostile or to retaliate: *the dog turned on the children.* **4.** (*tr., adv.*) *Informal.* to produce (charm, tears, etc.) suddenly or automatically. **5.** (*tr., adv.*) *Slang.* to arouse emotionally or sexually. **6.** (*intr., adv.*) *Slang.* to take or become intoxicated by drugs. **7.** (*tr., adv.*) *Slang.* to introduce (someone) to drugs. *~n.* **turn-on. 8.** *Slang.* a person or thing that causes emotional or sexual arousal.

turn out *vb.* (*adv.*) **1.** (*tr.*) to cause (something, esp. a light) to cease operating by or as if by turning a knob, etc. **2.** (*tr.*) to produce by an effort or process: *she turned out 50 units per hour.* **3.** (*tr.*) to dismiss, discharge, or expel: *the family had been turned out of their home.* **4.** (*tr.*) to empty the contents of, esp. in order to clean, tidy, or rearrange: *to turn out one's pockets.* **5.** (*copula*) **a.** to prove to be: *her work turned out to be badly done.* **b.** to end up; result: *it all turned out well.* **6.** (*tr.*) to fit as with clothes: *that woman turns her children out well.* **7.** (*intr.*) to assemble or gather: *a crowd turned out for the fair.* **8.** (of a soldier) to parade or to call (a soldier) to parade. **9.** (*intr.*) *Informal.* to get out of bed. *~n.* **turnout. 10.** the body of people appearing together at a gathering. **11.** the quantity or amount produced. **12.** an array of clothing or equipment. **13.** the manner in which a person or thing is arrayed or equipped.

turn over *vb.* (*adv.*) **1.** to change or cause to change position, esp. so as to reverse top and bottom. **2.** to start (an engine), esp. with a starting handle, or (of an engine) to start or function correctly. **3.** to shift or cause to shift position, as by rolling from side to side. **4.** (*tr.*) to deliver; transfer. **5.** (*tr.*) to consider carefully: *he turned over the problem for hours.* **6.** (*tr.*) **a.** to sell and replenish (stock in trade). **b.** to transact business and so generate gross revenue of (a specified sum). **7.** (*tr.*) to invest and recover (capital). **8.** (*tr.*) *Slang.* to rob. **9. turn over a new leaf.** to reform; resolve to improve one's behaviour. *~n.* **turnover. 10. a.** the amount of business, usually expressed in terms of gross revenue, transacted during a specified period. **b.** (*as modifier*): *a turnover tax.* **11.** the rate at which stock in trade is sold and replenished. **12.** a change or reversal of position. **13.** a small semicircular or triangular pastry case filled with fruit, jam, etc. **14. a.** the number of workers employed by a firm in a given period to replace those who have left. **b.** the ratio between this number and the average number of employees during the same period. **15.** *Banking.* the amount of capital funds loaned on call during a specified period. *~adj.* **16.** (*prenominal*) able or designed to be turned or folded over: *a turnover collar.*

turnpike ('tɜːnˌpaɪk) *n.* **1.** (between the mid-16th and late 19th centuries) **a.** gates or some other barrier set across a road to prevent passage until a toll had been paid. **b.** a road on which a turnpike was operated. **2.** an obsolete word for **turnstile** (sense 1). **3.** *U.S.* a motorway for use of which a toll is charged. [C15: from TURN + PIKE[2]]

turnround ('tɜːnˌraʊnd) *n.* **1. a.** the act or process in which a ship, aircraft, etc., unloads passengers and freight at the end of a trip and reloads for the next trip. **b.** the time taken for this. **2.** the total time taken by a ship, aircraft, or other vehicle in a round trip. **3.** a complete reversal of a situation or set of circumstances. ~Also called (esp. U.S. and Canadian): **turnaround.**

turnsole ('tɜːnˌsəʊl) *n.* **1.** any of various plants having flowers that are said to turn towards the sun. **2.** a euphorbiaceous plant, *Croton tinctoria,* of the Mediterranean region that yields a purple dye. **3.** the dye extracted from this plant. [C14: from Old French *tournesole,* from Old Italian *tornasole,* from *tornare* to TURN + *sole* sun, from Latin *sōl* sun]

turnspit ('tɜːnˌspɪt) *n.* **1.** (formerly) a servant or small dog whose job was to turn the spit on which meat, poultry, etc., was roasting. **2.** a spit that can be so turned.

turnstile ('tɜːnˌstaɪl) *n.* **1.** a mechanical gate or barrier with metal arms that are turned to admit one person at a time, usually in one direction only. **2.** any similar device that admits foot passengers but no large animals or vehicles. **3.** *Logic.* Also called: **gatepost.** a symbol of the form $\vdash$, $\models$, or $\Vdash$, used to represent logical consequence when inserted between expressions to form a sequent, or when prefixed to a single expression to indicate its status as a theorem.

turnstone ('tɜːnˌstəʊn) *n.* either of two shore birds of the genus *Arenaria,* esp. *A. interpres* (**ruddy turnstone**). They are related and similar to plovers and sandpipers. [C17: so called because it turns over stones in search of food]

turntable ('tɜːnˌteɪbᵊl) *n.* **1.** the circular horizontal platform that rotates a gramophone record while it is being played. **2.** a flat circular platform that can be rotated about its centre, used for turning locomotives and cars. **3.** the revolvable platform on a microscope on which specimens are examined. **4.** *Austral.* an area on a road, hill, etc., where a motor vehicle can turn round.

turntable ladder *n. Brit.* a power-operated extending ladder mounted on a fire engine. U.S. and Canadian name: **aerial ladder.**

turn to *vb.* (*intr., adv.*) to set about a task: *we must turn to and finish our work.*

turn up *vb.* (*adv.*) **1.** (*intr.*) to arrive or appear: *he turned up late at the party.* **2.** to find or be found, esp. by accident: *his book turned up in the cupboard.* **3.** (*tr.*) to increase the flow, volume, etc., of: *to turn up the radio.* **4.** (*tr.*) *Informal.* to cause to vomit. *~n.* **turn-up. 5.** (*often pl.*) *Brit.* the turned-up fold at the bottom of some trouser legs. U.S. and Canadian name: **cuff. 6.** *Informal.* an unexpected or chance occurrence.

turpentine ('tɜːpᵊnˌtaɪn) *n.* **1.** Also called: **gum turpentine.** any of various viscous oleoresins obtained from various coniferous trees, esp. from the longleaf pine, and used as the main source of commercial turpentine. **2.** a brownish-yellow sticky viscous oleoresin that exudes from the terebinth tree. **3.** Also called: **oil of turpentine, spirits of turpentine.** a colourless flammable volatile liquid with a pungent odour, distilled from turpentine oleoresin. It is an essential oil containing a mixture of terpenes and is used as a solvent for paints and in medicine as a rubefacient and expectorant. Sometimes shortened (esp. Brit.) to **turps. 4.** Also called: **turpentine substitute, white spirit.** (*not in technical usage*) any one of a number of thinners for paints and varnishes, consisting of fractions of petroleum. Related adj.: **terebinthine.** *~vb.* (*tr.*) **5.** to treat or saturate with turpentine. **6.** to extract crude turpentine from (trees). [C14 *terebentyne,* from Medieval Latin *terbentīna,* from Latin *terebinthīna* turpentine, from *terebinthus* the turpentine tree, TEREBINTH]

turpentine tree *n.* **1.** a tropical African leguminous tree, *Copaifera mopane,* yielding a hard dark wood and a useful resin. **2.** either of two Australian evergreen myrtaceous trees, *Syncarpia lilli* or *S. glomulifera,* that have durable wood and are sometimes planted as shade trees.

turpeth ('tɜːpɪθ) *n.* **1.** a convolvulaceous plant, *Operculina turpethum,* of the East Indies, having roots with purgative properties. **2.** the root of this plant or the drug obtained from it. [C14: from Medieval Latin *turbithum,* ultimately from Arabic *turbid*]

turpitude ('tɜːpɪˌtjuːd) *n.* base character or action; depravity. [C15: from Latin *turpitūdō* ugliness, from *turpis* base]

turps (tɜːps) *n.* (*functioning as sing.*) **1.** *Brit.* short for **turpentine** (sense 3). **2.** *Austral. and N.Z. slang.* alcoholic drink, esp. beer.

turquoise ('tɜːkwɔɪz, -kwɑːz) *n.* **1.** a greenish-blue fine-grained secondary mineral consisting of hydrated copper aluminium phosphate. It occurs in igneous rocks rich in aluminium and is used as a gemstone. Formula: $CuAl_6(PO_4)_4(OH)_8.4H_2O$. **2. a.** the colour of turquoise. **b.** (*as adj.*): *a turquoise dress.* [C14: from Old French *turqueise* Turkish (stone)]

turret ('tʌrɪt) *n.* **1.** a small tower that projects from the wall of a building, esp. a medieval castle. **2. a.** a self-contained structure, capable of rotation, in which weapons are mounted, esp. in tanks and warships. **b.** a similar structure on an aircraft that houses one or more guns and sometimes a gunner. **3.** a tall wooden tower on wheels used formerly by besiegers to scale the walls of a fortress. **4.** (on a machine tool) a turret-like steel structure with tools projecting radially that can be indexed round to bring each tool to bear on the work. [C14: from Old French *torete,* from *tor* tower, from Latin *turris*]

turreted ('tʌrɪtɪd), **turriculate** (tʌ'rɪkjʊlɪt, -ˌleɪt), *or* **turriculated** *adj.* **1.** having or resembling a turret or turrets. **2.** (of a gastropod shell) having the shape of a long spiral.

turret lathe *n.* another name for **capstan lathe.**

turtle[1] ('tɜːtᵊl) *n.* **1.** any of various aquatic chelonian reptiles, esp. those of the marine family *Chelonidae,* having a flattened shell enclosing the body and flipper-like limbs adapted for swimming. **2.** *U.S. and Canadian.* any of the chelonian reptiles, including the tortoises and terrapins. **3.** *Nautical.* a zip bag made as part of a spinnaker for holding the sail so that it can be set rapidly. **4. turn turtle.** to capsize. *~vb.* **5.** (*intr.*) to catch or hunt turtles. [C17: from French *tortue* TORTOISE (influenced by TURTLE[2])] —'**turtler** *n.*

turtle[2] ('tɜːtᵊl) *n.* an archaic name for **turtledove.** [Old English *turtla,* from Latin *turtur,* of imitative origin; related to German *Turteltaube*]

turtleback ('tɜːtᵊlˌbæk) *n.* **1.** an arched projection over the upper deck of a ship at the bow and sometimes at the stern for protection in heavy seas. **2.** (*now obsolete in archaeological usage*) a crude convex stone axe.

turtledove (ˈtɜːtᵊlˌdʌv) *n.* **1.** any of several Old World doves of the genus *Streptopelia,* having a brown plumage with speckled wings and a long dark tail. **2.** a gentle or loving person. [see TURTLE²]

turtleneck (ˈtɜːtᵊlˌnɛk) *n.* **a.** a round high close-fitting neck on a sweater or the sweater itself. **b.** (*as modifier*): *a turtleneck sweater.*

turves (tɜːvz) *n.* a plural of **turf.**

Tuscan (ˈtʌskən) *adj.* **1.** of or relating to the region of Tuscany in central Italy, its inhabitants, or their dialect of Italian. **2.** of, denoting, or relating to one of the five classical orders of architecture: characterized by a column with an unfluted shaft and a capital and base with mouldings but no decoration. See also **Ionic, Composite, Doric, Corinthian.** ~*n.* **3.** a native or inhabitant of Tuscany. **4.** any of the dialects of Italian spoken in Tuscany, esp. the dialect of Florence: the standard form of Italian.

Tuscarora (ˌtʌskəˈrɔːrə) *n.* **1.** (*pl.* **-ras** *or* **-ra**) a member of a North American Indian people formerly living in North Carolina, who later moved to New York State and joined the Iroquois. **2.** the language of this people, belonging to the Iroquoian family.

tusche (tʊʃ) *n.* a substance used in lithography for drawing the design and as a resist in silk-screen printing and lithography. [from German, from *tuschen* to touch up with colour or ink, from French *toucher* to TOUCH]

tush¹ (tʌʃ) *interj. Archaic.* an exclamation of disapproval or contempt. [C15: Middle English, of imitative origin]

tush² (tʌʃ) *n. Rare.* a tusk. [Old English *tūsc;* see TUSK]

tushery (ˈtʌʃərɪ) *n. Literary.* the use of affectedly archaic language in novels, etc. [coined by the British writer Robert Louis Stevenson (1850–94) from TUSH¹ + -ERY]

tusk (tʌsk) *n.* **1.** a pointed elongated usually paired tooth in the elephant, walrus, and certain other mammals that is specialized for fighting. **2.** the canine tooth of certain animals, esp. horses. **3.** a sharp pointed projection. **4.** Also called: **tusk tenon.** *Building trades.* a tenon shaped with an additional oblique shoulder to make a stronger joint. ~*vb.* **5.** to stab, tear, or gore with the tusks. [Old English *tūsc;* related to Old Frisian *tosk;* see TOOTH] —**tusked** *adj.* —ˈ**tusk**ˌ**like** *adj.*

tusker (ˈtʌskə) *n.* any animal with prominent tusks, esp. a wild boar or elephant.

tusk shell *n.* any of various burrowing sea-shore molluscs of the genus *Dentalium* and related genera that have a long narrow tubular shell open at both ends: class *Scaphopoda.* Also called: **tooth shell.**

tussis (ˈtʌsɪs) *n.* the technical name for a **cough.** See **pertussis.** [Latin: cough] —ˈ**tussal** *adj.* —ˈ**tussive** *adj.*

tussle (ˈtʌsᵊl) *vb.* **1.** (*intr.*) to fight or wrestle in a vigorous way; struggle. ~*n.* **2.** a vigorous fight; scuffle; struggle. [C15: related to Old High German *zūsen;* see TOUSLE]

tussock (ˈtʌsək) *n.* **1.** a dense tuft of vegetation, esp. of grass. **2.** *Austral. and N.Z.* **a.** short for **tussock grass. b. the.** country where tussock grass grows. [C16: perhaps related to TUSK] —ˈ**tussocky** *adj.*

tussock grass *n. Austral. and N.Z.* any of several pasture grasses of the genus *Poa.*

tussock moth *n.* any of various pale or dull-coloured moths of the family *Lymantriidae* (or *Laparidae*), the hairy caterpillars of which are pests of many trees. See also **gipsy moth, browntail moth, goldtail moth.** [C19: so named because of the tufts of hair on the caterpillars]

tussore (tʊˈsɔː, ˈtʌsə), **tusser** (ˈtʌsə), *or* (*chiefly U.S.*) **tussah** (ˈtʌsə) *n.* **1.** a strong coarse brownish Indian silk obtained from the cocoons of an Oriental saturniid silkworm, *Antheraea paphia.* **2.** a fabric woven from this silk. **3.** the silkworm producing this silk. [C17: from Hindi *tasar* shuttle, from Sanskrit *tasara* a wild silkworm]

tut *interj.* (*pronounced as an alveolar click; spelling pron.* tʌt), *n., vb.* **tuts, tutting, tutted.** short for **tut-tut.**

tutee (tjuːˈtiː) *n.* one who is tutored, esp. in a university.

tutelage (ˈtjuːtɪlɪdʒ) *n.* **1.** the act or office of a guardian or tutor. **2.** instruction or guidance, esp. by a tutor. **3.** the condition of being under the supervision of a guardian or tutor. [C17: from Latin *tūtēla* a caring for, from *tuērī* to watch over; compare TUITION]

tutelary (ˈtjuːtɪlərɪ) *or* **tutelar** (ˈtjuːtɪlə) *adj.* **1.** invested with the role of guardian or protector. **2.** of or relating to a guardian or guardianship. ~*n., pl.* **-laries** *or* **-lars. 3.** a tutelary person, deity, or saint.

tutiorism (ˈtjuːtɪəˌrɪzəm) *n.* (in Roman Catholic moral theology) the doctrine that in cases of moral doubt it is best to follow the safer course or that in agreement with the law. [C19: from Latin *tutior* safer, comparative of *tutus* safe] —ˈ**tutiorist** *n.*

tutor (ˈtjuːtə) *n.* **1.** a teacher, usually instructing individual pupils and often engaged privately. **2.** (at universities, colleges, etc.) a member of staff responsible for the teaching and supervision of a certain number of students. **3.** *Scots Law.* the guardian of a pupil. See **pupil¹** (sense 2). ~*vb.* **4.** to act as a tutor to (someone); instruct. **5.** (*tr.*) to act as guardian to; have care of. **6.** (*intr.*) *Chiefly U.S.* to study under a tutor. **7.** (*tr.*) *Rare.* to admonish, discipline, or reprimand. [C14: from Latin: a watcher, from *tuērī* to watch over] —ˈ**tutorage** *or* ˈ**tutor**ˌ**ship** *n.*

tutorial (tjuːˈtɔːrɪəl) *n.* **1.** a period of intensive tuition given by a tutor to an individual student or to a small group of students. ~*adj.* **2.** of or relating to a tutor.

tutorial system *n.* a system, mainly in universities, in which students receive guidance in academic or personal matters from tutors.

tutsan (ˈtʌtsən) *n.* a woodland shrub, *Hypericum androsaemum,* of Europe and W Asia, having yellow flowers and reddish-purple fruits: family *Hypericaceae.* See also **Saint John's wort.** [C15: from Old French *toute-saine* (unattested), literally: all healthy]

Tutsi (ˈtuːtsɪ) *n., pl.* **-si** *or* **-sis.** a member of a Bantu people of Rwanda in central Africa.

tutti (ˈtʊtɪ) *adj., adv. Music.* to be performed by the whole orchestra, choir, etc. Compare **soli.** [C18: from Italian, pl. of *tutto* all, from Latin *tōtus*]

tutti-frutti (ˈtuːtɪˈfruːtɪ) *n.* **1.** (*pl.* **-fruttis**) an ice cream or a confection containing small pieces of candied or fresh fruits. **2.** a preserve of chopped mixed fruits, often with brandy syrup. **3.** a flavour like that of many fruits combined. ~*adj.* **4.** having such a flavour. [from Italian, literally: all the fruits]

tut-tut *interj.* (*pronounced as alveolar clicks; spelling pron.* ˈtʌtˈtʌt). **1.** an exclamation of mild reprimand, disapproval, or surprise. ~*vb.* **-tuts, -tutting, -tutted. 2.** (*intr.*) to express disapproval by the exclamation of "tut-tut." ~*n.* **3.** the act of tut-tutting. ~Often shortened to **tut.**

tutty (ˈtʌtɪ) *n.* finely powdered impure zinc oxide obtained from the flues of zinc-smelting furnaces and used as a polishing powder. [C14: from Old French *tutie,* from Arabic *tūtiyā,* probably from Persian, from Sanskrit *tuttha*]

tutu¹ (ˈtuːtuː) *n.* a very short skirt worn by ballerinas, made of projecting layers of stiffened sheer material. [from French, changed from the nursery word *cucu* backside, from *cul,* from Latin *cūlus* the buttocks]

tutu² (ˈtuːtuː) *n.* a shrub, *Coriaria arborea,* of New Zealand, having seeds that are poisonous to farm animals. [Maori]

tu-whit tu-whoo (təˈwɪt təˈwuː) *interj.* an imitation or representation of the sound made by an owl.

tuxedo (tʌkˈsiːdəʊ) *n., pl.* **-dos.** the usual U.S. and Canadian name for **dinner jacket,** often shortened to **tux.** [C19: named after a country club in *Tuxedo Park,* New York]

tuyère (ˈtwiːɛə, ˈtwaɪə; *French* tyjɛr) *or* **twyer** (ˈtwaɪə) *n.* a water-cooled nozzle through which air is blown into a cupola, blast furnace, or forge. [C18: from French, from *tuyau* pipe, from Old French *tuel,* probably of Germanic origin]

TV *abbrev. for* television.

TVEI (in Britain) *Education. abbrev. for* technical and vocational educational initiative.

TV game *n.* a video game, such as tennis, football, or target practice, that is played on a domestic television screen by plugging in a special unit with manual controls for one or two players.

TVP *abbrev. for* textured vegetable protein: a protein obtained from soya beans or other vegetables that have been spun into fibres and flavoured: used esp. as a substitute for meat.

TVR *abbrev. for* television rating: a measurement of the popularity of a TV programme based on a survey.

TVRO *abbrev. for* television receive only: an antenna and associated apparatus for reception from a broadcasting satellite.

twa (twɔː) *or* **twae** (twe) *n., determiner.* a Scot. word for **two.**

twaddle (ˈtwɒdᵊl) *n.* **1.** silly, trivial, or pretentious talk or writing; nonsense. ~*vb.* **2.** to talk or write (something) in a silly or pretentious way. [C16 *twattle,* variant of *twittle* or *tittle;* see TITTLE-TATTLE] —ˈ**twaddler** *n.*

twain (tweɪn) *determiner, n.* an archaic word for **two.** [Old English *twēgen;* related to Old Saxon *twēne,* Old High German *zwēne,* Old Norse *tveir,* Gothic *twai*]

twang (twæŋ) *n.* **1.** a sharp ringing sound produced by or as if by the plucking of a taut string: *the twang of a guitar.* **2.** the act of plucking a string to produce such a sound. **3.** a strongly nasal quality in a person's speech, esp. in certain dialects. ~*vb.* **4.** to make or cause to make a twang: *to twang a guitar.* **5.** to strum (music, a tune, etc.): *to twang on a guitar.* **6.** to speak or utter with a sharp nasal voice. **7.** (*intr.*) to be released or move with a twang: *the arrow twanged away.* [C16: of imitative origin] —ˈ**twangy** *adj.*

'twas (twɒz; *unstressed* twəz) *Poetic or dialect. contraction of* it was.

twat (twæt, twɒt) *n. Taboo slang.* **1.** the female genitals. **2.** a girl or woman considered sexually. **3.** a foolish or despicable person. [of unknown origin]

twattle (ˈtwɒtᵊl) *n.* a rare word for **twaddle.**

twayblade (ˈtweɪˌbleɪd) *n.* any of various terrestrial orchids of the genera *Listera, Liparis, Ophrys,* etc., having a basal pair of oval unstalked leaves arranged opposite each other. [C16: translation of Medieval Latin *bifolium* having two leaves, from obsolete *tway* TWO + BLADE]

tweak (twiːk) *vb.* (*tr.*) **1.** to twist, jerk, or pinch with a sharp or sudden movement: *to tweak someone's nose.* **2.** *Motor racing slang.* to tune (a car or engine) for peak performance. ~*n.* **3.** an instance of tweaking. [Old English *twiccian;* related to Old High German *zwecchōn;* see TWITCH] —ˈ**tweaky** *adj.*

tweaker (ˈtwiːkə) *n. Slang.* an engineer's small screwdriver, used for fine adjustments.

twee (twiː) *adj. Brit.* excessively sentimental, sweet, or pretty. [C19: from *tweet*, mincing or affected pronunciation of SWEET] —ˈ**tweely** *adv.*

tweed (twiːd) *n.* **1. a.** a thick woollen often knobbly cloth produced originally in Scotland. **b.** (*as modifier*): *a tweed coat.* **2.** (*pl.*) clothes made of this cloth, esp. a man's or woman's suit. **3.** (*pl.*) *Austral. informal.* trousers. [C19: probably from *tweel*, a Scottish variant of TWILL, influenced by *Tweed*, a river in SE Scotland and NE England]

Tweedledum and Tweedledee (ˌtwiːdᵊlˈdʌm; ˌtwiːdᵊlˈdiː) *n.* any two persons or things that differ only slightly from each other; two of a kind. [C19: from the proverbial names of the rival musicians Handel and Buononcini, thought by some to be so similar that there was nothing to choose between them. The names were popularized by Lewis Carroll's use of them in *Through the Looking Glass* (1872)]

tweedy (ˈtwiːdɪ) *adj.* **tweedier, tweediest. 1.** of, made of, or resembling tweed. **2.** showing a fondness for a hearty outdoor life, usually associated with wearers of tweeds. —ˈ**tweediness** *n.*

ˈ**tween** (twiːn) *Poetic or dialect. contraction of* between.

ˈ**tween deck** *or* **decks** *n. Nautical.* a space between two continuous decks of a vessel.

tweeny (ˈtwiːnɪ) *n., pl.* **tweenies.** *Brit. informal, obsolete.* a maid who assists both cook and housemaid. [C19: shortened from BETWEEN (that is, a maid between cook and housemaid)]

tweet (twiːt) *interj.* **1.** (*often reiterated*) an imitation or representation of the thin chirping sound made by small or young birds. ~*vb.* **2.** (*intr.*) to make this sound. [C19: of imitative origin]

tweeter (ˈtwiːtə) *n.* a loudspeaker used in high-fidelity systems for the reproduction of high audio frequencies. It is usually employed in conjunction with a woofer and a crossover network. [C20: from TWEET]

tweeze (twiːz) *vb. Chiefly U.S.* to take hold of or pluck (hair, small objects, etc.) with or as if with tweezers. [C17: back formation from TWEEZERS]

tweezers (ˈtwiːzəz) *pl. n.* a small pincer-like instrument for handling small objects, plucking out hairs, etc. Also called: **pair of tweezers, tweezer** (esp. U.S.). [C17: plural of *tweezer* (on the model of *scissors*, etc.), from *tweeze* case of instruments, from French *étuis* cases (of instruments), from Old French *estuier* to preserve, from Vulgar Latin *studiāre* (unattested) to keep, from Latin *studēre* to care about]

twelfth (twɛlfθ) *adj.* **1.** (*usually prenominal*) **a.** coming after the eleventh in number or counting order, position, time, etc.; being the ordinal number of *twelve:* often written 12th. **b.** (*as n.*)*: the twelfth of the month.* ~*n.* **2. a.** one of 12 equal or nearly equal parts of an object, quantity, measurement, etc. **b.** (*as modifier*)*: a twelfth part.* **3.** the fraction equal to one divided by 12 (1/12). **4.** *Music.* **a.** an interval of one octave plus a fifth. **b.** one of two notes constituting such an interval in relation to the other. **c.** an organ stop sounding a note one octave and a fifth higher than that normally produced by the key depressed. [from Old English *twelfta*]

Twelfth Day *n.* **a.** Jan. 6, the twelfth day after Christmas and the feast of the Epiphany, formerly observed as the final day of the Christmas celebrations. **b.** (*as modifier*)*: Twelfth-Day celebrations.*

twelfth man *n.* a reserve player in a cricket team.

Twelfth Night *n.* **a.** the evening of Jan. 5, the eve of Twelfth Day, formerly observed with various festal celebrations. **b.** the evening of Twelfth Day itself. **c.** (*as modifier*)*: Twelfth-Night customs.*

Twelfthtide (ˈtwɛlfθˌtaɪd) *n.* **a.** the season of Epiphany. **b.** (*as modifier*)*: the Twelfthtide celebrations.*

twelve (twɛlv) *n.* **1.** the cardinal number that is the sum of ten and two. See also **number** (sense 1). **2.** a numeral, 12, XII, etc., representing this number. **3.** something represented by, representing, or consisting of 12 units. **4.** Also called: **twelve o'clock.** noon or midnight. ~*determiner.* **5. a.** amounting to twelve: *twelve loaves.* **b.** (*as pronoun*)*: twelve have arrived.* ~Related adj.: **duodecimal.** See also **dozen.** [Old English *twelf;* related to Old Frisian *twelif,* Old High German *zwelif,* Old Norse *tolf,* Gothic *twalif*]

twelve-inch *n.* a gramophone record 12 inches in diameter and played at 45 revolutions per minute, usually containing an extended remix of a single.

twelve-mile limit *n.* the offshore boundary 12 miles from the coast claimed by some states as marking the extent of their territorial jurisdiction.

twelvemo (ˈtwɛlvməʊ) *n., pl.* **-mos.** *Bookbinding.* another word for **duodecimo.**

twelvemonth (ˈtwɛlvˌmʌnθ) *n. Chiefly Brit.* an archaic or dialect word for a **year.**

twelve pitch *n.* another name for **elite** (sense 2).

twelve-tone *adj.* of, relating to, or denoting a type of serial music that uses as musical material a tone row formed by the 12 semitones of the chromatic scale, together with its inverted and retrograde versions. The technique has been applied in various ways by different composers and usually results in music in which there are few, if any, tonal centres. See **serialism.**

twentieth (ˈtwɛntɪɪθ) *adj.* **1.** (*usually prenominal*) **a.** coming after the nineteenth in numbering or counting order, position, time, etc.; being the ordinal number of *twenty:* often written 20th. **b.** (*as n.*)*: he left on the twentieth.* ~*n.* **2. a.** one of 20 approximately equal parts of something. **b.** (*as modifier*)*: a twentieth part.* **3.** the fraction that is equal to one divided by 20 (1/20). [from Old English *twentigotha*]

twentieth man *n. Australian Rules football.* the second reserve player.

twenty (ˈtwɛntɪ) *n., pl.* **-ties. 1.** the cardinal number that is the product of ten and two; a score. See also **number** (sense 1). **2.** a numeral, 20, XX, etc., representing this number. **3.** something representing, represented by, or consisting of 20 units. ~*determiner.* **4. a.** amounting to twenty: *twenty questions.* **b.** (*as pronoun*)*: to order twenty.* [Old English *twēntig;* related to Old High German *zweinzug,* German *zwanzig*]

twenty-one *n.* another name (esp. U.S.) for **pontoon**[2] (sense 1).

twenty-twenty *adj. Med.* (of vision) being of normal acuity: usually written 20/20.

ˈ**twere** (twɜː; *unstressed* twə) *Poetic or dialect. contraction of* it were.

twerp *or* **twirp** (twɜːp) *n. Informal.* a silly, weak-minded, or contemptible person. [C20: of unknown origin]

Twi (twiː) *n.* **1.** a language of S Ghana: one of the two chief dialects of Akan. Formerly called: **Ashanti.** Compare **Fanti. 2.** (*pl.* **Twi** *or* **Twis**) a member of the Negroid people who speak this language.

twibill *or* **twibil** (ˈtwaɪˌbɪl) *n.* **1.** a mattock with a blade shaped like an adze at one end and like an axe at the other. **2.** *Archaic.* a double-bladed battle-axe. [Old English, from *twi-* two, double + *bill* sword, BILL[3]]

twice (twaɪs) *adv.* **1.** two times; on two occasions or in two cases: *he coughed twice.* **2.** double in degree or quantity: *twice as long.* [Old English *twiwa;* related to Old Norse *tvisvar,* Middle Low German *twiges*]

twice-laid *adj.* **1.** made from strands of used rope. **2.** made from old or used material or retwisted yarn. [C16: from LAY[1] (in the sense: to twist together)]

twice-told *adj.* hackneyed through repeated use.

twiddle (ˈtwɪdᵊl) *vb.* **1.** (when *intr.*, often foll. by *with*) to twirl or fiddle (with), often in an idle way. **2. twiddle one's thumbs.** to do nothing; be unoccupied. **3.** (*intr.*) to turn, twirl, or rotate. **4.** (*intr.*) *Rare.* to be occupied with trifles. ~*n.* **5.** an act or instance of twiddling. [C16: probably a blend of TWIRL + FIDDLE] —ˈ**twiddler** *n.*

twig[1] (twɪg) *n.* **1.** any small branch or shoot of a tree or other woody plant. **2.** something resembling this, esp. a minute branch of a blood vessel. [Old English *twigge;* related to Old Norse *dvika* consisting of two, Old High German *zwīg* twig, Old Danish *tvige* fork] —ˈ**twigˌlike** *adj.*

twig[2] (twɪg) *vb.* **twigs, twigging, twigged.** *Brit. informal.* **1.** to understand (something). **2.** to find out or suddenly comprehend (something): *he hasn't twigged yet.* **3.** (*tr.*) *Rare.* to perceive (something). [C18: perhaps from Scottish Gaelic *tuig* I understand]

twiggy (ˈtwɪgɪ) *adj.* **-gier, -giest. 1.** of or relating to a twig or twigs. **2.** covered with twigs. **3.** slender or fragile.

twilight (ˈtwaɪˌlaɪt) *n.* **1.** the soft diffused light occurring when the sun is just below the horizon, esp. following sunset. Related adj.: **crepuscular. 2.** the period in which this light occurs. **3.** the period of time during which the sun is a specified angular distance below the horizon (6°, 12°, and 18° for **civil twilight, nautical twilight,** and **astronomical twilight,** respectively). **4.** any faint light. **5.** a period in which strength, importance, etc., are waning: *the twilight of his life.* **6.** (*modifier*) of or relating to twilight; dim. [C15: literally: half-light (between day and night), from Old English *twi-* half + LIGHT[1]] —**twilit** (ˈtwaɪˌlɪt) *adj.*

twilight sleep *n. Med.* a state of partial anaesthesia in which the patient retains a slight degree of consciousness.

twilight zone *n.* **1.** an area of a city or town, usually surrounding the central business district, where houses have become dilapidated. **2.** the lowest level of the ocean to which light can penetrate. **3.** any indefinite or transitional condition or area.

twill (twɪl) *adj.* **1.** (in textiles) of or designating a weave in which the weft yarns are worked around two or more warp yarns to produce an effect of parallel diagonal lines or ribs. ~*n.* **2.** any fabric so woven. ~*vb.* **3.** (*tr.*) to weave in this fashion. [Old English *twilic* having a double thread; related to Old High German *zwilīth* twill, Latin *bilīx* two-threaded]

ˈ**twill** (twɪl) *Poetic or dialect. contraction of* it will.

twin (twɪn) *n.* **1. a.** either of two persons or animals conceived at the same time. **b.** (*as modifier*)*: a twin brother.* See also **identical** (sense 3), **fraternal** (sense 3). **2. a.** either of two persons or things that are identical or very similar; counterpart. **b.** (*as modifier*)*: twin carburettors.* **3.** Also called: **macle.** a crystal consisting of two parts each of which has a definite orientation to the other. ~*vb.* **twins, twinning, twinned. 4.** to pair or be paired together; couple. **5.** (*intr.*) to bear twins. **6.** (*intr.*) (of a crystal) to form into a twin. **7.** (*intr.*) *Archaic.* to be born as a twin. **8. a.** (*tr.*) to create a reciprocal relation between (two towns in different countries); pair (a town) with another in a different country. **b.** (*intr.*) (of a town) to be paired with a town

in a different country. [Old English *twinn;* related to Old High German *zwiniling*, Old Norse *tvinnr* double] —'**twinning** *n.*
twin bed *n.* one of a pair of matching single beds.
twinberry ('twɪnbərɪ, -brɪ) *n., pl.* **-ries.** another name for **partridgeberry** (sense 1).
twin bill *n. U.S.* an informal name for **double feature** or **double-header** (sense 2).
twine (twaɪn) *n.* **1.** string made by twisting together fibres of hemp, cotton, etc. **2.** the act or an instance of twining. **3.** something produced or characterized by twining. **4.** a twist, coil, or convolution. **5.** a knot, tangle, or snarl. ~*vb.* **6.** (*tr.*) to twist together; interweave: *she twined the wicker to make a basket.* **7.** (*tr.*) to form by or as if by twining: *to twine a garland.* **8.** (when *intr.*, often foll. by *around*) to wind or cause to wind, esp. in spirals: *the creeper twines around the tree.* [Old English *twīn;* related to Old Frisian *twīne,* Dutch *twijn* twine, Lithuanian *dvynu* twins; see TWIN] —'**twiner** *n.*
twinflower ('twɪn,flaʊə) *n.* an evergreen caprifoliaceous trailing shrub, *Linnaea borealis,* of North America, having round leaves, white or pink fragrant bell-shaped flowers arranged in pairs, and yellow fruits.
twinge (twɪndʒ) *n.* **1.** a sudden brief darting or stabbing pain. **2.** a sharp emotional pang: *a twinge of conscience.* ~*vb.* **3.** to have or cause to have a twinge. **4.** (*tr.*) *Obsolete.* to pinch; tweak. [Old English *twengan* to pinch; related to Old High German *zwengen*]
twinkle ('twɪŋkᵊl) *vb.* (*mainly intr.*) **1.** to emit or reflect light in a flickering manner; shine brightly and intermittently; sparkle: *twinkling stars.* **2.** (of the eyes) to sparkle, esp. with amusement or delight. **3.** *Rare.* to move about quickly. **4.** (*also tr.*) *Rare.* to wink (the eyes); blink. ~*n.* **5.** an intermittent gleam of light; flickering brightness; sparkle or glimmer. **6.** an instant. **7.** a rare word for **wink**[1]. [Old English *twinclian;* related to Middle High German *zwinken* to blink] —'**twinkler** *n.*
twinkling ('twɪŋklɪŋ) *or* **twink** (twɪŋk) *n.* a very short time; instant; moment. Also called: **twinkling of an eye.**
twin-lens reflex *n.* See **reflex camera.**
twin paradox *n.* a phenomenon predicted by relativity. One of a pair of identical twins is supposed to live normally in an inertial system whilst the other is accelerated to a high speed in a spaceship, travels for a long time, and finally returns to rest beside his twin. The travelled twin will be found to be younger than his brother.
Twins (twɪnz) *pl. n.* **the.** the constellation Gemini, the third sign of the zodiac.
twin-screw *adj.* (of a vessel) having two propellers.
twinset ('twɪn,sɛt) *n. Brit.* a matching jumper and cardigan.
twin town *n. Brit.* a town that has civic associations, such as reciprocal visits and cultural exchanges, with a foreign town, usually of similar size and sometimes with other similarities, as in commercial activities.
twin-tub *n.* a type of washing machine that has two revolving drums, one for washing and the other for spin-drying.
twirl (twɜːl) *vb.* **1.** to move or cause to move around rapidly and repeatedly in a circle. **2.** (*tr.*) to twist, wind, or twiddle, often idly: *she twirled her hair around her finger.* **3.** (*intr.;* often foll. by *around* or *about*) to turn suddenly to face another way: *she twirled around angrily to face him.* ~*n.* **4.** an act of rotating or being rotated; whirl or twist. **5.** something wound around or twirled; coil. **6.** a written flourish or squiggle. [C16: perhaps a blend of TWIST + WHIRL] —'**twirler** *n.*
twirp (twɜːp) *n.* a variant spelling of **twerp.**
twist (twɪst) *vb.* **1.** to cause (one end or part) to turn or (of one end or part) to turn in the opposite direction from another; coil or spin. **2.** to distort or be distorted; change in shape. **3.** to wind or cause to wind; twine, coil, or intertwine: *to twist flowers into a wreath.* **4.** to force or be forced out of the natural form or position: *to twist one's ankle.* **5.** to change or cause to change for the worse in character, meaning, etc.; pervert: *his ideas are twisted; she twisted the statement.* **6.** to revolve or cause to revolve; rotate. **7.** (*tr.*) to wrench with a turning action: *to twist something from someone's grasp.* **8.** (*intr.*) to follow a winding course. **9.** (*intr.*) to squirm, as with pain. **10.** (*intr.*) to dance the twist. **11.** (*tr.*) *Brit. informal.* to cheat; swindle. **12. twist someone's arm.** to persuade or coerce someone. ~*n.* **13.** the act or an instance of twisting. **14.** something formed by or as if by twisting: *a twist of hair.* **15.** a decisive change of direction, aim, meaning, or character. **16.** (in a novel, play, etc.) an unexpected event, revelation, or other development. **17.** a bend: *a twist in the road.* **18.** a distortion of the original or natural shape or form. **19.** a jerky pull, wrench, or turn. **20.** a strange personal characteristic, esp. a bad one. **21.** a confused mess, tangle, or knot made by twisting. **22.** a twisted thread used in sewing where extra strength is needed. **23.** (in weaving) a specified direction of twisting the yarn. **24. the twist.** a modern dance popular in the 1960s, in which couples vigorously twist the hips in time to rhythmic music. **25.** a bread loaf or roll made of one or more pieces of twisted dough. **26.** a thin sliver of peel from a lemon, lime, etc., twisted and added to a drink. **27. a.** a cigar made by twisting three cigars around one another. **b.** chewing tobacco made in the form of a roll by twisting the leaves together. **28.** *Physics.* torsional deformation or shear stress or strain. **29.** *Sport, chiefly U.S. and Canadian.* spin given to a ball in various games, esp. baseball. **30.** the extent to which the grooves in the bore of a rifled firearm are spiralled. **31. round the twist.** *Brit. slang.* mad; eccentric. [Old English; related to German dialect *Zwist* a quarrel, Dutch *twisten* to quarrel] —'**twistable** *adj.* —,**twista'bility** *n.* —'**twisted** *adj.* —'**twisting** *adj.*
twist drill *n.* a drill bit having two helical grooves running from the point along the shank to clear swarf and cuttings.
twister ('twɪstə) *n.* **1.** *Brit.* a swindling or dishonest person. **2.** a person or thing that twists, such as a device used in making ropes. **3.** *U.S. and Canadian.* an informal name for **tornado. 4.** a ball moving with a twisting motion.
twist grip *n.* a handlebar control in the form of a ratchet-controlled rotating grip, used on some bicycles and motorcycles as a gear-change control and on motorcycles as an accelerator.
twit[1] (twɪt) *vb.* **twits, twitting, twitted. 1.** (*tr.*) to tease, taunt, or reproach, often in jest. ~*n.* **2.** *U.S. and Canadian informal.* a nervous or excitable state. **3.** *Rare.* a reproach; taunt. **4.** *Rare.* the act or an instance of teasing or taunting. [Old English *ætwītan,* from *æt* against + *wītan* to accuse; related to Old High German *wīzan* to punish]
twit[2] (twɪt) *n. Informal, chiefly Brit.* a foolish or stupid person; idiot. [C19: from TWIT[1] (originally in the sense: a person given to twitting)]
twitch (twɪtʃ) *vb.* **1.** to move or cause to move in a jerky spasmodic way. **2.** (*tr.*) to pull or draw (something) with a quick jerky movement. **3.** (*intr.*) to hurt with a sharp spasmodic pain. **4.** (*tr.*) *Rare.* to nip. ~*n.* **5.** a sharp jerking movement. **6.** a mental or physical twinge. **7.** a sudden muscular spasm, esp. one caused by a nervous condition. Compare **tic. 8.** a loop of cord used to control a horse by drawing it tight about its upper lip. [Old English *twiccian* to pluck; related to Old High German *zwecchōn* to pinch, Dutch *twicken*] —'**twitching** *adj., n.* —'**twitchy** *adj.*
twitcher ('twɪtʃə) *n.* **1.** a person or thing that twitches. **2.** *Informal.* a bird-watcher who tries to spot as many rare varieties as possible.
twitch grass *n.* another name for **couch grass.** Sometimes shortened to **twitch.** [C16: a variant of QUITCH GRASS]
twite (twaɪt) *n.* a N European finch, *Acanthis flavirostris,* with a brown streaked plumage. [C16: imitative of its cry]
twitter ('twɪtə) *vb.* **1.** (*intr.*) (esp. of a bird) to utter a succession of chirping sounds. **2.** (*intr.*) to talk or move rapidly and tremulously. **3.** (*intr.*) to giggle: *her schoolmates twittered behind their desks.* **4.** (*tr.*) to utter in a chirping way. ~*n.* **5.** a twittering sound, esp. of a bird. **6.** the act of twittering. **7.** a state of nervous excitement (esp. in the phrase **in a twitter**). [C14: of imitative origin] —'**twitterer** *n.* —'**twittery** *adj.*
'twixt *or* **twixt** (twɪkst) *Poetic contraction of* betwixt.
two (tuː) *n.* **1.** the cardinal number that is the sum of one and one. It is a prime number. See also **number** (sense 1). **2.** a numeral, 2, II, (ii), etc., representing this number. **3.** *Music.* the numeral 2 used as the lower figure in a time signature, indicating that the beat is measured in minims. **4.** something representing, represented by, or consisting of two units, such as a playing card with two symbols on it. **5.** Also called: **two o'clock.** two hours after noon or midnight. **6. in two.** in or into two parts: *break the bread in two.* **7. put two and two together.** to make an inference from available evidence, esp. an obvious inference. **8. that makes two of us.** the same applies to me. ~*determiner.* **9. a.** amounting to two: *two nails.* **b.** (*as pronoun*): *he bought two.* ~Related adjs.: **binary, double, dual.** Related prefixes: **di-, bi-.** [Old English *twā* (feminine); related to Old High German *zwā,* Old Norse *tvau,* Latin, Greek *duo*]
two-bit *adj.* (*prenominal*) *U.S. and Canadian slang.* worth next to nothing; cheap. [C20: from the phrase *two bits* a small sum]
two-by-four *n.* **1.** a length of untrimmed timber with a cross section that measures 2 inches by 4 inches. **2.** a trimmed timber joist with a cross section that measures 1½ inches by 3½ inches.
two-cycle *adj.* the U.S. and Canadian word for **two-stroke.**
two-dimensional *adj.* **1.** of, having, or relating to two dimensions, usually describable in terms of length and breadth or length and height. **2.** lying on a plane; having an area but not enclosing any volume. **3.** lacking in depth, as characters in a literary work. **4.** (of painting or drawing) lacking the characteristics of form or depth. —'**two-di,mension'ality** *n.* —'**two-di'mensionally** *adv.*
two-edged *adj.* **1.** having two cutting edges. **2.** (esp. of a remark) having two interpretations, such as *she looks nice when she smiles.*
two-faced *adj.* deceitful; insincere; hypocritical. —**two-facedly** ('tuː'feɪsɪdlɪ, -'feɪst-) *adv.* —'**two-'facedness** *n.*
twofold ('tuː,fəʊld) *adj.* **1.** equal to twice as many or twice as much; double: *a twofold increase.* **2.** composed of two parts; dual: *a twofold reason.* ~*adv.* **3.** doubly.
two-four time *n. Music.* a form of simple duple time in which there are two crotchet beats in each bar.
two-handed *adj.* **1.** requiring the use of both hands. **2.** ambidextrous. **3.** requiring the participation or cooperation of two people. —'**two-'handedly** *adv.*
two-hander (,tuː'hændə) *n.* a play for two actors.
two-line *n.* (*modifier*) (formerly) denoting double the normal size of printer's type: *two-line pica* (24 point).
two-name paper *n. U.S. finance.* a commercial paper signed by two persons both of whom accept full liability.

two-pack *adj.* (of a paint, filler, etc.) supplied as two separate components, for example a base and a catalyst, that are mixed together immediately before use.
two-party system *n.* a condition or system in which two major parties dominate a political unit.
twopence *or* **tuppence** ('tʌpəns) *n. Brit.* **1.** the sum of two pennies. **2.** (*used with a negative*) something of little value (in the phrase **not care** *or* **give twopence**). **3.** a former British silver coin, now only coined as Maundy money.
twopenny *or* **tuppenny** ('tʌpənɪ) *adj. Chiefly Brit.* **1.** Also: **twopenny-halfpenny.** cheap or tawdry. **2.** (intensifier): *a twopenny damn.* **3.** worth two pence.
two-phase *adj.* (of an electrical circuit, device, etc.) generating or using two alternating voltages of the same frequency, displaced in phase by 90°. Also: **quarter-phase.**
two-piece *adj.* **1.** consisting of two separate parts, usually matching, as of a garment. ~*n.* **2.** such an outfit.
two-ply *adj.* **1.** made of two thicknesses, layers, or strands. ~*n., pl.* **-plies.** **2.** a two-ply wood, knitting yarn, etc.
two-pot screamer *n. Austral. slang.* a person easily influenced by alcohol.
two-seater *n.* a vehicle providing seats for two people.
two-sided *adj.* **1.** having two sides or aspects. **2.** controversial; debatable: *a two-sided argument.*
twosome ('tu:səm) *n.* **1.** two together, esp. two people. **2.** a match between two people. **3.** (*modifier*) consisting of or played by two: *a twosome performance.*
two-spot *n.* a card with two pips; two; deuce.
two-step *n.* **1.** an old-time dance in duple time. **2.** a piece of music composed for or in the rhythm of such a dance.
two-stroke *adj.* relating to or designating an internal-combustion engine whose piston makes two strokes for every explosion. U.S. and Canadian word: **two-cycle.** Compare **four-stroke.**
two-tailed *adj. Statistics.* (of a significance test) concerned with the hypothesis that an observed value of a sampling statistic differs significantly from a given value, where an error in either direction is relevant: for instance, in testing the fairness of scales, an inspector will seek to exclude both overweight and underweight goods. Compare **one-tailed.**
two-tailed pasha *n.* a distinctive vanessid butterfly of S Europe, *Charaxes jasius,* having mottled brown wings with a yellow-orange margin and frilled hind edges.
two-tier *adj.* involving or comprising two levels of structure, policy, etc.
two-time *vb. Informal.* to deceive (someone, esp. a lover) by carrying on a relationship with another. —ˌ**two-'timer** *n.*
two-tone *adj.* **1.** of two colours or two shades of the same colour. **2.** (esp. of sirens, car horns, etc.) producing or consisting of two notes.
two-tooth *n., pl.* **-tooths.** *Austral. and N.Z.* a sheep between one and two years old with two permanent incisor teeth.
'twould (twʊd) *Poetic or dialect. contraction of* it would.
two-up *n. Chiefly Austral.* a gambling game in which two coins are tossed or spun. Bets are made on both coins landing with the same face uppermost.
two-way *adj.* **1.** moving, permitting movement, or operating in either of two opposite directions: *two-way traffic; a two-way valve.* **2.** involving two participants: *a two-way agreement.* **3.** involving reciprocal obligation or mutual action: *a two-way process.* **4.** (of a radio, telephone, etc.) allowing communications in two directions using both transmitting and receiving equipment.
two-way mirror *n.* a half-silvered sheet of glass that functions as a mirror when viewed from one side but is translucent from the other.
twp (tʊp) *adj.* (*predicative*) *South Wales dialect.* stupid; daft. [Welsh]
twyer ('twaɪə) *n.* a variant of **tuyère.**
TX *abbrev. for* Texas.
-ty^{1} *suffix of numerals.* denoting a multiple of ten: *sixty; seventy.* [from Old English *-tig* TEN]
-ty^{2} *suffix forming nouns.* indicating state, condition, or quality: *cruelty.* [from Old French *-te, -tet,* from Latin *-tās, -tāt-;* related to Greek *-tēs*]
tychism ('taɪkɪzəm) *n. Philosophy.* the theory that chance is an objective reality at work in the universe, esp. in evolutionary adaptations. [from Greek *tukhē* chance]
tycoon (taɪ'ku:n) *n.* **1.** a business man of great wealth and power. **2.** an archaic name for a **shogun.** [C19: from Japanese *taikun,* from Chinese *ta* great + *chün* ruler]
tyke *or* **tike** (taɪk) *n.* **1.** a dog, esp. a mongrel. **2.** *Informal.* a small or cheeky child: used esp. in affectionate reproof. **3.** *Brit. dialect.* a rough ill-mannered person. **4.** Also called: **Yorkshire tyke.** *Brit. slang, often offensive.* a person from Yorkshire. **5.** *Austral. slang, offensive.* a Roman Catholic. [C14: from Old Norse *tīk* bitch]
tylopod ('taɪləʊˌpɒd) *n.* any artiodactyl mammal of the suborder *Tylopoda,* having padded, rather than hoofed, digits: includes the camels and llamas. [C19: from New Latin, from Greek *tulos* knob or *tulē* cushion + -POD]
tylosis (taɪ'ləʊsɪs) *n. Botany.* a bladder-like outgrowth from certain cells in woody tissue that extends into and blocks adjacent conducting xylem cells. [C19: from Greek *tulōsis,* from *tulos* knob or *tulē* callus + -OSIS]
tymbal ('tɪmbᵊl) *n.* a variant spelling of **timbal.**
tympan ('tɪmpən) *n.* **1.** a membrane stretched over a frame or resonating cylinder, bowl, etc. **2.** *Printing.* packing interposed between the platen and the paper to be printed in order to provide an even impression. **3.** *Architect.* another name for **tympanum** (sense 3). [Old English *timpana,* from Latin; see TYMPANUM]
tympani ('tɪmpənɪ) *pl. n.* a variant spelling of **timpani.**
tympanic (tɪm'pænɪk) *adj.* **1.** *Anatomy, architect.* of, relating to, or having a tympanum. **2.** of, relating to, or resembling a drumhead.
tympanic bone *n.* the part of the temporal bone in the mammalian skull that surrounds the auditory canal.
tympanic membrane *n.* the thin translucent oval membrane separating the external ear from the middle ear. It transmits vibrations produced by sound waves, via the ossicles, to the cochlea. Also called: **tympanum.** Nontechnical name: **eardrum.**
tympanist ('tɪmpənɪst) *n.* a person who plays a drum, now specifically the kettledrum.
tympanites (ˌtɪmpə'naɪti:z) *n.* distension of the abdomen caused by an abnormal accumulation of gas in the intestinal or peritoneal cavity, as in peritonitis. Also called: **meteorism, tympany.** [C14: from Late Latin, from Greek *tumpanitēs* concerning a drum, from *tumpanon* drum] —**tympanitic** (ˌtɪmpə'nɪtɪk) *adj.*
tympanitis (ˌtɪmpə'naɪtɪs) *n.* inflammation of the eardrum. Also called: **otitis media.**
tympanum ('tɪmpənəm) *n., pl.* **-nums** *or* **-na** (-nə). **1. a.** the cavity of the middle ear. **b.** another name for **tympanic membrane.** **2.** any diaphragm resembling that in the middle ear in function. **3.** Also called: **tympan.** *Architect.* **a.** the recessed space bounded by the cornices of a pediment, esp. one that is triangular in shape and ornamented. **b.** the recessed space bounded by an arch and the lintel of a doorway or window below it. **4.** *Music.* a tympan or drum. **5.** a scoop wheel for raising water. [C17: from Latin, from Greek *tumpanon* drum; related to Greek *tuptein* to beat]
tympany ('tɪmpənɪ) *n., pl.* **-nies.** **1.** another name for **tympanites.** **2.** *Obsolete.* excessive pride or arrogance.
Tyndall effect ('tɪndᵊl) *n.* the phenomenon in which light is scattered by particles of matter in its path. It enables a beam of light to become visible by illuminating dust particles, etc. [C19: named after John *Tyndall* (1820–93), British physicist]
tyndallimetry (ˌtɪndᵊl'ɪmətrɪ) *n. Chem.* the determination of the concentration of suspended material in a liquid by measuring the amount of light scattered. [C20: from TYNDALL EFFECT + -METRY]
Tynwald ('tɪnwəld, 'taɪn-) *n.* **the.** the Parliament of the Isle of Man. Full name: **Tynwald Court.** [C15: from Old Norse *thingvollr* from *thing* assembly + *vollr* field]
typ., typo., *or* **typog.** *abbrev. for:* **1.** typographer. **2.** typographic(al). **3.** typography.
typal ('taɪpᵊl) *adj.* a rare word for **typical.**
type (taɪp) *n.* **1.** a kind, class, or category, the constituents of which share similar characteristics. **2.** a subdivision of a particular class of things or people; sort: *what type of shampoo do you use?* **3.** the general form, plan, or design distinguishing a particular group. **4.** *Informal.* a person who typifies a particular quality: *he's the administrative type.* **5.** *Informal.* a person, esp. of a specified kind: *he's a strange type.* **6. a.** a small block of metal or more rarely wood bearing a letter or character in relief for use in printing. **b.** such pieces collectively. **7.** characters printed from type; print. **8.** *Biology.* **a.** the taxonomic group the characteristics of which are used for defining the next highest group, for example *Rattus norvegicus* (brown rat) is the type species of the rat genus *Rattus.* **b.** (*as modifier*): *a type genus; a type species.* **9.** See **type specimen.** **10.** the characteristic device on a coin. **11.** *Linguistics.* a symbol regarded as standing for the class of all symbols identical to it. Compare **token** (sense 8). **12.** *Logic.* a class of expressions or of the entities they represent that can all enter into the same syntactic relations. The **theory of types** was advanced by Bertrand Russell to avoid the liar paradox, Russell's paradox, etc. **13.** *Philosophy.* a universal. If a sentence always has the same meaning whenever it is used, the meaning is said to be a property of the sentence-type. Compare **token** (sense 9). **14.** *Chiefly Christian theol.* a figure, episode, or symbolic factor resembling some future reality in such a way as to foreshadow or prefigure it. **15.** *Rare.* a distinctive sign or mark. ~*vb.* **16.** to write (copy) on a typewriter. **17.** (*tr.*) to be a symbol of; typify. **18.** (*tr.*) to decide the type of; clarify into a type. **19.** (*tr.*) *Med.* to determine the blood group of (a blood sample). **20.** (*tr.*) *Chiefly Christian theol.* to foreshadow or serve as a symbol of (some future reality). [C15: from Latin *typus* figure, from Greek *tupos* image, from *tuptein* to strike]
-type *n. combining form.* **1.** type or form: *archetype.* **2.** printing type or photographic process: *collotype.* [from Latin *-typus,* from Greek *-typos,* from *tupos* TYPE]
typebar ('taɪpˌbɑ:) *n.* one of the bars in a typewriter that carry the type and are operated by keys.
typecase ('taɪpˌkeɪs) *n.* a compartmental tray for storing printer's type.
typecast ('taɪpˌkɑ:st) *vb.* **-casts, -casting, -cast.** (*tr.*) to cast (an actor) in the same kind of role continually, esp. because of his

physical appearance or previous success in such roles. —**'type,caster** *n.*

typeface ('taɪp,feɪs) *n.* another name for **face** (sense 16).

type founder *n.* a person who casts metallic printer's type. —**type founding** *n.* —**type foundry** *n.*

type-high *adj.* having the height of a piece of type, standardized as 0.918 inches.

type metal *n. Printing.* an alloy of tin, lead, and antimony, from which type is cast.

type I error *n. Statistics.* the error of rejecting the null hypothesis when it is true, the probability of which is the significance level of a result.

typescript ('taɪp,skrɪpt) *n.* **1.** a typed copy of a document, literary script, etc. **2.** any typewritten material.

typeset ('taɪp,sɛt) *vb.* **-sets, -setting, -set.** (*tr.*) *Printing.* to set (textual matter) in type.

typesetter ('taɪp,sɛtə) *n.* **1.** a person who sets type; compositor. **2.** a typesetting machine.

type specimen *n. Biology.* the original specimen from which a description of a new species is made. Also called: **holotype.**

type II error *n. Statistics.* the error of not rejecting the null hypothesis when it is false. The probability of avoiding such an error is the power of the test and is a function of the alternative hypothesis.

typewrite ('taɪp,raɪt) *vb.* **-writes, -writing, -wrote, -written.** to write by means of a typewriter; type.

typewriter ('taɪp,raɪtə) *n.* **1.** a keyboard machine for writing mechanically in characters resembling print. It may be operated entirely by hand (**manual typewriter**) or be powered by electricity (**electric typewriter**). **2.** *Printing.* a style of type resembling typescript.

typewriting ('taɪp,raɪtɪŋ) *n.* **1.** the act or skill of using a typewriter. **2.** copy produced by a typewriter; typescript.

typhlitis (tɪf'laɪtɪs) *n.* **1.** inflammation of the caecum. **2.** an obsolete name for **appendicitis.** [C19: from New Latin, from Greek *tuphlon* the caecum, from *tuphlos* blind] —**typhlitic** (tɪf'lɪtɪk) *adj.*

typhlology (tɪf'lɒlədʒɪ) *n.* the branch of science concerned with blindness and the care of the blind. [C19: from Greek *tuphlos* blind]

typhogenic (,taɪfəʊ'dʒɛnɪk) *adj.* causing typhus or typhoid fever.

typhoid ('taɪfɔɪd) *Pathol.* ~*adj. also* **typhoidal. 1.** resembling typhus. ~*n.* **2.** short for **typhoid fever.**

typhoid fever *n.* an acute infectious disease characterized by high fever, rose-coloured spots on the chest or abdomen, abdominal pain, and occasionally intestinal bleeding. It is caused by the bacillus *Salmonella typhosa* ingested with food or water. Also called: **enteric fever.** [C19: from TYPHUS + -OID; so called because the symptoms resemble those of typhus]

typhoidin (taɪ'fɔɪdɪn) *n. Med.* a culture of dead typhoid bacillus for injection into the skin to test for typhoid fever.

typhoon (taɪ'fuːn) *n.* **1.** a small violent tropical storm or cyclone, esp. in the China seas and W Pacific. **2.** a violent storm of India. [C16: from Chinese *tai fung* great wind, from *tai* great + *fung* wind; influenced by Greek *tuphōn* whirlwind] —**typhonic** (taɪ'fɒnɪk) *adj.*

typhus ('taɪfəs) *n.* any one of a group of acute infectious rickettsial diseases characterized by high fever, skin rash, and severe headache. Also called: **typhus fever.** [C18: from New Latin *typhus,* from Greek *tuphos* fever; related to *tuphein* to smoke] —**'typhous** *adj.*

typical ('tɪpɪkᵊl) *adj.* **1.** being or serving as a representative example of a particular type; characteristic: *the painting is a typical Rembrandt.* **2.** considered to be an example of some undesirable trait: *that is typical of you!* **3.** of or relating to a representative specimen or type. **4.** conforming to a type. **5.** *Biology.* having most of the characteristics of a particular taxonomic group: *a typical species of a genus.* ~Also (poetic) **typic.** [C17: from Medieval Latin *typicālis,* from Late Latin *typicus* figurative, from Greek *tupikos,* from *tupos* TYPE] —**'typically** *adv.* —**'typicalness** *or* **,typi'cality** *n.*

typify ('tɪpɪ,faɪ) *vb.* **-fies, -fying, -fied.** (*tr.*) **1.** to be typical of; characterize. **2.** to symbolize or represent completely, by or as if by a type. [C17: from Latin *typus* TYPE + -IFY] —**,typifi'cation** *n.* —**'typi,fier** *n.*

typist ('taɪpɪst) *n.* a person who types, esp. for a living.

typo ('taɪpəʊ) *n., pl.* **-pos.** *Informal.* a typographical error. Also called (Brit.): **literal.**

typo. *or* **typog.** *abbrev.* variants of **typ.**

typographer (taɪ'pɒgrəfə) *n.* **1.** a person skilled in typography. **2.** another name for **compositor.**

typography (taɪ'pɒgrəfɪ) *n.* **1.** the art, craft, or process of composing type and printing from it. **2.** the planning, selection, and setting of type for a printed work. —**typographical** (,taɪpə'græfɪkᵊl) *or* **,typo'graphic** *adj.* —**,typo'graphically** *adv.*

typology (taɪ'pɒlədʒɪ) *n. Chiefly Christian theol.* the doctrine or study of types or of the correspondence between them and the realities which they typify. —**typological** (,taɪpə'lɒdʒɪkᵊl) *or* **,typo'logic** *adj.* —**,typo'logically** *adv.* —**ty'pologist** *n.*

typothetae (taɪ'pɒθɪ,tiː, ,taɪpə'θiːtiː) *pl. n. U.S.* printers collectively; used in the names of organized associations, as of master printers. [C19: New Latin: typesetters, from Greek *tupos* TYPE + *thetēs* one who places, from *tithenai* to place]

typw. *abbrev. for:* **1.** typewriter. **2.** typewritten.

tyramine ('taɪrə,miːn, 'tɪ-) *n.* a colourless crystalline amine derived from phenol and found in ripe cheese, ergot, decayed animal tissue, and mistletoe and used for its sympathomimetic action; 4-hydroxyphenethylamine. Formula: $(C_2H_4NH_2)C_6H_4OH$. [C20: from TYR(OSINE) + AMINE]

tyrannical (tɪ'rænɪkᵊl) *or* **tyrannic** *adj.* characteristic of or relating to a tyrant or to tyranny; oppressive. —**ty'rannically** *adv.* —**ty'rannicalness** *n.*

tyrannicide (tɪ'rænɪ,saɪd) *n.* **1.** the killing of a tyrant. **2.** a person who kills a tyrant. —**tyr,ranni'cidal** *adj.*

tyrannize *or* **tyrannise** ('tɪrə,naɪz) *vb.* (when *intr.,* often foll. by *over*) to rule or exercise power (over) in a cruel or oppressive manner. —**'tyran,nizer** *or* **'tyran,niser** *n.*

tyrannosaur (tɪ'rænə,sɔː) *or* **tyrannosaurus** (tɪ,rænə'sɔːrəs) *n.* any large carnivorous bipedal dinosaur of the genus *Tyrannosaurus,* common in North America in upper Jurassic and Cretaceous times: suborder *Theropoda* (theropods). [C19: from New Latin *Tyrannosaurus,* from Greek *turannos* TYRANT + -SAUR]

tyranny ('tɪrənɪ) *n., pl.* **-nies. 1. a.** government by a tyrant or tyrants; despotism. **b.** similarly oppressive and unjust government by more than one person. **2.** arbitrary, unreasonable, or despotic behaviour or use of authority: *the teacher's tyranny.* **3.** any harsh discipline or oppression: *the tyranny of the clock.* **4.** a political unit ruled by a tyrant. **5.** (esp. in ancient Greece) government by a usurper. **6.** a tyrannical act. [C14: from Old French *tyrannie,* from Medieval Latin *tyrannia,* from Latin *tyrannus* TYRANT] —**'tyrannous** *adj.* —**'tyrannously** *adv.* —**'tyrannousness** *n.*

tyrant ('taɪrənt) *n.* **1.** a person who governs oppressively, unjustly, and arbitrarily; despot. **2.** any person who exercises authority in a tyrannical manner. **3.** anything that exercises tyrannical influence. **4.** (esp. in ancient Greece) a ruler whose authority lacked the sanction of law or custom; usurper. [C13: from Old French *tyrant,* from Latin *tyrannus,* from Greek *turannos*]

tyrant flycatcher *n.* any passerine bird of the American family *Tyrannidae.* Often shortened to **flycatcher.**

tyre *or U.S.* **tire** ('taɪə) *n.* **1.** a rubber ring placed over the rim of a wheel of a road vehicle to provide traction and reduce road shocks, esp. a hollow inflated ring (**pneumatic tyre**) consisting of a reinforced outer casing enclosing an inner tube. See also **tubeless tyre, cross-ply, radial-ply. 2.** a ring of wear-resisting steel shrunk thermally onto a cast-iron railway wheel. **3.** a metal band or hoop attached to the rim of a wooden cartwheel. ~*vb.* **4.** (*tr.*) to fit a tyre or tyres to (a wheel, vehicle, etc.). [C18: variant of C15 *tire,* probably from TIRE[3]]

Tyrian ('tɪrɪən) *n.* **1.** a native or inhabitant of ancient Tyre, a major Phoenician seaport in present-day Lebanon. **2.** short for **Tyrian purple** (sense 2). ~*adj.* **3.** of or relating to ancient Tyre.

Tyrian purple *n.* **1.** a deep purple dye obtained from molluscs of the genus *Murex* and highly prized in antiquity. **2. a.** a vivid purplish-red colour. **b.** (*as adj.*): *a Tyrian-purple robe.* Sometimes shortened to **Tyrian.**

tyro *or* **tiro** ('taɪrəʊ) *n., pl.* **-ros.** a novice or beginner. [C17: from Latin *tīrō* recruit] —**tyronic** *or* **tironic** (taɪ'rɒnɪk) *adj.*

tyrocidine (,taɪrəʊ'saɪdiːn) *n.* an antibiotic that is the main constituent of tyrothricin. [C20: from TYRO(SINE) + -CID(E) + -INE[1]]

Tyrolese (,tɪrə'liːz) *or* **Tyrolean** (,tɪrə'lɪən) *adj.* **1.** of or relating to the Tyrol, a mountainous region of W Austria, or to its people or culture. ~*n.* **2.** a native or inhabitant of the Tyrol. ~Also: **Tirolese, Tirolean.**

Tyrolienne (tɪ,rəʊlɪ'ɛn) *n.* **1.** a gay peasant dance from the Tyrol. **2.** a song composed for or in the style of this dance, characterized by the yodel. [French: of the *Tyrol*]

tyropitta (tɪ'rɒpɪtə) *n.* a Greek cheese pie. [C20: from Modern Greek]

tyrosinase (,taɪrəʊsɪ'neɪz, ,tɪrəʊ-) *n.* an enzyme occurring in many organisms that is a catalyst in the conversion of tyrosine to the pigment melanin; inactivity of this enzyme results in albinism.

tyrosine ('taɪrə,siːn, -sɪn, 'tɪrə-) *n.* an aromatic nonessential amino acid; a component of proteins. It is a metabolic precursor of thyroxine, the pigment melanin, and other biologically important compounds. [C19: from Greek *turos* cheese + -INE[2]]

tyrothricin (,taɪrəʊ'θraɪsɪn) *n.* an antibiotic, obtained from the soil bacterium *Bacillus brevis,* consisting of tyrocidine and gramicidin and active against Gram-positive bacteria such as staphylococci and streptococci: applied locally for the treatment of ulcers and abscesses. [C20: from New Latin *Tyrothrix* (genus name), from Greek *turos* cheese + *thrix* hair]

tyum (tjʊm) *n. Dialect.* a variant spelling of **tum**[1].

tzar (zɑː) *n.* a less common spelling of **tsar.** —**'tzarism** *n.*

tzatziki (tsæt'sɪkɪ) *n.* a Greek dip made from yoghurt, chopped cucumber, and mint. [C20: from Modern Greek]

tzetze fly ('tsɛtsɪ) *n.* a variant spelling of **tsetse fly.**

Tzigane (tsɪ'gɑːn, sɪ-) *n.* **a.** a Gypsy, esp. a Hungarian one. **b.** (*as modifier*): *Tzigane music.* [C19: via French from Hungarian *czigány* Gypsy, of uncertain origin]

u *or* **U** (juː) *n., pl.* **u's, U's,** *or* **Us.** **1.** the 21st letter and fifth vowel of the modern English alphabet. **2.** any of several speech sounds represented by this letter, in English as in *mute, cut, hurt, sure, pull,* or *minus.* **3. a.** something shaped like a U. **b.** (*in combination*): *a U-bolt; a U-turn.*

U[1] *symbol for:* **1.** united. **2.** unionist. **3.** university. **4.** (in Britain) **a.** universal (used to describe a category of film certified as suitable for viewing by anyone). **b.** (*as modifier*): *a U film.* **5.** *Chem.* uranium. ~*adj.* **6.** *Brit. informal.* (esp. of language habits) characteristic of or appropriate to the upper class. Compare **non-U.** ~**7.** *international car registration for* Uruguay.

U[2] (uː) *n.* a Burmese title of respect for men, equivalent to *Mr.*

U. *abbrev. for:* **1.** *Maths.* union. **2.** unit. **3.** united. **4.** university. **5.** upper.

UAE *abbrev. for* United Arab Emirates.

UAM *abbrev. for* underwater-to-air missile.

UAR *abbrev. for* United Arab Republic.

UART (ˈjuːˌɑːt) *n. Electronics. acronym for* Universal Asynchronous Receiver Transmitter.

UB40 *n.* (in Britain) **1.** a registration card issued by the Department of Employment to a person registering as unemployed. **2.** *Informal.* a person registered as unemployed.

U-bend *n.* a U-shaped bend in a pipe or drain that traps water in the lower part of the U and prevents the escape of noxious fumes or vapours; trap.

Übermensch *German.* (ˈyːbərˌmɛnʃ) *n., pl.* **-menschen** (-mɛnʃən). (esp. in the writings of Nietzsche) the German word for **superman.** [literally: over-man]

uberrima fides (ˈjuːbəˌriːmə ˈfaɪdiːz, juːˈbɛrɪmə) *n.* another name for **utmost good faith.** [Latin: utmost good faith]

ubiety (juːˈbaɪɪtɪ) *n.* the condition of being in a particular place. [C17: from Latin *ubī* where + *-ety,* on the model of *society*]

ubiquinone (juːˈbɪkwɪˌnəʊn) *n.* another name for **coenzyme Q.**

ubiquitarian (juːˌbɪkwɪˈtɛərɪən) *n.* **1.** a member of the Lutheran church who holds that Christ is no more present in the elements of the Eucharist than elsewhere, as he is present in all places at all times. ~*adj.* **2.** denoting, relating to, or holding this belief. [C17: from Latin *ubīque* everywhere; see UBIQUITOUS] —**uˌbiquiˈtarianˌism** *n.*

ubiquitous (juːˈbɪkwɪtəs) *adj.* having or seeming to have the ability to be everywhere at once; omnipresent. [C14: from Latin *ubīque* everywhere, from *ubī* where] —**uˈbiquitously** *adv.* —**uˈbiquity** *or* **uˈbiquitousness** *n.*

ubi supra *Latin.* (ˈuːbɪ ˈsuːprɑː) where (mentioned or cited) above.

U-boat *n.* a German submarine, esp. in World Wars I and II. [from German *U-Boot,* abbreviation for *Unterseeboot,* literally: undersea boat]

U bolt *n.* a metal bar bent into the shape of a *U* and threaded at both ends to receive securing nuts: used to secure leaf springs, ring bolts, shackles, etc.

UC *abbrev. for* University College.

u.c. *Printing. abbrev. for* upper case.

UCATT (ˈʌkət) *n. acronym for* Union of Construction, Allied Trades and Technicians.

UCCA (ˈʌkə) *n.* (in Britain) *acronym for* Universities Central Council on Admissions.

UCW *abbrev. for* Union of Communication Workers.

UDA *abbrev. for* Ulster Defence Association.

udal (ˈjuːdᵊl) *n. Law.* a form of freehold possession of land existing in northern Europe before the introduction of the feudal system and still used in the Scottish islands of Orkney and Shetland. [C16: Orkney and Shetland dialect, from Old Norse *othal;* related to Old English *ēthel, ōethel,* Old High German *wodal*]

UDC (in Britain) *abbrev. for* Urban District Council.

udder (ˈʌdə) *n.* the large baglike mammary gland of cows, sheep, etc., having two or more teats. [Old English *ūder;* related to Old High German *ūtar,* Old Norse *jūr,* Latin *über,* Sanskrit *ūdhar*] —**ˈudder-ˌlike** *adj.*

UDF (in South Africa) *abbrev. for* United Democratic Front.

UDI *abbrev. for* Unilateral Declaration of Independence.

UDM (in Britain) *abbrev. for* Union of Democratic Mineworkers.

Udmurt (ˈʊdmʊət) *n.* another name for **Votyak.**

udo (ˈuːdəʊ) *n., pl.* **udos.** a stout araliaceous perennial plant, *Aralia cordata,* of Japan and China, having berry-like black fruits and young shoots that are edible when blanched. [from Japanese]

udometer (juːˈdɒmɪtə) *n.* another term for **rain gauge.** [C19: from French, from Latin *ūdus* damp]

UDR *abbrev. for* Ulster Defence Regiment.

UE (in New Zealand) *abbrev. for* university entrance (examination).

UEFA (juːˈeɪfə) *n. acronym for* Union of European Football Associations.

UFO (*sometimes* ˈjuːfəʊ) *abbrev. for* unidentified flying object.

ufology (ˌjuːˈfɒlədʒɪ) *n.* the study of UFOs. —**uˈfologist** *n.*

ugali (uːˈgaliː) *n. E African.* a type of stiff porridge made by mixing corn meal with boiling water: the basic starch constituent of a meal. [from Swahili]

Ugandan (juːˈgændən) *adj.* **1.** of or relating to Uganda, a republic in E Africa, its people, or its culture. ~*n.* **2.** a native or inhabitant of Uganda.

Ugaritic (ˌuːgəˈrɪtɪk) *n.* **1.** an extinct Semitic language of N Syria. ~*adj.* **2.** of or relating to this language. [C19: after *Ugarit* (modern name: Ras Shamra), an ancient Syrian city-state]

UGC (in Britain) *abbrev. for* University Grants Committee.

ugh (ʊx, ʊh, ʌh) *interj.* an exclamation of disgust, annoyance, or dislike.

ugli (ˈʌglɪ) *n., pl.* **-lis** *or* **-lies.** a large juicy yellow-skinned citrus fruit of the West Indies: a cross between a tangerine, grapefruit, and orange. Also called: **ugli fruit.** [C20: probably an alteration of UGLY, referring to its wrinkled skin]

uglify (ˈʌglɪˌfaɪ) *vb.* **-fies, -fying, -fied.** to make or become ugly or more ugly. —**ˌuglifiˈcation** *n.* —**ˈugliˌfier** *n.*

ugly (ˈʌglɪ) *adj.* **-lier, -liest.** **1.** of unpleasant or unsightly appearance. **2.** repulsive, objectionable, or displeasing in any way: *war is ugly.* **3.** ominous or menacing: *an ugly situation.* **4.** bad-tempered, angry, or sullen: *an ugly mood.* [C13: from Old Norse *uggligr* dreadful, from *ugga* fear] —**ˈuglily** *adv.* —**ˈugliness** *n.*

ugly duckling *n.* a person or thing, initially ugly or unpromising, that changes into something beautiful or admirable. [an allusion to *The Ugly Duckling,* a story by Hans Christian Andersen (1805–75), Danish writer]

Ugrian (ˈuːgrɪən, ˈjuː-) *adj.* **1.** of or relating to a light-haired subdivision of the Turanian people, who include the Samoyeds, Voguls, Ostyaks, and Magyars. ~*n.* **2.** a member of this group of peoples. **3.** another word for **Ugric.** [C19: from Old Russian *Ugre* Hungarians]

Ugric (ˈuːgrɪk, ˈjuː-) *n.* **1.** one of the two branches of the Finno-Ugric family of languages, including Hungarian and some languages of NW Siberia. Compare **Finnic.** ~*adj.* **2.** of or relating to this group of languages or their speakers.

UHF *Radio. abbrev. for* ultrahigh frequency.

uh-huh (əˈhə) *sentence substitute. Informal.* a less emphatic variant of **yes.**

uhlan *or* **ulan** (ˈuːlɑːn, ˈjuːlən) *n. History.* a member of a body of lancers first employed in the Polish army and later in W European armies. [C18: via German from Polish *ulan,* from Turkish *ōlan* young man]

UHT *abbrev. for* ultra heat treated.

uh-uh (ˈʌˈʌ) *sentence substitute. Informal, chiefly U.S.* a less emphatic variant of **no**[1].

uhuru (uːˈhuːruː) *n.* (esp. in E Africa) **1.** national independence. **2.** freedom. [C20: from Swahili]

Uigur *or* **Uighur** (ˈwiːgʊə) *n.* **1.** (*pl.* **-gur** *or* **-gurs**) a member of a Mongoloid people of NW China and adjacent parts of the former Soviet Union. **2.** the language of this people, belonging to the Turkic branch of the Altaic family. —**Uiˈgurian, Uiˈghurian** *or* **Uiˈguric, Uiˈghuric** *adj.*

uillean pipes (ˈuːlɪən) *pl. n.* bagpipes developed in Ireland and operated by squeezing bellows under the arm. Also called: **Irish pipes, union pipes.** [C19: Irish *píob uilleann,* from *píob* pipe + *uilleann* genitive sing. of *uille* elbow]

uintathere (juːˈɪntəˌθɪə) *n.* any of various extinct Tertiary rhinoceros-like mammals of North America, having six horny processes on the head. Also called: **dinoceras.** [from *Uinta,* a county in Wyoming, U.S. + Greek *thērion* wild animal]

uitlander (ˈeɪtˌlandə, -ˌlæn-, ˈɔɪt-) *n.* (*sometimes cap.*) *S. African.* a foreigner; alien. [C19: Afrikaans: outlander]

ujamaa village (uːdʒaˈma) *n.* (*sometimes caps.*) a communally organized village in Tanzania. [C20: *ujamaa* socialism, from Swahili: brotherhood]

UK *abbrev. for* United Kingdom.

UKAEA *abbrev. for* United Kingdom Atomic Energy Authority.

ukase (juːˈkeɪz) *n.* **1.** (in imperial Russia) an edict of the tsar. **2.** a rare word for **edict.** [C18: from Russian *ukaz,* from *ukazat* to command]

ukiyo-e (ˌuːkiːjəʊˈjeɪ) *n.* a school of Japanese painting depicting subjects from everyday life. [Japanese: pictures of the floating world]

Ukr. *abbrev. for* Ukraine.

Ukrainian (juːˈkreɪnɪən) *adj.* **1.** of or relating to Ukraine, a former Soviet republic in SE Europe, its people, or their language. ~*n.* **2.** the official language of Ukraine: an East Slavonic language closely related to Russian. **3.** a native or inhabitant of Ukraine. ~Formerly called: **Little Russian.**

ukulele *or* **ukelele** (ˌjuːkəˈleɪlɪ) *n.* a small four-stringed guitar, esp. of Hawaii. [C19: from Hawaiian, literally: jumping flea, from *'uku* flea + *lele* jumping]
ulan (ˈuːlɑːn, ˈjuːlən) *n.* a less common variant of **uhlan.**
ULCC *abbrev. for* ultralarge crude carrier.
ulcer (ˈʌlsə) *n.* **1.** a disintegration of the surface of the skin or a mucous membrane resulting in an open sore that heals very slowly. See also **peptic ulcer. 2.** a source or element of corruption or evil. [C14: from Latin *ulcus;* related to Greek *helkos* a sore]
ulcerate (ˈʌlsəˌreɪt) *vb.* to make or become ulcerous.
ulceration (ˌʌlsəˈreɪʃən) *n.* **1.** the development or formation of an ulcer. **2.** an ulcer or an ulcerous condition.
ulcerative (ˈʌlsərətɪv) *adj.* of, relating to, or characterized by ulceration: *ulcerative colitis.*
ulcerous (ˈʌlsərəs) *adj.* **1.** relating to, characteristic of, or characterized by an ulcer or ulcers. **2.** being or having a corrupting influence. —ˈ**ulcerously** *adv.* —ˈ**ulcerousness** *n.*
-ule *suffix forming nouns.* indicating smallness: *globule.* [from Latin *-ulus,* diminutive suffix]
ulema (ˈuːlɪmə) *n.* **1.** a body of Muslim scholars or religious leaders. **2.** a member of this body. [C17: from Arabic *'ulamā* scholars, from *'alama* to know]
-ulent *suffix forming adjectives.* abundant or full of: *fraudulent.* [from Latin *-ulentus*]
ullage (ˈʌlɪdʒ) *n.* **1.** the volume by which a liquid container falls short of being full. **2. a.** the quantity of liquid lost from a container due to leakage or evaporation. **b.** (in customs terminology) the amount of liquid remaining in a container after such loss. ~*vb.* (*tr.*) **3.** to create ullage in. **4.** to determine the amount of ullage in. **5.** to fill up ullage in. [C15: from Old French *ouillage* filling of a cask, from *ouiller* to fill a cask, from *ouil* eye, from Latin *oculus* eye] —ˈ**ullaged** *adj.*
ullage rocket *n.* a small hydrogen peroxide rocket engine that produces sufficient acceleration to keep propellants in their places when the main rocket is shut off.
ulmaceous (ʌlˈmeɪʃəs) *adj.* of, relating to, or belonging to the *Ulmaceae,* a temperate and tropical family of deciduous trees and shrubs having scaly buds, simple serrated leaves, and typically winged fruits: includes the elms. [C19: via New Latin *Ulmāceae,* from Latin *ulmus* elm tree]
ulna (ˈʌlnə) *n., pl.* **-nae** (-niː) *or* **-nas. 1.** the inner and longer of the two bones of the human forearm. **2.** the corresponding bone in other vertebrates. [C16: from Latin: elbow, ELL[1]] —ˈ**ulnar** *adj.*
ulnar nerve *n.* a nerve situated along the inner side of the arm and passing close to the surface of the skin near the elbow. See **funny bone.**
ulotrichous (juːˈlɒtrɪkəs) *adj.* having woolly or curly hair. [C19: from New Latin *Ulotrichī* (classification applied to humans having this type of hair), from Greek *oulothrix* from *oulos* curly + *thrix* hair] —**uˈlotrichy** *n.*
ulster (ˈʌlstə) *n.* a man's heavy double-breasted overcoat with a belt or half-belt at the back. [C19: so called because it was first produced in *Ulster,* a province of N Ireland]
Ulsterman (ˈʌlstəmən) *n., pl.* **-men.** a native or inhabitant of Ulster. —ˈ**Ulsterˌwoman** *fem. n.*
ult. *abbrev. for:* **1.** ultimate(ly). **2.** Also: **ulto.** ultimo.
ulterior (ʌlˈtɪərɪə) *adj.* **1.** lying beneath or beyond what is revealed, evident, or supposed: *ulterior motives.* **2.** succeeding, subsequent, or later. **3.** lying beyond a certain line or point. [C17: from Latin: further, from *ulter* beyond] —**ulˈteriorly** *adv.*
ultima (ˈʌltɪmə) *n.* the final syllable of a word. [from Latin: the last, feminine of *ultimus* last; see ULTIMATE]
ultimate (ˈʌltɪmɪt) *adj.* **1.** conclusive in a series or process; last; final: *an ultimate question.* **2.** the highest or most significant: *the ultimate goal.* **3.** elemental, fundamental, basic, or essential. ~*n.* **4.** the most significant, highest, furthest, or greatest thing. [C17: from Late Latin *ultimāre* to come to an end, from Latin *ultimus* last, from *ulter* distant] —ˈ**ultimateness** *n.*
ultimate constituent *n.* a constituent of something, such as a linguistic construction, that cannot be further subdivided in the terms of the analysis being undertaken. Compare **immediate constituent.**
ultimately (ˈʌltɪmɪtlɪ) *adv.* in the end; at last; finally.
ultimate strength *n.* the maximum tensile stress that a material can withstand before rupture.
ultima Thule (ˈθjuːlɪ) *n.* **1.** any distant or unknown region. **2.** a remote goal or aim. [Latin: the most distant Thule, a region believed by ancient geographers to be the northernmost land in the inhabited world]
ultimatum (ˌʌltɪˈmeɪtəm) *n., pl.* **-tums** *or* **-ta** (-tə). **1.** a final communication by a party, esp. a government, setting forth conditions on which it insists, as during negotiations on some topic. **2.** any final or peremptory demand, offer, or proposal. [C18: from New Latin, neuter of *ultimatus* ULTIMATE]
ultimo (ˈʌltɪˌməʊ) *adv. Now rare except when abbreviated in formal correspondence.* in or during the previous month: *a letter of the 7th ultimo.* Abbrev.: **ult.** Compare **instant, proximo.** [C16: from Latin *ultimō* on the last]
ultimogeniture (ˌʌltɪməʊˈdʒɛnɪtʃə) *n. Law.* **1.** a principle of inheritance whereby the youngest son succeeds to the estate of his ancestor. Compare **primogeniture. 2.** another name for **borough-English.** [C19: *ultimo-* from Latin *ultimus* last + Late Latin *genitura* a birth; compare PRIMOGENITURE]
ultra (ˈʌltrə) *adj.* **1.** extreme or immoderate, esp. in beliefs or opinions. ~*n.* **2.** an extremist. [C19: from Latin: beyond, from *ulter* distant]
ultra- *prefix.* **1.** beyond or surpassing a specified extent, range, or limit: *ultramicroscopic.* **2.** extreme or extremely: *ultramodern.* [from Latin *ultrā* beyond; see ULTRA]
ultrabasic (ˌʌltrəˈbeɪsɪk) *adj.* (of such igneous rocks as peridotite) containing less than 45 per cent silica.
ultracentrifuge (ˌʌltrəˈsɛntrɪˌfjuːdʒ) *Chem.* ~*n.* **1.** a high-speed centrifuge used to separate colloidal solutions. ~*vb.* **2.** (*tr.*) to subject to the action of an ultracentrifuge. —**ultracentrifugal** (ˌʌltrəsenˈtrɪfjʊgᵊl, -ˌsentrɪˈfjuːgᵊl) *adj.* —ˌ**ultracenˈtrifugally** *adv.* —**ultracentrifugation** (ˌʌltrəˌsɛntrɪfjʊˈgeɪʃən) *n.*
ultraconservative (ˌʌltrəkənˈsɜːvətɪv) *adj.* **1.** highly reactionary. ~*n.* **2.** a reactionary person.
ultra-distance *n.* (*modifier*) *Athletics.* covering a distance in excess of 30 miles, often as part of a longer race or competition: *an ultra-distance runner.*
ultrafiche (ˈʌltrəˌfiːʃ) *n.* a sheet of film, usually the size of a filing card, that is similar to a microfiche but has a much larger number of microcopies. [C20: from ULTRA- + French *fiche* small card. See MICROFICHE]
ultrafilter (ˌʌltrəˈfɪltə) *n.* a filter with small pores used to separate very small particles from a suspension or colloidal solution. —**ultrafiltration** (ˌʌltrəfɪlˈtreɪʃən) *n.*
ultra filtration *n. Engineering.* filtration that removes particles less than 10 microns (10^{-6}m) in diameter.
ultrahigh frequency (ˈʌltrəˌhaɪ) *n.* a radio-frequency band or radio frequency lying between 3000 and 300 megahertz. Abbrev.: **UHF.**
ultraism (ˈʌltrəˌɪzəm) *n.* extreme philosophy, belief, or action. —ˈ**ultraist** *n., adj.* —ˌ**ultraˈistic** *adj.*
ultralarge crude carrier (ˌʌltrəˈlɑːdʒ) *n. Oil industry.* an oil tanker with a capacity of over 400 000 tons.
ultramarine (ˌʌltrəməˈriːn) *n.* **1.** a blue pigment consisting of sodium and aluminium silicates and some sodium sulphide, obtained by powdering natural lapis lazuli or made synthetically: used in paints, printing ink, plastics, etc. **2.** a vivid blue colour. ~*adj.* **3.** of the colour ultramarine. **4.** from across the seas. [C17: from Medieval Latin *ultramarinus,* from *ultrā* beyond (see ULTRA-) + *mare* sea; so called because the lapis lazuli from which the pigment was made was imported from Asia]
ultramicrometer (ˌʌltrəmaɪˈkrɒmɪtə) *n.* a micrometer for measuring extremely small distances.
ultramicroscope (ˌʌltrəˈmaɪkrəˌskəʊp) *n.* a microscope used for studying colloids, in which the sample is illuminated from the side and colloidal particles are seen as bright points on a dark background. Also called: **dark-field microscope.**
ultramicroscopic (ˌʌltrəˌmaɪkrəˈskɒpɪk) *adj.* **1.** too small to be seen with an optical microscope. **2.** of or relating to an ultramicroscope. —**ultramicroscopy** (ˌʌltrəmaɪˈkrɒskəpɪ) *n.*
ultramodern (ˌʌltrəˈmɒdən) *adj.* extremely modern. —ˌ**ultraˈmodernism** *n.* —ˌ**ultraˈmodernist** *n.* —ˌ**ultraˌmodernˈistic** *adj.*
ultramontane (ˌʌltrəmɒnˈteɪn) *adj.* **1.** on the other side of the mountains, esp. the Alps, from the speaker or writer. Compare **cismontane. 2.** of or relating to a movement in the Roman Catholic Church which favours the centralized authority and influence of the pope as opposed to local independence. Compare **cisalpine** (sense 2). ~*n.* **3.** a resident or native from beyond the mountains, esp. the Alps. **4.** a member of the ultramontane party of the Roman Catholic Church.
ultramontanism (ˌʌltrəˈmɒntɪˌnɪzəm) *n. R.C. Church.* the doctrine of central papal supremacy. Compare **Gallicanism.** —ˌ**ultraˈmontanist** *n.*
ultramundane (ˌʌltrəˈmʌndeɪn) *adj.* extending beyond the world, this life, or the universe.
ultranationalism (ˌʌltrəˈnæʃnəˌlɪzəm) *n.* extreme devotion to one's own nation. —ˌ**ultraˈnational** *adj.* —ˌ**ultraˈnationalist** *adj., n.* —ˌ**ultraˌnationalˈistic** *adj.*
ultrared (ˌʌltrəˈrɛd) *adj.* an obsolete word for **infrared.**
ultrashort (ˌʌltrəˈʃɔːt) *adj.* (of a radio wave) having a wavelength shorter than 10 metres.
ultrasonic (ˌʌltrəˈsɒnɪk) *adj.* of, concerned with, or producing waves with the same nature as sound waves but frequencies above audio frequencies. See also **ultrasound.** —ˌ**ultraˈsonically** *adv.*
ultrasonic cleaning *n.* the use of ultrasound to vibrate a piece to be cleaned while the piece is immersed in a cleaning fluid. The process produces a very high degree of cleanliness, and is used for jewellery and ornately shaped items.
ultrasonics (ˌʌltrəˈsɒnɪks) *n.* (*functioning as sing.*) the branch of physics concerned with ultrasonic waves. Also called: **supersonics.**
ultrasonic testing *n. Engineering.* the scanning of material with an ultrasonic beam, during which reflections from faults in the material can be detected: a powerful nondestructive test method.
ultrasonic welding *n.* the use of high-energy vibration of ultrasonic frequency to produce a weld between two components which are held in close contact.

ultrasonography (ˌʌltrəsəˈnɒgrəfɪ) *n.* the technique of using ultrasound to produce pictures of structures within the body, as for example of a fetus.

ultrasound (ˌʌltrəˈsaʊnd) *n.* ultrasonic waves at frequencies above the audible range (above about 20 kHz), used in cleaning metallic parts, echo sounding, medical diagnosis and therapy, etc.

ultrasound scanner *n.* a device used to examine an internal bodily structure by the use of ultrasonic waves, esp. for the diagnosis of abnormality in a fetus.

ultrastructure (ˈʌltrəˌstrʌktʃə) *n.* the minute structure of an organ, tissue, or cell, as revealed by microscopy, esp. electron microscopy. —ˌ**ultraˈstructural** *adj.*

ultraviolet (ˌʌltrəˈvaɪəlɪt) *n.* **1.** the part of the electromagnetic spectrum with wavelengths shorter than light but longer than x-rays; in the range 0.4×10^{-6} and 1×10^{-8} metres. ~*adj.* **2.** of, relating to, or consisting of radiation lying in the ultraviolet: *ultraviolet radiation.*

ultraviolet astronomy *n.* the study of radiation from celestial sources in the wavelength range 25 to 350 nanometres.

ultra vires (ˈvaɪriːz) *adv., adj.* (*predicative*) *Law.* beyond the legal power or authority of a person, corporation, agent, etc. [Latin, literally: beyond strength]

ultravirus (ˌʌltrəˈvaɪrəs) *n.* a virus small enough to pass through the panes of the finest filter.

ululate (ˈjuːljʊˌleɪt) *vb.* (*intr.*) to howl or wail, as with grief. [C17: from Latin *ululāre* to howl, from *ulula* screech owl] —ˈ**ululant** *adj.* —ˌ**uluˈlation** *n.*

um (ʌm, ᵊm) *interj.* a representation of a common sound made when hesitating in speech.

umbel (ˈʌmbᵊl) *n.* a racemose inflorescence, characteristic of umbelliferous plants, in which the flowers arise from the same point in the main stem and have stalks of the same length, to give a cluster with the youngest flowers at the centre. [C16: from Latin *umbella* a sunshade, from *umbra* shade] —**umbellate** (ˈʌmbɪlɪt, -ˌleɪt), **umbellar** (ʌmˈbɛlə), *or* ˈ**umbelˌlated** *adj.* —ˈ**umbellately** *adv.*

umbelliferous (ˌʌmbɪˈlɪfərəs) *adj.* **1.** of, relating to, or belonging to the *Umbelliferae,* a family of herbaceous plants and shrubs, typically having hollow stems, divided or compound leaves, and flowers in umbels: includes fennel, dill, parsley, carrot, celery, and parsnip. **2.** designating any other plant bearing umbels. [C17: from New Latin *umbellifer,* from Latin *umbella* sunshade + *ferre* to bear] —**umˈbellifer** *n.*

umbellule (ʌmˈbɛljuːl, ˈʌmbɪˌljuːl) *n.* any of the small secondary umbels that make up a compound umbel. [C18: from New Latin *umbellula,* diminutive of Latin *umbella;* see UMBEL] —**umbellulate** (ʌmˈbɛljʊlɪt, -ˌleɪt) *adj.*

umber (ˈʌmbə) *n.* **1.** any of various natural brown earths containing ferric oxide together with lime and oxides of aluminium, manganese, and silicon. See also **burnt umber. 2.** any of the dark brown to greenish-brown colours produced by this pigment. **3.** short for **umber moth. 4.** *Obsolete.* **a.** shade or shadow. **b.** any dark, dusky, or indefinite colour. ~*adj.* **5.** of, relating to, or stained with umber. [C16: from French (*terre d'*) *ombre* or Italian (*terra di*) *ombra* shadow (earth), from Latin *umbra* shade]

umber moth *n.* any of various brownish geometrid moths, esp. the **waved umber** (*Menophra abruptaria*) and **small waved umber** (*Horisme vitalbata*), that are cryptically marked to merge with tree bark, and the **mottled umber** (*Erannis defoliaria*) whose looper larvae can strip branches and even trees. Often shortened to **umber.**

umbilical (ʌmˈbɪlɪkᵊl, ˌʌmbɪˈlaɪkᵊl) *adj.* **1.** of, relating to, or resembling the umbilicus or the umbilical cord. **2.** in the region of the umbilicus: *an umbilical hernia.* ~*n.* **3.** short for **umbilical cord.** —**umˈbilically** *adv.*

umbilical cord *n.* **1.** the long flexible tubelike structure connecting a fetus with the placenta: it provides a means of metabolic interchange with the mother. **2.** any flexible cord, tube, or cable used to transfer information, power, oxygen, etc., as between an astronaut walking in space and his spacecraft or a deep-sea diver and his craft.

umbilicate (ʌmˈbɪlɪkɪt, -ˌkeɪt) *adj.* **1.** having an umbilicus or navel. **2.** having a central depression: *an umbilicate leaf.* **3.** shaped like a navel, as some bacterial colonies.

umbilication (ʌmˌbɪlɪˈkeɪʃən) *n.* **1.** *Biology, anatomy.* a navel-like notch or depression, as in the centre of a vesicle. **2.** the condition of being umbilicated.

umbilicus (ʌmˈbɪlɪkəs, ˌʌmbɪˈlaɪkəs) *n., pl.* **-bilici** (-ˈbɪlɪˌsaɪ, -bəˈlaɪsaɪ). **1.** *Biology.* a hollow or navel-like structure, such as the cavity at the base of a gastropod shell. **2.** *Anatomy.* a technical name for the **navel.** [C18: from Latin: navel, centre; compare Latin *umbō* shield boss, Greek *omphalos* navel] —**umbiliform** (ʌmˈbɪlɪˌfɔːm) *adj.*

umble pie (ˈʌmbᵊl) *n.* See **humble pie** (sense 1).

umbles (ˈʌmbᵊlz) *pl. n.* another term for **numbles.**

umbo (ˈʌmbəʊ) *n., pl.* **umbones** (ʌmˈbəʊniːz) *or* **umbos. 1.** a small hump projecting from the centre of the cap in certain mushrooms. **2.** a hooked prominence occurring at the apex of each half of the shell of a bivalve mollusc. **3.** *Anatomy.* the slightly convex area at the centre of the outer surface of the eardrum, where the malleus is attached on the internal surface. **4.** a large projecting central boss on a shield, esp. on a Saxon shield. [C18: from Latin: boss of a shield, projecting piece] —**umbonate** (ˈʌmbənɪt, -ˌneɪt), **umbonal** (ˈʌmbənᵊl), *or* **umbonic** (ʌmˈbɒnɪk) *adj.*

umbra (ˈʌmbrə) *n., pl.* **-brae** (-briː) *or* **-bras. 1.** a region of complete shadow resulting from the total obstruction of light by an opaque object, esp. the shadow cast by the moon onto the earth during a solar eclipse. **2.** the darker inner region of a sunspot. ~Compare **penumbra.** [C16: from Latin: shade, shadow] —ˈ**umbral** *adj.*

umbrage (ˈʌmbrɪdʒ) *n.* **1.** displeasure or resentment; offence (in the phrase **give** *or* **take umbrage). 2.** the foliage of trees, considered as providing shade. **3.** *Rare.* shadow or shade. **4.** *Archaic.* a shadow or semblance. [C15: from Old French *umbrage,* from Latin *umbrāticus* relating to shade, from *umbra* shade, shadow]

umbrageous (ʌmˈbreɪdʒəs) *adj.* **1.** shady or shading. **2.** *Rare.* easily offended. —**umˈbrageously** *adv.* —**umˈbrageousness** *n.*

umbrella (ʌmˈbrɛlə) *n.* **1.** a portable device used for protection against rain, snow, etc., and consisting of a light canopy supported on a collapsible metal frame mounted on a central rod. **2.** the flattened cone-shaped contractile body of a jellyfish or other medusa. **3.** a protective shield or screen, esp. of aircraft or gunfire. **4.** anything that has the effect of a protective screen or cover. **5. a.** any system or agency that provides centralized organization or general cover for a group of related companies, organizations, etc.: *dance umbrella.* **b.** (*as modifier*): *an umbrella fund; umbrella group.* [C17: from Italian *ombrella,* diminutive of *ombra* shade; see UMBRA] —**umˈbrella-ˌlike** *adj.*

umbrella bird *n.* a black tropical American passerine bird, *Cephalopterus ornatus,* having a large overhanging crest and a long feathered wattle: family *Cotingidae* (cotingas).

umbrella pine *n.* another name for **stone pine.**

umbrella plant *n.* an African sedge, *Cyperus alternifolius,* having large umbrella-like whorls of slender leaves: widely grown as an ornamental water plant.

umbrella stand *n.* an upright rack or stand for umbrellas.

umbrella tree *n.* **1.** a North American magnolia, *Magnolia tripetala,* having long leaves clustered into an umbrella formation at the ends of the branches and unpleasant-smelling white flowers. **2.** Also called: **umbrella bush.** any of various other trees or shrubs having leaves shaped like an umbrella or growing in an umbrella-like cluster.

Umbrian (ˈʌmbrɪən) *adj.* **1.** of or relating to Umbria, a region of central Italy, or to its inhabitants, their dialect of Italian, or the ancient language once spoken there. **2.** of or relating to a Renaissance school of painting that included Raphael (1483–1520). ~*n.* **3.** a native or inhabitant of Umbria. **4.** an extinct language of ancient S Italy, belonging to the Italic branch of the Indo-European family. See also **Osco-Umbrian.**

umiak *or* **oomiak** (ˈuːmɪˌæk) *n.* a large open boat made of stretched skins, used by Eskimos. Compare **kayak.** [C18: from Greenland Eskimo: boat for the use of women]

UMIST (ˈjuːˌmɪst) *n. acronym for* University of Manchester Institute of Science and Technology.

umlaut (ˈʊmlaʊt) *n.* **1.** the mark (¨) placed over a vowel in some languages, such as German, indicating modification in the quality of the vowel. Compare **diaeresis. 2.** (esp. in Germanic languages) the change of a vowel within a word brought about by the assimilating influence of a vowel or semivowel in a preceding or following syllable. [C19: German, from *um* around (in the sense of changing places) + *Laut* sound]

umpire (ˈʌmpaɪə) *n.* **1.** an official who rules on the playing of a game, as in cricket or baseball. **2.** a person who rules on or judges disputes between contesting parties. ~*vb.* **3.** to act as umpire in (a game, dispute, or controversy). [C15: by mistaken division from *a noumpere,* from Old French *nomper* not one of a pair, from *nom-, non-* not + *per* equal, PEER] —ˈ**umpireship** *or* ˈ**umpirage** *n.*

umpteen (ˌʌmpˈtiːn) *determiner. Informal.* **a.** very many: *umpteen things to do.* **b.** (*as pronoun*): *umpteen of them came.* [C20: from *umpty* a great deal (perhaps from *-enty* as in *twenty*) + *-teen* ten] —ˌ**umpˈteenth** *n., adj.*

umpy (ˈʌmpɪ) *n., pl.* **umpies.** *Austral.* an informal word for **umpire.**

umwelt (ˈʊmvɛlt) *n. Biology, psychol.* the environmental factors, collectively, that are capable of affecting the behaviour of an animal or individual. [C20: from German *Umwelt* environment]

UN *abbrev. for* United Nations.

un-[1] *prefix.* (*freely used with adjectives, participles, and their derivative adverbs and nouns: less frequently used with certain other nouns*) not; contrary to; opposite of: *uncertain; uncomplaining; unemotionally; untidiness; unbelief; unrest; untruth.* [from Old English *on-, un-;* related to Gothic *on-,* German *un-,* Latin *in-*]

un-[2] *prefix forming verbs.* **1.** denoting reversal of an action or state: *uncover; untangle.* **2.** denoting removal from, release, or deprivation: *unharness; unman; unthrone.* **3.** (intensifier): *unloose.* [from Old English *un-, on-;* related to Gothic *and-,* German *ent-,* Latin *ante*]

'un *or* **un** (ən) *pron.* a spelling of **one** intended to reflect a dialectal or informal pronunciation: *that's a big 'un.*

UNA (in Britain) *abbrev. for* United Nations Association.

unabated (ˌʌnəˈbeɪtɪd) *adj.* without losing any original force or violence; undiminished. —ˌ**unaˈbatedly** *adv.*
unable (ʌnˈeɪbᵊl) *adj.* **1.** (*postpositive;* foll. by *to*) lacking the necessary power, ability, or authority (to do something); not able. **2.** *Archaic.* incompetent.
unaccommodated (ˌʌnəˈkɒməˌdeɪtɪd) *adj.* **1.** not suitable or apt; not adapted. **2.** unprovided for.
unaccompanied (ˌʌnəˈkʌmpənɪd) *adj.* **1.** not accompanied. **2.** *Music.* **a.** (of an instrument) playing alone. **b.** (of music for a group of singers) without instrumental accompaniment.
unaccomplished (ˌʌnəˈkɒmplɪʃt) *adj.* **1.** not accomplished or finished. **2.** lacking accomplishments.
unaccountable (ˌʌnəˈkaʊntəbᵊl) *adj.* **1.** allowing of no explanation; inexplicable. **2.** puzzling; extraordinary: *an unaccountable fear of hamburgers.* **3.** not accountable or answerable to. —ˌ**unacˈcountableness** *or* ˌ**unacˌcountaˈbility** *n.* —ˌ**unacˈcountably** *adv.*
unaccounted-for (ˌʌnəˈkaʊntɪdfɔː) *adj.* (*usually predicative*) not understood, explained, or taken into consideration.
unaccustomed (ˌʌnəˈkʌstəmd) *adj.* **1.** (foll. by *to*) not used (to): *unaccustomed to pain.* **2.** not familiar; strange or unusual. —ˌ**unacˈcustomedness** *n.*
una corda (ˈuːnə ˈkɔːdə) *adj., adv. Music.* (of the piano) to be played with the soft pedal depressed. [Italian, literally: one string; the pedal moves the mechanism so that only one string of the three tuned to each note is struck by the hammer]
unadopted (ˌʌnəˈdɒptɪd) *adj.* **1.** (of a child) not adopted. **2.** *Brit.* (of a road, etc.) not maintained by a local authority.
unadvised (ˌʌnədˈvaɪzd) *adj.* **1.** rash or unwise. **2.** not having received advice. —**unadvisedly** (ˌʌnədˈvaɪzɪdlɪ) *adv.* —ˌ**unadˈvisedness** *n.*
unaffected[1] (ˌʌnəˈfɛktɪd) *adj.* unpretentious, natural, or sincere. —ˌ**unafˈfectedly** *adv.* —ˌ**unafˈfectedness** *n.*
unaffected[2] (ˌʌnəˈfɛktɪd) *adj.* not affected.
unalienable (ʌnˈeɪljənəbᵊl) *adj. Law.* a variant of **inalienable.**
unalloyed (ˌʌnəˈlɔɪd) *adj.* not mixed or intermingled with any other thing; pure: *unalloyed metal; unalloyed pleasure.*
un-American *adj.* **1.** not in accordance with the aims, ideals, customs, etc., of the U.S. **2.** against the interests of the U.S. —ˌ**un-Aˈmericanism** *n.*
unaneled (ˌʌnəˈniːld) *adj. Archaic.* not having received extreme unction. [C17: from UN-[1] + ANELE]
unanimous (juːˈnænɪməs) *adj.* **1.** in complete or absolute agreement. **2.** characterized by complete agreement: *a unanimous decision.* [C17: from Latin *ūnanimus* from *ūnus* one + *animus* mind] —**uˈnanimously** *adv.* —**unanimity** (ˌjuːnəˈnɪmɪtɪ) *or* **uˈnanimousness** *n.*
unanswerable (ʌnˈɑːnsərəbᵊl) *adj.* **1.** incapable of being refuted. **2.** (of a question) not admitting of any answer. —**unˈanswerableness** *n.* —**unˈanswerably** *adv.*
unappealable (ˌʌnəˈpiːləbᵊl) *adj. Law.* (of a judgment, etc.) not capable of being appealed against. —ˌ**unapˈpealableness** *n.* —ˌ**unapˈpealably** *adv.*
unapproachable (ˌʌnəˈprəʊtʃəbᵊl) *adj.* **1.** discouraging intimacy, friendliness, etc.; aloof. **2.** inaccessible. **3.** not to be rivalled. —ˌ**unapˈproachableness** *n.* —ˌ**unapˈproachably** *adv.*
unappropriated (ˌʌnəˈprəʊprɪˌeɪtɪd) *adj.* **1.** not set aside for specific use. **2.** *Accounting.* designating that portion of the profits of a business enterprise that is retained in the business and not withdrawn by the proprietor. **3.** (of property) not having been taken into any person's possession or control.
unapt (ʌnˈæpt) *adj.* **1.** (*usually postpositive;* often foll. by *for*) not suitable or qualified; unfitted. **2.** mentally slow. **3.** (*postpositive; may take an infinitive*) not disposed or likely (to). —**unˈaptly** *adv.* —**unˈaptness** *n.*
unarguable (ʌnˈɑːgjʊəbᵊl) *adj.* **1.** incapable of being argued. **2.** incontestable; indisputable. —**unˈarguably** *adv.*
unarm (ʌnˈɑːm) *vb.* a less common word for **disarm.**
unarmed (ʌnˈɑːmd) *adj.* **1.** without weapons. **2.** (of animals and plants) having no claws, prickles, spines, thorns, or similar structures. **3.** of or relating to a projectile that does not use a detonator to initiate explosive action.
unary (ˈjuːnərɪ) *adj.* consisting of, or affecting, a single element or component; monadic. [C16 (in the obsolete sense: a unit): from Latin *unus* one + -ARY]
unashamed (ˌʌnəˈʃeɪmd) *adj.* **1.** lacking moral restraints. **2.** not embarrassed, contrite, or apologetic. —**unashamedly** (ˌʌnəˈʃeɪmɪdlɪ) *adv.* —ˌ**unaˈshamedness** *n.*
unasked (ʌnˈɑːskt) *adj.* **1.** not requested or demanded. **2.** not invited.
unassailable (ˌʌnəˈseɪləbᵊl) *adj.* **1.** not able to be attacked. **2.** undeniable or irrefutable. —ˌ**unasˈsailableness** *n.* —ˌ**unasˈsailably** *adv.*
unassuming (ˌʌnəˈsjuːmɪŋ) *adj.* modest or unpretentious. —ˌ**unasˈsumingly** *adv.* —ˌ**unasˈsumingness** *n.*
unattached (ˌʌnəˈtætʃt) *adj.* **1.** not connected with any specific thing, body, group, etc.; independent. **2.** not engaged or married. **3.** (of property) not seized or held as security or in satisfaction of a judgment.
unattended (ˌʌnəˈtɛndɪd) *adj.* **1.** not looked after or cared for. **2.** unaccompanied or alone. **3.** not listened to.
unau (ˈjuːnaʊ) *n.* another name for the **two-toed sloth** (see **sloth** (sense 1)). [C18: via French from Tupi]
unavailing (ˌʌnəˈveɪlɪŋ) *adj.* useless or futile. —ˌ**unaˈvailingly** *adv.*
unavoidable (ˌʌnəˈvɔɪdəbᵊl) *adj.* **1.** unable to be avoided; inevitable. **2.** *Law.* not capable of being declared null and void. —**unaˌvoidaˈbility** *or* ˌ**unaˈvoidableness** *n.* —ˌ**unaˈvoidably** *adv.*
unaware (ˌʌnəˈwɛə) *adj.* **1.** (*postpositive*) not aware or conscious (of): *unaware of the danger he ran across the road.* **2.** not fully cognizant of what is going on in the world: *he's the most unaware person I've ever met.* ~*adv.* **3.** a variant of **unawares.** —ˌ**unaˈwarely** *adv.* —ˌ**unaˈwareness** *n.*
▷**Usage.** Careful users of English distinguish between the adjective *unaware* (to be ignorant of) and the adverb *unawares* (by surprise): *they were unaware of the danger; the danger caught them unawares.*
unawares (ˌʌnəˈwɛəz) *adv.* **1.** without prior warning or plan; unexpectedly: *she caught him unawares.* **2.** without being aware of or knowing: *he lost it unawares.*
unb. *or* **unbd** *Bookbinding. abbrev. for* unbound.
unbacked (ʌnˈbækt) *adj.* **1.** (of a book, chair, etc.) not having a back. **2.** bereft of support, esp. on a financial basis. **3.** (of a horse) **a.** not supported by bets. **b.** never having been ridden.
unbalance (ʌnˈbæləns) *vb.* (*tr.*) **1.** to upset the equilibrium or balance of. **2.** to disturb the mental stability of (a person or his mind). ~*n.* **3.** imbalance or instability.
unbalanced (ʌnˈbælənst) *adj.* **1.** lacking balance. **2.** irrational or unsound; erratic. **3.** mentally disordered or deranged. **4.** biased; one-sided: *unbalanced reporting.* **5.** (in double-entry book-keeping) not having total debit balances equal to total credit balances. **6.** *Electronics.* (of signals or circuitry) not symmetrically disposed about earth or zero reference potential.
unbar (ʌnˈbɑː) *vb.* **-bars, -barring, -barred.** (*tr.*) **1.** to take away a bar or bars from. **2.** to unfasten bars, locks, etc., from (a door); open.
unbated (ʌnˈbeɪtɪd) *adj.* **1.** a less common spelling of **unabated.** **2.** *Archaic.* (of a sword, lance, etc.) not covered with a protective button.

ˌ**unaˈbashed** *adj.*
ˌ**unabˈbreviˌated** *adj.*
ˌ**unaˈbridged** *adj.*
ˌ**unabˈsorbed** *adj.*
ˌ**unacaˈdemic** *adj.*
ˌ**unacˈcented** *adj.*
ˌ**unacˈcentuˌated** *adj.*
ˌ**unacˈceptable** *adj.*
ˌ**unacˈclaimed** *adj.*
unacˈclimaˌtized *or* ˌ**unacˈclimaˌtised** *adj.*
ˌ**unacˈcommoˌdating** *adj.*
ˌ**unacˈcounted** *adj.*
ˌ**unacˈcredited** *adj.*
ˌ**unacˈknowledged** *adj.*
ˌ**unacˈquainted** *adj.*
ˌ**unacˈquitted** *adj.*
unˈacted *adj.*
unˈactionable *adj.*
unˈactuˌated *adj.*
ˌ**unaˈdaptable** *adj.*
ˌ**unaˈdapted** *adj.*
ˌ**unadˈdressed** *adj.*
ˌ**unadˈjourned** *adj.*
ˌ**unadˈjustable** *adj.*
ˌ**unaˈdorned** *adj.*
ˌ**unaˈdulterˌated** *adj.*
ˌ**unadvanˈtageous** *adj.*
ˌ**unadˈventurous** *adj.*
ˌ**unˈadverˌtised** *adj.*
ˌ**unadˈvisable** *adj.*
ˌ**unafˈfiliˌated** *adj.*
ˌ**unaˈfraid** *adj.*
ˌ**unagˈgressive** *adj.*
unˈaided *adj.*
unˈaimed *adj.*
unˈaired *adj.*
ˌ**unaˈlarmed** *adj.*
ˌ**unaˈligned** *adj.*
ˌ**unalˈlayed** *adj.*
ˌ**unalˈleviˌated** *adj.*
ˌ**unalˈlied** *adj.*
ˌ**unalˈlowable** *adj.*
unˈalterable *adj.*
unˈaltered *adj.*
ˌ**unamˈbiguous** *adj.*
ˌ**unamˈbitious** *adj.*
unˈamiable *adj.*
unˈamicable *adj.*
unˈampliˌfied *adj.*
ˌ**unaˈmused** *adj.*
unˈaniˌmated *adj.*
ˌ**unanˈnounced** *adj.*
unˈanswered *adj.*
ˌ**unanˈticiˌpated** *adj.*
ˌ**unaˌpoloˈgetic** *adj.*
ˌ**unapˈparent** *adj.*
ˌ**unapˈpealing** *adj.*
ˌ**unapˈpeasable** *adj.*
unˈappeˌtizing *or* **unˈappeˌtising** *adj.*
unˈapplicable *adj.*
ˌ**unapˈplied** *adj.*
ˌ**unapˈpointed** *adj.*
ˌ**unapˈportioned** *adj.*
ˌ**unapˈpreciˌated** *adj.*
ˌ**unapˈpreciative** *adj.*
ˌ**unappreˈhensive** *adj.*
ˌ**unapˈproved** *adj.*
ˌ**unarˈticuˌlated** *adj.*
ˌ**unarˈtistic** *adj.*
ˌ**unascerˈtainable** *adj.*
unˈaspiˌrated *adj.*
ˌ**unasˈpiring** *adj.*
ˌ**unasˈsailed** *adj.*
ˌ**unasˈsertive** *adj.*
ˌ**unasˈsessed** *adj.*
ˌ**unasˈsigned** *adj.*
ˌ**unasˈsimiˌlated** *adj.*
ˌ**unasˈsisted** *adj.*
ˌ**unasˈsorted** *adj.*
ˌ**unasˈsumed** *adj.*
ˌ**unaˈtoned** *adj.*
ˌ**unatˈtainable** *adj.*
ˌ**unatˈtained** *adj.*
ˌ**unatˈtempted** *adj.*
ˌ**unatˈtested** *adj.*
ˌ**unatˈtractive** *adj.*
ˌ**unausˈpicious** *adj.*
ˌ**unauˈthentic** *adj.*
ˌ**unauˈthentiˌcated** *adj.*
unˈauthorˌized *or* **unˈauthorˌised** *adj.*
ˌ**unaˈvailable** *adj.*
ˌ**unaˈvenged** *adj.*
ˌ**unbapˈtized** *or* ˌ**unbapˈtised** *adj.*

unbearable (ʌnˈbɛərəbᵊl) *adj.* not able to be borne or endured. —unˈ**bearableness** *n.* —unˈ**bearably** *adv.*
unbeatable (ʌnˈbiːtəbᵊl) *adj.* unable to be defeated or outclassed; surpassingly excellent.
unbeaten (ʌnˈbiːtᵊn) *adj.* **1.** having suffered no defeat. **2.** not worn down; untrodden. **3.** not mixed or stirred by beating: *unbeaten eggs.* **4.** not beaten or struck.
unbecoming (ˌʌnbɪˈkʌmɪŋ) *adj.* **1.** unsuitable or inappropriate, esp. through being unattractive: *an unbecoming hat.* **2.** (when *postpositive,* usually foll. by *of* or an object) not proper or seemly (for): *manners unbecoming a lady.* —ˌ**unbeˈcomingly** *adv.* —ˌ**unbeˈcomingness** *n.*
unbeknown (ˌʌnbɪˈnəʊn) *adv.* **1.** (*sentence modifier;* foll. by *to*) Also (esp. Brit.): ˌ**unbeˈknownst.** without the knowledge (of a person): *unbeknown to him she had left the country.* ~*adj.* **2.** (*postpositive;* usually foll. by *to*) *Rare.* not known (to). [C17: from the archaic *beknown* known; see BE-, KNOW]
unbelief (ˌʌnbɪˈliːf) *n.* disbelief or rejection of belief.
unbelievable (ˌʌnbɪˈliːvəbᵊl) *adj.* unable to be believed; incredible or astonishing. —ˌ**unbeˌlievaˈbility** *or* ˌ**unbeˈlievableness** *n.* —ˌ**unbeˈlievably** *adv.*
unbeliever (ˌʌnbɪˈliːvə) *n.* a person who does not believe or withholds belief, esp. in religious matters.
unbelieving (ˌʌnbɪˈliːvɪŋ) *adj.* **1.** not believing; sceptical. **2.** proceeding from or characterized by scepticism. —ˌ**unbeˈlievingly** *adv.* —ˌ**unbeˈlievingness** *n.*
unbelt (ʌnˈbɛlt) *vb.* (*tr.*) **1.** to unbuckle the belt of (a garment). **2.** to remove (something) from a belt.
unbend (ʌnˈbɛnd) *vb.* **-bends, -bending, -bent.** **1.** to release or be released from the restraints of formality and ceremony. **2.** *Informal.* to relax (the mind) or (of the mind) to become relaxed. **3.** to become or be made straightened out from an originally bent shape or position. **4.** (*tr.*) *Nautical.* **a.** to remove (a sail) from a stay, mast, yard, etc. **b.** to untie (a rope, etc.) or cast (a cable) loose. —unˈ**bendable** *adj.*
unbending (ʌnˈbɛndɪŋ) *adj.* **1.** rigid or inflexible. **2.** characterized by sternness or severity: *an unbending rule.* —unˈ**bendingly** *adv.* —unˈ**bendingness** *n.*
unbent (ʌnˈbɛnt) *vb.* **1.** the past tense and past participle of **unbend.** ~*adj.* **2.** not bent or bowed. **3.** not compelled to yield or give way by force.
unbiased *or* **unbiassed** (ʌnˈbaɪəst) *adj.* **1.** having no bias or prejudice; fair or impartial. **2.** *Statistics.* **a.** (of a sample) not affected by any extraneous factors, conflated variables, or selectivity which influence its distribution; random. **b.** (of an estimator) having an expected value equal to the parameter being estimated; having zero bias. **c.** Also called: **discriminatory.** (of a significance test). having a power greater than the predetermined significance level. —unˈ**biasedly** *or* unˈ**biassedly** *adv.* —unˈ**biasedness** *or* unˈ**biassedness** *n.*
unbidden (ʌnˈbɪdᵊn) *adj.* **1.** not ordered or commanded; voluntary or spontaneous. **2.** not invited or asked.
unbind (ʌnˈbaɪnd) *vb.* **binds, binding, bound.** (*tr.*) **1.** to set free from restraining bonds or chains; release. **2.** to unfasten or make loose (a bond, tie, etc.).
unbirthday (ˌʌnˈbɜːθdeɪ) *n. Brit., jocular.* **a.** any day other than one's birthday. **b.** (*as modifier*): *an unbirthday present.* [C19: coined by the British writer Lewis Carroll (1832–98) in *Through the Looking-Glass*]
unblenched (ʌnˈblɛntʃt) *adj. Obsolete.* undismayed. [C17: from UN-[1] + BLENCH[1]]
unblessed (ʌnˈblɛst) *adj.* **1.** deprived of blessing. **2.** unhallowed, cursed, or evil. **3.** unhappy or wretched. —**unblessedness** (ʌnˈblɛsɪdnɪs) *n.*
unblinking (ʌnˈblɪŋkɪŋ) *adj.* **1.** without blinking. **2.** showing no visible response or emotion. **3.** not wavering through trepidation or fear. —unˈ**blinkingly** *adv.*
unblown (ʌnˈbləʊn) *adj.* **1.** *Archaic.* (of a flower) still in the bud. **2.** not blown.
unblushing (ʌnˈblʌʃɪŋ) *adj.* immodest or shameless. —unˈ**blushingly** *adv.* —unˈ**blushingness** *n.*
unbolt (ʌnˈbəʊlt) *vb.* (*tr.*) **1.** to unfasten a bolt of (a door). **2.** to undo (the nut) on a bolt.
unbolted (ʌnˈbəʊltɪd) *adj.* (of grain, meal, or flour) not sifted.
unboned (ʌnˈbəʊnd) *adj.* **1.** (of meat, fish, etc.) not having had the bones removed. **2.** (of animals) having no bones.
unbonnet (ʌnˈbɒnɪt) *vb.* to remove a bonnet or hat from (one's head), esp. as a mark of respect.
unborn (ʌnˈbɔːn) *adj.* **1.** not yet born or brought to birth. **2.** still to come in the future: *the unborn world.*
unbosom (ʌnˈbʊzəm) *vb.* (*tr.*) to relieve (oneself) of (secrets, etc.) by telling someone. [C16: from UN-[2] + BOSOM (in the sense: seat of the emotions); compare Dutch *ontboezemen*] —unˈ**bosomer** *n.*
unbound (ʌnˈbaʊnd) *vb.* **1.** the past tense and past participle of **unbind.** ~*adj.* **2.** (of a book) not bound within a cover. **3.** not restrained or tied down by bonds. **4.** (of a morpheme) able to form a word by itself; free.
unbounded (ʌnˈbaʊndɪd) *adj.* having no boundaries or limits. —unˈ**boundedly** *adv.* —unˈ**boundedness** *n.*
unbowed (ʌnˈbaʊd) *adj.* **1.** not bowed or bent. **2.** free or unconquered.
unbrace (ʌnˈbreɪs) *vb.* (*tr.*) **1.** to remove tension or strain from; relax. **2.** to remove a brace or braces from.
unbred (ʌnˈbrɛd) *adj.* **1.** a less common word for **ill-bred.** **2.** not taught or instructed. **3.** *Obsolete.* not born.
unbridle (ʌnˈbraɪdᵊl) *vb.* (*tr.*) **1.** to remove the bridle from (a horse). **2.** to remove all controls or restraints from.
unbridled (ʌnˈbraɪdᵊld) *adj.* **1.** with all restraints removed. **2.** (of a horse, etc.) wearing no bridle. —unˈ**bridledly** *adv.* —unˈ**bridledness** *n.*
unbroken (ʌnˈbrəʊkən) *adj.* **1.** complete or whole. **2.** continuous or incessant. **3.** undaunted in spirit. **4.** (of animals, esp. horses) not tamed; wild. **5.** not disturbed or upset: *the unbroken quiet of the afternoon.* **6.** (of a record, esp. at sport) not improved upon. **7.** (of a contract, law, etc.) not broken or infringed. —unˈ**brokenly** *adv.* —unˈ**brokenness** *n.*
unbundle (ʌnˈbʌndᵊl) *vb.* (*tr.*) *Computer technol.* to separate (hardware from software) for sales purposes.
unbundling (ʌnˈbʌndlɪŋ) *n. Commerce.* the takeover of a large conglomerate with a view to retaining the core business and selling off some of the subsidiaries to help finance the takeover.
unburden (ʌnˈbɜːdᵊn) *vb.* (*tr.*) **1.** to remove a load or burden from. **2.** to relieve or make free (one's mind, oneself, etc.) of a worry, trouble, etc., by revelation or confession. ~Archaic spelling: **unburthen** (ʌnˈbɜːðən).
unbutton (ʌnˈbʌtᵊn) *vb.* **1.** to undo by unfastening (the buttons) of (a garment). **2.** *Informal.* to release or relax (oneself, tension, etc.).
unbuttoned (ʌnˈbʌtᵊnd) *adj.* **1.** with buttons not fastened. **2.** *Informal.* uninhibited; unrestrained: *hours of unbuttoned self-revelation.*
uncaged (ʌnˈkeɪdʒd) *adj.* at liberty.
uncalled-for (ˌʌnˈkɔːldfɔː) *adj.* unnecessary or unwarranted.
uncanny (ʌnˈkænɪ) *adj.* **1.** characterized by apparently supernatural wonder, horror, etc. **2.** beyond what is normal or expected; extreme: *uncanny accuracy.* —unˈ**cannily** *adv.* —unˈ**canniness** *n.*
uncap (ʌnˈkæp) *vb.* **-caps, -capping, -capped.** **1.** (*tr.*) to remove a cap or top from (a container): *to uncap a bottle.* **2.** to remove a cap from (the head).
uncared-for (ˌʌnˈkɛədfɔː) *adj.* not cared for; neglected.
uncaused (ʌnˈkɔːzd) *adj. Now rare.* not brought into existence by any cause; spontaneous or natural.
unceasing (ʌnˈsiːsɪŋ) *adj.* not ceasing or ending. —unˈ**ceasingly** *adv.* —unˈ**ceasingness** *n.*
unceremonious (ˌʌnsɛrɪˈməʊnɪəs) *adj.* without ceremony; informal, abrupt, rude, or undignified. —ˌ**uncereˈmoniously** *adv.* —ˌ**uncereˈmoniousness** *n.*
uncertain (ʌnˈsɜːtᵊn) *adj.* **1.** not able to be accurately known or predicted: *the issue is uncertain.* **2.** (when *postpositive,* often foll. by *of*) not sure or confident (about): *a man of uncertain opinion.* **3.** not precisely determined, established, or decided: *uncertain plans.* **4.** not to be depended upon; unreliable: *an uncertain vote.* **5.** liable to variation; changeable: *the weather is uncertain.* **6. in no uncertain terms. a.** unambiguously. **b.** forcefully. —unˈ**certainly** *adv.* —unˈ**certainness** *n.*
uncertainty (ʌnˈsɜːtᵊntɪ) *n., pl.* **-ties.** **1.** Also called: **uncertainness.** the state or condition of being uncertain. **2.** an uncertain matter, contingency, etc.
uncertainty principle *n.* **the.** the principle that energy and time or position and momentum, cannot both be accurately measured simultaneously. The product of their uncertainties is always greater than or equal to $h/4\pi$, where h is the Planck constant. Also called: **Heisenberg uncertainty principle, indeterminacy principle.**
unchain (ʌnˈtʃeɪn) *vb.* (*tr.*) **1.** to remove a chain or chains from. **2.** to set at liberty; make free.
unchancy (ʌnˈtʃɑːnsɪ) *adj. Scot.* unlucky, ill-omened, or dangerous. Compare **wanchancy.**
uncharged (ʌnˈtʃɑːdʒd) *adj.* **1.** (of land or other property) not subject to a charge. **2.** having no electric charge; neutral. **3.** *Archaic.* (of a firearm) not loaded.

ˌ**unbeˈfitting** *adj.*
ˌ**unbeˈfriended** *adj.*
ˌ**unbeˈgotten** *adj.*
ˌ**unbeˈholden** *adj.*
unˈ**bleached** *adj.*
unˈ**blemished** *adj.*
unˈ**block** *vb.*
unˈ**breakable** *adj.*
unˈ**bribable** *adj.*
unˈ**bruised** *adj.*
unˈ**brushed** *adj.*
unˈ**buckle** *vb.,* **-les, -ling, -led.**
unˈ**budgeted** *adj.*
unˈ**built** *adj.*
unˈ**buried** *adj.*
unˈ**cashed** *adj.*
ˌ**uncateˈgorical** *adj.*
unˈ**caught** *adj.*
unˈ**celeˌbrated** *adj.*
unˈ**censored** *adj.*
unˈ**censured** *adj.*
unˈ**certiˌfied** *adj.*
unˈ**challengeable** *adj.*
unˈ**challenged** *adj.*
unˈ**changeable** *adj.*
unˈ**changeableness** *n.*
unˈ**changeably** *adv.*
unˈ**changed** *adj.*
unˈ**changing** *adj.*
unˈ**chaperˌoned** *adj.*
ˌ**uncharacterˈistic** *adj.*

uncharted (ʌn'tʃɑːtɪd) *adj.* (of a physical or nonphysical region or area) not yet mapped, surveyed, or investigated: *uncharted waters; the uncharted depths of the mind.*

unchartered (ʌn'tʃɑːtəd) *adj.* **1.** not authorized by charter; unregulated. **2.** unauthorized, lawless, or irregular.

unchristian (ʌn'krɪstʃən) *adj.* **1.** not in accordance with the principles or ethics of Christianity. **2.** non-Christian or pagan. —**un'christianly** *adv.*

unchurch (ʌn'tʃɜːtʃ) *vb.* (*tr.*) **1.** to excommunicate. **2.** to remove church status from (a building).

uncial ('ʌnsɪəl) *adj.* **1.** of, relating to, or written in majuscule letters, as used in Greek and Latin manuscripts of the third to ninth centuries, that resemble modern capitals, but are characterized by much greater curvature and inclination and general inequality of height. **2.** pertaining to an inch or an ounce. **3.** pertaining to the duodecimal system. ~*n.* **4.** an uncial letter or manuscript. [C17: from Late Latin *unciāles litterae* letters an inch long, from Latin *unciālis,* from *uncia* one twelfth, inch, OUNCE] —'**uncially** *adv.*

unciform ('ʌnsɪˌfɔːm) *adj.* **1.** *Anatomy, zoology, etc.* having the shape of a hook. ~*n.* **2.** Also called: **hamate bone.** *Anatomy.* any hook-shaped structure or part, esp. a small bone of the wrist (**unciform bone**). [C18: from New Latin *unciformis,* from Latin *uncus* a hook]

uncinariasis (ˌʌnsɪnə'raɪəsɪs) *n.* the condition of being infested with hookworms; hookworm disease. [C20: via New Latin *Uncināria,* from Late Latin *uncīnus* a hook, from Latin *uncus*]

uncinate ('ʌnsɪnɪt, -ˌneɪt) *adj. Biology.* **1.** shaped like a hook: *the uncinate process of the ribs of certain vertebrates.* **2.** of, relating to, or possessing uncini. [C18: from Latin *uncīnātus,* from *uncīnus* a hook, from *uncus*]

uncinus (ʌn'saɪnəs) *n., pl.* **-cini** (-'saɪnaɪ). *Zoology.* a small hooked structure, such as any of the hooked chaetae of certain polychaete worms. [C19: from Late Latin: hook, from Latin *uncus*]

uncircumcised (ʌn'sɜːkəmˌsaɪzd) *adj.* **1.** not circumcised. **2.** not Jewish; gentile. **3.** *Theol.* not purified.

uncircumcision (ˌʌnsɜːkəm'sɪʒən) *n. Chiefly New Testament.* the state of being uncircumcised.

uncivil (ʌn'sɪvəl) *adj.* **1.** lacking civility or good manners. **2.** an obsolete word for **uncivilized.** —**uncivility** (ˌʌnsɪ'vɪlɪtɪ) *or* **un'civilness** *n.* —**un'civilly** *adv.*

uncivilized *or* **uncivilised** (ʌn'sɪvɪˌlaɪzd) *adj.* **1.** (of a tribe or people) not yet civilized, esp. preliterate. **2.** lacking culture or sophistication. —**uncivilizedly** *or* **uncivilisedly** (ʌn'sɪvɪˌlaɪzɪdlɪ) *adv.* —**un'civiˌlizedness** *or* **un'civiˌlisedness** *n.*

unclad (ʌn'klæd) *adj.* having no clothes on; naked.

unclasp (ʌn'klɑːsp) *vb.* **1.** (*tr.*) to unfasten the clasp of (something). **2.** to release one's grip (upon an object).

unclassified (ʌn'klæsɪˌfaɪd) *adj.* **1.** not arranged in any specific order or grouping. **2.** (of information) not possessing a security classification. **3.** (of football results) not arranged in any special order or in divisions.

uncle ('ʌŋkəl) *n.* **1.** a brother of one's father or mother. **2.** the husband of one's aunt. **3.** a term of address sometimes used by children for a male friend of their parents. **4.** *Slang.* a pawnbroker. ~Related adj.: **avuncular.** [C13: from Old French *oncle,* from Latin *avunculus;* related to Latin *avus* grandfather]

unclean (ʌn'kliːn) *adj.* lacking moral, spiritual, ritual, or physical cleanliness. —**un'cleanness** *n.*

uncleanly[1] (ʌn'kliːnlɪ) *adv.* in an unclean manner.

uncleanly[2] (ʌn'klɛnlɪ) *adj.* characterized by an absence of cleanliness; unclean. —**un'cleanliness** *n.*

unclear (ʌn'klɪə) *adj.* not clear or definite; ambiguous. —**un'clearly** *adv.* —**un'clearness** *n.*

Uncle Sam *n.* a personification of the government of the United States. [C19: apparently a humorous interpretation of the letters stamped on army supply boxes during the War of 1812 between Great Britain and the United States: *U.S.*]

Uncle Tom *n. Informal, derogatory.* a Negro whose behaviour towards white people is regarded as obsequious and servile. [C20: after the slave who is the main character of *Uncle Tom's Cabin* (1852), a novel by the U.S. writer Harriet Beecher Stowe] —'**Uncle 'Tomism** *n.*

unclog (ʌn'klɒg) *vb.* **-clogs, -clogging, -clogged.** (*tr.*) to remove an obstruction from (a drain, etc.).

unclose (ʌn'kləʊz) *vb.* **1.** to open or cause to open. **2.** to come or bring to light; reveal or be revealed.

unclothe (ʌn'kləʊð) *vb.* **-clothes, -clothing, -clothed** *or* **-clad.** (*tr.*) **1.** to take off garments from; strip. **2.** to uncover or lay bare.

unco ('ʌŋkəʊ) *Scot.* ~*adj.* **uncoer, uncoest. 1.** unfamiliar, strange, or odd. **2.** remarkable or striking. ~*adv.* **3.** very; extremely. **4. the unco guid.** narrow-minded, excessively religious, or self-righteous people. ~*n., pl.* **uncos** *or* **uncoes. 5.** a novel or remarkable person or thing. **6.** *Obsolete.* a stranger. **7.** (*pl.*) news. [C15: variant of UNCOUTH]

uncoil (ʌn'kɔɪl) *vb.* to unwind or become unwound; untwist.

uncoined (ʌn'kɔɪnd) *adj.* (of a metal) not made into coin.

uncomfortable (ʌn'kʌmftəbəl) *adj.* **1.** not comfortable. **2.** feeling or causing discomfort or unease; disquieting. —**un'comfortableness** *n.* —**un'comfortably** *adv.*

uncommercial (ˌʌnkə'mɜːʃəl) *adj.* **1.** not concerned with commerce or trade. **2.** not in accordance with the aims or principles of business or trade.

uncommitted (ˌʌnkə'mɪtɪd) *adj.* not bound or pledged to a specific opinion, course of action, or cause.

uncommon (ʌn'kɒmən) *adj.* **1.** outside or beyond normal experience, conditions, etc.; unusual. **2.** in excess of what is normal: *an uncommon liking for honey.* ~*adv.* **3.** an archaic word for **uncommonly** (sense 2). —**un'commonness** *n.*

uncommonly (ʌn'kɒmənlɪ) *adv.* **1.** in an uncommon or unusual manner or degree; rarely. **2.** (intensifier): *you're uncommonly friendly.*

uncommunicative (ˌʌnkə'mjuːnɪkətɪv) *adj.* disinclined to talk or give information or opinions. —ˌ**uncom'municatively** *adv.* —ˌ**uncom'municativeness** *n.*

uncompromising (ʌn'kɒmprəˌmaɪzɪŋ) *adj.* not prepared to give ground or to compromise. —**un'comproˌmisingly** *adv.* —**un'comproˌmisingness** *n.*

unconcern (ˌʌnkən'sɜːn) *n.* apathy or indifference.

unconcerned (ˌʌnkən'sɜːnd) *adj.* **1.** lacking in concern or involvement. **2.** not worried; untroubled. —**unconcernedly** (ˌʌnkən'sɜːnɪdlɪ) *adv.* —ˌ**uncon'cernedness** *n.*

unconditional (ˌʌnkən'dɪʃənəl) *adj.* **1.** without conditions or limitations; total: *unconditional surrender.* **2.** *Maths.* (of an equality) true for all values of the variable: *$(x+1)>x$ is an unconditional equality.* —ˌ**uncon'ditionally** *adv.* —ˌ**uncon'ditionalness** *or* ˌ**unconˌdition'ality** *n.*

unconditioned (ˌʌnkən'dɪʃənd) *adj.* **1.** *Psychol.* characterizing an innate reflex and the stimulus and response that form parts of it. Compare **conditioned** (sense 1). **2.** *Metaphysics.* unrestricted by conditions; infinite; absolute. **3.** without limitations; unconditional. —ˌ**uncon'ditionedness** *n.*

unconditioned response *n.* a reflex action innately elicited by a stimulus without the intervention of any learning process. Also called (esp. formerly): **unconditioned reflex.** Compare **conditioned response.**

unconditioned stimulus *n. Psychol.* any stimulus evoking an unlearnt response, esp. in the context of classical conditioning, in which the conditioned stimulus is followed by the unconditioned one.

unconformable (ˌʌnkən'fɔːməbəl) *adj.* **1.** not conformable or conforming. **2.** (of rock strata) consisting of a series of recent strata resting on different, much older rocks. —ˌ**unconˌforma'bility** *or* ˌ**uncon'formableness** *n.* —ˌ**uncon'formably** *adv.*

unconformity (ˌʌnkən'fɔːmɪtɪ) *n., pl.* **-ties. 1.** lack of conformity. **2.** the junction between recently deposited stratified rocks and much older or folded rocks.

unconnected (ˌʌnkə'nɛktɪd) *adj.* **1.** not linked; separate or independent. **2.** disconnected or incoherent. —ˌ**uncon'nectedly** *adv.* —ˌ**uncon'nectedness** *n.*

unconscionable (ʌn'kɒnʃənəbəl) *adj.* **1.** unscrupulous or unprincipled: *an unconscionable liar.* **2.** immoderate or excessive: *unconscionable demands.* —**un'conscionableness** *n.* —**un'conscionably** *adv.*

unconscious (ʌn'kɒnʃəs) *adj.* **1.** lacking normal sensory awareness of the environment; insensible. **2.** not aware of one's actions, behaviour, etc.: *unconscious of his bad manners.* **3.** characterized by lack of awareness or intention: *an unconscious blunder.* **4.** coming from or produced by the unconscious: *unconscious resentment.* ~*n.* **5.** *Psychoanal.* the part of the mind containing instincts, impulses, images, and ideas that are not available for direct examination. See also **collective unconscious.** Compare **subconscious, preconscious.** —**un'consciously** *adv.*

unconsciousness (ʌn'kɒnʃəsnɪs) *n.* the state of being without normal sensory awareness; insensibility.

un'charitable *adj.*
un'chaste *adj.*
un'checked *adj.*
un'chivalrous *adj.*
un'chosen *adj.*
un'christened *adj.*
un'claimed *adj.*
un'clariˌfied *adj.*
un'cleaned *adj.*
un'clouded *adj.*
un'cluttered *adj.*
ˌ**uncol'lected** *adj.*
un'coloured *adj.*
un'combed *adj.*
ˌ**uncom'bined** *adj.*
ˌ**uncom'mendable** *adj.*
ˌ**uncom'panionable** *adj.*
un'compenˌsated *adj.*
ˌ**uncom'petitive** *adj.*
ˌ**uncom'plaining** *adj.*
ˌ**uncom'pleted** *adj.*
ˌ**uncom'pliant** *adj.*
un'compliˌcated *adj.*
ˌ**uncompli'mentary** *adj.*
ˌ**uncom'pounded** *adj.*
ˌ**uncompre'hending** *adj.*
ˌ**uncompre'hensible** *adj.*
ˌ**uncon'cealed** *adj.*
ˌ**uncon'ceded** *adj.*
ˌ**uncon'certed** *adj.*
ˌ**uncon'cluded** *adj.*
ˌ**uncon'demned** *adj.*
ˌ**uncon'densed** *adj.*
ˌ**uncon'ducive** *adj.*
un'confident *adj.*
ˌ**uncon'fined** *adj.*
ˌ**uncon'firmed** *adj.*
ˌ**uncon'fused** *adj.*
ˌ**uncon'genial** *adj.*
un'conquered *adj.*
ˌ**unconsci'entious** *adj.*

unconsidered (ˌʌnkənˈsɪdəd) *adj.* **1.** not considered; disregarded. **2.** done without consideration.

unconstitutional (ˌʌnkɒnstɪˈtjuːʃənᵊl) *adj.* at variance with or not permitted by a constitution. —ˌ**unconstiˌtutionˈality** *n.*

unconstitutional strike *n.* a stoppage of work which violates the dispute procedure agreed between the employer and the trade union or trade unions concerned.

uncontrollable (ˌʌnkənˈtrəʊləbᵊl) *adj.* incapable of being controlled or managed. —ˌ**unconˌtrollaˈbility** *or* ˌ**unconˈtrollableness** *n.* —ˌ**unconˈtrollably** *adv.*

unconventional (ˌʌnkənˈvɛnʃənᵊl) *adj.* not conforming to accepted rules or standards. —ˌ**unconˌventionˈality** *n.* —ˌ**unconˈventionally** *adv.*

uncool (ʌnˈkuːl) *adj. Slang.* **1.** unsophisticated; unfashionable. **2.** excitable; tense; not cool.

uncoordinated (ˌʌnkəʊˈɔːdɪˌneɪtɪd) *adj.* **1.** lacking order, system, or organization. **2.** (of a person, action, etc.) lacking muscular or emotional coordination.

uncork (ʌnˈkɔːk) *vb.* (*tr.*) **1.** to draw the cork from (a bottle, etc.). **2.** to release or unleash (emotions, etc.).

uncountable (ʌnˈkaʊntəbᵊl) *adj.* **1.** too many to be counted; innumerable. **2.** *Linguistics.* denoting a noun that does not refer to an isolable object. See **mass noun.**

uncounted (ʌnˈkaʊntɪd) *adj.* **1.** unable to be counted; innumerable. **2.** not counted.

uncouple (ʌnˈkʌpᵊl) *vb.* **1.** to disconnect or unfasten or become disconnected or unfastened. **2.** (*tr.*) to set loose; release.

uncouth (ʌnˈkuːθ) *adj.* lacking in good manners, refinement, or grace. [Old English *uncūth*, from UN-[1] + *cūth* familiar; related to Old High German *kund* known, Old Norse *kunnr*] —**unˈcouthly** *adv.* —**unˈcouthness** *n.*

uncovenanted (ʌnˈkʌvɪnəntɪd) *adj. Law.* **1.** not guaranteed or promised by a covenant. **2.** not in accordance with or sanctioned by a covenant.

uncover (ʌnˈkʌvə) *vb.* **1.** (*tr.*) to remove the cover, cap, top, etc., from. **2.** (*tr.*) to reveal or disclose: *to uncover a plot.* **3.** to take off (one's head covering), esp. as a mark of respect.

uncovered (ʌnˈkʌvəd) *adj.* **1.** not covered; revealed or bare. **2.** not protected by insurance, security, etc. **3.** with hat removed as a mark of respect.

uncrowned (ʌnˈkraʊnd) *adj.* **1.** having the power of royalty without the title. **2.** not having yet assumed the crown. **3.** **uncrowned king** *or* **queen.** a man or woman of high status among a certain group.

UNCTAD *abbrev. for* United Nations Conference on Trade and Development.

unction (ˈʌŋkʃən) *n.* **1.** *Chiefly R.C. and Eastern Churches.* the act of anointing with oil in sacramental ceremonies, in the conferring of holy orders. **2.** excessive suavity or affected charm. **3.** an ointment or unguent. **4.** anything soothing or comforting. [C14: from Latin *unctiō* an anointing, from *ungere* to anoint; see UNGUENT] —ˈ**unctionless** *adj.*

unctuous (ˈʌŋktjʊəs) *adj.* **1.** slippery or greasy. **2.** affecting an oily charm. [C14: from Medieval Latin *unctuōsus*, from Latin *unctum* ointment, from *ungere* to anoint] —**unctuosity** (ˌʌŋktjʊˈɒsɪtɪ) *or* ˈ**unctuousness** *n.* —ˈ**unctuously** *adv.*

uncurl (ʌnˈkɜːl) *vb.* to move or cause to move out of a curled or rolled up position.

uncus (ˈʌŋkəs) *n., pl.* **unci** (ˈʌnsaɪ). *Zoology, anatomy.* a hooked part or process, as in the human cerebrum. [C19: from Latin: hook]

uncut (ʌnˈkʌt) *adj.* **1.** (of a book) not having the edges of its pages trimmed or slit. **2.** (of a gemstone) not cut and faceted. **3.** not abridged or shortened.

undamped (ʌnˈdæmpt) *adj.* **1.** (of an oscillating system) having unrestricted motion; not damped. **2.** not repressed, discouraged, or subdued; undiminished.

undaunted (ʌnˈdɔːntɪd) *adj.* not put off, discouraged, or beaten. —**unˈdauntedly** *adv.* —**unˈdauntedness** *n.*

undecagon (ʌnˈdɛkəˌgɒn) *n.* a polygon having eleven sides. [C18: from Latin *undecim* eleven (from *unus* one + *decem* ten) + -GON]

undeceive (ˌʌndɪˈsiːv) *vb.* (*tr.*) to reveal the truth to (someone previously misled or deceived); enlighten. —ˌ**undeˈceivable** *adj.* —ˌ**undeˈceiver** *n.*

undecided (ˌʌndɪˈsaɪdɪd) *adj.* **1.** not having made up one's mind. **2.** (of an issue, problem, etc.) not agreed or decided upon. —ˌ**undeˈcidedly** *adv.* —ˌ**undeˈcidedness** *n.*

undemonstrative (ˌʌndɪˈmɒnstrətɪv) *adj.* tending not to show the feelings; of a reserved nature. —ˌ**undeˈmonstratively** *adv.* —ˌ**undeˈmonstrativeness** *n.*

undeniable (ˌʌndɪˈnaɪəbᵊl) *adj.* **1.** unquestionably or obviously true. **2.** of unquestionable excellence: *a man of undeniable character.* **3.** unable to be resisted or denied. —ˌ**undeˈniableness** *n.* —ˌ**undeˈniably** *adv.*

under (ˈʌndə) *prep.* **1.** directly below; on, to, or beneath the underside or base of: *under one's feet.* **2.** less than: *under forty years.* **3.** lower in rank than: *under a corporal.* **4.** subject to the supervision, jurisdiction, control, or influence of. **5.** subject to (conditions); in (certain circumstances). **6.** within a classification of: *a book under theology.* **7.** known by: *under an assumed name.* **8.** planted with: *a field under corn.* **9.** powered by: *under sail.* **10.** *Astrology.* during the period that the sun is in (a sign of the zodiac): *born under Aries.* ~*adv.* **11.** below; to a position underneath something. **12.** **one degree under.** *Informal.* off colour; ill. [Old English; related to Old Saxon, Gothic *undar*, Old High German *untar*, Old Norse *undir*, Latin *infra*]

under- *prefix.* **1.** below or beneath: *underarm; underground.* **2.** of lesser importance or lower rank: *undersecretary.* **3.** to a lesser degree than is proper; insufficient or insufficiently: *undercharge; underemployed.* **4.** indicating secrecy or deception: *underhand.*

underachieve (ˌundərəˈtʃiːv) *vb.* (*intr.*) to fail to achieve a performance appropriate to one's age or talents. —ˌ**underaˈchiever** *n.* —ˌ**underaˈchievement** *n.*

underact (ˌʌndərˈækt) *vb. Theatre.* to play (a role) without adequate emphasis. Compare **overact.**

underage (ˌʌndərˈeɪdʒ) *adj.* below the required or standard age, esp. below the legal age for voting or drinking.

underarm (ˈʌndərˌɑːm) *adj.* **1.** (of a measurement) extending along the arm from wrist to armpit. **2.** *Cricket, tennis, etc.* of or denoting a style of throwing, bowling, or serving in which the hand is swung below shoulder level. **3.** below the arm. ~*adv.* **4.** in an underarm style.

underbelly (ˈʌndəˌbɛlɪ) *n., pl.* **-lies.** **1.** the part of an animal's belly nearest to the ground. **2.** a vulnerable or unprotected part, aspect, or region.

underbid (ˌʌndəˈbɪd) *vb.* **-bids, -bidding, -bid.** (*tr.*) **1.** to submit a bid lower than that of (others): *Irena underbid the other dealers.* **2.** to submit an excessively low bid for. **3.** *Bridge.* to make a bid that will win fewer tricks than is justified by the strength of the hand: *he underbid his hand.* —ˈ**underˌbidder** *n.*

underbody (ˈʌndəˌbɒdɪ) *n., pl.* **-bodies.** the underpart of a body, as of an animal or motor vehicle.

underbred (ˌʌndəˈbrɛd) *adj.* **1.** of impure stock; not thoroughbred. **2.** a less common word for **ill-bred.** —ˌ**underˈbreeding** *n.*

underbrush (ˈʌndəˌbrʌʃ) *or* **underbush** *n. Chiefly U.S. and Canadian.* undergrowth.

underbuy (ˌʌndəˈbaɪ) *vb.* **-buys, -buying, -bought.** **1.** to buy (stock in trade) in amounts lower than required. **2.** (*tr.*) to buy at a price below that paid by (others). **3.** (*tr.*) to pay a price less than the true value for.

undercapitalize *or* **undercapitalise** (ˌʌndəˈkæpɪtəˌlaɪz) *vb.* to provide or issue capital for (a commercial enterprise) in an amount insufficient for efficient operation.

undercarriage (ˈʌndəˌkærɪdʒ) *n.* **1.** Also called: **landing gear.** the assembly of wheels, shock absorbers, struts, etc., that supports an aircraft on the ground and enables it to take off and land. **2.** the framework that supports the body of a vehicle, carriage, etc.

undercart (ˈʌndəˌkɑːt) *n. Brit. informal.* another name for **undercarriage** (sense 1).

undercharge (ˌʌndəˈtʃɑːdʒ) *vb.* **1.** to charge too little (for). **2.** (*tr.*) to load (a gun, cannon, etc.,) with an inadequate charge. ~*n.* **3.** an insufficient charge.

underclass (ˈʌndəˌklɑːs) *n.* a class beneath the usual social scale consisting of the most disadvantaged people, such as the unemployed in inner cities.

underclay (ˈʌndəˌkleɪ) *n.* a grey or whitish clay rock containing fossilized plant roots and occurring beneath coal seams. When used as a refractory, it is known as fireclay.

unˈconseˌcrated *adj.*
ˌ**unconˈsenting** *adj.*
ˌ**unconˈsoled** *adj.*
ˌ**unconˈstrained** *adj.*
ˌ**unconˈstraint** *n.*
ˌ**unconˈstricted** *adj.*
unˈconsumˌmated *adj.*
ˌ**unconˈtamiˌnated** *adj.*
ˌ**unconˈtested** *adj.*
ˌ**uncontraˈdicted** *adj.*
ˌ**unconˈtrived** *adj.*
ˌ**unconˈtrolled** *adj.*
ˌ**uncontroˈversial** *adj.*
ˌ**unconˈversant** *adj.*
ˌ**unconˈverted** *adj.*
ˌ**unconˈvinced** *adj.*
ˌ**unconˈvincing** *adj.*
unˈcooked *adj.*
ˌ**uncoˈoperative** *adj.*
ˌ**uncorˈrectable** *adj.*
ˌ**uncorˈrected** *adj.*
ˌ**uncorˈroboˌrated** *adj.*
ˌ**uncorˈrupted** *adj.*
unˈcourteous *adj.*
unˈcourtly *adj.*
ˌ**uncreˈative** *adj.*
unˈcritical *adj.*
unˈcross *vb.*
unˈcrowded *adj.*
unˈcrown *vb.*
unˈcultiˌvated *adj.*
unˈcultured *adj.*
unˈcurbed *adj.*
unˈcured *adj.*
unˈcustomary *adj.*
unˈdamaged *adj.*
unˈdated *adj.*
ˌ**undeˈbatable** *adj.*
ˌ**undeˈcipherable** *adj.*
unˈdecked *adj.*
ˌ**undeˈclared** *adj.*
unˈdecoˌrated *adj.*
ˌ**undeˈfeated** *adj.*
ˌ**undeˈfended** *adj.*
ˌ**undeˈfiled** *adj.*
ˌ**undeˈfinable** *adj.*
ˌ**undeˈfined** *adj.*
ˌ**undeˈmanding** *adj.*
ˌ**undemoˈcratic** *adj.*
ˌ**undeˈmonstrable** *adj.*
ˌ**undeˈnied** *adj.*
ˌ**undeˈpendable** *adj.*
ˌ**underˈclad** *adj.*

underclothes ('ʌndə,kləʊðz) *pl. n.* a variant of **underwear.** Also called: **underclothing.**

undercoat ('ʌndə,kəʊt) *n.* **1.** a coat of paint or other substance applied before the top coat. **2.** a coat worn under an overcoat. **3.** *Zoology.* another name for **underfur. 4.** the U.S. name for **underseal.** ~*vb.* **5.** (*tr.*) to apply an undercoat to (a surface).

undercool (,ʌndə'ku:l) *vb.* a less common word for **supercool.**

undercover (,ʌndə'kʌvə) *adj.* done or acting in secret: *undercover operations.*

undercroft ('ʌndə,krɒft) *n.* an underground chamber, such as a church crypt, often with a vaulted ceiling. [C14: from *croft* a vault, cavern, from earlier *crofte,* ultimately from Latin *crypta* CRYPT]

undercurrent ('ʌndə,kʌrənt) *n.* **1.** a current that is not apparent at the surface or lies beneath another current. **2.** an opinion, emotion, etc., lying beneath apparent feeling or meaning. ~Also called: **underflow.**

undercut *vb.* (,ʌndə'kʌt, 'ʌndə,kʌt) **-cuts, -cutting, -cut. 1.** to charge less than (a competitor) in order to obtain trade. **2.** to cut away the under part of (something). **3.** *Golf, tennis, etc.* to hit (a ball) in such a way as to impart backspin. ~*n.* ('ʌndə,kʌt). **4.** the act or an instance of cutting underneath. **5.** a part that is cut away underneath. **6.** a tenderloin of beef, including the fillet. **7.** *Forestry, chiefly U.S. and Canadian.* a notch cut in a tree trunk, to ensure a clean break in felling. **8.** *Tennis, golf, etc.* a stroke that imparts backspin to the ball.

underdevelop (,ʌndədɪ'vɛləp) *vb.* (*tr.*) *Photog.* to process (a film, plate, or paper) in developer for less than the required time, or at too low a temperature, or in an exhausted solution. —,**underde'velopment** *n.*

underdeveloped (,ʌndədɪ'vɛləpt) *adj.* **1.** immature or undersized. **2.** relating to societies in which both the surplus capital and the social organization necessary to advance are lacking. **3.** *Photog.* (of a film, plate, or print) processed in developer for less than the required time, thus lacking in contrast.

underdog ('ʌndə,dɒg) *n.* **1.** the losing competitor in a fight or contest. **2.** a person in adversity or a position of inferiority.

underdone (,ʌndə'dʌn) *adj.* insufficiently or lightly cooked.

underdrain *n.* ('ʌndə,dreɪn). **1.** a drain buried below agricultural land. ~*vb.* (,ʌndə'dreɪn). **2.** to bury such drains below (agricultural land). —'**under,drainage** *n.*

underdressed (,ʌndə'drɛst) *adj.* wearing clothes that are not elaborate or formal enough for a particular occasion.

underemployed (,ʌndərɪm'plɔɪd) *adj.* not fully or adequately employed. —,**underem'ployment** *n.*

underestimate *vb.* (,ʌndər'ɛstɪ,meɪt). (*tr.*) **1.** to make too low an estimate of: *he underestimated the cost.* **2.** to think insufficiently highly of: *to underestimate a person.* ~*n.* (,ʌndər'ɛstɪmɪt). **3.** too low an estimate. —,**under,esti'mation** *n.*

underexpose (,ʌndərɪk'spəʊz) *vb.* (*tr.*) **1.** *Photog.* to expose (a film, plate, or paper) for too short a period or with insufficient light so as not to produce the required effect. **2.** (*often passive*) to fail to subject to appropriate or expected publicity.

underexposure (,ʌndərɪk'spəʊʒə) *n.* **1.** *Photog.* **a.** inadequate exposure to light. **b.** an underexposed negative, print, or transparency. **2.** insufficient attention or publicity.

underfeed *vb.* (,ʌndə'fi:d), **-feeds, -feeding, -fed.** (*tr.*) **1.** to give too little food to. **2.** to supply (a furnace, engine, etc.) with fuel from beneath. ~*n.* ('ʌndə,fi:d). **3.** an apparatus by which fuel, etc., is supplied from below.

underfelt ('ʌndə,fɛlt) *n.* thick felt laid between floorboards and carpet to increase insulation and resilience.

underfloor ('ʌndə,flɔ:) *adj.* situated beneath the floor: *underfloor heating.*

underflow ('ʌndə,fləʊ) *n.* **1.** another word for **undercurrent. 2.** *Computer technol.* a condition that occurs when arithmetic operations produce results too small to store in the available register.

underfoot (,ʌndə'fʊt) *adv.* **1.** underneath the feet; on the ground. **2.** in a position of subjugation or subservience. **3.** in the way.

underfur ('ʌndə,fɜ:) *n.* the layer of dense soft fur occurring beneath the outer coarser fur in certain mammals, such as the otter and seal. Also called: **undercoat.**

undergarment ('ʌndə,gɑ:mənt) *n.* any garment worn under the visible outer clothes, usually next to the skin.

undergird (,ʌndə'gɜ:d) *vb.* **-girds, -girding, -girded** *or* **-girt.** (*tr.*) to strengthen or reinforce by passing a rope, cable, or chain around the underside of (an object, load, etc.). [C16: from UNDER- + GIRD[1]]

underglaze ('ʌndə,gleɪz) *adj.* **1.** *Ceramics.* applied to pottery or porcelain before the application of glaze. ~*n.* **2.** a pigment, etc., applied in this way.

undergo (,ʌndə'gəʊ) *vb.* **-goes, -going, -went, -gone.** (*tr.*) to experience, endure, or sustain: *to undergo a change of feelings.* [Old English: earlier meanings were more closely linked with the senses of *under* and *go*] —'**under,goer** *n.*

undergraduate (,ʌndə'grædjʊɪt) *n.* a person studying in a university for a first degree. Sometimes shortened to **undergrad.** —,**under'graduateship** *n.*

underground *adj.* ('ʌndə,graʊnd), *adv.* (,ʌndə'graʊnd). **1.** occurring, situated, used, or going below ground level: *an underground tunnel; an underground explosion.* **2.** secret; hidden: *underground activities.* ~*n.* ('ʌndə,graʊnd). **3.** a space or region below ground level. **4. a.** a movement dedicated to overthrowing a government or occupation forces, as in the European countries occupied by the German army in World War II. **b.** (*as modifier*): *an underground group.* **5.** (often preceded by *the*) an electric passenger railway operated in underground tunnels. U.S. and Canadian equivalent: **subway. 6.** (usually preceded by *the*) **a.** any avant-garde, experimental, or subversive movement in popular art, films, music, etc. **b.** (*as modifier*): *the underground press; underground music.*

underground railroad *n.* (*often caps.*) (in the pre-Civil War U.S.) the system established by abolitionists to aid escaping slaves.

undergrown ('ʌndə,grəʊn, ,ʌndə'grəʊn) *adj.* **1.** not having the expected height. **2.** having undergrowth.

undergrowth ('ʌndə,grəʊθ) *n.* **1.** small trees, bushes, ferns, etc., growing beneath taller trees in a wood or forest. **2.** the condition of being undergrown. **3.** a growth of short fine hairs beneath longer ones; underfur.

underhand ('ʌndə,hænd) *adj. also* **underhanded. 1.** clandestine, deceptive, or secretive. **2.** *Sport.* another word for **underarm.** ~*adv.* **3.** in an underhand manner or style.

underhand chop *n. N.Z.* (in an axemen's competition) a chop where the axeman stands on the log, which is placed on the ground. Compare **standing chop.**

underhanded (,ʌndə'hændɪd) *adj.* another word for **underhand** or **short-handed.** —,**under'handedly** *adv.* —,**under'handedness** *n.*

underhung (,ʌndə'hʌŋ) *adj.* **1.** (of the lower jaw) projecting beyond the upper jaw; undershot. **2.** (of a sliding door, etc.) supported at its lower edge by a track or rail.

underlaid (,ʌndə'leɪd) *adj.* **1.** laid underneath. **2.** having an underlay or supporting layer underneath. ~*vb.* **3.** the past tense and past participle of **underlay.**

underlay *vb.* (,ʌndə'leɪ), **-lays, -laying, -laid.** (*tr.*) **1.** to place (something) under or beneath. **2.** to support by something laid beneath. **3.** to achieve the correct printing pressure all over (a forme block) or to bring (a block) up to type height by adding material, such as paper, to the appropriate areas beneath it. ~*n.* ('ʌndə,leɪ). **4.** a layer, lining, support, etc., laid underneath something else. **5.** *Printing.* material, such as paper, used to underlay a forme or block. **6.** felt, rubber, etc., laid beneath a carpet to increase insulation and resilience.

underlet (,ʌndə'lɛt) *vb.* **-lets, -letting, -let.** (*tr.*) **1.** to let for a price lower than expected or justified. **2.** a less common word for **sublet.** —'**under,letter** *n.*

underlie (,ʌndə'laɪ) *vb.* **-lies, -lying, -lay, -lain.** (*tr.*) **1.** to lie or be placed under or beneath. **2.** to be the foundation, cause, or basis of: *careful planning underlies all our decisions.* **3.** *Finance.* to take priority over (another claim, liability, mortgage, etc.): *a first mortgage underlies a second.* **4.** to be the root or stem from which (a word) is derived: *"happy" underlies "happiest".* —'**under,lier** *n.*

underline *vb.* (,ʌndə'laɪn). (*tr.*) **1.** to put a line under. **2.** to state forcibly; emphasize or reinforce. ~*n.* ('ʌndə,laɪn). **3.** a line underneath, esp. under written matter.

underlinen ('ʌndə,lɪnən) *n.* underclothes, esp. when made of linen.

underling ('ʌndəlɪŋ) *n.* a subordinate or lackey.

underlying (,ʌndə'laɪɪŋ) *adj.* **1.** concealed but detectable: *underlying guilt.* **2.** fundamental; basic. **3.** lying under. **4.** *Finance.* (of a claim, liability, etc.) taking precedence; prior.

undermentioned ('ʌndə,mɛnʃənd) *adj.* mentioned below or subsequently.

undermine (,ʌndə'maɪn) *vb.* (*tr.*) **1.** (of the sea, wind, etc.) to wear away the bottom or base of (land, cliffs, etc.). **2.** to weaken gradually or insidiously: *insults undermined her confidence.* **3.** to tunnel or dig beneath. —,**under'miner** *n.*

undermost ('ʌndə,məʊst) *adj.* **1.** being the furthest under; lowest. ~*adv.* **2.** in the lowest place.

underneath (,ʌndə'ni:θ) *prep., adv.* **1.** under; beneath. ~*adj.* **2.** lower. ~*n.* **3.** a lower part, surface, etc. [Old English *underneothan,* from UNDER + *neothan* below; related to Old Danish *underneden;* see BENEATH]

undernourish (,ʌndə'nʌrɪʃ) *vb.* (*tr.*) to deprive of or fail to provide with nutrients essential for health and growth. —,**under'nourishment** *n.*

underpainting ('ʌndə,peɪntɪŋ) *n.* the first layer in a painting, indicating the design and main areas of light and shade.

underpants ('ʌndə,pænts) *pl. n.* a man's undergarment covering the body from the waist or hips to the top of the thighs or knees. Often shortened to **pants.**

'**under,clerk** *n.*
,**under'clothed** *adj.*
,**under'cook** *vb.*
,**under'do** *vb.,* -'**does,** -'**doing,** -'**did,** -'**done.**
,**under'eat** *vb.,* -'**eats,** -'**eating,** -'**ate,** -'**eaten.**
,**under'edu,cated** *adj.*
,**under'funded** *adj.*
,**underin'sured** *adj.*
,**under'layer** *n.*
'**under,named** *adj.*
,**under'paid** *adj.*

underpass (ˈʌndəˌpɑːs) *n.* **1.** a section of a road that passes under another road, railway line, etc. **2.** another word for **subway** (sense 1).
underpay (ˌʌndəˈpeɪ) *vb.* **-pays, -paying, -paid.** to pay (someone) insufficiently. —ˌ**underˈpayment** *n.*
underpin (ˌʌndəˈpɪn) *vb.* **-pins, -pinning, -pinned.** (*tr.*) **1.** to support from beneath, esp. by a prop, while avoiding damaging or weakening the superstructure: *to underpin a wall.* **2.** to give corroboration, strength, or support to.
underpinning (ˈʌndəˌpɪnɪŋ) *n.* a structure of masonry, concrete, etc., placed beneath a wall to provide support.
underpinnings (ˈʌndəˌpɪnɪŋz) *pl. n.* any supporting structure or system.
underpitch vault (ˈʌndəˌpɪtʃ) *n. Architect.* a vault that is intersected by one or more vaults of lower pitch.
underplay (ˌʌndəˈpleɪ) *vb.* **1.** to play (a role) with restraint or subtlety. **2.** to achieve (an effect) by deliberate lack of emphasis. **3.** (*intr.*) *Cards.* to lead or follow suit with a lower card when holding a higher one.
underplot (ˈʌndəˌplɒt) *n.* **1.** a subsidiary plot in a literary or dramatic work. **2.** an undercover plot.
underprice (ˌʌndəˈpraɪs) *vb.* (*tr.*) to price (an article for sale) at too low a level or amount.
underprivileged (ˌʌndəˈprɪvɪlɪdʒd) *adj.* lacking the rights and advantages of other members of society; deprived.
underproduction (ˌʌndəprəˈdʌkʃən) *n. Commerce.* production below full capacity or below demand.
underproof (ˌʌndəˈpruːf) *adj.* (of a spirit) containing less than 57.1 per cent alcohol by volume.
underprop (ˌʌndəˈprɒp) *vb.* **-props, -propping, -propped.** (*tr.*) to prop up from beneath. —ˈ**underˌpropper** *n.*
underquote (ˌʌndəˈkwəʊt) *vb.* **1.** to offer for sale (securities, goods, or services) at a price lower than the market price. **2.** (*tr.*) to quote a price lower than that quoted by (another).
underrate (ˌʌndəˈreɪt) *vb.* (*tr.*) to underestimate.
undersaturated (ˌʌndəˈsætʃəˌreɪtɪd) *adj.* (of an igneous rock) having a low silica content.
underscore *vb.* (ˌʌndəˈskɔː). (*tr.*) **1.** to draw or score a line or mark under. **2.** to stress or reinforce. ~*n.* (ˈʌndəˌskɔː). **3.** a line drawn under written matter.
undersea (ˈʌndəˌsiː) *adj., adv. also* **underseas** (ˌʌndəˈsiːz). below the surface of the sea.
underseal (ˈʌndəˌsiːl) *Brit.* ~*n.* **1.** a coating of a tar or rubber-based material applied to the underside of a motor vehicle to retard corrosion. U.S. name: **undercoat.** ~*vb.* **2.** (*tr.*) to apply a coating of underseal to (a motor vehicle).
undersecretary (ˌʌndəˈsɛkrətrɪ) *n., pl.* **-taries. 1.** (in Britain) **a.** any of various senior civil servants in certain government departments. **b.** short for **undersecretary of state:** any of various high officials subordinate only to the minister in charge of a department. **2.** (in the U.S.) a high government official subordinate only to the secretary in charge of a department. —ˌ**underˈsecretaryˌship** *n.*
undersell (ˌʌndəˈsɛl) *vb.* **-sells, -selling, -sold. 1.** to sell for less than the usual or expected price. **2.** (*tr.*) to sell at a price lower than that of (another seller). **3.** (*tr.*) to advertise (merchandise) with moderation or restraint. —ˌ**underˈseller** *n.*
underset (ˈʌndəˌsɛt) *n.* **1.** an ocean undercurrent. **2.** an underlying vein of ore. ~*vb.* **-sets, -setting, -set. 3.** (*tr.*) to support from underneath.
undersexed (ˌʌndəˈsɛkst) *adj.* having weaker sex urges or responses than is considered normal.
undersheriff (ˈʌndəˌʃɛrɪf) *n.* a deputy sheriff.
undershirt (ˈʌndəˌʃɜːt) *n. Chiefly U.S. and Canadian.* an undergarment worn under a blouse or shirt. Brit. name: **vest.**
undershoot (ˌʌndəˈʃuːt) *vb.* **-shoots, -shooting, -shot. 1.** (of a pilot) to cause (an aircraft) to land short of (a runway) or (of an aircraft) to land in this way. **2.** to shoot a projectile so that it falls short of (a target).
undershorts (ˈʌndəˌʃɔːts) *pl. n.* another word for **shorts** (sense 2).
undershot (ˈʌndəˌʃɒt) *adj.* **1.** (of the lower jaw) projecting beyond the upper jaw; underhung. **2.** (of a water wheel) driven by a flow of water that passes under the wheel rather than over it. ~Compare **overshot.**
undershrub (ˈʌndəˌʃrʌb) *n.* another name for **subshrub.**
underside (ˈʌndəˌsaɪd) *n.* the bottom or lower surface.
undersigned (ˈʌndəˌsaɪnd) *n.* **1. the.** the person or persons who have signed at the foot of a document, statement, etc. ~*adj.* **2.** having signed one's name at the foot of a document, statement, etc. **3.** (of a document) signed at the foot. **4.** signed at the foot of a document.
undersized (ˌʌndəˈsaɪzd) *adj.* of less than usual size.
underskirt (ˈʌndəˌskɜːt) *n.* any skirtlike garment worn under a skirt.
underslung (ˌʌndəˈslʌŋ) *adj.* **1.** suspended below a supporting member, esp. (of a motor vehicle chassis) suspended below the axles. **2.** having a low centre of gravity.
undersoil (ˈʌndəˌsɔɪl) *n.* another word for **subsoil** (sense 1a).
understand (ˌʌndəˈstænd) *vb.* **-stands, -standing, -stood. 1.** (*may take a clause as object*) to know and comprehend the nature or meaning of: *I understand you; I understand what you mean.* **2.** (*may take a clause as object*) to realize or grasp (something): *he understands your position.* **3.** (*tr.; may take a clause as object*) to assume, infer, or believe: *I understand you are thinking of marrying.* **4.** (*tr.*) to know how to translate or read: *can you understand Spanish?* **5.** (*tr.; may take a clause as object; often passive*) to accept as a condition or proviso: *it is understood that children must be kept quiet.* **6.** (*tr.*) to be sympathetic to or compatible with: *we understand each other.* [Old English *understandan;* related to Old Frisian *understonda,* Middle High German *understān* step under; see UNDER, STAND] —ˌ**underˈstandable** *adj.* —ˌ**underˈstandably** *adv.*
understanding (ˌʌndəˈstændɪŋ) *n.* **1.** the ability to learn, judge, make decisions, etc.; intelligence or sense. **2.** personal opinion or interpretation of a subject: *my understanding of your predicament.* **3.** a mutual agreement or compact, esp. an informal or private one. **4.** *Chiefly Brit.* an unofficial engagement to be married. **5.** *Philosophy, archaic.* the mind, esp. the faculty of reason. **6. on the understanding that.** with the condition that; providing. ~*adj.* **7.** sympathetic, tolerant, or wise towards people. **8.** possessing judgment and intelligence. —ˌ**underˈstandingly** *adv.*
understate (ˌʌndəˈsteɪt) *vb.* **1.** to state (something) in restrained terms, often to obtain an ironic effect. **2.** to state that (something, such as a number) is less than it is. —ˌ**underˈstatement** *n.*
understeer (ˈʌndəˌstɪə) *vb.* (*intr.*) (of a vehicle) to turn less sharply, for a particular movement of the steering wheel, than anticipated.
understood (ˌʌndəˈstʊd) *vb.* **1.** the past tense and past participle of **understand.** ~*adj.* **2.** implied or inferred. **3.** taken for granted; assumed.
understorey (ˈʌndəˌstɔːrɪ) *n.* a lower tier of shrubs and small trees under the main canopy of forest trees.
understrapper (ˈʌndəˌstræpə) *n.* a less common word for **underling.** [C18: from STRAP (in the archaic sense: to work hard)]
understudy (ˈʌndəˌstʌdɪ) *vb.* **-studies, -studying, -studied. 1.** (*tr.*) to study (a role or part) so as to be able to replace the usual actor or actress if necessary. **2.** to act as understudy to (an actor or actress). ~*n., pl.* **-studies. 3.** an actor or actress who studies a part so as to be able to replace the usual actor or actress if necessary. **4.** anyone who is trained to take the place of another in case of need.
undertake (ˌʌndəˈteɪk) *vb.* **-takes, -taking, -took, -taken. 1.** (*tr.*) to contract to or commit oneself to (something) or (to do something): *to undertake a job; to undertake to deliver the goods.* **2.** (*tr.*) to attempt to; agree to start. **3.** (*tr.*) to take (someone) in charge. **4.** (*intr.;* foll. by *for*) *Archaic.* to make oneself responsible (for). **5.** (*tr.*) to promise.
undertaker (ˈʌndəˌteɪkə) *n.* a person whose profession is the preparation of the dead for burial or cremation and the management of funerals; funeral director.
undertaking (ˈʌndəˌteɪkɪŋ) *n.* **1.** something undertaken; task, venture, or enterprise. **2.** an agreement to do something. **3.** the business of an undertaker.
under the table *adj.* **1.** (**under-the-table** *when prenominal*) done illicitly and secretly. **2.** *Slang.* drunk.
underthings (ˈʌndəˌθɪŋz) *pl. n.* girls' or women's underwear.
underthrust (ˈʌndəˌθrʌst) *n. Geology.* a reverse fault in which the rocks on the lower surface of a fault plane have moved under the relatively static rocks on the upper surface. Compare **overthrust.**
undertint (ˈʌndəˌtɪnt) *n.* a slight, subdued, or delicate tint.
undertone (ˈʌndəˌtəʊn) *n.* **1.** a quiet or hushed tone of voice. **2.** an underlying tone or suggestion in words or actions: *his offer has undertones of dishonesty.* **3.** a pale or subdued colour.
undertook (ˌʌndəˈtʊk) *vb.* the past tense of **undertake.**
undertow (ˈʌndəˌtəʊ) *n.* **1.** the seaward undercurrent following the breaking of a wave on the beach. **2.** any strong undercurrent flowing in a different direction from the surface current.
undertrick (ˈʌndəˌtrɪk) *n. Bridge.* a trick by which a declarer falls short of making his contract.
undertrump (ˌʌndəˈtrʌmp) *vb.* (*intr.*) *Cards.* to play a lower trump on a trick to which a higher trump has already been played.
undervalue (ˌʌndəˈvæljuː) *vb.* **-values, -valuing, -valued.** (*tr.*) to value at too low a level or price. —ˌ**underˌvaluˈation** *n.* —ˌ**underˈvaluer** *n.*
undervest (ˈʌndəˌvɛst) *n. Brit.* another name for **vest** (sense 1).
underwater (ˈʌndəˈwɔːtə) *adj.* **1.** being, occurring, or going under the surface of the water, esp. the sea: *underwater exploration.* **2.** *Nautical.* below the water line of a vessel. ~*adv.* **3.** beneath the surface of the water.
under way *adj.* (*postpositive*) **1.** in progress; in operation: *the show was under way.* **2.** *Nautical.* in motion.

ˈ**underˌpart** *n.*
ˌ**underˈpeopled** *adj.*
ˌ**underˈpopuˌlated** *adj.*
ˌ**underˈpowered** *adj.*
ˌ**underˈpraise** *vb.*
ˌ**underproˈduce** *vb.*
ˌ**underˈripened** *adj.*
ˈ**underˌservant** *n.*
ˌ**underˈspend** *vb.,* **-ˈspends, -ˈspending, -ˈspent.**
ˌ**underˈstaffed** *adj.*
ˌ**undersupˈply** *vb.,* **-ˈplies, -ˈplying, -ˈplied.**
ˈ**underˌsurface** *n.*
ˌ**underˈtrained** *adj.*

underwear (ˈʌndəˌwɛə) *n.* clothing worn under the outer garments, usually next to the skin. Also called: **underclothes.**

underweight (ˌʌndəˈweɪt) *adj.* weighing less than is average, expected, or healthy.

underwent (ˌʌndəˈwɛnt) *vb.* the past tense of **undergo.**

underwhelm (ˌʌndəˈwɛlm) *vb.* (*tr.*) to make no positive impact or impression on; disappoint. [C20: originally a humorous coinage based on *overwhelm*] —ˌ**underˈwhelming** *adj.*

underwing (ˈʌndəˌwɪŋ) *n.* **1.** the hind wing of an insect, esp. when covered by the forewing. **2.** See **red underwing, yellow underwing.**

underwood (ˈʌndəˌwʊd) *n.* a less common word for **undergrowth.**

underworld (ˈʌndəˌwɜːld) *n.* **1. a.** criminals and their associates considered collectively. **b.** (*as modifier*): *underworld connections.* **2.** *Greek and Roman myth.* the regions below the earth's surface regarded as the abode of the dead; Hades. **3.** the antipodes.

underwrite (ˈʌndəˌraɪt, ˌʌndəˈraɪt) *vb.* **-writes, -writing, -wrote, -written.** (*tr.*) **1.** *Finance.* to undertake to purchase at an agreed price any unsold portion of (a public issue of shares, etc.). **2.** to accept financial responsibility for (a commercial project or enterprise). **3.** *Insurance.* **a.** to sign and issue (an insurance policy) thus accepting liability if specified losses occur. **b.** to insure (a property or risk). **c.** to accept liability up to (a specified amount) in an insurance policy. **4.** to write (words, a signature, etc.) beneath (other written matter); subscribe. **5.** to support or concur with (a decision, statement, etc.) by or as if by signature.

underwriter (ˈʌndəˌraɪtə) *n.* **1.** a person or enterprise that underwrites public issues of shares, bonds, etc. **2. a.** a person or enterprise that underwrites insurance policies. **b.** an employee or agent of an insurance company who assesses risks and determines the premiums payable.

undescended (ˌʌndɪˈsɛndɪd) *adj.* (of the testes) remaining in the abdominal cavity rather than descending to lie in the scrotum.

undesigned (ˌʌndɪˈzaɪnd) *adj.* **1.** (of an action) unintentional. **2.** not yet designed.

undesigning (ˌʌndɪˈzaɪnɪŋ) *adj.* (of a person) frank; straightforward.

undesirable (ˌʌndɪˈzaɪərəbᵊl) *adj.* **1.** not desirable or pleasant; objectionable. ~*n.* **2.** a person or thing that is considered undesirable. —ˌ**undeˌsiraˈbility** *or* ˌ**undeˈsirableness** *n.* —ˌ**undeˈsirably** *adv.*

undetermined (ˌʌndɪˈtɜːmɪnd) *adj.* **1.** not yet resolved; undecided. **2.** not known or discovered.

undid (ʌnˈdɪd) *vb.* the past tense of **undo.**

undies (ˈʌndɪz) *pl. n. Informal.* women's underwear.

undine (ˈʌndiːn) *n.* any of various female water spirits. [C17: from New Latin *undina,* from Latin *unda* a wave]

undirected (ˌʌndɪˈrɛktɪd, -daɪ-) *adj.* **1.** lacking a clear purpose or objective. **2.** (of a letter, parcel, etc.) having no address.

undisputed world champion *n. Boxing.* a boxer who holds the World Boxing Association and the World Boxing Council world championship titles simultaneously.

undistinguished (ˌʌndɪˈstɪŋgwɪʃt) *adj.* **1.** not particularly good or bad. **2.** without distinction: *undistinguished features.* **3.** *Rare.* indistinguishable.

undistributed (ˌʌndɪsˈtrɪbjʊtɪd) *adj.* **1.** *Logic.* (of a term) referring only to some members of the class designated by the term, as *doctors* in *some doctors are overworked.* **2.** *Business.* (of a profit) not paid in dividends to the shareholders of a company but retained to help finance its trading.

undo (ʌnˈduː) *vb.* **-does, -doing, -did, -done.** (*mainly tr.*) **1.** (*also intr.*) to untie, unwrap, or open or become untied, unwrapped, etc. **2.** to reverse the effects of. **3.** to cause the downfall of. **4.** *Obsolete.* to explain or solve. —**unˈdoer** *n.*

undoing (ʌnˈduːɪŋ) *n.* **1.** ruin; downfall. **2.** the cause of downfall: *drink was his undoing.*

undone[1] (ʌnˈdʌn) *adj.* not done or completed; unfinished.

undone[2] (ʌnˈdʌn) *adj.* **1.** ruined; destroyed. **2.** unfastened; untied.

undoubted (ʌnˈdaʊtɪd) *adj.* beyond doubt; certain or indisputable. —**unˈdoubtedly** *adv.*

undreamed (ʌnˈdriːmd) *or* **undreamt** (ʌnˈdrɛmt) *adj.* (often foll. by *of*) not thought of, conceived, or imagined.

undress *vb.* (ʌnˈdrɛs). **1.** to take off clothes from (oneself or another). **2.** (*tr.*) to strip of ornamentation. **3.** (*tr.*) to remove the dressing from (a wound). ~*n.* (ʌnˈdrɛs). **4.** partial or complete nakedness. **5.** informal or normal working clothes or uniform. ~*adj.* (ˈʌndrɛs). **6.** characterized by or requiring informal or normal working dress or uniform.

undressed (ʌnˈdrɛst) *adj.* **1.** partially or completely naked. **2.** (of an animal hide) not fully processed. **3.** (of food, esp. salad) not prepared with sauce or dressing.

UNDRO (ˈʌnˌdrəʊ) *n. acronym for* United Nations Disaster Relief Organization.

undue (ʌnˈdjuː) *adj.* **1.** excessive or unwarranted. **2.** unjust, improper, or illegal. **3.** (of a debt, bond, etc.) not yet payable.

undulant (ˈʌndjʊlənt) *adj. Rare.* resembling waves; undulating. —ˈ**undulance** *n.*

undulant fever *n.* another name for **brucellosis.** [C19: so called because the fever symptoms are intermittent]

undulate *vb.* (ˈʌndjʊˌleɪt). **1.** to move or cause to move in waves or as if in waves. **2.** to have or provide with a wavy form or appearance. ~*adj.* (ˈʌndjʊlɪt, -ˌleɪt), *also* **undulated. 3.** having a wavy or rippled appearance, margin, or form: *an undulate leaf.* [C17: from Latin *undulātus,* from *unda* a wave] —ˈ**unduˌlator** *n.*

undulation (ˌʌndjʊˈleɪʃən) *n.* **1.** the act or an instance of undulating. **2.** any wave or wavelike form, line, etc.

undulatory (ˈʌndjʊlətərɪ, -trɪ) *adj.* **1.** caused by or characterized by waves or undulations. **2.** having a wavelike motion or form.

unduly (ʌnˈdjuːlɪ) *adv.* **1.** immoderately; excessively. **2.** in contradiction of moral or legal standards.

undying (ʌnˈdaɪɪŋ) *adj.* unending; eternal. —**unˈdyingly** *adv.*

unearned (ʌnˈɜːnd) *adj.* **1.** not deserved. **2.** not yet earned.

unearned income *n.* income from property, investment, etc., comprising rent, interest, and dividends.

unearned increment *n.* a rise in the market value of landed property resulting from general economic factors.

unearth (ʌnˈɜːθ) *vb.* (*tr.*) **1.** to dig up out of the earth. **2.** to reveal or discover, esp. by exhaustive searching.

unearthly (ʌnˈɜːθlɪ) *adj.* **1.** ghostly; eerie; weird: *unearthly screams.* **2.** heavenly; sublime: *unearthly music.* **3.** ridiculous or unreasonable (esp. in the phrase **unearthly hour**). —**unˈearthliness** *n.*

uneasy (ʌnˈiːzɪ) *adj.* **1.** (of a person) anxious; apprehensive. **2.** (of a condition) precarious; uncomfortable: *an uneasy truce.* **3.** (of a thought, etc.) disturbing; disquieting. —**unˈease** *n.* —**unˈeasily** *adv.* —**unˈeasiness** *n.*

uneconomic (ˌʌniːkəˈnɒmɪk, ˌʌnɛkə-) *adj.* not economic; not profitable.

uneconomical (ˌʌniːkəˈnɒmɪkᵊl, -ɛkə-) *adj.* not economical; wasteful.

UNEF (ˈjuːˌnɛf) *n. acronym for* United Nations Emergency Force.

unemployable (ˌʌnɪmˈplɔɪəbᵊl) *adj.* unable or unfit to keep a job. —ˌ**unemˌployaˈbility** *n.*

unemployed (ˌʌnɪmˈplɔɪd) *adj.* **1. a.** without remunerative employment; out of work. **b.** (*as collective n.; preceded by the*): *the unemployed.* **2.** not being used; idle.

unemployment (ˌʌnɪmˈplɔɪmənt) *n.* **1.** the condition of being unemployed. **2.** the number of unemployed workers, often as a percentage of the total labour force.

unemployment benefit *n.* **1.** (in the British National Insurance scheme) a regular payment to a person who is out of work and has usually paid a fixed number of insurance contributions. Informal term: **dole. 2.** (in New Zealand) a means-tested monetary benefit paid weekly by the Social Security Department to the unemployed.

unemployment compensation *n.* (in the U.S.) payment by a governmental agency to unemployed people.

unequal (ʌnˈiːkwəl) *adj.* **1.** not equal in quantity, size, rank, value, etc. **2.** (foll. by *to*) inadequate; insufficient. **3.** not evenly balanced. **4.** (of character, quality, etc.) irregular; varying;

ˌ**undeˈserved** *adj.*
ˌ**undeˈserving** *adj.*
ˌ**undeˈsired** *adj.*
ˌ**undeˈstroyed** *adj.*
ˌ**undeˈtachable** *adj.*
ˌ**undeˈtached** *adj.*
ˌ**undeˈtected** *adj.*
ˌ**undeˈterred** *adj.*
ˌ**undeˈveloped** *adj.*
unˈdiagˌnosed *adj.*
ˌ**undifferˈentiˌated** *adj.*
ˌ**undiˈgested** *adj.*
unˈdigniˌfied *adj.*
ˌ**undiˈluted** *adj.*
ˌ**undiˈminished** *adj.*
unˈdimmed *adj.*
ˌ**undiploˈmatic** *adj.*
ˌ**undisˈcerning** *adj.*
ˌ**undisˈcharged** *adj.*
unˈdisciplined *adj.*
ˌ**undisˈclosed** *adj.*
ˌ**undisˈcouraged** *adj.*
ˌ**undisˈcovered** *adj.*
ˌ**undisˈcrimiˌnating** *adj.*
ˌ**undisˈguised** *adj.*
ˌ**undisˈmayed** *adj.*
ˌ**undisˈposed** *adj.*
ˌ**undisˈputed** *adj.*
ˌ**undisˈsociˌated** *adj.*
ˌ**undisˈsolved** *adj.*
ˌ**undisˈtinguishable** *adj.*
ˌ**undisˈtressed** *adj.*
ˌ**undisˈturbed** *adj.*
ˌ**undiˈversiˌfied** *adj.*
ˌ**undiˈvided** *adj.*
unˈdocuˌmented *adj.*
ˌ**undoˈmestiˌcated** *adj.*
unˈdoubtable *adj.*
unˈdrained *adj.*
ˌ**undraˈmatic** *adj.*
unˈdraped *adj.*
unˈdraw *vb.*
unˈdrinkable *adj.*
unˈdutiful *adj.*
unˈdyed *adj.*
unˈeatable *adj.*
unˈeaten *adj.*
unˈedible *adj.*
unˈediˌfying *adj.*
unˈedited *adj.*
unˈeducable *adj.*
unˈeduˌcated *adj.*
ˌ**uneˈlectable** *adj.*
ˌ**uneˈmanciˌpated** *adj.*
ˌ**unemˈbarrassed** *adj.*
ˌ**unemˈbellished** *adj.*
ˌ**uneˈmotional** *adj.*
ˌ**unemˈphatic** *adj.*
unˈemptied *adj.*
ˌ**unenˈclosed** *or* ˌ**uninˈclosed** *adj.*
ˌ**unenˈcumbered** *or* ˌ**uninˈcumbered** *adj.*
unˈending *adj.*
ˌ**unenˈdorsed** *or* ˌ**uninˈdorsed** *adj.*
ˌ**unenˈdowed** *adj.*
ˌ**unenˈdurable** *adj.*
ˌ**unenˈforced** *adj.*
ˌ**unenˈgaged** *adj.*
ˌ**unenˈjoyable** *adj.*
ˌ**unenˈlightened** *adj.*

inconsistent. 5. (of a contest, etc.) having competitors of different ability. 6. *Obsolete.* unjust. —**un'equally** *adv.*

unequalled *or U.S.* **unequaled** (ʌn'iːkwəld) *adj.* not equalled; unparalleled or unrivalled; supreme.

unequivocal (ˌʌnɪ'kwɪvəkᵊl) *adj.* not ambiguous; plain. —ˌ**une'quivocally** *adv.* —ˌ**une'quivocalness** *n.*

unerring (ʌn'ɜːrɪŋ) *adj.* 1. not missing the mark or target. 2. consistently accurate; certain. —**un'erringly** *adv.* —**un'erringness** *n.*

UNESCO (juː'nɛskəʊ) *n. acronym for* United Nations Educational, Scientific, and Cultural Organization.

unessential (ˌʌnɪ'sɛnʃəl) *adj.* 1. a less common word for **inessential.** ~*n.* 2. something that is not essential. —ˌ**unes'sentially** *adv.*

uneven (ʌn'iːvən) *adj.* 1. (of a surface, etc.) not level or flat. 2. spasmodic or variable. 3. not parallel, straight, or horizontal. 4. not fairly matched: *an uneven race.* 5. *Archaic.* not equal. 6. *Obsolete.* unjust. —**un'evenly** *adv.* —**un'evenness** *n.*

uneventful (ˌʌnɪ'vɛntfʊl) *adj.* ordinary, routine, or quiet. —ˌ**une'ventfully** *adv.* —ˌ**une'ventfulness** *n.*

unexampled (ˌʌnɪg'zɑːmpᵊld) *adj.* without precedent or parallel.

unexceptionable (ˌʌnɪk'sɛpʃənəbᵊl) *adj.* beyond criticism or objection. —ˌ**unex'ceptionableness** *or* ˌ**unexˌceptiona'bility** *n.* —ˌ**unex'ceptionably** *adv.*

unexceptional (ˌʌnɪk'sɛpʃənᵊl) *adj.* 1. usual, ordinary, or normal. 2. subject to or allowing no exceptions. 3. *Not standard.* another word for **unexceptionable.** —ˌ**unex'ceptionally** *adv.*

unexcited (ˌʌnɪk'saɪtɪd) *adj.* 1. not aroused to pleasure, interest, agitation, etc. 2. (of an atom, molecule, etc.) remaining in its ground state.

unexpected (ˌʌnɪk'spɛktɪd) *adj.* surprising or unforeseen. —ˌ**unex'pectedly** *adv.* —ˌ**unex'pectedness** *n.*

unexperienced (ˌʌnɪk'spɪərɪənst) *adj.* 1. (of a situation, sensation, fact, etc.) not having been undergone or known by experience. 2. inexperienced.

unexpressed (ˌʌnɪk'sprɛst) *adj.* 1. not expressed or said. 2. understood without being expressed.

unfailing (ʌn'feɪlɪŋ) *adj.* 1. not failing; unflagging. 2. continuous or unceasing. 3. sure; certain. —**un'failingly** *adv.* —**un'failingness** *n.*

unfair (ʌn'fɛə) *adj.* 1. characterized by inequality or injustice. 2. dishonest or unethical. —**un'fairly** *adv.* —**un'fairness** *n.*

unfaithful (ʌn'feɪθfʊl) *adj.* 1. not true to a promise, vow, etc. 2. not true to a wife, husband, lover, etc., esp. in having sexual intercourse with someone else. 3. inaccurate; inexact; unreliable; untrustworthy: *unfaithful copy.* 4. *Obsolete.* not having religious faith; infidel. 5. *Obsolete.* not upright; dishonest. —**un'faithfully** *adv.* —**un'faithfulness** *n.*

unfamiliar (ˌʌnfə'mɪljə) *adj.* 1. not known or experienced; strange. 2. (*postpositive;* foll. by *with*) not familiar. —**unfamiliarity** (ˌʌnfəˌmɪlɪ'ærɪtɪ) *n.* —ˌ**unfa'miliarly** *adv.*

unfasten (ʌn'fɑːsᵊn) *vb.* to undo, untie, or open or become undone, untied, or opened.

unfathered (ʌn'fɑːðəd) *adj.* 1. having no known father. 2. of unknown or uncertain origin. 3. *Archaic.* fatherless.

unfathomable (ʌn'fæðəməbᵊl) *adj.* 1. incapable of being fathomed; immeasurable. 2. incomprehensible. —**un'fathomableness** *n.* —**un'fathomably** *adv.*

unfavourable *or U.S.* **unfavorable** (ʌn'feɪvərəbᵊl, -'feɪvrə-) *adj.* not favourable; adverse or inauspicious. —**un'favourableness** *or U.S.* **un'favorableness** *n.* —**un'favourably** *or U.S.* **un'favorably** *adv.*

unfazed (ʌn'feɪzd) *adj. Informal.* not disconcerted; unperturbed.

unfeeling (ʌn'fiːlɪŋ) *adj.* 1. without sympathy; callous. 2. without physical feeling or sensation. —**un'feelingly** *adv.* —**un'feelingness** *n.*

unfetter (ʌn'fɛtə) *vb.* (*tr.*) 1. to release from fetters, bonds, etc. 2. to release from restraint or inhibition.

unfinished (ʌn'fɪnɪʃt) *adj.* 1. incomplete or imperfect. 2. (of paint, polish, varnish, etc.) without an applied finish; rough. 3. (of fabric) unbleached or not processed. 4. (of fabric) with a short nap.

unfit (ʌn'fɪt) *adj.* 1. (*postpositive;* often foll. by *for*) unqualified, incapable, or incompetent: *unfit for military service.* 2. (*postpositive;* often foll. by *for*) unsuitable or inappropriate: *the ground was unfit for football.* 3. in poor physical condition. ~*vb.* **-fits, -fitting, -fitted.** 4. (*tr.*) *Rare.* to disqualify or render unfit. —**un'fitly** *adv.* —**un'fitness** *n.*

unfix (ʌn'fɪks) *vb.* (*tr.*) 1. to unfasten, detach, or loosen. 2. to unsettle or disturb.

unflappable (ʌn'flæpəbᵊl) *adj. Informal.* hard to upset; imperturbable; calm; composed. —**unˌflappa'bility** *or* **un'flappableness** *n.* —**un'flappably** *adv.*

unfledged (ʌn'flɛdʒd) *adj.* 1. (of a young bird) not having developed adult feathers. 2. immature and undeveloped.

unflinching (ʌn'flɪntʃɪŋ) *adj.* not shrinking from danger, difficulty, etc. —**un'flinchingly** *adv.*

unfold (ʌn'fəʊld) *vb.* 1. to open or spread out or be opened or spread out from a folded state. 2. to reveal or be revealed: *the truth unfolds.* 3. to develop or expand or be developed or expanded. —**un'folder** *n.*

unforgettable (ˌʌnfə'gɛtəbᵊl) *adj.* impossible to forget; highly memorable. —ˌ**unfor'gettably** *adv.*

unformed (ʌn'fɔːmd) *adj.* 1. shapeless. 2. immature.

unfortunate (ʌn'fɔːtʃənɪt) *adj.* 1. causing or attended by misfortune. 2. unlucky, unsuccessful, or unhappy: *an unfortunate character.* 3. regrettable or unsuitable: *an unfortunate speech.* ~*n.* 4. an unlucky person. —**un'fortunately** *adv.* —**un'fortunateness** *n.*

unfounded (ʌn'faʊndɪd) *adj.* 1. (of ideas, allegations, etc.) baseless; groundless. 2. not yet founded or established. —**un'foundedly** *adv.* —**un'foundedness** *n.*

unfranked income (ʌn'fræŋkt) *n.* any income from an investment that does not qualify as franked investment income.

unfreeze (ʌn'friːz) *vb.* **-freezes, -freezing, -froze, -frozen.** 1. to thaw or cause to thaw. 2. (*tr.*) to relax governmental restrictions on (wages, prices, credit, etc.) or on the manufacture or sale of (goods, etc.).

unfriended (ʌn'frɛndɪd) *adj. Now rare.* without a friend or friends; friendless.

unfriendly (ʌn'frɛndlɪ) *adj.* **-lier, -liest.** 1. not friendly; hostile. 2. unfavourable or disagreeable. ~*adv.* 3. *Rare.* in an unfriendly manner. —**un'friendliness** *n.*

unfrock (ʌn'frɒk) *vb.* (*tr.*) to deprive (a person in holy orders) of ecclesiastical status.

unfruitful (ʌn'fruːtfʊl) *adj.* 1. barren, unproductive, or unprofitable. 2. failing to produce or develop into fruit. —**un'fruitfully** *adv.* —**un'fruitfulness** *n.*

unfunded debt (ʌn'fʌndɪd) *n.* a short-term floating debt not represented by bonds.

unfurl (ʌn'fɜːl) *vb.* to unroll, unfold, or spread out or be unrolled, unfolded, or spread out from a furled state.

ungainly (ʌn'geɪnlɪ) *adj.* **-lier, -liest.** 1. lacking grace when moving. 2. difficult to move or use; unwieldy. 3. *Rare.* crude or coarse. ~*adv.* 4. *Rare.* clumsily. [C17: from UN-[1] + obsolete or dialect GAINLY graceful] —**un'gainliness** *n.*

ungodly (ʌn'gɒdlɪ) *adj.* **-lier, -liest.** 1. a. wicked; sinful. b. (*as collective n.;* preceded by *the*): *the ungodly.* 2. *Informal.* unseemly; outrageous (esp. in the phrase **an ungodly hour**). —**un'godliness** *n.*

ungotten (ʌn'gɒtᵊn) *adj. Archaic.* not obtained or won.

ungovernable (ʌn'gʌvənəbᵊl) *adj.* not able to be disciplined, restrained, etc.: *an ungovernable temper.* —**un'governableness** *n.* —**un'governably** *adv.*

ungrateful (ʌn'greɪtfʊl) *adj.* 1. not grateful or thankful. 2. unrewarding or unpleasant; thankless. 3. (of land) failing to

un'entered *adj.*
un'enterˌprising *adj.*
ˌ**unenter'taining** *adj.*
ˌ**unenˌthusi'astic** *adj.*
un'enviable *adj.*
ˌ**une'quipped** *adj.*
ˌ**unes'capable** *adj.*
ˌ**unes'corted** *adj.*
ˌ**unes'tablished** *adj.*
un'estiˌmated *adj.*
un'ethical *adj.*
ˌ**une'vaded** *adj.*
ˌ**unex'aggerˌated** *adj.*
ˌ**unex'ceeded** *adj.*
ˌ**unex'celled** *adj.*
ˌ**unex'cused** *adj.*
un'exeˌcuted *adj.*
un'exerˌcised *adj.*
ˌ**unex'perienced** *adj.*
un'expiˌated *adj.*
ˌ**unex'pired** *adj.*
ˌ**unex'plainable** *adj.*
ˌ**unex'plained** *adj.*
ˌ**unex'plicit** *adj.*
ˌ**unex'ploited** *adj.*
ˌ**unex'plored** *adj.*
ˌ**unex'posed** *adj.*
ˌ**unex'pressive** *adj.*
un'expurˌgated *adj.*
ˌ**unex'tended** *adj.*
ˌ**unex'tinguished** *adj.*
un'fading *adj.*
un'fashionable *adj.*
un'fathomed *adj.*
ˌ**unfa'tigued** *adj.*
un'favoured *adj.*
un'feasible *adj.*
un'featured *adj.*
un'fed *adj.*
un'federˌated *adj.*
un'feigned *adj.*
un'felt *adj.*
un'feminine *adj.*
ˌ**unfer'mented** *adj.*
un'fertiˌlized *or* **un'fertiˌlised** *adj.*
un'filled *adj.*
un'filtered *adj.*
un'fired *adj.*
un'fitting *adj.*
un'flagging *adj.*
un'flattering *adj.*
un'flavoured *adj.*
ˌ**unfor'bearing** *adj.*
ˌ**unfor'bidden** *adj.*
un'forceable *adj.*
un'forced *adj.*
ˌ**unfore'seeable** *adj.*
ˌ**unfore'seen** *adj.*
un'forested *adj.*
ˌ**unfore'told** *adj.*
ˌ**unfor'givable** *adj.*
ˌ**unfor'given** *adj.*
ˌ**unfor'giving** *adj.*
ˌ**unfor'gotten** *adj.*
un'formuˌlated *adj.*
ˌ**unfor'saken** *adj.*
ˌ**unforth'coming** *adj.*
un'fortiˌfied *adj.*
un'fought *adj.*
un'found *adj.*
un'framed *adj.*
ˌ**unfre'quented** *adj.*
ˌ**unful'filled** *adj.*
un'funny *adj.*
un'furnished *adj.*
un'furrowed *adj.*
un'gallant *adj.*
un'gathered *adj.*
un'generous *adj.*
un'gentlemanly *adj.*
un'glazed *adj.*
un'governed *adj.*
un'graceful *adj.*
un'gracious *adj.*
un'graded *adj.*
ˌ**ungram'matical** *adj.*

increase fertility in response to cultivation. —**un'gratefully** *adv.* —**un'gratefulness** *n.*
ungrudging (ʌn'grʌdʒɪŋ) *adj.* liberal; unstinted; willing: *ungrudging support.* —**un'grudgingly** *adv.*
ungual ('ʌŋgwəl) *or* **ungular** ('ʌŋgjʊlə) *adj.* **1.** of, relating to, or affecting the fingernails or toenails. **2.** of or relating to an unguis. [C19: from Latin *unguis* nail, claw]
unguarded (ʌn'gɑːdɪd) *adj.* **1.** unprotected; vulnerable. **2.** guileless; open; frank. **3.** incautious or careless. —**un'guardedly** *adv.* —**un'guardedness** *n.*
unguent ('ʌŋgwənt) *n.* a less common name for an **ointment.** [C15: from Latin *unguentum,* from *unguere* to anoint] —**'unguentary** *adj.*
unguiculate (ʌŋ'gwɪkjʊlɪt, -ˌleɪt) *adj.* **1.** (of mammals) having claws or nails. **2.** (of petals) having a clawlike base. ~*n.* **3.** an unguiculate mammal. [C19: from New Latin *unguiculātus,* from Latin *unguiculus,* diminutive of *unguis* nail, claw]
unguinous ('ʌŋgwɪnəs) *adj. Obsolete.* fatty; greasy; oily. [C17: from Latin *unguinōsus* oily, from *unguin-, unguen* a fatty substance, from *unguere* to anoint, besmear]
unguis ('ʌŋgwɪs) *n., pl.* **-gues** (-gwiːz). **1.** a nail, claw, or hoof, or the part of the digit giving rise to it. **2.** the clawlike base of certain petals. [C18: from Latin]
ungula ('ʌŋgjʊlə) *n., pl.* **-lae** (-ˌliː). **1.** *Maths.* a truncated cone, cylinder, etc. **2.** a rare word for **hoof.** [C18: from Latin: hoof, from *unguis* nail] —**'ungular** *adj.*
ungulate ('ʌŋgjʊlɪt, -ˌleɪt) *n.* any of a large group of mammals all of which have hooves: divided into odd-toed ungulates (see **perissodactyl**) and even-toed ungulates (see **artiodactyl**). [C19: from Late Latin *ungulātus* having hooves, from UNGULA]
unguligrade ('ʌŋgjʊlɪˌgreɪd) *adj.* (of horses, etc.) walking on hooves. [C19: from Latin *ungula* hoof + -GRADE]
unhair (ʌn'hɛə) *vb.* to remove the hair from (a hide).
unhallow (ʌn'hæləʊ) *vb. (tr.) Archaic.* to desecrate.
unhallowed (ʌn'hæləʊd) *adj.* **1.** not consecrated or holy: *unhallowed ground.* **2.** sinful or profane.
unhand (ʌn'hænd) *vb. (tr.) Archaic or literary.* to release from the grasp.
unhandy (ʌn'hændɪ) *adj.* **1.** not skilful with one's hands; clumsy; awkward. **2.** inconvenient.
unhappy (ʌn'hæpɪ) *adj.* **-pier, -piest.** **1.** not joyful; sad or depressed. **2.** unfortunate or wretched: *an unhappy fellow.* **3.** tactless or inappropriate: *an unhappy remark.* **4.** *Archaic.* unfavourable. —**un'happily** *adv.* —**un'happiness** *n.*
unharness (ʌn'hɑːnɪs) *vb. (tr.)* **1.** to remove the harness from (a horse, etc.). **2.** *Archaic.* to remove the armour from.
unhealthy (ʌn'hɛlθɪ) *adj.* **-healthier, -healthiest.** **1.** characterized by ill-health; sick; unwell. **2.** characteristic of, conducive to, or resulting from ill-health: *an unhealthy complexion; an unhealthy climate.* **3.** morbid or unwholesome. **4.** *Informal.* dangerous; risky. —**un'healthily** *adv.* —**un'healthiness** *n.*
unheard (ʌn'hɜːd) *adj.* **1.** not heard; not perceived by the ear. **2.** not listened to or granted a hearing: *his warning went unheard.* **3.** *Archaic.* unheard-of.
unheard-of *adj.* **1.** previously unknown: *an unheard-of actress.* **2.** without precedent: *an unheard-of treatment.* **3.** highly offensive: *unheard-of behaviour.*
unhelm (ʌn'hɛlm) *vb.* to remove the helmet of (oneself or another). [C15: from UN-[2] + HELM[2]]
unhesitating (ʌn'hɛzɪˌteɪtɪŋ) *adj.* **1.** steadfast; unwavering: *unhesitating loyalty.* **2.** without hesitation; prompt. —**un'hesiˌtatingly** *adv.*
unhinge (ʌn'hɪndʒ) *vb. (tr.)* **1.** to remove (a door, gate, etc.) from its hinges. **2.** to derange or unbalance (a person, his mind, etc.). **3.** to disrupt or unsettle (a process or state of affairs). **4.** (usually foll. by *from*) to detach or dislodge.
unholy (ʌn'həʊlɪ) *adj.* **-lier, -liest.** **1.** not holy or sacred. **2.** immoral or depraved. **3.** *Informal.* outrageous or unnatural: *an unholy alliance.* —**un'holiness** *n.*
unhook (ʌn'hʊk) *vb.* **1.** *(tr.)* to remove (something) from a hook. **2.** *(tr.)* to unfasten the hook of (a dress, etc.). **3.** *(intr.)* to become unfastened or be capable of unfastening: *the dress wouldn't unhook.*
unhoped-for (ˌʌn'həʊptfɔː) *adj.* (esp. of something pleasant) not anticipated; unexpected.
unhorse (ʌn'hɔːs) *vb. (tr.)* **1.** *(usually passive)* to knock or throw from a horse. **2.** to overthrow or dislodge, as from a powerful position. **3.** *Now rare.* to unharness horses from (a carriage, etc.).
unhouseled (ʌn'haʊzəld) *adj. Archaic.* not having received the Eucharist. [C16: from *un-* + obsolete *housel* to administer the sacrament, from Old English *hūsl* (n.), *hūslian* (vb.), of unknown origin]
unhurried (ʌn'hʌrɪd) *adj.* leisurely or deliberate: *an unhurried walk.* —**un'hurriedly** *adv.*
uni ('juːnɪ) *n. Informal.* short for **university.**
uni- *combining form.* consisting of, relating to, or having only one: *unilateral; unisexual.* [from Latin *ūnus* one]
Uniat ('juːnɪˌæt) *or* **Uniate** ('juːnɪɪt, -ˌeɪt) *adj.* **1.** designating any of the Eastern Churches that retain their own liturgy but submit to papal authority. ~*n.* **2.** a member of one of these Churches. [C19: from Russian *uniyat,* from Polish *unja* union, from Late Latin *ūniō;* see UNION] —**'UniˌatismUn** *n.*
uniaxial (ˌjuːnɪ'æksɪəl) *adj.* **1.** (esp. of plants) having an unbranched main axis. **2.** (of a crystal) having only one direction along which double refraction of light does not occur. —ˌ**uni'axially** *adv.*
unicameral (ˌjuːnɪ'kæmərəl) *adj.* of or characterized by a single legislative chamber. —ˌ**uni'cameralism** *n.* —ˌ**uni'cameralist** *n.* —ˌ**uni'camerally** *adv.*
UNICEF ('juːnɪˌsɛf) *n. acronym for* United Nations Children's Fund (formerly, United Nations International Children's Emergency Fund).
unicellular (ˌjuːnɪ'sɛljʊlə) *adj.* (of organisms, such as protozoans and certain algae) consisting of a single cell. —ˌ**uniˌcellu'larity** *n.*
unicolour *or U.S.* **unicolor** (ˌjuːnɪ'kʌlə) *adj.* of one colour; monochromatic.
unicorn ('juːnɪˌkɔːn) *n.* **1.** an imaginary creature usually depicted as a white horse with one long spiralled horn growing from its forehead. **2.** *Old Testament.* a two-horned animal, thought to be either the rhinoceros or the aurochs (Deuteronomy 33:17): mistranslation in the Authorized Version of the original Hebrew. [C13: from Old French *unicorne,* from Latin *ūnicornis* one-horned, from *ūnus* one + *cornu* a horn]
unicostate (ˌjuːnɪ'kɒsteɪt) *adj. Biology.* having only one rib or riblike part: *unicostate leaves.*
unicycle ('juːnɪˌsaɪkəl) *n.* a one-wheeled vehicle driven by pedals, esp. one used in a circus, etc. Also called: **monocycle.** [from UNI- + CYCLE, on the model of TRICYCLE] —**'uniˌcyclist** *n.*
unidirectional (ˌjuːnɪdɪ'rɛkʃənəl, -daɪ-) *adj.* having, moving in, or operating in only one direction.
UNIDO (juː'niːdəʊ) *n. acronym for* United Nations Industrial Development Organization.
unific (juː'nɪfɪk) *adj. Rare.* unifying; uniting.
unification (ˌjuːnɪfɪ'keɪʃən) *n.* **1.** an act, instance, or process of uniting. **2.** the state of being united.
Unification Church *n.* a religious sect founded in 1954 by Sun Myung Moon (born 1920), South Korean industrialist and religious leader. See also **Moonie.**
unified atomic mass unit *n.* another name for **atomic mass unit.**
unified field theory *n.* any theory capable of describing in one set of equations the properties of gravitational fields, electromagnetic fields, and strong and weak nuclear interactions. No satisfactory theory has yet been found.
unified screw thread *n.* a screw thread system introduced for defence equipment (1939–44), in which the thread form and pitch were a compromise between British Standard Whitworth and American Standard Sellers: adopted by the International Standards Organization.
unifilar (ˌjuːnɪ'faɪlə) *adj. Rare.* composed of, having, or using only one wire, thread, filament, etc. [from UNI- + Latin *fīlum* thread; see FILAMENT, FILAR]
unifoliate (ˌjuːnɪ'fəʊlɪɪt, -ˌeɪt) *adj.* having a single leaf or leaflike part.
unifoliolate (ˌjuːnɪ'fəʊlɪəˌleɪt) *adj.* (of a compound leaf) having only one leaflet.
uniform ('juːnɪˌfɔːm) *n.* **1.** a prescribed identifying set of clothes for the members of an organization, such as soldiers or schoolchildren. **2.** a single set of such clothes. **3.** a characteristic feature or fashion of some class or group. ~*adj.* **4.** unchanging in form, quality, quantity, etc.; regular: *a uniform surface.* **5.** identical; alike or like: *a line of uniform toys.* ~*vb. (tr.)* **6.** to fit out (a body of soldiers, etc.) with uniforms. **7.** to make uniform. [C16: from Latin *ūniformis,* from *ūnus* one + *forma* shape] —**'uniˌformly** *adv.* —**'uniˌformness** *n.*
Uniform ('juːnɪˌfɔːm) *n. Communications.* a code word for the letter *u.*
uniformitarian (ˌjuːnɪˌfɔːmɪ'tɛərɪən) *adj.* **1.** of or relating to uniformitarianism. **2.** of, characterized by, or conforming to uniformity. ~*n.* **3.** a supporter of a theory of uniformity or of uniformitarianism.

un'gratiˌfying *adj.*
un'grounded *adj.*
un'guided *adj.*
un'hackneyed *adj.*
un'hailed *adj.*
un'hampered *adj.*
un'handiˌcapped *adj.*
un'hardened *adj.*
un'harmed *adj.*
un'harmful *adj.*
ˌ**unhar'monious** *adj.*
ˌ**unhar'moniously** *adv.*
un'harrowed *adj.*
un'harvested *adj.*
un'hatched *adj.*
un'healed *adj.*
un'heated *adj.*
un'heeded *adj.*
un'heededly *adv.*
un'heedful *adj.*
un'heeding *adj.*
un'helped *adj.*
un'helpful *adj.*
un'heralded *adj.*
ˌ**unhe'roic** *adj.*
un'hewn *adj.*
un'hindered *adj.*
un'hitch *vb.*
un'honoured *adj.*
un'housed *adj.*
un'human *adj.*
un'hurt *adj.*
ˌ**unhy'gienic** *adj.*
un'hyphenˌated *adj.*
ˌ**uni'deal** *adj.*
ˌ**uni'dentiˌfiable** *adj.*
ˌ**uni'dentiˌfied** *adj.*
ˌ**unidio'matic** *adj.*
ˌ**unidio'matically** *adv.*

uniformitarianism (ˌjuːnɪˌfɔːmɪˈtɛərɪəˌnɪzəm) *n.* the concept that the earth's surface was shaped in the past by gradual processes, such as erosion, and by small sudden changes, such as earthquakes, of the type acting today rather than by the sudden divine acts, such as Noah's flood, demanded by the doctrine of catastrophism.
uniformity (ˌjuːnɪˈfɔːmɪtɪ) *n., pl.* **-ties.** **1.** a state or condition in which everything is regular, homogeneous, or unvarying. **2.** lack of diversity or variation, esp. to the point of boredom or monotony; sameness.
unify (ˈjuːnɪˌfaɪ) *vb.* **-fies, -fying, -fied.** to make or become one; unite. [C16: from Medieval Latin *ūnificāre*, from Latin *ūnus* one + *facere* to make] —ˈ**uniˌfiable** *adj.* —ˈ**uniˌfier** *n.*
unijugate (ˌjuːnɪˈdʒuːgɪt, -ˌgeɪt) *adj.* (of a compound leaf) having only one pair of leaflets.
unilateral (ˌjuːnɪˈlætərəl) *adj.* **1.** of, having, affecting, or occurring on only one side. **2.** involving or performed by only one party of several: *unilateral disarmament.* **3.** *Law.* (of contracts, obligations, etc.) made by, affecting, or binding one party only and not involving the other party in reciprocal obligations. **4.** *Botany.* having or designating parts situated or turned to one side of an axis. **5.** *Sociol.* relating to or tracing the line of descent through ancestors of one sex only. Compare **bilateral** (sense 5). **6.** *Phonetics.* denoting an (l) sound produced on one side of the tongue only. —ˌ**uniˈlateralism** *or* ˌ**uniˌlaterˈality** *n.* —ˌ**uniˈlaterally** *adv.*
unilateral neglect *n.* a symptom of brain damage in which a person is unaware of one side of his body and of anything in the external world on the same side.
unilingual (ˌjuːnɪˈlɪŋgwəl) *adj.* of or having only one language.
uniliteral (ˌjuːnɪˈlɪtərəl) *adj.* consisting of one letter.
unilocular (ˌjuːnɪˈlɒkjʊlə) *adj.* (esp. of a plant ovary or anther) having or consisting of a single chamber or cavity.
unimpeachable (ˌʌnɪmˈpiːtʃəbᵊl) *adj.* unquestionable as to honesty, truth, etc. —ˌ**unimˌpeachaˈbility** *or* ˌ**unimˈpeachableness** *n.* —ˌ**unimˈpeachably** *adv.*
unimproved (ˌʌnɪmˈpruːvd) *adj.* **1.** not improved or made better. **2.** (of land) not cleared, drained, cultivated, etc. **3.** neglected; unused: *unimproved resources.*
unimproved value *n. N.Z.* the valuation of land for rating purposes, disregarding the value of buildings or other development.
unincorporated (ˌʌnɪnˈkɔːpəˌreɪtɪd) *adj.* **1.** *Law.* lacking corporate status. **2.** not unified or included.
uninspired (ˌʌnɪnˈspaɪəd) *adj.* dull or ordinary; unimaginative: *an uninspired painting.*
unintelligent (ˌʌnɪnˈtɛlɪdʒənt) *adj.* **1.** lacking intelligence; stupid; foolish. **2.** not endowed with a mind or intelligence. —ˌ**uninˈtelligence** *n.* —ˌ**uninˈtelligently** *adv.*
uninterested (ʌnˈɪntrɪstɪd, -tərɪs-) *adj.* indifferent; unconcerned. —**unˈinterestedly** *adv.* —**unˈinterestedness** *n.*
▷**Usage.** See at **disinterested.**
union (ˈjuːnjən) *n.* **1.** the condition of being united, the act of uniting, or a conjunction formed by such an act. **2.** an association, alliance, or confederation of individuals or groups for a common purpose, esp. political. **3.** agreement or harmony. **4.** short for **trade union.** **5.** the act or state of marriage or sexual intercourse. **6.** a device on a flag representing union, such as another flag depicted in the top left corner. **7.** a device for coupling or linking parts, such as pipes. **8.** (*often cap.*) **a.** an association of students at a university or college formed to look after the students' interests, provide facilities for recreation, etc. **b.** the building or buildings housing the facilities of such an organization. **9.** Also called: **join.** *Maths.* a set containing all members of two given sets. Symbol: ∪, as in $A \cup B$. **10.** (in 19th-century England) **a.** a number of parishes united for the administration of poor relief. **b.** a workhouse supported by such a combination. **11.** *Textiles.* a piece of cloth or fabric consisting of two different kinds of yarn. **12.** (*modifier*) of or related to a union, esp. a trade union. [C15: from Church Latin *ūniō* oneness, from Latin *ūnus* one]
Union (ˈjuːnjən) *n.* **the. 1.** *Brit.* **a.** the union of the English and Scottish crowns (1603–1707). **b.** the union of England and Scotland from 1707. **c.** the political union of Great Britain and Ireland (1801–1920). **d.** the union of Great Britain and Northern Ireland from 1920. **2.** *U.S.* **a.** the northern states of the U.S. during the Civil War (1861–65). **b.** (*as modifier*): *Union supporters.*
union card *n.* a membership card for a trade union.
union catalogue *n.* a catalogue listing every publication held at cooperating libraries.
unionism (ˈjuːnjəˌnɪzəm) *n.* **1.** the principles of trade unions. **2.** adherence to the principles of trade unions. **3.** the principle or theory of any union.
Unionism (ˈjuːnjəˌnɪzəm) *n.* (*sometimes not cap.*) the principles or adherence to the principles of Unionists.
unionist (ˈjuːnjənɪst) *n.* **1.** a supporter or advocate of unionism or union. **2.** a member of a trade union. ~*adj.* **3.** *Chiefly Brit.* of or relating to union or unionism, esp. trade unionism. —ˌ**unionˈistic** *adj.*
Unionist (ˈjuːnjənɪst) *n.* **1.** (*sometimes not cap.*) **a.** (before 1920) a supporter of the union of all Ireland and Great Britain. **b.** (since 1920) a supporter of union between Britain and Northern Ireland, esp. a member of a political party in Northern Ireland that favours union. ~*adj.* **2.** a supporter of the U.S. federal Union, esp. during the Civil War (1861–65). **3.** of, resembling, or relating to Unionists.
unionize *or* **unionise** (ˈjuːnjəˌnaɪz) *vb.* **1.** to organize (workers) into a trade union. **2.** to join or cause to join a trade union. **3.** (*tr.*) to subject to the rules or codes of a trade union. —ˌ**unioniˈzation** *or* ˌ**unioniˈsation** *n.*
Union Jack *n.* **1.** Also called: **Union flag.** the national flag of the United Kingdom, being a composite design composed of St George's Cross (England), Saint Andrew's Cross (Scotland), and Saint Patrick's Cross (Ireland). **2.** (*often not caps.*) a national flag flown at the jackstaff of a vessel.
union pipes *pl. n.* another name for **uillean pipes.**
union shop *n.* an establishment whose employment policy is governed by a contract between employer and a trade union permitting the employment of nonunion labour only on the condition that such labour joins the union within a specified time period. Compare **open shop, closed shop.**
union territory *n.* one of the 9 administrative territories that, with 21 states, make up the Indian Republic.
uniparous (juːˈnɪpərəs) *adj.* **1.** (of certain animals) producing a single offspring at each birth. **2.** (of a woman) having borne only one child. **3.** *Botany.* (of a cyme) giving rise to only one branch from each flowering stem.
unipersonal (ˌjuːnɪˈpɜːsənᵊl) *adj.* **1.** existing in the form of only one person or being. Compare **tripersonal.** **2.** (of a verb) existing or used in only one person; for example, *rain* is used only in the third person. —ˌ**uniˌpersonˈality** *n.*
uniplanar (ˌjuːnɪˈpleɪnə) *adj.* situated in one plane.
unipod (ˈjuːnɪˌpɒd) *n.* a one-legged support, as for a camera.
unipolar (ˌjuːnɪˈpəʊlə) *adj.* **1.** of, concerned with, or having a single magnetic or electric pole. **2.** (of a nerve cell) having a single process. **3.** (of a transistor) utilizing charge carriers of one polarity only, as in a field-effect transistor. ~Compare **bipolar.** —**unipolarity** (ˌjuːnɪpəʊˈlærɪtɪ) *n.*
unique (juːˈniːk) *adj.* **1.** being the only one of a particular type; single; sole. **2.** without equal or like; unparalleled. **3.** *Informal.* very remarkable or unusual. **4.** *Maths.* **a.** leading to only one result: *the sum of two integers is unique.* **b.** having precisely one value: *the unique positive square root of 4 is 2.* [C17: via French from Latin *ūnicus* unparalleled, from *ūnus* one] —**uˈniquely** *adv.* —**uˈniqueness** *n.*
▷**Usage.** Certain words in English, such as *unique, perfect,* and *simultaneous,* describe absolute states, that is to say, states that cannot be qualifed; something is either *unique* or it is *not unique,* but it cannot be, for example, *rather unique.* Careful users of English therefore avoid the use of comparatives or intensifiers where absolute states are concerned: *that is very exceptional* (not *very unique*); *this one comes nearer to perfection* (not *is more perfect*).
uniramous (ˌjuːnɪˈreɪməs) *adj.* (esp. of the appendages of crustaceans) consisting of a single branch; undivided. Also: **uniramose** (ˌjuːnɪˈreɪməʊs, -ræˈməʊs)
uniseptate (ˌjuːnɪˈsɛpteɪt) *adj. Biology.* having only one partition or septum: *a uniseptate fruit.*
uniserial (ˌjuːnɪˈsɪərɪəl) *adj.* in or relating to a single series.
uniseriate (ˌjuːnɪˈsɪərɪˌeɪt) *adj. Botany.* (of parts, cells, etc.) arranged in a single row, layer, or series.

ˌ**unilˈlumiˌnated** *adj.*
ˌ**unilˈlumiˌnating** *adj.*
unˈillusˌtrated *adj.*
ˌ**unimˈaginable** *adj.*
ˌ**unimˈaginably** *adv.*
ˌ**unimˈaginative** *adj.*
ˌ**unimˈaginatively** *adv.*
ˌ**unimˈagined** *adj.*
ˌ**unimˈbued** *adj.*
ˌ**unimˈpaired** *adj.*
ˌ**unimˈpassioned** *adj.*
ˌ**unimˈpeded** *adj.*
ˌ**unimˈportant** *adj.*
ˌ**unimˈposing** *adj.*
ˌ**unimˈpressed** *adj.*
ˌ**unimˈpressionable** *adj.*
ˌ**unimˈpressive** *adj.*
ˌ**unimˈpressively** *adv.*
ˌ**uninˈclosed** *adj.*
unˈincuˌbated *adj.*
ˌ**uninˈcumbered** *adj.*
ˌ**uninˈdemniˌfied** *adj.*
ˌ**uninˈdorsed** *adj.*
ˌ**uninˈfected** *adj.*
ˌ**uninˈflammable** *adj.*
ˌ**uninˈflected** *adj.*
unˈinfluenced *adj.*
ˌ**uninfluˈential** *adj.*
ˌ**uninˈformative** *adj.*
ˌ**uninˈformed** *adj.*
ˌ**uninˈhabitable** *adj.*
ˌ**uninˈhabited** *adj.*
ˌ**uninˈhibited** *adj.*
unˈinitiˌated *adj.*
unˈinjured *adj.*
ˌ**uninˈquisitive** *adj.*
ˌ**uninˈspiring** *adj.*
ˌ**uninˈspiringly** *adv.*
ˌ**uninˈstructed** *adj.*
ˌ**uninˈstructive** *adj.*
ˌ**uninˈsurable** *adj.*
ˌ**uninˈsured** *adj.*
ˌ**unintelˈlectual** *adj.*
ˌ**uninˈtelligible** *adj.*
ˌ**uninˈtended** *adj.*
ˌ**uninˈtendedly** *adv.*
ˌ**uninˈtentional** *adj.*
ˌ**uninˈtentionally** *adv.*
unˈinteresting *adj.*
ˌ**uninterˈrupted** *adj.*
ˌ**uninˈventive** *adj.*
ˌ**uninˈvested** *adj.*
ˌ**uninˈvestiˌgated** *adj.*
ˌ**uninˈvited** *adj.*
ˌ**uninˈviting** *adj.*
ˌ**uninˈvitingly** *adv.*
ˌ**uninˈvoked** *adj.*
ˌ**uninˈvolved** *adj.*
unˈironed *adj.*

unisex (ˈjuːnɪˌsɛks) *adj.* of or relating to clothing, a hairstyle, etc., that can be worn by either sex. [C20: from UNI- + SEX]

unisexual (ˌjuːnɪˈsɛksjʊəl) *adj.* **1.** of or relating to one sex only. **2.** (of some organisms) having either male or female reproductive organs but not both. —ˌ**uniˌsexuˈality** *n.* —ˌ**uniˈsexually** *adv.*

unison (ˈjuːnɪsᵊn, -zᵊn) *n.* **1.** *Music.* **a.** the interval between two notes of identical pitch. **b.** (*modifier*) played or sung at the same pitch: *unison singing.* **2.** complete agreement; harmony (esp. in the phrase **in unison**). [C16: from Late Latin *ūnisonus,* from UNI- + *sonus* sound] —**uˈnisonous, uˈnisonal,** *or* **uˈnisonant** *adj.*

unit (ˈjuːnɪt) *n.* **1.** a single undivided entity or whole. **2.** any group or individual, esp. when regarded as a basic element of a larger whole. **3.** a mechanical part or integrated assembly of parts that performs a subsidiary function: *a filter unit.* **4.** a complete system, apparatus, or establishment that performs a specific function: *a production unit.* **5.** a subdivision of a larger military formation. **6.** Also called: **unit of measurement.** a standard amount of a physical quantity, such as length, mass, energy, etc., specified multiples of which are used to express magnitudes of that physical quantity: *the second is a unit of time.* **7.** the amount of a drug, vaccine, etc., needed to produce a particular effect. **8.** a standard measure used in calculating alcohol intake and its effect. **9.** *Maths.* **a.** (*usually pl.*) the first position in a place-value counting system, representing a single-digit number: *in the decimal system the number 27 has 7 units and 2 tens.* **b.** (*modifier*) having a value defined as one for the system: *unit vector.* **10.** Also called: **unit set.** *Maths, logic.* a set having a single member. **11.** short for **home unit. 12.** short for **stock unit. 13.** *N.Z.* a self-propelled railcar. [C16: back formation from UNITY, perhaps on the model of *digit*]

Unit. *abbrev. for* Unitarian.

UNITA (juːˈniːtə) *n. acronym for* União Nacional para a Independencia Total de Angola. [Portuguese: National Union for the Total Independence of Angola]

unitarian (ˌjuːnɪˈtɛərɪən) *n.* **1.** a supporter of unity or centralization. ~*adj.* **2.** of or relating to unity or centralization. **3.** another word for **unitary.**

Unitarian (ˌjuːnɪˈtɛərɪən) *n.* **1.** *Theol.* a person who believes that God is one being and rejects the doctrine of the Trinity. **2.** *Ecclesiast.* an upholder of Unitarianism, esp. a member of the Church (**Unitarian Church**) that embodies this system of belief. ~*adj.* **3.** of or relating to Unitarians or Unitarianism.

unitarianism (ˌjuːnɪˈtɛərɪəˌnɪzəm) *n.* any unitary system, esp. of government.

Unitarianism (ˌjuːnɪˈtɛərɪəˌnɪzəm) *n.* a system of Christian belief that maintains the unipersonality of God, rejects the Trinity and the divinity of Christ, and takes reason, conscience, and character as the criteria of belief and practice.

unitary (ˈjuːnɪtərɪ, -trɪ) *adj.* **1.** of a unit or units. **2.** based on or characterized by unity. **3.** individual; whole. **4.** of or relating to a system of government in which all governing authority is held by the central government. Compare **federal.**

unitary matrix *n. Maths.* a square matrix that is the inverse of its Hermitian conjugate.

unit cell *n. Crystallog.* the smallest group of atoms, ions, or molecules that is characteristic of a particular crystal lattice.

unit character *n. Genetics.* a character inherited as a single unit and dependent on a single gene.

unit cost *n.* the actual cost of producing one article.

unite[1] (juːˈnaɪt) *vb.* **1.** to make or become an integrated whole or a unity; combine. **2.** to join, unify or be unified in purpose, action, beliefs, etc. **3.** to enter or cause to enter into an association or alliance. **4.** to adhere or cause to adhere; fuse. **5.** (*tr.*) to possess or display (qualities) in combination or at the same time: *he united charm with severity.* **6.** *Archaic.* to join or become joined in marriage. [C15: from Late Latin *ūnīre,* from *ūnus* one] —**uˈniter** *n.*

unite[2] (ˈjuːnaɪt, juːˈnaɪt) *n.* an English gold coin minted in the Stuart period, originally worth 20 shillings. [C17: from obsolete *unite* joined, alluding to the union of England and Scotland (1603)]

united (juːˈnaɪtɪd) *adj.* **1.** produced by two or more persons or things in combination or from their union or amalgamation: *a united effort.* **2.** in agreement. **3.** in association or alliance. —**uˈnitedly** *adv.* —**uˈnitedness** *n.*

United Church of Christ *n.* a U.S. Protestant denomination formed in 1957 from the Evangelical and Reformed Church and the Congregational Christian Church.

United Empire Loyalist *n. Canadian history.* any of the American colonists who settled in Canada during or after the War of American Independence (1775–81) because of loyalty to the British Crown.

United Nations *n.* (*functioning as sing. or pl.*) an international organization of independent states, with its headquarters in New York City, that was formed in 1945 to promote peace and international cooperation and security. Abbrev.: **UN.**

United Reformed Church *n.* (in England and Wales) a Protestant denomination formed from the union of the Presbyterian and Congregational churches in 1972.

unit factor *n. Genetics.* the gene responsible for the inheritance of a unit character.

unitive (ˈjuːnɪtɪv) *adj.* **1.** tending to unite or capable of uniting. **2.** characterized by unity. —**ˈunitively** *adv.*

unitize *or* **unitise** (ˈjuːnɪˌtaɪz) *vb.* (*tr.*) *Finance.* to convert (an investment trust) into a unit trust. —ˌ**unitiˈzation** *or* ˌ**unitiˈsation** *n.*

unit-linked policy *n.* a life-assurance policy the investment benefits of which are directly in proportion to the number of units in a unit trust purchased on the policyholder's behalf. Compare **traditional policy.**

unit magnetic pole *n.* the strength of a magnetic pole that will repel a similar pole 1 centimetre distant from it, in a vacuum, with a force of 1 dyne.

unit of account *n.* **1.** *Economics.* the function of money that enables the user to keep accounts, value transactions, etc. **2.** a monetary denomination used for accounting purposes, etc., but not necessarily corresponding to any real currency: *the ECU is the unit of account of the European Monetary Fund.* Also called (esp. U.S. and Canada): **money of account. 3.** the unit of currency of a country.

unit price *n.* a price for foodstuffs, etc., stated or shown as the cost per unit, as per pound, per kilogram, per dozen, etc.

unit pricing *n.* a system of pricing foodstuffs, etc., in which the cost of a single unit is shown to enable shoppers to see the advantage of buying multipacks.

unit process *n. Chemical engineering.* any of a number of standard operations, such as filtration or distillation, that are widely used in various chemical industries.

unit trust *n. Brit.* an investment trust that issues units for public sale, the holders of which are creditors and not shareholders with their interests represented by a trust company independent of the issuing agency.

unity (ˈjuːnɪtɪ) *n., pl.* **-ties. 1.** the state or quality of being one; oneness. **2.** the act, state, or quality of forming a whole from separate parts. **3.** something whole or complete that is composed of separate parts. **4.** mutual agreement; harmony or concord: *the participants were no longer in unity.* **5.** uniformity or constancy: *unity of purpose.* **6.** *Maths.* **a.** the number or numeral one. **b.** a quantity assuming the value of one: *the area of the triangle was regarded as unity.* **c.** the element of a set producing no change in a number following multiplication. **7.** the arrangement of the elements in a work of art in accordance with a single overall design or purpose. **8.** any one of the three principles of dramatic structure deriving from Aristotle's *Poetics* by which the action of a play should be limited to a single plot (unity of action), a single location (unity of place), and the events of a single day (unity of time). [C13: from Old French *unité,* from Latin *ūnitās,* from *ūnus* one]

unity of interest *n. Property law.* the equal interest in property held by joint tenants.

unity ticket *n. Austral.* a how-to-vote card in a union election associating Labor and Communist candidates.

univ. *abbrev. for:* **1.** universal(ly). **2.** university.

Univ. *abbrev. for:* **1.** Universalist. **2.** University.

univalent (ˌjuːnɪˈveɪlənt, juːˈnɪvələnt) *adj.* **1.** (of a chromosome during meiosis) not paired with its homologue. **2.** *Chem.* another word for **monovalent.** —ˌ**uniˈvalency** *n.*

univalve (ˈjuːnɪˌvælv) *Zoology.* ~*adj.* **1.** relating to, designating, or possessing a mollusc shell that consists of a single piece (valve). ~*n.* **2.** a gastropod mollusc or its shell.

universal (ˌjuːnɪˈvɜːsᵊl) *adj.* **1.** of, relating to, or typical of the whole of mankind or of nature. **2.** common to, involving, or proceeding from all in a particular group. **3.** applicable to or affecting many individuals, conditions, or cases; general. **4.** existing or prevailing everywhere. **5.** applicable or occurring throughout or relating to the universe; cosmic: *a universal constant.* **6.** (esp. of a language) capable of being used and understood by all. **7.** embracing or versed in many fields of knowledge, activity, interest, etc. **8.** *Machinery.* designed or adapted for a range of sizes, fittings, or uses. **9.** *Linguistics.* (of a constraint in a formal grammar) common to the grammatical description of all human languages, actual or possible. **10.** *Logic.* (of a statement or proposition) affirming or denying something about every member of a class, as in *all men are wicked.* Compare **particular** (sense 6). **11.** *Archaic.* entire; whole. ~*n.* **12.** *Philosophy.* **a.** a general term or concept or the type such a term signifies. **b.** a metaphysical entity taken to be the reference of a general term, as distinct from the class of individuals it describes. **c.** a Platonic Idea or Aristotelian form. **13.** *Logic.* **a.** a universal proposition, statement, or formula. **b.** a universal quantifier. **14.** a characteristic common to every member of a particular culture or to every human being. **15.** short for **universal joint.** —ˌ**uniˈversalness** *n.*

universal beam *n.* a broad-flanged rolled steel joist suitable for a stanchion (axial load) or beam (bending load).

universal class *or* **set** *n.* (in Boolean algebra) the class containing all points and including all other classes.

universal donor *n.* a person who has blood of group O and whose blood may be safely transfused to persons with most other blood types.

universal gas constant *n.* another name for **gas constant.**

universal grammar *n. Linguistics.* (in transformation linguistics) the abstract limitations on the formal grammatical description of all human languages, actual or possible, that make them human languages.

universalism (ˌjuːnɪˈvɜːsəˌlɪzəm) *n.* **1.** a universal feature or characteristic. **2.** another word for **universality.** **3.** *Social welfare.* the principle that welfare services should be available to all by right, according to need, and not restricted by individual ability to pay, but funded by general contributions through taxes, rates, or national insurance payments.

Universalism (ˌjuːnɪˈvɜːsəˌlɪzəm) *n.* a system of religious beliefs maintaining that all men are predestined for salvation. —ˌ**Uniˈversalist** *n., adj.*

universalist (ˌjuːnɪˈvɜːsəlɪst) *n.* **1.** a person who has a wide range of interests, knowledge, activities, etc. ~*adj.* **2.** characterized by universality. —ˌ**uniˌversalˈistic** *adj.*

universality (ˌjuːnɪvɜːˈsælɪtɪ) *n.* the state or quality of being universal.

universalizability *or* **universalisability** (ˌjuːnɪˌvɜːsəlaɪzəˈbɪlɪtɪ) *n.* *Ethics.* **1.** the thesis that any moral judgment must be equally applicable to every relevantly identical situation. **2.** the Kantian principle that if a course of action cannot be universally adopted it must be morally impermissible.

universalize *or* **universalise** (ˌjuːnɪˈvɜːsəˌlaɪz) *vb.* (*tr.*) to make universal. —ˌ**uniˌversaliˈzation** *or* ˌ**uniˌversaliˈsation** *n.*

universal joint *or* **coupling** *n.* a form of coupling between two rotating shafts allowing freedom of movement in all directions.

universally (ˌjuːnɪˈvɜːsəlɪ) *adv.* everywhere or in every case; without exception: *this principle applies universally.*

universal motor *n.* an electric motor capable of working on either direct current or single-phase alternating current at approximately the same speed and output.

universal quantifier *n.* *Logic.* a formal device indicating that the open sentence that follows is true of every member of the relevant universe of interpretation, as $(\forall x)(Fx \to Gx)$ or $(x)(Fx \to Gx)$, literally, for everything, if it is an F it is a G, that is, all Fs are Gs. Usual symbol: $\forall$

Universal Soul *or* **Spirit** *n.* *Hinduism.* Brahman in its aspect as the sacred syllable Om, the eternal and spiritual principle that permeates the universe.

universal time *n.* **1.** (until 1972) an internationally agreed basis for timekeeping based on Greenwich Mean Time. Abbrev.: **UT.** **2.** Also called: **universal time coordinated**, abbrev.: **UTC.** an internationally agreed basis for timekeeping introduced in 1972 and based on International Atomic Time, the SI unit of which is the second.

universe (ˈjuːnɪˌvɜːs) *n.* **1.** *Astronomy.* the aggregate of all existing matter, energy, and space. **2.** human beings collectively. **3.** a province or sphere of thought or activity. **4.** *Statistics.* another word for **population** (sense 7). [C16: from French *univers,* from Latin *ūniversum* the whole world, from *ūniversus* all together, from UNI- + *vertere* to turn]

universe of discourse *n.* *Logic.* the complete range of objects, events, attributes, relations, ideas, etc., that are expressed, assumed, or implied in a discussion.

university (ˌjuːnɪˈvɜːsɪtɪ) *n., pl.* **-ties.** **1.** an institution of higher education having authority to award bachelors' and higher degrees, usually having research facilities. **2.** the buildings, members, staff, or campus of a university. [C14: from Old French *universite,* from Medieval Latin *ūniversitās* group of scholars, from Late Latin: guild, society, body of men, from Latin: whole, totality, universe]

university entrance *n.* (in New Zealand) **a.** an examination taken by pupils of postprimary schools. **b.** the certificate issued to a successful candidate. ~Abbrev.: **UE.**

univocal (ˌjuːnɪˈvəʊkᵊl) *adj.* **1.** unambiguous or unmistakable. ~*n.* **2.** a word or term that has only one meaning. —ˌ**uniˈvocally** *adv.*

UNIX (ˈjuːnɪks) *n.* *Trademark.* a multi-user multitasking operating system found on many types of computer.

unjust (ʌnˈdʒʌst) *adj.* not in accordance with accepted standards of fairness or justice; unfair. —**unˈjustly** *adv.* —**unˈjustness** *n.*

unkempt (ʌnˈkɛmpt) *adj.* **1.** (of the hair) uncombed; dishevelled. **2.** ungroomed; slovenly: *unkempt appearance.* **3.** *Archaic.* crude or coarse. [Old English *uncembed;* from UN-[1] + *cembed,* past participle of *cemban* to COMB; related to Old Saxon *kembian,* Old High German *kemben* to comb] —**unˈkemptly** *adv.* —**unˈkemptness** *n.*

unkenned (ʌnˈkɛnd) *or* **unkent** (ʌnˈkɛnt) *adj.* *Scot. and northern English dialect.* unknown. [C14: from UN-[1] + KEN]

unkennel (ʌnˈkɛnᵊl) *vb.* **-nels, -nelling, -nelled** *or U.S.* **-nels, -neling, -neled.** (*tr.*) **1.** to release from a kennel. **2.** to drive from a hole or lair. **3.** *Rare.* to bring to light.

unkind (ʌnˈkaɪnd) *adj.* **1.** lacking kindness; unsympathetic or cruel. **2.** *Archaic or dialect.* **a.** (of weather) unpleasant. **b.** (of soil) hard to cultivate. —**unˈkindly** *adv.* —**unˈkindness** *n.*

unknit (ʌnˈnɪt) *vb.* **-knits, -knitting, -knitted** *or* **-knit.** **1.** to make or become undone, untied, or unravelled. **2.** (*tr.*) to loosen, weaken, or destroy: *to unknit an alliance.* **3.** (*tr.*) *Rare.* to smooth out (a wrinkled brow).

unknowable (ʌnˈnəʊəbᵊl) *adj.* **1.** incapable of being known or understood. **2. a.** beyond human understanding. **b.** (*as n.*): *the unknowable.* —**unˈknowableness** *or* **unˌknowaˈbility** *n.* —**unˈknowably** *adv.*

Unknowable (ʌnˈnəʊəbᵊl) *n.* **the.** *Philosophy.* the ultimate reality that underlies all phenomena but cannot be known.

unknowing (ʌnˈnəʊɪŋ) *adj.* **1.** not knowing; ignorant. **2.** (*postpositive;* often foll. by *of*) without knowledge or unaware (of). —**unˈknowingly** *adv.*

unknown (ʌnˈnəʊn) *adj.* **1.** not known, understood, or recognized. **2.** not established, identified, or discovered: *an unknown island.* **3.** not famous; undistinguished: *some unknown artist.* ~*n.* **4.** an unknown person, quantity, or thing. **5.** *Maths.* a variable, or the quantity it represents, the value of which is to be discovered by solving an equation; a variable in a conditional equation: *$3y = 4x + 5$ is an equation in two unknowns.* **6. unknown quantity.** a person or thing whose action, effect, etc., is unknown or unpredictable. —**unˈknownness** *n.*

Unknown Soldier *or* **Warrior** *n.* (in various countries) an unidentified soldier who has died in battle and for whom a tomb is established as a memorial to other unidentified dead of the nation's armed forces.

unlace (ʌnˈleɪs) *vb.* (*tr.*) **1.** to loosen or undo the lacing of (shoes, garments, etc.). **2.** to unfasten or remove garments of (oneself or another) by or as if by undoing lacing.

unlade (ʌnˈleɪd) *vb.* a less common word for **unload.**

unlash (ʌnˈlæʃ) *vb.* (*tr.*) to untie or unfasten.

unlatch (ʌnˈlætʃ) *vb.* to open or unfasten or come open or unfastened by the lifting or release of a latch.

unlawful (ʌnˈlɔːfʊl) *adj.* **1.** illegal. **2.** illicit; immoral: *unlawful love.* **3.** an archaic word for **illegitimate.** —**unˈlawfully** *adv.* —**unˈlawfulness** *n.*

unlawful assembly *n.* *Law.* a meeting of three or more people with the intent of carrying out any unlawful purpose.

unlay (ʌnˈleɪ) *vb.* **-lays, -laying, -laid.** (*tr.*) to untwist (a rope or cable) to separate its strands.

unlead (ʌnˈlɛd) *vb.* (*tr.*) **1.** to strip off lead. **2.** *Printing.* to remove the leads or spaces from between (lines of type).

unleaded (ʌnˈlɛdɪd) *adj.* **1.** (of petrol) containing a reduced amount of tetraethyl lead, in order to reduce environmental pollution. **2.** not covered or weighted with lead. **3.** *Printing.* (of lines of type, etc.) not spaced or separated with leads; solid. ~*n.* **4.** petrol containing a reduced amount of tetraethyl lead.

unlearn (ʌnˈlɜːn) *vb.* **-learns, -learning, -learnt** *or* **-learned** (-ˈlɜːnd). to try to forget (something learnt) or to discard (accumulated knowledge).

unlearned (ʌnˈlɜːnɪd) *adj.* ignorant or untaught. —**unˈlearnedly** *adv.*

unlearnt (ʌnˈlɜːnt) *or* **unlearned** (ʌnˈlɜːnd) *adj.* **1.** denoting knowledge or skills innately present and therefore not learnt. **2.** not learnt or taken notice of: *unlearnt lessons.*

unleash (ʌnˈliːʃ) *vb.* (*tr.*) **1.** to release from or as if from a leash. **2.** to free from restraint or control.

unleavened (ʌnˈlɛvənd) *adj.* (of bread, biscuits, etc.) made from a dough containing no yeast or leavening.

unless (ʌnˈlɛs) *conj.* **1.** (*subordinating*) except under the circumstances that; except on the condition that: *they'll sell it unless he hears otherwise.* ~*prep.* **2.** *Rare.* except. [C14: *onlesse,* from *on* ON + *lesse* LESS; compare French *à moins que,* literally: at less than]

unlettered (ʌnˈlɛtəd) *adj.* **1.** uneducated; illiterate. **2.** not marked with letters: *an unlettered tombstone.*

unlicensed (ʌnˈlaɪsənst) *adj.* **1.** having no licence: *an unlicensed restaurant.* **2.** without permission; unauthorized. **3.** unrestrained or lawless.

unlike (ʌnˈlaɪk) *adj.* **1.** not alike; dissimilar or unequal; different. **2.** *Archaic or northern English dialect.* unlikely. ~*prep.* **3.** not like; not typical of: *unlike his father he lacks intelligence.* —**unˈlikeness** *n.*

unlikely (ʌnˈlaɪklɪ) *adj.* not likely; improbable. —**unˈlikeliness** *or* **unˈlikelihood** *n.*

unlimber (ʌnˈlɪmbə) *vb.* **1.** (*tr.*) to disengage (a gun) from its limber. **2.** to prepare (something) for use.

unlimited (ʌnˈlɪmɪtɪd) *adj.* **1.** without limits or bounds: *unlimited knowledge.* **2.** not restricted, limited, or qualified: *unlimited power.* **3.** *Finance, Brit.* **a.** (of liability) not restricted to any unpaid portion of nominal capital invested in a business. **b.** (of

unˈjoined *adj.*
unˈjointed *adj.*
unˈjustiˌfiable *adj.*
unˈjustiˌfiably *adv.*
unˈjustiˌfied *adj.*
unˈkept *adj.*
unˈkindled *adj.*
unˈkingly *adj., adv.*
unˈkissed *adj.*
unˈknot *vb.,* **-ˈknots, -ˈknotting, -ˈknotted.**
unˈknowledgeable *or* **unˈknowledgable** *adj.*
unˈlabelled *adj.*
unˈlaboured *adj.*
unˈladen *adj.*
unˈladyˌlike *adj.*
unˈlaid *adj.*
ˌunlaˈmented *adj.*
unˈleased *adj.*
unˈliberˌated *adj.*
unˈlifeˌlike *adj.*
unˈlighted *adj.*
unˈlikable *or* **unˈlikeable** *adj.*
unˈlined *adj.*
unˈlink *vb.*

a business enterprise) having owners with such unlimited liability. —**un'limitedly** *adv.* —**un'limitedness** *n.*
unlisted (ʌn'lɪstɪd) *adj.* **1.** not entered on a list. **2.** *U.S. and Canadian.* (of a telephone number or telephone subscriber) not listed in a telephone directory. Brit. term: **ex-directory.**
unlisted securities market *n.* a market on the London Stock Exchange, established in 1981, for trading in shares of smaller companies, who do not wish to comply with the requirements for a full listing. Abbrev.: **USM.**
unlive (ʌn'lɪv) *vb.* (*tr.*) to live so as to nullify, undo, or live down (past events or times).
unload (ʌn'ləʊd) *vb.* **1.** to remove a load or cargo from (a ship, lorry, etc.). **2.** to discharge (cargo, freight, etc.). **3.** (*tr.*) to relieve of a burden or troubles. **4.** (*tr.*) to give vent to (anxiety, troubles, etc.). **5.** (*tr.*) to get rid of or dispose of (esp. surplus goods). **6.** (*tr.*) to remove the charge of ammunition from (a firearm). —**un'loader** *n.*
unlock (ʌn'lɒk) *vb.* **1.** (*tr.*) to unfasten (a lock, door, etc.). **2.** (*tr.*) to open, release, or let loose. **3.** (*tr.*) to disclose or provide the key to: *unlock a puzzle.* **4.** (*intr.*) to become unlocked. —**un'lockable** *adj.*
unlooked-for (ˌʌn'lʊktfɔː) *adj.* unexpected; unforeseen.
unloose (ʌn'luːs) *or* **unloosen** *vb.* (*tr.*) **1.** to set free; release. **2.** to loosen or relax (a hold, grip, etc.). **3.** to unfasten or untie.
unlovely (ʌn'lʌvlɪ) *adj.* **1.** unpleasant in appearance. **2.** unpleasant in character. —**un'loveliness** *n.*
unlucky (ʌn'lʌkɪ) *adj.* **1.** characterized by misfortune or failure: *an unlucky person; an unlucky chance.* **2.** ill-omened; inauspicious: *an unlucky date.* **3.** regrettable; disappointing. **4.** *Brit. dialect.* causing trouble; mischievous. —**un'luckily** *adv.* —**un'luckiness** *n.*
unmade (ʌn'meɪd) *vb.* **1.** the past tense and past participle of **unmake.** ~*adj.* **2.** not yet made. **3.** existing without having been made or created. **4.** *Falconry.* another word for **unmanned** (sense 4).
unmake (ʌn'meɪk) *vb.* **-makes, -making, -made.** (*tr.*) **1.** to undo or destroy. **2.** to depose from office, rank, or authority. **3.** to alter the nature of. —**un'maker** *n.*
unman (ʌn'mæn) *vb.* **-mans, -manning, -manned.** (*tr.*) **1.** to cause to lose courage or nerve. **2.** to make effeminate. **3.** to remove the men from. **4.** *Archaic.* to deprive of human qualities.
unmanly (ʌn'mænlɪ) *adj.* **1.** not masculine or virile. **2.** ignoble, cowardly, or dishonourable. ~*adv.* **3.** *Archaic.* in an unmanly manner. —**un'manliness** *n.*
unmanned (ʌn'mænd) *adj.* **1.** lacking personnel or crew: *an unmanned ship.* **2.** (of aircraft, spacecraft, etc.) operated by automatic or remote control. **3.** uninhabited. **4.** *Falconry.* (of a hawk or falcon) not yet trained to accept humans.
unmannered (ʌn'mænəd) *adj.* **1.** without good manners; coarse; rude. **2.** not affected; without mannerisms.
unmannerly (ʌn'mænəlɪ) *adj.* **1.** lacking manners; discourteous. ~*adv.* **2.** *Archaic.* rudely; discourteously. —**un'mannerliness** *n.*
unmarked (ʌn'mɑːkt) *adj.* **1.** not carrying a mark or marks. **2.** not noticed or observed.
unmarried (ʌn'mærɪd) *adj.* **1.** not married: *an unmarried mother.* **2.** *Films.* denoting a print of a cinematograph film in which the picture and sound recordings are on separate reels.
unmask (ʌn'mɑːsk) *vb.* **1.** to remove (the mask or disguise) from (someone or oneself). **2.** to appear or cause to appear in true character. **3.** (*tr.*) *Military.* to make evident the presence of (weapons), either by firing or by the removal of camouflage, etc. —**un'masker** *n.*
unmeaning (ʌn'miːnɪŋ) *adj.* **1.** having no meaning. **2.** showing no intelligence; vacant: *an unmeaning face.* —**un'meaningly** *adv.* —**un'meaningness** *n.*
unmeant (ʌn'mɛnt) *adj.* unintentional; accidental.
unmeasured (ʌn'mɛʒəd) *adj.* **1.** measureless; limitless. **2.** unrestrained; unlimited or lavish. **3.** *Music.* without bar lines and hence without a fixed pulse. —**un'measurable** *adj.* —**un'measurableness** *n.* —**un'measurably** *adv.* —**un'measuredly** *adv.*
unmeet (ʌn'miːt) *adj. Literary or archaic.* not meet; unsuitable. —**un'meetly** *adv.* —**un'meetness** *n.*
unmentionable (ʌn'mɛnʃənəbᵊl) *adj.* **a.** unsuitable or forbidden as a topic of conversation. **b.** (*as n.*): *the unmentionable.* —**un'mentionableness** *n.* —**un'mentionably** *adv.*
unmentionables (ʌn'mɛnʃənəbᵊlz) *pl. n. Chiefly humorous.* underwear.
unmerciful (ʌn'mɜːsɪfʊl) *adj.* **1.** showing no mercy; relentless. **2.** extreme or excessive. —**un'mercifully** *adv.* —**un'mercifulness** *n.*
unmindful (ʌn'maɪndfʊl) *adj.* (*usually postpositive* and foll. by *of*) careless, heedless, or forgetful. —**un'mindfully** *adv.* —**un'mindfulness** *n.*
unmissable (ʌn'mɪsəbᵊl) *adj.* (of a film, television programme, etc.) so good that it should not be missed.
unmistakable *or* **unmistakeable** (ˌʌnmɪs'teɪkəbᵊl) *adj.* not mistakable; clear, obvious, or unambiguous. —ˌ**unmis'takableness** *or* ˌ**unmis'takeableness** *n.* —ˌ**unmis'takably** *or* ˌ**unmis'takeably** *adv.*
unmitigated (ʌn'mɪtɪˌgeɪtɪd) *adj.* **1.** not diminished in intensity, severity, etc. **2.** (*prenominal*) (intensifier): *an unmitigated disaster.* —**un'mitiˌgatedly** *adv.*
unmoor (ʌn'mʊə, -'mɔː) *vb. Nautical.* **1.** to weigh the anchor or drop the mooring of (a vessel). **2.** (*tr.*) to reduce the mooring of (a vessel) to one anchor.
unmoral (ʌn'mɒrəl) *adj.* outside morality; amoral. —**unmorality** (ˌʌnmə'rælɪtɪ) *n.* —**un'morally** *adv.*
unmurmuring (ʌn'mɜːmərɪŋ) *adj.* not complaining.
unmusical (ʌn'mjuːzɪkᵊl) *adj.* **1.** not musical or harmonious. **2.** not talented in or appreciative of music. —**un'musically** *adv.* —**un'musicalness** *n.*
unmuzzle (ʌn'mʌzᵊl) *vb.* (*tr.*) **1.** to take the muzzle off (a dog, etc.). **2.** to free from control or censorship.
unnamed (ʌn'neɪmd) *adj.* **1.** having no name. **2.** not mentioned by name: *the culprit shall remain unnamed.*
unnatural (ʌn'nætʃərəl, -'nætʃrəl) *adj.* **1.** contrary to nature; abnormal. **2.** not in accordance with accepted standards of behaviour or right and wrong: *unnatural love.* **3.** uncanny; supernatural: *unnatural phenomena.* **4.** affected or forced: *an unnatural manner.* **5.** inhuman or monstrous; wicked: *an unnatural crime.* **6.** *Obsolete.* illegitimate. —**un'naturally** *adv.* —**un'naturalness** *n.*
unnecessary (ʌn'nɛsɪsərɪ, -ɪsrɪ) *adj.* not necessary. —**un'necessarily** *adv.* —**un'necessariness** *n.*
unnerve (ʌn'nɜːv) *vb.* (*tr.*) to cause to lose courage, strength, confidence, self-control, etc.
unnumbered (ʌn'nʌmbəd) *adj.* **1.** countless; innumerable. **2.** not counted or assigned a number.
UNO *abbrev. for* United Nations Organization.
unoccupied (ʌn'ɒkjuˌpaɪd) *adj.* **1.** (of a building) without occupants. **2.** unemployed or idle. **3.** (of an area or country) not overrun by foreign troops.
unofficial (ˌʌnə'fɪʃəl) *adj.* **1.** not official or formal: *an unofficial engagement.* **2.** not confirmed officially: *an unofficial report.* **3.** (of a strike) not approved by the strikers' trade union. **4.** (of a medicinal drug) not listed in a pharmacopoeia. —ˌ**unof'ficially** *adv.*
unorganized *or* **unorganised** (ʌn'ɔːgəˌnaɪzd) *adj.* **1.** not arranged into an organized system, structure, or unity. **2.** (of workers) not unionized. **3.** nonliving; inorganic.
unorthodox (ʌn'ɔːθəˌdɒks) *adj.* not conventional in belief, behaviour, custom, etc. —**un'orthoˌdoxly** *adv.*

un'lit *adj.*
un'livable *or* **un'liveable** *adj.*
ˌ**unlo'cated** *adj.*
un'locked *adj.*
un'lovable *or* **un'loveable** *adj.*
un'loved *adj.*
un'loving *adj.*
un'lubriˌcated *adj.*
un'magniˌfied *adj.*
un'manageable *adj.*
ˌ**unma'nipuˌlated** *adj.*
ˌ**unmanu'factured** *adj.*
un'marketable *adj.*
un'marred *adj.*
un'marriageable *adj.*
un'mastered *adj.*
un'matched *adj.*
ˌ**unma'tured** *adj.*
ˌ**unme'chanical** *adj.*
un'mediˌcated *adj.*
ˌ**unme'lodious** *adj.*
un'melted *adj.*
un'memorable *adj.*
un'memoˌrized *or* **un'memoˌrised** *adj.*
un'mended *adj.*
un'mentioned *adj.*
un'merchantable *adj.*
un'merited *adj.*
ˌ**unme'thodical** *adj.*
un'metrical *adj.*
un'military *adj.*
un'mingled *adj.*
ˌ**unmis'taken** *adj.*
un'mixed *adj.*
un'modiˌfied *adj.*
un'moduˌlated *adj.*
ˌ**unmo'lested** *adj.*
un'motiˌvated *adj.*
un'moulded *adj.*
un'mounted *adj.*
un'mourned *adj.*
un'movable *or* **un'moveable** *adj.*
un'moved *adj.*
un'moving *adj.*
un'mown *adj.*
un'muffle *vb.*
un'mystiˌfied *adj.*
un'namable *or* **un'nameable** *adj.*
un'navigable *adj.*
un'needed *adj.*
un'needful *adj.*
ˌ**unne'gotiable** *adj.*
ˌ**unne'gotiˌated** *adj.*
un'neighbourly *adj.*
un'noteˌworthy *adj.*
un'noticeable *adj.*
un'noticeably *adv.*
un'noticed *adj.*
un'nurtured *adj.*
ˌ**unob'jectionable** *adj.*
ˌ**uno'bliging** *adj.*
ˌ**unob'scured** *adj.*
ˌ**unob'servant** *adj.*
ˌ**unob'served** *adj.*
ˌ**unob'structed** *adj.*
ˌ**unob'tainable** *adj.*
ˌ**unob'tained** *adj.*
ˌ**unob'truding** *adj.*
ˌ**unob'trusive** *adj.*
ˌ**unob'trusively** *adv.*
ˌ**unob'trusiveness** *n.*
ˌ**unof'fended** *adj.*
ˌ**unof'fending** *adj.*
ˌ**unof'fensive** *adj.*
ˌ**unof'fensively** *adv.*
un'offered *adj.*
ˌ**unof'ficious** *adj.*
ˌ**unof'ficiously** *adv.*
un'open *adj.*
un'opened *adj.*
ˌ**unop'posed** *adj.*
ˌ**unop'pressed** *adj.*
ˌ**unop'pressive** *adj.*
ˌ**unop'pressively** *adv.*
ˌ**unor'dained** *adj.*
ˌ**uno'riginal** *adj.*
ˌ**unorna'mental** *adj.*

unpack (ʌn'pæk) *vb.* 1. to remove the packed contents of (a case, trunk, etc.). 2. (*tr.*) to take (something) out of a packed container. 3. (*tr.*) to remove a pack from; unload: *to unpack a mule.* —**un'packer** *n.*

unpaged (ʌn'peɪdʒd) *adj.* (of a book) having no page numbers.

unpaid (ʌn'peɪd) *adj.* 1. (of a bill, debt, etc.) not yet paid. 2. working without pay. 3. having wages outstanding.

unparalleled (ʌn'pærəˌlɛld) *adj.* unmatched; unequalled.

unparliamentary (ˌʌnpɑːlə'mɛntərɪ, -trɪ) *adj.* not consistent with parliamentary procedure or practice. —ˌ**unparlia'mentarily** *adv.* —ˌ**unparlia'mentariness** *n.*

unpeg (ʌn'pɛg) *vb.* **-pegs, -pegging, -pegged.** (*tr.*) 1. to remove the peg or pegs from, esp. to unfasten. 2. to allow (prices, wages, etc.) to rise and fall freely.

unpeople (ʌn'piːpᵊl) *vb.* (*tr.*) to empty of people.

unperforated (ʌn'pɜːfəˌreɪtɪd) *adj.* (of a stamp) not provided with perforations.

unperson ('ʌnpɜːsᵊn) *n.* a person whose existence is officially denied or ignored.

unpick (ʌn'pɪk) *vb.* (*tr.*) 1. to undo (the stitches) of (a piece of sewing). 2. to unravel or undo (a garment, etc.). 3. *Obsolete.* to open (a door, lock, etc.) by picking.

unpin (ʌn'pɪn) *vb.* **-pins, -pinning, -pinned.** (*tr.*) 1. to remove a pin or pins from. 2. to unfasten by removing pins.

unplaced (ʌn'pleɪst) *adj.* 1. not given or put in a particular place. 2. *Horse racing.* not in the first three (sometimes four) runners in a race.

unpleasant (ʌn'plɛzᵊnt) *adj.* not pleasant or agreeable. —**un'pleasantly** *adv.*

unpleasantness (ʌn'plɛzəntnɪs) *n.* 1. the state or quality of being unpleasant. 2. an unpleasant event, situation, etc. 3. a disagreement or quarrel.

unplug (ʌn'plʌg) *vb.* **-plugs, -plugging, -plugged.** (*tr.*) 1. to disconnect (an electrical appliance) by taking the plug out of the socket. 2. to remove a plug or obstruction from.

unplumbed (ʌn'plʌmd) *adj.* 1. unfathomed; unsounded. 2. not understood in depth. 3. (of a building) having no plumbing.

unpolitic (ʌn'pɒlɪtɪk) *adj.* another word for **impolitic.**

unpolled (ʌn'pəʊld) *adj.* 1. not included in an opinion poll. 2. not having voted. 3. *U.S.* not registered for an election: *unpolled votes.* 4. *Archaic.* uncut or unshorn.

unpopular (ʌn'pɒpjʊlə) *adj.* not popular with an individual or group of people. —**unpopularity** (ˌʌnpɒpjʊ'lærɪtɪ) *n.* —**un'popularly** *adv.*

unpractical (ʌn'præktɪkᵊl) *adj.* another word for **impractical.** —ˌ**unpracti'cality** *or* **un'practicalness** *n.* —**un'practically** *adv.*

unpractised *or U.S.* **unpracticed** (ʌn'præktɪst) *adj.* 1. without skill, training, or experience. 2. not used or done often or repeatedly. 3. not yet tested.

unprecedented (ʌn'prɛsɪˌdɛntɪd) *adj.* having no precedent; unparalleled. —**un'preceˌdentedly** *adv.*

unpredictable (ˌʌnprɪ'dɪktəbᵊl) *adj.* not capable of being predicted; changeable. —ˌ**unpreˌdicta'bility** *or* ˌ**unpre'dictableness** *n.* —ˌ**unpre'dictably** *adv.*

unprejudiced (ʌn'prɛdʒʊdɪst) *adj.* not prejudiced or biased; impartial. —**un'prejudicedly** *adv.*

unpremeditated (ˌʌnprɪ'mɛdɪˌteɪtɪd) *adj.* not planned beforehand; spontaneous. —ˌ**unpre'mediˌtatedly** *adv.* —ˌ**unpreˌmedi'tation** *n.*

unprepared (ˌʌnprɪ'pɛəd) *adj.* 1. having made inadequate preparations. 2. not made ready or prepared. 3. done without preparation; extemporaneous. —ˌ**unpre'paredly** *adv.* —ˌ**unpre'paredness** *n.*

unpriced (ʌn'praɪst) *adj.* 1. having no fixed or marked price. 2. *Poetic.* beyond price; priceless.

unprincipled (ʌn'prɪnsɪpᵊld) *adj.* 1. lacking moral principles; unscrupulous. 2. (foll. by *in*) *Archaic.* not versed in the principles of (a subject). —**un'principledness** *n.*

unprintable (ʌn'prɪntəbᵊl) *adj.* unsuitable for printing for reasons of obscenity, libel, bad taste, etc. —**un'printableness** *n.* —**un'printably** *adv.*

unproductive (ˌʌnprə'dʌktɪv) *adj.* 1. (often foll. by *of*) not productive of (anything). 2. not producing goods and services with exchange value. —ˌ**unpro'ductively** *adv.* —ˌ**unpro'ductiveness** *n.*

unprofessional (ˌʌnprə'fɛʃənᵊl) *adj.* 1. contrary to the accepted code of conduct of a profession. 2. amateur. 3. not belonging to or having the required qualifications for a profession. —ˌ**unpro'fessionally** *adv.*

unprofitable (ʌn'prɒfɪtəbᵊl) *adj.* 1. not making a profit. 2. not fruitful or beneficial. —**unˌprofita'bility** *or* **un'profitableness** *n.* —**un'profitably** *adv.*

unprovided (ˌʌnprə'vaɪdɪd) *adj.* (*postpositive*) 1. (foll. by *with*) not provided or supplied. 2. (often foll. by *for*) not prepared or ready. 3. **unprovided for.** without income or means. —ˌ**unpro'videdly** *adv.*

unputdownable (ˌʌnpʊt'daʊnəbᵊl) *adj.* (of a book, esp. a novel) so gripping as to be read right through at one sitting.

unqualified (ʌn'kwɒlɪˌfaɪd) *adj.* 1. lacking the necessary qualifications. 2. not restricted or modified: *an unqualified criticism.* 3. (*usually prenominal*) (intensifier): *an unqualified success.* —**un'qualiˌfiable** *adj.* —**un'qualiˌfiedly** *adv.* —**un'qualiˌfiedness** *n.*

unquestionable (ʌn'kwɛstʃənəbᵊl) *adj.* 1. indubitable or indisputable. 2. not admitting of exception or qualification: *an unquestionable ruling.* —**unˌquestiona'bility** *or* **un'questionableness** *n.* —**un'questionably** *adv.*

unquestioned (ʌn'kwɛstʃənd) *adj.* 1. accepted without question. 2. not admitting of doubt or question: *unquestioned power.* 3. not questioned or interrogated. 4. *Rare.* not examined or investigated.

unquiet (ʌn'kwaɪət) *Chiefly literary.* ~*adj.* 1. characterized by disorder, unrest, or tumult: *unquiet times.* 2. anxious; uneasy. 3. *Archaic.* noisy. ~*n.* 4. a state of unrest. —**un'quietly** *adv.* —**un'quietness** *n.*

unquote (ʌn'kwəʊt) *interj.* 1. an expression used parenthetically to indicate that the preceding quotation is finished. ~*vb.* 2. to close (a quotation), esp. in printing.

unravel (ʌn'rævᵊl) *vb.* **-els, -elling, -elled** *or U.S.* **-els, -eling, -eled.** 1. (*tr.*) to reduce (something knitted or woven) to separate strands. 2. (*tr.*) to undo or untangle (something tangled or knotted). 3. (*tr.*) to explain or solve: *the mystery was unravelled.* 4. (*intr.*) to become unravelled. —**un'raveller** *n.* —**un'ravelment** *n.*

unread (ʌn'rɛd) *adj.* 1. (of a book, newspaper, etc.) not yet read. 2. (of a person) having read little. 3. (*postpositive;* foll. by *in*) not versed (in a specified field).

unreadable (ʌn'riːdəbᵊl) *adj.* 1. illegible; undecipherable. 2. difficult or tedious to read. —**unˌreada'bility** *or* **un'readableness** *n.* —**un'readably** *adv.*

unready (ʌn'rɛdɪ) *adj.* 1. not ready or prepared. 2. slow or hesitant to see or act. 3. *Archaic or Brit. dialect.* not dressed. —**un'readily** *adv.* —**un'readiness** *n.*

unreal (ʌn'rɪəl) *adj.* 1. imaginary or fanciful or seemingly so: *an unreal situation.* 2. having no actual existence or substance. 3. insincere or artificial. —**un'really** *adv.*

unreality (ˌʌnrɪ'ælɪtɪ) *n.* 1. the quality or state of being unreal, fanciful, or impractical. 2. something that is unreal.

unreason (ʌn'riːzᵊn) *n.* 1. irrationality or madness. 2. something that lacks or is contrary to reason. 3. lack of order; chaos. ~*vb.* 4. (*tr.*) to deprive of reason.

unreasonable (ʌn'riːznəbᵊl) *adj.* 1. immoderate; excessive: *unreasonable demands.* 2. refusing to listen to reason. 3. lacking reason or judgment. —**un'reasonableness** *n.* —**un'reasonably** *adv.*

unreasonable behaviour *n. Law.* conduct by a spouse sufficient to cause the irretrievable breakdown of a marriage.

ˌ**unosten'tatious** *adj.*
ˌ**unosten'tatiously** *adv.*
un'owned *adj.*
un'paciˌfied *adj.*
un'paired *adj.*
un'palatable *adj.*
un'pardonable *adj.*
un'pasteurˌized *or* **un'pasteurˌised** *adj.*
un'patented *adj.*
ˌ**unpatri'otic** *adj.*
un'paved *adj.*
un'peaceful *adj.*
un'pensioned *adj.*
un'peppered *adj.*
ˌ**unper'ceived** *adj.*
ˌ**unper'ceptive** *adj.*
ˌ**unper'fected** *adj.*
ˌ**unper'formed** *adj.*
ˌ**unper'plexed** *adj.*
ˌ**unper'suaded** *adj.*
ˌ**unper'suasive** *adj.*
ˌ**unper'turbable** *adj.*
ˌ**unper'turbed** *adj.*
ˌ**unphilo'sophical** *adj.*
un'picked *adj.*
un'pitied *adj.*
un'pitying *adj.*
un'planned *adj.*
un'planted *adj.*
un'playable *adj.*
un'played *adj.*
un'pleasing *adj.*
un'pledged *adj.*
un'ploughed *adj.*
un'plucked *adj.*
ˌ**unpo'etic** *adj.*
un'pointed *adj.*
un'poised *adj.*
un'polarˌized *or* **un'polarˌised** *adj.*
un'polished *adj.*
ˌ**unpol'luted** *adj.*
un'polymerˌized *or* **un'polymerˌised** *adj.*
un'popuˌlated *adj.*
un'posed *adj.*
un'practicable *adj.*
ˌ**unpre'dicted** *adj.*
ˌ**unprepos'sessing** *adj.*
ˌ**unpre'scribed** *adj.*
ˌ**unpre'sentable** *adj.*
ˌ**unpre'served** *adj.*
un'pressed *adj.*
ˌ**unpre'sumptuous** *adj.*
ˌ**unpre'tending** *adj.*
ˌ**unpre'tentious** *adj.*
ˌ**unpre'vailing** *adj.*
un'processed *adj.*
ˌ**unpro'claimed** *adj.*
ˌ**unpro'curable** *adj.*
ˌ**unpro'fessed** *adj.*
ˌ**unpro'gressive** *adj.*
ˌ**unpro'hibited** *adj.*
un'promising *adj.*
un'prompted *adj.*
ˌ**unpro'nounceable** *adj.*
ˌ**unpro'nounced** *adj.*
ˌ**unpro'pitious** *adj.*
ˌ**unpro'posed** *adj.*
ˌ**unpro'tected** *adj.*
ˌ**unpro'testing** *adj.*
un'proved *adj.*
un'proven *adj.*
ˌ**unpro'voked** *adj.*
un'published *adj.*
un'punctual *adj.*
un'punished *adj.*
un'puriˌfied *adj.*
un'quantiˌfiable *adj.*
un'quelled *adj.*
un'quenched *adj.*
un'questioning *adj.*
un'quotable *adj.*
un'raised *adj.*
ˌ**unreal'istic** *adj.*
un'realˌized *or* **un'realˌised** *adj.*

unreasoning (ʌn'riːzənɪŋ) *adj.* not controlled by reason; irrational. —**un'reasoningly** *adv.*

unreckonable (ʌn'rɛkənəb^{ə}l) *adj.* incalculable; unlimited.

unreconstructed (ˌʌnriːkəns'trʌktɪd) *adj. Chiefly U.S.* unwilling to accept social and economic change, as exemplified by those White Southerners who refused to accept the reorganization and reintegration of the South into the Union after the American Civil War.

unreeve (ʌn'riːv) *vb.* **-reeves, -reeving, -rove** *or* **-reeved.** *Nautical.* to withdraw (a rope) from a block, thimble, etc. [C17: from UN-^{2} + REEVE]

unrefined (ˌʌnrɪ'faɪnd) *adj.* **1.** (of substances such as petroleum, ores, and sugar) not processed into a pure or usable form. **2.** coarse in manners or language.

unreflected (ˌʌnrɪ'flɛktɪd) *adj.* **1.** (foll. by *on* or *upon*) not considered. **2.** (of light, particles, etc., incident on a surface) not reflected; absorbed or transmitted.

unreflective (ˌʌnrɪ'flɛktɪv) *adj.* not reflective or thoughtful; rash; unthinking. —ˌ**unre'flectively** *adv.*

unregenerate (ˌʌnrɪ'dʒɛnərɪt) *adj. also* **unregenerated. 1.** unrepentant; unreformed. **2.** obstinately adhering to one's own views. ~*n.* **3.** an unregenerate person. —ˌ**unre'generacy** *n.* —ˌ**unre'generately** *adv.*

unrelenting (ˌʌnrɪ'lɛntɪŋ) *adj.* **1.** refusing to relent or take pity; relentless; merciless. **2.** not diminishing in determination, speed, effort, force, etc. —ˌ**unre'lentingly** *adv.* —ˌ**unre'lentingness** *n.*

unreligious (ˌʌnrɪ'lɪdʒəs) *adj.* **1.** another word for **irreligious. 2.** secular. —ˌ**unre'ligiously** *adv.*

unremitting (ˌʌnrɪ'mɪtɪŋ) *adj.* never slackening or stopping; unceasing; constant. —ˌ**unre'mittingly** *adv.* —ˌ**unre'mittingness** *n.*

unrepair (ˌʌnrɪ'pɛə) *n.* a less common word for **disrepair.** —ˌ**unre'paired** *adj.*

unrequited (ˌʌnrɪ'kwaɪtɪd) *adj.* (of love, affection, etc.) not reciprocated or returned.

unreserved (ˌʌnrɪ'zɜːvd) *adj.* **1.** without reserve; having an open manner. **2.** without reservation. **3.** not booked or bookable. —**unreservedly** (ˌʌnrɪ'zɜːvɪdlɪ) *adv.* —ˌ**unre'servedness** *n.*

unrest (ʌn'rɛst) *n.* **1.** a troubled or rebellious state of discontent. **2.** an uneasy or troubled state.

unrestrained (ˌʌnrɪ'streɪnd) *adj.* not restrained or checked; free or natural. —**unrestrainedly** (ˌʌnrɪ'streɪnɪdlɪ) *adv.*

unriddle (ʌn'rɪd^{ə}l) *vb. (tr.)* to solve or puzzle out. [C16: from UN-^{2} + RIDDLE^{1}] —**un'riddler** *n.*

unrifled (ʌn'raɪf^{ə}ld) *adj.* (of a firearm or its bore) not rifled; smoothbore.

unrig (ʌn'rɪg) *vb.* **-rigs, -rigging, -rigged. 1.** (*tr.*) to strip (a vessel) of standing and running rigging. **2.** *Archaic or dialect.* to undress (someone or oneself).

unrighteous (ʌn'raɪtʃəs) *adj.* **1. a.** sinful; wicked. **b.** (*as collective n.;* preceded by *the*): *the unrighteous.* **2.** not fair or right; unjust. —**un'righteously** *adv.* —**un'righteousness** *n.*

unrip (ʌn'rɪp) *vb.* **-rips, -ripping, -ripped.** (*tr.*) **1.** to rip open. **2.** *Obsolete.* to reveal; disclose.

unripe (ʌn'raɪp) *or* **unripened** *adj.* **1.** not fully matured. **2.** not fully prepared or developed; not ready. **3.** *Obsolete.* premature or untimely. —**un'ripeness** *n.*

unrivalled (ʌn'raɪv^{ə}ld) *adj.* having no equal; matchless.

unroll (ʌn'rəʊl) *vb.* **1.** to open out or unwind (something rolled, folded, or coiled) or (of something rolled, etc.) to become opened out or unwound. **2.** to make or become visible or apparent, esp. gradually; unfold.

unroot (ʌn'ruːt) *vb. (tr.) Chiefly U.S.* a less common word for **uproot.**

unrounded (ʌn'raʊndɪd) *adj. Phonetics.* articulated with the lips spread; not rounded.

unruffled (ʌn'rʌf^{ə}ld) *adj.* **1.** unmoved; calm. **2.** still: *the unruffled seas.* —**un'ruffledness** *n.*

unruly (ʌn'ruːlɪ) *adj.* **-lier, -liest.** disposed to disobedience or indiscipline. —**un'ruliness** *n.*

unruly certificate *n.* an informal name for **certificate of unruliness.**

UNRWA ('ʌnrə) *n. acronym for* United Nations Relief and Works Agency.

unsaddle (ʌn'sæd^{ə}l) *vb.* **1.** to remove the saddle from (a horse, mule, etc.). **2.** (*tr.*) to unhorse.

unsaddling enclosure *n.* the area at a racecourse where horses are unsaddled after a race and often where awards are given to owners, trainers, and jockeys.

unsaid (ʌn'sɛd) *adj.* not said or expressed; unspoken.

unsaturated (ʌn'sætʃəˌreɪtɪd) *adj.* **1.** not saturated. **2.** (of a chemical compound, esp. an organic compound) containing one or more double or triple bonds and thus capable of undergoing addition reactions. **3.** (of a fat, esp. a vegetable fat) containing a high proportion of fatty acids having double bonds. **4.** (of a solution) containing less solute than a saturated solution. —ˌ**unsatu'ration** *n.*

unsavoury *or U.S.* **unsavory** (ʌn'seɪvərɪ) *adj.* **1.** objectionable or distasteful: *an unsavoury character.* **2.** disagreeable in odour or taste. —**un'savourily** *or U.S.* **un'savorily** *adv.* —**un'savouriness** *or U.S.* **un'savoriness** *n.*

unsay (ʌn'seɪ) *vb.* **-says, -saying, -said.** (*tr.*) to retract or withdraw (something said or written).

unscathed (ʌn'skeɪðd) *adj.* not harmed or injured.

unschooled (ʌn'skuːld) *adj.* **1.** having received no training or schooling. **2.** spontaneous; natural: *unschooled talent.*

unscientific (ˌʌnsaɪən'tɪfɪk) *adj.* **1.** not consistent with the methods or principles of science, esp. lacking objectivity. **2.** ignorant of science. —ˌ**unscien'tifically** *adv.*

unscramble (ʌn'skræmb^{ə}l) *vb. (tr.)* **1.** to resolve from confusion or disorderliness. **2.** to restore (a scrambled message) to an intelligible form. —**un'scrambler** *n.*

unscratched (ʌn'skrætʃt) *adj.* quite unharmed.

unscreened (ʌn'skriːnd) *adj.* **1.** not sheltered or concealed by a screen. **2.** not passed through a screen; unsifted. **3.** (of a film) not yet on show to the public. **4.** not put through a security check.

unscrew (ʌn'skruː) *vb.* **1.** (*tr.*) to draw or remove a screw from (an object). **2.** (*tr.*) to loosen (a screw, lid, etc.) by rotating continuously, usually in an anticlockwise direction. **3.** (*intr.*) (esp. of an engaged threaded part) to become loosened or separated: *the lid wouldn't unscrew.*

unscripted (ʌn'skrɪptɪd) *adj.* (of a speech, play, etc.) not using or based on a script.

unscrupulous (ʌn'skruːpjʊləs) *adj.* without scruples; unprincipled. —**un'scrupulously** *adv.* —**un'scrupulousness** *or* **unscrupulosity** (ʌnˌskruːpjʊ'lɒsɪtɪ) *n.*

unseal (ʌn'siːl) *vb. (tr.)* **1.** to remove or break the seal of. **2.** to reveal or free (something concealed or closed as if sealed): *to unseal one's lips.* —**un'sealable** *adj.*

unseam (ʌn'siːm) *vb. (tr.)* to open or undo the seam of.

unseasonable (ʌn'siːzənəb^{ə}l) *adj.* **1.** (esp. of the weather) inappropriate for the season. **2.** untimely; inopportune. —**un'seasonableness** *n.* —**un'seasonably** *adv.*

unseasoned (ʌn'siːzənd) *adj.* **1.** (of persons) not sufficiently experienced: *unseasoned troops.* **2.** not matured or seasoned: *unseasoned timber.* **3.** (of food) not flavoured with seasoning. —**un'seasonedness** *n.*

unseat (ʌn'siːt) *vb. (tr.)* **1.** to throw or displace from a seat, saddle, etc. **2.** to depose from office or position.

unsecured (ˌʌnsɪ'kjʊəd) *adj.* **1.** *Finance.* **a.** (of a loan, etc.) secured only against general assets and not against a specific asset. **b.** (of a creditor) having no security against a specific asset and with a claim inferior to those of secure creditors. **2.** not made secure; loose.

un'reasoned *adj.*
ˌ**unre'buked** *adj.*
ˌ**unre'ceptive** *adj.*
ˌ**unre'ciproˌcated** *adj.*
un'reckoned *adj.*
un'recogˌnizable *or* **un'recogˌnisable** *adj.*
un'recogˌnized *or* **un'recogˌnised** *adj.*
ˌ**unrecom'mended** *adj.*
un'recomˌpensed *adj.*
un'reconˌciled *adj.*
ˌ**unre'corded** *adj.*
un'rectiˌfied *adj.*
ˌ**unre'deemed** *adj.*
un'reel *vb.*
ˌ**unre'flecting** *adj.*
ˌ**unre'freshed** *adj.*
un'regiˌmented *adj.*
un'registered *adj.*
un'reguˌlated *adj.*
ˌ**unre'hearsed** *adj.*
ˌ**unre'lated** *adj.*
ˌ**unre'liable** *adj.*
ˌ**unre'lieved** *adj.*
ˌ**unre'markable** *adj.*
un'remedied *adj.*
ˌ**unre'membered** *adj.*
ˌ**unre'mitted** *adj.*
ˌ**unre'morseful** *adj.*
ˌ**unre'munerative** *adj.*
un'rendered *adj.*
ˌ**unre'newed** *adj.*
ˌ**unre'nowned** *adj.*
un'rented *adj.*
ˌ**unre'pealed** *adj.*
ˌ**unre'peatable** *adj.*
ˌ**unre'pentant** *adj.*
ˌ**unre'placeable** *adj.*
ˌ**unre'ported** *adj.*
ˌ**unrepre'sentative** *adj.*
ˌ**unrepre'sented** *adj.*
ˌ**unre'proved** *adj.*
ˌ**unre'quested** *adj.*
ˌ**unre'sentful** *adj.*
ˌ**unre'sistant** *adj.*
ˌ**unre'sisted** *adj.*
ˌ**unre'sisting** *adj.*
ˌ**unre'solved** *adj.*
ˌ**unre'spectful** *adj.*
ˌ**unre'sponsive** *adj.*
un'rested *adj.*
ˌ**unre'stricted** *adj.*
ˌ**unre'turned** *adj.*
ˌ**unre'vealed** *adj.*
ˌ**unre'vealing** *adj.*
ˌ**unre'vised** *adj.*
ˌ**unre'voked** *adj.*
ˌ**unre'warded** *adj.*
ˌ**unre'warding** *adj.*
un'rhymed *adj.*
un'rhythmical *adj.*
un'ridden *adj.*
ˌ**unro'mantic** *adj.*
un'ruled *adj.*
un'safe *adj.*
un'saintly *adj.*
un'salaried *adj.*
un'saleable *adj.*
un'salted *adj.*
un'sanctiˌfied *adj.*
un'sanctioned *adj.*
un'sanitary *adj.*
un'sated *adj.*
ˌ**unsatis'factory** *adj.*
un'satisˌfied *adj.*
un'satisˌfying *adj.*
un'saved *adj.*
un'sayable *adj.*
un'scalable *adj.*
un'scanned *adj.*
un'scarred *adj.*
un'scented *adj.*
un'scheduled *adj.*
un'scholarly *adj.*
un'seaˌworthy *adj.*
ˌ**unse'cluded** *adj.*
un'seconded *adj.*

unseeded (ʌnˈsiːdɪd) *adj.* (of players in various sports) not assigned to a preferential position in the preliminary rounds of a tournament. See **seed** (sense 18).

unseemly (ʌnˈsiːmlɪ) *adj.* **1.** not in good style or taste; unbecoming. **2.** *Obsolete.* unattractive. ~*adv.* **3.** *Rare.* in an unseemly manner. —**unˈseemliness** *n.*

unseen (ʌnˈsiːn) *adj.* **1.** not observed or perceived; invisible. **2.** (of passages of writing) not previously seen or prepared. ~*n.* **3.** *Chiefly Brit.* a passage, not previously seen, that is presented to students for translation.

unselfish (ʌnˈsɛlfɪʃ) *adj.* not selfish or greedy; generous. —**unˈselfishly** *adv.* —**unˈselfishness** *n.*

unset (ʌnˈsɛt) *adj.* **1.** not yet solidified or firm. **2.** (of a gem) not yet in a setting. **3.** (of textual matter) not yet composed.

unsettle (ʌnˈsɛtᵊl) *vb.* **1.** (*usually tr.*) to change or become changed from a fixed or settled condition. **2.** (*tr.*) to confuse or agitate (emotions, the mind, etc.). —**unˈsettlement** *n.*

unsettled (ʌnˈsɛtᵊld) *adj.* **1.** lacking order or stability: *an unsettled era.* **2.** unpredictable; uncertain: *an unsettled climate.* **3.** constantly changing or moving from place to place: *an unsettled life.* **4.** (of controversy, etc.) not brought to an agreed conclusion. **5.** (of debts, law cases, etc.) not disposed of. **6.** (of regions, etc.) devoid of settlers. —**unˈsettledness** *n.*

unsex (ʌnˈsɛks) *vb.* (*tr.*) *Chiefly literary.* to deprive (a person) of the attributes of his or her sex, esp. to make a woman more callous.

unshakable *or* **unshakeable** (ʌnˈʃeɪkəbᵊl) *adj.* (of beliefs, convictions, etc.) utterly firm and unwavering. —**unˈshakableness** *or* **unˈshakeableness** *n.* —**unˈshakably** *or* **unˈshakeably** *adv.*

unshapen (ʌnˈʃeɪpᵊn) *adj.* **1.** having no definite shape; shapeless. **2.** deformed; misshapen.

unsheathe (ʌnˈʃiːð) *vb.* (*tr.*) to draw or pull out (something, esp. a weapon) from a sheath or other covering.

unship (ʌnˈʃɪp) *vb.* **-ships, -shipping, -shipped.** **1.** to be or cause to be unloaded, discharged, or disembarked from a ship. **2.** (*tr.*) *Nautical.* to remove from a regular place: *to unship oars.*

unsighted (ʌnˈsaɪtɪd) *adj.* **1.** not sighted. **2.** not having a clear view. **3. a.** (of a gun) not equipped with a sight. **b.** (of a shot) not aimed by means of a sight. —**unˈsightedly** *adv.*

unsightly (ʌnˈsaɪtlɪ) *adj.* unpleasant or unattractive to look at; ugly. —**unˈsightliness** *n.*

unsized[1] (ʌnˈsaɪzd) *adj.* not made or sorted according to size.

unsized[2] (ʌnˈsaɪzd) *adj.* (of a wall, etc.) not treated with size.

unskilful *or U.S.* **unskillful** (ʌnˈskɪlfʊl) *adj.* **1.** lacking dexterity or proficiency. **2.** (often foll. by *in*) *Obsolete.* ignorant (of). —**unˈskilfully** *or U.S.* **unˈskillfully** *adv.* —**unˈskilfulness** *or U.S.* **unˈskillfulness** *n.*

unskilled (ʌnˈskɪld) *adj.* **1.** not having or requiring any special skill or training: *unskilled workers; an unskilled job.* **2.** having or displaying no skill; inexpert: *he is quite unskilled at dancing.*

unslaked lime (ʌnˈsleɪkt) *n.* another name for **calcium oxide.** Compare **slaked lime.**

unsling (ʌnˈslɪŋ) *vb.* **-slings, -slinging, -slung.** (*tr.*) **1.** to remove or release from a slung position. **2.** to remove slings from.

unsnap (ʌnˈsnæp) *vb.* **-snaps, -snapping, -snapped.** (*tr.*) to unfasten (the snap or catch) of (something).

unsnarl (ʌnˈsnɑːl) *vb.* (*tr.*) to free from a snarl or tangle.

unsociable (ʌnˈsəʊʃəbᵊl) *adj.* **1.** (of a person) disinclined to associate or fraternize with others. **2.** unconducive to social intercourse: *an unsociable neighbourhood.* **3.** *Archaic.* incompatible. —**unˌsociaˈbility** *or* **unˈsociableness** *n.* —**unˈsociably** *adv.*

unsocial (ʌnˈsəʊʃəl) *adj.* **1.** not social; antisocial. **2.** (of the hours of work of certain jobs) falling outside the normal working day.

unsophisticated (ˌʌnsəˈfɪstɪˌkeɪtɪd) *adj.* **1.** lacking experience or worldly wisdom. **2.** marked by a lack of refinement or complexity: *an unsophisticated machine.* **3.** unadulterated or genuine. —ˌ**unsoˈphistiˌcatedly** *adv.* —ˌ**unsoˈphistiˌcatedness** *or* ˌ**unsoˌphistiˈcation** *n.*

unsound (ʌnˈsaʊnd) *adj.* **1.** diseased, weak, or unstable: *of unsound mind.* **2.** unreliable or fallacious: *unsound advice.* **3.** lacking solidity, strength, or firmness: *unsound foundations.* **4.** of doubtful financial or commercial viability: *an unsound enterprise.* **5.** (of fruit, timber, etc.) not in an edible or usable condition. —**unˈsoundly** *adv.* —**unˈsoundness** *n.*

unsparing (ʌnˈspɛərɪŋ) *adj.* **1.** not sparing or frugal; lavish; profuse. **2.** showing harshness or severity; unmerciful. —**unˈsparingly** *adv.* —**unˈsparingness** *n.*

unspeak (ʌnˈspiːk) *vb.* **-speaks, -speaking, -spoke, -spoken.** an obsolete word for **unsay.**

unspeakable (ʌnˈspiːkəbᵊl) *adj.* **1.** incapable of expression in words: *unspeakable ecstasy.* **2.** indescribably bad or evil. **3.** not to be uttered: *unspeakable thoughts.* —**unˈspeakableness** *n.* —**unˈspeakably** *adv.*

unsphere (ʌnˈsfɪə) *vb.* (*tr.*) *Chiefly poetic.* to remove from its, one's, etc., sphere or place.

unspoiled (ʌnˈspɔɪld) *or* **unspoilt** (ʌnˈspɔɪlt) *adj.* (of a village, town, etc.) having an unaltered character.

unspoken (ʌnˈspəʊkən) *adj.* **1.** understood without needing to be spoken; tacit. **2.** not uttered aloud.

unspotted (ʌnˈspɒtɪd) *adj.* **1.** without spots or stains. **2.** (esp. of reputations) free from moral stigma or blemish. —**unˈspottedness** *n.*

unstable (ʌnˈsteɪbᵊl) *adj.* **1.** lacking stability, fixity, or firmness. **2.** disposed to temperamental, emotional, or psychological variability. **3.** (of a chemical compound) readily decomposing. **4.** *Physics.* **a.** (of an elementary particle) having a very short lifetime. **b.** spontaneously decomposing by nuclear decay; radioactive: *an unstable nuclide.* **5.** *Electronics.* (of an electrical circuit, mechanical body, etc.) having a tendency to self-oscillation. —**unˈstableness** *n.* —**unˈstably** *adv.*

unsteady (ʌnˈstɛdɪ) *adj.* **1.** not securely fixed: *an unsteady foothold.* **2.** (of behaviour, etc.) lacking constancy; erratic. **3.** without regularity: *an unsteady rhythm.* **4.** (of a manner of walking, etc.) precarious or staggering, as from intoxication. ~*vb.* **-steadies, -steadying, -steadied.** **5.** (*tr.*) to make unsteady. —**unˈsteadily** *adv.* —**unˈsteadiness** *n.*

unsteel (ʌnˈstiːl) *vb.* (*tr.*) to make (the heart, feelings, etc.) more gentle or compassionate.

unstep (ʌnˈstɛp) *vb.* **-steps, -stepping, -stepped.** (*tr.*) *Nautical.* to remove (a mast) from its step.

unstick (ʌnˈstɪk) *vb.* **-sticks, -sticking, -stuck.** (*tr.*) to free or loosen (something stuck).

unstop (ʌnˈstɒp) *vb.* **-stops, -stopping, -stopped.** (*tr.*) **1.** to remove the stop or stopper from. **2.** to free from any stoppage or obstruction; open. **3.** to draw out the stops on (an organ).

unstoppable (ʌnˈstɒpəbᵊl) *adj.* not capable of being stopped; extremely forceful. —**unˈstoppably** *adv.*

unstopped (ʌnˈstɒpt) *adj.* **1.** not obstructed or stopped up. **2.** *Phonetics.* denoting a speech sound for whose articulation the closure is not complete, as in the pronunciation of a vowel, fricative, or continuant. **3.** *Prosody.* (of verse) having the sense of the line carried over into the next. **4.** (of an organ pipe or a string on a musical instrument) not stopped.

unstrained (ʌnˈstreɪnd) *adj.* **1.** not under strain; relaxed. **2.** not cleared or separated by passing through a strainer.

unstratified (ʌnˈstrætɪˌfaɪd) *adj.* (esp. of igneous rocks and rock formations) not occurring in distinct layers or strata; not stratified.

unstreamed (ʌnˈstriːmd) *adj. Brit. education.* (of children) not divided into groups or streams according to ability.

unstressed (ʌnˈstrɛst) *adj.* **1.** carrying relatively little stress; unemphasized. **2.** *Phonetics.* of, relating to, or denoting the weakest accent in a word or breath group, which in some languages, such as English or German, is also associated with a reduction in vowel quality to a centralized (i) or (a). **3.** *Prosody.* (of a syllable in verse) having no stress or accent.

unstriated (ʌnˈstraɪˌeɪtɪd) *adj.* (of muscle) composed of elongated cells that do not have striations; smooth.

unstring (ʌnˈstrɪŋ) *vb.* **-strings, -stringing, -strung.** (*tr.*) **1.** to remove the strings of. **2.** (of beads, pearls, etc.) to remove or take from a string. **3.** to weaken or enfeeble emotionally (a person or his nerves).

unstriped (ʌnˈstraɪpt) *adj.* (esp. of smooth muscle) not having stripes; unstriated.

unstructured (ʌnˈstrʌktʃəd) *adj.* **1.** without formal structure or systematic organization. **2.** without a preformed shape; (esp. of clothes) loose; untailored.

unstrung (ʌnˈstrʌŋ) *adj.* **1.** emotionally distressed; unnerved. **2.** (of a stringed instrument) with the strings detached.

ˌ**unseˈduced** *adj.*
unˈseeing *adj.*
unˈsegmented *adj.*
unˈsegreˌgated *adj.*
ˌ**unseˈlected** *adj.*
ˌ**unseˈlective** *adj.*
ˌ**unselfˈconscious** *adj.*
ˌ**unsentiˈmental** *adj.*
unˈsepaˌrated *adj.*
unˈserved *adj.*
unˈserviceable *adj.*
unˈshadowed *adj.*
unˈshaken *adj.*
unˈshapely *adj.*
unˈshared *adj.*
unˈshaved *adj.*
unˈshaven *adj.*
unˈshed *adj.*
unˈshelled *adj.*
unˈsheltered *adj.*
unˈshielded *adj.*
unˈshockable *adj.*
unˈshod *adj.*
unˈshrinkable *adj.*
unˈsigned *adj.*
unˈsilenced *adj.*
unˈsinkable *adj.*
unˈsmiling *adj.*
unˈsoiled *adj.*
unˈsold *adj.*
ˌ**unsoˈlicited** *adj.*
unˈsolvable *adj.*
unˈsolved *adj.*
unˈsorted *adj.*
unˈsought *adj.*
unˈsown *adj.*
unˈspecialˌized *or* **unˈspecialˌised** *adj.*
ˌ**unspeˈcific** *adj.*
unˈspeciˌfied *adj.*
ˌ**unspecˈtacular** *adj.*
unˈspiritual *adj.*
unˈsporting *adj.*
unˈsportsmanˌlike *adj.*
unˈstained *adj.*
unˈstamped *adj.*
unˈstandardˌized *or* **unˈstandardˌised** *adj.*
unˈstated *adj.*
unˈstatesmanˌlike *adj.*
unˈstemmed *adj.*
unˈsterile *adj.*
unˈsteriˌlized *or* **unˈsteriˌlised** *adj.*
unˈstinted *adj.*
unˈstrap *vb.*, **-ˈstraps, -ˈstrapping, -ˈstrapped.**

unstuck (ʌn'stʌk) *adj.* **1.** freed from being stuck, glued, fastened, etc. **2. come unstuck.** to suffer failure or disaster.

unstudied (ʌn'stʌdɪd) *adj.* **1.** natural; unaffected. **2.** (foll. by *in*) without knowledge or training.

unsubstantial (ˌʌnsəb'stænʃəl) *adj.* **1.** lacking weight, strength, or firmness. **2.** (esp. of an argument) of doubtful validity. **3.** of no material existence or substance; unreal. —**ˌunsubˌstanti'ality** *n.* —**ˌunsub'stantially** *adv.*

unsung (ʌn'sʌŋ) *adj.* **1.** not acclaimed or honoured; *unsung deeds.* **2.** not yet sung.

unsupportable (ˌʌnsə'pɔːtəbᵊl) *adj.* **1.** not able to be supported. **2.** not able to be defended: *unsupportable actions.*

unsure (ʌn'ʃʊə) *adj.* **1.** lacking assurance or self-confidence. **2.** (*usually postpositive*) without sure knowledge; uncertain: *unsure of her agreement.* **3.** precarious; insecure. **4.** not certain or reliable.

unsuspected (ˌʌnsə'spɛktɪd) *adj.* **1.** not under suspicion. **2.** not known to exist. —**ˌunsus'pectedly** *adv.* —**ˌunsus'pectedness** *n.*

unsuspecting (ˌʌnsə'spɛktɪŋ) *adj.* disposed to trust; not suspicious; trusting. —**ˌunsus'pectingly** *adv.*

unswear (ʌn'swɛə) *vb.* **-swears, -swearing, -swore, -sworn.** to retract or revoke (a sworn oath); abjure.

unswerving (ʌn'swɜːvɪŋ) *adj.* not turning aside; constant.

untangle (ʌn'tæŋgᵊl) *vb.* (*tr.*) **1.** to free from a tangled condition. **2.** to free from perplexity or confusion.

untaught (ʌn'tɔːt) *adj.* **1.** without training or education. **2.** attained or achieved without instruction.

unteach (ʌn'tiːtʃ) *vb.* **-teaches, -teaching, -taught.** (*tr.*) *Rare.* to cause to disbelieve (teaching).

untenable (ʌn'tɛnəbᵊl) *adj.* **1.** (of theories, propositions, etc.) incapable of being maintained, defended, or vindicated. **2.** unable to be maintained against attack. **3.** *Rare.* (of a house, etc.) unfit for occupation. —**unˌtena'bility** *or* **un'tenableness** *n.* —**un'tenably** *adv.*

unthink (ʌn'θɪŋk) *vb.* **-thinks, -thinking, -thought.** (*tr.*) **1.** to reverse one's opinion about. **2.** to dispel from the mind.

unthinkable (ʌn'θɪŋkəbᵊl) *adj.* **1.** not to be contemplated; out of the question. **2.** unimaginable; inconceivable. **3.** unreasonable; improbable. —**unˌthinka'bility** *or* **un'thinkableness** *n.* —**un'thinkably** *adv.*

unthinking (ʌn'θɪŋkɪŋ) *adj.* **1.** lacking thoughtfulness; inconsiderate. **2.** heedless; inadvertent: *it was done in an unthinking moment.* **3.** not thinking or able to think. —**un'thinkingly** *adv.* —**un'thinkingness** *n.*

unthought-of (ˌʌn'θɔːtɒv) *adj.* unimaginable; inconceivable.

unthread (ʌn'θrɛd) *vb.* (*tr.*) **1.** to draw out the thread or threads from (a needle, etc.). **2.** to disentangle.

unthrone (ʌn'θrəʊn) *vb.* (*tr.*) a less common word for **dethrone.**

untidy (ʌn'taɪdɪ) *adj.* **-dier, -diest.** **1.** not neat; slovenly. ~*vb.* **-dies, -dying, -died.** **2.** (*tr.*) to make untidy. —**un'tidily** *adv.* —**un'tidiness** *n.*

untie (ʌn'taɪ) *vb.* **-ties, -tying, -tied.** **1.** to unfasten or free (a knot or something that is tied) or (of a knot or something that is tied) to become unfastened. **2.** (*tr.*) to free from constraint or restriction.

until (ʌn'tɪl) *conj.* (*subordinating*) **1.** up to (a time) that: *he laughed until he cried.* **2.** (*used with a negative*) before (a time or event): *until you change, you can't go out.* ~*prep.* **3.** (often preceded by *up*) in or throughout the period before: *he waited until six.* **4.** (*used with a negative*) earlier than; before: *he won't come until tomorrow.* [C13 *untill;* related to Old High German *unt* unto, until, Old Norse *und;* see TILL[1]]

▷**Usage.** See at **till**[1].

untimely (ʌn'taɪmlɪ) *adj.* **1.** occurring before the expected, normal, or proper time: *an untimely death.* **2.** inappropriate to the occasion, time, or season: *his joking at the funeral was most untimely.* ~*adv.* **3.** prematurely or inopportunely. —**un'timeliness** *n.*

untitled (ʌn'taɪtᵊld) *adj.* **1.** without a title: *an untitled manuscript.* **2.** having no claim or title: *an untitled usurper.*

unto ('ʌntuː) *prep.* an archaic word for **to.** [C13: of Scandinavian origin; see UNTIL]

untogether (ˌʌntə'gɛðə) *adj. Slang.* incompetent or badly organized; mentally or emotionally unstable.

untold (ʌn'təʊld) *adj.* **1.** incapable of description or expression: *untold suffering.* **2.** incalculably great in number or quantity: *untold thousands.* **3.** not told.

untouchable (ʌn'tʌtʃəbᵊl) *adj.* **1.** lying beyond reach. **2.** above reproach, suspicion, or impeachment. **3.** unable to be touched. ~*n.* **4.** a member of the lowest class in India, whom those of the four main castes were formerly forbidden to touch. —**unˌtoucha'bility** *n.*

untouched (ʌn'tʌtʃt) *adj.* **1.** not used, handled, touched, etc. **2.** not injured or harmed. **3.** (*postpositive*) emotionally unmoved. **4.** not changed, modified, or affected. **5.** (of food or drink) left without being consumed. **6.** not mentioned or referred to: *he left the subject untouched.*

untoward (ˌʌntə'wɔːd, ʌn'təʊəd) *adj.* **1.** characterized by misfortune, disaster, or annoyance. **2.** not auspicious; adverse; unfavourable. **3.** unseemly or improper. **4.** out of the ordinary; out of the way. **5.** *Archaic.* refractory; perverse. **6.** *Obsolete.* awkward, ungainly, or uncouth. —**ˌunto'wardly** *adv.* —**ˌunto'wardness** *n.*

untravelled (ʌn'trævᵊld) *adj.* **1.** (of persons) not having travelled widely; narrow or provincial. **2.** (of a road) never travelled over.

untread (ʌn'trɛd) *vb.* **-treads, -treading, -trod, -trodden** *or* **-trod.** (*tr.*) *Rare.* to retrace (a course, path, etc.).

untried (ʌn'traɪd) *adj.* **1.** not tried, attempted, or proved; untested. **2.** not tried by a judge or court.

untrue (ʌn'truː) *adj.* **1.** incorrect or false. **2.** disloyal. **3.** diverging from a rule, standard, or measure; inaccurate. —**un'trueness** *n.* —**un'truly** *adv.*

untruss (ʌn'trʌs) *vb.* **1.** (*tr.*) to release from or as if from a truss; unfasten. **2.** *Obsolete.* to undress.

untruth (ʌn'truːθ) *n.* **1.** the state or quality of being untrue. **2.** a statement, fact, etc., that is not true.

untruthful (ʌn'truːθfʊl) *adj.* **1.** (of a person) given to lying. **2.** diverging from the truth; untrue. —**un'truthfully** *adv.* —**un'truthfulness** *n.*

untuck (ʌn'tʌk) *vb.* to become or cause to become loose or not tucked in: *to untuck the blankets.*

untutored (ʌn'tjuːtəd) *adj.* **1.** without formal instruction or education. **2.** lacking sophistication or refinement.

unused *adj.* **1.** (ʌn'juːzd). not being or never having been made use of. **2.** (ʌn'juːst). (*postpositive;* foll. by *to*) not accustomed or used (to something).

unusual (ʌn'juːʒʊəl) *adj.* out of the ordinary; uncommon; extraordinary: *an unusual design.* —**un'usually** *adv.* —**un'usualness** *n.*

unutterable (ʌn'ʌtərəbᵊl) *adj.* incapable of being expressed in words. —**un'utterableness** *n.* —**un'utterably** *adv.*

unvalued (ʌn'væljuːd) *adj.* **1.** not appreciated or valued. **2.** not assessed or estimated as to price or valuation. **3.** *Obsolete.* of great value.

unvarnished (ʌn'vɑːnɪʃt) *adj.* not elaborated upon or glossed; plain and direct: *the unvarnished truth.*

unveil (ʌn'veɪl) *vb.* **1.** (*tr.*) to remove the cover or shroud from, esp. in the ceremonial unveiling of a monument, etc. **2.** to remove the veil from (one's own or another person's face). **3.** (*tr.*) to make (something secret or concealed) known or public; divulge; reveal.

unveiling (ʌn'veɪlɪŋ) *n.* **1.** a ceremony involving the removal of a veil at the formal presentation of a statue, monument, etc., for the first time. **2.** the presentation of something, esp. for the first time.

unvoice (ʌn'vɔɪs) *vb.* (*tr.*) **1.** to pronounce without vibration of the vocal cords. **2.** another word for **devoice.**

unvoiced (ʌn'vɔɪst) *adj.* **1.** not expressed or spoken. **2.** articulated without vibration of the vocal cords; voiceless.

ˌunsub'dued *adj.*
ˌunsub'missive *adj.*
ˌunsub'stantiˌated *adj.*
un'subtle *adj.*
ˌunsuc'cessful *adj.*
un'suitable *adj.*
un'suited *adj.*
un'sullied *adj.*
un'superˌvised *adj.*
ˌunsup'ported *adj.*
ˌunsup'pressed *adj.*
ˌunsur'mountable *adj.*
ˌunsur'passable *adj.*
ˌunsur'passed *adj.*
ˌunsur'prised *adj.*
ˌunsus'ceptible *adj.*
ˌunsus'tained *adj.*
un'swathe *vb.*
un'swayed *adj.*
un'sweetened *adj.*
ˌunsym'metrical *adj.*
ˌunsympa'thetic *adj.*
ˌunsystem'atic *adj.*
un'tack *vb.*
un'tactful *adj.*
un'tainted *adj.*
un'talented *adj.*
un'tamable *or* **un'tameable** *adj.*
un'tamed *adj.*
un'tapped *adj.*
un'tarnished *adj.*
un'tasted *adj.*
un'taxed *adj.*
un'teachable *adj.*
un'tempered *adj.*
un'tempted *adj.*
un'tenanted *adj.*
un'tended *adj.*
un'tested *adj.*
un'tethered *adj.*
un'thanked *adj.*
un'thankful *adj.*
un'thoughtful *adj.*
un'tillable *adj.*
un'tilled *adj.*
un'tinged *adj.*
un'tiring *adj.*
un'traced *adj.*
un'tracked *adj.*
un'tractable *adj.*
un'trained *adj.*
un'trammelled *adj.*
ˌuntrans'ferable *adj.*
ˌuntrans'formed *adj.*
ˌuntrans'latable *adj.*
ˌuntrans'lated *adj.*
un'treated *adj.*
un'trodden *adj.*
un'troubled *adj.*
un'trustˌworthy *adj.*
un'tuneful *adj.*
un'turned *adj.*
un'twine *vb.*
un'twist *vb.*
un'typical *adj.*
un'usable *adj.*
un'uttered *adj.*
un'vacciˌnated *adj.*
un'vanquished *adj.*
un'varied *adj.*
un'varying *adj.*
un'ventiˌlated *adj.*
un'veriˌfiable *adj.*
un'veriˌfied *adj.*
un'versed *adj.*
un'viable *adj.*
un'visited *adj.*

unwaged (ʌnˈweɪdʒd) *adj.* of, relating to, or denoting a person who is not receiving pay because of either being unemployed or working in the home.
unwarrantable (ʌnˈwɒrəntəbᵊl) *adj.* incapable of vindication or justification. —**unˈwarrantableness** *n.* —**unˈwarrantably** *adv.*
unwarranted (ʌnˈwɒrəntɪd) *adj.* **1.** lacking justification or authorization. **2.** another word for **unwarrantable.**
unwary (ʌnˈwɛərɪ) *adj.* lacking caution or prudence; not vigilant or careful. —**unˈwarily** *adv.* —**unˈwariness** *n.*
unwashed (ʌnˈwɒʃt) *adj.* **1.** not washed. ~*n.* **2. the great unwashed.** *Informal and derogatory.* the masses.
unwatched (ʌnˈwɒtʃt) *adj.* (of an automatic device, such as a beacon) not manned.
unwearied (ʌnˈwɪərɪd) *adj.* **1.** not abating or tiring. **2.** not fatigued; fresh. —**unˈweariedly** *adv.* —**unˈweariedness** *n.*
unweighed (ʌnˈweɪd) *adj.* **1.** (of quantities purchased, etc.) not measured for weight. **2.** (of statements, etc.) not carefully considered.
unwelcome (ʌnˈwɛlkəm) *adj.* **1.** (of persons) not welcome. **2.** causing dissatisfaction or displeasure. —**unˈwelcomely** *adv.* —**unˈwelcomeness** *n.*
unwell (ʌnˈwɛl) *adj.* (*postpositive*) not well; ill.
unwept (ʌnˈwɛpt) *adj.* **1.** not wept for or lamented. **2.** *Rare.* (of tears) not shed.
unwholesome (ʌnˈhəʊlsəm) *adj.* **1.** detrimental to physical or mental health: *an unwholesome climate.* **2.** morally harmful or depraved: *unwholesome practices.* **3.** indicative of illness, esp. in appearance. **4.** (esp. of food) of inferior quality. —**unˈwholesomely** *adv.* —**unˈwholesomeness** *n.*
unwieldy (ʌnˈwiːldɪ) *or* **unwieldly** *adj.* **1.** too heavy, large, or awkwardly shaped to be easily handled. **2.** ungainly; clumsy. —**unˈwieldily** *or* **unˈwieldlily** *adv.* —**unˈwieldiness** *or* **unˈwieldliness** *n.*
unwilled (ʌnˈwɪld) *adj.* not intentional; involuntary.
unwilling (ʌnˈwɪlɪŋ) *adj.* **1.** unfavourably inclined; reluctant. **2.** performed, given, or said with reluctance. —**unˈwillingly** *adv.* —**unˈwillingness** *n.*
unwind (ʌnˈwaɪnd) *vb.* **-winds, -winding, -wound. 1.** to slacken, undo, or unravel or cause to slacken, undo, or unravel. **2.** (*tr.*) to disentangle. **3.** to make or become relaxed: *he finds it hard to unwind after a busy day at work.* —**unˈwindable** *adj.* —**unˈwinder** *n.*
unwinking (ʌnˈwɪŋkɪŋ) *adj.* vigilant; watchful.
unwise (ʌnˈwaɪz) *adj.* lacking wisdom or prudence; foolish. —**unˈwisely** *adv.* —**unˈwiseness** *n.*
unwish (ʌnˈwɪʃ) *vb.* (*tr.*) **1.** to retract or revoke (a wish). **2.** to desire (something) not to be or take place.
unwished (ʌnˈwɪʃt) *adj.* not desired; unwelcome.
unwitnessed (ʌnˈwɪtnɪst) *adj.* **1.** without the signature or attestation of a witness. **2.** not seen or observed.
unwitting (ʌnˈwɪtɪŋ) *adj.* (*usually prenominal*) **1.** not knowing or conscious. **2.** not intentional; inadvertent. [Old English *unwitende,* from UN-[1] + *witting,* present participle of *witan* to know; related to Old High German *wizzan* to know, Old Norse *vita*] —**unˈwittingly** *adv.* —**unˈwittingness** *n.*
unwonted (ʌnˈwəʊntɪd) *adj.* **1.** out of the ordinary; unusual. **2.** (usually foll. by *to*) *Archaic.* unaccustomed; unused. —**unˈwontedly** *adv.* —**unˈwontedness** *n.*
unworldly (ʌnˈwɜːldlɪ) *adj.* **1.** not concerned with material values or pursuits. **2.** lacking sophistication; naive. **3.** not of this earth or world. —**unˈworldliness** *n.*
unworthy (ʌnˈwɜːðɪ) *adj.* **1.** (often foll. by *of*) not deserving or worthy. **2.** (often foll. by *of*) beneath the level considered befitting (to): *that remark is unworthy of you.* **3.** lacking merit or value. **4.** (of treatment) not warranted or deserved. —**unˈworthily** *adv.* —**unˈworthiness** *n.*
unwound (ʌnˈwaʊnd) *vb.* the past tense and past participle of **unwind.**
unwrap (ʌnˈræp) *vb.* **-wraps, -wrapping, -wrapped.** to remove the covering or wrapping from (something) or (of something wrapped) to have the covering come off.
unwritten (ʌnˈrɪtᵊn) *adj.* **1.** not printed or in writing. **2.** effective only through custom; traditional. **3.** without writing upon it.
unwritten law *n.* **1.** the law based upon custom, usage, and judicial decisions, as distinguished from the enactments of a legislature, orders or decrees in writing, etc. **2. the.** the tradition that a person may avenge any insult to family integrity, as used to justify criminal acts of vengeance.
unyoke (ʌnˈjəʊk) *vb.* **1.** to release (an animal, etc.) from a yoke. **2.** (*tr.*) to set free; liberate. **3.** (*tr.*) to disconnect or separate. **4.** (*intr.*) *Archaic.* to cease working.
unzip (ʌnˈzɪp) *vb.* **-zips, -zipping, -zipped.** to unfasten the zip of (a garment) or (of a zip or garment with a zip) to become unfastened: *her skirt unzipped as she sat down.*
up (ʌp) *prep.* **1.** indicating movement from a lower to a higher position: *climbing up a mountain.* **2.** at a higher or further level or position in or on: *soot up the chimney; a shop up the road.* ~*adv.* **3.** (*often particle*) to an upward, higher, or erect position, esp. indicating readiness for an activity: *looking up at the stars; up and doing something.* **4.** (*particle*) indicating intensity or completion of an action: *he tore up the cheque; drink up now!* **5.** to the place referred to or where the speaker is: *the man came up and asked the way.* **6. a.** to a more important place: *up to London.* **b.** to a more northerly place: *up to Scotland.* **c.** (of a member of some British universities) to or at university. **d.** in a particular part of the country: *up north.* **7.** appearing for trial: *up before the magistrate.* **8.** having gained: *ten pounds up on the deal.* **9.** higher in price: *coffee is up again.* **10.** raised (for discussion, etc.): *the plan was up for consideration.* **11.** taught: *well up in physics.* **12.** (*functioning as imperative*) get, stand, etc., up: *up with you!* **13. all up with.** *Informal.* **a.** over; finished. **b.** doomed to die. **14. up with.** (*functioning as imperative*) wanting the beginning or continuation of: *up with the monarchy!* **15. something's up.** *Informal.* something strange is happening. **16. up against. a.** touching. **b.** having to cope with: *look what we're up against now.* **17. up for.** as a candidate or applicant for: *he's up for re-election again.* **18. up to. a.** devising or scheming; occupied with: *she's up to no good.* **b.** dependent or incumbent upon: *the decision is up to you.* **c.** equal to (a challenge, etc.) or capable of (doing, etc.): *are you up to playing in the final?* **d.** aware of: *up to a person's tricks.* **e.** as far as: *up to his waist in mud.* **f.** as many as: *up to two years waiting time.* **g.** comparable with: *not up to your normal standard.* **19. up top.** *Informal.* in the head or mind. **20. up yours.** *Slang.* a vulgar expression of contempt or refusal. **21. what's up?** *Informal.* **a.** what is the matter? **b.** what is happening? ~*adj.* **22.** (*predicative*) of a high or higher position. **23.** (*predicative*) out of bed; awake: *the children aren't up yet.* **24.** (*prenominal*) of or relating to a train or trains to a more important place or one regarded as higher: *the up platform.* ~*vb.* **ups, upping, upped. 25.** (*tr.*) to increase or raise. **26.** (*intr.*; foll. by *and* with a verb) *Informal.* to do (something) suddenly, unexpectedly, etc.: *she upped and married someone else.* ~*n.* **27.** high point; good or pleasant period (esp. in the phrase **ups and downs**). **28.** *Slang.* another word (esp. U.S.) for **upper** (sense 9). **29. on the up and up. a.** trustworthy or honest. **b.** *Brit.* on the upward trend or movement: *our firm's on the up and up.* [Old English *upp;* related to Old Saxon, Old Norse *up,* Old High German *ūf,* Gothic *iup*]
UP *abbrev. for:* **1.** United Press. **2.** Uttar Pradesh (Indian state).
up- *prefix.* up, upper, or upwards: *uproot; upmost; upthrust; upgrade; uplift.*
up-anchor *vb.* (*intr.*) *Nautical.* to weigh anchor.
up-and-coming *adj.* promising continued or future success; enterprising.
up-and-down *adj.* **1.** moving, executed, or formed alternately upwards and downwards. **2.** *Chiefly U.S.* very steep; vertical. ~*adv., prep.* **up and down. 3.** backwards and forwards (along).
up-and-over *adj.* (of a door, etc.) opened by being lifted and moved into a horizontal position.
up-and-under *n. Rugby League.* a high kick forwards followed by a charge to the place where the ball lands.
upas (ˈjuːpəs) *n.* **1.** a large moraceous tree of Java, *Antiaria toxicaria,* having whitish bark and poisonous milky sap. **2.** the sap of this tree, used as an arrow poison. ~Also called: **antiar.** [C19: from Malay: poison]
upbeat (ˈʌpˌbiːt) *n.* **1.** *Music.* **a.** a usually unaccented beat, esp. the last in a bar. **b.** the upward gesture of a conductor's baton indicating this. Compare **downbeat. 2.** an upward trend (in prosperity, etc.). ~*adj.* **3.** *Informal.* marked by cheerfulness or optimism.
up-bow (ˈʌpˌbəʊ) *n.* a stroke of the bow from its tip to its nut on a stringed instrument. Compare **down-bow.**
upbraid (ʌpˈbreɪd) *vb.* (*tr.*) **1.** to reprove or reproach angrily. **2.** to find fault with. [Old English *upbregdan;* related to Danish *bebreide;* see UP, BRAID] —**upˈbraider** *n.* —**upˈbraiding** *n.* —**upˈbraidingly** *adv.*
upbringing (ˈʌpˌbrɪŋɪŋ) *n.* the education of a person during his formative years. Also called: **bringing-up.**
upbuild (ʌpˈbɪld) *vb.* **-builds, -building, -built.** (*tr.*) to build up; enlarge, increase, etc. —**upˈbuilder** *n.*
upcast (ˈʌpˌkɑːst) *n.* **1.** material cast or thrown up. **2.** a ventilation shaft through which air leaves a mine. Compare **downcast** (sense 3). **3.** *Geology.* (in a fault) the section of strata that has been displaced upwards. ~*adj.* **4.** directed or thrown upwards. ~*vb.* **-casts, -casting, -cast. 5.** (*tr.*) to throw or cast up.
upcoming (ˌʌpˈkʌmɪŋ) *adj.* coming soon; forthcoming.
upcountry (ʌpˈkʌntrɪ) *adj.* **1.** of or coming from the interior of a country or region. **2.** *Disparaging.* lacking the sophistication associated with city-dwellers; countrified. ~*n.* **3.** the interior

unˈwanted *adj.*
unˈwarmed *adj.*
unˈwarned *adj.*
unˈwavering *adj.*
unˈweaned *adj.*
unˈweary *adj.*
unˈwearying *adj.*
unˈwedded *or* **unˈwed** *adj.*
unˈweeded *adj.*
unˈwished-for *adj.*
unˈwithered *adj.*
unˈwooded *adj.*
unˈworkable *adj.*
unˈworked *adj.*
unˈworkmanˌlike *adj.*
unˈworn *adj.*
unˈworried *adj.*
unˈwounded *adj.*
unˈyielding *adj.*

part of a region or country. ~*adv.* **4.** towards, in, or into the interior part of a country or region.

update *vb.* (ʌpˈdeɪt). (*tr.*) **1.** to bring up to date. ~*n.* (ˈʌpˌdeɪt). **2.** the act of updating or something that is updated. —**upˈdateable** *adj.* —**upˈdater** *n.*

updraught (ˈʌpˌdrɑːft) *n.* an upward movement of air or other gas.

upend (ʌpˈɛnd) *vb.* **1.** to turn or set or become turned or set on end. **2.** (*tr.*) to affect or upset drastically.

upfront (ˈʌpˈfrʌnt) *adj.* **1.** *Informal.* open, frank, honest. ~*adv., adj.* **2.** (of money) paid out at the beginning of a business arrangement.

upgrade *vb.* (ʌpˈgreɪd). (*tr.*) **1.** to assign or promote (a person or job) to a higher professional rank or position. **2.** to raise in value, importance, esteem, etc. **3.** to improve (a breed of livestock) by crossing with a better strain. ~*n.* (ˈʌpˌgreɪd). **4.** *U.S. and Canadian.* an upward slope. **5. on the upgrade.** improving or progressing, as in importance, status, health, etc. ~*adj.* **6.** *U.S. and Canadian.* going or sloping upwards. ~*adv.* (ˈʌpˈgreɪd). **7.** *U.S. and Canadian.* up an incline, hill, or slope. —**upˈgrader** *n.*

upgrowth (ˈʌpˌgrəʊθ) *n.* **1.** the process of developing or growing upwards. **2.** a result of evolution or growth.

upheaval (ʌpˈhiːvᵊl) *n.* **1.** a strong, sudden, or violent disturbance, as in politics, social conditions, etc. **2.** *Geology.* another word for **uplift** (sense 7).

upheave (ʌpˈhiːv) *vb.* **-heaves, -heaving, -heaved** *or* **-hove. 1.** to heave or rise upwards. **2.** *Geology.* to thrust (land) upwards or (of land) to be thrust upwards. **3.** (*tr.*) to disturb violently; throw into disorder.

upheld (ʌpˈhɛld) *vb.* the past tense and past participle of **uphold.**

uphill (ˈʌpˈhɪl) *adj.* **1.** inclining, sloping, or leading upwards. **2.** requiring arduous and protracted effort: *an uphill task.* **3.** *Rare.* located on or at a high place. ~*adv.* **4.** up an incline or slope; upwards. **5.** against difficulties. ~*n.* **6.** a rising incline; ascent.

uphold (ʌpˈhəʊld) *vb.* **-holds, -holding, -held.** (*tr.*) **1.** to maintain, affirm, or defend against opposition or challenge. **2.** to give moral support or inspiration to. **3.** *Rare.* to support physically. **4.** to lift up. —**upˈholder** *n.*

upholster (ʌpˈhəʊlstə) *vb.* (*tr.*) to fit (chairs, sofas, etc.) with padding, springs, webbing, and covering.

upholsterer (ʌpˈhəʊlstərə) *n.* a person who upholsters furniture as a profession. [C17: from *upholster* small furniture dealer; see UPHOLD, -STER, -ER[1]]

upholstery (ʌpˈhəʊlstərɪ) *n., pl.* **-steries. 1.** the padding, covering, etc., of a piece of furniture. **2.** the business, work, or craft of upholstering.

uphroe (ˈjuːfrəʊ) *n. Nautical.* a variant spelling of **euphroe.**

UPI *abbrev. for* United Press International.

upkeep (ˈʌpˌkiːp) *n.* **1.** the act or process of keeping something in good repair, esp. over a long period; maintenance. **2.** the cost of maintenance.

upland (ˈʌplənd) *n.* **1.** an area of high or relatively high ground. ~*adj.* **2.** relating to or situated in an upland.

upland cotton *n.* **1.** a tropical American cotton plant, *Gossypium hirsutum,* widely cultivated for its fibre. **2.** the fibre of this plant, or the fabric woven from it.

upland plover *or* **sandpiper** *n.* an American sandpiper, *Bartramia longicauda,* with a short slender bill and long tail.

uplift *vb.* (ʌpˈlɪft). (*tr.*) **1.** to raise; elevate; lift up. **2.** to raise morally, spiritually, culturally, etc. **3.** *Scot. and N.Z.* to collect (a passenger, parcel, etc.); pick up. ~*n.* (ˈʌpˌlɪft). **4.** the act, process, or result of lifting up. **5.** the act or process of bettering moral, social or cultural conditions, etc. **6. a.** a brassiere for lifting and supporting the breasts. **b.** (*as modifier*): *an uplift bra.* **7.** the process or result of land being raised to a higher level, as during a period of mountain building. —**upˈlifter** *n.* —**upˈlifting** *adj.*

uplighter (ˈʌpˌlaɪtə) *n.* a lamp or wall light designed or positioned to cast its light upwards.

uplink (ˈʌpˌlɪŋk) *n.* the transmitter on the ground that sends signals up to a communications satellite.

up-market *adj.* relating to commercial products, services, etc., that are relatively expensive and of superior quality.

upmost (ˈʌpˌməʊst) *adj.* another word for **uppermost.**

upon (əˈpɒn) *prep.* **1.** another word for **on. 2.** indicating a position reached by going up: *climb upon my knee.* **3.** imminent for: *the weekend was upon us again.* [C13: from UP + ON]

upper (ˈʌpə) *adj.* **1.** higher or highest in relation to physical position, wealth, rank, status, etc. **2.** (*cap. when part of a name*) lying farther upstream, inland, or farther north: *the upper valley of the Loire.* **3.** (*cap. when part of a name*) *Geology, archaeol.* denoting the late part or division of a period, system, formation, etc.: *Upper Palaeolithic.* **4.** *Maths.* (of a limit or bound) greater than or equal to one or more numbers or variables. ~*n.* **5.** the higher of two objects, people, etc. **6.** the part of a shoe above the sole, covering the upper surface of the foot. **7. on one's uppers.** extremely poor; destitute. **8.** *Informal.* any tooth of the upper jaw. **9.** Also called (esp. U.S.): **up.** *Slang.* any of various drugs having a stimulant or euphoric effect. Compare **downer.**

upper atmosphere *n. Meteorol.* that part of the atmosphere above the troposphere, esp. at heights that cannot be reached by balloon.

upper case *Printing.* ~*n.* **1.** the top half of a compositor's type case in which capital letters, reference marks, and accents are kept. ~*adj.* (**upper-case** *when prenominal*). **2.** of or relating to capital letters kept in this case and used in the setting or production of printed or typed matter. ~*vb.* **upper-case. 3.** (*tr.*) to print with upper-case letters; capitalize.

upper chamber *n.* another name for an **upper house.**

upper class *n.* **1.** the class occupying the highest position in the social hierarchy, esp. the wealthy or the aristocracy. ~*adj.* (**upper-class** *when prenominal*). **2.** of or relating to the upper class. **3.** *U.S. education.* of or relating to the junior or senior classes of a college or high school.

upper crust *n. Informal.* the upper class.

uppercut (ˈʌpəˌkʌt) *n.* **1.** a short swinging upward blow with the fist delivered at an opponent's chin. ~*vb.* **-cuts, -cutting, -cut. 2.** to hit (an opponent) with an uppercut.

upper hand *n.* **the.** the position of control; advantage (esp. in the phrases **have** *or* **get the upper hand**).

upper house *n.* (*often caps.*) one of the two houses of a bicameral legislature. Also called: **upper chamber.** Compare **lower house.**

upper mordent *n.* another name for **inverted mordent.**

uppermost (ˈʌpəˌməʊst) *adj. also* **upmost. 1.** highest in position, power, importance, etc. ~*adv.* **2.** in or into the highest position, etc.

Upper Palaeolithic *n.* **1.** the latest of the three periods of the Palaeolithic, beginning about 40 000 B.C. and ending, in Europe, about 12 000 B.C.: characterized by the emergence of modern man, *Homo sapiens.* ~*adj.* **2.** of or relating to this period.

upper regions *pl. n.* **the.** *Chiefly literary.* the sky; heavens.

upper school *n.* the senior pupils in a secondary school, usually those in the fourth and fifth years and above.

upper works *pl. n. Nautical.* the parts of a vessel above the waterline when fully laden.

uppish (ˈʌpɪʃ) *adj. Brit. informal.* snobbish, arrogant, or presumptuous. [C18: from UP + -ISH] —**ˈuppishly** *adv.* —**ˈuppishness** *n.*

uppity (ˈʌpɪtɪ) *adj. Informal.* **1.** not yielding easily to persuasion or control. **2.** another word for **uppish.** [from UP + fanciful ending, perhaps influenced by -ITY]

upraise (ʌpˈreɪz) *vb.* (*tr.*) **1.** *Chiefly literary.* to lift up; elevate. **2.** *Archaic.* to praise; exalt. —**upˈraiser** *n.*

uprate (ʌpˈreɪt) *vb.* **1.** raise the value, rate, or size of, upgrade. **2.** *Photog.* to increase the effective speed of (a film) by underexposing, usually up to two stops, and subsequently overdeveloping (pushing the processing).

uprear (ʌpˈrɪə) *vb.* (*tr.*) to lift up; raise.

upright (ˈʌpˌraɪt) *adj.* **1.** vertical or erect. **2.** honest, honourable, or just. ~*adv.* **3.** vertically. ~*n.* **4.** a vertical support, such as a stake or post. **5.** short for **upright piano. 6.** the state of being vertical. ~*vb.* **7.** (*tr.*) to make upright. —**ˈupˌrightly** *adv.* —**ˈupˌrightness** *n.*

upright piano *n.* a piano which has a rectangular vertical case. Compare **grand piano.**

uprise *vb.* (ʌpˈraɪz), **-rises, -rising, -rose, -risen. 1.** (*tr.*) to rise up. ~*n.* (ˈʌpˌraɪz). **2.** another word for **rise** (senses 24, 25, 30). —**upˈriser** *n.*

uprising (ˈʌpˌraɪzɪŋ, ʌpˈraɪzɪŋ) *n.* **1.** a revolt or rebellion. **2.** *Archaic.* an ascent.

upriver (ˈʌpˈrɪvə) *adj., adv.* **1.** towards or near the source of a river. ~*n.* **2.** an area located upstream.

uproar (ˈʌpˌrɔː) *n.* a commotion or disturbance characterized by loud noise and confusion; turmoil.

uproarious (ʌpˈrɔːrɪəs) *adj.* **1.** causing or characterized by an uproar; tumultuous. **2.** extremely funny; hilarious. **3.** (of laughter) loud and boisterous. —**upˈroariously** *adv.* —**upˈroariousness** *n.*

uproot (ʌpˈruːt) *vb.* (*tr.*) **1.** to pull up by or as if by the roots. **2.** to displace (a person or persons) from native or habitual surroundings. **3.** to remove or destroy utterly. —**upˈrootedness** *n.* —**upˈrooter** *n.*

uprouse (ʌpˈraʊz) *vb.* (*tr.*) *Rare.* to rouse or stir up; arouse.

uprush (ˈʌpˌrʌʃ) *n.* an upward rush, as of consciousness.

upsadaisy (ˈʌpsəˈdeɪzɪ) *interj.* a variant of **upsy-daisy.**

ups and downs *pl. n.* alternating periods of good and bad fortune, high and low spirits, etc.

upscale (ˈʌpˈskeɪl) *adj. Informal.* of or for the upper end of an economic or social scale; up-market.

upset *vb.* (ʌpˈsɛt), **-sets, -setting, -set.** (*mainly tr.*) **1.** (*also intr.*) to tip or be tipped over; overturn, capsize, or spill. **2.** to disturb the normal state, course, or stability of : *to upset the balance of nature.* **3.** to disturb mentally or emotionally. **4.** to defeat or overthrow, usually unexpectedly. **5.** to make physically ill: *seafood always upsets my stomach.* **6.** to thicken or spread (the end of a bar, rivet, etc.) by forging, hammering, or swagging. ~*n.* (ˈʌpˌsɛt). **7.** an unexpected defeat or reversal, as in a contest or plans. **8.** a disturbance or disorder of the emotions, body, etc. **9.** a tool used to upset a bar or rivet; swage. **10.** a forging or bar that has been upset in preparation for further processing. ~*adj.* (ʌpˈsɛt). **11.** overturned or capsized. **12.** emotionally or physically disturbed or distressed. **13.** disordered; confused. **14.** defeated or overthrown. [C14 (in the sense: to set up, erect; C19 in the sense: to overthrow); related to

Middle High German *ūfsetzen* to put on, Middle Dutch *opzetten*] —**up'settable** *adj.* —**up'setter** *n.* —**up'setting** *adj.* —**up'settingly** *adv.*

upset price ('ʌpˌsɛt) *n.* another name (esp. Scot., U.S., and Canadian) for **reserve price.**

upsetting (ʌp'sɛtɪŋ) *n. Metallurgy.* the process of hammering the end of a heated bar of metal so that its width is increased locally, as in the manufacture of bolts.

upshot ('ʌpˌʃɒt) *n.* **1.** the final result; conclusion; outcome. **2.** *Archery.* the final shot in a match. [C16: from UP + SHOT[1]]

upside ('ʌpˌsaɪd) *n.* the upper surface or part.

upside down *adj.* **1.** (*usually postpositive;* **upside-down** *when prenominal*) turned over completely; inverted. **2.** *Informal.* confused; topsy-turvy: *an upside-down world.* ~*adv.* **3.** in an inverted fashion. **4.** in a chaotic or crazy manner. [C16: variant, by folk etymology, of earlier *upsodown*] —ˌ**upside-'downness** *n.*

upside-down cake *n.* a sponge cake baked with sliced fruit at the bottom, then inverted before serving.

upsides ('ʌpˌsaɪdz) *adv. Informal, chiefly Brit.* (foll. by *with*) equal or level (with), as through revenge or retaliation.

upsilon ('ʌpsɪˌlɒn, juːp'saɪlən) *n.* the 20th letter in the Greek alphabet (Υ or υ) a vowel, transliterated as *y* or *u.* [C17: from Medieval Greek *u psilon* simple *u,* name adopted for graphic *u* to avoid confusion with graphic *oi,* since pronunciation was the same for both in Late Greek]

upspring *Archaic or literary.* ~*vb.* (ʌp'sprɪŋ). **-springs, -springing, -sprang** *or* **-sprung, -sprung. 1.** (*intr.*) to spring up or come into existence. ~*n.* ('ʌpˌsprɪŋ). **2.** a leap forwards or upwards. **3.** the act of coming into existence.

upstage ('ʌp'steɪdʒ) *adv.* **1.** on, at, or to the rear of the stage. ~*adj.* **2.** of or relating to the back half of the stage. **3.** *Informal.* haughty; supercilious; aloof. ~*vb.* (*tr.*) **4.** to move upstage of (another actor), thus forcing him to turn away from the audience. **5.** *Informal.* to draw attention to oneself from (someone else); steal the show from (someone). **6.** *Informal.* to treat haughtily. ~*n.* **7.** the back half of the stage.

upstairs ('ʌp'stɛəz) *adv.* **1.** up the stairs; to or on an upper floor or level. **2.** *Informal.* to or into a higher rank or office. **3.** *Informal.* in the mind: *a little weak upstairs.* **4. kick upstairs.** *Informal.* to promote to a higher rank or position, esp. one that carries less power. ~*n.* (*functioning as sing. or pl.*) **5. a.** an upper floor or level. **b.** (*as modifier*): *an upstairs room.* **6.** *Brit. informal.* the masters of a household collectively, esp. of a large house. Compare **downstairs** (sense 3).

upstanding (ʌp'stændɪŋ) *adj.* **1.** of good character. **2.** upright and vigorous in build. **3. be upstanding. a.** (in a court of law) a direction to all persons present to rise to their feet before the judge enters or leaves the court. **b.** (at a formal dinner) a direction to all persons present to rise to their feet for a toast. —**up'standingness** *n.*

upstart *n.* ('ʌpˌstɑːt). **1. a.** a person, group, etc., that has risen suddenly to a position of power or wealth. **b.** (*as modifier*): *an upstart tyrant; an upstart family.* **2. a.** an arrogant or presumptuous person. **b.** (*as modifier*): *his upstart ambition.* ~*vb.* (ʌp'stɑːt). **3.** (*intr.*) *Archaic.* to start up, as in surprise, etc.

upstate ('ʌp'steɪt) *U.S.* ~*adj., adv.* **1.** towards, in, from, or relating to the outlying or northern sections of a state, esp. of New York State. ~*n.* **2.** the outlying, esp. northern, sections of a state. —**'up'stater** *n.*

upstream ('ʌp'striːm) *adv., adj.* **1.** in or towards the higher part of a stream; against the current. **2.** (in the oil industry) of or for any of the stages prior to oil production, such as exploration or research. Compare **downstream** (sense 2).

upstretched (ʌp'strɛtʃt) *adj.* (esp. of the arms) stretched or raised up.

upstroke ('ʌpˌstrəʊk) *n.* **1. a.** an upward stroke or movement, as of a pen or brush. **b.** the mark produced by such a stroke. **2.** the upward movement of a piston in a reciprocating engine.

upsurge *vb.* (ʌp'sɜːdʒ). **1.** (*intr.*) *Chiefly literary.* to surge up. ~*n.* ('ʌpˌsɜːdʒ). **2.** a rapid rise or swell.

upsweep *n.* ('ʌpˌswiːp). **1.** a curve or sweep upwards. **2.** *U.S. and Canadian.* an upswept hairstyle. ~*vb.* (ʌp'swiːp), **-sweeps, -sweeping, -swept. 3.** to sweep, curve, or brush or be swept, curved, or brushed upwards.

upswell (ʌp'swɛl) *vb.* **-swells, -swelling, -swelled, -swelled** *or* **-swollen.** *Rare.* to swell up or cause to swell up.

upswing *n.* ('ʌpˌswɪŋ). **1.** *Economics.* a recovery period in the trade cycle. **2.** an upward swing or movement or any increase or improvement. ~*vb.* (ʌp'swɪŋ), **-swings, -swinging, -swung. 3.** (*intr.*) to swing or move up.

upsy-daisy ('ʌpsɪ'deɪzɪ) *or* **upsadaisy** *interj.* an expression, usually of reassurance, uttered as when someone, esp. a child, stumbles or is being lifted up. [C18 *up-a-daisy,* irregularly formed from UP (adv.)]

uptake ('ʌpˌteɪk) *n.* **1.** a pipe, shaft, etc., that is used to convey smoke or gases, esp. one that connects a furnace to a chimney. **2.** *Mining.* another term for **upcast** (sense 2). **3.** taking up or lifting up. **4.** the act of accepting or taking up something on offer or available. **5. quick** (*or* **slow**) **on the uptake.** *Informal.* quick (or slow) to understand or learn.

upthrow ('ʌpˌθrəʊ). *n.* **1.** *Geology.* the upward movement of rocks on one side of a fault plane relative to rocks on the other side. **2.** *Rare.* an upward thrust or throw; upheaval.

upthrust ('ʌpˌθrʌst) *n.* **1.** an upward push or thrust. **2.** *Geology.* a violent upheaval of the earth's surface.

uptight (ʌp'taɪt) *adj. Informal.* **1.** displaying tense repressed nervousness, irritability, or anger. **2.** unable to give expression to one's feelings, personality, etc.

uptilt (ʌp'tɪlt) *vb.* (*tr.*) to tilt up.

uptime ('ʌpˌtaɪm) *n. Commerce.* time during which a machine, such as a computer, actually operates.

up-to-date *adj.* **a.** modern, current, or fashionable: *an up-to-date magazine.* **b.** (*predicative*): *the magazine is up to date.* —**'up-to-'dately** *adv.* —**'up-to-'dateness** *n.*

uptown ('ʌp'taʊn) *U.S. and Canadian.* ~*adj., adv.* **1.** towards, in, or relating to some part of a town that is away from the centre. ~*n.* **2.** such a part of a town, esp. a residential part. —**'up'towner** *n.*

upturn *vb.* (ʌp'tɜːn). **1.** to turn or cause to turn up, over, or upside down. **2.** (*tr.*) to create disorder. **3.** (*tr.*) to direct upwards. ~*n.* ('ʌpˌtɜːn). **4.** an upward turn, trend, or improvement. **5.** an upheaval or commotion.

UPU *abbrev. for* Universal Postal Union.

upward ('ʌpwəd) *adj.* **1.** directed or moving towards a higher point or level. ~*adv.* **2.** a variant of **upwards.** —**'upwardly** *adv.* —**'upwardness** *n.*

upwardly mobile *adj.* (of a person or social group) moving or aspiring to move to a higher social class or to a position of increased status or power.

upward mobility *n. Sociol.* the movement of an individual, social group, or class to a position of increased status or power. Compare **downward mobility.** See also **horizontal mobility, vertical mobility.**

upwards ('ʌpwədz) *or* **upward** *adv.* **1.** from a lower to a higher place, level, condition, etc. **2.** towards a higher level, standing, etc.

upwind ('ʌp'wɪnd) *adv.* **1.** into or against the wind. **2.** towards or on the side where the wind is blowing; windward. ~*adj.* **3.** going against the wind: *the upwind leg of the course.* **4.** on the windward side: *the upwind side of the house has weathered.*

ur- *combining form.* a variant of **uro-**[1] and **uro-**[2] before a vowel.

Ur- *combining form.* original, primitive: *Ursprache.* [German]

uracil ('jʊərəsɪl) *n. Biochem.* a pyrimidine present in all living cells, usually in a combined form, as in RNA. Formula: $C_4H_4N_2O_2$. [C20: from URO-[1] + ACETIC + -ILE]

uraemia *or U.S.* **uremia** (jʊ'riːmɪə) *n. Pathol.* the accumulation of waste products, normally excreted in the urine, in the blood: causes severe headaches, vomiting, etc. Also called: **azotaemia.** [C19: from New Latin, from Greek *ouron* urine + *haima* blood] —**u'raemic** *or U.S.* **u'remic** *adj.*

uraeus (jʊ'riːəs) *n., pl.* **-uses.** the sacred serpent represented on the headdresses of ancient Egyptian kings and gods. [C19: from New Latin, from Greek *ouraios,* from Egyptian *uro* asp]

Ural-Altaic *n.* **1.** a postulated group of related languages consisting of the Uralic and Altaic families of languages. ~*adj.* **2.** of or relating to this group of languages, characterized by agglutination and vowel harmony.

Uralic (jʊ'rælɪk) *or* **Uralian** (jʊ'reɪlɪən) *n.* **1.** a superfamily of languages consisting of the Finno-Ugric family together with Samoyed. See also **Ural-Altaic.** ~*adj.* **2.** of or relating to these languages.

uralite ('jʊərəˌlaɪt) *n.* an amphibole mineral, similar to hornblende, that replaces pyroxene in some igneous and metamorphic rocks. [C19: from the *Ural* Mountains, bordering Europe and Asia, where it was first found + -ITE[1]] —**uralitic** (ˌjʊərə'lɪtɪk) *adj.*

uranalysis (ˌjʊərə'nælɪsɪs) *n., pl.* **-ses** (-ˌsiːz). *Med.* a variant spelling of **urinalysis.**

Uranian (jʊ'reɪnɪən) *adj.* **1.** of, occurring on, or relating to the planet Uranus. **2.** of the heavens; celestial. **3.** relating to astronomy; astronomical.

uranic[1] (jʊ'rænɪk) *adj.* of or containing uranium, esp. in a high valence state.

uranic[2] (jʊ'rænɪk) *adj. Obsolete.* astronomical or celestial. [C19: from Greek *ouranos* heaven]

uranide ('jʊərəˌnaɪd) *n.* any element having an atomic number greater than that of protactinium.

uraninite (jʊ'rænɪˌnaɪt) *n.* a blackish heavy radioactive mineral consisting of uranium oxide in cubic crystalline form together with radium, lead, helium, etc.: occurs in coarse granite. Formula: UO_2. [C19: see URANIUM, -IN, -ITE[1]]

uranism ('jʊərænɪzəm) *n.* a rare word for **homosexuality** (esp. male homosexuality). [C20: from German *Uranismus,* from Greek *ouranios* heavenly, i.e. spiritual]

uranite ('jʊərəˌnaɪt) *n.* any of various minerals containing uranium, esp. torbernite or autunite. —**uranitic** (ˌjʊərə'nɪtɪk) *adj.*

uranium (jʊ'reɪnɪəm) *n.* a radioactive silvery-white metallic element of the actinide series. It occurs in several minerals including pitchblende, carnotite, and autunite and is used chiefly as a source of nuclear energy by fission of the radioisotope **uranium-235.** Symbol: U; atomic no.: 92; atomic wt.: 238.03; half-life of most stable isotope, ^{238}U: 4.51×10^9 years; valency: 2-6; relative density: 18.95 (approx.); melting pt.: 1132°C; boiling pt.:

3818°C. [C18: from New Latin, from URANUS; from the fact that the element was discovered soon after the planet]
uranium series *n. Physics.* a radioactive series that starts with uranium-238 and proceeds by radioactive decay to lead-206.
urano- *combining form.* denoting the heavens: *uranography.* [from Greek *ouranos*]
uranography (ˌjʊərəˈnɒgrəfɪ) *n.* the branch of astronomy concerned with the description and mapping of the stars, galaxies, etc. —ˌ**uraˈnographer** *or* ˌ**uraˈnographist** *n.* —**uranographic** (ˌjʊərənəˈgræfɪk) *or* ˌ**uranoˈgraphical** *adj.*
uranous (ˈjʊərənəs) *adj.* of or containing uranium, esp. in a low valence state.
Uranus (jʊˈreɪnəs, ˈjʊrənəs) *n.* one of the giant planets, the seventh planet from the sun, sometimes visible to the naked eye. It has about 15 satellites, a ring system, and an axis of rotation almost lying in the plane of the orbit. Mean distance from sun: 2870 million km; period of revolution around sun: 84 years; period of axial rotation: 10.8 hours; diameter and mass: 3.7 and 14.5 times that of earth respectively. [C19: from Latin *Ūranus,* from Greek *Ouranos* heaven]
uranyl (ˈjʊərənɪl) *n.* (*modifier*) of, consisting of, or containing the divalent ion UO_2^{2+} or the group $-UO_2$. [C19: from URANIUM + -YL] —ˌ**uraˈnylic** *adj.*
urate (ˈjʊəreɪt) *n.* any salt or ester of uric acid. —**uratic** (jʊˈrætɪk) *adj.*
urban (ˈɜːbᵊn) *adj.* **1.** of, relating to, or constituting a city or town. **2.** living in a city or town. ~Compare **rural.** [C17: from Latin *urbānus,* from *urbs* city]
urban area *n.* (in population censuses) a city area considered as the inner city plus built-up environs, irrespective of local body administrative boundaries.
urban blues *n.* (*sometimes functioning as sing.*) an extrovert and rhythmic style of blues, usually accompanied by a band. Compare **country blues.**
urban district *n.* **1.** (in England and Wales from 1888 to 1974 and Northern Ireland from 1898 to 1973) an urban division of an administrative county with an elected council in charge of housing and environmental services: usually made up of one or more thickly populated areas but lacking a borough charter. **2.** (in the Republic of Ireland) any of 49 medium-sized towns with their own elected councils.
urbane (ɜːˈbeɪn) *adj.* characterized by elegance or sophistication. [C16: from Latin *urbānus* belonging to the town; see URBAN] —**urˈbanely** *adv.* —**urˈbaneness** *n.*
urban guerrilla *n.* a guerrilla who operates in a town or city, engaging in terrorism, kidnapping, etc.
urbanism (ˈɜːbəˌnɪzəm) *n. Chiefly U.S.* **1. a.** the character of city life. **b.** the study of this. **2.** a less common term for **urbanization.**
urbanite (ˈɜːbəˌnaɪt) *n.* a resident of an urban community; city dweller.
urbanity (ɜːˈbænɪtɪ) *n., pl.* **-ties. 1.** the quality of being urbane. **2.** (*usually pl.*) civilities or courtesies.
urbanize *or* **urbanise** (ˈɜːbəˌnaɪz) *vb.* (*tr.*) **1.** (*usually passive*) **a.** to make (esp. a predominantly rural area or country) more industrialized and urban. **b.** to cause the migration of an increasing proportion of (rural dwellers) into cities. **2.** *Rare.* to make urbane. —ˌ**urbaniˈzation** *or* ˌ**urbaniˈsation** *n.*
urban legend *n.* a story, esp. one with a shocking or amusing ending, related as having actually happened, usu. to someone vaguely connected with the teller.
urban renewal *n.* the process of redeveloping dilapidated or no longer functional urban areas.
urbi et orbi *Latin.* (ˈɜːbɪ ɛt ˈɔːbɪ) *adv. R.C. Church.* to the city and the world: a phrase qualifying the solemn papal blessing.
URC *abbrev. for* United Reformed Church.
urceolate (ˈɜːsɪəlɪt, -ˌleɪt) *adj. Biology.* shaped like an urn or pitcher: *an urceolate corolla.* [C18: via New Latin *urceolātus,* from Latin *urceolus* diminutive of *urceus* a pitcher]
urchin (ˈɜːtʃɪn) *n.* **1.** a mischievous roguish child, esp. one who is young, small, or raggedly dressed. **2.** See **sea urchin, heart urchin. 3.** an archaic or dialect name for a **hedgehog. 4.** either of the two cylinders in a carding machine that are covered with carding cloth. **5.** *Obsolete.* an elf or sprite. [C13: *urchon,* from Old French *heriçon,* from Latin *ēricius* hedgehog, from *ēr,* related to Greek *khēr* hedgehog]
urd (ɜːd) *n.* another name for **black gram** (see **gram**² (sense 1)). [Hindi]
urdé *or* **urdée** (ˈɜːdeɪ, -diː, -dɪ) *adj. Heraldry.* having points; pointed. [C16 *urdee:* probably a misreading and misunderstanding of French *vidée* in the phrase *croix aiquissée et vidée* cross sharply pointed and reduced]
Urdu (ˈʊəduː, ˈɜː-) *n.* an official language of Pakistan, also spoken in India. The script derives primarily from Persia. It belongs to the Indic branch of the Indo-European family of languages, being closely related to Hindi but containing many Arabic and Persian loan words. [C18: from Hindustani (*zabāni*) *urdū* (language of the) camp, from Persian *urdū* camp, from Turkish *ordū*]
-ure *suffix forming nouns.* **1.** indicating act, process, or result: *seizure.* **2.** indicating function or office: *legislature; prefecture.* [from French, from Latin *-ūra*]
urea (ˈjʊərɪə) *n.* a white water-soluble crystalline compound with a saline taste and often an odour of ammonia, produced by protein metabolism and excreted in urine. A synthetic form is used as a fertilizer, animal feed, and in the manufacture of synthetic resins. Formula: $CO(NH_2)_2$. Also called: **carbamide.** [C19: from New Latin, from French *urée,* from Greek *ouron* URINE] —**uˈreal** *or* **uˈreic** *adj.*
urea cycle *n.* the sequence of metabolic reactions leading in vertebrates to the synthesis of urea.
urea-formaldehyde resin *n.* any one of a class of rigid odourless synthetic materials that are made from urea and formaldehyde and are used in electrical fittings, adhesives, laminates, and finishes for textiles.
urease (ˈjʊərɪˌeɪs, -ˌeɪz) *n.* an enzyme occurring in many plants, esp. fungi, that converts urea to ammonium carbonate.
uredium (jʊˈriːdɪəm) *or* **uredinium** (ˌjʊərɪˈdɪnɪəm) *n., pl.* **-dia** (-dɪə) *or* **-dinia** (-ˈdɪnɪə). a spore-producing body of some rust fungi in which uredospores are formed. Also called: **uredosorus.** [C20: from New Latin, from UREDO] —**uˈredial** *adj.*
uredo (jʊˈriːdəʊ) *n., pl.* **uredines** (jʊˈriːdɪˌniːz). a less common name for **urticaria.** [C18: from Latin: burning itch, from *ūrere* to burn]
uredosorus (jʊˌriːdəʊˈsɔːrəs) *n., pl.* **-sori** (-ˈsɔːraɪ). another word for **uredium.** [from UREDO + SORUS]
uredospore (jʊˈriːdəʊˌspɔː) *n.* any of the brownish spores that are produced in each uredium of the rust fungi and spread the infection between hosts.
ureide (ˈjʊərɪˌaɪd) *n. Chem.* **1.** any of a class of organic compounds derived from urea by replacing one or more of its hydrogen atoms by organic groups. **2.** any of a class of derivatives of urea and carboxylic acids, in which one or more of the hydrogen atoms have been replaced by acyl groups: includes the cyclic ureides, such as alloxan.
uremia (jʊˈriːmɪə) *n.* the usual U.S. spelling of **uraemia.** —**uˈremic** *adj.*
-uret *suffix.* formerly used to form the names of binary chemical compounds. [from New Latin *-uretum*]
ureter (jʊˈriːtə) *n.* the tube that conveys urine from the kidney to the urinary bladder or cloaca. [C16: via New Latin from Greek *ourētēr,* from *ourein* to URINATE] —**uˈreteral** *or* **ureteric** (ˌjʊərɪˈtɛrɪk) *adj.*
urethane (ˈjʊərɪˌθeɪn) *or* **urethan** (ˈjʊərɪˌθæn) *n.* **1.** short for **polyurethane. 2.** another name for **ethyl carbamate.** [C19: from URO-¹ + ETHYL + -ANE]
urethra (jʊˈriːθrə) *n., pl.* **-thrae** (-θriː) *or* **-thras.** the canal that in most mammals conveys urine from the bladder out of the body. In human males it also conveys semen. [C17: via Late Latin from Greek *ourēthra,* from *ourein* to URINATE] —**uˈrethral** *adj.*
urethritis (ˌjʊərɪˈθraɪtɪs) *n.* inflammation of the urethra. [C19: from New Latin, from Late Latin URETHRA] —**urethritic** (ˌjʊərɪˈθrɪtɪk) *adj.*
urethroscope (jʊˈriːθrəˌskəʊp) *n.* a medical instrument for examining the urethra. [C20: see URETHRA, -SCOPE] —**urethroscopic** (jʊˌriːθrəˈskɒpɪk) *adj.* —**urethroscopy** (ˌjʊərɪˈθrɒskəpɪ) *n.*
uretic (jʊˈrɛtɪk) *adj.* of or relating to the urine. [C19: via Late Latin from Greek *ourētikos,* from *ouron* URINE]
urge (ɜːdʒ) *vb.* **1.** (*tr.*) to plead, press, or move (someone to do something): *we urged him to surrender.* **2.** (*tr.; may take a clause as object*) to advocate or recommend earnestly and persistently; plead or insist on: *to urge the need for safety.* **3.** (*tr.*) to impel, drive, or hasten onwards: *he urged the horses on.* **4.** (*tr.*) *Archaic or literary.* to stimulate, excite, or incite. ~*n.* **5.** a strong impulse, inner drive, or yearning. [C16: from Latin *urgēre*]
urgent (ˈɜːdʒənt) *adj.* **1.** requiring or compelling speedy action or attention: *the matter is urgent; an urgent message.* **2.** earnest and persistent. [C15: via French from Latin *urgent-, urgens,* present participle of *urgēre* to URGE] —**urgency** (ˈɜːdʒənsɪ) *n.* —ˈ**urgently** *adv.*
urger (ˈɜːdʒə) *n.* **1.** a person who urges. **2.** *Austral. slang.* a person who is unwilling to take risks, speculate, etc., on his own account, esp. one who encourages others to do so.
-urgy *n. combining form.* indicating technology concerned with a specified material: *metallurgy.* [from Greek *-urgia,* from *ergon* WORK]
-uria *n. combining form.* indicating a diseased or abnormal condition of the urine: *dysuria; pyuria.* [from Greek *-ouria,* from *ouron* urine] —**-uric** *adj. combining form.*
uric (ˈjʊərɪk) *adj.* of, concerning, or derived from urine. [C18: from URO-¹ + -IC]
uric acid *n.* a white odourless tasteless crystalline product of protein metabolism, present in the blood and urine; 2,6,8-trihydroxypurine. Formula: $C_5H_4N_4O_3$.
uridine (ˈjʊərɪˌdiːn) *n. Biochem.* a nucleoside present in all living cells in a combined form, esp. in RNA. [C20: from URO-¹ + -IDE + -INE²]
uridylic acid (ˌjuːrɪˈdɪlɪk) *n.* a nucleotide consisting of uracil, ribose, and a phosphate group. It is a constituent of RNA. Also called: **uridine monophosphate.**
urinal (jʊˈraɪnᵊl, ˈjʊərɪ-) *n.* **1.** a sanitary fitting, esp. one fixed to a wall, used by men for urination. **2.** a room containing urinals. **3.** any vessel for holding urine prior to its disposal.
urinalysis (ˌjʊərɪˈnælɪsɪs) *or* **uranalysis** *n., pl.* **-ses** (-ˌsiːz). *Med.* chemical analysis of the urine to test for the presence of disease.
urinant (ˈjʊərɪnənt) *adj. Heraldry.* having the head downwards. [C17: from Latin *ūrināri* to dive]

urinary ('jʊərɪnərɪ) *adj.* 1. *Anatomy.* of or relating to urine or to the organs and structures that secrete and pass urine. ~*n., pl.* **-naries.** 2. a reservoir for urine. 3. another word for **urinal.**

urinary bladder *n.* a distensible membranous sac in which the urine excreted from the kidneys is stored.

urinate ('jʊərɪˌneɪt) *vb.* (*intr.*) to excrete or void urine; micturate. —ˌ**uri'nation** *n.* —'**urinative** *adj.*

urine ('jʊərɪn) *n.* the pale yellow slightly acid fluid excreted by the kidneys, containing waste products removed from the blood. It is stored in the urinary bladder and discharged through the urethra. [C14: via Old French from Latin *ūrīna;* related to Greek *ouron,* Latin *ūrīnāre* to plunge under water]

uriniferous (ˌjʊərɪ'nɪfərəs) *adj.* conveying urine.

urinogenital (ˌjʊərɪnəʊ'dʒɛnɪtᵊl) *adj.* another word for **urogenital** or **genitourinary.**

urinometer (ˌjʊərɪ'nɒmɪtə) *n. Med.* an instrument for determining the specific gravity of urine.

urinous ('jʊərɪnəs) *or* **urinose** *adj.* of, resembling, or containing urine.

urn (ɜːn) *n.* 1. a vaselike receptacle or vessel, esp. a large bulbous one with a foot. 2. a vase used as a receptacle for the ashes of the dead. 3. a large vessel, usually of metal, with a tap, used for making and holding tea, coffee, etc. 4. *Botany.* the spore-producing capsule of a moss. [C14: from Latin *ūrna;* related to Latin *ūrere* to burn, *urceus* pitcher, Greek *hurkhē* jar] —'**urnˌlike** *adj.*

urnfield ('ɜːnˌfiːld) *n.* 1. a cemetery full of individual cremation urns. ~*adj.* 2. (of a number of Bronze Age cultures) characterized by cremation in urns, which began in E Europe about the second millennium B.C. and by the seventh century B.C. had covered almost all of mainland Europe.

urning ('ɜːnɪŋ) *n.* a rare word for **homosexual** (esp. a male homosexual). [C20: from German, from *Urania* (Aphrodite); compare URANISM]

uro-[1] *or before a vowel* **ur-** *combining form.* indicating urine or the urinary tract: *urochrome; urogenital; urolith; urology.* [from Greek *ouron* urine]

uro-[2] *or before a vowel* **ur-** *combining form.* indicating a tail: *urochord; uropod; urostyle.* [from Greek *oura*]

urobilin (ˌjʊərəʊ'baɪlɪn) *n.* a brownish pigment found in faeces and sometimes in urine. It is formed by oxidation of **urobilinogen,** a colourless substance produced by bacterial degradation of the bile pigment bilirubin in the intestine.

urochord ('jʊərəʊˌkɔːd) *n.* 1. the notochord of a larval tunicate, typically confined to the tail region. ~*n., adj.* 2. Also: **urochordate** (ˌjʊərəʊ'kɔːdeɪt). another word for **tunicate.** [C19: from URO-[2] + *chord,* a variant of CORD] —ˌ**uro'chordal** *adj.*

urochrome ('jʊərəʊˌkrəʊm) *n.* the yellowish pigment that colours urine. [C19: from URO-[1] + -CHROME]

urodele ('jʊərəʊˌdiːl) *n.* 1. any amphibian of the order *Urodela,* having a long body and tail and four short limbs: includes the salamanders and newts. ~*adj.* 2. of, relating to, or belonging to the *Urodela.* [C19: from French *urodèle,* from URO-[2] + *-dèle,* from Greek *dēlos* evident]

urodynamics (ˌjʊərəʊdaɪ'næmɪks) *n.* (*functioning as sing.*) the study and measurement of the flow of urine in the urinary tract.

urogenital (ˌjʊərəʊ'dʒɛnɪtᵊl) *or* **urinogenital** *adj.* of or relating to the urinary and genital organs and their functions. Also: **genitourinary.**

urogenital system *or* **tract** *n. Anatomy.* the urinary tract and reproductive organs.

urogenous (jʊ'rɒdʒɪnəs) *adj.* 1. producing or derived from urine. 2. involved in the secretion and excretion of urine.

urography (ˌjʊər'ɒgrəfɪ) *n.* another name for **pyelography.**

urolith ('jʊərəʊlɪθ) *n. Pathol.* a calculus in the urinary tract. [from URO-[1] + Greek *lithos* stone] —ˌ**uro'lithic** *adj.*

urology (jʊ'rɒlədʒɪ) *n.* the branch of medicine concerned with the study and treatment of diseases of the urogenital tract. —**urologic** (ˌjʊərə'lɒdʒɪk) *or* ˌ**uro'logical** *adj.* —**u'rologist** *n.*

uropod ('jʊərəʊˌpɒd) *n.* the paired appendage that arises from the last segment of the body in lobsters and related crustaceans and forms part of the tail fan. [C19: from URO-[2] + -POD] —**uropodal** (jʊ'rɒpədᵊl) *or* **u'ropodous** *adj.*

uropygial gland *n.* a gland, situated at the base of the tail in most birds, that secretes oil used in preening.

uropygium (ˌjʊərə'pɪdʒɪəm) *n.* the hindmost part of a bird's body, from which the tail feathers grow. [C19: via New Latin from Greek *ouropugion,* from URO-[2] + *pugē* rump] —ˌ**uro'pygial** *adj.*

uroscopy (jʊ'rɒskəpɪ) *n. Med.* examination of the urine. See also **urinalysis.** —**uroscopic** (ˌjʊərə'skɒpɪk) *adj.* —**u'roscopist** *n.*

urostyle ('jʊərəʊˌstaɪl) *n.* the bony rod forming the last segment of the vertebral column of frogs, toads, and related amphibians. [C19: from URO-[2] + Greek *stulos* pillar]

Ursa Major ('ɜːsə 'meɪdʒə) *n., Latin genitive* **Ursae Majoris** ('ɜːsiː mə'dʒɔːrɪs). an extensive conspicuous constellation in the N hemisphere, visible north of latitude 40°. The seven brightest stars form the **Plough.** A line through the two brightest stars points to the Pole Star lying in **Ursa Minor.** Also called: the **Great Bear,** the **Bear.** [Latin: greater bear]

Ursa Minor ('ɜːsə 'maɪnə) *n., Latin genitive* **Ursae Minoris** ('ɜːsiː mɪ'nɔːrɪs). a small faint constellation, the brightest star of which is the Pole Star, lying 1° from the true celestial pole. Also called: the **Little Bear,** the **Bear,** (U.S. and Canadian) the **Little Dipper.** [Latin: lesser bear]

ursine ('ɜːsaɪn) *adj.* of, relating to, or resembling a bear or bears. [C16: from Latin *ursus* a bear]

Ursprache *German.* ('uːrʃpraːxə) *n.* any hypothetical extinct and unrecorded language reconstructed from groups of related recorded languages. For example, Germanic is an Ursprache reconstructed by comparison of English, Dutch, German, the Scandinavian languages, and Gothic; Indo-European is an Ursprache reconstructed by comparison of the Germanic group, Latin, Sanskrit, etc. [from *ur-* primeval, original + *Sprache* language]

Ursuline ('ɜːsjʊˌlaɪn) *n.* a member of an order of nuns devoted to teaching in the Roman Catholic Church: founded in 1537 at Brescia, N Italy. [C16: named after St *Ursula,* patron saint of St Angela Merici, who founded the order]

Urtext *German.* ('uːrtɛkst) *n.* 1. the earliest form of a text as established by linguistic scholars as a basis for variants in later texts still in existence. 2. an edition of a musical score showing the composer's intentions without later editorial interpolation. [from *ur-* original + TEXT]

urticaceous (ˌɜːtɪ'keɪʃəs) *adj.* of, relating to, or belonging to the *Urticaceae,* a family of plants, having small flowers and, in many species, stinging hairs: includes the nettles and pellitory. [C18: via New Latin from Latin *urtīca* nettle, from *ūrere* to burn]

urticaria (ˌɜːtɪ'kɛərɪə) *n.* a skin condition characterized by the formation of itchy red or whitish raised patches, usually caused by an allergy. Nontechnical names: **hives, nettle rash.** [C18: from New Latin, from Latin *urtīca* nettle] —ˌ**urti'carial** *or* ˌ**urti'carious** *adj.*

urticate ('ɜːtɪˌkeɪt) *adj.* 1. Also: **urticant** ('ɜːtɪkənt). characterized by the presence of weals. ~*vb.* 2. to perform urtication. [C19: from Medieval Latin *urtīcāre* to sting, from Latin *urtīca* a nettle]

urtication (ˌɜːtɪ'keɪʃən) *n.* 1. a burning or itching sensation. 2. another name for **urticaria.** 3. a former method of producing counterirritation of the skin by beating the area with nettles.

Uru. *abbrev. for* Uruguay.

Uruguayan (ˌjʊərə'gwaɪən) *adj.* 1. of or relating to Uruguay, a republic in South America, or to its people or culture. ~*n.* 2. a native or inhabitant of Uruguay.

urus ('jʊərəs) *n., pl.* **uruses.** another name for the **aurochs.** [C17: from *ūrus,* of Germanic origin; compare Old High German *ūr,* Old Norse *urr,* Greek *ouros* aurochs]

urushiol ('uːrʊʃɪˌɒl, uː'ruː-) *n.* a poisonous pale yellow liquid occurring in poison ivy and the lacquer tree. [from Japanese *urushi* lacquer + -OL[2]]

us (ʌs) *pron.* (*objective*) 1. refers to the speaker or writer and another person or other people: *don't hurt us; to decide among us.* 2. refers to all people or people in general: *this table shows us the tides.* 3. an informal word for **me:** *give us a kiss!* 4. a formal word for **me** used by editors, monarchs, etc. 5. *Chiefly U.S.* a dialect word for **ourselves** when used as an indirect object: *we ought to get us a car.* [Old English *ūs;* related to Old High German *uns,* Old Norse *oss,* Latin *nōs,* Sanskrit *nas* we]

▷**Usage.** See at **me.**

u.s. *abbrev. for:* 1. ubi supra. 2. ut supra.

U.S. *or* **US** *abbrev. for* United States.

U/S *Informal. abbrev. for:* 1. unserviceable. 2. useless.

USA 1. *abbrev. for* United States Army. ~2. *international car registration for* United States of America.

U.S.A. *or* **USA** *abbrev. for* United States of America.

usable *or* **useable** ('juːzəbᵊl) *adj.* able to be used. —ˌ**usa'bility,** ˌ**usea'bility** *or* '**usableness,** '**useableness** *n.* —'**usably** *or* '**useably** *adv.*

USAF *abbrev. for* United States Air Force.

usage ('juːsɪdʒ, -zɪdʒ) *n.* 1. the act or a manner of using; use; employment. 2. constant use, custom, or habit. 3. something permitted or established by custom or practice. 4. what is actually said in a language, esp. as contrasted with what is prescribed. [C14: via Old French, from Latin *ūsus* USE (n.)]

usance ('juːzəns) *n.* 1. *Commerce.* the period of time permitted by commercial usage for the redemption of foreign bills of exchange. 2. *Rare.* unearned income. 3. an obsolete word for **usage, usury,** or **use.** [C14: from Old French, from Medieval Latin *ūsantia,* from *ūsāre* to USE]

USDAW ('ʌzˌdɔː) *n. acronym for* Union of Shop, Distributive, and Allied Workers.

use *vb.* (juːz). (*tr.*) 1. to put into service or action; employ for a given purpose: *to use a spoon to stir with.* 2. to make a practice or habit of employing; exercise: *he uses his brain.* 3. to behave towards: *to use a friend well.* 4. to behave towards in a particular way for one's own ends: *he uses people.* 5. to consume, expend, or exhaust: *the engine uses very little oil.* 6. *Chiefly U.S. and Canadian.* to partake of (alcoholic drink, drugs, etc.) or smoke (tobacco, marijuana, etc.). ~*n.* (juːs). 7. the act of using or the state of being used: *the carpet wore out through constant use.* 8. the ability, right, or permission to use. 9. the occasion to use; need: *I have no use for this paper.* 10. an instance or manner of using. 11. usefulness; advantage: *it is of no use to complain.* 12. custom; practice; habit: *long use has inured him to it.* 13. the purpose for which something is used; end. 14. *Christianity.* a distinctive form of liturgical or ritual observance, esp. one that is traditional in a Church or group of Churches. **15.** the enjoyment of property, land, etc., by occupation or by deriving revenue or other benefit from it. **16.** *Law.* the beneficial enjoyment of property the legal title to which is held by another person as trustee. **17.** *Law.* an archaic word for **trust** (sense 7). **18.** *Philosophy, logic, linguistics.* the occurrence of an expression in such a context that it performs its own linguistic function rather than being itself referred to. In *"Fido" refers to Fido,* the name *Fido* is used only on the second occurrence, first being mentioned. Compare **mention** (sense 7). See also **material mode.** **19. have no use for. a.** to have no need of. **b.** to have a contemptuous dislike for. **20. make use of. a.** to employ; use. **b.** to exploit (a person). ~See also **used to, use up.** [C13: from Old French *user* to use, from Latin *ūsus* having used, from *ūtī* to use]

used (juːzd) *adj.* bought or sold second-hand: *used cars.*

used to (juːst) *adj.* **1.** made familiar with; accustomed to: *I am used to hitchhiking.* ~*vb.* (*tr.*) **2.** (*takes an infinitive or implied infinitive*) used as an auxiliary to express habitual or accustomed actions, states, etc., taking place in the past but not continuing into the present: *I don't drink these days, but I used to; I used to fish here every day.*

useful (ˈjuːsfʊl) *adj.* **1.** able to be used advantageously, beneficially, or for several purposes; helpful or serviceable. **2.** *Informal.* commendable or capable: *a useful term's work.* ~*n.* **3.** *Austral. informal.* an odd-jobman or general factotum. —**ˈusefully** *adv.* —**ˈusefulness** *n.*

useless (ˈjuːslɪs) *adj.* **1.** having no practical use or advantage. **2.** *Informal.* ineffectual, weak, or stupid: *he's useless at history.* —**ˈuselessly** *adv.* —**ˈuselessness** *n.*

user (ˈjuːzə) *n.* **1.** *Law.* **a.** the continued exercise, use, or enjoyment of a right, esp. in property. **b.** a presumptive right based on long-continued use: *right of user.* **2.** (*often in combination*) a person or thing that uses: *a road-user.* **3.** *Informal.* a drug addict.

user-defined key *n.* a key on the keyboard of a computer that can be used to carry out any of a limited number of predefined actions as selected by the user.

user-friendly *adj.* **1.** easy to use or understand: *a user-friendly dictionary.* **2.** (of a computer system) easily operated and understood by means of a straightforward guide in jargon-free language. —**user-friendliness** *n.*

use up *vb.* (*tr., adv.*) **1.** to finish (a supply); consume completely. **2.** to exhaust; wear out.

usher (ˈʌʃə) *n.* **1.** an official who shows people to their seats, as in a church or theatre. **2.** a person who acts as doorkeeper, esp. in a court of law. **3.** (in England) a minor official charged with maintaining order in a court of law. **4.** an officer responsible for preceding persons of rank in a procession or introducing strangers at formal functions. **5.** *Brit., obsolete.* a teacher. ~*vb.* (*tr.*) **6.** to conduct or escort, esp. in a courteous or obsequious way. **7.** (usually foll. by *in*) to be a precursor or herald (of). [C14: from Old French *huissier* doorkeeper, from Vulgar Latin *ustiārius* (unattested), from Latin *ostium* door]

usherette (ˌʌʃəˈrɛt) *n.* a woman assistant in a cinema, theatre, etc., who shows people to their seats.

USM *abbrev. for:* **1.** *Stock Exchange.* unlisted securities market. **2.** underwater-to-surface missile.

USN *abbrev. for* United States Navy.

USO (in the U.S.) *abbrev. for* United Service Organization.

USP *abbrev. for* unique selling proposition: a characteristic of a product that can be used in advertising to differentiate it from its competitors.

usquebaugh (ˈʌskwɪˌbɔː) *n.* **1.** *Irish.* the former name for **whiskey.** **2.** *Scot.* the former name for **whisky.** **3.** an Irish liqueur flavoured with coriander. [C16: from Irish Gaelic *uisce beathadh* or Scot. Gaelic *uisge beatha* water of life]

USS *abbrev. for:* **1.** United States Senate. **2.** United States Ship.

USSR *abbrev. for* Union of Soviet Socialist Republics.

ustulation (ˌʌstjʊˈleɪʃən) *n.* the act or process of searing or burning. [C17: from Late Latin *ustulāre,* from Latin *ūrere* to burn]

usual (ˈjuːʒʊəl) *adj.* **1.** of the most normal, frequent, or regular type; customary: *that's the usual sort of application to send.* ~*n.* **2.** ordinary or commonplace events (esp. in the phrase **out of the usual**). **3. the usual.** *Informal.* the habitual or usual drink, meal, etc. [C14: from Late Latin *ūsuālis* ordinary, from Latin *ūsus* USE] —**ˈusually** *adv.* —**ˈusualness** *n.*

usufruct (ˈjuːsjʊˌfrʌkt) *n.* the right to use and derive profit from a piece of property belonging to another, provided the property itself remains undiminished and uninjured in any way. [C17: from Late Latin *ūsūfrūctus,* from Latin *ūsus* use + *frūctus* enjoyment] —**ˌusuˈfructuary** *n., adj.*

usurer (ˈjuːʒərə) *n.* **1.** a person who lends funds at an exorbitant rate of interest. **2.** *Obsolete.* a moneylender.

usurp (juːˈzɜːp) *vb.* to seize, take over, or appropriate (land, a throne, etc.) without authority. [C14: from Old French *usurper,* from Latin *ūsūrpāre* to take into use, probably from *ūsus* use + *rapere* to seize] —**ˌusurˈpation** *n.* —**uˈsurpative** *or* **uˈsurpatory** *adj.* —**uˈsurper** *n.*

usury (ˈjuːʒərɪ) *n., pl.* **-ries.** **1.** the act or practice of loaning money at an exorbitant rate of interest. **2.** an exorbitant or unlawfully high amount or rate of interest. **3.** *Obsolete.* moneylending. [C14: from Medieval Latin *ūsūria,* from Latin *ūsūra* usage, from *ūsus* USE] —**usurious** (juːˈʒʊərɪəs) *adj.*

USW *Radio. abbrev. for* ultrashort wave.

ut (ʌt, uːt) *n. Music.* **1.** the syllable used in the fixed system of solmization for the note C. **2.** the first note of a hexachord in medieval music. [C14: from Latin *ut;* see GAMUT]

UT *abbrev. for:* **1.** universal time. **2.** Utah.

UTC *abbrev. for* universal time coordinated. See **universal time.**

ut dict. (in prescriptions) *abbrev. for* as directed. [from Latin *ut dictum*]

ute (juːt) *n. Austral. and N.Z. informal.* short for **utility** (sense 6).

Ute (juːt, ˈjuːtɪ) *n.* **1.** (*pl.* **Utes** *or* **Ute**) a member of a North American Indian people of Utah, Colorado, and New Mexico, related to the Aztecs. **2.** the language of this people, belonging to the Shoshonean subfamily of the Uto-Aztecan family.

utensil (juːˈtɛnsəl) *n.* an implement, tool, or container for practical use: *writing utensils.* [C14 *utensele,* via Old French from Latin *ūtēnsilia* necessaries, from *ūtēnsilis* available for use, from *ūtī* to use]

uterine (ˈjuːtəˌraɪn) *adj.* **1.** of, relating to, or affecting the uterus. **2.** (of offspring) born of the same mother but not the same father: *uterine brothers.*

uterus (ˈjuːtərəs) *n., pl.* **uteri** (ˈjuːtəˌraɪ). **1.** *Anatomy.* a hollow muscular organ lying within the pelvic cavity of female mammals. It houses the developing fetus and by contractions aids in its expulsion at parturition. Nontechnical name: **womb.** **2.** the corresponding organ in other animals. [C17: from Latin; compare Greek *hustera* womb, *hoderos* belly, Sanskrit *udara* belly]

utile (ˈjuːtaɪl, -tɪl) *adj.* an obsolete word for **useful.** [C15: via Old French from Latin *ūtilis,* from *ūtī* to use]

utilitarian (juːˌtɪlɪˈtɛərɪən) *adj.* **1.** of or relating to utilitarianism. **2.** designed for use rather than beauty. ~*n.* **3.** a person who believes in utilitarianism.

utilitarianism (juːˌtɪlɪˈtɛərɪəˌnɪzəm) *n. Ethics.* **1.** the doctrine that the morally correct course of action consists in the greatest good for the greatest number, that is, in maximizing the total benefit resulting, without regard to the distribution of benefits and burdens. **2.** the theory that the criterion of virtue is utility.

utility (juːˈtɪlɪtɪ) *n., pl.* **-ties.** **1. a.** the quality of practical use; usefulness; serviceability. **b.** (*as modifier*): *a utility fabric.* **2.** something useful. **3. a.** a public service, such as the bus system; public utility. **b.** (*as modifier*): *utility vehicle.* **4.** *Economics.* **a.** the ability of a commodity to satisfy human wants. **b.** the amount of such satisfaction. **5.** *Statistics.* **a.** a measure of the total benefit or disadvantage attaching to each of a set of alternative courses of action. **b.** (*as modifier*): *utility function.* ~See also **expected utility, decision theory.** **6.** Also called: **utility truck,** (Informal) **ute.** *Austral. and N.Z.* a small truck with an open body and low sides, often with a removable tarpaulin cover; pick-up. [C14: from Old French *utelite,* from Latin *ūtilitās* usefulness, from *ūtī* to use]

utility function *n. Economics.* a function relating specific goods and services in an economy to individual preferences.

utility man *n. Chiefly U.S.* **1.** a worker who is expected to serve in any of several capacities. **2.** an actor who plays any of numerous small parts.

utility player *n. Sport.* a player who is capable of playing competently in any of several positions.

utility program *n.* computer software designed to do a routine task, such as examining files or copying data from one file to another.

utility room *n.* a room, esp. in a private house, used for storage, laundry, etc.

utility truck *n.* another name for **utility** (sense 6).

utilize *or* **utilise** (ˈjuːtɪˌlaɪz) *vb.* (*tr.*) to make practical or worthwhile use of. —**ˈutiˌlizable** *or* **ˈutiˌlisable** *adj.* —**ˌutiliˈzation** *or* **ˌutiliˈsation** *n.* —**ˈutiˌlizer** *or* **ˈutiˌliser** *n.*

ut infra *Latin.* (ʊt ˈɪnfrɑː) as below.

uti possidetis (ˈjuːtaɪ ˌpɒsɪˈdiːtɪs) *n. International law.* the rule that territory and other property remains in the hands of the belligerent state actually in possession at the end of a war unless otherwise provided for by treaty. [from Latin, literally: as you possess]

utmost (ˈʌtˌməʊst) *or* **uttermost** *adj.* (*prenominal*) **1.** of the greatest possible degree or amount: *the utmost degree.* **2.** at the furthest limit: *the utmost town on the peninsula.* ~*n.* **3.** the greatest possible degree, extent, or amount: *he tried his utmost.* [Old English *ūtemest,* from *ūte* out + *-mest* MOST]

utmost good faith *n.* a principle used in insurance contracts, legally obliging all parties to reveal to the others any information that might influence the others' decision to enter into the contract. Also called: ***uberrima fides.***

Uto-Aztecan (ˈjuːtəʊˈæztɛkən) *n.* **1.** a family of North and Central American Indian languages including Nahuatl, Shoshone, Pima, and Ute. ~*adj.* **2.** of or relating to this family of languages or the peoples speaking them.

Utopia (juːˈtəʊpɪə) *n.* (*sometimes not cap.*) any real or imaginary society, place, state, etc., considered to be perfect or ideal. [C16: from New Latin *Utopia* (coined by the English statesman and humanist Sir Thomas More in 1516 as the title of his book that described an imaginary island representing the perfect society), literally: no place, from Greek *ou* not + *topos* a place]

Utopian (juːˈtəʊpɪən) (*sometimes not cap.*) ~*adj.* **1.** of or relating to a perfect or ideal existence. ~*n.* **2.** an idealistic social reformer. —**Uˈtopianism** *n.*

utopian socialism *n.* (*sometimes caps.*) socialism established by the peaceful surrender of the means of production by capitalists moved by moral persuasion, example, etc. Compare **scientific socialism.**

utricle (ˈjuːtrɪkᵊl) *or* **utriculus** (juːˈtrɪkjʊləs) *n., pl.* **utricles** *or* **utriculi** (juːˈtrɪkjʊˌlaɪ). **1.** *Anatomy.* the larger of the two parts of the membranous labyrinth of the internal ear. Compare **saccule.** **2.** *Botany.* the bladder-like one-seeded indehiscent fruit of certain plants. [C18: from Latin *ūtriculus* diminutive of *ūter* bag] —**uˈtricular** *or* **uˈtriculate** *adj.*

utriculitis (juːˌtrɪkjʊˈlaɪtɪs) *n.* inflammation of the inner ear.

ut supra *Latin.* (ʊt ˈsuːprɑː) as above.

utter[1] (ˈʌtə) *vb.* **1.** to give audible expression to (something): *to utter a growl.* **2.** *Criminal law.* to put into circulation (counterfeit coin, forged banknotes, etc.). **3.** (*tr.*) to make publicly known; publish: *to utter slander.* **4.** *Obsolete.* to give forth, issue, or emit. [C14: probably originally a commercial term, from Middle Dutch *ūteren* (modern Dutch *uiteren*) to make known; related to Middle Low German *ūtern* to sell, show] —**ˈutterable** *adj.* —**ˈutterableness** *n.* —**ˈutterer** *n.* —**ˈutterless** *adj.*

utter[2] (ˈʌtə) *adj.* (*prenominal*) (intensifier): *an utter fool; utter bliss; the utter limit.* [C15: from Old English *utera* outer, comparative of *ūte* OUT (adv.); related to Old High German *ūzaro,* Old Norse *ūtri*]

utterance[1] (ˈʌtərəns) *n.* **1.** something uttered, such as a statement. **2.** the act or power of uttering or the ability to utter. **3.** *Logic, philosophy.* an element of spoken language, esp. a sentence. Compare **inscription** (sense 4).

utterance[2] (ˈʌtərəns) *n. Archaic or literary.* the bitter end (esp. in the phrase **to the utterance**). [C13: from Old French *oultrance,* from *oultrer* to carry to excess, from Latin *ultrā* beyond]

utter barrister *n. Law.* the full title of a barrister who is not a Queen's Counsel. See also **junior** (sense 6).

utterly (ˈʌtəlɪ) *adv.* (intensifier): *I'm utterly miserable.*

uttermost (ˈʌtəˌməʊst) *adj., n.* a variant of **utmost.**

U-turn *n.* **1.** a turn made by a vehicle in the shape of a U, resulting in a reversal of direction. **2.** a complete change in direction of political or other policy.

UU *abbrev. for* Ulster Unionist.

UV *abbrev. for* ultraviolet.

UV-A *or* **UVA** *abbrev. for* ultraviolet radiation with a range of 320–380 nanometres.

uvarovite (uːˈvɑːrəˌvaɪt) *n.* an emerald-green garnet found in chromium deposits: consists of calcium chromium silicate. Formula: $Ca_3Cr_2(SiO_4)_3$. [C19: from German *Uvarovit;* named after Count Sergei S. *Uvarov* (1785–1855), Russian author and statesman]

UV-B *or* **UVB** *abbrev. for* ultraviolet radiation with a range of 280–320 nanometres.

uvea (ˈjuːvɪə) *n.* the part of the eyeball consisting of the iris, ciliary body, and choroid. [C16: from Medieval Latin *ūvea,* from Latin *ūva* grape] —**ˈuveal** *or* **ˈuveous** *adj.*

uveitis (ˌjuːvɪˈaɪtɪs) *n.* inflammation of the uvea. —**uveitic** (ˌjuːvɪˈɪtɪk) *adj.*

UVF *abbrev. for* Ulster Volunteer Force.

uvula (ˈjuːvjʊlə) *n., pl.* **-las** *or* **-lae** (-ˌliː). a small fleshy finger-like flap of tissue that hangs in the back of the throat and is an extension of the soft palate. [C14: from Medieval Latin, literally: a little grape, from Latin *ūva* a grape]

uvular (ˈjuːvjʊlə) *adj.* **1.** of or relating to the uvula. **2.** *Phonetics.* articulated with the uvula and the back of the tongue, such as the (r) sound of Parisian French. ~*n.* **3.** a uvular consonant. —**ˈuvularly** *adv.*

uvulitis (ˌjuːvjʊˈlaɪtɪs) *n.* inflammation of the uvula.

UWIST (ˈjuːˌwɪst) *n. acronym for* University of Wales Institute of Science and Technology.

ux. *abbrev. for* uxor. [Latin: wife]

uxorial (ʌkˈsɔːrɪəl) *adj.* of or relating to a wife: *uxorial influence.* [C19: from Latin *uxor* wife] —**uxˈorially** *adv.*

uxoricide (ʌkˈsɔːrɪˌsaɪd) *n.* **1.** the act of killing one's wife. **2.** a man who kills his wife. [C19: from Latin *uxor* wife + -CIDE] —**uxˌoriˈcidal** *adj.*

uxorious (ʌkˈsɔːrɪəs) *adj.* excessively attached to or dependent on one's wife. [C16: from Latin *uxōrius* concerning a wife, from *uxor* wife] —**uxˈoriously** *adv.* —**uxˈoriousness** *n.*

Uzbek (ˈʊzbɛk, ˈʌz-) *n.* **1.** (*pl.* **-beks** *or* **-bek**) a member of a Mongoloid people of the former Soviet republic of Uzbekistan. **2.** the language of this people, belonging to the Turkic branch of the Altaic family.

v *or* **V** (viː) *n., pl.* **v's, V's,** *or* **Vs. 1.** the 22nd letter and 17th consonant of the modern English alphabet. **2.** a speech sound represented by this letter, in English usually a voiced labiodental fricative, as in *vote.* **3. a.** something shaped like a V. **b.** *(in combination): a V neck.* See also **V-sign.**

v *symbol for:* **1.** *Physics.* velocity. **2.** specific volume (of a gas).

V *symbol for:* **1.** (in transformational grammar) verb. **2.** volume (capacity). **3.** volt. **4.** *Chem.* vanadium. **5.** luminous efficiency. **6.** victory. ~**7.** *the Roman numeral for* five. See **Roman numerals.** ~**8.** *international car registration for* Vatican City.

v. *abbrev. for:* **1.** ventral. **2.** verb. **3.** verse. **4.** version. **5.** verso. **6.** *(usually italic)* versus. **7.** very. **8.** vide [Latin: see] **9.** violin. **10.** vocative. **11.** voice. **12.** volume. **13.** von.

V. *abbrev. for:* **1.** Venerable. **2.** (in titles) Very. **3.** (in titles) Vice. **4.** Viscount.

V-1 *n.* a robot bomb invented by the Germans in World War II: used esp. to bombard London. It was propelled by a pulsejet. Also called: **doodlebug, buzz bomb, flying bomb.** [from German *Vergeltungswaffe* revenge weapon]

V-2 *n.* a rocket-powered ballistic missile invented by the Germans in World War II: used esp. to bombard London. It used ethanol as fuel and liquid oxygen as the oxidizer. [see V-1]

V6 *n.* a car or internal-combustion engine having six cylinders arranged in the form of a V.

V8 *n.* a car or internal-combustion engine having eight cylinders arranged in the form of a V.

VA *abbrev. for:* **1.** (in the U.S.) Veterans' Administration. **2.** Vicar Apostolic. **3.** Vice Admiral. **4.** (Order of) Victoria and Albert. **5.** Virginia. **6.** volt-ampere.

Va. *abbrev. for* Virginia.

v.a. *abbrev. for* verb active.

vac (væk) *n. Brit. informal.* short for **vacation.**

vacancy (ˈveɪkənsɪ) *n., pl.* **-cies. 1.** the state or condition of being vacant or unoccupied; emptiness. **2.** an unoccupied post or office: *we have a vacancy in the accounts department.* **3.** an unoccupied room in a boarding house, hotel, etc.: *put the "No Vacancies" sign in the window.* **4.** lack of thought or intelligent awareness; inanity: *an expression of vacancy on one's face.* **5.** *Physics.* a defect in a crystalline solid caused by the absence of an atom, ion, or molecule from its position in the crystal lattice. **6.** *Obsolete.* idleness or a period spent in idleness.

vacant (ˈveɪkənt) *adj.* **1.** without any contents; empty. **2.** *(postpositive;* foll. by *of)* devoid (of something specified). **3.** having no incumbent; unoccupied: *a vacant post.* **4.** having no tenant or occupant: *a vacant house.* **5.** characterized by or resulting from lack of thought or intelligent awareness: *a vacant stare.* **6.** (of time, etc.) not allocated to any activity: *a vacant hour in one's day.* **7.** spent in idleness or inactivity: *a vacant life.* **8.** *Law.* (of an estate, etc.) having no heir or claimant. [C13: from Latin *vacāre* to be empty] —ˈ**vacantly** *adv.* —ˈ**vacantness** *n.*

vacant possession *n.* ownership of an unoccupied house or property, any previous owner or tenant having departed.

vacate (vəˈkeɪt) *vb. (mainly tr.)* **1.** to cause (something) to be empty, esp. by departing from or abandoning it: *to vacate a room.* **2.** *(also intr.)* to give up the tenure, possession, or occupancy of (a place, post, etc.); leave or quit. **3.** *Law.* **a.** to cancel or rescind. **b.** to make void or of no effect; annul. —**va**ˈ**catable** *adj.*

vacation (vəˈkeɪʃən) *n.* **1.** *Chiefly Brit.* a period of the year when the law courts or universities are closed. **2.** another word (esp. U.S. and Canadian) for **holiday. 3.** the act of departing from or abandoning property, etc. ~*vb.* **4.** *(intr.) U.S. and Canadian.* to take a vacation; holiday. [C14: from Latin *vacātiō* freedom, from *vacāre* to be empty] —**va**ˈ**cationless** *adj.*

vacationist (vəˈkeɪʃənɪst) *or* **vacationer** (vəˈkeɪʃənə) *n.* U.S. and Canadian words for **holiday-maker.**

vaccinal (ˈvæksɪnəl) *adj.* of or relating to vaccine or vaccination.

vaccinate (ˈvæksɪˌneɪt) *vb.* to inoculate (a person) with vaccine so as to produce immunity against a specific disease. —ˈ**vacci**ˌ**nator** *n.*

vaccination (ˌvæksɪˈneɪʃən) *n.* **1.** the act of vaccinating. **2.** the scar left following inoculation with a vaccine.

vaccine (ˈvæksiːn) *n. Med.* **1.** a suspension of dead, attenuated, or otherwise modified microorganisms (viruses, bacteria, or rickettsiae) for inoculation to produce immunity to a disease by stimulating the production of antibodies. **2.** a preparation of the virus of cowpox taken from infected cows and inoculated in humans to produce immunity to smallpox. **3.** *(modifier)* of or relating to vaccination or vaccinia. **4.** *Computer technol.* a piece of software designed to detect and remove computer viruses from a system. [C18: from New Latin *variolae vaccīnae* cowpox, title of medical treatise (1798) by the British physician Edward Jenner (1749–1823), from Latin *vacca* a cow]

vaccinia (vækˈsɪnɪə) *n.* a technical name for **cowpox.** [C19: New Latin, from Latin *vaccīnus* of cows] —**vac**ˈ**cinial** *adj.*

vacherin *French.* (vaʃrɛ̃) *n.* a dessert consisting of a meringue shell filled with whipped cream, ice cream, fruit, etc. [also in France a type of cheese, from French *vache* cow, from Latin *vacca*]

vacillate (ˈvæsɪˌleɪt) *vb. (intr.)* **1.** to fluctuate in one's opinions; be indecisive. **2.** to sway from side to side physically; totter or waver. [C16: from Latin *vacillāre* to sway, of obscure origin] —ˌ**vacil**ˈ**lation** *n.* —ˈ**vacil**ˌ**lator** *n.*

vacillating (ˈvæsɪˌleɪtɪŋ) *or (rarely)* **vacillant** (ˈvæsɪlənt) *adj.* inclined to waver; indecisive. —ˈ**vacil**ˌ**latingly** *adv.*

vacua (ˈvækjʊə) *n.* a plural of **vacuum.**

vacuity (væˈkjuːɪtɪ) *n., pl.* **-ties. 1.** the state or quality of being vacuous; emptiness. **2.** an empty space or void; vacuum. **3.** a lack or absence of something specified: *a vacuity of wind.* **4.** lack of normal intelligence or awareness; vacancy: *his stare gave an impression of complete vacuity.* **5.** something, such as a statement, saying, etc., that is inane or pointless. **6.** (in customs terminology) the difference in volume between the actual contents of a container and its full capacity. [C16: from Latin *vacuitās* empty space, from *vacuus* empty]

vacuole (ˈvækjʊˌəʊl) *n. Biology.* a fluid-filled cavity in the cytoplasm of a cell. [C19: from French, literally: little vacuum, from Latin VACUUM] —**vacuolar** (ˌvækjʊˈəʊlə) *adj.* —**vacuolate** (ˈvækjʊəlɪt, -ˌleɪt) *adj.* —**vacuolation** (ˌvækjʊəˈleɪʃən) *n.*

vacuous (ˈvækjʊəs) *adj.* **1.** containing nothing; empty. **2.** bereft of ideas or intelligence; mindless. **3.** characterized by or resulting from vacancy of mind: *a vacuous gaze.* **4.** indulging in no useful mental or physical activity; idle. **5.** *Logic, maths.* (of an operator or expression) having no import; idle: in *(x) (John is tall)* the quantifier *(x)* is vacuous. [C17: from Latin *vacuus* empty, from *vacāre* to be empty] —ˈ**vacuously** *adv.* —ˈ**vacuousness** *n.*

vacuum (ˈvækjʊəm) *n., pl.* **vacuums** *or* **vacua** (ˈvækjʊə). **1.** a region containing no matter; free space. Compare **plenum** (sense 3). **2.** a region in which gas is present at a low pressure. **3.** the degree of exhaustion of gas within an enclosed space: *a high vacuum; a perfect vacuum.* **4.** a sense or feeling of emptiness: *his death left a vacuum in her life.* **5.** short for **vacuum cleaner. 6.** *(modifier)* of, containing, measuring, producing, or operated by a low gas pressure: *a vacuum tube; a vacuum brake.* ~*vb.* **7.** to clean (something) with a vacuum cleaner: *to vacuum a carpet.* [C16: from Latin: an empty space, from *vacuus* empty]

vacuum activity *n. Ethology.* instinctive behaviour occurring in the absence of the appropriate stimulus.

vacuum brake *n.* a brake system, used on British and many overseas railways, in which the brake is held off by a vacuum on one side of the brake-operating cylinder. If the vacuum is destroyed by controlled leakage of air or a disruptive emergency the brake is applied. It is now largely superseded by the Westinghouse brake system.

vacuum cleaner *n.* an electrical household appliance used for cleaning floors, carpets, furniture, etc., by suction. —**vacuum cleaning** *n.*

vacuum distillation *n.* distillation in which the liquid distilled is enclosed at a low pressure in order to reduce its boiling point.

vacuum flask *n.* an insulating flask that has double walls, usually of silvered glass, with an evacuated space between them. It is used for maintaining substances at high or low temperatures. Also called: **Thermos, Dewar flask.**

vacuum forming *n.* a process in which a sheet of warmed thermoplastic is shaped by placing it in a mould and applying suction.

vacuum gauge *n.* any of a number of instruments for measuring pressures below atmospheric pressure.

vacuum-packed *adj.* packed in an airtight container or packet under low pressure in order to maintain freshness, prevent corrosion, etc.

vacuum pump *n.* a pump for producing a low gas pressure.

vacuum servo *n.* a servomechanism that is operated by the lowering of pressure in the intake duct of an internal-combustion engine.

vacuum tube *or* **valve** *n.* the U.S. and Canadian name for **valve** (sense 3).

VAD 1. *abbrev. for* Voluntary Aid Detachment. ~*n.* **2.** a nurse serving in the Voluntary Aid Detachment.

vade mecum (ˈvɑːdɪ ˈmeɪkʊm) *n.* a handbook or other aid carried on the person for immediate use when needed. [C17: from Latin, literally: go with me]

vadose (ˈveɪdəʊs) *adj.* of, relating to, designating, or derived from water occurring above the water table: *vadose water; vadose* *deposits.* [C19: from Latin *vadōsus* full of shallows, from *vadum* a ford]

vag (væg) *Austral. informal.* ~*n.* **1.** a vagrant. **2. the vag.** the Vagrancy Act: *the police finally got him on the vag.* ~*vb.* **vags, vagging, vagged.** **3.** (*tr.*) to arrest (someone) for vagrancy.

vagabond (ˈvægəˌbɒnd) *n.* **1.** a person with no fixed home. **2.** an idle wandering beggar or thief. **3.** (*modifier*) of or like a vagabond; shiftless or idle. [C15: from Latin *vagābundus* wandering, from *vagārī* to roam, from *vagus* VAGUE] —ˈ**vagaˌbondage** *n.* —ˈ**vagaˌbondish** *adj.* —ˈ**vagaˌbondism** *n.*

vagal (ˈveɪgᵊl) *adj. Anatomy.* of, relating to, or affecting the vagus nerve: *vagal inhibition.*

vagarious (vəˈgɛərɪəs) *adj. Rare.* characterized or caused by vagaries; irregular or erratic. —**vaˈgariously** *adv.*

vagary (ˈveɪgərɪ, vəˈgɛərɪ) *n., pl.* **-garies.** an erratic or outlandish notion or action; whim. [C16: probably from Latin *vagārī* to roam; compare Latin *vagus* VAGUE]

vagina (vəˈdʒaɪnə) *n., pl.* **-nas** *or* **-nae** (-niː). **1.** the moist canal in most female mammals, including humans, that extends from the cervix of the uterus to an external opening between the labia minora. **2.** *Anatomy, biology.* any sheath or sheathlike structure, such as a leaf base that encloses a stem. [C17: from Latin: sheath] —**vagˈinal** *adj.*

vaginate (ˈvædʒɪnɪt, -ˌneɪt) *adj.* (esp. of plant parts) having a vagina or sheath; sheathed: *a vaginate leaf.*

vaginectomy (ˌvædʒɪˈnɛktəmɪ) *n.* **1.** surgical removal of all or part of the vagina. **2.** surgical removal of part of the serous sheath surrounding the testis and epididymis.

vaginismus (ˌvædʒɪˈnɪzməs, -ˈnɪsməs) *n.* painful spasm of the vagina. [C19: from New Latin, from VAGINA + *-ismus;* see -ISM]

vaginitis (ˌvædʒɪˈnaɪtɪs) *n.* inflammation of the vagina.

vagotomy (væˈgɒtəmɪ) *n., pl.* **-mies.** surgical division of the vagus nerve, performed to limit gastric secretion in patients with severe peptic ulcers. [C19: from VAG(US) + -TOMY]

vagotonia (ˌveɪgəˈtəʊnɪə) *n.* pathological overactivity of the vagus nerve, affecting various bodily functions controlled by this nerve. [C19: from VAG(US) + *-tonia,* from Latin *tonus* tension, TONE]

vagotropic (ˌveɪgəˈtrɒpɪk) *adj. Physiol.* (of a drug) affecting the activity of the vagus nerve. [C20: from VAG(US) + -TROPIC]

vagrancy (ˈveɪgrənsɪ) *n., pl.* **-cies.** **1.** the state or condition of being a vagrant. **2.** the conduct or mode of living of a vagrant. **3.** *Rare.* digression in thought; mental lapse.

vagrant (ˈveɪgrənt) *n.* **1.** a person of no settled abode, income, or job; tramp. **2.** a migratory bird or insect that is off course. ~*adj.* **3.** wandering about; nomadic. **4.** of, relating to, or characteristic of a vagrant or vagabond. **5.** moving in an erratic fashion, without aim or purpose; wayward. **6.** (of plants) showing uncontrolled or straggling growth. ~Archaic equivalent: **vagrom** (ˈveɪgrəm). [C15: probably from Old French *waucrant* (from *wancrer* to roam, of Germanic origin), but also influenced by Old French *vagant* vagabond, from Latin *vagārī* to wander] —ˈ**vagrantly** *adv.* —ˈ**vagrantness** *n.*

vague (veɪg) *adj.* **1.** (of statements, meaning, etc.) not explicit; imprecise: *vague promises.* **2.** not clearly perceptible or discernible; indistinct: *a vague idea; a vague shape.* **3.** not clearly or definitely established or known: *a vague rumour.* **4.** (of a person or his expression) demonstrating lack of precision or clear thinking; absent-minded. [C16: via French from Latin *vagus* wandering, of obscure origin] —ˈ**vaguely** *adv.* —ˈ**vagueness** *n.*

vagus *or* **vagus nerve** (ˈveɪgəs) *n., pl.* **-gi** (-dʒaɪ). the tenth cranial nerve, which supplies the heart, lungs, and viscera. [C19: from Latin *vagus* wandering]

vahana (ˈvɑːhənə) *n. Indian myth.* a vehicle. [Hindi, from Sanskrit, from *vaha* to carry]

vail[1] (veɪl) *vb.* (*tr.*) *Obsolete.* **1.** to lower (something, such as a weapon), esp. as a sign of deference or submission. **2.** to remove (the hat, cap, etc.) as a mark of respect or meekness. [C14 *valen,* from obsolete *avalen,* from Old French *avaler* to let fall, from Latin *ad vallem,* literally: to the valley, that is, down, from *ad* to + *vallis* VALLEY]

vail[2] (veɪl) *n., vb.* an archaic word for **avail.**

vail[3] (veɪl) *n., vb.* an archaic spelling of **veil.**

vain (veɪn) *adj.* **1.** inordinately proud of one's appearance, possessions, or achievements. **2.** given to ostentatious display, esp. of one's beauty. **3.** worthless. **4.** senseless or futile. ~*n.* **5. in vain.** to no avail; fruitlessly. **6. take someone's name in vain. a.** to use the name of someone, esp. God, without due respect or reverence. **b.** *Jocular.* to mention someone's name. [C13: via Old French from Latin *vānus*] —ˈ**vainly** *adv.* —ˈ**vainness** *n.*

vainglory (ˌveɪnˈglɔːrɪ) *n.* **1.** boastfulness or vanity. **2.** ostentation. —ˌ**vainˈglorious** *adj.*

vair (vɛə) *n.* **1.** a fur, probably Russian squirrel, used to trim robes in the Middle Ages. **2.** one of the two principal furs used on heraldic shields, conventionally represented by white and blue skins in alternate lines. Compare **ermine** (sense 3). [C13: from Old French: of more than one colour, from Latin *varius* variegated, VARIOUS]

Vaishnava (ˈvɪʃnəvə) *n. Hinduism.* a member of a sect devoted to the cult of Vishnu, strongly anti-Brahminic and antipriestly in outlook and stressing devotion through image worship and simple ritual. [from Sanskrit *vaisnava* of VISHNU] —ˈ**Vaishnavism** *n.*

Vaisya (ˈvaɪsjə, ˈvaɪʃjə) *n.* the third of the four main Hindu castes, the traders. [C18: from Sanskrit, literally: settler, from *viś* settlement]

val. *abbrev. for:* **1.** valuation. **2.** value.

valance (ˈvæləns) *n.* a short piece of drapery hung along a shelf, canopy, or bed, or across a window, to hide structural detail. [C15: perhaps named after *Valence,* France, town noted for its textiles] —ˈ**valanced** *adj.*

vale[1] (veɪl) *n.* a literary word for **valley.** [C13: from Old French *val,* from Latin *vallis* valley]

vale[2] *Latin.* (ˈvɑːleɪ) *sentence substitute.* farewell; goodbye.

valediction (ˌvælɪˈdɪkʃən) *n.* **1.** the act or an instance of saying goodbye. **2.** any valedictory statement, speech, etc. [C17: from Latin *valedīcere,* from *valē* farewell + *dīcere* to say]

valedictory (ˌvælɪˈdɪktərɪ, -trɪ) *adj.* **1.** saying goodbye. **2.** of or relating to a farewell or an occasion of farewell. ~*n., pl.* **-ries.** **3.** a farewell address or speech. **4.** *U.S. and Canadian.* a farewell speech delivered at commencement by the most outstanding graduate.

valence (ˈveɪləns) *n. Chem.* **1.** another name (esp. U.S. and Canadian) for **valency.** **2.** the phenomenon of forming chemical bonds.

valence band *n.* See **energy band.**

valence-conduction band *n.* See **energy band.**

Valenciennes (ˌvælənsɪˈɛn) *n.* a flat bobbin lace typically having scroll and floral designs and originally made of linen, now often cotton. [named after *Valenciennes,* town in N France where it was originally made]

valency (ˈveɪlənsɪ) *or esp. U.S. and Canadian* **valence** *n., pl.* **-cies** *or* **-ces.** **1.** *Chem.* a property of atoms or groups, equal to the number of atoms of hydrogen that the atom or group could combine with or displace in forming compounds. **2.** *Linguistics.* the number of satellite noun phrases with which a verb combines: *the English verb "give" takes a subject and two objects, so it has a valency of three.* **3.** *Immunol.* **a.** the number of antigen-binding sites on an antibody molecule. **b.** the number of antigen-binding sites with which an antigen can combine. [C19: from Latin *valentia* strength, from *valēre* to be strong]

valency electron *n. Chem.* an electron in the outer shell of an atom, responsible for forming chemical bonds.

valency grammar *n.* a system of linguistic syntax, conceived by analogy with chemical valency, according to which verbs have valencies dependent on the number of noun phrases with which they combine. See **valency** (sense 2).

valentine (ˈvælənˌtaɪn) *n.* **1.** a card or gift expressing love or affection, sent, often anonymously, to one's sweetheart or satirically to a friend, on Saint Valentine's Day. **2.** a sweetheart selected for such a greeting.

valerian (vəˈlɪərɪən) *n.* **1.** Also called: **allheal.** any of various Eurasian valerianaceous plants of the genus *Valeriana,* esp. *V. officinalis,* having small white or pinkish flowers and a medicinal root. **2.** a sedative drug made from the dried roots of *V. officinalis.* [C14: via Old French from Medieval Latin *valeriana* (*herba*) (herb) of *Valerius,* unexplained Latin personal name]

valerianaceous (vəˌlɪərɪəˈneɪʃəs) *adj.* of, relating to, or belonging to the *Valerianaceae,* a family of herbaceous plants having the calyx of the flower reduced to a ring of hairs: includes valerian, spikenard, and corn salad. [C19: from New Latin; see VALERIAN]

valeric (vəˈlɛrɪk, -ˈlɪərɪk) *adj.* of, relating to, or derived from valerian.

valeric acid *n.* another name for **pentanoic acid.**

valet (ˈvælɪt, ˈvæleɪ) *n.* **1.** a manservant who acts as personal attendant to his employer, looking after his clothing, serving his meals, etc. French name: **valet de chambre.** **2.** a manservant who attends to the requirements of patrons in a hotel, passengers on board ship, etc.; steward. [C16: from Old French *vaslet* page, from Medieval Latin *vassus* servant; see VASSAL]

valet de chambre *French.* (valɛ də ʃɑ̃brə) *n., pl.* ***valets de chambre*** (valɛ də ʃɑ̃brə). the full French term for **valet** (sense 1).

valet parking *n.* a system at hotels, airports, etc., in which patrons' cars are parked by a steward.

valetudinarian (ˌvælɪˌtjuːdɪˈnɛərɪən) *or* **valetudinary** (ˌvælɪˈtjuːdɪnərɪ) *n., pl.* **-narians** *or* **-naries.** **1.** a person who is chronically sick; invalid. **2.** a person excessively worried about the state of his health; hypochondriac. **3.** an old person who is in good health. ~*adj.* **4.** relating to, marked by, or resulting from poor health. **5.** being a valetudinarian. **6.** trying to return to a healthy state. [C18: from Latin *valētūdō* state of health, from *valēre* to be well] —ˌ**valeˌtudiˈnarianism** *n.*

valgus (ˈvælgəs) *adj. Pathol.* displaced or twisted away from the midline of the body. See **hallux valgus.** [C19: from Latin: bow-legged]

valiant (ˈvæljənt) *adj.* **1.** courageous, intrepid, or stout-hearted; brave. **2.** marked by bravery or courage: *a valiant deed.* [C14: from Old French *vaillant,* from *valoir* to be of value, from Latin *valēre* to be strong] —ˈ**valiance** *or* ˈ**valiancy** *n.* —ˈ**valiantly** *adv.*

valid (ˈvælɪd) *adj.* **1.** having some foundation; based on truth. **2.** legally acceptable: *a valid licence.* **3. a.** having legal force; effective. **b.** having legal authority; binding. **4.** having some force or cogency: *a valid point in a debate.* **5.** *Logic.* (of an inference or argument) having premises and conclusion so related that whenever the former are true the latter must also be true, esp.

(formally valid) when the inference is justified by the form of the premises and conclusion alone. Thus *Tom is a bachelor; therefore Tom is unmarried* is valid but not formally so, while *today is hot and dry; therefore today is hot* is formally valid. Compare **invalid**^{2} (sense 2). **6.** *Archaic.* healthy or strong. [C16: from Latin *validus* robust, from *valēre* to be strong] —**'validly** *adv.* —**validity** (və'lɪdɪtɪ) *or* **'validness** *n.*

▷**Usage.** In everyday contexts *valid* is often used of a statement purely to mean correct, irrespective of its derivation by a logically valid argument, but in logic validity cannot be said to attach to a conclusion by itself. Nor should the classification of arguments as valid or invalid be confused with the classification of component statements as true or false; all combinations are possible except that of a valid argument with true premises and a false conclusion.

validate ('vælɪˌdeɪt) *vb.* (*tr.*) **1.** to confirm or corroborate. **2.** to give legal force or official confirmation to; declare legally valid. —**ˌvali'dation** *n.* —**'validatory** *adj.*

valine ('veɪliːn, 'væl-) *n.* an essential amino acid; a component of proteins. [C19: from VAL(ERIC ACID) + -INE^2]

valise (və'liːz) *n.* a small overnight travelling case. [C17: via French from Italian *valigia,* of unknown origin]

Valium ('vælɪəm) *n. Trademark.* a preparation of the drug diazepam used as a tranquillizer. See also **benzodiazepine.**

vallation (və'leɪʃən) *n.* **1.** the act or process of building fortifications. **2.** a wall or rampart. [C17: from Late Latin *vallātiō,* from *vallum* rampart]

vallecula (və'lɛkjʊlə) *n., pl.* **-lae** (-ˌliː). **1.** *Anatomy.* any of various natural depressions or crevices, such as certain fissures of the brain. **2.** *Botany.* a groove or furrow. [C19: from Late Latin: little valley, from Latin *vallis* valley] —**val'lecular** *or* **val'leculate** *adj.*

valley ('vælɪ) *n.* **1.** a long depression in the land surface, usually containing a river, formed by erosion or by movements in the earth's crust. **2.** the broad area drained by a single river system: *the Thames valley.* **3.** any elongated depression resembling a valley. **4.** the junction of a roof slope with another or with a wall. **5.** (*modifier*) relating to or proceeding by way of a valley: *a valley railway.* [C13: from Old French *valee,* from Latin *vallis*]

vallum ('væləm) *n. Archaeol.* a Roman rampart or earthwork.

Valois (*French* valwa) *adj.* denoting or relating to the royal house of France that ruled from 1328 to 1589: *the Valois lineage.*

valonia (və'ləʊnɪə) *n.* the acorn cups and unripe acorns of the Eurasian oak *Quercus aegilops,* used in tanning, dyeing, and making ink. [C18: from Italian *vallonia,* ultimately from Greek *balanos* acorn]

valorize *or* **valorise** ('vǽləˌraɪz) *vb.* (*tr.*) to fix and maintain an artificial price for (a commodity) by governmental action. [C20: back formation from *valorization;* see VALOUR] —**ˌvalori'zation** *or* **ˌvalori'sation** *n.*

valour *or U.S.* **valor** ('vælə) *n.* courage or bravery, esp. in battle. [C15: from Late Latin *valor,* from *valēre* to be strong] —**'valorous** *adj.* —**'valorously** *adv.*

valse *French.* (vals) *n.* the French word, esp. used in the titles of some pieces of music, for **waltz.**

valuable ('væljʊəbᵊl) *adj.* **1.** having considerable monetary worth. **2.** of considerable importance or quality: *a valuable friend; valuable information.* **3.** able to be valued. ~*n.* **4.** (*usually pl.*) a valuable article of personal property, esp. jewellery. —**'valuableness** *n.* —**'valuably** *adv.*

valuate ('væljʊˌeɪt) *vb. U.S.* another word for **value** (senses 10, 12) or **evaluate.**

valuation (ˌvæljʊ'eɪʃən) *n.* **1.** the act of valuing, esp. a formal assessment of the worth of property, jewellery, etc. **2.** the price arrived at by the process of valuing: *the valuation of this property is considerable; I set a high valuation on technical ability.* —**ˌvalu'ational** *adj.* —**ˌvalu'ationally** *adv.*

valuator ('væljʊˌeɪtə) *n.* a person who estimates the value of objects, paintings, etc.; appraiser.

value ('væljuː) *n.* **1.** the desirability of a thing, often in respect of some property such as usefulness or exchangeability: worth, merit, or importance. **2.** an amount, esp. a material or monetary one, considered to be a fair exchange in return for a thing; assigned valuation: *the value of the picture is £10 000.* **3.** reasonable or equivalent return; satisfaction: *value for money.* **4.** precise meaning or significance. **5.** (*pl.*) the moral principles and beliefs or accepted standards of a person or social group: *a person with old-fashioned values.* **6.** *Maths.* **a.** a particular magnitude, number, or amount: *the value of the variable was 7.* **b.** the particular quantity that is the result of applying a function or operation for some given argument: *the value of the function for x=3 was 9.* **7.** *Music.* short for **time value. 8.** (in painting, drawing, etc.) **a.** a gradation of tone from light to dark or of colour luminosity. **b.** the relation of one of these elements to another or to the whole picture. **9.** *Phonetics.* the quality or tone of the speech sound associated with a written character representing it: *"g" has the value* (dʒ) *in English "gem."* ~*vb.* **-ues, -uing, -ued.** (*tr.*) **10.** to assess or estimate the worth, merit, or desirability of; appraise. **11.** to have a high regard for, esp. in respect of worth, usefulness, merit, etc.; esteem or prize: *to value freedom.* **12.** (foll. by *at*) to fix the financial or material worth of (a unit of currency, work of art, etc.): *jewels valued at £40 000.* [C14: from Old French, from *valoir,* from Latin *valēre* to be worth, be strong] —**'valuer** *n.*

value added *n.* the difference between the total revenues of a firm, industry, etc., and its total purchases from other firms, industries, etc. The aggregate of values added throughout an economy (**gross value added**) represents that economy's gross domestic product.

value-added tax *n.* (in Britain) the full name for **VAT.**

value date *n.* the exact date on which a financial transaction, esp. in buying and selling foreign exchange, is deemed to take place: used for calculating exchange rates.

valued policy *n.* an insurance policy in which the amount payable in the event of a valid claim is agreed upon between the company and policyholder when the policy is issued and is not related to the actual value of a loss. Compare **open policy.**

value judgment *n.* a subjective assessment based on one's own code of values or that of one's class.

valueless ('væljʊlɪs) *adj.* having or possessing no value; worthless. —**'valuelessness** *n.*

valuer ('væljʊə) *n.* a person who assesses the monetary worth of a work of art, jewel, house, etc.; appraiser.

Valuer General *n. Austral.* a state official who values properties for rating purposes.

valuta (və'luːtə) *n. Rare.* the value of one currency in terms of its exchange rate with another. [C20: from Italian, literally: VALUE]

valvate ('vælveɪt) *adj.* **1.** furnished with a valve or valves. **2.** functioning as or resembling a valve. **3.** *Botany.* **a.** having or taking place by means of valves: *valvate dehiscence.* **b.** (of petals or sepals in the bud) having the margins touching but not overlapping.

valve (vælv) *n.* **1.** any device that shuts off, starts, regulates, or controls the flow of a fluid. **2.** *Anatomy.* a flaplike structure in a hollow organ, such as the heart, that controls the one-way passage of fluid through that organ. **3.** Also called: **tube.** an evacuated electron tube containing a cathode, anode, and, usually, one or more additional control electrodes. When a positive potential is applied to the anode, electrons emitted from the cathode are attracted to the anode, constituting a flow of current which can be controlled by a voltage applied to the grid to produce amplification, oscillation, etc. U.S. and Canadian name: **vacuum tube.** See also **diode** (sense 2), **triode** (sense 1), **tetrode, pentode. 4.** *Zoology.* any of the separable pieces that make up the shell of a mollusc. **5.** *Music.* a device on some brass instruments by which the effective length of the tube may be varied to enable a chromatic scale to be produced. **6.** *Botany.* **a.** any of the several parts that make up a dry dehiscent fruit, esp. a capsule. **b.** either of the two halves of a diatom cell wall. **7.** *Archaic.* a leaf of a double door or of a folding door. [C14: from Latin *valva* a folding door] —**'valveless** *adj.* —**'valveˌlike** *adj.*

valve gear *n.* a mechanism that operates the valves of a reciprocating engine, usually involving the use of cams, pushrods, rocker arms, etc.

valve-in-head engine *n.* the U.S. name for **overhead-valve engine.**

valve spring *n.* **1.** a helical spring used to hold closed a valve in the cylinder head of an internal-combustion engine. **2.** any spring that closes a valve after it has been opened mechanically or by flow pressure.

valvular ('vælvjʊlə) *adj.* **1.** of, relating to, operated by, or having a valve or valves. **2.** having the shape or function of a valve.

valvule ('vælvjuːl) *or* **valvelet** ('vælvlɪt) *n.* a small valve or a part resembling one. [C18: from New Latin *valvula,* diminutive of VALVE]

valvulitis (ˌvælvjʊ'laɪtɪs) *n.* inflammation of a bodily valve, esp. a heart valve. [C19: from VALVULE + -ITIS]

vambrace ('væmbreɪs) *n.* a piece of armour used to protect the arm. [C14: from Anglo-French *vauntbras,* from *vaunt-* (from Old French *avant-* fore-) + *bras* arm] —**'vambraced** *adj.*

vamoose (və'muːs) *vb.* (*intr.*) *Slang, chiefly U.S.* to leave a place hurriedly; decamp. [C19: from Spanish *vamos* let us go, from Latin *vādere* to go, walk rapidly]

vamp^1 (væmp) *Informal.* ~*n.* **1.** a seductive woman who exploits men by use of her sexual charms. ~*vb.* **2.** to exploit (a man) in the fashion of a vamp. [C20: short for VAMPIRE] —**'vamper** *n.* —**'vampish** *adj.*

vamp^2 (væmp) *n.* **1.** something patched up to make it look new. **2.** the reworking of a theme, story, etc. **3.** an improvised accompaniment, consisting largely of chords. **4.** the front part of the upper of a shoe. ~*vb.* **5.** (*tr.;* often foll. by *up*) to give a vamp to; make a renovation of. **6.** to improvise (an accompaniment) to (a tune). [C13: from Old French *avantpié* the front part of a shoe (hence, something patched), from *avant-* fore- + *pié* foot, from Latin *pēs*] —**'vamper** *n.*

vampire ('væmpaɪə) *n.* **1.** (in European folklore) a corpse that rises nightly from its grave to drink the blood of the living. **2.** See **vampire bat. 3.** a person who preys mercilessly upon others, such as a blackmailer. **4.** See **vamp**^{1} (sense 1). **5.** *Theatre.* a trapdoor on a stage. [C18: from French, from German *Vampir,* from Magyar; perhaps related to Turkish *uber* witch, Russian *upyr* vampire] —**vampiric** (væm'pɪrɪk) *or* **vampirish** ('væmpaɪərɪʃ) *adj.*

vampire bat *n.* any bat, esp. *Desmodus rotundus,* of the family *Desmodontidae* of tropical regions of Central and South America, having sharp incisor and canine teeth and feeding on the blood of birds and mammals. Compare **false vampire.**

vampirism ('væmpaɪəˌrɪzəm) *n.* **1.** belief in the existence of vampires. **2.** the actions of vampires; bloodsucking. **3.** the act of preying upon or exploiting others.

van[1] (væn) *n.* **1.** short for **caravan** (sense 1). **2.** a covered motor vehicle for transporting goods, etc., by road. **3.** *Brit.* a closed railway wagon in which the guard travels, for transporting goods, mail, etc. **4.** *Brit.* See **delivery van.**

van[2] (væn) *n.* short for **vanguard.**

van[3] (væn) *n. Tennis, chiefly Brit.* **1.** short for **advantage** (sense 3). Usual U.S. and Canadian word: **ad. 2. van in.** an advantage scored by the server. **3. van out.** an advantage scored by the receiver.

van[4] (væn) *n.* **1.** any device for winnowing corn. **2.** an archaic or poetic word for **wing.** [C17: variant of FAN[1]]

vanadate ('vænəˌdeɪt) *n.* any salt or ester of a vanadic acid.

vanadic (və'nædɪk, -'neɪdɪk) *adj.* of or containing vanadium, esp. in a trivalent or pentavalent state.

vanadic acid *n.* any one of various oxyacids of vanadium, such as H_3VO_4 **(orthovanadic acid),** HVO_4 **(metavanadic acid),** and $H_4V_2O_7$ **(pyrovanadic acid),** known chiefly in the form of their vanadate salts.

vanadinite (və'nædɪˌnaɪt) *n.* a red, yellow, or brownish mineral consisting of a chloride and vanadate of lead in hexagonal crystalline form. It results from weathering of lead ores in desert regions and is a source of vanadium. Formula: $Pb_5(VO_4)_3Cl$.

vanadium (və'neɪdɪəm) *n.* a toxic silvery-white metallic element occurring chiefly in carnotite and vanadinite and used in steel alloys, high-speed tools, and as a catalyst. Symbol: V; atomic no.: 23; atomic wt.: 50.94; valency: 2–5; relative density: 6.1; melting pt.: 1890° C; boiling pt.: 3380° C. [C19: New Latin, from Old Norse *Vanadis,* epithet of the goddess Freya + -IUM]

vanadium steel *n. Engineering.* steel containing up to 0.5 per cent vanadium, usually with 1.1–1.5 per cent chromium and 0.4–0.5 per cent carbon to increase its tensile strength and elasticity.

vanadous ('vænədəs) *adj.* of or containing vanadium, esp. in a divalent or trivalent state.

Van Allen belt (væn 'ælən) *n.* either of two regions of charged particles above the earth, the inner one extending from 2400 to 5600 kilometres above the earth and the outer one from 13 000 to 19 000 kilometres. The charged particles result from cosmic rays and are trapped by the earth's magnetic field. [C20: named after its discoverer, J. A. *Van Allen* (born 1914), U.S. physicist]

vanaspati (və'næspətɪ) *n.* a hydrogenated vegetable fat commonly used in India as a substitute for butter. [C20: the Sanskrit name of a forest plant, from *vana* forest + *pati* lord]

vanda ('vændə) *n.* any epiphytic orchid of the E hemisphere genus *Vanda,* having white, mauve, blue, or greenish fragrant flowers. [C19: New Latin, from Hindi *vandā* mistletoe, from Sanskrit]

V and A (in Britain) *abbrev. for* Victoria and Albert Museum.

vandal ('vændᵊl) *n.* **a.** a person who deliberately causes damage or destruction to personal or public property. **b.** (*as modifier*): *vandal instincts.* [C17: from VANDAL, from Latin *Vandallus,* of Germanic origin]

Vandal ('vændᵊl) *n.* a member of a Germanic people that raided Roman provinces in the 3rd and 4th centuries A.D. before devastating Gaul (406–409), conquering Spain and N Africa, and sacking Rome (455): crushed at Carthage (533). —**Vandalic** (væn'dælɪk) *adj.* —'**Vandal,ism** *n.*

vandalism ('vændəˌlɪzəm) *n.* the wanton or deliberate destruction caused by a vandal or an instance of such destruction. —ˌ**vandal'istic** *or* '**vandalish** *adj.*

vandalize *or* **vandalise** ('vændəˌlaɪz) *vb.* (*tr.*) to destroy or damage (something) by an act of vandalism.

Van de Graaff generator ('væn də ˌgrɑːf) *n.* a device for producing high electrostatic potentials (up to 15 million volts), consisting of a hollow metal sphere on which a charge is accumulated from a continuous moving belt of insulating material: used in particle accelerators. [C20: named after R. J. *Van de Graaff* (1901–67), U.S. physicist]

Van der Hum ('væn də ˌhʊm) *n. S. African.* a liqueur with tangerine flavouring. [of uncertain origin]

van der Waals equation ('væn də ˌwɑːlz) *n.* an equation of state for a fluid substance which is applicable approximately to both the liquid and the gaseous conditions. [named after J. D. *van der Waals* (1837–1923), Dutch physicist who proposed it]

van der Waals forces *pl. n.* weak electrostatic forces between atoms and molecules caused by transient dissymmetries in the distribution of electrons in the interacting atoms or molecules.

Vandyke beard ('vændaɪk) *n.* a short pointed beard. Often shortened to **Vandyke.** [C18: after Sir Anthony *Van Dyck* (1599–1641), Flemish painter]

Vandyke brown *n.* **1. a.** a moderate brown colour. **b.** (*as adj.*): *a Vandyke-brown suit.* **2.** any of various brown pigments, usually consisting of a mixture of ferric oxide and lampblack.

Vandyke collar *or* **cape** *n.* a large white collar with several very deep points. Often shortened to **Vandyke.**

vane (veɪn) *n.* **1.** Also called: **weather vane, wind vane.** a flat plate or blade of metal mounted on a vertical axis in an exposed position to indicate wind direction. **2.** any one of the flat blades or sails forming part of the wheel of a windmill. **3.** any flat or shaped plate used to direct fluid flow, esp. a stator blade in a turbine, etc. **4.** a fin or plate fitted to a projectile or missile to provide stabilization or guidance. **5.** *Ornithol.* the flat part of a feather, consisting of two rows of barbs on either side of the shaft. **6.** *Surveying.* **a.** a sight on a quadrant or compass. **b.** the movable marker on a levelling staff. [Old English *fana;* related to Old Saxon, Old High German *fano,* Old Norse *fani,* Latin *pannus* cloth] —**vaned** *adj.* —'**vaneless** *adj.*

vanessid (və'nɛsɪd) *n.* **1.** a butterfly belonging to any of several brightly coloured species, including admirals, tortoiseshells, and the Camberwell beauty, which with the fritillaries comprise the *Nymphalidae.* ~*adj.* **2.** of, relating to, or belonging to this group. [C20: from New Latin *vanessa*]

vang (væŋ) *n. Nautical.* **1.** a rope or tackle extended from the boom of a fore-and-aft mainsail to a deck fitting of a vessel when running, in order to keep the boom from riding up. **2.** a guy extending from the end of a gaff to the vessel's rail on each side, used for steadying the gaff. [C18: from Dutch, from *vangen* to catch]

vanguard ('vænˌgɑːd) *n.* **1.** the leading division or units of a military force. **2.** the leading position in any movement or field, or the people who occupy such a position: *the vanguard of modern literature.* [C15: from Old French *avant-garde,* from *avant-* fore- + *garde* GUARD]

vanilla (və'nɪlə) *n.* **1.** any tropical climbing orchid of the genus *Vanilla,* esp. *V. plonifolia,* having spikes of large fragrant greenish-yellow flowers and long fleshy pods containing the seeds (beans). **2.** the pod or bean of certain of these plants, used to flavour food, etc. **3.** a flavouring extract prepared from vanilla beans and used in cooking. ~*adj.* **4.** flavoured with or as if with vanilla: *vanilla ice cream.* **5.** *Computer technol. slang.* ordinary. [C17: from New Latin, from Spanish *vainilla* pod, from *vaina* a sheath, from Latin *vāgīna* sheath]

vanillic (və'nɪlɪk) *adj.* of, resembling, containing, or derived from vanilla or vanillin.

vanillin ('vænɪlɪn, və'nɪlɪn) *n.* a white crystalline aldehyde found in vanilla and many natural balsams and resins; 3-methoxy-4-hydroxybenzaldehyde. It is a by-product of paper manufacture and is used as a flavouring and in perfumes and pharmaceuticals. Formula: $(CH_3O)(OH)C_6H_3CHO$.

vanish ('vænɪʃ) *vb.* (*intr.*) **1.** to disappear, esp. suddenly or mysteriously. **2.** to cease to exist; fade away. **3.** *Maths.* to become zero. ~*n.* **4.** *Phonetics, rare.* the second and weaker of the two vowels in a falling diphthong. [C14 *vanissen,* from Old French *esvanir,* from Latin *ēvānēscere* to evaporate, from *ē-* EX-[1] + *vānēscere* to pass away, from *vānus* empty] —'**vanisher** *n.*

vanishing cream *n.* a cosmetic cream that is colourless once applied, used as a foundation for powder or as a cleansing or moisturizing cream.

vanishing point *n.* **1.** the point to which parallel lines appear to converge in the rendering of perspective, usually on the horizon. **2.** a point in space or time at or beyond which something disappears or ceases to exist.

vanity ('vænɪtɪ) *n., pl.* **-ties. 1.** the state or quality of being vain; excessive pride or conceit. **2.** ostentation occasioned by ambition or pride. **3.** an instance of being vain or something about which one is vain. **4.** the state or quality of being valueless, futile, or unreal. **5.** something that is worthless or useless. **6.** *N.Z.* short for **vanity unit.** [C13: from Old French *vanité,* from Latin *vānitās* emptiness, from *vānus* empty]

vanity bag, case, *or* **box** *n.* a woman's small bag or hand case used to carry cosmetics, etc.

Vanity Fair *n.* (*often not caps.*) *Literary.* the social life of a community, esp. of a great city, or the world in general, considered as symbolizing worldly frivolity. [from John Bunyan's *The Pilgrim's Progress* (1678)]

vanity unit *n.* a hand basin built into a wooden Formica-covered or tiled top, usually with a built-in cupboard below it. Also called (trademark): **Vanitory unit** ('vænɪtərɪ).

vanquish ('væŋkwɪʃ) *vb.* (*tr.*) **1.** to defeat or overcome in a battle, contest, etc.; conquer. **2.** to defeat or overcome in argument or debate. **3.** to conquer (an emotion). [C14 *vanquisshen,* from Old French *venquis* vanquished, from *veintre* to overcome, from Latin *vincere*] —'**vanquishable** *adj.* —'**vanquisher** *n.* —'**vanquishment** *n.*

vantage ('vɑːntɪdʒ) *n.* **1.** a state, position, or opportunity affording superiority or advantage. **2.** superiority or benefit accruing from such a position, state, etc. **3.** *Tennis.* short for **advantage.** [C13: from Old French *avantage* ADVANTAGE] —'**vantageless** *adj.*

vantage ground *n.* a position or condition affording superiority or advantage over or as if over an opponent.

vantage point *n.* a position or place that allows one a wide or favourable overall view of a scene or situation.

vanward ('vænwəd) *adj., adv.* in or towards the front.

vapid ('væpɪd) *adj.* **1.** bereft of strength, sharpness, flavour, etc.; flat. **2.** boring or dull; lifeless: *vapid talk.* [C17: from Latin *vapidus;* related to *vappa* tasteless or flat wine, and perhaps to *vapor* warmth] —**va'pidity** *n.* —'**vapidly** *adv.* —'**vapidness** *n.*

vapor ('veɪpə) *n.* the U.S. spelling of **vapour.**

vaporescence (ˌveɪpə'rɛsəns) *n.* the production or formation of vapour. —ˌ**vapor'escent** *adj.*

vaporetto (ˌveɪpəˈrɛtəʊ; *Italian* vapoˈrɛtto) *n., pl.* **-ti** (-tɪ; *Italian* -ti) *or* **-tos.** a steam-powered passenger boat, as used on the canals in Venice. [Italian, from *vapore* a steamboat]
vaporific (ˌveɪpəˈrɪfɪk) *adj.* **1.** producing, causing, or tending to produce vapour. **2.** of, concerned with, or having the nature of vapour. **3.** tending to become vapour; volatile. ~Also: **vaporous.** [C18: from New Latin *vaporificus,* from Latin *vapor* steam + *facere* to make]
vaporimeter (ˌveɪpəˈrɪmɪtə) *n.* an instrument for measuring vapour pressure, used to determine the volatility of oils or the amount of alcohol in alcoholic liquids.
vaporize *or* **vaporise** (ˈveɪpəˌraɪz) *vb.* **1.** to change or cause to change into vapour or into the gaseous state. **2.** to evaporate or disappear or cause to evaporate or disappear, esp. suddenly. **3.** to destroy or be destroyed by being turned into a gas as a result of the extreme heat generated by a nuclear explosion. **4.** (*intr.*) *Rare.* to brag. —ˈ**vaporˌizable** *or* ˈ**vaporˌisable** *adj.* —ˌ**vaporiˈzation** *or* ˌ**vaporiˈsation** *n.*
vaporizer *or* **vaporiser** (ˈveɪpəˌraɪzə) *n.* **1.** a substance that vaporizes or a device that causes vaporization. **2.** *Med.* a device that produces steam or atomizes medication for inhalation.
vaporous (ˈveɪpərəs) *adj.* **1.** resembling or full of vapour. **2.** another word for **vaporific. 3.** lacking permanence or substance; ephemeral or fanciful. **4.** given to foolish imaginings. **5.** dulled or obscured by an atmosphere of vapour. —ˈ**vaporously** *adv.* —ˈ**vaporousness** *or* **vaporosity** (ˌveɪpəˈrɒsɪtɪ) *n.*
vapour *or U.S.* **vapor** (ˈveɪpə) *n.* **1.** particles of moisture or other substance suspended in air and visible as clouds, smoke, etc. **2.** a gaseous substance at a temperature below its critical temperature. Compare **gas** (sense 3). **3.** a substance that is in a gaseous state at a temperature below its boiling point. **4.** *Rare.* something fanciful that lacks substance or permanence. **5. the vapours.** *Archaic.* a depressed mental condition believed originally to be the result of vaporous exhalations from the stomach. ~*vb.* **6.** to evaporate or cause to evaporate; vaporize. **7.** (*intr.*) to make vain empty boasts; brag. [C14: from Latin *vapor*] —ˈ**vapourable** *or U.S.* ˈ**vaporable** *adj.* —ˌ**vapouraˈbility** *or U.S.* ˌ**vaporaˈbility** *n.* —ˈ**vapourer** *or U.S.* ˈ**vaporer** *n.* —ˈ**vapourish** *or U.S.* ˈ**vaporish** *adj.* —ˈ**vapourless** *or U.S.* ˈ**vaporless** *adj.* —ˈ**vapour-ˌlike** *or U.S.* ˈ**vapor-ˌlike** *adj.* —ˈ**vapoury** *or U.S.* ˈ**vapory** *adj.*
vapour density *n.* the ratio of the density of a gas or vapour to that of hydrogen at the same temperature and pressure. See also **relative density.**
vapourer moth *n.* a tussock moth, *Orgyia antiqua,* of hedgerows and trees, the female of which is wingless and lays her eggs on her former cocoon.
vapour lock *n.* a stoppage in a pipe carrying a liquid caused by a bubble of gas, esp. such a stoppage caused by vaporization of the petrol in the pipe feeding the carburettor of an internal-combustion engine.
vapour pressure *n. Physics.* the pressure exerted by a vapour, esp. that exerted by a vapour in equilibrium with its solid or liquid phase at a particular temperature.
vapour trail *n.* a visible trail left by an aircraft flying at high altitude or through supercold air, caused by the deposition of water vapour in the engine exhaust as minute ice crystals. Also called: **condensation trail, contrail.**
var (vɑː) *n.* a unit of reactive power of an alternating current, equal to the product of the current measured in amperes and the voltage measured in volts. [from *v(olt-)a(mperes) r(eactive)*]
VAR *abbrev. for* visual aural range.
var. *abbrev. for:* **1.** variable. **2.** variant. **3.** variation. **4.** variety. **5.** various.
vara (ˈvɑːrə) *n.* a unit of length used in Spain, Portugal, and South America and having different values in different localities, usually between 32 and 43 inches (about 80 to 108 centimetres). [C17: via Spanish from Latin: wooden trestle, from *vārus* crooked]
varactor (ˈvɛəˌræktə) *n.* a semiconductor diode that acts as a voltage-dependent capacitor, being operated with a reverse bias. Compare **varistor.** [C20: probably a blend of *variable reactor*]
Varangian (vəˈrændʒɪən) *n.* **1.** one of the Scandinavians who invaded and settled parts of Russia and the Ukraine from the 8th to the 11th centuries, and who formed the bodyguard of the Byzantine emperor (**Varangian Guard**) in the late 10th and 11th centuries. ~*adj.* **2.** of or relating to the Varangians. [C18: from Medieval Latin *Varangus,* from Medieval Greek *Barangos,* from Old Norse *Væringi,* probably from *vār* pledge]
varec (ˈværɛk) *n.* **1.** another name for **kelp. 2.** the ash obtained from kelp. [C17: from French, from Old Norse *wrek* (unattested); see WRECK]
varia (ˈvɛərɪə) *pl. n.* a collection or miscellany, esp. of literary works. [Latin, neuter plural of *varius* VARIOUS]
variable (ˈvɛərɪəbᵊl) *adj.* **1.** liable to or capable of change: *variable weather.* **2.** (of behaviour, opinions, emotions, etc.) lacking constancy; fickle. **3.** *Maths.* having a range of possible values. **4.** (of a species, characteristic, etc.) liable to deviate from the established type. **5.** (of a wind) varying its direction and intensity. **6.** (of an electrical component or device) designed so that a characteristic property, such as resistance, can be varied: *variable capacitor.* ~*n.* **7.** something that is subject to variation. **8.** *Maths.* **a.** an expression that can be assigned any of a set of values. **b.** a symbol, esp. *x, y,* or *z,* representing an unspecified member of a class of objects, numbers, etc. See also **dependent variable, independent variable. 9.** *Logic.* a symbol, esp. *x, y, z,* representing any member of a class of entities. **10.** *Astronomy.* See **variable star. 11.** a variable wind. **12.** (*pl.*) a region where variable winds occur. [C14: from Latin *variābilis* changeable, from *variāre* to diversify] —ˌ**variaˈbility** *or* ˈ**variableness** *n.* —ˈ**variably** *adv.*
variable cost *n.* a cost that varies directly with output.
variable-density wind tunnel *n.* a closed-circuit wind tunnel entirely contained in a casing in which the pressure and therefore the density of the working fluid can be maintained at a preselected value.
variable-geometry *or* **variable-sweep** *adj.* denoting an aircraft in which the wings are hinged to give the variable aspect ratio colloquially known as a **swing-wing.**
variable star *n.* any star that varies considerably in brightness, either irregularly or in regular periods. **Intrinsic variables,** in which the variation is a result of internal changes, include novae, supernovae, and pulsating stars. See also **eclipsing binary.**
variance (ˈvɛərɪəns) *n.* **1.** the act of varying or the quality, state, or degree of being divergent; discrepancy. **2.** an instance of diverging; dissension: *our variance on this matter should not affect our friendship.* **3. at variance. a.** (often foll. by *with*) (of facts, etc.) not in accord; conflicting. **b.** (of persons) in a state of dissension. **4.** *Statistics.* a measure of dispersion obtained by taking the mean of the squared deviations of the observed values from their mean in a frequency distribution. **5.** a difference or discrepancy between two steps in a legal proceeding, esp. between a statement in a pleading and the evidence given to support it. **6.** (in the U.S. and Canada) a licence or authority to contravene the usual rule, esp. to build contrary to the provision of a zoning code. **7.** *Chem.* the number of degrees of freedom of a system, used in the phase rule. **8.** *Accounting.* the difference between actual and standard costs of production.
variant (ˈvɛərɪənt) *adj.* **1.** liable to or displaying variation. **2.** differing from a standard or type: *a variant spelling.* **3.** *Obsolete.* not constant; fickle. ~*n.* **4.** something that differs from a standard or type. **5.** *Statistics.* another word for **variate** (sense 1). [C14: via Old French from Latin *variāns,* from *variāre* to diversify, from *varius* VARIOUS]
variate (ˈvɛərɪɪt) *n.* **1.** *Statistics.* a random variable or a numerical value taken by it. **2.** a less common word for **variant** (sense 4). [C16: from Latin *variāre* to VARY]
variation (ˌvɛərɪˈeɪʃən) *n.* **1.** the act, process, condition, or result of changing or varying; diversity. **2.** an instance of varying or the amount, rate, or degree of such change. **3.** something that differs from a standard or convention. **4.** *Music.* **a.** a repetition of a musical theme in which the rhythm, harmony, or melody is altered or embellished. **b.** (*as modifier*): *variation form.* **5.** *Biology.* **a.** a marked deviation from the typical form or function. **b.** a characteristic or an organism showing this deviation. **6.** *Astronomy.* any change in or deviation from the mean motion or orbit of a planet, satellite, etc., esp. a perturbation of the moon. **7.** another word for **magnetic declination. 8.** *Ballet.* a solo dance. **9.** *Linguistics.* any form of morphophonemic change, such as one involved in inflection, conjugation, or vowel mutation. —ˌ**variˈational** *adj.* —ˌ**variˈationally** *adv.*
varicella (ˌværɪˈsɛlə) *n.* the technical name for **chickenpox.** [C18: New Latin, irregular diminutive of VARIOLA] —ˌ**variˈcellar** *adj.*
varicellate (ˌværɪˈsɛlɪt, -eɪt) *adj.* (of certain shells) marked on the surface with small ridges. [C19: from New Latin *varicella,* diminutive of Latin *varix* dilated vein, VARIX]
varicelloid (ˌværɪˈsɛlɔɪd) *adj.* resembling chickenpox.
varices (ˈværɪˌsiːz) *n.* the plural of **varix.**
varico- *or before a vowel* **varic-** *combining form.* indicating a varix or varicose veins: *varicotomy.* [from Latin *varix, varic-* distended vein]
varicocele (ˈværɪkəʊˌsiːl) *n. Pathol.* an abnormal distension of the veins of the spermatic cord in the scrotum.
varicoloured *or U.S.* **varicolored** (ˈvɛərɪˌkʌləd) *adj.* having many colours; variegated; motley.
varicose (ˈværɪˌkəʊs) *adj.* of or resulting from varicose veins: *a varicose ulcer.* [C18: from Latin *varicōsus,* from VARIX]
varicose veins *pl. n.* a condition in which the superficial veins, esp. of the legs, become tortuous, knotted, and swollen: caused by a defect in the venous valves or in the venous pump that normally moves the blood out of the legs when standing for long periods.
varicosis (ˌværɪˈkəʊsɪs) *n. Pathol.* any condition characterized by distension of the veins. [C18: from New Latin, from Latin: VARIX]
varicosity (ˌværɪˈkɒsɪtɪ) *n., pl.* **-ties.** *Pathol.* **1.** the state, condition, or quality of being varicose. **2.** an abnormally distended vein.
varicotomy (ˌværɪˈkɒtəmɪ) *n., pl.* **-mies.** surgical excision of a varicose vein.
varied (ˈvɛərɪd) *adj.* **1.** displaying or characterized by variety; diverse. **2.** modified or altered: *the amount may be varied without notice.* **3.** varicoloured; variegated. —ˈ**variedly** *adv.* —ˈ**variedness** *n.*
variegate (ˈvɛərɪˌgeɪt) *vb.* (*tr.*) **1.** to alter the appearance of, esp. by adding different colours. **2.** to impart variety to. [C17: from

Late Latin *variegāre*, from Latin *varius* diverse, VARIOUS + *agere* to make] —ˌvarieˈgation *n.*
variegated (ˈvɛərɪˌgeɪtɪd) *adj.* **1.** displaying differently coloured spots, patches, streaks, etc. **2.** (of foliage or flowers) having pale patches as a result of mutation, infection, etc.
varietal (vəˈraɪɪtᵊl) *adj.* **1.** of, relating to, characteristic of, designating, or forming a variety, esp. a biological variety. ~*n.* **2.** a wine labelled with the name of the grape from which it is pressed. —**vaˈrietally** *adv.*
variety (vəˈraɪɪtɪ) *n., pl.* **-ties. 1.** the quality or condition of being diversified or various. **2.** a collection of unlike things, esp. of the same general group; assortment. **3.** a different form or kind within a general category; sort: *varieties of behaviour.* **4. a.** *Taxonomy.* a race whose distinct characters are insufficient to justify classification as a separate species; a subspecies. **b.** *Horticulture, stockbreeding.* a strain of animal or plant produced by artificial breeding. **5. a.** entertainment consisting of a series of short unrelated performances or acts, such as comedy turns, songs, dances, sketches, etc. **b.** (*as modifier*): *a variety show.* [C16: from Latin *varietās*, from VARIOUS]
variety meat *n. Chiefly U.S.* processed meat, such as sausage, or offal.
variform (ˈvɛərɪˌfɔːm) *adj.* varying in form or shape. —**ˈvariˌformly** *adv.*
vario- *combining form.* indicating variety or difference: *variometer.* [from Latin *varius* VARIOUS]
variola (vəˈraɪələ) *n.* the technical name for **smallpox.** [C18: from Medieval Latin: disease marked by little spots, from Latin *varius* spotted] —**vaˈriolar** *adj.*
variolate (ˈvɛərɪəˌleɪt) *vb.* **1.** (*tr.*) to inoculate with the smallpox virus. ~*adj.* **2.** marked or pitted with or as if with the scars of smallpox. [C18: from VARIOLA] —ˌ**varioˈlation,** ˌ**varioliˈzation,** *or* ˌ**varioliˈsation** *n.*
variole (ˈvɛərɪˌəʊl) *n.* any of the rounded masses that make up the rock variolite. [C19: from French, from Medieval Latin; see VARIOLA]
variolite (ˈvɛərɪəˌlaɪt) *n.* any basic igneous rock containing rounded bodies (varioles) consisting of radiating crystal fibres. [C18: from VARIOLA, referring to the pockmarked appearance of the rock] —**variolitic** (ˌvɛərɪəˈlɪtɪk) *adj.*
varioloid (ˈvɛərɪəˌlɔɪd) *adj.* **1.** resembling smallpox. ~*n.* **2.** a mild form of smallpox occurring in persons with partial immunity.
variolous (vəˈraɪələs) *adj.* relating to or resembling smallpox; variolar.
variometer (ˌvɛərɪˈɒmɪtə) *n.* **1.** an instrument for measuring variations in a magnetic field, used esp. for studying the magnetic field of the earth. **2.** *Electronics.* a variable inductor consisting of a movable coil mounted inside and connected in series with a fixed coil. **3.** a sensitive rate-of-climb indicator, used mainly in gliders.
variorum (ˌvɛərɪˈɔːrəm) *adj.* **1.** containing notes by various scholars or critics or various versions of the text: *a variorum edition.* ~*n.* **2.** an edition or text of this kind. [C18: from Latin phrase *ēditiō cum notīs variōrum* edition with the notes of various commentators]
various (ˈvɛərɪəs) *determiner.* **1. a.** several different: *he is an authority on various subjects.* **b.** (*as pronoun;* foll. by *of*) *Not standard: various of them came.* ~*adj.* **2.** of different kinds, though often within the same general category; diverse: *various occurrences; his disguises are many and various.* **3.** (*prenominal*) relating to a collection of separate persons or things: *the various members of the club.* **4.** displaying variety; many-sided: *his various achievements are most impressive.* **5.** *Poetic.* variegated. **6.** *Obsolete.* inconstant. [C16: from Latin *varius* changing; perhaps related to Latin *vārus* crooked] —**ˈvariously** *adv.* —**ˈvariousness** *n.*
variscite (ˈværɪˌsaɪt) *n.* a green secondary mineral consisting of hydrated aluminium. [from Medieval Latin *Variscia*, the district of Vogtland in Saxony]
varistor (vəˈrɪstə) *n.* a two-electrode semiconductor device having a voltage-dependent nonlinear resistance. Compare **varactor.** [C20: a blend of *variable resistor*]
varitype (ˈvɛərɪˌtaɪp) *vb.* **1.** to produce (copy) on a Varityper. ~*n.* **2.** copy produced on a Varityper. —**ˈvariˌtypist** *n.*
Varityper (ˈvɛərɪˌtaɪpə) *n. Trademark.* a justifying typewriter used to produce copy in various type styles.
varix (ˈvɛərɪks) *n., pl.* **varices** (ˈværɪˌsiːz). *Pathol.* **a.** a tortuous dilated vein. See **varicose veins. b.** Also called: **arterial varix, varix lymphaticus.** a similar condition affecting an artery or lymphatic vessel. [C15: from Latin]
varlet (ˈvɑːlɪt) *n. Archaic.* **1.** a menial servant. **2.** a knight's page. **3.** a rascal. [C15: from Old French, variant of *vallet* VALET]
varletry (ˈvɑːlɪtrɪ) *n. Archaic.* **1. the.** rabble; mob. **2.** varlets collectively.
varmint (ˈvɑːmɪnt) *n. Informal.* an irritating or obnoxious person or animal. [C16: dialect variant of *varmin* VERMIN]
varna (ˈvɑːnə) *n.* any of the four Hindu castes; Brahman, Kshatriya, Vaisya, or Sudra. [from Sanskrit: class]
varnish (ˈvɑːnɪʃ) *n.* **1.** Also called: **oil varnish.** a preparation consisting of a solvent, a drying oil, and usually resin, rubber, bitumen, etc., for application to a surface where it polymerizes to yield a hard glossy, usually transparent, coating. **2.** a similar preparation consisting of a substance, such as shellac or cellulose ester, dissolved in a volatile solvent, such as alcohol. It hardens to a film on evaporation of the solvent. See also **spirit varnish. 3.** Also called: **natural varnish.** the sap of certain trees used to produce such a coating. **4.** a smooth surface, coated with or as with varnish. **5.** an artificial, superficial, or deceptively pleasing manner, covering, etc.; veneer. **6.** *Chiefly Brit.* another word for **nail polish.** ~*vb.* (*tr.*) **7.** to cover with varnish. **8.** to give a smooth surface to, as if by painting with varnish. **9.** to impart a more attractive appearance to. **10.** to make superficially attractive. [C14: from Old French *vernis*, from Medieval Latin *veronix* sandarac, resin, from Medieval Greek *berenikē*, perhaps from Greek *Berenikē*, city in Cyrenaica, Libya where varnishes were used] —**ˈvarnisher** *n.*
varnishing day *n.* (at an exhibition of paintings) the day before the opening when artists may varnish or retouch their pictures after they have been hung.
varnish tree *n.* any of various trees, such as the lacquer tree, yielding substances used to make varnish or lacquer.
varsity (ˈvɑːsɪtɪ) *n., pl.* **-ties.** *Brit. and N.Z. informal.* short for **university:** formerly used esp. at the universities of Oxford and Cambridge.
varus (ˈvɛərəs) *adj. Pathol.* turned inwards towards the midline of the body. [C19: from Latin: crooked, bent]
varve (vɑːv) *n. Geology.* **1.** a band of sediment deposited in glacial lakes, consisting of a light layer and a dark layer deposited at different seasons. **2.** either of the layers of sediment making up this band. [C20: from Swedish *varv* layer, from *varva*, from Old Norse *hverfa* to turn]
vary (ˈvɛərɪ) *vb.* **varies, varying, varied. 1.** to undergo or cause to undergo change, alteration, or modification in appearance, character, form, attribute, etc. **2.** to be different or cause to be different; be subject to change. **3.** (*tr.*) to give variety to. **4.** (*intr.;* foll. by *from*) to differ, as from a convention, standard, etc. **5.** (*intr.*) to change in accordance with another variable: *her mood varies with the weather; pressure varies directly with temperature and inversely with volume.* **6.** (*tr.*) *Music.* to modify (a theme) by the use of variation. [C14: from Latin *variāre*, from *varius* VARIOUS] —**ˈvarying** *adj.* —**ˈvaryingly** *adv.*
vas (væs) *n., pl.* **vasa** (ˈveɪsə). *Anatomy, zoology.* a vessel, duct, or tube that carries a fluid. [C17: from Latin: vessel]
vas- *combining form.* a variant of **vaso-** before a vowel.
vascular (ˈvæskjʊlə) *adj. Biology, anatomy.* of, relating to, or having vessels that conduct and circulate liquids: *a vascular bundle; the blood vascular system.* [C17: from New Latin *vāsculāris*, from Latin: VASCULUM] —**vascularity** (ˌvæskjʊˈlærɪtɪ) *n.* —**ˈvascularly** *adv.*
vascular bundle *n.* a longitudinal strand of vascular tissue in the stems and leaves of higher plants.
vascularization *or* **vascularisation** (ˌvæskjʊləraɪˈzeɪʃən) *n.* the development of blood vessels in an organ or part.
vascular ray *n.* another name for **medullary ray.**
vascular tissue *n.* tissue of higher plants consisting mainly of xylem and phloem and occurring as a continuous system throughout the plant: it conducts water, mineral salts, and synthesized food substances and provides mechanical support. Also called: **conducting tissue.**
vasculum (ˈvæskjʊləm) *n., pl.* **-la** (-lə) *or* **-lums.** a metal box used by botanists in the field for carrying botanical specimens. [C19: from Latin: little vessel, from VAS]
vas deferens (ˈvæs ˈdɛfəˌrɛnz) *n., pl.* **vasa deferentia** (ˈveɪsə ˌdɛfəˈrɛnʃɪə). *Anatomy.* the duct that conveys spermatozoa from the epididymis to the urethra. [C16: from New Latin, from Latin *vās* vessel + *deferēns*, present participle of *deferre* to bear away]
vase (vɑːz) *n.* a vessel used as an ornament or for holding cut flowers. [C17: via French from Latin *vās* vessel]
vasectomy (væˈsɛktəmɪ) *n., pl.* **-mies.** surgical removal of all or part of the vas deferens, esp. as a method of contraception.
Vaseline (ˈvæsɪˌliːn) *n.* a trademark for **petrolatum.**
vaso- *or before a vowel* **vas-** *combining form.* **1.** indicating a blood vessel: *vasodilator.* **2.** indicating the vas deferens: *vasectomy.* [from Latin *vās* vessel]
vasoactive (ˌveɪzəʊˈæktɪv) *adj.* affecting the diameter of blood vessels: *vasoactive peptides.*
vasoconstrictor (ˌveɪzəʊkənˈstrɪktə) *n.* **1.** a drug, agent, or nerve that causes narrowing (**vasoconstriction**) of the walls of blood vessels. ~*adj.* **2.** causing vasoconstriction. —ˌ**vasoconˈstrictive** *adj.*
vasodilator (ˌveɪzəʊdaɪˈleɪtə) *n.* **1.** a drug, agent, or nerve that can cause dilation (**vasodilation**) of the walls of blood vessels. ~*adj.* **2.** causing vasodilation.
vasoinhibitor (ˌveɪzəʊɪnˈhɪbɪtə) *n.* any of a group of drugs that reduce or inhibit the action of the vasomotor nerves. —**vasoinhibitory** (ˌveɪzəʊɪnˈhɪbɪtərɪ, -trɪ) *adj.*
vasomotor (ˌveɪzəʊˈməʊtə) *adj.* (of a drug, agent, nerve, etc.) relating to or affecting the diameter of blood vessels.
vasopressin (ˌveɪzəʊˈprɛsɪn) *n.* a polypeptide hormone secreted by the posterior lobe of the pituitary gland. It increases the reabsorption of water by the kidney tubules and increases blood pressure by constricting the arteries. Also called: **antidiuretic hormone.** Chemical name: **beta-hypophamine.** Compare **oxytocin.** [from *Vasopressin*, a trademark]

vasopressor (ˌveɪzəʊˈprɛsə) *Med.* ~*adj.* **1.** causing an increase in blood pressure by constricting the arteries. ~*n.* **2.** a substance that has such an effect.
vassal (ˈvæsᵊl) *n.* **1.** (in feudal society) a man who entered into a personal relationship with a lord to whom he paid homage and fealty in return for protection and often a fief. A **great vassal** was in vassalage to a king and a **rear vassal** to a great vassal. **2. a.** a person, nation, etc., in a subordinate, suppliant, or dependent position relative to another. **b.** (*as modifier*): *vassal status.* ~*adj.* **3.** of or relating to a vassal. [C14: via Old French from Medieval Latin *vassallus,* from *vassus* servant, of Celtic origin; compare Welsh *gwas* boy, Old Irish *foss* servant] —ˈ**vassal-less** *adj.*
vassalage (ˈvæsəlɪdʒ) *n.* **1.** (esp. in feudal society) **a.** the condition of being a vassal or the obligations to which a vassal was liable. **b.** the relationship between a vassal and his lord. **2.** subjection, servitude, or dependence in general. **3.** *Rare.* vassals collectively.
vassalize *or* **vassalise** (ˈvæsəˌlaɪz) *vb.* (*tr.*) to make a vassal of.
vast (vɑːst) *adj.* **1.** unusually large in size, extent, degree, or number; immense. **2.** (*prenominal*) (intensifier): *in vast haste.* ~*n.* **3. the vast.** *Chiefly poetic.* immense or boundless space. **4.** *Brit. dialect.* a very great amount or number. [C16: from Latin *vastus* deserted] —ˈ**vastity** *n.* —ˈ**vastly** *adv.* —ˈ**vastness** *n.*
vastitude (ˈvɑːstɪˌtjuːd) *n. Rare.* **1.** the condition or quality of being vast. **2.** a vast space, expanse, extent, etc.
vasty (ˈvɑːstɪ) *adj.* **vastier, vastiest.** an archaic or poetic word for **vast.**
vat (væt) *n.* **1.** a large container for holding or storing liquids. **2.** *Chem.* a preparation of reduced vat dye. ~*vb.* **vats, vatting, vatted. 3.** (*tr.*) to place, store, or treat in a vat. [Old English *fæt;* related to Old Frisian *fet,* Old Saxon, Old Norse *fat,* Old High German *faz*]
VAT (*sometimes* væt) (in Britain) *abbrev. for* value-added tax: a tax levied on the difference between the cost of materials and the selling price of a commodity or service.
Vat. *abbrev. for* Vatican.
vat dye *n.* a dye, such as indigo, that is applied by first reducing it to its leuco base, which is soluble in alkali, and then regenerating the insoluble dye by oxidation in the fibres of the material. —ˈ**vat-ˌdyed** *adj.*
vatic (ˈvætɪk) *adj. Rare.* of, relating to, or characteristic of a prophet; oracular. [C16: from Latin *vātēs* prophet]
Vatican (ˈvætɪkən) *n.* **a.** the authority of the Pope and the papal curia. **b.** (*as modifier*): *a Vatican edict.* [C16: after the principal residence of the popes in Rome, from Latin *Vāticānus mons* Vatican hill, on the western bank of the Tiber, of Etruscan origin]
Vaticanism (ˈvætɪkəˌnɪzəm) *n. Often derogatory.* the authority and policies of the Pope and the papal curia, esp. with regard to papal infallibility.
vaticide (ˈvætɪˌsaɪd) *n. Rare.* **a.** the murder of a prophet. **b.** a person guilty of this. [C18: from Latin *vātēs* prophet + -CIDE]
vaticinate (vəˈtɪsɪˌneɪt) *vb. Rare.* to foretell; prophesy. [C17: from Latin *vāticinārī* from *vātēs* prophet + *canere* to foretell] —**vaticination** (ˌvætɪsɪˈneɪʃən) *n.* —**vaˈticiˌnator** *n.* —**vaticinal** (vəˈtɪsɪnᵊl) *or* **vaˈticinatory** *adj.*
vaudeville (ˈvəʊdəvɪl, ˈvɔː-) *n.* **1.** *Chiefly U.S. and Canadian.* variety entertainment consisting of short acts such as acrobatic turns, song-and-dance routines, animal acts, etc., popular esp. in the early 20th century. **2.** a light or comic theatrical piece interspersed with songs and dances. [C18: from French, from *vaudevire* satirical folk song, shortened from *chanson du vau de Vire* song of the valley of Vire, a district in Normandy where this type of song flourished]
vaudevillian (ˌvəʊdəˈvɪlɪən, ˌvɔː-) *n. also* **vaudevillist. 1.** a person who writes for or performs in vaudeville. ~*adj.* **2.** of, characteristic of, or relating to vaudeville.
Vaudois (ˈvəʊdwɑː) *pl. n., sing.* **-dois.** another name for the **Waldenses.**
vault[1] (vɔːlt) *n.* **1.** an arched structure that forms a roof or ceiling. **2.** a room, esp. a cellar, having an arched roof down to floor level. **3.** a burial chamber, esp. when underground. **4.** a strongroom for the safe-deposit and storage of valuables. **5.** an underground room or part of such a room, used for the storage of wine, food, etc. **6.** *Anatomy.* any arched or domed bodily cavity or space: *the cranial vault.* **7.** something suggestive of an arched structure, as the sky. ~*vb.* **8.** (*tr.*) to furnish with or as if with an arched roof. **9.** (*tr.*) to construct in the shape of a vault. **10.** (*intr.*) to curve, arch, or bend in the shape of a vault. [C14 *vaute,* from Old French, from Vulgar Latin *volvita* (unattested) a turn, probably from Latin *volvere* to roll] —ˈ**vaultˌlike** *adj.*
vault[2] (vɔːlt) *vb.* **1.** to spring over (an object), esp. with the aid of a long pole or with the hands resting on the object. **2.** (*intr.*) to do, achieve, or attain something as if by a leap: *he vaulted to fame on the strength of his discovery.* **3.** *Dressage.* to perform or cause to perform a curvet. ~*n.* **4.** the act of vaulting. **5.** *Dressage.* a low leap; curvet. [C16: from Old French *voulter* to turn, from Italian *voltare* to turn, from Vulgar Latin *volvitāre* (unattested) to turn, leap; see VAULT[1]] —ˈ**vaulter** *n.*
vaulting[1] (ˈvɔːltɪŋ) *n.* one or more vaults in a building or such structures considered collectively.
vaulting[2] (ˈvɔːltɪŋ) *adj.* (*prenominal*) **1.** excessively confident; overreaching; exaggerated: *vaulting arrogance.* **2.** used to vault: *a vaulting pole.*
vaunt (vɔːnt) *vb.* **1.** (*tr.*) to describe, praise, or display (one's success, possessions, etc.) boastfully. **2.** (*intr.*) *Rare or literary.* to use boastful language; brag. ~*n.* **3.** a boast. **4.** *Archaic.* ostentatious display. [C14: from Old French *vanter,* from Late Latin *vānitāre* to brag, from Latin *vānus* VAIN] —ˈ**vaunter** *n.*
vaunt-courier *n. Archaic or poetic.* a person or thing that goes in advance; forerunner; herald. [C16: from French *avant-courrier;* see AVAUNT, COURIER]
v. aux. *abbrev. for* auxiliary verb.
vav (vɔːv) *n.* the sixth letter of the Hebrew alphabet (ו) transliterated as *v* or *w.* Also called: **waw.** [from Hebrew *wāw* a hook]
vavasor (ˈvævəˌsɔː) *or* **vavasour** (ˈvævəˌsʊə) *n.* (in feudal society) the noble or knightly vassal of a baron or great lord who also has vassals himself. Also: **vavassor.** [C13: from Old French *vavasour,* perhaps contraction of Medieval Latin *vassus vassōrum* vassal of vassals; see VASSAL]
vb *abbrev. for* verb.
VB (in transformational grammar) *abbrev. for* verbal constituent.
VC *abbrev. for:* **1.** Vice-chairman. **2.** Vice Chancellor. **3.** Vice Consul. **4.** Victoria Cross. **5.** Vietcong.
VCR *abbrev. for:* **1.** video cassette recorder. **2.** visual control room (at an airfield).
vd *abbrev. for* various dates.
VD *abbrev. for* venereal disease.
V-Day *n.* a day nominated to celebrate victory, as in V-E Day or V-J Day in World War II.
VDC *abbrev. for* Volunteer Defence Corps.
VDQS *abbrev. for* vins délimités de qualité supérieure: on a bottle of French wine, indicates that it contains high-quality wine from an approved regional vineyard: the second highest French wine classification. Compare **AOC,** ***vin de pays.***
VDT *Computer technol. abbrev. for* visual display terminal.
VDU *Computer technol. abbrev. for* visual display unit.
've *contraction of* have: *I've; you've.*
Veadar *Hebrew.* (ˈviːəˌdɑː, ˈveɪ-) *n. Judaism.* another term for **Adar Sheni:** see **Adar.** [from Hebrew *va'adhar,* literally: and Adar, that is, the extra Adar]
veal (viːl) *n.* **1.** the flesh of the calf used as food. **2.** Also called: **veal calf.** a calf, esp. one bred for eating. [C14: from Old French *veel,* from Latin *vitellus* a little calf, from *vitulus* calf]
vealer (ˈviːlə) *n.* **1.** *U.S., Canadian and Austral.* another name for **veal** (sense 2). **2.** *N.Z.* a young bovine animal of up to 14 months old grown for veal.
vector (ˈvɛktə) *n.* **1.** Also called: **polar vector.** *Maths.* a variable quantity, such as force, that has magnitude and direction and can be resolved into components that are odd functions of the coordinates. It is represented in print by a bold italic symbol: ***F*** or $\bar{F}$. Compare **pseudoscalar, pseudovector, scalar** (sense 1), **tensor** (sense 2). **2.** *Maths.* an element of a vector space. **3.** Also called: **carrier.** *Pathol.* an organism, esp. an insect, that carries a disease-producing microorganism from one host to another, either within or on the surface of its body. **4.** Also called: **cloning vector.** *Genetics.* an agent, such as a bacteriophage or a plasmid, by means of which a fragment of foreign DNA is inserted into a host cell to produce a gene clone in genetic engineering. **5.** the course or compass direction of an aircraft. **6.** any behavioural influence, force, or drive. ~*vb.* (*tr.*) **7.** to direct or guide (a pilot, aircraft, etc.) by directions transmitted by radio. **8.** to alter the direction of (the thrust of a jet engine) as a means of steering an aircraft. [C18: from Latin: carrier, from *vehere* to convey] —**vectorial** (vɛkˈtɔːrɪəl) *adj.* —**vecˈtorially** *adv.*
vector field *n.* a region of space under the influence of some vector quantity, such as magnetic field strength, in which each point can be described by a vector.
vector product *n.* the product of two vectors that is a pseudovector, whose magnitude is the product of the magnitudes of the given vectors and the sine of the angle between them. Its axis is perpendicular to the plane of the given vectors. Written: $\boldsymbol{A}\times\boldsymbol{B}$ or $\boldsymbol{A}\wedge\boldsymbol{B}$. Compare **scalar product.** Also called: **cross product.**
vector space *n. Maths.* a mathematical structure consisting of a set of objects (**vectors**) associated with a field of objects (**scalars**), such that the set constitutes an Abelian group and a further operation, scalar multiplication, is defined in which the product of a scalar and a vector is a vector. See also **scalar multiplication.**
vector sum *n.* a vector whose length and direction are represented by the diagonal of a parallelogram whose sides represent the given vectors. See also **resultant.**
Veda (ˈveɪdə) *n.* any or all of the most ancient sacred writings of Hinduism, esp. the Rig-Veda, Yajur-Veda, Sama-Veda, and Atharva-Veda. [C18: from Sanskrit: knowledge; related to *veda* I know] —**Vedaic** (vɪˈdeɪɪk) *adj.* —**Vedaism** (ˈveɪdəˌɪzəm) *n.*
vedalia (vɪˈdeɪlɪə) *n.* an Australian ladybird, *Rodolia cardinalis,* introduced elsewhere to control the scale insect *Icerya purchasi,* which is a pest of citrus fruits. [C20: from New Latin]
Vedanta (vɪˈdɑːntə, -ˈdæn-) *n.* one of the six main philosophical schools of Hinduism, expounding the monism regarded as implicit in the Veda in accordance with the doctrines of the Upani-

shads. It teaches that only Brahma has reality, while the whole phenomenal world is the outcome of illusion (maya). [C19: from Sanskrit, from VEDA + *ánta* end] —**Ve'dantic** *adj.* —**Ve'dantism** *n.* —**Ve'dantist** *n.*

V-E Day *n.* the day marking the Allied victory in Europe in World War II (May 8, 1945).

Vedda *or* **Veddah** ('vɛdə) *n., pl.* **-da, -das** *or* **-dah, -dahs.** a member of an aboriginal people of Sri Lanka, characterized by slender build, dark complexion, and wavy hair, noted for their Stone Age technology. [C17: from Sinhalese: hunter, of Dravidian origin]

Veddoid ('vɛdɔɪd) *adj.* **1.** of, relating to, or resembling the Vedda. ~*n.* **2.** a Vedda. **3.** a member of a postulated prehistoric race of S Asia, having slender build, dark complexion, and wavy hair: thought to be ancestors of the Vedda.

vedette (vɪ'dɛt) *n.* **1.** Also called: **vedette boat.** *Naval.* a small patrol vessel. **2.** Also called: **vidette.** *Military.* a mounted sentry posted forward of a formation's position. [C17: from French, from Italian *vedetta* (influenced by *vedere* to see), from earlier *veletta,* perhaps from Spanish *vela* watch, from *velar* to keep vigil, from Latin *vigilāre*]

Vedic ('veɪdɪk) *adj.* **1.** of or relating to the Vedas or the ancient form of Sanskrit in which they are written. **2.** of or relating to the ancient Indo-European settlers in India, regarded as the originators of many of the traditions preserved in the Vedas. ~*n.* **3.** the classical form of Sanskrit; the language of the Vedas.

veer[1] (vɪə) *vb.* **1.** to alter direction (of); swing around. **2.** (*intr.*) to change from one position, opinion, etc., to another. **3.** (*intr.*) (of the wind) **a.** to change direction clockwise in the northern hemisphere and anticlockwise in the southern. **b.** *Nautical.* to blow from a direction nearer the stern. Compare **haul** (sense 5). **4.** *Nautical.* to steer (a vessel) off the wind. ~*n.* **5.** a change of course or direction. [C16: from Old French *virer,* probably of Celtic origin; compare Welsh *gwyro* to diverge]

veer[2] (vɪə) *vb.* (*tr.*; often foll. by *out* or *away*) *Nautical.* to slacken or pay out (cable or chain). [C16: from Dutch *vieren,* from Old High German *fieren* to give direction]

veery ('vɪərɪ) *n., pl.* **veeries.** a tawny brown North American thrush, *Hylocichla fuscescens,* with a slightly spotted grey breast. [C19: probably imitative of its note]

veg (vɛdʒ) *n. Informal.* a vegetable or vegetables.

Vega ('viːgə) *n.* the brightest star in the constellation Lyra and one of the most conspicuous in the N hemisphere. It is part of an optical double star having a faint companion. Distance: 26 light years. [C17: from Medieval Latin, from Arabic (*al nasr*) *al wāqi,* literally: the falling (vulture), that is, the constellation Lyra]

vegan ('viːgən) *n.* a person who refrains from using any animal product whatever for food, clothing, or any other purpose.

vegeburger *or* **veggieburger** ('vɛdʒɪˌbɜːgə) *n.* a flat cake of chopped seasoned vegetables and pulses that is grilled or fried and often served in a bread roll.

Vegemite ('vɛdʒɪˌmaɪt) *n. Austral. trademark.* a vegetable extract used as a spread, flavouring, etc.

vegetable ('vɛdʒtəbᵊl) *n.* **1.** any of various herbaceous plants having parts that are used as food, such as peas, beans, cabbage, potatoes, cauliflower, and onions. **2.** *Informal.* a person who has lost control of his mental faculties, limbs, etc., as from an injury, mental disease, etc. **3. a.** a dull inactive person. **b.** (*as modifier*): *a vegetable life.* **4.** (*modifier*) consisting of or made from edible vegetables: *a vegetable diet.* **5.** (*modifier*) of, relating to, characteristic of, derived from, or consisting of plants or plant material: *vegetable oils; the vegetable kingdom.* **6.** *Rare.* any member of the plant kingdom. [C14 (adj.): from Late Latin *vegetābilis* animating, from *vegetāre* to enliven, from Latin *vegēre* to excite]

vegetable butter *n.* any of a group of vegetable fats having the consistency of butter.

vegetable ivory *n.* **1.** the hard whitish material obtained from the endosperm of the ivory nut: used to make buttons, ornaments, etc. **2.** another name for the **ivory nut.**

vegetable kingdom *n.* another name for **plant kingdom.**

vegetable marrow *n.* **1.** a cucurbitaceous plant, *Cucurbita pepo,* probably native to America but widely cultivated for its oblong green striped fruit, which is eaten as a vegetable. **2.** Also called (in the U.S.): **marrow squash.** the fruit of this plant. Often shortened to **marrow.**

vegetable oil *n.* any of a group of oils that are esters of fatty acids and glycerol and are obtained from plants.

vegetable oyster *n.* another name for **salsify** (sense 1).

vegetable sheep *n. N.Z.* any of various species of the genus *Raoulia,* esp. *R. mammillaris* or *R. eximia,* of New Zealand rocky mountains: a small low bush having white flowers and hairy leaves which, from a distance, make it look like a sheep.

vegetable silk *n.* any of various silky fibres obtained from the seed pods of certain plants. See also **kapok.**

vegetable sponge *n.* another name for **dishcloth gourd.**

vegetable tallow *n.* any of various types of tallow that are obtained from plants.

vegetable wax *n.* any of various waxes that occur on parts of certain plants, esp. the trunks of certain palms, and prevent loss of water from the plant.

vegetal ('vɛdʒɪtᵊl) *adj.* **1.** of, relating to, or characteristic of vegetables or plant life. **2.** of or relating to processes in plants and animals that do not involve sexual reproduction; vegetative. [C15: from Late Latin *vegetāre* to quicken; see VEGETABLE]

vegetarian (ˌvɛdʒɪ'tɛərɪən) *n.* **1.** a person who advocates or practises vegetarianism. ~*adj.* **2.** relating to, advocating, or practising vegetarianism. **3.** *Cookery.* strictly, consisting of vegetables and fruit only, but usually including milk, cheese, eggs, etc.

vegetarianism (ˌvɛdʒɪ'tɛərɪəˌnɪzəm) *n.* the principle or practice of excluding all meat and fish, and sometimes, in the case of vegans, all animal products (such as eggs, cheese, etc.) from one's diet.

vegetate ('vɛdʒɪˌteɪt) *vb.* (*intr.*) **1.** to grow like a plant; sprout. **2.** to lead a life characterized by monotony, passivity, or mental inactivity. **3.** *Pathol.* (of a wart, polyp, etc.) to develop fleshy outgrowths. [C17: from Late Latin *vegetāre* to invigorate]

vegetation (ˌvɛdʒɪ'teɪʃən) *n.* **1.** plant life as a whole, esp. the plant life of a particular region. **2.** the process of vegetating. **3.** *Pathol.* any abnormal growth, excrescence, etc. **4.** a vegetative existence. —ˌ**vege'tational** *adj.* —ˌ**vege'tatious** *adj.*

vegetative ('vɛdʒɪtətɪv) *adj.* **1.** of, relating to, or concerned with vegetation, plant life, or plant growth. **2.** (of reproduction) characterized by asexual processes. **3.** of or relating to functions such as digestion, growth, and circulation rather than sexual reproduction. **4.** (of a style of living) dull, stagnant, unthinking, or passive. —'**vegetatively** *adv.* —'**vegetativeness** *n.*

veggie ('vɛdʒɪ) *n., adj.* an informal word for **vegetarian.**

veg out *vb.* **vegges, vegging, vegged.** (*intr., adv.*) *Slang, chiefly U.S.* to relax in an inert passive way; vegetate: *vegging out in front of the television set.*

vehement ('viːɪmənt) *adj.* **1.** marked by intensity of feeling or conviction; emphatic. **2.** (of actions, gestures, etc.) characterized by great energy, vigour, or force; furious. [C15: from Latin *vehemēns* ardent; related to *vehere* to carry] —'**vehemence** *n.* —'**vehemently** *adv.*

vehicle ('viːɪkᵊl) *n.* **1.** any conveyance in or by which people or objects are transported, esp. one fitted with wheels. **2.** a medium for the expression, communication, or achievement of ideas, information, power, etc. **3.** *Pharmacol.* a therapeutically inactive substance mixed with the active ingredient to give bulk to a medicine. **4.** Also called: **base.** a painting medium, such as oil, in which pigments are suspended. **5.** (in the performing arts) a play, musical composition, etc., that enables a particular performer to display his talents. **6.** a rocket excluding its payload. [C17: from Latin *vehiculum,* from *vehere* to carry] —**vehicular** (vɪ'hɪkjʊlə) *adj.*

veil (veɪl) *n.* **1.** a piece of more or less transparent material, usually attached to a hat or headdress, used to conceal or protect a woman's face and head. **2.** part of a nun's headdress falling round the face onto the shoulders. **3.** something that covers, conceals, or separates; mask: *a veil of reticence.* **4. the veil.** the life of a nun in a religious order and the obligations entailed by it. **5. take the veil.** to become a nun. **6.** Also called: **velum.** *Botany.* a membranous structure, esp. the thin layer of cells covering a young mushroom. **7.** *Anatomy.* another word for **caul.** **8.** See **humeral veil.** ~*vb.* **9.** (*tr.*) to cover, conceal, or separate with or as if with a veil. **10.** (*intr.*) to wear or put on a veil. [C13: from Norman French *veile,* from Latin *vēla* sails, pl. of *vēlum* a covering] —'**veiler** *n.* —'**veilless** *adj.* —'**veil-ˌlike** *adj.*

veiled (veɪld) *adj.* **1.** disguised: *a veiled insult.* **2.** (of sound, tone, the voice, etc.) not distinct; muffled. —**veiledly** ('veɪlɪdlɪ) *adv.*

veiling ('veɪlɪŋ) *n.* a veil or the fabric used for veils.

vein (veɪn) *n.* **1.** any of the tubular vessels that convey oxygen-depleted blood to the heart. Compare **pulmonary vein, artery.** **2.** any of the hollow branching tubes that form the supporting framework of an insect's wing. **3.** any of the vascular bundles of a leaf. **4.** a clearly defined mass of ore, mineral, etc., typically occurring as a thin layer in a rock fissure or between rock strata. **5.** an irregular streak of colour or alien substance in marble, wood, or other material. **6.** a natural underground watercourse. **7.** a crack or fissure. **8.** a distinctive trait or quality in speech, writing, character, etc.; strain: *a vein of humour.* **9.** a temporary disposition, attitude, or temper; mood: *the debate entered a frivolous vein.* **10.** *Irish.* a parting in hair. ~*vb.* (*tr.*) **11.** to diffuse over or cause to diffuse over in streaked patterns. **12.** to fill, furnish, or mark with or as if with veins. [C13: from Old French *veine,* from Latin *vēna*] —'**veinal** *adj.* —'**veinless** *adj.* —'**veinˌlike** *adj.* —'**veiny** *adj.*

veining ('veɪnɪŋ) *n.* a pattern or network of veins or streaks.

veinlet ('veɪnlɪt) *n.* any small vein or venule.

veinstone ('veɪnˌstəʊn) *n.* another word for **gangue.**

veinule ('veɪnjuːl) *n.* a less common spelling of **venule.**

vel. *Bookbinding. abbrev. for* vellum.

Vela ('viːlə) *n., Latin genitive* **Velorum** (viː'lɔːrəm). a constellation in the S hemisphere, close to Puppis and Carina and crossed by the Milky Way, that has four second-magnitude stars.

velamen (və'leɪmɛn) *n., pl.* **-lamina** (-'læmɪnə). **1.** the thick layer of dead cells that covers the aerial roots of certain orchids and aroids and absorbs moisture from the surroundings. **2.** *Anatomy.* another word for **velum.** [C19: from Latin: a veil, from *vēlāre* to cover]

velar (ˈviːlə) *adj.* **1.** of, relating to, or attached to a velum: *velar tentacles.* **2.** *Phonetics.* articulated with the soft palate and the back of the tongue, as in the sounds (k), (g), or (ŋ). [C18: from Latin *vēlāris,* from *vēlum* VEIL]

velarium (vɪˈlɛərɪəm) *n., pl.* **-laria** (-ˈlɛərɪə). an awning used to protect the audience in ancient Roman theatres and amphitheatres. [C19: from Latin, from *vēlāre* to cover]

velarize *or* **velarise** (ˈviːləˌraɪz) *vb.* (*tr.*) *Phonetics.* to pronounce or supplement the pronunciation of (a speech sound) with articulation at the soft palate, as in dark (l) in English *tall.* —ˌ**velariˈzation** *or* ˌ**velariˈsation** *n.*

velate (ˈviːlɪt, -leɪt) *adj.* having or covered with velum.

Velcro (ˈvɛlkrəʊ) *n. Trademark.* a fastening consisting of two strips of nylon fabric, one having tiny hooked threads and the other a coarse surface, that form a strong bond when pressed together.

veld *or* **veldt** (fɛlt, vɛlt) *n.* elevated open grassland in Southern Africa. Compare **pampas, prairie, steppe.** [C19: from Afrikaans, from earlier Dutch *veldt* FIELD]

veldskoen (ˈfɛltˌskʊn, ˈvɛlt-) *n.* an ankle-length boot of soft but strong rawhide. [from Afrikaans, literally: field shoe]

veleta *or* **valeta** (vəˈliːtə) *n.* a ballroom dance in triple time. [from Spanish: weather vane]

veliger (ˈvɛlɪdʒə) *n.* the free-swimming larva of many molluscs, having a rudimentary shell and a ciliated velum used for feeding and locomotion. [C19: from New Latin, from VELUM + -GER(OUS)]

velites (ˈviːlɪˌtiːz) *pl. n.* light-armed troops in ancient Rome, drawn from the poorer classes. [C17: from Latin, pl. of *vēles* light-armed foot soldier; related to *volāre* to fly]

velleity (vɛˈliːɪtɪ) *n., pl.* **-ties.** *Rare.* **1.** the weakest level of desire or volition. **2.** a mere wish. [C17: from New Latin *velleitās,* from Latin *velle* to wish]

vellicate (ˈvɛlɪˌkeɪt) *vb. Rare.* to twitch, pluck, or pinch. [C17: from Latin *vellicāre,* from *vellere* to tear off] —ˌ**velliˈcation** *n.* —ˈ**vellicative** *adj.*

vellum (ˈvɛləm) *n.* **1.** a fine parchment prepared from the skin of a calf, kid, or lamb. **2.** a work printed or written on vellum. **3.** a creamy coloured heavy paper resembling vellum. ~*adj.* **4.** made of or resembling vellum. **5.** (of a book) bound in vellum. [C15: from Old French *velin,* from *velin* of a calf, from *veel* VEAL]

veloce (vɪˈləʊtʃɪ) *adj., adv. Music.* to be played rapidly. [from Italian, from Latin *vēlōx* quick]

velocipede (vɪˈlɒsɪˌpiːd) *n.* **1.** an early form of bicycle propelled by pushing along the ground with the feet. **2.** any early form of bicycle or tricycle. [C19: from French *vélocipède,* from Latin *vēlōx* swift + *pēs* foot] —**veˈlociˌpedist** *n.*

velocity (vɪˈlɒsɪtɪ) *n., pl.* **-ties. 1.** speed of motion, action, or operation; rapidity; swiftness. **2.** *Physics.* a measure of the rate of motion of a body expressed as the rate of change of its position in a particular direction with time. It is measured in metres per second, miles per hour, etc. Symbol: *u, v, w* **3.** *Physics.* (not in technical usage) another word for **speed** (sense 3). [C16: from Latin *vēlōcitās,* from *vēlōx* swift; related to *volāre* to fly]

velocity head *n.* the velocity of a fluid expressed in terms of the head or static pressure required to produce that velocity. It equals $\rho v/2$ where ρ is the density of the fluid and v is the velocity. In hydrology the density of water can be written $1/g$ where g is the gravitational constant.

velocity modulation *n.* the modulation in velocity of a beam of electrons or ions caused by passing the beam through a high-frequency electric field, as in a cavity resonator.

velocity of circulation *n. Economics.* the average number of times a unit of money is used in a given time, esp. calculated as the ratio of the total money spent in that time to the total amount of money in circulation.

velodrome (ˈviːləˌdrəʊm, ˈvɛl-) *n.* an arena with a banked track for cycle racing. [C20: from French *vélodrome,* from *vélo-* (from Latin *vēlōx* swift) + -DROME]

velours *or* **velour** (vɛˈlʊə) *n.* any of various fabrics with a velvet-like finish, used for upholstery, coats, hats, etc. [C18: from Old French *velous,* from Old Provençal *velos* velvet, from Latin *villosus* shaggy, from *villus* shaggy hair; compare Latin *vellus* a fleece]

velouté (vəˈluːteɪ) *n.* a rich white sauce or soup made from stock, egg yolks, and cream. [from French, literally: velvety, from Old French *velous;* see VELOURS]

velum (ˈviːləm) *n., pl.* **-la** (-lə). **1.** *Zoology.* any of various membranous structures, such as the ciliated oral membrane of certain mollusc larvae or the veil-like membrane running around the rim of a jellyfish. **2.** *Anatomy.* any of various veil-like bodily structures, esp. the soft palate. **3.** *Botany.* another word for **veil** (sense 6). [C18: from Latin: veil]

velure (vəˈlʊə) *n.* **1.** velvet or a similar fabric. **2.** a hatter's pad, used for smoothing silk hats. [C16: from Old French *velour,* from Old French *velous;* see VELOURS]

velutinous (vəˈluːtɪnəs) *adj.* covered with short dense soft hairs: *velutinous leaves.* [C19: from New Latin *velūtīnus* like velvet]

velvet (ˈvɛlvɪt) *n.* **1. a.** a fabric of silk, cotton, nylon, etc., with a thick close soft usually lustrous pile. **b.** (*as modifier*): *velvet curtains.* **2.** anything with a smooth soft surface. **3. a.** smoothness; softness. **b.** (*as modifier*): *velvet skin; a velvet night.* **4.** the furry covering of the newly formed antlers of a deer. **5.** *Slang, chiefly U.S.* **a.** gambling or speculative winnings. **b.** a gain, esp. when unexpectedly high. **6. on velvet.** *Slang.* in a condition of ease, advantage, or wealth. **7. velvet glove.** gentleness or caution, often concealing strength or determination (esp. in the phrase **an iron hand in a velvet glove**). [C14 *veluet,* from Old French *veluotte,* from *velu* hairy, from Vulgar Latin *villutus* (unattested), from Latin *villus* shaggy hair] —ˈ**velvet-ˌlike** *adj.* —ˈ**velvety** *adj.*

velvet ant *n.* a solitary digger wasp of the family *Mutillidae.* [C19: so named from the wingless female]

velveteen (ˌvɛlvɪˈtiːn) *n.* **1. a.** a cotton fabric resembling velvet with a short thick pile, used for clothing, etc. **b.** (*as modifier*): *velveteen trousers.* **2.** (*pl.*) trousers made of velveteen. —ˌ**velvetˈeened** *adj.*

velvet scoter *n.* a European sea duck, *Melanitta fusca,* the male of which has a black plumage with white patches below the eyes and on the wings.

velvet shank *n.* a bright yellow edible basidiomycetous fungus, *Flammulina velutipes,* common on trunks, stumps, or branches of broad-leaved trees in winter.

velvet stout *n.* a less common name for **black velvet.**

Ven. *abbrev. for* Venerable.

vena (ˈviːnə) *n., pl.* **-nae** (-niː). *Anatomy.* a technical word for **vein.** [C15: from Latin *vēna* VEIN]

vena cava (ˈkeɪvə) *n., pl.* **venae cavae** (ˈkeɪviː). either one of the two large veins that convey oxygen-depleted blood to the heart. [Latin: hollow vein]

venal (ˈviːnᵊl) *adj.* **1.** easily bribed or corrupted; mercenary: *a venal magistrate.* **2.** characterized by corruption: *a venal civilization.* **3.** open to purchase, esp. by bribery: *a venal contract.* [C17: from Latin *vēnālis,* from *vēnum* sale] —**veˈnality** *n.* —ˈ**venally** *adv.*

venatic (viːˈnætɪk) *or* **venatical** *adj.* **1.** of, relating to, or used in hunting. **2.** (of people) engaged in or given to hunting. [C17: from Latin *vēnāticus,* from *vēnārī* to hunt] —**veˈnatically** *adv.*

venation (viːˈneɪʃən) *n.* **1.** the arrangement of the veins in a leaf or in the wing of an insect. **2.** such veins collectively. —**veˈnational** *adj.*

vend (vɛnd) *vb.* **1.** to sell or be sold. **2.** to sell (goods) for a living. **3.** (*tr.*) *Rare.* to utter or publish (an opinion, etc.). [C17: from Latin *vendere,* contraction of *vēnum dare* to offer for sale] —**vendition** (vɛnˈdɪʃən) *n.*

Venda (ˈvɛndə) *n.* **1.** (*pl.* **-da** *or* **-das**) a member of a Negroid people of southern Africa, living chiefly in the N Transvaal. **2.** the language of this people, belonging to the Bantu group of the Niger-Congo family but not easily related to any other members of the group.

vendace (ˈvɛndeɪs) *n., pl.* **-daces** *or* **-dace.** either of two small whitefish, *Coregonus vandesius* (**Lochmaben vendace**) or *C. gracilior* (**Cumberland vendace**), occurring in lakes in Scotland and NW England respectively. See also **powan.** [C18: from New Latin *vandēsius,* from Old French *vandoise,* probably of Celtic origin]

vendee (vɛnˈdiː) *n. Chiefly law.* a person to whom something, esp. real property, is sold; buyer.

Vendémiaire *French.* (vɑ̃demjɛr) *n.* the month of the grape harvest: the first month of the French Revolutionary calendar, extending from Sept. 23 to Oct. 22. [C18: from French, from Latin *vindēmia* vintage, from *vīnum* wine + *dēmere* to take away]

vendetta (vɛnˈdɛtə) *n.* **1.** a private feud, originally between Corsican or Sicilian families, in which the relatives of a murdered person seek vengeance by killing the murderer or some member of his family. **2.** any prolonged feud, quarrel, etc. [C19: from Italian, from Latin *vindicta,* from *vindicāre* to avenge; see VINDICATE] —**venˈdettist** *n.*

vendible (ˈvɛndəbᵊl) *adj.* **1.** saleable or marketable. **2.** *Obsolete.* venal. ~*n.* **3.** (*usually pl.*) *Rare.* a saleable object. —ˌ**vendiˈbility** *or* ˈ**vendibleness** *n.*

vending machine *n.* a machine that automatically dispenses consumer goods such as cigarettes, food, or petrol, when money is inserted. Also called: **automat.**

vendor (ˈvɛndɔː) *or* **vender** (ˈvɛndə) *n.* **1.** *Chiefly law.* a person who sells something, esp. real property. **2.** another name for **vending machine.**

vendor placing *n. Finance.* a method of financing the purchase of one company by another in which the purchasing company pays for the target company in its own shares, on condition that the vendor places these shares with investors for cash payment.

vendue (ˈvɛndjuː) *n. U.S.* a public sale; auction. [C17: from Dutch *vendu,* from Old French *vendue* a sale, from *vendre* to sell, from Latin *vendere*]

veneer (vɪˈnɪə) *n.* **1.** a thin layer of wood, plastic, etc., with a decorative or fine finish that is bonded to the surface of a less expensive material, usually wood. **2.** a superficial appearance, esp. one that is pleasing: *a veneer of gentility.* **3.** any facing material that is applied to a different backing material. **4.** any one of the layers of wood that is used to form plywood. ~*vb.* (*tr.*) **5.** to cover (a surface) with a veneer. **6.** to bond together (thin layers of wood) to make plywood. **7.** to conceal (something) under a superficially pleasant surface. [C17: from German *furnieren* to veneer, from Old French *fournir* to FURNISH] —**veˈneerer** *n.*

veneering (vɪˈnɪərɪŋ) *n.* **1.** material used as veneer or a veneered surface. **2.** *Rare.* a superficial show.

venenose (ˈvɛnɪˌnəʊs) *adj. Rare.* poisonous. [C17: from Late Latin *venēnōsus,* from Latin *venēnum* poison]
venepuncture (ˈvɛnɪˌpʌŋktʃə) *n.* a variant spelling of **venipuncture.**
venerable (ˈvɛnərəbᵊl) *adj.* **1.** (esp. of a person) worthy of reverence on account of great age, religious associations, character, position, etc. **2.** (of inanimate objects) hallowed or impressive on account of historical or religious association. **3.** ancient: *venerable tomes.* **4.** *R.C. Church.* a title bestowed on a deceased person when the first stage of his canonization has been accomplished and his holiness has been recognized in a decree of the official Church. **5.** *Church of England.* a title given to an archdeacon. [C15: from Latin *venerābilis,* from *venerārī* to venerate] —ˌ**veneraˈbility** *or* ˈ**venerableness** *n.* —ˈ**venerably** *adv.*
venerate (ˈvɛnəˌreɪt) *vb.* (*tr.*) **1.** to hold in deep respect; revere. **2.** to honour in recognition of qualities of holiness, excellence, wisdom, etc. [C17: from Latin *venerārī,* from *venus* love] —ˈ**venerˌator** *n.*
veneration (ˌvɛnəˈreɪʃən) *n.* **1.** a feeling or expression of awe or reverence. **2.** the act of venerating or the state of being venerated. —ˌ**venerˈational** *adj.* —ˈ**venerativeness** *n.*
venereal (vɪˈnɪərɪəl) *adj.* **1.** of, relating to, or infected with venereal disease. **2.** (of a disease) transmitted by sexual intercourse. **3.** of, relating to, or involving the genitals. **4.** of or relating to sexual intercourse or erotic desire; aphrodisiac. [C15: from Latin *venereus* concerning sexual love, from *venus* sexual love, from *Venus,* Roman goddess of love]
venereal disease *n.* any of various diseases, such as syphilis or gonorrhoea, transmitted by sexual intercourse. Abbrev.: **VD.**
venereology (vɪˌnɪərɪˈɒlədʒɪ) *n.* the branch of medicine concerned with the study and treatment of venereal disease. —**veˌnereˈologist** *n.*
venery[1] (ˈvɛnərɪ, ˈviː-) *n. Archaic.* the pursuit of sexual gratification. [C15: from Medieval Latin *veneria,* from Latin *venus* love; see VENEREAL]
venery[2] (ˈvɛnərɪ, ˈviː-) *n.* the art, sport, lore, or practice of hunting, esp. with hounds; the chase. [C14: from Old French *venerie,* from *vener* to hunt, from Latin *vēnārī*]
venesection (ˈvɛnɪˌsɛkʃən) *n.* surgical incision into a vein. [C17: from New Latin *vēnae sectiō;* see VEIN, SECTION]
Venetian (vɪˈniːʃən) *adj.* **1.** of, relating to, or characteristic of Venice, a city and port in NE Italy, or its inhabitants. ~*n.* **2.** a native or inhabitant of Venice. **3.** See **Venetian blind. 4.** (*sometimes not cap.*) one of the tapes that join the slats of a Venetian blind. **5.** a cotton or woollen cloth used for linings.
Venetian blind *n.* a window blind consisting of a number of horizontal slats whose angle may be altered to let in more or less light.
Venetian glass *n.* fine ornamental glassware made in or near Venice, esp. on the island of Murano.
Venetian red *n.* **1.** natural or synthetic ferric oxide used as a red pigment. **2. a.** a moderate to strong reddish-brown colour. **b.** (*as adj.*): *a Venetian-red coat.*
Venetic (vɪˈnɛtɪk) *n.* an ancient language of NE Italy, usually regarded as belonging to the Italic branch of the Indo-European family. It is recorded in about 200 inscriptions and was extinct by the 2nd century A.D.
Venez. *abbrev. for* Venezuela.
Venezuelan (ˌvɛnɪˈzweɪlən) *adj.* **1.** of or relating to Venezuela, a republic in South America, or to its people, or culture. ~*n.* **2.** a native or inhabitant of Venezuela.
venge (vɛndʒ) *vb.* (*tr.*) an archaic word for **avenge.** [C13: from Old French *venger,* from Latin *vindicāre;* see VINDICATE]
vengeance (ˈvɛndʒəns) *n.* **1.** the act of or desire for taking revenge; retributive punishment. **2. with a vengeance.** (intensifier): *he's a coward with a vengeance.* [C13: from Old French, from *venger* to avenge, from Latin *vindicāre* to punish; see VINDICATE]
vengeful (ˈvɛndʒfʊl) *adj.* **1.** desiring revenge; vindictive. **2.** characterized by or indicating a desire for revenge: *a vengeful glance.* **3.** inflicting or taking revenge: *with vengeful blows.* —ˈ**vengefully** *adv.* —ˈ**vengefulness** *n.*
venial (ˈviːnɪəl) *adj.* easily excused or forgiven: *a venial error.* [C13: via Old French from Late Latin *veniālis,* from Latin *venia* forgiveness; related to Latin *venus* love] —ˌ**veniˈality** *n.* —ˈ**venially** *adv.*
venial sin *n. Christianity.* a sin regarded as involving only a partial loss of grace. Compare **mortal sin.**
venin (ˈvɛnɪn, ˈviː-) *n.* any of the poisonous constituents of animal venoms. [C20: from French *ven(in)* poison + -IN]
venipuncture *or* **venepuncture** (ˈvɛnɪˌpʌŋktʃə) *n. Med.* the puncturing of a vein, esp. to take a sample of venous blood or inject a drug.
venire facias (vɪˈnaɪrɪ ˈfeɪʃɪˌæs) *n. Law.* (formerly) a writ directing a sheriff to summon suitable persons to form a jury. [C15: Latin, literally: you must make come]
venireman (vɪˈnaɪərɪmən) *n., pl.* **-men.** (in the U.S. and formerly in England) a person summoned for jury service under a venire facias.
venison (ˈvɛnzən; ˈvɛnɪzᵊn, -sᵊn) *n.* **1.** the flesh of a deer, used as food. **2.** *Archaic.* the flesh of any game animal used for food. [C13: from Old French *venaison,* from Latin *vēnātiō* hunting, from *vēnārī* to hunt]
Venite (vɪˈnaɪtɪ) *n.* **1.** *Ecclesiast.* the opening word of the 95th psalm, an invitatory prayer at matins. **2.** a musical setting of this. [Latin: come ye]
Venn diagram (vɛn) *n. Maths, logic.* a diagram in which mathematical sets or terms of a categorial statement are represented by overlapping circles within a boundary representing the universal set, so that all possible combinations of the relevant properties are represented by the various distinct areas in the diagram. [C19: named after John *Venn* (1834–1923), British logician]
vennel (ˈvɛnᵊl) *n. Scot.* a lane; alley. [C15: from Old French *venelle,* from Latin *vēna* vein]
venography (vɪˈnɒgrəfɪ) *n. Med.* radiography of veins after injection of a contrast medium. Also called: **phlebography.**
venom (ˈvɛnəm) *n.* **1.** a poisonous fluid secreted by such animals as certain snakes and scorpions and usually transmitted by a bite or sting. **2.** malice; spite. **3.** *Archaic.* any kind of poison. [C13: from Old French *venim,* from Latin *venēnum* poison, love potion; related to *venus* sexual love] —ˈ**venomless** *adj.* —ˈ**venomous** *adj.* —ˈ**venomously** *adv.* —ˈ**venomousness** *n.*
venosclerosis (ˌviːnəʊsklɪˈrəʊsɪs) *n.* another name for **phlebosclerosis.**
venose (ˈviːnəʊs) *adj.* **1.** having veins; venous. **2.** (of a plant) covered with veins or similar ridges. [C17: via Latin *vēnōsus,* from *vēna* a VEIN]
venosity (vɪˈnɒsɪtɪ) *n.* **1.** an excessive quantity of blood in the venous system or in an organ or part. **2.** an unusually large number of blood vessels in an organ or part.
venous (ˈviːnəs) *adj.* **1.** *Physiol.* of or relating to the blood circulating in the veins. **2.** of or relating to the veins. [C17: see VENOSE] —ˈ**venously** *adv.* —ˈ**venousness** *n.*
vent[1] (vɛnt) *n.* **1.** a small opening for the passage or escape of fumes, liquids, etc. **2.** the shaft of a volcano or an aperture in the earth's crust through which lava and gases erupt. **3.** the external opening of the urinary or genital systems of lower vertebrates. **4.** a small aperture at the breech of old guns through which the charge was ignited. **5.** an exit, escape, or passage. **6. give vent to.** to release (an emotion, passion, idea, etc.) in an utterance or outburst. ~*vb.* (*mainly tr.*) **7.** to release or give expression or utterance to (an emotion, idea, etc.): *he vents his anger on his wife.* **8.** to provide a vent for or make vents in. **9.** to let out (steam, liquid, etc.) through a vent. [C14: from Old French *esventer* to blow out, from EX-[1] + *venter,* from Vulgar Latin *ventāre* (unattested) to be windy, from Latin *ventus* wind] —ˈ**venter** *n.* —ˈ**ventless** *adj.*
vent[2] (vɛnt) *n.* **1.** a vertical slit at the back or both sides of a jacket. ~*vb.* **2.** (*tr.*) to make a vent or vents in (a jacket). [C15: from Old French *fente* slit, from *fendre* to split, from Latin *findere* to cleave]
ventage (ˈvɛntɪdʒ) *n.* **1.** a small opening; vent. **2.** a finger hole in a musical instrument such as a recorder.
ventail (ˈvɛnteɪl) *n.* (in medieval armour) a covering for the lower part of the face. [C14: from Old French *ventaille* sluice, from *vent* wind, from Latin *ventus*]
venter (ˈvɛntə) *n.* **1.** *Anatomy, zoology.* **a.** the belly or abdomen of vertebrates. **b.** a protuberant structure or part, such as the belly of a muscle. **c.** *Rare.* the abdominal cavity. **2.** *Botany.* the swollen basal region of an archegonium, containing the developing ovum. **3.** *Law.* the womb. **4. in venter.** *Law.* conceived but not yet born. [C16: from Latin]
ventifact (ˈvɛntɪˌfækt) *n. Geology.* a pebble that has been shaped by wind-blown sand.
ventilate (ˈvɛntɪˌleɪt) *vb.* (*tr.*) **1.** to drive foul air out of (an enclosed area). **2.** to provide with a means of airing. **3.** to expose (a question, grievance, etc.) to public examination or discussion. **4.** *Physiol.* to oxygenate (the blood) in the capillaries of the lungs. **5.** to winnow (grain). [C15: from Latin *ventilāre* to fan, from *ventulus* diminutive of *ventus* wind] —ˈ**ventilable** *adj.*
ventilation (ˌvɛntɪˈleɪʃən) *n.* **1.** the act or process of ventilating or the state of being ventilated. **2.** an installation in a building that provides a supply of fresh air. —ˈ**ventiˌlative** *adj.* —ˈ**ventiˌlatory** *adj.*
ventilator (ˈvɛntɪˌleɪtə) *n.* **1.** an opening or device, such as a fan, used to ventilate a room, building, etc. **2.** *Med.* a machine that maintains a flow of air into and out of the lungs of a patient who is unable to breathe normally.
Ventôse *French.* (vɑ̃toz) *n.* the windy month: the sixth month of the French Revolutionary calendar, extending from Feb. 20 to March 21. [C18: from Latin *ventōsus* full of wind, from *ventus* wind]
ventral (ˈvɛntrəl) *adj.* **1.** relating to the front part of the body; towards the belly. Compare **dorsal. 2.** of, relating to, or situated on the upper or inner side of a plant organ, esp. a leaf, that is facing the axis. [C18: from Latin *ventrālis,* from *venter* abdomen] —ˈ**ventrally** *adv.*
ventral fin *n.* **1.** another name for **pelvic fin. 2.** any unpaired median fin situated on the undersurface of fishes and some other aquatic vertebrates.
ventricle (ˈvɛntrɪkᵊl) *n. Anatomy.* **1.** a chamber of the heart, having thick muscular walls, that receives blood from the atrium and pumps it to the arteries. **2.** any one of the four main cavities of the vertebrate brain, which contain cerebrospinal fluid. **3.**

any of various other small cavities in the body. [C14: from Latin *ventriculus*, diminutive of *venter* belly]

ventricose ('vɛntrɪˌkəʊs) *adj.* **1.** *Botany, zoology, anatomy.* having a swelling on one side; unequally inflated: *the ventricose corolla of many labiate plants.* **2.** another word for **corpulent.** [C18: from New Latin *ventricōsus*, from Latin *venter* belly] —**ventricosity** (ˌvɛntrɪ'kɒsɪtɪ) *n.*

ventricular (vɛn'trɪkjʊlə) *adj.* **1.** of, relating to, involving, or constituting a ventricle. **2.** having a belly. **3.** swollen or distended; ventricose.

ventriculography (vɛnˌtrɪkjʊ'lɒgrəfɪ) *n. Med.* **1.** radiography of the ventricles of the heart after injection of a contrast medium. **2.** radiography of the ventricles of the brain after injection of air or a radiopaque material.

ventriculus (vɛn'trɪkjʊləs) *n., pl.* **-li** (-ˌlaɪ). **1.** *Zoology.* **a.** the midgut of an insect, where digestion takes place. **b.** the gizzard of a bird. **2.** another word for **ventricle.** [C18: from Latin, diminutive of *venter* belly]

ventriloquism (vɛn'trɪləˌkwɪzəm) *or* **ventriloquy** *n.* the art of producing vocal sounds that appear to come from another source. [C18: from Latin *venter* belly + *loquī* to speak] —**ventriloquial** (ˌvɛntrɪ'ləʊkwɪəl) *or* **ventriloqual** (vɛn'trɪləkwəl) *adj.* —ˌ**ventri'loquially** *adv.* —**ven'triloquist** *n.* —**venˌtrilo'quistic** *adj.*

ventriloquize *or* **ventriloquise** (vɛn'trɪləˌkwaɪz) *vb.* to produce (sounds) in the manner of a ventriloquist.

venture ('vɛntʃə) *vb.* **1.** (*tr.*) to expose to danger; hazard: *he ventured his life.* **2.** (*tr.*) to brave the dangers of (something): *I'll venture the seas.* **3.** (*tr.*) to dare (to do something): *does he venture to object?* **4.** (*tr.; may take a clause as object*) to express in spite of possible refutation or criticism: *I venture that he is not that honest.* **5.** (*intr.*; often foll. by *out, forth,* etc.) to embark on a possibly hazardous journey, undertaking, etc.: *to venture forth upon the high seas.* ~*n.* **6.** an undertaking that is risky or of uncertain outcome. **7. a.** a commercial undertaking characterized by risk of loss as well as opportunity for profit. **b.** the merchandise, money, or other property placed at risk in such an undertaking. **8.** something hazarded or risked in an adventure; stake. **9.** *Archaic.* chance or fortune. **10. at a venture.** at random; by chance. [C15: variant of *aventure* ADVENTURE] —'**venturer** *n.*

venture capital *n.* **1.** capital that is provided for a new commercial enterprise by individuals or organizations other than those who own the new enterprise. **2.** another name for **risk capital.**

Venture Scout *or* **Venturer** *n. Brit.* a young man or woman, aged 16–20, who is a member of the senior branch of the Scouts. Former name: **Rover.** U.S. equivalent: **Explorer.**

venturesome ('vɛntʃəsəm) *or* **venturous** ('vɛntʃərəs) *adj.* **1.** willing to take risks; daring. **2.** hazardous.

Venturi tube (vɛn'tjʊərɪ) *n.* **1.** *Physics.* a device for measuring fluid flow, consisting of a tube so constricted that the pressure differential produced by fluid flowing through the constriction gives a measure of the rate of flow. **2.** Also called: **venturi.** a tube with a constriction used to reduce or control fluid flow, as one in the air inlet of a carburettor. [C19: named after G. B. *Venturi* (1746–1822), Italian physicist]

venue ('vɛnjuː) *n.* **1.** *Law.* **a.** the place in which a cause of action arises. **b.** the place fixed for the trial of a cause. **c.** the locality from which the jurors must be summoned to try a particular cause. **2.** a meeting place. **3.** any place where an organized gathering, such as a rock concert or public meeting, is held. **4.** *Chiefly U.S.* a position in an argument. [C14: from Old French, from *venir* to come, from Latin *venīre*]

venule ('vɛnjuːl) *n.* **1.** *Anatomy.* any of the small branches of a vein that receives oxygen-depleted blood from the capillaries and returns it to the heart via the venous system. **2.** any of the branches of a vein in an insect's wing. [C19: from Latin *vēnula* diminutive of *vēna* VEIN] —**venular** ('vɛnjʊlə) *adj.*

Venus ('viːnəs) *n.* **1.** one of the inferior planets and the second nearest to the sun, visible as a bright morning or evening star. Its surface is extremely hot (over 400°C) and is completely shrouded by dense cloud consisting principally of carbon dioxide. Mean distance from sun: 108 million km; period of revolution around sun: 225 days; period of axial rotation: 244.3 days (retrograde motion); diameter and mass: 96.5 and 81.5 per cent that of earth respectively. **2.** the alchemical name for **copper**[1].

Venusian (vɪ'njuːzɪən) *adj.* **1.** of, occurring on, or relating to the planet Venus. ~*n.* **2.** (in science fiction) an inhabitant of Venus.

Venus's flower basket *n.* any of several deep-sea sponges of the genus *Euplectella*, esp. *E. aspergillum*, having a skeleton composed of interwoven glassy six-rayed spicules. [after *Venus*, Roman goddess of love]

Venus's-flytrap *or* **Venus flytrap** *n.* an insectivorous plant, *Dionaea muscipula*, of Carolina, having hinged two-lobed leaves that snap closed when the sensitive hairs on the surface are touched: family *Droseraceae.* See also **sundew, pitcher plant, butterwort.**

Venus's-girdle *n.* a ctenophore, *Cestum veneris*, of warm seas, having an elongated ribbon-like body.

Venus's-hair *n.* a fragile maidenhair fern, *Adiantum capillus-veneris*, of tropical and subtropical America, having fan-shaped leaves and a black stem.

Venus shell *n.* a marine bivalve mollusc of the family *Veneridae*, typified by the intertidal *Venus gallina*, with somewhat rounded ribbed valves.

Venus's looking glass *n.* a purple-flowered campanulaceous plant, *Legousia hybrida*, of Europe, W Asia, and N Africa.

ver. *abbrev. for:* **1.** verse. **2.** version.

veracious (vɛ'reɪʃəs) *adj.* **1.** habitually truthful or honest. **2.** accurate; precise. [C17: from Latin *vērax*, from *vērus* true] —**ve'raciously** *adv.* —**ve'raciousness** *n.*

veracity (vɛ'ræsɪtɪ) *n., pl.* **-ties. 1.** truthfulness or honesty, esp. when consistent or habitual. **2.** precision; accuracy. **3.** something true; a truth. [C17: from Medieval Latin *vērācitās*, from Latin *vērax*; see VERACIOUS]

veranda *or* **verandah** (və'rændə) *n.* **1.** a porch or portico, sometimes partly enclosed, along the outside of a building. **2.** *N.Z.* a canopy sheltering pedestrians in a shopping street. [C18: from Portuguese *varanda* railing; related to Hindi *varandā* railing] —**ve'randaed** *or* **ve'randahed** *adj.*

verapamil (vɪ'ræpəˌmɪl) *n. Med.* a calcium antagonist used in the treatment of angina pectoris, hypertension, and irregular heart rhythm.

veratridine (vɪ'rætrɪˌdiːn) *n.* a yellowish-white amorphous alkaloid obtained from the seeds of sabadilla. Formula: $C_{36}H_{51}NO_{11}$. [C20: from VERATR(INE) + -ID[3] + -INE[2]]

veratrine ('vɛrəˌtriːn) *or* **veratrin** ('vɛrətrɪn) *n.* a white poisonous mixture obtained from the seeds of sabadilla, consisting of veratridine and several other alkaloids: formerly used in medicine as a counterirritant. [C19: from Latin *vērātrum* hellebore + -INE[2]]

verb (vɜːb) *n.* **1.** (in traditional grammar) any of a large class of words in a language that serve to indicate the occurrence or performance of an action, the existence of a state or condition, etc. In English, such words as *run, make, do,* and the like are verbs. **2.** (in modern descriptive linguistic analysis) **a.** a word or group of words that functions as the predicate of a sentence or introduces the predicate. **b.** (*as modifier*): *a verb phrase.* ~Abbrevs.: **vb, v.** [C14: from Latin *verbum* a word] —'**verbless** *adj.*

verbal ('vɜːbᵊl) *adj.* **1.** of, relating to, or using words, esp. as opposed to ideas, etc.: *merely verbal concessions.* **2.** oral rather than written: *a verbal agreement.* **3.** verbatim; literal: *an almost verbal copy.* **4.** *Grammar.* of or relating to verbs or a verb. ~*n.* **5.** *Grammar.* another word for **verbid. 6.** (*pl.*) *Slang.* a criminal's admission of guilt on arrest. ~*vb.* **-bals, -balling, -balled.** (*tr.*) **7.** *Slang.* (of the police) to implicate (someone) in a crime by quoting alleged admission of guilt in court. —'**verbally** *adv.*

verbalism ('vɜːbəˌlɪzəm) *n.* **1.** a verbal expression; phrase or word. **2.** an exaggerated emphasis on the importance of words by the uncritical acceptance of assertions in place of explanations, the use of rhetorical style, etc. **3.** a statement lacking real content, esp. a cliché.

verbalist ('vɜːbəlɪst) *n.* **1.** a person who deals with words alone, rather than facts, ideas, feeling, etc. **2.** a person skilled in the use of words.

verbalize *or* **verbalise** ('vɜːbəˌlaɪz) *vb.* **1.** to express (an idea, feeling, etc.) in words. **2.** to change (any word that is not a verb) into a verb or derive a verb from (any word that is not a verb). **3.** (*intr.*) to be verbose. —ˌ**verbali'zation** *or* ˌ**verbali'sation** *n.* —'**verbalˌizer** *or* '**verbalˌiser** *n.*

verbal noun *n.* a noun derived from a verb, such as *smoking* in the sentence *smoking is bad for you.* See also **gerund.**

verbascum (vɜː'bæskəm) *n.* See **mullein.** [Latin: mullein]

verbatim (vɜː'beɪtɪm) *adv., adj.* using exactly the same words; word for word. [C15: from Medieval Latin: word by word, from Latin *verbum* word]

verbena (vɜː'biːnə) *n.* **1.** any plant of the verbenaceous genus *Verbena*, chiefly of tropical and temperate America, having red, white, or purple fragrant flowers: much cultivated as garden plants. See also **vervain. 2.** any of various similar or related plants, esp. the lemon verbena. [C16: via Medieval Latin, from Latin: sacred bough used by the priest in religious acts, VERVAIN]

verbenaceous (ˌvɜːbɪ'neɪʃəs) *adj.* of, relating to, or belonging to the *Verbenaceae*, a family of herbaceous and climbing plants, shrubs, and trees, mostly of warm and tropical regions, having tubular typically two-lipped flowers: includes teak, lantana, vervain, and verbena. [C19: from New Latin *Verbēnāceae*, from Medieval Latin: VERBENA]

verbiage ('vɜːbɪɪdʒ) *n.* **1.** the excessive and often meaningless use of words; verbosity. **2.** *Rare.* diction; wording. [C18: from French, from Old French *verbier* to chatter, from *verbe* word, from Latin *verbum*]

verbid ('vɜːbɪd) *n. Grammar.* any nonfinite form of a verb or any nonverbal word derived from a verb: *participles, infinitives, and gerunds are all verbids.*

verbify ('vɜːbɪˌfaɪ) *vb.* **-fies, -fying, -fied.** another word for **verbalize** (senses 2, 3). —ˌ**verbifi'cation** *n.*

verbose (vɜː'bəʊs) *adj.* using or containing an excess of words, so as to be pedantic or boring; prolix. [C17: from Latin *verbōsus* from *verbum* word] —**ver'bosely** *adv.* —**verbosity** (vɜː'bɒsɪtɪ) *or* **ver'boseness** *n.*

verboten *German.* (fɛr'boːtən) *adj.* forbidden; prohibited.

verb phrase *n. Grammar.* a constituent of a sentence that contains the verb and any direct and indirect objects but not the subject. It is a controversial question in grammatical theory whether or not this constituent is to be identified with the predicate of the sentence. Abbrev.: **VP.**

verb. sap. *or* **sat.** *abbrev. for* verbum sapienti sat est. [Latin: a word is enough to the wise]

verdant ('vɜːdᵊnt) *adj.* **1.** covered with green vegetation. **2.** (of plants, etc.) green in colour. **3.** immature or unsophisticated; green. [C16: from Old French *verdoyant,* from *verdoyer* to become green, from Old French *verd* green, from Latin *viridis,* from *virēre* to be green] —'**verdancy** *n.* —'**verdantly** *adv.*

verd antique (vɜːd) *n.* **1.** a dark green mottled impure variety of serpentine marble. **2.** any of various similar marbles or stones. **3.** another name for **verdigris.** [C18: from French, from Italian *verde antico* ancient green]

verderer ('vɜːdərə) *n. English legal history.* a judicial officer responsible for the maintenance of law and order in the royal forests. [C16: from Anglo-French, from Old French *verdier,* from *verd* green, from Latin *viridis;* compare Latin *viridārium* plantation of trees]

verdict ('vɜːdɪkt) *n.* **1.** the findings of a jury on the issues of fact submitted to it for examination and trial; judgment. **2.** any decision, judgment, or conclusion. [C13: from Medieval Latin *vērdictum,* from Latin *vērē dictum* truly spoken, from *vērus* true + *dīcere* to say]

verdigris ('vɜːdɪgrɪs) *n.* **1.** a green or bluish patina formed on copper, brass, or bronze and consisting of a basic salt of copper containing both copper oxide and a copper salt. **2.** a green or blue crystalline substance obtained by the action of acetic acid on copper and used as a fungicide and pigment; basic copper acetate. [C14: from Old French *vert de Grice* green of Greece]

verdigris toadstool *n.* a basidiomycetous fungus, *Stropharia aeruginosa,* having a distinctive and unusual blue-green cap and paler shaggy stem.

verdin ('vɜːdɪn) *n.* a small W North American tit, *Auriparus flaviceps,* having a grey plumage with a yellow head. [French: yellowhammer]

verdure ('vɜːdʒə) *n.* **1.** flourishing green vegetation or its colour. **2.** a condition of freshness or healthy growth. [C14: from Old French *verd* green, from Latin *viridis*] —'**verdured** *adj.* —'**verdurous** *adj.*

verecund ('vɛrɪˌkʌnd) *adj. Rare.* shy or modest. [C16: from Latin *verēcundus* diffident, from *verērī* to fear]

verge[1] (vɜːdʒ) *n.* **1.** an edge or rim; margin. **2.** a limit beyond which something occurs; brink: *on the verge of ecstasy.* **3.** *Brit.* a grass border along a road. **4.** an enclosing line, belt, or strip. **5.** *Architect.* the edge of the roof tiles projecting over a gable. **6.** *Architect.* the shaft of a classical column. **7.** an enclosed space. **8.** *Horology.* the spindle of a balance wheel in a vertical escapement, found only in very early clocks. **9.** *English legal history.* **a.** the area encompassing the royal court that is subject to the jurisdiction of the Lord High Steward. **b.** a rod or wand carried as a symbol of office or emblem of authority, as in the Church. **c.** a rod held by a person swearing fealty to his lord on becoming a tenant, esp. of copyhold land. **10.** *Printing.* a trigger-like device for releasing the matrices on a Linotype machine. ~*vb.* **11.** (*intr.;* foll. by *on*) to be near (to): *to verge on chaos.* **12.** (when *intr.,* sometimes foll. by *on*) to serve as the edge of (something): *this narrow strip verges the road.* [C15: from Old French, from Latin *virga* rod]

verge[2] (vɜːdʒ) *vb.* (*intr.;* foll. by *to* or *towards*) to move or incline in a certain direction. [C17: from Latin *vergere*]

vergeboard ('vɜːdʒˌbɔːd) *n.* another name for **bargeboard.**

vergence ('vɜːdʒəns) *n.* the inward or outward turning movement of the eyes in convergence or divergence. [C19: from VERGE[2] + -ENCE]

verger ('vɜːdʒə) *n. Chiefly Church of England.* **1.** a church official who acts as caretaker and attendant, looking after the interior of a church and often the vestments and church furnishings. **2.** an official who carries the verge or rod of office before a bishop, dean, or other dignitary in ceremonies and processions. [C15: from Old French, from *verge,* from Latin *virga* rod, twig]

verglas ('vɛəglɑː) *n., pl.* **-glases** (-glɑː, -glɑːz). a thin film of ice on rock. [from Old French *verre-glaz* glass-ice, from *verre* glass (from Latin *vitrum*) + *glaz* ice (from Late Latin *glacia,* from Latin *glaciēs*)]

veridical (vɪ'rɪdɪkᵊl) *adj.* **1.** truthful. **2.** *Psychol.* of or relating to revelations in dreams, hallucinations, etc., that appear to be confirmed by subsequent events. [C17: from Latin *vēridicus,* from *vērus* true + *dīcere* to say] —**veˌridi'cality** *n.* —**ve'ridically** *adv.*

veriest ('vɛrɪɪst) *adj. Archaic.* (intensifier): *the veriest coward.*

verification (ˌvɛrɪfɪ'keɪʃən) *n.* **1.** establishment of the correctness of a theory, fact, etc. **2.** evidence that provides proof of an assertion, theory, etc. **3.** *Law.* **a.** (formerly) a short affidavit at the end of a pleading stating the pleader's readiness to prove his assertions. **b.** confirmatory evidence. —'**verifiˌcative** *or* '**verifiˌcatory** *adj.*

verification principle *n.* (in the philosophy of the logical positivists) the doctrine that nontautologous statements are meaningful only if it is in principle possible to establish empirically whether they are true or false.

verify ('vɛrɪˌfaɪ) *vb.* **-fies, -fying, -fied.** (*tr.*) **1.** to prove to be true; confirm; substantiate. **2.** to check or determine the correctness or truth of by investigation, reference, etc. **3.** *Law.* to add a verification to (a pleading); substantiate or confirm (an oath). [C14: from Old French *verifier,* from Medieval Latin *vērificāre,* from Latin *vērus* true + *facere* to make] —'**veriˌfiable** *adj.* —'**veriˌfiableness** *n.* —'**veriˌfiably** *adv.* —'**veriˌfier** *n.*

verily ('vɛrɪlɪ) *adv.* (*sentence modifier*) *Archaic.* in truth; truly: *verily, thou art a man of God.* [C13: from VERY + -LY[2]]

verisimilar (ˌvɛrɪ'sɪmɪlə) *adj.* appearing to be true; probable; likely. [C17: from Latin *vērīsimilis,* from *vērus* true + *similis* like] —ˌ**veri'similarly** *adv.*

verisimilitude (ˌvɛrɪsɪ'mɪlɪˌtjuːd) *n.* **1.** the appearance or semblance of truth or reality; quality of seeming true. **2.** something that merely seems to be true or real, such as a doubtful statement. [C17: from Latin *vērisimilitūdō,* from *vērus* true + *similitūdō* SIMILITUDE]

verism ('vɪərɪzəm) *n.* extreme naturalism in art or literature. [C19: from Italian *verismo,* from *vero* true, from Latin *vērus*] —'**verist** *n., adj.* —**ve'ristic** *adj.*

verismo (vɛ'rɪzməʊ; *Italian* ve'rismo) *n. Music.* a school of composition that originated in Italian opera towards the end of the 19th century, drawing its themes from real life and emphasizing naturalistic elements. [C19: from Italian; see VERISM]

veritable ('vɛrɪtəbᵊl) *adj.* (*prenominal*) **1.** (intensifier; *usually qualifying a word used metaphorically*): *he's a veritable swine!* **2.** *Rare.* genuine or true; proper: *I require veritable proof.* [C15: from Old French, from *vérité* truth; see VERITY] —'**veritableness** *n.* —'**veritably** *adv.*

verity ('vɛrɪtɪ) *n., pl.* **-ties.** **1.** the quality or state of being true, real, or correct. **2.** a true principle, statement, idea, etc.; a truth or fact. [C14: from Old French *vérité,* from Latin *vēritās,* from *vērus* true]

verjuice ('vɜːˌdʒuːs) *n.* **1. a.** the acid juice of unripe grapes, apples, or crab apples, formerly much used in making sauces, etc. **b.** (*as modifier*): *verjuice sauce.* **2.** *Rare.* **a.** sourness or sharpness of temper, looks, etc. **b.** (*as modifier*): *a verjuice old wife.* ~*vb.* **3.** (*tr.*) *Rare.* to make sour; embitter. [C14: from Old French *vert jus* green (unripe) juice, from Old French *vert* green (from Latin *viridis*) + *jus* juice (from Latin *jūs*)]

verkrampte (fə'krɑmtə) *n.* (in South Africa) **a.** an Afrikaner Nationalist absolutely opposed to any change towards liberal trends in government policy, esp. relating to racial questions. **b.** (*as modifier*): *verkrampte politics.* ~Compare **verligte.** [C20: from Afrikaans (adj.), literally: restricted]

verligte (fə'ləxtə) *n.* (in South Africa) **a.** a person of any of the White political parties who supports liberal trends in government policy. **b.** (*as modifier*): *verligte politics.* ~Compare **verkrampte.** [C20: from Afrikaans (adj.), literally: enlightened]

vermeil ('vɜːmeɪl) *n.* **1.** gilded silver, bronze, or other metal, used esp. in the 19th century. **2. a.** vermilion. **b.** (*as adj.*): *vermeil shoes.* [C15: from Old French, from Late Latin *vermiculus* insect (of the genus *Kermes*) or the red dye prepared from it, from Latin: little worm]

vermi- *combining form.* worm: *vermicide; vermiform; vermifuge.* [from Latin *vermis* worm]

vermicelli (ˌvɜːmɪ'sɛlɪ; *Italian* vermi'tʃɛlli) *n.* **1.** very fine strands of pasta, used in soups. **2.** tiny chocolate strands used to coat cakes, etc. [C17: from Italian: little worms, from *verme* a worm, from Latin *vermis*]

vermicide ('vɜːmɪˌsaɪd) *n.* any substance used to kill worms. —ˌ**vermi'cidal** *adj.*

vermicular (vɜː'mɪkjʊlə) *adj.* **1.** resembling the form, markings, motion, or tracks of worms. **2.** of or relating to worms or wormlike animals. [C17: from Medieval Latin *vermiculāris,* from Latin *vermiculus,* diminutive of *vermis* worm] —**ver'micularly** *adv.*

vermiculate *vb.* (vɜː'mɪkjʊˌleɪt). **1.** (*tr.*) to decorate with wavy or wormlike tracery or markings. ~*adj.* (vɜː'mɪkjʊlɪt, -ˌleɪt). **2.** vermicular; sinuous. **3.** worm-eaten or appearing as if worm-eaten. **4.** (of thoughts, etc.) insinuating; subtly tortuous. [C17: from Latin *vermiculātus* in the form of worms, from *vermis* worm]

vermiculation (vɜːˌmɪkjʊ'leɪʃən) *n.* **1.** *Physiol.* any wormlike movement, esp. of the intestines; peristalsis. **2.** decoration consisting of wormlike carving or marks. **3.** the state of being worm-eaten.

vermiculite (vɜː'mɪkjʊˌlaɪt) *n.* any of a group of micaceous minerals consisting mainly of hydrated silicate of magnesium, aluminium, and iron: on heating they expand and exfoliate and in this form are used in heat and sound insulation, fireproofing, and as a bedding medium for young plants. [C19: from VERMICUL(AR) + -ITE[1]]

vermiform ('vɜːmɪˌfɔːm) *adj.* resembling a worm.

vermiform appendix *or* **process** *n.* a wormlike pouch extending from the lower end of the caecum in some mammals. In man it is vestigial. Also called: **appendix.**

vermifuge ('vɜːmɪˌfjuːdʒ) *n.* any drug or agent able to destroy or expel intestinal worms. Also called: **anthelminthic, anthelmintic, helminthic.** —**vermifugal** (ˌvɜːmɪ'fjuːgᵊl) *adj.*

vermilion *or* **vermillion** (və'mɪljən) *n.* **1. a.** a bright red to reddish-orange colour. **b.** (*as adj.*): *a vermilion car.* **2.** mercuric sulphide, esp. when used as a bright red pigment; cinnabar. [C13: from Old French *vermeillon,* from VERMEIL]

vermin (ˈvɜːmɪn) *n.* **1.** (*functioning as pl.*) small animals collectively, esp. insects and rodents, that are troublesome to man, domestic animals, etc. **2.** (*pl.* **-min**) an unpleasant, obnoxious, or dangerous person. [C13: from Old French *vermine*, from Latin *vermis* a worm]

vermination (ˌvɜːmɪˈneɪʃən) *n.* the spreading of or infestation with vermin.

verminous (ˈvɜːmɪnəs) *adj.* relating to, infested with, or suggestive of vermin. —ˈ**verminously** *adv.* —ˈ**verminousness** *n.*

vermis (ˈvɜːmɪs) *n., pl.* **-mes** (-miːz). *Anatomy.* the middle lobe connecting the two halves of the cerebellum. [C19: via New Latin from Latin: worm]

vermivorous (vɜːˈmɪvərəs) *adj.* (of certain animals) feeding on worms.

vermouth (ˈvɜːməθ) *n.* any of several wines containing aromatic herbs and some other flavourings. [C19: from French, from German *Wermut* WORMWOOD (absinthe)]

vernacular (vəˈnækjʊlə) *n.* **1. the.** the commonly spoken language or dialect of a particular people or place. **2.** a local style of architecture, in which ordinary houses are built: *this group of architects have re-created a true English vernacular.* ~*adj.* **3.** relating to, using, or in the vernacular. **4.** designating or relating to the common name of an animal or plant. **5.** built in the local style of ordinary houses, rather than a grand architectural style. [C17: from Latin *vernāculus* belonging to a household slave, from *verna* household slave] —**ver**ˈ**nacularly** *adv.*

vernacularism (vəˈnækjʊləˌrɪzəm) *n.* the use of the vernacular or a term in the vernacular.

vernal (ˈvɜːnᵊl) *adj.* **1.** of or occurring in spring. **2.** *Poetic.* of or characteristic of youth; fresh. [C16: from Latin *vernālis*, from *vēr* spring] —ˈ**vernally** *adv.*

vernal equinox *n.* **1.** the time at which the sun crosses the plane of the equator towards the relevant hemisphere, making day and night of equal length. It occurs about March 21 in the N hemisphere (Sept. 23 in the S hemisphere). **2.** *Astronomy.* the point on the celestial sphere, lying in the constellation of Pisces, at which the celestial equator intersects the ecliptic.

vernal grass *n.* any of various Eurasian grasses of the genus *Anthoxanthum*, such as *A. odoratum* (**sweet vernal grass**), having the fragrant scent of coumarin.

vernalize *or* **vernalise** (ˈvɜːnəˌlaɪz) *vb.* to shorten the period between sowing and flowering in (plants), esp. by subjection of the seeds to low temperatures before planting. —ˌ**vernali**ˈ**zation** *or* ˌ**vernali**ˈ**sation** *n.*

vernation (vɜːˈneɪʃən) *n.* the way in which leaves are arranged in the bud. [C18: from New Latin *vernātiō*, from Latin *vernāre* to be springlike, from *vēr* spring]

Verner's law (ˈvɜːnəz) *n. Linguistics.* a modification of Grimm's law accommodating some of its exceptions. It states that non-initial voiceless fricatives in Proto-Germanic occurring as a result of Grimm's law became voiced fricatives if the previous syllable had been unstressed in Proto-Indo-European. [C19: named after Karl Adolph *Verner* (1846–96), Danish philologist, who formulated it] —**Vernerian** (vɜːˈnɛərɪən) *adj.*

vernier (ˈvɜːnɪə) *n.* **1.** a small movable scale running parallel to the main graduated scale in certain measuring instruments, such as theodolites, used to obtain a fractional reading of one of the divisions on the main scale. **2.** an auxiliary device for making a fine adjustment to an instrument, usually by means of a fine screw thread. **3.** (*modifier*) relating to or fitted with a vernier: *a vernier scale; a vernier barometer.* [C18: named after Paul *Vernier* (1580–1637), French mathematician, who described the scale]

vernier rocket *n.* another name for **thruster** (sense 2).

vernissage (ˌvɜːnɪˈsɑːʒ) *n.* **1.** a preview or the opening or first day of an exhibition of paintings. **2.** another term for **varnishing day.** [French, from *vernis* VARNISH]

Veronal (ˈvɛrənᵊl) *n.* a trademark for **barbitone.**

veronica[1] (vəˈrɒnɪkə) *n.* any scrophulariaceous plant of the genus *Veronica*, esp. the speedwells, of temperate and cold regions, having small blue, pink, or white flowers and flattened notched fruits. [C16: from Medieval Latin, perhaps from the name *Veronica*]

veronica[2] (vəˈrɒnɪkə) *n. R.C. Church.* **1.** the representation of the face of Christ that, according to legend, was miraculously imprinted upon the headcloth that Saint Veronica offered him on his way to his crucifixion. **2.** the cloth itself. **3.** any similar representation of Christ's face.

veronica[3] (vəˈrɒnɪkə) *n. Bullfighting.* a pass in which the matador slowly swings the cape away from the charging bull. [from Spanish, from the name *Veronica*]

verra (ˈvɛrə) *adj., adv.* a Scot. word for **very.**

verruca (vɛˈruːkə) *n., pl.* **-cae** (-siː) *or* **-cas. 1.** *Pathol.* a wart, esp. one growing on the hand or foot. **2.** *Biology.* a wartlike outgrowth, as in certain plants or on the skin of some animals. [C16: from Latin: wart]

verrucose (ˈvɛrʊˌkəʊs) *or* **verrucous** (ˈvɛrʊkəs, vɛˈruːkəs) *adj. Botany.* covered with warty processes. [C17: from Latin *verrūcōsus* full of warts, from *verrūca* a wart] —**verrucosity** (ˌvɛrʊˈkɒsɪtɪ) *n.*

vers *abbrev. for* versed sine.

versant (ˈvɜːsᵊnt) *n.* **1.** the side or slope of a mountain or mountain range. **2.** the slope of a region. [C19: from French, from *verser* to turn, from Latin *versāre*]

versatile (ˈvɜːsəˌtaɪl) *adj.* **1.** capable of or adapted for many different uses, skills, etc. **2.** variable or changeable. **3.** *Botany.* (of an anther) attached to the filament by a small area so that it moves freely in the wind. **4.** *Zoology.* able to turn forwards and backwards: *versatile antennae.* [C17: from Latin *versātilis* moving around, from *versāre* to turn] —ˈ**versa**ˌ**tilely** *adv.* —**versatility** (ˌvɜːsəˈtɪlɪtɪ) *n.*

vers de société *French.* (vɛr də sɔsjete) *n.* light, witty, and polished verse. [literally: society verse]

verse (vɜːs) *n.* **1.** (not in technical usage) a stanza or other short subdivision of a poem. **2.** poetry as distinct from prose. **3. a.** a series of metrical feet forming a rhythmical unit of one line. **b.** (*as modifier*): *verse line.* **4.** a specified type of metre or metrical structure: *iambic verse.* **5.** one of the series of short subsections into which most of the writings in the Bible are divided. **6.** a metrical composition; poem. ~*vb.* **7.** a rare word for **versify.** [Old English *vers*, from Latin *versus* a furrow, literally: a turning (of the plough), from *vertere* to turn]

versed (vɜːst) *adj.* (*postpositive;* foll. by *in*) thoroughly knowledgeable (about), acquainted (with), or skilled (in).

versed sine *n.* a trigonometric function equal to one minus the cosine of the specified angle. Abbrev.: **vers.** [C16: from New Latin *sinus versus*, from SINE[1] + *versus* turned, from *vertere* to turn]

versicle (ˈvɜːsɪkᵊl) *n.* **1.** a short verse. **2.** a short sentence recited or sung by the minister at a liturgical ceremony and responded to by the choir or congregation. [C14: from Latin *versiculus* a little line, from *versus* VERSE]

versicolour *or U.S.* **versicolor** (ˈvɜːsɪˌkʌlə) *adj.* of variable or various colours. [C18: from Latin *versicolor*, from *versāre* to turn + *color* COLOUR]

versicular (vɜːˈsɪkjʊlə) *adj. Rare.* of, relating to, or consisting of verses or versicles.

versification (ˌvɜːsɪfɪˈkeɪʃən) *n.* **1.** the technique or art of versifying. **2.** the form or metrical composition of a poem. **3.** a metrical version of a prose text.

versify (ˈvɜːsɪˌfaɪ) *vb.* **-fies, -fying, -fied. 1.** (*tr.*) to render (something) into metrical form or verse. **2.** (*intr.*) to write in verse. [C14: from Old French *versifier*, from Latin *versificāre*, from *versus* VERSE + *facere* to make] —ˈ**versi**ˌ**fier** *n.*

version (ˈvɜːʃən, -ʒən) *n.* **1.** an account of a matter from a certain point of view, as contrasted with others: *his version of the accident is different from the policeman's.* **2.** a translation, esp. of the Bible, from one language into another. **3.** a variant form of something; type. **4.** an adaptation, as of a book or play into a film. **5.** *Med.* manual turning of a fetus to correct an irregular position within the uterus. **6.** *Pathol.* an abnormal displacement of the uterus characterized by a tilting forwards (**anteversion**), backwards (**retroversion**), or to either side (**lateroversion**). [C16: from Medieval Latin *versiō* a turning, from Latin *vertere* to turn] —ˈ**versional** *adj.*

vers libre *French.* (vɛr librə) *n.* (in French poetry) another term for **free verse.**

verso (ˈvɜːsəʊ) *n., pl.* **-sos. 1. a.** the back of a sheet of printed paper. **b.** Also called: **reverso.** the left-hand pages of a book, bearing the even numbers. Compare **recto. 2.** the side of a coin opposite to the obverse; reverse. [C19: from the New Latin phrase *versō foliō* the leaf having been turned, from Latin *vertere* to turn + *folium* a leaf]

verst (vɛəst, vɜːst) *n.* a unit of length, used in Russia, equal to 1.067 kilometres (0.6629 miles). [C16: from French *verste* or German *Werst*, from Russian *versta* line]

versus (ˈvɜːsəs) *prep.* **1.** (esp. in a competition or lawsuit) against; in opposition to. Abbrev.: **v.,** (esp. U.S.) **vs. 2.** as opposed to; in contrast with. [C15: from Latin: turned (in the direction of), opposite, from *vertere* to turn]

vert (vɜːt) *n.* **1.** *English legal history.* **a.** the right to cut green wood in a forest. **b.** the wood itself. **2.** *Heraldry.* **a.** the colour green. **b.** (*as adj., usually postpositive*): *a table vert.* [C15: from Old French *verd*, from Latin *viridis* green, from *virēre* to grow green]

vert. *abbrev. for* vertical.

vertebra (ˈvɜːtɪbrə) *n., pl.* **-brae** (-briː) *or* **-bras.** one of the bony segments of the spinal column. [C17: from Latin: joint of the spine, from *vertere* to turn] —ˈ**vertebral** *adj.* —ˈ**vertebrally** *adv.*

vertebral column *n.* another name for **spinal column.**

vertebrate (ˈvɜːtɪˌbreɪt, -brɪt) *n.* **1.** any chordate animal of the subphylum *Vertebrata*, characterized by a bony or cartilaginous skeleton and a well-developed brain: the group contains fishes, amphibians, reptiles, birds, and mammals. ~*adj.* **2.** of, relating to, or belonging to the subphylum *Vertebrata.*

vertebration (ˌvɜːtɪˈbreɪʃən) *n.* the formation of vertebrae or segmentation resembling vertebrae.

vertex (ˈvɜːtɛks) *n., pl.* **-texes** *or* **-tices** (-tɪˌsiːz). **1.** the highest point. **2.** *Maths.* **a.** the point opposite the base of a figure. **b.** the point of intersection of two sides of a plane figure or angle. **c.** the point of intersection of a pencil of lines or three or more planes of a solid figure. **3.** *Astronomy.* a point in the sky towards which a star stream appears to move. 4. *Anatomy.* the crown of the head. [C16: from Latin: whirlpool, from *vertere* to turn]

vertical (ˈvɜːtɪkᵊl) *adj.* 1. at right angles to the horizon; perpendicular; upright: *a vertical wall.* Compare **horizontal** (sense 1). 2. extending in a perpendicular direction. 3. at or in the vertex or zenith; directly overhead. 4. *Economics.* of or relating to associated or consecutive, though not identical, stages of industrial activity: *vertical integration; vertical amalgamation.* 5. of or relating to the vertex. 6. *Anatomy.* of, relating to, or situated at the top of the head (vertex). ~*n.* 7. a vertical plane, position, or line. 8. a vertical post, pillar, or other structural member. [C16: from Late Latin *verticālis,* from Latin VERTEX] —ˌ**vertiˈcality** *n.* —ˈ**vertically** *adv.*

vertical angles *pl. n. Geometry.* the pair of equal angles between a pair of intersecting lines; opposite angles. Also called: **vertically opposite angles.**

vertical circle *n. Astronomy.* a great circle on the celestial sphere passing through the zenith and perpendicular to the horizon.

vertical grouping *n.* another term for **family grouping.**

vertical mobility *n. Sociol.* the movement of individuals or groups to positions in society that involve a change in class, status, and power. Compare **horizontal mobility.** See also **upward mobility, downward mobility.**

vertical stabilizer *n.* the U.S. name for **fin**[1] (sense 3a).

vertical union *n.* another name (esp. U.S.) for **industrial union.**

vertices (ˈvɜːtɪˌsiːz) *n.* a plural of **vertex** (in technical and scientific senses only).

verticil (ˈvɜːtɪsɪl) *n. Biology.* a circular arrangement of parts about an axis, esp. leaves around a stem. [C18: from Latin *verticillus* whorl (of a spindle), from VERTEX]

verticillaster (ˌvɜːtɪsɪˈlæstə) *n. Botany.* an inflorescence, such as that of the dead-nettle, that resembles a whorl but consists of two crowded cymes on either side of the stem. [C19: from New Latin; see VERTICIL, -ASTER] —**verticillastrate** (ˌvɜːtɪsɪˈlæsˌtreɪt, -trɪt) *adj.*

verticillate (vɜːˈtɪsɪlɪt, -ˌleɪt; ˌvɜːtɪˈsɪleɪt) *adj. Biology.* having or arranged in whorls or verticils. —**verˈticillately** *adv.* —**verˌticilˈlation** *n.*

vertiginous (vɜːˈtɪdʒɪnəs) *adj.* 1. of, relating to, or having vertigo. 2. producing dizziness. 3. whirling. 4. changeable; unstable. [C17: from Latin *vertīginōsus,* from VERTIGO] —**verˈtiginously** *adv.* —**verˈtiginousness** *n.*

vertigo (ˈvɜːtɪˌɡəʊ) *n., pl.* **vertigoes** *or* **vertigines** (vɜːˈtɪdʒɪˌniːz). *Pathol.* a sensation of dizziness or abnormal motion resulting from a disorder of the sense of balance. [C16: from Latin: a whirling round, from *vertere* to turn]

vertu (vɜːˈtuː) *n.* a variant spelling of **virtu.**

vervain (ˈvɜːveɪn) *n.* any of several verbenaceous plants of the genus *Verbena,* having square stems and long slender spikes of purple, blue, or white flowers. [C14: from Old French *verveine,* from Latin *verbēna* sacred bough; see VERBENA]

verve (vɜːv) *n.* 1. great vitality, enthusiasm, and liveliness; sparkle. 2. a rare word for **talent.** [C17: from Old French: garrulity, from Latin *verba* words, chatter]

vervet (ˈvɜːvɪt) *n.* a variety of a South African guenon monkey, *Cercopithecus aethiops,* having dark hair on the hands and feet and a reddish patch beneath the tail. Compare **green monkey, grivet.** [C19: from French, from *vert* green, but influenced by GRIVET]

very (ˈverɪ) *adv.* 1. (intensifier) used to add emphasis to adjectives that are able to be graded: *very good; very tall.* ~*adj.* (*prenominal*) 2. (intensifier) used with nouns preceded by a definite article or possessive determiner, in order to give emphasis to the significance, appropriateness or relevance of a noun in a particular context, or to give exaggerated intensity to certain nouns: *the very man I want to see; his very name struck terror; the very back of the room.* 3. (intensifier) used in metaphors to emphasize the applicability of the image to the situation described: *he was a very lion in the fight.* 4. *Archaic.* a. real or true; genuine: *the very living God.* b. lawful: *the very vengeance of the gods.* [C13: from Old French *verai* true, from Latin *vērax* true, from *vērus* true]

▷**Usage.** In strict usage adverbs of degree such as *very, too, quite, really,* and *extremely* are used only to qualify adjectives: *he is very happy; she is too sad.* By this rule, these words should not be used to qualify past participles that follow the verb *to be,* since they would then be technically qualifying verbs. With the exception of certain participles, such as *tired* or *disappointed,* that have come to be regarded as adjectives, all other past participles are qualified by adverbs such as *much, greatly, seriously,* or *excessively: he has been much* (not *very*) *inconvenienced; she has been excessively* (not *too*) *criticized.*

very high frequency *n.* a radio-frequency band or radio frequency lying between 300 and 30 megahertz. Abbrev.: **VHF.**

very large-scale integration *n. Computer technol.* the process of integrating many thousands of circuits on a single silicon chip. Abbrev.: **VLSI.**

Very light (ˈverɪ) *n.* a coloured flare fired from a special pistol (**Very pistol**) for signalling at night, esp. at sea. [C19: named after Edward W. *Very* (1852–1910), U.S. naval ordnance officer]

very low frequency *n.* a radio-frequency band or radio frequency lying between 30 and 3 kilohertz. Abbrev.: **VLF.**

Very Reverend *n.* a title of respect for a variety of ecclesiastical officials, such as deans and the superiors of some religious houses.

vesica (ˈvesɪkə) *n., pl.* **-cae** (-ˌsiː). 1. *Anatomy.* a technical name for **bladder** (sense 1). 2. (in medieval sculpture and painting) an aureole in the shape of a pointed oval. [C17: from Latin: bladder, sac, blister]

vesical (ˈvesɪkᵊl) *adj.* of or relating to a vesica, esp. the urinary bladder.

vesicant (ˈvesɪkənt) *or* **vesicatory** (ˈvesɪˌkeɪtərɪ) *n., pl.* **-cants** *or* **-catories.** 1. any substance that causes blisters, used in medicine and in chemical warfare. ~*adj.* 2. acting as a vesicant. [C19: see VESICA]

vesicate (ˈvesɪˌkeɪt) *vb.* to blister. [C17: from New Latin *vēsīcāre* to blister; see VESICA] —ˌ**vesiˈcation** *n.*

vesicle (ˈvesɪkᵊl) *n.* 1. *Pathol.* a. any small sac or cavity, esp. one containing serous fluid. b. a blister. 2. *Geology.* a rounded cavity within a rock formed during solidification by expansion of the gases present in the magma. 3. *Botany.* a small bladder-like cavity occurring in certain seaweeds and aquatic plants. 4. any small cavity or cell. [C16: from Latin *vēsīcula,* diminutive of VESICA] —**vesicular** (veˈsɪkjʊlə) *adj.* —**veˈsicularly** *adv.*

vesiculate *vb.* (veˈsɪkjʊˌleɪt). 1. to make (an organ or part) vesicular or (of an organ or part) to become vesicular. ~*adj.* (veˈsɪkjʊlɪt, -ˌleɪt). 2. containing, resembling, or characterized by a vesicle or vesicles. —**veˌsicuˈlation** *n.*

vesper (ˈvespə) *n.* 1. an evening prayer, service, or hymn. 2. an archaic word for **evening.** 3. (*modifier*) of or relating to vespers. ~See also **vespers.** [C14: from Latin: evening, the evening star; compare Greek *hesperos* evening; see WEST]

Vesper (ˈvespə) *n.* the planet Venus, when appearing as the evening star.

vesperal (ˈvespərəl) *n. Christianity.* 1. a liturgical book containing the prayers, psalms, and hymns used at vespers. 2. the part of the antiphonary containing these. 3. a cloth laid over the altar cloth between offices or services.

vespers (ˈvespəz) *n.* (*functioning as sing.*) 1. *Chiefly R.C. Church.* the sixth of the seven canonical hours of the divine office, originally fixed for the early evening and now often made a public service on Sundays and major feast days. 2. another word for **evensong** (sense 1).

vespertilionine (ˌvespəˈtɪlɪəˌnaɪn, -nɪn) *adj.* of, relating to, or belonging to the *Vespertilionidae,* a family of common and widespread bats. [C17: from Latin *vespertīliō* a bat, from *vesper* evening] —**vespertilionid** (ˌvespəˈtɪlɪənɪd) *adj., n.*

vespertine (ˈvespəˌtaɪn) *adj.* 1. *Botany, zoology.* appearing, opening, or active in the evening: *vespertine flowers.* 2. occurring in the evening or (esp. of stars) appearing or setting in the evening.

vespiary (ˈvespɪərɪ) *n., pl.* **-aries.** a nest or colony of social wasps or hornets. [C19: from Latin *vespa* a wasp, on the model of *apiary*]

vespid (ˈvespɪd) *n.* 1. any hymenopterous insect of the family *Vespidae,* including the common wasps and hornets. ~*adj.* 2. of, relating to, or belonging to the family *Vespidae.* [C19: from New Latin *Vespidae,* from Latin *vespa* a wasp]

vespine (ˈvespaɪn) *adj.* of, relating to, or resembling a wasp or wasps. [C19: from Latin *vespa* a wasp]

vessel (ˈvesᵊl) *n.* 1. any object used as a container, esp. for a liquid. 2. a passenger or freight-carrying ship, boat, etc. 3. an aircraft, esp. an airship. 4. *Anatomy.* a tubular structure that transports such body fluids as blood and lymph. 5. *Botany.* a tubular element of xylem tissue consisting of a row of cells in which the connecting cell walls have broken down. 6. *Rare.* a person regarded as an agent or vehicle for some purpose or quality: *she was the vessel of the Lord.* [C13: from Old French *vaissel,* from Late Latin *vascellum* urn, from Latin *vās* vessel]

vest (vest) *n.* 1. an undergarment covering the body from the shoulders to the hips, made of cotton, nylon, etc. U.S. and Canadian equivalent: **T-shirt, undershirt.** Austral. equivalent: **singlet.** 2. the usual U.S., Canadian, and Austral. word for **waistcoat.** 3. *Obsolete.* any form of dress, esp. a long robe. ~*vb.* 4. (*tr.;* foll. by *in*) to place or settle (power, rights, etc., in): *power was vested in the committee.* 5. (*tr.;* foll. by *with*) to bestow or confer (on): *the company was vested with authority.* 6. (usually foll. by *in*) to confer (a right, title, property, etc., upon) or (of a right, title, etc.) to pass (to) or devolve (upon). 7. (*tr.*) to clothe or array. 8. (*intr.*) to put on clothes, ecclesiastical vestments, etc. [C15: from Old French *vestir* to clothe, from Latin *vestīre,* from *vestis* clothing] —ˈ**vestless** *adj.* —ˈ**vestˌlike** *adj.*

vesta (ˈvestə) *n.* a short friction match, usually of wood. [C19: named after the goddess *Vesta;* see VESTAL]

vestal (ˈvestᵊl) *adj.* 1. chaste or pure; virginal. ~*n.* 2. Also: **vestal virgin.** (in ancient Rome) one of the four, later six, virgin priestesses whose lives were dedicated to Vesta, goddess of the hearth, and to maintaining the sacred fire in her temple. 3. a chaste woman; virgin. 4. a rare word for **nun**[1] (sense 1).

vested (ˈvestɪd) *adj. Property law.* having a present right to the immediate or future possession and enjoyment of property. Compare **contingent.**

vested interest *n.* 1. *Property law.* an existing and disposable right to the immediate or future possession and enjoyment of property. 2. a strong personal concern in a state of affairs, system, etc., usually resulting in private gain. **3.** a person or group that has such an interest.

vestiary ('vɛstɪərɪ) *n., pl.* **-aries.** **1.** *Obsolete.* a room for storing clothes or dressing in, such as a vestry. ~*adj.* **2.** *Rare.* of or relating to clothes. [C17: from Late Latin *vestiārius,* from *vestis* clothing]

vestibular system *n.* the sensory mechanism in the inner ear that detects movement of the head and helps to control balance.

vestibule ('vɛstɪˌbjuːl) *n.* **1.** a small entrance hall or anteroom; lobby. **2.** any small bodily cavity or space at the entrance to a passage or canal. [C17: from Latin *vestibulum*] —**vestibular** (vɛ'stɪbjʊlə) *adj.*

vestige ('vɛstɪdʒ) *n.* **1.** a small trace, mark, or amount; hint: *a vestige of truth; no vestige of the meal.* **2.** *Biology.* an organ or part of an organism that is a small nonfunctioning remnant of a functional organ in an ancestor. [C17: via French from Latin *vestīgium* track]

vestigial (vɛ'stɪdʒɪəl) *adj.* **1.** of, relating to, or being a vestige. **2.** (of certain organs or parts of organisms) having attained a simple structure and reduced size and function during the evolution of the species: *the vestigial pelvic girdle of a snake.* —**ves'tigially** *adv.*

vestment ('vɛstmənt) *n.* **1.** a garment or robe, esp. one denoting office, authority, or rank. **2.** any of various ceremonial garments worn by the clergy at religious services. [C13: from Old French *vestiment,* from Latin *vestīmentum* clothing, from *vestīre* to clothe] —**vestmental** (vɛst'mɛntᵊl) *adj.* —**'vestmented** *adj.*

vest-pocket *n.* (*modifier*) *Chiefly U.S.* small enough to fit into a waistcoat pocket.

vestry ('vɛstrɪ) *n., pl.* **-tries.** **1.** a room in or attached to a church in which vestments, sacred vessels, etc., are kept. **2.** a room in or attached to some churches, used for Sunday school, meetings, etc. **3. a.** *Church of England.* a meeting of all the members of a parish or their representatives, to transact the official and administrative business of the parish. **b.** the body of members meeting for this; the parish council. **4.** *Episcopalian (U.S.) and Anglican (Canadian) Churches.* a committee of vestrymen chosen by the congregation to manage the temporal affairs of their church. [C14: probably from Old French *vestiarie;* see VEST] —**'vestral** *adj.*

vestryman ('vɛstrɪmən) *n., pl.* **-men.** a member of a church vestry.

vesture ('vɛstʃə) *n.* **1.** *Archaic.* a garment or something that seems like a garment: *a vesture of cloud.* **2.** *Law.* **a.** everything except trees that grows on the land. **b.** a product of the land, such as grass, wheat, etc. ~*vb.* **3.** (*tr.*) *Archaic.* to clothe. [C14: from Old French, from *vestir,* from Latin *vestīre,* from *vestis* clothing] —**'vestural** *adj.*

vesuvian (vɪ'suːvɪən) *n.* **1.** (esp. formerly) a match for lighting cigars; fusee. **2.** another name for **vesuvianite.** [C18 (the mineral), C19 (the match): both named after *Vesuvius,* a volcano in SW Italy]

vesuvianite (vɪ'suːvɪəˌnaɪt) *n.* a green, brown, or yellow mineral consisting of a hydrated silicate of calcium, magnesium, iron, and aluminium: it occurs as tetragonal crystals in limestones and is used as a gemstone. Formula: $Ca_{10}Al_4(MgFe)_2Si_9O_{34}(OH)_4$. Also called: **idocrase, vesuvian.** [C19: first found in the lava of *Vesuvius*]

vet[1] (vɛt) *n.* **1.** short for **veterinary surgeon.** ~*vb.* **vets, vetting, vetted.** **2.** (*tr.*) *Chiefly Brit.* to make a prior examination and critical appraisal of (a person, document, scheme, etc.): *the candidates were well vetted.* See also **positive vetting.** **3.** to examine, treat, or cure (an animal).

vet[2] (vɛt) *n. U.S. and Canadian.* short for **veteran** (senses 2, 3).

vet. *abbrev. for:* **1.** veteran. **2.** veterinarian. **3.** veterinary. ~Also (for senses 2, 3): **veter.**

vetch (vɛtʃ) *n.* **1.** any of various climbing papilionaceous plants of the temperate genus *Vicia,* esp. *V. sativa,* having pinnate leaves, typically blue or purple flowers, and tendrils on the stems. **2.** any of various similar and related plants, such as *Lathyrus sativus,* cultivated in parts of Europe, and the kidney vetch. **3.** the beanlike fruit of any of these plants. [C14 *fecche,* from Old French *veche,* from Latin *vicia*]

vetchling ('vɛtʃlɪŋ) *n.* any of various papilionaceous tendril-climbing plants of the genus *Lathyrus,* esp. *L. pratensis* (**meadow vetchling**), mainly of N temperate regions, having winged or angled stems and showy flowers. See also **sweet pea.**

veteran ('vɛtərən, 'vɛtrən) *n.* **1. a.** a person or thing that has given long service in some capacity. **b.** (*as modifier*): *veteran firemen.* **2. a.** a soldier who has seen considerable active service. **b.** (*as modifier*): *veteran soldier.* **3.** *U.S. and Canadian.* a person who has served in the military forces. **4.** See **veteran car.** [C16: from Latin *veterānus,* from *vetus* old]

veteran car *n. Brit.* a car constructed before 1919, esp. one constructed before 1905. Compare **vintage car.**

Veterans Day *n.* the U.S. equivalent of **Armistice Day.**

veterinarian (ˌvɛtərɪ'nɛərɪən, ˌvɛtrɪ-) *n.* the U.S. and Canadian term for **veterinary surgeon.**

veterinary ('vɛtərɪnərɪ, 'vɛtrɪnrɪ) *adj.* of or relating to veterinary science. [C18: from Latin *veterīnārius* concerning draught animals, from *veterīnae* draught animals; related to *vetus* mature (hence able to bear a burden)]

veterinary science *or* **medicine** *n.* the branch of medicine concerned with the health of animals and the treatment of injuries or diseases that affect them.

veterinary surgeon *n. Brit.* a person skilled in the practice of veterinary medicine. U.S. and Canadian term: **veterinarian.**

vetiver ('vɛtɪvə) *n.* **1.** a tall hairless grass, *Vetiveria zizanioides,* of tropical and subtropical Asia, having aromatic roots and stiff long narrow ornamental leaves. **2.** the root of this plant used for making screens, mats, etc., and yielding a fragrant oil used in perfumery, medicine, etc. [C19: from French *vétiver,* from Tamil *vettivēru*]

veto ('viːtəʊ) *n., pl.* **-toes.** **1.** the power to prevent legislation or action proposed by others; prohibition: *the presidential veto.* **2.** the exercise of this power. **3.** Also called: **veto message.** *U.S. government.* a document containing the reasons why a chief executive has vetoed a measure. ~*vb.* **-toes, -toing, -toed.** (*tr.*) **4.** to refuse consent to (a proposal, esp. a government bill). **5.** to prohibit, ban, or forbid: *her parents vetoed her trip.* [C17: from Latin: I forbid, from *vetāre* to forbid] —**'vetoer** *n.* —**'vetoless** *adj.*

vex (vɛks) *vb.* (*tr.*) **1.** to anger or annoy. **2.** to confuse; worry. **3.** *Archaic.* to agitate. [C15: from Old French *vexer,* from Latin *vexāre* to jolt (in carrying), from *vehere* to convey] —**'vexer** *n.* —**'vexing** *adj.* —**'vexingly** *adv.*

vexation (vɛk'seɪʃən) *n.* **1.** the act of vexing or the state of being vexed. **2.** something that vexes.

vexatious (vɛk'seɪʃəs) *adj.* **1.** vexing or tending to vex. **2.** vexed. **3.** *Law.* (of a legal action or proceeding) instituted without sufficient grounds, esp. so as to cause annoyance or embarrassment to the defendant: *vexatious litigation.* —**vex'atiously** *adv.* —**vex'atiousness** *n.*

vexed (vɛkst) *adj.* **1.** annoyed, confused, or agitated. **2.** much debated and discussed (esp. in the phrase **a vexed question**). —**vexedly** ('vɛksɪdlɪ) *adv.* —**'vexedness** *n.*

vexillology (ˌvɛksɪ'lɒlədʒɪ) *n.* the study and collection of information about flags. [C20: from Latin *vexillum* flag + -LOGY] —ˌ**vexil'lologist** *n.*

vexillum (vɛk'sɪləm) *n., pl.* **-la** (-lə). **1.** *Ornithol.* the vane of a feather. **2.** *Botany.* another name for **standard** (sense 15). [C18: from Latin: banner, perhaps from *vēlum* sail] —**'vexillary** *or* **vex'illar** *adj.* —**'vexillate** *adj.*

VF *abbrev. for* video frequency.

VFA (in Australia) *abbrev. for* Victorian Football Association.

VFL (in Australia) *abbrev. for* Victorian Football League.

vg *abbrev. for* very good.

VG *abbrev. for* Vicar General.

VHF *or* **vhf** *Radio. abbrev. for* very high frequency.

VHS *abbrev. for* video home system: a video cassette recording system using ½″ magnetic tape.

vi *abbrev. for* vide infra.

VI *abbrev. for:* **1.** Vancouver Island. **2.** Virgin Islands.

via ('vaɪə) *prep.* by way of; by means of; through: *to London via Paris.* [C18: from Latin *viā,* from *via* way]

viable ('vaɪəbᵊl) *adj.* **1.** capable of becoming actual, useful, etc.; practicable: *a viable proposition.* **2.** (of seeds, eggs, etc.) capable of normal growth and development. **3.** (of a fetus) having reached a stage of development at which further development can occur independently of the mother. [C19: from French, from *vie* life, from Latin *vīta*] —ˌ**via'bility** *n.*

Via Dolorosa ('viːə ˌdɒlə'rəʊsə) *n.* an arduous or distressing course or experience. [Latin, literally: sorrowful road, originally the route followed by Christ from the place of his condemnation to Calvary for his crucifixion]

viaduct ('vaɪəˌdʌkt) *n.* a bridge, esp. for carrying a road or railway across a valley, etc., consisting of a set of arches supported by a row of piers or towers. [C19: from Latin *via* way + *dūcere* to bring, on the model of *aqueduct*]

vial ('vaɪəl, vaɪl) *n.* a less common variant of **phial.** [C14 *fiole,* from Old French, from Old Provençal *fiola,* from Latin *phiala,* from Greek *phialē;* see PHIAL]

via media *Latin.* ('vaɪə 'miːdɪə) *n.* a compromise between two extremes; middle course.

viand ('viːənd, 'vaɪ-) *n.* **1.** a type of food, esp. a delicacy. **2.** (*pl.*) provisions. [C14: from Old French *viande,* ultimately from Latin *vīvenda* things to be lived on, from *vīvere* to live]

viaticum (vaɪ'ætɪkəm) *n., pl.* **-ca** (-kə) *or* **-cums.** **1.** *Christianity.* Holy Communion as administered to a person dying or in danger of death. **2.** *Rare.* provisions or a travel allowance for a journey. [C16: from Latin, from *viāticus* belonging to a journey, from *viāre* to travel, from *via* way]

viator (vaɪ'eɪtɔː) *n., pl.* **viatores** (ˌvaɪə'tɔːriːz). *Rare.* a traveller. [C16: from Latin, from *viāre* to travel]

vibes (vaɪbz) *pl. n.* **1.** *Informal.* (esp. in jazz) short for **vibraphone.** **2.** *Slang.* short for **vibrations.**

vibist ('vaɪbɪst) *n. Informal.* a person who plays a vibraphone in a jazz band or group.

vibraculum (vaɪ'brækjʊləm) *n., pl.* **-la** (-lə). *Zoology.* any of the specialized bristle-like polyps in certain bryozoans, the actions of which prevent parasites from settling on the colony. [C19: from New Latin, from Latin *vibrāre* to brandish] —**vi'bracular** *adj.* —**vi'bracuˌloid** *adj.*

Vibram (ˈvaɪbrəm) *n. Trademark.* a special type of moulded rubber sole, widely used for climbing and walking boots. [C20: from *Vi(tale) Bram(ini)*, Italian climber who devised the product]

vibrant (ˈvaɪbrənt) *adj.* **1.** characterized by or exhibiting vibration; pulsating or trembling. **2.** giving an impression of vigour and activity. **3.** caused by vibration; resonant. **4.** *Phonetics.* trilled or rolled. ~*n.* **5.** a vibrant speech sound, such as a trilled (r). [C16: from Latin *vibrāre* to agitate] —ˈ**vibrancy** *n.* —ˈ**vibrantly** *adv.*

vibraphone (ˈvaɪbrəˌfəʊn) *or esp. U.S.* **vibraharp** (ˈvaɪbrəˌhɑːp) *n.* a percussion instrument, used esp. in jazz, consisting of a set of metal bars placed over tubular metal resonators, which are made to vibrate electronically. —ˈ**vibraˌphonist** *n.*

vibrate (vaɪˈbreɪt) *vb.* **1.** to move or cause to move back and forth rapidly; shake, quiver, or throb. **2.** (*intr.*) to oscillate. **3.** to send out (a sound) by vibration; resonate or cause to resonate. **4.** (*intr.*) to waver. **5.** *Physics.* to undergo or cause to undergo an oscillatory or periodic process, as of an alternating current; oscillate. **6.** (*intr.*) *Rare.* to respond emotionally; thrill. [C17: from Latin *vibrāre*] —**vibratile** (ˈvaɪbrəˌtaɪl) *adj.* —**viˈbrating** *adj.* —**viˈbratingly** *adv.* —ˈ**vibratory** *adj.*

vibration (vaɪˈbreɪʃən) *n.* **1.** the act or an instance of vibrating. **2.** *Physics.* **a.** a periodic motion about an equilibrium position, such as the regular displacement of air in the propagation of sound. **b.** a single cycle of such a motion. **3.** the process or state of vibrating or being vibrated. —**viˈbrational** *adj.* —**viˈbrationless** *adj.*

vibrations (vaɪˈbreɪʃənz) *pl. n. Slang.* **1.** instinctive feelings supposedly influencing human communication. **2.** a characteristic atmosphere felt to be emanating from places or objects. ~Often shortened to **vibes.**

vibrato (vɪˈbrɑːtəʊ) *n., pl.* **-tos.** *Music.* **1.** a slight, rapid, and regular fluctuation in the pitch of a note produced on a stringed instrument by a shaking movement of the hand stopping the strings. **2.** an oscillatory effect produced in singing by fluctuation in breath pressure or pitch. ~Compare **tremolo.** [C19: from Italian, from Latin *vibrāre* to VIBRATE]

vibrator (vaɪˈbreɪtə) *n.* **1. a.** a device for producing a vibratory motion, such as one used in massage. **b.** such a device with a vibrating part or tip, used as a dildo. **2.** a device in which a vibrating conductor interrupts a circuit to produce a pulsating current from a steady current, usually so that the current can then be amplified or the voltage transformed. See also **chopper** (sense 6).

vibrio (ˈvɪbrɪˌəʊ) *n., pl.* **-os.** any curved or spiral rodlike Gram-negative bacterium of the genus *Vibrio,* esp. the comma bacillus: family *Spirillaceae.* [C19: from New Latin, from Latin *vibrāre* to VIBRATE] —ˈ**vibriˌoid** *adj.*

vibrissa (vaɪˈbrɪsə) *n., pl.* **-sae** (-siː). (*usually pl.*) **1.** any of the bristle-like sensitive hairs on the face of many mammals; a whisker. **2.** any of the specialized bristle-like feathers around the beak in certain insectivorous birds. [C17: from Latin, probably from *vibrāre* to shake] —**viˈbrissal** *adj.*

vibronic (vaɪˈbrɒnɪk) *adj. Physics.* of, concerned with, or involving both electronic and vibrational energy levels: *a vibronic spectrum; a vibronic transition.* [C20: from *vibr(atory* + *electr)onic*]

Vibropac block (ˈvaɪbrəʊˌpæk) *n. N.Z. trademark.* a precast concrete building block.

viburnum (vaɪˈbɜːnəm) *n.* **1.** any of various temperate and subtropical caprifoliaceous shrubs or trees of the genus *Viburnum,* such as the wayfaring tree, having small white flowers and berry-like red or black fruits. **2.** the dried bark of several species of this tree, sometimes used in medicine. [C18: from Latin: wayfaring tree]

Vic. *Austral. abbrev. for* Victoria (the state).

vicar (ˈvɪkə) *n.* **1.** *Church of England.* **a.** (in Britain) a clergyman appointed to act as priest of a parish from which, formerly, he did not receive tithes but a stipend. **b.** a clergyman who acts as assistant to or substitute for the rector of a parish at Communion. **c.** (in the U.S.) a clergyman in charge of a chapel. **2.** *R.C. Church.* a bishop or priest representing the pope or the ordinary of a diocese and exercising a limited jurisdiction. **3.** Also called: **lay vicar, vicar choral.** *Church of England.* a member of a cathedral choir appointed to sing certain parts of the services. **4.** a person appointed to do the work of another. [C13: from Old French *vicaire,* from Latin *vicārius* (n.) a deputy, from *vicārius* (adj.) VICARIOUS] —ˈ**vicarly** *adj.*

vicarage (ˈvɪkərɪdʒ) *n.* **1.** the residence or benefice of a vicar. **2.** a rare word for **vicariate** (sense 1).

vicar apostolic *n. R.C. Church.* a titular bishop having jurisdiction in non-Catholic or missionary countries where the normal hierarchy has not yet been established.

vicar forane (fɒˈreɪn) *n., pl.* **vicars forane.** *R.C. Church.* a priest or bishop appointed by the ordinary of the diocese to exercise a limited jurisdiction in a locality at some distance from the ordinary's official see. [*forane,* from Late Latin *forāneus* in a foreign land, from Latin *forās* outside]

vicar general *n., pl.* **vicars general.** an official, usually a layman, appointed to assist the bishop of a diocese in discharging his administrative or judicial duties.

vicarial (vɪˈkɛərɪəl, vaɪ-) *adj.* **1.** of or relating to a vicar, vicars, or a vicariate. **2.** holding the office of a vicar. **3.** vicarious: used esp. of certain ecclesiastical powers.

vicariate (vɪˈkɛərɪɪt, vaɪ-) *n.* **1.** Also called: **vicarship** (ˈvɪkəʃɪp). the office, rank, or authority of a vicar. **2.** the district that a vicar holds as his pastoral charge.

vicarious (vɪˈkɛərɪəs, vaɪ-) *adj.* **1.** obtained or undergone at second hand through sympathetic participation in another's experiences. **2.** suffered, undergone, or done as the substitute for another: *vicarious punishment.* **3.** delegated: *vicarious authority.* **4.** taking the place of another. **5.** *Pathol.* (of menstrual bleeding) occurring at an abnormal site. See **endometriosis.** [C17: from Latin *vicārius* substituted, from *vicis* interchange; see VICE[3], VICISSITUDE] —**viˈcariously** *adv.* —**viˈcariousness** *n.*

Vicar of Christ *n. R.C. Church.* the pope when regarded as Christ's earthly representative.

vice[1] (vaɪs) *n.* **1.** an immoral, wicked, or evil habit, action, or trait. **2.** habitual or frequent indulgence in pernicious, immoral, or degrading practices. **3.** a specific form of pernicious conduct, esp. prostitution or sexual perversion. **4.** a failing or imperfection in character, conduct, etc.: *smoking is his only vice.* **5.** *Pathol., obsolete.* any physical defect or imperfection. **6.** a bad trick or disposition, as of horses, dogs, etc. [C13: via Old French from Latin *vitium* a defect] —ˈ**viceless** *adj.*

vice[2] *or U.S.* (*often*) **vise** (vaɪs) *n.* **1.** an appliance for holding an object while work is done upon it, usually having a pair of jaws. ~*vb.* **2.** (*tr.*) to grip (something) with or as if with a vice. [C15: from Old French *vis* a screw, from Latin *vītis* vine, plant with spiralling tendrils (hence the later meaning)] —ˈ**viceˌlike** *or U.S.* (*often*) ˈ**viseˌlike** *adj.*

vice[3] (vaɪs) *adj.* **1. a.** (*prenominal*) serving in the place of or as a deputy for. **b.** (*in combination*): *viceroy.* ~*n.* **2.** *Informal.* a person who serves as a deputy to another. [C18: from Latin *vice,* from *vicis* interchange]

vice[4] (ˈvaɪsɪ) *prep.* instead of; as a substitute for. [C16: from Latin, ablative of *vicis* change]

vice admiral *n.* a commissioned officer of flag rank in certain navies, junior to an admiral and senior to a rear admiral. —ˌ**vice-ˈadmiralty** *n.*

vice-chairman *n., pl.* **-men.** a person who deputizes for a chairman and serves in his place during his absence or indisposition. —ˌ**vice-ˈchairmanship** *n.*

vice chancellor *n.* **1.** the chief executive or administrator at some British universities. Compare **chancellor** (sense 3). **2.** (in the U.S.) a judge in courts of equity subordinate to the chancellor. **3.** (formerly in England) a senior judge of the court of chancery who acted as assistant to the Lord Chancellor. **4.** a person serving as the deputy of a chancellor. —ˌ**vice-ˈchancellorship** *n.*

vicegerent (ˌvaɪsˈdʒɛrənt) *n.* **1.** a person appointed to exercise all or some of the authority of another, esp. the administrative powers of a ruler; deputy. **2.** *R.C. Church.* the pope or any other representative of God or Christ on earth, such as a bishop. ~*adj.* **3.** invested with or characterized by delegated authority. [C16: from New Latin *vicegerēns,* from VICE[3] + Latin *gerere* to manage] —ˌ**viceˈgeral** *adj.* —ˌ**viceˈgerency** *n.*

vicenary (ˈvɪsɪnərɪ) *adj.* **1.** relating to or consisting of 20. **2.** *Maths.* having or using a base 20. [C17 (in the sense: one who has charge over twenty persons): from Latin *vīcēnārius,* from *vīcēnī* twenty each, from *vīgintī* twenty]

vicennial (vɪˈsɛnɪəl) *adj.* **1.** occurring every 20 years. **2.** relating to or lasting for a period of 20 years. [C18: from Late Latin *vīcennium* period of twenty years, from Latin *vīciēs* twenty times + *-ennium,* from *annus* year]

vice president *n.* an officer ranking immediately below a president and serving as his deputy. A vice president takes the president's place during his absence or incapacity, after his death, and in certain other circumstances. Abbrevs.: **VP, V. Pres.** —ˌ**vice-ˈpresidency** *n.* —ˌ**vice-ˌpresiˈdential** *adj.*

viceregal (ˌvaɪsˈriːgəl) *adj.* **1.** of or relating to a viceroy or his viceroyalty. **2.** *Chiefly Austral. and N.Z.* of or relating to a governor or governor general. —ˌ**viceˈregally** *adv.*

viceregal assent *n. Austral.* the formal signing of an act of parliament by a governor general, by which it becomes law.

vicereine (ˌvaɪsˈreɪn) *n.* **1.** the wife of a viceroy. **2.** a female viceroy. [C19: from French, from VICE[3] + *reine* queen, from Latin *rēgīna*]

viceroy (ˈvaɪsrɔɪ) *n.* a governor of a colony, country, or province who acts for and rules in the name of his sovereign or government. Related adj.: **viceregal.** [C16: from French, from VICE[3] + *roy* king, from Latin *rex*] —ˈ**viceroyˌship** *n.*

viceroyalty (ˌvaɪsˈrɔɪəltɪ) *n., pl.* **-ties.** **1.** the office, authority, or dignity of a viceroy. **2.** the domain governed by a viceroy. **3.** the term of office of a viceroy.

vice squad *n.* a police division to which is assigned the enforcement of gaming and prostitution laws.

vice versa (ˈvaɪsɪ ˈvɜːsə) *adv.* with the order reversed; the other way around. [C17: from Latin: relations being reversed, from *vicis* change + *vertere* to turn]

vichyssoise (*French* viʃiswaz) *n.* a thick soup made from leeks, potatoes, chicken stock, and cream, usually served chilled. [French, from (*crème*) *Vichyssoise* (*glacée*) (ice-cold cream) from *Vichy,* a town and spa in central France]

vichy water *n.* 1. (*sometimes cap.*) a natural mineral water from springs at Vichy in France, reputed to be beneficial to the health. 2. any sparkling mineral water resembling this. ~Often shortened to **vichy.**

vicinage ('vɪsənɪdʒ) *n. Now rare.* 1. the residents of a particular neighbourhood. 2. a less common word for **vicinity.** [C14: from Old French *vicenage,* from *vicin* neighbouring, from Latin *vīcīnus;* see VICINITY]

vicinal ('vɪsɪn°l) *adj.* 1. neighbouring. 2. (esp. of roads) of or relating to a locality or neighbourhood. 3. *Chem.* relating to or designating two adjacent atoms to which groups are attached in a chain. [C17: from Latin *vīcīnālis* nearby, from *vīcīnus,* from *vīcus* a neighbourhood]

vicinity (vɪ'sɪnɪtɪ) *n., pl.* **-ties.** 1. a surrounding, adjacent, or nearby area; neighbourhood. 2. the fact or condition of being close in space or relationship. [C16: from Latin *vīcīnitās,* from *vīcīnus* neighbouring, from *vīcus* village]

vicious ('vɪʃəs) *adj.* 1. wicked or cruel; villainous: *a vicious thug.* 2. characterized by violence or ferocity: *a vicious blow.* 3. *Informal.* unpleasantly severe; harsh: *a vicious wind.* 4. characterized by malice: *vicious lies.* 5. (esp. of dogs, horses, etc.) ferocious or hostile; dangerous. 6. characterized by or leading to vice. 7. invalidated by defects; unsound: *a vicious inference.* 8. *Obsolete.* noxious or morbid: *a vicious exhalation.* [C14: from Old French *vicieus,* from Latin *vitiōsus* full of faults, from *vitium* a defect] —'**viciously** *adv.* —'**viciousness** *n.*

vicious circle *n.* 1. a situation in which an attempt to resolve one problem creates new problems that lead back to the original situation. 2. *Logic.* **a.** a form of reasoning in which a conclusion is inferred from premises the truth of which cannot be established independently of that conclusion. **b.** an explanation given in terms that cannot be understood independently of that which was to be explained. **c.** a situation in which some statement is shown to entail its negation and vice versa, as *this statement is false* is true only if false and false only if true. 3. *Med.* a condition in which one disease or disorder causes another, which in turn aggravates the first condition.

vicissitude (vɪ'sɪsɪˌtjuːd) *n.* 1. variation or mutability in nature or life, esp. successive alternation from one condition or thing to another. 2. a variation in circumstance, fortune, character, etc. [C16: from Latin *vicissitūdō,* from *vicis* change, alternation] —**viˌcissi'tudinary** *or* **viˌcissi'tudinous** *adj.*

vicomte (*French* vikɔ̃t) *or* (*fem.*) **vicomtesse** (*French* vikɔ̃tɛs) *n.* a French noble holding a rank corresponding to that of a British viscount or viscountess.

Victa ('vɪktə) *n. Austral. trademark.* a type of rotary lawnmower first manufactured in 1952. [C20: named after Mervyn *Victor* Richardson, who invented it]

victim ('vɪktɪm) *n.* 1. a person or thing that suffers harm, death, etc., from another or from some adverse act, circumstance, etc.: *victims of tyranny.* 2. a person who is tricked or swindled; dupe. 3. a living person or animal sacrificed in a religious rite. [C15: from Latin *victima*]

victimize *or* **victimise** ('vɪktɪˌmaɪz) *vb.* (*tr.*) 1. to punish or discriminate against selectively or unfairly. 2. to make a victim of. 3. to kill as or in a manner resembling a sacrificial victim. —ˌ**victimi'zation** *or* ˌ**victimi'sation** *n.* —'**victimˌizer** *or* '**victimˌiser** *n.*

victor ('vɪktə) *n.* 1. **a.** a person, nation, etc., that has defeated an adversary in war, etc. **b.** (*as modifier*): *the victor army.* 2. the winner of any contest, conflict, or struggle. [C14: from Latin, from *vincere* to conquer]

Victor ('vɪktə) *n. Communications.* a code word for the letter *v.*

victoria (vɪk'tɔːrɪə) *n.* 1. a light four-wheeled horse-drawn carriage with a folding hood, two passenger seats, and a seat in front for the driver. 2. Also called: **victoria plum.** *Brit.* a large sweet variety of plum, red and yellow in colour. 3. any South American giant water lily of the genus *Victoria,* having very large floating leaves and large white, red, or pink fragrant flowers: family *Euryalaceae.* [C19: all named after Queen *Victoria;* see VICTORIAN]

Victoria Cross (vɪk'tɔːrɪə) *n.* the highest decoration for gallantry in the face of the enemy awarded to the British and Commonwealth armed forces: instituted in 1856 by Queen Victoria.

Victoria Day *n.* the Monday preceding May 24: observed in Canada as a national holiday in commemoration of the birthday of Queen Victoria.

Victorian (vɪk'tɔːrɪən) *adj.* 1. of, relating to, or characteristic of the British monarch Queen Victoria (1819–1901) or the period of her reign (1837–1901). 2. exhibiting the characteristics popularly attributed to the Victorians, esp. prudery, bigotry, or hypocrisy. Compare **Victorian values.** 3. denoting, relating to, or having the style of architecture used in England during the reign of Queen Victoria, characterized by massive construction and elaborate ornamentation. ~*n.* 4. a person who lived during the reign of Queen Victoria. —**Vic'torianˌism** *n.*

Victoriana (vɪkˌtɔːrɪ'ɑːnə) *n.* objects, ornaments, etc., of the Victorian period.

Victorian values *pl. n.* qualities considered to characterize the Victorian period, including enterprise and initiative and the importance of the family. Compare **Victorian** (sense 2).

victorious (vɪk'tɔːrɪəs) *adj.* 1. having defeated an adversary: *the victorious nations.* 2. of, relating to, indicative of, or characterized by victory: *a victorious conclusion.* —**vic'toriously** *adv.* —**vic'toriousness** *n.*

victory ('vɪktərɪ) *n., pl.* **-ries.** 1. final and complete superiority in a war. 2. a successful military engagement. 3. a success attained in a contest or struggle or over an opponent, obstacle, or problem. 4. the act of triumphing or state of having triumphed. [C14: from Old French *victorie,* from Latin *victōria,* from *vincere* to subdue]

victory roll *n.* a roll of an aircraft made by a pilot to announce or celebrate the shooting down of an enemy plane or other cause for celebration.

victual ('vɪt°l) *vb.* **-uals, -ualling, -ualled** *or U.S.* **-uals, -ualing, -ualed.** 1. to supply with or obtain victuals. 2. (*intr.*) *Rare.* (esp. of animals) to partake of victuals. ~See also **victuals.** [C14: from Old French *vitaille,* from Late Latin *victualia* provisions, from Latin *victuālis* concerning food, from *victus* sustenance, from *vīvere* to live] —'**victual-less** *adj.*

victualage ('vɪtəlɪdʒ) *n.* a rare word for **victuals.**

victualler ('vɪtələ, 'vɪtlə) *n.* 1. a supplier of victuals, as to an army; sutler. 2. *Brit.* a licensed purveyor of spirits; innkeeper. 3. a supply ship, esp. one carrying foodstuffs.

victuals ('vɪt°lz) *pl. n.* (*sometimes sing.*) food or provisions.

vicuña (vɪ'kuːnjə) *or* **vicuna** (vɪ'kjuːnə) *n.* 1. a tawny-coloured cud-chewing Andean artiodactyl mammal, *Vicugna vicugna,* similar to the llama: family *Camelidae.* 2. the fine light wool or cloth obtained from this animal. [C17: from Spanish *vicuña,* from Quechuan *wikúña*]

vid (vɪd) *n. Informal.* short for **video** (sense 4).

vide ('vaɪdɪ) (used to direct a reader to a specified place in a text, another book, etc.) refer to, see (often in the phrases **vide ante** (see before), **vide infra** (see below), **vide post** (see after), **vide supra** (see above), **vide ut supra** (see as above), etc.). Abbrev.: **v., vid.** [C16: from Latin]

videlicet (vɪ'diːlɪˌsɛt) *adv.* namely: used to specify items, examples, etc. Abbrev.: **viz.** [C15: from Latin]

video ('vɪdɪˌəʊ) *adj.* 1. relating to or employed in the transmission or reception of a televised image. 2. of, concerned with, or operating at video frequencies. ~*n., pl.* **-os.** 3. the visual elements of a television broadcast. 4. a film recorded on a video cassette. 5. short for **video cassette, video cassette recorder.** 6. *Informal.* the quality of the visual image in a television. 7. *U.S.* an informal name for **television.** ~*vb.* **videos, videoing, videoed.** 8. to record (a television programme, etc.) on a video cassette recorder. ~Compare **audio.** [C20: from Latin *vidēre* to see, on the model of AUDIO]

video cassette *n.* a cassette containing video tape.

video cassette recorder *n.* a tape recorder for vision and sound signals using magnetic tape in closed plastic cassettes: used for recording and playing back television programmes and films. Often shortened to **video.** Abbrev.: **VCR.**

video conferencing *n.* a facility enabling participants in distant locations to take part in a conference by means of electronic sound and video communication.

videodisk ('vɪdɪəʊˌdɪsk) *n.* another name for **optical disk.**

video frequency *n.* the frequency of a signal conveying the image and synchronizing pulses in a television broadcasting system. It lies in the range from about 50 hertz to 8 megahertz.

video game *n.* any of various games that can be played by using an electronic control to move points of light or graphical symbols on the screen of a visual display unit. Some are ball-and-racket type games, others are computerized giving greater scope for variety. See also **TV game.**

video jockey *n.* a person who introduces and plays videos, esp. of pop songs, on a television programme.

video nasty *n.* a film, usually specially made for video, that is explicitly horrific, brutal, and pornographic.

videophone ('vɪdɪəˌfəʊn) *n.* a telephonic device in which there is both verbal and visual communication between parties. —**videophonic** (ˌvɪdɪə'fɒnɪk) *adj.*

video tape *n.* 1. magnetic tape used mainly for recording the video-frequency signals of a television programme or film for subsequent transmission. ~*vb.* **video-tape.** 2. to record (a programme, film, etc.) on video tape.

video tape recorder *n.* a tape recorder for vision signals and sometimes accompanying sound, using magnetic tape on open spools: used in television broadcasting. Abbrev.: **VTR.**

Videotex ('vɪdɪəʊˌtɛks) *n. Trademark.* an information system that displays information from a distant computer on a television screen. See also **Teletext, Viewdata.**

videotext ('vɪdɪəʊˌtɛkst) *n.* a means of providing a written or graphical representation of computerized information on a television screen.

vidette (vɪ'dɛt) *n.* a variant spelling of **vedette.**

vidicon ('vɪdɪˌkɒn) *n.* a small television camera tube, used in closed-circuit television and outside broadcasts, in which incident light forms an electric charge pattern on a photoconductive surface. Scanning by a low-velocity electron beam discharges the surface, producing a current in an adjacent conducting layer. See also **Plumbicon.** [C20: from VID(EO) + ICON(OSCOPE)]

vie (vaɪ) *vb.* **vies, vying, vied.** 1. (*intr.;* foll. by *with* or *for*) to contend for superiority or victory (with) or strive in competition (for). **2.** (*tr.*) *Archaic.* to offer, exchange, or display in rivalry. [C15: probably from Old French *envier* to challenge, from Latin *invītāre* to INVITE] —'**vier** *n.* —'**vying** *adj., n.*

Viennese (ˌvɪəˈniːz) *adj.* **1.** of, relating to, or characteristic of Vienna, capital of Austria. ~*n., pl.* **-nese. 2.** a native or inhabitant of Vienna.

vi et armis *Latin.* (ˈvaɪ ɛt ˈɑːmɪs) *n. Legal history.* a kind of trespass accompanied by force and violence. [literally: by force and arms]

Vietnamese (ˌvjɛtnəˈmiːz) *adj.* **1.** of, relating to, or characteristic of the republic of Vietnam in SE Asia, its people, or their language. ~*n.* **2.** (*pl.* **-ese**) a native or inhabitant of Vietnam. **3.** the language of Vietnam, probably related to the Mon-Khmer languages.

vieux jeu *French.* (vjø ʒø) *adj.* old-fashioned. [literally: old game]

view (vjuː) *n.* **1.** the act of seeing or observing; an inspection. **2.** vision or sight, esp. range of vision: *the church is out of view.* **3.** a scene, esp. of a fine tract of countryside: *the view from the top was superb.* **4.** a pictorial representation of a scene, such as a photograph. **5.** (*sometimes pl.*) opinion; thought: *my own view on the matter differs from yours.* **6.** chance or expectation: *the policy has little view of success.* **7.** (foll. by *to*) a desired end or intention: *he has a view to securing further qualifications.* **8.** a general survey of a topic, subject, etc.: *a comprehensive view of Shakespearean literature.* **9.** visual aspect or appearance: *they look the same in outward view.* **10.** *Law.* **a.** a formal inspection by a jury of the place where an alleged crime was committed. **b.** a formal inspection of property in dispute. **11.** a sight of a hunted animal before or during the chase. **12. in view of.** taking into consideration. **13. on view.** exhibited to the public gaze. **14. take a dim** *or* **poor view of.** to regard (something) with disfavour or disapproval. **15. with a view to. a.** with the intention of. **b.** in anticipation or hope of. ~*vb.* **16.** (*tr.*) to look at. **17.** (*tr.*) to consider in a specified manner: *they view the growth of Communism with horror.* **18.** (*tr.*) to examine or inspect carefully: *to view the accounts.* **19.** (*tr.*) to survey mentally; contemplate: *to view the difficulties.* **20.** to watch (television). **21.** (*tr.*) to sight (a hunted animal) before or during the chase. [C15: from Old French *veue,* from *veoir* to see, from Latin *vidēre*] —'**viewable** *adj.*

Viewdata (ˈvjuːˌdeɪtə) *n. Trademark.* an interactive form of Videotex that sends information from a distant computer along telephone lines, enabling shopping, booking theatre and airline tickets, and banking transactions to be conducted from the home.

viewer (ˈvjuːə) *n.* **1.** a person who views something, esp. television. **2.** any optical device by means of which something is viewed, esp. one used for viewing photographic transparencies. **3.** *Law.* a person appointed by a court to inspect and report upon property, etc. —'**viewership** *n.*

viewfinder (ˈvjuːˌfaɪndə) *n.* a device on a camera, consisting of a lens system and sometimes a ground-glass screen, enabling the user to see what will be included in his photograph. Sometimes shortened to **finder.**

view halloo *interj.* **1.** a huntsman's cry uttered when the quarry is seen breaking cover or shortly afterwards. ~*n.* **2.** a shout indicating an abrupt appearance.

viewing (ˈvjuːɪŋ) *n.* **1.** the act of watching television. **2.** television programmes collectively: *late-night viewing.*

viewless (ˈvjuːlɪs) *adj.* **1.** (of windows, etc.) not affording a view. **2.** having no opinions. **3.** *Poetic.* invisible.

viewpoint (ˈvjuːˌpɔɪnt) *n.* **1.** the mental attitude that determines a person's opinions or judgments; point of view. **2.** a place from which something can be viewed.

viewy (ˈvjuːɪ) *adj.* **viewier, viewiest.** *Informal, rare.* **1.** having fanciful opinions or ideas; visionary. **2.** characterized by ostentation; showy. —'**viewiness** *n.*

VIFF (vɪf) *n.* a technique used in flying VTOL aircraft to change direction suddenly by swivelling the jet engine nozzles. [C20: *v(ectoring) i(n) f(orward) f(light)*]

vigesimal (vaɪˈdʒɛsɪməl) *adj.* **1.** relating to or based on the number 20. **2.** taking place or proceeding in intervals of 20. **3.** twentieth. [C17: from Latin *vīgēsimus,* variant (influenced by *vīgintī* twenty) of *vīcēsimus* twentieth]

vigia (ˈvɪdʒɪə) *n. Nautical.* a navigational hazard marked on a chart although its existence and nature has not been confirmed. [C19: from Spanish *vigía,* reef, from Latin *vigilāre* to keep watch]

vigil (ˈvɪdʒɪl) *n.* **1.** a purposeful watch maintained, esp. at night, to guard, observe, pray, etc. **2.** the period of such a watch. **3.** *R.C. Church, Church of England.* the eve of certain major festivals, formerly observed as a night spent in prayer: often marked by fasting and abstinence and a special Mass and divine office. **4.** a period of sleeplessness; insomnia. [C13: from Old French *vigile,* from Medieval Latin *vigilia* watch preceding a religious festival, from Latin: vigilance, from *vigil* alert, from *vigēre* to be lively]

vigilance (ˈvɪdʒɪləns) *n.* **1.** the fact, quality, or condition of being vigilant. **2.** the abnormal state or condition of being unable to sleep.

vigilance committee *n.* (in the U.S.) a self-appointed body of citizens organized to maintain order, punish crime, etc., where an efficient system of courts does not exist.

vigilant (ˈvɪdʒɪlənt) *adj.* keenly alert to or heedful of trouble or danger, as while others are sleeping or unsuspicious. [C15: from Latin *vigilāns* keeping awake, from *vigilāre* to be watchful; see VIGIL] —'**vigilantly** *adv.* —'**vigilantness** *n.*

vigilante (ˌvɪdʒɪˈlæntɪ) *n.* **1.** one of an organized group of citizens who take upon themselves the protection of their district, properties, etc. **2.** Also called: **vigilance man.** *U.S.* a member of a vigilance committee. [C19: from Spanish, from Latin *vigilāre* to keep watch]

vigilantism (ˌvɪdʒɪˈlæntɪzəm) *n. U.S.* the methods, conduct, attitudes, etc., associated with vigilantes, esp. militancy, bigotry, or suspiciousness.

vigil light *n. Chiefly R.C. Church.* **1.** a small candle lit as an act of personal devotion before a shrine or statue, usually in a church. **2.** a small lamp kept permanently burning before such a shrine or statue.

vigneron (ˈviːnjərɒn; *French* viɲrɔ̃) *n.* a person who grows grapes for winemaking. [French, from *vigne* vine]

vignette (vɪˈnjɛt) *n.* **1.** a small illustration placed at the beginning or end of a book or chapter. **2.** a short graceful literary essay or sketch. **3.** a photograph, drawing, etc., with edges that are shaded off. **4.** *Architect.* a carved ornamentation that has a design based upon tendrils, leaves, etc. **5.** any small endearing scene, view, picture, etc. ~*vb.* (*tr.*) **6.** to finish (a photograph, picture, etc.) with a fading border in the form of a vignette. **7. a.** to decorate with vignettes. **b.** to portray in or as in a vignette. [C18: from French, literally: little vine, from *vigne* VINE; with reference to the vine motif frequently used in embellishments to a text] —**vi'gnettist** *n.*

vignetting (vɪˈnjɛtɪŋ) *n.* **1.** the technique of producing a photographic vignette, esp. a portrait, by progressively reducing the amount of light falling on the photographic surface towards the edges. **2.** the reduction in area of a light beam passing through a camera lens as the obliquity of the beam is increased.

vigoro (ˈvɪgəˌrəʊ) *n. Austral. sport.* a women's game similar to cricket with paddle-shaped bats, introduced into Australia in 1919. [C20: from VIGOUR]

vigorous (ˈvɪgərəs) *adj.* **1.** endowed with bodily or mental strength or vitality; robust. **2.** displaying, involving, characterized by, or performed with vigour: *vigorous growth.* —'**vigorously** *adv.* —'**vigorousness** *n.*

vigour *or U.S.* **vigor** (ˈvɪgə) *n.* **1.** exuberant and resilient strength of body or mind; vitality. **2.** substantial effective energy or force: *the vigour of the tempest.* **3.** forcefulness; intensity: *I was surprised by the vigour of her complaints.* **4.** the capacity for survival or strong healthy growth in a plant or animal: *hybrid vigour.* **5.** the most active period or stage of life, manhood, etc.; prime. **6.** *Chiefly U.S.* legal force or effectiveness; validity (esp. in the phrase **in vigour**). [C14: from Old French *vigeur,* from Latin *vigor* activity, from *vigēre* to be lively]

vihuela (*Spanish* biˈwela) *n.* an obsolete plucked stringed instrument of Spain, related to the guitar. [from Spanish]

Viking (ˈvaɪkɪŋ) *n.* (*sometimes not cap.*) **1.** Also called: **Norseman, Northman.** any of the Danes, Norwegians, and Swedes who raided by sea most of N and W Europe from the 8th to the 11th centuries, later often settling, as in parts of Britain. **2.** any sea rover, plunderer, or pirate. **3.** (*modifier*) of, relating to, or characteristic of a Viking or Vikings: *a Viking ship.* [C19: from Old Norse *vīkingr,* probably from *vīk* creek, sea inlet + *-ingr* (see -ING[3]); perhaps related to Old English *wīc* camp]

vil. *abbrev. for* village.

vilayet (vɪˈlɑːjɛt) *n.* a major administrative division of Turkey. [C19: from Turkish, from Arabic *wilāyat,* from *walīy* governor]

vile (vaɪl) *adj.* **1.** abominably wicked; shameful or evil: *the vile development of slavery appalled them.* **2.** morally despicable; ignoble: *vile accusations.* **3.** disgusting to the senses or emotions; foul: *a vile smell; vile epithets.* **4.** tending to humiliate or degrade: *only slaves would perform such vile tasks.* **5.** unpleasant or bad: *vile weather.* **6.** paltry: *a vile reward.* [C13: from Old French *vil,* from Latin *vīlis* cheap] —'**vilely** *adv.* —'**vileness** *n.*

vilify (ˈvɪlɪˌfaɪ) *vb.* **-fies, -fying, -fied.** (*tr.*) **1.** to revile with abusive or defamatory language; malign. **2.** *Rare.* to make vile; debase; degrade. [C15: from Late Latin *vīlificāre,* from Latin *vīlis* worthless + *facere* to make] —**vilification** (ˌvɪlɪfɪˈkeɪʃən) *n.* —'**viliˌfier** *n.*

vilipend (ˈvɪlɪˌpɛnd) *vb.* (*tr.*) *Rare.* **1.** to treat or regard with contempt. **2.** to speak slanderously or slightingly of. [C15: from Late Latin *vīlipendere,* from Latin *vīlis* worthless + *pendere* to esteem] —'**viliˌpender** *n.*

villa (ˈvɪlə) *n.* **1.** (in ancient Rome) a country house, usually consisting of farm buildings and residential quarters around a courtyard. **2.** a large and usually luxurious country residence. **3.** *Brit.* a detached or semidetached suburban house. **4.** *N.Z.* a medium-sized suburban house standing in its own grounds. [C17: via Italian from Latin; related to Latin *vīcus* a village] —'**villa-ˌlike** *adj.*

village (ˈvɪlɪdʒ) *n.* **1.** a small group of houses in a country area, larger than a hamlet. **2.** the inhabitants of such a community collectively. **3.** an incorporated municipality smaller than a town in various parts of the U.S. and Canada. **4.** a group of habitats of certain animals. **5.** *N.Z.* a self-contained city area having its own shops, etc. **6.** (*modifier*) of, relating to, or characteristic of a village: *a village green.* [C15: from Old French, from *ville* farm, from Latin: VILLA] —'**village-ˌlike** *adj.*

village college *n. Brit.* a centre, often for a group of villages, with educational and recreational facilities for the whole neighbourhood. Also called: **community college.**
villager ('vɪlɪdʒə) *n.* **1.** an inhabitant of a village. *~adj.* **2.** *E African.* backward, unsophisticated, or illiterate.
villa home *n. Austral.* one of a set of suburban bungalows built compactly on the one allotment, esp. on the former site of a single bungalow.
villain ('vɪlən) *n.* **1.** a wicked or malevolent person. **2.** (in a novel, play, film, etc.) the main evil character and antagonist to the hero. **3.** *Often jocular.* a mischievous person; rogue. **4.** *Brit. police slang.* a criminal. **5.** *History.* a variant spelling of **villein. 6.** *Obsolete.* an uncouth person; boor. [C14: from Old French *vilein* serf, from Late Latin *vīllānus* worker on a country estate, from Latin: VILLA] —'**villainess** *fem. n.*
villainage ('vɪlənɪdʒ) *n.* a variant spelling of **villeinage.**
villainous ('vɪlənəs) *adj.* **1.** of, like, or appropriate to a villain. **2.** very bad or disagreeable: *a villainous climate.* —'**villainously** *adv.* —'**villainousness** *n.*
villainy ('vɪlənɪ) *n., pl.* **-lainies. 1.** conduct befitting a villain; vicious behaviour or action. **2.** an evil, abhorrent, or criminal act or deed. **3.** the fact or condition of being villainous. **4.** *English history.* a rare word for **villeinage.**
villanella (ˌvɪlə'nɛlə) *n., pl.* **-las.** a type of part song originating in Naples in SW Italy during the 16th century. [C16: from Italian, from *villano* rustic, from Late Latin *vīllānus;* see VILLAIN]
villanelle (ˌvɪlə'nɛl) *n.* a verse form of French origin consisting of 19 lines arranged in five tercets and a quatrain. The first and third lines of the first tercet recur alternately at the end of each subsequent tercet and both together at the end of the quatrain. [C16: from French, from Italian VILLANELLA]
Villanovan (ˌvɪlə'nəʊvᵊn) *adj.* **1.** of or relating to an early Iron Age culture near Bologna, Italy, characterized by the use of bronze and the primitive use of iron. *~n.* **2.** a member of this culture. [C19: named after the NE Italian town of *Villanova,* where the first remains of the culture were excavated in 1853]
villatic (vɪ'lætɪk) *adj. Literary.* of or relating to a villa, village, or farm; rustic; rural. [C17: from Latin *vīllaticus,* from *villa* a farm]
-ville *n. and adj. combining form. Slang, chiefly U.S.* (denoting) a place, condition, or quality with a character as specified: *dragsville; squaresville.*
villein *or* **villain** ('vɪlən) *n.* (in medieval Europe) a peasant personally bound to his lord, to whom he paid dues and services, sometimes commuted to rents, in return for his land. [C14: from Old French *vilein* serf; see VILLAIN]
villeinage *or* **villainage** ('vɪlənɪdʒ) *n.* (in medieval Europe) **1.** the status and condition of a villein. **2.** the tenure by which a villein held his land.
villi ('vɪlaɪ) *n.* the plural of **villus.**
villiform ('vɪlɪˌfɔːm) *adj.* having the form of a villus or a series of villi. [C19: from New Latin *villiformis,* from Latin *villus* shaggy hair + -FORM]
villosity (vɪ'lɒsɪtɪ) *n., pl.* **-ties. 1.** the state of being villous. **2.** a villous coating or surface. **3.** a villus or a collection of villi.
villous ('vɪləs) *adj.* **1.** (of plant parts) covered with long hairs. **2.** of, relating to, or having villi. [C14: from Latin *villōsus,* from *villus* tuft of hair] —'**villously** *adv.*
villus ('vɪləs) *n., pl.* **villi** ('vɪlaɪ). (*usually pl.*) **1.** *Zoology, anatomy.* any of the numerous finger-like projections of the mucous membrane lining the small intestine of many vertebrates. **2.** any similar membranous process, such as any of those in the mammalian placenta. **3.** *Botany.* any of various hairlike outgrowths, as from the stem of a moss. [C18: from Latin: shaggy hair]
vim (vɪm) *n. Slang.* exuberant vigour and energy. [C19: from Latin, from *vīs;* related to Greek *is* strength]
vimen ('vaɪmɛn) *n., pl.* **vimina** ('vɪmɪnə). a long flexible shoot that occurs in certain plants. [C19: from Latin: a pliant twig, osier]
vimineous (vɪ'mɪnɪəs) *adj. Botany.* having, producing, or resembling long flexible shoots. [C17: from Latin *vīmineus* made of osiers, from *vīmen* flexible shoot]
vin- *combining form.* a variant of **vini-** before a vowel.
vina ('viːnə) *n.* a stringed musical instrument, esp. of India, related to the sitar. [C18: from Hindi *bīnā,* from Sanskrit *vīnā*]
vinaceous (vaɪ'neɪʃəs) *adj.* **1.** of, relating to, or containing wine. **2.** having a colour suggestive of red wine. [C17: from Late Latin *vīnāceus,* from Latin *vīnum* wine]
vinaigrette (ˌvɪneɪ'grɛt) *n.* **1.** Also called: **vinegarette.** a small decorative bottle or box with a perforated top, used for holding smelling salts, etc. **2.** Also called: **vinaigrette sauce.** a salad dressing made from oil and vinegar with seasonings; French dressing. *~adj.* **3.** served with vinaigrette. [C17: from French, from *vinaigre* VINEGAR]
vinasse (vɪ'næs) *n.* the residue left in a still after distilling spirits, esp. brandy. [C20: from French]
vinblastine (vɪn'blæstiːn) *n.* a cytotoxic drug used in the treatment of lymphomas, derived as an alkaloid from the tropical shrub Madagascar periwinkle (*Vinca rosea*). [C20: shortened from *vincaleukoblastine,* from VINCA + *leukoblast,* from *leukocyte* + -BLAST + -INE[2]]
vinca ('vɪŋkə) *n.* See **periwinkle**[2]. [New Latin, from Latin *pervinca* periwinkle]
vinca alkaloid *n. Med.* any of a group of alkaloids obtained from the periwinkle *Vinca rosea,* such as vinblastine and vincristine, that interfere with cell division and are used in the treatment of cancer.
Vincent's angina *or* **disease** ('vɪnsənts) *n.* an ulcerative bacterial infection of the mouth, esp. involving the throat and tonsils. [C20: named after J. H. *Vincent* (died 1950), French bacteriologist]
vincible ('vɪnsɪbᵊl) *adj. Rare.* capable of being defeated or overcome. [C16: from Latin *vincibilis,* from *vincere* to conquer] —ˌ**vinci'bility** *or* '**vincibleness** *n.*
vincristine (vɪn'krɪstiːn) *n.* a cytotoxic drug used in the treatment of leukaemia, derived as an alkaloid from the tropical shrub Madagascar periwinkle (*Vinca rosea*). [C20: from New Latin VINCA + Latin *crista* crest + -INE[2]]
vinculum ('vɪŋkjʊləm) *n., pl.* **-la** (-lə). **1.** a horizontal line drawn above a group of mathematical terms, used as an alternative to parentheses in mathematical expressions, as in $x + \overline{y - z}$ which is equivalent to $x + (y - z)$. **2.** *Anatomy.* **a.** any bandlike structure, esp. one uniting two or more parts. **b.** another name for **ligament. 3.** *Rare.* a unifying bond; tie. [C17: from Latin: bond, from *vincīre* to bind]
vin de pays *French.* (vɛ̃ də pei) *n., pl.* ***vins de pays*** (vɛ̃ də pei). the third highest French wine classification: indicates that the wine meets certain requirements concerning area of production, strength, etc. Also called: ***vin du pays.*** Abbrev.: **VDP.** Compare **AOC, VDQS.** [literally: local wine]
vindicable ('vɪndɪkəbᵊl) *adj.* capable of being vindicated; justifiable. —ˌ**vindica'bility** *n.*
vindicate ('vɪndɪˌkeɪt) *vb.* (*tr.*) **1.** to clear from guilt, accusation, blame, etc., as by evidence or argument. **2.** to provide justification for: *his promotion vindicated his unconventional attitude.* **3.** to uphold, maintain, or defend (a cause, etc.): *to vindicate a claim.* **4.** *Roman law.* to bring an action to regain possession of (property) under claim of legal title. **5.** *Rare.* to claim, as for oneself or another. **6.** *Obsolete.* to take revenge on or for; punish. **7.** *Obsolete.* to set free. [C17: from Latin *vindicāre,* from *vindex* claimant] —'**vindiˌcator** *n.* —'**vindiˌcatory** *adj.*
vindication (ˌvɪndɪ'keɪʃən) *n.* **1.** the act of vindicating or the condition of being vindicated. **2.** a means of exoneration from an accusation. **3.** a fact, evidence, circumstance, etc., that serves to vindicate a theory or claim.
vindictive (vɪn'dɪktɪv) *adj.* **1.** disposed to seek vengeance. **2.** characterized by spite or rancour. **3.** *English law.* (of damages) in excess of the compensation due to the plaintiff and imposed in punishment of the defendant. [C17: from Latin *vindicta* revenge, from *vindicāre* to VINDICATE] —**vin'dictively** *adv.* —**vin'dictiveness** *n.*
vin du pays *French.* (vɛ̃ du pei) *n., pl.* ***vins du pays.*** a variant spelling of ***vin de pays.***
vine (vaɪn) *n.* **1.** any of various plants, esp. the grapevine, having long flexible stems that creep along the ground or climb by clinging to a support by means of tendrils, leafstalks, etc. **2.** the stem of such a plant. [C13: from Old French *vine,* from Latin *vīnea* vineyard, from *vīneus* belonging to wine, from *vīnum* wine] —**vined** *adj.* —'**vineless** *adj.* —'**vineˌlike** *adj.* —'**viny** *adj.*
vinedresser ('vaɪnˌdrɛsə) *n.* a person who prunes, tends, or cultivates grapevines.
vinegar ('vɪnɪgə) *n.* **1.** a sour-tasting liquid consisting of impure dilute acetic acid, made by oxidation of the ethyl alcohol in beer, wine, or cider. It is used as a condiment or preservative. **2.** sourness or peevishness of temper, countenance, speech, etc. **3.** *Pharmacol.* a medicinal solution in dilute acetic acid. **4.** *U.S. and Canadian informal.* vitality. *~vb.* **5.** (*tr.*) to apply vinegar to. [C13: from Old French *vinaigre,* from *vin* WINE + *aigre* sour, from Latin *acer* sharp] —'**vinegarish** *adj.* —'**vinegar-ˌlike** *adj.* —'**vinegary** *adj.*
vinegar eel *n.* a nematode worm, *Anguillula aceti,* that feeds on the organisms that cause fermentation in vinegar and other liquids. Also called: **vinegar worm, eelworm.**
vinegarette (ˌvɪnɪgə'rɛt) *n.* a variant spelling of **vinaigrette** (sense 1).
vinegar fly *n.* any of various dipterous flies of the genus *Drosophila.* See **drosophila.**
vinegarroon (ˌvɪnɪgə'ruːn) *n.* a large whip scorpion, *Mastigoproctus giganteus,* of the southwestern U.S. and Mexico that emits a vinegary odour when alarmed. [from Mexican Spanish *vinagrón,* from Spanish *vinagre* VINEGAR]
vinery ('vaɪnərɪ) *n., pl.* **-eries. 1.** a hothouse for growing grapes. **2.** another name for a **vineyard. 3.** vines collectively.
vineyard ('vɪnjəd) *n.* a plantation of grapevines, esp. where wine grapes are produced. [Old English *wīngeard;* see VINE, YARD[2]; related to Old High German *wīngart,* Old Norse *vingarthr*] —'**vineyardist** *n.*
vingt-et-un *French.* (vɛ̃teœ̃) *n.* another name for **pontoon**[2]. [literally: twenty-one]
vinho verde (ˌviːnjəʊ 'vɜːdɪ) *n.* any of a variety of light, slightly sharp-tasting wines made from early-picked grapes in the Minho region of NW Portugal. [Portuguese, literally: green (or young) wine]
vini- *or before a vowel* **vin-** *combining form.* indicating wine: *viniculture.* [from Latin *vīnum*]
vinic ('vaɪnɪk, 'vɪnɪk) *adj.* of, relating to, or contained in wine. [C19: from Latin *vīnum* wine]

viniculture ('vɪnɪˌkʌltʃə) *n.* the process or business of growing grapes and making wine. —ˌ**vini'cultural** *adj.* —ˌ**vini'culturist** *n.*

viniferous (vɪ'nɪfərəs) *adj.* wine-producing.

vinificator ('vɪnɪfɪˌkeɪtə) *n.* a condenser that collects the alcohol vapour escaping from fermenting wine. [C19: from Latin *vīnum* wine + *facere* to make]

vino ('viːnəʊ) *n., pl.* **-nos.** an informal word for **wine.** [jocular use of Italian or Spanish *vino*]

vin ordinaire *French.* (vɛ̃n ɔrdinɛr) *n., pl.* ***vins ordinaires*** (vɛ̃z ɔrdinɛr). cheap table wine, esp. French.

vinosity (vɪ'nɒsɪtɪ) *n.* the distinctive and essential quality and flavour of wine. [C17: from Late Latin *vīnōsitas,* from Latin *vīnōsus* VINOUS]

vinous ('vaɪnəs) *adj.* **1.** of, relating to, or characteristic of wine. **2.** indulging in or indicative of indulgence in wine: *a vinous complexion.* [C17: from Latin *vīnōsus,* from *vīnum* WINE]

vintage ('vɪntɪdʒ) *n.* **1.** the wine obtained from a harvest of grapes, esp. in an outstandingly good year, referred to by the year involved, the district, or the vineyard. **2.** the harvest from which such a wine is obtained. **3. a.** the harvesting of wine grapes. **b.** the season of harvesting these grapes or for making wine. **4.** a time of origin: *a car of Edwardian vintage.* **5.** *Informal.* a group of people or objects of the same period: *a fashion of last season's vintage.* ~*adj.* **6.** (of wine) of an outstandingly good year. **7.** representative of the best and most typical: *vintage Shakespeare.* **8.** of lasting interest and importance; venerable; classic: *vintage films.* **9.** old-fashioned; dated. ~*vb.* **10.** (*tr.*) to gather (grapes) or make (wine). [C15: from Old French *vendage* (influenced by *vintener* VINTNER), from Latin *vindēmia,* from *vīnum* WINE, grape + *dēmere* to take away (from *dē-* away + *emere* to take)]

vintage car *n. Chiefly Brit.* an old car, esp. one constructed between 1919 and 1930. Compare **veteran car.**

vintager ('vɪntɪdʒə) *n.* a grape harvester.

vintner ('vɪntnə) *n.* a wine merchant. [C15: from Old French *vinetier,* from Medieval Latin *vīnētārius,* from Latin *vīnētum* vineyard, from *vīnum* WINE]

vinyl ('vaɪnɪl) *n.* **1.** (*modifier*) of, consisting of, or containing the monovalent group of atoms CH_2CH-: *a vinyl polymer; vinyl chloride.* **2.** (*modifier*) of, consisting of, or made of a vinyl resin: *a vinyl raincoat.* **3.** any vinyl polymer, resin, or plastic, esp. PVC. **4.** (collectively) conventional records made of vinyl as opposed to compact discs. [C19: from VINI- + -YL]

vinyl acetate *n.* a colourless volatile liquid unsaturated ester that polymerizes readily in light and is used for making polyvinyl acetate. Formula: CH_2:$CHOOCCH_3$.

vinyl chloride *n.* a colourless flammable gaseous unsaturated compound made by the chlorination of ethylene and used as a refrigerant and in the manufacture of PVC; chloroethylene; chloroethene. Formula: CH:CHCl.

vinylidene (vaɪ'nɪlɪˌdiːn) *n.* (*modifier*) of, consisting of, or containing the group CH_2:C: *a vinylidene group or radical; vinylidene chloride; a vinylidene resin.* [C20: from VINYL + -IDE + -ENE]

vinyl resin *or* **polymer** *n.* any one of a class of thermoplastic materials, esp. PVC and polyvinyl acetate, made by polymerizing vinyl compounds.

viol ('vaɪəl) *n.* any of a family of stringed musical instruments that preceded the violin family, consisting of a fretted fingerboard, a body rather like that of a violin but having a flat back and six strings, played with a curved bow. They are held between the knees when played and have a quiet yet penetrating tone; they were much played, esp. in consorts, in the 16th and 17th centuries. [C15: from Old French *viole,* from Old Provençal *viola;* see VIOLA[1]]

viola[1] (vɪ'əʊlə) *n.* **1.** a bowed stringed instrument, the alto of the violin family; held beneath the chin when played. It is pitched and tuned an octave above the cello. **2.** any of various instruments of the viol family, such as the viola da gamba. [C18: from Italian *viola,* probably from Old Provençal *viola,* of uncertain origin; perhaps related to Latin *vītulārī* to rejoice]

viola[2] ('vaɪələ, vaɪ'əʊ-) *n.* any temperate perennial herbaceous plant of the violaceous genus *Viola,* the flowers of which have showy irregular petals, white, yellow, blue, or mauve in colour. See also **violet** (sense 1), **pansy** (sense 1). [C15: from Latin: violet]

violaceous (ˌvaɪə'leɪʃəs) *adj.* **1.** of, relating to, or belonging to the *Violaceae,* a family of herbaceous plants and shrubs including the violets and pansies. **2.** of the colour violet. [C17: from Latin *violāceus,* from *viola* VIOLET]

viola clef *n.* another term for **alto clef.**

viola da braccio (vɪ'əʊlə də 'brætʃɪˌəʊ) *n.* **1.** an old name for **viola**[1] (sense 1). **2.** a type of viol held on the shoulder, from which the modern viola was developed. [from Italian, literally: viol for the arm]

viola da gamba (vɪ'əʊlə də 'gæmbə) *n.* the second largest and lowest member of the viol family. See **viol.** [C18: from Italian, literally: viol for the leg]

viola d'amore (vɪ'əʊlə dæ'mɔːrɪ) *n.* an instrument of the viol family having no frets, seven strings, and a set of sympathetic strings. It was held under the chin when played. [C18: from Italian, literally: viol of love]

violate ('vaɪəˌleɪt) *vb.* (*tr.*) **1.** to break, disregard, or infringe (a law, agreement, etc.). **2.** to rape or otherwise sexually assault. **3.** to disturb rudely or improperly; break in upon. **4.** to treat irreverently or disrespectfully; outrage: *he violated a sanctuary.* **5.** *Obsolete.* to mistreat physically. ~*adj.* **6.** *Archaic.* violated or dishonoured. [C15: from Latin *violāre* to do violence to, from *vīs* strength] —'**violable** *adj.* —ˌ**viola'bility** *or* '**violableness** *n.* —'**violably** *adv.* —ˌ**vio'lation** *n.* —'**violative** *adj.* —'**vioˌlator** *or* '**vioˌlater** *n.*

violence ('vaɪələns) *n.* **1.** the exercise or an instance of physical force, usually effecting or intended to effect injuries, destruction, etc. **2.** powerful, untamed, or devastating force: *the violence of the sea.* **3.** great strength of feeling, as in language, etc.; fervour. **4.** an unjust, unwarranted, or unlawful display of force, esp. such as tends to overawe or intimidate. **5. do violence to. a.** to inflict harm upon; damage or violate: *they did violence to the prisoners.* **b.** to distort or twist the sense or intention of: *the reporters did violence to my speech.* [C13: via Old French from Latin *violentia* impetuosity, from *violentus* VIOLENT]

violent ('vaɪələnt) *adj.* **1.** marked or caused by great physical force or violence: *a violent stab.* **2.** (of a person) tending to the use of violence, esp. in order to injure or intimidate others. **3.** marked by intensity of any kind: *a violent clash of colours.* **4.** characterized by an undue use of force; severe; harsh. **5.** caused by or displaying strong or undue mental or emotional force: *a violent tongue.* **6.** tending to distort the meaning or intent: *a violent interpretation of the text.* [C14: from Latin *violentus,* probably from *vīs* strength] —'**violently** *adv.*

violent storm *n.* a wind of force 11 on the Beaufort scale, reaching speeds of 64–72 mph.

violet ('vaɪəlɪt) *n.* **1.** any of various temperate perennial herbaceous plants of the violaceous genus *Viola,* such as *V. odorata* (**sweet** (or **garden**) **violet**), typically having mauve or bluish flowers with irregular showy petals. **2.** any other plant of the genus *Viola,* such as the wild pansy. **3.** any of various similar but unrelated plants, such as the African violet. **4. a.** any of a group of colours that vary in saturation but have the same purplish-blue hue. They lie at one end of the visible spectrum, next to blue; approximate wavelength range 445–390 nanometres. **b.** (*as adj.*): *a violet dress.* **5.** a dye or pigment of or producing these colours. **6.** violet clothing: *dressed in violet.* **7. shrinking violet.** *Informal.* a shy person. [C14: from Old French *violete* a little violet, from *viole,* from Latin *viola* violet] —'**violet-ˌlike** *adj.*

violin (ˌvaɪə'lɪn) *n.* a bowed stringed instrument, the highest member of the violin family, consisting of a fingerboard, a hollow wooden body with waisted sides, and a sounding board connected to the back by means of a soundpost that also supports the bridge. It has two f-shaped sound holes cut in the belly. The instrument, noted for its fine and flexible tone, is the most important of the stringed instruments. It is held under the chin when played. Range: roughly three and a half octaves upwards from G below middle C. [C16: from Italian *violino* a little viola, from VIOLA[1]]

violinist (ˌvaɪə'lɪnɪst) *n.* a person who plays the violin.

violist[1] (vɪ'əʊlɪst) *n. U.S.* a person who plays the viola.

violist[2] ('vaɪəlɪst) *n.* a person who plays the viol.

violoncello (ˌvaɪələn'tʃɛləʊ) *n., pl.* **-los.** the full name for **cello.** [C18: from Italian, from VIOLONE + *-cello,* diminutive suffix] —ˌ**violon'cellist** *n.*

violone ('vaɪəˌləʊn) *n.* the double-bass member of the viol family lying an octave below the viola da gamba. It corresponds to the double bass in the violin family. [C18: from Italian, from VIOLA[1] + *-one,* augmentative suffix]

VIP *abbrev. for:* **1.** very important person. **2.** vasoactive intestinal peptide: a polypeptide secreted by the small intestine during digestion and also found in the brain as a neurotransmitter: large amounts in the blood cause diarrhoea.

viper ('vaɪpə) *n.* **1.** any venomous Old World snake of the family *Viperidae,* esp. any of the genus *Vipera* (the adder and related forms), having hollow fangs in the upper jaw that are used to inject venom. **2.** any of various other snakes, such as the horned viper. **3.** See **pit viper. 4.** a malicious or treacherous person. [C16: from Latin *vīpera,* perhaps from *vīvus* living + *parere* to bear, referring to a tradition that the viper was viviparous] —'**viper-ˌlike** *adj.*

viperous ('vaɪpərəs) *or* **viperish** *adj.* **1.** Also: **viperine** ('vaɪpəˌraɪn). of, relating to, or resembling a viper. **2.** malicious. —'**viperously** *or* '**viperishly** *adv.*

viper's bugloss *n.* a Eurasian boraginaceous weed, *Echium vulgare,* having blue flowers and pink buds. Also called: (U.S.) **blueweed,** (Austral.) **Paterson's curse,** (South Australia) **Salvation Jane.** See also **echium.**

VIR *abbrev. for* Victoria Imperatrix Regina. [Latin: Victoria, Empress and Queen]

virago (vɪ'rɑːgəʊ) *n., pl.* **-goes** *or* **-gos. 1.** a loud, violent, and ill-tempered woman; scold; shrew. **2.** *Archaic.* a strong, brave, or warlike woman; amazon. [Old English, from Latin: a man-like maiden, from *vir* a man] —**viraginous** (vɪ'rædʒɪnəs) *adj.* —**vi'rago-ˌlike** *adj.*

viral ('vaɪrəl) *adj.* of, relating to, or caused by a virus.

Vir Chakra (ˈviːr ˈtʃʌkrə) *n.* an award made to distinguished soldiers by the Government of India. [Hindi: *vir* brave man + *chakra* wheel]

virelay (ˈvɪrɪˌleɪ) *n.* **1.** an old French verse form, rarely used in English, consisting of short lines arranged in stanzas having only two rhymes, and two opening lines recurring at intervals. **2.** any of various similar forms. [C14: from Old French *virelai,* probably from *vireli* (associated with *lai* LAY[4]), meaningless word used as a refrain]

virement (ˈvɪəmɑ̃) *n.* an administrative transfer of funds from one part of a budget to another. [from French, from Middle French: act of turning, from *virer* to turn]

vireo (ˈvɪrɪəʊ) *n., pl.* **vireos.** any insectivorous American songbird of the family *Vireonidae,* esp. those of the genus *Vireo,* having an olive-grey back with pale underparts. [C19: from Latin: a bird, probably a greenfinch; compare *virēre* to be green]

virescence (vɪˈrɛsəns) *n.* **1.** (in plants) the state of becoming green, esp. by the action of disease, etc., in parts not normally green. **2.** the condition of being or the process of becoming green. [C19: see VIRESCENT]

virescent (vɪˈrɛsᵊnt) *adj.* greenish or becoming green. [C19: from Latin *virescere* to grow green, from *virēre* to be green]

virga (ˈvɜːgə) *n.* (*sometimes functioning as pl.*) *Meteorol.* wisps of rain or snow, seen trailing from clouds, that evaporate before reaching the earth. [C20: from Latin: streak]

virgate[1] (ˈvɜːgɪt, -geɪt) *adj.* long, straight, and thin; rod-shaped: *virgate stems.* [C19: from Latin *virgātus* made of twigs, from *virga* a rod]

virgate[2] (ˈvɜːgɪt, -geɪt) *n. Brit.* an obsolete measure of land area, usually taken as equivalent to 30 acres. [C17: from Medieval Latin *virgāta* (*terrae*) a rod's measurement (of land), from Latin *virga* rod; the phrase is a translation of Old English *gierd landes* a yard of land]

virgin (ˈvɜːdʒɪn) *n.* **1.** a person, esp. a woman, who has never had sexual intercourse. **2.** an unmarried woman who has taken a religious vow of chastity in order to dedicate herself totally to God. **3.** any female animal that has never mated. **4.** a female insect that produces offspring by parthenogenesis. ~*adj.* (*usually prenominal*) **5.** of, relating to, resembling, suitable for, or characteristic of a virgin or virgins; chaste. **6.** pure and natural, uncorrupted, unsullied, or untouched: *virgin purity.* **7.** not yet cultivated, explored, exploited, etc., by man: *virgin territories.* **8.** being the first or happening for the first time. **9.** (of vegetable oils) obtained directly by the first pressing of fruits, leaves, or seeds of plants without applying heat. **10.** (of a metal) made from an ore rather than from scrap. **11.** occurring naturally in a pure and uncombined form: *virgin silver.* **12.** *Physics.* (of a neutron) not having experienced a collision. [C13: from Old French *virgine,* from Latin *virgō* virgin]

Virgin[1] (ˈvɜːdʒɪn) *n.* a statue or other artistic representation of the Virgin Mary, the mother of Christ.

Virgin[2] (ˈvɜːdʒɪn) *n.* **the.** the constellation Virgo, the sixth sign of the zodiac.

virginal[1] (ˈvɜːdʒɪnᵊl) *adj.* **1.** of, relating to, characterized by, proper to, or maintaining a state of virginity; chaste. **2.** extremely pure or fresh; untouched; undefiled. [C15: from Latin *virginālis* maidenly, from *virgō* virgin] —ˈ**virginally** *adv.*

virginal[2] (ˈvɜːdʒɪnᵊl) *n.* (*often pl.*) a smaller version of the harpsichord, but oblong in shape, having one manual and no pedals. [C16: probably from Latin *virginālis* VIRGINAL[1], perhaps because it was played largely by young ladies] —ˈ**virginalist** *n.*

virgin birth *n.* another name for **parthenogenesis** (sense 2).

Virgin Birth *n.* the doctrine that Jesus Christ had no human father but was conceived solely by the direct intervention of the Holy Spirit so that Mary remained miraculously a virgin during and after his birth.

virgin forest *n.* a forest in its natural state, before it has been explored or exploited by man.

Virginia (vəˈdʒɪnɪə) *n.* (*sometimes not cap.*) a type of flue-cured tobacco grown originally in the state of Virginia in the eastern U.S.

Virginia creeper *n.* **1.** Also called (U.S.): **American ivy, woodbine.** a vitaceous woody vine, *Parthenocissus quinquefolia,* of North America, having tendrils with adhesive tips, bluish-black berry-like fruits, and compound leaves that turn red in autumn: widely planted for ornament. **2.** Also called: **Japanese ivy.** a similar related plant, *Parthenocissus tricuspidata,* of SE Asia, having trilobed leaves and purple berries. U.S. name: **Boston ivy.**

Virginia deer *n.* another name for **white-tailed deer.**

Virginia reel *n.* **1.** an American country dance. **2.** music written for or in the manner of this dance.

Virginia stock *n.* a Mediterranean cruciferous plant, *Malcomia maritima,* cultivated for its white and pink flowers.

virginity (vəˈdʒɪnɪtɪ) *n.* **1.** the condition or fact of being a virgin; maidenhood; chastity. **2.** the condition of being untouched, unsullied, etc.

virginium (vəˈdʒɪnɪəm) *n. Chem.* a former name for **francium.**

virgin's-bower *n.* any of several American clematis plants, esp. *Clematis virginiana,* of E North America, which has clusters of small white flowers.

virgin soil *n.* **1.** soil that has not been cultivated before. **2.** a person or thing that is as yet undeveloped.

virgin wool *n.* wool that is being processed or woven for the first time.

Virgo (ˈvɜːgəʊ) *n., Latin genitive* **Virginis** (ˈvɜːdʒɪnɪs). **1.** *Astronomy.* a large zodiacal constellation on the celestial equator, lying between Leo and Libra. It contains the star Spica and a cluster of several thousand galaxies, the **Virgo cluster,** lying 20 million light years away. **2.** *Astrology.* **a.** Also called: the **Virgin.** the sixth sign of the zodiac, symbol ♍, having a mutable earth classification and ruled by the planet Mercury. The sun is in this sign between about Aug. 23 and Sept. 22. **b.** Also called: **Virgoan** (vɜːˈgəʊən). a person born when the sun is in this sign. ~*adj.* **3.** Also: **Virgoan.** *Astrology.* born under or characteristic of Virgo. [C14: from Latin]

virgo intacta (ˈvɜːgəʊ ɪnˈtæktə) *n.* a girl or woman whose hymen has not been broken. [Latin, literally: untouched virgin]

virgulate (ˈvɜːgjʊlɪt, -ˌleɪt) *adj.* rod-shaped or rodlike. [C19: from Latin *virgula* a little rod, from *virga* rod]

virgule (ˈvɜːgjuːl) *n. Printing.* another name for **solidus.** [C19: from French: comma, from Latin *virgula* a little rod, from *virga* rod]

viridescent (ˌvɪrɪˈdɛsᵊnt) *adj.* greenish or tending to become green. [C19: from Late Latin *viridescere* to grow green, from Latin *viridis* green] —ˌ**viriˈdescence** *n.*

viridian (vɪˈrɪdɪən) *n.* a green pigment consisting of a hydrated form of chromic oxide. [C19: from Latin *viridis* green]

viridity (vɪˈrɪdɪtɪ) *n.* **1.** the quality or state of being green; greenness; verdancy. **2.** innocence, youth, or freshness. [C15: from Latin *viriditās,* from *viridis* green]

virile (ˈvɪraɪl) *adj.* **1.** of, relating to, or having the characteristics of an adult male. **2.** (of a male) possessing high sexual drive and capacity for sexual intercourse. **3.** of or capable of copulation or procreation. **4.** strong, forceful, or vigorous. [C15: from Latin *virīlis* manly, from *vir* a man; related to Old English *wer* man and probably to Latin *vis* strength] —**virility** (vɪˈrɪlɪtɪ) *n.*

virilism (ˈvɪrɪˌlɪzəm) *n. Med.* the abnormal development in a woman of male secondary sex characteristics.

virino (vɪˈriːnəʊ) *n.* an entity postulated to be the causative agent of BSE and related diseases, said to consist of a fragment of nucleic acid surrounded by a protein coat derived from the host cell. [C20: from VIRUS + *-ino* diminutive form]

virion (ˈvaɪrɪɒn) *n.* a virus in infective form, consisting of an RNA particle within a protein covering. [C20: from VIR(US) + ION]

viroid (ˈvaɪrɔɪd) *n.* any of various infective RNA particles, smaller than a virus and known to cause some plant diseases. [C20: from VIR(US) + -OID]

virology (vaɪˈrɒlədʒɪ) *n.* the branch of medicine concerned with the study of viruses and the diseases they cause. —**virological** (ˌvaɪrəˈlɒdʒɪkᵊl) *adj.* —**viˈrologist** *n.*

virtu *or* **vertu** (vɜːˈtuː) *n.* **1.** a taste or love for curios or works of fine art; connoisseurship. **2.** such objects collectively. **3.** the quality of being rare, beautiful, or otherwise appealing to a connoisseur (esp. in the phrases **articles of virtu; objects of virtu**). [C18: from Italian *virtù;* see VIRTUE]

virtual (ˈvɜːtʃʊəl) *adj.* **1.** having the essence or effect but not the appearance or form of: *a virtual revolution.* **2.** *Physics.* being, relating to, or involving a virtual image: *a virtual focus.* **3.** *Computer technol.* of or relating to virtual storage: *virtual memory.* **4.** *Rare.* capable of producing an effect through inherent power or virtue. **5.** *Physics.* designating or relating to a particle exchanged between other particles that are interacting by a field of force: *a virtual photon.* See also **exchange force.** [C14: from Medieval Latin *virtuālis* effective, from Latin *virtūs* VIRTUE] —ˌ**virtuˈality** *n.*

virtual image *n.* an optical image formed by the apparent divergence of rays from a point, rather than their actual divergence from a point.

virtually (ˈvɜːtʃʊəlɪ) *adv.* in effect though not in fact; practically; nearly.

virtual reality *n.* a computer-generated environment that, to the person experiencing it, closely resembles reality.

virtual storage *or* **memory** *n.* a computer system in which the size of the memory is effectively increased by automatically transferring sections of a program from a large capacity backing store, such as a disk, into the smaller core memory as they are required.

virtue (ˈvɜːtjuː, -tʃuː) *n.* **1.** the quality or practice of moral excellence or righteousness. **2.** a particular moral excellence: *the virtue of tolerance.* **3.** any of the cardinal virtues (prudence, justice, fortitude, and temperance) or theological virtues (faith, hope, and charity). **4.** any admirable quality, feature, or trait. **5.** chastity, esp. in women. **6.** *Archaic.* an effective, active, or inherent power or force. **7. by** *or* **in virtue of.** on account of or by reason of. **8. make a virtue of necessity.** to acquiesce in doing something unpleasant with a show of grace because one must do it in any case. [C13 *vertu,* from Old French, from Latin *virtūs* manliness, courage, from *vir* man] —ˈ**virtueless** *adj.*

virtues (ˈvɜːtjuːz, -tʃuːz) *pl. n.* (*often cap.*) the fifth of the nine orders into which the angels are traditionally divided in medieval angelology.

virtuoso (ˌvɜːtjuˈəʊzəʊ, -səʊ) *n., pl.* **-sos** *or* **-si** (-siː). **1.** a consummate master of musical technique and artistry. **2.** a person who has a masterly or dazzling skill or technique in any field of activity. **3.** a connoisseur, dilettante, or collector of art objects.

4. *Obsolete.* a scholar or savant. 5. (*modifier*) showing masterly skill or brilliance: *a virtuoso performance.* [C17: from Italian: skilled, from Late Latin *virtuōsus* good, virtuous; see VIRTUE] —**virtuosic** (ˌvɜːtjuˈɒsɪk) *adj.* —ˌ**virtuˈosity** *n.*

virtuous (ˈvɜːtʃuəs) *adj.* 1. characterized by or possessing virtue or moral excellence; righteous; upright. 2. (of women) chaste or virginal. 3. *Archaic.* efficacious; potent. —ˈ**virtuously** *adv.* —ˈ**virtuousness** *n.*

virulence (ˈvɪrʊləns) *or* **virulency** *n.* 1. the quality of being virulent. 2. the capacity of a microorganism for causing disease.

virulent (ˈvɪrʊlənt) *adj.* 1. a. (of a microorganism) extremely infective. b. (of a disease) having a rapid course and violent effect. 2. extremely poisonous, injurious, etc. 3. extremely bitter, hostile, etc. [C14: from Latin *vīrulentus* full of poison, from *vīrus* poison; see VIRUS] —ˈ**virulently** *adv.*

virus (ˈvaɪrəs) *n., pl.* **-ruses.** 1. any of a group of submicroscopic entities consisting of a single nucleic acid surrounded by a protein coat and capable of replication only within the cells of animals and plants: many are pathogenic. 2. *Informal.* a disease caused by a virus. 3. any corrupting or infecting influence. 4. *Computer technol.* an unauthorized program that inserts itself into a computer system and then propagates itself to other computers via networks or disks; when activated it interferes with the operation of the computer. [C16: from Latin: slime, poisonous liquid; related to Old English *wāse* marsh, Greek *ios* poison] —ˈ**virus-ˌlike** *adj.*

vis *Latin.* (vɪs) *n., pl.* ***vires*** (ˈvaɪriːz). power, force, or strength.

Vis. *abbrev. for* Viscount *or* Viscountess.

visa (ˈviːzə) *n., pl.* **-sas.** 1. an endorsement in a passport or similar document, signifying that the document is in order and permitting its bearer to travel into or through the country of the government issuing it. 2. any sign or signature of approval. ~*vb.* **-sas, -saing, -saed.** (*tr.*) 3. to enter a visa into (a passport). 4. to endorse or ratify. [C19: via French from Latin *vīsa* things seen, from *vīsus,* past participle of *vidēre* to see]

visage (ˈvɪzɪdʒ) *n. Chiefly literary.* 1. face or countenance. 2. appearance; aspect. [C13: from Old French: aspect, from *vis* face, from Latin *vīsus* appearance, from *vidēre* to see]

-visaged *adj.* (*in combination*) having a visage as specified: *flat-visaged.*

visagiste (ˌviːzɑːˈʒiːst) *n.* a person who designs and applies face make-up; make-up artist. [C20: from French, from *visage* face + *-iste* -ist]

vis-à-vis (ˌviːzɑːˈviː) *prep.* 1. in relation to; regarding. 2. face to face with; opposite. ~*adv., adj.* 3. face to face; opposite. ~*n., pl.* **vis-à-vis.** 4. a person or thing that is situated opposite to another. 5. a person who corresponds to another in office, capacity, etc.; counterpart. 6. an upholstered sofa; tête-à-tête. 7. a type of horse-drawn carriage in which the passengers sit opposite one another. 8. a coin having an obverse upon which two portraits appear facing each other. [C18: French, from *vis* face]

Visayan (vɪˈsɑːjən) *or* **Bisayan** *n., pl.* **-yans** *or* **-yan.** 1. a member of the most numerous indigenous people of the Philippines in SE Asia. ~*adj.* 2. of or relating to this people.

Visc. *abbrev. for* Viscount *or* Viscountess.

viscacha *or* **vizcacha** (vɪsˈkætʃə) *n.* 1. a gregarious burrowing hystricomorph rodent, *Lagostomus maximus,* of southern South America, similar to but larger than the chinchillas: family *Chinchillidae.* 2. **mountain viscacha.** another name for **mountain chinchilla** (see **chinchilla** (sense 3)). [C17: from Spanish, from Quechuan *wiskácha*]

viscaria (vɪsˈkeərɪə) *n.* any plant of the Eurasian perennial genus *Viscaria,* closely related to genus *Lychnis,* in which it is sometimes included: low-growing, with pink, white, or purple flowers: family *Carophyllaceae.* [New Latin, from *viscum* birdlime (from the viscid stems)]

viscera (ˈvɪsərə) *pl. n., sing.* **viscus** (ˈvɪskəs). 1. *Anatomy.* the large internal organs of the body collectively, esp. those in the abdominal cavity. 2. (less formally) the intestines; guts. [C17: from Latin: entrails, pl. of *viscus* internal organ]

visceral (ˈvɪsərəl) *adj.* 1. of, relating to, or affecting the viscera. 2. characterized by intuition or instinct rather than intellect. —ˈ**viscerally** *adv.*

visceromotor (ˈvɪsərəʊˌməʊtə) *adj. Physiol.* relating to or controlling movements of the viscera.

viscerotonia (ˌvɪsərəʊˈtəʊnɪə) *n.* a personality type characterized by hedonism and conviviality: said to be correlated with an endomorph body type. Compare **cerebrotonia, somatotonia.**

viscid (ˈvɪsɪd) *adj.* 1. cohesive and sticky; glutinous; viscous. 2. (esp. of a leaf) covered with a sticky substance. [C17: from Late Latin *viscidus* sticky, from Latin *viscum* mistletoe or birdlime] —**visˈcidity** *or* ˈ**viscidness** *n.* —ˈ**viscidly** *adv.*

viscoelastic (ˌvɪskəʊɪˈlæstɪk) *adj. Physics.* (of a solid or liquid) exhibiting both viscous and elastic behaviour when deformed. —ˌ**viscoelasˈticity** *n.*

viscoid (ˈvɪskɔɪd) *or* **viscoidal** (vɪsˈkɔɪdᵊl) *adj.* (of a fluid) somewhat viscous.

viscometer (vɪsˈkɒmɪtə) *or* **viscosimeter** (ˌvɪskəʊˈsɪmɪtə) *n.* any device for measuring viscosity. —**viscometric** (ˌvɪskəˈmɛtrɪk) *or* ˌ**viscoˈmetrical** *adj.* —**visˈcometry** *n.*

viscose (ˈvɪskəʊs) *n.* 1. a. a viscous orange-brown solution obtained by dissolving cellulose in sodium hydroxide and carbon disulphide. It can be converted back to cellulose by an acid, as in the manufacture of rayon and cellophane. b. (*as modifier*): *viscose rayon.* 2. rayon made from this material. ~*adj.* 3. another word for **viscous.** [C19: from Late Latin *viscōsus* full of birdlime, sticky, from *viscum* birdlime; see VISCID]

viscosity (vɪsˈkɒsɪtɪ) *n., pl.* **-ties.** 1. the state or property of being viscous. 2. *Physics.* a. the extent to which a fluid resists a tendency to flow. b. Also called: **absolute viscosity.** a measure of this resistance, equal to the tangential stress on a liquid undergoing streamline flow divided by its velocity gradient. It is measured in newton seconds per metre squared. Symbol: η See also **kinematic viscosity, specific viscosity.**

viscount (ˈvaɪkaʊnt) *n.* 1. (in the British Isles) a nobleman ranking below an earl and above a baron. 2. (in various countries) a son or younger brother of a count. See also **vicomte.** 3. (in medieval Europe) the deputy of a count. [C14: from Old French *visconte,* from Medieval Latin *vicecomes,* from Late Latin *vice-* VICE[3] + *comes* COUNT[2]]

viscountcy (ˈvaɪkaʊntsɪ) *or* **viscounty** *n.* the rank or position of a viscount.

viscountess (ˈvaɪkaʊntɪs) *n.* 1. the wife or widow of a viscount. 2. a woman who holds the rank of viscount in her own right.

viscous (ˈvɪskəs) *or* **viscose** *adj.* 1. (of liquids) thick and sticky; viscid. 2. having or involving viscosity. [C14: from Late Latin *viscōsus;* see VISCOSE] —ˈ**viscously** *adv.* —ˈ**viscousness** *n.*

viscous flow *n.* another name for **streamline flow.**

Visct *abbrev. for* Viscount *or* Viscountess.

viscus (ˈvɪskəs) *n.* the singular of **viscera.**

vise (vaɪs) *n., vb. U.S.* a variant spelling of **vice**[2].

Vishnu (ˈvɪʃnuː) *n. Hinduism.* the Pervader or Sustainer, originally a solar deity occupying a secondary place in the Hindu pantheon, later one of the three chief gods, the second member of the Trimurti, and, later still, the saviour appearing in many incarnations. [C17: from Sanskrit *Viṣṇu,* literally: the one who works everywhere] —ˈ**Vishnuism** *n.*

visibility (ˌvɪzɪˈbɪlɪtɪ) *n.* 1. the condition or fact of being visible. 2. clarity of vision or relative possibility of seeing. 3. the range of vision: *visibility is 500 yards.*

visible (ˈvɪzɪbᵊl) *adj.* 1. capable of being perceived by the eye. 2. capable of being perceived by the mind; evident: *no visible dangers.* 3. available: *the visible resources.* 4. (of an index or file) using a flexible display system for the contents. 5. of or relating to the balance of trade: *visible transactions.* 6. represented by visible symbols. ~*n.* 7. a visible item of trade; product. [C14: from Latin *vīsibilis,* from *vidēre* to see] —ˈ**visibleness** *n.* —ˈ**visibly** *adv.*

visible balance *n.* another name for **balance of trade.**

visible radiation *n.* electromagnetic radiation that causes the sensation of sight; light. It has wavelengths between about 380 and 780 nanometres.

visible speech *n.* a system of phonetic notation that utilized symbols based on the schematic representation of the articulations used for each speech sound.

Visigoth (ˈvɪzɪˌgɒθ) *n.* a member of the western group of the Goths, who were driven into the Balkans in the late 4th century A.D. Moving on, they sacked Rome (410) and established a kingdom in present-day Spain and S France that lasted until 711. [C17: from Late Latin *Visigothī* (pl.), of Germanic origin, *visi-* perhaps meaning: west] —ˌ**Visiˈgothic** *adj.*

vision (ˈvɪʒən) *n.* 1. the act, faculty, or manner of perceiving with the eye; sight. 2. a. the image on a television screen. b. (*as modifier*): *vision control.* 3. the ability or an instance of great perception, esp. of future developments: *a man of vision.* 4. mystical or religious experience of seeing some supernatural event, person, etc.: *the vision of St John of the Cross.* 5. that which is seen, esp. in such a mystical experience. 6. (*sometimes pl.*) a vivid mental image produced by the imagination: *he had visions of becoming famous.* 7. a person or thing of extraordinary beauty. ~*vb.* 8. (*tr.*) to see or show in or as if in a vision. [C13: from Latin *vīsiō* sight, from *vidēre* to see] —ˈ**visionless** *adj.*

visional (ˈvɪʒənᵊl) *adj.* of, relating to, or seen in a vision, apparition, etc. —ˈ**visionally** *adv.*

visionary (ˈvɪʒənərɪ) *adj.* 1. marked by vision or foresight: *a visionary leader.* 2. incapable of being realized or effected; unrealistic. 3. (of people) characterized by idealistic or radical ideas, esp. impractical ones. 4. given to having visions. 5. of, of the nature of, or seen in visions. ~*n., pl.* **-aries.** 6. a visionary person. —ˈ**visionariness** *n.*

vision mixer *n. Television.* 1. the person who selects and manipulates the television signals from cameras, film, and other sources, to make the composite programme. 2. the equipment used for vision mixing.

visit (ˈvɪzɪt) *vb.* **-its, -iting, -ited.** 1. to go or come to see (a person, place, etc.). 2. to stay with (someone) as a guest. 3. to go or come to (an institution, place, etc.) for the purpose of inspecting or examining. 4. (*tr.*) (of a disease, disaster, etc.) to assail; afflict. 5. (*tr.;* foll. by *upon* or *on*) to inflict (punishment, etc.): *the judge visited his full anger upon the defendant.* 6. (*tr.;* usually foll. by *with*) *Archaic.* to afflict or plague (with punishment, etc.). 7. (often foll. by *with*) *U.S. and Canadian informal.* to chat or converse (with someone). ~*n.* **8.** the act or an instance of visiting. **9.** a stay as a guest. **10.** a professional or official call. **11.** a formal call for the purpose of inspection or examination. **12.** *International law.* the right of an officer of a belligerent state to stop and search neutral ships in war to verify their nationality and ascertain whether they carry contraband: *the right of visit and search.* **13.** *U.S. and Canadian informal.* a friendly talk or chat. [C13: from Latin *vīsitāre* to go to see, from *vīsere* to examine, from *vidēre* to see] —'**visitable** *adj.*

visitant ('vɪzɪtənt) *n.* **1.** a supernatural being; ghost; apparition. **2.** a visitor or guest, usually from far away. **3.** a pilgrim or tourist. **4.** Also called: **visitor.** a migratory bird that is present in a particular region only at certain times: *a summer visitant.* ~*adj.* **5.** *Archaic.* paying a visit; visiting. [C16: from Latin *vīsitāns* going to see, from *vīsitāre;* see VISIT]

visitation (ˌvɪzɪ'teɪʃən) *n.* **1.** an official call or visit for the purpose of inspecting or examining an institution, esp. such a visit made by a bishop to his diocese. **2.** a visiting of punishment or reward from heaven. **3.** any disaster or catastrophe: *a visitation of the plague.* **4.** an appearance or arrival of a supernatural being. **5.** any call or visit. **6.** *Informal.* an unduly prolonged social call. —ˌ**visit'ational** *adj.*

Visitation (ˌvɪzɪ'teɪʃən) *n.* a Church festival, held on July 2, commemorating the visit made by the Virgin Mary to her cousin Elizabeth (Luke 1:39–56).

visitatorial (ˌvɪzɪtə'tɔːrɪəl) *or* **visitorial** *adj.* **1.** of, relating to, or for an official visitation or visitor. **2.** empowered to make official visitations.

visiting card *n. Brit.* a small card bearing the name and usually the address of a person, esp. for giving to business or social acquaintances. U.S. and Canadian term: **calling card.**

visiting fireman *n. U.S. informal.* a visitor whose presence is noticed because he is an important figure, a lavish spender, etc.

visiting nurse *n.* (in the U.S.) a registered nurse employed by a community, hospital, etc., to visit and nurse the sick in their homes or to promote public health.

visiting professor *n.* a professor invited to teach in a college or university other than his own, often in another country, for a certain period, such as a term or year.

visitor ('vɪzɪtə) *n.* **1.** a person who pays a visit; caller, guest, tourist, etc. **2.** another name for **visitant** (sense 4). —ˌ**visi'torial** *adj.*

visitor centre *n.* another term for **interpretive centre.**

visitor's passport *n.* (in Britain) a passport, valid for one year, that can be purchased from post offices. It grants entry to certain countries, usually for a restricted period of time. Also called: **British Visitor's Passport.**

vis major ('vɪs 'meɪdʒə) *n.* See **force majeure.** [from Latin, literally: greater force]

visor *or* **vizor** ('vaɪzə) *n.* **1.** a transparent flap on a helmet that can be pulled down to protect the face. **2.** a piece of armour fixed or hinged to the helmet to protect the face and furnished with slits for the eyes. **3.** another name for **peak** (on a cap). **3.** a small movable screen used as protection against glare from the sun, esp. one attached above the windscreen of a motor vehicle. **5.** *Archaic or literary.* a mask or any other means of disguise or concealment. ~*vb.* **6.** *(tr.)* to cover, provide, or protect with a visor; shield. [C14: from Anglo-French *viser,* from Old French *visiere,* from *vis* face; see VISAGE] —'**visored** *or* '**vizored** *adj.* —'**visorless** *or* '**vizorless** *adj.*

vista ('vɪstə) *n.* **1.** a view, esp. through a long narrow avenue of trees, buildings, etc., or such a passage or avenue itself; prospect: *a vista of arches.* **2.** a comprehensive mental view of a distant time or a lengthy series of events: *the vista of the future.* [C17: from Italian: a view, from *vedere* to see, from Latin *vidēre*] —'**vistaed** *adj.* —'**vistaless** *adj.*

VISTA ('vɪstə) *n.* (in the U.S.) *acronym for* Volunteers in Service to America.

visual ('vɪʒʊəl, -zjʊ-) *adj.* **1.** of, relating to, done by, or used in seeing: *visual powers; visual steering.* **2.** another word for **optical.** **3.** capable of being seen; visible. **4.** of, occurring as, or induced by a mental image. ~*n.* **5.** a sketch to show the proposed layout of an advertisement, as in a newspaper. **6.** *(often pl.)* a photograph, film, or other display material. [C15: from Late Latin *vīsuālis,* from Latin *vīsus* sight, from *vidēre* to see] —'**visually** *adv.*

visual aids *pl. n.* devices, such as films, slides, models, and blackboards, that display in visual form material to be understood or remembered.

visual angle *n.* the angle subtended by an object at the lens of the eye.

visual arts *pl. n.* the arts of painting, sculpting, engraving, etc., as opposed to music, drama, and literature.

visual display unit *n. Computer technol.* a device incorporating a cathode-ray tube that displays characters or line drawings representing data in a computer memory. It usually has a keyboard or light pen for the input of information or inquiries. Abbrev.: **VDU.**

visual field *n.* the whole extent of the image falling on the retina when the eye is fixating a given point in space.

visualize *or* **visualise** ('vɪʒʊəˌlaɪz, -zjʊ-) *vb.* **1.** to form a mental image of (something incapable of being viewed or not at that moment visible). **2.** *Med.* to view by means of an x-ray the outline of (a bodily organ, structure, or part). —ˌ**visuali'zation** *or* ˌ**visuali'sation** *n.* —'**visualˌizer** *or* '**visualˌiser** *n.*

visually handicapped *adj.* **a.** unable to carry out normal activities because of defects of vision, including blindness. **b.** *(as collective n.;* preceded by *the): the visually handicapped.* —**visual handicap** *n.*

visually impaired *adj.* **a.** having any defect of vision, whether disabling or not. **b.** *(as collective n.;* preceded by *the): the visually impaired.* ~Compare **partially sighted.** —**visual impairment** *n.*

visual magnitude *n. Astronomy.* the magnitude of a star as determined by visual observation. Compare **photographic magnitude.**

visual purple *n.* another name for **rhodopsin.**

visual violet *n.* another name for **iodopsin.**

vita ('viːtə, 'vaɪ-) *n., pl.* **vitae** ('viːtaɪ, 'vaɪtiː). *U.S. and Canadian.* a less common term for **curriculum vitae.** [from Latin: life]

vitaceous (vaɪ'teɪʃəs) *adj.* of, relating to, or belonging to the *Vitaceae,* a family of tropical and subtropical flowering plants having a climbing habit and berry-like fruits: includes the grapevine and Virginia creeper. [C19: via New Latin *Vītāceae,* from Latin: vine]

vital ('vaɪtᵊl) *adj.* **1.** essential to maintain life: *the lungs perform a vital function.* **2.** forceful, energetic, or lively: *a vital person.* **3.** of, relating to, having, or displaying life: *a vital organism.* **4.** indispensable or essential: *books vital to this study.* **5.** of great importance; decisive: *a vital game.* **6.** *Archaic.* influencing the course of life, esp. negatively: *a vital treachery.* ~*n.* **7.** *(pl.)* **a.** the bodily organs, such as the brain, liver, heart, lungs, etc., that are necessary to maintain life. **b.** the organs of reproduction, esp. the male genitals. **8.** *(pl.)* the essential elements of anything. [C14: via Old French from Latin *vītālis* belonging to life, from *vīta* life] —'**vitally** *adv.*

vital capacity *n. Physiol.* the volume of air that can be exhaled from the lungs after the deepest possible breath has been taken: a measure of lung function.

vital force *n.* (esp. in early biological theory) a hypothetical force, independent of physical and chemical forces, regarded as being the causative factor of the evolution and development of living organisms.

vitalism ('vaɪtəˌlɪzəm) *n.* the philosophical doctrine that the phenomena of life cannot be explained in purely mechanical terms because there is something immaterial which distinguishes living from inanimate matter. Compare **dynamism, mechanism.** —'**vitalist** *n., adj.* —ˌ**vital'istic** *adj.*

vitality (vaɪ'tælɪtɪ) *n., pl.* **-ties.** **1.** physical or mental vigour, energy, etc. **2.** the power or ability to continue in existence, live, or grow: *the vitality of a movement.* **3.** a less common name for **vital force.**

vitalize *or* **vitalise** ('vaɪtəˌlaɪz) *vb. (tr.)* to make vital, living, or alive; endow with life or vigour. —ˌ**vitali'zation** *or* ˌ**vitali'sation** *n.* —'**vitalˌizer** *or* '**vitalˌiser** *n.*

vital staining *n.* the technique of treating living cells and tissues with dyes that do not immediately kill them, facilitating observation under a microscope.

vital statistics *pl. n.* **1.** quantitative data concerning human life or the conditions and aspects affecting it, such as the death rate. **2.** *Informal.* the measurements of a woman's bust, waist, and hips.

vitamin ('vɪtəmɪn, 'vaɪ-) *n.* any of a group of substances that are essential, in small quantities, for the normal functioning of metabolism in the body. They cannot usually be synthesized in the body but they occur naturally in certain foods: insufficient supply of any particular vitamin results in a deficiency disease. [C20 *vit-* from Latin *vīta* life + *-amin* from AMINE; so named by the U.S. biochemist Casimir Funk (1884–1967), who believed the substances to be amines] —ˌ**vita'minic** *adj.*

vitamin A *n.* a fat-soluble yellow unsaturated alcohol occurring in green and yellow vegetables (esp. carrots), butter, egg yolk, and fish-liver oil (esp. halibut oil). It is essential for the prevention of night blindness and the protection of epithelial tissue. Formula: $C_{20}H_{30}O$. Also called: **vitamin A_1, retinol.**

vitamin A_2 *n.* a vitamin that occurs in the tissues of freshwater fish and has a function similar to that of vitamin A. Formula: $C_{20}H_{28}O$. Also called: **dehydroretinol.**

vitamin B *n., pl.* **B vitamins.** any of the vitamins in the vitamin B complex.

vitamin B_1 *n.* another name for **thiamine.**

vitamin B_2 *n.* another name for **riboflavin.**

vitamin B_6 *n.* another name for **pyridoxine.**

vitamin B_{12} *n.* another name for **cyanocobalamin.**

vitamin B complex *n.* a large group of water-soluble vitamins occurring esp. in liver and yeast: includes thiamine, riboflavin, nicotinic acid, pyridoxine, pantothenic acid, biotin, choline, folic acid, and cyanocobalamin. Sometimes shortened to **B complex.**

vitamin C *n.* another name for **ascorbic acid.**

vitamin D *n., pl.* **D vitamins.** any of the fat-soluble vitamins, including calciferol and cholecalciferol, occurring in fish-liver oils (esp. cod-liver oil), milk, butter, and eggs: used in the treatment of rickets and osteomalacia.

vitamin D_1 *n.* the first isolated form of vitamin D, consisting of calciferol and its precursor, lumisterol.

vitamin D_2 *n.* another name for **calciferol.**

vitamin D$_3$ *n.* another name for **cholecalciferol.**
vitamin E *n.* another name for **tocopherol.**
vitamin G *n.* another name (esp. U.S. and Canadian) for **riboflavin.**
vitamin H *n.* another name (esp. U.S. and Canadian) for **biotin.**
vitamin K *n., pl.* **K vitamins.** any of the fat-soluble vitamins, including phylloquinone and the menaquinones, which are essential for the normal clotting of blood.
vitamin K$_1$ *n.* another name for **phylloquinone.**
vitamin K$_2$ *n.* another name for **menaquinone.**
vitamin K$_3$ *n.* a former name for **menadione.**
vitamin P *n., pl.* **P vitamins.** any of a group of water-soluble crystalline substances occurring mainly in citrus fruits, blackcurrants, and rosehips: they regulate the permeability of the blood capillaries. Also called: **citrin, bioflavonoid.**
Vitaphone ('vaɪtəˌfəʊn) *n. Trademark.* an early technique in commercial film-making in which the accompanying sound was produced by discs.
vitascope ('vaɪtəˌskəʊp) *n.* an early type of film projector. [C19: from Latin *vīta* life + -SCOPE]
vitellin (vɪ'tɛlɪn) *n. Biochem.* a phosphoprotein that is the major protein in egg yolk. [C19: from VITELLUS + -IN]
vitelline (vɪ'tɛlɪn, -aɪn) *adj. Zoology.* **1.** of or relating to the yolk of an egg: *the vitelline gland.* **2.** having the yellow colour of an egg yolk. [C15: from Medieval Latin *vitellīnus,* from Latin *vitellus* the yolk of an egg; see VITELLUS]
vitelline membrane *n. Zoology.* a membrane that surrounds a fertilized ovum and prevents the entry of other spermatozoa.
vitellogenic (ˌvɪtələʊ'dʒɛnɪk) *or* **vitelligenous** (ˌvɪtə'lɪdʒɪnəs) *adj. Zoology.* producing or stimulating the formation of yolk. [C20: from VITELLUS + -GENIC] —ˌ**vitello'genesis** *n.*
vitellus (vɪ'tɛləs) *n., pl.* **-luses** *or* **-li** (-laɪ). *Zoology, rare.* the yolk of an egg. [C18: from Latin, literally: little calf, later: yolk of an egg, from *vitulus* calf]
vitiate ('vɪʃɪˌeɪt) *vb. (tr.)* **1.** to make faulty or imperfect. **2.** to debase, pervert, or corrupt. **3.** to destroy the force or legal effect of (a deed, etc.): *to vitiate a contract.* [C16: from Latin *vitiāre* to injure, from *vitium* a fault] —'**vitiable** *adj.* —ˌ**viti'ation** *n.* —'**vitiˌator** *n.*
viticulture ('vɪtɪˌkʌltʃə) *n.* **1.** the science, art, or process of cultivating grapevines. **2.** the study of grapes and the growing of grapes. [C19: *viti-,* from Latin *vītis* vine] —ˌ**viti'cultural** *adj.* —ˌ**viti'culturer** *or* ˌ**viti'culturist** *n.*
vitiligo (ˌvɪtɪ'laɪgəʊ) *n.* another name for **leucoderma.** [C17: from Latin: a skin disease, probably from *vitium* a blemish]
vitrain ('vɪtreɪn) *n.* a type of coal occurring as horizontal glassy bands of a nonsoiling friable material. [C20: from Latin *vitrum* glass + *-ain,* as in FUSAIN]
vitreous ('vɪtrɪəs) *adj.* **1.** of, relating to, or resembling glass. **2.** made of, derived from, or containing glass. **3.** of or relating to the vitreous humour or vitreous body. [C17: from Latin *vitreus* made of glass, from *vitrum* glass; probably related to *vidēre* to see] —'**vitreously** *adv.*
vitreous body *n.* a transparent gelatinous substance, permeated by fine fibrils, that fills the interior of the eyeball between the lens and the retina.
vitreous humour *n.* the aqueous fluid contained within the interstices of the vitreous body.
vitreous silica *n.* another name for **silica glass.**
vitrescence (vɪ'trɛsəns) *n.* **1.** the quality or condition of being or becoming vitreous. **2.** the process of producing a glass or turning a crystalline material into glass.
vitrescent (vɪ'trɛsᵊnt) *adj.* **1.** tending to turn into glass. **2.** capable of being transformed into glass.
vitric ('vɪtrɪk) *adj.* of, relating to, resembling, or having the nature of glass; vitreous.
vitrification (ˌvɪtrɪfɪ'keɪʃən) *n.* **1.** the process or act of vitrifying or the state of being vitrified. **2.** something that is or has been vitrified.
vitriform ('vɪtrɪˌfɔːm) *adj.* having the form or appearance of glass.
vitrify ('vɪtrɪˌfaɪ) *vb.* **-fies, -fying, -fied.** to convert or be converted into glass or a glassy substance. [C16: from French *vitrifier,* from Latin *vitrum* glass] —'**vitriˌfiable** *adj.* —ˌ**vitriˌfia'bility** *n.*
vitrine ('vɪtriːn) *n.* a glass display case or cabinet for works of art, curios, etc. [C19: from French, from *vitre* pane of glass, from Latin *vitrum* glass]
vitriol ('vɪtrɪˌɒl) *n.* **1.** another name for **sulphuric acid. 2.** any one of a number of sulphate salts, such as ferrous sulphate (**green vitriol**), copper sulphate (**blue vitriol**), or zinc sulphate (**white vitriol**). **3.** speech, writing, etc., displaying rancour, vituperation, or bitterness. ~*vb.* **-ols, -oling, -oled** *or* **-olling, -olled.** *(tr.)* **4.** to attack or injure with or as if with vitriol. **5.** to treat with vitriol. [C14: from Medieval Latin *vitriolum,* from Late Latin *vitriolus* glassy, from Latin *vitrum* glass, referring to the glossy appearance of the sulphates]
vitriolic (ˌvɪtrɪ'ɒlɪk) *adj.* **1.** (of a substance, esp. a strong acid) highly corrosive. **2.** severely bitter or caustic; virulent: *vitriolic criticism.*
vitriolize *or* **vitriolise** ('vɪtrɪəˌlaɪz) *vb. (tr.)* **1.** to convert into or treat with vitriol. **2.** to burn or injure with vitriol. —ˌ**vitrioli'zation** *or* ˌ**vitrioli'sation** *n.*
vitta ('vɪtə) *n., pl.* **-tae** (-tiː). **1.** any of numerous tubelike cavities containing oil or resin that occur in the fruits of certain plants, esp. of parsley and related plants. **2.** *Biology.* a band or stripe of colour. [C17: from Latin: headband; related to *viēre* to plait] —'**vittate** *adj.*
vittle ('vɪtᵊl) *n., vb.* an obsolete or dialect spelling of **victual.**
vituline ('vɪtjʊˌlaɪn, -lɪn) *adj.* of or resembling a calf or veal. [C17: from Latin *vitulīnus,* from *vitulus* a calf]
vituperate (vɪ'tjuːpəˌreɪt) *vb.* to berate or rail (against) abusively; revile. [C16: from Latin *vituperāre* to blame, from *vitium* a defect + *parāre* to make] —**vi'tuperˌator** *n.*
vituperation (vɪˌtjuːpə'reɪʃən) *n.* **1.** abusive language or venomous censure. **2.** the act of vituperating. —**vituperative** (vɪ'tjuːpərətɪv, -prətɪv) *adj.* —**vi'tuperatively** *adv.*
viva[1] ('viːvə) *interj.* long live; up with (a specified person or thing). [C17: from Italian, literally: may (he) live! from *vivere* to live, from Latin *vīvere*]
viva[2] ('vaɪvə) *Brit.* ~*n.* **1.** an oral examination. ~*vb.* **-vas, -vaing, -vaed.** *(tr.)* **2.** to examine orally. [shortened from VIVA VOCE]
vivace (vɪ'vɑːtʃɪ) *adj., adv. Music.* to be performed in a brisk lively manner. [C17: from Italian, from Latin *vīvax* long-lived, vigorous, from *vīvere* to live]
vivacious (vɪ'veɪʃəs) *adj.* **1.** full of high spirits and animation; lively or vital. **2.** *Obsolete.* having or displaying tenacity of life. [C17: from Latin *vīvax* lively; see VIVACE] —**vi'vaciously** *adv.* —**vi'vaciousness** *n.*
vivacity (vɪ'væsɪtɪ) *n., pl.* **-ties. 1.** the quality or condition of being vivacious. **2.** *(often pl.) Rare.* a vivacious act or expression.
vivandière *French.* (vivɑ̃djɛr) *n.* (formerly) a female sutler or victualler offering extra provisions and spirits to soldiers, esp. those of the French and British armies. [C16: see VIAND]
vivarium (vaɪ'vɛərɪəm) *n., pl.* **-iums** *or* **-ia** (-ɪə). a place where live animals are kept under natural conditions for study, research, etc. [C16: from Latin: enclosure where live fish or game are kept, from *vīvus* alive]
viva voce ('vaɪvə 'vəʊtʃɪ) *adv., adj.* **1.** by word of mouth. ~*n., vb.* **2.** the full form of **viva**[2]. [C16: from Medieval Latin, literally: with living voice]
vive (viːv) *interj.* long live; up with (a specified person or thing). [from French]
viverrine (vaɪ'vɛraɪn) *adj.* **1.** of, relating to, or belonging to the *Viverridae,* a family of small to medium-sized predatory mammals of Eurasia and Africa, including genets, civets and mongooses: order *Carnivora* (carnivores). ~*n.* **2.** any animal belonging to the family *Viverridae.* [C19: from New Latin *viverrīnus,* from Latin *viverra* a ferret]
vivid ('vɪvɪd) *adj.* **1.** (of a colour) very bright; having a very high saturation or purity; produced by a pure or almost pure colouring agent. **2.** brilliantly coloured: *vivid plumage.* **3.** conveying to the mind striking realism, freshness, or trueness to life; graphic: *a vivid account.* **4.** (of a recollection, memory, etc.) remaining distinct in the mind. **5.** (of the imagination, etc.) prolific in the formation of lifelike images. **6.** making a powerful impact on the emotions or senses: *a vivid feeling of shame.* **7.** uttered, operating, or acting with vigour: *vivid expostulations.* **8.** full of life or vitality: *a vivid personality.* [C17: from Latin *vīvidus* animated, from *vīvere* to live] —'**vividly** *adv.* —'**vividness** *n.*
vivify ('vɪvɪˌfaɪ) *vb.* **-fies, -fying, -fied.** *(tr.)* **1.** to bring to life; animate. **2.** to make more vivid or striking. [C16: from Late Latin *vīvificāre,* from Latin *vīvus* alive + *facere* to make] —ˌ**vivifi'cation** *n.* —'**viviˌfier** *n.*
viviparous (vɪ'vɪpərəs) *adj.* **1.** (of most mammals) giving birth to living offspring that develop within the uterus of the mother. Compare **oviparous, ovoviviparous. 2.** (of seeds) germinating before separating from the parent plant. **3.** (of plants) producing bulbils or young plants instead of flowers. [C17: from Latin *vīviparus,* from *vīvus* alive + *parere* to bring forth] —**viviparity** (ˌvɪvɪ'pærɪtɪ), **vi'vipary, vi'viparism,** *or* **vi'viparousness** *n.* —**vi'viparously** *adv.*
vivisect ('vɪvɪˌsɛkt, ˌvɪvɪ'sɛkt) *vb.* to subject (an animal) to vivisection. [C19: back formation from VIVISECTION] —'**viviˌsector** *n.*
vivisection (ˌvɪvɪ'sɛkʃən) *n.* the act or practice of performing experiments on living animals, involving cutting into or dissecting the body. [C18: from *vivi-,* from Latin *vivus* living + SECTION, as in DISSECTION] —ˌ**vivi'sectional** *adj.* —ˌ**vivi'sectionally** *adv.*
vivisectionist (ˌvɪvɪ'sɛkʃənɪst) *n.* **1.** a person who practises vivisection. **2.** a person who advocates the practice of vivisection as being useful or necessary to science.
vivo ('viːvəʊ) *adj., adv. Music. (in combination)* with life and vigour: *allegro vivo.* [Italian: lively]
vixen ('vɪksən) *n.* **1.** a female fox. **2.** a quarrelsome or spiteful woman. [C15 *fixen;* related to Old English *fyxe,* feminine of FOX; compare Old High German *fuhsīn*] —'**vixenish** *adj.* —'**vixenishly** *adv.* —'**vixenishness** *n.* —'**vixenly** *adv., adj.*
Viyella (vaɪ'ɛlə) *n. Trademark.* a soft fabric made of wool and cotton, used esp. for blouses and shirts.
viz *abbrev. for* videlicet.

vizard ('vɪzəd) *n. Archaic or literary.* a means of disguise; mask; visor. [C16: variant of VISOR] —'**vizarded** *adj.*
vizcacha (vɪs'kætʃə) *n.* a variant spelling of **viscacha.**
vizier (vɪ'zɪə) *n.* a high official in certain Muslim countries, esp. in the former Ottoman Empire. Viziers served in various capacities, such as that of provincial governor or chief minister to the sultan. [C16: from Turkish *vezīr,* from Arabic *wazīr* porter, from *wazara* to bear a burden] —**vi'zierial** *or* **vi'zirial** *adj.* —**vi'ziership** *n.*
vizierate (vɪ'zɪərɪt, -eɪt) *n.* **1.** the position, rank, or authority of a vizier. **2.** the term of office of a vizier.
vizor ('vaɪzə) *n., vb.* a variant spelling of **visor.**
vizsla ('vɪʒlə) *n.* a breed of Hungarian hunting dog with a smooth rusty-gold coat. [C20: named after *Vizsla,* Hungary]
VJ *abbrev. for:* **1.** video jockey. **2.** *Austral.* Vaucluse Junior: a type of small yacht.
V-J Day *n.* the day marking the Allied victory over Japan in World War II (Aug. 15, 1945).
vl *abbrev. for* variant reading. [from Latin *varia lectio*]
VL *abbrev. for* Vulgar Latin.
Vlach (vlɑːk) or **Walach** ('wɑːlɒk) *n.* **1.** a member of a people scattered throughout SE Europe in the early Middle Ages, speaking a Romanic dialect. ~*adj.* **2.** of or relating to Vlachs or their dialect.
VLCC *Oil industry. abbrev. for* very large crude carrier: an oil tanker with a capacity between 200 000 and 400 000 tons.
vlei (fleɪ, vleɪ) *n.* **1.** *S. African.* an area of low marshy ground, esp. one that feeds a stream. **2.** *Northern U.S. dialect.* a marsh. [C19: from Afrikaans (for sense 1); from obsolete N American Dutch dialect (for sense 2): VALLEY]
VLF *or* **vlf** *Radio. abbrev. for* very low frequency.
VLSI *Computer technol. abbrev. for* very large-scale integration.
VMD *abbrev. for* Doctor of Veterinary Medicine. [Latin *veterinariae medicinae doctor*]
VN *international car registration for* Vietnam.
V neck *n.* a neck on a garment that comes down to a point on the throat or chest, resembling the shape of the letter "V". —'**V-ˌneck** *or* '**V-ˌnecked** *adj.*
VO *abbrev. for:* **1.** very old: used to imply that a brandy or whisky is old, now often extended to port and other dessert wines. **2.** Royal Victorian Order.
vo. *abbrev. for* verso.
voc. *or* **vocat.** *abbrev. for* vocative.
vocab ('vəʊkæb) *n.* short for **vocabulary.**
vocable ('vəʊkəbᵊl) *n.* **1.** any word, either written or spoken, regarded simply as a sequence of letters or spoken sounds, irrespective of its meaning. **2.** a vocal sound; vowel. ~*adj.* **3.** capable of being uttered. [C16: from Latin *vocābulum* a designation, from *vocāre* to call] —'**vocably** *adv.*
vocabulary (və'kæbjʊlərɪ) *n., pl.* **-laries. 1.** a listing, either selective or exhaustive, containing the words and phrases of a language, with meanings or translations into another language; glossary. **2.** the aggregate of words in the use or comprehension of a specified person, class, profession, etc. **3.** all the words contained in a language. **4.** a range or system of symbols, qualities, or techniques constituting a means of communication or expression, as any of the arts or crafts: *a wide vocabulary of textures and colours.* [C16: from Medieval Latin *vocābulārium,* from *vocābulārius* concerning words, from Latin *vocābulum* VOCABLE]
vocal ('vəʊkᵊl) *adj.* **1.** of, relating to, or designed for the voice: *vocal music.* **2.** produced or delivered by the voice: *vocal noises.* **3.** connected with an attribute or the production of the voice: *vocal organs.* **4.** frequently disposed to outspoken speech, criticism, etc.: *a vocal minority.* **5.** full of sound or voices: *a vocal assembly.* **6.** endowed with a voice. **7.** eloquent or meaningful. **8.** *Phonetics.* **a.** of or relating to a speech sound. **b.** of or relating to a voiced speech sound, esp. a vowel. ~*n.* **9.** a piece of jazz or pop music that is sung. **10.** a performance of such a piece of music. [C14: from Latin *vōcālis* possessed of a voice, from *vōx* voice] —**vocality** (vəʊ'kælɪtɪ) *n.* —'**vocally** *adv.*
vocal cords *pl. n.* either of two pairs of mucomembranous folds in the larynx. The upper pair (**false vocal cords**) are not concerned with vocal production; the lower pair (**true vocal cords** or **vocal folds**) can be made to vibrate and produce sound when air from the lungs is forced over them. See also **glottis.**
vocal folds *pl. n.* See **vocal cords.**
vocalic (vəʊ'kælɪk) *adj. Phonetics.* of, relating to, or containing a vowel or vowels.
vocalise (ˌvəʊkə'liːz) *n.* a musical passage sung upon one vowel as an exercise to develop flexibility and control of pitch and tone; solfeggio.
vocalism ('vəʊkəˌlɪzəm) *n.* **1.** the exercise of the voice, as in singing or speaking. **2.** singing, esp. in respect to technique or skill. **3.** *Phonetics.* **a.** a voiced speech sound, esp. a vowel. **b.** a system of vowels as used in a language.
vocalist ('vəʊkəlɪst) *n.* a singer, esp. one who regularly appears with a jazz band or pop group.
vocalize *or* **vocalise** ('vəʊkəˌlaɪz) *vb.* **1.** to express with or use the voice; articulate (a speech, song, etc.). **2.** (*tr.*) to make vocal or articulate. **3.** (*tr.*) *Phonetics.* **a.** to articulate (a speech sound) with voice. **b.** to change (a consonant) into a vowel. **4.** another word for **vowelize. 5.** (*intr.*) to sing a melody on a vowel, etc. —ˌ**vocali'zation** *or* ˌ**vocali'sation** *n.* —'**vocalˌizer** *or* '**vocalˌiser** *n.*
vocal sac *n. Zoology.* either of the loose folds of skin on each side of the mouth in many male frogs that can be inflated and act as resonators.
vocal score *n.* a musical score that shows voice parts in full and orchestral parts in the form of a piano transcription.
vocation (vəʊ'keɪʃən) *n.* **1.** a specified occupation, profession, or trade. **2. a.** a special urge, inclination, or predisposition to a particular calling or career, esp. a religious one. **b.** such a calling or career. [C15: from Latin *vocātiō* a calling, from *vocāre* to call]
vocational (vəʊ'keɪʃənᵊl) *adj.* **1.** of or relating to a vocation or vocations. **2.** of or relating to applied educational courses concerned with skills needed for an occupation, trade, or profession: *vocational training.* —**vo'cationally** *adv.*
vocational guidance *n.* a guidance service based on psychological tests and interviews to find out what career or occupation may best suit a person.
vocative ('vɒkətɪv) *adj.* **1.** relating to, used in, or characterized by calling. **2.** *Grammar.* denoting a case of nouns, in some inflected languages, used when the referent of the noun is being addressed. ~*n.* **3.** *Grammar.* **a.** the vocative case. **b.** a vocative noun or speech element. [C15: from Latin phrase *vocātīvus cāsus* the calling case, from *vocāre* to call] —'**vocatively** *adv.*
voces ('vəʊsiːz) *n.* the plural of **vox.**
vociferant (vəʊ'sɪfərənt) *adj.* **1.** a less common word for **vociferous.** ~*n.* **2.** *Rare.* a vociferous person. [C17: from Latin *vōciferārī* to bawl; see VOCIFERATE] —**vo'ciferance** *n.*
vociferate (vəʊ'sɪfəˌreɪt) *vb.* to exclaim or cry out about (something) clamorously, vehemently, or insistently. [C17: from Latin *vōciferārī* to clamour, from *vōx* voice + *ferre* to bear] —**voˌcifer'ation** *n.* —**vo'ciferˌator** *n.*
vociferous (vəʊ'sɪfərəs) *adj.* **1.** characterized by vehemence, clamour, or noisiness: *vociferous protests.* **2.** making an outcry or loud noises; clamorous: *a vociferous mob.* —**vo'ciferously** *adv.* —**vo'ciferousness** *n.*
vocoder ('vəʊ'kəʊdə) *n. Music.* a type of synthesizer that uses the human voice as an oscillator.
vodka ('vɒdkə) *n.* an alcoholic drink originating in Russia, made from grain, potatoes, etc., usually consisting only of rectified spirit and water. [C19: from Russian, diminutive of *voda* water; related to Sanskrit *udan* water, Greek *hudōr*]
voe (vəʊ; *Scot.* vo) *n.* (in Orkney and Shetland) a small bay or narrow creek. [C17: from Old Norse *vagr*]
voetsek ('fʊtsɛk, 'vʊt-) *interj. S. African slang.* an expletive used when chasing animals away: offensive when addressed to people. [from Afrikaans, from the phrase *voort se ek* away say I]
voetstoots *or* **voetstoets** ('fʊtstʊts, 'vʊt-) *S. African.* ~*adj.* **1.** denoting a sale in which the vendor is freed from all responsibility for the condition of the goods being sold. ~*adv.* **2.** without responsibility for the condition of the goods sold. [Afrikaans, from Dutch]
vogue (vəʊg) *n.* **1.** the popular style at a specified time (esp. in the phrase **in vogue**). **2.** a period of general or popular usage or favour: *the vogue for such dances is now over.* ~*adj.* **3.** (*usually prenominal*) popular or fashionable: *a vogue word.* [C16: from French: a rowing, fashion, from Old Italian *voga,* from *vogare* to row, of unknown origin] —'**voguish** *adj.*
vogueing ('vəʊgɪŋ) *n.* a dance style of the late 1980s, in which a fashion model's movements and postures are imitated in a highly stylized manner. [C20: from *Vogue* magazine]
Vogul ('vəʊgᵊl) *n.* **1.** (*pl.* **-gul** *or* **-guls**) a member of a people living in W Siberia and NE Europe. **2.** the language of this people, belonging to the Finno-Ugric family: related to Hungarian.
voice (vɔɪs) *n.* **1.** the sound made by the vibration of the vocal cords, esp. when modified by the resonant effect of the tongue and mouth. See also **speech. 2.** the natural and distinctive tone of the speech sounds characteristic of a particular person: *nobody could mistake his voice.* **3.** the condition, quality, effectiveness, or tone of such sounds: *a hysterical voice.* **4.** the musical sound of a singing voice, with respect to its quality or tone: *she has a lovely voice.* **5.** the ability to speak, sing, etc.: *he has lost his voice.* **6.** a sound resembling or suggestive of vocal utterance: *the voice of the sea; the voice of hard experience.* **7.** written or spoken expression, as of feeling, opinion, etc. (esp. in the phrase **give voice to**). **8.** a stated choice, wish, or opinion or the power or right to have an opinion heard and considered: *to give someone a voice in a decision.* **9.** an agency through which is communicated another's purpose, policy, etc.: *such groups are the voice of our enemies.* **10.** *Music.* **a.** musical notes produced by vibrations of the vocal chords at various frequencies and in certain registers: *a tenor voice.* **b.** (in harmony) an independent melodic line or part: *a fugue in five voices.* **11.** *Phonetics.* the sound characterizing the articulation of several speech sounds, including all vowels or sonants, that is produced when the vocal cords make loose contact with each other and are set in vibration by the breath as it forces its way through the glottis. **12.** *Grammar.* a category of the verb or verbal inflections that expresses whether the relation between the subject and the verb is that of agent and action, action and recipient, or some other relation. See **active** (sense 5), **passive** (sense 5), **middle** (sense 5). **13.**

Obsolete. rumour. **14.** (foll. by *of*) *Obsolete.* fame; renown. **15. in voice.** in a condition to sing or speak well. **16. out of voice.** with the voice temporarily in a poor condition, esp. for singing. **17. with one voice.** unanimously. ~*vb.* (*tr.*) **18.** to utter in words; give expression to: *to voice a complaint.* **19.** to articulate (a speech sound) with voice. **20.** *Music.* to adjust (a wind instrument or organ pipe) so that it conforms to the correct standards of tone colour, pitch, etc. [C13: from Old French *voiz,* from Latin *vōx*] —'**voicer** *n.*

voice box *n.* **1.** another word for the **larynx. 2.** Also called: **talkbox.** an electronic guitar attachment with a tube into the player's mouth to modulate the sound vocally.

voiced (vɔɪst) *adj.* **1.** declared or expressed by the voice. **2.** (*in combination*) having a voice as specified: *loud-voiced.* **3.** *Phonetics.* articulated with accompanying vibration of the vocal cords: *in English* (b) *is a voiced consonant.* Compare **voiceless.**

voiceful ('vɔɪsful) *adj. Poetic.* **1.** endowed with a voice, esp. of loud quality. **2.** full of voices. —'**voicefulness** *n.*

voice input *n.* the control and operation of computer systems by spoken commands.

voice-leading ('vɔɪs,liːdɪŋ) *n. U.S.* another term for **part-writing.**

voiceless ('vɔɪslɪs) *adj.* **1.** without a voice; mute. **2.** not articulated: *voiceless misery.* **3.** lacking a musical voice. **4.** silent. **5.** without the power or right to express an opinion. **6.** *Phonetics.* articulated without accompanying vibration of the vocal cords: *In English* (p) *is a voiceless consonant.* —'**voicelessly** *adv.* —'**voicelessness** *n.*

voice-over *n.* the voice of an unseen commentator heard during a film, television programme, etc.

voice part *n.* a melodic line written for the voice.

voiceprint ('vɔɪs,prɪnt) *n.* a graphic representation of a person's voice recorded electronically, usually having time plotted along the horizontal axis and the frequency of the speech on the vertical axis.

voice recognition *n.* the control of a computer system by a voice or voices that the computer has been instructed to accept.

voice response *n.* output of information from a computer system in the form of speech rather than displayed text.

voice vote *n.* a vote taken in a legislative body by calling for the ayes and the noes and estimating which faction is more numerous from the volume of the noise.

void (vɔɪd) *adj.* **1.** without contents; empty. **2.** not legally binding: *null and void.* **3.** (of an office, house, position, etc.) without an incumbent; unoccupied. **4.** (*postpositive;* foll. by *of*) destitute or devoid: *void of resources.* **5.** having no effect; useless: *all his efforts were rendered void.* **6.** (of a card suit or player) having no cards in a particular suit: *his spades were void.* ~*n.* **7.** an empty space or area: *the huge desert voids of Asia.* **8.** a feeling or condition of loneliness or deprivation: *his divorce left him in a void.* **9.** a lack of any cards in one suit: *to have a void in spades.* **10.** Also called: **counter.** the inside area of a character of type, such as the inside of an *o.* ~*vb.* (*mainly tr.*) **11.** to make ineffective or invalid. **12.** to empty (contents, etc.) or make empty of contents. **13.** (*also intr.*) to discharge the contents of (the bowels or urinary bladder). **14.** *Archaic.* to vacate (a place, room, etc.). **15.** *Obsolete.* to expel. [C13: from Old French *vuide,* from Vulgar Latin *vocītus* (unattested), from Latin *vacuus* empty, from *vacāre* to be empty] —'**voider** *n.* —'**voidness** *n.*

voidable ('vɔɪdəbᵊl) *adj.* **1.** capable of being voided. **2.** capable of being legally annulled or made void. —'**voidableness** *n.*

voidance ('vɔɪdᵊns) *n.* **1.** an annulment, as of a contract. **2.** the condition of being vacant, as an office, benefice, etc. **3.** the act of voiding, ejecting, or evacuating. [C14: variant of AVOIDANCE]

voided ('vɔɪdɪd) *adj.* **1.** *Heraldry.* (of a design) with a hole in the centre of the same shape as the design: *a voided lozenge.* **2.** *Rare.* having a void or made void.

voile (vɔɪl; *French* vwal) *n.* a light semitransparent fabric of silk, rayon, cotton, etc., used for dresses, scarves, shirts, etc. [C19: from French: VEIL]

voir dire (vwɑː 'dɪə) *n. Law.* **1.** the preliminary examination on oath of a proposed witness by the judge. **2.** the oath administered to such a witness. [C17: from Old French: to speak the truth]

voix céleste (vwɑː sɛ'lɛst) *n.* an organ stop which produces a tremolo effect through the acoustic phenomenon of beats. [from French: heavenly voice]

vol. *abbrev. for:* **1.** volcano. **2.** volume. **3.** volunteer.

Volans ('vəʊlænz) *n., Latin genitive* **Volantis** (vəʊ'læntɪs). a small constellation in the S hemisphere lying between Carina and Hydrus. [C19: from Latin, literally: flying, from *volāre* to fly]

volant ('vəʊlənt) *adj.* **1.** (*usually postpositive*) *Heraldry.* in a flying position. **2.** *Rare.* flying or capable of flight. **3.** *Poetic.* moving lightly or agilely; nimble. [C16: from French: flying, from *voler* to fly, from Latin *volāre*]

Volapuk *or* **Volapük** ('vɒlə,pʊk) *n.* an artificial language based on English, French, German, Latin, etc., invented in 1880. [C19: from *vol,* based on WORLD + euphonic *-a-* + *pük* speech, based on SPEAK]

volar[1] ('vəʊlə) *adj. Anatomy.* of or relating to the palm of the hand or the sole of the foot. [C19: from Latin *vola* hollow of the hand, palm, sole of the foot]

volar[2] ('vəʊlə) *adj. Rare.* relating to or employed in flying. [C19: from Latin *volāre* to fly]

volatile ('vɒlə,taɪl) *adj.* **1.** (of a substance) capable of readily changing from a solid or liquid form to a vapour; having a high vapour pressure and a low boiling point. **2.** (of persons) disposed to caprice or inconstancy; fickle; mercurial. **3.** (of circumstances) liable to sudden, unpredictable, or explosive change. **4.** lasting only a short time: *volatile business interests.* **5.** *Computer technol.* (of a memory) not retaining stored information when the power supply is cut off. **6.** *Obsolete.* flying or capable of flight; volant. ~*n.* **7.** a volatile substance. **8.** *Rare.* a winged creature. [C17: from Latin *volātilis* flying, from *volāre* to fly] —'**volatileness** *or* **volatility** (,vɒlə'tɪlɪtɪ) *n.*

volatile oil *n.* another name for **essential oil.**

volatile salt *n.* another name for **sal volatile.**

volatilize *or* **volatilise** (vɒ'lætɪ,laɪz) *vb.* to change or cause to change from a solid or liquid to a vapour. —**vo'lati,lizable** *or* **vo'lati,lisable** *adj.* —**vo,latiliz'ation** *or* **vo,latilis'ation** *n.*

vol-au-vent (*French* vɔlovɑ̃) *n.* a very light puff pastry case filled either with a savoury mixture in a richly flavoured sauce or sometimes with fruit. [C19: from French, literally: flight in the wind]

volcanic (vɒl'kænɪk) *adj.* **1.** of, relating to, produced by, or characterized by the presence of volcanoes: *a volcanic region.* **2.** suggestive of or resembling an erupting volcano: *a volcanic era.* **3.** another word for **extrusive** (sense 2). —**vol'canically** *adv.* —**volcanicity** (,vɒlkə'nɪsɪtɪ) *n.*

volcanic bomb *n.* See **bomb** (sense 4).

volcanic glass *n.* any of several glassy volcanic igneous rocks, such as obsidian and pitchstone.

volcanism ('vɒlkə,nɪzəm) *or* **vulcanism** *n.* those processes collectively that result in the formation of volcanoes and their products.

volcanize *or* **volcanise** ('vɒlkə,naɪz) *vb.* (*tr.*) to subject to the effects of or change by volcanic heat. —,**volcani'zation** *or* ,**volcani'sation** *n.*

volcano (vɒl'keɪnəʊ) *n., pl.* **-noes** *or* **-nos. 1.** an opening in the earth's crust from which molten lava, rock fragments, ashes, dust, and gases are ejected from below the earth's surface. **2.** a mountain formed from volcanic material ejected from a vent in a central crater. [C17: from Italian, from Latin *Volcānus* Vulcan, Roman god of fire and metalworking, whose forges were believed to be responsible for volcanic rumblings]

volcanology (,vɒlkə'nɒlədʒɪ) *or* **vulcanology** *n.* the study of volcanoes and volcanic phenomena. —**volcanological** (,vɒlkənə'lɒdʒɪkᵊl) *or* ,**vulcano'logical** *adj.* —,**volcan'ologist** *or* ,**vulcan'ologist** *n.*

vole[1] (vəʊl) *n.* any of numerous small rodents of the genus *Microtus* and related genera, mostly of Eurasia and North America and having a stocky body, short tail, and inconspicuous ears: family *Cricetidae.* See also **water vole.** [C19: short for *volemouse,* from Old Norse *vollr* field + *mus* MOUSE; related to Icelandic *vollarmus*]

vole[2] (vəʊl) *n.* (in some card games, such as écarté) the taking of all the tricks in a deal, thus scoring extra points. [C17: from French, from *voler* to fly, from Latin *volāre*]

volitant ('vɒlɪtənt) *adj.* **1.** flying or moving about rapidly. **2.** capable of flying. [C19: from Latin *volitāre* to flit, from *volāre* to fly]

volition (və'lɪʃən) *n.* **1.** the act of exercising the will: *of one's own volition.* **2.** the faculty or capability of conscious choice, decision, and intention; the will. **3.** the resulting choice or resolution. **4.** *Philosophy.* an act of will as distinguished from the physical movement it intends to bring about. [C17: from Medieval Latin *volitiō,* from Latin *vol-* as in *volō* I will, present stem of *velle* to wish] —**vo'litional** *or* **vo'litionary** *adj.* —**vo'litionally** *adv.*

volitive ('vɒlɪtɪv) *adj.* **1.** of, relating to, or emanating from the will. **2.** *Grammar.* another word for **desiderative.**

volk (fɔlk) *n. S. African.* the people or nation, esp. the nation of Afrikaners. [Afrikaans]

Völkerwanderung *German.* ('fœlkərvandərʊŋ) *n.* the migration of peoples, esp. of Germanic and Slavic peoples into S and W Europe from 2nd to 11th centuries. [literally: nations wandering, German translation of Latin *migrātiō gentium*]

Volkslied *German.* ('fɔlksliːt) *n., pl.* **-lieder** (-liːdər). a type of popular German folk song. [literally: folk song]

volley ('vɒlɪ) *n.* **1.** the simultaneous discharge of several weapons, esp. firearms. **2.** the projectiles or missiles so discharged. **3.** a burst of oaths, protests, etc., occurring simultaneously or in rapid succession. **4.** *Sport.* a stroke, shot, or kick at a moving ball before it hits the ground. Compare **half volley. 5.** *Cricket.* the flight of such a ball or the ball itself. **6.** the simultaneous explosion of several blastings of rock. ~*vb.* **7.** to discharge (weapons, etc.) in or as if in a volley or (of weapons, etc.) to be discharged. **8.** (*tr.*) to utter vehemently or sound loudly and continuously. **9.** (*tr.*) *Sport.* to strike or kick (a moving ball) before it hits the ground. **10.** (*intr.*) to issue or move rapidly or indiscriminately. [C16: from French *volée* a flight, from *voler* to fly, from Latin *volāre*] —'**volleyer** *n.*

volleyball ('vɒlɪ,bɔːl) *n.* **1.** a game in which two teams hit a large ball back and forth over a high net with their hands. **2.** the ball used in this game.

volost ('vəʊlɒst) *n.* **1.** (in the former Soviet Union) a rural soviet. **2.** (in tsarist Russia) a peasant community consisting of several villages or hamlets. [from Russian]

vols. *abbrev. for* volumes.

Volscian ('vɒlskɪən) *n.* **1.** a member of the Volsci, a warlike people of ancient Latium in W central Italy. **2.** the extinct language of the Volsci, closely related to Umbrian. ~*adj.* **3.** of or relating to the Volsci or their language.

volt[1] (vəʊlt) *n.* the derived SI unit of electric potential; the potential difference between two points on a conductor carrying a current of 1 ampere, when the power dissipated between these points is 1 watt. Symbol: V [C19: named after Count Alessandro *Volta* (1745–1827), Italian physicist]

volt[2] *or* **volte** (vɒlt) *n.* **1.** a small circle of determined size executed in dressage. **2.** a leap made in fencing to avoid an opponent's thrust. [C17: from French *volte,* from Italian *volta* a turn, ultimately from Latin *volvere* to turn]

volta ('vɒltə; *Italian* 'vɔlta) *n., pl.* **-te** (*Italian* -te). **1.** a quick-moving Italian dance popular during the 16th and 17th centuries. **2.** a piece of music written for or in the rhythm of this dance, in triple time. [C17: from Italian: turn; see VOLT[2]]

voltage ('vəʊltɪdʒ) *n.* an electromotive force or potential difference expressed in volts.

voltage divider *n.* another name for a **potential divider.**

voltaic (vɒl'teɪɪk) *adj.* another word for **galvanic** (sense 1).

Voltaic (vɒl'teɪɪk) *adj.* **1.** of or relating to Burkina-Faso in W Africa, formerly known as Upper Volta. **2.** denoting, belonging to, or relating to the Gur group of African languages. ~*n.* **3.** this group of languages. See also **Gur.**

voltaic cell *n.* another name for **primary cell.**

voltaic couple *n. Physics.* a pair of dissimilar metals in an electrolyte with a potential difference between the metals resulting from chemical action.

voltaic pile *n.* an early form of battery consisting of a pile of paired plates of dissimilar metals, such as zinc and copper, each pair being separated from the next by a pad moistened with an electrolyte. Also called: **pile, galvanic pile, Volta's pile.**

voltaism ('vɒltəˌɪzəm) *n.* another name for **galvanism.**

voltameter (vɒl'tæmɪtə) *n.* another name for **coulometer.** —**voltametric** (ˌvɒltə'mɛtrɪk) *adj.*

voltammeter (ˌvəʊlt'æmˌmiːtə) *n.* a dual-purpose instrument that can measure both potential difference and electric current, usually in volts and amperes respectively.

volt-ampere ('vəʊlt'æmpɛə) *n.* the product of the potential in volts across an electrical circuit and the resultant current in amperes. Abbrev.: **VA.**

volte (vɒlt) *n.* a variant spelling of **volt**[2].

volte-face ('vɒlt'fɑːs) *n., pl.* **volte-face.** **1.** a reversal, as in opinion or policy. **2.** a change of position so as to look, lie, etc., in the opposite direction. [C19: from French, from Italian *volta-faccia,* from *volta* a turn + *faccia* face]

voltmeter ('vəʊltˌmiːtə) *n.* an instrument for measuring potential difference or electromotive force.

voluble ('vɒljʊb[ə]l) *adj.* **1.** talking easily, readily, and at length; fluent. **2.** *Archaic.* easily turning or rotating, as on an axis. **3.** *Rare.* (of a plant) twining or twisting. [C16: from Latin *volūbilis* turning readily, fluent, from *volvere* to turn] —ˌ**volu'bility** *or* '**volubleness** *n.* —'**volubly** *adv.*

volume ('vɒljuːm) *n.* **1.** the magnitude of the three-dimensional space enclosed within or occupied by an object, geometric solid, etc. Symbol: *V* **2.** a large mass or quantity: *the volume of protest.* **3.** an amount or total: *the volume of exports.* **4.** fullness or intensity of tone or sound. **5.** the control on a radio, etc., for adjusting the intensity of sound. **6.** a bound collection of printed or written pages; book. **7.** any of several books either bound in an identical format or part of a series. **8.** the complete set of issues of a periodical over a specified period, esp. one year. **9.** *History.* a roll or scroll of parchment, papyrus, etc. **10. speak volumes.** to convey much significant information. ~Abbrevs. (for senses 6–8): **v., vol.** [C14: from Old French *volum,* from Latin *volūmen* a roll, book, from *volvere* to roll up]

volumed ('vɒljuːmd) *adj.* **1.** (of literary works) **a.** consisting of or being in volumes. **b.** (*in combination*): *a three-volumed history.* **2.** *Rare.* having bulk or volume. **3.** *Poetic.* forming a rounded mass.

volumeter (vɒ'ljuːmɪtə) *n.* any instrument for measuring the volume of a solid, liquid, or gas.

volumetric (ˌvɒljʊ'mɛtrɪk) *adj.* of, concerning, or using measurement by volume: *volumetric analysis; volumetric efficiency.* Compare **gravimetric.** —ˌ**volu'metrically** *adv.* —**volumetry** (vɒ'ljuːmɪtrɪ) *n.*

volumetric analysis *n. Chem.* **1.** quantitative analysis of liquids or solutions by comparing the volumes that react with known volumes of standard reagents, usually by titration. Compare **gravimetric analysis. 2.** quantitative analysis of gases by volume.

volumetric displacement *n.* the volume of air per revolution that passes through a mechanical pump when the pressure at the intake and the exhaust is the same as that of the atmosphere. Also called: **swept volume.**

volumetric efficiency *n.* **1.** the ratio of fluid delivered by a piston or ram pump per stroke to the displacement volume of the piston or ram. **2.** the ratio of air or gas-air mixture drawn into the cylinder of an internal-combustion engine to the volumetric displacement of the piston.

voluminous (və'luːmɪnəs) *adj.* **1.** of great size, quantity, volume, or extent. **2.** (of writing) consisting of or sufficient to fill volumes. **3.** prolific in writing or speech. **4.** *Obsolete.* winding. [C17: from Late Latin *volūminōsus* full of windings, from *volūmen* VOLUME] —**voluminosity** (vəˌluːmɪ'nɒsɪtɪ) *or* **vo'luminousness** *n.* —**vo'luminously** *adv.*

voluntarism ('vɒləntəˌrɪzəm) *n.* **1.** *Philosophy.* the theory that the will rather than the intellect is the ultimate principle of reality. **2.** a doctrine or system based on voluntary participation in a course of action. **3.** the belief that the state, government, and the law should not interfere with the procedures of collective bargaining and of trade union organization. **4.** another name for **voluntaryism.** —'**voluntarist** *n., adj.* —ˌ**volunta'ristic** *adj.*

voluntary ('vɒləntərɪ, -trɪ) *adj.* **1.** performed, undertaken, or brought about by free choice, willingly, or without being asked: *a voluntary donation.* **2.** (of persons) serving or acting in a specified function of one's own accord and without compulsion or promise of remuneration: *a voluntary social worker.* **3.** done by, composed of, or functioning with the aid of volunteers: *a voluntary association.* **4.** endowed with, exercising, or having the faculty of willing: *a voluntary agent.* **5.** arising from natural impulse; spontaneous: *voluntary laughter.* **6.** *Law.* **a.** acting or done without legal obligation, compulsion, or persuasion. **b.** made without payment or recompense in any form: *a voluntary conveyance.* **7.** (of the muscles of the limbs, neck, etc.) having their action controlled by the will. **8.** maintained or provided by the voluntary actions or contributions of individuals and not by the state: *voluntary schools; the voluntary system.* ~*n., pl.* **-taries. 9.** *Music.* a composition or improvisation, usually for organ, played at the beginning or end of a church service. **10.** work done without compulsion. **11.** *Obsolete.* a volunteer, esp. in an army. [C14: from Latin *voluntārius,* from *voluntās* will, from *velle* to wish] —'**voluntarily** *adv.* —'**voluntariness** *n.*

voluntary arrangement *n. Law.* a procedure enabling an insolvent company to come to an arrangement with its creditors and resolve its financial problems, often in compliance with a court order.

voluntaryism ('vɒləntərɪˌɪzəm, -trɪ-) *or* **voluntarism** *n.* **1.** the principle of supporting churches, schools, and various other institutions by voluntary contributions rather than with state funds. **2.** any system based on this principle. —'**voluntaryist** *or* '**voluntarist** *n.*

voluntary retailer *n.* another name for **symbol retailer.**

volunteer (ˌvɒlən'tɪə) *n.* **1. a.** a person who performs or offers to perform voluntary service. **b.** (*as modifier*): *a volunteer system; volunteer advice.* **2.** a person who freely undertakes military service, esp. temporary or special service. **3.** *Law.* **a.** a person who does some act or enters into a transaction without being under any legal obligation to do so and without being promised any remuneration for his services. **b.** *Property law.* a person to whom property is transferred without his giving any valuable consideration in return, as a legatee under a will. **4. a.** a plant that grows from seed that has not been deliberately sown. **b.** (*as modifier*): *a volunteer plant.* ~*vb.* **5.** to offer (oneself or one's services) for an undertaking by choice and without request or obligation. **6.** (*tr.*) to perform, give, or communicate voluntarily: *to volunteer help; to volunteer a speech.* **7.** (*intr.*) to enlist voluntarily for military service. [C17: from French *volontaire,* from Latin *voluntārius* willing; see VOLUNTARY]

volunteer bureau *n.* (*often caps.*) (in Britain) *Social welfare.* an agency that matches up people wishing to do voluntary work with appropriate voluntary organizations.

voluptuary (və'lʌptjʊərɪ) *n., pl.* **-aries. 1.** a person devoted or addicted to luxury and sensual pleasures. ~*adj.* **2.** of, relating to, characterized by, or furthering sensual gratification or luxury. [C17: from Late Latin *voluptuārius* delightful, from Latin *voluptās* pleasure]

voluptuous (və'lʌptjʊəs) *adj.* **1.** relating to, characterized by, or consisting of pleasures of the body or senses; sensual. **2.** disposed, devoted, or addicted to sensual indulgence or luxurious pleasures. **3.** provocative and sexually alluring, esp. through shapeliness or fullness: *a voluptuous woman.* [C14: from Latin *voluptuōsus* full of gratification, from *voluptās* pleasure] —**vo'luptuously** *adv.* —**vo'luptuousness** *n.*

volute ('vɒljuːt, və'luːt) *n.* **1.** a spiral or twisting turn, form, or object; spiral; whorl. **2.** Also called: **helix.** a carved ornament, esp. as used on an Ionic capital, that has the form of a spiral scroll. **3.** any of the whorls of the spirally coiled shell of a snail or similar gastropod mollusc. **4.** any tropical marine gastropod mollusc of the family *Volutidae,* typically having a spiral shell with beautiful markings. **5.** a tangential part, resembling the volute of a snail's shell, that collects the fluids emerging from the periphery of a turbine, impeller pump, etc. ~*adj. also* **voluted** (və'luːtɪd). **6.** having the form of a volute; spiral. **7.** *Machinery.* moving in a spiral path. [C17: from Latin *volūta* a spiral decoration, from *volūtus* rolled, from *volvere* to roll up]

volution (və'luːʃən) *n.* **1.** a rolling, revolving, or spiral form or motion. **2.** a whorl of a spiral gastropod shell.

volva ('vɒlvə) *n., pl.* **-vae** (-viː) *or* **-vas.** *Botany.* a cup-shaped structure that sheathes the base of the stalk of certain mushrooms. [C18: from Latin: a covering, from *volvere* to wrap] —**volvate** (ˈvɒlvɪt, -veɪt) *adj.*

volvox (ˈvɒlvɒks) *n.* any freshwater flagellate protozoan of the genus *Volvox,* occurring in colonies in the form of hollow multicellular spheres: class *Mastigophora* (or *Flagellata*). [C18: from New Latin, from Latin *volvere* to roll]

volvulus (ˈvɒlvjʊləs) *n., pl.* **-luses.** *Pathol.* an abnormal twisting of the intestines causing obstruction. [C17: from New Latin, from Latin *volvere* to twist]

vomer (ˈvəʊmə) *n.* the thin flat bone forming part of the separation between the nasal passages in mammals. [C18: from Latin: ploughshare] —**vomerine** (ˈvəʊməˌraɪn, -rɪn, ˈvɒm-) *adj.*

vomit (ˈvɒmɪt) *vb.* **-its, -iting, -ited. 1.** to eject (the contents of the stomach) through the mouth as the result of involuntary muscular spasms of the stomach and oesophagus. **2.** to eject or be ejected forcefully; spew forth. ~*n.* **3.** the matter ejected in vomiting. **4.** the act of vomiting. **5.** a drug or agent that induces vomiting; emetic. [C14: from Latin *vomitāre* to vomit repeatedly, from *vomere* to vomit] —ˈ**vomiter** *n.*

vomitory (ˈvɒmɪtərɪ, -trɪ) *adj.* **1.** Also: **vomitive** (ˈvɒmɪtɪv). causing vomiting; emetic. ~*n., pl.* **-ries. 2.** Also called: **vomitive.** a vomitory agent. **3.** *Rare.* a container for receiving vomitus. **4.** Also called: **vomitorium** (ˌvɒmɪˈtɔːrɪəm). a passageway in an ancient Roman amphitheatre that connects an outside entrance to a tier of seats. **5.** an opening through which matter is ejected.

vomiturition (ˌvɒmɪtjʊˈrɪʃən) *n.* the act of retching.

vomitus (ˈvɒmɪtəs) *n., pl.* **-tuses. 1.** matter that has been vomited. **2.** the act of vomiting. [Latin: a vomiting]

voodoo (ˈvuːduː) *n., pl.* **-doos. 1.** Also called: **voodooism.** a religious cult involving witchcraft and communication by trance with ancestors and animistic deities, common among Negroes in Haiti and other Caribbean islands. **2.** a person who practises voodoo. **3.** a charm, spell, or fetish involved in voodoo worship and ritual. ~*adj.* **4.** relating to or associated with voodoo. ~*vb.* **-doos, -dooing, -dooed. 5.** (*tr.*) to affect by or as if by the power of voodoo. [C19: from Louisiana French *voudou,* ultimately of West African origin; compare Ewe *vodu* guardian spirit] —ˈ**voodooist** *n.* —ˌ**voodooˈistic** *adj.*

voorkamer (ˈfʊəˌkɑːmə) *n. S. African.* the front room, esp. of a Cape Dutch house or farmhouse. [from Afrikaans *voor* front + *kamer* room]

Voortrekker (ˈfʊəˌtrɛkə, ˈvʊə-) *n.* (in South Africa) **1.** one of the original Afrikaner settlers of the Transvaal and the Orange Free State who migrated from the Cape Colony in the 1830s. **2.** a member of the Afrikaner youth movement founded in 1931. [C19: from Dutch, from *voor-* FORE- + *trekken* to TREK]

voracious (vɒˈreɪʃəs) *adj.* **1.** devouring or craving food in great quantities. **2.** very eager or unremitting in some activity: *voracious reading.* [C17: from Latin *vorāx* swallowing greedily, from *vorāre* to devour] —**voˈraciously** *adv.* —**voracity** (vɒˈræsɪtɪ) *or* **voˈraciousness** *n.*

Vorlage *German.* (ˈfoːrlaːgə) *n. Skiing.* a position in which a skier leans forward but keeps his heels on the skis. [from *vor* before, in front of + *Lage* position, stance]

-vorous *adj. combining form.* feeding on or devouring: *carnivorous.* [from Latin *-vorus;* related to *vorāre* to swallow up, DEVOUR] —**-vore** *n. combining form.*

vortex (ˈvɔːtɛks) *n., pl.* **-texes** *or* **-tices** (-tɪˌsiːz). **1.** a whirling mass or motion of liquid, gas, flame, etc., such as the spiralling movement of water around a whirlpool. **2.** any activity, situation, or way of life regarded as irresistibly engulfing. [C17: from Latin: a whirlpool; variant of VERTEX] —**vortical** (ˈvɔːtɪkᵊl) *adj.* —ˈ**vortically** *adv.*

vortex drag *n.* See **trailing vortex drag.**

vortex ring *n.* a stable perturbation in a fluid that takes the form of a torus in which the flow rotates in the section of the torus so that the pressure difference between the inside and outside of the torus balances body forces. The best-known vortex ring is a smoke ring.

vortex shedding *n.* the process by which vortices formed continuously by the aerodynamic conditions associated with a solid body in a gas or air stream are carried downstream by the flow in the form of a vortex street. See also **vortex street.**

vortex street *n.* a regular stream of vortices or parallel streams of vortices carried downstream by the flow of a fluid over a body. These are sometimes made visible by vapour condensation as in the vortex trails from the wing tips of an aeroplane. See also **Karmen vortex street, vortex shedding.**

vorticella (ˌvɔːtɪˈsɛlə) *n., pl.* **-lae** (-liː). any protozoan of the genus *Vorticella,* consisting of a goblet-shaped ciliated cell attached to the substratum by a long contractile stalk. [C18: from New Latin, literally: a little eddy, from VORTEX]

vorticism (ˈvɔːtɪˌsɪzəm) *n.* an art movement initiated in England in 1913, combining the techniques of cubism with the concern for the problems of the machine age evinced in futurism. [C20: referring to the "vortices" of modern life on which the movement was based] —ˈ**vorticist** *n.*

vorticose (ˈvɔːtɪˌkəʊs) *adj. Rare.* rotating quickly; whirling. [C18: from Latin *vorticōsus,* variant of *verticōsus* full of whirlpools; see VERTEX]

vortiginous (vɔːˈtɪdʒɪnəs) *adj.* like a vortex; vortical; whirling. [C17: variant of VERTIGINOUS]

vostro account (ˈvɒstrəʊ) *n.* a bank account held by a foreign bank with a British bank, usually in sterling. Compare **nostro account.**

votary (ˈvəʊtərɪ) *n., pl.* **-ries,** *also* **votarist. 1.** *R.C. Church, Eastern Churches.* a person, such as a monk or nun, who has dedicated himself or herself to religion by taking vows. **2.** a devoted adherent of a religion, cause, leader, pursuit, etc. ~*adj.* **3.** ardently devoted to the services or worship of God, a deity, or a saint. [C16: from Latin *vōtum* a vow, from *vovēre* to vow] —ˈ**votaress** *or* ˈ**votress** *fem. n.*

vote (vəʊt) *n.* **1.** an indication of choice, opinion, or will on a question, such as the choosing of a candidate, by or as if by some recognized means, such as a ballot: *10 votes for Jones.* **2.** the opinion of a group of persons as determined by voting: *it was put to the vote; do not take a vote; it came to a vote.* **3.** a body of votes or voters collectively: *the Jewish vote.* **4.** the total number of votes cast: *the vote decreased at the last election.* **5.** the ticket, ballot, etc., by which a vote is expressed. **6. a.** the right to vote; franchise; suffrage. **b.** a person regarded as the embodiment of this right. **7.** a means of voting, such as a ballot. **8.** *Chiefly Brit.* a grant or other proposition to be voted upon. ~*vb.* **9.** (when *tr., takes a clause as object or an infinitive*) to express or signify (one's preference, opinion, or will) (for or against some question, etc.): *to vote by ballot; we voted that it was time to adjourn; vote for me!* **10.** (*intr.*) to declare oneself as being (something or in favour of something) by exercising one's vote: *to vote socialist.* **11.** (*tr.;* foll. by *into* or *out of,* etc.) to appoint or elect (a person to or from a particular post): *they voted him into the presidency; he was voted out of office.* **12.** (*tr.*) to determine the condition of in a specified way by voting: *the court voted itself out of existence.* **13.** (*tr.*) to authorize, confer, or allow by voting: *vote us a rise.* **14.** (*tr.*) *Informal.* to declare by common opinion: *the party was voted a failure.* **15.** (*tr.*) to influence or control the voting of: *do not try to vote us!* [C15: from Latin *vōtum* a solemn promise, from *vovēre* to vow] —ˈ**votable** *or* ˈ**voteable** *adj.* —ˈ**voteless** *adj.*

vote down *vb.* (*tr., adv.*) to decide against or defeat in a vote: *the bill was voted down.*

vote of no confidence *n. Parliament.* a vote on a motion put by the Opposition censuring an aspect of the Government's policy; if the motion is carried the Government is obliged to resign. Also called: **vote of censure.**

voter (ˈvəʊtə) *n.* a person who can or does vote.

voting machine *n.* (esp. in the U.S.) a machine at a polling station that voters operate to register their votes and that mechanically or electronically counts all votes cast.

votive (ˈvəʊtɪv) *adj.* **1.** offered, given, undertaken, performed or dedicated in fulfilment of or in accordance with a vow. **2.** *R.C. Church.* optional; not prescribed; having the nature of a voluntary offering: *a votive Mass; a votive candle.* [C16: from Latin *vōtīvus* promised by a vow, from *vōtum* a vow] —ˈ**votively** *adv.* —ˈ**votiveness** *n.*

Votyak (ˈvəʊtɪˌæk) *n.* **1.** (*pl.* **-aks** *or* **-ak**) a member of a Finnish people living chiefly in W central Russia, in the former Udmurt ASSR. **2.** the language of this people, belonging to the Finno-Ugric family. ~Also called: **Udmurt.**

vouch (vaʊtʃ) *vb.* **1.** (*intr.;* usually foll. by *for*) to give personal assurance; guarantee: *I'll vouch for his safety.* **2.** (when *tr., usually takes a clause as object;* when *intr.,* usually foll. by *for*) to furnish supporting evidence (for) or function as proof (of). **3.** (*tr.*) *English legal history.* to summon (a person who had warranted title to land) to defend that title or give up land of equal value. **4.** (*tr.*) *Archaic.* to cite (authors, principles, etc.) in support of something. **5.** (*tr.*) *Obsolete.* to assert. ~*n.* **6.** *Obsolete.* the act of vouching; assertion or allegation. [C14: from Old French *vocher* to summon, ultimately from Latin *vocāre* to call]

voucher (ˈvaʊtʃə) *n.* **1.** a document serving as evidence for some claimed transaction, as the receipt or expenditure of money. **2.** *Brit.* a ticket or card serving as a substitute for cash: *a gift voucher.* **3.** a person or thing that vouches for the truth of some statement, etc. **4.** any of certain documents that various groups of British nationals born outside Britain must obtain in order to settle in Britain. **5.** *English law, obsolete.* **a.** the summoning into court of a person to warrant a title to property. **b.** the person so summoned. [C16: from Anglo-French, noun use of Old French *voucher* to summon; see VOUCH]

vouchsafe (ˌvaʊtʃˈseɪf) *vb.* (*tr.*) **1.** to give or grant or condescend to give or grant: *she vouchsafed no reply; he vouchsafed me no encouragement.* **2.** (*may take a clause as object or an infinitive*) to agree, promise, or permit, often graciously or condescendingly: *he vouchsafed to come yesterday.* **3.** *Obsolete.* **a.** to warrant as being safe. **b.** to bestow as a favour (upon). [C14 *vouchen sauf;* see VOUCH, SAFE] —ˌ**vouchˈsafement** *n.*

vouge (vuːʒ) *n.* a form of pike or halberd used by foot soldiers in the 14th century and later. [from Old French *voulge, vouge* (Medieval Latin *vanga*), of obscure origin]

voussoir (vuːˈswɑː) *n.* a wedge-shaped stone or brick that is used with others to construct an arch or vault. [C18: from French, from Vulgar Latin *volsōrium* (unattested), ultimately from Latin *volvere* to turn, roll]

Vouvray (ˈvuːvreɪ; *French* vuvrɛ) *n.* a dry white wine, which can be still, sparkling, or semisparkling, produced in France around Touraine in the Loire Valley.

vow (vaʊ) *n.* **1.** a solemn or earnest pledge or promise binding the person making it to perform a specified act or behave in a certain way. **2.** a solemn promise made to a deity or saint, by which the promiser pledges himself to some future act, course of action, or way of life. **3. take vows.** to enter a religious order and commit oneself to its rule of life by the vows of poverty, chastity, and obedience, which may be taken for a limited period as **simple vows** or as a perpetual and still more solemn commitment as **solemn vows.** ~*vb.* **4.** (*tr.; may take a clause as object or an infinitive*) to pledge, promise, or undertake solemnly: *he vowed that he would continue; he vowed to return.* **5.** (*tr.*) to dedicate or consecrate to God, a deity, or a saint. **6.** (*tr.; usually takes a clause as object*) to assert or swear emphatically. **7.** (*intr.*) *Archaic.* to declare solemnly. [C13: from Old French *vou,* from Latin *vōtum* a solemn promise, from *vovēre* to vow] —'**vower** *n.* —'**vowless** *adj.*

vowel ('vaʊəl) *n.* **1.** *Phonetics.* a voiced speech sound whose articulation is characterized by the absence of friction-causing obstruction in the vocal tract, allowing the breath stream free passage. The timbre of a vowel is chiefly determined by the position of the tongue and the lips. **2.** a letter or character representing a vowel. [C14: from Old French *vouel,* from Latin *vocālis littera* a vowel, from *vocālis* sonorous, from *vox* a voice] —'**vowel-less** *adj.* —'**vowel-ˌlike** *adj.*

vowel gradation *n.* another name for **ablaut.** See **gradation** (sense 5).

vowelize *or* **vowelise** ('vaʊəˌlaɪz) *vb.* (*tr.*) to mark the vowel points in (a Hebrew word or text). Also: **vocalize.** —ˌ**voweli'zation** *or* ˌ**voweli'sation** *n.*

vowel mutation *n.* another name for **umlaut.**

vowel point *n.* any of several marks or points placed above or below consonants, esp. those evolved for Hebrew or Arabic, in order to indicate vowel sounds.

vox (vɒks) *n., pl.* **voces** ('vəʊsiːz). a voice or sound. [Latin: voice]

vox angelica (æn'dʒɛlɪkə) *n.* an organ stop with a soft tone, often similar to the voix céleste. [C18: from Latin: angelic voice]

vox humana (hjuː'mɑːnə) *n.* a reed stop on an organ supposedly imitative of the human voice. [C18: from Latin: human voice]

vox pop *n.* interviews with members of the public on a radio or television programme. [C20: shortened from VOX POPULI]

vox populi ('pɒpjʊˌlaɪ) *n.* the voice of the people; popular or public opinion. [Latin]

voyage ('vɔɪɪdʒ) *n.* **1.** a journey, travel, or passage, esp. one to a distant land or by sea or air. **2.** *Obsolete.* an ambitious project. ~*vb.* **3.** to travel over or traverse (something): *we will voyage to Africa.* [C13: from Old French *veiage,* from Latin *viāticum* provision for travelling, from *viāticus* concerning a journey, from *via* a way] —'**voyager** *n.*

voyage charter *n.* the hire of a ship or aircraft for a specified number of voyages. Compare **time charter.**

voyageur (ˌvɔɪə'dʒɜː) *n. Canadian.* **1.** *History.* a boatman employed by one of the early fur-trading companies, esp. in the interior. **2.** a woodsman, guide, trapper, boatman, or explorer, esp. in the North. [C19: from French: traveller, from *voyager* to VOYAGE]

voyeur (vwaɪ'ɜː; *French* vwajœr) *n.* a person who obtains sexual pleasure or excitement from the observation of someone undressing, having intercourse, etc. [C20: French, literally: one who sees, from *voir* to see, from Latin *vidēre*] —**vo'yeurism** *n.* —ˌ**voyeur'istic** *adj.* —ˌ**voyeur'istically** *adv.*

VP *abbrev. for* **1.** Vice President. **2.** verb phrase.

VR *abbrev. for:* **1.** variant reading. **2.** Victoria Regina. [Latin: Queen Victoria] **3.** Volunteer Reserve.

vraisemblance (ˌvreɪsɒm'blɒns; *French* vrɛsɑ̃blɑ̃s) *n.* verisimilitude; appearance of truth. [French, from *vrai* true + SEMBLANCE]

V. Rev. *abbrev. for* Very Reverend.

VRI *abbrev. for* Victoria Regina et Imperatrix. [Latin: Victoria, Queen and Empress]

vroom (vruːm, vrʊm) *interj.* an exclamation imitative of a car engine revving up, as for high-speed motor racing.

vs *abbrev. for* versus.

VS *abbrev. for* Veterinary Surgeon.

v.s. *abbrev. for* vide supra. See **vide.**

vsb *abbrev. for* vestigial sideband: a transmission in an amplitude-modulated signal in which one complete sideband is transmitted, but only part of the other.

V-sign *n.* **1.** (in Britain) an offensive gesture made by sticking up the index and middle fingers with the palm of the hand inwards as an indication of contempt, defiance, etc. **2.** a similar gesture with the palm outwards meaning victory or peace.

VSO *abbrev. for:* **1.** very superior old: used to indicate that a brandy, port, etc., is between 12 and 17 years old. **2.** (in Britain) Voluntary Service Overseas.

VSOP *abbrev. for* very special (or superior) old pale: used to indicate that a brandy, port, etc., is between 20 and 25 years old.

Vt. *or* **VT** *abbrev. for* Vermont.

VTOL ('viːtɒl) *n.* **1.** vertical takeoff and landing; a system in which an aircraft can take off and land vertically. **2.** an aircraft that uses this system. Compare **STOL.**

VTR *abbrev. for* video tape recorder.

V-type engine *n.* a type of internal-combustion engine having two cylinder blocks attached to a single crankcase, the angle between the two blocks forming a V.

vug, vugg, *or* **vugh** (vʌg) *n. Mining.* a small cavity in a rock or vein, usually lined with crystals. [C19: from Cornish *vooga* cave] —'**vuggy** *or* '**vughy** *adj.*

Vul. *abbrev. for* Vulgate.

vulcanian (vʌl'keɪnɪən) *adj. Geology.* **a.** of or relating to a volcanic eruption characterized by the explosive discharge of gases, fine ash, and viscous lava that hardens in the crater. **b.** a less common word for **volcanic.**

vulcanism ('vʌlkəˌnɪzəm) *n.* a variant spelling of **volcanism.**

vulcanite ('vʌlkəˌnaɪt) *n.* a hard usually black rubber produced by vulcanizing natural rubber with large amounts of sulphur. It is resistant to chemical attack: used for chemical containers, electrical insulators, etc. Also called: **ebonite.**

vulcanize *or* **vulcanise** ('vʌlkəˌnaɪz) *vb.* (*tr.*) **1.** to treat (rubber) with sulphur or sulphur compounds under heat and pressure to improve elasticity and strength or to produce a hard substance such as vulcanite. **2.** to treat (substances other than rubber) by a similar process in order to improve their properties. —'**vulcanˌizable** *or* '**vulcanˌisable** *adj.* —ˌ**vulcani'zation** *or* ˌ**vulcani'sation** *n.* —'**vulcanˌizer** *or* '**vulcanˌiser** *n.*

vulcanology (ˌvʌlkə'nɒlədʒɪ) *n.* a variant spelling of **volcanology.** —**vulcanological** (ˌvʌlkənə'lɒdʒɪkᵊl) *adj.* —ˌ**vulcan'ologist** *n.*

vulg. *abbrev. for* vulgar(ly).

Vulg. *abbrev. for* Vulgate.

vulgar ('vʌlgə) *adj.* **1.** marked by lack of taste, culture, delicacy, manners, etc.: *vulgar behaviour; vulgar language.* **2.** (*often cap.; usually prenominal*) denoting a form of a language, esp. of Latin, current among common people, esp. at a period when the formal language is archaic and not in general spoken use. **3.** *Archaic.* **a.** of, relating to, or current among the great mass of common people, in contrast to the educated, cultured, or privileged; ordinary. **b.** (*as collective n.; preceded by the*): *the vulgar.* [C14: from Latin *vulgāris* belonging to the multitude, from *vulgus* the common people] —'**vulgarly** *adv.*

vulgar fraction *n.* another name for **simple fraction.**

vulgarian (vʌl'gɛərɪən) *n.* a vulgar person, esp. one who is rich or has pretensions to good taste.

vulgarism ('vʌlgəˌrɪzəm) *n.* **1.** a coarse, crude, or obscene expression. **2.** a word or phrase found only in the vulgar form of a language. **3.** another word for **vulgarity.**

vulgarity (vʌl'gærɪtɪ) *n., pl.* **-ties.** **1.** the condition of being vulgar; lack of good manners. **2.** a vulgar action, phrase, etc.

vulgarize *or* **vulgarise** ('vʌlgəˌraɪz) *vb.* (*tr.*) **1.** to make commonplace or vulgar; debase. **2.** to make (something little known or difficult to understand) widely known or popular among the public; popularize. —ˌ**vulgari'zation** *or* ˌ**vulgari'sation** *n.* —'**vulgarˌizer** *or* '**vulgarˌiser** *n.*

Vulgar Latin *n.* any of the dialects of Latin spoken in the Roman Empire other than classical Latin. The Romance languages developed from them.

vulgate ('vʌlgeɪt, -gɪt) *Rare.* ~*n.* **1.** a commonly recognized text or version. **2.** everyday or informal speech; the vernacular. ~*adj.* **3.** generally accepted; common.

Vulgate ('vʌlgeɪt, -gɪt) *n.* **a.** (from the 13th century onwards) the fourth-century version of the Bible produced by the monk and scholar Saint Jerome, partly by translating the original languages, and partly by revising the earlier Latin text based on the Greek versions. **b.** (*as modifier*): *the Vulgate version.* [C17: from Medieval Latin *Vulgāta,* from Late Latin *vulgāta editiō* popular version (of the Bible), from Latin *vulgāre* to make common, from *vulgus* the common people]

vulnerable ('vʌlnərəbᵊl) *adj.* **1.** capable of being physically or emotionally wounded or hurt. **2.** open to temptation, persuasion, censure, etc. **3.** *Military.* liable or exposed to attack. **4.** *Bridge.* (of a side who have won one game towards rubber) subject to increased bonuses or penalties. [C17: from Late Latin *vulnerābilis,* from Latin *vulnerāre* to wound, from *vulnus* a wound] —ˌ**vulnera'bility** *or* '**vulnerableness** *n.* —'**vulnerably** *adv.*

vulnerary ('vʌlnərərɪ) *Med.* ~*adj.* **1.** of, relating to, or used to heal a wound. ~*n., pl.* **-aries.** **2.** a vulnerary drug or agent. [C16: from Latin *vulnerārius* belonging to wounds, from *vulnus* a wound]

Vulpecula (vʌl'pɛkjʊlə) *n., Latin genitive* **Vulpeculae** (vʌl'pɛkjʊˌliː). a faint constellation in the N hemisphere lying between Cygnus and Aquila. [C19: from Latin: a little fox, from *vulpēs* a fox]

vulpine ('vʌlpaɪn) *adj.* **1.** Also: **vulpecular** (vʌl'pɛkjʊlə). of, relating to, or resembling a fox. **2.** possessing the characteristics often attributed to foxes; crafty, clever, etc. [C17: from Latin *vulpīnus* foxlike, from *vulpēs* a fox]

vulture ('vʌltʃə) *n.* **1.** any of various very large diurnal birds of prey of the genera *Neophron, Gyps, Gypaetus,* etc., of Africa, Asia, and warm parts of Europe, typically having broad wings and soaring flight and feeding on carrion: family *Accipitridae* (hawks). See also **griffon**[1] (sense 2), **lammergeier.** **2.** any similar bird of the family *Cathartidae* of North, Central, and South America. See also **condor, turkey buzzard.** **3.** a person or thing that preys greedily and ruthlessly on others, esp. the helpless. [C14: from Old French *voltour,* from Latin *vultur;* perhaps related to Latin *vellere* to pluck, tear] —'**vulture-ˌlike** *adj.*

vulturine ('vʌltʃəˌraɪn) *adj.* **1.** of, relating to, or resembling a vulture. **2.** Also: '**vulturous.** rapacious, predatory, or greedy.

vulva ('vʌlvə) *n., pl.* **-vae** (-viː) *or* **-vas.** the external genitals of human females, including the labia, mons veneris, clitoris, and the vaginal orifice. [C16: from Latin: covering, womb, matrix] —'**vulval,** '**vulvar,** *or* **vulvate** ('vʌlveɪt) *adj.* —**vulviform** ('vʌlvɪˌfɔːm) *adj.*

vulvitis (vʌl'vaɪtɪs) *n.* inflammation of the vulva.

vulvovaginitis (ˌvʌlvəʊˌvædʒɪ'naɪtɪs) *n.* inflammation of the vulva and vagina or of the small glands (**vulvovaginal glands**) on either side of the lower part of the vagina.

vv *abbrev. for* vice versa.

vv. *abbrev. for:* **1.** versus. **2.** *Music.* volumes.

VW *abbrev. for* **1.** Very Worshipful. **2.** Volkswagen.

VX *n.* a U.S. lethal nerve gas.

w *or* **W** ('dʌbᵊl,juː) *n., pl.* **w's, W's,** *or* **Ws. 1.** the 23rd letter and 18th consonant of the modern English alphabet. **2.** a speech sound represented by this letter, in English usually a bilabial semivowel, as in *web.*

W *symbol for:* **1.** watt. **2.** West. **3.** *Physics.* work. **4.** *Chem.* tungsten [from New Latin *wolframium,* from German *Wolfram*] **5.** women's (size).

w. *abbrev. for:* **1.** week. **2.** weight. **3.** width. **4.** wife. **5.** with. **6.** *Cricket.* **a.** wide. **b.** wicket.

W. *abbrev. for:* **1.** Wales. **2.** Warden. **3.** Welsh.

WA *abbrev. for* **1.** Washington (state). **2.** Western Australia.

WAAAF *abbrev. for* Women's Auxiliary Australian Air Force.

WAAC (wæk) *n.* **1.** *acronym for* Women's Army Auxiliary Corps. **2.** Also called: **waac.** a member of this corps.

WAAF (wæf) *n.* **1.** *acronym for:* **a.** Women's Auxiliary Air Force. **b.** Women's Auxiliary Australian Air Force. **2.** Also called: **Waaf.** a member of either of these forces.

wabbit ('wæbɪt) *adj. Scot.* weary; exhausted. [C19: from earlier *wobart* withered, feeble]

wabble ('wɒbᵊl) *vb., n.* a variant spelling of **wobble.** —'**wabbler** *n.* —'**wabbly** *adj.*

wack (wæk) *or* **wacker** ('wækə) *n. Liverpool and Midlands dialect.* friend; pal: used chiefly as a term of address. [perhaps from dialect *wack* or *whack* to share out, hence one who shares, a friend]

wacke ('wækə) *n. Obsolete.* any of various soft earthy rocks that resemble or are derived from basaltic rocks. [C18: from German: rock, gravel, basalt]

wacky ('wækɪ) *adj.* **wackier, wackiest.** *Slang.* eccentric, erratic, or unpredictable. [C19 (in dialect sense: a fool, an eccentric): from WHACK (hence, a *whacky,* a person who behaves as if he had been whacked on the head)] —'**wackily** *adv.* —'**wackiness** *n.*

wad[1] (wɒd) *n.* **1.** a small mass or ball of fibrous or soft material, such as cotton wool, used esp. for packing or stuffing. **2. a.** a plug of paper, cloth, leather, etc., pressed against a charge to hold it in place in a muzzle-loading cannon. **b.** a disc of paper, felt, pasteboard, etc., used to hold in place the powder and shot in a shotgun cartridge. **3.** a roll or bundle of something, esp. of banknotes. **4.** *U.S. and Canadian slang.* a large quantity, esp. of money. **5.** *Brit. dialect.* a bundle of hay or straw. **6.** *Brit. military slang.* a bun: *char and a wad.* ~*vb.* **wads, wadding, wadded. 7.** to form (something) into a wad. **8.** (*tr.*) to roll into a wad or bundle. **9.** (*tr.*) **a.** to hold (a charge) in place with a wad. **b.** to insert a wad into (a gun). **10.** (*tr.*) to pack or stuff with wadding; pad. [C14: from Late Latin *wadda;* related to German *Watte* cotton wool] —'**wadder** *n.*

wad[2] (wɒd) *n.* a soft dark earthy amorphous material consisting of decomposed manganese minerals: occurs in damp marshy areas. [C17: of unknown origin]

wadding ('wɒdɪŋ) *n.* **1. a.** any fibrous or soft substance used as padding, stuffing, etc., esp. sheets of carded cotton prepared for the purpose. **b.** a piece of this. **2.** material for wads used in cartridges or guns.

waddle ('wɒdᵊl) *vb.* (*intr.*) **1.** to walk with short steps, rocking slightly from side to side. ~*n.* **2.** a swaying gait or motion. [C16: probably frequentative of WADE] —'**waddler** *n.* —'**waddling** *adj.* —'**waddly** *adj.*

waddy ('wɒdɪ) *n., pl.* **-dies. 1.** a heavy wooden club used as a weapon by Australian Aborigines. ~*vb.* **-dies, -dying, -died. 2.** (*tr.*) to hit with a waddy. [C19: from a native Australian language, perhaps based on English WOOD]

wade (weɪd) *vb.* **1.** to walk with the feet immersed in (water, a stream, etc.): *the girls waded the river at the ford.* **2.** (*intr.*; often foll. by *through*) to proceed with difficulty: *to wade through a book.* **3.** (*intr.*; foll. by *in* or *into*) to attack energetically. ~*n.* **4.** the act or an instance of wading. [Old English *wadan;* related to Old Frisian *wada,* Old High German *watan,* Old Norse *vatha,* Latin *vadum* FORD] —'**wadable** *or* '**wadeable** *adj.*

wader ('weɪdə) *n.* **1.** a person or thing that wades. **2.** Also called: **wading bird.** any of various long-legged birds, esp. those of the order *Ciconiiformes* (herons, storks, etc.), that live near water and feed on fish, etc. **3.** a Brit. name for **shore bird.**

waders ('weɪdəz) *pl. n.* long waterproof boots, sometimes extending to the chest like trousers, worn by anglers.

wadi *or* **wady** ('wɒdɪ) *n., pl.* **-dies.** a watercourse in N Africa and Arabia, dry except in the rainy season. [C19: from Arabic]

wadmal ('wɒdməl) *n.* a coarse thick woollen fabric, formerly woven esp. in Orkney and Shetland, for outer garments. [C14: from Old Norse *vathmal,* from *vath* cloth + *mal* measure]

wadset ('wɒd,sɛt) *Scots Law.* ~*n.* **1.** another name for **mortgage.** ~*vb.* **-sets, -setting, -setted. 2.** (*tr.*) to pledge or mortgage. [C14: *wad,* a Scottish variant of WED + SET; compare Old English *wedd settan* to deposit a pledge]

wae (weɪ) *n., interj. Scot. and northern English* a dialect word for **woe.**

wafer ('weɪfə) *n.* **1.** a thin crisp sweetened biscuit with different flavourings, served with ice cream, etc. **2.** *Christianity.* a thin disc of unleavened bread used in the Eucharist as celebrated by the Western Church. **3.** *Pharmacol.* an envelope of rice paper enclosing a medicament. **4.** *Electronics.* a small thin slice of semiconductor material, such as silicon, that is separated into numerous individual components or circuits. **5.** a small thin disc of adhesive material used to seal letters, documents, etc. ~*vb.* **6.** (*tr.*) to seal, fasten, or attach with a wafer. [C14: from Old Northern French *waufre,* from Middle Low German *wāfel;* related to WAFFLE] —'**wafer-,like** *or* '**wafery** *adj.*

waff (wæf, wɑːf) *n. Scot. and northern English dialect.* **1.** a gust or puff of air. **2.** a glance; glimpse. ~*vb.* **3.** to flutter or cause to flutter. [C16: Scottish and northern English variant of WAVE]

waffle[1] ('wɒfᵊl) *n. Chiefly U.S. and Canadian.* **a.** a crisp golden-brown pancake with deep indentations on both sides. **b.** (*as modifier*): *waffle iron.* [C19: from Dutch *wafel* (earlier *wæfel*), of Germanic origin; related to Old High German *wabo* honeycomb]

waffle[2] ('wɒfᵊl) *Informal, chiefly Brit.* ~*vb.* **1.** (*intr.*; often foll. by *on*) to speak or write in a vague and wordy manner: *he waffled on for hours.* ~*n.* **2.** vague and wordy speech or writing. [C19: of unknown origin] —'**waffler** *n.* —'**waffling** *adj., n.* —'**waffly** *adj.*

waft (wɑːft, wɒft) *vb.* **1.** to carry or be carried gently on or as if on the air or water. ~*n.* **2.** the act or an instance of wafting. **3.** something, such as a scent, carried on the air. **4.** a wafting motion. **5.** Also called: **waif.** *Nautical.* (formerly) a signal flag hoisted furled to signify various messages depending on where it was flown. [C16 (in obsolete sense: to convey by ship): back formation from C15 *wafter* a convoy vessel, from Middle Dutch *wachter* guard, from *wachten* to guard; influenced by WAFF] —'**waftage** *n.*

wafter ('wɑːftə, 'wɒf-) *n.* a device that causes a draught.

wafture ('wɑːftʃə, 'wɒf-) *n. Archaic.* **1.** the act of wafting or waving. **2.** anything that is wafted.

wag[1] (wæg) *vb.* **wags, wagging, wagged. 1.** to move or cause to move rapidly and repeatedly from side to side or up and down. **2.** to move (the tongue) or (of the tongue) to be moved rapidly in talking, esp. in idle gossip. **3.** to move (the finger) or (of the finger) to be moved from side to side, in or as in admonition. **4.** *Slang.* to play truant (esp. in the phrase **wag it**). ~*n.* **5.** the act or an instance of wagging. [C13: from Old English *wagian* to shake; compare Old Norse *vagga* cradle]

wag[2] (wæg) *n.* a humorous or jocular person; wit. [C16: of uncertain origin] —'**waggery** *n.* —'**waggish** *adj.* —'**waggishly** *adv.* —'**waggishness** *n.*

WAG *international car registration for* West Africa Gambia.

wage (weɪdʒ) *n.* **1. a.** (*often pl.*) payment in return for work or services, esp. that made to workmen on a daily, hourly, weekly, or piece-work basis. Compare **salary. b.** (*as modifier*): *wage freeze.* **2.** (*pl.*) *Economics.* the portion of the national income accruing to labour as earned income, as contrasted with the unearned income accruing to capital in the form of rent, interest, and dividends. **3.** (*often pl.*) recompense, return, or yield. **4.** an obsolete word for **pledge.** ~*vb.* (*tr.*) **5.** to engage in. **6.** *Obsolete.* to pledge or wager. **7.** *Obsolete or Brit. dialect.* another word for **hire** (senses 1, 2). [C14: from Old Northern French *wagier* to pledge, from *wage,* of Germanic origin; compare Old English *weddian* to pledge, WED] —'**wageless** *adj.* —'**wagelessness** *n.*

wage determination *n.* the process of setting wage rates or establishing wage structures in particular situations.

wage differential *n.* the difference in wages between workers with different skills in the same industry or between those with comparable skills in different industries or localities.

wage earner *or U.S.* **wage worker** *n.* **1.** a person who works for wages, esp. as distinguished from one paid a salary. **2.** the person who earns money to support a household by working.

wage incentive *n.* additional wage payments intended to stimulate improved work performance.

wage-plug *n. Austral. informal, often derogatory.* a wage earner.

wager ('weɪdʒə) *n.* **1.** an agreement or pledge to pay an amount of money as a result of the outcome of an unsettled matter. **2.** an amount staked on the outcome of such a matter or event. **3. wager of battle.** (in medieval Britain) a pledge to do battle for a cause, esp. to decide guilt or innocence by single combat. **4. wager of law.** *English legal history.* a form of trial in which the accused offered to make oath of his innocence, supported by the oaths of 11 of his neighbours declaring their belief in his statements. ~*vb.* **5.** (when *tr., may take a clause as object*) to risk or bet (something) on the outcome of an unsettled matter. **6.** (*tr.*) *History.* to pledge oneself to (battle). [C14: from Anglo-French *wageure* a pledge, from Old Northern French *wagier* to pledge; see WAGE] —'**wagerer** *n.*

wage scale *n.* **1.** a schedule of wages paid to workers for various jobs in an industry, company, etc. **2.** an employer's schedule of wages.

wages council *n.* (in Britain) a statutory body empowered to fix minimum wages in an industry.

wage slave *n. Ironical.* a person dependent on a wage or salary.

wagga ('wɒgə) *n. Austral.* a blanket or bed covering made out of sacks stitched together. [C19: named after *Wagga Wagga*, city in New South Wales]

waggle ('wægᵊl) *vb.* **1.** to move or cause to move with a rapid shaking or wobbling motion. ~*n.* **2.** a rapid shaking or wobbling motion. [C16: frequentative of WAG] —'**wagglingly** *adv.* —'**waggly** *adj.*

waggler ('wæglə) *n. Angling.* a float only the bottom of which is attached to the line.

waggon ('wægən) *n., vb.* a variant spelling (esp. Brit.) of **wagon.**

Wagnerian (vɑːg'nɪərɪən) *adj.* **1.** of or suggestive of the dramatic musical compositions of the German composer Richard Wagner (1813–83), their massive scale, dramatic and emotional intensity, etc. **2.** denoting or relating to a singer who has a voice suitable for singing Wagner. **3.** of or relating to a big, powerful, or domineering woman: *a Wagnerian maiden.* ~*n. also* **Wagnerite. 4.** a follower or disciple of the music or theories of Richard Wagner.

wagon *or* **waggon** ('wægən) *n.* **1.** any of various types of wheeled vehicles, ranging from carts to lorries, esp. a vehicle with four wheels drawn by a horse, tractor, etc., and used for carrying crops, heavy loads, etc. **2.** *Brit.* a railway freight truck, esp. an open one. **3.** *U.S. and Canadian.* a child's four-wheeled cart. **4.** *U.S. and Canadian.* a police van for transporting prisoners and those arrested. **5.** *Chiefly U.S. and Canadian.* See **station wagon. 6.** an obsolete word for **chariot. 7. on** (*or* **off**) **the wagon.** *Informal.* abstaining (or no longer abstaining) from alcoholic drinks. ~*vb.* **8.** (*tr.*) to transport by wagon. [C16: from Dutch *wagen* WAIN] —'**wagonless** *or* '**waggonless** *adj.*

Wagon *or* **Waggon** ('wægən) *n.* **the.** another name for the **Plough.**

wagoner *or* **waggoner** ('wægənə) *n.* a person who drives a wagon.

wagonette *or* **waggonette** (ˌwægə'nɛt) *n.* a light four-wheeled horse-drawn vehicle with two lengthwise seats facing each other behind a crosswise driver's seat.

wagon-lit (*French* vagɔ̃li) *n., pl.* **wagons-lits** (vagɔ̃li). **1.** a sleeping car on a European railway. **2.** a compartment on such a car. [C19: from French, from *wagon* railway coach + *lit* bed]

wagonload *or* **waggonload** ('wægənˌləʊd) *n.* the load that is or can be carried by a wagon.

wagon soldier *n. U.S. slang.* a soldier belonging to the field artillery.

wagon train *n.* a supply train of horses and wagons, esp. one going over rough terrain.

wagon vault *n.* another name for **barrel vault.**

wagtail ('wægˌteɪl) *n.* any of various passerine songbirds of the genera *Motacilla* and *Dendronanthus*, of Eurasia and Africa, having a very long tail that wags when the bird walks: family *Motacillidae.*

Wahhabi *or* **Wahabi** (wə'hɑːbɪ) *n., pl.* **-bis.** a member of a strictly conservative Muslim sect founded in the 18th century with the aim of eliminating all innovations later than the 3rd century of Islam. —**Wah'habism** *or* **Wa'habism** *n.*

wahine (wɑː'hiːnɪ) *n.* (esp. in the Pacific islands) **1.** a Polynesian or Maori woman. **2.** an attractive girl, esp. one who visits beaches. [from Maori and Hawaiian]

wahoo[1] (wɑː'huː, 'wɑːhuː) *n., pl.* **-hoos.** an elm, *Ulmus alata*, of SE North America having twigs with winged corky edges. Also called: **winged elm.** [from Creek *ŭhawhu* cork elm]

wahoo[2] (wɑː'huː, 'wɑːhuː) *n., pl.* **-hoos.** an E North American shrub or small tree, *Euonymus atropurpureus*, with scarlet capsules and seeds. Also called: **burning bush.** [C19: from Dakota *wāhu* arrowwood]

wahoo[3] (wɑː'huː, 'wɑːhuː) *n., pl.* **-hoos.** a large fast-moving food and game fish, *Acanthocybium solandri*, of tropical seas: family *Scombridae* (mackerels and tunnies). [of unknown origin]

wah-wah ('wɑːˌwɑː) *n.* **1.** the sound made by a trumpet, cornet, etc., when the bell is alternately covered and uncovered: much used in jazz. **2.** an electronic attachment for an electric guitar, etc., that simulates this effect. [C20: of imitative origin]

waif (weɪf) *n.* **1.** a person, esp. a child, who is homeless, friendless, or neglected. **2.** anything found and not claimed, the owner being unknown. **3.** *Nautical.* another name for **waft** (sense 5). **4.** *Law, obsolete.* a stolen article thrown away by a thief in his flight and forfeited to the Crown or to the lord of the manor. [C14: from Anglo-Norman, variant of Old Northern French *gaif*, of Scandinavian origin; related to Old Norse *veif* a flapping thing] —'**waifˌlike** *adj.*

wail (weɪl) *vb.* **1.** (*intr.*) to utter a prolonged high-pitched cry, as of grief or misery. **2.** (*intr.*) to make a sound resembling such a cry: *the wind wailed in the trees.* **3.** (*tr.*) to lament, esp. with mournful sounds. ~*n.* **4.** a prolonged high-pitched mournful cry or sound. [C14: of Scandinavian origin; related to Old Norse *vǣla* to wail, Old English *wā* WOE] —'**wailer** *n.* —'**wailful** *adj.* —'**wailfully** *adv.*

wain (weɪn) *n. Chiefly poetic.* a farm wagon or cart. [Old English *wægn*; related to Old Frisian *wein*, Old Norse *vagn*]

wainscot ('weɪnskət) *n.* **1.** Also called: **wainscoting** *or* **wainscotting.** a lining applied to the walls of a room, esp. one of wood panelling. **2.** the lower part of the walls of a room, esp. when finished in a material different from the upper part. **3.** fine quality oak used as wainscot. ~*vb.* **4.** (*tr.*) to line (a wall of a room) with a wainscot. [C14: from Middle Low German *wagenschot*, perhaps from *wagen* WAGON + *schot* planking, related to German *Scheit* piece of wood]

wainwright ('weɪnˌraɪt) *n.* a person who makes wagons.

wairsh (werʃ) *adj. Scot.* a variant spelling of **wersh.**

waist (weɪst) *n.* **1.** *Anatomy.* the constricted part of the trunk between the ribs and hips. **2.** the part of a garment covering the waist. **3.** the middle part of an object that resembles the waist in narrowness or position. **4.** the middle part of a ship. **5.** Also called: **centre section.** the middle section of an aircraft fuselage. **6.** the constriction between the thorax and abdomen in wasps and similar insects. [C14: origin uncertain; related to Old English *wæstm* WAX[2]] —'**waistless** *adj.*

waistband ('weɪstˌbænd) *n.* an encircling band of material to finish and strengthen a skirt or trousers at the waist.

waistcloth ('weɪstˌklɒθ) *n. Obsolete.* another word for **loincloth.**

waistcoat ('weɪsˌkəʊt) *n.* **1.** a man's sleeveless waistlength garment worn under a suit jacket, usually buttoning up the front. U.S. and Canadian name: **vest. 2.** a man's garment worn under a doublet in the 16th century. —'**waistˌcoated** *adj.*

waisted ('weɪstɪd) *adj.* **a.** having a waist or waistlike part: *a waisted air-gun pellet.* **b.** (*in combination*): *high-waisted.*

waistline ('weɪstˌlaɪn) *n.* **1.** a line or indentation around the body at the narrowest part of the waist. **2.** the intersection of the bodice and the skirt of a dress, etc., or the level of this: *a low waistline.*

wait (weɪt) *vb.* **1.** (when *intr.*, often foll. by *for, until,* or *to*) to stay in one place or remain inactive in expectation (of something); hold oneself in readiness (for something). **2.** to delay temporarily or be temporarily delayed: *that work can wait.* **3.** (when *intr.*, usually foll. by *for*) (of things) to be in store (for a person): *success waits you in your new job.* **4.** (*intr.*) to act as a waiter or waitress. ~*n.* **5.** the act or an instance of waiting. **6.** a period of waiting. **7.** (*pl.*) *Rare.* a band of musicians who go around the streets, esp. at Christmas, singing and playing carols. **8.** an interlude or interval between two acts or scenes in a play, etc. **9. lie in wait.** to prepare an ambush (for someone). ~See also **wait on, wait up.** [C12: from Old French *waitier*; related to Old High German *wahtēn* to WAKE]

wait-a-bit *n.* any of various plants having sharp hooked thorns or similar appendages, esp. the greenbrier and the grapple plant.

Waitangi Day (waɪ'tʌŋiː) *n.* the national day of New Zealand (Feb. 6), commemorating the signing of the **Treaty of Waitangi** (1840) by Maori chiefs and a representative of the British Government. The treaty provided the basis for the British annexation of New Zealand.

waiter ('weɪtə) *n.* **1.** a man whose occupation is to serve at table, as in a restaurant. **2.** an attendant at the London Stock Exchange or Lloyd's who carries messages: the modern equivalent of waiters who performed these duties in the 17th-century London coffee houses in which these institutions originated. **3.** a person who waits. **4.** a tray or salver on which dishes, etc., are carried.

waiting game *n.* the postponement of action or decision in order to gain the advantage.

waiting list *n.* a list of people waiting to obtain some object, treatment, status, etc.

waiting room *n.* a room in which people may wait, as at a railway station, doctor's or dentist's office, etc.

wait on *vb.* (*intr., prep.*) **1.** to serve at the table of. **2.** to act as an attendant or servant to. **3.** *Archaic.* to visit. ~*interj.* **4.** *Austral. and N.Z.* stop! hold on! ~Also (for senses 1, 2, 3) **wait upon.**

waitress ('weɪtrɪs) *n.* a woman who serves at table, as in a restaurant.

wait up *vb.* (*intr., adv.*) **1.** to delay going to bed in order to await some event. **2.** *Informal, chiefly U.S. and Canadian.* to halt and pause in order that another person may catch up.

waive (weɪv) *vb.* (*tr.*) **1.** to set aside or relinquish: *to waive one's right to something.* **2.** to refrain from enforcing or applying (a law, penalty, etc.). **3.** to defer. [C13: from Old Northern French *weyver*, from *waif* abandoned; see WAIF]

waiver ('weɪvə) *n.* **1.** the voluntary relinquishment, expressly or by implication, of some claim or right. **2.** the act or an instance of relinquishing a claim or right. **3.** a formal statement in writing of such relinquishment. [C17: from Old Northern French *weyver* to relinquish, WAIVE]

Wakashan (wɑː'kæʃən, 'wɔːkəˌʃæn) *n.* **1.** a family of North American Indian languages of British Columbia and Washington, including Kwakiutl and Nootka. **2.** a speaker of any of these languages.

wake[1] (weɪk) *vb.* **wakes, waking, woke, woken. 1.** (often foll. by *up*) to rouse or become roused from sleep. **2.** (often foll. by *up*) to rouse or become roused from inactivity. **3.** (*intr.*; often foll. by *to* or *up to*) to become conscious or aware: *at last he woke* *to the situation.* **4.** (*intr.*) to be or remain awake. **5.** *Dialect.* to hold a wake over (a corpse). **6.** *Archaic or dialect.* to keep watch over. ~*n.* **7.** a watch or vigil held over the body of a dead person during the night before burial. **8.** (in Ireland) festivities held after a funeral. **9.** the patronal or dedication festival of English parish churches. **10.** a solemn or ceremonial vigil. **11.** (*usually pl.*) an annual holiday in any of various towns in northern England, when the local factory or factories close, usually for a week or two weeks. **12.** *Rare.* the state of being awake. [Old English *wacian;* related to Old Frisian *wakia,* Old High German *wahtēn*] —'**waker** *n.*

▷**Usage.** Where there is an object and the sense is the literal one *wake* (*up*) and *waken* are the commonest forms: *I wakened him; I woke him* (*up*). Both verbs are also commonly used without an object: *I woke up. Awake* and *awaken* are preferred to other forms of *wake* where the sense is a figurative one: *he awoke to the danger.*

wake[2] (weɪk) *n.* **1.** the waves or track left by a vessel or other object moving through water. **2.** the track or path left by anything that has passed: *wrecked houses in the wake of the hurricane.* [C16: of Scandinavian origin; compare Old Norse *vaka, vök* hole cut in ice, Swedish *vak,* Danish *vaage;* perhaps related to Old Norse *vökr,* Middle Dutch *wak* wet]

wakeful ('weɪkfʊl) *adj.* **1.** unable or unwilling to sleep. **2.** sleepless. **3.** alert. —'**wakefully** *adv.* —'**wakefulness** *n.*

wakeless ('weɪklɪs) *adj.* (of sleep) deep or unbroken.

waken ('weɪkən) *vb.* to rouse or be roused from sleep or some other inactive state. —'**wakener** *n.*

▷**Usage.** See at **wake**[1].

wakerife ('weɪkˌraɪf) *adj. Scot. and northern English dialect.* wakeful. [C15: from WAKE[1] + RIFE] —'**wakeˌrifeness** *n.*

wake-robin *n.* **1.** any of various North American herbaceous plants of the genus *Trillium,* such as *T. grandiflorum,* having a whorl of three leaves and three-petalled solitary flowers: family *Trilliaceae.* **2.** *U.S.* any of various aroid plants, esp. the cuckoopint.

wake-up *n. Austral. informal.* **1.** an alert or intelligent person. **2. a wake-up to.** fully alert to (a person, thing, action, etc.).

WAL *international car registration for* Sierra Leone. [from *W*(*est*) *A*(*frica*) *L*(*eone*)]

Wal. *abbrev. for* Walloon.

Walach ('wɑːlɒk) *n., adj.* a variant spelling of **Vlach.**

Waldenses (wɒl'dɛnsiːz) *pl. n.* the members of a small sect founded as a reform movement within the Roman Catholic Church by Peter Waldo, a merchant of Lyons in the late 12th century, which in the 16th century joined the Reformation movement. Also called: **Vaudois.** —**Waldensian** (wɒl'dɛnsɪən) *n., adj.*

waldgrave ('wɔːldˌgreɪv) *n.* (in medieval Germany) an officer with jurisdiction over a royal forest. [from German *Waldgraf,* from *Wald* forest + *Graf* count]

waldo ('wɔːldəʊ) *n., pl.* **-dos** *or* **-does.** a gadget for manipulating objects by remote control. [C20: named after *Waldo* F. Jones, inventor in a science-fiction story by Robert Heinlein]

Waldorf salad ('wɔːldɔːf) *n.* a salad of diced apples, celery, and walnuts mixed with mayonnaise. [C20: named after the *Waldorf-Astoria Hotel* in New York City]

waldsterben ('wɔːldˌstɜːbən) *n. Ecology.* the symptoms of tree decline in central Europe from the 1970s, considered to be caused by atmospheric pollution. [C20: from German *Wald* forest + *sterben* to die]

wale[1] (weɪl) *n.* **1.** the raised mark left on the skin after the stroke of a rod or whip. **2. a.** the weave or texture of a fabric, such as the ribs in corduroy. **b.** a vertical row of stitches in knitting. Compare **course** (sense 14). **3.** *Nautical.* **a.** a ridge of planking along the rail of a ship. **b.** See **gunwale.** ~*vb.* (*tr.*) **4.** to raise a wale or wales on by striking. **5.** to weave with a wale. [Old English *walu* WEAL; related to Old Norse *vala* knuckle, Dutch *wäle*]

wale[2] (weɪl) *Scot. and northern English dialect.* ~*n.* **1.** a choice. **2.** anything chosen as the best. ~*adj.* **3.** choice. ~*vb.* **4.** (*tr.*) to choose. [C14: from Old Norse *val* choice, related to German *Wahl*]

Waler ('weɪlə) *n. Chiefly Austral.* a saddle horse originating in New South Wales. [C19: from *Wales,* in *New South Wales*]

walk (wɔːk) *vb.* **1.** (*intr.*) to move along or travel on foot at a moderate rate; advance in such a manner that at least one foot is always on the ground. **2.** (*tr.*) to pass through, on, or over on foot, esp. habitually. **3.** (*tr.*) to cause, assist, or force to move along at a moderate rate: *to walk a dog.* **4.** (*tr.*) to escort or conduct by walking: *to walk someone home.* **5.** (*intr.*) (of ghosts, spirits, etc.) to appear or move about in visible form. **6.** (of inanimate objects) to move or cause to move in a manner that resembles walking. **7.** (*intr.*) to follow a certain course or way of life: *to walk in misery.* **8.** (*tr.*) to bring into a certain condition by walking: *I walked my shoes to shreds.* **9.** (*tr.*) to measure, survey, or examine by walking. **10.** (*intr.*) *Basketball.* to take more than two steps without passing or dribbling the ball. **11.** to disappear or be stolen: *where's my pencil? It seems to have walked.* **12. walk it.** to win easily. **13. walk the plank.** See **plank** (sense 4). **14. walk on air.** to be delighted or exhilarated. **15. walk tall.** *Chiefly U.S. and Canadian informal.* to have self-respect or pride. **16. walk the streets. a.** to be a prostitute. **b.** to wander round a town or city, esp. when looking for work or having nowhere to stay. ~*n.* **17.** the act or an instance of walking. **18.** the distance or extent walked. **19.** a manner of walking; gait. **20.** a place set aside for walking; promenade. **21.** a chosen profession or sphere of activity (esp. in the phrase **walk of life**). **22.** a foot race in which competitors walk. **23. a.** an arrangement of trees or shrubs in widely separated rows. **b.** the space between such rows. **24.** an enclosed ground for the exercise or feeding of domestic animals, esp. horses. **25.** *Chiefly Brit.* the route covered in the course of work, as by a tradesman or postman. **26.** a procession; march: *Orange walk.* **27.** *Obsolete.* the section of a forest controlled by a keeper. ~See also **walk away, walk into, walk off, walk out, walkover, walk through.** [Old English *wealcan;* related to Old High German *walchan,* Sanskrit *valgati* he moves] —'**walkable** *adj.*

walkabout ('wɔːkəˌbaʊt) *n.* **1.** a periodic nomadic excursion into the Australian bush made by an Aborigine. **2.** a walking tour. **3.** *Chiefly journalistic.* an occasion when celebrities, royalty, etc., walk among and meet the public. **4. go walkabout.** *Austral.* **a.** to wander through the bush. **b.** *Informal.* to be lost or misplaced. **c.** *Informal.* to lose one's concentration.

walk away *vb.* (*intr., adv.*) **1.** to leave, esp. callously and disregarding someone else's distress. **2. walk away with.** to achieve or win easily.

walker ('wɔːkə) *n.* **1.** a person who walks. **2.** Also called: **baby walker.** a tubular frame on wheels or castors to support a baby learning to walk. **3.** a similar support for walking, often with rubber feet, for use by disabled or infirm people.

walkie-talkie *or* **walky-talky** (ˌwɔːkɪ'tɔːkɪ) *n., pl.* **-talkies.** a small combined radio transmitter and receiver, usually operating on shortwave, that can be carried around by one person: widely used by the police, medical services, etc.

walk-in *adj.* **1.** (of a cupboard) large enough to allow a person to enter and move about in. **2.** *U.S.* (of a building or apartment) located so as to admit of direct access from the street. **3.** (of a flat or house) in a suitable condition for immediate occupation.

walking ('wɔːkɪŋ) *adj.* (of a person) considered to possess the qualities of something inanimate as specified: *he is a walking encyclopedia.*

walking bass (beɪs) *n. Jazz.* a simple accompaniment played by the double bass at medium tempo, usually consisting of ascending and descending tones or semitones, one to each beat.

walking delegate *n.* **1.** (in the U.S.) an agent appointed by a trade union to visit branches, check whether agreements are observed, and negotiate with employers. **2.** (in N.Z.) a trade union official who visits dispersed working areas on a wharf.

walking dragline *n.* a very large-capacity dragline mounted on feet or pads instead of tracks. See **dragline** (sense 2).

walking fern *or* **leaf** *n.* a North American fern, *Camptosorus rhizophyllus,* having sword-shaped fronds, the tips of which take root when in contact with the ground: family *Aspleniaceae.*

walking papers *pl. n. Slang, chiefly U.S. and Canadian.* notice of dismissal.

walking stick *n.* **1.** a stick or cane carried in the hand to assist walking. **2.** the usual U.S. name for **stick insect.**

walk into *vb.* (*intr., prep.*) to meet with unwittingly: *to walk into a trap.*

Walkman ('wɔːkmən) *n.. Trademark.* a small portable cassette player with light headphones.

walk off *vb.* **1.** (*intr.*) to depart suddenly. **2.** (*tr., adv.*) to get rid of by walking: *to walk off an attack of depression.* **3. walk (a person) off his feet.** to make (a person) walk so fast that he is exhausted. **4. walk off with. a.** to steal. **b.** to win, esp. easily.

walk-on *n.* **1. a.** a small part in a play or theatrical entertainment, esp. one without any lines. **b.** (*as modifier*): *a walk-on part.* ~*adj.* **2.** (of an aircraft or air service) having seats to be booked immediately before departure rather than in advance.

walk out *vb.* (*intr., adv.*) **1.** to leave without explanation, esp. in anger. **2.** to go on strike. **3. walk out on.** *Informal.* to abandon or desert. **4. walk out with.** *Brit., obsolete or dialect.* to court or be courted by. ~*n.* **walkout. 5.** a strike by workers. **6.** the act of leaving a meeting, conference, etc., as a protest.

walkover ('wɔːkˌəʊvə) *n.* **1.** *Informal.* an easy or unopposed victory. **2.** *Horse racing.* **a.** the running or walking over the course by the only contestant entered in a race at the time of starting. **b.** a race won in this way. ~*vb.* **walk over.** (*intr., mainly prep.*) **3.** (*also adv.*) to win a race by a walkover. **4.** *Informal.* to beat (an opponent) conclusively or easily. **5.** *Informal.* to take advantage of (someone).

walk socks *pl. n. N.Z.* knee-length stockings.

walk through *Theatre.* ~*vb.* **1.** (*tr.*) to act or recite (a part) in a perfunctory manner, as at a first rehearsal. ~*n.* **walk-through. 2.** a rehearsal of a part.

walk-up *n. U.S. and Canadian informal.* **a.** a block of flats having no lift. **b.** (*as modifier*): *a walk-up block.*

walkway ('wɔːkˌweɪ) *n.* **1.** a path designed, and sometimes landscaped, for pedestrian use. **2.** a passage or path connecting buildings. **3.** a passage or path, esp. one for walking over machinery, etc.

wall (wɔːl) *n.* **1. a.** a vertical construction made of stone, brick, wood, etc., with a length and height much greater than its thickness, used to enclose, divide, or support. **b.** (*as modifier*): *wall hangings.* Related adj.: **mural. 2.** (*often pl.*) a structure or rampart built to protect and surround a position or place for defensive purposes. 3. *Anatomy.* any lining, membrane, or investing part that encloses or bounds a bodily cavity or structure: *abdominal wall.* Technical name: **paries.** Related adj.: **parietal.** 4. *Mountaineering.* a vertical or almost vertical smooth rock face. 5. anything that suggests a wall in function or effect: *a wall of fire; a wall of prejudice.* 6. **bang one's head against a brick wall.** to try to achieve something impossible. 7. **drive** (*or* **push**) **to the wall.** to force into an awkward situation. 8. **go to the wall.** to be ruined; collapse financially. 9. **go** (*or* **drive**) **up the wall.** *Slang.* to become (or cause to become) crazy or furious. 10. **have one's back to the wall.** to be in a very difficult situation. 11. See **off-the-wall.** 12. See **wall-to-wall.** ~*vb.* (*tr.*) 13. to protect, provide, or confine with or as if with a wall. 14. (often foll. by *up*) to block (an opening) with a wall. 15. (often foll. by *in* or *up*) to seal by or within a wall or walls. [Old English *weall,* from Latin *vallum* palisade, from *vallus* stake] —**walled** *adj.* —ˈ**wall-less** *adj.* —ˈ**wall-ˌlike** *adj.*

wallaby (ˈwɒləbɪ) *n., pl.* **-bies** *or* **-by.** 1. any of various herbivorous marsupials of the genera *Lagorchestes* (**hare wallabies**), *Petrogale* (**rock wallabies**), *Protemnodon,* etc., of Australia and New Guinea, similar to but smaller than kangaroos: family *Macropodidae.* 2. **on the wallaby (track).** *Austral. slang.* (of a person) wandering about looking for work. [C19: from native Australian *wolabā*]

Wallaby (ˈwɒləbɪ) *n., pl.* **-bies.** a member of the international Rugby Union football team of Australia.

Wallace's line (ˈwɒlɪsɪz) *n.* the hypothetical boundary between the Oriental and Australasian zoogeographical regions, which runs between the Indonesian islands of Bali and Lombok, through the Macassar Strait, and SE of the Philippines. [C20: named after A. R. *Wallace* (1823–1913), British naturalist]

wallah *or* **walla** (ˈwɒlə) *n.* (*usually in combination*) *Informal.* a person involved with or in charge of (a specified thing): *the book wallah.* [C18: from Hindi *-wālā* from Sanskrit *pāla* protector]

wallaroo (ˌwɒləˈruː) *n., pl.* **-roos** *or* **-roo.** a large stocky Australian kangaroo, *Macropus* (or *Osphranter*) *robustus,* of rocky regions. [C19: from native Australian *wolarū*]

wall bars *pl. n.* a series of horizontal bars attached to a wall and used in gymnastics.

wallboard (ˈwɔːlˌbɔːd) *n.* a thin board made of materials, such as compressed wood fibres or gypsum plaster, between stiff paper, and used to cover walls, partitions, etc.

wall brown *n.* any of three species of brown butterfly, esp. the common *Lasiommata megera,* that habitually sun themselves on rocks and walls.

wall creeper *n.* a pink-and-grey woodpecker-like songbird, *Tichodroma muraria,* of Eurasian mountain regions: family *Sittidae* (nuthatches).

walled plain *n.* any of the largest of the lunar craters, having diameters between 50 and 300 kilometres.

wallet (ˈwɒlɪt) *n.* 1. a small folding case, usually of leather, for holding paper money, documents, etc. 2. a bag used to carry tools. 3. *Archaic, chiefly Brit.* a rucksack or knapsack. [C14: of Germanic origin; compare Old English *weallian,* Old High German *wallōn* to roam, German *wallen* to go on a pilgrimage]

walleye (ˈwɔːlˌaɪ) *n., pl.* **-eyes** *or* **-eye.** 1. a divergent squint. 2. opacity of the cornea. 3. an eye having a white or light-coloured iris. 4. (in some collies) an eye that is particoloured white and blue. 5. Also called: **walleyed pike.** a North American pike-perch, *Stizostedion vitreum,* valued as a food and game fish. 6. any of various other fishes having large staring eyes. [back formation from earlier *walleyed,* from Old Norse *vagleygr,* from *vage,* perhaps: a film over the eye (compare Swedish *vagel* sty in the eye) + *-eygr* -eyed, from *auga* eye; modern form influenced by WALL] —ˈ**wallˌeyed** *adj.*

wallflower (ˈwɔːlˌflaʊə) *n.* 1. Also called: **gillyflower.** a cruciferous plant, *Cheiranthus cheiri,* of S Europe, grown for its clusters of yellow, orange, brown, red, or purple fragrant flowers and naturalized on old walls, cliffs, etc. 2. any of numerous other cruciferous plants of the genera *Cheiranthus* and *Erysimum,* having orange or yellow flowers. 3. *Informal.* a person who stays on the fringes of a dance or party on account of lacking a partner or being shy.

wall fruit *n.* fruit grown on trees trained against a wall for the shelter and warmth it provides.

wall game *n.* a type of football played at Eton against a wall.

wallies (ˈwælɪz) *pl. n. Central Scot. dialect.* false teeth; dentures. [see WALLY[2]]

wall knot *n.* a knot forming a knob at the end of a rope, made by unwinding the strands and weaving them together.

wall lizard *n.* a small mottled grey lizard, *Lacerta muralis,* of Europe, N Africa, and SW Asia: family *Lacertidae.*

wall mustard *n.* another name for **stinkweed** (sense 1).

wall of death *n.* (at a fairground) a giant cylinder round the inside walls of which a motorcyclist rides.

Walloon (wɒˈluːn) *n.* 1. a member of a French-speaking people living chiefly in S Belgium and adjacent parts of France. Compare **Fleming.** 2. the French dialect of Belgium. ~*adj.* 3. of, relating to, or characteristic of the Walloons or their dialect. [C16: from Old French *Wallon,* from Medieval Latin: foreigner, of Germanic origin; compare Old English *wealh* foreign, WELSH]

wallop (ˈwɒləp) *vb.* **-lops, -loping, -loped.** 1. (*tr.*) *Informal.* to beat soundly; strike hard. 2. (*tr.*) *Informal.* to defeat utterly. 3. (*intr.*) *Dialect.* to move in a clumsy manner. 4. (*intr.*) (of liquids) to boil violently. ~*n.* 5. *Informal.* a hard blow. 6. *Informal.* the ability to hit powerfully, as of a boxer. 7. *Informal.* a forceful impression. 8. *Brit.* a slang word for **beer.** ~*vb., n.* 9. an obsolete word for **gallop.** [C14: from Old Northern French *waloper* to gallop, from Old French *galoper,* of unknown origin]

walloper (ˈwɒləpə) *n.* 1. a person or thing that wallops. 2. *Austral. slang.* a policeman.

walloping (ˈwɒləpɪŋ) *Informal.* ~*n.* 1. a thrashing. ~*adj.* 2. (intensifier): *a walloping drop in sales.*

wallow (ˈwɒləʊ) *vb.* (*intr.*) 1. (esp. of certain animals) to roll about in mud, water, etc., for pleasure. 2. to move about with difficulty. 3. to indulge oneself in possessions, emotion, etc.: *to wallow in self-pity.* 4. (of smoke, waves, etc.) to billow. ~*n.* 5. the act or an instance of wallowing. 6. a muddy place or depression where animals wallow. [Old English *wealwian* to roll (in mud); related to Latin *volvere* to turn, Greek *oulos* curly, Russian *valun* round pebble] —ˈ**wallower** *n.*

wallpaper (ˈwɔːlˌpeɪpə) *n.* 1. paper usually printed or embossed with designs for pasting onto walls and ceilings. ~*vb.* 2. to cover (a surface) with wallpaper.

wall pass *n. Soccer.* a movement in which one player passes the ball to another and sprints forward to receive the quickly played return. Also called: **one-two.**

wall pellitory *n.* See **pellitory** (sense 1).

wall pepper *n.* a small Eurasian crassulaceous plant, *Sedum acre,* having creeping stems, yellow flowers, and acrid-tasting leaves.

wall plate *n.* a horizontal timber member placed along the top of a wall to support the ends of joists, rafters, etc., and distribute the load.

wallposter (ˈwɔːlˌpəʊstə) *n.* (in China) a bulletin or political message painted in large characters on walls.

wall rock *n.* rock that is immediately adjacent to a mineral vein, fault, or igneous intrusion.

wall rocket *n.* any of several yellow-flowered European cruciferous plants of the genus *Diplotaxis,* such as *D. muralis,* that grow on old walls and in waste places.

wall rue *n.* a delicate fern, *Asplenium ruta-muraria,* that grows in rocky crevices and walls in North America and Eurasia.

Wall Street *n.* the embodiment of American finance. [from the name of the main street of the financial district of New York City]

wall-to-wall *adj.* 1. (of carpeting) completely covering a floor. 2. *Informal.* as far as the eye can see; widespread: *wall-to-wall sales in the high street shops.*

wally[1] (ˈweɪlɪ) *adj. Scot. archaic.* 1. fine, pleasing, or splendid. 2. robust or strong. [C16: of obscure origin]

wally[2] (ˈwælɪ) *adj. Central Scot. dialect.* 1. made of china: *a wally dug; a wally vase.* 2. lined with ceramic tiles: *a wally close.* ~See also **wallies.** [from obsolete dialect *wallow* faded, adjectival use of *wallow* to fade, from Old English *wealwian*]

wally[3] (ˈwɒlɪ) *n., pl.* **-lies.** *Slang.* a stupid person. [C20: shortened form of the given name *Walter*]

walnut (ˈwɔːlˌnʌt) *n.* 1. any juglandaceous deciduous tree of the genus *Juglans,* of America, SE Europe, and Asia, esp. *J. regia,* which is native to W Asia but introduced elsewhere. They have aromatic leaves and flowers in catkins and are grown for their edible nuts and for their wood. 2. the nut of any of these trees, having a wrinkled two-lobed seed and a hard wrinkled shell. 3. the wood of any of these trees, used in making furniture, panelling, etc. 4. a light yellowish-brown colour. ~*adj.* 5. made from the wood of a walnut tree: *a walnut table.* 6. of the colour walnut. [Old English *walh-hnutu,* literally: foreign nut; compare Old French *noux gauge* walnut, probably translation of Vulgar Latin phrase *nux gallica* (unattested) Gaulish (hence, foreign) nut]

Walpurgis Night (vælˈpʊəgɪs) *n.* the eve of May 1, believed in German folklore to be the night of a witches' sabbath on the Brocken, in the Harz Mountains. [C19: translation of German *Walpurgisnacht,* the eve of the feast day of St Walpurga, 8th-century abbess in Germany]

walrus (ˈwɔːlrəs, ˈwɒl-) *n., pl.* **-ruses** *or* **-rus.** a pinniped mammal, *Odobenus rosmarus,* of northern seas, having a tough thick skin, upper canine teeth enlarged as tusks, and coarse whiskers and feeding mainly on shellfish: family *Odobenidae.* [C17: probably from Dutch, from Scandinavian; compare Old Norse *hrosshvalr* (literally: horse whale) and Old English *horschwæl;* see HORSE, WHALE]

walrus moustache *n.* a long thick moustache drooping at the ends.

waltz (wɔːls) *n.* 1. a ballroom dance in triple time in which couples spin around as they progress round the room. 2. a piece of music composed for or in the rhythm of this dance. ~*vb.* 3. to dance or lead (someone) in or as in a waltz: *he waltzed her off her feet.* 4. (*intr.*) to move in a sprightly and self-assured manner. 5. (*intr.*) *Informal.* to succeed easily. [C18: from German *Walzer,* from Middle High German *walzen* to roll; compare WELTER] —ˈ**waltzˌlike** *adj.*

waltzer (ˈwɔːlsə) *n.* **1.** a person who waltzes. **2.** a fairground roundabout on which people are spun round and moved up and down as it revolves.

waltz Matilda *vb. Austral.* See **Matilda.**

wambenger (wɒmˈbɛŋə) *n. Austral.* another name for **tuan**[2]. [from a native Australian language]

wamble (ˈwɒmbəl) *Dialect, chiefly Brit.* ~*vb.* (*intr.*) **1.** to move unsteadily. **2.** to twist the body. **3.** to feel nausea. ~*n.* **4.** an unsteady movement. **5.** a sensation of nausea. [C14 *wamelen* to feel ill, perhaps of Scandinavian origin; compare Norwegian *vamla* to stagger] —ˈ**wambliness** *n.* —ˈ**wambly** *adj.*

wame (weɪm) *n. Scot. and northern English dialect.* the belly, abdomen, or womb. [C14: northern variant of WOMB]

wampum (ˈwɒmpəm) *n.* **1.** (formerly) money used by North American Indians, made of cylindrical shells strung or woven together, esp. white shells rather than the more valuable black or purple ones. **2.** *U.S. and Canadian informal.* money or wealth. ~Also called: **peag, peage.** [C17: short for *wampumpeag,* from Narraganset *wampompeag,* from *wampan* light + *api* string + *-ag* plural suffix]

wan (wɒn) *adj.* **wanner, wannest. 1.** unnaturally pale esp. from sickness, grief, etc. **2.** characteristic or suggestive of ill health, unhappiness, etc. **3.** (of light, stars, etc.) faint or dim. ~*vb.* **wans, wanning, wanned. 4.** to make or become wan. [Old English *wann* dark; related to *wanian* to WANE] —ˈ**wanly** *adv.* —ˈ**wanness** *n.*

WAN *abbrev. for:* **1.** wide area network. ~**2.** *international car registration for* (West Africa) Nigeria.

wanchancy (wɒnˈtʃænsɪ) *adj. Scot.* **1.** unlucky. **2.** dangerous; risky. **3.** uncanny; eerie. ~Compare **unchancy.** [C18: from *wanchance* ill luck, from *wan-* prefix expressing negation or privation + CHANCE]

wand (wɒnd) *n.* **1.** a slender supple stick or twig. **2.** a thin rod carried as a symbol of authority. **3.** a rod used by a magician, water diviner, etc. **4.** *Informal.* a conductor's baton. **5.** *Archery.* a marker used to show the distance at which the archer stands from the target. [C12: from Old Norse *vōndr;* related to Gothic *wandus* and English WEND] —ˈ**wand,like** *adj.*

wander (ˈwɒndə) *vb.* (*mainly intr.*) **1.** (*also tr.*) to move or travel about, in, or through (a place) without any definite purpose or destination. **2.** to proceed in an irregular course; meander. **3.** to go astray, as from a path or course. **4.** (of the mind, thoughts, etc.) to lose concentration or direction. **5.** to think or speak incoherently or illogically. ~*n.* **6.** the act or an instance of wandering. [Old English *wandrian;* related to Old Frisian *wandria,* Middle Dutch, Middle High German *wanderen*] —ˈ**wanderer** *n.* —ˈ**wandering** *adj., n.* —ˈ**wanderingly** *adv.*

wandering albatross *n.* a large albatross, *Diomedea exulans,* having a very wide wingspan and a white plumage with black wings.

wandering Jew *n.* **1.** any of several related creeping or trailing plants of tropical America, esp. *Tradescantia fluminensis* and *Zebrina pendula:* family *Commelinaceae.* **2.** *Austral.* a similar creeping plant of the genus *Commelina.*

Wanderjahr *German.* (ˈvandərjaːr) *n., pl.* ***-jahre*** (-jaːrə). (formerly) a year in which an apprentice travelled to improve his skills. [German, literally: wander year]

wanderlust (ˈwɒndə,lʌst) *n.* a great desire to travel and rove about. [German, literally: wander desire]

wanderoo (,wɒndəˈruː) *n., pl.* **-deroos.** a macaque monkey, *Macaca silenus,* of India and Sri Lanka, having black fur with a ruff of long greyish fur on each side of the face. [C17: from Sinhalese *vanduru* monkeys, literally: forest-dwellers, from Sanskrit *vānara* monkey, from *vana* forest]

wander plug *n.* an electrical plug on the end of a flexible wire, for insertion into any of a number of sockets.

wandoo (ˈwɒnduː) *n.* a eucalyptus tree, *Eucalyptus redunca,* of W Australia, having white bark and durable wood. [from a native Australian language]

wane (weɪn) *vb.* (*intr.*) **1.** (of the moon) to show a gradually decreasing portion of illuminated surface, between full moon and new moon. Compare **wax**[2] (sense 2). **2.** to decrease gradually in size, strength, power, etc. **3.** to draw to a close. ~*n.* **4.** a decrease, as in size, strength, power, etc. **5.** the period during which the moon wanes. **6.** the act or an instance of drawing to a close. **7.** a rounded surface or defective edge of a plank, where the bark was. **8. on the wane.** in a state of decline. [Old English *wanian* (vb.); related to *wan-,* prefix indicating privation, *wana* defect, Old Norse *vana*] —ˈ**waney** *or* ˈ**wany** *adj.*

wangle (ˈwæŋgᵊl) *Informal.* ~*vb.* **1.** (*tr.*) to use devious or illicit methods to get or achieve (something) for (oneself or another): *he wangled himself a salary increase.* **2.** to manipulate or falsify (a situation, action, etc.). ~*n.* **3.** the act or an instance of wangling. [C19: originally printers' slang, perhaps a blend of WAGGLE and dialect *wankle* wavering, from Old English *wancol;* compare Old High German *wankōn* to waver] —ˈ**wangler** *n.*

wank (wæŋk) *Taboo slang.* ~*vb.* **1.** (*intr.*) to masturbate. ~*n.* **2.** an instance of wanking. [of uncertain origin]

Wankel engine (ˈwæŋkᵊl) *n.* a type of four-stroke internal-combustion engine without reciprocating parts. It consists of one or more approximately elliptical combustion chambers within which a curved triangular-shaped piston rotates, by the explosion of compressed gas, dividing the combustion chamber into three gastight sections. [C20: named after Felix *Wankel* (1902–88), German engineer who invented it]

wanker (ˈwæŋkə) *n.* **1.** *Taboo slang.* a person who wanks; masturbator. **2.** *Derogatory slang.* a worthless fellow.

wanna (ˈwɒnə) *vb.* a spelling of **want to** intended to reflect a dialectal or informal pronunciation: *I wanna go home.*

want (wɒnt) *vb.* **1.** (*tr.*) to feel a need or longing for: *I want a new hat.* **2.** (when *tr., may take a clause as object or an infinitive*) to wish, need, or desire (something or to do something): *he wants to go home.* **3.** (*intr.;* usually used with a negative and often foll. by *for*) to be lacking or deficient (in something necessary or desirable): *the child wants for nothing.* **4.** (*tr.*) to feel the absence of: *lying on the ground makes me want my bed.* **5.** (*tr.*) to fall short by (a specified amount). **6.** (*tr.*) *Chiefly Brit.* to have need of or require (doing or being something): *your shoes want cleaning.* **7.** (*intr.*) to be destitute. **8.** (*tr.; often passive*) to seek or request the presence of: *you're wanted upstairs.* **9.** (*intr.*) to be absent. **10.** (*tr.; takes an infinitive*) *Informal.* should or ought (to do something): *you don't want to go out so late.* **11. want in** (*or* **out**). *Informal.* to wish to be included in (or excluded from) a venture. ~*n.* **12.** the act or an instance of wanting. **13.** anything that is needed, desired, or lacked: *to supply someone's wants.* **14.** a lack, shortage, or absence: *for want of common sense.* **15.** the state of being in need; destitution: *the state should help those in want.* **16.** a sense of lack; craving. [C12 (vb., in the sense: it is lacking), C13 (n.): from Old Norse *vanta* to be deficient; related to Old English *wanian* to WANE] —ˈ**wanter** *n.*

want ad *n. Informal.* a classified advertisement in a newspaper, magazine, etc., for something wanted, such as property or employment.

wanting (ˈwɒntɪŋ) *adj.* (*postpositive*) **1.** lacking or absent; missing. **2.** not meeting requirements or expectations: *you have been found wanting.* ~*prep.* **3.** without. **4.** *Archaic.* minus.

wanton (ˈwɒntən) *adj.* **1.** dissolute, licentious, or immoral. **2.** without motive, provocation, or justification: *wanton destruction.* **3.** maliciously and unnecessarily cruel or destructive. **4.** unrestrained: *wanton spending.* **5.** *Archaic or poetic.* playful or capricious. **6.** *Archaic.* (of vegetation, etc.) luxuriant or superabundant. ~*n.* **7.** a licentious person, esp. a woman. **8.** a playful or capricious person. ~*vb.* **9.** (*intr.*) to behave in a wanton manner. **10.** (*tr.*) to squander or waste. [C13 *wantowen* (in the obsolete sense: unmanageable, unruly): from *wan-* (prefix equivalent to UN-[1]; related to Old English *wanian* to WANE) + *-towen,* from Old English *togen* brought up, from *tēon* to bring up] —ˈ**wantonly** *adv.* —ˈ**wantonness** *n.*

wapentake (ˈwɒpən,teɪk, ˈwæp-) *n. English legal history.* a subdivision of certain shires or counties, esp. in the Midlands and North of England, corresponding to the hundred in other shires. [Old English *wǣpen(ge)tæc,* from Old Norse *vāpnatak,* from *vápn* WEAPON + *tak* TAKE]

wapiti (ˈwɒpɪtɪ) *n., pl.* **-tis.** a large deer, *Cervus canadensis,* with large much-branched antlers, native to North America and now also common in the South Island of New Zealand. Also called: **American elk.** [C19: from Shawnee, literally: white deer, from *wap* (unattested) white; from the animal's white tail and rump]

wappenshaw (ˈwæpənʃɔː, ˈwɒp-) *n.* (formerly) a muster of men in a particular area in Scotland to show that they were properly armed. [C16: from Northern English *wapen,* from Old Norse *vápn* WEAPON + *schaw* SHOW]

war (wɔː) *n.* **1.** open armed conflict between two or more parties, nations, or states. Related adj.: **belligerent. 2.** a particular armed conflict: *the 1973 war in the Middle East.* **3.** the techniques of armed conflict as a study, science, or profession. **4.** any conflict or contest: *a war of wits; the war against crime.* **5.** (*modifier*) of, relating to, resulting from, or characteristic of war: *a war hero; war damage; a war story.* **6. to have had a good war.** to have fulfilled one's potential for courageous, decisive, or heroic action or other qualities by wartime service, esp. in the armed forces. **7. in the wars.** *Informal.* (esp. of a child) hurt or knocked about, esp. as a result of quarrelling and fighting. ~*vb.* **wars, warring, warred. 8.** (*intr.*) to conduct a war. [C12: from Old Northern French *werre* (variant of Old French *guerre*), of Germanic origin; related to Old High German *werra*]

War. *abbrev. for* Warwickshire.

waragi (ˈwaragɪ, -dʒɪ) *n.* a Ugandan alcoholic drink made from bananas. [from Luganda]

waratah (,wɒrəˈtɑː) *n. Austral.* a proteaceous shrub, *Telopea speciosissima,* the floral emblem of New South Wales, having dark green leaves and large clusters of crimson flowers. [from a native Australian language]

warb (wɔːb) *n. Austral. slang.* a dirty or insignificant person. [C20: of unknown origin] —ˈ**warby** *adj.*

war baby *n.* a child born in wartime, esp. the illegitimate child of a soldier.

warble[1] (ˈwɔːbᵊl) *vb.* **1.** to sing (words, songs, etc.) with trills, runs, and other embellishments. **2.** (*tr.*) to utter in a song. **3.** *U.S.* another word for **yodel.** ~*n.* **4.** the act or an instance of warbling. [C14: via Old French *werbler* from Germanic; compare Frankish *hwirbilōn* (unattested), Old High German *wirbil* whirlwind; see WHIRL]

warble[2] (ˈwɔːbᵊl) *n. Vet. science.* **1.** a small lumpy abscess under the skin of cattle caused by infestation with larvae of the warble fly. **2.** a hard tumorous lump of tissue on a horse's back, caused by prolonged friction of a saddle. [C16: of uncertain origin] —'**warbled** *adj.*

warble fly *n.* any of various hairy beelike dipterous flies of the genus *Hypoderma* and related genera, the larvae of which produce warbles in cattle: family *Oestridae*.

warbler ('wɔːblə) *n.* **1.** a person or thing that warbles. **2.** any small active passerine songbird of the Old World subfamily *Sylviinae:* family *Muscicapidae*. They have a cryptic plumage and slender bill and are arboreal insectivores. **3.** Also called: **wood warbler.** any small bird of the American family *Parulidae*, similar to the Old World forms but often brightly coloured.

war bonnet *n.* a headband with trailing feathers, worn by certain North American Indian warriors as a headdress.

war bride *n.* a soldier's bride met as a result of troop movements in wartime, esp. a foreign national.

war chest *n. U.S.* a fund collected for a specific purpose, such as an election campaign.

war correspondent *n.* a journalist who reports on a war from the scene of action.

war crime *n.* a crime committed in wartime in violation of the accepted rules and customs of war, such as genocide, ill-treatment of prisoners of war, etc. —**war criminal** *n.*

war cry *n.* **1.** a rallying cry used by combatants in battle. **2.** a cry, slogan, etc., used to rally support for a cause.

ward (wɔːd) *n.* **1.** (in many countries) a district into which a city, town, parish, or other area is divided for administration, election of representatives, etc. **2.** a room in a hospital, esp. one for patients requiring similar kinds of care: *a maternity ward.* **3.** one of the divisions of a prison. **4.** an open space enclosed within the walls of a castle. **5.** *Law.* **a.** Also called: **ward of court.** a person, esp. a minor or one legally incapable of managing his own affairs, placed under the control or protection of a guardian or of a court. **b.** guardianship, as of a minor or legally incompetent person. **6.** the state of being under guard or in custody. **7.** a person who is under the protection or in the custody of another. **8.** a means of protection. **9. a.** an internal ridge or bar in a lock that prevents an incorrectly cut key from turning. **b.** a corresponding groove cut in a key. **10.** a less common word for **warden.** ~*vb.* **11.** (*tr.*) *Archaic.* to guard or protect. ~See also **ward off.** [Old English *weard* protector; related to Old High German *wart,* Old Saxon *ward,* Old Norse *vorthr*. See GUARD] —'**wardless** *adj.*

-ward *suffix.* **1.** (*forming adjectives*) indicating direction towards: *a backward step; heavenward progress.* **2.** (*forming adverbs*) a variant and the usual U.S. and Canadian form of **-wards.** [Old English *-weard* towards]

war dance *n.* **1.** a ceremonial dance performed before going to battle or after victory, esp. by certain North American Indian peoples. **2.** a dance representing warlike action.

warded ('wɔːdɪd) *adj.* (of locks, keys, etc.) having wards.

warden[1] ('wɔːdᵊn) *n.* **1.** a person who has the charge or care of something, esp. a building, or someone. **2.** *Archaic.* any of various public officials, esp. one responsible for the enforcement of certain regulations. **3.** *Chiefly U.S. and Canadian.* the chief officer in charge of a prison. **4.** *Brit.* the principal or president of any of various universities or colleges. **5.** See **churchwarden** (sense 1). [C13: from Old Northern French *wardein,* from *warder* to guard, of Germanic origin; see GUARD] —'**wardenry** *n.*

warden[2] ('wɔːdᵊn) *n.* a variety of pear that has crisp firm flesh and is used for cooking. [C15: of obscure origin]

warder[1] ('wɔːdə) *or* (*fem.*) **wardress** *n.* **1.** *Chiefly Brit.* an officer in charge of prisoners in a jail. **2.** a person who guards or has charge of something. [C14: from Anglo-French *wardere,* from Old French *warder* to GUARD, of Germanic origin] —'**wardership** *n.*

warder[2] ('wɔːdə) *n.* (formerly) a staff or truncheon carried by a ruler as an emblem of authority and used to signal his wishes or intentions. [C15: perhaps from Middle English *warden* to WARD]

ward heeler *n. U.S. politics, disparaging.* a party worker who canvasses votes and performs chores for a political boss. Also called: **heeler.**

wardian case ('wɔːdɪən) *n.* a type of glass container used for housing delicate ferns and similar plants. [C19: named after N. B. *Ward* (died 1868), English botanist]

wardmote ('wɔːdməʊt) *n. Brit.* an assembly of the citizens or liverymen of a ward. [C14: see WARD, MOOT]

ward off *vb.* (*tr., adv.*) to turn aside or repel; avert.

Wardour Street English ('wɔːdə) *n.* affectedly archaic speech or writing. [after a street in Soho, London, formerly noted for shops selling antiques]

wardrobe ('wɔːdrəʊb) *n.* **1.** a tall closet or cupboard, with a rail or hooks on which to hang clothes. **2.** the total collection of articles of clothing belonging to one person. **3.** the collection of costumes belonging to a theatre or theatrical company. [C14: from Old Northern French *warderobe,* from *warder* to GUARD + *robe* ROBE]

wardrobe mistress *n.* a person responsible for maintaining and sometimes making the costumes in a theatre.

wardrobe trunk *n.* a large upright rectangular travelling case, usually opening longitudinally, with one side having a hanging rail, the other having drawers or compartments.

wardroom ('wɔːdˌruːm, -ˌrʊm) *n.* **1.** the quarters assigned to the officers (except the captain) of a warship. **2.** the officers of a warship collectively, excepting the captain.

-wards *or* **-ward** *suffix forming adverbs.* indicating direction towards: *a step backwards; to sail shorewards.* Compare **-ward.** [Old English *-weardes* towards]

wardship ('wɔːdʃɪp) *n.* the state of being a ward.

ware[1] (wɛə) *n.* (*often in combination*) **1.** (*functioning as sing.*) articles of the same kind or material: *glassware; silverware.* **2.** porcelain or pottery of a specified type: *agateware; jasper ware.* ~See also **wares.** [Old English *waru;* related to Old Frisian *were,* Old Norse *vara,* Middle Dutch *Ware*]

ware[2] (wɛə) *Archaic.* ~*vb.* **1.** another word for **beware.** ~*adj.* **2.** another word for **wary** or **wise.** [Old English *wær;* related to Old Saxon, Old High German *giwar,* Old Norse *varr,* Gothic *war,* Latin *vereor*. See AWARE, BEWARE]

ware[3] (wɛə) *vb.* (*tr.*) *Northern Brit. dialect.* to spend or squander. [C15: of Scandinavian origin; related to Icelandic *verja*]

warehouse *n.* ('wɛəˌhaʊs). **1.** a place where goods are stored prior to their use, distribution, or sale. **2.** See **bonded warehouse.** **3.** *Chiefly Brit.* a large commercial, esp. wholesale, establishment. ~*vb.* ('wɛəˌhaʊz, -ˌhaʊs). **4.** (*tr.*) to store or place in a warehouse, esp. a bonded warehouse.

warehouseman ('wɛəˌhaʊsmən) *n., pl.* **-men.** a person who manages, is employed in, or owns a warehouse.

warehouse party *n.* a professionally organized large-scale party for young people, held in a disused warehouse. Compare **Acid-House party.**

warehousing ('wɛəˌhaʊzɪŋ) *n. Stock Exchange.* an attempt to maintain the price of a company's shares or to gain a significant stake in a company without revealing the true identity of the purchaser. Shares are purchased through an insurance company, a unit trust, or nominees.

wares (wɛəz) *pl. n.* **1.** articles of manufacture considered as being for sale. **2.** any talent or asset regarded as a commercial or saleable commodity. **3.** *Caribbean.* earthenware.

war establishment *n.* the full wartime complement of men, equipment, and vehicles of a military unit.

warfare ('wɔːˌfɛə) *n.* **1.** the act, process, or an instance of waging war. **2.** conflict, struggle, or strife.

warfarin ('wɔːfərɪn) *n.* a crystalline insoluble optically active compound, used as a rodenticide and, in the form of its sodium salt, as a medical anticoagulant. Formula: $C_{19}H_{16}O_4$. [C20: from the patent owners *W(isconsin) A(lumni) R(esearch) F(oundation)* + (COUM)ARIN]

war game *n.* **1.** a notional tactical exercise for training military commanders, in which no military units are actually deployed. **2.** a game in which model soldiers are used to create battles, esp. past battles, in order to study tactics.

warhead ('wɔːˌhɛd) *n.* the part of the fore end of a missile or projectile that contains explosives.

warhorse ('wɔːˌhɔːs) *n.* **1.** a horse used in battle. **2.** *Informal.* a veteran soldier, politician, or elderly person, esp. one who is aggressive.

warison ('wærɪsən) *n.* (esp. formerly) a bugle note used as an order to a military force to attack. [C13: from Old Northern French, from *warir* to protect, of Germanic origin; compare Old English *warian* to defend]

wark (wɑːrk, wɔːrk) *n.* a Scot. word for **work.**

Warks *abbrev. for* Warwickshire.

warlike ('wɔːˌlaɪk) *adj.* **1.** of, relating to, or used in war. **2.** hostile or belligerent. **3.** fit or ready for war.

warlock ('wɔːˌlɒk) *n.* **1.** a man who practises black magic; sorcerer. **2.** a fortune-teller, conjurer, or magician. [Old English *wǣrloga* oath breaker, from *wǣr* oath + *-loga* liar, from *lēogan* to LIE[1]]

warlord ('wɔːˌlɔːd) *n.* a military leader of a nation or part of a nation, esp. one who is accountable to nobody when the central government is weak: *the Chinese warlords.*

Warlpiri ('walpri) *n.* an Aboriginal language of central Australia.

warm (wɔːm) *adj.* **1.** characterized by or having a moderate degree of heat; moderately hot. **2.** maintaining or imparting heat: *a warm coat.* **3.** having or showing ready affection, kindliness, etc. *a warm personality.* **4.** lively, vigorous, or passionate: *a warm debate.* **5.** cordial or enthusiastic; ardent: *warm support.* **6.** quickly or easily aroused: *a warm temper.* **7.** (of colours) predominantly red or yellow in tone. **8.** (of a scent, trail, etc.) recently made; strong. **9.** near to finding a hidden object or discovering or guessing facts, as in children's games. **10.** *Informal.* uncomfortable or disagreeable, esp. because of the proximity of danger. ~*vb.* **11.** (sometimes foll. by *up*) to raise or be raised in temperature; make or become warm or warmer. **12.** (when *intr.,* often foll. by *to*) to make or become excited, enthusiastic, etc. (about): *he warmed to the idea of buying a new car.* **13.** (*intr.;* often foll. by *to*) to feel affection, kindness, etc. (for someone): *I warmed to her mother from the start.* **14.** (*tr.*) *Brit.* to give a caning to: *I'll warm you in a minute.* ~*n.* **15.** *Informal.* a warm place or area: *come into the warm.* **16.** *Informal.* the act or an instance of warming or being warmed. ~See also **warm over, warm up.** [Old English *wearm;* related to Old Frisian, Old Saxon *warm,* Old Norse *varmr*] —'**warmer** *n.* —'**warmish** *adj.* —'**warmly** *adv.* —'**warmness** *n.*

warm-blooded *adj.* **1.** ardent, impetuous, or passionate. **2.** *Zoology.* the nontechnical term for **homoiothermic.** —ˌ**warm-ˈbloodedness** *n.*
war memorial *n.* a monument, usually an obelisk or cross, to those who die in a war, esp. those from a particular locality.
warm front *n. Meteorol.* the boundary between a warm air mass and the cold air above, which is rising at a less steep angle than at the cold front. Compare **cold front, occluded front.**
warm-hearted *adj.* kindly, generous, or readily sympathetic. —ˌ**warm-ˈheartedly** *adv.* —ˌ**warm-ˈheartedness** *n.*
warming pan *n.* a pan, often of copper and having a long handle, filled with hot coals or hot water and formerly drawn over the sheets to warm a bed.
warmonger (ˈwɔːˌmʌŋgə) *n.* a person who fosters warlike ideas or advocates war. —ˈ**warˌmongering** *n.*
warm over *vb. (tr., adv.)* **1.** *U.S. and Canadian.* to reheat (food). **2.** *Informal.* to present (an idea, etc.) again, esp. without freshness or originality.
warm sector *n. Meteorol.* a wedge of warm air between the warm and cold fronts of a depression, which is eventually occluded. See also **cold front, warm front.**
warmth (wɔːmθ) *n.* **1.** the state, quality, or sensation of being warm. **2.** intensity of emotion: *he denied the accusation with some warmth.* **3.** affection or cordiality.
warm up *vb. (adv.)* **1.** to make or become warm or warmer. **2.** *(intr.)* to exercise in preparation for and immediately before a game, contest, or more vigorous exercise. **3.** to get ready for something important; prepare. **4.** to run or operate (an engine, etc.) until the normal working temperature or condition is attained, or (of an engine, etc.) to undergo this process. **5.** to make or become more animated or enthusiastic: *the party warmed up when Tom came.* **6.** to reheat (already cooked food) or (of such food) to be reheated. **7.** *(tr.)* to make (an audience) relaxed and receptive before a show, esp. a television comedy show. ~*n.* **warm-up. 8.** the act or an instance of warming up. **9.** a preparatory exercise routine.
warn (wɔːn) *vb.* **1.** to notify or make (someone) aware of danger, harm, etc. **2.** *(tr.; often takes a negative and an infinitive)* to advise or admonish (someone) as to action, conduct, etc.: *I warn you not to do that again.* **3.** *(takes a clause as object or an infinitive)* to inform (someone) in advance: *he warned them that he would arrive late.* **4.** *(tr.;* usually foll. by *away, off,* etc.) to give notice to go away, be off, etc.: *he warned the trespassers off his ground.* [Old English *wearnian;* related to Old High German *warnēn,* Old Norse *varna* to refuse] —ˈ**warner** *n.*
warning (ˈwɔːnɪŋ) *n.* **1.** a hint, intimation, threat, etc., of harm or danger. **2.** advice to beware or desist. **3.** an archaic word for **notice** (sense 6). ~*adj.* **4.** *(prenominal)* intended or serving to warn: *a warning look.* **5.** (of the coloration of certain distasteful or poisonous animals) having conspicuous markings, which predators recognize and learn to avoid; aposematic. —ˈ**warningly** *adv.*
war of nerves *n.* the use of psychological tactics against an opponent, such as shattering his morale by the use of propaganda.
warp (wɔːp) *vb.* **1.** to twist or cause to twist out of shape, as from heat, damp, etc. **2.** to turn or cause to turn from a true, correct, or proper course; pervert or be perverted. **3.** *(tr.)* to prepare (yarn) as a warp. **4.** *Nautical.* to move (a vessel) by hauling on a rope fixed to a stationary object ashore or (of a vessel) to be moved thus. **5.** *(tr.)* (formerly) to curve or twist (an aircraft wing) in order to assist control in flight. **6.** *(tr.)* to flood (land) with water from which alluvial matter is deposited. ~*n.* **7.** the state or condition of being twisted out of shape. **8.** a twist, distortion, or bias. **9.** a mental or moral deviation. **10.** the yarns arranged lengthways on a loom, forming the threads through which the weft yarns are woven. **11.** the heavy threads used to reinforce the rubber in the casing of a pneumatic tyre. **12.** *Nautical.* a rope used for warping a vessel. **13.** alluvial sediment deposited by water. [Old English *wearp* a throw; related to Old High German *warf,* Old Norse *varp* throw of a dragging net, Old English *weorpan* to throw] —ˈ**warpage** *n.* —**warped** *adj.* —ˈ**warper** *n.*
war paint *n.* **1.** painted decoration of the face and body applied by certain North American Indians before battle. **2.** *Informal.* finery or regalia. **3.** *Informal.* cosmetics.
warpath (ˈwɔːˌpɑːθ) *n.* **1.** the route taken by North American Indians on a warlike expedition. **2. on the warpath. a.** preparing to engage in battle. **b.** *Informal.* in a state of anger.
warplane (ˈwɔːˌpleɪn) *n.* any aircraft designed for and used in warfare. Also called (U.S.): **battle plane.**
warrant (ˈwɒrənt) *n.* **1.** anything that gives authority for an action or decision; authorization; sanction. **2.** a document that certifies or guarantees, such as a receipt for goods stored in a warehouse, a licence, or a commission. **3.** *Law.* an authorization issued by a magistrate or other official allowing a constable or other officer to search or seize property, arrest a person, or perform some other specified act. **4.** (in certain armed services) the official authority for the appointment of warrant officers. **5.** a security that functions as a stock option by giving the owner the right to buy ordinary shares in a company at a specified date, often at a specified price. ~*vb. (tr.)* **6.** to guarantee the quality, condition, etc., of (something). **7.** to give authority or power to. **8.** to attest to or assure the character, worthiness, etc., of. **9.** to guarantee (a purchaser of merchandise) against loss of, damage to, or misrepresentation concerning the merchandise. **10.** *Law.* to guarantee (the title to an estate or other property). **11.** to declare confidently. [C13: from Anglo-French *warrant,* variant of Old French *guarant,* from *guarantir* to guarantee, of Germanic origin; compare GUARANTY] —ˈ**warrantable** *adj.* —ˌ**warrantaˈbility** *n.* —ˈ**warrantably** *adv.* —ˈ**warranter** *n.* —ˈ**warrantless** *adj.*
warrantee (ˌwɒrənˈtiː) *n.* a person to whom a warranty is given.
warrant officer *n.* an officer in certain armed services who holds a rank between those of commissioned and noncommissioned officers. In the British army, the rank has two classes: see **regimental sergeant major, company sergeant major.**
Warrant of Fitness *n. N.Z.* a six-monthly certificate required for motor vehicles certifying mechanical soundness.
warrantor (ˈwɒrənˌtɔː) *n.* an individual or company that provides a warranty.
warrant sale *n. Scots Law.* a sale of someone's personal belongings or household effects that have been seized to meet unpaid debts.
warranty (ˈwɒrəntɪ) *n., pl.* **-ties. 1.** *Property law.* a covenant, express or implied, by which the vendor of real property vouches for the security of the title conveyed. **2.** *Contract law.* an express or implied term in a contract collateral to the main purpose, such as an undertaking that goods contracted to be sold shall meet specified requirements as to quality, etc. **3.** *Insurance law.* an undertaking by the party insured that the facts given regarding the risk are as stated. **4.** the act of warranting. [C14: from Anglo-French *warantie,* from *warantir* to warrant, variant of Old French *guarantir;* see WARRANT]
warren (ˈwɒrən) *n.* **1.** a series of interconnected underground tunnels in which rabbits live. **2.** a colony of rabbits. **3.** an overcrowded area or dwelling. **4. a.** *Chiefly Brit.* an enclosed place where small game animals or birds are kept, esp. for breeding, or a part of a river or lake enclosed by nets in which fish are kept (esp. in the phrase **beasts** or **fowls of warren**). **b.** *English legal history.* a franchise permitting one to keep animals, birds, or fish in this way. [C14: from Anglo-French *warenne,* of Germanic origin; compare Old High German *werien* to preserve]
warrener (ˈwɒrənə) *n. Obsolete.* a gamekeeper or keeper of a warren (sense 4).
warrigal (ˈwɒrɪgæl) *Austral.* ~*n.* **1.** a dingo. **2.** a wild horse. **3.** a wild Aboriginal. ~*adj.* **4.** untamed or wild. [C19: from a native Australian language]
warrior (ˈwɒrɪə) *n.* **a.** a person engaged in, experienced in, or devoted to war. **b.** *(as modifier): a warrior nation.* [C13: from Old Northern French *werreieor,* from *werre* WAR]
warship (ˈwɔːˌʃɪp) *n.* a vessel armed, armoured, and otherwise equipped for naval warfare.
warsle (ˈwɑːsəl) *n., vb.* a Scot. and northern English dialect word for **wrestle.** Also: **warstle.** —ˈ**warsler** *n.*
wart (wɔːt) *n.* **1.** Also called: **verruca.** *Pathol.* any firm abnormal elevation of the skin caused by a virus. **2.** *Botany.* a small rounded outgrowth. **3. warts and all.** with all blemishes evident. [Old English *weart(e);* related to Old High German *warza,* Old Norse *varta*] —ˈ**warted** *adj.* —ˈ**wartˌlike** *adj.* —ˈ**warty** *adj.*
wart cress *n.* either of two prostrate cruciferous annuals, *Coronopus squamatus* and *C. didymus,* having small white flowers. Also called: **swine's cress.**
wart hog *n.* a wild pig, *Phacochoerus aethiopicus,* of southern and E Africa, having heavy tusks, wartlike protuberances on the face, and a mane of coarse hair.
wartime (ˈwɔːˌtaɪm) *n.* **a.** a period or time of war. **b.** *(as modifier): wartime conditions.*
war whoop *n.* the yell or howl uttered, esp. by North American Indians, while making an attack.
wary (ˈwɛərɪ) *adj.* **warier, wariest. 1.** watchful, cautious, or alert. **2.** characterized by caution or watchfulness. [C16: from WARE^2 + -Y^1] —ˈ**warily** *adv.* —ˈ**wariness** *n.*
was (wɒz; *unstressed* wəz) *vb.* (used with *I, he, she, it,* and with singular nouns) **1.** the past tense (indicative mood) of **be. 2.** *Not standard.* a form of the subjunctive mood used in place of *were,* esp. in conditional sentences: *if the film was to be with you, would you be able to process it?* [Old English *wæs,* from *wesan* to be; related to Old Frisian, Old High German *was,* Old Norse *var*]
wash (wɒʃ) *vb.* **1.** to apply water or other liquid, usually with soap, to (oneself, clothes, etc.) in order to cleanse. **2.** *(tr.;* often foll. by *away, from, off,* etc.) to remove by the application of water or other liquid and usually soap: *she washed the dirt from her clothes.* **3.** *(intr.)* to be capable of being washed without damage or loss of colour. **4.** (of an animal such as a cat) to cleanse (itself or another animal) by licking. **5.** *(tr.)* to cleanse from pollution or defilement. **6.** *(tr.)* to make wet or moist. **7.** (often foll. by *away,* etc.) to move or be moved by water: *the flood washed away the bridge.* **8.** (esp. of waves) to flow or sweep against or over (a surface or object), often with a lapping sound. **9.** to form by erosion or be eroded: *the stream washed a ravine in the hill.* **10.** *(tr.)* to apply a thin coating of paint, metal, etc., to. **11.** *(tr.)* to separate (ore, precious stones, etc.) from (gravel, earth, or sand) by immersion in water. **12.** *(intr.; usually used with a negative) Informal, chiefly Brit.* to admit of testing or proof: *your excuses*

won't wash. **13. wash one's hands. a.** *Euphemistic.* to go to the lavatory. **b.** (usually foll. by *of*) to refuse to have anything more to do (with). ~*n.* **14.** the act or process of washing; ablution. **15.** a quantity of articles washed together. **16.** a preparation or thin liquid used as a coating or in washing: *a thin wash of paint; a hair wash.* **17.** *Med.* **a.** any medicinal or soothing lotion for application to a part of the body. **b.** (*in combination*): *an eyewash.* **18.** the flow of water, esp. waves, against a surface, or the sound made by such a flow. **19. a.** the technique of making wash drawings. **b.** See **wash drawing. 20.** the erosion of soil by the action of flowing water. **21.** a mass of alluvial material transported and deposited by flowing water. **22.** land that is habitually washed by tidal or river waters. **23.** the disturbance in the air or water produced at the rear of an aircraft, boat, or other moving object. **24.** gravel, earth, etc., from which valuable minerals may be washed. **25.** waste liquid matter or liquid refuse, esp. as fed to pigs; swill. **26.** an alcoholic liquid resembling strong beer, resulting from the fermentation of wort in the production of whisky. **27. come out in the wash.** *Informal.* to become known or apparent in the course of time. ~See also **wash down, wash out, wash up.** [Old English *wæscan, waxan;* related to Old High German *wascan;* see WATER]

Wash. *abbrev. for* Washington.

washable ('wɒʃəbᵊl) *adj.* (esp. of fabrics or clothes) capable of being washed without deteriorating. —,**washa'bility** *n.*

wash-and-wear *adj.* (of fabrics, garments, etc.) requiring only light washing, short drying time, and little or no ironing.

washaway ('wɒʃə,weɪ) *n. Austral.* another word for **washout** (sense 4).

washbasin ('wɒʃ,beɪsᵊn) *n.* a basin or bowl for washing the face and hands. Also called: **washbowl.**

washboard ('wɒʃ,bɔːd) *n.* **1.** a board having a surface, usually of corrugated metal, on which esp. formerly, clothes were scrubbed. **2.** such a board used as a rhythm instrument played with the fingers in skiffle, Country and Western music, etc. **3.** a less common U.S. word for **skirting board. 4.** *Nautical.* **a.** a vertical planklike shield fastened to the gunwales of a boat to prevent water from splashing over the side. **b.** Also called: **splashboard.** a shield under a port for the same purpose.

washcloth ('wɒʃ,klɒθ) *n.* **1.** another name for **dishcloth. 2.** the U.S. and Canadian word for **face cloth.**

washday ('wɒʃ,deɪ) *n.* a day on which clothes and linen are washed, often the same day each week.

wash down *vb.* (*tr., adv.*) **1.** to wash completely, esp. from top to bottom. **2.** to take drink with or after (food or another drink).

wash drawing *n.* a pen-and-ink drawing that has been lightly brushed over with water to soften the lines.

washed out *adj.* (**washed-out** *when prenominal*). **1.** faded or colourless. **2.** exhausted, esp. when being pale in appearance.

washed up *adj.* (**washed-up** *when prenominal*). *Informal, chiefly U.S., Canadian, and N.Z.* **1.** no longer useful, successful, hopeful, etc.: *our hopes for the new deal are all washed up.* **2.** exhausted.

washer ('wɒʃə) *n.* **1.** a person or thing that washes. **2.** a flat ring or drilled disc of metal used under the head of a bolt or nut to spread the load when tightened. **3.** any flat ring of rubber, felt, metal, etc., used to provide a seal under a nut or in a tap or valve seat. **4.** See **washing machine. 5.** *Chemical engineering.* a device for cleaning or washing gases or vapours; scrubber. **6.** *Austral.* a face cloth; flannel.

washerwoman ('wɒʃə,wʊmən), **washwoman,** *or* (*masc.*) **washerman** *n., pl.* **-women** *or* **-men.** a person who washes clothes for a living.

washery ('wɒʃərɪ) *n.* a plant at a mine where water or other liquid is used to remove dirt from a mineral, esp. coal.

wash house *n.* (formerly) a building or outbuilding in which laundry was done.

washin ('wɒʃɪn) *n. Aeronautics.* an increase in the angle of attack of an aircraft wing towards the wing tip. [C20: from WASH (flow) + IN]

washing ('wɒʃɪŋ) *n.* **1.** articles that have been or are to be washed together on a single occasion. **2.** liquid in which an article has been washed. **3.** something, such as gold dust or metal ore, that has been obtained by washing. **4.** a thin coat of something applied in liquid form.

washing machine *n.* a mechanical apparatus, usually powered by electricity, for washing clothing, linens, etc.

washing powder *n.* powdered detergent for washing fabrics.

washing soda *n.* the crystalline decahydrate of sodium carbonate, esp. when used as a cleansing agent.

Washington palm ('wɒʃɪŋtən) *n.* a palm tree, *Washingtonia filifera,* of California and Florida, having large fan-shaped leaves and small black fruits. Also called: **desert palm.**

washing-up *n. Brit.* **1.** the washing of dishes, cutlery, etc., after a meal. **2.** dishes and cutlery waiting to be washed up. **3.** (*as modifier*): *a washing-up machine.*

wash out *vb.* (*adv.*) **1.** (*tr.*) to wash (the inside of something) so as to remove (dirt). **2.** Also: **wash off.** to remove or be removed by washing: *grass stains don't wash out easily.* **3.** (*tr.*) to cancel or abandon (a sporting event). ~*n.* **washout. 4.** *Geology.* **a.** erosion of the earth's surface by the action of running water. **b.** a narrow channel produced by this erosion. **5.** *Informal.* **a.** a total failure or disaster. **b.** an incompetent person. **6.** *Aeronautics.* a decrease in the angle of attack of an aircraft wing towards the wing tip.

washrag ('wɒʃ,ræg) *n. U.S.* another word for **flannel** (sense 4).

washroom ('wɒʃ,ruːm, -,rʊm) *n.* **1.** a room, esp. in a factory or office block, in which lavatories, washbasins, etc., are situated. **2.** *U.S. and Canadian.* a euphemism for **lavatory.**

wash sale *n. U.S.* the illegal stock-exchange practice of buying and selling the same securities at an inflated price through a colluding broker to give the impression that the security has a strong market.

washstand ('wɒʃ,stænd) *n.* a piece of furniture designed to hold a basin, etc., for washing the face and hands.

washtub ('wɒʃ,tʌb) *n.* a tub or large container used for washing anything, esp. clothes.

wash up *vb.* (*adv.*) **1.** *Chiefly Brit.* to wash (dishes, cutlery, etc.) after a meal. **2.** (*intr.*) *U.S.* to wash one's face and hands. ~*n.* **washup. 3.** *Austral.* the end, outcome of a process: *in the washup, three candidates were elected.*

washwoman ('wɒʃ,wʊmən) *n., pl.* **-women.** a less common word for **washerwoman.**

washy ('wɒʃɪ) *adj.* **washier, washiest. 1.** overdiluted, watery, or weak. **2.** lacking intensity or strength. —'**washily** *adv.* —'**washiness** *n.*

wasn't ('wɒzᵊnt) *vb. contraction of* was not.

wasp (wɒsp) *n.* **1.** any social hymenopterous insect of the family *Vespidae,* esp. *Vespula vulgaris* (**common wasp**), typically having a black-and-yellow body and an ovipositor specialized for stinging. See also **potter wasp, hornet. 2.** any of various solitary hymenopterans, such as the digger wasp and gall wasp. [Old English *wæsp;* related to Old Saxon *waspa,* Old High German *wefsa,* Latin *vespa*] —'**wasp,like** *adj.* —'**waspy** *adj.* —'**waspily** *adv.* —'**waspiness** *n.*

Wasp *or* **WASP** (wɒsp) *n. U.S. and Canadian, often derogatory.* a person descended from N European, usually Protestant stock, forming a group often considered the most dominant, privileged, and influential in American society. [C20: *W(hite) A(nglo-) S(axon) P(rotestant)*]

waspish ('wɒspɪʃ) *adj.* **1.** relating to or suggestive of a wasp. **2.** easily annoyed or angered. —'**waspishly** *adv.* —'**waspishness** *n.*

wasp waist *n.* a very slender waist, esp. one that is tightly corseted. —'**wasp-,waisted** *adj.*

wassail ('wɒseɪl) *n.* **1.** (formerly) a toast or salutation made to a person at festivities. **2.** a festivity when much drinking takes place. **3.** alcoholic drink drunk at such a festivity, esp. spiced beer or mulled wine. **4.** the singing of Christmas carols, going from house to house. **5.** *Archaic.* a drinking song. ~*vb.* **6.** to drink the health of (a person) at a wassail. **7.** (*intr.*) to go from house to house singing carols at Christmas. [C13: from Old Norse *ves heill* be in good health; related to Old English *wes hāl;* see HALE[1]] —'**wassailer** *n.*

Wassermann test *or* **reaction** ('wæsəmən; *German* 'vasərman) *n. Med.* a diagnostic test for syphilis. See **complement fixation test.** [C20: named after August von *Wassermann* (1866–1925), German bacteriologist]

wast (wɒst; *unstressed* wəst) *vb. Archaic or dialect.* (used with the pronoun *thou* or its relative equivalent) a singular form of the past tense (indicative mood) of **be.**

wastage ('weɪstɪdʒ) *n.* **1.** anything lost by wear or waste. **2.** the process of wasting. **3.** reduction in size of a workforce by retirement, voluntary resignation, etc. (esp. in the phrase **natural wastage**).

waste (weɪst) *vb.* **1.** (*tr.*) to use, consume, or expend thoughtlessly, carelessly, or to no avail. **2.** (*tr.*) to fail to take advantage of: *to waste an opportunity.* **3.** (when *intr.,* often foll. by *away*) to lose or cause to lose bodily strength, health, etc. **4.** to exhaust or become exhausted. **5.** (*tr.*) to ravage. **6.** (*tr.*) *Informal.* to murder or kill: *I want that guy wasted by tomorrow.* ~*n.* **7.** the act of wasting or state of being wasted. **8.** a failure to take advantage of something. **9.** anything unused or not used to full advantage. **10.** anything or anyone rejected as useless, worthless, or in excess of what is required. **11.** garbage, rubbish, or trash. **12.** a land or region that is devastated or ruined. **13.** a land or region that is wild or uncultivated. **14.** *Physiol.* **a.** the useless products of metabolism. **b.** indigestible food residue. **15.** disintegrated rock material resulting from erosion. **16.** *Law.* reduction in the value of an estate caused by act or neglect, esp. by a life-tenant. ~*adj.* **17.** rejected as useless, unwanted, or worthless. **18.** produced in excess of what is required. **19.** not cultivated, inhabited, or productive: *waste land.* **20. a.** of or denoting the useless products of metabolism. **b.** of or denoting indigestible food residue. **21.** destroyed, devastated, or ruined. **22.** designed to contain or convey waste products. **23. lay waste.** to devastate or destroy. [C13: from Anglo-French *waster,* from Latin *vastāre* to lay waste, from *vastus* empty] —'**wastable** *adj.*

wastebasket ('weɪst,bɑːskɪt) *n.* another term (esp. U.S. and Canadian) for **wastepaper basket.**

wasted ('weɪstɪd) *adj.* **1.** not exploited or taken advantage of: *a wasted opportunity.* **2.** useless or unprofitable: *wasted effort.* **3.** physically enfeebled and emaciated: *a thin wasted figure.* **4.** *Slang.* showing signs of habitual drug abuse.

waste disposal unit *n.* an electrically operated fitment in the plughole of a kitchen sink that breaks up food refuse so that it goes down the waste pipe.
wasteful ('weɪstfʊl) *adj.* **1.** tending to waste or squander; extravagant. **2.** causing waste, destruction, or devastation. —'**wastefully** *adv.* —'**wastefulness** *n.*
waste heat recovery *n.* the use of heat that is produced in a thermodynamic cycle, as in a furnace, combustion engine, etc., in another process, such as heating feedwater or air.
wasteland ('weɪstˌlænd) *n.* **1.** a barren or desolate area of land, not or no longer used for cultivation or building. **2.** a region, period in history, etc., that is considered spiritually, intellectually, or aesthetically barren or desolate: *American television is a cultural wasteland.*
wastelot ('weɪstˌlɒt) *n. Chiefly Canadian.* a piece of waste ground in a city.
wastepaper ('weɪstˌpeɪpə) *n.* paper discarded after use.
wastepaper basket *or* **bin** *n.* an open receptacle for paper and other dry litter. Usual U.S. and Canadian word: **wastebasket.**
waste pipe *n.* a pipe to take excess or used water away, as from a sink to a drain.
waster ('weɪstə) *n.* **1.** a person or thing that wastes. **2.** a ne'er-do-well; wastrel. **3.** an article spoiled in manufacture.
wasteweir ('weɪstˌwɪə) *n.* another name for **spillway.**
wasting ('weɪstɪŋ) *adj.* (*prenominal*) reducing the vitality, strength, or robustness of the body: *a wasting disease.* —'**wastingly** *adv.*
wasting asset *n.* an unreplaceable business asset of limited life, such as a coal mine or an oil well.
wastrel ('weɪstrəl) *n.* **1.** a wasteful person; spendthrift; prodigal. **2.** an idler or vagabond.
wat (wɑːt) *n.* a Thai Buddhist monastery or temple. [Thai, from Sanskrit *vāta* enclosure]
watap (wæ'tɑːp, wɑː-) *n.* a stringy thread made by North American Indians from the roots of various conifers and used for weaving and sewing. [C18: from Canadian French, from Cree *watapiy*]
watch (wɒtʃ) *vb.* **1.** to look at or observe closely or attentively. **2.** (*intr.*; foll. by *for*) to wait attentively or expectantly. **3.** to guard or tend (something) closely or carefully. **4.** (*intr.*) to keep vigil. **5.** (*tr.*) to maintain an interest in: *to watch the progress of a child at school.* **6. watch it!** be careful! look out! ~*n.* **7. a.** a small portable timepiece, usually worn strapped to the wrist (a **wristwatch**) or in a waistcoat pocket. **b.** (*as modifier*): *a watch spring.* **8.** the act or an instance of watching. **9.** a period of vigil, esp. during the night. **10.** (formerly) one of a set of periods of any of various lengths into which the night was divided. **11.** *Nautical.* **a.** any of the usually four-hour periods beginning at midnight and again at noon during which part of a ship's crew are on duty. **b.** those officers and crew on duty during a specified watch. **12.** the period during which a guard is on duty. **13.** (formerly) a watchman or band of watchmen. **14. on the watch.** on the lookout; alert. ~See also **watch out.** [Old English *wæccan* (vb.), *wæcce* (n.); related to WAKE[1]]
-watch *suffix of nouns.* indicating a regular television programme or newspaper feature on the topic specified: *Crimewatch.*
watchable ('wɒtʃəbᵊl) *adj.* **1.** capable of being watched. **2.** interesting, enjoyable, or entertaining: *a watchable television documentary.*
watchband ('wɒtʃˌbænd) *n.* a U.S., Canadian, and Australian word for **watchstrap.**
watch cap *n.* a knitted navy-blue woollen cap worn by seamen in cold weather.
watchcase ('wɒtʃˌkeɪs) *n.* a protective case for a watch, generally of metal such as gold, silver, brass, or gunmetal.
watch chain *n.* a chain used for fastening a pocket watch to the clothing. See also **fob**[1].
watchdog ('wɒtʃˌdɒg) *n.* **1.** a dog kept to guard property. **2. a.** a person or group of persons that acts as a protector or guardian against inefficiency, illegal practices, etc. **b.** (*as modifier*): *a watchdog committee.*
watcher ('wɒtʃə) *n.* **1.** a person who watches. **2.** a person who maintains a vigil at the bedside of an invalid. **3.** *U.S.* a representative of a candidate or party stationed at a poll on election day to watch out for fraud.
watch fire *n.* a fire kept burning at night as a signal or for warmth and light by a person keeping watch.
watchful ('wɒtʃfʊl) *adj.* **1.** vigilant or alert. **2.** *Archaic.* not sleeping. —'**watchfully** *adv.* —'**watchfulness** *n.*
watch-glass *n.* **1.** a curved glass disc that covers the dial of a watch. **2.** a similarly shaped piece of glass used in laboratories for evaporating small samples of a solution, etc.
watchmaker ('wɒtʃˌmeɪkə) *n.* a person who makes or mends watches. —'**watchˌmaking** *n.*
watchman ('wɒtʃmən) *n., pl.* **-men. 1.** a person employed to guard buildings or property. **2.** (formerly) a man employed to patrol or guard the streets at night.
watch night *n.* **1.** (in Protestant churches) the night of December 31, during which a service is held to mark the passing of the old year and the beginning of the new. **2.** the service held on this night.
watch out *vb.* **1.** (*intr., adv.*) to be careful or on one's guard. ~*n.* **watchout. 2.** a less common word for **lookout** (sense 1).
watchstrap ('wɒtʃˌstræp) *n.* a strap of leather, cloth, etc., attached to a watch for fastening it around the wrist. Also called (U.S. and Canadian): **watchband.**
watchtower ('wɒtʃˌtaʊə) *n.* a tower on which a sentry keeps watch.
watchword ('wɒtʃˌwɜːd) *n.* **1.** another word for **password. 2.** a rallying cry or slogan.
water ('wɔːtə) *n.* **1.** a clear colourless tasteless odourless liquid that is essential for plant and animal life and constitutes, in impure form, rain, oceans, rivers, lakes, etc. It is a neutral substance, an effective solvent for many compounds, and is used as a standard for many physical properties. Formula: H_2O. Related adj.: **aqueous.** Related combining form: **hydro-. 2. a.** any body or area of this liquid, such as a sea, lake, river, etc. **b.** (*as modifier*): *water sports; water transport; a water plant.* Related adj.: **aquatic. 3.** the surface of such a body or area: *fish swam below the water.* **4.** any form or variety of this liquid, such as rain. **5.** See **high water, low water. 6.** any of various solutions of chemical substances in water: *lithia water; ammonia water.* **7.** *Physiol.* **a.** any fluid secreted from the body, such as sweat, urine, or tears. **b.** (*usually pl.*) the amniotic fluid surrounding a fetus in the womb. **8.** a wavy lustrous finish on some fabrics, esp. silk. **9.** *Archaic.* the degree of brilliance in a diamond. See also **first water. 10.** excellence, quality, or degree (in the phrase **of the first water**). **11.** *Finance.* **a.** capital stock issued without a corresponding increase in paid-up capital, so that the book value of the company's capital is not fully represented by assets or earning power. **b.** the fictitious or unrealistic asset entries that reflect such inflated book value of capital. **12.** (*modifier*) *Astrology.* of or relating to the three signs of the zodiac Cancer, Scorpio, and Pisces. Compare **air** (sense 18), **earth** (sense 10), **fire** (sense 24). **13. above the water.** *Informal.* out of trouble or difficulty, esp. financial trouble. **14. hold water.** to prove credible, logical, or consistent: *the alibi did not hold water.* **15. in deep water.** in trouble or difficulty. **16. make water. a.** to urinate. **b.** (of a boat, hull, etc.) to let in water. **17. pass water.** to urinate. **18. test the water.** See **test**[1] (sense 4). **19. throw** (*or* **pour**) **cold water on.** *Informal.* to be unenthusiastic about or discourage. **20. water under the bridge.** events that are past and done with. ~*vb.* **21.** (*tr.*) to sprinkle, moisten, or soak with water. **22.** (*tr.*; often foll. by *down*) to weaken by the addition of water. **23.** (*intr.*) (of the eyes) to fill with tears. **24.** (*intr.*) (of the mouth) to salivate, esp. in anticipation of food (esp. in the phrase **make one's mouth water**). **25.** (*tr.*) to irrigate or provide with water: *to water the land; he watered the cattle.* **26.** (*intr.*) to drink water. **27.** (*intr.*) (of a ship, etc.) to take in a supply of water. **28.** (*tr.*) *Finance.* to raise the par value of (issued capital stock) without a corresponding increase in the real value of assets. **29.** (*tr.*) to produce a wavy lustrous finish on (fabrics, esp. silk). ~See also **water down.** [Old English *wæter,* of Germanic origin; compare Old Saxon *watar,* Old High German *wazzar,* Gothic *watō,* Old Slavonic *voda;* related to Greek *hudōr*] —'**waterer** *n.* —'**waterish** *adj.* —'**waterless** *adj.* —'**water-ˌlike** *adj.*
waterage ('wɔːtərɪdʒ) *n. Brit.* the transportation of cargo by means of ships, or the charges for such transportation.
water back *n.* the U.S. name for **back boiler.**
water bag *n.* a bag, sometimes made of skin, leather, etc., but in Australia always canvas, for holding, carrying, and keeping water cool.
water bailiff *n.* an official responsible for enforcing laws on river management and fishing.
water-bath *n. Chem.* a vessel containing heated water, used for heating substances.
water bear *n.* another name for a **tardigrade.**
water bed *n.* a waterproof mattress filled with water.
water beetle *n.* any of various beetles of the families *Dysticidae, Hydrophilidae,* etc., that live most of the time in freshwater ponds, rivers, etc. See **whirligig beetle.**
water bird *n.* any aquatic bird, including the wading and swimming birds.
water biscuit *n.* a thin crisp plain biscuit, usually served with butter or cheese.
water blister *n.* a blister containing watery or serous fluid, without any blood or pus.
water boatman *n.* any of various aquatic bugs of the families *Notonectidae* and *Corixidae,* having a flattened body and oarlike hind legs, adapted for swimming.
waterborne ('wɔːtəˌbɔːn) *adj.* **1.** floating or travelling on water. **2.** (of a disease, etc.) transported or transmitted by water.
water bottle *n.* any of various types of container for drinking water, such as a skin or leather bag used in some countries, a glass bottle for table use, or a flask used by soldiers or travellers.
waterbrain ('wɔːtəˌbreɪn) *n. Vet. science.* another name for **gid.**
water brash *n. Pathol.* another term for **heartburn.**
waterbuck ('wɔːtəˌbʌk) *n.* any of various antelopes of the genus *Kobus,* esp. *K. ellipsiprymnus,* of swampy areas of Africa, having long curved ridged horns.
water buffalo *or* **ox** *n.* a member of the cattle tribe, *Bubalus bubalis,* of swampy regions of S Asia, having widely spreading back-curving horns. Domesticated forms are used as draught

animals. Also called: **Asiatic buffalo, Indian buffalo, carabao.**

water bug *n.* any of various heteropterous insects adapted to living in the water or on its surface, esp. any of the family *Belostomatidae* (**giant water bugs**), of North America, India, and southern Africa, which have flattened hairy legs.

water butt *n.* a barrel for collecting rainwater, esp. from a drainpipe.

water cannon *n.* an apparatus for pumping water through a nozzle at high pressure, used in quelling riots.

Water Carrier *or* **Bearer** *n.* **the.** the constellation Aquarius, the 11th sign of the zodiac.

water chestnut *n.* **1.** Also called: **water caltrop.** a floating aquatic onagraceous plant, *Trapa natans,* of Asia, having four-pronged edible nutlike fruits. **2. Chinese water chestnut.** a Chinese cyperaceous plant, *Eleocharis tuberosa,* with an edible succulent corm. **3.** the corm of the Chinese water chestnut, used in Oriental cookery.

water chinquapin *n.* a North American aquatic plant, *Nelumbo lutea,* having large umbrella-shaped leaves, pale yellow flowers, and edible nutlike seeds: family *Nelumbonaceae.* Compare **chinquapin.**

water clock *or* **glass** *n.* any of various devices for measuring time that use the escape of water as the motive force.

water closet *n.* **1.** a lavatory flushed by water. **2.** a small room that has a lavatory. ~Usually abbreviated to **WC.**

watercolour *or U.S.* **watercolor** (ˈwɔːtəˌkʌlə) *n.* **1. a.** Also called: **pure watercolour.** water-soluble pigment, applied in transparent washes and without the admixture of white pigment in the lighter tones. **b.** any water-soluble pigment, including opaque kinds such as gouache and tempera. **2. a.** a painting done in watercolours. **b.** (*as modifier*): *a watercolour masterpiece.* **3.** the art or technique of painting with such pigments. —ˈ**waterˌcolourist** *or U.S.* ˈ**waterˌcolorist** *n.*

water-cool *vb.* (*tr.*) to cool (an engine, etc.) by a flow of water circulating in an enclosed jacket. Compare **air-cool.** —ˈ**water-ˌcooled** *adj.* —ˈ**water-ˌcooling** *adj.*

water cooler *n.* a device for cooling and dispensing drinking water.

watercourse (ˈwɔːtəˌkɔːs) *n.* **1.** a stream, river, or canal. **2.** the channel, bed, or route along which this flows.

watercraft (ˈwɔːtəˌkrɑːft) *n.* **1.** a boat or ship or such vessels collectively. **2.** skill in handling boats or in water sports.

water crake *n.* another name for **spotted crake** and **dipper** (the bird).

watercress (ˈwɔːtəˌkrɛs) *n.* **1.** an Old World cruciferous plant, *Rorippa nasturtium-aquaticum* (or *Nasturtium officinale*), of clear ponds and streams, having pungent leaves that are used in salads and as a garnish. **2.** any of several similar or related plants.

water cure *n.* **1.** *Med.* a nontechnical name for **hydropathy** or **hydrotherapy. 2.** *Informal.* a form of torture in which the victim is forced to drink very large amounts of water.

water cycle *n.* the circulation of the earth's water, in which water evaporates from the sea into the atmosphere, where it condenses and falls as rain or snow, returning to the sea by rivers or returning to the atmosphere by evapotranspiration. Also called: **hydrologic cycle.**

water diviner *n. Brit.* a person able to locate the presence of water, esp. underground, with a divining rod. U.S. name: **waterfinder.**

water dog *n.* **1.** a dog trained to hunt in water. **2.** *Informal.* a dog or person who enjoys going in or on the water.

water down *vb.* (*tr., adv.*) **1.** to dilute or weaken with water. **2.** to modify or adulterate, esp. so as to omit anything harsh, unpleasant, or offensive: *to water down the truth.* —ˌ**watered-ˈdown** *adj.*

water dropwort *n.* See **dropwort** (sense 2).

waterfall (ˈwɔːtəˌfɔːl) *n.* a cascade of falling water where there is a vertical or almost vertical step in a river.

water flea *n.* any of numerous minute freshwater branchiopod crustaceans of the order *Cladocera,* which swim by means of hairy branched antennae. See also **daphnia.**

waterfowl (ˈwɔːtəˌfaʊl) *n.* **1.** any aquatic freshwater bird, esp. any species of the family *Anatidae* (ducks, geese, and swans). **2.** such birds collectively.

waterfront (ˈwɔːtəˌfrʌnt) *n.* the area of a town or city alongside a body of water, such as a harbour or dockyard.

water gap *n.* a deep valley in a ridge, containing a stream.

water gas *n.* a mixture of hydrogen and carbon monoxide produced by passing steam over hot carbon, used as a fuel and raw material. See also **producer gas.**

water gate *n.* **1.** a gate in a canal, leat, etc. that can be opened or closed to control the flow of water. **2.** a gate through which access may be gained to a body of water.

Watergate (ˈwɔːtəˌgeɪt) *n.* a public scandal, esp. involving politicians or a possible cover-up. See also **-gate.** [after the break-in at the Democratic Party headquarters in the *Watergate* building, Washington, DC, during the 1972 U.S. presidential campaign, that forced the resignation of President Richard Nixon]

water gauge *n.* an instrument that indicates the presence or the quantity of water in a tank, reservoir, or boiler feed. Also called: **water glass.**

water glass *n.* **1.** a viscous syrupy solution of sodium silicate in water: used as a protective coating for cement and a preservative, esp. for eggs. **2.** another name for **water clock** or **water gauge.**

water gum *n.* **1.** any of several gum trees, esp. *Nyssa biflora* (or *tupelo*), of swampy areas of North America: family *Nyssaceae.* **2.** any of several Australian myrtaceous trees, esp. *Tristania laurina,* of swampy ground.

water gun *n.* another term (esp. U.S.) for **water pistol.**

water hammer *n.* a sharp concussion produced when the flow of water in a pipe is suddenly blocked.

water hemlock *n.* another name for **cowbane** (sense 1).

water hen *n.* another name for **gallinule.**

water hole *n.* **1.** a depression, such as a pond or pool, containing water, esp. one used by animals as a drinking place. **2.** a source of drinking water in a desert.

water hyacinth *n.* a floating aquatic plant, *Eichhornia crassipes,* of tropical America, having showy bluish-purple flowers and swollen leafstalks: family *Pontederiaceae.* It forms dense masses in rivers, ponds, etc., and is a serious pest in the southern U.S., Java, Australia, New Zealand, and parts of Africa.

water ice *n.* an ice cream made from a frozen sugar syrup flavoured with fruit juice or purée; sorbet.

watering can *n.* a container with a handle and a spout with a perforated nozzle used to sprinkle water over plants.

watering hole *n.* **1.** a pool where animals drink; water hole. **2.** *Facetious slang.* a pub.

watering place *n.* **1.** a place where drinking water for men or animals may be obtained. **2.** *Brit.* a spa. **3.** *Brit.* a seaside resort.

watering pot *n.* another name (U.S.) for **watering can.**

water jacket *n.* a water-filled envelope or container surrounding a machine, engine, or part for cooling purposes, esp. the casing around the cylinder block of a pump or internal-combustion engine. Compare **air jacket.**

water jump *n.* a ditch, brook, or pond over which athletes or horses must jump in a steeplechase or similar contest.

water level *n.* **1.** the level reached by the surface of a body of water. **2.** the water line of a boat or ship.

water lily *n.* **1.** any of various aquatic plants of the genus *Nymphaea* and related genera, of temperate and tropical regions, having large leaves and showy flowers that float on the surface of the water: family *Nymphaeaceae.* **2.** any of various similar and related plants, such as the yellow water lily.

water line *n.* **1.** a line marked at the level around a vessel's hull to which the vessel will be immersed when afloat. **2.** a line marking the level reached by a body of water.

waterlogged (ˈwɔːtəˌlɒgd) *adj.* **1.** saturated with water. **2.** (of a vessel still afloat) having taken in so much water as to be unmanageable.

Waterloo (ˌwɔːtəˈluː) *n.* a total or crushing defeat (esp. in **meet one's Waterloo**). [after the battle (1815) fought near the Belgian town of Waterloo in which British and Prussian forces routed the French under Napoleon]

water louse *n.* an aquatic isopod of the genus *Asellus,* common in weedy water. Also called: **water slater.**

water main *n.* a principal supply pipe in an arrangement of pipes for distributing water.

waterman (ˈwɔːtəmən) *n., pl.* **-men.** a skilled boatman. —ˈ**watermanˌship** *n.*

watermark (ˈwɔːtəˌmɑːk) *n.* **1.** a distinguishing mark impressed on paper during manufacture, visible when the paper is held up to the light. **2.** another word for **water line** (senses 1, 2). ~*vb.* (*tr.*) **3.** to mark (paper) with a watermark.

water meadow *n.* a meadow that remains fertile by being periodically flooded by a stream.

water measurer *n.* a slender heteropterous bug, *Hydrometra stagnorum,* that has a greatly elongated head and is found on still or sluggish water where it preys on water fleas, mosquito larvae, etc.

watermelon (ˈwɔːtəˌmɛlən) *n.* **1.** an African melon, *Citrullus vulgaris,* widely cultivated for its large edible fruit. **2.** the fruit of this plant, which has a hard green rind and sweet watery reddish flesh.

water meter *n.* a device for measuring the quantity or rate of water flowing through a pipe.

water milfoil *n.* any of various pond plants of the genus *Myriophyllum,* having feathery underwater leaves and small inconspicuous flowers: family *Haloragidaceae.*

water mill *n.* a mill operated by a water wheel.

water mint *n.* a Eurasian mint plant, *Mentha aquatica,* of marshy places, having scented leaves and whorls of small flowers.

water moccasin *n.* a large dark grey venomous snake, *Agkistrodon piscivorus,* of swamps in the southern U.S.: family *Crotalidae* (pit vipers). Also called: **cottonmouth.**

water nymph *n.* **1.** any fabled nymph of the water. **2.** any of various aquatic plants, esp. a water lily or a naiad.

water of crystallization *n.* water present in the crystals of certain compounds. It is chemically combined in stoichiometric amounts, usually by coordinate or hydrogen bonds, but can often be easily expelled.

water ouzel *n.* another name for **dipper** (the bird).

water ox *n.* another term for **water buffalo.**

water paint *n.* any water-based paint, such as an emulsion or an acrylic paint.

water parting *n.* another term (esp. U.S.) for **watershed** (sense 1).

water pepper *n.* any of several polygonaceous plants of the genus *Polygonum*, esp. *P. hydropiper*, of marshy regions, having reddish stems, clusters of small greenish flowers, and acrid-tasting leaves.

water pimpernel *n.* another name for **brookweed.**

water pipe *n.* **1.** a pipe for water. **2.** another name for **hookah.**

water pistol *n.* a toy pistol that squirts a stream of water or other liquid. Also called (U.S.): **water gun.**

water plantain *n.* any of several marsh plants of the genus *Alisma*, esp. *A. plantago-aquatica*, of N temperate regions and Australia, having clusters of small white or pinkish flowers and broad pointed leaves: family *Alismataceae.*

water polo *n.* a game played in water by two teams of seven swimmers in which each side tries to throw or propel an inflated ball into the opponents' goal.

water power *n.* **1.** the power latent in a dynamic or static head of water as used to drive machinery, esp. for generating electricity. **2.** a source of such power, such as a drop in the level of a river, etc. **3.** the right to the use of water for such a purpose, as possessed by a water mill.

waterproof (ˈwɔːtəˌpruːf) *adj.* **1.** not penetrable by water. Compare **water-repellent, water-resistant.** *~n.* **2.** *Chiefly Brit.* a waterproof garment, esp. a raincoat. *~vb. (tr.)* **3.** to make (a fabric, item of clothing, etc.) waterproof.

water purslane *n.* **1.** an onagraceous marsh plant, *Ludwigia palustris*, of temperate and warm regions, having reddish stems and small reddish flowers. **2.** any of several lythraceous plants of wet places that resemble purslane, such as *Peplis portular* of Europe, which has small pinkish flowers, and *Didiplis diandris* of North America, which has small greenish flowers.

water rail *n.* a large Eurasian rail, *Rallus aquaticus*, of swamps, ponds, etc., having a long red bill.

water rat *n.* **1.** any of several small amphibious rodents, esp. the water vole or the muskrat. **2.** any of various amphibious rats of the subfamily *Hydromyinae*, of New Guinea, the Philippines, and Australia. **3.** *Informal.* a person who is very fond of water sports.

water-repellent *adj.* (of fabrics, garments, etc.) having a finish that resists the absorption of water.

water-resistant *adj.* (esp. of fabrics) designed to resist but not entirely prevent the penetration of water.

water right *n.* the right to make use of a water supply, as for irrigation.

water sapphire *n.* a deep blue variety of the mineral cordierite that occurs in Sri Lanka: used as a gemstone.

waterscape (ˈwɔːtəˌskeɪp) *n.* a picture, view, or representation of a body of water.

water scorpion *n.* any of various long-legged aquatic insects of the heteropterous family *Nepidae*, which breathe by means of a long spinelike tube that projects from the rear of the body and penetrates the surface of the water.

water seal *n.* a small amount of water contained in the trap of a drain to prevent the passage of foul smells.

watershed (ˈwɔːtəˌʃɛd) *n.* **1.** the dividing line between two adjacent river systems, such as a ridge. **2.** an important period or factor that serves as a dividing line.

water shield *n.* **1.** a North American nymphaeaceous plant, *Brasenia schreberi*, with floating oval leaves and purple flowers. **2.** any of several similar and related plants of the genus *Cabomba.*

water shrew *n.* either of two small amphibious shrews, *Neomys fodiens* (**European water shrew**) or *N. anomalus* (**Mediterranean water shrew**), having a dark pelage with paler underparts.

water-sick *adj.* (of land) made infertile or uncultivable by excessive irrigation.

waterside (ˈwɔːtəˌsaɪd) *n.* **a.** the area of land beside a body of water. **b.** (*as modifier*): *waterside houses.*

watersider (ˈwɔːtəˌsaɪdə) *n. Austral. and N.Z.* a wharf labourer.

water-ski *n. also* **water ski. 1.** a type of ski used for planing or gliding over water. *~vb.* **-skis, -skiing, -skied** *or* **-ski'd. 2.** (*intr.*) to ride over water on a water-ski or water-skis while holding a rope towed by a speedboat. —**ˈwater-ˌskier** *n.* —**ˈwater-ˌskiing** *n.*

water snake *n.* any of various colubrid snakes that live in or near water, esp. any of numerous harmless North American snakes of the genus *Natrix*, such as *N. sipedon.*

water-soak *vb. (tr.)* to soak or drench with or in water.

water softener *n.* **1.** any substance that lessens the hardness of water, usually by precipitating or absorbing calcium and magnesium ions. **2.** a tank, apparatus, or chemical plant that is used to filter or treat water to remove chemicals that cause hardness.

water soldier *n.* an aquatic plant, *Stratiotes aloides*, of Europe and NW Asia, having rosettes of large leaves and large three-petalled white flowers: family *Hydrocharitaceae.*

water spaniel *n.* either of two large curly-coated breeds of spaniel (the Irish and the American), which are used for hunting waterfowl. See also **Irish water spaniel.**

water spider *n.* a Eurasian spider, *Argyroneta aquatica*, that spins a web in the form of an air-filled chamber in which it lives submerged in streams and ponds.

water splash *n.* a place where a stream runs over a road.

water sports *pl. n.* various sports, such as swimming, water-skiing, or windsurfing, that take place in or on water.

waterspout (ˈwɔːtəˌspaʊt) *n.* **1.** *Meteorol.* **a.** a tornado occurring over water that forms a column of water and mist extending between the surface and the clouds above. **b.** a sudden downpour of heavy rain. **2.** a pipe or channel through which water is discharged, esp. one used for drainage from the gutters of a roof.

water starwort *n.* See **starwort** (sense 2).

water stick insect *n.* a slender sticklike flightless water bug, *Ranatra linearis*, that is predatory on small creatures such as water fleas.

water strider *or* **skater** *n.* another name for a **pond-skater.**

water supply *n.* **1.** an arrangement of reservoirs, purification plant, distribution pipes, etc., for providing water to a community. **2.** the supply of treated and purified water for a community.

water system *n.* **1.** a river and all its tributaries. **2.** a system for supplying water to a community.

water table *n.* **1.** the surface of the water-saturated part of the ground, usually following approximately the contours of the overlying land surface. **2.** an offset or string course that has a moulding designed to throw rainwater clear of the wall below.

water thrush *n.* either of two North American warblers, *Seiurus motacilla* or *S. noveboracensis*, having a brownish back and striped underparts and occurring near water.

watertight (ˈwɔːtəˌtaɪt) *adj.* **1.** not permitting the passage of water either in or out: *a watertight boat.* **2.** without loopholes: *a watertight argument.* **3.** kept separate from other subjects or influences: *different disciplines are often thought of in watertight compartments.* —**ˈwaterˌtightness** *n.*

water torture *n.* any of various forms of torture using water, esp. one in which water drips or is slowly poured onto the victim's forehead.

water tower *n.* a reservoir or storage tank mounted on a tower-like structure at the summit of an area of high ground in a place where the water pressure would otherwise be inadequate for distribution at a uniform pressure.

water tube boiler *n.* a steam generator consisting of water drums and steam drums connected by banks of tubes through which the water is circulated. The tubes are exposed to the hot gases of the furnace and the heat transfer rate is high.

water vapour *n.* water in the gaseous state, esp. when due to evaporation at a temperature below the boiling point. Compare **steam.**

water vole *n.* a large amphibious vole, *Arvicola terrestris*, of Eurasian river banks: family *Cricetidae.* Also called: **water rat.**

water wagtail *n.* another name for **pied wagtail.**

waterway (ˈwɔːtəˌweɪ) *n.* a river, canal, or other navigable channel used as a means of travel or transport.

waterweed (ˈwɔːtəˌwiːd) *n.* **1.** any of various weedy aquatic plants. **2.** another name for **pondweed** (sense 2).

water wheel *n.* **1.** a simple water-driven turbine consisting of a wheel having vanes set axially across its rim, used to drive machinery. **2.** a wheel with buckets attached to its rim for raising water from a stream, pond, etc.

water wings *pl. n.* an inflatable rubber device shaped like a pair of wings, which is placed round the front of the body and under the arms of a person learning to swim.

water witch *n.* a person who claims the ability to detect water underground by means of a divining rod.

waterworks (ˈwɔːtəˌwɜːks) *n.* **1.** (*functioning as sing.*) an establishment for storing, purifying, and distributing water for community supply. **2.** (*functioning as pl.*) a display of water in movement, as in fountains. **3.** (*functioning as pl.*) *Brit. informal euphemism.* the urinary system, esp. with reference to its normal functioning: *he has trouble with his waterworks.* **4.** (*functioning as pl.*) *Informal.* crying; tears.

waterworn (ˈwɔːtəˌwɔːn) *adj.* worn smooth by the action or passage of water.

watery (ˈwɔːtərɪ) *adj.* **1.** relating to, consisting of, containing, or resembling water. **2.** discharging or secreting water or a water-like fluid: *a watery wound.* **3.** tearful; weepy. **4.** insipid, thin, or weak. —**ˈwateriness** *n.*

watt (wɒt) *n.* the derived SI unit of power, equal to 1 joule per second; the power dissipated by a current of 1 ampere flowing across a potential difference of 1 volt. 1 watt is equivalent to 1.341×10^{-3} horsepower. Symbol: W [C19: named after James *Watt* (1736–1819), British engineer and inventor]

wattage (ˈwɒtɪdʒ) *n.* **1.** power, esp. electric power, measured in watts. **2.** the power rating, measured in watts, of an electrical appliance.

Watteau back (ˈwɒtəʊ) *n.* a section at the back of a woman's dress that is caught in pleats or gathers at the neck and falls unbelted to the floor. [from its resemblance to the costumes depicted by Antoine *Watteau* (1684–1721), French painter]

watt-hour *n.* a unit of energy equal to a power of one watt operating for one hour. 1 watt-hour equals 3600 joules.

wattle (ˈwɒtᵊl) *n.* **1.** a frame of rods or stakes interwoven with twigs, branches, etc., esp. when used to make fences. **2.** the material used in such a construction. **3.** a loose fold of skin, often brightly coloured, hanging from the neck or throat of certain birds, lizards, etc. **4.** any of various chiefly Australian acacia trees having spikes of small brightly coloured flowers and flexible branches, which were used by early settlers for making fences. See also **golden wattle.** **5.** a southern African caesalpinaceous tree, *Peltophorum africanum,* with yellow flowers. *~vb.* (*tr.*) **6.** to construct from wattle. **7.** to bind or frame with wattle. **8.** to weave or twist (branches, twigs, etc.) into a frame. *~adj.* **9.** made of, formed by, or covered with wattle. [Old English *watol;* related to *wethel* wrap, Old High German *wadal,* German *Wedel*] —'**wattled** *adj.*

wattle and daub *n.* **a.** a form of wall construction consisting of interwoven twigs plastered with a mixture of clay, lime, water, and sometimes dung and chopped straw. **b.** (*as modifier*): *a wattle-and-daub hut.*

wattlebird ('wɒtᵊl,bɜːd) *n.* **1.** any of various Australian honeyeaters of the genus *Anthochaera,* such as *A. paradoxa* (**yellow wattlebird**), that have red or yellow wattles on both sides of the head. **2.** any arboreal New Zealand songbird of the family *Callaeidae,* having wattles on both sides of the bill.

wattmeter ('wɒt,miːtə) *n.* a meter for measuring electric power in watts.

Watusi (wə'tuːzɪ) *or* **Watutsi** (wə'tʊtsɪ) *n., pl.* **-sis** *or* **-si.** a member of a cattle-owning Negroid people of Rwanda and Burundi in Africa.

wauk[1] (wɔːk) *vb.* a Scot. word for **wake**[1].

wauk[2] *or* **waulk** (wɔːk) *vb.* (*tr.*) *Scot.* to full (cloth). [C15: variant of WALK]

waukrife ('wɔːk,raɪf) *adj. Scot.* a variant of **wakerife.**

waul *or* **wawl** (wɔːl) *vb.* (*intr.*) to cry or wail plaintively like a cat. [C16: of imitative origin]

waur[1] (wɔːr) *adj., n., adv.* a Scot. word for **worse.**

waur[2] (wɔːr) *adj.* a Scot. word for **wary.**

wave (weɪv) *vb.* **1.** to move or cause to move freely to and fro: *the banner waved in the wind.* **2.** (*intr.*) to move the hand to and fro as a greeting. **3.** to signal or signify by or as if by waving something. **4.** (*tr.*) to direct to move by or as if by waving something: *he waved me on.* **5.** to form or be formed into curves, undulations, etc. **6.** (*tr.*) to give a wavy or watered appearance to (silk, etc.). **7.** (*tr.*) to set waves in (the hair). *~n.* **8.** one of a sequence of ridges or undulations that moves across the surface of a body of a liquid, esp. the sea: created by the wind or a moving object and gravity. **9.** any undulation on or at the edge of a surface reminiscent of such a wave: *a wave across the field of corn.* **10. the waves.** the sea. **11.** anything that suggests the movement of a wave, as by a sudden rise: *a crime wave.* **12.** a widespread movement that advances in a body: *a wave of settlers swept into the country.* **13.** the act or an instance of waving. **14.** *Physics.* an oscillation propagated through a medium or space such that energy is periodically interchanged between two kinds of disturbance. For example, an oscillating electric field generates a magnetic oscillation and vice versa, hence an electromagnetic wave is produced. Similarly a wave on a liquid comprises vertical and horizontal displacements. See also **antinode, longitudinal wave, node, standing wave, transverse wave.** **15.** *Physics.* a graphical representation of a wave obtained by plotting the magnitude of the disturbance against time at a particular point in the medium or space; waveform. **16.** a prolonged spell of some weather condition: *a heat wave.* **17.** an undulating curve or series of curves or loose curls in the hair. **18.** an undulating pattern or finish on a fabric. **19.** short for **wave moth.** **20. make waves.** to cause trouble; disturb the status quo. [Old English *wafian* (vb.); related to Old High German *weban* to WEAVE, Old Norse *vafra;* see WAVER; C16 (n.) changed from earlier *wāwe,* probably from Old English *wǣg* motion; compare WAG[1]] —'**waveless** *adj.* —'**wave,like** *adj.*

waveband ('weɪv,bænd) *n.* a range of wavelengths or frequencies used for a particular type of radio transmission.

wave-cut platform *n.* a flat surface at the base of a cliff formed by erosion by waves.

wave down *vb.* (*tr., adv.*) to signal with a wave to (a driver or vehicle) to stop.

wave energy *n.* energy obtained by harnessing wave power.

wave equation *n. Physics.* a partial differential equation describing wave motion. It has the form $\nabla^2\phi = (1/c^2) \times (\partial^2\phi/\partial t^2)$, where ∇^2 is the Laplace operator, t the time, c the velocity of propagation, and ϕ is a function characterizing the displacement of the wave.

waveform ('weɪv,fɔːm) *n. Physics.* the shape of the graph of a wave or oscillation obtained by plotting the value of some changing quantity against time.

wavefront ('weɪv,frʌnt) *n. Physics.* a surface associated with a propagating wave and passing through all points in the wave that have the same phase. It is usually perpendicular to the direction of propagation.

wave function *n. Physics.* a mathematical function of position and sometimes time, used in wave mechanics to describe the state of a physical system. Symbol: ψ

waveguide ('weɪv,gaɪd) *n. Electronics.* a solid rod of dielectric or a hollow metal tube, usually of rectangular cross section, used as a path to guide microwaves.

wavelength ('weɪv,lɛŋθ) *n.* **1.** the distance, measured in the direction of propagation, between two points of the same phase in consecutive cycles of a wave. Symbol: λ **2.** the wavelength of the carrier wave used by a particular broadcasting station. **3. on someone's** (*or* **the same**) **wavelength.** *Informal.* having similar views, feelings, or thoughts (as someone else).

wavelet ('weɪvlɪt) *n.* a small wave.

wavellite ('weɪvə,laɪt) *n.* a greyish-white, yellow, or brown mineral consisting of hydrated basic aluminium phosphate in radiating clusters of small orthorhombic crystals. Formula: $Al_3(OH)_3(PO_4)_2.5H_2O$. [C19: named after William *Wavell* (died 1829), British physician]

wave mechanics *n.* (*functioning as sing.*) *Physics.* the formulation of quantum mechanics in which the behaviour of systems, such as atoms, is described in terms of their wave functions.

wavemeter ('weɪv,miːtə) *n.* an instrument for measuring the frequency or wavelength of radio waves.

wave moth *n.* any of several small geometrid moths with wavy markings, such as the **common wave** (*Deilinia exanthemata*), with grey-marked wings, and the lighter **common white wave** (*D. pusaria*). Often shortened to **wave.**

wave number *n. Physics.* the reciprocal of the wavelength of a wave. Symbol: ν, σ

waveoff ('weɪv,ɒf) *n.* a signal or instruction to an aircraft not to land.

wave power *n.* power extracted from the motion of sea waves at the coast.

waver ('weɪvə) *vb.* (*intr.*) **1.** to be irresolute; hesitate between two possibilities. **2.** to become unsteady. **3.** to fluctuate or vary. **4.** to move back and forth or one way and another. **5.** (of light) to flicker or flash. *~n.* **6.** the act or an instance of wavering. [C14: from Old Norse *vafra* to flicker; related to German *wabern* to move about] —'**waverer** *n.* —'**wavering** *adj.* —'**waveringly** *adv.*

WAVES *or* **Waves** (weɪvz) *n.* (in the U.S.) *acronym for* Women Accepted for Volunteer Emergency Service; the women's reserve of the U.S. navy.

wave speed *or* **velocity** *n.* other names for **phase speed.**

wave theory *n.* **1.** the theory proposed by the Dutch physicist Christiaan Huygens (1629–95) that light is transmitted by waves. **2.** any theory that light or other radiation is transmitted as waves. See **electromagnetic wave.** ~Compare **corpuscular theory.**

wave train *n. Physics.* a series of waves travelling in the same direction and spaced at regular intervals.

wavey ('weɪvɪ) *n. Canadian.* a snow goose or other wild goose. Also called: **wawa.** [via Canadian French from Algonquian (Cree *wehwew*)]

wavy ('weɪvɪ) *adj.* **wavier, waviest.** **1.** abounding in or full of waves. **2.** moving or proceeding in waves or undulations. **3.** (of hair) set in or having waves and curls. **4.** unstable or wavering. —'**wavily** *adv.* —'**waviness** *n.*

waw (wɔː) *n.* another name for **vav.**

wawa[1] ('wɑː,wɑː) *Canadian W coast slang.* *~n.* **1.** speech; language. *~vb.* **2.** (*intr.*) to speak. [C19: from Chinook Jargon; probably of imitative origin]

wawa[2] ('wɑː,wɑː, 'wɑːwə) *n. Canadian.* a variant of **wavey.**

wawl (wɔːl) *vb.* a variant spelling of **waul.**

wax[1] (wæks) *n.* **1.** any of various viscous or solid materials of natural origin: characteristically lustrous, insoluble in water, and having a low softening temperature, they consist largely of esters of fatty acids. **2.** any of various similar substances, such as paraffin wax or ozocerite, that have a mineral origin and consist largely of hydrocarbons. **3.** short for **beeswax** or **sealing wax.** **4.** *Physiol.* another name for **cerumen.** **5.** a resinous preparation used by shoemakers to rub on thread. **6. bone wax.** a mixture of wax, oil, and carbolic acid applied to the cut surface of a bone to prevent bleeding. **7.** any substance or object that is pliable or easily moulded: *he was wax in the hands of the political bosses.* **8.** (*modifier*) made of or resembling wax: *a wax figure.* **9. put on wax.** to make a gramophone record of. *~vb.* **10.** (*tr.*) to coat, polish, etc., with wax. **11.** (*tr.*) *Informal.* to make a gramophone record of. [Old English *weax,* related to Old Saxon, Old High German *wahs,* Old Norse *vax*] —'**waxer** *n.* —'**wax,like** *adj.*

wax[2] (wæks) *vb.* (*intr.*) **1.** to become larger, more powerful, etc. **2.** (of the moon) to show a gradually increasing portion of illuminated surface, between new moon and full moon. Compare **wane** (sense 1). **3.** *Archaic.* to become as specified: *the time waxed late.* [Old English *weaxan;* related to Old Frisian *waxa,* Old Saxon, Old High German *wahsan,* Gothic *wahsjan*]

wax[3] (wæks) *n. Informal, chiefly Brit.* a fit of rage or temper: *he's in a wax today.* [of obscure origin; perhaps from the phrase *to wax angry*]

wax bean *n. U.S.* any of certain string beans that have yellow waxy pods and are grown in the U.S.

waxberry ('wæksbərɪ, -brɪ) *n., pl.* **-ries.** the waxy fruit of the wax myrtle or the snowberry.

waxbill ('wæks,bɪl) *n.* any of various chiefly African finchlike weaverbirds of the genus *Estrilda* and related genera, having a brightly coloured bill and plumage.

wax cap *n.* any fungus of the basidiomycetous family Hygrophoraceae, having thick waxy gills. Many are brightly coloured, like the **parrot toadstool** (*Hygrophorus psittacinus*), which is yellow with a covering of green slime, and the orange-red *H. conicus*.

waxcloth (ˈwæksˌklɒθ) *n.* **1.** another name for **oilcloth. 2.** another name for **linoleum.**

waxen[1] (ˈwæksən) *adj.* **1.** made of, treated with, or covered with wax. **2.** resembling wax in colour or texture.

waxen[2] (ˈwæksən) *vb. Archaic.* a past participle of **wax**[2].

waxeye (ˈwæksˌaɪ) *n. Austral. and N.Z.* another name for **white-eye.**

wax flower *n. Austral.* any of several rutaceous shrubs of the genus *Eriostemon,* having waxy pink-white five-petalled flowers.

wax insect *n.* any of various scale insects that secrete wax or a waxy substance, esp. the oriental species *Ceroplastes ceriferus,* which produces Chinese wax.

wax light *n.* a candle or taper of wax.

wax moth *n.* a brown pyralid moth, *Galleria mellonella,* the larvae of which feed on the combs of beehives. Also called: **honeycomb moth, bee moth.**

wax myrtle *n.* a shrub, *Myrica cerifera,* of SE North America, having evergreen leaves and a small berry-like fruit with a waxy coating: family *Myricaceae.* Also called: **bayberry, candleberry, waxberry.**

wax palm *n.* **1.** a tall Andean palm tree, *Ceroxylon andicola,* having pinnate leaves that yield a resinous wax used in making candles. **2.** another name for **carnauba** (sense 1).

wax paper *n.* paper treated or coated with wax or paraffin to make it waterproof.

waxplant (ˈwæksˌplɑːnt) *n.* **1.** a climbing asclepiadaceous shrub, *Hoya carnosa,* of E Asia and Australia, having fleshy leaves and clusters of small waxy white pink-centred flowers. **2.** any of various similar plants of the genus *Hoya.*

wax tree *n.* a Japanese anacardiaceous tree, *Rhus succedanea,* having white berries that yield wax.

waxwing (ˈwæksˌwɪŋ) *n.* any of several gregarious passerine songbirds of the genus *Bombycilla,* esp. *B. garrulus,* having red waxy wing tips and crested heads: family *Bombycillidae.*

waxwork (ˈwæksˌwɜːk) *n.* **1.** an object reproduced in wax, esp. as an ornament. **2.** a life-size lifelike figure, esp. of a famous person, reproduced in wax. **3.** (*pl.; functioning as sing. or pl.*) a museum or exhibition of wax figures or objects. —ˈ**waxˌworker** *n.*

waxy[1] (ˈwæksɪ) *adj.* **waxier, waxiest. 1.** resembling wax in colour, appearance, or texture. **2.** made of, covered with, or abounding in wax. —ˈ**waxily** *adv.* —ˈ**waxiness** *n.*

waxy[2] (ˈwæksɪ) *adj.* **waxier, waxiest.** *Brit. slang.* bad-tempered or irritable; angry.

way (weɪ) *n.* **1.** a manner, method, or means: *a way of life; a way of knowing.* **2.** a route or direction: *the way home.* **3. a.** a means or line of passage, such as a path or track. **b.** (*in combination*): *waterway.* **4.** space or room for movement or activity (esp. in the phrases **make way, in the way, out of the way**). **5.** distance, usually distance in general: *you've come a long way.* **6.** a passage or journey: *on the way.* **7.** characteristic style or manner: *I did it in my own way.* **8.** (*often pl.*) habits; idiosyncrasies: *he has some offensive ways.* **9.** an aspect of something; particular: *in many ways he was right.* **10. a.** a street in or leading out of a town. **b.** (*cap. when part of a street name*): *Icknield Way.* **11.** something that one wants in a determined manner (esp. in the phrases **get** *or* **have one's (own) way**). **12.** the experience or sphere in which one comes into contact with things (esp. in the phrase **come one's way**). **13.** *Informal.* a state or condition, usually financial or concerning health (esp. in the phrases **in a good** (*or* **bad**) **way**). **14.** *Informal.* the area or direction of one's home: *drop in if you're ever over my way.* **15.** movement of a ship or other vessel. **16.** a right of way in law. **17.** a guide along which something can be moved, such as the surface of a lathe along which the tailstock slides. **18.** (*pl.*) the wooden or metal tracks down which a ship slides to be launched. **19.** a course of life including experiences, conduct, etc.: *the way of sin.* **20.** *Archaic.* calling or trade. **21. by the way.** (*sentence modifier*) in passing or incidentally. **22. by way of. a.** via. **b.** serving as: *by way of introduction.* **c.** in the state or condition of: *by way of being an artist.* **23. each way.** (of a bet) laid on a horse, dog, etc., to win or gain a place. **24. give way. a.** to collapse or break down. **b.** to withdraw or yield. **25. give way to. a.** to step aside for or stop for. **b.** to give full rein to (emotions, etc.). **26. go out of one's way.** to take considerable trouble or inconvenience oneself. **27. have a way with.** to have such a manner or skill as to handle successfully. **28. have it both ways.** to enjoy two things that would normally contradict each other or be mutually exclusive. **29. in a way.** in some respects. **30. in no way.** not at all. **31. lead the way. a.** to go first. **b.** to set an example or precedent. **32. make one's way. a.** to proceed or advance. **b.** to achieve success in life. **33. no way.** *Informal.* that is impossible. **34. on the way out.** *Informal.* **a.** becoming unfashionable, obsolete, etc. **b.** dying. **35. out of the way. a.** removed or dealt with so as to be no longer a hindrance. **b.** remote. **c.** unusual and sometimes improper. **36. pay one's way.** See **pay** (sense 11). **37. see one's way (clear).** to find it possible and be willing (to do something). **38. the way.** *Irish.* so that: *I left early the way I would avoid the traffic.* **39. under way.** having started moving or making progress. ~*adv.* **40.** *Informal.* **a.** at a considerable distance or extent: *way over yonder.* **b.** very far; considerably: *they're way up the mountain.* [Old English *weg;* related to Old Frisian *wei,* Old Norse *vegr,* Gothic *wigs*]

▷**Usage.** The use of *the way* for *as* in sentences such as *he does not write the way his father did* is well established in the U.S. and is common in British informal usage. Careful writers, however, prefer *as* in formal contexts.

waybill (ˈweɪˌbɪl) *n.* a document attached to goods in transit specifying their nature, point of origin, and destination as well as the route to be taken and the rate to be charged.

wayfarer (ˈweɪˌfɛərə) *n.* a person who goes on a journey. —ˈ**wayˌfaring** *n., adj.*

wayfaring tree *n.* a caprifoliaceous shrub, *Viburnum lantana,* of Europe and W Asia, having white flowers and berries that turn from red to black.

waylay (weɪˈleɪ) *vb.* **-lays, -laying, -laid.** (*tr.*) **1.** to lie in wait for and attack. **2.** to await and intercept unexpectedly. [C16: from WAY + LAY[1]] —**way**ˈ**layer** *n.*

wayleave (ˈweɪˌliːv) *n.* access to property granted by a landowner for payment, for example to allow a contractor access to a building site.

wayleggo (ˌweɪleˈgəʊ) *interj. N.Z.* away here! let go!; a shepherd's call to a dog on completion of a task.

waymark (ˈweɪˌmɑːk) *n.* a symbol or signpost marking the route of a footpath. —ˈ**wayˌmarked** *adj.*

way-out *adj. Informal.* **1.** extremely unconventional or experimental; avant-garde. **2.** excellent or amazing.

-ways *suffix forming adverbs.* indicating direction or manner: *sideways.* [Old English *weges,* literally: of the way, from *weg* WAY]

ways and means *pl. n.* **1.** the revenues and methods of raising the revenues needed for the functioning of a state or other political unit. **2.** (*usually cap.*) a standing committee of the U.S. House of Representatives that supervises all financial legislation. **3.** the methods and resources for accomplishing some purpose.

wayside (ˈweɪˌsaɪd) *n.* **1. a.** the side or edge of a road. **b.** (*modifier*) situated by the wayside: *a wayside inn.* **2. fall by the wayside.** to cease or fail to continue doing something: *of the nine starters, three fell by the wayside.* **3. go by the wayside.** to be put aside on account of something more urgent.

wayward (ˈweɪwəd) *adj.* **1.** wanting to have one's own way regardless of the wishes or good of others. **2.** capricious, erratic, or unpredictable. **3.** *Archaic.* unwelcome or unwanted. [C14: changed from *awayward* turned or turning away] —ˈ**waywardly** *adv.* —ˈ**waywardness** *n.*

wayworn (ˈweɪˌwɔːn) *adj. Rare.* worn or tired by travel.

wayzgoose (ˈweɪzˌguːs) *n.* a works outing made annually by a printing house. [C18: from earlier *waygoose,* of unknown origin]

wb *abbrev. for:* **1.** water ballast. **2.** Also: **W/B, WB** waybill. **3.** westbound.

Wb *Physics. symbol for* weber.

WBA *abbrev. for* World Boxing Association.

WBC *abbrev. for* World Boxing Council.

W boson *n. Physics.* another name for **W particle.**

wc *abbrev. for:* **1.** water closet. **2.** without charge.

WC *abbrev. for:* **1.** water closet. **2.** (in London postal code) West Central.

WCC *abbrev. for* World Council of Churches.

wd *abbrev. for:* **1.** ward. **2.** wood. **3.** word.

WD *abbrev. for:* **1.** War Department. **2.** Works Department. **3.** *international car registration for* (Windward Islands) Dominica.

WDM *or* **wdm** *abbrev. for* wavelength division multiplex: a system in which several independent signals may be sent down an optical fibre link by monitoring them on light-carriers of different wavelengths.

we (wiː) *pron.* (*subjective*) **1.** refers to the speaker or writer and another person or other people: *we should go now.* **2.** refers to all people or people in general: *the planet on which we live.* **3. a.** a formal word for **I** used by editors or other writers, and formerly by monarchs. **b.** (*as n.*): *he uses the royal we in his pompous moods.* **4.** *Informal.* used instead of *you* with a tone of persuasiveness, condescension, or sarcasm: *how are we today?* [Old English *wē,* related to Old Saxon *wī,* Old High German *wir,* Old Norse *vēr,* Danish, Swedish *vi,* Sanskrit *vayam*]

WEA (in Britain) *abbrev. for* Workers' Educational Association.

weak (wiːk) *adj.* **1.** lacking in physical or mental strength or force; frail or feeble. **2.** liable to yield, break, or give way: *a weak link in a chain.* **3.** lacking in resolution or firmness of character. **4.** lacking strength, power, or intensity: *a weak voice.* **5.** lacking strength in a particular part: *a team weak in defence.* **6. a.** not functioning as well as normal: *weak eyes.* **b.** easily upset: *a weak stomach.* **7.** lacking in conviction, persuasiveness, etc.: *a weak argument.* **8.** lacking in political or strategic strength: *a weak state.* **9.** lacking the usual, full, or desirable strength of flavour: *weak tea.* **10.** *Grammar.* **a.** denoting or belonging to a class of verbs, in certain languages including the Germanic languages, whose conjugation relies on inflectional endings rather than internal vowel gradation, as *look, looks, looking, looked.* **b.** belonging to any part-of-speech class, in any of various languages, whose inflections follow the more regular of two possible patterns. Compare **strong** (sense 13). **11.** (of a syllable) not accented or stressed. **12.** (of a fuel-air mixture) containing a relatively low proportion of fuel. Compare **rich** (sense 13). **13.** *Photog.* having low density or contrast; thin. **14.** (of an industry, market, currency, securities, etc.) falling in price or characterized by falling prices. [Old English *wāc* soft, miserable; related to Old Saxon *wēk*, Old High German *weih*, Old Norse *veikr*] —ˈ**weakish** *adj.* —ˈ**weakishly** *adv.* —ˈ**weakishness** *n.*

weaken (ˈwiːkən) *vb.* to become or cause to become weak or weaker. —ˈ**weakener** *n.*

weaker sex (ˈwiːkə) *n.* the female sex.

weakfish (ˈwiːkˌfɪʃ) *n., pl.* **-fish** *or* **-fishes.** any of several sciaenid sea trouts, esp. *Cynoscion regalis*, a food and game fish of American Atlantic coastal waters.

weak interaction *or* **force** *n. Physics.* an interaction between elementary particles that is responsible for certain decay processes, operates at distances less than about 10^{-15} metres, and is 10^{12} times weaker than the strong interaction. Also called: **weak nuclear interaction** *or* **force.** See **interaction** (sense 2), **electroweak interaction.**

weak-kneed *adj. Informal.* yielding readily to force, persuasion, intimidation, etc. —ˌ**weak-ˈkneedly** *adv.* —ˌ**weak-ˈkneedness** *n.*

weakling (ˈwiːklɪŋ) *n.* a person or animal that is lacking in strength or weak in constitution or character.

weakly (ˈwiːklɪ) *adj.* **-lier, -liest. 1.** sickly; feeble. ~*adv.* **2.** in a weak or feeble manner. —ˈ**weakliness** *n.*

weak-minded *adj.* **1.** lacking in stability of mind or character. **2.** another word for **feeble-minded.** —ˌ**weak-ˈmindedly** *adv.* —ˌ**weak-ˈmindedness** *n.*

weakness (ˈwiːknɪs) *n.* **1.** the state or quality of being weak. **2.** a deficiency or failing, as in a person's character. **3.** a self-indulgent fondness or liking: *a weakness for chocolates.*

weak sister *n. U.S. informal.* a person in a group who is regarded as weak or unreliable.

weak-willed *adj.* lacking strength of will.

weal[1] (wiːl) *n.* a raised mark on the surface of the body produced by a blow. Also called: **wale, welt, wheal.** [C19: variant of WALE[1], influenced in form by WHEAL]

weal[2] (wiːl) *n.* **1.** *Archaic.* prosperity or wellbeing (now esp. in the phrases **the public weal, the common weal**). **2.** *Obsolete.* the state. **3.** *Obsolete.* wealth. [Old English *wela*; related to Old Saxon *welo*, Old High German *wolo*]

weald (wiːld) *n. Brit. archaic.* open or forested country. [Old English; related to Old Saxon, Old High German *wald*, Old Norse *vollr*, probably related to WILD]

wealth (wɛlθ) *n.* **1.** a large amount of money and valuable material possessions. **2.** the state of being rich. **3.** a great profusion: *a wealth of gifts.* **4.** *Economics.* all goods and services with monetary, exchangeable, or productive value. [C13 *welthe*, from WEAL[2]; related to WELL[1]] —ˈ**wealthless** *adj.*

wealth tax *n.* a tax on personal property; capital levy.

wealthy (ˈwɛlθɪ) *adj.* **wealthier, wealthiest. 1.** possessing wealth; affluent; rich. **2.** of, characterized by, or relating to wealth. **3.** abounding: *wealthy in friends.* —ˈ**wealthily** *adv.* —ˈ**wealthiness** *n.*

wean[1] (wiːn) *vb.* (*tr.*) **1.** to cause (a child or young mammal) to replace mother's milk by other nourishment. **2.** (usually foll. by *from*) to cause to desert former habits, pursuits, etc. [Old English *wenian* to accustom; related to German *gewöhnen* to get used to] —**weanedness** (ˈwiːnɪdnɪs, ˈwiːnd-) *n.*

wean[2] (weɪn; wiːn) *n. Scot. and northern English dialect.* a child; infant. [a contraction of *wee ane* or perhaps a shortened form of WEANLING]

weaner (ˈwiːnə) *n.* **1.** a person or thing that weans. **2.** a pig that has just been weaned and weighs less than 40 kg. **3.** *Austral. and N.Z.* a lamb, pig, or calf in the year in which it is weaned.

weanling (ˈwiːnlɪŋ) *n.* **a.** a child or young animal recently weaned. **b.** (*as modifier*): *a weanling calf.* [C16: from WEAN[1] + -LING[1]]

weapon (ˈwɛpən) *n.* **1.** an object or instrument used in fighting. **2.** anything that serves to outwit or get the better of an opponent: *his power of speech was his best weapon.* **3.** any part of an animal that is used to defend itself, to attack prey, etc., such as claws, teeth, horns, or a sting. **4.** a slang word for **penis.** [Old English *wǣpen*; related to Old Norse *vápn*, Old Frisian *wēpen*, Old High German *wāffan*] —ˈ**weaponed** *adj.* —ˈ**weaponless** *adj.*

weaponeer (ˌwɛpəˈnɪə) *n.* (formerly) a person associated with the use or maintenance of weapons, esp. nuclear weapons.

weaponry (ˈwɛpənrɪ) *n.* weapons regarded collectively.

weapon system *n. Military.* a weapon and the components necessary to its proper function, such as targeting and guidance devices.

wear[1] (wɛə) *vb.* **wears, wearing, wore, worn. 1.** (*tr.*) to carry or have (a garment, etc.) on one's person as clothing, ornament, etc. **2.** (*tr.*) to carry or have on one's person habitually: *she wears a lot of red.* **3.** (*tr.*) to have in one's aspect: *to wear a smile.* **4.** (*tr.*) to display, show, or fly: *a ship wears its colours.* **5.** to deteriorate or cause to deteriorate by constant use or action. **6.** to produce or be produced by constant rubbing, scraping, etc.: *to wear a hole in one's trousers.* **7.** to bring or be brought to a specified condition by constant use or action: *to wear a tyre to shreds.* **8.** (*intr.*) to submit to constant use or action in a specified way: *his suit wears well.* **9.** (*tr.*) to harass or weaken. **10.** (when *intr.*, often foll. by *on*) (of time) to pass or be passed slowly. **11.** (*tr.*) *Brit. slang.* to accept: *Larry won't wear that argument.* **12.** **wear ship.** to change the tack of a sailing vessel, esp. a square-rigger, by coming about so that the wind passes astern. ~*n.* **13.** the act of wearing or state of being worn. **14. a.** anything designed to be worn: *leisure wear.* **b.** (*in combination*): *nightwear.* **15.** deterioration from constant or normal use or action. **16.** the quality of resisting the effects of constant use. ~See also **wear down, wear off, wear out.** [Old English *werian*; related to Old High German *werien*, Old Norse *verja*, Gothic *vasjan*] —ˈ**wearer** *n.*

wear[2] (wɛə) *vb.* **wears, wearing, wore, worn.** *Nautical.* to tack by gybing instead of by going through stays. [C17: from earlier *weare*, of unknown origin]

wearable (ˈwɛərəbᵊl) *adj.* **1.** suitable for wear or able to be worn. ~*n.* **2.** (*often pl.*) any garment that can be worn. —ˌ**wearaˈbility** *n.*

wear and tear *n.* damage, depreciation, or loss resulting from ordinary use.

wear down *vb.* (*adv.*) **1.** to consume or be consumed by long or constant wearing, rubbing, etc. **2.** to overcome or be overcome gradually by persistent effort.

weariless (ˈwɪərɪlɪs) *adj.* not wearied or able to be wearied. —ˈ**wearilessly** *adv.*

wearing (ˈwɛərɪŋ) *adj.* causing fatigue or exhaustion; tiring. —ˈ**wearingly** *adv.*

wearing course *n.* the top layer of a road that carries the traffic; road surface.

wearisome (ˈwɪərɪsəm) *or* **weariful** *adj.* causing fatigue or annoyance; tedious. —ˈ**wearisomely** *or* ˈ**wearifully** *adv.* —ˈ**wearisomeness** *or* ˈ**wearifulness** *n.*

wear off *vb.* (*adv.*) **1.** (*intr.*) to decrease in intensity gradually: *the pain will wear off in an hour.* **2.** to disappear or cause to disappear gradually through exposure, use, etc.: *the pattern on the ring had been worn off.*

wear out *vb.* (*adv.*) **1.** to make or become unfit or useless through wear. **2.** (*tr.*) to exhaust or tire.

wearproof (ˈwɛəˌpruːf) *adj.* resistant to damage from normal wear or usage.

weary (ˈwɪərɪ) *adj.* **-rier, -riest. 1.** tired or exhausted. **2.** causing fatigue or exhaustion. **3.** caused by or suggestive of weariness: *a weary laugh.* **4.** (*postpositive*; often foll. by *of* or *with*) discontented or bored, esp. by the long continuance of something. ~*vb.* **-ries, -rying, -ried. 5.** to make or become weary. **6.** to make or become discontented or impatient, esp. by the long continuance of something. [Old English *wērig*; related to Old Saxon *wōrig*, Old High German *wuorag* drunk, Greek *hōrakian* to faint] —ˈ**wearily** *adv.* —ˈ**weariness** *n.* —ˈ**wearying** *adj.* —ˈ**wearyingly** *adv.*

weasand (ˈwiːzənd) *n.* a former name for the **trachea.** [Old English *wǣsend, wāsend*; related to Old Frisian *wāsenda*, Old High German *weisont* vein, Danish *vissen*]

weasel (ˈwiːzᵊl) *n., pl.* **-sel** *or* **-sels. 1.** any of various small predatory musteline mammals of the genus *Mustela* and related genera, esp. *M. nivalis* **(European weasel)**, having reddish-brown fur, an elongated body and neck, and short legs. **2.** *Informal.* a sly or treacherous person. **3.** *Chiefly U.S.* a motor vehicle for use in snow, esp. one with caterpillar tracks. [Old English *weosule, wesle*; related to Old Norse *visla*, Old High German *wisula*, Middle Dutch *wesel*] —ˈ**weaselly** *adj.*

weasel out *vb.* (*intr., adv.*) *Informal, chiefly U.S. and Canadian.* **1.** to go back on a commitment. **2.** to evade a responsibility, esp. in a despicable manner.

weasel words *pl. n. Informal.* intentionally evasive or misleading speech; equivocation. [C20: alluding to the weasel's supposed ability to suck an egg out of its shell without seeming to break the shell] —ˈ**weasel-ˌworded** *adj.*

weather (ˈwɛðə) *n.* **1. a.** the day-to-day meteorological conditions, esp. temperature, cloudiness, and rainfall, affecting a specific place. Compare **climate** (sense 1). **b.** (*modifier*): relating to the forecasting of weather: *a weather ship.* **2.** a prevailing state or condition. **3. make heavy weather. a.** (of a vessel) to roll and pitch in heavy seas. **b.** (foll. by *of*) to carry out with great difficulty or unnecessarily great effort. **4. under the weather.** *Informal.* **a.** not in good health. **b.** intoxicated. ~*adj.* **5.** (*prenominal*) on or at the side or part towards the wind; windward: *the weather anchor.* Compare **lee** (sense 4). ~*vb.* **6.** to expose or be exposed to the action of the weather. **7.** to undergo or cause to undergo changes, such as discoloration, due to the action of the weather. **8.** (*intr.*) to withstand the action of the weather. **9.** (when *intr.*, foll. by *through*) to endure (a crisis, danger, etc.). **10.** (*tr.*) to slope (a surface, such as a roof, sill, etc.) so as to throw rainwater clear. **11.** (*tr.*) to sail to the windward of: *to weather a point.* [Old English *weder*; related to Old Saxon *wedar*, Old High German *wetar*, Old Norse *vethr*] —ˌ**weatheraˈbility** *n.* —ˈ**weatherer** *n.*

weather-beaten *adj.* **1.** showing signs of exposure to the weather. **2.** tanned or hardened by exposure to the weather.

weatherboard (ˈwɛðəˌbɔːd) *n.* **1.** a timber board, with a groove (rabbet) along the front of its top edge and along the back of its lower edge, that is fixed horizontally with others to form an exterior cladding on a wall or roof. Compare **clapboard.** **2.** a

sloping timber board fixed at the bottom of a door to deflect rain. **3.** the windward side of a vessel. **4.** Also called: **weatherboard house.** *Chiefly Austral. and N.Z.* a house having walls made entirely of weatherboarding.
weatherboarding ('wɛðəˌbɔːdɪŋ) *n.* **1.** an area or covering of weatherboards. **2.** weatherboards collectively.
weather-bound *adj.* (of a vessel, aircraft, etc.) delayed by bad weather.
weathercock ('wɛðəˌkɒk) *n.* **1.** a weather vane in the form of a cock. **2.** a person who is fickle or changeable. ~*vb.* **3.** (*intr.*) (of an aircraft) to turn or tend to turn into the wind.
weathered ('wɛðəd) *adj.* **1.** affected by exposure to the action of the weather. **2.** (of rocks and rock formations) eroded, decomposed, or otherwise altered by the action of wind, frost, heat, etc. **3.** (of a sill, roof, etc.) having a sloped surface so as to allow rainwater to run off. **4.** (of wood) artificially stained so as to appear weather-beaten.
weather eye *n.* **1.** the vision of a person trained to observe changes in the weather. **2.** *Informal.* an alert or observant gaze. **3. keep one's weather eye open.** to stay on the alert.
weatherglass ('wɛðəˌglɑːs) *n.* any of various instruments, esp. a barometer, that measure atmospheric conditions.
weather house *n.* a model house with two human figures, one that comes out to foretell bad weather and the other to foretell good weather.
weathering ('wɛðərɪŋ) *n.* the mechanical and chemical breakdown of rocks by the action of rain, snow, cold, etc.
weatherly ('wɛðəlɪ) *adj.* (of a sailing vessel) making very little leeway when close-hauled, even in a stiff breeze. —'**weatherliness** *n.*
weatherman ('wɛðəˌmæn) *n., pl.* **-men.** a person who forecasts the weather, esp. one who works in a meteorological office.
Weatherman ('wɛðəˌmæn) *n., pl.* **-men.** *U.S.* a member of a militant revolutionary group active in the U.S. during the 1970s. [C20: name adopted from a line in Bob Dylan's song "Subterranean Homesick Blues": "You don't need a weatherman To know which way the wind blows."]
weather map *or* **chart** *n.* a synoptic chart showing weather conditions, compiled from simultaneous observations taken at various weather stations.
weatherproof ('wɛðəˌpruːf) *adj.* **1.** designed or able to withstand exposure to weather without deterioration. ~*vb.* **2.** (*tr.*) to render (something) weatherproof. —'**weatherˌproofness** *n.*
weather station *n.* one of a network of meteorological observation posts where weather data is recorded.
weather strip *n.* a thin strip of compressible material, such as spring metal, felt, etc., that is fitted between the frame of a door or window and the opening part to exclude wind and rain. Also called: **weatherstripping.**
weather vane *n.* a vane designed to indicate the direction in which the wind is blowing.
weather window *n.* a limited interval when weather conditions can be expected to be suitable for a particular project, such as laying offshore pipelines, reaching a high mountain summit, launching a satellite, etc.
weather-wise *adj.* **1.** skilful or experienced in predicting weather conditions. **2.** skilful or experienced in predicting trends in public opinion, reactions, etc.
weatherworn ('wɛðəˌwɔːn) *adj.* another word for **weather-beaten.**
weave (wiːv) *vb.* **weaves, weaving, wove** *or* **weaved; woven** *or* **weaved. 1.** to form (a fabric) by interlacing (yarn, etc.), esp. on a loom. **2.** (*tr.*) to make or construct by such a process: *to weave a shawl.* **3.** (*tr.*) to make or construct (an artefact, such as a basket) by interlacing (a pliable material, such as cane). **4.** (of a spider) to make (a web). **5.** (*tr.*) to construct by combining separate elements into a whole. **6.** (*tr.;* often foll. by *in, into, through,* etc.) to introduce: *to weave factual details into a fiction.* **7.** to create (a way, etc.) by moving from side to side: *to weave through a crowd.* **8. get weaving.** *Informal.* to hurry; start to do something. ~*n.* **9.** the method or pattern of weaving or the structure of a woven fabric: *a twill weave; an open weave.* [Old English *wefan;* related to Old High German *weban,* Old Norse *vefa,* Greek *hyphos,* Sanskrit *vābhis;* compare WEB, WEEVIL, WASP]
weaver ('wiːvə) *n.* **1.** a person who weaves, esp. as a means of livelihood. **2.** short for **weaverbird.**
weaverbird ('wiːvəˌbɜːd) *or* **weaver** *n.* **1.** any small Old World passerine songbird of the chiefly African family *Ploceidae,* having a short thick bill and a dull plumage and building covered nests: includes the house sparrow and whydahs. **2.** any similar bird of the family *Estrildae,* of warm regions of the Old World: includes the waxbills, grassfinches, and Java sparrow. Also called: **weaver finch.**
weaver's hitch *or* **knot** *n.* another name for **sheet bend.**
web (wɛb) *n.* **1.** any structure, construction, fabric, etc., formed by or as if by weaving or interweaving. **2.** a mesh of fine tough scleroprotein threads built by a spider from a liquid secreted from its spinnerets and used to trap insects. See also **cobweb** (sense 1). **3.** a similar network of threads spun by certain insect larvae, such as the silkworm. **4.** a fabric, esp. one in the process of being woven. **5.** a membrane connecting the toes of some aquatic birds or the digits of such aquatic mammals as the otter. **6.** the vane of a bird's feather. **7.** *Architect.* the surface of a ribbed vault that lies between the ribs. **8.** the central section of an I-beam or H-beam that joins the two flanges of the beam. **9.** the radial portion of a crank that connects the crankpin to the crankshaft. **10.** a thin piece of superfluous material left attached to a forging; fin. **11. a.** a continuous strip of paper as formed on a paper machine or fed from a reel into some printing presses. **b.** (*as modifier*): *web offset; a web press.* **12.** the woven edge, without pile, of some carpets. **13.** any structure, construction, etc., that is intricately formed or complex: *a web of intrigue.* ~*vb.* **webs, webbing, webbed. 14.** (*tr.*) to cover with or as if with a web. **15.** (*tr.*) to entangle or ensnare. **16.** (*intr.*) to construct a web. [Old English *webb;* related to Old Saxon, Old High German *webbi,* Old Norse *vefr*] —'**webless** *adj.* —'**webˌlike** *adj.*
webbed (wɛbd) *adj.* **1.** (of the feet of certain animals) having the digits connected by a thin fold of skin; palmate. **2.** having, consisting of, or resembling a web.
webbing ('wɛbɪŋ) *n.* **1.** a strong fabric of hemp, cotton, jute, etc., woven in strips and used under springs in upholstery or for straps, etc. **2.** the skin that unites the digits of a webbed foot. **3.** anything that forms a web.
webby ('wɛbɪ) *adj.* **-bier, -biest.** of, relating to, resembling, or consisting of a web.
weber ('veɪbə) *n.* the derived SI unit of magnetic flux; the flux that, when linking a circuit of one turn, produces in it an emf of 1 volt as it is reduced to zero at a uniform rate in one second. 1 weber is equivalent to 10^8 maxwells. Symbol: Wb [C20: named after W. E. *Weber* (1804–91), German physicist]
webfoot ('wɛbˌfʊt) *n.* **1.** *Zoology.* a foot having the toes connected by folds of skin. **2.** *Anatomy.* a foot having an abnormal membrane connecting adjacent toes.
web-footed *or* **web-toed** *adj.* (of certain animals) having webbed feet that facilitate swimming.
web spinner *n.* any small fragile dull-coloured typically tropical insect of the order *Embioptera,* which has biting mouthparts and constructs silken tunnels in which to live.
webster ('wɛbstə) *n.* an archaic word for **weaver** (sense 1). [Old English *webbestre,* from *webba* a weaver, from *webb* WEB]
webwheel ('wɛbˌwiːl) *n.* **1.** a wheel containing a plate or web instead of spokes. **2.** a wheel of which the rim, spokes, and centre are in one piece.
wed (wɛd) *vb.* **weds, wedding, wedded** *or* **wed. 1.** to take (a person of the opposite sex) as a husband or wife; marry. **2.** (*tr.*) to join (two people) in matrimony. **3.** (*tr.*) to unite closely. [Old English *weddian;* related to Old Frisian *weddia,* Old Norse *vethja,* Gothic *wadi* pledge] —'**wedded** *adj.*
we'd (wiːd; *unstressed* wɪd) *contraction of* we had *or* we would.
Wed. *abbrev. for* Wednesday.
wedding ('wɛdɪŋ) *n.* **1. a.** the act of marrying or the celebration of a marriage. **b.** (*as modifier*): *wedding day.* **2.** the anniversary of a marriage (in such combinations as **silver wedding** or **diamond wedding**). **3.** the combination or blending of two separate elements.
wedding breakfast *n.* the meal usually served after a wedding ceremony or just before the bride and bridegroom leave for their honeymoon.
wedding cake *n.* a rich fruit cake, with one, two, or more tiers, covered with almond paste and decorated with royal icing, which is served at a wedding reception.
wedding ring *n.* a band ring with parallel sides, typically of precious metal, worn to indicate married status.
wedeln ('veɪdəln) *n.* a succession of high-speed turns performed in skiing. [from German, literally: to wag]
wedge (wɛdʒ) *n.* **1.** a block of solid material, esp. wood or metal, that is shaped like a narrow V in cross section and can be pushed or driven between two objects or parts of an object in order to split or secure them. **2.** any formation, structure, or substance in the shape of a wedge: *a wedge of cheese.* **3.** something such as an idea, action, etc., that tends to cause division. **4.** a shoe with a wedge heel. **5.** *Golf.* a club, a No. 10 iron with a face angle of more than 50°, used for bunker shots (**sand wedge**) or pitch shots (**pitching wedge**). **6.** a wedge-shaped extension of the high pressure area of an anticyclone, narrower than a ridge. **7.** *Mountaineering.* a wedge-shaped device, formerly of wood, now usually of hollow steel, for hammering into a crack to provide an anchor point. **8.** any of the triangular characters used in cuneiform writing. **9.** (formerly) a body of troops formed in a V-shape. **10.** *Photog.* a strip of glass coated in such a way that it is clear at one end but becomes progressively more opaque towards the other end: used in making measurements of transmission density. **11. thin end of the wedge.** anything unimportant in itself that implies the start of something much larger. ~*vb.* **12.** (*tr.*) to secure with or as if with a wedge. **13.** to squeeze or be squeezed like a wedge into a narrow space. **14.** (*tr.*) to force apart or divide with or as if with a wedge. [Old English *wecg;* related to Old Saxon *weggi,* Old High German *wecki,* Old Norse *veggr* wall] —'**wedgeˌlike** *adj.* —'**wedgy** *adj.*
wedge heel *n.* **1.** a raised shoe heel with the heel and sole forming a solid block. **2.** a shoe with such a heel.
wedge-tailed eagle *n.* a large brown Australian eagle, *Aquila audax,* having a wedge-shaped tail and a wingspan of 3 m. Also called: **eaglehawk.**

Wedgwood (ˈwɛdʒwʊd) *n.* **1.** *Trademark.* **a.** pottery produced, esp. during the late 18th and early 19th centuries, at the Wedgwood factories near Stoke-on-Trent in Staffordshire. **b.** such pottery having applied classical decoration in white on a blue or other coloured ground. ~*adj.* **2.** relating to or characteristic of such pottery: *Wedgwood blue.* [named after Josiah *Wedgwood* (1730–95), British potter and founder of the factories]

Wedgwood blue *n.* **a.** a pale blue or greyish-blue colour. **b.** (*as adj.*): *a Wedgwood-blue door.*

wedlock (ˈwɛdlɒk) *n.* **1.** the state of being married. **2. born** *or* **conceived out of wedlock.** born or conceived when one's parents are not legally married. [Old English *wedlāc,* from *wedd* pledge + *-lāc,* suffix denoting activity, perhaps from *lāc* game, battle (related to Gothic *laiks* dance, Old Norse *leikr*)]

Wednesday (ˈwɛnzdɪ) *n.* the fourth day of the week; third day of the working week. [Old English *Wōdnes dæg* Woden's day (Woden being the foremost Anglo-Saxon god), translation of Latin *mercurii dies* Mercury's day; related to Old Frisian *wōnsdei,* Middle Dutch *wōdensdach* (Dutch *woensdag*)]

wee[1] (wiː) *adj.* **1.** very small; tiny; minute. ~*n.* **2.** *Chiefly Scot.* a short time (esp. in the phrase **bide a wee.**). [C13: from Old English *wǣg* WEIGHT]

wee[2] (wiː) *Informal, chiefly Brit.* ~*n.* **1. a.** the act or an instance of urinating. **b.** urine. ~*vb.* **2.** (*intr.*) to urinate. ~Also: **wee-wee.** [of unknown origin]

weed[1] (wiːd) *n.* **1.** any plant that grows wild and profusely, esp. one that grows among cultivated plants, depriving them of space, food, etc. **2.** *Slang.* **a. the weed.** tobacco. **b.** marijuana. **3.** *Informal.* a thin or unprepossessing person. **4.** an inferior horse, esp. one showing signs of weakness of constitution. ~*vb.* **5.** to remove (useless or troublesome plants) from (a garden, etc.). [Old English *weod;* related to Old Saxon *wiod,* Old High German *wiota* fern] —ˈ**weeder** *n.* —ˈ**weedless** *adj.* —ˈ**weed,like** *adj.*

weed[2] (wiːd) *n. Rare.* a black crepe band worn to indicate mourning. See also **weeds.** [Old English *wǣd, wēd;* related to Old Saxon *wād,* Old High German *wāt,* Old Norse *vāth*]

weedkiller (ˈwiːdˌkɪlə) *n.* a substance, usually a chemical or hormone, used for killing weeds.

weed out *vb.* (*tr., adv.*) to separate out, remove, or eliminate (anything unwanted): *to weed out troublesome students.*

weeds (wiːdz) *pl. n.* **1.** Also called: **widow's weeds.** a widow's black mourning clothes. **2.** *Obsolete.* any clothing. [pl. of WEED[2]]

weedy (ˈwiːdɪ) *adj.* **weedier, weediest. 1.** full of or containing weeds: *weedy land.* **2.** (of a plant) resembling a weed in rapid or straggling growth. **3.** *Informal.* thin or weakly in appearance. —ˈ**weedily** *adv.* —ˈ**weediness** *n.*

Wee Free *n. Informal, often derogatory.* a member of the minority of the Free Church of Scotland that refused to be joined with the United Free Church in 1900.

week (wiːk) *n.* **1.** a period of seven consecutive days, esp., one beginning with Sunday. Related adj.: **hebdomadal. 2.** a period of seven consecutive days beginning from or including a specified day: *Easter week; a week from Wednesday.* **3.** the period of time within a week devoted to work. **4.** a week devoted to the celebration of a cause. ~*adv.* **5.** *Chiefly Brit.* seven days before or after a specified day: *I'll visit you Wednesday week.* [Old English *wice, wicu, wucu;* related to Old Norse *vika,* Gothic *wikō* order]

weekday (ˈwiːkˌdeɪ) *n.* any day of the week other than Sunday and, often, Saturday.

weekend *n.* (ˌwiːkˈɛnd). **1. a.** the end of the week, esp. the period from Friday night until the end of Sunday. **b.** (*as modifier*): *a weekend party.* ~*vb.* (ˈwiːkˌɛnd). **2.** (*intr.*) *Informal.* to spend or pass a weekend. ~See also **weekends.**

weekender (ˌwiːkˈɛndə) *n.* **1.** a person spending a weekend holiday in a place, esp. habitually. **2.** *Austral.* a house, shack, etc., occupied only at weekends, for holidays, etc.

weekends (ˌwiːkˈɛndz) *adv. Informal.* at the weekend, esp. regularly or during every weekend.

weekly (ˈwiːklɪ) *adj.* **1.** happening or taking place once a week or every week. **2.** determined or calculated by the week. ~*adv.* **3.** once a week or every week. ~*n., pl.* **-lies. 4.** a newspaper or magazine issued every week.

weeknight (ˈwiːkˌnaɪt) *n.* the evening or night of a weekday.

weel (wiːl) *adv., adj., interj., sentence connector.* a Scot. word for **well**[1].

ween (wiːn) *vb. Archaic.* to think or imagine (something). [Old English *wēnan;* related to Old Saxon *wānian,* Gothic *wēnjan,* German *wähnen* to assume wrongly]

weeny (ˈwiːnɪ) *or* **weensy** (ˈwiːnzɪ) *adj.* **-nier, -niest** *or* **-sier, -siest.** *Informal.* very small; tiny. [C18: from WEE[1] with the ending *-ny* as in TINY]

weeny-bopper *n. Informal.* a child of 8 to 12 years, esp. a girl, who is a keen follower of pop music. [C20: formed on the model of TEENYBOPPER, from *weeny,* as in *teeny-weeny* very small]

weep (wiːp) *vb.* **weeps, weeping, wept. 1.** to shed (tears) as an expression of grief or unhappiness. **2.** (*tr.;* foll. by *out*) to utter, shedding tears. **3.** (when *intr.,* foll. by *for*) to mourn or lament (for something). **4.** to exude (drops of liquid). **5.** (*intr.*) (of a wound, etc.) to exude a watery or serous fluid. ~*n.* **6.** a spell of weeping. [Old English *wēpan;* related to Gothic *wōpjan,* Old High German *wuofan,* Old Slavonic *vabiti* to call]

weeper (ˈwiːpə) *n.* **1.** a person who weeps, esp. a hired mourner. **2.** something worn as a sign of mourning. **3.** a hole through a wall, to allow water to drain away.

weeping (ˈwiːpɪŋ) *adj.* (of plants) having slender hanging branches. —ˈ**weepingly** *adv.*

weeping ivy *n.* a climbing plant, *Ficus benjamina,* of the fig family, grown as a greenhouse or house plant for its graceful glossy leaves on slender drooping branches.

weeping willow *n.* a Chinese willow tree, *Salix babylonica,* having long hanging branches: widely planted for ornament.

weepy (ˈwiːpɪ) *Informal.* ~*adj.* **weepier, weepiest. 1.** liable or tending to weep. ~*n., pl.* **weepies. 2.** a romantic and sentimental film or book. —ˈ**weepily** *adv.* —ˈ**weepiness** *n.*

weever (ˈwiːvə) *n.* any small marine percoid fish of the family *Trachinidae,* such as *Trachinus vipera* of European waters, having venomous spines around the gills and the dorsal fin. [C17: from Old Northern French *wivre* viper, ultimately from Latin *vīpera* VIPER]

weevil (ˈwiːvɪl) *n.* **1.** Also called: **snout beetle.** any beetle of the family *Curculionidae,* having an elongated snout (rostrum): they are pests, feeding on plants and plant products. See also **boll weevil. 2.** Also called: **pea** or **bean weevil.** any of various beetles of the family *Bruchidae* (or *Lariidae*), the larvae of which live in the seeds of leguminous plants. **3.** any of various similar or related beetles. [Old English *wifel;* related to Old High German *wibil;* compare Old Norse *tordȳfill* dungbeetle] —ˈ**weevily** *adj.*

wee-wee *n., vb.* a variant of **wee**[2].

w.e.f. *abbrev. for* with effect from.

weft (wɛft) *n.* the yarn woven across the width of the fabric through the lengthwise warp yarn. Also called: **filling, woof.** [Old English, related to Old Norse *veptr;* see WEAVE]

weigela (waɪˈgiːlə, -ˈdʒiː-; ˈwaɪgɪlə) *n.* any caprifoliaceous shrub of the Asian genus *Weigela,* having clusters of pink, purple, red, or white showy bell-shaped flowers. [C19: from New Latin, named after C. E. *Weigel* (1748–1831), German physician]

weigh[1] (weɪ) *vb.* **1.** (*tr.*) to measure the weight of. **2.** (*intr.*) to have weight or be heavy: *she weighs more than her sister.* **3.** (*tr.;* often foll. by *out*) to apportion according to weight. **4.** (*tr.*) to consider carefully: *to weigh the facts of a case.* **5.** (*intr.*) to be influential: *his words weighed little with the jury.* **6.** (*intr.;* often foll. by *on*) to be oppressive or burdensome (to). **7.** *Obsolete.* to regard or esteem. **8. weigh anchor.** to raise a vessel's anchor or (of a vessel) to have its anchor raised preparatory to departure. ~See also **weigh down, weigh in, weigh up.** [Old English *wegan;* related to Old Frisian *wega,* Old Norse *vega,* Gothic *gawigan,* German *wiegen*] —ˈ**weighable** *adj.* —ˈ**weigher** *n.*

weigh[2] (weɪ) *n.* **under weigh.** a variant spelling of **under way.** [C18: variation due to the influence of phrases such as *to weigh anchor*]

weighbridge (ˈweɪˌbrɪdʒ) *n.* a machine for weighing vehicles, etc., by means of a metal plate set into a road.

weigh down *vb.* (*adv.*) to press (a person) down by or as if by weight: *his troubles weighed him down.*

weigh in *vb.* (*intr., adv.*) **1. a.** (of a boxer or wrestler) to be weighed before a bout. **b.** (of a jockey) to be weighed after, or sometimes before, a race. **2.** *Informal.* to contribute, as in a discussion, etc.: *he weighed in with a few sharp comments.* ~*n.* **weigh-in. 3.** the act of checking a competitor's weight, as in boxing, horse racing, etc.

weight (weɪt) *n.* **1.** a measure of the heaviness of an object; the amount anything weighs. **2.** *Physics.* the vertical force experienced by a mass as a result of gravitation. It equals the mass of the body multiplied by the acceleration of free fall. Its units are units of force (such as newtons or poundals) but is often given as a mass unit (kilogram or pound). Symbol: *W* **3.** a system of units used to express the weight of a substance: *troy weight.* **4.** a unit used to measure weight: *the kilogram is the weight used in the metric system.* **5.** any mass or heavy object used to exert pressure or weigh down. **6.** an oppressive force: *the weight of cares.* **7.** any heavy load: *the bag was such a weight.* **8.** the main or greatest force: preponderance: *the weight of evidence.* **9.** importance, influence, or consequence: *his opinion carries weight.* **10.** *Statistics.* one of a set of coefficients assigned to items of a frequency distribution that are analysed in order to represent the relative importance of the different items. **11.** *Printing.* the apparent blackness of a printed typeface. **12.** *Slang.* a pound of a drug, esp. cannabis. **13. pull one's weight.** *Informal.* to do one's full or proper share of a task. **14. throw one's weight around.** *Informal.* to act in an overauthoritarian or aggressive manner. ~*vb.* (*tr.*) **15.** to add weight to. **16.** to burden or oppress. **17.** to add importance, value, etc., to one side rather than another; bias; favour: *a law weighted towards landlords.* **18.** *Statistics.* to attach a weight or weights to. **19.** to make (fabric, threads, etc.) heavier by treating with mineral substances, etc. [Old English *wiht;* related to Old Frisian, Middle Dutch *wicht,* Old Norse *vētt,* German *Gewicht*] —ˈ**weighter** *n.*

weighted average *n.* an average calculated by taking into account not only the frequencies of the values of a variable but also some other factor such as their variance. The weighted average of observed data is the result of dividing the sum of the products of each observed value, the number of times it occurs, and this other factor by the total number of observations.

weighting (ˈweɪtɪŋ) *n.* **1.** a factor by which some quantity is multiplied in order to make it comparable with others. See also **weighted average. 2.** an increase in some quantity, esp. an additional allowance paid to compensate for higher living costs: *a London weighting.*

weightlessness (ˈweɪtlɪsnɪs) *n.* a state in which an object has no actual weight (because it is in space and unaffected by gravitational attraction) or no apparent weight (because the gravitational attraction equals the centripetal force and the object is in free fall). —ˈ**weightless** *adj.*

weightlifting (ˈweɪtˌlɪftɪŋ) *n.* the sport of lifting barbells of specified weights in a prescribed manner for competition or exercise. —ˈ**weightˌlifter** *n.*

weight training *n.* physical exercise involving lifting weights to improve muscle performance.

weight watcher *n.* a person who tries to lose weight, esp. by dieting.

weighty (ˈweɪtɪ) *adj.* **weightier, weightiest. 1.** having great weight. **2.** important or momentous. **3.** causing anxiety or worry. —ˈ**weightily** *adv.* —ˈ**weightiness** *n.*

weigh up *vb. (tr., adv.)* to make an assessment of (a person, situation, etc.); judge.

Weil's disease (vaɪlz) *n.* another name for **leptospirosis.** [named after Adolf *Weil* (1848–1916), German physician]

Weimaraner (ˈvaɪməˌrɑːnə, ˈwaɪməˌrɑː-) *n.* a breed of hunting dog, having a very short sleek grey coat and short tail. [C20: named after *Weimar*, a city in Germany where the breed was developed]

weir (wɪə) *n.* **1.** a low dam that is built across a river to raise the water level, divert the water, or control its flow. **2.** a series of traps or enclosures placed in a stream to catch fish. [Old English *wer;* related to Old Norse *ver,* Old Frisian *were,* German *Wehr*]

weird (wɪəd) *adj.* **1.** suggestive of or relating to the supernatural; eerie. **2.** strange or bizarre. **3.** *Archaic.* of or relating to fate or the Fates. ~*n.* **4.** *Archaic, chiefly Scot.* **a.** fate or destiny. **b.** one of the Fates. **5. dree one's weird.** *Scot.* see **dree.** ~*vb. (tr.)* **6.** *Scot.* to destine or ordain by fate; predict. [Old English *(ge)wyrd* destiny; related to *weorthan* to become, Old Norse *urthr* bane, Old Saxon *wurd;* see WORTH[2]] —ˈ**weirdly** *adv.* —ˈ**weirdness** *n.*

weirdo (ˈwɪədəʊ) *or* **weirdie** (ˈwɪədɪ) *n., pl.* **-dos** *or* **-dies.** *Informal.* a person who behaves in a bizarre or eccentric manner.

Weismannism (ˈvaɪsmənˌɪzəm) *n.* the doctrine of the continuity of the germ plasm. This theory of heredity states that all inheritable characteristics are transmitted by the reproductive cells and that characteristics acquired during the lifetime of the organism are not inherited. [C19: named after August *Weismann* (1834–1914), German biologist]

weka (ˈweɪkə, ˈwiːkə) *n.* any flightless New Zealand rail of the genus *Gallirallus,* having a mottled brown plumage and rudimentary wings. Also called: **Maori hen, wood hen.** [C19: from Maori, of imitative origin]

welch (wɛlʃ) *vb.* a variant spelling of **welsh.** —ˈ**welcher** *n.*

Welch (wɛlʃ) *adj.* an archaic spelling of **Welsh**[1].

welcome (ˈwɛlkəm) *adj.* **1.** gladly and cordially received or admitted: *a welcome guest.* **2.** bringing pleasure or gratitude: *a welcome gift.* **3.** freely permitted or invited: *you are welcome to call.* **4.** under no obligation (only in such phrases as **you're welcome** or **he's welcome,** as conventional responses to thanks). ~*sentence substitute.* **5.** an expression of cordial greeting, esp. to a person whose arrival is desired or pleasing. ~*n.* **6.** the act of greeting or receiving a person or thing; reception: *the new theory had a cool welcome.* **7. wear out one's welcome.** to come more often or stay longer than is acceptable or pleasing. ~*vb. (tr.)* **8.** to greet the arrival of (visitors, guests, etc.) cordially or gladly. **9.** to receive or accept, esp. gladly. [C12: changed (through influence of WELL[1]) from Old English *wilcuma* (agent noun referring to a welcome guest), *wilcume* (a greeting of welcome), from *wil* WILL[2] + *cuman* to COME] —ˈ**welcomely** *adv.* —ˈ**welcomeness** *n.* —ˈ**welcomer** *n.*

weld[1] (wɛld) *vb.* **1.** *(tr.)* to unite (pieces of metal or plastic) together, as by softening with heat and hammering or by fusion. **2.** to bring or admit of being brought into close association or union. ~*n.* **3.** a joint formed by welding. [C16: variant probably based on past participle of WELL[2] in obsolete sense to boil, heat] —ˈ**weldable** *adj.* —ˌ**weldaˈbility** *n.* —ˈ**welder** *or* ˈ**weldor** *n.* —ˈ**weldless** *adj.*

weld[2] (wɛld), **wold,** *or* **woald** (wəʊld) *n.* **1.** a yellow dye obtained from the plant dyer's rocket. **2.** another name for **dyer's rocket.** [C14: from Low German; compare Middle Low German *walde, waude,* Dutch *wouw*]

welding rod *n. Electrical engineering.* filler metal supplied in the form of a rod, usually coated with flux.

welfare (ˈwɛlˌfɛə) *n.* **1.** health, happiness, prosperity, and well-being in general. **2. a.** financial and other assistance given to people in need. **b.** *(as modifier): welfare services.* **3.** Also called: **welfare work.** plans or work to better the social or economic conditions of various underprivileged groups. **4. the welfare.** *Informal, chiefly Brit.* the public agencies involved with giving such assistance. **5. on welfare.** *Chiefly U.S. and Canadian.* in receipt of financial aid from a government agency or other source. [C14: from the phrase *wel fare;* related to Old Norse *velferth,* German *Wohlfahrt;* see WELL[1], FARE]

welfare economics *n. (functioning as sing.)* the aspects of economic theory concerned with the welfare of society and priorities to be observed in the allocation of resources.

welfare state *n.* **1.** a system in which the government undertakes the chief responsibility for providing for the social and economic security of its population, usually through unemployment insurance, old-age pensions, and other social-security measures. **2.** a social system characterized by such policies.

welfarism (ˈwɛlˌfɛərɪzəm) *n.* policies or attitudes associated with a welfare state. —ˈ**welˌfarist** *n.*

welkin (ˈwɛlkɪn) *n. Archaic.* the sky, heavens, or upper air. [Old English *wolcen, welcen;* related to Old Frisian *wolken,* Old Saxon, Old High German *wolcan*]

well[1] (wɛl) *adv.* **better, best. 1.** *(often used in combination)* in a satisfactory manner: *the party went very well.* **2.** *(often used in combination)* in a good, skilful, or pleasing manner: *she plays the violin well.* **3.** in a correct or careful manner: *listen well to my words.* **4.** in a comfortable or prosperous manner: *to live well.* **5.** *(usually used with auxiliaries)* suitably; fittingly: *you can't very well say that.* **6.** intimately: *I knew him well.* **7.** in a kind or favourable manner: *she speaks well of you.* **8.** to a great or considerable extent; fully: *to be well informed.* **9.** by a considerable margin: *let me know well in advance.* **10.** (preceded by *could, might,* or *may*) indeed: *you may well have to do it yourself.* **11.** *Informal.* (intensifier): *well safe.* **12. all very well.** used ironically to express discontent, dissent, etc. **13. as well. a.** in addition; too. **b.** (preceded by *may* or *might*) with equal effect: *you might as well come.* **14. as well as.** in addition to. **15. (just) as well.** preferable or advisable: *it would be just as well if you paid me now.* **16. leave well (enough) alone.** to refrain from interfering with something that is satisfactory. **17. well and good.** used to indicate calm acceptance, as of a decision: *if you accept my offer, well and good.* **18. well up in.** well acquainted with (a particular subject); knowledgeable about. ~*adj. (usually postpositive)* **19.** (when *prenominal, usually used with a negative*) in good health: *I'm very well, thank you; he's not a well man.* **20.** satisfactory, agreeable, or pleasing. **21.** prudent; advisable: *it would be well to make no comment.* **22.** prosperous or comfortable. **23.** fortunate or happy: *it is well that you agreed to go.* ~*interj.* **24. a.** an expression of surprise, indignation, or reproof. **b.** an expression of anticipation in waiting for an answer or remark. ~*sentence connector.* **25.** an expression used to preface a remark, gain time, etc.: *well, I don't think I will come.* [Old English *wel;* related to Old High German *wala, wola* (German *wohl*), Old Norse *val,* Gothic *waila*]

well[2] (wɛl) *n.* **1.** a hole or shaft that is excavated, drilled, bored, or cut into the earth so as to tap a supply of water, oil, gas, etc. **2.** a natural pool where ground water comes to the surface. **3. a.** a cavity, space, or vessel used to contain a liquid. **b.** *(in combination): an inkwell.* **4.** an open shaft through the floors of a building, such as one used for a staircase. **5.** a deep enclosed space in a building or between buildings that is open to the sky to permit light and air to enter. **6. a.** a bulkheaded compartment built around a ship's pumps for protection and ease of access. **b.** another word for **cockpit. 7.** a perforated tank in the hold of a fishing boat for keeping caught fish alive. **8.** (in England) the open space in the centre of a law court. **9.** a source, esp. one that provides a continuous supply: *he is a well of knowledge.* ~*vb.* **10.** to flow or cause to flow upwards or outwards: *tears welled from her eyes.* [Old English *wella;* related to Old High German *wella* (German *Welle* wave), Old Norse *vella* boiling heat]

we'll (wiːl) *contraction of* we will *or* we shall.

well-advised *adj.* (**well advised** *when postpositive*). **1.** acting with deliberation or reason. **2.** well thought out; considered: *a well-advised plan.*

well-affected *adj.* (**well affected** *when postpositive*). favourably disposed (towards); steadfast or loyal.

well-appointed *adj.* (**well appointed** *when postpositive*). well equipped or furnished; properly supplied.

wellaway (ˈwɛləˈweɪ) *interj. Archaic.* woe! alas! [Old English, from *wei lā wei,* variant of *wā lā wā,* literally: woe! lo woe]

well-balanced *adj.* (**well balanced** *when postpositive*). **1.** having good balance or proportions. **2.** of balanced mind; sane or sensible.

ˈ**well-acˈcepted** *adj.*
ˈ**well-acˈcomplished** *adj.*
ˈ**well-acˈcustomed** *adj.*
ˈ**well-acˈknowledged** *adj.*
ˈ**well-acˈquainted** *adj.*
ˈ**well-ˈacted** *adj.*
ˈ**well-aˈdapted** *adj.*
ˈ**well-adˈjusted** *adj.*
ˈ**well-adˈministered** *adj.*
ˈ**well-ˈadverˌtised** *adj.*
ˈ**well-ˈaimed** *adj.*
ˈ**well-ˈaired** *adj.*
ˈ**well-apˈplied** *adj.*
ˈ**well-ˈargued** *adj.*
ˈ**well-ˈarmed** *adj.*
ˈ**well-arˈranged** *adj.*
ˈ**well-asˈsorted** *adj.*
ˈ**well-asˈsured** *adj.*
ˈ**well-atˈtended** *adj.*
ˈ**well-atˈtested** *adj.*
ˈ**well-atˈtired** *adj.*
ˈ**well-auˈthentiˌcated** *adj.*
ˈ**well-aˈware** *adj.*

wellbeing ('wɛl'biːɪŋ) *n.* the condition of being contented, healthy, or successful; welfare.
well-bred *adj.* (**well bred** *when postpositive*). **1.** Also: **well-born.** of respected or noble lineage. **2.** indicating good breeding: well-bred manners. **3.** of good thoroughbred stock: a well-bred spaniel.
well-chosen *adj.* (**well chosen** *when postpositive*). carefully selected to produce a desired effect; apt: *a few well-chosen words may be more effective than a long speech.*
well-connected *adj.* (**well connected** *when postpositive*). having influential or important relatives or friends.
well-disposed *adj.* (**well disposed** *when postpositive*). inclined to be sympathetic, kindly, or friendly: *he was never well disposed towards her relatives.*
well-done *adj.* (**well done** *when postpositive*). **1.** (of food, esp. meat) cooked thoroughly. **2.** made or accomplished satisfactorily.
well dressing *n.* the decoration of wells with flowers, etc.: a traditional annual ceremony of great antiquity in some parts of Britain, originally associated with the cult of water deities.
well-favoured *adj.* (**well favoured** *when postpositive*). having good features; good-looking.
well-fed *adj.* (**well fed** *when postpositive*). **1.** having a nutritious diet; well nourished. **2.** plump; fat.
well-formed *adj. Logic, linguistics.* (of a formula, expression, etc.) constructed in accordance with the syntactic rules of a particular system; grammatically correct. —**well-formedness** *n.*
well-found *adj.* (**well found** *when postpositive*). furnished or supplied with all or most necessary things.
well-founded *adj.* (**well founded** *when postpositive*). having good grounds: *well-founded rumours.*
well-groomed *adj.* (**well groomed** *when postpositive*). **1.** (of a person) having a tidy pleasing appearance. **2.** kept tidy and neat: *a well-groomed garden.* **3.** well turned out and tended: *a well-groomed horse.*
well-grounded *adj.* (**well grounded** *when postpositive*). **1.** well instructed in the basic elements of a subject. **2.** another term for **well-founded.**
wellhead ('wɛl,hɛd) *n.* **1.** the source of a well or stream. **2.** a source, fountainhead, or origin.
well-heeled *adj.* (**well heeled** *when postpositive*). *Informal.* rich; prosperous; wealthy.
well-hung *adj.* (**well hung** *when postpositive*). **1.** (of game) hung for a sufficient length of time. **2.** *Taboo slang.* (of a man) having large genitals.
wellies ('wɛlɪz) *pl. n. Brit. informal.* Wellington boots.
well in *adj.* (*postpositive*) **1.** (often foll. by *with*) *Brit. informal.* on good terms (with): *the foreman was well in with the management.* **2.** *Austral. informal.* rich; prosperous.
well-informed *adj.* (**well informed** *when postpositive*). **1.** having knowledge about a great variety of subjects: *he seems to be a well-informed person.* **2.** possessing reliable information on a particular subject.
Wellington boots ('wɛlɪŋtən) *pl. n.* **1.** Also called: **gumboots, wellingtons.** *Brit.* knee-length or calf-length rubber or rubberized boots, worn esp. in wet conditions. Often shortened to **wellies. 2.** military leather boots covering the front of the knee but cut away at the back to allow easier bending of the knee. [C19: named after the 1st Duke of *Wellington* (1769–1852), British soldier and statesman]
wellingtonia (,wɛlɪŋ'təʊnɪə) *n.* another name for **big tree.** [C19: named after the 1st Duke of *Wellington*]
well-intentioned *adj.* (**well intentioned** *when postpositive*). having or indicating benevolent intentions, usually with unfortunate results.
well-knit *adj.* (**well knit** *when postpositive*). strong, firm, or sturdy.
well-known *adj.* (**well known** *when postpositive*). **1.** widely known; famous; celebrated. **2.** known fully or clearly.
well-mannered *adj.* (**well mannered** *when postpositive*). having good manners; courteous; polite.
well-meaning *adj.* (**well meaning** *when postpositive*). having or indicating good or benevolent intentions, usually with unfortunate results.
well-nigh *adv.* nearly; almost: *it's well-nigh three o'clock.*
▷**Usage.** In strict usage, *well-nigh* is an adverb meaning *nearly* or *almost* and not a preposition meaning *near: he well-nigh cried; he was near* (not *well-nigh*) *death.*
well-off *adj.* (**well off** *when postpositive*). **1.** in a comfortable or favourable position or state. **2.** financially well provided for; moderately rich.
well-oiled *adj.* (**well oiled** *when postpositive*). *Informal.* drunk.
well-ordered *adj. Logic, maths.* (of a relation) having the property that every nonempty subset of its field has a least member under the relation: *less than* is well-ordered on the natural numbers but not on the reals, since an open set has no least member.
well-padded *adj.* (**well padded** *when postpositive*). (of a person) corpulent; portly; fat.
well-preserved *adj.* (**well preserved** *when postpositive*). **1.** kept in a good condition. **2.** continuing to appear youthful: *she was a well-preserved old lady.*
well-read ('wɛl'rɛd) *adj.* (**well read** *when postpositive*). having read widely and intelligently; erudite.
well-rounded *adj.* (**well rounded** *when postpositive*). **1.** rounded in shape or well developed: *a well-rounded figure.* **2.** full, varied, and satisfying: *a well-rounded life.* **3.** well planned and balanced: *a well-rounded programme.*
well-set *adj.* (**well set** *when postpositive*). **1.** firmly established. **2.** (of a person) strongly built.
well-spoken *adj.* (**well spoken** *when postpositive*). **1.** having a clear, articulate, and socially acceptable accent and way of speaking. **2.** spoken satisfactorily or pleasingly.
wellspring ('wɛl,sprɪŋ) *n.* **1.** the source of a spring or stream; fountainhead. **2.** a source of continual or abundant supply. [Old English *welspryng, wylspring;* see WELL², SPRING]
well-stacked *adj.* (**well stacked** *when postpositive*). *Brit. slang.* (of a woman) of voluptuous proportions.
well sweep *n.* a device for raising buckets from and lowering them into a well, consisting of a long pivoted pole, the bucket being attached to one end by a long rope.
well-tempered *adj.* (**well tempered** *when postpositive*). (of a musical scale or instrument) conforming to the system of equal temperament. See **temperament** (sense 4).
well-thought-of *adj.* having a good reputation; respected.
well-thought-out *adj.* (**well thought out** *when postpositive*). carefully planned.
well-thumbed *adj.* (**well thumbed** *when postpositive*). (of a copy of a book) having the pages marked from frequent turning.
well-to-do *adj.* moderately wealthy.
well-turned *adj.* (**well turned** *when postpositive*). **1.** (of a phrase, speech, etc.) apt and pleasingly sonorous. **2.** having a pleasing shape: *a well-turned leg.*
well-upholstered *adj.* (**well upholstered** *when postpositive*) *Informal.* (of a person) fat.

'well-be'haved *adj.*
'well-be'loved *adj., n.*
'well-'blessed *adj.*
'well-'built *adj.*
'well-'calcu,lated *adj.*
'well-'clothed *adj.*
'well-'coached *adj.*
'well-'compen,sated *adj.*
'well-con'cealed *adj.*
'well-con'ditioned *adj.*
'well-con'ducted *adj.*
'well-con'firmed *adj.*
'well-con'sidered *adj.*
'well-con'structed *adj.*
'well-con'tented *adj.*
'well-con'trolled *adj.*
'well-'cooked *adj.*
'well-'covered *adj.*
'well-'culti,vated *adj.*
'well-de'fended *adj.*
'well-de'fined *adj.*
'well-'demon,strated *adj.*
'well-de'scribed *adj.*
'well-de'served *adj.*
'well-de'veloped *adj.*
'well-de'vised *adj.*
'well-di'gested *adj.*
'well-'disciplined *adj.*
'well-'docu,mented *adj.*
'well-'dressed *adj.*
'well-'earned *adj.*
'well-'edu,cated *adj.*
'well-em'ployed *adj.*
'well-en'dowed *adj.*
'well-e'quipped *adj.*
'well-es'tablished *adj.*
'well-es'teemed *adj.*
'well-fi'nanced *adj.*
'well-'finished *adj.*
'well-'fitted *adj.*
'well-'forti,fied *adj.*
'well-'fought *adj.*
'well-'furnished *adj.*
'well-'governed *adj.*
'well-'guarded *adj.*
'well-'handled *adj.*
'well-'hidden *adj.*
'well-'housed *adj.*
'well-'illus,trated *adj.*
'well-in'clined *adj.*
'well-'judged *adj.*
'well-'justi,fied *adj.*
'well-'kept *adj.*
'well-'liked *adj.*
'well-'loved *adj.*
'well-'made *adj.*
'well-'managed *adj.*
'well-'marked *adj.*
'well-'matched *adj.*
'well-'merited *adj.*
'well-'mixed *adj.*
'well-'moti,vated *adj.*
'well-'noted *adj.*
'well-'organ,ized *or* **'well-'organ,ised** *adj.*
'well-'paid *adj.*
'well-'phrased *adj.*
'well-'placed *adj.*
'well-'planned *adj.*
'well-'played *adj.*
'well-'pleased *adj.*
'well-'practised *adj.*
'well-pre'pared *adj.*
'well-pro'portioned *adj.*
'well-pro'tected *adj.*
'well-pro'vided *adj.*
'well-'quali,fied *adj.*
'well-'reasoned *adj.*
'well-re'ceived *adj.*
'well-recom'mended *adj.*
'well-re'garded *adj.*
'well-'regu,lated *adj.*
'well-re'hearsed *adj.*
'well-re'membered *adj.*
'well-repre'sented *adj.*
'well-re'spected *adj.*
'well-re'viewed *adj.*
'well-'ripened *adj.*
'well-'satis,fied *adj.*
'well-'schooled *adj.*
'well-'seasoned *adj.*
'well-se'cured *adj.*
'well-'shaped *adj.*
'well-'situ,ated *adj.*
'well-'spent *adj.*
'well-'stated *adj.*
'well-'stocked *adj.*
'well-'suited *adj.*
'well-sup'plied *adj.*
'well-sup'ported *adj.*
'well-sus'tained *adj.*
'well-'taught *adj.*
'well-'timed *adj.*
'well-'trained *adj.*
'well-'travelled *adj.*
'well-'treated *adj.*
'well-'tried *adj.*
'well-'trodden *adj.*
'well-under'stood *adj.*

well-wisher *n.* a person who shows benevolence or sympathy towards a person, cause, etc. —ˈ**well-ˌwishing** *adj., n.*

well-woman *n., pl.* **-women.** *Social welfare.* **a.** a woman who, although not ill, attends a health-service clinic for preventive monitoring, health education, and advice. **b.** (*as modifier*): *well-woman clinic.*

well-worn *adj.* (**well worn** *when postpositive*). **1.** so much used as to be affected by wear: *a well-worn coat.* **2.** used too often; hackneyed: *a well-worn phrase.*

welly *or* **welly boot** (ˈwɛlɪ) *n., pl.* **wellies** *or* **welly boots.** *Informal.* a Wellington boot.

Welsbach burner (ˈwɛlzbæk; *German* ˈvɛlsbax) *n. Trademark.* a type of gaslight in which a mantle containing thorium and cerium compounds becomes incandescent when heated by a gas flame. [C19: named after Carl Auer, Baron von *Welsbach* (1858–1929), Austrian chemist, who invented it]

welsh *or* **welch** (wɛlʃ) *vb.* (*intr.*; often foll. by *on*) *Slang.* **1.** to fail to pay a gambling debt. **2.** to fail to fulfil an obligation. [C19: of unknown origin] —ˈ**welsher** *or* ˈ**welcher** *n.*

Welsh[1] (wɛlʃ) *adj.* **1.** of, relating to, or characteristic of Wales, its people, their Celtic language, or their dialect of English. ~*n.* **2.** a language of Wales, belonging to the S Celtic branch of the Indo-European family. Welsh shows considerable diversity between dialects. **3. the Welsh.** (*functioning as pl.*) the natives or inhabitants of Wales collectively. ~Also (rare): **Welch.** [Old English *Wēlisc, Wǣlisc;* related to *wealh* foreigner, Old High German *walahisc* (German *welsch*), Old Norse *valskr,* Latin *Volcae*]

Welsh[2] (wɛlʃ) *n.* a white long-bodied lop-eared breed of pig, kept chiefly for bacon.

Welsh corgi *n.* another name for **corgi.**

Welsh dresser *n.* a sideboard with drawers and cupboards below and open shelves above.

Welsh harp *n.* a type of harp in which the strings are arranged in three rows, used esp. for the accompaniment of singing, improvisation on folk tunes, etc.

Welshman (ˈwɛlʃmən) *or* (*fem.*) **Welshwoman** *n., pl.* **-men** *or* **-women.** a native or inhabitant of Wales.

Welshman's button *n.* an angler's name for a species of caddis fly, *Sericostoma personatum.*

Welsh Mountain *n.* a common breed of small hardy sheep kept mainly in the mountains of Wales.

Welsh mountain pony *n.* a small sturdy but graceful breed of pony used mostly for riding, originally from Wales.

Welsh poppy *n.* a perennial W European papaveraceous plant, *Meconopsis cambrica,* with large yellow flowers.

Welsh rabbit *n.* a savoury dish consisting of melted cheese sometimes mixed with milk, seasonings, etc., on hot buttered toast. Also called: **Welsh rarebit, rarebit.** [C18: a fanciful coinage; *rarebit* is a later folk-etymological variant]

Welsh springer spaniel *n.* See **springer spaniel.**

Welsh terrier *n.* a wire-haired breed of terrier with a black-and-tan coat.

welt (wɛlt) *n.* **1.** a raised or strengthened seam or edge, sewn in or on a knitted garment. **2.** another word for **weal**[1]. **3.** (in shoemaking) a strip of leather, etc., put in between the outer sole and the inner sole and upper. ~*vb.* (*tr.*) **4.** to put a welt in (a garment, etc.). **5.** to beat or flog soundly. [C15: origin unknown]

Weltanschauung *German.* (ˈvɛltanʃauʊŋ) *n.* a comprehensive view or personal philosophy of human life and the universe. [from *Welt* world + *Anschauung* view]

welter (ˈwɛltə) *vb.* (*intr.*) **1.** to roll about, writhe, or wallow. **2.** (esp. of the sea) to surge, heave, or toss. **3.** to lie drenched in a liquid, esp. blood. ~*n.* **4.** a rolling motion, as of the sea. **5.** a confused mass; jumble. [C13: from Middle Low German, Middle Dutch *weltern;* related to Old High German *walzan, welzen* to roll]

welterweight (ˈwɛltəˌweɪt) *n.* **1. a.** a professional boxer weighing 140–147 pounds (63.5–66.5 kg). **b.** an amateur boxer weighing 63.5–67 kg (140–148 pounds). **c.** (*as modifier*): *a great welterweight era.* **2.** a wrestler in a similar weight category (usually 154–172 pounds (70–78 kg)).

Weltpolitik *German.* (ˈvɛltpolitiːk) *n.* the policy of participation in world affairs. [literally: world politics]

Weltschmerz *German.* (ˈvɛltʃmɛrts) *n.* sadness or melancholy at the evils of the world; world-weariness. [literally: world pain]

welwitschia (wɛlˈwɪtʃɪə) *n.* a gymnosperm plant, *Welwitschia mirabilis,* of arid regions of tropical and southern Africa, consisting of two large woody leaves lying on the ground with a conelike structure arising between them: order *Gnetales.* [C19: named after F. M. J. *Welwitsch* (1807–72), Portuguese botanist, born in Austria]

wen[1] (wɛn) *n.* **1.** *Pathol.* a sebaceous cyst, esp. one occurring on the scalp. **2.** a large overcrowded city (esp. London in the phrase **the great wen**). [Old English *wenn;* related to Danish dialect *van, væne,* Dutch *wenn*]

wen[2] (wɛn) *n.* a rune having the sound of Modern English *w.* [Old English *wen, wyn*]

wench (wɛntʃ) *n.* **1.** a girl or young woman, esp. a buxom or lively one: now used facetiously. **2.** *Archaic.* a female servant. **3.** *Archaic.* a prostitute. ~*vb.* (*intr.*) **4.** *Archaic.* to frequent the company of prostitutes. [Old English *wencel* child, from *wancol* weak; related to Old High German *wanchal, wankōn*] —ˈ**wencher** *n.*

wend (wɛnd) *vb.* to direct (one's course or way); travel. [Old English *wendan;* related to Old High German *wenten,* Gothic *wandjan;* see WIND[2]]

Wend (wɛnd) *n.* (esp. in medieval European history) a Sorb; a member of the Slavonic people who inhabited the area in present-day Germany between the Rivers Saale and Oder in the early Middle Ages and were conquered by Germanic invaders by the 12th century. See also **Lusatian.**

Wendish (ˈwɛndɪʃ) *adj.* **1.** of or relating to the Wends. ~*n.* **2.** the West Slavonic language of the Wends. See also **Sorbian.**

Wendy house (ˈwɛndɪ) *n.* a small model house that children can enter and play in. [C20: named after the house built for *Wendy,* the girl in J. M. Barrie's play *Peter Pan* (1904)]

wensleydale (ˈwɛnzlɪˌdeɪl) *n.* **1.** a type of white cheese with a flaky texture. **2.** a breed of sheep with long woolly fleece. [named after *Wensleydale,* North Yorkshire]

went (wɛnt) *vb.* the past tense of **go.**

wentletrap (ˈwɛntᵊlˌtræp) *n.* any marine gastropod mollusc of the family *Epitoniidae,* having a long pointed pale-coloured longitudinally ridged shell. [C18: from Dutch *winteltrap* spiral shell, from *wintel,* earlier *windel,* from *wenden* to wind + *trap* a step, stairs]

Wentworth scale (ˈwɛntwəθ) *n. Geology.* a scale for specifying the sizes (diameters) of sedimentary particles, ranging from clay particles (less than 1/256 mm) to boulders (over 256 mm). [after C. K. *Wentworth* (1891–1969), U.S. geologist]

wept (wɛpt) *vb.* the past tense and past participle of **weep.**

were (wɜː; *unstressed* wə) *vb.* the plural form of the past tense (indicative mood) of **be** and the singular form used with *you.* It is also used as a subjunctive, esp. in conditional sentences. [Old English *wērun, wǣron* past tense plural of *wesan* to be; related to Old Norse *vera,* Old Frisian *weria,* Old High German *werōn* to last]

▷**Usage.** *Were,* as a remnant of the past subjunctive in English, is used in formal contexts in clauses expressing hypotheses (*if he were to die, she would inherit everything*), suppositions contrary to fact (*if I were you, I would be careful*), and desire (*I wish he were there now*). In informal speech, however, *was* is often used instead.

we're (wɪə) *contraction of* we are.

weren't (wɜːnt) *vb. contraction of* were not.

werewolf (ˈwɪəˌwʊlf, ˈwɛə-) *n., pl.* **-wolves.** a person fabled in folklore and superstition to have been changed into a wolf by being bewitched or said to be able to assume wolf form at will. [Old English *werewulf,* from *wer* man + *wulf* WOLF; related to Old High German *werwolf,* Middle Dutch *weerwolf*]

wergild, weregild (ˈwɜːˌgɪld, ˈwɛə-), *or* **wergeld** (ˈwɜːˌgɛld, ˈwɛə-) *n.* the price set on a man's life in successive Anglo-Saxon and Germanic law codes, to be paid as compensation by his slayer. [Old English *wergeld,* from *wer* man (related to Old Norse *ver,* Latin *vir*) + *gield* tribute (related to Gothic *gild,* Old High German *gelt* payment); see YIELD]

wernerite (ˈwɜːnəˌraɪt) *n.* another name for **scapolite.** [C19: named after A.G. *Werner* (1750–1817), German mineralogist]

wersh (wɜːʃ; *Scot.* wɛrʃ) *adj. Scot.* **1.** tasteless; insipid. **2.** sour; bitter. [C16: perhaps alteration of dialect *wearish,* probably of Germanic origin]

wert (wɜːt; *unstressed* wət) *vb. Archaic or dialect.* (used with the pronoun *thou* or its relative equivalent) a singular form of the past tense (indicative mood) of **be.**

weskit (ˈwɛskɪt) *n.* an informal word for **waistcoat.**

Wesleyan (ˈwɛzlɪən) *adj.* **1.** of, relating to, or deriving from John Wesley (1703–91), English preacher who founded Methodism. **2.** of, relating to, or characterizing Methodism, esp. in its original form or as upheld by the branch of the Methodist Church known as the **Wesleyan Methodists.** ~*n.* **3.** a follower of John Wesley. **4.** a member of the Methodist Church or (formerly) of the Wesleyan Methodists. —ˈ**Wesleyanism** *n.*

west (wɛst) *n.* **1.** one of the four cardinal points of the compass, 270° clockwise from north and 180° from east. **2.** the direction along a parallel towards the sunset, at 270° clockwise from north. **3. the west.** (*often cap.*) any area lying in or towards the west. Related adjs.: **Hesperian, Occidental.** **4.** *Cards.* (*usually cap.*) the player or position at the table corresponding to west on the compass. ~*adj.* **5.** situated in, moving towards, or facing the west. **6.** (esp. of the wind) from the west. ~*adv.* **7.** in, to, or towards the west. **8.** *Archaic.* (of the wind) from the west. **9. go west.** *Informal.* **a.** to be lost or destroyed irrevocably. **b.** to die. ~Symbol: W [Old English; related to Old Norse *vestr,* Sanskrit *avāstāt,* Latin *vesper* evening, Greek *hésperos*]

West (wɛst) *n.* **the.** **1.** the western part of the world contrasted historically and culturally with the East or Orient; the Occident. **2.** (formerly) the non-Communist countries of Europe and

ˈ**well-ˈused** *adj.*
ˈ**well-ˈveriˌfied** *adj.*
ˈ**well-ˈwooded** *adj.*
ˈ**well-ˈworded** *adj.*
ˈ**well-ˈwritten** *adj.*
ˈ**well-ˈwrought** *adj.*

America contrasted with the Communist states of the East. Compare **East** (sense 2). **3. a.** of or denoting the western part of a specified country, area, etc. **b.** (*as part of a name*): *the West Coast.*

West Atlantic *n.* **1.** a branch of the Niger-Congo family of African languages, spoken in Senegal and in scattered areas eastwards, including Fulani and Wolof. *~adj.* **2.** relating to or belonging to this group of languages.

westbound ('wɛstˌbaʊnd) *adj.* going or leading towards the west.

west by north *n.* **1.** one point on the compass north of west, 281° 15′ clockwise from north. *~adj., adv.* **2.** in, from, or towards this direction.

west by south *n.* **1.** one point on the compass south of west, 258° 45′ clockwise from north. *~adj., adv.* **2.** in, from, or towards this direction.

West Coast jazz *n.* a type of cool jazz displaying a soft intimate sound, regular rhythms, and a tendency to incorporate academic classical devices into jazz, such as fugue.

wester ('wɛstə) *vb.* **1.** (*intr.*) (of the sun, moon, or a star) to move or appear to move towards the west. *~n.* **2.** a strong wind or storm from the west.

westering ('wɛstərɪŋ) *adj. Poetic.* moving towards the west: *the westering star.*

Westerlies ('wɛstəlɪz) *pl. n. Meteorol.* the prevailing winds blowing from the west on the poleward sides of the horse latitudes, often bringing depressions and anticyclones.

westerly ('wɛstəlɪ) *adj.* **1.** of, relating to, or situated in the west. *~adv., adj.* **2.** towards or in the direction of the west. **3.** (esp. of the wind) from the west. *~n., pl.* **-lies. 4.** a wind blowing from the west. —'**westerliness** *n.*

western ('wɛstən) *adj.* **1.** situated in or towards or facing the west. **2.** going or directed to or towards the west. **3.** (of a wind, etc.) coming or originating from the west. **4.** native to, inhabiting, or growing in the west. **5.** *Music.* See **country and western.**

Western ('wɛstən) *adj.* **1.** of, relating to, or characteristic of the West. **2.** of, relating to, or characteristic of the western states of the U.S. *~n.* **3.** a film, book, etc., concerned with life in the western states of the U.S., esp. during the era of exploration and early development.

Western Church *n.* **1.** the part of Christendom that derives its liturgy, discipline, and traditions principally from the patriarchate of Rome, as contrasted with the part that derives these from the other ancient patriarchates, esp. that of Constantinople. **2.** the Roman Catholic Church, sometimes together with the Anglican Communion of Churches.

westerner ('wɛstənə) *n.* (*sometimes cap.*) a native or inhabitant of the west of any specific region, esp. of the western states of the U.S. or of the western hemisphere.

western hemisphere *n.* (*often caps.*) **1.** that half of the globe containing the Americas, lying to the west of the Greenwich or another meridian. **2.** the lands contained in this, esp. the Americas.

western hemlock *n.* a North American coniferous evergreen tree, *Tsuga heterophylla,* having hanging branches and oblong cones: family *Pinaceae.*

westernism ('wɛstəˌnɪzəm) *n.* a word, habit, practice, etc., characteristic of western people or of the western U.S.

westernize *or* **westernise** ('wɛstəˌnaɪz) *vb.* (*tr.*) to influence or make familiar with the customs, practices, etc., of the West. —ˌ**westerni'zation** *or* ˌ**westerni'sation** *n.*

western larch *n.* a North American larch, *Larix occidentalis,* having oval cones and found mainly in S British Columbia.

westernmost ('wɛstənˌməʊst) *adj.* situated or occurring farthest west.

western red cedar *n.* **1.** a large North American arbor vitae, *Thuja plicata,* found along and near the Pacific coast. **2.** the wood of this tree, used by North American Indians for building and for carving totem poles.

western roll *n.* a technique in high-jumping in which the jumper executes a half-turn of the body to clear the bar.

western swing *n.* a 1930s jazz-influenced style of country music.

West Germanic *n.* a subbranch of the Germanic languages that consists of English, Frisian, Dutch, Flemish, Afrikaans, Low German, German, Yiddish, and their associated dialects.

West Highland white terrier *n.* a small pure white terrier having a hard straight coat and erect ears and tail.

West Indian *n.* **1.** a native or inhabitant of any of the islands making up the West Indies, in the Atlantic Ocean off Central America. **2.** an emigrant from the West Indies or a descendant of one. *~adj.* **3.** of or relating to the West Indies, West Indians, or their culture.

westing ('wɛstɪŋ) *n. Navigation.* movement, deviation, or distance covered in a westerly direction, esp. as expressed in the resulting difference in longitude.

Westinghouse brake ('wɛstɪŋˌhaʊs) *n.* a braking system and adopted by U.S. railways, in which the brakes are held off by compressed air in the operating cylinder: controlled leakage of the air or a disruptive emergency causes the brakes to be applied. The system is used on most heavy vehicles and is replacing the vacuum system on many railways. [named after its U.S. inventor, George *Westinghouse* (1846–1914)]

Westm. *abbrev. for* Westminster.

west-northwest *n.* **1.** the point on the compass or the direction midway between west and northwest, 292° 30′ clockwise from north. *~adj., adv.* **2.** in, from, or towards this direction. *~Symbol:* WNW

Weston standard cell ('wɛstən) *n.* a primary cell used as a standard of emf, producing 1.018636 volts: consists of a mercury anode and a cadmium amalgam cathode in an electrolyte of saturated cadmium sulphate. Former name: **cadmium cell.** [C20: from a trademark]

West Saxon (in Anglo-Saxon England) *~adj.* **1.** of or relating to the kingdom of Wessex in S and SW England, its inhabitants, or their dialect. *~n.* **2.** the dialect of Old English spoken in Wessex: the chief literary dialect of Old English. See also **Anglian, Kentish. 3.** an inhabitant of Wessex.

west-southwest *n.* **1.** the point on the compass or the direction midway between southwest and west, 247° 30′ clockwise from north. *~adj., adv.* **2.** in, from, or towards this direction. *~Symbol:* WSW

westward ('wɛstwəd) *adj.* **1.** moving, facing, or situated in the west. *~adv.* **2.** Also: **westwards.** towards the west. *~n.* **3.** the westward part, direction, etc.; the west. —'**westwardly** *adj., adv.*

wet (wɛt) *adj.* **wetter, wettest. 1.** moistened, covered, saturated, etc., with water or some other liquid. **2.** not yet dry or solid: *wet varnish.* **3.** rainy, foggy, misty, or humid: *wet weather.* **4.** employing a liquid, usually water: *a wet method of chemical analysis.* **5.** *Chiefly U.S. and Canadian.* characterized by or permitting the free sale of alcoholic beverages: *a wet state.* **6.** *Brit. informal.* feeble or foolish. **7. wet behind the ears.** *Informal.* immature or inexperienced; naive. *~n.* **8.** wetness or moisture. **9.** damp or rainy weather. **10.** *Brit. informal.* a Conservative politician who is considered not to be a hard-liner. Compare **dry** (sense 21). **11.** *Brit. informal.* a feeble or foolish person. **12.** *Chiefly U.S. and Canadian.* a person who advocates free sale of alcoholic beverages. **13. the wet.** *Austral.* (in northern and central Australia) the rainy season. *~vb.* **wets, wetting, wet** *or* **wetted. 14.** to make or become wet. **15.** to urinate on (something). **16.** (*tr.*) *Dialect.* to prepare (tea) by boiling or infusing. **17. wet one's whistle.** *Informal.* to take an alcoholic drink. [Old English *wǣt;* related to Old Frisian *wēt,* Old Norse *vātr,* Old Slavonic *vedro* bucket] —'**wetly** *adv.* —'**wetness** *n.* —ˌ**wetta'bility** *n.* —'**wettable** *adj.* —'**wetter** *n.* —'**wettish** *adj.*

weta ('wɛtə) *n.* any of various wingless insects of the family *Stenopelmatidae* of New Zealand, with long spiny legs. [Maori]

wet-and-dry-bulb thermometer *n.* another name for **psychrometer.**

wetback ('wɛtˌbæk) *n. U.S. informal.* a Mexican labourer who enters the U.S. illegally.

wet blanket *n. Informal.* a person whose low spirits or lack of enthusiasm have a depressing effect on others.

wet-bulb thermometer *n.* a thermometer the bulb of which is covered by a moist muslin bag, used together with a dry-bulb thermometer to measure humidity.

wet cell *n.* a primary cell in which the electrolyte is a liquid. Compare **dry cell.**

wet dream *n.* an erotic dream accompanied by an emission of semen during or just after sleep.

wet fish *n.* **a.** fresh fish as opposed to frozen or cooked fish. **b.** (*as modifier*): *a wet-fish shop.*

wet fly *n. Angling.* **a.** an artificial fly designed to float or ride below the water surface. **b.** (*as modifier*): *wet-fly fishing.* ~Compare **dry fly.**

wether ('wɛðə) *n.* a male sheep, esp. a castrated one. [Old English *hwæther;* related to Old Frisian *hweder,* Old High German *hwedar,* Old Norse *hvatharr*]

wetland ('wɛtlənd) *n.* (*sometimes pl.*) **a.** an area of swampy or marshy land, esp. considered as part of an ecological system. **b.** (*as modifier*): *wetland species.*

wet look *n.* a shiny finish given to certain clothing and footwear materials, esp. plastic and leather.

wet nurse *n.* **1.** a woman hired to suckle the child of another. *~vb.* **wet-nurse.** (*tr.*) **2.** to act as a wet nurse to (a child). **3.** *Informal.* to attend with great devotion.

wet pack *n. Med.* a hot or cold damp sheet or blanket for wrapping around a patient.

wet rot *n.* **1.** a state of decay in timber caused by various fungi, esp. *Coniophora puteana.* The hyphal strands of the fungus are seldom visible and affected timber turns dark brown. **2.** any of the fungi causing this decay.

wet steam *n.* steam, usually low-pressure, that contains water droplets in suspension.

wet suit *n.* a close-fitting rubber suit used by skin divers, yachtsmen, etc., to retain body heat when they are immersed in water or sailing in cold weather.

wetting agent *n. Chem.* any substance added to a liquid to lower its surface tension and thus increase its ability to spread across or penetrate into a solid.

WEU *abbrev. for* Western European Union.

we've (wiːv) *contraction of* we have.

wf *Printing. abbrev. for* wrong fount.

WFF *Logic. abbrev. for* well-formed formula.

WFTU *abbrev. for* World Federation of Trade Unions.

wg *or* **WG** *abbrev. for:* **1.** water gauge. **2.** wire gauge.
WG *international car registration for* (Windward Islands) Grenada.
W. Glam. *abbrev. for* West Glamorgan.
wh. *abbrev. for* white.
wha (hwɔː) *or* **whae** (hwe) *pron.* a Scot. word for **who.**
whack (wæk) *vb. (tr.)* **1.** to strike with a sharp resounding blow. **2.** *(usually passive) Brit. informal.* to exhaust completely. *~n.* **3.** a sharp resounding blow or the noise made by such a blow. **4.** *Informal.* a share or portion. **5.** *Informal.* a try or attempt (esp. in the phrase **have a whack at**). *~interj.* **6.** an exclamation imitating the noise of a sharp resounding blow. [C18: perhaps a variant of THWACK, ultimately of imitative origin] —**'whacker** *n.*
whacking ('wækɪŋ) *Informal, chiefly Brit.* *~adj.* **1.** enormous. *~adv.* **2.** (intensifier): *a whacking big lie.*
whacko ('wækəʊ) *interj. Slang.* an exclamation of happiness, delight, etc. [C20: from WHACK]
whack off *vb. (intr., adv) Taboo slang.* to masturbate.
whacky ('wækɪ) *adj.* **whackier, whackiest.** *U.S. slang.* a variant spelling of **wacky.**
whale[1] (weɪl) *n., pl.* **whales** *or* **whale. 1.** any of the larger cetacean mammals, excluding dolphins, porpoises, and narwhals. They have flippers, a streamlined body, and a horizontally flattened tail and breathe through a blowhole on the top of the head. **2.** any cetacean mammal. See also **toothed whale, whalebone whale. 3. a whale of a.** *Informal.* an exceptionally large, fine, etc., example of a (person or thing): *we had a whale of a time on holiday.* [Old English *hwæl;* related to Old Saxon, Old High German *hwal,* Old Norse *hvalr,* Latin *squalus* seapig]
whale[2] (weɪl) *vb. (tr.)* to beat or thrash soundly. [C18: variant of WALE[1]]
whaleback ('weɪlˌbæk) *n.* **1.** something shaped like the back of a whale. **2.** a steamboat having a curved upper deck.
whaleboat ('weɪlˌbəʊt) *n.* a narrow boat from 20 to 30 feet long having a sharp prow and stern, formerly used in whaling. Also called: **whaler.**
whalebone ('weɪlˌbəʊn) *n.* **1.** Also called: **baleen.** a horny elastic material forming a series of numerous thin plates that hang from the upper jaw on either side of the palate in the toothless (whalebone) whales and strain plankton from water entering the mouth. **2.** a thin strip of this substance, used in stiffening corsets, bodices, etc.
whalebone whale *n.* any whale belonging to the cetacean suborder *Mysticeti,* having a double blowhole and strips of whalebone between the jaws instead of teeth: includes the rorquals, right whales, and the blue whale. Compare **toothed whale.**
whale catcher *n.* a vessel engaged in the actual harpooning of whales.
whale oil *n.* oil obtained either from the blubber of whales (train oil) or the head of the sperm whale (sperm oil).
whaler ('weɪlə) *n.* **1.** Also called (U.S.): **whaleman.** a person employed in whaling. **2.** a vessel engaged in whaling. See **factory ship, whale catcher. 3.** another word for **whaleboat. 4.** *Austral.* a nomad surviving in the bush without working.
whale shark *n.* a large spotted whalelike shark, *Rhincodon typus,* of warm seas, that feeds on plankton and small animals: family *Rhincodontidae.*
whaling ('weɪlɪŋ) *n.* **1.** the work or industry of hunting and processing whales for food, oil, etc. *~adv.* **2.** *Informal.* (intensifier): *a whaling good time.*
wham (wæm) *n.* **1.** a forceful blow or impact or the sound produced by such a blow or impact. *~interj.* **2.** an exclamation imitative of this sound. *~vb.* **whams, whamming, whammed. 3.** to strike or cause to strike with great force. [C20: of imitative origin]
whanau ('fɑːnaʊ) *n. N.Z.* a family, esp. an extended family. [Maori]
whang[1] (wæŋ) *vb.* **1.** to strike or be struck so as to cause a resounding noise. *~n.* **2.** the resounding noise produced by a heavy blow. **3.** a heavy blow. [C19: of imitative origin]
whang[2] (wæŋ) *n. Scot.* **1.** a leather thong. *~vb.* **2.** *(tr.)* to strike with or as if with a thong. [C17: variant of THONG]
whangee (wæŋ'iː) *n.* **1.** any tall woody grass of the S and SE Asian genus *Phyllostachys,* grown for its stems, which are used for bamboo canes and as a source of paper pulp. **2.** a cane or walking stick made from the stem of any of these plants. [C19: probably from Chinese (Mandarin) *huangli,* from *huang* yellow + *li* bamboo cane]
whap (wɒp) *vb.* **whaps, whapping, whapped,** *n.* a less common spelling of **whop.**
whare ('wɔːrɪ; *Maori* 'fɒrɛ) *n. N.Z.* **1.** a Maori hut or dwelling place. **2.** any simple dwelling place, esp. at a beach or in the bush. [from Maori]
wharepuni ('fɒrɛˌpʊnɪ) *n. N.Z.* another name for **meeting house** (sense 2).
wharf (wɔːf) *n., pl.* **wharves** (wɔːvz) *or* **wharfs. 1.** a platform of timber, stone, concrete, etc., built parallel to the waterfront at a harbour or navigable river for the docking, loading, and unloading of ships. **2. the wharves.** *N.Z.* the working area of a dock. **3.** an obsolete word for **shore.** *~vb. (tr.)* **4.** to moor or dock at a wharf. **5.** to provide or equip with a wharf or wharves. **6.** to store or unload on a wharf. [Old English *hwearf* heap; related to Old Saxon *hwarf,* Old High German *hwarb* a turn, Old Norse *hvarf* circle]
wharfage ('wɔːfɪdʒ) *n.* **1.** accommodation for ships at wharves. **2.** a charge for use of a wharf. **3.** wharves collectively.
wharfie ('wɔːfɪ) *n. Austral. and N.Z.* a wharf labourer; docker.
wharfinger ('wɔːfɪndʒə) *n.* an owner or manager of a wharf. [C16: probably alteration of *wharfager* (see WHARFAGE, -ER[1]); compare HARBINGER]
wharf rat *n.* **1.** any rat, usually a brown rat, that infests wharves. **2.** *Informal.* a person who haunts wharves, usually for dishonest purposes.
wharve (wɔːv) *n.* a wooden disc or wheel on a shaft serving as a flywheel or pulley. [Old English *hweorfa,* from *hweorfan* to revolve; related to Old Saxon *hwervo* axis, Old High German *hwerbo* a turn]
what (wɒt; *unstressed* wət) *determiner.* **1. a.** used with a noun in requesting further information about the identity or categorization of something: *what job does he do?* **b.** *(as pronoun): what is her address?* **c.** *(used in indirect questions): does he know what man did this? tell me what he said.* **2. a.** the (person, thing, persons, or things) that: *we photographed what animals we could see.* **b.** *(as pronoun): bring me what you've written; come what may.* **3.** (intensifier; used in exclamations): *what a good book!* *~adv.* **4.** in what respect? to what degree?: *what do you care?* *~pron.* **5.** *Not standard.* which, who, or that, when used as relative pronouns: *this is the man what I saw in the park yesterday.* **6. what about.** what do you think, know, feel, etc., concerning? **7. what for. a.** for what purpose? why? **b.** *Informal.* a punishment or reprimand (esp. in the phrase **give (a person) what for**). **8. what have you.** someone, something, or somewhere unknown or unspecified: *cars, motorcycles, or what have you.* **9. what if. a.** what would happen if? **b.** what difference would it make if? **10. what matter.** what does it matter? **11. what's what.** *Informal.* the true or real state of affairs. *~interj.* **12.** *Informal.* don't you think? don't you agree?: *splendid party, what?* [Old English *hwæt;* related to Old Frisian *whet,* Old High German *hwaz* (German *was*), Old Norse *hvatr*]
whatever (wɒt'ɛvə, wət-) *pron.* **1.** everything or anything that: *do whatever he asks you to.* **2.** no matter what: *whatever he does, he is forgiven.* **3.** *Informal.* an unknown or unspecified thing or things: *take a hammer, chisel, or whatever.* **4.** an intensive form of *what,* used in questions: *whatever can he have said to upset her so much?* *~determiner.* **5.** an intensive form of *what: use whatever tools you can get hold of.* *~adj.* **6.** *(postpositive)* absolutely; whatsoever: *I saw no point whatever in continuing.*
whatnot ('wɒtˌnɒt) *n.* **1.** Also called: **what-d'you-call-it.** *Informal.* a person or thing the name of which is unknown, temporarily forgotten, or deliberately overlooked. **2.** *Informal.* unspecified assorted material. **3.** a portable stand with shelves, used for displaying ornaments, etc.
whatsit ('wɒtsɪt), **whatsitsname,** *(masc.)* **whatshisname,** *or (fem.)* **whatshername** *n. Informal.* a person or thing the name of which is unknown, temporarily forgotten, or deliberately overlooked.
whatsoever (ˌwɒtsəʊ'ɛvə) *adj.* **1.** *(postpositive)* at all: used as an intensifier with indefinite pronouns and determiners such as *none, any, no one, anybody,* etc. *~pron.* **2.** an archaic word for **whatever.**
whaup (wɔːp; *Scot.* hwɔːp) *n. Chiefly Scot.* a popular name for the **curlew.** [C16: related to Old English *huilpe,* ultimately imitative of the bird's cry; compare Low German *regenwilp* sandpiper]
whaur (hwɔːr) *adv., pron., conj., n.* a Scot. word for **where.**
wheal (wiːl) *n.* a variant spelling of **weal**[1].
wheat (wiːt) *n.* **1.** any annual or biennial grass of the genus *Triticum,* native to the Mediterranean region and W Asia but widely cultivated, having erect flower spikes and light brown grains. **2.** the grain of any of these grasses, used in making flour, pasta, etc. ~See also **emmer, durum.** [Old English *hwǣte,* related to Old Frisian, Old Saxon *hwēti,* Old High German *hweizi,* Old Norse *hveiti;* see WHITE]
wheatear ('wiːtˌɪə) *n.* any small northern songbird of the genus *Oenanthe,* esp. *O. oenanthe,* a species having a pale grey back, black wings and tail, white rump, and pale brown underparts: subfamily *Turdinae* (thrushes). [C16: back formation from *wheatears* (wrongly taken as plural), probably from WHITE + ARSE; compare Dutch *witstaart,* French *culblanc* white tail]
wheaten ('wiːtᵊn) *adj.* **1.** made of the grain or flour of wheat: *wheaten bread.* **2.** of a pale yellow colour.
wheat germ *n.* the vitamin-rich embryo of the wheat kernel, which is largely removed before milling and is used in cereals, as a food supplement, etc.
wheatmeal ('wiːtˌmiːl) *n.* **a.** a brown flour intermediate between white flour and wholemeal flour. **b.** *(as modifier): a wheatmeal loaf.*
wheat rust *n.* **1.** a rust fungus, *Puccinia graminis,* that attacks cereals, esp. wheat, and the barberry. **2.** the disease caused by this fungus.
Wheatstone bridge ('wiːtstən) *n.* a device for determining the value of an unknown resistance by comparison with a known standard resistance. [C19: named after Sir Charles *Wheatstone* (1802–75), British physicist and inventor]
wheatworm ('wiːtˌwɜːm) *n.* a parasitic nematode worm, *Anguina tritici,* that forms galls in the seeds of wheat.

whee (wiː) *interj.* an exclamation of joy, thrill, etc.

wheedle (ˈwiːdᵊl) *vb.* **1.** to persuade or try to persuade (someone) by coaxing words, flattery, etc. **2.** (*tr.*) to obtain by coaxing and flattery: *she wheedled some money out of her father.* [C17: perhaps from German *wedeln* to wag one's tail, from Old High German *wedil, wadil* tail] —ˈ**wheedler** *n.* —ˈ**wheedling** *adj.* —ˈ**wheedlingly** *adv.*

wheel (wiːl) *n.* **1.** a solid disc, or a circular rim joined to a hub by radial or tangential spokes, that is mounted on a shaft about which it can turn, as in vehicles and machines. **2.** anything like a wheel in shape or function. **3.** a device consisting of or resembling a wheel or having a wheel as its principal component: *a steering wheel; a water wheel.* **4.** (usually preceded by *the*) a medieval torture consisting of a wheel to which the victim was tied and then had his limbs struck and broken by an iron bar. **5.** short for **wheel of fortune** or **potter's wheel. 6.** the act of turning. **7.** a pivoting movement of troops, ships, etc. **8.** a type of firework coiled to make it rotate when let off. **9.** a set of short rhyming lines, usually four or five in number, forming the concluding part of a stanza. Compare **bob**[2] (sense 7). **10.** the disc in which the ball is spun in roulette. **11.** *U.S. and Canadian.* an informal word for **bicycle. 12.** *Archaic.* a refrain. **13.** *Informal, chiefly U.S. and Canadian.* a person of great influence (esp. in the phrase **big wheel**). **14. at the wheel. a.** driving or steering a vehicle or vessel. **b.** in charge. ~*vb.* **15.** (when *intr.* sometimes foll. by *about* or *round*) to turn or cause to turn on or as if on an axis. **16.** to move or cause to move on or as if on wheels; roll. **17.** (*tr.*) to perform with or in a circular movement. **18.** (*tr.*) to provide with a wheel or wheels. **19.** (*intr.*; often foll. by *about*) to change one's mind or opinion. **20. wheel and deal.** *Informal.* to be a free agent, esp. to advance one's own interests. ~See also **wheels.** [Old English *hweol, hweowol;* related to Old Norse *hvēl,* Greek *kuklos,* Middle Low German *wēl,* Dutch *wiel*] —ˈ**wheel-less** *adj.*

wheel and axle *n.* a simple machine for raising weights in which a rope unwinding from a wheel is wound onto a cylindrical drum or shaft coaxial with or joined to the wheel to provide mechanical advantage.

wheel animalcule *n.* another name for **rotifer.**

wheelbarrow (ˈwiːlˌbærəʊ) *n.* **1.** a simple vehicle for carrying small loads, typically being an open container supported by a wheel at the front and two legs behind. ~*vb.* **2.** (*tr.*) to convey in a wheelbarrow.

wheelbase (ˈwiːlˌbeɪs) *n.* the distance between the front and back axles of a motor vehicle.

wheel bug *n.* a large predatory North American heteropterous insect, *Arilus cristatus,* having a semicircular thoracic projection: family *Reduviidae* (assassin bugs).

wheelchair (ˈwiːlˌtʃɛə) *n. Med.* a special chair mounted on large wheels, for use by invalids or others for whom walking is impossible or temporarily inadvisable.

wheelchair housing *n. Social welfare.* housing designed or adapted for a chairbound person. See also **mobility housing.**

wheel clamp *n.* a device fixed onto one wheel of an illegally parked car in order to immobilize it. The driver has to pay to have it removed.

wheeled (wiːld) *adj.* **a.** having or equipped with a wheel or wheels. **b.** (*in combination*): *four-wheeled.*

wheeler (ˈwiːlə) *n.* **1.** Also called: **wheel horse.** a horse or other draught animal nearest the wheel. **2.** (*in combination*) something equipped with a specified sort or number of wheels: *a three-wheeler.* **3.** a person or thing that wheels.

wheeler-dealer *n. Informal.* a person who wheels and deals.

wheel horse *n.* **1.** another word for **wheeler** (sense 1). **2.** *U.S. and Canadian.* a person who works steadily or hard.

wheelhouse (ˈwiːlˌhaʊs) *n.* another term for **pilot house.**

wheelie (ˈwiːlɪ) *n., pl.* **-ies.** a manoeuvre on a bicycle or motorbike in which the front wheel is raised off the ground.

wheel lock *n.* **1.** a gunlock formerly in use in which the firing mechanism was activated by sparks produced by friction between a small steel wheel and a flint. **2.** a gun having such a lock.

wheel man *n.* **1.** a cyclist. **2.** Also called: **wheelsman.** *U.S.* a helmsman.

wheel of fortune *n.* (in mythology and literature) a revolving device spun by a deity of fate selecting random changes in the affairs of man. Often shortened to **wheel.**

wheels (wiːlz) *pl. n.* **1.** the main directing force behind an organization, movement, etc.: *the wheels of government.* **2.** an informal word for **car. 3. wheels within wheels.** a series of intricately connected events, plots, etc.

wheel window *n.* another name for **rose window.**

wheel wobble *n.* an oscillation of the front wheels of a vehicle caused by a defect in the steering gear, unbalanced wheels, etc.

wheelwork (ˈwiːlˌwɜːk) *n.* an arrangement of wheels in a machine, esp. a train of gears.

wheelwright (ˈwiːlˌraɪt) *n.* a person who makes or mends wheels as a trade.

wheen (wiːn; *Scot.* hwiːn) *determiner. Scot. and northern English dialect.* **1.** few; some. **2.** (preceded by *a*) **a.** a small number of. **b.** a good number of. **c.** (*as pronoun; functioning as pl.*): *a wheen of years.* [Old English *hwēne,* instrumental of *hwōn* few, a few]

wheesh (hwiːʃ) *or* **wheesht** (hwiːʃt) *Scot.* ~*interj.* **1.** a plea or demand for silence; hush. ~*vb.* **2.** to silence (a person, noise, etc.) or to be silent. ~*n.* **3.** silence; hush. **4. haud your wheesht!** be silent! hush! [of imitative origin; compare HUSH]

wheeze (wiːz) *vb.* **1.** to breathe or utter (something) with a rasping or whistling sound. **2.** (*intr.*) to make or move with a noise suggestive of wheezy breathing. ~*n.* **3.** a husky, rasping, or whistling sound or breathing. **4.** *Brit. slang.* a trick, idea, or plan (esp. in the phrase **good wheeze**). **5.** *Informal.* a hackneyed joke or anecdote. [C15: probably from Old Norse *hvǣsa* to hiss] —ˈ**wheezer** *n.* —ˈ**wheezy** *adj.* —ˈ**wheezily** *adv.* —ˈ**wheeziness** *n.*

whelk[1] (wɛlk) *n.* any carnivorous marine gastropod mollusc of the family *Buccinidae,* of coastal waters and intertidal regions, having a strong snail-like shell. [Old English *weoloc;* related to Middle Dutch *willok,* Old Norse *vil* entrails]

whelk[2] (wɛlk) *n.* a raised lesion on the skin; wheal. [Old English *hwylca,* of obscure origin] —ˈ**whelky** *adj.*

whelm (wɛlm) *vb.* (*tr.*) *Archaic.* **1.** to engulf entirely with or as if with water. **2.** another word for **overwhelm.** [C13: *whelmen* to turn over, of uncertain origin]

whelp (wɛlp) *n.* **1.** a young offspring of certain animals, esp. of a wolf or dog. **2.** *Disparaging.* a young man or youth. **3.** *Jocular.* a young child. **4.** *Nautical.* any of the ridges, parallel to the axis, on the drum of a capstan to keep a rope, cable, or chain from slipping. ~*vb.* **5.** (of an animal or, disparagingly, a woman) to give birth to (young). [Old English *hwelp(a);* related to Old High German *hwelf,* Old Norse *hvelpr,* Danish *hvalp*]

when (wɛn) *adv.* **1. a.** at what time? over what period?: *when is he due?* **b.** (*used in indirect questions*): *ask him when he's due.* **2. say when.** to state when an action is to be stopped or begun, as when someone is pouring a drink. ~*conj.* **3.** (*subordinating*) at a time at which; at the time at which; just as; after: *I found it easily when I started to look seriously.* **4.** although: *he drives when he might walk.* **5.** considering the fact that: *how did you pass the exam when you'd not worked for it?* ~*pron.* **6.** at which (time); over which (period): *an age when men were men.* ~*n.* **7.** (*usually pl.*) a question as to the time of some occurrence. [Old English *hwanne, hwænne;* related to Old High German *hwanne, hwenne,* Latin *cum*]

▷**Usage.** Care should be taken so that *when* and *where* refer explicitly to time or place, and are not used loosely to substitute for *in which* after the verb *to be: paralysis is a condition in which* (not *when* or *where*) *parts of the body cannot be moved.*

whenas (wɛnˈæz) *conj.* **1.** *Archaic.* **a.** when; whenever. **b.** inasmuch as; while. **2.** *Obsolete.* whereas; although.

whence (wɛns) *Archaic or formal.* ~*adv.* **1.** from what place, cause, or origin? ~*pron.* **2.** (*subordinating*) from what place, cause, or origin. [C13 *whannes,* adverbial genitive of Old English *hwanon;* related to Old Frisian *hwana,* Old High German *hwanan*]

▷**Usage.** Careful users of English avoid the expression *from whence,* since *whence* already means from which place: *the tradition whence* (not *from whence*) *such ideas flow.*

whencesoever (ˌwɛnssəʊˈɛvə) *conj.* (*subordinating*), *adv. Archaic.* out of whatsoever place, cause, or origin.

whene'er (wɛnˈɛə) *adv., conj.* a poetic contraction of **whenever.**

whenever (wɛnˈɛvə) *conj.* **1.** (*subordinating*) at every or any time that; when: *I laugh whenever I see that.* ~*adv. also* **when ever. 2.** no matter when: *it'll be here, whenever you decide to come for it.* **3.** *Informal.* at an unknown or unspecified time: *I'll take it if it comes today, tomorrow, or whenever.* **4.** an intensive form of *when,* used in questions: *whenever did he escape?*

whensoever (ˌwɛnsəʊˈɛvə) *conj., adv. Rare.* an intensive form of **whenever.**

whenua (fɛnˈuə) *n. N.Z.* land. [Maori]

where (wɛə) *adv.* **1. a.** in, at, or to what place, point, or position?: *where are you going?* **b.** (*used in indirect questions*): *I don't know where they are.* ~*pron.* **2.** in, at, or to which (place): *the hotel where we spent our honeymoon.* ~*conj.* **3.** (*subordinating*) in the place at which: *where we live it's always raining.* ~*n.* **4.** (*usually pl.*) a question as to the position, direction, or destination of something. [Old English *hwǣr, hwār(a);* related to Old Frisian *hwēr,* Old Saxon, Old High German *hwār,* Old Norse, Gothic *hvar*]

▷**Usage.** See at **when.**

whereabouts (ˈwɛərəˌbaʊts) *adv.* **1.** Also: **whereabout.** at what approximate location or place; where: *whereabouts are you?* **2.** *Obsolete.* about or concerning which. ~*n.* **3.** (*functioning as sing. or pl.*) the place, esp. the approximate place, where a person or thing is.

whereafter (ˌwɛərˈɑːftə) *sentence connector. Archaic or formal.* after which.

whereas (wɛərˈæz) *conj.* **1.** (*coordinating*) but on the other hand: *I like to go swimming whereas Sheila likes to sail.* ~*sentence connector.* **2.** (in formal documents to begin sentences) it being the case that; since.

whereat (wɛərˈæt) *Archaic.* ~*adv.* **1.** at or to which place. ~*sentence connector.* **2.** upon which occasion.

whereby (wɛəˈbaɪ) *pron.* **1.** by or because of which: *the means whereby he took his life.* ~*adv.* **2.** *Archaic.* how? by what means?: *whereby does he recognize me?*

where'er (wɛərˈɛə) *adv., conj.* a poetic contraction of **wherever.**

wherefore (ˈwɛəˌfɔː) *n.* **1.** (*usually pl.*) an explanation or reason (esp. in the phrase **the whys and wherefores**). ~*adv.* **2.** *Ar-*

chaic. for what reason? why? *~sentence connector.* **3.** *Archaic or formal.* for which reason: used as an introductory word in legal preambles.

wherefrom (wɛəˈfrɒm) *Archaic.* *~adv.* **1.** from what or where? whence? *~pron.* **2.** from which place; whence.

wherein (wɛərˈɪn) *Archaic or formal.* *~adv.* **1.** in what place or respect? *~pron.* **2.** in which place, thing, etc.

whereinto (wɛərˈɪntuː) *Archaic.* *~adv.* **1.** into what place? *~pron.* **2.** into which place.

whereof (wɛərˈɒv) *Archaic or formal.* *~adv.* **1.** of what or which person or thing? **2.** of which (person or thing): *the man whereof I speak is no longer alive.*

whereon (wɛərˈɒn) *Archaic.* *~adv.* **1.** on what thing or place? *~pron.* **2.** on which thing, place, etc.

wheresoever (ˌwɛəsəʊˈɛvə) *conj.* (*subordinating*), *adv., pron. Rare.* an intensive form of **wherever**.

whereto (wɛəˈtuː) *Archaic or formal.* *~adv.* **1.** towards what (place, end, etc.)? *~pron.* **2.** to which. *~*Also (archaic): **whereunto.**

whereupon (ˌwɛərəˈpɒn) *sentence connector.* **1.** at which; at which point; upon which. *~adv.* **2.** *Archaic.* upon what?

wherever (wɛərˈɛvə) *pron.* **1.** at, in, or to every place or point which; where: *wherever she went, he would be there.* *~conj.* **2.** (*subordinating*) in, to, or at whatever place: *wherever we go the weather is always bad.* *~adv. also* **where ever. 3.** no matter where: *I'll find you, wherever you are.* **4.** *Informal.* at, in, or to an unknown or unspecified place: *I'll go anywhere to escape: London, Paris, or wherever.* **5.** an intensive form of *where,* used in questions: *wherever can they be?*

wherewith (wɛəˈwɪθ, -ˈwɪð) *Archaic or formal.* *~pron.* **1.** (*often foll. by an infinitive*) with or by which: *the pen wherewith I am wont to write.* **2.** something with which: *I have not wherewith to buy my bread.* *~adv.* **3.** with what? *~sentence connector.* **4.** with or after that; whereupon.

wherewithal *n.* (ˈwɛəwɪðˌɔːl). **1. the wherewithal.** necessary funds, resources, or equipment (for something or to do something): *these people lack the wherewithal for a decent existence.* *~pron.* (ˌwɛəwɪðˈɔːl). **2.** a less common word for **wherewith** (senses 1, 2).

wherret (ˈwɛrət) *Dialect.* *~vb.* **1.** (*tr.*) to strike (someone) a blow. *~n.* **2.** a blow, esp. a slap on the face; stroke. [probably of imitative origin]

wherrit (ˈwɛrɪt) *vb.* **1.** to worry or cause to worry. **2.** (*intr.*) to complain or moan. [perhaps from *thwert,* obsolete variant of THWART; compare WORRIT]

wherry (ˈwɛrɪ) *n., pl.* **-ries. 1.** any of certain kinds of half-decked commercial boats, such as barges, used in Britain. **2.** a light rowing boat used in inland waters and harbours. [C15: origin unknown] —ˈ**wherryman** *n.*

whet (wɛt) *vb.* **whets, whetting, whetted.** (*tr.*) **1.** to sharpen, as by grinding or friction. **2.** to increase or enhance (the appetite, desire, etc.); stimulate. *~n.* **3.** the act of whetting. **4.** a person or thing that whets. [Old English *hwettan;* related to *hwæt* sharp, Old High German *hwezzen,* Old Norse *hvetja,* Gothic *hvatjan*] —ˈ**whetter** *n.*

whether (ˈwɛðə) *conj.* **1.** (*subordinating*) used to introduce an indirect question or a clause after a verb expressing or implying doubt or choice in order to indicate two or more alternatives, the second or last of which is introduced by *or* or *or whether: he doesn't know whether she's in Britain or whether she's gone to France.* **2.** (*subordinating;* often foll. by *or not*) used to introduce any indirect question: *he was not certain whether his friend was there or not.* **3.** (*coordinating*) another word for **either** (sense 3): *any man, whether liberal or conservative, would agree with me.* **4.** (*coordinating*) *Archaic.* used to introduce a direct question consisting of two alternatives, the second of which is introduced by *or* or *or whether: whether does he live at home or abroad.* **5. whether or no. a.** used as a conjunction as a variant of **whether** (sense 1). **b.** under any circumstances: *he will be here tomorrow, whether or no.* **6. whether...or (whether).** if on the one hand...or even if on the other hand: *you'll eat that, whether you like it or not.* *~determiner, pron.* **7.** *Obsolete.* which (of two): used in direct or indirect questions. [Old English *hwæther, hwether;* related to Old Frisian *hweder, hoder,* Old High German *hwedar,* Old Norse *hvatharr, hvarr,* Gothic *hwathar*]

whetstone (ˈwɛtˌstəʊn) *n.* **1.** a stone used for sharpening edged tools, knives, etc. **2.** something that sharpens.

whew (hwjuː) *interj.* an exclamation or sharply exhaled breath expressing relief, surprise, delight, etc.

whey (weɪ) *n.* the watery liquid that separates from the curd when the milk is clotted, as in making cheese. [Old English *hwǣg;* related to Middle Low German *wei, heie,* Dutch *hui*] —ˈ**wheyey,** ˈ**wheyish,** *or* ˈ**whey,like** *adj.*

wheyface (ˈweɪˌfeɪs) *n.* **1.** a pale bloodless face. **2.** a person with such a face. —ˈ**wheyˌfaced** *adj.*

whf *abbrev. for* wharf.

which (wɪtʃ) *determiner.* **1. a.** used with a noun in requesting that its referent be further specified, identified, or distinguished from the other members of a class: *which house did you want to buy?* **b.** (*as pronoun*): *which did you find?* **c.** (*used in indirect questions*): *I wondered which apples were cheaper.* **2. a.** whatever of a class; whichever: *bring which car you want.* **b.** (*as pronoun*): *choose which of the cars suits you.* *~pron.* **3.** used in relative clauses with inanimate antecedents: *the house, which is old, is in poor repair.* **4.** as; and that: used in relative clauses with verb phrases or sentences as their antecedents: *he died of cancer, which is what I predicted.* **5. the which.** *Archaic.* a longer form of **which,** often used as a sentence connector. [Old English *hwelc, hwilc;* related to Old High German *hwelīh* (German *welch*) Old Norse *hvelīkr,* Gothic *hvileiks,* Latin *quis, quid*]

▷**Usage.** See at **that.**

whichever (wɪtʃˈɛvə) *determiner.* **1. a.** any (one, two, etc., out of several): *take whichever car you like.* **b.** (*as pronoun*): *choose whichever appeals to you.* **2. a.** no matter which (one or ones): *whichever card you pick you'll still be making a mistake.* **b.** (*as pronoun*): *it won't make any difference, whichever comes first.*

whichsoever (ˌwɪtʃsəʊˈɛvə) *pron.* an archaic or formal word for **whichever.**

whicker (ˈwɪkə) *vb.* (*intr.*) (of a horse) to whinny or neigh; nicker. [C17: of imitative origin]

whidah (ˈwɪdə) *n.* a variant spelling of **whydah.**

whiff[1] (wɪf) *n.* **1.** a passing odour. **2.** a brief gentle gust of air. **3.** a single inhalation or exhalation from the mouth or nose. *~vb.* **4.** to come, convey, or go in whiffs; puff or waft. **5.** to take in or breathe out (tobacco smoke, air, etc.). **6.** (*tr.*) to sniff or smell. **7.** (*intr.*) *Brit. slang.* to have an unpleasant smell; stink. [C16: of imitative origin] —ˈ**whiffer** *n.*

whiff[2] (wɪf) *n. Chiefly Brit.* a narrow clinker-built skiff having outriggers, for one oarsman. [C19: special use of WHIFF[1]]

whiffle (ˈwɪfᵊl) *vb.* **1.** (*intr.*) to think or behave in an erratic or unpredictable way. **2.** to blow or be blown fitfully or in gusts. **3.** (*intr.*) to whistle softly. [C16: frequentative of WHIFF[1]]

whiffler[1] (ˈwɪflə) *n.* a person who whiffles.

whiffler[2] (ˈwɪflə) *n. Archaic.* an attendant who cleared the way for a procession. [C16: from *wifle* battle-axe, from Old English *wifel,* of Germanic origin; the attendants originally carried weapons to clear the way]

whiffletree (ˈwɪfᵊlˌtriː) *n.* another name (esp. U.S.) for **swingletree.** [C19: variant of WHIPPLETREE]

whiffy (ˈwɪfɪ) *adj.* **-fier, -fiest.** *Slang.* smelly.

Whig (wɪg) *n.* **1.** a member of the English political party or grouping that opposed the succession to the throne of James, Duke of York (1679–80), on the grounds that he was a Catholic. The Whigs subsequently represented the great aristocracy and the moneyed middle class and, later, the reforming industrialists and Dissenters: they provided the core of the Liberal Party. **2.** (in the U.S.) a supporter of the War of American Independence (1775–81) against British rule. Compare **Tory. 3.** a member of the American political party that opposed the Democrats from about 1834 to 1855 and represented propertied and professional interests. **4.** a person who advocates and believes in an unrestricted laissez-faire economy. **5.** *History.* a 17th-century Scottish Presbyterian, esp. one in rebellion against the Crown. *~adj.* **6.** of, characteristic of, or relating to Whigs. [C17: probably shortened from *whiggamore,* one of a group of 17th-century Scottish rebels who joined in an attack on Edinburgh known as *the whiggamore raid;* probably from Scottish *whig* to drive (of obscure origin) + *more, mer, maire* horse, MARE] —ˈ**Whiggery** *or* ˈ**Whiggism** *n.* —ˈ**Whiggish** *adj.* —ˈ**Whiggishly** *adv.* —ˈ**Whiggishness** *n.*

whigmaleerie (ˌhwɪgməˈliːrɪ) *n. Scot.* **1.** a trinket, whimsical ornament, or trifle. **2.** a whim or caprice. [C18: of unknown origin]

while (waɪl) *conj. also* **whilst** (waɪlst). **1.** (*subordinating*) at the same time that: *please light the fire while I'm cooking.* **2.** (*subordinating*) all the time that: *I stay inside while it's raining.* **3.** (*subordinating*) in spite of the fact that: *while I agree about his brilliance I still think he's rude.* **4.** (*coordinating*) whereas; and in contrast: *flats are expensive, while houses are cheap.* **5.** (*subordinating; used with a gerund*) during the activity of: *while walking I often whistle.* *~prep., conj.* **6.** *Scot. and northern English dialect.* another word for **until:** *you'll have to wait while Monday for these sheets; you'll never make any progress while you listen to me.* *~n.* **7.** (*usually used in adverbial phrases*) a period or interval of time: *once in a long while.* **8.** trouble or time (esp. in the phrase **worth one's while**): *it's hardly worth your while to begin work today.* **9. the while.** at that time: *he was working the while.* *~*See also **whiles.** [Old English *hwīl;* related to Old High German *hwīla* (German *Weile*), Gothic *hveila,* Latin *quiēs* peace, *tranquīlus* TRANQUIL]

▷**Usage.** The main sense of *while* is *during the time that.* However, many careful users of English would now accept as established the use of *while* to mean *although: while he disliked working, he was obliged to do so.* In careful usage, *while* is not used to mean *whereas* or *and: he thought that they were in Paris, whereas* (not *while*) *they had gone on to Rome; his friends went to Paris for their holiday, his brother to Rome, and* (not *while*) *his parents went to Berlin.* Careful writers try to avoid any ambiguity that may result from the possibility of two interpretations of *while* in context: *while* (*although* or *during the time that*) *his brother worked in the park, he refused to do any gardening at home.*

while away *vb.* (*tr., adv.*) to pass (time) idly and usually pleasantly.

whiles (waɪlz; *Scot.* hwəɪlz) *Archaic or dialect.* *~adv.* **1.** at times; occasionally. *~conj.* **2.** while; whilst.

whilk (hwɪlk) *pron.* an archaic and dialect word for **which.**

whilom ('waɪləm) *Archaic.* ~*adv.* **1.** formerly; once. ~*adj.* **2.** (*prenominal*) one-time; former. [Old English *hwīlum,* dative plural of *hwīl* WHILE; related to Old High German *hwīlōm,* German *weiland* of old]

whilst (waɪlst) *conj. Chiefly Brit.* another word for **while** (senses 1–5). [C13: from WHILES + *-t* as in *amidst*]

whim (wɪm) *n.* **1.** a sudden, passing, and often fanciful idea; impulsive or irrational thought. **2.** a horse-drawn winch formerly used in mining to lift ore or water. [C17: from WHIM-WHAM]

whimbrel ('wɪmbrəl) *n.* a small European curlew, *Numenius phaeopus,* with a striped head. [C16: from dialect *whimp* or from WHIMPER, alluding to its cry]

whimper ('wɪmpə) *vb.* **1.** (*intr.*) to cry, sob, or whine softly or intermittently. **2.** to complain or say (something) in a whining plaintive way. ~*n.* **3.** a soft plaintive whine. [C16: from dialect *whimp,* of imitative origin] —'**whimperer** *n.* —'**whimpering** *n.* —'**whimperingly** *adv.*

whimsical ('wɪmzɪkᵊl) *adj.* **1.** spontaneously fanciful or playful. **2.** given to whims; capricious. **3.** quaint, unusual, or fantastic. —**whimsicality** (ˌwɪmzɪ'kælɪtɪ) *n.* —'**whimsically** *adv.* —'**whimsicalness** *n.*

whimsy *or* **whimsey** ('wɪmzɪ) *n., pl.* **-sies** *or* **-seys. 1.** a capricious idea or notion. **2.** light or fanciful humour. **3.** something quaint or unusual. ~*adj.* **-sier, -siest. 4.** quaint, comical, or unusual, often in a tasteless way. [C17: from WHIM; compare FLIMSY]

whim-wham *n. Archaic.* something fanciful; a trifle. [C16: of unknown origin; compare FLIMFLAM]

whin[1] (wɪn) *n.* another name for **gorse.** [C11: from Scandinavian; compare Old Danish *hvine* (*græs*), Norwegian *hvine,* Swedish *hven*]

whin[2] (wɪn) *n.* short for **whinstone.** [C14 *quin,* of obscure origin]

whinchat ('wɪnˌtʃæt) *n.* an Old World songbird, *Saxicola rubetra,* having a mottled brown-and-white plumage with pale cream underparts: subfamily *Turdinae* (thrushes). [C17: from WHIN[1] + CHAT]

whine (waɪn) *n.* **1.** a long high-pitched plaintive cry or moan. **2.** a continuous high-pitched sound. **3.** a peevish complaint, esp. one repeated. ~*vb.* **4.** to make a whine or utter in a whine. [Old English *hwīnan;* related to Old Norse *hvīna,* Swedish *hvija* to scream] —'**whiner** *n.* —'**whining** *adj.* —'**whiningly** *adv.* —'**whiny** *adj.*

whinge (wɪndʒ) *Informal.* ~*vb.* (*intr.*) **1.** to cry in a fretful way. **2.** to complain. ~*n.* **3.** a complaint. [from a Northern variant of Old English *hwinsian* to whine; related to Old High German *winsan, winisan,* whence Middle High German *winsen*] —'**whingeing** *n., adj.*

whinny ('wɪnɪ) *vb.* **-nies, -nying, -nied.** (*intr.*) **1.** (of a horse) to neigh softly or gently. **2.** to make a sound resembling a neigh, such as a laugh. ~*n., pl.* **-nies. 3.** a gentle or low-pitched neigh. [C16: of imitative origin]

whinstone ('wɪnˌstəʊn) *n.* any dark hard fine-grained rock, such as basalt. [C16: from WHIN[2] + STONE]

whip (wɪp) *vb.* **whips, whipping, whipped. 1.** to strike (a person or thing) with several strokes of a strap, rod, etc. **2.** (*tr.*) to punish by striking in this manner. **3.** (*tr.;* foll. by *out, away,* etc.) to pull, remove, etc., with sudden rapid motion: *to whip out a gun.* **4.** (*intr.;* foll. by *down, into, out of,* etc.) *Informal.* to come, go, etc., in a rapid sudden manner: *they whipped into the bar for a drink.* **5.** to strike or be struck as if by whipping: *the tempest whipped the surface of the sea.* **6.** (*tr.*) to criticize virulently. **7.** (*tr.*) to bring, train, etc., forcefully into a desired condition (esp. in the phrases **whip into line** and **whip into shape**). **8.** (*tr.*) *Informal.* to overcome or outdo: *I know when I've been whipped.* **9.** (*tr.;* often foll. by *on, out,* or *off*) to drive, urge, compel, etc., by or as if by whipping. **10.** (*tr.*) to wrap or wind (a cord, thread, etc.) around (a rope, cable, etc.) to prevent chafing or fraying. **11.** (*tr.*) *Nautical.* to hoist by means of a rope through a single pulley. **12.** (*tr.*) (in fly-fishing) to cast the fly repeatedly onto (the water) in a whipping motion. **13.** (*tr.*) (in sewing) to join, finish, or gather with whipstitch. **14.** to beat (eggs, cream, etc.) with a whisk or similar utensil to incorporate air and produce expansion. **15.** (*tr.*) to spin (a top). **16.** (*tr.*) *Informal.* to steal: *he whipped her purse.* ~*n.* **17.** a device consisting of a lash or flexible rod attached at one end to a stiff handle and used for driving animals, inflicting corporal punishment, etc. **18.** a whipping stroke or motion. **19.** a person adept at handling a whip, as a coachman, etc. **20.** (in a legislative body) **a.** a member of a party chosen to organize and discipline the members of his faction, esp. in voting and to assist in the arrangement of the business. **b.** a call issued to members of a party, insisting with varying degrees of urgency upon their presence or loyal voting behaviour. **c.** (in the Brit. Parliament) a schedule of business sent to members of a party each week. Each item on it is underlined to indicate its importance: one line means that no division is expected, two lines means that the item is fairly important, and three lines means that the item is very important and every member must attend and vote according to the party line. **21.** an apparatus for hoisting, consisting of a rope, pulley, and snatch block. **22.** any of a variety of desserts made from egg whites or cream beaten stiff, sweetened, and flavoured with fruit, fruit juice, etc. **23.** See **whipper-in. 24.** a windmill vane. **25.** transient elastic movement of a structure or part, such as a shaft, when subjected to sudden loads or dynamic excitation. **26.** a percussion instrument consisting of two strips of wood, joined forming the shape of a V, and clapped loudly together. **27.** flexibility, as in the shaft of a golf club, etc. **28.** a ride in a funfair involving bumper cars that move with sudden jerks. **29.** a wrestling throw in which a wrestler seizes his opponent's arm and spins him to the floor. **30. a fair crack of the whip.** *Informal.* a fair chance or opportunity. ~See also **whip in, whip-round, whips, whip up.** [C13: perhaps from Middle Dutch *wippen* to swing; related to Middle Dutch *wipfen* to dance, German *Wipfel* tree top] —'**whipˌlike** *adj.* —'**whipper** *n.*

whip bird *n. Austral.* **1.** any of several birds of the genus *Psophodes,* esp. *P. olivaceus* (**eastern whip bird**) and *P. nigrogularis* (**black-throated whip bird**), having a whistle ending in a whipcrack note. **2.** any of various other birds, such as *Pachycephala pectoralis* and *P. rufiventris* (**mock whip bird**).

whipcord ('wɪpˌkɔːd) *n.* **1.** a strong worsted or cotton fabric with a diagonally ribbed surface. **2.** a closely twisted hard cord used for the lashes of whips, etc.

whip graft *n. Horticulture.* a graft made by inserting a tongue cut on the sloping base of the scion into a slit on the sloping top of the stock.

whip hand *n.* (usually preceded by *the*) **1.** (in driving horses) the hand holding the whip. **2.** advantage or dominating position.

whip in *vb.* (*adv.*) **1.** (*intr.*) to perform the duties of a whipper-in to a pack of hounds. **2.** (*tr.*) *Chiefly U.S.* to keep (members of a political party, etc.) together.

whiplash ('wɪpˌlæʃ) *n.* **1.** a quick lash or stroke of a whip or like that of a whip. **2.** *Med.* See **whiplash injury.**

whiplash injury *n. Med. informal.* any injury to the neck resulting from a sudden thrusting forwards and snapping back of the unsupported head. Technical name: **hyperextension-hyperflexion injury.**

whipper-in *n., pl.* **whippers-in.** a person employed to assist the huntsman managing the hounds.

whippersnapper ('wɪpəˌsnæpə) *n.* an insignificant but pretentious or cheeky person, often a young one. Also called: **whipster.** [C17: probably from *whipsnapper* a person who snaps whips, influenced by earlier *snippersnapper,* of obscure origin]

whippet ('wɪpɪt) *n.* a small slender breed of dog similar to a greyhound in appearance. [C16: of uncertain origin; perhaps based on the phrase *whip it!* move quickly!]

whipping ('wɪpɪŋ) *n.* **1.** a thrashing or beating with a whip or similar implement. **2.** cord or twine used for binding or lashing.

whipping boy *n.* a person of little importance who is blamed for the errors, incompetence, etc., of others, esp. his superiors; scapegoat. [C17: originally referring to a boy who was educated with a prince and who received punishment for any faults committed by the prince]

whipping cream *n.* cream that contains just enough butterfat to allow it to be whipped until stiff.

whippletree ('wɪpᵊlˌtriː) *n.* another name for **swingletree.** [C18: apparently from WHIP]

whippoorwill ('wɪpʊˌwɪl) *n.* a nightjar, *Caprimulgus vociferus,* of North and Central America, having a dark plumage with white patches on the tail. [C18: imitative of its cry]

whip-round *Informal, chiefly Brit.* ~*n.* **1.** an impromptu collection of money. ~*vb.* **whip round. 2.** (*intr., adv.*) to make such a collection of money.

whips (wɪps) *pl. n.* (often foll. by *of*) *Austral. informal.* a large quantity: *I've got whips of cash at the moment.*

whipsaw ('wɪpˌsɔː) *n.* **1.** any saw with a flexible blade, such as a bandsaw. ~*vb.* **-saws, -sawing, -sawed, -sawed** *or* **-sawn.** (*tr.*) **2.** to saw with a whipsaw. **3.** *U.S.* to defeat in two ways at once.

whip scorpion *n.* any nonvenomous arachnid of the order *Uropygi* (or *Pedipalpi*), typically resembling a scorpion but lacking a sting. See also **vinegarroon.**

whip snake *n.* **1.** any of several long slender fast-moving nonvenomous snakes of the colubrid genus *Coluber,* such as *C. hippocrepis* (**horseshoe whipsnake**) of Eurasia. **2.** any of various other slender nonvenomous snakes, such as *Masticophis flagellum* (**coachwhip snake**) of the U.S.

whipstall ('wɪpˌstɔːl) *n.* a stall in which an aircraft goes into a nearly vertical climb, pauses, slips backwards momentarily, and drops suddenly with its nose down.

whipstitch ('wɪpˌstɪtʃ) *n.* **1.** a sewing stitch passing over an edge. **2.** *U.S. slang.* an instant; moment. ~*vb.* **3.** (*tr.*) to sew (an edge) using whipstitch; overcast.

whipstock ('wɪpˌstɒk) *n.* a whip handle.

whip up *vb.* (*tr., adv.*) **1.** to excite; arouse: *to whip up a mob; to whip up discontent.* **2.** *Informal.* to prepare quickly: *to whip up a meal.*

whipworm ('wɪpˌwɜːm) *n.* any of several parasitic nematode worms of the genus *Trichuris,* esp. *T. trichiura,* having a whiplike body and living in the intestines of mammals.

whir *or* **whirr** (wɜː) *n.* **1.** a prolonged soft swish or buzz, as of a motor working or wings flapping. **2.** a bustle or rush. ~*vb.* **whirs** *or* **whirrs, whirring, whirred. 3.** to make or cause to make a whir. [C14: probably from Scandinavian; compare Norwegian *kvirra,* Danish *hvirre;* see WHIRL]

whirl (wɜːl) *vb.* **1.** to spin, turn, or revolve or cause to spin, turn, or revolve. **2.** (*intr.*) to turn around or away rapidly. **3.** (*intr.*) to have a spinning sensation, as from dizziness, etc. **4.** to move or drive or be moved or driven at high speed. ~*n.* **5.** the act or an instance of whirling; swift rotation or a rapid whirling movement. **6.** a condition of confusion or giddiness: *her accident left me in a whirl.* **7.** a swift round, as of events, meetings, etc. **8.** a tumult; stir. **9.** *Informal.* a brief trip, dance, etc. **10. give (something) a whirl.** *Informal.* to attempt or give a trial to (something). [C13: from Old Norse *hvirfla* to turn about; related to Old High German *wirbil* whirlwind] —'**whirler** *n.* —'**whirling** *adj.* —'**whirlingly** *adv.*

whirlabout ('wɜːləˌbaʊt) *n.* **1.** anything that whirls around; whirligig. **2.** the act or an instance of whirling around.

whirligig ('wɜːlɪˌgɪg) *n.* **1.** any spinning toy, such as a top. **2.** another name for **merry-go-round. 3.** anything that whirls about, spins, or moves in a circular or giddy way: *the whirligig of social life.* **4.** another name for **windmill** (the toy). [C15 *whirlegigge,* from WHIRL + GIG[1]]

whirligig beetle *n.* any flat-bodied water beetle of the family *Gyrinidae,* which circles rapidly on the surface of the water.

whirlpool ('wɜːlˌpuːl) *n.* **1.** a powerful circular current or vortex of water, usually produced by conflicting tidal currents or by eddying at the foot of a waterfall. **2.** something resembling a whirlpool in motion or the power to attract into its vortex.

whirlpool bath *n.* a bath having a device for maintaining the water in a swirling motion.

whirlwind ('wɜːlˌwɪnd) *n.* **1.** a column of air whirling around and towards a more or less vertical axis of low pressure, which moves along the land or ocean surface. **2. a.** a motion or course resembling this, esp. in rapidity. **b.** (*as modifier*): *a whirlwind romance.* **3.** an impetuously active person.

whirlybird ('wɜːlɪˌbɜːd) *n.* an informal word for **helicopter.**

whish (wɪʃ) *n., vb.* a less common word for **swish.**

whisht (hwɪʃt) *or* **whist** (hwɪst) *Scot., or archaic, or dialect.* ~*interj.* **1.** hush! be quiet! ~*adj.* **2.** silent or still. ~*vb.* **3.** to make or become silent. ~See also **wheesh.** [C14: compare HIST; also obsolete v. *whist* to become silent]

whisk (wɪsk) *vb.* **1.** (*tr.;* often foll. by *away* or *off*) to brush, sweep, or wipe off lightly. **2.** (*tr.*) to move, carry, etc., with a light or rapid sweeping motion: *the taxi whisked us to the airport.* **3.** (*intr.*) to move, go, etc., quickly and nimbly: *to whisk downstairs for a drink.* **4.** (*tr.*) to whip (eggs, cream, etc.) to a froth. ~*n.* **5.** the act of whisking. **6.** a light rapid sweeping movement or stroke. **7.** a utensil, often incorporating a coil of wires, for whipping eggs, etc. **8.** a small brush or broom. **9.** a small bunch or bundle, as of grass, straw, etc. [C14: from Old Norse *visk* wisp; related to Middle Dutch *wisch,* Old High German *wisc*]

whisker ('wɪskə) *n.* **1.** any of the stiff sensory hairs growing on the face of a cat, rat, or other mammal. Technical name: **vibrissa. 2.** any of the hairs growing on a person's face, esp. on the cheeks or chin. **3.** (*pl.*) a beard or that part of it growing on the sides of the face. **4.** (*pl.*) *Informal.* a moustache. **5.** Also called: **whisker boom, whisker pole.** any light spar used for extending the clews of a sail, esp. in light airs. **6.** *Chem.* a very fine filamentary crystal having greater strength than the bulk material since it is a single crystal. Such crystals often show unusual electrical properties. **7.** a person or thing that whisks. **8.** a narrow margin; a small distance: *he escaped death by a whisker.* —'**whiskered** *or* '**whiskery** *adj.*

whiskey ('wɪskɪ) *n.* the usual Irish and U.S. spelling of **whisky.**

Whiskey ('wɪskɪ) *n. Communications.* a code word for the letter *w.*

whiskey sour *n. U.S.* a mixed drink of whisky and lime or lemon juice, sometimes sweetened.

whisky ('wɪskɪ) *n., pl.* **-kies.** a spirit made by distilling fermented cereals, which is matured and often blended. [C18: shortened from *whiskybae,* from Scottish Gaelic *uisge beatha,* literally: water of life; see USQUEBAUGH]

whisky mac *n. Brit.* a drink consisting of whisky and ginger wine.

whisper ('wɪspə) *vb.* **1.** to speak or utter (something) in a soft hushed tone, esp. without vibration of the vocal cords. **2.** (*intr.*) to speak secretly or furtively, as in promoting intrigue, gossip, etc. **3.** (*intr.*) (of leaves, trees, etc.) to make a low soft rustling sound. **4.** (*tr.*) to utter or suggest secretly or privately: *to whisper treason.* ~*n.* **5.** a low soft voice: *to speak in a whisper.* **6.** something uttered in such a voice. **7.** a low soft rustling sound. **8.** a trace or suspicion. **9.** *Informal.* a rumour or secret. [Old English *hwisprian;* related to Old Norse *hvīskra,* Old High German *hwispalōn,* Dutch *wispern*] —'**whisperer** *n.*

whispering campaign *n. Chiefly U.S. and Canadian.* the organized diffusion by word of mouth of defamatory rumours designed to discredit a person, group, etc.

whispering gallery *n.* a gallery or dome with acoustic characteristics such that a sound made at one point is audible at distant points.

whist[1] (wɪst) *n.* a card game for four in which the two sides try to win the balance of the 13 tricks: forerunner of bridge. [C17: perhaps changed from WHISK, referring to the sweeping up or whisking up of the tricks]

whist[2] (hwɪst) *interj., adj., vb.* a variant of **whisht.**

whist drive *n.* a social gathering where whist is played; the winners of each hand move to different tables to play the losers of the previous hand.

whistle ('wɪsᵊl) *vb.* **1.** to produce (shrill or flutelike musical sounds), as by passing breath through a narrow constriction most easily formed by the pursed lips: *he whistled a melody.* **2.** (*tr.*) to signal, summon, or command by whistling or blowing a whistle: *the referee whistled the end of the game.* **3.** (of a kettle, train, etc.) to produce (a shrill sound) caused by the emission of steam through a small aperture. **4.** (*intr.*) to move with a whistling sound caused by rapid passage through the air. **5.** (of animals, esp. birds) to emit (a shrill sound) resembling human whistling. ~*n.* **6.** a device for making a shrill high-pitched sound by means of air or steam under pressure. **7.** a shrill sound effected by whistling. **8.** a whistling sound, as of a bird, bullet, the wind, etc. **9.** a signal, warning, command, etc., transmitted by or as if by a whistle. **10.** the act of whistling. **11.** *Music.* any pipe that is blown down its end and produces sounds on the principle of a flue pipe, usually having as a mouthpiece a fipple cut in the side. **12. wet one's whistle.** *Informal.* to take an alcoholic drink. **13. blow the whistle.** (usually foll. by *on*) *Informal.* **a.** to inform (on). **b.** to bring a stop (to). **14. whistle in the dark.** to try to keep up one's confidence in spite of fear. ~See also **whistle for, whistle up.** [Old English *hwistlian;* related to Old Norse *hvīsla*]

whistle-blower *n. Informal.* a person who informs on someone or puts a stop to something.

whistle for *vb.* (*intr., prep.*) *Informal.* to seek or expect in vain.

whistler ('wɪslə) *n.* **1.** a person or thing that whistles. **2.** *Radio.* an atmospheric disturbance picked up by radio receivers, characterized by a whistling sound of decreasing pitch. It is caused by the electromagnetic radiation produced by lightning. **3.** any of various birds having a whistling call, such as certain Australian flycatchers (see **thickhead** (sense 2)) and the goldeneye. **4.** any of various North American marmots of the genus *Marmota,* esp. *M. caligata* (**hoary marmot**). **5.** *Vet. science.* a horse affected with whistling.

whistle stop *n.* **1.** *U.S. and Canadian.* **a.** a minor railway station where trains stop only on signal. **b.** a small town having such a station. **2. a.** a brief appearance in a town, esp. by a political candidate in order to make a speech, shake hands, etc. **b.** (*as modifier*): *a whistle-stop tour.* ~*vb.* **whistle-stop, -stops, -stopping, -stopped. 3.** (*intr.*) to campaign for office by visiting many small towns to give short speeches.

whistle up *vb.* (*tr., adv.*) to call or summon (a person or animal) by whistling.

whistling ('wɪslɪŋ) *n. Vet. science.* a breathing defect of horses characterized by a high-pitched sound with each intake of air. Compare **roaring** (sense 6).

whistling swan *n.* a white North American swan, *Cygnus columbianus,* with a black bill and straight neck. Compare **mute swan.**

whit (wɪt) *n.* (*usually used with a negative*) the smallest particle; iota; jot: *he has changed not a whit.* [C15: probably variant of WIGHT[1]]

Whit (wɪt) *n.* **1.** See **Whitsuntide.** ~*adj.* **2.** of or relating to Whitsuntide.

white (waɪt) *adj.* **1.** having no hue due to the reflection of all or almost all incident light. Compare **black** (sense 1). **2.** (of light, such as sunlight) consisting of all the colours of the spectrum or produced by certain mixtures of three additive primary colours, such as red, green, and blue. **3.** comparatively white or whitish-grey in colour or having parts of this colour: *white clover.* **4.** (of an animal) having pale-coloured or white skin, fur, or feathers. **5.** bloodless or pale, as from pain, emotion, etc. **6.** (of hair, a beard, etc.) silvery or grey, usually from age. **7.** benevolent or without malicious intent: *white magic.* **8.** colourless or transparent: *white glass.* **9.** capped with or accompanied by snow: *a white Christmas.* **10.** (*sometimes cap.*) counterrevolutionary, very conservative, or royalist. Compare **Red** (sense 2). **11.** blank, as an unprinted area of a page. **12.** (of wine) made from pale grapes or from black grapes separated from their skins. **13. a.** (of coffee or tea) with milk or cream. **b.** (of bread) made with white flour. **14.** *Physics.* having or characterized by a continuous distribution of energy, wavelength, or frequency: *white noise.* **15.** *Informal.* honourable or generous. **16.** (of armour) made completely of iron or steel (esp. in the phrase **white harness**). **17.** *Rare.* morally unblemished. **18.** *Rare.* (of times, seasons, etc.) auspicious; favourable. **19.** *Poetic or archaic.* having a fair complexion; blond. **20. bleed white.** to deprive slowly of resources. ~*n.* **21.** a white colour. **22.** the condition or quality of being white; whiteness. **23.** the white or lightly coloured part or area of something. **24.** (usually preceded by *the*) the viscous fluid that surrounds the yolk of a bird's egg, esp. a hen's egg; albumen. **25.** *Anatomy.* the white part (sclera) of the eyeball. **26.** any of various butterflies of the family *Pieridae.* See **large white, small white,** and also **cabbage white. 27.** *Chess, draughts.* **a.** a white or light-coloured piece or square. **b.** (*usually cap.*) the player playing with such pieces. **28.** anything that has or is characterized by a white colour, such as a white paint or pigment, a white cloth, a white ball in billiards. **29.** an unprinted area of a page. **30.** *Archery.* **a.** the outer ring of the target, having the lowest score. **b.** a shot or arrow hitting this ring. **31.** *Poetic.* fairness of complexion. **32. in the white.** (of wood or furniture) left unpainted or unvarnished. *~vb.* **33.** (usually foll. by *out*) to create or leave white spaces in (printed or other matter). **34.** *Obsolete.* to make or become white. ~See also **white out, whites.** [Old English *hwīt;* related to Old Frisian *hwīt,* Old Saxon *hwīt,* Old Norse *hvītr,* Gothic *hveits,* Old High German *hwīz* (German *weiss*)] —'**whitely** *adv.* —'**whiteness** *n.* —'**whitish** *adj.*

White (waɪt) *n.* **1.** a member of the Caucasoid race. **2.** a person of European ancestry. *~adj.* **3.** denoting or relating to a White or Whites.

white admiral *n.* a nymphalid butterfly, *Limenitis camilla,* of Eurasia, having brown wings with white markings. See also **red admiral.**

white alkali *n.* **1.** refined sodium carbonate. **2.** any of several mineral salts, esp. sodium sulphate, sodium chloride, and magnesium sulphate, that often appear on the surface of soils as a whitish layer in dry conditions.

white ant *n.* another name for **termite.**

white area *n.* an area of land for which no specific planning proposal has been adopted.

whitebait ('waɪtˌbeɪt) *n.* **1.** the young of herrings, sprats, etc., cooked and eaten whole as a delicacy. **2.** any of various small silvery fishes, such as *Galaxias attenuatus* of Australia and New Zealand and *Allosmerus elongatus* of North American coastal regions of the Pacific. [C18: from its formerly having been used as bait]

whitebeam ('waɪtˌbiːm) *n.* a N temperate rosaceous tree, *Sorbus aria,* having leaves that are densely hairy on the undersurface and hard timber.

white bear *n.* another name for **polar bear.**

white birch *n.* any of several birch trees with white bark, such as the silver birch of Europe and the paper birch of North America. See also **birch** (sense 1).

white blood cell *n.* a nontechnical name for **leucocyte.**

white book *n.* an official government publication in some countries.

Whiteboy ('waɪtbɔɪ) *n. Irish history.* a member of a secret society of violent agrarian protest, formed around 1760. [C18: adopted from the earlier use of the phrase as a term of endearment for a boy or man]

white bryony *n.* a climbing herbaceous cucurbitaceous plant, *Bryonia dioica,* of Europe and North Africa, having greenish flowers and red berries. Also called: **red bryony.** See also **black bryony, bryony.**

whitecap ('waɪtˌkæp) *n.* **1.** a wave with a white broken crest. **2.** *U.S.* a member of a vigilante organization that attempts to control a community.

white cedar *n.* **1.** a coniferous tree, *Chamaecyparis thyoides,* of swampy regions in North America, having scalelike leaves and boxlike cones: family *Cupressaceae.* See also **cypress**[1] (sense 2). **2.** the wood of this tree, which is used for building boats, etc. **3.** a coniferous tree, *Thuja occidentalis,* of NE North America, having scalelike leaves: family *Cupressaceae.* See also **arbor vitae.** **4.** the wood of this tree, much used for telegraph poles.

Whitechapel ('waɪtˌtʃæpᵊl) *n. Billiards.* the act of potting one's opponent's white ball. [C19: slang use of *Whitechapel,* a district of London]

white clover *n.* a Eurasian clover plant, *Trifolium repens,* with rounded white flower heads: cultivated as a forage plant.

white coal *n.* water, esp. when flowing and providing a potential source of usable power.

white-collar *adj.* of, relating to, or designating nonmanual and usually salaried workers employed in professional and clerical occupations: *white-collar union.* Compare **blue-collar.**

white currant *n.* a cultivated N temperate shrub, *Ribes sativum,* having small rounded white edible berries: family *Grossulariaceae.*

whitedamp ('waɪtˌdæmp) *n.* a mixture of poisonous gases, mainly carbon monoxide, occurring in coal mines. See also **afterdamp.**

whited sepulchre ('waɪtɪd) *n.* a hypocrite. [from Matthew 23:27]

white dwarf *n.* one of a large class of small faint stars of enormous density (on average 10^8 kg/m^3) known to cause an Einstein shift of spectral lines. It is thought to mark the final stage in a star's evolution.

white elephant *n.* **1.** a rare albino or pale grey variety of the Indian elephant, regarded as sacred in parts of S Asia. **2.** a possession that is unwanted by its owner. **3.** an elaborate venture, construction, etc., that proves useless. **4.** a rare or valuable possession the upkeep of which is very expensive.

White Ensign *n.* the ensign of the Royal Navy and the Royal Yacht Squadron, having a red cross on a white background with the Union Jack at the upper corner of the vertical edge alongside the hoist. Compare **Red Ensign, Blue Ensign.**

white-eye *n.* **1.** Also called (N.Z.): **blighty, silvereye, waxeye.** any songbird of the family *Zosteropidae* of Africa, Australia, New Zealand, and Asia, having a greenish plumage with a white ring around each eye. **2.** any of certain other birds having a white ring or patch around the eye.

white feather *n.* **1.** a symbol or mark of cowardice. **2. show the white feather.** to act in a cowardly manner. [from the belief that a white feather in a gamecock's tail was a sign of a poor fighter]

whitefish ('waɪtˌfɪʃ) *n., pl.* **-fish** *or* **-fishes.** any herring-like salmonoid food fish of the genus *Coregonus* and family *Coregonidae,* typically of deep cold lakes of the N hemisphere, having large silvery scales and a small head.

white fish *n.* (in the British fishing industry) any edible marine fish or invertebrate in which the main reserves of fat are in the liver, excluding herring, trout, sprat, mackerel, salmon, and shellfish.

white flag *n.* a white flag or a piece of white cloth hoisted to signify surrender or request a truce.

white flint *n.* another name for **flint** (sense 4).

white flour *n.* flour that consists substantially of the starchy endosperm of wheat, most of the bran and the germ having been removed by the milling process.

whitefly ('waɪtˌflaɪ) *n., pl.* **-flies.** any hemipterous insect of the family *Aleyrodidae,* typically having a body covered with powdery wax. Many are pests of greenhouse crops.

white-footed mouse *n.* any of various mice of the genus *Peromyscus,* esp. *P. leucopus,* of North and Central America, having brownish fur with white underparts: family *Cricetidae.* See also **deer mouse.**

white fox *n.* another name for **arctic fox.**

white friar *n.* a Carmelite friar, so called because of the white cloak that forms part of the habit of this order.

white frost *n.* another term for **hoarfrost.**

white gold *n.* any of various white lustrous hard-wearing alloys containing gold together with platinum and palladium and sometimes smaller amounts of silver, nickel, or copper: used in jewellery.

white goods *pl. n.* **1.** household linen such as sheets, towels, tablecloths, etc. **2.** *Marketing.* large household appliances, such as refrigerators or cookers. Compare **brown goods.**

white gum *n.* any of various Australian eucalyptus trees with whitish bark.

white-haired boy *or* **white-headed boy** *n.* a favourite; darling.

Whitehall ('waɪtˌhɔːl) *n.* the British Government or its central administration. [after the street in London that is the site of the main government offices]

white heat *n.* **1.** intense heat or a very high temperature, characterized by emission of white light. **2.** *Informal.* a state of intense excitement or activity.

white hole *n. Astronomy.* a hypothetical reversal of a black hole from which matter and radiation are emitted, now believed not to exist.

white hope *n. Informal.* a person who is expected to bring honour or glory to his group, team, etc.

white horse *n.* **1.** the outline of a horse carved into the side of a chalk hill, usually dating to the Neolithic, Bronze, or Iron Ages, such as that at Uffington, Berkshire. **2.** (*usually pl.*) a wave with a white broken crest.

white-hot *adj.* **1.** at such a high temperature that white light is emitted. **2.** *Informal.* in a state of intense emotion.

White House *n.* **the.** the U.S. presidency. [after the official Washington residence of the president of the U.S.]

white knight *n.* a champion or rescuer, esp. a person or organization that rescues a company from financial difficulties, an unwelcome takeover bid, etc.

white-knuckle *adj.* causing or experiencing fear or anxiety: *a white-knuckle ride.*

white lady *n.* **1.** a cocktail consisting of gin, Cointreau, and lemon juice. **2.** *Austral. informal.* methylated spirits as a drink, sometimes mixed with shoe polish or other additives.

white lead (lɛd) *n.* **1.** Also called: **ceruse.** a white solid usually regarded as a mixture of lead carbonate and lead hydroxide; basic lead carbonate: used in paint and in making putty and ointments for the treatment of burns. Formula: $2PbCO_3.Pb(OH)_2$. **2.** either of two similar white pigments based on lead sulphate or lead silicate. **3.** a type of putty made by mixing white lead with boiled linseed oil.

white lead ore (lɛd) *n.* another name for **cerussite.**

white leather *n.* leather that has been treated with a chemical, such as alum or salt, to make it white. Also called: **whitleather** ('wɪtˈlɛðə).

white leg *n.* another name for **milk leg.**

white lias *n.* a type of rock composed of pale-coloured limestones and marls. See also **Lias.**

white lie *n.* a minor or unimportant lie, esp. one uttered in the interests of tact or politeness.

white light *n.* light that contains all the wavelengths of visible light at approximately equal intensities, as in sunlight or the light from white-hot solids.

white line *n.* **1.** a line or strip of white in the centre of a road to separate traffic going in different directions. **2.** *Printing.* a line of spaces without letters or other characters. **3.** a white lamination in the hoof of a horse.

white-livered *adj.* **1.** lacking in spirit or courage. **2.** pallid and unhealthy in appearance.

White man's burden *n.* the supposed duty of the White race to bring education and Western culture to the non-White inhabitants of their colonies.

white matter *n.* the whitish tissue of the brain and spinal cord, consisting mainly of myelinated nerve fibres. Technical name: **substantia alba.** Compare **grey matter.**

white meat *n.* any meat that is light in colour, such as veal or the breast of turkey. Compare **red meat.**

white metal *n.* any of various alloys, such as Babbitt metal, used for bearings. Also called: **antifriction metal.**

white meter *n. Brit.* an electricity meter used to record the consumption of off-peak electricity.

white mustard *n.* a Eurasian cruciferous plant, *Brassica hirta* (or *Sinapis alba*), having clusters of yellow flowers and pungent seeds from which the condiment mustard is made.

whiten ('waɪtᵊn) *vb.* to make or become white or whiter; bleach. —'**whitener** *n.* —'**whitening** *n.*

white noise *n.* **a.** sound or electrical noise that has a relatively wide continuous range of frequencies of uniform intensity. **b.** noise containing all frequencies rising in level by six decibels every octave.

white oak *n.* **1.** a large oak tree, *Quercus alba,* of E North America, having pale bark, leaves with rounded lobes, and heavy light-coloured wood. **2.** any of several other oaks, such as the roble.

white out *vb.* (*adv.*) **1.** (*intr.*) to lose or lack daylight visibility owing to snow or fog. **2.** (*tr.*) to create or leave white spaces in (printed or other matter). **3.** (*tr.*) to delete (typewritten words or characters) with a white correcting fluid. *~n.* **whiteout. 4.** an atmospheric condition consisting of loss of visibility and sense of distance and direction due to a uniform whiteness of a heavy cloud cover and snow-covered ground, which reflects almost all the light it receives.

white paper *n.* (*often caps.*) an official government report in any of a number of countries, including Britain, Australia, New Zealand, and Canada, which sets out the government's policy on a matter that is or will come before Parliament.

white pepper *n.* a condiment, less pungent than black pepper, made from the husked dried beans of the pepper plant *Piper nigrum,* used either whole or ground.

white pine *n.* **1.** a North American coniferous tree, *Pinus strobus,* having blue-green needle-like leaves, hanging brown cones, and rough bark: family *Pinaceae.* **2.** the light-coloured wood of this tree, much used commercially. **3.** another name for **kahikatea.**

white plague *n. Informal.* tuberculosis of the lungs.

white poplar *n.* **1.** Also called: **abele.** a Eurasian salicaceous tree, *Populus alba,* having leaves covered with dense silvery-white hairs. **2.** another name for **tulipwood** (sense 1).

white potato *n.* another name for **potato** (sense 1).

white pudding *n.* (in Britain) a kind of sausage made like black pudding but without pigs' blood.

white rainbow *n.* another name for **fogbow.**

white rat *n.* a white variety of the brown rat (*Rattus norvegicus*), used extensively in scientific research.

white rose *n. English history.* a widely used emblem or badge of the Yorkists. See also **red rose.**

White Russian *adj., n.* another term for **Byelorussian.**

whites (waɪts) *pl. n.* **1.** household linen or cotton goods, such as sheets. **2.** white or off-white clothing, such as that worn for playing cricket. **3.** an informal name for **leucorrhoea.**

white sale *n.* a sale of household linens at reduced prices.

white sapphire *n.* a white pure variety of corundum, used as a gemstone.

white sauce *n.* a thick sauce made from flour, butter, seasonings, and milk or stock.

white settler *n.* a well-off incomer to a district who takes advantage of what it has to offer without regard to the local inhabitants. [C20: from earlier colonial sense]

white slave *n.* a girl or woman forced or sold into prostitution. —**white slavery** *n.*

white-slaver *n.* a person who procures or forces women to become prostitutes.

whitesmith ('waɪtˌsmɪθ) *n.* a person who finishes and polishes metals, particularly tin plate and galvanized iron.

white spirit *n.* a colourless liquid obtained from petroleum and used as a substitute for turpentine.

white spruce *n.* a N North American spruce tree, *Picea glauca,* having grey bark, pale brown oblong cones, and bluish-green needle-like leaves.

white squall *n.* a violent highly localized weather disturbance at sea, in which the surface of the water is whipped to a white spray by the winds.

white stick *n.* a walking stick used by a blind person for feeling the way: painted white as a sign to others that the person is blind.

White supremacy *n.* the theory or belief that White people are innately superior to people of other races. —**White supremacist** *n., adj.*

white-tailed deer *n.* a deer, *Odocoileus virginianus,* of North America and N South America: the coat varies in colour, being typically reddish-brown in the summer, and the tail is white. Also called: **Virginia deer.**

whitethorn ('waɪtˌθɔːn) *n.* another name for **hawthorn.**

whitethroat ('waɪtˌθrəʊt) *n.* either of two Old World warblers, *Sylvia communis* or *S. curruca* (**lesser whitethroat**), having a greyish-brown plumage with a white throat and underparts.

white tie *n.* **1.** a white bow tie worn as part of a man's formal evening dress. **2. a.** formal evening dress for men. **b.** (*as modifier*): *a white-tie occasion.*

white vitriol *n.* another name for **zinc sulphate.**

whitewall ('waɪtˌwɔːl) *n.* a pneumatic tyre having white sidewalls.

white walnut *n.* another name for **butternut** (senses 1–4).

whitewash ('waɪtˌwɒʃ) *n.* **1.** a substance used for whitening walls and other surfaces, consisting of a suspension of lime or whiting in water, often with other substances, such as size, added. **2.** *Informal.* deceptive or specious words or actions intended to conceal defects, gloss over failings, etc. **3.** *Informal.* a game in which the loser fails to score. *~vb.* (*tr.*) **4.** to cover or whiten with whitewash. **5.** *Informal.* to conceal, gloss over, or suppress. **6.** *Informal.* to defeat (someone) in a game by preventing him from scoring. —'**whiteˌwasher** *n.*

white water *n.* **1.** a stretch of water with a broken foamy surface, as in rapids. **2.** light-coloured sea water, esp. over shoals or shallows.

white whale *n.* a small white toothed whale, *Delphinapterus leucas,* of northern waters: family *Monodontidae.* Also called: **beluga.**

whitewood ('waɪtˌwʊd) *n.* **1.** any of various trees with light-coloured wood, such as the tulip tree, basswood, and cottonwood. **2.** the wood of any of these trees.

whitey *or* **whity** ('waɪtɪ) *n. Chiefly U.S.* (used contemptuously by Negroes) a White man.

whither ('wɪðə) *Archaic or poetic.* *~adv.* **1.** to what place? **2.** to what end or purpose? *~conj.* **3.** to whatever place, purpose, etc. [Old English *hwider, hwæder;* related to Gothic *hvadrē;* modern English form influenced by HITHER]

whithersoever (ˌwɪðəsəʊ'ɛvə) *adv., conj. Archaic or poetic.* to whichever place.

whitherward ('wɪðəwəd) *adv. Archaic or poetic.* in which direction.

whiting[1] ('waɪtɪŋ) *n.* **1.** an important gadoid food fish, *Merlangius* (or *Gadus*) *merlangus,* of European seas, having a dark back with silvery sides and underparts. **2.** any of various similar fishes, such as *Merluccius bilinearis,* a hake of American Atlantic waters, and any of several Atlantic sciaenid fishes of the genus *Menticirrhus.* **3.** *Austral.* any of several marine food fishes of the genus *Sillago.* **4. whiting pout.** another name for **bib** (the fish). [C15: perhaps from Old English *hwītling;* related to Middle Dutch *wijting.* See WHITE, -ING[3]]

whiting[2] ('waɪtɪŋ) *n.* white chalk that has been ground and washed, used in making whitewash, metal polish, etc. Also called: **whitening.**

whitlow ('wɪtləʊ) *n.* any pussy inflammation of the end of a finger or toe. [C14: changed from *whitflaw,* from WHITE + FLAW[1]]

whitlow grass *n.* any of various grasses of the genera *Draba* and *Erophila,* once thought to cure whitlows.

Whit Monday *n.* the Monday following Whit Sunday.

Whitsun ('wɪtsᵊn) *n.* **1.** short for **Whitsuntide.** *~adj.* **2.** of or relating to Whit Sunday or Whitsuntide.

Whitsunday (ˌhwɪt'sʌndɪ, ˌwɪt-) *n.* (in Scotland) May 15, one of the four quarter days.

Whit Sunday *n.* the seventh Sunday after Easter, observed as a feast in commemoration of the descent of the Holy Spirit on the apostles 50 days after Easter. Also called: **Pentecost.** [Old English *hwīta sunnandæg* white Sunday, probably named after the ancient custom of wearing white robes at or after baptism]

Whitsuntide ('wɪtsᵊnˌtaɪd) *n.* the week that begins with Whit Sunday, esp. the first three days.

whitter ('wɪtə) *vb., n.* a variant spelling of **witter.**

whittle ('wɪtᵊl) *vb.* **1.** to cut or shave strips or pieces from (wood, a stick, etc.), esp. with a knife. **2.** (*tr.*) to make or shape by paring or shaving. **3.** (*tr.;* often foll. by *away, down, off,* etc.) to reduce, destroy, or wear away gradually: *~n.* **4.** *Brit. dialect.* a knife, esp. a large one. [C16: variant of C15 *thwittle* large knife, from Old English *thwitel,* from *thwītan* to cut; related to Old Norse *thveitr* cut, *thveita* to beat] —'**whittler** *n.*

whittlings ('wɪtlɪŋz) *pl. n.* chips or shavings whittled off from an object.

whittret ('wɪtrət) *or* **whitrick** ('wɪtrɪk) *n. Dialect.* a male weasel. [Old English *whytrate, whittratt;* perhaps from *hwīt* WHITE + *rætt* RAT]

Whitworth screw thread ('wɪtwəθ) *n.* a thread form and system of standard sizes, proposed by Whitworth in 1841 and adopted as standard in the U.K., having a flank angle of 55° and a rounded top and foot. [named after Sir Joseph *Whitworth* (1803–87), British engineer]

whity ('waɪtɪ) *n., pl.* **whities 1.** *Informal.* a variant spelling of **whitey.** *~adj.* **2. a.** whitish in colour. **b.** (*in combination*): *whity-brown.*

whiz *or* **whizz** (wɪz) *vb.* **whizzes, whizzing, whizzed. 1.** to make or cause to make a loud humming or buzzing sound. **2.** to move or cause to move with such a sound. **3.** (*intr.*) *Informal.* to move or go rapidly. *~n.* **4.** a loud humming or buzzing sound. **5.** *Informal.* a person who is extremely skilful at some activity. [C16: of imitative origin]

whiz-bang *or* **whizz-bang** *n.* **1.** a small-calibre World War I shell that, when discharged, travelled at such a high velocity that the sound of its flight was heard only an instant, if at all, before the sound of its explosion. *~adj.* **2.** *Informal.* excellent or first-rate.

whiz kid, whizz kid, *or* **wiz kid** *n. Informal.* a person who is pushing, enthusiastic, and outstandingly successful for his or her age. [C20: from WHIZ, perhaps influenced by WIZARD]

who (huː) *pron.* **1.** which person? what person? used in direct and indirect questions: *he can't remember who did it; who met you?* **2.** used to introduce relative clauses with antecedents referring to human beings: *the people who lived here have left.* **3.** the one or ones who; whoever: *bring who you want.* [Old English *hwā;* related to Old Saxon *hwē,* Old High German *hwer,* Gothic *hvas,* Lithuanian *kàs,* Danish *hvo*]

▷**Usage.** See at **whom.**

WHO *abbrev. for* World Health Organization.

whoa (wəʊ) *interj.* a command used esp. to horses to stop or slow down. [C19: variant of HO]

who'd (huːd) *contraction of* who had *or* who would.

who-does-what *adj.* (of a dispute, strike, etc.) relating to the separation of kinds of work performed by different trade unions.

whodunit *or* **whodunnit** (huːˈdʌnɪt) *n. Informal.* a novel, play, etc., concerned with a crime, usually murder.

whoever (huːˈɛvə) *pron.* **1.** any person who; anyone that: *whoever wants it can have it.* **2.** no matter who: *I'll come round tomorrow, whoever may be here.* **3.** an intensive form of *who,* used in questions: *whoever could have thought that?* **4.** *Informal.* an unknown or unspecified person: *give those to John, or Cathy, or whoever.*

whole (həʊl) *adj.* **1.** containing all the component parts necessary to form a total; complete: *a whole apple.* **2.** constituting the full quantity, extent, etc. **3.** uninjured or undamaged. **4.** healthy. **5.** having no fractional or decimal part; integral: *a whole number.* **6.** of, relating to, or designating a relationship established by descent from the same parents; full: *whole brothers.* **7. out of whole cloth.** *U.S. and Canadian informal.* entirely without a factual basis. *~adv.* **8.** in an undivided or unbroken piece: *to swallow a plum whole.* *~n.* **9.** all the parts, elements, etc., of a thing. **10.** an assemblage of parts viewed together as a unit. **11.** a thing complete in itself. **12. as a whole.** considered altogether; completely. **13. on the whole. a.** taking all things into consideration. **b.** in general. [Old English *hāl, hǣl;* related to Old Frisian *hāl, hēl,* Old High German *heil,* Gothic *hails;* compare HALE[1]] —ˈ**wholeness** *n.*

whole blood *n.* blood obtained from a donor for transfusion from which none of the elements has been removed.

wholefood (ˈhəʊlˌfuːd) *n.* (*sometimes pl.*) **a.** food that has been refined or processed as little as possible and is eaten in its natural state, such as brown rice, wholemeal flour, etc. **b.** (*as modifier*): *a wholefood restaurant.*

whole gale *n.* a wind of force ten on the Beaufort scale, seldom experienced inland.

wholehearted (ˌhəʊlˈhɑːtɪd) *adj.* done, acted, given, etc., with total sincerity, enthusiasm, or commitment. —ˌ**whole**ˈ**heartedly** *adv.* —ˌ**whole**ˈ**heartedness** *n.*

whole hog *n. Slang.* the whole or total extent (esp. in the phrase **go the whole hog**).

wholemeal (ˈhəʊlˌmiːl) *adj. Brit.* (of flour, bread, etc.) made from the entire wheat kernel. U.S. and Canadian term: **whole-wheat.**

whole milk *n.* milk from which no constituent has been removed. Compare **skim milk.**

whole note *n.* the usual U.S. and Canadian name for **semibreve.**

whole number *n.* **1.** an integer. **2.** a natural number.

wholesale (ˈhəʊlˌseɪl) *n.* **1.** the business of selling goods to retailers in larger quantities than they are sold to final consumers but in smaller quantities than they are purchased from manufacturers. Compare **retail** (sense 1). **2. at wholesale. a.** in large quantities. **b.** at wholesale prices. *~adj.* **3.** of, relating to, or engaged in such business. **4.** made, done, etc., on a large scale or without discrimination. *~adv.* **5.** on a large scale or without discrimination. *~vb.* **6.** to sell (goods) at wholesale. —ˈ**whole**ˌ**saler** *n.*

wholesale price index *n.* an indicator of price changes in the wholesale market.

wholesome (ˈhəʊlsəm) *adj.* **1.** conducive to health or physical wellbeing. **2.** conducive to moral wellbeing. **3.** characteristic or suggestive of health or wellbeing, esp. in appearance. [C12: from WHOLE (healthy) + -SOME[1]; related to German *heilsam* healing] —ˈ**wholesomely** *adv.* —ˈ**wholesomeness** *n.*

whole tone *or U.S. and Canadian* **whole step** *n.* an interval of two semitones; a frequency difference of 200 cents in the system of equal temperament. Often shortened to **tone.**

whole-tone scale *n.* either of two scales, consisting of six degrees to the octave, produced by commencing on one of any two notes a chromatic semitone apart and proceeding upwards or downwards in whole tones for an octave.

whole-wheat *adj.* another term (esp. U.S. and Canadian) for **wholemeal.**

who'll (huːl) *contraction of* who will *or* who shall.

wholly (ˈhəʊllɪ) *adv.* **1.** completely, totally, or entirely. **2.** without exception; exclusively.

whom (huːm) *pron.* the objective form of *who,* used when *who* is not the subject of its own clause: *whom did you say you had seen? he can't remember whom he saw.* [Old English *hwām,* dative of *hwā* WHO]

▷**Usage.** In formal English, careful writers always use *whom* when the objective form of *who* is required. In informal contexts, however, many careful speakers consider *whom* to be unnatural, esp. at the beginning of a sentence: *who were you looking for?* Careful speakers usually prefer *whom* where it closely follows a preposition: *to whom did you give it?* as contrasted with *who did you give it to?*

whomever (huːmˈɛvə) *pron.* the objective form of *whoever: I'll hire whomever I can find.*

whomsoever (ˌhuːmsəʊˈɛvə) *pron. Archaic or formal.* the objective form of *whosoever: to whomsoever it may concern.*

whoop (wuːp) *vb.* **1.** to utter (speech) with loud cries, as of enthusiasm or excitement. **2.** *Med.* to cough convulsively with a crowing sound made at each inspiration. **3.** (of certain birds) to utter (a hooting cry). **4.** (*tr.*) to urge on or call with or as if with whoops. **5.** (wʊp, wuːp). **whoop it up.** *Informal.* **a.** to indulge in a noisy celebration. **b.** *U.S.* to arouse enthusiasm. *~n.* **6.** a loud cry, esp. one expressing enthusiasm or excitement. **7.** *Med.* the convulsive crowing sound made during a paroxysm of whooping cough. **8. not worth a whoop.** *Informal.* worthless. ~See also **whoops.** [C14: of imitative origin]

whoopee *Informal.* *~interj.* (wʊˈpiː). **1.** an exclamation of joy, excitement, etc. *~n.* (ˈwʊpiː). **2. make whoopee. a.** to engage in noisy merrymaking. **b.** to make love.

whoopee cushion *n.* a joke cushion that emits a sound like the breaking of wind when someone sits on it.

whooper *or* **whooper swan** (ˈwuːpə) *n.* a large white Old World swan, *Cygnus cygnus,* having a black bill with a yellow base and a noisy whooping cry.

whooping cough (ˈhuːpɪŋ) *n.* an acute infectious disease characterized by coughing spasms that end with a shrill crowing sound on inspiration: caused by infection with the bacillus *Bordetella pertussis.* Technical name: **pertussis.**

whooping crane *n.* a rare North American crane, *Grus americana,* having a white plumage with black wings and a red naked face.

whoops (wʊps) *interj.* an exclamation of surprise, as when a person falls over, or of apology.

whoosh *or* **woosh** (wʊʃ) *n.* **1.** a hissing or rushing sound. *~vb.* **2.** (*intr.*) to make or move with such a sound.

whop, wop, *or* (*less commonly*) **whap** (wɒp) *Informal.* *~vb.* **whops, whopping, whopped. 1.** (*tr.*) to strike, beat, or thrash. **2.** (*tr.*) to defeat utterly. **3.** (*intr.*) to drop or fall. *~n.* **4.** a heavy blow or the sound made by such a blow. [C14: variant of *wap,* perhaps of imitative origin]

whopper (ˈwɒpə) *n. Informal.* **1.** anything uncommonly large of its kind. **2.** a big lie. [C18: from WHOP]

whopping (ˈwɒpɪŋ) *adj. Informal.* uncommonly large.

whore (hɔː) *n.* **1.** a prostitute or promiscuous woman: often a term of abuse. *~vb.* (*intr.*) **2.** to be or act as a prostitute. **3.** (of a man) to have promiscuous sexual relations, esp. with prostitutes. **4.** (often foll. by *after*) to seek that which is immoral, idolatrous, etc. [Old English *hōre;* related to Old Norse *hōra,* Old High German *hvora,* Latin *carus* dear] —ˈ**whorish** *adj.* —ˈ**whorishly** *adv.* —ˈ**whorishness** *n.*

whoredom (ˈhɔːdəm) *n.* **1.** the activity of whoring or state of being a whore. **2.** a biblical word for **idolatry.**

whorehouse (ˈhɔːˌhaʊs) *n.* another word for **brothel.**

whoremaster (ˈhɔːˌmɑːstə) *n. Archaic.* a person who consorts with or procures whores. —ˈ**whore**ˌ**mastery** *n.*

whoremonger (ˈhɔːˌmʌŋgə) *n.* a person who consorts with whores; lecher. —ˈ**whore**ˌ**mongery** *n.*

whoreson (ˈhɔːsən) *Archaic.* *~n.* **1.** a bastard. **2.** a scoundrel; wretch. *~adj.* **3.** vile or hateful.

whorl (wɜːl) *n.* **1.** *Botany.* a radial arrangement of three or more petals, stamens, leaves, etc., around a stem. **2.** *Zoology.* a single turn in a spiral shell. **3.** one of the basic patterns of the human fingerprint, formed by several complete circular ridges one inside another. Compare **arch**[1] (sense 4b.), **loop**[1] (sense 10a.). **4.** anything shaped like a coil. [C15: probably variant of *wherville* WHIRL, influenced by Dutch *worvel*] —**whorled** *adj.*

whortleberry (ˈwɜːtᵊlˌbɛrɪ) *n., pl.* **-ries. 1.** Also called: **bilberry, blaeberry, huckleberry** and (dialect) **hurt, whort.** a small Eurasian ericaceous shrub, *Vaccinium myrtillus,* greenish-pink flowers and edible sweet blackish berries. **2.** the fruit of this shrub. **3. bog whortleberry.** a related plant, *V. uliginosum,* of mountain regions, having pink flowers and black fruits. [C16: southwestern English dialect form of *hurtleberry;* of unknown origin]

who's (huːz) *contraction of* who is.

whose (huːz) *determiner* **1. a.** of who? belonging to who? used in direct and indirect questions: *I told him whose fault it was; whose car is this?* **b.** (*as pronoun*): *whose is that?* **2.** of who; belonging to who; of which; belonging to which: used as a relative pronoun: *a house whose windows are broken; a man whose reputation has suffered.* [Old English *hwæs,* genitive of *hwā* WHO and *hwæt* WHAT]

whoso (ˈhuːsəʊ) *pron.* an archaic word for **whoever.**

whosoever (ˌhuːsəʊˈɛvə) *pron.* an archaic or formal word for **whoever.**

who's who *n.* a book or list containing the names and short biographies of famous people.

WH question *n.* a question in English to which an appropriate answer is to give information rather than to answer "yes" or "no": typically introduced by the word *who, which, what, where, when,* or *how.* Also called: **information question.**

Whr *abbrev. for* watt-hour.

whsle *abbrev. for* wholesale.

why (waɪ) *adv.* **1. a.** for what reason, purpose, or cause?: *why are you here?* **b.** (*used in indirect questions*): *tell me why you're here.* ~*pron.* **2.** for or because of which: *there is no reason why he shouldn't come.* ~*n., pl.* **whys. 3.** (*usually pl.*) the reason, purpose, or cause of something (esp. in the phrase **the whys and wherefores**). ~*interj.* **4.** an introductory expression of surprise, disagreement, indignation, etc.: *why, don't be silly!* [Old English *hwī;* related to Old Norse *hvī,* Gothic *hveileiks* what kind of, Latin *quī*]

whydah *or* **whidah** ('wɪdə) *n.* any of various predominantly black African weaverbirds of the genus *Vidua* and related genera, the males of which grow very long tail feathers in the breeding season. Also called: **whydah bird, whidah bird, widow bird.** [C18: after the name of a town in Benin, W Africa]

WI *abbrev. for:* **1.** West Indian. **2.** West Indies. **3.** Wisconsin. **4.** (in Britain) Women's Institute.

Wicca ('wɪkə) *n.* (*sometimes not cap.*) the cult or practice of witchcraft. [C20: revival of Old English *wicca* witch]

wick[1] (wɪk) *n.* **1.** a cord or band of loosely twisted or woven fibres, as in a candle, cigarette lighter, etc., that supplies fuel to a flame by capillary action. **2. get on (someone's) wick.** *Brit. slang.* to cause irritation to (a person). [Old English *weoce;* related to Old High German *wioh,* Middle Dutch *wēke* (Dutch *wiek*)] —'**wicking** *n.*

wick[2] (wɪk) *n. Archaic.* a village or hamlet. [Old English *wīc;* related to *-wich* in place names, Latin *vīcus,* Greek *oikos*]

wick[3] (wɪk) *adj. Northern English dialect.* **1.** lively or active. **2.** alive or crawling: *wick with fleas.* [dialect variant of QUICK alive]

wicked ('wɪkɪd) *adj.* **1. a.** morally bad in principle or practice. **b.** (*as collective n.* preceded by *the*): *the wicked.* **2.** mischievous or roguish, esp. in a playful way: *a wicked grin.* **3.** causing injury or harm. **4.** troublesome, unpleasant, or offensive. **5.** *Slang.* very good. [C13: from dialect *wick,* from Old English *wicca* sorcerer, *wicce* WITCH] —'**wickedly** *adv.* —'**wickedness** *n.*

wicker ('wɪkə) *n.* **1.** a slender flexible twig or shoot, esp. of willow. **2.** short for **wickerwork.** ~*adj.* **3.** made, consisting of, or constructed from wicker. [C14: from Scandinavian; compare Swedish *viker,* Danish *viger* willow, Swedish *vika* to bend]

wickerwork ('wɪkəˌwɜːk) *n.* **a.** a material consisting of wicker. **b.** (*as modifier*): *a wickerwork chair.*

wicket ('wɪkɪt) *n.* **1.** a small door or gate, esp. one that is near to or part of a larger one. **2.** *U.S.* a small window or opening in a door, esp. one fitted with a grating or glass pane, used as a means of communication in a ticket office, bank, etc. **3.** a small sluicegate, esp. one in a canal lock gate or by a water wheel. **4.** *U.S.* a croquet hoop. **5. a.** *Cricket.* either of two constructions, placed 22 yards apart, consisting of three pointed stumps stuck parallel in the ground with two wooden bails resting on top, at which the batsman stands. **b.** the strip of ground between these. **c.** a batsman's turn at batting or the period during which two batsmen bat: *a third-wicket partnership.* **d.** the act or instance of a batsman being got out: *the bowler took six wickets.* **6. keep wicket.** to act as a wicketkeeper. **7. on a good, sticky,** *etc.,* **wicket.** *Informal.* in an advantageous, awkward, etc., situation. [C18: from Old Northern French *wiket;* related to Old Norse *vikja* to move]

wicketkeeper ('wɪkɪtˌkiːpə) *n. Cricket.* the player on the fielding side positioned directly behind the wicket.

wicket maiden *n. Cricket.* an over in which no runs are scored with the bat and at least one wicket is taken by the bowler. See also **maiden over.**

wickiup, wikiup, *or* **wickyup** ('wɪkɪˌʌp) *n. U.S. and Canadian.* a crude shelter made of brushwood, mats, or grass and having an oval frame, esp. of a kind used by nomadic Indians now in Oklahoma and neighbouring states of the U.S. [C19: from Sac, Fox, and Kickapoo *wikiyap;* compare WIGWAM]

wickthing ('wɪkˌθɪŋ) *n. Lancashire dialect.* a creeping animal, such as a woodlouse. [from WICK[3] + THING]

wicopy ('wɪkəpɪ) *n., pl.* **-pies.** *U.S.* any of various North American trees, shrubs, or herbaceous plants, esp. the leatherwood, various willowherbs, and the basswood. [C18: from Cree *wikupiy* inner bark, willow bark]

widdershins ('wɪdəˌʃɪnz; *Scot.* 'wɪdər-) *adv. Chiefly Scot.* a variant spelling of **withershins.**

wide (waɪd) *adj.* **1.** having a great extent from side to side. **2.** of vast size or scope; spacious or extensive. **3. a.** (*postpositive*) having a specified extent, esp. from side to side: *two yards wide.* **b.** (*in combination*): covering or extending throughout: *nationwide.* **4.** distant or remote from the desired point, mark, etc.: *your guess is wide of the mark.* **5.** (of eyes) opened fully. **6.** loose, full, or roomy: *wide trousers.* **7.** exhibiting a considerable spread, as between certain limits: *a wide variation.* **8.** *Phonetics.* another word for **lax** (sense 4) or **open** (sense 34). **9.** *Brit. slang.* unscrupulous and astute: *a wide boy.* ~*adv.* **10.** over an extensive area: *to travel far and wide.* **11.** to the full extent: *he opened the door wide.* **12.** far from the desired point, mark, etc. ~*n.* **13.** (in cricket) a bowled ball that is outside the batsman's reach and scores a run for the batting side. **14.** *Archaic or poetic.* a wide space or extent. **15. to the wide.** completely. [Old English *wīd;* related to Old Norse *vīthr,* Old High German *wīt*] —'**widely** *adv.* —'**wideness** *n.* —'**widish** *adj.*

wide-angle lens *n.* a lens system on a camera that can cover an angle of view of 60° or more and therefore has a fairly small focal length. See also **fish-eye lens.**

wide area network *n. Computer technol.* the linking over a large area of a number of different devices by cable. Abbrev.: **WAN.**

wide-awake *adj.* (**wide awake** *when postpositive*). **1.** fully awake. **2.** keen, alert, or observant. ~*n.* **3.** Also called: **wide-awake hat.** a hat with a low crown and very wide brim. —'**wide-a'wakeness** *n.*

wide-body *adj.* (of an aircraft) having a wide fuselage, esp. wide enough to contain three rows of seats abreast.

wide-eyed *adj.* innocent or credulous.

widen ('waɪdᵊn) *vb.* to make or become wide or wider. —'**widener** *n.*

wide-open *adj.* (**wide open** *when postpositive*). **1.** open to the full extent. **2.** (*postpositive*) exposed to attack; vulnerable. **3.** uncertain as to outcome. **4.** *U.S. informal.* (of a town or city) lax in the enforcement of certain laws, esp. those relating to the sale and consumption of alcohol, gambling, the control of vice, etc.

wide receiver *n. American football.* a player whose function is to catch long passes from the quarterback.

wide-screen *adj.* of or relating to a form of film projection in which the screen has much greater width than height.

widespread ('waɪdˌsprɛd) *adj.* **1.** extending over a wide area. **2.** accepted by or occurring among many people.

widgeon ('wɪdʒən) *n.* a variant spelling of **wigeon.**

widget ('wɪdʒɪt) *n. Informal.* any small mechanism or device, the name of which is unknown or temporarily forgotten. [C20: changed from GADGET]

widgie ('wɪdʒɪ) *n. Austral. slang.* a female larrikin or bodgie. [C20: alteration of BODGIE]

widow ('wɪdəʊ) *n.* **1.** a woman who has survived her husband, esp. one who has not remarried. **2.** (*usually with a modifier*) *Informal.* a woman whose husband frequently leaves her alone while he indulges in a sport, etc.: *a golf widow.* **3.** *Printing.* a short line at the end of a paragraph, esp. one that occurs as the top line of a page or set of column. **4.** (in some card games) an additional hand or set of cards exposed on the table. ~*vb.* (*tr.; usually passive*) **5.** to cause to become a widow. **6.** to deprive of something valued or desirable. [Old English *widuwe;* related to German *Witwe,* Latin *vidua* (feminine of *viduus* deprived), Sanskrit *vidhavā*] —'**widowhood** *n.*

widow bird *n.* another name for **whydah.**

widower ('wɪdəʊə) *n.* a man whose wife has died and who has not remarried.

widow's benefit *n.* (in the British National Insurance scheme) a weekly payment made to a widow.

widow's cruse *n.* an endless or unfailing source of supply. [allusion to I Kings 17:16]

widow's mite *n.* a small contribution given by a person who has very little. [allusion to Mark 12:43]

widow's peak *n.* a V-shaped point in the hairline in the middle of the forehead. [from the belief that it presaged early widowhood]

widow woman *n. Archaic or dialect.* another term for **widow** (sense 1).

width (wɪdθ) *n.* **1.** the linear extent or measurement of something from side to side, usually being the shortest dimension or (for something fixed) the shortest horizontal dimension. **2.** the state or fact of being wide. **3.** a piece or section of something at its full extent from side to side: *a width of cloth.* **4.** the distance across a rectangular swimming bath, as opposed to its length. [C17: from WIDE + -TH[1], analogous to BREADTH]

widthwise ('wɪdθˌwaɪz) *or* **widthways** ('wɪdθˌweɪz) *adv.* in the direction of the width; from side to side.

wield (wiːld) *vb.* (*tr.*) **1.** to handle or use (a weapon, tool, etc.). **2.** to exert or maintain (power or authority). **3.** *Obsolete.* to rule. [Old English *wieldan, wealdan;* related to Old Norse *valda,* Old Saxon *waldan,* German *walten,* Latin *valēre* to be strong] —'**wieldable** *adj.* —'**wielder** *n.*

wieldy ('wiːldɪ) *adj.* **wieldier, wieldiest.** easily handled, used, or managed.

wiener ('wiːnə) *or* **wienerwurst** ('wiːnəˌwɜːst) *n. U.S. and Canadian.* a kind of smoked beef or pork sausage, similar to a frankfurter. Also called: **wienie, weenie** ('wiːnɪ). [C20: shortened from German *Wiener Wurst* Viennese sausage]

Wiener schnitzel ('viːnə 'ʃnɪtsəl) *n.* a large thin escalope of veal, coated in egg and crumbs, fried, and traditionally served with a garnish. [German: Viennese cutlet]

wife (waɪf) *n., pl.* **wives** (waɪvz). **1.** a man's partner in marriage; a married woman. Related adj.: **uxorial. 2.** an archaic or dialect word for **woman. 3. take to wife.** to marry (a woman). [Old English *wīf;* related to Old Norse *vīf* (perhaps from *vīfathr* veiled), Old High German *wīb* (German *Weib*)] —'**wifehood** *n.* —'**wifeless** *adj.* —'**wifeˌlike** *adj.* —'**wifeliness** *n.* —'**wifely** *adj.*

wife swapping *n.* **a.** the temporary exchange of wives between married couples for sexual relations. **b.** (*as modifier*): *a wife-swapping party.*

wig (wɪg) *n.* **1.** an artificial head of hair, either human or synthetic, worn to disguise baldness, as part of a theatrical or ceremonial dress, as a disguise, or for adornment. ~*vb.* **wigs, wigging, wigged.** (*tr.*) **2.** *Obsolete.* to furnish with a wig. **3.** *Brit. slang.* to berate severely. [C17: shortened from PERIWIG] —**wigged** *adj.* —**'wigless** *adj.* —**'wig,like** *adj.*

Wig. *abbrev. for* Wigtownshire.

wigeon *or* **widgeon** ('wɪdʒən) *n.* **1.** a Eurasian duck, *Anas penelope,* of marshes, swamps, etc., the male of which has a reddish-brown head and chest and grey and white back and wings. **2.** **American wigeon.** Also called: **baldpate.** a similar bird, *Anas americana,* of North America, the male of which has a white crown. [C16: of uncertain origin]

wigging ('wɪgɪŋ) *n.* **1.** *Brit. slang.* a rebuke or reprimand. **2.** *N.Z.* the shearing of wool from the head of a sheep.

wiggle ('wɪgᵊl) *vb.* **1.** to move or cause to move with jerky movements, esp. from side to side. ~*n.* **2.** the act or an instance of wiggling. **3.** **get a wiggle on.** *Slang, chiefly U.S.* to hurry up. [C13: from Middle Low German, Middle Dutch *wiggelen*] —**'wiggler** *n.* —**'wiggly** *adj.*

wight[1] (waɪt) *n. Archaic.* a human being. [Old English *wiht;* related to Old Frisian *āwet* something, Old Norse *vǣttr* being, Gothic *waihts* thing, German *Wicht* small person]

wight[2] (waɪt) *adj. Archaic.* strong and brave; valiant. [C13: from Old Norse *vigt;* related to Old English *wīg* battle, Latin *vincere* to conquer]

wigwag ('wɪg,wæg) *vb.* **-wags, -wagging, -wagged.** **1.** to move (something) back and forth. **2.** to communicate with (someone) by means of a flag semaphore. ~*n.* **3. a.** a system of communication by flag semaphore. **b.** the message signalled. [C16: from obsolete *wig,* probably short for WIGGLE + WAG] —**'wig,wagger** *n.*

wigwam ('wɪg,wæm) *n.* **1.** any dwelling of the North American Indians, esp. one made of bark, rushes, or skins spread over or enclosed by a set of arched poles lashed together. Compare **tepee.** **2.** a similar structure for children. [from Abnaki and Massachuset *wīkwām,* literally: their abode]

wikiup ('wɪkɪ,ʌp) *n.* a variant spelling of **wickiup.**

wilco (,wɪl'kəʊ) *interj.* an expression in signalling, telecommunications, etc., indicating that a message just received will be complied with. Compare **roger.** [C20: abbreviation for *I will comply*]

Wilcoxon test (wɪl'kɒksᵊn) *n.* **a.** Also called: **Wilcoxon matched-pairs signed-ranks test.** a statistical test for the relative size of the scores of the same or matched subjects under two experimental conditions by comparing the distributions for positive and negative differences of the ranks of their absolute values. **b.** **Wilcoxon Mann-Whitney test.** See **Mann-Whitney test.** [named after Frank *Wilcoxon* (1892–1965), Irish mathematician and statistician]

wild (waɪld) *adj.* **1.** (of animals) living independently of man; not domesticated or tame. **2.** (of plants) growing in a natural state; not cultivated. **3.** uninhabited or uncultivated; desolate: *a wild stretch of land.* **4.** living in a savage or uncivilized way: *wild tribes.* **5.** lacking restraint or control: *wild merriment.* **6.** of great violence or intensity: *a wild storm.* **7.** disorderly or chaotic: *wild thoughts; wild talk.* **8.** dishevelled; untidy: *wild hair.* **9.** in a state of extreme emotional intensity: *wild with anger.* **10.** reckless: *wild speculations.* **11.** not calculated; random: *a wild guess.* **12.** unconventional; fantastic; crazy: *wild friends.* **13.** (*postpositive;* foll. by *about*) *Informal.* intensely enthusiastic or excited: *I'm wild about my new boyfriend.* **14.** (of a card, such as a joker or deuce in some games) able to be given any value the holder pleases: *jacks are wild.* **15. wild and woolly. a.** rough; untamed; barbarous. **b.** (of theories, plans, etc.) not fully thought out. ~*adv.* **16.** in a wild manner. **17. run wild. a.** to grow without cultivation or care: *the garden has run wild.* **b.** to behave without restraint: *he has let his children run wild.* ~*n.* **18.** (*often pl.*) a desolate, uncultivated, or uninhabited region. **19. the wild. a.** a free natural state of living. **b.** the wilderness. [Old English *wilde;* related to Old Saxon, Old High German *wildi,* Old Norse *villr,* Gothic *wiltheis*] —**'wildish** *adj.* —**'wildly** *adv.* —**'wildness** *n.*

wild boar *n.* a wild pig, *Sus scrofa,* of parts of Europe and central Asia, having a pale grey to black coat, thin legs, a narrow body, and prominent tusks.

wild brier *n.* another name for **wild rose.**

wild card *n.* **1.** See **wild** (sense 14). **2.** *Sport.* a player or team that has not qualified for a competition but is allowed to take part, at the organizers' discretion, after all the regular places have been taken. **3.** an unpredictable element in a situation.

wild carrot *n.* an umbelliferous plant, *Daucus carota,* of temperate regions, having clusters of white flowers and hooked fruits. Also called: **Queen Anne's lace.**

wildcat ('waɪld,kæt) *n., pl.* **-cats** *or* **-cat.** **1.** a wild European cat, *Felis silvestris,* that resembles the domestic tabby but is larger and has a bushy tail. **2.** any of various other felines, esp. of the genus *Lynx,* such as the lynx and the caracal. **3.** *U.S. and Canadian.* another name for **bobcat.** **4.** *Informal.* a savage or aggressive person. **5.** an exploratory drilling for petroleum or natural gas. **6.** *U.S. and Canadian.* an unsound commercial enterprise. **7.** the U.S. and Canadian name for **light engine.** **8.** (*modifier*) *U.S. and Canadian.* **a.** of or relating to an unsound business enterprise: *wildcat stock.* **b.** financially or commercially unsound: *a wildcat project.* **9.** (*modifier*) *U.S. and Canadian.* (of a train) running without permission or outside the timetable. ~*vb.* **-cats, -catting, -catted.** **10.** (*intr.*) to drill for petroleum or natural gas in an area having no known reserves. —**'wild,catting** *n., adj.*

wildcat strike *n.* a strike begun by workers spontaneously or without union approval.

wildcatter ('waɪld,kætə) *n. U.S. and Canadian informal.* a prospector for oil or ores in areas having no proved resources.

wild celery *n.* a strongly scented umbelliferous plant, *Apium graveolens,* of temperate regions: the ancestor of cultivated celery. Archaic name: **smallage.**

wild cherry *n.* another name for **gean** (sense 1).

wild dog *n.* another name for **dingo.**

wildebeest ('wɪldɪ,bi:st, 'vɪl-) *n., pl.* **-beests** *or* **-beest.** another name for **gnu.** [C19: from Afrikaans, literally: wild beast]

wilder ('wɪldə) *vb. Archaic.* **1.** to lead or be led astray. **2.** to bewilder or become bewildered. [C17: of uncertain origin] —**'wilderment** *n.*

wilderness ('wɪldənɪs) *n.* **1.** a wild, uninhabited, and uncultivated region. **2.** any desolate tract or area. **3.** a confused mass or collection. **4. a voice (crying) in the wilderness.** a person, group, etc., making a suggestion or plea that is ignored. [Old English *wildēornes,* from *wildēor* wild beast (from WILD + *dēor* beast, DEER) + -NESS; related to Middle Dutch *wildernisse,* German *Wildernis*]

wild-eyed *adj.* **1.** glaring in an angry, distracted, or wild manner. **2.** ill-conceived or totally impracticable.

wildfire ('waɪld,faɪə) *n.* **1.** a highly flammable material, such as Greek fire, formerly used in warfare. **2. a.** a raging and uncontrollable fire. **b.** anything that is disseminated quickly (esp. in the phrase **spread like wildfire**). **3.** lightning without audible thunder. **4.** another name for **will-o'-the-wisp.**

wild flower *n.* **1.** any flowering plant that grows in an uncultivated state. **2.** the flower of such a plant.

wildfowl ('waɪld,faʊl) *n.* **1.** any bird that is hunted by man, esp. any duck or similar aquatic bird. **2.** such birds collectively. —**'wild,fowler** *n.* —**'wild,fowling** *adj., n.*

wild ginger *n.* a North American plant, *Asarum canadense,* having a solitary brownish flower and an aromatic root: family *Aristolochiaceae.* See also **asarabacca, asarum.**

wild-goose chase *n.* an absurd or hopeless pursuit, as of something unattainable.

wild hyacinth *n.* another name for **bluebell** (sense 1).

wild indigo *n.* any of several North American leguminous plants of the genus *Baptisia,* esp. *B. tinctoria,* which has yellow flowers and three-lobed leaves.

wilding ('waɪldɪŋ) *n.* **1.** an uncultivated plant, esp. the crab apple, or a cultivated plant that has become wild. **2.** a wild animal. ~Also called: **'wildling.**

wild Irishman *n. N.Z.* another name for **matagouri.**

wild lettuce *n.* any of several uncultivated lettuce plants, such as *Lactuca serriola* (or *L. scariola*) of Eurasia and *L. canadensis* (**horseweed**) of North America, which grow as weeds and have yellow or blue flowers, milky juice in the stem, and prickly leaves: family *Compositae* (composites).

wildlife ('waɪld,laɪf) *n.* wild animals and plants collectively.

wild liquorice *n.* **1.** another name for *Astragalus glycyphyllos:* see **milk vetch.** **2.** another name for **liquorice** (sense 1). **3.** a North American plant, *Glycyrrhiza lepidota,* that is related to true liquorice and has similar properties.

wild man *n.* **1.** a savage. **2.** an extremist in politics.

wild mustard *n.* another name for **charlock** (sense 1).

wild oat *n.* any of several temperate annual grasses of the genus *Avena,* esp. *A. fatua,* that grow as weeds and have long bristles on their flower spikes.

wild oats *pl. n. Slang.* the indiscretions of youth, esp. dissoluteness before settling down (esp. in the phrase **sow one's wild oats**).

wild olive *n.* any of various trees or shrubs that resemble the olive tree or bear olive-like fruits, esp. the oleaster.

wild pansy *n.* **1.** Also called: **heartsease, love-in-idleness,** and (in the U.S.) **Johnny-jump-up.** a Eurasian violaceous plant, *Viola tricolor,* having purple, yellow, and pale mauve spurred flowers. **2.** any of various similar plants of the genus *Viola.*

wild parsley *n.* any of various uncultivated umbelliferous plants that resemble parsley.

wild parsnip *n.* a strong-smelling umbelliferous plant, *Pastinaca sativa,* that has an inedible root: the ancestor of the cultivated parsnip.

wild rice *n.* another name for **Indian rice.**

wild rose *n.* any of numerous roses, such as the dogrose and sweetbrier, that grow wild and have flowers with only one whorl of petals.

wild rubber *n.* rubber obtained from uncultivated rubber trees.

wild rye *n.* any of various perennial grasses of the N temperate genus *Elymus,* resembling cultivated rye in having paired bristly ears or spikes and flat leaves.

wild silk *n.* **1.** silk produced by wild silkworms. **2.** a fabric made from this, or from short fibres of silk designed to imitate it.

wild Spaniard *n.* any of various subalpine perennials of the genus *Aciphylla* of New Zealand, with sharp leaves. Often shortened to **Spaniard.**

wild track *n.* a soundtrack recorded other than with a synchronized picture, usually carrying sound effects, random dialogue, etc.

wild type *n. Biology.* the typical form of a species of organism resulting from breeding under natural conditions.

wild water *n.* **a.** turbulent water in a river, esp. as an area for navigating in a canoe as a sport. **b.** (*as modifier*): *wild-water racing.*

Wild West show *n. U.S.* a show or circus act presenting feats of horsemanship, shooting, etc.

wildwood ('waɪldˌwʊd) *n. Archaic.* a wood or forest growing in a natural uncultivated state.

wile (waɪl) *n.* **1.** trickery, cunning, or craftiness. **2.** (*usually pl.*) an artful or seductive trick or ploy. ~*vb.* **3.** (*tr.*) to lure, beguile, or entice. [C12: from Old Norse *vel* craft; probably related to Old French *wīle,* Old English *wīgle* magic. See GUILE]

wilful *or U.S.* **willful** ('wɪlfʊl) *adj.* **1.** intent on having one's own way; headstrong or obstinate. **2.** willed or intentional: *wilful murder.* —'**wilfully** *or U.S.* '**willfully** *adv.* —'**wilfulness** *or U.S.* '**willfulness** *n.*

wilga ('wɪlgə) *n.* a small drought-resistant tree, *Geijera parviflora,* of Australia, having hard aromatic wood and foliage that resembles that of the willow. [C19: from a native Australian language]

will[1] (wɪl) *vb. past* **would.** (takes an infinitive without *to* or an implied infinitive) used as an auxiliary. **1.** (esp. with *you, he, she, it, they,* or a noun as subject) to make the future tense. Compare **shall** (sense 1). **2.** to express resolution on the part of the speaker: *I will buy that radio if it's the last thing I do.* **3.** to indicate willingness or desire: *will you help me with this problem?* **4.** to express compulsion, as in commands: *you will report your findings to me tomorrow.* **5.** to express capacity or ability: *this rope will support a load.* **6.** to express probability or expectation on the part of the speaker: *that will be Jim telephoning.* **7.** to express customary practice or inevitability: *boys will be boys.* **8.** (*with the infinitive always implied*) to express desire: usually in polite requests: *stay if you will.* **9. what you will.** whatever you like. **10. will do.** *Informal.* a declaration of willingness to do what is requested. [Old English *willan;* related to Old Saxon *willian,* Old Norse *vilja,* Old High German *wollen,* Latin *velle* to wish, will]

▷**Usage.** See at **shall.**

will[2] (wɪl) *n.* **1.** the faculty of conscious and deliberate choice of action; volition. Related adj.: **voluntary. 2.** the act or an instance of asserting a choice. **3. a.** the declaration of a person's wishes regarding the disposal of his property after his death. **b.** a revocable instrument by which such wishes are expressed. **4.** anything decided upon or chosen, esp. by a person in authority; desire; wish. **5.** determined intention: *where there's a will there's a way.* **6.** disposition or attitude towards others: *he bears you no ill will.* **7. at will.** at one's own desire, inclination, or choice. **8. with a will.** heartily; energetically. **9. with the best will in the world.** even with the best of intentions. ~*vb.* (*mainly tr.; often takes a clause as object or an infinitive*) **10.** (*also intr.*) to exercise the faculty of volition in an attempt to accomplish (something): *he willed his wife's recovery from her illness.* **11.** to give (property) by will to a person, society, etc.: *he willed his art collection to the nation.* **12.** (*also intr.*) to order or decree: *the king wills that you shall die.* **13.** to choose or prefer: *wander where you will.* **14.** to yearn for or desire: *to will that one's friends be happy.* [Old English *willa;* related to Old Norse *vili,* Old High German *willeo* (German *Wille*), Gothic *wilja,* Old Slavonic *volja*] —'**willer** *n.*

willable ('wɪləbᵊl) *adj.* able to be wished or determined by the will.

willed (wɪld) *adj.* (*in combination*) having a will as specified: *weak-willed.*

willemite ('wɪləˌmaɪt) *n.* a secondary mineral consisting of zinc silicate in hexagonal crystalline form. It is white, colourless, or coloured by impurities and is found in veins of zinc ore. Formula: Zn_2SiO_4. [C19: from Dutch *willemit,* named after *Willem* I of the Netherlands (1772–1834)]

willet ('wɪlɪt) *n.* a large American shore bird, *Catoptrophorus semipalmatus,* having a long stout bill, long legs, and a grey plumage with black-and-white wings: family *Scolopacidae* (sandpipers, etc.), order *Charadriiformes.* [short for *pill-will-willet* imitation of its cry]

willful ('wɪlfʊl) *adj.* the U.S. spelling of **wilful.**

Williams pear ('wɪljəmz) *n.* a variety of pear that has large yellow juicy sweet fruit. Also called: **William's Bon Chrétien.**

willie ('wɪlɪ) *n. Brit. informal.* a childish or jocular term for **penis.**

willies ('wɪlɪz) *pl. n.* **the.** *Slang.* nervousness, jitters, or fright (esp. in the phrase **give** (*or* **get**) **the willies**). [C20: of unknown origin]

willing ('wɪlɪŋ) *adj.* **1.** favourably disposed or inclined; ready. **2.** cheerfully or eagerly compliant. **3.** done, given, accepted, etc., freely or voluntarily. —'**willingly** *adv.* —'**willingness** *n.*

willing horse *n.* a person prepared to work hard.

williwaw ('wɪlɪˌwɔː) *n. U.S. and Canadian.* **1.** a sudden strong gust of cold wind blowing offshore from a mountainous coast. **2.** a state of great turmoil. [C19: of unknown origin]

will-o'-the-wisp (ˌwɪləðə'wɪsp) *n.* **1.** Also called: **friar's lantern, ignis fatuus, jack-o'-lantern.** a pale flame or phosphorescence sometimes seen over marshy ground at night. It is believed to be due to the spontaneous combustion of methane or other hydrocarbons originating from decomposing organic matter. **2.** a person or thing that is elusive or allures and misleads. [C17: originally *Will with the wisp,* from *Will* short for *William* and *wisp* in former sense of a twist of hay or straw burning as a torch] —ˌ**will-o'-the-'wispish** *or* ˌ**will-o'-the-'wispy** *adj.*

willow ('wɪləʊ) *n.* **1.** any of numerous salicaceous trees and shrubs of the genus *Salix,* such as the weeping willow and osiers of N temperate regions, which have graceful flexible branches and flowers in catkins. **2.** the whitish wood of certain of these trees. **3.** something made of willow wood, such as a cricket or baseball bat. **4.** a machine having a system of revolving spikes for opening and cleaning raw textile fibres. [Old English *welig;* related to *wilige* wicker basket, Old Saxon *wilgia,* Middle High German *wilge,* Greek *helikē* willow, *helix* twisted] —'**willowish** *or* '**willow-ˌlike** *adj.*

willow fly *n.* a stonefly, *Leuctra geniculata,* of the English chalk streams, esteemed by trout and therefore by anglers.

willow grouse *n.* a N European grouse, *Lagopus lagopus,* with a reddish-brown plumage and white wings: now regarded as the same species as the red grouse (*L. lagopus scoticus*) of Britain.

willowherb ('wɪləʊˌhɜːb) *n.* **1.** any of various temperate and arctic onagraceous plants of the genus *Epilobium,* having narrow leaves and terminal clusters of pink, purplish, or white flowers. **2.** short for **rosebay willowherb** (see **rosebay**). **3.** (not in botanical usage) another name for **purple loosestrife** (see **loosestrife**). **4. hairy willowherb.** See **codlins-and-cream.**

willow pattern *n.* **a.** a pattern incorporating a willow tree, river, bridge, and figures, typically in blue on a white ground, used on pottery and porcelain. **b.** (*as modifier*): *a willow-pattern plate.*

willow tit *n.* a small tit, *Parus montanus,* of marshy woods in Europe, having a greyish-brown body and dull black crown.

willow warbler *n.* an Old World warbler, *Phylloscopus trochilis,* of Eurasian woodlands.

willowy ('wɪləʊɪ) *adj.* **1.** slender and graceful. **2.** flexible or pliant. **3.** covered or shaded with willows.

willpower ('wɪlˌpaʊə) *n.* **1.** the ability to control oneself and determine one's actions. **2.** firmness of will.

willy-nilly ('wɪlɪ'nɪlɪ) *adv.* **1.** whether desired or not. ~*adj.* **2.** occurring or taking place whether desired or not. [Old English *wile hē, nyle hē,* literally: will he or will he not; *nyle,* from *ne* not + *willan* to WILL[1]]

willy wagtail *n. Austral.* a black-and-white flycatcher, *Rhipidura leucophrys,* having white feathers over the brows.

willy-willy ('wɪlɪ'wɪlɪ) *n. Austral.* a tropical cyclone or duststorm. [from a native Australian language]

Wilson cloud chamber ('wɪlsən) *n.* the full name for **cloud chamber.**

Wilson's petrel *n.* a common storm petrel, *Oceanites oceanicus,* that breeds around Antarctica but is often seen in the Atlantic. See **storm petrel.**

Wilson's snipe *n.* another name for the **common snipe.** See **snipe** (sense 1).

wilt[1] (wɪlt) *vb.* **1.** to become or cause to become limp, flaccid, or drooping: *insufficient water makes plants wilt.* **2.** to lose or cause to lose courage, strength, etc. ~*n.* **3.** the act of wilting or state of becoming wilted. **4.** any of various plant diseases characterized by permanent wilting, usually caused by fungal parasites attacking the roots. [C17: perhaps variant of *wilk* to wither, from Middle Dutch *welken*]

wilt[2] (wɪlt) *vb. Archaic or dialect.* (used with the pronoun *thou* or its relative equivalent) a singular form of the present tense (indicative mood) of **will**[1].

Wilton ('wɪltən) *n.* a kind of carpet with a close velvet pile of cut loops. [C18: named after *Wilton,* Wiltshire, noted for carpet manufacture]

Wilts (wɪlts) *abbrev. for* Wiltshire.

wily ('waɪlɪ) *adj.* **wilier, wiliest.** characterized by or proceeding from wiles; sly or crafty. —'**wiliness** *n.*

wimble ('wɪmbᵊl) *n.* **1.** any of a number of hand tools, such as a brace and bit or a gimlet, used for boring holes. ~*vb.* **2.** to bore (a hole) with or as if with a wimble. [C13: from Middle Dutch *wimmel* auger]

wimp (wɪmp) *n. Informal.* a feeble ineffective person. [C20: of unknown origin] —'**wimpish** *or* '**wimpy** *adj.*

WIMP *acronym for* windows, icons, menus (*or* mice), pointers: denoting a type of user-friendly screen display used on small computers: *a WIMP system.*

wimple ('wɪmpᵊl) *n.* **1.** a piece of cloth draped around the head to frame the face, worn by women in the Middle Ages and still a part of the habit of some nuns. **2.** *Scot.* a curve or bend, as in a river. ~*vb.* **3.** *Rare.* to ripple or cause to ripple or undulate. **4.** (*tr.*). *Archaic.* to cover with or put a wimple on. **5.** *Archaic.* (esp. of a veil) to lie or cause to lie in folds or pleats. [Old English *wimpel;* related to Old Saxon *wimpal,* Middle Dutch *wumpel,* Middle High German *bewimpfen* to veil]

wimp out *vb.* (*intr., adv.*) *Slang.* to fail to do or complete something through fear or lack of conviction.

Wimpy ('wɪmpɪ) *n. Trademark.* a hamburger served in a soft bread roll.

Wimshurst machine ('wɪmzhɜːst) *n.* a type of electrostatic generator with two parallel insulating discs revolving in different directions, each being in contact with a thin metal wiper that produces a charge on the disc: usually used for demonstration purposes. [C19: named after J. *Wimshurst* (1832–1903), British engineer]

win[1] (wɪn) *vb.* **wins, winning, won.** 1. (*intr.*) to achieve first place in a competition. 2. (*tr.*) to gain or receive (a prize, first place, etc.) in a competition. 3. (*tr.*) to succeed in or gain (something) with an effort: *we won recognition.* 4. **win one's spurs. a.** to achieve recognition in some field of endeavour. **b.** *History.* to be knighted. 5. to gain victory or triumph in (a battle, argument, etc.). 6. (*tr.*) to earn or procure (a living, etc.) by work. 7. (*tr.*) to take possession of, esp. violently; capture: *the Germans never won Leningrad.* 8. (when *intr.*, foll. by *out, through,* etc.) to reach with difficulty (a desired condition or position) or become free, loose, etc., with effort: *the boat won the shore; the boat won through to the shore.* 9. (*tr.*) to turn someone into (a supporter, enemy, etc.): *you have just won an ally.* 10. (*tr.*) to gain (the sympathy, loyalty, etc.) of someone. 11. (*tr.*) to obtain (a woman, etc.) in marriage. 12. (*tr.*) **a.** to extract (ore, coal, etc.) from a mine. **b.** to extract (metal or other minerals) from ore. **c.** to discover and make (a mineral deposit) accessible for mining. 13. **you can't win.** *Informal.* an expression of resignation after an unsuccessful attempt to overcome difficulties. ~*n.* 14. *Informal.* a success, victory, or triumph. 15. profit; winnings. 16. the act or fact of reaching the finishing line or post first. ~See also **win out.** [Old English *winnan;* related to Old Norse *vinna,* German *gewinnen*] —'**winnable** *adj.*

win[2] (wɪn) *vb.* **wins, winning, won** *or* **winned.** (*tr.*) *Irish, Scot., and northern English dialect.* 1. to dry (grain, hay, peat, etc.) by exposure to sun and air. 2. a less common word for **winnow.** [Old English, perhaps a variant of WINNOW]

wince[1] (wɪns) *vb.* 1. (*intr.*) to start slightly, as with sudden pain; flinch. ~*n.* 2. the act of wincing. [C18 (earlier (C13) meaning: to kick): via Old French *wencier, guenchir* to avoid, from Germanic; compare Old Saxon *wenkian,* Old High German *wenken*] —'**wincer** *n.*

wince[2] (wɪns) *n.* a roller for transferring pieces of cloth between dyeing vats. [C17: variant of WINCH]

wincey ('wɪnsɪ) *n. Brit.* a plain- or twill-weave cloth, usually having a cotton or linen warp and a wool filling. [C19: of Scottish origin, probably an alteration of *woolsey* as in LINSEY-WOOLSEY]

winceyette (ˌwɪnsɪ'ɛt) *n. Brit.* a plain-weave cotton fabric with slightly raised two-sided nap.

winch[1] (wɪntʃ) *n.* 1. a windlass driven by a hand- or power-operated crank. 2. a hand- or power-operated crank by which a machine is driven. ~*vb.* 3. (*tr.;* often foll. by *up* or *in*) to pull (in a rope) or lift (a weight) using a winch. [Old English *wince* pulley; related to WINK] —'**wincher** *n.*

winch[2] (wɪntʃ) *vb.* (*intr.*) an obsolete word for **wince**[1].

winchester ('wɪntʃɪstə) *n.* (*sometimes cap.*) a large cylindrical bottle with a narrow neck used for transporting chemicals. It contains about 2.5 litres. [after *Winchester,* Hampshire]

Winchester disk *n.* a type of hard disk in which disks are permanently sealed, together with read-write heads, in an airtight container to keep dust out. [C20: named after the 3030 WINCHESTER RIFLE, as the original device would have had 3030 as its IBM number]

Winchester rifle *n. Trademark.* a breech-loading slide-action repeating rifle with a tubular magazine under the barrel. Often shortened to **Winchester.** [C19: named after O. F. *Winchester* (1810–80), U.S. manufacturer]

wind[1] (wɪnd) *n.* 1. a current of air, sometimes of considerable force, moving generally horizontally from areas of high pressure to areas of low pressure. See also **Beaufort scale.** 2. *Chiefly poetic.* the direction from which a wind blows, usually a cardinal point of the compass. 3. air artificially moved, as by a fan, pump, etc. 4. any sweeping and destructive force. 5. a trend, tendency, or force: *the winds of revolution.* 6. *Informal.* a hint; suggestion: *we got wind that you were coming.* 7. something deemed insubstantial: *his talk was all wind.* 8. breath, as used in respiration or talk: *you're just wasting wind.* 9. (often used in sports) the power to breathe normally: *his wind is weak.* See also **second wind.** 10. *Music.* **a.** a wind instrument or wind instruments considered collectively. **b.** (*often pl.*) the musicians who play wind instruments in an orchestra. **c.** (*modifier*): of, relating to, or composed of wind instruments: *a wind ensemble.* 11. an informal name for **flatus.** 12. the air on which the scent of an animal is carried to hounds or on which the scent of a hunter is carried to his quarry. 13. **between wind and water. a.** the part of a vessel's hull below the water line that is exposed by rolling or by wave action. **b.** any point particularly susceptible to attack or injury. 14. **break wind.** to release intestinal gas through the anus. 15. **get** *or* **have the wind up.** *Informal.* to become frightened. 16. **have in the wind.** to be in the act of following (quarry) by scent. 17. **how** *or* **which way the wind blows** *or* **lies.** what appears probable. 18. **in the wind.** about to happen. 19. **in the wind** *or* **three sheets in the wind.** *Informal.* intoxicated; drunk. 20. **in the teeth** (*or* **eye**) **of the wind.** directly into the wind. 21. **into the wind.** against the wind or upwind. 22. **off the wind.** *Nautical.* away from the direction from which the wind is blowing. 23. **on the wind.** *Nautical.* as near as possible to the direction from which the wind is blowing. 24. **put the wind up.** *Informal.* to frighten or alarm. 25. **raise the wind.** *Brit. informal.* to obtain the necessary funds. 26. **sail close** *or* **near to the wind. a.** to come near the limits of danger or indecency. **b.** to live frugally or manage one's affairs economically. 27. **take the wind out of someone's sails.** to destroy someone's advantage; disconcert or deflate. ~*vb.* (*tr.*) 28. to cause (someone) to be short of breath: *the blow winded him.* 29. **a.** to detect the scent of. **b.** to pursue (quarry) by following its scent. 30. to cause (a baby) to bring up wind after feeding by patting or rubbing on the back. 31. to expose to air, as in drying, ventilating, etc. [Old English *wind;* related to Old High German *wint,* Old Norse *vindr,* Gothic *winds,* Latin *ventus*] —'**windless** *adj.* —'**windlessly** *adv.* —'**windlessness** *n.*

wind[2] (waɪnd) *vb.* **winds, winding, wound.** 1. (often foll. by *around, about, or upon*) to turn or coil (string, cotton, etc.) around some object or point or (of string, etc.) to be turned etc., around some object or point: *he wound a scarf around his head.* 2. (*tr.*) to twine, cover, or wreathe by or as if by coiling, wrapping, etc.; encircle: *we wound the body in a shroud.* 3. (*tr.;* often foll. by *up*) to tighten the spring of (a clockwork mechanism). 4. (*tr.;* foll. by *off*) to remove by uncoiling or unwinding. 5. (*usually intr.*) to move or cause to move in a sinuous, spiral, or circular course: *the river winds through the hills.* 6. (*tr.*) to introduce indirectly or deviously: *he is winding his own opinions into the report.* 7. (*tr.*) to cause to twist or revolve: *he wound the handle.* 8. (*tr.;* usually foll. by *up* or *down*) to move by cranking: *please wind up the window.* 9. (*tr.*) to haul, lift, or hoist (a weight, etc.) by means of a wind or windlass. 10. (*intr.*) (of a board, etc.) to be warped or twisted. 11. (*intr.*) *Archaic.* to proceed deviously or indirectly. ~*n.* 12. the act of winding or state of being wound. 13. a single turn, bend, etc.: *a wind in the river.* 14. Also called: **winding.** a twist in a board or plank. ~See also **wind down, wind up.** [Old English *windan;* related to Old Norse *vinda,* Old High German *wintan* (German *winden*)] —'**windable** *adj.*

wind[3] (waɪnd) *vb.* **winds, winding, winded** *or* **wound.** (*tr.*) *Poetic.* to blow (a note or signal) on (a horn, bugle, etc.). [C16: special use of WIND[1]]

windage ('wɪndɪdʒ) *n.* 1. **a.** a deflection of a projectile as a result of the effect of the wind. **b.** the degree of such deflection. **c.** the extent to which it is necessary to adjust the wind gauge of a gun sight in order to compensate for such deflection. 2. the difference between a firearm's bore and the diameter of its projectile. 3. *Nautical.* the exposed part of the hull of a vessel responsible for wind resistance. 4. the retarding force upon a rotating machine resulting from the drag of the air.

windbag ('wɪndˌbæg) *n.* 1. *Slang.* a voluble person who has little of interest to communicate. 2. the bag in a set of bagpipes, which provides a continuous flow of air to the pipes.

windblown ('wɪndˌbləʊn) *adj.* 1. blown by the wind. 2. (of a woman's hair style) cut short and combed to look as though it has been dishevelled by the wind. 3. (of trees, shrubs, etc.) growing in a shape determined by the prevailing winds. 4. *N.Z.* (of trees) felled by the wind.

wind-borne *adj.* (esp. of plant seeds or pollen) transported by wind.

windbound ('wɪndˌbaʊnd) *adj.* (of a sailing vessel) prevented from sailing by an unfavourable wind.

windbreak ('wɪndˌbreɪk) *n.* a fence, line of trees, etc., serving as a protection from the wind by breaking its force.

wind-broken *adj.* (of a horse) asthmatic or heaving.

windburn ('wɪndˌbɜːn) *n.* irritation and redness of the skin caused by prolonged exposure to winds of high velocity. —'**windˌburnt** *or* '**windˌburned** *adj.*

windcheater ('wɪndˌtʃiːtə) *or* **windjammer** *n.* a warm jacket, usually with a close-fitting knitted neck, cuffs, and waistband. U.S. name (trademark): **Windbreaker** ('wɪndˌbreɪkə).

wind chest (wɪnd) *n.* a box in an organ in which air from the bellows is stored under pressure before being supplied to the pipes or reeds.

wind-chill (wɪnd-) *n.* **a.** the serious chilling effect of wind and low temperature: it is measured on a scale that runs from hot to fatal to life and allows for varying combinations of air temperature and wind speed. **b.** (*as modifier*): *wind-chill factor.*

wind chimes (wɪnd) *pl. n.* a decorative arrangement of small discs of metal, shell, etc., hung near a window or door, that shake together with a tinkling sound in a draught.

wind cone (wɪnd) *n.* another name for **windsock.**

wind down (waɪnd) *vb.* (*adv.*) 1. (*tr.*) to lower or move down by cranking. 2. (*intr.*) (of a clock spring) to become slack. 3. (*intr.*) to diminish gradually in force or power; relax.

winded ('wɪndɪd) *adj.* 1. out of breath, as from strenuous exercise. 2. (*in combination*) having breath or wind as specified: *broken-winded; short-winded.*

winder ('waɪndə) *n.* 1. a person or device that winds, as an engine for hoisting the cages in a mine shaft or a device for winding the yarn in textile manufacture. 2. an object, such as a bobbin, around which something is wound. 3. a knob or key used to wind up a clock, watch, or similar mechanism. **4.** any plant that twists itself around a support. **5.** a step of a spiral staircase.

windfall (ˈwɪndˌfɔːl) *n.* **1.** a piece of unexpected good fortune, esp. financial gain. **2.** something blown down by the wind, esp. a piece of fruit. **3.** *Chiefly U.S. and Canadian.* a plot of land covered with trees blown down by the wind.

wind farm *n.* a large group of wind-driven generators for electricity supply.

windflower (ˈwɪndˌflaʊə) *n.* any of various anemone plants, such as the wood anemone.

windgall (ˈwɪndˌgɔːl) *n. Vet. science.* a soft swelling in the area of the fetlock joint of a horse. [C16: from WIND[1] + GALL[2]] —**ˈwindˌgalled** *adj.*

wind gap (wɪnd) *n.* a narrow dry valley on a mountain or ridge.

wind gauge (wɪnd) *n.* **1.** another name for **anemometer** (sense 1). **2.** a scale on a gun sight indicating the amount of deflection necessary to allow for windage. **3.** *Music.* a device for measuring the wind pressure in the bellows of an organ.

wind harp (wɪnd) *n.* a less common name for **aeolian harp.**

windhover (ˈwɪndˌhɒvə) *n. Brit.* a dialect name for a **kestrel.**

winding (ˈwaɪndɪŋ) *n.* **1.** a curving or sinuous course or movement. **2.** anything that has been wound or wrapped around something. **3.** a particular manner or style in which something has been wound. **4.** a curve, bend, or complete turn in wound material, a road, etc. **5.** (*often pl.*) devious thoughts or behaviour: *the tortuous windings of political argumentation.* **6.** one or more turns of wire forming a continuous coil through which an electric current can pass, as used in transformers, generators, etc. **7.** another name for **wind**[2] (sense 14). **8.** a coil of tubing in certain brass instruments, esp. the French horn. *~adj.* **9.** curving; sinuous: *a winding road.* —**ˈwindingly** *adv.*

winding drum (ˈwaɪndɪŋ) *n.* a rotating drum usually grooved to nest a wire rope which is wound onto it as part of the mechanism of a hoist.

winding sheet *n.* a sheet in which a corpse is wrapped for burial; shroud.

winding staircase *n.* another word for **spiral staircase.**

winding-up *n.* the process of finishing or closing something, esp. the process of closing down a business.

wind instrument (wɪnd) *n.* any musical instrument sounded by the breath, such as the woodwinds and brass instruments of an orchestra.

windjammer (ˈwɪndˌdʒæmə) *n.* **1.** a large merchant sailing ship. **2.** another name for **windcheater.**

windlass (ˈwɪndləs) *n.* **1.** a machine for raising weights by winding a rope or chain upon a barrel or drum driven by a crank, motor, etc. *~vb.* **2.** (*tr.*) to raise or haul (a weight, etc.) by means of a windlass. [C14: from Old Norse *vindáss,* from *vinda* to WIND[2] + *ass* pole; related to Old French *guindas,* Middle Low German, Dutch *windas*]

windlestraw (ˈwɪndᵊlˌstrɔː) *n. Irish, Scot., and English dialect.* **1.** the dried stalk of any of various grasses. **2.** anything weak or feeble, esp. a thin unhealthy person. [Old English *windelstrēaw,* from *windel* basket, from *windan* to WIND[2] + *strēaw* STRAW]

wind machine (wɪnd) *n.* a machine used, esp. in the theatre, to produce wind or the sound of wind.

windmill (ˈwɪndˌmɪl, ˈwɪnˌmɪl) *n.* **1.** a machine for grinding or pumping driven by a set of adjustable vanes or sails that are caused to turn by the force of the wind. **2.** the set of vanes or sails that drives such a mill. **3.** Also called: **whirligig.** *Brit.* a toy consisting of plastic or paper vanes attached to a stick in such a manner that they revolve like the sails of a windmill. U.S. and Canadian name: **pinwheel.** **4.** an imaginary opponent or evil (esp. in the phrase **tilt at** *or* **fight windmills**). **5.** a small air-driven propeller fitted to a light aircraft to drive auxiliary equipment. Compare **ram-air turbine.** **6.** an informal name for **helicopter.** **7.** an informal name for **propeller** (sense 1). *~vb.* **8.** to move or cause to move like the arms of a windmill. **9.** (*intr.*) (of an aircraft propeller, rotor of a turbine, etc.) to rotate as a result of the force of a current of air rather than under power.

window (ˈwɪndəʊ) *n.* **1.** a light framework, made of timber, metal, or plastic, that contains glass or glazed opening frames and is placed in a wall or roof to let in light or air or to see through. Related adj.: **fenestral.** **2.** an opening in the wall or roof of a building that is provided to let in light or air or to see through. **3.** See **windowpane.** **4.** the display space in and directly behind a shop window: *the dress in the window.* **5.** any opening or structure resembling a window in function or appearance, such as the transparent area of an envelope revealing an address within. **6.** an opportunity to see or understand something usually unseen: *a window on the workings of Parliament.* **7.** a period of unbooked time in a diary, schedule, etc. **8.** short for **launch window** or **weather window.** **9.** *Physics.* a region of the spectrum in which a medium transmits electromagnetic radiation. See also **radio window.** **10.** *Computer technol.* an area of a VDU display that may be manipulated separately from the rest of the display area; typically different files can be displayed simultaneously in different overlapping windows. **11.** (*modifier*): of or relating to a window or windows: *a window ledge.* **12. out of the window.** *Informal.* dispensed with; disregarded. *~vb.* **13.** (*tr.*) to furnish with or as if with windows. [C13: from Old Norse *vindauga,* from *vindr* WIND[1] + *auga* EYE]

window box *n.* **1.** a long narrow box, placed on or outside a windowsill, in which plants are grown. **2.** either of a pair of vertical boxes, attached to the sides of a sash window frame, that enclose a sash cord and counterbalancing weight.

window-dresser *n.* a person employed to design and build up a display in a shop window.

window-dressing *n.* **1.** the ornamentation of shop windows, designed to attract customers. **2.** the pleasant, showy, or false aspect of an idea, policy, etc., which is stressed to conceal the real or unpleasant nature; façade.

window envelope *n.* a type of envelope, esp. for business use, having a transparent area that reveals the address within.

windowpane (ˈwɪndəʊˌpeɪn) *n.* a sheet of glass in a window.

window sash *n.* a glazed window frame, esp. one that opens.

window seat *n.* **1.** a seat below a window, esp. in a bay window. **2.** a seat beside a window in a bus, train, etc.

window-shop *vb.* **-shops, -shopping, -shopped.** (*intr.*) to look at goods in shop windows without buying them. —**ˈwindowˌshopper** *n.* —**ˈwindow-ˌshopping** *n.*

windowsill (ˈwɪndəʊˌsɪl) *n.* a sill below a window.

window tax *n. History.* a tax on windows in houses levied between 1695 and 1851.

windpipe (ˈwɪndˌpaɪp) *n.* a nontechnical name for **trachea** (sense 1).

wind-pollinated *adj.* (of certain plants) pollinated by wind-borne pollen. —**ˈwind-ˌpolliˈnation** *n.*

wind power (wɪnd) *n.* power produced from windmills and wind turbines.

wind rose (wɪnd) *n.* a diagram with radiating lines showing the frequency and strength of winds from each direction affecting a specific place.

windrow (ˈwɪndˌrəʊ, ˈwɪnˌrəʊ) *n.* **1.** a long low ridge or line of hay or a similar crop, designed to achieve the best conditions for drying or curing. **2.** a line of leaves, snow, dust, etc., swept together by the wind. *~vb.* **3.** (*tr.*) to put (hay or a similar crop) into windrows. —**ˈwindˌrower** *n.*

windsail (ˈwɪndˌseɪl) *n.* **1.** a sail rigged as an air scoop over a hatch or companionway to catch breezes and divert them below. **2.** any of the vanes or sails of a windmill.

wind scale (wɪnd) *n.* a numerical scale of wind force, such as the Beaufort scale.

windscreen (ˈwɪndˌskriːn) *n. Brit.* the sheet of flat or curved glass that forms a window of a motor vehicle, esp. the front window. U.S. and Canadian name: **windshield.**

windscreen wiper *n. Brit.* an electrically operated blade with a rubber edge that wipes a windscreen clear of rain, snow, etc. U.S. and Canadian name: **windshield wiper.**

wind shake (wɪnd) *n.* a crack between the annual rings in wood: caused by strong winds bending the tree trunk.

wind shear (wɪnd) *n.* stress on an aircraft in an area in which winds of different speeds and directions are close together.

windshield (ˈwɪndˌʃiːld) *n.* **1.** the U.S. and Canadian name for **windscreen.** **2.** an object designed to shield something from the wind.

windsock (ˈwɪndˌsɒk) *n.* a truncated cone of textile mounted on a mast so that it is free to rotate about a vertical axis: used, esp. at airports, to indicate the local wind direction. Also called: **air sock, drogue, wind sleeve, wind cone.**

Windsor chair (ˈwɪnzə) *n.* a simple wooden chair, popular in England and America from the 18th century, usually having a shaped seat, splayed legs, and a back of many spindles. [named after *Windsor,* a town in SE England]

Windsor knot *n.* a wide triangular knot, produced by making extra turns in tying a tie.

Windsor rocker *n. U.S. and Canadian.* a Windsor chair on rockers.

Windsor tie *n.* a wide silk tie worn in a floppy bow.

windstorm (ˈwɪndˌstɔːm) *n.* a storm consisting of violent winds.

wind-sucking *n.* a harmful habit of horses in which the animal arches its neck and swallows a gulp of air. —**ˈwindˌsucker** *n.*

windsurf (ˈwɪndˌsɜːf) *vb.* (*intr.*) to take part in the sport of windsurfing. —**ˈwindˌsurfer** *n.*

windsurfing (ˈwɪndˌsɜːfɪŋ) *n.* the sport of sailing standing up on a sailboard that is equipped with a mast, sail, and wishbone boom. Also called: **boardsailing, sailboarding.**

wind surge (wɪnd) *n.* a wind-induced rise in the water level at the coast or the shore of an inland expanse of water. It has a definite frequency and if this is close to the tidal frequency serious flooding can result.

windswept (ˈwɪndˌswɛpt) *adj.* **1.** open to or swept by the wind. **2.** another word for **windblown** (sense 2).

wind tee (wɪnd) *n.* a large weather vane shaped like a *T,* located at an airfield to indicate the wind direction.

wind tunnel (wɪnd) *n.* a chamber for testing the aerodynamic properties of aircraft, aerofoils, etc., in which a current of air can be maintained at a constant velocity.

wind up (waɪnd) *vb.* (*adv.*) **1.** to bring to or reach a conclusion: *he wound up the proceedings.* **2.** (*tr.*) to tighten the spring of (a clockwork mechanism). **3.** (*tr.; usually passive*) *Informal.* to make nervous, tense, etc.; excite: *he was all wound up before the big fight.* **4.** (*tr.*) to roll (thread, etc.) into a ball. **5.** an informal word for **liquidate** (sense 2). **6.** (*intr.*) *Informal.* to end up (in a specified state): *you'll wind up without any teeth.* **7.** (*tr.; usually* *passive*) to involve; entangle: *they were wound up in three different scandals.* **8.** (*tr.*) to hoist or haul up. **9.** (*tr.*) *Brit. slang.* to tease (someone). ~*n.* **wind-up. 10.** the act of concluding. **11.** the finish; end.

windward (ˈwɪndwəd) *Chiefly nautical.* ~*adj.* **1.** of, in, or moving to the quarter from which the wind blows. **2. to windward of.** advantageously situated with respect to. ~*n.* **3.** the windward point. **4.** the side towards the wind. ~*adv.* **5.** towards the wind. ~Compare **leeward.**

windy (ˈwɪndɪ) *adj.* **windier, windiest. 1.** of, characterized by, resembling, or relating to wind; stormy. **2.** swept by or open to powerful winds. **3.** marked by or given to empty, prolonged, and often boastful speech; bombastic: *windy orations.* **4.** void of substance. **5.** an informal word for **flatulent. 6.** *Slang.* afraid; frightened; nervous. —ˈ**windily** *adv.* —ˈ**windiness** *n.*

wine (waɪn) *n.* **1. a.** an alcoholic drink produced by the fermenting of grapes with water and sugar. **b.** an alcoholic drink produced in this way from other fruits, flowers, etc.: *elderberry wine.* **2. a.** a dark red colour, sometimes with a purplish tinge. **b.** (*as adj.*): *wine-coloured.* **3.** anything resembling wine in its intoxicating or invigorating effect. **4.** *Pharmacol.* fermented grape juice containing medicaments. **5. Adam's wine.** *Brit.* a dialect word for **water. 6. new wine in old bottles.** something new added to or imposed upon an old or established order. ~*vb.* **7.** (*intr.*) to drink wine. **8. wine and dine.** to entertain or be entertained with wine and fine food. [Old English *wīn*, from Latin *vīnum;* related to Greek *oinos*, of obscure origin] —ˈ**wineless** *adj.*

wine bar *n.* a bar in a restaurant, etc., or an establishment that specializes in serving wine and usually food.

wineberry (ˈwaɪnˌbɛrɪ) *n., pl.* **-ries.** *N.Z.* another name for **mako**[2] (sense 1).

winebibber (ˈwaɪnˌbɪbə) *n.* a person who drinks a great deal of wine. —ˈ**wineˌbibbing** *n.*

wine box *n.* wine sold in a cubic carton, usually of three-litre capacity, having a plastic lining and a tap for dispensing.

wine cellar *n.* **1.** a place, such as a dark cool cellar, where wine is stored. **2.** the stock of wines stored there.

wine cooler *n.* **1.** a bucket-like vessel containing ice in which a bottle of wine is placed to be cooled. **2.** the full name for **cooler** (sense 3).

wine gallon *n. Brit.* a former unit of capacity equal to 231 cubic inches.

wineglass (ˈwaɪnˌglɑːs) *n.* **1.** a glass drinking vessel, typically having a small bowl on a stem, with a flared foot. **2.** Also called: **wineglassful.** the amount that such a glass will hold.

wine grower *n.* a person engaged in cultivating vines in order to make wine. —**wine growing** *n.*

wine palm *n.* any of various palm trees, the sap of which is used, esp. when fermented, as a drink. See **toddy** (sense 2). Also called: **toddy palm.**

winepress (ˈwaɪnˌprɛs) *n.* any equipment used for squeezing the juice from grapes in order to make wine.

winery (ˈwaɪnərɪ) *n., pl.* **-eries.** *Chiefly U.S. and Canadian.* a place where wine is made.

wineskin (ˈwaɪnˌskɪn) *n.* the skin of a sheep or goat sewn up and used as a holder for wine.

wine tasting *n.* an occasion for sampling a number of wines. —**wine taster** *n.*

wing (wɪŋ) *n.* **1.** either of the modified forelimbs of a bird that are covered with large feathers and specialized for flight in most species. **2.** one of the organs of flight of an insect, consisting of a membranous outgrowth from the thorax containing a network of veins. **3.** either of the organs of flight in certain other animals, esp. the forelimb of a bat. **4. a.** a half of the main supporting surface on an aircraft, confined to one side of it. **b.** the full span of the main supporting surface on both sides of an aircraft. **c.** an aircraft designed as one complete wing. **d.** a position in flight formation, just to the rear and to one side of an aircraft. **5. a.** an organ or apparatus resembling a wing. **b.** *Anatomy.* any bodily structure resembling a wing: *the wings of a sphenoid bone.* Technical name: **ala. 6.** anything suggesting a wing in form, function, or position, such as a sail of a windmill or a ship. **7.** *Botany.* **a.** either of the lateral petals of a sweetpea or related flower. **b.** any of various outgrowths of a plant part, esp. the process on a wind-dispersed fruit or seed. **8.** a means or cause of flight or rapid motion; flight: *fear gave wings to his feet.* **9.** the act or manner of flying: *a bird of strong wing.* **10.** *Brit.* the part of a car body that surrounds the wheels. U.S. and Canadian name: **fender. 11.** any affiliate of or subsidiary to a parent organization. **12.** *Soccer, hockey, etc.* **a.** either of the two sides of the pitch near the touchline. **b.** a player stationed in such a position; winger. **13.** a faction or group within a political party or other organization. See also **left wing, right wing. 14.** a part of a building that is subordinate to the main part. **15.** (*pl.*) the space offstage to the right or left of the acting area in a theatre. **16. in** *or* **on the wings.** ready to step in when needed. **17.** *Fortifications.* a side connecting the main fort and an outwork. **18.** a folding panel, as of a double door or a movable partition. **19.** either of the two pieces that project forwards from the sides of some chairbacks. **20.** the U.S. name for **quarterlight. 21.** a surface fitted to a racing car to produce aerodynamic download to hold it on the road at high speed. **22.** (*pl.*) an insignia in the form of stylized wings worn by a qualified aircraft pilot. **23.** a tactical formation in some air forces, consisting of two or more squadrons. **24.** any of various flattened organs or extensions in lower animals, esp. when used in locomotion. **25.** the side of a hold alongside a ship's hull. **26.** the outside angle of the cutting edge on the share and mouldboard of a plough. **27.** a jetty or dam for narrowing a channel of water. **28.** *Rare.* the feather of an arrow. **29. on the wing. a.** flying. **b.** travelling. **c.** about to leave. **30. take wing. a.** to lift off or fly away. **b.** to depart in haste. **c.** to become joyful. **31. under one's wing.** in one's care or tutelage. **32. clip (someone's) wings. a.** to restrict (someone's) freedom. **b.** to thwart (someone's) ambition. **33. on wings.** flying or as if flying. **34. spread** *or* **stretch one's wings.** to make full use of one's abilities. ~*vb.* (*mainly tr.*) **35.** (*also intr.*) to make (one's way) swiftly on or as if on wings. **36.** to shoot or wound (a bird, person, etc.) superficially, in the wing or arm, etc. **37.** to cause to fly or move swiftly: *to wing an arrow.* **38.** to fit (an arrow) with a feather. **39.** to provide with wings. **40.** (of buildings, altars, etc.) to provide with lateral extensions. **41.** (*tr.*) *Theatre, informal.* to perform (a part) without having fully learned one's lines. [C12: from Scandinavian; compare Old Norse *vængir* (plural), Norwegian *veng*] —ˈ**wingˌlike** *adj.*

wing and wing *adv.* with sails extended on both sides by booms.

wing beat *n.* a complete cycle of moving the wing by a bird when flying.

wing bow (bəʊ) *n.* a distinctive band of colour marking the wing of a domestic fowl.

wing-case *n.* the nontechnical name for **elytron.**

wing chair *n.* an easy chair having wings on each side of the back.

wing collar *n.* a stiff turned-up shirt collar worn with the points turned down over the tie.

wing commander *n.* an officer holding commissioned rank in certain air forces, such as the Royal Air Force: junior to a group captain and senior to a squadron leader.

wing covert *n.* any of the covert feathers of the wing of a bird, occurring in distinct rows.

wingding (ˈwɪŋˌdɪŋ) *n. Slang, chiefly U.S. and Canadian.* **1. a.** a noisy lively party or festivity. **b.** (*as modifier*): *a real wingding party.* **2.** a real or pretended fit or seizure. [C20: of unknown origin]

winged (wɪŋd) *adj.* **1.** furnished with wings: *winged god; winged horse.* **2.** flying straight and true as if by wing: *winged words.*

winger (ˈwɪŋə) *n. Soccer, hockey, etc.* a player stationed on the wing.

wing-footed *adj. Archaic.* fleet; swift.

wingless (ˈwɪŋlɪs) *adj.* **1.** having no wings or vestigial wings. **2.** designating primitive insects of the subclass *Apterygota*, characterized by small size, lack of wings, and larvae resembling the adults: includes the springtails and bristletails. —ˈ**winglessness** *n.*

winglet (ˈwɪŋlɪt) *n.* **1.** a small wing, esp. the bastard wing of a bird. **2.** a small wing placed at the tip of the main wing of an aircraft and perpendicular to it designed to reduce the aircraft's vortex drag.

wing loading *n.* the total weight of an aircraft divided by its wing area.

wingman (ˈwɪŋmæn) *n., pl.* **-men.** a player in the wing position in Australian Rules.

wing nut *n.* a threaded nut tightened by hand by means of two flat lugs or wings projecting from the central body. Also called: **butterfly nut.**

wingover (ˈwɪŋˌəʊvə) *n.* a manoeuvre in which the direction of flight of an aircraft is reversed by putting it into a climbing turn until nearly stalled, the nose then being allowed to fall while continuing the turn.

wing shot *n.* **1.** a shot taken at a bird in flight. **2.** an expert at shooting birds in flight.

wingspan (ˈwɪŋˌspæn) *or* **wingspread** (ˈwɪŋˌsprɛd) *n.* the distance between the wing tips of an aircraft, bird, etc.

wing tip *n.* the outermost edge of a wing.

wink[1] (wɪŋk) *vb.* **1.** (*intr.*) to close and open one eye quickly, deliberately, or in an exaggerated fashion to convey friendliness, etc. **2.** to close and open (an eye or the eyes) momentarily. **3.** (*tr.;* foll. by *away, back,* etc.) to force away (tears, etc.) by winking. **4.** (*tr.*) to signal with a wink. **5.** (*intr.*) (of a light) to gleam or flash intermittently. ~*n.* **6.** a winking movement, esp. one conveying a signal, etc., or such a signal. **7.** an interrupted flashing of light. **8.** a brief moment of time; instant. **9.** *Informal.* the smallest amount, esp. of sleep. See also **forty winks. 10. tip the wink.** *Brit. informal.* to give a hint. [Old English *wincian;* related to Old Saxon *wincon*, Old High German *winchan*, German *winken* to wave. See WENCH, WINCH]

wink[2] (wɪŋk) *n.* a disc used in the game of tiddlywinks. [C20: shortened from TIDDLYWINKS]

wink at *vb.* (*intr., prep.*) to connive at; disregard: *the authorities winked at corruption.*

winker (ˈwɪŋkə) *n.* **1.** a person or thing that winks. **2.** *U.S. and Canadian slang, English dialect.* an eye, eyelash, or eyelid. **3.** another name for **blinker** (sense 1).

winkle (ˈwɪŋkᵊl) *n.* **1.** See **periwinkle**[1]. ~*vb.* **2.** (*tr.*; usually foll. by *out, out of,* etc.) *Informal, chiefly Brit.* to extract or prise out. [C16: shortened from PERIWINKLE[1]]

winkle-pickers *pl. n.* shoes or boots with very pointed narrow toes, popular in the mid-20th century.

Winnebago (ˌwɪnɪˈbeɪgəʊ) *n.* **1.** (*pl.* **-gos** *or* **-go**) a member of a North American Indian people living in Wisconsin and Nebraska. **2.** the language of this people, belonging to the Siouan family.

winner (ˈwɪnə) *n.* **1.** a person or thing that wins. **2.** *Informal.* a person or thing that seems sure to win or succeed.

winner's enclosure *or* **circle** *n.* See **unsaddling enclosure.**

winning (ˈwɪnɪŋ) *adj.* **1.** (of a person, character, etc.) charming, engaging, or attractive: *winning ways; a winning smile.* **2.** gaining victory: *the winning stroke.* ~*n.* **3. a.** a shaft or seam of coal. **b.** the extraction of coal or ore from the ground. **4.** (*pl.*) money, prizes, or valuables won, esp. in gambling. —ˈ**winningly** *adv.* —ˈ**winningness** *n.*

winning gallery *n. Real Tennis.* the gallery farthest from the net on either side of the court, into which any shot played wins a point.

winning opening *n. Real Tennis.* the grille, dedans, or winning gallery, into which any shot played wins a point.

winning post *n.* the post marking the finishing line on a racecourse.

Winnipeg couch (ˈwɪnɪˌpɛg) *n. Canadian.* a couch with no arms or back, opening out into a double bed.

winnow (ˈwɪnəʊ) *vb.* **1.** to separate (grain) from (chaff) by means of a wind or current of air. **2.** (*tr.*) to examine in order to select the desirable elements. **3.** (*tr.*) *Archaic.* to beat (the air) with wings. **4.** (*tr.*) *Rare.* to blow upon; fan. ~*n.* **5. a.** a device for winnowing. **b.** the act or process of winnowing. [Old English *windwian;* related to Old High German *wintōn,* Gothic *diswinthjan,* Latin *ventilāre.* See WIND[1]] —ˈ**winnower** *n.*

wino (ˈwaɪnəʊ) *n., pl.* **-os.** *Informal.* a person who habitually drinks wine as a means of getting drunk.

win out *vb.* (*intr., adv.*) *Informal.* to succeed or prevail as if in a contest: *sanity rarely wins out over prejudice.*

win over *vb.* (*tr., adv.*) to gain the support or consent of (someone). Also: **win round.**

winsome (ˈwɪnsəm) *adj.* charming; winning; engaging: *a winsome smile.* [Old English *wynsum,* from *wynn* joy (related to Old High German *wunnia,* German *Wonne*) + *-sum* -SOME[1]] —ˈ**winsomely** *adv.* —ˈ**winsomeness** *n.*

winter (ˈwɪntə) *n.* **1. a.** (*sometimes cap.*) the coldest season of the year, between autumn and spring, astronomically from the December solstice to the March equinox in the N hemisphere and at the opposite time of year in the S hemisphere. **b.** (*as modifier*): *winter pasture.* **2.** the peri d of cold weather associated with the winter. **3.** a time of decline, decay, etc. **4.** *Chiefly poetic.* a year represented by this season: *a man of 72 winters.* Related adjs.: **hibernal, hiemal.** ~*vb.* **5.** (*intr.*) to spend the winter in a specified place. **6.** to keep or feed (farm animals, etc.) during the winter or (of farm animals) to be kept or fed during the winter. [Old English; related to Old Saxon, Old High German *wintar,* Old Norse *vetr,* Gothic *wintrus*] —ˈ**winterer** *n.* —ˈ**winterish** *or* ˈ**winter-ˌlike** *adj.* —ˈ**winterless** *adj.*

winter aconite *n.* a small Old World ranunculaceous herbaceous plant, *Eranthis hyemalis,* cultivated for its yellow flowers, which appear early in spring.

winterbourne (ˈwɪntəˌbɔːn) *n.* a stream flowing only after heavy rainfall, esp. in winter. [Old English *winterburna;* see WINTER, BURN[2]]

winter cherry *n.* **1.** a Eurasian solanaceous plant, *Physalis alkekengi,* cultivated for its ornamental inflated papery orange-red calyx. **2.** the calyx of this plant. ~See also **Chinese lantern, ground cherry.**

wintercress (ˈwɪntəˌkrɛs) *n.* **1.** a bitter-tasting yellow-flowered perennial, *Barbarea vulgaris,* somewhat resembling mustard. **2.** a commercial hybrid, *Rorippa* × *sterilis,* between watercress and *R. microphylla.*

winterfeed (ˈwɪntəˌfiːd) *vb.* **-feeds, -feeding, -fed.** to feed (livestock) in winter when the grazing is not rich enough.

winter garden *n.* **1.** a garden of evergreen plants. **2.** a conservatory in which flowers are grown in winter.

wintergreen (ˈwɪntəˌgriːn) *n.* **1.** Also called: **boxberry, checkerberry, teaberry, spiceberry, partridgeberry.** any of several evergreen ericaceous shrubs of the genus *Gaultheria,* esp. *G. procumbens,* of E North America, which has white bell-shaped flowers and edible red berries. **2. oil of wintergreen.** an aromatic compound, formerly made from this and various other plants but now synthesized: used medicinally and for flavouring. **3.** any of various plants of the genus *Pyrola,* esp. *P. minor* (**common wintergreen**), of temperate and arctic regions, having rounded leaves and small pink globose flowers: family *Pyrolaceae.* Usual U.S. name: **shinleaf. 4.** any of several plants of the genera *Orthilia* and *Moneses:* family *Pyrolaceae.* **5. chickweed wintergreen.** a primulaceous plant, *Trientalis europaea,* of N Europe and N Asia, having white flowers and leaves arranged in a whorl. [C16: from Dutch *wintergroen* or German *Wintergrün;* see WINTER, GREEN]

winter hedge *n. West Yorkshire, south Lancashire, and Derbyshire dialect.* a clothes horse. [so called in contrast to a hedge on which clothes are dried in summer]

winter heliotrope *n.* a creeping perennial, *Petasites fragrans,* related to the butterbur, having lilac to heliotrope coloured flowers smelling of vanilla: found chiefly on road verges.

winterize *or* **winterise** (ˈwɪntəˌraɪz) *vb.* (*tr.*) *U.S. and Canadian.* to prepare (a house, car, etc.) to withstand winter conditions. —ˌ**winteriˈzation** *or* ˌ**winteriˈsation** *n.*

winter jasmine *n.* a jasmine shrub, *Jasminum nudiflorum,* widely cultivated for its winter-blooming yellow flowers.

winterkill (ˈwɪntəˌkɪl) *vb. Chiefly U.S. and Canadian.* to kill (crops or other plants) by exposure to frost, cold, etc., or (of plants) to die by this means. —ˈ**winterˌkilling** *adj., n.*

winter melon *n.* a variety of muskmelon, *Cucumis melo inodorus,* that has sweet fruit with pale orange flesh and an unridged rind. Also called: **Persian melon.**

winter moth *n.* a brown geometrid moth, *Operophtera brumata,* of which the male is often seen against lighted windows in winter, the female being wingless.

Winter Olympic Games *n.* (*functioning as sing. or pl.*) an international contest of winter sports, esp. skiing, held in the year of the Olympic Games. Also called: **Winter Olympics.**

winter quarters *pl. n.* housing or accommodation for the winter, esp. for military personnel.

winter rose *n.* another name for **Christmas rose.**

winter solstice *n.* **1.** the time at which the sun is at its southernmost point in the sky (northernmost point in the S hemisphere) appearing at noon at its lowest altitude above the horizon. It occurs about December 22 (June 21 in the S hemisphere). **2.** *Astronomy.* the point on the celestial sphere, opposite the **summer solstice,** at which the ecliptic is furthest south from the celestial equator. Right ascension: 18 hours; declination: –23.5°.

winter sports *pl. n.* sports held in the open air on snow or ice, esp. skiing.

wintertime (ˈwɪntəˌtaɪm) *n.* the winter season. Also (archaic): ˈ**winterˌtide.**

winterweight (ˈwɪntəˌweɪt) *adj.* (of clothes) suitable in weight for wear in the winter; relatively heavy.

winter wheat *n.* a type of wheat that is planted in the autumn and is harvested the following summer.

wintry (ˈwɪntrɪ), **wintery** (ˈwɪntərɪ, -trɪ), *or* (*less commonly*) **winterly** *adj.* **-trier, -triest. 1.** (esp. of weather) of or characteristic of winter. **2.** lacking cheer or warmth; bleak. —ˈ**wintrily** *adv.* —ˈ**wintriness,** ˈ**winteriness,** *or* (*less commonly*) ˈ**winterliness** *n.*

winy (ˈwaɪnɪ) *adj.* **winier, winiest.** having the taste or qualities of wine, esp. in being intoxicating; heady.

winze (wɪnz) *n. Mining.* a steeply inclined shaft, as for ventilation between levels. [C18: from earlier *winds,* probably from C14 *wynde* windlass, from Middle Dutch or Middle Low German *winde;* related to Danish *vinde* pulley]

wipe (waɪp) *vb.* (*tr.*) **1.** to rub (a surface or object) lightly, esp. with (a cloth, hand, etc.), as in removing dust, water, grime, etc. **2.** (usually foll. by *off, away, from, up,* etc.) to remove by or as if by rubbing lightly: *he wiped the dirt from his hands.* **3.** to eradicate or cancel (a thought, memory, etc.). **4.** to erase a recording from (an audio or video tape). **5.** *Austral. informal.* to abandon or reject (a person). **6.** to apply (oil, grease, etc.) by wiping. **7.** to form (a joint between two lead pipes) with solder or soft lead. **8. wipe the floor with (someone).** *Informal.* to defeat decisively. ~*n.* **9.** the act or an instance of wiping. **10.** (in film editing) an effect causing the transition from one scene to the next in which the image of the first scene appears to be wiped off the screen by that of the second. **11.** *Dialect.* a sweeping blow or stroke. **12.** *Brit. dialect.* a gibe or jeer. **13.** *Obsolete.* a slang name for **handkerchief.** [Old English *wīpian,* related to Middle Low German *wīpen, wīp* bundle (of cloth), Old High German *wīffa, wīfan* to wind, Gothic *weipan* to wreathe]

wipe out *vb.* (*adv.*) **1.** (*tr.*) to destroy completely; eradicate. **2.** (*tr.*) *Informal.* to murder or kill. **3.** (*intr.*) to fall or jump off a surfboard or skateboard. ~*n.* **wipeout. 4.** an act or instance of wiping out. **5.** the interference of one radio signal by another so that reception is impossible.

wiper (ˈwaɪpə) *n.* **1.** any piece of cloth, such as a handkerchief, towel, etc., used for wiping. **2.** a cam rotated to ease a part and allow it to fall under its own weight, as used in stamping machines, etc. **3.** See **windscreen wiper. 4.** *Electrical engineering.* a movable conducting arm, esp. one in a switching or selecting device, that makes contact with a row or ring of contacts.

WIPO *or* **Wipo** (ˈwaɪpəʊ) *n. acronym for* World Intellectual Property Organization.

wire (waɪə) *n.* **1.** a slender flexible strand or rod of metal. **2.** a cable consisting of several metal strands twisted together. **3.** a flexible metallic conductor, esp. one made of copper, usually insulated, and used to carry electric current in a circuit. **4.** (*modifier*) of, relating to, or made of wire: *a wire fence; a wire stripper.* **5.** anything made of wire, such as wire netting, a barbed wire fence, etc. **6.** a long continuous wire or cable connecting points in a telephone or telegraph system. **7.** *Old-fashioned.* **a.** an informal name for **telegram** or **telegraph. b.**

the wire. an informal name for **telephone.** **8.** a metallic string on a guitar, piano, etc. **9.** *U.S. and Canadian horse racing.* the finishing line on a racecourse. **10.** a wire-gauze screen upon which pulp is spread to form paper during the manufacturing process. **11.** anything resembling a wire, such as a hair. **12.** a snare made of wire for rabbits and similar animals. **13. down to the wire.** *Informal, chiefly U.S. and Canadian.* right up to the last moment. **14. get in under the wire.** *Informal, chiefly U.S. and Canadian.* to accomplish something with little time to spare. **15. get one's wires crossed.** *Informal.* to misunderstand. **16. pull wires.** *Chiefly U.S. and Canadian.* to exert influence behind the scenes, esp. through personal connections; pull strings. ~*vb.* (*mainly tr.*) **17.** (*also intr.*) to send a telegram to (a person or place). **18.** to send (news, a message, etc.) by telegraph. **19.** to equip (an electrical system, circuit, or component) with wires. **20.** to fasten or furnish with wire. **21.** (often foll. by *up*) to provide (an area) with fibre optic cabling to receive cable television. **22.** to string (beads, etc.) on wire. **23.** *Croquet.* to leave (a player's ball) so that a hoop or peg lies between it and the other balls. **24.** to snare with wire. **25. wire in.** *Informal.* to set about (something, esp. food) with enthusiasm. [Old English *wīr;* related to Old High German *wiara,* Old Norse *vīra,* Latin *viriae* bracelet] —'**wire,like** *adj.*

wire brush *n.* a brush having wire bristles, used for cleaning metal, esp. for removing rust, or for brushing against a cymbal.

wire cloth *n.* a mesh or netting woven from fine wire, used in window screens, strainers, etc.

wired (waɪəd) *adj. Slang.* edgy from stimulant intake.

wiredraw ('waɪə,drɔː) *vb.* **-draws, -drawing, -drew, -drawn.** to convert (metal) into wire by drawing through successively smaller dies.

wire entanglement *n.* a barrier or obstruction of barbed wire used in warfare.

wire-gauge *n.* **1.** a flat plate with slots in which standard wire sizes can be measured. **2.** a standard system of sizes for measuring the diameters of wires.

wire gauze *n.* a stiff meshed fabric woven of fine wires.

wire glass *n.* a sheet glass that contains a layer of reinforcing wire netting within it.

wire grass *n.* any of various grasses, such as Bermuda grass, that have tough wiry roots or rhizomes.

wire-guided *adj.* (of a missile) controlled by signals transmitted through fine wires uncoiled during the missile's flight.

wire-haired *adj.* (of an animal) having a rough wiry coat.

wireless ('waɪəlɪs) *n., vb. Chiefly Brit., old-fashioned.* another word for **radio.**

wireless telegraphy *n.* another name for **radiotelegraphy.**

wireless telephone *n.* another name for **radiotelephone.** —**wireless telephony** *n.*

wireman ('waɪəmən) *n., pl.* **-men.** *Chiefly U.S.* a person who installs and maintains electric wiring, cables, etc.

wire netting *n.* a net made of wire, often galvanized, that is used for fencing, as a light reinforcement, etc.

wirephoto ('waɪə,fəʊtəʊ) *n., pl.* **-tos.** a facsimile of a photograph transmitted electronically via a telephone system.

wirepuller ('waɪə,pʊlə) *n. Chiefly U.S. and Canadian.* a person who uses private or secret influence for his own ends. —'**wire,pulling** *n.*

wirer ('waɪərə) *n.* a person who sets or uses wires to snare rabbits and similar animals.

wire recorder *n.* an early type of magnetic recorder in which sounds were recorded on a thin steel wire magnetized by an electromagnet. Compare **tape recorder.** —**wire recording** *n.*

wire rope *n.* rope made of strands of wire twisted together.

wire service *n. Chiefly U.S. and Canadian.* an agency supplying news, etc., to newspapers, radio and television stations, etc.

wiretap ('waɪə,tæp) *vb.* **-taps, -tapping, -tapped.** to make a connection to a telegraph or telephone wire in order to obtain information secretly. —'**wire,tapper** *n.*

wirewalker ('waɪə,wɔːkə) *n. Chiefly U.S.* another name for **tightrope walker.**

wire wheel *n.* **1.** a wheel in which the rim is held to the hub by wire spokes, esp. one used on a sports car. Compare **disc wheel. 2.** a power-driven rotary wire brush for scaling or burnishing.

wire wool *n.* a mass of fine wire, used esp. to clean kitchen articles.

wirework ('waɪə,wɜːk) *n.* **1.** functional or decorative work made of wire. **2.** objects made of wire, esp. netting. **3.** the work performed by acrobats on a tightrope.

wireworks ('waɪə,wɜːks) *n.* (*functioning as sing. or pl.*) a factory where wire or articles of wire are made.

wireworm ('waɪə,wɜːm) *n.* the wormlike larva of various elaterid beetles, which feeds on the roots of many crop plants and is a serious agricultural pest.

wire-wove *adj.* **1.** of, relating to, or comprising a high-grade glazed paper, usually for writing. **2.** woven of wire.

wiring ('waɪərɪŋ) *n.* **1.** the network of wires used in an electrical system, device, or circuit. **2.** the quality or condition of such a network. ~*adj.* **3.** used in wiring.

wirra ('wɪrə) *interj. Irish.* an exclamation of sorrow or deep concern. [C19: shortened from Irish Gaelic *a Muire!* O Mary! as invocation to the Virgin Mary]

wirrah ('wɪrə) *n.* a saltwater fish, *Acanthistius serratus,* of Australia, with bright blue spots. [from a native Australian language]

wiry ('waɪərɪ) *adj.* **wirier, wiriest. 1.** (of people or animals) slender but strong in constitution. **2.** made of or resembling wire, esp. in stiffness: *wiry hair.* **3.** (of a sound) produced by or as if by a vibrating wire. —'**wirily** *adv.* —'**wiriness** *n.*

wis (wɪs) *vb. Archaic.* to know or suppose (something). [C17: a form derived from IWIS, mistakenly interpreted as *I wis* I know, as if from Old English *witan* to know]

Wis. *abbrev. for* Wisconsin.

Wisd. *abbrev. for* Wisdom of Solomon.

wisdom ('wɪzdəm) *n.* **1.** the ability or result of an ability to think and act utilizing knowledge, experience, understanding, common sense, and insight. **2.** accumulated knowledge, erudition, or enlightenment. **3.** *Archaic.* a wise saying or wise sayings or teachings. **4.** *Obsolete.* soundness of mind. ~Related adj.: **sagacious.** [Old English *wīsdōm;* see WISE[1], -DOM]

wisdom tooth *n.* **1.** any of the four molar teeth, one at the back of each side of the jaw, that are the last of the permanent teeth to erupt. Technical name: **third molar. 2. cut one's wisdom teeth.** to arrive at the age of discretion.

wise[1] (waɪz) *adj.* **1.** possessing, showing, or prompted by wisdom or discernment. **2.** prudent; sensible. **3.** shrewd; crafty: *a wise plan.* **4.** well-informed; erudite. **5.** aware, informed, or knowing (esp. in the phrase **none the wiser**). **6.** *Slang.* (*postpositive;* often foll. by *to*) in the know, esp. possessing inside information (about). **7.** *Archaic or Brit. dialect.* possessing powers of magic. **8.** *Slang, chiefly U.S. and Canadian.* cocksure or insolent. **9. be** *or* **get wise.** (often foll. by *to*) *Informal.* to be or become aware or informed (of something) or to face up (to facts). **10. put wise.** (often foll. by *to*) *Slang.* to inform or warn (of). ~*vb.* **11.** See **wise up.** [Old English *wīs;* related to Old Norse *vīss,* Gothic *weis,* German *weise*] —'**wisely** *adv.* —'**wiseness** *n.*

wise[2] (waɪz) *n. Archaic.* way, manner, fashion, or respect (esp. in the phrases **any wise, in no wise**). [Old English *wīse* manner; related to Old Saxon *wīsa,* German *Weise,* Old Norse *vīsa* verse, Latin *vīsus* face]

wise[3] (waɪz) *vb.* (*tr.*) *Scot. and northern English dialect.* to direct or lead. [Old English *wīsian;* related to Old Norse *vīsa,* Old Saxon *wīsōn,* German *weisen,* Old Frisian *wīsia* to turn around]

-wise *adv. combining form.* **1.** Also: **-ways.** indicating direction or manner: *clockwise; likewise.* **2.** with reference to: *profitwise; businesswise.* [Old English *-wisan;* see WISE[2]]

▷**Usage.** The addition of *-wise* to a noun as a replacement for a lengthier phrase (such as *as far as...is concerned*) is considered unacceptable by most careful speakers and writers: *talentwise, he's a little weak* (he's a little weak as regards talent); *the company is thriving profitwise* (as far as profits are concerned, the company is thriving).

wiseacre ('waɪz,eɪkə) *n.* **1.** a person who wishes to seem wise. **2.** a wise person: often used facetiously or contemptuously. [C16: from Middle Dutch *wijsseggher* soothsayer; related to Old High German *wīssaga,* German *Weissager.* See WISE[1], SAY]

wisecrack ('waɪz,kræk) *Informal.* ~*n.* **1.** a flippant gibe or sardonic remark. ~*vb.* **2.** to make a wisecrack. —'**wise,cracker** *n.*

wise guy *n. Informal.* a person who is given to making conceited, sardonic, or insolent comments.

wisent ('wiːzᵊnt) *n.* another name for **European bison.** See **bison** (sense 2). [German, from Old High German *wisunt* BISON]

wise up *vb.* (*adv.*) *Slang, chiefly U.S. and Canadian.* (often foll. by *to*) to become or cause to become aware or informed (of).

wish (wɪʃ) *vb.* **1.** (when *tr., takes a clause as object or an infinitive;* when *intr.,* often foll. by *for*) to want or desire (something, often that which cannot be or is not the case): *I wish I lived in Italy; to wish for peace.* **2.** (*tr.*) to feel or express a desire or hope concerning the future or fortune of: *I wish you well.* **3.** (*tr.*) to desire or prefer to be as specified. **4.** (*tr.*) to greet as specified; bid: *he wished us good afternoon.* **5.** (*tr.*) *Formal.* to order politely: *I wish you to come at three o'clock.* ~*n.* **6.** the act of wishing; the expression of some desire or mental inclination: *to make a wish.* **7.** something desired or wished for: *he got his wish.* **8.** (*usually pl.*) expressed hopes or desire, esp. for someone's welfare, health, etc. **9.** (*often pl.*) *Formal.* a polite order or request. ~See also **wish on.** [Old English *wȳscan;* related to Old Norse *öskja,* German *wünschen,* Dutch *wenschen*] —'**wisher** *n.* —'**wishless** *adj.*

wishbone ('wɪʃ,bəʊn) *n.* the V-shaped bone above the breastbone in most birds consisting of the fused clavicles; furcula. [C17: from the custom of two people breaking apart the bone after eating: the person with the longer part makes a wish]

wishbone boom *n.* a boom on a sailboard having two arms that are joined at the mast and at the foot of the sail. The windsurfer holds onto it for support and to steer the sailboard.

wishful ('wɪʃfʊl) *adj.* having wishes or characterized by wishing. —'**wishfully** *adv.* —'**wishfulness** *n.*

wish fulfilment *n.* (in Freudian psychology) any successful attempt to fulfil a wish stemming from the unconscious mind, whether in fact, in fantasy, or by such disguised means as sublimation. See also **pleasure principle.**

wishful thinking *n.* the erroneous belief that one's wishes are in accordance with reality. —**wishful thinker** *n.*

wish on *vb.* (*tr., prep.*) to hope that (someone or something) should be imposed (on someone); foist: *I wouldn't wish my cold on anyone.*

wish-wash *n. Informal.* **1.** any thin weak drink. **2.** rubbishy talk or writing.

wishy-washy (ˈwɪʃɪˌwɒʃɪ) *adj. Informal.* **1.** lacking in substance, force, colour, etc. **2.** watery; thin. —ˈ**wishy-ˌwashily** *adv.* —ˈ**wishy-ˌwashiness** *n.*

wisp (wɪsp) *n.* **1.** a thin, light, delicate, or fibrous piece or strand, such as a streak of smoke or a lock of hair. **2.** a small bundle, as of hay or straw. **3.** anything slender and delicate: *a wisp of a girl.* **4.** a mere suggestion or hint. **5.** a flock of birds, esp. snipe. ~*vb.* **6.** (*intr.;* often foll. by *away*) to move or act like a wisp. **7.** (*tr.*) *Chiefly Brit. dialect.* to twist into a wisp. **8.** (*tr.*) *Chiefly Brit.* to groom (a horse) with a wisp of straw, etc. [C14: variant of *wips,* of obscure origin; compare WIPE] —ˈ**wispˌlike** *adj.*

wispy (ˈwɪspɪ) *adj.* **wispier, wispiest.** wisplike; delicate, faint, light, etc. —ˈ**wispily** *adv.* —ˈ**wispiness** *n.*

wist (wɪst) *vb. Archaic.* the past tense and past participle of **wit**[2].

wisteria (wɪˈstɪərɪə) *n.* any twining leguminous woody climbing plant of the genus *Wisteria,* of E Asia and North America, having blue, purple, or white flowers in large drooping clusters. [C19: from New Latin, named after Caspar *Wistar* (1761–1818), American anatomist]

wistful (ˈwɪstfʊl) *adj.* sadly pensive, esp. about something yearned for. —ˈ**wistfully** *adv.* —ˈ**wistfulness** *n.*

wit[1] (wɪt) *n.* **1.** the talent or quality of using unexpected associations between contrasting or disparate words or ideas to make a clever humorous effect. **2.** speech or writing showing this quality. **3.** a person possessing, showing, or noted for such an ability, esp. in repartee. **4.** practical intelligence (esp. in the phrase **have the wit to**). **5.** *Scot. and northern English dialect.* information or knowledge (esp. in the phrase **get wit of**). **6.** *Archaic.* mental capacity or a person possessing it. **7.** *Obsolete.* the mind or memory. ~See also **wits.** [Old English *witt;* related to Old Saxon *giwitt,* Old High German *wizzi* (German *Witz*), Old Norse *vit,* Gothic *witi.* See WIT[2]]

wit[2] (wɪt) *vb.* **1.** *Archaic.* to be or become aware of (something). ~*adv.* **2. to wit.** that is to say; namely (used to introduce statements, as in legal documents). [Old English *witan;* related to Old High German *wizzan* (German *wissen*), Old Norse *vita,* Latin *vidēre* to see]

witan (ˈwɪtᵊn) *n.* (in Anglo-Saxon England) **1.** an assembly of higher ecclesiastics and important laymen, including king's thegns, that met to counsel the king on matters such as judicial problems. **2.** the members of this assembly. ~Also called: **witenagemot.** [Old English *witan,* plural of *wita* wise man; see WIT[2], WITNESS]

witblits (ˈvɪtˌblɪts) *n. S. African.* an extremely potent illegally distilled spirit. [from Afrikaans *wit* white + *blits* lightning]

witch[1] (wɪtʃ) *n.* **1.** a person, usually female, who practises or professes to practise magic or sorcery, esp. black magic, or is believed to have dealings with the devil. **2.** an ugly or wicked old woman. **3.** a fascinating or enchanting woman. **4.** short for **water witch.** ~*vb.* **5.** (*tr.*) to cause or change by or as if by witchcraft. **6.** a less common word for **bewitch.** [Old English *wicca;* related to Middle Low German *wicken* to conjure, Swedish *vicka* to move to and fro] —ˈ**witchˌlike** *adj.*

witch[2] (wɪtʃ) *n.* a flatfish, *Pleuronectes* (or *Glyptocephalus*) *cynoglossus,* of N Atlantic coastal waters, having a narrow greyish-brown body marked with tiny black spots: family *Pleuronectidae* (plaice, flounders, etc.). [C19: perhaps from WITCH[1], alluding to the appearance of the fish]

witch- *or* **wych-** *prefix.* having pliant branches: *witch-elm.* [Old English *wice* and *wic;* probably from Germanic *wik-* bend]

witchcraft (ˈwɪtʃˌkrɑːft) *n.* **1.** the art or power of bringing magical or preternatural power to bear or the act or practice of attempting to do so. **2.** the influence of magic or sorcery. **3.** fascinating or bewitching influence or charm.

witch doctor *n.* **1.** Also called: **shaman, medicine man.** a man in certain societies, esp. preliterate ones, who appears to possess magical powers, used esp. to cure sickness but also to harm people. **2.** a person who seeks out or hunts witches in some African tribal cultures.

witch-elm *n.* a variant spelling of **wych-elm.**

witchery (ˈwɪtʃərɪ) *n., pl.* **-eries.** **1.** the practice of witchcraft. **2.** magical or bewitching influence or charm.

witches'-broom, witchbroom (ˈwɪtʃˌbruːm), *or* **witches'-besom** *n.* a dense abnormal growth of shoots on a tree or other woody plant, usually caused by parasitic fungi of the genus *Taphrina.*

witches' butter *n.* See **jelly fungus.**

witches' Sabbath *n.* See **Sabbath** (sense 4).

witchetty grub (ˈwɪtʃɪtɪ) *n.* the wood-boring edible caterpillar of an Australian moth, *Xyleutes leucomochla:* family *Cossidae.* [C19 *witchetty,* from a native Australian language]

witch hazel *or* **wych-hazel** *n.* **1.** any of several trees and shrubs of the genus *Hamamelis,* esp. *H. virginiana,* of North America, having ornamental yellow flowers and medicinal properties: family *Hamamelidaceae.* **2.** an astringent medicinal solution containing an extract of the bark and leaves of *H. virginiana,* applied to treat bruises, inflammation, etc.

witch-hunt *n.* a rigorous campaign to round up or expose dissenters on the pretext of safeguarding the public welfare. —ˈ**witch-ˌhunter** *n.* —ˈ**witch-ˌhunting** *n., adj.*

witching (ˈwɪtʃɪŋ) *adj.* **1.** relating to or appropriate for witchcraft. **2.** *Now rare.* bewitching. ~*n.* **3.** witchcraft; magic. —ˈ**witchingly** *adv.*

witching hour *n.* **the.** the hour at which witches are supposed to appear, usually midnight.

witch of Agnesi (ɑːnˈjeɪzɪ) *n. Maths.* a plane curve, symmetrical about the *y*-axis, having the equation $x^2y = 4a^2(2a - y)$. Sometimes shortened to **witch.** [C19: named after Maria Gaetana *Agnesi* (1718–99), Italian mathematician; probably so called from the resemblance of the curve to the outline of a witch's hat]

wite (waɪt) *n. Scot. and northern English dialect.* reproach, blame, or fault. [Old English *wīte;* related to Old Saxon *wīti,* Old High German *wīzzi,* Old Norse *vīti*]

witenagemot (ˌwɪtɪnəgɪˈməʊt) *n.* another word for **witan.** [Old English *witena,* genitive plural of *wita* councillor + *gemōt* meeting, MOOT]

with (wɪð, wɪθ) *prep.* **1.** using; by means of: *he killed her with an axe.* **2.** accompanying; in the company of: *the lady you were with.* **3.** possessing; having: *a man with a red moustache.* **4.** concerning or regarding: *be patient with her.* **5.** in spite of: *with all his talents, he was still humble.* **6.** used to indicate a time or distance by which something is away from something else: *with three miles to go, he collapsed.* **7.** in a manner characterized by: *writing with abandon.* **8.** caused or prompted by: *shaking with rage.* **9.** often used with a verb indicating a reciprocal action or relation between the subject and the preposition's object: *agreeing with me; chatting with the troops.* **10. not with you.** *Informal.* not able to grasp or follow what you are saying. **11. with it.** *Informal.* **a.** fashionable; in style. **b.** comprehending what is happening or being said. **12. with that.** after that; having said or done that. [Old English; related to Old Norse *vith,* Gothic *withra,* Latin *vitricus* stepfather, Sanskrit *vitarám* wider]

withal (wɪˈðɔːl) *adv.* **1.** *Literary.* as well; likewise. **2.** *Literary.* nevertheless. **3.** *Archaic.* therewith. ~*prep.* **4.** (*postpositive*) an archaic word for **with.** [C12: from WITH + ALL]

withdraw (wɪðˈdrɔː) *vb.* **-draws, -drawing, -drew, -drawn.** **1.** (*tr.*) to take or draw back or away; remove. **2.** (*tr.*) to remove from deposit or investment in a bank, building society, etc. **3.** (*tr.*) to retract or recall (a statement, promise, etc.). **4.** (*intr.*) to retire or retreat: *the troops withdrew.* **5.** (*intr.;* often foll. by *from*) to back out (of) or depart (from): *he withdrew from public life.* **6.** (*intr.*) to detach oneself socially, emotionally, or mentally. [C13: from WITH (in the sense: away from) + DRAW] —**withˈdrawable** *adj.* —**withˈdrawer** *n.*

withdrawal (wɪðˈdrɔːəl) *n.* **1.** an act or process of withdrawing; retreat, removal, or detachment. **2.** the period a drug addict goes through following abrupt termination in the use of narcotics, usually characterized by physical and mental symptoms (**withdrawal symptoms**).

withdrawing room *n.* an archaic term for **drawing room.**

withdrawn (wɪðˈdrɔːn) *vb.* **1.** the past participle of **withdraw.** ~*adj.* **2.** unusually reserved, introverted, or shy. **3.** secluded or remote. —**withˈdrawnness** *n.*

withdrew (wɪðˈdruː) *vb.* the past tense of **withdraw.**

withe (wɪθ, wɪð, waɪð) *n.* **1.** a strong flexible twig, esp. of willow, suitable for binding things together; withy. **2.** a band or rope of twisted twigs or stems. **3.** a handle made of elastic material, fitted on some tools to reduce the shock during use. **4.** a wall with a thickness of half a brick, such as a leaf of a cavity wall, or a division between two chimney flues. ~*vb.* **5.** (*tr.*) to bind with withes. [Old English *withthe;* related to Old Norse *vithja,* Old High German *witta, widi,* Gothic *wida*]

wither (ˈwɪðə) *vb.* **1.** (*intr.*) (esp. of a plant) to droop, wilt, or shrivel up. **2.** (*intr.;* often foll. by *away*) to fade or waste: *all hope withered away.* **3.** (*intr.*) to decay, decline, or disintegrate. **4.** (*tr.*) to cause to wilt, fade, or lose vitality. **5.** (*tr.*) to abash, esp. with a scornful look. **6.** (*tr.*) to harm or damage. [C14: perhaps variant of WEATHER (vb.); related to German *verwittern* to decay] —ˈ**withered** *adj.* —ˈ**witherer** *n.* —ˈ**withering** *adj.* —ˈ**witheringly** *adv.*

witherite (ˈwɪðəˌraɪt) *n.* a white, grey, or yellowish mineral consisting of barium carbonate in orthorhombic crystalline form: occurs in veins of lead ore. Formula: $BaCO_3$. [C18: named after W. *Withering* (1741–99), British scientist, who first described it]

withers (ˈwɪðəz) *pl. n.* the highest part of the back of a horse, behind the neck between the shoulders. [C16: short for *widersones,* from *wider* WITH + *-sones,* perhaps variant of SINEW; related to German *Widerrist,* Old English *withre* resistance]

withershins (ˈwɪðəˌʃɪnz; *Scot.* ˈwɪdər-) *or* **widdershins** *adv. Chiefly Scot.* **1.** in the direction contrary to the apparent course of the sun; anticlockwise. **2.** in a direction contrary to the usual; in the wrong direction. Compare **deasil.** [C16: from Middle Low German *weddersinnes,* from Middle High German, literally: opposite course, from *wider* against + *sinnes,* genitive of *sin* course]

withhold (wɪðˈhəʊld) *vb.* **-holds, -holding, -held.** **1.** (*tr.*) to keep back; refrain from giving: *he withheld his permission.* **2.** (*tr.*) to hold back; restrain. **3.** (*tr.*) to deduct (taxes, etc.) from a salary or wages. **4.** (*intr.;* usually foll. by *from*) to refrain or forbear. —**withˈholder** *n.*

withholding tax *n.* 1. tax deducted at source from income, esp. from dividends, paid to nonresidents of a country, which may be reclaimed if a double-taxation agreement exists between the country in which the income is paid and the country of residence of the recipient. 2. *U.S.* a portion of an employee's tax liability paid directly to the government by the employer.

within (wɪˈðɪn) *prep.* 1. in; inside; enclosed or encased by. 2. before (a period of time) has elapsed: *within a week.* 3. not beyond the limits of; not differing by more than (a specified amount) from: *live within your means; within seconds of the world record.* ~*adv.* 4. *Formal.* inside; internally.

withindoors (ˈwɪðɪnˈdɔːz) *adv.* an obsolete word for **indoors.**

within-subjects design *n.* (*modifier*) *Statistics.* (of an experiment) concerned with measuring the value of the dependent variable for the same subjects under the various experimental conditions. Compare **between-subjects design, matched-pairs design.**

without (wɪˈðaʊt) *prep.* 1. not having: *a traveller without much money.* 2. not accompanied by: *he came without his wife.* 3. not making use of: *it is not easy to undo screws without a screwdriver.* 4. (*foll. by a verbal noun or noun phrase*) not, while not, or after not: *she can sing for two minutes without drawing breath.* 5. *Archaic.* on the outside of: *without the city walls.* ~*adv.* 6. *Formal.* outside; outwardly. ~*conj.* 7. *Not standard.* unless: *don't come without you have some money.*

withoutdoors (ˈwɪðaʊtˈdɔːz) *adv.* an obsolete word for **outdoors.**

withstand (wɪðˈstænd) *vb.* **-stands, -standing, -stood.** 1. (*tr.*) to stand up to forcefully; resist. 2. (*intr.*) to remain firm in endurance or opposition. —**withˈstander** *n.*

withy (ˈwɪðɪ) *n., pl.* **withies.** 1. a variant spelling of **withe** (senses 1, 2). 2. a willow tree, esp. an osier. ~*adj.* 3. (of people) tough and agile. 4. *Rare.* resembling a withe in strength or flexibility. [Old English *wīdig(e);* related to Old Norse *vīthir,* Old High German *wīda,* Latin *vītis* vine, Sanskrit *vītika* fetter. See WITHE, WIRE]

witless (ˈwɪtlɪs) *adj.* lacking wit, intelligence, or sense; stupid. —ˈ**witlessly** *adv.* —ˈ**witlessness** *n.*

witling (ˈwɪtlɪŋ) *n. Archaic.* a person who thinks himself witty.

witness (ˈwɪtnɪs) *n.* 1. a person who has seen or can give first-hand evidence of some event. 2. a person or thing giving or serving as evidence. 3. a person who testifies, esp. in a court of law, to events or facts within his own knowledge. 4. a person who attests to the genuineness of a document, signature, etc., by adding his own signature. 5. **bear witness. a.** to give written or oral testimony. **b.** to be evidence or proof of. ~Related adj.: **testimonial.** ~*vb.* 6. (*tr.*) to see, be present at, or know at first hand. 7. to give or serve as evidence (of). 8. (*tr.*) to be the scene or setting of: *this field has witnessed a battle.* 9. (*intr.*) to testify, esp. in a court of law, to events within a person's own knowledge. 10. (*tr.*) to attest to the genuineness of (a document, signature, etc.) by adding one's own signature. [Old English *witnes* (meaning both *testimony* and *witness*), from *witan* to know, WIT[2] + -NESS; related to Old Norse *vitni*] —ˈ**witnessable** *adj.* —ˈ**witnesser** *n.*

witness box *or esp. U.S.* **witness stand** *n.* the place in a court of law in which witnesses stand to give evidence.

wits (wɪts) *pl. n.* 1. (*sometimes sing.*) the ability to reason and act, esp. quickly (esp. in the phrase **have one's wits about one**). 2. (*sometimes sing.*) right mind, sanity (esp. in the phrase **out of one's wits**). 3. **at one's wits' end.** at a loss to know how to proceed. 4. **five wits.** *Obsolete.* the five senses or mental faculties. 5. **live by one's wits.** to gain a livelihood by craftiness rather than by hard work.

-witted *adj.* (*in combination*) having wits or intelligence as specified: *slow-witted; dim-witted.*

witter (ˈwɪtə) *Informal.* ~*vb.* 1. (*intr.,* often foll. by *on*) to chatter or babble pointlessly or at unnecessary length. ~*n.* 2. pointless chat; chatter. [C20: from dialect; compare TWITTER]

Wittgensteinian (ˈvɪtgənˌʃtaɪnɪən, -ˌstaɪnɪən) *adj.* (of a philosophical position or argument) derived from or related to the work of Austrian-born British philosopher Ludwig Wittgenstein (1889–1951), esp. the later work in which he attacks essentialism and stresses the open texture and variety of use of ordinary language.

witticism (ˈwɪtɪˌsɪzəm) *n.* a clever or witty remark. [C17: from WITTY; coined (1677) by the English poet, dramatist, and critic John Dryden by analogy with *criticism*]

witting (ˈwɪtɪŋ) *adj. Rare.* 1. deliberate; intentional: *a witting insult.* 2. aware; knowing. —ˈ**wittingly** *adv.*

wittol (ˈwɪtᵊl) *n. Obsolete.* a man who tolerates his wife's unfaithfulness. [C15 *wetewold,* from *witen* to know (see WIT[2]) + *-wold,* perhaps from *cokewold* CUCKOLD]

witty (ˈwɪtɪ) *adj.* **-tier, -tiest.** 1. characterized by clever humour or wit. 2. *Archaic or dialect.* intelligent or sensible. —ˈ**wittily** *adv.* —ˈ**wittiness** *n.*

wive (waɪv) *vb. Archaic.* 1. to marry (a woman). 2. (*tr.*) to supply with a wife. [Old English *gewīfian,* from *wīf* WIFE]

wivern (ˈwaɪvən) *n.* a less common spelling of **wyvern.**

wives (waɪvz) *n.* the plural of **wife.**

wiz (wɪz) *n. Informal.* a variant spelling of **whiz** (sense 5).

wizard (ˈwɪzəd) *n.* 1. a male witch or a man who practises or professes to practise magic or sorcery. 2. a person who is outstandingly clever in some specified field; expert. 3. *Obsolete.* a wise man. ~*adj.* 4. *Informal, chiefly Brit.* superb; outstanding. 5. of or relating to a wizard or wizardry. [C15: variant of *wissard,* from WISE[1] + -ARD] —ˈ**wizardly** *adj.*

wizardry (ˈwɪzədrɪ) *n.* the art, skills, and practices of a wizard, sorcerer, or magician.

wizen[1] (ˈwɪzᵊn) *vb.* 1. to make or become shrivelled. ~*adj.* 2. a variant of **wizened.** [Old English *wisnian;* related to Old Norse *visna,* Old High German *wesanēn*]

wizen[2] (ˈwiːzᵊn) *n.* an archaic word for **weasand** (the gullet).

wizened (ˈwɪzᵊnd) *or* **wizen** *adj.* shrivelled, wrinkled, or dried up, esp. with age.

wk *abbrev. for:* 1. (*pl.* **wks**) week. 2. work. 3. weak.

wkly *abbrev. for* weekly.

WL *international car registration for* (Windward Islands) St Lucia.

w.l. *or* **WL** *abbrev. for* water line.

WLM *abbrev. for* women's liberation movement.

wmk *abbrev. for* watermark.

WMO *abbrev. for* World Meteorological Organization.

WNW *symbol for* west-northwest.

wo (wəʊ) *n., pl.* **wos.** an archaic spelling of **woe.**

WO *abbrev. for:* 1. War Office. 2. Warrant Officer. 3. wireless operator.

w/o *abbrev. for:* 1. without. 2. written off.

woad (wəʊd) *n.* 1. a European cruciferous plant, *Isatis tinctoria,* formerly cultivated for its leaves, which yield a blue dye. See also **dyer's-weed, dyer's rocket.** 2. the dye obtained from this plant, used esp. by the ancient Britons, as a body dye. [Old English *wād;* related to Old High German *weit;* Middle Dutch *wēd,* Latin *vitrum*]

woaded (ˈwəʊdɪd) *adj.* coloured blue with woad.

woadwaxen (ˈwəʊdˌwæksən) *n.* another name for **dyer's-greenweed.**

woald (wəʊld) *n.* another name for **weld**[2]**.**

wobbegong (ˈwɒbɪˌgɒŋ) *n.* any of various carpet sharks of the family *Orectolobidae,* of Australian waters, having a richly patterned brown-and-white skin. [from a native Australian language]

wobble (ˈwɒbᵊl) *vb.* 1. (*intr.*) to move, rock, or sway unsteadily. 2. (*intr.*) to tremble or shake: *her voice wobbled with emotion.* 3. (*intr.*) to vacillate with indecision. 4. (*tr.*) to cause to wobble. ~*n.* 5. a wobbling movement, motion, or sound. ~Also: **wabble.** [C17: variant of *wabble,* from Low German *wabbeln;* related to Middle High German *wabelen* to WAVER] —ˈ**wobbler** *n.*

wobble board *n. Austral.* a piece of fibreboard used as a musical instrument, producing a characteristic sound when flexed.

wobble plate *n.* another name for **swash plate.**

wobbly (ˈwɒblɪ) *adj.* **-blier, -bliest.** 1. unsteady. 2. trembling, shaking. ~*n.* 3. **throw a wobbly.** *Slang.* to become suddenly very agitated or angry. —ˈ**wobbliness** *n.*

wodge (wɒdʒ) *n. Brit. informal.* a thick lump or chunk cut or broken off something. [C20: alteration of WEDGE]

woe (wəʊ) *n.* 1. *Literary.* intense grief or misery. 2. (*often pl.*) affliction or misfortune. 3. **woe betide (someone).** misfortune will befall (someone): *woe betide you if you arrive late.* ~*interj.* 4. Also: **woe is me.** *Archaic.* an exclamation of sorrow or distress. [Old English *wā, wǣ;* related to Old Saxon, Old High German *wē,* Old Norse *vei,* Gothic *wai,* Latin *vae,* Sanskrit *uvē;* see WAIL]

woebegone (ˈwəʊbɪˌgɒn) *adj.* 1. sorrowful or sad in appearance. 2. *Archaic.* afflicted with woe. [C14: from a phrase such as *me is wo begon* woe has beset me]

woeful (ˈwəʊfᵊl) *adj.* 1. expressing or characterized by sorrow. 2. bringing or causing woe. 3. pitiful; miserable: *a woeful standard of work.* —ˈ**woefully** *adv.* —ˈ**woefulness** *n.*

WOF (in New Zealand) *abbrev. for* Warrant of Fitness.

wog[1] (wɒg) *n. Brit. slang, derogatory.* a foreigner, esp. one who is not White. [probably from GOLLIWOG]

wog[2] (wɒg) *n. Slang, chiefly Austral.* influenza or any similar illness. [C20: of unknown origin]

woggle (ˈwɒgᵊl) *n.* the ring of leather through which a Scout neckerchief is threaded. [C20: of unknown origin]

wok (wɒk) *n.* a large metal Chinese cooking pot having a curved base like a bowl and traditionally with a wooden handle. [from Chinese (Cantonese)]

woke (wəʊk) *vb.* a past tense of **wake.**

woken (ˈwəʊkən) *vb.* a past participle of **wake.**

wokka board (ˈwɒkə) *n. Austral.* another name for **wobble board.**

wold[1] (wəʊld) *n. Chiefly literary.* a tract of open rolling country, esp. upland. [Old English *weald* bush; related to Old Saxon *wald,* German *Wald* forest, Old Norse *vollr* ground; see WILD]

wold[2] (wəʊld) *n.* another name for **weld**[2]**.**

wolf (wʊlf) *n., pl.* **wolves** (wʊlvz). 1. a predatory canine mammal, *Canis lupus,* which hunts in packs and was formerly widespread in North America and Eurasia but is now less common. See also **timber wolf.** Related adj.: **lupine.** 2. any of several similar and related canines, such as the red wolf and the coyote (**prairie wolf**). 3. the fur of any such animal. 4. **Tasmanian wolf.** another name for the **thylacine.** 5. a voracious, grabbing, or fiercely cruel person or thing. 6. *Informal.* a man who habitually tries to seduce women. 7. *Informal.* the destructive larva of any of various moths and beetles. 8. Also called: **wolf note.**

Music. **a.** an unpleasant sound produced in some notes played on the violin, cello, etc., owing to resonant vibrations of the belly. **b.** an out-of-tune effect produced on keyboard instruments accommodated esp. to the system of mean-tone temperament. See **temperament** (sense 4). **9. cry wolf.** to give a false alarm. **10. have** *or* **hold a wolf by the ears.** to be in a desperate situation. **11. keep the wolf from the door.** to ward off starvation or privation. **12. lone wolf.** a person or animal who prefers to be alone. **13. throw to the wolves.** to abandon or deliver to destruction. **14. wolf in sheep's clothing.** a malicious person in a harmless or benevolent disguise. ~*vb.* **15.** (*tr.*; often foll. by *down*) to gulp (down). **16.** (*intr.*) to hunt wolves. [Old English *wulf*; related to Old High German *wolf*, Old Norse *ulfr*, Gothic *wulfs*, Latin *lupus* and *vulpēs* fox] —'**wolfish** *adj.* —'**wolf,like** *adj.*

Wolf Cub *n. Brit.* the former name for **Cub Scout.**

wolfer ('wʊlfə) *n.* a less common spelling of **wolver.**

Wolffian body ('vɒlfɪən) *n. Embryol.* another name for **mesonephros.** [C19: named after K. F. *Wolff* (1733–94), German embryologist]

wolffish ('wʊlf,fɪʃ) *n., pl.* **-fish** *or* **-fishes.** any large northern deep-sea blennioid fish of the family *Anarhichadidae*, such as *Anarhichas lupus.* They have large sharp teeth and no pelvic fins and are used as food fishes. Also called: **catfish.**

wolfhound ('wʊlf,haʊnd) *n.* the largest breed of dog, used formerly to hunt wolves.

wolfram ('wʊlfrəm) *n.* another name for **tungsten.** [C18: from German, originally perhaps from the proper name, *Wolfram*, used pejoratively of tungsten because it was thought inferior to tin]

wolframite ('wʊlfrə,maɪt) *n.* a black to reddish-brown mineral consisting of tungstates of iron and manganese in monoclinic crystalline form: it occurs mainly in quartz veins and is the chief ore of tungsten. Formula: $(Fe,Mn)WO_4$.

Wolf-Rayet star ('wʊlf'reɪət) *n.* any of over 100 very hot intensely luminous stars surrounded by a rapidly expanding envelope of gas. Sometimes shortened to **W star.** [C19: named after Charles *Wolf* (1827–1918) and Georges *Rayet* (1839–1906), French astronomers]

wolfsbane *or* **wolf's-bane** ('wʊlfs,beɪn) *n.* any of several poisonous N temperate plants of the ranunculaceous genus *Aconitum*, esp. *A. lycoctonum*, which has yellow hoodlike flowers.

wolf spider *n.* any spider of the family *Lycosidae*, which chase their prey to catch it. Also called: **hunting spider.**

wolf whistle *n.* **1.** a whistle made by a man to express admiration of a woman's appearance. ~*vb.* **wolf-whistle. 2.** (when *intr.*, sometimes foll. by *at*) to make such a whistle (at someone).

wollastonite ('wʊləstə,naɪt) *n.* a white or grey mineral consisting of calcium silicate in triclinic crystalline form: occurs in metamorphosed limestones. Formula: $CaSiO_3$. [C19: named after W. H. *Wollaston* (1766–1828), British physicist]

wolly ('wɒlɪ) *n., pl.* **-lies.** *East London dialect.* a pickled cucumber or olive. [perhaps from OLIVE]

Wolof ('wɒlɒf) *n.* **1.** (*pl.* **-of** *or* **-ofs**) a member of a Negroid people of W Africa living chiefly in Senegal. **2.** the language of this people, belonging to the West Atlantic branch of the Niger-Congo family.

wolver ('wʊlvə) *or* **wolfer** *n.* a person who hunts wolves.

wolverine ('wʊlvə,riːn) *n.* a large musteline mammal, *Gulo gulo*, of northern forests of Eurasia and North America having dark very thick water-resistant fur. Also called: **glutton.** [C16 *wolvering*, from WOLF + -ING[3] (later altered to *-ine*)]

wolves (wʊlvz) *n.* the plural of **wolf.**

woman ('wʊmən) *n., pl.* **women** ('wɪmɪn). **1.** an adult female human being. **2.** (*modifier*) female or feminine: *a woman politician; woman talk.* **3.** women collectively; womankind. **4.** (usually preceded by *the*) feminine nature or feelings: *babies bring out the woman in her.* **5.** a female servant or domestic help. **6.** a man considered as having female characteristics, such as meekness or cowardliness. **7.** *Informal.* a wife, mistress, or girlfriend. **8. the little woman.** *Informal.* one's wife. **9. woman of the streets.** a prostitute. ~*vb.* (*tr.*) **10.** *Rare.* to provide with women. **11.** *Obsolete.* to make effeminate. [Old English *wīfmann, wimman*; from WIFE + MAN (human being)] —'**womanless** *adj.* —'**woman-,like** *adj.*

womanhood ('wʊmən,hʊd) *n.* **1.** the state or quality of being a woman or being womanly. **2.** women collectively.

womanish ('wʊmənɪʃ) *adj.* **1.** having qualities or characteristics regarded as unsuitable to a strong character of either sex, esp. a man. **2.** characteristic of or suitable for a woman. —'**womanishly** *adv.* —'**womanishness** *n.*

womanize *or* **womanise** ('wʊmə,naɪz) *vb.* **1.** (*intr.*) (of a man) to indulge in many casual affairs with women; philander. **2.** (*tr.*) to make effeminate. —'**woman,izer** *or* '**woman,iser** *n.*

womankind ('wʊmən,kaɪnd) *n.* the female members of the human race; women collectively.

womanly ('wʊmənlɪ) *adj.* **1.** possessing qualities, such as warmth, attractiveness, etc., generally regarded as typical of a woman, esp. a mature woman. **2.** characteristic of or belonging to a woman. —'**womanliness** *n.*

womb (wuːm) *n.* **1.** the nontechnical name for **uterus. 2.** a hollow space enclosing something, esp. when dark, warm, or sheltering. **3.** a place where something is conceived: *the Near East is the womb of western civilization.* **4.** *Obsolete.* the belly. [Old English *wamb*; related to Old Norse *vomb*, Gothic *wamba*, Middle Low German *wamme*, Swedish *våmm*] —**wombed** *adj.* —'**womblike** *adj.*

wombat ('wɒmbæt) *n.* either of two burrowing herbivorous Australian marsupials, *Vombatus ursinus* or *Lasiorhinus latifrons*, constituing the family *Vombatidae* (or *Phascolomidae*) and having short limbs, a heavy body, and coarse dense fur. [C18: from a native Australian language]

women ('wɪmɪn) *n.* the plural of **woman.**

womenfolk ('wɪmɪn,fəʊk) *or U.S.* (*sometimes*) **womenfolks** *pl. n.* **1.** women collectively. **2.** a group of women, esp. the female members of one's family.

women's liberation *n.* a movement directed towards the removal of attitudes and practices that preserve inequalities based upon the assumption that men are superior to women. Also called: **women's lib.**

women's refuge *n. Social welfare.* a house where battered women and their children can go for protection from their oppressors.

women's studies *pl. n.* courses in history, literature, psychology, etc., that are particularly concerned with women's roles, experiences, and achievements.

women's suffrage *n.* the right of women to vote. See also **suffragette.**

womera ('wʊmərə) *n.* a variant spelling of **woomera.**

won[1] (wʌn) *vb.* the past tense of **win**[1].

won[2] (wɒn) *n., pl.* **won. 1.** the standard monetary unit of North Korea, divided into 100 chon. **2.** the standard monetary unit of South Korea, divided into 100 chon. ~Also called: **hwan.** [Korean *wǎn*]

won[3] (wʌn, wʊn, wəʊn) *vb.* **wons, wonning, wonned.** (*intr.*) *Archaic.* to live or dwell. [Old English *wunian* to become accustomed to; related to WIN[1]]

wonder ('wʌndə) *n.* **1.** the feeling excited by something strange; a mixture of surprise, curiosity, and sometimes awe. **2.** something that causes such a feeling, such as a miracle. **3.** (*modifier*) exciting wonder by virtue of spectacular results achieved, feats performed, etc.: *a wonder drug; a wonder horse.* **4. do** *or* **work wonders.** to achieve spectacularly fine results. **5. for a wonder.** surprisingly or amazingly. **6. nine days' wonder.** a subject that arouses general surprise or public interest for a short time. **7. no wonder.** (*sentence connector*) (I am) not surprised at all (that): *no wonder he couldn't come.* **8. small wonder.** (*sentence connector*) (I am) hardly surprised (that): *small wonder he couldn't make it tonight.* ~*vb.* (when *tr., may take a clause as object*) **9.** (when *intr.*, often foll. by *about*) to indulge in speculative inquiry, often accompanied by an element of doubt (concerning something): *I wondered about what she said; I wonder what happened.* **10.** (when *intr.*, often foll. by *at*) to be amazed (at something): *I wonder at your impudence.* [Old English *wundor*; related to Old Saxon *wundar*, Old Norse *undr*, German *Wunder*] —'**wonderer** *n.* —'**wonderless** *adj.*

wonderful ('wʌndəfʊl) *adj.* **1.** exciting a feeling of wonder; marvellous or strange. **2.** extremely fine; excellent. —'**wonderfully** *adv.* —'**wonderfulness** *n.*

wonderland ('wʌndə,lænd) *n.* **1.** an imaginary land of marvels or wonders. **2.** an actual place or scene of great or strange beauty or wonder.

wonderment ('wʌndəmənt) *n.* **1.** rapt surprise; awe. **2.** puzzled interest. **3.** something that excites wonder.

wonderwork ('wʌndə,wɜːk) *n.* something done or made that excites wonder; miracle or wonder. —'**wonder-,worker** *n.* —'**wonder-,working** *n., adj.*

wondrous ('wʌndrəs) *Archaic or literary.* ~*adj.* **1.** exciting wonder; marvellous. ~*adv.* **2.** (intensifier): *it is wondrous cold.* —'**wondrously** *adv.* —'**wondrousness** *n.*

wonga-wonga ('wɒŋə'wɒŋə) *n.* **1.** a large Australian pigeon, *Leucosarcia melanoleuca.* **2.** an Australian evergreen vine of the genus *Pandorea* or *Tecoma*, esp. *T. australis.* [from a native Australian language]

wonky ('wɒŋkɪ) *adj.* **-kier, -kiest.** *Brit. informal.* **1.** shaky or unsteady. **2.** not in correct alignment; askew. **3.** liable to break down or develop a fault. [C20: variant of dialect *wanky*, from Old English *wancol*]

wont (wəʊnt) *adj.* **1.** (*postpositive*) accustomed (to doing something): *he was wont to come early.* ~*n.* **2.** a manner or action habitually employed by or associated with someone (often in the phrases **as is my wont, as is his wont,** etc.). ~*vb.* **3.** (when *tr., usually passive*) to become or cause to become accustomed. [Old English *gewunod*, past participle of *wunian* to be accustomed to; related to Old High German *wunēn* (German *wohnen*), Old Norse *una* to be satisfied; see WEAN, WISH, WINSOME]

won't (wəʊnt) *vb. contraction of* will not.

wonted ('wəʊntɪd) *adj.* **1.** (*postpositive*) accustomed or habituated (to doing something). **2.** (*prenominal*) customary; usual: *she is in her wonted place.*

won ton ('wɒn 'tɒn) *n. Chinese cookery.* **1.** a dumpling filled with spiced minced pork, usually served in soup. **2.** soup containing such dumplings. [from Chinese (Cantonese) *wan t'an* pastry]

woo (wuː) *vb.* **woos, wooing, wooed. 1.** to seek the affection, favour, or love of (a woman) with a view to marriage. **2.** (*tr.*) to seek after zealously or hopefully: *to woo fame.* **3.** (*tr.*) to bring upon oneself (good or evil results) by one's own action. **4.** (*tr.*)

to beg or importune (someone). [Old English *wōgian,* of obscure origin] —'**wooer** *n.* —'**wooing** *n.*

wood[1] (wʊd) *n.* **1.** the hard fibrous substance consisting of xylem tissue that occurs beneath the bark in trees, shrubs, and similar plants. **2.** the trunks of trees that have been cut and prepared for use as a building material. **3.** a collection of trees, shrubs, herbs, grasses, etc., usually dominated by one or a few species of tree: usually smaller than a forest: *an oak wood.* Related adj.: **sylvan.** **4.** fuel; firewood. **5.** *Golf.* **a.** a long-shafted club with a wooden head, used for driving: numbered from 1 to 5 according to size, angle of face, etc. **b.** (*as modifier*): *a wood shot.* **6.** *Tennis, etc.* the frame of a racket: *he hit a winning shot off the wood.* **7.** one of the biased wooden bowls used in the game of bowls. **8.** *Music.* short for **woodwind.** See also **woods** (sense 3). **9. a.** casks, barrels, etc., made of wood. **b. from the wood.** (of a beverage) from a wooden container rather than a metal or glass one. **10. have (got) the wood on.** *Austral. and N.Z. informal.* to have an advantage over. **11. out of the wood** *or* **woods.** clear of or safe from dangers or doubts: *we're not out of the wood yet.* **12. see the wood for the trees.** (*used with a negative*) to obtain a general view of a situation, problem, etc., without allowing details to cloud one's analysis: *he can't see the wood for the trees.* **13.** (*modifier*) made of, used for, employing, or handling wood: *a wood fire.* **14.** (*modifier*) dwelling in, concerning, or situated in a wood: *a wood nymph.* ~*vb.* **15.** (*tr.*) to plant a wood upon. **16.** to supply or be supplied with fuel or firewood. ~See also **woods.** [Old English *widu, wudu;* related to Old High German *witu,* Old Norse *vithr*] —'**woodless** *adj.*

wood[2] (wʊd) *adj. Obsolete.* raging or raving like a maniac. [Old English *wōd;* related to Old High German *wuot* (German *Wut*), Old Norse *ōthr,* Gothic *wōths,* Latin *vātēs* seer]

wood alcohol *n.* another name for **methanol.**

wood-and-water joey *n. Austral. informal.* a person employed to carry out menial tasks. [from the biblical phrase "hewers of wood and drawers of water" (Joshua 9:21) and JOEY]

wood anemone *n.* any of several woodland anemone plants, esp. *Anemone quinquefolia* of E North America and *A. nemorosa* of Europe, having finely divided leaves and solitary white flowers. Also called: **windflower.**

wood ant *n.* a reddish-brown European ant, *Formica rufa,* typically living in anthills in woodlands.

wood avens *n.* another name for **herb bennet.**

woodbine ('wʊd,baɪn) *n.* **1.** a honeysuckle, *Lonicera periclymenum,* of Europe, SW Asia, and N Africa, having fragrant yellow flowers. **2. American woodbine.** a related North American plant, *L. caprifolium.* **3.** *U.S.* another name for **Virginia creeper** (sense 1). **4.** *Austral. slang.* an Englishman. [sense 4 from the English brand of cigarettes so named]

wood block *n.* **1.** a small rectangular flat block of wood that is laid with others as a floor surface. **2.** *Music.* another word for **Chinese block.**

woodborer ('wʊd,bɔːrə) *n.* **1.** any of various beetles of the families *Anobiidae, Buprestidae,* etc., the larvae of which bore into and damage wood. **2.** any of various other unrelated invertebrates that bore into wood.

woodcarving ('wʊd,kɑːvɪŋ) *n.* **1.** the act of carving wood, esp. as an art form. **2.** a work of art produced by carving wood. —'**wood,carver** *n.*

woodchat *or* **woodchat shrike** ('wʊd,tʃæt) *n.* a songbird, *Lanius senator,* of Europe and N Africa, having a black-and-white plumage with a reddish-brown crown and a hooked bill: family *Laniidae* (shrikes).

woodchop ('wʊd,tʃɒp) *n. Austral.* a wood-chopping competition, esp. at a show.

woodchuck ('wʊd,tʃʌk) *n.* a North American marmot, *Marmota monax,* having coarse reddish-brown fur. Also called: **groundhog.** [C17: by folk etymology from Cree *otcheck* fisher, marten]

wood coal *n.* another name for **lignite** or **charcoal.**

woodcock ('wʊd,kɒk) *n.* **1.** an Old World game bird, *Scolopax rusticola,* resembling the snipe but larger and having shorter legs and neck: family *Scolopacidae* (sandpipers, etc.), order *Charadriiformes.* **2.** a related North American bird, *Philohela minor.* **3.** *Obsolete.* a simpleton.

woodcraft ('wʊd,krɑːft) *n. Chiefly U.S. and Canadian.* **1.** ability and experience in matters concerned with living in a wood or forest. **2.** ability or skill at woodwork, carving, etc. **3.** skill in caring for trees. —'**wood,craftsman** *n.*

woodcut ('wʊd,kʌt) *n.* **1.** a block of wood cut along the grain and with a design, illustration, etc., incised with a knife, from which prints are made. **2.** a print from a woodcut.

woodcutter ('wʊd,kʌtə) *n.* **1.** a person who fells trees or chops wood. **2.** a person who makes woodcuts. —'**wood,cutting** *n.*

wood duck *n.* a duck, *Aix sponsa,* of wooded swamps, lakes, etc., in North America, having a very brightly coloured plumage in the male.

wooded ('wʊdɪd) *adj.* **1.** covered with or abounding in woods or trees. **2.** (*in combination*) having wood of a specified character: *a soft-wooded tree.*

wooden ('wʊdᵊn) *adj.* **1.** made from or consisting of wood. **2.** awkward or clumsy. **3.** bereft of spirit or animation: *a wooden expression.* **4.** obstinately unyielding: *a wooden attitude.* **5.** mentally slow or dull. **6.** not highly resonant: *a wooden thud.* ~*vb.* **7.** (*tr.*) *Austral. slang.* to fell or kill (a person or animal). —'**woodenly** *adv.* —'**woodenness** *n.*

wood engraving *n.* **1.** the art of engraving pictures or designs on wood for printing by incising them with a burin on a block of wood cut across the grain. **2.** a block of wood so engraved or a print taken from it. —**wood engraver** *n.*

woodenhead ('wʊdᵊn,hɛd) *n. Informal.* a dull, foolish, or unintelligent person. —,**wooden'headed** *adj.* —,**wooden'headedness** *n.*

wooden spoon *n.* a booby prize, esp. in sporting contests.

woodfree ('wʊd,friː) *adj.* (of high-quality paper) made from pulp that has been treated chemically, removing impurities.

woodgrouse ('wʊd,graʊs) *n.* another name for **capercaillie.**

wood hedgehog *n.* a pale-buff basidiomycetous fungus, *Hydnum repandum,* found in broad-leaved woodlands, having a spiny underside to the cap.

woodhen ('wʊd,hɛn) *n. N.Z.* another name for **weka.**

wood hyacinth *n.* another name for **bluebell** (sense 1).

wood ibis *n.* any of several storks having a downward-curved bill, esp. *Mycteria americana* of America and *Ibis ibis* of Africa.

woodland ('wʊdlənd) *n.* **a.** land that is mostly covered with woods or dense growths of trees and shrubs. **b.** (*as modifier*): *woodland fauna.* —'**woodlander** *n.*

woodlark ('wʊd,lɑːk) *n.* an Old World lark, *Lullula arborea,* similar to but slightly smaller than the skylark.

woodlot ('wʊd,lɒt) *n.* an area restricted to the growing of trees. Also called (esp. Canadian): **bush lot.**

woodlouse ('wʊd,laʊs) *n., pl.* **-lice** (-,laɪs). any of various small terrestrial isopod crustaceans of the genera *Oniscus, Porcellio,* etc., which have a flattened segmented body and occur in damp habitats. See also **pill bug.**

woodman ('wʊdmən) *n., pl.* **-men.** **1.** a person who looks after and fells trees used for timber. **2.** another word for **woodsman.** **3.** *Obsolete.* a hunter who is knowledgeable about woods and the animals living in them.

woodnote ('wʊd,nəʊt) *n.* a natural musical note or song, like that of a wild bird.

wood nymph *n.* one of a class of nymphs fabled to inhabit the woods, such as a dryad.

wood opal *n.* a form of petrified wood impregnated by common opal.

wood owl *n.* another name for **tawny owl.**

woodpecker ('wʊd,pɛkə) *n.* any climbing bird of the family *Picidae,* typically having a brightly coloured plumage and strong chisel-like bill with which they bore into trees for insects: order *Piciformes.*

wood pigeon *n.* a large Eurasian pigeon, *Columba palumbus,* having white patches on the wings and neck. Also called: **ringdove, cushat.**

woodpile ('wʊd,paɪl) *n.* **1.** a pile or heap of firewood. **2. nigger in the woodpile.** See **nigger** (sense 3).

wood pitch *n.* the dark viscid residue left after the distillation of wood tar: used as a binder in briquettes.

wood preservative *n.* a coating applied to timber as a protection against decay, insects, weather, etc.

woodprint ('wʊd,prɪnt) *n.* another name for **woodcut** (sense 2).

wood pulp *n.* **1.** wood that has been ground to a fine pulp for use in making newsprint and other cheap forms of paper. **2.** finely pulped wood that has been digested by a chemical, such as caustic soda, and sometimes bleached: used in making paper.

wood rat *n.* another name for **pack rat.**

woodruff ('wʊdrʌf) *n.* any of several rubiaceous plants of the genus *Asperula,* esp. *A. odorata* (or *Galium odoratum*) (**sweet woodruff**), of Eurasia, which has small sweet-scented white flowers and whorls of narrow fragrant leaves used to flavour wine and liqueurs and in perfumery. [Old English *wudurofe,* from WOOD[1] + *rōfe,* related to Old High German *ruoba,* Middle Low German *rōve* (beet)root, Latin *rēpere* to creep]

Woodruff key ('wʊdrʌf) *n. Engineering.* a semicircular key restrained in a curved keyway in a shaft. [C19: named after the *Woodruff Manufacturing Co.,* in Hartford, Connecticut, who first manufactured it in 1892]

woodrush ('wʊd,rʌʃ) *n.* any of various juncaceous plants of the genus *Luzula,* chiefly of cold and temperate regions of the N hemisphere, having grasslike leaves and small brown flowers.

woods (wʊdz) *pl. n.* **1.** closely packed trees forming a forest or wood, esp. a specific one. **2.** another word for **backwoods** (sense 2). **3.** the woodwind instruments in an orchestra. See also **wood**[1] (sense 8). **4. this (that, our,** etc.) **neck of the woods.** *Informal.* this particular area or piece of territory.

wood sage *n.* a downy labiate perennial, *Teucrium scorodonia,* having spikes of green-yellow flowers: common on acid heath and scree.

woodscrew ('wʊd,skruː) *n.* a metal screw that tapers to a point so that it can be driven into wood by a screwdriver.

Woodser ('wʊdzə) *n.* See **Jimmy Woodser.**

woodshed ('wʊd,ʃɛd) *n.* a small outbuilding where firewood, garden tools, etc., are stored.

woodsia ('wʊdzɪə) *n.* any small fern of the genus *Woodsia,* of temperate and cold regions, having tufted rhizomes and numerous wiry fronds: family *Polypodiaceae.*

woodsman ('wʊdzmən) *n., pl.* **-men.** a person who lives in a wood or who is skilled in woodcraft. Also called: **woodman.**

wood sorrel *n.* a Eurasian plant, *Oxalis acetosella,* having trifoliate leaves, an underground creeping stem, and white purple-veined flowers: family *Oxalidaceae.*

wood spirit *n. Chem.* another name for **methanol.**

wood sugar *n. Chem.* another name for **xylose.**

woodswallow ('wʊd,swɒləʊ) *n.* any of several insectivorous birds of the genus *Artamus* of Australia.

woodsy ('wʊdzɪ) *adj.* **woodsier, woodsiest.** *U.S. and Canadian informal.* of, reminiscent of, or connected with woods.

wood tar *n.* any tar produced by the destructive distillation of wood: used in producing tarred cord and rope and formerly in medicine as disinfectants and antiseptics.

wood vinegar *n.* another name for **pyroligneous acid.**

wood warbler *n.* **1.** a European woodland warbler, *Phylloscopus sibilatrix,* with a dull yellow plumage. **2.** another name for the **American warbler.** See **warbler** (sense 3).

wood wasp *n.* another name for the **horntail.**

woodwaxen ('wʊd,wæksᵊn) *n.* another name for **dyer's-greenweed.**

woodwind ('wʊd,wɪnd) *Music.* ~*adj.* **1.** of, relating to, or denoting a type of wind instrument, excluding the brass instruments, formerly made of wood but now often made of metal, such as the flute or clarinet. ~*n.* **2.** (*functioning as pl.*) woodwind instruments collectively.

wood woollyfoot ('wʊlɪ,fʊt) *n.* a common yellowish basidiomycetous fungus, *Collybia peronata,* of broad-leaved woodland, having a hairy tuft at the foot of the stem.

woodwork ('wʊd,wɜːk) *n.* **1.** the art, craft, or skill of making things in wood; carpentry. **2.** components made of wood, such as doors, staircases, etc.

woodworker ('wʊd,wɜːkə) *n.* a person who works in wood, such as a carpenter, joiner, or cabinet-maker.

woodworking ('wʊd,wɜːkɪŋ) *n.* **1.** the process of working wood. ~*adj.* **2.** of, relating to, or used in woodworking.

woodworm ('wʊd,wɜːm) *n.* **1.** any of various insect larvae that bore into wooden furniture, beams, etc., esp. the larvae of the furniture beetle, *Anobium punctatum,* and the deathwatch beetle. **2.** the condition caused in wood by any of these larvae.

woody ('wʊdɪ) *adj.* **woodier, woodiest.** **1.** abounding in or covered with forest or woods. **2.** connected with, belonging to, or situated in a wood. **3.** consisting of or containing wood or lignin: *woody tissue; woody stems.* **4.** resembling wood in hardness or texture. —'**woodiness** *n.*

woodyard ('wʊd,jɑːd) *n.* a place where timber is cut and stored.

woody nightshade *n.* a scrambling woody Eurasian solanaceous plant, *Solanum dulcamara,* having purple flowers with recurved petals and a protruding cone of yellow anthers and producing poisonous red berry-like fruits. Also called: **bittersweet.**

woof[1] (wuːf) *n.* **1.** the crosswise yarns that fill the warp yarns in weaving; weft. **2.** a woven fabric or its texture. [Old English *ōwef,* from *ō-,* perhaps from ON, + *wef* WEB (see WEAVE); modern form influenced by WARP]

woof[2] (wʊf) *interj.* **1.** an imitation of the bark or growl of a dog. ~*vb.* **2.** (*intr.*) (of dogs) to bark or growl.

woofer ('wuːfə) *n.* a loudspeaker used in high-fidelity systems for the reproduction of low audio frequencies.

wool (wʊl) *n.* **1.** the outer coat of sheep, yaks, etc., which consists of short curly hairs. **2.** yarn spun from the coat of sheep, etc., used in weaving, knitting, etc. **3. a.** cloth or a garment made from this yarn. **b.** (*as modifier*): *a wool dress.* **4.** any of certain fibrous materials: *glass wool; steel wool.* **5.** *Informal.* short thick curly hair. **6.** a tangled mass of soft fine hairs that occurs in certain plants. **7. dyed in the wool.** confirmed in one's beliefs or opinions. **8. lose** (*or* **keep**) **one's wool.** *Brit. informal.* to lose (or keep) one's temper. **9. pull the wool over someone's eyes.** to deceive or delude someone. [Old English *wull;* related to Old Frisian, Middle Dutch *wulle,* Old High German *wolla* (German *Wolle*), Old Norse *ull,* Latin *lāna* and *vellus* fleece] —'**wool-,like** *adj.*

wool bale *n. Austral. and N.Z.* a standard-sized jute, flax, etc., cubical container of compressed wool weighing over 100 kg when containing fleece or lamb's wool and weighing 204 kg when containing oddments.

wool cheque *n. N.Z.* the annual return for a sheep farmer.

wool classing *n. Austral. and N.Z.* the grading and grouping together of similar types of wool.

wool clip *n.* the total amount of wool shorn from a particular flock, or from flocks in a particular region or country, in one year.

wool fat *or* **grease** *n.* another name for **lanolin.**

woolfell ('wʊl,fɛl) *n. Obsolete.* the skin of a sheep or similar animal with the fleece still attached.

woolgathering ('wʊl,gæðərɪŋ) *n.* idle or absent-minded indulgence in fantasy; daydreaming. —'**wool,gatherer** *n.*

woolgrower ('wʊl,grəʊə) *n.* a person who keeps sheep for their wool. —'**wool,growing** *n., adj.*

woolled (wʊld) *adj.* **1.** (of animals) having wool. **2.** having wool as specified: *coarse-woolled.*

woollen *or U.S.* **woolen** ('wʊlən) *adj.* **1.** relating to or consisting partly or wholly of wool. ~*n.* **2.** (*often pl.*) a garment or piece of cloth made wholly or partly of wool, esp. a knitted one.

woolly *or U.S.* (*often*) **wooly** ('wʊlɪ) *adj.* **woollier, woolliest.** **1.** consisting of, resembling, or having the nature of wool. **2.** covered or clothed in wool or something resembling it. **3.** lacking clarity or substance: *woolly thinking.* **4.** *Botany.* covered with long soft whitish hairs: *woolly stems.* **5.** *U.S.* recalling the rough and lawless period of the early West of America (esp. in the phrase **wild and woolly**). ~*n., pl.* **-lies.** **6.** (*often pl.*) a garment, such as a sweater, made of wool or something similar. **7.** *Western U.S. and Austral.* (*usually pl.*) a slang word for **sheep.** —'**woollily** *adv.* —'**woolliness** *n.*

woolly bear *n.* the caterpillar of any of various tiger moths, esp. *Arctia caja* of Europe and *Isia isabella* of North America, having a dense covering of soft hairs.

woollybutt ('wʊlɪ,bʌt) *n. Austral.* any of several eucalyptus trees, esp. *Eucalyptus longifolia,* having loose fibrous bark around the base of the trunk.

woolly-minded *adj.* showing a vague, ill-defined, or muddled way of thinking.

woolpack ('wʊl,pæk) *n.* **1.** the cloth or canvas wrapping used to pack a bale of wool. **2.** a bale of wool.

woolsack ('wʊl,sæk) *n.* **1.** a sack containing or intended to contain wool. **2.** (in Britain) the seat of the Lord Chancellor in the House of Lords, formerly made of a large square sack of wool.

woolshed ('wʊl,ʃɛd) *n. Austral. and N.Z.* a shearing shed.

wool-sorter's disease *n.* another name for **anthrax.**

wool stapler *n.* a person who sorts wool into different grades or classifications. —'**wool-,stapling** *n., adj.*

wool store *n. Austral. and N.Z.* a building where bales of wool are stored and made available to prospective buyers for inspection.

wool table *n. N.Z.* a slatted wooden table in a shearing shed where fleeces are skirted and classed.

woomera *or* **womera** ('wʊmərə) *n. Austral.* a type of notched stick used by Australian Aborigines to increase leverage and propulsion in the throwing of a spear. [from a native Australian language]

Woop Woop ('wuːp ,wuːp) *n. Austral. slang.* a jocular name for any backward or remote town or district.

woorali (wʊ'rɑːlɪ) *n.* a less common name for **curare.** [C18: from the native S American name]

woosh (wʊʃ) *n., vb.* a variant spelling of **whoosh.**

woozy ('wuːzɪ) *adj.* **woozier, wooziest.** *Informal.* **1.** dazed or confused. **2.** experiencing dizziness, nausea, etc. [C19: perhaps from a blend of *woolly* + *muzzy* or *dizzy*] —'**woozily** *adv.* —'**wooziness** *n.*

wop[1] (wɒp) *n. Slang, derogatory.* a member of a Latin people, esp. an Italian. [C20: probably from southern Italian dialect *guappo* dandy, braggart, from Spanish *guapo*]

wop[2] (wɒp) *vb.* **wops, wopping, wopped,** *n.* a variant spelling of **whop.**

wop-wops ('wɒp,wɒps) *n.* (*functioning as pl. or sing.*) **the.** *N.Z. informal.* the backblocks, the back of beyond.

Worcester china *or* **porcelain** ('wʊstə) *n.* porcelain articles made in Worcester, central England, from 1751 in a factory that became, in 1862, the Royal Worcester Porcelain Company. Sometimes shortened to **Worcester.**

Worcester sauce *or* **Worcestershire sauce** *n.* a commercially prepared piquant sauce, made from a basis of soy sauce, with vinegar, spices, etc.

Worcs *abbrev. for* Worcestershire.

word (wɜːd) *n.* **1.** one of the units of speech or writing that native speakers of a language usually regard as the smallest isolable meaningful element of the language, although linguists would analyse these further into morphemes. **2.** an instance of vocal intercourse; chat, talk, or discussion: *to have a word with someone.* **3.** an utterance or expression, esp. a brief one: *a word of greeting.* **4.** news or information: *he sent word that he would be late.* **5.** a verbal signal for action; command: *when I give the word, fire!* **6.** an undertaking or promise: *I give you my word; he kept his word.* **7.** an autocratic decree or utterance; order: *his word must be obeyed.* **8.** a watchword or slogan, as of a political party: *the word now is "freedom".* **9.** *Computer technol.* a set of bits used to store, transmit, or operate upon an item of information in a computer, such as a program instruction. **10. as good as one's word.** doing what one has undertaken or promised to do. **11. at a word.** at once. **12. by word of mouth.** orally rather than by written means. **13. in a word.** briefly or in short. **14. my word! a.** an exclamation of surprise, annoyance, etc. **b.** *Austral.* an exclamation of agreement. **15. of one's word.** given to or noted for keeping one's promises: *I am a man of my word.* **16. put in a word** *or* **good word for.** to make favourable mention of (someone); recommend. **17. take someone at his** *or* **her word.** to assume that someone means, or will do, what he or she says: *when he told her to go, she took him at his word and left.* **18. take someone's word for it.** to accept or believe what someone says. **19. the last word. a.** the closing remark of a conversation or argument, esp. a remark that supposedly settles an issue. **b.** the latest or most fashionable design, make, or model: *the last word in bikinis.* **c.** the finest example (of some quality, condition, etc.); *the last word in luxury.* **20. the word.** the proper or most fitting expression: *cold is not the word for it, it's freezing!* **21. upon my word! a.** *Archaic.* on my honour. **b.** an exclamation of surprise, annoyance, etc. **22. word for word.**

a. (of a report, transcription, etc.) using exactly the same words as those employed in the situation being reported; verbatim. **b.** translated by substituting each word in the new text for each corresponding word in the original rather than by general sense. **23. word of honour.** a promise; oath. **24.** (*modifier*) of, relating to, or consisting of words: *a word list.* ~*vb.* **25.** (*tr.*) to state in words, usually specially selected ones; phrase. **26.** (*tr.; often foll. by up*) *Austral. informal.* to inform or advise (a person). ~See also **words.** [Old English *word;* related to Old High German *wort,* Old Norse *orth,* Gothic *waurd,* Latin *verbum,* Sanskrit *vratá* command]

Word (wɜːd) *n.* **the. 1.** *Christianity.* the 2nd person of the Trinity. **2.** Scripture, the Bible, or the Gospels as embodying or representing divine revelation. Often called: **the Word of God.** [translation of Greek *logos,* as in John 1:1]

wordage (ˈwɜːdɪdʒ) *n.* words considered collectively, esp. a quantity of words.

word association *n.* an early method of psychoanalysis in which the patient thinks of the first word that comes into consciousness on hearing a given word. In this way it was claimed that aspects of the unconscious could be revealed before defence mechanisms intervene.

word blindness *n.* the nontechnical name for **alexia** and **dyslexia.** —ˈ**word-ˌblind** *adj.*

wordbook (ˈwɜːdˌbʊk) *n.* **1.** a book containing words, usually with their meanings. **2.** a libretto for an opera.

wordbreak (ˈwɜːdˌbreɪk) *n. Printing.* the point at which a word is divided when it runs over from one line of print to the next.

word class *n. Linguistics.* a form class in which the members are words. See **part of speech.**

word deafness *n.* loss of ability to understand spoken words, esp. as the result of a cerebral lesion. Also called: **auditory aphasia.** —ˈ**word-ˌdeaf** *adj.*

word game *n.* any game involving the formation, discovery, or alteration of a word or words.

wording (ˈwɜːdɪŋ) *n.* **1.** the way in which words are used to express a statement, report, etc., esp. a written one. **2.** the words themselves, as used in a written statement or a sign.

wordless (ˈwɜːdlɪs) *adj.* **1.** inarticulate or silent. **2.** *Music.* of or relating to vocal music that is not provided with an articulated text: *a wordless chorus.* —ˈ**wordlessly** *adv.* —ˈ**wordlessness** *n.*

word order *n.* the arrangement of words in a phrase, clause, or sentence. In many languages, including English, word order plays an important part in determining meanings expressed in other languages by inflections.

word-perfect *or U.S.* **letter-perfect** *adj.* **1.** correct in every detail. **2.** (of a speech, part in a play, etc.) memorized perfectly. **3.** (of a speaker, actor, etc.) knowing one's speech, role, etc., perfectly.

word picture *n.* a verbal description, esp. a vivid one.

wordplay (ˈwɜːdˌpleɪ) *n.* verbal wit based on the meanings and ambiguities of words; puns, clever repartee, etc.

word processing *n.* the storage and organization of written text by electronic means, esp. for business purposes.

word processor *n.* an installation for word processing, typically consisting of a keyboard and a VDU incorporating a microprocessor, with storage and processing capabilities.

words (wɜːdz) *pl. n.* **1.** the text of a part of an actor, etc. **2.** the text or lyrics of a song, as opposed to the music. **3.** angry speech (esp. in the phrase **have words with someone**). **4. eat one's words.** to retract a statement. **5. for words.** (preceded by *too* and an adj. or adv.) indescribably; extremely: *the play was too funny for words.* **6. have no words for.** to be incapable of describing. **7. in other words.** expressing the same idea but differently. **8. in so many words.** explicitly or precisely. **9. of many** (*or* **few**) **words.** (not) talkative. **10. put into words.** to express in speech or writing as well as thought. **11. say a few words.** to give a brief speech. **12. take the words out of one's** (*or* **someone's**) **mouth.** to say exactly what someone else was about to say. **13. words fail me.** I am too happy, sad, amazed, etc., to express my thoughts.

wordsmith (ˈwɜːdˌsmɪθ) *n.* a person skilled in using words.

word square *n.* a puzzle in which the player must fill a square grid with words that read the same across as down.

word stress *n.* the stress accent on the syllables of individual words either in a sentence or in isolation.

Wordsworthian (ˌwɜːdzˈwɜːðɪən) *adj.* **1.** of, relating to, or characteristic of the British poet William Wordsworth (1770–1850) or his works. ~*n.* **2.** a student of or specialist in Wordsworth's works.

word wrapping *n. Computer technol.* the automatic shifting of a word at the end of a line to a new line in order to keep within preset margins.

wordy (ˈwɜːdɪ) *adj.* **wordier, wordiest. 1.** using, inclined to use, or containing an excess of words: *a wordy writer; a wordy document.* **2.** of the nature of or relating to words; verbal. —ˈ**wordily** *adv.* —ˈ**wordiness** *n.*

wore (wɔː) *vb.* the past tense of **wear.**

work (wɜːk) *n.* **1.** physical or mental effort directed towards doing or making something. **2.** paid employment at a job or a trade, occupation, or profession. **3.** a duty, task, or undertaking. **4.** something done, made, etc., as a result of effort or exertion: *a work of art.* **5.** materials or tasks on which to expend effort or exertion. **6.** another word for **workmanship** (sense 3). **7.** the place, office, etc., where a person is employed. **8.** any piece of material that is undergoing a manufacturing operation or process; workpiece. **9. a.** decoration or ornamentation, esp. of a specified kind. **b.** (in combination): *wirework; woolwork.* **10.** an engineering structure such as a bridge, building, etc. **11.** *Physics.* the transfer of energy expressed as the product of a force and the distance through which its point of application moves in the direction of the force. Abbrevs.: *W, w* **12.** a structure, wall, etc., built or used as part of a fortification system. **13. at work. a.** at one's job or place of employment. **b.** in action; operating. **14. make short work of.** *Informal.* to handle or dispose of very quickly. **15.** (*modifier*) of, relating to, or used for work: *work clothes; a work permit.* ~*vb.* **16.** (*intr.*) to exert effort in order to do, make, or perform something. **17.** (*intr.*) to be employed. **18.** (*tr.*) to carry on operations, activity, etc., in (a place or area): *that salesman works the southern region.* **19.** (*tr.*) to cause to labour or toil: *he works his men hard.* **20.** to operate or cause to operate, esp. properly or effectively: *to work a lathe; that clock doesn't work.* **21.** (*tr.*) to till or cultivate (land). **22.** to handle or manipulate or be handled or manipulated: *to work dough.* **23.** to shape, form, or process or be shaped, formed, or processed: *to work copper.* **24.** to reach or cause to reach a specific condition, esp. gradually: *the rope worked loose.* **25.** (*tr.*) *Chiefly U.S. and Canadian.* to solve (a mathematical problem). **26.** (*intr.*) to move in agitation: *his face worked with anger.* **27.** (*tr.; often foll. by up*) to provoke or arouse: *to work someone into a frenzy.* **28.** (*tr.*) to effect or accomplish: *to work one's revenge.* **29.** to make (one's way) with effort: *he worked his way through the crowd.* **30.** (*tr.*) to make or decorate by hand in embroidery, tapestry, etc.: *she was working a sampler.* **31.** (*intr.*) (of a mechanism) to move in a loose or otherwise imperfect fashion. **32.** (*intr.*) (of liquids) to ferment, as in brewing. **33.** (*tr.*) *Informal.* to manipulate or exploit to one's own advantage. **34.** (*tr.*) *Slang.* to cheat or swindle. ~See also **work back, work in, work off, work on, work out, work over, works, work up.** [Old English *weorc* (n.), *wircan, wyrcan* (vb.); related to Old High German *wurchen,* German *wirken,* Old Norse *yrkja,* Gothic *waurkjan*] —ˈ**workless** *adj.* —ˈ**worklessness** *n.*

workable (ˈwɜːkəbᵊl) *adj.* **1.** practicable or feasible. **2.** able to be worked. —ˌ**workaˈbility** *or* ˈ**workableness** *n.*

workaday (ˈwɜːkəˌdeɪ) *adj.* (*usually prenominal*) **1.** being a part of general human experience; ordinary. **2.** suitable for working days; everyday or practical.

workaholic (ˌwɜːkəˈhɒlɪk) *n.* a person obsessively addicted to work. [C20: from WORK + -HOLIC, coined in 1971 by Wayne Oates, U.S. author]

work back *vb.* (*intr., adv.*) *Austral. informal.* to work overtime.

workbag (ˈwɜːkˌbæg) *n.* a container for implements, tools, or materials, esp. sewing equipment. Also called: **work basket, workbox.**

workbench (ˈwɜːkˌbɛntʃ) *n.* a heavy table at which work is done by a carpenter, mechanic, toolmaker, etc.

workbook (ˈwɜːkˌbʊk) *n.* **1.** an exercise book or textbook used for study, esp. a textbook with spaces for answers. **2.** a book of instructions for some process. **3.** a book in which is recorded all work done or planned.

work camp *n.* a camp set up for young people who voluntarily do manual work on a worthwhile project.

workday (ˈwɜːkˌdeɪ) *n.* **1.** the usual U.S. term for **working day.** ~*adj.* **2.** another word for **workaday.**

worked (wɜːkt) *adj.* made or decorated with evidence of workmanship; wrought, as with embroidery or tracery.

worked up *adj.* agitated or excited.

worker (ˈwɜːkə) *n.* **1.** a person or thing that works, usually at a specific job: *a good worker; a research worker.* **2.** an employee in an organization, as opposed to an employer or manager. **3.** a manual labourer or other employee working in a manufacturing or other industry. **4.** any other member of the working class. **5.** a sterile female member of a colony of bees, ants, or wasps that forages for food, cares for the larvae, etc. —ˈ**workerless** *adj.*

worker director *n.* a worker elected to the governing board of a business concern to represent the interests of the employees in decision making.

worker participation *n.* a process by which subordinate employees, either individually or collectively, become involved in one or more aspects of organizational decision making within the enterprises in which they work.

worker-priest *n.* a Roman Catholic priest who has full-time or part-time employment in a secular job to be more closely in touch with the problems of the laity.

workers' cooperative *n.* See **cooperative** (sense 4).

work ethic *n.* a belief in the moral value of work (often in the phrase **Protestant work ethic**).

workfare (ˈwɜːkˌfɛə) *n.* a scheme under which the government of a country requires unemployed people to do community work or undergo job training in return for social-security payments. [C20: from WORK + (WEL)FARE]

workfolk (ˈwɜːkˌfəʊk) *or U.S.* (*informal*) **workfolks** *pl. n.* working people, esp. labourers on a farm.

workforce (ˈwɜːkˌfɔːs) *n.* **1.** the total number of workers employed by a company on a specific job, project, etc. **2.** the total

number of people who could be employed: *the country's workforce is growing rapidly.*
work function *n.* **1.** *Physics.* the minimum energy required to transfer an electron from a point within a solid to a point just outside its surface. Symbol: ϕ or Φ **2.** *Thermodynamics.* another name (not now used because of confusion with sense 1) for **Helmholtz function.**
work-harden *vb.* (*tr.*) to increase the strength or hardness of (a metal) by a mechanical process, such as tension, compression, or torsion. —ˈ**work-ˌhardening** *n.*
workhorse (ˈwɜːkˌhɔːs) *n.* **1.** a horse used for nonrecreational activities. **2.** *Informal.* a person who takes on the greatest amount of work in a project or job.
workhouse (ˈwɜːkˌhaʊs) *n.* **1.** (formerly in England) an institution maintained at public expense where able-bodied paupers did unpaid work in return for food and accommodation. **2.** (in the U.S.) a prison for petty offenders serving short sentences at manual labour.
work in *vb.* (*adv.*) **1.** to insert or become inserted: *she worked the patch in carefully.* **2.** (*tr.*) to find space for: *I'll work this job in during the day.* ~*n.* **work-in. 3.** a form of industrial action in which a factory that is to be closed down is occupied and run by its workers.
working (ˈwɜːkɪŋ) *n.* **1.** the operation or mode of operation of something. **2.** the act or process of moulding something pliable. **3.** a convulsive or jerking motion, as from excitement. **4.** (*often pl.*) a part of a mine or quarry that is being or has been worked. **5.** (*pl.*) the whole system of excavations in a mine. **6.** a record of the steps by which the result of a calculation or the solution of a problem is obtained: *all working is to be submitted to the examiners.* **7.** *Rare.* slow advance against or as if against resistance. ~*adj.* (*prenominal*) **8.** relating to or concerned with a person or thing that works: *a working man.* **9.** concerned with, used in, or suitable for work: *working clothes.* **10.** (of a meal or occasion) during which business discussions are carried on: *working lunch; working breakfast.* **11.** capable of being operated or used: *a working model.* **12.** sufficiently large or accurate to be useful or to accomplish a desired end: *a working majority; a working knowledge of German.* **13.** (of a theory, etc.) providing a basis, usually a temporary one, on which operations or procedures may be carried out.
working bee *n. N.Z.* a voluntary group doing a job for charity.
working capital *n.* **1.** *Accounting.* current assets minus current liabilities. **2.** current or liquid assets. **3.** that part of the capital of a business enterprise available for operations.
working class *n.* **1.** Also called: **proletariat.** the social stratum, usually of low status, that consists of those who earn wages, esp. as manual workers. Compare **lower class, middle class, upper class.** ~*adj.* **working-class. 2.** of, relating to, or characteristic of the working class.
working day *or esp. U.S.* **workday** *n.* **1.** a day on which work is done, esp. for an agreed or stipulated number of hours in return for a salary or wage. **2.** the part of the day allocated to work: *a seven-hour working day.* **3.** (*often pl.*) *Commerce.* any day of the week except Sunday, public holidays, and, in some cases, Saturday.
working dog *n.* a dog of suitable breed or training kept for its practical use, such as herding sheep, rather than as a pet or for showing.
working drawing *n.* a scale drawing of a part or assembly that provides a guide for manufacture.
working memory *n. Psychol.* the current contents of consciousness.
working papers *pl. n.* **1.** papers or notes showing the intermediate stages of a proposal, solution, etc., arrived at or being worked on. **2.** legal documents that certain people in some countries must possess to be allowed to work.
working party *n.* **1.** a committee established to investigate a problem, question, etc. **2.** a group of soldiers or prisoners assigned to perform some manual task or duty.
working substance *or* **fluid** *n.* the fluid, esp. water, steam, or compressed air, that operates an engine, etc.
working week *or esp. U.S. and Canadian* **workweek** (ˈwɜːkˌwiːk) *n.* the number of hours or days in a week actually or officially allocated to work: *a four-day working week.*
work-in-progress *n. Book-keeping.* the value of work begun but not completed, as shown in a profit-and-loss account.
workload (ˈwɜːkˌləʊd) *n.* the amount of work to be done, esp. in a specified period by a person, machine, etc.
workman (ˈwɜːkmən) *n., pl.* **-men. 1.** a man who is employed in manual labour or who works an industrial machine. **2.** a craftsman of skill as specified: *a bad workman.*
workmanlike (ˈwɜːkmənˌlaɪk) *or* (*less commonly*) **workmanly** (ˈwɜːkmənlɪ) *adj.* appropriate to or befitting a good workman.
workmanship (ˈwɜːkmənʃɪp) *n.* **1.** the art or skill of a workman. **2.** the art or skill with which something is made or executed. **3.** the degree of art or skill exhibited in the finished product. **4.** the piece of work so produced.
workmate (ˈwɜːkˌmeɪt) *n.* a person who works with another; fellow worker.
workmen's compensation *n.* compensation for death, injury, or accident suffered by a workman in the course of his employment and paid to him or his dependents.
work of art *n.* **1.** a piece of fine art, such as a painting or sculpture. **2.** something that may be likened to a piece of fine art, esp. in beauty, intricacy, etc.
work off *vb.* (*tr., adv.*) **1.** to get rid of or dissipate, as by effort: *he worked off some of his energy by digging the garden.* **2.** to discharge (a debt) by labour rather than payment.
work on *vb.* (*intr., prep.*) to persuade or influence or attempt to persuade or influence.
work out *vb.* (*adv.*) **1.** (*tr.*) to achieve or accomplish by effort. **2.** (*tr.*) to solve or find out by reasoning or calculation: *to work out an answer; to work out a sum.* **3.** (*tr.*) to devise or formulate: *to work out a plan.* **4.** (*intr.*) to prove satisfactory or effective: *did your plan work out?* **5.** (*intr.*) to happen as specified: *it all worked out well.* **6.** (*intr.*) to take part in physical exercise, as in training. **7.** (*tr.*) to remove all the mineral in (a mine, body of ore, etc.) that can be profitably exploited. **8.** (*intr.*; often foll. by *to* or *at*) to reach a total: *your bill works out at a pound.* **9.** (*tr.*) *Informal.* to understand the real nature of: *I shall never work you out.* ~*n.* **work-out. 10.** a session of physical exercise, esp. for training or practice.
work over *vb.* **1.** (*tr., adv.*) to do again; repeat. **2.** (*intr., prep.*) to examine closely and thoroughly. **3.** (*tr., adv.*) *Slang.* to assault or thrash.
workpeople (ˈwɜːkˌpiːpᵊl) *pl. n.* the working members of a population, esp. those employed in manual tasks.
workpiece (ˈwɜːkˌpiːs) *n.* a piece of metal or other material that is in the process of being worked on or made or has actually been cut or shaped by a hand tool or machine.
workplace (ˈwɜːkˌpleɪs) *n.* a place, such as a factory or office, where people work.
workroom (ˈwɜːkˌruːm, -ˌrʊm) *n.* **1.** a room in which work, usually manual labour, is done. **2.** a room in a house set aside for a hobby, such as sewing.
works (wɜːks) *pl. n.* **1.** (*often functioning as sing.*) a place where a number of people are employed, such as a factory. **2.** the sum total of a writer's or artist's achievements, esp. when considered together: *the works of Shakespeare.* **3.** the deeds of a person, esp. virtuous or moral deeds performed as religious acts: *works of charity.* **4.** the interior parts of the mechanism of a machine, etc.: *the works of a clock.* **5. in the works.** *Informal.* in preparation. **6. spanner in the works.** See **spanner** (sense 2). **7. the works.** *Slang.* **a.** full or extreme treatment. **b.** a very violent physical beating: *to give someone the works.* **8.** *Slang.* a syringe. **9.** (*modifier*) of or denoting a racing car, etc., that is officially entered by a manufacturer in an event: *a works entry.*
works council *n. Chiefly Brit.* **1.** a council composed of both employer and employees convened to discuss matters of common interest concerning a factory, plant, business policy, etc., not covered by regular trade union agreements. **2.** a body representing the workers of a plant, factory, etc., elected to negotiate with the management about working conditions, wages, etc. ~Also called: **works committee.**
work-sharing *n.* an arrangement whereby one full-time job may be carried out by two people working part time. —ˈ**work-ˌsharer** *n.*
work sheet *n.* **1.** a sheet of paper used for the preliminary or rough draft of a problem, design, etc. **2.** a piece of paper recording work being planned or already in progress.
workshop (ˈwɜːkˌʃɒp) *n.* **1.** a room or building in which manufacturing or other forms of manual work are carried on. **2.** a room in a private dwelling, school, etc., set aside for crafts. **3.** a group of people engaged in study or work on a creative project or subject: *a music workshop.*
workshy (ˈwɜːkˌʃaɪ) *adj.* not inclined to work.
work station *n.* **1.** an area in an office where one person works. **2.** *Computer technol.* a device or component of an electronic office system consisting of a display screen and keyboard used to handle electronic office work.
work-study *n.* an examination of ways of finding the most efficient method of doing a job, esp. in terms of time and effort.
worktable (ˈwɜːkˌteɪbᵊl) *n.* **a.** any table at which writing, sewing, or other work may be done. **b.** (in English cabinetwork) a small elegant table fitted with sewing accessories.
work through *vb.* (*tr., adv.*) *Psychol.* to resolve (a problem, esp. an emotional one), by thinking about it repeatedly and hence lessening its intensity either by gaining insight or by becoming bored by it.
worktop (ˈwɜːkˌtɒp) *n.* a surface in a kitchen, often made of heat-resistant laminated plastic, that is used for food preparation.
work-to-rule *n.* **1.** a form of industrial action in which employees adhere strictly to all the working rules laid down by their employers, with the deliberate intention of reducing the rate of working. ~*vb.* **work to rule. 2.** (*intr.*) to decrease the rate of working by this means.
work up *vb.* (*tr., mainly adv.*) **1.** to arouse the feelings of; excite. **2.** to cause to grow or develop: *to work up a hunger.* **3.** (*also prep.*) to move or cause to move gradually upwards. **4.** to manipulate or mix into a specified object or shape. **5.** to gain knowledge of or skill at (a subject).
workwear (ˈwɜːkˌwɛə) *n.* clothes, such as overalls, as worn for work in a factory, shop, etc.; working clothes.
workweek (ˈwɜːkˌwiːk) *n.* the usual U.S. and Canadian term for **working week.**

world (wɜːld) *n.* **1.** the earth as a planet, esp. including its inhabitants. **2.** mankind; the human race. **3.** people generally; the public: *in the eyes of the world.* **4.** social or public life: *to go out into the world.* **5.** the universe or cosmos; everything in existence. **6.** a complex united whole regarded as resembling the universe. **7.** any star or planet, esp. one that might be inhabited. **8.** (*often cap.*) a division or section of the earth, its history, or its inhabitants: *the Western World; the Ancient World; the Third World.* **9.** an area, sphere, or realm considered as a complete environment: *the animal world.* **10.** any field of human activity or way of life or those involved in it: *the world of television.* **11.** a period or state of existence: *the next world.* **12.** the total circumstances and experience of an individual that make up his life, esp. that part of it relating to happiness: *you have shattered my world.* **13.** a large amount, number, or distance: *worlds apart.* **14.** worldly or secular life, ways, or people. **15.** *Logic.* See **possible world.** **16. all the world and his wife.** a large group of people of various kinds. **17. bring into the world. a.** (of a midwife, doctor, etc.) to deliver (a baby). **b.** to give birth to. **18. come into the world.** to be born. **19. dead to the world.** *Informal.* unaware of one's surroundings, esp. fast asleep or very drunk. **20. for the world.** (*used with a negative*) for any inducement, however great. **21. for all the world.** in every way; exactly. **22. give to the world.** to publish. **23. in the world.** (intensifier; *usually used with a negative*): *no-one in the world can change things.* **24. man** (*or* **woman**) **of the world.** a man (or woman) experienced in social or public life. **25. not long for this world.** nearing death. **26. on top of the world.** *Informal.* exultant, elated, or very happy. **27. out of this world.** *Informal.* wonderful; excellent. **28. set the world on fire.** to be exceptionally or sensationally successful. **29. the best of both worlds.** the benefits from two different or opposed ways of life, philosophies, etc. **30. think the world of.** to be extremely fond of or hold in very high esteem. **31. world of one's own.** a state of mental detachment from other people. **32. world without end.** for ever. **33.** (*modifier*) of or concerning most or all countries; worldwide: *world politics; a world record.* **34.** (*in combination*) throughout the world: *world-famous.* [Old English *w(e)orold,* from *wer* man + *ald* age, life; related to Old Frisian *warld, wrald,* Old Norse *verold,* Old High German *wealt* (German *Welt*)]

world-beater *n.* a person or thing that surpasses all others in its category; champion. —ˈ**world-ˌbeating** *n., adj.*

world-class *adj.* of or denoting someone with a skill or attribute that puts him or her in the highest class in the world: *a world-class swimmer.*

World Cup *n.* an international association football championship competition held between national teams selected through preliminary tournaments. It has been held in different countries every four years since 1930, except during World War II.

world language *n.* **1.** a language spoken and known in many countries, such as English. **2.** an artificial language for international use, such as Esperanto.

world-line *n. Physics.* a line on a space–time path that shows the path of a body.

worldling (ˈwɜːldlɪŋ) *n.* a person who is primarily concerned with worldly matters or material things.

worldly (ˈwɜːldlɪ) *adj.* **-lier, -liest. 1.** not spiritual; mundane or temporal. **2.** Also: **worldly-minded.** absorbed in or concerned with material things or matters that are immediately relevant. **3.** Also: **worldly-wise.** versed in the ways of the world; sophisticated. **4.** *Archaic.* existing on or relating to the earth. **5.** *Obsolete.* secular; lay. ~*adv.* **6.** *Archaic.* in a worldly manner. —ˈ**worldliness** *n.*

world music *n.* popular music of various ethnic origins and styles outside the tradition of Western pop and rock music.

world power *n.* a state that possesses sufficient power to influence events throughout the world.

World Series *or* **World's Series** *n. Baseball.* (in the U.S.) a best-of-seven playoff for the world championship between the two winning teams in the major leagues at the end of the season.

world-shaking *adj.* of enormous significance; momentous.

world-view *n.* another word for **Weltanschauung.**

world-weary *adj.* no longer finding pleasure in living; tired of the world. —ˈ**world-ˌweariness** *n.*

worldwide (ˈwɜːldˈwaɪd) *adj.* applying or extending throughout the world; universal.

worm (wɜːm) *n.* **1.** any of various invertebrates, esp. the annelids (earthworms, etc.), nematodes (roundworms), and flatworms, having a slender elongated body. **2.** any of various insect larvae having an elongated body, such as the silkworm and wireworm. **3.** any of various unrelated animals that resemble annelids, nematodes, etc., such as the glow-worm and shipworm. **4.** a gnawing or insinuating force or agent that torments or slowly eats away. **5.** a wretched or spineless person. **6.** anything that resembles a worm in appearance or movement. **7.** a shaft on which a helical groove has been cut, as in a gear arrangement in which such a shaft meshes with a toothed wheel. **8.** a spiral pipe cooled by air or flowing water, used as a condenser in a still. **9.** a nontechnical name for **lytta. 10.** *Anatomy.* any wormlike organ, structure, or part, such as the middle lobe of the cerebellum (*vermis cerebelli*). Technical name: **vermis. 11.** *Computer technol.* a program that duplicates itself many times and prevents its destruction. It often carries a logic bomb or virus. ~*vb.* **12.** to move, act, or cause to move or act with the slow sinuous movement of a worm. **13.** (foll. by *in, into, out of,* etc.) to make (one's way) slowly and stealthily; insinuate (oneself). **14.** (*tr.;* often foll. by *out of* or *from*) to extract (information, a secret, etc.) from by persistent questioning. **15.** (*tr.*) to free from or purge of worms. **16.** (*tr.*) *Nautical.* to wind yarn around (a rope) so as to fill the spaces between the strands and render the surface smooth for parcelling and serving. ~See also **worms.** [Old English *wyrm;* related to Old Frisian *wirm,* Old High German *wurm,* Old Norse *ormr,* Gothic *waurms,* Latin *vermis,* Greek *romos* woodworm] —ˈ**wormer** *n.* —ˈ**wormˌlike** *or* ˈ**wormish** *adj.*

WORM (wɜːm) *n. Computers. acronym for* write once read many times: an optical disk that enables users to store their own data.

wormcast (ˈwɜːmˌkɑːst) *n.* a coil of earth or sand that has been egested by a burrowing earthworm or lugworm.

worm conveyor *n.* another name for **screw conveyor.**

worm-eaten *adj.* **1.** eaten into by worms: *a worm-eaten table.* **2.** decayed; rotten. **3.** old-fashioned; antiquated.

wormery (ˈwɜːmərɪ) *n., pl.* **-eries. 1.** a piece of apparatus, having a glass side or sides, in which worms are kept for study. **2.** a container in which worms are kept and bred, esp. for fishing bait.

wormfly (ˈwɜːmˌflaɪ) *n. Angling.* a type of lure dressed on a double hook, the barbs of which sit one above the other and back-to-back.

worm gear *n.* **1.** a device consisting of a threaded shaft (**worm**) that mates with a gearwheel (**worm wheel**) so that rotary motion can be transferred between two shafts at right angles to each other. **2.** Also called: **worm wheel.** a gearwheel driven by a threaded shaft or worm.

wormhole (ˈwɜːmˌhəʊl) *n.* **1.** a hole made by a worm in timber, plants, etc. **2.** *Physics.* a tunnel in the geometry of space–time postulated to connect different parts of the universe. —ˈ**wormˌholed** *adj.*

worm lizard *n.* any wormlike burrowing legless lizard of the family *Amphisbaenidae,* of Africa, South and Central America, and S Europe.

worms (wɜːmz) *n.* (*functioning as sing.*) any disease or disorder, usually of the intestine, characterized by infestation with parasitic worms.

wormseed (ˈwɜːmˌsiːd) *n.* **1.** any of various plants having seeds or other parts used in medicine to treat worm infestation, esp. an American chenopodiaceous plant, *Chenopodium anthelminticum* (or *C. ambrosioides*) (**American wormseed**), and the santonica plant. **2.** the part of any of these plants that is used as an anthelmintic.

worm's eye view *n.* a view seen from below or from a more lowly or humble point.

wormwood (ˈwɜːmˌwʊd) *n.* **1.** Also called: **absinthe.** any of various plants of the chiefly N temperate genus *Artemisia,* esp. *A. absinthium,* a European plant yielding a bitter extract used in making absinthe: family *Compositae* (composites). **2.** something that embitters, such as a painful experience. [C15: changed (through influence of WORM and WOOD[1]) from Old English *wormōd, wermōd;* related to Old High German *werrnuata,* German *Wermut;* see VERMOUTH]

wormy (ˈwɜːmɪ) *adj.* **wormier, wormiest. 1.** worm-infested or worm-eaten. **2.** resembling a worm in appearance, ways, or condition. **3.** (of wood) having irregular small tunnels bored into it and tracked over its surface, made either by worms or artificially. **4.** low or grovelling. —ˈ**worminess** *n.*

worn (wɔːn) *vb.* **1.** the past participle of **wear.** ~*adj.* **2.** affected, esp. adversely, by long use or action: *a worn suit.* **3.** haggard; drawn. **4.** exhausted; spent. —ˈ**wornness** *n.*

worn-out *adj.* (**worn out** *when postpositive*). **1.** worn or used until threadbare, valueless, or useless. **2.** exhausted; very weary.

worriment (ˈwʌrɪmənt) *n. Informal, chiefly U.S. and Canadian.* anxiety or the trouble that causes it; worry.

worrisome (ˈwʌrɪsəm) *adj.* **1.** causing worry; vexing. **2.** tending to worry. —ˈ**worrisomely** *adv.*

worrit (ˈwʌrɪt) *vb.* (*tr.*) *Dialect.* to tease or worry. [probably variant of WORRY, but compare WHERRIT]

worry (ˈwʌrɪ) *vb.* **-ries, -rying, -ried. 1.** to be or cause to be anxious or uneasy, esp. about something uncertain or potentially dangerous. **2.** (*tr.*) to disturb the peace of mind of; bother: *don't worry me with trivialities.* **3.** (*intr.;* often foll. by *along* or *through*) to proceed despite difficulties. **4.** (*intr.;* often foll. by *away*) to struggle or work: *to worry away at a problem.* **5.** (*tr.*) (of a dog, wolf, etc.) to lacerate or kill by biting, shaking, etc. **6.** (when *intr.,* foll. by *at*) to bite, tear, or gnaw (at) with the teeth: *a dog worrying a bone.* **7.** (*tr.*) to move as specified, esp. by repeated pushes: *they worried the log into the river.* **8.** (*tr.*) to touch or poke repeatedly and idly. **9.** *Obsolete.* to choke or cause to choke. **10. not to worry.** *Informal.* you need not worry. ~*n., pl.* **-ries. 11.** a state or feeling of anxiety. **12.** a person or thing that causes anxiety. **13.** an act of worrying. [Old English *wyrgan;* related to Old Frisian *wergia* to kill, Old High German *wurgen* (German *(er)würgen* to strangle), Old Norse *virgill, urga* rope] —ˈ**worried** *adj.* —ˈ**worriedly** *adv.* —ˈ**worrying** *adj.* —ˈ**worryingly** *adv.*

worry beads *pl. n.* a string of beads that when fingered or played with supposedly relieves nervous tension.

worryguts (ˈwʌrɪˌgʌts) *or* **worrywart** (ˈwʌrɪˌwɔːt) *n. Informal.* a person who tends to worry, esp. about insignificant matters.

worse (wɜːs) *adj.* 1. the comparative of **bad.** 2. **none the worse for.** not harmed by (adverse events or circumstances). 3. **the worse for wear. a.** shabby or worn. **b.** a slang term for **drunk.** 4. **worse luck!** *Informal.* unhappily; unfortunately. 5. (*postpositive*) **worse off.** in a worse, esp. a worse financial, condition. ~*n.* 6. something that is worse. 7. **for the worse.** into a less desirable or inferior state or condition: *a change for the worse.* 8. **go from bad to worse.** to deteriorate even more. ~*adv.* 9. in a more severe or unpleasant manner. 10. in a less effective or successful manner. [Old English *wiersa;* related to Old Frisian *werra,* Old High German *wirsiro,* Old Norse *verri,* Gothic *wairsiza*]

worsen (ˈwɜːsᵊn) *vb.* to grow or cause to grow worse.

worser (ˈwɜːsə) *adj.* an archaic or nonstandard word for **worse.**

worship (ˈwɜːʃɪp) *vb.* **-ships, -shipping, -shipped** *or U.S.* **-ships, -shiping, -shiped.** 1. (*tr.*) to show profound religious devotion and respect to; adore or venerate (God or any person or thing considered divine). 2. (*tr.*) to be devoted to and full of admiration for. 3. (*intr.*) to have or express feelings of profound adoration. 4. (*intr.*) to attend services for worship. 5. (*tr.*) *Obsolete.* to honour. ~*n.* 6. religious adoration or devotion. 7. the formal expression of religious adoration; rites, prayers, etc. 8. admiring love or devotion. 9. *Archaic.* dignity or standing. [Old English *weorthscipe,* from WORTH + -SHIP] —ˈ**worshipable** *adj.* —ˈ**worshipper** *n.*

Worship (ˈwɜːʃɪp) *n. Chiefly Brit.* (preceded by *Your, His,* or *Her*) a title used to address or refer to a mayor, magistrate, or a person of similar high rank.

worshipful (ˈwɜːʃɪpfʊl) *adj.* 1. feeling or showing reverence or adoration. 2. (*often cap.*) *Chiefly Brit.* a title used to address or refer to various people or bodies of distinguished rank, such as mayors and certain ancient companies of the City of London. —ˈ**worshipfully** *adv.* —ˈ**worshipfulness** *n.*

worst (wɜːst) *adj.* 1. the superlative of **bad.** ~*adv.* 2. in the most extreme or bad manner or degree. 3. least well, suitably, or acceptably. 4. (*in combination*) in or to the smallest degree or extent; least: *worst-loved.* ~*n.* 5. **the worst.** the least good or most inferior person, thing, or part in a group, narrative, etc. 6. (often preceded by *at*) the most poor, unpleasant, or unskilled quality or condition: *television is at its worst these days.* 7. the greatest amount of damage or wickedness of which a person or group is capable: *the invaders came and did their worst.* 8. the weakest effort or poorest achievement that a person or group is capable of making: *the applicant did his worst at the test because he did not want the job.* 9. **at worst. a.** in the least favourable interpretation or view. **b.** under the least favourable conditions. 10. **if the worst comes to the worst.** if all the more desirable alternatives become impossible or if the worst possible thing happens. 11. **come off worst** *or* **get the worst of it.** to enjoy the least benefit from an issue or be defeated in it. 12. **give (someone) the worst of it.** to defeat (someone) soundly. ~*vb.* 13. (*tr.*) to get the advantage over; defeat or beat. [Old English *wierrest;* related to Old Frisian *wersta,* Old Saxon, Old High German *wirsisto,* Old Norse *verstr*]

worst case *n.* **a.** a situation in which the most unfavourable conditions prevail. **b.** (*as modifier*): *a worst-case projection of a massive accident.*

worsted (ˈwʊstɪd) *n.* 1. a closely twisted yarn or thread made from combed long-staple wool. 2. a fabric made from this, with a hard smooth close-textured surface and no nap. 3. (*modifier*) made of this yarn or fabric: *a worsted suit.* [C13: named after *Worstead,* a district in Norfolk, E England]

wort (wɜːt) *n.* 1. (*in combination*) any of various unrelated plants, esp. ones formerly used to cure diseases: *liverwort; spleenwort.* 2. the sweet liquid obtained from the soaked mixture of warm water and ground malt, used to make a malt liquor. [Old English *wyrt* root, related to Old High German *warz,* Gothic *waurts* root]

worth[1] (wɜːθ) *adj.* (governing a noun with prepositional force) 1. worthy of; meriting or justifying: *it's not worth discussing; an idea worth some thought.* 2. having a value of: *the book is worth 30 pounds.* 3. **for all one is worth.** to the utmost; to the full extent of one's powers or ability. 4. **worth one's weight in gold.** extremely helpful, kind, etc. ~*n.* 5. high quality; excellence. 6. value, price. 7. the amount or quantity of something of a specified value: *five pounds worth of petrol.* [Old English *weorth;* related to Old Saxon, Old High German *werth* (German *Wert*), Old Norse *verthr,* Gothic *wairths*]

worth[2] (wɜːθ) *vb.* (*intr.*) *Archaic.* to happen or betide (esp. in the phrase **woe worth the day**). [Old English *weorthan;* related to Old Frisian *wertha,* Old Saxon, Old High German *werthan* (German *werden*), Old Norse *vertha,* Gothic *wairthan,* Latin *vertere* to turn]

worthless (ˈwɜːθlɪs) *adj.* 1. without practical value or usefulness. 2. without merit; good-for-nothing. —ˈ**worthlessly** *adv.* —ˈ**worthlessness** *n.*

worthwhile (ˌwɜːθˈwaɪl) *adj.* sufficiently important, rewarding, or valuable to justify time or effort spent.

worthy (ˈwɜːðɪ) *adj.* **-thier, -thiest.** 1. (*postpositive;* often foll. by *of* or an infinitive) having sufficient merit or value (for something or someone specified); deserving. 2. having worth, value, or merit. ~*n., pl.* **-thies.** 3. *Often facetious.* a person of distinguished character, merit, or importance. —ˈ**worthily** *adv.* —ˈ**worthiness** *n.*

wot (wɒt) *vb. Archaic or dialect.* (used with *I, she, he, it,* or a singular noun) a form of the present tense (indicative mood) of **wit**[2].

wotcher (ˈwɒtʃə) *sentence substitute.* a slang term of greeting (esp. in the phrase **wotcher cock!**). [C19: Cockney for *what cheer?*]

would (wʊd; *unstressed* wəd) *vb.* (takes an infinitive without *to* or an implied infinitive) used as an auxiliary: 1. to form the past tense or subjunctive mood of **will**[1]. 2. (with *you, he, she, it, they,* or a noun as subject) to indicate willingness or desire in a polite manner: *would you help me, please?* 3. to describe a past action as being accustomed or habitual: *every day we would go for walks.* 4. I wish: *would that he were here.*

▷**Usage.** See at **should.**

would-be *adj.* (*prenominal*) 1. *Usually derogatory.* wanting or professing to be: *a would-be politician.* 2. intended to be: *would-be generosity.* ~*n.* 3. *Derogatory.* a person who wants or professes to be something that he is not.

wouldn't (ˈwʊdᵊnt) *vb. contraction of* would not.

wouldst (wʊdst) *vb. Archaic or dialect.* (used with the pronoun *thou* or its relative equivalent) a singular form of the past tense of **will.**

Woulfe bottle (wʊlf) *n. Chem.* a bottle with more than one neck, used for passing gases through liquids. [C18: named after Peter *Woulfe* (?1727–1803), British chemist]

wound[1] (wuːnd) *n.* 1. any break in the skin or an organ or part as the result of violence or a surgical incision. 2. an injury to plant tissue. 3. any injury or slight to the feelings or reputation. ~*vb.* 4. to inflict a wound or wounds upon (someone or something). [Old English *wund;* related to Old Frisian *wunde,* Old High German *wunta* (German *Wunde*), Old Norse *und,* Gothic *wunds*] —ˈ**woundable** *adj.* —ˈ**wounder** *n.* —ˈ**wounding** *adj.* —ˈ**woundingly** *adv.* —ˈ**woundless** *adj.*

wound[2] (waʊnd) *vb.* the past tense and past participle of **wind**[2].

wounded (ˈwuːndɪd) *adj.* 1. **a.** suffering from wounds; injured, esp. in a battle or fight. **b.** (*as collective n.;* preceded by *the*): *the wounded.* 2. (of feelings) damaged or hurt.

woundwort (ˈwuːndˌwɜːt) *n.* 1. any of various plants of the genus *Stachys,* such as *S. arvensis* (**field woundwort**), having purple, scarlet, yellow, or white flowers and formerly used for dressing wounds: family *Labiatae* (labiates). 2. any of various other plants used in this way.

wove (wəʊv) *vb.* a past tense of **weave.**

woven (ˈwəʊvᵊn) *vb.* a past participle of **weave.**

wove paper *n.* paper with a very faint mesh impressed on it by the dandy roller on the paper-making machine. Compare **laid paper.**

wow[1] (waʊ) *interj.* 1. an exclamation of admiration, amazement, etc. ~*n.* 2. *Slang.* a person or thing that is amazingly successful, attractive, etc. ~*vb.* 3. (*tr.*) *Slang.* to arouse great enthusiasm in. [C16: originally Scottish, expressive of surprise, amazement, etc.]

wow[2] (waʊ, wəʊ) *n.* a slow variation or distortion in pitch that occurs at very low audio frequencies in sound-reproducing systems, such as a record player, usually due to variation in speed of the turntable, etc. See also **flutter** (sense 14). [C20: of imitative origin]

WOW *abbrev. for* waiting on weather: used esp. in the oil industry.

wowser (ˈwaʊzə) *n. Austral. and N.Z. slang.* 1. a fanatically puritanical person. 2. a teetotaller. [C20: from English dialect *wow* to whine, complain]

WP *abbrev. for:* 1. weather permitting. 2. word processing. 3. word processor.

WPA (in the U.S.) *abbrev. for* Work Projects Administration or Works Progress Administration.

W particle *n. Physics.* a type of elementary particle with either a positive or negative charge considered to transmit the weak interaction between other elementary particles. W particles have a rest mass of about 10^{-25} kg. Also called: **W boson.** See also **Z particle.**

WPB *or* **wpb** *abbrev. for* waste paper basket.

WPC (in Britain) *abbrev. for* woman police constable.

wpm *abbrev. for* words per minute.

WR *abbrev. for* Western Region.

Wraac (ræk) *n.* a member of the Women's Royal Australian Army Corps.

WRAAC *abbrev. for* Women's Royal Australian Army Corps.

WRAAF *abbrev. for* Women's Royal Australian Air Force.

WRAC (in Britain) *abbrev. for* Women's Royal Army Corps.

wrack[1] *or* **rack** (ræk) *n.* 1. collapse or destruction (esp. in the phrase **wrack and ruin**). 2. something destroyed or a remnant of such. [Old English *wræc* persecution, misery; related to Gothic *wraka,* Old Norse *rāk.* Compare WRECK, WRETCH]

wrack[2] (ræk) *n.* 1. seaweed or other marine vegetation that is floating in the sea or has been cast ashore. 2. any of various seaweeds of the genus *Fucus,* such as *F. serratus* (**serrated wrack**). 3. *Literary or dialect.* **a.** a wreck or piece of wreckage. **b.** a remnant or fragment of something destroyed. ~*vb.* 4. *Archaic.* to be or cause to be wrecked. [C14 (in the sense: a wrecked ship, wreckage, hence later applied to marine vegetation washed ashore): perhaps from Middle Dutch *wrak* wreckage; the term corresponds to Old English *wræc* WRACK[1]]

WRAF (in Britain) *abbrev. for* Women's Royal Air Force.

wraith (reɪθ) *n.* **1.** the apparition of a person living or thought to be alive, supposed to appear around the time of his death. **2.** a ghost or any apparition. **3.** an insubstantial copy of something. **4.** something pale, thin, and lacking in substance, such as a column of smoke. [C16: Scottish, of unknown origin] —**'wraith,like** *adj.*

Wran (ræn) *n.* a member of the Women's Royal Australian Naval Service.

wrang (ræŋ) *adj., adv., n., vb.* a Scot. word for **wrong.**

wrangle ('ræŋgᵊl) *vb.* **1.** (*intr.*) to argue, esp. noisily or angrily. **2.** (*tr.*) to encourage, persuade, or obtain by argument. **3.** (*tr.*) *Western U.S. and Canadian.* to herd (cattle or horses). ~*n.* **4.** a noisy or angry argument. [C14: from Low German *wrangeln;* related to Norwegian *vrangla*]

wrangler ('ræŋglə) *n.* **1.** one who wrangles. **2.** *Western U.S. and Canadian.* a herder; cowboy. **3.** *Brit.* (at Cambridge University) a candidate who has obtained first-class honours in Part II of the mathematics tripos. The wrangler with the highest marks is called the **senior wrangler.**

WRANS *abbrev. for* Women's Royal Australian Naval Service.

wrap (ræp) *vb.* **wraps, wrapping, wrapped.** (*mainly tr.*) **1.** to fold or wind (paper, cloth, etc.) around (a person or thing) so as to cover. **2.** (often foll. by *up*) to fold paper, etc., around to fasten securely. **3.** to surround or conceal by surrounding. **4.** to enclose, immerse, or absorb: *wrapped in sorrow.* **5.** to fold, wind, or roll up. **6.** (*intr.;* often foll. by *about, around,* etc.) to be or become wound or extended. **7.** (often foll. by *up*) Also: **rap.** *Austral. informal.* to praise (someone). ~*n.* **8.** a garment worn wrapped around the body, esp. the shoulders, such as a shawl or cloak. **9.** short for **wrapround** (sense 5). **10.** *Chiefly U.S.* wrapping or a wrapper. **11.** Also called: **rap.** *Austral. informal.* a commendation. **12. keep under wraps.** to keep secret. **13. take the wraps off.** to reveal. [C14: origin unknown]

wraparound ('ræpə,raʊnd) *n. Computer technol.* another name for **word wrapping.**

wrapover ('ræp,əʊvə) *or* **wrapround** *adj.* **1.** (of a garment, esp. a skirt) not sewn up at one side, but worn wrapped round the body and fastened so that the open edges overlap. ~*n.* **2.** such a garment.

wrapped (ræpt) *vb.* **1.** the past tense and past participle of **wrap.** ~*adj.* **2.** Also: **rapt.** *Austral. informal.* very pleased: delighted. **3. wrapped up in.** *Informal.* **a.** completely absorbed or engrossed in. **b.** implicated or involved in.

wrapper ('ræpə) *n.* **1.** the cover, usually of paper or cellophane, in which something is wrapped. **2.** a dust jacket of a book. **3.** the ripe firm tobacco leaf forming the outermost portion of a cigar and wound around its body. **4.** a loose negligee or dressing gown, esp. in the 19th century.

wrapping ('ræpɪŋ) *n.* the material used to wrap something.

wrapround ('ræp,raʊnd) *or* **wraparound** ('ræpə,raʊnd) *adj.* **1.** made so as to be wrapped round something: *a wrapround skirt.* **2.** surrounding, curving round, or overlapping. **3.** curving round in one continuous piece: *a wrapround windscreen.* ~*n.* **4.** *Printing.* a flexible plate of plastic, metal, or rubber that is made flat but used wrapped round the plate cylinder of a rotary press. **5.** Also called: **outsert.** *Printing.* a separately printed sheet folded around a section for binding. Sometimes shortened to **wrap. 6.** a slip of paper folded round the dust jacket of a book to announce a price reduction, special offer, etc. **7.** another name for **wrapover.**

wrap up *vb.* (*adv.*) **1.** (*tr.*) to fold paper around. **2.** to put warm clothes on. **3.** (*usually imperative*) *Slang.* to be silent. **4.** (*tr.*) *Informal.* **a.** to settle the final details of. **b.** to make a summary of.

wrasse (ræs) *n.* any marine percoid fish of the family *Labridae,* of tropical and temperate seas, having thick lips, strong teeth, and usually a bright coloration: many are used as food fishes. [C17: from Cornish *wrach;* related to Welsh *gwrach* old woman]

wrath (rɒθ) *n.* **1.** angry, violent, or stern indignation. **2.** divine vengeance or retribution. **3.** *Archaic.* a fit of anger or an act resulting from anger. ~*adj.* **4.** *Obsolete.* incensed; angry. [Old English *wrǣththu;* see WROTH] —**'wrathless** *adj.*

wrathful ('rɒθfʊl) *adj.* **1.** full of wrath; raging or furious. **2.** resulting from or expressing wrath. ~Also (informal): **'wrathy.** —**'wrathfully** *adv.* —**'wrathfulness** *n.*

wreak (ri:k) *vb.* (*tr.*) **1.** to inflict (vengeance, etc.) or to cause (chaos, etc.): *to wreak havoc on the enemy.* **2.** to express, or gratify (anger, hatred, etc.). **3.** *Archaic.* to take vengeance for. [Old English *wrecan;* related to Old Frisian *wreka,* Old High German *rehhan* (German *rächen*), Old Norse *reka,* Latin *urgēre* to push] —**'wreaker** *n.*

wreath (ri:θ) *n., pl.* **wreaths** (ri:ðz, ri:θs). **1.** a band of flowers or foliage intertwined into a ring, usually placed on a grave as a memorial or worn on the head as a garland or a mark of honour. **2.** any circular or spiral band or formation. **3.** a spiral or circular defect appearing in porcelain and glassware. [Old English *wrǣth, wrǣd;* related to Middle Low German *wrēden* to twist. See WRITHE] —**'wreathless** *adj.* —**'wreath,like** *adj.*

wreathe (ri:ð) *vb.* **1.** to form into or take the form of a wreath by intertwining or twisting together. **2.** (*tr.*) to decorate, crown, or encircle with wreaths. **3.** to move or cause to move in a twisting way: *smoke wreathed up to the ceiling.* [C16: perhaps back formation from *wrēthen,* from Old English *writhen,* past participle of *wrīthan* to WRITHE; see WREATH]

wreck (rɛk) *vb.* **1.** to involve in or suffer disaster or destruction. **2.** (*tr.*) to cause the wreck of (a ship). ~*n.* **3. a.** the accidental destruction of a ship at sea. **b.** the ship so destroyed. **4.** *Maritime law.* goods cast ashore from a wrecked vessel. **5.** a person or thing that has suffered ruin or dilapidation. **6.** Also called: **'wreckage.** the remains of something that has been destroyed. **7.** Also called: **'wreckage.** the act of wrecking or the state of being wrecked; ruin or destruction. [C13: from Scandinavian; compare Icelandic *rek.* See WRACK[2], WREAK]

wrecked (rɛkt) *adj. Slang.* in a state of intoxication, stupor, or euphoria, induced by drugs or alcohol.

wrecker ('rɛkə) *n.* **1.** a person or thing that ruins or destroys. **2.** *Chiefly U.S. and Canadian.* a person whose job is to demolish buildings or dismantle cars. **3.** (formerly) a person who lures ships to destruction to plunder the wreckage. **4.** a U.S. and Canadian name for **breakdown van.**

wreckfish ('rɛk,fɪʃ) *n., pl.* **-fish** *or* **-fishes.** another name for **stone bass.** [so called because it is often found near wrecked ships]

wreckful ('rɛkfʊl) *adj. Poetic.* causing wreckage.

wrecking bar *n.* a short crowbar, forked at one end and slightly angled at the other to make a fulcrum.

Wrekin ('ri:kɪn) *n.* **(all) round the Wrekin.** *Midland English dialect.* the long way round: *he went all round the Wrekin instead of explaining clearly.* [referring to an isolated hill in Shropshire]

wren (rɛn) *n.* **1.** any small brown passerine songbird of the chiefly American family *Troglodytidae,* esp. *Troglodytes troglodytes* (**wren** in Britain, **winter wren** in the U.S. and Canada). They have a slender bill and feed on insects. **2.** any of various similar birds of the families *Muscicapidae* (Australian warblers), *Xenicidae* (New Zealand wrens), etc. [Old English *wrenna, werna;* related to Old High German *wrendo, rentilo,* Old Norse *rindill*]

Wren (rɛn) *n. Informal.* (in Britain and certain other nations) a member of the Women's Royal Naval Service. [C20: from the abbreviation *WRNS*]

wrench (rɛntʃ) *vb.* **1.** to give (something) a sudden or violent twist or pull esp. so as to remove (something) from that to which it is attached: *to wrench a door off its hinges.* **2.** (*tr.*) to twist suddenly so as to sprain (a limb): *to wrench one's ankle.* **3.** (*tr.*) to give pain to. **4.** (*tr.*) to twist from the original meaning or purpose. **5.** (*intr.*) to make a sudden twisting motion. ~*n.* **6.** a forceful twist or pull. **7.** an injury to a limb, caused by twisting. **8.** sudden pain caused esp. by parting. **9.** a parting that is difficult or painful to make. **10.** a distorting of the original meaning or purpose. **11.** a spanner, esp. one with adjustable jaws. See also **torque wrench.** [Old English *wrencan;* related to Old High German *renken,* Lithuanian *rangyti* to twist. See WRINKLE[1]]

wrest (rɛst) *vb.* (*tr.*) **1.** to take or force away by violent pulling or twisting. **2.** to seize forcibly by violent or unlawful means. **3.** to obtain by laborious effort. **4.** to distort in meaning, purpose, etc. ~*n.* **5.** the act or an instance of wresting. **6.** *Archaic.* a small key used to tune a piano or harp. [Old English *wrǣstan;* related to Old Norse *reista.* See WRITHE] —**'wrester** *n.*

wrestle ('rɛsᵊl) *vb.* **1.** to fight (another person) by holding, throwing, etc., without punching with the closed fist. **2.** (*intr.*) to participate in wrestling. **3.** (when *intr.,* foll. by *with* or *against*) to fight with (a person, problem, or thing): *wrestle with one's conscience.* **4.** (*tr.*) to move laboriously, as with wrestling movements. **5.** (*tr.*) *U.S. and Canadian.* to throw (an animal) for branding. ~*n.* **6.** the act of wrestling. **7.** a struggle or tussle. [Old English *wrǣstlian;* related to Middle Dutch *wrastelen* (Dutch *worstelen*), Old Norse *rost* current, race] —**'wrestler** *n.*

wrestling ('rɛslɪŋ) *n.* any of certain sports in which the contestants fight each other according to various rules governing holds and usually forbidding blows with the closed fist. The principal object is to overcome the opponent either by throwing or pinning him to the ground or by causing him to submit. See **freestyle, Graeco-Roman, sumo.**

wrest pin *n.* (on a piano, harp, etc.) a pin around which one end of a string is wound: it may be turned by means of a tuning key to alter the tension of the string. In a piano the wrest pin is embedded in the **wrest plank.**

wretch (rɛtʃ) *n.* **1.** a despicable person. **2.** a person pitied for his misfortune. [Old English *wrecca;* related to Old Saxon *wrekkeo,* Old High German *reccheo* (German *Recke* warrior), Old Norse *rek(n)ingr*]

wretched ('rɛtʃɪd) *adj.* **1.** in poor or pitiful circumstances. **2.** characterized by or causing misery. **3.** despicable; base. **4.** poor, inferior, or paltry. **5.** (*prenominal*) (intensifier qualifying something undesirable): *a wretched nuisance.* —**'wretchedly** *adv.* —**'wretchedness** *n.*

wrick (rɪk) *vb.* a variant spelling (chiefly Brit.) of **rick**[2]. [C19: earlier *rick;* perhaps from Middle Low German *wricken* to move jerkily, sprain]

wrier *or* **wryer** ('raɪə) *adj.* the comparative of **wry.**

wriest *or* **wryest** ('raɪɪst) *adj.* the superlative of **wry.**

wriggle (ˈrɪgᵊl) *vb.* **1.** to make or cause to make twisting movements. **2.** (*intr.*) to progress by twisting and turning. **3.** (*intr.; foll. by into or out of*) to manoeuvre oneself by clever or devious means: *wriggle out of an embarrassing situation.* ~*n.* **4.** a wriggling movement or action. **5.** a sinuous marking or course. [C15: from Middle Low German; compare Dutch *wriggelen*] —ˈ**wriggler** *n.* —ˈ**wriggly** *adj.*

wright (raɪt) *n.* (*now chiefly in combination*) a person who creates, builds, or repairs something specified: *a playwright; a shipwright.* [Old English *wryhta, wyrhta;* related to Old Frisian *wrichta,* Old Saxon, Old High German *wurhtio.* See WORK]

wring (rɪŋ) *vb.* **wrings, wringing, wrung. 1.** (often foll. by *out*) to twist and compress to squeeze (a liquid) from (cloth, etc.). **2.** (*tr.*) to twist forcibly: *wring its neck.* **3.** (*tr.*) to clasp and twist (one's hands), esp. in anguish. **4.** (*tr.*) to distress: *wring one's heart.* **5.** (*tr.*) to grip (someone's hand) vigorously in greeting. **6.** (*tr.*) to obtain by or as if by forceful means: *wring information out of.* **7.** (*intr.*) to writhe with or as if with pain. **8. wringing wet.** soaking; drenched. ~*n.* **9.** an act or the process of wringing. [Old English *wringan;* related to Old High German *ringan* (German *wringen*), Gothic *wrungō* snare. See WRANGLE, WRONG]

wringer (ˈrɪŋə) *n.* another name for **mangle**[2] (sense 1).

wring together *vb.* (*tr., adv.*) *Engineering.* to join (two smooth flat surfaces, esp. slip gauges) by hand pressure and a slight twisting movement.

wrinkle[1] (ˈrɪŋkᵊl) *n.* **1.** a slight ridge in the smoothness of a surface, such as a crease in the skin as a result of age. ~*vb.* **2.** to make or become wrinkled, as by crumpling, creasing, or puckering. [C15: back formation from *wrinkled,* from Old English *gewrinclod,* past participle of *wrinclian* to wind around; related to Swedish *vrinka* to sprain, Lithuanian *reñgti* to twist. See WRENCH] —ˈ**wrinkleless** *adj.* —ˈ**wrinkly** *adj.*

wrinkle[2] (ˈrɪŋkᵊl) *n. Informal.* a clever or useful trick, hint, or dodge. [Old English *wrenc* trick; related to Middle Low German *wrank* struggle, Middle High German *ranc* sudden turn. See WRENCH]

wrinklies (ˈrɪŋklɪz) *pl. n. Informal, derogatory.* old people.

wrist (rɪst) *n.* **1.** *Anatomy.* the joint between the forearm and the hand. Technical name: **carpus. 2.** the part of a sleeve or glove that covers the wrist. **3.** *Machinery.* **a.** See **wrist pin. b.** a joint in which a wrist pin forms the pivot. [Old English; related to Old High German, Old Norse *rist.* See WRIGGLE, WRY]

wristband (ˈrɪstˌbænd) *n.* **1.** a band around the wrist, esp. one attached to a watch or forming part of a long sleeve. **2.** a sweatband around the wrist.

wrist-drop *n.* paralysis of the extensor muscles of the wrist and fingers.

wristlet (ˈrɪstlɪt) *n.* a band or bracelet worn around the wrist.

wristlock (ˈrɪstˌlɒk) *n.* a wrestling hold in which a wrestler seizes his opponent's wrist and exerts pressure against the joints of his hand, arm, or shoulder.

wrist pin *n.* **1.** a cylindrical boss or pin attached to the side of a wheel parallel with the axis, esp. one forming a bearing for a crank. **2.** the U.S. and Canadian name for **gudgeon pin.**

wristwatch (ˈrɪstˌwɒtʃ) *n.* a watch worn strapped around the wrist.

wristy (ˈrɪstɪ) *adj.* (of a player's style of hitting the ball in cricket, tennis, etc.) characterized by considerable movement of the wrist.

writ[1] (rɪt) *n.* **1.** a document under seal, issued in the name of the Crown or a court, commanding the person to whom it is addressed to do or refrain from doing some specified act. **2.** *Archaic.* a piece or body of writing: *Holy Writ.* [Old English; related to Old Norse *rit,* Gothic *writs* stroke, Old High German *riz* (German *Riss* a tear). See WRITE]

writ[2] (rɪt) *vb.* **1.** *Archaic or dialect.* a past tense and past participle of **write. 2. writ large.** plain to see; very obvious.

write (raɪt) *vb.* **writes, writing, wrote, written. 1.** to draw or mark (symbols, words, etc.) on a surface, usually paper, with a pen, pencil, or other instrument. **2.** to describe or record (ideas, experiences, etc.) in writing. **3.** to compose (a letter) to or correspond regularly with (a person, organization, etc.). **4.** (*tr.; may take a clause as object*) to say or communicate by letter: *he wrote that he was on his way.* **5.** (*tr.*) *Informal, chiefly U.S. and Canadian.* to send a letter to (a person, etc.). **6.** to write (words) in cursive as opposed to printed style. **7.** (*tr.*) to be sufficiently familiar with (a specified style, language, etc.) to use it in writing. **8.** to be the author or composer of (books, music, etc.). **9.** (*tr.*) to fill in the details for (a document, form, etc.). **10.** (*tr.*) to draw up or draft. **11.** (*tr.*) to produce by writing: *he wrote ten pages.* **12.** (*tr.*) to show clearly: *envy was written all over his face.* **13.** (*tr.*) to spell, inscribe, or entitle. **14.** (*tr.*) to ordain or prophesy: *it is written.* **15.** (*intr.*) to produce writing as specified. **16.** *Computer technol.* to record (data) in a location in a storage device. Compare **read**[1] (sense 16). **17.** (*tr.*) See **underwrite** (sense 3a). ~See also **write down, write in, write off, write out, write up.** [Old English *wrītan* (originally: to scratch runes into bark); related to Old Frisian *wrīta,* Old Norse *rīta,* Old High German *rīzan* (German *reissen* to tear)] —ˈ**writable** *adj.*

write down *vb.* (*adv.*) **1.** (*tr.*) to set down in writing. **2.** (*tr.*) to harm or belittle by writing about (a person) in derogatory terms. **3.** (*intr.; foll. by to or for*) to write in a simplified way (to a supposedly less cultured readership). **4.** (*tr.*) *Accounting.* to decrease the book value of (an asset). ~*n.* **write-down. 5.** *Accounting.* a reduction made in the book value of an asset.

write in *vb.* (*tr.*) **1.** to insert in (a document, form, etc.) in writing. **2.** (*adv.*) *U.S.* **a.** to vote for (a person not on a ballot) by writing in his name. **b.** to cast (a vote) for such a person by writing in his name. ~*n.* **write-in.** *U.S.* **3.** the act of voting for a person by writing his name on a ballot. **4.** a candidate or vote that has been written in. **5.** (*as modifier*): *a write-in campaign.*

write off *vb.* (*tr., adv.*) **1.** *Accounting.* **a.** to cancel (a bad debt or obsolete asset) from the accounts. **b.** to consider (a transaction, etc.) as a loss or set off (a loss) against revenues. **c.** to depreciate (an asset) by periodic charges. **d.** to charge (a specified amount) against gross profits as depreciation of an asset. **2.** to cause or acknowledge the complete loss of. **3.** to send a written order for (something): *she wrote off for a brochure.* **4.** *Informal.* to damage (something, esp. a car) beyond repair. ~*n.* **write-off. 5.** *Accounting.* **a.** the act of cancelling a bad debt or obsolete asset from the accounts. **b.** the bad debt or obsolete asset cancelled. **c.** the amount cancelled against gross profits, corresponding to the book value of the bad debt or obsolete asset. **6.** *Informal.* something damaged beyond repair, esp. a car.

write out *vb.* (*tr., adv.*) **1.** to put into writing or reproduce in full form in writing. **2.** to exhaust (oneself or one's creativity) by excessive writing. **3.** to remove (a character) from a television or radio series.

writer (ˈraɪtə) *n.* **1.** a person who writes books, articles, etc., esp. as an occupation. **2.** the person who has written something specified. **3.** a person who is able to write or write well. **4.** a scribe or clerk. **5.** a composer of music. **6.** *Scot.* a legal practitioner, such as a notary or solicitor. **7. Writer to the Signet.** (in Scotland) a member of an ancient society of solicitors, now having the exclusive privilege of preparing crown writs.

writer's cramp *n.* a muscular spasm or temporary paralysis of the muscles of the thumb and first two fingers caused by prolonged writing.

write up *vb.* (*tr., adv.*) **1.** to describe fully, complete, or bring up to date in writing: *write up a diary.* **2.** to praise or bring to public notice in writing. **3.** *Accounting, U.S.* **a.** to place an excessively high value on (an asset). **b.** to increase the book value of (an asset) in order to reflect more accurately its current worth in the market. ~*n.* **write-up. 4.** a published account of something, such as a review in a newspaper or magazine. **5.** *Accounting, U.S.* **a.** an excessive or illegally high valuation of corporate assets. **b.** a raising of the book value of an asset.

writhe (raɪð) *vb.* **1.** to twist or squirm in or as if in pain. **2.** (*intr.*) to move with such motions. **3.** (*intr.*) to suffer acutely from embarrassment, revulsion, etc. ~*n.* **4.** the act or an instance of writhing. [Old English *wrīthan;* related to Old High German *rīdan,* Old Norse *rītha.* See WRATH, WREATH, WRIST, WROTH] —ˈ**writher** *n.*

writhen (ˈrɪðən) *Archaic or poetic.* ~*vb.* **1.** a past participle of **writhe.** ~*adj.* **2.** twisted; distorted.

writing (ˈraɪtɪŋ) *n.* **1.** a group of letters or symbols written or marked on a surface as a means of communicating ideas by making each symbol stand for an idea, concept, or thing (see **ideogram**), by using each symbol to represent a set of sounds grouped into syllables (**syllabic writing**), or by regarding each symbol as corresponding roughly or exactly to each of the sounds in the language (**alphabetic writing**). **2.** short for **handwriting. 3.** anything expressed in letters, esp. a literary composition. **4.** the work of a writer. **5.** literary style, art, or practice. **6.** written form: *give it to me in writing.* **7.** (*modifier*): related to or used in writing: *writing ink.* **8. writing on the wall.** a sign or signs of approaching disaster. [sense 8: allusion to Daniel 5:5]

writing case *n.* a portable folder with compartments for holding writing materials.

writing desk *n.* a piece of furniture with a writing surface and drawers and compartments for papers, writing materials, etc.

writing paper *n.* paper sized to take writing ink and used for letters and other manuscripts.

Writings (ˈraɪtɪŋz) *pl. n.* **the.** another term for the **Hagiographa.**

writing table *n.* a table designed or used for writing at.

writ of execution *n. Law.* a writ ordering that a judgment be enforced.

written (ˈrɪtᵊn) *vb.* **1.** the past participle of **write.** ~*adj.* **2.** taken down in writing; transcribed: *written evidence; the written word.* Compare **spoken** (sense 2).

Written Law *n. Judaism.* another name for the **Torah.**

WRNS *abbrev. for* Women's Royal Naval Service. See also **Wren.**

wrnt *abbrev. for* warrant.

wrong (rɒŋ) *adj.* **1.** not correct or truthful: *the wrong answer.* **2.** acting or judging in error: *you are wrong to think that.* **3.** (*postpositive*) immoral; bad: *it is wrong to cheat.* **4.** deviating from or unacceptable to correct or conventional laws, usage, etc. **5.** not intended or wanted: *the wrong road.* **6.** (*postpositive*) not working properly; amiss: *something is wrong with the engine.* **7.** (of a side, esp. of a fabric) intended to face the inside so as not to be seen. **8. get on the wrong side of** *or* (*U.S.*) **get in wrong with.** *Informal.* to come into disfavour with. **9. go down the wrong way.** (of food) to pass into the windpipe instead of the gullet. **10. wrong in the** (*or* **one's**) **head.** *Informal.* mad; crazy. ~*adv.* **11.** in the wrong direction or manner. **12. go wrong. a.**

to turn out other than intended. **b.** to make a mistake. **c.** (of a machine, etc.) to cease to function properly. **d.** to go astray morally. **13. get wrong. a.** to fail to understand properly. **b.** to fail to provide the correct answer to. *~n.* **14.** a bad, immoral, or unjust thing or action. **15.** *Law.* **a.** an infringement of another person's rights, rendering the offender liable to a civil action, as for breach of contract or tort: *a private wrong.* **b.** a violation of public rights and duties, affecting the community as a whole and actionable at the instance of the Crown: *a public wrong.* **16. in the wrong.** mistaken or guilty. *~vb. (tr.)* **17.** to treat unjustly. **18.** to discredit, malign, or misrepresent. **19.** to seduce or violate. [Old English *wrang* injustice, from Old Norse *vrang;* see WRING] —ˈ**wronger** *n.* —ˈ**wrongly** *adv.* —ˈ**wrongness** *n.*

wrongdoer (ˈrɒŋˌduːə) *n.* a person who acts immorally or illegally. —ˈ**wrongˌdoing** *n.*

wrong-foot *vb. (tr.)* **1.** *Tennis, etc.* to play a shot in such a way as to cause (one's opponent) to be off balance. **2.** to take by surprise so as to place in an embarrassing or disadvantageous situation.

wrong fount *n. Printing.* an error in composition in which a type of the wrong face or size is used. Abbrev.: **wf.**

wrongful (ˈrɒŋfʊl) *adj.* immoral, unjust, or illegal. —ˈ**wrongfully** *adv.* —ˈ**wrongfulness** *n.*

wrong-headed *adj.* **1.** constantly wrong in judgment. **2.** foolishly stubborn; perverse; obstinate. —ˌ**wrong-**ˈ**headedly** *adv.* —ˌ**wrong-**ˈ**headedness** *n.*

wrong number *n.* a telephone number wrongly connected or dialled in error or the person so contacted.

wrote (rəʊt) *vb.* the past tense of **write.**

wroth (rəʊθ, rɒθ) *adj. Archaic or literary.* angry; irate. [Old English *wrāth;* related to Old Saxon *wrēth,* Old Norse *reithr,* Old High German *reid* curly haired]

wrought (rɔːt) *vb.* **1.** *Archaic.* a past tense and past participle of **work.** *~adj.* **2.** *Metallurgy.* shaped by hammering or beating. **3.** (*often in combination*) formed, fashioned, or worked as specified: *well-wrought.* **4.** decorated or made with delicate care. [C16: variant of *worht,* from Old English *geworht,* past participle of *(ge)wyrcan* to WORK]

wrought iron *n.* **a.** a pure form of iron having a low carbon content and a fibrous microstructure. It is made by various processes and is often used for decorative work. **b.** (*as modifier*): *wrought-iron gates.*

wrought-up *adj.* agitated or excited.

wrung (rʌŋ) *vb.* the past tense and past participle of **wring.**

WRVS *abbrev. for* Women's Royal Voluntary Service.

wry (raɪ) *adj.* **wrier, wriest** *or* **wryer, wryest. 1.** twisted, contorted, or askew. **2.** (of a facial expression) produced or characterized by contorting of the features, usually indicating dislike. **3.** dryly humorous; sardonic. **4.** warped, misdirected, or perverse. **5.** (of words, thoughts, etc.) unsuitable or wrong. *~vb.* **wries, wrying, wried. 6.** *(tr.)* to twist or contort. [C16: from dialect *wry* to twist, from Old English *wrīgian* to turn; related to Old Frisian *wrīgia* to bend, Old Norse *riga* to move, Middle Low German *wrīch* bent, stubborn] —ˈ**wryly** *adv.* —ˈ**wryness** *n.*

wrybill (ˈraɪˌbɪl) *n.* a New Zealand plover, *Anarhynchus frontalis,* having its bill deflected to one side enabling it to search for food beneath stones.

wryneck (ˈraɪˌnɛk) *n.* **1.** either of two cryptically coloured Old World woodpeckers, *Jynx torquilla* or *J. ruficollis,* which do not drum on trees. **2.** another name for **torticollis. 3.** *Informal.* a person who has a twisted neck.

WS **1.** *abbrev. for* Writer to the Signet. *~***2.** *international car registration for* Western Samoa.

W star *n.* short for **Wolf-Rayet star.**

WSW *symbol for* west-southwest.

wt. *abbrev. for* weight.

Wu (wuː) *n.* a group of dialects of Chinese spoken around the Yangtze delta near Shanghai.

wulfenite (ˈwʊlfəˌnaɪt) *n.* a yellow, orange, red, or grey lustrous secondary mineral consisting of lead molybdate in the form of platelike tetragonal crystals. It occurs with lead ores and is a source of molybdenum. Formula: $PbMoO_4$. [C19: from German *Wulfenit,* named after F. X. von *Wulfen* (1728–1805), Austrian mineralogist]

wunderkind (ˈwʌndəˌkɪnd; *German* ˈvʊndərˌkɪnt) *n., pl.* **-kinds** *or* **-kinder** (*German* -kɪndər). **1.** a child prodigy. **2.** a person who is exceptionally successful in his field while still young. [C20: German, literally: wonder child]

wurley *or* **wurlie** (ˈwɜːlɪ) *n. Austral.* an Aboriginal hut. [from a native Australian language]

Würm (vʊəm, wɜːm) *n.* the fourth and final Pleistocene glaciation in Alpine Europe. See also **Günz, Riss, Mindel.** [C20: named after the river *Würm* in Bavaria, Germany]

wurst (wɜːst, wʊəst, vʊəst) *n.* a large sausage, esp. of a type made in Germany, Austria, etc. [from German, literally: something rolled; related to Latin *vertere* to turn]

wus (wʌs) *n. South Wales dialect.* a casual term of address: *fancy a drink, wus?* [from Welsh *was,* variant of *gwas* servant]

wuthering (ˈwʌðərɪŋ) *adj. Northern English dialect.* **1.** (of a wind) blowing strongly with a roaring sound. **2.** (of a place) characterized by such a sound. [variant of *whitherin,* from *whither* blow, from Old Norse *hvithra;* related to *hvitha* squall of wind, Old English *hweothu* wind]

WV **1.** *abbrev. for* West Virginia. *~***2.** *international car registration for* (Windward Islands) St Vincent.

W. Va. *abbrev. for* West Virginia.

WVS (formerly, in Britain) *abbrev. for* Women's Voluntary Service, since 1966 **WRVS.**

WWF *abbrev. for* Worldwide Fund for Nature.

WY *or* **Wy.** *abbrev. for* Wyoming.

Wyandotte (ˈwaɪənˌdɒt) *n.* a heavy American breed of domestic fowl with many different varieties. [C19: from *Wyandot,* a N American Indian people]

wych- *prefix.* a variant of **witch-.**

wych-elm *or* **witch-elm** (ˈwɪtʃˌɛlm) *n.* **1.** Eurasian elm tree, *Ulmus glabra,* having a rounded shape, longish pointed leaves, clusters of small flowers, and winged fruits. **2.** the wood of this tree. [C17: from Old English *wice* wych-elm]

wych-hazel *n.* a variant spelling of **witch hazel.**

Wycliffite *or* **Wyclifite** (ˈwɪklɪˌfaɪt) *English history.* *~n.* **1.** a follower of the English religious reformer John Wycliffe (?1330–84) or an adherent of his religious ideas; a Lollard. *~adj.* **2.** of or relating to Wycliffe, his followers, or his religious ideas. —ˈ**Wycliffism** *or* ˈ**Wyclifism** *n.*

Wykehamist (ˈwɪkəmɪst) *n.* a pupil or former pupil of Winchester College, the oldest English public school, founded (1382) by William of Wykeham (1324–1404), English prelate and statesman.

wynd (waɪnd) *n. Scot.* a narrow lane or alley. [C15: from the stem of WIND[2]]

Wyo. *abbrev. for* Wyoming.

WYSIWYG (ˈwɪzɪˌwɪg) *n., adj. Computers. acronym for* what you see is what you get: referring to what is displayed on the screen being the same as what will be printed out.

wyvern *or* (*less commonly*) **wivern** (ˈwaɪvən) *n.* a heraldic beast having a serpent's tail and a dragon's head and a body with wings and two legs. [C17: variant of earlier *wyver,* from Old French, from Latin *vīpera* VIPER]

x *or* **X** (ɛks) *n., pl.* **x's, X's,** *or* **Xs. 1.** the 24th letter and 19th consonant of the modern English alphabet. **2.** a speech sound sequence represented by this letter, in English pronounced as *ks* or *gz* or, in initial position, *z*, as in *xylophone.*
x *symbol for:* **1.** *Commerce, finance, etc.* ex. **2.** *Maths.* the *x*-axis or a coordinate measured along the *x*-axis in a Cartesian coordinate system. **3.** an algebraic variable.
X *symbol:* **1. a.** (in Britain, formerly) indicating a film that may not be publicly shown to anyone under 18. Since 1982 replaced by symbol 18. **b.** (*as modifier*): *an X film.* **2.** denoting any unknown, unspecified, or variable factor, number, person, or thing. **3.** (on letters, cards, etc.) denoting a kiss. **4.** (on ballot papers, etc.) indicating choice. **5.** (on examination papers, etc.) indicating error. **6.** for Christ; Christian. [from the form of the Greek letter khi (X), first letter of *Khristos* Christ] ~**7.** *the Roman numeral for* ten. See **Roman numerals.**
xanthate ('zænθeɪt) *n.* any salt or ester of xanthic acid. —**xan'thation** *n.*
xanthein ('zænθiːɪn) *n.* the soluble part of the yellow pigment that is found in the cell sap of some flowers.
xanthene ('zænθiːn) *n.* a yellowish crystalline heterocyclic compound used as a fungicide; benzo-1,4-pyran. Its molecular structural unit is found in many dyes, such as rhodamine and fluorosein. Formula: $CH_2(C_6H_4)_2O$.
xanthic ('zænθɪk) *adj.* **1.** of, containing, or derived from xanthic acid. **2.** *Botany, rare.* having a yellow colour.
xanthic acid *n.* any of a class of organic sulphur-containing acids with the general formula ROC(S)SH, where R is an organic group. Their salts are the xanthates.
xanthin ('zænθɪn) *n.* any of a group of yellow or orange carotene derivatives that occur in the fruit and flowers of certain plants.
xanthine ('zænθiːn, -θaɪn) *n.* **1.** a crystalline compound related in structure to uric acid and found in urine, blood, certain plants, and certain animal tissues. Formula: $C_5H_4N_4O_2$. **2.** any substituted derivative of xanthine, esp. one of the three pharmacologically active methylated xanthines, caffeine, theophylline, or theobromine, which act as stimulants and diuretics.
Xanthippe (zæn'θɪpɪ) *or* **Xantippe** (zæn'tɪpɪ) *n.* a nagging, peevish, or irritable woman. [after the nagging wife of the ancient Greek philosopher Socrates]
xanthism ('zæn,θɪzəm) *n.* a condition of skin, fur, or feathers in which yellow coloration predominates.
xantho- *or before a vowel* **xanth-** *combining form.* indicating yellow: *xanthophyll.* [from Greek *xanthos*]
xanthochroid ('zænθəʊ,krɔɪd) *adj. Rare.* of, relating to, or designating races having light-coloured hair and a pale complexion. [C19: New Latin *xanthochroi,* from XANTHO- + Greek *ōkhros* pale]
xanthochroism (zæn'θɒkrəʊ,ɪzəm) *n.* a condition in certain animals, esp. aquarium goldfish, in which all skin pigments other than yellow and orange disappear. [C19: from Greek *xanthokhro(os)* yellow-skinned (from *xanthos* yellow + *khroia* skin) + -ISM]
xanthoma (zæn'θəʊmə) *n. Pathol.* the presence in the skin of fatty yellow or brownish plaques or nodules, esp. on the eyelids, caused by a disorder of lipid metabolism.
xanthophyll *or esp. U.S.* **xanthophyl** ('zænθəʊfɪl) *n.* any of a group of yellow carotenoid pigments occurring in plant and animal tissue. —,**xantho'phyllous** *adj.*
xanthous ('zænθəs) *adj.* of, relating to, or designating races with yellowish hair and a light complexion.
***x*-axis** *n.* a reference axis, usually horizontal, of a graph or two- or three-dimensional Cartesian coordinate system along which the *x*-coordinate is measured.
X-chromosome *n.* the sex chromosome that occurs in pairs in the diploid cells of the females of many animals, including humans, and as one of a pair with the Y-chromosome in those of males. Compare **Y-chromosome.**
Xe *the chemical symbol for* xenon.
xebec, zebec, *or* **zebeck** ('ziːbɛk) *n.* a small three-masted Mediterranean vessel with both square and lateen sails, formerly used by Algerian pirates and later used for commerce. [C18: earlier *chebec* from French, ultimately from Arabic *shabbāk;* present spelling influenced by Catalan *xabec,* Spanish *xabeque* (now *jabeque*)]
xenia ('ziːnɪə) *n. Botany.* the influence of pollen upon the form of the fruit developing after pollination. [C19: from New Latin, from Greek: hospitality, from *xenos* guest] —**'xenial** *adj.*
xeno- *or before a vowel* **xen-** *combining form.* indicating something strange, different, or foreign: *xenogamy.* [from Greek *xenos* strange]
xenocryst ('zɛnə,krɪst) *n.* a crystal included within an igneous rock as the magma cooled but not formed from it. [C20: from XENO- + CRYST(AL)]
xenogamy (zɛ'nɒgəmɪ) *n. Botany.* another name for **allogamy.** —**xe'nogamous** *adj.*
xenogeneic (,zɛnəʊdʒɪ'neɪɪk) *adj. Med.* derived from an individual of a different species: *a xenogeneic tissue graft.*
xenogenesis (,zɛnə'dʒɛnɪsɪs) *n.* **1.** the supposed production of offspring completely unlike either parent. **2.** another name for **abiogenesis** or **alternation of generations.** —**xenogenetic** (,zɛnəʊdʒɪ'nɛtɪk) *or* ,**xeno'genic** *adj.*
xenoglossia (,zɛnə'glɒsɪə) *or* **xenoglossy** ('zɛnə,glɒsɪ) *n.* an ability claimed by some mediums, clairvoyants, etc., to speak a language with which they are unfamiliar. [C20: from Greek, from XENO- + Attic Greek *glossa* tongue, language]
xenograft ('zɛnəʊ,grɑːft) *n.* another word for **heterograft.**
xenolith ('zɛnəlɪθ) *n.* a fragment of rock differing in origin, composition, structure, etc., from the igneous rock enclosing it. —,**xeno'lithic** *adj.*
xenomorphic (,zɛnə'mɔːfɪk) *adj.* (of a mineral constituent of an igneous rock) not having its characteristic crystal shape because of deforming pressure from adjacent minerals. —,**xeno'morphically** *adv.*
xenon ('zɛnɒn) *n.* a colourless odourless gaseous element occurring in trace amounts in air; formerly considered inert it is now known to form compounds and is used in radio valves, stroboscopic and bactericidal lamps, and bubble chambers. Symbol: Xe; atomic no.: 54; atomic wt.: 131.30; density: 5.887 kg/m^3; melting pt.: –111.9°C; boiling pt.: –107.1°C. [C19: from Greek: something strange]
xenophile ('zɛnə,faɪl) *n.* a person who likes foreigners or things foreign. [C19: from Greek, from XENO- + -PHILE]
xenophobe ('zɛnə,fəʊb) *n.* a person who hates or fears foreigners or strangers. [C20: from Greek, from XENO- + -PHOBE]
xenophobia (,zɛnə'fəʊbɪə) *n.* hatred or fear of foreigners or strangers or of their politics or culture. —,**xeno'phobic** *adj.*
xeranthemum (zɪə'rænθəməm) *n.* any of a Mediterranean genus of plants having flower heads that are dry and retain their colour and shape for years: family *Compositae* (composites). See also **immortelle.** [C18: New Latin, from Greek XERO- + *anthemon* flower]
xerarch ('zɪərɑːk) *adj. Ecology.* (of a sere) having its origin in a dry habitat. [from XER(O)- + Greek *arkhē* a beginning, from *arkhein* to begin]
xeric ('zɪərɪk) *adj. Ecology.* of, relating to, or growing in dry conditions. —**'xerically** *adv.*
xero- *or before a vowel* **xer-** *combining form.* indicating dryness: *xeroderma.* [from Greek *xēros* dry]
xeroderma (,zɪərəʊ'dɜːmə) *or* **xerodermia** (,zɪərəʊ'dɜːmɪə) *n. Pathol.* **1.** any abnormal dryness of the skin as the result of diminished secretions from the sweat or sebaceous glands. **2.** another name for **ichthyosis.** —**xerodermatic** (,zɪərəʊdə'mætɪk) *or* ,**xero'dermatous** *adj.*
xerography (zɪ'rɒgrəfɪ) *n.* a photocopying process in which an electrostatic image is formed on a selenium plate or cylinder. The plate or cylinder is dusted with a resinous powder, which adheres to the charged regions, and the image is then transferred to a sheet of paper on which it is fixed by heating. —**xe'rographer** *n.* —**xerographic** (,zɪərə'græfɪk) *adj.* —,**xero'graphically** *adv.*
xeromorphic (,zɪərə'mɔːfɪk) *adj.* (of plants or plant parts) having characteristics that serve as protection against excessive loss of water.
xerophilous (zɪ'rɒfɪləs) *adj.* (of plants or animals) adapted for growing or living in dry surroundings. —**xerophile** ('zɪərəʊ,faɪl) *n.* —**xe'rophily** *n.*
xerophthalmia (,zɪərɒf'θælmɪə) *n. Pathol.* excessive dryness of the cornea and conjunctiva, caused by a deficiency of vitamin A. Also called: **xeroma** (zɪ'rəʊmə). —,**xeroph'thalmic** *adj.*
xerophyte ('zɪərə,faɪt) *n.* a xerophilous plant, such as a cactus. —**xerophytic** (,zɪərə'fɪtɪk) *adj.* —,**xero'phytically** *adv.* —**'xero,phytism** *n.*
xerosere ('zɪərə,sɪə) *n. Ecology.* a sere that originates in dry surroundings.
xerosis (zɪ'rəʊsɪs) *n. Pathol.* abnormal dryness of bodily tissues, esp. the skin, eyes, or mucous membranes. —**xerotic** (zɪ'rɒtɪk) *adj.*
xerostomia (,zɪːrə'stəʊmɪə) *n.* abnormal lack of saliva; dryness of the mouth. [C19: from XERO- + -STOM(E) + -IA]
Xerox ('zɪərɒks) *n.* **1.** *Trademark.* **a.** a xerographic copying process. **b.** a machine employing this process. **c.** a copy produced by this process. ~*vb.* **2.** to produce a copy of (a document, illustration, etc.) by this process.
Xhosa ('kɔːsə) *n.* **1.** (*pl.* **-sa** *or* **-sas**) a member of a cattle-rearing Negroid people of southern Africa, living chiefly in Cape Province of the Republic of South Africa. **2.** the language of this

people, belonging to the Bantu group of the Niger-Congo family: closely related to Swazi and Zulu and characterized by several clicks in its sound system. —'**Xhosan** *adj.*

xi (zaɪ, saɪ, ksaɪ, ksiː) *n., pl.* **xis.** the 14th letter in the Greek alphabet (Ξ, ξ), a composite consonant, transliterated as *x.*

xiphi- *or before a vowel* **xiph-** *combining form.* indicating a sword, esp. something shaped like or resembling a sword: *xiphisternum; xiphoid.* [from Greek *xiphos* sword]

xiphisternum (ˌzɪfɪ'stɜːnəm) *n., pl.* **-na** (-nə). *Anatomy, zoology.* the cartilaginous process forming the lowermost part of the breastbone (sternum). Also called: **xiphoid, xiphoid process.**

xiphoid ('zɪfɔɪd) *adj.* **1.** *Biology.* shaped like a sword. **2.** of or relating to the xiphisternum. *~n.* **3.** Also called: **xiphoid process.** another name for **xiphisternum.**

xiphosuran (ˌzɪfə'sjuərən) *n.* **1.** any chelicerate arthropod of the subclass *Xiphosura,* including the horseshoe crabs and many extinct forms. *~adj.* **2.** of, relating to, or belonging to the subclass *Xiphosura.* [C19: from New Latin *Xiphosura,* irregularly from Greek *xiphos* sword + *oura* tail]

XL *symbol for* extra large.

Xmas ('ɛksməs, 'krɪsməs) *n. Informal.* short for **Christmas.** [C16: from symbol X for Christ + -MAS]

Xn *or* **Xtian** *abbrev. for* Christian.

Xnty *or* **Xty** *abbrev. for* Christianity.

xoanon ('zəuəˌnɒn) *n., pl.* **-na** (-nə). a primitive image of a god, carved, esp. originally, in wood, and supposed to have fallen from heaven. [C18: from Greek, from *xuō* to scrape, smooth]

XP *n.* the Christian monogram made up of the Greek letters *khi* and *rho,* the first two letters of *Khristos,* the Greek form of Christ's name.

x-radiation *n.* another term for **x-ray.**

x-ray *or* **X-ray** *n.* **1. a.** electromagnetic radiation emitted when matter is bombarded with fast electrons. X-rays have wavelengths shorter than that of ultraviolet radiation, that is less than about 1×10^{-8} metres. They extend to indefinitely short wavelengths, but below about 1×10^{-11} metres they are often called gamma radiation or bremsstrahlung. **b.** (*as modifier*): *x-ray astronomy.* **2.** a picture produced by exposing photographic film to x-rays: used in medicine as a diagnostic aid as parts of the body, such as bones, absorb x-rays and so appear as opaque areas on the picture. **3.** (*usually cap.*) *Communications.* a code word for the letter *x.* *~vb.* (*tr.*) **4.** to photograph (part of the body, etc.) using x-rays. **5.** to treat or examine by means of x-rays. [C19: partial translation of German *X-Strahlen* (from *Strahl* ray), coined by the German physicist W. K. Röntgen, who discovered x-rays in 1895]

x-ray astronomy *n.* the branch of astronomy concerned with the detection and measurement of x-rays emitted by certain celestial bodies. As x-rays are absorbed by the atmosphere, satellites and rockets are used.

x-ray crystallography *n.* the study and practice of determining the structure of a crystal by passing a beam of x-rays through it and observing and analysing the diffraction pattern produced.

x-ray star *n.* a star that emits x-rays, as well as other types of radiation. The x-rays are detected by instruments carried in satellites and space probes.

x-ray therapy *n. Med.* the therapeutic use of x-rays.

x-ray tube *n.* an evacuated tube containing a metal target onto which is directed a beam of electrons at high energy for the generation of x-rays.

Xt *abbrev. for* Christ. [representing the initial letter (chi) and the t (tau) of Greek *Khristos*]

x-unit *n.* a unit of length equal to $0.100\,202 \times 10^{-12}$ metre, for expressing the wavelengths of x-rays and gamma rays.

xylan ('zaɪlæn) *n. Biochem.* a yellow polysaccharide consisting of xylose units: occurs in straw husks and other woody tissue.

xylem ('zaɪləm, -lɛm) *n.* a plant tissue that conducts water and mineral salts from the roots to all other parts, provides mechanical support, and forms the wood of trees and shrubs. It is of two types (see **protoxylem, metaxylem**), both of which are made up of vessels, tracheids, and other elements. [C19: from Greek *xulon* wood]

xylene ('zaɪliːn) *n.* an aromatic hydrocarbon existing in three isomeric forms, all three being colourless flammable volatile liquids used as solvents and in the manufacture of synthetic resins, dyes, and insecticides; dimethylbenzene. Formula: $C_6H_4(CH_3)_2$. Also called: **xylol.**

xylidine ('zaɪlɪˌdiːn, -ˌdaɪn, 'zɪlɪ-) *n.* **1.** a mixture of six isomeric amines derived from xylene and used in dyes. Formula: $(CH_3)_2C_6H_3NH_2$. **2.** any one of these isomers.

xylo- *or before a vowel* **xyl-** *combining form.* **1.** indicating wood: *xylophone.* **2.** indicating xylene: *xylidine.* [from Greek *xulon* wood]

xylocarp ('zaɪləˌkɑːp) *n. Botany.* a fruit, such as a coconut, having a hard woody pericarp. —ˌ**xylo'carpous** *adj.*

xylogenous (zaɪ'lɒdʒɪnəs) *adj. Biology.* living in or on wood. Also: **xylophilous** (zaɪ'lɒfɪləs).

xylograph ('zaɪləˌgrɑːf, -ˌgræf) *n.* **1.** an engraving in wood. **2.** a print taken from a wood block. *~vb.* **3.** (*tr.*) to print (a design, illustration, etc.) from a wood engraving.

xylography (zaɪ'lɒgrəfɪ) *n.* the art, craft, or process of printing from wooden blocks. —**xy'lographer** *n.* —**xylographic** (ˌzaɪlə'græfɪk) *or* ˌ**xylo'graphical** *adj.*

xyloid ('zaɪlɔɪd) *adj. Botany.* of, relating to, or resembling wood; woody.

xylol ('zaɪlɒl) *n.* another name (not in technical usage) for **xylene.**

xylophagous (zaɪ'lɒfəgəs) *adj.* (of certain insects, crustaceans, etc.) feeding on or living within wood.

xylophone ('zaɪləˌfəun) *n. Music.* a percussion instrument consisting of a set of wooden bars of graduated length. It is played with hard-headed hammers. [C19: from XYLO- + -PHONE] —**xylophonic** (ˌzaɪlə'fɒnɪk) *adj.* —**xylophonist** (zaɪ'lɒfənɪst) *n.*

xylorimba (ˌzaɪlə'rɪmbə) *n.* a large xylophone with an extended range of five octaves. [C20: XYLO(PHONE) + (MA)RIMBA]

xylose ('zaɪləuz, -ləus) *n.* a white crystalline dextrorotatory sugar found in the form of xylan in wood and straw. It is extracted by hydrolysis with acids and used in dyeing, tanning, and in foods for diabetics. Formula: $C_5H_{10}O_5$.

xylotomous (zaɪ'lɒtəməs) *adj.* (of certain insects, insect larvae, etc.) cutting or boring into wood.

xylotomy (zaɪ'lɒtəmɪ) *n.* the preparation of sections of wood for examination by microscope. —**xy'lotomist** *n.*

xylyl ('zaɪlɪl) *n.* (*modifier*) of, containing, or denoting the group of atoms $(CH_3)_2C_6H_3$-, derived from xylene.

xyst (zɪst), **xystus,** *or* **xystos** ('zɪstəs) *n.* **1.** a long portico, esp. one used in ancient Greece for athletics. **2.** (in ancient Rome) a covered garden walk or one lined with trees. [C17: from Latin *xystus,* from Greek *xustos,* literally: smoothed, polished (area), from *xuein* to scrape, make smooth]

xyster ('zɪstə) *n.* a surgical instrument for scraping bone; surgical rasp or file. [C17: via New Latin from Greek: tool for scraping, from *xuein* to scrape, make smooth]

y *or* **Y** (waɪ) *n., pl.* **y's, Y's,** *or* **Ys.** 1. the 25th letter of the modern English alphabet. 2. a speech sound represented by this letter, in English usually a semivowel, as in *yawn*, or a vowel, as in *symbol* or *shy*. 3. a. something shaped like a Y. b. (*in combination*): *a Y-cross.*

y *Maths. symbol for:* 1. the *y*-axis or a coordinate measured along the *y*-axis in a Cartesian coordinate system. 2. an algebraic variable.

Y *symbol for:* 1. any unknown, unspecified, or variable factor, number, person, or thing. 2. *Chem.* yttrium. 3. *Currency.* a. yen. b. yuan.

y. *abbrev. for* year.

Y. *abbrev. for* YMCA or YWCA.

-y[1] *or* **-ey** *suffix forming adjectives.* 1. (*from nouns*) characterized by; consisting of; filled with; relating to; resembling: *sunny; sandy; smoky; classy.* 2. (*from verbs*) tending to; acting or existing as specified: *leaky; shiny.* [from Old English *-ig, -ǣg*]

-y[2], **-ie,** *or* **-ey** *suffix of nouns. Informal.* 1. denoting smallness and expressing affection and familiarity: *a doggy; a bunny; a granny; Jamie.* 2. a person or thing concerned with or characterized by being: *a groupie; a goalie; a fatty.* [C14: from Scottish *-ie, -y*, familiar suffix occurring originally in names, as in *Jamie* (*James*)]

-y[3] *suffix forming nouns.* 1. (*from verbs*) indicating the act of doing what is indicated by the verbal element: *inquiry.* 2. (*esp. with combining forms of Greek, Latin, or French origin*) indicating state, condition, or quality: *geography; jealousy.* [from Old French *-ie*, from Latin *-ia*]

yabber ('jæbə) *Informal, chiefly Austral.* ~*vb.* 1. (*intr.*) to talk or jabber. ~*n.* 2. talk or jabber. [C19: from a native Australian language *yabba* talk, probably influenced by JABBER]

yabby *or* **yabbie** ('jæbɪ) *Austral.* ~*n., pl.* **-bies.** 1. a small freshwater crayfish of the genus *Cherax.* 2. a marine prawn used as bait. ~*vb.* **-bies, -bying, -bied.** 3. (*intr.*) to go out to catch yabbies. [from a native Australian language]

yacht (jɒt) *n.* 1. a vessel propelled by sail or power, used esp. for pleasure cruising, racing, etc. 2. short for **sand yacht** or **ice yacht.** ~*vb.* 3. (*intr.*) to sail or cruise in a yacht. [C16: from obsolete Dutch *jaghte*, short for *jahtschip*, from *jagen* to chase + *schip* SHIP]

yachtie ('jɒtɪ) *n. Austral. and N.Z. informal.* a yachtsman; sailing enthusiast.

yachting ('jɒtɪŋ) *n.* a. the sport or practice of navigating a yacht. b. (*as modifier*): *yachting clothes.*

yachtsman ('jɒtsmən) *or* (*fem.*) **yachtswoman** *n., pl.* **-men** *or* **-women.** a person who sails a yacht or yachts. —**'yachtsman,ship** *n.*

yack (jæk) *n., vb.* a variant spelling of **yak**[2].

yackety-yak (ˌjækɪtɪ'jæk) *n. Slang.* noisy, continuous, and trivial talk or conversation. Sometimes shortened to **yak.** [of imitative origin]

yae (je) *adj. Scot.* a variant of **ae.**

yaffle ('jæfᵊl) *n.* another name for **green woodpecker.** [C18: imitative of its cry]

Yagi aerial ('jɑːgɪ, 'jægɪ) *n.* a sharply directional aerial, used esp. in television and radio astronomy, consisting of three or more elements lying parallel to each other, the principal direction of radiation being along the line of the centres. [C20: named after Hidetsugu *Yagi* (1886–1976), Japanese engineer]

yah (jɑː, jɛə) *sentence substitute.* 1. an informal word for **yes,** often used to indicate derision or contempt. ~*interj.* 2. an exclamation of derision or disgust.

yahoo (jə'huː) *n., pl.* **-hoos.** a crude, brutish, or obscenely coarse person. [C18: from the name of a race of brutish creatures resembling men in Jonathan Swift's *Gulliver's Travels* (1726)] —**ya'hooism** *n.*

Yahrzeit ('jɔːtsaɪt) *n. Judaism.* the anniversary of the death of a close relative, on which it is customary to kindle a light and recite the Kaddish and also, in some communities, to observe a fast. [Yiddish, from Middle High German *jārzīt* anniversary; see YEAR, TIDE[1]]

Yahweh, Jahweh ('jɑːweɪ) *or* **Yahveh, Jahveh** ('jɑːveɪ) *n. Old Testament.* a vocalization of the Tetragrammaton, used esp. by Christian theologians. [from Hebrew, from YHVH, with conjectural vowels; perhaps related to *hāwāh* to be; see also JEHOVAH]

Yahwism, Jahwism ('jɑːwɪzəm) *or* **Yahvism, Jahvism** ('jɑːvɪzəm) *n.* the use of the name Yahweh, esp. in parts of the Old Testament, as the personal name of God.

Yahwist, Jahwist ('jɑːwɪst) *or* **Yahvist, Jahvist** ('jɑːvɪst) *n. Bible.* **the.** a. the conjectured author or authors of the earliest of four main sources or strands of tradition of which the Pentateuch is composed and in which God is called *Yahweh* throughout. b. (*as modifier*): *the Yahwist source.*

Yahwistic, Jahwistic (jɑː'wɪstɪk) *or* **Yahvistic, Jahvistic** (jɑː'vɪstɪk) *adj. Bible.* of or relating to Yahwism, the Yahwist, or Yahweh.

Yajur-Veda ('jʌdʒʊə'veɪdə) *n. Hinduism.* the second Veda, consisting of prayers and sacrificial formulas primarily for use by the priests. [from Sanskrit, from *yajur* sacred, holy (compare Greek *hagios* holy) + VEDA]

yak[1] (jæk) *n.* a wild and domesticated type of cattle, *Bos grunniens*, of Tibet, having long horns and long shaggy hair. [C19: from Tibetan *gyag*]

yak[2] (jæk) *Slang.* ~*n.* 1. noisy, continuous, and trivial talk or conversation. ~*vb.* **yaks, yakking, yakked.** 2. (*intr.*) to chatter or talk in this way; jabber. ~Also: **yakety-yak** (ˌjækɪtɪ'jæk). [C20: of imitative origin]

yakka, yakker, *or* **yacker** ('jækə) *n. Austral. and N.Z. informal.* work. [C19: from a native Australian language]

Yakut (jæ'kʊt) *n.* 1. (*pl.* **-kuts** *or* **-kut**) a native or inhabitant of the former Yakut ASSR, in NE Siberia. 2. the language of this people, belonging to the Turkic branch of the Altaic family.

Yale lock (jeɪl) *n. Trademark.* a type of cylinder lock using a flat serrated key.

yam (jæm) *n.* 1. any of various twining plants of the genus *Dioscorea*, of tropical and subtropical regions, cultivated for their edible tubers: family *Dioscoreaceae.* 2. the starchy tuber of any of these plants, which is eaten as a vegetable. 3. *Southern U.S.* any of certain large varieties of sweet potato. 4. a former Scot. name for the (common) **potato.** [C17: from Portuguese *inhame*, ultimately of West African origin; compare Senegal *nyami* to eat]

yamen ('jɑːmɛn) *n.* (in imperial China) the office or residence of a public official. [C19: from Chinese, from *ya* general's office + *mĕn* gate]

Yamim Nora'im (jɑ'mim nɔrɑ'im) *or* **Yomim Noro'im** ('jɔmim nəʊ'roim) *pl. n.* another name for **High Holidays.** [Hebrew, literally: Days of Awe]

yammer ('jæmə) *Informal.* ~*vb.* 1. to utter or whine in a complaining or peevish manner. 2. to make (a complaint) loudly or persistently. 3. (*intr.*) (esp. of an animal) to howl or wail plaintively or distressingly; yelp or yowl. ~*n.* 4. a yammering sound, wail, or utterance. 5. nonsense; jabber. [Old English *geōmrian* to grumble, complain; related to Old High German *iāmar* misery, lamentation, Old Norse *amra* to howl] —**'yammerer** *n.*

Yang (jæŋ) *n.* See **Yin and Yang.**

yank (jæŋk) *vb.* 1. to pull, jerk, or move with a sharp movement; tug. ~*n.* 2. a sharp jerking movement; tug. [C19: of unknown origin]

Yank (jæŋk) *n.* 1. a slang word for an American. 2. *U.S. informal.* short for **Yankee.**

Yankee ('jæŋkɪ) *or* (*informal*) **Yank** *n.* 1. *Often disparaging.* a native or inhabitant of the U.S.; American. 2. a native or inhabitant of New England, the NE part of the U.S. 3. a native or inhabitant of the Northern U.S., esp. a Northern soldier in the Civil War (1861–65). 4. *Communications.* a code word for the letter *y.* 5. *Finance.* a bond issued in the U.S. by a foreign borrower. ~*adj.* 6. of, relating to, or characteristic of Yankees. [C18: perhaps from Dutch *Jan Kees* John Cheese, nickname used derisively by Dutch settlers in New York to designate English colonists in Connecticut]

Yankee Doodle *n.* 1. an American song, popularly regarded as a characteristically national melody. 2. another name for **Yankee.**

Yankeeism ('jæŋkɪɪzəm) *n.* 1. Yankee character, behaviour, or attitudes. 2. a typical Yankee word, expression, or trait.

yap (jæp) *vb.* **yaps, yapping, yapped.** (*intr.*) 1. (of a dog) to bark in quick sharp bursts; yelp. 2. *Informal.* to talk at length in an annoying or stupid way; jabber. ~*n.* 3. a high-pitched or sharp bark; yelp. 4. *Slang.* annoying or stupid speech; jabber. 5. *Slang.* a derogatory word for **mouth.** ~*interj.* 6. (*usually reiterated*) an imitation or representation of the sound of a dog yapping or people jabbering. [C17: of imitative origin] —**'yapper** *n.* —**'yappy** *adj.*

yapok (jə'pɒk) *n.* an amphibious nocturnal opossum, *Chironectes minimus*, of Central and South America, having dense fur and preying on shrimps, crayfish, etc. Also called: **water opossum.** [C19: named after *Oyapok*, a river flowing between French Guiana and Brazil]

yapon ('jɔːpᵊn) *n.* a variant spelling of **yaupon.**

yarborough ('jɑːbərə, -brə) *n. Bridge, whist.* a hand of 13 cards in which no card is higher than nine. [C19: supposed to be named after the second Earl of *Yarborough* (died 1897), who is said to have bet a thousand to one against the occurrence of such a hand]

yard[1] (jɑːd) *n.* **1.** a unit of length equal to 3 feet and defined in 1963 as exactly 0.9144 metre. Abbrev.: **yd. 2.** a cylindrical wooden or hollow metal spar, tapered at the ends, slung from a mast of a square-rigged or lateen-rigged vessel and used for suspending a sail. **3.** short for **yardstick** (sense 2). [Old English *gierd* rod, twig; related to Old Frisian *jerde,* Old Saxon *gerdia,* Old High German *gertia,* Old Norse *gaddr*]

yard[2] (jɑːd) *n.* **1.** a piece of enclosed ground, usually either paved or laid with concrete and often adjoining or surrounded by a building or buildings. **2. a.** an enclosed or open area used for some commercial activity, for storage, etc.: *a railway yard.* **b.** (*in combination*): *a brickyard; a shipyard.* **3.** a U.S. and Canadian word for **garden** (sense 1). **4.** an area having a network of railway tracks and sidings, used for storing rolling stock, making up trains, etc. **5.** *U.S. and Canadian.* the winter pasture of deer, moose, and similar animals. **6.** *Austral. and N.Z.* an enclosed area used to draw off part of a herd, etc. **7.** *N.Z.* short for **saleyard** or **stockyard.** ~*vb.* (*tr.*) **8.** to draft (animals), esp. to a saleyard. [Old English *geard;* related to Old Saxon *gard,* Old High German *gart,* Old Norse *garthr* yard, Gothic *gards* house, Old Slavonic *gradu* town, castle, Albanian *garth* hedge]

yardage[1] (ˈjɑːdɪdʒ) *n.* a length measured in yards.

yardage[2] (ˈjɑːdɪdʒ) *n.* **1.** the use of a railway yard in the transportation of cattle. **2.** the charge for this.

yardarm (ˈjɑːdˌɑːm) *n. Nautical.* the two tapering outer ends of a ship's yard.

yardbird (ˈjɑːdˌbɜːd) *n. U.S. military.* an inexperienced, untrained, or clumsy soldier, esp. one employed on menial duties.

yard grass *n.* an Old World perennial grass, *Eleusine indica,* with prostrate leaves, growing as a troublesome weed on open ground, yards, etc. Also called: **wire grass.**

Yardie (ˈjɑːdɪ) *n.* a member of a Black criminal syndicate originally based in Jamaica. [origin unknown]

yarding (ˈjɑːdɪŋ) *n.* a group of animals displayed for sale: *a good yarding.*

yard of ale *n.* **1.** the beer or ale contained in a narrow horn-shaped drinking glass, usually about one yard long and holding between two and three pints. **2.** such a drinking glass itself.

yardstick (ˈjɑːdˌstɪk) *n.* **1.** a measure or standard used for comparison: *on what kind of yardstick is he basing his criticism?* **2.** a graduated stick, one yard long, used for measurement.

yare (jɛə) *adj.* **yarer, yarest. 1.** *Archaic or dialect.* ready, brisk, or eager. **2.** (of a vessel) answering swiftly to the helm; easily handled. ~*adv.* **3.** *Obsolete.* readily or eagerly. [Old English *gearu* ready; related to Old Saxon, Old High German *garo* ready, prepared, Old Norse *gorr*] —ˈ**yarely** *adv.*

yarmulke (ˈjɑːməlkə) *n. Judaism.* a skullcap worn by orthodox male Jews at all times, and by others during prayer. [from Yiddish, from Ukrainian and Polish *yarmulka* cap, probably from Turkish *yağmurluk* raincoat, from *yağmur* rain]

yarn (jɑːn) *n.* **1.** a continuous twisted strand of natural or synthetic fibres, used in weaving, knitting, etc. **2.** *Informal.* a long and often involved story or account, usually telling of incredible or fantastic events. **3. spin a yarn.** *Informal.* **a.** to tell such a story. **b.** to make up or relate a series of excuses. ~*vb.* **4.** (*intr.*) to tell such a story or stories. [Old English *gearn;* related to Old High German *garn* yarn, Old Norse *görn* gut, Greek *khordē* string, gut]

yarn-dyed *adj.* (of fabric) dyed while still in yarn form, before being woven. Compare **piece-dyed.**

Yarra-banker *n. Austral. slang.* a soapbox orator on the banks of the Yarra River in Melbourne.

yarraman (ˈjærəmən) *n., pl.* **-mans** *or* **-men.** *Austral.* a horse. [C19: from a native Australian language]

yarran (ˈjærən) *n.* a small hardy tree, *Acacia homalophylla,* of inland Australia: useful as fodder and for firewood. [from a native Australian language]

yarrow (ˈjærəʊ) *n.* any of several plants of the genus *Achillea,* esp. *A. millefolium,* of Eurasia, having finely dissected leaves and flat clusters of white flower heads: family *Compositae* (composites). Also called: **milfoil.** See also **sneezewort.** [Old English *gearwe;* related to Old High German *garwa,* Dutch *gerwe*]

yashmak *or* **yashmac** (ˈjæʃmæk) *n.* the face veil worn by Muslim women when in public. [C19: from Arabic]

yataghan (ˈjætəgən) *or* **ataghan** *n.* a Turkish sword with a curved single-edged blade. [C19: from Turkish *yatağan*]

yate (jeɪt) *n. Austral.* any of several small eucalyptus trees, esp. *Eucalyptus cornuta,* yielding a very hard timber. [from a native Australian language]

yatter (ˈjætə; *Scot.* ˈjɑtər) *Scot.* ~*vb.* (*intr.*) **1.** to talk at length; chatter. ~*n.* **2.** continuous chatter. [of imitative origin]

yauld (jɔːd, jɑːd, jɑːld) *adj. Scot. and northern English dialect.* alert, sprightly, or nimble. [C18: of unknown origin]

yaup (jɔːp) *vb., n.* a variant spelling of **yawp.** —ˈ**yauper** *n.*

yaupon *or* **yapon** (ˈjɔːpᵊn) *n.* a southern U.S. evergreen holly shrub, *Ilex vomitoria,* with spreading branches, scarlet fruits, and oval leaves: used as a substitute for tea. [from Catawba *yopun* shrub, diminutive of *yop* tree]

yautia (ˈjɔːtɪə) *n.* **1.** any of several West Indian aroid plants of the genus *Xanthosoma,* such as *X. sagittifolium,* cultivated for their edible leaves and underground stems. **2.** the leaves or underground stems of these plants, which can be eaten as vegetables. [C19: American Spanish, from Taino]

yaw (jɔː) *vb.* **1.** (*intr.*) (of an aircraft, missile, etc.) to turn about its vertical axis. Compare **pitch**[1] (sense 10), **roll** (sense 14). **2.** (*intr.*) (of a ship, etc.) to deviate temporarily from a straight course. **3.** (*tr.*) to cause (an aircraft, ship, etc.) to yaw. ~*n.* **4.** the angular movement of an aircraft, missile, etc., about its vertical axis. **5.** the deviation of a vessel from a straight course. [C16: of unknown origin]

yawl[1] (jɔːl) *n.* **1.** a two-masted sailing vessel, rigged fore-and-aft, with a large mainmast and a small mizzenmast stepped aft of the rudderpost. Compare **ketch, sloop. 2.** a ship's small boat, usually rowed by four or six oars. [C17: from Dutch *jol* or Middle Low German *jolle,* of unknown origin]

yawl[2] (jɔːl) *vb.* (*intr.*) *Brit. dialect.* to howl, weep, or scream harshly; yowl. [C14: from Low German *jaulen;* see YOWL]

yawn (jɔːn) *vb.* **1.** (*intr.*) to open the mouth wide and take in air deeply, often as in involuntary reaction to tiredness, sleepiness, or boredom. **2.** (*tr.*) to express or utter while yawning. **3.** (*intr.*) to be open wide as if threatening to engulf (someone or something): *the mine shaft yawned below.* ~*n.* **4.** the act or an instance of yawning. [Old English *gionian;* related to Old Saxon *ginōn,* Old High German *ginēn* to yawn, Old Norse *gjā* gap] —ˈ**yawner** *n.* —ˈ**yawning** *adj.* —ˈ**yawningly** *adv.*

yawp (jɔːp) *Dialect and U.S. and Canadian informal.* ~*vb.* (*intr.*) **1.** to gape or yawn, esp. audibly. **2.** to shout, cry, or talk noisily; bawl. **3.** to bark, yelp, or yowl. ~*n.* **4.** a shout, bark, yelp, or cry. **5.** a noisy, foolish, or raucous utterance. [C15 *yolpen,* probably of imitative origin; see YAP, YELP] —ˈ**yawper** *n.*

yaws (jɔːz) *n.* (*usually functioning as sing.*) an infectious non-venereal disease of tropical climates with early symptoms resembling syphilis, characterized by red skin eruptions and, later, pain in the joints: it is caused by the spiral bacterium *Treponema pertenue.* Also called: **framboesia.** [C17: of Carib origin]

***y*-axis** *n.* a reference axis, usually vertical, of a graph or two- or three-dimensional Cartesian coordinate system along which the *y*-coordinate is measured.

Yb *the chemical symbol for* ytterbium.

YC (in Britain) *abbrev. for* Young Conservative.

Y-chromosome *n.* the sex chromosome that occurs as one of a pair with the X-chromosome in the diploid cells of the males of many animals, including humans. Compare **X-chromosome.**

yclept (ɪˈklɛpt) *Obsolete.* ~*vb.* **1.** a past participle of **clepe.** ~*adj.* **2.** having the name of; called. [Old English *gecleopod,* past participle of *cleopian* to call]

Y connection *n. Electrical engineering.* a three-phase star connection.

yd *or* **yd.** *abbrev. for* yard (measure).

ye[1] (jiː; *unstressed* jɪ) *pron.* **1.** *Archaic or dialect.* refers to more than one person including the person addressed but not including the speaker. **2.** Also: **ee** (iː). *Dialect.* refers to one person addressed: *I tell ye.* [Old English *gē;* related to Dutch *gij,* Old Norse *ēr,* Gothic *jus*]

ye[2] (ðiː; *spelling pron.* jiː) *determiner.* a form of **the**[1], used as a supposed archaism, esp. in conjunction with other putative archaic spellings: *ye olde oake.* [from a misinterpretation of *the* as written in some Middle English texts. The runic letter thorn (Þ, representing *th*) was incorrectly transcribed as *y* because of a resemblance in their shapes],

yea (jeɪ) *sentence substitute.* **1.** a less common word for **aye** (yes). ~*adv.* **2.** (*sentence modifier*) *Archaic or literary.* indeed; truly: *yea, though my enemies spurn me, I shall prevail.* [Old English *gēa;* related to Old Frisian *jē,* Old Saxon, Old Norse, Old High German *jā,* Gothic *jai*]

yeah (jɛə) *sentence substitute.* an informal word for **yes.**

yean (jiːn) *vb.* (of a sheep or goat) to give birth to (offspring). [Old English *geēanian;* related to Dutch *oonen* to bring forth young, Latin *agnus* lamb; see EWE]

yeanling (ˈjiːnlɪŋ) *n.* the young of a goat or sheep.

year (jɪə) *n.* **1.** Also called: **civil year.** the period of time, the **calendar year,** containing 365 days or in a **leap year** 366 days. It is based on the Gregorian calendar, being divided into 12 calendar months, and is reckoned from January 1 to December 31. **2.** a period of twelve months from any specified date, such as one based on the four seasons. **3.** a specific period of time, usually occupying a definite part or parts of a twelve-month period, used for some particular activity: *a school year.* **4.** Also called: **astronomical year, tropical year, equinoctial year.** the period of time, the **solar year,** during which the earth makes one revolution around the sun, measured between two successive vernal equinoxes: equal to 365.242 19 days. **5.** the period of time, the **sidereal year,** during which the earth makes one revolution around the sun, measured between two successive conjunctions of a particular star: equal to 365.256 36 days. **6.** the period of time, the **lunar year,** containing 12 lunar months and equal to 354.3671 days. **7.** the period of time taken by a specified planet to complete one revolution around the sun: *the Martian year.* **8.** (*pl.*) age, esp. old age: *a man of his years should be more careful.* **9.** (*pl.*) time: *in years to come.* **10.** a group of pupils or students, who are taught or study together, divided into classes at school: *they are the best year we've ever had for history.* **11. the year dot.** *Informal.* as long ago as can be remembered. **12. year and a day.** *English law.* a period fixed by law to ensure the completion of a full year. It is applied for certain purposes, such as to determine the time within which wrecks must be claimed. **13. year in, year out.** regularly or monotonously, over a long period. ~Related adj.: **annual.** [Old English *gear;* related to Gothic *jēr,* Old Saxon, Old High German *jār,* Old Norse *ār* year, Polish *jar* springtime, Latin *hōrnus* of this year]

▷ **Usage.** In writing spans of years, it is important to choose a style that avoids ambiguity. The practice adopted in this dictionary is, in four-figure dates, to specify the last two digits of the second date if it falls within the same century as the first: *1801–08; 1850–51; 1899–1901.* In writing three-figure B.C. dates, it is advisable to give both dates in full: *159–156* B.C., not *159–56* B.C. unless of course the span referred to consists of 103 years rather than three years. It is also advisable to specify B.C. or A.D. in years under 1000 unless the context makes this self-evident.

yearbook ('jɪəˌbʊk) *n.* an almanac or other reference book published annually and containing details of events of the previous year.

yearling ('jɪəlɪŋ) *n.* **1.** the young of any of various animals, including the antelope and buffalo, between one and two years of age. **2.** a thoroughbred racehorse counted for racing purposes as being one year old until the second Jan. 1 following its birth. **3. a.** a bond that is intended to mature after one year. **b.** (*as modifier*): *yearling bonds.* ~*adj.* **4.** being a year old.

yearlong ('jɪə'lɒŋ) *adj.* throughout a whole year.

yearly ('jɪəlɪ) *adj.* **1.** occurring, done, appearing, etc., once a year or every year; annual. **2.** lasting or valid for a year; annual: *a yearly subscription.* ~*adv.* **3.** once a year; annually. ~*n., pl.* **-lies. 4.** a publication, event, etc., that occurs once a year.

yearn (jɜːn) *vb.* (*intr.*) **1.** (usually foll. by *for* or *after* or an infinitive) to have an intense desire or longing (for); hanker or pine (for). **2.** to feel tenderness or affection. [Old English *giernan;* related to Old Saxon *girnian,* Old Norse *girna,* Gothic *gairnjan,* Old High German *gerōn* to long for, Sanskrit *haryati* he likes] —'**yearner** *n.*

yearning ('jɜːnɪŋ) *n.* an intense or overpowering longing, desire, or need; craving. —'**yearningly** *adv.*

year of grace *n.* any year of the Christian era, as dated from the presumed date of Christ's birth.

year-round *adj.* open, in use, operating, etc., throughout the year.

yeast (jiːst) *n.* **1.** any of various single-celled ascomycetous fungi of the genus *Saccharomyces* and related genera, which reproduce by budding and are able to ferment sugars: a rich source of vitamins of the B complex. **2.** a commercial preparation containing yeast cells and inert material such as meal, used in raising dough for bread or for fermenting beer, whisky, etc. See also **brewer's yeast. 3.** a preparation containing yeast cells, used to treat diseases caused by vitamin B deficiency. **4.** froth or foam, esp. on beer. ~*vb.* **5.** (*intr.*) to froth or foam. [Old English *giest;* related to Old Norse *jostr,* Old High German *jesan,* Swedish *esa,* Norwegian *asa,* Sanskrit *yasati*] —'**yeastless** *adj.* —'**yeastˌlike** *adj.*

yeast cake *n. Chiefly U.S. and Canadian.* living yeast cells compressed with a little starch into a small cake, suitable for use in baking or brewing.

yeasty ('jiːstɪ) *adj.* **yeastier, yeastiest. 1.** of, resembling, or containing yeast. **2.** fermenting or causing fermentation. **3.** tasting of or like yeast. **4.** insubstantial or frivolous. **5.** restless, agitated, or unsettled. **6.** covered with or containing froth or foam. —'**yeastily** *adv.* —'**yeastiness** *n.*

yegg (jɛg) *n. Slang, chiefly U.S.* a burglar or safe-breaker. [C20: perhaps from the surname of a burglar]

yeld (jɛld) *adj. Scot. and northern English dialect.* **1.** (of an animal) barren or too young to bear young. **2.** (of a cow) not yielding milk. [Old English *gelde* barren; related to GELD[1]]

yelk (jɛlk) *n.* a dialect word for **yolk** (of an egg).

yell (jɛl) *vb.* **1.** to shout, scream, cheer, or utter in a loud or piercing way. ~*n.* **2.** a loud piercing inarticulate cry, as of pain, anger, or fear. **3.** *U.S. and Canadian.* a rhythmic cry of words or syllables, used in cheering in unison. [Old English *giellan;* related to Old Saxon *gellon,* Old High German *gellan,* Old Norse *gjalla;* see NIGHTINGALE] —'**yeller** *n.*

yellow ('jɛləʊ) *n.* **1.** any of a group of colours that vary in saturation but have the same hue. They lie in the approximate wavelength range 585–575 nanometres. Yellow is the complementary colour of blue and with cyan and magenta forms a set of primary colours. Related adj.: **xanthous. 2.** a pigment or dye of or producing these colours. **3.** yellow cloth or clothing: *dressed in yellow.* **4.** the yolk of an egg. **5.** a yellow ball in snooker, etc. **6.** any of a group of pieridine butterflies the males of which have yellow or yellowish wings, esp. the clouded yellows (*Colias* spp.) and the brimstone. ~*adj.* **7.** of the colour yellow. **8.** yellowish in colour or having parts or marks that are yellowish: *yellow jasmine.* **9.** having a yellowish skin; Mongoloid. **10.** *Informal.* cowardly or afraid. **11.** offensively sensational, as a cheap newspaper (esp. in the phrase **yellow press**). ~*vb.* **12.** to make or become yellow. See also **yellows.** [Old English *geolu;* related to Old Saxon, Old High German *gelo,* Old Norse *gulr,* Latin *helvus*] —'**yellowish** *adj.* —'**yellowly** *adv.* —'**yellowness** *n.* —'**yellowy** *adj.*

yellow archangel *n.* See **archangel** (sense 3).

yellowbark ('jɛləʊˌbɑːk) *n.* another name for **calisaya.**

yellow belly *n.* **1.** *Dialect.* a native of Lincolnshire, esp. of the fens. **2.** *Austral.* any of several freshwater food fishes with yellow underparts.

yellow-belly *n., pl.* **-lies.** a slang word for **coward.** —'**yellow-ˌbellied** *adj.*

yellow bile *n. Archaic.* one of the four bodily humours, choler.

yellowbird ('jɛləʊˌbɜːd) *n.* any of various birds having a yellow plumage, such as the American goldfinch.

yellow brain fungus *n.* See **jelly fungus.**

yellow cake *n. Informal.* semirefined uranium ore.

yellow card *n. Soccer.* a card of a yellow colour displayed by a referee to indicate that a player has been officially cautioned for some offence.

yellow cress *n.* any of various species of cress (*Rorippa*) that are related to watercress and have yellow flowers. They are not confined to water margins and some are garden weeds.

yellow-dog contract *n. U.S.* a contract with an employer, now illegal, in which an employee agreed not to join a trade union during his employment. [C20: from U.S. *yellow-dog* anti-trade union, from *yellow dog* mongrel, contemptible person]

yellow fever *n.* an acute infectious disease of tropical and subtropical climates, characterized by fever, haemorrhages, vomiting of blood, and jaundice: caused by a virus transmitted by the bite of a female mosquito of the species *Aedes aegypti.* Also called: **yellow jack, black vomit.**

yellow flag *n.* **1.** another name for **quarantine flag. 2.** See **flag**[2] (sense 1).

yellowhammer ('jɛləʊˌhæmə) *n.* **1.** a European bunting, *Emberiza citrinella,* having a yellowish head and body and brown streaked wings and tail. **2.** *U.S. and Canadian.* an informal name for the **yellow-shafted flicker,** an American woodpecker (see **flicker**[2]). [C16: of uncertain origin]

yellowhead ('jɛləʊˌhɛd) *n.* a small bush bird, *Mohoua ochrocephala,* of South Island, New Zealand, having a yellow head and breast.

yellow jack *n.* **1.** *Pathol.* another name for **yellow fever. 2.** another name for **quarantine flag. 3.** any of certain large yellowish carangid food fishes, esp. *Caranx bartholomaei,* of warm and tropical Atlantic waters.

yellow jacket *n. U.S. and Canadian.* any of several social wasps of the genus *Vespa,* having yellow markings on the body.

yellow jasmine *n.* a climbing shrub, *Gelsemium sempervirens,* of the southeastern U.S., having fragrant funnel-shaped yellow flowers: family *Loganiaceae.* See also **gelsemium.**

yellow jersey *n.* (in the Tour de France) a yellow jersey awarded as a trophy to the cyclist with the fastest time in each stage of the race.

yellow journalism *n.* the type of journalism that relies on sensationalism and lurid exaggeration to attract readers. [C19: perhaps shortened from the phrase *Yellow Kid journalism,* referring to the *Yellow Kid,* a cartoon (1895) in the *New York World,* a newspaper having a reputation for sensationalism]

yellowlegs ('jɛləʊˌlɛgz) *n.* (*functioning as sing.*) either of two North American sandpipers, *Tringa melanoleuca* (or *Totanus melanoleucus*) **(greater yellowlegs)** or *T. flavipes* **(lesser yellowlegs)**, having bright yellow legs.

yellow line *n. Brit.* a yellow line painted along the edge of a road indicating waiting restrictions.

yellow metal *n.* **1.** a type of brass having about 60 per cent copper and 40 per cent zinc. **2.** another name for **gold.**

Yellow Pages *pl. n. Trademark.* a classified telephone directory, often printed on yellow paper, that lists subscribers by the business or service provided.

yellow peril *n.* the power or alleged power of Asiatic peoples, esp. the Chinese, to threaten or destroy the supremacy of White or Western civilization.

yellow poplar *n.* another name for **tulip tree** (sense 1) or **tulipwood** (sense 1).

yellow rain *n.* a type of yellow precipitation described in parts of SE Asia and alleged by some to be evidence of chemical warfare using mycotoxins.

yellow rattle *n.* See **rattle**[1] (sense 10).

yellows ('jɛləʊz) *n.* (*functioning as sing.*) **1.** any of various fungal or viral diseases of plants, characterized by yellowish discoloration and stunting. **2.** *Vet. science.* another name for **jaundice.**

yellow sally *n.* an angler's name for either of two small yellow stoneflies: *Isoperla grammatica* of chalk streams and *Chloroperla torrentium* of upland streams.

yellow spot *n. Anatomy.* another name for **macula lutea.**

yellow streak *n. Informal.* a cowardly or weak trait, characteristic, or flaw in a person's nature.

yellowtail ('jɛləʊˌteɪl) *n., pl.* **-tails** *or* **-tail. 1.** a carangid game fish, *Seriola dorsalis,* of coastal waters of S California and Mexico, having a yellow tail fin. **2.** any of various similar fishes. **3.** Also called: **yellowtail moth.** another name for **goldtail moth.**

yellow underwing *n.* any of several species of noctuid moths (*Noctua* and *Anarta* species), the hind wings of which are yellow with a black bar.

yellow water lily *n.* an aquatic nymphaeaceous plant, *Nuphar lutea,* of Europe and N Asia, having floating heart-shaped leaves and yellow flowers. Also called: **brandy bottle.**

yellowweed ('jɛləʊˌwiːd) *n.* any of various yellow-flowered plants, such as the ragwort in Europe and some species of goldenrod in the U.S.

yellowwood ('jɛləʊˌwʊd) *n.* **1.** Also called (U.S.): **gopherwood.** any of several leguminous trees of the genus *Cladrastis,* esp. *C. lutea,* of the southeastern U.S., having clusters of white flowers and yellow wood yielding a yellow dye. **2.** Also called: **West Indian satinwood.** a rutaceous tree, *Zanthoxylum flavum,* of the West Indies, with smooth hard wood. **3.** any of several other trees with yellow wood, esp. *Podocarpus falcatus,* a conifer of southern Africa: family *Podocarpaceae.* **4.** the wood of any of these trees.

yellowwort ('jɛləʊˌwɜːt) *n.* a gentianaceous perennial, *Blackstonia perfoliata,* that is related to centaury and has waxy grey foliage and yellow flowers: characteristically found on chalk turf.

yellow-yite *n.* a Scot. word for **yellowhammer** (sense 1). Also called: **yite, yitie.**

yelp (jɛlp) *vb.* (*intr.*) **1.** (esp. of a dog) to utter a sharp or high-pitched cry or bark, often indicating pain. *~n.* **2.** a sharp or high-pitched cry or bark. [Old English *gielpan* to boast; related to Low German *galpen* to croak, Danish *gylpe* to croak] —'**yelper** *n.*

Yemeni ('jɛmənɪ) *n.* **1.** a native or inhabitant of Yemen, a republic in SW Arabia, formed in 1990 from the union of North Yemen and South Yemen. *~adj.* **2.** of or relating to Yemen or its people.

yen[1] (jɛn) *n., pl.* **yen.** the standard monetary unit of Japan, (formerly) divided into 100 sen. [C19: from Japanese *en,* from Chinese *yüan* circular object, dollar]

yen[2] (jɛn) *Informal.* *~n.* **1.** a passionate, ardent, or intense longing or desire. *~vb.* **yens, yenning, yenned. 2.** (*intr.*) to yearn. [perhaps from Chinese (Cantonese) *yǎn* a craving, addiction]

yeoman ('jəʊmən) *n., pl.* **-men. 1.** *History.* **a.** a member of a class of small freeholders of common birth who cultivated their own land. **b.** an assistant or other subordinate to an official, such as a sheriff, or to a craftsman or trader. **c.** an attendant or lesser official in a royal or noble household. **2.** (in Britain) another name for **yeoman of the guard. 3.** (*modifier*) characteristic of or relating to a yeoman. **4.** a petty officer or noncommissioned officer in the Royal Navy or Marines in charge of signals. [C15: perhaps from *yongman* young man]

yeomanly ('jəʊmənlɪ) *adj.* **1.** of, relating to, or like a yeoman. **2.** having the virtues attributed to yeomen, such as staunchness, loyalty, and courage. *~adv.* **3.** in a yeomanly manner, as in being brave, staunch, or loyal.

yeoman of the guard *n.* a member of the bodyguard (**Yeomen of the Guard**) of the English monarch. This unit was founded in 1485 and now retains ceremonial functions only.

yeomanry ('jəʊmənrɪ) *n.* yeomen collectively.

yep (jɛp) *sentence substitute.* an informal word for **yes.**

yerba *or* **yerba maté** ('jɛəbə, 'jɜːbə) *n.* another name for **maté.** [from Spanish *yerba maté* herb maté]

yes (jɛs) *sentence substitute.* **1.** used to express acknowledgment, affirmation, consent, agreement, or approval or to answer when one is addressed. **2.** used, often with interrogative intonation, to signal someone to speak or keep speaking, enter a room, or do something. *~n.* **3.** an answer or vote of *yes.* **4.** (*often pl.*) a person who votes in the affirmative. ~Compare **no**[1]. [Old English *gēse,* from *iā sīe* may it be; see YEA]

yeshiva (jə'ʃiːvə; *Hebrew* jə'ʃiːva) *n., pl.* **-vahs** *or* **-voth** (*Hebrew* -vɔt). **1.** a traditional Jewish school devoted chiefly to the study of rabbinic literature and the Talmud. **2.** a school run by Orthodox Jews for children of elementary school age, providing both religious and secular instruction. [from Hebrew *yěshībhāh* a sitting, seat, hence, an academy]

yes man *n.* a servile, submissive, or acquiescent subordinate, assistant, or associate; sycophant.

yes/no question *n. Grammar.* a question inviting the answer "yes" or "no". Compare **WH question.**

yester ('jɛstə) *adj. Archaic.* of or relating to yesterday: *yester sun.* Also: **yestern** ('jɛstən). [Old English *geostror;* related to Old High German *gestaron,* Gothic *gistra,* Old Norse *ī gœr*]

yester- *prefix.* **1.** indicating the day before today: *yesterday.* **2.** indicating a period of time before the present one: *yesteryear.* [Old English *geostran;* compare German *gestern,* Latin *hesternus* of yesterday]

yesterday ('jɛstədɪ, -ˌdeɪ) *n.* **1.** the day immediately preceding today. **2.** (*often pl.*) the recent past. *~adv.* **3.** on or during the day before today. **4.** in the recent past.

yesteryear ('jɛstəˌjɪə) *Formal or literary.* *~n.* **1.** last year or the past in general. *~adv.* **2.** during last year or the past in general.

yestreen (jɛ'striːn) *adv. Scot.* yesterday evening. [C14: from YEST(E)R- + E(V)EN[2]]

yet (jɛt) *sentence connector.* **1.** nevertheless; still; in spite of that: *I want to and yet I haven't the courage; she is strange yet kind.* *~adv.* **2.** (*usually used with a negative or interrogative*) so far; up until then or now: *they're not home yet; is it teatime yet?* **3.** (often preceded by *just; usually used with a negative*) now (as contrasted with later): *we can't stop yet.* **4.** (*often used with a comparative*) even; still: *yet more potatoes for sale; yet another problem family.* **5.** eventually, in spite of everything: *we'll convince him yet.* **6. as yet.** so far; up until then or now. [Old English *gēta;* related to Old Frisian *jēta*]

yeti ('jɛtɪ) *n.* another term for **abominable snowman.** [C20: from Tibetan]

yett (jɛt) *n. Scot.* a gate or door. [Old English variant of GATE[1]]

yew (juː) *n.* **1.** any coniferous tree of the genus *Taxus,* of the Old World and North America, esp. *T. baccata,* having flattened needle-like leaves, fine-grained elastic wood, and cuplike red waxy cones resembling berries: family *Taxaceae.* **2.** the wood of any of these trees, used to make bows for archery. **3.** *Archery.* a bow made of yew. [Old English *īw;* related to Old High German *īwa,* Old Norse *ȳr* yew, Latin *ūva* grape, Russian *iva* willow]

Yezidis ('jɛzɪdɪz) *pl. n.* a religious sect based around Mosul, Iraq, that combines elements of Islam and Christianity and incorporates worship of the devil as an agent of God. [C19: perhaps from *Yazid,* native name for the devil]

Y-fronts *pl. n. Trademark.* boys' or men's underpants having a front opening within an inverted Y shape.

YHA (in Britain) *abbrev. for* Youth Hostels Association.

YHVH, YHWH, JHVH, *or* **JHWH** *Old Testament.* the letters of the **Tetragrammaton.** See also **Yahweh, Jehovah.**

yid (jɪd) *n. Slang.* a derogatory word for a Jew. [C20: probably from *Yiddish,* from Middle High German *Jude* JEW]

Yiddish ('jɪdɪʃ) *n.* **1.** a language spoken as a vernacular by Jews in Europe and elsewhere by Jewish emigrants, usually written in the Hebrew alphabet. Historically, it is a dialect of High German with an admixture of words of Hebrew, Romance, and Slavonic origin, developed in central and E Europe during the Middle Ages. *~adj.* **2.** in or relating to this language. [C19: from German *jüdisch,* from *Jude* JEW]

Yiddisher ('jɪdɪʃə) *adj.* **1.** in or relating to Yiddish. **2.** Jewish *~n.* **3.** a speaker of Yiddish; Jew.

yield (jiːld) *vb.* **1.** to give forth or supply (a product, result, etc.), esp. by cultivation, labour, etc.; produce or bear. **2.** (*tr.*) to furnish as a return: *the shares yielded three per cent.* **3.** (*tr.; often* foll. by *up*) to surrender or relinquish, esp. as a result of force, persuasion, etc. **4.** (*intr.;* sometimes foll. by *to*) to give way, submit, or surrender, as through force or persuasion: *she yielded to his superior knowledge.* **5.** (*intr.;* often foll. by *to*) to agree; comply; assent: *he eventually yielded to their request for money.* **6.** (*tr.*) to grant or allow; concede: *to yield right of way.* **7.** (*tr.*) *Obsolete.* to pay or repay: *God yield thee!* *~n.* **8.** the result, product, or amount yielded. **9.** the profit or return, as from an investment or tax. **10.** the annual income provided by an investment, usually expressed as a percentage of its cost or of its current value: *the yield on these shares is 15 per cent at today's market value.* **11.** the energy released by the explosion of a nuclear weapon expressed in terms of the amount of TNT necessary to produce the same energy. **12.** *Chem.* the quantity of a specified product obtained in a reaction or series of reactions, usually expressed as a percentage of the quantity that is theoretically obtainable. [Old English *gieldan;* related to Old Frisian *jelda,* Old High German *geltan,* Old Norse *gjalda,* Gothic *gildan*] —'**yieldable** *adj.* —'**yielder** *n.*

yielding ('jiːldɪŋ) *adj.* **1.** compliant, submissive, or flexible. **2.** pliable or soft: *a yielding material.* —'**yieldingly** *adv.* —'**yieldingness** *n.*

yield point *n.* the stress at which an elastic material under increasing stress ceases to behave elastically; under conditions of tensile strength the elongation is greater than the increase in stress. Also called: **yield stress, yield strength.**

yield stress *n.* the stress level at which a metal or other material ceases to behave elastically. The stress divided by the strain is no longer constant. The point at which this occurs is known as the yield point. Compare **proof stress.**

yike (jaɪk) *Austral. informal.* *~n.* **1.** an argument, squabble, or fight. *~vb.* (*intr.*) **2.** to argue, squabble, or fight. [origin unknown]

yin (jɪn) *determiner, pron., n.* a Scot. word for **one.**

Yin and Yang (jɪn) *n.* two complementary principles of Chinese philosophy: Yin is negative, dark, and feminine, Yang positive, bright, and masculine. Their interaction is thought to maintain the harmony of the universe and to influence everything within it. [from Chinese (Peking) *yin* dark + *yang* bright]

Yinglish ('jɪŋglɪʃ) *n.* a dialect of English spoken esp. by Jewish immigrants to New York, and heavily influenced by Yiddish constructions and loan words. Also: **Yenglish.** [from YI(DDISH) + (E)NGLISH]

yippee (jɪ'piː) *interj.* an exclamation of joy, pleasure, anticipation, etc.

yips (jɪps) *pl. n.* **the.** *Informal.* (in sport, originally esp. golf) nervous twitching or tension that destroys concentration and spoils performance. [C20: of unknown origin]

yirr (jɜː) *vb.* (*intr.*) *Dialect, chiefly Scot.* to snarl, growl, or yell. [C18: perhaps from Old English *georran, gyrran* to growl, of imitative origin]

yite (jaɪt) *or* **yitie** ('jaɪtɪ) *n.* Scot. words for **yellowhammer** (sense 1). Also called: **yellow-yite.** [C19: of unknown origin]

Yizkor ('jizkor) *n. Judaism.* a memorial prayer included in the liturgy for certain festivals. [from Hebrew, literally: let him remember]

-yl *suffix of nouns.* (in chemistry) indicating a group or radical: *methyl; carbonyl.* [from Greek *hulē* wood, matter]

ylang-ylang *or* **ilang-ilang** ('iːlæŋ'iːlæŋ) *n.* **1.** an aromatic Asian tree, *Cananga odorata* (or *Canangium odoratum*), with fragrant greenish-yellow flowers yielding a volatile oil: family *Annonaceae.* **2.** the oil obtained from this tree, used in perfumery. [C19: from Tagalog *ilang-ilang*]

ylem ('aɪləm) *n.* the original matter from which the basic elements are said to have been formed following the explosion postulated in the big bang theory of cosmology. [Middle English, from Old French *ilem,* from Latin *hӯlē* stuff, matter, from Greek *hulē* wood, matter]

Y-level *n. Surveying.* a level mounted on a Y-shaped support that can be rotated.

YMCA *abbrev. for* Young Men's Christian Association.

YMHA *abbrev. for* Young Men's Hebrew Association.

-yne *suffix forming nouns.* denoting an organic chemical containing a triple bond: *alkyne.* [alteration of -INE[2]]

yo (jəʊ) *sentence substitute.* an expression used as a greeting, to attract someone's attention, etc. [C20: of unknown origin]

yob (jɒb) *or* **yobbo** ('jɒbəʊ) *n., pl.* **yobs** *or* **yobbos.** *Brit. slang.* an aggressive and surly youth, esp. a teenager. [C19: perhaps back slang for BOY] —'**yobbish** *adj.* —'**yobbery** *n.*

yod *or* **yodh** (jʊd) *n.* the tenth letter in the Hebrew alphabet (י), transliterated as *y.* [C18: from Hebrew, literally: hand]

yodel ('jəʊdᵊl) *n.* **1.** an effect produced in singing by an abrupt change of register from the chest voice to falsetto, esp. in popular folk songs of the Swiss Alps. ~*vb.* **-dels, -delling, -delled** *or U.S.* **-dels, -deling, -deled. 2.** to sing (a song) in which a yodel is used. [C19: from German *jodeln,* of imitative origin] —'**yodeller** *n.*

yodle ('jəʊdᵊl) *n.* a variant spelling of **yodel.** —'**yodler** *n.*

yoga ('jəʊgə) *n.* (*often cap.*) **1.** a Hindu system of philosophy aiming at the mystical union of the self with the Supreme Being in a state of complete awareness and tranquillity through certain physical and mental exercises. **2.** any method by which such awareness and tranquillity are attained, esp. a course of related exercises and postures designed to promote physical and spiritual wellbeing. See **hatha yoga, raja yoga.** [C19: from Sanskrit: a yoking, union, from *yunakti* he yokes] —**yogic** ('jəʊgɪk) *adj.*

yogh (jɒg) *n.* **1.** a character (ȝ) used in Old and Middle English to represent a palatal fricative very close to the semivowel sound of Modern English *y,* as in Old English *ȝeong* (young). **2.** this same character as used in Middle English for both the voiced and voiceless palatal fricatives; when final or in a closed syllable in medial position the sound approached that of German *ch* in *ich,* as in *knyȝt* (knight). After the 14th century this symbol became the modern consonantal (semivocalic) *y* when initial or commencing a syllable, and though no longer pronounced in medial position it is preserved in many words by a modern *gh,* as in *thought.* [C14: perhaps from *yok* YOKE, referring to the letter's shape]

yoghurt, yogurt, *or* **yoghourt** ('jəʊgət, 'jɒg-) *n.* a thick custard-like food prepared from milk that has been curdled by bacteria, often sweetened and flavoured with fruit, chocolate, etc. [C19: from Turkish *yoğurt*]

yogi ('jəʊgɪ) *n., pl.* **-gis** *or* **-gin** (-gɪn). a person who is a master of yoga. —**yogini** (jəʊ'giːniː) *fem. n.*

yo-heave-ho (ˌjəʊhiːv'həʊ) *interj.* a cry formerly used by sailors while pulling or lifting together in rhythm.

yohimbine (jəʊ'hɪmbiːn) *n.* an alkaloid found in the bark of the tree *Corynanthe yohimbe.* It is used in medicine as an adrenergic blocking agent. Formula: $C_{21}H_{26}N_2O_3$. [C19: from Bantu *yohimbé* a tropical African tree + -INE[1]]

yo-ho-ho *interj.* **1.** an exclamation to call attention. **2.** another word for **yo-heave-ho.**

yoicks (haɪk; *spelling pron.* jɔɪks) *interj.* a cry used by huntsmen to urge on the hounds to the fox.

yoke (jəʊk) *n., pl.* **yokes** *or* **yoke. 1.** a wooden frame, usually consisting of a bar with an oxbow or similar collar-like piece at either end, for attaching to the necks of a pair of draught animals, esp. oxen, so that they can be worked as a team. **2.** something resembling a yoke in form or function, such as a frame fitting over a person's shoulders for carrying buckets suspended at either end. **3.** a fitted part of a garment, esp. around the neck, shoulders, and chest or around the hips, to which a gathered, pleated, flared, or unfitted part is attached. **4.** an immense oppressive force or burden: *under the yoke of a tyrant.* **5.** a pair of oxen or other draught animals joined together by a yoke. **6.** a part, esp. one of relatively thick cross section, that secures two or more components so that they move together. **7.** a crosshead that transmits the drive of an opposed piston engine from the upper of a pair of linked pistons to the crankshaft through a connecting rod. **8.** a steel framework around the formwork during the casting of concrete. **9.** *Nautical.* a crossbar fixed athwartships to the head of a rudderpost in a small boat, to which are attached ropes or cables for steering. **10.** a Y-shaped cable, rope, or chain, used for holding, towing, etc. **11.** (in the ancient world) a symbolic reconstruction of a yoke, consisting of two upright spears with a third lashed across them, under which conquered enemies were compelled to march, esp. in Rome. **12.** a mark, token, or symbol of slavery, subjection, or suffering. **13.** *Now rare.* a link, tie, or bond: *the yoke of love.* **14.** *Brit. dialect.* a period of steady work, esp. the time during which a ploughman and his team work at a stretch. **15.** *Irish.* any device, unusual object, or gadget: *where's the yoke for opening tins?* ~*vb.* **16.** (*tr.*) to secure or harness (a draught animal) to (a plough, vehicle, etc.) by means of a yoke. **17.** to join or be joined by means of a yoke; couple, unite, or link. **18.** (*tr.*) *Obsolete.* to oppress, burden, or enslave. [Old English *geoc;* related to Old High German *ioh,* Old Norse *ok,* Gothic *juk,* Latin *iugum,* Sanskrit *yugam*] —'**yokeless** *adj.*

yokefellow ('jəʊkˌfɛləʊ) *n. Archaic.* a working companion or associate.

yokel ('jəʊkᵊl) *n. Disparaging.* (used chiefly by townspeople) a person who lives in the country, esp. one who is simple and old-fashioned. [C19: perhaps from dialect *yokel* green woodpecker, yellowhammer] —'**yokelish** *adj.*

yolk (jəʊk) *n.* **1.** the substance in an animal ovum consisting of protein and fat that nourishes the developing embryo. **2.** a greasy substance secreted by the skin of a sheep and present in the fleece. [Old English *geoloca,* from *geolu* YELLOW] —'**yolkless** *adj.* —'**yolky** *adj.*

yolk sac *n. Zoology.* **1.** the membranous sac that is attached to the ventral surface of the embryos of birds, reptiles, and some fishes and contains yolk. **2.** the corresponding part in the embryo of mammals, which contains no yolk.

Yom Kippur (jɒm 'kɪpə; *Hebrew* jɔm ki'pur) *n.* an annual Jewish holiday celebrated on Tishri 10 as a day of fasting, on which prayers of penitence are recited in the synagogue throughout the day. Also called: **Day of Atonement.** [from Hebrew, from *yōm* day + *kippūr* atonement]

yomp (jɒmp) *vb.* (*intr.*) to walk or trek laboriously, esp. heavily laden and over difficult terrain. [C20: military slang, of uncertain origin]

yom tov ('jɔm 'tɔv, 'jɔmtəv) *n., pl.* **yamin tovim** (jɑ'min tɔ'vim). *Judaism.* a festival, esp. that of Passover, Shabuoth, Sukkoth, or Rosh Hashana.

yon (jɒn) *or* **yond** (jɒnd) *determiner.* **1.** *Chiefly Scot. and northern English* **a.** an archaic or dialect word for **that:** *yon man.* **b.** (*as pronoun*): *yon's a fool.* **2.** variants of **yonder.** [Old English *geon;* related to Old Frisian *jen,* Old High German *jenēr,* Old Norse *enn,* Gothic *jains*]

yonder ('jɒndə) *adv.* **1.** at, in, or to that relatively distant place; over there. ~*determiner.* **2.** being at a distance, either within view or as if within view: *yonder valleys.* [C13: from Old English *geond* yond; related to Old Saxon *jendra,* Old High German *jenēr,* Gothic *jaind*]

yoni ('jəʊnɪ) *n. Hinduism.* **1.** the female genitalia, regarded as a divine symbol of sexual pleasure and matrix of generation and the visible form of the female principle Sakti. **2.** an image of these as an object of worship. [C18: from Sanskrit, literally: vulva, womb]

yonks (jɒŋks) *pl. n. Informal.* a very long time; ages: *I haven't seen him for yonks.* [C20: of unknown origin]

yonnie ('jɒnɪ) *n. Austral. children's slang.* a stone. [from a native Australian language]

yoo-hoo ('juːˌhuː) *interj.* a call to attract a person's attention.

YOP (jɒp) *n.* (in Britain) **1. a.** *acronym for* Youth Opportunities Programme. **b.** (*as modifier*): *a YOP scheme.* **2.** Also called: '**yopper.** *Informal.* a young person employed through this government programme.

yore (jɔː) *n.* **1.** time long past (now only in the phrase **of yore**). ~*adv.* **2.** *Obsolete.* in the past; long ago. [Old English *geāra,* genitive plural of *gēar* YEAR; see HOUR]

york (jɔːk) *vb.* (*tr.*) *Cricket.* to bowl or try to bowl (a batsman) by pitching the ball under or just beyond the bat. [C19: back formation from YORKER]

yorker (jɔːkə) *n. Cricket.* a ball bowled so as to pitch just under or just beyond the bat. [C19: probably named after the *Yorkshire* County Cricket Club]

yorkie ('jɔːkɪ) *n.* another name for **Yorkshire terrier.**

Yorkist ('jɔːkɪst) *English history* ~*n.* **1.** a member or adherent of the royal house of York (reigned 1461–85), esp. during the Wars of the Roses (1455–85) in England. ~*adj.* **2.** of, belonging to, or relating to the supporters or members of the house of York.

Yorks. (jɔːks) *abbrev. for* Yorkshire.

Yorkshire fog ('jɔːkˌʃɪə, -ʃə) *n.* a common tufted grass, *Holcus lanatus,* having downy leaves and flower heads that are white or pink and branched, with spikelets carrying the flowers.

Yorkshire pudding *n. Chiefly Brit.* a light puffy baked pudding made from a batter of flour, eggs, and milk, traditionally served with roast beef.

Yorkshire terrier *n.* a very small breed of terrier with a long straight glossy coat of steel-blue and tan. Also called: **yorkie.**

Yoruba ('jɒrʊbə) *n.* **1.** (*pl.* **-bas** *or* **-ba**) a member of a Negroid people of W Africa, living chiefly in the coastal regions of SW Nigeria: noted for their former city states and complex material culture, particularly as evidenced in their music, art, and sculpture. **2.** the language of this people, belonging to the Kwa branch of the Niger-Congo family. —'**Yoruban** *adj.*

you (juː; *unstressed* jʊ) *pron.* (*subjective or objective*) **1.** refers to the person addressed or to more than one person including the person or persons addressed but not including the speaker: *you know better; the culprit is among you.* **2.** Also: **one.** refers to an unspecified person or people in general: *you can't tell the boys from the girls.* **3.** *Chiefly U.S.* a dialect word for **yourself** or **yourselves** when used as an indirect object: *you should get you a wife now.* ~*n.* **4.** *Informal.* the personality of the person being addressed or something that expresses it: *that hat isn't really you.* **5. you know what** *or* **who.** a thing or person that the speaker cannot or does not want to specify. [Old English *ēow,* dative and accusative of *gē* YE[1]; related to Old Saxon *eu,* Old High German *iu,* Gothic *izwis*]

▷**Usage.** See at **me.**

you-all *pron.* a U.S., esp. Southern, word for **you,** esp. when addressing more than one person.

you'd (juːd; *unstressed* jʊd) *contraction of* you had *or* you would.

you'll (juːl; *unstressed* jʊl) *contraction of* you will *or* you shall.

young (jʌŋ) *adj.* **younger** (ˈjʌŋgə), **youngest** (ˈjʌŋgɪst). **1. a.** having lived, existed, or been made or known for a relatively short time: *a young man; a young movement; a young country.* **b.** (*as collective n.;* preceded by *the*): *the young.* **2.** youthful or having qualities associated with youth; vigorous or lively: *she's very young for her age.* **3.** of or relating to youth: *in my young days.* **4.** having been established or introduced for a relatively short time: *a young member.* **5.** in an early stage of progress or development; not far advanced: *the day was young.* **6.** *Geography.* **a.** (of mountains) formed in the Alpine orogeny and still usually rugged in outline. **b.** another term for **youthful** (sense 4). **7.** (*often cap.*) of or relating to a rejuvenated group or movement or one claiming to represent the younger members of the population, esp. one adhering to a political ideology: *Young England; Young Socialists.* ~*n.* **8.** (*functioning as pl.*) offspring, esp. young animals: *a rabbit with her young.* **9. with young.** (of animals) pregnant. [Old English *geong;* related to Old Saxon, Old High German *iung,* Old Norse *ungr,* Latin *iuvenis,* Sanskrit *yuvan*] —ˈ**youngish** *adj.*

youngberry (ˈjʌŋbərɪ, -brɪ) *n., pl.* **-ries. 1.** a trailing bramble of the southwestern U.S. that is a hybrid of a blackberry and dewberry with large sweet dark purple fruits. **2.** the fruit of this plant. [C20: named after B. M. *Young,* U.S. fruit-grower who was first to cultivate it (circa 1900)]

young blood *n.* young, fresh, or vigorous new people, ideas, attitudes, etc.

Young Fogey *n.* a young or fairly young person who adopts the conservative values of an older generation.

young lady *n.* a girlfriend; sweetheart.

youngling (ˈjʌŋlɪŋ) *n.* **1.** *Literary.* **a.** a young person, animal, or plant. **b.** (*as modifier*): *a youngling brood.* **2.** *Rare.* a beginner; novice. [Old English *geongling*]

young man *n.* a boyfriend; sweetheart.

Young's modulus *n.* a modulus of elasticity, applicable to the stretching of a wire etc., equal to the ratio of the applied load per unit area of cross section to the increase in length per unit length. Symbol: *E* [C19: named after Thomas *Young* (1773–1829), British physicist and physician]

youngster (ˈjʌŋstə) *n.* **1.** a young person; child or youth. **2.** a young animal, esp. a horse.

Young Turk *n.* **1.** a progressive, revolutionary, or rebellious member of an organization, political party, etc., esp. one agitating for radical reform. **2.** a member of an abortive reform movement in the Ottoman Empire, originally made up of exiles in W Europe who advocated liberal reforms. The movement fell under the domination of young Turkish army officers of a nationalist bent, who wielded great influence in the government between 1908 and 1918.

younker (ˈjʌŋkə) *n.* **1.** *Archaic or literary.* a young man; lad. **2.** *Obsolete.* a young gentleman or knight. [C16: from Dutch *jonker,* from Middle Dutch *jonc* YOUNG]

your (jɔː, jʊə; *unstressed* jə) *determiner.* **1.** of, belonging to, or associated with you: *your nose; your house; your first taste of freedom.* **2.** belonging to or associated with an unspecified person or people in general: *the path is on your left heading north; this lotion is for your head only.* **3.** *Informal.* used to indicate all things or people of a certain type: *your part-time worker is a problem.* **4. your actual.** *Brit. informal.* (intensifier): *here is your actual automatic tin-opener.* [Old English *eower,* genitive of *gē* YE[1]; related to Old Frisian *jūwe,* Old Saxon *euwa,* Old High German *iuwēr*]

you're (jʊə, jɔː; *unstressed* jə) *contraction of* you are.

yours (jɔːz, jʊəz) *pron.* **1.** something or someone belonging to or associated in some way with you: *I've eaten yours.* **2.** your family: *greetings to you and yours.* **3.** used in conventional closing phrases at the end of a letter: *yours sincerely, yours faithfully.* **4. of yours.** belonging to or associated with you. **5. what's yours?** *Jocular.* what would you like to drink?

yourself (jɔːˈsɛlf, jʊə-) *pron., pl.* **-selves. 1. a.** the reflexive form of *you.* **b.** (intensifier): *you yourself control your destiny.* **2.** (*preceded by a copula*) your normal or usual self: *you're not yourself these days.*

▷**Usage.** See at **myself.**

yours truly *pron.* an informal term for *I, myself,* or *me.* [from the conventional closing phrase used at the end of letters]

yous *or* **youse** (juːz) *pron. Dialect or nonstandard.* refers to more than one person including the person or persons addressed but not including the speaker: *yous have all had it now; I'm fed up with yous.*

youth (juːθ) *n., pl.* **youths** (juːðz). **1.** the quality or condition of being young, immature, or inexperienced: *his youth told against him in the contest.* **2.** the period between childhood and maturity, esp. adolescence and early adulthood. **3.** the freshness, vigour, or vitality characteristic of young people: *youth shone out from her face.* **4.** any period of early development: *the project was in its youth.* **5.** a young person, esp. a young man or boy. **6.** young people collectively: *youth everywhere is rising in revolt.* [Old English *geogoth;* related to Old Frisian *jogethe,* Old High German *iugund,* Gothic *junda,* Latin *juventus*] —ˈ**youthless** *adj.*

youth club *n.* a centre providing leisure activities for young people, often associated with a church or community centre.

youth custody *n.* (in Britain) a sentence of from four to eighteen months' detention passed on a person aged 15 to 21.

youth custody centre *n.* (in Britain) a place where offenders aged 15 to 21 may be detained and given training, instruction, and work. Former name: **borstal.**

youthful (ˈjuːθfʊl) *adj.* **1.** of, relating to, possessing, or characteristic of youth. **2.** fresh, vigorous, or active: *he's surprisingly youthful for his age.* **3.** in an early stage of development: *a youthful culture.* **4.** Also: **young.** (of a river, valley, or land surface) in the early stage of the cycle of erosion, characterized by steep slopes, lack of flood plains, and V-shaped valleys. Compare **mature** (sense 6), **old** (sense 18). —ˈ**youthfully** *adv.* —ˈ**youthfulness** *n.*

youth hostel *n.* one of a chain of inexpensive lodging places for young people travelling cheaply. Often shortened to **hostel.**

you've (juːv; *unstressed* jʊv) *contraction of* you have.

yowe (jaʊ) *n.* a Scot. word for **ewe.**

yowl (jaʊl) *vb.* **1.** to express with or produce a loud mournful wail or cry; howl. ~*n.* **2.** a loud mournful cry; wail or howl. [C13: from Old Norse *gaula;* related to German *jaulen;* see YAWL[2]] —ˈ**yowler** *n.*

yo-yo (ˈjəʊjəʊ) *n., pl.* **-yos. 1.** a toy consisting of a spool attached to a string, the end of which is held while it is repeatedly spun out and reeled in. **2.** *U.S. and Canadian slang.* a stupid person, esp. one who is easily manipulated. ~*vb.* **yo-yos, yo-yoing, yo-yoed.** (*intr.*) **3.** *Informal.* to change repeatedly from one position to another; fluctuate. ~*adj.* **4.** *Informal.* changing repeatedly; fluctuating. [from Filipino *yo yo,* come come, a weapon consisting of a spindle attached to a thong]

Yquem (iːˈkɛm) *n.* a sweet white table wine produced at Yquem, a French vineyard of the Sauternes area of Bordeaux. Also called: **Château d'Yquem.**

yr *abbrev. for:* **1.** (*pl.* **yrs**) year. **2.** younger. **3.** your.

yrs *abbrev. for:* **1.** years. **2.** yours.

Yt *the former chemical symbol for* yttrium (now **Y**).

YT *abbrev. for* Yukon Territory.

YTS (in Britain) *abbrev. for* Youth Training Scheme.

ytterbia (ɪˈtɜːbɪə) *n.* another name for **ytterbium oxide.** [C19: New Latin, named after *Ytterby,* Swedish quarry where it was discovered]

ytterbite (ɪˈtɜːbaɪt) *n.* another name for **gadolinite.**

ytterbium (ɪˈtɜːbɪəm) *n.* a soft malleable silvery element of the lanthanide series of metals that occurs in monazite and is used to improve the mechanical properties of steel. Symbol: Yb; atomic no.: 70; atomic wt.: 173.04; valency: 2 or 3; relative density: 6.97 or 6.54; melting pt.: 824°C; boiling pt.: 1193°C. [C19: New Latin; see YTTERBIA]

ytterbium oxide *n.* a colourless weakly basic hygroscopic substance used in certain alloys and ceramics. Formula: Yb_2O_3. Also called: **ytterbia.**

yttria (ˈɪtrɪə) *n.* another name for **yttrium oxide.** [C19: New Latin, named after *Ytterby;* see YTTERBIA]

yttriferous (ɪˈtrɪfərəs) *adj.* containing or yielding yttrium.

yttrium (ˈɪtrɪəm) *n.* a silvery metallic element occurring in monazite and gadolinite and used in various alloys, in lasers, and as a catalyst. Symbol: Y; atomic no.: 39; atomic wt.: 88.90; valency: 3; relative density: 4.46; melting pt.: 1523°C; boiling pt.: 3337°C. [C19: New Latin; see YTTERBIA] —ˈ**yttric** *adj.*

yttrium metal *n. Chem.* any one of a group of elements including yttrium and the related lanthanides, holmium, erbium, thulium, ytterbium, and lutecium.

yttrium oxide *n.* a colourless or white insoluble solid used mainly in incandescent mantles. Formula: Y_2O_3. Also called: **yttria.**

YU *international car registration for* Yugoslavia.

yuan (ˈjuːˈæn) *n., pl.* **-an. 1.** the standard monetary unit of the People's Republic of China, divided into 100 fen. **2.** the former name for **dollar** (sense 2). [from Chinese *yüan* round object; see YEN[1]]

Yüan (ˈjuːˈæn) *adj.* of or relating to the imperial dynasty of China from 1279 to 1368, esp. to the Chinese porcelain produced during this period, characterized by the appearance of underglaze blue-and-white ware.

Yuan Tan (ˈjuːˈæn ˈtæn) *n.* an annual Chinese festival marking the Chinese New Year. It can last over three days and includes the exchange of gifts, firework displays, and dancing.

yucca (ˈjʌkə) *n.* any of several liliaceous plants of the genus *Yucca,* of tropical and subtropical America, having stiff lancelike leaves and spikes of white flowers. See also **Adam's-needle, Spanish bayonet.** [C16: from American Spanish *yuca,* ultimately from an American Indian word]

yuck *or* **yuk** (jʌk) *interj. Slang.* an exclamation indicating contempt, dislike, or disgust.

yucky *or* **yukky** (ˈjʌkɪ) *adj.* **yuckier, yuckiest** *or* **yukkier, yukkiest.** *Slang.* disgusting; sickening; nasty.
Yuga (ˈjugə) *n.* (in Hindu cosmology) one of the four ages of mankind, together lasting over 4 million years and marked by a progressive decline in the vitality and morals of men. [C18: from Sanskrit: yoke, race of men, era; see YOKE]
yugarie (ˈjuːgərɪ) *n.* a variant spelling of **eugarie.**
Yugo. *abbrev. for* Yugoslavia.
Yugoslav *or* **Jugoslav** (ˈjuːgəʊˌslɑːv) *n.* **1.** a native, inhabitant, or citizen of Yugoslavia, a republic in SE Europe on the Adriatic Sea. **2.** (not in technical use) another name for **Serbo-Croatian** (the language). *~adj.* **3.** of, relating to, or characteristic of Yugoslavia or its people. ~Also (senses 1 and 3): ˌ**Yugoˈslavian,** ˌ**Jugoˈslavian.**
yulan (ˈjuːlæn) *n.* a Chinese magnolia, *Magnolia denudata,* that is often cultivated for its showy white flowers. [C19: from Chinese, from *yu* a gem + *lan* plant]
yule (juːl) *n.* (*sometimes cap.*) *Literary, archaic, or dialect.* **a.** Christmas, the Christmas season, or Christmas festivities. **b.** (*in combination*): *yuletide.* [Old English *geōla,* originally a name of a pagan feast lasting 12 days; related to Old Norse *jōl,* Swedish *jul,* Gothic *jiuleis*]
yule log *n.* a large log of wood traditionally used as the foundation of a fire in the hearth at Christmas.
Yuman (ˈjuːmən) *n.* **1.** a family of North American Indian languages spoken chiefly in Arizona, California, and Mexico. *~adj.* **2.** relating to or belonging to this family of languages.
yummy (ˈjʌmɪ) *Slang.* *~interj.* **1.** Also: **yum-yum.** an exclamation indicating pleasure or delight, as in anticipation of delicious food. *~adj.* **-mier, -miest.** **2.** delicious, delightful, or attractive. [C20: from *yum-yum,* of imitative origin]
yup (jʌp) *sentence substitute.* an informal word for **yes.**
Yupik (ˈjuːpɪk) *n.* a western Eskimo, of Alaska or Asia. Compare **Inuit.**
yuppie *or* **yuppy** (ˈjʌpɪ) (*sometimes cap.*) *~n.* **1.** *acronym for* young urban (*or* upwardly mobile) professional. *~adj.* **2.** typical of or reflecting the values characteristic of yuppies. —ˈ**yuppiedom** *n.*
yuppie disease *or* **flu** *n.* *Informal.* any of a number of debilitating long-lasting viral disorders associated with stress, such as myalgic encephalomyelitis, whose symptoms include muscle weakness, chronic tiredness, and depression.
yuppify (ˈjʌpɪˌfaɪ) *vb.* (*tr.*) **-fies, -fying, -fied.** to make yuppie in nature. —ˌ**yuppifiˈcation** *n.*
yurt (juət) *n.* a circular tent consisting of a framework of poles covered with felt or skins, used by Mongolian and Turkic nomads of E and central Asia. [from Russian *yurta,* of Turkic origin; compare Turkish *yurt* abode, home]
YV *international car registration for* Venezuela.
YWCA *abbrev. for* Young Women's Christian Association.
YWHA *abbrev. for* Young Women's Hebrew Association.
ywis (ɪˈwɪs) *adv.* a variant spelling of **iwis.**

Z

z *or* **Z** (zɛd; *U.S.* ziː) *n., pl.* **z's, Z's,** *or* **Zs.** **1.** the 26th and last letter and the 20th consonant of the modern English alphabet. **2.** a speech sound represented by this letter, in English usually a voiced alveolar fricative, as in *zip.* **3. a.** something shaped like a Z. **b.** *(in combination): a Z-bend in a road.*

z *Maths. symbol for:* **1.** the *z*-axis or a coordinate measured along the *z*-axis in a Cartesian or cylindrical coordinate system. **2.** an algebraic variable.

Z *symbol for:* **1.** any unknown, variable, or unspecified factor, number, person, or thing. **2.** *Chem.* atomic number. **3.** *Physics.* impedance. **4.** zone. **5.** *Currency.* zaïre. ~ **6.** *international car registration for* Zambia.

z. *abbrev. for:* **1.** zero. **2.** zone.

ZA *international car registration for* South Africa. [from Afrikaans *Zuid Afrika*]

zabaglione (ˌzæbəˈljəʊnɪ) *n.* a light foamy dessert made of egg yolks, sugar, and marsala, whipped together and served warm in a glass. [Italian; probably related to Late Latin *sabaia* Illyrian drink made from grain]

zaffer *or* **zaffre** (ˈzæfə) *n.* impure cobalt oxide, used to impart a blue colour to enamels. [C17: from Italian *zaffera;* perhaps related to Latin *sapphīrus* SAPPHIRE]

zaibatsu (ˈzaɪbætˈsuː) *n.* *(functioning as sing. or pl.)* the group or combine comprising a few wealthy families that controls industry, business, and finance in Japan. [from Japanese, from *zai* wealth, from Chinese *ts'ai* + *batsu* family, person of influence, from Chinese *fa*]

zaïre (zɑːˈɪə) *n., pl.* **-ïre.** the standard monetary unit of Zaïre.

Zaïrian (zɑːˈɪərɪən) *or* **Zaïrese** (ˌzɑːɪəˈriːz) *adj.* **1.** of or relating to Zaïre, a republic in S central Africa, or its people or culture. ~*n.* **2.** a native or inhabitant of Zaïre.

zakuski *or* **zakouski** (zæˈkʊskɪ) *pl. n., sing.* **-ka** (-kə). *Russian cookery.* hors d'oeuvres, consisting of tiny open sandwiches spread with caviar, smoked sausage, etc., or a cold dish such as radishes in sour cream, all usually served with vodka. [Russian, from *zakusit'* to have a snack]

Zambian (ˈzæmbɪən) *adj.* **1.** of or relating to Zambia, a republic in southern Africa, or its people or culture. ~*n.* **2.** a native or inhabitant of Zambia.

zambuck (ˈzæmbʌk) *n. Austral. and N.Z. informal.* a St John ambulance attendant, esp. at a sports meeting. [C20: from *Zambuck,* the trade name of an ointment which comes in a black-and-white container, black and white being the colours of the St John uniform]

zamia (ˈzeɪmɪə) *n.* any cycadaceous plant of the genus *Zamia,* of tropical and subtropical America, having a short thick trunk, palmlike leaves, and short stout cones. [C19: from New Latin, from Latin *zamiae,* erroneous reading of phrase *nucēs azāniae* pine cones, probably from Greek *azainein* to dry up]

zamindar *or* **zemindar** (zəmiːnˈdɑː) *n.* (in India) the owner of an agricultural estate. [via Hindi from Persian: landholder, from *zamīn* land + *-dār* holder]

zamindari *or* **zemindari** (zəmiːnˈdɑːrɪ) *n., pl.* **-is.** (in India) a large agricultural estate.

zander (ˈzændə) *n., pl.* **zander** *or* **zanders.** a freshwater teleost pikeperch of Europe, *Stizostedion lucioperca,* valued as a food fish.

zanthoxylum (zænˈθɒksɪləm) *n.* any rutaceous shrub or tree of the genus *Zanthoxylum,* of temperate and subtropical E Asia and North America: includes the prickly ash and the West Indian yellowwood (or satinwood). [C19 *zantho-* variant of XANTHO- + Greek *xulon* wood]

Zanu(PF) (ˌzænuː (ˌpiːˈɛf)) *n. acronym for* Zimbabwe African National Union (Patriotic Front).

zany (ˈzeɪnɪ) *adj.* **-nier, -niest.** **1.** comical in an endearing way; imaginatively funny or comical, esp. in behaviour. ~*n., pl.* **-nies.** **2.** a clown or buffoon, esp. one in old comedies who imitated other performers with ludicrous effect. **3.** a ludicrous or foolish person. [C16: from Italian *zanni,* from dialect (Venice and Lombardy) *Zanni,* nickname for *Giovanni* John; one of the traditional names for a clown] —ˈ**zanily** *adv.* —ˈ**zaniness** *n.* —ˈ**zanyism** *n.*

Zanzibari (ˌzænzɪˈbɑːrɪ) *adj.* **1.** of or relating to the island of Zanzibar, part of Tanzania off the E coast of Africa, or to its people or culture. ~*n.* **2.** a native or inhabitant of Zanzibar.

zap (zæp) *Slang.* ~*vb.* **zaps, zapping, zapped.** **1.** *(tr.)* to attack, kill, or destroy, as with a sudden bombardment. **2.** *(intr.)* to move quickly; rush. **3.** *(tr.) Computer technol.* **a.** to clear from the screen. **b.** to erase. **4.** *(intr.) Television.* to change channels rapidly by remote control. ~*n.* **5.** energy, vigour, or pep. ~*interj.* **6.** an exclamation used to express sudden or swift action. [of imitative origin]

zapateado *Spanish.* (θapateˈaðo) *n., pl.* **-dos** (-ðos). a Spanish dance with stamping and very fast footwork. [from *zapatear* to tap with the shoe, from *zapato* shoe]

Zapotec (ˈzɑːpəˌtɛk) *n.* **1.** *(pl.* **-tecs** *or* **-tec)** Also called: **Zapotecan** (ˌzæpəʊˈtɛkən, ˌzɑː-). any member of a large tribe of central American Indians inhabiting S Mexico, esp. the Mexican state of Oaxaca. **2.** the group of languages spoken by this people. **3.** Also: **Zapotecan.** of or relating to this people or their language. [from Spanish *Zapoteca,* from Nahuatl *Tzapoteca,* literally: people of the land of the sapodillas, from *tzapotl* sapodilla]

zappy (ˈzæpɪ) *adj.* **zappier, zappiest.** *Slang.* full of energy; snappy; zippy.

ZAPU (ˈzæpuː) *n. acronym for* Zimbabwe African People's Union.

zaratite (ˈzærəˌtaɪt) *n.* a green amorphous mineral consisting of hydrated nickel carbonate. Formula: $NiCO_3.2Ni(OH)_2.4H_2O$. [C19: from Spanish *zaratita,* named after G. *Zárate,* 19th-century Spaniard]

zareba *or* **zareeba** (zəˈriːbə) *n.* (in northern E Africa, esp. formerly) **1.** a stockade or enclosure of thorn bushes around a village or campsite. **2.** the area so protected or enclosed. [C19: from Arabic *zarībah* cattlepen, from *zarb* sheepfold]

zarf (zɑːf) *n.* (esp. in the Middle East) a holder, usually ornamental, for a hot coffee cup. [from Arabic: container, sheath]

zarzuela (zɑːˈzweɪlə) *n.* **1.** a type of Spanish vaudeville or operetta, usually satirical in nature. **2.** a seafood stew. [from Spanish, from *La Zarzuela,* name of the palace near Madrid where such vaudeville was first performed (1629)]

zastruga (zəˈstruːgə, zæ-) *n.* a variant spelling of **sastruga.**

zax (zæks) *n.* a variant of **sax**[1].

z-axis *n.* a reference axis of a three-dimensional Cartesian coordinate system along which the *z*-coordinate is measured.

zayin (ˈzɑːjɪn) *n.* the seventh letter of the Hebrew alphabet (ז), transliterated as *z.* [from Hebrew, literally: weapon]

Z boson *n. Physics.* another name for **Z particle.**

ZB station *n.* (in New Zealand) a radio station of a commercial network.

Z chart *n. Statistics.* a chart often used in industry and constructed by plotting on it three series: monthly, weekly, or daily data, the moving annual total, and the cumulative total dating from the beginning of the current year.

zeal (ziːl) *n.* fervent or enthusiastic devotion, often extreme or fanatical in nature, as to a religious movement, political cause, ideal, or aspiration. [C14: from Late Latin *zēlus,* from Greek *zēlos*]

zealot (ˈzɛlət) *n.* an immoderate, fanatical, or extremely zealous adherent to a cause, esp. a religious one. [C16: from Late Latin *zēlōtēs,* from Greek, from *zēloun* to be zealous, from *zēlos* ZEAL]

Zealot (ˈzɛlət) *n.* any of the members of an extreme Jewish sect or political party that resisted all aspects of Roman rule in Palestine in the 1st century A.D.

zealotry (ˈzɛlətrɪ) *n.* extreme or excessive zeal or devotion.

zealous (ˈzɛləs) *adj.* filled with or inspired by intense enthusiasm or zeal; ardent; fervent. —ˈ**zealously** *adv.* —ˈ**zealousness** *n.*

zebec *or* **zebeck** (ˈziːbɛk) *n.* variant spellings of **xebec.**

zebra (ˈziːbrə, ˈzɛbrə) *n., pl.* **-ras** *or* **-ra.** any of several mammals of the horse family *(Equidae),* such as *Equus burchelli* (the **common zebra**), of southern and eastern Africa, having distinctive black-and-white striped hides. [C16: via Italian from Old Spanish: wild ass, probably from Vulgar Latin *eciferus* (unattested) wild horse, from Latin *equiferus,* from *equus* horse + *ferus* wild] —ˈ**zebra-ˌlike** *or* **zebraic** (zɪˈbreɪɪk) *adj.* —**zebrine** (ˈziːbraɪn, ˈzɛb-) *or* ˈ**zebroid** *adj.*

Zebra (ˈziːbrə, ˈzɛbrə) *n. Finance.* a noninterest-paying bond in which the accrued income is taxed annually rather than on redemption. Compare **zero** (sense 12). [C20: from *zero-coupon bond*]

zebra crossing *n. Brit.* a pedestrian crossing marked on a road by broad alternate black and white stripes. Once on the crossing the pedestrian has right of way.

zebra finch *n.* any of various Australasian songbirds with zebra-like markings, such as the grassfinch *Poephila castanotis.*

zebra plant *n.* See **calathea.**

zebrawood (ˈzɛbrəˌwʊd, ˈziː-) *n.* **1.** a tree, *Connarus guianensis,* of tropical America, Asia, and Africa, yielding striped hardwood used in cabinetwork: family *Connaraceae.* **2.** any of various other trees or shrubs having striped wood. **3.** the wood of any of these trees.

zebu (ˈziːbuː) *n.* a domesticated ox, *Bos indicus,* having a humped back, long horns, and a large dewlap: used in India and E Asia as a draught animal. [C18: from French *zébu,* perhaps of Tibetan origin]

zecchino (zɛˈkiːnəʊ) *n., pl.* **-ni** (-nɪ). another word for **sequin** (the coin). [C18: from Italian; see SEQUIN]

Zech. *Bible. abbrev. for* Zechariah.
zed (zɛd) *n.* the Brit. spoken form of the letter *z.* U.S. word: **zee.** [C15: from Old French *zede,* via Late Latin from Greek *zēta*]
zedoary ('zɛdəʊərɪ) *n.* the dried rhizome of the tropical Asian plant *Curcuma zedoaria,* used as a stimulant and a condiment: family *Zingiberaceae.* [C15: from Medieval Latin *zedoaria,* from Arabic *zadwār,* of Persian origin]
zee (ziː) *n.* the U.S. word for **zed** (letter *z*).
Zeeman effect ('ziːmən) *n.* the splitting of a spectral line of a substance into several closely spaced lines when the substance is placed in a magnetic field. [C20: named after Pieter *Zeeman* (1865–1943), Dutch physicist]
zein ('ziːɪn) *n.* a protein of the prolamine group occurring in maize and used in the manufacture of plastics, paper coatings, adhesives, etc. [C19: from New Latin *zēa* maize, from Latin: a kind of grain, from Greek *zeia* barley]
Zeitgeist *German.* ('tsaitgaist) *n.* the spirit, attitude, or general outlook of a specific time or period, esp. as it is reflected in literature, philosophy, etc. [German, literally: time spirit; see TIDE[1], GHOST]
zemindar (zəmiːn'dɑː) *n.* a variant spelling of **zamindar.** —**zemin'dari** *n.*
zemstvo ('zɛmstvəʊ; *Russian* 'zjɛmstvə) *n., pl.* **-stvos.** (in tsarist Russia) an elective provincial or district council established in most provinces of Russia by Alexander II in 1864 as part of his reform policy. [C19: from Russian, from *zemlya* land; related to Latin *humus* earth, Greek *khamai* on the ground]
Zen (zɛn) *Buddhism.* ~*n.* **1.** a Japanese school, of 12th-century Chinese origin, teaching that contemplation of one's essential nature to the exclusion of all else is the only way of achieving pure enlightenment. **2.** (*modifier*) of or relating to this school: *Zen Buddhism.* [from Japanese, from Chinese *ch'an* religious meditation, from Pali *jhāna,* from Sanskrit *dhyāna*] —'**Zenic** *adj.* —'**Zenist** *n.*
zenana (zɛ'nɑːnə) *n.* (in the East, esp. in Muslim and Hindu homes) part of a house reserved for the women and girls of a household. [C18: from Hindi *zanāna,* from Persian, from *zan* woman]
Zend (zɛnd) *n.* **1.** a former name for **Avestan. 2.** short for **Zend-Avesta. 3.** an exposition of the Avesta in the Middle Persian language (Pahlavi). [C18: from Persian *zand* commentary, exposition; used specifically of the Middle Persian commentary on the Avesta, hence of the language of the Avesta itself] —'**Zendic** *adj.*
Zend-Avesta (ˌzɛndə'vɛstə) *n.* the Avesta together with the traditional interpretative commentary known as the Zend, esp. as preserved in the Avestan language among the Parsees. [from Avestan, representing *Avesta'-va-zend* Avesta with interpretation] —**Zend-Avestaic** (ˌzɛndəvɛs'teɪɪk) *adj.*
Zener diode ('ziːnə) *n.* a semiconductor diode that exhibits a sharp increase in reverse current at a well-defined reverse voltage: used as a voltage regulator. [C20: named after C. M. *Zener* (born 1905), U.S. physicist]
zenith ('zɛnɪθ; *U.S.* 'ziːnɪθ) *n.* **1.** *Astronomy.* the point on the celestial sphere vertically above an observer. **2.** the highest point; peak; acme: *the zenith of someone's achievements.* ~Compare **nadir.** [C17: from French *cenith,* from Medieval Latin, from Old Spanish *zenit,* based on Arabic *samt,* as in *samt arrās* path over one's head, from *samt* way, path + *al* the + *rās* head] —'**zenithal** *adj.*
zenithal projection *n.* a type of map projection in which part of the earth's surface is projected onto a plane tangential to it, either at one of the poles (**polar zenithal**), at the equator (**equatorial zenithal**), or between (**oblique zenithal**).
zenith telescope *n.* an instrument used to determine the latitude of stars, similar to the meridian circle but fitted with an extremely sensitive level and a declination micrometer.
zeolite ('ziːəˌlaɪt) *n.* **1.** any of a large group of glassy secondary minerals consisting of hydrated aluminium silicates of calcium, sodium, or potassium: formed in cavities in lava flows and plutonic rocks. **2.** any of a class of similar synthetic materials used in ion exchange and as selective absorbents. See **molecular sieve.** [C18 *zeo-,* from Greek *zein* to boil + -LITE; from the swelling up that occurs under the blowpipe] —**zeolitic** (ˌziːə'lɪtɪk) *adj.*
Zeph. *Bible. abbrev. for* Zephaniah.
zephyr ('zɛfə) *n.* **1.** a soft or gentle breeze. **2.** any of several delicate soft yarns, fabrics, or garments, usually of wool. [C16: from Latin *zephyrus,* from Greek *zephuros* the west wind; probably related to Greek *zophos* darkness, west]
zeppelin ('zɛpəlɪn) *n.* (*sometimes cap.*) a large cylindrical rigid airship built from 1900 to carry passengers, and used in World War I for bombing and reconnaissance. [C20: named after Count von *Zeppelin* (1838–1917), German aeronautical pioneer who designed it]
zero ('zɪərəʊ) *n., pl.* **-ros** *or* **-roes. 1.** the symbol 0, indicating an absence of quantity or magnitude; nought. Former name: **cipher. 2.** the integer denoted by the symbol 0; nought. **3.** the ordinal number between +1 and −1. **4.** nothing; nil. **5.** a person or thing of no significance; nonentity. **6.** the lowest point or degree: *his prospects were put at zero.* **7.** the line or point on a scale of measurement from which the graduations commence. **8. a.** the temperature, pressure, etc., that registers a reading of zero on a scale. **b.** the value of a variable, such as temperature, obtained under specified conditions. **9.** a gunsight setting in which accurate allowance has been made for both windage and elevation for a specified range. **10.** *Maths.* **a.** the cardinal number of a set with no members. **b.** the identity element of addition. **11.** *Linguistics.* **a.** an allomorph with no phonetic realization, as the plural marker of English *sheep.* **b.** (*as modifier*): *a zero form.* **12.** *Finance.* Also called **zero-coupon bond.** a bond that pays no interest, the equivalent being paid in its redemption value. Compare **Zebra.** ~*adj.* **13.** having no measurable quantity, magnitude, etc. **14.** *Meteorol.* **a.** (of a cloud ceiling) limiting visibility to 15 metres (50 feet) or less. **b.** (of horizontal visibility) limited to 50 metres (165 feet) or less. ~*vb.* **-roes, -roing, -roed. 15.** (*tr.*) to adjust (an instrument, apparatus, etc.) so as to read zero or a position taken as zero. ~*determiner.* **16.** *Informal, chiefly U.S.* no (thing) at all: *this job has zero interest.* [C17: from Italian, from Medieval Latin *zephirum,* from Arabic *sifr* empty, CIPHER]
zero gravity *n.* the state or condition of weightlessness.
zero grazing *n.* a type of dairy farming in which the cattle are fed with cut grass.
zero hour *n.* **1.** *Military.* the time set for the start of an attack or the initial stage of an operation. **2.** *Informal.* a critical time, esp. at the commencement of an action.
zero in *vb.* (*adv.*) **1.** (often foll. by *on*) to bring (a weapon) to bear (on a target), as while firing repeatedly. **2.** (*intr.*; foll. by *on*) *Informal.* to bring one's attention to bear (on a problem, etc.). **3.** (*intr.*; foll. by *on*) *Informal.* to converge (upon): *the police zeroed in on the site of the crime.*
zero option *n.* (in international nuclear arms negotiations) an offer to remove all shorter-range nuclear missiles or, in the case of the **zero-zero option** all intermediate-range nuclear missiles, if the other side will do the same.
zero-rated *adj.* denoting goods on which the buyer pays no value-added tax although the seller can claim back any tax he has paid.
zero stage *n.* a solid-propellant rocket attached to a liquid-propellant rocket to provide greater thrust at liftoff.
zero-sum game *n.* (in game theory) a contest in which one person's loss is equal to the other person's gain.
zeroth ('zɪərəʊθ) *adj.* denoting a term in a series that precedes the term otherwise regarded as the first term. [C20: from ZERO + -TH[2]]
zest (zɛst) *n.* **1.** invigorating or keen excitement or enjoyment: *a zest for living.* **2.** added interest, flavour, or charm; piquancy: *her presence gave zest to the occasion.* **3.** something added to give flavour or relish. **4.** the peel or skin of an orange or lemon, used as flavouring in drinks, etc. ~*vb.* **5.** (*tr.*) to give flavour, interest, or piquancy to. [C17: from French *zeste* peel of citrous fruits used as flavouring, of unknown origin] —'**zestful** *adj.* —'**zestfully** *adv.* —'**zestfulness** *n.* —'**zestless** *adj.* —'**zesty** *adj.*
zeta ('ziːtə) *n.* the sixth letter in the Greek alphabet (Ζ, ζ), a consonant, transliterated as *z.* [from Greek, of Semitic origin; compare Hebrew *sādhē*]
Zeta ('ziːtə) *n.* (*foll. by the genitive case of a specified constellation*) the sixth brightest star in a constellation: *Zeta Tauri.*
ZETA ('ziːtə) *n.* a torus-shaped apparatus used for research on controlled thermonuclear reactions and plasma physics. [C20: from *z*(*ero-*)*e*(*nergy*) *t*(*hermonuclear*) *a*(*pparatus*)]
zetetic (zə'tɛtɪk) *adj.* proceeding by inquiry; investigating. [C17: from New Latin, from Greek *zētētikos,* from *zēteō* to seek]
zeugma ('zjuːgmə) *n.* a figure of speech in which a word is used to modify or govern two or more words although appropriate to only one of them or making a different sense with each, as in the sentence *Mr. Pickwick took his hat and his leave* (Charles Dickens). [C16: via Latin from Greek: a yoking, from *zeugnunai* to yoke] —**zeugmatic** (zjuːg'mætɪk) *adj.* —**zeug'matically** *adv.*
zho (zəʊ) *n., pl.* **zhos** *or* **zho.** a variant spelling of **zo.**
Zhou (dʒəʊ) *n.* the Pinyin transliteration of the Chinese name for **Chou.**
zibeline ('zɪbəˌlaɪn, -lɪn) *n.* **1.** a sable or the fur of this animal. **2.** a thick cloth made of wool or other animal hair, having a long nap and a dull sheen. ~*adj.* **3.** of, relating to, or resembling a sable. [C16: from French, from Old Italian *zibellino,* ultimately of Slavonic origin; compare SABLE]
zibet ('zɪbɪt) *n.* a large civet, *Viverra zibetha,* of S and SE Asia, having tawny fur marked with black spots and stripes. [C16: from Medieval Latin *zibethum,* from Arabic *zabād* CIVET]
zidovudine (zaɪ'dɒvjʊˌdiːn) *n.* a drug that prolongs life and alleviates symptoms among some AIDS sufferers. Also called: **AZT.**
Ziegler catalyst ('ziːglə) *n.* any of a group of catalysts, such as titanium trichloride ($TiCl_3$) and aluminium alkyl ($Al(CH_3)_3$), that produce stereospecific polymers. [C20: named after Carl *Ziegler* (1898–1973), German chemist]
ziff (zɪf) *n. Austral. informal.* a beard. [C20: of unknown origin]
ziggurat ('zɪgʊˌræt), **zikkurat,** *or* **zikurat** ('zɪkʊˌræt) *n.* a type of rectangular temple tower or tiered mound erected by the Sumerians, Akkadians, and Babylonians in Mesopotamia. The tower of Babel is thought to be one of these. [C19: from Assyrian *ziqqurati* summit, height]
zigzag ('zɪgˌzæg) *n.* **1.** a line or course characterized by sharp turns in alternating directions. **2.** one of the series of such turns. **3.** something having the form of a zigzag. ~*adj.* **4.**

(*usually prenominal*) formed in or proceeding in a zigzag. **5.** (of sewing machine stitches) produced in a zigzag by a swing needle: used for joining stretch fabrics, neatening raw edges, etc. ~*adv.* **6.** in a zigzag manner. ~*vb.* **-zags, -zagging, -zagged. 7.** to proceed or cause to proceed in a zigzag. **8.** (*tr.*) to form into a zigzag. [C18: from French, from German *zickzack*, from *Zacke* point, jagged projection; see TACK[1]] —**'zig,zaggedness** *n.*

zila, zilla, *or* **zillah** ('zɪlɑː) *n.* an administrative district in India. [C19: from Hindi *dilah* division, from Arabic *dil'* part]

zila parishad ('pʌrɪʃəd) *n.* a district council in India. [Hindi, from *zila'* district (from Arabic *dil'* part) + *parishad* assembly, council]

zilch (zɪltʃ) *n. Chiefly U.S. and Canadian slang.* nothing. [C20: of uncertain origin]

zillion ('zɪljən) *Informal.* ~*n., pl.* **-lions** *or* **-lion. 1.** (*often pl.*) an extremely large but unspecified number, quantity, or amount: *zillions of flies in this camp.* ~*determiner.* **2. a.** amounting to a zillion: *a zillion different problems.* **b.** (*as pronoun*): *I found a zillion under the sink.* [on the model of *million*]

Zimbabwean (zɪm'bɑːbwɪən, -weɪən) *n.* **1.** a native or inhabitant of Zimbabwe, a country in SE Africa. ~*adj.* **2.** of or relating to Zimbabwe or its people.

zimmer ('zɪmə) *n. Trademark.* another name for **walker** (sense 3). Also called: **zimmer aid.**

zinc (zɪŋk) *n.* **1.** a brittle bluish-white metallic element that becomes coated with a corrosion-resistant layer in moist air and occurs chiefly in sphalerite and smithsonite. It is a constituent of several alloys, esp. brass and nickel-silver, and is used in die-casting, galvanizing metals, and in battery electrodes. Symbol: Zn; atomic no.: 30; atomic wt.: 65.37; valency: 2; relative density: 7.133; melting pt.: 419.58°C; boiling pt.: 907°C. **2.** *Informal.* corrugated galvanized iron. [C17: from German *Zink*, perhaps from *Zinke* prong, from its jagged appearance in the furnace] —**'zincic, 'zincous,** *or* **'zincoid** *adj.* —**'zincky, 'zincy,** *or* **'zinky** *adj.*

zincate ('zɪŋkeɪt) *n.* any of a class of salts derived from the amphoteric hydroxide of zinc, $Zn(OH)_2$, often thought of as the acid H_2ZnO_2.

zinc blende *n.* another name for **sphalerite.**

zinc chloride *n.* a white odourless soluble poisonous granular solid used in manufacturing parchment paper and vulcanized fibre and in preserving wood. It is also a soldering flux, embalming agent, and a medical astringent and antiseptic. Formula: $ZnCl_2$ Also called: **butter of zinc.**

zinciferous (zɪŋ'kɪfərəs) *adj.* containing or yielding zinc.

zincite ('zɪŋkaɪt) *n.* a red or yellow mineral consisting of zinc oxide in hexagonal crystalline form. It occurs in metamorphosed limestone. Formula: ZnO.

zinckenite ('zɪŋkə,naɪt) *n.* a variant spelling of **zinkenite.**

zinco ('zɪŋkəʊ) *n., pl.* **-cos.** short for **zincograph** (sense 1).

zincograph ('zɪŋkə,grɑːf, -,græf) *n.* **1.** a printing plate made by zincography. **2.** a print taken from such a plate.

zincography (zɪŋ'kɒgrəfɪ) *n.* the art or process of etching on zinc to form a printing plate. —**zin'cographer** *n.* —**zincographic** (,zɪŋkə'græfɪk) *or* **,zinco'graphical** *adj.*

zinc ointment *n.* a medicinal ointment consisting of zinc oxide, petrolatum, and paraffin, used to treat certain skin diseases.

zinc oxide *n.* a white insoluble powder used as a pigment in paints (**zinc white** or **Chinese white**), cosmetics, glass, and printing inks. It is an antiseptic and astringent and is used in making zinc ointment. Formula: ZnO. Also called: **flowers of zinc, philosopher's wool.**

zinc sulphate *n.* a colourless soluble crystalline substance usually existing as the heptahydrate or monohydrate: used as a mordant, in preserving wood and skins, and in the electrodeposition of zinc. Formula: $ZnSO_4$. Also called: **white vitriol, zinc vitriol.**

zinc white *n.* another name for **Chinese white.**

zindabad ('zɪndɑː,bɑːd) *vb.* (*tr.*) *Indian.* long live: used as part of a slogan in India, Pakistan, etc. Compare **murdabad.** [Hindi, from Persian]

Zinfandel ('zɪnfən,dɛl) *n.* a Californian wine grape originally transplanted from Europe and producing a quick-maturing fruity red wine. [C19: of unknown origin]

zing (zɪŋ) *n. Informal.* **1.** a short high-pitched buzzing sound, as of a bullet or vibrating string. **2.** vitality; zest. ~*vb.* **3.** (*intr.*) to make or move with or as if with a high-pitched buzzing sound. [C20: of imitative origin] —**'zingy** *adj.*

zingaro ('dzingaro) *or* (*fem.*) ***zingara*** ('dzingara) *Italian. n., pl.* ***-ri*** (-ri) *or* ***-re*** (-re). an Italian Gypsy. [C16: ultimately from Greek *Athinganoi*, name of an oriental people]

zingiberaceous (,zɪndʒɪbə'reɪʃəs) *adj.* of, relating to, or belonging to the *Zingiberaceae*, a family of tropical aromatic plants that typically have fleshy rhizomes and flowers in spikes or clusters: includes ginger and the plants yielding arrowroot and turmeric. [C19: via New Latin from *zingiber* GINGER]

zinjanthropus (zɪn'dʒænθrəpəs) *n.* a type of australopithecine, *Australopithecus boisei* (formerly *Zinjanthropus boisei*), remains of which were discovered in the Olduvai Gorge in Tanzania in 1959. [C20: New Latin, from Arabic *Zinj* East Africa + Greek *anthrōpos* man]

zinkenite *or* **zinckenite** ('zɪŋkə,naɪt) *n.* a steel-grey metallic mineral consisting of a sulphide of lead and antimony. Formula: $PbSb_2S_4$. [C19: named after J. K. L. *Zincken* (1790–1862), German mineralogist]

zinnia ('zɪnɪə) *n.* any annual or perennial plant of the genus *Zinnia*, of tropical and subtropical America, having solitary heads of brightly coloured flowers: family *Compositae* (composites). [C18: named after J. G. *Zinn* (died 1759), German botanist]

Zion ('zaɪən) *or* **Sion** *n.* **1.** *Judaism.* **a.** the ancient Israelites of the Bible. **b.** the modern Jewish nation. **2.** *Christianity.* heaven regarded as the city of God and the final abode of his elect. **3.** any form of social organization, way of life, or life after death regarded as an ultimate goal. **4. a.** a religious community or its site, regarded as chosen by God and under his special protection. **b.** an ideal theocratic community, esp. any of the Christian Churches regarded as such a community.

Zionism ('zaɪə,nɪzəm) *n.* **1.** a political movement for the establishment and support of a national homeland for Jews in Palestine, now concerned chiefly with the development of the modern state of Israel. **2.** a policy or movement for Jews to return to Palestine from the Diaspora. —**'Zionist** *n., adj.* —**,Zion'istic** *adj.*

zip (zɪp) *n.* **1. a.** Also called: **zip fastener.** a fastening device operating by means of two parallel rows of metal or plastic teeth on either side of a closure that are interlocked by a sliding tab. U.S. and Canadian term: **zipper. b.** (*modifier*) having or equipped with such a device: *a zip bag.* **2.** a short sharp whizzing sound, as of a passing bullet. **3.** *Informal.* energy; vigour; vitality. **4.** *N.Z. trademark.* an electric water heater. ~*vb.* **zips, zipping, zipped. 5.** (*tr.*; often foll. by *up*) to fasten (clothing, a bag, etc.) with a zip. **6.** (*intr.*) to move with a zip: *the bullet zipped past.* **7.** (*intr.*; often foll. by *along, through*, etc.) to hurry; rush: *they zipped through town.* [C19: of imitative origin]

zip code *n.* the U.S. equivalent of **postcode.** [C20: from *z(one) i(mprovement) p(lan)*]

zip gun *n. U.S. and Canadian slang.* a crude homemade pistol, esp. one powered by a spring or rubber band.

zipper ('zɪpə) *n.* the U.S. and Canadian word for **zip** (sense 1a).

zippy ('zɪpɪ) *adj.* **-pier, -piest.** *Informal.* full of energy; lively.

zircalloy (zɜːk'ælɔɪ) *n.* an alloy of zirconium containing small amounts of tin, chromium, and nickel. It is used in pressurized-water reactors.

zircon ('zɜːkɒn) *n.* a reddish-brown, grey, green, blue, or colourless hard mineral consisting of zirconium silicate in tetragonal crystalline form with hafnium and some rare earths as impurities. It occurs principally in igneous rocks and is an important source of zirconium, zirconia, and hafnia: it is used as a gemstone and a refractory. Formula: $ZrSiO_4$. [C18: from German *Zirkon*, from French *jargon*, via Italian and Arabic, from Persian *zargūn* golden]

zirconia (zɜː'kəʊnɪə) *n.* another name (not in technical usage) for **zirconium oxide.**

zirconium (zɜː'kəʊnɪəm) *n.* a greyish-white metallic element, occurring chiefly in zircon, that is exceptionally corrosion-resistant and has low neutron absorption. It is used as a coating in nuclear and chemical plants, as a deoxidizer in steel, and alloyed with niobium in superconductive magnets. Symbol: Zr; atomic no.: 40; atomic wt.: 91.22; valency: 2, 3, or 4; relative density: 6.51; melting pt.: 1852°C; boiling pt.: 4377°C. [C19: from New Latin; see ZIRCON] —**zirconic** (zɜː'kɒnɪk) *adj.*

zirconium oxide *n.* a white amorphous powder that is insoluble in water and highly refractory, used as a pigment for paints, a catalyst, and an abrasive. Formula: ZrO_2. Also called: **zirconia.**

zit (zɪt) *n. U.S. slang.* a pimple. [of unknown origin]

zither ('zɪðə) *n.* a plucked musical instrument consisting of numerous strings stretched over a resonating box, a few of which may be stopped on a fretted fingerboard. [C19: from German, from Latin *cithara*, from Greek *kithara*] —**'zitherist** *n.*

zizith ('tsɪtsɪs, tsiː'tsiːt) *n.* (*functioning as sing. or pl.*) *Judaism.* a variant spelling of **tsitsith.**

zizz (zɪz) *Brit. informal.* ~*n.* **1.** a short sleep; nap ~*vb.* (*intr.*). **2.** to take a short sleep, snooze. [C20: of imitative origin]

Zl *symbol for* zloty.

zloty ('zlɒtɪ) *n., pl.* **-tys** *or* **-ty.** the standard monetary unit of Poland, divided into 100 groszy. [from Polish: golden, from *zlyoto* gold; related to Russian *zoloto* gold]

Zn *the chemical symbol for* zinc.

zo, zho, *or* **dzo** (zəʊ) *n., pl.* **zos, zhos, dzos** *or* **zo, zho, dzo.** a Tibetan breed of cattle, developed by crossing the yak with common cattle. [C20: from Tibetan]

zo- *combining form.* a variant of **zoo-** before a vowel.

zoa ('zəʊə) *n.* the plural of **zoon.**

-zoa *suffix forming plural proper nouns.* indicating groups of animal organisms: *Protozoa.* [from New Latin, from Greek *zōia*, plural of *zōion* animal, living being]

zoaea (zəʊ'iːə) *n., pl.* **zoaeae** (zəʊ'iːiː) *or* **zoaeas.** a variant spelling of **zoea.**

zod. *abbrev. for* zodiac.

zodiac ('zəʊdɪ,æk) *n.* **1.** an imaginary belt extending 8° either side of the ecliptic, which contains the 12 **zodiacal constellations** and within which the moon and planets appear to move. It is divided into 12 equal areas, called **signs of the zodiac,** each named after the constellation which once lay in it. **2.** *Astrology.* a diagram, usually circular, representing this belt and showing the symbols, illustrations, etc., associated with each of the 12 signs of the zodiac, used to predict the future. **3.** *Rare.* a complete circuit; circle. [C14: from Old French *zodiaque,* from Latin *zōdiacus,* from Greek *zōidiakos* (*kuklos*) (circle) of signs, from *zōidion* animal sign, carved figure, from *zōion* animal] —**zodiacal** (zəʊ'daɪəkəl) *adj.*

zodiacal constellation *n.* any of the 12 constellations after which the signs of the zodiac are named: Aries, Taurus, Gemini, Cancer, Leo, Virgo, Libra, Scorpio, Sagittarius, Capricorn, Aquarius, or Pisces.

zodiacal light *n.* a very faint cone of light in the sky, visible in the east just before sunrise and in the west just after sunset. It is probably due to the reflection of sunlight from cosmic dust in the plane of the ecliptic.

zoea *or* **zoaea** (zəʊ'iːə) *n., pl.* **zoeae, zoaeae** (zəʊ'iːiː) *or* **zoeas, zoaeas.** the free-swimming larva of a crab or related crustacean, which has well-developed abdominal appendages and may bear one or more spines. [C20: New Latin, from Greek *zōē* life]

Zohar ('zəʊhɑː) *n. Judaism.* a mystical work, consisting of a commentary on parts of the Pentateuch and the Hagiographa, probably composed in the 2nd century A.D.

zoic ('zəʊɪk) *adj.* **1.** relating to or having animal life. **2.** *Geology.* (of rocks, strata, etc.) containing fossilized animals. [C19: from New Latin, from Greek *zōion* animal]

-zoic *adj. and n. combining form.* indicating a geological era: *Palaeozoic.* [from Greek *zōē* life + -IC]

zoisite ('zɔɪˌsaɪt) *n.* a grey, brown, or pink mineral consisting of hydrated calcium aluminium silicate in orthorhombic crystalline form. Formula: $Ca_2Al_3(SiO_4)_3(OH)$. [C19: from German *Zoisit;* named after Baron Sigismund *Zois* von Edelstein (1747–1819), Slovenian nobleman; see -ITE[1]]

zombie *or* **zombi** ('zɒmbɪ) *n., pl.* **-bies** *or* **-bis. 1.** a person who is or appears to be lifeless, apathetic, or totally lacking in independent judgment; automaton. **2.** a supernatural spirit that reanimates a dead body. **3.** a corpse brought to life in this manner. [from Kongo *zumbi* good-luck fetish] —'**zombiism** *n.*

zonal ('zəʊnᵊl) *or* (*less commonly*) **zonary** ('zəʊnərɪ) *adj.* of, relating to, or of the nature of a zone. —'**zonally** *adv.*

zonal soil *n.* soil having a profile determined mainly by the local climate and vegetation. Compare **azonal soil, intrazonal soil.**

zonate ('zəʊneɪt) *or* **zonated** *adj.* marked with, divided into, or arranged in zones.

zonation (zəʊ'neɪʃən) *n.* arrangement in zones; zonate formation.

zone (zəʊn) *n.* **1.** a region, area, or section characterized by some distinctive feature or quality. **2.** a sphere of thought, disagreement, argument, etc. **3.** an area subject to a particular political, military, or government function, use, or jurisdiction: *a demilitarized zone.* **4.** (*often cap.*) *Geography.* one of the divisions of the earth's surface, esp. divided into latitudinal belts according to temperature. See **Torrid Zone, Temperate Zone. 5.** *Geology.* a distinctive layer or region of rock, characterized by particular fossils (**zone fossils**), metamorphism, structural deformity, etc. **6.** *Ecology.* an area, esp. a belt of land, having a particular flora and fauna determined by the prevailing environmental conditions. **7.** *Maths.* a portion of a sphere between two parallel planes intersecting the sphere. **8.** *Sport.* **a.** a period during which a competitor is performing particularly well: *McEnroe is in the zone at the moment.* **b.** (*modifier*) of or relating to competitive performance that depends on the mood or state of mind of the participant: *a zone player.* **9.** *Archaic or literary.* a girdle or belt. **10.** *N.Z.* a section on a transport route; fare stage. **11.** *N.Z.* a catchment area for pupils for a specific school. ~*vb.* (*tr.*) **12.** to divide into zones, as for different use, jurisdiction, activities, etc. **13.** to designate as a zone. **14.** to mark with or divide into zones. **15.** *N.Z.* to establish (an area) as a zone for a specific school. [C15: from Latin *zōna* girdle, climatic zone, from Greek *zōnē*] —'**zoning** *n.*

zone of saturation *n.* the ground below the water table.

zone refining *n.* a technique for producing solids of extreme purity, esp. for use in semiconductors. The material, in the form of a bar, is melted in one small region that is passed along the solid. Impurities concentrate in the melt and are moved to the end of the bar.

zonetime ('zəʊnˌtaɪm) *n.* the standard time of the time zone in which a ship is located at sea, each zone extending 7½° to each side of a meridian.

zonked (zɒŋkt) *adj. Slang.* **1.** highly intoxicated from drugs or alcohol. **2.** utterly exhausted. [C20: of imitative origin]

zonule ('zɒnjuːl) *n.* a small zone, band, or area. [C19: from New Latin *zōnula* a little ZONE] —**zonular** ('zɒnjʊlə) *adj.*

zoo (zuː) *n., pl.* **zoos.** a place where live animals are kept, studied, bred, and exhibited to the public. Formal term: **zoological garden.** [C19: shortened from *zoological gardens* (originally applied to those in London)]

zoo- *or before a vowel* **zo-** *combining form.* indicating animals: *zooplankton.* [from Greek *zōion* animal]

zoobiotic (ˌzəʊəbaɪ'ɒtɪk) *adj. Biology.* parasitic on or living in association with an animal.

zoochemistry (ˌzəʊə'kɛmɪstrɪ) *n.* the branch of biochemistry that is concerned with the constituents of an animal's body. —ˌ**zoo'chemical** *adj.*

zoochore ('zəʊəˌkɔː) *n.* a plant the spores or seeds of which are dispersed by animals. [from ZOO- + -CHORE] —ˌ**zoo'chorous** *adj.*

zoogeography (ˌzəʊədʒɪ'ɒgrəfɪ) *n.* the branch of zoology concerned with the geographical distribution of animals. —ˌ**zooge'ographer** *n.* —**zoogeographic** (ˌzəʊəˌdʒɪə'græfɪk) *or* ˌ**zooˌgeo'graphical** *adj.* —ˌ**zooˌgeo'graphically** *adv.*

zoogloea (ˌzəʊə'gliːə) *n.* a mass of bacteria adhering together by a jelly-like substance derived from their cell walls. [C19: ZOO- + New Latin *gloea* glue, from Greek *gloia*] —ˌ**zoo'gloeal** *adj.*

zoography (zəʊ'ɒgrəfɪ) *n.* the branch of zoology concerned with the description of animals. —**zo'ographer** *n.* —**zoographic** (ˌzəʊə'græfɪk) *or* ˌ**zoo'graphical** *adj.*

zooid ('zəʊɔɪd) *n.* **1.** any independent animal body, such as an individual of a coelenterate colony. **2.** a motile cell or body, such as a gamete, produced by an organism. —**zo'oidal** *adj.*

zool. *abbrev. for:* **1.** zoological. **2.** zoology.

zoolatry (zəʊ'ɒlətrɪ) *n.* **1.** (esp. in ancient or primitive religions) the worship of animals as the incarnations of certain deities, symbols of particular qualities or natural forces, etc. **2.** extreme or excessive devotion to animals, particularly domestic pets. —**zo'olater** *n.* —**zo'olatrous** *adj.*

zoological garden *n.* the formal term for **zoo.**

zoology (zəʊ'ɒlədʒɪ, zuː-) *n., pl.* **-gies. 1.** the study of animals, including their classification, structure, physiology, and history. **2.** the biological characteristics of a particular animal or animal group. **3.** the fauna characteristic of a particular region. **4.** a book, treatise, etc., dealing with any aspect of the study of animals. —**zoological** (ˌzəʊə'lɒdʒɪkᵊl, ˌzuːə-) *adj.* —**zo'ologist** *n.*

zoom (zuːm) *vb.* **1.** to make or cause to make a continuous buzzing or humming sound. **2.** to move or cause to move with such a sound. **3.** (*intr.*) to move very rapidly; rush: *we zoomed through town.* **4.** to cause (an aircraft) to climb briefly at an unusually steep angle, or (of an aircraft) to climb in this way. **5.** (*intr.*) (of prices) to rise rapidly. ~*n.* **6.** the sound or act of zooming. **7.** See **zoom lens.** [C20: of imitative origin]

zoometry (zəʊ'ɒmɪtrɪ) *n.* the branch of zoology concerned with the relative length or size of the different parts of an animal or animals. —**zoometric** (ˌzəʊə'mɛtrɪk) *or* ˌ**zoo'metrical** *adj.*

zoom in *or* **out** *vb.* (*intr., adv.*) *Photog., films, television.* to rapidly increase or decrease the magnification of the image of a distant object by means of a zoom lens.

zoom lens *n.* a lens system that allows the focal length of a camera lens to be varied continuously without altering the sharpness of the image. See also **telephoto lens.**

zoomorphism (ˌzəʊə'mɔːfɪzəm) *n.* **1.** the conception or representation of deities in the form of animals. **2.** the use of animal forms or symbols in art, literature, etc. —ˌ**zoo'morphic** *adj.*

zoon ('zəʊɒn) *n., pl.* **zoa** ('zəʊə) *or* **zoons.** a less common term for **zooid** (sense 1). [C19: from New Latin, from Greek *zōion* animal; related to Greek *zōē* life] —**zo'onal** *adj.*

-zoon *n. combining form.* indicating an individual animal or an independently moving entity derived from an animal: *spermatozoon.* [from Greek *zōion* animal]

zoonosis (zəʊ'ɒnəsɪs, ˌzəʊə'nəʊsɪs) *n., pl.* **-ses** (-siːz). *Pathol.* any infection or disease that is transmitted to man from lower vertebrates. [from ZOO- + Greek *nosos* disease]

zoophagous (zəʊ'ɒfəgəs) *adj.* feeding on animals.

zoophile ('zəʊəˌfaɪl) *n.* a person who is devoted to animals and their protection from practices such as vivisection. —**zoophilic** (ˌzəʊə'fɪlɪk) *adj.*

zoophilia (ˌzəʊə'fɪlɪə) *n.* a morbid condition in which a person has a sexual attraction to animals; bestiality.

zoophilism (zəʊ'ɒfɪˌlɪzəm) *n.* the tendency to be emotionally attached to animals.

zoophilous (zəʊ'ɒfɪləs) *adj.* **1.** (of plants) pollinated by animals. **2.** of, characterized by, or relating to zoophilism.

zoophobia (ˌzəʊə'fəʊbɪə) *n.* an unusual or morbid dread of animals. —**zoophobous** (zəʊ'ɒfəbəs) *adj.*

zoophyte ('zəʊəˌfaɪt) *n.* any animal resembling a plant, such as a sea anemone. —**zoophytic** (ˌzəʊə'fɪtɪk) *or* ˌ**zoo'phytical** *adj.*

zooplankton (ˌzəʊə'plæŋktən) *n.* the animal constituent of plankton, which consists mainly of small crustaceans and fish larvae. Compare **phytoplankton.**

zooplasty ('zəʊəˌplæstɪ) *n.* the surgical transplantation to man of animal tissues. —ˌ**zoo'plastic** *adj.*

zoosperm ('zəʊəˌspɜːm) *n.* another word for **spermatozoon.** —**zoospermatic** (ˌzəʊəspɜː'mætɪk) *adj.*

zoosporangium (ˌzəʊəspɔː'rændʒɪəm) *n., pl.* **-gia** (-dʒɪə). *Botany.* a sporangium that produces zoospores. —ˌ**zoospo'rangial** *adj.*

zoospore ('zəʊəˌspɔː) *n.* **1.** an asexual spore of some algae and fungi that moves by means of flagella. **2.** one of several spores produced in a saclike body (sporocyst) by some parasitic protozoans. —ˌ**zoo'sporic** *or* **zoosporous** (zəʊ'ɒspərəs, ˌzəʊə'spɔːrəs) *adj.*

zoosterol (zəʊ'ɒstəˌrɒl) *n.* any of a group of animal sterols, such as cholesterol.

zootechnics (ˌzəʊə'tɛknɪks) *n.* (*functioning as sing.*) the science concerned with the domestication and breeding of animals.

zootomy (zəʊ'ɒtəmɪ) *n.* the branch of zoology concerned with the dissection and anatomy of animals. —**zootomic** (ˌzəʊə'tɒmɪk) *or* ˌ**zoo'tomical** *adj.* —ˌ**zoo'tomically** *adv.* —**zo'otomist** *n.*
zootoxin (ˌzəʊə'tɒksɪn) *n.* a toxin, such as snake venom, that is produced by an animal. Compare **phytotoxin.** —ˌ**zoo'toxic** *adj.*
zoot suit (zuːt) *n. Slang.* a man's suit consisting of baggy trousers with very tapered bottoms and a long jacket with wide padded shoulders, popular esp. in the U.S. in the 1940s. [C20: of uncertain origin; perhaps an arbitrary rhyme on *suit*] —'**zoot**ˌ**suiter** *n.*
zorilla (zə'rɪlə) *or* **zorille** (zə'rɪl) *n.* a skunk-like African musteline mammal, *Ictonyx striatus,* having a long black-and-white coat. [C18: from French, from Spanish *zorrillo* a little fox, from *zorro* fox]
Zoroastrian (ˌzɒrəʊ'æstrɪən) *adj.* **1.** of or relating to Zoroastrianism or its founder Zoroaster. ~*n.* **2.** a follower of Zoroaster or adherent of Zoroastrianism: in modern times a Gabar or a Parsee.
Zoroastrianism (ˌzɒrəʊ'æstrɪənˌɪzəm) *or* **Zoroastrism** *n.* the dualistic religion founded by the Persian prophet Zoroaster in the late 7th or early 6th centuries B.C. and set forth in the sacred writings of the Zend-Avesta. It is based on the concept of a continuous struggle between Ormazd (or Ahura Mazda), the god of creation, light, and goodness, and his arch enemy, Ahriman, the spirit of evil and darkness, and it includes a highly developed ethical code. Also called: **Mazdaism.**
zoster ('zɒstə) *n. Pathol.* short for **herpes zoster.** [C18: from Latin: shingles, from Greek *zōster* girdle]
Zouave (zuː'ɑːv, zwɑːv) *n.* **1.** (formerly) a member of a body of French infantry composed of Algerian recruits noted for their dash, hardiness, and colourful uniforms. **2.** a member of any body of soldiers wearing a similar uniform or otherwise modelled on the French Zouaves, esp. a volunteer in such a unit of the Union Army in the American Civil War (1861–65). [C19: from French, from *Zwāwa,* tribal name in Algeria]
zouk (zuːk) *n.* a style of dance music that combines African and Latin American rhythms and uses electronic instruments and modern studio technology. [C20: from West Indian Creole *zouk* to have a good time]
zounds (zaʊndz) *or* **swounds** (zwaʊndz, zaʊndz) *interj. Archaic.* a mild oath indicating surprise, indignation, etc. [C16: euphemistic shortening of *God's wounds*]
zoysia ('zɔɪzɪə) *n.* any creeping perennial grass of the genus *Zoysia,* of warm dry regions, having short stiffly pointed leaves: often used for lawns. [C19: from New Latin, named after Karl von *Zois* (died 1800), German botanist]
Z particle *n. Physics.* a type of neutral elementary particle considered to transmit the weak interaction between other elementary particles. Z particles have a rest mass of about 10^{-24} kg. Also called: **Z boson.** See also **W particle.**
ZPG *abbrev. for* zero population growth.
Zr *the chemical symbol for* zirconium.
zucchetto (tsuː'ketəʊ, suː-, zuː-) *n., pl.* **-tos.** *R.C. Church.* a small round skullcap worn by certain ecclesiastics and varying in colour according to the rank of the wearer, the Pope wearing white, cardinals red, bishops violet, and others black. [C19: from Italian, from *zucca* a gourd, head, from Late Latin *cucutia* gourd, probably from Latin *cucurbita*]
zucchini (tsuː'kiːnɪ, zuː-) *n., pl.* **-ni** *or* **-nis.** the U.S. and Canadian name for **courgette.** [Italian, pl. of *zucchino,* literally: a little gourd, from *zucca* gourd; see ZUCCHETTO]
zugzwang (*German* 'tsuːktsvaŋ) *Chess.* ~*n.* **1.** a position in which one player can move only with loss or severe disadvantage. ~*vb.* **2.** (*tr.*) to manoeuvre (one's opponent) into a zugzwang. [from German, from *Zug* a pull, tug + *Zwang* force, compulsion]
Zulu ('zuːlʊ -luː) *n.* **1.** (*pl.* **-lus** *or* **-lu**) a member of a tall Negroid people of SE Africa, living chiefly in N Natal in South Africa, who became dominant during the 19th century due to a warrior-clan system. **2.** the language of this people, belonging to the Bantu group of the Niger-Congo family, closely related to Swazi and Xhosa. **3.** *Communications.* a code word for the letter *z.*
Zuñi ('zuːnjiː, 'suː-) *n.* **1.** (*pl.* **-ñis** *or* **-ñi**) a member of a North American Indian people of W New Mexico. **2.** the language of this people, a member of the Penutian phylum of languages. —'**Zuñian** *adj., n.*
zwieback ('zwaɪˌbæk, 'zwiː-; *German* 'tsviːbak) *n.* a small type of rusk, which has been baked first as a loaf, then sliced and toasted, usually bought ready-made. [German: twice-baked]
Zwinglian ('zwɪŋglɪən, 'swɪŋg-, 'tsvɪŋ-) *n.* **1.** an upholder of the religious doctrines or movement of the Swiss Reformation leader Ulrich Zwingli (1484–1531). ~*adj.* **2.** of or relating to Zwingli, his religious movement, or his doctrines, esp. his denial of the Eucharistic presence. —'**Zwinglianism** *n.* —'**Zwinglianist** *n.*
zwischenzug ('zvɪʃənzuːg) *n. Chess.* a tactical move interpolated into an exchange or series of exchanges to improve the outcome. [C20: German: in-between move]
zwitterion ('tsvɪtərˌaɪən) *n. Chem.* an ion that carries both a positive and a negative charge. [C20: from German *Zwitter* hermaphrodite + ION] —**zwitterionic** (ˌtsvɪtəraɪ'ɒnɪk) *adj.*
zydeco ('zaɪdəˌkəʊ) *n.* a type of Black Cajun music.
zygapophysis (ˌzɪgə'pɒfɪsɪs, ˌzaɪgə-) *n., pl.* **-ses** (-ˌsiːz). *Anatomy, zoology.* one of several processes on a vertebra that articulates with the corresponding process on an adjacent vertebra. [C19: from ZYGO- + APOPHYSIS] —**zygapophyseal** (ˌzɪgæpə'fɪzɪəl) *adj.*
zygo- *or before a vowel* **zyg-** *combining form.* indicating a pair or a union: *zygodactyl; zygospore.* [from Greek *zugon* yoke]
zygodactyl (ˌzaɪgəʊ'dæktɪl, ˌzɪgə-) *adj. also* **zygodactylous. 1.** (of the feet of certain birds) having the first and fourth toes directed backwards and the second and third forwards. ~*n.* **2.** a zygodactyl bird. ~Compare **heterodactyl.** —ˌ**zygo'dactylism** *n.*
zygoma (zaɪ'gəʊmə, zɪ-) *n., pl.* **-mata** (-mətə). another name for **zygomatic arch.** [C17: via New Latin from Greek, from *zugon* yoke] —**zygomatic** (ˌzaɪgəʊ'mætɪk, ˌzɪg-) *adj.*
zygomatic arch *n.* the slender arch of bone that forms a bridge between the cheekbone and the temporal bone on each side of the skull of mammals. Also called: **zygoma.**
zygomatic bone *n.* either of two bones, one on each side of the skull, that form part of the side wall of the eye socket and part of the zygomatic arch; cheekbone. Also called: **malar, malar bone.**
zygomatic process *n.* a slender bony process of the temporal bone that forms part of the zygomatic arch.
zygomorphic (ˌzaɪgəʊ'mɔːfɪk, ˌzɪg-) *or* **zygomorphous** *adj.* (of a flower) capable of being cut in only one plane so that the two halves are mirror images. See also **actinomorphic.** —ˌ**zygo'morphism** *or* '**zygo**ˌ**morphy** *n.*
zygophyllaceous (ˌzaɪgəʊfɪ'leɪʃəs, ˌzɪg-) *adj.* of, relating to, or belonging to the *Zygophyllaceae,* an Old World family of flowering plants having pinnate leaves and capsules as fruits: includes the bean caper and guaiacum.
zygophyte ('zaɪgəʊˌfaɪt, 'zɪg-) *n.* a plant, such as an alga, that reproduces by means of zygospores.
zygosis (zaɪ'gəʊsɪs, zɪ-) *n. Biology.* another name for **conjugation.** —**zygose** ('zaɪgəʊs, 'zɪg-) *adj.*
zygospore ('zaɪgəʊˌspɔː, 'zɪg-) *n.* a thick-walled sexual spore formed from the zygote of some fungi and algae. —ˌ**zygo'sporic** *adj.*
zygote ('zaɪgəʊt, 'zɪg-) *n.* **1.** the cell resulting from the union of an ovum and a spermatozoon. **2.** the organism that develops from such a cell. [C19: from Greek *zugōtos* yoked, from *zugoun* to yoke] —**zygotic** (zaɪ'gɒtɪk, zɪ-) *adj.* —**zy'gotically** *adv.*
zygotene ('zaɪgəˌtiːn, 'zɪg-) *n.* the second stage of the prophase of meiosis, during which homologous chromosomes become associated in pairs (bivalents).
zymase ('zaɪmeɪs) *n.* a mixture of enzymes that is obtained as an extract from yeast and ferments sugars.
zymo- *or before a vowel* **zym-** *combining form.* indicating fermentation: *zymology.* [from Greek *zumē* leaven]
zymogen ('zaɪməʊˌdʒen) *n. Biochem.* any of a group of compounds that are inactive precursors of enzymes and are activated by a kinase.
zymogenesis (ˌzaɪməʊ'dʒenɪsɪs) *n.* the conversion of a zymogen into an enzyme.
zymogenic (ˌzaɪməʊ'dʒenɪk) *adj.* **1.** of, or relating to a zymogen. **2.** capable of causing zymogenesis.
zymology (zaɪ'mɒlədʒɪ) *n.* the chemistry of fermentation. —**zymologic** (ˌzaɪməʊ'lɒdʒɪk) *or* ˌ**zymo'logical** *adj.* —**zy'mologist** *n.*
zymolysis (zaɪ'mɒlɪsɪs) *n.* the process of fermentation. Also called: **zymosis.** —**zymolytic** (ˌzaɪməʊ'lɪtɪk) *adj.*
zymometer (zaɪ'mɒmɪtə) *n.* an instrument for estimating the degree of fermentation.
zymosis (zaɪ'məʊsɪs) *n., pl.* **-ses** (-siːz). **1.** *Med.* **a.** any infectious disease. **b.** the development process or spread of such a disease. **2.** another name for **zymolysis.**
zymotic (zaɪ'mɒtɪk) *adj.* **1.** of, relating to, or causing fermentation. **2.** relating to or caused by infection; denoting or relating to an infectious disease. —**zy'motically** *adv.*
zymurgy ('zaɪmɜːdʒɪ) *n.* the branch of chemistry concerned with fermentation processes in brewing, etc.
Zyrian ('zɪrɪən) *n.* **1.** the language of the Komi people, belonging to the Finno-Ugric family; Komi. ~*adj.* **2.** of or relating to this language or its speakers.

SUPPLEMENTS

Languages and alphabets

A simplified tree of Indo-European languages

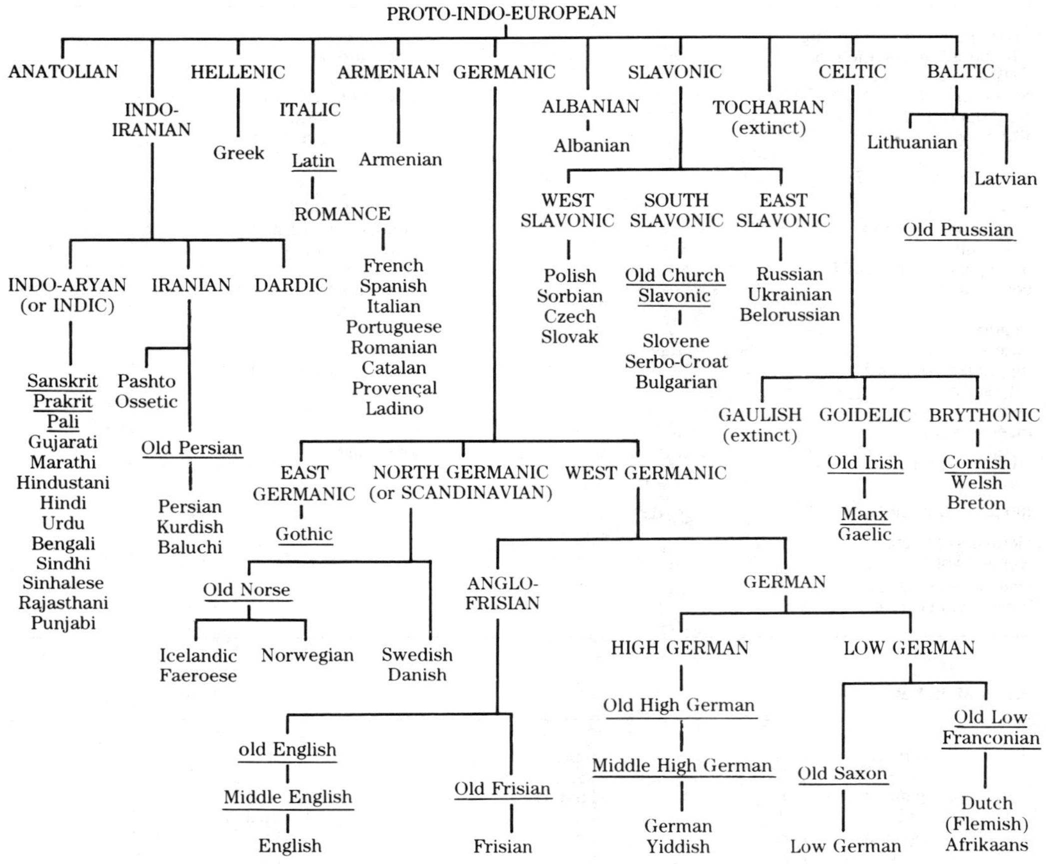

Note: underlined languages are no longer spoken

The development of the modern Roman alphabet

Phoenician	𐤀	𐤁	𐤂	𐤃	𐤄	𐤅	𐤂	𐤇	𐤉	𐤉	𐤊	𐤋	𐤌	𐤍	𐤏	𐤐	𐤒	𐤓	𐤔	𐤕	𐤅	𐤅	𐤅	𐤎	[illegible]	𐤆
Early Hebrew	𐤀	𐤁	𐤂	𐤃	𐤄	𐤅	𐤂	𐤇	𐤉	𐤉	𐤊	𐤋	𐤌	𐤍	𐤏	𐤐	𐤒	𐤓	𐤔	𐤕	𐤅	𐤅	𐤅	𐤎	[illegible]	𐤆
Early Aramaic	𐤀	𐤁	𐤂	𐤃	𐤄	𐤅	𐤂	𐤇	𐤉	𐤉	𐤊	𐤋	𐤌	𐤍	𐤏	𐤐	𐤒	𐤓	𐤔	𐤕	𐤅	𐤅	𐤅	𐤎	[illegible]	[illegible]
Early Greek	A	8	1	Δ	∃	ᖷ	1	B	≷	≷	ꓘ	1	M	ᴎ	O	1	Φ	4	ϟ	X	Y	Y	Y	☰		I
Classical Greek	A	B	Γ	Δ	E		Γ	H	I	I	K	Λ	M	N	O	Π		P	Σ	T	Y	Y	Y	Ξ		Z
Etruscan	A	8	1	ᗡ	∃	ᖷ	1	⊟	I	I	ꓘ	√	M	ᴎ	O	1	P	4	ϟ	T	Y	Y	[illegible]	X		I
Early Latin	A	B	<	D	E	F	<	H	I	I	K	L	M	N	O	Γ	Q	P	ϟ	T	V	V	V	X	Y	Z
Classical Latin	A	B	C	D	E	F	G	H	I	I	K	L	M	N	O	P	Q	R	S	T	V	V	V	X	Y	Z
Russian-Cyrillic	А	Б	Г	Д	Е	Ф	Г	И	I		К	Л	М	Н	О	П		Р	С	Т	У					З
Modern Roman	A	B	C	D	E	F	G	H	I	J	K	L	M	N	O	P	Q	R	S	T	U	V	W	X	Y	Z

Symbols used in mathematics, logic and electronics

Operation	*Symbol*	*Operation*	*Symbol*
AND operation, conjunction	$\wedge$.	equivalence	$\leftrightarrow \equiv$
OR operation, disjunction	$\vee$ +	biconditional	$\leftrightarrow \equiv$
NOT operation, negation	′ — ~	conditional	$\rightarrow \Rightarrow$
NAND operation	$\mid \Delta$	general binary operation	$\circ$
NOR operation	$\uparrow \nabla$	universal quantifier	$\forall$
EXOR operation	$\veebar$	existential quantifier	$\exists$
For set S and/or set T:			
x is a member of S	$x \in S$	union of S and T	$S \cup T$
x is not a member of S	$x \notin S$	intersection of S and T	$S \cap T$
S is a subset of T	$S \subseteq T$	Cartesian product of S and T	$S \times T$
S is a proper subset of T	$S \subset T$		
complement of S	S' $\sim S$ $\bar{S}$	set of all x for which $p(x)$ is true	$\{x \mid p(x)\}$
relation	R		
function of x	$f(x)$	greater than	$>$
function f from set X to set Y	$f: X \rightarrow Y$	greater than or equal to	$\geqslant$
		less than	$<$
inverse function	f^{-1}	less than or equal to	$\leqslant$
inverse relation	R^{-1}	approx. equal to	$\cong$
sum, with limits	$\sum_{i=1}^{n}$	not equal to	$\neq$
		infinity	∞
integral, with limits	$\int_b^a dx$		
elements of vector v	v_1		
elements of matrix A	a_{ij}		
transpose of matrix A	A^T		
inverse of matrix A	A^{-1}		

Greek alphabet

alpha	α, A	iota	ι, I	rho	ρ, P
beta	β, B	kappa	κ, K	sigma	σ, Σ
gamma	γ, Γ	lambda	λ, Λ	tau	τ, T
delta	δ, Δ	mu	μ, M	upsilon	υ, Y
epsilon	ϵ, E	nu	ν, N	phi	ϕ, Φ
zeta	ζ, Z	xi	ξ, Ξ	chi	χ, X
eta	η, H	omikron	o, O	psi	ψ, Ψ
theta	θ, Θ	pi	π, Π	omega	ω, Ω

Electronics

AC	heater	resistor
AND gate	inductor	sawtooth wave
capacitor	lamp	sine wave
cathode	meter	square wave
connector terminals	meter *or* motor	switch
crystal	negative pulse	transformer
DC	neon bulb	transistor (NPN)
diode	NOT gate (inverter)	triangle wave
earth	operational amplifier	tunnel diode
electrolytic capacitor	OR gate	XOR gate
flip-flop	positive pulse	Zener diode

Symbols for physical quantities

Quantity	Symbol
absorptance	α
acceleration	a
activity	A
admittance	Y
amount of substance	n
ampere turn	At
angular acceleration	a
angular displacement	θ
angular frequency	ω
angular magnification	M
angular momentum	L
angular velocity	ω
atomic number, proton number	Z
Bragg angle	θ
Brewster angle	i
bulk modulus	K
capacitance	C
centripetal acceleration	a
centripetal force	F
characteristic temperature	θ
charge	Q
charge density	ρ
coefficient of friction	μ
concentration	c
conductance	G
conductivity, electrical	σ
conductivity, thermal	λ
cubic expansion coefficient	γ
current	i
current density	j
decay constant	λ
declination	c
degeneracy of an energy level	g
density	ρ
diameter	d
diffusion coefficient	D
displacement	s
efficiency	η
electric displacement	D
electric field strength	E
electric flux	ψ
electric potential	V
electrochemical equivalent	Z
electromotive force	E
emessivity	ϵ
energy	W, E
enthalpy	H
entropy	S
exitance	M
force	F
frequency	f, v
half-life	$T_{1/2}$
heat	Q, H
heat capacity	C
horizontal intensity	B
illumination, illuminance	E
impedance	Z
inclination	δ
internal energy	U, E
ionization potential	I
irradiance	E
kinematic viscosity	ν
kinetic energy	T, E_K, K
linear expansion coefficient	α
luminance	L
luminous flux	ϕ
luminous intensity	I
magnetic field strength	H
magnetic flux	Φ
magnetic flux density	B
magnetic moment	m
magnetic susceptibility	χ
magnetomotive force	F
magnification	m
mass	m
mean free path	λ
mean life	τ
molar heat capacity	C_m
moment of force	M
moment of inertia	I
momentum, linear	p
Néel temperature	θ_N
neutron number	N
nucleon number	A
optical path	d
osmotic pressure	Π
parity	P
period	T
permeability	μ
permittivity	ϵ
potential difference	V
potential energy	V
power	P
pressure	p
proton number, atomic number	Z
radiance	L_e
radiant flux	Φ_e
radiant intensity	I_e
radius	r
radius of curvature	r
radius of gyration	k
reactance	X
reflectance	ρ
refractive constant	n
relative atomic mass	A_r
relative density	d
relative molecular mass	M_r
reluctance	R
resistance	R
resistivity	ρ
restitution, coefficient of	e
rest mass	m_0
shear modulus	G
solid angle	Ω
specific heat capacity	c
specific rotary power	a_m
speed	u
surface tension	γ
susceptance	B
susceptibility	χ
temperature	T, t
thermodynamic temperature	T
time	t
torque	T
velocity	v
viscosity	η
voltage	V
volume	V
wavelength	λ
wave number	σ
weight	W
work	W
work function	Φ
Young modulus	E

Chemistry and physics

Periodic table of the elements

1A	2A	3B	4B	5B	6B	7B	8			1B	2B	3A	4A	5A	6A	7A	0
1 H																	2 He
3 Li	4 Be											5 B	6 C	7 N	8 O	9 F	10 Ne
11 Na	12 Mg	← transition elements →										13 Al	14 Si	15 P	16 S	17 Cl	18 Ar
19 K	20 Ca	21 Sc	22 Ti	23 V	24 Cr	25 Mn	26 Fe	27 Co	28 Ni	29 Cu	30 Zn	31 Ga	32 Ge	33 As	34 Se	35 Br	36 Kr
37 Rb	38 Sr	39 Y	40 Zr	41 Nb	42 Mo	43 Tc	44 Ru	45 Rh	46 Pd	47 Ag	48 Cd	49 In	50 Sn	51 Sb	52 Te	53 I	54 Xe
55 Cs	56 Ba	57* La	72 Hf	73 Ta	74 W	75 Re	76 Os	77 Ir	78 Pt	79 Au	80 Hg	81 Tl	82 Pb	83 Bi	84 Po	85 At	86 Rn
87 Fr	38 Ra	89† Ac															
*Lanthanides			57 La	58 Ce	59 Pr	60 Nd	61 Pm	62 Sm	63 Eu	64 Gd	65 Tb	66 Dy	67 Ho	68 Er	69 Tm	70 Yb	71 Lu
†Actinides			89 Ac	90 Th	91 Pa	92 U	93 Np	94 Pu	95 Am	96 Cm	97 Bk	98 Cf	99 Es	100 Fm	101 Md	102 No	103 Lr

Fundamental constants

Constant	*Symbol*	*Value in SI units*
acceleration of free fall	g	$9.806\,65$ m s^{-2}
Avogrado constant	L, N_A	$6.022\,52 \times 10^{23}$ mol^{-1}
electric constant	ϵ_0	8.854×10^{-12} F m^{-1}
electronic charge	e	$1.602\,10 \times 10^{-19}$ C
electronic rest mass	m_e	$9.109\,08 \times 10^{-31}$ kg
gas constant	R_0	$8.314\,34$ J K^{-1} mol^{-1}
gravitational constant	G	6.672×10^{-11} N m^2 kg^{-2}
magnetic constant	μ_0	$4\pi \times 10^{-7}$ H m^{-1}
neutron rest mass	m_n	$1.674\,82 \times 10^{-27}$ kg
Planck constant	h	$6.625\,59 \times 10^{-34}$ J s
proton rest mass	m_p	$1.672\,52 \times 10^{-27}$ kg
speed of light	c	$2.997\,924\,58 \times 10^{8}$ m s^{-1}

SI units

Base and supplementary SI units

Physical quantity	*SI unit*	*Symbol*
length	metre	m
mass	kilogram	kg
time	second	s
electric current	ampere	A
thermodynamic temperature	kelvin	K
luminous intensity	candela	cd
amount of substance	mole	mol
plane angle (supplementary unit)	radian	rad
solid angle (supplementary unit)	steradian	sr

Derived SI units with special names

Physical quantity	*SI unit*	*Symbol*
frequency	hertz	Hz
energy	joule	J
force	newton	N
power	watt	W
pressure	pascal	Pa
electric charge	coulomb	C
electric potential difference	volt	V
electric resistance	ohm	Ω
electric conductance	siemens	S
electric capacitance	farad	F
magnetic flux	weber	Wb
inductance	henry	H
magnetic flux density (magnetic induction)	tesla	T
luminous flux	lumen	lm
illuminance	lux	lx
absorbed dose	gray	Gy
activity	becquerel	Bq
dose equivalent	sievert	Sv

Decimal multiples and submultiples used with SI units

Submultiple	*Prefix*	*Symbol*	*Multiple*	*Prefix*	*Symbol*
10^{-1}	deci–	d	10	*deca–*	da
10^{-2}	cent–	c	10^{2}	*hecto–*	h
10^{-3}	milli–	m	10^{3}	*kilo–*	k
10^{-6}	micro–	μ	10^{6}	*mega–*	M
10^{-9}	nano–	n	10^{9}	*giga–*	G
10^{-12}	pico–	p	10^{12}	*tera–*	T
10^{-15}	femto–	f	10^{15}	*peta–*	P
10^{-18}	atto–	a	10^{18}	*exa–*	E

Unit conversion tables

Length

	metre	centimetre	inch	foot	yard
1 metre	1	100	39.3701	3.28084	1.09361
1 centimetre	0.01	1	0.393701	0.0328084	0.0109361
1 inch	0.0254	2.54	1	0.0833333	0.0277778
1 foot	0.3048	30.48	12	1	0.333333
1 yard	0.9144	91.44	36	3	1

	kilometre	mile	nautical mile
1 kilometre	1	0.621371	0.539957
1 mile	1.60934	1	0.868976
1 nautical mile	1.85200	1.15078	1

Area

	m^2	cm^2	in^2	ft^2
1 square metre	1	10^4	1550	10.7639
1 square centimetre	10^{-4}	1	0.155	1.07639×10^{-3}
1 square inch	6.4516×10^{-4}	6.4516	1	6.94444×10^{-3}
1 square foot	9.2903×10^{-2}	929.03	144	1

	m^2	km^2	yd^2	mi^2	acre
1 square metre	1	10^{-6}	1.19599	3.86019×10^{-7}	2.47105×10^{-4}
1 square kilometre	10^6	1	1.19599×10^6	0.386019	247.105
1 square yard	0.836127	8.36127×10^{-7}	1	3.22831×10^{-7}	2.06612×10^{-4}
1 square mile	2.58999×10^6	2.58999	3.0976×10^6	1	640
1 acre	4.04686×10^3	4.04686×10^{-3}	4840	1.5625×10^{-3}	1

Volume

	m^3	cm^3	in^3	ft^3	gallons
1 cubic metre	1	10^6	6.10236×10^4	35.3146	219.969
1 cubic centimetre	10^{-6}	1	0.0610236	3.53146×10^{-5}	2.19969×10^{-4}
1 cubic inch	1.63871×10^{-5}	16.3871	1	5.78704×10^{-4}	3.60464×10^{-3}
1 cubic foot	0.0283168	28316.8	1728	1	6.22882
1 gallon (UK)	4.54609×10^{-3}	4546.09	277.42	0.160544	1

Speed

	m/sec	km/hr	mi/hr	ft/sec
1 metre per second	1	3.6	2.23694	3.28084
1 kilometre per hour	0.277778	1	0.621371	0.911346
1 mile per hour	0.44704	1.609344	1	1.46667
1 foot per second	0.3048	1.09728	0.681817	1

Mass

	kg	g	lb
1 kilogram	1	1000	2.20462
1 gram	10^{-3}	1	2.20462×10^{-3}
1 pound	0.453592	453.592	1

Density

	kg/m^3	g/m^3	lb/ft^3
1 kilogram per cubic metre	1	10^{-3}	0.062428
1 gram per cubic centimetre	1000	1	62.428
1 pound per cubic foot	16.0185	0.0160185	1

Force

	N	kg	dyne	poundal	lb
1 newton	1	0.101972	10^5	7.23300	0.224809
1 kilogram force	9.80665	1	9.80665×10^5	70.9316	2.20462
1 dyne	10^{-5}	1.01972×10^{-6}	1	7.23300×10^{-5}	2.4809×10^{-6}
1 poundal	0.138255	1.40981×10^{-2}	1.38255×10^4	1	0.031081
1 pound force	4.44822	0.453592	4.44823×10^5	32.174	1

Pressure

	N/m^2(Pa)	kg/cm^2	lb/in^2	atmos
1 newton per square metre (pascal)	1	1.01972×10^{-5}	1.45038×10^{-4}	9.86923×10^{-6}
1 kilogram per square centimetre	980.665×10^2	1	14.2234	0.967841
1 pound per square inch	6.89476×10^3	0.0703068	1	0.068046
1 atmosphere	1.01325×10^5	1.03323	14.6959	1

Work and Energy

	J	cal_{IT}	kWhr	btu_{IT}
1 joule	1	0.238846	2.77778×10^{-7}	9.47813×10^{-4}
1 calorie (IT)	4.1868	1	1.16300×10^{-6}	3.96831×10^{-3}
1 kilowatt hour	3.6×10^6	8.59845×10^5	1	3412.14
1 British Thermal Unit (IT)	1055.06	251.997	2.93071×10^{-4}	1

Geological time scale

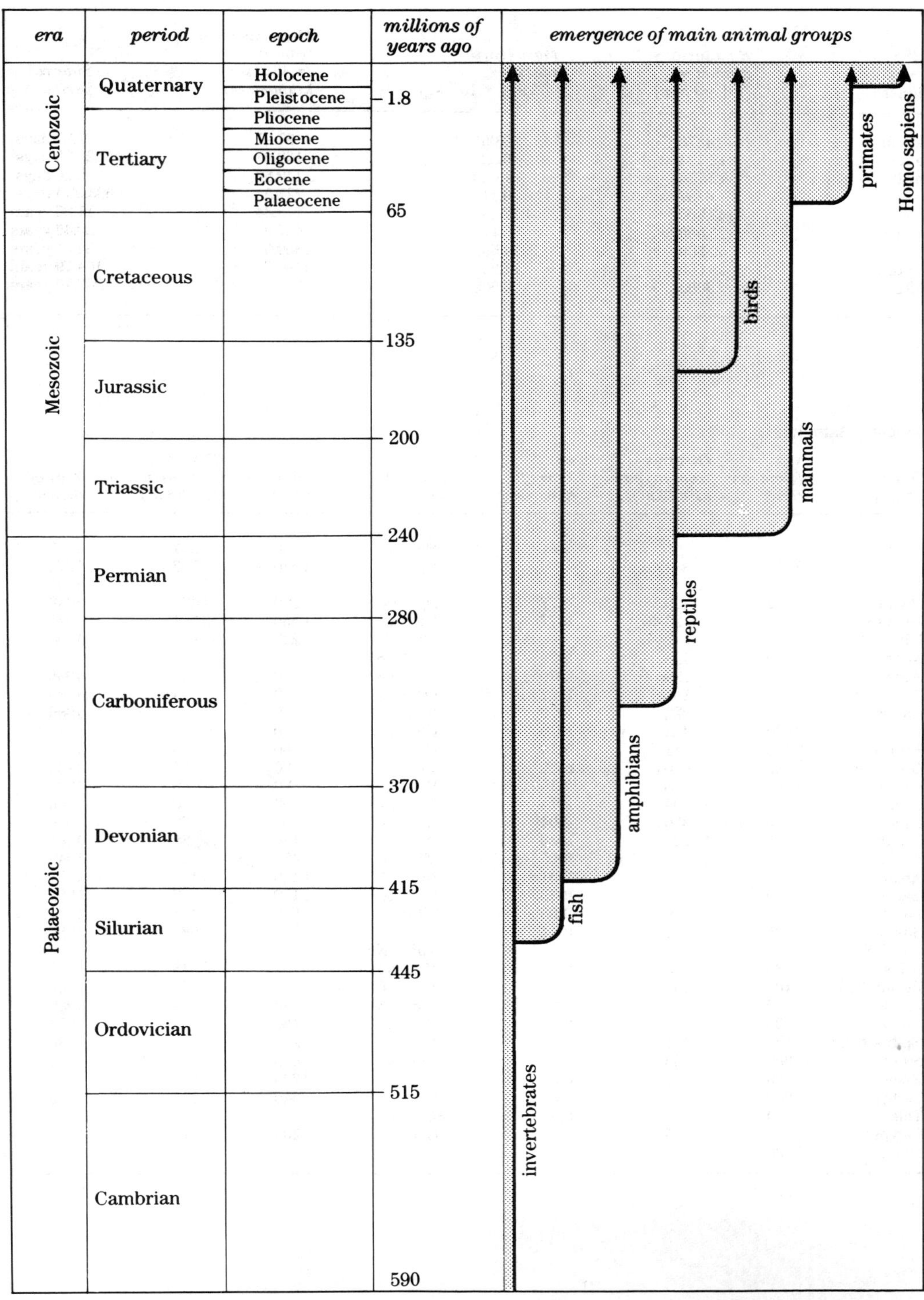

era
period
epoch
millions of years ago
emergence of main animal groups
Cenozoic
Mesozoic
Palaeozoic
Quaternary
Tertiary
Cretaceous
Jurassic
Triassic
Permian
Carboniferous
Devonian
Silurian
Ordovician
Cambrian
Holocene
Pleistocene
Pliocene
Miocene
Oligocene
Eocene
Palaeocene
1.8
65
135
200
240
280
370
415
445
515
590
invertebrates
fish
amphibians
reptiles
mammals
birds
primates
Homo sapiens

The solar system

The Planets

Planet	*Equatorial diameter (kilometres)*	*Mass (earth masses = 5.974 × 10^{24} kg)*	*Mean distance from sun (millions of kilometres)*	*Sidereal period*
Mercury	4878	0.06	57.91	87.97 days
Venus	12 104	0.82	108.21	224.70 days
Earth	12 756	1.000	149.60	365.26 days
Mars	6787	0.11	227.94	686.980 days
Jupiter	142 800	317.83	778.34	11.86 years
Saturn	120 000	95.17	1427.01	29.46 years
Uranus	50 800	14.50	2869.6	84.01 years
Neptune	48 600	17.20	4496.7	164.79 years
Pluto	3000?	0.002	5907	247.70 years

Planetary Satellites

Planet & satellite	*Diameter (km)*	*Distance from primary (1000km)*	*Year of discovery*
EARTH			
Moon	3476	384.40	–
MARS			
Phobos	22	9.38	1877
Deimos	13	23.46	1877
JUPITER			
Metis	40	128	1979
Adrastea	20	129	1979
Amalthea	190	181	1892
Thebe	100	222	1979
Io	3630	422	1610
Europa	3140	671	1610
Ganymede	5260	1070	1610
Callisto	4800	1883	1610
Leda	15	11094	1974
Himalia	185	11480	1904
Lysithea	35	11720	1938
Elara	75	11737	1905
Ananke	30	21200	1951
Carme	40	22600	1938
Pasiphae	50	23500	1908
Sinope	35	23700	1914
SATURN			
Atlas	30	138	1980
Prometheus	105	139	1980
Pandora	90	142	1980
Janus	90	151	1966
Epimetheus	120	151	1966
Mimas	390	186	1789
Enceladus	500	238	1789
Tethys	1060	295	1684
Telesto	30	295	1980
Calypso	25	295	1980
Dione	1120	377	1684
Helene	30	377	1980
Rhea	1530	527	1672
Titan	5150	1222	1655
Hyperion	290	1481	1848
Iapetus	1460	3561	1671
Phoebe	220	12952	1898
URANUS			
Cordelia	40	50	1986
Ophelia	50	54	1986
Bianca	50	59	1986
Cressida	60	62	1986
Desdemona	60	63	1986
Juliet	80	64	1986
Portia	90	66	1986
Rosalind	60	70	1986
Belinda	50	75	1986
Puck	170	86	1985
Miranda	480	129	1948
Ariel	1160	191	1851
Umbriel	1190	266	1851
Titania	1610	436	1787
Oberon	1550	584	1787
NEPTUNE			
1989 N6	50	48	1989
1989 N5	90	50	1989
1989 N3	140	53	1989
1989 N4	160	62	1989
1989 N2	200	74	1989
1989 N1	420	118	1989
Triton	2720	354	1846
Nereid	340	5511	1949
PLUTO			
Charon	1200	19	1978

The plant kingdom

A simplified classification

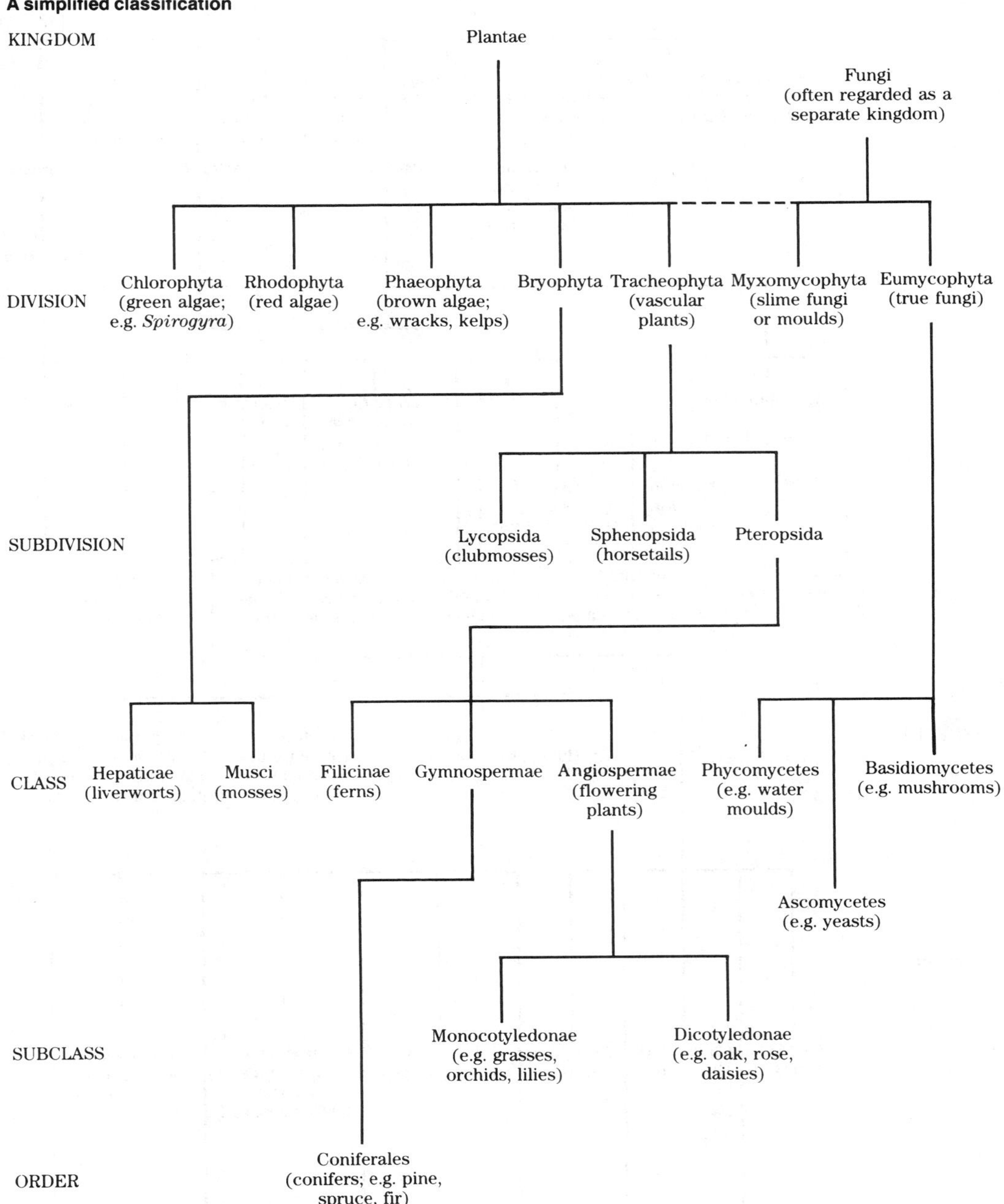
KINGDOM
Plantae
Fungi (often regarded as a separate kingdom)
DIVISION
Chlorophyta (green algae; e.g. Spirogyra)
Rhodophyta (red algae)
Phaeophyta (brown algae; e.g. wracks, kelps)
Bryophyta
Tracheophyta (vascular plants)
Myxomycophyta (slime fungi or moulds)
Eumycophyta (true fungi)
SUBDIVISION
Lycopsida (clubmosses)
Sphenopsida (horsetails)
Pteropsida
CLASS
Hepaticae (liverworts)
Musci (mosses)
Filicinae (ferns)
Gymnospermae
Angiospermae (flowering plants)
Phycomycetes (e.g. water moulds)
Basidiomycetes (e.g. mushrooms)
Ascomycetes (e.g. yeasts)
SUBCLASS
Monocotyledonae (e.g. grasses, orchids, lilies)
Dicotyledonae (e.g. oak, rose, daisies)
ORDER
Coniferales (conifers; e.g. pine, spruce, fir)

The animal kingdom

A simplified classification

- KINGDOM: Animalia
  - PHYLUM: Protozoa (e.g. *Amoeba*, *Plasmodium*)
  - PHYLUM: Porifera (sponges)
  - PHYLUM: Coelenterata (e.g. jellyfish, sea anemones, corals)
  - PHYLUM: Platyhelminthes (flatworms; e.g. flukes, tapeworms)
  - PHYLUM: Nematoda (roundworms)
  - PHYLUM: Mollusca
    - CLASS: Gastropoda (e.g. snails, slugs)
    - CLASS: Lamellibranchia (e.g. oysters mussels, clams)
    - CLASS: Cephalopoda (e.g. squids, octopuses)
  - PHYLUM: Annelida (segmented worms; e.g. earthworms, lugworms, leeches)
  - PHYLUM: Arthropoda
    - CLASS: Arachnida (e.g. spiders, scorpions, mites)
    - CLASS: Crustacea (e.g. shrimps, crabs, lobsters)
    - CLASS: Insecta
      - ORDER: Hemiptera (bugs)
      - ORDER: Diptera (flies)
      - ORDER: Lepidoptera (butterflies and moths)
      - ORDER: Hymenoptera (ants, bees, wasps)
      - ORDER: Coleoptera (beetles)
    - CLASS: Myriapoda (centipedes and millipedes)
  - PHYLUM: Echinodermata (e.g. starfish, sea urchins, brittlestars)
  - PHYLUM: Chordata
    - SUBPHYLUM: Vertebrata
      - CLASS: Agnatha (jawless fish; e.g. lampreys, hagfish)
      - CLASS: Elasmobranchii (cartilaginous fish; e.g. sharks, rays)
      - CLASS: Osteichthyes (bony fish)
        - SUBCLASS: Dipnoi (lungfish)
        - SUBCLASS: Teleostei (e.g. salmon, plaice, eel)
      - CLASS: Amphibia (e.g. frogs, toads)
      - CLASS: Reptilia (e.g. crocodiles, snakes, lizards)
      - CLASS: Aves (birds)
      - CLASS: Mammalia
        - SUBCLASS: Prototheria (monotremes; e.g. duckbilled platypus)
        - SUBCLASS: Metatheria (marsupial mammals; e.g. kangaroo, wombat)
        - SUBCLASS: Eutheria (placental mammals)
          - ORDER: Chiroptera (bats)
          - ORDER: Primates (monkeys, apes, man, etc.)
          - ORDER: Cetacea (whales)
          - ORDER: Rodentia (rats, mice, squirrels, porcupines, etc.)
          - ORDER: Carnivora (cats, dogs, bears, weasels, badgers, etc.)
          - ORDER: Perissodactyla (horses, rhinos, etc.)
          - ORDER: Artiodactyla (pigs, hippos, deer, antelopes, cattle, etc.)

The human body

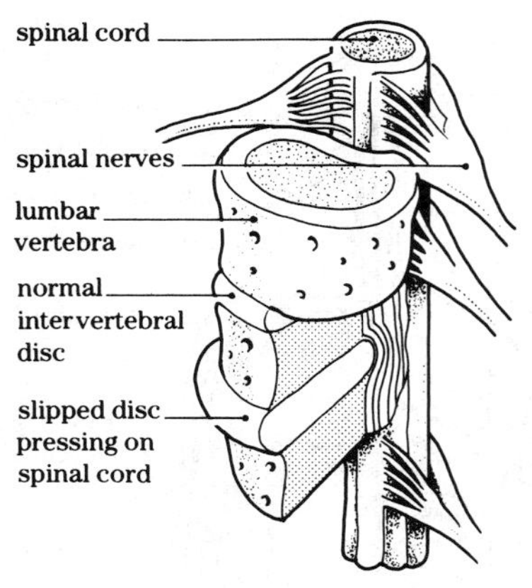

Skeleton (left) and muscular system (right)

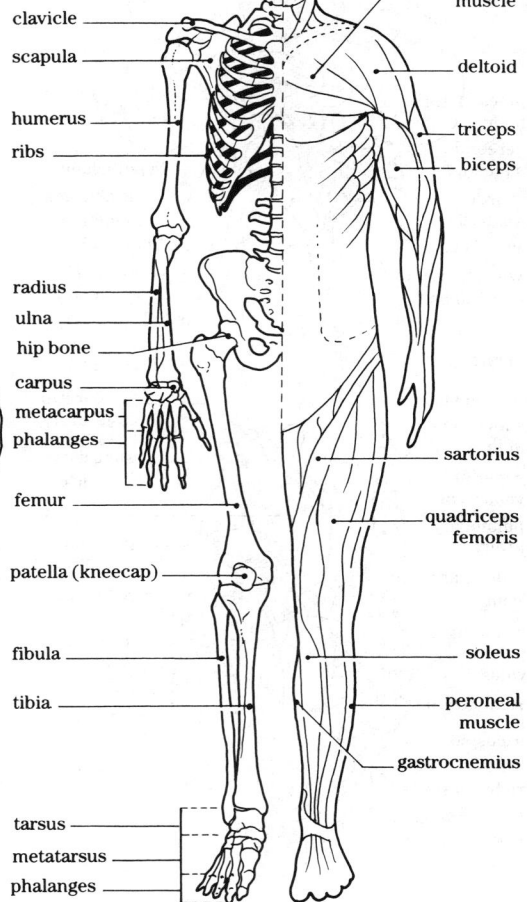

cranium
clavicle
scapula
humerus
ribs
radius
ulna
hip bone
carpus
metacarpus
phalanges
femur
patella (kneecap)
fibula
tibia
tarsus
metatarsus
phalanges
pectoral muscle
deltoid
triceps
biceps
sartorius
quadriceps femoris
soleus
peroneal muscle
gastrocnemius

Muscles and bones of the arm

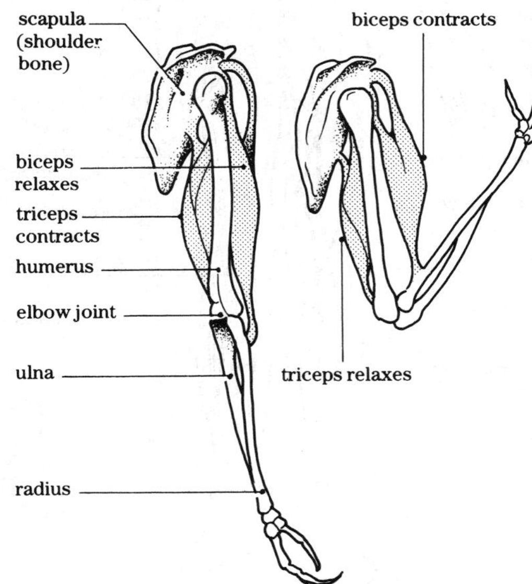

Male reproductive system

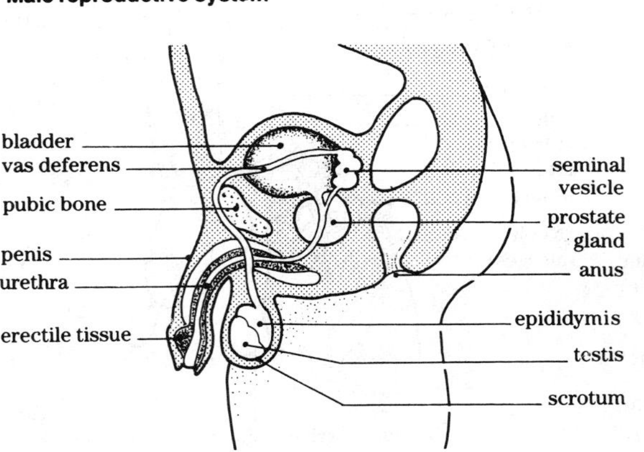

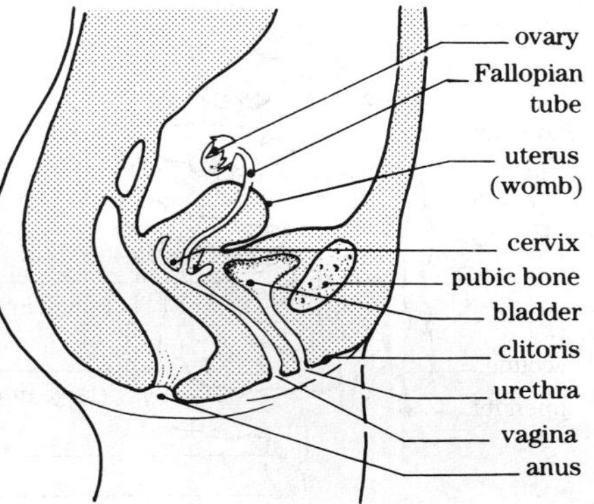

The human body

Brain

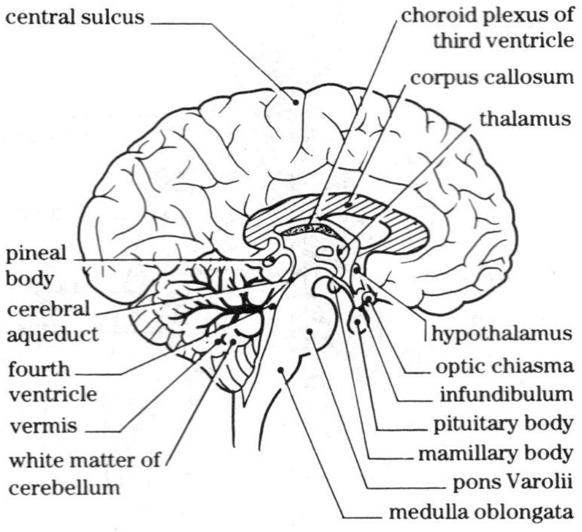
central sulcus
choroid plexus of third ventricle
corpus callosum
thalamus
pineal body
cerebral aqueduct
fourth ventricle
vermis
white matter of cerebellum
hypothalamus
optic chiasma
infundibulum
pituitary body
mamillary body
pons Varolii
medulla oblongata

Heart

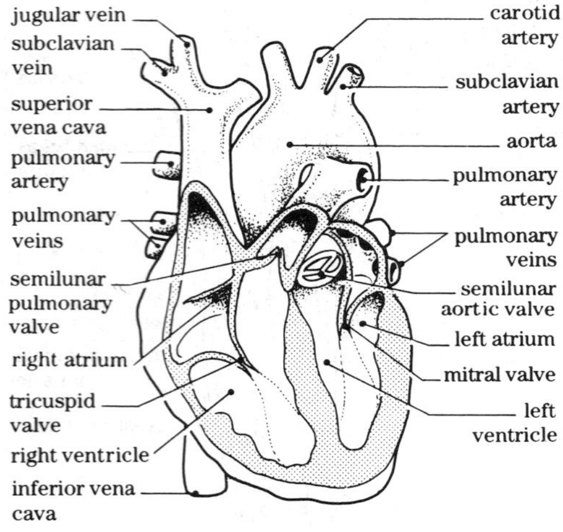
jugular vein
subclavian vein
superior vena cava
pulmonary artery
pulmonary veins
semilunar pulmonary valve
right atrium
tricuspid valve
right ventricle
inferior vena cava
carotid artery
subclavian artery
aorta
pulmonary artery
pulmonary veins
semilunar aortic valve
left atrium
mitral valve
left ventricle

Alimentary canal

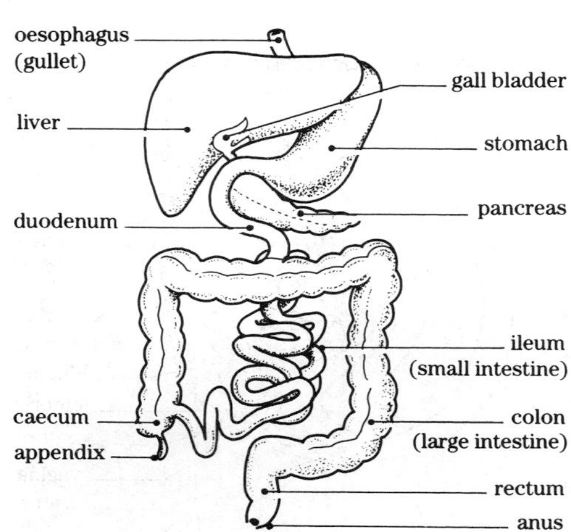
oesophagus (gullet)
liver
duodenum
caecum
appendix
gall bladder
stomach
pancreas
ileum (small intestine)
colon (large intestine)
rectum
anus

Nervous system (left) and circulatory system (right)

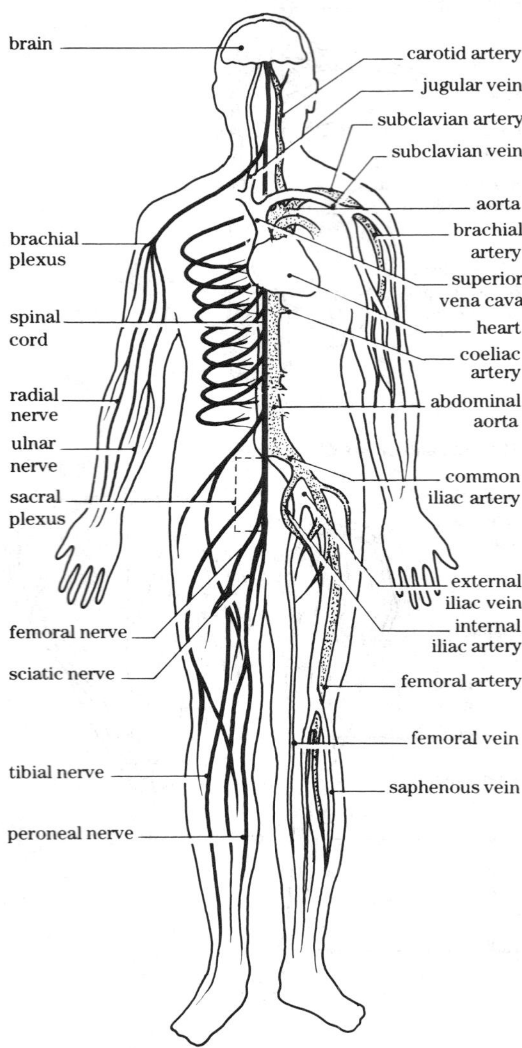
brain
brachial plexus
spinal cord
radial nerve
ulnar nerve
sacral plexus
femoral nerve
sciatic nerve
tibial nerve
peroneal nerve
carotid artery
jugular vein
subclavian artery
subclavian vein
aorta
brachial artery
superior vena cava
heart
coeliac artery
abdominal aorta
common iliac artery
external iliac vein
internal iliac artery
femoral artery
femoral vein
saphenous vein

Lungs

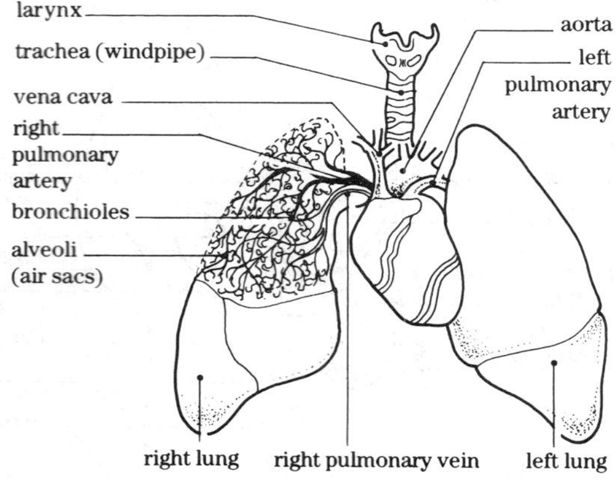
larynx
trachea (windpipe)
vena cava
right pulmonary artery
bronchioles
alveoli (air sacs)
aorta
left pulmonary artery
right lung
right pulmonary vein
left lung

Music symbols etc.

Notes and rests

Note	Rest	British	American
		breve	double-whole note
		semibreve	whole note
		minim	half note
	or	crotchet	quarter note
		quaver	eighth note
		semiquaver	sixteenth note
		demisemiquaver	thirty-second note
		hemidemisemiquaver	sixty-fourth note

Clefs

Fixed note	Position of middle C	Clef
		G *or* treble clef
		F *or* bass clef
		C (soprano) clef
		C (alto) clef
		C (tenor) clef

Accidentals

sharp; raising note one semitone

double sharp; raising note one tone

flat; lowering note one semitone

double flat; lowering note one tone

natural; restoring note to normal pitch after sharp or flat

Ornaments and decorations

Staccato marks and signs of accentuation

or *mezzo-staccato:* shorten note by about ¼

staccato: shorten note by about ½

staccatissimo: shorten note by about ¾

detached: accented

attack

Time signatures

Simple duple:

2/2 *or* ¢ two minim beats

2/4 two crotchet beats

2/8 two quaver beats

Compound duple:

6/4 two dotted minim beats

6/8 two dotted crotchet beats

6/16 two dotted quaver beats

Simple triple:

3/2 three minim beats

3/4 three crotchet beats

3/8 three quaver beats

Compound triple:

9/4 three dotted minim beats

9/8 three dotted crotchet beats

9/16 three dotted quaver beats

Simple quadruple:

4/2 four minim beats

4/4 *or* C four crotchet beats

4/8 four quaver beats

Compound quadruple:

12/4 four dotted minim beats

12/8 four dotted crotchet beats

12/16 four dotted quaver beats

Irregular rhythms

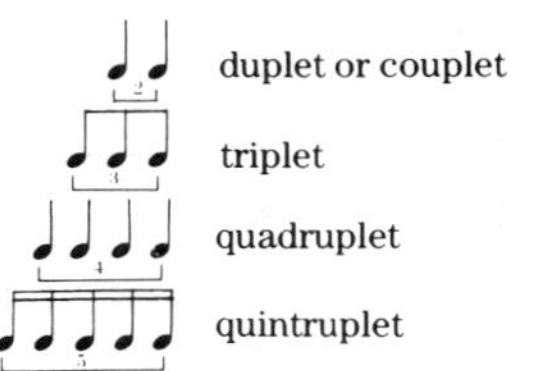

Dynamics

crescendo

diminuendo

Curved lines

tie or bind; two notes played as one

slur or legato; play smoothly (in one bow on stringed instrument)

Other

repeat preceding section

end of section or piece

pause

8^e^ play an octave above notes written

Music symbols etc.

Range of some musical instruments

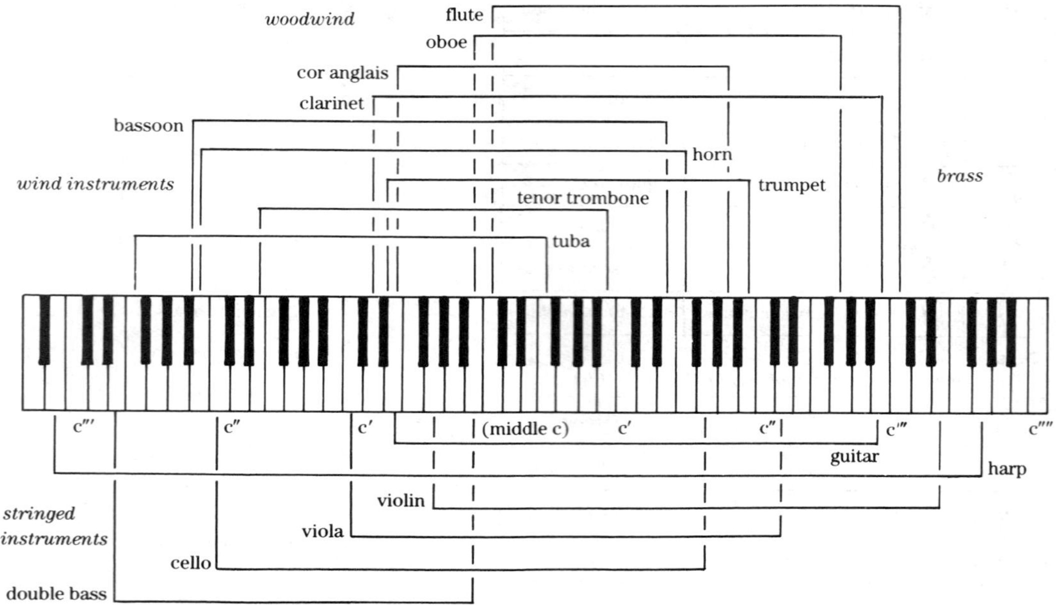

Keys and key signatures

Major key	*Relative minor key*	*Key signature (sharp keys)*	*Key signature (flat keys)*
C	A		
G	E		
D	B		
A	F♯		
E	C♯		
B = C♭	G♯		
F♯ = G♭	E♭		
C♯ = D♭	B♭		
A♭	F		
E♭	C		
B♭	G		
F	D		

Sports pitches

American Football

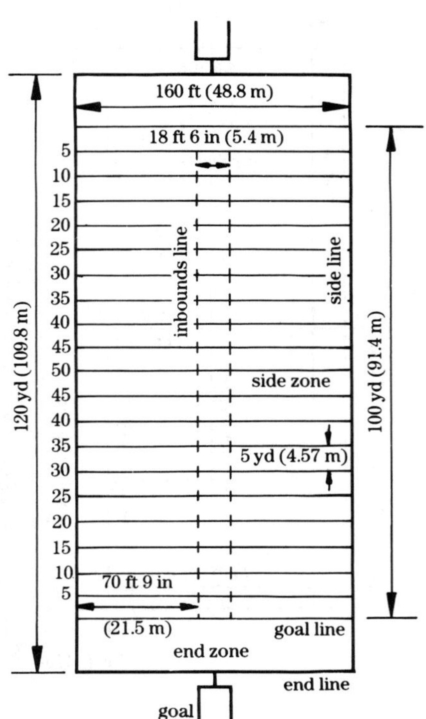

Association Football

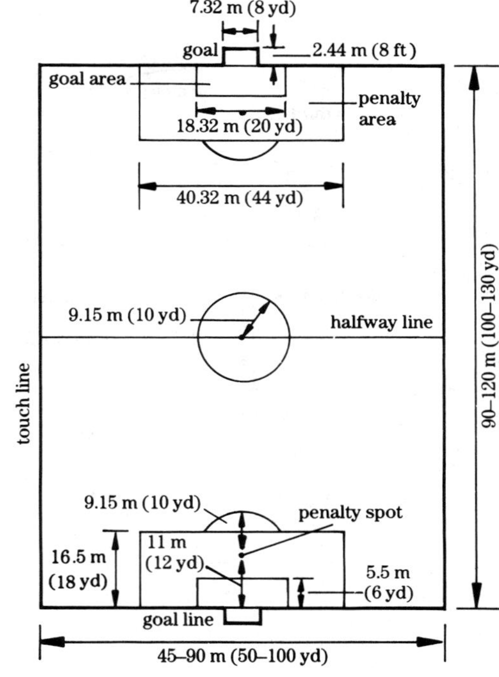

Rugby Union

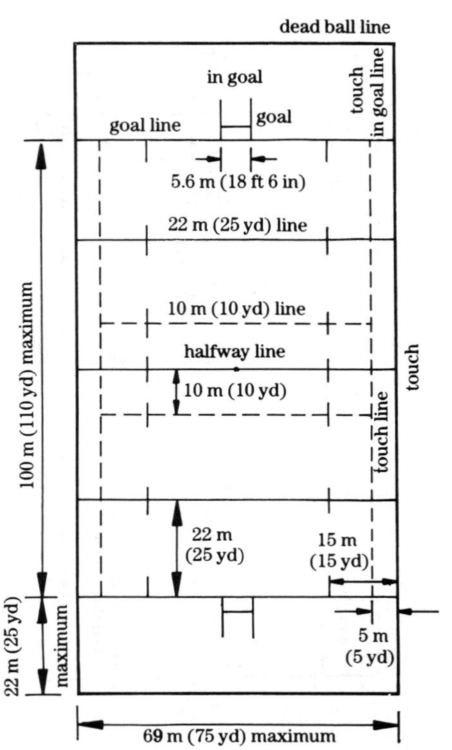

Australian Rules

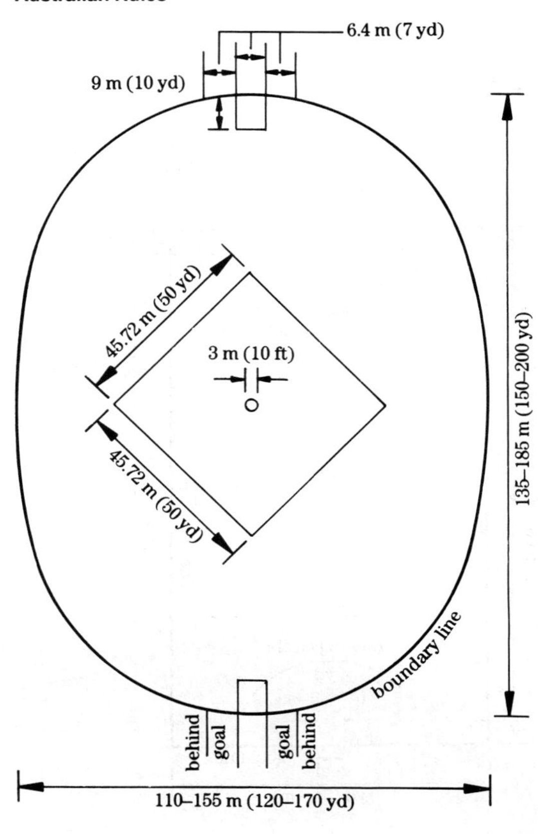

Sports pitches

Cricket; fielding positions (right-handed batsman)

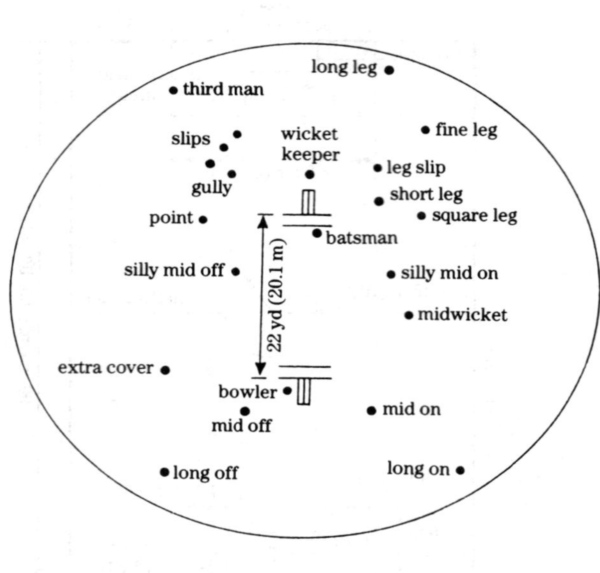

Tennis

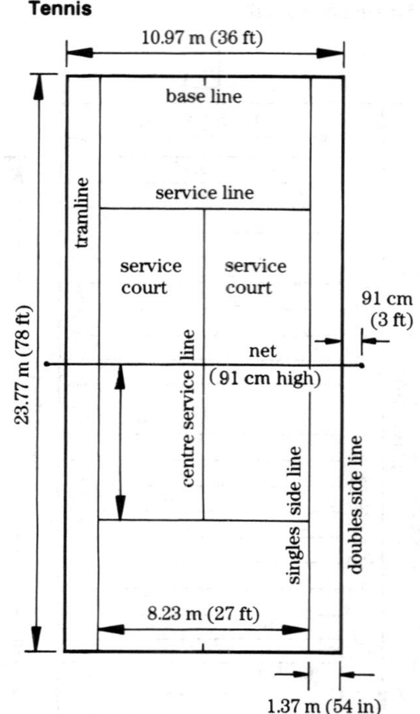

Hockey

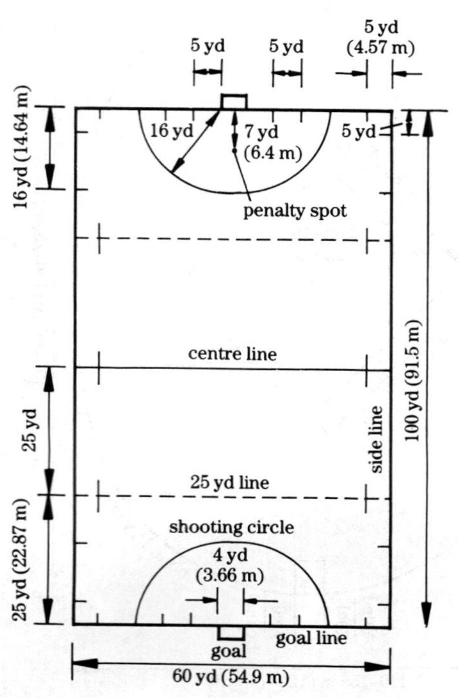

Basketball

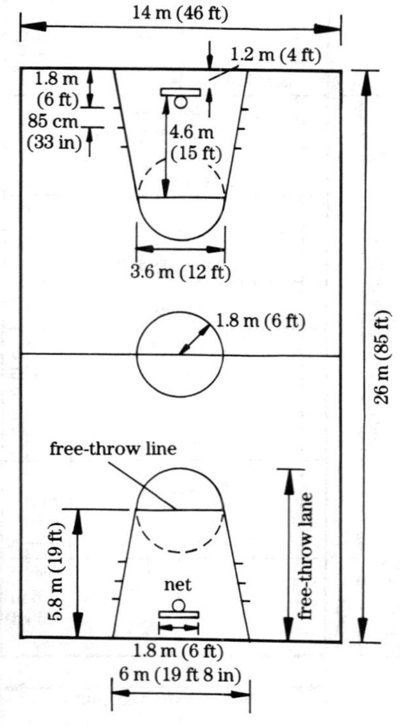

Political Britain

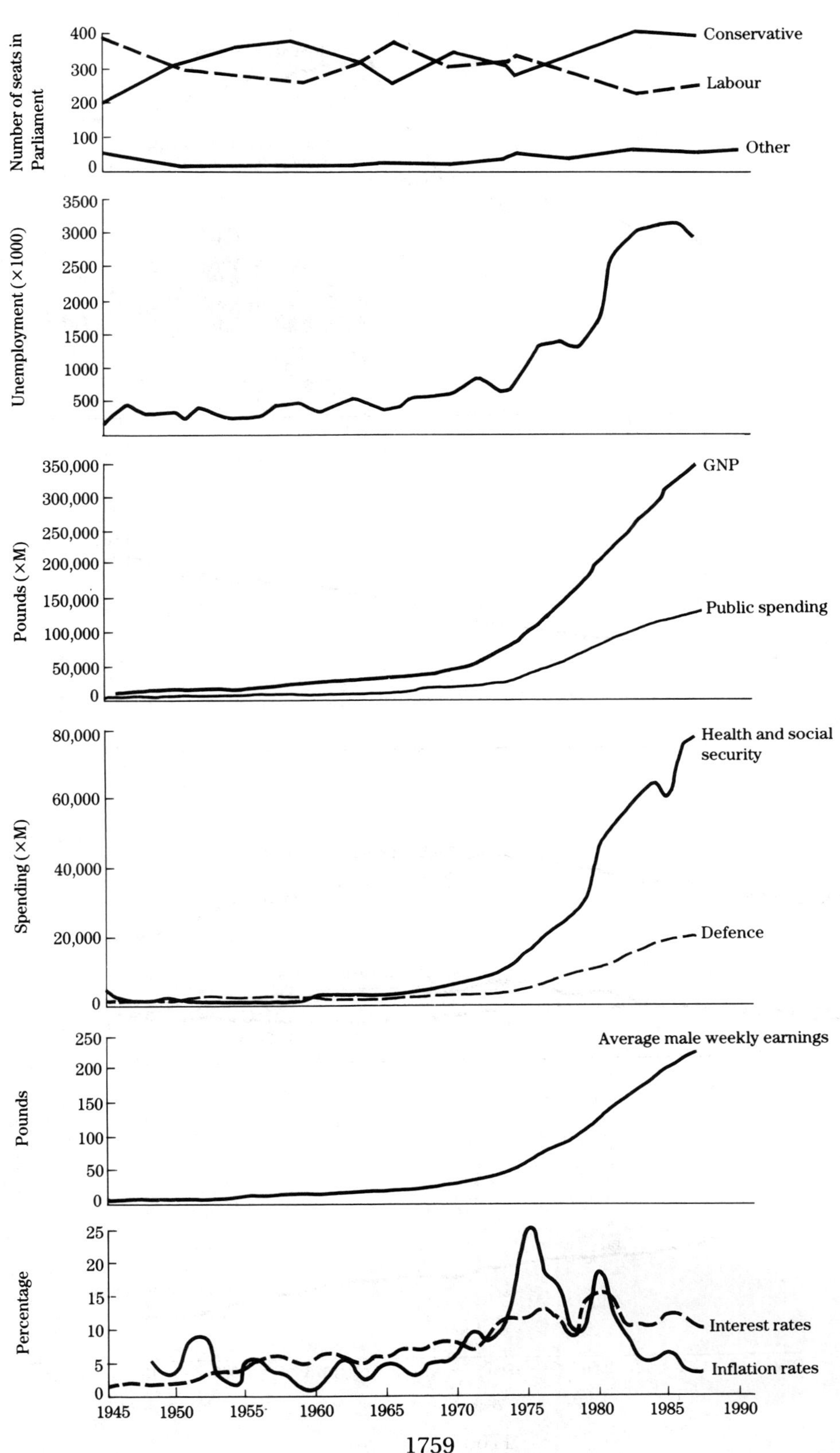

Causes of death in Britain

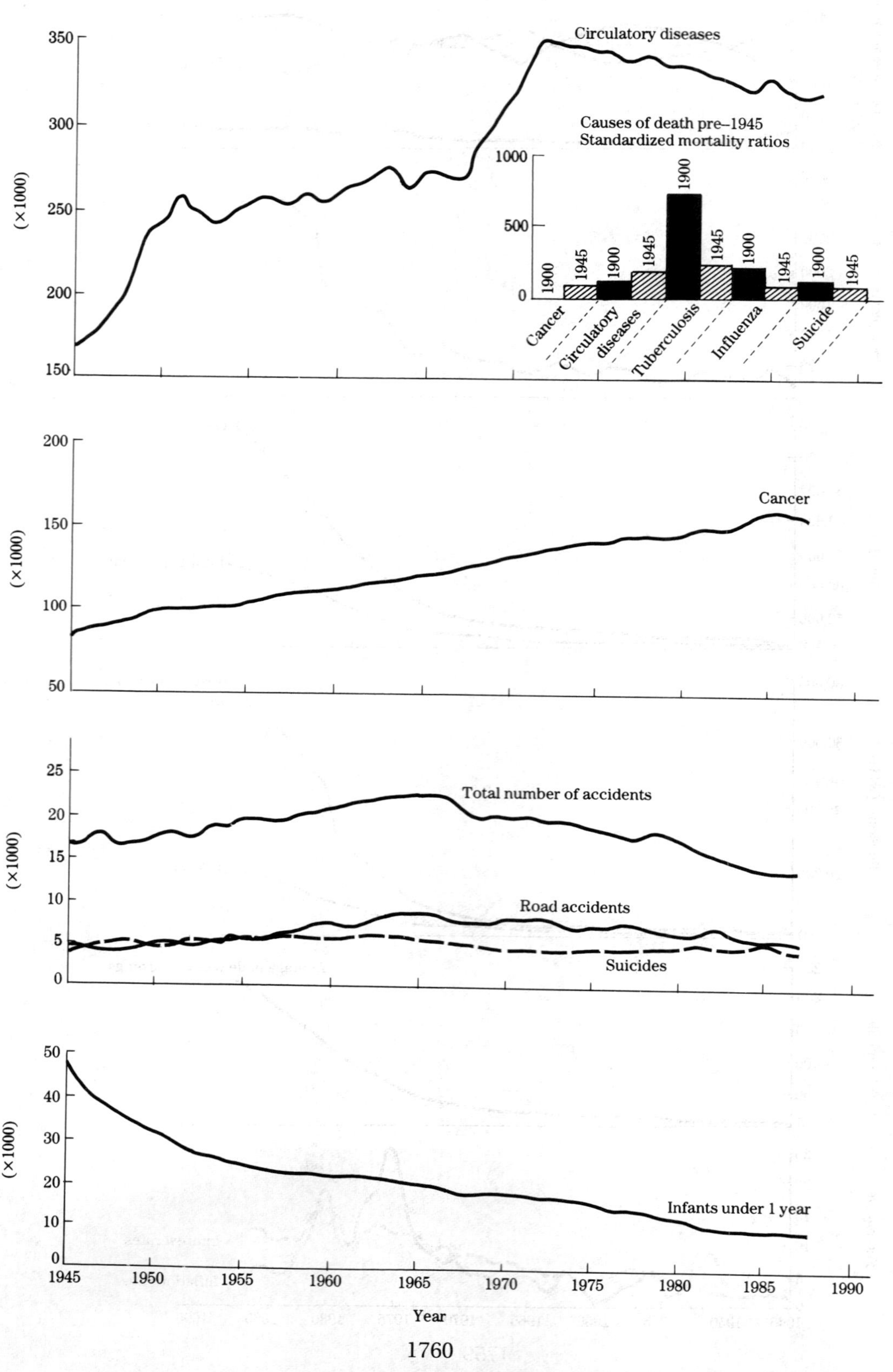

The British family

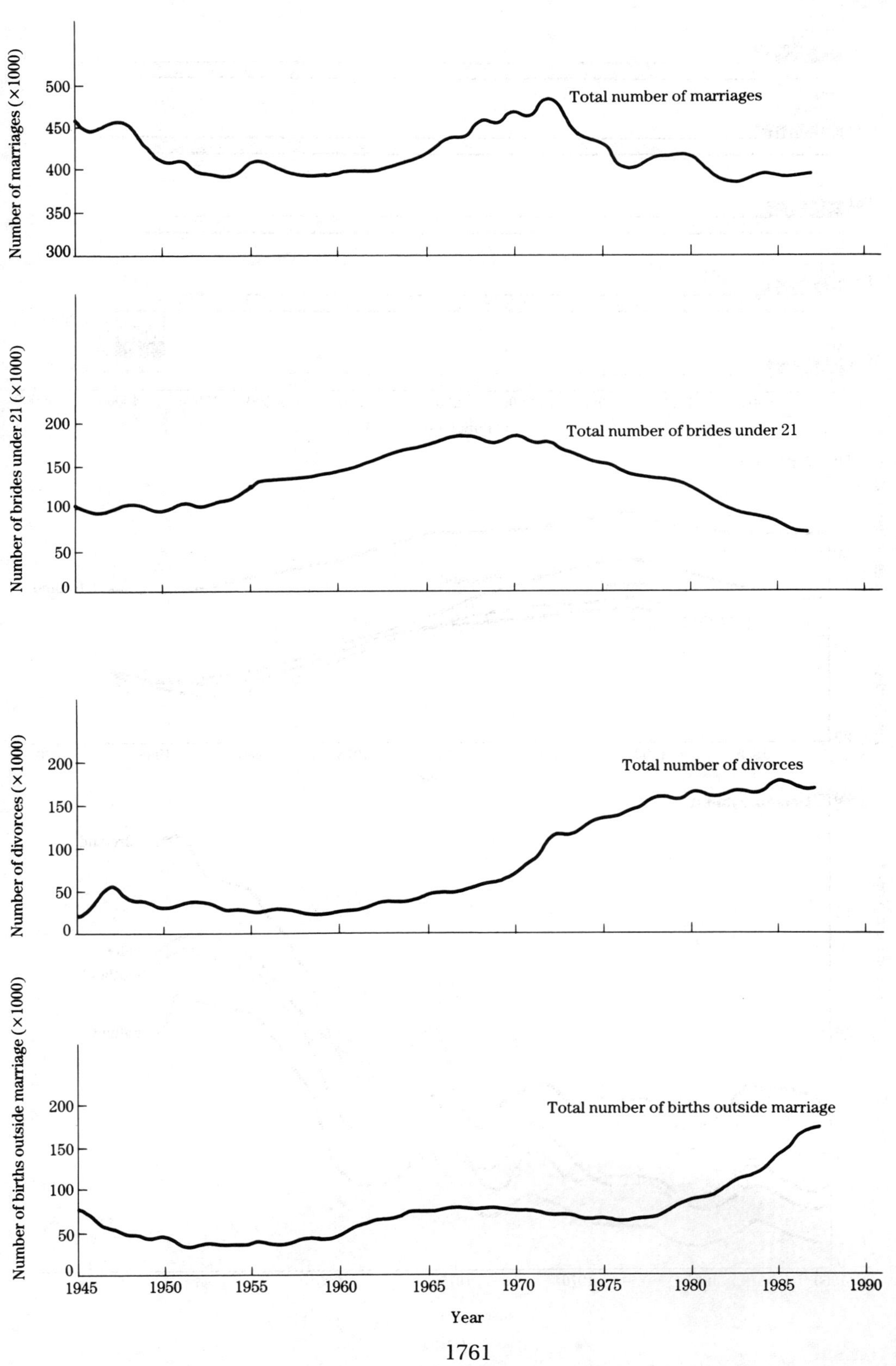

The four nations

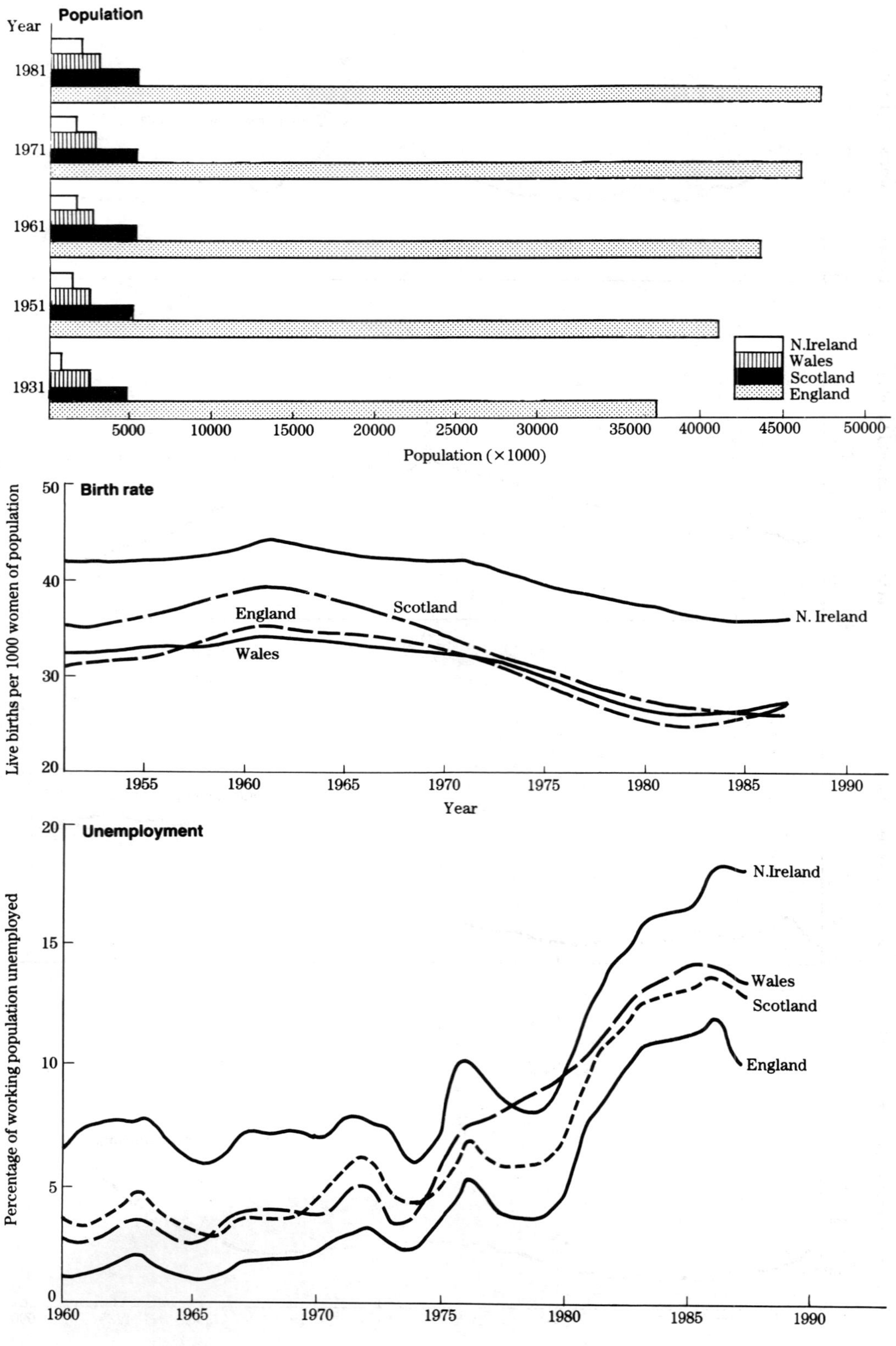

Consumer durables

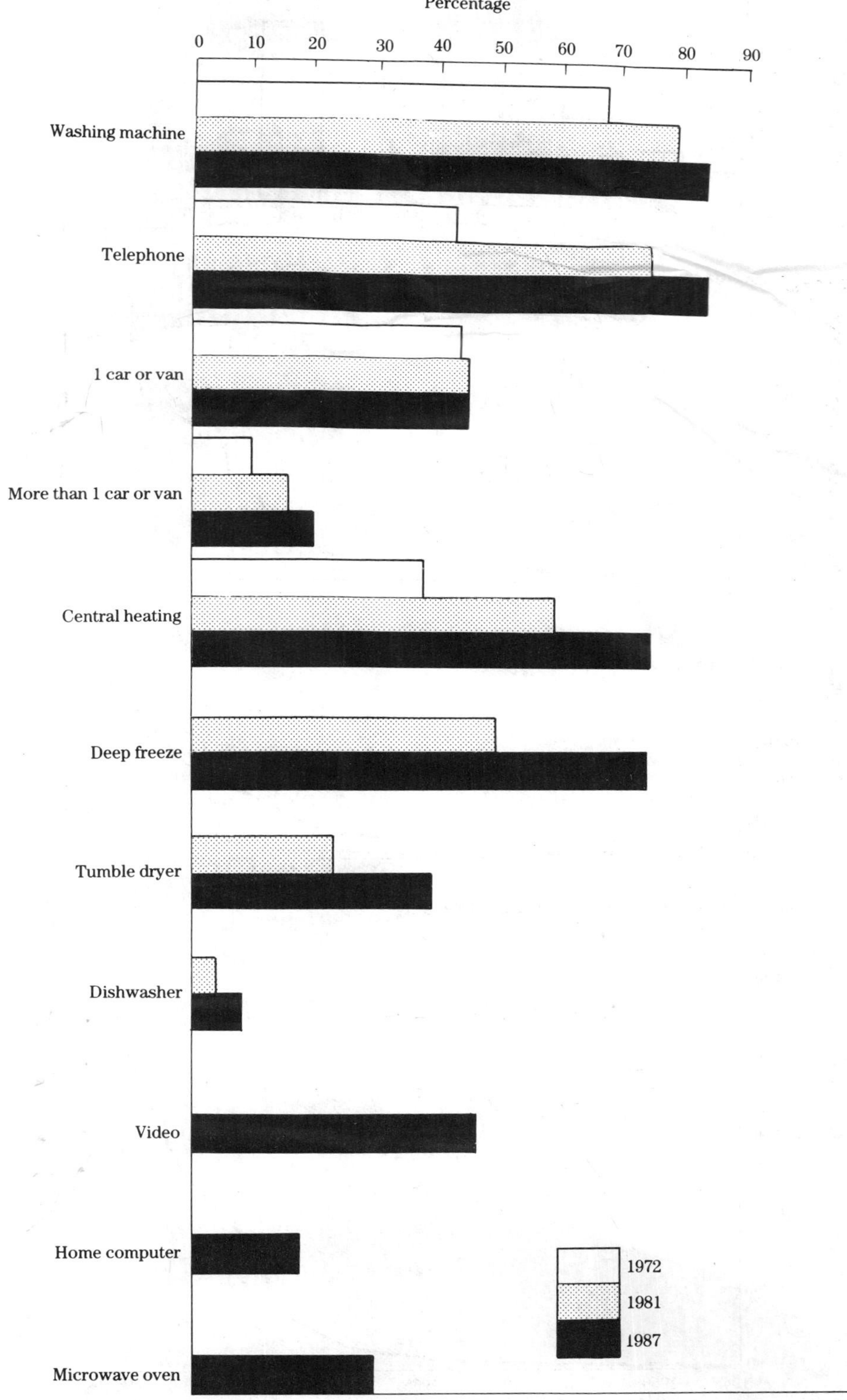

Australia

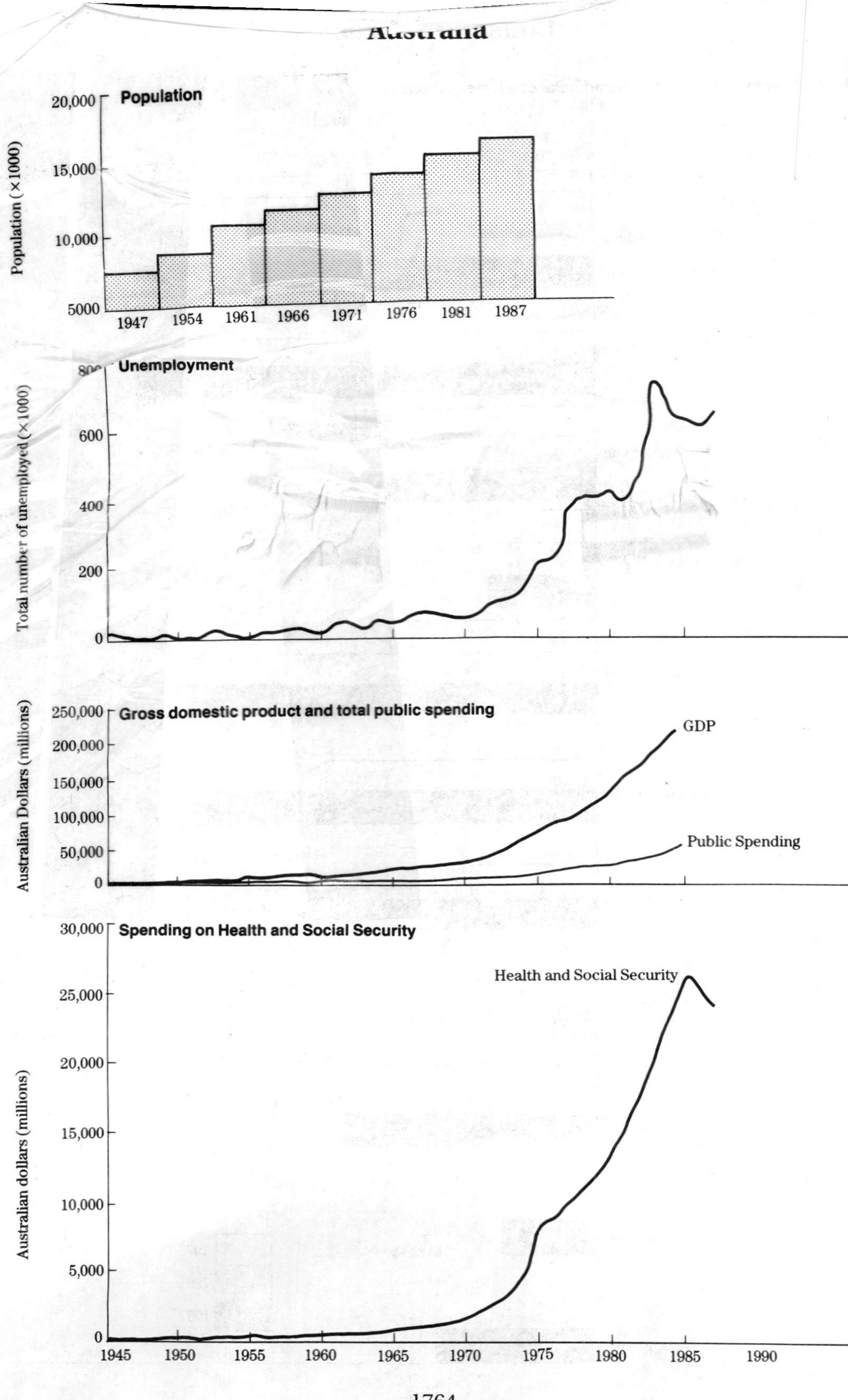

Population
Population (×1000)
20,000
15,000
10,000
5000
1947
1954
1961
1966
1971
1976
1981
1987
Unemployment
Total number of unemployed (×1000)
800
600
400
200
0
Gross domestic product and total public spending
Australian Dollars (millions)
250,000
200,000
150,000
100,000
50,000
0
GDP
Public Spending
Spending on Health and Social Security
Australian dollars (millions)
30,000
25,000
20,000
15,000
10,000
5,000
0
Health and Social Security
1945
1950
1955
1960
1965
1970
1975
1980
1985
1990